LAROUSSE

CONCISE DICTIONARY

SPANISH
ENGLISH

ENGLISH
SPANISH

LAROUSSE

LAROUSSE

DICCIONARIO COMPACT

ESPAÑOL INGLÉS

INGLÉS ESPAÑOL

LAROUSSE

Third Edition/Tercera Edición

Project Management/Dirección
Sharon J. Hunter

Editors/Redacción
Antonio Fortin, José A. Gálvez, Carol Styles Carvajal
David Tarradas Agea

Typesetting/Composición
APS – Chromostyle

Second Edition/Segunda Edición

Project Management/Dirección
José A. Gálvez
Sharon J. Hunter

Editors/Redacción
Joaquín A. Blasco
Dileri Borunda Johnston
Isabel Ferrer Marrades
Ana Cristina Llompart Lucas
Julie Muleba
Victoria Ordóñez Diví
José María Ruiz Vaca
Carol Styles Carvajal
Eduardo Vallejo

First Edition/Primera Edición

Montserrat Alberte Montserrat
José María Díaz de Mendívil
Elena Estremera Paños
Isabel Ferrer Marrades
Carmen González Bodeguero
Anna Jené Palat
Salut Llonch Soler
Judith Medall Cirera
Victoria Ordóñez Diví
Malihe Forghani-Nowbari
Núria Vilanova Pous

Tom Bartlett
Claire Evans Calder
Margaret Jull Costa
Gilla Evans
Wendy Lee
Hilary Macartney
Hugh O'Donnell
Kathryn Phillips–Miles
Clare Plater
Leane Shanks
Patrick White

CONTENTS
ÍNDICE

© Larousse, 2009

ISBN 978–203–541010–8 (hardback edition)

ISBN 978–203–541009–2 (paperback edition)

Larousse, 21 rue du Montparnasse, 75283 Paris Cedex 06

Distribución/Sales: Houghton Mifflin Company, Boston

4500627684
Manufactured in the USA

ISBN 978–84–8016–726–0
LAROUSSE EDITORIAL, S.L.
C/Mallorca, 45, 3ª planta
08029 Barcelona
larousse@larousse.es/www.larousse.es

TO OUR READERS

This new edition of the LAROUSSE COMPACT Dictionary continues to be a reliable and user–friendly tool for use in all language situations. It provides accurate and up–to–date information on written and spoken Spanish and English as they are used today and covers all of the most important American and European variants for both English and Spanish.

Containing more than 100,000 words and phrases and over 130,000 translations the COMPACT gives you access to Spanish texts of all types. The dictionary aims to be as comprehensive as possible in a book of this size, and includes many proper names and abbreviations, as well as a selection of the most common terms from computing, business and current affairs.

Carefully constructed entries and a clear page design help you to find the translation that you are looking for fast. Examples (from basic constructions and common phrases to idioms) have been included to help put a word in context and give a clear picture of how it is used.

The dictionary provides extra help for students of Spanish with the inclusion of boxes on life and culture in Spain and Latin America that appear within the dictionary text itself.

A NUESTROS LECTORES

El Diccionario COMPACT LAROUSSE es la herramienta de trabajo ideal en una amplia gama de circunstancias, desde el aprendizaje de idiomas en la escuela y en casa hasta el uso diario en la oficina.

El COMPACT español–inglés está pensado para responder rápida y eficazmente a los diferentes problemas que plantea la lectura del inglés actual y la redacción de trabajos escolares, cartas e informes.

Con sus más de 100.000 palabras y expresiones y un número de traducciones superior a 130.000, este diccionario permitirá al lector comprender con claridad un amplio espectro de textos literarios y periodísticos, entender documentos comerciales, folletos o manuales, y realizar resúmenes y traducciones con rapidez y corrección.

De entre las características de esta obra, cabe destacar el tratamiento totalmente actualizado de siglas y abreviaturas, nombres propios y términos comerciales e informáticos de uso frecuente.

Con la ayuda de un tratamiento claro y detallado del vocabulario básico, de ejemplos de construcciones gramaticales y modismos, así como de los indicadores de sentido que guían hacia la traducción más adecuada, el usuario podrá escribir en inglés con precisión y seguridad.

Se ha puesto especial cuidado en la presentación de las entradas, tanto desde el punto de vista de su estructura como de la tipografía empleada. Para aquellos lectores que hayan superado el primer nivel de aprendizaje de inglés, pero no aspiren a alcanzar un grado de especialización en esta lengua, el COMPACT es el diccionario ideal.

ABBREVIATIONS

ABREVIATURAS

abbreviation	*abbr/abrev*	abreviatura
adjective	*adj*	adjetivo
adverb	*adv*	adverbio
Latin American Spanish	*Amér*	español latinoamericano
Central American Spanish	*Amér C*	español de Centroamérica
Andean Spanish	*Andes*	español de los Andes
Argentinian Spanish	*Arg*	español de Argentina
before noun	*antes de s*	antes de sustantivo
article	*art*	artículo
auxiliary	*aux*	auxiliar
Bolivian Spanish	*Bol*	español de Bolivia
Caribbean Spanish	*Caribe*	español del Caribe
Chilean Spanish	*Chile*	español de Chile
Colombian Spanish	*Col*	español de Colombia
comparative	*comp(ar)*	comparativo
conjunction	*conj*	conjunción
continuous	*cont*	continuo
Costa Rican Spanish	*C Rica*	español de Costa Rica
Cono Sur Spanish	*C Sur*	español del Cono Sur
Cuban Spanish	*Cuba*	español de Cuba
definite	*def*	determinado
demonstrative	*demos*	demostrativo
pejorative	*despec*	despectivo
dated	*desus*	desusado
Ecudorian Spanish	*Ecuad*	español de Ecuador
especially	*esp*	especialmente
euphemism	*euph/eufem*	eufemismo
exclamation	*excl*	interjeccíon
feminine noun	*f*	sustantivo femenino
informal	*fam*	familiar
figurative	*fig*	figurado
formal	*fml*	formal, culto
inseparable	*fus*	inseparable
generally	*gen*	generalmente
Guatemalan Spanish	*Guat*	español de Guatemala
humorous	*hum*	humorístico
impersonal verb	*impers vb*	verbo impersonal
indefinite	*indef*	indeterminado
informal	*inf*	familiar
inseparable	*insep*	inseperable
exclamation	*interj*	interjección
invariable	*inv*	invariable
ironic	*iro/irón*	irónico
literal	*lit*	literal
literally	*liter*	literalmente
phrase(s)	*loc*	locución, locuciones
masculine noun	*m*	sustantivo masculino
Mexican Spanish	*Méx*	español de México
noun	*n*	sustantivo
Nicaraguan Spanish	*Nic*	español de Nicaragua
proper noun	*n pr*	nombre propio
numeral	*num/núm*	número

ABBREVIATIONS

ABREVIATURAS

oneself	*o.s*	
Panamanian Spanish	*Pan*	español de Panamá
pejorative	*pej*	despectivo
personal	*pers*	personal
Peruvian Spanish	*Perú*	español de Perú
phrase(s)	*phr*	locución, locuciones
plural	*pl*	plural
possessive	*poss/poses*	posesivo
past participle	*pp*	participio pasado
preposition	*prep*	preposición
proper noun	*pr n*	nombre propio
Porto Rican Spanish	*P Rico*	español de Puerto Rico
pronoun	*pron*	pronombre
proverb	*prov*	proverbio
past tense	*pt*	pasado, pretérito
registered trademark	®	marca registrada
Dominican Republic Spanish	*R Dom*	español de República Dominicana
relative	*relat*	relativo
River Plate Spanish	*R Plata*	español del Río de la Plata
noun	*s*	sustantivo
someone, somebody	*sb*	
Scottish English	*Scot*	inglés de Escocia
separable	*sep*	separable
singular	*sing*	singular
slang	*sl*	argot
something	*sthg*	
subject	*subj/suj*	sujeto
superlative	*superl*	superlativo
uncountable noun	*U*	sustantivo 'incontable'
British English	*UK*	inglés británico
Uruguayan Spanish	*Urug*	español de Uruguay
American English	*US*	inglés americano
verb	*vb/v*	verbo
Venezuelan Spanish	*Ven*	español de Venezuela
intransitive verb	*vi*	verbo intransitivo
impersonal verb	*v impers*	verbo impersonal
pronominal verb	*vprnl*	verbo pronominal
transitive verb	*vt*	verbo transitivo
vulgar	*vulg*	vulgar
cultural equivalent	≃	equivalente cultural

FIELD LABELS

CAMPOS SEMÁNTICOS

administration	**ADMIN**	administración
aeronautics, aviation	**AERON**	aeronáutica
agriculture	**AGRIC**	agricultura
anatomy	**ANAT**	anatomía
archeology	**ARCHAEOL**	arqueología
architecture	**ARCHIT/ARQUIT**	arquitectura
astrology	**ASTROL**	astrología
astronomy	**ASTRON**	astronomía
automobile, cars	**AUT(O)**	automóviles
biology	**BIOL**	biología
botany	**BOT**	botánica
chemistry	**CHEM**	química
cinema, film–making	**CIN(E)**	cine
commerce, business	**COM(M)**	comercio
information technology	**COMPUT**	informática
construction, building	**CONSTR**	construcción
culinary, cooking	**CULIN**	cocina
sport	**DEP**	deporte
juridical, legal	**DER**	derecho
ecology	**ECOLOG**	ecología
economics	**ECON**	economía
school, education	**EDUC**	educación, escuela
electricity	**ELEC(TR)**	electricidad
electronics	**ELECTRON/ELECTRÓN**	electrónica
pharmacology, pharmaceuticals	**FARM**	farmacología, farmacia
railways	**FERROC**	ferrocarril
finance, financial	**FIN**	finanzas
physics	**FÍS**	física
photography	**FOTO**	fotografía
soccer	**FTBL**	fútbol
geography	**GEOG(R)**	geografía
geology, geological	**GEOL**	geología
geometry	**GEOM**	geometría
grammar	**GRAM**	gramática
history	**HIST**	historia
industry	**INDUST**	industria
information technology	**INFORM**	informática
linguistics	**LING**	lingüística
literature	**LIT(ER)**	literatura
mathematics	**MAT(HS)**	matemáticas
mechanical engineering	**MEC(ÁN)**	mecánica
medicine	**MED**	medicina
weather, meteorology	**METEOR**	meteorología
military	**MIL**	militar
music	**MUS/MÚS**	música
mythology	**MYTH/MITOL**	mitología
nautical, maritime	**NAUT/NÁUT**	náutica
pharmacology, pharmaceuticals	**PHARM**	farmacología, farmacia
photography	**PHOT**	fotografía
physics	**PHYS**	física
politics	**POL(ÍT)**	política
psychology	**PSYCHOL/PSICOL**	psicología

FIELD LABELS

CAMPOS SEMÁNTICOS

chemistry	**QUÍM**	química
railways	**RAIL**	ferrocarril
religion	**RELIG**	religión
school, education	**SCH**	educación, escuela
sociology	**SOCIOL**	sociología
Stock Exchange	**ST EX**	bolsa
bullfighting	**TAUROM**	tauromaquia
theatre	**TEATR**	teatro
technical, technology	**TECH/TECNOL**	técnico, tecnología
telecommunications	**TELEC(OM)**	telecomunicaciones
printing, typography	**TYPO**	imprenta
television	**TV**	televisión
university	**UNIV**	universidad
veterinary science	**VETER**	veterinaria
zoology	**ZOOL**	zoología

LA ORDENACIÓN ALFABÉTICA EN ESPAÑOL

En este diccionario se ha seguido la ordenación alfabética internacional. Esto significa que las entradas con **ch** aparecerán después de **cg** y no al final de **c**; del mismo modo las entradas con **ll** vendrán después de **lk** y no al final de **l**. Adviértase, sin embargo, que la letra **ñ** *sí* se considera letra aparte y sigue a la **n**.

SPANISH ALPHABETICAL ORDER

The dictionary follows international alphabetical order. Thus entries with **ch** appear after **cg** and not at the end of **c**. Similarly, entries with **ll** appear after **lk** and not at the end of **l**. Note, however, that **ñ** *is* treated as a separate letter and follows **n**.

LOS COMPUESTOS EN INGLÉS

En inglés se llama compuesto a una locución sustantiva de significado único pero formada por más de una palabra; p.ej. **point of view, kiss of life** o **virtual reality**. Uno de los rasgos distintivos de este diccionario es la inclusión de estos compuestos con entrada propia y en riguroso orden alfabético. De esta forma **blood test** vendrá después de **bloodshot**, el cual sigue a **blood pressure**.

ENGLISH COMPOUNDS

A compound is a word or expression which has a single meaning but is made up of more than one word, e.g. **point of view, kiss of life** and **virtual reality**. It is a feature of this dictionary that English compounds appear in the A–Z list in strict alphabetical order. The compound **blood test** will therefore come after **bloodshot** which itself follows **blood pressure**.

TRADEMARKS

Words considered to be trademarks are marked with the symbol ®. However, neither the presence nor the absence of such designation should be regarded as affecting the legal status of any trademark.

SPANISH VERBS

Spanish verbs have a number (from [1] to [81]), which refers to the conjugation table given at the back of the dictionary. This number is not repeated for reflexive verbs when they are sub-entries.

NOMBRES DE MARCAS

Los nombres de marca aparecen señalados en este diccionario con el símbolo ®. Sin embargo, ni este símbolo ni su ausencia son representativos de la situación legal de la marca.

VERBOS ESPAÑOLES

Los verbos españoles llevan un número (del [1] al [81]) que hace referencia a la tabla de conjugación que aparece al final de la obra. El número no se repite en los verbos pronominales cuando son subentradas.

PHONETICS

English vowels

[ɪ] pit, big, rid
[e] pet, tend
[æ] pat, bag, mad
[ʌ] run, cut
[ɒ] pot, log
[ʊ] put, full
[ə] mother, suppose

[iː] bean, weed
[ɑː] barn, car, laugh
[ɔː] born, lawn
[uː] loop, loose
[ɜː] burn, learn, bird

English diphthongs

[eɪ] bay, late, great
[aɪ] buy, light, aisle
[ɔɪ] boy, foil
[əʊ] no, road, blow
[aʊ] now, shout, town
[ɪə] peer, fierce, idea
[eə] pair, bear, share
[ʊə] poor, sure, tour

English semi-vowels

[j] you, spaniel
[w] wet, why, twin

English consonants

[p] pop, people
[b] bottle, bib
[t] train, tip
[d] dog, did
[k] come, kitchen
[g] gag, great
[tʃ] chain, wretched
[dʒ] jet, fridge
[f] fib, physical
[v] vine, live

FONÉTICA

Vocales españolas

[i] piso, imagen
[e] tela, eso
[a] pata, amigo
[o] bola, otro
[u] luz, luna

Diptongos españoles

[ei] ley, peine
[ai] aire, caiga
[oi] soy, boina
[au] causa, aula
[eu] Europa, deuda

Semivocales españoles

[j] hierba, miedo
[w] agua, hueso

Consonantes españoles

[p] papá, campo
[b] vaca, bomba
[β] curvo, caballo
[t] toro, pato
[d] donde, caldo
[k] que, cosa
[g] grande, guerra
[ɣ] aguijón, iglesia
[tʃ] ocho, chusma
[f] fui, afán

[θ]	think, fifth		[θ]	cera, paz
[ð]	this, with		[ð]	cada, pardo
[s]	seal, peace		[s]	solo, paso
[z]	zip, his		[z]	andinismo
[ʃ]	sheep, machine		[x]	gemir, jamón
[ʒ]	usual, measure		[m]	madre, cama
[h]	how, perhaps		[n]	no, pena
[m]	metal, comb		[ŋ]	banca, encanto
[n]	night, dinner		[ɳ]	caña
[ŋ]	sung, parking		[l]	ala, luz
[l]	little, help		[ɾ]	atar, paro
[r]	right, carry		[r]	perro, rosa
			[ʎ]	llave, collar

Los símbolos ['] y [ˌ] indican que la sílaba siguiente lleva un acento primario o secundario respectivamente.

The symbol ['] indicates that the following syllable carries primary stress and the symbol [ˌ] that the following syllable carries secondary stress.

El símbolo [ʳ] en fonética inglesa indica que la r al final de palabra se pronuncia sólo cuando precede a una palabra que comienza por vocal. Adviértase que casi siempre se pronuncia en inglés americano.

The symbol [ʳ] in English phonetics indicates that the final r is pronounced only when followed by a word beginning with a vowel. Note that it is nearly always pronounced in American English.

HOW TO USE THE DICTIONARY

How to find the word or expression you are looking for:

First ask yourself some basic questions:

Is it a single word, a hyphenated word or an abbreviation?
Is it a compound noun?
Is it a phrase?
Is it a reflexive verb?
Is it a Spanish irregular verb form?

Single words, hyphenated words and abbreviations

As a rule, you can find the word you are looking for in its alphabetical order. If you want to translate an English word into Spanish, you should look on the English–Spanish side of the dictionary, and if you want to know what a Spanish term means, you should look on the Spanish–English side. The word in **bold** at the start of each entry is called the 'headword'.

Entries beginning with a **capital** appear after those spelled the same way but with a small letter.

> **ad** [æd] (*abbr of* **advertisement**) *n* anuncio *m*.
> **AD** (*abbr of* **Anno Domini**) d. C.

Words with a **hyphen**, a **full stop** or an **apostrophe** come after those spelled the same way but without any of these punctuation marks.

> **its** [ɪts] *poss adj* su, sus (*pl*); **the dog broke its leg** el perro se rompió la pata.
> **it's** [ɪts] - **1.** (*abbr of* = **it is**), ▷ **be** - **2.** (*abbr of* = **it has**), ▷ **have**.

In some cases, the entry is followed by a number in **superscript**. This means that just before or just after there is another entry, also followed by a number, which is written the same way but which has a completely different meaning or pronunciation. You must take care not to choose the wrong entry.

> **sino**[1] *sm* fate, destiny.
> **sino**[2] *conj* - **1.** [para contraponer] but; **no lo hizo él, sino ella** he didn't do it, she did; **no sólo es listo, sino también trabajador** he's not only clever but also hardworking - **2.** [para exceptuar] except, but; **¿quién sino tú lo haría?** who else but you would do it?; **no quiero sino que se haga justicia** I only want justice to be done.

> ◆ **go after** *vt insep* ir a por OR detrás de.
> ◆ **go against** *vt insep* - **1.** [conflict with, be unfavourable to] ir en contra de - **2.** [act contrary to] actuar en contra de.

You will sometimes see words followed by a grey lozenge, called sub-entries. English phrasal verbs fall into this category.

> **afternoon** [,ɑːftə'nuːn] *n* tarde *f*; **in the afternoon** por la tarde; **at three in the afternoon** a las tres de la tarde; **good afternoon** buenas tardes.
> ◆ **afternoons** *adv* US por las tardes.

If you are looking up a noun which has a form with an initial capital which has a different meaning from the form without a capital, you should look at the form without a capital.

> **salvador, ra** ⋄ *adj* saving. ⋄ *sm, f* [persona] saviour.
> ➤ **Salvador** *sm* - **1.** RELIG: **el Salvador** the Saviour - **2.** GEOGR: **El Salvador** El Salvador.

If you are looking up a noun which, in the plural, has a different meaning from the noun in its singular form (like glass/glasses in English), you will find it under the singular form; the plural form will be there as a sub-entry, indicated by the symbol ➤.

> **glass** [glɑːs] ⋄ *n* - **1.** [material] vidrio *m*, cristal *m* - **2.** [drinking vessel, glassful] vaso *m*; [with stem] copa *f* - **3.** *(U)* [glassware] cristalería *f*. ⋄ *comp* de vidrio OR cristal.
> ➤ **glasses** *npl* [spectacles] gafas *fpl*.

Some plural nouns appear as headwords in their own right when they are never or rarely used in the singular (e.g. **gafas** in Spanish, **scissors** in English).

Compound nouns

A compound is a word or expression which has a single meaning but is made up of more than one word, e.g. **point of order, kiss of life, virtual reality, International Monetary Fund**. It is a feature of this dictionary that English compounds appear in the A–Z list in strict alphabetical order. The compound **blood donor** will therefore come after **bloodcurdling** which itself follows **blood count**.

> **blood count** *n* recuento *m* de glóbulos.
> **bloodcurdling** ['blʌd,kɜːdlɪŋ] *adj* espeluznante.
> **blood donor** *n* donante *mf* de sangre.

On the Spanish-English side however you should look under the first element of the compound. So, for example, you will find **billete sencillo** at the entry **billete**. If there is more than one compound within an entry they will appear in their alphabetical order within the entry, regardless of any preposition between the two parts of the compound. So at **billete** you will find **billete de ida** after **billete de andén** and before **billete sencillo**.

Some compounds that have distinct meanings from the main entry are treated separately as sub-entries, preceded by a black lozenge.

> **bóveda** *sf* ARQUIT vault.
> ➤ **bóveda celeste** *sf* firmament.
> ➤ **bóveda craneal** *sf* cranial vault.

Phrases

If looking for a phrase, you should look first under the noun that is used in the phrase. If there is no noun, then you should look under the adjective, and if there is no adjective, under the verb. Phrases appear in entries in bold, the symbol ~ standing for the headword.

Some very fixed phrases like **in spite of** in English or **a pesar de** in Spanish are entered under the first important element and preceded by ➡.

time [taɪm] ◇ *n* - **1.** [gen] tiempo *m*; **a good time to go** un buen momento de irnos; **ahead of time** temprano; **in good time** con tiempo; **on time** puntualmente; **to take time** llevar tiempo; **it's (about) time to...** ya es hora de...; **to get the time to do sthg** coger el tiempo para hacer algo; **it's high time...** ya va siendo hora de...; **to get time and a half** recibir el pago establecido más la mitad de éste; **to have no time for** no poder con...

spite [spaɪt] ◇ *n* rencor *m*; **to do sthg out of** OR **from spite** hacer algo por despecho. ◇ *vt* fastidiar, molestar.
➡ **in spite of** *prep* a pesar de; **I did it in spite of myself** [unintentionally] lo hice muy a pesar mío.

pesar ◇ *sm* - **1.** [tristeza] grief - **2.** [arrepentimiento] remorse - **3.** *loc:* **a pesar mío** against my will. ◇ *vt* - **1.** [determinar el peso de] to weigh - **2.** [examinar] to weigh up. ◇ *vi* - **1.** [tener peso] to weigh - **2.** [ser pesado] to be heavy - **3.** [importar] to play an important part - **4.** [molestar]: **me pesa tener que hacerlo** it grieves me to have to do it; **pese a quien pese** in spite of everything - **5.** [entristecer]: **me pesa tener que decirte esto** I'm sorry to have to tell you this.
➡ **pesarse** *vprnl* to weigh o.s.
➡ **a pesar de** *loc prep* despite; **a pesar de todo** in spite of everything.
➡ **a pesar de que** *loc conj* in spite of the fact that.

Reflexive verbs

Spanish reflexive verbs are entered under the main form, after the symbol ➡.

patear ◇ *vt* [dar un puntapié] to kick; [pisotear] to stamp on. ◇ *vi* - **1.** [patalear] to stamp one's feet - **2.** *fam fig* [andar] to tramp.
➡ **patearse** *vprnl* [recorrer] to tramp.

Irregular forms

Irregular forms of nouns, adjectives and verbs appear in the dictionary as entries with cross-references to the main form.

ate [UK et, US eɪt] *pt* ▷ **eat**.

Set phrases

Set phrases appear on a separate line, preceded by the symbol ▸▸▸.

> **beside** [bɪ'saɪd] *prep* - **1.** [next to] al lado de, junto a - **2.** [compared with] comparado(da) con ▸▸▸ **that's beside the point** eso no importa, eso no viene al caso; **to be beside o.s. with rage** estar fuera de sí; **to be beside o.s. with joy** estar loco(ca) de alegría.

How to find the right translation

Once you have found the word or phrase that you are looking for, there may be several different translations given from which to choose. However, all the necessary information to help you find the right translation is given.

Step 1 Imagine that you want to translate *he accepted the blame* into Spanish.

Go first to the entry **accept** on the English-Spanish side of the dictionary. At sense 3 you will find the verb used in this context: **asumir**.

> **accept** [ək'sept] ◇ *vt* - **1.** [gen] aceptar - **2.** [difficult situation, problem] asimilar - **3.** [defeat, blame, responsibility] asumir, admitir - **4.** [agree]: **to accept that** admitir que - **5.** [subj: machine - coins, tokens] funcionar con, admitir. ◇ *vi* aceptar.

Step 2 Go now to the entry for the second word that needs to be translated, **blame**.

NB It is important first to find the correct grammatical category (each new category is introduced by ◇). **Blame** is a noun in this example and so you should look under the noun category (labelled **n**).

> **blame** [bleɪm] ◇ *n* culpa *f*; **to take the blame for** hacerse responsable de; **to be to blame for** ser el culpable de. ◇ *vt* echar la culpa a, culpar; **to blame sthg on sthg/sb, to blame sthg/sb for sthg** culpar algo/a alguien de algo.

Step 3 On examining the noun category, you will find that the translation used is **culpa**.

Step 4 The words selected can now be put together in the phrase to be translated, to give: **asumió la culpa**.

Cultural information

An appreciation of the culture of a foreign country is key to being able to understand and speak its language well. Cultural information on Spain and Latin America is provided in this dictionary in boxes on the Spanish–English side of the dictionary.

As **A level** are part of an education system unique to the UK, there is no real equivalent in Spanish and a box is required to explain it.

> **A level** (*abbr of* **Advanced level**) *n* UK SCH *nivel escolar necesario para acceder a la universidad.*
>
> **A level**
>
> ▦▦▦ Exámenes de acceso a la universidad en el Reino Unido. Se caracterizan por un alto grado de especialización ya que no se hacen en más de dos o tres asignaturas (excepcionalmente cuatro). Asimismo, las notas son decisivas a la hora de acceder al centro donde se desea cursar estudios.

CÓMO UTILIZAR ESTE DICCIONARIO LAROUSSE

¿Cómo podemos encontrar la palabra o la expresión que buscamos?

De entrada, hay que preguntarse:

¿Es una palabra o una abreviatura?
¿Es un nombre compuesto?

¿Es una expresión o una locución?

¿Es un verbo con preposición?
¿Es un verbo pronominal?
¿Es una forma verbal irregular?

Palabras y abreviaturas

Por regla general, encontraremos la palabra que buscamos en el lugar que le corresponde en el orden alfabético. Si queremos traducir una palabra española al inglés, miraremos en la parte español–inglés del diccionario y, si ignoramos el sentido de una palabra inglesa, miraremos en la parte inglés–español. La palabra en **negrita** que aparece al principio de cada artículo se llama "entrada".

Las entradas que empiezan con **mayúscula** aparecen después de las que se escriben igual pero empiezan con minúscula.

ad [æd] (*abbr of* **advertisement**) *n* anuncio *m*.
AD (*abbr of* **Anno Domini**) d. C.

Las palabras con **guión, apóstrofo** o **puntos** aparecen después de las que se escriben igual pero sin ninguno de estos signos.

its [ɪts] *poss adj* su, sus (*pl*); **the dog broke its leg** el perro se rompió la pata.
it's [ɪts] **- 1.** (*abbr of* = it is), ▷ **be - 2.** (*abbr of* = it has), ▷ **have**.

Las entradas con **acento ortográfico** se encuentran después de las que se escriben igual pero sin acento.

papa *sf* potato; **no saber ni papa** *fam* not to have a clue.
◆ **Papa** *sm* Pope.
papá *sm fam* dad, daddy, pop *US*; **papá grande** *Méx* grandpa.

En algunos casos, la entrada va seguida de un número **superíndice.** Esto quiere decir que, inmediatamente antes o inmediatamente después, hay otra entrada, también con un número, que se escribe igual pero que tiene un significado o una pronunciación completamente distintos. Son lo que llamamos homógrafos. Atención: ¡tenemos que asegurarnos de que no nos equivocamos de entrada! Hay que prestar mucha atención a la categoría gramatical.

sino[1] *sm* fate, destiny.
sino[2] *conj* **- 1.** [para contraponer] but; **no lo hizo él, sino ella** he didn't do it, she did; **no sólo es listo, sino también trabajador** he's not only clever but also hardworking **- 2.** [para exceptuar] except, but; **¿quién sino tú lo haría?** who else but you would do it?; **no quiero sino que se haga justicia** I only want justice to be done.

A veces, encontraremos palabras precedidas por un **rombo negro** (◆), llamadas "subentradas". Los verbos frasales ingleses, así como los verbos pronominales españoles entran dentro de esta categoría.

◆ **go after** *vt insep* ir a por *OR* detrás de.
◆ **go against** *vt insep* **- 1.** [conflict with, be unfavourable to] ir en contra de **- 2.** [act contrary to] actuar en contra de.

Si lo que buscamos es una palabra que posee una forma con **mayúscula** inicial con un sentido distinto al de la forma con minúscula inicial, la encontraremos bajo la forma sin mayúscula pero precedida por un rombo negro.

---

salvador, ra ◇ *adj* saving. ◇ *sm, f* [persona] saviour.
◆ **Salvador** *sm* - **1.** RELIG: **el Salvador** the Saviour - **2.** GEOGR: **El Salvador** El Salvador.

Igualmente, si buscamos un nombre que, en plural, tiene un significado distinto del singular (como **padre/padres** en español), la encontraremos bajo la forma en singular: la palabra en plural aparece como subentrada precedida por el símbolo (◆).

---

padre ◇ *sm* [gen & RELIG] father; **padre de familia** head of the family; **padre espiritual** confessor; **padre soltero** single parent; **de padre y muy señor mío** incredible, tremendous. ◇ *adj inv* - **1.** *Esp fam* [enorme] incredible, tremendous - **2.** *Méx fam* [estupendo] fantastic, great.
◆ **padres** *smpl* - **1.** [padre y madre] parents - **2.** [antepasados] ancestors, forefathers.
◆ **Padres de la Iglesia** *smpl* RELIG Fathers of the Christian Church.
◆ **Santo Padre** *sm* RELIG Holy Father, Pope.

Algunos nombres aparecen directamente en **plural** en la lista alfabética, ya sea porque no existen en singular o porque este último es poco frecuente (**scissors** en inglés, **gafas** en español).

Nombres compuestos

Un nombre compuesto es una expresión que tiene un significado global pero que está formada por varias palabras (p. ej. **billete sencillo** o **joint venture**). En la parte español-inglés, encontraremos estos compuestos en la entrada correspondiente a su primer elemento. Así, **billete sencillo** aparecerá en **billete**. Los distintos nombres compuestos **billete de andén**, **billete de ida**, **billete kilométrico**, etc. aparecen

---

billete *sm* - **1.** [dinero] note *UK*, bill *US* - **2.** [de rifa, transporte, cine etc] ticket; **'no hay billetes'** TEATRO 'sold out'; **billete de andén** platform ticket; **billete de ida** single (ticket); **billete de ida y vuelta** return (ticket) *UK*, round-trip (ticket) *US*; **billete kilométrico** *ticket to travel a set distance*; **billete sencillo** single (ticket) *UK*, one-way (ticket) *US* - **3.** [de lotería] lottery ticket.

---

ordenados alfabéticamente, sin tener en cuenta la preposición que los une (por ejemplo **de** en **billete de ida**). En la sección de inglés-español, los compuestos ingleses aparecen en estricto orden alfabético. Así que el compuesto **blood donor** aparece después de **bloodcurdling**, el cual viene después de **blood count**.

Cuando el compuesto en español está muy lexicalizado, es decir, cuando se considera más una unidad que la suma de dos o más palabras, se trata aparte, precedido por un rombo negro, con el fin de ponerlo en relieve.

---

bóveda *sf* ARQUIT vault.
◆ **bóveda celeste** *sf* firmament.
◆ **bóveda craneal** *sf* cranial vault.

Expresiones y locuciones

Deberemos buscar todas las expresiones y locuciones bajo el primer nombre que las forman. Si en la expresión no hay ningún nombre, la buscaremos bajo el verbo. En el interior de cada artículo, las expresiones aparecen en negrita y el símbolo ~ representa la entrada.

> **time** [taɪm] ⟐ *n* - **1.** [gen] tiempo *m*; **a good time to go** un buen momento de irnos; **ahead of time** temprano; **in good time** con tiempo; **on time** puntualmente; **to take time** llevar tiempo; **it's (about) time to...** ya es hora de...; **to get the time to do sthg** coger el tiempo para hacer algo; **it's high time...** ya va siendo hora de...; **to get time and a half** recibir el pago establecido más la mitad de éste; **to have no time for** no poder con...

Algunas expresiones ya hechas que tienen un valor gramatical global (locuciones), tales como **a pesar de** en español o **in spite of** en inglés, aparecen bajo el primer elemento importante precedidas por el símbolo (◆).

> **spite** [spaɪt] ⟐ *n* rencor *m*; **to do sthg out of** OR **from spite** hacer algo por despecho. ⟐ *vt* fastidiar, molestar.
> ◆ **in spite of** *prep* a pesar de; **I did it in spite of myself** [unintentionally] lo hice muy a pesar mío.

Este sistema permite poner de relieve la diferencia de sentido y función gramatical entre la locución y la entrada bajo la que aparece.

> **pesar** ⟐ *sm* - **1.** [tristeza] grief - **2.** [arrepentimiento] remorse - **3.** *loc*: **a pesar mío** against my will. ⟐ *vt* - **1.** [determinar el peso de] to weigh - **2.** [examinar] to weigh up. ⟐ *vi* - **1.** [tener peso] to weigh - **2.** [ser pesado] to be heavy - **3.** [importar] to play an important part - **4.** [molestar]: **me pesa tener que hacerlo** it grieves me to have to do it; **pese a quien pese** in spite of everything - **5.** [entristecer]: **me pesa tener que decirte esto** I'm sorry to have to tell you this.
> ◆ **pesarse** *vprnl* to weigh o.s.
> ◆ **a pesar de** *loc prep* despite; **a pesar de todo** in spite of everything.
> ◆ **a pesar de que** *loc conj* in spite of the fact that.

Verbos pronominales

La mayoría de los verbos pronominales aparecen bajo la forma principal que les corresponde, precedidos por el símbolo (◆).

> **conformar** *vt* [configurar] to shape.
> ◆ **conformarse con** *vprnl* [suerte, destino] to resign o.s. to; [apañárselas con] to make do with; [contentarse con] to settle for.

Formas irregulares

Si ignoramos a qué infinitivo corresponde una determinada forma verbal, es posible que se trate de una forma irregular. La tabla

> **obligue** *etc* ⊳ **obligar**.

de conjugación (al final de la obra) nos permitirá encontrar el infinitivo, pero si, además, buscamos la forma en cuestión en el cuerpo del diccionario, también la encontraremos.

Las frases hechas aparecen en una línea aparte, precedidas por el símbolo ▶▶.

> **miedo** *sm* fear; **coger miedo a algo** to develop a fear of sthg; **dar miedo** to be frightening; **me de miedo conducir** I'm afraid o frightened of driving; **meter miedo a** to frighten; **por miedo a** for fear of; **por miedo de que...** for fear that...; **temblar de miedo** to tremble with fear; **tener miedo** to be frightened o scared; **tener miedo a** o **de (hacer algo)** to be afraid of (doing sthg); **miedo cerval** terrible fear, terror ▶▶ **de miedo** *fam*: **esta película está de miedo** this film is brilliant; **lo pasamos de miedo** we had a whale of a time; **estar cagado de miedo** *vulg* to be shit-scared; **morirse de miedo** to die of fright, to be terrified.

Cómo encontrar la traducción correcta

Una vez localizada la palabra o la expresión buscada, es posible que tenga varias traducciones. No importa, encontraremos en el diccionario todos los elementos necesarios para identificar la traducción que estamos buscando.

> **accept** [ək'sept] ◇ *vt* **- 1.** [gen] aceptar **- 2.** [difficult situation, problem] asimilar **- 3.** [defeat, blame, responsibility] asumir, admitir **- 4.** [agree]: **to accept that** admitir que **- 5.** [subj: machine - coins, tokens] funcionar con, admitir. ◇ *vi* aceptar.

1er Paso Imaginemos que queremos traducir **he accepted the blame**.
Examinemos primero el artículo **accept** de la parte inglés-español.
Tras el número **3**, encontraremos la palabra que se utiliza en este sentido.

2° Paso Pasemos ahora a la segunda palabra que debemos buscar: **blame**. Examinemos el artículo **blame**.

> **blame** [bleɪm] ◇ *n* culpa *f*; **to take the blame for** hacerse responsable de; **to be to blame for** ser el culpable de. ◇ *vt* echar la culpa a, culpar; **to blame sthg on sthg/sb, to blame sthg/sb for sthg** culpar algo/a alguien de algo.

Atención: Es importante buscar en primer lugar la categoría gramatical correcta. Cada cambio de categoría aparece introducido por un rombo blanco (◇). En este caso debemos buscar en la categoría gramatical **n**.

3er Paso Al leer las traducciones propuestas para el sentido número **3** de **accept**, encontraremos la palabra que debemos utilizar para describir **culpabilidad**: la traducción será **asumir**.

4° Paso Ahora deberemos aplicar las traducciones elegidas a la frase que queremos traducir: **asumió la culpa**.

Información de tipo cultural

Con el fin de comprender y hablar mejor una lengua extranjera, es necesario obtener información sobre las especificidades culturales del país en cuestión. Sin embargo, el lugar apropiado para este tipo de información no es el interior de una entrada de diccionario. Así pues, el lector español encontrará en la parte inglés-español unos recuadros que le informarán sobre las particularidades culturales de Gran Bretaña o Estados Unidos.

El recuadro de **A level** nos explica un sistema educativo propio de Gran Bretaña que en España no cuenta con un equivalente.

A level (*abbr of* **Advanced level**) *n* UK SCH *nivel escolar necesario para acceder a la universidad.*

A level

Exámenes de acceso a la universidad en el Reino Unido. Se caracterizan por un alto grado de especialización ya que no se hacen en más de dos o tres asignaturas (excepcionalmente cuatro). Asimismo, las notas son decisivas a la hora de acceder al centro donde se desea cursar estudios.

LISTA DE RECUADROS CULTURALES ESPAÑOLES
LIST OF SPANISH CULTURAL BOXES

ALBURES
APELLIDOS
AUTONOMÍA
AVE
BOE
CAJA DE AHORROS
CALENDARIO LABORAL
CASA ROSADA
CASTELLANO
CATALÁN
COLEGIO DE MÉXICO
DENOMINACIÓN DE
  ORIGEN
DOCUMENTO NACIONAL
  DE IDENTIDAD
ESO

EUSKERA
FIESTAS
GALLEGO
GUARANÍ
GUARDIA CIVIL
HORA INGLESA
JORNADA CONTINUA
LATIFUNDIO
MAQUILADORA
MATE
LA MONCLOA
LA MONEDA
NÁHUATL
ONCE
OPERACIÓN RETORNO
OPOSICIONES

PAGA EXTRA
PARADOR NACIONAL
PEMEX
LOS PINOS
PREJUBILACIÓN
PUENTE
QUECHUA
RAE
SISTEMA EDUCATIVO
SMI
SPANGLISH
TRATAMIENTO
UNIÓN DE HECHO
VOSEO
VOSOTROS

LISTA DE RECUADROS CULTURALES INGLESES
LIST OF ENGLISH CULTURAL BOXES

AFFIRMATIVE ACTION
A LEVEL
CHURCH
COMMONWEALTH
CONGRESS
CONSTITUTION
DEVOLUTION
DOWNING STREET
FIFTH AMENDMENT
FLEET STREET
FORT KNOX
FOURTH OF JULY
-GATE
GREEN CARD
HOLIDAYS
HONOURS LIST

HOUSE OF COMMONS
HOUSE OF LORDS
IVY LEAGUE
LABOR DAY
LICENSING HOURS
MEDICAID/MEDICARE
MINIMUM WAGE
NATIONAL INSURANCE
NHS
NORTH-SOUTH DIVIDE
OXBRIDGE
PLEDGE OF ALLEGIANCE
POLITICAL CORRECTNESS
PRIVATE EDUCATION
PUBLIC ACCESS
  TELEVISION

QUEEN'S SPEECH
SAT
STARS AND STRIPES
STATE OF THE UNION
  ADDRESS
STATE SCHOOLS
TABLOIDS
THANKSGIVING
UNITED KINGDOM
WASP
WHITE HOUSE
WORKING HOURS
WORLD SERIES
YANKEE
YEARBOOK

ESPAÑOL–INGLÉS
SPANISH–ENGLISH

a¹ *(pl* aes), **A** *(pl* Aes) *sf* [letra] a, A.

a² *prep* *(a + el = al)* **- 1.** [periodo de tiempo]: **a las pocas semanas** a few weeks later; **al mes de casados** a month after they were married; **al día siguiente** the following day **- 2.** [momento preciso] at; **a las siete** at seven o'clock; **a los 11 años** at the age of 11; **al caer la noche** at nightfall; **al oír la noticia, se desmayó** on hearing the news, she fainted **- 3.** [frecuencia]: **40 horas a la semana** 40 hours per *o* a week; **tres veces al día** three times a day **- 4.** [dirección] to; **voy a Sevilla** I'm going to Seville; **me voy al extranjero** I'm going abroad; **llegó a Barcelona/la fiesta** he arrived in Barcelona/at the party **- 5.** [posición]: **a la puerta** at the door; **está a la derecha/izquierda** it's on the right/left; **a orillas del mar** by the sea **- 6.** [distancia]: **está a más de cien kilómetros de aquí** it's more than a hundred kilometres from here **- 7.** [con complemento indirecto] to; **dáselo a Juan** give it to Juan; **dile a Juan que venga** tell Juan to come **- 8.** [con complemento directo]: **quiere a sus hijos/su gato** she loves her children/her cat **- 9.** [cantidad, medida, precio]: **a cientos/miles/docenas** by the hundred/thousand/dozen; **a 90 km por hora** (at) 90 km per hour; **¿a cuánto están las peras?** how much are the pears?; **tiene las peras a tres euros** she's selling pears for *o* at three euros; **ganaron tres a cero** they won three nil **- 10.** [modo]: **lo hace a la antigua** he does it the old way; **a lo bestia** rudely; **a lo grande** *fam* in style; **a lo Mozart** in Mozart's style; **a cuadros** checked; **a escondidas** secretly; **poco a poco** little by little; **me quieren como a una madre** they love me like a mother **- 11.** [instrumento]: **escribir a máquina** to use a typewriter; **a lápiz** in pencil; **a mano** by hand; **olla a presión** pressure cooker **- 12.** *(después de v y antes de infinitivo)* [finalidad] to; **entró a pagar** he came in to pay; **aprender a nadar** to learn to swim **- 13.** *(después de s y antes de infinitivo)* [complemento de nombre]: **sueldo a convenir** salary to be agreed; **temas a tratar** matters to be discussed **- 14.** *(antes de infinitivo)* [condición]: **a no ser por mí, hubieses fracasado** you wouldn't have done it if it hadn't been for me **- 15.** [en oraciones imperativas]: **¡a la cama!** go to bed!; **¡a callar todo el mundo!** quiet, everyone!; **¡a bailar!** let's dance! **- 16.** *(antes de 'por')* [en busca de]: **ir a por pan** to go for some bread **- 17.** [indica desafío]: **¿a que no lo haces?** I bet you won't do it!

AA *(abrev de* **Alcohólicos Anónimos)** *smpl* AA.

AA EE *sm abrev de* **Asuntos Exteriores.**

ábaco *sm* abacus.

abad, esa *sm, f* abbot *(f* abbess).

abadía *sf* abbey.

abajo ◇ *adv* **- 1.** [posición - gen] below; [- en edificio] downstairs; **vive (en el piso de) abajo** she lives downstairs; **está aquí/allí abajo** it's down here/there; **abajo del todo** right at the bottom; **más abajo** further down **- 2.** [dirección] down; **ve abajo** [en edificio] go downstairs; **hacia/para abajo** down, downwards; **calle/escaleras abajo** down the street/stairs; **río abajo** downstream **- 3.** [en un texto] below. ◇ *interj*: **¡abajo...!** down with...!; **¡abajo la dictadura!** down with the dictatorship!

➤ **abajo de** *loc prep* less than.

➤ **de abajo** *loc adj* bottom; **el estante de abajo** the bottom shelf.

abalanzarse **[13]** *vprnl*: **abalanzarse sobre** to fall upon; **abalanzarse hacia** to rush towards.

abalear *vt Andes, Amér C & Ven* to shoot at.

abalorio *sm* *(gen pl)* - **1.** [cuenta] glass bead - **2.** [bisutería] trinket.

abanderado *sm* *lit & fig* standard-bearer.

abandonado, **da** *adj* - **1.** [desierto] deserted - **2.** [desamparado] abandoned - **3.** [descuidado - persona] unkempt; [- jardín, casa] neglected; **dejar abandonado** to abandon.

abandonar *vt* - **1.** [gen] to abandon; [lugar, profesión, cónyuge] to leave - **2.** [desatender - obligaciones, estudios] to neglect.

abandonarse *vprnl* - **1.** [de aspecto] to neglect o.s., to let o.s. go - **2.** [a una emoción]: **abandonarse a** [desesperación, dolor] to succumb to; [bebida, drogas] to give o.s. over to.

abandono *sm* - **1.** [acción - gen] abandonment; [- de lugar, profesión, cónyuge] leaving; [- de obligaciones, estudios] neglect - **2.** [estado] state of abandon - **3.** DEP: **ganar por abandono** to win by default.

abanicar [10] *vt* to fan.

abanicarse *vprnl* to fan o.s.

abanico *sm* - **1.** [para dar aire] fan - **2.** *fig* [gama] range.

abaratar *vt* to reduce the price of.

abaratarse *vprnl* to go down in price, to become cheaper.

abarcar [10] *vt* - **1.** [incluir] to embrace, to cover; **abarca varios siglos** it covers several centuries; **quien mucho abarca poco aprieta** *prov* don't bite off more than you can chew - **2.** [ver] to be able to see, to have a view of; **desde aquí se abarca todo el valle** you can see the whole valley from here.

abarque *etc* ⊳ **abarcar**.

abarrotado, **da** *adj*: **abarrotado (de)** [teatro, autobús] packed (with); [desván, baúl] crammed (with); **el cine estaba abarrotado** the cinema was packed.

abarrotar *vt*: **abarrotar algo (de o con)** [teatro, autobús] to pack sthg (with); [desván, baúl] to cram sthg full (of).

abarrotería *sf* *Amér C & Méx* grocer's (shop) *UK*, grocery store *US*.

abarrotero, **ra** *sm, f* *Amér C & Méx* grocer.

abarrotes *smpl* *Amér* groceries.

abastecer [30] *vt*: **abastecer algo/a alguien (de)** to supply sthg/sb (with).

abastecerse *vprnl*: **abastecerse (de algo)** to stock up (on sthg).

abastecimiento *sm* [cantidad] supply; [acción] supplying; **abastecimiento de agua** water supply.

abasto *sm*: **no dar abasto para hacer algo** to be unable to cope with doing sthg; **no doy abasto con tanto trabajo** I can't cope with all this work.

abatible *adj* reclining; **de alas abatibles** gatelegged.

abatido, **da** *adj* dejected.

abatir *vt* - **1.** [derribar - muro] to knock down; [- avión] to shoot down - **2.** [desanimar] to depress.

abatirse *vprnl*: **abatirse (sobre)** to swoop (down on).

abdicación *sf* abdication.

abdicar [10] ⟨⟩ *vt*: **abdicar el trono (en alguien)** to abdicate the throne (in favour of sb). ⟨⟩ *vi* to abdicate; **abdicar de algo** *fig* to renounce sthg.

abdomen *sm* abdomen.

abdominal *adj* abdominal.

abdominales *smpl*: **hacer abdominals** to do sit-ups.

abecé *sm* *lit & fig* ABC.

abecedario *sm* - **1.** [alfabeto] alphabet - **2.** [libro] spelling book.

abedul *sm* birch (tree).

abeja *sf* bee; **abeja obrera** worker bee; **abeja reina** queen bee.

abejorro *sm* bumblebee.

aberración *sf* aberration; **eso es una aberración** that's absurd.

aberrante *adj* aberrant.

abertura *sf* opening.

abertzale [aβer'tʃale] *adj & smf* Basque nationalist.

abeto *sm* fir (tree).

abierto, **ta** ⟨⟩ *pp* ⊳ **abrir**. ⟨⟩ *adj* - **1.** [gen] open; **dejar el grifo abierto** to leave the tap on; **llevas la bragueta abierta** your flies are undone; **estar abierto a** to be open to; **bien o muy abierto** wide open - **2.** *fig* [liberal] open-minded.

abigarrado, **da** *adj* multi-coloured; *fig* motley.

abisal *adj* [fosa] deep-sea.

abismal *adj* vast, colossal.

abismar *vt* - **1.** [hundir] to engulf - **2.** [abatir]: **abismar a alguien en algo** to plunge sb into sthg.

abismarse *vprnl*: **abismarse en** [lectura] to be engrossed o absorbed in; [dolor] to abandon o.s. to.

abismo *sm* - **1.** [profundidad] abyss; **estar al borde del abismo** to be on the brink of ruin - **2.** *fig* [diferencia] gulf; **salvar el abismo** to bridge the gulf.

Abiyán *n pr* Abidjan.

abjurar *culto* ⟨⟩ *vt* to abjure. ⟨⟩ *vi*: **abjurar de algo** to abjure sthg.

ablandamiento *sm* softening.

ablandar *vt* - **1.** [material] to soften - **2.** *fig* [persona] to move; [ira] to calm.
◆ **ablandarse** *vprnl* - **1.** [material] to soften, to become softer - **2.** *fig* [persona] to be moved; [ira] to cool off.

ablativo *sm* ablative; **ablativo absoluto** ablative absolute.

ablución *sf (gen pl)* ablution.

ablusado, da *adj* loose, baggy.

abnegación *sf* abnegation, self-denial.

abnegarse [35] *vprnl* to deny o.s.

abobado, da *adj* - **1.** [estupefacto] bewildered - **2.** [estúpido] stupid.

abocado, da *adj*: **abocado a** destined *o* doomed to.

abochornar *vt* to embarrass.
◆ **abochornarse** *vprnl* to get embarrassed.

abofetear *vt* to slap; **abofetear la cara a alguien** to slap sb in the face.

abogacía *sf* legal profession.

abogado, da *sm, f* - **1.** lawyer, attorney *US*; **abogado defensor** counsel for the defence; **abogado del estado** public prosecutor; **abogado laboralista** labour lawyer; **abogado de oficio** legal aid lawyer - **2.** *fig* [intercesor] intermediary; [defensor] advocate; **abogado del diablo** devil's advocate.

abogar [16] *vi* - **1.** DER to plead - **2.** *fig* [defender]: **abogar por algo** to advocate sthg; **abogar por alguien** to stand up for sb.

abolengo *sm* lineage; **de (rancio) abolengo** of ancient lineage.

abolición *sf* abolition.

abolicionismo *sm* abolitionism.

abolicionista *adj* & *smf* abolitionist.

abolir [78] *vt* to abolish.

abolladura *sf* dent.

abollar *vt* to dent.
◆ **abollarse** *vprnl* to get dented.

abombado, da *adj* buckled *o* bulging outwards.

abominable *adj* abominable.

abominación *sf* abomination.

abominar <> *vt* - **1.** [condenar] to condemn - **2.** [detestar] to abhor, to abominate. <> *vi*: **abominar de alguien/algo** [condenar] to condemn sb/sthg.

abonado, da *sm, f* [de teléfono, revista] subscriber; [al fútbol, teatro, transporte] season-ticket holder.

abonar *vt* - **1.** [pagar] to pay; **abonar algo en la cuenta de alguien** to credit sb's account with sthg - **2.** [tierra] to fertilize.
◆ **abonarse** *vprnl*: **abonarse (a)** [revista] to subscribe (to); [fútbol, teatro, transporte] to buy a season ticket (for).

abonero, ra *sm, f Méx* hawker, street trader.

abono *sm* - **1.** [pase] season ticket - **2.** [fertilizante] fertilizer - **3.** [pago] payment - **4.** *Méx* [plazo] instalment; **pagar en abonos** to pay by instalments.

abordable *adj* [persona] approachable; [tema] that can be tackled; [tarea] manageable.

abordaje *sm* NÁUT boarding.

abordar *vt* - **1.** [embarcación] to board - **2.** *fig* [persona] to approach - **3.** *fig* [tema, tarea] to tackle.

aborigen *adj* [indígena] indigenous; [de Australia] aboriginal.
◆ **aborígenes** *smf pl* [población indígena] indigenous population *sing*; [de Australia] aborigines.

aborrecer [30] *vt* [actividad] to abhor; [persona] to loathe.

aborrecible *adj* abhorrent, loathsome.

abortar <> *vi* [MED - espontáneamente] to have a miscarriage, to miscarry; [- intencionadamente] to have an abortion. <> *vt fig* [hacer fracasar] to foil.

abortista *adj* & *smf* abortionist.

abortivo *sm* abortifacient.

aborto *sm* - **1.** [MED - espontáneo] miscarriage; [- intencionado] abortion - **2.** *fam despec* [persona fea] freak.

abotargarse [16] *vprnl* to swell (up).

abotonar *vt* to button up.
◆ **abotonarse** *vprnl* to do one's buttons up; [abrigo, camisa] to button up.

abovedado, da *adj* arched, vaulted.

abr. (*abrev de* **abril**) Apr.

abracadabra *sm* abracadabra.

abrace *etc* ▷ **abrazar**.

abrasador, ra *adj* burning.

abrasar <> *vt* - **1.** [quemar - casa, bosque] to burn down; [- persona, mano, garganta] to burn; **murieron abrasados** they were burned to death - **2.** [desecar - suj: sol, calor, lejía] to scorch; [- suj: sed] to parch. <> *vi* [café etc] to be burning *o* boiling hot.
◆ **abrasarse** *vprnl* [casa, bosque] to burn down; [persona] to burn o.s.; [tierra, planta] to get scorched.

abrasivo, va *adj* abrasive.
◆ **abrasivo** *sm* abrasive.

abrazadera *sf* TECNOL brace, bracket; [en carpintería] clamp.

abrazar [13] *vt* - **1.** [con los brazos] to hug, to embrace; **abrazar fuerte a alguien** to hold sb tight - **2.** *fig* [doctrina] to embrace.
◆ **abrazarse** *vprnl* to hug *o* embrace (each other).

abrazo *sm* embrace, hug; **'un (fuerte) abrazo'** [en cartas] 'best wishes'.

abrebotellas *sm inv* bottle opener.

abrecartas *sm inv* paper knife, letter opener.

abrelatas *sm inv* tin opener *UK*, can opener *US*.

abrevadero *sm* [pila] drinking trough; [natural] watering place.

abrevar *vt* to water, to give water to.

abreviación *sf* [de texto] abridgement; [de viaje, estancia] cutting short.

abreviado, da *adj* [texto] abridged; [viaje, estancia] interrupted.

abreviar [8] ◇ *vt* [gen] to shorten; [texto] to abridge; [palabra] to abbreviate; [viaje, estancia] to cut short. ◇ *vi*: **para abreviar** [al hacer algo] to keep it quick; [al contar algo] to cut a long story short.

abreviatura *sf* abbreviation.

abridor *sm* - **1.** [abrebotellas] (bottle) opener - **2.** [abrelatas] (tin) opener *UK*, (can) opener *US*.

abrigar [16] *vt* - **1.** [arropar - suj: persona] to wrap up; [- suj: ropa] to keep warm - **2.** *fig* [albergar - esperanza] to cherish; [- sospechas, malas intenciones] to harbour.
◆ **abrigarse** *vprnl* - **1.** [arroparse] to wrap up - **2.** [resguardarse]: **abrigarse de** to shelter from.

abrigo *sm* - **1.** [prenda] coat, overcoat - **2.** [refugio] shelter; **al abrigo de** [árbol] under the shelter of; [peligro, ataque] safe from; [lluvia, viento] sheltered from; [ley] under the protection of.

abrigue *etc* ▷ **abrigar**.

abril *sm* April; **tiene 17 abriles** she is 17 (years of age); *ver también* **septiembre**.

abrillantador *sm* polish.

abrillantar *vt* to polish.

abrir ◇ *vt* - **1.** [gen] to open; [alas] to spread; [melón] to cut open - **2.** [agua, gas] to turn on; [luz] to switch on - **3.** [puerta] to unlock, to open; [pestillo] to pull back; [grifo] to turn on; [cremallera] to undo - **4.** [túnel] to dig; [canal, camino] to build; [agujero, surco] to make - **5.**: **abrir el apetito** to whet one's appetite - **6.** [encabezar - lista] to head; [- manifestación] to lead. ◇ *vi* [establecimiento] to open.
◆ **abrirse** *vprnl* - **1.** [sincerarse]: **abrirse a alguien** to open up to sb, to confide in sb - **2.** [comunicarse]: **abrirse (con)** to be more open (with) - **3.** [posibilidades] to open up - **4.** [cielo] to clear - **5.** *mfam* [irse] to clear off.

abrochar *vt* [camisa, botón] to do up; [cinturón] to fasten.
◆ **abrocharse** *vprnl* to do up; [cinturón] to fasten; **¡abróchate!** [el abrigo] do your coat up!

abrogar [16] *vt* to abrogate, to repeal.

abroncar [10] *vt fam* - **1.** [reprender] to tick off, to tell off - **2.** [abuchear] to boo.

abrumador, ra *adj* overwhelming.

abrumar *vt* [agobiar] to overwhelm.

abrupto, ta *adj* [escarpado] sheer; [accidentado] rugged.

ABS (*abrev de* **Antiblockiersystem**) *sm* ABS; **frenos ABS** ABS brakes.

absceso *sm* abscess.

abscisa *sf* x-axis.

absentismo *sm* - **1.** [de trabajador]: **absentismo laboral** [justificado] absence from work; [injustificado] absenteeism - **2.** [de terrateniente] absentee landownership.

ábside *sm* apse.

absolución *sf* - **1.** DER acquittal - **2.** RELIG absolution.

absolutismo *sm* absolutism.

absolutista *adj* & *smf* absolutist.

absoluto, ta *adj* [gen] absolute; [silencio, obediencia] total.
◆ **en absoluto** *loc adv* [en negativas] at all; [tras pregunta] not at all; **¿te gusta? – en absoluto** do you like it? – not at all; **nada en absoluto** nothing at all.

absolver [24] *vt*: **absolver a alguien (de algo)** DER to acquit sb (of sthg); RELIG to absolve sb (of sthg).

absorbente *adj* - **1.** [que empapa] absorbent - **2.** [persona, carácter] demanding - **3.** [actividad] absorbing.

absorber *vt* - **1.** [gen] to absorb - **2.** [ocupar el tiempo de] to take up the time of - **3.** [consumir, gastar] to soak up.

absorción *sf* absorption.

absorto, ta *adj*: **absorto (en)** absorbed o engrossed (in).

abstemio, mia ◇ *adj* teetotal. ◇ *sm, f* teetotaller.

abstención *sf* abstention.

abstencionismo *sm* abstentionism.

abstenerse [72] *vprnl*: **abstenerse (de algo/de hacer algo)** to abstain (from sthg/from doing sthg); **le han recomendado que se abstenga del alcohol** she has been advised to stay off the alcohol.

abstinencia *sf* abstinence.

abstracción *sf* - **1.** [gen] abstraction - **2.** [concentración] concentration.

abstracto, ta *adj* abstract.
◆ **en abstracto** *loc adv* in the abstract.

abstraer [73] *vt* to consider separately, to detach.
◆ **abstraerse** *vprnl*: **abstraerse (de)** to detach o.s. (from).

abstraído, da *adj* lost in thought, engrossed.

abstuviera *etc* ▷ **abstenerse**.

absuelto, **ta** *pp* ▷ **absolver**.

absuelva *etc* ▷ **absolver**.

absurdo, **da** *adj* absurd; **lo absurdo sería que no lo hicieras** it would be absurd for you not to do it.
◆ **absurdo** *sm*: **decir/hacer un absurdo** to say/do something ridiculous.

abubilla *sf* hoopoe.

abuchear *vt* to boo.

abucheo *sm* booing.

abuelo, **la** *sm, f* - **1**. [familiar] grandfather (*f* grandmother); **¡cuéntaselo a tu abuela!** *fam* pull the other one!; **éramos pocos y parió la abuela** *fam* that was all we needed; **no necesitar abuela** *fam* to be full of o.s. - **2**. [anciano] old person, old man (*f* old woman).
◆ **abuelos** *smpl* grandparents.

abuhardillado, **da** *adj* attic *(antes de s)*.

abulia *sf* apathy, lethargy.

abúlico, **ca** ◇ *adj* apathetic, lethargic. ◇ *sm, f* apathetic o lethargic person.

abultado, **da** *adj* [paquete] bulky; [labios] thick; [cantidad, cifra] inflated.

abultar ◇ *vt* - **1**. [hinchar] to swell - **2**. [suj: lente] to magnify - **3**. [exagerar] to blow up. ◇ *vi* - **1**. [ser muy grande] to be bulky - **2**. [tener forma de bulto] to bulge.

abundancia *sf* - **1**. [gran cantidad] abundance; **en abundancia** in abundance - **2**. [riqueza] plenty, prosperity; **nadar** o **vivir en la abundancia** to be filthy rich.

abundante *adj* abundant.

abundar *vi* - **1**. [ser abundante] to abound; **abundaban los niños** there were lots of children there - **2**. [estar de acuerdo]: **abundar en** to agree completely with; [insistir] to go into detail about.

abundoso, **sa** *adj Amér* abundant.

aburguesado, **da** *adj* bourgeois.

aburguesarse *vprnl* to adopt middle-class ways.

aburrido, **da** ◇ *adj* - **1**. [harto, fastidiado] bored; **estar aburrido de hacer algo** to be fed up with doing sthg - **2**. [que aburre] boring. ◇ *sm, f* bore.

aburrimiento *sm* boredom; **¡qué aburrimiento!** what a bore!

aburrir *vt* to bore; **me aburre** I'm bored of it.
◆ **aburrirse** *vprnl* to get bored; [estar aburrido] to be bored.

abusado, **da** *adj Méx* astute, shrewd.

abusar *vi* - **1**. [excederse] to go too far; **abusar de algo** to abuse sthg; **abusar del alcohol** to drink too much; **abusar de alguien** to take advantage of sb - **2**. [forzar sexualmente]: **abusar de alguien** to sexually abuse sb.

abusivo, **va** *adj* [trato] very bad, appalling; [precio] extortionate.

abuso *sm* - **1**. [uso excesivo]: **abuso (de)** abuse (of); **abuso de confianza** breach of confidence; **abusos deshonestos** sexual abuse *(U)* - **2**. [escándalo] scandal.

abusón, **ona** ◇ *adj* self-seeking. ◇ *sm, f* self-seeking person.

abyección *sf culto* abjection.

abyecto, **ta** *adj culto* vile, wretched.

a. C. (*abrev de* antes de Cristo) BC.

acá *adv* - **1**. [lugar] here; **de acá para allá** back and forth; **más acá** closer; **¡ven acá!** come here! - **2**. [tiempo]: **de una semana acá** during the last week; **de un tiempo acá** recently.

acabado, **da** *adj* - **1**. [completo] perfect, consummate - **2**. [fracasado] finished, ruined.
◆ **acabado** *sm* [de producto] finish; [de piso] décor.

acabar ◇ *vt* - **1**. [concluir] to finish - **2**. [consumir - provisiones, dinero] to use up; [- comida] to finish. ◇ *vi* - **1**. [gen] to finish, to end; **la espada acaba en punta** the sword ends in a point; **el asunto acabó mal** the affair finished o ended badly; **cuando acabes, avísame** tell me when you've finished; **acabar de hacer algo** to finish doing sthg - **2**. [haber hecho recientemente]: **acabar de hacer algo** to have just done sthg; **acabo de llegar** I've just arrived - **3**. [terminar por - persona]: **acabar por hacer algo**, **acabar haciendo algo** to end up doing sthg - **4**. [destruir]: **acabar con** [gen] to destroy; [salud] to ruin; [paciencia] to exhaust; [violencia, crimen] to put an end to - **5**. [matar]: **acabar con alguien** to kill sb; *fig* to be the death of sb - **6**. (con adjetivos) to end up; **acabar loco** to go mad - **7**. (en frase negativa): **no acabo de entenderlo** I can't quite understand it; **no acaba de parecerme bien** I don't really think it's a very good idea - **8**. *loc*: **de nunca acabar** never-ending.
◆ **acabarse** *vprnl* - **1**. [agotarse] to be used up, to be gone; **se nos ha acabado el petróleo** we're out of petrol; **se ha acabado la comida** there's no more food left, all the food has gone - **2**. [concluir] to finish, to be over - **3**. *loc*: **¡se acabó!** [¡basta ya!] that's enough!; [se terminó] that's it, then!

acabose *sm fam*: **¡es el acabose!** it really is the limit!

acacia *sf* acacia.

academia *sf* - **1**. [para aprender] school - **2**. [institución] academy.

➤ **Real Academia Española** *sf institution that sets lexical and syntactical standards for Spanish.*

académico, ca ◇ *adj* academic. ◇ *sm, f* academician.

acaecer *v impers culto* to take place, to occur.

acallar *vt* to silence.

acalorado, da *adj* - **1.** [por cansancio] flushed (with effort) - **2.** [por calor] hot - **3.** [apasionado - debate] heated; [- persona] hot under the collar; [- defensor] fervent.

acalorar *vt* - **1.** [dar calor] to (make) warm - **2.** [enfadar]: **acalorar a alguien** to make sb hot under the collar.

➤ **acalorarse** *vprnl* - **1.** [calentarse] to get hot - **2.** [enfadarse] to get aroused *o* excited.

acampada *sf* - **1.** [acción] camping - **2.** [lugar] camp site.

acampanado, da *adj* flared.

acampar *vi* to camp.

acanalado, da *adj* [columna] fluted; [tejido] ribbed; [hierro, uralita] corrugated.

acanalar *vt* - **1.** [terreno] to dig channels in - **2.** [tejado] to corrugate.

acantilado *sm* cliff.

acanto *sm* acanthus.

acaparador, ra *adj* greedy.

acaparamiento *sm* monopolization.

acaparar *vt* - **1.** [monopolizar] to monopolize; [mercado] to corner; **acaparaba las miradas de todos** all eyes were on her - **2.** [guardarse] to hoard.

acápite *sm Amér* paragraph.

acaramelado, da *adj* - **1.** [con caramelo] covered in caramel - **2.** *fig* [pegajoso] sickly sweet - **3.** *fig* [cariñoso] starry-eyed; **estaban acaramelados** they were all lovey-dovey.

acaramelar *vt* to cover in caramel.

➤ **acaramelarse** *vprnl* to be starry-eyed.

acariciar [8] *vt* - **1.** [persona] to caress; [animal] to stroke - **2.** *fig* [idea, proyecto] to cherish.

➤ **acariciarse** *vprnl* to caress (each other).

acarrear *vt* - **1.** [transportar] to carry; [carbón] to haul - **2.** *fig* [ocasionar] to bring, to give rise to.

acartonarse *vprnl fam* to become wizened.

acaso *adv* perhaps; **¿acaso no lo sabías?** are you trying to tell me you didn't know?; **por si acaso** (just) in case; **¿acaso es culpa mía?** is it my fault?

➤ **si acaso** ◇ *loc adv* [en todo caso] if anything. ◇ *loc conj* [en caso de que] if.

acatamiento *sm* respect, compliance.

acatar *vt* to respect, to comply with.

acatarrarse *vprnl* to catch a cold.

acaudalado, da *adj* well-to-do, wealthy.

acaudillar *vt* to lead.

acceder *vi* - **1.** [consentir]: **acceder (a algo/hacer algo)** to agree (to sthg/to do sthg) - **2.** [tener acceso]: **acceder a** to enter - **3.** [alcanzar]: **acceder a** [trono] to accede to; [poder] to come to; [cargo] to obtain.

accesible *adj* - **1.** [lugar] accessible - **2.** [persona] approachable.

accésit *sm inv* runners-up prize, consolation prize.

acceso *sm* - **1.** [entrada]: **acceso (a)** entrance (to) - **2.** [paso]: **acceso (a)** access (to); **acceso a Internet** Internet access; **acceso remoto** remote access - **3.** [carretera] access road, ramp *US* - **4.** *fig & MED* [de tos] fit; [de fiebre, gripe] bout.

accesorio, ria *adj* incidental.

➤ **accesorio** *(gen pl) sm* accessory.

accidentado, da ◇ *adj* - **1.** [vida, viaje] eventful - **2.** [terreno, camino] rough, rugged. ◇ *sm, f* injured person, victim.

accidental *adj* - **1.** [no esencial] incidental - **2.** [imprevisto] accidental; [encuentro] chance.

accidentarse *vprnl* to be involved in *o* have an accident.

accidente *sm* - **1.** [desgracia] accident; **accidente de avión/coche** plane/car crash; **accidente laboral/mortal** industrial/fatal accident; **accidente de tráfico** road accident - **2.** *(gen pl)* [del terreno] unevenness *(U)* - **3.** *GRAM* accidence.

acción *sf* - **1.** [gen] action; **entrar en acción** to go into action; **película de acción** action film *UK o* movie *US* - **2.** [hecho] deed, act; **acción de gracias** *RELIG* thanksgiving - **3.** *FIN* share; **acción ordinaria/preferente** ordinary/preference share; **acciones en cartera** shares in portfolio.

accionar *vt* to activate.

accionariado *sm* shareholders *pl*.

accionista *smf* shareholder.

acebo *sm* - **1.** [hoja] holly - **2.** [árbol] holly (bush).

acechanza *sf* observation, surveillance.

acechar *vt* - **1.** [vigilar] to observe, to keep under surveillance; [suj: cazador] to stalk - **2.** [amenazar] to be lying in wait for.

acecho *sm* observation, surveillance; **estar al acecho de** to lie in wait for; *fig* to be on the lookout for.

acedera *sf* sorrel.

acéfalo, la *adj* [estado, organización] leaderless.

aceitar *vt* [motor] to lubricate; [comida] to pour oil onto.

aceite *sm* oil; **aceite de colza/girasol/oliva** rapeseed/sunflower/olive oil; **aceite de ricino/de hígado de bacalao** castor/cod-liver oil.

aceitera *sf* oil can.

➤ **aceiteras** *sfpl* cruet *sing*.

aceitoso, **sa** *adj* oily.

aceituna *sf* olive; **aceituna rellena** stuffed olive.

aceitunado, **da** *adj* olive.

aceitunero, **ra** *sm*, *f* - **1.** [campesino] olive picker - **2.** [vendedor] olive merchant.

aceituno *sm* olive tree.

aceleración *sf* acceleration.

acelerado, **da** *adj* rapid, quick; FÍS accelerated.

acelerador, **ra** *adj* accelerating.

➤ **acelerador** *sm* accelerator.

acelerar ◇ *vt* - **1.** [avivar] to speed up; TECNOL to accelerate - **2.** [adelantar] to bring forward. ◇ *vi* to accelerate.

➤ **acelerarse** *vprnl* to hurry up.

acelerón *sm*: **dar un acelerón** AUTO to put one's foot down.

acelga *sf* chard.

acendrado, **da** *adj* untarnished, pure.

acendrar *vt* - **1.** [metal] to purify - **2.** *fig* [cualidad, sentimiento] to refine.

acento *sm* - **1.** [gen] accent; **acento agudo/circunflejo/grave** acute/circumflex/grave accent; **acento ortográfico** (written) accent - **2.** [intensidad] stress, accent.

acentuación *sf* accentuation.

acentuado, **da** *adj* - **1.** [con acento gráfico] stressed - **2.** [marcado] marked, distinct.

acentuar [6] *vt* - **1.** [palabra, letra - al escribir] to accent, to put an accent on; [- al hablar] to stress - **2.** *fig* [realzar] to accentuate - **3.** *fig* [intensificar] to increase.

➤ **acentuarse** *vprnl* [intensificarse] to deepen, to increase.

acepción *sf* meaning, sense.

aceptable *adj* acceptable.

aceptación *sf* - **1.** [aprobación] acceptance - **2.** [éxito] success, popularity.

aceptar *vt* to accept.

acequia *sf* irrigation channel.

acera *sf* - **1.** [para peatones] pavement UK, sidewalk US; **ser de la otra acera, ser de la acera de enfrente** *fam despec* to be one of them, to be queer - **2.** [lado de la calle] side of the street.

acerado, **da** *adj* - **1.** [cortante] sharp - **2.** [con acero] containing steel - **3.** *fig* [fuerte, resistente] steely, tough - **4.** [mordaz] cutting, biting.

acerar *vt* - **1.** [pavimentar] to pave - **2.** [convertir en acero] to turn into steel - **3.** [recubrir de acero] to steel.

acerbo, **ba** *adj* *culto* - **1.** [áspero] bitter - **2.** [mordaz] caustic, cutting.

acerca ➤ **acerca de** *loc adv* about.

acercamiento *sm* [de personas, estados] rapprochement; [de suceso, fecha] approach.

acercar [10] *vt* to bring nearer o closer; **¡acércame el pan!** could you pass me the bread?

➤ **acercarse** *vprnl* - **1.** [arrimarse - viniendo] to come closer; [- yendo] to go over - **2.** [ir] to go; [venir] to come; [a casa de alguien] to come/go round - **3.** [tiempo] to draw nearer, to approach.

acería *sf* steelworks *sing*.

acero *sm* steel; **acero inoxidable** stainless steel.

acerque *etc* ➡ **acercar**.

acérrimo, **ma** *adj* [defensor] diehard *(antes de s)*; [enemigo] bitter.

acertado, **da** *adj* - **1.** [con acierto - respuesta] correct; [- disparo] on target; [- comentario] appropriate - **2.** [oportuno] good, clever.

acertante ◇ *adj* winning. ◇ *smf* winner.

acertar [19] ◇ *vt* - **1.** [adivinar] to guess (correctly) - **2.** [el blanco] to hit - **3.** [elegir bien] to choose well. ◇ *vi* - **1.** [atinar]: **acertar (al hacer algo)** to be right (to do sthg) - **2.** [conseguir]: **acertar a hacer algo** to manage to do sthg; **acertaba a pasar por allí** *fig* she happened to pass that way; **no acierto a comprenderlo** I just can't understand it - **3.** [hallar]: **acertar con** to find.

acertijo *sm* riddle.

acervo *sm* [patrimonio] heritage.

acetato *sm* acetate.

acético, **ca** *adj* acetic.

acetileno *sm* acetylene.

acetona *sf* acetone.

achacar [10] *vt*: **achacar algo a alguien/algo** to attribute sthg to sb/sthg.

achacoso, **sa** *adj* - **1.** [persona] frail - **2.** [cosa] faulty, defective.

achampañado, **da** *adj* sparkling.

achantar *vt* *fam* to put the wind up.

➤ **achantarse** *vprnl* *fam* to get the wind up.

achaparrado, **da** *adj* squat.

achaque ◇ *sm* ailment. ◇ *v* ➡ **achacar**.

achatado, **da** *adj* flattened.

achatar *vt* to flatten.

➤ **achatarse** *vprnl* to level out.

achicar [10] *vt* - **1.** [tamaño] to make smaller - **2.** [agua - de barco] to bale out; [- de mina] to drain - **3.** *fig* [acobardar] to intimidate.

achicarse *vprnl* [acobardarse] to become intimidated.

achicharrar ◇ *vt* [chamuscar] to burn. ◇ *vi* [sol, calor] to be scorching.

◆ **achicharrarse** *vprnl* - **1.** *fig* [de calor] to fry, to roast - **2.** [chamuscarse] to burn.

achicoria *sf* chicory.

achinado, **da** *adj* - **1.** [ojos] slanting - **2.** [persona] Chinese-looking - **3.** *R Dom* [como indio] Indian-looking.

achique *etc* ⊳ **achicar**.

achispar *vt* to make tipsy.

◆ **achisparse** *vprnl* to get tipsy.

achuchado, **da** *adj fam* hard, tough.

achuchar *vt fam* - **1.** [abrazar] to hug - **2.** *fig* [presionar] to be on at, to badger.

achuchón *sm fam* - **1.** [abrazo] big hug - **2.** [indisposición] mild illness; **le dio un achuchón** he took sick.

achunchar *vt Andes* [avergonzar] to shame.

◆ **achuncharse** *vprnl* [avergonzarse] to be shamed.

aciago, **ga** *adj culto* black, fateful.

acicalado, **da** *adj* neat and tidy.

acicalar *vt* [arreglar] to do up.

◆ **acicalarse** *vprnl* to do o.s. up.

acicate *sm* - **1.** [espuela] spur - **2.** *fig* [estímulo] incentive.

acidez *sf* - **1.** [cualidad] acidity - **2.** MED: **acidez (de estómago)** heartburn.

ácido, **da** *adj* - **1.** QUÍM acidic - **2.** [bebida, sabor, carácter] acid, sour.

◆ **ácido** *sm* - **1.** QUÍM acid; **ácido clorhídrico/ desoxirribonucleico/ribonucleico/sulfúrico** hydrochloric/deoxyribonucleic/ribonucleic/ sulphuric acid - **2.** *fam* [droga] acid.

acierta *etc* ⊳ **acertar**.

acierto *sm* - **1.** [a pregunta] correct answer - **2.** [en quinielas] correct entry - **3.** [habilidad, tino] good *o* sound judgment - **4.** [éxito] success.

ácimo, **ázimo** *adj* [pan] unleavened.

acimut (*pl* **acimutes**), **azimut** (*pl* **azimutes**) *sm* azimuth.

aclamación *sf* [ovación] acclamation, acclaim; **por aclamación** unanimously; **entre aclamaciones** to great acclaim.

aclamar *vt* to acclaim.

aclaración *sf* explanation.

aclarado *sm* rinsing, rinse.

aclarar ◇ *vt* - **1.** [ropa] to rinse - **2.** [explicar] to clarify, to explain - **3.**: **aclarar la voz** [carraspeando] to clear one's throat - **4.** [lo oscuro] to make lighter - **5.** [lo espeso - chocolate, sopa] to thin (down); [- bosque] to thin out.

◇ *v impers* - **1.** [amanecer] to get light - **2.** [clarear, despejarse] to clear up.

◆ **aclararse** *vprnl* - **1.** [entender] to understand - **2.** [explicarse] to explain o.s. - **3.** [ver claro] to see clearly.

aclaratorio, **ria** *adj* explanatory.

aclimatación *sf* acclimatization.

aclimatar *vt* - **1.** [al clima]: **aclimatar algo/a alguien (a)** to acclimatize sthg/sb (to) - **2.** [al ambiente]: **aclimatar algo/a alguien a algo** to get sthg/sb used to sthg.

◆ **aclimatarse** *vprnl* - **1.** [al clima]: **aclimatarse (a algo)** to acclimatize (to sthg) - **2.** [al ambiente] to settle in; **aclimatarse a algo** to get used to sthg.

acné *sm* acne.

acobardar *vt* to frighten, to scare.

◆ **acobardarse** *vprnl* to get frightened *o* scared; **acobardarse ante** to shrink back from.

acodado, **da** *adj* [cañería] elbowed.

acodarse *vprnl*: **acodarse (en)** to lean (on).

acogedor, **ra** *adj* [país, persona] friendly, welcoming; [casa, ambiente] cosy.

acoger [14] *vt* - **1.** [recibir] to welcome - **2.** [dar refugio] to take in - **3.** *fig* [idea, noticia etc] to receive; [campeonato] to host.

◆ **acogerse a** *vprnl* [inmunidad parlamentaria etc] to take refuge in; [ley] to have recourse to.

acogida *sf* reception; **acogida familiar** fostering.

acoja *etc* ⊳ **acoger**.

acojonante *adj vulg* - **1.** [impresionante] bloody incredible - **2.** [que da miedo] shit scary.

acojonar *vulg* ◇ *vt* - **1.** [asustar] to scare shitless - **2.** [impresionar] to gobsmack. ◇ *vi* [asustar] to be shit scary.

◆ **acojonarse** *vprnl vulg* to be shit scared.

acolchado, **da** *adj* padded.

acolchar *vt* to pad.

acólito *sm* - **1.** [seguidor] acolyte - **2.** [monaguillo] altar boy.

acometer ◇ *vt* - **1.** [atacar] to attack; **le acometieron las dudas** he was assailed by doubts - **2.** [emprender] to undertake. ◇ *vi* [embestir]: **acometer contra** to hurtle into.

acometida *sf* - **1.** [ataque] attack, charge - **2.** [de luz, gas etc] (mains) connection.

acomodadizo, **za** *adj* accommodating.

acomodado, **da** *adj* - **1.** [rico] well-off, well-to-do - **2.** [instalado] ensconced.

acomodador, **ra** *sm, f* usher (*f* usherette).

acomodar *vt* - **1.** [instalar - persona] to seat, to instal; [- cosa] to place - **2.** [adaptar] to fit.

➡ **acomodarse** *vprnl* - **1.** [instalarse] to make o.s. comfortable; **acomodarse en** to settle down in - **2.** [conformarse]: **acomodarse a** to adapt to.

acomodaticio, **cia** *adj* [complaciente] accommodating.

acomodo *sm* [alojamiento] accommodation.

acompañamiento *sm* - **1.** [comitiva - en entierro] cortege; [- de rey] retinue - **2.** CULIN & MÚS accompaniment.

acompañante *smf* [compañero] companion; MÚS accompanist.

acompañar ⟨⟩ *vt* - **1.** [ir con]: **acompañar a alguien** [gen] to go with *o* accompany sb; [a la puerta] to show sb out; [a casa] to walk sb home; **te acompaño** I'll come with you - **2.** [estar con]: **acompañar a alguien** to keep sb company - **3.** [compartir emociones con]: **acompañar en algo a alguien** to be with sb in sthg; **lo acompaño en el sentimiento** please accept my condolences - **4.** [adjuntar] to enclose - **5.** MÚS to accompany - **6.** [coexistir con] to accompany - **7.** CULIN: **acompañar algo con algo** to serve sthg with sthg. ⟨⟩ *vi* [hacer compañía] to provide company.

➡ **acompañarse** *vprnl* MÚS: **acompañarse con** to accompany o.s. on.

acompasado, **da** *adj* [movimiento] steady, rhythmic; [pasos] measured.

acompasar *vt*: **acompasar algo (a)** to synchronize sthg (with).

acomplejado, **da** ⟨⟩ *adj* inhibited, having a complex. ⟨⟩ *sm*, *f* inhibited person, person with a complex.

acomplejar *vt* to give a complex.

➡ **acomplejarse** *vprnl* to develop a complex.

acondicionado, **da** *adj* equipped; **estar bien/mal acondicionado** to be in a fit/no fit state; **aire acondicionado** air conditioned.

acondicionador *sm* - **1.** [de aire] (air) conditioner - **2.** [de pelo] conditioner.

acondicionamiento *sm* conditioning, conversion, upgrading.

acondicionar *vt* - **1.** [reformar] to condition, to convert, to upgrade - **2.** [preparar] to prepare, to get ready.

aconfesional *adj* with no official religion.

acongojar *vt* to distress, to cause anguish to.

➡ **acongojarse** *vprnl* to be distressed.

aconsejable *adj* advisable.

aconsejar *vt* - **1.** [dar consejos]: **aconsejar a alguien (que haga algo)** to advise sb (to do sthg); **te aconsejo que vayas al médico** I'd advise you to see a doctor - **2.** [hacer aconsejable] to make advisable.

acontecer *v impers* to take place, to happen.

acontecimiento *sm* event; **adelantarse** *o* **anticiparse a los acontecimientos** to jump the gun; [prevenir] to take preemptive measures.

acopiar [8] *vt* [juntar] to gather; [acaparar] to buy up.

acopio *sm* stock, store; **hacer acopio de** [existencias, comestibles] to stock up on; [valor, paciencia] to summon up.

acoplable *adj*: **acoplable (a)** attachable (to).

acoplamiento *sm* [de piezas] attachment, connection; [de módulo espacial] docking.

acoplar *vt* - **1.** [encajar] to attach, to fit together - **2.** FERROC to couple - **3.** *fig* [adaptar] to adapt, to fit.

➡ **acoplarse** *vprnl* - **1.** [adaptarse] to adjust to each other; **acoplarse a** to adjust to - **2.** [encajar] to fit together.

acoquinar *vt fam* to put the wind up.

➡ **acoquinarse** *vprnl fam* to get the wind up.

acorazado, **da** *adj* armour-plated.

➡ **acorazado** *sm* battleship.

acorazar [13] *vt* to armour-plate, to armour.

acordar [23] *vt*: **acordar algo/hacer algo** to agree on sthg/to do sthg.

➡ **acordarse** *vprnl*: **acordarse (de algo/de hacer algo)** to remember (sthg/to do sthg); **acordarse de haber hecho algo** to remember doing sthg.

acorde ⟨⟩ *adj* - **1.** [conforme] in agreement - **2.** [en consonancia]: **acorde con** in keeping with. ⟨⟩ *sm* MÚS chord.

acordeón *sm* accordion.

acordonado, **da** *adj* cordoned off.

acordonar *vt* - **1.** [zapatos] to do *o* lace up - **2.** [lugar] to cordon off.

acornear *vt* to gore.

acorralamiento *sm* [de malhechor, animal de caza] cornering.

acorralar *vt lit & fig* to corner.

acortar *vt* - **1.** [falda, pantalón etc] to take up; [cable] to shorten - **2.** [plazo, vacaciones] to cut short - **3.** [extensión] to shorten.

➡ **acortarse** *vprnl* [días] to get shorter; [reunión] to end early.

acosador, **ra** *adj* relentless, persistent.

acosamiento *sm* harassment.

acosar *vt* - **1.** [hostigar] to harass - **2.** [perseguir] to pursue relentlessly.

acoso *sm* - **1.** [hostigamiento] harassment; **acoso sexual** sexual harassment - **2.** [persecución] relentless pursuit.

acostar [23] *vt* - **1.** [en la cama] to put to bed - **2.** NÁUT to bring alongside.

◆ **acostarse** *vprnl* - **1.** [irse a la cama] to go to bed - **2.** [tumbarse] to lie down - **3.** *fam* [tener relaciones sexuales]: **acostarse con alguien** to sleep with sb.

acostumbrado, da *adj* - **1.** [habitual] usual - **2.** [habituado]: **estamos acostumbrados** we're used to it; **estar acostumbrado a** to be used to.

acostumbrar ◇ *vt* [habituar]: **acostumbrar a alguien a algo/a hacer algo** to get sb used to sthg/to doing sthg. ◇ *vi* [soler]: **acostumbrar a hacer algo** to be in the habit of doing sthg; **acostumbro a levantarme temprano** I usually get up early.

◆ **acostumbrarse** *vprnl* [habituarse]: **terminé acostumbrándome** I got used to it eventually; **acostumbrarse a algo/a hacer algo** to get used to sthg/to doing sthg.

acotación *sf* - **1.** [nota] note in the margin - **2.** TEATRO stage direction.

acotado, da *adj* enclosed.

acotamiento *sm* - **1.** [de terreno, campo] enclosing, demarcation - **2.** *Méx* [arcén] hard shoulder.

acotar *vt* - **1.** [terreno, campo] to enclose, to demarcate; *fig* [tema etc] to delimit - **2.** [texto] to write notes in the margin of.

acotejar *vt* *Amér* to arrange.

ácrata *adj* & *smf* anarchist.

acre ◇ *adj* - **1.** [olor] acrid, pungent - **2.** [sabor] bitter - **3.** *fig* [brusco, desagradable] caustic. ◇ *sm* acre.

acrecentar [19] *vt* to increase.

◆ **acrecentarse** *vprnl* to increase.

acreditación *sf* [credencial] credential.

acreditado, da *adj* - **1.** [médico, abogado etc] distinguished; [marca] reputable - **2.** [embajador, representante] accredited.

acreditar *vt* - **1.** [certificar] to certify; [autorizar] to authorize - **2.** [confirmar] to confirm - **3.** [dar fama] to be a credit to - **4.** [embajador] to accredit - **5.** FIN to credit.

acreedor, ra ◇ *adj*: **hacerse acreedor de algo** to earn sthg, to show o.s. to be worthy of sthg. ◇ *sm, f* creditor.

acribillar *vt* - **1.** [agujerear] to perforate - **2.** [herir]: **acribillar (a)** to pepper *o* riddle (with); **acribillar a balazos** to riddle with bullets; **me han acribillado los mosquitos** the mosquitoes have bitten me all over - **3.** *fam fig* [molestar]: **acribillar a alguien a preguntas** to pester sb with questions.

acrílico, ca *adj* acrylic.

acrimonia = **acritud**.

acristalar *vt* to glaze.

acritud, acrimonia *sf* - **1.** [de olor] acridity, pungency; [de sabor] bitterness - **2.** *fig* [mordacidad] venom - **3.** [desavenencia] acrimony.

acrobacia *sf* - **1.** [en circo] acrobatics *pl* - **2.** [de avión] aerobatic manoeuvre.

acróbata *smf* acrobat.

acrobático, ca *adj* acrobatic.

acrónimo *sm* acronym.

acrópolis *sf inv* acropolis.

acta *sf (el)* - **1.** [de junta, reunión] minutes *pl*; **constar en acta** to be recorded in the minutes; **levantar acta** to take the minutes - **2.** [de defunción etc] certificate; **acta notarial** affidavit - **3.**: **acta (de nombramiento)** certificate of appointment.

◆ **actas** *sfpl* minutes.

actitud *sf* - **1.** [disposición de ánimo] attitude - **2.** [postura] posture, position.

activación *sf* activation.

activar *vt* - **1.** [gen] to activate - **2.** [explosivo] to detonate - **3.** [estimular] to stimulate; [acelerar] to speed up.

actividad *sf* [acción] activity; [trabajo] work; **desplegar una gran actividad** to be in a flurry of activity; **en actividad** active; **actividades extraescolares** extracurricular activities.

activismo *sm* activism.

activista *smf* activist.

activo, va *adj* - **1.** [gen & GRAM] active - **2.** [trabajador] hard-working - **3.** [que trabaja] working; **en activo** [en funciones] on active service - **4.** [rápido] fast-acting.

◆ **activo** *sm* FIN assets *pl*; **activo fijo/líquido/financiero** fixed/liquid/financial assets; **activo y pasivo** assets and liabilities.

acto *sm* - **1.** [acción] act; **hacer acto de presencia** to show one's face; **acto reflejo** reflex action; **acto sexual** sexual act, sexual intercourse *(U)*; **acto de solidaridad** show of solidarity - **2.** [ceremonia] ceremony - **3.** TEATRO act.

◆ **acto seguido** *loc adv* immediately after.

◆ **en el acto** *loc adv* on the spot, there and then; **'fotos de carné en el acto'** 'passport photos while you wait'; **murió en el acto** she died instantly.

actor, triz *sm, f* actor (*f* actress).

actuación *sf* - **1.** [conducta, proceder] conduct, behaviour - **2.** [interpretación] performance - **3.** DER proceedings *pl*.

actual *adj* - **1.** [existente] present, current - **2.** [de moda] modern, present-day - **3.** [de actualidad] topical.

actualidad *sf* - **1.** [momento presente] current situation; **de actualidad** [moderno] in fashion; [de interés actual] topical; **en la actualidad** at the present time, these days - **2.** [vigencia] relevance to modern society - **3.** [noticia] news *(U)*; **ser actualidad** to be making the news.

actualización *sf* [de información] updating; [de tecnología, industria] modernization; INFORM upgrade.

actualizar [**13**] *vt* [información] to update; [tecnología, industria] to modernize; INFORM to upgrade.

actualmente *adv* [hoy día] these days, nowadays; [en este momento] at the (present) moment.

actuar [**6**] *vi* - **1.** [gen] to act; **actuar de** to act as - **2.** DER to undertake proceedings.

actuario, ria *sm, f* - **1.** DER clerk of the court - **2.** FIN: **actuario de seguros** actuary.

acuarela *sf* watercolour.

acuarelista *smf* watercolourist.

acuario *sm* aquarium.

◆ **acuario** ⟨⟩ *sm* [zodiaco] Aquarius; **ser acuario** to be (an) Aquarius. ⟨⟩ *smf* [persona] Aquarius.

acuartelamiento *sm* - **1.** [acción] confinement to barracks - **2.** [lugar] barracks *pl*.

acuartelar *vt* to confine to barracks.

acuático, ca *adj* aquatic.

acuchillar *vt* - **1.** [apuñalar] to stab - **2.** [mueble, parqué] to grind down.

acuciante *adj culto* urgent, pressing.

acuciar [**8**] *vt culto* [suj: persona] to goad; [suj: necesidad, deseo] to press.

acuclillarse *vprnl* to squat (down).

acudir *vi* - **1.** [ir] to go; [venir] to come - **2.** [recurrir]: **acudir a** to go o turn to - **3.** [presentarse]: **acudir (a)** [escuela, iglesia] to attend; [cita, examen] to turn up (for); *fig* [memoria, mente] to come (to).

acueducto *sm* aqueduct.

acuerda *etc* ⊳ **acordar**.

acuerdo *sm* agreement; **de acuerdo** all right, O.K.; **de acuerdo con** [conforme a] in accordance with; **estar de acuerdo (con alguien/en hacer algo)** to agree (with sb/to do sthg); **llegar a un acuerdo, ponerse de acuerdo** to reach agreement; **por común acuerdo** by common consent; **acuerdo marco** framework agreement; **acuerdo de paz** peace agreement.

acuesta *etc* ⊳ **acostar**.

acumulación *sf* accumulation.

acumulador *sm* accumulator.

acumular *vt* to accumulate.

◆ **acumularse** *vprnl* to accumulate, to build up.

acunar *vt* to rock.

acuñar *vt* - **1.** [moneda] to mint - **2.** [palabra] to coin.

acuoso, sa *adj* watery.

acupuntor, ra *sm, f* acupuncturist.

acupuntura *sf* acupuncture.

acurrucarse [**10**] *vprnl* [por frío] to huddle up; [en sitio agradable] to curl up.

acusación *sf* - **1.** [inculpación] charge - **2.** [abogado]: **la acusación** the prosecution.

acusado, da ⟨⟩ *adj* [marcado] marked, distinct. ⟨⟩ *sm, f* [procesado] accused, defendant.

acusador, ra *adj* accusing.

acusar *vt* - **1.** [culpar] to accuse; DER to charge; **acusar a alguien de algo** [gen] to accuse sb of sthg; DER to charge sb with sthg - **2.** [mostrar] to show - **3.** [padecer] to be susceptible to - **4.** [recibo] to acknowledge.

◆ **acusarse** *vprnl* - **1.** [mutuamente] to blame one another - **2.** [uno mismo]: **acusarse de haber hecho algo** to confess to having done sthg.

acusativo *sm* accusative.

acusatorio, ria *adj* DER accusatory.

acuse ◆ **acuse de recibo** *sm* acknowledgement of receipt.

acusica *smf fam* telltale.

acústico, ca *adj* acoustic.

◆ **acústica** *sf* - **1.** [ciencia] acoustics *(U)* - **2.** [de local] acoustics *pl*.

AD *sf* (*abrev de* **Acción Democrática**) Venezuelan political party.

adagio *sm* - **1.** [sentencia breve] adage - **2.** MÚS adagio.

adalid *sm* champion.

adaptación *sf* - **1.** [aclimatación]: **adaptación (a)** adjustment (to) - **2.** [modificación] adaptation.

adaptado, da *adj*: **adaptado (a)** suited (to).

adaptador *smf* ELECTR adapter.

adaptar *vt* - **1.** [acomodar, ajustar] to adjust - **2.** [modificar] to adapt.

◆ **adaptarse** *vprnl*: **adaptarse (a)** to adjust (to).

adecentar *vt* to tidy up.

◆ **adecentarse** *vprnl* to make o.s. decent.

adecuado, da *adj* appropriate, suitable.

adecuar [**7**] *vt* to adapt.

◆ **adecuarse a** *vprnl* - **1.** [ser adecuado] to be appropriate for - **2.** [adaptarse] to adjust to.

adefesio *sm fam* - **1.** [persona fea] fright, sight - **2.** [cosa fea] eyesore, monstrosity.

a. de JC., a.JC. (*abrev de* antes de Jesucristo) BC.

adelantado, da *adj* advanced; **llevo el reloj adelantado** my watch is fast; **por adelantado** in advance.

adelantamiento *sm* AUTO overtaking.

adelantar ◇ *vt* - **1.** [dejar atrás] to overtake - **2.** [mover hacia adelante] to move forward; [pie, reloj] to put forward - **3.** [en el tiempo - trabajo, viaje] to bring forward; [- dinero] to pay in advance - **4.** [conseguir]: **¿qué adelantas con eso?** what do you hope to gain *o* achieve by that? ◇ *vi* - **1.** [progresar] to make progress - **2.** [reloj] to be fast.
◆ **adelantarse** *vprnl* - **1.** [en el tiempo] to be early; [frío, verano] to arrive early; [reloj] to gain; **adelantarse a alguien** to beat sb to it - **2.** [en el espacio] to go on ahead.

adelante ◇ *adv* forward, ahead; **(de ahora) en adelante** from now on, in future; **más adelante** [en el tiempo] later (on); [en el espacio] further on. ◇ *interj*: **¡adelante!** [¡siga!] go ahead!; [¡pase!] come in!

adelanto *sm* advance.

adelfa *sf* oleander.

adelgazamiento *sm* slimming.

adelgazante *adj* slimming.

adelgazar [13] ◇ *vi* to lose weight, to slim. ◇ *vt* to lose.

ademán *sm* [gesto - con manos etc] gesture; [- con cara] face, expression; **en ademán de** as if to.
◆ **ademanes** *smpl* [modales] manners.

además *adv* [con énfasis] moreover, besides; [también] also; **además de** as well as, in addition to.

adentrarse *vprnl*: **adentrarse en** [jungla etc] to enter the heart of; [tema etc] to study in depth.

adentro *adv* inside; **tierra adentro** inland; **mar adentro** out to sea.
◆ **adentros** *smpl*: **para mis/tus** etc **adentros** to myself/yourself etc.

adepto, ta ◇ *adj* [partidario] supporting; **ser adepto a** to be a follower of. ◇ *sm, f*: **adepto (a)** follower (of).

aderezar [13] *vt* - **1.** [sazonar - ensalada] to dress; [- comida] to season - **2.** [adornar] to deck out.

aderezo *sm* - **1.** [aliño - de ensalada] dressing; [- de comida] seasoning - **2.** [adorno] adornment.

adeudar *vt* - **1.** [deber] to owe - **2.** COM to debit.
◆ **adeudarse** *vprnl* to get into debt.

adherencia *sf* [de sellos, pegatina] stickiness, adhesion; [de ruedas] roadholding.

adherente *adj* adhesive, sticky.

adherir [27] *vt* to stick.
◆ **adherirse** *vprnl* - **1.** [pegarse] to stick - **2.** [mostrarse de acuerdo]: **adherirse a** to adhere to - **3.** [afiliarse]: **adherirse a** to join.

adhesión *sf* [apoyo] support.

adhesivo, va *adj* adhesive.
◆ **adhesivo** *sm* - **1.** [pegatina] sticker - **2.** [sustancia] adhesive.

adhiera etc ⊳ **adherir**.

adhiriera etc ⊳ **adherir**.

adicción *sf*: **adicción (a)** addiction (to).

adición *sf* addition.

adicional *adj* additional.

adicionar *vt* to add.

adicto, ta ◇ *adj*: **adicto (a)** addicted (to). ◇ *sm, f*: **adicto (a)** addict (of).

adiestramiento *sm* training.

adiestrar *vt* to train; **adiestrar a alguien en algo/para hacer algo** to train sb in sthg/to do sthg.

adinerado, da *adj* wealthy.

adiós ◇ *sm* goodbye. ◇ *interj*: **¡adiós!** goodbye!; [al cruzarse con alguien] hello!

adiposidad *sf* adiposity.

adiposo, sa *adj* adipose.

aditamento *sm* - **1.** [complemento] accessory - **2.** [cosa añadida] addition.

aditivo *sm* additive.

adivinador, ra *sm, f* fortune-teller.

adivinanza *sf* riddle.

adivinar *vt* - **1.** [predecir] to foretell; [el futuro] to tell - **2.** [acertar] to guess (correctly) - **3.** [intuir] to suspect.
◆ **adivinarse** *vprnl* [vislumbrarse] to be visible.

adivino, na *sm, f* fortune-teller.

adjetivo, va *adj* adjectival.
◆ **adjetivo** *sm* adjective; **adjetivo calificativo/demostrativo/numeral** qualifying/demonstrative/quantitative adjective.

adjudicación *sf* awarding.

adjudicar [10] *vt* [asignar] to award.
◆ **adjudicarse** *vprnl* [apropiarse] to take for o.s.; **adjudicarse un premio** to win a prize.

adjuntar *vt* to enclose.

adjunto, ta ◇ *adj* - **1.** [incluido] enclosed; **'adjunto le remito...'** 'please find enclosed...' - **2.** [auxiliar] assistant *(antes de s)*. ◇ *sm, f* [auxiliar] assistant.

adminículo *sm* gadget.

administración *sf* - **1.** [suministro] supply; [de medicamento, justicia] administering - **2.** [gestión] administration - **3.** [gerentes] management; [oficina] manager's office.
◆ **Administración** *sf* [gobierno] administration; **Administración local** local government; **Administración pública** civil service.

administrador, ra *sm, f* - **1.** [de empresa] manager - **2.** [de bienes ajenos] administrator.

administrar *vt* - **1.** [gestionar - empresa, finca etc] to manage, to run; [- casa] to run - **2.** [país] to run the affairs of - **3.** [suministrar] to administer - **4.** [racionar] to use sparingly.
➥ **administrarse** *vprnl* [emplear dinero] to organize one's finances.

administrativo, **va** ⬦ *adj* administrative. ⬦ *sm, f* office clerk.

admirable *adj* admirable.

admiración *sf* - **1.** [sentimiento] admiration; **causar admiración** to be admired; **sentir admiración por alguien** to admire sb - **2.** [signo ortográfico] exclamation mark.

admirador, **ra** *sm, f* admirer.

admirar *vt* - **1.** [gen] to admire; **ser de admirar** to be admirable - **2.** [sorprender] to amaze.
➥ **admirarse** *vprnl*: **admirarse (de)** to be amazed (by).

admisible *adj* acceptable.

admisión *sf* - **1.** [de persona] admission - **2.** [de solicitudes etc] acceptance; **prueba de admisión** entrance exam.

admitir *vt* - **1.** [acoger, reconocer] to admit; **admitir a alguien en** to admit sb to - **2.** [aceptar] to accept - **3.** [permitir, tolerar] to allow, to permit.

admón. (*abrev de* **administración**) admin.

admonición *sf* warning.

ADN (*abrev de* **ácido desoxirribonucleico**) *sm* DNA.

adobar *vt* to marinate.

adobe *sm* adobe.

adobo *sm* - **1.** [acción] marinating - **2.** [salsa] marinade.

adocenado, **da** *adj* mediocre, run-of-the-mill.

adocenarse *vprnl* to lapse into mediocrity.

adoctrinar *vt* to instruct.

adolecer [30] ➥ **adolecer de** *vi* to suffer from.

adolescencia *sf* adolescence.

adolescente *adj & smf* adolescent.

adonde *adv* where; **la ciudad adonde vamos** the city we are going to, the city where we are going.

adónde *adv* where.

adondequiera *adv* wherever.

adonis *sm inv fig* Adonis, handsome young man.

adopción *sf* [de hijo, propuesta] adoption; [de ley] passing.

adoptar *vt* [hijo, propuesta] to adopt; [ley] to pass.

adoptivo, **va** *adj* [hijo, país] adopted; [padre] adoptive.

adoquín (*pl* **adoquines**) *sm* cobblestone.

adoquinado, **da** *adj* cobbled.
➥ **adoquinado** *sm* - **1.** [suelo] cobbles *pl* - **2.** [acción] cobbling.

adoquinar *vt* to cobble.

adorable *adj* [persona] adorable; [ambiente, película] wonderful.

adoración *sf* adoration; **sentir adoración por alguien** to worship sb.

adorar *vt* - **1.** [dios, ídolo] to worship - **2.** [persona, comida] to adore.

adormecer [30] *vt* - **1.** [producir sueño] to lull to sleep - **2.** *fig* [aplacar] to calm - **3.** [entumecer] to numb.
➥ **adormecerse** *vprnl* to nod off, to drop off.

adormidera *sf* poppy.

adormilarse *vprnl* to doze.

adornar ⬦ *vt* to decorate. ⬦ *vi* to serve as decoration.

adorno *sm* decoration; **de adorno** [árbol, figura] decorative, ornamental; [person] serving no useful purpose.

adosado, **da** *adj* [casa] semi-detached.

adosar *vt*: **adosar algo a algo** to push sthg up against sthg.

adquirir [22] *vt* - **1.** [comprar] to acquire, to purchase - **2.** [conseguir - conocimientos, hábito, cultura] to acquire; [- éxito, popularidad] to achieve; [- compromiso] to undertake.

adquisición *sf* - **1.** [compra, cosa comprada] purchase; **ser una buena/mala adquisición** to be a good/bad buy - **2.** [obtención] acquisition - **3.** [de costumbres] adoption.

adquisitivo, **va** *adj* purchasing (*antes de s*).

adrede *adv* on purpose, deliberately.

adrenalina *sf* adrenalin.

Adriático *sm*: **el (mar) Adriático** the Adriatic (Sea).

adscribir *vt* - **1.** [asignar] to assign - **2.** [destinar] to appoint *o* assign to.
➥ **adscribirse** *vprnl*: **adscribirse (a)** [grupo, partido] to become a member (of); [ideología] to subscribe (to).

adscrito, **ta** ⬦ *pp* ⊳ **adscribir**. ⬦ *adj* assigned.

aduana *sf* - **1.** [administración] customs *pl*; **pasar por la aduana** to go through customs - **2.** [oficina] customs (office) - **3.** [derechos] customs duty.

aducir [33] *vt* to adduce.

adueñarse ➥ **adueñarse de** *vprnl* - **1.** [apoderarse] to take over, to take control of - **2.** [dominar] to take hold of.

adujera *etc* ⊳ **aducir**.

adulación *sf* flattery.

adulador, ra ◇ *adj* flattering. ◇ *sm, f* flatterer.

adular *vt* to flatter.

adulón, ona *sm, f* toady.

adulteración *sf* adulteration.

adulterar *vt* - **1.** [alimento] to adulterate - **2.** [falsear] to doctor, to distort.

adulterio *sm* adultery.

adúltero, ra ◇ *adj* adulterous. ◇ *sm, f* adulterer (*f* adulteress).

adulto, ta *adj* & *sm, f* adult.

adusto, ta *adj* dour.

aduzca *etc* ⊳ **aducir**.

advenedizo, za *adj* & *sm, f* parvenu (*f* parvenue).

advenimiento *sm* [llegada] advent; [al trono] accession.

adverbial *adj* adverbial.

adverbio *sm* adverb; **adverbio de cantidad/lugar/modo/tiempo** adverb of degree/place/manner/time.

adversario, ria *sm, f* adversary.

adversativo, va *adj* adversative.

adversidad *sf* adversity.

adverso, sa *adj* [gen] adverse; [destino] unkind; [suerte] bad; [viento] unfavourable.

advertencia *sf* warning; **servir de advertencia** to serve as a warning; **hacer una advertencia a alguien** to warn sb.

advertir [27] *vt* - **1.** [notar] to notice - **2.** [prevenir, avisar] to warn; **te advierto que no deberías hacerlo** I'd advise against you doing it; **te advierto que no me sorprende** mind you, it doesn't surprise me.

adviento *sm* Advent.

advierta *etc* ⊳ **advertir**.

advirtiera *etc* ⊳ **advertir**.

adyacente *adj* adjacent.

AEE (*abrev de* **Agencia Espacial Europea**) *sf* ESA.

aéreo, a *adj* - **1.** [del aire] aerial - **2.** AERON air (*antes de s*).

aerobio, bia *adj* aerobic.

aeroclub (*pl* **aeroclubes**) *sm* flying club.

aerodeslizador *sm* hovercraft.

aerodinámico, ca *adj* - **1.** FÍS aerodynamic - **2.** [forma, línea] streamlined.
  ◆ **aerodinámica** *sf* aerodynamics (*U*).

aeródromo *sm* airfield, aerodrome.

aeroespacial *adj* aerospace (*antes de s*).

aerofaro *sm* beacon (*at airport*).

aerógrafo *sm* airbrush.

aerolínea *sf* airline.

aerolito *sm* aerolite.

aeromodelismo *sm* airplane modelling.

aeromozo, za *sm, f* Amér air steward (*f* air hostess).

aeronauta *smf* aeronaut.

aeronáutico, ca *adj* aeronautic.
  ◆ **aeronáutica** *sf* aeronautics (*U*).

aeronaval *adj* air and sea (*antes de s*).

aeronave *sf* [gen] aircraft; [dirigible] airship.

aeroplano *sm* aeroplane.

aeropuerto *sm* airport.

aerosol *sm* aerosol.

aerostático, ca *adj* aerostatic.

aeróstato *sm* hot-air balloon.

aerotaxi *sm* light aircraft (*for hire*).

aerotransportado, da *adj* airborne.

afabilidad *sf* affability.

afable *adj* affable.

afamado, da *adj* famous.

afán *sm* - **1.** [esfuerzo] hard work (*U*) - **2.** [anhelo] urge; **tener afán de algo** to be eager for sthg; **afán de conocimiento** thirst for knowledge.

afanador, ra *sm, f* Méx cleaner.

afanar *vt fam* [robar] to pinch, to swipe.
  ◆ **afanarse** *vprnl* [esforzarse]**: afanarse (por hacer algo)** to do everything one can (to do sthg).

afanoso, sa *adj* - **1.** [trabajoso] hard, demanding - **2.** [que se afana] keen, eager.

afasia *sf* aphasia.

afear *vt* to make ugly.

afección *sf* - **1.** MED complaint, disease - **2.** [afecto] affection.

afectación *sf* affectation.

afectado, da ◇ *adj* - **1.** [gen] affected - **2.** [afligido] upset, badly affected. ◇ *sm, f* [víctima] victim.

afectar *vt* - **1.** [gen] to affect - **2.** [afligir] to upset, to affect badly.

afectísimo, ma *adj* [en cartas]**: 'suyo afectísimo'** 'yours faithfully'.

afectivo, va *adj* - **1.** [emocional] emotional - **2.** [cariñoso] affectionate, loving.

afecto *sm* affection, fondness; **sentir afecto por alguien, tenerle afecto a alguien** to be fond of sb.

afectuoso, sa *adj* affectionate, loving.

afeitado *sm* - **1.** [de pelo, barba] shave - **2.** TAUROM *blunting of bull's horns for safety reasons.*

afeitar *vt* - **1.** [pelo, barba] to shave - **2.** TAUROM *to blunt bull's horns for safety reasons.*
  ◆ **afeitarse** *vprnl* to shave.

afeite *sm* - **1.** [acicalamiento] toilet, washing and dressing - **2.** [cosmético] make-up (*U*).

afelpado, da *adj* plush.

afeminado, **da** *adj* effeminate.
◆ **afeminado** *sm* effeminate man.
afeminarse *vprnl* to become effeminate.
aferrarse *vprnl*: **aferrarse a** *lit & fig* to cling to.
Afganistán *n pr* Afghanistan.
afgano, **na** *adj* & *sm, f* Afghan.
AFI (*abrev de* **alfabeto fonético internacional**)
IPA.
afianzar [13] *vt* - **1.** [teoría, diagnóstico] to reinforce - **2.** [objeto] to secure.
◆ **afianzarse** *vprnl* to steady o.s.; **afianzarse
en algo** [opinión etc] to become sure o convinced of sthg; [cargo, liderazgo] to consolidate
sthg.
afiche *sm Amér* poster.
afición *sf* - **1.** [inclinación] fondness, liking; **tener afición a algo** to be keen on sthg - **2.** [en
tiempo libre] hobby; **por afición** as a hobby
- **3.** [aficionados] fans *pl*.
aficionado, **da** ◇ *adj* - **1.** [interesado] keen;
ser aficionado a algo to be keen on sthg
- **2.** [no profesional] amateur. ◇ *sm, f* - **1.** [in-
teresado] fan; **aficionado al cine** film buff
- **2.** [amateur] amateur.
aficionar *vt*: **aficionar a alguien a algo** to
make sb keen on sthg.
◆ **aficionarse** *vprnl*: **aficionarse a algo** to become keen on sthg.
afijo, **ja** *adj* affixed.
◆ **afijo** *sm* affix.
afilado, **da** *adj* - **1.** [borde, filo] sharp; [dedos]
pointed - **2.** *fig* [hiriente, mordaz] cutting.
◆ **afilado** *sm* sharpening.
afilador, **ra** ◇ *adj* sharpening. ◇ *sm, f* [per-
sona] knifegrinder.
◆ **afiladora** *sf* [objeto] grindstone, sharpener.
afilalápices *sm inv* pencil sharpener.
afilar *vt* to sharpen.
◆ **afilarse** *vprnl fig* to become pointed, to
taper.
afiliación *sf* - **1.** [acción] joining - **2.** [pertenen-
cia] membership.
afiliado, **da** *sm, f*: **afiliado (a)** member (of).
afiliarse [8] *vprnl*: **afiliarse a** to join, to become a member of.
afín *adj* - **1.** [semejante] similar, like - **2.** [con-
tiguo] neighbouring.
afinar *vt* - **1.** MÚS [instrumento] to tune; **afinar la
voz** to sing in tune - **2.** [perfeccionar, mejorar] to
fine-tune - **3.** [pulir] to refine.
afincar [10] *vi* to buy land.
◆ **afincarse** *vprnl*: **afincarse en** to settle in.
afinidad *sf* - **1.** [gen & QUÍM] affinity - **2.** [par-
entesco]: **por afinidad** by marriage.
afinque *etc* ▷ **afincar**.
afirmación *sf* statement, assertion.

afirmar *vt* - **1.** [confirmar] to confirm - **2.** [de-
cir] to say, to declare - **3.** [consolidar] to reaffirm
- **4.** CONSTR to reinforce.
◆ **afirmarse** *vprnl* - **1.** [asegurarse] to be confirmed - **2.** [ratificarse]: **afirmarse en algo** to reaffirm sthg.
afirmativo, **va** *adj* affirmative.
◆ **afirmativa** *sf* affirmative.
aflicción *sf* suffering, sorrow.
afligir [15] *vt* [afectar] to afflict; [causar pena] to
distress.
◆ **afligirse** *vprnl* to be distressed.
aflojar ◇ *vt* - **1.** [destensar] to loosen; [cuerda]
to slacken - **2.** *fam* [dinero] to fork out. ◇ *vi*
- **1.** [disminuir] to abate, to die down - **2.** *fig*
[ceder] to ease off.
◆ **aflojarse** *vprnl* [gen] to come loose; [cuerda]
to slacken.
aflorar *vi* - **1.** *fig* [surgir] to (come to the) surface, to show - **2.** [masa mineral] to outcrop.
afluencia *sf* stream, volume.
afluente *sm* tributary.
afluir [51] ◆ **afluir a** *vi* - **1.** [gente] to flock to
- **2.** [río] to flow into - **3.** [sangre, fluido] to flow
to.
afluya *etc* ▷ **afluir**.
afluyera *etc* ▷ **afluir**.
afma. (*abrev de* **afectísima**) *abrev de* **afectísimo**.
afmo. (*abrev de* **afectísimo**) *abrev de* **afectísimo**.
afonía *sf* loss of voice.
afónico, **ca** *adj*: **quedarse afónico** to lose
one's voice.
aforar *vt* TECNOL to gauge.
aforismo *sm* aphorism.
aforo *sm* [cabida] seating capacity.
afortunadamente *adv* fortunately.
afortunado, **da** ◇ *adj* - **1.** [agraciado] lucky,
fortunate - **2.** [oportuno] happy, felicitous.
◇ *sm, f* [gen] lucky person; [en lotería] lucky
winner.
afrancesado, **da** ◇ *adj* Frenchified.
◇ *sm, f* HIST *supporter of the French during
the Peninsular War*.
afrenta *sf* - **1.** [vergüenza] disgrace - **2.** [ofensa,
agravio] affront.
África *n pr* Africa.
africado, **da** *adj* LING affricate.
africanismo *sm* Africanism.
africano, **na** *adj* & *sm, f* African.
afro *adj inv* afro.
afroamericano, **na** *adj* Afro-American.
afrodisiaco, **ca** *adj* aphrodisiac.
◆ **afrodisíaco** *sm* aphrodisiac.

afrontar *vt* - **1.** [hacer frente a] to face - **2.** [carear] to bring face to face.

afrutado, **da** *adj* fruity.

afuera *adv* outside; **por (la parte de) afuera** on the outside.

➤ **afueras** *sfpl*: **las afueras** the outskirts.

afuerita *adv* Amér fam right outside.

afusilar *vt* Amér fam to shoot.

agachar *vt* to lower; [la cabeza] to bow.

➤ **agacharse** *vprnl* [acuclillarse] to crouch down; [inclinar la cabeza] to stoop.

agalla *sf* ZOOL gill.

➤ **agallas** *sfpl* fig guts; **tener agallas** to have guts.

ágape *sm* culto banquet, feast.

agarrada *sf* ▷ agarrado.

agarradero *sm* - **1.** [asa] hold - **2.** fam fig [pretexto] pretext, excuse.

agarrado, **da** *adj* - **1.** [asido]: **agarrado (de)** gripped (by); **agarrados del brazo** arm in arm; **agarrados de la mano** hand in hand - **2.** fam [tacaño] tight, stingy.

➤ **agarrado** *sm* fam smooch.

➤ **agarrada** *sf* fam row, bust-up.

agarrar ⬦ *vt* - **1.** [asir] to grab - **2.** [pillar - ladrón, resfriado] to catch; Amér [- tomar] to take; **agarrarla** fam fig to get pissed. ⬦ *vi* [tinte] to take; [planta] to take root.

➤ **agarrarse** *vprnl* - **1.** [sujetarse] to hold on; **agarrarse de** o **a algo** to hold on to o clutch sthg - **2.** [pegarse] to stick - **3.** fam fig [pelearse] to scrap, to have a fight - **4.** fig [pretextar]: **agarrarse a algo** to use sthg as an excuse.

agarrón *sm* - **1.** [tirón] pull, tug - **2.** fam [pelea] row, bust-up.

agarrotar *vt* [parte del cuerpo] to cut off the circulation in; [mente] to numb.

➤ **agarrotarse** *vprnl* - **1.** [parte del cuerpo] to go numb - **2.** [mecanismo] to seize up.

agasajar *vt* to lavish attention on, to treat like a king; **agasajar a alguien con algo** to lavish sthg upon sb.

agasajo *sm* lavish attention.

ágata *sf* (el) agate.

agazaparse *vprnl* - **1.** [para esconderse] to crouch - **2.** [agacharse] to bend down.

agencia *sf* - **1.** [empresa] agency; **agencia de noticias** o **prensa** news agency; **agencia de aduanas** customs agent's; **agencia inmobiliaria** estate agent's *UK*, real estate office *US*; **agencia matrimonial** marriage bureau; **agencia de publicidad** advertising agency; **agencia de viajes** travel agency - **2.** [sucursal] branch.

agenciar [8] *vt*: **agenciar algo a alguien** to fix sb up with sthg.

➤ **agenciarse** *vprnl* to get hold of, to fix o.s. up with.

agenda *sf* - **1.** [de notas, fechas] diary; [de teléfonos, direcciones] book; **agenda electrónica** electronic organizer - **2.** [de trabajo] agenda.

agente ⬦ *sm, f* [persona] agent; **agente de policía** o **de la autoridad** policeman (*f* policewoman); **agente de aduanas** customs officer; **agente de cambio (y bolsa)** stockbroker; **agente comercial** broker; **agente secreto** secret agent; **agentes económicos** ECON social partners. ⬦ *sm* - **1.** [causa activa] agent - **2.** GRAM ▷ complemento.

agigantar *vt* to blow up, to magnify.

ágil *adj* - **1.** [movimiento, persona] agile - **2.** [estilo, lenguaje] fluent; [respuesta, mente] nimble, sharp.

agilidad *sf* agility.

agilizar [13] *vt* to speed up.

agio *sm* ECON agio.

agiotaje *sm* ECON agiotage, speculation.

agitación *sf* - **1.** [movimiento - de botella] shaking; [- de líquido] stirring; [- de brazos] waving - **2.** [intranquilidad] restlessness - **3.** [jaleo] racket, commotion - **4.** [conflicto] unrest.

agitador, **ra** ⬦ *adj* [viento] gusty. ⬦ *sm, f* agitator.

agitanado, **da** *adj* gypsy-like.

agitar *vt* - **1.** [mover - botella] to shake; [- líquido] to stir; [- brazos] to wave - **2.** [inquietar] to perturb, to worry - **3.** [alterar, perturbar] to stir up.

➤ **agitarse** *vprnl* [inquietarse] to get worried.

aglomeración *sf* build-up; [de gente] crowd.

aglomerar *vt* to bring together.

➤ **aglomerarse** *vprnl* to amass.

aglutinante *adj* - **1.** [adherente] agglutinant - **2.** LING agglutinative.

aglutinar *vt* - **1.** [pegar] to agglutinate - **2.** MED to bind - **3.** fig [aunar, reunir - personas] to unite; [- ideas, esfuerzos] to pool.

agnóstico, **ca** *adj* & *sm, f* agnostic.

ago. (*abrev de* **agosto**) Aug.

agobiado, **da** *adj*: **agobiado (de)** [trabajo] snowed under (with); [problemas] weighed down (with).

agobiante *adj* [presión, trabajo, persona] overwhelming; [calor] oppressive.

agobiar [8] *vt* to overwhelm.

➤ **agobiarse** *vprnl* to feel overwhelmed, to let things get one down.

agobio *sm* - **1.** [físico] choking, suffocation - **2.** [psíquico] pressure.

agolparse *vprnl* - **1.** [gente] to crowd round; [sangre] to rush - **2.** fig [problemas] to come to a head.

agonía *sf* - **1.** [pena] agony - **2.** [ansia] desperation - **3.** [del moribundo] death throes *pl* - **4.** *fig* [decadencia] decline, dying days *pl*.

agonizante *adj* dying.

agonizar [13] *vi* - **1.** [expirar] to be dying - **2.** *fig* [extinguirse] to fizzle out - **3.** *fig* [sufrir] to be in agony.

agorafobia *sf* agoraphobia.

agorero, **ra** *sm*, *f* prophet of doom.

agosto *sm* - **1.** [mes] August - **2.** *fig* [cosecha] harvest (time) - **3.** *loc*: **hacer su agosto** to line one's pockets; *ver también* **septiembre**.

agotado, **da** *adj* - **1.** [cansado]**: agotado (de)** exhausted (from) - **2.** [producto] out of stock, sold out - **3.** [pila, batería] flat.

agotador, **ra** *adj* exhausting.

agotamiento *sm* - **1.** [cansancio] exhaustion - **2.** [de producto] selling-out.

agotar *vt* [gen] to exhaust; [producto] to sell out of; [agua] to drain.

➤ **agotarse** *vprnl* - **1.** [cansarse] to tire o.s. out - **2.** [acabarse] to run out; [libro, disco, entradas] to be sold out; [pila, batería] to go flat.

agraciado, **da** ◇ *adj* - **1.** [atractivo] attractive, fetching - **2.** [afortunado]**: agraciado con algo** lucky enough to win sthg. ◇ *sm*, *f* [afortunado] lucky winner.

agraciar [8] *vt* - **1.** [embellecer] to make more attractive o fetching - **2.** [conceder una gracia] to pardon - **3.** *culto* [premiar] to reward.

agradable *adj* pleasant.

agradar ◇ *vi* to be pleasant; **no me agrada** I don't like it. ◇ *vt* to please.

agradecer [30] *vt* - **1.** [suj: persona]**: agradecer algo a alguien** [dar las gracias] to thank sb for sthg; [estar agradecido] to be grateful to sb for sthg - **2.** [suj: cosas] to be thankful for.

➤ **agradecerse** *v impers* to be nice.

agradecido, **da** *adj* [ser] grateful; [estar] appreciative.

agradecimiento *sm* gratitude.

agrado *sm* - **1.** [gusto] pleasure; **esto no es de mi agrado** this is not to my liking - **2.** [afabilidad] kindness.

agrandar *vt* to make bigger.

agrario, **ria** *adj* [reforma] agrarian; [producto, política] agricultural.

agravación *sf* worsening, exacerbation.

agravamiento *sm* = agravación.

agravante ◇ *adj* aggravating. ◇ *sm o sf* - **1.** [problema] additional problem - **2.** DER aggravating circumstance.

agravar *vt* [situación] to aggravate; [impuestos etc] to increase (the burden of).

➤ **agravarse** *vprnl* to get worse, to worsen.

agraviar [8] *vt* to offend.

agravio *sm* - **1.** [ofensa] offence, insult - **2.** [perjuicio] wrong.

agredido, **da** *sm*, *f* victim *(of an attack)*.

agredir [78] *vt* to attack.

agregado, **da** ◇ *adj* [añadido] added on. ◇ *sm*, *f* - **1.** EDUC assistant teacher - **2.** [de embajada] attaché; **agregado cultural** cultural attaché.

➤ **agregado** *sm* - **1.** [añadido] addition - **2.** ECON aggregate.

agregar [16] *vt*: agregar (algo a algo) to add (sthg to sthg).

➤ **agregarse** *vprnl*: agregarse a algo to join (sthg).

agresión *sf* [ataque] act of aggression, attack.

agresividad *sf* aggression.

agresivo, **va** *adj* *lit & fig* aggressive.

agresor, **ra** *sm*, *f* attacker, assailant.

agreste *adj* - **1.** [abrupto, rocoso] rough, rugged - **2.** [rural] country *(antes de s)*, rural - **3.** *fig* [basto, rudo] coarse, uncouth.

agriar [9] *vt* - **1.** [vino, leche] to (turn) sour - **2.** *fig* [carácter] to sour, to embitter.

➤ **agriarse** *vprnl* *lit & fig* to turn sour.

agrícola *adj* agricultural; [pueblo] farming *(antes de s)*.

agricultor, **ra** *sm*, *f* farmer.

agricultura *sf* agriculture; **agricultura extensiva/intensiva** extensive/intensive farming.

agridulce *adj* bittersweet; CULIN sweet and sour.

agrietar *vt* - **1.** [muro, tierra] to crack - **2.** [labios, manos] to chap.

➤ **agrietarse** *vprnl* [la piel] to chap.

agrio, **agria** *adj* - **1.** [ácido] sour - **2.** *fig* [áspero] acerbic, bitter.

➤ **agrios** *smpl* citrus fruits.

agriparse *vprnl* *Andes & Méx* to catch the flu.

agro *sm* farmland.

agronomía *sf* agronomy.

agrónomo, **ma** *sm*, *f* agronomist.

agropecuario, **ria** *adj* farming and livestock *(antes de s)*.

agrupación *sf* - **1.** [asociación] group, association - **2.** [agrupamiento] grouping.

agrupamiento *sm* [concentración] grouping.

agrupar *vt* to group (together).

➤ **agruparse** *vprnl* - **1.** [congregarse] to gather (round) - **2.** [unirse] to form a group.

agua *sf (el)* water; **agua bendita/dulce/destilada/potable/salada** holy/fresh/distilled/drinking/salt water; **agua mineral sin gas/con gas** still/sparkling mineral water; **claro como el agua** as clear as day; **estar con el agua al cuello** to be up to one's neck (in it);

hacerse agua en la boca to melt in one's mouth; **quedar en agua de borrajas** to come to nothing; **venir como agua de mayo** to be a godsend.

◆ **aguas** *sfpl* - **1.** [manantial] waters, spring *sing*; **aguas termales** thermal o hot springs - **2.** [de río, mar] waters; **aguas territoriales** o **jurisdiccionales** territorial waters; **aguas internacionales** international waters - **3.** [de tejado] slope - **4.** [de diamantes, telas] water *(U)* - **5.** *loc:* **hacer aguas** NÁUT to leak; *fig* to go under; **nadar entre dos aguas** to sit on the fence; **ha roto aguas** her waters have broken.

◆ **agua de colonia** *sf* eau de cologne.

◆ **agua oxigenada** *sf* hydrogen peroxide.

◆ **aguas menores** *sfpl* water *(U)*, urine *(U)*.

◆ **aguas residuales** *sfpl* sewage *(U)*.

aguacate *sm* - **1.** [fruto] avocado (pear) - **2.** [árbol] avocado.

aguacero *sm* shower.

aguachirle *sf* dishwater *(U)*, revolting drink.

aguado, da *adj* - **1.** [con demasiada agua] watery; [diluido a propósito] watered-down - **2.** *fig* [estropeado] ruined.

◆ **aguada** *sf* ARTE gouache.

aguafiestas *smf inv* spoilsport.

aguafuerte *sm* etching.

aguaitada *sf* *Amér fam* glance; **echar una aguaitada a algo** to have a look at sthg.

aguaitar *vt* *Amér fam* - **1.** [mirar] to look at - **2.** [acechar] to spy on.

aguamarina *sf* aquamarine.

aguamiel *sf* *Amér* [bebida] *water mixed with honey or cane syrup*; *Caribe & Méx* [jugo] maguey juice.

aguanieve *sf* sleet.

aguantar *vt* - **1.** [sostener] to hold - **2.** [resistir - peso] to bear - **3.** [tolerar, soportar] to bear, to stand; **no sé cómo la aguantas** I don't know how you put up with her - **4.** [contener - risa] to contain; [- respiración] to hold - **5.** [esperar - tiempo] to hold out for, to wait for.

◆ **aguantarse** *vprnl* - **1.** [contenerse] to restrain o.s., to hold o.s. back - **2.** [resignarse]: **no quiere aguantarse** he refuses to put up with it.

aguante *sm* - **1.** [paciencia] self-restraint, tolerance - **2.** [resistencia] strength; [de persona] stamina.

aguar [45] *vt* - **1.** [mezclar con agua] to water down - **2.** *fig* [estropear] to spoil, to ruin.

◆ **aguarse** *vprnl* to be spoiled.

aguardar *vt* to wait for, to await.

aguardiente *sm* spirit, liquor.

aguarrás *sm* turpentine.

aguatero *sm* *Amér* water carrier.

aguce *etc* ▷ **aguzar**.

agudeza *sf* - **1.** [gen] sharpness - **2.** [dicho ingenioso] witticism.

agudizar [13] *vt* - **1.** [afilar] to sharpen - **2.** *fig* [acentuar] to exacerbate, to make worse.

◆ **agudizarse** *vprnl* - **1.** [crisis] to get worse - **2.** [ingenio] to get sharper.

agudo, da *adj* - **1.** [gen] sharp; [crisis, problema, enfermedad] serious, acute - **2.** *fig* [perspicaz] keen, sharp - **3.** *fig* [ingenioso] witty - **4.** GRAM oxytone - **5.** MÚS [nota, voz] high, high-pitched.

agüe *etc* ▷ **aguar**.

agüero *sm*: **de buen/mal agüero** that bodes well/ill.

aguerrido, da *adj* *culto* - **1.** [valiente] battle-hardened - **2.** *fig* [experimentado] veteran *(antes de s)*.

aguijar *vt* [caballo] to spur; [buey] to goad.

aguijón *sm* - **1.** [de insecto] sting - **2.** [de planta] thorn - **3.** *fig* [estímulo] spur, stimulus.

aguijonear *vt* - **1.** [espolear]: **aguijonear a alguien para que haga algo** to goad sb into doing sthg - **2.** *fig* [estimular] to drive on.

águila *sf (el)* - **1.** [ave] eagle - **2.** *fig* [vivo, listo] sharp o perceptive person; **¿águila o sol?** *Méx* heads or tails?

aguileño, ña *adj* aquiline.

aguilucho *sm* eaglet.

aguinaldo *sm* Christmas box.

aguja *sf* - **1.** [de coser, jeringuilla] needle; [de hacer punto] knitting needle; **aguja hipodérmica** hypodermic needle; **es como buscar una aguja en un pajar** it's like looking for a needle in a haystack - **2.** [de reloj] hand; [de brújula] pointer; [de iglesia] spire - **3.** FERROC point - **4.** [de tocadiscos] stylus, needle.

◆ **agujas** *sfpl* [de res] ribs.

agujerear *vt* to make a hole o holes in.

agujero *sm* hole; **agujero negro** ASTRON black hole.

agujetas *sfpl*: **tener agujetas** to feel stiff.

agustino, na *sm, f* Augustinian.

aguzar [13] *vt* - **1.** [afilar] to sharpen - **2.** *fig* [apetito] to whet; [ingenio] to sharpen.

ah *interj*: **¡ah!** [admiración] ooh!; [sorpresa] oh!; [pena] ah!

ahí *adv* there; **vino por ahí** he came that way; **la solución está ahí** that's where the solution lies; **¡ahí tienes!** here you are!, there you go!; **de ahí que** [por eso] and consequently, so; **está por ahí** [en lugar indefinido] he/she is around (somewhere); [en la calle] he/she is out; **por ahí, por ahí** *fig* something like that; **por ahí va la cosa** you're not too far wrong.

ahijado, da *sm, f* - **1.** [de padrinos] godson (*f* goddaughter) - **2.** *fig* [protegido] protégé.

ahijar *vt* to adopt.

ahínco *sm* enthusiasm, devotion.

ahíto, ta *adj* - **1.** *culto* [saciado]: **estar ahíto** to be full - **2.** *fig* [fastidiado]: **ahíto (de)** fed up (with).

ahogado, da <> *adj* - **1.** [en el agua] drowned - **2.** [falto de aliento - respiración] laboured; [- persona] out of breath; [- grito] muffled - **3.** [estrecho] cramped - **4.** *fig* [agobiado] overwhelmed, swamped. <> *sm, f* drowned person.

ahogar [16] *vt* - **1.** [en el agua] to drown; [asfixiar] to smother, to suffocate - **2.** [estrangular] to strangle - **3.** [extinguir] to extinguish, to put out - **4.** *fig* [controlar - levantamiento] to put down, to quell; [- pena] to hold back, to contain - **5.** [motor] to flood.
◆ **ahogarse** *vprnl* - **1.** [en el agua] to drown - **2.** [asfixiarse] to suffocate - **3.** *fig* [de calor] to be stifled.

ahogo *sm* - **1.** [asfixia] breathlessness, difficulty in breathing - **2.** *fig* [angustia] anguish, distress - **3.** *fig* [económico] financial difficulty.

ahogue *etc* ▷ **ahogar**.

ahondar *vi* [profundizar] to go into detail; **ahondar en** [penetrar] to penetrate deep into; [profundizar] to study in depth.

ahora <> *adv* - **1.** [en el presente] now; **ahora mismo** right now; **por ahora** for the time being; **de ahora en adelante** from now on - **2.** [pronto] in a second o moment; **¡hasta ahora!** see you in a minute! <> *conj* - **1.** [ya... ya]: **ahora habla, ahora canta** one minute she's talking, the next she's singing - **2.** [pero] but, however; **ahora que** but, though; **ahora bien** but, however.

ahorcado, da *sm, f* hanged man (f hanged woman).

ahorcar [10] *vt* to hang.
◆ **ahorcarse** *vprnl* to hang o.s.

ahorita, ahoritita *adv Amér C & Méx fam* right now.

ahorque *etc* ▷ **ahorcar**.

ahorrador, ra <> *adj* thrifty, careful with money. <> *sm, f* thrifty person.

ahorrar *vt* to save.
◆ **ahorrarse** *vprnl*: **ahorrarse algo** to save o spare o.s. sthg.

ahorro *sm* - **1.** [gen] saving - **2.** *(gen pl)* [cantidad ahorrada] savings *pl*.

ahuecar [10] <> *vt* - **1.** [poner hueco - manos] to cup; [- tronco] to hollow out - **2.** [mullir - colchón] to plump up; [- tierra] to hoe. <> *vi fam* [irse] to clear off.
◆ **ahuecarse** *vprnl fam fig* to puff up o swell with pride.

ahuevado, da *adj Andes & Amér C fam* [tonto] daft.

ahumado, da *adj* smoked.
◆ **ahumado** *sm* smoking.

ahumar *vt* - **1.** [jamón, pescado] to smoke - **2.** [habitación etc] to fill with smoke.
◆ **ahumarse** *vprnl* - **1.** [saber a humo] to acquire a smoky taste - **2.** [ennegrecerse de humo] to become blackened with smoke.

ahuyentar *vt* - **1.** [espantar, asustar] to scare away - **2.** *fig* [apartar] to drive away.

airado, da *adj* angry.

airar *vt* to anger, to make angry.
◆ **airarse** *vprnl* to get angry.

aire *sm* - **1.** [fluido] air; **al aire** exposed; **al aire libre** in the open air; **cambiar de aires** to have a change of scene; **dejar algo en el aire** to leave sthg up in the air; **estar en el aire** to be in the air; **saltar o volar por los aires** to be blown sky high, to explode; **tomar el aire** to go for a breath of fresh air - **2.** [viento] wind; [corriente] draught; **hoy hace (mucho) aire** it's (very) windy today - **3.** *fig* [aspecto] air, appearance - **4.** *fig* [parecido]: **tiene un aire a su madre** she has something of her mother about her - **5.** *fig* [gracia] grace, elegance - **6.** *loc*: **a mi/tu aire** my/your etc (own) way.
◆ **aires** *smpl* [vanidad] airs (and graces); **darse aires** to put on airs.
◆ **aire (acondicionado)** *sm* air-conditioning.

aireación *sf* ventilation.

airear *vt* - **1.** [ventilar] to air - **2.** *fig* [contar] to air (publicly).
◆ **airearse** *vprnl* to get a breath of fresh air.

airoso, sa *adj* - **1.** [garboso] graceful, elegant - **2.** [triunfante]: **salir airoso de algo** to come out of sthg with flying colours.

aislacionismo *sm* isolationism.

aislado, da *adj* - **1.** [gen] isolated - **2.** TECNOL insulated.

aislamiento *sm* - **1.** [gen] isolation - **2.** TECNOL insulation.

aislante *adj* insulating.

aislar *vt* - **1.** [gen] to isolate - **2.** TECNOL to insulate.

aizkolari *sm competitor in the rural Basque sport of chopping felled tree-trunks.*

ajá *interj*: **¡ajá!** [sorpresa] aha!; *fam* [aprobación] great!

ajar *vt* [flores] to wither, to cause to fade; [piel] to wrinkle; [colores] to make faded; [ropa] to wear out.
◆ **ajarse** *vprnl* [flores] to fade, to wither; [piel] to wrinkle, to become wrinkled.

ajardinado, da *adj* landscaped.

ajedrecista *smf* chess player.

ajedrez *sm inv* chess.

ajenjo *sm* - **1.** BOT wormwood, absinth - **2.** [licor] absinth.

ajeno, na *adj* - **1.** [de otro] of others; **jugar en campo ajeno** to play away from home - **2.** [extraño]: **ajeno a** having nothing to do with; **ajeno a nuestra voluntad** beyond our control - **3.** *fig* [libre]: **ajeno de** free from.

ajetreo *sm* - **1.** [tarea] running around, hard work - **2.** [animación] (hustle and) bustle.

ají *sm Andes & R Dom* chilli (pepper).

ajiaceite *sm garlic mayonnaise.*

ajiaco *sm Andes & Caribe* chilli-based stew.

ajillo ➟ **al ajillo** *loc adj* CULIN *in a sauce made with oil, garlic and chilli.*

ajo *sm* garlic; **ajo blanco** CULIN cold garlic soup; **ajo tierno** young garlic; **andar** *o* **estar en el ajo** *fig* to be in on it.

ajuntarse *vprnl fam* to live together.

ajustado, da *adj* - **1.** [ceñido - ropa] tight-fitting; [- tuerca, pieza] tight; [- resultado, final] close - **2.** [justo] correct, right; [precio] reasonable.

➟ **ajustado** *sm* fitting.

ajustador, ra ◇ *adj* adjusting. ◇ *sm, f* typesetter.

ajustar *vt* - **1.** [arreglar] to adjust - **2.** [apretar] to tighten - **3.** [encajar - piezas de motor] to fit; [- puerta, ventana] to push to - **4.** [pactar - matrimonio] to arrange; [- pleito] to settle; [- paz] to negotiate; [- precio] to fix, to agree.

➟ **ajustarse a** *vprnl* - **1.** [adaptarse] to adapt to - **2.** [conformarse] to fit in with.

ajuste *sm* [de pieza] fitting; [de mecanismo] adjustment; [de salario] agreement; **ajuste de cuentas** *fig* settling of scores.

al *prep* ▷ **a**.

ala *sf (el)* - **1.** ZOOL & POLÍT wing; **ahuecar el ala** *fam* to clear off, to hop it; **cortar las alas a alguien** to clip sb's wings - **2.** [parte lateral - de tejado] eaves *pl*; [- de sombrero] brim; [- de nariz] side; [- de mesa] leaf - **3.** DEP winger, wing.

➟ **ala delta** *sf* [aparato] hang glider.

alabanza *sf* praise.

alabar *vt* to praise.

alabastro *sm* alabaster.

alacena *sf* kitchen cupboard.

alacrán *sm* [animal] scorpion.

alado, da *adj* - **1.** [con alas] winged - **2.** *fig* [ligero] swift, fleet.

alambicado, da *adj* elaborate, involved.

alambicar [**10**] *vt* - **1.** [destilar] to distil - **2.** *fig* [complicar] to over-complicate.

alambique *sm* still.

alambrada *sf* wire-fence.

alambre *sm* wire; **alambre de espino** *o* **púas** barbed wire.

alameda *sf* - **1.** [sitio con álamos] poplar grove - **2.** [paseo] tree-lined avenue.

álamo *sm* poplar.

alano *sm* [perro] mastiff.

alar *sm* eaves *pl*.

alarde *sm*: **alarde (de)** show *o* display (of); **hacer alarde de algo** to show sthg off, to flaunt sthg.

alardear *vi*: **alardear de** to show off about.

alargador, ra *adj* extension *(antes de s)*.

➟ **alargador** *sm* extension lead.

alargamiento *sm* extension, lengthening.

alargar [**16**] *vt* - **1.** [ropa] to lengthen - **2.** [viaje, visita, plazo] to extend; [conversación] to spin out - **3.** [pasar]: **alargar algo a alguien** to pass sthg (over) to sb.

➟ **alargarse** *vprnl* - **1.** [hacerse más largo - días] to get longer; [- reunión] to be prolonged - **2.** *fig* [hacerse muy largo] to go on for ages.

alarido *sm* shriek, howl.

alarma *sf* - **1.** [gen] alarm; **dar la alarma** to raise the alarm; **alarma de coche** car alarm - **2.** MIL call to arms.

alarmante *adj* alarming.

alarmar *vt* - **1.** [avisar] to alert - **2.** *fig* [asustar] to alarm.

➟ **alarmarse** *vprnl* [inquietarse] to be alarmed.

Alaska *n pr* Alaska.

alazán, ana *adj* chestnut.

alba *sf (el)* - **1.** [amanecer] dawn, daybreak; **al alba** at dawn - **2.** [vestidura] alb.

albacea *smf* executor (*f* executrix).

albahaca *sf* basil.

albanés, esa *adj & sm, f* Albanian.

➟ **albanés** *sm* [lengua] Albanian.

Albania *n pr* Albania.

albañil *sm* bricklayer.

albañilería *sf* - **1.** [arte] bricklaying - **2.** [obra] brickwork.

albarán *sm* delivery note.

albaricoque *sm* apricot.

albatros *sm inv* albatross.

albedrío *sm* [antojo, elección] fancy, whim; **a su albedrío** as takes his/her fancy; **libre albedrío** free will; **a su libre albedrío** of his/her own free will.

alberca *sf* - **1.** [depósito] water tank - **2.** *Méx* [piscina] swimming pool.

albergar [**16**] *vt* - **1.** [personas] to accommodate, to put up - **2.** [odio] to harbour; [esperanzas] to cherish.

➟ **albergarse** *vprnl* to stay.

albergue *sm* accommodation *(U)*, lodgings *pl*; [de montaña] shelter, refuge; **albergue de juventud** *O* **juvenil** youth hostel.

albino, na *adj* & *sm, f* albino.

albis ➡ **in albis** *loc adv*: **estar in albis** to be in the dark; **quedarse in albis** not to have a clue *O* the faintest idea.

albóndiga *sf* meatball.

albor *sm* **- 1.** [blancura] whiteness **- 2.** [luz del alba] first light of day **- 3.** *(gen pl) fig* [principio] dawn, earliest days *pl*.

alborada *sf* **- 1.** [amanecer] dawn, daybreak **- 2.** MÚS *popular song sung at dawn* **- 3.** MIL reveille.

alborear *v impers*: **empezaba a alborear** dawn was breaking.

albornoz *sm* bathrobe.

alborotador, ra <> *adj* rowdy. <> *sm, f* troublemaker.

alborotar <> *vi* to be noisy *O* rowdy. <> *vt* **- 1.** [perturbar] to disturb, to unsettle **- 2.** [amotinar] to stir up, to rouse **- 3.** [desordenar] to mess up.

➡ **alborotarse** *vprnl* [perturbarse] to get worked up.

alboroto *sm* **- 1.** [ruido] din **- 2.** [jaleo] fuss, to-do; **armar un alboroto** to cause a commotion **- 3.** [desorden] mess.

alborozar [13] *vt* to delight.

alborozo *sm* delight, joy.

albricias *interj*: ¡albricias! great (news)!

albufera *sf* lagoon.

álbum *(pl* álbumes) *sm* album.

albúmina *sf* albumin.

albuminoide *adj* albuminoid.

albur *sm* Méx [juego de palabras] *play on words*.

Albures

Albures are a distinctive feature of male Mexican lower-class speech. They are rapid-fire puns, chiefly of a sexual nature, which can be stretched into extensive exchanges as each participant tries to top the last speaker's remark. Non-native speakers, no matter how fluent their Spanish, are unlikely to make much sense of an exchange of **albures**, let alone be able to participate. Indeed, they can be largely incomprehensible even to many Mexicans.

ALCA *sf (abrev de* **Área de Libre Comercio de América)** LAFTA.

alcachofa *sf* **- 1.** BOT artichoke **- 2.** [pieza - de regadera] rose, sprinkler; [- de ducha] shower head.

alcahuete, ta *sm, f* **- 1.** [mediador] go-between **- 2.** [chismoso] gossipmonger.

alcaide *sm* prison governor.

alcalde, esa *sm, f* mayor (*f* mayoress).

alcaldía *sf* **- 1.** [cargo] mayoralty **- 2.** [lugar] mayor's office **- 3.** [jurisdicción] municipality.

álcali *sm* alkali.

alcalino, na *adj* alkaline.

alcaloide *sm* alkaloid.

alcance *sm* **- 1.** [de arma, misil, emisora] range; **de corto/largo alcance** short-/long-range **- 2.** [de persona]: **a mi/a tu** *etc* **alcance** within my/your *etc* reach; **al alcance de la vista** within sight; **dar alcance a alguien** to catch up with sb; **fuera del alcance de** beyond the reach of **- 3.** [de reformas etc] scope, extent; **de alcance** important, far-reaching **- 4.** [talento]: **de pocos alcances** slow, dim-witted.

alcancía *sf* Amér money box.

alcanfor *sm* camphor.

alcantarilla *sf* sewer; [boca] drain.

alcantarillado *sm* sewers *pl*.

alcanzar [13] <> *vt* **- 1.** [llegar a] to reach **- 2.** [igualarse con] to catch up with **- 3.** [agarrar] to take **- 4.** [entregar] to pass **- 5.** [suj: bala etc] to hit **- 6.** [lograr] to obtain **- 7.** [afectar] to affect **- 8.** [autobús, tren] to manage to catch. <> *vi* **- 1.** [ser suficiente]: **alcanzar para algo/ hacer algo** to be enough for sthg/to do sthg **- 2.** [poder]: **alcanzar a hacer algo** to be able to do sthg.

alcaparra *sf* caper.

alcatraz *sm* gannet.

alcaucil *sm* Amér [alcachofa] artichoke.

alcayata *sf* hook.

alcazaba *sf* citadel.

alcázar *sm* fortress.

alce <> *sm* elk, moose. <> *v* ▷ **alzar**.

alcista *adj* FIN bullish; [mercado] bull *(antes de s)*.

alcoba *sf* bedroom.

alcohol *sm* alcohol; **alcohol etílico** QUÍM ethyl alcohol; **alcohol de quemar** methylated spirits *pl*.

alcoholemia *sf* blood alcohol level.

alcohólico, ca *adj* & *sm, f* alcoholic.

alcoholímetro *sm* **- 1.** [para bebida] alcoholo-meter **- 2.** [para la sangre] Breathalyzer® *UK*, drunkometer *US*.

alcoholismo *sm* alcoholism.

alcoholizar [13] *vt* to turn into an alcoholic. ➡ **alcoholizarse** *vprnl* to become an alcoholic.

alcohotest *(pl* alcohotests) *sm* Breathalyzer® *UK*, drunkometer *US*.

alcornoque *sm* - **1.** [árbol] cork oak - **2.** [madera] cork, corkwood - **3.** *fig* [persona] idiot, fool.

alcurnia *sf* lineage, descent.

aldaba *sf* - **1.** [llamador] doorknocker - **2.** [pestillo] latch.

aldea *sf* small village.

aldeano, na *sm, f* villager.

ale *interj*: ¡ale! come on!

aleación *sf* - **1.** [acción] alloying - **2.** [producto] alloy; **aleación ligera** light alloy.

alear *vt* to alloy.

aleatorio, ria *adj* [número] random; [suceso] chance *(antes de s)*.

alebrestarse *vprnl* Col [ponerse nervioso] to get nervous.

aleccionador, ra *adj* - **1.** [instructivo] instructive - **2.** [ejemplar] exemplary.

aleccionar *vt* to instruct, to teach.

aledaño, ña *adj* adjacent.

➤ **aledaños** *smpl* surrounding area *sing*.

alegación *sf* allegation.

alegar [16] *vt* [motivos, pruebas] to put forward; **alegar que** to claim (that).

alegato *sm* - **1.** *fig* & DER plea - **2.** [ataque] diatribe.

alegoría *sf* allegory.

alegórico, ca *adj* allegorical.

alegrar *vt* - **1.** [persona] to cheer up, to make happy; **me alegra que me lo preguntes** I'm glad you asked me that; [fiesta] to liven up - **2.** *fig* [habitación etc] to brighten up - **3.** *fig* [emborrachar] to make tipsy.

➤ **alegrarse** *vprnl* - **1.** [sentir alegría]: **alegrarse (de algo/por alguien)** to be pleased (about sthg/for sb) - **2.** *fig* [emborracharse] to get tipsy.

alegre *adj* - **1.** [contento] happy - **2.** [que da alegría] cheerful, bright - **3.** *fig* [arriesgado] happy-go-lucky - **4.** *fam* [borracho] tipsy - **5.** *fig* [deshonesto] loose.

alegría *sf* - **1.** [gozo] happiness, joy - **2.** [motivo de gozo] joy - **3.** *fig* [irresponsabilidad] rashness, recklessness.

alegue *etc* ⊳ **alegar**.

alejamiento *sm* - **1.** [distancia] distance - **2.** [separación - de objetos etc] separation; [- entre personas] estrangement.

alejar *vt* - **1.** [poner más lejos] to move away - **2.** *fig* [ahuyentar] to drive out.

➤ **alejarse** *vprnl*: **alejarse (de)** [ponerse más lejos] to go o move away (from); [retirarse] to leave.

alelado, da *adj* stupid.

alelar *vt* to daze, to stupefy.

aleluya ◇ *sm* o *sf* hallelujah. ◇ *interj*: ¡aleluya! Hallelujah!

alemán, ana *adj* & *sm, f* German.

➤ **alemán** *sm* [lengua] German.

Alemania *n pr* Germany.

alentador, ra *adj* encouraging.

alentar [19] *vt* to encourage.

alergia *sf* *lit* & *fig* allergy; **tener alergia a algo** to be allergic to sthg; **alergia primaveral** hay fever.

alérgico, ca *adj* *lit* & *fig*: **alérgico (a)** allergic (to).

alero *sm* - **1.** [del tejado] eaves *pl* - **2.** DEP winger, wing - **3.** AUTO wing - **4.** *loc*: **estar en el alero** to be (hanging) in the balance.

alerón *sm* aileron.

alerta ◇ *adj inv* & *adv* alert. ◇ *sf* alert; **alerta roja** red alert. ◇ *interj*: ¡alerta! watch o look out!

alertar *vt* to alert.

aleta *sf* - **1.** [de pez] fin; **aleta dorsal** dorsal fin - **2.** [de buzo, foca] flipper - **3.** [de coche] wing - **4.** [de nariz] flared part.

aletargar [16] *vt* to make drowsy, to send to sleep.

➤ **aletargarse** *vprnl* to become drowsy o sleepy.

aletear *vi* to flap o flutter its wings.

alevín *sm* - **1.** [cría de pez] fry, young fish - **2.** *fig* [persona] novice, beginner.

alevosía *sf* - **1.** [traición] treachery - **2.** [premeditación] premeditation.

alevoso, sa *adj* - **1.** [traidor] treacherous - **2.** [premeditado] premeditated.

alfa *(el) sf* FÍS & MAT alpha; **alfa y omega** beginning and end, alpha and omega.

alfabético, ca *adj* alphabetical.

alfabetización *sf* - **1.** [de personas - acción] teaching to read and write; [- estado] literacy - **2.** [ordenación] alphabetization.

alfabetizar [13] *vt* - **1.** [personas] to teach to read and write - **2.** [ordenar] to put into alphabetical order.

alfabeto *sm* alphabet; **alfabeto Morse** Morse code.

alfalfa *sf* alfalfa, lucerne.

alfanumérico, ca *adj* INFORM alphanumeric.

alfaque *sm* sandbank, bar.

alfarería *sf* - **1.** [técnica] pottery - **2.** [lugar] potter's, pottery shop.

alfarero, ra *sm, f* potter.

alféizar *sm* window-sill.

alfeñique *sm* *fam fig* [persona] weakling.

alférez *sm* ≈ second lieutenant.

alfil *sm* bishop.

alfiler *sm* - **1.** [aguja] pin; **alfiler de gancho** *Andes, R Dom & Ven* safety pin; **alfiler de seguri-**

dad *Méx & Pan* safety pin; **no cabe ni un alfiler** it's jam-packed; **prendido con alfileres** *fig* sketchy **- 2.** [joya] brooch, pin; **alfiler de corbata** tie-pin.

alfiletero *sm* pin box.

alfombra *sf* [grande] carpet; [pequeña] rug.

alfombrar *vt* to carpet.

alfombrilla *sf* **- 1.** [alfombra pequeña] rug **- 2.** [felpudo] doormat **- 3.** [del baño] bathmat **- 4.** INFORM: **alfombrilla (del ratón)** mouse mat.

alforja *sf (gen pl)* **- 1.** [mochila] knapsack **- 2.** [de caballo] saddlebag.

alga *sf (el)* [de mar] seaweed *(U)*; [de río] algae *pl*.

algarabía *sf* **- 1.** [habla confusa] gibberish **- 2.** [alboroto] racket.

algarada *sf* racket, din.

algarroba *sf* **- 1.** [planta] vetch **- 2.** [fruto] carob *o* locust bean.

algarrobo *sm* carob *o* locust tree.

algazara *sf* racket, uproar.

álgebra *sf (el)* algebra.

algebraico, ca *adj* algebraic.

álgido, da *adj* [culminante] critical.

algo ◇ *pron* **- 1.** [alguna cosa] something; [en interrogativas] anything; **¿te pasa algo?** is anything the matter?; **algo es algo** something is better than nothing; **por algo lo habrá dicho** he must have said it for a reason; **o algo así** or something like that **- 2.** [cantidad pequeña] a bit, a little; **algo de** some, a little **- 3.** *fig* [cosa importante] something; **se cree que es algo** he thinks he's something (special). ◇ *adv* [un poco] rather, somewhat. ◇ *sm*: **tiene un algo** there's something attractive about him.

algodón *sm* cotton; **algodón (hidrófilo)** cotton wool *UK*, absorbent cotton *US*; **criado entre algodones** *fig* pampered, mollycoddled.

algodonero, ra *adj* cotton *(antes de s)*.

algoritmo *sm* INFORM algorithm.

alguacil *sm* **- 1.** [del ayuntamiento] *mayor's assistant* **- 2.** [del juzgado] bailiff.

alguacilillo *sm mounted official at bullfight*.

alguien *pron* **- 1.** [alguna persona] someone, somebody; [en interrogativas] anyone, anybody; **¿hay alguien ahí?** is anyone there? **- 2.** *fig* [persona de importancia] somebody; **se cree alguien** she thinks she's somebody (special).

alguno, na ◇ *adj (antes de sm: algún)* **- 1.** [indeterminado] some; [en interrogativas] any; **¿tienes algún libro?** do you have any books?; **algún día** some *o* one day; **ha surgido algún (que otro) problema** the odd problem has come up **- 2.** *(después de s)* [ninguno] any; **no tengo interés alguno** I have no interest, I haven't any interest. ◇ *pron* **- 1.** [persona]

someone, somebody; *(pl)* some people; [en interrogativas] anyone, anybody; **¿conocisteis a algunos?** did you get to know any?; **algunos de, algunos (de) entre** some *o* a few of **- 2.** [cosa] the odd one, some *pl*, a few *pl*; [en interrogativas] any; **me salió mal alguno** I got the odd one wrong.

alhaja *sf* **- 1.** [joya] jewel **- 2.** [objeto de valor] treasure **- 3.** *fig* [persona] gem.

alhelí *(pl* alhelíes) *sm* wallflower.

aliado, da *adj* allied.

➤ **Aliados** *smpl*: **los Aliados** the Allies.

alianza *sf* **- 1.** [pacto, parentesco] alliance **- 2.** [anillo] wedding ring.

aliar [9] *vt* **- 1.** [naciones] to ally **- 2.** [cualidades etc] to combine.

➤ **aliarse** *vprnl* to form an alliance.

alias ◇ *adv* alias. ◇ *sm inv* alias; [entre amigos] nickname.

alicaído, da *adj* **- 1.** [triste] depressed **- 2.** *fig* [débil] weak.

alicatado *sm* tiling.

alicatar *vt* to tile.

alicates *smpl* pliers.

aliciente *sm* **- 1.** [incentivo] incentive **- 2.** [atractivo] attraction.

alícuota *adj* MAT aliquot.

alienación *sf* **- 1.** [gen] alienation **- 2.** [trastorno psíquico] derangement, madness.

alienante *adj* alienating.

alienar *vt* **- 1.** [enajenar] to derange, to drive mad **- 2.** FILOS to alienate.

alienígena *smf* alien.

alienta *etc* ▷ **alentar**.

aliento *sm* **- 1.** [respiración] breath; **tener mal aliento** to have bad breath; **cobrar aliento** to catch one's breath; **sin aliento** breathless **- 2.** *fig* [ánimo] strength.

aligerar *vt* **- 1.** [peso] to lighten **- 2.** [ritmo] to speed up; [el paso] to quicken **- 3.** *fig* [aliviar] to relieve, to ease.

alijo *sm* contraband *(U)*; **alijo de drogas** consignment of drugs.

alimaña *sf* pest *(fox, weasel etc)*.

alimentación *sf* **- 1.** [acción] feeding **- 2.** [comida] food **- 3.** [régimen alimenticio] diet **- 4.** TECNOL feed, input.

alimentador, ra *adj* TECNOL feeding.

➤ **alimentador** *sm* TECNOL feed, feeder; **alimentador de papel** INFORM paper feed.

alimentar ◇ *vt* [gen] to feed; [motor, coche] to fuel. ◇ *vi* [nutrir] to be nourishing.

➤ **alimentarse** *vprnl* [comer]: **alimentarse de** to live on.

alimentario, ria *adj* food *(antes de s)*.

alimenticio, cia *adj* nourishing; **productos alimenticios** foodstuffs; **valor alimenticio** food value.

alimento *sm* [gen] food; [valor nutritivo] nourishment; **alimentos transgénicos** GM foods.

alimón ➡ **al alimón** *loc adv* jointly, together.

alineación *sf* - **1.** [en el espacio] alignment - **2.** DEP line-up.

alineado, da *adj* - **1.** [en el espacio] lined up - **2.** DEP selected.

➡ **no alineado, da** *adj* POLÍT non-aligned.

alineamiento *sm* alignment.

➡ **no alineamiento** *sm* POLÍT non-alignment.

alinear *vt* - **1.** [en el espacio] to line up - **2.** DEP to select.

➡ **alinearse** *vprnl* POLÍT to align.

aliñar *vt* [ensalada] to dress; [carne] to season.

aliño *sm* [para ensalada] dressing; [para carne] seasoning.

alioli *sm* garlic mayonnaise.

alirón *interj*: ¡alirón! hooray!

alisar *vt* to smooth (down).

alisio ⊏▷ **viento**.

aliso *sm* alder.

alistamiento *sm* enlistment.

alistarse *vprnl* to enlist; *Amér* [aprontarse] to get ready.

aliteración *sf* alliteration.

aliviar [8] *vt* - **1.** [atenuar] to soothe - **2.** [aligerar - persona] to relieve; [- carga] to lighten.

alivio *sm* relief; ¡qué alivio! what a relief!

➡ **de alivio** *loc adj* [terrible] dreadful.

aljibe *sm* - **1.** [de agua] cistern - **2.** NÁUT tanker.

allá *adv* - **1.** [espacio] over there; **allá abajo/arriba** down/up there; **más allá** further on; **más allá de** beyond; ¡**allá voy!** I'm coming! - **2.** [tiempo]: **allá por los años cincuenta** back in the 50s; **allá para el mes de agosto** around August some time - **3.** *loc*: **allá él/ella** *etc* that's his/her *etc* problem.

➡ **el más allá** *sm* the great beyond.

allanamiento *sm* forceful entry; **allanamiento de morada** breaking and entering.

allanar *vt* - **1.** [terreno] to flatten, to level - **2.** *fig* [dificultad] to overcome - **3.** [irrumpir en] to break into.

allegado, da ◇ *adj* close. ◇ *sm, f* - **1.** [familiar] relative - **2.** [amigo] close friend.

allende *adv* beyond.

allí *adv* there; **allí abajo/arriba** down/up there; **allí mismo** right there; **está por allí** it's around there somewhere; **hasta allí** up until then.

alma *sf (el)* - **1.** [gen] soul - **2.** *fig* [catalizador - de negocio, equipo] backbone; **el alma de la fiesta** the life and soul of the party - **3.** [de bastón, ovillo] core - **4.** *loc*: **se le cayó el alma a los pies** his heart sank; **en el alma** truly, from the bottom of one's heart; **ir con el alma en pena, ser como un alma en pena** to go about like a lost soul; **llegar al alma a alguien** to touch sb's heart; **partir el alma a alguien** to break sb's heart; **sentirlo en el alma** to be truly sorry; **ser un alma de cántaro** to be thoughtless o uncaring; ¡**alma mía!** my love!

almacén *sm* warehouse.

➡ **(grandes) almacenes** *smpl* department store *sing*.

almacenamiento *sm* [gen & INFORM] storage.

almacenar *vt* - **1.** [gen & INFORM] to store - **2.** [reunir] to collect.

almendra *sf* almond.

almendrado, da *adj* almond-shaped.

➡ **almendrado** *sm* CULIN almond paste.

almendro *sm* almond (tree).

almíbar *sm* syrup.

almibarado, da *adj* - **1.** [con almíbar] covered in syrup - **2.** *fig* [afectado] syrupy, sugary.

almibarar *vt* to cover in syrup.

almidón *sm* starch.

almidonado, da *adj* starched.

➡ **almidonado** *sm* starching.

almidonar *vt* to starch.

alminar *sm* minaret.

almirantazgo *sm* - **1.** [dignidad] admiralty - **2.** [de la Armada] Admiralty.

almirante *sm* admiral.

almirez *sm* mortar.

almizcle *sm* musk.

almizclero *sm* musk deer.

almohada *sf* pillow; **consultarlo con la almohada** *fig* to sleep on it.

almohadilla *sf* [gen, TECNOL & ZOOL] pad; [cojín] small cushion.

almohadillado, da *adj* padded.

almohadón *sm* cushion.

almoneda *sf* - **1.** [venta] sale - **2.** [subasta] auction.

almorávide *adj* & *smf* Almoravid.

almorrana *sf (gen pl)* piles *pl*.

almorzar [37] ◇ *vt* - **1.** [al mediodía] to have for lunch - **2.** [a media mañana] to have as a mid-morning snack. ◇ *vi* - **1.** [al mediodía] to have lunch - **2.** [a media mañana] to have a mid-morning snack.

almuerzo *sm* - **1.** [al mediodía] lunch - **2.** [a media mañana] mid-morning snack - **3.** [al comenzar el día] breakfast.

aló *interj Andes & Caribe* [al teléfono] hello?

alocado, da *sm, f* crazy person.

alocución *sf* address, speech.

alojamiento *sm* accommodation; **buscar alojamiento** to look for accommodation; **dar alojamiento a** to put up.

alojar *vt* to put up.

◆ **alojarse** *vprnl* - **1.** [hospedarse] to stay - **2.** [introducirse] to lodge.

alondra *sf* lark.

alopecia *sf* alopecia.

alpaca *sf* alpaca.

alpargata *sf* (gen pl) espadrille.

Alpes *smpl*: **los Alpes** the Alps.

alpinismo *sm* mountaineering.

alpinista *smf* mountaineer.

alpino, **na** *adj* Alpine.

alpiste *sm* - **1.** [planta] canary grass - **2.** [semilla] birdseed.

alquería *sf* farmstead.

alquilar *vt* [casa, TV, oficina] to rent; [coche] to hire.

◆ **alquilarse** *vprnl* [casa, TV, oficina] to be for rent; [coche] to be for hire; **'se alquila'** 'to let'.

alquiler *sm* - **1.** [acción - de casa, TV, oficina] renting; [- de coche] hiring *UK*, rental *US*; **de alquiler** [- casa] rented; [- coche] hire *(antes de s) UK*, rental *(antes de s) US*; **tenemos pisos de alquiler** we have flats to let *UK*, we have apartments to rent *US* - **2.** [precio - de casa, oficina] rent; [- de televisión] rental; [- de coche] hire *UK*, rental *US*.

alquimia *sf* alchemy.

alquimista *smf* alchemist.

alquitrán *sm* tar.

alquitranar *vt* to tar.

alrededor *adv* - **1.** [en torno] around; **mira a tu alrededor** look around you; **de alrededor** surrounding - **2.** [aproximadamente]: **alrededor de** around, about.

◆ **alrededores** *smpl* surrounding area *sing*; **en los alrededores de Londres** in the area around London.

◆ **alrededor de** *loc prep* around.

alta *sf* ▷ **alto**.

altanería *sf* haughtiness.

altanero, **ra** *adj* haughty.

altar *sm* altar; **altar mayor** high altar; **conducir** *o* **llevar a alguien al altar** *fig* to lead sb down the aisle.

altavoz *sm* [gen] speaker; [para anuncios] loudspeaker.

alteración *sf* - **1.** [cambio] alteration - **2.** [excitación] agitation - **3.** [alboroto] disturbance; **alteración del orden público** breach of the peace.

alterar *vt* - **1.** [cambiar] to alter - **2.** [perturbar - persona] to agitate, to fluster; [- orden público] to disrupt - **3.** [estropear] to spoil; [leche] to turn.

◆ **alterarse** *vprnl* - **1.** [perturbarse] to get agitated *o* flustered - **2.** [estropearse] to spoil, to go off; [leche] to turn.

altercado *sm* argument, row.

alternador *sm* ELECTR alternator.

alternancia *sf* alternation.

alternar ◇ *vt* to alternate. ◇ *vi* - **1.** [relacionarse]: **alternar (con)** to mix (with), to socialize (with) - **2.** [sucederse]: **alternar con** to alternate with.

◆ **alternarse** *vprnl* - **1.** [en el tiempo] to take turns - **2.** [en el espacio] to alternate.

alternativa *sf* ▷ **alternativo**.

alternativamente *adv* [moverse] alternately.

alternativo, **va** *adj* - **1.** [movimiento] alternating - **2.** [posibilidad] alternative.

◆ **alternativa** *sf* - **1.** [opción] alternative; **alternativa de poder** POLÍT succession of power - **2.** TAUROM *ceremony in which bullfighter shares the kill with his novice, accepting him as a professional*; **tomar la alternativa** to become a professional bullfighter.

alterne *sm practice whereby women encourage people to drink in return for a commission*; **bar de alterne** singles bar.

alterno, **na** *adj* alternate; ELECTR alternating.

alteza *sf fig* [de sentimientos] loftiness.

◆ **Alteza** *sf* [tratamiento] Highness; **Su Alteza Real** His Royal Highness (*f* Her Royal Highness).

altibajos *smpl* - **1.** [del terreno] unevenness *sing* - **2.** *fig* [de vida etc] ups and downs.

altillo *sm* - **1.** [armario] *small cupboard usually found above another cupboard* - **2.** [cerro] hillock.

altímetro *sm* altimeter.

altiplano *sm* high plateau.

altísimo ◆ **Altísimo** *sm*: **el Altísimo** the Most High.

altisonante *adj* high-sounding.

altitud *sf* altitude.

altivez *sf* haughtiness.

altivo, **va** *adj* haughty.

alto, **ta** *adj* - **1.** [gen] high; [persona, árbol, edificio] tall; [piso] top, upper; **alta fidelidad** high fidelity; **altos hornos** blast furnace - **2.** [ruidoso] loud - **3.** [avanzado] late; **a altas horas de la noche** late at night, in the small hours - **4.** GEOGR upper, northern.

◆ **alto** ◇ *sm* - **1.** [altura] height; **mide dos metros de alto** [cosa] it's two metres high; [persona] he's two metres tall - **2.** [interrupción] stop; **hacer un alto** to make a stop - **3.** [lugar elevado] height; **en lo alto de** at the top of - **4.** MÚS alto - **5.** *loc*: **pasar por alto algo** to pass over sthg; **por todo lo alto** [lujoso] grand, luxurious; [a lo grande] in (great) style. ◇ *adv* **- 1.** [arriba] high (up) **- 2.** [hablar etc] loud. ◇ *interj*: ¡alto! halt!, stop!

◆ **alta** *sf (el)* **- 1.** [del hospital] discharge; **dar de alta** *o* **el alta a alguien** to discharge sb (from hospital) **- 2.** [documento médico] certificate of discharge **- 3.** [en una asociación] membership; **darse de alta** to become a member.

altoparlante *sm* Amér loudspeaker.

altozano *sm* hillock.

altramuz *sm* lupin.

altruismo *sm* altruism.

altruista ◇ *adj* altruistic. ◇ *smf* altruist.

altura *sf* **- 1.** [gen] height; [en el mar] depth; **volar a gran altura** to fly at altitude; **ganar altura** to climb; **tiene dos metros de altura** [gen] it's two metres high; [persona] he's two metres tall; **Viella está a 1.000 m de altura** Viella is 1,000 metres above sea level **- 2.** [nivel] level; **está a la altura del ayuntamiento** it's next to the town hall **- 3.** [latitud] latitude **- 4.** [valor] value; **a la altura de** on a par with **- 5.** *fig* [de persona] stature **- 6.** *fig* [de sentimientos, espíritu] loftiness.

◆ **alturas** *sfpl* [el cielo] Heaven *sing*; **a estas alturas** *fig* this far on, this late.

alubia *sf* bean.

alucinación *sf* hallucination.

alucinado, **da** *adj* **- 1.** MED hallucinating **- 2.** *fam* [sorprendido] gobsmacked.

alucinante *adj* **- 1.** MED hallucinatory **- 2.** *fam* [extraordinario] amazing.

alucinar ◇ *vi* **- 1.** MED to hallucinate **- 2.** *fam* [equivocarse]: **¡no alucines!** come off it! ◇ *vt* *fam* fig [seducir] to hypnotize, to captivate.

alucinógeno, **na** *adj* hallucinogenic.

◆ **alucinógeno** *sm* hallucinogen.

alud *sm* lit & fig avalanche.

aludido, **da** *sm*, *f*: **el aludido** the aforesaid; **darse por aludido** [ofenderse] to take it personally; [reaccionar] to take the hint.

aludir *vi*: **aludir a** [sin mencionar] to allude to; [mencionando] to refer to.

alumbrado *sm* lighting; **alumbrado público** street lighting.

alumbramiento *sm* **- 1.** [iluminación] lighting **- 2.** [parto] delivery.

alumbrar ◇ *vt* **- 1.** [iluminar] to light up **- 2.** [instruir] to enlighten **- 3.** [dar a luz] to give birth to. ◇ *vi* [iluminar] to give light.

aluminio *sm* aluminium.

aluminosis *sf inv* CONSTR *collapse of buildings as a result of inadequate building materials containing aluminium.*

alumnado *sm* [de escuela] pupils *pl*; [de universidad] students *pl*.

alumno, **na** *sm*, *f* [de escuela, profesor particular] pupil; [de universidad] student.

alunizaje *sm* landing on the moon.

alunizar [13] *vi* to land on the moon.

alusión *sf* [sin mencionar] allusion; [mencionando] reference; **hacer alusión a** [sin mencionar] to allude to; [mencionando] to refer to.

alusivo, **va** *adj* allusive.

aluvión *sm* **- 1.** [gen] flood **- 2.** GEOL alluvium.

alvéolo, **alveolo** *sm* **- 1.** [de panal] cell **- 2.** ANAT alveolus.

alza *sf (el)* rise; **en alza** FIN rising; *fig* gaining in popularity; **jugar al alza** FIN to bull the market.

alzacuello *sm* RELIG dog collar.

alzado, **da** *adj* **- 1.** [gen] raised **- 2.** [comerciante] fraudulent **- 3.** [precio] fixed.

◆ **alzado** *sm* ARQUIT elevation.

◆ **alzada** *sf* **- 1.** [de caballo] height **- 2.** DER appeal.

alzamiento *sm* uprising, revolt.

alzar [13] *vt* **- 1.** [levantar] to lift, to raise; [voz] to raise; [vela] to hoist; [cuello de abrigo] to turn up; [mangas] to pull up **- 2.** [aumentar] to raise **- 3.** [construir] to erect **- 4.** [sublevar] to stir up, to raise.

◆ **alzarse** *vprnl* **- 1.** [levantarse] to rise **- 2.** [sublevarse] to rise up, to revolt **- 3.** [conseguir]: **alzarse con** [victoria] to win; [botín] to make off with; [premio] to carry off.

a.m. (*abrev de* ante merídiem) a.m.

AM (*abrev de* amplitude modulation) *sf* AM.

ama ⊳ amo.

amabilidad *sf* kindness; **¿tendría la amabilidad de...?** would you be so kind as to...?

amabilísimo, **ma** *superl* = amable.

amable *adj* kind; **¿sería tan amable de...?** would you be so kind as to...?

amado, **da** *sm*, *f* loved one.

amaestrado, **da** *adj* [gen] trained; [en circo] performing.

amaestrar *vt* to train.

amagar [16] ◇ *vt* **- 1.** [dar indicios de] to show signs of **- 2.** [mostrar intención] to threaten; **le amagó un golpe** he threatened to hit him. ◇ *vi* [tormenta] to be imminent, to threaten.

amago *sm* **- 1.** [indicio] sign, hint **- 2.** [amenaza] threat.

amague *etc* ⊳ amagar.

amainar ◇ *vt* NÁUT to take in. ◇ *vi* lit & fig to abate, to die down.

amalgama *sf* fig & QUÍM amalgam.

amalgamar *vt* fig & QUÍM to amalgamate.

amamantar *vt* [animal] to suckle; [bebé] to breastfeed.

amancebamiento *sm* living together, cohabitation.

amancebarse *vprnl* to live together, to cohabit.

amanecer [30] ⬦ *sm* dawn; **al amanecer** at dawn. ⬦ *v impers*: **amaneció a las siete** dawn broke at seven. ⬦ *vi* [en un lugar] to see in the dawn.

amanerado, da *adj* - **1.** [afeminado] effeminate - **2.** [afectado] mannered, affected.

amaneramiento *sm* - **1.** [afeminamiento] effeminacy - **2.** [afectación] affectation.

amanerarse *vprnl* - **1.** [afeminarse] to become effeminate - **2.** [volverse afectado] to become affected.

amanita *sf* amanita.

amansar *vt* - **1.** [animal] to tame - **2.** *fig* [persona] to calm down - **3.** *fig* [pasiones] to calm.
◆ **amansarse** *vprnl* to calm down.

amante *smf* - **1.** [querido] lover - **2.** *fig* [aficionado]: **ser amante de algo/hacer algo** to be keen on sthg/doing sthg; **los amantes del arte** art lovers.

amanuense *smf* scribe.

amañar *vt* [falsear] to fix; [elecciones, resultado] to rig; [documento] to doctor.
◆ **amañarse** *vprnl*: **amañárselas** to manage.

amaño *sm* (gen pl) [treta] ruse, trick.

amapola *sf* poppy.

amar [1] *vt* to love.

amaraje *sm* [de hidroavión] landing at sea; [de vehículo espacial] splashdown.

amaranto *sm* amaranth.

amarar *vi* [hidroavión] to land at sea; [vehículo espacial] to splash down.

amargado, da ⬦ *adj* [resentido] bitter.
⬦ *sm, f* bitter person.

amargar [16] *vt* to make bitter; *fig* to spoil, to ruin.
◆ **amargarse** *vprnl* [suj: alimento, persona] to become bitter.

amargo, ga *adj lit & fig* bitter.

amargor *sm* [sabor] bitterness.

amargoso, sa *adj Amér* bitter.

amargue *etc* ▷ **amargar**.

amargura *sf* [sentimiento] sorrow.

amariconado, da *adj fam despec* poofy.
◆ **amariconado** *sm fam despec* pansy.

amarillento, ta *adj* yellowish.

amarillo, lla *adj* - **1.** [color] yellow - **2.** PRENSA sensationalist - **3.** [sindicato] conservative.
◆ **amarillo** *sm* [color] yellow.

amarilloso, sa *adj Amér* yellowish.

amariposado, da *adj* [afeminado] effeminate.

amarra *sf* mooring rope o line; **largar** o **soltar amarras** to cast off.
◆ **amarras** *sfpl fig* [contactos] connections, friends in high places.

amarrar *vt* - **1.** NÁUT to moor - **2.** [atar] to tie (up); **amarrar algo/a alguien a algo** to tie sthg/sb to sthg.
◆ **amarrarse** *vprnl Amér salvo R Plata* - **1.** [pelo] to tie up - **2.** [zapatos] to tie.

amarre *sm* mooring.

amarrete *adj Andes & R Plata fam despec* mean, tight.

amartillar *vt* [arma] to cock.

amasar *vt* - **1.** [masa] to knead; [yeso] to mix - **2.** *fam fig* [riquezas] to amass.

amasia *sf C Rica, Méx & Perú* mistress.

amasiato *sm Andes, C Rica & Méx* living in sin.

amasijo *sm fam fig* [mezcla] hotchpotch.

amateur [ama'ter] (*pl* **amateurs**) *adj inv & smf* amateur.

amateurismo [amate'rismo] *sm* amateur nature.

amatista *sf* amethyst.

amazacotado, da *adj* - **1.** [comida] stodgy - **2.** *fig* [pasajeros] packed, crammed.

amazona *sf* - **1.** *fig* [jinete] horsewoman - **2.** MITOL Amazon.

Amazonas *sm*: **el Amazonas** the Amazon.

amazónico, ca *adj* [gen] Amazon (antes de s); [tribu, cultura] Amazonian.

ambages *smpl*: **sin ambages** without beating about the bush, in plain English.

ámbar *sm* amber.

ambición *sf* ambition.

ambicionar *vt* to have as one's ambition.

ambicioso, sa ⬦ *adj* ambitious. ⬦ *sm, f* ambitious person.

ambidextro, tra ⬦ *adj* ambidextrous.
⬦ *sm, f* ambidextrous person.

ambientación *sf* - **1.** CINE, LITER & TEATRO setting - **2.** RADIO & TV sound effects *pl*.

ambientador *sm* air freshener.

ambiental *adj* - **1.** [físico, atmosférico] ambient - **2.** [ecológico] environmental.

ambientar *vt* - **1.** CINE, LITER & TEATRO to set - **2.** [animar] to liven up.
◆ **ambientarse** *vprnl* to settle down.

ambiente ⬦ *adj* ambient. ⬦ *sm* - **1.** [aire] air, atmosphere - **2.** [circunstancias] environment - **3.** [ámbito] world, circles *pl* - **4.** [animación] life, atmosphere - **5.** *Andes & R Dom* [habitación] room.

ambigüedad *sf* ambiguity.

ambiguo, **gua** *adj* - **1.** [gen] ambiguous - **2.** GRAM that may be either masculine or feminine.

ámbito *sm* - **1.** [espacio, límites] confines *pl*; **una ley de ámbito provincial** an act which is provincial in its scope - **2.** [ambiente] world, circles *pl*.

ambivalencia *sf* ambivalence.

ambivalente *adj* ambivalent.

ambos, **bas** ◇ *adj pl* both. ◇ *pron pl* both (of them).

ambulancia *sf* ambulance.

ambulante *adj* travelling; [biblioteca] mobile.

ambulatorio *sm* state-run surgery o clinic.

ameba *sf* amoeba.

amedrentar *vt* to scare, to frighten.

➡ **amedrentarse** *vprnl* to get scared o frightened.

amén *adv* [en plegaria] amen; **en un decir amén** *fig* in the twinkling of an eye; **decir amén a** *fig* to accept unquestioningly.

➡ **amén de** *loc prep* - **1.** [además de] in addition to - **2.** [excepto] except for, apart from.

amenaza *sf* threat; **amenaza de bomba** bomb scare; **amenaza de muerte** death threat.

amenazar [13] *vt* to threaten; **amenazar a alguien con hacerle algo** to threaten to do sthg to sb; **amenazar a alguien con hacer algo** to threaten sb with doing sthg; **amenazar a alguien de muerte/con el despido** to threaten to kill/sack sb; **amenaza lluvia** it's threatening to rain.

amenidad *sf* - **1.** [entretenimiento] entertaining qualities *pl* - **2.** [agrado] pleasantness.

amenizar [13] *vt fig* to liven up.

ameno, **na** *adj* - **1.** [entretenido] entertaining - **2.** [placentero] pleasant.

amenorrea *sf* amenorrhea.

América *n pr* America; **América del Sur** South America; **América Central** Central America.

americana *sf* ⊳ **americano**.

americanismo *sm* - **1.** [carácter] American character - **2.** LING Americanism.

americanizar [13] *vt* to americanize.

➡ **americanizarse** *vprnl* to become americanized.

americano, **na** *adj* & *sm, f* American.

➡ **americana** *sf* [chaqueta] jacket.

amerindio, **dia** *adj* & *sm, f* American Indian, Amerindian.

ameritar *vt Amér* to deserve.

amerizaje *sm* [de hidroavión] landing at sea; [de vehículo espacial] splashdown.

amerizar [13] *vi* [hidroavión] to land at sea; [vehículo espacial] to splash down.

ametralladora *sf* machine gun.

ametrallar *vt* - **1.** [con ametralladora] to machinegun - **2.** [con metralla] to shower with shrapnel.

amianto *sm* asbestos.

amigable *adj* amicable.

amígdala *sf* tonsil.

amigdalitis *sf inv* tonsillitis.

amigo, **ga** ◇ *adj* - **1.** [gen] friendly - **2.** [aficionado]: **amigo de algo/hacer algo** keen on sthg/doing sthg; **amigo de la buena mesa** partial to good food. ◇ *sm, f* - **1.** [persona] friend; **hacerse amigo de** to make friends with; **hacerse amigos** to become friends; **amigo íntimo** close friend - **2.** *fam* [compañero, novio] partner; [amante] lover - **3.** [tratamiento] (my) friend; **'Querido amigo'** [en carta] 'Dear friend'.

amigote, **amiguete** *sm fam* pal, mate *UK*.

amiguismo *sm*: **hay mucho amiguismo** there are always jobs for the boys.

amilanar *vt* [asustar] to terrify.

➡ **amilanarse** *vprnl* [desanimarse] to be discouraged, to lose heart.

aminoácido *sm* amino acid.

aminorar ◇ *vt* to reduce. ◇ *vi* to decrease, to diminish.

amistad *sf* friendship; **hacer** o **trabar amistad (con)** to make friends (with).

➡ **amistades** *sfpl* friends.

amistoso, **sa** *adj* friendly.

amnesia *sf* amnesia.

amnésico, **ca** ◇ *adj* amnesic. ◇ *sm, f* amnesiac.

amniótico, **ca** *adj* amniotic.

amnistía *sf* amnesty; **Amnistía Internacional** Amnesty International.

amnistiar [9] *vt* to grant amnesty to.

amo, **ama** *sm, f* - **1.** [gen] owner - **2.** [de criado, situación etc] master (*f* mistress).

➡ **ama de casa** *sf* housewife.

➡ **ama de cría** *sf* wet nurse.

➡ **ama de llaves** *sf* housekeeper.

amodorrado, **da** *adj* drowsy.

amodorrarse *vprnl* to get drowsy.

amoldable *adj* adaptable; **ser amoldable a** to be able to adapt to.

amoldar *vt* [adaptar]: **amoldar (a)** to adapt (to).

➡ **amoldarse** *vprnl* [adaptarse]: **amoldarse (a)** to adapt (to).

amonal *sm* ammonal.

amonestación *sf* - **1.** [reprimenda] reprimand - **2.** DEP warning.

➤ **amonestaciones** *sfpl* [para matrimonio] banns.

amonestar *vt* - **1.** [reprender] to reprimand - **2.** DEP to warn - **3.** [para matrimonio] to publish the banns of.

amoníaco, amoniaco *sm* - **1.** [gas] ammonia - **2.** [disolución] liquid ammonia.

amontonar *vt* - **1.** [apilar] to pile up - **2.** [reunir] to accumulate.

➤ **amontonarse** *vprnl* - **1.** [personas] to form a crowd - **2.** [problemas, trabajo] to pile up; [ideas, solicitudes] to come thick and fast.

amor *sm* love; **amor libre/platónico** free/platonic love; **de mil amores** with pleasure, gladly; **hacer el amor** to make love; **por amor al arte** for the love of it; **¡por el amor de Dios!** for God's sake!

➤ **amor propio** *sm* pride.

amoral *adj* amoral.

amoralidad *sf* amorality.

amoratado, da *adj* [de frío] blue; [por golpes] black and blue.

amoratar *vt* [suj: el frío] to turn blue; [suj: persona] to bruise.

➤ **amoratarse** *vprnl* [por el frío] to turn blue; [por golpes] to turn black and blue.

amordazar [13] *vt* [persona] to gag; [perro] to muzzle.

amorfo, fa *adj* - **1.** [sin forma] amorphous - **2.** *fig* [persona] lacking in character.

amorío *sm fam* [romance] fling.

amoroso, sa *adj* - **1.** [gen] loving; [carta, relación] love *(antes de s)* - **2.** *C Sur* [encantador] charming.

amortajar *vt* [difunto] to shroud.

amortiguación *sf* - **1.** [de ruido] muffling; [de golpe] softening, cushioning - **2.** AUTO suspension, shock absorbers *pl*.

amortiguador, ra *adj* [de ruido] muffling; [de golpe] softening, cushioning.

➤ **amortiguador** *sm* AUTO shock absorber.

amortiguar [45] *vt* [ruido] to muffle; [golpe] to soften, to cushion.

➤ **amortiguarse** *vprnl* [ruido] to die away; [golpe] to be cushioned.

amortizable *adj* ECON [bonos, acciones] redeemable.

amortización *sf* ECON [de deuda, préstamo] amortization, paying-off; [de inversión, capital] recouping; [de bonos, acciones] redemption; [de bienes de equipo] depreciation.

amortizar [13] *vt* - **1.** [sacar provecho] to get one's money's worth out of - **2.** [ECON - deuda, préstamo] to amortize, to pay off; [- inversión, capital] to recoup; [- bonos, acciones] to redeem; [- bienes de equipo] to depreciate.

amoscarse [10] *vprnl fam* to get in a huff.

amotinado, da *adj* & *sm, f* rebel, insurgent.

amotinamiento *sm* rebellion, uprising; [de marineros] mutiny.

amotinar *vt* to incite to riot; [a marineros] to incite to mutiny.

➤ **amotinarse** *vprnl* to riot; [marineros] to mutiny.

amovible *adj* - **1.** [pieza] detachable - **2.** [cargo] revocable.

amparar *vt* - **1.** [proteger] to protect - **2.** [dar cobijo a] to give shelter to, to take in.

➤ **ampararse** *vprnl* - **1.** *fig* [apoyarse]: **ampararse en** [ley] to have recourse to; [excusas] to draw on - **2.** [cobijarse]: **ampararse de** o **contra** to (take) shelter from.

amparo *sm* [protección] protection; **al amparo de** [persona, caridad] with the help of; [ley] under the protection of.

amperaje *sm* amperage.

amperímetro *sm* ammeter.

amperio *sm* amp, ampere.

ampliable *adj* - **1.** [gen] expandable - **2.** FOTO enlargeable - **3.** [plazo] extendible.

ampliación *sf* - **1.** [aumento] expansion; [de edificio, plazo] extension; **ampliación de capital** ECON increase in capital - **2.** FOTO enlargement.

ampliadora *sf* FOTO enlarger.

ampliar [9] *vt* - **1.** [gen] to expand; [local] to add an extension to; [plazo] to extend - **2.** FOTO to enlarge, to blow up - **3.** [estudios] to further, to continue.

amplificación *sf* amplification.

amplificador *sm* ELECTRÓN amplifier.

amplificar [10] *vt* to amplify.

amplio, plia *adj* - **1.** [sala etc] roomy, spacious; [avenida, gama] wide - **2.** [ropa] loose - **3.** [explicación etc] comprehensive; **en el sentido más amplio de la palabra** in the broadest sense of the word - **4.** [mentalidad etc] broad.

amplitud *sf* - **1.** [espaciosidad] roominess, spaciousness; [de avenida] wideness - **2.** [de ropa] looseness - **3.** *fig* [extensión] extent, comprehensiveness; **amplitud de miras** broadmindedness.

ampolla *sf* - **1.** [en piel] blister - **2.** [para inyecciones] ampoule - **3.** [frasco] phial.

ampuloso, sa *adj* pompous.

amputación *sf* amputation.

amputar *vt* to amputate.

amueblado, da *adj* [apartamento] furnished.

➤ **amueblado** *sm R Dom* room hired for sex.

amueblar *vt* to furnish.

amuleto *sm* amulet.

amurallado, da *adj* walled.

amurallar *vt* to build a wall around.

anabolizante <> *adj* anabolic. <> *sm* anabolic steroid.

anacarado, da *adj* pearly.

anacardo *sm* cashew.

anacoreta *smf* anchorite, hermit.

anacrónico, ca *adj* anachronistic.

anacronismo *sm* anachronism.

ánade *sm culto* duck.

anaerobio, bia *adj* anaerobic.

anagrama *sm* anagram.

anal *adj* ANAT anal.

anales *smpl lit & fig* annals.

analfabetismo *sm* illiteracy.

analfabeto, ta *adj & sm, f* illiterate.

analgésico, ca *adj* analgesic.
➤ **analgésico** *sm* analgesic.

análisis *sm inv* analysis; **análisis clínico** (clinical) test; **análisis gramatical** sentence analysis, parsing; **análisis de orina** urine analysis; **análisis de sangre** blood test.

analista *smf* - **1.** [gen] analyst - **2.** INFORM (computer) analyst; **analista programador/de sistemas** programmer/systems analyst.

analítico, ca *adj* analytical.
➤ **analítica** *sf* MED clinical testing.

analizar [13] *vt* to analyse.

analogía *sf* similarity; **por analogía** by analogy.

analógico, ca *adj* - **1.** [análogo] analogous, similar - **2.** INFORM & TECNOL analogue, analog - **3.** ⊳ **reloj**.

análogo, ga *adj*: **análogo (a)** analogous *o* similar (to).

ananá, ananás *sm R Dom* pineapple.

anaquel *sm* shelf.

anaranjado, da *adj* orange.

anarco *fam* <> *adj* anarchistic. <> *smf* anarchist.

anarcosindicalismo *sm* anarchosyndicalism.

anarcosindicalista *adj & smf* anarchosyndicalist.

anarquía *sf* - **1.** [falta de gobierno] anarchy - **2.** [doctrina política] anarchism - **3.** *fig* [desorden] chaos, anarchy.

anárquico, ca *adj* anarchic.

anarquismo *sm* anarchism.

anarquista *adj & smf* anarchist.

anatema *sm* [maldición] curse, anathema.

anatomía *sf* anatomy.

anatómico, ca *adj* - **1.** ANAT anatomical - **2.** [asiento, calzado] orthopaedic.

anca *sf (el)* haunch; **ancas de rana** frogs' legs.

ancestral *adj* ancestral; [costumbre] age-old.

ancestro *sm* ancestor.

ancho, cha *adj* [gen] wide; [prenda] loose-fitting; **te va** *o* **está ancho** it's too big for you; **a mis/tus** *etc* **anchas** *fig* at ease; **quedarse tan ancho** not to care less; **lo dijo delante de todos y se quedó tan ancho** he said it in front of everyone, just like that.
➤ **ancho** *sm* width; **a lo ancho** crosswise; **cinco metros de ancho** five metres wide; **a lo ancho de** across (the width of); **ancho de vía** gauge.

anchoa *sf* anchovy *(salted)*.

anchura *sf* - **1.** [medida] width - **2.** [de ropa] bagginess.

anciano, na <> *adj* old. <> *sm, f* old person, old man (*f* old woman).
➤ **anciano** *sm* [de tribu] elder.

ancla *sf (el)* anchor; **echar/levar anclas** to drop/weigh anchor.

anclar *vi* to anchor.

áncora *(el) sf* anchor.

andadas *sfpl*: **volver a las andadas** *fam fig* to return to one's evil ways.

andaderas *sfpl* baby-walker *sing*.

andador, ra, andarín, ina *adj* fond of walking.
➤ **andadores** *smpl* [para niño] harness *sing*.

andadura *sf* walking.

ándale *interj Amér C & Méx fam* come on!

Andalucía *n pr* Andalusia.

andalucismo *sm* - **1.** [doctrina] *doctrine favouring Andalusian autonomy* - **2.** LING *Andalusian word or expression*.

andaluz, za *adj & sm, f* Andalusian.

andamiaje *sm* scaffolding.

andamio *sm* scaffold.

andanada *sf* - **1.** *fig & MIL* broadside - **2.** TAUROM *covered stand in a bullring*.

andando *interj*: **¡andando!** come on!, let's get a move on!

andante *adj* - **1.** [que anda] walking - **2.** MÚS andante.

andanza *sf (gen pl)* [aventura] adventure.

andar [52] <> *vi* - **1.** [caminar] to walk; [moverse] to move - **2.** [funcionar] to work, to go; **el reloj no anda** the clock has stopped; **las cosas andan mal** things are going badly - **3.** [estar] to be; **andar preocupado** to be worried; **andar mal de dinero** to be short of money; **creo que anda por el almacén** I think he is somewhere in the warehouse; **andar tras algo/alguien** *fig* to be after sthg/sb - **4.** *(antes de gerundio)*: **andar haciendo algo** to be doing sthg; **anda echando broncas a todos** he's going round telling everybody off; **anda explicando sus**

aventuras he's talking about his adventures; **anda buscando algo** he's looking for sthg **- 5.** [ocuparse]: **andar en** [asuntos, líos] to be involved in; [papeleos, negocios] to be busy with **- 6.** [hurgar]: **andar en** to rummage around in; **¿has andado en mis papeles?** have you been fiddling with my papers? **- 7.** *(antes de a y s pl)* [expresa acción]: **en ese país andan a tiros** in that country they go round shooting one another; **andar gritando** to be always shouting **- 8.** [alcanzar, rondar]: **andar por** to be about; **anda por los 60** he's about sixty **- 9.** *fam* [enredar]: **andar con algo** to play with sthg **- 10.** *loc:* **quien mal anda mal acaba** *prov* everyone gets his just deserts. ⬦ *vt* **- 1.** [recorrer] to go, to travel **- 2.** *Amér C* [llevar puesto] to wear. ⬦ *sm* gait, walk.

➤ **andarse** *vprnl* [obrar]: **andarse con cuidado/misterios** to be careful/secretive.

➤ **andares** *smpl* [de persona] gait *sing*; **tener andares de** to walk like.

➤ **anda** *interj*: **¡anda!** [sorpresa, desilusión] oh!; [¡vamos!] come on!; [¡por favor!] go on!; **¡anda ya!** [incredulidad] come off it!

andarín, ina = andador.

andas *sfpl*: **llevar a alguien en andas** *fig* to be all over sb.

andén *sm* **- 1.** FERROC platform **- 2.** *Andes & Amér C* [acera] pavement *UK*, sidewalk *US* **- 3.** *Andes & Amér C* [bancal de tierra] terrace.

Andes *smpl*: **los Andes** the Andes.

andinismo *sm* *Amér* mountaineering.

andinista *smf* *Amér* mountaineer.

andino, na *adj & sm, f* Andean.

Andorra *n pr* Andorra.

andorrano, na *adj & sm, f* Andorran.

andrajo *sm* **- 1.** [harapo] rag **- 2.** *fig & despec* [persona] good-for-nothing.

andrajoso, sa ⬦ *adj* ragged. ⬦ *sm, f* person dressed in rags.

andrógino, na *adj* androgynous.

➤ **andrógino** *sm* hermaphrodite.

androide ⬦ *adj* [masculino] masculine. ⬦ *sm* [autómata] android.

andurriales *smpl* remote place *sing*; **¿qué haces por estos andurriales?** what are you doing as far off the beaten track as this?

anduviera *etc* ⊳ andar.

anécdota *sf* anecdote.

anecdotario *sm* collection of anecdotes.

anecdótico, ca *adj* **- 1.** [con historietas] anecdotal **- 2.** [no esencial] incidental.

anegar [16] *vt* **- 1.** [inundar] to flood **- 2.** [ahogar - planta] to drown.

➤ **anegarse** *vprnl* **- 1.** [inundarse] to flood; **sus ojos se anegaron de lágrimas** tears welled up in his eyes **- 2.** [ahogarse] to drown.

anejo, ja *adj*: **anejo (a)** [edificio] connected (to); [documento] attached (to).

➤ **anejo** *sm* annexe.

anemia *sf* anaemia.

anémico, ca ⬦ *adj* anaemic. ⬦ *sm, f* anaemia sufferer.

anémona *sf* anemone.

anestesia *sf* anaesthesia; **anestesia general/local** general/local anaesthesia.

anestesiar [8] *vt* to anaesthetize, to place under anaesthetic.

anestésico, ca *adj* anaesthetic.

➤ **anestésico** *sm* anaesthetic.

anestesista *smf* anaesthetist.

Aneto *sm*: **el Aneto** Aneto.

aneurisma *sm* aneurysm.

anexar *vt* [documento] to attach.

anexión *sf* annexation.

anexionar *vt* to annex.

anexionista *smf* annexationist.

anexo, xa *adj* [edificio] connected; [documento] attached.

➤ **anexo** *sm* annexe.

anfeta *sf* *fam* pep pill.

anfetamina *sf* amphetamine.

anfibio, bia *adj* *lit & fig* amphibious.

➤ **anfibio** *sm* amphibian.

anfiteatro *sm* **- 1.** CINE & TEATRO circle **- 2.** [edificio] amphitheatre.

anfitrión, ona ⬦ *adj* host *(antes de s)*. ⬦ *sm, f* host (*f* hostess).

ánfora *sf* *(el)* [cántaro] amphora.

ángel *sm* *lit & fig* angel; **ángel custodio** *o* **de la guarda** guardian angel; **tener ángel** to have something special.

angelical *adj* angelic.

ángelus *sm* *inv* RELIG angelus.

angina *sf* *(gen pl)* [amigdalitis] sore throat; **tener anginas** to have a sore throat.

➤ **angina de pecho** *sf* angina (pectoris).

anglicanismo *sm* Anglicanism.

anglicano, na *adj & sm, f* Anglican.

anglicismo *sm* anglicism.

angloamericano, na *adj & sm, f* Anglo-American.

anglófilo, la *adj & sm, f* anglophile.

anglófobo, ba *adj & sm, f* anglophobe.

anglófono, na, angloparlante ⬦ *adj* English-speaking, anglophone. ⬦ *sm, f* English speaker, anglophone.

anglosajón, ona *adj & sm, f* Anglo-Saxon.

Angola *n pr* Angola.

angolano, na adj & sm, f Angolan.
angora sf [de conejo] angora; [de cabra] mohair.
angosto, ta adj culto narrow.
angostura sf - **1.** [estrechez] narrowness - **2.** [bebida] angostura.
anguila sf eel; **anguila de mar** conger eel.
angula sf elver.
angular adj angular.
➠ **gran angular** sm FOTO wide-angle lens.
ángulo sm - **1.** [gen] angle; **ángulo agudo/obtuso/recto** acute/obtuse/right angle; **ángulo de mira** [para disparar] line of sight; **ángulo de tiro** [para disparar] elevation - **2.** [rincón] corner.
anguloso, sa adj angular.
angustia sf - **1.** [aflicción] anxiety - **2.** PSICOL distress.
angustiar [8] vt to distress.
➠ **angustiarse** vprnl [agobiarse]: **angustiarse (por)** to get worried (about).
angustioso, sa adj [espera, momentos] anxious; [situación, noticia] distressing.
anhelante adj: **anhelante (por algo/hacer algo)** longing (for sthg/to do sthg), desperate (for sthg/to do sthg).
anhelar vt to long o wish for; **anhelar hacer algo** to long to do sthg.
anhelo sm longing.
anhídrido sm anhydride; **anhídrido carbónico** carbon dioxide.
anidar vi - **1.** [pájaro] to nest - **2.** fig [sentimiento]: **anidar en** to find a place in.
anilla sf ring.
➠ **anillas** sfpl DEP rings.
anillo sm - **1.** [gen & ASTRON] ring; **anillo de boda** wedding ring; **ir** o **venir como anillo al dedo** fam [persona] to be just the right person; [cosa] to be just what one needed; **no se me van a caer los anillos** fam it won't hurt me (to do it) - **2.** ZOOL annulus.
ánima sf (el) soul; **ánima bendita** soul in Purgatory.
animación sf - **1.** [alegría] liveliness - **2.** [bullicio] hustle and bustle, activity - **3.** CINE animation.
animado, da adj - **1.** [con buen ánimo] cheerful - **2.** [divertido] lively - **3.** CINE animated.
animador, ra sm, f - **1.** [en espectáculo] compere - **2.** [en fiesta de niños] children's entertainer - **3.** [en béisbol etc] cheerleader.
animadversión sf animosity.
animal ◇ adj - **1.** [reino, funciones] animal (antes de s) - **2.** fam [persona - basto] rough; [- ignorante] ignorant. ◇ smf fam fig [persona] animal, brute. ◇ sm animal; **animal doméstico** [de granja etc] domestic animal; [de compañía] pet; **animal de tiro** draught animal.

animalada sf fam fig: **decir/hacer una animalada** to say/do something mindless.
animalucho sm fig & despec disgusting creature.
animar vt - **1.** [estimular] to encourage; **animar a alguien** a o **para hacer algo** to encourage sb to do sthg - **2.** [alegrar - persona] to cheer up - **3.** [avivar - fuego, diálogo, fiesta] to liven up; [comercio] to stimulate.
➠ **animarse** vprnl - **1.** [alegrarse - persona] to cheer up; [- fiesta etc] to liven up - **2.** [decidir]: **animarse (a hacer algo)** to finally decide (to do sthg).
anímico, ca adj mental.
ánimo ◇ sm - **1.** [valor] courage - **2.** [aliento] encouragement; **dar ánimos a alguien** to encourage sb - **3.** [intención]: **con/sin ánimo de** with/without the intention of; **lo hice sin ánimo de ofenderte** I didn't mean to offend you - **4.** [humor] disposition - **5.** [alma] mind. ◇ interj [para alentar]: **¡ánimo!** come on!
animosidad sf animosity.
animoso, sa adj [valiente] courageous; [decidido] undaunted.
aniñado, da adj [comportamiento] childish; [voz, rostro] childlike.
aniquilación sf annihilation.
aniquilar vt to annihilate, to wipe out.
anís (pl anises) sm - **1.** [planta] anise - **2.** [grano] aniseed - **3.** [licor] anisette.
anisete sm anisette.
aniversario sm [gen] anniversary; [cumpleaños] birthday.
ano sm anus.
anoche adv last night, yesterday evening; **antes de anoche** the night before last.
anochecer [30] ◇ sm dusk, nightfall; **al anochecer** at dusk. ◇ v impers to get dark. ◇ vi: **anochecer en algún sitio** to be somewhere at nightfall.
anodino, na adj - **1.** [sin gracia] dull, insipid - **2.** [insustancial] lacking in substance.
ánodo sm anode.
anomalía sf anomaly.
anómalo, la adj anomalous.
anonadar vt - **1.** [sorprender] to astonish, to bewilder - **2.** [abatir] to stun.
➠ **anonadarse** vprnl - **1.** [sorprenderse] to be astonished o bewildered - **2.** [abatirse] to be stunned.
anonimato sm anonymity; **permanecer en el anonimato** to remain nameless; **vivir en el anonimato** to live out of the public eye.
anónimo, ma adj anonymous.
➠ **anónimo** sm anonymous letter.
anorak (pl anoraks) sm anorak.

anorexia *sf* anorexia.

anormal ◇ *adj* - **1.** [anómalo] abnormal - **2.** *despec* [deficiente] subnormal. ◇ *smf despec* subnormal person.

anormalidad *sf* - **1.** [anomalía] abnormality - **2.** [defecto físico o psíquico] handicap, disability.

anotación *sf* [gen] note; [en registro] entry; anotación al margen marginal note; **anotación contable** COM book entry.

anotar *vt* - **1.** [apuntar] to note down, to make a note of - **2.** [tantear] to notch up.

◆ **anotarse** *vprnl* [matricularse] to enrol.

anovulatorio, ria *adj* anovulatory.

◆ **anovulatorio** *sm* anovulant.

anquilosamiento *sm* - **1.** [estancamiento] stagnation - **2.** MED paralysis.

anquilosarse *vprnl* - **1.** [estancarse] to stagnate - **2.** MED to become paralysed.

ánsar *sm* [ave] goose.

ansia *sf (el)* - **1.** [afán]: **ansia de** longing *o* yearning for - **2.** [ansiedad] anxiousness; [angustia] anguish; **comer con ansia** to eat ravenously.

◆ **ansias** *sfpl* [náuseas] sickness *(U)*, nausea *(U)*.

ansiar [9] *vt*: **ansiar hacer algo** to long *o* be desperate to do sthg.

ansiedad *sf* - **1.** [inquietud] anxiety; **con ansiedad** anxiously - **2.** PSICOL nervous tension.

ansiolítico, ca *adj* sedative.

◆ **ansiolítico** *sm* sedative.

ansioso, sa *adj* - **1.** [impaciente] impatient; **estar ansioso por** *o* **de hacer algo** to be impatient to do sthg - **2.** [angustiado] in anguish.

antagónico, ca *adj* antagonistic.

antagonismo *sm* antagonism.

antagonista *smf* opponent.

antaño *adv* in days gone by.

antártico, ca *adj* Antarctic.

◆ **Antártico** *sm*: **el Antártico** the Antarctic; **el océano Glacial Antártico** the Antarctic Ocean.

Antártida *sf*: **la Antártida** the Antarctic.

ante¹ *sm* - **1.** [piel] suede - **2.** [animal] elk, moose.

ante² *prep* - **1.** [delante de, en presencia de] before - **2.** [frente a - hecho, circunstancia] in the face of - **3.** [respecto de] compared to; **su opinión prevaleció ante la mía** his opinion prevailed over mine.

◆ **ante todo** *loc adv* - **1.** [sobre todo] above all - **2.** [en primer lugar] first of all.

anteanoche *adv* the night before last.

anteayer *adv* the day before yesterday.

antebrazo *sm* forearm.

antecámara *sf* antechamber.

antecedente ◇ *adj* preceding, previous. ◇ *sm* - **1.** [precedente] precedent - **2.** GRAM & MAT antecedent.

◆ **antecedentes** *smpl* [de persona] record *sing*; [de asunto] background *sing*; **poner a alguien en antecedentes de** [informar] to fill sb in on; **una persona sin antecedentes** a person with a clean record; **antecedentes penales** criminal record *sing*.

anteceder *vt* to come before, to precede.

antecesor, ra *sm, f* [predecesor] predecessor.

◆ **antecesores** *smpl* [antepasados] ancestors.

antedicho, cha *adj* aforementioned.

antediluviano, na *adj lit & fig* antediluvian.

antefirma *sf* title of the signatory.

antelación *sf*: **con antelación** in advance, beforehand; **con dos horas de antelación** two hours in advance.

antemano ◆ **de antemano** *loc adv* beforehand, in advance.

antemeridiano, na *adj* morning *(antes de s)*.

antena *sf* - **1.** RADIO & TV aerial *UK*, antenna *US*; **estar/salir en antena** to be/go on the air; **antena colectiva** *aerial shared by all the inhabitants of a block of flats*; **antena parabólica** satellite dish - **2.** ZOOL antenna.

anteojos *smpl Amér* glasses.

antepasado, da *sm, f* ancestor.

antepecho *sm* [de puente] parapet; [de ventana] sill.

antepenúltimo, ma *adj & sm, f* last but two.

anteponer [65] *vt*: **anteponer algo a algo** to put sthg before sthg.

◆ **anteponerse** *vprnl*: **anteponerse a** to come before.

anteproyecto *sm* draft; **anteproyecto de ley** draft bill.

antepuesto, ta *pp* ▷ **anteponer**.

anterior *adj* - **1.** [previo]: **anterior (a)** previous (to); **el día anterior** the day before - **2.** [delantero] front *(antes de s)*.

anterioridad *sf*: **con anterioridad** beforehand; **con anterioridad a** before, prior to.

anteriormente *adv* previously.

antes *adv* - **1.** [gen] before; **no importa si venís antes** it doesn't matter if you come earlier; **ya no nado como antes** I can't swim as I used to; **mucho/poco antes** long/shortly before; **lo antes posible** as soon as possible; **mi coche de antes** my old car - **2.** [primero] first; **esta señora está antes** this lady is first - **3.** [expresa preferencial: **antes... que** rather... than; **prefiero la sierra antes que el mar** I like the mountains better than the sea; **iría a la cárcel antes que mentir** I'd rather go to prison than lie.

➡ **antes de** *loc prep* before; **antes de hacer algo** before doing sthg.

➡ **antes (de) que** *loc conj* before; **antes (de) que llegarais** before you arrived.

antesala *sf* anteroom; **estar en la antesala de** *fig* to be on the verge of; **hacer antesala** [esperar] to wait.

antevíspera *sf* day before yesterday.

antiabortista ◇ *adj* anti-abortion, pro-life. ◇ *smf* anti-abortion o pro-life campaigner.

antiácido, da *adj* antacid.
➡ **antiácido** *sm* antacid.

antiadherente *adj* non-stick.

antiaéreo, a *adj* anti-aircraft.

antiarrugas *adj inv* anti-wrinkle.

antibala, antibalas *adj inv* bullet-proof.

antibiótico, ca *adj* antibiotic.
➡ **antibiótico** *sm* antibiotic.

antichoque *adj* shockproof.

anticiclón *sm* anticyclone.

anticipación *sf* earliness; **con anticipación** in advance; **con un mes de anticipación** a month in advance; **con anticipación a** prior to.

anticipado, da *adj* [elecciones] early; [pago] advance; **por anticipado** in advance.

anticipar *vt* - **1.** [prever] to anticipate - **2.** [adelantar] to bring forward - **3.** [dinero] to pay in advance - **4.** [información]: **no te puedo anticipar nada** I can't tell you anything just now.
➡ **anticiparse** *vprnl* - **1.** [suceder antes] to arrive early; **se anticipó a su tiempo** he was ahead of his time - **2.** [adelantarse]: **anticiparse a alguien** to beat sb to it.

anticipo *sm* - **1.** [de dinero] advance - **2.** [presagio] foretaste.

anticlerical *adj* anticlerical.

anticlericalismo *sm* anticlericalism.

anticoagulante *adj* & *sm* anticoagulant.

anticomunismo *sm* anti-communism.

anticomunista *adj* & *smf* anti-communist.

anticoncepción *sf* contraception.

anticonceptivo, va *adj* contraceptive.
➡ **anticonceptivo** *sm* contraceptive.

anticonformismo *sm* non-conformism.

anticongelante *adj* & *sm* antifreeze.

anticonstitucional *adj* unconstitutional.

anticonstitucionalidad *sf* unconstitutional nature.

anticorrosivo, va *adj* anticorrosive.
➡ **anticorrosivo** *sm* anticorrosive substance.

anticristo *sm* Antichrist.

anticuado, da *adj* old-fashioned.

anticuario, ria *sm, f* [comerciante] antique dealer; [experto] antiquarian.
➡ **anticuario** *sm* [tienda] antique shop.

anticuerpo *sm* antibody.

antidemocrático, ca *adj* undemocratic.

antideportivo, va *adj* unsporting, unsportsmanlike.

antidepresivo, va *adj* antidepressant.
➡ **antidepresivo** *sm* antidepressant (drug).

antideslizante *adj* anti-skid; [ruedas] non-skid.

antideslumbrante *adj* anti-dazzle.

antidisturbios *smpl* [policía] riot police.

antidopaje *sm* doping tests *pl*.

antidoping [anti'ðopin] *adj* doping *(antes de s)*.

antídoto *sm* antidote.

antier *adv* *Amér fam* the day before yesterday.

antiestético, ca *adj* unsightly.

antifascista *adj* & *smf* anti-fascist.

antifaz *sm* mask.

antigás *adj inv* gas *(antes de s)*.

antígeno *sm* antigen.

antiglobalización *sf* antiglobalization.

antigripal ◇ *adj* designed to combat flu, flu *(antes de s)*. ◇ *sm* flu remedy.

antigualla *sf* *despec* [cosa] museum piece; [persona] old fogey, old fossil.

antiguamente *adv* [hace mucho] long ago; [previamente] formerly.

Antigua y Barbuda *n pr* Antigua and Barbuda.

antigubernamental *adj* anti-government.

antigüedad *sf* - **1.** [gen] antiquity - **2.** [veteranía] seniority.
➡ **antigüedades** *sfpl* [objetos] antiques; **tienda de antigüedades** antique shop.

antiguo, gua *adj* - **1.** [viejo] old; [inmemorial] ancient - **2.** [anterior, previo] former - **3.** [veterano] senior - **4.** [pasado de moda] old-fashioned; **a la antigua** in an old-fashioned way.
➡ **antiguos** *smpl* HIST ancients.

antihéroe *sm* antihero.

antihigiénico, ca *adj* unhygienic.

antihistamínico *sm* antihistamine.

antiinflacionista *adj* anti-inflationary.

antiinflamatorio *sm* anti-inflammatory drug.

antílope *sm* antelope.

antimateria *sf* antimatter.

antimilitarismo *sm* antimilitarism.

antimilitarista *adj* & *smf* antimilitarist.

antimisil *sm* antimissile.

antimonopolio *adj inv* ECON antitrust *(antes de s)*.

antinatural *adj* unnatural.

antiniebla ▷ **faro**.

antioxidante ◇ *adj* anti-rust. ◇ *sm* rust-proofing agent.

antipapa *sm* antipope.

antiparasitario *sm* - **1.** [veterinaria] flea collar - **2.** TELECOM suppressor.

antiparras *sfpl fam* specs.

antipatía *sf* dislike; **tener antipatía a alguien** to dislike sb.

antipático, ca ◇ *adj* unpleasant. ◇ *sm, f* unpleasant person.

antipirético, ca *adj* antipyretic.
➤ **antipirético** *sm* antipyretic.

antípodas *sfpl*: **las antípodas** the Antipodes.

antiquísimo, ma *superl* = **antiguo**.

antirreflectante *adj* non-reflective.

antirrobo ◇ *adj inv* antitheft *(antes de s)*. ◇ *sm* [en coche] antitheft device; [en edificio] burglar alarm.

antisemita ◇ *adj* anti-Semitic. ◇ *smf* anti-Semite.

antiséptico, ca *adj* antiseptic.
➤ **antiséptico** *sm* antiseptic.

antisocial *adj* antisocial.

antiterrorismo *sm* fight against terrorism.

antiterrorista *adj* anti-terrorist.

antítesis *sf inv* antithesis.

antitetánico, ca *adj* anti-tetanus *(antes de s)*.

antitético, ca *adj culto* antithetical.

antivirus *sm inv* - **1.** MED vaccine - **2.** INFORM antivirus system.

antojadizo, za *adj* capricious.

antojarse *vprnl* - **1.** [capricho]: **se le antojaron esos zapatos** he fancied those shoes; **se le ha antojado ir al cine** he felt like going to the cinema; **cuando se me antoje** when I feel like it - **2.** [posibilidad]: **se me antoja que...** I have a feeling that...

antojitos *smpl Méx* snacks, appetizers.

antojo *sm* - **1.** [capricho] whim; [de embarazada] craving; **a mi/tu** *etc* **antojo** my/your *etc* (own) way; **tener un antojo** [embarazada] to have a craving - **2.** [en la piel] birthmark.

antología *sf* anthology; **de antología** memorable, unforgettable.

antológico, ca *adj* - **1.** [recopilador] anthological - **2.** [inolvidable] memorable, unforgettable.

antónimo *sm* antonym.

antonomasia *sf*: **por antonomasia** par excellence.

antorcha *sf* torch.

antracita *sf* anthracite.

ántrax *sm inv* anthrax.

antro *sm despec* dive, dump.

antropocentrismo *sm* anthropocentrism.

antropofagia *sf* anthropophagy, cannibalism.

antropófago, ga ◇ *adj* anthropophagous. ◇ *sm, f* cannibal.

antropología *sf* anthropology.

antropólogo, ga *sm, f* anthropologist.

anual *adj* annual.

anualidad *sf* annuity, yearly payment.

anuario *sm* yearbook.

anudar *vt* to knot, to tie in a knot.
➤ **anudarse** *vprnl* - **1.** [atarse] to get into a knot - **2.** [entorpecerse]: **se le anudó la voz** he got a lump in his throat.

anulación *sf* - **1.** [cancelación] cancellation; [de ley] repeal; [de matrimonio, contrato] annulment - **2.** [DEP - de un partido] calling-off; [- de un gol] disallowing; [- de un resultado] declaration as void.

anular[1] ◇ *adj* [en forma de anillo] annular. ◇ *sm* ⊏ **dedo**.

anular[2] *vt* - **1.** [cancelar - gen] to cancel; [- ley] to repeal; [- matrimonio, contrato] to annul - **2.** [DEP - partido] to call off; [- gol] to disallow; [- resultado] to declare void - **3.** [reprimir] to repress.

anunciación *sf* announcement.
➤ **Anunciación** *sf* RELIG Annunciation.

anunciante ◇ *adj* advertising *(antes de s)*. ◇ *smf* advertiser.

anunciar [8] *vt* - **1.** [notificar] to announce - **2.** [hacer publicidad de] to advertise - **3.** [presagiar] to herald.
➤ **anunciarse** *vprnl*: **anunciarse en** to advertise in, to put an advert in.

anuncio *sm* - **1.** [notificación] announcement; [cartel, aviso] notice; [póster] poster - **2.**: **anuncio (publicitario)** advertisement, advert; **anuncios por palabras** classified adverts - **3.** [presagio] sign, herald.

anverso *sm* [de moneda] head, obverse; [de hoja] front.

anzuelo *sm* - **1.** [para pescar] (fish) hook - **2.** *fam* [señuelo] bait; **picar** *o* **morder el anzuelo** to take the bait.

añadido, da *adj*: **añadido (a)** added (to).
➤ **añadido** *sm* addition.

añadidura *sf* addition; **por añadidura** in addition, what is more.

añadir *vt* to add.

añejo, ja *adj* - **1.** [vino, licor] mature; [tocino] cured - **2.** [costumbre] age-old.

añicos *smpl*: **hacer** *o* **hacerse añicos** to shatter.

añil *adj* & *sm* [color] indigo.

año *sm* year; **en el año 1939** in 1939; **los años 30** the thirties; **año académico/escolar/fiscal** academic/school/tax year; **año bisiesto/solar**

leap/solar year; **año nuevo** New Year; **¡Feliz Año Nuevo!** Happy New Year!; **año sabático** sabbatical; **el año de la nana** *fam* the year dot.

◆ **años** *smpl* [edad] age *sing*; **¿cuántos años tienes? – tengo 17 años** how old are you? – I'm 17 (years old); **los de 25 años** the 25-year-olds; **cumplir años** to have one's birthday; **cumplo años el 25** it's my birthday on the 25th; **estar entrado** *o* **metido en años** to be getting on; **te has quitado años de encima** [rejuvenecer] you look much younger.

◆ **año luz** (*pl* **años luz**) *sm* light year; **estar a años luz de** *fig* to be light years away from.

añoranza *sf*: **añoranza (de)** [gen] nostalgia (for); [hogar, patria] homesickness (for).

añorar *vt* to miss.

aorta *sf* aorta.

aovado, da *adj* egg-shaped.

aovar *vi* to lay eggs; [peces] to spawn.

ap. *abrev de* **aparte**.

APA (*abrev de* **asociación de padres de alumnos**) *sf* Spanish association for parents of schoolchildren, ≃ PTA.

apabullar *vt* to overwhelm.

◆ **apabullarse** *vprnl* to be overwhelmed.

apacentar [19] *vt* to graze.

apache *adj* & *smf* Apache.

apacible *adj* [gen] mild, gentle; [lugar, ambiente] pleasant.

apacienta *etc* ▷ **apacentar**.

apaciguador, ra *adj* calming.

apaciguar [45] *vt* - **1.** [tranquilizar] to calm down - **2.** [aplacar - dolor etc] to soothe.

◆ **apaciguarse** *vprnl* - **1.** [tranquilizarse] to calm down - **2.** [aplacarse - dolor etc] to abate.

apadrinar *vt* - **1.** [niño] to act as a godparent to - **2.** [artista] to sponsor.

apagado, da *adj* - **1.** [luz, fuego] out; [aparato] off - **2.** [color, persona] subdued - **3.** [sonido] dull, muffled; [voz] low, quiet.

apagar [16] *vt* - **1.** [extinguir - fuego] to put out; [- luz] to put off; [- vela] to extinguish - **2.** [desconectar] to turn *o* switch off; **apaga y vámonos** *fig* we have nothing more to talk about - **3.** [aplacar - sed] to quench; [- dolor] to get rid of - **4.** [rebajar - color] to soften; [- sonido] to muffle.

◆ **apagarse** *vprnl* - **1.** [extinguirse - fuego, vela, luz] to go out; [- dolor, ilusión, rencor] to die down; [- sonido] to die away - **2.** [morir] to pass away.

apagón *sm* power cut.

apague *etc* ▷ **apagar**.

apaisado, da *adj* oblong.

apalabrar *vt* [concertar] to make a verbal agreement regarding; [contratar] to engage on the basis of a verbal agreement.

apalancar [10] *vt* [para abrir] to lever open; [para mover] to lever.

◆ **apalancarse** *vprnl* *mfam* [apoltronarse] to install o.s.

apalear *vt* to beat up.

apañado, da *adj* *fam* [hábil, mañoso] clever, resourceful; **estar apañado** *fig* to have had it.

apañar *vt* *fam* - **1.** [reparar] to mend - **2.** [amañar] to fix, to arrange.

◆ **apañárselas** *vprnl* *fam* to cope, to manage; **apañárselas (para hacer algo)** to manage (to do sthg).

apaño *sm* *fam* - **1.** [reparación] patch - **2.** [chanchullo] fix, shady deal - **3.** [acuerdo] compromise.

apapachado, da *adj* *Méx* pampered, spoilt.

apapachador, ra *adj* *Méx* comforting.

apapachar *vt* *Méx* [mimar] to cuddle; [consentir] to spoil.

aparador *sm* - **1.** [mueble] sideboard - **2.** [escaparate] shop window.

aparato *sm* - **1.** [máquina] machine; [de laboratorio] apparatus *(U)*; [electrodoméstico] appliance; **aparato de radio** radio; **aparato de televisión** television set - **3.** [teléfono]: **¿quién está al aparato?** who's speaking? - **4.** [avión] plane - **5.** [MED - prótesis] aid; [- para dientes] brace - **6.** ANAT system - **7.** POLÍT machinery - **8.** [ostentación] pomp, ostentation.

aparatoso, sa *adj* - **1.** [ostentoso] ostentatious, showy - **2.** [espectacular] spectacular.

aparcamiento *sm* - **1.** [acción] parking - **2.** [parking] car park *UK*, parking lot *US*; [hueco] parking place.

aparcar [10] ◇ *vt* - **1.** [estacionar] to park - **2.** [posponer] to shelve. ◇ *vi* [estacionar] to park.

aparcero, ra *sm, f* sharecropper.

aparear *vt* [animales] to mate.

◆ **aparearse** *vprnl* [animales] to mate.

aparecer [30] *vi* - **1.** [gen] to appear - **2.** [acudir]: **aparecer por (un lugar)** to turn up at (a place) - **3.** [ser encontrado] to turn up.

◆ **aparecerse** *vprnl* to appear.

aparecido, da *sm, f* ghost.

aparejador, ra *sm, f* quantity surveyor.

aparejar *vt* - **1.** [preparar] to get ready, to prepare - **2.** [caballerías] to harness - **3.** NÁUT to rig (out).

aparejo *sm* - **1.** [de caballerías] harness - **2.** MECÁN block and tackle - **3.** NÁUT rigging.

aparejos *smpl* equipment *(U)*; [de pesca] tackle *(U)*.

aparentar ◇ *vt* - **1.** [fingir] to feign - **2.** [edad] to look. ◇ *vi* [presumir] to show off.

aparente *adj* - **1.** [falso, supuesto] apparent - **2.** [visible] visible - **3.** [llamativo] striking.

aparición *sf* - **1.** [gen] appearance - **2.** [de ser sobrenatural] apparition.

apariencia *sf* - **1.** [aspecto] appearance; **en apariencia** apparently, outwardly; **guardar las apariencias** to keep up appearances; **las apariencias engañan** appearances can be deceptive - **2.** [falsedad] illusion.

aparque *etc* ⊳ **aparcar**.

apartado, da *adj* - **1.** [separado]: **apartado de** away from - **2.** [alejado] remote.

apartado *sm* [párrafo] paragraph; [sección] section.

apartado de correos *sm* PO Box.

apartamento *sm* apartment, flat *UK*.

apartar *vt* - **1.** [alejar] to move away; [quitar] to remove - **2.** [separar] to separate - **3.** [escoger] to take, to select.

apartarse *vprnl* - **1.** [hacerse a un lado] to move to one side, to move out of the way - **2.** [separarse] to separate; **apartarse de** [gen] to move away from; [tema] to get away from; [mundo, sociedad] to cut o.s. off from.

aparte ◇ *adv* - **1.** [en otro lugar, a un lado] aside, to one side; **bromas aparte** joking apart; **dejar algo aparte** to leave sthg aside; **poner algo aparte** to put sthg aside; **impuestos aparte** [además] besides - **2.** [además] besides; **aparte de fea...** besides being ugly... - **3.** [por separado] separately. ◇ *adj inv* separate; **ser caso aparte** to be a different matter. ◇ *sm* - **1.** [párrafo] new paragraph - **2.** TEATRO aside.

aparte de *loc prep* [excepto] apart from, except from.

apartheid [apar'teid] *sm* apartheid.

apartotel, aparthotel *sm* hotel apartments *pl*.

apasionado, da ◇ *adj* passionate. ◇ *sm, f* lover, enthusiast.

apasionante *adj* fascinating.

apasionar *vt* to fascinate; **le apasiona la música** he's mad about music.

apasionarse *vprnl* to get excited; **apasionarse por** *o* **con** to be mad about.

apatía *sf* apathy.

apático, ca ◇ *adj* apathetic. ◇ *sm, f* apathetic person.

apátrida ◇ *adj* stateless. ◇ *smf* stateless person.

apdo. *abrev de* **apartado**.

apeadero *sm* [de tren] halt.

apear *vt* - **1.** [bajar] to take down - **2.** *fam* [disuadir]: **apear a alguien de** to talk sb out of.

apearse *vprnl* - **1.** [bajarse]: **apearse (de)** [tren] to alight (from), to get off; [coche] to get out (of); [caballo] to dismount (from) - **2.** *fam* [disuadirse]: **apearse de** to back down on.

apechugar [16] *vi*: **apechugar con** to put up with, to live with.

apedrear ◇ *vt* [persona] to stone; [cosa] to throw stones at. ◇ *v impers* to hail.

apegarse [16] *vprnl*: **apegarse a** to become fond of *o* attached to.

apego *sm* fondness, attachment; **tener/tomar apego a** to be/become fond of.

apelación *sf* appeal.

apelar *vi* - **1.** DER (to lodge an) appeal; **apelar ante/contra** to appeal to/against - **2.** [recurrir]: **apelar a** [persona] to go to; [sentido común, bondad] to appeal to; [violencia] to resort to.

apelativo *sm* name.

apellidarse *vprnl*: **se apellida Suárez** her surname is Suárez.

apellido *sm* surname.

Apellidos

In the Spanish-speaking world people commonly use the last name of both their father and their mother (in that order). Thus, if Pedro García Fernández and María Piñedo Saavedra have a daughter called Eva, she will be known as Eva García Piñedo. This custom is followed in all official documents, though in everyday use many people use only their first surname. When a woman gets married she usually keeps her full maiden name, rather than adopting her husband's, so she can be known by her husband's name. So, if Eva García Piñedo married Carlos Hernández Río, she could either keep her own name intact, or be known as Señora de Hernández Río. In Latin America she might also be known as Eva García Piñedo de Hernández.

apelmazado, da *adj* - **1.** [jersey] shrunk - **2.** [arroz, bizcocho] stodgy.

apelmazar [13] *vt* - **1.** [jersey] to shrink - **2.** [arroz, bizcocho] to make stodgy.

apelmazarse *vprnl* - **1.** [jersey] to shrink - **2.** [arroz, bizcocho] to go stodgy.

apelotonar *vt* to bundle up.

apelotonarse *vprnl* [gente] to crowd together.

apenado, da *adj Andes, Amér C, Caribe & Méx* [avergonzado] ashamed, embarrassed.

apenar *vt* to sadden.

apenarse *vprnl* - **1.** to be saddened - **2.** *Andes, Amér C, Caribe & Méx* [avergonzarse] to be ashamed, to be embarrassed.

apenas *adv* - **1.** [casi no] scarcely, hardly; **apenas me puedo mover** I can hardly move - **2.** [tan sólo] only; **apenas hace dos minutos** only two minutes ago - **3.** [tan pronto como] as soon as; **apenas llegó, sonó el teléfono** no sooner had he arrived than the phone rang.

apencar [10] *vi fam*: **apencar con** [trabajo] to take on; [responsabilidad] to shoulder; [consecuencias, dificultad] to live with.

apéndice *sm* appendix.

apendicitis *sf inv* appendicitis.

apenque *etc* ▷ **apencar**.

apercibir *vt* - **1.** [darse cuenta de] to notice - **2.** [amonestar] to reprimand, to give a warning to - **3.** DER to issue with a warning.

◆ **apercibirse de** *vprnl* to notice.

apergaminarse *vprnl fam* to become wrinkled o wizened.

aperitivo *sm* [bebida] aperitif; [comida] appetizer.

apero *sm* (gen pl) tool; **aperos de labranza** farming implements.

aperrearse *vprnl fam* to refuse to change one's mind.

apertura *sf* - **1.** [gen] opening; [de año académico, temporada] start - **2.** [DEP - en rugby] kick-off; [- en ajedrez] opening (move) - **3.** POLÍT [liberalización] liberalization *(especially that introduced in Spain by the Franco regime after 1970)*.

aperturismo *sm* progressive policies *pl*.

aperturista *adj & smf* progressive.

apesadumbrar *vt* to weigh down.

◆ **apesadumbrarse** *vprnl* to be weighed down.

apestar ◇ *vi*: **apestar (a)** to stink (of). ◇ *vt* - **1.** [hacer que huela mal] to infest, to stink out - **2.** [contagiar peste] to infect with the plague.

apestoso, sa *adj* foul.

apetecer [30] ◇ *vi*: **¿te apetece un café?** do you fancy a coffee?; **me apetece salir** I feel like going out. ◇ *vt*: **tenían todo cuanto apetecían** they had everything they wanted.

apetecible *adj* [comida] appetizing, tempting; [vacaciones etc] desirable.

apetito *sm* appetite; **abrir el apetito** to whet one's appetite; **perder el apetito** to lose one's appetite; **tener apetito** to be hungry.

apetitoso, sa *adj* - **1.** [comida] appetizing - **2.** [oferta, empleo] tempting.

apiadar *vt* to earn the pity of.

◆ **apiadarse** *vprnl* to show compassion; **apiadarse de** to take pity on.

ápice *sm* - **1.** [pizca] iota; **ni un ápice** not a single bit; **no ceder un ápice** not to budge an inch - **2.** [vértice - de montaña] peak; [- de hoja, lengua] tip; [- de edificio] top - **3.** [punto culminante] peak, height.

apicultor, ra *sm, f* beekeeper.

apicultura *sf* beekeeping.

apilar *vt* to pile up.

◆ **apilarse** *vprnl* to pile up.

apiñado, da *adj* [apretado] packed, crammed.

apiñar *vt* to pack o cram together.

◆ **apiñarse** *vprnl* to crowd together; [para protegerse, por miedo] to huddle together.

apio *sm* celery.

apisonadora *sf* steamroller.

aplacar [10] *vt* to placate; [hambre] to satisfy; [sed] to quench.

◆ **aplacarse** *vprnl* to calm down; [dolor] to abate.

aplace *etc* ▷ **aplazar**.

aplanar *vt* to level.

aplaque *etc* ▷ **aplacar**.

aplastante *adj fig* [apabullante] overwhelming, devastating.

aplastar *vt* - **1.** [por el peso] to flatten - **2.** [derrotar] to crush.

aplatanado, da *adj fam* listless.

aplatanar *vt fam* to make listless.

◆ **aplatanarse** *vprnl fam* to become listless.

aplaudir *vt & vi* to applaud.

aplauso *sm* - **1.** [ovación] round of applause; **aplausos** applause *(U)* - **2.** *fig* [alabanza] applause.

aplazamiento *sm* postponement.

aplazar [13] *vt* - **1.** [retrasar] to postpone - **2.** *R Plata* [suspender] to fail.

aplicación *sf* - **1.** [gen & INFORM] application - **2.** [decoración] appliqué.

aplicado, da *adj* - **1.** [estudioso] diligent - **2.** [ciencia] applied.

aplicar [10] *vt* [gen] to apply; [nombre, calificativo] to give.

◆ **aplicarse** *vprnl* - **1.** [esmerarse]: **aplicarse (en algo)** to apply o.s. (to sthg) - **2.** [concernir]: **aplicarse a** to apply to.

aplique *sm* wall lamp.

aplomo *sm* composure; **perder el aplomo** to lose one's composure.

apocado, da *adj* timid.

apocalipsis *sm inv* calamity.

◆ **Apocalipsis** *sm* Apocalypse.

apocalíptico, ca *adj* apocalyptic.

apocamiento *sm* timidity.

apocarse [10] *vprnl* [intimidarse] to be frightened o scared; [humillarse] to humble o.s.

apocopar *vt* to apocopate.
apócope *sf* apocopation.
apócrifo, **fa** *adj* apocryphal.
apodar *vt* to nickname.
◆ **apodarse** *vprnl* to be nicknamed.
apoderado, **da** *sm*, *f* - **1.** [representante] (official) representative - **2.** TAUROM agent, manager.
apoderar *vt* [gen] to authorize, to empower; DER to grant power of attorney to.
◆ **apoderarse de** *vprnl* - **1.** [adueñarse de] to seize - **2.** *fig* [dominar] to take hold of, to grip.
apodo *sm* nickname.
apogeo *sm* *fig* height, apogee; **estar en (pleno) apogeo** to be at its height.
apolillado, **da** *adj* moth-eaten.
apolillar *vt* to eat holes in.
◆ **apolillarse** *vprnl* to get moth-eaten.
apolítico, **ca** *adj* apolitical.
apología *sf* apology, eulogy; **apología del terrorismo** defence of terrorism.
apoltronarse *vprnl* - **1.** [apalancarse]: **apoltronarse (en)** to become lazy *o* idle (in) - **2.** [acomodarse]: **apoltronarse en** to lounge in.
apoplejía *sf* apoplexy.
apoquinar *vt* & *vi* *fam* to fork out.
aporrear *vt* to bang.
aportación *sf* - **1.** [proporcionamiento] provision - **2.** [contribución] contribution; **hacer una aportación** to contribute.
aportar *vt* - **1.** [proporcionar] to provide - **2.** [contribuir con] to contribute.
aposentar *vt* to put up, to lodge.
◆ **aposentarse** *vprnl* to take up lodgings.
aposento *sm* - **1.** [habitación] room; **retirarse a sus aposentos** *desus* & *hum* to withdraw (to one's chamber) - **2.** [alojamiento] lodgings *pl*.
aposición *sf* apposition.
apósito *sm* dressing.
aposta *adv* on purpose, intentionally.
apostante *smf* person who places a bet.
apostar [23] ◇ *vt* - **1.** [jugarse] to bet - **2.** [emplazar] to post. ◇ *vi*: **apostar (por)** to bet (on); **apuesto a que no viene** I bet he doesn't come.
◆ **apostarse** *vprnl* - **1.** [jugarse] to bet; **apostarse algo con alguien** to bet sb sthg - **2.** [colocarse] to post o.s.
apóstata *smf* apostate.
apostilla *sf* note.
apostillar *vt* to annotate.
apóstol *sm* *lit* & *fig* apostle.
apostolado *sm* - **1.** [de apóstol] apostolate - **2.** [de ideales] mission.
apostólico, **ca** *adj* apostolic.

apostolizar [13] *vt* to convert to Christianity.
apóstrofe *sm o sf* LITER apostrophe.
apóstrofo *sm* GRAM apostrophe.
apostura *sf* [garbo] dashing nature.
apoteósico, **ca** *adj* tremendous.
apoteosis *sf inv* [final] grand finale.
apoyacabezas *sm inv* headrest.
apoyar *vt* - **1.** [inclinar] to lean, to rest - **2.** *fig* [basar, respaldar] to support.
◆ **apoyarse** *vprnl* - **1.** [sostenerse]: **apoyarse en** to lean on - **2.** *fig* [basarse]: **apoyarse en** [suj: tesis, conclusiones] to be based on, to rest on; [suj: persona] to base one's arguments on - **3.** [respaldarse] to support one another.
apoyo *sm* *lit* & *fig* support.
APRA *sf* (*abrev de* **Alianza Popular Revolucionaria Americana**), *Peruvian political party*.
apreciable *adj* - **1.** [perceptible] appreciable, significant - **2.** *fig* [estimable] worthy.
apreciación *sf* [consideración] appreciation; [estimación] evaluation.
apreciar [8] *vt* - **1.** [valorar] to appreciate; [sopesar] to appraise, to evaluate - **2.** [sentir afecto por] to think highly of - **3.** [percibir] to tell, to make out - **4.** [opinar]: **apreciar que** to consider (that).
aprecio *sm* esteem; **sentir aprecio por alguien** to think highly of sb.
aprehender *vt* - **1.** [coger - persona] to apprehend; [- alijo, mercancía] to seize - **2.** [comprender] to take in.
aprehensión *sf* [de persona] arrest, capture; [de alijo, mercancía] seizure.
apremiante *adj* pressing, urgent.
apremiar [8] ◇ *vt* - **1.** [meter prisa]: **apremiar a alguien para que haga algo** to urge sb to do sthg - **2.** [obligar]: **apremiar a alguien a hacer algo** to compel sb to do sthg. ◇ *vi* [ser urgente] to be pressing.
apremio *sm* - **1.** [urgencia] urgency - **2.** DER writ.
aprender ◇ *vt* - **1.** [estudiar] to learn - **2.** [memorizar] to memorize. ◇ *vi*: **aprender (a hacer algo)** to learn (to do sthg); **¡para que aprendas!** that'll teach you!
◆ **aprenderse** *vprnl* - **1.** [estudiar] to learn - **2.** [memorizar] to memorize.
aprendiz, **za** *sm*, *f* - **1.** [ayudante] apprentice, trainee - **2.** [novato] beginner.
aprendizaje *sm* - **1.** [acción] learning - **2.** [tiempo, situación] apprenticeship.
aprensión *sf*: **aprensión (por)** [miedo] apprehension (about); [escrúpulo] squeamishness (about).

aprensivo, **va** *adj* - **1.** [miedoso] apprehens-ive - **2.** [escrupuloso] squeamish - **3.** [hipocondríaco] hypochondriac.

apresar *vt* [suj: animal] to catch; [suj: persona] to capture.

aprestar *vt* - **1.** [preparar] to prepare, to get ready - **2.** [tela] to size.
➡ **aprestarse a** *vprnl*: **aprestarse a hacer algo** to get ready to do sthg.

apresto *sm* size.

apresurado, **da** *adj* hasty, hurried.

apresuramiento *sm* haste.

apresurar *vt* to hurry along, to speed up; **apresurar a alguien para que haga algo** to try to make sb do sthg more quickly.
➡ **apresurarse** *vprnl* to hurry; **apresurarse a hacer algo** to do sthg quickly.

apretado, **da** *adj* - **1.** [gen] tight; [triunfo] narrow; [esprint] close; [caligrafía] cramped - **2.** [apiñado] packed.

apretar [19] <> *vt* - **1.** [oprimir - botón, tecla] to press; [- gatillo] to pull, to squeeze; [- nudo, tuerca, cinturón] to tighten; **el zapato me aprieta** my shoe is pinching - **2.** [estrechar] to squeeze; [abrazar] to hug - **3.** [comprimir - ropa, objetos] to pack tight - **4.** [juntar - dientes] to grit; [- labios] to press together - **5.** *fig* [el paso, la marcha] to quicken - **6.** *fig* [presionar] to press. <> *vi* [calor, lluvia] to get worse, to intensify; **apretar a correr** *fam* to run off.
➡ **apretarse** *vprnl* [agolparse] to crowd together; [acercarse] to squeeze up.

apretón *sm* [estrechamiento] squeeze; **apretón de manos** handshake.
➡ **apretones** *smpl* [aglomeración] crush *sing*.

apretujar *vt* - **1.** [gen] to squash - **2.** [hacer una bola con] to screw up.
➡ **apretujarse** *vprnl* [en banco, autobús] to squeeze together; [por frío] to huddle up.

apretujón *sm fam* [abrazo] bearhug.

aprieta *etc* ⊳ **apretar**.

aprieto *sm fig* fix, difficult situation; **poner en un aprieto a alguien** to put sb in a difficult position; **verse** *o* **estar en un aprieto** to be in a fix.

aprisa *adv* quickly.

aprisionar *vt* - **1.** [encarcelar] to imprison - **2.** [inmovilizar - atando, con camisa de fuerza] to strap down; [- suj: viga etc] to trap.

aprobación *sf* approval.

aprobado, **da** *adj* [aceptado] approved.
➡ **aprobado** *sm* EDUC pass.

aprobar [23] *vt* - **1.** [proyecto, moción, medida] to approve; [ley] to pass - **2.** [comportamiento etc] to approve of - **3.** [examen, asignatura] to pass.

apropiación *sf* [robo] theft.

apropiado, **da** *adj* suitable, appropriate.

apropiar [8] *vt*: **apropiar (a)** to adapt (to).
➡ **apropiarse de** *vprnl lit & fig* to appropriate.

aprovechable *adj* usable.

aprovechado, **da** <> *adj* - **1.** [caradura]: **es muy aprovechado** he's always sponging off other people - **2.** [bien empleado - tiempo] well-spent; [- espacio] well-planned - **3.** [aplicado] diligent. <> *sm, f* [caradura] sponger.

aprovechamiento *sm* - **1.** [utilización] use - **2.** [en el estudio] progress, improvement.

aprovechar <> *vt* - **1.** [gen] to make the most of; [oferta, ocasión] to take advantage of; [conocimientos, experiencia] to use, to make use of; **aprovechar que...** to make the most of the fact that... - **2.** [lo inservible] to put to good use. <> *vi* - **1.** [ser provechoso] to be beneficial; **¡que aproveche!** enjoy your meal! - **2.** [mejorar] to make progress.
➡ **aprovecharse** *vprnl*: **aprovecharse (de)** to take advantage (of).

aprovisionamiento *sm* supplying.

aprovisionar *vt* to supply.

aprox. (*abrev de* **aproximadamente**) approx.

aproximación *sf* - **1.** [acercamiento] approach - **2.** [en cálculo] approximation - **3.** [en lotería] *in lotteries, consolation prize given to numbers immediately before and after the winning number* - **4.** *fig* [de países] rapprochement; [de puntos de vista] converging.

aproximadamente *adv* approximately.

aproximado, **da** *adj* approximate.

aproximar *vt* to move closer.
➡ **aproximarse** *vprnl* to come closer.

aprueba *etc* ⊳ **aprobar**.

aptitud *sf* ability, aptitude; **tener aptitud para algo** to have an aptitude for sthg.

apto, **ta** *adj* - **1.** [adecuado, conveniente]: **apto (para)** suitable (for) - **2.** [capacitado - intelectualmente] capable, able; [- físicamente] fit - **3.** CINE: **apto/no apto para menores** suitable/unsuitable for children.

apto. (*abrev de* **apartamento**) Apt.

apuesta <> *sf* bet. <> *v* ⊳ **apostar**.

apuesto, **ta** *adj* dashing.

apuntador, **ra** *sm, f* prompter.

apuntalamiento *sm lit & fig* underpinning.

apuntalar *vt lit & fig* to underpin.

apuntar <> *vt* - **1.** [anotar] to make a note of, to note down; **apuntar a alguien** [en lista] to put sb down; **apúntamelo (en la cuenta)** put it on my account - **2.** [dirigir - dedo] to point; [- arma] to aim; **apuntar a alguien** [- con el dedo] to point at sb; [- con un arma] to aim at sb - **3.** TEATRO to prompt - **4.** *fig* [sugerir] to hint at

- 5. *fig* [indicar] to point out. ◇ *vi* **- 1.** [vislumbrarse] to appear; [día] to break **- 2.** *fig* [indicar]: **apuntar a** to point to, to suggest.

◆ **apuntarse** *vprnl* **- 1.** [en lista] to put one's name down; [en curso] to enrol **- 2.** [participar]: **apuntarse (a hacer algo)** to join in (doing sthg); **yo me apunto** I'm in.

apunte *sm* **- 1.** [nota] note **- 2.** [boceto] sketch **- 3.** COM entry **- 4.** TEATRO prompt.

◆ **apuntes** *smpl* EDUC notes; **tomar apuntes** to take notes.

apuñalar *vt* to stab.

apurado, da *adj* **- 1.** [necesitado] in need; **apurado de** short of **- 2.** [avergonzado] embarrassed **- 3.** [difícil] awkward **- 4.** *Amér* [con prisa]: **estar apurado** to be in a hurry.

apurar *vt* **- 1.** [agotar] to finish off; [existencias, la paciencia] to exhaust **- 2.** [meter prisa] to hurry **- 3.** [preocupar] to trouble **- 4.** [avergonzar] to embarrass **- 5.** [barba] to shave closely.

◆ **apurarse** *vprnl* **- 1.** [preocuparse]: **apurarse (por)** to worry (about) **- 2.** [darse prisa] to hurry.

apuro *sm* **- 1.** [dificultad] fix, difficult situation; **estar en apuros** to be in a tight spot **- 2.** [penuria] hardship *(U)*; **pasar apuros** to be hard up **- 3.** [vergüenza] embarrassment; **me da apuro (decírselo)** I'm embarrassed (to tell her) **- 4.** *Amér* [prisa] rush; **tener apuro** to be in a rush.

aquejado, da *adj*: **aquejado de** suffering from.

aquejar *vt* to afflict; **le aquejan varias enfermedades** he suffers from a number of illnesses.

aquel, aquella *(mpl* **aquellos**, *fpl* **aquellas)** *adj demos* that *(pl* those).

aquél, aquélla *(mpl* **aquéllos**, *fpl* **aquéllas)** *pron demos* **- 1.** [ése] that (one), those (ones) *pl*; **este cuadro me gusta pero aquél del fondo no** I like this picture, but I don't like that one at the back; **aquél fue mi último día en Londres** that was my last day in London **- 2.** [nombrado antes] the former; **teníamos un coche y una moto, ésta estropeada y aquél sin gasolina** we had a car and a motorbike, the former was out of petrol, the latter had broken down **- 3.** [con oraciones relativas] whoever, anyone who; **aquél que quiera hablar que levante la mano** whoever wishes *o* anyone wishing to speak should raise their hand; **aquéllos que...** those who...

aquelarre *sm* coven.

aquella ▷ **aquel**.

aquélla ▷ **aquél**.

aquello *pron demos (neutro)* that; **no consiguió saber si aquello lo dijo en serio** he never found out whether she meant those words *o* that seriously; **aquello de su mujer es una mentira** all that about his wife is a lie.

aquellos, aquellas ▷ **aquel**.

aquéllos, aquéllas ▷ **aquél**.

aquí *adv* **- 1.** [gen] here; **aquí abajo/arriba** down/up here; **aquí dentro/fuera** in/out here; **aquí mismo** right here; **aquí y allá** here and there; **de aquí para allá** [de un lado a otro] to and fro; **por aquí** over here **- 2.** [ahora] now; **de aquí a mañana** between now and tomorrow; **de aquí a poco** shortly, soon; **de aquí a un mes** a month from now, in a month **- 3.** [en tiempo pasado]: **aquí empezaron los problemas** that was when the problems started.

◆ **de aquí que** *loc conj* [por eso] hence, therefore.

aquietar *vt* to calm down.

◆ **aquietarse** *vprnl* to calm down.

aquilatar *vt* **- 1.** [metales, joyas] to assay **- 2.** *fig* [examinar] to assess.

ara *sf (el)* **- 1.** *culto* [piedra] altar stone **- 2.** [altar] altar.

◆ **en aras de** *loc prep culto* for the sake of.

árabe ◇ *adj* Arab, Arabian. ◇ *smf* [persona] Arab. ◇ *sm* [lengua] Arabic.

arabesco *sm* arabesque.

Arabia Saudí, Arabia Saudita *n pr* Saudi Arabia.

arábigo, ga *adj* **- 1.** [de Arabia] Arab, Arabian **- 2.** [numeración] Arabic.

arado *sm* plough.

Aragón *n pr* Aragon.

aragonés, esa *adj* & *sm, f* Aragonese.

arameo *sm* [lengua] Aramaic.

arancel *sm* tariff.

arancelario, ria *adj* tariff *(antes de s)*.

arándano *sm* bilberry, blueberry *US*.

arandela *sf* TECNOL washer.

araña *sf* **- 1.** [animal] spider; **araña de mar** spider crab **- 2.** [lámpara] chandelier.

arañar *vt* **- 1.** [gen] to scratch **- 2.** *fig* [reunir] to scrape together.

arañazo *sm* scratch.

arar *vt* to plough.

arbitraje *sm* **- 1.** [DEP - en fútbol etc] refereeing; [- en tenis, cricket] umpiring **- 2.** DER arbitration.

arbitral *adj* DEP of the referee.

arbitrar ◇ *vt* **- 1.** [DEP - en fútbol etc] to referee; [- en tenis, cricket] to umpire **- 2.** [medidas, recursos] to bring together **- 3.** DER to arbitrate. ◇ *vi* **- 1.** [DEP - en fútbol etc] to referee; [- en tenis, cricket] to umpire **- 2.** DER to arbitrate.

arbitrariedad *sf* **- 1.** [cualidad] arbitrariness **- 2.** [acción] arbitrary action.

arbitrario, **ria** *adj* arbitrary.

arbitrio *sm* [decisión] judgment; **dejar algo al arbitrio de alguien** to leave sthg to sb's discretion; **libre arbitrio** free will.

➤ **arbitrios** *smpl* [impuestos] taxes.

árbitro *sm* - **1.** [DEP - en fútbol etc] referee; **árbitro asistente** asisstant referee; [- en tenis, cricket] umpire - **2.** DER arbitrator.

árbol *sm* - **1.** BOT tree; **árbol de Navidad** Christmas tree - **2.** TECNOL shaft; **árbol de levas** camshaft - **3.** NÁUT mast.

➤ **árbol genealógico** *sm* family tree.

arbolado, **da** *adj* - **1.** [terreno] wooded; [calle] tree-lined - **2.** [mar] tempestuous.

➤ **arbolado** *sm* woodland (U).

arboladura *sf* NÁUT masts and spars *pl*.

arbolar *vt* - **1.** [barco] to mast - **2.** [bandera] to raise, to hoist - **3.** [mar] to whip up.

➤ **arbolarse** *vprnl* to rear up.

arboleda *sf* grove.

arbotante *sm* flying buttress.

arbusto *sm* bush, shrub.

arca *sf (el)* - **1.** [arcón] chest - **2.** [barco]: **arca de Noé** Noah's Ark.

➤ **arcas** *sfpl* coffers; **arcas públicas** Treasury *sing*.

arcabuz *sm* arquebus.

arcada *sf* - **1.** *(gen pl)* [de estómago] retching (U); **me dieron arcadas** I retched - **2.** [ARQUIT - arcos] arcade; [- de puente] arch.

arcaico, **ca** *adj* archaic.

arcaísmo *sm* archaism.

arcángel *sm* archangel.

arcano, **na** *adj* arcane.

➤ **arcano** *sm* - **1.** [carta] arcana - **2.** [misterio] mystery.

arce *sm* maple.

arcén *sm* [de autopista] hard shoulder UK, shoulder US; [de carretera] verge.

archiconocido, **da** *adj fam* very well-known.

archiduque, **esa** *sm*, *f* archduke (*f* archduchess).

archimillonario, **ria** *sm*, *f* multimillionaire.

archipiélago *sm* archipelago.

archisabido, **da** *adj* very well-known.

archivador, **ra** *sm*, *f* archivist.

➤ **archivador** *sm* filing cabinet.

archivar *vt* - **1.** [guardar - documento, fichero etc] to file - **2.** *fig* [olvidar - suceso etc] to push to the back of one's mind.

archivo *sm* - **1.** [lugar] archive; [documentos] archives *pl*; **imágenes de archivo** TV library pictures - **2.** [informe, ficha] file - **3.** INFORM file; **archivo batch** batch file.

arcilla *sf* clay.

arcipreste *sm* archpriest.

arco *sm* - **1.** GEOM arc - **2.** ARQUIT arch; **arco de herradura** horseshoe arch; **arco triunfal** O de **triunfo** triumphal arch - **3.** DEP, MIL & MÚS bow - **4.** *Amér* [portería] goal, goalmouth.

➤ **arco iris** *sm* rainbow.

arcón *sm* large chest.

arder *vi* to burn; [sin llama] to smoulder; **arder de** *fig* to burn with; **está que arde** [persona] he's fuming; [reunión] it's getting pretty heated.

ardid *sm* ruse, trick.

ardiente *adj* [gen] burning; [líquido] scalding; [admirador, defensor] ardent.

ardilla *sf* squirrel.

ardite *sm*: **no vale un ardite** *fam* it isn't worth a brass farthing.

ardor *sm* - **1.** [calor] heat - **2.** [quemazón] burning (sensation); **ardor de estómago** heartburn - **3.** *fig* [entusiasmo] fervour.

arduo, **dua** *adj* arduous.

área *sf (el)* - **1.** [gen] area; **área metropolitana/de servicio** metropolitan/service area; **área de libre cambio** ECON free exchange area - **2.** DEP: **área (de castigo** O **penalti)** (penalty) area.

arena *sf* - **1.** [de playa etc] sand; **arenas movedizas** quicksand (U) - **2.** [para luchar] arena - **3.** TAUROM bullring.

ARENA *sf* (*abrev de* **Alianza Republicana Nacionalista**) *Salvadorean political party*.

arenal *sm* sandy ground (U).

arenga *sf* harangue.

arengar **[16]** *vt* to harangue.

arenilla *sf* [polvo] dust.

➤ **arenillas** *sfpl* MED kidney stones.

arenisca *sf* sandstone.

arenoso, **sa** *adj* sandy.

arenque *sm* herring.

aretes *smpl* *Andes & Cuba* earrings.

argamasa *sf* mortar.

Argelia *n pr* Algeria.

Argentina *n pr* Argentina.

argentinismo *sm* word peculiar to Argentinian Spanish.

argentino, **na** *adj* & *sm*, *f* Argentinian.

argolla *sf* - **1.** [aro] (large) ring - **2.** *Andes & Cuba* [alianza] wedding ring.

argonauta *sm* Argonaut.

argot *sm* - **1.** [popular] slang - **2.** [técnico] jargon.

argucia *sf* sophism.

argüir **[44]** ⇔ *vt culto* - **1.** [argumentar] to argue - **2.** [demostrar] to prove, to demonstrate - **3.** [deducir] to deduce. ⇔ *vi* [argumentar] to argue.

argumentación *sf* line of argument.

argumentar *vt* - **1.** [teoría, opinión] to argue - **2.** [razones, excusas] to allege.

argumento *sm* - **1.** [razonamiento] argument - **2.** [trama] plot.

arguya *etc* ▷ **argüir**.

arguyera *etc* ▷ **argüir**.

aria *sf* MÚS aria.

aridez *sf* [gen] dryness; [de zona, clima] aridity.

árido, **da** *adj* [gen] dry; [zona, clima] arid.
➡ **áridos** *smpl* dry goods.

Aries ◇ *sm* [zodiaco] Aries; **ser Aries** to be (an) Aries. ◇ *smf* [persona] Aries.

ariete *sm* - **1.** HIST & MIL battering ram - **2.** DEP centre forward.

ario, **ria** *adj* & *sm, f* Aryan.

arisco, **ca** *adj* surly.

arista *sf* edge.

aristocracia *sf* aristocracy.

aristócrata *smf* aristocrat.

aristocrático, **ca** *adj* aristocratic.

aristotélico, **ca** *adj* & *sm, f* Aristotelian.

aritmético, **ca** *adj* arithmetic.
➡ **aritmética** *sf* arithmetic.

arlequín *sm* harlequin.

arma *sf* (el) - **1.** [instrumento] arm, weapon; **presentar/rendir armas** to present/surrender arms; **arma biológica/nuclear/química** biological/nuclear/chemical weapon; **armas de destrucción masiva** weapons of mass destruction; **arma blanca** blade, weapon with a sharp blade; **arma de fuego** firearm; **arma homicida** murder weapon - **2.** *fig* [medio] weapon - **3.** *loc*: **alzarse en armas** to rise up; **arma de dos filos** o **doble filo** double-edged sword; **ser de armas tomar** to be sb to be reckoned with, to be formidable.
➡ **armas** *sfpl* [profesión] military career *sing*.

armada *sf* ▷ **armado**.

armadillo *sm* armadillo.

armado, **da** *adj* - **1.** [con armas] armed - **2.** [con armazón] reinforced.
➡ **armada** *sf* [marina] navy; [escuadra] fleet.
➡ **Armada** *sf*: **la Armada Invencible** the Spanish Armada.

armador, **ra** *sm, f* shipowner.

armadura *sf* - **1.** [de barco, tejado] framework; [de gafas] frame - **2.** [de guerrero] armour.

armamentista, armamentístico, ca *adj* arms (antes de s).

armamento *sm* - **1.** [armas] arms *pl* - **2.** [acción] armament, arming.

armañac *sm* armagnac.

armar *vt* - **1.** [montar - mueble etc] to assemble; [- tienda] to pitch - **2.** [ejército, personas] to arm - **3.** [fusil, pistola] to load - **4.** *fam fig* [provocar] to cause; **armarla** *fam* to cause trouble.
➡ **armarse** *vprnl* - **1.** [con armas] to arm o.s. - **2.** [prepararse]: **armarse de** [valor, paciencia] to summon up - **3.** *loc*: **se armó la gorda** o **la de San Quintín** o **la de Dios es Cristo** *fam* all hell broke loose.

armario *sm* [para objetos] cupboard, closet US; [para ropa] wardrobe UK, closet US; **armario empotrado** fitted cupboard/wardrobe; **salir del armario** *fam* to come out of the closet.

armatoste *sm* [mueble, objeto] unwieldy object; [máquina] contraption.

armazón *sf* [gen] framework, frame; [de avión, coche] chassis; [de edificio] skeleton.

Armenia *n pr* Armenia.

armenio, **nia** *adj* & *sm, f* Armenian.

armería *sf* - **1.** [museo] military o war museum - **2.** [depósito] armoury - **3.** [tienda] gunsmith's (shop) - **4.** [arte] gunsmith's craft.

armero *sm* - **1.** [fabricante] gunsmith - **2.** MIL armourer.

armiño *sm* [piel] ermine; [animal] stoat.

armisticio *sm* armistice.

armonía *sf* harmony.

armónico, **ca** *adj* harmonic.
➡ **armónico** *sm* harmonic.
➡ **armónica** *sf* harmonica.

armonio *sm* harmonium.

armonioso, **sa** *adj* harmonious.

armonizar [13] ◇ *vt* - **1.** [concordar] to match - **2.** MÚS to harmonize. ◇ *vi* [concordar]: **armonizar con** to match.

ARN (*abrev de* **ácido ribonucleico**) *sm* RNA.

arnés *sm* armour.
➡ **arneses** *smpl* [de animales] trappings, harness (U).

árnica *sf* arnica.

aro *sm* - **1.** [círculo] hoop; TECNOL ring; **los aros olímpicos** the Olympic rings; **entrar** o **pasar por el aro** to knuckle under - **2.** [servilletero] napkin o serviette ring - **3.** [alianza] ring - **4.** *Amér* [pendiente] earring.

aroma *sm* [gen] aroma; [de vino] bouquet; CULIN flavouring.

aromático, **ca** *adj* aromatic.

aromatizador *sm* air freshener.

aromatizar [13] *vt* to perfume; CULIN to flavour.

arpa *sf* (el) harp.

arpía *sf* - **1.** MITOL harpy - **2.** *fig* [mujer] old hag.

arpillera *sf* sackcloth, hessian.

arpón *sm* harpoon.

arponear *vt* to harpoon.

arquear *vt* [gen] to bend; [cejas, espalda, lomo] to arch.
◆ **arquearse** *vprnl* to bend.

arqueo *sm* **- 1.** [curvamiento] bending; [de cejas, espalda, lomo] arching **- 2.** COM cashing up **- 3.** NÁUT registered tonnage.

arqueología *sf* archeology.

arqueológico, **ca** *adj* archeological.

arqueólogo, **ga** *sm, f* archeologist.

arquero *sm* **- 1.** DEP & MIL archer **- 2.** [tesorero] treasurer **- 3.** *Amér* [portero de fútbol] goalkeeper.

arquetipo *sm* archetype.

arquitecto, **ta** *sm, f* architect.

arquitectónico, **ca** *adj* architectural.

arquitectura *sf* lit & fig architecture.

arquitrabe *sm* architrave.

arquivolta *sf* archivolt.

arrabal *sm* [barrio pobre] slum *(on city outskirts)*; [barrio periférico] outlying district.

arrabalero, **ra** ◇ *adj* **- 1.** [periférico] outlying **- 2.** [barriobajero] rough, coarse. ◇ *sm, f* [barriobajero] rough o coarse person.

arracimarse *vprnl* to cluster together.

arraigado, **da** *adj* [costumbre, idea] deeply rooted; [persona] established.

arraigar [16] ◇ *vt* to establish. ◇ *vi* lit & fig to take root.
◆ **arraigarse** *vprnl* [establecerse] to settle down.

arraigo *sm* roots *pl*; **tener mucho arraigo** to be deeply rooted.

arrancada *sf* sudden start.

arrancar [10] ◇ *vt* **- 1.** [desarraigar - árbol] to uproot; [- malas hierbas, flor] to pull up **- 2.** [quitar, separar] to tear o rip off; [cable, página, pelo] to tear out; [cartel, cortinas] to tear down; [muela] to pull out, to extract; [ojos] to gouge out **- 3.** [arrebatar]: **arrancar algo a alguien** to grab o snatch sthg from sb **- 4.** AUTO & TECNOL to start; INFORM to start up **- 5.** fig [obtener]: **arrancar algo a alguien** [confesión, promesa, secreto] to extract sthg from sb; [sonrisa, dinero, ovación] to get sthg out of sb; [suspiro, carcajada] to bring sthg from sb **- 6.** fig [mover]: **arrancar a alguien de un sitio** to shift sb from somewhere. ◇ *vi* **- 1.** [partir] to set off **- 2.** [suj: máquina, coche] to start **- 3.** [provenir]: **arrancar de** to stem from.
◆ **arrancarse** *vprnl*: **arrancarse a hacer algo** to begin o start to do sthg.

arranque *sm* **- 1.** [comienzo] start **- 2.** AUTO starter motor **- 3.** fig [arrebato] fit.

arras *sfpl* **- 1.** [fianza] deposit *sing* **- 2.** [en boda] *coins given by the bridegroom to the bride.*

arrasar *vt* to destroy, to devastate.

arrastrado, **da** *adj* fam miserable, wretched.

arrastrar ◇ *vt* **- 1.** [gen] to drag o pull along; [pies] to drag; [carro, vagón] to pull; [suj: corriente, aire] to carry away **- 2.** fig [convencer] to win over, to sway; **arrastrar a alguien a algo/a hacer algo** to lead sb into sthg/to do sthg; **dejarse arrastrar por algo/alguien** to allow o.s. to be swayed by sthg/sb **- 3.** INFORM to drag; **arrastrar y soltar algo** to drag and drop sthg **- 4.** fig [producir] to bring **- 5.** fig [soportar - vida] to lead; [- deudas, penas] to have hanging over one. ◇ *vi* [rozar el suelo] to drag (along) the ground.
◆ **arrastrarse** *vprnl* to crawl; fig to grovel.

arrastre *sm* **- 1.** [acarreo] dragging **- 2.** [pesca] trawling **- 3.** *Esp* fam: **estar para el arrastre** to have had it **- 4.** *R Dom* fam: **tener arrastre** to be popular with members of the opposite sex.

arrayán *sm* myrtle.

arre *interj*: **¡arre!** gee up!

arrear *vt* **- 1.** [azuzar] to gee up **- 2.** fam [propinar] to give **- 3.** [poner arreos] to harness.

arrebatado, **da** *adj* **- 1.** [impetuoso] impulsive, impetuous **- 2.** [ruborizado] flushed **- 3.** [iracundo] enraged.

arrebatador, **ra** *adj* captivating.

arrebatar *vt* **- 1.** [arrancar]: **arrebatar algo a alguien** to snatch sthg from sb **- 2.** fig [cautivar] to captivate.
◆ **arrebatarse** *vprnl* [enfurecerse] to get furious.

arrebato *sm* **- 1.** [arranque] fit, outburst; **un arrebato de amor** a crush **- 2.** [furia] rage, fury.

arrebujar *vt* **- 1.** [amontonar] to bundle (up) **- 2.** [arropar] to wrap up (warmly).
◆ **arrebujarse** *vprnl* [arroparse] to wrap o.s. up.

arrechar *vt Amér C, Col & Méx* mfam to make horny, to turn on.
◆ **arrecharse** *vprnl Amér C, Col & Méx* mfam to get horny.

arrecho, **cha** *adj Amér C, Col & Méx* mfam horny, randy.

arrechucho *sm* fam funny turn.

arreciar [8] *vi* **- 1.** [temporal etc] to get worse **- 2.** fig [críticas etc] to intensify.

arrecife *sm* reef.

arredrarse *vprnl*: **arredrarse ante** to be frightened of, to be intimidated by.

arreglado, **da** *adj* **- 1.** [reparado] fixed, repaired; [ropa] mended **- 2.** [ordenado] tidy **- 3.** [bien vestido] smart **- 4.** [solucionado] sorted out **- 5.** fig [precio] reasonable **- 6.** loc: **estamos arreglados** we're really done for **- 7.**: **arreglado a algo** in accordance with sthg.

arreglar *vt* **- 1.** [reparar] to fix, to repair; [ropa] to mend **- 2.** [ordenar] to tidy (up) **- 3.** [solucionar] to sort out **- 4.** MÚS to arrange **- 5.** [acicalar] to smarten up; [cabello] to do **- 6.** [adornar - cuarto etc] to decorate, to fit out **- 7.** *fam* [escarmentar]: **¡ya te arreglaré!** I'm going to sort you out!

◆ arreglarse *vprnl* **- 1.** [apañarse]: **arreglarse (con algo)** to make do (with sthg); **arreglárselas (para hacer algo)** to manage (to do sthg) **- 2.** [acicalarse] to smarten up.

arreglista *smf* MÚS (musical) arranger.

arreglo *sm* **- 1.** [reparación] mending, repair; [de ropa] mending **- 2.** [solución] settlement **- 3.** MÚS (musical) arrangement **- 4.** [acuerdo] agreement; **llegar a un arreglo** to reach agreement; **con arreglo a** in accordance with **- 5.** [decoración] decoration, doing up.

arrejuntar *vt fam* [cosas] to put together.

◆ arrejuntarse *vprnl fam* [amantes] to shack up together.

arrellanarse *vprnl* to settle back.

arremangado, da *adj* rolled-up.

arremangar = remangar.

arremeter ◆ arremeter contra *vi* to attack.

arremetida *sf* attack.

arremolinarse *vprnl* **- 1.** *fig* [personas]: **arremolinarse alrededor de** to crowd around **- 2.** [agua, hojas] to swirl (about).

arrendador, ra *sm, f* lessor.

arrendamiento, arriendo *sm* **- 1.** [acción] renting, leasing **- 2.** [precio] rent, lease.

arrendar [19] *vt* **- 1.** [dar en arriendo] to let, to lease **- 2.** [tomar en arriendo] to rent, to lease.

arrendatario, ria ⬦ *adj* leasing *(antes de s).* ⬦ *sm, f* leaseholder, tenant.

arreos *smpl* harness *(U).*

arrepanchingarse [16] *vprnl fam* to stretch out, to sprawl.

arrepentido, da ⬦ *adj* repentant. ⬦ *sm, f* **- 1.** [gen] penitent **- 2.** POLÍT *person who renounces terrorist activities.*

arrepentimiento *sm* regret, repentance.

arrepentirse [27] *vprnl* to repent; **arrepentirse de algo/de haber hecho algo** to regret sthg/having done sthg.

arrestado, da ⬦ *adj* under arrest. ⬦ *sm, f* detainee, person under arrest.

arrestar *vt* to arrest.

arresto *sm* [detención] arrest; **arresto domiciliario** house arrest.

◆ arrestos *smpl* courage *(U).*

arriar [9] *vt* to lower.

arriate *sm* (flower) bed.

arriba ⬦ *adv* **- 1.** [posición - gen] above; *Amér* [- encima de] above; [- en edificio] upstairs; **vive (en el piso de) arriba** she lives upstairs; **está aquí/allí arriba** it's up here/there; **arriba del todo** right at the top; **más arriba** further up

- 2. [dirección] up; **ve arriba** [en edificio] go upstairs; **hacia/para arriba** up, upwards; **calle/escaleras arriba** up the street/stairs; **río arriba** upstream **- 3.** [en un texto] above; **'el arriba mencionado...'** 'the above-mentioned...' **- 4.** *loc*: **de arriba abajo** [cosa] from top to bottom; [persona] from head to toe O foot; **mirar a alguien de arriba abajo** [con desdén] to look sb up and down. ⬦ *prep*: **arriba (de)** *Amér* [encima de] on top of. ⬦ *interj*: **¡arriba...!** up (with)...!; **¡arriba los mineros!** up (with) the miners!; **¡arriba las manos!** hands up!

◆ arriba de *loc prep* more than.

◆ de arriba *loc adj* top; **el estante de arriba** the top shelf.

arribar *vi* to arrive; NÁUT to reach port.

arribeño, ña *sm, f Amér fam* highlander.

arribista *adj* & *smf* arriviste.

arrienda *etc* ➪ **arrendar.**

arriendo *sm* = arrendamiento.

arriero, ra *sm, f* muleteer.

arriesgado, da *adj* **- 1.** [peligroso] risky **- 2.** [osado] daring.

arriesgar [16] *vt* to risk; [hipótesis] to venture, to suggest.

◆ arriesgarse *vprnl* to take risks/a risk.

arrimar *vt* **- 1.** [acercar] to move O bring closer; **arrimar algo a** [pared, mesa] to move sthg up against **- 2.** *fig* [arrinconar] to put away.

◆ arrimarse *vprnl* **- 1.** [acercarse] to come closer O nearer; **arrimaos que no cabemos** move up or we won't all fit in; **arrimarse a algo** [acercándose] to move closer to sthg; [apoyándose] to lean on sthg **- 2.** *fig* [ampararse]: **arrimarse a alguien** to seek sb's protection.

arrinconado, da *adj* **- 1.** [en una esquina] in a corner **- 2.** [abandonado] discarded, forgotten.

arrinconar *vt* **- 1.** [apartar] to put in a corner **- 2.** [abandonar] to discard, to put away **- 3.** *fig* [persona - dar de lado] to cold-shoulder; [- acorralar] to corner.

arritmia *sf* arrhythmia.

arrítmico, ca *adj* arrythmic.

arroba *sf* [peso] = 11.5 *kg*; **por arrobas** *fig* by the sackful.

arrobamiento *sm* ecstasy, rapture.

arrobar *vt* to captivate.

◆ arrobarse *vprnl* to go into raptures.

arrocero, ra ⬦ *adj* rice *(antes de s).* ⬦ *sm, f* rice grower.

arrodillarse *vprnl* to kneel down; *fig* to go down on one's knees, to grovel.

arrogancia *sf* arrogance.

arrogante *adj* arrogant.

arrogarse [16] *vprnl* to assume, to claim for o.s.

arrojado, **da** *adj* bold, fearless.

arrojar *vt* - **1.** [lanzar] to throw; [con violencia] to hurl, to fling - **2.** [despedir - humo] to send out; [- olor] to give off; [- lava] to spew out - **3.** [echar]: **arrojar a alguien de** to throw sb out of - **4.** [resultado] to produce, to yield - **5.** [vomitar] to throw up.

◆ **arrojarse** *vprnl* to hurl o.s.

arrojo *sm* courage, fearlessness.

arrollador, **ra** *adj* overwhelming; [belleza, personalidad] dazzling.

arrollar *vt* - **1.** [enrollar] to roll (up) - **2.** [atropellar] to knock down, to run over - **3.** [tirar - suj: agua, viento] to sweep away - **4.** [vencer] to crush.

arropar *vt* - **1.** [con ropa] to wrap up; [en cama] to tuck up - **2.** *fig* [proteger] to protect.

◆ **arroparse** *vprnl* to wrap o.s. up.

arrostrar *vt* to face up to.

arroyo *sm* - **1.** [riachuelo] stream - **2.** *loc*: **poner a alguien en el arroyo** to throw sb out into the street; **sacar a alguien del arroyo** to drag sb out of the gutter.

arroz *sm* rice; **arroz blanco** white rice; **arroz integral** brown rice; **arroz con leche** rice pudding.

arrozal *sm* paddy field, rice field.

arruga *sf* - **1.** [en ropa, papel] crease - **2.** [en piel] wrinkle, line.

arrugar [16] *vt* - **1.** [ropa, papel] to crease, to crumple - **2.** [piel] to wrinkle.

◆ **arrugarse** *vprnl* - **1.** [ropa] to get creased - **2.** [piel] to get wrinkled - **3.** *fam* [acobardarse]: **arrugarse ante** to shrink from.

arruinado, **da** *adj* ruined.

arruinar *vt* *lit & fig* to ruin.

◆ **arruinarse** *vprnl* to go bankrupt, to be ruined.

arrullar *vt* to lull to sleep.

◆ **arrullarse** *vprnl* - **1.** [animales] to coo - **2.** *fam fig* [personas] to whisper sweet nothings.

arrullo *sm* - **1.** [de palomas] cooing - **2.** [nana] lullaby - **3.** *fig* [de agua, olas] murmur.

arrumaco *sm* (*U*) *fam*: **arrumacos** affection, lovey-dovey behaviour.

arrumar *vt Andes & Ven* to pile up.

arrumbar *vt* to put aside.

arrume *sm Col & Ven* pile.

arsenal *sm* - **1.** [de barcos] shipyard - **2.** [de armas] arsenal - **3.** [de cosas] array - **4.** *fig* [de conocimientos] fount, store.

arsénico *sm* arsenic.

art. (*abrev de* **artículo**) art.

arte *sm o sf* (*en sing gen m; en pl f*) - **1.** [gen] art; **arte abstracto/figurativo** abstract/figurative art; **arte dramático** drama - **2.** [don] artistry

- **3.** [astucia] artfulness, cunning; **malas artes** trickery (*U*) - **4.** *loc*: **no tener arte ni parte en** to have nothing whatsoever to do with; **como por arte de birlibirloque** o **de encantamiento** o **de magia** as if by magic.

◆ **artes** *sfpl* arts; **artes gráficas/plásticas** graphic/plastic arts; **artes liberales** liberal arts; **artes marciales** martial arts; **artes y oficios** ≃ technical college *UK*; **bellas artes** fine arts.

artefacto *sm* [aparato] device; [máquina] machine.

arteria *sf* *lit & fig* artery.

arterial *adj* arterial.

arterioesclerosis, arteriosclerosis *sf inv* arteriosclerosis.

artesa *sf* trough.

artesanal *adj* [hecho a mano] handmade.

artesanía *sf* craftsmanship; **de artesanía** [producto] handmade.

artesano, **na** *sm, f* craftsman (*f* craftswoman).

artesonado *sm* coffered ceiling.

ártico, **ca** *adj* arctic.

◆ **Ártico** *sm*: **el Ártico** the Arctic; **el océano Glacial Ártico** the Arctic Ocean.

articulación *sf* - **1.** ANAT & TECNOL joint - **2.** LING articulation - **3.** [estructuración] coordination.

articulado, **da** *adj* articulated.

articular *vt* - **1.** [palabras, piezas] to articulate - **2.** [ley, contrato] to break down into separate articles - **3.** [plan, proyecto] to coordinate.

articulista *smf* feature writer.

artículo *sm* - **1.** [gen] article; **artículo definido** o **determinado** definite article; **artículo indefinido** o **indeterminado** indefinite article; **artículo básico** ECON basic product; **artículo de fondo** editorial, leader; **artículo de importación** import; **artículo líder** ECON product leader; **artículo de primera necesidad** basic commodity - **2.** [de diccionario] entry.

◆ **artículo de fe** *sm* RELIG article of faith; *fig* gospel (truth) (*U*).

artífice *smf* *fig* architect.

artificial *adj* artificial.

artificiero *sm* - **1.** [pirotécnico] explosives expert - **2.** [desactivador] bomb disposal expert.

artificio *sm* - **1.** [aparato] device - **2.** *fig* [falsedad] artifice; [artimaña] trick.

artificioso, **sa** *adj* *fig* [engañoso] deceptive.

artillería *sf* artillery.

artillero *sm* artilleryman.

artilugio *sm* gadget, contrivance.

artimaña *sf* (*gen pl*) trick, ruse.

artista *smf* - **1.** [gen] artist - **2.** [de espectáculos] artiste; **artista de cine** movie actor (*f* actress).

artístico, **ca** *adj* artistic.

artritis *sf inv* arthritis.

artrosis *sf inv* arthrosis.

arveja *sf Andes, Col, C Sur & Ven* pea.

arzobispo *sm* archbishop.

as *sm* - **1.** [carta, dado] ace - **2.** [campeón]: **un as del volante** an ace driver; **ser un as** to be brilliant.

asa *sf (el)* handle.

asado, **da** *adj* roasted.

◆ **asado** *sm* - **1.** [carne] roast - **2.** *Col & C Sur* [barbacoa] barbecue.

asador *sm* - **1.** [aparato] roaster - **2.** [varilla] spit.

asaduras *sfpl* offal *(U)*; [de pollo, pavo] giblets.

asalariado, **da** ◇ *adj* wage-earning. ◇ *sm, f* wage earner.

asalariar [8] *vt* to take on.

asalmonado, **da** *adj* salmon (pink).

asaltante *smf* [agresor] attacker; [atracador] robber.

asaltar *vt* - **1.** [atacar] to attack; [castillo, ciudad etc] to storm - **2.** [robar] to rob - **3.** *fig* [suj: dudas etc] to assail - **4.** [importunar] to plague.

asalto *sm* - **1.** [ataque] attack; [de castillo, ciudad] storming - **2.** [robo] robbery - **3.** DEP round.

asamblea *sf* assembly; POLÍT mass meeting.

asar *vt* - **1.** [alimentos - al horno] to bake; [- a la parrilla] to grill; [- en asador] to roast - **2.** *fig* [importunar]: **asar a alguien a preguntas** to plague sb with questions.

◆ **asarse** *vprnl fig* to be boiling hot.

ascendencia *sf* - **1.** [linaje] descent - **2.** [extracción social] extraction - **3.** *fig* [influencia] ascendancy.

ascendente ◇ *adj* rising. ◇ *sm* ASTROL ascendant.

ascender [20] ◇ *vi* - **1.** [subir] to go up, to climb - **2.** [aumentar, elevarse] to rise, to go up - **3.** [en empleo, deportes]: **ascender (a)** to be promoted (to) - **4.** [totalizar - precio etc]: **ascender a** to come O amount to. ◇ *vt*: **ascender a alguien (a)** to promote sb (to).

ascendiente ◇ *smf* [antepasado] ancestor. ◇ *sm* [influencia] influence.

ascensión *sf* ascent.

◆ **Ascensión** *sf* RELIG Ascension.

ascenso *sm* - **1.** [en empleo, deportes] promotion - **2.** [escalada] ascent - **3.** [de precios, temperaturas] rise.

ascensor *sm* lift *UK*, elevator *US*.

ascensorista *smf* lift attendant *UK*, elevator attendant *US*.

ascético, **ca** *adj* ascetic.

ascetismo *sm* asceticism.

ASCII (*abrev de* **American Standard Code for Information Interchange**) *sm* INFORM ASCII.

asco *sm* [sensación] revulsion; **siento asco** I feel sick; **¡qué asco de tiempo!** what foul weather!; **me da asco** I find it disgusting; **¡qué asco!** how disgusting O revolting!; **tener asco a algo** to find sthg disgusting O revolting; **hacer ascos a** to turn one's nose up at; **estar hecho un asco** *fam* [cosa] to be filthy; [persona] to be a real sight; **ser un asco** *fam* to be the pits.

ascua *sf (el)* ember; **arrimar uno el ascua a su sardina** to put o.s. first, to look after number one; **en** O **sobre ascuas** on tenterhooks.

aseado, **da** *adj* [limpio] clean; [arreglado] smart.

asear *vt* to clean.

◆ **asearse** *vprnl* to get washed and dressed.

asechanza *sf* snare.

asediar [8] *vt* to lay siege to; *fig* to pester, to badger.

asedio *sm* siege; *fig* pestering, badgering.

asegurado, **da** *sm, f* policy-holder.

asegurador, **ra** ◇ *adj* insurance *(antes de s)*. ◇ *sm, f* insurer.

asegurar *vt* - **1.** [fijar] to secure - **2.** [garantizar] to assure; **te lo aseguro** I assure you; **asegurar a alguien que...** to assure sb that... - **3.** COM: **asegurar (contra)** to insure (against); **asegurar algo en** [cantidad] to insure sthg for.

◆ **asegurarse** *vprnl* - **1.** [cerciorarse]: **asegurarse de que...** to make sure that...; **asegúrate de cerrar la puerta** make sure you close the door - **2.** COM to insure o.s., to take out an insurance policy.

asemejar ◆ **asemejar a** *vi* to be similar to, to be like. ◆ **asemejarse** *vprnl* to be similar O alike; **asemejarse a** to be similar to, to be like.

asentado, **da** *adj fig* [establecido] settled, established.

asentamiento *sm* - **1.** MECÁN securing - **2.** [campamento] settlement.

asentar [19] *vt* - **1.** [instalar - empresa, campamento] to set up; [- comunidad, pueblo] to settle - **2.** [asegurar] to secure; [cimientos] to lay.

◆ **asentarse** *vprnl* - **1.** [instalarse] to settle down - **2.** [sedimentarse] to settle.

asentimiento *sm* approval, assent.

asentir [27] *vi* - **1.** [estar conforme]: **asentir (a)** to agree (to) - **2.** [afirmar con la cabeza] to nod.

aseo *sm* - **1.** [limpieza - acción] cleaning; [- cualidad] cleanliness - **2.** [habitación] bathroom.

◆ **aseos** *smpl* toilets *UK*, restroom *sing US*.

asepsia *sf* - **1.** MED asepsis - **2.** *fig* [indiferencia] detachment.

aséptico, **ca** *adj* - **1.** MED aseptic - **2.** *fig* [indiferente] detached.

asequible *adj* - **1.** [accesible, comprensible] accessible - **2.** [precio, producto] affordable.

aserción *sf* assertion.

aserradero *sm* sawmill.

aserrar [19] *vt* to saw.

aserto *sm* assertion.

asesinar *vt* to murder; [rey, jefe de estado] to assassinate.

asesinato *sm* murder; [de rey, jefe de estado] assassination.

asesino, na <> *adj lit & fig* murderous. <> *sm, f* murderer (*f* murderess); [de rey, jefe de estado] assassin; **asesino a sueldo** hired assassin; **asesino profesional** professional killer; **asesino en serie** serial killer.

asesor, ra *sm, f* adviser; FIN consultant; **asesor fiscal** tax consultant.

asesoramiento *sm* advice; FIN consultancy.

asesorar *vt* to advise; FIN to provide with consultancy services.

◆ **asesorarse** *vprnl* to seek advice; **asesorarse de** to consult.

asesoría *sf* - **1.** [oficio] consultancy - **2.** [oficina] consultant's office.

asestar *vt* [golpe] to deal; [tiro] to fire.

aseveración *sf* assertion.

aseverar *vt* to assert.

asexuado, da *adj* sexless.

asexual *adj* asexual.

asfaltado *sm* [acción] asphalting, surfacing; [asfalto] asphalt, (road) surface.

asfaltadora *sf* (road) surfacer.

asfaltar *vt* to asphalt, to surface.

asfalto *sm* asphalt.

asfixia *sf* asphyxiation, suffocation.

asfixiante *adj* asphyxiating; *fig* [calor] stifling.

asfixiar [8] *vt* - **1.** [ahogar] to asphyxiate, to suffocate - **2.** *fig* [agobiar] to overwhelm.

◆ **asfixiarse** *vprnl* - **1.** [ahogarse] to asphyxiate, to suffocate - **2.** *fig* [agobiarse] to be overwhelmed; [por calor] to be stifling.

asga *etc* ▷ **asir**.

así <> *adv* [de este modo] in this way, like this; [de ese modo] in that way, like that; **era así de largo** it was this/that long; **así es/era/fue como...** that is how...; **así así** [no muy bien] so so; **algo así** [algo parecido] something like that; **algo así como** [algo igual a] something like; **así es** [para asentir] that is correct, yes; **y así todos los días** and the same thing happens day after day; **así como** [también] as well as, and also; [tal como] just as, exactly as; **así no más** *Amér fam* [de repente] just like that. <> *conj* - **1.** [de modo que]: **así (es) que** so - **2.** [aunque] although

- **3.** [tan pronto como]: **así que** as soon as - **4.** *Amér* [aun si] even if. <> *adj inv* [como éste] like this; [como ése] like that.

◆ **así pues** *loc adv* so, therefore.

◆ **así y todo, aun así** *loc adv* even so.

Asia *n pr* Asia.

asiático, ca *adj & sm, f* Asian, Asiatic.

asidero *sm* - **1.** [agarradero] handle - **2.** *fig* [apoyo] support.

asiduidad *sf* frequency.

asiduo, dua *adj & sm, f* regular.

asienta *etc* ▷ **asentar**. ▷ **asentir**.

asiento *sm* - **1.** [en casa, teatro] seat; **tomar asiento** to sit down; **asiento abatible** tip-up seat - **2.** [base] bottom - **3.** [excavación arqueológica] site - **4.** COM entry; **asiento contable** book entry.

asierra *etc* ▷ **aserrar**.

asignable *adj*: **asignable a** that can be given to.

asignación *sf* - **1.** [atribución] allocation - **2.** [sueldo] salary.

asignar *vt* - **1.** [atribuir]: **asignar algo a alguien** to assign o allocate sthg to sb - **2.** [destinar]: **asignar a alguien a** to send sb to.

asignatura *sf* EDUC subject; **asignatura pendiente** failed subject; *fig* unresolved matter.

asilado, da *sm, f person living in an old people's home, convalescent home etc*; **asilado político** political refugee.

asilar *vt* [huérfano, anciano] to put into a home; [refugiado político] to grant political asylum to.

asilo *sm* - **1.** [hospicio] home; **asilo de ancianos** old people's home - **2.** *fig* [amparo] asylum; **asilo político** political asylum - **3.** [hospedaje] accommodation.

asimetría *sf* asymmetry.

asimilación *sf* - **1.** [gen & LING] assimilation - **2.** [comparación] comparison - **3.** [equiparación] granting of equal rights.

asimilar *vt* - **1.** [gen] to assimilate - **2.** [comparar] to compare - **3.** [equiparar] to grant equal rights to.

◆ **asimilarse** *vprnl* LING to become assimilated.

asimismo *adv* [también] also, as well; *(a principio de frase)* likewise.

asintiera *etc* ▷ **asentir**.

asir [53] *vt* to grasp, to take hold of.

◆ **asirse a** *vprnl lit & fig* to cling to.

asisito *adv Amér fam* so so.

asistencia *sf* - **1.** [presencia - acción] attendance; [- hecho] presence - **2.** [ayuda] assistance; **asistencia letrada** o **jurídica** legal advice; **asistencia médica** medical attention; **asistencia pública** social security; **asistencia**

sanitaria health care; **asistencia social** social work; **asistencia técnica** technical assistance **- 3.** [afluencia] audience **- 4.** DEP assist.

asistencial *adj* MED healthcare *(antes de s)*.

asistenta *sf* cleaning lady.

asistente *smf* **- 1.** [ayudante] assistant, helper; **asistente personal** INFORM personal digital assistant; **asistente social** social worker **- 2.** [presente] person present; **los asistentes** the audience *sing*.

asistido, **da** *adj* AUTO power *(antes de s)*; INFORM computer-assisted.

asistir <> *vt* **- 1.** [ayudar] to attend to **- 2.** [acompañar] to accompany. <> *vi*: **asistir a** to attend, to go to.

asma *sf (el)* asthma.

asmático, **ca** *adj* & *sm, f* asthmatic.

asno *sm lit & fig* ass.

asociación *sf* association; **asociación de consumidores** consumer association; **asociación de ideas** association of ideas; **asociación de padres de alumnos** parent-teacher association; **asociación de vecinos** residents' association.

asociado, **da** <> *adj* **- 1.** [relacionado] associated **- 2.** [miembro] associate. <> *sm, f* **- 1.** [miembro] associate, partner **- 2.** EDUC associate lecturer.

asocial *adj* asocial.

asociar [8] *vt* **- 1.** [relacionar] to associate **- 2.** COM to take into partnership.
➤ **asociarse** *vprnl* to form a partnership.

asociativo, **va** *adj* associative.

asolar [23] *vt* to devastate.

asomar <> *vi* [gen] to peep up; [del interior de algo] to peep out. <> *vt* to stick; **asomar la cabeza por la ventana** to stick one's head out of the window.
➤ **asomarse a** *vprnl* [ventana] to stick one's head out of; [balcón] to come/go out onto.

asombrar *vt* [causar admiración] to amaze; [causar sorpresa] to surprise.
➤ **asombrarse** *vprnl*: **asombrarse (de)** [sentir admiración] to be amazed (at); [sentir sorpresa] to be surprised (at).

asombro *sm* [admiración] amazement; [sorpresa] surprise.

asombroso, **sa** *adj* [sensacional] amazing; [sorprendente] surprising.

asomo *sm* [indicio] trace, hint; [de esperanza] glimmer; **ni por asomo** not under any circumstances.

asonancia *sf* assonance.

asonante *adj* assonant.

aspa *sf (el)* X-shaped cross; [de molino] arms *pl*.

aspaviento *sm (gen pl)* furious gesticulations *pl*.

aspecto *sm* **- 1.** [apariencia] appearance; **tener buen/mal aspecto** [persona] to look well/awful; [cosa] to look nice/horrible **- 2.** [faceta] aspect; **bajo este aspecto** from this angle; **en todos los aspectos** in every respect.

aspereza *sf* roughness; *fig* sharpness, sourness; **limar asperezas** to smooth things over.

áspero, **ra** *adj* **- 1.** [rugoso] rough **- 2.** [acre] sour **- 3.** *fig* [desagradable] sharp, sour.

aspersión *sf* [de jardín] sprinkling; [de cultivos] spraying.

aspersor *sm* [para jardín] sprinkler; [para cultivos] sprayer.

aspiración *sf* **- 1.** [ambición & LING] aspiration **- 2.** [de aire - por una persona] breathing in; [- por una máquina] suction.

aspirador *sm* = **aspiradora**.

aspiradora *sf* vacuum cleaner, hoover®; **pasar la aspiradora** to vacuum, to hoover.

aspirante <> *adj* [persona] aspiring. <> *smf*: **aspirante (a)** candidate (for); [en deportes, concursos] contender (for).

aspirar <> *vt* **- 1.** [aire - suj: persona] to breathe in, to inhale; [- suj: máquina] to suck in **- 2.** LING to aspirate. <> *vi*: **aspirar a algo** [ansiar] to aspire to sthg.

aspirina® *sf* aspirin.

asquear *vt* to disgust, to make sick.

asquerosidad *sf* disgusting o revolting thing.

asqueroso, **sa** *adj* disgusting, revolting.

asta *sf (el)* **- 1.** [de bandera] flagpole, mast; **a media asta** at half-mast **- 2.** [de lanza] shaft; [de brocha] handle **- 3.** [de toro] horn.

astado *sm* TAUROM bull.

asterisco *sm* asterisk.

asteroide *sm* asteroid.

astigmatismo *sm* astigmatism.

astil *sm* [de hacha, pico] haft; [de azada] handle.

astilla *sf* splinter; **hacer astillas** *fig* to smash to smithereens.

astillar *vt* to splinter; [tronco] to chop up.
➤ **astillarse** *vprnl* to splinter.

astillero *sm* shipyard.

astracán *sm* astrakhan.

astral *adj* astral.

astringente *adj* astringent.

astro *sm* ASTRON heavenly body; *fig* star.

astrofísica *sf* astrophysics *(U)*.

astrología *sf* astrology.

astrólogo, **ga** *sm, f* astrologer.

astronauta *smf* astronaut.

astronáutica *sf* astronautics *(U)*.

astronave *sf* spacecraft, spaceship.

astronomía *sf* astronomy.

astronómico, ca *adj* lit & fig astronomical.

astrónomo, ma *sm, f* astronomer.

astucia *sf* - **1.** [picardía] cunning, astuteness - **2.** *(gen pl)* [treta] cunning trick.

asturiano, na *adj & sm, f* Asturian.

Asturias *n pr* Asturias.

astuto, ta *adj* [ladino, tramposo] cunning; [sagaz, listo] astute.

asuela *etc* ⊳ **asolar**.

asueto *sm* break, rest; **unos días de asueto** a few days off.

asumir *vt* - **1.** [gen] to assume - **2.** [aceptar] to accept.

asunción *sf* assumption.
⟜ **Asunción** *sf*: **la Asunción** RELIG the Assumption.

Asunción *n pr* GEOGR Asunción.

asunto *sm* - **1.** [tema - general] subject; [- específico] matter; [- de obra, libro] theme; **asuntos a tratar** agenda *sing* - **2.** [cuestión, problema] issue - **3.** [negocio] affair, business *(U)*; **no es asunto tuyo** it's none of your business - **4.** *fam* [romance] affair.
⟜ **asuntos** *smpl* POLÍT affairs; **asuntos exteriores** foreign affairs.

asustadizo, za *adj* easily frightened.

asustado, da *adj* frightened, scared.

asustar *vt* to frighten, to scare.
⟜ **asustarse** *vprnl*: **asustarse (de)** to be frightened *o* scared (of).

atacante ⟨⟩ *adj* attacking. ⟨⟩ *smf* [agresor] attacker. ⟨⟩ *sm* DEP forward.

atacar [10] *vt* - **1.** [gen] to attack; **me ataca los nervios** *fig* it gets on my nerves - **2.** [sobrevenir]: **le atacó la risa/fiebre** he had a fit of laughter/bout of fever - **3.** *fig* [acometer] to set about.

atado *sm* - **1.** [conjunto, montón] bundle - **2.** *R Plata* [cajetilla] packet of cigarettes.

atadura *sf* lit & fig tie.

atajar ⟨⟩ *vi* [acortar]: **atajar (por)** to take a short cut (through). ⟨⟩ *vt* - **1.** [contener] to put a stop to; [hemorragia, inundación] to stem - **2.** *fig* [interrumpir] to cut short.

atajo *sm* - **1.** [camino corto, medio rápido] short cut; **coger** *o* **tomar un atajo** to take a short cut - **2.** *despec* [panda] bunch.

atalaya *sf* - **1.** [torre] watchtower - **2.** [altura] vantage point.

atañer *vi* - **1.** [concernir]: **atañer a** to concern; **en lo que atañe a este asunto** as far as this subject is concerned - **2.** [corresponder]: **atañer a** to be the responsibility of.

ataque ⟨⟩ *sm* - **1.** [gen & DEP] attack - **2.** *fig* [acceso] fit, bout; **ataque cardíaco** *o* **al corazón** heart attack; **ataque de nervios** nervous breakdown. ⟨⟩ *v* ⊳ **atacar**.

atar *vt* - **1.** [unir] to tie (up) - **2.** *fig* [relacionar] to link together - **3.** *fig* [constreñir] to tie down; **atar corto a alguien** *fam* to keep a tight rein on sb.
⟜ **atarse** *vprnl* - **1.** [comprometerse] to tie o.s. up in knots - **2.** [ceñirse]: **atarse a** to become tied to.

atarazana *sf* shipyard.

atardecer [30] ⟨⟩ *sm* dusk; **al atardecer** at dusk. ⟨⟩ *v impers* to get dark.

atareado, da *adj* busy.

atascar [10] *vt* to block (up).
⟜ **atascarse** *vprnl* - **1.** [obstruirse] to get blocked up - **2.** *fig* [detenerse] to get stuck; [al hablar] to dry up.

atasco *sm* - **1.** [obstrucción] blockage - **2.** AUTO traffic jam - **3.** [impedimento] hindrance, obstacle.

atasque *etc* ⊳ **atascar**.

ataúd *sm* coffin.

ataviar [9] *vt* [cosa] to deck out; [persona] to dress up.
⟜ **ataviarse** *vprnl* to dress up.

atávico, ca *adj* atavistic.

atavío *sm* - **1.** [adorno] adornment - **2.** [indumentaria] attire *(U)*.

ate *sm* Méx quince jelly.

ateísmo *sm* atheism.

atemorizar [13] *vt* to frighten.
⟜ **atemorizarse** *vprnl* to get frightened.

atenazar [13] *vt* - **1.** [sujetar] to clench - **2.** *fig* [suj: dudas] to torment, to rack; [suj: miedo, nervios] to grip.

atención ⟨⟩ *sf* - **1.** [interés] attention; **a la atención de** for the attention of; **llamar la atención** [atraer] to attract attention; **llamar la atención a alguien** [amonestar] to tell sb off; **poner** *o* **prestar atención** to pay attention; **atención al cliente** customer service department; **atención personalizada** personalized service; **atención psiquiátrica** psychiatric treatment - **2.** [cortesía] attentiveness *(U)*; **en atención a** [teniendo en cuenta] out of consideration for; [en honor a] in honour of. ⟨⟩ *interj*: **¡atención!** [en aeropuerto, conferencia] your attention please!
⟜ **atenciones** *sfpl* attentions, attentiveness *(U)*.

atender [20] ⟨⟩ *vt* - **1.** [satisfacer - petición, ruego] to attend to; [- consejo, instrucciones] to heed; [- propuesta] to agree to - **2.** [cuidar de - necesitados, invitados] to look after; [- enfermo] to care for; [- cliente] to serve; **¿le atienden?** are you being served? <> **vi - 1.** [estar atento]: **atender (a)** to pay attention (to) **- 2.** [tener en cuenta]: **atendiendo a** taking into account, bearing in mind **- 3.** [responder]: **atender por** to answer to the name of.

ateneo *sm* athenaeum.

atenerse **[72]** ◆ atenerse a *vprnl* **- 1.** [promesa, orden] to stick to; [ley, normas] to observe, to abide by **- 2.** [consecuencias] to bear in mind.

ateniense *adj* & *smf* Athenian.

atentado *sm*: **atentado contra alguien** attempt on sb's life; **atentado contra algo** crime against sthg; **atentado terrorista** terrorist attack.

atentamente *adv* **- 1.** [con atención, cortesía] attentively; **mire atentamente** watch carefully **- 2.** [en cartas] Yours sincerely o faithfully.

atentar *vi*: **atentar contra (la vida de) alguien** to make an attempt on sb's life; **atentar contra algo** [principio etc] to be a crime against sthg.

atento, ta *adj* **- 1.** [pendiente] attentive; **estar atento a** [explicación, programa, lección] to pay attention to; [ruido, sonido] to listen out for; [acontecimientos, cambios, avances] to keep up with **- 2.** [cortés] considerate, thoughtful.

atenuante *sm* DER extenuating circumstance.

atenuar **[6]** *vt* [gen] to diminish; [dolor] to ease; [luz] to filter.

ateo, a <> *adj* atheistic. <> *sm, f* atheist.

aterido, da *adj* freezing.

aterirse *vprnl* to be freezing.

aterrador, ra *adj* terrifying.

aterrar *vt* to terrify.

aterrizaje *sm* landing; **aterrizaje de emergencia** o **forzoso** emergency landing.

aterrizar **[13]** *vi* **- 1.** [avión] to land **- 2.** *fig* [persona] to turn up.

aterrorizar **[13]** *vt* to terrify; [suj: agresor] to terrorize.

◆ **aterrorizarse** *vprnl* to be terrified.

atesorar *vt* **- 1.** [riquezas] to amass **- 2.** *fig* [virtudes] to be blessed with.

atestado *sm* official report.

atestar *vt* **- 1.** [llenar] to pack, to cram **- 2.** DER to testify to.

atestiguar **[45]** *vt* to testify to.

atezado, da *adj* tanned.

atiborrar *vt* to stuff full.

◆ **atiborrarse** *vprnl*: **atiborrarse (de)** *fam fig* to stuff one's face (with).

atice *etc* ▷ **atizar**.

ático *sm* [para vivir] penthouse; [desván] attic.

atienda *etc* ▷ **atender**.

atildar *vt* [acicalar] to smarten up.

atinar *vi* [adivinar] to guess correctly; [dar en el blanco] to hit the target; **atinar a hacer algo** to succeed in doing sthg; **atinar con** to hit upon.

atingencia *sf Amér* [relación] connection.

atípico, ca *adj* atypical.

atiplado, da *adj* shrill.

atisbar *vt* **- 1.** [divisar, prever] to make out **- 2.** [acechar] to observe, to spy on.

atisbo *sm* (*gen pl*) trace, hint; [de esperanza] glimmer.

atizador *sm* poker.

atizar **[13]** *vt* **- 1.** [fuego] to poke, to stir **- 2.** *fig* [sospechas, discordias etc] to fan **- 3.** *fam* [puñetazo, patada] to land, to deal.

◆ **atizarse** *vprnl fam* [comida, bebida] to guzzle.

atlante *sm* ARQUIT atlas, telamon.

atlántico, ca *adj* Atlantic.

◆ **Atlántico** *sm*: **el (océano) Atlántico** the Atlantic (Ocean).

atlantismo *sm* POLÍT doctrine followed by NATO.

atlas *sm inv* atlas.

atleta *smf* athlete.

atlético, ca *adj* athletic.

atletismo *sm* athletics (*U*).

atmósfera *sf lit & fig* atmosphere.

atmosférico, ca *adj* atmospheric.

atole *sm Amér C & Méx* drink made of corn meal.

atolladero *sm* [apuro] fix, jam; **meter en/sacar de un atolladero a alguien** to put sb in/get sb out of a tight spot.

atolón *sm* atoll.

atolondrado, da <> *adj* **- 1.** [precipitado] hasty, disorganized **- 2.** [aturdido] bewildered. <> *sm, f* [precipitado] hasty o disorganized person.

atolondramiento *sm* **- 1.** [precipitación] haste, disorganization **- 2.** [aturdimiento] bewilderment.

atómico, ca *adj* atomic; [central, armas] nuclear.

atomizador *sm* atomizer, spray.

atomizar **[13]** *vt fig* [fragmentar] to break down (into constituent parts).

átomo *sm lit & fig* atom; **átomo gramo** gram atom; **ni un átomo de** without a trace of.

atónito, ta *adj* astonished, astounded.

átono, na *adj* atonic.

atontado, da *adj* **- 1.** [aturdido] dazed **- 2.** [tonto] stupid.

atontar *vt* **- 1.** [aturdir] to daze **- 2.** [alelar] to dull the mind of.

atormentar *vt* to torture; *fig* to torment.

atornillar *vt* to screw.

atorón *sm* Méx traffic jam.

atorrante *adj* R Dom [holgazán] lazy.

atosigar [16] *vt* fig to harass.

atracadero *sm* landing stage.

atracador, ra *sm, f* [de banco] armed robber; [en la calle] mugger.

atracar [10] ◇ *vi* NÁUT: atracar (en) to dock (at). ◇ *vt* [banco] to rob; [persona] to mug.

◆ **atracarse** *vprnl*: atracarse de to eat one's fill of.

atracción *sf* - **1.** [gen] attraction - **2.** [atractivo] attractiveness, charm - **3.** [espectáculo] act - **4.** fig [centro de atención] centre of attention - **5.** (gen pl) [atracción de feria] fairground attraction.

atraco *sm* robbery; **atraco a mano armada** armed robbery.

atracón *sm* fam feast; **darse un atracón** to stuff one's face.

atractivo, va *adj* attractive.

◆ **atractivo** *sm* [de persona] attractiveness, charm; [de cosa] attraction.

atraer [73] *vt* - **1.** [gen] to attract - **2.** fig [ocasionar] to bring.

atragantarse *vprnl*: atragantarse (con) to choke (on); **se me ha atragantado este libro/tipo** fig I can't stand that book/guy.

atraiga, atrajera etc ▷ **atraer**.

atrancar [10] *vt* - **1.** [cerrar] to bar - **2.** [obturar] to block.

◆ **atrancarse** *vprnl* - **1.** [encerrarse] to lock o.s. in - **2.** [atascarse] to get blocked - **3.** fig [al hablar, escribir] to dry up.

atrapar *vt* - **1.** [agarrar, alcanzar] to catch - **2.** fam [conseguir] to get o.s.

atraque etc ▷ **atracar**.

atrás ◇ *adv* - **1.** [detrás - posición] behind, at the back; [- movimiento] backwards; **echarse para atrás** to move backwards; **quedarse atrás** fig to fall behind - **2.** [antes] earlier, before. ◇ *interj*: ¡atrás! get back!

atrasado, da *adj* - **1.** [en el tiempo] delayed; [reloj] slow; [pago] overdue, late; [número, copia] back (antes de s) - **2.** [en evolución, capacidad] backward.

atrasar ◇ *vt* to put back. ◇ *vi* to be slow.

◆ **atrasarse** *vprnl* - **1.** [demorarse] to be late - **2.** [quedarse atrás] to fall behind.

atraso *sm* - **1.** [del reloj] slowness - **2.** [de evolución] backwardness.

◆ **atrasos** *smpl* fam arrears.

atravesar [19] *vt* - **1.** [interponer] to put across - **2.** [cruzar] to cross - **3.** [perforar] to go through - **4.** fig [vivir] to go through.

◆ **atravesarse** *vprnl* [interponerse] to be in the way; **se me ha atravesado la vecina** fig I can't stand my neighbour.

atrayente *adj* attractive.

atrechar *vi* P Rico fam to take a short cut.

atreverse *vprnl*: atreverse (a hacer algo) to dare (to do sthg); **atreverse a algo** to be bold enough for sthg; **atreverse con alguien** to take sb on; **se atreve con todo** he can tackle anything.

atrevido, da ◇ *adj* [osado] daring; [caradura] cheeky. ◇ *sm, f* [osado] daring person; [caradura] cheeky person.

atrevimiento *sm* - **1.** [osadía] daring - **2.** [insolencia] cheek.

atrezo *sm* props pl.

atribución *sf* - **1.** [imputación] attribution - **2.** [competencia] responsibility, duty.

atribuir [51] *vt* [imputar]: atribuir algo a to attribute sthg to.

◆ **atribuirse** *vprnl* [méritos] to claim for o.s.; [poderes] to assume; **atribuirse la responsibilidad** to claim responsibility.

atribular culto *vt* to distress.

◆ **atribularse** *vprnl* to be distressed.

atributo *sm* attribute.

atril *sm* [para libros] bookrest; MÚS music stand.

atrincherarse *vprnl* - **1.** MIL to entrench o.s. - **2.** fig [escudarse]: atrincherarse en to hide behind.

atrio *sm* - **1.** [pórtico] portico - **2.** [claustro] cloister.

atrocidad *sf* - **1.** [crueldad] atrocity - **2.** fig [necedad] stupid thing.

atrofia *sf* MED atrophy; fig deterioration.

atrofiar [8] *vt* MED to atrophy; fig to weaken.

◆ **atrofiarse** *vprnl* MED to atrophy; fig to deteriorate.

atronador, ra *adj* deafening.

atropellado, da *adj* hasty.

atropellar *vt* - **1.** [suj: vehículo] to run over - **2.** fig [suj: persona] to trample on.

◆ **atropellarse** *vprnl* [al hablar] to trip over one's words.

atropello *sm* - **1.** [por vehículo] running over - **2.** fig [moral] abuse.

atroz *adj* atrocious; [dolor] awful.

ATS (abrev de **ayudante técnico sanitario**) *smf* Esp qualified nurse.

atte. abrev de **atentamente**.

atuendo *sm* attire.

atufar ◇ *vi* to stink. ◇ *vt* [suj: olor, humo - persona] to overpower; [- lugar] to stink out.

atún *sm* tuna.

aturdido, da *adj* dazed.

aturdimiento *sm* - **1.** [desconcierto] bewilderment, confusion - **2.** [irreflexión] thoughtlessness.

aturdir *vt* [gen] to stun; [suj: alcohol] to fuddle; [suj: ruido, luz] to confuse, to bewilder.

➤ **aturdirse** *vprnl* [gen] to be stunned; [por alcohol] to get fuddled; [con ruido, luz] to get confused.

aturullar, aturrullar *fam vt* to fluster.

➤ **aturullarse, aturrullarse** *vprnl* to get flustered.

audacia *sf* [intrepidez] daring.

audaz *adj* [intrépido] daring.

audible *adj* audible.

audición *sf* - **1.** [gen] hearing - **2.** MÚS & TEATRO audition.

audiencia *sf* - **1.** [público, recepción] audience; **dar audiencia** to grant an audience; **índice de audiencia** audience ratings - **2.** [DER - juicio] hearing; [- tribunal, edificio] court; **audiencia provincial** provincial court; **audiencia pública** public hearing.

audífono *sm* hearing aid.

audiómetro *sm* audiometer.

audiovisual *adj* audiovisual.

auditar *vt* FIN to audit.

auditivo, va *adj* ear *(antes de s)*.

auditor, ra *sm, f* FIN auditor.

auditoría *sf* - **1.** FIN [profesión] auditing - **2.** FIN [despacho] auditing company - **3.** FIN [balance] audit; **auditoría externa/interna** external/internal audit.

auditorio *sm* - **1.** [público] audience - **2.** [lugar] auditorium.

auge *sm* [gen & ECON] boom; **estar en (pleno) auge** to be booming.

augurar *vt* [suj: persona] to predict; [suj: suceso] to augur.

augurio *sm* omen, sign.

augusto, ta *adj* august.

aula *sf (el)* [de escuela] classroom; [de universidad] lecture room; **aula magna** great hall.

aullar *vi* to howl.

aullido *sm* howl.

aumentar ◇ *vt* - **1.** [gen] to increase; [peso] to put on - **2.** [en óptica] to magnify - **3.** [sonido] to amplify. ◇ *vi* to increase; [precios] to rise.

aumentativo, va *adj* augmentative.

➤ **aumentativo** *sm* augmentative.

aumento *sm* - **1.** [incremento] increase; [de sueldo, precios] rise; **ir en aumento** to be on the increase; **aumento de sueldo** pay rise o raise US - **2.** [en óptica] magnification.

aun ◇ *adv* even. ◇ *conj*: **aun estando cansado, lo hizo** even though he was tired, he did it; **ni aun puesta de puntillas llega** she can't reach it, even on tiptoe; **aun cuando** even though; **aun así** even so.

aún *adv* [todavía] still; *(en negativas)* yet, still; **no ha llegado aún** he hasn't arrived yet, he still hasn't arrived.

aunar *vt* to join, to pool.

➤ **aunarse** *vprnl* [aliarse] to unite.

aunque *conj* - **1.** [a pesar de que] even though, although; [incluso si] even if - **2.** [pero] although.

aúpa *interj*: ¡aúpa! [¡levántate!] get up!; ¡aúpa el Atleti! up the Athletic!

➤ **de aúpa** *loc adj fam*: **un susto de aúpa** a real fright; **una caravana de aúpa** a hell of a queue.

au pair [o'per] *sf* au pair.

aupar *vt* to help up; *fig* [animar] to cheer on.

➤ **auparse** *vprnl* to climb up.

aura *sf (el)* - **1.** [halo] aura - **2.** [viento] gentle breeze.

áureo, a *adj* golden.

aureola *sf* - **1.** ASTRON & RELIG halo - **2.** *fig* [fama] aura.

aurícula *sf* auricle.

auricular ◇ *adj* auricular. ◇ *sm* [de teléfono] receiver.

➤ **auriculares** *smpl* [cascos] headphones.

aurora *sf* first light of dawn; **al despuntar** o **romper la aurora** at dawn; **aurora boreal** aurora borealis, northern lights *pl*.

auscultar *vt* to sound *(with a stethoscope)*.

ausencia *sf* absence; **brillar por su ausencia** to be conspicuous by one's/its absence.

ausentarse *vprnl* to go away.

ausente ◇ *adj* - **1.** [no presente] absent; **estará ausente todo el día** he'll be away all day - **2.** [distraído] absent-minded. ◇ *smf* - **1.** [no presente]: **hay varios ausentes** there are a number of absentees; **criticó a los ausentes** he criticized the people who weren't there - **2.** DER missing person.

auspiciar [8] *vt* - **1.** [apoyar] to back - **2.** [patrocinar] to sponsor.

auspicio *sm* [protección] protection; **bajo los auspicios de** under the auspices of.

➤ **auspicios** *smpl* [señales] omens.

austeridad *sf* austerity.

austero, ra *adj* - **1.** [gen] austere - **2.** [moderado] sober.

austral ◇ *adj* southern. ◇ *sm* [moneda] austral.

Australia *n pr* Australia.

australiano, na *adj & sm, f* Australian.

Austria *n pr* Austria.

austriaco, ca, austríaco, ca *adj & sm, f* Austrian.

autarquía *sf* - **1.** POLÍT autarchy - **2.** ECON autarky.

autárquico, ca *adj* - **1.** POLÍT autarchical - **2.** ECON autarkic.

autenticidad *sf* authenticity.

auténtico, ca *adj* [gen] genuine; [piel, joyas] genuine, real; **un auténtico imbécil** a real idiot; **es un tío auténtico** he's a genuine bloke.

autentificar [10] *vt* to authenticate.

autismo *sm* autism.

autista <> *adj* autistic. <> *smf* autistic person.

auto *sm* - **1.** *fam* [coche] car; *C Sur* [vehículo] car - **2.** DER judicial decree; **auto de procesamiento** indictment - **3.** LITER (mystery) play.
◆ **autos** *smpl* DER case documents; **constar en autos** to be recorded in the case documents.
◆ **auto de fe** *sm* auto-da-fé.
◆ **de autos** *loc adj* DER: **la noche de autos** the night of the crime.

autoabastecimiento *sm* self-sufficiency.

autoadhesivo, va *adj* self-adhesive.

autoalimentación *sf* INFORM automatic paper feed.

autobiografía *sf* autobiography.

autobiográfico, ca *adj* autobiographical.

autobombo *sm fam*: **darse autobombo** to blow one's own trumpet.

autobús *sm* bus.

autocar *sm Esp* coach.

autocartera *sf shares in a company held by that same company.*

autocensura *sf* self-censorship.

autocine *sm* drive-in (cinema).

autocomplacencia *sf* self-satisfaction.

autocontrol *sm* self-control.

autocracia *sf* autocracy.

autocrítica *sf* self-criticism.

autóctono, na <> *adj* indigenous, native. <> *sm, f* native.

autodefensa *sf* self-defence.

autodestrucción *sf* self-destruction.

autodeterminación *sf* self-determination.

autodidacta <> *adj* self-taught. <> *smf* self-taught person.

autodirigido, da *adj* guided.

autodisciplina *sf* self-discipline.

autódromo *sm* motor racing circuit.

autoedición *sf* INFORM desktop publishing.

autoencendido *sm* AUTO automatic ignition.

autoescuela *sf* driving school.

autoestima *sf* self-esteem.

autoestop, autostop *sm* hitch-hiking; **hacer autoestop** to hitch-hike.

autoestopista, autostopista *smf* hitchhiker.

autofinanciación *sf* self-financing.

autogestión *sf* self-management.

autogobierno *sm* self-government, self-rule.

autógrafo *sm* autograph.

autómata *sm lit & fig* automaton.

automático, ca *adj* automatic.
◆ **automático** *sm* [botón] press-stud.

automatismo *sm* automatism.

automatización *sf* automation.

automatizar [13] *vt* to automate.

automedicarse [10] *vprnl* to self-administer medicine.

automotor, triz *adj* self-propelled.

automóvil *sm* car UK, automobile US.

automovilismo *sm* motoring; DEP motor racing.

automovilista *smf* motorist, driver.

automovilístico, ca *adj* motor *(antes de s)*; DEP motor-racing *(antes de s)*.

autonomía *sf* - **1.** [POLÍT - facultad] autonomy; [- territorio] autonomous region - **2.** [de persona] independence - **3.** [de vehículo] range; [de videocámara] recording time; [de pila] battery life; **autonomía de vuelo** range.

Autonomía

The Spanish Constitution of 1978 approved the reorganization of Spain into autonomous regions corresponding to traditional geographical and/or cultural divisions. Each region has devolved authority in defined areas, exercised by an elected assembly. Regions with a strong sense of distinct identity such as Catalonia, Galicia and the Basque Country (which each have their own language) have extended these devolved powers and now have control over their own education, health, police and public services (and certain tax-raising powers). Other regions, however, still retain the initial more limited powers.

autonómico, ca *adj* autonomous.

autónomo, ma <> *adj* - **1.** POLÍT autonomous - **2.** [trabajador] self-employed; [traductor, periodista] freelance. <> *sm, f* self-employed person; [traductor, periodista] freelance.

autopista *sf* motorway UK, freeway US; **autopista de peaje** toll motorway UK, tollway US.

autopropulsado, da *adj* self-propelled.

autopropulsión *sf* self-propulsion.

autopsia *sf* autopsy, post-mortem.

autor, ra *sm, f* **- 1.** LITER author **- 2.** [de crimen] perpetrator; **autor material del hecho** DER actual perpetrator of the crime.

autoría *sf* LITER authorship; [de crimen] perpetration; [de atentado] responsibility.

autoridad *sf* **- 1.** [gen] authority; **imponer su autoridad** to impose one's authority **- 2.** [ley]: **la autoridad** the authorities *pl.*

autoritario, ria *adj* & *sm, f* authoritarian.

autoritarismo *sm* authoritarianism.

autorización *sf* authorization; **dar autorización a alguien (para hacer algo)** to authorize sb (to do sthg).

autorizado, da *adj* **- 1.** [permitido] authorized **- 2.** [digno de crédito] authoritative.

autorizar [13] *vt* **- 1.** [dar permiso] to allow; [en situaciones oficiales] to authorize **- 2.** [capacitar] to allow, to entitle.

autorradio *sm* car radio.

autorretrato *sm* self-portrait.

autoservicio *sm* **- 1.** [tienda] self-service shop **- 2.** [restaurante] self-service restaurant.

autostop = autoestop.

autostopista = autoestopista.

autosuficiencia *sf* self-sufficiency.

autosuficiente *adj* self-sufficient.

autosugestión *sf* autosuggestion.

autovacuna *sf* autoinoculation.

autovía *sf* dual carriageway UK, state highway US.

auxiliar [8] <> *adj* [gen & GRAM] auxiliary. <> *smf* assistant; **auxiliar administrativo** office clerk; **auxiliar de vuelo** air steward (*f* air hostess UK, air stewardess). <> *vt* to assist, to help.

auxilio *sm* assistance, help; **pedir/prestar auxilio** to call for/give help; **primeros auxilios** first aid *(U)*; **¡socorro, auxilio!** help! help!

av., avda. (*abrev de* **avenida**) Ave.

aval *sm* **- 1.** [persona] guarantor **- 2.** [documento] guarantee, reference; **aval bancario** banker's reference.

avalancha *sf* lit & fig avalanche.

avalar *vt* to endorse, to guarantee.

avalista *smf* guarantor.

avance <> *sm* **- 1.** [gen] advance **- 2.** FIN [anticipo] advance payment **- 3.** RADIO & TV [- meteorológico etc] summary; [- de futura programación] preview; **avance informativo** news *(U)* in brief. <> *v* ▷ **avanzar**.

avanzada *sf* ▷ **avanzado**.

avanzadilla *sf* MIL advance patrol.

avanzado, da <> *adj* **- 1.** [gen] advanced **- 2.** [progresista] progressive. <> *sm, f* person ahead of his/her time.

▶ **avanzada** *sf* MIL advance patrol.

avanzar [13] <> *vi* to advance. <> *vt* **- 1.** [adelantar] to move forward **- 2.** [anticipar] to tell in advance.

avaricia *sf* greed, avarice; **la avaricia rompe el saco** *prov* greed doesn't pay; **ser feo/pesado con avaricia** to be ugly/boring in the extreme.

avaricioso, sa <> *adj* avaricious, miserly. <> *sm, f* miser.

avariento, ta <> *adj* avaricious, miserly. <> *sm, f* miser.

avaro, ra <> *adj* miserly, mean. <> *sm, f* miser.

avasallador, ra *adj* overwhelming.

avasallar *vt* **- 1.** [arrollar] to overwhelm **- 2.** [someter] to subjugate.

avatar *sm* (*gen pl*) vagary, sudden change; **los avatares de la vida** the ups and downs of life.

avda. (*abrev de* **avenida**), = av.

ave *sf* (*el*) **- 1.** [gen] bird; **ave del paraíso** bird of paradise; **ave rapaz** *o* **de rapiña** bird of prey; **ser un ave pasajera** *o* **de paso** *fig* to be a rolling stone **- 2.** *Amér* [pollo] chicken.

AVE (*abrev de* **alta velocidad española**) *sm* Spanish high-speed train.

AVE

The AVE is Spain's most modern train, and is designed to travel at speeds of over to 300Km/h. It is a development of the French TGV, and Spanish, German and French companies are involved in its manufacture. It runs on a separate track from ordinary Spanish rolling stock, as the latter has a wider gauge than the European standard of the AVE track. The first AVE line was opened from Madrid to Seville to coincide with the Expo '92 in the latter city. The final section of the line from Madrid to Barcelona is under construction, and this will eventually extend to the French border. A further line is also being built between the capital and the northern city of Valladolid, and eventually it is intended that a single high-speed network will connect the cities of the Atlantic and Mediterranean coasts via Madrid.

avecinarse *vprnl* to be on the way.

avefría *sf* lapwing.

avejentar *culto vt* to age, to put years on. ▶ **avejentarse** *vprnl* to age.

avellana *sf* hazelnut.

avellano *sm* hazel (tree).

avemaría *sf* (*el*) [oración] Hail Mary.

avena *sf* **- 1.** [planta] oat **- 2.** [grano] oats *pl.*

avenencia *sf* [acuerdo] compromise.

avenida *sf* avenue.

avenido, da *adj*: **bien/mal avenidos** on good/bad terms.

avenirse [75] *vprnl* - **1.** [llevarse bien] to get on (well) - **2.** [ponerse de acuerdo] to come to an agreement; **avenirse a algo/a hacer algo** to agree on sthg/to do sthg.

aventajado, da *adj* [adelantado] outstanding.

aventajar *vt* [rebasar] to overtake; [estar por delante de] to be ahead of; **aventajar a alguien en algo** to surpass sb in sthg.

aventar [19] *vt* - **1.** [abanicar] to fan - **2.** [trigo] to winnow - **3.** *Andes, Amér C & Méx* [empujar] to push, to shove; [tirar] to throw.

aventón *sm Amér C, Méx & Perú*: **dar aventón a alguien** to give sb a lift.

aventura *sf* - **1.** [gen] adventure; **correr aventuras** to have adventures - **2.** [relación amorosa] affair.

aventurado, da *adj* risky.

aventurarse *vprnl* to take a risk *o* risks; **aventurarse a hacer algo** to dare to do sthg.

aventurero, ra <> *adj* adventurous. <> *sm, f* adventurer (*f* adventuress).

avergonzar [38] *vt* - **1.** [deshonrar] to shame - **2.** [abochornar] to embarrass.
➡ **avergonzarse** *vprnl*: **avergonzarse (de)** [por culpa] to be ashamed (of); [por timidez] to be embarrassed (about).

avería *sf* [de máquina] fault; AUTO breakdown.

averiado, da *adj* [máquina] out of order; [coche] broken down.

averiar [9] *vt* to damage.
➡ **averiarse** *vprnl* [máquina] to be out of order; AUTO to break down.

averiguación *sf* investigation; **hacer averiguaciones** to make inquiries.

averiguar [45] *vt* to find out.

aversión *sf* aversion; **tener aversión a** to feel aversion towards.

avestruz *sm* ostrich.

aviación *sf* - **1.** [navegación] aviation - **2.** [ejército] airforce.

aviador, ra *sm, f* aviator.

aviar [9] *vt* - **1.** [maleta] to pack; [habitación] to tidy up - **2.** [comida] to prepare.

avícola *adj* poultry (antes de s).

avicultura *sf* poultry farming.

avidez *sf* eagerness.

ávido, da *adj*: **ávido de** eager for.

avienta *etc* ➡ **aventar**.

avieso, sa *adj* - **1.** [torcido] twisted - **2.** *fig* [malo] evil.

avinagrado, da *adj lit & fig* sour.

avinagrarse *vprnl* to go sour; *fig* to become sour.

avío *sm* [preparativo] preparation.
➡ **avíos** *smpl* - **1.** *fam* [equipo] things, kit (U) - **2.** [víveres] provisions *pl*.

avión *sm* plane, airplane *US*; **en avión** by plane; **por avión** [en un sobre] airmail; **avión nodriza** supply plane; **avión a reacción** jet; **avión de papel** paper aeroplane.

avioneta *sf* light aircraft.

avisar *vt* - **1.** [informar]: **avisar a alguien** to let sb know, to tell sb - **2.** [advertir]: **avisar (de)** to warn (of) - **3.** [llamar] to call, to send for.

aviso *sm* - **1.** [advertencia, amenaza] warning; **andar** *o* **estar sobre aviso** to be on the alert; **poner sobre aviso a alguien** to warn sb - **2.** *Amér* [anuncio] advertisement, advert; **aviso clasificado** classified advertisement - **3.** [notificación] notice; [en teatros, aeropuertos] call; **hasta nuevo aviso** until further notice; **sin previo aviso** without notice; **aviso de vencimiento** COM due-date reminder - **4.** TAUROM *warning to matador not to delay the kill any longer.*

avispa *sf* wasp.

avispado, da *adj fam* sharp, quick-witted.

avispero *sm* - **1.** [nido] wasp's nest - **2.** *fam fig* [lío] mess; **meterse en un avispero** to get into a mess.

avistar *vt* to sight, to make out.

avitaminosis *sf inv* vitamin deficiency.

avituallamiento *sm* provisioning.

avituallar *vt* to provide with food.

avivar *vt* - **1.** [sentimiento] to rekindle - **2.** [color] to brighten - **3.** [fuego] to stoke up.

avutarda *sf* great bustard.

axial *adj* axial.

axila *sf* armpit.

axioma *sm* axiom.

ay (*pl* **ayes**) <> *sm* groan. <> *interj*: **¡ay!** [dolor físico] ouch!; [sorpresa, pena] oh!; **¡ay de ti si te cojo!** Heaven help you if I catch you!

aya ➡ **ayo**.

ayatolá *sm* ayatollah.

ayer <> *adv* yesterday; *fig* in the past; **ayer (por la) noche** last night; **ayer por la mañana** yesterday morning; **antes de ayer** the day before yesterday. <> *sm fig* yesteryear.

ayo, aya *sm, f* [tutor] tutor (*f* governess).

ayuda *sf* help, assistance; ECON & POLÍT aid; **acudir en ayuda de alguien** to go to sb's assistance; **ayuda en carretera** breakdown service; **ayuda humanitaria** humanitarian aid.

ayudante *adj & smf* assistant.

ayudar *vt* to help; **ayudar a alguien a hacer algo** to help sb (to) do sthg; **¿en qué puedo ayudarle?** how can I help you?

➡ **ayudarse** *vprnl*: **ayudarse de** to make use of.

ayunar *vi* to fast.

ayunas *sfpl*: **en ayunas** [sin comer] without having eaten; *fig* [sin enterarse] in the dark.

ayuno *sm* fast; **hacer ayuno** to fast.

ayuntamiento *sm* - **1.** [corporación] ≃ town council - **2.** [edificio] town hall *UK*, city hall *US*.

azabache *sm* jet; **negro como el azabache** jet-black.

azada *sf* hoe.

azafata *sf*: **azafata (de vuelo)** air hostess *UK*, air stewardess; **azafata de exposiciones y congresos** hostess; **azafata de tierra** stewardess.

azafate *sm* *Amér C, Caribe, Méx & Perú* [bandeja] tray.

azafrán *sm* saffron, crocus.

azahar *sm* [del naranjo] orange blossom; [del limonero] lemon blossom.

azalea *sf* azalea.

azar *sm* chance, fate; **al azar** at random; **por (puro) azar** by (pure) chance.

azaroso, sa *adj* [vida, viaje] eventful.

ázimo *adj* = **ácimo**.

azimut = **acimut**.

azogue *sm* mercury.

azor *sm* goshawk.

azoramiento *sm* embarrassment.

azorar *vt* to embarrass.

➡ **azorarse** *vprnl* to be embarrassed.

Azores *sfpl*: **las Azores** the Azores.

azotaina *sf* *fam* slapping, smacking.

azotar *vt* - **1.** [suj: persona] to beat; [en el trasero] to smack, to slap; [con látigo] to whip - **2.** *fig* [suj: calamidad] to devastate.

azote *sm* - **1.** [golpe] blow; [en el trasero] smack, slap; [latigazo] lash - **2.** *fig* [calamidad] scourge.

azotea *sf* [de edificio] terraced roof; **estar mal de la azotea** *fam fig* to be funny in the head.

AZT (*abrev de* **azidothymidine**) *sm* AZT.

azteca ⬦ *adj* & *smf* Aztec. ⬦ *sm* [lengua] Aztec.

azúcar *sm o sf* sugar; **azúcar blanquilla/moreno** refined/brown sugar; **azúcar cande** *o* **candi** sugar candy; **azúcar glas** *o* **de lustre** icing sugar *UK*, confectioner's sugar *US*.

azucarado, da *adj* sweet, sugary.

azucarero, ra *adj* sugar *(antes de s)*.

➡ **azucarero** *sm* sugar bowl.

➡ **azucarera** *sf* sugar factory.

azucarillo *sm* - **1.** *CULIN* lemon candy - **2.** [terrón] sugar lump.

azuce *etc* ➪ **azuzar**.

azucena *sf* white lily.

azufre *sm* sulphur.

azul *adj* & *sm* blue; **azul celeste/marino/eléctrico** sky/navy/electric blue; **azul turquesa** turquoise.

azulado, da *adj* bluish.

azulejo *sm* (glazed) tile.

azulete *sm* [para lavar] blue.

azulgrana *adj inv* *DEP* Barcelona football club *(antes de s)*.

azuzar [13] *vt* - **1.** [animal] to set on - **2.** *fig* [persona] to egg on.

B

b, B *sf* [letra] b, B.

baba *sf* - **1.** [saliva - de niño] dribble; [- de adulto] spittle, saliva; [- de perro] slobber; **echar babas** to drool - **2.** [de caracol etc] slime - **3.** *loc*: **se le cae la baba con su hija** *fam* she drools over her daughter; **tener mala baba** *fam* to be bad-tempered.

babear *vi* [niño] to dribble; [adulto, animal] to slobber; *fig* to drool.

babel *sm o sf* *fam fig* bedlam.

babero *sm* bib.

babi *sm* child's overall.

babia *sf*: **estar** *o* **quedarse en babia** to have one's head in the clouds.

babilónico, ca *adj* - **1.** *HIST* Babylonian - **2.** [fastuoso] lavish.

bable *sm* Asturian dialect.

babor *sm*: **a babor** to port.

babosada *sf* *Amér C & Méx fam* daft thing.

baboso, sa ⬦ *adj* *Amér fam* [tonto] daft, stupid; [niño] dribbly; [adulto, animal] slobbering. ⬦ *sm, f* *Amér fam* [tonto] twit, idiot.

➡ **babosa** *sf* *ZOOL* slug.

babucha *sf* slipper.

baca *sf* roof *o* luggage rack.

bacaladero, ra *adj* cod-fishing *(antes de s)*.

➡ **bacaladero** *sm* cod-fishing boat.

bacalao *sm* [fresco] cod; [salado] dried salted cod; **bacalao a la vizcaína** CULIN *Basque dish of salt cod cooked in a thick sauce of olive oil, onions, tomato and red peppers*; **bacalao al pil-pil** CULIN *Basque dish of salt cod cooked slowly in an earthenware dish with olive oil and garlic*; **partir** o **cortar el bacalao** *fam fig* to be the boss.

bacán R *Dom* ◇ *adj* fine. ◇ *sm* toff; **como un bacán** like a real gentleman.

bacanal *sf* orgy.

bacarrá, bacará *sm* baccarat.

bache *sm* - **1.** [en carretera] pothole - **2.** *fig* [dificultades] bad patch - **3.** [en un vuelo] air pocket.

bachillerato *sm* *Spanish two-year course of secondary studies for academically orientated 16-18-year-olds*; **bachillerato unificado polivalente** ⊏⊐ BUP.

bacilo *sm* bacillus; **bacilo de Koch** tubercle bacillus.

bacín *sm* chamber pot.

bacinica *sf* *Amér* chamber pot.

backgammon *sm inv* backgammon.

backup [ba'kap] (*pl* **backups**) *sm* INFORM backup.

bacon ['beikon] *sm inv* bacon.

bacteria *sf* germ; **bacterias** bacteria.

bacteriano, na *adj* bacterial.

bactericida *adj* bactericidal.

bacteriología *sf* bacteriology.

bacteriológico, ca *adj* [guerra] germ *(antes de s)*.

bacteriólogo, ga *sm, f* bacteriologist.

báculo *sm* - **1.** [de obispo] crosier - **2.** *fig* [sostén] support.

badajo *sm* clapper *(of bell)*.

badén *sm* - **1.** [de carretera] ditch - **2.** [cauce] channel.

bádminton ['baðminton] *sm inv* badminton.

bafle, baffle *sm* loudspeaker.

bagaje *sm* *fig* background; **bagaje cultural** cultural baggage.

bagatela *sf* trifle.

Bahamas *sfpl*: **las Bahamas** the Bahamas.

bahía *sf* bay.

bailaor, ra *sm, f* flamenco dancer.

bailar ◇ *vt* to dance; **que me quiten lo bailado** *fam* no one can take away the good times. ◇ *vi* - **1.** [danzar] to dance; **es otro que tal baila** *fam* he's just the same, he's no different - **2.** [no encajar] to be loose; **los pies me bailan (en los zapatos)** my shoes are too big.

bailarín, ina *sm, f* dancer; [de ballet] ballet dancer; **prima bailarina** prima ballerina.

baile *sm* - **1.** [gen] dance; **baile clásico** ballet; **baile de salón** ballroom dancing - **2.** [fiesta] ball - **3.** COM: **baile de cifras** number transposition.
➤ **baile de San Vito** *sm* St Vitus' dance.

bailongo *sm* *fam* dance.

bailotear *vi* *fam* to boogie, to bop.

bailoteo *sm* *fam* bopping.

baja *sf* ⊏⊐ bajo.

bajada *sf* - **1.** [descenso] descent; **bajada de bandera** [de taxi] minimum fare - **2.** [pendiente] (downward) slope - **3.** [disminución] decrease, drop.

bajamar *sf* low tide.

bajar ◇ *vt* - **1.** [poner abajo - libro, cuadro etc] to take/bring down; [- telón, ventanilla, mano] to lower - **2.** [descender - montaña, escaleras] to go/come down - **3.** [precios, inflación, hinchazón] to reduce; [música, volumen, radio] to turn down; [fiebre] to bring down - **4.** [ojos, cabeza, voz] to lower. ◇ *vi* - **1.** [descender] to go/come down; **bajar por algo** to go/come down to get sthg; **bajar corriendo** to run down - **2.** [disminuir] to fall, to drop; [fiebre, hinchazón] to go/come down; [Bolsa] to suffer a fall.
➤ **bajarse** *vprnl*: **bajarse (de)** [coche] to get out (of); [moto, tren, avión] to get off; [árbol, escalera, silla] to get/come down (from).

bajel *sm* *culto* vessel, ship.

bajero, ra *adj* lower.

bajeza *sf* - **1.** [cualidad] baseness - **2.** [acción] nasty deed.

bajial *sm* *Méx & Perú* lowland.

bajío *sm* sandbank.

bajista ◇ *adj* FIN bearish; [mercado] bear *(antes de s)*. ◇ *smf* MÚS bassist.

bajo, ja *adj* - **1.** [gen] low; [persona] short; [planta] ground *(antes de s)*; [sonido] soft, faint; **en voz baja** in a low voice - **2.** [territorio, época] lower; **el bajo Amazonas** the lower Amazon - **3.** [pobre] lower-class - **4.** [vil] base.
➤ **bajo** ◇ *sm* - **1.** (*gen pl*) [dobladillo] hem - **2.** [piso] ground floor flat - **3.** [MÚS - instrumento, cantante] bass; [- instrumentista] bassist. ◇ *adv* - **1.** [gen] low - **2.** [hablar] quietly, softly. ◇ *prep* - **1.** [gen] under - **2.** [con temperaturas] below.
➤ **baja** *sf* - **1.** [descenso] drop, fall; **jugar a la baja** FIN to bear the market - **2.** [cese] **dar de baja a alguien** [en una empresa] to lay sb off; [en un club, sindicato] to expel sb; **darse de baja (de)** [dimitir] to resign (from); [salirse] to drop out (of) - **3.** [por enfermedad - permiso] sick leave (*U*); [- documento] sick note, doctor's certificate; **estar/darse de baja** to be on/to take sick leave; **baja por maternidad/paternidad** maternity/paternity leave - **4.** MIL loss, casualty.

bajos *smpl* [planta] ground floor *sing*.

bajón *sm* slump; **dar un bajón** to slump; [suj - mercado, producción] to slump; [- persona] to go downhill.

bajorrelieve *sm* bas-relief.

bajura ▷ **pesca**.

bala *sf* - **1.** [proyectil] bullet; **como una bala** *fig* like a shot - **2.** [fardo] bale.

◆ **bala perdida** *sm fam* ne'er-do-well.

balacear *vt* Amér [tirotear] to shoot.

balacera *sf* Amér shootout.

balada *sf* ballad.

baladí (*pl* **baladíes**) *adj* trivial.

baladronada *sf* boast.

balance *sm* - **1.** [COM - operación] balance; [- documento] balance sheet; **balance consolidado** consolidated balance sheet - **2.** [resultado] outcome; **hacer balance (de)** to take stock (of).

balancear *vt* [cuna] to rock; [columpio] to swing.

◆ **balancearse** *vprnl* [en cuna, mecedora] to rock; [en columpio] to swing; [barco] to roll.

balanceo *sm* - **1.** [gen] swinging; [de cuna, mecedora] rocking; [de barco] roll - **2.** Amér AUTO wheel balance.

balancín *sm* - **1.** [mecedora] rocking chair; [en jardín] swing hammock - **2.** [columpio] seesaw - **3.** AUTO rocker arm.

balandro *sm* yacht.

balanza *sf* - **1.** [báscula] scales *pl*; **balanza de cocina** kitchen scales; **balanza de precisión** precision balance; **la balanza se inclinó a nuestro favor** the balance o scales tipped in our favour - **2.** COM: **balanza comercial/de pagos** balance of trade/payments.

balar *vi* to bleat.

balarrasa *sm* ne'er-do-well.

balaustrada *sf* balustrade.

balazo *sm* [disparo] shot; [herida] bullet wound.

balbucear = **balbucir**.

balbuceo *sm* babbling.

balbucir [79], **balbucear** *vi* & *vt* to babble.

Balcanes *smpl*: **los Balcanes** the Balkans.

balcánico, **ca** *adj* Balkan.

balcón *sm* - **1.** [terraza] balcony - **2.** [mirador] vantage point.

balda *sf* shelf.

baldado, **da** *adj* - **1.** [tullido] crippled - **2.** [exhausto] shattered.

balde *sm* pail, bucket.

◆ **de balde** *loc adv* free (of charge); **estar de balde** [sobrar] to be getting in the way.

◆ **en balde** *loc adv* in vain; **no ha sido en balde** it wasn't in vain.

baldío, **día** *adj* - **1.** [sin cultivar] uncultivated; [no cultivable] waste *(antes de s)* - **2.** [inútil] fruitless.

baldón *sm* insult.

baldosa *sf* [en casa, edificio] floor tile; [en la acera] paving stone.

baldosín *sm* tile.

balear ◇ *vt* Amér to shoot. ◇ *adj* Balearic. ◇ *smf* native/inhabitant of the Balearic Islands.

Baleares *sfpl*: **las (islas) Baleares** the Balearic Islands.

baleárico, **ca** *adj* Balearic.

baleo *sm* Amér shootout.

balido *sm* bleat, bleating *(U)*.

balín *sm* pellet.

balístico, **ca** *adj* ballistic.

◆ **balística** *sf* ballistics *(U)*.

baliza *sf* NÁUT marker buoy; AERON beacon.

ballena *sf* - **1.** [animal] whale - **2.** [varilla - de corsé] stay; [- de paraguas] spoke.

ballenato *sm* whale calf.

ballenero, **ra** *adj* whaling *(antes de s)*.

◆ **ballenero** *sm* [barco] whaler, whaling ship.

ballesta *sf* - **1.** HIST crossbow - **2.** AUTO (suspension) spring.

ballet [ba'le] (*pl* **ballets**) *sm* ballet.

balneario *sm* - **1.** [con baños termales] spa - **2.** Amér [con piscinas, etc] ≈ lido.

balompié *sm* football.

balón *sm* - **1.** [pelota] ball; **echar balones fuera** to evade the issue; **balón de reglamento** regulation ball - **2.** [recipiente] bag; **balón de oxígeno** oxygen bag; *fig* shot in the arm - **3.** [en tebeos] (speech) balloon.

baloncestista *smf* basketball player.

baloncesto *sm* basketball.

balonmano *sm* handball.

balonvolea *sm* volleyball.

balotaje *sm* second round of voting.

balsa *sf* - **1.** [embarcación] raft - **2.** [estanque] pond, pool - **3.** *loc*: **ser una balsa de aceite** [mar] to be as calm as a millpond; [reunión] to go smoothly.

balsámico, **ca** *adj* balsamic.

bálsamo *sm* - **1.** [medicamento] balsam - **2.** [alivio] balm.

balsero, **ra** *sm*, *f* Cuba refugee fleeing Cuba on a raft.

Báltico *sm*: **el (mar) Báltico** the Baltic (Sea).

baluarte *sm* - **1.** [fortificación] bulwark - **2.** *fig* [bastión] bastion, stronghold.

bamba *sm* bamba.

bambalina *sf* backdrop; **entre bambalinas** *fig* backstage.

bambolear *vi* to shake.

➤ **bambolearse** *vprnl* [gen] to sway; [mesa, silla] to wobble.

bambú (*pl* bambúes *o* bambús) *sm* bamboo.

banal *adj* banal.

banalidad *sf* banality.

banalizar [13] *vt* to trivialize.

banana *sf Amér* banana.

bananero, ra *adj* banana (antes de s).

➤ **bananero** *sm* [árbol] banana tree.

banano *sm* banana tree.

banca *sf* - **1.** [actividad] banking; **banca electrónica** electronic banking; **banca por Internet** Internet banking; **banca en línea** online banking; **banca telefónica** telephone banking - **2.** [institución]: **la banca** the banks *pl* - **3.** [en juegos] bank; **hacer saltar la banca** to break the bank - **4.** [asiento] bench - **5.** *Andes & R Plata* [escaño] seat.

bancario, ria *adj* banking (antes de s).

bancarrota *sf* bankruptcy; **en bancarrota** bankrupt; **declararse en bancarrota** to go bankrupt.

banco *sm* - **1.** [asiento] bench; [de iglesia] pew - **2.** FIN bank; **banco central/comercial/emisor/industrial/de inversiones** central/commercial/issuing/industrial/investment bank; **Banco Central Europeo** European Central Bank - **3.** [de peces] shoal - **4.** [de ojos, semen etc] bank - **5.** [de carpintero, artesano etc] workbench.

➤ **banco azul** *sm* POLÍT ≃ front bench *UK*.

➤ **banco de arena** *sm* sandbank.

➤ **banco de datos** *sm* INFORM data bank.

➤ **banco de pruebas** *sm* MECÁN test bench; *fig* testing ground.

➤ **Banco Mundial** *sm*: **el Banco Mundial** the World Bank.

banda *sf* - **1.** [cuadrilla] gang; **banda terrorista** terrorist organization - **2.** MÚS band - **3.** [faja] sash - **4.** [cinta] ribbon - **5.** [franja] stripe - **6.** RADIO waveband; **banda de frecuencias** frequency (band) - **7.** [margen] side; [en billar] cushion; [en fútbol] touchline; **fuera de banda** out of play; **sacar de banda** to throw the ball in - **8.** *loc*: **cerrarse en banda** to dig one's heels in.

➤ **banda ancha** *sf* INFORM broadband.

➤ **banda magnética** *sf* magnetic strip.

➤ **banda sonora** *sf* soundtrack.

bandada *sf* [de aves] flock; [de peces] shoal.

bandazo *sm* [del barco] lurch; **dar bandazos** [barco, borracho] to lurch; *fig* [ir sin rumbo] to chop and change; **dar un bandazo** [con el volante] to swerve violently.

bandeja *sf* tray; **servir** *o* **dar algo a alguien en bandeja** *fig* to hand sthg to sb on a plate; **bandeja de entrada** INFORM inbox; **bandeja de salida** INFORM outbox.

bandera *sf* flag; **jurar bandera** to swear allegiance (to the flag); **bandera blanca** white flag; **estar hasta la bandera** to be packed.

➤ **de bandera** *loc adj fam* [magnífico] fantastic, terrific.

banderilla *sf* - **1.** TAUROM banderilla (barbed dart thrust into bull's back) - **2.** [aperitivo] savoury hors d'œuvre on a stick.

banderillero, ra *sm, f* TAUROM banderillero (bullfighter's assistant who sticks 'banderillas' into the bull).

banderín *sm* - **1.** [bandera] pennant - **2.** MIL pennant-bearer.

banderola *sf* pennant.

bandido, da *sm, f* - **1.** [delincuente] bandit - **2.** [granuja] rascal.

bando *sm* - **1.** [facción] side; **pasarse al otro bando** to change sides - **2.** [de alcalde] edict.

bandolero, ra *sm, f* bandit.

➤ **bandolera** *sf* [correa] bandoleer; **en bandolera** slung across one's chest.

bandurria *sf* small 12-stringed guitar.

banjo ['baɲʝo] *sm* banjo.

banquero, ra *sm, f* banker.

banqueta *sf* - **1.** [asiento] stool - **2.** *Amér C & Méx* [acera] pavement *UK*, sidewalk *US*.

banquete *sm* [comida] banquet; **banquete de boda** wedding breakfast; **banquete eucarístico** holy communion.

banquillo *sm* - **1.** [asiento] low stool; **banquillo de los acusados** DER dock - **2.** DEP bench.

bañadera *sf Arg* [bañera] bath.

bañador *sm* [for women] swimsuit; [for men] swimming trunks *pl*.

bañar *vt* - **1.** [asear] to bath; MED to bathe - **2.** [sumergir] to soak, to submerge - **3.** [revestir] to coat - **4.** [suj: río] to flow through; [suj: mar] to wash the coast of - **5.** [suj: sol, luz] to bathe.

➤ **bañarse** *vprnl* - **1.** [en el baño] to have *o* take a bath, to bathe *US* - **2.** [en playa, piscina] to go swimming.

bañera *sf* bathtub, bath; **bañera de hidromasaje** whirlpool bath.

bañista *smf* bather.

baño *sm* - **1.** [acción - en bañera] bath; [en playa, piscina] swim; **darse un baño** [en bañera] to have *o* take a bath; [en playa, piscina] to go for a swim; **baño de asiento** hip bath; **baño de sol** sunbathing (*U*); **dar un baño a alguien** *fig* to knock the spots off sb - **2.** [bañera] bathtub, bath - **3.** [cuarto de aseo] bathroom - **4.** [vahos] inhalation (*U*) - **5.** [capa] coat.

◆ **baño María** *sm* bain Marie.

◆ **baños** *smpl* [balneario] spa *sing*.

baptismo *sm* baptism.

baptista *adj* & *smf* Baptist.

baptisterio *sm* baptistry.

baquelita *sf* Bakelite®.

baquetear *vi* [equipaje etc] to bump up and down.

bar *sm* bar.

barahúnda *sf* racket, din.

baraja *sf* pack (of cards); **jugar con dos barajas** *fig* to play a double game.

barajar *vt* - **1.** [cartas] to shuffle - **2.** [considerar - nombres, posibilidades] to consider; [- datos, cifras] to marshal, to draw on.

baranda, barandilla *sf* [de escalera] handrail; [de balcón] rail.

barata *sf* ⊏▷ **barato**.

baratero, ra *sm, f* *Amér* [comerciante] discount retailer.

baratija *sf* trinket, knick-knack.

baratillo *sm* - **1.** [género] junk - **2.** [tienda] junkshop; [mercadillo] flea market.

barato, ta *adj* cheap.

◆ **barato** *adv* cheap, cheaply; **de barato** for free.

◆ **barata** *sf* - **1.** *Méx* [rebaja] sale - **2.** *Chile* [insecto] cockroach.

barba *sf* beard; **barba incipiente** stubble; **apurarse la barba** to shave close; **dejarse barba** to let one's beard grow; **por barba** [cada uno] per head; **hacer algo en las barbas de alguien** *o* **en sus propias barbas** to do sthg under sb's nose; **reírse de alguien en sus propias barbas** to laugh in sb's face.

◆ **barbas** *sfpl* [de pez] barbel *sing*.

barbacoa *sf* barbecue.

Barbados *n pr* Barbados.

barbaridad *sf* - **1.** [cualidad] cruelty; **¡qué barbaridad!** how terrible! - **2.** [disparate] nonsense *(U)* - **3.** [montón]: **una barbaridad (de)** tons (of); **se gastó una barbaridad** she spent a fortune.

barbarie *sf* - **1.** [crueldad - cualidad] cruelty, savagery; [- acción] atrocity - **2.** [incultura] barbarism.

barbarismo *sm* - **1.** [extranjerismo] foreign word - **2.** [incorrección] substandard usage.

bárbaro, ra ⟨▷ *adj* - **1.** HIST barbarian - **2.** [cruel] barbaric, cruel - **3.** [bruto] uncouth, coarse - **4.** *fam* [extraordinario] brilliant, great. ⟨▷ *sm, f* HIST barbarian.

◆ **bárbaro** *adv* *fam* [magníficamente]: **pasarlo bárbaro** to have a wild time.

barbecho *sm* fallow (land); **estar en barbecho** to be left fallow.

barbería *sf* barber's (shop).

barbero, ra *sm, f* barber.

barbilampiño, ña *adj* smooth-faced, beardless.

◆ **barbilampiño** *sm* beardless man.

barbilla *sf* chin.

barbitúrico *sm* barbiturate.

barbo *sm* barbel; **barbo de mar** red mullet.

barbotar *vi* & *vt* to mutter.

barbudo, da ⟨▷ *adj* bearded. ⟨▷ *sm* bearded man.

barbullar *vi* to jabber.

barca *sf* dinghy, small boat.

barcaza *sf* barge.

Barcelona *n pr* Barcelona.

barcelonés, esa ⟨▷ *adj* of/relating to Barcelona. ⟨▷ *sm, f* native/inhabitant of Barcelona.

barco *sm* [gen] boat; [de gran tamaño] ship; **en barco** by boat; **barco cisterna** tanker; **barco de guerra** warship; **barco mercante** cargo ship; **barco de vapor** steamer, steamboat; **barco de vela** sailing boat, sail boat *US*.

bardo *sm* bard.

baremo *sm* [escala] scale.

bario *sm* barium.

barítono *sm* baritone.

barlovento *sm* windward.

barman ['barman] (*pl* **barmans**) *sm* barman, bartender *US*.

barniz *sm* [para madera] varnish; [para loza, cerámica] glaze; **barniz de uñas** nail varnish.

barnizar **[13]** *vt* [madera] to varnish; [loza, cerámica] to glaze.

barómetro *sm* barometer.

barón, onesa *sm, f* baron (*f* baroness).

barquero, ra *sm, f* boatman (*f* boatwoman).

barquilla *sf* [de globo] basket.

barquillo *sm* CULIN cornet, cone.

barra *sf* - **1.** [gen] bar; [de hielo] block; [para cortinas] rod; [en bicicleta] crossbar; **la barra** [de tribunal] the bar; **barra de labios** lipstick; **barra de pan** baguette, French stick - **2.** [de bar, café] bar (*counter*); **barra americana** singles bar; **barra libre** *unlimited drink for a fixed price* - **3.** [para bailarines] barre - **4.** [signo gráfico] slash, oblique stroke - **5.** *Andes* & *R Plata* [de amigos] gang; **barra brava** *R Dom* group of violent soccer fans - **6.** INFORM: **barra de estado** status bar; **barra de herramientas** tool bar; **barra de menús** menu bar - **7.** *loc*: **sin pararse en barras** stopping at nothing.

barrabasada *sf* *fam* mischief *(U)*.

barraca *sf* - **1.** [chabola] shack - **2.** [caseta de feria] stall - **3.** [en Valencia y Murcia] thatched farmhouse.

barracón *sm* large hut.

barranco *sm* - **1.** [precipicio] precipice - **2.** [cauce] ravine.

barraquismo *sm* shanty towns *pl*.

barrena *sf* drill; **entrar en barrena** AERON to go into a spin; *fig* [persona, gobierno] to totter.

barrenar *vt* - **1.** [taladrar] to drill - **2.** [frustrar] to scupper.

barrendero, ra *sm, f* street sweeper.

barreno *sm* - **1.** [instrumento] large drill - **2.** [agujero - para explosiones] blast hole.

barreño *sm* washing-up bowl.

barrer <> *vt* - **1.** [con escoba, reflectores] to sweep - **2.** [suj: viento, olas] to sweep away - **3.** *fam* [derrotar] to thrash, to annihilate. <> *vi*: **barrer con** [llevarse] to finish off, to make short work of; **barrer hacia** o **para adentro** *fig* to look after number one.

barrera *sf* - **1.** [gen] barrier; FERROC crossing gate; [de campo, casa] fence; **poner barreras a algo** *fig* to erect barriers against sthg, to hinder sthg - **2.** TAUROM *barrier around the edge of a bull ring* - **3.** DEP wall.
➤ **barrera de seguridad** *sf* [en carretera] safety barrier.
➤ **barrera del sonido** *sf* sound barrier.

barriada *sf* - **1.** neighbourhood, area - **2.** *Amér* [pobre] shanty town.

barrica *sf* keg.

barricada *sf* barricade.

barrido *sm* - **1.** [con escoba] sweep, sweeping *(U)*; **dar un barrido (a algo)** to sweep (sthg); **servir** o **valer tanto para un barrido como para un fregado** [persona] to be a jack-of-all-trades - **2.** TECNOL scan, scanning *(U)* - **3.** CINE pan, panning *(U)*.

barriga *sf* belly; **echar barriga** to get a paunch; **rascarse** o **tocarse la barriga** *fig* to twiddle one's thumbs, to laze around.

barrigazo *sm fam*: **darse un barrigazo** to fall flat on one's face.

barrigón, ona <> *adj* paunchy. <> *sm, f* [persona] portly person.
➤ **barrigón** *sm* [barriga] big belly.

barril *sm* barrel; **de barril** [bebida] draught.

barrilete *sm* - **1.** [de revólver] chamber - **2.** *Amér* [cometa] kite.

barrio *sm* - **1.** [vecindario] area, neighborhood *US*; **barrio comercial/periférico** shopping/outlying district; **barrio chino** red light district; **mandar a alguien al otro barrio** *fam fig* to do sb in, to finish sb off - **2.** *Amér* [arrabal] shanty town.

barriobajero, ra *despec* <> *adj* low-life *(antes de s)*. <> *sm, f* common person.

barrizal *sm* mire.

barro *sm* - **1.** [fango] mud - **2.** [arcilla] clay - **3.** [grano] blackhead - **4.** *loc*: **arrastrarse por el barro** to abase o.s.

barroco, ca *adj* - **1.** ARTE baroque - **2.** [recargado] ornate.
➤ **barroco** *sm* ARTE baroque.

barroquismo *sm* ARTE baroque style.

barrote *sm* bar.

barruntar *vt* - **1.** [presentir] to suspect - **2.** [ser indicio de] to suggest, to hint at.

barrunto *sm* - **1.** [presentimiento] suspicion - **2.** [indicio] sign, indication.

bartola ➤ **a la bartola** *loc adv fam*: **tumbarse a la bartola** to lounge around.

bártulos *smpl* things, bits and pieces; **liar los bártulos** *fam fig* to pack one's bags.

barullo *sm fam* - **1.** [ruido] din, racket; **armar barullo** to raise hell - **2.** [desorden] mess.

basa *sf* ARQUIT base.

basalto *sm* basalt.

basamento *sm* ARQUIT base, plinth.

basar *vt* [fundamentar] to base.
➤ **basarse en** *vprnl* [suj: teoría, obra etc] to be based on; [suj: persona] to base one's argument on.

basca *sf* - **1.** *fam* [de amigos] pals *pl*, mates *pl* - **2.** [náusea] nausea.

báscula *sf* scales *pl*; **báscula de baño/de precisión** bathroom/precision scales.

basculador *sm* dumper truck.

bascular *vi* to tilt.

base *sf* - **1.** [gen, MAT & MIL] base; [de edificio] foundations *pl*; **base aérea** air base; **base espacial** space station; **base de lanzamiento** launch site; **base de operaciones** operational base; **base naval** naval base - **2.** [fundamento, origen] basis; **sentar las bases para** to lay the foundations of - **3.** [de partido, sindicato]: **las bases** the grass roots *pl*, the rank and file; **de base** grassroots *(antes de s)* - **4.** *loc*: **a base de** (means of]; **me alimento a base de verduras** I live on vegetables; **a base de bien** extremely well; **a base de trabajar mucho** by working hard.
➤ **base de datos** *sf* INFORM database; **base de datos documental/relacional** documentary/relational database.
➤ **base imponible** *sf* taxable income.

BASIC ['beisik] *sm* INFORM BASIC.

básico, ca *adj* basic; **lo básico de** the basics of.

basílica *sf* basilica.

basilisco *sm*: **ponerse hecho un basilisco** *fam fig* to go mad, to fly into a rage.

básquetbol *sm Amér* basketball.

basquetbolista *smf Amér* basketball player.

basta *interj*: **¡basta!** that's enough!; **¡basta de chistes/tonterías!** that's enough jokes/of this nonsense!

bastante <> *adv* - **1.** [suficientemente] enough; **es lo bastante lista para...** she's smart enough to... - **2.** [considerablemente - antes de adj o adv] quite, pretty; [- después de verbo] quite a lot; **me gustó bastante** I quite enjoyed it, I enjoyed it quite a lot. <> *adj* - **1.** [suficiente] enough; **no tengo dinero bastante** I haven't enough money - **2.** [mucho]: **éramos bastantes** there were quite a few of us; **tengo bastante frío** I'm quite *o* pretty cold.

bastar *vi* to be enough; **basta con que se lo digas** it's enough for you to tell her; **con ocho basta** eight is enough; **baste decir que...** suffice it to say that...; **con la intención basta** it's the thought that counts.
➤ **bastarse** *vprnl* to be self-sufficient.

bastardía *sf* bastardy.

bastardilla ▷ **letra**.

bastardo, da <> *adj* - **1.** [hijo etc] bastard *(antes de s)* - **2.** [animal] crossbred - **3.** *despec* [innoble] mean, base. <> *sm, f* bastard.

bastidor *sm* - **1.** [armazón] frame - **2.** AUTO chassis - **3.** NÁUT screw propeller's frame.
➤ **bastidores** *smpl* TEATRO wings; **entre bastidores** *fig* behind the scenes.

bastión *sm lit & fig* bastion.

basto, ta *adj* coarse.
➤ **bastos** *smpl* [naipes] ≈ clubs.

bastón *sm* - **1.** [para andar] walking stick - **2.** [de mando] baton; **empuñar el bastón** *fig* to take the helm - **3.** [para esquiar] ski stick.

bastonazo *sm* blow (with a stick).

basura *sf lit & fig* rubbish *UK*, garbage *US*, trash *US*; **tirar algo a la basura** to throw sthg away; **basura radiactiva** radioactive waste.

basurero *sm* - **1.** [persona] dustman *UK*, garbage man *US* - **2.** [vertedero] rubbish dump.

bata *sf* - **1.** [de casa] housecoat; [para baño, al levantarse] dressing gown, robe *US* - **2.** [de médico] white coat; [de laboratorio] lab coat.

batacazo *sm* bump, bang.

batalla *sf* battle; **batalla campal** pitched battle; **de batalla** [de uso diario] everyday.

batallador, ra *adj* battling *(antes de s)*.

batallar *vi* - **1.** [con armas] to fight - **2.** *fig* [por una cosa] to battle.

batallón *sm* - **1.** MIL batallion - **2.** *fig* [grupo numeroso] crowd.

batata *sf* sweet potato.

bate *sm* DEP bat.

batea *sf Amér* washing trough.

bateador, ra *sm, f* batsman (*f* batswoman).

batear <> *vt* to hit. <> *vi* to bat.

batería <> *sf* - **1.** ELECTR & MIL battery; **batería solar** solar cell - **2.** MÚS drums *pl* - **3.** TEATRO floodlights *pl* - **4.** [conjunto] set; [de preguntas] barrage; **batería de cocina** pots *pl* and pans - **5.** *loc*: **aparcado en batería** parked at an angle to the pavement. <> *smf* drummer.

baterista *smf Amér* drummer.

batiborrillo, batiburrillo *sm* jumble.

batido, da *adj* - **1.** [nata] whipped; [clara] whisked - **2.** [senda, camino] well-trodden.
➤ **batido** *sm* - **1.** [acción de batir] beating - **2.** [bebida] milkshake.
➤ **batida** *sf* - **1.** [de caza] beat - **2.** [de policía] combing, search.

batidor *sm* - **1.** [aparato manual] whisk - **2.** [en caza] beater - **3.** MIL scout.

batidora *sf* [eléctrica] mixer.

batiente *sm* - **1.** [de puerta] jamb; [de ventana] frame - **2.** [costa] shoreline.

batín *sm* short dressing gown.

batir <> *vt* - **1.** [gen] to beat; [nata] to whip; [récord] to break - **2.** [suj: olas, lluvia, viento] to beat against - **3.** [derribar] to knock down - **4.** [explorar - suj: policía etc] to comb, to search. <> *vi* [suj: sol, lluvia] to beat down.
➤ **batirse** *vprnl* [luchar] to fight.

batiscafo *sm* bathyscaphe.

batista *sf* batiste, cambric.

baturro, rra <> *adj* Aragonese. <> *sm, f* Aragonese peasant.

batuta *sf* baton; **llevar la batuta** *fig* to call the tune.

baúl *sm* - **1.** [cofre] trunk - **2.** *Arg & Col* [maletero] boot *UK*, trunk *US*.

bautismal *adj* baptismal.

bautismo *sm* baptism.

bautizar [13] *vt* - **1.** RELIG to baptize, to christen - **2.** *fig* [denominar, poner mote] to christen - **3.** *fam fig* [aguar] to dilute.

bautizo *sm* - **1.** RELIG baptism, christening - **2.** [fiesta] christening party.

bauxita *sf* bauxite.

baya *sf* berry.

bayeta *sf* - **1.** [tejido] flannel - **2.** [para fregar] cloth; [de gamuza] chamois.

bayo, ya *adj* bay.

bayoneta *sf* bayonet.

baza *sf* - **1.** [en naipes] trick - **2.** [ventaja] advantage - **3.** *loc*: **meter baza en algo** to butt in on sthg; **no pude meter baza (en la**

conversación) I couldn't get a word in edge-ways; **no jugó bien su baza** he didn't play his cards right.

bazar *sm* bazaar.

bazo *sm* ANAT spleen.

bazofia *sf* - **1.** [comida] pigswill *(U)* - **2.** *fig* [libro, película etc] rubbish *(U)*.

bazuca, bazooka *sm* bazooka.

BCE (*abrev de* **Banco Central Europeo**) *sm* ECB.

be *sf* Amér: **be larga** o **grande** b.

beatería *sf* devoutness.

beatificación *sf* beatification.

beatificar [10] *vt* to beatify.

beatitud *sf* beatitude.

beato, ta ◇ *adj* - **1.** [beatificado] blessed - **2.** [piadoso] devout - **3.** *fig* [santurrón] sanctimonious. ◇ *sm, f* - **1.** RELIG beatified person - **2.** [piadoso] devout person - **3.** *fig* [santurrón] sanctimonious person.

bebe, ba *sm, f* C Sur fam baby.

bebé *sm* baby; **bebé probeta** test-tube baby.

bebedero *sm* - **1.** [de jaula] water dish - **2.** [abrevadero] drinking trough.

bebedizo *sm* [medicinal] potion; [de amor] love potion.

bebedor, ra *sm, f* heavy drinker.

beber ◇ *vt* - **1.** [líquido] to drink - **2.** *fig* [absorber - palabras, consejos] to lap up; [- sabiduría, información] to draw, to acquire. ◇ *vi* - **1.** [tomar líquido] to drink - **2.** *fig* [emborracharse] to drink (heavily) - **3.** [brindar]: **beber a** o **por** to drink to.

bebida *sf* drink; **darse** o **entregarse a la bebida** to take to the bottle; **bebida alcohólica** alcoholic drink.

bebido, da *adj* drunk.

bebito, ta *sm, f* Amér little baby.

beca *sf* [del gobierno] grant; [de organización privada] scholarship; **beca de investigación** research grant.

becar [10] *vt* [suj: gobierno] to award a grant to; [suj: organización privada] to award a scholarship to.

becario, ria *sm, f* - **1.** [del gobierno] grant holder; [de organización privada] scholarship holder - **2.** [en prácticas] *person on a work placement*, intern *US*.

becerrada *sf* bullfight with young bulls.

becerro, rra *sm, f* calf.

bechamel [betʃa'mel] = **besamel**.

bedel *sm* janitor.

beduino, na *adj* & *sm, f* Bedouin.

befa *sf* jeer; **hacer befa de** to jeer at.

begonia *sf* begonia.

beige [beis] *adj inv* & *sm inv* beige.

béisbol *sm* baseball.

beldad *sf* culto fairness, beauty.

belén *sm* - **1.** [de Navidad] crib, Nativity scene - **2.** *fam* [desorden] bedlam *(U)* - **3.** (*gen pl*) *fig* [embrollo] mess *(U)*.

Belén *n pr* Bethlehem.

belfo, fa *adj* thick-lipped.
➡ **belfo** *sm* horse's lip.

belga *adj* & *smf* Belgian.

Bélgica *n pr* Belgium.

Belice *n pr* Belize.

beliceño, ña *adj* & *sm, f* Belizean.

belicismo *sm* warmongering.

belicista ◇ *adj* belligerent. ◇ *smf* warmonger.

bélico, ca *adj* [gen] war (*antes de s*); [actitud] bellicose, warlike.

belicoso, sa *adj* bellicose; *fig* aggressive.

beligerancia *sf* belligerence.

beligerante *adj* & *smf* belligerent.

bellaco, ca *sm, f* villain, scoundrel.

belladona *sf* belladonna, deadly nightshade.

bellaquería *sf* wickedness, roguery.

belleza *sf* beauty.

bello, lla *adj* beautiful.

bellota *sf* acorn.

bemol ◇ *adj* flat. ◇ *sm* MÚS flat; **doble bemol** double flat; **tener (muchos) bemoles** [ser difícil] to be tricky; [tener valor] to have guts; [ser un abuso] to be a bit rich o much.

benceno *sm* benzene.

bencina *sf* Chile petrol *UK*, gas *US*.

bencinera *sf* Chile petrol station *UK*, gas station *US*.

bendecir [66] *vt* to bless.

bendición *sf* blessing.
➡ **bendiciones nupciales** *sfpl* wedding sing.

bendiga, bendijera *etc* ▷ **bendecir**.

bendito, ta ◇ *adj* - **1.** [santo] holy; [alma] blessed; **¡bendito sea Dios!** *fam fig* thank goodness! - **2.** [dichoso] lucky - **3.** [para enfatizar] damned. ◇ *sm, f* simple soul; **dormir como un bendito** to sleep like a baby.

benedictino, na *adj* & *sm, f* Benedictine.

benefactor, ra ◇ *adj* beneficent. ◇ *sm, f* benefactor (*f* benefactress).

beneficencia *sf* charity.

beneficiar [8] *vt* to benefit.
➡ **beneficiarse** *vprnl* to benefit; **beneficiarse de algo** to do well out of sthg.

beneficiario, ria *sm, f* [de herencia, póliza] beneficiary; [de cheque] payee.

beneficio sm - **1.** [bien] benefit; **a beneficio de** [gala, concierto] in aid of; **en beneficio de** for the good of; **en beneficio de todos** in everyone's interest; **en beneficio propio** for one's own good - **2.** [ganancia] profit; **beneficio bruto/neto** gross/net profit.

beneficioso, sa adj: **beneficioso (para)** beneficial (to).

benéfico, ca adj - **1.** [favorable] beneficial - **2.** [rifa, función] charity (antes de s); [organización] charitable.

benemérito, ta adj worthy.
➨ **Benemérita** sf: **la Benemérita** another name for the 'Guardia Civil'.

beneplácito sm consent.

benevolencia sf benevolence.

benevolente, benévolo, la adj benevolent.

bengala sf - **1.** [para pedir ayuda, iluminar etc] flare - **2.** [fuego artificial] sparkler.

benigno, na adj - **1.** [gen] benign - **2.** [clima, temperatura] mild.

benjamín, ina sm, f youngest child.

benzol sm benzol.

beodo, da adj & sm, f drunk.

beque etc ⊳ **becar**.

berberecho sm cockle.

berenjena sf aubergine UK, eggplant US.

berenjenal sm fam [enredo] mess; **meterse en un berenjenal** to get o.s. into a right mess.

bergantín sm brigantine.

beriberi sm beriberi.

berilio sm beryllium.

berlina sf four-door saloon.

bermejo, ja adj reddish.

bermellón adj inv & sm vermilion.

bermudas sfpl Bermuda shorts.

berrear vi - **1.** [animal] to bellow - **2.** [persona] to howl.

berrido sm - **1.** [del becerro] bellow, bellowing (U) - **2.** [de persona] howl, howling (U).

berrinche sm fam tantrum; **coger** o **agarrarse un berrinche** to throw a tantrum.

berro sm watercress.

bertsolari sm in Basque culture, poet who extemporizes poems at gatherings and literary competitions.

berza sf cabbage.

berzotas smf inv fam thickhead.

besamel, bechamel sf béchamel sauce.

besar vt to kiss.
➨ **besarse** vprnl to kiss.

beso sm kiss; **dar un beso a alguien** to kiss sb, to give sb a kiss; **comerse a besos a alguien** to smother sb with kisses.

bestia ⊳ adj - **1.** [ignorante] thick, stupid - **2.** [torpe] clumsy - **3.** [maleducado] rude. ⊳ smf - **1.** [ignorante, torpe] brute - **2.** [maleducado] rude person. ⊳ sf [animal] beast; **bestia de carga** beast of burden.

bestial adj - **1.** [brutal] animal, brutal; [apetito] tremendous - **2.** fam [formidable] terrific.

bestialidad sf - **1.** [brutalidad] brutality - **2.** fam [tontería] rubbish (U), nonsense (U) - **3.** fam [montón]: **una bestialidad de** tons pl o stacks pl of.

bestiario sm LITER bestiary.

best-seller [bes'seler] (pl **best-sellers**) sm best-seller.

besucón, ona fam ⊳ adj kissy. ⊳ sm, f kissy person.

besugo sm - **1.** [pez] sea bream - **2.** fam [persona] idiot.

besuquear fam vt to smother with kisses.
➨ **besuquearse** vprnl fam to smooch.

beta adj beta (antes de s).

bético, ca adj - **1.** [andaluz] Andalusian - **2.** DEP of or relating to Real Betis Football Club.

betún sm - **1.** [para calzado] shoe polish - **2.** QUÍM bitumen; **betún de Judea** asphalt.

bianual adj - **1.** [dos veces al año] biannual, twice-yearly - **2.** [cada dos años] biennial.

biberón sm (baby's) bottle; **dar el biberón a** to bottle-feed.

Biblia sf Bible; **ser la Biblia en verso** fig to be endless.

bíblico, ca adj biblical.

bibliófilo, la sm, f - **1.** [coleccionista] book collector - **2.** [lector] book lover.

bibliografía sf bibliography.

bibliográfico, ca adj bibliographic.

bibliógrafo, fa sm, f bibliographer.

bibliorato sm R Dom lever arch file.

biblioteca sf - **1.** [gen] library; **biblioteca ambulante/pública** mobile/public library - **2.** [mueble] bookcase.

bibliotecario, ria sm, f librarian.

bicameral adj bicameral, two-chamber (antes de s).

bicarbonato sm - **1.** [medicamento] bicarbonate of soda - **2.** QUÍM bicarbonate.

bicentenario sm bicentenary.

bíceps sm inv biceps.

bicha sf fam snake.

bicharraco sm fam - **1.** [animal] disgusting creature - **2.** [persona mala] nasty piece of work.

bicho sm - **1.** [animal] beast, animal; [insecto] bug - **2.** fam [persona mala]: **(mal) bicho** nasty piece of work; **bicho raro** weirdo; **todo bicho**

viviente every Tom, Dick and Harry; **bicho malo nunca muere** ill weeds grow apace - **3.** [pillo] little terror.

bici *sf fam* bike.

bicicleta *sf* bicycle.

bicoca *sf fam* [compra, alquiler] bargain; [trabajo] cushy number.

bicolor *adj* two-coloured.

bidé *sm* bidet.

bidimensional *adj* two-dimensional.

bidón *sm* drum *(for oil etc)*; [lata] can, canister; [de plástico] (large) bottle.

biela *sf* connecting rod.

bien ◇ *adv* - **1.** [como es debido, adecuado] well; **has hecho bien** you did the right thing; **habla inglés bien** she speaks English well; **cierra bien la puerta** shut the door properly; **hiciste bien en decírmelo** you were right to tell me - **2.** [expresa opinión favorable]: **estar bien** [de aspecto] to be nice; [de salud] to be *o* feel well; [de calidad] to be good; [de comodidad] to be comfortable; **está bien que te vayas, pero antes despídete** it's all right for you to go, but say goodbye first; **oler bien** to smell nice; **pasarlo bien** to have a good time; **sentar bien a alguien** [ropa] to suit sb; [comida] to agree with sb; [comentario] to please sb - **3.** [muy, bastante] very; **hoy me he levantado bien temprano** I got up nice and early today; **quiero un vaso de agua bien fría** I'd like a nice cold glass of water - **4.** [vale, de acuerdo] all right, OK; **¿nos vamos? – bien** shall we go? – all right *o* OK - **5.** [de buena gana, fácilmente] quite happily; **ella bien que lo haría, pero no la dejan** she'd be happy to do it, but they won't let her - **6.** *loc*: **¡bien por...!** three cheers for...!; **¡está bien!** [bueno, vale] all right then!; [es suficiente] that's enough!; **¡ya está bien!** that's enough!; **estar a bien con alguien** to be on good terms with sb; **¡muy bien!** very good!, excellent!; **¡pues (sí que) estamos bien!** that's all we needed!; **tener a bien hacer algo** to be good enough to do sthg. ◇ *adj inv* [adinerado] well-to-do. ◇ *conj*: **bien... bien** either... or; **dáselo bien a mi hermano, bien a mi padre** either give it to my brother or my father. ◇ *sm* good; **el bien y el mal** good and evil; **hacer el bien** to do good (deeds); **por el bien de** for the sake of; **lo hice por tu bien** I did it for your own good.

➤ **bienes** *smpl* - **1.** [patrimonio] property *(U)*; **bienes inmuebles** *o* **raíces** real estate *(U)*; **bienes gananciales** shared possessions; **bienes muebles** personal property *(U)* - **2.** [productos] goods; **bienes de consumo** consumer goods; **bienes de equipo** capital goods; **bienes de producción** industrial goods.

➤ **más bien** *loc adv* rather; **no estoy contento, más bien estupefacto** I'm not so much happy as stunned.

➤ **no bien** *loc adv* no sooner, as soon as; **no bien me había marchado cuando empezaron a...** no sooner had I gone than they started...

➤ **si bien** *loc conj* although, even though.

bienal ◇ *adj* biennial. ◇ *sf* biennial exhibition.

bienaventurado, da *sm, f* RELIG blessed person.

bienaventuranza *sf* - **1.** RELIG divine vision - **2.** [felicidad] happiness.

➤ **bienaventuranzas** *sfpl* RELIG Beatitudes.

bienestar *sm* wellbeing.

bienhechor, ra ◇ *adj* beneficial. ◇ *sm, f* benefactor *(f* benefactress).

bienintencionado, da *adj* well-intentioned.

bienio *sm* - **1.** [periodo] two years *pl* - **2.** [en sueldo] two-yearly increment.

bienvenido, da ◇ *adj* welcome. ◇ *interj*: **¡bienvenido!** welcome!

➤ **bienvenida** *sf* welcome; **dar la bienvenida a alguien** to welcome sb.

bies *sm inv* bias binding; **al bies** [costura] on the bias; [sombrero] at an angle.

bifásico, ca *adj* two-phase *(antes de s)*.

bife *sm* Andes & R Plata steak.

bífido, da *adj* forked.

bifocal *adj* bifocal.

biftec = **bistec**.

bifurcación *sf* [entre calles] fork; TECNOL bifurcation.

bifurcarse [10] *vprnl* to fork.

bigamia *sf* bigamy.

bígamo, ma ◇ *adj* bigamous. ◇ *sm, f* bigamist.

bígaro *sm* winkle.

big bang [biban] *(pl* **big bangs**) *sm* big bang.

bigote *sm* moustache; **de bigotes** *fig* fantastic.

bigotudo, da *adj* with a big moustache.

bigudí *(pl* **bigudíes** *o* **bigudís**) *sm* curler.

bikini = **biquini**.

bilateral *adj* bilateral.

biliar *adj* bile *(antes de s)*.

bilingüe *adj* bilingual.

bilingüismo *sm* bilingualism.

bilioso, sa *adj* lit & fig bilious.

bilirrubina *sf* bilirubin.

bilis *sf inv* lit & fig bile; **tragar bilis** *fig* to bite one's tongue.

billar *sm* - **1.** [juego] billiards *(U)*; **billar americano** ≃ pool; **billar romano** bar billiards - **2.** [mesa] billiard table - **3.** [sala] billiard hall.

billete *sm* - **1.** [dinero] note *UK*, bill *US* - **2.** [de rifa, transporte, cine etc] ticket; **'no hay billetes'** TEATRO 'sold out'; **billete de andén** platform ticket; **billete de ida** single (ticket); **billete de ida y vuelta** return (ticket) *UK*, round-trip (ticket) *US*; **billete kilométrico** *ticket to travel a set distance*; **billete sencillo** single (ticket) *UK*, one-way (ticket) *US* - **3.** [de lotería] lottery ticket.

billetera *sf* wallet.

billetero *sm* = billetera.

billón *num* billion *UK*, trillion *US*; *ver también* **seis**.

bimensual *adj* twice-monthly.

bimestral *adj* two-monthly.

bimestre *sm* two months *pl*.

bimotor ◇ *adj* twin-engine *(antes de s)*. ◇ *sm* twin-engined plane.

binario, ria *adj* [gen & INFORM] binary.

bingo *sm* - **1.** [juego] bingo - **2.** [sala] bingo hall - **3.** [premio] (full) house.

binoculares *smpl* binoculars; TEATRO opera glasses.

binóculo *sm* pince-nez.

binomio *sm* - **1.** MAT binomial - **2.** *fig* [de personas] duo.

biocombustible *sm* biofuel.

biodegradable *adj* biodegradable.

bioética *sf* bioethics.

biofeedback [bio'fidbak] *sm inv* PSICOL biofeedback.

biofísico, ca *adj* biophysical. ➤ **biofísica** *sf* biophysics *(U)*.

biogenético, ca *adj* genetic. ➤ **biogenética** *sf* genetics *(U)*.

biografía *sf* biography.

biografiar [9] *vt* to write the biography of.

biográfico, ca *adj* biographical.

biógrafo, fa *sm, f* [persona] biographer. ➤ **biógrafo** *sm Amér* [cine] cinema.

bioingeniería *sf* bioengineering.

biología *sf* biology.

biológico, ca *adj* biological.

biólogo, ga *sm, f* biologist.

biomasa *sf* biomass.

biombo *sm* (folding) screen.

biometría *sf* biometry.

biónico, ca *adj* bionic. ➤ **biónica** *sf* bionics.

biopsia *sf* biopsy.

bioquímico, ca ◇ *adj* biochemical. ◇ *sm, f* [persona] biochemist. ➤ **bioquímica** *sf* [ciencia] biochemistry.

biorritmo *sm* biorhythm.

biosfera *sf* biosphere.

biotecnología *sf* biotechnology.

bioterapia *sf* biotherapy.

bioterrorismo *sm* bioterrorism.

bióxido *sm* dioxide.

bipartidismo *sm* two-party system.

bipartidista *adj* two-party *(antes de s)*.

bipartito, ta *adj* bipartite.

bípedo, da *adj* biped.

biplano *sm* biplane.

biplaza ◇ *adj* two-seater *(antes de s)*. ◇ *sm* two-seater.

bipolar *adj* bipolar.

biquini, bikini *sm* [bañador] bikini.

birlar *vt fam* to pinch, to nick.

birlibirloque ⊳ **arte**.

Birmania *n pr* Burma.

birmano, na *adj & sm, f* Burmese. ➤ **birmano** *sm* [lengua] Burmese.

birra *sf fam* beer.

birreactor, ra *adj* twin-jet *(antes de s)*. ➤ **birreactor** *sm* twin-jet aircraft.

birrete *sm* - **1.** [de clérigo] biretta - **2.** [de catedrático] mortarboard - **3.** [de abogados, jueces] *cap worn by judges and lawyers*.

birria *sf fam* - **1.** [fealdad - persona] sight, fright; [- cosa] monstrosity - **2.** [cosa sin valor] rubbish *(U)*.

bis *(pl* bises) ◇ *adj inv*: **viven en el 150 bis** they live at 150a. ◇ *sm* encore. ◇ *adv* MÚS [para repetir] bis.

bisabuelo, la *sm, f* great-grandfather (*f* great-grandmother); **bisabuelos** great-grandparents.

bisagra *sf* hinge.

bisbisar, bisbisear *vt fam* to mutter.

bisbiseo *sm* muttering.

bisección *sf* bisection.

bisectriz *sf* bisector.

bisel *sm* bevel.

biselado *sm* bevelling.

biselar *vt* to bevel.

bisemanal *adj* twice-weekly.

bisexual *adj & smf* bisexual.

bisiesto ⊳ **año**.

bisílabo, ba *adj* two-syllabled.

bisnieto, ta *sm, f* great-grandchild, great-grandson (*f* great-granddaughter).

bisonte *sm* bison.

bisoñé *sm* toupée.

bisoño, **ña** *sm, f* novice.

bistec, **biftec** *sm* steak.

bisturí (*pl* **bisturíes** o **bisturís**) *sm* scalpel.

bisutería *sf* imitation jewellery.

bit [bit] (*pl* **bits**) *sm* INFORM bit.

bitácora *sf* - **1.** binnacle - **2.** INFORM blog.

bíter, **bitter** *sm* bitters *(U)*.

bizantino, **na** ◇ *adj* - **1.** HIST Byzantine - **2.** [discusión, razonamiento] hair-splitting. ◇ *sm, f* Byzantine.

bizarría *sf* - **1.** [valor] bravery - **2.** [generosidad] generosity.

bizarro, **rra** *adj* - **1.** [valiente] brave, valiant - **2.** [generoso] generous.

bizco, **ca** ◇ *adj* cross-eyed. ◇ *sm, f* cross-eyed person.

bizcocho *sm* [de repostería] sponge.

bizquear *vi* to squint.

bizquera *sf* squint.

blablablá *sm* *fam* blah, blah, blah.

blanco, **ca** ◇ *adj* white. ◇ *sm, f* [persona] white (person).

➤ **blanco** *sm* - **1.** [color] white - **2.** [diana] target; **dar en el blanco** DEP & MIL to hit the target; *fig* to hit the nail on the head - **3.** *fig* [objetivo] target; [de miradas] object - **4.** [espacio vacío] blank (space).

➤ **blanca** *sf* MÚS minim; **estar** o **quedarse sin blanca** *fig* to be flat broke.

➤ **blanco del ojo** *sm* white of the eye.

➤ **en blanco** *loc adv* - **1.** [gen] blank; **se quedó con la mente en blanco** his mind went blank - **2.** [sin dormir]: **una noche en blanco** a sleepless night.

blancura *sf* whiteness.

blancuzco, **ca** *adj* off-white.

blandengue *adj* *lit & fig* weak.

blandir [78] *vt* to brandish.

blando, **da** *adj* - **1.** [gen] soft; [carne] tender - **2.** *fig* [persona - débil] weak; [- indulgente] lenient, soft.

blandura *sf* - **1.** [gen] softness; [de carne] tenderness - **2.** *fig* [debilidad] weakness; [indulgencia] leniency.

blanqueador, **ra** ◇ *adj* whitening *(antes de s)*. ◇ *sm, f* whitewasher.

blanquear *vt* - **1.** [ropa] to whiten; [con lejía] to bleach - **2.** [con cal] to whitewash - **3.** *fig* [dinero] to launder.

blanquecino, **na** *adj* off-white.

blanqueo *sm* - **1.** [de ropa] whitening; [con lejía] bleaching - **2.** [encalado] whitewashing - **3.** *fig* [de dinero] laundering.

blanquillo *sm* *Amér C & Méx* [huevo] egg.

blasfemar *vi* - **1.** RELIG: **blasfemar (contra)** to blaspheme (against) - **2.** [maldecir] to swear, to curse.

blasfemia *sf* - **1.** RELIG blasphemy - **2.** [palabrota] curse - **3.** *fig* [injuria]: **es una blasfemia hablar así de...** it's sacrilege to talk like that about...

blasfemo, **ma** ◇ *adj* blasphemous. ◇ *sm, f* blasphemer.

blasón *sm* - **1.** [escudo] coat of arms - **2.** *fig* [orgullo] honour, glory.

bledo *sm*: **me importa un bledo (lo que diga)** *fam* I don't give a damn (about what he says).

blindado, **da** *adj* armour-plated; [coche] armoured.

blindaje *sm* armour-plating; [de coche] armour.

blindar *vt* to armour-plate.

bloc [blok] (*pl* **blocs**) *sm* pad; **bloc de dibujo** sketchpad; **bloc de notas** notepad.

blocar [10] *vt* DEP to block.

blonda *sf* [para tartas etc] doily.

bloomers ['blumers] *smpl* *Col* knickers.

bloque ◇ *sm* - **1.** [gen & INFORM] block - **2.** POLÍT bloc; **en bloque** en masse; [votación] block *(antes de s)* - **3.** MECÁN cylinder block. ◇ *v* ➤ **blocar**.

bloquear *vt* - **1.** [gen & DEP] to block - **2.** [aislar - suj: ejército, barcos] to blockade; [- suj: nieve, inundación] to cut off - **3.** FIN to freeze - **4.** AUTO to lock.

➤ **bloquearse** *vprnl* [persona] to have a mental block.

bloqueo *sm* - **1.** [gen & DEP] blocking; **bloqueo mental** mental block - **2.** ECON & MIL blockade - **3.** FIN freeze, freezing *(U)* - **4.** AUTO locking.

blues [blus] *sm inv* MÚS blues.

blúmer *sm* *Amér C & Caribe* knickers.

blusa *sf* blouse.

blusón *sm* [camisa] long shirt; [de pintor] smock.

bluyín *sm* jeans *pl*.

bluyines *Amér, Andes & Ven smpl* = **bluyín**.

boa ◇ *sf* ZOOL boa; **boa constrictor** boa constrictor. ◇ *sm* [prenda] (feather) boa.

boato *sm* show, ostentation.

bobada *sf* *fam*: **decir bobadas** to talk nonsense; **hacer bobadas** to mess about.

bobalicón, **ona** *fam* ◇ *adj* simple. ◇ *sm, f* simpleton.

bobina *sf* - **1.** [gen] reel; [en máquina de coser] bobbin - **2.** ELECTR coil.

bobinar *vt* to wind.

bobo, **ba** ◇ *adj* - **1.** [tonto] stupid, daft - **2.** [ingenuo] naïve, simple. ◇ *sm, f* - **1.** [tonto] fool, idiot - **2.** [ingenuo] simpleton.

bobsleigh [boβs'leix] (*pl* **bobsleighs**) *sm* bobsleigh.

boca *sf* - **1.** [gen] mouth; **boca arriba/abajo** face up/down; **abrir** *o* **hacer boca** to whet one's appetite; **andar** *o* **ir de boca en boca** to be on everyone's lips; **a pedir de boca** perfectly; **cerrar la boca a alguien** to make sb shut up; **se fue de la boca** he let the cat out of the bag; **me lo has quitado de la boca** you took the words right out of my mouth; **meterse en la boca del lobo** to put one's head into the lion's mouth; **no decir esta boca es mía** not to open one's mouth; **por la boca muere el pez** *prov* silence is golden; **quedarse con la boca abierta** to be left speechless; **se me hace la boca agua** it makes my mouth water; **tapar la boca a alguien** to silence sb - **2.** [entrada] opening; [de cañón] muzzle; **boca del estómago** pit of the stomach; **boca de metro** tube *o* underground entrance *UK*, subway entrance *US*; **boca de riego** hydrant.
◆ **boca a boca** *sm* mouth-to-mouth (resuscitation).
◆ **a boca de jarro** *loc adv* point-blank.

bocacalle *sf* [entrada] entrance (*to a street*); [calle] side street; **gire en la tercera bocacalle** take the third turning.

bocadillo *sm* - **1.** CULIN sandwich - **2.** [en cómic] speech bubble, balloon.

bocado *sm* - **1.** [comida] mouthful; **no probar bocado** [por estar desganado] not to touch one's food; [no haber podido comer] not to have a bite (to eat) - **2.** [mordisco] bite.
◆ **bocado de Adán** *sm* Adam's apple.

bocajarro ◆ **a bocajarro** *loc adv* [disparar] point-blank; **se lo dije a bocajarro** I told him to his face.

bocamanga *sf* cuff.

bocanada *sf* [de líquido] mouthful; [de humo] puff; [de viento] gust.

bocata *sm fam* sarnie.

bocazas *smf inv fam despec* big mouth, blabbermouth.

boceto *sm* sketch, rough outline.

bocha *sf* [bolo] bowl.
◆ **bochas** *sfpl* [juego] bowls (*U*).

bochinche *sm fam* commotion, uproar.

bochorno *sm* - **1.** [calor] stifling *o* muggy heat - **2.** [vergüenza] embarrassment.

bochornoso, sa *adj* - **1.** [tiempo] stifling, muggy - **2.** [vergonzoso] embarrassing.

bocina *sf* - **1.** AUTO & MÚS horn - **2.** [megáfono] megaphone, loudhailer.

bocinazo *sm* AUTO hoot.

bocio *sm* goitre.

bock (*pl* **bocks**) *sm* stein.

boda *sf* [ceremonia] wedding; [convite] reception; **bodas de diamante/oro/plata** diamond/golden/silver wedding *sing*.

bodega *sf* - **1.** [cava] wine cellar - **2.** [tienda] wine shop; [bar] bar - **3.** [en buque, avión] hold - **4.** *Amér* [colmado] small grocery store - **5.** *Méx* [almacén] store.

bodegón *sm* - **1.** ARTE still life - **2.** [taberna] tavern, inn.

bodeguero, ra *sm, f* [dueño] owner of a wine cellar; [encargado] cellarman.

bodrio *sm fam despec* [gen] rubbish (*U*); [comida] pigswill (*U*); **¡qué bodrio!** what a load of rubbish!

body ['boði] (*pl* **bodies**) *sm* body.

BOE (*abrev de* **Boletín Oficial del Estado**) *sm official Spanish gazette.*

BOE

The **Boletín Oficial del Estado** is the official Spanish state gazette, which publishes the text of new laws and decrees, the outcome of public tenders, details of government grants and other matters which are legally required to be published. The judgements handed down by Spain's Constitutional Court are also published in separate supplements to the **BOE**. All texts published in the **BOE** are regarded as definitive and carry the force of law.

---

bofetada *sf* slap (in the face); **dar una bofetada a alguien** to slap sb (in the face); **darse de bofetadas** to come to blows.

bofetón *sm* hard slap (in the face).

bofia *sf*: **la bofia** *fam* the cops *pl*.

boga *sf*: **estar en boga** to be in vogue.

bogar [16] *vi* - **1.** [remar] to row - **2.** [navegar] to sail.

bogavante *sm* lobster.

Bogotá *n pr* Bogotá.

bogotano, na *adj* of/relating to Bogotá.

bogue *etc* ⊳ **bogar**.

Bohemia *n pr* Bohemia.

bohemio, mia ⬦ *adj* - **1.** [vida etc] bohemian - **2.** [de Bohemia] Bohemian. ⬦ *sm, f* - **1.** [artista] bohemian - **2.** [de Bohemia] Bohemian.
◆ **bohemia** *sf*: **la bohemia** the bohemian lifestyle.

bohío *sm Caribe* hut.

boicot (*pl* **boicots**) *sm* boycott.

boicotear *vt* to boycott.

boicoteo *sm* boycotting.

boina *sf* beret.

boj *(pl* bojes*) sm* - **1.** [árbol] box - **2.** [madera] boxwood.

bol *(pl* boles*) sm* bowl.

bola *sf* - **1.** [gen] ball; [canica] marble; **bola de cristal** crystal ball; **bola del mundo** globe; **bola de nieve** snowball; **bolas de naftalina** mothballs; **convertirse en una bola de nieve** *fig* to snowball - **2.** *fam* [mentira] fib - **3.** *Amér* [rumor] rumour - **4.** *loc*: **en bolas** *fam* starkers; **no rascar bola** *fam* to get everything wrong.

bolada *sf R Dom fam* opportunity.

bolchevique *adj* & *smf* Bolshevik.

bolchevismo *sm* Bolshevism.

bolea *sf* DEP volley.

bolear *vt Méx* [embetunar] to shine, to polish.

bolera *sf* bowling alley.

bolería *sf Méx* shoeshine store.

bolero, ra *sm, f Méx* shoeshine, bootblack *UK*.
◆ **bolero** *sm* [baile y música] bolero.

boleta *sf Amér* [recibo] receipt; *Amér C & C Sur* [multa] parking ticket; *Cuba & Méx* [para voto] ballot, voting slip.

boletería *sf Amér* [de cine, teatro] box office; [de estacíon] ticket office.

boletero, ra *sm, f Amér* box office attendant.

boletín *sm* journal, periodical; **boletín de noticias** *o* **informativo** news bulletin; **boletín meteorológico** weather forecast; **boletín de prensa** press release; **boletín de subscripción** subscription form; **Boletín Oficial del Estado** *official Spanish gazette.*

boleto *sm* - **1.** [de lotería, rifa] ticket; [de quinielas] coupon; **boleto de apuestas** betting slip - **2.** *Amér* [para medio de transporte] ticket.

boli *sm fam* Biro®.

boliche *sm* - **1.** [en la petanca] jack - **2.** [bolos] ten-pin bowling - **3.** [bolera] bowling alley - **4.** *Amér* [tienda] small grocery store - **5.** *C Sur fam* [bar] *cheap bar o café.*

bólido *sm* racing car; **ir como un bólido** *fig* to go like the clappers.

bolígrafo *sm* ballpoint pen, Biro®.

bolillo *sm* - **1.** [en costura] bobbin - **2.** *Méx* [panecillo] bread roll.

bolívar *sm* bolivar.

Bolivia *n pr* Bolivia.

boliviano, na *adj* & *sm, f* Bolivian.

bollería *sf* - **1.** [tienda] cake shop - **2.** [productos] cakes *pl.*

bollo *sm* - **1.** [para comer - de pan] (bread) roll; [- dulce] bun - **2.** [abolladura] dent; [abultamiento] bump.

bolo *sm* - **1.** DEP [pieza] skittle - **2.** [actuación] show - **3.** *Amér C fam* [borracho] boozer.
◆ **bolos** *smpl* [deporte] skittles.

bolsa *sf* - **1.** [gen] bag; **bolsa de agua caliente** hot-water bottle; **bolsa de aire** air pocket; **bolsa de basura** bin liner; **bolsa de deportes** holdall, sports bag; **bolsa de plástico** [en tiendas] carrier *o* plastic bag; **bolsa de viaje** travel bag; **bolsa de patatas fritas** packet of crisps - **2.** FIN: **bolsa (de valores)** stock exchange, stock market; **la bolsa ha subido/bajado** share prices have gone up/down; **jugar a la bolsa** to speculate on the stock market - **3.** [acumulación de mineral] pocket - **4.** ANAT sac - **5.** *R Dom* [saco de dormir] sleeping bag.
◆ **bolsa de trabajo** *sf* employment bureau, labour exchange.

bolsillo *sm* pocket; **de bolsillo** pocket *(antes de s)*; **lo pagué de mi bolsillo** I paid for it out of my own pocket; **meterse** *o* **tener a alguien en el bolsillo** to have sb eating out of one's hand; **rascarse el bolsillo** *fam* to fork out.

bolso *sm* bag; [de mujer] handbag, purse *US*.

boludear *vi R Dom fam* [decir tonterías] to talk nonsense; [hacer tonterías, perder el tiempo] to mess about *o* around.

boludo, da *sm, f R Dom fam* [estúpido] prat *UK*, jerk *US*; [perezoso] lazy slob.

bomba ◇ *sf* - **1.** [explosivo] bomb; **bomba atómica** atom *o* nuclear bomb; **bomba H** *o* **de hidrógeno** H *o* hydrogen bomb; **bomba de humo** [gen] smoke bomb; *fig* smokescreen; **bomba lacrimógena** tear gas grenade; **bomba de mano** (hand) grenade; **bomba de neutrones** neutron bomb; **bomba de relojería** time bomb - **2.** [máquina] pump; **bomba de cobalto** MED cobalt bomb; **bomba hidráulica** hydraulic pump - **3.** *fig* [acontecimiento] bombshell; **caer como una bomba** to be a bombshell - **4.** *Chile, Col, Ecuad & Ven* [surtidor de gasolina] petrol station *UK*, gas station *US* - **5.** *loc*: **pasarlo bomba** *fam* to have a great time. ◇ *adj inv fam* astounding.

bombachos *smpl* baggy trousers.

bombardear *vt lit & fig* to bombard.

bombardeo *sm* bombardment; **bombardeo aéreo** air raid; **bombardeo atómico** FÍS bombardment in a particle accelerator.

bombardero *sm* [avión] bomber.

bombazo *sm* - **1.** [explosión] explosion, blast - **2.** *fig* [noticia] bombshell.

bombear *vt* [gen & DEP] to pump.

bombeo *sm* - **1.** [de líquido] pumping - **2.** [abombamiento] bulge.

bombero, ra *sm, f* - **1.** [de incendios] fireman *(f* firewoman) - **2.** *Ven* [de gasolinera] petrol-pump *UK o* gas-pump *US* attendant.

bombilla *sf* - **1.** [de lámpara] light bulb - **2.** *R Plata* [para mate] tube for drinking maté tea.

bombillo *sm* Amér C, Col & Méx light bulb.

bombín *sm* bowler (hat).

bombo *sm* - **1.** MÚS bass drum; **estar con bombo** *fam fig* to be in the family way - **2.** *fam fig* [elogio] hype; **a bombo y platillo** with a lot of hype - **3.** MECÁN drum.

bombón *sm* - **1.** [golosina] chocolate - **2.** *fam fig* [mujer] peach.

bombona *sf* cylinder; **bombona de butano** (butane) gas cylinder.

bonachón, ona *fam* <> *adj* kindly. <> *sm, f* kindly person.

bonaerense *adj* of/relating to Buenos Aires.

bonancible *adj* [tiempo] fair; [mar] calm.

bonanza *sf* - **1.** [de tiempo] fair weather; [de mar] calm at sea - **2.** *fig* [prosperidad] prosperity.

bondad *sf* [cualidad] goodness; [inclinación] kindness; **tener la bondad de hacer algo** to be kind enough to do sthg.

bondadoso, sa *adj* kind, good-natured.

bonete *sm* [eclesiástico] biretta; [universitario] mortarboard.

bongo, bongó *sm* bongo (drum).

boniato *sm* sweet potato.

bonificación *sf* - **1.** [descuento] discount - **2.** [mejora] improvement.

bonificar [10] *vt* - **1.** [descontar] to give a discount of - **2.** [mejorar] to improve.

bonito, ta *adj* pretty; [bueno] nice.
◆ **bonito** *sm* bonito (tuna).

bono *sm* - **1.** [vale] voucher - **2.** COM bond; **bono basura** junk bond; **bono de caja** short-term bond; **bono del Estado/del tesoro** government/treasury bond.

bonobús *sm* ten-journey bus ticket.

bonoloto *sm* Spanish state-run lottery.

bonsai *sm* bonsai.

boñiga *sf* cowpat.

boom [bum] *sm* boom.

boquerón *sm* (fresh) anchovy.

boquete *sm* hole.

boquiabierto, ta *adj* open-mouthed; *fig* astounded, speechless.

boquilla *sf* - **1.** [para fumar] cigarette holder - **2.** [de pipa, instrumento musical] mouthpiece - **3.** [de tubo, aparato] nozzle.
◆ **de boquilla** *loc adv*: **ser todo de boquilla** *fam* to be all hot air.

borbónico, ca *adj* Bourbon.

borbotear, borbotar *vi* to bubble.

borbotón *sm*: **salir a borbotones** to gush out.

borda *sf* NÁUT gunwale; **tirar** *o* **echar algo por la borda** *fig* to throw sthg overboard.

◆ **fuera borda** *sm* [barco] outboard motorboat; [motor] outboard motor.

bordado, da *adj* embroidered.
◆ **bordado** *sm* embroidery.

bordadura *sf* embroidery.

bordar *vt* - **1.** [al coser] to embroider - **2.** *fig* [hacer bien] to do excellently.

borde <> *adj fam* [antipático] stroppy, miserable. <> *smf fam* [antipático] stroppy person. <> *sm* [gen] edge; [de carretera] side; [del mar] shore, seaside; [de río] bank; [de vaso, botella] rim; **al borde de** *fig* on the verge o brink of.

bordear *vt* - **1.** [estar alrededor de] to border; [moverse alrededor de] to skirt (round) - **2.** *fig* [rozar] to be close to.

bordillo *sm* kerb.

bordo ◆ **a bordo** *loc adv* on board.

boreal *adj* northern.

borgoña *sm* burgundy.

bórico *adj* boric.

borla *sf* tassel; [pompón] pompom.

borne *sm* terminal.

boro *sm* boron.

borrachera *sf* - **1.** [embriaguez] drunkenness (U); **agarrar** *o Esp* **coger una borrachera** to get drunk - **2.** *fig* [emoción] intoxication.

borrachín, ina *sm, f fam* boozer.

borracho, cha <> *adj* - **1.** [ebrio] drunk - **2.** *fig* [emocionado]: **borracho de** drunk o intoxicated with. <> *sm, f* [persona] drunk.
◆ **borracho** *sm* [bizcocho] *sponge soaked in alcohol*, ≃ rum baba.

borrador *sm* - **1.** [de escrito] rough draft; [de dibujo] sketch - **2.** [goma de borrar] rubber UK, eraser US.

borraja *sf* borage.

borrar *vt* - **1.** [hacer desaparecer - con goma] to rub out UK, to erase US; [- en ordenador] to delete; [- en casete] to erase - **2.** [tachar] to cross out; *fig* [de lista etc] to take off - **3.** *fig* [olvidar] to erase.
◆ **borrarse** *vprnl* - **1.** [desaparecer] to disappear - **2.** *fig* [olvidarse] to be wiped away.

borrasca *sf* area of low pressure.

borrascoso, sa *adj* stormy.

borrego, ga *sm, f* - **1.** [animal] lamb - **2.** *fam despec* [persona] cretin, moron.

borrico, ca *sm, f* donkey; *fig* ass.

borriquero ▷ cardo.

borrón *sm* blot; *fig* blemish; **hacer borrón y cuenta nueva** to wipe the slate clean.

borroso, sa *adj* [foto, visión] blurred; [escritura, texto] smudgy.

Bosnia *n pr* Bosnia.

bosnio, **nia** *adj* & *sm, f* Bosnian.

bosque *sm* [pequeño] wood; [grande] forest.

bosquejar *vt* - **1.** [esbozar] to sketch (out) - **2.** *fig* [dar una idea de] to give a rough outline of.

bosquejo *sm* - **1.** [esbozo] sketch - **2.** *fig* [de idea, tema, situación] rough outline.

bossa-nova *sf* bossa nova.

bostezar [13] *vi* to yawn.

bostezo *sm* yawn.

bota *sf* - **1.** [calzado] boot; **botas camperas/de montar** cowboy/riding boots; **botas de agua** o **de lluvia** wellingtons; **botas de goma** gumboots; **morir con las botas puestas** *fam* to die with one's boots on; **ponerse las botas** *fam* [comiendo] to stuff one's face; [ganando dinero] to make a fortune - **2.** [de vino] *small leather container in which wine is kept.*

botadura *sf* launching.

botafumeiro *sm* censer.

botana *sf* *Méx* snack, appetizer.

botánico, **ca** <> *adj* botanical. <> *sm, f* [persona] botanist.
◆ **botánica** *sf* [ciencia] botany.

botanista *smf* botanist.

botar <> *vt* - **1.** NÁUT to launch - **2.** *fam* [despedir] to throw o kick out - **3.** [pelota] to bounce - **4.** DEP [córner etc] to take - **5.** *Andes, Amér C, Caribe* & *Méx* [tirar] to throw away. <> *vi* - **1.** [saltar] to jump; **está que bota** *fam fig* he/she is hopping mad - **2.** [pelota] to bounce.

botarate *sm* *fam despec* madcap.

botavara *sf* boom.

bote *sm* - **1.** [tarro] jar; **bote de humo** smoke canister - **2.** [lata] can - **3.** [botella de plástico] bottle - **4.** [barca] boat; **bote salvavidas** lifeboat - **5.** [para propinas] tips box; [fondo común] kitty; **poner un bote** to have a kitty; **hay un bote de 100.000 euros** the jackpot is 100,000 euros - **6.** [salto] jump; **dar botes** [gen] to jump up and down; [en tren, coche] to bump up and down - **7.** [de pelota] bounce; **dar botes** to bounce - **8.** *Méx* & *Ven fam* [cárcel] nick *UK*, joint *US* - **9.** *Méx* [de la basura] rubbish bin *UK*, trash can *US* - **10.** *loc*: **chupar del bote** *fam* to feather one's nest; **tener a alguien en el bote** *fam* to have sb eating out of one's hand.
◆ **a bote pronto** *loc adv* - **1.** DEP on the rebound - **2.** *fig* [sin pensar] off the top of one's head.
◆ **de bote en bote** *loc adv* chock-a-block.

botella *sf* bottle; **de botella** bottled; **botella de oxígeno** oxygen cylinder; *Cuba*: **pedir botella** to hitchhike; **dar botella a alguien** to give sb a ride, to give sb a lift.

botellazo *sm* blow with a bottle.

botellero *sm* wine rack.

botellín *sm* small bottle.

botica *sf* *desus* pharmacy, chemist's (shop) *UK*.

boticario, **ria** *sm, f* *desus* pharmacist, chemist *UK*.

botijo *sm* earthenware jug.

botín *sm* - **1.** [de guerra, atraco] plunder, loot - **2.** [calzado] ankle boot.

botiquín *sm* [caja] first-aid kit; [mueble] first-aid cupboard; [enfermería] first-aid post.

botón *sm* button; **botón de marcado abreviado** TELECOM speed-dial button.
◆ **botones** *sm inv* [de hotel] bellboy, bellhop *US*; [de oficinas etc] errand boy.
◆ **botón de muestra** *sm* sample.

botonadura *sf* buttons *pl*.

botulismo *sm* botulism.

boulder ['bulder] *sm* DEP bouldering.

bourbon ['burbon] *sm* bourbon.

boutique [bu'tik] *sf* boutique.

bóveda *sf* ARQUIT vault.
◆ **bóveda celeste** *sf* firmament.
◆ **bóveda craneal** *sf* cranial vault.

bovino, **na** *adj* bovine.
◆ **bovinos** *smpl* cattle (*U*).

box (*pl* boxes) *sm* - **1.** [de caballo] stall - **2.** [de coches] pit; **entrar en boxes** to make a pit stop - **3.** *Amér* boxing.

boxeador, **ra** *sm, f* boxer.

boxear *vi* to box.

boxeo *sm* boxing.

bóxer (*pl* boxers) *sm* boxer.

boya *sf* - **1.** [en el mar] buoy - **2.** [de una red] float.

boyante *adj* - **1.** [feliz] happy - **2.** [próspero - empresa, negocio] prosperous; [- economía, comercio] buoyant.

boy scout ['bojes'kaut] *sm* boy scout.

bozal *sm* - **1.** [gen] muzzle - **2.** *Amér* [cabestro] halter.

bracear *vi* - **1.** [mover los brazos] to wave one's arms about - **2.** [nadar] to swim.

bracero *sm* day labourer.

braga (*gen pl*) *sf* knickers *pl*.

bragazas *sm inv* *fam despec* henpecked man.

braguero *sm* truss.

bragueta *sf* flies *pl UK*, zipper *US*; **tienes la bragueta abierta** your flies are undone.

braguetazo *sm* *fam* marriage for money.

braille ['braile] *sm* Braille.

brainstorming [breins'tormin] (*pl* brainstormings) *sm* brainstorming session.

bramante *sm* string.

bramar *vi* - **1.** [animal] to bellow - **2.** [persona - de dolor] to groan; [- de ira] to roar.

bramido *sm* - **1.** [de animal] bellow - **2.** [de persona - de dolor] groan; [- de ira] roar.

brandy *sm* brandy.

branquia *(gen pl)* *sf* gill.

brasa *sf* ember; **a la brasa** CULIN barbecued.

brasear *vt* to barbecue.

brasero *sm* brazier.

brasier, brassier *sm* *Caribe, Col & Méx* bra.

Brasil *n pr* Brazil.

brasileño, ña, brasilero, ra *adj & sm, f* *Andes, C Sur & Ven* Brazilian.

brassier = brasier.

bravata *(gen pl)* *sf* - **1.** [amenaza] threat - **2.** [fanfarronería] bravado *(U)*.

braveza *sf* bravery.

bravío, a *adj* [salvaje] wild; [feroz] fierce.

bravo, va *adj* - **1.** [valiente] brave - **2.** [animal] wild - **3.** [mar] rough.
➧ **bravo** ⬦ *sm* [aplauso] cheer. ⬦ *interj*: ¡**bravo!** bravo!
➧ **por las bravas** *loc adv* by force.

bravucón, ona *despec* ⬦ *adj* swaggering. ⬦ *sm, f* braggart.

bravuconada *sf despec* show of bravado.

bravuconear *vi despec* to brag.

bravuconería *sf despec* bravado.

bravura *sf* - **1.** [de persona] bravery - **2.** [de animal] ferocity.

braza *sf* - **1.** DEP breaststroke; **nadar a braza** to swim breaststroke - **2.** [medida] fathom.

brazada *sf* stroke.

brazalete *sm* - **1.** [en la muñeca] bracelet - **2.** [en el brazo] armband.

brazo *sm* - **1.** [gen & ANAT] arm; [de animal] foreleg; **cogidos del brazo** arm in arm; **en brazos** in one's arms; **luchar a brazo partido** [con empeño] to fight tooth and nail; **con los brazos abiertos** with open arms; **quedarse** *o* **estarse con los brazos cruzados** *fig* to sit around doing nothing; **no dar su brazo a torcer** not to give an inch; **ser el brazo derecho de alguien** to be sb's right-hand man (*f* woman) - **2.** [de árbol, río, candelabro] branch; [de grúa] boom, jib - **3.** *fig* [trabajador] hand.
➧ **brazo de gitano** *sm* ≈ swiss roll.
➧ **brazo de mar** *sm* GEOGR arm (of the sea).

brea *sf* - **1.** [sustancia] tar - **2.** [para barco] pitch.

brear *vt fam fig* [a palos] to bash in; [a preguntas] to bombard.

brebaje *sm* concoction, foul drink.

brecha *sf* - **1.** [abertura] hole, opening - **2.** MIL breach - **3.** *fig* [impresión] impression - **4.** *loc*:

estar siempre en la brecha [amigo etc] always to be there (when one is needed); [socio, empleado] to work tirelessly; [deportista, artista] always to be up there with the best.

brécol *sm* broccoli.

brega *sf* [lucha] struggle, fight.

bregar [16] *vi* - **1.** [luchar] to struggle - **2.** [trabajar] to work hard - **3.** [reñir] to quarrel.

brete *sm* fix, difficulty; **estar en un brete** to be in a fix; **poner a alguien en un brete** to put sb in a difficult position.

breva *sf* - **1.** [fruta] early fig - **2.** [cigarro] flat cigar - **3.** *loc*: ¡**no caerá esa breva!** *fam* some chance (of that happening)!

breve ⬦ *adj* brief; **en breve** [pronto] shortly; [en pocas palabras] in short. ⬦ *sf* MÚS breve.

brevedad *sf* shortness; **a** *o* **con la mayor brevedad** as soon as possible.

breviario *sm* - **1.** RELIG breviary - **2.** [compendio] compendium.

brezo *sm* heather.

bribón, ona *sm, f* scoundrel, rogue.

bricolaje *sm* D.I.Y., do-it-yourself.

brida *sf* - **1.** [de caballo] bridle - **2.** [de tubo] bracket, collar - **3.** MED adhesion.

bridge [britʃ] *sm* bridge.

brigada ⬦ *sm* MIL ≈ warrant officer. ⬦ *sf* - **1.** MIL brigade - **2.** [equipo] squad, team; **brigada antidisturbios/antidroga** riot/drug squad.

brigadier *sm* brigadier.

brillante ⬦ *adj* - **1.** [reluciente - luz, astro] shining; [- metal, zapatos, pelo] shiny; [- ojos, sonrisa, diamante] sparkling - **2.** [magnífico] brilliant. ⬦ *sm* diamond.

brillantez *sf fig* brilliance.

brillantina *sf* brilliantine, Brylcreem®.

brillar *vi lit & fig* to shine.

brillo *sm* - **1.** [resplandor - de luz] brilliance; [- de estrellas] shining; [- de zapatos] shine; **sacar brillo a** to polish, to shine - **2.** [lucimiento] splendour, brilliance.

brilloso, sa *adj Amér* shining.

brincar [10] *vi* - **1.** [saltar] to skip (about); **brincar de alegría** to jump for joy - **2.** *fig* [enfadarse]: **está que brinca** he's hopping mad.

brinco *sm* jump; **en un brinco** *fig* in a second, quickly.

brindar ⬦ *vi* to drink a toast; **brindar por algo/alguien** to drink to sthg/sb. ⬦ *vt* to offer.
➧ **brindarse** *vprnl*: **brindarse a hacer algo** to offer to do sthg.

brindis *sm inv* toast.

brinque *etc* ▷ brincar.

brío *sm* [energía, decisión] spirit, verve.

brioso, sa *adj* spirited, lively.

brisa *sf* breeze.

británico, ca ◇ *adj* British. ◇ *sm, f* British person, Briton; **los británicos** the British.

brizna *sf* - **1.** [filamento - de hierba] blade; [- de tabaco] strand - **2.** *fig* [un poco] trace, bit.

broca *sf* (drill) bit.

brocado *sm* brocade.

brocal *sm* curb, parapet.

brocha *sf* brush; **brocha de afeitar** shaving brush.

brochazo *sm* brushstroke.

broche *sm* - **1.** [cierre] clasp, fastener - **2.** [joya] brooch - **3.** *R Plata* [para papeles] staple - **4.** *Méx & Urug* [para el cabello] hair slide *UK*, barrette *US* - **5.** *Arg* [para ropa] clothespin.
◆ **broche de oro** *sm fig* final flourish.

brocheta *sf* CULIN shish kebab; [aguja] skewer.

broma *sf* [ocurrencia, chiste] joke; [jugarreta] prank, practical joke; **en broma** as a joke; **gastar una broma a alguien** to play a joke *O* prank on sb; **tomar algo a broma** not to take sthg seriously; **broma de mal gusto** bad joke; **broma pesada** nasty practical joke; **ni en broma** *fig* no way, not on your life.

bromear *vi* to joke.

bromista ◇ *adj* fond of playing jokes. ◇ *smf* joker.

bromo *sm* bromine.

bromuro *sm* bromide.

bronca *sf* ▷ **bronco**.

bronce *sm* - **1.** [aleación] bronze - **2.** [estatua] bronze (statue).

bronceado, da *adj* tanned.
◆ **bronceado** *sm* tan.

bronceador, ra *adj* tanning *(antes de s)*, suntan *(antes de s)*.
◆ **bronceador** *sm* [loción] suntan lotion; [leche] suntan cream.

broncear *vt* to tan.
◆ **broncearse** *vprnl* to get a tan.

bronco, ca *adj* - **1.** [tosco] rough; [paisaje, peñascos] rugged - **2.** [grave - voz] harsh; [- tos] throaty - **3.** *fig* [brusco] gruff, surly.
◆ **bronca** *sf* - **1.** [jaleo] row; **armar (una) bronca** to kick up a row; **buscar bronca** to look for trouble - **2.** [regañina] scolding, telling-off; **echar una bronca a alguien** to give sb a row, to tell sb off - **3.** *R Dom fam* [rabia]: **me da bronca** it hacks me off; **el jefe le tiene bronca** the boss has got it in for her.

bronquial *adj* bronchial.

bronquio *sm* bronchial tube.

bronquitis *sf inv* bronchitis.

broquel *sm* - **1.** [escudo] small shield - **2.** *fig* [amparo] shield.

brotar *vi* - **1.** [planta] to sprout, to bud - **2.** [agua, sangre etc]: **brotar de** to well out of - **3.** *fig* [esperanza, sospechas, pasiones] to stir - **4.** [en la piel]: **le brotó un sarpullido** he broke out in a rash.

brote *sm* - **1.** [de planta] bud, shoot - **2.** *fig* [inicios] sign, hint.

broza *sf* - **1.** [maleza] brush, scrub - **2.** *fig* [relleno] waffle.

bruces ◆ **de bruces** *loc adv* face down; **se cayó de bruces** he fell headlong, he fell flat on his face.

bruja *sf* ▷ **brujo**.

brujería *sf* witchcraft, sorcery.

brujo, ja *adj* [hechicero] enchanting, captivating.
◆ **brujo** *sm* wizard, sorcerer.
◆ **bruja** ◇ *sf* - **1.** [hechicera] witch, sorceress - **2.** [mujer fea] hag - **3.** [mujer mala] (old) witch. ◇ *adj inv Méx*: **estar bruja** *fam* to be broke.

brújula *sf* compass.

bruma *sf* [niebla] mist; [en el mar] sea mist.

brumoso, sa *adj* misty.

bruñido *sm* polishing.

bruñir *vt* to polish.

brusco, ca *adj* - **1.** [repentino, imprevisto] sudden, abrupt - **2.** [tosco, grosero] brusque.

brusquedad *sf* - **1.** [imprevisión] suddenness, abruptness - **2.** [grosería] brusqueness.

brut *sm inv* brut.

brutal *adj* - **1.** [violento] brutal - **2.** *fam* [extraordinario] tremendous.

brutalidad *sf* - **1.** [cualidad] brutality - **2.** [acción] brutal act.

bruto, ta ◇ *adj* - **1.** [torpe] clumsy; [ignorante] thick, stupid; [maleducado] rude - **2.** [sin tratar]: **en bruto** [diamante] uncut; [petróleo] crude - **3.** [sueldo, peso etc] gross. ◇ *sm, f* brute.

bucanero *sm* buccaneer.

buceador, ra *sm, f* (underwater) diver.

bucear *vi* - **1.** [en agua] to dive, to swim underwater - **2.** *fig* [investigar]: **bucear en** to delve into.

buceo *sm* (underwater) diving.

buche *sm* - **1.** [de ave] crop - **2.** [de animal] maw - **3.** *fam* [de persona] belly.

bucle *sm* - **1.** [rizo] curl, ringlet - **2.** AERON & INFORM loop.

bucólico, ca *adj* - **1.** [campestre] country *(antes de s)* - **2.** LITER bucolic.

budín *sm* pudding.

budismo *sm* Buddhism.

budista *adj* & *smf* Buddhist.

buen ⊳ bueno.

buenamente *adv*: hice lo que buenamente pude I did what I could, I did as much as I could.

buenas ⊳ bueno.

buenaventura *sf* - **1.** [adivinación] fortune; leer la buenaventura a alguien to tell sb's fortune - **2.** [suerte] good luck.

bueno, na *(mejor es el comparativo y el superlativo de* bueno*) adj (antes de s m* buen*)* - **1.** [gen] good - **2.** [bondadoso] kind, good; **ser bueno con alguien** to be good to sb - **3.** [curado, sano] well, all right - **4.** [apacible - tiempo, clima] nice, fine - **5.** [aprovechable] all right; [comida] fresh - **6.** [uso enfático]: **ese buen hombre** that good man; **un buen día** one fine day - **7.** *loc*: **de buen ver** good-looking, attractive; **de buenas a primeras** [de repente] all of a sudden; [a simple vista] at first sight, on the face of it; **estar bueno** *fam* [persona] to be a bit of all right, to be tasty; **estar de buenas** to be in a good mood; **estaría bueno** *irón* that would really cap it all; **librarse de una buena** to have a narrow escape; **lo bueno es que...** the best thing about it is that...; **poner bueno a alguien** *irón* to criticize sb harshly; **por las buenas** willingly.
◆ **bueno** ◇ *sm* CINE: **el bueno** the goody. ◇ *adv* - **1.** [vale, de acuerdo] all right, O.K. - **2.** [pues] well. ◇ *interj* Méx [al teléfono]: **¡bueno!** hello.
◆ **buenas** *interj*: **¡buenas!** hello!; *Col* & *Méx*: **¿bueno?** [al teléfono] hello.

Buenos Aires *n pr* Buenos Aires.

buey *(pl* bueyes*) sm* ox.

bueyada *sf* Amér drove of oxen.

búfalo *sm* buffalo.

bufanda *sf* scarf.

bufar *vi* - **1.** [toro, caballo] to snort - **2.** *fig* [persona] to be furious.

bufé, buffet *(pl* buffets*) sm* - **1.** [en restaurante] buffet - **2.** [mueble] sideboard.

bufete *sm* lawyer's practice.

buffer ['bafer] *(pl* buffers*) sm* INFORM buffer.

buffet = bufé.

bufido *sm* - **1.** [de toro, caballo] snort - **2.** *fam* [de persona] fit of rage.

bufo, fa *adj* [gen & MÚS] comic.

bufón *sm* buffoon, jester.

bufonada *sf* *fig* clowning.

bug [buk] *sm* INFORM bug.

buganvilla *sf* bougainvillea.

buhardilla *sf* - **1.** [habitación] attic - **2.** [ventana] dormer (window).

búho *sm* owl.

buhonero, ra *sm, f* hawker, pedlar.

buitre *sm* *lit* & *fig* vulture.

bujía *sf* AUTO spark plug.

bula *sf* [documento] (papal) bull.

bulbo *sm* ANAT & BOT bulb; **bulbo raquídeo** rachidian bulb.

buldog *(pl* buldogs*)*, **bulldog** *(pl* bulldogs*)* [bul'doɣ] *sm* bulldog.

buldozer *(pl* buldozers*)*, **bulldozer** *(pl* bulldozers*)* [bul'doθer] *sm* bulldozer.

bulerías *sfpl* *popular Andalusian song and dance.*

bulevar *(pl* bulevares*) sm* boulevard.

Bulgaria *n pr* Bulgaria.

búlgaro, ra *adj* & *sm, f* Bulgarian.
◆ **búlgaro** *sm* [lengua] Bulgarian.

bulimia *sf* bulimia.

bulín *sm* R Dom bachelor pad.

bulla *sf* racket, uproar; **armar bulla** to kick up a racket.

bullabesa *sf* CULIN bouillabaisse.

bullanguero, ra ◇ *adj* noisy, rowdy. ◇ *sm, f* noisy o boisterous person.

bulldog = buldog.

bulldozer = buldozer.

bullicio *sm* [de ciudad, mercado] hustle and bustle; [de multitud] hubbub.

bullicioso, sa ◇ *adj* - **1.** [agitado - reunión, multitud] noisy; [- calle, mercado] busy, bustling - **2.** [inquieto] rowdy, boisterous. ◇ *sm, f* boisterous person.

bullir *vi* - **1.** [hervir] to boil; [burbujear] to bubble - **2.** *fig* [multitud] to bustle; [ratas, hormigas etc] to swarm; [mar] to boil; **bullir de** to seethe with.

bulo *sm* false rumour.

bulto *sm* - **1.** [volumen] bulk, size; **a bulto** approximately, roughly; **hacer mucho bulto** to take up a lot of space; **de bulto** glaringly obvious; **escurrir el bulto** [trabajo] to shirk; [cuestión] to evade the issue - **2.** [abombamiento - en rodilla, superficie etc] bump; [- en maleta, bolsillo etc] bulge - **3.** [forma imprecisa] blurred shape - **4.** [paquete] package; [maleta] item of luggage; [fardo] bundle; **bulto de mano** piece o item of hand luggage.

bumerán *(pl* bumeranes*)*, **bumerang** *(pl* bumerangs*) sm* boomerang.

bungalow [buŋga'lo] *(pl* bungalows*) sm* bungalow.

búnquer *(pl* bunquers*)*, **bunker** *(pl* bunkers*) sm* - **1.** [refugio] bunker - **2.** POLÍT reactionary forces *pl*.

buñuelo *sm* [CULIN - dulce] ≃ doughnut; [- de bacalao etc] ≃ dumpling; **buñuelo de viento** doughnut.

BUP *sm academically oriented secondary-school course formerly taught in Spain for pupils aged 14-17, now known as the bachillerato.*

buque *sm* ship; **buque de carga** cargo ship; **buque de guerra** warship; **buque nodriza** supply ship; **buque de pasajeros** passenger ship, liner; **buque de vapor** streamer, streamship.

buqué, bouquet [bu'ke] *sm* bouquet.

burbuja *sf* bubble; **con burbujas** fizzy; **hacer burbujas** to bubble.

burbujear *vi* to bubble.

burbujeo *sm* bubbling.

burdel *sm* brothel.

burdeos ◇ *adj inv* maroon. ◇ *sm inv* Bordeaux.

burdo, da *adj* [gen] crude; [tela] coarse.

burgués, esa ◇ *adj* middle-class, bourgeois. ◇ *sm, f* member of the middle class; HIST & POLÍT member of the bourgeoisie.

burguesía *sf* middle class; HIST & POLÍT bourgeoisie; **alta burguesía** upper middle class; HIST & POLÍT haute bourgeoisie.

burla *sf* - **1.** [mofa] taunt; **hacer burla de** to mock - **2.** [broma] joke; **burlas aparte** joking aside - **3.** [engaño] trick.
➤ **burlas** *sfpl* ridicule *(U)*, mockery *(U)*.

burladero *sm* TAUROM *wooden board behind which bullfighter can hide from bull.*

burlador *sm* Casanova, Don Juan.

burlar *vt* [esquivar] to evade; [ley] to flout; **burla burlando** *fig* without anyone noticing.
➤ **burlarse de** *vprnl* to mock, to make fun of.

burlesco, ca *adj* [tono] jocular; LITER burlesque.

burlete *sm* draught excluder.

burlón, ona *adj* - **1.** [bromista] waggish, fond of telling jokes - **2.** [sarcástico] mocking.

buró *sm* - **1.** [escritorio] bureau, writing desk - **2.** POLÍT executive committee - **3.** *Méx* bedside table.

burocracia *sf* bureaucracy.

burócrata *smf* bureaucrat.

burocrático, ca *adj* bureaucratic.

burocratizar [13] *vt* to bureaucratize.

burrada *sf* - **1.** [acción, dicho]: **hacer burradas** to act stupidly; **decir burradas** to talk nonsense - **2.** *fam* [cantidad]: **una burrada (de)** tons *pl* (of), masses *pl* (of).

burro, rra ◇ *adj* [necio] stupid, dim. ◇ *sm, f* - **1.** [animal] donkey; **apearse** *o* **bajarse del bu-** rro *fam* to back down; **no ver tres en un burro** *fam* to be as blind as a bat - **2.** *fam* [necio] ass, dimwit - **3.** *fam* [trabajador]: **burro (de carga)** workhorse.
➤ **burro** *sm* - **1.** *Caribe & Méx* [escalera] stepladder - **2.** *Méx* [tabla de planchar] ironing board.

bursátil *adj* stock-market *(antes de s).*

bus *(pl* buses*) sm* AUTO & INFORM bus.

busca ◇ *sf* search; **en busca de** in search of; **la busca de** the search for; **andar a la busca** *fig* to find a way of getting by. ◇ *sm* = **buscapersonas**.

buscador, ra *sm, f* hunter; **buscador de oro** gold prospector.

buscapersonas, busca *sm inv* bleeper, pager.

buscapiés *sm inv* firecracker, jumping jack.

buscapleitos *smf inv* troubleseeker.

buscar [10] ◇ *vt* - **1.** [gen] to look for; [provecho, beneficio propio] to seek; **voy a buscar el periódico** I'm going for the paper *o* to get the paper; **ir a buscar a alguien** to pick sb up; **'se busca camarero'** 'waiter wanted' - **2.** [en diccionario, índice, horario] to look up - **3.** INFORM to search for - **4.** *fam* [provocar] to push, to try the patience of. ◇ *vi* to look.
➤ **buscarse** *vprnl*: **buscársela** to be asking for it.

buscavidas *smf inv fam* - **1.** [ambicioso] go-getter - **2.** [entrometido] nosy parker *UK*.

buscón, ona *sm, f* [estafador] swindler.
➤ **buscona** *sf fam despec* [prostituta] whore.

busque *etc* ➭ **buscar**.

búsqueda *sf* search.

busto *sm* - **1.** [pecho] chest; [de mujer] bust - **2.** [escultura] bust.

butaca *sf* - **1.** [mueble] armchair - **2.** [en cine] seat.

butacón *sm* large easy chair.

butano *sm* butane (gas).

buten ➤ **de buten** *loc adj fam* wicked, terrific.

butifarra *sf type of Catalan pork sausage.*

buzo *sm* - **1.** [persona] diver - **2.** *Arg & Col* [sudadera] sweatshirt - **3.** *Arg, Chile & Perú* [chándal] tracksuit - **4.** *Urug* [suéter] sweater, jumper *UK*.

buzón *sm* letter box; **echar algo al buzón** to post sthg; **buzón electrónico** electronic mailbox; **buzón de sugerencias** suggestion box; **buzón de voz** voice mail.

byte [bait] *sm* INFORM byte.

c, C *sf* [letra] c, C.

c. (*abrev de* **calle**) St.

c/ - 1. (*abrev de* **calle**) St. **- 2.** (*abrev de* **cuenta**) a/c.

cabal *adj* **- 1.** [honrado] upright, honest **- 2.** [exacto] exact; [completo] complete; **a los nueve meses cabales** at exactly nine months.

▸ **cabales** *smpl*: **no estar en sus cabales** not to be in one's right mind.

cábala *sf* **- 1.** [doctrina] cabbala **- 2.** (*gen pl*) [conjeturas] guess; **hacer cábalas** to speculate, to guess.

cabalgadura *sf* mount.

cabalgar [16] *vi* to ride.

cabalgata *sf* cavalcade, procession.

cabalístico, ca *adj* **- 1.** [de cábala] cabbalistic **- 2.** *fig* [oculto] mysterious.

▸ **cabalística** *sf* cabbalism.

caballa *sf* mackerel.

caballar *adj* equine, horse (*antes de s*).

caballeresco, ca *adj* **- 1.** [persona, modales] chivalrous **- 2.** [literatura] chivalric.

caballería *sf* **- 1.** [animal] mount, horse **- 2.** [cuerpo militar] cavalry.

caballeriza *sf* stable.

caballerizo *sm* groom, stable lad.

caballero ◇ *adj* [cortés] gentlemanly. ◇ *sm* **- 1.** [gen] gentleman; [al dirigir la palabra] sir; **ser todo un caballero** to be a real gentleman; **'caballeros'** [en aseos] 'gents'; [en grandes almacenes] 'menswear' **- 2.** [miembro de una orden] knight; **caballero andante** knight errant **- 3.** [noble] nobleman.

caballerosidad *sf* gentlemanliness.

caballeroso, sa *adj* gentlemanly.

caballete *sm* **- 1.** [de lienzo] easel **- 2.** [de mesa] trestle **- 3.** [de nariz] bridge **- 4.** [de tejado] ridge.

caballito *sm* small horse, pony.

▸ **caballitos** *smpl* [de feria] merry-go-round *sing*.

▸ **caballito de mar** *sm* sea horse.

caballo *sm* **- 1.** [animal] horse; **montar a caballo** to ride **- 2.** [pieza de ajedrez] knight **- 3.** [naipe] ≃ queen **- 4.** MECÁN: **caballo (de fuerza** o

de vapor) horsepower **- 5.** *mfam* [heroína] smack **- 6.** *loc*: **estar a caballo entre dos cosas** to be halfway between two things; **a caballo regalado no le mires el diente** o **el dentado** *prov* don't look a gift horse in the mouth.

▸ **caballo de batalla** *sm* **- 1.** [dificultad, escollo] bone of contention **- 2.** [objetivo, obsesión] hobbyhorse.

▸ **caballo de Troya** *sm* Trojan horse.

▸ **caballo marino** *sm* sea horse.

cabaña *sf* **- 1.** [choza] hut, cabin **- 2.** [ganado] livestock (*U*).

cabaré *sm* cabaret.

cabaretera *sf* cabaret girl.

cabecear *vi* **- 1.** [persona - negando] to shake one's head; [- afirmando] to nod one's head **- 2.** [caballo] to toss its head **- 3.** [dormir] to nod (off) **- 4.** [en fútbol] to head the ball **- 5.** [balancearse - coche] to lurch; [- barco] to pitch.

cabecera *sf* **- 1.** [gen] head; [de cama] headboard **- 2.** [de texto] heading; [de periódico] headline **- 3.** [de río] headwaters *pl*.

cabecilla *smf* ringleader.

cabellera *sf* long hair (*U*).

cabello *sm* hair (*U*).

▸ **cabello de ángel** *sm* CULIN pumpkin and syrup preserve.

cabelludo, da *adj* hairy.

caber [54] *vi* **- 1.** [gen] to fit; **no cabe nadie más** there's no room for anyone else; **no me cabe en el dedo** it won't fit my finger; **caber por** to go through **- 2.** MAT: **nueve entre tres caben a tres** three into nine goes three (times) **- 3.** [ser posible] to be possible; **cabe destacar que...** it's worth pointing out that...; **cabe preguntarse si...** one might ask whether... **- 4.** *loc*: **dentro de lo que cabe** as far as possible; **no caber en sí de gozo/celos** to be beside o.s. with joy/jealousy.

cabestrante, cabrestante *sm* capstan.

cabestrillo ▸ **en cabestrillo** *loc adj* in a sling.

cabestro *sm* **- 1.** [cuerda] halter **- 2.** [animal] leading ox.

cabeza *sf* **- 1.** [gen] head; **cabeza abajo** upside down; **cabeza arriba** the right way up; **por cabeza** per head; **obrar con cabeza** to use one's head; **tirarse de cabeza (a)** to dive (into); **venir a la cabeza** to come to mind; **cabeza (lectora)** [gen] head; [de tocadiscos] pickup **- 2.** [pelo] hair **- 3.** [posición] front, head; **a la** o **en cabeza** [en competición etc] in front, in the lead; [en lista] at the top o head **- 4.** [ciudad] main town; **cabeza de partido** ≃ county town **- 5.** *loc*: **alzar** o **levantar cabeza** to get back on one's feet, to recover; **andar** o **estar mal de la cabeza** to be funny in the head; **ir de cabeza a** to head straight for; **meterle algo en la cabeza a alguien** to get sthg into sb's head; **se le ha metido en la cabeza que...** he has got it into his head that...; **se me pasó por la cabeza** it crossed my mind; **perder la cabeza** to lose one's head; **romperse la cabeza** to rack one's brains; **sentar la cabeza** to settle down; **se le subió a la cabeza** it went to his head; **traer de cabeza a alguien** to drive sb mad.

◆ **cabeza de ajo** sf head of garlic.

◆ **cabeza de chorlito** sm scatterbrain.

◆ **cabeza de familia** sm head of the family.

◆ **cabeza de lista** sm POLÍT person who heads a party's list of candidates.

◆ **cabeza rapada** smf skinhead.

◆ **cabeza de turco** sf scapegoat.

cabezada sf - **1.** [de sueño] nod, nodding (U); **dar cabezadas** to nod off; **echar o dar una cabezada** to have a nap - **2.** [golpe] butt.

cabezal sm - **1.** [de aparato] head - **2.** [almohada] bolster.

cabezazo sm - **1.** [golpe - que se da] head butt; [- que se recibe] blow o bump on the head - **2.** DEP header.

cabezón, **ona** ⬦ adj - **1.** [de cabeza grande] with a big head - **2.** [terco] pigheaded, stubborn. ⬦ sm, f [terco] pigheaded o stubborn person.

cabezonería sf fam pigheadedness, stubbornness.

cabezota fam ⬦ adj pigheaded. ⬦ smf pigheaded o stubborn person.

cabezudo, **da** fam ⬦ adj pigheaded, stubborn. ⬦ sm, f pigheaded o stubborn person.

◆ **cabezudo** sm [en fiesta] giant-headed carnival figure.

cabida sf capacity; **dar cabida a, tener cabida para** to hold, to have room for.

cabildo sm - **1.** [municipio] ≈ district council - **2.** [de eclesiásticos] chapter - **3.** [sala] chapterhouse.

cabina sf - **1.** [locutorio] booth, cabin; **cabina de prensa** press box - **2.**: **cabina de proyección** projection room; **cabina telefónica** phone box UK, phone booth US - **3.** [de avión] cockpit; [de camión] cab; **cabina de mandos** flight deck - **4.** [vestuario - en playa] bathing hut; [- en piscina] changing cubicle.

cabizbajo, **ja** adj crestfallen, downcast.

cable sm cable; **echar un cable** fam fig to help out, to lend a hand; **televisión por cable** cable television.

cableado, **da** adj INFORM hardwired.

◆ **cableado** sm INFORM hardwiring.

cablegrafiar [9] vt to cable.

cablevisión sf cable television.

cabo sm - **1.** GEOGR cape - **2.** NÁUT cable, rope - **3.** MIL corporal; **cabo primero** military rank between corporal and sergeant - **4.** [trozo] bit, piece; [trozo final] stub, stump; [de cuerda] end - **5.** loc: **atar cabos** to put two and two together; **no dejar ningún cabo suelto** to tie up all the loose ends; **estar al cabo de la calle** to be well-informed; **llevar algo a cabo** to carry sthg out.

◆ **cabo suelto** sm loose end.

◆ **al cabo de** loc prep after.

◆ **de cabo a rabo** loc adv from beginning to end.

cabotaje sm coastal shipping.

Cabo Verde n pr Cape Verde.

cabra sf - **1.** [animal] goat; **cabra montés** wild goat; **estar como una cabra** fam to be off one's head; **la cabra siempre tira al monte** prov you can't make a leopard change his spots - **2.** [piel] goatskin.

cabrales sm inv Asturian cheese similar to Roquefort.

cabré ⟼ caber.

cabrear vt mfam: **cabrear a alguien** to get sb's goat, to annoy sb.

◆ **cabrearse** vprnl mfam: **cabrearse (con)** to get really narked UK o pissed US (with).

cabreo sm mfam rage, fit; **cogerse o coger un cabreo** to get really narked UK o pissed US.

cabrero, **ra** sm, f goatherd.

cabrestante = cabestrante.

cabría ⟼ caber.

cabrío ⟼ macho.

cabriola sf prance; **hacer cabriolas** to prance about.

cabritilla sf kid, kidskin.

cabrito sm - **1.** [animal] kid (goat) - **2.** mfam [cabrón] bastard, bugger UK.

cabro, **bra** sm, f Chile fam kid.

cabrón, **ona** vulg ⬦ adj: **¡qué cabrón eres!** you bastard! ⬦ sm, f bastard (f bitch).

◆ **cabrón** sm - **1.** vulg [cornudo] cuckold - **2.** [animal] billy goat.

cabronada sf: **hacerle una cabronada a alguien** vulg to be a bastard to sb.

cabronazo sm vulg bastard.

cabuya sf Amér C, Col & Ven rope.

caca sf fam - **1.** [excremento] pooh; **hacer caca** to do a pooh - **2.** [cosa sucia] nasty o dirty thing - **3.** fig [desastre] crap (U).

cacahuate sm Amér C & Méx peanut.

cacahuete sm - **1.** [fruto] peanut - **2.** [planta] groundnut.

cacao *sm* - **1.** [bebida] cocoa - **2.** [semilla] cocoa bean - **3.** [árbol] cacao - **4.** *fam* [confusión] chaos, mess; [jaleo] fuss, rumpus; **cacao mental** mental confusion.

cacarear ◇ *vt fam* - **1.** [jactarse de] to boast about - **2.** [pregonar] to blab about. ◇ *vi* [gallo] to cluck, to cackle.

cacatúa *sf* - **1.** [ave] cockatoo - **2.** *fam* [mujer vieja] old bat.

cace *etc* ▷ **cazar**.

cacería *sf* hunt.

cacerola *sf* pot, pan.

cacha *sf* - **1.** *fam* [muslo] thigh - **2.** [mango - de cuchillo] handle; [- de pistola] butt.

◆ **cachas** *adj inv fam* [hombre fuerte] he-man; **un tío cacha** a strong man; **estar cachas** to be well-built.

cachalote *sm* sperm whale.

cachar *vt* - **1.** *Ecuad & R Plata* [burlarse de] to tease - **2.** *Amér* [cornear] to gore - **3.** *Amér fam* [agarrar] to grab - **4.** *Amér fam* [sorprender, atrapar] to catch - **5.** *Andes fam* [entender] to understand, to get.

cacharro *sm* - **1.** [recipiente] pot; **fregar los cacharros** to do the dishes - **2.** *fam* [trasto] junk *(U)*, rubbish *(U)* - **3.** [máquina] crock; [coche] banger.

cachaza *sf fam*: **tener cachaza** to be cool.

cachear *vt* to frisk.

cachemir *sm* cashmere.

cachemira *sf* = **cachemir**.

cacheo *sm* frisk, frisking *(U)*.

cachet [ka'tʃe] *sm* - **1.** [distinción] cachet - **2.** [cotización de artista] fee.

cachetada *sf fam* smack.

cachete *sm* - **1.** [moflete] chubby cheek - **2.** [bofetada] slap.

cachetear *vt* to slap.

cachiporra *sf* club, cudgel; [de policía] truncheon.

cachirulo *sm* - **1.** [chisme] thingamajig - **2.** [pañuelo] *headscarf worn by men as part of traditional Aragonese costume*.

cachivache *sm fam* knick-knack.

cacho *sm* - **1.** *fam* [pedazo] piece, bit - **2.** *Andes & Ven* [asta] horn.

cachondearse *vprnl*: **cachondearse (de)** *fam* to take the mickey (out of).

cachondeo *sm fam* - **1.** [diversión] lark; **irse de cachondeo** to go out on the town - **2.** *despec* [cosa poco seria] joke; **tomarse algo a cachondeo** to treat sthg as a joke.

cachondo, da *fam* ◇ *adj* - **1.** [divertido] funny - **2.** [salido] randy. ◇ *sm, f*: **cachondo (mental)** joker.

cachorro, rra *sm, f* [de perro] pup, puppy; [de león, lobo, oso] cub.

cacique *sm* - **1.** [persona influyente] cacique, local political boss - **2.** *despec & fig* [despota] despot - **3.** [jefe indio] chief, cacique.

caciquil *adj fig* despotic.

caciquismo *sm* caciquism.

caco *sm fam* thief.

cacofonía *sf* cacophony.

cacofónico, ca *adj* cacophonous.

cacto, cactus *(pl* **cactus)** *sm* cactus.

cacumen *sm* - **1.** [ingenio] brains *pl*, wits *pl* - **2.** *fam* [cabeza] nut, head.

CAD *(abrev de* **computer-aided design)** *sm* CAD.

cada *adj inv* - **1.** [gen] each; [con números, tiempo] every; **cada dos meses** every two months; **cada cosa a su tiempo** one thing at a time; **cada cual** each one, every one; **cada uno de** each of - **2.** [valor progresivo]: **cada vez más** more and more; **cada vez más largo** longer and longer; **cada día más** more and more each day - **3.** [valor enfático] such; **¡se pone cada sombrero!** she wears such hats!

cadalso *sm* scaffold.

cadáver *sm* corpse, (dead) body; **antes pasarán por encima de mi cadáver** over my dead body.

cadavérico, ca *adj* cadaverous; [pálido] deathly pale.

caddie = **cadi**.

cadena *sf* - **1.** [gen] chain; **en cadena** [accidente] multiple; **tirar de la cadena** to pull the chain, to flush the toilet; **cadena alimenticia** food chain; **cadena de tiendas** chain of stores; **romper sus cadenas** to break out of one's chains - **2.** TV channel - **3.** [RADIO - emisora] station; [- red de emisoras] network - **4.** [de proceso industrial] line; **cadena de montaje** assembly line - **5.** [aparato de música] sound system - **6.** GEOGR range - **7.** *fig* [sujeción] chains *pl*, bonds *pl*.

◆ **cadenas** *sfpl* AUTO (tyre) chains.

◆ **cadena perpetua** *sf* life imprisonment.

cadencia *sf* - **1.** [ritmo] rhythm, cadence - **2.** LITER & MÚS cadence.

cadencioso, sa *adj* rhythmical.

cadeneta *sf* chain stitch.

cadera *sf* hip.

cadete *sm* - **1.** cadet - **2.** *R Dom* [recadero] errand boy, office junior.

cadi, caddie *sm* caddie.

cadmio *sm* cadmium.

caducar [10] *vi* - **1.** [carné, ley, pasaporte etc] to expire - **2.** [medicamento] to pass its use-by date; [alimento] to pass its sell-by date.

caducidad *sf* expiry.

caduco, **ca** adj - **1.** [viejo] decrepit; [idea] out-moded - **2.** [perecedero] transitory - **3.** [desfasa-do] no longer valid - **4.** BOT deciduous.

caduque etc ⊳ **caducar**.

caer [55] vi - **1.** [gen] to fall; [diente, pelo] to fall out; **dejar caer algo** to drop sthg; **caer bajo** to sink (very) low; **estar al caer** to be about to arrive - **2.** [al perder equilibrio] to fall over O down; **caer de un tejado/caballo** to fall from a roof/horse - **3.** fig [abalanzarse]: **caer sobre** to fall O descend upon - **4.** fig [aparecer]: **dejar-se caer por casa de alguien** to drop by sb's house - **5.** fig [sentar]: **caer bien/mal (a al-guien)** [comentario, noticia etc] to go down well/badly (with sb) - **6.** fig [mostrarse]: **me cae bien/mal** I like/don't like him - **7.** fig [estar situado]: **cae cerca de aquí** it's not far from here - **8.** fig [recordar]: **caer (en algo)** to be able to remem-ber (sthg); **no caigo** I can't remember.
◆ **caer en** vi - **1.** [entender] to get, to under-stand; [solución] to hit upon - **2.** [coincidir - fecha] to fall on; **cae en domingo** it falls on a Sunday - **3.** [incurrir] to fall into.
◆ **caerse** vprnl - **1.** [persona] to fall over O down; **caerse de** to fall from; **caerse de inge-nuo/listo** fig to be incredibly naive/clever - **2.** [objetos] to drop, to fall - **3.** [desprenderse - diente, pelo etc] to fall out; [- botón] to fall off; [- cuadro] to fall down - **4.** [falda, pantalones etc] to fall down; **se te caen los pantalones** your trousers are falling down.

café ◇ sm - **1.** [gen] coffee; **café solo/con le-che** black/white coffee; **café instantáneo** O **soluble** instant coffee; **café americano** large weak black coffee; **café expreso** expresso; **ca-fé irlandés** Irish coffee; **café molido** ground coffee - **2.** [establecimiento] cafe. ◇ adj inv [co-lor] coffee-coloured.

cafeína sf caffeine.

cafetal sm coffee plantation.

cafetera sf ⊳ **cafetero**.

cafetería sf cafe.

cafetero, **ra** ◇ adj - **1.** [de café] coffee (antes de s); [país] coffee-producing - **2.** [bebedor de ca-fé] fond of coffee. ◇ sm, f - **1.** [cultivador] coffee grower - **2.** [comerciante] coffee merchant.
◆ **cafetera** sf - **1.** [gen] coffee pot - **2.** [en bares] expresso machine; [eléctrica] percolator, coffee machine - **3.** fam [aparato viejo] old crock.

cafeto sm coffee bush.

cafiche sm Andes fam pimp.

cafre ◇ adj brutish. ◇ smf brute.

cagado, **da** sm, f vulg [cobarde] yellow-belly, chicken.
◆ **cagada** sf vulg - **1.** [equivocación] cock-up - **2.** [excremento] shit - **3.** [desastre] crap.

cagar [16] vulg ◇ vi [defecar] to shit, to crap. ◇ vt [estropear] to bugger up; **cagarla** fig to cock it up.
◆ **cagarse** vprnl vulg lit & fig to shit o.s.

cagón, **ona** adj vulg - **1.** [que caga] shitty - **2.** [miedica] chicken, cowardly.

cague etc ⊳ **cagar**.

cagueta vulg ◇ adj chicken, cowardly. ◇ smf coward, chicken.

caído, **da** adj - **1.** [árbol, hoja] fallen - **2.** [decaí-do] low.
◆ **caída** sf - **1.** [gen] fall, falling (U); [de diente, pelo] loss - **2.** [de paro, precios, terreno]: **caída (de)** drop (in) - **3.** [de falda, vestido etc] drape - **4.** loc: **a la caída del sol** at sunset; **a la caída de la tarde** at nightfall.
◆ **caídos** smpl: **los caídos** the fallen.
◆ **caída de ojos** sf droop of one's eyelids.

caiga etc ⊳ **caer**.

caimán sm - **1.** [animal] alligator, cayman - **2.** fig [persona] sly fox.

caja sf - **1.** [gen] box; [para transporte, embalaje] crate; **caja de zapatos** shoebox; **una caja de cervezas** a crate of beer; **caja torácica** thorax - **2.** [de reloj] case; [de engranajes etc] housing; **caja de cambios** gearbox - **3.** [ataúd] coffin - **4.** [de dinero] cash box; **caja fuerte** O **de cau-dales** safe, strongbox - **5.** [en tienda, supermer-cado] till; [en banco] cashier's desk - **6.** [banco]: **caja (de ahorros)** savings bank, ≈ savings and loan association US - **7.** [hueco - de escalera] well; [- de chimenea, ascensor] shaft - **8.** IMPR case - **9.** [de instrumento musical] body; **caja de reso-nancia** sound box; **caja de ritmos** drum ma-chine - **10.** COM [cuenta contable] cash account.
◆ **caja de música** sf music box.
◆ **caja de reclutamiento** O **de reclutas** sf re-cruiting office.
◆ **caja negra** sf black box.
◆ **caja registradora** sf cash register.

Caja de Ahorros

In Spain, apart from the conventional banks, there are also **cajas de ahor-ros** (savings banks). These usually carry the name of the region or province where they are based, e.g. "Caja Soria", "Caja de Andalu-cía". They differ from conventional banks in that part of their profits has to be reinvested in social projects or cultural events which benefit their region.

cajero, **ra** sm, f [en tienda] cashier; [en banco] teller.
◆ **cajero** sm: **cajero (automático)** cash ma-chine, cash dispenser, ATM US.

cajetilla sf - **1.** [de cigarrillos] packet - **2.** [de ce-rillas] box - **3.** Amér [petimetre] fop, dandy.

cajón *sm* - **1.** [de mueble] drawer - **2.** [recipiente] crate, case - **3.** *loc*: **eso es de cajón** *fam* that goes without saying.
➤ **cajón de sastre** *sm* muddle, jumble.

cajuela *sf Méx* boot *UK*, trunk *US*.

cal *sf* lime; **cal viva** quicklime; **cerrar a cal y canto** to shut tight *o* firmly; **dar una de cal y otra de arena** to be inconsistent.

cala *sf* - **1.** [bahía pequeña] cove - **2.** [del barco] hold - **3.** [de fruta] sample slice - **4.** BOT arum lily - **5.** *fam* [dinero] peseta.

calabacín *sm* courgette *UK*, zucchini *US*.

calabaza *sf* pumpkin, squash *US*, gourd; **dar calabazas a alguien** *fam* [a pretendiente] to turn sb down; [en exámenes] to fail sb.

calabobos *sm inv* drizzle.

calabozo *sm* cell.

calada *sf* ▷ **calado**.

caladero *sm* fishing grounds *pl*.

calado, da *adj* soaked.
➤ **calado** *sm* - **1.** NÁUT draught - **2.** AUTO stalling - **3.** [bordado] openwork.
➤ **calada** *sf* - **1.** [en agua] soaking - **2.** [de cigarrillo] drag; **dar una calada** to take a drag.

calafatear *vt* to caulk.

calamar *sm* squid.

calambre *sm* - **1.** [descarga eléctrica] (electric) shock - **2.** [contracción muscular] cramp (*U*).

calamidad *sf* calamity; **pasar calamidades** to suffer great hardship; **ser una calamidad** *fig* to be a dead loss.

calamitoso, sa *adj* calamitous.

calandria *sf* - **1.** [pájaro] calandra lark - **2.** [para papel y telas] calender.

calaña *sf*: **de esa calaña** *despec* of that ilk.

calar ◇ *vt* - **1.** [empapar] to soak - **2.** *fig* [persona] to see through - **3.** [gorro, sombrero] to jam on - **4.** [tela] to do openwork embroidery on - **5.** [sandía, melón] to cut a sample of - **6.** [perforar] to perforate, to pierce. ◇ *vi* - **1.** NÁUT to draw - **2.** *fig* [penetrar]: **calar en** to have an impact on.
➤ **calarse** *vprnl* - **1.** [empaparse] to get soaked - **2.** [motor] to stall.

calato, ta *adj Andes & R Dom* [desnudo] naked.

calavera ◇ *sf* [cráneo] skull. ◇ *sm fig* madcap, crazy person.
➤ **calaveras** *sfpl Méx* [luces] tail lights.

calcado, da *adj* traced; **ser calcado a alguien** to be the spitting image of sb.

calcañar *sm* heel.

calcar [10] *vt* - **1.** [dibujo] to trace - **2.** [imitar] to copy.

calcáreo, a *adj* calcareous.

calce ◇ *sm* - **1.** [cuña] wedge - **2.** *Guat, Méx & P Rico* DER footnote. ◇ *v* ▷ **calzar**.

calceta *sf* stocking; **hacer calceta** to knit.

calcetín *sm* sock.

calcificarse [10] *vprnl* to calcify.

calcinación *sf* burning.

calcinar *vt* - **1.** [quemar] to burn, to char - **2.** TECNOL to calcine.

calcio *sm* calcium.

calco *sm* - **1.** [reproducción] tracing - **2.** *fig* [imitación] carbon copy - **3.** LING calque, loan translation.

calcografía *sf* chalcography.

calcomanía *sf* transfer.

calculador, ra *adj lit & fig* calculating.
➤ **calculadora** *sf* calculator; **calculadora de bolsillo** pocket calculator.

calcular *vt* - **1.** [cantidades] to calculate - **2.** [suponer] to reckon; **le calculo sesenta años** I reckon he's about sixty.

cálculo *sm* - **1.** [operación] calculation; **cálculo mental** mental arithmetic (*U*) - **2.** [ciencia] calculus; **cálculo diferencial/infinitesimal/integral** differential/infinitesimal/integral calculus - **3.** [evaluación] estimate; **cálculo de probabilidades** probability theory - **4.** MED stone, calculus.

caldas *sfpl* hot springs.

caldear *vt* - **1.** [calentar] to heat (up) - **2.** *fig* [excitar] to warm up, to liven up.

caldera *sf* - **1.** [recipiente] cauldron - **2.** [máquina] boiler; **caldera de vapor** steam boiler.

calderero, ra *sm, f* boilermaker.

caldereta *sf* CULIN [de pescado] fish stew; [de carne] meat stew.

calderilla *sf* small change, coppers *pl UK*.

caldero *sm* cauldron.

calderón *sm* MÚS pause.

caldillo *sm* stock.

caldo *sm* - **1.** [sopa] broth - **2.** [caldillo] stock - **3.** [vino] wine - **4.** [aceite] oil.
➤ **caldo de cultivo** *sm* - **1.** BIOL culture medium - **2.** *fig* [condición idónea] breeding ground.

caldoso, sa *adj* [sopa] watery; [arroz] soggy.

calé *adj* & *smf* gypsy.

calefacción *sf* heating; **calefacción central** central heating.

calefactor *sm* heater.

caleidoscopio, calidoscopio *sm* kaleidoscope.

calendario sm calendar; **calendario escolar/laboral** school/working year.

Calendario Laboral

The **calendario laboral** lists the 15 public holidays a year in Spain. There are eight official national holidays, some of which are religious: Good Friday, the Assumption (15 August), All Saints' (1 November), the Immaculate Conception (8 December), Christmas; others are required by labour legislation: New Year, Labour Day (1 May), Day of the Constitution (6 December). A further five national holidays are optional (in that regional authorities can substitute them with other days): Epiphany (6 January), St Joseph (19 March), Holy Thursday, Feast of Santiago (25 July), Spanish National Day (12 October). There are two further holidays, one to be decided by each autonomous region, and one by each province.

calentador sm - **1.** [aparato] heater - **2.** [prenda] legwarmer.

calentamiento sm - **1.** [subida de temperatura] heating; **calentamiento global** global warming - **2.** [ejercicios] warm-up.

calentar [19] ◇ vt - **1.** [subir la temperatura de] to heat (up), to warm (up) - **2.** fig [animar] to liven up - **3.** fig [pegar] to hit, to strike - **4.** mfam fig [sexualmente] to turn on. ◇ vi [entrenarse] to warm up.

➡ **calentarse** vprnl - **1.** [por calor - suj: persona] to warm o.s., to get warm; [- suj: cosa] to heat up - **2.** mfam fig [sexualmente] to get randy UK o horny.

calentón, ona sm, f mfam randy UK o horny person.

calentura sf - **1.** [fiebre] fever, temperature - **2.** [herida] cold sore.

calenturiento, ta adj - **1.** [con fiebre] feverish - **2.** fig [incontrolado] wild; [sexualmente] filthy.

calesa sf calash.

calibración sf = calibrado.

calibrado sm - **1.** [gen] calibration - **2.** [de arma] boring.

calibrador sm callipers pl.

calibrar vt - **1.** [medir] to calibrate, to gauge - **2.** [dar calibre a - arma] to bore - **3.** fig [juzgar] to gauge.

calibre sm - **1.** [diámetro - de pistola] calibre; [- de alambre] gauge; [- de tubo] bore - **2.** [instrumento] gauge - **3.** fig [tamaño] size - **4.** fig [importancia] importance, significance.

calidad sf - **1.** [gen] quality; **de calidad** quality (antes de s); **calidad de vida** quality of life - **2.** [clase] class - **3.** [condición]: **en calidad de** in one's capacity as.

cálido, da adj warm.

calidoscopio = caleidoscopio.

calienta ⊳ calentar.

calientapiés sm inv foot warmer.

calientaplatos sm inv hotplate.

caliente ◇ adj - **1.** [gen] hot; [templado] warm; **en caliente** fig in the heat of the moment - **2.** fig [acalorado] heated - **3.** mfam [excitado] randy UK, horny. ◇ v ⊳ **calentar**.

califa sm caliph.

califato sm caliphate.

calificación sf - **1.** [de película] rating - **2.** EDUC mark.

calificado, da adj - **1.** [importante] eminent - **2.** [apto] qualified.

calificar [10] vt - **1.** [denominar]: **calificar a alguien de algo** to call sb sthg, to describe sb as sthg - **2.** EDUC to mark - **3.** GRAM to qualify.

calificativo, va adj qualifying.
➡ **calificativo** sm epithet.

caligrafía sf - **1.** [arte] calligraphy - **2.** [tipo de letra] handwriting.

calígrafo, fa sm, f calligrapher.

calina sf haze, mist.

calipso sm calypso.

cáliz sm - **1.** RELIG chalice - **2.** ANAT & BOT calyx.

calizo, za adj chalky.
➡ **caliza** sf limestone.

callado, da adj quiet, silent.

callandito adv fam on the quiet.

callar ◇ vi - **1.** [no hablar] to keep quiet, to be silent; **quien calla otorga** prov silence signifies consent - **2.** [dejar de hablar] to be quiet, to stop talking. ◇ vt - **1.** [ocultar] to keep quiet about; [secreto] to keep - **2.** [acallar] to silence.
➡ **callarse** vprnl - **1.** [no hablar] to keep quiet, to be silent - **2.** [dejar de hablar] to be quiet, to stop talking; **¡cállate!** shut up! - **3.** [ocultar] to keep quiet about; [secreto] to keep.

calle sf - **1.** [vía de circulación] street, road; **calle arriba/abajo** up/down the street; **calle de dirección única** one-way street; **calle peatonal** pedestrian precinct; **calle sin salida** dead end, blind alley - **2.** DEP lane - **3.** Amér [callejón] cul-de-sac - **4.** loc: **dejar a alguien en la calle** to put sb out of a job; **echar a alguien a la calle** [de un trabajo] to sack sb; [de un lugar público] to kick o throw sb out; **echarse a la calle** [manifestarse] to take to the streets; **hacer la calle** to walk the streets; **llevarse a alguien de calle** to win sb over; **traer o llevar a alguien por la calle de la amargura** to make sb's life a misery.

callejear *vi* to wander the streets.

callejero, **ra** *adj* - **1.** [gen] street *(antes de s)*; [perro] stray - **2.** [persona] fond of being out and about.

➤ **callejero** *sm* [guía] street map.

callejón *sm* alley; **callejón sin salida** cul-de-sac; *fig* blind alley, impasse.

callejuela *sf* backstreet, side street.

callista *smf* chiropodist.

callo *sm* - **1.** [dureza] callus; [en el pie] corn; **dar el callo** *fam fig* to slog - **2.** *fam fig* [persona fea] sight, fright.

➤ **callos** *smpl* CULIN tripe *(U)*.

callosidad *sf* callus, hard skin *(U)*.

calloso, **sa** *adj* calloused.

calma *sf* - **1.** [sin ruido o movimiento] calm; **en calma** calm; **calma chicha** dead calm - **2.** [sosiego] tranquility; **perder la calma** to lose one's composure; **tómatelo con calma** take it easy - **3.** [apatía] sluggishness, indifference.

calmante ⇔ *adj* sedative, soothing. ⇔ *sm* sedative.

calmar *vt* - **1.** [mitigar] to relieve - **2.** [tranquilizar] to calm, to soothe.

➤ **calmarse** *vprnl* to calm down; [dolor, tempestad] to abate.

calmoso, **sa** *adj* calm.

caló *sm* gypsy dialect.

calor *sm* - **1.** [gen] heat; [sin quemar] warmth; **entrar en calor** [gen] to get warm; [público, deportista] to warm up; **hacer calor** to be warm o hot; **tener calor** to be warm o hot; **calor corporal** body heat; **calor específico** FÍS specific heat - **2.** *fig* [afecto, entusiasmo] warmth; **al calor de** under the wing of.

caloría *sf* calorie.

calórico, **ca** *adj* caloric.

calorífero, **ra** *adj* [que da calor] heat-producing.

calorífico, **ca** *adj* calorific.

calostro *sm* colostrum.

calote *sm Amér* swindle.

calque *etc* ➞ **calcar**.

calumnia *sf* [oral] slander; [escrita] libel.

calumniar *vt* [oralmente] to slander; [por escrito] to libel.

calumnioso, **sa** *adj* [de palabra] slanderous; [por escrito] libellous.

caluroso, **sa** *adj* - **1.** [gen] hot; [templado] warm - **2.** *fig* [afectuoso] warm.

calva *sf* ➞ **calvo**.

calvados *sm inv* Calvados.

calvario *sm* - **1.** [vía crucis] Calvary, stations *pl* of the Cross - **2.** *fig* [sufrimiento] ordeal.

calvicie *sf* baldness.

calvinista *adj* Calvinist.

calvo, **va** ⇔ *adj* bald; **ni tanto ni tan calvo** neither one extreme nor the other. ⇔ *sm*, *f* bald person.

➤ **calva** *sf* - **1.** [en la cabeza] bald patch - **2.** [en tejido, terreno] bare patch.

calza *sf* - **1.** [cuña] wedge, block - **2.** *desus* [media] stocking - **3.** *Col* [empaste] filling *(in tooth)*.

calzado, **da** *adj* - **1.** [con zapatos] shod - **2.** [ave] feather-legged.

➤ **calzado** *sm* footwear.

➤ **calzada** *sf* road.

calzar [13] *vt* - **1.** [poner calzado] to put on - **2.** [proveer de calzado] to provide shoes for - **3.** [llevar un calzado] to wear; **¿qué número calza?** what size do you take? - **4.** [poner cuña a] to wedge, to block - **5.** *Col* [empastar] to fill *(a tooth)*.

➤ **calzarse** *vprnl* to put on.

calzo *sm* [cuña] wedge.

calzón *sm* - **1.** *Esp* [deportivo] shorts - **2.** *Andes, Méx & R Plata* [braga] knickers *UK*, panties *US*.

calzonazos *sm inv fam* henpecked husband.

calzoncillo *sm (gen pl)* underpants *pl*, shorts *pl US*.

cama *sf* bed; **estar en** o **guardar cama** to be in bed; **hacer la cama** to make the bed; **cama individual/de matrimonio** single/double bed; **cama de agua** water bed; **cama nido** truckle bed; **cama turca** divan bed; **hacerle** o **ponerle la cama a alguien** *fig* to plot against sb.

camada *sf* litter.

camafeo *sm* cameo.

camaleón *sm lit & fig* chameleon.

camaleónico, **ca** *adj fig* fickle.

cámara ⇔ *sf* - **1.** [gen & TECNOL] chamber; **cámara alta/baja** upper/lower house; **cámara de aire/gas** air/gas chamber; **cámara de Comercio** Chamber of Commerce; **cámara de compensación** clearing house; **cámara frigorífica** cold-storage room; **cámara mortuoria** funeral chamber - **2.** CINE, FOTO & TV camera; **a cámara lenta** *lit & fig* in slow motion; **cámara digital** digital camera; **cámara oscura** camera obscura; **cámara de seguridad** security camera; **cámara de vídeo** video camera; **cámara web** web camera - **3.** [de balón, neumático] inner tube - **4.** [habitáculo] cabin. ⇔ *smf* [persona] cameraman *(f* camerawoman*)*.

➤ **de cámara** *loc adj* MÚS chamber *(antes de s)*.

camarada *smf* - **1.** POLÍT comrade - **2.** [compañero] colleague.

camaradería *sf* camaraderie.

camarero, **ra** *sm*, *f* - **1.** [de restaurante] waiter *(f* waitress*)*; [de hotel] steward *(f* chambermaid*)* - **2.** [de rey etc] chamberlain *(f* lady-in-waiting*)*.

➤ **camarera** *sf Amér* [azafata] air hostess.

camarilla *sf* clique; POLÍT lobby, pressure group.

camarón *sm* shrimp.

camarote *sm* cabin.

camastro *sm* ramshackle bed.

cambalache *sm fam* - **1.** [trueque] swap - **2.** *R Dom* [tienda] junk shop.

cambiante *adj* changeable.

cambiar [8] ◇ *vt* - **1.** [gen] to change; **cambiar libras por euros** to change pounds into euros - **2.** [canjear]: **cambiar algo (por)** to exchange sthg (for). ◇ *vi* - **1.** [gen] to change; **cambiar de** [gen] to change; **cambiar de casa** to move house; **cambiar de trabajo** to move jobs - **2.** AUTO: **cambiar de marcha** to change gear.

◆ **cambiarse** *vprnl*: **cambiarse (de)** [ropa] to change; [casa] to move; **cambiarse de vestido** to change one's dress.

cambiazo *sm fam* - **1.** [cambio grande] radical change - **2.** [sustitución] switch *(in order to steal bag etc)*; **dar el cambiazo** *fig* to do a switch.

cambio *sm* - **1.** [gen] change; **a las primeras de cambio** at the first opportunity; **cambio climático** climate change; **cambio de domicilio** change of address; **cambio de guardia** changing of the guard - **2.** [trueque] exchange; **a cambio (de)** in exchange *o* return (for) - **3.** [FIN - de acciones] price; [- de divisas] exchange rate; **'cambio'** 'bureau de change'; **cambio base** base rate - **4.** AUTO: **cambio automático** automatic transmission; **cambio de marchas** *o* **velocidades** gear change; **cambio de sentido** U-turn.

◆ **cambio de rasante** *sm* brow of a hill.

◆ **libre cambio** *sm* - **1.** ECON [librecambismo] free trade - **2.** FIN [de divisas] floating exchange rates *pl*.

◆ **en cambio** *loc adv* - **1.** [por otra parte] on the other hand, however - **2.** [en su lugar] instead.

cambista *smf* money changer.

Camboya *n pr* Cambodia.

camboyano, **na** *adj* & *sm*, *f* Cambodian.

cambujo, **ja** *adj Amér* [oscuro] dark.

cambur *sm Amér* - **1.** [empleo] job - **2.** [empleado] clerk - **3.** *Ven* banana.

camelar *vt fam* - **1.** [seducir, engañar] to butter up, to win over - **2.** [enamorar] to flirt with.

camelia *sf* camellia.

camello, **lla** *sm*, *f* [animal] camel.

◆ **camello** *sm fam* [traficante] drug pusher *o* dealer.

camellón *sm Col & Méx* central reservation UK, median (strip) US.

camelo *sm fam* - **1.** [engaño] humbug *(U)* - **2.** [noticia falsa] hoax.

camerino *sm* dressing room.

Camerún *n pr* Cameroon.

camerunés, **esa** ◇ *adj* of/relating to Cameroon. ◇ *sm*, *f* native/inhabitant of Cameroon.

camilla ◇ *sf* [gen] stretcher; [de psiquiatra, dentista] couch. ◇ *adj* ⊳ **mesa**.

camillero, **ra** *sm*, *f* stretcher-bearer.

caminante *smf* walker.

caminar ◇ *vi* - **1.** [a pie] to walk - **2.** *fig* [ir]: **caminar (hacia)** to head (for). ◇ *vt* [una distancia] to travel, to cover.

caminata *sf* long walk.

camino *sm* - **1.** [sendero] path, track; [carretera] road; **camino de herradura** bridle path; **camino de montaña** mountain path; **abrir camino a** to clear the way for; **abrirse camino** to get on *o* ahead - **2.** [ruta] way; **a medio camino** halfway; **estar a medio camino** to be halfway there; **quedarse a medio camino** to stop halfway through; **camino de** on the way to; **en el** *o* **de camino** on the way; **ir camino de** to be heading for - **3.** [viaje] journey; **ponerse en camino** to set off - **4.** *fig* [medio] way.

◆ **camino de Santiago** *sm* - **1.** ASTRON the Milky Way - **2.** RELIG pilgrimage route to Santiago de Compostela.

◆ **camino trillado** *sm fig* well-trodden path.

camión *sm* - **1.** [de mercancías] lorry UK, truck US; **camión articulado** articulated lorry UK *o* truck US; **camión cisterna** tanker; **camión de la mudanza** removal van - **2.** *Amér C & Méx* [bus] bus.

camionero, **ra** ◇ *adj Amér C & Méx* bus. ◇ *sm*, *f* lorry driver UK, trucker US.

camioneta *sf* van.

camisa *sf* - **1.** [prenda] shirt - **2.** TECNOL lining - **3.** ZOOL slough, skin - **4.** BOT skin - **5.** *loc*: **jugarse hasta la camisa** to stake one's shirt; **meterse en camisa de once varas** to complicate matters unnecessarily; **mudar** *o* **cambiar de camisa** to change sides; **no le llega la camisa al cuerpo** she's scared stiff.

◆ **camisa de fuerza** *sf* straitjacket.

camisería *sf* [tienda] shirt shop, outfitter's.

camisero, **ra** ◇ *adj* shirt *(antes de s)*. ◇ *sm*, *f* - **1.** [que confecciona] shirtmaker - **2.** [que vende] outfitter.

camiseta *sf* - **1.** [prenda interior] vest UK, undershirt US - **2.** [de verano] T-shirt - **3.** [DEP - de tirantes] vest; [- de mangas] shirt.

camisola *sf* - **1.** [prenda interior] camisole - **2.** *Amér* DEP sports shirt.

camisón *sm* nightdress.

camomila *sf* camomile.

camorra *sf* trouble; **buscar camorra** to look for trouble.

camorrista ⟷ *adj* belligerent, quarrelsome. ⟷ *smf* troublemaker.

campal ⊳ **batalla**.

campamento *sm* camp.

campana *sf* bell; **campana de buzo** o **de salvamento** diving bell; **campana extractora de humos** extractor hood; **echar las campanas al vuelo** *fam* to jump for joy; **oír campanas y no saber dónde** not to know what one is talking about.

campanada *sf* - **1.** [de campana] peal - **2.** [de reloj] stroke - **3.** *fig* [suceso] sensation.

campanario *sm* belfry, bell tower.

campanilla *sf* - **1.** [de la puerta] (small) bell; [con mango] handbell - **2.** ANAT uvula - **3.** [flor] campanula, bellflower.

campanilleo *sm* tinkling *(U)*.

campante *adj*: **estar** o **quedarse tan campante** *fam* to remain quite unruffled.

campaña *sf* - **1.** [gen & INFORM] campaign; **hacer campaña (de/contra)** to campaign (for/against); **de campaña** MIL field *(antes de s)* - **2.** [campo llano] open countryside - **3.** *R Dom* [campo] countryside.

campechano, **na** *adj*   *fam*   genial, good-natured.

campeón, **ona** *sm*, *f* champion.

campeonato *sm* championship; **de campeonato** *fig* terrific, great.

campero, **ra** *adj* country *(antes de s)*; [al aire libre] open-air.

◆ **campero** *sm Amér* jeep.

◆ **campera** *sf* - **1.** [bota] ≃ cowboy boot - **2.** *R Dom* [chaqueta] jacket.

campesinado *sm* peasants *pl*, peasantry.

campesino, **na** ⟷ *adj* country *(antes de s)*, rural. ⟷ *sm*, *f* [gen] farmer; [muy pobre] peasant.

campestre *adj* country *(antes de s)*.

campiña *sf* countryside.

camping ['kampin] *(pl* **campings)** *sm* - **1.** [actividad] camping; **ir de camping** to go camping - **2.** [lugar de acampada] campsite.

campista *smf* camper.

campo *sm* - **1.** [gen & INFORM] field; **campo de aviación** airfield; **campo de batalla** battlefield; **campo magnético** magnetic field; **campo de tiro** firing range; **dejar el campo libre** *fig* to leave the field open - **2.** [campiña] country, countryside; **campo abierto** open countryside; **a campo traviesa** cross country - **3.** [DEP - de fútbol] pitch; [- de tenis] court; [- de

golf] course; **jugar en campo propio** to play at home - **4.** *C Sur* [hacienda] cattle ranch - **5.** *Andes* [lugar] room, space.

◆ **campo de concentración** *sm* concentration camp.

◆ **campo de trabajo** *sm* [de vacaciones] work camp; [para prisioneros] labour camp.

◆ **campo visual** *sm* field of vision.

camposanto *sm* cemetery.

campus *sm inv* campus.

camuflaje *sm* camouflage.

camuflar *vt* to camouflage.

can *sm* hound, dog.

cana *sf* ⊳ **cano**.

Canadá *n pr*: **(el) Canadá** Canada.

canadiense *adj* & *smf* Canadian.

canal ⟷ *sm* - **1.** [cauce artificial] canal; **canal de riego** irrigation channel - **2.** GEOGR channel, strait - **3.** RADIO & TV channel; **canal por cable** cable channel - **4.** ANAT canal, duct - **5.** [de agua, gas] conduit, pipe - **6.** *fig* [medio, vía] channel; **canal de comercialización** ECON distribution channel - **7.** [res] carcass; **abrir en canal** to slit open; *fig* to tear apart. ⟷ *sm* o *sf* [de un tejado] (valley) gutter.

canalé *sm* ribbed knitwear.

canalización *sf* - **1.** [encauzamiento] piping - **2.** *(gen pl)* [cañería] pipes *pl* - **3.** *fig* [orientación] channelling.

canalizar [13] *vt* - **1.** [territorio] to canalize; [agua] to channel - **2.** [cauce] to deepen the course of - **3.** *fig* [orientar] to channel.

canalla *smf* swine, dog.

canallada *sf* [acto] dirty trick.

canalón *sm* [de tejado] gutter; [en la pared] drainpipe.

canapé *sm* - **1.** CULIN canapé - **2.** [sofá] sofa, couch.

Canarias *sfpl*: **las (islas) Canarias** the Canary Islands, the Canaries.

canario, **ria** ⟷ *adj* of the Canary Islands. ⟷ *sm*, *f* [persona] Canary Islander.

◆ **canario** *sm* [pájaro] canary.

canasta *sf* - **1.** [gen & DEP] basket - **2.** [juego de naipes] canasta.

canastilla *sf* - **1.** [cesto pequeño] basket - **2.** [de bebé] layette.

canasto *sm* large basket.

cancán, **cancanes** *sm* o *sf R Dom* tights *UK*, pantyhose *US*.

cancela *sf* wrought-iron gate.

cancelación *sf* cancellation.

cancelar *vt* - **1.** [anular] to cancel - **2.** [deuda] to pay, to settle - **3.** *Chile & Perú* [cuenta] to pay.

cáncer *sm fig* & MED cancer.

Cáncer <> *sm* [zodiaco] Cancer; **ser Cáncer** to be (a) Cancer. <> *smf* [persona] Cancer, Cancerian.

cancerígeno, na *adj* carcinogenic.

cancerología *sf* oncology.

cancerológico, ca *adj* oncological.

cancerólogo, ga *sm, f* cancer specialist, oncologist.

canceroso, sa <> *adj* [úlcera, tejido] cancerous; [enfermo] suffering from cancer. <> *sm, f* [enfermo] cancer patient.

canciller *sm* - **1.** [de gobierno, embajada] chancellor - **2.** [de asuntos exteriores] foreign minister.

cancillería *sf* - **1.** [de gobierno] chancellorship - **2.** [de embajada] chancellery - **3.** [de asuntos exteriores] foreign ministry.

canción *sf* song; **canción de cuna** lullaby; **la misma canción** *fig* the same old story.

cancionero *sm* songbook.

candado *sm* padlock.

candela *sf* - **1.** [vela] candle - **2.** *fam fig* [lumbre] light - **3.** *Amér* [fuego] fire.

candelabro *sm* candelabra.

candelero *sm* candlestick; **estar en el candelero** *fig* to be in the limelight.

candente *adj* - **1.** [incandescente] red-hot - **2.** *fig* [actual] burning *(antes de s)*.

candidato, ta *sm, f* candidate.

candidatura *sf* - **1.** [para un cargo] candidacy; **presentar alguien su candidatura (a)** to put o.s. forward as a candidate (for) - **2.** [lista] list of candidates.

candidez *sf* ingenuousness.

cándido, da *adj* ingenuous, simple.

candil *sm* - **1.** [lámpara] oil lamp - **2.** *Méx* [araña] chandelier.

candilejas *sfpl* footlights.

candor *sm* ingenuousness, simplicity.

candoroso, sa *adj* ingenuous, simple.

caneca *sf Col* rubbish bin *UK*, trashcan *US*.

canelo, la *adj* - **1.** [caballo, perro] cinnamon-coloured - **2.** *fam fig* [inocentón] gullible.

canela *sf* cinnamon; **ser canela fina** *fig* to be sheer class.

canelón *sm* CULIN cannelloni *pl*.

canesú *(pl canesúes o canesús) sm* - **1.** [de vestido] bodice - **2.** [de blusa] yoke.

cangrejo *sm* crab; **cangrejo de río** crayfish.

canguelo *sm*: **le entró canguelo** *fam* she got the wind up.

canguro <> *sm* [animal] kangaroo. <> *smf fam* [persona] babysitter; **hacer de canguro** to babysit.

caníbal <> *adj* cannibalistic. <> *smf* cannibal.

canibalismo *sm* cannibalism.

canica *sf* [pieza] marble.

canicas *sfpl* [juego] marbles.

caniche *sm* poodle.

canícula *sf* dog o hottest days *pl*.

canijo, ja <> *adj* sickly. <> *sm, f* sickly person.

canilla *sf* - **1.** [espinilla] shinbone - **2.** [bobina] bobbin - **3.** *R Dom* [grifo] tap *UK*, faucet *US* - **4.** *Amér* [pierna] leg.

canillita *sm R Dom fam* newspaper vendor.

canino, na *adj* canine.

canino *sm* [diente] canine (tooth).

canje *sm* exchange.

canjeable *adj* exchangeable.

canjear *vt* to exchange.

cannabis *sm inv* cannabis.

cano, na *adj* grey.

cana *sf* grey hair; **echar una cana al aire** *fig* to let one's hair down.

canoa *sf* canoe.

canódromo *sm* greyhound track.

canon *sm* - **1.** [norma] canon; **como mandan los cánones** according to the rules - **2.** [modelo] ideal - **3.** [impuesto] tax - **4.** MÚS canon.

cánones *smpl* DER canon law (U).

canónico, ca *adj* canonical; [derecho] canon *(antes de s)*.

canónigo *sm* canon.

canonizar [13] *vt* to canonize.

canoso, sa *adj* [pelo] grey; [persona] grey-haired.

cansado, da *adj* - **1.** [agotado] tired; **cansado de algo/de hacer algo** tired of sthg/of doing sthg - **2.** [pesado, cargante] tiring.

cansador, ra *adj Andes & R Plata* [que cansa] tiring; [que aburre] tiresome, boring.

cansancio *sm* tiredness.

cansar <> *vt* to tire (out). <> *vi* to be tiring.

cansarse *vprnl*: **cansarse (de)** *lit & fig* to get tired (of).

cansino, na *adj* lethargic.

Cantabria *n pr* Cantabria.

Cantábrico *sm*: **el (mar) Cantábrico** the Cantabrian Sea.

cántabro, bra *adj & sm, f* Cantabrian.

cantaleta *sf Amér* nagging.

cantamañanas *smf inv* unreliable person.

cantante <> *adj* singing. <> *smf* singer.

cantaor, ra *sm, f* flamenco singer.

cantar <> *vt* - **1.** [canción] to sing - **2.** [bingo, línea, el gordo] to call (out); **cantar victoria** to claim victory; **cantar a alguien las cuarenta** to give sb a piece of one's mind. <> *vi* - **1.** [persona, ave] to sing; [gallo] to crow; [grillo] to chirp

- 2. *fam fig* [confesar] to talk **- 3.** *fam fig* [apestar] to whiff, to pong **- 4.** *fam fig* [desentonar] to stick out like a sore thumb **- 5.** *fig* [alabar]: **cantar a** to sing the praises of. ◇ *sm* LITER poem; **eso es otro cantar** that's another story; **cantar de gesta** chanson de geste.

cántara *sf* large pitcher.

cántaro *sm* large pitcher; **a cántaros** in torrents; **llover a cántaros** to rain cats and dogs.

cantata *sf* cantata.

cantautor, ra *sm, f* singer-songwriter.

cante *sm*: **cante (jondo** O **hondo)** flamenco singing; **dar el cante** *fam* to call attention to o.s.

cantera *sf* **- 1.** [de piedra] quarry **- 2.** *fig* [de profesionales, jugadores] young blood *(U)*.

cantero *sm* C Sur & Cuba [de flores] flowerbed.

cántico *sm* canticle.

cantidad ◇ *sf* **- 1.** [medida] quantity **- 2.** [abundancia] abundance, large number; **en cantidad** in abundance; **cantidad de** lots of; **en cantidads industriales** in industrial quantities **- 3.** [número] number **- 4.** [suma de dinero] sum (of money). ◇ *adv fam* really; **me gusta cantidad** I don't half like it.

cantiga, cántiga *sf* ballad.

cantilena, cantinela *sf*: **la misma cantilena** *fig* the same old story.

cantimplora *sf* water bottle.

cantina *sf* [de soldados] mess; [en fábrica] canteen; [en estación de tren] buffet; [bar] snack bar.

cantinela = **cantilena**.

cantinero, ra *sm, f* [de bar] publican.

canto *sm* **- 1.** [acción, arte] singing **- 2.** [canción] song; **canto del cisne** swansong; **canto de sirena** wheedling **- 3.** *fig* [alabanza] hymn **- 4.** [lado, borde] edge; **de canto** edgeways; **darse con un canto en los dientes** to consider o.s. lucky; **por el canto de un duro** by a hair's breadth **- 5.** [de cuchillo] blunt edge **- 6.** [guijarro] pebble; **canto rodado** [pequeño] pebble; [grande] boulder.

cantón *sm* [territorio] canton.

cantor, ra ◇ *adj* singing *(antes de s)*. ◇ *sm, f* singer.

cantoral *sm* choir book.

canturrear *vt & vi fam* to sing softly.

canutas *sfpl*: **pasarlas canutas** *fam* to have a rough time.

canutillo *sm* glass tube.

canuto *sm* **- 1.** [tubo] tube **- 2.** *fam* [porro] joint.

caña *sf* **- 1.** BOT cane; **caña de azúcar** sugarcane **- 2.** [de río, estanque] reed **- 3.** [tuétano] bone marrow **- 4.** [de la bota, del calcetín] leg **- 5.** *Esp* [de cerveza] half; **una caña** one beer **- 6.** *Andes, Cuba & R Plata* [aguardiente] *type of rum*

made using sugar cane spirit **- 7.** *loc*: **darle** O **meterle caña a algo** *fam* to get a move on with sthg.

◆ **caña de pescar** *sf* fishing rod.

cañabrava *sf Cuba & R Dom kind of cane.*

cañada *sf* gorge, ravine.

cáñamo *sm* hemp.

cañamón *sm* hempseed.

cañaveral *sm* reedbed.

cañería *sf* pipe.

cañero, ra *sm, f Amér* [trabajador] sugar plantation worker.

cañizo *sm* wattle.

caño *sm* [de fuente] jet.

cañón *sm* **- 1.** [arma] gun; HIST cannon; **cañón antiaéreo** anti-aircraft gun; **cañón de nieve** snow cannon **- 2.** [de fusil] barrel; [de chimenea] flue; [de órgano] pipe **- 3.** GEOGR canyon **- 4.** *loc*: **estar cañón** *fam* to be gorgeous.

cañonazo *sm* **- 1.** [disparo de cañón] gunshot **- 2.** [en fútbol] powerful shot.

cañonear *vt* to shell.

cañonera *sf* gunboat.

caoba *sf* mahogany.

caos *sm inv* chaos.

caótico, ca *adj* chaotic.

cap. *(abrev de* **capítulo)** ch.

CAP *(abrev de* **Certificado de Aptitud Pedagógica)** *sm Spanish teaching certificate needed to teach in secondary education.*

capa *sf* **- 1.** [manto] cloak, cape; **andar de capa caída** to be in a bad way; **de capa y espada** cloak and dagger; **defender a capa y espada** to defend tooth and nail; **hacer de su capa un sayo** to do as one pleases **- 2.** [baño - de barniz, pintura] coat; [- de chocolate etc] coating **- 3.** [estrato] layer; GEOL stratum, layer; **capa atmosférica** atmosphere; **capa de ozono** ozone layer; **capa terrestre** earth's surface; **capa de hielo** sheet of ice **- 4.** [grupo social] stratum, class **- 5.** TAUROM cape.

capacho *sm* wicker basket.

capacidad *sf* **- 1.** [gen] capacity; **con capacidad para 500 personas** with a capacity of 500 **- 2.** [aptitud] ability; **no tener capacidad para algo/para hacer algo** to be no good at sthg/at doing sthg.

◆ **capacidad adquisitiva** *sf* purchasing power.

◆ **capacidad de decisión** *sf* decision-making ability.

◆ **capacidad de trabajo** *sf* capacity for hard work.

capacitación *sf* training.

capacitar vt: **capacitar a alguien para algo** [habilitar] to qualify sb for sthg; [formar] to train sb for sthg.

capar vt to castrate.

caparazón sm lit & fig shell.

capataz sm, f foreman (f forewoman).

capaz adj - **1.** [gen] capable; **capaz de algo/ de hacer algo** capable of sthg/of doing sthg - **2.** DER competent - **3.** [atrevido]: **ser capaz** to dare; **ser capaz de hacer algo** to bring oneself to do sthg - **4.** [espacioso]: **muy/poco capaz** with a large/small capacity; **capaz para** with room for.

capazo sm large wicker basket.

capcioso, sa adj [pregunta] trick (antes de s).

capea sf TAUROM bullfight with young bulls.

capear vt fig [eludir] to get out of.

capellán sm chaplain.

caperuza sf - **1.** [gorro] hood - **2.** [capuchón] top, cap.

capicúa ◇ adj inv reversible. ◇ sm inv reversible number.

capilar ◇ adj - **1.** [del cabello] hair (antes de s) - **2.** ANAT & FÍS capillary. ◇ sm ANAT capillary.

capilaridad sf FÍS capillarity, capillary action.

capilla sf chapel; **capilla ardiente** funeral chapel; **estar en capilla** fig [condenado a muerte] to be awaiting execution; fam [en ascuas] to be on tenterhooks.

capirotazo sm flick.

capirote sm - **1.** [gorro] hood - **2.** ➭ **tonto**.

cápita ➧ **per cápita** loc adj per capita.

capital ◇ adj - **1.** [importante] supreme - **2.** [principal] main. ◇ sm ECON capital; **capital circulante/fijo/social** working/fixed/ share capital; **capital escriturado** declared capital, capital stock; **capital líquido** liquid assets pl; **capital bajo riesgo** sum at risk; **capital de riesgo** venture capital. ◇ sf [ciudad] capital; **soy de Barcelona capital** I'm from the city of Barcelona.

capitalidad sf capital status.

capitalismo sm capitalism.

capitalista adj & smf capitalist.

capitalización sf capitalization.

capitalizar [13] vt - **1.** ECON to capitalize - **2.** fig [sacar provecho] to capitalize on.

capitán, ana sm, f captain; **capitán general** MIL ≃ field marshal UK, general of the army US.
➧ **capitana** sf NÁUT flagship.

capitanear vt - **1.** DEP & MIL to captain - **2.** [dirigir] to head, to lead.

capitanía sf - **1.** MIL [empleo] captaincy - **2.** MIL [oficina] military headquarters; **capitanía general** Captaincy General.

capitel sm capital.

capitolio sm - **1.** [edificio] capitol - **2.** [acrópolis] acropolis.

capitoste smf despec big wheel, big boss.

capitulación sf capitulation, surrender.
➧ **capitulaciones matrimoniales** sfpl marriage settlement sing.

capitular vi to capitulate, to surrender.

capítulo sm - **1.** [sección, división] chapter - **2.** fig [tema] subject; **ser capítulo aparte** to be another matter (altogether).

capó, capot [ka'po] sm bonnet UK, hood US.

capón sm - **1.** [animal] capon - **2.** [golpe] rap on the head.

caporal sm MIL ≃ corporal.

capot = **capó**.

capota sf hood UK, top US.

capotazo sm TAUROM pass with the cape.

capote sm - **1.** [capa] cape with sleeves; [militar] greatcoat - **2.** TAUROM cape - **3.** loc: **echar un capote a alguien** to give sb a (helping) hand.

capricho sm - **1.** [antojo] whim, caprice; **darse un capricho** to treat o.s. - **2.** MÚS & ARTE caprice.

caprichoso, sa adj capricious.

Capricornio ◇ sm [zodiaco] Capricorn; **ser Capricornio** to be (a) Capricorn. ◇ smf [persona] Capricorn.

cápsula sf - **1.** [gen & ANAT] capsule - **2.** [tapón] cap.
➧ **cápsula espacial** sf space capsule.

captar vt - **1.** [atraer - simpatía] to win; [- interés] to gain, to capture - **2.** [entender] to grasp - **3.** [sintonizar] to pick up, to receive - **4.** [aguas] to collect.
➧ **captarse** vprnl [atraer] to win, to attract.

captura sf capture.

capturar vt to capture.

capucha sf hood.

capuchino, na adj Capuchin.
➧ **capuchino** sm - **1.** [fraile] Capuchin - **2.** [café] cappuccino.

capuchón sm cap, top.

capullo, lla vulg ◇ adj bloody stupid. ◇ sm, f [persona] prat.
➧ **capullo** sm - **1.** [de flor] bud - **2.** [de gusano] cocoon - **3.** vulg [de pene] head.

caqui, kaki ◇ adj inv [color] khaki. ◇ sm - **1.** BOT kaki - **2.** [color] khaki.

cara sf - **1.** [rostro, aspecto] face; **a cara descubierta** openly; **cara a** [frente a] facing; **cara a cara** face to face; **de cara** [sol, viento] in one's face; **poner cara de tonto** to pull a stupid face; **tener buena/mala cara** [persona] to look well/ awful; **tener cara de enfadado** to look angry;

tiene cara de ponerse a llover it looks as if it's going to rain - **2.** [lado] side; GEOM face - **3.** [de moneda] heads *(U)*; **cara o cruz** heads or tails; **echar algo a cara o cruz** to toss (a coin) for sthg - **4.** *fam* [osadía] cheek; **tener (mucha) cara, tener la cara muy dura** to have a cheek - **5.** [parte frontal] front - **6.** *loc*: **se le cayó la cara de vergüenza** she blushed with shame; **cruzar la cara a alguien** to slap sb in the face; **dar la cara por alguien** to make excuses for sb; **de cara a** with a view to; **decir algo a alguien en *o* a la cara** to say sthg to sb's face; **echar en cara algo a alguien** to reproach sb for sthg; **hacer cara a** to stand up to; **por su linda cara, por su cara bonita** because his/her face fits; **romper *o* partir la cara a alguien** to smash sb's face in; **tener dos caras** to be two-faced; **verse las caras** [pelearse] to have it out; [enfrentarse] to fight it out.

carabela *sf* caravel.

carabina *sf* - **1.** [arma] carbine, rifle - **2.** *fam fig* [mujer] chaperone.

Caracas *n pr* Caracas.

caracol *sm* - **1.** [animal] snail - **2.** [concha] shell - **3.** [rizo] curl.
● **escalera de caracol** *sf* spiral staircase.
● **caracoles** *interj*: **¡caracoles!** *fam desus* good grief!

caracola *sf* conch.

carácter (*pl* caracteres) *sm* - **1.** [de persona] character; **tener buen/mal carácter** to be good-natured/bad-tempered - **2.** [índole] nature; **con carácter de urgencia** as a matter of urgency; **una reunión de carácter privado/oficial** a private/official meeting - **3.** INFORM character; **carácter alfanumérico** alphanumeric character; **caracteres de imprenta** typeface *sing* - **4.** BIOL trait.

característico, ca *adj* characteristic.
● **característica** *sf* characteristic.

caracterización *sf* - **1.** [gen] characterization - **2.** [maquillaje] make-up.

caracterizar [13] *vt* - **1.** [definir] to characterize - **2.** [representar] to portray - **3.** [maquillar] to make up.
● **caracterizarse por** *vprnl* to be characterized by.

caradura *fam* ⇔ *adj* cheeky. ⇔ *smf* cheeky person.

carajillo *sm* coffee with a dash of liqueur.

carajo *mfam* ⇔ *sm*: **me importa un carajo** I couldn't give a monkey's; **irse al carajo** to go down the tubes; **¡vete al carajo!** go to hell! ⇔ *interj*: **¡carajo!** damn it!

caramba *interj*: **¡caramba!** [sorpresa] good heavens!; [enfado] for heaven's sake!

carámbano *sm* icicle.

carambola *sf* - **1.** cannon *(in billiards)*; **por carambola** by a fluke - **2.** [fruta] starfruit.
● **carambolas** *interj* *Amér*: **¡carambolas!** good heavens!

caramelo *sm* - **1.** [golosina] sweet - **2.** [azúcar fundido] caramel; **de caramelo** *fig* great.

carantoñas *sfpl*: **hacer carantoñas a alguien** to butter sb up.

caraota *sf* *Ven* bean.

caraqueño, ña ⇔ *adj* of/relating to Caracas. ⇔ *sm, f* native/inhabitant of Caracas.

carátula *sf* - **1.** [de libro] front cover; [de disco] sleeve - **2.** [máscara] mask - **3.** *Méx* [de reloj] dial.

caravana *sf* - **1.** [gen] caravan *UK*, trailer *US* - **2.** [de coches] tailback.
● **caravanas** *sfpl* *Amér* [pendientes] earrings.

caravaning [kara'βanin] *sm* caravanning.

caray *interj*: **¡caray!** [sorpresa] good heavens!; [enfado] damn it!

carbón *sm* - **1.** [para quemar] coal; **negro como el carbón** [negro] black as coal; [bronceado] brown as a berry; **carbón de leña *o* vegetal** charcoal; **carbón mineral *o* de piedra** coal - **2.** [para dibujar] charcoal.

carbonatado, da *adj* carbonated.

carbonato *sm* carbonate.

carboncillo *sm* charcoal; **al carboncillo** in charcoal.

carbonero, ra ⇔ *adj* coal *(antes de s)*. ⇔ *sm, f* [persona] coal merchant.
● **carbonera** *sf* - **1.** [lugar] coal bunker - **2.** [de leña] charcoal stack.

carbónico, ca *adj* carbonic.

carbonilla *sf* - **1.** [ceniza] cinder - **2.** [carbón pequeño] small coal.

carbonizar [13] *vt* to char, to carbonize; **morir carbonizado** to burn to death.
● **carbonizarse** *vprnl* to carbonize.

carbono *sm* carbon; **carbono 14** carbon 14.

carburador *sm* carburettor.

carburante *sm* fuel.

carburar ⇔ *vt* to carburate. ⇔ *vi* *fam* to work.

carburo *sm* carbide.

carca *fam despec* ⇔ *adj* old-fashioned. ⇔ *smf* old fogey.

carcaj (*pl* carcajes) *sm* quiver.

carcajada *sf* guffaw; **reír a carcajadas** to roar with laughter.

carcajearse *vprnl* to roar with laughter.

carcamal *smf* *fam despec* old crock.

cárcel *sf* prison; **estar en la cárcel** to be in prison; **meter a alguien en la cárcel** to put sb in prison; **cárcel de alta seguridad** top security prison.

carcelario, **ria** *adj* prison *(antes de s)*.

carcelero, **ra** *sm*, *f* warder, jailer.

carcoma *sf* - **1.** [insecto] woodworm - **2.** [polvo] wood dust.

carcomer *vt lit & fig* to eat away at.
- **carcomerse** *vprnl fig* [consumirse] to be eaten up o consumed.

cardado *sm* - **1.** [de lana] carding - **2.** [del pelo] backcombing.

cardán *sm* cardan joint.

cardar *vt* - **1.** [lana] to card - **2.** [pelo] to backcomb.

cardenal *sm* - **1.** RELIG cardinal - **2.** [hematoma] bruise.

cardenalicio, **cia** *adj* cardinal's *(antes de s)*.

cárdeno, **na** *adj* purple.
- **cárdeno** *sm* [color] purple.

cardiaco, **ca**, **cardíaco**, **ca** *adj* cardiac, heart *(antes de s)*.

cárdigan, **cardigán** *sm* cardigan.

cardinal *adj* cardinal.

cardiograma *sm* cardiogram.

cardiología *sf* cardiology.

cardiólogo, **ga** *sm*, *f* cardiologist.

cardiopatía *sf* heart condition.

cardiovascular *adj* cardiovascular.

cardo *sm* - **1.** [planta] thistle; **cardo borriquero** cotton thistle - **2.** *fam fig* [persona] prickly customer.

carear *vt* DER to bring face to face.

carecer [30] *vi*: **carecer de algo** to lack sthg.

carencia *sf* [ausencia] lack; [defecto] deficiency.

carente *adj*: **carente de** lacking (in).

careo *sm* DER confrontation.

carero, **ra** *adj fam* pricey.

carestía *sf* - **1.** [escasez] scarcity, shortage - **2.** [encarecimiento]: **la carestía de la vida** the high cost of living.

careta *sf* - **1.** [máscara] mask; **careta antigás** gas mask - **2.** *fig* [engaño] front.

carey *sm* - **1.** [tortuga] sea turtle - **2.** [material] tortoiseshell.

carga *sf* - **1.** [acción] loading; **de carga frontal** front-loading - **2.** [cargamento - de avión, barco] cargo; [- de tren] freight; [- de camión] load - **3.** [peso] load - **4.** *fig* [sufrimiento] burden - **5.** [ataque, explosivo] charge; **carga de profundidad** depth charge; **volver a la carga** *fig* to persist - **6.** [de batería, condensador] charge - **7.** [para mechero, bolígrafo] refill - **8.** *fig* [componente] charge; **tiene una fuerte carga emocional** it's heavily charged with emotion - **9.** [impuesto] tax; **cargas sociales** social security contributions; **carga fiscal** tax burden.

cargado, **da** *adj* - **1.** [abarrotado]: **cargado (de)** loaded (with); **estar cargado de** *fam* to have loads of; **un árbol cargado de fruta** a tree laden with fruit - **2.** [arma] loaded - **3.** [bebida] strong - **4.** [bochornoso - habitación] stuffy; [- tiempo] sultry, close; [- cielo] overcast - **5.**: **cargado de hombros** round-shouldered *(s)*.

cargador *sm* - **1.** [de arma] chamber - **2.** [persona] loader; **cargador de muelle** docker, stevedore - **3.** ELECTR charger.

cargamento *sm* cargo.

cargante *adj fam fig* annoying.

cargar [16] <> *vt* - **1.** [gen] to load; [pluma, mechero] to refill - **2.** [peso encima] to throw over one's shoulder - **3.** ELECTR to charge; INFORM to load - **4.** *fig* [responsabilidad, tarea] to give, to lay upon; **cargar a alguien de deudas** to encumber sb with debts - **5.** *fam fig* [molestar] to annoy - **6.** [producir pesadez - suj: humo] to make stuffy; [- suj: comida] to bloat - **7.** [gravar]: **cargar un impuesto a algo/alguien** to tax sthg/sb - **8.** [importe, factura, deuda]: **cargar algo (a)** to charge sthg (to); **cárguelo a mi cuenta** charge it to my account. <> *vi* - **1.** [recaer]: **cargar sobre alguien** to fall on sb - **2.** [atacar]: **cargar (contra)** to charge.
- **cargar con** *vi* - **1.** [paquete etc] to carry away - **2.** *fig* [coste, responsabilidad] to bear; [consecuencias] to accept; [culpa] to get.
- **cargarse** *vprnl* - **1.** *fam* [romper] to break - **2.** *fam* [suspender] to fail - **3.** *fam* [matar - persona] to bump off; [- animal] to kill - **4.** [de humo] to get stuffy - **5.** [colmarse]: **cargarse de** to be loaded down with - **6.** ELECTR to become charged; INFORM to load - **7.** *loc*: **¡te la vas a cargar!** *fam* you're in for it!

cargo *sm* - **1.** [gen, ECON & DER] charge; **con cargo a** charged to; **sin cargo** free of charge; **correr a cargo de** to be borne by; **estar a cargo de algo**, **tener algo a cargo de uno** to be in charge of sthg; **las personas a mi cargo** the people in my care; **hacerse cargo de** [asumir el control de] to take charge of; [ocuparse de] to take care of; [comprender] to understand; **tener cargo de conciencia** to feel pangs of conscience, to feel remorse - **2.** [empleo] post, position; **alto cargo** high-ranking official; **es un cargo público** he holds public office.

cargosear *vt* C Sur to annoy, to pester.

cargoso, **sa** *adj* C Sur annoying.

carguero *sm* cargo boat.

cariacontecido, **da** *adj* crestfallen.

cariado, **da** *adj* decayed.

cariar [8] *vt* to decay.
- **cariarse** *vprnl* to decay.

cariátide *sf* caryatid.

Caribe *sm*: el (mar) Caribe the Caribbean (Sea).

caribeño, ña <> *adj* Caribbean. <> *sm, f* native/inhabitant of the Caribbean Islands.

caricatura *sf* - **1.** [de personaje, situación] caricature - **2.** *Méx* [dibujos animados] cartoon.

caricaturesco, ca *adj* caricature *(antes de s)*.

caricaturista *smf* caricaturist.

caricaturizar [13] *vt* to caricature.

caricia *sf* [a persona] caress; [a perro, gato etc] stroke.

caridad *sf* charity.

caries *sf inv* tooth decay; **tengo dos caries** I have two cavities.

carillón *sm* carillon.

cariñena *sm wine from Cariñena, in the province of Zaragoza.*

cariño *sm* - **1.** [afecto] affection; **tomar cariño a** to grow fond of; **con mucho cariño** with great affection - **2.** [cuidado] loving care - **3.** [apelativo] love.

cariñoso, sa *adj* affectionate.

carioca <> *adj* of/relating to Rio de Janeiro. <> *smf* native/inhabitant of Rio de Janeiro.

carisma *sm* charisma.

carismático, ca *adj* charismatic.

Cáritas *sf charitable organization run by the Catholic Church.*

caritativo, va *adj* charitable.

cariz *sm* look, appearance; **tomar mal/buen cariz** to take a turn for the worse/better.

carlinga *sf* [AERON - para piloto] cockpit; [- para pasajeros] cabin.

carlista *adj & smf* Carlist.

carmelita *adj & smf* Carmelite.

carmesí (*pl* carmesíes o carmesís) *adj & sm* crimson.

carmín <> *adj* [color] carmine. <> *sm* - **1.** [color] carmine - **2.** [lápiz de labios] lipstick.

carnada *sf lit & fig* bait.

carnal <> *adj* - **1.** [de la carne] carnal - **2.** [primo] first *(antes de s)*. <> *sm Méx fam* [amigo] mate.

carnaval *sm* carnival.

carnavalada *sf fam* farce.

carnavalesco, ca *adj* carnival *(antes de s)*.

carnaza *sf lit & fig* bait.

carne *sf* - **1.** [de persona, fruta] flesh; **en carne viva** raw; **entrado** o **metido en carnes** plump; **ser de carne y hueso** *fig* to be human - **2.** [alimento] meat; **carne de cerdo** pork; **carne de cordero** lamb; **carne picada** mince; **carne de ternera** veal; **carne de vaca** beef; **poner toda la carne en el asador** *fig* to go for broke; **ser**

carne de cañón to be cannon fodder; **poner la carne de gallina a alguien** [de frío] to give sb goose pimples; [de miedo] to give sb the creeps.

➡ **carne de membrillo** *sf* quince jelly.

carné, carnet (*pl* carnets) *sm* - **1.** [documento] card; **carné de conducir** driving licence; **carné de identidad** identity card; **carné de estudiante** student card; **carné de prensa** press pass - **2.** [agenda] notebook.

carnear *vt Andes & R Dom* to slaughter, to butcher.

carnet *sm* = carné.

carnicería *sf* - **1.** [tienda] butcher's - **2.** *fig* [destrozo] butchery *(U)* - **3.** *fig* [masacre] carnage *(U)*.

carnicero, ra <> *adj* [animal] carnivorous. <> *sm, f lit & fig* [persona] butcher.

➡ **carnicero** *sm* ZOOL carnivore.

cárnico, ca *adj* meat *(antes de s)*.

carnitas *sfpl Méx small pieces of braised pork.*

carnívoro, ra *adj* carnivorous.

➡ **carnívoro** *sm* carnivore.

carnosidad *sf* - **1.** [de una herida] proud flesh *(U)* - **2.** [gordura] fleshy part.

carnoso, sa *adj* fleshy; [labios] full.

caro, ra *adj* - **1.** [precio] expensive - **2.** *culto* [querido] cherished, fond.

➡ **caro** *adv*: **costar caro** to be expensive; *fig* to cost dear; **vender caro algo** to sell sthg at a high price; *fig* not to give sthg up easily; **pagar caro algo** *fig* to pay dearly for sthg; **salir caro** to be expensive; *fig* to cost dear.

carolingio, gia *adj & sm, f* Carolingian.

carota *smf fam* cheeky so-and-so.

carótida *adj & sf* carotid.

carozo *sm R Dom* stone, pit *US*.

carpa *sf* - **1.** [pez] carp - **2.** [de circo] big top; [para fiestas etc] marquee - **3.** *Amér* [tienda de campaña] tent.

carpanta *sf fam* ravenous hunger.

Cárpatos *smpl*: los Cárpatos the Carpathians.

carpeta *sf* file, folder.

carpetazo *sm*: **dar carpetazo a algo** to shelve sthg.

carpetovetónico, ca *adj* deeply Spanish.

carpintería *sf* - **1.** [arte] carpentry; [de puertas y ventanas] joinery - **2.** [taller] carpenter's/joiner's shop.

carpintero, ra *sm, f* carpenter; [de puertas y ventanas] joiner.

carraca *sf* - **1.** [instrumento] rattle - **2.** *fig* [cosa vieja] old crock.

carrara *sm* Carrara marble.

carraspear *vi* - **1.** [hablar ronco] to speak with a hoarse voice - **2.** [toser] to clear one's throat.

carraspera *sf* hoarseness.

carrera *sf* - **1.** [acción de correr] run, running *(U)* - **2.** *fig* & DEP race; **carrera armamentística** o **de armamentos** arms race; **carrera contra reloj** race against the clock; **carrera ciclista** cycle race; **carrera de coches** motor race; **carrera de obstáculos** steeplechase - **3.** [trayecto] route - **4.** [de taxi] ride - **5.** [estudios] university course; **hacer la carrera de derecho** to study law (at university) - **6.** [profesión] career; **hacer carrera** [triunfar] to succeed (in life) - **7.** [en medias] ladder UK, run US - **8.** [calle] street; **hacer la carrera** [prostituirse] to walk the streets.

carrerilla *sf*: **coger** o **tomar carrerilla** to take a run-up.
➤ **de carrerilla** *loc adv* by heart.

carreta *sf* cart.

carrete *sm* - **1.** [de hilo] bobbin, reel; [de alambre] coil - **2.** FOTO roll (of film) - **3.** [para pescar] reel - **4.** [de máquina de escribir] spool - **5.** *loc*: **dar carrete a alguien** to draw sb out.

carretera *sf* road; **viaje por carretera** road journey; **carretera de circunvalación** ring road; **carretera comarcal** ≃ B road UK; **carretera de cuota** *Méx* toll road; **carretera nacional** ≃ A road UK, state highway US; *Méx*: **carretera de cuota** toll road.

carretero, **ra** ⬦ *sm, f* [conductor] carter; **fumar como un carretero** *fig* to smoke like a chimney. ⬦ *adj Amér* road; **un accidente carretero** a road accident; **tráfico carretero** road traffic.
➤ **carretero** *sm Amér* [carretera] road.

carretilla *sf* wheelbarrow.

carril *sm* - **1.** [de carretera] lane; **carril de aceleración** fast lane; **carril bici** cycle lane; **carril bus** bus lane - **2.** [de vía de tren] rail - **3.** [de ruedas] rut.

carrillo *sm* cheek; **comer a dos carrillos** *fig* to cram one's face with food.

carrito *sm* trolley UK, cart US.

carro *sm* - **1.** [vehículo] cart; **carro de combate** MIL tank; **¡para el carro!** [espera un momento] hang on a minute! - **2.** [de máquina de escribir] carriage - **3.** *Andes, Amér C, Caribe* & *Méx* [automóvil] car - **4.** *Méx*: **carro comedor** [en tren] dining car, restaurant car.

carrocería *sf* bodywork UK, body.

carromato *sm* - **1.** [carro] wagon - **2.** [coche viejo] old car.

carroña *sf* carrion.

carroza ⬦ *sf* [vehículo] carriage. ⬦ *smf fam* [viejo] old fogey.

carruaje *sm* carriage.

carrusel *sm* - **1.** [tiovivo] carousel, merry-go-round - **2.** [de caballos] mounted patrol.

carta *sf* - **1.** letter; **echar una carta** to post a letter; **carta certificada/urgente** registered/express letter; **carta de presentación** letter of introduction; **carta de recomendación** reference (letter) - **2.** [naipe] (playing) card; **echar las cartas a alguien** to tell sb's fortune *(with cards)* - **3.** [en restaurante] menu; **carta de vinos** wine list - **4.** [mapa] map; NÁUT chart; **carta astral** star chart - **5.** [documento] charter; **carta de crédito** COM letter of credit; **carta de naturaleza** naturalization papers *pl*; **carta de pago** COM receipt; **carta de trabajo** work permit; **carta verde** green card; **cartas credenciales** letters of credence - **6.** *loc*: **a carta cabal** through and through; **jugarse la última carta** to play one's last card; **jugarse todo a una carta** to put all one's eggs in one basket; **no saber a qué carta quedarse** to be unsure; **poner las cartas boca arriba** o **sobre la mesa** to put one's cards on the table; **tomar cartas en un asunto** to intervene in a matter; **dar carta blanca a alguien** to give sb carte blanche.
➤ **carta de ajuste** *sf* test card.
➤ **Carta de Derechos** *sf* Bill of Rights.
➤ **Carta Magna** *sf* Constitution.

cartabón *sm* set square.

cartapacio *sm* - **1.** [carpeta] folder - **2.** [cuaderno] note book.

cartearse *vprnl* to correspond.

cartel *sm* - **1.** [póster] poster; **'prohibido fijar carteles'** 'billposters will be prosecuted' - **2.** [letrero] sign - **3.** *fig* [fama]: **de cartel** famous, star *(antes de s)*; **tener cartel** to be all the rage.

cártel *sm* cartel.

cartelero, **ra** *adj* popular, big-name.

cartelera *sf* - **1.** [tablón] hoarding, billboard - **2.** PRENSA entertainments page; **estar en cartelera** to be showing; **lleva un año en cartelera** it's been running for a year.

cartelista *smf* poster artist.

carteo *sm* correspondence.

cárter *sm* AUTO housing.

cartera *sf* - **1.** [para dinero] wallet - **2.** [para documentos] briefcase; [sin asa] portfolio; [de colegial] satchel; **tener algo en cartera** *fig* to have sthg in the pipeline - **3.** COM, FIN & POLÍT portfolio; **cartera de pedidos** [pedidos pendientes] orders *pl* in hand; [pedidos atrasados] backlog; **cartera de valores** portfolio - **4.** [bolsillo] pocket flap - **5.** *Andes* & *C Sur* [bolso] handbag UK, purse US.

carterista *smf* pickpocket.

cartero, **ra** *sm, f* postman (*f* postwoman).

cartesiano, **na** *adj* & *sm, f* FILOS Cartesian.

cartilaginoso, **sa** *adj* cartilaginous.

cartílago *sm* cartilage.

cartilla *sf* - **1.** [documento] book; **cartilla (de ahorros)** savings book; **cartilla militar** *booklet to say one has completed one's military service*; **cartilla del paro** ≃ UB40 *UK, registration card issued to the unemployed*; **cartilla de la seguridad social** social security card - **2.** [para aprender a leer] primer - **3.** *loc*: **leerle la cartilla a alguien** to read sb the riot act; **no saberse la cartilla** not to have a clue.

cartografía *sf* cartography.

cartógrafo, **fa** *sm, f* cartographer.

cartomancia *sf* cartomancy.

cartón *sm* - **1.** [material] cardboard; **cartón piedra** papier mâché - **2.** [de cigarrillos, leche] carton; [de huevos] box.

cartoné ➤ **en cartoné** *loc adv* bound in boards.

cartuchera *sf* cartridge belt.

cartucho *sm* - **1.** [de arma] cartridge; **quemar el último cartucho** *fig* to play one's last card - **2.** [envoltorio - de monedas] roll; [- de avellanas etc] paper cone.

cartujo, **ja** *adj* Carthusian.
➤ **cartujo** *sm* - **1.** [religioso] Carthusian - **2.** *fig* [persona retraída] hermit.
➤ **cartuja** *sf* charterhouse.

cartulina *sf* card; **cartulina amarilla/roja** FÚT yellow/red card.

casa *sf* - **1.** [edificio] house; **casa adosada** semi-detached house; **casa de campo** country house; **casa unifamiliar** *house (usually detached)* on an estate; **se le cae la casa encima** [se deprime] it's the end of the world for him; **echar** *o* **tirar la casa por la ventana** to spare no expense; **empezar la casa por el tejado** to put the cart before the horse; **ser de andar por casa** [sencillo] to be simple *o* basic; **en casa del herrero cuchillo de palo** *prov* the shoemaker's wife is always worst shod - **2.** [hogar] home; **en casa** at home; **ir a casa** to go home; **pásate por mi casa** come round to my place; **jugar en casa/fuera de casa** to play at home/away - **3.** [familia] family - **4.** [linaje] house - **5.** [empresa] company; **vino de la casa** house wine; **casa de empeño** *o* **préstamo** pawnshop; **casa de citas** brothel; **casa discográfica** record company - **6.** [organismo]: **casa Consistorial** town hall; **casa de huéspedes** guesthouse; **casa de juego** gambling house; **casa de putas** brothel; **casa de socorro** first-aid post.

Casa Rosada

Casa Rosada (the "pink house") in Buenos Aires, is the name of the Argentinian Presidential Palace. Its pink colour was originally chosen (for an earlier building) by president Domingo Sarmiento (1868-74) to represent a combination betweeen the two feuding political traditions of nineteenth century Argentina - red for the Federalists and white for the Unitarians. Argentina's presidents have addressed the people from the balcony of the palace, but the most famous orator to use it was Evita Peron, so there was a huge controversy when film director Alan Parker obtained permission to use the balcony when filming his musical "Evita" in 1997, with Madonna in the title role.

casaca *sf* frock coat.

casación *sf* annulment.

casadero, **ra** *adj* marriageable.

casado, **da** ◇ *adj*: **casado (con)** married (to). ◇ *sm, f* married man (*f* married woman); **los recién casados** the newly-weds.

casamentero, **ra** ◇ *adj* matchmaking. ◇ *sm, f* matchmaker.

casamiento *sm* wedding, marriage.

casanova *sm* Casanova.

casar ◇ *vt* - **1.** [en matrimonio] to marry - **2.** [unir] to fit together. ◇ *vi* to match.
➤ **casarse** *vprnl*: **casarse (con)** to get married (to); **casarse por la iglesia/lo civil** to have a church/civil wedding; **no casarse con nadie** *fig* to be totally impartial.

cascabel *sm* (small) bell; **poner el cascabel al gato** *fig* to dare to go ahead.

cascado, **da** *adj* - **1.** *fam* [estropeado] bust; [persona, ropa] worn-out - **2.** [ronco] rasping.
➤ **cascada** *sf* [de agua] waterfall; **en cascada** one after another.

cascanueces *sm inv* nutcracker.

cascar [10] ◇ *vt* - **1.** [romper] to crack - **2.** *fam* [dañar] to damage, to harm; **cascarla** *fig* to kick the bucket - **3.** *fam* [la voz] to make hoarse - **4.** *fam* [pegar] to thump. ◇ *vi fam* [hablar] to witter on.
➤ **cascarse** *vprnl* [romperse] to crack; **cascársela** *vulg* to jerk off.

cáscara *sf* - **1.** [de almendra, huevo etc] shell - **2.** [de limón, naranja] skin, peel - **3.** [de plátano] skin.

cascarilla *sf* husk.

cascarón *sm* eggshell; **salir del cascarón** *fig* to leave the nest.

cascarrabias *smf inv* grouch, misery guts *sing*.

casco *sm* - **1.** [para la cabeza] helmet; [de motorista] crash helmet - **2.** [de barco] hull - **3.** [de ciudad]: **casco antiguo** old (part of) town; **casco urbano** city centre - **4.** [de caballo] hoof - **5.** [envase] empty bottle - **6.** [pedazo - de objeto] fragment, piece; [- de cebolla] segment.

cascos *smpl fam* [cabeza] nut *sing*; **calentarse** *o* **romperse los cascos** to rack one's brains; **ser alegre** *o* **ligero de cascos** to be scatter-brained; [auriculares] headphones.

cascote *sm* piece of rubble.

caserío *sm* - **1.** [pueblecito] hamlet - **2.** [casa de campo] country house.

casero, ra <> *adj* - **1.** [de casa - comida] homemade; [- trabajos] domestic; [- reunión, velada] at home; [de la familia] family *(antes de s)* - **2.** [hogareño] home-loving. <> *sm, f* - **1.** [propietario] landlord (*f* landlady) - **2.** [encargado] house agent.

caserón *sm* large, rambling house.

caseta *sf* - **1.** [casa pequeña] hut - **2.** [en la playa] bathing hut - **3.** [de feria] stall, booth - **4.** [para perro] kennel - **5.** *Méx*: **caseta de cobro** tollbooth; **caseta telefónica** phone box, phone booth *US*.

casete, cassette [ka'sete] <> *sf* [cinta] cassette. <> *sm* [aparato] cassette recorder.

casi *adv* almost; **casi me muero** I almost *o* nearly died; **casi no dormí** I hardly slept at all; **casi, casi** almost, just about; **casi nunca** hardly ever; **casi nada** hardly anything.

casilla *sf* - **1.** [taquilla] box office - **2.** [de caja, armario] compartment; [para cartas] pigeonhole; **casilla de correos** *Andes & R Dom* PO Box; **casilla postal** *Amér C, Caribe & Méx* PO Box - **3.** [en un impreso] box - **4.** [de ajedrez etc] square - **5.** *Méx* [de votación] polling booth - **6.** *loc*: **sacar a alguien de sus casillas** to drive sb mad; **salir** *o* **salirse de sus casillas** to fly off the handle.

casillero *sm* - **1.** [mueble] set of pigeonholes - **2.** [casilla] pigeonhole.

casino *sm* - **1.** [para jugar] casino - **2.** [asociación] (social) club.

casis ['kasis] *sm inv* - **1.** [arbusto] blackcurrant bush - **2.** [fruto] blackcurrant - **3.** [licor] cassis.

caso *sm* - **1.** [gen, DER & GRAM] case; **el caso es que...** the fact is (that)...; **en el mejor/peor de los casos** at best/worst; **en todo caso** in any case; **caso de conciencia** matter of conscience; **caso de fuerza mayor** force (*U*) of circumstance; **caso clínico** clinical case - **2.** [ocasión] occasion; **en caso de** in the event of; **en caso de que** if; **(en) caso de que venga** should she come; **en cualquier** *o* **todo caso** in any event *o* case - **3.** *loc*: **hacer caso a** to pay attention to; **hacer caso omiso de** to ignore; **ir al caso** to get to the point; **no hacer** *o* **venir al caso** to be irrelevant; **ser un caso** *fam* to be a case, to be a right one; **ser un caso perdido** to be a lost cause; **tú ni caso** take no notice.

caspa *sf* dandruff.

Caspio *sm*: **el (mar) Caspio** the Caspian Sea.

cáspita *interj*: **¡cáspita!** *desus* [sorpresa] my word!; [enfado] dash it!

casque *etc* ▷ **cascar**.

casquete *sm* [gorro] skullcap.

casquete esférico *sm* segment of a sphere.

casquete polar *sm* polar cap.

casquillo *sm* [de munición] case; **casquillo de bala** bullet shell.

casquivano, na *adj fam* harebrained.

cassette = casete.

casta *sf* ▷ **casto**.

castaña *sf* ▷ **castaño**.

castañazo *sm fam* bash.

castañetear <> *vt* [dedos] to snap. <> *vi* [dientes] to chatter.

castañeteo *sm* - **1.** [de castañuelas] clacking - **2.** [de dientes] chattering - **3.** [de dedos] snapping.

castaño, ña *adj* [color] chestnut.

castaño *sm* - **1.** [color] chestnut; **pasar de castaño oscuro** *fig* to be beyond a joke - **2.** [árbol] chestnut (tree); **castaño de Indias** horse-chestnut (tree) - **3.** [madera] chestnut.

castaña *sf* - **1.** [fruto] chestnut; **sacarle a alguien las castañas del fuego** *fam* to get sb out of trouble - **2.** *fam* [golpe] thump - **3.** *fam* [borrachera]: **agarrarse una castaña** to get legless.

castañuela *sf* castanet; **estar como unas castañuelas** to be very happy.

castellanizar [13] *vt* to hispanicize.

castellano, na *adj & sm, f* Castilian.

castellano *sm* [lengua] (Castilian) Spanish.

Castellano ▬▬▬

♠♠♠ Castellano (Castilian) is the official term for Spanish used in the Spanish Constitution of 1978, but español (Spanish) and lengua española (Spanish language) are often used when referring to Spanish as opposed to French, Italian or German, and also in linguistic or academic contexts. Elsewhere, the term español is often avoided because of its associations with either the former colonizing country (in the case of Latin America) or (in Spain) with the domination of Spanish over the other languages spoken in Spain.

casticismo *sm* purism.

castidad *sf* chastity.

castigador, **ra** *fam* ◇ *adj* seductive. ◇ *sm, f* ladykiller (*f* man-eater).

castigar [16] *vt* - **1.** [imponer castigo] to punish - **2.** DEP to penalize - **3.** [maltratar] to damage - **4.** *fig* [enamorar] to seduce.

castigo *sm* - **1.** [sanción] punishment; **castigo ejemplar** exemplary punishment - **2.** [sufrimiento] suffering *(U)*; [daño] damage *(U)* - **3.** DEP penalty.

castillo *sm* - **1.** [edificio] castle; **castillos en el aire** o **de naipes** *fig* castles in the air; **castillo de naipes** house of cards - **2.** NÁUT: **castillo de popa** quarterdeck; **castillo de proa** forecastle.

castizo, **za** *adj* pure; [autor] purist.

casto, **ta** *adj* chaste.
◆ **casta** *sf* - **1.** [linaje] stock, lineage - **2.** [especie, calidad] breed - **3.** [en la India] caste.

castor *sm* beaver.

castración *sf* castration.

castrar *vt* - **1.** [animal, persona] to castrate; [gato] to doctor - **2.** *fig* [debilitar] to sap, to impair.

castrense *adj* military.

castrista *adj* & *smf* Castroist.

casual *adj* chance, accidental.

casualidad *sf* coincidence; **fue pura casualidad** it was sheer coincidence; **dio la casualidad de que...** it so happened that...; **por casualidad** by chance; **¡qué casualidad!** what a coincidence!

casualmente *adv* by chance.

casuístico, **ca** *adj* casuistic.
◆ **casuística** *sf* casuistry.

casulla *sf* chasuble.

cata *sf* tasting; **cata de vino** wine tasting.

catabolismo *sm* catabolism.

cataclismo *sm* cataclysm.

catacumbas *sfpl* catacombs.

catador, **ra** *sm, f* taster.

catadura *sf* *fig* look, appearance.

catafalco *sm* catafalque.

catalán, **ana** *adj* & *sm, f* Catalan, Catalonian.
◆ **catalán** *sm* [lengua] Catalan.

Catalán

Catalan is one of several official languages in Spain in addition to Castilian Spanish. Like Spanish (**castellano**) and Galician (**gallego**) it developed from late Latin. It is spoken by about six million people in Catalonia in northeastern Spain. Close relatives of Catalan are spoken in the Balearic Islands (**mallorquín**) and the Valencian region (**valenciano**), though whether they are dialects of Catalan or separate languages remains an issue of political as much as linguistic controversy. Catalonia's economic development in the latter part of the 19th century encouraged a renaissance in the use of the language as a literary medium. During Franco's dictatorship (1939-75), Catalan was effectively banned for official purposes, but it continued to be used in everyday life as well as in literature. Since the return of democracy, Catalonia's regional government has promoted Catalan as the official language for use in education and public administration.

catalanismo *sm* - **1.** [palabra] Catalanism - **2.** POLÍT Catalan nationalism.

catalejo *sm* telescope.

catalepsia *sf* catalepsy.

catalítico, **ca** *adj* QUÍM catalytic.

catalizador, **ra** *adj* - **1.** QUÍM catalytic - **2.** *fig* [impulsor] catalysing *(antes de s)*.
◆ **catalizador** *sm* - **1.** *fig* & QUÍM catalyst - **2.** AUTO catalytic converter.

catalizar [13] *vt* - **1.** QUÍM to catalyse - **2.** *fig* [impulsar] to provoke.

catalogación *sf* cataloguing.

catalogar [16] *vt* - **1.** [en catálogo] to catalogue - **2.** [clasificar]: **catalogar a alguien (de)** to class sb (as).

catálogo *sm* catalogue.

Cataluña *n pr* Catalonia.

catamarán *sm* catamaran.

cataplasma *sf* - **1.** MED poultice - **2.** *fam fig* [pesado] bore.

catapulta *sf* catapult.

catapultar *vt* to catapult.

catar *vt* to taste.

catarata *sf* - **1.** [de agua] waterfall; **las cataratas del Iguazú** the Iguaçu Falls; **las cataratas del Niágara** the Niagara Falls - **2.** *(gen pl)* MED cataract.

catarro *sm* cold.

catarsis *sf inv* catharsis.

catártico, **ca** *adj* cathartic.

catastro *sm* land registry.

catástrofe *sf* catastrophe; [accidente] disaster; **catástrofe aérea** air disaster; **catástrofe natural** natural disaster.

catastrófico, **ca** *adj* catastrophic.

catastrofismo *sm* [pesimismo] scaremongering, alarmism.

catastrofista *adj* & *smf* alarmist.

catch [katʃ] *sm* DEP all-in wrestling.

cátcher ['katʃer] (*pl* catchers) *sm* DEP catcher.

catchup ['katʃup], **ketchup** *sm inv* ketchup.

cate *sm fam* fail.

catear *vt fam* - **1.** *Esp*: **he cateado las matemáticas** I failed *o* flunked *US* maths - **2.** *Amér* [registrar] to search.

catecismo *sm* catechism.

Catedr. (*abrev de* catedrático) Prof.

cátedra *sf* - **1.** [cargo - en universidad] chair; [- en instituto] post of head of department - **2.** [departamento] department - **3.** *loc*: **poner** *o* **sentar cátedra** to lay down the law.

catedral *sf* cathedral.

catedralicio, **cia** *adj* cathedral (*antes de s*).

catedrático, **ca** *sm*, *f* [de universidad] professor; [de instituto] head of department.

categoría *sf* - **1.** [gen] category; **categoría gramatical** part of speech - **2.** [posición social] standing; **de categoría** important - **3.** [calidad] quality; **de (primera) categoría** first-class.

categórico, **ca** *adj* categorical.

catequesis *sf inv* catechesis.

catequizar [13] *vt* - **1.** [enseñar religión] to instruct in the Christian doctrine - **2.** *fig* [adoctrinar] to convert.

caterva *sf* host, multitude.

cateto, **ta** *despec* ◇ *adj* uncultured, uncouth. ◇ *sm*, *f* country bumpkin.

cateto *sm* GEOM cathetus.

catire, **ra** *adj Caribe* blond (*f* blonde).

cátodo *sm* cathode.

catolicismo *sm* Catholicism.

católico, **ca** ◇ *adj* Catholic; **no estar muy católico** *fam fig* to be under the weather. ◇ *sm*, *f* Catholic.

catorce *num* fourteen; *ver también* **seis**.

catorceavo, **va** *num* fourteenth; **una catorceava parte** a fourteenth.

catre *sm* [cama] camp bed; **irse al catre** *fam* to hit the sack.

catrín, **ina** *sm*, *f Amér C & Méx fam* toff.

caucásico, **ca** *adj* & *sm*, *f* Caucasian.

cauce *sm* - **1.** *fig* & AGRIC channel - **2.** [de río] river-bed; **volver a su cauce** to return to normal.

caucho *sm* - **1.** [sustancia] rubber; **caucho sintético** synthetic rubber; **caucho vulcanizado** vulcanized rubber - **2.** [planta] rubber tree.

caudal *sm* - **1.** [cantidad de agua] flow, volume - **2.** [capital, abundancia] wealth.

caudaloso, **sa** *adj* - **1.** [río] with a large flow - **2.** [persona] wealthy, rich.

caudillaje *sm* leadership.

caudillo *sm* [en la guerra] leader, head.

Caudillo *sm*: **el Caudillo** HIST *title used to refer to Franco.*

causa *sf* - **1.** [origen, ideal] cause; **por una buena causa** for a good cause - **2.** [razón] reason; **a causa de** because of - **3.** DER case.

causal *adj* causal.

causalidad *sf* causality.

causante ◇ *adj*: **la razón causante** the cause. ◇ *smf* cause.

causar *vt* [gen] to cause; [impresión] to make; [placer] to give; **causar asombro a alguien** to amaze sb.

causticidad *sf lit & fig* causticity.

cáustico, **ca** *adj lit & fig* caustic.

cautela *sf* caution, cautiousness; **con cautela** cautiously.

cauteloso, **sa** ◇ *adj* cautious, careful. ◇ *sm*, *f* cautious person.

cauterizar [13] *vt* to cauterize.

cautivador, **ra** ◇ *adj* captivating, enchanting. ◇ *sm*, *f* charmer.

cautivar *vt* - **1.** [apresar] to capture - **2.** [seducir] to captivate, to enchant.

cautiverio *sm* captivity; **vivir en cautiverio** to live in captivity.

cautividad *sf* = cautiverio.

cautivo, **va** *adj* & *sm*, *f* captive.

cauto, **ta** *adj* cautious, careful.

cava ◇ *sm* [bebida] cava. ◇ *sf* - **1.** [bodega] wine cellar - **2.** [excavación] digging.

cavar *vt* & *vi* [gen] to dig; [con azada] to hoe.

caverna *sf* cave; [más grande] cavern.

cavernícola *smf* caveman (*f* cavewoman).

cavernoso, **sa** *adj* cavernous; [voz, tos] hollow.

caviar *sm* caviar.

cavidad *sf* cavity; [formada con las manos] cup.

cavilación *sf* deep thought, pondering.

cavilar *vi* to think deeply, to ponder.

caviloso, **sa** *adj* thoughtful, pensive.

cayado *sm* - **1.** [de pastor] crook - **2.** [de obispo] crozier.

cayera *etc* ▷ **caer**.

caza <> *sf* **- 1.** [acción de cazar] hunting; **dar caza a** to hunt down; **salir** *o* **ir de caza** to go hunting; **caza de brujas** *fig* witch-hunt; **caza furtiva** poaching **- 2.** [animales, carne] game; **caza mayor/menor** big/small game. <> *sm* fighter (plane).

cazabombardero *sm* fighter-bomber.

cazador, ra <> *adj* hunting. <> *sm, f* [persona] hunter; **cazador furtivo** poacher.

➤ **cazadora** *sf* [prenda] bomber jacket.

cazadotes *sm inv* fortune hunter.

cazalla *sf* [bebida] aniseed-flavoured spirit.

cazar [13] *vt* **- 1.** [animales etc] to hunt **- 2.** *fig* [pillar, atrapar] to catch; [en matrimonio] to trap.

cazo *sm* saucepan.

cazoleta *sf* **- 1.** [recipiente] pot **- 2.** [de pipa] bowl.

cazuela *sf* **- 1.** [recipiente] pot; [de barro] earthenware pot; [para el horno] casserole (dish) **- 2.** [guiso] casserole, stew; **a la cazuela** casseroled.

cazurro, rra <> *adj* [bruto] stupid. <> *sm, f* [bruto] idiot, fool.

cc - 1. (*abrev de* **centímetro cúbico**) cc (*cubic centimetre*) **- 2.** (*abrev de* **copia de carbón**) cc (*carbon copy*).

c/c (*abrev de* **cuenta corriente**) a/c.

CC (*abrev de* **corriente continua**) DC.

CC OO (*abrev de* **Comisiones Obreras**) *sfpl* Spanish Communist-inspired trade union.

CD *sm* **- 1.** (*abrev de* **compact disc**) CD **- 2.** (*abrev de* **club deportivo**) sports club; [en fútbol] FC **- 3.** (*abrev de* **cuerpo diplomático**) CD.

CDI (*abrev de* **compact disc interactive**) *sm* IN-FORM CDI.

CD-ROM (*abrev de* **compact disc read only memory**) *sm* CD–ROM.

ce *sf*: **ce por be** *fig* in great detail.

CE <> *sm* (*abrev de* **Consejo de Europa**) CE. <> *sf* **- 1.** (*abrev de* **Comunidad Europea**) EC **- 2.** (*abrev de* **Comisión Europea**) EC **- 3.** (*abrev de* **constitución española**) Spanish Constitution.

cebada *sf* barley.

cebador *sm* **- 1.** [de fluorescente] ballast **- 2.** [de pólvora] primer.

cebar *vt* **- 1.** [sobrealimentar] to fatten (up) **- 2.** [máquina, arma] to prime **- 3.** [anzuelo] to bait **- 4.** *R Dom* [mate] to prepare, to brew.

➤ **cebarse en** *vprnl* to take it out on.

cebo *sm* **- 1.** [para cazar] bait **- 2.** [para alimentar] feed, food **- 3.** *fig* [para atraer] incentive.

cebolla *sf* onion.

cebolleta *sf* **- 1.** BOT spring onion **- 2.** [en vinagre] pickled onion; [muy pequeña] silverskin onion.

cebollino *sm* **- 1.** BOT chive; [cebolleta] spring onion **- 2.** *fam* [necio] idiot.

cebón, ona *adj* fattened.

➤ **cebón** *sm* pig.

cebra *sf* zebra.

cebú (*pl* cebúes *o* cebús) *sm* zebu.

ceca *sf* mint.

➤ **Ceca** *sf*: **ir de la Ceca a la Meca** *fig* to go here, there and everywhere.

CECA (*abrev de* **Comunidad Europea del Carbón y del Acero**) *sf* ECSC (*European Coal & Steel Community*).

cecear *vi* to lisp.

ceceo *sm* lisp.

cecina *sf* dried, salted meat.

cedazo *sm* sieve.

ceder <> *vt* **- 1.** [traspasar, transferir] to hand over **- 2.** [conceder] to give up; **'ceda el paso'** 'give way'; **ceder la palabra a alguien** to give the floor to sb. <> *vi* **- 1.** [venirse abajo] to give way **- 2.** [destensarse] to give, to become loose **- 3.** [disminuir] to abate **- 4.** [rendirse] to give up; **ceder a** to give in to; **ceder en** to give up on **- 5.** [ensancharse] to stretch.

cedilla *sf* cedilla.

cedro *sm* cedar.

cédula *sf* document; **cédula de citación** summons *sing*; **cédula de habitabilidad** *certificate stating that a place is habitable*; **cédula hipotecaria** mortgage bond; **cédula (de identidad)** *Amér* identity card; **cédula de vecindad** identity card.

cefalea *sf* MED headache, cephalalgia.

cefalópodo *sm* cephalopod.

cegador, ra *adj* blinding.

cegar [35] <> *vt* **- 1.** [gen] to blind **- 2.** [tapar - ventana] to block off; [- tubo] to block up. <> *vi* to be blinding.

➤ **cegarse** *vprnl lit & fig* to be blinded.

cegato, ta *fam* <> *adj* short-sighted. <> *sm, f* short-sighted person.

cegué *etc* ⊳ **cegar**.

ceguera *sf lit & fig* blindness.

Ceilán *n pr* Ceylon.

ceja *sf* **- 1.** ANAT eyebrow; **quemarse las cejas** *fam* to burn the midnight oil; **se le metió entre ceja y ceja** *fam* he got it into his head; **tener a alguien entre ceja y ceja** *fam* not to be able to stand the sight of sb **- 2.** [borde] border, edging **- 3.** [MÚS - puente] bridge; [- cejilla] capo.

cejar *vi*: **cejar en** to give up on.

cejijunto, ta *adj* **- 1.** [persona] bushy-eyebrowed **- 2.** [gesto] frowning.

cejilla *sf* MÚS capo.

celada *sf* [trampa] trick, trap.

celador, ra *sm, f* [de colegio, hospital] porter; [de prisión] warder; [de museo] attendant.

CELAM *sm* (*abrev de* **Consejo Episcopal Latinoamericano**), *Latin American Episcopal Council*.

celda *sf* cell; **celda de castigo** solitary confinement cell.

celdilla *sf* cell.

celebérrimo, ma *superl* = **célebre**.

celebración *sf* - **1.** [festejo] celebration - **2.** [realización] holding.

celebrar *vt* - **1.** [festejar] to celebrate - **2.** [llevar a cabo] to hold; [oficio religioso] to celebrate - **3.** [alegrarse de] to be delighted with - **4.** [alabar] to praise, to applaud.

← **celebrarse** *vprnl* - **1.** [festejarse] to be celebrated; **esa fiesta se celebra el 24 de julio** that festivity falls on 24th July - **2.** [llevarse a cabo] to take place, to be held.

célebre *adj* famous, celebrated.

celebridad *sf* - **1.** [fama] fame - **2.** [persona famosa] celebrity.

celeridad *sf* speed.

celeste *adj* - **1.** [del cielo] celestial, heavenly - **2.** ▷ **azul**.

celestial *adj* celestial, heavenly.

celestina *sf* lovers' go-between.

celibato *sm* celibacy.

célibe *adj* & *smf* celibate.

celo *sm* - **1.** [esmero] zeal, keenness - **2.** [devoción] devotion - **3.** [de animal] heat; **en celo** on heat, in season - **4.** [cinta adhesiva] Sellotape® UK, Scotch tape® US.

← **celos** *smpl* jealousy (U); **dar celos a alguien** to make sb jealous; **tener celos de alguien** to be jealous of sb.

celofán *sm* cellophane.

celosía *sf* lattice window, jalousie.

celoso, sa ◇ *adj* - **1.** [con celos] jealous - **2.** [cumplidor] keen, eager. ◇ *sm, f* [con celos] jealous person.

celta ◇ *adj* Celtic. ◇ *smf* [persona] Celt. ◇ *sm* [lengua] Celtic.

celtíbero, ra, celtibero, ra *adj* & *sm, f* Celtiberian.

céltico, ca *adj* Celtic.

célula *sf* cell.

← **célula fotoeléctrica** *sf* photoelectric cell, electric eye.

← **célula fotovoltaica** *sf* photovoltaic cell.

← **célula madre** *sf* stem cell.

celular ◇ *adj* cellular, cell (*antes de s*). ◇ *sm* Amér mobile UK o cell US phone.

celulitis *sf inv* cellulitis.

celuloide *sm* - **1.** QUÍM celluloid - **2.** [película] movie, film UK.

celulosa *sf* cellulose.

cementerio *sm* - **1.** [para personas] cemetery, graveyard - **2.** [de cosas inutilizables] dump; **cementerio de automóviles** o **coches** scrapyard; **cementerio nuclear** o **radioactivo** nuclear dumping ground.

cemento *sm* [gen] cement; [hormigón] concrete; **cemento armado** reinforced concrete.

cena *sf* dinner, evening meal; **dar una cena** to give a dinner party; **cena de despedida** farewell dinner; **cena de negocios** business dinner.

← **Última Cena** *sf*: **la Última Cena** the Last Supper.

cenáculo *sm* culto & fig [círculo] circle.

cenador *sm* arbour, bower.

cenagal *sm* bog, marsh.

cenagoso, sa *adj* muddy, boggy.

cenar ◇ *vt* to have for dinner. ◇ *vi* to have dinner.

cencerro *sm* cowbell; **estar como un cencerro** fam fig to be as mad as a hatter.

cenefa *sf* border.

cenicero *sm* ashtray.

ceniciento, ta *adj* ashen, ash-grey.

← **cenicienta** *sf* fig Cinderella.

cenit, zenit *sm* lit & fig zenith.

cenital *adj* midday (*antes de s*).

cenizo, za *adj* ashen, ash-grey.

← **cenizo** *sm* - **1.** [mala suerte] bad luck - **2.** [gafe] jinx.

← **ceniza** *sf* ash.

← **cenizas** *sfpl* [de cadáver] ashes.

censar *vt* to take a census of.

censo *sm* - **1.** [padrón] census; **censo de población** population census; **censo electoral** electoral roll - **2.** [tributo] tax - **3.** DER lease.

censor, ra *sm, f* - **1.** [funcionario] censor - **2.** [crítico] critic.

← **censor de cuentas** *sm* ECON auditor.

censura *sf* - **1.** [prohibición] censorship - **2.** [organismo] censors pl - **3.** [reprobación] censure, severe criticism.

censurable *adj* censurable.

censurar *vt* - **1.** [prohibir] to censor - **2.** [reprobar] to criticize severely, to censure.

centauro *sm* centaur.

centavo, va *num* hundredth.

← **centavo** *sm* [moneda - en países anglosajones] cent; [- en países latinoamericanos] centavo; **sin un centavo** penniless.

centella *sf* - **1.** [rayo] flash - **2.** [chispa] spark - **3.** *fig* [cosa, persona]**: es una centella** he's like lightning; **rápido como una centella** quick as a flash.

centellear *vi* [luz] to sparkle; [estrella] to twinkle.

centelleo *sm* [de luz] sparkle, sparkling *(U)*; [de estrella] twinkle, twinkling *(U)*.

centena *sf* hundred; **una centena de** a hundred.

centenar *sm* hundred; **un centenar de** a hundred; **a centenares** by the hundred.

centenario, ria *adj* [persona] in one's hundreds; [cifra] three-figure *(antes de s)*.
➤ **centenario** *sm* centenary; **quinto centenario** five hundredth anniversary.

centeno *sm* rye.

centésimo, ma *num* hundredth.

centígrado, da *adj* centigrade.
➤ **centígrado** *sm* centigrade.

centigramo *sm* centigram.

centilitro *sm* centilitre.

centímetro *sm* centimetre.

céntimo *sm* [moneda] cent; **estar sin un céntimo** *fig* to be flat broke.

centinela *sm* sentry.

centollo *sm* spider crab.

centrado, da *adj* - **1.** [basado]**: centrado en** based on - **2.** [equilibrado] stable, steady - **3.** [rueda, cuadro etc] centred.

central <> *adj* central. <> *sm* DEP central defender. <> *sf* - **1.** [oficina] headquarters, head office; [de correos, comunicaciones] main office; **central telefónica** telephone exchange - **2.** [de energía] power station; **central eólica** wind farm; **central hidroeléctrica** *o* **hidráulica/nuclear/térmica** hydroelectric/nuclear/thermal power station; **central camionera** *Méx* bus station.

centralismo *sm* centralism.

centralista *adj* & *smf* centralist.

centralita *sf* switchboard.

centralización *sf* centralization.

centralizar [13] *vt* to centralize.

centrar *vt* - **1.** [gen & DEP] to centre - **2.** [arma] to aim - **3.** [persona] to steady, to make stable - **4.** [atención, interés] to be the centre of.
➤ **centrarse** *vprnl* - **1.** [concentrarse]**: centrarse en** to concentrate *o* focus on - **2.** [equilibrarse] to find one's feet.

céntrico, ca *adj* central.

centrifugadora *sf* - **1.** [máquina centrífuga] centrifuge - **2.** [para secar ropa] spin-dryer.

centrifugar [16] *vt* - **1.** TECNOL to centrifuge - **2.** [ropa] to spin-dry.

centrífugo, ga *adj* centrifugal.

centrípeto, ta *adj* centripetal.

centrista <> *adj* centre *(antes de s)*. <> *smf* centrist.

centro *sm* - **1.** [gen] centre; **ser de centro** POLÍT to be at the centre of the political spectrum; **centro docente** *o* **de enseñanza** educational institution; **centro nervioso/óptico** nerve/optic centre; **centro de cálculo** computer centre; **centro de desintoxicación** detoxication centre; **centro de planificación familiar** family planning clinic; **centro social** community centre - **2.** [de ciudad] town centre; **me voy al centro** I'm going to town; **centro urbano** town centre.
➤ **centro comercial** *sm* shopping centre.
➤ **centro de atracción** *sm* centre of attraction.
➤ **centro de gravedad** *sm* centre of gravity.
➤ **centro de mesa** *sm* centrepiece.
➤ **centro de salud** *sm* health centre.

Centroamérica *sf* Central America.

centroamericano, na *adj* Central American.

centrocampista *smf* DEP midfielder.

centuplicar [10] *vt* to increase a hundredfold.

centuria *sf* century.

ceñido, da *adj* tight.

ceñidor *sm* belt.

ceñir [26] *vt* - **1.** [apretar] to be tight on - **2.** [abrazar] to embrace - **3.** *fig* [amoldar]**: ceñir a** to keep *o* restrict to.
➤ **ceñirse** *vprnl* - **1.** [apretarse] to tighten - **2.** [limitarse]**: ceñirse a** to keep *o* stick to.

ceño *sm* frown, scowl; **fruncir el ceño** to frown, to knit one's brow.

cepa *sf* *lit* & *fig* stock; **de pura cepa** [auténtico] real, genuine; [pura sangre] thoroughbred.

cepillado *sm* - **1.** [de ropa, pelo, dientes] brush, brushing *(U)* - **2.** [de madera] planing.

cepillar *vt* - **1.** [ropa, pelo, dientes] to brush - **2.** [madera] to plane - **3.** *fam* [birlar] to pinch - **4.** *fam* [adular] to butter up, to flatter.
➤ **cepillarse** *vprnl* - **1.** [pelo, dientes] to brush - **2.** *fam* [comida, trabajo etc] to polish off - **3.** *fam* [suspender] to fail - **4.** *mfam* [matar] to bump off - **5.** *vulg* [fornicar] to screw.

cepillo *sm* - **1.** [para limpiar] brush; [para pelo] hairbrush; **cepillo de dientes** toothbrush - **2.** [de carpintero] plane - **3.** [de donativos] collection box, poor box.

cepo *sm* - **1.** [para cazar] trap - **2.** [para vehículos] wheel clamp - **3.** [para sujetar] clamp - **4.** [para presos] stocks *pl*.

ceporro *sm* *fam* idiot, blockhead.

CEPSA (*abrev de* **Compañía Española de Petróleos, SA**) *sf* Spanish petroleum company.

CEPYME (*abrev de* **Confederación Española de la Pequeña y Mediana Empresa**) *sf Spanish confederation of SME's.*

cera *sf* [gen] wax; [de abeja] beeswax; **hacerse la cera en las piernas** to wax one's legs; **cera depilatoria** hair-removing wax.

cerámica *sf* - **1.** [arte] ceramics *(U)*, pottery - **2.** [objeto] piece of pottery.

ceramista *smf* potter.

cerbatana *sf* blowpipe.

cebiche = **ceviche**.

cerca ⬦ *sf* - **1.** [valla] fence - **2.** [muro] wall. ⬦ *adv* near, close; **por aquí cerca** nearby; **de cerca** [examinar, ver] closely; [afectar, vivir] deeply.
➤ **cerca de** *loc prep* - **1.** [en el espacio] near, close to - **2.** [aproximadamente] nearly, about.

cercado *sm* - **1.** [valla] fence - **2.** [lugar] enclosure.

cercanía *sf* [proximidad] nearness, closeness.
➤ **cercanías** *sfpl* [de ciudad] outskirts, suburbs.

cercano, na *adj* - **1.** [pueblo, lugar] nearby - **2.** [tiempo] near - **3.** [pariente, fuente de información]: **cercano (a)** close (to).

cercar [10] *vt* - **1.** [vallar] to fence (off) - **2.** [rodear, acorralar] to surround.

cercenar *vt culto* - **1.** [extremidad] to amputate - **2.** [restringir] to cut back, to curtail.

cerciorar *vt* to assure; **cerciorarse (de)** to make sure (of).

cerco *sm* - **1.** [gen] circle, ring - **2.** [de puerta, ventana] frame - **3.** [de astro] halo - **4.** [asedio] siege; **poner cerco a** to lay siege to - **5.** *Amér* [valla] fence.

cerda *sf* ➤ **cerdo**.

cerdada *sf fam* dirty trick.

Cerdeña *n pr* Sardinia.

cerdo, da *sm, f* - **1.** [animal] pig (*f* sow) - **2.** *fam fig* [persona] pig, swine.
➤ **cerdo** *sm* [carne] pork.
➤ **cerda** *sf* [pelo - de cerdo, jabalí] bristle; [- de caballo] horsehair.

cereal *sm* cereal; **cereales** (breakfast) cereal *(U)*.

cerebral *adj* - **1.** [del cerebro] brain *(antes de s)*, cerebral - **2.** [racional] cerebral.

cerebro *sm* - **1.** [gen] brain - **2.** *fig* [cabecilla] brains *sing* - **3.** *fig* [inteligencia] brains *pl*.
➤ **cerebro electrónico** *sm* electronic brain.

ceremonia *sf* ceremony.

ceremonial *adj & sm* ceremonial.

ceremonioso, sa *adj* ceremonious.

céreo, a *adj* wax *(antes de s)*.

cereza *sf* cherry.

cerezo *sm* - **1.** [árbol] cherry tree - **2.** [madera] cherry (wood).

cerilla *sf* match.

cerillo *sm Amér C, Ecuad & Méx* match.

cerner [20], **cernir** *vt* [cribar] to sieve, to sift.
➤ **cernerse** *vprnl* - **1.** [ave, avión] to hover - **2.** *fig* [amenaza, peligro] to loom.

cernícalo *sm* - **1.** [ave] kestrel - **2.** *fam* [bruto] brute.

cernir = **cerner**.

cero ⬦ *adj inv* zero. ⬦ *sm* - **1.** [signo] nought, zero; [en fútbol] nil; [en tenis] love; **dos goles a cero** two goals to nil, two nil - **2.** [cantidad] nothing - **3.** FÍS & METEOR zero; **sobre/bajo cero** above/below zero; **cero absoluto** absolute zero - **4.** *loc*: **ser un cero a la izquierda** *fam* [un inútil] to be useless; [un don nadie] to be a nobody; **partir de cero** to start from scratch; *ver también* **seis**.

cerque *etc* ➤ **cercar**.

cerquillo *sm Amér* fringe *UK*, bangs *US pl*.

cerrado, da *adj* - **1.** [al exterior] closed, shut; [con llave, pestillo etc] locked; **cerrado a** closed to - **2.** [tiempo, cielo] overcast; **era noche cerrada** it was completely dark - **3.** [mentalidad, sociedad]: **cerrado (a)** closed (to) - **4.** [rodeado] surrounded; [por montañas] walled in - **5.** [circuito] closed - **6.** [curva] sharp, tight - **7.** [vocal] close - **8.** [acento, deje] broad, thick.

cerradura *sf* lock.

cerrajería *sf* - **1.** [oficio] locksmithery - **2.** [local] locksmith's (shop).

cerrajero, ra *sm, f* locksmith.

cerrar ⬦ *vt* - **1.** [gen] to close; [puerta, cajón, boca] to shut, to close; [puños] to clench; [con llave, pestillo etc] to lock - **2.** [tienda, negocio - definitivamente] to close down - **3.** [apagar] to turn off - **4.** [bloquear - suj: accidente, inundación etc] to block; [- suj: policía etc] to close off - **5.** [tapar - agujero, hueco] to fill, to block (up); [- bote] to put the lid o top on - **6.** [cercar] to fence (off), to enclose - **7.** [cicatrizar] to heal, to close up - **8.** [ir último en] to bring up the rear of - **9.: cerrar un trato** to seal a deal. ⬦ *vi* to close, to shut; [con llave, pestillo etc] to lock up.
➤ **cerrarse** *vprnl* - **1.** [al exterior] to close, to shut - **2.** [incomunicarse] to clam up; **cerrarse a** to close one's mind to; **cerrarse en banda** to close ranks - **3.** [herida] to heal, to close up - **4.** [acto, debate, discusión etc] to (come to a) close.

cerrazón *sf fig* stubbornness, obstinacy.

cerril *adj* - **1.** [animal] wild - **2.** *fam fig* [obstinado] stubborn, obstinate; [tosco, grosero] ignorant, rude.

cerro *sm* hill; **irse por los cerros de Úbeda** to stray from the point.

cerrojazo *sm* - **1.** [cierre brusco] slamming - **2.** *fig* [interrupción] sudden interruption.

cerrojo *sm* bolt; **echar el cerrojo** to bolt the door.

certamen *sm* competition, contest.

certero, **ra** *adj* **- 1.** [tiro] accurate **- 2.** [opinión, respuesta etc] correct.

certeza *sf* certainty; **tener la certeza de que** to be certain (that).

certidumbre *sf* certainty.

certificación *sf* **- 1.** [hecho] certification **- 2.** [documento] certificate.

certificado, **da** *adj* [gen] certified; [carta, paquete] registered.

◆ **certificado** *sm* certificate; **certificado de calidad** quality guarantee; **certificado de depósito** BANCA certificate of deposit; **certificado de estudios** school-leaving certificate; **certificado médico** medical certificate; **certificado de origen** COM certificate of origin.

certificar **[10]** *vt* **- 1.** [constatar] to certify **- 2.** *fig* [sospechas, inocencia] to confirm **- 3.** [en correos] to register.

cerumen *sm* earwax.

cerval *adj*: **miedo cerval** terror.

cervantino, **na** *adj* Cervantine.

cervatillo *sm* (small) fawn.

cervato *sm* fawn.

cervecería *sf* **- 1.** [fábrica] brewery **- 2.** [bar] bar.

cervecero, **ra** ⬦ *adj* beer *(antes de s).* ⬦ *sm, f* [que hace cerveza] brewer.

cerveza *sf* beer; **cerveza de barril** draught beer; **cerveza negra** stout; **cerveza rubia** lager.

cervical ⬦ *adj* cervical, neck *(antes de s).* ⬦ *sf* (gen pl) back of the neck.

cerviz *sf* ANAT nape, back of the neck.

cesante ⬦ *adj* **- 1.** [destituido] sacked; [ministro] removed from office **- 2.** *C Sur & Méx* [en paro] unemployed. ⬦ *smf* sacked person; [ministro] person removed from office.

cesantear *vt Chile & R Dom* to make redundant.

cesantía *sf* **- 1.** [destitución] sacking; [de ministro] removal from office **- 2.** *Chile & R Dom* [desempleo] unemployment.

cesar ⬦ *vt* [destituir] to sack; [ministro] to remove from office. ⬦ *vi* **- 1.** [parar]: **cesar (de hacer algo)** to stop *O* cease (doing sthg); **no cesaba de llorar** he didn't stop crying; **no cesa de intentarlo** she keeps trying; **sin cesar** nonstop, incessantly **- 2.** [dimitir]: **cesar (de *O* en)** to resign (from).

cesárea *sf* caesarean (section).

cese *sm* **- 1.** [detención, paro] stopping, ceasing **- 2.** [destitución] sacking; [de ministro] removal from office.

cesio *sm* caesium.

cesión *sf* cession, transfer; **cesión de bienes** surrender of property.

césped *sm* **- 1.** [hierba] lawn, grass *(U)* **- 2.** DEP field, pitch.

◆ **césped artificial** *sm* artificial turf.

cesta *sf* basket.

◆ **cesta de la compra** *sf* **- 1.** *fig* cost of living **- 2.** [para compras en Internet] shopping basket.

◆ **cesta de Navidad** *sf* Christmas hamper.

cestería *sf* **- 1.** [oficio] basketmaking **- 2.** [tienda] basket shop.

cesto *sm* **- 1.** [cesta] (large) basket **- 2.** DEP basket.

cetáceos *smpl* cetaceans.

cetrería *sf* falconry.

cetrino, **na** *adj culto* sallow.

cetro *sm* **- 1.** [vara] sceptre **- 2.** *fig* [reinado] reign **- 3.** *fig* [superioridad]: **ostentar el cetro de** to hold the crown of.

ceviche, **cebiche** *sm* (*abrev de* Méx) *dish with raw fish or seafood, marinated in onion, lemon juice and pepper.*

cf., **cfr.** (*abrev de* **confróntese**) cf.

cg (*abrev de* **centigramo**) cg.

CG (*abrev de* **cuartel general**) *sm* HQ.

CH (*abrev de* **Confederación Helvética**) *sf* CH.

chabacanada *sf* vulgar thing.

chabacanería *sf* **- 1.** [acción, comentario]: **lo que hizo/dijo fue una chabacanería** what he did/said was vulgar **- 2.** [cualidad] vulgarity.

chabacano, **na** *adj* vulgar.

◆ **chabacano** *sm* Méx [fruto] apricot.

chabola *sf* shack; **barrios de chabolas** shanty town *sing.*

chabolismo *sm* shanty towns *pl.*

chabolista *smf* shanty town dweller.

chacal *sm* jackal.

chacarero, **ra** *sm, f* Andes & R Plata [agricultor] farmer.

chacha *sf* maid.

chachachá *sm* cha-cha.

cháchara *sf fam* chatter, nattering; **estar de cháchara** to have a natter.

chacina *sf* cured *O* prepared pork.

chacolí (*pl* chacolíes *O* chacolís) *sm light wine from the Basque Country.*

chacota *sf*: **tomar algo a chacota** to take sthg as a joke.

chacra *sf* Andes & R Plata farm.

Chad *sm*: **el Chad** Chad.

chafar *vt* **- 1.** [aplastar] to flatten **- 2.** [arrugar] to crease **- 3.** *fig* [estropear] to spoil, to ruin **- 4.** *fig* [abatir] to depress; **dejar a alguien chafado** to crush sb.

◆ **chafarse** *vprnl* [estropearse] to be ruined.

chaflán *sm* - **1.** [de edificio] corner - **2.** GEOM bevel.

chagra *Amér* ◇ *smf* peasant, person from the country. ◇ *sf* farm.

chal *sm* shawl.

chalado, da *fam* ◇ *adj* crazy, mad; **estar chalado por algo/alguien** *fig* to be crazy about sthg/sb. ◇ *sm, f* nutter.

chaladura *sf fam* - **1.** [locura] craziness, madness - **2.** [enamoramiento] crazy infatuation.

chalán, ana *sm, f fig* & *despec* shark, wheeler-dealer.

chalana *sf* NÁUT barge.

chalar *vt* to drive round the bend.

chalé, chalet (*pl* **chalets**) *sm* [gen] detached house (with garden); [en el campo] cottage; [de alta montaña] chalet; **chalé adosado** luxury terraced house; **chalé pareado** semi-detached house.

chaleco *sm* waistcoat, vest *US*; [de punto] tank-top; **chaleco antibalas** bullet-proof vest; **chaleco salvavidas** life jacket.

chalet = **chalé**.

chalupa *sf* - **1.** NÁUT small boat - **2.** *Méx* [plato] *small tortilla with a raised rim to contain a filling*.

chamaco, ca *sm, f Méx fam* kid.

chamán *sm* shaman.

chamarileo *sm* dealing in second-hand goods.

chamarra *sf* sheepskin jacket.

chamba *sf Amér C, Méx, Perú & Ven fam* odd job.

chambelán *sm* chamberlain.

chamiza *sf* - **1.** [hierba] thatch - **2.** [leña] brushwood.

chamizo *sm* - **1.** [leña] half-burnt wood (*U*) - **2.** [casa] thatched hut - **3.** *fam despec* [lugar] hovel, dive.

champa *sf Amér C* - **1.** [tienda de campaña] tent - **2.** [cobertizo] shed.

champán, champaña *sm* champagne.

champiñón *sm* mushroom.

champú (*pl* **champús** o **champúes**) *sm* shampoo.

chamuscar [10] *vt* to scorch; [cabello, barba, tela] to singe.

◆ **chamuscarse** *vprnl* [cabello, barba, tela] to get singed.

chamusquina *sf* scorch, scorching (*U*); **me huele a chamusquina** *fam fig* it smells a bit fishy to me.

chance ◇ *sf Amér* opportunity, chance. ◇ *adv Méx* maybe.

chanchada *sf Amér* [trastada] dirty trick.

chancho, cha *Amér adj* [sucio] filthy.

chancho *sm* - **1.** [animal] pig (*f* sow) - **2.** [persona] slob - **3.** [carne] pork.

chanchullero, ra *fam* ◇ *adj* crooked, dodgy. ◇ *sm, f* trickster, crook.

chanchullo *sm fam* fiddle, racket.

chancla *sf* - **1.** *despec* [calzado viejo] old shoe - **2.** [chancleta] low sandal; [para la playa] flip-flop.

chancleta *sf* low sandal; [para la playa] flip-flop.

chanclo *sm* - **1.** [de madera] clog - **2.** [de plástico] galosh.

chándal (*pl* **chándales** o **chandals**), **chandal** (*pl* **chandals**) *sm* tracksuit.

changarro *sm Méx* small store.

changurro *sm typical Basque dish of dressed crab*.

chantaje *sm* blackmail; **hacer chantaje a** to blackmail; **chantaje emocional** emotional blackmail.

chantajear *vt* to blackmail.

chantajista *smf* blackmailer.

chantillí, chantilly *sm* whipped cream.

chanza *sf* joke; **estar de chanza** to be joking.

chao *interj*: ¡chao! *fam* bye!, see you!

chapa *sf* - **1.** [lámina - de metal] sheet, plate; [- de madera] board; **de tres chapas** three-ply - **2.** [tapón] top, cap - **3.** [insignia] badge - **4.** [ficha de guardarropa] metal token o disc - **5.** *Col, Cuba & Méx* [cerradura] lock - **6.** *R Dom* [de matrícula] number plate *UK*, license plate *US*.

◆ **chapas** *sfpl* [juego] *children's game played with bottle tops*.

chapado, da *adj* [con metal] plated; [con madera] veneered; **chapado a la antigua** *fig* stuck in the past, old-fashioned.

◆ **chapado** *sm* [metal] plate; [madera] veneer.

chapar *vt* [con metal] to plate; [con madera] to veneer.

chaparro, rra ◇ *adj* short and squat. ◇ *sm, f* [persona] short, squat person.

◆ **chaparro** *sm* BOT dwarf oak.

chaparrón *sm* downpour; *fam fig* [gran cantidad] torrent.

chapata *sf* ciabatta.

chapear *vt* - **1.** [con metal] to plate; [con madera] to veneer - **2.** *Amér* [escardar] to clear with a machete.

chapela *sf* beret.

chapista *smf* AUTO panel beater.

chapopote *sm Caribe & Méx* bitumen, pitch.

chapotear *vi* to splash about.

chapucear *vt* to botch (up).

chapucería *sf* botch (job).

chapucero, ra ◇ *adj* [trabajo] shoddy, sloppy; [persona] bungling. ◇ *sm, f* bungler.

chapulín *sm Amér C & Méx* - **1.** [saltamontes] grasshopper - **2.** *fam* [niño] kid.

chapurrear, chapurrar *vt* to speak badly.

chapurreo *sm* jabbering.

chapuza *sf* - **1.** [trabajo mal hecho] botch (job) - **2.** [trabajo ocasional] odd job.

chapuzón *sm* dip; **darse un chapuzón** to go for a dip.

chaqué *sm* morning coat.

chaqueta *sf* jacket; [de punto] cardigan; **cambiarse de chaqueta** *fig* to change sides.

chaqueteo *sm* changing sides.

chaquetero, ra *adj & sm, f* turncoat.

chaquetilla *sf* short jacket.

chaquetón *sm* short coat.

charada *sf newspaper puzzle in which a word must be guessed, with its meaning and certain syllables given as clues.*

charanga *sf* - **1.** [banda] brass band - **2.** *fam* [fiesta] party.

charca *sf* pool, pond.

charco *sm* puddle; **cruzar el charco** *fig* to cross the pond *o* Atlantic.

charcutería *sf* - **1.** [tienda] *shop selling cold cooked meats and cheeses,* ≃ delicatessen - **2.** [productos] cold cuts *pl* and cheese.

charcutero, ra *sm, f owner of "charcutería".*

charla *sf* - **1.** [conversación] chat - **2.** [conferencia] talk.

charlar *vi* to chat.

charlatán, ana ⬦ *adj* talkative. ⬦ *sm, f* - **1.** [hablador] chatterbox - **2.** [mentiroso] trickster, charlatan - **3.** [vendedor] travelling salesman (*f* travelling saleswoman).

charlatanería *sf* - **1.** [locuacidad] talkativeness - **2.** [palabrería] spiel.

charlestón *sm* charleston.

charlotada *sf* - **1.** [payasada] clowning around (*U*) - **2.** TAUROM slapstick bull-fight.

charlotear *vi* to chat.

charloteo *sm* chat, chatting (*U*).

charnego, ga *sm, f pejorative term referring to immigrant to Catalonia from another part of Spain.*

charol *sm* - **1.** [piel] patent leather - **2.** [barniz] shiny varnish - **3.** *Andes* [bandeja] tray.

charola *sf Bol, Amér C & Méx* tray.

charretera *sf* epaulette.

charro, rra ⬦ *adj* - **1.** [salmantino] Salamancan - **2.** *fig* [recargado] gaudy, showy. ⬦ *sm, f* Salamancan.

charrúa *Amér adj inv & smf inv* Uruguayan.

chárter ⬦ *adj inv* charter (*antes de s*). ⬦ *sm* charter plane.

chasca *sf Andes* [greña] mop of hair.

chascar [10] ⬦ *vt* - **1.** [lengua] to click - **2.** [dedos] to snap. ⬦ *vi* - **1.** [madera] to crack - **2.** [lengua] to click.

chascarrillo *sm fam* funny story.

chasco *sm* - **1.** [decepción] disappointment; **llevarse un chasco** to be disappointed - **2.** [burla] trick; **dar un chasco a alguien** to play a trick on sb.

chasis *sm inv* - **1.** AUTO chassis - **2.** FOTO plate-holder - **3.** *fam* [esqueleto] body.

chasque *etc* ▷ **chascar**.

chasquear ⬦ *vt* - **1.** [látigo] to crack - **2.** [la lengua] to click - **3.** *fig* [engañar] to play a trick on. ⬦ *vi* [madera] to crack.

chasquido *sm* [de látigo, madera, hueso] crack; [de lengua, arma] click; [de dedos] snap.

chasquillas *sfpl Chile* fringe *sing* UK, bangs US.

chatarra *sf* - **1.** [metal] scrap (metal) - **2.** [objetos, piezas] junk - **3.** *fam despec* [joyas] cheap and nasty jewellery; [condecoraciones] brass, medals *pl* - **4.** *fam* [monedas] small change.

chatarrería *sf* scrapyard.

chatarrero, ra *sm, f* scrap (metal) dealer.

chatear *vi* [en bar] to go out drinking; INFORM to chat.

chateo *sm* - **1.** [en bar] pub crawl, pub crawling (*U*); **ir de chateo** to go out drinking - **2.** INFORM chatting.

chato, ta ⬦ *adj* - **1.** [nariz] snub; [persona] snub-nosed - **2.** [aplanado] flat - **3.** *R Dom* [mediocre] commonplace. ⬦ *sm, f* - **1.** [persona] snub-nosed person - **2.** *fam* [apelativo] love, dear.
➦ **chato** *sm* [de vino] small glass of wine.

chau, chaucito *interj Bol, C Sur & Perú fam* bye!, see you!

chaucha *sf* - **1.** *Andes & R Dom* [moneda] coin of little value - **2.** *Andes* [patata] early potato - **3.** *Bol & R Dom* [judía verde] green bean.

chauvinismo = **chovinismo**.

chauvinista = **chovinista**.

chaval, la *sm, f fam* kid, lad (*f* lass).

chavalería *sf fam* kids *pl*.

chavalo, la *sm, f Amér fam* lad (*f* lass).

chaveta *sf* - **1.** [clavija] cotter pin - **2.** *fam* [cabeza] nut, head; **perder la chaveta** to go off one's rocker - **3.** *Andes* [navaja] penknife.

chavo, va *fam sm, f Méx* [joven] boy (*f* girl).
➦ **chavo** *sm* [dinero]: **no tener un chavo** to be penniless.

che *interj R Dom fam*: **¿como andás, che?** hey, how's it going?; **¡che, vení para acá!** hey, over here, you!

checar *vt Amér C, Andes & Méx* - **1.** [comprobar] to check - **2.** [vigilar] to keep an eye on.

Chechenia Chechnya.

checheno *adj* & *sm, f* Chechen.

checo, ca *adj* & *sm, f* Czech.

➤ **checo** *sm* [lengua] Czech.

chef [tʃef] (*pl* **chefs**) *sm* chef.

chele, la *Amér C* <> *adj* [rubio] blond (*f* blonde); [de piel blanca] fair-skinned. <> *sm, f* [rubio] blond(e); [de piel blanca] fair-skinned person.

cheli *sm fam modern Spanish slang used by young people.*

chelín *sm* shilling.

chelo, la <> *adj Amér* blond (*f* blonde). <> *sm, f* MÚS [instrumentista] cellist.

➤ **chelo** *sm* MÚS [instrumento] cello.

chepa *sf fam* hump.

cheposo, sa <> *adj* hunchbacked. <> *sm, f* hunchback.

cheque *sm* cheque *UK*, check *US*; **extender un cheque** to make out a cheque; **cheque en blanco/sin fondos** blank/bad cheque; **cheque cruzado** o **barrado** crossed cheque; **cheque (de) gasolina** petrol voucher; **cheque nominativo** cheque in favour of a specific person; **cheque al portador** cheque payable to the bearer; **cheque de viaje** o **de viajero** traveller's cheque; **cheque regalo** gift voucher.

chequear *vt* - **1.** MED: **chequear a alguien** to examine sb, to give sb a checkup - **2.** [comprobar] to check.

chequeo *sm* - **1.** MED checkup - **2.** [comprobación] check, checking *(U)*.

chequera *sf* chequebook *UK*, checkbook *US*.

chévere *adj Andes, Amér C, Caribe* & *Méx fam* great, fantastic.

cheviot (*pl* **cheviots**) *sm* cheviot.

chic *adj inv* chic.

chica *sf* - **1.** [criada] maid - **2.** *ver también* **chico**.

➤ **chica de alterne** *sf* girl who works in bars encouraging customers to drink in return for a commission.

chicano, na *adj* & *sm, f* Chicano, Mexican-American.

➤ **chicano** *sm* [lengua] Chicano.

chicarrón, ona *sm, f* strapping lad (*f* strapping lass).

chicha *sf* - **1.** *Esp fam* [para comer] meat - **2.** *Esp fam* [de persona] flesh - **3.** *loc:* **no ser ni chicha ni limonada** o **limoná** not to be one thing or the other.

chícharo *sm Amér C* & *Méx* pea.

chicharra *sf* - **1.** ZOOL cicada - **2.** *Méx* & *R Plata* [timbre] electric buzzer.

chicharro *sm* - **1.** [alimento] pork crackling - **2.** [pez] horse mackerel.

chicharrón *sm* [frito] pork crackling.

➤ **chicharrones** *smpl* [embutido] *cold processed meat made from pork.*

chiche *sm* - **1.** *Andes* & *R Dom* [adorno] adornment - **2.** *C Sur* [juguete] toy - **3.** *Amér C* & *Méx mfam* [pecho] tit.

chichón *sm* bump.

chichonera *sf* helmet.

chicle *sm* chewing gum.

chiclé, chicler *sm* AUTO jet.

chico, ca <> *adj* [pequeño] small; [joven] young; **cuando era chico** when I was little. <> *sm, f* - **1.** [joven] boy (*f* girl) - **2.** [tratamiento - hombre] sonny, mate; [- mujer] darling.

➤ **chico** *sm* [recadero] messenger, office-boy.

chicote *sm Amér* [látigo] whip.

chifla *sf* - **1.** [silbido] whistle - **2.** [burla] mockery.

chiflado, da *fam* <> *adj* crazy, mad. <> *sm, f* nutter.

chifladura *sf* - **1.** [locura] madness - **2.** [pasión] craze, craziness *(U)*.

chiflar <> *vt fam* [encantar]: **me chiflan las patatas fritas** I'm mad about chips. <> *vi* [silbar] to whistle.

➤ **chiflarse** *vprnl*: **chiflarse por algo** o **alguien** *fam* to go crazy about sthg o sb.

chiflido *sm Amér* whistling.

chigüín, güina *sm, f Amér C fam* kid.

chihuahua *sm* chihuahua.

chiíta *adj* & *smf* Shi'ite.

chilaba *sf* jellaba.

chile *sm* chilli; **chile con carne** CULIN chilli con carne.

Chile *n pr* Chile.

chileno, na *adj* & *sm, f* Chilean.

chilindrón *sm* CULIN *seasoning made of tomatoes and peppers.*

chillar <> *vi* - **1.** [gritar - personas] to scream, to yell; [- ave, mono] to screech; [- cerdo] to squeal; [- ratón] to squeak - **2.** [chirriar] to screech; [puerta, madera] to creak; [bisagras] to squeak. <> *vt fam* [reñir] to yell at.

chillido *sm* [de persona] scream, yell; [de ave, mono] screech; [de cerdo] squeal; [de ratón] squeak.

chillón, ona <> *adj* - **1.** [voz] piercing - **2.** [persona] noisy, screeching - **3.** [color] loud, gaudy. <> *sm, f* noisy person.

chimenea *sf* - **1.** [hogar] fireplace - **2.** [en tejado] chimney.

chimpancé *sm* chimpanzee.

china ▷ **chino**.

China *n pr*: **(la) China** China.

chinchar *vt fam* to pester, to bug.

◆ **chincharse** *vprnl fam* to get cross; **ahora te chinchas** now you can lump it.

chinche ◇ *adj fam fig* annoying. ◇ *sf* - **1.** [insecto] bedbug - **2.** *Amér* [para clavar] drawing pin *UK*, thumbtack *US*. ◇ *smf fam fig* [persona] pest, pain.

chincheta *sf* drawing pin *UK*, thumbtack *US*.

chinchilla *sf* chinchilla.

chinchín *sm* - **1.** [ruido] noise of a brass band - **2.** [brindis] toast; **¡chinchín!** cheers!; **hacer chinchín por alguien** to toast sb.

chinchón *sm* strong aniseed liquor.

chinchorro *sm* - **1.** *Méx* [red] net - **2.** *Chile & Ven* [hamaca] hammock.

chinchoso, sa ◇ *adj* annoying. ◇ *sm, f* pest, pain.

chinga *sf Méx mfam* [paliza]: **me dieron una chinga** they kicked the shit out of me; [trabajo duro]: **es una chinga** it's a bitch of a job.

chingado, da *adj* - **1.** *fam* [enfadado] cheesed off - **2.** *Esp & Méx* [estropeado] bust, knackered *UK* - **3.** *Méx vulg* [jodido] fucking.

◆ **chingada** *sf Méx vulg*: **¡vete a la chingada!** fuck off!; **¡hijo de la chingada!** bastard!

chingar [16] *Esp & Méx* ◇ *vt* - **1.** *mfam* [molestar]: **chingar a alguien** to get up sb's nose, to piss sb off - **2.** *mfam* [estropear] to bust, to knacker *UK* - **3.** *vulg* [acostarse con] to screw, to fuck. ◇ *vi vulg* [fornicar] to screw, to fuck.

chino, na *adj & sm, f* - **1.** Chinese; **engañar a alguien como a un chino** *fig* to take sb for a ride; **trabajar como un chino** *fig* to slave away - **2.** *Andes & R Plata* [mestizo] person of mixed ancestry.

◆ **chino** *sm* - **1.** [lengua] Chinese - **2.** [instrumento] sieve - **3.** [piedra] pebble.

◆ **china** *sf* - **1.** [piedra] small stone, pebble; **tocarle a alguien la china** to have bad luck - **2.** [porcelana] china - **3.** *Amér* [india] Indian woman - **4.** *Amér* [criada] maid.

◆ **chinos** *smpl* [juego] game in which each player must guess the number of coins or pebbles in the other's hand.

chip (*pl* chips) *sm* INFORM chip.

chipé, chipén *adj inv fam* brilliant, terrific; **ser de chipé** to be brilliant o terrific.

chipirón *sm* baby squid.

Chipre *n pr* Cyprus.

chipriota *adj & smf* Cypriot.

chiquero *sm* TAUROM bull-pen.

chiquillada *sf* childish thing.

chiquillería *sf* kids *pl*.

chiquillo, lla *sm, f* kid.

chiquitín, ina ◇ *adj* tiny. ◇ *sm, f* tiny tot.

chiquito, ta *adj* tiny; **no andarse con chiquitas** *fig* not to mess about.

◆ **chiquito** *sm* [de vino] small glass of wine.

chiribita *sf* [chispa] spark.

◆ **chiribitas** *sfpl fam* [en los ojos] spots in front of one's eyes.

chirigota *sf fam* - **1.** [broma] joke - **2.** [en carnavales] group of disguised people singing satirical songs.

chirimbolo *sm fam* thingamajig, whatsit.

chirimía *sf* shawm.

chirimoya *sf* custard apple.

chiringuito *sm fam* - **1.** [bar] refreshment stall - **2.** [negocio]: **montarse un chiringuito** to set up a little business.

chiripa *sf fam fig* fluke; **de** o **por chiripa** by luck.

chirivía *sf* BOT parsnip.

chirla *sf* small clam.

chirona *sf fam* clink, slammer; **en chirona** in the clink.

chirriar [9] *vi* [gen] to screech; [puerta, madera] to creak; [bisagra, muelles] to squeak.

chirrido *sm* [gen] screech; [de puerta, madera] creak; [de bisagra, muelles] squeak.

chis, chist *interj* ¡chis! ssh!

chisme *sm* - **1.** [cotilleo] rumour, piece of gossip - **2.** *fam* [cosa] thingamajig, thingy.

chismorrear *vi* to spread rumours, to gossip.

chismorreo *sm* gossip.

chismoso, sa ◇ *adj* gossipy. ◇ *sm, f* gossip, scandalmonger.

chispa *sf* - **1.** [de fuego, electricidad] spark; **echar chispas** *fam* to be hopping mad - **2.** [de lluvia] spot (of rain) - **3.** *fig* [pizca] bit; **una chispa de sal** a pinch of salt - **4.** *fig* [agudeza] sparkle.

chispazo *sm lit & fig* spark.

chispeante *adj* - **1.** [que chispea] that gives off sparks - **2.** *fig* [conversación, discurso, mirada] sparkling.

chispear ◇ *vi* - **1.** [chisporrotear] to spark - **2.** [relucir] to sparkle. ◇ *v impers* [llover] to spit (with rain).

chisporrotear *vi* [fuego, leña] to crackle; [aceite] to splutter; [comida] to sizzle.

chisporroteo *sm* [de fuego, leña] crackling; [de aceite] spluttering; [de comida] sizzling.

chist = **chis**.

chistar *vi*: **me fui sin chistar** I left without a word.

chiste *sm* joke; **contar chistes** to tell jokes; **chiste verde** dirty joke.

chistera *sf* [sombrero] top hat.

chistorra *sf* type of cured pork sausage typical of Aragon and Navarre.

chistoso, sa ◇ *adj* funny. ◇ *sm, f* amusing o funny person.

chistu *sm* Basque flute.

chistulari smf "chistu" player.

chita ➡ **a la chita callando** loc adv fam quietly, on the quiet.

chitón interj: ¡chitón! quiet!

chivar vt fam to whisper, to tell secretly.
➡ **chivarse** vprnl fam: **chivarse (de/a)** [niños] to split (on/to); [delincuentes] to grass (on/to).

chivatazo sm fam tip-off; **dar el chivatazo** to grass.

chivato, ta sm, f fam [delator] grass, informer; [acusica] telltale.
➡ **chivato** sm - **1.** [luz] warning light; [alarma] alarm bell - **2.** Ven fam [pez gordo] big cheese.

chivo, va sm, f kid, young goat; **ser el chivo expiatorio** fig to be the scapegoat.

choc (pl **chocs**), **choque, shock** [tʃok] sm shock.

chocante adj startling.

chocar [10] ◇ vi - **1.** [colisionar]: **chocar (contra)** to crash (into), to collide (with) - **2.** fig [enfrentarse] to clash. ◇ vt - **1.**: **chocar la mano de alguien** to shake hands with sb; ¡chócala! put it there! - **2.** [copas, vasos] to clink - **3.** fig [sorprender] to startle.

chochear vi - **1.** [viejo] to be senile - **2.** fam fig [de cariño]: **chochear por alguien** to dote on sb.

chochez sf - **1.** [vejez] senility - **2.** [dicho, hecho]: **decir/hacer chocheces** to say/do senile things.

chocho, cha adj - **1.** [viejo] senile - **2.** fam fig [encariñado] soft, doting.
➡ **chocho** sm - **1.** vulg [órgano] cunt - **2.** fam [altramuz] lupin.

choclo sm Andes & R Plata corncob, ear of maize O corn US.

choclón sm Chile fam crowd.

chocolate sm - **1.** [para comer, beber] chocolate; **chocolate (a la taza)** thick drinking chocolate; **chocolate blanco** white chocolate; **chocolate con leche** milk chocolate - **2.** fam [para fumar] hash.

chocolatera sf ▷ **chocolatero.**

chocolatería sf - **1.** [fábrica] chocolate factory - **2.** [establecimiento] café where drinking chocolate is served.

chocolatero, ra sm, f - **1.** [oficio] chocolate maker O seller - **2.** [aficionado al chocolate] chocoholic, person fond of chocolate.
➡ **chocolatera** sf [recipiente] = pot for making drinking chocolate.

chocolatina sf chocolate bar.

chófer (pl **chóferes**) smf - **1.** [como oficio - de automóvil] chauffeur; [- de autobús] driver - **2.** Amér [conductor] driver.

chollo sm fam [producto, compra] bargain; [trabajo, situación] cushy number.

cholo, la Amér ◇ adj mestizo, mixed race. ◇ sm, f - **1.** [mestizo] person of mixed race - **2.** [indio] country bumpkin.

chomba, chompa sf Andes sweater.

chompipe sm Amér C & Méx turkey.

chonchón sm Chile lamp.

chongo sm Méx [moño] bun.

chopera sf poplar grove.

chopito sm CULIN baby squid in batter.

chopo sm poplar.

choque ◇ sm - **1.** [impacto] impact; [de coche, avión etc] crash; **choque frontal** head-on collision - **2.** fig [enfrentamiento] clash; **choque cultural** culture shock - **3.** = **choc**. ◇ v ▷ **chocar.**

choriceo sm fam [robo] robbery; [timo] rip-off.

chorizar [13] vt fam to nick, to pinch.

chorizo sm - **1.** [embutido] highly seasoned pork sausage - **2.** fam [ladrón] thief.

chorlito sm - **1.** ZOOL plover - **2.** ▷ **cabeza.**

choro sm Andes mussel.

chorra ▷ **chorro.**

chorrada sf mfam rubbish (U); **eso es una chorrada** that's rubbish; **decir chorradas** to talk rubbish.

chorrear ◇ vi - **1.** [gotear - gota a gota] to drip; [- en un hilo] to trickle - **2.** [brotar] to spurt (out), to gush (out). ◇ vt [suj: jersey etc] to drip; [suj: persona] to drip with.

chorreo sm - **1.** [goteo - gota a gota] dripping; [- en un hilo] trickling - **2.** [brote] spurting, gushing - **3.** [de dinero] trickle.

chorreras sfpl frill sing.

chorro[1] sm - **1.** [de líquido - borbotón] jet, spurt; [- hilo] trickle; **salir a chorros** to spurt O gush out; **chorro de vapor** steam jet - **2.** fig [de luz, gente etc] stream; **tiene un chorro de dinero** she has loads of money; **a chorros** in abundance - **3.** loc: **como los chorros del oro** as clean as a new pin.

chorro[2], rra sm, f R Dom fam [ladrón] thief.
➡ **chorra** mfam ◇ smf [tonto] wally, idiot; **hacer el chorra** to muck about. ◇ sf [suerte] luck.

chotearse vprnl fam: **chotearse (de)** to make fun (of).

choteo sm fam joking, kidding; **tomar algo a choteo** to take sthg as a joke.

chotis sm inv dance typical of Madrid.

choto, ta sm, f - **1.** [cabrito] kid, young goat - **2.** [ternero] calf.

chovinismo, chauvinismo [tʃoβi'nismo] sm chauvinism.

chovinista, chauvinista [tʃoβi'nista] ◇ adj chauvinistic. ◇ smf chauvinist.

choza sf hut.

christmas = crismas.

chubasco *sm* shower.

chubasquero *sm* raincoat, mac.

chúcaro, **ra** *adj Andes, Amér C & R Plata fam* [animal] wild; [persona] unsociable.

chuchería *sf* - **1.** [golosina] sweet - **2.** [objeto] trinket.

chucho *sm fam* mutt, dog.

chueco, **ca** *adj Amér* [torcido] twisted; *Méx fam* [proyecto, razonamiento] shady; *Amér* [patizambo] bowlegged.

chufa *sf* - **1.** [planta] chufa - **2.** [tubérculo] tiger nut.

chulada *sf* - **1.** [bravuconada] swaggering *(U)* - **2.** *fam* [cosa bonita] delight, gorgeous thing.

chulapo, **pa**, **chulapón**, **ona** *sm, f* HIST lower-class native of Madrid.

chulear *fam* ⟨> *vt*: **chulear a una mujer** to live off a woman. ⟨> *vi* [fanfarronear]: **chulear (de)** to be cocky (about).

chulería *sf* - **1.** [descaro] cockiness - **2.** [salero] charm, winning ways *pl*; **¡qué chulería!** that's really nice!

chuleta ⟨> *sf* - **1.** [de carne] chop; **chuleta de cordero** lamb chop - **2.** *fam* [en exámenes] crib note. ⟨> *smf fam* [chulo] cocky person. ⟨> *adj fam* [chulo] cocky.

chulo, **la** ⟨> *adj* - **1.** [descarado] cocky; **ponerse chulo** to get cocky - **2.** *fam* [bonito] lovely. ⟨> *sm, f* - **1.** [descarado] cocky person - **2.** [madrileño] working-class native of Madrid.

➤ **chulo** *sm* [proxeneta] pimp.

chumba ▷ higuera.

chumbera *sf* prickly pear.

chumbo ▷ higo.

chuminada *sf fam* silly thing.

chungo, **ga** *adj fam* [persona] horrible, nasty; [cosa] lousy.

➤ **chunga** *sf*: **tomarse algo a chunga** *fam* to take sthg as a joke.

chupa *sf fam*: **chupa de cuero** leather jacket.

chupachup® *(pl* chupachups*) sm* lollipop.

chupado, **da** *adj* - **1.** [delgado] skinny - **2.** *fam* [fácil]: **estar chupado** to be dead easy *o* a piece of cake.

➤ **chupada** *sf* [gen] suck; [fumando] puff, drag.

chupar *vt* - **1.** [succionar] to suck; [fumando] to puff at - **2.** [absorber] to soak up - **3.** [quitar]: **chuparle algo a alguien** to milk sb for sthg; **chuparle la sangre a alguien** *fig* to bleed sb dry.

➤ **chuparse** *vprnl* - **1.** [adelgazar] to get thinner - **2.** *fam* [aguantar] to put up with - **3.** *loc*: **¡chúpate esa!** take that!; **estar para chuparse los dedos** to be absolutely delicious.

chupatintas *smf inv despec* pen-pusher.

chupe *sm Andes & Arg* stew.

chupete *sm* dummy *UK*, pacifier *US*.

chupetear *vt* to suck on *o* away at.

chupi *adj fam* great, brill.

chupinazo *sm* - **1.** [cañonazo] cannon shot - **2.** [en fútbol] hard kick.

chupón, **ona** *sm*, *f fam* [gorrón] sponger, cadger.

➤ **chupón** *sm Méx* [chupete] dummy *UK*, pacifier *US*.

chupóptero, **ra** *sm, f fam* parasite.

churrería *sf* shop selling "churros".

churrero, **ra** *sm, f* "churros" seller.

churrete *sm* spurt; [de grasa] stain.

churrigueresco, **ca** *adj* churrigueresque.

churro *sm* - **1.** [para comer] *dough formed into sticks or rings and fried in oil* - **2.** [fracaso] botch - **3.** *fam* [suerte] fluke, stroke of luck.

churrusco *sm* piece of burnt toast.

churumbel *sm fam* kid.

chusco, **ca** *adj* funny.

➤ **chusco** *sm fam* bread bun.

chusma *sf* rabble, mob.

chut *(pl* chuts*) sm* kick.

chutar *vi* - **1.** [lanzar] to shoot - **2.** *fam* [funcionar] to work; **esto va que chuta** it's going very well; **con diez euros ya va que chuta** ten euros is more than enough.

➤ **chutarse** *vprnl mfam* to shoot up.

chute *sm* - **1.** FÚT shot - **2.** *mfam* [de droga] fix.

chuzo *sm*: **llover a chuzos, caer chuzos de punta** *fig* to rain cats and dogs.

CI *(abrev de* cociente intelectual*) sm* IQ.

CIA *(abrev de* Central Intelligence Agency*) sf* CIA.

cía., Cía. *(abrev de* compañía*)* Co.

cianuro *sm* cyanide.

ciático, **ca** *adj* sciatic.

➤ **ciática** *sf* sciatica.

cibercafé *sm* cybercafe, Internet cafe.

ciberespacio *sm* cyberspace.

cibernético, **ca** *adj* cybernetic.

➤ **cibernética** *sf* cybernetics *(U)*.

cicatería *sf* stinginess, meanness.

cicatero, **ra** ⟨> *adj* stingy, mean. ⟨> *sm, f* skinflint, miser.

cicatriz *sf lit & fig* scar.

cicatrización *sf* scarring.

cicatrizante ⟨> *adj* healing. ⟨> *sm* healing substance.

cicatrizar [13] ⟨> *vi* to form a scar, to heal (up). ⟨> *vt fig* to heal.

cicerón *sm* eloquent speaker.

cicerone *smf* guide.

cíclico, **ca** *adj* cyclical.

ciclismo *sm* cycling.

ciclista <> *adj* cycling *(antes de s)*. <> *smf* cyclist.

ciclo *sm* - **1.** [gen] cycle; **ciclo vital** life cycle - **2.** [de conferencias, actos] series - **3.** [de enseñanza] stage.

ciclocrós *sm* cyclo-cross.

ciclomotor *sm* moped.

ciclón *sm* cyclone.

cíclope *sm* Cyclops.

ciclópeo, **a** *adj* culto & fig [enorme] colossal, massive.

cicuta *sf* hemlock.

ciega ⊳ **cegar**.

ciego, **ga** <> *adj* - **1.** [invidente] blind; **quedarse ciego** to go blind; **a ciegas** *lit & fig* blindly - **2.** *fig* [enloquecido]: **ciego (de)** blinded (by) - **3.** [pozo, tubería] blocked (up) - **4.** *mfam* [drogado] stoned; **ponerse ciego de algo** to get stoned on sthg. <> *sm, f* [invidente] blind person; **los ciegos** the blind; **hacerse el ciego** to turn a blind eye.
◆ **ciego** *sm* - **1.** ANAT caecum - **2.** *mfam* [de droga] trip.

ciegue *v* ⊳ **cegar**.

cielo *sm* - **1.** [gen] sky; **a cielo abierto** [gen] in the open; [mina] opencast - **2.** RELIG heaven - **3.** *fig* [Dios]: **el cielo** the Good Lord - **4.** [nombre cariñoso] my love, my dear - **5.** [parte superior] roof; **cielo del paladar** roof of the mouth; **cielo raso** ceiling - **6.** *loc*: **me viene caído del cielo** it's a godsend (to me); **clama al cielo** it's outrageous; **como llovido del cielo** [inesperadamente] out of the blue; [oportunamente] at just the right moment; **estar en el séptimo cielo** to be in seventh heaven; **se le juntó el cielo con la tierra** he lost his nerve; **mover cielo y tierra** to move heaven and earth; **ser un cielo** to be an angel; **ver el cielo abierto** to see one's way out.
◆ **cielos** *interj*: ¡cielos! good heavens!

ciempiés *sm inv* centipede.

cien - **1.** ⊳ **ciento** - **2.**: **poner a alguien a cien** *fam* [excitar] to make sb feel horny *fam*.

ciénaga *sf* marsh, bog.

ciencia *sf* - **1.** [gen] science; **ciencias económicas** economics *(U)*; **ciencias exactas** exact *o* pure sciences; **ciencias naturales/sociales** natural/social sciences; **ciencias ocultas** occult sciences - **2.** *fig* [habilidad] learning, knowledge; **ciencia infusa** *fig* intuitive knowledge.
◆ **ciencias** *sfpl* EDUC science *(U)*.
◆ **ciencia ficción** *sf* science fiction.
◆ **a ciencia cierta** *loc adv* for certain.

cieno *sm* mud, sludge.

cientificismo *sm* over-emphasis on scientific ideas.

científico, **ca** <> *adj* scientific. <> *sm, f* scientist.

cientista *smf C Sur*: **cientista social** social scientist.

ciento, **cien** *num* a *o* one hundred; **ciento cincuenta** a *o* one hundred and fifty; **cien mil** a *o* one hundred thousand; **cientos de** hundreds of; **por ciento** per cent; **ciento por ciento, cien por cien** a hundred per cent; **cientos de veces** hundreds of times; **a cientos** by the hundred; **darle ciento y raya a alguien** to run rings around sb; **eran ciento y la madre** everybody and his dog was there; *ver también* **seis**.

cierna *etc* ⊳ **cerner**.

cierne ◆ **en ciernes** *loc adv*: **estar en ciernes** to be in its infancy; **una campeona en ciernes** a budding champion.

cierre *sm* - **1.** [gen] closing, shutting; [con llave] locking; [de fábrica] shutdown; RADIO & TV closedown; **cierre centralizado** AUTO central locking; **cierre patronal** lockout - **2.** [mecanismo] fastener; **cierre metálico** [de tienda etc] metal shutter; **cierre relámpago** *Andes, Arg & Méx* [cremallera] zip *UK*, zipper *US*.

cierto, **ta** *adj* - **1.** [verdadero] true; **estar en lo cierto** to be right; **lo cierto es que...** the fact is that... - **2.** [seguro] certain, definite - **3.** [algún] certain; **cierto hombre** a certain man; **en cierta ocasión** once, on one occasion; **durante cierto tiempo** for a while.
◆ **cierto** *adv* right, certainly.
◆ **por cierto** *loc adv* by the way.

ciervo, **va** *sm, f* deer, stag (*f* hind).

cierzo *sm* north wind.

CIF (*abrev de* **código de identificación fiscal**) *sm* tax code.

cifra *sf* - **1.** [gen] figure; **cifra de negocios** ECON turnover; **cifra de ventas** sales figures - **2.** [clave]: **en cifra** in code.

cifrado, **da** *adj* coded, in code.

cifrar *vt* - **1.** [codificar] to code - **2.** *fig* [centrar] to concentrate, to centre.
◆ **cifrarse en** *vprnl* to come to, to amount to.

cigala *sf* Dublin Bay prawn.

cigarra *sf* cicada.

cigarrero, **ra** *sm, f* [persona] cigar maker.
◆ **cigarrera** *sf* [caja] cigar case.

cigarrillo *sm* cigarette.

cigarro *sm* - **1.** [habano] cigar - **2.** [cigarrillo] cigarette.

cigüeña *sf* stork.

cigüeñal *sm* crankshaft.

cilantro *sm* coriander *UK*, cilantro *US*.

cilicio *sm* hair shirt.
cilindrada *sf* cylinder capacity.
cilíndrico, **ca** *adj* cylindrical.
cilindro *sm* [gen] cylinder; [de imprenta] roller.
cima *sf* - **1.** [punta - de montaña] peak, summit; [- de árbol] top - **2.** *fig* [apogeo] peak, high point.
cimarrón, **ona** *sm*, *f* Amér runaway slave.
címbalo *(gen pl) sm* cymbal.
cimbreante *adj* swaying.
cimbrear *vt* - **1.** [vara] to waggle - **2.** [caderas] to sway.
cimentación *sf* - **1.** [acción] laying of the foundations - **2.** [cimientos] foundations *pl*.
cimentar [19] *vt* - **1.** [edificio] to lay the foundations of; [ciudad] to found, to build - **2.** *fig* [idea, paz, fama] to cement, to consolidate.
cimero, **ra** *adj* - **1.** [alto] topmost - **2.** *fig* [sobresaliente] foremost, most outstanding.
cimienta *etc* ⊳ **cimentar**.
cimiento *sm (gen pl)* - **1.** CONSTR foundation; **echar los cimientos** *lit & fig* to lay the foundations - **2.** *fig* [base] basis.
cimitarra *sf* scimitar.
cinabrio *sm* cinnabar.
cinc, **zinc** *sm* zinc.
cincel *sm* chisel.
cincelar *vt* to chisel.
cincha *sf* girth.
cincho *sm* - **1.** [cinturón] belt - **2.** [aro de hierro] hoop.
cinco *num* five; **¡choca esos cinco!** *fig* put it there!; **estar sin cinco** *fig* to be broke; *ver también* **seis**.
cincuenta *num* fifty; **los (años) cincuenta** the fifties; *ver también* **seis**.
cincuentenario *sm* fiftieth anniversary.
cincuentón, **ona** *sm*, *f* fifty-year-old.
cine *sm* cinema; **hacer cine** to make films; **cine de estreno/de verano** first-run/open-air cinema; **cine de terror** horror films; **cine mudo** silent films *pl*; **cine sonoro** talking pictures *pl*, talkies *pl*.
◆ **cine fórum** *sm* film with discussion group.
cineasta *smf* film maker o director.
cineclub *sm* - **1.** [asociación] film society - **2.** [sala] club cinema.
cinéfilo, **la** *sm*, *f* film buff.
cinegético, **ca** *adj* hunting *(antes de s)*.
◆ **cinegética** *sf* hunting.
cinemascope *sm* cinemascope.
cinemateca *sf* film library.
cinemática *sf* kinematics *(U)*.
cinematografía *sf* cinematography, film-making.
cinematográfico, **ca** *adj* film *(antes de s)*.

cinematógrafo *sm* - **1.** [aparato] film projector - **2.** [local] cinema.
cinerama *sm* cinerama.
cinético, **ca** *adj* kinetic.
◆ **cinética** *sf* kinetics *(U)*.
cíngaro, **ra**, **zíngaro**, **ra** *adj* & *sm*, *f* Tzigane.
cínico, **ca** ◇ *adj* cynical. ◇ *sm*, *f* cynic.
cinismo *sm* cynicism.
cinta *sf* - **1.** [tira - de plástico, papel] strip, band; [- de tela] ribbon; **cinta adhesiva** o **autoadhesiva** adhesive o sticky tape; **cinta aislante** o **aisladora** insulating tape; **cinta de impresora** printer ribbon; **cinta métrica** tape measure; **cinta perforada** punched tape - **2.** [de imagen, sonido, ordenadores] tape; **cinta digital/magnética** digital/magnetic tape; **cinta limpiadora** head-cleaning tape; **cinta magnetofónica** recording tape; **cinta de vídeo** videotape - **3.** [mecanismo] belt; **cinta transportadora** conveyor belt; **cinta de equipajes** baggage carousel - **4.** [película] film.
cinto *sm* belt.
cintura *sf* waist; **meter en cintura** to bring under control.
cinturilla *sf* waistband.
cinturón *sm* - **1.** [cinto] belt; **cinturón negro** DEP black belt; **apretarse el cinturón** to tighten one's belt - **2.** AUTO ring road - **3.** [cordón] cordon.
◆ **cinturón de castidad** *sm* chastity belt.
◆ **cinturón de seguridad** *sm* seat o safety belt.
◆ **cinturón de miseria** *sm* Amér slum or shanty town area round a large city.
ciña, **ciñera** *etc* ⊳ **ceñir**.
cipote, **ta** *sm*, *f* Amér lad (*f* lass).
◆ **cipote** *sm* vulg prick, cock.
ciprés *sm* cypress.
circense *adj* circus *(antes de s)*.
circo *sm* - **1.** [gen] circus - **2.** GEOGR cirque, corrie.
circuito *sm* - **1.** DEP & ELECTRÓN circuit; **circuito impreso/integrado** printed/integrated circuit; **circuito cerrado** closed circuit; **corto circuito** short-circuit - **2.** [contorno] belt - **3.** [recorrido] tour.
circulación *sf* - **1.** [gen] circulation; **circulación de la sangre** circulation of the blood; **circulación fiduciaria** o **monetaria** paper currency - **2.** [tráfico] traffic - **3.** [conducción] driving.
circular ◇ *adj* & *sf* circular. ◇ *vi* - **1.** [pasar]: **circular (por)** [líquido] to flow o circulate (through); [persona] to move o walk (around); [vehículos] to drive (along); **este autobús no cir-**

cula hoy this bus doesn't run today **- 2.** [de mano en mano] to circulate; [moneda] to be in circulation **- 3.** [difundirse] to go round.

circulatorio, **ria** adj circulatory.

círculo sm lit & fig circle.

➤ **círculos** smpl [medios] circles.

➤ **círculo polar** sm polar circle; **el círculo polar ártico/antártico** the Arctic/Antarctic Circle.

➤ **círculo vicioso** sm vicious circle.

circuncidar vt to circumcise.

circuncisión sf circumcision.

circundante adj surrounding.

circundar vt to surround.

circunferencia sf circumference.

circunflejo ▷ **acento**.

circunlocución sf circumlocution.

circunloquio sm circumlocution.

circunnavegar [16] vt to circumnavigate, to sail round.

circunscribir vt **- 1.** [limitar] to restrict, to confine **- 2.** GEOM to circumscribe.

➤ **circunscribirse a** vprnl to confine o.s. to.

circunscripción sf **- 1.** [limitación] limitation **- 2.** [distrito] district; MIL division; POLÍT constituency.

circunscrito, **ta** ◇ pp ▷ **circunscribir**. ◇ adj restricted, limited.

circunspección sf culto **- 1.** [comedimiento] circumspection **- 2.** [seriedad] graveness, seriousness.

circunspecto, **ta** adj culto **- 1.** [comedido] circumspect **- 2.** [serio] grave, serious.

circunstancia sf circumstance; **en estas circunstancias** under the circumstances; **circunstancia atenuante/agravante/eximente** DER extenuating/aggravating/exonerating circumstance.

circunstancial adj **- 1.** [accidental] chance (antes de s) **- 2.** GRAM ▷ **complemento**.

circunvalación sf [carretera] ring road.

circunvalar vt to go round.

cirílico, **ca** adj Cyrillic.

cirio sm (wax) candle; **cirio pascual** paschal candle; **montar un cirio** to make a row.

cirrosis sf inv cirrhosis.

ciruela sf plum; **ciruela claudia** greengage; **ciruela pasa** prune.

ciruelo sm plum tree.

cirugía sf surgery; **cirugía estética** o **plástica** cosmetic o plastic surgery.

cirujano, **na** sm, f surgeon.

cisco sm **- 1.** [carbón] slack; **hecho cisco** fig shattered **- 2.** fam [alboroto] row, rumpus.

cisma sm **- 1.** [separación] schism **- 2.** [discordia] split.

cismático, **ca** adj & sm, f schismatic.

cisne sm swan.

cisterciense adj & smf Cistercian.

cisterna sf **- 1.** [de retrete] cistern **- 2.** [aljibe, tanque] tank.

cistitis sf inv cystitis.

cita sf **- 1.** [entrevista] appointment; [de novios] date; **concertar una cita** to make an appointment; **darse cita** to meet; **tener una cita** to have an appointment **- 2.** [referencia] quotation.

citación sf DER summons sing.

citar vt **- 1.** [convocar] to make an appointment with **- 2.** [aludir] to mention; [textualmente] to quote **- 3.** DER to summons.

➤ **citarse** vprnl: **citarse (con alguien)** to arrange to meet (sb).

cítara sf zither.

citología sf **- 1.** [análisis] smear test **- 2.** BIOL cytology.

citoplasma sm cytoplasm.

cítrico, **ca** adj citric.

➤ **cítricos** smpl citrus fruits.

CiU (abrev de **Convergència i Unió**) sf Catalan coalition party to the centre-right of the political spectrum.

ciudad sf **- 1.** [localidad] city; [pequeña] town; **ciudad dormitorio/satélite** commuter/satellite town; **ciudad jardín** garden city **- 2.** [instalaciones] complex; **ciudad deportiva** sports complex; **ciudad sanitaria** hospital complex; **ciudad universitaria** university campus.

➤ **Ciudad del Cabo** sf Cape Town.

➤ **Ciudad del Vaticano** sf Vatican City.

➤ **Ciudad de México** sf Mexico City.

➤ **Ciudad Eterna** sf: **la Ciudad Eterna** the Eternal City.

➤ **Ciudad Santa** sf: **la Ciudad Santa** the Holy City.

ciudadanía sf **- 1.** [nacionalidad] citizenship **- 2.** [población] public, citizens pl.

ciudadano, **na** ◇ adj city (antes de s); [orgullo, deberes etc] civic. ◇ sm, f citizen; **el ciudadano de a pie** the man in the street.

ciudadela sf citadel, fortress.

cívico, **ca** adj civic; [conducta] public-spirited.

civil ◇ adj lit & fig civil. ◇ sm **- 1.** [no militar] civilian **- 2.** fam [Guardia Civil] member of "Guardia Civil".

civilización sf civilization.

civilizado, **da** adj civilized.

civilizar [13] vt to civilize.

➤ **civilizarse** vprnl to become civilized.

civismo *sm* - **1.** [urbanidad] community spirit - **2.** [cortesía] civility, politeness.

cizalla *sf* - **1.** [herramienta] shears *pl*, metal cutters *pl* - **2.** [recortes] metal cuttings *pl*.

cizaña *sf* BOT darnel; **meter** *o* **sembrar cizaña** to sow discord; **separar la cizaña del buen grano** to separate the wheat from the chaff.

cl (*abrev de* **centilitro**) cl.

clamar ◇ *vt* - **1.** [expresar] to exclaim - **2.** [exigir] to cry out for. ◇ *vi* - **1.** [implorar] to appeal - **2.** [protestar] to cry out.

clamor *sm* clamour.

clamoroso, sa *adj* - **1.** [rotundo] resounding - **2.** [vociferante] loud, clamorous.

clan *sm* - **1.** [tribu, familia] clan - **2.** [banda] faction.

clandestinidad *sf* secrecy; **en la clandestinidad** underground.

clandestino, na *adj* clandestine; POLÍT underground.

claque *sf* claque.

claqué *sm* tap dancing.

claqueta *sf* clapperboard.

clara *sf* ▷ **claro**.

claraboya *sf* skylight.

clarear ◇ *vt* to light up. ◇ *v impers* - **1.** [amanecer]: **empezaba a clarear** dawn was breaking - **2.** [despejarse] to clear up, to brighten up.

clarearse *vprnl* [transparentarse] to be see-through.

clarete ▷ **vino**.

claridad *sf* - **1.** [transparencia] clearness, clarity - **2.** [luz] light - **3.** [franqueza] candidness; **ser de una claridad meridiana** to be crystal clear - **4.** [lucidez] clarity; **explicar algo con claridad** to explain sthg clearly.

clarificación *sf* clarification.

clarificador, ra *adj* clarifying.

clarificar [10] *vt* - **1.** [gen] to clarify; [misterio] to clear up - **2.** [purificar] to refine.

clarín ◇ *sm* [instrumento] bugle. ◇ *smf* [persona] bugler.

clarinete ◇ *sm* [instrumento] clarinet. ◇ *smf* [persona] clarinettist.

clarinetista *smf* clarinettist.

clarividencia *sf* farsightedness, perception.

clarividente ◇ *adj* farsighted, perceptive. ◇ *smf* perceptive person.

claro, ra *adj* - **1.** [gen] clear; **claro está que...** of course...; **dejar algo claro** to make sthg clear; **a las claras** clearly; **pasar una noche en claro** to spend a sleepless night; **poner algo en claro** to get sthg clear, to clear sthg up; **sacar algo en claro (de)** to make sthg out (from);

tener algo claro to be sure of sthg - **2.** [luminoso] bright - **3.** [color] light - **4.** [diluido - té, café] weak; [- salsa] thin - **5.** [poco tupido] thin, sparse.

◆ **claro** ◇ *sm* - **1.** [en bosque] clearing; [en multitud, texto] space, gap - **2.** METEOR bright spell - **3.** [en pintura] highlight. ◇ *adv* clearly. ◇ *interj*: **¡claro!** of course!; **¡claro que no!** of course not!; **¡claro que sí!** yes, of course.

◆ **clara** *sf* - **1.** [de huevo] white - **2.** [bebida] shandy - **3.** [calvicie] bald patch.

◆ **claro de luna** *sm* moonlight.

claroscuro *sm* chiaroscuro.

clase *sf* - **1.** [gen] class; **clase alta/media** upper/middle class; **clase obrera** *o* **trabajadora** working class; **clase social** social class; **clase preferente/turista** club/tourist *o* coach US class; **clase salón** *Amér* FERROC first class; **primera clase** first class; **clases pasivas** pensioners - **2.** [tipo] sort, kind; **toda clase de** all sorts *o* kinds of - **3.** [EDUC - asignatura, alumnos] class; [- aula] classroom; **dar clases** [- en un colegio] to teach; [- en una universidad] to lecture; **clases particulares** private classes *o* lessons; **clases de recuperación** *extra lessons for pupils who have failed their exams.*

clasicismo *sm* - **1.** ARTE & LITER classicism - **2.** [tradicionalismo] classical nature.

clásico, ca ◇ *adj* - **1.** [de la Antigüedad] classical - **2.** [ejemplar, prototípico] classic - **3.** [peinado, estilo, música etc] classical - **4.** [habitual] customary - **5.** [peculiar]: **clásico de** typical of. ◇ *sm, f* [persona] classic.

◆ **clásicas** *sfpl* [estudios] classics.

clasificación *sf* classification; DEP (league) table.

clasificador, ra *adj* classifying.

◆ **clasificador** *sm* [mueble] filing cabinet.

◆ **clasificadora** *sf* [máquina] sorter.

clasificar [10] *vt* to classify.

◆ **clasificarse** *vprnl* - **1.** [ganar acceso]: **clasificarse (para)** to qualify (for); DEP to get through (to) - **2.** [llegar]: **se clasificó en segundo lugar** she came second.

clasismo *sm* class discrimination.

clasista ◇ *adj* class-conscious; *despec* snobbish. ◇ *smf* class-conscious person; *despec* snob.

claudia ▷ **ciruela**.

claudicación *sf* withdrawal.

claudicar [10] *vi* - **1.** [ceder] to give in - **2.** [renunciar]: **claudicar de** to renounce.

claustro *sm* - **1.** ARQUIT & RELIG cloister - **2.** [de universidad] senate.

◆ **claustro materno** *sm* womb.

claustrofobia *sf* claustrophobia.

cláusula *sf* clause.

clausura *sf* - **1.** [acto solemne] closing cere- mony - **2.** [cierre] closing down - **3.** [aislamiento] enclosed life, enclosure - **4.** RELIG religious se- clusion.

clausurar *vt* - **1.** [acto] to close, to conclude - **2.** [local] to close down.

clavadista *smf Amér C & Méx* diver.

clavado, da *adj* - **1.** [con clavos] nailed - **2.** [en punto - hora] on the dot - **3.** [a la medida] just right - **4.** [parecido] almost identical; **ser clava- do a alguien** to be the spitting image of sb - **5.** [fijo] fixed.
◆ **clavada** *sf mfam* [estafa] rip-off.

clavar *vt* - **1.** [clavo, estaca etc] to drive; [cuchillo] to thrust; [chincheta, alfiler] to stick - **2.** [cartel, placa etc] to nail, to fix - **3.** *fig* [mirada, atención] to fix, to rivet; **clavar los ojos en** to stare at - **4.** *mfam* [estafar] to sting, to rip off; **me han cla- vado cien euros** they stung me for a hundred euros.
◆ **clavarse** *vprnl* [hincarse]: **me clavé un cristal en el pie** I got a splinter of glass in my foot.

clave ◇ *adj inv* key; **palabra clave** keyword. ◇ *sm* MÚS harpsichord. ◇ *sf* - **1.** [código] code; **en clave** in code - **2.** *fig* [solución] key; **la clave del problema** the key to the problem - **3.** MÚS clef; **clave de sol** treble clef - **4.** INFORM key; **clave de acceso** access key.

clavecín *sm* spinet.

clavel *sm* carnation.

claveteado *sm* studding.

clavetear *vt* - **1.** [adornar con clavos] to stud (with nails) - **2.** [poner clavos] to nail roughly.

clavicémbalo *sm* harpsichord.

clavicordio *sm* clavichord.

clavícula *sf* collar bone.

clavija *sf* - **1.** ELECTR & TECNOL pin; [de auriculares, teléfono] jack - **2.** MÚS peg; **apretar las clavijas a alguien** to put the screws on sb.

clavo *sm* - **1.** [pieza metálica] nail; **agarrarse a un clavo ardiendo** to clutch at straws; **estaré allí como un clavo** I'll be there on the dot; **dar en el clavo** to hit the nail on the head; **rema- char el clavo** to make matters worse; **¡por los clavos de Cristo!** for heaven's sake - **2.** BOT & CULIN clove - **3.** MED [para huesos] pin.

claxon® (*pl* **cláxones**) *sm* horn; **tocar el cla- xon** to sound the horn.

clemencia *sf* mercy, clemency.

clemente *adj* - **1.** [persona] merciful, clement - **2.** *fig* [invierno etc] mild.

clementina *sf* clementine.

cleptomanía *sf* kleptomania.

cleptómano, na *sm, f* kleptomaniac.

clerecía *sf* - **1.** [clero] clergy - **2.** [oficio] priest- hood.

clerical ◇ *adj* clerical. ◇ *smf* clericalist.

clérigo *sm* [católico] priest; [anglicano] clergy- man.

clero *sm* clergy.

clic *sm* INFORM click; **hacer clic en algo** to click on sthg.

cliché, clisé *sm* - **1.** FOTO negative - **2.** IMPR plate - **3.** *fig* [tópico] cliché.

cliente, ta *sm, f* [de tienda, garaje, bar] custom- er; [de banco, abogado etc] client; [de hotel] guest; **cliente habitual** regular customer.

clientela *sf* [de tienda, garaje] customers *pl*; [de banco, abogado etc] clients *pl*; [de hotel] guests *pl*; [de bar, restaurante] clientele.

clima *sm lit & fig* climate; **clima mediterráneo/ tropical** Mediterranean/tropical climate.

climaterio *sm* climacteric.

climático, ca *adj* climatic.

climatización *sf* air conditioning.

climatizado, da *adj* air-conditioned.

climatizar [13] *vt* to air-condition.

climatología *sf* - **1.** [tiempo] weather - **2.** [ciencia] climatology.

climatológico, ca *adj* climatological.

clímax *sm inv* climax.

clínico, ca *adj* clinical.
◆ **clínica** *sf* clinic.

clip *sm* - **1.** [para papel] paper clip - **2.** [para el pelo] hairclip - **3.** [videoclip] (video) clip.

clíper *sm* clipper.

clisé = **cliché**.

clítoris *sm inv* clitoris.

cloaca *sf* sewer.

clon *sm* clone.

clonar *vt* to clone.

clónico, ca *adj* clonic.

cloquear *vi* to cluck.

cloración *sf* chlorination.

clorato *sm* chlorate.

clorhídrico ▷ **ácido**.

cloro *sm* - **1.** QUÍM chlorine - **2.** *Amér C & Chile* [lejía] bleach.

clorofila *sf* chlorophyll.

cloruro *sm* chloride; **cloruro de cal** bleach- ing powder; **cloruro de sodio** o **sódico** sodium chloride.

clóset, closets *sm Amér* fitted cupboard.

clown [klawn] *sm* clown.

club (*pl* **clubes** o **clubs**) *sm* club; **club de fans** fan club; **club de fútbol** football club; **club náutico** yacht club; **club nocturno** nightclub.

clueca *adj* broody.

cm (*abrev de* **centímetro**) cm.

CNA (*abrev de* **Congreso Nacional Africano**) *sm* ANC.

CNT (*abrev de* **Confederación Nacional del Trabajo**) *sf Spanish anarchist trade union federation created in 1911.*

Co. (*abrev de* **compañía**) Co.

coacción *sf* coercion.

coaccionar *vt* to coerce.

coactivo, **va** *adj* coercive.

coagulación *sf* clotting, coagulation.

coagulante <> *adj* clotting. <> *sm* clotting agent.

coagular *vt* [gen] to coagulate; [sangre] to clot; [leche] to curdle.

◆ **coagularse** *vprnl* [gen] to coagulate; [sangre] to clot; [leche] to curdle.

coágulo *sm* clot.

coalición *sf* coalition; **formar una coalición** to form a coalition.

coaligar *vt* = **coligar**.

coartada *sf* alibi.

coartar *vt* to limit, to restrict.

coautor, **ra** *sm, f* coauthor.

coaxial *adj* coaxial.

coba *sf fam* [halago] flattery; **dar coba a alguien** [hacer la pelota] to suck up *o* crawl to sb; [aplacar] to soft-soap sb.

cobalto *sm* cobalt.

cobarde <> *adj* cowardly. <> *smf* coward.

cobardía *sf* cowardice.

cobaya *sm o sf* guinea pig.

cobertizo *sm* - **1.** [tejado adosado] lean-to - **2.** [barracón] shed.

cobertura *sf* - **1.** [gen] cover - **2.** [de un edificio] covering - **3.** PRENSA: **cobertura informativa** news coverage - **4.** TELECOM: **no tengo cobertura** my network doesn't cover this area.

cobija *sf Amér* [manta] blanket.

cobijar *vt* - **1.** [albergar] to house - **2.** [proteger] to shelter.

◆ **cobijarse** *vprnl* to take shelter.

cobijo *sm* shelter; **dar cobijo a alguien** to give shelter to sb, to take sb in.

cobista *smf fam* creep.

COBOL *sm* INFORM COBOL.

cobra *sf* cobra.

cobrador, **ra** *sm, f* [del autobús] conductor (*f* conductress); [de deudas, recibos] collector.

cobrar <> *vt* - **1.** [COM - dinero] to charge; [- cheque] to cash; [- deuda] to collect; **cantidades por cobrar** amounts due; **¿me cobra, por favor?** how much do I owe you? - **2.** [en el trabajo] to earn, to be paid - **3.** [adquirir - importancia] to get, to acquire; **cobrar fama** to become famous - **4.** [sentir - cariño, afecto] to start to feel;

cobrarle afecto a alguien to take a liking to sb. <> *vi* - **1.** [en el trabajo] to get paid - **2.** *fam* [recibir una paliza] to catch it; **¡vas a cobrar!** you'll be in for it!

◆ **cobrarse** *vprnl*: **el accidente se cobró nueve vidas** nine people were killed in the crash.

cobre *sm* copper; **no tener un cobre** *Amér* to be flat broke.

cobrizo, **za** *adj* - **1.** [color, piel] copper (*antes de s*) - **2.** [de cobre - metal] containing copper.

cobro *sm* [de talón] cashing; [de pago] collection; **llamada a cobro revertido** reverse charge call *UK*, collect call *US*; **llamar a cobro revertido** to reverse the charges *UK*, to call collect *US*.

coca *sf* - **1.** [planta] coca - **2.** *fam* [cocaína] coke.

cocaína *sf* cocaine.

cocainómano, **na** *sm, f* cocaine addict.

cocción *sf* [gen] cooking; [en agua] boiling; [en horno] baking.

cóccix, **coxis** *sm inv* coccyx.

cocear *vi* to kick.

cocer [41] *vt* - **1.** [gen] to cook; [hervir] to boil; [en horno] to bake - **2.** [cerámica, ladrillos] to fire.

◆ **cocerse** *vprnl* - **1.** [gen] to cook; [hervir] to boil; [en horno] to bake - **2.** *fig* [plan] to be afoot.

cochambre *sf fam* - **1.** [suciedad] filth - **2.** [cosa de mala calidad] rubbish.

cochambroso, **sa** *adj fam* filthy.

cochayuyo *sm Andes* seaweed.

coche *sm* - **1.** [automóvil] car, automobile *US*; **ir en coche** [montado] to go by car; [conduciendo] to drive; **coche de alquiler** hire car; **coche blindado** armoured car; **coche de bomberos** fire engine; **coche de carreras** racing car; **coche celular** police van; **coche deportivo** sports car; **coche familiar** estate car *UK*, station wagon *US*; **coche fúnebre** hearse; **coche grúa** breakdown van *o* lorry *UK* *o* truck *US*; **coche patrulla** patrol car, squad car *US* - **2.** [de tren] coach, carriage; **coche cama** sleeping car, sleeper; **coche restaurante** restaurant *o* dining car - **3.** [de caballos] carriage - **4.** *loc*: **ir en el coche de San Fernando** *fam hum* to go on foot.

◆ **coche bomba** *sm* car bomb.

cochera *sf* [para coches] garage; [de autobuses, tranvías] depot.

cochero *sm* coachman.

cochinada *sf fam fig* [guarrería] dirty *o* filthy thing; [grosería] obscenity, dirty word; **decir cochinadas** to use foul language; [mala jugada] dirty trick.

cochinilla *sf* - **1.** [crustáceo] woodlouse - **2.** [insecto] cochineal.

cochinillo *sm* sucking pig.

cochino, na <> *adj* - **1.** [persona] filthy
- **2.** [tiempo, dinero] lousy. <> *sm, f* [animal - macho] pig; [- hembra] sow.

cocido *sm* stew; **cocido madrileño** CULIN *stew made with chickpeas, bacon, meat and root vegetables, typical of Madrid.*

cociente *sm* quotient; **cociente intelectual** intelligence quotient, I.Q.

cocina *sf* - **1.** [habitación] kitchen - **2.** [electrodoméstico] cooker, stove; **cocina eléctrica/de gas** electric/gas cooker - **3.** [arte] cooking; **alta cocina** haute cuisine; **cocina casera** home cooking; **cocina española** Spanish cuisine o cooking; **libro/clase de cocina** cookery book/class.

cocinar *vt & vi* to cook.

cocinero, ra *sm, f* cook; **haber sido cocinero antes que fraile** to know what one is talking about.

cocker *sm* cocker spaniel.

coco *sm* - **1.** [árbol] coconut palm; [fruto] coconut - **2.** *fam* [cabeza] nut, head; **comerse el coco** to worry (one's head); **comer el coco a alguien** [convencer] to brainwash sb - **3.** *fam* [fantasma] bogeyman - **4.** BOT [bacteria] coccus.

cococha *sf* barbel.

cocodrilo *sm* crocodile.

cocotero *sm* coconut palm.

cóctel, coctel *sm* - **1.** [bebida, comida] cocktail; **cóctel de gambas** prawn cocktail - **2.** [reunión] cocktail party.

➥ **cóctel molotov** *sm* Molotov cocktail.

coctelera *sf* cocktail shaker.

cód. *abrev de* **código**.

coda *sf* coda.

codazo *sm* nudge, jab *(with one's elbow)*; **abrirse paso a codazos** to elbow one's way through; **dar un codazo a alguien** [con disimulo] to give sb a nudge, to nudge sb; [con fuerza] to elbow sb.

codearse *vprnl*: **codearse (con)** to rub shoulders (with).

codeína *sf* codeine.

codera *sf* elbow patch.

códice *sm* codex.

codicia *sf* - **1.** [avaricia] greed - **2.** [de lo ajeno] covetousness.

codiciar [8] *vt* to covet.

codicioso, sa *adj* greedy.

codificación *sf* - **1.** [de norma, ley] codification - **2.** [de mensaje en clave] encoding - **3.** INFORM coding.

codificador, ra <> *adj* codifying. <> *sm, f* INFORM [profesional] encoder.

➥ **codificador** *sm* [aparato] encoder.

codificar [10] *vt* - **1.** [ley] to codify - **2.** [un mensaje] to encode - **3.** INFORM to code.

código *sm* [gen & INFORM] code; **código postal** post UK o zip US code; **código territorial** area code; **código mercantil** o **de comercio** commercial law; **código de barras/de señales** bar/signal code; **código de circulación** highway code; **código civil/penal** civil/penal code; **código ASCII** ASCII code; **código máquina** machine code; **código Morse** Morse code; **código territorial** dialling code UK, area code US.

codillo *sm* - **1.** [en un cuadrúpedo] upper foreleg - **2.** [de jamón] shoulder - **3.** [de un tubo] elbow, bend.

codirector, ra *sm, f* co-director.

codo *sm* - **1.** [en brazo, tubería] elbow; **estaba de codos sobre la mesa** she was leaning (with her elbows) on the table; **dar con el codo** to nudge - **2.** [medida] cubit - **3.** *loc*: **se sacó la carrera a base de codos** she got her degree by sheer hard work; **codo con codo, codo a codo** side by side; **empinar el codo** *fam* to booze; **hablar por los codos** *fam* to talk nineteen to the dozen, to be a chatterbox; **hincar los codos** *fam* to swot.

codorniz *sf* quail.

coeficiente *sm* - **1.** [gen] coefficient; **coeficiente de caja** BANCA cash ratio; **coeficiente intelectual** o **de inteligencia** intelligence quotient, I.Q. - **2.** [índice] rate.

coercer [11] *vt* to restrict, to constrain.

coerción *sf* coercion.

coerza *etc* ▷ **coercer**.

coetáneo, a *adj & sm, f* contemporary.

coexistencia *sf* coexistence; **coexistencia pacífica** peaceful coexistence.

coexistente *adj* coexisting.

coexistir *vi* to coexist.

cofia *sf* [de enfermera, camarera] cap; [de monja] coif.

cofrade *sm, f* - **1.** [de cofradía religiosa] brother (*f* sister) - **2.** [de cofradía no religiosa] member.

cofradía *sf* - **1.** [religiosa] brotherhood (*f* sisterhood) - **2.** [no religiosa] guild.

cofre *sm* - **1.** [arca] chest, trunk - **2.** [para joyas] jewel box.

coger [14] <> *vt* - **1.** [asir, agarrar] to take; **coger a alguien de** o **por la mano** to take sb by the hand - **2.** [atrapar - ladrón, pez, pájaro] to catch - **3.** [alcanzar - persona, vehículo] to catch up with - **4.** [recoger - frutos, flores] to pick - **5.** [quedarse con - propina, empleo, piso] to take - **6.** [contratar - personal] to take on - **7.** [quitar]: **coger algo (a alguien)** to take sthg (from sb) - **8.** [tren, autobús] to take, to catch; **no me gusta coger el avión** I don't like flying - **9.** [contraer - gripe, resfriado] to catch, to get; **coger una borrachera** to get drunk - **10.** [sentir - manía, odio, afecto] to start to feel; **coger cariño/mie-**

do a to become fond/scared of - **11.** [suj: coche] to knock over, to run over; [suj: toro] to gore - **12.** [oír] to catch; [entender] to get; **no cogió el chiste** he didn't get the joke - **13.** [sorprender, encontrar]: **coger a alguien haciendo algo** to catch sb doing sthg; **lo cogieron robando** they caught him stealing - **14.** [sintonizar - canal, emisora] to get, to receive - **15.** [abarcar - espacio] to cover, to take up - **16.** *Méx, R Plata & Ven vulg* [tener relaciones sexuales con] to screw, to fuck. <> *vi* - **1.** [situarse] to be; **coge muy cerca de aquí** it's not very far from here - **2.** [dirigirse]: **coger a la derecha/la izquierda** to turn right/left - **3.** *loc*: **cogió y se fue** he upped and went; **de pronto cogió y me insultó** he turned round and insulted me.

➤ **cogerse** *vprnl* - **1.** [agarrarse]: **cogerse de** o **a algo** to cling to o clutch sthg - **2.** [pillarse]: **cogerse los dedos/la falda en la puerta** to catch one's fingers/skirt in the door.

cogestión *sf* copartnership.

cogida *sf* [de torero]: **sufrir una cogida** to be gored.

cognac = **coñac.**

cogollo *sm* - **1.** [de lechuga] heart - **2.** [brote - de árbol, planta] shoot.

cogorza *sf fam*: **agarrarse una cogorza** to get smashed, to get blind drunk; **llevar una cogorza** to be smashed, to be blind drunk.

cogotazo *sm* rabbit punch.

cogote *sm* nape, back of the neck.

cohabitación *sf* cohabitation.

cohabitar *vi* to cohabit, to live together.

cohecho *sm* bribery.

coherencia *sf* - **1.** [de razonamiento] coherence - **2.** FÍS cohesion.

coherente *adj* coherent.

cohesión *sf* cohesion.

cohete *sm* rocket.

cohibición *sf* inhibition.

cohibido, da *adj* inhibited.

cohibir *vt* to inhibit.

➤ **cohibirse** *vprnl* to become inhibited.

cohorte *sf* cohort.

COI (*abrev de* **Comité Olímpico Internacional**) *sm* IOC.

coima *sf Andes & R Dom fam* bribe, backhander *UK*.

coincidencia *sf* coincidence; **¡qué coincidencia!** what a coincidence!

coincidir *vi* - **1.** [superficies, versiones, gustos] to coincide - **2.** [personas - encontrarse] to meet; [- estar de acuerdo] to agree; **coincidimos en una fiesta** we saw each other at a party.

coito *sm* (sexual) intercourse.

coja ➤ **coger.**

cojear *vi* - **1.** [persona] to limp - **2.** [mueble] to wobble - **3.** *fig* [adolecer] to falter, to flounder.

cojera *sf* [acción] limp; [estado] lameness.

cojín *sm* cushion.

cojinete *sm* [en eje] bearing; [en un riel de ferrocarril] chair.

cojo, ja <> *adj* - **1.** [persona] lame - **2.** [mueble] wobbly - **3.** *fig* [razonamiento, frase] faulty. <> *sm, f* cripple; **no ser cojo ni manco** *fig* to know a thing or two. <> *v* ➤ **coger.**

cojón *sm* (*gen pl*) *vulg* ball; **¡ahora lo vas a hacer por cojones!** you bloody well are going to do it!; **tener cojones** to have balls o guts.

➤ **cojones** *interj vulg*: **¡cojones!** [enfado] for fuck's sake!

cojonudo, da *adj vulg* bloody brilliant.

cojudear *vt Andes & R Dom fam* - **1.** [hacer tonterías] to piss about, to muck about - **2.** [engañar] to trick.

cojudez *sf Andes mfam*: **¡que cojudez!** [acto] what a bloody *UK* o goddamn *US* stupid thing to do!; [dicho] what a bloody *UK* o goddamn *US* stupid thing to say!

cojudo, da *adj Andes mfam* bloody *UK* o goddamn *US* stupid.

col *sf* cabbage; **col de Bruselas** Brussels sprout; **col lombarda** red cabbage; **entre col y col, lechuga** *fam* variety is the spice of life.

cola *sf* - **1.** [de animal, avión] tail - **2.** [de vestido de novia] train - **3.** [fila] queue *UK*, line *US*; **¡a la cola!** get in the queue! *UK*, get in line! *US*; **hacer cola** to queue (up) *UK*, to stand in line *US*; **ponerse a la cola** to join the end of the queue *UK* o line *US*; **cola de impresión** INFORM printout queue - **4.** [de clase, lista] bottom; [de desfile] end - **5.** [pegamento] glue - **6.** [bebida] cola - **7.** [peinado]: **cola (de caballo)** pony tail - **8.** *Esp fam* [pene] willy *UK*, peter *US* - **9.** *Amér fam* [nalgas] bum *UK*, fanny *US* - **10.** *loc*: **no pegan ni con cola** *fam* they don't match at all; **tener** o **traer cola** *fam* to have serious consequences o repercussions.

colaboración *sf* - **1.** [gen] collaboration - **2.** [de prensa] contribution, article.

colaboracionismo *sm* collaborationism.

colaboracionista <> *adj* collaborationist. <> *smf* collaborator.

colaborador, ra <> *adj* cooperative. <> *sm, f* - **1.** [gen] collaborator - **2.** [de prensa] contributor, writer.

colaborar *vi* - **1.** [ayudar] to collaborate - **2.** [en prensa]: **colaborar en** o **con** to write for, to work for - **3.** [contribuir] to contribute.

colación *sf*: **sacar** o **traer algo a colación** [tema] to bring sthg up.

coladero *sm fam* easy way through.

colado, **da** *adj* - **1.** [líquido] strained - **2.** [enamorado]: **estar colado por alguien** *fam* to have a crush on sb.

➤ **colada** *sf* [ropa] laundry; **hacer la colada** to do the washing.

colador *sm* [para líquidos] strainer, sieve; [para verdura] colander.

colágeno *sm* collagen.

colapsar ◇ *vt* to bring to a halt, to stop. ◇ *vi* to come o grind to a halt.

colapso *sm* - **1.** MED collapse, breakdown; **sufrir un colapso** to collapse; **colapso nervioso** nervous breakdown - **2.** [de actividad] stoppage; [de tráfico] traffic jam, hold-up.

colar [23] ◇ *vt* - **1.** [verdura, té] to strain; [café] to filter - **2.** [dinero falso] to pass off as genuine; [mentira] to slip through - **3.** [por un sitio estrecho] to slip, to squeeze. ◇ *vi fam* [pasar por bueno]: **esto no colará** this won't wash.

➤ **colarse** *vprnl* - **1.** [líquido]: **colarse por** to seep through - **2.** [persona] to slip, to sneak; [en una cola] to jump the queue *UK* o line *US*; **colarse en una fiesta** to gatecrash a party - **3.** *fam* [por error] to slip up - **4.** *loc*: **colarse por alguien** *fam* to fall for sb.

colateral *adj* - **1.** [lateral] on either side - **2.** [pariente] collateral.

colcha *sf* bedspread.

colchón *sm* - **1.** [de cama] mattress; **colchón inflable** air bed - **2.** INFORM buffer.

colchoneta *sf* [para playa] beach mat; [en gimnasio] mat.

cole *sm fam* school.

colear *vi* - **1.** [animal] to wag its tail - **2.** *fig* [asunto, problema] to drag on.

colección *sf lit & fig* collection.

coleccionable ◇ *adj* collectable. ◇ *sm* special supplement in serialized form.

coleccionar *vt* to collect.

coleccionista *smf* collector.

colecta *sf* collection.

colectividad *sf* community.

colectivismo *sm* collectivism.

colectivización *sf* collectivization.

colectivizar [13] *vt* to collectivize.

colectivo, **va** *adj* collective.

➤ **colectivo** *sm* - **1.** [grupo] group - **2.** *Andes* [taxi] collective taxi - **3.** *Andes & Bol* [autobús] bus.

colector, **ra** *adj* collecting.

➤ **colector** *sm* - **1.** [sumidero] sewer; **colector de basuras** chute - **2.** MECÁN [de motor] manifold - **3.** [de transistor] collector.

colega *smf* - **1.** [compañero profesional] colleague - **2.** [homólogo] counterpart, opposite number - **3.** *fam* [amigo] mate.

colegiado, **da** *adj* who belongs to a professional association.

➤ **colegiado** *sm* DEP referee.

colegial, **la** *sm, f* schoolboy (*f* schoolgirl).

➤ **colegial** *adj* school (*antes de s*).

colegiarse [8] *vprnl* to become a member of a professional association.

colegiata *sf* collegiate church.

colegio *sm* - **1.** [escuela] school; **colegio concertado** private school with state subsidy; **colegio de curas** school run by priests; **colegio de monjas** convent school; **colegio de pago** fee-paying o private school - **2.** [de profesionales]: **colegio (profesional)** professional association.

➤ **colegio electoral** *sm* [lugar] polling station; [votantes] ward.

➤ **colegio mayor** *sm* hall of residence.

Colegio de México

The **Colegio de México** is an institution dedicated to research and graduate teaching in the Social Sciences and Humanities, and has exercised a leading influence on intellectual and academic life in Mexico since its foundation in 1940. It developed from the "Casa de España", which was set up in 1938 as a refuge for exiled Spanish academics during the Spanish Civil War, and of which the Mexican writer Alfonso Reyes was one of the first directors. The early work of the Colegio concentrated on historical, literary and linguistic research, but in time it grew to encompass economics, demographics and sociology, as well as Asian and African and International studies. Although it is a small institution compared with the large public universities, it has one of the most important libraries in Latin America (the Biblioteca Cosío Villegas), and publishes about 100 books a year.

colegir [42] ➤ **colegir de** *vi* to infer from, to gather from. ➤ **colegirse de** *vprnl* to be inferred from.

coleópteros *smpl* coleoptera.

cólera ◇ *sm* MED cholera. ◇ *sf* [ira] anger, rage; **montar en cólera** to get angry, to lose one's temper.

colérico, **ca** *adj* - **1.** [carácter] bad-tempered - **2.** MED cholera (*antes de s*).

colesterol *sm* cholesterol.

coleta *sf* pigtail; **cortarse la coleta** to call it a day, to retire.

coletazo *sm* flick o swish of the tail; **está dando (los últimos) coletazos** it's in its death throes.

coletilla *sf* postscript.

colgado, **da** *adj* - **1.** [cuadro, jamón etc]: **colgado (de)** hanging (from) - **2.** [teléfono] on the hook - **3.** *fam fig* [abandonado]: **dejar colgado a alguien** to leave sb in the lurch - **4.** *fam* [enganchado]: **quedarse colgado (con)** to get hooked (on).

colgador *sm* hanger, coathanger.

colgajo *sm* - **1.** [de ropa] hanging piece of material - **2.** [de piel] flap.

colgante <> *adj* hanging. <> *sm* pendant.

colgar [39] <> *vt* - **1.** [suspender, ahorcar] to hang; **colgar el teléfono** to hang up - **2.** [imputar]: **colgar algo a alguien** to blame sthg on sb - **3.** [suspender en los estudios] to fail - **4.** [abandonar] to give up. <> *vi* - **1.** [pender]: **colgar (de)** to hang (from) - **2.** [hablando por teléfono] to hang up, to put the phone down.
  colgarse *vprnl*: **colgarse (de)** [gen] to hang (from); [ahorcarse] to hang o.s. (from).

colibrí *sm* hummingbird.

cólico *sm* stomachache; **cólico hepático** biliary colic; **cólico nefrítico** o **renal** renal colic.

coliflor *sf* cauliflower.

coligar, coaligar [16] *vt* to ally, to unite.
  coligarse *vprnl* to unite, to join together.

colige, coligió *etc* ⊳ **colegir**.

coligue *etc* ⊳ **coligar**.

colija *etc* ⊳ **colegir**.

colilla *sf* (cigarette) butt o stub.

colimba *sf* *Arg fam* military service.

colina *sf* hill.

colindante *adj* neighbouring, adjacent.

colindar *vi* to be adjacent, to adjoin.

colirio *sm* eyewash, eyedrops *pl*.

coliseo *sm* coliseum.

colisión *sf* [de automóviles] collision, crash; [de ideas, intereses] clash.

colisionar *vi* - **1.** [coche]: **colisionar (contra)** to collide (with), to crash (into) - **2.** *fig* [ideas] to clash.

colista *smf* [en liga de fútbol etc] bottom team; [en carreras] tailender.

colitis *sf inv* stomach infection.

collado *sm* [colina] hill.

collage [koˈlaʃ] *sm* collage.

collar *sm* - **1.** [de personas] necklace - **2.** [para animales] collar - **3.** [abrazadera] collar, ring.

collarín *sm* surgical collar.

collera *sf Andes* cuff link.

colmado, **da** *adj*: **colmado (de)** full to the brim (with).
  colmado *sm* grocer's (shop).

colmar *vt* - **1.** [recipiente] to fill (to the brim) - **2.** *fig* [aspiración, deseo] to fulfil; **colmar a alguien de regalos/elogios** to shower gifts/praise on sb.

colmena *sf* beehive.

colmenar *sm* apiary.

colmillo *sm* - **1.** [de persona] canine, eye-tooth - **2.** [de perro] fang; [de elefante] tusk - **3.** *loc*: **enseñar los colmillos** to show one's teeth.

colmo *sm* height; **para colmo de desgracias** to crown it all; **es el colmo de la locura** it's sheer madness; **¡eso es el colmo!** *fam* that's the last straw!

colocación *sf* - **1.** [acción] placing, positioning; [situación] place, position - **2.** [empleo] position, job.

colocado, **da** *adj* - **1.** [gen] placed; **estar muy bien colocado** to have a very good job - **2.** *fam* [borracho] legless; [drogado] high, stoned.

colocar [10] *vt* - **1.** [en su sitio] to place, to put - **2.** [en una posición]: **colocar los brazos en alto** to raise one's arms - **3.** [en un empleo] to find a job for - **4.** [casar] to marry off - **5.** [invertir] to place, to invest.
  colocarse *vprnl* - **1.** [en un trabajo] to get a job - **2.** *fam* [emborracharse] to get legless; [drogarse] to get high o stoned.

colofón *sm* - **1.** [remate, fin] climax, culmination - **2.** [de libro] colophon.

Colombia *n pr* Colombia.

colombianismo *sm* Colombian expression.

colombiano, **na** *adj* & *sm, f* Colombian.

colombofilia *sf* pigeon-fancying.

colon *sm* colon.

colón *sm* colon (*unit of currency in Costa Rica and El Salvador*).

colonia *sf* - **1.** [gen] colony - **2.** [de niños]: **colonia (de verano)** (summer) camp; **ir de colonias** to go to summer camp - **3.** [perfume] eau de cologne - **4.** *Méx* [barrio] district; **colonia proletaria** shanty town, slum area.

colonial *adj* colonial.

colonialismo *sm* colonialism.

colonialista *adj* & *smf* colonialist.

colonización *sf* colonization.

colonizador, **ra** <> *adj* colonizing. <> *sm, f* colonizer, colonist.

colonizar [13] *vt* to colonize.

colono *sm* settler, colonist.

coloque *etc* ⊳ **colocar**.

coloquial *adj* colloquial.

coloquio *sm* - **1.** [conversación] conversation - **2.** [debate] discussion, debate.

color *sm* - **1.** [gen] colour; **color rojo** red; **color azul** blue; **¿de qué color?** what colour?; **una falda de color rosa** a pink skirt; **color local**

local colour; **a todo color** in full colour; **de color** [persona] coloured; **en color** [foto, televisor] colour; **color primario** primary colour; **colores complementarios** complementary colours **- 2.** fig [aspecto] tone **- 3.** [en los naipes] suit **- 4.** loc: **dar color a algo** to colour sthg in; fig to brighten o liven sthg up; **no hay color** it's no contest; **ponerse de mil colores** to flush; **sacarle a alguien los colores (a la cara)** to make sb blush; **ver las cosas de color de rosa** to see things through rose-coloured o rose-tinted spectacles.

colorado, da adj [color] red; **ponerse colorado** to blush, to go red.

➤ **colorado** sm [color] red.

colorante sm colouring.

colorear vt to colour (in).

colorete sm rouge, blusher.

colorido sm colours pl.

colorín (gen pl) sm bright colour; **colorín colorado, este cuento se ha acabado** and they all lived happily ever after.

colorista adj colouristic.

colosal adj **- 1.** [estatura, tamaño] colossal **- 2.** [extraordinario] great, enormous.

coloso sm **- 1.** [estatua] colossus **- 2.** fig [cosa, persona] giant.

colt® sm Colt®.

columna sf **- 1.** [gen] column; **quinta columna** fifth column **- 2.** fig [pilar] pillar.

➤ **columna vertebral** sf spinal column.

columnata sf colonnade.

columnista smf columnist.

columpiar [8] vt to swing.

➤ **columpiarse** vprnl to swing.

columpio sm swing.

colza sf BOT rape.

coma ◇ sm MED coma; **en coma** in a coma. ◇ sf **- 1.** GRAM comma **- 2.** MAT ≃ decimal point.

comadre sf **- 1.** [mujer chismosa] gossip, gossipmonger; [vecina] neighbour **- 2.** Amér C & Méx [amiga] friend.

comadrear vi to gossip.

comadreja sf weasel.

comadreo sm gossip.

comadrona sf midwife.

comandancia sf **- 1.** [rango] command **- 2.** [edificio] command headquarters.

comandante sm [MIL - rango] major; [- de un puesto] commander, commandant; **comandante en jefe** commander-in-chief.

comandar vt MIL to command.

comando sm MIL commando; **comando terrorista** terrorist unit.

comarca sf region, area.

comarcal adj district (antes de s), local.

comatoso, sa adj comatose.

comba sf **- 1.** [juego] skipping; **jugar** o **saltar a la comba** to skip **- 2.** [cuerda] skipping rope.

combado, da adj curved.

combar vt to bend.

➤ **combarse** vprnl [gen] to bend; [madera] to warp; [pared] to bulge.

combate sm [gen] fight; [batalla] battle; **dejar a alguien fuera de combate** [en boxeo] to knock sb out; fig to put sb out of the running.

combatiente smf combatant, fighter.

combatir ◇ vt to combat, to fight. ◇ vi: **combatir (contra)** to fight (against).

combatividad sf fighting spirit.

combativo, va adj aggressive, combative.

combi sm [frigorífico] fridge-freezer.

combinación sf **- 1.** [gen] combination **- 2.** [de bebidas] cocktail **- 3.** QUÍM compound **- 4.** [prenda] slip **- 5.** [plan] scheme **- 6.** [de medios de transporte] connections pl.

combinado sm **- 1.** [bebida] cocktail **- 2.** DEP combined team **- 3.** Amér [radiograma] radiogram.

combinar vt **- 1.** [gen] to combine **- 2.** [bebidas] to mix **- 3.** [colores] to match **- 4.** [planificar] to arrange, to organize.

combinatoria sf MAT combinatorial analysis.

combustible ◇ adj combustible. ◇ sm fuel.

combustión sf combustion.

comecocos sm inv fam **- 1.** [para convencer]: **este panfleto es un comecocos** this pamphlet is designed to brainwash you **- 2.** [cosa difícil de comprender] mind-bending problem o puzzle etc.

comedero sm trough.

comedia sf **- 1.** [obra, película, género] comedy; **comedia musical** musical (comedy) **- 2.** fig [engaño] farce; **hacer la comedia** to pretend, to make believe.

comediante, ta sm, f actor (f actress); fig [farsante] fraud.

comedido, da adj moderate, restrained.

comedimiento sm moderation, restraint.

comediógrafo, fa sm, f playwright, dramatist.

comedirse [26] vprnl to be restrained.

comedor sm **- 1.** [habitación - de casa] dining room; [- de fábrica] canteen **- 2.** [muebles] dining-room suite.

comensal smf fellow diner.

comentar vt [opinar sobre] to comment on; [hablar de] to discuss.

comentario *sm* - **1.** [observación] comment, remark - **2.** [crítica] commentary.

➥ **comentarios** *smpl* [murmuraciones] gossip *(U)*.

comentarista *smf* commentator.

comenzar [34] <> *vt* to start, to begin; **comenzar a hacer algo** to start doing *o* to do sthg; **comenzar diciendo que...** to start *o* begin by saying that... <> *vi* to start, to begin.

comer <> *vi* [ingerir alimentos - gen] to eat; [- al mediodía] to have lunch. <> *vt* - **1.** [alimentos] to eat - **2.** [colores] to fade - **3.** [en juegos de tablero] to take, to capture - **4.** *fig* [consumir] to eat up - **5.** *loc:* **sin comerlo ni beberlo** through no fault of one's own.

➥ **comerse** *vprnl* - **1.** [alimentos] to eat - **2.** [desgastar - recursos] to eat up; [- metal] to corrode - **3.** [en los juegos de tablero] to take, to capture - **4.** *fam* [palabras] to swallow - **5.** *Amér vulg* [fornicar] to fuck.

comercial <> *adj* commercial. <> *sm Amér* [anuncio] advert.

comercialización *sf* marketing.

comercializar [13] *vt* to market.

comerciante *smf* tradesman (*f* tradeswoman); [tendero] shopkeeper.

comerciar [8] *vi* to trade, to do business.

comercio *sm* - **1.** [de productos] trade; **comercio electrónico** e-business; **comercio exterior/interior** foreign/domestic trade; **comercio justo** fair trade; **libre comercio** free trade - **2.** [actividad] business, commerce - **3.** [tienda] shop.

comestible *adj* edible, eatable.

➥ **comestibles** *smpl* [gen] food *(U)*; [en una tienda] groceries.

cometa <> *sm* ASTRON comet. <> *sf* kite.

cometer *vt* [crimen] to commit; [error] to make.

cometido *sm* - **1.** [objetivo] mission, task - **2.** [deber] duty.

comezón *sf* - **1.** [picor] itch, itching *(U)* - **2.** *fig* [remordimiento] twinge; [deseo] urge, itch.

cómic (*pl* **comics**) *sm* (adult) comic.

comicidad *sf* humorousness.

comicios *smpl* elections.

cómico, ca <> *adj* - **1.** [de la comedia] comedy (antes de s), comic - **2.** [gracioso] comic, comical. <> *sm, f* [actor de teatro] actor (*f* actress); [humorista] comedian (*f* comedienne), comic.

comida *sf* - **1.** [alimento] food *(U)*; **comida basura** junk food; **comida chatarra** *Amér* junk food; **comida rápida** fast food - **2.** [almuerzo, cena etc] meal - **3.** [al mediodía] lunch; **comida de negocios** business lunch.

comidiera *etc* ▷ **comedirse**.

comidilla *sf*: **ser/convertirse en la comidilla del pueblo** *fam* to be/to become the talk of the town.

comidió ▷ **comedirse**.

comience *etc* ▷ **comenzar**.

comienzo *sm* start, beginning; **a comienzos de los años 50** in the early 1950s; **dar comienzo** to start, to begin.

comillas *sfpl* inverted commas, quotation marks; **entre comillas** in inverted commas.

comilón, ona *fam* <> *adj* greedy. <> *sm, f* [persona] greedy pig, glutton.

comilona *sf fam* [festín] blow-out.

comino *sm* [planta] cumin, cummin; **me importa un comino** *fam* I don't give a damn; **no valer un comino** *fam* not to be worth tuppence.

comisaría *sf* police station, precinct *US*.

comisario, ria *sm, f* - **1.**: **comisario (de policía)** police superintendent - **2.** [delegado] commissioner; **comisario político** political commissar.

comisión *sf* - **1.** [de un delito] perpetration - **2.** COM commission; **(trabajar) a comisión** (to work) on a commission basis; **comisión fija** ECON flat fee - **3.** [delegación] commission, committee; **Comisión Europea** European Comission; **comisión investigadora** committee of inquiry; **comisión parlamentaria** parliamentary committee; **comisión permanente** standing commission; **comisión de servicio** special assignment; **Comisiones Obreras** Spanish Communist-inspired trade union.

comisionado, da *sm, f* committee member.

comisionar *vt* to commission.

comisionista *smf* commission agent.

comisura *sf* corner (of mouth, eyes).

comité *sm* committee; **comité ejecutivo** executive committee; **comité de empresa** works council.

comitiva *sf* retinue.

como <> *adv* - **1.** *(compar)*: **tan... como...** as... as...; **es (tan) negro como el carbón** it's as black as coal; **ser como algo** to be like sthg; **vive como un rey** he lives like a king; **lo que dijo fue como para ruborizarse** his words were enough to make you blush - **2.** [de la manera que] as; **lo he hecho como es debido** I did it as *o* the way it should be done; **me encanta como bailas** I love the way you dance - **3.** [según] as; **como te decía ayer...** as I was telling you yesterday... - **4.** [en calidad de] as; **trabaja como bombero** he works as a fireman; **dieron el dinero como anticipo** they gave the money as an advance - **5.** [aproximadamente] about; **me quedan como cien euros** I've got about a hundred euros left; **estamos como a mitad de camino** we're about halfway there;

tiene un sabor como a naranja it tastes a bit like an orange. <> *conj* - **1.** [ya que] as, since; **como no llegabas, nos fuimos** as o since you didn't arrive, we left - **2.** [si] if; **como no me hagas caso, lo pasarás mal** if you don't listen to me, there will be trouble - **3.** [que] that; **después de tantas veces como te lo he explicado** after all the times (that) I've explained it to you.

◆ **como que** *loc conj* - **1.** [que] that; **le pareció como que lloraban** it seemed to him (that) they were crying - **2.** [expresa causa]: **pareces cansado – como que he trabajado toda la noche** you seem tired – well, I've been up all night working - **3.** [expresa incredulidad]: **como que te voy a creer a ti que eres un mentiroso** as if I'd believe a liar like you!

◆ **como quiera** *loc adv* [de cualquier modo] anyway, anyhow.

◆ **como quiera que** *loc conj* - **1.** [de cualquier modo que] whichever way, however; **como quiera que sea** whatever the case may be - **2.** [dado que] since, given that.

◆ **como si** *loc conj* as if.

cómo <> *adv* - **1.** [de qué modo, por qué motivo] how; **¿cómo lo has hecho?** how did you do it?; **¿cómo son?** what are they like?; **no sé cómo has podido decir eso** I don't know how you could say that; **¿cómo que no la has visto nunca?** what do you mean you've never seen her?; **¿a cómo están los tomates?** how much are the tomatoes?; **¿cómo?** *fam* [¿qué dices?] sorry?, what?; **¿cómo es eso?** *fam* [¿por qué?] how come? - **2.** [exclamativo] how; **¡cómo pasan los años!** how time flies!; **¡cómo no!** of course!; **está lloviendo, ¡y cómo!** it isn't half raining! <> *sm*: **el cómo y el porqué** the whys and wherefores.

cómoda *sf* chest of drawers.

comodidad *sf* comfort, convenience (U); **para su comodidad** for your convenience.
◆ **comodidades** *sfpl* comforts.

comodín *sm* - **1.** [naipe] joker - **2.** *fig* [cosa] multi-purpose gadget; [persona] jack-of-all-trades.

cómodo, da *adj* - **1.** [confortable] comfortable; **ponte cómodo** make yourself comfortable, make yourself at home; **sentirse cómodo con alguien** to feel comfortable with sb - **2.** [útil] convenient - **3.** [oportuno, fácil] easy.

comodón, ona <> *adj* [amante de la comodidad] comfort-loving; [vago] laid-back; **no seas comodón** don't be lazy. <> *sm, f* [amante de la comodidad] comfort-lover; [vago] laid-back person.

comodoro *sm* commodore.

comoquiera *adv*: **comoquiera que** [de cualquier manera que] whichever way, however; [dado que] since, seeing as.

compa *smf fam* pal, mate *UK*, buddy *US*.

compactación *sf* INFORM compression; **compactación de ficheros** file compression.

compactar *vt* to compress.

compact disk, compact disc *sm* compact disc.

compacto, ta *adj* compact.

compactoteca *sf* compact disc library.

compadecer [30] *vt* to pity, to feel sorry for.
◆ **compadecerse de** *vprnl* to pity, to feel sorry for.

compadre *sm fam* [amigo] friend, mate *UK*, buddy *US*.

compadrear *vi R Dom fam* to brag, to boast.

compadreo *sm fam* [amistad] friendship.

compaginación *sf* - **1.** [combinación] reconciling - **2.** [en imprenta] page make-up.

compaginar *vt* - **1.** [combinar] to reconcile - **2.** [en imprenta] to make up.
◆ **compaginarse** *vprnl*: **compaginarse con** to square with, to go together with.

compañerismo *sm* comradeship.

compañero, ra *sm, f* - **1.** [acompañante] companion - **2.** [pareja] partner; **compañero sentimental** partner - **3.** [colega] colleague; **compañero de clase** classmate; **compañero de piso** flatmate - **4.** [par]: **el compañero de este guante** the other glove of this pair.

compañía *sf* company; **le perdieron las malas compañías** he was led astray by the bad company he kept; **en compañía de** accompanied by, in the company of; **hacer compañía a alguien** to keep sb company; **compañía de seguros** insurance company; **compañía teatral** o **de teatro** theatre company.

comparación *sf* comparison; **en comparación con** in comparison with, compared to.

comparado, da *adj* comparative.

comparar *vt*: **comparar algo (con)** to compare sthg (to).

comparativo, va *adj* comparative.
◆ **comparativo** *sm* GRAM comparative.

comparecencia *sf* appearance.

comparecer [30] *vi* to appear.

comparsa <> *sf* - **1.** TEATRO extras *pl* - **2.** [en carnaval] *group of people at carnival in same costume and with masks.* <> *smf* - **1.** TEATRO extra - **2.** *fig* [en carreras, competiciones] also-ran; [en organizaciones, empresas] nobody.

compartimentar *vt* to compartmentalize.

compartimento, compartimiento *sm* compartment; **compartimiento estanco** watertight compartment; **compartimiento de fumadores** smoking compartment.

compartir *vt* - **1.** [ganancias] to share (out) - **2.** [piso, ideas] to share.

compás *sm* - **1.** [instrumento] pair of compasses - **2.** NÁUT [brújula] compass - **3.** [MÚS - periodo] bar; [- ritmo] rhythm, beat; **al compás (de la música)** in time (with the music); **llevar el compás** to keep time; **perder el compás** to lose the beat.

◆ **compás de espera** *sm* pause, interlude.

compasión *sf* compassion, pity; **¡por compasión!** for pity's sake!; **tener compasión de** to feel sorry for.

compasivo, va *adj* compassionate, sympathetic.

compatibilidad *sf* [gen & INFORM] compatibility.

compatibilizar [13] *vt* to make compatible.

compatible *adj* [gen & INFORM] compatible.

compatriota *smf* compatriot, fellow countryman (*f* fellow countrywoman).

compeler *vt* to compel, to force.

compendiar [8] *vt* [cualidades, características] to summarize; [libro, historia] to abridge.

compendio *sm* - **1.** [libro] compendium - **2.** *fig* [síntesis] epitome, essence.

compenetración *sf* mutual understanding.

compenetrarse *vprnl* to understand each other.

compensación *sf* - **1.** [gen] compensation; **en compensación (por)** in return (for); **compensación económica** financial compensation - **2.** BANCA compensation; **compensación bancaria** bank clearing.

compensar *vt* - **1.** [valer la pena] to make up for; **no me compensa (perder tanto tiempo)** it's not worth my while (wasting all that time) - **2.** [indemnizar]: **compensar a alguien (de o por)** to compensate sb (for).

competencia *sf* - **1.** [entre personas, empresas] competition; **hacer la competencia a** to compete with; **competencia desleal** ECON unfair competition, dumping - **2.** [incumbencia] field, province - **3.** [aptitud, atribuciones] competence.

competente *adj* competent; **competente en materia de** responsible for.

competer ◆ **competer a** *vi* [gen] to be up to, to be the responsibility of; [una autoridad] to come under the jurisdiction of.

competición *sf* competition.

competidor, ra ◇ *adj* rival, competing. ◇ *sm, f* competitor.

competir [26] *vi*: **competir (con/por)** to compete (with/for).

competitividad *sf* competitiveness.

competitivo, va *adj* competitive.

compilación *sf* [acción] compiling; [colección] compilation.

compilador, ra ◇ *adj* compiling (*antes de s*). ◇ *sm, f* [persona] compiler.

◆ **compilador** *sm* INFORM compiler.

compilar *vt* [gen & INFORM] to compile.

compinche *smf* *fam* crony.

compita, compitiera *etc* ▷ **competir.**

complacencia *sf* pleasure, satisfaction.

complacer [29] *vt* to please.

complaciente *adj* - **1.** [amable] obliging, helpful - **2.** [indulgente] indulgent.

complejidad *sf* complexity.

complejo, ja *adj* complex.

◆ **complejo** *sm* complex; **complejo de Edipo/de inferioridad/de superioridad** Oedipus/inferiority/superiority complex; **complejo deportivo** sports complex; **complejo hotelero** hotel complex; **complejo industrial** industrial park; **complejo turístico** tourist development; **complejo vitamínico** vitamin complex.

complementar *vt* to complement.

◆ **complementarse** *vprnl* to complement each other.

complementario, ria *adj* complementary.

complemento *sm* - **1.** [añadido] complement, complement - **2.** GRAM object, complement; **complemento agente** agent; **complemento circunstancial** adjunct; **complemento directo/indirecto** direct/indirect object.

completamente *adv* completely, totally.

completar *vt* to complete.

◆ **completarse** *vprnl* to be completed.

completo, ta *adj* - **1.** [entero, perfecto] complete; **por completo** completely; **un deportista muy completo** an all-round sportsman - **2.** [lleno] full.

complexión *sf* build; **de complexión atlética** with an athletic build; **de complexión fuerte** well-built, with a strong constitution.

complicación *sf* - **1.** [gen] complication - **2.** [complejidad] complexity.

complicado, da *adj* - **1.** [difícil] complicated - **2.** [implicado]: **complicado (en)** involved (in).

complicar [10] *vt* - **1.** [dificultar] to complicate - **2.** [comprometer]: **complicar a alguien (en)** to involve sb (in).

◆ **complicarse** *vprnl* [problema] to become complicated; [enfermedad] to get worse.

cómplice *smf* accomplice.

complicidad *sf* complicity.

complot, compló *sm* plot, conspiracy.

componenda *sf* shady deal.

componente ◇ *adj* component, constituent. ◇ *sm* [gen & ELECTR] component. ◇ *smf* [persona] member.

componer [65] *vt* - **1.** [constituir, ser parte de] to make up - **2.** [música, versos] to compose - **3.** [arreglar - algo roto] to repair - **4.** [texto - en imprenta] to set, to compose.
➤ **componerse** *vprnl* - **1.** [estar formado]: **componerse de** to be made up of, to consist of - **2.** [engalanarse] to dress up - **3.** *loc:* **allá se las compongan** that's their problem; **componérselas (para hacer algo)** to manage (to do sthg).

comportamiento *sm* behaviour.

comportar *vt* to involve, to entail.
➤ **comportarse** *vprnl* to behave.

composición *sf* composition; **hacer** *o* **hacerse una composición de lugar** to size up the situation.

compositor, ra *sm, f* composer.

compostelano, na *adj* of/relating to Santiago de Compostela.

compostura *sf* - **1.** [reparación] repair - **2.** [de persona, rostro] composure - **3.** [en comportamiento] restraint; **guardar la compostura** to show restraint.

compota *sf* CULIN compote, stewed fruit (*U*).

compra *sf* purchase; **ir de compras** to go shopping; **ir a** *o* **hacer la compra** to do the shopping; **compra al contado** cash purchase; **compra a plazos** hire purchase.

comprador, ra ◇ *adj* buying, purchasing. ◇ *sm, f* [gen] buyer, purchaser; [en una tienda] shopper, customer.

comprar *vt* - **1.** [adquirir] to buy, to purchase; **comprar algo a alquien** to buy sthg from sb - **2.** [sobornar] to buy (off), to bribe.

compraventa *sf* buying and selling, trading.

comprender *vt* - **1.** [incluir] to include, to comprise - **2.** [entender] to understand; **hacerse comprender** to make o.s. understood.
➤ **comprenderse** *vprnl* [personas] to understand each other.

comprensible *adj* understandable, comprehensible.

comprensión *sf* understanding.

comprensivo, va *adj* understanding.

compresa *sf* - **1.** [para menstruación] sanitary towel UK, sanitary napkin US - **2.** [para herida] compress.

compresión *sf* compression.

compresor, ra *adj* compressing.
➤ **compresor** *sm* compressor.

comprimido, da *adj* compressed.
➤ **comprimido** *sm* pill, tablet.

comprimir *vt* to compress.

comprobación *sf* checking.

comprobante *sm* [documento] supporting document, proof; [recibo] receipt.

comprobar [23] *vt* [averiguar] to check; [demostrar] to prove.

comprometedor, ra *adj* compromising.

comprometer *vt* - **1.** [poner en peligro - éxito etc] to jeopardize; [- persona] to compromise - **2.** [avergonzar] to embarrass - **3.** [hacer responsable]: **comprometer a alguien (a hacer algo)** to oblige *o* compel sb (to do sthg).
➤ **comprometerse** *vprnl* - **1.** [hacerse responsable]: **comprometerse (a hacer algo)** to commit o.s. (to doing sthg) - **2.** [ideológicamente, moralmente]: **comprometerse (en algo)** to become involved (in sthg).

comprometido, da *adj* - **1.** [con una idea] committed - **2.** [difícil] compromising, awkward.

compromisario *sm* delegate, representative (*in an election*).

compromiso *sm* - **1.** [obligación] commitment; [acuerdo] agreement - **2.** [cita] engagement; **sin compromiso** without obligation - **3.** [de matrimonio] engagement; **compromiso matrimonial** engagement - **4.** [dificultad, aprieto] compromising *o* difficult situation; **me pones en un compromiso** you're putting me in an awkward position.

compuerta *sf* sluice, floodgate.

compuesto, ta ◇ *pp* ▷ **componer**. ◇ *adj* - **1.** [formado]: **compuesto de** composed of, made up of - **2.** [palabra] compound (*antes de s*) - **3.** [arreglado - persona] dressed up.
➤ **compuesto** *sm* GRAM & QUÍM compound.

compulsar *vt* to check against the original.

compulsivo, va *adj* compulsive, urgent.

compungido, da *adj* contrite, remorseful.

compusiera *etc* ▷ **componer**.

computable *adj* computable.

computador *sm* = **computadora**.

computadora *sf* computer.

computar *vt* - **1.** [calcular] to compute, to calculate - **2.** [considerar] to count, to regard as valid.

computarizar [13] *vt* to computerize.

cómputo *sm* calculation.

comulgar [16] *vi* - **1.** RELIG to take communion - **2.** *fig* [estar de acuerdo]: **comulgar con algo** to share sthg.

común *adj* - **1.** [gen] common; **por lo común** generally; **poco común** unusual - **2.** [compartido - amigo, interés] mutual; [- bienes, pastos] communal; **tener algo en común** to have sthg in common; **hacer algo en común** to do sthg together **- 3.** [ordinario - vino etc] ordinary, average; **común y corriente** perfectly ordinary.

comuna *sf* **- 1.** commune **- 2.** *Amér* [municipalidad] municipality.

comunal *adj* communal.

comunicación *sf* **- 1.** [gen] communication; **ponerse en comunicación con alguien** to get in touch with sb; **medios de comunicación de masas** mass media **- 2.** [escrito oficial] communiqué; [informe] report.

➠ **comunicaciones** *sfpl* communications.

comunicado, da *adj*: **bien comunicado** [lugar] well-served, with good connections.

➠ **comunicado** *sm* announcement, statement; **comunicado oficial** communiqué; **comunicado a la prensa** press release.

comunicante ◇ *adj* communicating. ◇ *smf* informant.

comunicar [10] ◇ *vt* **- 1.** [transmitir - sentimientos, ideas] to convey; [- movimiento, virus] to transmit **- 2.** [información]: **comunicar algo a alguien** to inform sb of sthg, to tell sb sthg. ◇ *vi* **- 1.** [hablar - gen] to communicate; [- al teléfono] to get through; [escribir] to get in touch **- 2.** [dos lugares]: **comunicar con algo** to connect with sthg, to join sthg **- 3.** [suj: el teléfono] to be engaged *UK*, to be busy *US*.

➠ **comunicarse** *vprnl* **- 1.** [hablarse] to communicate (with each other) **- 2.** [dos lugares] to be connected **- 3.** [propagarse] to spread.

comunicativo, va *adj* communicative, open.

comunidad *sf* community; **comunidad autónoma** autonomous region; **comunidad de bienes** co-ownership *(between spouses)*; **comunidad de propietarios** residents' association; **Comunidad Económica Europea** HIST European Economic Community.

comunión *sf* *lit & fig* communion; **hacer la primera comunión** to take one's First Communion.

comunismo *sm* communism.

comunista *adj* & *smf* communist.

comunitario, ria *adj* **- 1.** [de la comunidad] community *(antes de s)* **- 2.** [de la UE] Community *(antes de s)*, of the European Community; **política comunitaria** EU *o* Community policy.

con *prep* **- 1.** [gen] with; **¿con quién vas?** who are you going with?; **lo ha conseguido con su esfuerzo** he has achieved it through his own efforts; **una cartera con varios documentos** a briefcase containing several documents; **con el tiempo lo olvidé** in time I forgot it **- 2.** [a pesar de] in spite of; **con todo** despite everything; **con lo estudioso que es, lo suspendieron** for all his hard work, they still failed him **- 3.** [ha-

cia]: **para con** towards; **es amable para con todos** she is friendly towards *o* with everyone **- 4.** *(+ infinitivo)* [para introducir una condición] by *(+ gerundio)*; **con hacerlo así** by doing it this way; **con salir a las diez es suficiente** if we leave at ten, we'll have plenty of time **- 5.** [a condición de que]: **con (tal) que** *(+ subjuntivo)* as long as; **con que llegue a tiempo me conformo** I don't mind as long as he arrives on time **- 6.** [para expresar queja o decepción]: **mira que perder, ¡con lo bien que jugaste!** it's bad luck you lost, you played really well!

conato *sm* attempt; **conato de robo** attempted robbery; **un conato de incendio** the beginnings of a fire.

concadenar *vt* = concatenar.

concatenación *sf* succession.

concatenar, concadenar *vt* to link together.

concavidad *sf* **- 1.** [cualidad] concavity **- 2.** [lugar] hollow.

cóncavo, va *adj* concave.

concebir [26] ◇ *vt* [plan, hijo] to conceive; [imaginar] to imagine. ◇ *vi* to conceive.

conceder *vt* **- 1.** [dar] to grant; [premio] to award **- 2.** [asentir] to admit, to concede.

concejal, la *sm, f* (town) councillor.

concejalía *sf* seat on the town council.

concejo *sm* (town) council.

concelebrar *vt* to concelebrate.

concentración *sf* **- 1.** [gen] concentration **- 2.** [de gente] gathering; **concentración parcelaria** ECON land consolidation **- 3.** DEP training camp.

concentrado *sm* concentrate.

concentrar *vt* **- 1.** [gen] to concentrate **- 2.** [reunir - gente] to bring together; [- tropas] to assemble.

➠ **concentrarse** *vprnl* to concentrate.

concéntrico, ca *adj* concentric.

concepción *sf* conception.

concepto *sm* **- 1.** [idea] concept **- 2.** [opinión] opinion; **te tiene en muy buen concepto** she thinks highly of you **- 3.** [motivo]: **bajo ningún concepto** under no circumstances; **en concepto de** by way of, as **- 4.** [de una cuenta] heading, item.

conceptual *adj* conceptual.

conceptuar [6] *vt* to consider, to judge.

concerniente *adj*: **concerniente a** concerning, regarding.

concernir [21] *v impers* to concern; **en lo que concierne a** as regards; **por lo que a mí me concierne** as far as I'm concerned.

concertación *sf* settlement.

concertado, da *adj* [centro de enseñanza] state-assisted, ≃ grant-maintained *UK*; **hospital concertado** *private hospital that has been contracted to provide free treatment for social security patients.*

concertar [19] ◇ *vt* [precio] to agree on; [cita] to arrange; [pacto] to reach. ◇ *vi* [concordar]: **concertar (con)** to tally (with), to fit in (with).

concertina *sf* concertina.

concertino *sm* first violin.

concertista *smf* soloist.

concesión *sf* - **1.** [de préstamo etc] granting; [de premio] awarding - **2.** *fig* & COM concession.

concesionario, ria ◇ *adj* concessionary. ◇ *sm, f* [persona con derecho exclusivo de venta] licensed dealer; [titular de una concesión] concessionaire, licensee.

concha *sf* - **1.** [de los animales] shell - **2.** [material] tortoiseshell - **3.** *Ven* [de frutas] peel, rind - **4.** *Andes & R Plata vulg* [vulva] cunt.

◆ **concha de su madre** *smf Andes & R Plata vulg* motherfucker.

conchabarse *vprnl:* **conchabarse (contra)** *fam* to gang up (on).

conchudo, da *adj Perú & R Dom vulg* bloody stupid.

conciba, concibiera *etc* ▷ **concebir**.

conciencia, consciencia *sf* - **1.** [conocimiento] consciousness, awareness; **tener/tomar conciencia de** to be/become aware of; **conciencia de clase** class consciousness; **conciencia social** social conscience - **2.** [moral, integridad] conscience; **a conciencia** conscientiously; **me remuerde la conciencia** I have a guilty conscience; **tener la conciencia tranquila** to have a clear conscience.

concienciar [8] *vt* to make aware.

◆ **concienciarse** *vprnl* to become aware.

concientizar *Amér vt:* **concientizar a alguien de algo** to make sb aware of sthg.

◆ **concientizarse** *vprnl:* **concientizarse (de)** to become aware (of).

concienzudo, da *adj* conscientious.

concierna *etc* ▷ **concernir**.

concierta *etc* ▷ **concertar**.

concierto *sm* - **1.** [actuación] concert - **2.** [composición] concerto - **3.** [acuerdo] agreement - **4.** [orden] order.

conciliación *sf* [en un litigio] reconciliation; [en un conflicto laboral] conciliation.

conciliar [8] ◇ *adj* conciliar. ◇ *vt* to reconcile; **conciliar el sueño** to get to sleep.

concilio *sm* council; **concilio ecuménico** ecumenical council.

concisión *sf* conciseness.

conciso, sa *adj* concise.

concitar *vt* to stir up, to arouse.

conciudadano, na *sm, f* fellow citizen.

cónclave, conclave *sm* conclave.

concluir [51] ◇ *vt* to conclude; **concluir haciendo o por hacer algo** to end up doing sthg. ◇ *vi* to (come to an) end.

conclusión *sf* conclusion; **llegar a una conclusión** to come to o to reach a conclusion; **en conclusión** in conclusion.

concluyente *adj* conclusive.

concomerse *vprnl:* **concomerse de** [envidia] to be green with; [arrepentimiento] to be consumed with; [impaciencia] to be itching with.

concordancia *sf* [gen & GRAM] agreement.

concordar [23] ◇ *vt* to reconcile. ◇ *vi* - **1.** [estar de acuerdo]: **concordar (con)** to agree o tally (with) - **2.** GRAM: **concordar (con)** to agree (with).

concordato *sm* concordat.

concordia *sf* harmony.

concreción *sf* - **1.** [acción y efecto] precision - **2.** [de partículas] concretion.

concretar *vt* - **1.** [precisar] to specify, to state exactly - **2.** [reducir a lo esencial] to summarize.

◆ **concretarse** *vprnl* - **1.** [limitarse]: **concretarse a hacer algo** to confine o limit o.s. to doing sthg - **2.** [materializarse] to take shape.

concreto, ta *adj* specific, particular; **en concreto** [en resumen] in short; [específicamente] specifically; **nada en concreto** nothing definite.

◆ **concreto armado** *sm Amér* reinforced concrete.

concubina *sf* concubine.

concuerda ▷ **concordar**.

concuñado, da *sm, f* [hermano del cuñado] brother or sister of one's brother-in-law or sister-in-law; [cónyuge del cuñado] spouse of one's brother-in-law or sister-in-law.

concurrencia *sf* - **1.** [asistencia] attendance; [espectadores] crowd, audience - **2.** [de sucesos] concurrence - **3.** COM competition; **no concurrencia** DER non-competition clause.

concurrente ◇ *adj* concurrent. ◇ *smf* person present.

concurrido, da *adj* [bar, calle] crowded, busy; [espectáculo] well-attended.

concurrir *vi* - **1.** [reunirse]: **concurrir a algo** to go to sthg, to attend sthg - **2.** [influir]: **concurrir (a)** to contribute (to) - **3.** [participar]: **concurrir a** [concurso] to take part in, to compete in; [examen] to sit *UK*, to take.

concursante *smf* [en concurso] competitor, contestant; [en oposiciones] candidate.

concursar *vi* [competir] to compete, to participate; [en oposiciones] to be a candidate.

concurso *sm* - **1.** [prueba - literaria, deportiva] competition; [- de televisión] game show; **fuera de concurso** out of the running; **concurso de belleza** beauty contest - **2.** [para una obra] tender; **salir a concurso** to be put out to tender - **3.** [ayuda] cooperation.

condado *sm* [territorio] county.

condal *adj*: **la Ciudad Condal** Barcelona.

conde, esa *sm, f* count (*f* countess).

condecoración *sf* - **1.** [insignia] medal - **2.** [acto] decoration.

condecorar *vt* to decorate.

condena *sf* sentence; **cumplir condena** to serve a sentence; **imponer una condena** to impose a sentence.

condenable *adj* condemnable.

condenado, da <> *adj* - **1.** [a una pena] convicted, sentenced; [a un sufrimiento] condemned - **2.** *fam* [maldito] damned, wretched. <> *sm, f* convicted person; [a muerte] condemned person; **trabajar como un condenado** to work like a slave.

condenar *vt* - **1.** [declarar culpable] to convict - **2.** [castigar]: **condenar a alguien a algo** to sentence sb to sthg - **3.** [predestinar]: **estar condenado a** to be doomed to - **4.** [recriminar] to condemn.

◆ **condenarse** *vprnl* to be damned.

condensación *sf* condensation.

condensado, da *adj* condensed.

condensador, ra *adj* condensing.

◆ **condensador** *sm* condenser.

condensar *vt lit & fig* to condense.

condescendencia *sf* [benevolencia] graciousness, kindness; [altivez] condescension.

condescender [20] *vi*: **condescender a** [con amabilidad] to consent to, to accede to; [con desprecio] to deign to, to condescend to.

condescendiente *adj* obliging.

condición *sf* - **1.** [gen] condition; **condiciones de un contrato** terms of a contract; **a** *o* **con la condición de que alguien haga algo** on condition that sb does sthg; **con una sola condición** on one condition; **sin condiciones** unconditional - **2.** [naturaleza] nature - **3.** [clase social] social class; **de condición humilde** of humble circumstances.

◆ **condiciones** *sfpl* - **1.** [aptitud] talent *(U)*, ability *(U)* - **2.** [circunstancias] conditions; **condiciones atmosféricas/de vida** weather/living conditions - **3.** [estado] condition *(U)*; **estar en condiciones de** *o* **para hacer algo** [físicamente] to be in a fit state to do sthg; [por la situación] to be in a position to do sthg; **estar en buenas condiciones** [casa, coche] to be in good condi-

tion; [carne, pescado] to be fresh; **estar en malas condiciones** [casa, coche] to be in bad condition; [carne, pescado] to be off.

condicionado, da *adj* conditioned.

condicional *adj* & *sm* conditional.

condicionamiento *sm* conditioning.

condicionante *sm* determinant.

condicionar *vt*: **condicionar algo a algo** to make sthg dependent on sthg.

condimentación *sf* seasoning.

condimentar *vt* to season.

condimento *sm* seasoning *(U)*.

condiscípulo, la *sm, f* schoolmate.

condolencia *sf* condolence.

condolerse [24] *vprnl*: **condolerse (de)** to feel pity (for).

condominio *sm* - **1.** [de un territorio] condominium; [de una cosa] joint ownership - **2.** *Amér* [edificio] block of flats *UK*, condominium *US*.

condón *sm* condom.

condonar *vt* - **1.** [deuda, pena] to remit - **2.** [violencia, terrorismo] to condone.

cóndor *sm* condor.

conducción *sf* - **1.** [de vehículo] driving - **2.** [por tubería] piping; [por cable] wiring - **3.** [conducto - de agua, gas] pipe; [- de electricidad] cable - **4.** *fig* [dirección] management, running.

conducir [33] <> *vt* - **1.** [vehículo] to drive - **2.** [dirigir - empresa] to manage, to run; [- ejército] to lead; [- asunto] to handle - **3.** [a una persona a un lugar] to lead - **4.** [por tubería, cable - calor] to conduct; [- líquido] to convey; [- electricidad] to carry. <> *vi* - **1.** [en vehículo] to drive - **2.** [a sitio, situación]: **conducir a** to lead to.

◆ **conducirse** *vprnl* to behave.

conducta *sf* behaviour, conduct.

conductismo *sm* PSICOL behaviourism.

conductividad *sf* FÍS conductivity.

conducto *sm* - **1.** [de fluido] pipe - **2.** *fig* [vía] channel; **por conducto de** through - **3.** ANAT duct.

conductor, ra <> *adj* FÍS conductive. <> *sm, f* - **1.** [de vehículo] driver - **2.** FÍS conductor.

conduela *etc* ⊳ **condolerse**.

conectado, da *adj* - **1.** ELECTR: **conectado (a)** connected (to) - **2.** INFORM on-line.

conectar <> *vt*: **conectar algo (a** *o* **con)** to connect sthg (to *o* up to). <> *vi*: **conectar con** RADIO & TV to go over to; [persona] to contact.

◆ **conectarse** *vprnl*: **conectarse a Internet** to get connected to the Internet.

conejera *sf* [madriguera] (rabbit) warren; [jaula] rabbit hutch.

conejillo ← conejillo de Indias *sm* guinea pig.

conejo, ja *sm, f* rabbit (*f* doe); **conejo a la cazadora** CULIN *rabbit cooked in olive oil with chopped onion, garlic and parsley.*

conexión *sf* - **1.** [gen] connection - **2.** RADIO & TV link-up; **conexión a Internet** Internet connection; **conexión vía satélite** satellite link.
← **conexiones** *sfpl* [influencia] connections.

conexo, xa *adj* related, connected.

confabulación *sf* conspiracy.

confabular ← **confabularse** *vprnl*: **confabularse (para)** to plot *o* conspire (to).

confección *sf* - **1.** [de ropa] tailoring, dressmaking; **de confección** off-the-peg - **2.** [de comida] preparation, making; [de lista] drawing up.

confeccionar *vt* - **1.** [ropa] to make (up); [lista] to draw up - **2.** [plato] to prepare; [bebida] to mix.

confederación *sf* confederation.

confederado, da *adj* confederate.
← **confederado** *sm* HIST Confederate.

confederarse *vprnl* to confederate, to form a confederation.

conferencia *sf* - **1.** [charla] lecture; **dar una conferencia** to give a talk *o* lecture; **conferencia de prensa** press conference - **2.** [reunión] conference - **3.** [por teléfono] (long-distance) call; **poner una conferencia** to make a long-distance call; **conferencia a cobro revertido** reverse-charge call *UK*, collect call *US*.

conferenciante *smf* lecturer.

conferenciar [8] *vi* to have a discussion.

conferir [27] *vt* - **1.**: **conferir algo a alguien** [honor, dignidad] to confer *o* bestow sthg upon sb; [responsabilidades] to give sthg to sb - **2.** [cualidad] to give.

confesar [19] *vt* [gen] to confess; [debilidad] to admit.
← **confesarse** *vprnl* RELIG: **confesarse (de algo)** to confess (sthg).

confesión *sf* - **1.** [gen] confession - **2.** [credo] religion, (religious) persuasion.

confesional *adj* denominational; **estado confesional** *country with an official state religion.*

confesionario *sm* confessional.

confeso, sa *adj* self-confessed.

confesor *sm* confessor.

confeti *sm* confetti (*U*).

confiado, da *adj* [seguro] confident; [crédulo] trusting.

confianza *sf* - **1.** [seguridad]: **confianza (en)** confidence (in); **confianza en uno mismo** self-confidence - **2.** [fe] trust; **de confianza** trust-worthy; **ser digno de confianza** to be trust-worthy - **3.** [familiaridad] familiarity; **tengo mucha confianza con él** I am very close to him; **amigo de confianza** close *o* intimate friend; **con toda confianza** in all confidence; **puedes hablar con toda confianza** you can talk quite freely; **en confianza** in confidence; **en confianza, no creo que apruebe** don't tell anyone I said this, but I doubt she'll pass.

confiar [9] *vt* - **1.** [secreto] to confide - **2.** [responsabilidad, persona, asunto]: **confiar algo a alguien** to entrust sthg to sb.
← **confiar en** *vi* - **1.** [tener fe] to trust in - **2.** [suponer]: **confiar en que** to be confident that.
← **confiarse** *vprnl* - **1.** [despreocuparse] to be too sure (of o.s.), to be overconfident - **2.** [sincerarse]: **confiarse a** to confide in.

confidencia *sf* confidence, secret; **hacer confidencias a alguien** to confide in sb.

confidencial *adj* confidential.

confidente *smf* - **1.** [amigo] confidant (*f* confidante) - **2.** [soplón] informer.

confiera *etc* ▷ **conferir**.

confiesa *etc* ▷ **confesar**.

configuración *sf* - **1.** [gen & INFORM] configuration - **2.** [del terreno] lie; [de la costa] outline, shape; [de ciudad] layout.

configurar *vt* - **1.** [formar] to shape, to form - **2.** INFORM to configure.

confín *(gen pl)* *sm* - **1.** [límite] border, boundary - **2.** [extremo - del reino, universo] outer reaches *pl*; **en los confines de** on the very edge of.

confinamiento *sm* - **1.** [de un detenido]: **confinamiento (en)** confinement (to) - **2.** [de un desterrado]: **confinamiento (en)** banishment (to).

confinar *vt* - **1.** [detener]: **confinar (en)** to confine (to) - **2.** [desterrar]: **confinar (en)** to banish (to).

confiriera *etc* ▷ **conferir**.

confirmación *sf* [gen & RELIG] confirmation.

confirmar *vt* to confirm.

confiscar [10] *vt* to confiscate.

confitado, da *adj* candied; **frutas confitadas** crystallized fruit.

confitar *vt* to candy.

confite *sm* sweet *UK*, candy *US*.

confitería *sf* - **1.** [tienda] sweetshop, confectioner's - **2.** *R Dom* [café] cafe.

confitero, ra *sm, f* confectioner.

confitura *sf* preserve, jam.

conflictividad *sf* conflict; **conflictividad laboral** industrial unrest.

conflictivo, va *adj* [asunto] controversial; [situación] troubled; [trabajador] difficult.

conflicto *sm* [gen] conflict; [de intereses, opiniones] clash; **estar en conflicto** to be in conflict; **conflicto armado** armed conflict; **conflicto generacional** generation gap; **conflicto laboral** industrial dispute.

confluencia *sf* confluence; **la confluencia de las dos calles** the place where the two roads meet.

confluir [51] *vi* - **1.** [corriente, cauce]: **confluir (en)** to converge o meet (at) - **2.** [personas]: **confluir (en)** to come together o to gather (in).

conformar *vt* [configurar] to shape.
➤ **conformarse con** *vprnl* [suerte, destino] to resign o.s. to; [apañárselas con] to make do with; [contentarse con] to settle for.

conforme ⬦ *adj* - **1.** [acorde]: **conforme a** in accordance with - **2.** [de acuerdo]: **conforme (con)** in agreement (with) - **3.** [contento]: **conforme (con)** happy (with). ⬦ *adv* - **1.** [gen] as; **conforme envejecía** as he got older; **te lo cuento conforme lo vi** I'm telling you exactly what I saw - **2.** [en cuanto] as soon as; **conforme amanezca, iré** I'll leave as soon as it gets light; **conforme a** in accordance o keeping with.

conformidad *sf* [aprobación]: **conformidad (con)** approval (of); **dar uno su conformidad** to give one's consent.

conformismo *sm* conformity.

conformista *adj & smf* conformist.

confort (*pl* **conforts**) *sm* comfort; **'todo confort'** 'all mod cons'.

confortable *adj* comfortable.

confortar *vt* to console, to comfort.

confraternidad *sf* brotherhood.

confraternizar [13] *vi* to get along (like brothers).

confrontación *sf* - **1.** [enfrentamiento] confrontation - **2.** [comparación] comparison.

confrontar *vt* - **1.** [enfrentar] to confront - **2.** [comparar] to compare.

confundir *vt* - **1.** [trastocar]: **confundir una cosa con otra** to mistake one thing for another; **confundir dos cosas** to get two things mixed up - **2.** [liar] to confuse - **3.** [mezclar] to mix up - **4.** [abrumar] to embarrass, to overwhelm.
➤ **confundirse** *vprnl* - **1.** [equivocarse] to make a mistake; **confundirse de piso** to get the wrong flat; **se ha confundido** [al teléfono] you've got the wrong number - **2.** [liarse] to get confused; **me confundo con tanta información** I get confused by all that information - **3.** [mezclarse - colores, siluetas]: **confundirse (en)** to merge (into); [- personas]: **confundirse entre la gente** to lose o.s. in the crowd.

confusión *sf* - **1.** [gen] confusion - **2.** [error] mix-up; **ha habido una confusión** there has been a bit of a mix-up.

confusionismo *sm* confusion.

confuso, sa *adj* - **1.** [incomprensible - estilo, explicación] obscure - **2.** [poco claro - rumor] muffled; [- clamor, griterío] confused; [- contorno, forma] blurred - **3.** [turbado] confused, bewildered.

conga *sf* conga.

congelación *sf* - **1.** [de alimentos] freezing - **2.** ECON [de precios, salarios] freeze.

congelador *sm* freezer.

congelados *smpl* frozen foods.

congelar *vt* [gen & ECON] to freeze.
➤ **congelarse** *vprnl* to freeze.

congénere *smf* kind o sort (of person).

congeniar [8] *vi*: **congeniar (con)** to get on (with).

congénito, ta *adj* [enfermedad] congenital; [talento] innate.

congestión *sf* congestion.

congestionar *vt* to block.
➤ **congestionarse** *vprnl* - **1.** AUTO & MED to become congested - **2.** [cara - de rabia etc] to flush, to turn purple.

conglomerado *sm* - **1.** GEOL & TECNOL conglomerate - **2.** *fig* [mezcla] combination.

conglomerar *vt* - **1.** TECNOL to conglomerate - **2.** *fig* [intereses etc] to unite.

Congo *sm*: **el Congo** (the) Congo.

congoja *sf* anguish.

congraciarse [8] *vprnl*: **congraciarse con alguien** to win sb over.

congratular *vt*: **congratular a alguien (por)** to congratulate sb (on).
➤ **congratularse** *vprnl*: **congratularse (por)** to be pleased (about).

congregación *sf* congregation.

congregar [16] *vt* to assemble, to bring together.

congresista *smf* - **1.** [en un congreso] delegate - **2.** [político] congressman (*f* congresswoman).

congreso *sm* - **1.** [de una especialidad] congress - **2.** [asamblea nacional] **congreso de diputados** [en España] *lower house of Spanish Parliament*; UK ≃ House of Commons; US ≃ House of Representatives; **el Congreso** [en Estados Unidos] Congress - **3.** [edificio] parliament building.

congrio *sm* conger eel.

congruente *adj* consistent, congruous.

cónico, ca *adj* conical.

conjetura *sf* conjecture; **hacer conjeturas, hacerse una conjetura** to conjecture.

conjeturar *vt* to conjecture about, to make predictions about.

conjugación *sf* - **1.** GRAM conjugation - **2.** [de opiniones] combination; [de esfuerzos, ideas] pooling.

conjugar [16] *vt* - **1.** GRAM to conjugate - **2.** [opiniones] to bring together, to combine; [esfuerzos, ideas] to pool.

conjunción *sf* - **1.** ASTRON & GRAM conjunction - **2.** [de hechos, esfuerzos] combination.

conjuntado, **da** *adj* coordinated.

conjuntar *vt* to coordinate.

conjuntiva *sf* ⊳ conjuntivo.

conjuntivitis *sf inv* conjunctivitis.

conjuntivo, **va** *adj* conjunctive.
➠ **conjuntiva** *sf* ANAT conjunctiva.

conjunto, **ta** *adj* [gen] joint; [hechos, acontecimientos] combined.
➠ **conjunto** *sm* - **1.** [gen] set, collection; **un conjunto de circunstancias** a number of reasons; **conjunto urbanístico** housing estate - **2.** [de ropa] outfit - **3.** [MÚS - de rock] group, band; [- de música clásica] ensemble - **4.** [totalidad] whole; **en conjunto** overall, as a whole - **5.** MAT set.

conjura *sf* conspiracy, plot.

conjurar ◇ *vi* [conspirar] to conspire, to plot. ◇ *vt* - **1.** [exorcizar] to exorcize - **2.** [evitar - un peligro] to ward off, to avert.

conjuro *sm* spell, incantation.

conllevar *vt* - **1.** [implicar] to involve, to entail - **2.** [soportar] to bear.

conmemoración *sf* commemoration; **en conmemoración de** in commemoration of.

conmemorar *vt* to commemorate.

conmemorativo, **va** *adj* commemorative.

conmensurable *adj* measurable.

conmigo *pron pers* with me; **conmigo mismo/misma** with myself.

conminar *vt*: **conminar a alguien a hacer algo** to order sb to do sthg.

conmiseración *sf* compassion, pity.

conmoción *sf* - **1.** [física o psíquica] shock; **conmoción cerebral** concussion - **2.** *fig* [trastorno, disturbio] upheaval.

conmocionar *vt* - **1.** [psíquicamente] to shock, to stun - **2.** [físicamente] to concuss.

conmovedor, **ra** *adj* moving, touching.

conmover [24] *vt* - **1.** [emocionar] to move, to touch - **2.** [sacudir] to shake.
➠ **conmoverse** *vprnl* - **1.** [emocionarse] to be moved, to be touched - **2.** [sacudirse] to be shaken.

conmutación *sf* DER commutation.

conmutador *sm* - **1.** ELECTR switch - **2.** *Amér* [centralita] switchboard.

conmutar *vt* to commute.

connotación *sf* connotation; **una connotación irónica** a hint of irony.

connotar *vt* to suggest, to have connotations of.

cono *sm* cone.

conocedor, **ra** *sm, f*: **conocedor (de)** [gen] expert (on); [de vinos] connoisseur (of).

conocer [31] *vt* - **1.** [gen] to know; **darse a conocer** to make o.s. known; **conocer bien un tema** to know a lot about a subject; **conocer alguien de vista** to know sb by sight; **conocer a alguien de oídas** to have heard of sb - **2.** [descubrir - lugar, país] to get to know - **3.** [a una persona - por primera vez] to meet - **4.** [reconocer]: **conocer a alguien (por algo)** to recognize sb (by sthg).
➠ **conocerse** ◇ *vprnl* - **1.** [a uno mismo] to know o.s. - **2.** [dos o más personas - por primera vez] to meet, to get to know each other; [- desde hace tiempo] to know each other. ◇ *v impers* [parecer]: **se conoce que...** apparently...

conocido, **da** ◇ *adj* well-known. ◇ *sm, f* acquaintance.

conocimiento *sm* - **1.** [gen] knowledge; **hablar/actuar con conocimiento de causa** to know what one is talking about/doing - **2.** MED [sentido] consciousness; **perder/recobrar el conocimiento** to lose/regain consciousness.
➠ **conocimientos** *smpl* knowledge (U); **tener muchos conocimientos** to be very knowledgeable.

conozca *etc* ⊳ conocer.

conque *conj* so; **¿conque te has cansado?** so you're tired, are you?

conquista *sf* - **1.** [de tierras, persona] conquest - **2.** *fig* [de libertad, derecho] winning.

conquistador, **ra** ◇ *adj* [seductor] seductive. ◇ *sm, f* - **1.** [de tierras] conqueror - **2.** HIST conquistador - **3.** *fig* [persona seductora] Casanova, womanizer (*f* man-eater).

conquistar *vt* - **1.** [tierras] to conquer - **2.** *fig* [libertad, derechos, simpatía] to win - **3.** *fig* [seducir] to win the heart of.

consabido, **da** *adj* [conocido] well-known; [habitual] usual.

consagración *sf* - **1.** RELIG consecration - **2.** [dedicación] dedication - **3.** [reconocimiento] recognition.

consagrado, **da** *adj* - **1.** RELIG consecrated - **2.** [dedicado] dedicated - **3.** [reconocido] recognized, established.

consagrar *vt* - **1.** RELIG to consecrate - **2.** [dedicar]: **consagrar algo a algo/alguien** [tiempo, espacio] to devote sthg to sthg/sb; [monumento, lápida] to dedicate sthg to sthg/sb - **3.** [acreditar, confirmar] to confirm, to establish.

consagrarse *vprnl* - **1.** [dedicarse]: **consagrarse (a)** to devote o dedicate o.s. (to) - **2.** [alcanzar reconocimiento] to establish o.s.

consanguíneo, nea *adj* related by blood; **hermano consanguíneo** half-brother *(of same father)*.

consciencia = conciencia.

consciente *adj* conscious; **ser consciente de** to be aware of; **estar consciente** [físicamente] to be conscious.

consecución *sf* [de un deseo] realization; [de un objetivo] attainment; [de un premio] winning.

consecuencia *sf* - **1.** [resultado] consequence; **a** o **como consecuencia de** as a consequence o result of; **atenerse a las consecuencias** to accept the consequences; **en consecuencia** consequently; **tener consecuencias** to have consequences; **traer como consecuencia** to result in - **2.** [coherencia] consistency.

consecuente *adj* [coherente] consistent.

consecutivo, va *adj* consecutive.

conseguir [43] *vt* [gen] to obtain, to get; [un objetivo] to achieve; **conseguir hacer algo** to manage to do sthg; **conseguir que alguien haga algo** to get sb to do sthg.

consejería *sf* POLÍT [en España] ministry *(in an autonomous government)*.

consejero, ra *sm, f* - **1.** [en asuntos personales] counsellor; [en asuntos técnicos] adviser, consultant - **2.** [de un consejo de administración] member; POLÍT [en España] minister *(in an autonomous government)*.

consejo *sm* - **1.** [advertencia] advice *(U)*; **dar un consejo** to give some advice; **te voy a dar un consejo** I've got a piece of advice for you - **2.** [organismo] council; **consejo de administración** board of directors - **3.** [reunión] meeting.

➤ **Consejo de Europa** *sm* Council of Europe.

➤ **consejo de guerra** *sm* court martial.

➤ **consejo de ministros** *sm* cabinet.

consenso *sm* [acuerdo] consensus; [consentimiento] consent.

consensuar [6] *vt* to approve by consensus.

consentido, da ◇ *adj* spoilt, spoiled. ◇ *sm, f* spoiled brat.

consentimiento *sm* consent.

consentir [27] ◇ *vt* - **1.** [tolerar] to allow, to permit - **2.** [mimar] to spoil. ◇ *vi*: **consentir en algo/en hacer algo** to agree to sthg/to do sthg; **consintió en que se quedaran** he agreed to let them stay.

conserje *smf* [portero] porter; [encargado] caretaker.

conserjería *sf* - **1.** [de un hotel] reception desk - **2.** [de un edificio público o privado] porter's lodge.

conserva *sf* tinned o canned food; **conserva de carne** tinned meat; **en conserva** tinned, canned.

conservación *sf* - **1.** [gen] conservation; [alimentos] preservation - **2.** [mantenimiento] maintenance.

conservacionismo *sm* conservationism.

conservacionista ◇ *adj* conservation *(antes de s)*. ◇ *smf* conservationist.

conservadurismo *sm* conservatism.

conservante *smf* preservative.

conservar *vt* - **1.** [gen & CULIN] to preserve; [amistad] to sustain, to keep up; [salud] to look after; [calor] to retain - **2.** [guardar - libros, cartas, secreto] to keep.

➤ **conservarse** *vprnl* to keep; **se conserva bien** he's keeping well.

conservatorio *sm* conservatoire.

conservero, ra *adj* canning *(antes de s)*; **industria conservera** canning industry.

considerable *adj* [gen] considerable; [importante, eminente] notable.

consideración *sf* - **1.** [valoración] consideration; **tomar en consideración** to take into consideration - **2.** [respeto] respect; **tratar a alguien con consideración** to be nice to sb; **tratar a alguien sin consideración** to show no consideration to sb; **en consideración a algo** in recognition of sthg - **3.** [importancia]: **de consideración** serious; **hubo varios heridos de consideración** several people were seriously injured.

considerado, da *adj* [atento] considerate, thoughtful; [respetado] respected, highly-regarded.

considerar *vt* - **1.** [valorar] to consider - **2.** [juzgar, estimar] to think - **3.** [respetar] to esteem, to treat with respect.

➤ **considerarse** *vprnl* to consider o.s.; **me considero feliz** I consider myself happy.

consienta *etc* ➤ consentir.

consiga *etc* ➤ conseguir.

consigna *sf* - **1.** [órdenes] instructions *pl* - **2.** [para el equipaje] left-luggage office *UK*, checkroom *US*.

consignar *vt* - **1.** [poner por escrito] to record, to write down - **2.** [asignar] to allocate - **3.** [enviar - mercancía] to consign, to dispatch - **4.** [equipaje] to deposit in the left-luggage office.

consignatario, ria *sm, f* - **1.** [de una mercancía] consignee - **2.** [representante]: **consignatario de buques** shipping agent.

consigo ◇ *pron pers* with him/her, *pl* with them; [con usted] with you; [con uno mismo] with o.s.; **lleva siempre la pistola consigo** she always carries the gun with her; **consigo mismo/misma** with himself/herself; **hablar consigo mismo** to talk to o.s. ◇ *v* ⯈ **conseguir**.

consiguiente *adj* consequent; **por consiguiente** consequently, therefore.

consiguiera *etc* ⯈ **conseguir**.

consintiera *etc* ⯈ **consentir**.

consistencia *sf lit & fig* consistency.

consistente *adj* - **1.** [sólido - material] solid - **2.** [coherente - argumento] sound, convincing - **3.** [compuesto]: **consistente en** consisting of.

consistir ⬤ **consistir en** *vi* - **1.** [gen] to consist of - **2.** [deberse a] to lie in, to be based on.

consistorial *adj* of a town hall; **casa consistorial** town hall.

consistorio *sm* town council.

consola *sf* - **1.** [mesa] console table - **2.** INFORM & TECNOL console; **consola de videojuegos** video console.

consolación *sf* consolation.

consolador, ra *adj* consoling, comforting.

consolar [23] *vt* to console.
⬤ **consolarse** *vprnl* to console o.s., to take comfort.

consolidación *sf* consolidation.

consolidar *vt* to consolidate.

consomé *sm* consommé.

consonancia *sf* harmony; **en consonancia con** in keeping with.

consonante *sf* consonant.

consonántico, ca *adj* consonantal.

consorcio *sm* consortium; **consorcio bancario** bankers' consortium.

consorte *smf* spouse; **príncipe consorte** prince consort.

conspicuo, cua *adj* [evidente] conspicuous; [ilustre] eminent.

conspiración *sf* plot, conspiracy.

conspirador, ra *sm, f* conspirator, plotter.

conspirar *vi* to conspire, to plot.

constancia *sf* - **1.** [perseverancia - en una empresa] perseverance; [- en las ideas, opiniones] steadfastness; **hacer algo con constancia** to persevere with sthg - **2.** [testimonio] record; **dejar constancia de algo** [registrar] to put sthg on record; [probar] to demonstrate sthg.

constante ◇ *adj* - **1.** [persona - en una empresa] persistent; [- en ideas, opiniones] steadfast - **2.** [acción] constant. ◇ *sf* constant; **mantener las constantes vitales de alguien** MED to keep sb alive.

constar *vi* - **1.** [una información]: **constar (en)** to appear (in), to figure (in); **constarle a alguien** to be clear to sb; **me consta que...** I am quite sure that...; **que conste que...** let it be clearly understood that..., let there be no doubt that...; **hacer constar** to put on record; **hacer constar por escrito** to confirm in writing - **2.** [estar constituido por]: **constar de** to consist of.

constatar *vt* [observar] to confirm; [comprobar] to check.

constelación *sf* constellation.

consternación *sf* consternation, dismay.

constipado, da *adj*: **estar constipado** to have a cold.
⬤ **constipado** *sm* cold; **coger un constipado** to catch a cold.

constiparse *vprnl* to catch a cold.

constitución *sf* constitution.
⬤ **Constitución** *sf* [de un Estado] Constitution.

constitucional *adj* constitutional.

constitucionalidad *sf* constitutionality.

constituir [51] *vt* - **1.** [componer] to make up - **2.** [ser] to be - **3.** [crear] to set up, to constitute.

constitutivo, va *adj* constituent; **ser constitutivo de algo** to constitute sthg.

constituyente *adj & sm* constituent.

constreñir *vt* - **1.** [obligar]: **constreñir a alguien a hacer algo** to compel *o* force sb to do sthg - **2.** [oprimir, limitar] to restrict.

construcción *sf* - **1.** [gen] construction; **en construcción** under construction - **2.** [edificio] building.

constructivo, va *adj* constructive.

constructor, ra *adj* building *(antes de s)*, construction *(antes de s)*.
⬤ **constructor** *sm* [de edificios] builder.

construir [51] *vt* [edificio, barco] to build; [aviones, coches] to manufacture; [frase, teoría] to construct.

consuegro, gra *sm, f* father-in-law *o* mother-in-law of one's son or daughter.

consuela *etc* ⯈ **consolar**.

consuelo *sm* consolation, solace.

cónsul, consulesa *sm, f* consul.

consulado *sm* [oficina] consulate; [cargo] consulship.

consular *adj* consular.

consulta *sf* - **1.** [pregunta] consultation; **hacer una consulta a alguien** to seek sb's advice; **consulta popular** referendum, plebiscite - **2.** [despacho de médico] consulting room; **horas de consulta** surgery hours; **pasar consulta** to hold a surgery.

consultar ◇ *vt* [dato, fecha] to look up; [libro, persona] to consult. ◇ *vi*: **consultar con** to consult, to seek advice from.

consultivo, va *adj* consultative, advisory; **órgano consultivo** consultative body.

consultor, ra *sm, f* consultant.

consultoría *sf* consultancy firm.

consultorio *sm* - **1.** [de un médico] consulting room - **2.** [en periódico] problem page; [en radio] *programme answering listeners' questions* - **3.** [asesoría] advice bureau.

consumación *sf* [gen] consummation; [de un crimen] perpetration.

consumado, da *adj* consummate, perfect; **es un granuja consumado** he's a complete scoundrel.

consumar *vt* [gen] to complete; [un crimen] to perpetrate; [el matrimonio] to consummate.

consumición *sf* - **1.** [acción] consumption; **está prohibida la consumición de bebidas alcohólicas** the consumption of alcohol is prohibited - **2.** [bebida] drink; [comida] food; **consumición mínima** cover charge.

consumido, da *adj* [flaco] emaciated.

consumidor, ra *sm, f* [gen] consumer; [en un bar, restaurante] patron.

consumir ⬦ *vt* - **1.** [gen] to consume; **consumieron los refrescos en el bar** they had their drinks at the bar - **2.** [destruir - suj: fuego] to destroy; [- suj: enfermedad] to eat away at. ⬦ *vi* to consume.

◆ **consumirse** *vprnl* - **1.** [persona] to waste away - **2.** [fuego] to burn out.

consumismo *sm* consumerism.

consumo *sm* consumption; **no apto para el consumo** unfit for human consumption; **bienes/sociedad de consumo** consumer goods/society; **consumo de drogas** taking of drugs.

contabilidad *sf* - **1.** [oficio] accountancy - **2.** [de persona, empresa] bookkeeping, accounting; **llevar la contabilidad** to do the accounts; **doble contabilidad** double-entry bookkeeping.

contabilización *sf* COM entering.

contabilizar [13] *vt* COM to enter.

contable *smf* accountant.

contactar ◆ **contactar con** *vi* to contact.

contacto *sm* - **1.** [gen] contact; **estar en contacto con** to be in touch with; **ponerse en contacto con** to get in touch with; **perder el contacto** to lose touch - **2.** AUTO ignition.

contado, da *adj* - **1.** [raro] rare, infrequent; **contadas veces** very rarely - **2.** [enumerado] counted.

◆ **al contado** *loc adv*: **pagar al contado** to pay (in) cash.

contador, ra *sm, f* Amér [contable] accountant; **contador público** chartered accountant UK, certified public accountant US.

◆ **contador** *sm* [aparato] meter; **contador de revoluciones** rev counter.

contaduría *sf* Amér: **contaduría general** audit office.

contagiar [8] *vt* [persona] to infect; [enfermedad] to transmit.

◆ **contagiarse** *vprnl* [enfermedad, risa] to be contagious; [persona] to become infected; **contagiarse de algo** to become infected with sthg, to catch sthg.

contagio *sm* infection, contagion.

contagioso, sa *adj* [enfermedad] contagious, infectious; [risa etc] infectious.

container = **contenedor**.

contaminación *sf* [gen] contamination; [del medio ambiente] pollution; **contaminación acústica** noise pollution.

contaminante *adj* contaminating, polluting.

◆ **contaminantes** *smpl* pollutants.

contaminar *vt* - **1.** [gen] to contaminate; [el medio ambiente] to pollute - **2.** *fig* [pervertir] to corrupt.

contante ⊳ **dinero**.

contar [23] ⬦ *vt* - **1.** [enumerar, incluir] to count - **2.** [narrar] to tell; **¡a mí me lo vas a contar!** you're telling me!, tell me about it! ⬦ *vi* to count.

◆ **contar con** *vi* - **1.** [confiar en] to count on - **2.** [tener, poseer] to have; **cuenta con dos horas para hacerlo** he has two hours to do it - **3.** [tener en cuenta] to take into account; **con esto no contaba** I hadn't reckoned with that.

contemplación *sf* contemplation.

◆ **contemplaciones** *sfpl* consideration (U); **no andarse con contemplaciones** not to beat about the bush; **tener demasiadas contemplaciones con alguien** to be too soft on sb.

contemplar *vt* [mirar, considerar] to contemplate.

contemplativo, va *adj* contemplative.

contemporáneo, a *adj* & *sm, f* contemporary.

contemporizar [13] *vi* to be accommodating.

contención *sf* - **1.** CONSTR: **muro de contención** retaining wall - **2.** [moderación] restraint, self-restraint.

contencioso, sa *adj* - **1.** [tema, cuestión] contentious - **2.** DER litigious.

◆ **contencioso** *sm* dispute, conflict.

contender [20] *vi* [competir] to contend; [pelear] to fight.

contendiente ⬦ *adj* [en una competición] contending *(antes de s)*; [en una guerra] warring *(antes de s)*. ⬦ *smf* [en una competición] contender; [en una guerra] warring faction.

contenedor, ra *adj* containing.

contenedor, container *sm* [gen] container; [para escombros] skip; **contenedor de basura** *large rubbish bin for collecting rubbish from blocks of flats etc*; **contenedor de vidrio reciclable** bottle bank.

contener [72] *vt* - **1.** [encerrar] to contain - **2.** [detener, reprimir] to restrain, to hold back.

contenerse *vprnl* to restrain o.s., to hold o.s. back.

contenido *sm* [gen] contents *pl*; [de discurso, redacción] content.

contentar *vt* to please, to keep happy.

contentarse *vprnl*: **contentarse con** to make do with.

contento, ta *adj* [alegre] happy; [satisfecho] pleased; **estar contento con alguien/algo** to be pleased withsb/sthg; **tener contento a alguien** to keep sb happy.

contento *sm* happiness, joy; **no caber en sí de contento** to be beside o.s. with joy.

contertulio, lia *sm, f* companion *(at a social gathering)*.

contestación *sf* answer.

contestador **contestador (automático)** *sm* answering machine.

contestar *vt* to answer; **contestó que vendría** she answered that she'd come. *vi* - **1.** [responder] to answer; **no contestan** there's no answer - **2.** [replicar] to answer back; **no contestes a tu madre** don't answer back to your mother.

contestatario, ria *adj* anti-establishment.

contexto *sm* context.

contextualizar [13] *vt* to contextualize.

contextura *sf* [textura] texture; [complexión] build.

contienda *sf* [competición, combate] contest; [guerra] conflict, war. *v* contender.

contiene contener.

contigo *pron pers* with you; **contigo mismo/misma** with yourself.

contiguo, gua *adj* adjacent.

continencia *sf* continence, self-restraint.

continental *adj* continental.

continente *sm* - **1.** GEOGR continent - **2.** [recipiente] container.

contingencia *sf* [eventualidad] eventuality; [imprevisibilidad] unpredictability.

contingente *adj* unforeseeable. *sm* - **1.** [grupo] contingent - **2.** COM quota.

continuación *sf* continuation; **a continuación** next, then.

continuar [6] *vt* to continue, to carry on with. *vi* to continue, to go on; **continuar haciendo algo** to continue doing o to do sthg; **continúa lloviendo** it's still raining; **'continuará'** 'to be continued'.

continuidad *sf* [en una sucesión] continuity; [permanencia] continuation.

continuo, nua *adj* - **1.** [ininterrumpido] continuous - **2.** [constante, perseverante] continual.

contonearse *vprnl* [hombre] to swagger; [mujer] to swing one's hips.

contoneo *sm* [de hombre] swagger; [de mujer] sway of the hips.

contornear *vt* [seguir el contorno de] to go round; [perfilar] to outline.

contorno *sm* - **1.** GEOGR contour; [línea] outline - **2.** *(gen pl)* [vecindad] neighbourhood; [de una ciudad] outskirts *pl*.

contorsión *sf* contortion.

contorsionarse *vprnl* [gen] to do contortions; [de dolor] to writhe.

contorsionista *smf* contortionist.

contra *prep* against; **un jarabe contra la tos** a cough syrup; **en contra** against; **en contra de algo** to be opposed to sthg; **en contra de** [a diferencia de] contrary to. *sm*: **los pros y los contras** the pros and cons.

contraatacar [10] *vt* to counterattack.

contraataque *sm* counterattack.

contrabajo *sm* - **1.** [instrumento] double-bass - **2.** [voz, cantante] low bass. *smf* [instrumentista] double-bass player.

contrabandista *smf* smuggler.

contrabando *sm* [acto] smuggling; [mercancías] contraband; **pasar algo de contrabando** to smuggle sthg in; **contrabando de armas** gunrunning; **tabaco de contrabando** contraband cigarettes.

contracción *sf* contraction.

contracepción *sf* contraception.

contraceptivo, va *adj* contraceptive *(antes de s)*.

contrachapado, da *adj* made of plywood.

contrachapado *sm* plywood.

contracorriente *sf* crosscurrent; **ir a contracorriente** to go against the current o tide.

contracultura *sf* counter-culture.

contracultural *adj* counter-culture *(antes de s)*.

contradecir [66] *vt* to contradict.

contradecirse *vprnl* to contradict o.s.

contradicción *sf* contradiction; **estar en contradicción con** to be in (direct) contradiction to.

contradicho, cha *pp* contradecir.

contradictorio, ria *adj* contradictory.

contraer [73] *vt* - **1.** [gen] to contract - **2.** [costumbre, acento etc] to acquire - **3.** [enfermedad] to catch.
➡ **contraerse** *vprnl* to contract.

contraespionaje *sm* counterespionage.

contrafuerte *sm* - **1.** ARQUIT buttress - **2.** [del calzado] heel reinforcement - **3.** GEOGR foothill.

contragolpe *sm* counter-attack.

contrahecho, cha *adj* deformed.

contraindicación *sf*: 'contraindicaciones:...' 'not to be taken with...'

contraindicado, da *adj*: **está contraindicado beber durante el embarazo** alcohol should be avoided during pregnancy.

contralmirante *sm* rear admiral.

contralor *sm Chile* inspector of public spending.

contraloría *sf Méx & R Dom* office controlling public spending.

contralto <> *sm* [voz] contralto. <> *smf* [cantante] counter tenor (*f* contralto).

contraluz *sm* back lighting; **a contraluz** against the light.

contramaestre *sm* - **1.** NÁUT boatswain; MIL warrant officer - **2.** [capataz] foreman.

contraofensiva *sf* counteroffensive.

contraorden *sf* countermand.

contrapartida *sf* compensation; **como contrapartida** to make up for it.

contrapelo ➡ **a contrapelo** *loc adv* - **1.** [acariciar] the wrong way - **2.** [vivir, actuar] against the grain.

contrapesar *vt* - **1.** [físicamente] to counterbalance - **2.** *fig* [contrarrestar] to compensate for.

contrapeso *sm* - **1.** [en ascensores, poleas] counterweight - **2.** *fig* [fuerza que iguala] counterbalance.

contraponer [65] *vt* - **1.** [oponer]: **contraponer (a)** to set up (against) - **2.** [cotejar] to compare.
➡ **contraponerse** *vprnl* to oppose.

contraportada *sf* [de periódico, revista] back page; [de libro, disco] back cover.

contraposición *sf* - **1.** [oposición] conflict - **2.** [comparación] comparison.

contraproducente *adj* counterproductive.

contrapuesto, ta <> *pp* ⊳ **contraponer**. <> *adj* conflicting.

contrapunto *sm* - **1.** MÚS counterpoint - **2.** *fig* [contraste] contrast.

contrariado, da *adj* upset.

contrariar [9] *vt* - **1.** [contradecir] to go against - **2.** [disgustar] to upset.

contrariedad *sf* - **1.** [dificultad] setback - **2.** [disgusto] annoyance - **3.** [oposición] contrary o opposing nature.

contrario, ria *adj* - **1.** [opuesto - dirección, sentido] opposite; [- parte] opposing; [- opinión] contrary; **ser contrario a algo** to be opposed to sthg - **2.** [perjudicial]: **contrario a** contrary to - **3.** *loc*: **llevar la contraria** to be awkward o contrary.
➡ **contrario** *sm* - **1.** [rival] opponent - **2.** [opuesto] opposite; **al contrario, por el contrario** on the contrary; **de lo contrario** otherwise; **todo lo contrario** quite the contrary.

contrarreembolso = **contrarrembolso**.

contrarreforma *sf* Counter-Reformation.

contrarreloj *adj inv*: **etapa contrarreloj** time trial; **ir contrarreloj** to be working against the clock.

contrarrembolso, contrarreembolso *sm* cash on delivery.

contrarrestar *vt* [neutralizar] to counteract.

contrarrevolución *sf* counterrevolution.

contrarrevolucionario, ria *adj* & *sm, f* counterrevolutionary.

contrasentido *sm* nonsense *(U)*; **es un contrasentido hacer eso** it doesn't make sense to do that.

contraseña *sf* password.

contrastar <> *vi* to contrast. <> *vt* - **1.** [probar - hechos] to check, to verify - **2.** [resistir] to resist.

contraste *sm* contrast; **hacer contraste con algo** to contrast with sthg; **en contraste con** in contrast to; **por contraste** in contrast.

contrata *sf* (fixed price) contract.

contratación *sf* [de personal] hiring.

contratante *smf* contracting party.

contratar *vt* - **1.** [obreros, personal, detective] to hire; [deportista] to sign - **2.** [servicio, obra, mercancía]: **contratar algo a alguien** to contract for sthg with sb.

contraterrorismo *sm* counterterrorism.

contraterrorista *adj* & *smf* counterterrorist.

contratiempo *sm* [accidente] mishap; [dificultad] setback.

contratista *smf* contractor; **contratista de obras** building contractor.

contrato *sm* contract; **bajo contrato** under contract; **contrato indefinido/laboral/mercantil** indefinite/work/commercial contract; **contrato administrativo** administrative contract; **contrato basura** short-term contract *(with poor conditions)*; **contrato de arrendamiento** lease; **contrato de compraventa** contract of sale; **contrato matrimonial** marriage contract; **contrato temporal** temporary *o* short-term contract; **contrato verbal** oral contract.

contravenir [75] *vi*: **contravenir a** to contravene.

contraventana *sf* shutter.

contrayente *smf person getting married.*

contribución *sf* - **1.** [gen] contribution - **2.** [impuesto] tax; **contribución directa/indirecta** direct/indirect tax; **contribución urbana** ≃ council tax *UK*.

contribuir [51] *vi* - **1.** [gen]: **contribuir (a)** to contribute (to); **contribuir con algo para** to contribute sthg towards - **2.** [pagar impuestos] to pay taxes.

contribuyente *smf* taxpayer.

contrincante *smf* rival, opponent.

contrito, ta *adj* - **1.** [arrepentido] contrite - **2.** *fig* [triste, compungido] downcast.

control *sm* - **1.** [gen] control; **bajo control** under control; **fuera de control** out of control; **perder el control** to lose one's temper; **control del estrés** stress management; **control de cambios** ECON foreign exchange regulation; **control de natalidad** birth control; **control remoto** remote control - **2.** [verificación] examination, inspection; **(bajo) control médico** (under) medical supervision; **control antidoping** dope test; **control de calidad** quality control - **3.** [puesto policial] checkpoint; **control de pasaportes** passport control.

controlador, ra *sm, f* [gen & INFORM] controller; **controlador aéreo** air traffic controller.

➠ **controlador de disco** *sm* disk controller.

controlar *vt* - **1.** [gen] to control; [cuentas] to audit - **2.** [comprobar] to check - **3.** [vigilar] to watch, to keep an eye on.

➠ **controlarse** *vprnl* to control o.s., to restrain o.s.

controversia *sf* controversy.

contubernio *sm fig* conspiracy.

contumaz *adj* stubborn, obstinate.

contundencia *sf* - **1.** [de golpes, patadas] force - **2.** *fig* [de palabras, argumentos] forcefulness.

contundente *adj* - **1.** [arma, objeto] blunt; [golpe] thudding - **2.** *fig* [razonamiento, argumento] forceful.

contusión *sf* bruise.

contusionar *vt* to bruise.

contuviera *etc* ▷ **contener.**

conurbación *sf* conurbation.

convalecencia *sf* convalescence.

convalecer [30] *vi*: **convalecer (de)** to convalesce (after).

convaleciente *adj* convalescent.

convalidación *sf* [de estudios] recognition; [de asignaturas] validation.

convalidar *vt* [estudios] to recognize; [asignaturas] to validate.

convección *sf* convection.

convector *sm* convector.

convencer [11] *vt* to convince; **convencer a alguien de algo** to convince sb of sthg.

➠ **convencerse** *vprnl*: **convencerse de** to become convinced of.

convencimiento *sm* [certeza] conviction; [acción] convincing.

convención *sf* convention.

convencional *adj* conventional.

convencionalismo *sm* conventionality.

conveniencia *sf* - **1.** [utilidad] usefulness; [oportunidad] suitability - **2.** [interés] convenience; **sólo mira su conveniencia** he only looks after his own interests.

➠ **conveniencias** *sfpl* conventions.

conveniente *adj* [útil] useful; [oportuno] suitable, appropriate; [lugar, hora] convenient; [aconsejable] advisable; **sería conveniente asistir** it would be a good idea to go.

convenio *sm* agreement; **convenio colectivo** collective bargaining.

convenir [75] ◇ *vi* - **1.** [venir bien] to be suitable; **conviene analizar la situación** it would be a good idea to analyse the situation; **no te conviene hacerlo** you shouldn't do it - **2.** [acordar]: **convenir en** to agree on. ◇ *vt* to agree on.

convento *sm* [de monjas] convent; [de monjes] monastery.

convergencia *sf* [gen, en UE] convergence.

convergente *adj* converging, convergent.

converger [14] *vi* to converge.

conversación *sf* conversation; **cambiar de conversación** to change the subject; **dar conversación a alguien** to keep sb talking; **trabar conversación con alguien** to strike up a conversation with sb.

➠ **conversaciones** *sfpl* [negociaciones] talks.

conversada *sf Amér* chat.

conversador, ra ◇ *adj* talkative. ◇ *sm, f* conversationalist.

conversar *vi* to talk, to converse.

conversión *sf* conversion.

converso, sa ◇ *adj* converted. ◇ *sm, f* convert.

convertibilidad *sf* ECON convertibility.

convertible *adj* convertible.

convertir [21] *vt* - **1.** RELIG to convert - **2.** [transformar]: **convertir algo/a alguien en** to convert sthg/sb into, to turn sthg/sb into.

convertirse *vprnl* - **1.** RELIG: **convertirse (a)** to convert (to) - **2.** [transformarse]: **convertirse en** to become, to turn into.

convexo, **xa** *adj* convex.

convicción *sf* conviction; **tener la convicción de que** to be convinced that.

convicto, **ta** *adj* convicted.

convidado, **da** *sm, f* guest; **como el convidado de piedra** silent as the grave.

convidar *vt* [invitar] to invite.

➤ **convidar a** *vi* [mover, incitar] to be conducive to.

conviene *etc* ➢ **convenir**.

convierta *etc* ➢ **convertir**.

convincente *adj* convincing.

conviniera *etc* ➢ **convenir**.

convite *sm* - **1.** [invitación] invitation - **2.** [fiesta] banquet.

convivencia *sf* living together.

➤ **convivencias** *sfpl*: **irse de convivencias** [gen] to go to camp; RELIG to go on a retreat.

convivir *vi* to live together; **convivir con** to live with.

convocar [10] *vt* [reunión] to convene; [huelga, elecciones] to call.

convocatoria *sf* - **1.** [anuncio, escrito] notice - **2.** [de examen] diet.

convoy (*pl* **convoyes**) *sm* - **1.** [gen] convoy - **2.** [tren] train.

convulsión *sf* - **1.** [de músculos] convulsion - **2.** [política, social] upheaval *(U)* - **3.** [de tierra] tremor.

convulsionar *vt* to convulse.

convulso, **sa** *adj* convulsed.

conyugal *adj* conjugal; **vida conyugal** married life.

cónyuge *smf* spouse; **los cónyuges** husband and wife.

coña *sf fam* - **1.** [guasa] joke; **está de coña** she's joking - **2.** [molestia] drag, pain.

coñac (*pl* **coñacs**), **cognac** (*pl* **cognacs**) *sm* brandy, cognac.

coñazo *sm fam* pain, drag; **dar el coñazo** to be a pain.

coño *vulg* ➢ *sm* - **1.** [genital] cunt - **2.** [para enfatizar]: **¿dónde/qué coño...?** where/what the fuck...? ➢ *interj* - **1.** [enfado]: **¡coño!** for fuck's sake! - **2.** [asombro]: **¡coño!** fucking hell!

cooperación *sf* cooperation.

cooperador, **ra** *adj* cooperative.

cooperante *adj* cooperating.

cooperar *vi*: **cooperar (con alguien en algo)** to cooperate (with sb in sthg).

cooperativa *sf* ➢ **cooperativo**.

cooperativismo *sm* cooperative movement.

cooperativo, **va** *adj* cooperative.

➤ **cooperativa** *sf* cooperative; **cooperativa agrícola** farming cooperative.

coordenada (*gen pl*) *sf* coordinate.

coordinación *sf* coordination.

coordinado, **da** *adj* coordinated.

coordinador, **ra** ➢ *adj* coordinating. ➢ *sm, f* coordinator.

coordinar *vt* - **1.** [movimientos, gestos] to coordinate - **2.** [esfuerzos, medios] to combine, to pool.

copa *sf* - **1.** [vaso] glass; **ir de copas** to go out drinking; **¿quieres (tomar) una copa?** would you like (to have) a drink?; **lleva unas copas de más** she's had one too many - **2.** [de árbol] top; **es un profesional como la copa de un pino** *fam* he's a consummate professional; **es una mentira como la copa de un pino** *fam* it's a whopper of a lie - **3.** [de sombrero] crown - **4.** [en deporte] cup.

➤ **copas** *sfpl* [naipes] *suit with pictures of goblets in Spanish playing cards*, ≃ hearts.

copar *vt fig* - **1.** [puestos - en competición] to win - **2.** [cargos] to monopolize.

copear *vi* to have a few drinks.

copeo *sm* drinking.

copero, **ra** *adj* [competición, partido] cup *(antes de s)*; [equipo] cupwinning *(antes de s)*.

copete *sm* - **1.** [de ave] crest - **2.** [de pelo] tuft - **3.** *loc*: **de alto copete** upper-class.

copetín *sm Amér* [bebida] aperitif; [comida] appetizer.

copia *sf* - **1.** [reproducción] copy; **sacar una copia** to make a copy; **copia al carbón** carbon copy; **copia de seguridad** INFORM backup; **hacer una copia de seguridad de algo** to back sthg up, to make a back-up of sthg - **2.** [acción] copying - **3.** [persona] (spitting) image.

copiador, **ra** *adj* copying.

copiar [8] ➢ *vt* [gen] to copy; [al dictado] to take down. ➢ *vi* [en examen] to cheat, to copy.

copiloto *smf* copilot.

copión, **ona** *sm, f* [imitador] copycat; [en examen] cheat.

copioso, **sa** *adj* copious.

copista *smf* copyist.

copla *sf* - **1.** [canción] folksong, popular song - **2.** [estrofa] verse, stanza.

copo *sm* - **1.** [de nieve, cereales] flake; **copos de avena** rolled oats; **copos de maíz** cornflakes - **2.** [de algodón] ball.

copón *sm* ciborium; **un lío del copón** *fam* a hell of a mess.

coprocesador *sm* INFORM coprocessor; **coprocesador matemático** maths chip *o* coprocessor.

coproducción *sf* coproduction.

copropiedad *sf* joint ownership.

copropietario, ria *sm, f* co-owner, joint owner.

cópula *sf* - **1.** [sexual] copulation - **2.** GRAM copula.

copulación *sf* copulation.

copular *vi* to copulate.

copulativo, va *adj* copulative.

coque *sm* coke.

coqueta ⊳ **coqueto**.

coquetear *vi* to flirt.

coquetería *sf* coquetry.

coqueto, ta *adj* - **1.** [persona - que flirtea] flirtatious, coquettish; [- que se arregla mucho] concerned with one's appearance - **2.** [cosa] charming, delightful.
◆ **coqueta** *sf* [tocador] dressing table.

coraje *sm* - **1.** [valor] courage - **2.** [rabia] anger; **me da mucho coraje** it makes me furious.

coral ◇ *adj* choral. ◇ *sm* coral. ◇ *sf* - **1.** [coro] choir - **2.** [composición] chorale.

coralino, na *adj* coral.

Corán *sm*: **el Corán** the Koran.

coraza *sf* - **1.** [de soldado] cuirasse, armour - **2.** [de tortuga] shell - **3.** *fig* [protección] shield.

corazón *sm* - **1.** [órgano] heart; **cirugía a corazón abierto** open-heart surgery; **sufrir del corazón** to have heart trouble - **2.** [centro - de ciudad, alcachofa] heart; [- de manzana] core - **3.** ⊳ **dedo** - **4.** *loc*: **con el corazón en la mano** frankly, openly; **de buen corazón** kindhearted; **de (todo) corazón** from the bottom of one's heart, quite sincerely; **se me encoge el corazón al ver...** it breaks my heart to see...; **llevar el corazón en la mano** to wear one's heart on one's sleeve; **no tener corazón** to have no heart, to be heartless; **romper o partir el corazón a alguien** to break sb's heart; **tener un corazón de oro** to have a heart of gold.
◆ **Sagrado Corazón** *sm* Sacred Heart.

corazonada *sf* - **1.** [presentimiento] feeling, hunch - **2.** [impulso] sudden impulse.

corbata *sf* tie; **corbata de pajarita** bow tie.

corbeta *sf* corvette.

Córcega *n pr* Corsica.

corcel *sm culto* steed.

corchea *sf* quaver.

corchera *sf* rope with cork floats to divide lanes in swimming pool.

corchete *sm* - **1.** [broche] hook and eye - **2.** [signo ortográfico] square bracket - **3.** *Chile* [grapa] staple.

corcho *sm* cork.

córcholis *interj* - **1.** [para expresar sorpresa]: **¡córcholis!** good heavens! - **2.** [para expresar enfado]: **¡córcholis!** for Heaven's sake!

cordada *sf* roped party of mountaineers.

cordaje *sm* - **1.** [de guitarra, raqueta] strings *pl* - **2.** NÁUT rigging.

cordel *sm* cord.

cordero, ra *sm, f lit & fig* lamb; **cordero lechal** suckling lamb.

cordial *adj* cordial.

cordialidad *sf* cordiality.

cordillera *sf* mountain range; **la cordillera Cantábrica** the Cantabrian Mountains.

cordón *sm* - **1.** [gen & ANAT] cord; [de zapato] lace; **cordón umbilical** umbilical cord - **2.** [cable eléctrico] flex - **3.** *fig* [para protección, vigilancia] cordon; **cordón sanitario** cordon sanitaire - **4.** *C Sur* [de la vereda] kerb *UK*, curb *US*; **aparcar en cordón** to park end-to-end.

cordura *sf* [juicio] sanity; [sensatez] sense; **con cordura** sensibly.

Corea *n pr*: **Corea del Norte/Sur** North/South Korea.

corear *vt* to chorus.

coreografía *sf* choreography.

coreógrafo, fa *sm, f* choreographer.

corintio, tia *adj* & *sm, f* Corinthian.

corista ◇ *smf* [en coro] chorus singer. ◇ *sf* [en cabaré] chorus girl.

cormorán *sm* cormorant.

cornada *sf* goring; **dar una cornada a alguien** to gore sb.

cornamenta *sf* - **1.** [de toro] horns *pl*; [de ciervo] antlers *pl* - **2.** *fam* [del marido engañado] cuckold's horns *pl*.

cornamusa *sf* - **1.** [trompeta] hunting horn - **2.** [gaita] bagpipe.

córnea *sf* cornea.

cornear, acornear *vt* to gore.

córner *sm* corner (kick); **lanzar o sacar un córner** to take a corner.

corneta ◇ *sf* [instrumento] bugle. ◇ *smf* [persona] bugler.

cornete *sm* - **1.** ANAT turbinate bone - **2.** [helado] cornet, cone.

cornetín ◇ *sm* [instrumento] cornet. ◇ *smf* [persona] cornet player.

cornflakes® ['konfleiks] *smpl* Cornflakes®.

cornisa *sf* - **1.** ARQUIT cornice - **2.** GEOGR: **la cornisa cantábrica** the Cantabrian Coast.

cornudo, da *adj* - **1.** [animal] horned - **2.** *fam fig* [cónyuge] cuckolded.
◆ **cornudo** *sm fam fig* [marido] cuckold.

coro *sm* - **1.** [gen] choir; **contestar a coro** to answer all at once - **2.** [de obra musical] chorus.

corola *sf* corolla.

corona *sf* - **1.** [gen] crown - **2.** [de flores] garland; **corona fúnebre/de laurel** funeral/laurel wreath - **3.** [de santos] halo - **4.** [de comida] ring.

coronación *sf* - **1.** [de monarca] coronation - **2.** *fig* [remate, colmo] culmination.

coronamiento *sm* - **1.** *fig* [remate, fin] culmination - **2.** ARQUIT crown.

coronar *vt* - **1.** [persona] to crown - **2.** *fig* [terminar] to complete; [culminar] to crown, to cap - **3.** *fig* [cima] to reach.

coronario, ria *adj* coronary.

coronel *sm* colonel.

coronilla *sf* crown (of the head); **estar hasta la coronilla (de)** to be sick and tired (of).

corotos *smpl Caribe* things, whatnots.

corpiño *sm* - **1.** bodice - **2.** *Arg* [sostén] bra.

corporación *sf* corporation.

corporal *adj* corporal.

corporativo, va *adj* corporate.

corpulencia *sf* corpulence.

corpulento, ta *adj* corpulent.

Corpus Christi ['korpus'kristi] *sm* Corpus Christi.

corpúsculo *sm* corpuscle.

corral *sm* - **1.** [gen] yard; [para cerdos, ovejas] pen - **2.** [para teatro] *open-air theatre in courtyard.*

correa *sf* - **1.** [de bolso, reloj] strap; [de pantalón] belt; [de perro] lead, leash - **2.** TECNOL belt; **correa del ventilador** fan belt.

correaje *sm* [de un caballo] harness.

corrección *sf* - **1.** [de errores] correction; **corrección de pruebas** proofreading - **2.** [de exámenes] marking - **3.** [de texto] revision - **4.** [de comportamiento] correctness, courtesy - **5.** [reprimenda] reprimand.

correccional *sm* reformatory, reform school.

correctivo, va *adj* corrective.

➤ **correctivo** *sm* punishment.

correcto, ta *adj* - **1.** [resultado, texto, respuesta] correct - **2.** [persona] polite; [conducta] proper.

corrector, ra <> *adj* corrective. <> *sm, f:* **corrector (de pruebas)** proofreader.

➤ **corrector** *sm* INFORM: **corrector de estilo** stylechecker; **corrector de gramática** grammar checker; **corrector ortográfico** spellchecker; **pasar el corrector ortográfico a** to spellcheck.

corredero, ra *adj* sliding.

➤ **corredera** *sf* [ranura] runner; **puerta de corredera** sliding door.

corredizo, za *adj* sliding *(antes de s).*

corredor, ra <> *adj* running *(s).* <> *sm, f* - **1.** [deportista] runner - **2.** [intermediario]: **corredor de bolsa** stockbroker; **corredor de comercio** COM registered broker; **corredor de fincas** land agent; **corredor de seguros** COM insurance broker.

➤ **corredor** *sm* [pasillo] corridor, passage.

corregir [42] *vt* - **1.** [gen] to correct; [exámenes] to mark - **2.** [reprender] to reprimand.

➤ **corregirse** *vprnl* to change for the better.

correlación *sf* correlation.

correlativo, va *adj* correlative.

correligionario, ria *adj* [en religión] fellow *(antes de s)*; [en política, ideología] like-minded.

correo <> *sm* post UK, mail US; **echar al correo** to post; **a vuelta de correo** by return (of post); **correo aéreo** air mail; **correo basura** INFORM spam; **correo certificado** registered post O mail; **correo comercial** direct mail; **correo electrónico** e-mail; **correo urgente** special delivery; **correo de voz** voice mail. <> *adj*: **tren correo** mail train.

➤ **Correos** *sm* [organismo] the post office.

correoso, sa *adj* leathery.

correr <> *vi* - **1.** [andar de prisa] to run; **a todo correr** at full speed O pelt; **(ella) corre que se las pela** she runs like the wind - **2.** [conducir de prisa] to drive fast - **3.** [pasar por - río] to flow; [- camino, agua del grifo] to run; **deja correr el agua del grifo** leave the tap running - **4.** [el tiempo, las horas] to pass, to go by - **5.** [propagarse - noticia etc] to spread - **6.** [ser válido - moneda] to be legal tender - **7.** [encargarse de]: **correr con** [los gastos] to bear; [la cuenta] to pay; **correr a cargo de** to be taken care of by; **la comida corre a cargo de la empresa** the meal is on the company - **8.** [sueldo etc] to be payable. <> *vt* - **1.** [recorrer - una distancia] to cover; **corrió los 100 metros** he ran the 100 metres - **2.** [deslizar - mesa, silla] to move O pull up - **3.** [cortinas] to draw; **correr el pestillo** to bolt the door - **4.** [experimentar - aventuras, vicisitudes] to have; [- riesgo] to run; **correrla** *fam* to go out on the town - **5.** *Amér fam* [despedir] to throw out.

➤ **correrse** *vprnl* - **1.** [desplazarse - persona] to move over; [- cosa] to slide - **2.** [pintura, colores] to run - **3.** *Andes, Cuba & Esp mfam* [tener un orgasmo] to come.

correría *sf* foray.

correspondencia *sf* - **1.** [gen] correspondence; **curso por correspondencia** correspondence course - **2.** [de metro, tren] connection.

corresponder *vi* - **1.** [compensar]: **corresponder (con algo) a alguien/algo** to repay sb/sthg (with sthg) - **2.** [pertenecer] to belong - **3.** [coincidir]: **corresponder (a/con)** to correspond (to/with) - **4.** [tocar]: **corresponderle a alguien hacer algo** to be sb's responsibility to do sthg - **5.** [a un sentimiento] to reciprocate.

◆ **corresponderse** *vprnl* - **1.** [escribirse] to correspond - **2.** [amarse] to love each other.

correspondiente *adj* - **1.** [gen]: **correspondiente (a)** corresponding (to) - **2.** [respectivo] respective.

corresponsal *smf* - **1.** PRENSA correspondent - **2.** COM agent.

corresponsalía *sf* post of correspondent.

corretear *vi* - **1.** [correr] to run about - **2.** *fam* [vagar] to hang about.

correveidile *smf* gossip.

corrido, da *adj* - **1.** [cortinas] drawn - **2.** [avergonzado] embarrassed - **3.** [continuo] continuous.

◆ **corrida** *sf* - **1.** TAUROM bull fight - **2.** [acción de correr] run; **dar una corrido** to make a dash; **en una corrido** inan instant O a flash.

◆ **de corrido** *loc prep* by heart; **recitar algo de corrido** to recite sthg parrot-fashion.

corriente ◇ *adj* - **1.** [normal] ordinary, normal; **corriente y moliente** run-of-the-mill - **2.** [agua] running - **3.** [mes, año, cuenta] current. ◇ *sf* - **1.** [de río, electricidad] current; **corriente alterna/continua** alternating/direct current - **2.** [de aire] draught - **3.** *fig* [tendencia] trend, current; [de opinión] tide - **4.** *loc*: **dejarse llevar de** O **por la corriente** to follow the crowd; **ir contra corriente** to go against the tide; **llevarle** O **seguirle la corriente a alguien** to humour sb. ◇ *sm*: **estar al corriente de** to be up to date with; **poner al corriente** to bring up to date; **ponerse al corriente** to bring o.s. up to date; **tener a alguien al corriente** to keep sb informed.

corrige, corrigió *etc* ⊏▷ **corregir**.

corrillo *sm* knot O small group of people.

corrimiento *sm* shift, slipping; **corrimiento de tierras** landslide.

corro *sm* - **1.** [círculo] circle, ring; **en corro** in a circle; **hacer corro** to form a circle - **2.** FIN [cotizaciones] stocks *pl*.

corroborar *vt* to corroborate.

corroer [69] *vt* - **1.** [gen] to corrode; GEOL to erode - **2.** *fig* [consumir] to consume, to eat away at.

corromper *vt* - **1.** [pudrir - madera] to rot; [- alimentos] to turn bad, to spoil - **2.** [pervertir] to corrupt - **3.** [sobornar] to bribe.

◆ **corromperse** *vprnl* - **1.** [pudrirse] to rot - **2.** [pervertirse] to become corrupted.

corrosión *sf* [gen] corrosion; [de un metal] rust; GEOL erosion.

corrosivo, va *adj* *lit & fig* corrosive.

corrupción *sf* - **1.** [gen] corruption; **corrupción de menores** corruption of minors - **2.** [soborno] bribery - **3.** [de una substancia] decay.

corruptela *sf* corruption.

corrupto, ta *adj* corrupt.

corruptor, ra ◇ *adj* corrosive. ◇ *sm, f* corrupter.

corrusco *sm* hard crust.

corsario, ria *adj* pirate *(antes de s)*.

◆ **corsario** *sm* corsair, pirate.

corsé *sm* corset.

corsetería *sf* ladies' underwear shop.

cortacésped (*pl* **cortacéspedes**) *sm* lawnmower.

cortacircuitos *sm inv* circuit breaker.

cortado, da *adj* - **1.** [labios, manos] chapped - **2.** [leche] sour, off; [salsa] curdled - **3.** *fam fig* [tímido] inhibited; **quedarse cortado** to be left speechless.

◆ **cortado** *sm* [café] *small coffee with just a little milk*.

cortadura *sf* cut.

cortafuego *sm* firebreak.

cortafuegos *sm inv* INFORM firewall.

cortante *adj* - **1.** [afilado] sharp - **2.** *fig* [frase] cutting; [viento] biting; [frío] bitter.

cortapisa *sf* limitation, restriction; **poner cortapisas a algo** to hinder sb.

cortaplumas *sm inv* penknife.

cortar ◇ *vt* - **1.** [seccionar - pelo, uñas] to cut; [- papel] to cut up; [- ramas] to cut off; [- árbol] to cut down - **2.** [amputar] to amputate, to cut off - **3.** [tela, figura de papel] to cut out - **4.** [interrumpir - retirada, luz, teléfono] to cut off; [- carretera] to block (off); [- hemorragia] to stop, to staunch; [- discurso, conversación] to interrupt - **5.** [atravesar - calle, territorio] to cut across - **6.** [labios, piel] to crack, to chap - **7.** [hender - aire, olas] to slice through - **8.** [alimento] to curdle - **9.** [recortar - gastos etc] to cut back - **10.** [poner fin a - beca etc] to cut; [- abusos etc] to put a stop to - **11.** [avergonzar]: **este hombre me corta un poco** I find it hard to be myself when that man's around - **12.** [censurar] to censor; [película] to cut - **13.** INFORM to cut off. ◇ *vi* - **1.** *R Dom* [comunicación] to hang up - **2.** [producir un corte] to cut - **3.** [atajar] to take a short cut; **cortar por** to take a short cut through - **4.** [cesar una relación] to break O split up; **he cortado con mi novio** I've split up with my boyfriend.

◆ **cortarse** *vprnl* - **1.** [herirse] to cut o.s.; **cortarse el pelo** to have a haircut - **2.** [labios, piel] to become chapped O cracked - **3.** [alimento] to curdle - **4.** [comunicación] to get cut off - **5.** *fam* [turbarse] to become tongue-tied.

cortaúñas *sm inv* nail clippers *pl*.

corte ◇ *sm* - **1.** [raja] cut; [en pantalones, camisa etc] tear; **corte y confección** [para mujeres] dressmaking; [para hombres] tailoring - **2.** [de pelo] haircut; **corte a la navaja** razor cut - **3.** [retal de tela] length - **4.** [contorno] shape - **5.** [interrupción]: **corte de digestión** stomach cramps; **corte de luz** power cut - **6.** [sección] section - **7.** [concepción, estilo] style - **8.** [pausa] break - **9.** [filo] (cutting) edge - **10.** *fam* [respuesta ingeniosa] put-down; **dar un corte a alguien** to cut sb dead; **hacer un corte de mangas** ≃ to stick two fingers up, ≃ to make a V-sign - **11.** *fam* [vergüenza] embarrassment; **dar corte a alguien** to embarrass sb. ◇ *sf* [palacio] court; **hacer la corte a alguien** *fig* to court sb.

◆ **Cortes** *sfpl* POLÍT the Spanish parliament.

cortedad *sf* - **1.** [de extensión] shortness - **2.** *fig* [timidez] shyness.

cortejar *vt* to court.

cortejo *sm* retinue; **cortejo fúnebre** funeral cortège O procession.

cortés *adj* polite, courteous.

cortesano, na ◇ *adj* [fiestas, vida] court *(antes de s)*; [modales] courtly. ◇ *sm, f* [personaje de la corte] courtier.

◆ **cortesana** *sf* [meretriz] courtesan.

cortesía *sf* courtesy; **de cortesía** courtesy; **por cortesía de** courtesy of.

corteza *sf* - **1.** [del árbol] bark - **2.** [de pan] crust; [de queso, tocino, limón] rind; [de naranja etc] peel - **3.** [terrestre] crust - **4.** ANAT cortex.

cortical *adj* cortical.

corticoide *sm* corticoid.

cortijo *sm* [finca] farm; [casa] farmhouse.

cortina *sf* [de tela] curtain; *fig*: **cortina de agua** sheet of water; **cortina de humo** smoke screen.

cortinaje *sm* curtains *pl*.

cortisona *sf* cortisone.

corto, ta *adj* - **1.** [gen] short - **2.** [escaso - raciones] small, meagre; [- disparo] short of the target; **corto de** [dinero etc] short of; **corto de vista** short-sighted - **3.** *fig* [bobo] dim, simple - **4.** *loc*: **a la corta o a la larga** sooner or later; **ni corto ni perezoso** as bold as brass; **quedarse corto** [al calcular] to underestimate; **decir que es bueno es quedarse corto** it's an understatement to call it good.

◆ **corto** *sm* CINE short (film).

cortocircuito *sm* short circuit.

cortometraje *sm* short (film).

corvo, va *adj* [gen] curved; [nariz] hooked.

◆ **corva** *sf* back of the knee.

corzo, za *sm, f* roe buck (*f* roe deer).

cosa *sf* - **1.** [gen] thing; **¿queréis alguna cosa?** is there anything you want?; **no es gran cosa** it's not important, it's no big deal; **poca cosa** nothing much - **2.** [asunto] matter; **esto es otra cosa** that's another matter; **no es cosa de risa** it's no laughing matter - **3.** [ocurrencia] funny remark; **¡qué cosas tienes!** you do say some funny things! - **4.** *loc*: **¡a otra cosa, mariposa!** let's change the subject!; **como si tal cosa** as if nothing had happened; **decir cuatro cosas a alguien** to give sb a piece of one's mind; **eso es cosa mía** that's my affair O business; **hacer algo como quien no quiere la cosa** [disimuladamente] to do sthg as if one wasn't intending to; [sin querer] to do sthg almost without realizing it; **¡lo que son las cosas!** it's a funny old world!; **no sea cosa que** just in case; **son cosas de mamá** that's just the way Mum is, that's just one of Mum's little idiosyncrasies; **son las cosas de la vida** that's life.

◆ **cosa de** *loc adv* about; **es cosa de tres semanas** it takes about three weeks.

cosaco, ca *adj* & *sm, f* Cossack; **beber como un cosaco** to drink like a fish.

coscorrón *sm* bump on the head.

cosecha *sf* - **1.** [gen] harvest; **ser de la (propia) cosecha de alguien** to be made up O invented by sb - **2.** [del vino] vintage.

cosechadora *sf* combine harvester.

cosechar ◇ *vt* - **1.** [cultivar] to grow - **2.** [recolectar] to harvest - **3.** *fig* [obtener] to win, to reap. ◇ *vi* to (bring in the) harvest.

cosechero, ra *sm, f* [de cereales] harvester, reaper; [de frutos] picker.

coseno *sm* cosine.

coser ◇ *vt* - **1.** [con hilo] to sew; **coser un botón** to sew on a button - **2.** [con grapas] to staple (together). ◇ *vi* to sew; **coser a balazos** to riddle with bullets; **coser a cuchilladas** to stab repeatedly; **ser cosa de coser y cantar** to be child's play O a piece of cake.

cosido *sm* stitching.

cosmético, ca *adj* cosmetic *(antes de s)*.

◆ **cosmético** *sm* cosmetic.

◆ **cosmética** *sf* cosmetics (U).

cósmico, ca *adj* cosmic.

cosmonauta *smf* cosmonaut.

cosmopolita *adj* & *smf* cosmopolitan.

cosmos *sm inv* cosmos.

coso *sm* - **1.** [plaza] bullring - **2.** C Sur [objeto] whatnot, thing.

cosquillas *sfpl*: **hacer cosquillas** to tickle; **tener cosquillas** to be ticklish; **buscarle las cosquillas a alguien** to wind sb up, to irritate sb.

cosquilleo *sm* tickling sensation.

costa *sf* GEOGR coast.

◆ **costas** *sfpl* DER costs.

◆ **Costa Azul** *sf*: **la Costa Azul** the Côte d'Azur.

◆ **Costa Brava** *sf*: **la Costa Brava** the Costa Brava.

◆ **a costa de** *loc prep* at the expense of; **lo hizo a costa de grandes esfuerzos** he did it by dint of much effort; **vive a costa de sus padres** she lives off her parents.

◆ **a toda costa** *loc prep* at all costs.

Costa de Marfil *n pr* Ivory Coast.

costado *sm* side; **es francés por los cuatro costados** he's French through and through.

costal *sm* sack.

costalada *sf* = costalazo.

costalazo *sm* heavy fall.

costanera *sf C Sur* promenade.

costar [23] ⬦ *vt* - **1.** [dinero] to cost; **¿cuánto cuesta?** how much is it? - **2.** [tiempo] to take - **3.** *loc*: **cueste lo que cueste** whatever the cost; **le costó la vida** it cost him his life; **costar un ojo de la cara** *o* **un riñón** to cost an arm and a leg. ⬦ *vi* (ser difícil): **costarle a alguien hacer algo** to be difficult for sb to do sthg; **costar caro a alguien** to cost sb dear.

Costa Rica *n pr* Costa Rica.

costarricense, costarriqueño, **ña** *adj* & *sm, f* Costa Rican.

coste *sm* [de producción] cost; [de un objeto] price; **coste de la vida** cost of living; **coste unitario** ECON unit cost.

costear *vt* - **1.** [pagar] to pay for - **2.** NÁUT [la costa] to hug, to keep close to.

◆ **costearse** *vprnl*: **costearse algo** [pagárselo] to pay for sthg o.s.; [permitírselo] to be able to afford sthg.

costeño, ña, costero, ra *adj* [gen] coastal; [pueblo] seaside (antes de s).

◆ **costera** *sf Méx* promenade.

costilla *sf* - **1.** [de persona, barco] rib - **2.** [de animal] cutlet - **3.** *fam fig* [cónyuge] better half.

◆ **costillas** *sfpl fam* [espalda] back *sing*.

costillar *sm* [de persona] ribs *pl*, rib cage; [de carne] side.

costo *sm* [de una mercancía] price; [de un producto, de la vida] cost.

costoso, sa *adj* - **1.** [operación, maquinaria] expensive - **2.** *fig* [trabajo] exhausting; [triunfo] costly.

costra *sf* - **1.** [de pan] crust; [de queso] rind - **2.** [de herida] scab.

costumbre *sf* habit, custom; **coger/perder la costumbre de hacer algo** to get into/out of the habit of doing sthg; **como de costumbre** as usual; **por costumbre** through force of habit, out of habit.

◆ **costumbres** *sfpl* [de país, cultura] customs; [de persona] habits.

costumbrista *adj* describing the customs of a country or region.

costura *sf* - **1.** [labor] sewing, needlework - **2.** [puntadas] seam - **3.** [oficio] dressmaking; **alta costura** haute couture.

costurera *sf* dressmaker, seamstress.

costurero *sm* [caja] sewing box.

cota *sf* - **1.** [altura] altitude, height above sea level - **2.** [armadura]: **cota de mallas** coat of mail - **3.** *fig* [nivel] level, height.

cotarro *sm* riotous gathering; **alborotar el cotarro** to stir up trouble; **dirigir el cotarro** to rule the roost, to be the boss.

cotejar *vt* to compare.

cotejo *sm* comparison.

cotice *etc* ⬧ cotizar.

cotidianidad *sf* [vida cotidiana] everyday life; [monotonía] monotony.

cotidiano, na *adj* daily.

cotilla *smf fam* gossip, busybody.

cotillear *vi fam* to gossip.

cotilleo *sm fam* gossip, tittle-tattle.

cotillón *sm* New Year's Eve party.

cotizable *adj* quotable.

cotización *sf* - **1.** [valor] price - **2.** [en Bolsa] quotation, price.

cotizado, da *adj* - **1.** [en la Bolsa] quoted - **2.** [persona] sought-after.

cotizar [13] ⬦ *vt* - **1.** [valorar] to quote, to price - **2.** [pagar] to pay. ⬦ *vi* to pay contributions.

◆ **cotizarse** *vprnl* - **1.** [estimarse - persona] to be valued *o* prized - **2.**: **cotizarse a** [producto] to sell for, to fetch; [bonos, valores] to be quoted at.

coto *sm* preserve; **coto de caza** game preserve; **poner coto a** to put a stop to.

cotorra *sf* - **1.** [ave] parrot - **2.** *fam fig* [persona] chatterbox; **hablar como una cotorra** to talk nineteen to the dozen.

cotorrear *vi* to chatter.

COU (abrev de Curso de Orientación Universitaria) *sm* formerly, a one-year course which prepared pupils aged 17-18 for Spanish university entrance examinations.

covacha *sf* hovel.

coxis = cóccix.

coyote *sm* - **1.** [animal] coyote - **2.** *Méx fam* [guía] guide - **3.** *Méx fam* [intermediario] fixer, middleman.

coyuntura *sf* - **1.** [situación] moment; **la coyuntura económica** the economic situation - **2.** ANAT joint.

coyuntural *adj* transitional.

coz *sf* kick; **tratar a alguien a coces** *fam fig* to treat sb like dirt.

cozamos ⊳ cocer.

CPU (*abrev de* **central processing unit**) *sf* IN-FORM CPU.

crac (*pl* cracs), **crack** (*pl* cracks) *sm* FIN crash.

crack (*pl* cracks) *sm* - **1.** *fig* [estrella] star, superstar - **2.** FIN = crac - **3.** [droga] crack.

craneal *adj* cranial.

cráneo *sm* cranium, skull; **ir de cráneo** *fam* to be doing badly.

crápula *smf* libertine.

craso, sa *adj fig* gross, crass; **¡craso error!** no debió hacerlo that was a big mistake! he shouldn't have done it.

cráter *sm* crater.

creación *sf* creation.

creador, ra ⟡ *adj* creative. ⟡ *sm, f* creator; **creador gráfico** creator (*of cartoon etc*).
◆ **Creador** *sm*: **el Creador** the Creator.

crear *vt* - **1.** [gen] to create - **2.** [inventar] to invent - **3.** [fundar - una academia] to found.

creatividad *sf* creativity.

creativo, va ⟡ *adj* creative. ⟡ *sm, f* [en publicidad] ideas man (*f* ideas woman).

crecer [30] *vi* - **1.** [persona, planta] to grow - **2.** [días, noches] to grow longer - **3.** [río, marea] to rise - **4.** [aumentar - animosidad etc] to grow, to increase; [- rumores] to spread - **5.** [la luna] to wax.
◆ **crecerse** *vprnl* to become more self-confident.

creces ◆ **con creces** *adv* with interest.

crecido, da *adj* [cantidad] large; [hijo] grown-up.
◆ **crecida** *sf* spate, flood.

creciente ⟡ *adj* [gen] growing; [luna] crescent. ⟡ *sm* crescent.

crecimiento *sm* [gen] growth; [de precios] rise; **crecimiento económico** ECON economic growth.

credencial ⟡ *adj* accrediting. ⟡ *sf* - **1.** [de acceso a un lugar] pass - **2.** [documento identificador] ID card.
◆ **credenciales** *sfpl* [diplomáticas] credentials.

credibilidad *sf* credibility.

crediticio, cia *adj* credit (*antes de s*).

crédito *sm* - **1.** [préstamo] loan; **a crédito** on credit; **crédito al consumo** ECON consumer credit; **crédito blando** ECON soft loan; **crédito a la exportación** ECON export credit; **crédito hipotecario** ECON mortgage credit; **crédito oficial** ECON official credit; **crédito personal** ECON personal loan - **2.** [plazo de préstamo] credit - **3.** [confianza] trust, belief; **digno de crédito** trustworthy; **dar crédito a algo** to believe sthg - **4.** [fama] standing, reputation - **5.** [en universidad] credit.

credo *sm* - **1.** [religioso] creed - **2.** [ideológico, político] credo.

credulidad *sf* credulity.

crédulo, la *adj* credulous.

creencia *sf* belief.

creer [50] *vt* - **1.** [gen] to believe; **¡ya lo creo!** of course!, I should say so! - **2.** [suponer] to think; **creo que no** I don't think so; **creo que sí** I think so; **según creo** to the best of my knowledge - **3.** [estimar] to think; **lo creo muy capaz de hacerlo** I think he's quite capable of doing it.
◆ **creer en** *vi* to believe in.
◆ **creerse** *vprnl* - **1.** [considerarse] to believe o.s. to be; **¿qué se cree?** who does he think he is? - **2.** [dar por cierto] to believe completely.

creíble *adj* credible, believable.

creído, da *sm, f* [presumido] conceited.

crema ⟡ *sf* - **1.** [gen] cream; **crema batida** whipped cream; **la crema del mundo literario** the cream of the literary world - **2.** [cosmético, betún] cream; **crema de afeitar** shaving cream; **crema dental** toothpaste; **crema depilatoria** hair remover; **crema facial** face cream; **crema hidratante** moisturizer - **3.** [licor] crème - **4.** [dulce, postre] custard. ⟡ *adj* cream (*antes de s*).

cremación *sf* cremation.

cremallera *sf* - **1.** [para cerrar] zip (fastener), zipper US - **2.** TECNOL rack.

crematístico, ca *adj* financial.

crematorio, ria *adj*: **horno   crematorio** cremator.
◆ **crematorio** *sm* crematorium.

cremoso, sa *adj* creamy.

crepe [krep] *sf* crepe.

crepé *sm* [tejido] crepe.

crepitar *vi* to crackle.

crepuscular *adj* crepuscular, twilight (*antes de s*).

crepúsculo *sm* - **1.** [al amanecer] first light; [al anochecer] twilight, dusk - **2.** *fig* [fin] twilight.

crescendo [kresˈtʃendo] *sm* crescendo.
◆ **in crescendo** *adv* growing.

crespo, pa *adj* tightly curled, frizzy.

crespón *sm* crepe.

cresta *sf* - **1.** [gen] crest; **estar en la cresta (de la ola)** to be riding high - **2.** [del gallo] comb.

creta *sf* chalk.

cretino, na *sm, f* cretin.

cretona *sf* cretonne.

creyente *smf* believer.

creyera *etc* ⊳ creer.

crezca *etc* ⊳ crecer.

cría ⊳ crío.

criadero *sm* - **1.** [de animales] farm *(breeding place)*; [de árboles, plantas] nursery - **2.** [de mineral] seam.

criadillas *sfpl* bull's testicles.

criado, da ◇ *adj* brought up; **niño mal criado** spoilt child. ◇ *sm, f* servant (*f* maid).

criador, ra ◇ *adj* producing. ◇ *sm, f* [de animales] breeder; [de vinos] grower.

crianza *sf* - **1.** [de bebé] nursing, breastfeeding - **2.** [de animales] breeding, rearing - **3.** [del vino] vintage - **4.** [educación] breeding.

criar [9] *vt* - **1.** [amamantar - suj: mujer] to breastfeed; [- suj: animal] to suckle - **2.** [animales] to breed, to rear; [flores, árboles] to grow - **3.** [vino] to mature, to make - **4.** [educar] to bring up.

◆ **criarse** *vprnl* - **1.** [crecer] to grow up - **2.** [reproducirse] to breed.

criatura *sf* - **1.** [niño] child; [bebé] baby - **2.** [ser vivo] creature.

criba *sf* - **1.** [tamiz] sieve - **2.** [selección] screening.

cribar *vt* - **1.** [con el tamiz] to sieve - **2.** [seleccionar] to screen out, to select.

cricket ['kriket] *sm* cricket.

crimen *sm* crime; **cometer un crimen** to commit a crime; **crimen de guerra** war crime; **crimen organizado** organized crime; **crimen pasional** crime of passion; **crímenes contra la humanidad** crimes against humanity.

criminal *adj* & *smf* criminal; **criminal de guerra** war criminal.

criminalidad *sf* - **1.** [cualidad] criminality - **2.** [número de crímenes]: **(índice de) criminalidad** crime rate.

criminalista ◇ *adj* criminal. ◇ *smf* criminal lawyer.

criminología *sf* criminology.

crin *sf* mane.

crío, cría *sm, f* [niño] kid.

◆ **cría** *sf* - **1.** [hijo del animal] young - **2.** [crianza - de animales] breeding; [- de plantas] growing.

criogenia *sf* cryogenics *(sing)*.

criollo, lla ◇ *adj* - **1.** [persona] native to Latin America - **2.** [comida, lengua] creole. ◇ *sm, f* [persona] *person (black or white) born in Latin America.*

◆ **criollo** *sm* [idioma] creole.

cripta *sf* crypt.

críptico, ca *adj* cryptic.

criptograma *sm* cryptogram.

crisálida *sf* chrysalis.

crisantemo *sm* chrysanthemum.

crisis *sf inv* - **1.** [gen] crisis; **crisis cardíaca** cardiac arrest, heart failure; **crisis de los cuaren-** ta midlife crisis; **crisis económica** recession; **crisis nerviosa** nervous breakdown - **2.** [escasez] shortage.

crisma *sf fam* bonce, nut; **romperle la crisma a alguien** to bash sb's head in; **romperse la crisma** to crack one's head open.

crismas, christmas *sm inv* Christmas card.

crisol *sm* - **1.** [de metales] crucible - **2.** *fig* [lugar donde se mezclan cosas] melting pot.

crispación *sf* [de nervios] tension; [de músculos] tenseness.

crispar *vt* [los nervios] to set on edge; [los músculos] to tense; [las manos] to clench.

◆ **crisparse** *vprnl* to become tense.

cristal *sm* - **1.** [material] glass *(U)*; [vidrio fino] crystal; **cristal ahumado** smoked glass; **cristal blindado** bullet-proof glass; **cristal de roca** rock crystal - **2.** [en la ventana] (window) pane - **3.** [en mineralogía] crystal.

cristalera *sf* [puerta] French window; [techo] glass roof; [armario] glass-fronted cabinet.

cristalería *sf* - **1.** [objetos] glassware - **2.** [tienda] glassware shop; [fábrica] glassworks *sing*.

cristalero *sm* glazier.

cristalino, na *adj* crystalline.

◆ **cristalino** *sm* crystalline lens.

cristalización *sf lit & fig* crystallization.

cristalizar [13] *vt* - **1.** [una sustancia] to crystallize - **2.** *fig* [un asunto] to bring to a head.

◆ **cristalizarse** *vprnl* to crystallize.

◆ **cristalizarse en** *vprnl fig* to develop into.

cristiandad *sf* Christianity.

cristianismo *sm* Christianity.

cristianización *sf* Christianization, conversion to Christianity.

cristianizar [13] *vt* to Christianize, to convert to Christianity.

cristiano, na *adj* & *sm, f* Christian.

◆ **cristiano** *sm*: **hablar en cristiano** *fam* to speak (proper) Spanish.

cristo *sm* crucifix.

◆ **Cristo** *sm* Christ; **armar un Cristo** *fam* to kick up a fuss; **donde Cristo dio las tres voces/perdió el gorro** *fam* in the back of beyond; **estar hecho un Cristo** *fam* to be a pitiful sight.

criterio *sm* - **1.** [norma] criterion; **criterios de convergencia** [en UE] convergence criteria - **2.** [juicio] taste, discernment - **3.** [opinión] opinion.

crítica ▷ **crítico**.

criticable *adj* censurable, open to criticism.

criticar [10] *vt* - **1.** [enjuiciar - literatura, arte] to review - **2.** [censurar] to criticize.

crítico, ca ◇ *adj* critical. ◇ *sm, f* [persona] critic.

◆ **crítica** *sf* - **1.** [juicio - sobre arte, literatura] review - **2.** [conjunto de críticos]: **la crítico** the critics *pl* - **3.** [ataque] criticism.

criticón, ona ◇ *adj* nit-picking, over-critical. ◇ *sm, f* nitpicker.

Croacia *n pr* Croatia.

croar *vi* to croak.

croata ◇ *adj* Croatian. ◇ *smf* Croat, Croatian.

croché [kro'tʃe], **crochet** *sm* crochet.

croissant = **cruasán**.

croissantería = **cruasantería**.

crol *sm* DEP crawl.

cromado *sm* chromium-plating.

cromar *vt* to chrome, to chromium-plate.

cromático, ca *adj* chromatic.

cromatismo *sm* colouring.

cromo *sm* - **1.** [metal] chrome - **2.** [estampa] picture card; **ir hecho un cromo** to be dressed up to the nines.

cromosoma *sm* chromosome.

crónico, ca *adj* chronic.

◆ **crónica** *sf* - **1.** [de la historia] chronicle - **2.** [de un periódico] column; [de la televisión] feature, programme.

cronista *smf* [historiador] chronicler; [periodista] columnist.

crono *sm* DEP time.

cronología *sf* chronology.

cronológico, ca *adj* chronological.

cronometrador, ra *sm, f* timekeeper.

cronometraje *sm* timing.

cronometrar *vt* to time.

cronómetro *sm* DEP stopwatch; TECNOL chronometer.

croquet *sm* croquet.

croqueta *sf* croquette.

croquis *sm inv* sketch.

cross *sm inv* [carrera] cross-country race; [deporte] cross-country (running).

crótalo *sm* rattlesnake.

croupier = **crupier**.

cruasán, croissant [krwa'san] (*pl* **croissants**) *sm* croissant.

cruasantería, croissantería [krwasante'ria] *sf shop selling filled croissants.*

cruce ◇ *sm* - **1.** [de líneas] crossing, intersection; [de carreteras] crossroads - **2.** [paso] crossing; **cruce a nivel** level crossing *UK*, grade crossing *US*; **cruce de peatones** pedestrian crossing - **3.** [de animales] cross, crossbreeding (*U*) - **4.** [de teléfono] crossed line. ◇ *v* ▷ **cruzar.**

crucero *sm* - **1.** [viaje] cruise - **2.** [barco] cruiser - **3.** [de iglesias] transept.

crucial *adj* crucial.

crucificar [10] *vt* - **1.** [en una cruz] to crucify - **2.** *fig* [atormentar] to torment.

crucifijo *sm* crucifix.

crucifixión *sf* crucifixion.

crucigrama *sm* crossword (puzzle).

cruda *sf* ▷ **crudo.**

crudeza *sf* - **1.** [gen] harshness; **con crudeza** harshly - **2.** [de descripción, imágenes] brutality, harsh realism.

crudo, da *adj* - **1.** [natural] raw; [petróleo] crude - **2.** [sin cocer completamente] undercooked - **3.** [realidad, clima, tiempo] harsh; [novela] harshly realistic, hard-hitting - **4.** [cruel] cruel - **5.** [color] beige.

◆ **crudo** *sm* crude (oil).

◆ **cruda** *sf Guat & Méx fam* [resaca] hangover.

cruel *adj* [gen] cruel.

crueldad *sf* - **1.** [gen] cruelty - **2.** [acción cruel] act of cruelty.

crujido *sm* [de madera] creak, creaking (*U*); [de hojas secas] crackle, crackling (*U*).

crujiente *adj* [madera] creaky; [hojas secas] rustling; [patatas fritas] crunchy.

crujir *vi* [madera] to creak; [patatas fritas, nieve] to crunch; [hojas secas] to crackle; [dientes] to grind.

crupier, croupier [kru'pjer] *sm* croupier.

crustáceo *sm* crustacean.

cruz *sf* - **1.** [gen] cross; **cruz gamada** swastika - **2.** [de una moneda] tails (*U*) - **3.** *fig* [aflicción] burden, torment - **4.** *loc*: **hacer cruz y raya** to break off relations.

◆ **Cruz Roja** *sf* Red Cross.

cruza *sf Amér* cross, crossbreed.

cruzado, da *adj* - **1.** [cheque, piernas, brazos] crossed - **2.** [atravesado]: **cruzado en la carretera** blocking the road - **3.** [animal] crossbred - **4.** [abrigo, chaqueta] double-breasted.

◆ **cruzado** *sm* crusader.

◆ **cruzada** *sf lit & fig* crusade.

cruzar [13] *vt* - **1.** [gen] to cross; **cruzar los dedos** to cross one's fingers - **2.** [unas palabras] to exchange.

◆ **cruzarse** *vprnl* - **1.** [gen] to cross; **cruzarse de brazos** to fold one's arms - **2.** [personas]: **cruzarse con alguien** to pass sb.

CSIC (*abrev de* **Consejo Superior de Investigaciones Científicas**) *sm Spanish council for scientific research.*

CSN (*abrev de* **Consejo de Seguridad Nuclear**) *sm* AEC (*Atomic Energy Commission*).

cta. (*abrev de* **cuenta**) a/c.

cte. (*abrev de* **corriente**) inst.

cuaderno *sm* [gen] notebook; [en el colegio] exercise book.

◆ **cuaderno de bitácora** *sm* logbook.

cuadra *sf* - **1.** [de caballos] stable - **2.** *fam* [lugar sucio] pigsty - **3.** *Amér* [en calle] block.

cuadrado, da *adj* - **1.** [gen & MAT] square; **elevar al cuadrado** to square - **2.** [persona] square-built, stocky.

◆ **cuadrado** *sm* square.

cuadrafónico, ca *adj* quadraphonic.

cuadragésimo, ma *num* fortieth.

cuadrangular *adj* quadrangular.

cuadrángulo *sm* quadrangle.

cuadrante *sm* - **1.** [gen] quadrant - **2.** [reloj de sol] sundial.

cuadrar ◇ *vi* - **1.** [información, hechos]: **cuadrar (con)** to square *o* agree (with) - **2.** [números, cuentas] to tally, to add up. ◇ *vt* - **1.** [gen] to square - **2.** *Amér* [aparcar] to park.

◆ **cuadrarse** *vprnl* - **1.** MIL to stand to attention - **2.** [mostrar firmeza] to make a stand.

cuadratura *sf* GEOM quadrature; **la cuadratura del círculo** *fam* squaring the circle.

cuádriceps *sm inv* quadriceps.

cuadrícula *sf* grid.

cuadriculado, da *adj* squared.

cuadricular *vt* to divide into squares.

cuadriga, cuádriga *sf* four-in-hand.

cuadrilátero *sm* - **1.** GEOM quadrilateral - **2.** DEP ring.

cuadrilla *sf* - **1.** [de amigos, trabajadores] group; [de maleantes] gang - **2.** [de un torero] *team of helpers.*

cuadro *sm* - **1.** [pintura] painting, picture - **2.** [escena] scene, spectacle - **3.** [descripción] portrait - **4.** [cuadrado] square; **a cuadros** check *(antes de s)*; **quedarse a cuadros** *fam* to be gobsmacked, to be flabbergasted; **quedarse en cuadros** to be down to a skeleton staff - **5.** [equipo] team; **cuadros medios** middle management - **6.** [gráfico] chart, diagram; **cuadro sinóptico** (synoptic) chart - **7.** [de la bicicleta] frame - **8.** [de un aparato]: **cuadro de distribución** switchboard; **cuadro de mandos** control panel - **9.** TEATRO scene; **cuadro flamenco** flamenco group.

cuadrúpedo *sm* quadruped.

cuádruple *sm* quadruple.

cuadruplicar [10] *vt* to quadruple.

cuádruplo *sm* quadruple.

cuajado, da *adj* - **1.** [leche] curdled; [huevo] set - **2.** [lleno]: **cuajado de** full of.

◆ **cuajada** *sf* curd (cheese).

cuajar ◇ *vt* [solidificar - leche] to curdle; [- huevo] to set; [- sangre] to clot, to coagulate. ◇ *vi*

- **1.** [lograrse - acuerdo] to be settled; [- negocio] to take off, to get going - **2.** [ser aceptado - persona] to fit in; [- moda] to catch on - **3.** [nieve] to settle.

◆ **cuajarse** *vprnl* [leche] to curdle; [sangre] to clot, to coagulate.

cuajo *sm* rennet.

◆ **de cuajo** *loc adv*: **arrancar de cuajo** [árbol] to uproot; [brazo etc] to tear right off.

cual *pron relat*: **el/la cual** *etc* [de persona] *(sujeto)* who, *(complemento)* whom; [de cosa] which; **lo cual** which; **conoció a una española, la cual vivía en Buenos Aires** he met a Spanish girl who lived in Buenos Aires; **está muy enfadada, lo cual es comprensible** she's very angry, which is understandable; **todo lo cual** all of which; **sea cual sea** *o* **fuere su decisión** whatever his decision (may be); **los tres son a cual más inteligente** all three are equally intelligent.

cuál *pron* - **1.** *(interrogativo)* what; [en concreto, especificando] which one; **¿cuál es tu nombre?** what is your name?; **¿cuál es la diferencia?** what's the difference?; **no sé cuáles son mejores** I don't know which are best; **¿cuál prefieres?** which one do you prefer? - **2.** *(en oraciones distributivas)*: **todos contribuyeron, cuál más, cuál menos** everyone contributed, although some more than others.

cualesquiera ⊳ cualquiera.

cualidad *sf* quality.

cualificación *sf* degree of skill *(of a worker)*.

cualificado, da *adj* skilled.

cualificar [10] *vt* to qualify.

cualitativo, va *adj* qualitative.

cualquiera (*pl* **cualesquiera**) ◇ *adj* (*antes de s*: **cualquier**) any; **cualquier día vendré a visitarte** I'll drop by one of these days; **en cualquier momento** at any time; **en cualquier lugar** anywhere. ◇ *pron* anyone; **cualquiera te lo dirá** anyone will tell you; **cualquiera que** [persona] anyone who; [cosa] whatever; **cualquiera que te vea se reiría** anyone who saw you would laugh; **cualquiera que sea la razón** whatever the reason (may be). ◇ *sm, f* [don nadie] nobody. ◇ *sf fam* [prostituta] tart.

cuan *adv* [todo lo que]: **se desplomó cuan largo era** he fell flat on the ground.

cuán *adv* how.

cuando ◇ *adv* when; **de cuando en cuando** from time to time; **de vez en cuando** now and again. ◇ *conj* - **1.** [de tiempo] when; **cuando llegue el verano iremos de viaje** when summer comes we'll go travelling - **2.** [si] if; **cuando tú lo dices será verdad** it must be true if you say so - **3.** *(después de 'aun')* [aunque]: **no**

mentiría aun cuando le fuera en ello la vida she wouldn't lie even if her life depended on it.

◆ **cuando más** *loc adv* at the most.

◆ **cuando menos** *loc adv* at least.

◆ **cuando quiera que** *loc conj* whenever.

cuándo ◇ *adv* when; **¿cuándo vas a venir?** when are you coming?; **quisiera saber cuándo sale el tren** I'd like to know when O at what time the train leaves. ◇ *sm*: **ignorará el cómo y el cuándo de la operación** he won't know how or when the operation will take place.

cuantía *sf* [suma] amount, quantity; [alcance] extent.

cuántico, ca, quántico, ca *adj* quantum.

cuantificable *adj* quantifiable.

cuantificar [10] *vt* to quantify.

cuantioso, sa *adj* large, substantial.

cuantitativo, va *adj* quantitative.

cuanto, ta ◇ *adj* - **1.** [todo]: **despilfarra cuanto dinero gana** he squanders all the money he earns; **soporté todas cuantas críticas me hizo** I put up with every single criticism he made of me - **2.** *(antes de adv)* [compara cantidades] **cuantas más mentiras digas, menos te creerán** the more you lie, the less people will believe you. ◇ *pron relat (gen pl)* [de personas] everyone who; [de cosas] everything (that); **cuantos fueron alabaron el espectáculo** everyone who went said the show was excellent; **dio las gracias a todos cuantos le ayudaron** he thanked everyone who helped him.

◆ **cuanto** ◇ *pron relat (neutro)* - **1.** [todo lo que] everything, as much as; **come cuanto quieras** eat as much as you like; **comprendo cuanto dice** I understand everything he says; **todo cuanto** everything - **2.** [compara cantidades]: **cuanto más se tiene, más se quiere** the more you have, the more you want. ◇ *adv* [compara cantidades]: **cuanto más come, más gordo está** the more he eats, the fatter he gets.

◆ **cuanto antes** *loc adv* as soon as possible.

◆ **en cuanto** ◇ *loc conj* [tan pronto como] as soon as; **en cuanto acabe** as soon as I've finished. ◇ *loc prep* [en calidad de] as; **en cuanto cabeza de familia** as head of the family.

◆ **en cuanto a** *loc prep* as regards; **en cuanto a tu petición** as regards your request, as far as your request is concerned.

cuánto, ta ◇ *adj* - **1.** *(interrogativo)* how much (*pl* how many); **¿cuántas manzanas tienes?** how many apples do you have?; **¿cuánto pan quieres?** how much bread do you want?; **no sé cuántos hombres había** I don't know how many men were there - **2.** *(exclamativo)* what a lot of; **¡cuánta gente (había)!** what a lot of people (were there)! ◇ *pron (gen pl)* - **1.** *(interrogativo)* how much (*pl* how many); **¿cuántos han venido?** how many came?; **dime cuántas quieres** tell me how many you want - **2.** *(exclamativo)*: **¡cuántos quisieran conocerte!** there are so many people who would like to meet you!

◆ **cuánto** *pron (neutro)* - **1.** *(interrogativo)* how much; **¿cuánto quieres?** how much do you want?; **me gustaría saber cuánto te costarán** I'd like to know how much they'll cost you - **2.** *(exclamativo)*: **¡cuánto han cambiado las cosas!** how things have changed!; **¡cuánto me gusta!** I really like it!

cuarenta *num* forty; **los (años) cuarenta** the forties; **cantar a alguien las cuarenta** to give sb a piece of one's mind; *ver también* **seis**.

cuarentena *sf* - **1.** [por epidemia] quarantine; **poner en cuarentena** [enfermos] to (put in) quarantine; [noticia] to put on hold - **2.** [cuarenta unidades] forty; **una cuarentena de personas** about forty people.

cuarentón, ona *sm, f* person in his/her forties.

cuaresma *sf* Lent.

cuartear *vt* to cut O chop up.

◆ **cuartearse** *vprnl* to crack.

cuartel *sm* - **1.** MIL barracks *pl*; **cuartel general** headquarters *pl* - **2.** *fig* [piedad]: **sin cuartel** [guerra] all-out; **lucha sin cuartel** fight to the death.

cuartelazo *sm Amér* military uprising, revolt.

cuartelillo *sm* [de policía] police station.

cuarteto *sm* quartet.

cuartilla *sf* sheet of quarto.

cuarto, ta *num* fourth; **la cuarta parte** a quarter.

◆ **cuarto** *sm* - **1.** [parte] quarter; **un cuarto de hora** a quarter of an hour; **son las dos y cuarto** it's a quarter past UK O after US two; **son las dos menos cuarto** it's a quarter to UK O of US two; **cuarto creciente/menguante** first/last quarter; **ser tres cuartos de lo mismo** to be exactly the same O no different - **2.** [habitación] room; **cuarto de aseo** washroom, small bathroom; **cuarto de baño** bathroom; **cuarto de estar** living room; **cuarto de huéspedes** guestroom; **cuarto oscuro** FOTO darkroom; **cuarto secreto** *R Dom* voting booth - **3.** *loc*: **estar sin un cuarto** to be skint.

◆ **cuartos** *smpl* - **1.** *fam* [dinero] dough *(U)*, readies - **2.** DEP: **cuartos de final** quarter finals.

◆ **cuarta** *sf* [palmo] span.

cuarzo *sm* quartz.

cuate, ta *sm, f* Amér C, Ecuad & Méx *fam* pal, mate UK, buddy US.

cuaternario, ria *adj* Quaternary.

☛ **cuaternario** *sm*: **el cuaternario** the Quaternary (era).

cuatrero, ra *sm, f* [de caballos] horse thief; [de ganado] cattle rustler.

cuatrillizo, za *sm, f* quadruplet, quad.

cuatrimestral *adj* - **1.** [en frecuencia] four-monthly - **2.** [en duración] four-month *(antes de s)*, lasting four months.

cuatrimestre *sm* period of four months.

cuatrimotor *sm* four-engined plane.

cuatripartito, ta *adj* four-part.

cuatro <> *num* four; **más de cuatro** quite a few. <> *adj fig* [poco] a few; **hace cuatro días** a few days ago; *ver también* **seis**.

cuatrocientos, tas *num* four hundred; *ver también* **seis**.

cuba *sf* barrel, cask; **beber como una cuba** to drink like a fish; **estar como una cuba** to be legless o blind drunk.

Cuba *n pr* Cuba.

cubalibre *sm* rum and coke.

cubano, na *adj* & *sm, f* Cuban.

cubata *sm fam* rum and coke.

cubero *sm*: **a ojo de buen cubero** roughly.

cubertería *sf* set of cutlery, cutlery (U).

cubeta *sf* [cuba pequeña] bucket, pail; FOTO tray.

cúbico, ca *adj* cubic.

cubierto, ta <> *pp* ☞ **cubrir**. <> *adj* - **1.** [gen]: **cubierto (de)** covered (with); **estar a cubierto** [protegido] to be under cover; [con saldo acreedor] to be in the black; **ponerse a cubierto** to take cover - **2.** [cielo] overcast - **3.** [vacante] filled.

☛ **cubierto** *sm* - **1.** [pieza de cubertería] piece of cutlery - **2.** [juego de cubertería] set of cutlery - **3.** [para cada persona] place setting - **4.** [comida] set menu.

☛ **cubierta** *sf* - **1.** [gen] cover - **2.** [de neumático] tyre - **3.** [de barco] deck.

cubil *sm* - **1.** [de animales] den, lair - **2.** *fig* [de personas] poky room.

cubilete *sm* [en juegos] cup.

cubismo *sm* cubism.

cubista *adj* & *smf* cubist.

cubito *sm* - **1.** [de hielo] ice cube - **2.** [de caldo] stock cube.

cúbito *sm* ulna.

cubo *sm* - **1.** [recipiente] bucket; **cubo de la basura** rubbish bin UK, trashcan US, garbage can US - **2.** GEOM & MAT cube; **elevar al cubo** to cube - **3.** [de rueda] hub.

cubrecama *sm* bedspread.

cubrir *vt* - **1.** [gen] to cover - **2.** [proteger] to protect - **3.** [disimular] to cover up, to hide - **4.** [puesto, vacante] to fill.

☛ **cubrir de** *vt*: **cubrir de algo a alguien** to heap sthg on sb.

☛ **cubrirse** *vprnl* - **1.** [taparse]: **cubrirse (de)** to become covered (with) - **2.** [protegerse]: **cubrirse (de)** to shelter (from) - **3.** [con sombrero] to put one's hat on - **4.** [con ropa]: **cubrirse (con)** to cover o.s. (with) - **5.** [cielo] to cloud over - **6.** *loc*: **cubrirse de gloria** [triunfar] to cover o.s. in o with glory; *irón* to land o.s. in it.

cuca *sf* ☞ **cuco**.

cucaña *sf* greasy pole.

cucaracha *sf* cockroach UK, roach US.

cuchara *sf* - **1.** [para comer] spoon; **cuchara de palo** wooden spoon; **cuchara de postre** dessert spoon; **meter la cuchara** *fam* to butt in - **2.** [cucharada] spoonful.

cucharada *sf* spoonful.

cucharilla *sf* teaspoon.

cucharón *sm* ladle.

cuchichear *vi* to whisper.

cuchicheo *sm* whispering.

cuchilla *sf* blade; **cuchilla de afeitar** razor blade.

cuchillada *sf* [golpe] stab; [herida] stab wound.

cuchillo *sm* knife; **cuchillo de cocina** kitchen knife; **cuchillo eléctrico** electric carving knife; **cuchillo de trinchar** carving knife.

cuchitril *sm* hovel.

cuchufleta *sf fam* joke.

cuclillas ☛ **en cuclillas** *loc adv* squatting; **ponerse en cuclillas** to squat (down).

cuclillo *sm* cuckoo.

cuco, ca *adj fam* - **1.** [bonito] pretty - **2.** [astuto] shrewd, canny.

☛ **cuco** *sm* cuckoo.

☛ **cuca** *sf fam* peseta.

cucú *sm* - **1.** [canto] cuckoo - **2.** [reloj] cuckoo clock.

cucurucho *sm* - **1.** [de papel] paper cone - **2.** [para helado] cornet, cone - **3.** [gorro] pointed hat.

cuece ☞ **cocer**.

cuela *etc* ☞ **colar**.

cuelga *etc* ☞ **colgar**.

cuello *sm* - **1.** [gen] neck; **alargar el cuello** to stretch o crane one's neck; **cuello de botella** bottleneck; **cuello uterino** cervix - **2.** [de prendas] collar; **cuello de pajarita** wing collar; **cuello de pico** V-neck; **cuello alto** o **de cisne** polo neck UK, turtleneck US; **hablar para el cuello de su camisa** *fam* to talk to o.s.

cuenca *sf* - **1.** [de río] basin - **2.** [del ojo] (eye) socket - **3.** [región minera] coalfield.

cuenco *sm* earthenware bowl.

cuenta ◇ *sf* - **1.** [acción de contar] count; **echar cuentas** to reckon up; **llevar/perder la cuenta de** to keep/lose count of; **cuenta atrás** countdown - **2.** [cálculo] sum; **cuenta de la vieja** *fam* counting on one's fingers - **3.** BANCA & COM account; **abonar algo en cuenta a alguien** to credit sthg to sb's account; **abrir una cuenta** to open an account; **cuenta de gastos** expenditure account; **llevar las cuentas** to keep the books; **pagar mil euros a cuenta** to pay a thousand euros down; **cuenta de ahorros** savings account; **cuenta de ahorro vivienda** home loan; **cuenta corriente** current account *UK*, checking account *US*; **cuenta de crédito** current account with an overdraft facility; **cuenta deudora** overdrawn account; **cuenta de explotación** operating statement; **cuenta a plazo fijo** deposit account - **4.** [factura] bill *UK*, check *US*; **domiciliar una cuenta** to pay an account by standing order/direct debit; **pasar la cuenta** to send the bill; **cuenta por cobrar/pagar** account receivable/payable - **5.** [obligación, cuidado] responsibility; **déjalo de mi cuenta** leave it to me - **6.** [bolita - de collar, rosario] bead - **7.** *loc:* **a fin de cuentas** in the end; **ajustarle a alguien las cuentas** to settle an account *O* a score with sb; **caer en la cuenta de algo** to realize sthg; **dar cuenta de algo** [comunicar] to report sthg; [terminar] to account for sthg, to finish sthg off; **darse cuenta de algo** to realize sthg; **en resumidas cuentas** in short; **más de la cuenta** too much; **pedir cuentas a alguien** to call sb to account; **por mi/tu** *etc* **cuenta** on my/your *etc* own; **salir de cuentas** to be due to give birth; **tener en cuenta algo** to bear sthg in mind. ◇ *v* ▷ **contar**.

cuentagotas *sm inv* dropper; **a** *O* **con cuentagotas** in dribs and drabs.

cuentakilómetros *sm inv* [de distancia recorrida] ≃ milometer; [de velocidad] speedometer.

cuentarrevoluciones *sm inv* tachometer, rev counter.

cuentista *smf* - **1.** [escritor] short story writer - **2.** [mentiroso] fibber, story-teller.

cuento *sm* - **1.** [fábula] tale; **cuento de hadas** fairy tale; **el cuento de la lechera** *fig* wishful thinking - **2.** [narración] short story - **3.** [mentira, exageración] story, lie; **¡puro cuento!** what nonsense!; **cuento chino** tall story - **4.** *loc:* **quitarse** *O* **dejarse de cuentos** to stop beating about the bush; **ser el cuento de nunca acabar** to be the same old story; **tener cuento** to put it on; **venir a cuento** to be relevant; **venir con cuentos** to tell fibs *O* stories; **vivir del cuento** to live by one's wits.

cuerda *sf* - **1.** [para atar - fina] string; [- más gruesa] rope; **cuerda floja** tightrope - **2.** [de instrumento] string - **3.** [de reloj] spring; **dar cuerda a** [reloj] to wind up - **4.** GEOM chord - **5.** *loc:* **bajo cuerda** secretly, in an underhand manner; **estar en la cuerda floja** to be hanging by a thread; **tener mucha cuerda, tener cuerda para rato** to go on and on; **tirar de la cuerda** to go too far, to push it.
◆ **cuerdas vocales** *sfpl* vocal cords.

cuerdo, da ◇ *adj* - **1.** [sano de juicio] sane - **2.** [sensato] sensible. ◇ *sm, f* sane person.

cueriza *sf Andes fam* beating, leathering.

cuerno *sm* [gen] horn; [de ciervo] antler; **mandar al cuerno a alguien** *fam* to send sb packing; **saber a cuerno quemado** *fam* to be fishy; **¡vete al cuerno!** *fam* go to hell!
◆ **cuernos** *smpl fam:* **poner cuernos a alguien** to be unfaithful to sb; [a un hombre] to cuckold sb.

cuero *sm* - **1.** [piel de animal] skin; [piel curtida] hide; **cuero cabelludo** scalp; **en cueros, en cueros vivos** stark naked - **2.** [material] leather - **3.** *Amér vulg* [prostituta] whore.

cuerpo *sm* - **1.** [gen] body; **cuerpo celeste** heavenly body; **cuerpo extraño** foreign body; **de cuerpo entero** [persona] complete, consummate; [retrato] full-length; **a cuerpo** without a coat on; **luchar cuerpo a cuerpo** to fight hand-to-hand; **tomar cuerpo** to take shape; **vivir a cuerpo de rey** to live like a king; **en cuerpo y alma** body and soul - **2.** [tronco] trunk - **3.** [parte principal] main body - **4.** [grosor] thickness - **5.** [cadáver] corpse; **de cuerpo presente** (lying) in state - **6.** [corporación consular, militar etc] corps; **cuerpo de bomberos** fire brigade; **cuerpo diplomático** diplomatic corps; **cuerpo de policía** police force - **7.** [parte de armario, edificio] section.

cuervo *sm* crow.

cuesco *sm fam* fart.

cuesta ◇ *sf* slope; **cuesta arriba** uphill; **cuesta abajo** downhill; **a cuestas** on one's back, over one's shoulders; **hacérsele cuesta arriba a alguien** to be hard going *O* an uphill struggle for sb; **ir cuesta abajo** to decline, to go downhill. ◇ *v* ▷ **costar**.

cueste ▷ **costar**.

cuestión *sf* - **1.** [pregunta] question - **2.** [problema] problem - **3.** [asunto] matter, issue; **en cuestión** in question, at issue; **en cuestión de** [en materia de] as regards; **en cuestión de una hora** in no more than an hour; **ser cuestión de** to be a question of.

cuestionable *adj* questionable, debatable.

cuestionar *vt* to question.
◆ **cuestionarse** *vprnl* to (call into) question.

cuestionario *sm* questionnaire.

cueva *sf* cave; **cueva de ladrones** den of thieves.

cueza *etc* ⊳ **cocer**.

cuico *sm Méx fam* cop.

cuidado ⟨⟩ *sm* care; **con cuidado** [con esmero] carefully; [con cautela] cautiously; **de cuidado** [criminal, enemigo] dangerous; [accidente, problema] serious; **estar al cuidado de** to be in charge of; **tener cuidado con** to be careful with; **cuidados intensivos** intensive care *(U)*; **eso me tiene** o **trae sin cuidado** I couldn't care less about that. ⟨⟩ *interj*: ¡**cuidado!** careful!, look out!

cuidador, ra *sm, f* DEP trainer.

cuidadoso, sa *adj* careful.

cuidar *vt* [gen] to look after; [estilo etc] to take care over; [detalles] to pay attention to.
➤ **cuidar de** *vi* to look after; **cuida de que no lo haga** make sure she doesn't do it.
➤ **cuidarse** *vprnl* to take care of o to look after o.s.; **cuidarse de** to worry about.

culata *sf* - **1.** [de arma] butt - **2.** [de animal] hindquarters - **3.** [de motor] cylinder head.

culatazo *sm* [golpe] *blow with the butt of a rifle*; [retroceso] recoil, kick.

culé *(pl* **culés***) adj fam* DEP of/relating to the Barcelona Football Club.

culebra *sf* snake.

culebrón *sm* TV soap opera.

culinario, ria *adj* culinary.

culminación *sf* culmination.

culminante *adj* culminating; **punto culminante** high point.

culminar ⟨⟩ *vt*: **culminar (con)** to crown (with). ⟨⟩ *vi* to finish, to culminate.

culo *sm fam* - **1.** [de personas] backside, bum *UK*; **caerse de culo** *fam* to be flabbergasted, to be gobsmacked; **estar en el culo del mundo** *fam* to be in the back of beyond; **lamer el culo a alguien** *fam* to lick sb's arse *UK*, to lick sb's ass *US*; **ser un culo de mal asiento** to be fidgety - **2.** [de objetos] bottom - **3.** [líquido]: **queda un culo** there are a few drops left in the bottom.

culpa *sf* - **1.** [responsabilidad] fault; **tener la culpa de algo** to be to blame for sthg; **echar la culpa a alguien (de)** to blame sb (for); **por culpa de** because of - **2.** [falta]: **culpas** sins.

culpabilidad *sf* guilt.

culpabilizar [13] *vt* to blame.
➤ **culpabilizarse** *vprnl*: **culpabilizarse (de)** to accept the blame (for).

culpable ⟨⟩ *adj*: **culpable (de)** guilty (of); **declarar culpable a alguien** to find sb guilty; **declararse culpable** to plead guilty. ⟨⟩ *smf* DER guilty party; **tú eres el culpable** you're to blame.

culpar *vt*: **culpar a alguien (de)** [atribuir la culpa] to blame sb (for); [acusar] to accuse sb (of).

cultivable *adj* cultivable, arable.

cultivado, da *adj* cultivated.

cultivador, ra *sm, f* grower.

cultivar *vt* - **1.** [tierra] to farm, to cultivate; [plantas] to grow - **2.** [amistad, inteligencia] to cultivate - **3.** [arte] to practise - **4.** [germen] to culture.
➤ **cultivarse** *vprnl* [persona] to improve o.s.

cultivo *sm* - **1.** [de tierra] farming; [de plantas] growing - **2.** [plantación] crop - **3.** [de gérmenes] culture.

culto, ta *adj* [persona] cultured, educated; [estilo] refined; [palabra] literary, learned.
➤ **culto** *sm* - **1.** [devoción] worship; **libertad de culto** freedom of worship; **rendir culto a** [dios etc] to worship; [persona, valentía etc] to pay homage o tribute to - **2.** [religión] cult.

cultura *sf* - **1.** [de sociedad] culture - **2.** [sabiduría] learning, knowledge; **cultura general** general knowledge.

cultural *adj* cultural.

culturismo *sm* body-building.

culturista *smf* body-builder.

culturizar [13] *vt* to educate.

cumbia *sf Colombian dance*.

cumbre ⟨⟩ *adj* greatest. ⟨⟩ *sf* - **1.** [de montaña] summit - **2.** *fig* [punto culminante] peak, pinnacle - **3.** POLÍT summit (conference).

cumpleaños *sm inv* birthday.

cumplido, da *adj* - **1.** [acabado - orden] carried out; [- promesa, deber, profecía] fulfilled; [- plazo] expired - **2.** [completo, lleno] full, complete - **3.** [cortés] courteous.
➤ **cumplido** *sm* compliment; **andarse con cumplidos** to stand on ceremony; **visita de cumplido** courtesy call.

cumplidor, ra ⟨⟩ *adj* reliable, dependable. ⟨⟩ *sm, f* reliable o dependable person.

cumplimentar *vt* - **1.** [saludar] to greet - **2.** [felicitar] to congratulate - **3.** [cumplir - orden] to carry out; [- contrato] to fulfil.

cumplimiento *sm* [de un deber] performance; [de contrato, promesa] fulfilment; [de la ley] observance; [de órdenes] carrying out; [de condena] completion; [de plazo] expiry.

cumplir ⟨⟩ *vt* - **1.** [orden] to carry out; [promesa] to keep; [ley] to observe; [contrato] to fulfil - **2.** [años] to reach; **mañana cumplo los 20** I'm 20 o it's my 20th birthday tomorrow - **3.** [condena] to serve; [servicio militar] to do.

◇ **vi - 1.** [plazo, garantía] to expire **- 2.** [realizar el deber] to do one's duty; **cumplir con alguien** to do one's duty by sb; **para** o **por cumplir** out of politeness; **cumplir con el deber** to do one's duty; **cumplir con la palabra** to keep one's word.

cúmulo *sm* **- 1.** [de objetos] pile, heap **- 2.** [nube] cumulus **- 3.** *fig* [de asuntos, acontecimientos] accumulation, series.

cuna *sf* **- 1.** [para dormir] cot, cradle **- 2.** *fig* [de movimiento, civilización] cradle; [de persona] birthplace.

cundir *vi* **- 1.** [propagarse] to spread **- 2.** [dar de sí - comida, reservas, tiempo] to go a long way; [- trabajo, estudio] to go well.

cuneta *sf* [de una carretera] ditch; [de una calle] gutter.

cuña *sf* **- 1.** [pieza] wedge **- 2.** [de publicidad] commercial break **- 3.** [orinal] bedpan **- 4.** *Andes & R Plata fam*: **tener cuña** to have friends in high places.

cuñado, da *sm, f* brother-in-law (*f* sister-in-law).

cuño *sm* **- 1.** [troquel] die **- 2.** [sello, impresión] stamp **- 3.** *loc*: **ser de nuevo cuño** to be a new coinage.

cuota *sf* **- 1.** [contribución - a entidad, club] membership fee, subscription; [- a Hacienda] tax (payment); **cuota de entrada** admission fee **- 2.** [cupo] quota **- 3.** *Méx* [peaje] toll.

➤ **cuota de mercado** *sf* ECON market share.

➤ **cuota de pantalla** *sf* TV audience share.

cupido *sm* *fig* lady's man.

cupiera *etc* ▷ **caber.**

cupo ◇ *sm* **- 1.** [cantidad máxima] quota **- 2.** [cantidad proporcional] share; [de una cosa racionada] ration **- 3.** *Amér* [cabida] capacity. ◇ *v* ▷ **caber.**

cupón *sm* [gen] coupon; [de lotería, rifa] ticket.

cúpula *sf* **- 1.** ARQUIT dome, cupola **- 2.** *fig* [mandos] leaders *pl*.

cura ◇ *sm* priest. ◇ *sf* **- 1.** [curación] recovery; **tener cura** to be curable **- 2.** [tratamiento] treatment, cure; **necesitar una cura de sueño** to need a good sleep; **cura de emergencia** first aid; **cura de reposo** rest cure **- 3.** *loc*: **no tener cura** [ser incurable] to be incurable; *fam* [ser incorregible] to be incorrigible.

curación *sf* **- 1.** [de un enfermo - recuperación] recovery; [- tratamiento] treatment; [de una herida] healing **- 2.** [de jamón] curing.

curado, da *adj* [alimento] cured; [pieles] tanned; **curado de espanto** unshockable.

➤ **curado** *sm* [de alimentos] curing; [de pieles] tanning.

curandero, ra *sm, f* quack.

curar ◇ *vt* **- 1.** [gen] to cure **- 2.** [herida] to dress **- 3.** [pieles] to tan. ◇ *vi* [enfermo] to get well, to recover; [herida] to heal up.

➤ **curarse** *vprnl* **- 1.** [sanar]: **curarse (de)** to recover (from); **curarse en salud** to play safe **- 2.** [alimento] to cure.

curativo, va *adj* curative.

curco *sm* *Amér* **- 1.** [joroba] hump **- 2.** [jorobado] hunchback.

curcucho *sm* *Amér* hunchback.

curcuncho, cha ◇ *adj* *Andes fam* [jorobado] hunchbacked. ◇ *sm* [joroba] hump; [jorobado] hunchback.

curda *fam* ◇ *sf*: **coger** o **agarrar una curda** to get plastered. ◇ *adj* *Amér* drunk. ◇ *smf* *Amér* boozer, wino.

curdo, da ◇ *adj* Kurdish. ◇ *sm, f* [persona] Kurd.

➤ **curdo** *sm* [lengua] Kurdish.

curia *sf* **- 1.** HIST & RELIG curia **- 2.** DER court.

curiosear ◇ *vi* [fisgonear] to nose around; [por una tienda] to browse round. ◇ *vt* [libros, revistas] to browse through.

curiosidad *sf* curiosity; **sentir** o **tener curiosidad por** to be curious about.

curioso, sa ◇ *adj* **- 1.** [por saber, averiguar] curious, inquisitive **- 2.** [raro] odd, strange **- 3.** [limpio] neat, tidy; [cuidadoso] careful. ◇ *sm, f* onlooker.

curita *sm* *Amér* sticking plaster, Band-Aid® *US*.

currante ◇ *adj* *fam* hard-working. ◇ *smf* worker.

currar, currelar *vi* *fam* to work.

curre = curro.

currelar = currar.

currículum (vitae) [ku'rrikulum('bite)] (*pl* currícula (vitae) o currículums), **currículo** (*pl* currículos) *sm* curriculum vitae *UK*, résumé *US*.

curro, curre *sm* *fam* work.

curruscar [10] *vi* to crunch.

cursar *vt* **- 1.** [estudiar] to study **- 2.** [enviar] to send **- 3.** [dar - órdenes etc] to give, to issue **- 4.** [tramitar] to submit.

cursi ◇ *adj* *fam* [vestido, canción etc] naff, tacky; [modales, persona] affected. ◇ *smf* *fam* affected o pretentious person.

cursilada *sf* [acto, comportamiento] pretentious o affected act; [comentario] naff remark; [decoración, objeto] tacky thing.

cursilería *sf* **- 1.** [objeto] tacky thing; [comentario] naff remark; [acto, comportamiento] pretentious o affected act **- 2.** [cualidad] tackiness, naffness.

cursillo *sm* - **1.** [curso] short course - **2.** [conferencias] series of lectures.

cursiva ⊳ **letra**.

curso *sm* - **1.** [año académico] year - **2.** [lecciones] course; **curso intensivo** crash course; **curso por correspondencia** correspondence course - **3.** [texto, manual] textbook - **4.** [dirección - de río, acontecimientos] course; [- de la economía] trend; **seguir su curso** to go on, to continue; **el resfriado debe seguir su curso** you should allow the cold to run its course; **en el curso de** during (the course of); **en curso** [- mes, año] current; [- trabajo] in progress; **dar curso a algo** [- dar rienda suelta] to give free rein to sthg; [- tramitar] to process *o* deal with sthg - **5.** [circulación]: **moneda de curso legal** legal tender.

cursor *sm* INFORM cursor.

curtido, **da** *adj* - **1.** [piel, cuero] tanned - **2.** *fig* [experimentado] seasoned.
◆ **curtido** *sm* tanning.

curtir *vt* - **1.** [piel] to tan - **2.** *fig* [persona] to harden.
◆ **curtirse** *vprnl* - **1.** [piel] to tan - **2.** *fig* [persona] to become hardened.

curva ⊳ **curvo**.

curvado, **da** *adj* [gen] curved; [doblado] bent.

curvar *vt* to bend; [espalda, cejas] to arch.
◆ **curvarse** *vprnl* to become bent.

curvatura *sf* curvature.

curvilíneo, **a** *adj* [gen] curved; [cuerpo] curvaceous.

curvo, **va** *adj* [gen] curved; [doblado] bent.
◆ **curva** *sf* [gen] curve; [en carretera] bend; **curva cerrada** sharp bend; **curva de la felicidad** *fig* [barriga] paunch; **curva de nivel** contour line.

cuscurro *sm* [trozo de pan frito] crouton; [punta de pan] end *(of baguette)*.

cúspide *sf* - **1.** [de montaña] summit, top - **2.** *fig* [apogeo] peak, height - **3.** GEOM apex.

custodia *sf* - **1.** [de cosas] safekeeping - **2.** [de personas] custody; **estar bajo la custodia de** to be in the custody of; **custodia preventiva** protective custody.

custodiar [8] *vt* - **1.** [vigilar] to guard - **2.** [proteger] to look after.

custodio *sm* guard.

cutáneo, **a** *adj* skin *(antes de s)*.

cutícula *sf* cuticle.

cutis *sm inv* skin, complexion.

cutre *adj fam* - **1.** [de bajo precio, calidad] cheap and nasty - **2.** [sórdido] shabby - **3.** [tacaño] tight, stingy.

cutter *(pl* **cutters***) sm* (artist's) scalpel *(with retractable blade)*.

cuyo, **ya** *adj* [posesión - por parte de personas] whose; [- por parte de cosas] of which, whose; **ésos son los amigos en cuya casa nos hospedamos** those are the friends in whose house we spent the night; **ese señor, cuyo hijo conociste ayer** that man, whose son you met yesterday; **un equipo cuya principal estrella...** a team, the star player of which *o* whose star player...; **en cuyo caso** in which case.

CV (*abrev de* **currículum vitae**) *sm* CV.

d, D *sf* [letra] d, D.

D. *abrev de* **don**.

dactilar ⊳ **huella**.

dactilografía *sf* typing.

dádiva *sf* [regalo] gift; [donativo] donation.

dadivoso, **sa** *adj* generous.

dado, **da** *adj* given; **en un momento dado** at a certain point; **ser dado a** to be fond of.
◆ **dado** *sm* dice, die; **echar** *o* **tirar los dados** to throw the dice; **jugar a los dados** to play dice.
◆ **dado que** *loc conj* since, seeing as.

dador, **ra** *sm, f* - **1.** [de letra de cambio] drawer - **2.** [de carta] bearer.

daga *sf* dagger.

daguerrotipo *sm* daguerreotype.

dal (*abrev de* **decalitro**) dal.

dale *interj*: ¡dale! - ¡otra vez con lo mismo! there you go again!

dalia *sf* dahlia.

dálmata *adj* & *smf* - **1.** [persona] Dalmatian - **2.** [perro] Dalmatian.

daltónico, **ca** ◇ *adj* colour-blind. ◇ *sm, f* person with colour blindness.

daltonismo *sm* colour blindness.

dama *sf* - **1.** [mujer] lady; **dama de honor** [de novia] bridesmaid; [de reina] lady-in-waiting; **primera dama** TEATRO leading lady; POLÍT first lady *US* - **2.** [en damas] king; [en ajedrez, naipes] queen.
◆ **damas** *sfpl* [juego] draughts *(U) UK*, checkers *(U) US*.

damasco *sm* - **1.** [tela] damask - **2.** *Andes & R Dom* [albaricoque] apricot.

damero *sm* draughts board.

damisela *sf desus* damsel.

damnificado, **da** ◇ *adj* affected, damaged. ◇ *sm, f* victim.

damnificar [10] *vt* [cosa] to damage; [persona] to harm, to injure.

dance *etc* ▷ **danzar**.

dandi, dandy *sm* dandy.

danés, **esa** ◇ *adj* Danish. ◇ *sm, f* [persona] Dane.

◆ **danés** *sm* [lengua] Danish.

dantesco, **ca** *adj lit & fig* Dantesque.

Danubio *sm*: **el Danubio** the (River) Danube.

danza *sf* [gen] dancing; [baile] dance; **estar siempre en danza** to be always on the go *o* doing sthg; **estar metido en danza** to be up to no good.

danzar [13] *vi* - **1.** [bailar] to dance - **2.** *fig* [ir de un sitio a otro] to run about.

danzarín, **ina** *sm, f* dancer.

dañar *vt* [vista, cosecha] to harm, to damage; [persona] to hurt; [pieza, objeto] to damage.

◆ **dañarse** *vprnl* [persona] to hurt o.s.; [cosa] to become damaged.

dañino, **na** *adj* harmful.

daño *sm* - **1.** [dolor] pain, hurt; **hacer daño a alguien** to hurt sb; **hacerse daño** to hurt o.s. - **2.** [perjuicio - a algo] damage; [- a persona] harm; **daños colaterales** collateral damage; **daños y perjuicios** damages.

dar [56] ◇ *vt* - **1.** [gen] to give; [baile, fiesta] to hold, to give; [naipes] to deal; **dar algo a alguien** to give sthg to sb, to give sb sthg - **2.** [producir - gen] to give, to produce; [- frutos, flores] to bear; [- beneficios, intereses] to yield - **3.** [suj: reloj] to strike; **el reloj ha dado las doce** the clock struck twelve - **4.** [suministrar luz etc - por primera vez] to connect; [- tras un corte] to turn back on; [encender] to turn *o* switch on - **5.** CINE, TEATRO & TV to show; [concierto, interpretación] to give - **6.** [mostrar - señales etc] to show; **dar pruebas de sensatez** to show good sense - **7.** [untar con] to apply; **dar barniz a una silla** to varnish a chair - **8.** [provocar - gusto, escalofríos etc] to give; **me da vergüenza/pena** it makes me ashamed/sad; **me da risa** it makes me laugh; **me da miedo** it frightens me; **si no se calla me va a dar algo** *fam* if he doesn't shut up soon, I'll go mad; **si sigues trabajando así te va a dar algo** *fam* you can't go on working like that - **9.** *fam* [fastidiar] to ruin; **es tan pesado que me dio la tarde** he's so boring that he ruined the afternoon for me - **10.** [expresa acción]: **dar un grito** to give a cry; **dar un vistazo a** to have a look at; **darle un golpe/una puña-**lada a alguien to hit/stab sb; **voy a dar un paseo** I'm going (to go) for a walk - **11.** [considerar]: **dar algo por** to consider sthg as; **eso lo doy por hecho** I take that for granted; **dar a alguien por muerto** to give sb up for dead - **12.** *loc*: **donde las dan las toman** you get what you deserve; **no dar una** to get everything wrong. ◇ *vi* - **1.** [repartir - en naipes] to deal - **2.** [horas] to strike; **han dado las tres en el reloj** three o'clock struck - **3.** [golpear]: **le dieron en la cabeza** they hit him on the head; **la piedra dio contra el cristal** the stone hit the window - **4.** [accionar]: **dar a** [llave de paso] to turn; [botón, timbre] to press - **5.** [estar orientado]: **dar a** [suj: ventana, balcón] to look out onto, to overlook; [suj: pasillo, puerta] to lead to; [suj: casa, fachada] to face - **6.** [encontrar]: **dar con algo/alguien** to find sthg/sb; **he dado con la solución** I've hit upon the solution - **7.** [proporcionar]: **dar de beber a alguien** to give sb sthg to drink; **le da de mamar a su hijo** she breastfeeds her son - **8.** [ser suficiente]: **dar para** to be enough for - **9.** [motivar]: **dar que hablar** to set people talking; **aquello me dio que pensar** that made me think - **10.** [expresa repetición]: **le dieron de palos** they beat him repeatedly with a stick - **11.** [coger costumbre]: **darle a uno por hacer algo** to get it into one's head to do sthg; **le dio por la gimnasia** she's taken it into her head to start gymnastics - **12.** *loc*: **dar de sí** [ropa, calzado] to give, to stretch; **no dar más de sí** *o* **para más** [persona, animal] not to be up to much any more; **te digo que pares y tú ¡dale (que dale)!** I've told you to stop, but you just carry on and on!

◆ **darse** *vprnl* - **1.** [suceder] to occur, to happen; **se da pocas veces** it rarely happens - **2.** [entregarse]: **darse a** [droga etc] to take to - **3.** [golpearse]: **darse contra** to bump into - **4.** [tener aptitud]: **se me da bien/mal el latín** I'm good/bad at Latin - **5.** [considerarse]: **darse por** to consider o.s. (to be); **darse por vencido** to give in - **6.** *loc*: **dársela a alguien** [engañar] to take sb in; **se las da de listo** he makes out (that) he is clever.

dardo *sm* dart.

dársena *sf* dock.

darvinismo *sm* Darwinism.

datar *vt* to date.

◆ **datar de** *vi* to date back to, to date from.

dátil *sm* BOT & CULIN date.

◆ **dátiles** *smpl fam* [dedos] fingers.

◆ **dátil (de mar)** *sm* date mussel.

dato *sm* - **1.** [gen] piece of information, fact; **datos** [gen] information; INFORM data; **datos personales** personal details; **datos bancarios** bank details - **2.** MAT datum.

dcha. (*abrev de* **derecha**) rt.

d. de JC., d.JC. (abrev de después de Jesucristo) AD.

de prep (de + el = **del**) **- 1.** [posesión, pertenencia] of; **el coche de mi padre/mis padres** my father's/parents' car; **es de ella** it's hers; **la pata de la mesa** the table leg **- 2.** [materia] (made) of; **un vaso de plástico** a plastic cup; **un reloj de oro** a gold watch **- 3.** [en descripciones]: **un vaso de agua** a glass of water; **de fácil manejo** user-friendly; **la señora de verde** the lady in green; **el chico de la coleta** the boy with the ponytail; **he comprado las peras de dos euros el kilo** I bought the pears that were o at two euros a kilo; **un sello de 50 céntimos** a 50 cent stamp **- 4.** [asunto] about; **hablábamos de ti** we were talking about you; **libros de historia** history books **- 5.** [uso]: **una bici de carreras** a racer; **ropa de deporte** sportswear **- 6.** [en calidad de] as; **trabaja de bombero** he works as a fireman **- 7.** [tiempo - desde] from; [- durante] in; **trabaja de nueve a cinco** she works from nine to five; **de madrugada** early in the morning; **a las cuatro de la tarde** at four in the afternoon; **trabaja de noche y duerme de día** he works at night and sleeps during the day **- 8.** [procedencia, distancia] from; **salir de casa** to leave home; **soy de Bilbao** I'm from Bilbao; **de la playa al apartamento hay 100 metros** it's 100 metres from the beach to the apartment **- 9.** [causa, modo] with; **morirse de hambre** to die of hunger; **llorar de alegría** to cry with joy; **de una patada** with a kick; **de una sola vez** in one go **- 10.** [con superlativos]: **el mejor de todos** the best of all; **el más importante del mundo** the most important in the world **- 11.** [en comparaciones]: **más/menos de...** more/less than... **- 12.** (antes de infinitivo) [condición] if; **de querer ayudarme, lo haría** if she wanted to help me, she'd do it; **de no ser por ti, me hubiese hundido** if it hadn't been for you, I wouldn't have made it **- 13.** (después de adj y antes de s) [enfatiza cualidad]: **el idiota de tu hermano** your stupid brother **- 14.** (adj): **es difícil de creer** it's hard to believe.

dé ▷ **dar**.

deambular vi to wander (about).

debacle sf debacle.

debajo adv underneath; **debajo de** underneath, under; **por debajo de lo normal** below normal.

debate sm debate.

debatir vt to debate.
◆ **debatirse** vprnl [luchar] to struggle; **se debate la vida y la muerte** she's fighting for her life.

debe sm debit (side); **debe y haber** debit and credit.

deber ◇ vt [adeudar] to owe; **deber algo a alguien** to owe sb sthg, to owe sthg to sb. ◇ vi **- 1.** (después de adj y antes de infinitivo) [expresa obligación]: **debo hacerlo** I have to do it, I must do it; **deberían abolir esa ley** they ought to o should abolish that law; **debes dominar tus impulsos** you must o should control your impulses **- 2.** [expresa posibilidad]: **deber de: el tren debe de llegar alrededor de las diez** the train should arrive at about ten; **deben de ser las diez** it must be ten o'clock; **no debe de ser muy mayor** she can't be very old. ◇ sm duty.
◆ **deberse a** vprnl **- 1.** [ser consecuencia de] to be due to **- 2.** [dedicarse a] to have a responsibility towards.
◆ **deberes** smpl [trabajo escolar] homework (U); **hacer los deberes** to do one's homework.

debidamente adv properly.

debido, da adj **- 1.** [adeudado] owing **- 2.** [justo, conveniente] due, proper; **a su debido tiempo** in due course; **como es debido** properly.
◆ **debido a** loc conj (a principio de frase) owing to; (en mitad de frase) due to.

débil ◇ adj **- 1.** [persona - sin fuerzas] weak; [- condescendiente] lax, lenient **- 2.** [voz, sonido] faint; [luz] dim **- 3.** GRAM weak. ◇ smf weak person.

debilidad sf **- 1.** [gen] weakness; **tener debilidad por** to have a soft spot for **- 2.** [condescendencia] laxness.

debilitación sf weakening.

debilitar vt to weaken.
◆ **debilitarse** vprnl to become o grow weak.

débito sm [debe] debit; [deuda] debt.

debut sm [de persona] debut; [de obra] premiere.

debutante smf person making his/her debut.

debutar vi to make one's debut.

década sf decade; **la década de los sesenta** the sixties.

decadencia sf [gen] decadence; **en decadencia** [moda] on the way out; [cultura, sociedad] in decline.

decadente adj decadent.

decaer [55] vi [gen] to decline; [enfermo] to get weaker; [salud] to fail; [entusiasmo] to flag; [restaurante etc] to go downhill; **¡que no decaiga!** don't lose heart!

decágono sm decagon.

decaído, da adj [desalentado] gloomy, downhearted; [débil] frail.

decaiga etc ▷ **decaer**.

decaimiento sm [desaliento] gloominess; [decadencia] decline; [falta de fuerzas] weakness.

decalitro sm decalitre.

decálogo *sm* - **1.** RELIG Decalogue - **2.** *fig* [normas] golden *o* basic rules *pl.*

decámetro *sm* decametre.

decanato *sm* - **1.** [cargo] deanship - **2.** [despacho] dean's office.

decano, na *sm, f* - **1.** [de corporación, facultad] dean - **2.** [veterano] doyen (*f* doyenne), senior member.

decantar *vt* to decant.

➤ **decantarse** *vprnl* - **1.** [inclinarse]: **decantarse (a)** to lean (towards) - **2.** [optar]: **decantarse por** to opt for.

decapitar *vt* to decapitate, to behead.

decatlón, decathlón *sm* decathlon.

decayera *etc* ⊳ **decaer.**

deceleración *sf* deceleration.

decena *sf* ten; **una decena de veces** about ten times.

decencia *sf* - **1.** [gen] decency; [en el vestir] modesty - **2.** [dignidad] dignity.

decenio *sm* decade.

decente *adj* - **1.** [gen] decent - **2.** [en el comportamiento] proper; [en el vestir] modest - **3.** [limpio] clean.

decepción *sf* disappointment; **llevarse una decepción** to be disappointed.

decepcionante *adj* disappointing.

decepcionar *vt* to disappoint.

deceso *sm* decease, death.

dechado *sm*: **ser un dechado de virtudes** to be a paragon of virtue.

decibelio *sm* decibel.

decidido, da *adj* determined.

decidir ⬦ *vt* - **1.** [gen] to decide; **decidir hacer algo** to decide to do sthg - **2.** [determinar] to determine. ⬦ *vi* to decide, to choose.

➤ **decidirse** *vprnl* to decide, to make up one's mind; **decidirse a hacer algo** to decide to do sthg; **decidirse por** to decide on, to choose.

decigramo *sm* decigram.

decilitro *sm* decilitre.

décima ⊳ **décimo.**

decimal ⬦ *adj* - **1.** [sistema] decimal - **2.** [parte] tenth. ⬦ *sm* decimal.

decímetro *sm* decimetre.

décimo, ma *num* tenth; **la décima parte** a tenth.

➤ **décimo** *sm* - **1.** [fracción] tenth - **2.** [en lotería] *tenth part of a lottery ticket.*

➤ **décima** *sf* [en medidas] tenth; **tiene 3 décimas de fiebre** she has a slight fever; **una décima de segundo** a tenth of a second.

decimoctavo, va *num* eighteenth.

decimocuarto, ta *num* fourteenth.

decimonónico, ca *adj* - **1.** [del siglo XIX] nineteenth-century - **2.** [anticuado] old-fashioned.

decimonoveno, na *num* nineteenth.

decimoquinto, ta *num* fifteenth.

decimoséptimo, ma *num* seventeenth.

decimosexto, ta *num* sixteenth.

decimotercero, ra *num* thirteenth.

decir [57] ⬦ *vt* - **1.** [gen] to say; **decir que sí/no** to say yes/no; **dice que no viene** she says (that) she is not coming; **¿cómo se dice "estación" en inglés?** how do you say "estación" in English?; **¿diga?, ¿dígame?** [al teléfono] hello? - **2.** [contar, ordenar] to tell; **decir a alguien que haga algo** to tell sb to do sthg; **se dice que** they *o* people say (that); **decir la verdad** to tell the truth - **3.** [recitar] to recite, to read - **4.** *fig* [revelar] to tell, to show; **eso lo dice todo** that says it all - **5.** [llamar] to call - **6.** *loc*: **como quien no dice nada** as if it were nothing; **como quien dice, como si dijéramos** so to speak; **decir para sí** to say to o.s.; **decirle a alguien cuatro verdades** to tell sb a few home truths; **preocuparse por el qué dirán** to worry about what people will say; **es decir** that is, that's to say; **ni que decir tiene** needless to say; **¡no me digas!** no!, never!; **¡no me digas que no te gusta!** don't tell me you don't like it!; **no me dice nada el tenis** tennis doesn't do anything for me; **no hay más que decir** that's all there is to it, that's that; **(o) mejor dicho** or rather; **por decirlo así, por así decirlo** in other words, so to speak; **no llueve mucho que digamos** it's not exactly raining; **querer decir** to mean; **¿qué quieres decir con eso?** what do you mean by that?; **¡y que lo digas!** you can say that again! ⬦ *sm*: **es un decir** it's not strictly true.

decisión *sf* - **1.** [dictamen, resolución] decision; **tomar una decisión** to make *o* take a decision - **2.** [empeño, tesón] determination, resolve; [seguridad, resolución] decisiveness.

decisivo, va *adj* decisive.

declamar *vt* & *vi* to declaim, to recite.

declaración *sf* - **1.** [gen] statement; [de amor, guerra] declaration; **prestar declaración** to give evidence; **tomar declaración** to take (down) a statement; **declaración de derechos** bill of rights - **2.** [de impuestos] tax return; **tengo que hacer la declaración** I have to do my tax return; **declaración conjunta** joint tax return; **declaración del impuesto sobre la renta** income tax return - **3.** [comienzo - de incendio] outbreak.

declarar ⬦ *vt* [gen] to declare; [afirmar] to state, to say; **declarar la verdad** to tell the truth; **declarar culpable/inocente a alguien** to find sb guilty/not guilty. ⬦ *vi* DER to testify, to give evidence.

◆ **declararse** *vprnl* - **1.** [incendio, epidemia] to break out - **2.** [confesar el amor] to declare one's feelings *o* love - **3.** [dar una opinión]: **declararse a favor de algo** to say that one supports sthg; **declararse en contra de algo** to say that one is opposed to sthg; **declararse culpable/inocente** to plead guilty/not guilty.

declinación *sf* - **1.** [caída] decline - **2.** GRAM declension.

declinar ⬦ *vt* [gen & GRAM] to decline; [responsabilidad] to disclaim. ⬦ *vi* [día, tarde] to draw to a close; [fiebre] to subside, to abate; [economía] to decline.

declive *sm* - **1.** [decadencia] decline, fall; **en declive** in decline - **2.** [pendiente] slope.

decodificador = **descodificador**.

decodificar = **descodificar**.

decolaje *sm Amér* take-off.

decolar *vi Amér* to take off.

decolorante ⬦ *adj* bleaching. ⬦ *sm* bleaching agent.

decolorar *vt* to bleach.

◆ **decolorarse** *vprnl* to fade.

decomisar *vt* to confiscate, to seize.

decoración *sf* - **1.** [acción] decoration; [efecto] décor - **2.** [adorno] decorations *pl* - **3.** TEATRO set, scenery.

decorado *sm* CINE & TEATRO set.

decorador, ra *sm, f* interior designer; TEATRO set designer.

decorar *vt* to decorate.

decorativo, va *adj* decorative.

decoro *sm* - **1.** [pudor] decency, decorum - **2.** [dignidad] dignity; **vivir con decoro** to live decently.

decoroso, sa *adj* [decente] decent; [correcto] seemly, proper.

decrecer [30] *vi* [gen] to decrease, to decline; [caudal del río] to go down.

decreciente *adj* declining, decreasing.

decrépito, ta *adj despec* decrepit.

decretar *vt* to decree.

decreto *sm* decree; **por real decreto** by royal decree; **decreto ley** decree, ≈ order in council UK.

dedal *sm* thimble.

dedicación *sf* dedication; **con dedicación (en) exclusiva** full-time.

dedicar [10] *vt* - **1.** [tiempo, dinero, energía] to devote - **2.** [libro, monumento] to dedicate.

◆ **dedicarse a** *vprnl* - **1.** [a una profesión]: **¿a qué se dedica usted?** what do you do for a living?; **se dedica a la enseñanza** she works as a

teacher - **2.** [a una actividad, persona] to spend time on; **los domingos me dedico al estudio** I spend Sundays studying.

dedicatoria *sf* dedication.

dedillo *sm*: **saber algo al dedillo** *fam* to know sthg (off) by heart.

dedique *etc* ➪ **dedicar**.

dedo *sm* - **1.** [de la mano] finger; **contar con los dedos** to count on one's fingers; **dos dedos de whisky** two fingers of whisky; **meterse el dedo en la nariz** to pick one's nose; **dedo anular/corazón** ring/middle finger; **dedo gordo** *o* **pulgar** thumb; **dedo índice/meñique** index/little finger - **2.** [del pie] toe; **dedo gordo/pequeño** big/little toe - **3.** *loc*: **escaparse de entre los dedos** to slip through one's fingers; **estar a dos dedos de** to be within an inch of; **estar para chuparse los dedos** to be mouthwatering; **hacer dedo** *fam* to hitchhike; **mamarse** *o* **chuparse el dedo** to be a fool; **no creas que me chupo el dedo** I wasn't born yesterday, you know; **nombrar a alguien a dedo** to handpick sb; **no mover un dedo** not to lift a finger; **no tener dos dedos de frente** to be as thick as two short planks; **pillarse** *o* **cogerse los dedos** *fig* to get one's fingers burnt; **poner el dedo en la llaga** to put one's finger on it; **señalar a alguien con el dedo** to criticize sb.

deducción *sf* deduction; **deducción fiscal** ECON tax-deductible expenditure.

deducible *adj* - **1.** [idea] deducible - **2.** [dinero] deductible.

deducir [33] *vt* - **1.** [inferir] to guess, to deduce - **2.** [descontar] to deduct.

deductivo, va *adj* deductive.

dedujera, deduzca *etc* ➪ **deducir**.

defecar [10] *vi* to defecate.

defecto *sm* [físico] defect; [moral] fault, shortcoming; **defecto de forma** administrative error; **defecto de pronunciación** speech defect.

◆ **por defecto** *loc adv* by default.

defectuoso, sa *adj* [mercancía] defective, faulty; [trabajo] inaccurate.

defender [20] *vt* - **1.** [gen] to defend; [amigo etc] to stand up for - **2.** [proteger - del frío etc]: **defender a alguien (de)** to protect sb (against).

◆ **defenderse** *vprnl* - **1.** [protegerse]: **defenderse (de)** to defend o.s. (against) - **2.** *fig* [apañarse] to get by; **se defiende con su trabajo** he's getting along okay at work.

defensa ⬦ *sf* defence; **en defensa propia, en legítima defensa** in self-defence; **en defensa de** in defence of; **defensa personal** self-defence. ⬦ *smf* DEP defender; **defensa central** centre-back.

◆ **defensas** *sfpl* MED defences; **estoy baja de defensas** my body's defences are low.

defensiva, va *adj* defensive.

◆ **defensiva** *sf*: **ponerse/estar a la defensiva** to go/be on the defensive.

defensor, ra ◇ *adj* ▷ **abogado**. ◇ *sm, f* [gen] defender; [abogado] counsel for the defence; [adalid] champion; **defensor del pueblo** ≈ ombudsman.

defeque *etc* ▷ **defecar**.

deferencia *sf* deference; **por deferencia a** in deference to.

deferir [27] ◇ *vi*: **deferir (a)** to defer (to). ◇ *vt* DER to refer.

deficiencia *sf* [defecto] deficiency, shortcoming; [insuficiencia] lack.

deficiente *adj* - **1.** [defectuoso - gen] deficient; [audición, vista] defective - **2.** [mediocre] poor, unsatisfactory; **deficiente en** lacking *o* deficient in.

◆ **deficiente (mental)** *smf* mentally handicapped person.

◆ **muy deficiente** *sm* EDUC very poor, ≈ E (grade).

déficit *sm inv* - **1.** ECON deficit - **2.** [falta] lack, shortage.

deficitario, ria *adj* [empresa, operación] lossmaking; [balance] negative, showing a deficit.

defienda *etc* ▷ **defender**.

defiera *etc* ▷ **deferir**.

definición *sf* - **1.** [gen] definition; **por definición** by definition - **2.** [descripción] description - **3.** [en televisión] resolution; **alta definición** high resolution.

definido, da *adj* - **1.** [gen] defined - **2.** GRAM ▷ **artículo**.

definir *vt* - **1.** [gen] to define - **2.** [describir] to describe.

◆ **definirse** *vprnl* to take a clear stance.

definitivamente *adv* - **1.** [sin duda] definitely - **2.** [para siempre] for good.

definitivo, va *adj* [texto etc] definitive; [respuesta] definite; **en definitiva** in short, anyway.

defiriera *etc* ▷ **deferir**.

deforestación *sf* deforestation.

deformación *sf* [de huesos, objetos etc] deformation; [de la verdad etc] distortion; **deformación física** (physical) deformity; **tener deformación profesional** *to be always acting as if one were still at work*.

deformar *vt* - **1.** [huesos, objetos etc] to deform - **2.** *fig* [la verdad etc] to distort.

◆ **deformarse** *vprnl* to go out of shape.

deforme *adj* [cuerpo] deformed, disfigured; [imagen] distorted; [objeto] misshapen.

deformidad *sf* deformity.

defraudación *sf* [fraude] tax evasion.

defraudar *vt* - **1.** [decepcionar] to disappoint - **2.** [estafar] to defraud; **defraudar a Hacienda** to practise tax evasion.

defunción *sf* decease, death.

degeneración *sf* degeneration.

degenerado, da *adj* & *sm, f* degenerate.

degenerar *vi*: **degenerar (en)** to degenerate (into).

degollar [23] *vt* [cortar la garganta] to cut *o* slit the throat of; [decapitar] to behead.

degradación *sf* - **1.** [moral] (moral) degradation - **2.** [de un cargo] demotion.

degradante *adj* degrading.

degradar *vt* - **1.** [moralmente] to degrade, to debase - **2.** [de un cargo] to demote.

◆ **degradarse** *vprnl* to degrade *o* lower o.s.

degüella *etc* ▷ **degollar**.

degustación *sf* tasting (*of wines etc*).

degustar *vt* to taste (*wines etc*).

dehesa *sf* meadow.

dejada ▷ **dejado**.

dejadez *sf* neglect; [en aspecto] slovenliness.

dejado, da ◇ *adj* careless; [aspecto] slovenly. ◇ *sm, f* [persona] slovenly person.

◆ **dejada** *sf* [en tenis] drop shot.

dejar ◇ *vt* - **1.** [gen] to leave; **deja esa pera en el plato** put that pear on the plate; **deja el abrigo en la percha** leave your coat on the hanger; **dejar a alguien en algún sitio** [con el coche] to drop sb off somewhere; **deja algo de café para mí** leave some coffee for me; **dejar algo/a alguien a alguien** [encomendar] to leave sthg/sb with sb - **2.** [prestar]: **dejar algo a alguien** to lend sb sthg, to lend sthg to sb - **3.** [abandonar - casa, trabajo, país] to leave; [- tabaco, estudios] to give up; [- familia] to abandon; **dejar algo por imposible** to give sthg up as a lost cause; **dejar a alguien atrás** to leave sb behind - **4.** [permitir]: **dejar a alguien hacer algo** to let sb do sthg, to allow sb to do sthg; **sus gritos no me dejaron dormir** his cries prevented me from sleeping; **deja que tu hijo venga con nosotros** let your son come with us; **dejar correr algo** *fig* to let sthg be - **5.** [omitir] to leave out; **dejar algo por** *o* **sin hacer** to fail to do sthg; **dejó lo más importante por resolver** he left the most important question unsolved - **6.** (en imperativo) [prescindir de] to forget (about); **déjalo, no importa** forget it, it doesn't matter - **7.** (en imperativo) [no molestar] to leave alone *o* in peace; **¡déjame!, que tengo trabajo** leave me alone, I'm busy!; **déjame tranquilo** leave me alone *o* in peace - **8.** [esperar]: **dejar que** to wait until; **dejó que acabara de llover para salir** he waited until it had stopped raining before going out. ⟨> *vi* - **1.** [parar]: **dejar de hacer algo** to stop doing sthg; **no deja de venir ni un solo día** he never fails to come - **2.** [expresando promesa]: **no dejar de** to be sure to; **¡no dejes de escribirme!** be sure to write to me! - **3.** *loc*: **dejar (mucho** o **bastante) que desear** to leave a lot to be desired.

◆ **dejarse** *vprnl* - **1.** [olvidar]: **dejarse algo en algún sitio** to leave sthg somewhere - **2.** [permitir]: **dejarse engañar** to allow o.s. to be taken in - **3.** [cesar]: **dejarse de hacer algo** to stop doing sthg; **¡déjate de tonterías!** stop messing about! - **4.** [descuidarse] to let o.s. go - **5.** *loc*: **dejarse llevar (por algo)** to get carried away (with sthg).

deje *sm* - **1.** [acento] accent - **2.** *fig* [resabio] touch, hint.

dejo *sm* - **1.** [acento] accent - **2.** [sabor] aftertaste.

del ⊳ **de**.

delantal *sm* apron.

delante *adv* - **1.** [en primer lugar, en la parte delantera] in front; **el de delante** the one in front; **el asiento de delante** the seat in front - **2.** [enfrente] opposite - **3.** [presente] present.

◆ **delante de** *loc prep* in front of.

delantero, ra ⟨> *adj* front. ⟨> *sm, f* DEP forward; **delantero centro** centre forward.

◆ **delantera** *sf* - **1.** DEP forwards *pl*, attack - **2.** *fam* [de una mujer] bust - **3.** *loc*: **coger** o **tomar la delantera** to take the lead; **coger** o **tomar la delantera a alguien** to beat sb to it; **llevar la delantera** to be in the lead.

delatar *vt* to denounce; *fig* [suj: sonrisa, ojos etc] to betray, to give away; **le delaté a la policía** I reported him to the police.

◆ **delatarse** *vprnl* to give o.s. away.

delator, ra *sm, f* informer.

delco *sm* distributor.

delegación *sf* - **1.** [autorización, embajada] delegation; **delegación de poderes** devolution (of power) - **2.** [sucursal] branch - **3.** [oficina pública] local office - **4.** *Méx* [comisaría] police station, precinct US, station house US.

delegado, da *sm, f* - **1.** [gen] delegate; **delegado de curso** class representative - **2.** COM representative.

delegar [16] *vt*: **delegar algo (en** o **a)** to delegate sthg (to).

deleitar *vt* to delight.

◆ **deleitarse** *vprnl*: **deleitarse con** o **en algo** to take pleasure in sthg; **deleitarse haciendo algo** to take pleasure in o enjoy doing sthg.

deleite *sm* delight.

deletrear *vt* to spell (out).

deleznable *adj fig* [malo - clima, libro, actuación] appalling; [- excusa, razón] contemptible.

delfín *sm* - **1.** [animal] dolphin - **2.** [título] dauphin.

delgadez *sf* [gen] thinness; [esbeltez] slimness.

delgado, da *adj* [gen] thin; [esbelto] slim.

deliberación *sf* deliberation.

deliberado, da *adj* deliberate.

deliberar *vi* to deliberate.

delicadeza *sf* - **1.** [miramiento - con cosas] care; [- con personas] kindness, attentiveness; **tener la delicadeza de** to be thoughtful enough to - **2.** [finura - de perfume, rostro] delicacy; [- de persona] sensitivity - **3.** [de un asunto, situación] delicacy.

delicado, da *adj* - **1.** [gen] delicate; [perfume, gusto] subtle; [paladar] refined - **2.** [persona - sensible] sensitive; [- muy exigente] fussy; [- educado] polite; **estar delicado de salud** to be very weak.

delicia *sf* delight; **hacer las delicias de alguien** to delight sb.

delicioso, sa *adj* [comida] delicious; [persona] lovely, delightful.

delictivo, va *adj* criminal.

delimitar *vt* [finca etc] to set out the boundaries of; [funciones etc] to define.

delincuencia *sf* crime; **delincuencia juvenil** juvenile delinquency.

delincuente *smf* criminal; **delincuente habitual** habitual offender; **delincuente juvenil** juvenile delinquent.

delineante *sm, f* draughtsman (*f* draughtswoman).

delinear *vt* to draw; *fig* to outline.

delinquir [18] *vi* to commit a crime.

delirante *adj* - **1.** [gen] delirious - **2.** [idea] wild, crazy.

delirar *vi* [un enfermo] to be delirious; [desbarrar] to talk nonsense.

delirio *sm* [por la fiebre] delirium; [de un enfermo mental] ravings *pl*; **delirios de grandeza** delusions of grandeur; **con delirio** madly.

delito *sm* crime, offence; **cometer un delito** to commit a crime o an offence; **delito común** common law offence; **delito ecológico** ecological crime; **delito fiscal** tax offence; **delito informático** computer crime.

delta ⟨> *sm* delta. ⟨> *sf* delta.

demacrado, da *adj* gaunt.

demagogia *sf* demagoguery.

demagogo, ga *sm, f* demagogue.

demanda *sf* - **1.** [petición] request; [reivindicación] demand; **demanda salarial** wage claim; **en demanda de** asking for - **2.** ECON demand - **3.** DER lawsuit; [por daños y perjuicios] claim; **presentar una demanda contra** to take legal action against.

demandado, **da** *sm, f* defendant.

demandante *smf* plaintiff.

demandar *vt* - **1.** DER: **demandar a alguien (por)** to sue sb (for) - **2.** [pedir] to ask for, to seek.

demarcación *sf* - **1.** [señalización] demarcation - **2.** [territorio demarcado] area; [jurisdicción] district.

demás ◇ *adj* other; **los demás invitados** the other O remaining guests. ◇ *pron*: **lo demás** the rest; **todo lo demás** everything else; **los/las demás** the others, the rest; **por lo demás** apart from that, otherwise; **y demás** and so on.

demasía ► **en demasía** *loc adv* in excess, too much.

demasiado, **da** ◇ *adj* too much (*pl* too many); **demasiada comida** too much food; **demasiados niños** too many children. ◇ *adv* [gen] too much; *(antes de adj o adv)* too; **habla demasiado** she talks too much; **iba demasiado rápido** he was going too fast.

demencia *sf* madness, insanity; **demencia senil** senile dementia.

demencial *adj* [disparatado] chaotic.

demente ◇ *adj* mad. ◇ *smf* MED mental patient; [loco] lunatic.

democracia *sf* democracy.

demócrata ◇ *adj* democratic. ◇ *smf* democrat.

democratacristiano, **na**, **democristiano**, **na** *adj & sm, f* Christian Democrat.

democrático, **ca** *adj* democratic.

democratización *sf* democratization.

democratizar [13] *vt* to democratize.

democristiano, **na** = democratacristiano.

demografía *sf* demography.

demográfico, **ca** *adj* [estudio, instituto] demographic; [concentración, explosión] population *(antes de s)*.

demoledor, **ra** *adj* [huracán, críticas] devastating; [razones] overwhelming.

demoler [24] *vt* [edificio] to demolish, to pull down; *fig* to destroy.

demolición *sf* demolition.

demoniaco, **ca**, **demoníaco**, **ca** *adj* devilish, diabolic.

demonio *sm* - **1.** *lit & fig* devil; **un pesado de mil demonios** one hell of a bore; **saber a demonios** to taste disgusting - **2.** [para enfatizar]: **¿qué/dónde demonios...?** what/where the hell...?

► **demonios** *interj*: **¡demonios!** damn (it)!

demora *sf* delay.

demorar ◇ *vt* - **1.** to delay - **2.** *Amér* [tardar]: **demoraron 3 días en hacerlo** it took them

three days to do it; **demora una hora para vestirse** it takes her one hour to get dressed. ◇ *vi Amér* [tardar]: **¡no demores!** don't be late!

► **demorarse** *vprnl* - **1.** [retrasarse] to be delayed - **2.** [detenerse] to stop (somewhere).

demostración *sf* - **1.** [gen] demonstration; **hacer una demostración** [de cómo funciona algo] to demonstrate; [de gimnasia etc] to put on a display; **demostración de afecto** show of affection - **2.** [de un teorema] proof - **3.** [exhibición] display; [señal] sign; [prueba] proof.

demostrar [23] *vt* - **1.** [hipótesis, teoría, verdad] to prove - **2.** [alegría, impaciencia, dolor] to show - **3.** [funcionamiento, procedimiento] to demonstrate, to show.

demostrativo, **va** *adj* - **1.** [representativo] representative - **2.** GRAM demonstrative.

demuela *etc* ▷ **demoler**.

demuestra *etc* ▷ **demostrar**.

denegar [35] *vt* to turn down, to reject.

denigrante *adj* [humillante] degrading; [insultante] insulting.

denigrar *vt* [humillar] to denigrate, to vilify; [insultar] to insult.

denominación *sf* naming; **'denominación de origen'** 'appellation d'origine'.

Denominación de origen

🄰🄰🄰 Originally designed as a guarantee of the place of origin and quality of wine, the Denominación de Origen is now also used for other products such as cheeses, vegetables, olive oil, fruit and meat, especially where the production of a particular region is highly regarded (as in the case of olive oil from Jaén, Manchego cheese, or Jabugo cured ham). EU law now regulates the use of such labelling.

---

denominador *sm* denominator; **denominador común** *fig & MAT common denominator.

denominar *vt* to call.

denotar *vt* to indicate, to show.

densidad *sf* [gen & INFORM] density; **densidad de población** population density; **alta/doble densidad** INFORM high/double density.

denso, **sa** *adj* [gen] dense; [líquido] thick.

dentado, **da** *adj* [rueda] cogged, toothed; [filo, cuchillo] serrated; [sello] perforated; [hojas] dentate.

dentadura *sf* teeth *pl*; **dentadura postiza** false teeth *pl*, dentures *pl*.

dental *adj* dental.

dentellada *sf* - **1.** [mordisco] bite; **a dentelladas** with one's teeth - **2.** [herida] toothmark.

dentera *sf*: **dar dentera a alguien** to set sb's teeth on edge.

dentición *sf* - **1.** [proceso] teething - **2.** [conjunto] teeth *pl*.

dentífrico, ca *adj* tooth *(antes de s)*.
- **dentífrico** *sm* toothpaste.

dentista *smf* dentist.

dentística *sf Amér* dentistry.

dentro *adv* inside; **está ahí dentro** it's in there; **de dentro** inside; **el bolsillo de dentro** the inside pocket; **hacia/para dentro** inwards; **por dentro** (on the) inside; *fig* inside, deep down.
- **dentro de** *loc prep* in; **dentro del coche** in o inside the car; **dentro de poco/un año** in a while/a year; **dentro de un año terminaré los estudios** I'll have finished my studies within a year; **dentro de lo posible** as far as possible.

denuesta *etc* ⊳ **denostar**.

denuncia *sf* [acusación] accusation; [condena] denunciation; [a la policía] complaint; **presentar una denuncia contra** to file a complaint against.

denunciante *smf* person who reports a crime.

denunciar [8] *vt* to denounce; [delito] to report.

deparar *vt* [gen] to bring; [oportunidad, placer] to afford.

departamento *sm* - **1.** [gen] department - **2.** [división territorial] administrative district; [en Francia] department - **3.** [de maleta, cajón, tren] compartment - **4.** *Arg* [apartamento] flat *UK*, apartment *US*.

departir *vi* to chat, to talk.

dependencia *sf* - **1.** [de una persona] dependence; [de país, drogas, alcohol] dependency - **2.** [departamento] section; [sucursal] branch.
- **dependencias** *sfpl* [habitaciones] rooms; [edificios] outbuildings.

depender *vi* to depend; **depende...** it depends...
- **depender de** *vi*: **depender de algo** to depend on sthg; **depender de alguien** to be dependent on sb; **depende de ti** it's up to you.

dependienta *sf* shop assistant, saleswoman.

dependiente ⬦ *adj* dependent; **un organismo dependiente del gobierno central** a body which forms part of the central government. ⬦ *sm* salesman, shop assistant *UK*, salesclerk *US*.

depilación *sf* hair removal; **depilación a la cera** waxing.

depilar *vt* [gen] to remove the hair from; [cejas] to pluck; [con cera] to wax.
- **depilarse** *vprnl* [gen] to remove one's body hair; [las piernas] to wax one's legs.

depilatorio, ria *adj* hair-removing.
- **depilatorio** *sm* hair-remover.

deplorable *adj* [suceso, comportamiento] deplorable; [aspecto] sorry, pitiful.

deplorar *vt* to regret deeply.

deponer [65] *vt* - **1.** [abandonar - actitud] to drop, to set aside; [las armas] to lay down - **2.** [destituir - ministro, secretario] to remove from office; [- líder, rey] to depose; **deponer a alguien de su cargo** to strip sb of his/her office.

deportación *sf* deportation.

deportar *vt* to deport.

deporte *sm* sport; **hacer deporte** to do o practise sports; **hacer deporte es bueno para la salud** sport is good for your health; **practicar un deporte** to do a sport; **deportes de competición** competitive sports; **deportes extremos** extreme sports; **deportes náuticos** water sports; **hacer algo por deporte** to do sthg as a hobby.

deportista ⬦ *adj* sporty, sports-loving. ⬦ *sm, f* sportsman (*f* sportswoman).

deportividad *sf* sportsmanship.

deportivo, va *adj* - **1.** [revista, evento] sports *(antes de s)* - **2.** [conducta, espíritu] sportsmanlike.
- **deportivo** *sm* sports car.

deposición *sf* - **1.** [destitución - de ministro, secretario] removal from office; [- de líder, rey] overthrow - **2.** [defecación] defecation.

depositar *vt* - **1.** [gen] to place; **depositar algo en alguien** [confianza, ilusiones] to place sthg in sb - **2.** [en el banco etc] to deposit.
- **depositarse** *vprnl* [asentarse] to settle.

depositario, ria *sm, f* - **1.** [de dinero] trustee - **2.** [de confianza etc] repository - **3.** [de mercancías etc] depositary.

depósito *sm* - **1.** [almacén - de mercancías] store, warehouse; [- de armas] dump, arsenal; **depósito de cadáveres** morgue, mortuary; **depósito de equipaje** left luggage office *UK*, baggage room *US* - **2.** [recipiente] tank; **depósito de agua** [cisterna] water tank; [embalse] reservoir; **depósito de gasolina** petrol tank *UK*, gas tank *US* - **3.** [de dinero] deposit.
- **depósito legal** *sm copy of a publication legally required to be sent to the authorities.*

depravación *sf* depravity.

depravado, da ⬦ *adj* depraved. ⬦ *sm, f* depraved person.

depravar *vt* to corrupt, to deprave.
- **depravarse** *vprnl* to become depraved.

depreciación *sf* depreciation.

depreciar [8] *vt* to (cause to) depreciate.
- **depreciarse** *vprnl* to depreciate.

depredador, ra ⬦ *adj* predatory. ⬦ *sm, f* predator.

depresión *sf* - **1.** [gen] depression; **depresión nerviosa** nervous breakdown; **depresión posparto** postnatal depression - **2.** [en superficie, terreno] hollow, depression.

depresivo, va ◇ *adj* PSICOL depressive; [deprimente] depressing. ◇ *sm, f* depressive.

deprimente *adj* depressing.

deprimido, da *adj* depressed.

deprimir *vt* to depress.

◆ **deprimirse** *vprnl* to get depressed.

deprisa, de prisa *adv* fast, quickly; **¡deprisa!** quick!

depuesto, ta ◇ *pp* ▷ **deponer**. ◇ *adj* [destituido - ministro, secretario] removed from office; [- líder, rey] deposed.

depuración *sf* - **1.** [de agua, metal, gas] purification - **2.** *fig* [de organismo, sociedad] purge.

depurador, ra *adj* purifying.

◆ **depurador** *sm* purifier.

◆ **depuradora** *sf* purifier.

depurar *vt* - **1.** [agua, metal, gas] to purify - **2.** *fig* [organismo, sociedad] to purge - **3.** [estilo, gusto] to refine.

depusiera *etc* ▷ **deponer**.

derby *sm* - **1.** [en hípica] derby - **2.** [en fútbol] (local) derby.

derecha ▷ **derecho**.

derechazo *sm* [en boxeo] right.

derechista ◇ *adj* right-wing. ◇ *smf* right-winger.

derecho, cha ◇ *adj* - **1.** [diestro] right; **el margen derecho** the right-hand margin - **2.** [vertical] upright; **siempre anda muy derecha** she always walks with a very upright posture - **3.** [recto] straight. ◇ *adv* - **1.** [en posición vertical] upright - **2.** [en línea recta] straight; **todo derecho** straight ahead; **siga todo derecho y llegará al museo** continue straight ahead and you'll come to the museum - **3.** [directamente] straight; **se fue derecha a casa** she went straight home.

◆ **derecho** *sm* - **1.** [leyes, estudio] law; **un estudiante de derecho** a law student; **derecho administrativo/mercantil** administrative/mercantile law; **derecho canónico/fiscal** canon/tax law; **derecho civil/penal** civil/criminal law; **derecho natural** natural law - **2.** [prerrogativa] right; **con derecho a** with a right to; **de pleno derecho** fully-fledged; **el derecho al voto** the right to vote; **hacer valer sus derechos** to exercise one's rights; **¡no hay derecho!** it's not fair!; **reservado el derecho de admisión** the management reserves the right of admission; **tener derecho a algo** to have a right to sthg; **tener derecho a hacer algo** to have the right to do sthg; **derecho de asilo** right of asylum; **derecho de réplica** right

to reply; **derecho de retención** ECON right of retention; **derechos civiles/humanos** civil/human rights; **me queda el derecho al pataleo** all I can do now is complain - **3.** [de una tela, prenda] right side; **del derecho** right side out.

◆ **derecha** *sf* - **1.** [contrario de izquierda] right, right-hand side; **a la derecha** to the right; **girar a la derecha** to turn right - **2.** POLÍT right (wing); **ser de derechas** to be right-wing - **3.** *loc*: **no hacer nada a derechas** to do nothing right.

◆ **derechos** *smpl* [tasas] duties, taxes; [profesionales] fees; **derechos de aduana** customs duty *(U)*; **derechos de inscripción** membership fee *sing*; **derechos de autor** [potestad] copyright *(U)*; [dinero] royalties; **derechos reales** death duty *(U)*.

deriva *sf* drift; **a la deriva** adrift; **ir a la deriva** to drift.

derivación *sf* - **1.** [cable, canal, carretera] branch - **2.** ELECTR shunt - **3.** GRAM derivation.

derivado, da *adj* GRAM derived.

◆ **derivado** *sm* - **1.** [producto] by-product; **derivados lácteos** dairy products - **2.** QUÍM derivative.

◆ **derivada** *sf* MAT derivative.

derivar ◇ *vt* - **1.** [desviar] to divert - **2.** MAT to derive. ◇ *vi* [desviarse] to change direction, to drift.

◆ **derivar de** *vi* - **1.** [proceder] to derive from - **2.** GRAM to be derived from.

◆ **derivar en** *vi* to result in, to lead to.

dermatología *sf* dermatology.

dermatológico, ca *adj* dermatological.

dermatólogo, ga *sm, f* dermatologist.

dérmico, ca *adj* skin *(antes de s)*.

dermis *sf inv* dermis.

derogación *sf* repeal.

derogar [16] *vt* [ley] to repeal; [contrato] to rescind.

derramamiento *sm* spilling; **derramamiento de sangre** bloodshed.

derramar *vt* [por accidente] to spill; [verter] to pour; **derramar lágrimas/sangre** to shed tears/blood.

◆ **derramarse** *vprnl* [por accidente] to spill.

derrame *sm* - **1.** MED discharge; **derrame cerebral** brain haemorrhage; **derrame sinovial** water on the knee - **2.** [de líquido] spilling; [de sangre] shedding.

derrapar *vi* to skid.

derrengar *vt* [cansar] to exhaust, to tire out.

derretir [26] *vt* [gen] to melt; [hielo, nieve] to thaw.

◆ **derretirse** *vprnl* - **1.** [metal, mantequilla] to melt; [hielo, nieve] to thaw - **2.** *fam fig* [enamorarse]: **derretirse (por alguien)** to be madly in love (with sb).

derribar *vt* - **1.** [construcción] to knock down, to demolish - **2.** [hacer caer - árbol] to cut down, to fell; [- avión] to bring down - **3.** [gobierno, gobernante] to overthrow.

derribo *sm* - **1.** [de edificio] demolition; [de árbol] felling; [de avión] bringing down; [de gobierno, gobernante] overthrow - **2.** [material] rubble.

derrita, derritiera *etc* ⊳ **derretir**.

derrocar [10] *vt* [gobierno] to bring down, to overthrow; [ministro] to oust.

derrochador, ra ◇ *adj* wasteful. ◇ *sm, f* spendthrift.

derrochar *vt* - **1.** [malgastar] to squander - **2.** [rebosar de] to ooze, to be full of.

derroche *sm* - **1.** [malgaste] waste, squandering - **2.** [abundancia] profusion.

derrota *sf* - **1.** [fracaso] defeat - **2.** NÁUT [rumbo] course.

derrotar *vt* to defeat.

derrotero *sm* - **1.** [camino] direction; **tomar diferentes derroteros** to follow a different course - **2.** NÁUT course.

derrotista *adj* & *smf* defeatist.

derruir [51] *vt* to demolish, to knock down.

derrumbamiento *sm* - **1.** [de puente, edificio - por accidente] collapse; [- intencionado] demolition - **2.** *fig* [de imperio] fall; [de empresa etc] collapse - **3.** *fig* [de persona] devastation.

derrumbar *vt* - **1.** [puente, edificio] to demolish - **2.** [persona - moralmente] to destroy, to devastate.
➤ **derrumbarse** *vprnl* - **1.** [puente, edificio] to collapse; [techo] to fall *o* cave in - **2.** [persona] to be devastated; [esperanzas] to be shattered.

derrumbe *sm* collapse.

desabastecido, da *adj* without supplies; **desabastecido de** short *o* out of.

desaborido, da *fam* ◇ *adj* boring, dull. ◇ *sm, f* bore.

desabotonar *vt* to unbutton.
➤ **desabotonarse** *vprnl* [suj: persona] to undo one's buttons; [suj: ropa] to come undone.

desabrido, da *adj* - **1.** [tiempo] unpleasant, bad - **2.** [persona] surly; [tono] harsh.

desabrigar [16] *vt* to wrap up insufficiently.
➤ **desabrigarse** *vprnl* - **1.** [al salir a la calle]: **¡no te desabrigues!** make sure you wrap up warmly! - **2.** [en la cama] to throw off the covers.

desabrochar *vt* to undo.
➤ **desabrocharse** *vprnl* [suj: persona] to undo one's buttons; [suj: ropa] to come undone.

desacatar *vt* [ley, regla] to disobey; [costumbre, persona] not to respect.

desacato *sm* - **1.** [gen]: **desacato (a)** lack of respect (for), disrespect (for) - **2.** DER contempt of court.

desacertado, da *adj* [inoportuno] unwise, ill-considered; [erróneo] mistaken, wrong.

desacierto *sm* [error] error.

desaconsejar *vt*: **desaconsejar algo (a alguien)** to advise (sb) against sthg; **desaconsejar a alguien que haga algo** to advise sb not to do sthg.

desacoplar *vt* ELECTR to disconnect; TECNOL to uncouple.

desacostumbrado, da *adj* unusual, uncommon.

desacreditar *vt* to discredit.
➤ **desacreditarse** *vprnl* to become discredited.

desactivar *vt* to defuse.

desacuerdo *sm* disagreement; **estar en desacuerdo (con)** to disagree (with).

desafiante *adj* defiant.

desafiar [9] *vt* - **1.** [persona] to challenge; **desafiar a alguien a algo/a que haga algo** to challenge sb to sthg/to do sthg - **2.** [peligro] to defy.

desafinado, da *adj* out of tune.

desafinar *vi* MÚS to be out of tune.

desafío *sm* challenge.

desaforadamente *adv*: **gritar desaforadamente** to shout one's head off, to shout at the top of one's voice.

desaforado, da *adj* - **1.** [excesivo - apetito] uncontrolled - **2.** [furioso - grito] furious, wild.

desafortunadamente *adv* unfortunately.

desafortunado, da ◇ *adj* - **1.** [gen] unfortunate - **2.** [sin suerte] unlucky. ◇ *sm, f* unlucky person.

desagradable *adj* unpleasant.

desagradar *vi* to displease; **su actitud le desagradó** he was displeased at her attitude.

desagradecido, da *sm, f* ungrateful person.

desagrado *sm* displeasure; **con desagrado** reluctantly.

desagraviar [8] *vt*: **desagraviar a alguien por algo** [por una ofensa] to make amends to sb for sthg; [por un perjuicio] to compensate sb for sthg.

desagravio *sm*: **en señal de desagravio** (in order) to make amends.

desaguar [45] *vi* [bañera, agua] to drain; [río]: **desaguar en** to flow into.

desagüe *sm* [vaciado] drain; [cañería] drainpipe.

desaguisado *sm* [destrozo] damage *(U)*.

desahogado, **da** *adj* - **1.** [de espacio] spacious, roomy - **2.** [de dinero] well-off, comfortable.

desahogar [16] *vt* [ira] to vent; [pena] to relieve, to ease.

◆ **desahogarse** *vprnl* - **1.** [contar penas]: **desahogarse con alguien** to pour out one's woes o to tell one's troubles to sb - **2.** [desfogarse] to let off steam.

desahogo *sm* - **1.** [moral] relief, release - **2.** [de espacio] space, room - **3.** [económico] ease; **vivir con desahogo** to be comfortably off.

desahuciar [8] *vt* - **1.** [inquilino] to evict - **2.** [enfermo]: **desahuciar a alguien** to give up all hope of saving sb.

desahucio *sm* eviction.

desairado, **da** *adj* - **1.** [poco airoso - actuación] unimpressive, unsuccessful - **2.** [humillado] spurned.

desairar *vt* [person] to snub, to slight; [cosa] not to think much of, to be unimpressed by.

desaire *sm* snub, slight; **hacer un desaire a alguien** to snub sb; **sufrir un desaire** to receive a rebuff.

desajustar *vt* - **1.** [piezas] to disturb, to knock out of place - **2.** [planes] to upset.

desajuste *sm* - **1.** [de piezas] misalignment; [de máquina] breakdown - **2.** [de declaraciones] inconsistency; [económico etc] imbalance.

desalentar [19] *vt* to dishearten, to discourage.

◆ **desalentarse** *vprnl* to be discouraged, to lose heart.

desaliento *sm* dismay, dejection.

desaliñado, **da** *adj* scruffy.

desaliño *sm* scruffiness.

desalmado, **da** <> *adj* heartless. <> *sm, f* heartless person.

desalojar *vt* - **1.** [por una emergencia - edificio, personas] to evacuate - **2.** [por la fuerza - suj: policía, ejército] to clear; [- inquilinos etc] to evict - **3.** [por propia voluntad] to abandon, to move out of.

desamarrar *vt* to cast off.

desambientado, **da** *adj* [persona] out of place.

desamor *sm* [falta de afecto] indifference, coldness; [odio] dislike.

desamortización *sf* disentailment, alienation.

desamortizar [13] *vt* to disentail, to alienate.

desamparado, **da** <> *adj* [niño] helpless; [lugar] desolate, forsaken. <> *sm, f* helpless person.

desamparar *vt* to abandon.

desamparo *sm* [abandono] abandonment; [aflicción] helplessness.

desandar [52] *vt* to go back over; **desandar lo andado** to retrace one's steps.

desangelado, **da** *adj* [casa, habitación] dull, uninspiring.

desangrar *vt* - **1.** [animal, persona] to bleed - **2.** *fig* [económicamente] to bleed dry.

◆ **desangrarse** *vprnl* to lose a lot of blood.

desanimado, **da** *adj* - **1.** [persona] downhearted - **2.** [fiesta, lugar] quiet, lifeless.

desanimar *vt* to discourage.

◆ **desanimarse** *vprnl* to get downhearted o discouraged.

desánimo *sm* [gen] dejection; [depresión] depression.

desanudar *vt* to untie.

desapacible *adj* unpleasant.

desaparecer [30] *vi* - **1.** [gen] to disappear - **2.** [en guerra, accidente] to go missing.

desaparecido, **da** *sm, f* missing person.

desaparición *sf* disappearance.

desapasionado, **da** *adj* dispassionate.

desapego *sm* indifference.

desapercibido, **da** *adj*: **pasar desapercibido** to go unnoticed.

desaprensión *sf* unscrupulousness.

desaprensivo, **va** *sm, f* unscrupulous person.

desaprobación *sf* disapproval.

desaprobar [23] *vt* [gen] to disapprove of; [un plan etc] to reject.

desaprovechado, **da** *adj* - **1.** [estudiante] lacking in application, idle - **2.** [tiempo, ocasión] wasted; [casa, jardín] not properly used.

desaprovechamiento *sm* - **1.** [de estudiante] lack of application, idleness - **2.** [de tiempo, ocasión] waste; [de casa, jardín] failure to exploit fully.

desaprovechar *vt* to waste.

desarmador *sm* *Méx* - **1.** [herramienta] screwdriver - **2.** [cóctel] vodka and orange.

desarmar *vt* - **1.** [gen] to disarm - **2.** [desmontar] to take apart, to dismantle.

desarme *sm* MIL disarmament; **desarme nuclear** nuclear disarmament.

desarraigar [16] *vt* - **1.** [vicio, costumbre] to root out - **2.** [persona, pueblo] to banish, to drive (out).

desarraigo *sm* [de árbol] uprooting; [de vicio, costumbre] rooting out; [de persona, pueblo] banishment.

desarreglado, **da** *adj* [cuarto, armario, persona] untidy; [vida] disorganized.

desarreglar vt [armario, pelo] to mess up; [planes, horario] to upset.

desarreglo sm [de cuarto, persona] untidiness; [de vida] disorder.

desarrollado, da adj developed.

desarrollar vt - **1.** [mejorar - crecimiento, país] to develop - **2.** [exponer - teoría, tema, fórmula] to expound, to explain - **3.** [realizar - actividad, trabajo] to carry out - **4.** MAT to expand.
 ◆ **desarrollarse** vprnl - **1.** [crecer, mejorar] to develop - **2.** [suceder - reunión] to take place; [- película] to be set.

desarrollismo sm policy of development at all costs.

desarrollo sm - **1.** [mejora] development; **países en vías de desarrollo** developing countries - **2.** [crecimiento] growth, development - **3.** [de idea, argumento, acontecimiento] development.

desarticulación sf - **1.** [de huesos] dislocation - **2.** fig [de organización, banda] breaking up.

desarticular vt - **1.** [huesos] to dislocate - **2.** fig [organización, banda] to break up; [plan] to foil.

desaseado, da adj [sucio] dirty; [desarreglado] untidy.

desasosegar [35] vt to disturb, to make uneasy.
 ◆ **desasosegarse** vprnl to become uneasy.

desasosiego sm - **1.** [mal presentimiento] unease - **2.** [nerviosismo] restlessness.

desastrado, da adj [desaseado] scruffy; [sucio] dirty.

desastre sm disaster; **su madre es un desastre** her mother is hopeless; **¡vaya desastre!** what a shambles!; **desastre natural** natural disaster.

desastroso, sa adj disastrous.

desatar vt - **1.** [nudo, lazo] to untie; [paquete] to undo; [animal] to unleash - **2.** fig [tormenta, iras, pasión] to unleash; [entusiasmo] to arouse; [lengua] to loosen.
 ◆ **desatarse** vprnl - **1.** [nudo, lazo] to come undone - **2.** fig [desencadenarse - tormenta] to break; [- ira, cólera] to erupt.

desatascar [10] vt to unblock.

desatención sf [falta de atención] lack of attention; [descortesía] discourtesy, impoliteness.

desatender [20] vt - **1.** [obligación, persona] to neglect - **2.** [ruegos, consejos] to ignore.

desatento, ta adj - **1.** [distraído] inattentive - **2.** [descortés] impolite.

desatino sm - **1.** [locura] foolishness - **2.** [desacierto] foolish act.

desatrancar [10] vt [puerta, ventana] to unbolt; [tubería] to unblock.

desautorizar [13] vt - **1.** [desmentir - noticia] to deny - **2.** [prohibir - manifestación, huelga] to ban - **3.** [desacreditar] to discredit.

desavenencia sf [desacuerdo] friction, tension; [riña] quarrel.

desavenirse [75] vprnl to fall out.

desayunar <> vi to have breakfast. <> vt to have for breakfast.

desayuno sm breakfast; **desayuno continental** continental breakfast; **desayuno de trabajo** working breakfast.

desazón sf unease, anxiety.

desbancar [10] vt fig [ocupar el puesto de] to oust, to replace.

desbandada sf breaking up, scattering; **a la desbandada** in great disorder.

desbandarse vprnl to scatter.

desbarajuste sm disorder, confusion; **¡vaya desbarajuste!** what a mess!

desbaratar vt to ruin, to wreck.

desbarrar vi to talk nonsense.

desbloquear vt [cuenta] to unfreeze; [país] to lift the blockade on; [negociación] to end the deadlock in.

desbocado, da adj - **1.** [caballo] runaway - **2.** [prenda de vestir] stretched around the neck.

desbocarse [10] vprnl [caballo] to bolt.

desbole sm R Dom fam mess, chaos.

desbordamiento sm [de río] overflowing.

desbordar vt - **1.** [cauce, ribera] to overflow, to burst - **2.** [límites, previsiones] to exceed; [paciencia] to push beyond the limit - **3.** [contrario, defensa] to get past, to pass.
 ◆ **desbordar de** vi to overflow with.
 ◆ **desbordarse** vprnl - **1.** [líquido]: **desbordarse (de)** to overflow (from) - **2.** [río] to overflow - **3.** fig [sentimiento] to erupt.

descabalgar [16] vi to dismount.

descabellado, da adj crazy.

descabellar vt TAUROM to give the coup de grâce to.

descabezar [13] vt - **1.** [quitar la cabeza a - persona] to behead; [- cosa] to break the head off - **2.** [quitar la punta a - planta, árbol] to top.

descacharrar vt fam to smash up.

descafeinado, da adj - **1.** [sin cafeína] decaffeinated - **2.** fig [sin fuerza] watered down.
 ◆ **descafeinado** sm decaffeinated coffee.

descafeinar vt - **1.** [quitar cafeína] to decaffeinate - **2.** fig [quitar fuerza a] to water down.

descalabrar vt - **1.** [herir] to wound in the head - **2.** fam fig [perjudicar] to harm, to damage.
 ◆ **descalabrarse** vprnl to hurt one's head.

descalabro sm setback, damage (U).

descalcificar [10] *vt* to decalcify.
◆ **descalcificarse** *vprnl* to decalcify.

descalificar [10] *vt* - **1.** [en una competición] to disqualify - **2.** [desprestigiar] to discredit.

descalzar [13] *vt*: **descalzar a alguien** to take sb's shoes off.
◆ **descalzarse** *vprnl* to take off one's shoes.

descalzo, za *adj* barefoot.

descaminado, da *adj* - **1.** *fig* [equivocado]: **andar** o **ir descaminado** to be on the wrong track - **2.** [caminante, excursionista] heading in the wrong direction.

descaminar *vt* [suj: malas compañías] to lead astray; [suj: guía] to take the wrong way.
◆ **descaminarse** *vprnl* [por malas compañías] to go astray; [en una excursión] to go the wrong way.

descamisado, da <> *adj* - **1.** [sin camisa] barechested - **2.** *fig* [pobre] wretched. <> *sm, f* poor wretch.

descampado *sm* open country.

descansar <> *vi* - **1.** [reposar] to rest - **2.** [dormir] to sleep; **¡que descanses!** sleep well! - **3.** *fig* [viga, teoría etc]: **descansar en** to rest on - **4.** [estar enterrado]: **descanse en paz** rest in peace; **aquí descansan las víctimas de la guerra** here lie the victims of the war. <> *vt* - **1.** to rest; **descansar la vista** to rest one's eyes; **descansa la cabeza en mi hombro** rest your head on my shoulder - **2.** [dormir] to sleep - **3.** *fig* [viga, teoría etc]: **descansar en** to rest on.

descansillo *sm* landing.

descanso *sm* - **1.** [reposo] rest; **tomarse un descanso** to take a rest; **día de descanso** day off - **2.** [pausa] break; CINE & TEATRO interval; DEP half-time, interval - **3.** *fig* [alivio] relief - **4.** [calzado] *boot worn after skiing* - **5.** MIL: **adoptar la posición de descanso** to stand at ease.

descapitalizar [13] *vt* COM to undercapitalize.
◆ **descapitalizarse** *vprnl* to be undercapitalized.

descapotable *adj* & *sm* convertible.

descarado, da <> *adj* - **1.** [desvergonzado - persona] cheeky, impertinent - **2.** [flagrante - intento etc] barefaced, blatant; **¡es un robo descarado!** it's daylight robbery! <> *sm, f* cheeky devil.

descarga *sf* - **1.** [de mercancías] unloading - **2.** [de electricidad] shock - **3.** [disparo] firing, shots *pl* - **4.** INFORM download.

descargar [16] <> *vt* - **1.** [vaciar - mercancías, pistola] to unload - **2.** [disparar - munición, arma, ráfaga]: **descargar (sobre)** to fire (at) - **3.** [puntapié, puñetazo] to deal, to land - **4.** ELECTR to run down - **5.** [exonerar]: **descargar a alguien de**

algo to free o release sb from sthg - **6.** DER [absolver]: **descargar a alguien de algo** to clear sb of sthg. <> *vi* to burst; [tormenta] to break.
◆ **descargarse** *vprnl* - **1.** [desahogarse]: **descargarse con alguien** to take it out on sb - **2.** DER: **descargarse (de)** to clear oneself (of) - **3.** ELECTR to go flat.

descargo *sm* - **1.** [excusa]: **descargo a** argument against - **2.** DER defence; **en su descargo** in his/her defence - **3.** [COM - de deuda] discharge; [- recibo] receipt.

descarnado, da *adj* - **1.** [descripción] brutal - **2.** [persona, animal] scrawny.

descaro *sm* cheek, impertinence.

descarriarse [9] *vprnl* - **1.** [ovejas, ganado] to stray - **2.** *fig* [pervertirse] to lose one's way, to go astray.

descarrilamiento *sm* derailment.

descarrilar *vi* to be derailed.

descartar *vt* [ayuda] to refuse, to reject; [posibilidad] to rule out.
◆ **descartarse** *vprnl*: **descartarse (de)** to discard.

descarte *sm* [de naipes] discard.

descendencia *sf* - **1.** [hijos] offspring; **morir sin descendencia** to die without issue - **2.** [linaje] lineage, descent.

descendente *adj* [gen] descending; [movimiento, posición] downward.

descender [20] *vi* - **1.** [en estimación] to go down; **descender a segunda** to be relegated to the second division - **2.** [cantidad, valor, temperatura, nivel] to fall, to drop.
◆ **descender de** *vi* - **1.** [avión] to get off - **2.** [linaje] to be descended from.

descenso *sm* - **1.** [en el espacio] descent - **2.** [de cantidad, valor, temperatura, nivel] drop - **3.** [en esquí] downhill - **4.** [en fútbol etc] relegation.

descentrado, da *adj* - **1.** [geométricamente] off-centre - **2.** [mentalmente] unsettled, disorientated.

descentralización *sf* decentralization.

descentralizar [13] *vt* to decentralize.

descentrar *vt* - **1.** [sacar del centro] to knock off-centre - **2.** *fig* [desconcentrar] to distract.

descienda *etc* ⊳ **descender**.

descifrable *adj* [mensaje, jeroglífico] decipherable; [letra] legible.

descifrar *vt* - **1.** [clave, mensaje] to decipher - **2.** [motivos, intenciones] to work out; [misterio] to solve; [problemas] to puzzle out.

descodificador, decodificador *sm* decoder.

descodificar, decodificar [10] *vt* to decode.

descojonarse *vprnl vulg*: **descojonarse (de)** to piss oneself laughing (at).

descolgar [39] *vt* - **1.** [una cosa colgada] to take down - **2.** [teléfono] to pick up, to take off the hook.
  descolgarse *vprnl* - **1.** [bajar]: **descolgarse (por algo)** to let oneself down o to slide down (sthg) - **2.** DEP: **descolgarse de** to break away from - **3.** *fam* [mencionar]: **descolgarse con que** to come out with the idea that.

descollar *vi fig* [sobresalir] to stand out.

descolonización *sf* decolonization.

descolonizar [13] *vt* to decolonize.

descolorido, da *adj* faded.

descomedido, da *adj* excessive, uncontrollable.

descompasado, da *adj* excessive, uncontrollable.

descompensación *sf* imbalance.

descompensar *vt* to unbalance.

descomponer [65] *vt* - **1.** [pudrir - fruta] to rot; [- cadáver] to decompose - **2.** [dividir] to break down; **descomponer algo en** to break sthg down into - **3.** [desordenar] to mess up - **4.** [estropear] to damage, to break - **5.** *fig* [enojar] to annoy.
  descomponerse *vprnl* - **1.** [pudrirse - fruta] to rot; [- cadáver] to decompose - **2.** [irritarse] to get annoyed - **3.** [averiarse] to break down.

descomposición *sf* - **1.** [de elementos] decomposition - **2.** [putrefacción - de fruta] rotting; [- de cadáver] decomposition - **3.** [alteración] distortion - **4.** [diarrea] diarrhoea.

descompostura *sf* - **1.** [falta de mesura] lack of respect, rudeness - **2.** *Méx & R Dom* [avería] breakdown - **3.** *Amér* [malestar] sickness - **4.** *Amér* [diarrea] diarrhoea - **5.** *Méx & R Plata* [avería] breakdown.

descompresión *sf* decompression.

descompuesto, ta ⬦ *pp* ▷ **descomponer**. ⬦ *adj* - **1.** [putrefacto - fruta] rotten; [- cadáver] decomposed - **2.** [alterado - rostro] distorted, twisted - **3.** *Méx & R Plata* [mecanismo, máquina] broken, broken down.

descomunal *adj* tremendous, enormous.

desconcentrar *vt* to distract.
  desconcentrarse *vprnl* to get distracted.

desconcertante *adj* disconcerting.

desconcertar [19] *vt* to disconcert, to throw.
  desconcertarse *vprnl* to be thrown o bewildered.

desconchado *sm* [de pintura] peeling paint; [de enyesado] peeling plaster.

desconchar *vt* to chip.
  desconcharse *vprnl* [pintura] to flake off; [pared, loza] to chip.

desconcierto *sm* [desorden] disorder; [desorientación, confusión] confusion.

desconectar *vt* [aparato] to switch off; [línea] to disconnect; [desenchufar] to unplug.
  desconectarse *vprnl fig* [aislarse, olvidarse] to forget about one's worries; **desconectarse de algo** to shut sthg out, to forget (about) sthg.

desconfiado, da ⬦ *adj* distrustful. ⬦ *sm, f* distrustful person.

desconfianza *sf* distrust.

desconfiar [9] ▬ **desconfiar de** *vi* - **1.** [sospechar de] to distrust; **desconfía de él** don't trust him - **2.** [no confiar en] to have no faith in.

descongelar *vt* - **1.** [producto] to thaw; [nevera] to defrost - **2.** *fig* [precios] to free; [créditos, salarios] to unfreeze.

descongestionar *vt* - **1.** MED to clear - **2.** *fig* [calle, centro de ciudad] to make less congested; **descongestionar el tráfico** to reduce congestion.

desconocer [31] *vt* [ignorar] not to know.

desconocido, da ⬦ *adj* - **1.** [no conocido] unknown - **2.** [muy cambiado]: **estar desconocido** to have changed beyond all recognition. ⬦ *sm, f* stranger.

desconocimiento *sm* ignorance, lack of knowledge.

desconsideración *sf* thoughtlessness.

desconsiderado, da ⬦ *adj* thoughtless, inconsiderate. ⬦ *sm, f* thoughtless o inconsiderate person.

desconsolado, da *adj* disconsolate.

desconsolar [23] *vt* to distress.

desconsuelo *sm* distress, grief.

descontado, da *adj* discounted.
  por descontado *loc adv* obviously, needless to say; **dar algo por descontado** to take sthg for granted.

descontar [23] *vt* - **1.** [una cantidad] to deduct - **2.** COM to discount.

descontentar *vt* to upset, to make unhappy.

descontento, ta *adj* unhappy, dissatisfied.
  descontento *sm* dissatisfaction.

descontrol *sm* lack of control.

descontrolarse *vprnl* [coche, inflación] to go out of control; [persona] to lose control.

desconvocar [10] *vt* to cancel, to call off.

descorazonador, ra *adj* discouraging.

descorazonamiento *sm* discouragement.

descorazonar *vt* to discourage.
  descorazonarse *vprnl* to be discouraged, to lose heart.

descorchar *vt* to uncork.

descorrer *vt* - **1.** [cortinas] to draw back, to open - **2.** [cerrojo, pestillo] to draw back.

descortés *adj* rude.

descortesía *sf* discourtesy.

descoser *vt* to unstitch.

➻ **descoserse** *vprnl* to come unstitched.

descosido, da *adj* unstitched.

➻ **descosido** *sm* [roto - a propósito] open seam; [- por accidente] tear; **como un descosido** [- hablar] endlessly, non-stop; [- beber, comer] to excess; [- gritar] wildly.

descoyuntar *vt* to dislocate.

➻ **descoyuntarse** *vprnl* to dislocate; **descoyuntarse de risa** *fam* to split one's sides laughing.

descrédito *sm* discredit; **ir en descrédito de algo/alguien** to count against sthg/sb; **estar en descrédito** to be discredited.

descreído, da *sm, f* non-believer, disbeliever.

descremado, da *adj* skimmed.

descremar *vt* to skim.

describir *vt* to describe.

descripción *sf* description.

descriptivo, va *adj* descriptive.

descrito, ta *pp* ▷ **describir**.

descuajaringar [16] *vt* to break into pieces.

➻ **descuajaringarse** *vprnl* - **1.** [descomponerse] to fall apart o to pieces - **2.** [troncharse de risa] to fall about laughing.

descuartizar [13] *vt* [persona] to quarter; [res] to carve up.

descubierto, ta ◇ *pp* ▷ **descubrir**. ◇ *adj* - **1.** [gen] uncovered; [coche] open - **2.** [cielo] clear - **3.** [sin sombrero] bareheaded.

➻ **descubierto** *sm* [FIN - de empresa] deficit; [- de cuenta bancaria] overdraft.

➻ **al descubierto** *loc adv* - **1.** [al raso] in the open - **2.** BANCA overdrawn; **quedar al descubierto** *fig* to be exposed o uncovered.

➻ **en descubierto** *loc adv* BANCA overdrawn.

descubridor, ra *sm, f* discoverer.

descubrimiento *sm* - **1.** [de continentes, invenciones] discovery - **2.** [de placa, busto] unveiling - **3.** [de complots] uncovering; [de asesinos] detection.

descubrir *vt* - **1.** [gen] to discover; [petróleo] to strike; [complot] to uncover - **2.** [destapar - estatua, placa] to unveil - **3.** [vislumbrar] to spot, to spy - **4.** [delatar] to give away.

➻ **descubrirse** *vprnl* - **1.** [quitarse el sombrero] to take one's hat off; **descubrirse ante algo** *fig* to take one's hat off to sthg - **2.** [cielo, horizonte] to clear.

descuelga *etc* ▷ **descolgar**.

descuenta *etc* ▷ **descontar**.

descuento *sm* discount; **hacer descuento** to give a discount; **con descuento** at a discount; **un descuento del 10%** a 10% discount.

descuerar *vt* Chile to slam, to criticize.

descuidado, da *adj* - **1.** [desaseado - persona, aspecto] untidy; [- jardín] neglected - **2.** [negligente] careless - **3.** [distraído] off one's guard.

descuidar ◇ *vt* [desatender] to neglect. ◇ *vi* [no preocuparse] not to worry; **descuida, que yo me encargo** don't worry, I'll take care of it.

➻ **descuidarse** *vprnl* - **1.** [abandonarse] to neglect one's appearance; **descuidarse de algo/ de hacer algo** to neglect sthg/to do sthg - **2.** [despistarse] not to be careful.

descuido *sm* - **1.** [falta de aseo] carelessness - **2.** [olvido] oversight; [error] slip; **al menor descuido** if you let your attention wander for even a moment; **en un descuido** by mistake.

desde *prep* - **1.** [tiempo] since; **no lo veo desde el mes pasado/desde ayer** I haven't seen him since last month/yesterday; **desde ahora** from now on; **desde hace mucho/un mes** for ages/a month; **desde... hasta...** from... until...; **desde el lunes hasta el viernes** from Monday till Friday; **desde entonces** since then; **desde que** since; **desde que murió mi madre** since my mother died; **desde ya** [inmediatamente] right now - **2.** [espacio] from; **desde... hasta...** from... to...; **desde aquí hasta el centro** from here to the centre.

➻ **desde luego** *loc adv* - **1.** [por supuesto] of course - **2.** [en tono de reproche] for goodness' sake!; **¡desde luego tienes cada idea!** you really come out with some funny ideas!

desdecir [66] ➻ **desdecir de** *vi* [desmerecer] to be unworthy of; [no cuadrar con] not to go with, to clash with. ➻ **desdecirse** *vprnl* to go back on one's word; **desdecirse de** to go back on.

desdén *sm* disdain, scorn.

desdentado, da *adj* toothless.

desdeñable *adj* contemptible; **una cantidad nada desdeñable** a considerable amount.

desdeñar *vt* to scorn.

desdeñoso, sa *adj* scornful, disdainful.

desdibujado, da *adj* blurred.

desdibujarse *vprnl* to blur, to become blurred.

desdice ▷ **desdecir**.

desdicha *sf* [desgracia - situación] misery; [- suceso] misfortune; **por desdicha** unfortunately.

desdichado, da ◇ *adj* [decisión, situación] unfortunate; [persona - sin suerte] unlucky; [- sin felicidad] unhappy. ◇ *sm, f* poor wretch.

desdicho, cha *pp* ▷ **desdecir**.

desdienta *etc* ▷ **desdentar**.

desdiga, desdijera *etc* ▷ **desdecir**.

desdoblamiento *sm* - **1.** [de objeto] unfolding - **2.** [de imagen, personalidad] splitting.

desdoblar *vt* - **1.** [servilleta, carta] to unfold; [alambre] to straighten out - **2.** *fig* [dividir] to split.

desdramatizar [13] *vt* to play down.

deseable *adj* desirable.

desear *vt* - **1.** [querer] to want; [anhelar] to wish; **¿qué desea?** [en tienda] what can I do for you?; **desearía estar allí** I wish I was there; **estoy deseando que llegue** I can't wait for her to arrive; **dejar mucho/no dejar nada que desear** to leave much/nothing to be desired - **2.** [sexualmente] to desire.

desecar [10] *vt* to dry out.

➤ **desecarse** *vprnl* to dry out.

desechable *adj* disposable.

desechar *vt* - **1.** [tirar - ropa, piezas] to throw out, to discard - **2.** [rechazar - ayuda, oferta] to refuse, to turn down - **3.** [desestimar - idea] to reject; [- plan, proyecto] to drop - **4.** to ignore, to take no notice of.

desecho *sm* - **1.** [objeto usado] unwanted object; [ropa] castoff; **material de desecho** [gen] waste products *pl*; [metal] scrap - **2.** [escoria] dregs *pl*.

➤ **desechos** *smpl* [basura] rubbish *(U)*; [residuos] waste products; **desechos radiactivos** radioactive waste *(U)*.

desembalar *vt* to unpack.

desembarazar [13] *vt* to clear.

➤ **desembarazarse** *vprnl*: **desembarazarse de** to get rid of.

desembarazo *sm* ease.

desembarcadero *sm* pier, landing stage.

desembarcar [10] ➤ *vt* [pasajeros] to disembark; [mercancías] to unload. ➤ *vi* - **1.** [de barco, avión] to disembark - **2.** *Amér* [de autobús, tren] to get off.

➤ **desembarcarse** *vprnl Amér* to get off.

desembarco *sm* - **1.** [de pasajeros] disembarkation - **2.** MIL landing.

desembarque *sm* [de mercancías] unloading.

desembarrancar [10] *vt* to refloat.

desembocadura *sf* [de río] mouth; [de calle] opening.

desembocar [10] ➤ **desembocar en** *vi* - **1.** [río] to flow into - **2.** [calle] to lead onto - **3.** [asunto] to lead to, to result in.

desembolsar *vt* to pay out.

desembolso *sm* payment; **desembolso inicial** down payment.

desembozar [13] *vt* - **1.** [rostro] to unmask, to uncover - **2.** [cañería] to unblock.

desembragar [16] *vi* AUTO to disengage the clutch, to declutch.

desembrollar *vt fam* [lío, malentendido] to straighten out; [ovillo] to disentangle.

desembuchar *vi fam* to spit it out; **¡desembucha!** spit it out!, out with it!

desempacar [10] *vt* to unpack.

desempalmar *vt* to disconnect.

desempañar *vt* [con trapo etc] to wipe the steam off; [electrónicamente] to demist.

desempaquetar *vt* [paquete] to unwrap; [caja] to unpack.

desempatar *vi* to decide the contest; **jugar para desempatar** to have a play-off.

desempate *sm* final result; **partido de desempate** decider.

desempeñar *vt* - **1.** [función, misión] to carry out; [cargo, puesto] to hold - **2.** [papel] to play - **3.** [joyas] to redeem.

➤ **desempeñarse** *vprnl* to get oneself out of debt.

desempeño *sm* - **1.** [de función] carrying out - **2.** [de papel] performance - **3.** [de objeto] redemption.

desempleado, da ◇ *adj* unemployed. ◇ *sm, f* unemployed person.

desempleo *sm* - **1.** [falta de empleo] unemployment - **2.** [subsidio] unemployment benefit; **cobrar el desempleo** to receive unemployment benefit.

desempolvar *vt* - **1.** [mueble, jarrón] to dust - **2.** *fig* [recuerdos] to revive.

desencadenar *vt* - **1.** [preso, perro] to unchain - **2.** *fig* [suceso, polémica] to give rise to, to spark off; [pasión, furia] to unleash.

➤ **desencadenarse** *vprnl* - **1.** [pasiones, odios, conflicto] to erupt; [guerra] to break out - **2.** [viento] to blow up; [tormenta] to burst; [terremoto] to strike.

desencajar *vt* - **1.** [mecanismo, piezas - sin querer] to knock out of place; [- intencionadamente] to take apart - **2.** [hueso] to dislocate.

➤ **desencajarse** *vprnl* - **1.** [piezas] to come apart - **2.** [rostro] to distort, to become distorted.

desencantar *vt* [decepcionar] to disappoint.

➤ **desencantarse** *vprnl* to be disappointed.

desencanto *sm* disappointment.

desencapotarse *vprnl* to clear.

desenchufar *vt* to unplug.

desenfadado, da *adj* [persona, conducta] relaxed, easy-going; [comedia, programa de TV] light-hearted; [estilo] light; [en el vestir] casual.

desenfado *sm* [seguridad en sí mismo] self-assurance; [desenvoltura] ease; [desparpajo] forwardness, uninhibited nature.

desenfocado, da *adj* [imagen] out of focus; [visión] blurred.

desenfocar [10] *vt* [objeto] to focus incorrectly; [foto] to take out of focus.

desenfrenado, da *adj* [ritmo, baile] frantic, frenzied; [comportamiento] uncontrolled; [apetito] insatiable.

desenfrenar *vt* [coche] to take the brake off; [caballo] to unbridle.

◆ **desenfrenarse** *vprnl* [persona] to lose one's self-control.

desenfreno *sm* **- 1.** [gen] lack of restraint **- 2.** [vicio] debauchery.

desenfundar *vt* **- 1.** [pistola] to draw **- 2.** [mueble] to uncover.

desenganchar *vt* **- 1.** [vagón] to uncouple **- 2.** [caballo] to unhitch **- 3.** [pelo, jersey] to free.

◆ **desengancharse** *vprnl fam* [de un vicio] to kick the habit.

desengañado, da *adj*: desengañado (de) disillusioned (with).

desengañar *vt* **- 1.** [a persona equivocada]: **desengañar a alguien** to reveal the truth to sb **- 2.** [a persona esperanzada] to disillusion.

◆ **desengañarse** *vprnl*: desengañarse (de) to become disillusioned (with); **desengáñate** stop kidding yourself.

desengaño *sm* disappointment; **llevarse un desengaño con alguien** to be disappointed in sb; **desengaño amoroso** unhappy affair.

desengrasar *vt* to remove the grease from.

desenlace *sm* denouement, ending.

desenlazar [13] *vt* to undo.

desenmarañar *vt* **- 1.** [ovillo, pelo] to untangle **- 2.** *fig* [asunto] to sort out; [problema] to resolve.

desenmascarar *vt* [descubrir] to unmask.

desenredar *vt* **- 1.** [hilos, pelo] to untangle **- 2.** *fig* [asunto] to sort out; [problema] to resolve.

◆ **desenredarse** *vprnl*: desenredarse (de algo) to extricate oneself (from sthg); **desenredarse el pelo** to unknot one's hair.

desenrollar *vt* [hilo, cinta] to unwind; [persiana] to roll down; [pergamino, papel] to unroll.

desenroscar [10] *vt* to unscrew.

desensillar *vt* to unsaddle.

desentenderse [20] *vprnl* to pretend not to hear/know *etc*; **desentenderse de** to refuse to have anything to do with.

desenterrar [19] *vt* **- 1.** [cadáver] to disinter; [tesoro, escultura] to dig up **- 2.** *fig* [recordar]: **desenterrar algo (de)** to recall *o* revive sthg (from).

desentonar *vi* **- 1.** [MÚS - cantante] to sing out of tune; [- instrumento] to be out of tune **- 2.** [color, cortinas, edificio]: **desentonar (con)** to clash (with) **- 3.** [persona, modales] to be out of place.

desentrañar *vt* to unravel, to figure out.

desentrenado, da *adj* [bajo de forma] out of training; [falto de práctica] out of practice.

desentubar *vt fam*: **desentubar a alguien** to switch off sb's life-support machine.

desentumecer [30] *vt* to stretch.

◆ **desentumecerse** *vprnl* to loosen up.

desenvainar *vt* to draw.

desenvoltura *sf* [al moverse, comportarse] ease; [al hablar] fluency.

desenvolver [24] *vt* to unwrap.

◆ **desenvolverse** *vprnl* **- 1.** [asunto, proceso] to progress; [trama] to unfold **- 2.** [persona] to cope, to manage.

desenvuelto, ta ◇ *pp* ▷ desenvolver. ◇ *adj* [al moverse, comportarse] natural; [al hablar] fluent.

deseo *sm* **- 1.** [anhelo] wish, desire; **su deseo se hizo realidad** her wish came true; **arder en deseos de hacer algo** to be burning with desire to do sthg; **buenos deseos** good intentions; **pedir un deseo** to make a wish **- 2.** [apetito sexual] desire.

deseoso, sa *adj*: **estar deseoso de algo/hacer algo** to long for sthg/to do sthg.

deseque *etc* ▷ desecar.

desequilibrado, da ◇ *adj* **- 1.** [persona] unbalanced **- 2.** [balanza, eje] off-centre. ◇ *sm, f* unbalanced person.

desequilibrar *vt* **- 1.** [persona] to unbalance **- 2.** [objeto] to knock off balance.

◆ **desequilibrarse** *vprnl* **- 1.** [persona] to become mentally unbalanced *o* unstable **- 2.** [objeto] to lose its balance.

desequilibrio *sm* [mecánico] lack of balance; [mental] mental instability.

deserción *sf* desertion.

desertar *vi* to desert.

desértico, ca *adj* [del desierto] desert *(antes de s)*; [despoblado] deserted.

desertización *sf* [del terreno] desertification; [de la población] depopulation.

desertor, ra *sm, f* deserter.

desescolarización *sf* lack of schooling.

desesperación *sf* **- 1.** [falta de esperanza] despair, desperation; **con desesperación** in despair **- 2.** *fig* [enojo]: **es una desesperación lo lento que van los trenes** it's maddening how slowly the trains go.

desesperado, da *adj* [persona, intento] desperate; [estado, situación] hopeless; [esfuerzo] furious; **(hacer algo) a la desesperada** (to do sthg) in desperation.

desesperante *adj* infuriating.

desesperar ◇ *vt* to exasperate, to drive mad. ◇ *vi* to despair, to give up *o* lose hope.

➤ **desesperarse** *vprnl* - **1.** [perder la esperanza] to be driven to despair - **2.** [irritarse, enojarse] to get mad *o* exasperated.

desestabilizar [13] *vt* to destabilize.

desestatización *sf* Amér privatization.

desestatizar *vt* Amér to privatize, to sell off.

desestimar *vt* - **1.** [rechazar] to turn down - **2.** [despreciar] to turn one's nose up at.

desfachatez *sf* fam cheek.

desfalcar [10] *vt* to embezzle.

desfalco *sm* embezzlement.

desfallecer [30] *vi* - **1.** [debilitarse] to be exhausted; **desfallecer de** to feel faint from - **2.** [desmayarse] to faint.

desfallecimiento *sm* - **1.** [desmayo] fainting fit - **2.** [debilidad] faintness.

desfasado, da *adj* [persona] out of touch; [libro, moda] out of date.

desfasar *vt* ELECTR to phase out; **estar desfasado** *fig* to be out of touch.

desfase *sm* [diferencia] gap; **desfase horario** jet lag.

desfavorable *adj* unfavourable.

desfavorecer [30] *vt* - **1.** [perjudicar] to go against the interest of - **2.** [sentar mal] not to suit.

desfiguración *sf* [de rostro, cuerpo] disfigurement; [de la verdad] distortion.

desfigurar *vt* - **1.** [rostro, cuerpo] to disfigure - **2.** *fig* [la verdad] to distort.

desfiladero *sm* narrow mountain pass.

desfilar *vi* - **1.** MIL to parade - **2.** *fig* [marcharse] to head off, to leave.

desfile *sm* MIL parade; [de carrozas] procession; **desfile de modelos** fashion show.

desflorar *vt* to deflower.

desfogar [16] *vt* to vent.

➤ **desfogarse** *vprnl* to let off steam.

desfondar *vt* - **1.** [caja, bolsa] to knock the bottom out of - **2.** [agotar] to wear out.

➤ **desfondarse** *vprnl* [persona] to become completely exhausted.

desforestación *sf* deforestation.

desforestar *vt* to deforest.

desgajar *vt* [página] to tear out; [rama] to break off; [libro, periódico] to rip up; [naranja] to split into segments.

➤ **desgajarse** *vprnl* [rama] to break off; [hoja] to fall.

desgana *sf* - **1.** [falta de hambre] lack of appetite - **2.** [falta de ánimo] lack of enthusiasm; **con desgana** unwillingly, reluctantly.

desganado, da *adj* - **1.** [sin apetito]: **estar desganado** to be off one's food - **2.** [sin ganas] listless, apathetic.

desgañitarse *vprnl* to scream oneself hoarse.

desgarbado, da *adj* clumsy, ungainly.

desgarrador, ra *adj* harrowing.

desgarrar *vt* to rip; **desgarrar el corazón** to break one's heart.

➤ **desgarrarse** *vprnl* to rip.

desgarro *sm* tear.

desgarrón *sm* big tear.

desgastar *vt* to wear out.

➤ **desgastarse** *vprnl* to wear o.s. out.

desgaste *sm* - **1.** [de tela, muebles etc] wear and tear; [de roca] erosion; [de pilas] running down; [de cuerdas] fraying; [de metal] corrosion - **2.** [de persona] wear and tear; **desgaste político** erosion of voter confidence.

desglosar *vt* to break down.

desglose *sm* breakdown.

desgobernar [19] *vt* [país] to govern badly.

desgobierno *sm* [de país] misgovernment, misrule.

desgracia *sf* - **1.** [mala suerte] misfortune; **por desgracia** unfortunately; **tener la desgracia de** to be unfortunate enough to - **2.** [catástrofe] disaster; **desgracias personales** casualties; **es una desgracia que...** it's a terrible shame that... - **3.** *loc*: **caer en desgracia** to fall into disgrace; **las desgracias nunca vienen solas** it never rains but it pours.

desgraciadamente *adv* unfortunately.

desgraciado, da ⬦ *adj* - **1.** [gen] unfortunate - **2.** [sin suerte] unlucky - **3.** [infeliz] unhappy. ⬦ *sm, f* - **1.** [persona sin suerte] born loser - **2.** *fig* [pobre infeliz] miserable wretch.

desgraciar [8] *vt* to spoil.

➤ **desgraciarse** *vprnl* [plan, proyecto] to be a complete disaster, to fall through.

desgranar *vt* - **1.** [insultos, frases, oraciones] to spout, to come out with - **2.** [maíz, trigo] to thresh.

desgravable *adj* tax-deductible.

desgravación *sf* deduction; **desgravación fiscal** tax deduction, tax relief (*U*).

desgravar *vt* to deduct from one's tax bill.

desgreñado, da *adj* dishevelled.

desguace *sm* [de coches] scrapping; [de buques] breaking.

desguarnecer [30] *vt* - **1.** [quitar los adornos de] to strip - **2.** MIL to leave unprotected *o* without troops.

desguazar [13] *vt* [coche] to scrap; [buque] to break up.

deshabitado, da *adj* uninhabited.

deshabitar *vt* - **1.** [casa] to leave - **2.** [territorio] to depopulate, to empty of people.

deshabituar [6] *vt*: deshabituar a alguien **(de)** to get sb out of the habit (of).

  deshabituarse *vprnl*: deshabituarse **(de)** to break the habit (of).

deshacer [60] *vt* - **1.** [costura, nudo, paquete] to undo; [maleta] to unpack; [castillo de arena] to destroy - **2.** [disolver - helado, mantequilla] to melt; [- pastilla, terrón de azúcar] to dissolve - **3.** [poner fin a - contrato, negocio] to cancel; [- pacto, tratado] to break; [- plan, intriga] to foil; [- organización] to dissolve - **4.** [destruir - enemigo] to rout; [- matrimonio] to ruin - **5.** INFORM to undo - **6.** *fig* [afligir] to devastate.

  deshacerse *vprnl* - **1.** [desvanecerse] to disappear - **2.** [afligirse] to be devastated - **3.** *fig* [librarse]: **deshacerse de** to get rid of - **4.** *fig*: **deshacerse en algo (con o hacia alguien)** [cumplidos] to lavish sthg (on sb); [insultos] to heap sthg (on sb) - **5.** *fig*: **deshacerse por alguien** [desvivirse] to bend over backwards for sb; [estar enamorado] to be madly in love with sb.

desharrapado, da ◇ *adj* ragged. ◇ *sm, f* person dressed in rags.

deshecho, cha ◇ *pp* ▷ **deshacer**. ◇ *adj* - **1.** [costura, nudo, paquete] undone; [cama] unmade; [maleta] unpacked - **2.** [enemigo] destroyed; [tarta, matrimonio] ruined - **3.** [derretido - pastilla, terrón de azúcar] dissolved; [- helado, mantequilla] melted - **4.** [anulado - contrato, negocio] cancelled; [- pacto, tratado] broken; [- plan, intriga] foiled; [- organización] dissolved - **5.** [afligido] devastated - **6.** [cansado] tired out.

deshelar [19] *vt* [nieve, lago, hielo] to thaw, to melt; [parabrisas] to de-ice.

  deshelarse *vprnl* to thaw, to melt.

desheredado, da ◇ *adj* [excluido de herencia] disinherited; *fig* [indigente] underprivileged. ◇ *sm, f* [indigente] deprived person; **los desheredados** the underprivileged.

desheredar *vt* to disinherit.

deshice *etc* ▷ **deshacer**.

deshidratación *sf* dehydration.

deshidratar *vt* to dehydrate.

  deshidratarse *vprnl* to become dehydrated.

deshiela *etc* ▷ **deshelar**.

deshielo *sm* thaw.

deshilachar *vt* to unravel.

  deshilacharse *vprnl* to fray.

deshilar *vt* to unravel.

deshilvanado, da *adj* - **1.** [tela] untacked - **2.** *fig* [discurso, guión] disjointed.

deshilvanar *vt* to untack.

deshinchar *vt* - **1.** [globo, rueda] to let down, to deflate - **2.** [hinchazón] to reduce the swelling in.

  deshincharse *vprnl* - **1.** [globo, hinchazón] to go down; [neumático] to go flat - **2.** *fig* [desanimarse] to get off one's high horse.

deshizo ▷ **deshacer**.

deshojar *vt* [árbol] to strip the leaves off; [flor] to pull the petals off; [libro] to pull the pages out of.

  deshojarse *vprnl* [árbol] to shed its leaves; [flor] to drop its petals.

deshollinar *vt* to sweep.

deshonestidad *sf* dishonesty.

deshonesto, ta *adj* [sin honradez] dishonest; [sin pudor] indecent.

deshonor *sm* dishonour.

deshonra *sf* = **deshonor**.

deshonrar *vt* to dishonour.

  deshonrarse *vprnl* to be shamed.

deshonroso, sa *adj* dishonourable, shameful.

deshora   a deshora, a deshoras *loc adv* [en momento inoportuno] at a bad time; [en horas poco habituales] at an unearthly hour.

deshuesar *vt* [carne] to bone; [fruto] to stone.

deshumanizar [13] *vt* to dehumanize.

  deshumanizarse *vprnl* to become dehumanized, to lose one's humanity.

desidia *sf* [en el trabajo] neglect; [en el aspecto] slovenliness.

desierto, ta *adj* - **1.** [gen] deserted - **2.** [vacante - concurso] void; [- premio] deferred.

  desierto *sm* desert; **el desierto de Gobi** the Gobi Desert; **es como predicar en el desierto** it's like talking to a brick wall.

designación *sf* - **1.** [nombre] designation - **2.** [nombramiento] appointment.

designar *vt* - **1.** [nombrar] to appoint - **2.** [fijar, determinar] to name, to fix.

designio *sm* intention, plan.

desigual *adj* - **1.** [diferente] different; [terreno] uneven - **2.** [tiempo, persona, humor] changeable; [alumno, actuación] inconsistent; [lucha] unevenly matched, unequal; [tratamiento] unfair, unequal.

desigualdad *sf* [gen] inequality; [diferencia] difference; [del terreno] roughness; [de carácter] changeability; [de actuación, rendimiento] inconsistency.

desilusión *sf* disappointment, disillusionment *(U)*; **llevarse una desilusión** to be disappointed.

desilusionar *vt* [desengañar] to reveal the truth to; [decepcionar] to disappoint, to disillusion.

  desilusionarse *vprnl* [decepcionarse] to be disappointed o disillusioned; [desengañarse] to realize the truth.

desincrustar *vt* to descale.

desinencia *sf* ending.

desinfección *sf* disinfection.

desinfectante ◇ *adj* disinfectant *(antes de s)*. ◇ *sm* disinfectant.

desinfectar *vt* to disinfect.

desinflar *vt* - **1.** [quitar aire a] to let down, to deflate - **2.** *fig* [quitar importancia a] to play down - **3.** [desanimar] to depress.

◆ **desinflarse** *vprnl* - **1.** [perder aire - gen] to go down; [- neumático] to go flat - **2.** [desanimarse] to get depressed.

desinformación *sf* misinformation.

desinformar *vi* to misinform.

desinstalar *vt* INFORM uninstall.

desintegración *sf* - **1.** [de objetos] disintegration; **desintegración nuclear** nuclear fission - **2.** [de grupos, organizaciones] breaking up.

desintegrar *vt* - **1.** [objetos] to disintegrate; [átomo] to split - **2.** [grupos, organizaciones] to break up.

◆ **desintegrarse** *vprnl* - **1.** [objetos] to disintegrate - **2.** [grupos, organizaciones] to break up.

desinterés *sm* - **1.** [indiferencia] disinterest, lack of interest - **2.** [generosidad] unselfishness.

desinteresado, **da** *adj* unselfish.

desinteresarse *vprnl*: **desinteresarse de** *o* **por algo** to lose interest in sthg.

desintoxicación *sf* detoxification.

desintoxicar [10] *vt* to detoxify.

◆ **desintoxicarse** *vprnl* to detoxify oneself.

desistir *vi*: **desistir (de hacer algo)** to give up *o* to stop (doing sthg).

desleal *adj* [competencia] unfair; **desleal (con)** disloyal (to).

deslealtad *sf* disloyalty.

desleír [28] *vt* [sólido] to dissolve; [líquido] to dilute.

deslenguado, **da** *adj fig* foul-mouthed.

deslía ▷ **desleír**.

desliar [9] *vt* to unwrap.

deslíe *etc* ▷ **desleír**.

desligar [16] *vt* - **1.** [desatar] to untie - **2.** *fig* [separar]: **desligar algo (de)** to separate sthg (from).

◆ **desligarse** *vprnl* - **1.** [desatarse] to untie oneself - **2.** *fig* [separarse]: **desligarse de** to become separated from; **desligarse de un grupo** to distance o.s. from a group.

deslindar *vt* - **1.** [limitar] to mark out (the boundaries of) - **2.** *fig* [separar] to define.

deslió ▷ **desleír**.

desliz *sm* slip, error; **tener** *o* **cometer un desliz** to slip up.

deslizante *adj* slippery.

deslizar [13] *vt* - **1.** [mano, objeto]: **deslizar algo en** to slip sthg into; **deslizar algo por algo** to slide sthg along sthg - **2.** [indirecta, comentario] to let slip in.

◆ **deslizarse** *vprnl* - **1.** [resbalar]: **deslizarse por** to slide along - **2.** [introducirse]: **deslizarse en** [persona] to slip into; [error] to creep into - **3.** [tiempo] to slip away *o* by.

deslomar *vt* [a golpes] to thrash.

◆ **deslomarse** *vprnl fam* to break one's back, to wear oneself out.

deslucido, **da** *adj* - **1.** [sin brillo] faded; [plata] tarnished - **2.** [sin gracia - acto, ceremonia] dull; [- actuación] uninspired.

deslucir [32] *vt* [espectáculo] to spoil, to ruin.

deslumbrante *adj* dazzling.

deslumbrar *vt lit & fig* to dazzle.

deslustrar *vt* [zapatos etc] to take the shine off.

desmadejar *vt* to wear *o* tire out.

desmadrarse *vprnl fam* to go wild.

desmadre *sm fam* chaos, utter confusion.

desmán *sm* - **1.** [con la bebida, comida etc] excess - **2.** [abuso de poder] abuse (of power).

desmandado, **da** *adj* [desobediente] unruly.

desmandarse *vprnl* - **1.** [desobedecer] to be disobedient - **2.** [insubordinarse] to get out of hand.

desmano ◆ **a desmano** *loc adv* [fuera de alcance] out of reach; [fuera del camino seguido] out of the way.

desmantelado, **da** *adj* dismantled.

desmantelamiento *sm* [de casa, fábrica] stripping; [de organización] disbanding; [de arsenal, andamiaje] dismantling; [de barco] unrigging.

desmantelar *vt* [casa, fábrica] to clear out, to strip; [organización] to disband; [arsenal, andamio] to dismantle; [barco] to unrig.

desmaquillador *sm* make-up remover.

desmaquillar *vt* to remove the make-up from.

◆ **desmaquillarse** *vprnl* to take one's make-up off.

desmarcar [10] *vt* DEP to draw the marker away from.

◆ **desmarcarse** *vprnl* DEP to lose one's marker.

desmayado, **da** *adj* - **1.** [persona] unconscious; **caer desmayado** to faint - **2.** [color] pale.

desmayar *vi* to lose heart.

◆ **desmayarse** *vprnl* to faint.

desmayo *sm* - **1.** [físico] fainting fit; **sufrir desmayos** to have fainting fits - **2.** [moral] loss of heart; **sin desmayo** unfalteringly.

desmedido, **da** *adj* excessive, disproportionate.

desmedirse [26] *vprnl* to go too far, to go over the top.

desmejorar <> *vt* to spoil. <> *vi* to go downhill, to deteriorate.

◆ **desmejorarse** *vprnl* to go downhill, to deteriorate.

desmelenado, da *adj* - **1.** [persona] reckless, wild - **2.** [cabello] tousled, dishevelled.

desmelenar *vt* [cabello] to dishevel.

◆ **desmelenarse** *vprnl* to go wild.

desmembramiento *sm* [de cuerpo] dismemberment; [de miembro, extremidad] loss; [de estados, partidos] breaking up.

desmembrar [19] *vt* - **1.** [trocear - cuerpo] to dismember; [- miembro, extremidad] to cut off - **2.** [disgregar] to break up.

desmemoriado, da <> *adj* forgetful. <> *sm, f* forgetful person.

desmentido *sm* denial.

desmentir [27] *vt* - **1.** [negar] to deny - **2.** [no corresponder] to belie.

desmenuzar [13] *vt* - **1.** [trocear - pan, pastel, roca] to crumble; [- carne] to chop up; [- papel] to tear up into little pieces - **2.** *fig* [examinar, analizar] to scrutinize.

desmerecer [30] <> *vt* not to deserve, to be unworthy of. <> *vi* to lose value; **desmerecer (en algo) de alguien** to be inferior to sb (in sthg).

desmesurado, da *adj* [excesivo] excessive, disproportionate; [enorme] enormous.

desmida, desmidiera *etc* ▷ **desmedirse**.

desmienta *etc* ▷ **desmentir**.

desmigajar *vt* to crumble.

◆ **desmigajarse** *vprnl* to crumble.

desmilitarizar [13] *vt* to demilitarize.

desmintiera *etc* ▷ **desmentir**.

desmitificar [10] *vt* to demythologize.

desmontable *adj* that can be dismantled; **una librería desmontable** a self-assembly bookcase.

desmontar <> *vt* - **1.** [desarmar - máquina] to take apart o to pieces; [- motor] to strip down; [- piezas] to dismantle; [- rueda] to remove, to take off; [- tienda de campaña] to take down; [- arma] to uncock - **2.** [jinete - suj: caballo] to unseat; [- suj: persona] to help down. <> *vi*: **desmontar de** [caballo] to dismount from; [moto, bicicleta] to get off; [coche] to get out of.

◆ **desmontarse** *vprnl*: **desmontarse de** [caballo] to dismount from; [moto, bicicleta] to get off; [coche] to get out of.

desmonte *sm* - **1.** *(gen pl)* [terreno] levelled ground *(U)* - **2.** [allanamiento] levelling - **3.** [de bosque] clearing.

desmoralización *sf* demoralization.

desmoralizador, ra *adj* demoralizing.

desmoralizar [13] *vt* to demoralize.

◆ **desmoralizarse** *vprnl* to become demoralized.

desmoronamiento *sm* [de edificios, rocas, ideales] crumbling; [de imperios] fall.

desmoronar *vt* [edificios, rocas] to cause to crumble.

◆ **desmoronarse** *vprnl* - **1.** [edificio, roca, ideales] to crumble - **2.** *fig* [persona] to be devastated; [imperio] to fall.

desmovilizar [13] *vt* to demobilize.

desnacionalizar [13] *vt* to denationalize, to privatize.

desnatado, da *adj* skimmed.

desnatar *vt* to skim.

desnaturalizado, da *adj* - **1.** [sustancia] adulterated; [alcohol] denatured - **2.** [persona] inhuman.

desnaturalizar [13] *vt* - **1.** [sustancia] to adulterate - **2.** [persona] to deny the natural rights of.

desnivel *sm* - **1.** [cultural, social etc] difference, inequality - **2.** [del terreno] irregularity, unevenness *(U)*.

desnivelar *vt* to make uneven; [balanza] to tip.

◆ **desnivelarse** *vprnl* to become uneven.

desnucar [10] *vt* to break the neck of.

◆ **desnucarse** *vprnl* to break one's neck.

desnuclearizar [13] *vt* to make nuclear-free.

desnudar *vt* to undress.

◆ **desnudarse** *vprnl* to undress, to get undressed.

desnudez *sf* [de persona] nakedness, nudity; [de cosa] bareness.

desnudo, da *adj* - **1.** [persona, cuerpo] naked - **2.** *fig* [salón, hombro, árbol] bare; [verdad] plain; [paisaje] bare, barren.

◆ **desnudo** *sm* nude.

desnutrición *sf* malnutrition.

desnutrido, da *adj* undernourished.

desnutrirse *vprnl* to suffer from malnutrition.

desobedecer [30] *vt* to disobey.

desobediencia *sf* disobedience; **desobediencia civil** civil disobedience.

desobediente *adj* disobedient.

desocupado, da *adj* - **1.** [persona - ocioso] free, unoccupied; [- sin empleo] unemployed - **2.** [lugar] vacant, unoccupied.

desocupar *vt* [edificio] to vacate; [habitación, mesa] to leave.

desodorante *sm* deodorant.

desodorizar [13] *vt* to deodorize.

desoír *vt* not to listen to, to take no notice of.

desolación *sf* **- 1.** [destrucción] desolation **- 2.** [desconsuelo] distress, grief.

desolador, ra *adj* [imagen, espectáculo] desolate; [noticia etc] devastating.

desolar [80] *vt* **- 1.** [destruir] to devastate, to lay waste **- 2.** [afligir] to cause anguish to.

➡ **desolarse** *vprnl* to be devastated.

desollar [23] *vt* **- 1.** [despellejar] to skin **- 2.**: **desollar vivo a alguien** [criticar] to skin sb alive; [hacer pagar mucho] to fleece sb, to rip sb off.

desorbitado, da *adj* **- 1.** [gen] disproportionate; [precio] exorbitant **- 2.** *loc*: **con los ojos desorbitados** pop-eyed.

desorbitar *vt* *fig* [exagerar] to exaggerate, to blow out of proportion.

desorden *sm* **- 1.** [confusión] disorder, chaos; [falta de orden] mess; **en desorden** topsy-turvy; **poner en desorden** to upset, to disarrange **- 2.** [disturbio] disturbance.

desordenado, da *adj* **- 1.** [habitación, persona] untidy, messy; [documentos, fichas] jumbled (up) **- 2.** *fig* [vida] chaotic.

desordenar *vt* [habitación, cajón] to mess up; [documentos, fichas] to jumble up; [pelo] to ruffle.

desorganización *sf* disorganization.

desorganizar [13] *vt* to disrupt, to disorganize.

desorientación *sf* **- 1.** [en el espacio] disorientation **- 2.** *fig* [aturdimiento] confusion.

desorientar *vt* **- 1.** [en el espacio] to disorientate, to mislead **- 2.** *fig* [aturdir] to confuse.

➡ **desorientarse** *vprnl* **- 1.** [en el espacio] to lose one's way *o* bearings **- 2.** *fig* [aturdirse] to get confused.

desovar *vi* [peces, anfibios] to spawn; [insectos] to lay eggs.

desoxirribonucleico ⊳ **ácido**.

despabilado, da *adj* **- 1.** [despierto] wide-awake **- 2.** [listo] smart, quick.

despabilar *vt* **- 1.** [despertar] to wake up **- 2.** [hacer más avispado] to make streetwise.

➡ **despabilarse** *vprnl* **- 1.** [despertarse] to wake up **- 2.** [darse prisa] to hurry up.

despachar ⇔ *vt* **- 1.** [mercancía] to dispatch **- 2.** [en tienda - cliente] to serve; [- entradas, bebidas etc] to sell **- 3.** *fam fig* [terminar - trabajo, discurso] to finish off; [- comida] to polish off **- 4.** [del trabajo]: **despachar a alguien (de)** to dismiss *o* sack sb (from) **- 5.** [asunto, negocio] to settle **- 6.** *Amér* [equipaje] to check in. ⇔ *vi* **- 1.** [sobre un asunto] to do business **- 2.** [en una tienda] to serve.

➡ **despacharse** *vprnl* **- 1.** [hablar francamente]: **despacharse con alguien** to give sb a piece of one's mind **- 2.** [desembarazarse]: **despacharse de** to get rid of.

despacho *sm* **- 1.** [oficina] office; [en casa] study **- 2.** [muebles] set of office furniture **- 3.** [comunicación oficial] dispatch **- 4.** [venta] sale; [lugar de venta]: **despacho de billetes/localidades** ticket/box office.

despachurrar *vt* *fam* to squash.

despacio ⇔ *adv* **- 1.** [lentamente] slowly **- 2.** *esp Amér* [en voz baja] quietly. ⇔ *interj*: **¡despacio!** take it easy!

despampanante *adj* stunning.

despanzurrar *vt* *fam* to cause to burst open.

desparejar *vt* to mix up.

desparpajo *sm* *fam* forwardness, self-assurance.

desparramar *vt* **- 1.** [líquido] to spill; [objetos] to spread, to scatter **- 2.** *fig* [dinero] to squander.

➡ **desparramarse** *vprnl* [líquido] to spill; [objetos, personas] to scatter, to spread out.

despatarrarse *vprnl* to open one's legs wide.

despavorido, da *adj* terrified.

despavorir [80] *vt* to terrify.

despecharse *vprnl* to get angry.

despecho *sm* [rencor, venganza] spite; [desengaño] bitterness; **(hacer algo) por despecho** (to do sthg) out of spite.

➡ **a despecho de** *loc prep* in spite of, despite.

despechugarse [16] *vprnl* *fam fig* to bare one's breast.

despectivo, va *adj* **- 1.** [despreciativo] scornful, contemptuous **- 2.** GRAM pejorative.

➡ **despectivo** *sm* GRAM pejorative.

despedazar [13] *vt* **- 1.** [físicamente] to tear apart **- 2.** *fig* [moralmente] to shatter.

despedida *sf* **- 1.** [adiós] goodbye, farewell **- 2.** [fiesta] farewell party; **despedida de soltera** hen party; **despedida de soltero** stag *o* bachelor US party.

despedir [26] *vt* **- 1.** [decir adiós a] to say goodbye to; **fuimos a despedirle a la estación** we went to see him off at the station **- 2.** [echar - de un empleo] to dismiss, to sack; [- de un club] to throw out **- 3.** [lanzar, arrojar] to fling; **salir despedido de/por/hacia algo** to fly out of/through/towards sthg **- 4.** *fig* [difundir, desprender] to give off.

➡ **despedirse** *vprnl*: **despedirse (de)** to say goodbye (to).

despegado, da *adj* *fig* cold, detached.

despegar [16] ⇔ *vt* to unstick. ⇔ *vi* [avión] to take off.

➡ **despegarse** *vprnl* **- 1.** [etiqueta, pegatina, sello] to come unstuck **- 2.** [alejarse - persona]: **despegarse de alguien** to break away *o* withdraw from sb.

despego *sm* detachment, indifference.

despegue *sm* takeoff; **despegue vertical** vertical takeoff; **despegue económico** economic takeoff.

despeinar *vt* [pelo] to ruffle; **despeinar a alguien** to mess up sb's hair.

➤ **despeinarse** *vprnl* to mess up one's hair.

despejado, **da** *adj* - **1.** [tiempo, día] clear - **2.** *fig* [persona, mente] alert - **3.** [espacio - ancho] spacious; [- sin estorbos] clear, uncluttered.

despejar *vt* - **1.** [gen] to clear - **2.** MAT [incógnita] to find.

➤ **despejarse** *vprnl* - **1.** [persona - espabilarse] to clear one's head; [- despertarse] to wake o.s. up - **2.** [tiempo] to clear up; [cielo] to clear.

despeje *sm* DEP clearance.

despellejar *vt* - **1.** [animal] to skin - **2.** *fig* [criticar] to pull to pieces.

despelotarse *vprnl fam* - **1.** [desnudarse] to strip - **2.** [mondarse]: **despelotarse (de risa)** to laugh one's head off.

despelote *sm fam* - **1.** [desmadre] chaos (U) - **2.** [desnudo] strip.

despenalización *sf* decriminalization.

despenalizar [13] *vt* to decriminalize.

despensa *sf* larder, pantry.

despeñadero *sm* precipice.

despeñar *vt* to throw over a cliff.

➤ **despeñarse** *vprnl* to fall over a cliff.

desperdiciar [8] *vt* [tiempo, comida] to waste; [dinero] to squander; [ocasión] to throw away.

desperdicio *sm* - **1.** [acción] waste - **2.** [residuo]: **desperdicios** scraps - **3.** *loc*: **no tener desperdicio** to be excellent from start to finish.

desperdigar [16] *vt* to scatter, to disperse.

➤ **desperdigarse** *vprnl* to scatter.

desperezarse [13] *vprnl* to stretch.

desperfecto *sm* [deterioro] damage (U); [defecto] flaw, imperfection; **sufrir desperfectos** to get damaged.

despersonalizar [13] *vt* to depersonalize.

despertador *sm* alarm clock.

despertar [19] ⟨⟩ *vt* - **1.** [persona, animal] to wake (up) - **2.** *fig* [reacción] to arouse - **3.** *fig* [recuerdo] to revive, to awaken. ⟨⟩ *vi* to wake up. ⟨⟩ *sm* awakening.

➤ **despertarse** *vprnl* to wake up.

despiadado, **da** *adj* pitiless, merciless.

despida, **despidiera** *etc* ⊳ **despedir**.

despido *sm* dismissal, sacking; **despido colectivo** collective dismissal; **despido improcedente** wrongful dismissal.

despiece *sm* cutting-up.

despierta *etc* ⊳ **despertar**.

despierto, **ta** *adj* - **1.** [sin dormir] awake - **2.** *fig* [espabilado, listo] bright, sharp.

despilfarrar *vt* [dinero] to squander; [electricidad, agua etc] to waste.

despilfarro *sm* [de dinero] squandering; [de energía, agua etc] waste.

despintar *vt* to take the paint off.

despiole *sm* R Dom fam rumpus, shindy.

despistado, **da** ⟨⟩ *adj* absent-minded. ⟨⟩ *sm, f* scatterbrain; **hacerse el despistado** to pretend not to notice.

despistar *vt* - **1.** [dar esquinazo a] to throw off the scent - **2.** *fig* [confundir] to mislead.

➤ **despistarse** *vprnl* - **1.** [perderse] to lose one's way, to get lost - **2.** *fig* [distraerse] to get confused.

despiste *sm* - **1.** [distracción] absent-mindedness; [error] mistake, slip - **2.** [persona]: **Marta es un despiste** Marta is very absent-minded.

desplante *sm* rude remark; **hacer un desplante a alguien** to snub sb.

desplazado, **da** *adj fig* [persona] out of place.

desplazamiento *sm* - **1.** [viaje] journey; [traslado] move - **2.** NÁUT displacement.

desplazar [13] *vt* - **1.** [trasladar] to move - **2.** *fig* [desbancar] to take the place of; **desplazar a alguien/algo de** to remove sb/sthg from.

➤ **desplazarse** *vprnl* [viajar] to travel.

desplegar [35] *vt* - **1.** [tela, periódico, mapa] to unfold; [alas] to spread, to open; [bandera] to unfurl - **2.** [cualidad] to display - **3.** MIL to deploy.

despliegue *sm* - **1.** [de cualidad] display - **2.** MIL deployment; **despliegue de misiles** missile deployment.

desplomarse *vprnl* [gen] to collapse; [techo] to fall in.

desplumar *vt* - **1.** [ave] to pluck - **2.** *fig* [estafar] to fleece.

despoblación *sf* depopulation.

despoblado, **da** *adj* unpopulated, deserted.

➤ **despoblado** *sm* deserted spot.

despojar *vt*: **despojar a alguien de algo** to strip sb of sthg.

➤ **despojarse** *vprnl*: **despojarse de algo** [bienes, alimentos] to give sthg up; [abrigo, chandal] to take sthg off.

despojo *sm* [acción] stripping, plundering.

➤ **despojos** *smpl* - **1.** [sobras, residuos] leftovers - **2.** [de animales] offal (U) - **3.** [restos mortales] remains.

despolitizar [13] *vt* to depoliticize.

desposar *vt* to marry.

➤ **desposarse** *vprnl* to get married, to marry.

desposeer [50] *vt*: **desposeer a alguien de** to dispossess sb of.

déspota *smf* despot.

despotismo *sm* despotism; **despotismo ilustrado** enlightened despotism.

despotricar [10] *vi*: despotricar (contra) to rant on (at).

despreciar [8] *vt* - **1.** [desdeñar] to scorn - **2.** [rechazar] to spurn.

desprecio *sm* scorn, contempt; **hacer un desprecio a alguien** to snub sb.

desprender *vt* - **1.** [lo que estaba fijo] to remove, to detach - **2.** [olor, luz] to give off.

◆ **desprenderse** *vprnl* - **1.** [caerse, soltarse] to come o fall off - **2.** *fig* [deducirse]: **de sus palabras se desprende que...** from his words it is clear o it can be seen that... - **3.** [librarse]: **desprenderse de** to get rid of - **4.** [renunciar]: **desprenderse de algo** to part with sthg, to give sthg up.

desprendido, da *adj* [generoso] generous.

desprendimiento *sm* - **1.** [separación] detachment; **desprendimiento de tierras** landslide; **desprendimiento de retina** detachment of the retina - **2.** *fig* [generosidad] generosity.

despreocupado, da ◇ *adj* [libre de preocupaciones] unworried, unconcerned; [en el vestir] casual. ◇ *sm, f* [en el vestir] *person who doesn't care too much about his/her appearance.*

despreocuparse ◆ **despreocuparse de** *vprnl* - **1.** [asunto] to stop worrying about - **2.** [persona] to be neglectful of.

desprestigiar [8] *vt* to discredit.

desprestigio *sm* discredit.

desprevenido, da *adj* unprepared; **coger o pillar desprevenido a alguien** to catch sb unawares, to take sb by surprise.

desprolijo, ja *adj* *Amér* [casa, cuaderno] untidy; [persona] unkempt, dishevelled.

desproporción *sf* disproportion.

desproporcionado, da *adj* disproportionate.

despropósito *sm* stupid remark, nonsense (U).

desprovisto, ta *adj*: **desprovisto de** lacking in, devoid of.

después *adv* - **1.** [en el tiempo - más tarde] afterwards, later; [- entonces] then; [- justo lo siguiente] next; **poco después** soon after; **años después** years later; **ellos llegaron después** they arrived later; **llamé primero y después entré** I knocked first and then I went in; **yo voy después** it's my turn next - **2.** [en el espacio] next, after; **¿qué viene después?** what comes next o after?; **hay una farmacia y después está mi casa** there's a chemist's and then there's my house; **varias manzanas después** several blocks further on - **3.** [en una lista] further down.

◆ **después de** *loc prep* after; **llegó después de ti** she arrived after you; **después de él, nadie lo ha conseguido** since he did it, no one else has; **después de hacer algo** after doing sthg.

◆ **después de que** *loc conj* after; **después de que amanezca** after dawn; **después de que te fueras a la cama** after you went to bed; **después de que lo hice** after I did it, after doing it.

◆ **después de todo** *loc adv* after all.

despuntar ◇ *vt* [romper] to break the point off; [desgastar] to blunt. ◇ *vi* - **1.** [brotar - flor, capullo] to bud; [- planta] to sprout - **2.** *fig* [persona] to excel, to stand out - **3.** [alba] to break; [día] to dawn.

desquiciar [8] *vt* - **1.** [puerta, ventana] to unhinge - **2.** *fig* [desequilibrar] to derange, to disturb mentally; [sacar de quicio] to drive mad.

desquitarse *vprnl*: **desquitarse (de algo/alguien)** to get one's own back (for sthg/on sb).

desquite *sm* revenge.

desratizar [13] *vt* to clear of rats.

desriñonarse *vprnl* to break one's back.

destacado, da *adj* - **1.** [notable - persona] distinguished, prominent; [- acto] outstanding - **2.** MIL detached; **destacado en** stationed in.

destacamento *sm* detachment; **destacamento de tropas** task force.

destacar [10] ◇ *vt* - **1.** [poner de relieve] to emphasize, to highlight; **cabe destacar que...** it is important to point out that... - **2.** MIL to detach, to detail - **3.** ARTE to cause to stand out, to highlight. ◇ *vi* [sobresalir] to stand out.

◆ **destacarse** *vprnl*: **destacarse (de/por)** to stand out (from/because of).

destajo *sm* piecework; **trabajar a destajo** [por trabajo hecho] to do piecework; *fig* [afanosamente] to work flat out.

destapador *sm* *Amér* bottle opener.

destapar *vt* - **1.** [abrir - caja, botella] to open; [olla] to take the lid off; [descorchar] to uncork - **2.** [descubrir] to uncover - **3.** *R Dom* [desobstruir] to unblock.

◆ **destaparse** *vprnl* - **1.** [desabrigarse] to lose the covers - **2.** *fig* [revelarse] to open up.

destape *sm* [en revistas] nude photos *pl*; [en películas, teatro etc] striptease.

destartalado, da *adj* [viejo, deteriorado] dilapidated; [desordenado] untidy.

destellar *vi* [diamante, ojos] to sparkle; [estrellas] to twinkle.

destello *sm* - **1.** [de luz, brillo] sparkle; [de estrella] twinkle - **2.** *fig* [manifestación momentánea] glimmer.

destemplado, **da** *adj* - **1.** [persona] out of sorts, off colour - **2.** [instrumento] out of tune - **3.** [tiempo, clima] unpleasant - **4.** [carácter, actitud] irritable - **5.** [voz] sharp.

destemplar *vt* [instrumento] to put out of tune.
◆ **destemplarse** *vprnl* - **1.** [coger frío] to catch a chill - **2.** [irritarse] to get upset.

desteñir ◇ *vt* to fade, to bleach. ◇ *vi* to run, not to be colour fast.
◆ **desteñirse** *vprnl* to fade.

desternillarse *vprnl*: **desternillarse de risa** to split one's sides laughing *o* with laughter.

desterrar [19] *vt* - **1.** [persona] to banish, to exile - **2.** *fig* [idea] to dismiss - **3.** *fig* [costumbre, hábito] to do away with.

destetar *vt* to wean.

destete *sm* weaning.

destiempo ◆ **a destiempo** *loc adv* at the wrong time.

destierra *etc* ▷ **desterrar**.

destierro *sm* exile; **en el destierro** in exile.

destilación *sf* distillation.

destilar ◇ *vt* - **1.** [agua, petróleo] to distil - **2.** [sangre, pus] to ooze - **3.** *fig* [cualidad, sentimiento] to exude, to ooze. ◇ *vi* [gotear] to trickle, to drip.

destilería *sf* distillery; **destilería de petróleo** oil refinery.

destinar *vt* - **1.**: **destinar algo a** *o* **para** [cantidad, edificio] to set sthg aside for; [empleo, cargo] to assign sthg to; [carta] to address sthg to; [medidas, programa, publicación] to aim sthg at - **2.**: **destinar a alguien a** [cargo, empleo] to appoint sb to; [plaza, lugar] to post sb to.

destinatario, **ria** *sm, f* addressee.

destino *sm* - **1.** [sino] destiny, fate - **2.** [rumbo] destination; **(ir) con destino a** (to be) bound for *o* going to; **un vuelo con destino a...** a flight to... - **3.** [empleo, plaza] position, post - **4.** [finalidad] use, function.

destitución *sf* dismissal.

destituir [51] *vt* to dismiss.

destornillador *sm* screwdriver.

destornillar *vt* to unscrew.

destreza *sf* skill, dexterity.

destripar *vt* - **1.** [sacar las tripas a - animal, persona] to disembowel; [- pescado] to gut - **2.** *fig* [despanzurrar] to rip open.

destronar *vt* [rey] to dethrone, to depose; *fig* [rival] to unseat, to replace at the top.

destrozar [13] *vt* - **1.** [físicamente - romper] to smash; [- estropear] to ruin - **2.** [moralmente - persona] to shatter, to devastate; [- vida] to ruin.

destrozo *sm* damage *(U)*; **ocasionar grandes destrozos** to cause a lot of damage.

destrucción *sf* destruction.

destructivo, **va** *adj* destructive.

destructor, **ra** *adj* destructive.
◆ **destructor** *sm* destroyer.

destruir [51] *vt* - **1.** [gen] to destroy; [casa, argumento] to demolish - **2.** [proyecto] to ruin, to wreck; [ilusión] to dash.

desuella *etc* ▷ **desollar**.

desunión *sf* - **1.** [separación] separation - **2.** [división, discordia] disunity.

desunir *vt* - **1.** [separar] to separate - **2.** [enemistar - grupos] to divide, to cause a rift between.

desusado, **da** *adj* - **1.** [pasado de moda] old-fashioned, obsolete - **2.** [desacostumbrado] unusual.

desuso *sm* disuse; **caer en desuso** to become obsolete, to fall into disuse.

desvaído, **da** *adj* [color] pale, washed-out; [forma, contorno] blurred; [mirada] vague.

desvalido, **da** ◇ *adj* needy, destitute. ◇ *sm, f* needy *o* destitute person.

desvalijar *vt* [casa] to burgle, to burglarize *US*; [persona] to rob.

desvalorizar [13] *vt* to devalue.

desván *sm* attic, loft.

desvanecer [30] *vt* - **1.** [humo, nubes] to dissipate - **2.** [sospechas, temores] to dispel.
◆ **desvanecerse** *vprnl* - **1.** [desmayarse] to faint - **2.** [disiparse - humo, nubes] to clear, to disappear; [- sonido, sospechas, temores] to fade away.

desvanecimiento *sm* [desmayo] fainting fit.

desvariar [9] *vi* [delirar] to be delirious; [decir locuras] to talk nonsense, to rave.

desvarío *sm* - **1.** [dicho] raving; [hecho] act of madness - **2.** [delirio] delirium.

desvelar *vt* - **1.** [quitar el sueño a] to keep awake - **2.** [noticia, secreto etc] to reveal, to tell.
◆ **desvelarse** *vprnl Amér C & Méx* [quedarse despierto] to stay up *o* awake.
◆ **desvelarse por** *vprnl*: **desvelarse por hacer algo** to make every effort to do sthg.

desvelo *sm* - **1.** [insomnio] sleeplessness, insomnia - **2.** [esfuerzo] effort.

desvencijado, **da** *adj* [silla, mesa] rickety; [camión, coche] battered.

desvencijar *vt* [romper] to break; [desencajar] to cause to come apart.

desventaja *sf* disadvantage; **en desventaja** at a disadvantage.

desventura *sf* misfortune.

desventurado, **da** ◇ *adj* unfortunate. ◇ *sm, f* poor wretch.

desvergonzado, **da** ◇ *adj* shameless, insolent. ◇ *sm, f* shameless person.

desvergüenza *sf* - **1.** [atrevimiento, frescura] shamelessness - **2.** [dicho] shameless remark; [hecho] shameless act; **¡qué desvergüenza!** what a nerve!

desvestir [26] *vt* to undress.

◆ **desvestirse** *vprnl* to undress (o.s.)

desviación *sf* - **1.** [de dirección, cauce, norma] deviation - **2.** [en la carretera] diversion, detour - **3.** MED: **desviación de columna** slipped disc.

desviacionismo *sm* deviationism.

desviar [9] *vt* [río, carretera, tráfico] to divert; [dirección] to change; [golpe] to parry; [pelota, disparo] to deflect; [pregunta] to evade; [conversación] to change the direction of; [mirada, ojos] to avert.

◆ **desviarse** *vprnl* - **1.** [cambiar de dirección - conductor] to take a detour; [- avión, barco] to go off course; **desviarse de** to turn off - **2.** [cambiar]: **desviarse de** [tema] to wander o digress from; [propósito, idea] to lose sight of.

desvincular *vt*: **desvincular a alguien de** to release o discharge sb from.

◆ **desvincularse de** *vprnl* to cut oneself off from.

desvío *sm* diversion, detour.

desvirgar [16] *vt* to deflower.

desvirtuar [6] *vt* [gen] to detract from; [estropear] to spoil; [verdadero sentido] to distort.

desvista, desvistiera *etc* ▷ **desvestir**.

desvivirse *vprnl*: **desvivirse (por alguien/algo)** to do everything one can (for sb/sthg); **desvivirse por hacer algo** to bend over backwards to do sthg.

detalladamente *adv* in (great) detail.

detallado, da *adj* detailed, thorough.

detallar *vt* [historia, hechos] to detail, to give a rundown of; [cuenta, gastos] to itemize.

detalle *sm* - **1.** [gen] detail; **con detalle** in detail; **entrar en detalles** to go into detail - **2.** [atención] kind gesture o thought; **¡qué detalle!** what a kind gesture!, how thoughtful!; **tener un detalle con alguien** to be thoughtful o considerate to sb.

◆ **al detalle** *loc adv* COM retail.

detallista ◇ *adj* - **1.** [meticuloso] painstaking - **2.** [atento] thoughtful. ◇ *smf* COM retailer.

detección *sf* detection.

detectar *vt* to detect.

detective *smf* detective; **detective privado** private detective.

detector, ra *adj* detecting *(antes de s)*.

◆ **detector** *sm* detector; **detector de incendios** fire detector; **detector de mentiras** lie detector; **detector de metales** metal detector.

detención *sf* - **1.** [arresto] arrest; **detención domiciliaria** house arrest; **detención preventiva** protective custody - **2.** [parada] stopping, holding-up.

detener [72] *vt* - **1.** [arrestar] to arrest - **2.** [parar] to stop; [retrasar] to hold up - **3.** [entretener] to keep, to delay.

◆ **detenerse** *vprnl* - **1.** [pararse] to stop; **detenerse a hacer algo** to stop to do sthg - **2.** [demorarse] to hang about, to linger.

detenidamente *adv* carefully, thoroughly.

detenido, da ◇ *adj* - **1.** [detallado] careful, thorough - **2.** [arrestado]: **(estar) detenido** (to be) under arrest. ◇ *sm, f* prisoner, person under arrest.

detenimiento ◆ **con detenimiento** *loc adv* carefully, thoroughly.

detentar *vt* to hold unlawfully.

detergente *sm* detergent.

deteriorar *vt* to damage, to spoil.

◆ **deteriorarse** *vprnl* *fig* [empeorar] to deteriorate, to get worse.

deterioro *sm* [daño] damage; [empeoramiento] deterioration.

determinación *sf* - **1.** [fijación - de precio etc] settling, fixing - **2.** [resolución] determination, resolution - **3.** [decisión]: **tomar una determinación** to take a decision.

determinado, da *adj* - **1.** [concreto] specific; [en particular] particular - **2.** [resuelto] determined - **3.** GRAM definite.

determinante ◇ *adj* decisive, determining. ◇ *sm* - **1.** GRAM determiner - **2.** MAT determinant.

determinar *vt* - **1.** [fijar - fecha, precio] to settle, to fix - **2.** [averiguar] to determine; **determinar las causas de la muerte** to establish the cause of death - **3.** [motivar] to cause, to bring about - **4.** [decidir] to decide; **determinar hacer algo** to decide to do sthg.

◆ **determinarse** *vprnl*: **determinarse a hacer algo** to make up one's mind to do sthg.

determinismo *sm* determinism.

detestable *adj* detestable.

detestar *vt* to detest.

detiene ▷ **detener**.

detonación *sf* [acción] detonation; [sonido] explosion.

detonador *sm* detonator.

detonante ◇ *adj* explosive. ◇ *sm* - **1.** [explosivo] explosive - **2.** *fig* [desencadenante]: **ser el detonante de algo** to spark sthg off.

detonar *vi* to detonate, to explode.

detractor, ra ◇ *adj*: **detractor (de)** disparaging (about). ◇ *sm, f* detractor.

detrás *adv* - **1.** [en el espacio] behind; **tus amigos vienen detrás** your friends are coming on behind; **el interruptor está detrás** the switch is at the back - **2.** [en el orden] then, afterwards; **Portugal y detrás Puerto Rico** Portugal and then Puerto Rico.

 detrás de *loc prep* - **1.** [gen] behind - **2.** [a espaldas de]: **detrás de alguien** behind sb's back.

 por detrás *loc adv* at the back; **hablar de alguien por detrás** to talk about sb behind his/her back.

detrimento *sm* damage; **en detrimento de** to the detriment of.

detrito *sm* BIOL detritus.

 detritos *smpl* [residuos] waste *(U)*.

detuviera *etc* ▷ **detener**.

deuda *sf* debt; **contraer una deuda** to get into debt; **estar en deuda con alguien** *fig* [moral] to be indebted to sb; **deuda exterior** ECON foreign debt; **deuda pública** ECON national debt *UK*, public debt *US*.

deudor, ra ◇ *adj* [saldo] debit *(antes de s)*; [entidad] indebted. ◇ *sm, f* debtor.

devaluación *sf* devaluation.

devaluar [6] *vt* to devalue.

 devaluarse *vprnl* to go down in value.

devaneos *smpl* - **1.** [distracción] idle pursuits - **2.** [amoríos] affairs; [coqueteos] flirting *(U)*.

devastador, ra *adj* devastating.

devastar *vt* to devastate.

devengar [16] *vt* [intereses] to yield, to earn; [sueldo] to earn.

devoción *sf*: **devoción (por)** devotion (to).

devolución *sf* [gen] return; [de dinero] refund; **devolución fiscal** tax rebate *o* refund.

devolver [24] ◇ *vt* - **1.** [restituir]: **devolver algo (a)** [coche, dinero etc] to give sthg back (to); [producto defectuoso, carta] to return sthg (to) - **2.** [restablecer, colocar en su sitio]: **devolver algo a** to return sthg to - **3.** [favor, agravio] to pay back for; [visita] to return - **4.** [vomitar] to bring *o* throw up. ◇ *vi* to throw up.

 devolverse *vprnl Andes, Amér, Caribe & Méx* to come back.

devorar *vt lit & fig* to devour; **la culpabilidad le devora** he is consumed with guilt.

devoto, ta ◇ *adj* - **1.** [piadoso] devout; **ser devoto de** to have a devotion for - **2.** [admirador]: **devoto (de alguien)** devoted (to sb) - **3.** [imagen, templo, lugar] devotional. ◇ *sm, f* - **1.** [beato]: **los devotos** the faithful - **2.** [admirador] devotee.

devuelto, ta *pp* ▷ **devolver**.

devuelva *etc* ▷ **devolver**.

dg (*abrev de* **decigramo**) dg.

di *etc* ▷ **dar**. ▷ **decir**.

día *sm* - **1.** [gen] day; **me voy el día ocho** I'm going on the eighth; **¿a qué día estamos?** what day is it today?; **¿qué tal día hace?** what's the weather like today?; **todos los días** every day; **el día que se entere nos mata** when he finds out, he'll kill us; **día de deuda** COM pay-by date; **día de la Madre** Mother's Day; **día de los enamorados** St Valentine's Day; **día de los inocentes** *28th December,* ≃ April Fools' Day; **día de pago** payday; **día festivo** (public) holiday; **día hábil** *o* **laborable** *o* **de trabajo** working day; **día lectivo** school *o* teaching day; **día libre** day off; **de día en día** from day to day, day by day; **del día** fresh; **en su día** in due course; **hoy (en) día** nowadays; **todo el (santo) día** all day long; **el día de mañana** in the future; **al día siguiente** on the following day; **un día sí y otro no** every other day; **menú del día** today's menu - **2.** [luz] daytime, day; **es de día** it's daytime; **hacer algo de día** to do sthg in the daytime *o* during the day; **día y noche** day and night; **en pleno día, a plena luz del día** in broad daylight - **3.** *loc*: **dar el día a alguien** to ruin sb's day (for them); **mañana será otro día** tomorrow is another day; **no pasar los días para alguien** not to look one's age; **tener días** to have one's good days and one's bad days; **un día es un día** this is a special occasion; **el día menos pensado** when you least expect it; **estar/ponerse al día (de)** to be/get up to date (with); **poner algo/a alguien al día** to update sthg/sb; **vivir al día** to live from hand to mouth.

 días *smpl* - **1.** [vida] days, life *sing* - **2.** [época]: **en mis días** in my day; **en aquellos días de felicidad** in those happy times.

 buen día *interj Amér*: **¡buen día!** good morning!

 buenos días *interj*: **¡buenos días!** [gen] hello!; [por la mañana] good morning!

diabetes *sf inv* diabetes *(U)*.

diabético, ca *adj & sm, f* diabetic.

diablo *sm lit & fig* devil; **pobre diablo** poor devil; **tener el diablo en el cuerpo, ser la piel del diablo** to be a little devil; **mandar al diablo a alguien** to send sb packing; **más sabe el diablo por viejo que por diablo** experience is what really counts.

 diablos *fam* ◇ *smpl* [para enfatizar]: **¿dónde/cómo diablos...?** where/how the hell...? ◇ *interj*: **¡diablos!** damn it!

diablura *sf* prank.

diabólico, ca *adj* - **1.** [del diablo] diabolic - **2.** *fig* [muy malo, difícil] diabolical.

diadema *sf* [para el pelo] hairband.

diáfano, na *adj* - **1.** [transparente] transparent, diaphanous - **2.** *fig* [claro] clear.

diafragma *sm* diaphragm.

diagnosis *sf inv* diagnosis.

diagnosticar [10] *vt* to diagnose.

diagnóstico *sm* diagnosis; **diagnóstico precoz** early diagnosis.

diagonal *adj* & *sf* diagonal.

diagrama *sm* diagram; **diagrama de flujo** IN-FORM flow chart o diagram.

dial *sm* dial.

dialecto *sm* dialect.

diálisis *sf inv* dialysis.

dialogante *adj*: **persona dialogante** interlocutor.

dialogar [16] *vi*: **dialogar (con)** [hablar] to have a conversation (with), to talk (to); [negociar] to hold a dialogue o talks (with).

diálogo *sm* [conversación] conversation; LITER & POLÍT dialogue; **diálogo de besugos** mindless chatter *(U)*; **fue un diálogo de sordos** nobody listened to anyone else.

diamante *sm* [piedra preciosa] diamond; **diamante en bruto** uncut diamond; **ser un diamante en bruto** *fig* to have a lot of potential.
◆ **diamantes** *smpl* [naipes] diamonds.

diametralmente *adv* diametrically; **diametralmente opuesto a** diametrically opposed to.

diámetro *sm* diameter.

diana *sf* - **1.** [en blanco de tiro] bull's-eye, bull; **hacer diana** to hit the bull's-eye - **2.** [en cuartel] reveille; **tocar diana** to sound the reveille.

diapasón *sm* tuning fork.

diapositiva *sf* slide, transparency.

diariero, ra *sm, f Andes & R Plata* newspaper seller.

diario, ria *adj* daily; **a diario** every day; **de diario** daily, everyday; **ropa de diario** everyday clothes.
◆ **diario** *sm* - **1.** [periódico] newspaper, daily; **diario hablado/televisado** radio/television news (bulletin) - **2.** [relación día a día] diary; **diario de a bordo** logbook; **diario de sesiones** parliamentary report; **diario de vuelo** log, logbook.

diarrea *sf* diarrhoea; **tener diarrea mental** *fam* not to be thinking straight.

dibujante *sm, f* [gen] drawer, sketcher; [de dibujos animados] cartoonist; [de dibujo técnico] draughtsman (*f* draughtswoman).

dibujar *vt* & *vi* to draw, to sketch.

dibujo *sm* - **1.** [gen] drawing; **no se le da bien el dibujo** he's no good at drawing; **dibujos animados** cartoons; **dibujo artístico** art; **dibujo lineal** technical drawing; **dibujo al natural** drawing from life - **2.** [de tela, prenda etc] pattern.

dic., dicbre. (*abrev de* **diciembre**) Dec.

dicción *sf* diction.

diccionario *sm* dictionary.

dice ▷ **decir**.

dicha *sf* - **1.** [alegría] joy - **2.** [suerte] good fortune.

dicharachero, ra *adj fam* talkative.

dicho, cha ◇ *pp* ▷ **decir**. ◇ *adj* said, aforementioned; **dichos hombres** the said men, these men; **lo dicho** what I/we *etc* said; **o mejor dicho** or rather; **dicho y hecho** no sooner said than done.
◆ **dicho** *sm* saying; **del dicho al hecho hay un gran o mucho trecho** it's easier said than done.

dichoso, sa *adj* - **1.** [feliz] happy; [afortunado] fortunate - **2.** [para enfatizar - maldito] blessed, confounded.

diciembre *sm* December; *ver también* **septiembre**.

dictado *sm* dictation; **escribir al dictado** to take dictation.
◆ **dictados** *smpl* [órdenes] dictates.

dictador, ra *sm, f* dictator.

dictadura *sf* dictatorship; **dictadura del proletariado** dictatorship of the proletariat.

dictamen *sm* [opinión] opinion, judgment; [informe] report; **dictamen facultativo** o **médico** medical report.

dictar *vt* - **1.** [texto] to dictate - **2.** [emitir - sentencia, fallo] to pronounce, to pass; [- ley] to enact; [- decreto] to issue.

didáctico, ca *adj* didactic.
◆ **didáctica** *sf* didactics *(U)*.

diecinueve *num* nineteen; *ver también* **seis**.

diecinueveavo, va *num* nineteenth; **la diecinueveava parte** a nineteenth.

dieciocho *num* eighteen; *ver también* **seis**.

dieciochoavo, va *num* eighteenth; **la dieciochoava parte** an eighteenth.

dieciséis *num* sixteen; *ver también* **seis**.

dieciseisavo, va *num* sixteenth; **la dieciseisava parte** a sixteenth.

diecisiete *num* seventeen; *ver también* **seis**.

diecisieteavo, va *num* seventeenth; **la diecisieteava parte** a seventeenth.

diente *sm* tooth; **está echando** o **le están saliendo los dientes** she's teething; **diente de leche** milk tooth; **diente incisivo** incisor; **diente molar** molar; **dientes postizos** false teeth; **armado hasta los dientes** armed to the teeth; **enseñar los dientes** to bare one's teeth; **hablar entre dientes** to mumble, to mutter; **hincar el diente a algo** to sink one's teeth into sthg; *fig* to get one's teeth into sthg; **ponerle a**

alguien los dientes largos to turn sb green with envy; **me rechinan los dientes** it sets my teeth on edge; **reírse entre dientes** to chuckle.

◆ **diente de ajo** sm clove of garlic.

◆ **diente de león** sm dandelion.

diera ▷ **dar**.

diéresis sf inv diaeresis.

dieron etc ▷ **dar**.

diesel, diésel adj diesel.

diestro, tra adj [hábil]: **diestro (en)** skilful (at); **a diestro y siniestro** fig left, right and centre, all over the place.

◆ **diestro** sm TAUROM matador.

◆ **diestra** sf right hand; **a la diestra** on the right o right-hand side.

dieta sf MED diet; **estar/ponerse a dieta** to be/go on a diet; **dieta blanda** soft-food diet; **dieta equilibrada** balanced diet; **dieta mediterránea** Mediterranean diet.

◆ **dietas** sfpl COM expenses.

dietético, ca adj dietetic, dietary.

◆ **dietética** sf dietetics (U).

dietista smf Amér dietician.

diez ◇ num ten. ◇ sm [en la escuela] A, top marks pl; ver también **seis**.

diezmar vt to decimate.

difamación sf [verbal] slander; [escrita] libel.

difamar vt [verbalmente] to slander; [por escrito] to libel.

difamatorio, ria adj [declaraciones, críticas] defamatory; [texto, carta, escrito] libellous.

diferencia sf difference; **a diferencia de** unlike; **con diferencia** by a long chalk, by far; **es, con diferencia, el más listo** he's the smartest by far; **establecer** o **hacer una diferencia entre** to make a distinction between; **limar diferencias** to settle one's differences; **partir la diferencia** to split the difference; **diferencia horaria** time difference.

diferencial ◇ adj distinguishing. ◇ sm MECÁN differential. ◇ sf MAT differential.

diferenciar [7] ◇ vt: **diferenciar (de)** to distinguish (from). ◇ vi: **diferenciar (entre)** to distinguish o differentiate (between).

◆ **diferenciarse** vprnl - **1.** [diferir]: **diferenciarse (de/en)** to differ (from/in), to be different (from/in) - **2.** [descollar]: **diferenciarse de** to stand out from.

diferente ◇ adj: **diferente (de** o **a)** different (from o to). ◇ adv differently.

diferido ◆ **en diferido** loc adv TV recorded.

diferir [27] ◇ vt [posponer] to postpone, to put off. ◇ vi [diferenciarse] to differ, to be different; **diferir de alguien en algo** to differ from sb in sthg.

difícil adj difficult; **difícil de hacer** difficult to do; **es difícil que ganen** they are unlikely to win.

dificultad sf - **1.** [calidad de difícil] difficulty - **2.** [obstáculo] problem; **poner dificultades** to raise objections.

◆ **dificultades** sfpl [problemas] trouble (U); **pasar dificultades** to suffer hardship.

dificultar vt [estorbar] to hinder; [obstruir] to obstruct.

difiera, difiriera etc ▷ **diferir**.

difteria sf diphtheria.

difuminar vt to blur.

difundir vt - **1.** [noticia, doctrina, epidemia] to spread - **2.** [luz, calor] to diffuse; [emisión radiofónica] to broadcast.

◆ **difundirse** vprnl - **1.** [noticia, doctrina, epidemia] to spread - **2.** [luz, calor] to be diffused.

difunto, ta ◇ adj [gen] deceased, dead; **el difunto Sr. Pérez** the late Mr Pérez. ◇ sm, f: **el difunto** the deceased.

difusión sf - **1.** [de cultura, noticia, doctrina] dissemination - **2.** [de luz, calor, ondas] diffusion - **3.** [de programa] broadcasting.

difuso, sa adj [luz] diffuse; [estilo, explicación] wordy.

difusor, ra ◇ adj [medio, agencia] broadcasting. ◇ sm, f propagator.

diga ▷ **decir**.

digerir [27] vt to digest; fig [hechos] to assimilate, to take in.

digestión sf digestion; **hacer la digestión** to digest one's food.

digestivo, va adj digestive.

◆ **digestivo** sm digestive (drink).

digiera, digiriera etc ▷ **digerir**.

digital adj - **1.** [del dedo] finger (antes de s) - **2.** INFORM & TECNOL digital.

digitalización sf INFORM digitizing.

digitalizar vt INFORM to digitize.

dígito sm digit.

dignarse vprnl: **dignarse a** to deign to.

dignatario, ria sm, f dignitary.

dignidad sf - **1.** [cualidad] dignity - **2.** [cargo] office - **3.** [persona] dignitary.

dignificar [10] vt to dignify.

digno, na adj - **1.** [noble - actitud, respuesta] dignified; [- persona] honourable, noble - **2.** [merecedor]: **digno de** worthy of; **digno de elogio** praiseworthy; **digno de mención/de ver** worth mentioning/seeing - **3.** [adecuado]: **digno de** appropriate for, fitting for - **4.** [decente - sueldo, actuación etc] decent, good.

digo ▷ **decir**.

dije adj Amér nice, pleasant.

dijera *etc* ⊳ **decir**.

dilapidar *vt* to squander, to waste.

dilatación *sf* [gen] expansion; [de retina, útero] dilation.

dilatar *vt* - **1.** [extender] to expand; [retina, útero] to dilate - **2.** [prolongar] to prolong - **3.** [demorar] to delay.

◆ **dilatarse** *vprnl* - **1.** [extenderse] to expand; [retina, útero] to dilate - **2.** [prolongarse] to be prolonged, to go on - **3.** [demorarse] to be delayed.

dilema *sm* dilemma.

diligencia *sf* - **1.** [esmero, cuidado] diligence - **2.** [prontitud] speed - **3.** [trámite, gestión] business *(U)*; **hacer una diligencia** to run an errand - **4.** [vehículo] stagecoach.

◆ **diligencias** *sfpl* DER proceedings; **instruir diligencias** to start proceedings.

diligente *adj* diligent.

diluir [51] *vt* to dilute.

◆ **diluirse** *vprnl* to dissolve.

diluviar [8] *v impers* to pour with rain.

diluvio *sm* lit & fig flood; **el Diluvio Universal** the Flood.

diluya, diluyera *etc* ⊳ **diluir**.

dimensión *sf* dimension; **las dimensiones de la tragedia** the extent of the tragedy.

diminutivo *sm* diminutive.

diminuto, ta *adj* tiny, minute.

dimisión *sf* resignation; **presentar la dimisión** to hand in one's resignation.

dimitir *vi*: **dimitir (de)** to resign (from).

dimos ⊳ **dar**.

Dinamarca *n pr* Denmark.

dinámico, ca *adj* dynamic.

◆ **dinámica** *sf* - **1.** [gen] dynamics *pl*; **dinámica de grupo** group dynamics *pl* - **2.** FÍS dynamics *(U)*.

dinamismo *sm* dynamism.

dinamita *sf* dynamite.

dinamitar *vt* to dynamite.

dinamizar [13] *vt* to speed up.

dinamo, dínamo *sf* dynamo.

dinastía *sf* dynasty.

dineral *sm* fam fortune.

dinero *sm* money; **andar bien/mal de dinero** to be well off for/short of money; **hacer dinero** to make money; **tirar el dinero** to throw money away; **una familia de dinero** a family of means; **dinero circulante** ECON money in circulation; **dinero contante (y sonante)** hard cash; **dinero de curso legal** legal tender; **dinero en metálico** cash; **dinero negro** *o* **sucio** illegally obtained money; **dinero suelto** loose change.

dinosaurio *sm* dinosaur.

dintel *sm* ARQUIT lintel.

diñar *vt fam*: **diñarla** to snuff it.

dio ⊳ **dar**.

diócesis *sf* diocese.

dioptría *sf* dioptre.

dios, osa *sm, f* god (*f* goddess).

◆ **Dios** *sm* God; **¡a Dios gracias!** thank heavens!; **a la buena de Dios** any old how; **a Dios rogando y con el mazo dando** *prov* God helps those who help themselves; **¡anda** *o* **ve con Dios!** God be with you!; **armar la de Dios es Cristo** to raise hell, to make an almighty racket; **como Dios le da a entender** as best one can; **como Dios manda** properly; **para comer como Dios manda hay que sentarse en la mesa** to eat properly, you have to sit down at a table first; **Dios dirá** it's in the lap of the gods; **Dios los cría y ellos se juntan** *prov* birds of a feather flock together *prov*; **¡Dios me libre!** God *o* heaven forbid!; **Dios mediante, si Dios quiere** God willing; **¡Dios mío!** good God!, (oh) my God!; **Dios sabe, sabe Dios** God (alone) knows; **¡que Dios se lo pague!** God bless you!; **necesitar Dios y ayuda** to have one's work cut out; **¡por Dios!** for God's sake!; **sin encomendarse a Dios ni al diablo** throwing caution to the winds; **¡válgame Dios!** goodness gracious!, bless my soul!; **¡vaya por Dios!** for Heaven's sake!, honestly!

diploma *sm* diploma.

diplomacia *sf* - **1.** [gen] diplomacy - **2.** [carrera] diplomatic service.

diplomado, da ◇ *adj* qualified. ◇ *sm, f* holder of a diploma.

diplomático, ca ◇ *adj* lit & fig diplomatic. ◇ *sm, f* diplomat.

diptongo *sm* diphthong.

diputación *sf* - **1.** [corporación] committee; **diputación permanente** standing committee; **diputación provincial** *governing body of each province of an autonomous region in Spain*, ≃ county council *UK* - **2.** [cargo] post of member of parliament.

diputado, da *sm, f* ≃ Member of Parliament, MP *UK*, representative *US*.

dique *sm* - **1.** [en río] dike; **dique de contención** dam - **2.** [en puerto] dock; **dique flotante** floating docks; **dique seco** dry dock; **estar en (el) dique seco** fig to be out of action.

dirá ⊳ **decir**.

dirección *sf* - **1.** [sentido, rumbo] direction; **calle de dirección única** one-way street; **'dirección prohibida'** 'no entry'; **en dirección a** towards, in the direction of - **2.** [domicilio] address; **dirección comercial** business address; **dirección electrónica** *o* **de correo elec-**

trónico e-mail address; **dirección particular** home address **- 3.** [mando - de empresa, hospital] management; [- de partido] leadership; [- de colegio] headship; [- de periódico] editorship; [- de película] direction; [- de obra de teatro] production; [- de orquesta] conducting **- 4.** [junta directiva] management; **dirección comercial** commercial department; **dirección general** head office **- 5.** [de vehículo] steering; **dirección asistida** power steering.

◆ **Dirección** sf: **Dirección General de Tráfico** traffic department (part of the Ministry of the Interior).

direccional <> adj directional. <> sm Amér AUTO indicator.

direccionar vt INFORM to address.

directivo, va <> adj managerial. <> sm, f [jefe] manager.

◆ **directiva** sf [junta] board (of directors).

directo, ta adj **- 1.** [gen] direct **- 2.** [derecho] straight.

◆ **directo** <> sm [tren] through train. <> adv straight; **directo a** straight to.

◆ **directa** sf AUTO top gear; **poner** o **meter la directa** to go into top gear; fig to really get a move on.

◆ **en directo** loc adv live.

director, ra adj, sm, f **- 1.** [de empresa] director; [de hotel, hospital] manager (f manageress); [de periódico] editor; [de cárcel] governor; **director ejecutivo** executive director; **director general** general manager; **director gerente** managing director **- 2.** [de obra artística]: **director de cine** film director; **director de escena** producer, stage manager; **director de orquesta** conductor **- 3.** [de colegio] headmaster (f headmistress) **- 4.** [de tesis, trabajo de investigación] supervisor; **director espiritual** father confessor; **director técnico** DEP trainer.

directorio sm **- 1.** [gen & INFORM] directory; **directorio raíz** root directory **- 2.**: **directorio telefónico** Andes, Amér C, Caribe & Méx directory.

directriz sf GEOM directrix.

◆ **directrices** sfpl [normas] guidelines.

diría ▷ decir.

dirigente <> adj [en partido] leading; [en empresa] management (antes de s). <> smf [de partido político] leader; [de empresa] manager.

dirigible sm airship.

dirigir [15] vt **- 1.** [conducir - coche, barco] to steer; [- avión] to pilot; fig [- mirada] to direct **- 2.** [llevar - empresa, hotel, hospital] to manage; [- colegio, cárcel, periódico] to run; [- partido, revuelta] to lead; [- expedición] to head **- 3.** [película, obra de teatro] to direct; [orquesta] to conduct

- 4. [carta, paquete] to address **- 5.** [guiar - persona] to guide **- 6.** [dedicar]: **dirigir algo a** to aim sthg at.

◆ **dirigirse** vprnl **- 1.** [encaminarse]: **dirigirse a** o **hacia** to head for **- 2.** [hablar]: **dirigirse a** to address, to speak to **- 3.** [escribir]: **dirigirse a** to write to.

dirija etc ▷ dirigir.

discar [10] vt Andes & R Dom to dial.

discapacidad sf disability.

discernimiento sm discernment.

discernir [21] vt to discern, to distinguish; **discernir algo de algo** to distinguish sthg from sthg.

disciplina sf discipline.

disciplinar vt to discipline.

disciplinario, ria adj disciplinary.

discípulo, la sm, f disciple.

disc-jockey [dis'jokei] smf disc jockey.

disco sm **- 1.** ANAT, ASTRON & GEOM disc **- 2.** [de música] record; **parecer un disco rayado** fam to go on like a cracked record; **disco compacto** compact disc; **disco de larga duración** LP, long-playing record **- 3.** [semáforo] (traffic) light; **saltarse un disco rojo** to jump a red light UK, to to run a red light US **- 4.** DEP discus **- 5.** INFORM disk; **disco de arranque/del sistema** startup/system disk; **disco duro/flexible** hard/floppy disk; **disco magnético** magnetic disk; **disco óptico** optical disk, CD-ROM; **disco removible/rígido** removable/hard disk; **disco virtual** virtual disk; **disco Zip®** Zip® disk **- 6.** [del teléfono] dial.

discografía sf records previously released (by an artist or group).

discográfico, ca adj record (antes de s).

disconforme adj in disagreement; **estar disconforme con** to disagree with.

discontinuo, nua adj [esfuerzo] intermittent; [línea] broken, dotted.

discordante adj [sonidos] discordant; [opiniones] clashing.

discordia sf discord.

discoteca sf **- 1.** [local] disco, discotheque **- 2.** [colección] record collection.

discotequero, ra <> adj disco (antes de s). <> sm, f nightclubber.

discreción sf discretion.

◆ **a discreción** loc adv as much as one wants, freely.

discrecional adj [gen] optional; [parada] request (antes de s).

discrepancia sf [diferencia] difference, discrepancy; [desacuerdo] disagreement.

discrepar vi: **discrepar (de)** [diferenciarse] to differ (from); [disentir] to disagree (with).

discreto, **ta** *adj* - **1.** [prudente] discreet - **2.** [cantidad] moderate, modest - **3.** [no extravagante] modest - **4.** [normal - actuación] fair, reasonable.

discriminación *sf* discrimination; **discriminación racial/sexual** racial/sexual discrimination.

discriminar *vt* - **1.** [cosa]: **discriminar algo de** to discriminate *o* distinguish sthg from - **2.** [persona, colectividad] to discriminate against.

discriminatorio, **ria** *adj* discriminatory.

disculpa *sf* [pretexto] excuse; [excusa, perdón] apology; **dar disculpas** to make excuses; **pedir disculpas a alguien (por)** to apologize to sb (for).

disculpar *vt* to excuse; **disculpar a alguien (de** *o* **por algo)** to forgive sb (for sthg).
➤ **disculparse** *vprnl*: **disculparse (de** *o* **por algo)** to apologize (for sthg).

discurrir ◇ *vi* - **1.** [pasar - personas] to wander, to walk; [- tiempo, vida, sesión] to go by, to pass; [- río, tráfico] to flow - **2.** [pensar] to think, to reflect. ◇ *vt* to come up with.

discurso *sm* speech; **pronunciar un discurso** to make a speech.

discusión *sf* - **1.** [conversación] discussion; **estar en discusión** to be under discussion - **2.** [pelea] argument.

discutible *adj* debatable.

discutir ◇ *vi* - **1.** [hablar] to discuss - **2.** [pelear]: **discutir (de)** to argue (about). ◇ *vt* [hablar] to discuss; [contradecir] to dispute.

disecar [10] *vt* [animal] to stuff; [planta] to dry.

diseminar *vt* [semillas] to scatter; [ideas] to disseminate.

disentería *sf* dysentery.

disentir [27] *vi*: **disentir (de/en)** to disagree (with/on).

diseñador, **ra** *sm, f* designer; **diseñador gráfico** graphic designer; **diseñador industrial** industrial designer; **diseñador de modas** fashion designer; **diseñador de páginas web** web designer.

diseñar *vt* to design.

diseño *sm* design; **ropa de diseño** designer clothes; **diseño asistido por ordenador** INFORM computer-aided design; **diseño gráfico** graphic design; **diseño industrial** industrial design.

diseque *etc* ▷ **disecar**.

disertación *sf* [oral] lecture, discourse; [escrita] dissertation.

disertar *vi*: **disertar (sobre)** to speak *o* to lecture (on).

disfraz *sm* [gen] disguise; [para baile, fiesta etc] fancy dress (*U*).

disfrazar [13] *vt* to disguise; **disfrazar a alguien de** to dress sb up as.
➤ **disfrazarse** *vprnl* to disguise o.s.; **disfrazarse de** to dress up as.

disfrutar ◇ *vi* - **1.** [sentir placer] to enjoy o.s. - **2.** [disponer de]: **disfrutar de algo** to enjoy sthg. ◇ *vt* to enjoy.

disfrute *sm* - **1.** [placer] enjoyment - **2.** [provecho] benefit, use.

disgregar [16] *vt* - **1.** [multitud, manifestación] to disperse, to break up - **2.** [roca, imperio, estado] to break up; [átomo] to split.
➤ **disgregarse** *vprnl* - **1.** [multitud, manifestación] to disperse, to break up - **2.** [roca, imperio, estado] to break up.

disgustar *vt* - **1.** [suj: comentario, críticas, noticia] to upset - **2.** [suj: mal olor] to disgust.
➤ **disgustarse** *vprnl*: **disgustarse (con alguien/por algo)** [sentir enfado] to get upset (with sb/about sthg); [enemistarse] to fall out (with sb/over sthg).

disgusto *sm* - **1.** [enfado] annoyance; [pesadumbre] sorrow, grief; **dar un disgusto a alguien** to upset sb; **llevarse un disgusto** to be upset; **matar a alguien a disgustos** to worry sb to death - **2.** [desinterés, incomodidad]: **hacer algo a disgusto** to do sthg unwillingly *o* reluctantly; **estar a disgusto** to feel uncomfortable *o* uneasy - **3.** [pelea]: **tener un disgusto con alguien** to have a quarrel with sb.

disidencia *sf* [política, religiosa] dissidence; [desacuerdo] disagreement.

disidente ◇ *adj* [en política] dissident; [en religión] dissenting. ◇ *smf* [político] dissident; [religioso] dissenter.

disienta *etc* ▷ **disentir**.

disimulado, **da** *adj* hidden, concealed; **hacerse el disimulado** to pretend not to notice.

disimular ◇ *vt* to hide, to conceal. ◇ *vi* to pretend.

disimulo *sm* pretence, concealment; **con disimulo** furtively.

disintiera *etc* ▷ **disentir**.

disipar *vt* - **1.** [dudas, sospechas] to dispel; [ilusiones] to shatter - **2.** [fortuna, herencia] to squander, to throw away - **3.** [niebla, humo, vapor] to drive *o* blow away.
➤ **disiparse** *vprnl* - **1.** [dudas, sospechas] to be dispelled; [ilusiones] to be shattered - **2.** [niebla, humo, vapor] to vanish.

diskette = **disquete**.

dislexia *sm* dyslexia.

disléxico, **ca** *adj* & *sm, f* dyslexic.

dislocación *sf* dislocation.

dislocar [10] *vt* to dislocate.
◆ **dislocarse** *vprnl* to dislocate.
disminución *sf* decrease, drop; **ir en disminución** to be on the decrease.
disminuido, da ◇ *adj* handicapped. ◇ *sm, f* handicapped person; **disminuido físico** physically-handicapped person; **disminuido psíquico** mentally-handicapped person.
disminuir [51] ◇ *vt* to reduce, to decrease. ◇ *vi* [gen] to decrease; [precios, temperatura] to drop, to fall; [vista, memoria] to fail; [días] to get shorter; [beneficios] to fall off.
disociar [8] *vt*: **disociar (de)** to dissociate (from).
disolución *sf* - **1.** [en un líquido] dissolving - **2.** [de matrimonio, sociedad, partido] dissolution - **3.** [mezcla] solution.
disolvente *adj* & *sm* solvent.
disolver [24] *vt* - **1.** [gen] to dissolve - **2.** [reunión, manifestación, familia] to break up.
◆ **disolverse** *vprnl* - **1.** [gen] to dissolve - **2.** [reunión, manifestación, familia] to break up.
disparado, da *adj*: **salir/entrar disparado** to shoot out/in.
disparador *sm* - **1.** [de armas] trigger - **2.** FOTO shutter release.
disparar ◇ *vt* to shoot; [pedrada] to throw. ◇ *vi* to shoot, to fire.
◆ **dispararse** *vprnl* - **1.** [arma] to go off - **2.** [precipitarse - persona] to rush off; [- caballo] to bolt - **3.** [perder los estribos] to get carried away - **4.** [precios, inflación] to shoot up.
disparatado, da *adj* absurd, crazy.
disparatar *vi* [decir tonterías] to talk nonsense; [hacer tonterías] to behave foolishly.
disparate *sm* - **1.** [acción] silly thing; [comentario] foolish remark; [idea] crazy idea; **hacer disparates** to do silly things; **decir disparates** to make foolish remarks, to talk nonsense - **2.** [cantidad excesiva]: **gastar un disparate** to spend a ridiculous amount.
disparo *sm* shot; **disparo de advertencia** warning shot; **disparo de salida** starting shot.
dispensar *vt* - **1.** [disculpar] to excuse, to forgive - **2.** [rendir]: **dispensar algo (a alguien)** [honores] to confer sthg (upon sb); [bienvenida, ayuda] to give sthg (to sb) - **3.** [eximir]: **dispensar a alguien de** to excuse *o* exempt sb from.
dispensario *sm* dispensary.
dispersar *vt* - **1.** [esparcir - objetos] to scatter - **2.** [disolver - gentío] to disperse; [- manifestación] to break up; [- esfuerzos] to dissipate.
◆ **dispersarse** *vprnl* to scatter.
dispersión *sf* - **1.** [de objetos] scattering - **2.** [de gentío, luz] scattering; [de manifestación] breaking up.

disperso, sa *adj* scattered.
display [dis'plei] *sm* INFORM display.
displicencia *sf* - **1.** [desagrado] contempt - **2.** [negligencia] carelessness; [desgana] lack of enthusiasm.
displicente *adj* - **1.** [desagradable] contemptuous - **2.** [negligente] careless; [desganado] unenthusiastic.
disponer [65] ◇ *vt* - **1.** [gen] to arrange - **2.** [cena, comida] to lay on - **3.** [decidir - suj: persona] to decide; [suj: ley] to stipulate. ◇ *vi* - **1.** [poseer]: **disponer de** to have - **2.** [usar]: **disponer de** to make use of.
◆ **disponerse a** *vprnl*: **disponerse a hacer algo** to prepare *o* get ready to do sthg.
disponibilidad *sf* - **1.** [gen] availability - **2.** [a ayudar] readiness to help.
◆ **disponibilidades** *sfpl* [medios] financial resources.
disponible *adj* [gen] available; [tiempo] free, spare.
disposición *sf* - **1.** [colocación] arrangement, layout - **2.** [estado]: **estar *o* hallarse en disposición de hacer algo** to be prepared *o* ready to do sthg - **3.** [orden] order; [de ley] provision - **4.** [uso]: **a disposición de** at the disposal of; **pasar a disposición policial** to be brought before the judge - **5.** *fig* [aptitud] talent.
dispositivo *sm* device; **dispositivo intrauterino** intrauterine device, IUD.
dispuesto, ta ◇ *pp* ▷ **disponer**. ◇ *adj* - **1.** [preparado] ready; **estar dispuesto a hacer algo** to be prepared to do sthg; **estar poco dispuesto a hacer algo** to be reluctant to do sthg - **2.** [capaz] capable; [a ayudar] ready to help.
dispusiera *etc* ▷ **disponer**.
disputa *sf* dispute.
disputar *vt* - **1.** [cuestión, tema] to argue about - **2.** [trofeo, puesto] to compete for, to dispute; [carrera, partido] to compete in.
disquete, diskette [dis'kete] *sm* INFORM diskette, floppy disk.
disquetera *sf* INFORM disk drive.
distancia *sf* - **1.** [gen] distance; **a distancia** from a distance; **mantener a distancia** to keep at a distance; **mantener las distancias** to keep one's distance; **recorrer una gran distancia** to cover a lot of ground; **distancia de seguridad** safe distance - **2.** [en el tiempo] gap, space - **3.** [diferencia] difference - **4.** *loc*: **acortar las distancias** to come closer (to an agreement); **guardar las distancias** to keep one's distance; **salvando las distancias** only up to a point.
distanciamiento *sm* [afectivo] distance, coldness.
distanciar [8] *vt* [gen] to drive apart; [rival] to forge ahead of.

◆ **distanciarse** *vprnl* [alejarse - afectivamente] to grow apart; [- físicamente] to distance o.s.

distante *adj* - **1.** [en el espacio]: **distante (de)** far away (from) - **2.** [en el trato] distant.

distar *vi* - **1.** [hallarse a]: **ese sitio dista varios kilómetros de aquí** that place is several kilometres away from here - **2.** *fig* [diferenciarse]: **distar de** to be far from.

diste *etc* ⊳ **dar.**

distender [20] *vt* [situación, relaciones] to ease; [cuerda] to slacken.

distendido, da *adj* [informal] relaxed, informal.

distensión *sf* - **1.** [entre países] détente; [entre personas] easing of tension - **2.** [de arco, cuerda] slackening - **3.** MED strain.

distienda *etc* ⊳ **distender.**

distinción *sf* - **1.** [diferencia] distinction; **a distinción de** in contrast to, unlike; **sin distinción** alike; **hacer distinciones** not to treat everyone the same - **2.** [privilegio] privilege - **3.** [elegancia] refinement.

distinguido, da *adj* - **1.** [notable] distinguished - **2.** [elegante] refined.

distinguir [17] *vt* - **1.** [diferenciar] to distinguish; **distinguir algo de algo** to tell sthg from sthg - **2.** [separar] to pick out - **3.** [caracterizar] to characterize - **4.** [premiar] to honour - **5.** [vislumbrar] to make out.

◆ **distinguirse** *vprnl* - **1.** [destacarse] to stand out - **2.** [vislumbrarse] to be visible.

distintivo, va *adj* distinctive; [señal] distinguishing.

◆ **distintivo** *sm* badge.

distinto, ta *adj* [diferente] different.

◆ **distintos, tas** *adj pl* [varios] various.

distorsión *sf* [de tobillo, rodilla] sprain; [de imágenes, sonidos, palabras] distortion.

distorsionar *vt* to distort.

distracción *sf* - **1.** [entretenimiento] entertainment; [pasatiempo] hobby, pastime - **2.** [despiste] slip; [falta de atención] absent-mindedness.

distraer [73] *vt* - **1.** [divertir] to amuse, to entertain - **2.** [despistar] to distract.

◆ **distraerse** *vprnl* - **1.** [divertirse] to enjoy o.s.; [pasar el tiempo] to pass the time - **2.** [despistarse] to let one's mind wander.

distraído, da ◇ *adj* - **1.** [entretenido] amusing, entertaining - **2.** [despistado] absent-minded. ◇ *sm, f* daydreamer, absent-minded person; **hacerse el distraído** to pretend not to notice.

distribución *sf* - **1.** [gen] distribution; **distribución de premios** prizegiving - **2.** [de correo, mercancías] delivery; **distribución comercial** commercial distribution - **3.** [de casa, habitaciones] layout.

distribuidor, ra ◇ *adj* [entidad] wholesale; [red] supply *(antes de s)*. ◇ *sm, f* [persona] deliveryman (*f* deliverywoman).

◆ **distribuidor** *sm* [aparato] vending machine.

◆ **distribuidora** *sf* [firma] wholesaler, supplier.

distribuir [51] *vt* - **1.** [gen] to distribute; [carga, trabajo] to spread; [pastel, ganancias] to divide up - **2.** [correo, mercancías] to deliver - **3.** [casa, habitaciones] to arrange.

distributivo, va *adj* distributive.

distrito *sm* district; **distrito electoral** constituency; **distrito postal** postal district.

disturbio *sm* disturbance; [violento] riot; **disturbios raciales** race riots.

disuadir *vt*: **disuadir (de)** to dissuade (from).

disuasión *sf* deterrence.

disuasivo, va *adj* deterrent.

disuelto, ta *pp* ⊳ **disolver.**

disuelva *etc* ⊳ **disolver.**

disyuntivo, va *adj* GRAM disjunctive.

◆ **disyuntiva** *sf* straight choice.

DIU (*abrev de* **dispositivo intrauterino**) *sm* IUD.

diurético, ca *adj & sm* diuretic.

diurno, na *adj* [gen] daytime *(antes de s)*; [planta, animal] diurnal.

diva ⊳ **divo.**

divagación *sf* digression.

divagar [16] *vi* to digress.

diván *sm* divan; [de psiquiatra] couch.

divergencia *sf* - **1.** [de líneas] divergence - **2.** [de opinión] difference of opinion.

divergir [15] *vi* - **1.** [calles, líneas] to diverge - **2.** *fig* [opiniones]: **divergir (en)** to differ (on).

diversidad *sf* diversity.

diversificación *sf* diversification.

diversificar [10] *vt* to diversify.

◆ **diversificarse** *vprnl* to grow apart.

diversión *sf* entertainment, amusement.

diverso, sa *adj* [diferente] different.

◆ **diversos, sas** *adj pl* [varios] several, various.

divertido, da *adj* [entretenido - película, libro] entertaining; [- fiesta] enjoyable; [que hace reír] funny.

divertir [27] *vt* to entertain, to amuse.

◆ **divertirse** *vprnl* to enjoy o.s.

dividendo *sm* FIN & MAT dividend; **dividendo a cuenta** interim dividend.

dividir *vt*: **dividir (en)** to divide (into); **dividir entre** [gen] to divide between; MAT to divide by.

divierta *etc* ⊳ **divertir.**

divinidad *sf* divinity, god.

divino, na *adj* lit & fig divine.

divirtiera *etc* ⊳ **divertir.**

divisa *sf* - **1.** *(gen pl)* [moneda] foreign currency; **divisa convertible** convertible currency - **2.** [distintivo] emblem.

divisar *vt* to spy, to make out.

división *sf* [gen] division; [partición] splitting up; **división del trabajo** ECON division of labour.

divisor *sm* MAT divisor; **máximo común divisor** highest common factor.

divisorio, ria *adj* dividing.

divo, va *sm, f* - **1.** [MÚS - mujer] diva, prima donna; [- hombre] opera singer - **2.** [celebridad] star.

divorciado, da <> *adj* divorced. <> *sm, f* divorcé (*f* divorcée).

divorciar [8] *vt* lit & fig to divorce.
◆ **divorciarse** *vprnl* to get divorced.

divorcio *sm* - **1.** DER divorce - **2.** fig [diferencia] difference, inconsistency.

divulgación *sf* [de noticia, secreto] revelation; [de rumor] spreading; [de cultura, ciencia, doctrina] popularization.

divulgar [16] *vt* [noticia, secreto] to reveal; [rumor] to spread; [cultura, ciencia, doctrina] to popularize.

dl (*abrev de* **decilitro**) dl.

dm (*abrev de* **decímetro**) dm.

DNI (*abrev de* **documento nacional de identidad**) *sm* ID card.

Dña *abrev de* **doña**.

do *sm* MÚS C; [en solfeo] doh; **dar el do de pecho** fam fig to give one's all.

dobladillo *sm* [de traje, vestido] hem; [de pantalón] turn-up UK, cuff US; **hacer un dobladillo** to turn up, to hem.

doblado, da *adj* - **1.** [papel, camisa] folded - **2.** [voz, película] dubbed.

doblaje *sm* dubbing.

doblar <> *vt* - **1.** [duplicar] to double - **2.** [plegar] to fold - **3.** [torcer] to bend - **4.** [esquina] to turn, to go round - **5.** [voz, actor] to dub. <> *vi* - **1.** [girar] to turn - **2.** [campanas] to toll.
◆ **doblarse** *vprnl* [someterse]: **doblarse a** to give in to.

doble <> *adj* double; **tiene doble número de habitantes** it has double o twice the number of inhabitants; **es doble de ancho** it's twice as wide; **una frase de doble sentido** a phrase with a double meaning; **doble clic** INFORM double click. <> *smf* [gen & CINE] double. <> *sm* [duplo]: **el doble** twice as much; **gana el doble que yo** she earns twice as much as I do, she earns double what I do. <> *adv* double; **trabajar doble** to work twice as hard.
◆ **dobles** *smpl* DEP doubles.

doblegar [16] *vt* [someter] to bend, to cause to give in.
◆ **doblegarse** *vprnl*: **doblegarse (ante)** to give in o yield (to).

doblete *sm* [joya] fake, imitation; LING doublet.

doblez <> *sm* [pliegue] fold, crease. <> *sm o sf* fig [falsedad] deceit.

doc. (*abrev de* **documento**) doc.

doce *num* twelve; *ver también* **seis**.

doceavo, va *num* twelfth; **la doceava parte** a twelfth.

docena *sf* dozen; **a** o **por docenas** by the dozen.

docencia *sf* teaching.

docente <> *adj* teaching; **centro docente** educational institution. <> *smf* teacher.

dócil *adj* obedient.

docilidad *sf* obedience.

doctor, ra *sm, f*: **doctor (en)** doctor (of).

doctorado *sm* doctorate.

doctoral *adj* doctoral.

doctorar *vt* to confer a doctorate on.
◆ **doctorarse** *vprnl*: **doctorarse (en)** to get one's doctorate (in).

doctrina *sf* doctrine.

doctrinal *adj* doctrinal.

documentación *sf* - **1.** [en archivos] documentation - **2.** [identificación personal] papers *pl*.

documentado, da *adj* - **1.** [informado - película, informe] researched; [- persona] informed - **2.** [con papeles encima] having identification.

documental *adj* & *sm* documentary.

documentar *vt* - **1.** [evidenciar] to document - **2.** [informar] to brief.
◆ **documentarse** *vprnl* to do research.

documento *sm* - **1.** [escrito] document; **documento nacional de identidad** identity card - **2.** [testimonio] record.

Documento Nacional de Identidad

It is mandatory in many countries to carry a national identity card or Documento Nacional de Identidad ("DNI") showing the bearer's personal details and a photo. In Spain it is also called a "carné", and all Spanish citizens have to carry one from the age of fourteen. The card is renewed every five or ten years at police stations, and must be shown to police upon demand. A similar document, the "Cédula (Nacional) de Identidad" is carried in Colombia, Paraguay, Uruguay, Venezuela, Argentina and Chile. It is called the "Documento Nacional de Identidad" in Peru.

dodecaedro *sm* dodecahedron.

dogma *sm* dogma.

dogmático, ca *adj* dogmatic.

dogmatismo *sm* dogmatism.

dogmatizar [13] *vi* to see everything in a dogmatic way.

dogo *smf* bull mastiff.

dólar *sm* dollar.

dolencia *sf* pain.

doler [24] *vi* to hurt; **me duele la pierna** my leg hurts; **¿te duele?** does it hurt?; **me duele la garganta/la cabeza** I have a sore throat/a headache; **me duele ver tanta injusticia** it pains me to see so much injustice; **¡ahí le duele!** that has really got him/her *etc*!

◆ **dolerse** *vprnl*: **dolerse de** o **por algo** [quejarse] to complain about sthg; [arrepentirse] to be sorry about sthg.

dolido, da *adj* hurt.

dolmen *sm* dolmen.

dolor *sm* - **1.** [físico] pain; **siento un dolor en el brazo** I have a pain in my arm; (tener) **dolor de cabeza** (to have a) headache; **dolor de estómago** stomachache; **dolor de muelas** toothache - **2.** [moral] grief, sorrow.

dolorido, da *adj* [físicamente] sore; [moralmente] grieving, sorrowing.

doloroso, sa *adj* [físicamente] painful; [moralmente] distressing.

doma *sf* taming; [de caballos] breaking-in.

domador, ra *sm, f* [de caballos] breaker; [de leones] tamer.

domar *vt* [gen] to tame; [caballo] to break in; *fig* [personas] to control.

domesticar [10] *vt lit & fig* to tame.

doméstico, ca *adj* domestic.

domiciliación *sf*: **domiciliación (bancaria)** standing order, direct debit *(U)*.

domiciliar [8] *vt* - **1.** [pago] to pay by direct debit o standing order - **2.** [persona] to put up.

domiciliario, ria *adj* house *(antes de s)*.

domicilio *sm* - **1.** [vivienda] residence, home; **servicio a domicilio** home delivery; **venta a domicilio** door-to-door selling; **domicilio particular** private residence - **2.** [dirección] address; **sin domicilio fijo** of no fixed abode; **domicilio fiscal** registered office; **domicilio social** head office - **3.** [localidad] residence.

dominación *sf* rule, dominion.

dominante ◇ *adj* - **1.** [nación, religión, tendencia] dominant; [vientos] prevailing - **2.** [persona] domineering. ◇ *sf* predominant feature.

dominar ◇ *vt* - **1.** [controlar - país, territorio] to dominate, to rule (over); [- pasión, nervios, caballo] to control; [- situación] to be in control of; [- incendio] to bring under control; [- rebelión] to put down - **2.** [divisar] to overlook - **3.** [conocer - técnica, tema] to master; [- lengua] to be fluent in. ◇ *vi* [predominar] to predominate.

◆ **dominarse** *vprnl* to control o.s.

domingo *sm* Sunday; **domingo de Ramos** Palm Sunday; **domingo de Resurrección** o **de Pascua** Easter Sunday; *ver también* **sábado**.

dominguero, ra ◇ *adj fam despec* Sunday *(antes de s)*. ◇ *sm, f* Sunday tripper/driver *etc*.

dominical *adj* Sunday *(antes de s)*.

dominicano, na *adj* & *sm, f* Dominican.

dominico, ca *adj* & *sm, f* Dominican.

dominio *sm* - **1.** [dominación, posesión]: **dominio (sobre)** control (over); **dominio de** o **sobre sí mismo** self-control - **2.** [autoridad] authority, power - **3.** *fig* [territorio] domain; [ámbito] realm - **4.** [conocimiento - de arte, técnica] mastery; [- de idiomas] command - **5.** INFORM domain - **6.** *loc*: **ser del dominio público** to be public knowledge.

◆ **dominios** *smpl* [territorio] dominions.

dominó *sm* - **1.** [juego] dominoes *(U)* - **2.** [fichas] set of dominoes.

don *sm* - **1.** [tratamiento]: **don Luis García** [gen] Mr Luis García; [en cartas] Luis García Esquire; **don Luis** *not translated in modern English or translated as 'Mr' + surname, if known* - **2.** [habilidad] gift; **don de mando** leadership qualities; **el don de la palabra** the gift of the gab; **tener don de gentes** to have a way with people.

donación *sf* donation.

donaire *sm* [al expresarse] wit; [al andar etc] grace.

donante *smf* donor; **donante de sangre** blood donor.

donar *vt* to donate.

donativo *sm* donation.

doncella *sf* maid.

donde ◇ *adv* where; **el bolso está donde lo dejaste** the bag is where you left it; **puedes marcharte donde quieras** you can go wherever you want; **hasta donde** as far as, up to where; **llegaré hasta donde pueda** I'll get as far as I can; **por donde** wherever; **iré por donde me manden** I'll go wherever they send me. ◇ *pron* where; **la casa donde nací** the house where I was born; **la ciudad de donde viene** the town (where) she comes from, the town from which she comes; **hacia donde** towards where, towards which; **hasta donde** as far as where, as far as which.

◆ **de donde** *loc adv* [de lo cual] from which.

dónde *adv (interrogativo)* where; **¿dónde está el niño?** where's the child?; **no sé dónde se ha-**

brá metido I don't know where she can be; **¿a dónde vas?** where are you going?; **¿de dónde eres?** where are you from?; **¿hacia dónde vas?** where are you heading?; **¿por dónde?** whereabouts?; **¿por dónde se va al teatro?** how do you get to the theatre from here?

dondequiera ➤ **dondequiera que** *adv* wherever.

doña *sf*: **doña Luisa García** Mrs Luisa García; **doña Luisa** *not translated in modern English or translated as 'Mrs' + surname, if known.*

dopado, **da** *adj* having taken performance-enhancing drugs.

dopar *vt* to dope.

➤ **doparse** *vprnl* to take artificial stimulants.

doping ['dopin] *sm* doping.

doquier ➤ **por doquier** *loc adv* everywhere.

dorado, **da** *adj lit & fig* golden.

➤ **dorado** *sm* [material] gilt.

➤ **dorada** *sf* [pez] gilthead.

dorar *vt* - **1.** [cubrir con oro] to gild - **2.** [alimento] to brown - **3.** [piel] to turn golden brown.

➤ **dorarse** *vprnl* - **1.** [comida] to glaze - **2.** [piel] to tan.

dórico, **ca** *adj* Doric.

dormilón, **ona** *fam* ◇ *adj* fond of sleeping. ◇ *sm, f* [persona] sleepyhead.

➤ **dormilona** *sf* Ven [prenda] nightshirt, nightdress.

dormir [25] ◇ *vt* [niño, animal] to put to bed; **dormir la siesta** to have an afternoon nap; **dormirla** *fam* to sleep it off. ◇ *vi* to sleep.

➤ **dormirse** *vprnl* - **1.** [persona] to fall asleep - **2.** [brazo, mano] to go to sleep - **3.** *fig* [despistarse] to be slow to react.

dormitar *vi* to doze.

dormitorio *sm* - **1.** [de casa] bedroom; [de colegio] dormitory - **2.** [muebles] bedroom suite.

dorsal ◇ *adj* dorsal. ◇ *sm* number *(on player's back).*

dorso *sm* back; **al dorso, en el dorso** on the back; **'véase al dorso'** 'see overleaf'; **dorso de la mano** back of one's hand.

dos *num* two; **de dos en dos** in twos, two by two; **en un dos por tres** in no time at all; **cada dos por tres** every five minutes, continually; *ver también* **seis**.

DOS (*abrev de* **disk operating system**) *sm* DOS.

doscientos, **tas** *num* two hundred; *ver también* **seis**.

dosel *sm* canopy.

dosificador *sm* dispenser.

dosificar [10] *vt* - **1.** QUÍM to measure out - **2.** *fig* [fuerzas, palabras] to use sparingly.

dosis *sf inv lit & fig* dose; **en pequeñas dosis** in small doses.

dossier [do'sjer] *sm inv* dossier, file.

dotación *sf* - **1.** [de dinero, armas, medios] amount granted - **2.** [personal] staff, personnel; [tripulantes] crew; [patrulla] squad.

dotado, **da** *adj* gifted; **dotado de** [persona] blessed with; [edificio, instalación, aparato] equipped with.

dotar *vt* - **1.** [proveer]: **dotar algo de** to provide sthg with - **2.** [tripular]: **dotar algo de** to man sthg with - **3.** *fig* [suj: la naturaleza]: **dotar a algo/alguien de** to endow sthg/sb with - **4.** [dar una dote] to give a dowry to.

dote *sf* [en boda] dowry.

➤ **dotes** *sfpl* [dones] qualities; **dotes de mando** leadership qualities.

doy ➩ **dar.**

Dr. (*abrev de* **doctor**) Dr.

Dra. (*abrev de* **doctora**) Dr.

draconiano, **na** *adj fig* draconian.

draga *sf* [máquina] dredge; [barco] dredger.

dragado *sm* dredging.

dragaminas *sm inv* minesweeper.

dragar [16] *vt* to dredge.

dragón *sm* dragon.

drague *etc* ➩ **dragar.**

drama *sm* [gen] drama; [obra] play.

dramático, **ca** *adj* dramatic.

dramatismo *sm* dramatic nature, drama.

dramatizar [13] *vt* to dramatize.

dramaturgo, **ga** *sm, f* playwright, dramatist.

dramón *sm fam* melodrama.

drástico, **ca** *adj* drastic.

drenaje *sm* drainage.

drenar *vt* to drain.

driblar *vt* DEP to dribble.

drive [draif] *sm* DEP drive.

droga *sf* drug; **la droga** drugs *pl*; **droga blanda/dura** soft/hard drug; **droga de diseño** designer drug.

drogadicción *sf* drug addiction.

drogadicto, **ta** ◇ *adj* addicted to drugs. ◇ *sm, f* drug addict.

drogar [16] *vt* to drug.

➤ **drogarse** *vprnl* to take drugs.

drogodependencia *sf* drug dependence, drug addiction.

drogue *etc* ➩ **drogar.**

droguería *sf* - **1.** [tienda] *shop selling paint, cleaning materials etc* - **2.** Col [farmacia] pharmacy, drugstore US - **3.** Amér C, Andes & R Plata [distribuidora] pharmaceutical wholesalers.

droguero, **ra** *sm, f* *owner of a shop selling paint, cleaning materials etc.*

dromedario *sm* dromedary.

dto. *abrev de* **descuento**.

dual *adj* dual.

dualidad *sf* duality.

dualismo *sm* dualism.

dubitativo, va *adj* hesitant.

Dublín *n pr* Dublin.

dublinés, esa ◇ *adj* of/relating to Dublin.
◇ *sm, f* Dubliner.

ducado *sm* - **1.** [tierras] duchy - **2.** [moneda]
ducat.

ducha *sf* shower; **tomar** *o* **darse una ducha** to
have *o* take a shower; **una ducha de agua fría**
fam fig a bucket of cold water; **ducha de teléfono** hand-held shower.

duchar *vt* to shower.
◆ **ducharse** *vprnl* to have a shower.

ducho, cha *adj*: **ser ducho en** [entendido] to
know a lot about; [diestro] to be skilled at.

dúctil *adj* - **1.** [metal] ductile - **2.** [persona] malleable.

ductilidad *sf* - **1.** [de metal] ductility - **2.** [de
persona] malleability.

duda *sf* doubt; **poner algo en duda** to call sthg
into question; **sacar a alguien de la duda** to
remove sb's doubts; **salir de dudas** to set one's
mind at rest; **sin duda** doubtless, undoubtedly; **sin la menor duda** without the
slightest doubt; **sin sombra de duda** beyond
the shadow of a doubt; **tener uno sus dudas** to
have one's doubts; **no cabe duda** there is no
doubt about it; **no te quepa duda** don't doubt
it, make no mistake about it.

dudar ◇ *vi* - **1.** [desconfiar]: **dudar de algo/
alguien** to have one's doubts about sthg/sb
- **2.** [no estar seguro]: **dudar sobre algo** to be
unsure about sthg - **3.** [vacilar] to hesitate; **dudar entre hacer una cosa u otra** to be unsure
whether to do one thing or another. ◇ *vt* to
doubt; **dudo que venga** I doubt whether he'll
come.

dudoso, sa *adj* - **1.** [improbable]: **ser dudoso
(que)** to be doubtful (whether), to be unlikely
(that) - **2.** [vacilante] hesitant, indecisive
- **3.** [sospechoso] questionable, suspect.

duela *etc* ▷ **doler**.

duelo *sm* - **1.** [combate] duel; **batirse en duelo**
to fight a duel - **2.** [sentimiento] grief, sorrow;
en señal de duelo to show one's grief.

duende *sm* - **1.** [personaje] imp, goblin - **2.** *fig*
[encanto] charm.

dueño, ña *sm, f* [gen] owner; [de piso etc] landlord (*f* landlady); **cambiar de dueño** to change
hands; **hacerse dueño de algo** to take control

of sthg; **ser dueño de sí mismo** to be self-possessed; **ser muy dueño de hacer algo** to be
free to do sthg.

duerma *etc* ▷ **dormir**.

Duero *sm*: **el Duero** the Douro.

dueto *sm* duet.

dulce ◇ *adj* - **1.** [gen] sweet - **2.** [agua] fresh
- **3.** [mirada] tender. ◇ *sm* [caramelo, postre]
sweet; [pastel] cake, pastry; **a nadie le amarga
un dulce** *fig* anything's better than nothing.

dulcificar [10] *vt* - **1.** [endulzar] to sweeten
- **2.** *fig* [suavizar] to soften.

dulzura *sf* - **1.** [gen] sweetness - **2.** [palabra ca-
riñosa] sweet nothing.

duna *sf* dune.

dúo *sm* - **1.** MÚS duet - **2.** [pareja] duo; **a dúo**
together.

duodécimo, ma *num* twelfth.

duodeno *sm* duodenum.

dúplex, duplex *sm inv* - **1.** [piso] duplex
- **2.** ELECTRÓN linkup.

duplicado, da *adj* in duplicate.
◆ **duplicado** *sm*: **(por) duplicado** (in) duplicate.

duplicar [10] *vt* - **1.** [cantidad] to double
- **2.** [documento] to duplicate.
◆ **duplicarse** *vprnl* to double.

duplicidad *sf* - **1.** [repetición] duplication
- **2.** [falsedad] duplicity.

duplo, pla *adj & sm* double.

duque, esa *sm, f* duke (*f* duchess).

duración *sf* length; **de larga duración** [pila,
bombilla] long-life; [parado] long-term; [disco]
long-playing.

duradero, ra *adj* [gen] lasting; [ropa, zapatos]
hard-wearing.

duralex® *sm* *resistant glass-like plastic
used for making glasses, dishes etc*.

durante *prep* during; **le escribí durante las
vacaciones** I wrote to him during the holidays;
estuve escribiendo durante una hora I was
writing for an hour; **durante toda la semana**
all week.

durar *vi* [gen] to last; [permanecer, subsistir] to remain, to stay; [ropa] to wear well; **aún dura la
fiesta** the party's still going on.

durazno *sm* *Amér* peach.

dureza *sf* - **1.** [de objeto, metal etc] hardness
- **2.** [de clima, persona] harshness - **3.** [callosidad]
callus, hard skin (*U*).

durmiente *adj* sleeping; **la Bella Durmiente**
Sleeping Beauty.

durmiera *etc* ▷ **dormir**.

duro, ra *adj* - **1.** [gen] hard; [carne] tough
- **2.** [resistente] tough - **3.** [palabras, clima] harsh
- **4.** *loc*: **estar a las duras y a las maduras** [sin

rendirse] to be there through thick and thin; [sin quejarse] to take the rough with the smooth; **ser duro de pelar** to be a hard nut to crack.

◆ **duro** ◇ *sm* - **1.** [moneda] five-peseta piece; **estar sin un duro** to be flat broke - **2.** [persona] tough guy - **3.** *loc*: **lo que faltaba para el duro** that's all I/we *etc* need. ◇ *adv* hard.

DVD (*abrev de* digital versatile disk) *sm* DVD.

DVD-ROM (*abrev de* **digital versatile disk read only memory**) *sm* DVD ROM.

e¹, E *sf* [letra] e, E.

◆ **E** *sm* (*abrev de* este) E.

e² *conj* (*en lugar de 'y' ante palabras que empiecen por 'i' o 'hi'*) and.

EAO *sf* (*abrev de* **enseñanza asistida por ordenador**) CAI.

EAU (*abrev de* **Emiratos Árabes Unidos**) *smpl* UAE.

ebanista *smf* cabinet-maker.

ebanistería *sf* - **1.** [oficio] cabinet-making - **2.** [taller] cabinet-maker's.

ébano *sm* ebony.

ebonita *sf* ebonite, vulcanite.

ebrio, ebria *adj* - **1.** [borracho] drunk - **2.** *fig* [ofuscado]: **ebrio de** blind with.

Ebro *sm*: **el Ebro** the Ebro.

ebullición *sf* boiling; **punto de ebullición** boiling point.

eccema *sm* eczema.

ECG (*abrev de* **electrocardiograma**) *sm* ECG.

echar ◇ *vt* - **1.** [tirar] to throw; [red] to cast - **2.** [meter] to put - **3.** [añadir]: **echar algo (a o en algo)** [vino etc] to pour sthg (into sthg); [sal, azúcar etc] to add sthg (to sthg) - **4.** [decir - discurso] to give; [- reprimenda] to dish out - **5.** [carta, postal] to post - **6.** [humo, vapor, chispas] to give off, to emit - **7.** [hojas, flores] to sprout, to shoot - **8.** [expulsar]: **echar a alguien (de)** to throw sb out (of) - **9.** [despedir]: **echar a alguien (de)** to sack sb (from) - **10.** [accionar]: **echar la llave/el**

cerrojo to lock/bolt the door; **echar el freno** to brake, to put the brakes on - **11.** [acostar] to lie (down) - **12.** [condena] to give, to slap on - **13.** [calcular]: **¿cuántos años le echas?** how old do you reckon he is? - **14.** *fam* [en televisión, cine] to show; **¿qué echan esta noche en la tele?** what's on telly tonight? - **15.** [buenaventura] to tell - **16.** *loc*: **echar abajo** [edificio] to pull down, to demolish; [gobierno] to bring down; [proyecto] to ruin; **echar a perder** [vestido, alimentos, plan] to ruin; [ocasión] to waste; **echar de menos** to miss. ◇ *vi* - **1.** [dirigirse]: **echar por** to go o head along - **2.** [empezar]: **echar a hacer algo** to begin to do sthg, to start doing sthg; **echar a correr** to break into a run; **echar a llorar** to burst into tears; **echar a reír** to burst out laughing.

◆ **echarse** *vprnl* - **1.** [lanzarse]: **echarse a** to throw o.s. o jump into - **2.** [acostarse] to lie down - **3.** [empezar]: **echarse a hacer algo** to begin to do sthg, to start doing sthg - **4.** [apartarse]: **echarse (a un lado)** to move (aside); **echarse atrás** *fig* to back out - **5.** [obtener]: **echarse (un) novio** to get o.s. a boyfriend - **6.** *loc*: **echarse a perder** [comida] to go off, to spoil; [plan] to fall through.

echarpe *sm* shawl.

eclecticismo *sm* eclecticism.

ecléctico, ca *adj* & *sm, f* eclectic.

eclesiástico, ca *adj* ecclesiastical.

◆ **eclesiástico** *sm* clergyman.

eclipsar *vt* *lit & fig* to eclipse.

eclipse *sm* eclipse; **eclipse lunar** o **de luna** lunar eclipse, eclipse of the moon; **eclipse solar** o **de sol** solar eclipse, eclipse of the sun; **eclipse total** total eclipse.

eclosión *sf* *culto* emergence.

eco *sm* - **1.** [gen] echo; **hacerse eco de** to report; **tener eco** to arouse interest - **2.** [rumor] rumour; **ecos de sociedad** society column *sing*.

ecografía *sf* ultrasound scanning.

ecología *sf* ecology.

ecológico, ca *adj* [gen] ecological; [alimentos] organic.

ecologismo *sm* Green movement.

ecologista ◇ *adj* environmental, ecological. ◇ *smf* environmentalist, ecologist.

economato *sm* company cooperative shop.

economía *sf* - **1.** [gen] economy; **economía doméstica** housekeeping; **economía de libre mercado** free-market economy; **economía de mercado** market economy; **economía mixta** mixed economy; **economía planificada** planned economy; **economía sumergida** black economy o market - **2.** [estudio] economics (*U*); **economía aplicada** applied economics;

economía familiar home economics; **economía política** political economy - **3.** [ahorro] saving.

económico, ca adj - **1.** [problema, doctrina etc] economic - **2.** [barato] cheap, low-cost - **3.** [que gasta poco - motor etc] economical; [- persona] thrifty.

economista smf economist.

economizar [13] vt lit & fig to save.

ecosistema sm ecosystem.

ecotasa sf ecotax.

ecoturismo sm ecotourism.

ecuación sf equation; **ecuación de segundo grado** quadratic equation.

ecuador sm equator; **pasar el ecuador** to pass the halfway mark.

Ecuador n pr Ecuador.

ecualizador sm equalizer.

ecuánime adj - **1.** [en el ánimo] level-headed, even - **2.** [en el juicio] impartial, fair.

ecuanimidad sf - **1.** [del ánimo] equanimity, composure - **2.** [del juicio] impartiality, fairness.

ecuatorial adj equatorial.

ecuatoriano, na adj & sm, f Ecuadorian, Ecuadoran.

ecuestre adj equestrian.

ecuménico, ca adj ecumenical.

ed. - 1. (abrev de **editor**) ed. - **2.** (abrev de **edición**) edit. - **3.** abrev de **editorial**.

edad sf age; **¿qué edad tienes?** how old are you?; **tiene 25 años de edad** she's 25 (years old); **una persona de edad** an elderly person; **edad adulta** adulthood; **edad avanzada** old age; **edad del juicio** o **de la razón** age of reason; **edad escolar** school age; **Edad Media** Middle Ages pl; **edad mental** mental age; **edad del pavo** awkward age; **Edad de piedra** Stone Age; **la tercera edad** [ancianos] senior citizens pl; **estar en edad de merecer** hum to be of marriageable age.

edecán sm Méx assistant, aide.

edema sm oedema.

edén sm RELIG Eden; fig paradise.

edición sf - **1.** [acción - IMPR] publication; IN-FORM, RADIO & TV editing - **2.** [ejemplares] edition; **edición extraordinaria/de bolsillo** special/pocket edition; **edición crítica** critical edition; **edición pirata** pirate edition - **3.** [celebración periódica] staging.

edicto sm edict.

edificación sf building.

edificante adj [conducta] exemplary; [libro, discurso] edifying.

edificar [10] vt - **1.** [construir] to build - **2.** [aleccionar] to edify.

edificio sm building; **edificio inteligente** intelligent building.

edil sm (town) councillor.

Edimburgo n pr Edinburgh.

editar vt - **1.** [libro, periódico] to publish; [disco] to release - **2.** INFORM, RADIO & TV to edit.

editor, ra <> adj publishing (antes de s). <> sm, f - **1.** [de libro, periódico] publisher - **2.** RADIO & TV editor.

◆ **editor** sm INFORM editor; **editor de textos** text editor.

editorial <> adj publishing (antes de s). <> sm editorial, leader. <> sf publisher, publishing house.

edredón sm eiderdown, comforter US; **edredón nórdico** duvet.

educación sf - **1.** [enseñanza] education; **escuela de educación especial** special school; **educación física/sexual** physical/sex education; **educación primaria/secundaria** primary/secondary education - **2.** [modales] good manners pl; **¡qué poca educación!** how rude!; **mala educación** bad manners pl.

educado, da adj polite, well-mannered; **mal educado** rude, ill-mannered.

educador, ra sm, f teacher.

educar [10] vt - **1.** [enseñar] to educate - **2.** [criar] to bring up - **3.** [cuerpo, voz, oído] to train.

educativo, va adj [juego, libro, método] educational; [sistema] education (antes de s).

edulcorante <> adj sweetening (antes de s). <> sm sweetener.

edulcorar vt to sweeten.

eduque etc ▷ **educar**.

EEB (abrev de **encefalopatía espongiforme bovina**) sf BSE.

EE UU (abrev de **Estados Unidos**) smpl USA.

efectista adj designed for effect, dramatic.

efectivamente adv [en respuestas] precisely, exactly.

efectividad sf effectiveness.

efectivo, va adj - **1.** [útil] effective - **2.** [real] actual, true; **hacer efectivo** [gen] to carry out; [promesa] to keep; [dinero, crédito] to pay; [cheque] to cash.

◆ **efectivo** sm [dinero] cash; **en efectivo** in cash; **efectivo en caja** cash in hand.

◆ **efectivos** smpl [personal] forces.

efecto sm - **1.** [gen] effect; **de efecto retardado** delayed-action; **hacer** o **surtir efecto** to have the desired effect; **tener efecto** [vigencia] to come into o take effect; **efecto 2000** IN-FORM millennium bug; **efecto dominó** domino effect; **efecto invernadero** greenhouse effect; **efecto óptico** optical illusion; **efectos sono-**

ros/visuales sound/visual effects; **efectos especiales** special effects; **efectos secundarios** side effects **- 2.** [finalidad] aim, purpose; **a tal efecto** to that end; **a efectos** o **para los efectos de algo** as far as sthg is concerned **- 3.** [impresión] impression; **producir buen/mal efecto** to make a good/bad impression **- 4.** [de balón, bola] spin; **dar efecto a** to put spin on **- 5.** COM [documento] bill; **efecto de comercio** commercial paper; **efecto de favor** accommodation bill.

➡ **efectos personales** smpl personal possessions o effects.

➡ **en efecto** loc adv indeed.

efectuar [6] vt [gen] to carry out; [compra, pago, viaje] to make.

➡ **efectuarse** vprnl to take place.

efeméride sf [suceso] major event; [conmemoración] anniversary.

➡ **efemérides** sfpl PRENSA list of the day's anniversaries published in a newspaper.

efervescencia sf **- 1.** [de líquido] effervescence; [de bebida] fizziness **- 2.** fig [agitación, inquietud] unrest.

efervescente adj [bebida] fizzy.

eficacia sf [eficiencia] efficiency; [efectividad] effectiveness.

eficaz adj **- 1.** [eficiente] efficient **- 2.** [efectivo] effective.

eficiencia sf efficiency.

eficiente adj efficient.

efigie sf [gen] effigy; [en monedas etc] image, picture.

efímero, **ra** adj ephemeral.

efluvio sm [emanación] vapour; [aroma] scent.

efusión sf [cordialidad] effusiveness, warmth.

efusividad sf effusiveness.

efusivo, **va** adj effusive.

EGB (abrev de Educación General Básica) sf former Spanish primary education system.

egipcio, **cia** adj & sm, f Egyptian.

Egipto n pr Egypt.

égloga sf eclogue.

ego sm ego.

egocéntrico, **ca** ◇ adj egocentric, self-centred. ◇ sm, f egocentric o self-centred person.

egocentrismo sm egocentricity.

egoísmo sm selfishness, egoism.

egoísta ◇ adj egoistic, selfish. ◇ smf egoist, selfish person.

ególatra ◇ adj egotistical. ◇ smf egotist.

egolatría sf egotism.

egregio, **gia** adj culto egregious, illustrious.

egresado, **da** sm, f Amér graduate.

egresar vi Amér to graduate.

egreso sm Amér graduation.

eh interj: ¡eh! hey!

ej. abrev de ejemplo.

eje sm **- 1.** [de rueda] axle; [de máquina] shaft **- 2.** GEOM axis **- 3.** fig [idea central] central idea, basis.

ejecución sf **- 1.** [realización] carrying out **- 2.** [de condenado] execution **- 3.** [de concierto] performance, rendition **- 4.** INFORM [de un programa] execution.

ejecutar vt **- 1.** [realizar] to carry out **- 2.** [condenado] to execute **- 3.** [concierto] to perform **- 4.** INFORM [programa] to execute, to run.

ejecutivo, **va** ◇ adj executive. ◇ sm, f [persona] executive; **ejecutivo agresivo** thrusting executive; **ejecutivo de cuentas** account administrator.

➡ **ejecutivo** sm POLÍT: **el ejecutivo** the government.

➡ **ejecutiva** sf [junta] executive.

ejecutor, **ra** sm, f **- 1.** DER executor **- 2.** [verdugo] executioner.

ejem interj: ¡ejem! [expresa duda] um!; [expresa ironía] ahem!

ejemplar ◇ adj exemplary. ◇ sm [de libro] copy; [de revista] issue; [de moneda] example; [de especie, raza] specimen; **ejemplar de muestra** specimen copy.

ejemplificar [10] vt to exemplify.

ejemplo sm example; **por ejemplo** for example; **dar ejemplo** to set an example; **predicar con el ejemplo** to practise what one preaches.

ejercer [11] ◇ vt **- 1.** [profesión] to practise; [cargo] to hold **- 2.** [poder, derecho] to exercise; [influencia, dominio] to exert; **ejercer presión sobre** to put pressure on. ◇ vi to practise (one's profession); **ejercer de** to practise o work as.

ejercicio sm **- 1.** [gen] exercise; **hacer ejercicio** to (do) exercise; **ejercicio escrito** written exercise; **ejercicio físico** physical exercise; **ejercicios de calentamiento** warm-up exercises; **ejercicios de mantenimiento** keep-fit exercises **- 2.** [de profesión] practising; [de cargo, funciones] carrying out **- 3.** [de poder, derecho] exercising **- 4.** MIL drill **- 5.** ECON: **ejercicio económico/fiscal** financial/tax year.

➡ **ejercicios espirituales** smpl retreat (U).

ejercitar vt [derecho] to exercise.

➡ **ejercitarse** vprnl: **ejercitarse (en)** to train (in).

ejército sm fig & MIL army.

ejerza etc ⊏➤ ejercer.

ejote sm Amér C & Méx green bean.

el, **la** (*mpl* **los**, *fpl* **las**) *art* (**el** *antes de sf que empiece por 'a' o 'ha' tónica; a + el = al; de + el = del*) - **1.** [gen] the; [en sentido genérico] *no se traduce*; **el coche** the car; **la casa** the house; **los niños** the children; **el agua/hacha/águila** the water/axe/eagle; **fui a recoger a los niños** I went to pick up the children; **los niños imitan a los adultos** children copy adults - **2.** [con sustantivo abstracto] *no se traduce*; **el amor** love; **la vida** life - **3.** [indica posesión, pertenencia]: **se partió la pierna** he broke his leg; **se quitó los zapatos** she took her shoes off; **tiene el pelo oscuro** he has dark hair - **4.** [con días de la semana]: **vuelven el sábado** they're coming back on Saturday - **5.** [con nombres propios geográficos] the; **el Sena** the (River) Seine; **el Everest** (Mount) Everest; **la España de la postguerra** post-war Spain - **6.** *fam* [con nombre propio de persona]: **llama a la María** call Maria - **7.** [con complemento de nombre, especificativo]: **el de** the one; **he perdido el tren, cogeré el de las nueve** I've missed the train, I'll get the nine o'clock one; **el de azul** the one in blue - **8.** [con complemento de nombre, posesivo]: **mi hermano y el de Juan** my brother and Juan's - **9.** [antes de frase]: **el que** [cosa] the one, whichever; [persona] whoever; **coge el que quieras** take whichever you like; **el que más corra** whoever runs fastest - **10.** [antes de adjetivo]: **prefiero el rojo al azul** I prefer the red one to the blue one.

él, **ella** *pron pers* - **1.** [sujeto, predicado - persona] he (*f* she); [- animal, cosa] it; **mi hermana es ella** she's the one who is my sister - **2.** *(después de prep)* [complemento] him (*f* her); **voy a ir de vacaciones con ella** I'm going on holiday with her; **díselo a ella** tell her it - **3.** [posesivo]: **de él** his; **de ella** hers.

elaboración *sf* [de producto] manufacture; [de idea] working out; [de plan, informe] drawing up; **de elaboración casera** home-made.

elaborar *vt* [producto] to make, to manufacture; [idea] to work out; [plan, informe] to draw up.

elasticidad *sf* - **1.** [gen] elasticity - **2.** *fig* [falta de rigor] flexibility.

elástico, **ca** *adj* - **1.** [gen] elastic - **2.** *fig* [sin rigor] flexible.
◆ **elástico** *sm* [cinta] elastic.
◆ **elásticos** *smpl* [tirantes] braces.

elección *sf* - **1.** [nombramiento] election - **2.** [opción] choice.
◆ **elecciones** *sfpl* POLÍT election *sing*; **elecciones autonómicas** *elections to the regional parliament*; **elecciones generales** general election; **elecciones municipales** local elections.

electo, **ta** *adj* elect; **el presidente electo** the president elect.

elector, **ra** *sm, f* voter, elector.

electorado *sm* electorate.

electoral *adj* electoral.

electoralismo *sm* electioneering.

electoralista *adj* electioneering *(antes de s)*.

electricidad *sf* electricity; **electricidad estática** static electricity.

electricista ◇ *adj* electrical. ◇ *smf* electrician.

eléctrico, **ca** *adj* electric.

electrificar [10] *vt* to electrify.

electrizar [13] *vt fig* [exaltar] to electrify.

electrocardiograma *sm* electrocardiogram.

electrochoque, **electroshock** [elektroˈɪok] (*pl* **electroshocks**) *sm* electric shock therapy.

electrocución *sf* electrocution.

electrocutar *vt* to electrocute.
◆ **electrocutarse** *vprnl* to electrocute o.s.

electrodo *sm* electrode.

electrodoméstico *(gen pl)* *sm* electrical household appliance.

electroencefalograma *sm* electroencephalogram.

electrógeno, **na** *adj* generating.
◆ **electrógeno** *sm* generator.

electrólisis *sf inv* electrolysis.

electrólito *sm* electrolyte.

electromagnético, **ca** *adj* electromagnetic.

electromagnetismo *sm* electromagnetism.

electrón *sm* electron.

electrónico, **ca** *adj* - **1.** [de la electrónica] electronic - **2.** [del electrón] electron *(antes de s)*.
◆ **electrónica** *sf* electronics (U).

electroscopio *sm* electroscope.

electroshock = **electrochoque**.

electrostático, **ca** *adj* electrostatic.
◆ **electrostática** *sf* electrostatics (U).

elefante, **ta** *sm, f* elephant.
◆ **elefante marino** *sm* sea cow, walrus.

elegancia *sf* elegance.

elegante *adj* - **1.** [persona, traje, estilo] elegant - **2.** [conducta, actitud, respuesta] dignified.

elegantoso, **sa** *adj* Amér elegant.

elegía *sf* elegy.

elegiaco, **ca**, **elegíaco**, **ca** *adj* elegiac.

elegible *adj* eligible.

elegido, **da** *adj* [escogido] selected, chosen; POLÍT elected.

elegir [42] *vt* - **1.** [escoger] to choose, to select - **2.** [por votación] to elect.

elemental *adj* - **1.** [básico] basic - **2.** [obvio] obvious.

elemento ⬦ *sm* - **1.** [gen] element; **estar (uno) en su elemento** to be in one's element - **2.** [factor] factor - **3.** [persona - en equipo, colectivo] individual. ⬦ *smf fam*: **una elementa de cuidado** a bad lot; **¡menudo elemento está hecho tu sobrino!** your nephew is a real tearaway!

➡ **elementos** *smpl* [fundamentos] rudiments.

elenco *sm* - **1.** [reparto] cast - **2.** [catálogo] list, index.

elepé *sm* LP (record).

elevación *sf* - **1.** [de pesos, objetos etc] lifting; [de nivel, altura, precios] rise - **2.** [de terreno] elevation, rise.

elevado, **da** *adj* [alto] high; *fig* [sublime] lofty.

elevador *sm* - **1.** [montacargas] hoist - **2.** *Méx* [ascensor] lift *UK*, elevator *US*.

elevadorista *smf Amér* lift operator *UK*, elevator operator *US*.

elevalunas *sm inv* window winder; **elevalunas eléctrico** electric window.

elevar *vt* - **1.** [gen & MAT] to raise; [peso, objeto] to lift - **2.** [ascender]: **elevar a alguien (a)** to elevate sb (to) - **3.** *fig* [propuesta, quejas] to present.

➡ **elevarse** *vprnl* [gen] to rise; [edificio, montaña] to rise up; **elevarse a** [altura] to reach; [gastos, daños] to amount o come to.

elidir *vt* to elide.

elige, eligió ▷ **elegir**.

eliminación *sf* elimination.

eliminar *vt* [gen] to eliminate; [contaminación, enfermedad] to get rid of.

eliminatorio, **ria** *adj* qualifying *(antes de s)*.

➡ **eliminatoria** *sf* [gen] qualifying round; [en atletismo] heat.

elipse *sf* ellipse.

elipsis *sf inv* ellipsis.

elíptico, **ca** *adj* elliptical.

élite, elite *sf* elite.

elitismo *sm* elitism.

elitista *adj* & *smf* elitist.

elixir, elíxir *sm* - **1.** [producto medicinal]: **elixir bucal** mouthwash - **2.** *fig* [remedio milagroso] elixir.

ella ▷ **él**.

ellas *sfpl* ▷ **ellos**.

ello *pron pers (neutro)* it; **no nos llevamos bien, pero ello no nos impide formar un buen equipo** we don't get on very well, but it o that doesn't stop us making a good team; **no quiero hablar de ello** I don't want to talk about it; **por ello** for that reason.

ellos, ellas *pron pers* - **1.** [sujeto, predicado] they; **los invitados son ellos** they are the guests, it is they who are the guests - **2.** *(después de prep)* [complemento] them; **me voy al bar con ellas** I'm going with them to the bar; **díselo a ellos** tell them it - **3.** [posesivo]: **de ellos/ellas** theirs.

elocuencia *sf* eloquence.

elocuente *adj* eloquent; **se hizo un silencio elocuente** the silence said it all.

elogiar [8] *vt* to praise.

elogio *sm* praise.

elogioso, sa *adj* [palabras] appreciative, eulogistic.

elote *sm Amér C & Méx* corncob, ear of maize o corn *US*.

El Salvador *n pr* El Salvador.

elucidar *vt* to elucidate, to throw light upon.

elucubración *sf* - **1.** [reflexión] reflection, meditation - **2.** *despec* [divagación] mental meandering.

elucubrar *vt* - **1.** [reflexionar] to reflect o meditate upon - **2.** *despec* [divagar] to theorize about.

eludir *vt* [gen] to avoid; [perseguidores] to escape.

emanación *sf* emanation, emission.

emanar ➡ **emanar de** *vi* to emanate from.

emancipación *sf* [de mujeres, esclavos] emancipation; [de menores de edad] coming of age; [de países] obtaining of independence.

emancipar *vt* [gen] to emancipate, to free; [países] to grant independence (to).

➡ **emanciparse** *vprnl* to free o.s., to become independent.

embadurnar *vt*: **embadurnar algo (de)** to smear sthg (with).

➡ **embadurnarse** *vprnl*: **embadurnarse (de)** to smear o.s. (with).

embajada *sf* - **1.** [edificio] embassy - **2.** [cargo] ambassadorship - **3.** [empleados] embassy staff.

embajador, ra *sm, f* ambassador.

embalaje *sm* - **1.** [acción] packing - **2.** [caja] packaging.

embalar *vt* to wrap up, to pack.

➡ **embalarse** *vprnl* - **1.** [acelerar - corredor] to race away; [- vehículo] to pick up speed - **2.** *fig* [entusiasmarse] to get carried away.

embaldosar *vt* [piso] to tile; [calle] to pave.

embalsamar *vt* to embalm.

embalsar *vt* to dam (up).

➡ **embalsarse** *vprnl* to collect, to form puddles.

embalse *sm* reservoir.

embarazada ⬦ *adj f* pregnant; **dejar embarazada a alguien** to get sb pregnant; **estar**

embarazada de ocho meses to be eight months pregnant; **quedarse embarazada** to get pregnant. <> *sf* pregnant woman.

embarazar [13] *vt* - **1.** [preñar] to get pregnant - **2.** [impedir] to restrict - **3.** [cohibir] to inhibit.

embarazo *sm* - **1.** [preñez] pregnancy; **interrumpir un embarazo** to terminate a pregnancy; **prueba del embarazo** pregnancy test; **embarazo ectópico** *o* **extrauterino** ectopic pregnancy - **2.** [timidez] embarrassment.

embarazoso, sa *adj* awkward, embarrassing.

embarcación *sf* - **1.** [barco] craft, boat; **embarcación pesquera** fishing boat; **embarcación de recreo** pleasure boat - **2.** [embarque] embarkation.

embarcadero *sm* jetty.

embarcar [10] <> *vt* - **1.** [personas] to board; [mercancías] to ship - **2.** *fig* [involucrar]: **embarcar a alguien en algo** to involve sb in sthg. <> *vi* to board.

◆ **embarcarse** *vprnl* - **1.** [para viajar] to board - **2.** *fig* [aventurarse]: **embarcarse en algo** to become involved in sthg.

embargar [16] *vt* - **1.** DER to seize - **2.** [suj: emoción etc] to overcome.

embargo *sm* - **1.** DER seizure - **2.** ECON embargo.

◆ **sin embargo** *loc adv* however, nevertheless.

embarque *sm* [de personas] boarding; [de mercancías] embarkation.

embarrancar [10] *vi* to run aground.

◆ **embarrancarse** *vprnl* [barco] to run aground; [coche etc] to get stuck.

embarrar *vt* to cover with mud.

◆ **embarrarse** *vprnl* to get covered in mud.

embarullar *vt* *fam* to mess up.

◆ **embarullarse** *vprnl* *fam* to get into a muddle.

embaucador, ra <> *adj* deceitful. <> *sm, f* swindler.

embaucar [10] *vt* to swindle, to deceive.

embeber *vt* to soak up.

◆ **embeberse** *vprnl*: **embeberse (en algo)** [ensimismarse] to become absorbed (in sthg); *fig* [empaparse] to immerse o.s. (in sthg).

embelesar *vt* to captivate.

◆ **embelesarse** *vprnl* to be captivated.

embellecedor *sm* [adorno] go-faster stripes *pl*; [tapacubos] hubcap.

embellecer [30] *vt* to adorn, to embellish.

embellecimiento *sm* embellishment.

embestida *sf* [gen] attack; [de toro] charge.

embestir [26] *vt* [gen] to attack; [toro] to charge.

emblanquecer [30] *vt* to whiten.

emblema *sm* - **1.** [divisa, distintivo] emblem, badge - **2.** [símbolo] symbol.

embobar *vt* to captivate.

◆ **embobarse** *vprnl* to be captivated.

embocadura *sf* - **1.** [de río, puerto] mouth - **2.** [de instrumento] mouthpiece.

embocar [10] *vt* to enter *(a narrow space)*, to squeeze into.

emboce *etc* ⊳ **embozar**.

embolado *sm* *fam* jam, mess; **meter a alguien en un embolado** to land sb in it; **meterse en un embolado** to get oneself into a fine mess.

embolador *sm* *Col* boot black, shoeshine boy.

embolia *sf* embolism.

émbolo *sm* AUTO piston.

embolsarse *vprnl* [ganar] to make, to earn.

embonar *vt* *Andes, Cuba & Méx fam* - **1.** [ajustar] to suit - **2.** [abonar] to manure - **3.** [ensamblar] to join.

emboque *etc* ⊳ **embocar**.

emborrachar *vt* to make drunk.

◆ **emborracharse** *vprnl* to get drunk.

emborrascarse [10] *vprnl* to cloud over, to turn black.

emborronar *vt* - **1.** [garabatear] to scribble on; [manchar] to smudge - **2.** [escribir de prisa] to scribble.

emboscada *sf lit & fig* ambush; **tender una emboscada** to lay an ambush.

emboscar [10] *vt* to ambush.

embotamiento *sm* dullness.

embotar *vt* [sentidos] to dull.

embotellado, da *adj* bottled.

◆ **embotellado** *sm* bottling.

embotellamiento *sm* - **1.** [de tráfico] traffic jam - **2.** [de líquidos] bottling.

embotellar *vt* - **1.** [tráfico] to block - **2.** [líquido] to bottle.

embozo *sm* [de sábana] turnover.

embragar [16] *vi* to engage the clutch.

embrague *sm* clutch; **embrague automático** automatic clutch.

embravecer [30] *vt* to enrage.

◆ **embravecerse** *vprnl* - **1.** [animal] to become enraged - **2.** [mar] to become rough.

embriagador, ra *adj* intoxicating.

embriagar [16] *vt* - **1.** [extasiar] to intoxicate - **2.** [emborrachar] to make drunk.

◆ **embriagarse** *vprnl* - **1.** [extasiarse]: **embriagarse (de)** to become drunk (with) - **2.** [emborracharse]: **embriagarse (con)** to get drunk (on).

embriaguez *sf* - **1.** [borrachera] drunkenness - **2.** [éxtasis] intoxication.

embrión *sm* embryo.

embrollar *vt* [asunto] to confuse, to complicate; [hilos] to tangle up.
◆ **embrollarse** *vprnl* to get muddled up *o* confused.
embrollo *sm* **- 1.** [de hilos] tangle **- 2.** *fig* [lío] mess; [mentira] lie.
embromado, da *adj Andes, Caribe & R Plata fam* [complicado] tricky.
embromar *vt* **- 1.** [burlarse de] to tease **- 2.** *Andes, Caribe & R Plata* [fastidiar] to annoy, to bother **- 3.** *Andes, Caribe & R Plata* [estropear - máquina, objeto] to break; [- fiesta, vacaciones] to spoil, to ruin.
embrujamiento *sm* bewitchment.
embrujar *vt lit & fig* to bewitch.
embrujo *sm* [maleficio] curse, spell; *fig* [de ciudad, ojos] charm, magic.
embrutecer [30] *vt* to brutalize.
◆ **embrutecerse** *vprnl* to become brutalized.
embrutecimiento *sm* [acción] brutalization; [cualidad] brutishness.
embuchado, da *adj*: **carne embuchada** cured cold meat.
embuchar *vt* **- 1.** *fam* [comer] to wolf down, to gobble up **- 2.** [embutir] to process into sausages.
embudo *sm* funnel.
embuste *sm* lie.
embustero, ra ⬦ *adj* lying. ⬦ *sm, f* liar.
embute *sm Amér fam* bribe.
embutido *sm* **- 1.** [comida] cold cured meat **- 2.** [acción] sausage-making, stuffing.
embutir *vt lit & fig* to stuff.
emergencia *sf* **- 1.** [urgencia] emergency; **en caso de emergencia** in case of emergency **- 2.** [brote] emergence.
emergente *adj* emerging.
emerger [14] *vi* [salir del agua] to emerge; [aparecer] to come into view, to appear.
emérito, ta *adj* emeritus.
emerja *etc* ▷ **emerger**.
emigración *sf* **- 1.** [de personas] emigration; [de aves] migration **- 2.** [grupo de personas] emigrant community.
emigrado, da *sm, f* emigrant; **emigrado político** émigré.
emigrante *adj & smf* emigrant.
emigrar *vi* [persona] to emigrate; [ave] to migrate.
eminencia *sf* [persona] eminent figure, leading light; **eminencia gris** éminence grise.
◆ **Eminencia** *sf*: **Su Eminencia** His Eminence.
eminente *adj* **- 1.** [distinguido] eminent **- 2.** [elevado] high.
emir *sm* emir.

emirato *sm* emirate.
Emiratos Árabes Unidos *smpl*: **los Emiratos Árabes Unidos** United Arab Emirates.
emisario, ria *sm, f* emissary.
emisión *sf* **- 1.** [de energía, rayos etc] emission **- 2.** [de bonos, sellos, monedas] issue; **emisión de obligaciones** COM debentures issue **- 3.** RADIO & TV [- transmisión] broadcasting; [- programa] programme, broadcast.
emisor, ra *adj* transmitting *(antes de s)*.
◆ **emisor** *sm* transmitter.
◆ **emisora** *sf* radio station; **emisora pirata** pirate radio station.
emitir ⬦ *vt* **- 1.** [rayos, calor, sonidos] to emit **- 2.** [moneda, sellos, bonos] to issue **- 3.** [expresar - juicio, opinión] to express; [- fallo] to pronounce **- 4.** RADIO & TV to broadcast. ⬦ *vi* to broadcast.
emoción *sf* **- 1.** [conmoción, sentimiento] emotion **- 2.** [expectación] excitement; **¡qué emoción!** how exciting!
emocional *adj* emotional.
emocionante *adj* **- 1.** [conmovedor] moving, touching **- 2.** [apasionante] exciting, thrilling.
emocionar *vt* **- 1.** [conmover] to move **- 2.** [excitar, apasionar] to thrill, to excite.
◆ **emocionarse** *vprnl* **- 1.** [conmoverse] to be moved **- 2.** [excitarse, apasionarse] to get excited.
emolumento *(gen pl) sm* emolument.
emotividad *sf* emotional impact, emotiveness.
emotivo, va *adj* [persona] emotional; [escena, palabras] moving.
empacar *vi Amér* to pack.
empachar *vt* to give indigestion to.
◆ **empacharse** *vprnl* [hartarse] to stuff o.s.; [sufrir indigestión] to get indigestion.
empacho *sm* **- 1.** [indigestión] upset stomach, indigestion **- 2.** *fig* [hartura]: **tener un empacho de** to have had one's fill *o* enough of.
empadronamiento *sm* ≃ registration on the electoral roll.
empadronar *vt* ≃ to register on the electoral roll.
◆ **empadronarse** *vprnl* ≃ to register on the electoral roll.
empalagar [16] *vt*: **los bombones me empalagan** I find chocolates sickly.
◆ **empalagarse** *vprnl*: **empalagarse de** *o* **con** to get sick of.
empalago *sm* cloying taste.
empalagoso, sa *adj* sickly, cloying.
empalizada *sf* [cerca] fence; MIL stockade.
empalmar ⬦ *vt* **- 1.** [tubos, cables] to connect, to join **- 2.** [planes, ideas] to link **- 3.** [en fútbol]

to volley. ◇ vi - **1.** [autocares, trenes] to connect - **2.** [carreteras] to link o join (up) - **3.** [sucederse]: **empalmar (con)** to follow on (from).

empalme sm - **1.** [entre cables, tubos] joint, connection - **2.** [de líneas férreas, carreteras] junction.

empanada sf pasty; **tener una empanada mental** fam to be in a real muddle, not to be able to think straight.

empanadilla sf small pasty.

empanar vt CULIN to coat in breadcrumbs.

empantanar vt to flood.

◆ **empantanarse** vprnl - **1.** [inundarse] to be flooded o waterlogged - **2.** fig [atascarse] to get bogged down.

empañado, da adj - **1.** [cristal] misted o steamed up - **2.** [reputación] tarnished.

empañar vt - **1.** [cristal] to mist o steam up - **2.** fig [reputación] to tarnish.

◆ **empañarse** vprnl to mist o steam up.

empapar vt - **1.** [mojar] to soak - **2.** [absorber] to soak up.

◆ **empaparse** vprnl - **1.** [mojarse] to get soaked - **2.** [enterarse bien]: **se empapó de sociología antes de dar la conferencia** she did a lot of reading up about sociology before giving her speech; **¡para que te empapes!** fam so there!

empapelado sm - **1.** [acción] papering - **2.** [papel] wallpaper.

empapelar vt - **1.** [pared] to paper - **2.** fam fig [procesar] to have up (before the courts).

empaque sm Méx [en paquetes, bolsas, cajas] packing; [en latas] canning; [en botellas] bottling.

empaquetar vt to pack, to package.

emparedado, da adj confined.

◆ **emparedado** sm sandwich.

emparedar vt to shut up, to lock away.

emparejamiento sm pairing.

emparejar vt - **1.** [aparejar - personas] to pair off; [- zapatos etc] to match (up) - **2.** [nivelar] to make level.

◆ **emparejarse** vprnl [personas] to find a partner.

emparentar [19] vi: **emparentar con** to marry into.

emparrado sm [pérgola] bower.

emparrar vt to train.

empastar vt to fill.

empaste sm filling.

empatar ◇ vi DEP to draw; [en elecciones etc] to tie; **empatar a cero** to draw nil-nil. ◇ vt Andes & Ven to join, to link.

empate sm - **1.** [resultado] draw; **un empate a cero/dos** a goalless/two-all draw - **2.** Andes & Ven [empalme] joint, link.

empecé etc ▷ empezar.

empecinado, da adj stubborn.

empecinarse vprnl: **empecinarse (en hacer algo)** to insist (on doing sthg).

empedernido, da adj [bebedor, fumador] heavy; [criminal, jugador] hardened.

empedrado sm paving.

empedrar [19] vt to pave.

empeine sm [de pie, zapato] instep.

empellón sm push, shove; **abrirse paso a empellones** to shove o push one's way through.

empeñado, da adj - **1.** [en préstamo] in pawn - **2.** [obstinado] determined; **estar empeñado en hacer algo** to be determined to do sthg.

empeñar vt - **1.** [joyas etc] to pawn - **2.** [palabra, honor] to give.

◆ **empeñarse** vprnl - **1.** [obstinarse] to insist; **empeñarse en hacer algo** [obstinarse] to insist on doing sthg; [persistir] to persist in doing sthg - **2.** [endeudarse] to get into debt.

empeño sm - **1.** [de joyas etc] pawning; **casa de empeños** pawnshop - **2.** [obstinación] determination; **poner mucho empeño en algo** to put a lot of effort into sthg; **tener empeño en hacer algo** to be determined to do sthg; **en el empeño** in the attempt.

empeoramiento sm worsening, deterioration.

empeorar vi to get worse, to deteriorate.

empequeñecer [30] vt [quitar importancia a] to diminish; [en una comparación] to overshadow, to dwarf.

emperador, emperatriz sm, f emperor (f empress).

◆ **emperador** sm [pez] swordfish.

emperifollar vt fam to doll o tart up.

◆ **emperifollarse** vprnl fam to doll o tart o.s. up.

emperrarse vprnl: **emperrarse (en hacer algo)** to insist (on doing sthg).

empezar [34] ◇ vt to begin, to start. ◇ vi: **empezar (a hacer algo)** to begin o start (to do sthg); **empezar (por hacer algo)** to begin o start (by doing sthg); **para empezar** to begin o start with; **por algo se empieza** you've got to start somewhere.

empiedra etc ▷ empedrar.

empiezo ▷ empezar.

empinado, da adj steep.

empinar vt - **1.** [inclinar] to tip up - **2.** [levantar] to raise.

◆ **empinarse** vprnl - **1.** [animal] to stand up on its hind legs - **2.** [persona] to stand on tiptoe - **3.** mfam [pene]: **se le empinó** he got a hard-on.

empingorotado, da adj stuck-up, posh.

empírico, ca ◇ adj empirical. ◇ sm, f empiricist.

empirismo *sm* empiricism.

emplasto *sm* poultice.

emplazamiento *sm* - **1.** [ubicación] location - **2.** DER summons.

emplazar [13] *vt* - **1.** [situar] to locate; MIL to position - **2.** [citar] to summon; DER to summons.

empleado, da *sm, f* [gen] employee; [de banco, administración, oficina] clerk; **empleada de hogar** maid.

empleador, ra *sm, f* employer.

emplear *vt* - **1.** [usar - objetos, materiales etc] to use; [- tiempo] to spend; **emplear algo en hacer algo** to use sthg to do sthg - **2.** [contratar] to employ - **3.** *loc:* **lo tiene** o **le está bien empleado** he deserves it, it serves him right.

➤ **emplearse** *vprnl* - **1.** [colocarse] to find a job - **2.** [usarse] to be used.

empleo *sm* - **1.** [uso] use; **'modo de empleo'** 'instructions for use' - **2.** [trabajo] employment; [puesto] job; **estar sin empleo** to be out of work; **empleo comunitario** community service; **empleo juvenil** youth employment; **pleno empleo** full employment.

emplomadura *sf* R Dom [de diente] filling.

emplomar *vt* - **1.** [cubrir con plomo] to lead - **2.** R Dom [diente] to fill.

empobrecer [30] *vt* to impoverish.

➤ **empobrecerse** *vprnl* to get poorer.

empobrecimiento *sm* impoverishment.

empollar ◇ *vt* - **1.** [huevo] to incubate - **2.** *fam* [estudiar] to swot up on. ◇ *vi fam* to swot.

➤ **empollarse** *vprnl fam* to swot up on.

empollón, ona *fam* ◇ *adj* swotty. ◇ *sm, f* swot.

empolvarse *vprnl* to powder one's face.

emporrado, da *adj fam* stoned.

emporrarse *vprnl fam* to get stoned (on cannabis).

empotrado, da *adj* fitted, built-in.

empotrar *vt* to fit, to build in.

emprendedor, ra *adj* enterprising.

emprender *vt* - **1.** [trabajo] to start; [viaje, marcha] to set off on; **emprender vuelo** to fly off - **2.** *loc:* **emprenderla con alguien** to take it out on sb; **emprenderla a golpes con alguien** to start hitting sb.

empresa *sf* - **1.** [sociedad] company; **empresa de seguridad** security firm; **empresa de servicios** service company; **empresa mixta/privada** mixed/private company; **empresa filial** subsidiary; **empresa libre, libre empresa** free enterprise; **empresa matriz** parent company; **pequeña y mediana empresa** small and medium-sized business; **empresa pública** public sector firm; **empresa de trabajo temporal** temping agency - **2.** [acción] enterprise, undertaking.

empresariado *sm* employers *pl.*

empresarial *adj* management *(antes de s)*.

➤ **empresariales** *sfpl* business studies.

empresario, ria *sm, f* [patrono] employer; [hombre, mujer de negocios] businessman (*f* businesswoman); [de teatro] impresario; **pequeño empresario** small businessman.

empréstito *sm* debenture loan.

empujar *vt* to push; **empujar a alguien a que haga algo** to push sb into doing sthg.

empuje *sm* - **1.** [presión] pressure - **2.** [energía] energy, drive.

empujón *sm* - **1.** [empellón] shove, push; **dar un empujón a alguien** to give sb a push o a shove; **abrirse paso a empujones** to shove o push one's way through - **2.** *fig* [impulso] effort; **dar un último empujón a** to make one last effort with.

empuñadura *sf* handle; [de espada] hilt.

empuñar *vt* to take hold of, to grasp.

emulación *sf* [gen & INFORM] emulation.

emulador *sm* INFORM emulator.

emular *vt* [gen & INFORM] to emulate.

emulsión *sf* emulsion.

en *prep* - **1.** [lugar - en el interior de] in; [- sobre la superficie de] on; [- en un punto concreto de] at; **viven en la capital** they live in the capital; **tiene el dinero en el banco** he keeps his money in the bank; **en la mesa/el plato** on the table/plate; **en casa/el trabajo** at home/work - **2.** [dirección] into; **el avión cayó en el mar** the plane fell into the sea; **entraron en la habitación** they came into the room - **3.** [tiempo - mes, año etc] in; [- día] on; **nació en 1940/mayo** he was born in 1940/May; **en aquel día** on that day; **en Nochebuena** on Christmas Eve; **en Navidades** at Christmas; **en aquella época** at that time, in those days; **en un par de días** in a couple of days - **4.** [medio de transporte] by; **ir en tren/coche/avión/barco** to go by train/car/plane/boat - **5.** [modo] in; **en voz baja** in a low voice; **lo dijo en inglés** she said it in English; **pagar en libras** to pay in pounds; **la inflación aumentó en un 10%** inflation increased by 10%; **todo se lo gasta en ropa** he spends everything on clothes - **6.** [precio] in; **las ganancias se calculan en millones** profits are calculated in millions; **te lo dejo en 5.000** I'll let you have it for 5,000 - **7.** [tema]: **es un experto en la materia** he's an expert on the subject; **es doctor en medicina** he's a doctor of medicine - **8.** [causa] from; **lo detecté en su forma de hablar** I could tell from the way he was speaking - **9.** [materia] in, made of; **en se-**

da in silk - **10.** [cualidad] in terms of; **le supera en inteligencia** she is more intelligent than he is.

enagua *sf* (gen pl) petticoat.

enajenación *sf* - **1.** [locura] mental derangement, insanity; [éxtasis] rapture - **2.** [de una propiedad] transfer of ownership, alienation.

enajenamiento *sm* = enajenación.

enajenar *vt* - **1.** [volver loco] to drive mad; [extasiar] to enrapture - **2.** [propiedad] to transfer ownership of, to alienate.

enaltecer [30] *vt* to praise.

enamoradizo, za ◇ *adj* who falls in love easily. ◇ *sm, f* person who falls in love easily.

enamorado, da ◇ *adj*: enamorado (de) in love (with). ◇ *sm, f* lover.

enamoramiento *sm* falling in love.

enamorar *vt* to win the heart of.
➡ **enamorarse** *vprnl*: enamorarse (de) to fall in love (with).

enano, na *adj & sm, f* dwarf; **disfrutar como un enano** *fam* to have a whale of a time.

enarbolar *vt* [bandera] to raise, to hoist; [pancarta] to hold up; [arma] to brandish.

enardecer [30] *vt* [gen] to inflame; [persona, multitud] to fill with enthusiasm.

enarque *etc* ⊳ enarcar.

encabezamiento *sm* [de carta, escrito] heading; [de artículo periodístico] headline; [preámbulo] foreword.

encabezar [13] *vt* - **1.** [artículo de periódico] to headline; [libro] to write the foreword for - **2.** [lista, carta] to head - **3.** [marcha, expedición] to lead.

encabritarse *vprnl* - **1.** [caballo, moto] to rear up - **2.** *fam* [persona] to get shirty.

encabronarse *vprnl* *vulg* to get pissed off.

encadenado *sm* - **1.** CINE fade, dissolve - **2.** CONSTR buttress.

encadenamiento *sm* linking.

encadenar *vt* - **1.** [atar] to chain (up) - **2.** [enlazar] to link (together) - **3.** *fig* [esclavizar] to chain.

encajar ◇ *vt* - **1.** [meter ajustando]: encajar (en) to fit (into) - **2.** [meter con fuerza]: encajar (en) to push (in) - **3.** [hueso dislocado] to set - **4.** [recibir - golpe, noticia, críticas] to take - **5.** [soltar]: encajar algo a alguien [discurso] to force sb to listen to o sit through sthg; [insultos] to hurl sthg at sb; **encajarle un golpe a alguien** to land sb a blow. ◇ *vi* - **1.** [piezas, objetos] to fit - **2.** [hechos, declaraciones, datos]: encajar (con) to square (with), to match - **3.** [ser oportuno, adecuado]: encajar (con) to fit nicely (with).

encaje *sm* - **1.** [ajuste] insertion, fitting-in - **2.** [tejido] lace.

encajonar *vt* - **1.** [en cajas, cajones] to pack, to put in boxes - **2.** [en sitio estrecho]: encajonar algo/a alguien (en) to squeeze sthg/sb (into).

encalado *sm* whitewash.

encalar *vt* to whitewash.

encallar *vi* - **1.** [barco] to run aground - **2.** *fig* [solicitud, proyecto] to founder.

encamarse *vprnl* - **1.** [enfermo] to take to one's bed - **2.** *fam* [pareja]: encamarse con alguien to sleep with sb.

encaminar *vt* - **1.** [persona, pasos] to direct - **2.** [medidas, leyes, actividades] to aim; encaminado a aimed at.
➡ **encaminarse** *vprnl*: encaminarse a/hacia to set off for/towards.

encamotarse *vprnl Andes & Amér C fam* to fall in love.

encandilar *vt* to dazzle, to impress greatly.
➡ **encandilarse** *vprnl* to be dazzled.

encanecer [30] *vi* to go grey.
➡ **encanecerse** *vprnl* to go grey.

encantado, da *adj* - **1.** [contento] delighted; **estar encantado con algo/alguien** to be delighted with sthg/sb; **encantado de conocerle** pleased to meet you - **2.** [hechizado - casa, lugar] haunted; [- persona] bewitched.

encantador, ra *adj* delightful, charming.

encantamiento *sm* enchantment.

encantar *vt* - **1.** [gustar]: encantarle a alguien algo/hacer algo to love sthg/doing sthg; **me encanta el chocolate** I love chocolate; **le encanta bailar** she loves dancing - **2.** [embrujar] to bewitch, to cast a spell on.

encanto *sm* - **1.** [atractivo] charm; **ser un encanto** to be a treasure o a delight - **2.** [apelativo cariñoso] darling - **3.** [hechizo] spell; **como por encanto** as if by magic.

encañonar *vt* [persona] to point a gun at.

encapotado, da *adj* overcast.

encapotarse *vprnl* to cloud over.

encapricharse *vprnl* - **1.** [obstinarse]: encapricharse con algo/hacer algo to set one's mind on sthg/doing sthg - **2.** [enamorarse]: encapricharse (con alguien) to become infatuated (with sb).

encapuchado, da ◇ *adj* hooded. ◇ *sm, f* hooded person.

encarado, da *adj*: bien encarado good-looking; mal encarado plain, ugly.

encaramar *vt* to lift up.
➡ **encaramarse** *vprnl*: encaramarse (a o en) to climb up (onto).

encarar *vt* - **1.** [hacer frente a] to confront, to face up to - **2.** [poner frente a frente] to bring face to face.

◆ **encararse** *vprnl* [enfrentarse]: **encararse a** *o* **con** to stand up to.

encarcelamiento *sm* imprisonment.

encarcelar *vt* to imprison.

encarecer [30] *vt* - **1.** [productos, precios] to make more expensive - **2.** [rogar]: **encarecer a alguien que haga algo** to beg *o* implore sb to do sthg.

◆ **encarecerse** *vprnl* to become more expensive.

encarecidamente *adv* earnestly.

encarecimiento *sm* - **1.** [de producto, coste] increase in price - **2.** [empeño]: **con encarecimiento** insistently.

encargado, da ◇ *adj*: **encargado (de)** responsible (for), in charge (of). ◇ *sm, f* [gen] person in charge; COM manager (*f* manageress); **encargado de negocios** POLÍT chargé d'affaires.

encargar [16] *vt* - **1.** [poner al cargo]: **encargar a alguien de algo** to put sb in charge of sthg; **encargar a alguien que haga algo** to tell sb to do sthg - **2.** [pedir] to order.

◆ **encargarse** *vprnl* - **1.** [ocuparse]: **encargarse de** to be in charge of; **yo me encargaré de eso** I'll take care of *o* see to that - **2.** [pedir] to order.

encargo *sm* - **1.** [pedido] order; **por encargo** to order; **es como hecho de encargo** it's tailor-made - **2.** [recado] errand - **3.** [tarea] task, assignment.

encariñarse *vprnl*: **encariñarse con** to become fond of.

encarnación *sf* [personificación - cosa] embodiment; [- persona] personification.

◆ **Encarnación** *sf* RELIG Incarnation.

encarnado, da *adj* - **1.** [personificado] incarnate - **2.** [color] red.

◆ **encarnado** *sm* red.

encarnar ◇ *vt* [ideal, doctrina] to embody; [personaje, papel] to play. ◇ *vi* RELIG to become flesh.

encarnizado, da *adj* bloody, bitter.

encarnizarse [13] *vprnl*: **encarnizarse con** [presa] to fall upon; [prisionero, enemigo] to treat savagely.

encarpetar *vt* to file away.

encarrilar *vt* - **1.** [tren] to put back on the rails; [coche] to put back on the road - **2.** *fig* [negocio, situación] to put on the right track, to point in the right direction.

◆ **encarrilarse** *vprnl* [persona] to find out what one wants to do in life.

encarte *sm* [en naipes] lead.

encasillado *sm* grid.

encasillamiento *sm* pigeonholing.

encasillar *vt* - **1.** [clasificar] to pigeonhole; TEATRO to typecast - **2.** [poner en casillas] to put in a box, to enter into a grid.

encasquetar *vt* - **1.** [imponer]: **encasquetar algo a alguien** [idea, teoría] to drum sthg into sb; [discurso, lección] to force sb to sit through sthg - **2.** [sombrero] to pull on - **3.** [endilgar - bultos, objetos]: **encasquetar algo a alguien** to lumber sb with sthg.

◆ **encasquetarse** *vprnl* [sombrero] to pull on.

encasquillarse *vprnl* to get jammed.

encausar *vt* to prosecute.

encauzar [13] *vt* - **1.** [corriente] to channel - **2.** [orientar] to direct.

encefálico, ca *adj* brain *(antes de s)*.

encéfalo *sm* encephalon.

encefalograma *sm* encephalogram.

encendedor *sm* lighter.

encender [20] *vt* - **1.** [vela, cigarro, chimenea] to light - **2.** [aparato] to switch on - **3.** *fig* [avivar - entusiasmo, ira] to arouse; [- pasión, discusión] to inflame.

◆ **encenderse** *vprnl* - **1.** [fuego, gas] to ignite; [luz, estufa] to come on - **2.** *fig* [ojos] to light up; [persona, rostro] to go red, to blush; [de ira] to flare up.

encendido, da *adj* - **1.** [luz, colilla] burning; **la luz está encendida** the light is on - **2.** *fig* [deseos, mirada, palabras] passionate, ardent - **3.** [mejillas] red, flushed.

◆ **encendido** *sm* AUTO ignition; **encendido electrónico** electronic ignition.

encerado, da *adj* waxed, polished.

◆ **encerado** *sm* - **1.** [acción] waxing, polishing - **2.** [pizarra] blackboard.

encerar *vt* to wax, to polish.

encerrar [19] *vt* - **1.** [recluir - gen] to shut (up *o* in); [- con llave] to lock (up *o* in); [- en la cárcel] to lock away *o* up - **2.** [contener] to contain.

◆ **encerrarse** *vprnl* [gen] to shut o.s. away; [con llave] to lock o.s. away.

encerrona *sf* - **1.** [trampa] trap - **2.** TAUROM private bullfight.

encestar *vt* & *vi* to score *(in basketball)*.

enceste *sm* basket.

enchapado *sm* veneer.

encharcamiento *sm* flooding, swamping.

encharcar [10] *vt* to waterlog.

◆ **encharcarse** *vprnl* - **1.** [terreno] to become waterlogged - **2.** [pulmones] to become flooded.

enchilada *sf* Méx *filled tortilla*.

enchilarse *vprnl* Méx *fam* [enfadarse] to get angry.

enchinar vt Méx to curl.

enchironar vt fam to (put in the) nick.

enchufado, da ⬦ adj fam: **estar enchufado** to get where one is through connections. ⬦ sm, f fam person who got where they are through connections; **ser el enchufado de la clase** to be the teacher's pet.

enchufar vt - **1.** [aparato] to plug in - **2.** fam [a una persona] to pull strings for.

enchufe sm - **1.** [ELECTR - macho] plug; [- hembra] socket; **enchufe múltiple** adapter - **2.** fam [recomendación] connections pl; **obtener algo por enchufe** to get sthg by pulling strings o through one's connections.

enchufismo sm fam string-pulling.

encía sf gum.

encíclica sf encyclical.

enciclopedia sf encyclopedia.

enciclopédico, ca adj encyclopedic.

encienda etc ⊳ encender.

encierra etc ⊳ encerrar.

encierro sm - **1.** [protesta] sit-in - **2.** TAUROM running of the bulls.

encima adv - **1.** [arriba] on top; **yo vivo encima** I live upstairs; **por encima** [superficialmente] superficially - **2.** [además] on top of that - **3.** [sobre sí]: **lleva un abrigo encima** she has a coat on; **¿llevas dinero encima?** have you got any money on you?

➤ **encima de** loc prep - **1.** [en lugar superior que] above; **vivo encima de tu casa** I live upstairs from you - **2.** [sobre, en] on (top of); **el pan está encima de la mesa** the bread is on (top of) the table; **estar encima de alguien** fig to be on at sb - **3.** [además] on top of; **encima de ser tonto, es feo** on top of being stupid, he's also ugly.

➤ **por encima de** loc prep - **1.** [gen] over; **vive por encima de sus posibilidades** he lives beyond his means - **2.** fig [más que] more than; **por encima de todo** more than anything else.

encimero, ra adj top.

➤ **encimera** sf worktop.

encina sf holm oak.

encinta adj f pregnant.

enclaustrar vt to shut up in a convent.

➤ **enclaustrarse** vprnl to shut o.s. up in a convent; fig [encerrarse] to lock o.s. up in a room.

enclavado, da adj set, situated.

enclavar vt [clavar] to nail.

enclave sm enclave.

enclenque adj sickly, frail.

encoger [14] ⬦ vt - **1.** [ropa] to shrink - **2.** [miembro, músculo] to contract. ⬦ vi to shrink.

➤ **encogerse** vprnl - **1.** [ropa] to shrink; [músculos etc] to contract; **encogerse de hombros** to shrug one's shoulders - **2.** fig [apocarse] to cringe.

encogido, da adj [tímido] shy; [pusilánime] fearful, faint-hearted.

encoja etc ⊳ encoger.

encolado sm [de silla etc] glueing; [de pared] sizing.

encolar vt [silla etc] to glue; [pared] to size, to paste.

encolerizar [13] vt to infuriate, to enrage.

➤ **encolerizarse** vprnl to get angry.

encomendar [19] vt to entrust.

➤ **encomendarse** vprnl: **encomendarse a** [persona] to entrust o.s. to; [Dios, santos] to put one's trust in.

encomiar [8] vt to praise, to extol.

encomienda sf - **1.** [encargo] assignment, mission - **2.** Amér [paquete] package, parcel.

encomio sm praise.

enconado, da adj [lucha] bitter; [partidario] passionate, ardent.

enconar vt to inflame.

➤ **enconarse** vprnl - **1.** [persona] to get angry - **2.** [herida] to become inflamed.

encono sm rancour, animosity.

encontradizo, za adj: **hacerse el encontradizo** to contrive a meeting.

encontrado, da adj conflicting.

encontrar [23] vt - **1.** [gen] to find - **2.** [dificultades] to encounter - **3.** [persona] to meet, to come across.

➤ **encontrarse** vprnl - **1.** [hallarse] to be; **se encuentra en París** she's in Paris - **2.** [coincidir]: **encontrarse (con alguien)** to meet (sb); **me encontré con Juan** I ran into o met Juan - **3.** [de ánimo] to feel; **¿cómo te encuentras?** how do you feel?, how are you feeling?; **encontrarse bien/mal** to feel fine/ill - **4.** [chocar] to collide.

encontronazo sm collision, crash.

encopetado, da adj posh, upper-class.

encorsetar vt to straitjacket.

encorvar vt to bend.

➤ **encorvarse** vprnl to bend down o over.

encrespar vt - **1.** [pelo] to curl; [mar] to make choppy o rough - **2.** [irritar] to irritate.

➤ **encresparse** vprnl - **1.** [mar] to get rough - **2.** [persona] to get irritated.

encrucijada sf lit & fig crossroads sing.

encuadernación sf binding; **encuadernación en cuero** leather binding; **encuadernación en tela** cloth binding.

encuadernador, ra sm, f bookbinder.

encuadernar vt to bind.

encuadrar *vt* - **1.** [enmarcar - cuadro, tema] to frame - **2.** [encerrar] to contain - **3.** [encajar] to fit.

encuadre *sm* FOTO composition.

encubierto, ta ◇ *pp* ▷ **encubrir**. ◇ *adj* [intento] covert; [insulto, significado] hidden.

encubridor, ra *sm, f*: **encubridor (de)** accessory (to).

encubrimiento *sm* [de delito] concealment; [de persona] harbouring.

encubrir *vt* [delito] to conceal; [persona] to harbour.

encuentra *etc* ▷ **encontrar**.

encuentro *sm* - **1.** [acción] meeting, encounter; **un encuentro casual** o **fortuito** a chance meeting; **salir al encuentro de alguien** [para recibir] to go to meet sb; [para atacar] to confront sb - **2.** DEP game, match - **3.** [hallazgo] find.

encuesta *sf* - **1.** [de opinión] survey, opinion poll - **2.** [investigación] investigation, inquiry.

encuestado, da *sm, f* person polled.

encuestador, ra *sm, f* pollster.

encuestar *vt* to poll.

encumbrado, da *adj* exalted, distinguished.

encumbramiento *sm* [acción] rise; [posición] distinguished o exalted position.

encumbrar *vt* to elevate o raise to a higher position.
➡ **encumbrarse** *vprnl* to rise to a higher position.

encurtidos *smpl* pickles.

encurtir *vt* to pickle.

endeble *adj* [persona, argumento] weak, feeble; [objeto] fragile.

endemia *sf* endemic disease.

endémico, ca *adj* MED endemic.

endemoniado, da ◇ *adj* - **1.** *fam* [molesto - niño] wicked; [- trabajo] very tricky - **2.** [desagradable] terrible, foul - **3.** [poseído] possessed (of the devil). ◇ *sm, f* person possessed of the devil.

endenantes *adv* Amér fam before.

enderezamiento *sm* [acción de poner derecho] straightening; [acción de poner vertical] putting upright.

enderezar [13] *vt* - **1.** [poner derecho] to straighten - **2.** [poner vertical] to put upright - **3.** *fig* [corregir] to set right, to straighten out.
➡ **enderezarse** *vprnl* [sentado] to sit up straight; [de pie] to stand up straight.

endeudamiento *sm* debt.

endeudarse *vprnl* to get into debt.

endiablado, da *adj* [persona] wicked; [tiempo, genio] foul; [problema, crucigrama] fiendishly difficult.

endibia, endivia *sf* endive.

endilgar [16] *vt fam*: **endilgar algo a alguien** [sermón, bronca] to dish sthg out to sb; [bulto, tarea] to lumber sb with sthg.

endiñar *vt fam*: **endiñar algo a alguien** [golpe] to land o deal sb sthg; [trabajo, tarea] to lumber sb with sthg.

endiosamiento *sm* self-importance, conceit.

endivia = **endibia**.

endocrino, na ◇ *adj* endocrine *(antes de s)*. ◇ *sm, f* endocrinologist.

endocrinología *sf* endocrinology.

endocrinólogo, ga *sm, f* endocrinologist.

endogamia *sf* endogamy.

endógeno, na *adj* endogamous.

endomingado, da *adj*   *fam*   dressed-up, dolled-up.

endomingar [16] *vt fam* to dress o doll up.
➡ **endomingarse** *vprnl fam* to get dressed o dolled up in one's best clothes.

endorfina *sf* MED endorphin.

endosar *vt* - **1.** [tarea, trabajo]: **endosar algo a alguien** to lumber sb with sthg - **2.** COM to endorse.

endoscopia *sf* endoscopy.

endoso *sm* COM endorsement.

endulzar [13] *vt* [con azúcar] to sweeten; *fig* [hacer agradable] to ease, to make more bearable.

endurecer [30] *vt* - **1.** [gen] to harden - **2.** [fortalecer] to strengthen.

endurecimiento *sm lit & fig* hardening.

enebro *sm* juniper.

enema *sf* enema.

enemigo, ga ◇ *adj* enemy *(antes de s)*; **ser enemigo de algo** to hate sthg. ◇ *sm, f* enemy; **pasarse al enemigo** to go over to the enemy.

enemistad *sf* enmity.

enemistar *vt* to make enemies of.
➡ **enemistarse** *vprnl*: **enemistarse (con)** to fall out (with).

energético, ca *adj* energy *(antes de s)*.
➡ **energética** *sf* energetics *(U)*.

energía *sf* - **1.** [gen] energy; **energía atómica** o **nuclear** nuclear power; **energía eléctrica/eólica/hidráulica** electric/wind/water power; **energía solar** solar energy o power - **2.** [fuerza] strength; **hay que empujar con energía** you have to push hard.

enérgico, ca *adj* [gen] energetic; [carácter] forceful; [gesto, medida] vigorous; [decisión, postura] emphatic.

energúmeno, na *sm, f* madman (*f* madwoman); **gritaba como un energúmeno** he was screaming like one possessed.

enero *sm* January; *ver también* **septiembre**.

enervante *adj* [debilitador] draining; [exasperante] exasperating.

enervar *vt* - **1.** [debilitar] to sap, to weaken - **2.** [poner nervioso] to exasperate.

enésimo, ma *adj* - **1.** MAT nth - **2.** *fig* umpteenth; **por enésima vez** for the umpteenth time.

enfadado, da *adj* angry.

enfadar *vt* to anger.

◔ **enfadarse** *vprnl*: **enfadarse (con)** to get angry (with).

enfado *sm* anger.

enfangar [16] *vt* to cover in mud.

◔ **enfangarse** *vprnl* - **1.** [con fango] to get covered in mud - **2.** *fam fig* [en un asunto sucio] to get mixed up in shady business.

énfasis *sm inv* emphasis; **poner énfasis en algo** to emphasize sthg.

enfático, ca *adj* emphatic.

enfatizar [13] *vt* to emphasize, to stress.

enfermar ◇ *vt* - **1.** [causar enfermedad a] to make ill - **2.** *fig* [irritar] to make sick. ◇ *vi* to fall ill; **enfermar del pecho** to develop a chest complaint.

enfermedad *sf* illness; **contraer una enfermedad** to catch an illness; **enfermedad contagiosa** contagious disease; **enfermedad de Creutzfeldt-Jakob** Creutzfeldt-Jakob disease, CJD; **enfermedad infecciosa/venérea** infectious/venereal disease; **enfermedad mental** mental illness; **enfermedad profesional** occupational disease; **enfermedad terminal** terminal illness.

enfermera ▷ **enfermero**.

enfermería *sf* sick bay.

enfermero, ra *sm, f* male nurse (*f* nurse).

enfermizo, za *adj* *lit & fig* unhealthy.

enfermo, ma ◇ *adj* ill, sick; **caer enfermo** to fall ill. ◇ *sm, f* [gen] invalid, sick person; [en el hospital] patient; **enfermo terminal** terminally ill patient.

enfervorizar [13] *vt* to inflame, to rouse.

enfilar ◇ *vt* - **1.** [ir por - camino] to go *o* head straight along - **2.** [apuntar - arma] to aim. ◇ *vi*: **enfilar hacia** to go *o* head straight towards.

enfisema *sm* emphysema.

enflaquecer [30] ◇ *vt* to make thin. ◇ *vi* to grow thin, to lose weight.

enfocar [10] *vt* - **1.** [imagen, objetivo] to focus - **2.** [suj: luz, foco] to shine on - **3.** [tema, asunto] to approach, to look at.

enfoque *sm* - **1.** [de imagen] focus - **2.** [de asunto] approach, angle; **dar un enfoque nuevo a algo** to adopt a new approach to sthg.

enfrascado, da *adj*: **estar enfrascado (en)** to be totally absorbed (in).

enfrascar [10] *vt* to bottle.

◔ **enfrascarse en** *vprnl* [riña] to get embroiled in; [lectura, conversación] to become engrossed in.

enfrentamiento *sm* confrontation.

enfrentar *vt* - **1.** [hacer frente a] to confront, to face - **2.** [poner frente a frente] to bring face to face.

◔ **enfrentarse** *vprnl* - **1.** [luchar, encontrarse] to meet, to clash - **2.** [oponerse]: **enfrentarse con alguien** to confront sb.

enfrente *adv* - **1.** [delante] opposite; **la tienda de enfrente** the shop across the road; **enfrente de** opposite - **2.** [en contra]: **tiene a todos enfrente** everyone's against her.

enfriamiento *sm* - **1.** [catarro] cold - **2.** [acción] cooling.

enfriar [9] *vt* *lit & fig* to cool.

◔ **enfriarse** *vprnl* - **1.** [líquido, pasión, amistad] to cool down - **2.** [quedarse demasiado frío] to go cold - **3.** MED to catch a cold.

enfundar *vt* [espada] to sheathe; [pistola] to put away.

◔ **enfundarse** *vprnl*: **enfundarse algo** to wrap o.s. up in sthg.

enfurecer [30] *vt* to infuriate, to madden.

◔ **enfurecerse** *vprnl* - **1.** [gen] to get furious - **2.** *fig* [mar] to become rough.

enfurecimiento *sm* anger.

enfurruñarse *vprnl* *fam* to sulk.

engalanar *vt* to decorate.

◔ **engalanarse** *vprnl* to dress up.

enganchar *vt* - **1.** [agarrar - vagones] to couple; [- remolque, caballos] to hitch up; [- pez] to hook - **2.** [colgar de un gancho] to hang up - **3.** *fam fig* [atraer]: **enganchar a alguien para que haga algo** to rope sb into doing sthg - **4.** [pillar - empleo, marido] to land (o.s.)

◔ **engancharse** *vprnl* - **1.** [prenderse]: **engancharse algo con algo** to catch sthg on sthg - **2.** [alistarse] to enlist, to join up - **3.** [hacerse adicto]: **engancharse (a)** to get hooked (on).

enganche *sm* - **1.** [de trenes] coupling - **2.** [gancho] hook - **3.** [reclutamiento] enlistment - **4.** *Méx* [depósito] deposit.

enganchón *sm* [de ropa etc] snag.

engañabobos *sm inv* - **1.** [cosa] con (trick) - **2.** [persona] con man, con artist.

engañar *vt* - **1.** [gen] to deceive; **engaña a su marido** she cheats on her husband - **2.** [estafar] to cheat, to swindle - **3.** [hacer más llevadero] to appease; **engañar el hambre** to cheat one's stomach.

◔ **engañarse** *vprnl* - **1.** [hacerse ilusiones] to delude o.s. - **2.** [equivocarse] to be wrong.

engañifa *sf fam* [gen] trick; [estafa] swindle.

engaño *sm* [gen] deceit; [estafa] swindle; **llamarse a engaño** to claim one has been cheated.

engañoso, sa *adj* [persona, palabras] deceitful; [aspecto, apariencia] deceptive; [consejo] misleading.

engarce *sm* setting.

engarzar [13] *vt* - **1.** [encadenar - abalorios] to thread; [- perlas] to string - **2.** [engastar] to set - **3.** [enlazar - palabras] to string together.

engatusador, ra *fam* ◇ *adj* coaxing, cajoling. ◇ *sm, f* coaxer.

engatusamiento *sm fam* coaxing, cajoling.

engatusar *vt fam* to get round; **engatusar a alguien para que haga algo** to coax *o* cajole sb into doing sthg.

engendrar *vt* - **1.** [procrear] to give birth to, to beget - **2.** [originar] to give rise to.

engendro *sm* - **1.** [obra de mala calidad] monstrosity - **2.** [ser deforme] freak, deformed creature; [niño] malformed child.

englobar *vt* to bring together.

engomar *vt* to stick, to glue.

engordar ◇ *vt* - **1.** [cebar] to fatten up - **2.** *fig* [aumentar] to swell. ◇ *vi* to put on weight.

engorde *sm* fattening (up).

engorro *sm* nuisance.

engorroso, sa *adj* bothersome.

engranaje *sm* - **1.** [acción] gearing - **2.** [piezas - de reloj, piñón] cogs *pl*; AUTO gears *pl* - **3.** *fig* [enlace - de ideas] chain, sequence - **4.** [aparato - político, burocrático] machinery.

engranar *vt* - **1.** [piezas] to engage - **2.** *fig* [ideas] to link, to connect.

engrandecer [30] *vt* - **1.** *fig* [enaltecer] to exalt - **2.** [aumentar] to increase, to enlarge.

engrandecimiento *sm* - **1.** [enaltecimiento] enhancement - **2.** [aumento] increase.

engrapar *vt Amér* [grapar] to staple.

engrasar *vt* [gen] to lubricate; [bisagra, mecanismo] to oil; [eje, bandeja] to grease.

engrase *sm* - **1.** [acción - gen] lubrication; [- de goznes] oiling; [- de bandeja] greasing - **2.** [sustancia] lubricant.

engreído, da ◇ *adj* conceited, full of one's own importance. ◇ *sm, f* conceited person.

engrosar [23] *vt* - **1.** *fig* [aumentar] to swell - **2.** [engordar - animal] to fatten; [- texto] to bump up the size of.

engrudo *sm* paste.

engruesa *etc* ▷ **engrosar**.

engullir *vt* to gobble up, to wolf down.

enharinar *vt* to flour.

enhebrar *vt* - **1.** [gen] to thread; [perlas] to string - **2.** *fig* [palabras] to string together.

enhorabuena ◇ *sf* congratulations *pl*; **dar la enhorabuena a alguien** to congratulate sb. ◇ *interj*: ¡enhorabuena (por...)! congratulations (on...)!

enigma *sm* enigma.

enigmático, ca *adj* enigmatic.

enjabonado, da *adj* soapy.
◆ **enjabonado** *sm* washing.

enjabonar *vt* - **1.** [con jabón] to soap - **2.** [dar coba a] to soft-soap.

enjambre *sm lit & fig* swarm.

enjaular *vt* [en jaula] to cage; *fam* [en prisión] to jail, to lock up.

enjoyar *vt* to adorn with jewels.
◆ **enjoyarse** *vprnl* to put on (one's) jewels.

enjuagar [16] *vt* to rinse.
◆ **enjuagarse** *vprnl* to rinse o.s./one's mouth/one's hands *etc*.

enjuague *sm* rinse.

enjugar [16] *vt* - **1.** [secar] to dry, to wipe away - **2.** [pagar - deuda] to pay off; [- déficit] to cancel out.

enjuiciamiento *sm* - **1.** DER trial - **2.** [opinión] judgment.

enjuiciar [8] *vt* - **1.** DER to try - **2.** [opinar] to judge.

enjuto, ta *adj* [delgado] lean.

enlace *sm* - **1.** [acción] link - **2.** [persona] go-between; **enlace sindical** shop steward - **3.** QUÍM bond - **4.** [casamiento]: **enlace (matrimonial)** marriage - **5.** [de trenes] connection; **estación de enlace** junction; **vía de enlace** crossover - **6.** INFORM: **enlace de datos** data link; **enlace hipertextual** *o* **de hipertexto** hypertext link; ▷ **enlazar**.

enladrillado *sm* brick paving.

enladrillar *vt* to pave with bricks.

enlatar *vt* to can, to tin.

enlazar [13] ◇ *vt*: **enlazar algo a** [atar] to tie sthg up to; [trabar, relacionar] to link *o* connect sthg with. ◇ *vi*: **enlazar en** [trenes] to connect at.
◆ **enlazarse** *vprnl* to become linked.

enlodar *vt* to cover in mud.

enloquecedor, ra *adj* maddening.

enloquecer [30] ◇ *vt* - **1.** [volver loco] to drive mad - **2.** *fig* [gustar mucho] to drive wild *o* crazy. ◇ *vi* to go mad.

enloquecimiento *sm* madness.

enlosar *vt* to tile.

enlutado, da *adj* in mourning.

enmaderar *vt* [pared] to panel; [suelo] to lay the floorboards of.

enmadrarse *vprnl* to become too tied to one's mother.

enmarañar *vt* - **1.** [enredar] to tangle (up) - **2.** [complicar] to complicate, to confuse.

➤ **enmarañarse** *vprnl* - **1.** [enredarse] to become tangled - **2.** [complicarse] to become confused o complicated.

enmarcar [10] *vt* to frame.

enmascarado, **da** ◇ *adj* masked. ◇ *sm, f* masked man (*f* masked woman).

enmascarar *vt* [rostro] to mask; *fig* [encubrir] to disguise.

enmendar [19] *vt* [error] to correct; [ley, dictamen] to amend; [comportamiento] to mend; [daño, perjuicio] to redress.

➤ **enmendarse** *vprnl* to mend one's ways.

enmienda *sf* - **1.** [acción]: **hacer propósito de enmienda** to promise to mend one's ways - **2.** [en un texto] corrections *pl* - **3.** POLÍT amendment.

enmiende ▷ **enmendar**.

enmohecer [30] *vt* [gen] to turn mouldy; [metal] to rust.

➤ **enmohecerse** *vprnl* [gen] to grow mouldy; [metal, conocimientos] to go rusty.

enmohecimiento *sm* [gen] mould; [de metal] rust.

enmoquetado *sm* carpeting.

enmoquetar *vt* to carpet.

enmudecer [30] ◇ *vt* to silence. ◇ *vi* [callarse] to fall silent, to go quiet; [perder el habla] to be struck dumb.

ennegrecer [30] *vt* [gen] to blacken; [suj: nubes] to darken.

➤ **ennegrecerse** *vprnl* [gen] to become blackened; [nublarse] to darken, to grow dark.

ennoblecer [30] *vt* - **1.** *fig* [dignificar] to lend distinction to - **2.** [dar un título a] to ennoble.

enojadizo, **za** *adj* irritable, touchy.

enojar *vt* [enfadar] to anger; [molestar] to annoy.

➤ **enojarse** *vprnl*: **enojarse (con)** [enfadarse] to get angry (with); [molestarse] to get annoyed (with).

enojo *sm* [enfado] anger; [molestia] annoyance.

enojoso, **sa** *adj* [molesto] annoying; [delicado, espinoso] awkward.

enología *sf* oenology, study of wine.

enólogo, **ga** *sm, f* oenologist, wine expert.

enorgullecer [30] *vt* to fill with pride.

➤ **enorgullecerse de** *vprnl* to be proud of.

enorme *adj* [en tamaño] enormous, huge; [en gravedad] monstrous.

enormidad *sf* - **1.** [de tamaño] enormity, hugeness - **2.** *fig* [despropósito] crass remark/mistake *etc.*

enquistado, **da** *adj*: **tiene la mano enquistada** he has a cyst on his hand.

enquistarse *vprnl* to develop into a cyst.

enraizar [13] *vi* [árbol] to take root; [persona] to put down roots.

enramada *sf* - **1.** [espesura] branches *pl*, canopy - **2.** [cobertizo] bower.

enrarecer [30] *vt* - **1.** [contaminar] to pollute - **2.** [rarificar] to rarefy.

➤ **enrarecerse** *vprnl* - **1.** [contaminarse] to become polluted - **2.** [rarificarse] to become rarefied - **3.** *fig* [situación, ambiente] to become tense.

enredadera *sf* creeper.

enredador, **ra** ◇ *adj* [travieso] naughty, mischievous; [chismoso] gossiping. ◇ *sm, f* [travieso] mischief-maker; [chismoso] gossip.

enredar ◇ *vt* - **1.** [madeja, pelo] to tangle up; [situación, asunto] to complicate, to confuse - **2.** [implicar]: **enredar a alguien (en)** to embroil sb (in), to involve sb (in) - **3.** [entretener] to bother, to annoy. ◇ *vi* to get up to mischief.

➤ **enredarse** *vprnl* - **1.** [plantas] to climb; [madeja, pelo] to get tangled up; [situación, asunto] to become confused - **2.** [empezar]: **enredarse en algo** to get involved in sthg; **enredarse a hacer algo** to start doing sthg - **3.** *fam* [amancebarse]: **enredarse con** to get involved o have an affair with.

enredo *sm* - **1.** [maraña] tangle, knot - **2.** [lío] mess, complicated affair; [asunto ilícito] shady affair - **3.** [amoroso] (love) affair - **4.** LITER plot.

enrejado *sm* - **1.** [barrotes - de balcón, verja] railings *pl*; [- de jaula, celda, ventana] bars *pl* - **2.** [de cañas] trellis.

enrevesado, **da** *adj* complex, complicated.

enriquecedor, **ra** *adj* enriching.

enriquecer [30] *vt* - **1.** [hacer rico] to bring wealth to, to make rich - **2.** *fig* [engrandecer] to enrich.

➤ **enriquecerse** *vprnl* to get rich.

enriquecimiento *sm* enrichment.

enrojecer [30] ◇ *vt* [gen] to redden, to turn red; [rostro, mejillas] to cause to blush. ◇ *vi* [por calor] to flush; [por turbación] to blush.

➤ **enrojecerse** *vprnl* [por calor] to flush; [por turbación] to blush.

enrojecimiento *sm* - **1.** [rubor] blushing - **2.** [irritación] redness, red mark.

enrolar *vt* to enlist.

➤ **enrolarse en** *vprnl* [la marina] to enlist in; [un buque] to sign up for.

enrollado, **da** *adj* - **1.** [en forma de rollo] in a roll, rolled up - **2.** *fam* [interesante, animado] fun - **3.** *fam* [en relaciones amorosas]: **estar enrollado con alguien** to be involved with sb.

enrollar *vt* - **1.** [arrollar] to roll up - **2.** *fam* [gustar]: **me enrolla mucho** I love it, I think it's great.
➡ **enrollarse** *vprnl* - **1.** *fam* [tener relaciones]: **enrollarse (con)** to get involved o have an affair (with) - **2.** [hablar] to go on (and on).

enroscar [10] *vt* - **1.** [atornillar] to screw in - **2.** [enrollar] to roll up; [cuerpo, cola] to curl up.

ensaimada *sf* *cake made of sweet coiled pastry.*

ensalada *sf* - **1.** [de lechuga etc] salad; **ensalada de frutas** fruit salad; **ensalada mixta** mixed salad; **ensalada rusa** Russian salad - **2.** *fam fig* [lío] mishmash.

ensaladera *sf* salad bowl.

ensaladilla *sf*: **ensaladilla (rusa)** Russian salad.

ensalzar [13] *vt* to praise.

ensamblado *sm* assembly.

ensamblador, ra *sm, f* [persona] joiner.
➡ **ensamblador** *sm* INFORM assembler.

ensambladura *sf* = ensamblaje.

ensamblaje *sm* [acción] assembly; [pieza] joint.

ensamblar *vt* [gen & INFORM] to assemble; [madera] to join.

ensanchamiento *sm* [de orificio, calle] widening; [de ropa] letting out.

ensanchar *vt* [orificio, calle] to widen; [ropa] to let out; [ciudad] to expand.

ensanche *sm* - **1.** [de calle etc] widening - **2.** [en la ciudad] new suburb.

ensangrentado, da *adj* bloodstained.

ensangrentar [19] *vt* to cover with blood.

ensañamiento *sm* ferocity.

ensañarse *vprnl*: **ensañarse con** to torment, to treat cruelly.

ensartar *vt* - **1.** [perlas] to string; [aguja] to thread - **2.** [atravesar - torero] to gore; [puñal] to plunge, to bury.

ensayar *vt* - **1.** [gen] to test - **2.** TEATRO to rehearse.

ensayista *smf* essayist.

ensayo *sm* - **1.** TEATRO rehearsal; **ensayo general** dress rehearsal - **2.** [prueba] test; **ensayo nuclear** nuclear test - **3.** LITER essay - **4.** [en rugby] try.

enseguida *adv* [inmediatamente] immediately, at once; [pronto] very soon; **llegará enseguida** he'll be here any minute now.

ensenada *sf* cove, inlet.

enseña *sf* ensign.

enseñante *smf* teacher.

enseñanza *sf* [gen] education; [instrucción] teaching; **enseñanza estatal** o **pública** state education; **enseñanza privada** private (sector) education; **enseñanza superior/universitaria** higher/university education; **enseñanza primaria/secundaria** primary/secondary education; **enseñanza personificada** personal o individual tutoring.
➡ **enseñanzas** *sfpl* [de maestro] teachings.

enseñar *vt* - **1.** [instruir, aleccionar] to teach; **enseñar a alguien a hacer algo** to teach sb (how) to do sthg - **2.** [mostrar] to show.

enseres *smpl* - **1.** [efectos personales] belongings - **2.** [utensilios] equipment *(U)*; **enseres domésticos** household goods.

ensillado, da *adj* saddled.

ensillar *vt* to saddle up.

ensimismado, da *adj* [enfrascado] absorbed; [pensativo] lost in thought.

ensimismamiento *sm* absorption.

ensimismarse *vprnl* [enfrascarse] to become absorbed; [abstraerse] to be lost in thought.

ensombrecer [30] *vt lit & fig* to cast a shadow over.
➡ **ensombrecerse** *vprnl* to darken.

ensoñación *sf* daydream.

ensopar *vt Andes, R Plata & Ven* to soak.

ensordecedor, ra *adj* deafening.

ensordecer [30] ◇ *vt* - **1.** [causar sordera a] to cause to go deaf - **2.** [suj: sonido] to deafen. ◇ *vi* to go deaf.

ensordecimiento *sm* deafness.

ensuciar [8] *vt* to (make) dirty; *fig* [desprestigiar] to sully, to tarnish.
➡ **ensuciarse** *vprnl* to get dirty.

ensueño *sm lit & fig* dream; **de ensueño** dream *(antes de s)*, ideal.

entablado *sm* [armazón] wooden platform; [suelo] floorboards *pl*.

entablar *vt* - **1.** [suelo] to put down floorboards on - **2.** [iniciar - conversación, amistad] to strike up; [- negocio] to start up - **3.** [entablillar] to put in a splint.

entablillar *vt* to put in a splint.

entallar ◇ *vt* - **1.** [prenda] to cut, to tailor - **2.** [madera] to carve, to sculpt. ◇ *vi* to fit.

entarimado *sm* [plataforma] wooden platform; [suelo] floorboards *pl*.

entarimar *vt* [suelo] to put down floorboards on.

ente *sm* - **1.** [ser] being - **2.** [corporación] body, organization; **ente público** [gen] state-owned body o institution; [televisión] Spanish state broadcasting company - **3.** *fam* [personaje] odd bod.

entendederas *sfpl fam* brains; **ser corto de entendederas** to be a bit dim.

entendedor, **ra** *sm, f*: al buen entendedor sobran las palabras o pocas palabras bastan a word to the wise is sufficient.

entender [20] <> *vt* - **1.** [gen] to understand; ¿tú qué entiendes por 'amistad'? what do you understand by 'friendship'?; **dar algo a entender** to imply sthg; **dar a entender que...** to imply (that)... - **2.** [darse cuenta] to realize - **3.** [oír] to hear - **4.** [juzgar] to think; **yo no lo entiendo así** I don't see it that way. <> *vi* - **1.** [comprender] to understand - **2.** [saber]: **entender de** o **en algo** to be an expert on sthg; **entender poco/algo de** to know very little/a little about. <> *sm*: **a mi entender...** the way I see it...

◆ **entenderse** *vprnl* - **1.** [comprenderse - uno mismo] to know what one means; [- dos personas] to understand each other - **2.** [llevarse bien] to get on - **3.** [ponerse de acuerdo] to reach an agreement - **4.** [comunicarse] to communicate (with each other) - **5.** [amorosamente]: **entenderse (con)** to have an affair (with).

entendido, **da** <> *adj* - **1.** [comprendido] understood; **tener entendido que** to understand that - **2.** [versado] expert. <> *sm, f*: **entendido (en)** expert (on).

◆ **entendido** *interj*: ¡entendido! all right!, okay!

entendimiento *sm* - **1.** [comprensión] understanding; [juicio] judgment; [inteligencia] mind, intellect - **2.** [acuerdo] understanding; **llegar a un entendimiento** to come to o reach an understanding.

entente *sf* POLÍT entente cordiale; COM agreement.

enterado, **da** <> *adj*: **enterado (en)** well-informed (about); **estar enterado de algo** to be aware of sthg; **darse por enterado** to get the message; **no darse por enterado** to turn a deaf ear. <> *sm, f* expert.

enterarse *vprnl* - **1.** [descubrir]: **enterarse (de)** to find out (about) - **2.** *fam* [comprender] to get it, to understand - **3.** [darse cuenta]: **enterarse (de algo)** to realize (sthg) - **4.** *loc*: ¡para que te enteres! I'll have you know!, as a matter of fact!; ¡te vas a enterarse! you'll know all about it!, you'll catch it!

entereza *sf* [serenidad] composure; [honradez] integrity; [firmeza] firmness.

enternecedor, **ra** *adj* touching.

enternecer [30] *vt* to move, to touch.
◆ **enternecerse** *vprnl* to be moved.

enternecimiento *sm* compassion.

entero, **ra** *adj* - **1.** [completo] whole; **por entero** entirely, completely - **2.** [sereno] composed - **3.** [honrado] upright, honest.

◆ **entero** *sm* - **1.** [en la bolsa] point - **2.** C Sur [de trabajo] overalls *UK pl*, coveralls *US pl*; [sin mangas] dungarees *UK pl*, overalls *US pl*; [para bebé] rompers *pl*.

enterrador, **ra** *sm, f* gravedigger.

enterramiento *sm* burial.

enterrar [19] *vt* - **1.** [gen] to bury - **2.** *fig* [olvidar] to forget about.
◆ **enterrarse** *vprnl fig* to hide o.s. away.

entibiar [8] *vt* - **1.** [enfriar] to cool - **2.** [templar] to warm.
◆ **entibiarse** *vprnl* [sentimiento] to cool.

entidad *sf* - **1.** [corporación] body; [empresa] firm, company; **entidad bancaria** bank - **2.** FILOS entity - **3.** [importancia] importance.

entienda *etc* ▷ entender.

entierra *etc* ▷ enterrar.

entierro *sm* [acción] burial; [ceremonia] funeral.

entlo. *abrev de* entresuelo.

entoldado *sm* [toldo] awning; [para fiestas, bailes] marquee.

entoldar *vt* to cover with an awning.

entomología *sf* entomology.

entonación *sf* intonation.

entonar <> *vt* - **1.** [cantar] to sing - **2.** [tonificar] to pick up. <> *vi* - **1.** [al cantar] to sing in tune - **2.** [armonizar]: **entonar (con algo)** to match (sthg).

entonces <> *adv* then; **desde entonces** since then; **en** o **por aquel entonces** at that time. <> *interj*: ¡entonces! well, then!

entontecer [30] *vt*: **entontecer a alguien** to dull sb's brain.

entornar *vt* to half-close.

entorno *sm* - **1.** [ambiente] environment, surroundings *pl* - **2.** INFORM environment; **entorno gráfico** graphic environment; **entorno de programación** programming environment.

entorpecer [30] *vt* - **1.** [debilitar - movimientos] to hinder; [- miembros] to numb; [- mente] to cloud - **2.** [dificultar] to obstruct, to hinder.

entorpecimiento *sm* - **1.** [debilitamiento - físico] numbness; [- mental] haziness - **2.** [dificultad] hindrance.

entrada *sf* - **1.** [acción] entry; [llegada] arrival; **'prohibida la entrada'** 'no entry' - **2.** [lugar] entrance; [puerta] doorway; **'entrada'** 'way in', 'entrance'; **entrada principal** main entrance; **entrada de servicio** tradesman's entrance - **3.** TECNOL inlet, intake; **entrada de aire** air intake - **4.** [en espectáculos - billete] ticket; [- recaudación] receipts *pl*, takings *pl*; **entrada gratuita** admission free; **entrada libre** admission free; **sacar una entrada** to buy a ticket - **5.** [público] audience; DEP attendance - **6.** [pago inicial] down payment - **7.** [en contabilidad] income - **8.** [plato] starter - **9.** [en la frente]: **tener entradas** to have a receding hairline - **10.** [en un diccionario] entry - **11.** [principio] beginning, start; **de entrada** right from the beginning *o* the word go - **12.** INFORM input.

entrado, da *adj* - **1.** [gen]: **entrado el otoño** once autumn has started; **entrado en años** elderly; **entrado en carnes** portly, rather large - **2.** INFORM input.

entramado *sm* framework.

entramar *vt* to make the framework of.

entrante ◇ *adj* [año, mes] coming; [presidente, gobierno] incoming. ◇ *sm* - **1.** [plato] starter - **2.** [hueco] recess.

entraña *(gen pl)* *sf* - **1.** [víscera] entrails *pl*, insides *pl* - **2.** *fig* [centro, esencia] heart - **3.** *loc*: **arrancársele a uno las entrañas** to break sb's heart; **no tener entrañas** to be heartless.

entrañable *adj* intimate.

entrañar *vt* to involve.

entrar ◇ *vi* - **1.** [introducirse - viniendo] to enter, to come in; [- yendo] to enter, to go in; **entrar en algo** to enter sthg, to come/go into sthg; **entré por la ventana** I got in through the window - **2.** [penetrar - clavo etc] to go in; **entrar en algo** to go into sthg - **3.** [caber]: **entrar (en)** to fit (in); **este anillo no te entra** this ring won't fit you - **4.** [incorporarse]: **entrar (en algo)** [colegio, empresa] to start (at sthg); [club, partido político] to join (sthg); **entrar de** [botones etc] to start off as - **5.** [empezar]: **entrar a hacer algo** to start doing sthg - **6.** [participar] to join in; **entrar en** [discusión, polémica] to join in; [negocio] to get in on - **7.** [estar incluido]: **entrar en** to be included in - **8.** [figurar]: **entrar en** to belong to; **entro en el grupo de los disconformes** I number among the dissidents - **9.** [estado físico o de ánimo]: **le entraron ganas de hablar** he suddenly felt like talking; **me está entrando frío** I'm getting cold; **me entró mucha pena** I was filled with pity - **10.** [periodo de tiempo] to start; **el verano entra el 21 de junio** summer starts on 21st June; **entrar en** [edad, vejez] to reach; [año nuevo] to enter - **11.** [cantidad]: **¿cuántos entran en un kilo?** how many do you get to the kilo? - **12.** [concepto, asignatura etc]: **no le entra la geometría** he can't get the hang of geometry - **13.** AUTO to engage; **no entra la tercera** it won't go into third gear. ◇ *vt* - **1.** [introducir] to bring in - **2.** [prenda de vestir] to take in - **3.** [acometer] to approach, to deal with; **a ése no hay por donde entrarle** there's no way of getting through to him.

entre *prep* - **1.** [gen] between; **entre nosotros** [en confianza] between you and me, between ourselves; **era un color entre verde y azul** the colour was somewhere between green and blue; **su estado de ánimo estaba entre la ale-**

gría y la emoción his state of mind was somewhere between *o* was a mixture of joy and excitement; **entre una cosa y otra** what with one thing and another - **2.** [en medio de muchos] among, amongst; **estaba entre los asistentes** she was among those present; **estuvo entre los mejores** he was one of *o* amongst the best; **entre hombres y mujeres somos más de cien** there are over a hundred of us, men and women together; **entre sí** amongst themselves; **discutían entre sí** they were arguing with each other.

entreabierto, ta *pp* ▷ **entreabrir**.

entreabrir *vt* to half-open.

entreacto *sm* interval.

entrecejo *sm* space between the brows; **fruncir el entrecejo** to frown.

entrecerrar [19] *vt* to half-close.

entrecomillado, da *adj* in quotation marks. ➤ **entrecomillado** *sm* text in quotation marks.

entrecomillar *vt* to put in quotation marks.

entrecortado, da *adj* [voz, habla] faltering; [respiración] laboured; [señal, sonido] intermittent.

entrecot, entrecote *sm* entrecôte.

entrecruzar [13] *vt* to interweave; [miradas] to meet; [dedos] to link together. ➤ **entrecruzarse** *vprnl* to interweave; [miradas, caminos] to meet.

entredicho *sm*: **estar en entredicho** to be in doubt; **poner en entredicho** to question, to call into question.

entrega *sf* - **1.** [gen] handing over; [de pedido, paquete] delivery; [de premios] presentation; **hacer entrega de algo a alguien** to hand sthg over to sb; **entrega a domicilio** home delivery - **2.** [dedicación]: **entrega (a)** devotion (to) - **3.** [fascículo] instalment; **publicar por entregas** to serialize.

entregar [16] *vt* [gen] to hand over; [pedido, paquete] to deliver; [examen, informe] to hand in; [persona] to turn over. ➤ **entregarse** *vprnl* [rendirse - soldado, ejército] to surrender; [- criminal] to turn o.s. in. ➤ **entregarse a** *vprnl* - **1.** [persona, trabajo] to devote o.s. to - **2.** [vicio, pasión] to give o.s. over to.

entreguerras ➤ **de entreguerras** *loc adj* between the wars.

entrelazar [13] *vt* to interlace, to interlink.

entremedio, entremedias *adv* in between.

entremés *sm (gen pl)* CULIN hors d'œuvres.

entremeter *vt* to insert, to put in. ➤ **entremeterse** *vprnl* [inmiscuirse]: **entremeterse (en)** to meddle (in).

entremetido, da ◇ *adj* meddling. ◇ *sm, f* meddler.

entremezclar *vt* to mix up.
◆ **entremezclarse** *vprnl* to mix.

entrenador, ra *sm, f* coach; [seleccionador] manager.

entrenamiento *sm* training.

entrenar *vt & vi* to train.
◆ **entrenarse** *vprnl* to train.

entrepierna *sf* crotch.

entresacar [10] *vt* to pick out.

entresijos *smpl* ins and outs.

entresuelo *sm* mezzanine.

entretanto ◇ *adv* meanwhile. ◇ *sm*: **en el entretanto** in the meantime.

entretecho *sm* *Chile & Col* loft, attic.

entretela *sf* [de ropa] inner lining.
◆ **entretelas** *sfpl fig* innermost heart *sing*.

entretención *sf Chile* entertainment.

entretener [72] *vt* - **1.** [despistar] to distract - **2.** [retrasar] to hold up, to keep - **3.** [divertir] to entertain - **4.** [mantener] to keep alive, to sustain.
◆ **entretenerse** *vprnl* - **1.** [despistarse] to get distracted - **2.** [divertirse] to amuse o.s. - **3.** [retrasarse] to be held up.

entretenido, da *adj* entertaining, enjoyable.

entretenimiento *sm* - **1.** [acción] entertainment - **2.** [pasatiempo] pastime.

entretiempo *sm*: **de entretiempo** mild-weather *(antes de s)*.

entrever [76] *vt* - **1.** [vislumbrar] to barely make out; [por un instante] to glimpse - **2.** *fig* [adivinar] to see signs of.
◆ **entreverse** *vprnl* to be barely visible; **no se entreve una solución** *fig* there's no sign of a solution.

entreverar *C Sur vt* to mix.
◆ **entreverarse** *vprnl* to get tangled.

entrevero *sm C Sur* [lío] tangle, mess; [pelea] brawl.

entrevista *sf* - **1.** [periodística, de trabajo] interview; **hacer una entrevista a alguien** to interview sb; **entrevista de selección** job interview - **2.** [reunión] meeting.

entrevistador, ra *sm, f* interviewer.

entrevistar *vt* to interview.
◆ **entrevistarse** *vprnl*: **entrevistarse (con)** to have a meeting (with).

entrevisto, ta *pp* ⊳ **entrever**.

entristecer [30] *vt* to make sad.
◆ **entristecerse** *vprnl* to become sad.

entristecimiento *sm* sadness.

entrometerse *vprnl*: **entrometerse (en)** to interfere (in).

entrometido, da ◇ *adj* interfering. ◇ *sm, f* meddler.

entrometimiento *sm* meddling.

entromparse *vprnl fam* to get legless.

entroncar [10] *vi* - **1.** [emparentarse]: **entroncar (con)** to become related (to) - **2.** [trenes etc] to connect - **3.** *fig* [relacionarse]: **entroncar (con)** to be related (to).

entronizar [13] *vt* to crown.

entubar *vt* to fit tubes to, to tube.

entuerto *sm* wrong, injustice; **deshacer entuertos** to right wrongs.

entumecer [30] *vt* to numb.
◆ **entumecerse** *vprnl* to become numb.

entumecido, da *adj* numb.

entumecimiento *sm* numbness.

enturbiar [8] *vt lit & fig* to cloud.
◆ **enturbiarse** *vprnl lit & fig* to become cloudy.

entusiasmar *vt* - **1.** [animar] to fill with enthusiasm - **2.** [gustar]: **le entusiasma la música** he loves music.
◆ **entusiasmarse** *vprnl*: **entusiasmarse (con)** to get excited (about).

entusiasmo *sm* enthusiasm; **con entusiasmo** enthusiastically.

entusiasta ◇ *adj* enthusiastic. ◇ *smf* enthusiast.

enumeración *sf* enumeration, listing.

enumerar *vt* to enumerate, to list.

enunciación, enunciado *sf* formulation, enunciation.

enunciar [8] *vt* to formulate, to enunciate.

envainar *vt* to sheathe.

envalentonamiento *sm* boldness.

envalentonar *vt* to urge on, to fill with courage.
◆ **envalentonarse** *vprnl* to become daring.

envanecer [30] *vt* to make vain.
◆ **envanecerse** *vprnl* to become vain.

envanecimiento *sm* vanity.

envarado, da ◇ *adj* stiff, formal. ◇ *sm, f* stiff o formal person.

envasado *sm* [en botellas] bottling; [en latas] canning; [en paquetes] packing.

envasar *vt* [en botellas] to bottle; [en latas] to can; [en paquetes] to pack.

envase *sm* - **1.** [envasado - en botellas] bottling; [- en latas] canning; [- en paquetes] packing - **2.** [recipiente] container; [botella] bottle; **envase desechable** disposable container; **envase retornable** returnable bottle; **envase sin retorno** non-returnable bottle.

envejecer [30] ◇ *vi* [hacerse viejo] to grow old; [parecer viejo] to age. ◇ *vt* to age.

envejecido, **da** adj [de edad] old; [de aspecto] aged.

envejecimiento sm ageing.

envenenamiento sm poisoning.

envenenar vt to poison.

envergadura sf - **1.** [importancia] size, extent; [complejidad] complexity; **una reforma de gran envergadura** a wide-ranging reform - **2.** [anchura] span.

envés sm reverse (side), back; [de tela] wrong side.

enviado, **da** sm, f POLÍT envoy; PRENSA correspondent; **enviado especial** PRENSA special correspondent.

enviar [9] vt to send; **enviar a alguien a hacer algo** to send sb to do sthg.

enviciar [8] vt to addict, to get hooked.
➡ **enviciarse** vprnl to become addicted.

envidia sf envy; **era la envidia de todos** it was the envy of everyone; **dar envidia a alguien** to make sb jealous o envious; **tener envidia de alguien/algo** to envy sb/sthg, to be jealous o envious of sb/sthg; **morirse de envidia** to be green with envy.

envidiable adj enviable.

envidiar [8] vt to envy.

envidioso, **sa** ◇ adj envious. ◇ sm, f envious person.

envilecer [30] vt to debase.
➡ **envilecerse** vprnl to become debased.

envilecimiento sm debasement.

envío sm - **1.** COM dispatch; [de correo] delivery; [de víveres, mercancías] consignment; **gastos de envío** postage and packing UK, postage and handling US; **envío a domicilio** home delivery; **envío contra reembolso** cash on delivery - **2.** [paquete] package.

enviudar vi to be widowed.

envoltorio sm wrapper, wrapping.

envoltura sf = envoltorio.

envolvente adj enveloping.

envolver [24] vt - **1.** [embalar] to wrap (up) - **2.** [enrollar] to wind - **3.** [implicar]: **envolver a alguien en** to involve sb in.
➡ **envolverse** vprnl: **envolverse en** o **con algo** to wrap o.s. in sthg.

envuelto, **ta** pp ▷ envolver.

envuelva etc ▷ envolver.

enyesar vt - **1.** MED to put in plaster - **2.** CONSTR to plaster.

enzarzar [13] vt to entangle, to embroil.
➡ **enzarzarse** vprnl: **enzarzarse en** to get entangled o embroiled in.

enzima sf enzyme.

eólico, **ca** adj wind (antes de s).

epatar vt to shock.

e.p.d. (abrev de en paz descanse) RIP.

épica ▷ épico.

epicentro sm epicentre.

épico, **ca** adj epic.
➡ **épica** sf epic.

epicúreo, **a** adj & sm, f Epicurean.

epidemia sf epidemic.

epidémico, **ca** adj epidemic.

epidemiología sf epidemiology.

epidérmico, **ca** adj epidermic.

epidermis sf inv epidermis.

Epifanía sf Epiphany.

epígrafe sm heading.

epilepsia sf epilepsy.

epiléptico, **ca** adj & sm, f epileptic.

epílogo sm epilogue.

episcopado sm - **1.** [gen] episcopate, episcopacy - **2.** [territorio] diocese.

episcopal adj episcopal.

episodio sm - **1.** [gen] episode - **2.** [suceso] event.

epístola sf culto [carta] epistle; RELIG Epistle.

epistolar adj culto epistolary.

epistolario sm collected letters pl.

epitafio sm epitaph.

epitelio sm epithelium.

epíteto sm epithet.

época sf period; [estación] season; **de época** period (antes de s); **en aquella época** at that time; **hacer época** to become a symbol of its time; **época dorada** golden age.

epopeya sf - **1.** [gen] epic - **2.** fig [hazaña] feat.

equidad sf fairness.

equidistante adj equidistant.

equidistar vi: **equidistar (de)** to be equidistant (from).

équidos smpl members of the horse family.

equilátero, **ra** adj equilateral.

equilibrado, **da** adj - **1.** [gen] balanced - **2.** [sensato] sensible.

equilibrar vt to balance.
➡ **equilibrarse** vprnl to balance.

equilibrio sm balance; **mantener algo en equilibrio** to balance sthg; **mantenerse/perder el equilibrio** to keep/lose one's balance; **equilibrio ecológico** ecological balance; **equilibrio de poderes** balance of power; **hacer equilibrios** fig to perform a balancing act.

equilibrismo sm [en trapecio] trapeze; [funambulismo] tightrope walking.

equilibrista smf [trapecista] trapeze artist; [funambulista] tightrope walker.

equino, **na** adj equine.

equinoccio *sm* equinox.

equipaje *sm* luggage *UK*, baggage *US*; **hacer el equipaje** to pack; **equipaje de mano** hand luggage.

equipamiento *sm* [acción] equipping; [equipo] equipment.

equipar *vt*: **equipar (de)** [gen] to equip (with); [ropa] to fit out (with).
- **equiparse** *vprnl* to equip o.s.

equiparable *adj*: **equiparable (a)** comparable (to).

equiparar *vt* to compare.
- **equipararse** *vprnl* to be compared.

equipo *sm* - **1.** [equipamiento] equipment; **equipo de oficina** office equipment; **caerse con todo el equipo** *fam* to get it in the neck - **2.** [uniforme - de novia] trousseau; [- de solda-do] kit; [- de colegial] uniform - **3.** [personas, ju-gadores] team; **equipo de rescate** rescue team - **4.** [de música] system; **equipo de sonido** sound system.

equis *adj* X; **un número equis de personas** x number of people.

equitación *sf* [arte] equestrianism; [actividad] horse riding.

equitativo, va *adj* fair, even-handed.

equivalencia *sf* equivalence.

equivalente *adj* & *sm* equivalent.

equivaler [74] ● **equivaler a** *vi* to be equi-valent to; *fig* [significar] to amount to.

equivocación *sf* mistake; **por equivocación** by mistake.

equivocado, da *adj* mistaken.

equivocar [10] *vt* to choose wrongly; **equivo-car algo con algo** to mistake sthg for sthg.
- **equivocarse** *vprnl* to be wrong; **equivocar-se en** to make a mistake in; **se equivocó en la suma** she got the total wrong; **se equivocó de nombre** he got the wrong name.

equívoco, ca *adj* - **1.** [ambiguo] ambiguous, equivocal - **2.** [sospechoso] suspicious.
- **equívoco** *sm* misunderstanding.

era *sf* - **1.** [periodo] era; **era atómica/espacial/glacial** atomic/space/ice age; **era cristiana/geológica** Christian/geological era - **2.** [cam-po] threshing floor; ▷ **ser**.

erario *sm* funds *pl*; **erario público** exchequer.

ERASMUS (*abrev de* **European Action Scheme for the Mobility of University Stu-dents**) *sm* ERASMUS.

erección *sf* erection.

eréctil *adj* erectile.

erecto, ta *adj* erect.

eremita *smf* hermit.

eres ▷ **ser**.

ergonomía *sf* ergonomics *(U)*.

ergonómico, ca *adj* ergonomic.

erguir [58] *vt* to raise.
- **erguirse** *vprnl* to rise up.

erial ◇ *adj* uncultivated. ◇ *sm* uncultivated land.

erice *etc* ▷ **erizar**.

erigir [15] *vt* - **1.** [construir] to erect, to build - **2.** [nombrar] to name.
- **erigirse en** *vprnl* to set o.s. up as.

eritema *sm* skin rash.

erizado, da *adj* - **1.** [de punta] on end; [con púas o espinas] spiky - **2.** *fig* [lleno]: **erizado de** plagued with.

erizar [13] *vt* to cause to stand on end.
- **erizarse** *vprnl* [pelo] to stand on end; [perso-na] to stiffen.

erizo *sm* - **1.** [mamífero] hedgehog - **2.** [pez] globefish; **erizo de mar** sea urchin.

ermita *sf* hermitage.

ermitaño, ña *sm, f* hermit.

erógeno, na *adj* erogenous.

erosión *sf* erosion.

erosionar *vt* to erode.
- **erosionarse** *vprnl* to erode.

erosivo, va *adj* erosive.

erótico, ca *adj* erotic.
- **erótica** *sf*: **la erótica del poder** the thrill of power.

erotismo *sm* eroticism.

erradicación *sf* eradication.

erradicar [10] *vt* to eradicate.

errado, da *adj* [disparo] wide of the mark, missed; [razonamiento] mistaken.

errante *adj* wandering.

errar [47] ◇ *vt* [vocación, camino] to choose wrongly; [disparo, golpe] to miss. ◇ *vi* - **1.** [va-gar] to wander - **2.** [equivocarse] to make a mis-take - **3.** [al disparar] to miss.

errata *sf* misprint.

errático, ca *adj* [errante] wandering; MED er-ratic.

erre *sf*: **erre que erre** stubbornly.

erróneo, a *adj* mistaken.

error *sm* mistake, error; **cometer un error** to make a mistake; **estar en un error** to be mis-taken; **por error** by mistake; **salvo error u omisión** errors and omissions excepted; **error de cálculo** miscalculation; **error humano** hu-man error; **error de imprenta** misprint; **error judicial** miscarriage of justice; **error tipográ-fico** typo, typographical error.

ertzaina [er'tʃaina] *sf member of Basque re-gional police force.*

ertzaintza [er'tʃaintʃa] *sf Basque regional po-lice force.*

eructar *vi* to belch.

eructo *sm* belch.

erudición *sf* erudition.

erudito, ta ⬦ *adj* erudite. ⬦ *sm, f* scholar.

erupción *sf* - **1.** GEOL eruption; **en erupción** erupting; **entrar en erupción** to erupt - **2.** MED rash.

eruptivo, va *adj* [roca] volcanic; [volcán] active.

es ▷ **ser**.

esa ▷ **ese**.

ésa ▷ **ése**.

esbeltez *sf* slenderness, slimness.

esbelto, ta *adj* slender, slim.

esbirro *sm* henchman.

esbozar [13] *vt* to sketch, to outline; [sonrisa] to give a hint of.

esbozo *sm* sketch, outline.

escabechado, da *adj* CULIN marinated.
➥ **escabechado** *sm* CULIN marinade.

escabechar *vt* CULIN to marinate.

escabeche *sm* CULIN marinade.

escabechina *sf* destruction; [en examen] huge number of failures.

escabroso, sa *adj* - **1.** [abrupto] rough - **2.** [obsceno] risqué - **3.** [espinoso] awkward, thorny.

escabullirse *vprnl* - **1.** [desaparecer]: **escabullirse (de)** to slip away (from) - **2.** [escurrirse]: **escabullírsele a alguien** to slip out of sb's hands.

escacharrar *vt fam* to knacker.
➥ **escacharrarse** *vprnl fam* to get knackered.

escafandra *sf* diving suit; **escafandra espacial** spacesuit.

escafandrista *smf* diver.

escala *sf* - **1.** [gen] scale; [de colores] range; **a escala** [gráfica] to scale; **a escala mundial** *fig* on a worldwide scale; **a gran escala** on a large scale; **a pequeña escala** small-scale; **en pequeña escala** on a small scale; **escala de popularidad** popularity stakes *pl*; **escala salarial** salary scale - **2.** [en un viaje] stopover; **hacer escala** to stop over; **escala técnica** refuelling stop UK, refueling stop US - **3.** [escalera] ladder.

escalada *sf* - **1.** [de montaña] climb; **escalada libre** free climbing - **2.** [de violencia, precios] escalation, rise.

escalador, ra ⬦ *adj* climbing *(antes de s)*. ⬦ *sm, f* - **1.** [alpinista] climber - **2.** *fam* [de puestos] careerist.

escalafón *sm* scale, ladder.

escalar *vt* to climb.

escaldado, da *adj* - **1.** CULIN scalded - **2.** *fig* [receloso] wary.

escaldar *vt* to scald.
➥ **escaldarse** *vprnl* to get burned.

escaleno *adj* scalene.

escalera *sf* - **1.** [gen] stairs *pl*, staircase; [escala] ladder; **escalera mecánica** o **automática** escalator; **escalera de caracol** spiral staircase; **escalera de incendios** fire escape; **escalera de mano** ladder; **escalera de servicio** service stairs *pl*; **escalera de tijera** step ladder - **2.** [en naipes] run; **escalera de color** straight flush.

escalerilla *sf* [de avión] stairs *pl*.

escalfar *vt* to poach.

escalinata *sf* staircase.

escalofriante *adj* spine-chilling.

escalofrío *(gen pl) sm* shiver; **dar escalofríos a alguien** to give sb the shivers; **tener escalofríos** to have the shivers.

escalón *sm* step; *fig* grade.

escalonado, da *adj* - **1.** [en el tiempo] spread out - **2.** [terreno] terraced; [pelo] layered.

escalonar *vt* - **1.** [gen] to spread out - **2.** [terreno] to terrace.

escalope *sm* escalope.

escalpelo *sm* scalpel.

escama *sf* - **1.** [de peces, reptiles] scale - **2.** [de jabón, en la piel] flake.

escamado, da *adj fam* suspicious, wary.

escamar *vt* - **1.** [pescado] to scale - **2.** *fam fig* [mosquear] to make suspicious.
➥ **escamarse** *vprnl fam* to smell a rat, to get suspicious.

escamotear *vt*: **escamotear algo a alguien** [estafar] to do o swindle sb out of sthg; [hurtar] to rob sb of sthg.

escampar *v impers* to clear up, to stop raining.

escanciar [8] *vt* to serve, to pour out.

escandalizar [13] *vt* to scandalize, to shock.
➥ **escandalizarse** *vprnl* to be shocked.

escándalo *sm* - **1.** [inmoralidad] scandal; [indignación] outrage - **2.** [alboroto] uproar, racket; **armar un escándalo** to kick up a fuss.

escandaloso, sa ⬦ *adj* - **1.** [inmoral] outrageous, shocking - **2.** [ruidoso] very noisy. ⬦ *sm, f* very noisy o loud person.

Escandinavia *n pr* Scandinavia.

escandinavo, va *adj & sm, f* Scandinavian.

escanear *vt* to scan.

escáner *(pl escaners) sm* - **1.** [aparato] scanner - **2.** [exploración] scan; **hacerse un escáner** to have a scan.

escaño *sm* - **1.** [cargo] seat *(in parliament)* - **2.** [asiento] bench *(in parliament)*.

escapada *sf* - **1.** [huida] escape, flight; DEP breakaway - **2.** [viaje] quick trip.

escapar *vi* - **1.** [huir]: **escapar (de)** to get away *o* escape (from) - **2.** [quedar fuera del alcance]: **escapar a alguien** to be beyond sb.
◆ **escaparse** *vprnl* - **1.** [huir]: **escaparse (de)** to get away *o* escape (from); **escaparse de casa** to run away from home - **2.** [salir - gas, agua etc] to leak - **3.** [perder]: **se me escapó la risa/un taco** I let out a laugh/an expletive; **se me escapó el tren** I missed the train; **se me escapó la ocasión** the opportunity slipped by.

escaparate *sm* - **1.** [de tienda] (shop) window - **2.** *Cuba & Ven* [ropero] wardrobe.

escaparatista *smf* window dresser.

escapatoria *sf* - **1.** [fuga] escape; **no tener escapatoria** to have no way out - **2.** *fam* [evasiva] way (of getting) out.

escape *sm* [de gas etc] leak; [de coche] exhaust; **a escape** in a rush, at high speed.

escapismo *sm* escapism.

escapista *adj* escapist.

escaquearse *vprnl fam* to duck out; **escaquearse de algo/de hacer algo** to worm one's way out of sthg/doing sthg.

escarabajo *sm* beetle.

escaramuza *sf fig* & MIL skirmish.

escarapela *sf* rosette, cockade.

escarbar *vt* to scratch, to scrape.

escarceos *smpl* forays; **escarceos amorosos** flirtations.

escarcha *sf* frost.

escarchado, da *adj* [fruta] candied, crystallized.

escarchar *v impers* to freeze (over).

escarlata *adj* & *sm* scarlet.

escarlatina *sf* scarlet fever.

escarmentar **[19]** *vi* to learn (one's lesson); **¡no escarmienta!** he never learns!; **¡para que escarmientes!** that'll teach you!

escarmiento *sm* lesson; **servir de escarmiento** to serve as a lesson.

escarnecer **[30]** *vt* to mock, to ridicule.

escarnio *sm* mockery, ridicule.

escarola *sf* endive.

escarpado, da *adj* [inclinado] steep; [abrupto] craggy.

escasear *vi* to be scarce, to be in short supply.

escasez *sf* [insuficiencia] shortage; [pobreza] poverty.

escaso, sa *adj* - **1.** [insuficiente - conocimientos, recursos] limited, scant; [- tiempo] short; [- cantidad, número] low; [- víveres, trabajo] scarce, in short supply; [- visibilidad, luz] poor; **andar escaso de** to be short of - **2.** [casi completo]: **un metro escaso** barely a metre.

escatimar *vt* [gastos, comida] to be sparing with, to skimp on; [esfuerzo, energías] to use as little as possible; **no escatimar gastos** to spare no expense.

escay, skai *sm* Leatherette®.

escayola *sf* CONSTR plaster of Paris; MED plaster.

escayolar *vt* to put in plaster.

escena *sf* - **1.** [gen] scene; **hacer una escena** to make a scene; **escena retrospectiva** flashback - **2.** [escenario] stage; **llevar a la escena** to dramatize; **poner en escena** to stage; **salir a escena** to go on stage.

escenario *sm* - **1.** [tablas, escena] stage; CINE & TEATRO [lugar de la acción] setting - **2.** *fig* [de suceso] scene.

escénico, ca *adj* scenic.

escenificación *sf* [de novela] dramatization; [de obra de teatro] staging.

escenificar **[10]** *vt* [novela] to dramatize; [obra de teatro] to stage.

escenografía *sf* set design.

escenógrafo, fa *sm, f* set designer.

escepticismo *sm* scepticism.

escéptico, ca ◇ *adj* - **1.** FILOS sceptic - **2.** [incrédulo] sceptical. ◇ *sm, f* sceptic.

escindir *vt* to split.
◆ **escindirse** *vprnl*: **escindirse (en)** to split (into).

escisión *sf* [del átomo] splitting; [de partido político] split.

esclarecedor, ra *adj* illuminating.

esclarecer **[30]** *vt* to clear up, to shed light on.

esclarecimiento *sm* clearing up, elucidation.

esclava ▷ **esclavo**.

esclavitud *sf lit & fig* slavery.

esclavizar **[13]** *vt lit & fig* to enslave.

esclavo, va ◇ *adj* enslaved. ◇ *sm, f lit & fig* [persona] slave; **es un esclavo del trabajo** he's a slave to his work.
◆ **esclava** *sf* [pulsera] bangle, bracelet.

esclerosis *sf inv* MED sclerosis; **esclerosis múltiple** multiple sclerosis.

esclusa *sf* [de canal] lock; [compuerta] floodgate.

escoba *sf* broom; **pasar la escoba** to sweep (up).

escobazo *sm* blow with a broom; **echar a alguien a escobazos** to kick sb out.

escobilla *sf* - **1.** brush - **2.** *Chile* [de dientes] toothbrush.

escobillar *vt Amér* [cepillar] to brush.

escocedura *sf* - **1.** [herida] sore - **2.** [sensación] smarting, stinging.

escocer [41] *vi lit & fig* to sting.
➤ **escocerse** *vprnl* [piel] to get sore.

escocés, esa <> *adj* [gen] Scottish; [whisky] Scotch; [tejido] tartan, plaid. <> *sm, f* [persona] Scot, Scotsman (*f* Scotswoman); **los escoceses** the Scottish, the Scots.
➤ **escocés** *sm* [lengua] Scots (*U*).

Escocia *n pr* Scotland.

escoger [14] *vt* to choose.

escogido, da *adj* [elegido] selected, chosen; [selecto] choice, select.

escoja *etc* ▷ **escoger**.

escolar <> *adj* school (*antes de s*). <> *sm, f* pupil, schoolboy (*f* schoolgirl).

escolaridad *sf* schooling.

escolarización *sf* schooling.

escolarizar [13] *vt* to provide with schooling.

escollera *sf* breakwater.

escollo *sm* - **1.** [en el mar] reef - **2.** *fig* stumbling block.

escolta *sf* escort.

escoltar *vt* to escort.

escombros *smpl* rubble (*U*), debris (*U*).

esconder *vt* to hide, to conceal.
➤ **esconderse** *vprnl*: **esconderse (de)** to hide (from).

escondido, da *adj* [lugar] secluded.
➤ **a escondidas** *loc adv* in secret; **hacer algo a escondidas de alguien** to do sthg behind sb's back.

escondite *sm* - **1.** [lugar] hiding place - **2.** [juego] hide-and-seek.

escondrijo *sm* hiding place.

escoñar *vt fam* to knacker, to break.
➤ **escoñarse** *vprnl fam* to get knackered.

escopeta *sf* shotgun; **escopeta de aire comprimido** air gun; **escopeta de cañones recortados** sawn-off shotgun.

escopetazo *sm* [disparo] gunshot; [herida] gunshot wound.

escorar *vi* NÁUT to list.

escorbuto *sm* scurvy.

escoria *sf fig* dregs *pl*, scum.

Escorpio, Escorpión <> *sm* [zodiaco] Scorpio; **ser Escorpio** to be (a) Scorpio. <> *smf* [persona] Scorpio.

escorpión *sm* scorpion.
➤ **Escorpión** = **Escorpio**.

escotado, da *adj* low-cut, low-necked.

escote *sm* [de prendas] neckline; [de persona] neck; **pagar a escote** to go Dutch; **escote en pico** V-neck; **escote redondo** round neck.

escotilla *sf* hatch, hatchway.

escozamos ▷ **escocer**.

escozor *sm* stinging.

escribanía *sf Andes, C Rica & R Plata* [notaría] ≃ notary public's office.

escribano, na *sm, f Andes, C Rica & R Plata* [notario] notary (public).

escribir *vt & vi* to write; **escribir a lápiz** to write in pencil; **escribir a mano** to write by hand, to write in longhand; **escribir a máquina** to type.
➤ **escribirse** *vprnl* - **1.** [personas] to write to one another - **2.** [palabras]: **se escribe con 'h'** it is spelt with an 'h'.

escrito, ta <> *pp* ▷ **escribir**. <> *adj* written; **por escrito** in writing.
➤ **escrito** *sm* [gen] text; [documento] document; [obra literaria] writing, work.

escritor, ra *sm, f* writer.

escritorio *sm* - **1.** [mueble] desk, bureau - **2.** [habitación] office.

escritura *sf* - **1.** [arte] writing - **2.** [sistema de signos] script - **3.** DER deed.
➤ **Sagrada Escritura** (*gen pl*) *sf*: **La Sagrada Escritura** Holy Scripture.

escriturar *vt* to execute by deed.

escroto *sm* scrotum.

escrúpulo *sm* - **1.** [duda, recelo] scruple; **sin escrúpulos** unscrupulous - **2.** [minuciosidad] scrupulousness, great care - **3.** [aprensión] qualm; **le da escrúpulo** he has qualms about it.

escrupuloso, sa *adj* - **1.** [gen] scrupulous - **2.** [aprensivo] particular, fussy.

escrutar *vt* [con la mirada] to scrutinize, to examine; [votos] to count.

escrutinio *sm* count (*of votes*).

escuadra *sf* - **1.** GEOM square - **2.** [de buques] squadron - **3.** [de soldados] squad.

escuadrilla *sf* squadron.

escuadrón *sm* squadron; **escuadrón de la muerte** death squad.

escuálido, da *adj culto* emaciated.

escucha *sf* listening-in, monitoring; **estar** *o* **permanecer a la escucha** to listen in; **escuchas telefónicas** telephone tapping (*U*).

escuchar <> *vt* to listen to. <> *vi* to listen.

escuchimizado, da <> *adj* skinny, thin as a rake. <> *sm, f* skinny person.

escudar *vt fig* to shield.
➤ **escudarse** *vprnl*: **escudarse en algo** *fig* to hide behind sthg, to use sthg as an excuse.

escudería *sf* team (*in motor racing*).

escudero *sm* squire.

escudo *sm* - **1.** [arma] shield - **2.** [moneda] escudo - **3.** [emblema] coat of arms.

escudriñar *vt* [examinar] to scrutinize, to examine; [otear] to search.

escuece ▷ **escocer**.

escuela *sf* school; **escuela normal** teacher training college; **escuela nocturna** night school; **escuela parroquial** parish school; **escuela privada** private school, public school UK; **escuela pública** state school; **escuela universitaria** *university which awards degrees after three years of study*; **formar** *o* **hacer escuela** to have a following; **ser de la vieja escuela** to be of the old school.

escueto, ta *adj* [sucinto] concise; [sobrio] plain, unadorned.

escueza *etc v* ▷ **escocer**.

escuincle, cla *sm, f Méx fam* [muchacho] nipper, kid.

esculpir *vt* to sculpt, to carve.

escultor, ra *sm, f* sculptor (*f* sculptress).

escultura *sf* sculpture.

escultural *adj* - **1.** ARTE sculptural - **2.** [atractivo] statuesque.

escupir ◇ *vi* to spit. ◇ *vt* [suj: persona, animal] to spit out; [suj: volcán, chimenea etc] to belch out.

escupitajo *sm* gob, spit.

escurreplatos *sm inv* dish rack.

escurridero *sm* draining board.

escurridizo, za *adj lit & fig* slippery.

escurrido, da *adj* - **1.** [ropa - en lavadora] spundry; [- estrujando] wrung-out - **2.** [verdura] drained.

escurridor *sm* colander.

escurrir ◇ *vt* [gen] to drain; [ropa] to wring out; [en lavadora] to spin-dry. ◇ *vi* [gotear] to drip.
➤ **escurrirse** *vprnl* [resbalarse] to slip.

escúter (*pl* escuters), **scooter** (*pl* scooters) *sm* (motor) scooter.

esdrújulo, la *adj* proparoxytone.

ese[1] *sf* [figura] zigzag; **hacer eses** [en carretera] to zigzag; [al andar] to stagger about.

ese[2] (*pl* esos), **esa** (*pl* esas) *adj demos* - **1.** [gen] that (*pl* those) - **2.** *(después de s) fam despec* that (*pl* those); **el hombre ese no me inspira confianza** I don't trust that guy.

ése (*pl* ésos), **ésa** (*pl* ésas) *pron demos* - **1.** [gen] that one (*pl* those ones) - **2.** [mencionado antes] the former - **3.** *fam despec:* **ése fue el que me pegó** that's the guy who hit me - **4.** *loc:* **¡a ése!** stop that man!; **ni por ésas** not even then; **no me lo vendió ni por ésas** even then he wouldn't sell me it.

esencia *sf* essence; **quinta esencia** quintessence.

esencial *adj* essential; **lo esencial** the fundamental thing.

esfera *sf* - **1.** [gen] sphere; **esfera celeste** celestial sphere; **esfera terrestre** (terrestrial) globe - **2.** [de reloj] face - **3.** [círculo social] circle; **esfera de influencia** sphere of influence - **4.** INFORM: **esfera de arrastre** *o* **de desplazamiento** trackball.

esférico, ca *adj* spherical.
➤ **esférico** *sm* DEP ball.

esfinge *sf* sphinx; **parecer una esfinge** to be inscrutable.

esfínter (*pl* esfínteres) *sm* sphincter.

esforzar [37] *vt* [voz] to strain.
➤ **esforzarse** *vprnl* to make an effort; **esforzarse en** *o* **por hacer algo** to try very hard to do sthg, to do one's best to do sthg.

esfuerzo *sm* effort; **hacer un esfuerzo** to make an effort, to try hard; **sin esfuerzo** effortlessly.

esfumarse *vprnl* [esperanzas, posibilidades] to fade away; [persona] to vanish, to disappear.

esgrima *sf* fencing.

esgrimir *vt* - **1.** [arma] to brandish, to wield - **2.** [argumento, hecho, idea] to use, to employ.

esguince *sm* sprain.

eslabón *sm* link; **el eslabón perdido** the missing link.

eslalon (*pl* eslalons), **slalom** (*pl* slaloms) *sm* slalom.

eslavo, va ◇ *adj* slav, Slavonic. ◇ *sm, f* [persona] Slav.
➤ **eslavo** *sm* [lengua] Slavonic.

eslogan (*pl* eslóganes), **slogan** (*pl* slogans) *sm* slogan.

eslora *sf* NÁUT length.

eslovaco, ca *adj & sm, f* Slovak, Slovakian.
➤ **eslovaco** *sm* [lengua] Slovak.

Eslovaquia *n pr* Slovakia.

esloveno *adj & sm, f* Slovene.

esmaltado, da *adj* enamelled.
➤ **esmaltado** *sm* enamelling.

esmaltar *vt* to enamel.

esmalte *sm* - **1.** [sustancia - en dientes, cerámica etc] enamel; [- de uñas] (nail) varnish *o* polish - **2.** [objeto, joya etc] enamelwork.

esmerado, da *adj* [persona] painstaking, careful; [trabajo] carefully done, polished.

esmeralda ◇ *sf* emerald. ◇ *adj & sm inv* emerald.

esmerarse *vprnl:* **esmerarse (en algo/hacer algo)** [esforzarse] to take great pains (over sthg/doing sthg).

esmerilado, da *adj* [pulido] polished with emery; [translúcido] ground.

esmerilar *vt* [pulir] to polish with emery.

esmero *sm* great care.

esmirriado, da *adj* puny, weak.

esmoquin (*pl* **esmóquines**), **smoking** (*pl* **smokings**) *sm* dinner jacket *UK*, tuxedo *US*.

esnifada *sf fam* sniff (*of a drug*).

esnifar *vt* fam to sniff (*drugs*).

esnob (*pl* **esnobs**), **snob** (*pl* **snobs**) ⬦ *adj inv* trying to be trendy. ⬦ *sm, f* person who wants to be trendy.

esnobismo, snobismo *sm* desire to be trendy.

eso *pron demos* (*neutro*) that; **eso es la Torre Eiffel** that's the Eiffel Tower; **eso es lo que yo pienso** that's just what I think; **eso que propones es irrealizable** what you're proposing is impossible; **eso de vivir solo no me gusta** I don't like the idea of living on my own; **¡eso, eso!** that's right!, yes!; **¡eso es!** that's it; **¿cómo es eso?, ¿y eso?** [¿por qué?] how come?; **para eso es mejor no ir** if that's all it is, you might as well not go; **por eso vine** that's why I came.

➤ **a eso de** *loc prep* (at) about *o* around.

➤ **en eso** *loc adv* just then, at that very moment.

➤ **y eso que** *loc conj* even though.

ESO (*abrev de* **enseñanza secundaria obligatoria**) *sf* mainstream secondary education for pupils aged 12-16.

ESO

Mandatory secondary education or ESO ("Enseñanza Secundaria Obligatoria") in Spain lasts four years, from the age of twelve to sixteen. It is divided into two two-year cycles. At the end of the second cycle (equivalent to junior year in high school), students can either go on to two years of further study if they want to go to college, or take vocational and technical courses.

esófago *sm* oesophagus.

esos, esas ➡ ese.

ésos, ésas ➡ ése.

esotérico, ca *adj* esoteric.

esoterismo *sm* - **1.** [impenetrabilidad] esoteric nature - **2.** [ciencias ocultas] esotericism.

espabilar *vt* - **1.** [despertar] to wake up - **2.** [avispar]: **espabilar a alguien** to sharpen sb's wits.

➤ **espabilarse** *vprnl* - **1.** [despertarse] to wake up, to brighten up - **2.** [darse prisa] to get a move on - **3.** [avisparse] to sharpen one's wits.

espachurrar *fam vt* to squash.

➤ **espachurrarse** *vprnl* to get squashed.

espaciado, da *adj* at regular intervals.

espaciador *sm* space bar.

espacial *adj* space (*antes de s*).

espaciar [8] *vt* to space out.

espacio *sm* - **1.** [gen] space; **no tengo mucho espacio** I don't have much room; **a doble espacio** double-spaced; **por espacio de** over a period of; **espacio aéreo** air space; **espacio en blanco** blank; **espacio verde** park; **espacio vital** living space - **2.** RADIO & TV programme; **espacio publicitario** advertising spot.

espacioso, sa *adj* spacious.

espada ⬦ *sf* [arma] sword; **espada de dos filos** *fig* double-edged sword; **estar entre la espada y la pared** to be between the devil and the deep blue sea. ⬦ *sm* TAUROM matador.

➤ **espadas** *sfpl* [naipes] ≃ spades.

espadachín *sm* swordsman.

espagueti, spaghetti *sm* spaghetti (*U*).

espalda *sf* - **1.** [gen] back; **caer de espaldas** to fall flat on one's back; **cargado de espaldas** round-shouldered; **de espaldas a alguien** with one's back turned on sb; **espalda con espalda** back to back; **por la espalda** from behind; *fig* behind one's back; **tumbarse de espaldas** to lie on one's back; **cubrirse las espaldas** to cover o.s.; **echarse algo sobre las espaldas** to take sthg on; **hablar de alguien a sus espaldas** to talk about sb behind their back; **hacer algo a espaldas de alguien** to do sthg behind sb's back; **tener buenas espaldas** to be mentally tough; **tirar *o* tumbar de espaldas** to be amazing *o* stunning; **volver la espalda a alguien** to turn one's back on sb - **2.** [en natación] backstroke.

espaldarazo *sm* blow to the back; **eso le dio el espaldarazo (definitivo)** that finally earned her widespread recognition.

espalderas *sfpl* wall bars.

espaldilla *sf* shoulder (of lamb *etc*).

espantada *sf* stampede; [de caballo] bolt.

espantadizo, za *adj* nervous, easily frightened.

espantajo *sm* - **1.** [espantapájaros] scarecrow - **2.** [persona fea] fright, sight.

espantapájaros *sm inv* scarecrow.

espantar *vt* - **1.** [ahuyentar] to frighten *o* scare away - **2.** [asustar] to frighten, to scare.

➤ **espantarse** *vprnl* to get frightened *o* scared.

espanto *sm* fright; **¡qué espanto!** how terrible!; **estar curado de espantos** to be unshockable.

espantoso, sa *adj* - **1.** [terrorífico] horrific - **2.** [enorme] terrible - **3.** [feísimo] frightful, horrible.

España *n pr* Spain.

español, la ⬦ *adj* Spanish. ⬦ *sm, f* [persona] Spaniard.
➤ **español** *sm* [lengua] Spanish.
españolada *sf despec* exaggerated portrayal of Spain.
españolismo *sm* - **1.** [apego, afecto] affinity for things Spanish - **2.** [carácter, naturaleza] Spanishness, Spanish character.
españolizar [13] *vt* to make Spanish, to hispanicize.
➤ **españolizarse** *vprnl* to adopt Spanish ways.
esparadrapo *sm* (sticking) plaster, Band-Aid® *US.*
esparcido, da *adj* scattered.
esparcimiento *sm* - **1.** [diseminación] scattering - **2.** [ocio] relaxation, time off.
esparcir [12] *vt* [gen] to spread; [semillas, papeles, objetos] to scatter.
➤ **esparcirse** *vprnl* to spread (out).
espárrago *sm* asparagus *(U)*; **espárrago triguero** wild asparagus; **mandar a alguien a freír espárragos** *fam* to tell sb to get lost.
esparraguera *sf* asparagus (plant).
espartano, na ⬦ *adj* - **1.** [de Esparta] Spartan - **2.** *fig* [severo] spartan. ⬦ *sm, f* Spartan.
esparto *sm* esparto (grass).
espasmo *sm* spasm.
espasmódico, ca *adj* spasmodic.
espatarrarse *vprnl fam* to sprawl (with one's legs wide open).
espátula *sf* - **1.** CULIN & MED spatula; ARTE palette knife; CONSTR bricklayer's trowel; [de empapelado] stripping knife - **2.** [animal] spoonbill.
especia *sf* spice.
especial *adj* - **1.** [gen] special; **especial para** specially for; **en especial** especially, particularly; **¿alguno en especial?** any one in particular? - **2.** [peculiar - carácter, gusto, persona] peculiar, strange.
especialidad *sf* speciality, specialty *US*; **especialidad de la casa** house speciality.
especialista ⬦ *adj*: **especialista (en)** specializing (in). ⬦ *sm, f* - **1.** [experto]: **especialista (en)** specialist (in) - **2.** CINE stuntman (*f* stuntwoman).
especialización *sf* specialization.
especializado, da *adj*: **especializado en** specialized (in).
especializar [13] *vt* to specialize.
➤ **especializarse** *vprnl*: **especializarse (en)** to specialize (in).
especie *sf* - **1.** BIOL species *sing*; **especie en vías de extinción** endangered species; **espe-**

cie protegida protected species - **2.** [clase] kind, sort; **pagar en especie** *o* **especies** to pay in kind.
especificación *sf* specification.
especificar [10] *vt* to specify.
específico, ca *adj* specific.
➤ **específicos** *smpl* [medicamentos] patent medicines.
espécimen (*pl* **especímenes**) *sm* specimen.
espectacular *adj* spectacular.
espectacularidad *sf* spectacular nature.
espectáculo *sm* - **1.** [diversión] entertainment - **2.** [función] show, performance; **espectáculo de variedades** variety show - **3.** [suceso, escena] sight - **4.** *loc*: **dar el espectáculo** to cause a scene.
espectador, ra *sm, f* TV viewer; CINE & TEATRO member of the audience; DEP spectator; [de suceso, discusión] onlooker.
➤ **espectadores** *smpl* TV viewers; CINE & TEATRO audience *sing*; DEP spectators; [de suceso, discusión] onlookers.
espectral *adj* - **1.** FÍS spectral - **2.** *fig* ghostly.
espectro *sm* - **1.** [fantasma] spectre, ghost - **2.** FÍS & MED spectrum.
especulación *sf* speculation.
especulador, ra ⬦ *adj* speculating. ⬦ *sm, f* speculator.
especular *vi*: **especular (sobre)** to speculate (about); **especular en** COM to speculate on.
especulativo, va *adj* speculative.
espejismo *sm* mirage; *fig* illusion.
espejo *sm lit & fig* mirror; **mirarse al espejo** to look at o.s. in the mirror; **espejo de cuerpo entero** full-length mirror; **espejo retrovisor** rear-view mirror.
espeleología *sf* potholing.
espeleólogo, ga *sm, f* potholer.
espeluznante *adj* hair-raising, lurid.
espera *sf* - **1.** [acción] wait; **en espera de, a la espera de** waiting for, awaiting; **seguimos a la espera de su respuesta** [en cartas] we await your reply - **2.** [paciencia] patience.
esperanto *sm* Esperanto.
esperanza *sf* [deseo, ganas] hope; [confianza, expectativas] expectation; **dar esperanzas** to encourage, to give hope to; **perder la esperanza** to lose hope; **tener esperanza de hacer algo** to hope to be able to do sthg; **esperanza de vida** life expectancy.
esperanzador, ra *adj* encouraging, hopeful.
esperanzar [13] *vt* to give hope to, to encourage.
➤ **esperanzarse** *vprnl* to be encouraged.
esperar ⬦ *vt* - **1.** [aguardar] to wait for; **esperar a que alguien haga algo** to wait for sb to

do sthg **- 2.** [tener esperanza de]: **esperar que** to hope that; **espero que sí** I hope so; **espero que no** I hope not; **esperar hacer algo** to hope to do sthg **- 3.** [tener confianza en] to expect; **esperar que** to expect (that); **esperar algo de alguien** to expect sthg from sb, to hope for sthg from sb **- 4.** [ser inminente para] to await, to be in store for; **nos esperan muchas dificultades** many difficulties await us. <> *vi* [aguardar] to wait; **espera y verás** wait and see; **como era de esperar** as was to be expected; **hacer esperar a alguien** to keep sb waiting, to make sb wait; **quien espera desespera** *prov* a watched pot never boils *prov*.

➡ **esperarse** *vprnl* **- 1.** [imaginarse, figurarse] to expect **- 2.** [aguardar] to wait; **esperarse a que alguien haga algo** to wait for sb to do sthg.

esperma <> *sm o sf* BIOL sperm. <> *sf* *Amér* [vela] candle.

espermatozoide, espermatozoo *sm* sperm, spermatozoon.

esperpéntico, ca *adj* grotesque.

esperpento *sm* [persona] grotesque sight; [cosa] absurdity, piece of nonsense.

espesar *vt* to thicken.

espeso, sa *adj* [gen] thick; [bosque, niebla] dense; [nieve] deep.

espesor *sm* **- 1.** [grosor] thickness; **tiene 2 metros de espesor** it's 2 metres thick **- 2.** [densidad - de niebla, bosque] density; [- de nieve] depth.

espesura *sf* **- 1.** [vegetación] thicket **- 2.** [grosor] thickness; [densidad] density.

espetar *vt* **- 1.** [palabras] to blurt out, to tell straight out **- 2.** [carne] to skewer.

espía *smf* spy.

espiar [9] *vt* to spy on.

espiga *sf* **- 1.** [de trigo etc] ear **- 2.** [en telas] herringbone **- 3.** [pieza - de madera] peg; [- de hierro] pin.

espigado, da *adj* **- 1.** [persona] tall and slim **- 2.** [planta] ripe.

espigarse [16] *vprnl* **- 1.** [persona] to shoot up **- 2.** [planta] to go to seed.

espigón *sm* breakwater.

espigue *etc* ▷ **espigarse**.

espiguilla *sf* herringbone.

espina *sf* [de pez] bone; [de planta] thorn; **me da mala espina** it makes me uneasy, there's something fishy about it; **tener una espina clavada** to bear a great burden; **sacarse la espina** to get even.

➡ **espina dorsal** *sf* spine.

➡ **espina bífida** *sf* spina bifida.

espinaca *(gen pl)* *sf* spinach *(U)*.

espinal *adj* spinal.

espinazo *sm* spine, backbone; **doblar el espinazo** *fig* [humillarse] to kow-tow.

espinilla *sf* **- 1.** [hueso] shin, shinbone **- 2.** [grano] blackhead.

espino *sm* **- 1.** [planta] hawthorn **- 2.** [alambre] barbed wire.

espinoso, sa *adj* *lit & fig* thorny.

espionaje *sm* espionage; **espionaje industrial** industrial espionage.

espiración *sf* exhalation, breathing out.

espiral *sf* *lit & fig* spiral; **en espiral** [escalera, forma] spiral; **espiral inflacionaria** ECON inflationary spiral.

espirar *vi* & *vt* to exhale, to breathe out.

espiritismo *sm* spiritualism.

espiritista *adj* spiritualist.

espíritu *sm* **- 1.** [gen] spirit; RELIG soul; **espíritu de equipo** team spirit **- 2.** [fantasma] ghost **- 3.** [modo de pensar] attitudes *pl*.

➡ **Espíritu Santo** *sm* Holy Ghost.

espiritual *adj* & *sm* spiritual.

espiritualidad *sf* spirituality.

espita *sf* spigot, tap, faucet *US*.

espléndido, da *adj* **- 1.** [magnífico] splendid, magnificent **- 2.** [generoso] generous, lavish.

esplendor *sm* **- 1.** [magnificencia] splendour **- 2.** [apogeo] greatness.

esplendoroso, sa *adj* magnificent.

espliego *sm* lavender.

espolear *vt* *lit & fig* to spur on.

espoleta *sf* [de proyectil] fuse.

espolón *sm* **- 1.** [de ave] spur **- 2.** ARQUIT buttress; [de puente] cutwater.

espolvorear *vt* to dust, to sprinkle.

esponja *sf* sponge; **esponja vegetal** loofah, vegetable sponge; **beber como una esponja** *fam* to drink like a fish; **tirar la esponja** to throw in the towel.

esponjar *vt* to fluff up.

esponjosidad *sf* sponginess.

esponjoso, sa *adj* spongy.

esponsales *smpl* betrothal *sing*.

espontaneidad *sf* spontaneity.

espontáneo, a <> *adj* spontaneous. <> *sm, f* spectator who tries to join in a bullfight.

esporádico, ca *adj* sporadic.

esposa ▷ **esposo**.

esposado, da *adj* handcuffed.

esposar *vt* to handcuff.

esposo, sa *sm, f* [persona] husband (*f* wife).

➡ **esposas** *sfpl* [objeto] handcuffs.

espot *(pl* espots*)* = **spot**.

espray *(pl* esprays*)* *sm* spray.

esprint *(pl* esprints*)* *sm* sprint.

esprínter (*pl* **esprínters**) *sm, f* sprinter.

espuela *sf* - **1.** [gen] spur - **2.** *fam fig* [última copa]: **tomar la espuela** to have one for the road.

espuerta *sf* [recipiente] basket.

➤ **a espuertas** *loc adv* by the sackful *o* bucket.

espuma *sf* - **1.** [gen] foam; [de cerveza] head; [de jabón] lather; [de olas] surf; [de caldo] scum; **hacer espuma** to foam; **crecer como la espuma** to mushroom; **espuma de afeitar** shaving foam; **espuma seca** carpet shampoo - **2.** [para pelo] (styling) mousse.

espumadera *sf* skimmer.

espumar *vt* to skim.

espumarajo *sm* froth, foam; **echar espumarajos** to foam at the mouth.

espumoso, sa *adj* [gen] foamy, frothy; [vino] sparkling; [jabón] lathery.

➤ **espumoso** *sm* sparkling wine.

esputo *sm* [gen] spittle; MED sputum.

esqueje *sm* cutting.

esquela *sf* obituary.

esquelético, ca *adj* ANAT skeletal; *fam* [muy delgado] skinny.

esqueleto *sm* - **1.** [de persona] skeleton; **menear** *o* **mover el esqueleto** *fam* to boogie (on down) - **2.** [armazón] framework.

esquema *sm* [gráfico] diagram; [resumen] outline; **su respuesta me rompe los esquemas** her answer has thrown all my plans up in the air.

esquemático, ca *adj* schematic.

esquí (*pl* **esquís**), **ski** (*pl* **skis**) *sm* - **1.** [tabla] ski - **2.** [deporte] skiing; **esquí de fondo** *o* **nórdico** cross-country skiing; **esquí náutico** *o* **acuático** water-skiing; **esquí alpino** downhill skiing.

esquiador, ra *sm, f* skier.

esquiar [9] *vi* to ski.

esquilador, ra *sm, f* sheepshearer.

esquilar *vt* to shear.

esquimal ◇ *adj* & *smf* Eskimo. ◇ *sm* [lengua] Eskimo.

esquina *sf* corner; **a la vuelta de la esquina** just round the corner; **doblar la esquina** to turn the corner; **hacer esquina (con)** to be on the corner (of).

esquinado, da *adj* on the corner.

esquinazo *sm* corner; **dar (el) esquinazo a alguien** to give sb the slip.

esquirla *sf* splinter.

esquirol *sm* *fam* blackleg, scab.

esquivar *vt* [gen] to avoid; [golpe] to dodge.

esquivo, va *adj* shy.

esquizofrenia *sf* schizophrenia.

esquizofrénico, ca *adj* & *sm, f* schizophrenic.

esta ▷ **este**.

ésta ▷ **éste**.

estabilidad *sf* stability; **estabilidad de precios** price stability.

estabilización *sf* stabilization.

estabilizador, ra *adj* stabilizing.

➤ **estabilizador** *sm* stabilizer.

estabilizar [13] *vt* to stabilize.

➤ **estabilizarse** *vprnl* to stabilize, to become stable.

estable *adj* - **1.** [firme] stable - **2.** [permanente - huésped] permanent; [- cliente] regular.

establecer [30] *vt* - **1.** [gen] to establish; [récord] to set - **2.** [negocio, campamento] to set up - **3.** [inmigrantes etc] to settle.

➤ **establecerse** *vprnl* - **1.** [instalarse] to settle - **2.** [poner un negocio] to set up a business.

establecimiento *sm* - **1.** [gen] establishment; [de récord] setting - **2.** [de negocio, colonia] setting up - **3.** [de emigrantes, colonos] settlement.

establo *sm* cowshed.

estaca *sf* - **1.** [para clavar, delimitar] stake; [de tienda de campaña] peg - **2.** [garrote] cudgel.

estacada *sf* [valla] picket fence; MIL stockade, palisade; **dejar a alguien en la estacada** to leave sb in the lurch.

estación *sf* - **1.** [gen & INFORM] station; **estación de autocares/de tren** coach/railway station; **estación de esquí** ski resort; **estación de gasolina** petrol station; **estación de servicio** service station; **estación de trabajo** workstation; **estación meteorológica** weather station - **2.** [del año, temporada] season.

estacionamiento *sm* AUTO parking; **estacionamiento indebido** parking offence.

estacionar *vt* AUTO to park.

estacionario, ria *adj* [gen] stationary; ECON stagnant.

estadía *sf* C Sur stay, stop.

estadio *sm* - **1.** DEP stadium - **2.** [fase] stage.

estadista *smf* statesman (*f* stateswoman).

estadístico, ca *adj* statistical.

➤ **estadística** *sf* - **1.** [ciencia] statistics (U) - **2.** [datos] statistics *pl*.

estado *sm* state; **su estado es grave** his condition is serious; **estar en buen/mal estado** [coche, terreno etc] to be in good/bad condition; [alimento, bebida] to be fresh/off; **estado de ánimo** state of mind; **estado civil** marital status; **estado de bienestar** welfare state; **estado de cuentas** statement of accounts; **estado de excepción** *o* **emergencia** state of emergency; **estado de salud** (state of) health; **estado de sitio**

state of siege; **en estado de guerra** at war; **estar en estado (de esperanza** o **buena esperanza)** to be expecting.

➤ **Estado** *sm* [gobierno] State; **Estado Mayor** MIL general staff.

➤ **Estados Unidos (de América)** *n pr* United States (of America).

estadounidense <> *adj* United States *(antes de s)*. <> *smf* United States citizen.

estafa *sf* [gen] swindle; COM fraud.

estafador, ra *sm, f* swindler.

estafar *vt* [gen] to swindle; COM to defraud.

estafeta *sf* sub-post office.

estafilococo *sm* staphylococcus.

estalactita *sf* stalactite.

estalagmita *sf* stalagmite.

estalinismo *sm* Stalinism.

estalinista *adj* & *smf* Stalinist.

estallar *vi* - **1.** [reventar - bomba] to explode; [- neumático] to burst; [- volcán] to erupt; [- cristal] to shatter - **2.** [sonar - ovación] to break out; [- látigo] to crack - **3.** [guerra, epidemia etc] to break out - **4.** [persona]: **estallar en sollozos** to burst into tears; **estallar en una carcajada** to burst out laughing.

estallido *sm* - **1.** [de bomba] explosion; [de trueno] crash; [de látigo] crack - **2.** [de guerra etc] outbreak.

Estambul *n pr* Istanbul.

estamento *sm* stratum, class.

estampa *sf* - **1.** [imagen, tarjeta] print - **2.** [aspecto] appearance - **3.** [retrato, ejemplo] image.

estampado, da *adj* printed.

➤ **estampado** *sm* - **1.** [acción] printing - **2.** [dibujo] (cotton) print.

estampar *vt* - **1.** [imprimir - gen] to print; [- metal] to stamp - **2.** [escribir]: **estampar la firma** to sign one's name - **3.** *fig* [arrojar]: **estampar algo/a alguien contra** to fling sthg/sb against, to hurl sthg/sb against - **4.** *fig* [dar - beso] to plant; [- bofetada] to land.

estampida *sf* stampede; **de estampida** suddenly, in a rush.

estampido *sm* report, bang.

estampilla *sf* - **1.** [para marcar] rubber stamp - **2.** *Amér* [sello de correos] stamp.

estampillar *vt* [gen] to stamp; [documentos] to rubber-stamp.

estampita ▷ **timo**.

estancado, da *adj* [agua] stagnant; [situación, proyecto] at a standstill.

estancamiento *sm* stagnation.

estancarse [10] *vprnl* [líquido] to stagnate, to become stagnant; [situación] to come to a standstill.

estancia *sf* - **1.** [tiempo] stay - **2.** [habitación] room - **3.** C Sur [hacienda] cattle ranch.

estanciero *sm* C Sur ranch owner.

estanco, ca *adj* watertight.

➤ **estanco** *sm* tobacconist's.

estándar (*pl* **estándares**), **standard** (*pl* **standards**) *adj inv* & *sm* standard.

estandarización *sf* standardization.

estandarizar [13] *vt* to standardize.

estandarte *sm* standard, banner.

estanque *sm* - **1.** [alberca] pond; [para riego] reservoir - **2.** *Amér* [depósito] tank *(of petrol)*.

estanquero, ra *sm, f* tobacconist.

estante *sm* shelf.

estantería *sf* [gen] shelves *pl*, shelving *(U)*; [para libros] bookcase.

estañar *vt* to tin-plate.

estaño *sm* tin.

estar [59] <> *vi* - **1.** [hallarse] to be; **¿dónde está la llave?** where is the key?; **¿está María?** is María in?; **no está** she's not in - **2.** [con fechas]: **¿a qué estamos hoy?** what's the date today?; **hoy estamos a martes/a 15 de julio** today is Tuesday/the 15th of July; **estábamos en octubre** it was October - **3.** [quedarse] to stay, to be; **estaré un par de horas y me iré** I'll stay a couple of hours and then I'll go - **4.** *(antes de 'a')* [expresa valores, grados]: **estamos a veinte grados** it's twenty degrees here; **están a dos euros el kilo** they're two euros a kilo - **5.** [hallarse listo] to be ready; **¿aún no está ese trabajo?** is that piece of work still not ready? - **6.** [servir]: **estar para** to be (there) for; **para eso están los amigos** that's what friends are for; **para eso estoy** that's what I'm there for - **7.** *(antes de gerundio)* [expresa duración] to be; **están golpeando la puerta** they're banging on the door - **8.** *(antes de sin + infinitivo)* [expresa negación]: **estoy sin dormir desde ayer** I haven't slept since yesterday; **está sin acabar** it's not finished - **9.** [faltar]: **eso está aún por escribir** that has yet to be written - **10.** [hallarse a punto de]: **estar por hacer algo** to be on the verge of doing sthg; **estuve por pegarle** I was on the verge of hitting him - **11.** [expresa disposición]: **estar para algo** to be in the mood for sthg; **no estoy para bromas** I'm not in the mood for jokes. <> *v cop* - **1.** *(antes de adj)* [expresa cualidad, estado]* to be; **los pasteles están ricos** the cakes are delicious; **esta calle está sucia** this street is dirty - **2.** *(antes de con* o *sin + s)* [expresa estado] to be; **estamos sin agua** we have no water, we're without water - **3.** [expresa situación, acción]: **estar de: estar de camarero** to work as a waiter, to be a waiter; **estar de vacaciones** to be on holiday; **estar de viaje** to be on a trip; **estar de mudanza** to be (in the process of) moving; **estamos de suerte** we're in luck - **4.** [expresa permanencia]: **estar en uso** to be in use; **estar en guardia** to be on guard - **5.** [expresa apoyo, predilección]: **estar por** to be in favour of - **6.** [expresa ocupación]: **estar como** to be; **está como cajera** she's a checkout girl - **7.** [consistir]: **estar en** to be, to lie in; **el problema está en la fecha** the problem is the date - **8.** [sentar - ropa]: **este traje te está bien** this suit looks good on you - **9.** *(antes de 'que' + v)* [expresa actitud]: **está que muerde porque ha suspendido** he's furious because he failed.

➤ **estarse** *vprnl* [permanecer] to stay; **te puedes estar con nosotros unos días** you can stay O spend a few days with us.

estarcir *vt* to stencil.

estárter (*pl* **estárters**), **starter** (*pl* **starters**) *sm* starter.

estatal *adj* state *(antes de s)*.

estático, ca *adj* - **1.** FÍS static - **2.** [inmóvil] stock-still.

estatización *sf* Amér nationalization.

estatizar *vt* Amér to nationalize.

estatua *sf* statue.

estatura *sf* height; **de estatura media** O **mediana** of average O medium height.

estatus, status *sm inv* status.

estatuto *sm* [gen] statute; [de empresa] article (of association); [de ciudad] by-law.

este[1] ◇ *adj* [posición, parte] east, eastern; [dirección, viento] easterly. ◇ *sm* east; **los países del Este** the Eastern bloc countries.

este[2] (*pl* **estos**), **esta** *adj demos* - **1.** [gen] this (*pl* these); **esta camisa** this shirt; **este año** this year - **2.** *fam despec* that (*pl* those); **no soporto a la niña esta** I can't stand that girl.

éste (*pl* **éstos**), **ésta** *pron demos* - **1.** [gen] this one (*pl* these ones); **dame otro boli; éste no funciona** give me another pen; this one doesn't work; **aquellos cuadros no están mal, aunque éstos me gustan más** those paintings aren't bad, but I like these (ones) better; **ésta ha sido la semana más feliz de mi vida** this has been the happiest week of my life - **2.** [recién mencionado] the latter; **entraron Juan y Pedro, éste con un abrigo verde** Juan and Pedro came in, the latter wearing a green coat - **3.** *fam despec*: **éste es el que me pegó** this is the guy who hit me; **éstos son los culpables de todo lo ocurrido** it's this lot who are to blame for everything.

➤ **en éstas** *loc adv fam* just then, at that very moment.

estela *sf* - **1.** [de barco] wake; [de avión, estrella fugaz] trail - **2.** *fig* [rastro] trail.

estelar *adj* - **1.** ASTRON stellar - **2.** CINE & TEATRO star *(antes de s)*.

estelaridad *sf* Amér popularity.

estenografía *sf* shorthand.

estentóreo, a *adj* [culto] stentorian.

estepa *sf* steppe.

estepario, ria *adj* steppe *(antes de s)*.

estera *sf* [tejido] matting; [alfombrilla] mat.

estercolero *sm* dunghill; *fig* [lugar sucio] pigsty.

estéreo, stereo *adj inv* & *sm* stereo.

estereofonía *sf* stereo.

estereofónico, ca *adj* stereophonic, stereo.

estereoscopio *sm* stereoscope.

estereotipado, da *adj* stereotyped, stereotypical.

estereotipar *vt* to stereotype.

estereotipo *sm* stereotype.

estéril *adj* - **1.** [persona, terreno, imaginación] sterile - **2.** [gasa] sterilized - **3.** [inútil] futile, fruitless.

esterilidad *sf* sterility.

esterilización *sf* sterilization.

esterilizar [13] *vt* to sterilize.

esterilla *sf* small mat.

esterlina ⊳ **libra**.

esternón *sm* breastbone, sternum.

esteroides *smpl* steroids.

estertor *sm* death rattle.

estética ⊳ **estético**.

esteticista, esthéticienne [esteti'θjen] *sf* beautician.

estético, ca *adj* aesthetic.

➤ **estética** *sf* - **1.** FILOS aesthetics (U) - **2.** [belleza] beauty.

estetoscopio *sm* stethoscope.

esthéticienne = esteticista.

estiba *sf* stowage.

estibador, ra *sm, f* stevedore.

estibar *vt* to stow.

estiércol *sm* [excrementos] dung; [abono] manure.

estigma *sm* - **1.** [marca] mark, scar - **2.** *fig* [deshonor] stigma.

➤ **estigmas** *smpl* RELIG stigmata.

estigmatización *sf* [marca] branding; *fig* [deshonra] stigmatization.

estigmatizar [13] *vt* - **1.** [marcar] to scar; [con hierro candente] to brand - **2.** *fig* [deshonrar] to stigmatize.

estilarse *vprnl fam* to be in (fashion).

estilete *sm* - **1.** [daga] stiletto - **2.** MED stylet.

estilismo *sm* stylism.

estilista *smf* - **1.** [escritor] stylist - **2.** [de moda, accesorios] fashion designer.

estilístico, ca *adj* stylistic.

➤ **estilística** *sf* stylistics (U).

estilizar [13] *vt* to stylize.

estilo *sm* - **1.** [gen] style; **al estilo de** in the style of; **estilo de vida** lifestyle - **2.** [en natación] stroke - **3.** GRAM speech; **estilo directo/indirecto** direct/indirect speech - **4.** *loc*: **algo por el estilo** something of the sort; **ser por el estilo a** to be similar to.

estilográfica *sf* fountain pen.

estima *sf* esteem, respect.

estimable *adj* [cantidad] considerable; [digno de estimación] worthy of appreciation.

estimación *sf* - **1.** [aprecio] esteem, respect - **2.** [valoración] valuation - **3.** [en impuestos] assessment.

estimado, da *adj* [querido] esteemed, respected; **Estimado señor** Dear Sir.

estimar *vt* - **1.** [valorar - gen] to value; [- valor] to estimate - **2.** [apreciar] to think highly of - **3.** [creer] to consider, to think.
➡ **estimarse** *vprnl* [tener dignidad] to have self-respect.

estimativo, va *adj* approximate, rough.

estimulador, ra *adj* encouraging.

estimulante ⬦ *adj* - **1.** [que anima] encouraging - **2.** [que excita] stimulating. ⬦ *sm* stimulant.

estimular *vt* - **1.** [animar] to encourage - **2.** [excitar] to stimulate.

estímulo *sm* - **1.** [aliciente] incentive; [ánimo] encouragement - **2.** [de un órgano] stimulus.

estío *sm culto* summer.

estipulación *sf* - **1.** [acuerdo] agreement - **2.** DER stipulation.

estipular *vt* to stipulate.

estirado, da *adj* - **1.** [persona - altanero] haughty; [- adusto] uptight - **2.** [brazos, piernas] outstretched.

estiramiento *sm* stretching.

estirar ⬦ *vt* - **1.** [alargar - gen] to stretch; [- cuello] to crane; **estirar las piernas** to stretch one's legs - **2.** [desarrugar] to straighten - **3.** *fig* [dinero etc] to make last; [discurso, tema] to spin out. ⬦ *vi*: **estirar (de)** to pull.
➡ **estirarse** *vprnl* - **1.** [desperezarse] to stretch - **2.** [tumbarse] to stretch out - **3.** [crecer] to shoot up.

estirón *sm* - **1.** [acción] tug, pull - **2.** [al crecer]: **dar** o **pegar un estirón** to shoot up suddenly.

estirpe *sf* stock, lineage.

estival *adj* summer *(antes de s)*.

esto *pron demos (neutro)* this thing; **esto es tu regalo de cumpleaños** this is your birthday present; **esto que acabas de decir no tiene sentido** what you just said doesn't make sense; **esto de trabajar de noche no me gusta** I don't like this business of working at night; **esto es** that is (to say).
➡ **a todo esto** *loc adv* meanwhile, in the meantime.
➡ **en esto** *loc adv* just then, at that very moment.

estocada *sf* [en esgrima] stab; TAUROM (sword) thrust.

estofa *sf*: **de baja estofa** [gente] low-class; [cosas] poor-quality.

estofado *sm* stew.

estofar *vt* CULIN to stew.

estoicismo *sm* stoicism.

estoico, ca *adj* stoic, stoical.

estola *sf* stole.

estomacal ⬦ *adj* [dolencia] stomach *(antes de s)*; [bebida] digestive. ⬦ *sm* digestive *(drink)*.

estómago *sm* stomach; **revolver el estómago a alguien** to turn sb's stomach; **tener buen estómago** to be tough, to be able to stand a lot.

Estonia *n pr* Estonia.

estonio, nia *adj* & *sm, f* Estonian.

estop = stop.

estopa *sf* [fibra] tow; [tela] burlap.

estoque *sm* rapier.

estoquear *vt* to stab.

estor *sm* Venetian blind.

estorbar ⬦ *vt* [obstaculizar] to hinder; [molestar] to bother. ⬦ *vi* [estar en medio] to be in the way.

estorbo *sm* [obstáculo] hindrance; [molestia] nuisance.

estornino *sm* starling.

estornudar *vi* to sneeze.

estornudo *sm* sneeze.

estos, tas ▷ **este**.

éstos, tas ▷ **éste**.

estoy ▷ **estar**.

estrábico, ca ⬦ *adj* squint-eyed. ⬦ *sm, f* person with a squint.

estrabismo *sm* squint.

estrado *sm* platform.

estrafalario, ria *adj* outlandish, eccentric.

estragón *sm* tarragon.

estragos *smpl*: **causar** o **hacer estragos en** [físicos] to wreak havoc with; [morales] to destroy, to ruin.

estrambótico, ca *adj* outlandish.

estrangulador, ra *sm, f* strangler.

estrangulamiento *sm* strangulation.

estrangular *vt* - **1.** [ahogar] to strangle; MED to strangulate - **2.** [proyecto] to stifle, to nip in the bud.
➡ **estrangularse** *vprnl* to strangle o.s.

estraperlista *smf* black marketeer.

estraperlo *sm* black market; **de estraperlo** black market *(antes de s)*.

estratagema *sf* MIL stratagem; *fig* [astucia] artifice, trick.

estratega *smf* strategist.

estrategia *sf* strategy.

estratégico, **ca** *adj* strategic.

estratificación *sf* stratification.

estratificar [10] *vt* to stratify.

➤ **estratificarse** *vprnl* to form strata.

estrato *sm* *fig* & GEOL stratum.

estratosfera *sf* stratosphere.

estrechamiento *sm* - **1.** [de calle, tubo] narrowing - **2.** *fig* [de relaciones] rapprochement, tightening.

estrechar *vt* - **1.** [hacer estrecho - gen] to narrow; [- ropa] to take in - **2.** *fig* [relaciones] to make closer - **3.** [apretar] to squeeze, to hug; **estrechar la mano a alguien** to shake sb's hand.

➤ **estrecharse** *vprnl* - **1.** [hacerse estrecho] to narrow - **2.** [abrazarse] to embrace - **3.** [apretarse] to squeeze up.

estrechez *sf* - **1.** [falta de anchura] narrowness; [falta de espacio] lack of space; [de ropa] tightness; **estrechez de miras** narrow-mindedness - **2.** *fig* [falta de dinero] hardship; **pasar estrecheces** to be hard up - **3.** [intimidad] closeness.

estrecho, **cha** ◇ *adj* - **1.** [no ancho - gen] narrow; [- ropa] tight; [- habitación] cramped; **estrecho de miras** narrow-minded - **2.** *fig* [íntimo] close. ◇ *sm, f fam* [persona] prude.

➤ **estrecho** *sm* GEOGR strait.

estrella ◇ *adj inv (después de s)* star *(antes de s)*. ◇ *sf* - **1.** [gen] star; *fig* [destino] fate; **estrella de cine** film star *UK*, movie star *US*; **estrella fugaz** shooting star; **estrella polar** Pole Star; **ver las estrellas** to see stars - **2.** *loc*: **tener buena/mala estrella** to be lucky/unlucky.

➤ **estrella de mar** *sf* starfish.

estrellado, **da** *adj* - **1.** [con estrellas] starry - **2.** [por la forma] star-shaped - **3.** [que ha chocado] smashed.

estrellar *vt* [arrojar] to smash.

➤ **estrellarse** *vprnl* - **1.** [chocar]: **estrellarse (contra)** [gen] to smash (against); [avión, coche] to crash (into) - **2.** *fig* [fracasar] to come to nothing.

estrellato *sm* stardom.

estrellón *sm* *Amér* crash.

estremecer [30] *vt* to shake.

➤ **estremecerse** *vprnl*: **estremecerse (de)** [horror, miedo] to tremble *o* shudder (with); [frío] to shiver (with).

estremecimiento *sm* [de miedo] shudder; [de frío] shiver.

estrenar *vt* - **1.** [gen] to use for the first time; [ropa] to wear for the first time; [piso] to move into - **2.** CINE to release, to show for the first time; TEATRO to premiere.

➤ **estrenarse** *vprnl* [persona] to make one's debut, to start.

estreno *sm* [de espectáculo] premiere, first night; [de cosa] first use; [en un empleo] debut.

estreñido, **da** *adj* constipated.

estreñimiento *sm* constipation.

estreñir *vt* to constipate.

estrépito *sm* [ruido] racket, din; *fig* [ostentación] fanfare.

estrepitoso, **sa** *adj* - **1.** [gen] noisy; [aplausos] deafening - **2.** [derrota] resounding; [fracaso] spectacular.

estrés, **stress** *sm inv* stress.

estresado, **da** *adj* suffering from stress.

estresante *adj* stressful.

estresar *vt* to cause stress to.

estría *sf* [gen] groove; [en la piel] stretch mark.

estribar ➤ **estribar en** *vi* to be based on, to lie in.

estribillo *sm* - **1.** MÚS chorus; LITER refrain - **2.** *fam* [coletilla] pet word *o* phrase.

estribo *sm* - **1.** [de montura] stirrup - **2.** [de coche, tren] step - **3.** *loc*: **estar con un pie en el estribo** to be ready to leave; **perder los estribos** to fly off the handle.

estribor *sm* starboard; **a estribor** (to) starboard.

estricnina *sf* strychnine.

estricto, **ta** *adj* strict.

estridencia *sf* - **1.** [ruido] stridency, shrillness - **2.** *fig* [de colores] loudness.

estridente *adj* - **1.** [ruido] strident, shrill - **2.** [color] garish, loud.

estrofa *sf* stanza, verse.

estrógeno, **na** *adj* oestrogenic.

➤ **estrógeno** *sm* oestrogen.

estroncio *sm* strontium.

estropajo *sm* scourer.

estropajoso, **sa** *adj* - **1.** [habla] indistinct, mumbled - **2.** [persona - andrajoso] ragged - **3.** [filete] tough, chewy.

estropear *vt* - **1.** [averiar] to break - **2.** [dañar] to damage - **3.** [echar a perder] to ruin, to spoil.

➤ **estropearse** *vprnl* - **1.** [máquina] to break down - **2.** [comida] to go off, to spoil; [piel] to get damaged - **3.** [plan] to fall through.

estropicio *sm*: **hacer** *o* **causar un estropicio** to wreak havoc.

estructura *sf* structure; **estructura profunda/superficial** deep/surface structure.

estructuración *sf* structuring, organization.

estructural *adj* structural.

estructurar *vt* to structure, to organize.

estruendo *sm* - **1.** [estrépito] din, roar; [de trueno] crash - **2.** [alboroto] uproar, tumult.

estrujar *vt* - **1.** [limón] to squeeze; [trapo, ropa] to wring (out); [papel] to screw up; [caja] to crush - **2.** [abrazar - persona, mano] to squeeze - **3.** *fig* [sacar partido de] to bleed dry.
➤ **estrujarse** *vprnl* [apretujarse] to huddle together.

estuario *sm* estuary.

estucado *sm* stucco, stuccowork.

estucar [10] *vt* to stucco.

estuche *sm* - **1.** [caja] case; [de joyas] jewellery box - **2.** [utensilios] set.

estuco *sm* stucco.

estudiado, da *adj* studied.

estudiante *smf* student.

estudiantil *adj* student *(antes de s)*.

estudiar [8] ◇ *vt* - **1.** [gen] to study - **2.** [observar] to observe. ◇ *vi* to study; **estudiar para médico** to be studying to be a doctor.

estudio *sm* - **1.** [gen] study; **estar en estudio** to be under consideration; **estudio de mercado** [técnica] market research; [investigación] market survey - **2.** [oficina] study; [de fotógrafo, pintor] studio - **3.** [apartamento] studio apartment - **4.** *(gen pl)* CINE, RADIO & TV studio.
➤ **estudios** *smpl* [serie de cursos] studies; [educación] education *(U)*; **dar estudios a alguien** to pay for sb's education; **tener estudios** to be well-educated; **estudios primarios/secundarios** primary/secondary education.

estudioso, sa ◇ *adj* studious. ◇ *sm, f* [especialista] specialist, expert.

estufa *sf* - **1.** [calefacción] heater, fire; **estufa de gas** gas heater; **estufa eléctrica** electric heater - **2.** *Col & Méx* [cocina] cooker.

estupa *sm fam* drug squad detective.

estupefacción *sf* astonishment.

estupefaciente *sm* narcotic, drug.

estupefacto, ta *adj* astonished.

estupendamente *adv* wonderfully; **estoy estupendamente** I feel wonderful.

estupendo, da *adj* great, fantastic.
➤ **estupendo** *interj*: ¡estupendo! great!

estupidez *sf* stupidity; **decir/hacer una estupidez** to say/do sthg stupid.

estúpido, da ◇ *adj* stupid. ◇ *sm, f* idiot.

estupor *sm* astonishment.

estupro *sm* rape of a minor.

estuque *etc* ➞ **estucar**.

esturión *sm* sturgeon.

estuviera *etc* ➞ **estar**.

esvástica *sf* swastika.

ETA *(abrev de Euskadi ta Askatasuna) sf* ETA.

etano *sm* ethane.

etapa *sf* stage; **por etapas** in stages; **quemar etapas** to come on in leaps and bounds, to progress rapidly.

etarra ◇ *adj* ETA *(antes de s)*. ◇ *smf* member of ETA.

etc. *(abrev de etcétera)* etc.

etcétera ◇ *adv* etcetera. ◇ *sm*: **y un largo etcétera de...** and a long list of...

éter *sm* ether.

etéreo, a *adj* - **1.** QUÍM etheric - **2.** *fig* ethereal.

eternidad *sf* eternity; **hace una eternidad que no la veo** *fam* it's ages since I last saw her.

eternizar [13] *vt*: **eternizar algo** to make sthg last forever.
➤ **eternizarse** *vprnl*: **eternizarse (haciendo algo)** to spend ages (doing sthg).

eterno, na *adj* eternal; *fam* [larguísimo] never-ending, interminable.

ético, ca *adj* ethical.
➤ **ética** *sf* - **1.** FILOS ethics *(U)* - **2.** [moralidad] ethics *pl*; **ética profesional** (professional) ethics.

etileno *sm* ethylene.

etílico, ca *adj* QUÍM ethyl *(antes de s)*; **intoxicación etílica** alcohol poisoning.

etilismo *sm* intoxication.

etilo *sm* ethyl.

etimología *sf* etymology.

etimológico, ca *adj* etymological.

etiología *sf* MED etiology.

etíope *adj* & *smf* Ethiopian.

Etiopía *n pr* Ethiopia.

etiqueta *sf* - **1.** [gen & INFORM] label; **etiqueta autoadhesiva** sticky label; **etiqueta del precio** price tag - **2.** [ceremonial] etiquette; **de etiqueta** formal; **vestir de etiqueta** to wear formal dress.

etiquetado *sm* labelling.

etiquetar *vt lit & fig* to label; **etiquetar a alguien de algo** to label sb sthg.

etnia *sf* ethnic group.

étnico, ca *adj* ethnic.

etnocentrismo *sm* ethnocentrism.

etnografía *sf* ethnography.

etnología *sf* ethnology.

etnólogo, ga *sm, f* ethnologist.

etrusco, ca *adj* & *sm, f* Etruscan.

ETS *(abrev de enfermedad de transmisión sexual) sf* STD.

EUA (*abrev de* **Estados Unidos de América**) *smpl* USA.

eucalipto *sm* eucalyptus.

eucaristía *sf*: **la Eucaristía** the Eucharist.

eucarístico, ca *adj* Eucharistic.

eufemismo *sm* euphemism.

euforia *sf* euphoria, elation.

eufórico, ca *adj* euphoric, elated.

eunuco *sm* eunuch.

eureka *interj*: ¡eureka! eureka!

euro *sm* [unidad monetaria] euro.

Eurocámara *sf* European Parliament.

eurocheque *sm* eurocheque *UK*, eurocheck *US*.

eurocomunismo *sm* Eurocommunism.

eurocomunista *adj* & *smf* Eurocommunist.

eurócrata *adj* & *smf* Eurocrat.

eurodiputado, da *sm, f* Euro-M.P., M.E.P.

eurodivisa *sf* ECON eurocurrency.

Europa *n pr* Europe.

euroescéptico, ca *sm, f* Eurosceptic.

europeidad *sf* Europeanness.

europeísmo *sm* Europeanism.

europeísta *adj* & *smf* pro-European.

europeización *sf* Europeanization.

europeizar [13] *vt* to Europeanize.

europeo, a *adj* & *sm, f* European.

eurovisión *sf* Eurovision.

Euskadi *n pr* the Basque Country.

euskara, euskera *sm* Basque.

Euskera

> Euskera (or Basque) is one of the official languages spoken in Spain. It is spoken by about one million people in the northern Spanish region of Euskadi (the Basque Country), in the neighbouring province of Navarra, and in the Basque region of France. Its origin is unknown as it is not an Indo-European language. For decades Euskera was either banned or officially unrecognized, and as a consequence it was mainly spoken only in rural areas. However, it is now being promoted as the official language for use in education and public administration and a growing number of schoolchildren can now speak the language.

eutanasia *sf* euthanasia.

evacuación *sf* evacuation.

evacuado, da <> *adj* evacuated. <> *sm, f* evacuee.

evacuador, ra *adj* evacuative.

evacuar [7] *vt* [gen] to evacuate; [vientre] to empty, to void.

evadido, da <> *adj* [persona] escaped; [divisas, impuestos] evaded. <> *sm, f* escapee, fugitive.

evadir *vt* to evade; [respuesta, peligro] to avoid.

◆ **evadirse** *vprnl*: **evadirse (de)** to escape (from).

evaluable *adj* calculable.

evaluación *sf* - **1.** [gen] evaluation - **2.** [EDUC - examen] assessment; [- periodo] *period of continuous assessment*.

evaluador, ra *adj* evaluating, evaluative.

evaluar [6] *vt* to evaluate, to assess.

evanescencia *sf culto* evanescence.

evanescente *adj culto* evanescent.

evangélico, ca *adj* & *sm, f* evangelical.

evangelio *sm* gospel.

evangelista *sm* Evangelist.

evangelización *sf* evangelization, evangelizing.

evangelizar [13] *vt* to evangelize.

evaporación *sf* evaporation.

evaporar *vt* to evaporate.

◆ **evaporarse** *vprnl* - **1.** [líquido etc] to evaporate - **2.** *fam fig* [persona] to disappear into thin air.

evaporizar [13] *vt* to vaporize.

evasión *sf* - **1.** [huida] escape - **2.** [de dinero]: **evasión de capitales** *o* **divisas** capital flight; **evasión fiscal** tax evasion - **3.** [entretenimiento] amusement, recreation; [escapismo] escapism; **de evasión** escapist.

evasivo, va *adj* evasive.

◆ **evasiva** *sf* evasive answer; **responder con evasivas** not to give a straight answer.

evasor, ra *sm, f*: **evasor de impuestos** tax evader.

evento *sm* event.

eventual *adj* - **1.** [no fijo - trabajador] temporary, casual; [- gastos] incidental - **2.** [posible] possible.

eventualidad *sf* - **1.** [temporalidad] temporariness - **2.** [hecho incierto] eventuality; [posibilidad] possibility.

evidencia *sf* - **1.** [prueba] evidence, proof; **negar la evidencia** to refuse to accept the obvious; **rendirse ante la evidencia** to bow to the evidence - **2.** [claridad] obviousness; **poner algo en evidencia** to demonstrate sthg; **poner a alguien en evidencia** to show sb up.

evidenciar [8] *vt* to show, to demonstrate.

◆ **evidenciarse** *vprnl* to be obvious *o* evident.

evidente *adj* evident, obvious.

evitar *vt* [gen] to avoid; [desastre, accidente] to avert; **evitar hacer algo** to avoid doing sthg; **evitar que alguien haga algo** to prevent sb from doing sthg.

evocación *sf* recollection, evocation.

evocador, ra *adj* evocative.

evocar [10] *vt* - **1.** [recordar] to evoke - **2.** [espíritu] to invoke, to call up.

evolución *sf* - **1.** [gen] evolution; [de enfermedad] development, progress - **2.** MIL manoeuvre.

evolucionar *vi* - **1.** [gen] to evolve; [enfermedad] to develop, to progress; [cambiar] to change - **2.** MIL to carry out manoeuvres.

evolucionismo *sm* evolutionism.

evolucionista *adj* & *smf* evolutionist.

evolutivo, va *adj* evolutionary.

evoque *etc* ▷ **evocar**.

ex ◇ *smf* [cónyuge etc] ex. ◇ *prep* ex; **el ex presidente** the ex-president, the former president.

exabrupto *sm* sharp word *o* remark.

exacerbar *vt* - **1.** [agudizar] to exacerbate, to aggravate - **2.** [irritar] to irritate, to infuriate.

exactamente *adv* exactly, precisely.

exactas *sfpl* ▷ **exacto**.

exactitud *sf* accuracy, precision.

exacto, ta *adj* - **1.** [justo - cálculo, medida] exact; **tres metros exactos** exactly three metres - **2.** [preciso] accurate, precise; [correcto] correct, right; **para ser exactos** to be precise - **3.** [idéntico]: **exacto (a)** identical (to), exactly the same (as).
➤ **exacto** *interj*: ¡**exacto!** exactly!, precisely!
➤ **exactas** *sfpl* exact *o* pure sciences.

exageración *sf* exaggeration; **este precio es una exageración** this price is over the top.

exagerado, da *adj* [gen] exaggerated; [persona] overly dramatic; [precio] exorbitant; [gesto] flamboyant.

exagerar *vt* & *vi* to exaggerate.

exaltación *sf* - **1.** [júbilo] elation, intense excitement; [acaloramiento] overexcitement - **2.** [ensalzamiento] exaltation.

exaltado, da ◇ *adj* [jubiloso] elated; [acalorado - persona] worked up; [- discusión] heated; [excitable] hotheaded. ◇ *sm, f* [fanático] fanatic; POLÍT extremist.

exaltar *vt* - **1.** [elevar] to promote, to raise - **2.** [glorificar] to exalt.
➤ **exaltarse** *vprnl* to get excited *o* worked up.

examen *sm* - **1.** [ejercicio] exam, examination; **presentarse a un examen** to sit an exam; **examen de conducir** driving test; **examen de ingreso** entrance examination; **examen final/oral** final/oral (exam); **examen parcial** ≃ end-of-term exam - **2.** [indagación] consideration, examination; **hacer examen de conciencia** to take a good look at o.s.; **someter algo a examen** to examine sthg, to subject sthg

to examination; **examen médico** medical examination *o* check-up; **libre examen** personal interpretation.

examinador, ra *sm, f* examiner.

examinar *vt* to examine.
➤ **examinarse** *vprnl* to sit *o* take an exam.

exánime *adj* - **1.** [muerto] dead - **2.** [desmayado] lifeless - **3.** *fig* [agotado] exhausted, worn-out.

exasperación *sf* exasperation.

exasperante *adj* exasperating, infuriating.

exasperar *vt* to exasperate, to infuriate.
➤ **exasperarse** *vprnl* to get exasperated.

excarcelar *vt* to release (from prison).

excavación *sf* - **1.** [acción] excavation - **2.** [lugar] dig, excavation.

excavador, ra ◇ *adj* excavating, digging. ◇ *sm, f* [persona] excavator, digger.
➤ **excavadora** *sf* [máquina] digger.

excavar *vt* [gen] to dig; [en arqueología] to excavate.

excedencia *sf* leave (of absence); EDUC sabbatical; **excedencia por maternidad** maternity leave.

excedente ◇ *adj* - **1.** [producción etc] surplus - **2.** [funcionario etc] on leave; EDUC on sabbatical. ◇ *sm* COM surplus. ◇ *smf* [persona] person on leave; **excedente de cupo** *person excused from military service because there are already enough new recruits*.

exceder ◇ *vt* to exceed, to surpass. ◇ *vi* to be greater; **exceder a** *o* **de** to exceed.
➤ **excederse** *vprnl* - **1.** [pasarse de la raya]: **excederse (en)** to go too far *o* overstep the mark (in) - **2.** [rebasar el límite]: **se excede en el peso** it's too heavy.

excelencia *sf* [cualidad] excellence; **por excelencia** par excellence.
➤ **Su Excelencia** *sm, f* His Excellency (*f* Her Excellency).

excelente *adj* excellent.

excelentísimo, ma *adj* most excellent.

excelso, sa *adj culto* sublime, elevated.

excentricidad *sf* eccentricity.

excéntrico, ca *adj* & *sm, f* eccentric.

excepción *sf* exception; **a** *o* **con excepción de** with the exception of, except for; **hacer una excepción** to make an exception; **la excepción confirma la regla** *prov* the exception proves the rule.
➤ **de excepción** *loc adj* exceptional.

excepcional *adj* exceptional.

excepto *adv* except (for).

exceptuar [6] *vt*: **exceptuar (de)** [excluir] to exclude (from); [eximir] to exempt (from); **exceptuando a...** excluding...

exceptuarse *v impers*: se exceptúa a los menores de 16 años children under the age of 16 are exempt.

excesivo, va *adj* excessive.

exceso *sm* [demasía] excess; **en exceso** excessively, to excess; **exceso de equipaje** excess baggage; **exceso de peso** [obesidad] excess weight; **exceso de velocidad** speeding.

excisión *sf* MED excision.

excitación *sf* - **1.** [nerviosismo] agitation; [por enfado, sexo] arousal - **2.** BIOL & ELECTR excitation.

excitado, da *adj* [nervioso] agitated; [por enfado, sexo] aroused.

excitante <> *adj* [emocionante] exciting; [sexualmente] arousing; [café, tabaco] stimulating. <> *sm* stímulant.

excitar *vt* - **1.** [inquietar] to upset, to agitate - **2.** [incitar]: **excitar a** to incite to - **3.** [estimular - sentidos] to stimulate; [- apetito] to whet; [- pasión, curiosidad, persona] to arouse.

excitarse *vprnl* [alterarse] to get worked up O excited.

exclamación *sf* [interjección] exclamation; [grito] cry.

exclamar *vt* & *vi* to exclaim, to shout out.

exclamativo, va *adj* exclamatory.

excluir [51] *vt* to exclude; [hipótesis, opción] to rule out; [hacer imposible] to preclude; **excluir a alguien de algo** to exclude sb from sthg.

exclusión *sf* exclusion.

exclusiva ▷ **exclusivo**.

exclusive *adv* exclusive.

exclusividad *sf* - **1.** [gen] exclusiveness - **2.** [privilegio] exclusive O sole right.

exclusivo, va *adj* exclusive.

exclusiva *sf* - **1.** PRENSA exclusive - **2.** COM exclusive O sole right.

excluyente *adj* excluding.

Excma. *abrev de* **excelentísimo**.

Excmo. *abrev de* **excelentísimo**.

excombatiente *smf* ex-serviceman (*f* ex-servicewoman) *UK*, war veteran *US*.

excomulgar [16] *vt* to excommunicate.

excomunión *sf* excommunication.

excremento (*gen pl*) *sm* excrement (*U*).

excretar <> *vt* [soltar] to secrete. <> *vi* [evacuar] to excrete.

excretorio, ria *adj* excretory.

exculpación *sf* exoneration; DER acquittal.

exculpatorio, ria *adj* exonerative.

excursión *sf* - **1.** [viaje] excursion, trip; **ir de excursión** to go on an outing O a trip - **2.** *fam* [paseo] walk, stroll.

excursionismo *sm* rambling; [de montaña] hiking.

excursionista *smf* [en la ciudad] sightseer, tripper; [en el campo] rambler; [en la montaña] hiker.

excusa *sf* - **1.** [gen] excuse; **¡nada de excusas!** no excuses!; **buscar una excusa** to look for an excuse; **dar excusas** to make excuses - **2.** [petición de perdón] apology; **presentar uno sus excusas** to apologize, to make one's excuses.

excusado, da *adj* - **1.** [disculpado] excused - **2.** [secreto] secret.

excusado *sm* bathroom, lavatory.

excusar *vt* - **1.** [disculpar a] to excuse; [disculparse por] to apologize for - **2.** [evitar] to avoid.

excusarse *vprnl* to apologize, to excuse o.s.

execrable *adj culto* abominable, execrable.

exención *sf* exemption; **exención fiscal** tax exemption.

exento, ta *adj* exempt; **exento de** [sin] free from, without; [eximido de] exempt from; **exento de impuestos** tax free.

exequias *sfpl* funeral *sing*, funeral rites.

exfoliación *sf* exfoliation.

exfoliante <> *adj* exfoliating. <> *sm* exfoliating cream/lotion *etc*.

exhalación *sf* - **1.** [emanación] exhalation, vapour; [suspiro] breath - **2.** [centella]: **como una exhalación** as quick as a flash.

exhalar *vt* - **1.** [aire] to exhale, to breathe out; [suspiros] to heave; **exhalar el último suspiro** to breathe one's last (breath) - **2.** [olor] to give off - **3.** [quejas] to utter.

exhaustivo, va *adj* exhaustive.

exhausto, ta *adj* exhausted.

exhibición *sf* - **1.** [demostración] show, display - **2.** [deportiva, artística etc] exhibition - **3.** [de películas] showing.

exhibicionismo *sm* exhibitionism.

exhibicionista *adj* & *smf* exhibitionist.

exhibir *vt* - **1.** [exponer - cuadros, fotografías] to exhibit; [- modelos] to show; [- productos] to display - **2.** [lucir - joyas, cualidades etc] to show off - **3.** [película] to show, to screen.

exhibirse *vprnl* [alardear] to show off.

exhortación *sf* exhortation.

exhortar *vt*: **exhortar a alguien a** to exhort sb to.

exhumación *sf* exhumation, disinterment.

exhumar *vt* to exhume, to disinter.

exigencia *sf* - **1.** [obligación] demand, requirement - **2.** [capricho] fussiness (*U*).

exigente ⬦ *adj* demanding. ⬦ *smf* demanding person.

exigir [15] ⬦ *vt* **- 1.** [gen] to demand; **exigir algo de** o **a alguien** to demand sthg from sb **- 2.** [requerir, necesitar] to call for, to require. ⬦ *vi* to be demanding.

exiguo, gua *adj* [escaso] meagre, paltry; [pequeño] minute.

exija *etc* ▷ **exigir**.

exiliado, da ⬦ *adj* exiled, in exile. ⬦ *sm, f* exile.

exiliar [8] *vt* to exile.
➡ **exiliarse** *vprnl* to go into exile.

exilio *sm* exile.

eximente ⬦ *adj* absolutory, absolving. ⬦ *sf* case for acquittal.

eximio, mia *adj culto* eminent, illustrious.

eximir *vt*: **eximir (de)** to exempt (from).

existencia *sf* existence.
➡ **existencias** *sfpl* COM stock *(U)*; **en existencias** in stock; **reponer las existencias** to restock.

existencial *adj* existential.

existencialismo *sm* existentialism.

existencialista *adj* & *smf* existentialist.

existente *adj* existing, existent.

existir *vi* to exist; **existe mucha pobreza** there is a lot of poverty.

éxito *sm* **- 1.** [gen] success; **con éxito** successfully; **tener éxito** to be successful **- 2.** [libro] bestseller; [canción] hit.

exitoso, sa *adj* successful.

éxodo *sm* exodus.

exonerar *vt culto*: **exonerar a alguien (de)** [culpa, responsabilidad] to exonerate sb (from); [carga, obligación] to free sb (from); [empleo, cargo] to dismiss o remove sb (from).

exorbitante *adj* exorbitant.

exorbitar *vt* to exaggerate.

exorcismo *sm* exorcism.

exorcista *smf* exorcist.

exorcizar [13] *vt* to exorcize.

exótico, ca *adj* exotic.

exotismo *sm* exoticism.

expandir *vt* to spread; FÍS to expand.
➡ **expandirse** *vprnl* to spread; FÍS to expand.

expansión *sf* **- 1.** FÍS expansion **- 2.** ECON growth; **en expansión** expanding **- 3.** *fig* [difusión] spread, spreading **- 4.** [recreo] relaxation, amusement.

expansionarse *vprnl* **- 1.** [desahogarse]: **expansionarse (con)** to open one's heart (to) **- 2.** [divertirse] to relax, to let off steam **- 3.** [desarrollarse] to expand.

expansionismo *sm* expansionism.

expansionista *adj* expansionist.

expansivo, va *adj* **- 1.** [gen] expansive **- 2.** [persona] open, frank.

expatriación *sf* expatriation; [exilio] exile.

expatriado, da ⬦ *adj* expatriate *(antes de s)*; [exiliado] exiled. ⬦ *sm, f* expatriate; [exiliado] exile.

expatriar [9] *vt* to expatriate; [exiliar] to exile.
➡ **expatriarse** *vprnl* to leave one's country, to emigrate; [exiliarse] to go into exile.

expectación *sf* expectancy, anticipation.

expectante *adj* expectant.

expectativa *sf* [espera] expectation; [esperanza] hope; [perspectiva] prospect; **estar a la expectativa** to wait and see; **estar a la expectativa de** [atento] to be on the lookout for; [a la espera] to be hoping for; **expectativa de vida** life expectancy.

expectoración *sf* **- 1.** [acción] expectoration **- 2.** [esputo] sputum *(U)*.

expectorante *adj* & *sm* expectorant.

expectorar *vi* to expectorate.

expedición *sf* **- 1.** [viaje, grupo] expedition; **expedición militar** military expedition; **expedición de salvamento** rescue mission **- 2.** [envío] shipment, sending.

expedicionario, ria *adj* expeditionary.

expedidor, ra *sm, f* sender, dispatcher.

expedientar *vt* [castigar] to take disciplinary action against; [investigar] to start proceedings against.

expediente *sm* **- 1.** [documentación] documents *pl*; [ficha] file **- 2.** [historial] record; **expediente académico** academic record *UK*, transcript *US* **- 3.** [investigación] inquiry; **abrir expediente a alguien** [castigar] to take disciplinary action against sb; [investigar] to start proceedings against sb **- 4.** ECON: **expediente de regulación de empleo** streamlining (of the workforce) **- 5.** *loc*: **cubrir el expediente** *fam* to do the bare minimum.

expedir [26] *vt* [carta, pedido] to send, to dispatch; [pasaporte, decreto] to issue; [contrato, documento] to draw up.

expeditivo, va *adj* expeditious.

expedito, ta *adj* clear, free.

expeler *vt* [humo - suj: persona] to blow out; [- suj: chimenea, tubo de escape] to emit; [- suj: extractor, volcán] to expel.

expendedor, ra ⬦ *adj* [máquina] vending *(antes de s)*; [taquilla, establecimiento] sales *(antes de s)*. ⬦ *sm, f* dealer, retailer; [de lotería] seller, vendor.

expendeduría *sf* [de tabaco] tobacconist's *UK*, cigar store *US*.

expender *vt* to sell, to retail.

expensas *sfpl* [gastos] expenses, costs.
➤ **a expensas de** *loc prep* at the expense of.
experiencia *sf* - **1.** [gen] experience; **por (propia) experiencia** from (one's own) experience - **2.** [experimento] experiment.
experimentación *sf* experimentation.
experimentado, da *adj* [persona] experienced; [método] tried and tested.
experimentador, ra ⬦ *adj* experimenting. ⬦ *sm, f* experimenter.
experimental *adj* experimental.
experimentar *vt* - **1.** [gen] to experience; [derrota, pérdidas] to suffer - **2.** [probar] to test; [hacer experimentos con] to experiment with O on.
experimento *sm* experiment.
experto, ta *adj* & *sm, f* expert; **ser experto en la materia** to be a specialist in the subject; **ser experto en hacer algo** to be an expert at doing sthg.
expiación *sf* atonement, expiation.
expiar [9] *vt* to atone for, to expiate.
expiatorio, ria *adj* expiatory.
expida, expidiera *etc* ➪ **expedir**.
expiración *sf* expiry.
expirar *vi* to expire.
explanada *sf* - **1.** [llanura] flat O level ground (U) - **2.** [paseo marítimo] esplanade.
explayar *vt* to extend.
➤ **explayarse** *vprnl* - **1.** [divertirse] to amuse o.s., to enjoy o.s. - **2.** [hablar mucho] to talk at length - **3.** [desahogarse]: **explayarse (con)** to pour out one's heart (to).
explicación *sf* explanation; **dar/pedir explicaciones** to give/demand an explanation.
explicar [10] *vt* - **1.** [gen] to explain; [teoría] to expound - **2.** [enseñar] to teach, to lecture in.
➤ **explicarse** *vprnl* - **1.** [comprender] to understand; **no me lo explico** I can't understand it - **2.** [dar explicaciones] to explain o.s. - **3.** [expresarse] to make o.s. understood.
explicativo, va *adj* explanatory.
explícito, ta *adj* explicit.
exploración *sf* - **1.** [gen & MED] exploration - **2.** [de yacimientos] prospecting.
explorador, ra *sm, f* explorer; [scout] boy scout (f girl guide).
explorar *vt* - **1.** [gen] to explore; MIL to scout - **2.** [en yacimientos] to prospect - **3.** MED to examine; [internamente] to explore, to probe.
exploratorio, ria *adj* exploratory; [conversaciones] preliminary.
explosión *sf* lit & fig explosion; **hacer explosión** to explode; **explosión atómica/termonuclear** atomic/thermonuclear explosion; **explosión demográfica** population explosion.
explosionar *vt* & *vi* to explode, to blow up.

explosivo, va *adj* - **1.** [gen] explosive - **2.** GRAM plosive.
➤ **explosivo** *sm* explosive.
explotación *sf* - **1.** [acción] exploitation; [de fábrica etc] running; [de yacimiento minero] mining; [agrícola] farming; [de petróleo] drilling - **2.** [instalaciones]: **explotación agrícola** farm; **explotación minera** mine; **explotación petrolífera** oil field.
explotador, ra ⬦ *adj* exploiting. ⬦ *sm, f* exploiter.
explotar ⬦ *vt* - **1.** [gen] to exploit - **2.** [fábrica] to run, to operate; [terreno] to farm; [mina] to work. ⬦ *vi* to explode.
expoliación *sf* pillaging, plundering.
expoliar [8] *vt* to pillage, to plunder.
expolio *sm* pillaging, plundering.
exponencial *adj* & *sf* exponential.
exponente *sm* fig & MAT exponent.
exponer [65] *vt* - **1.** [gen] to expose - **2.** [teoría] to expound; [ideas, propuesta] to set out, to explain - **3.** [cuadro, obra] to exhibit; [objetos en vitrinas] to display - **4.** [vida, prestigio] to risk.
➤ **exponerse** *vprnl* [arriesgarse]: **exponerse (a)** [gen] to run the risk (of); [a la muerte] to expose o.s. (to).
exportación *sf* - **1.** [acción] export - **2.** [mercancías] exports pl; **exportaciones invisibles** invisible exports.
exportador, ra ⬦ *adj* exporting (antes de s). ⬦ *sm, f* exporter.
exportar *vt* COM & INFORM to export.
exposición *sf* - **1.** [gen & FOTO] exposure - **2.** [de arte etc] exhibition; [de objetos en vitrina] display; **exposición universal** world fair - **3.** [de teoría] exposition; [de ideas, propuesta] setting out, explanation.
expositivo, va *adj* explanatory.
expósito, ta ⬦ *adj* foundling (antes de s). ⬦ *sm, f* foundling.
expositor, ra ⬦ *adj* exponent. ⬦ *sm, f* [de arte] exhibitor; [de teoría] exponent.
exprés ⬦ *adj* - **1.** [tren] express - **2.** [café] espresso. ⬦ *sm* = **expreso**.
expresamente *adv* [a propósito] expressly; [explícitamente] explicitly, specifically.
expresar *vt* to express; [suj: rostro] to show.
➤ **expresarse** *vprnl* to express o.s.
expresión *sf* expression; **reducir a la mínima expresión** to cut down to the bare minimum.
expresionismo *sm* expressionism.
expresionista *adj* & *smf* expressionist.
expresividad *sf* expressiveness.
expresivo, va *adj* expressive; [cariñoso] affectionate.

expreso, **sa** *adj* [explícito] specific; [deliberado] express; [claro] clear.
➤ **expreso** <> *sm* - **1.** [tren] express train - **2.** [café] expresso. <> *adv* on purpose, expressly.

exprimelimones *sm inv* lemon squeezer.

exprimidor *sm* squeezer.

exprimir *vt* - **1.** [fruta] to squeeze; [zumo] to squeeze out - **2.** *fig* to exploit.

expropiación *sf* expropriation.

expropiar [8] *vt* to expropriate.

expuesto, **ta** <> *pp* ⊳ **exponer**. <> *adj* - **1.** [dicho] stated, expressed - **2.** [desprotegido]: **expuesto (a)** exposed (to) - **3.** [arriesgado] dangerous, risky - **4.** [exhibido] on display.

expulsar *vt* - **1.** [persona - de clase, local, asociación] to throw out; [- de colegio] to expel - **2.** DEP to send off - **3.** [humo] to emit, to give off.

expulsión *sf* [gen] expulsion; [de clase, local, asociación] throwing-out; DEP sending-off.

expulsor, **ra** *adj* ejector *(antes de s)*.
➤ **expulsor** *sm* ejector.

expurgación *sf* expurgation.

expurgar [16] *vt* to expurgate.

expusiera *etc* ⊳ **exponer**.

exquisitez *sf* - **1.** [cualidad] exquisiteness - **2.** [cosa] exquisite thing; [comida] delicacy.

exquisito, **ta** *adj* exquisite; [comida] delicious, sublime.

extasiarse [9] *vprnl*: **extasiarse (ante** O **con)** to go into ecstasies (over).

éxtasis *sm inv* ecstasy.

extender [20] *vt* - **1.** [desplegar - tela, plano, alas] to spread (out); [- brazos, piernas] to stretch out - **2.** [esparcir - mantequilla] to spread; [- pintura] to smear; [- objetos etc] to spread out - **3.** [ampliar - castigo, influencia etc] to extend, to widen - **4.** [documento] to draw up; [cheque] to make out; [pasaporte, certificado] to issue.
➤ **extenderse** *vprnl* - **1.** [ocupar]: **extenderse (por)** to stretch O extend across - **2.** [hablar mucho]: **extenderse (en)** to enlarge O expand (on) - **3.** [durar] to extend, to last - **4.** [difundirse]: **extenderse (por)** to spread (across) - **5.** [tenderse] to stretch out.

extensión *sf* - **1.** [superficie - de terreno etc] area, expanse - **2.** [amplitud - de país etc] size; [- de conocimientos] extent - **3.** [duración] duration, length - **4.** [sentido - de concepto, palabra] range of meaning; **en toda la extensión de la palabra** in every sense of the word; **por extensión** by extension - **5.** INFORM & TELECOM extensión.

extensivo, **va** *adj* extensive; **hacer algo extensivo a** to extend sthg to.

extenso, **sa** *adj* extensive; [país] vast; [libro, película] long.

extensor *sm* - **1.** [aparato] chest expander - **2.** [músculo] extensor.

extenuación *sf* severe exhaustion *(U)*.

extenuado, **da** *adj* completely exhausted, drained.

extenuante *adj* completely exhausting, draining.

extenuar [6] *vt* to exhaust completely, to drain.
➤ **extenuarse** *vprnl* to exhaust o.s., to tire o.s. out.

exterior <> *adj* - **1.** [de fuera] outside; [capa] outer, exterior - **2.** [visible] outward - **3.** [extranjero] foreign. <> *sm* - **1.** [superficie] outside; **en el exterior** outside - **2.** [extranjero] foreign countries *pl*; **en el exterior** abroad - **3.** [aspecto] appearance.
➤ **exteriores** *smpl* CINE outside shots; **rodar en exteriores** to film on location.

exteriorización *sf* outward demonstration, manifestation.

exteriorizar [13] *vt* to show, to reveal.

exterminación *sf* extermination.

exterminador, **ra** *adj* exterminating.

exterminar *vt* - **1.** [aniquilar] to exterminate - **2.** [devastar] to destroy, to devastate.

exterminio *sm* extermination.

externalización *sf* outsourcing.

externalizar *vt* to outsource.

externo, **na** *adj* - **1.** [gen] external; [parte, capa] outer; [influencia] outside; [signo, aspecto] outward - **2.** [alumno] day *(antes de s)*.

extienda *etc* ⊳ **extender**.

extinción *sf* - **1.** [gen] extinction; [de esperanzas] loss - **2.** [de plazos, obligaciones] termination, end.

extinguir [17] *vt* [incendio] to put out, to extinguish; [raza] to wipe out; [afecto, entusiasmo] to put an end to.
➤ **extinguirse** *vprnl* [fuego, luz] to go out; [animal, raza] to become extinct, to die out; [ruido] to die out; [afecto] to die.

extinto, **ta** *adj* extinguished; [animal, volcán] extinct.

extintor *sm* fire extinguisher.

extirpación *sf* MED removal; *fig* eradication, stamping out.

extirpar *vt* [tumor] to remove; [muela] to extract; *fig* to eradicate, to stamp out.

extorsión *sf* - **1.** [molestia] trouble, bother - **2.** DER extortion.

extorsionar *vt* - **1.** [perjudicar - persona] to inconvenience; [- plan] to mess up - **2.** DER to extort.

extorsionista *smf* extortionist.

extra ◇ *adj* - **1.** [adicional] extra - **2.** [de gran calidad] top quality, superior. ◇ *smf* CINE extra. ◇ *sm* [gasto etc] extra. ◇ *sf* ▷ **paga**.

extracción *sf* - **1.** [gen] extraction - **2.** [en sorteos] draw - **3.** [de carbón] mining.

extractar *vt* to summarize, to shorten.

extracto *sm* - **1.** [resumen] summary, résumé; **extracto de cuentas** statement (of account) - **2.** [concentrado] extract.

extractor, ra *adj* extractor *(antes de s)*.
➡ **extractor** *sm* extractor fan.

extracurricular *adj* extracurricular.

extradición *sf* extradition.

extraditar *vt* to extradite.

extraer [73] *vt*: **extraer (de)** [gen] to extract (from); [sangre] to draw (from); [carbón] to mine (from); [conclusiones] to come to o draw (from).

extrafino, na *adj* top quality, de luxe.

extrajudicial *adj* extrajudicial.

extralegal *adj* extralegal.

extralimitación *sf* abuse *(of power, authority)*.

extralimitarse *vprnl* fig to go too far.

extramuros *adv* outside the city o town.

extranjería *sf* foreign status.

extranjerismo *sm* foreign word.

extranjerizar [13] *vt* to introduce foreign customs to.

extranjero, ra ◇ *adj* foreign. ◇ *sm, f* [persona] foreigner.
➡ **extranjero** *sm* [territorio] foreign countries *pl*; **estar en el/ir al extranjero** to be/go abroad.

extranjis ➡ **de extranjis** *loc adv* fam on the quiet.

extrañamiento *sm* banishment.

extrañar *vt* - **1.** [sorprender] to surprise; **me extraña (que digas esto)** I'm surprised (that you should say that) - **2.** [echar de menos] to miss - **3.** [desterrar] to banish.
➡ **extrañarse de** *vprnl* [sorprenderse de] to be surprised at.

extrañeza *sf* - **1.** [sorpresa] surprise - **2.** [rareza] strangeness *(U)*.

extraño, ña ◇ *adj* - **1.** [raro] strange; **¡qué extraño!** how odd o strange! - **2.** [ajeno] detached, uninvolved - **3.** MED foreign. ◇ *sm, f* stranger.

extraoficial *adj* unofficial.

extraordinario, ria *adj* - **1.** [gen] extraordinary; **no tiene nada de extraordinario** there's nothing extraordinary about that - **2.** [gastos] additional; [edición, suplemento] special - **3.** ▷ **paga**.

➡ **extraordinario** *sm* - **1.** CULIN special dish - **2.** PRENSA special edition - **3.** [correo] special delivery.

extraparlamentario, ria *adj* non-parliamentary.

extraplano, na *adj* super-slim, extra-thin.

extrapolación *sf* generalization.

extrapolar *vt* to generalize about, to jump to conclusions about.

extrarradio *sm* outskirts *pl*, suburbs *pl*.

extraterrestre *adj* & *smf* extraterrestrial.

extraterritorial *adj* extraterritorial.

extraterritorialidad *sf* extraterritorial rights *pl*.

extravagancia *sf* eccentricity.

extravagante *adj* eccentric, outlandish.

extraversión, extroversión *sf* extroversion.

extravertido, da, extrovertido, da *adj* & *sm, f* extrovert.

extraviado, da *adj* [perdido] lost; [animal] stray.

extraviar [9] *vt* - **1.** [objeto] to lose, to mislay - **2.** [excursionista] to mislead, to cause to lose one's way - **3.** [mirada, vista] to allow to wander.
➡ **extraviarse** *vprnl* - **1.** [persona] to get lost - **2.** [objeto] to be mislaid, to go missing.

extravío *sm* - **1.** [pérdida] loss, mislaying - **2.** [desenfreno] excess.

extremado, da *adj* extreme.

Extremadura *n pr* Estremadura.

extremar *vt* to maximize.
➡ **extremarse** *vprnl* to take great pains o care.

extremaunción *sf* extreme unction.

extremeño, ña *adj* & *sm, f* Estremaduran.

extremidad *sf* [extremo] end.
➡ **extremidades** *sfpl* ANAT extremities.

extremismo *sm* extremism.

extremista *adj* & *smf* extremist.

extremo, ma *adj* [gen] extreme; [en el espacio] far, furthest.
➡ **extremo** *sm* - **1.** [punta] end - **2.** [límite] extreme; **en último extremo** as a last resort; **ir** o **pasar de un extremo al otro** to go from one extreme to the other; **ser el extremo opuesto** to be the complete opposite - **3.** DEP: **extremo derecho/izquierdo** outside right/left.
➡ **extremos** *smpl* [efusiones] exaggerations.

extrínseco, ca *adj* extrinsic.

extroversión = **extraversión**.

extrovertido, da = **extravertido**.

exuberancia *sf* exuberance.

exuberante *adj* exuberant.

exudación *sf* exudation.

exudado, **da** *adj* exuding, oozing.

exudar *vt* to exude, to ooze.

exultación *sf* exultation.

exultante *adj* exultant.

exultar ⟶ **exultar de** *vi* to exult with, to rejoice with.

exvoto *sm* votive offering, ex voto.

eyaculación *sf* ejaculation; **eyaculación precoz** premature ejaculation.

eyacular *vi* to ejaculate.

eyección *sf* ejection, expulsion.

eyectar *vt* to eject, to expel.

eyector *sm* [de armas] ejector; [de aire, gases] extractor.

f, F *sf* [letra] f, F.
⟶ **23 F** *sm* 23rd February, day of the failed coup d'état in Spain in 1981.

f. - **1.** (*abrev de* **factura**) inv. - **2.** (*abrev de* **folio**) f.

fa *sm* MÚS F; [en solfeo] fa.

fabada *sf* Asturian stew made of beans, pork sausage and bacon.

fábrica *sf* - **1.** [establecimiento] factory; **fábrica de cerveza** brewery; **fábrica de conservas** canning plant, cannery; **fábrica de papel** paper mill; **fábrica siderúrgica** iron and steelworks *sing* - **2.** [fabricación] manufacture.

fabricación *sf* manufacture; **de fabricación casera** home-made; **fabricación en serie** mass production.

fabricante ⟨⟩ *adj* manufacturing (*antes de s*). ⟨⟩ *smf* manufacturer.

fabricar [10] *vt* - **1.** [producir] to manufacture, to make - **2.** [construir] to build, to construct - **3.** *fig* [inventar] to fabricate, to make up.

fabril *adj* manufacturing (*antes de s*).

fábula *sf* - **1.** LITER fable; [leyenda] legend, myth - **2.** [rumor] piece of gossip.

fabular *vi* to make things up.

fabulista *smf* author of fables.

fabuloso, **sa** *adj* - **1.** [ficticio] mythical, fantastic - **2.** [muy bueno] fabulous, fantastic.

facción *sf* POLÍT faction.
⟶ **facciones** *sfpl* [rasgos] features.

faccioso, **sa** ⟨⟩ *adj* factious, rebellious. ⟨⟩ *sm*, *f* rebel.

faceta *sf* facet.

facha ⟨⟩ *sf* - **1.** [aspecto] appearance, look - **2.** [mamarracho] mess; **vas hecho una facha** you look a mess. ⟨⟩ *smf fam despec* [ultra derechista] fascist pig.

fachada *sf* - **1.** ARQUIT façade - **2.** *fig* [apariencia] outward appearance; **es pura fachada** it's just a show.

facial *adj* facial.

fácil *adj* - **1.** [gen] easy; **fácil de hacer** easy to do - **2.** [tratable] easy-going - **3.** [probable] probable, likely.

facilidad *sf* - **1.** [simplicidad] ease, easiness; **con facilidad** easily; **con la mayor facilidad** with the greatest of ease - **2.** [aptitud] aptitude; **tener facilidad para algo** to have a gift for sthg.
⟶ **facilidades** *sfpl* [comodidades] facilities; **dar facilidades a alguien para algo** to make sthg easy for sb; **facilidades de pago** easy (payment) terms.

facilitar *vt* - **1.** [simplificar] to facilitate, to make easy; [posibilitar] to make possible - **2.** [proporcionar] to provide; **facilitar algo a alguien** to provide *o* supply sb with sthg.

facilón, **ona** *adj fam* dead easy.

facineroso, **sa** *sm*, *f* miscreant, criminal.

facsímil, facsímile *sm* facsimile.

factible *adj* feasible.

fáctico ⟳ **poder**.

factor *sm* - **1.** [gen] factor; **factor humano** human factor; **factor de riesgo** risk factor - **2.** FERROC luggage clerk.

factoría *sf* - **1.** [fábrica] factory - **2.** COM outlet, agency.

factura *sf* - **1.** [por mercancías, trabajo realizado] invoice; **pasar** *o* **presentar una factura** to send an invoice; **factura pro forma** *o* **proforma** COM proforma invoice - **2.** [de gas, teléfono] bill; [en tienda, hotel] bill - **3.** *Arg* [repostería] cakes and pastries.

facturación *sf* - **1.** [cobro] invoicing - **2.** [ventas] turnover *UK*, net revenue *US* - **3.** [de equipaje - en aeropuerto] checking-in; [- en estación] registration; **mostrador de facturación** check-in desk.

facturar *vt* - **1.** [cobrar]: **facturarle a alguien algo** to invoice *o* bill sb for sthg - **2.** [vender] to turn over - **3.** [equipaje - en aeropuerto] to check in; [- en estación] to register.

facultad *sf* - **1.** [capacidad & UNIV] faculty; **facultades mentales** mental faculties - **2.** [poder] power, right.

facultar *vt* to authorize.

facultativo, va <> *adj* - **1.** [voluntario] optional - **2.** [médico] medical. <> *sm, f* doctor.

faena *sf* - **1.** [tarea] task, work *(U)*; **estar en plena faena** to be hard at work; **faenas domésticas** housework *(U)*, household chores; **hacerle una (mala) faena a alguien** to play a dirty trick on sb - **2.** TAUROM bullfighter's performance.

faenar *vi* to fish.

fagot <> *sm* [instrumento] bassoon. <> *smf* [músico] bassoonist.

faisán *sm* pheasant.

faja *sf* - **1.** [prenda de mujer, terapéutica] corset; [banda] sash, cummerbund - **2.** [de terreno - pequeña] strip; [- grande] belt - **3.** [de libro] band *(around new book)*.

fajín *sm* sash.

fajo *sm* [de billetes, papel] wad; [de leña, cañas] bundle.

fakir = **faquir.**

falacia *sf* deceit, trick.

falange *sf* - **1.** ANAT & MIL phalanx - **2.** POLÍT: **la Falange (Española)** the Falange.

falangismo *sm* Falangist movement.

falangista *adj* & *smf* Falangist.

falda *sf* - **1.** [prenda] skirt; **estar pegado** O **cosido a las faldas de su madre** to to be tied to one's mother's apron strings; **falda escocesa** kilt; **falda pantalón** culottes *pl*; **falda plisada** O **tableada** pleated skirt - **2.** [de montaña] slope, mountainside - **3.** [regazo] lap - **4.** [de mesa camilla] cover.

➤ **faldas** *sfpl fam* [mujeres] women; **aficionado a las faldas** womanizer, ladies' man.

faldero, ra *adj* - **1.** [dócil]: **perro faldero** lapdog - **2.** [mujeriego] keen on women.

faldón *sm* - **1.** [de ropa] tail; [de cortina, mesa camilla] folds *pl* - **2.** [de tejado] gable.

falible *adj* fallible.

fálico, ca *adj* phallic.

falla *sf* [gen & GEOL] fault.

➤ **fallas** *sfpl* [fiesta] *celebrations in Valencia during which cardboard figures are burnt.*

fallar <> *vt* - **1.** [sentenciar] to pass sentence on; [premio] to award - **2.** [equivocar - respuesta] to get wrong; [- tiro] to miss. <> *vi* - **1.** [equivocarse] to get it wrong; [no acertar] to miss - **2.** [fracasar, flaquear] to fail; [plan] to go wrong - **3.** [decepcionar]: **fallarle a alguien** to let sb down - **4.** [quebrarse, ceder] to give way - **5.** [sentenciar]: **fallar a favor/en contra de** to find in favour of/against.

fallecer [30] *vi* to pass away, to die.

fallecimiento *sm* decease, death.

fallero, ra *adj relating to the celebrations in Valencia during which cardboard figures are burnt.*

fallido, da *adj* [esfuerzo, intento] unsuccessful, failed; [esperanza] vain; [disparo] missed.

fallo *sm* - **1.** [error] mistake; DEP miss; **¡qué fallo!** what a stupid mistake!; **fallo humano** human error - **2.** [sentencia - de juez, jurado] verdict - **3.** [opinión] judgment.

falluto, ta <> *adj* R Dom fam phoney, hypocritical. <> *sm, f* hypocrite.

falo *sm* phallus.

falsario, ria <> *adj* false. <> *sm, f* liar.

falsear *vt* [hechos, historia] to falsify, to distort; [moneda, firma] to forge.

falsedad *sf* - **1.** [falta de verdad, autenticidad] falseness - **2.** [mentira] falsehood, lie.

falsete *sm* falsetto.

falsificación *sf* forgery.

falsificador, ra *sm, f* forger.

falsificar [10] *vt* to forge.

falsilla *sf* guide sheet *(for writing paper).*

falso, sa *adj* - **1.** [rumor, excusa etc] false, untrue - **2.** [dinero, firma, cuadro] forged; [joyas] fake; **jurar en falso** to commit perjury - **3.** [hipócrita] deceitful - **4.** [inadecuado] wrong, incorrect.

falta *sf* - **1.** [carencia] lack; **hacer falta** to be necessary; **me hace falta suerte** I need some luck; **por falta de** for want O lack of - **2.** [escasez] shortage - **3.** [ausencia] absence; **echar en falta algo/a alguien** [notar la ausencia de] to notice that sthg/sb is missing; [echar de menos] to miss sthg/sb - **4.** [imperfección] fault; [error] mistake; **falta de educación** bad manners *pl*; **falta de ortografía** spelling mistake; **falta de respeto** disrespect, lack of respect - **5.** DEP foul; [en tenis] fault; **doble falta** double fault; **falta libre directa** direct free kick offence; **falta personal** personal foul - **6.** DER offence - **7.** [en la menstruación] missed period.

➤ **a falta de** *loc prep* in the absence of; **a falta de pan, buenas son tortas** *prov* half a loaf is better than none.

➤ **sin falta** *loc adv* without fail.

faltante *sm Amér* deficit.

faltar *vi* - **1.** [no haber] to be lacking, to be needed; **falta aire** there's not enough air; **falta sal** it needs a bit of salt - **2.** [estar ausente] to be absent O missing; **falta Elena** Elena is missing - **3.** [carecer]: **le faltan las fuerzas** he lacks O doesn't have the strength - **4.** [hacer falta] to be necessary; **me falta tiempo** I need time - **5.** [quedar]: **falta un mes para las vacaciones** there's a month to go till the holidays;

sólo te falta firmar all you have to do is sign; ¿cuánto falta para Leeds? how much further is it to Leeds?; **falta mucho por hacer** there is still a lot to be done; **falta poco para que llegue** it won't be long till he arrives; **faltó poco para que le matase** I very nearly killed him **- 6.** *loc:* ¡**no faltaba** o **faltaría más!** [asentimiento] of course!; [rechazo] that tops it all!, that's a bit much!

faltar a *vi* **- 1.** [palabra, promesa] to break, not to keep; [deber, obligación] to neglect **- 2.** [cita, trabajo] not to turn up at; ¡**no faltes (a la cita)!** don't miss it!, be there! **- 3.** [no respetar] to be disrespectful towards; **faltar a alguien en algo** to offend sb in sthg **- 4.** [defraudar] to betray, to disappoint.

falto, **ta** *adj:* **falto de** lacking in, short of.

fama *sf* **- 1.** [renombre] fame; **tener fama** to be famous **- 2.** [reputación] reputation; **tener buena/mala fama** to have a good/bad reputation; **cría fama y échate a dormir** *prov* build yourself a good reputation, then you can rest on your laurels.

famélico, **ca** *adj* starving, famished.

familia *sf* family; **en familia** privately, in private; **ser de buena familia** to come from a good family; **ser como de la familia** to be like one of the family; **familia de acogida** host family; **familia monoparental** one-parent family; **familia numerosa** large family; **familia política** in-laws *pl;* **familia real** royal family.

familiar ◇ *adj* **- 1.** [de familia] family *(antes de s)* **- 2.** [en el trato - agradable] friendly; [- en demasía] overly familiar **- 3.** [lenguaje, estilo] informal, colloquial **- 4.** [conocido] familiar. ◇ *smf* relative, relation.

familiaridad *sf* familiarity.

familiarizar [13] *vt:* **familiarizar (con)** to familiarize (with).

familiarizarse *vprnl:* **familiarizarse con** [estudiar] to familiarize o.s. with; [acostumbrarse a] to get used to.

famoso, **sa** ◇ *adj* famous. ◇ *sm, f* famous person, celebrity.

fan *smf* fan.

fanático, **ca** ◇ *adj* fanatical. ◇ *sm, f* [gen] fanatic; DEP fan.

fanatismo *sm* fanaticism.

fanatizar [13] *vt* to arouse fanaticism in.

fandango *sm* [baile] fandango.

fandanguillo *sm type of fandango.*

fané *adj Amér* worn out.

fanega *sf grain measure which varies from region to region.*

fanfarria *sf* **- 1.** *fam* [jactancia] boasting, bragging **- 2.** [pieza musical] fanfare; [banda] brass band.

fanfarrón, **ona** ◇ *adj* boastful. ◇ *sm, f* braggart, show-off.

fanfarronada *sf* brag.

fanfarronear *vi:* **fanfarronear (de)** to boast o brag (about).

fanfarronería *sf* showing-off, bragging.

fango *sm* mud.

fangoso, **sa** *adj* muddy.

fantasear ◇ *vi* to fantasize. ◇ *vt* to imagine, to fantasize about.

fantasía *sf* **- 1.** [imaginación] imagination; [cosa imaginada] fantasy; **de fantasía** [ropa] fancy; [bisutería] imitation, costume *(antes de s)* **- 2.** MÚS fantasia.

fantasioso, **sa** *adj* imaginative.

fantasma ◇ *sm* [espectro] ghost, phantom. ◇ *smf fam* [fanfarrón] show-off.

fantasmada *sf fam* brag.

fantasmal *adj* ghostly.

fantasmón, **ona** *sm, f fam* show-off.

fantástico, **ca** *adj* fantastic.

fantochada *sf* crazy o mad thing.

fantoche *sm* **- 1.** [títere] puppet **- 2.** [mamarracho] (ridiculous) sight.

FAO *sf (abrev de* **fabricación asistida por ordenador)** CAM.

faquir, **fakir** *sm* fakir.

faradio *sm* farad.

farándula *sf:* **la farándula** the theatre, the stage.

faraón *sm* pharaoh.

faraónico, **ca** *adj* pharaonic; *fig* [fastuoso] lavish, magnificent.

fardada *sf fam* showing-off *(U).*

fardar *vi fam:* **fardar (de algo)** to show (sthg) off.

fardo *sm* bundle.

fardón, **ona** *fam* ◇ *adj* flashy. ◇ *sm, f* flash Harry.

farero, **ra** *sm, f* lighthouse keeper.

farfullar *vt* & *vi* to gabble, to splutter.

faringe *sf* pharynx.

faringitis *sf inv* sore throat.

fariseo, **a** *sm, f* **- 1.** HIST Pharisee **- 2.** *fig* [hipócrita] hypocrite.

farmacéutico, **ca** ◇ *adj* pharmaceutical. ◇ *sm, f* chemist, pharmacist.

farmacia *sf* **- 1.** [ciencia] pharmacy **- 2.** [establecimiento] chemist's (shop) *UK*, pharmacy, drugstore *US*; **farmacia de turno** o **de guardia** duty chemist's.

fármaco *sm* medicine, drug.

farmacología *sf* pharmacology.

faro *sm* - **1.** [para barcos] lighthouse - **2.** [de coche] headlight, headlamp; **faro antiniebla** foglamp.

farol *sm* - **1.** [farola] street lamp o light; [linterna] lantern, lamp - **2.** [en el juego] bluff - **3.** *fam* [mentira] fib, lie.

farola *sf* [farol] street lamp o light; [poste] lamppost.

farolear *vi fam* to fib.

farolero, ra <> *adj fam* boastful. <> *sm, f* - **1.** [oficio] lamplighter - **2.** *fam* [fanfarrón] show-off.

farolillo *sm* - **1.** [de papel] paper o Chinese lantern - **2.** [planta] Canterbury bell.

farra *sf fam* binge, spree; **ir de farra** to paint the town red.

farragoso, sa *adj* confused, rambling.

farruco, ca *adj* [valiente] cocky.

farsa *sf lit & fig* farce.

farsante <> *adj* deceitful. <> *smf* deceitful person.

fascículo *sm* part, instalment *(of serialization).*

fascinación *sf* fascination.

fascinante *adj* fascinating.

fascinar *vt* to fascinate.

fascismo *sm* fascism.

fascista *adj & smf* fascist.

fase *sf* phase; **en fase terminal** in terminal phase.

fastidiado, da *adj* [de salud] ill; **ando fastidiado del estómago** I've got a bad stomach.

fastidiar [8] <> *vt* - **1.** [estropear - fiesta etc] to spoil, to ruin; [- máquina, objeto etc] to break - **2.** [molestar] to annoy, to bother. <> *vi:* **¡no fastidies!** you're having me on!
* **fastidiarse** *vprnl* - **1.** [estropearse - fiesta etc] to be ruined; [- máquina] to break down - **2.** [aguantarse] to put up with it.

fastidio *sm* - **1.** [molestia] nuisance, bother; **¡qué fastidio!** what a nuisance! - **2.** [enfado] annoyance - **3.** [aburrimiento] bore.

fastidioso, sa *adj* - **1.** [molesto] annoying - **2.** [aburrido] boring, tedious.

fasto *sm* pomp, extravagance.

fastuosidad *sf* lavishness, sumptuousness.

fastuoso, sa *adj* lavish, sumptuous.

fatal <> *adj* - **1.** [mortal] fatal - **2.** [muy malo] terrible, awful - **3.** [inevitable] inevitable - **4.** [seductor]: **mujer fatal** femme fatale. <> *adv* terribly; **pasarlo fatal** to have an awful time; **sentirse fatal** to feel terrible.

fatalidad *sf* - **1.** [destino] fate, destiny - **2.** [desgracia] misfortune.

fatalismo *sm* fatalism.

fatalista <> *adj* fatalistic. <> *smf* fatalist.

fatídico, ca *adj* fateful, ominous.

fatiga *sf* [cansancio] tiredness, fatigue.
* **fatigas** *sfpl* [penas] troubles, hardships.

fatigado, da *adj* tired, weary.

fatigante *adj* tiring.

fatigar [16] *vt* to tire, to weary.
* **fatigarse** *vprnl* to get tired.

fatigoso, sa *adj* tiring, fatiguing.

fatigue *etc* ⊳ **fatigar**.

fatuidad *sf* - **1.** [necedad] fatuousness, foolishness - **2.** [vanidad] conceit.

fatuo, tua *adj* - **1.** [necio] fatuous, foolish - **2.** [engreído] conceited.

fauces *sfpl fig* jaws.

fauna *sf* fauna.

fausto, ta *adj* happy, fortunate.

favor *sm* favour; **a favor de** in favour of; **hacerle un favor a alguien** [ayudar a] to do sb a favour; *fam fig* [acostarse con] to go to bed with sb; **hágame el favor de cerrar la puerta** would you mind shutting the door, please?; **pedir un favor a alguien** to ask sb a favour; **tener a** o **en su favor a alguien** to enjoy sb's support.
* **favores** *smpl* [de una mujer] favours.
* **por favor** *loc adv* please.

favorable *adj* favourable; **ser favorable a algo** to be in favour of sthg.

favorecedor, ra *adj* flattering, becoming.

favorecer [30] *vt* - **1.** [gen] to favour; [ayudar] to help, to assist - **2.** [sentar bien] to suit.

favoritismo *sm* favouritism.

favorito, ta *adj & sm, f* favourite.

fax *sm inv* - **1.** [aparato] fax (machine); **mandar algo por fax** to fax sthg - **2.** [documento] fax.

fayuquero, ra *sm, f Méx fam* smuggler.

faz *sf culto* - **1.** [cara] countenance, face - **2.** [del mundo, de la tierra] face.

fe *sf* - **1.** [gen] faith; **hacer algo de buena fe** to do sthg in good faith; **tener fe en** to have faith in, to believe in - **2.** [documento] certificate; **fe de bautismo** certificate of baptism; **fe de erratas** errata *pl* - **3.** *loc*: **dar fe de que** to testify that; **la fe mueve montañas** faith can move mountains.

fealdad *sf* - **1.** [de rostro etc] ugliness - **2.** [de conducta etc] unworthiness.

feb., febr. *(abrev de* **febrero)** Feb.

febrero *sm* February; *ver también* **septiembre**.

febril *adj* feverish; *fig* [actividad] hectic.

fecal *adj* faecal.

fecha *sf* [gen] date; [momento actual] current date; **a partir de esta fecha** from today; **en fecha próxima** in the next few days; **hasta la**

fecha to date, so far; **ocurrió por estas fechas** it happened around this time of year; **fecha de caducidad** [de alimentos] sell-by date; [de carné, pasaporte] expiry date; [de medicamento] 'use before' date; **fecha de nacimiento** date of birth; **fecha tope** o **límite** deadline.

fechar *vt* to date.

fechoría *sf* bad deed, misdemeanour.

fécula *sf* starch (*in food*).

fecundación *sf* fertilization; **fecundación artificial** artificial insemination; **fecundación asistida** assisted fertilization; **fecundación in vitro** in vitro fertilization.

fecundar *vt* - **1.** [fertilizar] to fertilize - **2.** [hacer productivo] to make fertile.

fecundidad *sf* - **1.** [fertilidad] fertility - **2.** [productividad] productiveness.

fecundo, da *adj* [gen] fertile; [artista] prolific.

federación *sf* federation.

federal *adj* & *smf* federal.

federalismo *sm* federalism.

federalista *adj* & *smf* federalist.

federar *vt* to federate.

➡ **federarse** *vprnl* - **1.** [formar federación] to become o form a federation - **2.** [ingresar en federación] to join a federation.

federativo, va ◇ *adj* federative. ◇ *sm, f* member of a federation.

felación *sf* fellatio.

feldespato *sm* feldspar.

felicidad *sf* happiness.

➡ **felicidades** *interj*: ¡felicidades! [gen] congratulations!; [en cumpleaños] happy birthday!

felicitación *sf* - **1.** [acción]: **felicitaciones** congratulations - **2.** [postal] greetings card; **felicitación de Navidad** Christmas card.

felicitar *vt* to congratulate; ¡te felicito! congratulations!; **felicitar a alguien por algo** to congratulate sb on sthg.

➡ **felicitarse** *vprnl*: **felicitarse (por)** to be pleased o glad (about).

félidos *smpl* felines.

feligrés, esa *sm, f* parishioner.

felino, na *adj* feline.

➡ **felino** *sm* feline, cat.

feliz *adj* - **1.** [dichoso] happy; **hacer feliz a alguien** to make sb happy - **2.** [afortunado] lucky - **3.** [oportuno] timely.

felonía *sf* [traición] treachery, betrayal; [infamia] vile deed.

felpa *sf* [de seda] plush; [de algodón] towelling.

felpudo *sm* doormat.

femenino, na *adj* [gen] feminine; BOT & ZOOL female.

➡ **femenino** *sm* GRAM feminine.

fémina *sf* woman, female.

feminidad, femineidad *sf* femininity.

feminismo *sm* feminism.

feminista *adj* & *smf* feminist.

feminizar [13] *vt* to make feminine.

femoral ◇ *adj* femoral. ◇ *sf* femoral artery.

fémur (*pl* fémures) *sm* femur, thighbone.

fenicio, cia *adj* & *sm, f* Phoenician.

➡ **fenicio** *sm* [lengua] Phoenician.

fénix *sm inv* [ave] phoenix.

fenomenal *adj* [magnífico] wonderful, fantastic.

fenómeno ◇ *sm* - **1.** [gen] phenomenon - **2.** [monstruo] freak. ◇ *adv fam* brilliantly, fantastically; **pasarlo fenómeno** to have a great time. ◇ *interj*: ¡fenómeno! great!, terrific!

fenotipo *sm* phenotype.

feo, a ◇ *adj* - **1.** [persona] ugly; **le tocó bailar con la más fea** he drew the short straw; **ser más feo que Picio** to be as ugly as sin - **2.** [aspecto, herida, conducta] nasty; **es feo escupir** it's rude to spit - **3.** [tiempo] foul, horrible; **la tarde se ha puesto fea** the weather has turned nasty this afternoon. ◇ *sm, f* [persona] ugly person.

➡ **feo** *sm* [desaire] slight, insult; **hacer un feo a alguien** to offend o slight sb.

féretro *sm* coffin.

feria *sf* - **1.** [gen] fair; **feria (de muestras)** trade fair - **2.** [fiesta popular] festival.

feriado *sm* Amér (public) holiday.

ferial *adj* fair (antes de s); **recinto ferial** fairground.

feriante *smf* [vendedor] trader; [comprador] fairgoer.

fermentación *sf* fermentation.

fermentar *vt* & *vi* to ferment.

fermento *sm* ferment.

ferocidad *sf* ferocity, fierceness.

feroz *adj* - **1.** [animal, bestia] fierce, ferocious - **2.** *fig* [criminal, asesino] cruel, savage - **3.** *fig* [dolor, angustia] terrible - **4.** *fig* [enorme] massive.

férreo, a *adj lit* & *fig* iron (antes de s).

ferretería *sf* ironmonger's (shop) UK, hardware store.

ferretero, ra *sm, f* ironmonger, hardware dealer.

ferrocarril *sm* [sistema, medio] railway, railroad US; [tren] train; **por ferrocarril** by train.

ferroso, sa *adj* ferrous.

ferroviario, ria ◇ *adj* railway (antes de s) UK, rail (antes de s), railroad (antes de s) US. ◇ *sm, f* railway worker.

ferry sm ferry.

fértil adj lit & fig fertile.

fertilidad sf lit & fig fertility.

fertilización sf fertilization; **fertilización in vitro** in vitro fertilization.

fertilizante ◇ adj fertilizing. ◇ sm fertilizer.

fertilizar [13] vt to fertilize.

ferviente adj fervent.

fervor sm fervour.

fervoroso, sa adj fervent.

festejar vt - **1.** [celebrar] to celebrate - **2.** [agasajar] to entertain.

◆ **festejarse** vprnl [celebrarse] to be celebrated.

festejo sm - **1.** [fiesta] party - **2.** [agasajo] entertaining.

◆ **festejos** smpl [fiestas] public festivities.

festín sm banquet, feast.

festival sm festival.

festividad sf festivity.

festivo, va adj - **1.** [de fiesta] festive; **día festivo** (public) holiday - **2.** [alegre] cheerful, jolly; [chistoso] funny, witty.

festón sm [en costura] scallop.

festonear vt [en costura] to scallop.

fetal adj foetal.

fetén adj inv fam brilliant, great.

fetiche sm fetish.

fetichismo sm fetishism.

fetichista ◇ adj fetishistic. ◇ smf fetishist.

fétido, da adj fetid, foul-smelling.

feto sm foetus.

feudal adj feudal.

feudalismo sm feudalism.

feudo sm HIST fief; fig [dominio] domain, area of influence.

FF AA (abrev de **Fuerzas Armadas**) sfpl Spanish armed forces.

fiabilidad sf reliability.

fiable adj [máquina] reliable; [persona] trustworthy.

fiador, ra sm, f guarantor, surety; **salir fiador por** to vouch for.

fiambre sm - **1.** [comida] cold meat UK, cold cuts US - **2.** fam [cadáver] stiff, corpse.

fiambrera sf lunch O sandwich box.

fianza sf - **1.** [depósito] deposit - **2.** DER bail; **bajo fianza** on bail - **3.** [garantía] security, bond.

fiar [9] ◇ vt COM to sell on credit. ◇ vi COM to sell on credit; **ser de fiar** to be trustworthy.

◆ **fiarse** vprnl: **¡no te fíes!** don't be too sure (about it)!; **fiarse de algo/alguien** to trust sthg/sb.

fibra sf - **1.** [gen] fibre; [de madera] grain; **fibra de vidrio** fibreglass; **fibra óptica** INFORM optic fibre - **2.** [energía] character, vigour.

fibroma sm fibroma.

fibrosis sf inv fibrosis.

fibroso, sa adj fibrous.

ficción sf - **1.** [gen] fiction - **2.** [simulación] pretence, make-believe.

ficha sf - **1.** [tarjeta] (index) card; [con detalles personales] file, record card - **2.** [de guardarropa, aparcamiento] ticket - **3.** [de teléfono] token - **4.** [de juego - gen] counter; [en ajedrez] piece; [en casino] chip; **mover ficha** to act - **5.** DEP [contrato] contract - **6.** INFORM card; **ficha perforada** perforated card.

fichaje sm DEP [contratación] signing (up); [importe] transfer fee.

fichar ◇ vt - **1.** [archivar] to note down on an index card, to file - **2.** [suj: policía] to put on police files O records - **3.** DEP to sign up - **4.** fam [calar] to suss out, to see through. ◇ vi - **1.** [suj: trabajador - al entrar] to clock in; [- al salir] to clock out - **2.** DEP: **fichar (por)** to sign up (for).

fichero sm - **1.** [mueble] filing cabinet - **2.** INFORM file.

ficticio, cia adj - **1.** [imaginario] fictitious - **2.** [convencional] imaginary.

ficus sm inv rubber plant.

fidedigno, na adj reliable.

fidelidad sf - **1.** [lealtad] loyalty; [de cónyuge, perro] faithfulness - **2.** [precisión] accuracy; **alta fidelidad** high fidelity.

fideo sm noodle; **estar** O **quedarse como un fideo** to be as thin as a rake.

fiebre sf fever; **tener fiebre** to have a temperature; **fiebre aftosa** foot-and-mouth disease; **fiebre amarilla/de Malta** yellow/Malta fever; **fiebre del heno** hay fever; **fiebre reumática/tifoidea** rheumatic/typhoid fever; **la fiebre del oro** the gold rush.

fiel ◇ adj - **1.** [leal - amigo, seguidor] loyal; [- cónyuge, perro] faithful - **2.** [preciso] accurate. ◇ sm [de balanza] needle, pointer.

◆ **fieles** smpl RELIG: **los fieles** the faithful.

fieltro sm felt.

fiero, ra adj savage, ferocious.

◆ **fiera** sf - **1.** [animal] wild animal - **2.** fig [persona - genial] demon; [- cruel] brute; **estar/ponerse hecho una fiera** to be/go wild with anger; **ser una fiera para** to be brilliant at.

fierro sm Amér - **1.** [hierro] iron - **2.** [navaja] penknife.

fiesta sf - **1.** [reunión] party; [de pueblo etc] (local) festivities pl; **fiesta benéfica** fête; **fiesta de disfraces** fancy-dress party; **fiesta mayor** local celebrations for the festival of a town's *patron saint*; **la fiesta nacional** bull fighting; **aguar la fiesta a alguien** to spoil sb's fun; **no estar para fiestas** to be in no mood for joking **- 2.** [día] public holiday; **ser fiesta** to be a public holiday; **hacer fiesta** to be on holiday.

⬥ **fiestas** *sfpl* [vacaciones] holidays.

Fiestas

The Spanish word **fiesta** has long since entered the vocabulary of English, largely due to the centrality of such celebrations in the Spanish-speaking world. There are a number of national holidays when offices are likely to be closed or short-staffed - notably during "Semana Santa" (Easter) and in August. There are also annual regional and local celebrations, and these can also mean little important business can be done. For example, Valencia has its "Fallas" (a week-long celebration based on fireworks and bonfires) in March, while Pamplona has its nine day "Sanfermines" (with the famous running of the bulls through the streets) in July.

FIFA (*abrev de* **Federación Internacional de Fútbol Asociado**) *sf* FIFA.

fifí *sm Amér fam* playboy.

figura *sf* **- 1.** [gen] figure; [forma] shape; **tener buena figura** to have a good figure; **figura geométrica** geometric figure; **figura paterna** father figure **- 2.** [en naipes] picture card.

figuraciones *sfpl* imaginings; **son figuraciones tuyas** it's all in your imagination.

figurado, da *adj* figurative.

figurante, ta *sm, f* extra.

figurar ⬦ *vi* **- 1.** [aparecer]: **figurar (en)** to appear (in), to figure (in) **- 2.** [ser importante] to be prominent *o* important. ⬦ *vt* **- 1.** [representar] to represent **- 2.** [simular] to feign, to simulate.

⬥ **figurarse** *vprnl* [imaginarse] to imagine; **ya me lo figuraba yo** I thought as much.

figurativo, va *adj* ARTE figurative.

figurín *sm* fashion sketch; **ir/estar hecho un figurín** *fig* to be dressed up to the nines.

figurón *sm* poseur.

fijación *sf* **- 1.** [gen & FOTO] fixing **- 2.** [obsesión] fixation.

⬥ **fijaciones** *sfpl* [en esquí] bindings.

fijador *sm* **- 1.** [líquido] fixative; **fijador de pelo** [crema] hair gel; [espray] hair spray **- 2.** [en esquí] ski-clip.

fijar *vt* **- 1.** [gen] to fix; [asegurar] to fasten; [cartel] to stick up; [sello] to stick on **- 2.** [significado] to establish; **fijar el domicilio** to take up residence; **fijar la mirada/la atención en** to fix one's gaze/attention on.

⬥ **fijarse** *vprnl* to pay attention; **fijarse en algo** [darse cuenta] to notice sthg; [prestar atención] to pay attention to sthg.

fijeza *sf* firmness.

⬥ **con fijeza** *loc adv* **- 1.** [con seguridad] definitely, for sure **- 2.** [con persistencia] fixedly.

fijo, ja ⬦ *adj* **- 1.** [gen] fixed; [sujeto] secure **- 2.** [cliente] regular **- 3.** [fecha] firm, definite **- 4.** [empleado, trabajo] permanent. ⬦ *adv fam* definitely.

fila *sf* **- 1.** [hilera - gen] line; [- de asientos] row; **en fila, en fila india** in line, in single file; **ponerse en fila** to line up **- 2.** MIL rank **- 3.** [manía] dislike.

⬥ **filas** *sfpl* MIL ranks; **en filas** doing military service; **incorporarse a filas** to join up; **llamar a filas a alguien** to call sb up; **romper filas** to fall out; **cerrar filas** *fig* to close ranks.

filamento *sm* filament.

filantropía *sf* philanthropy.

filantrópico, ca *adj* philanthropic.

filántropo, pa *sm, f* philanthropist.

filarmónico, ca *adj* philharmonic.

⬥ **filarmónica** *sf* philharmonic (orchestra).

filatelia *sf* philately.

filatélico, ca ⬦ *adj* philatelic. ⬦ *sm, f* philatelist.

filete *sm* **- 1.** [CULIN - grueso] (fillet) steak; [- delgado] fillet; [solomillo] sirloin **- 2.** [de tornillo] thread.

filiación *sf* **- 1.** [ficha militar, policial] record, file **- 2.** POLÍT affiliation **- 3.** [parentesco] relationship.

filial ⬦ *adj* **- 1.** [de hijo] filial **- 2.** [de empresa] subsidiary. ⬦ *sf* subsidiary.

filigrana *sf* **- 1.** [en orfebrería] filigree **- 2.** *fig* [habilidad] skilful work **- 3.** [en billetes] watermark.

Filipinas *sfpl*: **(las) Filipinas** the Philippines *sing*.

filipino, na *adj & sm, f* Filipino.

⬥ **filipino** *sm* [lengua] Filipino.

filisteo, a *adj & sm, f* Philistine.

film = filme.

filmación *sf* filming, shooting.

filmador, ra *adj* film (*antes de s*).

⬥ **filmadora** *sf* [cámara] cine camera.

filmar *vt* to film, to shoot.

filme, film (*pl* films) *sm* film *UK*, movie *US*.

filmografía *sf* filmography.

filmoteca *sf* [archivo] film library; [sala de cine] film institute.

filo *sm* (cutting) edge; **de doble filo, de dos filos** *lit & fig* double-edged.

⬥ **al filo de** *loc prep* just before.

filología *sf* - **1.** [ciencia] philology - **2.** [carrera] language and literature.

filológico, ca *adj* philological.

filólogo, ga *sm, f* philologist.

filón *sm* - **1.** [de carbón etc] seam - **2.** *fig* [mina] gold mine.

filoso, sa, filudo, da *adj* *Amér* sharp.

filosofar *vi* to philosophize.

filosofía *sf* - **1.** [ciencia] philosophy - **2.** [resignación]**: tomarse algo con filosofía** to be philosophical about sthg.

filosófico, ca *adj* philosophical.

filósofo, fa *sm, f* philosopher.

filtración *sf* - **1.** [de agua] filtration - **2.** *fig* [de noticia etc] leak.

filtrar *vt* - **1.** [tamizar] to filter - **2.** *fig* [datos, noticia] to leak.

➤ **filtrarse** *vprnl* - **1.** [penetrar]**: filtrarse (por)** to filter o seep (through) - **2.** *fig* [datos, noticia] to be leaked.

filtro *sm* [gen] filter; [de cigarrillo] filter, filter tip; **filtro del aceite** oil filter.

filudo, da = **filoso**.

fimosis *sf inv* phimosis.

fin *sm* - **1.** [final] end; **dar** o **poner fin a algo** to put an end to sthg; **tocar a su fin** to come to a close; **fin de fiesta** grand finale; **fin de semana** weekend; **a fines de** at the end of; **al o por fin** at last, finally; **a fin de cuentas** after all; **al fin y al cabo** after all; **sin fin** endless; **al fin del mundo** to the end of the earth (and back) - **2.** [objetivo] aim, goal; **el fin justifica los medios** *prov* the end justifies the means.

➤ **a fin de** *loc conj* in order to.

➤ **a fin de que** *loc conj* so that.

➤ **en fin** *loc adv* anyway.

finado, da *sm, f*: **el finado** the deceased.

final ◇ *adj* final, end *(antes de s)*. ◇ *sm* end; **final feliz** happy ending; **a finales de** at the end of; **al final** [en conclusión] in the end; **al final de** at the end of. ◇ *sf* final.

finalidad *sf* aim, purpose.

finalista ◇ *adj* amongst the finalists. ◇ *smf* finalist.

finalización *sf* [gen] end; [de contrato] termination.

finalizar [13] ◇ *vt* to finish, to complete. ◇ *vi*: **finalizar (con)** to end o finish (in).

financiación *sf* financing.

financiar [8] *vt* to finance.

financiero, ra ◇ *adj* financial. ◇ *sm, f* [persona] financier.

➤ **financiera** *sf* [firma] finance company.

financista *smf* *Amér* financier.

finanzas *sfpl* finance *(U)*.

finca *sf* [gen] property; [casa de campo] country residence.

fineza *sf* - **1.** [cualidad] (fine) quality - **2.** [cortesía] courtesy.

fingido, da *adj* feigned, apparent.

fingimiento *sm* pretence.

fingir [15] ◇ *vt* to feign; **fingir hacer algo** to pretend to do sthg. ◇ *vi* to pretend.

finiquitar *vt* to settle.

finiquito *sm* settlement.

finito, ta *adj* finite.

finja *etc* ▷ **fingir**.

finlandés, esa ◇ *adj* Finnish. ◇ *sm, f* [persona] Finn.

➤ **finlandés** *sm* [lengua] Finnish.

Finlandia *n pr* Finland.

fino, na *adj* - **1.** [gen] fine; [delgado] thin; [cintura] slim - **2.** [cortés] refined - **3.** [agudo - oído, olfato] sharp, keen; [- gusto, humor, ironía] refined.

➤ **fino** *sm* dry sherry.

finolis *fam* ◇ *adj inv* affected. ◇ *smf inv* affected person.

finura *sf* [gen] fineness; [delgadez] thinness; [cortesía] refinement; [de oído, olfato] sharpness, keenness; [de gusto, humor, ironía] refinement.

fiordo *sm* fiord.

firma *sf* - **1.** [rúbrica] signature; [acción] signing; **estampar la firma** to sign, to write one's signature - **2.** [empresa] firm.

firmamento *sm* firmament.

firmante ◇ *adj* signatory. ◇ *smf* signatory; **el abajo firmante** the undersigned.

firmar *vt* to sign; **firmar algo en blanco** *fig* to rubber-stamp sthg.

firme ◇ *adj* - **1.** [gen] firm; [mueble, andamio, edificio] stable - **2.** [argumento, base] solid - **3.** [carácter, actitud, paso] resolute. ◇ *adv* hard; **mantenerse firme en** to hold fast to. ◇ *sm* road surface.

➤ **firmes** *interj*: **¡firmes!** MIL attention!

firmeza *sf* - **1.** [gen] firmness; [de mueble, edificio] stability - **2.** [de argumento] solidity - **3.** [de carácter, actitud] resolution.

fiscal ◇ *adj* tax *(antes de s)*, fiscal. ◇ *smf* public prosecutor *UK*, district attorney *US*.

fiscalía *sf* - **1.** [cargo] post of public prosecutor *UK* - **2.** [oficina] office of public prosecutor *UK* o district attorney *US*.

fiscalización *sf* investigation, inquiry.

fiscalizar [13] *vt* to inquire into o investigate the affairs of.

fisco *sm* treasury, exchequer.

fisgar [16], **fisgonear** *vi* [gen] to pry; [escuchando] to eavesdrop.

fisgón, ona ◇ *adj* nosey, prying. ◇ *sm, f* busybody, nosy parker.

fisgonear = **fisgar**.

fisgoneo *sm* prying.

fisgue *etc* ⊏▷ **fisgar**.

físico, ca ◇ *adj* physical. ◇ *sm, f* [persona] physicist.
➡ **físico** *sm* [complexión] physique.
➡ **física** *sf* [ciencia] physics *(U)*.

fisiología *sf* physiology.

fisiológico, ca *adj* physiological.

fisión *sf* fission.

fisionomía = **fisonomía**.

fisionomista = **fisonomista**.

fisioterapeuta *smf* physiotherapist.

fisioterapia *sf* physiotherapy.

fisonomía, fisionomía *sf* features *pl*, appearance.

fisonomista, fisionomista *smf* person who is good at remembering faces.

fístula *sf* fistula.

fisura *sf* - **1.** [grieta] fissure - **2.** *fig* weakness, weak point.

fitología *sf* botany.

flacidez, flaccidez *sf* flabbiness.

flácido, da, fláccido, da *adj* flaccid, flabby.

flaco, ca ◇ *adj* thin, skinny. ◇ *sm, f* Amér [como apelativo]**: ¿cómo estás, flaca?** hey, how are you doing?

flagelación *sf* flagellation.

flagelar *vt* to flagellate.
➡ **flagelarse** *vprnl* to flagellate o.s.

flagrante *adj* flagrant.

flamante *adj* [vistoso] resplendent; [nuevo] brand-new.

flambear *vt* to flambé.

flamear ◇ *vi* - **1.** [fuego] to blaze o flare (up) - **2.** [bandera, vela] to flap. ◇ *vt* to sterilize by passing through a flame.

flamenco, ca ◇ *adj* - **1.** MÚS flamenco *(antes de s)* - **2.** [de Flandes] Flemish - **3.** [achulado] cocky; **ponerse flamenco** to get cocky. ◇ *sm, f* [de Flandes] Fleming.
➡ **flamenco** *sm* - **1.** [ave] flamingo - **2.** [lengua] Flemish - **3.** MÚS flamenco.

flamencología *sf* study of flamenco.

flan *sm* crème caramel; **estar hecho** o **como un flan** to shake like a jelly, to be a bundle of nerves.

flanco *sm* flank.

flanera *sf* crème caramel mould.

flanquear *vt* to flank.

flaquear *vi* to weaken; *fig* to flag.

flaqueza *sf* weakness.

flash [flaʃ] *(pl* **flashes)** *sm* - **1.** FOTO flash - **2.** [informativo] newsflash - **3.** *fam* [imagen mental] flash of inspiration.

flato *sm***: tener flato** to have a stitch.

flatulencia *sf* flatulence, wind.

flatulento, ta *adj* flatulent.

flauta ◇ *sf* flute; **flauta dulce** recorder; **sonó la flauta (por casualidad)** it was sheer fluke; **de la gran flauta** Chile & R Dom *fig* tremendous. ◇ *interj*: **¡(la gran) flauta!** Chile & R Dom good grief!, good heavens!

flautín *sm* piccolo.

flautista *smf* flautist.

flebitis *sf inv* phlebitis.

flecha ◇ *sf* [gen] arrow; ARQUIT spire; **salir como una flecha** to shoot out, to fly out. ◇ *smf fam*: **ser un flecha** to be red hot, to be extremely good.

flechazo *sm* - **1.** [disparo] arrow shot; [herida] arrow wound - **2.** *fam fig* [amoroso]**: fue un flechazo** it was love at first sight.

fleco *sm* - **1.** [adorno] fringe - **2.** [de tela gastada] frayed edge.

flema *sf* phlegm.

flemático, ca *adj* - **1.** [con mucosidad] phlegmy - **2.** [tranquilo] phlegmatic.

flemón *sm* gumboil.

flequillo *sm* fringe, bangs *pl US*.

fletamiento *sm* [alquiler] charter, chartering *(U)*.

fletar *vt* - **1.** [alquilar] to charter - **2.** [cargar] to load.

flete *sm* - **1.** [precio] freightage - **2.** [carga] cargo, freight.

flexibilidad *sf* flexibility.

flexibilizar [13] *vt* to make flexible.

flexible *adj* flexible.

flexión *sf* - **1.** [doblegamiento] bending; **hacer flexiones** [de brazos] to do press-ups *UK*, to do push-ups *US*; [de piernas] to do squats - **2.** GRAM inflection.

flexionar *vt* to bend.

flexo *sm* adjustable table lamp o light.

flexor, ra *adj* flexional.
➡ **flexor** *sm* flexor.

flipado, da *adj fam* [drogado] stoned, high; [asombrado] gobsmacked.

flipar *fam* ◇ *vi* - **1.** [disfrutar] to have a wild time - **2.** [asombrarse] to be gobsmacked - **3.** [con una droga] to be stoned o high. ◇ *vt* [gustar]**: me flipan los videojuegos** I'm wild about video games.
➡ **fliparse** *fam vprnl* - **1.** [disfrutar]**: fliparse (con)** to go wild (about) - **2.** [drogarse] to get stoned o high.

flirtear *vi* to flirt.

flirteo *sm* flirtation, flirting *(U)*.

flojear *vi* - **1.** [decaer - piernas, fuerzas etc] to weaken; [- memoria] to be failing; [- película, libro] to flag; [- calor, trabajo] to ease off; [- ventas] to fall off - **2.** [no ser muy apto]: **flojear en algo** to get worse at sthg - **3.** *Andes* [holgazanear] to laze about *o* around.

flojedad *sf* weakness.

flojera *sf* lethargy, feeling of weakness.

flojo, ja *adj* - **1.** [suelto] loose - **2.** [débil - persona, bebida] weak; [- sonido] faint; [- tela] thin; [- salud] poor; [- viento] light - **3.** [sin calidad, aptitudes] poor; **estar flojo en algo** to be poor *o* weak at sthg - **4.** [inactivo - mercado, negocio] slack.

flor *sf* - **1.** BOT flower; **de flores** flowered; **en flor** in flower; **flor de lis** fleur-de-lis; **echar flores a alguien** to pay sb compliments; **no tener ni flores (de)** *fam* not to have a clue (about); **ser flor de un día** *fig* to be a flash in the pan - **2.** [lo mejor]: **la flor (y nata)** the crème de la crème, the cream; **en la flor de la edad** *o* **de la vida** in the prime of life.
◆ **a flor de** *loc adv*: **a flor de agua/tierra** at water/ground level; **a flor de piel** *fig* just below the surface.

flora *sf* flora; **flora intestinal** *o* **microbiana** microbes *pl*.

floración *sf* flowering, blossoming.

floral *adj* floral.

floreado, da *adj* flowery.

florecer [30] *vi* to flower; *fig* to flourish.

floreciente *adj fig* flourishing.

florecimiento *sm* flowering; *fig* flourishing.

florero *sm* vase.

floricultor, ra *sm, f* flower grower.

floricultura *sf* flower growing.

florido, da *adj* [con flores] flowery; [estilo, lenguaje] florid.

florín *sm* florin.

florista *smf* florist.

floristería *sf* florist's (shop).

floritura *sf* flourish.

flota *sf* fleet; **flota mercante** merchant fleet; **flota pesquera** fishing fleet.

flotabilidad *sf* - **1.** [en el agua] buoyancy - **2.** ECON floatability.

flotación *sf* [gen & ECON] flotation.

flotador *sm* - **1.** [para nadar] rubber ring - **2.** [de caña de pescar] float - **3.** [de cisternas] ballcock.

flotante *adj* [gen & ECON] floating.

flotar *vi* [gen & ECON] to float; [banderas] to flutter.

flote ◆ **a flote** *loc adv* afloat; **mantenerse a flote** to stay afloat; **sacar algo a flote** *fig* to get sthg back on its feet; **salir a flote** *fig* to get back on one's feet.

flotilla *sf* flotilla.

fluctuación *sf* - **1.** [variación] fluctuation - **2.** [vacilación] wavering.

fluctuante *adj* fluctuating.

fluctuar [6] *vi* - **1.** [variar] to fluctuate - **2.** [vacilar] to waver.

fluidez *sf* - **1.** [gen] fluidity; [del tráfico] free flow; [de relaciones] smoothness - **2.** *fig* [en el lenguaje] fluency.

fluido, da *adj* - **1.** [gen] fluid; [tráfico] free-flowing - **2.** [relaciones] smooth - **3.** *fig* [lenguaje] fluent.
◆ **fluido** *sm* fluid; **fluido eléctrico** electric current *o* power.

fluir [51] *vi* to flow.

flujo *sm* flow; **flujo de caja** cash flow; **flujo menstrual** menstrual flow; **flujo sanguíneo** bloodstream.

flúor *sm* fluorine.

fluorescencia *sf* fluorescence.

fluorescente ◇ *adj* fluorescent. ◇ *sm* strip light.

fluoruro *sm* fluoride.

fluvial *adj* river *(antes de s)*.

fluya, fluyera ▷ **fluir**.

FM *(abrev de frecuencia modulada)* *sf* FM.

FMI *(abrev de Fondo Monetario Internacional)* *sm* IMF.

fobia *sf* phobia.

foca *sf* seal.

focal *adj* focal.

focalizar [13] *vt* to focus.

foco *sm* - **1.** *fig* [centro] centre, focal point - **2.** [lámpara - para un punto] spotlight; [- para una zona] floodlight - **3.** FÍS & GEOM focus - **4.** *Col, Ecuad, Méx & Perú* [bombilla] light bulb - **5.** *Amér* [farola] street light - **6.** *Amér* AUTO (car) headlight.

fofo, fa *adj* flabby.

fogata *sf* bonfire, fire.

fogón *sm* - **1.** [para cocinar] stove - **2.** [de máquina de vapor] firebox.

fogonazo *sm* flash.

fogonero, ra *sm, f* stoker.

fogosidad *sf* passion.

fogoso, sa *adj* passionate.

fogueo *sm*: **de fogueo** blank.

foie-gras [fwa'ɣras] *sm* (pâté de) foie-gras.

folclore, folclor, folklor *sm* folklore.

folclórico, ca ⬦ *adj* traditional, popular. ⬦ *sm, f* flamenco singer.

folclorismo *sm* folklore.

foliación *sf* foliation.

folículo *sm* follicle.

folio *sm* [hoja] leaf, sheet; [tamaño] folio.

folklor = folclore.

follaje *sm* foliage.

follar *vi vulg* to fuck.

folletín *sm* [dramón] melodrama.

folletinesco, ca *adj* melodramatic.

folleto *sm* [turístico, publicitario] brochure; [explicativo, de instrucciones] leaflet.

follón *sm fam* - **1.** [discusión] row; **se armó follón** there was an almighty row - **2.** [lío] mess; **¡vaya follón!** what a mess!

fomentar *vt* to encourage, to foster.

fomento *sm* encouragement, fostering.

fonación *sf* phonation.

fonda *sf* boarding house.

fondeadero *sm* anchorage.

fondear ⬦ *vi* to anchor. ⬦ *vt* [sondear] to sound; [registrar - barco] to search.

fondista *smf* - **1.** [propietario de fonda] landlord (*f* landlady) - **2.** [DEP - corredor] long-distance runner; [- nadador] long-distance swimmer; [- esquiador] cross-country skier.

fondo *sm* - **1.** [de recipiente, mar, piscina] bottom; **sin fondo** bottomless; **tocar fondo** [embarcación] to scrape along the sea/river bed; *fig* to hit rock bottom; **doble fondo** false bottom - **2.** [de habitación etc] back; **al fondo de** [calle, pasillo] at the end of; [sala] at the back of - **3.** [dimensión] depth - **4.** [de tela, cuadro, foto] background; **al fondo** in the background - **5.** *R Dom* [patio] back patio - **6.** [de asunto, tema] heart, bottom; **llegar al fondo de** to get to the heart o bottom of - **7.** [de una persona]: **tener buen fondo** to have a good heart - **8.** [de obra literaria] substance - **9.** ECON fund; **a fondo perdido** nonreturnable; **fondo común** kitty; **fondo de amortización/de inversión/de pensiones** ECON sinking/investment/pension fund; **fondo de garantía de depósito** BANCA deposit guarantee fund - **10.** [fundamento] reason, basis - **11.** [de biblioteca, archivo] catalogue, collection; **fondo editorial** collection of published works - **12.** DEP stamina; **de fondo** long-distance; **de medio fondo** middle-distance - **13.** *Méx* [combinación] petticoat.

➤ **fondos** *smpl* - **1.** ECON [capital] funds; **estar mal de fondos** [persona] to be badly off; [empresa] to be short of funds; **recaudar fondos** to raise funds; **fondos públicos** public funds - **2.** [de embarcación] bottom *sing*.

➤ **bajos fondos** *smpl* underworld *(U).*

➤ **a fondo** ⬦ *loc adv* thoroughly; **emplearse a fondo** *fig* to do one's utmost. ⬦ *loc adj* thorough.

➤ **en el fondo** *loc adv* - **1.** [en lo más íntimo] deep down - **2.** [en lo esencial] basically.

fonético, ca *adj* phonetic.

➤ **fonética** *sf* - **1.** [ciencia] phonetics *(U)* - **2.** [sonidos] sound.

fónico, ca *adj* phonic.

fono *sm Amér fam* phone.

fonógrafo *sm* gramophone, phonograph *US*.

fonología *sf* phonology.

fonoteca *sf* record library.

fontanería *sf* plumbing.

fontanero, ra *sm, f* plumber.

football = fútbol.

footing ['futin] *sm* jogging; **hacer footing** to go jogging.

FOP (*abrev de* **Fuerzas de Orden Público**) *sfpl* police *(force).*

forajido, da *sm, f* outlaw.

foral *adj relating to ancient regional laws still existing in some parts of Spain.*

foráneo, a *adj* foreign.

forastero, ra *sm, f* stranger.

forcé ▷ forzar.

forcejear *vi* to struggle.

forcejeo *sm* struggle.

forcemos ▷ forzar.

fórceps *sm inv* forceps.

forense ⬦ *adj* forensic. ⬦ *smf* pathologist.

forestal *adj* forest *(antes de s).*

forfait [for'fe] *sm* - **1.** DEP default - **2.** [abono] pass - **3.** [precio invariable] fixed rate; **a forfait** fixed price.

forja *sf* [fragua] forge; [forjadura] forging.

forjado, da *adj* wrought.

forjar *vt* - **1.** [metal] to forge - **2.** *fig* [inventarse] to invent; [crear] to build up.

➤ **forjarse** *vprnl fig* [labrarse] to carve out for o.s.

forma *sf* - **1.** [gen] shape, form; **dar forma a** to shape, to form; **en forma de** in the shape of; **tomar forma** to take shape; **guardar las formas** to keep up appearances - **2.** [manera] way,

manner; **de cualquier forma, de todas formas** anyway, in any case; **de esta forma** in this way; **de forma que** in such a way that, so that; **forma de pago** method of payment - **3.** ARTE & LITER form - **4.** [condición física] fitness; **estar en forma** to be fit; **estar bajo de forma, estar en baja forma** to be in poor shape - **5.** RELIG host.
→ **formas** sfpl - **1.** [silueta] figure sing, curves - **2.** [modales] manners, social conventions.

formación sf - **1.** [gen & MIL] formation - **2.** [educación] training; **formación profesional** vocational training - **3.** [conjunto] grouping.

formal adj - **1.** [gen] formal - **2.** [que se porta bien] well-behaved, good - **3.** [de confianza] reliable - **4.** [serio] serious.

formalidad sf - **1.** [gen] formality - **2.** [educación] (good) manners pl - **3.** [fiabilidad] reliability - **4.** [seriedad] seriousness.

formalismo sm formalism.

formalista ◇ adj formal. ◇ smf formalist.

formalización sf formalization.

formalizar [13] vt to formalize.

formar ◇ vt - **1.** [gen] to form - **2.** [educar] to train, to educate - **3.** MIL to form up. ◇ vi MIL to fall in.
→ **formarse** vprnl - **1.** [gen] to form - **2.** [educarse] to be trained o educated.

formatear vt INFORM to format.

formateo sm INFORM formatting.

formativo, va adj formative.

formato sm [gen & INFORM] format.

formica® sf Formica®.

formidable adj [enorme] tremendous; [extraordinario] amazing, fantastic.

formol sm formalin.

fórmula sf formula; **fórmula magistral** magistral formula; **fórmula uno** formula one; **por pura fórmula** purely as a matter of form.

formulación sf formulation.

formular ◇ vt to formulate; **formular una pregunta** to ask a question. ◇ vi to write formulae.

formulario sm form; **rellenar un formulario** to fill in a form.

formulismo sm [apego - a las formas] formalism; [- a las normas] sticking to the rules.

fornicar [10] vi culto to fornicate.

fornido, da adj well-built.

foro sm - **1.** [tribunal] court (of law) - **2.** TEATRO back of the stage; **desaparecer por el foro** to slip away unnoticed - **3.** [debate] forum; **foro de discusión** INFORM forum.

forofo, fa sm, f fam fan, supporter.

forrado, da adj [libro] covered; [ropa] lined; [asiento] upholstered; **estar forrado** fam to be rolling in it.

forraje sm fodder.

forrar vt: **forrar (de)** [libro] to cover (with); [ropa] to line (with); [asiento] to upholster (with).
→ **forrarse** vprnl fam to make a packet.

forro sm - **1.** [de libro] cover; [de ropa] lining; [de asiento] upholstery; **forro polar** fleece; **ni por el forro** fam at all - **2.** R Dom fam [preservativo] rubber, johnny UK.

fortachón, ona adj strapping, well-built.

fortalecer [30] vt to strengthen.

fortalecimiento sm strengthening.

fortaleza sf - **1.** [gen] strength - **2.** [recinto] fortress.

fortificación sf fortification.

fortificar [10] vt to fortify.

fortín sm small fort.

fortuito, ta adj chance (antes de s).

fortuna sf - **1.** [suerte] (good) luck; **por fortuna** fortunately, luckily; **probar fortuna** to try one's luck - **2.** [destino] fortune, fate - **3.** [riqueza] fortune.

forúnculo, furúnculo sm boil.

forzado, da adj forced.

forzar [37] vt - **1.** [gen] to force; **forzar a alguien a hacer algo** to force sb to do sthg; **forzar la vista** to strain one's eyes - **2.** [violar] to rape.

forzoso, sa adj [obligatorio] obligatory, compulsory; [inevitable] inevitable; [necesario] necessary.

forzudo, da ◇ adj strong. ◇ sm, f strong man (f strong woman).

fosa sf - **1.** [sepultura] grave; **fosa común** common grave - **2.** ANAT cavity; **fosas nasales** nostrils - **3.** [hoyo] pit; **fosa marina** ocean trough; **fosa séptica** septic tank.

fosfatar vt [fertilizar] to fertilize with phosphates.

fosfato sm phosphate.

fosforescencia sf phosphorescence.

fosforescente adj phosphorescent.

fósforo sm - **1.** QUÍM phosphorus - **2.** [cerilla] match.

fósil ◇ adj fossil (antes de s). ◇ sm - **1.** GEOL fossil - **2.** fam [viejo] old fossil.

fosilización sf fossilization.

fosilizarse [13] vprnl - **1.** GEOL to fossilize - **2.** fig [persona] to turn into an old fossil.

foso *sm* [hoyo] ditch; [de fortaleza] moat; [de garaje] pit; DEP & TEATRO pit.

foto *sf* photo, picture; **hacer** o **sacar** o **tomar una foto** to take a photo o picture; **foto de carné** passport photo.

fotocomponedora *sf* IMPR typesetter, typesetting machine.

fotocomponer *vt* IMPR to typeset.

fotocomposición *sf* IMPR typesetting.

fotocopia *sf* - **1.** [objeto] photocopy - **2.** [procedimiento] photocopying.

fotocopiadora *sf* photocopier.

fotocopiar [8] *vt* to photocopy.

fotoeléctrico, **ca** *adj* photoelectric.

fotofobia *sf* photophobia.

fotogenia *sf* photogenic qualities *pl*.

fotogénico, **ca** *adj* photogenic.

fotograbado *sm* photogravure.

fotografía *sf* - **1.** [arte] photography - **2.** [imagen] photograph; **hacer** o **sacar** o **tomar una fotografía** to take a photograph; **fotografía de carné** passport photograph.

fotografiar [9] *vt* to photograph, to take a photograph of.

fotográfico, **ca** *adj* photographic.

fotógrafo, **fa** *sm, f* photographer.

fotograma *sm* still.

fotolito *sm* photolithograph.

fotomatón *sm* passport photo machine.

fotometría *sf* photometry.

fotómetro *sm* light meter.

fotomodelo *smf* photographic model.

fotomontaje *sm* photomontage.

fotonovela *sf* photo story.

fotorrobot (*pl* **fotorrobots**) *sf* Identikit® picture.

fotosensible *adj* photosensitive.

fotosíntesis *sf inv* photosynthesis.

fotuto *sm* *Cuba* AUTO horn.

foulard = **fular**.

foxterrier [fokste'rrjer] *sm* fox terrier.

FP (*abrev de* **formación profesional**) *sf* *vocational training*.

frac (*pl* **fracs**) *sm* tails *pl*, dress coat.

fracasado, **da** ◇ *adj* failed. ◇ *sm, f* failure.

fracasar *vi*: **fracasar (en/como)** to fail (at/as).

fracaso *sm* failure; **todo fue un fracaso** the whole thing was a disaster; **fracaso escolar** school failure.

fracción *sf* - **1.** [gen] fraction; **en una fracción de segundo** in a split second; **fracción decimal** decimal fraction - **2.** POLÍT faction.

fraccionamiento *sm* - **1.** [división] division, breaking up - **2.** *Méx* [urbanización] housing estate.

fraccionar *vt* to divide, to break up.

fraccionario, **ria** *adj* fractional; **moneda fraccionaria** small change.

fractura *sf* fracture.

fracturarse *vprnl* to fracture.

fragancia *sf* fragrance.

fragante *adj* fragrant.

fraganti ➧ **in fraganti** *loc adv*: **coger a alguien in fraganti** to catch sb red-handed o in the act.

fragata *sf* frigate.

frágil *adj* [objeto] fragile; [persona] frail.

fragilidad *sf* [de objeto] fragility; [de persona] frailty.

fragmentación *sf* [rotura] fragmentation; [división] division.

fragmentar *vt* [romper] to fragment; [dividir] to divide.

fragmentario, **ria** *adj* [incompleto] fragmentary.

fragmento *sm* fragment, piece; [de obra] excerpt.

fragor *sm* [de batalla] clamour; [de trueno] crash.

fragua *sf* forge.

fraguar [45] ◇ *vt* - **1.** [forjar] to forge - **2.** *fig* [idear] to think up. ◇ *vi* to set, to harden.
➧ **fraguarse** *vprnl* to be in the offing.

fraile *sm* friar.

frambuesa *sf* raspberry.

francés, **esa** ◇ *adj* French. ◇ *sm, f* Frenchman (*f* Frenchwoman); **los franceses** the French; **marcharse** o **despedirse a la francesa** to leave without even saying goodbye.
➧ **francés** *sm* [lengua] French.

franchute, **ta** *sm, f despec* Frog.

Francia *n pr* France.

franciscano, **na** *adj* & *sm, f* Franciscan.

franco, **ca** ◇ *adj* - **1.** [sincero] frank, open; [directo] frank - **2.** [sin obstáculos, gastos] free - **3.** *C Sur* [de permiso]: **me dieron el día franco** they gave me the day off - **4.** HIST Frankish. ◇ *sm, f* HIST Frank.
➧ **franco** *sm* - **1.** [moneda] franc - **2.** [lengua] Frankish.

francófono, **na** ◇ *adj* francophone. ◇ *sm, f* Francophone.

francotirador, **ra** *sm, f* - **1.** MIL sniper - **2.** *fig* [rebelde] maverick.

franela *sf* flannel.

franja *sf* strip; [en bandera, uniforme] stripe; **franja horaria** time zone.

franquear *vt* - **1.** [paso, camino] to clear - **2.** [río, montaña etc] to negotiate, to cross - **3.** [correo] to frank.

franqueo *sm* postage.

franqueza *sf* - **1.** [sinceridad] frankness, openness - **2.** [confianza] familiarity.

franquicia *sf* exemption.

franquismo *sm*: **el franquismo** [régimen] the Franco regime; [doctrina] Franco's doctrine.

franquista ◇ *adj* pro-Franco. ◇ *smf* supporter of Franco.

frasco *sm* small bottle.

frase *sf* - **1.** [oración] sentence - **2.** [locución] expression; **frase hecha** [modismo] set phrase; [tópico] cliché.

fraternal *adj* brotherly, fraternal.

fraternidad, **fraternización** *sf* brotherhood, fraternity.

fraternizar [13] *vi* to get on like brothers.

fraterno, **na** *adj* brotherly, fraternal.

fratricida ◇ *adj* fratricidal. ◇ *smf* fratricide.

fratricidio *sm* fratricide.

fraude *sm* fraud; **fraude electoral** election O electoral fraud; **fraude fiscal** tax evasion.

fraudulento, **ta** *adj* fraudulent.

frazada *sf Amér* blanket; **frazada eléctrica** electric blanket.

frecuencia *sf* frequency; **con frecuencia** often; **alta/baja frecuencia** high/low frequency; **frecuencia modulada**, **modulación de frecuencia** frequency modulation.

frecuentación *sf* frequenting.

frecuentado, **da** *adj* popular.

frecuentar *vt* [lugar] to frequent; [persona] to see, to visit.

frecuente *adj* [reiterado] frequent; [habitual] common.

fregadero *sm* (kitchen) sink.

fregado, **da** *adj Andes, Méx & Ven fam* [persona - ser] annoying; [- estar]: **perdí las llaves, ¡estoy fregada!** I've lost my keys, I've had it!; [roto] bust.
➤ **fregado** *sm* - **1.** [lavado - gen] wash; [- frotando] scrub - **2.** *fam* [lío] mess; **meterse en un fregado** to get into a mess - **3.** *fam* [discusión] row, rumpus.

fregar [35] *vt* - **1.** [limpiar] to wash; **fregar los platos** to do the washing-up - **2.** [frotar] scrub - **3.** *Amér fam* [molestar] to bother, to pester - **4.** *Andes, Méx & Ven* [estropear]: **vas a fregar la televisión** you're going to bust the television.

fregona *sf* - **1.** *despec* [criada] skivvy - **2.** *despec* [mujer vulgar]: **es una fregona** she's as common as muck - **3.** [utensilio] mop; **pasar la fregona** to mop.

fregotear *vt* to give a quick wash O wipe.

fregué *etc* ▷ **fregar**.

freidora *sf* [gen] deep fat fryer; [para patatas fritas] chip pan.

freiduría *sf shop where fried food, especially fish, is cooked and served.*

freír [28] *vt* - **1.** CULIN to fry - **2.** *fam* [molestar]: **freír a alguien (a)** to pester sb (with) - **3.** *fam* [matar]: **freír a alguien (a tiros)** to gun sb down.
➤ **freírse** *vprnl* to be frying.

fréjol *sm Andes, Amér C & Méx* bean.

frenado *sm* braking.

frenar ◇ *vt* - **1.** AUTO to brake - **2.** [contener] to check. ◇ *vi* to stop; AUTO to brake.

frenazo *sm* - **1.** AUTO: **dar un frenazo** to brake hard - **2.** *fig* [parón] sudden stop.

frenesí (*pl* **frenesíes** O **frenesís**) *sm* frenzy.

frenético, **ca** *adj* - **1.** [colérico] furious, mad - **2.** [enloquecido] frenzied, frantic.

frenillo *sm* fraenum.

freno *sm* - **1.** AUTO brake; **freno automático** automatic brake; **freno de mano** handbrake; **frenos ABS** ABS brakes; **frenos de disco** disc brakes - **2.** [de caballerías] bit - **3.** *fig* [contención] check; **poner freno a** to put a stop to.

frente ◇ *sf* forehead; **arrugar la frente** to knit one's brow, to frown; **frente a frente** face to face; **con la frente muy alta** with one's head held high. ◇ *sm* front; **estar al frente (de)** to be at the head (of); **hacer frente a** to face up to; **frente cálido/frío** warm/cold front.
➤ **de frente** *loc adv* - **1.** [hacia delante] forwards - **2.** [uno contra otro] head on.
➤ **en frente** *loc adv* opposite.
➤ **en frente de** *loc adv* opposite.
➤ **frente a** *loc prep* - **1.** [enfrente de] opposite - **2.** [con relación a] towards.

fresa *sf* - **1.** [planta, fruto] strawberry - **2.** [herramienta - de dentista] drill; [- de orfebre etc] milling cutter.

fresco, **ca** ◇ *adj* - **1.** [gen] fresh; [temperatura] cool; [pintura, tinta] wet - **2.** [caradura] cheeky; **¡qué fresco!** what a nerve! - **3.** *loc*: **quedarse tan fresco** not to bat an eyelid. ◇ *sm, f* [caradura] cheeky person.

fresco *sm* - **1.** ARTE fresco; **al fresco** in fresco - **2.** [frescor] coolness; **hace fresco** it's chilly; **tomar el fresco** to get a breath of fresh air.

fresca *sf* [insolencia]: **soltarle una fresca** o **cuatro frescas a alguien** to tell sb a few home truths.

frescor *sm* coolness, freshness.

frescura *sf* - **1.** [gen] freshness - **2.** [descaro] cheek, nerve; **¡qué frescura!** what a cheek!

fresno *sm* ash (tree).

fresón *sm* large strawberry.

freudiano, na [froi'ðjano, na] *adj* Freudian.

fría ▷ freír.

frialdad *sf lit & fig* coldness.

fricativo, va *adj* fricative.

fricativa *sf* fricative.

fricción *sf* [gen] friction; [friega] rub, massage.

friccionar *vt* to rub, to massage.

fríe ▷ freír.

friega *sf* rub, massage; ▷ **fregar**.

friera *etc* ▷ freír.

frígida *adj f* frigid.

frigidez *sf* frigidity.

frigorífico, ca *adj* [camión] refrigerator *(antes de s)*; [cámara] cold.

frigorífico *sm* refrigerator, fridge *UK*, icebox *US*.

frijol, fríjol *sm Andes, Amér C, Caribe & Méx* bean.

frió ▷ freír.

frío, a *adj* [gen] cold; [inmutable] cool; **dejar a alguien frío** to leave sb cold.

frío *sm* cold; **coger frío** to catch a chill; **hace frío** it's cold; **hacer un frío que pela** to be freezing cold; **pelarse de frío** to be freezing to death; **tener frío** to be cold; **coger a alguien en frío** *fig* to catch sb on the hop; **no darle a alguien ni frío ni calor** *fig* to leave sb cold.

friolento, ta *Amér* ◇ *adj* sensitive to the cold. ◇ *sm, f*: **es un friolento** he really feels the cold.

friolero, ra ◇ *adj* sensitive to the cold. ◇ *sm, f* person who feels the cold.

friolera *sf fam*: **costó la friolera de 20.000 euros** it cost a cool 20,000 euros.

friso *sm* - **1.** ARQUIT frieze - **2.** [zócalo] skirting board.

fritada *sf* fry-up, dish of fried food.

frito, ta ◇ *pp* ▷ freír. ◇ *adj* - **1.** [alimento] fried - **2.** *fam fig* [persona - harta] fed up (to the back teeth); [- dormida] flaked out, asleep.

frito *(gen pl) sm* fried food *(U)*.

fritura *sf* fry-up, dish of fried food.

frivolidad *sf* frivolity.

frívolo, la *adj* frivolous.

frondosidad *sf* leafiness.

frondoso, sa *adj* leafy.

frontal *adj* frontal.

frontera *sf* border; *fig* [límite] bounds *pl*.

fronterizo, za *adj* border *(antes de s)*.

frontis *sm inv* façade.

frontispicio *sm* - **1.** [de edificio - fachada] façade; [- remate] pediment - **2.** [de libro] frontispiece.

frontón *sm* - **1.** [deporte] pelota; [cancha] pelota court - **2.** ARQUIT pediment.

frotamiento *sm* rubbing.

frotar *vt* to rub.

frotarse *vprnl*: **frotarse las manos** to rub one's hands.

fructífero, ra *adj* fruitful.

fructificar [10] *vi lit & fig* to bear fruit.

fructosa *sf* fructose.

frugal *adj* frugal.

frugalidad *sf* frugality.

fruición *sf* gusto, delight.

fruncir [12] *vt* - **1.** [labios] to purse; **fruncir el ceño** to frown - **2.** [tela] to gather.

fruslería *sf* triviality, trifle.

frustración *sf* frustration.

frustrado, da *adj* frustrated; [fracasado] failed.

frustrante *adj* frustrating.

frustrar *vt* - **1.** [persona] to frustrate - **2.** [posibilidades, ilusiones] to thwart, to put paid to.

frustrarse *vprnl* - **1.** [persona] to get frustrated - **2.** [ilusiones] to be thwarted; [proyecto] to fail.

fruta *sf* fruit; **fruta confitada** candied fruit; **fruta de la pasión** passion fruit; **fruta del tiempo** seasonal fruit.

frutal ◇ *adj* fruit *(antes de s)*. ◇ *sm* fruit tree.

frutería *sf* fruit shop.

frutero, ra ◇ *adj* fruit *(antes de s)*. ◇ *sm, f* [persona] fruiterer.

frutero *sm* [recipiente] fruit bowl.

fruticultura *sf* fruit farming.

frutilla *sf Bol, C Sur & Ecuad* strawberry.

fruto *sm* - **1.** [naranja, plátano etc] fruit; [nuez, avellana etc] nut; **frutos secos** dried fruit and nuts - **2.** [resultado] fruit; **dar fruto** to bear fruit; **sacar fruto a** o **de algo** to profit from sthg.

FSLN *sm (abrev de* **Frente Sandinista de Liberación Nacional)** SNLF.

fu ▷ **ni fu ni fa** *loc adv* so-so.

fucsia ◇ *sf* [planta] fuchsia. ◇ *adj inv* & *sm inv* [color] fuchsia.

fue ▷ ir. ▷ ser.

fuego *sm* **- 1.** [gen & MIL] fire; [de cocina, fogón] ring, burner; **a fuego lento/vivo** CULIN over a low/high heat; **abrir fuego** to open fire; **atizar el fuego** to poke the fire; **pegar fuego a algo** to set sthg on fire, to set fire to sthg; **pedir/dar fuego** to ask for/give a light; **¿tiene fuego?** have you got a light?; **fuego fatuo** will-o'-the-wisp; **fuegos artificiales** fireworks; **echar fuego por los ojos** to look daggers; **estar entre dos fuegos** to be between the devil and the deep blue sea; **jugar con fuego** to play with fire **- 2.** [apasionamiento] passion, ardour **- 3.** [sensación de ardor] heat, burning.

fuel, fuel-oil *sm* fuel oil.

fuelle *sm* **- 1.** [gen] bellows *pl* **- 2.** [de maleta, bolso] accordion pleats *pl* **- 3.** [entre vagones] connecting corridor, concertina vestibule.

fuel-oil = **fuel**.

fuente *sf* **- 1.** [manantial] spring **- 2.** [construcción] fountain **- 3.** [bandeja] (serving) dish **- 4.** [origen] source; **fuentes oficiales** official sources; **fuente de información/ingresos** source of information/income **- 5.** ELECTRÓN: **fuente de alimentación** feed source **- 6.**: **fuente de soda** *Caribe, Chile, Col & Méx* cafe.

fuera ◇ *adv* **- 1.** [en el exterior] outside; **le echó fuera** she threw him out; **hacia fuera** outwards; **por fuera** (on the) outside **- 2.** [en otro lugar] away; [en el extranjero] abroad; **de fuera** [extranjero] from abroad **- 3.** *fig* [alejado]: **fuera de** [alcance, peligro] out of; [cálculos, competencia] outside; **estar fuera de sí** to be beside o.s. (with rage) **- 4.** DEP: **fuera de banda** out of play; **fuera de combate** knocked out; *fig* out of action; **fuera de juego** offside. ◇ *interj*: ¡**fuera!** [gen] (get) out!; [en el teatro] (get) off!; ¡**fuera de aquí!** get out of my sight! ▷ ir. ▷ ser.

➤ **fuera de** *loc prep* [excepto] except for, apart from.

➤ **fuera de serie** ◇ *adj* exceptional, out of the ordinary. ◇ *smf*: **ser un fuera de serie** to be one of a kind.

fueraborda *sm inv* outboard motor o engine.

fuerce ▷ forzar.

fuero *sm* **- 1.** *(gen pl)* [ley local] *ancient regional law still existing in some parts of Spain* **- 2.** [jurisdicción] code of laws **- 3.** *loc*: **en el fuero interno de alguien** in sb's heart of hearts, deep down.

fuerte ◇ *adj* **- 1.** [gen] strong **- 2.** [carácter] strong **- 3.** [frío, dolor, color] intense; [lluvia] heavy; [ruido] loud; [golpe, pelea] hard **- 4.** [comida, salsa] rich **- 5.** [nudo] tight **- 6.** [grave]: **esto es fuerte** that's a bit much **- 7.**: **estar fuerte en algo** [suj: estudiante] to be good at sthg. ◇ *adv* **- 1.** [intensamente - gen] hard; [- abrazar,

agarrar] tight **- 2.** [abundantemente] a lot **- 3.** [en voz alta] loudly. ◇ *sm* **- 1.** [fortificación] fort **- 2.** [punto fuerte] strong point, forte.

fuerza *sf* **- 1.** [gen] strength; [violencia] force; [de sonido] loudness; [de dolor] intensity; **cobrar fuerza** to gather strength; **por fuerza** of necessity; **tener fuerza** to be strong; **tener fuerzas para** to have the strength to; **fuerza mayor** DER force majeure; [en seguros] act of God; **no llegué por un caso de fuerza mayor** I didn't make it due to circumstances beyond my control; **a fuerza de** by dint of; **a la fuerza** [contra la voluntad] by force; [por necesidad] of necessity; **por la fuerza** by force; **írsele a alguien la fuerza por la boca** to be all talk and no action, to be all mouth; **sacar fuerzas de flaqueza** to screw up one's courage; **fuerza bruta** brute force; **fuerza de voluntad** willpower **- 2.** FÍS & MIL force; **fuerza aérea** airforce; **fuerza disuasoria** deterrent; **fuerza de la gravedad** force of gravity; **fuerza motriz** [gen] motive power; *fig* driving force; **fuerzas armadas** armed forces; **fuerzas del orden público** police *pl*; **fuerzas de seguridad** security forces **- 3.** ELECTR power; **fuerza hidráulica** water power; ▷ forzar.

➤ **fuerzas** *sfpl* [grupo] forces.

fuese ▷ ir. ▷ ser.

fuga *sf* **- 1.** [huida] escape; **darse a la fuga** to take flight; **fuga de capitales** flight of capital; **fuga de cerebros** brain drain **- 2.** [escape] leak **- 3.** MÚS fugue.

fugacidad *sf* fleeting nature.

fugarse [16] *vprnl* to escape; **fugarse de casa** to run away from home; **fugarse con alguien** to run off with sb.

fugaz *adj* fleeting.

fugitivo, va ◇ *adj* **- 1.** [en fuga] fleeing **- 2.** [fugaz] fleeting. ◇ *sm, f* fugitive.

fugue *etc* ▷ fugarse.

fui ▷ ir. ▷ ser.

fulano, na *sm, f* what's his/her name, so-and-so.

➤ **fulana** *sf* [prostituta] tart, whore.

fular, foulard [fu'lar] *sm* headscarf.

fulero, ra ◇ *adj* **- 1.** [chapucero] shoddy **- 2.** [tramposo] dishonest. ◇ *sm, f* trickster.

fulgor *sm* shining; [de disparo] flash.

fulgurante *adj* **- 1.** [rápido] rapid **- 2.** [resplandeciente] flashing.

fulgurar *vi* to gleam; [intermitentemente] to flash.

fullero, ra ◇ *adj* cheating, dishonest. ◇ *sm, f* cheat.

fulminante *adj* **- 1.** *fig* [despido, muerte] sudden; [enfermedad] devastating; [mirada] withering **- 2.** [explosivo] fulminating.

fulminar *vt* [suj: enfermedad] to strike down; **un rayo la fulminó** she was struck by lightning; **fulminar a alguien con la mirada** to look daggers at sb.

fumador, **ra** *sm, f* smoker; **fumador empedernido** chain-smoker; **fumador pasivo** passive smoker; **no fumador** nonsmoker.

fumar *vt* & *vi* to smoke.

fumeta *smf fam* pot-head, pot smoker.

fumigación *sf* fumigation.

fumigador *sm* fumigator.

fumigar [16] *vt* to fumigate.

funámbulo, **la** *sm, f* tightrope walker.

función *sf* - **1.** [gen] function; [trabajo] duty; **director en funciones** acting director; **entrar en funciones** to take up one's duties - **2.** CINE & TEATRO show.

◆ **en función de** *loc prep* depending on.

funcional *adj* functional.

funcionalidad *sf* functional qualities *pl*.

funcionamiento *sm* operation, functioning; **entrar/estar en funcionamiento** to come into/be in operation; **poner algo en funcionamiento** to start sthg (working).

funcionar *vi* to work; **funcionar con gasolina** to run on petrol; **'no funciona'** 'out of order'.

funcionariado *sm* civil service.

funcionario, **ria** *sm, f* civil servant.

funda *sf* [de sofá, máquina de escribir] cover; [de almohada] case; [de disco] sleeve; [de pistola] sheath.

fundación *sf* foundation.

fundado, **da** *adj* well-founded.

fundador, **ra** ◇ *adj* founding. ◇ *sm, f* founder.

fundamentación *sf* foundation, basis.

fundamental *adj* fundamental.

fundamentalismo *sm* fundamentalism.

fundamentalista *adj* & *smf* fundamentalist; **fundamentalista islámico** Islamic fundamentalist.

fundamentar *vt* - **1.** *fig* [basar] to base - **2.** CONSTR to lay the foundations of.

◆ **fundamentarse en** *vprnl fig* [basarse] to be based o founded on.

fundamento *sm* - **1.** [base] foundation, basis - **2.** [razón] reason, grounds *pl*; **sin fundamento** unfounded, groundless.

◆ **fundamentos** *smpl* - **1.** [principios] basic principles - **2.** [cimientos] foundations.

fundar *vt* - **1.** [crear] to found - **2.** [basar]: **fundar (en)** to base (on).

◆ **fundarse** *vprnl* [basarse]: **fundarse (en)** to be based (on).

fundición *sf* - **1.** [fusión - de vidrio] melting; [- de metal] smelting - **2.** [taller] foundry.

fundido *sm* [apareciendo] fade-in; [desapareciendo] fade-out.

fundir *vt* - **1.** [metalurgia] [plomo] to melt; [hierro] to smelt - **2.** ELECTR to fuse; [bombilla, fusible] to blow - **3.** *fig* & COM to merge.

◆ **fundirse** *vprnl* - **1.** ELECTR to blow - **2.** [derretirse] to melt - **3.** *fig* & COM to merge - **4.** *Amér* [arruinarse] to go bust.

fúnebre *adj* funeral *(antes de s)*.

funeral *(gen pl) sm* funeral.

funerario, **ria** *adj* funeral *(antes de s)*.

◆ **funeraria** *sf* undertaker's *UK*, mortician's *US*.

funesto, **ta** *adj* fateful, disastrous.

fungir *vi Méx* & *Perú*: **fungir (de** o **como)** to act (as), to serve (as).

funicular ◇ *adj* funicular. ◇ *sm* - **1.** [por tierra] funicular - **2.** [por aire] cable car.

furcia *sf vulg* slag, whore.

furgón *sm* AUTO van; FERROC wagon, van; **furgón celular** o **policial** police van; **furgón de cola** guard's van *UK*, caboose *US*.

furgoneta *sf* van.

furia *sf* fury; **estar hecho una furia** to be furious; **ponerse hecho una furia** to fly into a rage.

furibundo, **da** *adj* furious.

furioso, **sa** *adj* furious.

furor *sm* - **1.** [enfado] fury, rage - **2.** [ímpetu] fever, urge - **3.** *loc*: **hacer furor** to be all the rage.

furtivo, **va** *adj* [mirada, sonrisa] furtive.

furúnculo = **forúnculo**.

fuselaje *sm* fuselage.

fusible ◇ *adj* fusible. ◇ *sm* fuse.

fusil *sm* rifle.

fusilamiento *sm* - **1.** [ejecución] execution by firing squad - **2.** *fam* [plagio] plagiarism.

fusilar *vt* - **1.** [ejecutar] to execute by firing squad, to shoot - **2.** *fam* [plagiar] to plagiarize.

fusión *sf* - **1.** [agrupación] merging - **2.** [de empresas, bancos] merger - **3.** [derretimiento] melting - **4.** FÍS fusion; **fusión nuclear** nuclear fusion.

fusionar ◇ *vt* - **1.** [gen & ECON] to merge - **2.** FÍS to fuse. ◇ *vi* to fuse.

◆ **fusionarse** *vprnl* ECON to merge.

fusta *sf* riding crop.

fustán *sm Amér* petticoat.

fuste *sm* shaft.

fustigar [16] *vt* - **1.** [azotar] to whip - **2.** [censurar] to criticize harshly.

fútbol, futbol *Amér C* & *Méx* ['fudbol] *sm* football, soccer *US*; **fútbol sala** indoor five-a-side.

futbolero, **ra** *adj* football-crazy.

futbolín *sm* table football.

futbolista *smf* footballer.

futbolístico, ca *adj* football *(antes de s)*.

fútil *adj* trivial.

futilidad *sf* triviality.

futón *sm* futon.

futurible *adj* potential.

futuro, ra ◇ *adj* future. ◇ *adv*: **a futuro** C *Sur & Méx* in the future.

➡ **futuro** *sm* [gen & GRAM] future; **en un futuro próximo** in the near future; **futuro perfecto** future perfect.

➡ **futuros** *smpl* ECON futures.

futurología *sf* futurology.

futurólogo, ga *sm, f* futurologist.

G

g¹, G *sf* [letra] g, G.

g² *(abrev de* **gramo***)* g.

g/ *abrev de* **giro**.

gabacho, cha *fam despec* ◇ *adj* Froggy. ◇ *sm, f* Frog.

gabán *sm* overcoat.

gabardina *sf* - **1.** [tela] gabardine - **2.** [prenda] raincoat, mac.

gabinete *sm* - **1.** [gobierno] cabinet - **2.** [despacho] office; **gabinete de prensa** press office - **3.** [sala] study.

gacela *sf* gazelle.

gaceta *sf* gazette.

gachas *sfpl* CULIN (corn) porridge *(U)*.

gachí *sf fam* bird, chick.

gacho, cha *adj* drooping.

gachó *sm fam* bloke *UK*, guy.

gaélico, ca *adj* Gaelic.

➡ **gaélico** *sm* [lengua] Gaelic.

gafar *vt fam* to jinx, to bring bad luck to.

gafas *sfpl* glasses; **gafas bifocales** bifocals; **gafas graduadas** prescription glasses; **gafas de sol** sunglasses; **gafas submarinas** [para submarinismo] diving mask; [para nadar] goggles.

gafe ◇ *adj* jinxed; **ser gafe** to be jinxed. ◇ *smf* jinxed person.

gag *sm inv* gag.

gaita *sf* - **1.** [instrumento] bagpipes *pl* - **2.** *fam* [pesadez] drag, pain.

gaitero, ra *sm, f* piper.

gajes *smpl*: **gajes del oficio** occupational hazards.

gajo *sm* - **1.** [trozo de fruta] segment - **2.** [racimo] bunch - **3.** [rama] broken-off branch.

gala *sf* - **1.** [fiesta] gala; **ropa/uniforme de gala** [ropa] full dress/uniform; **cena de gala** black tie dinner, formal dinner - **2.** [ropa]: **galas** finery *(U)*, best clothes - **3.** [actuación] show - **4.** *loc*: **hacer gala de algo** [preciarse] to be proud of sthg; [exhibir] to demonstrate sthg; **tener a gala algo** to be proud of sthg.

galáctico, ca *adj* galactic.

galaico, ca *adj culto* Galician.

galán *sm* - **1.** [hombre atractivo] attractive young man - **2.** TEATRO leading man, lead.

galante *adj* gallant.

galantear *vt* to court, to woo.

galanteo *sm* courting, wooing.

galantería *sf* - **1.** [cualidad] politeness - **2.** [acción] gallantry, compliment.

galápago *sm* turtle.

galardón *sm* award, prize.

galardonado, da *adj* award-winning, prize-winning.

galardonar *vt* to award a prize to.

galaxia *sf* galaxy.

galeón *sm* galleon.

galera *sf* galley.

galería *sf* - **1.** [gen] gallery; [corredor descubierto] verandah - **2.** [para cortinas] curtain rail - **3.** [vulgo] masses *pl*; **hacer algo para la galería** to play to the gallery.

➡ **galerías (comerciales)** *sfpl* shopping arcade *sing*.

galerna *sf* strong north-west wind.

Gales *n pr*: **(el país de) Gales** Wales.

galés, esa ◇ *adj* Welsh. ◇ *sm, f* Welshman *m* (Welshwoman *f*); **los galeses** the Welsh.

➡ **galés** *sm* [lengua] Welsh.

galgo *sm* greyhound; **¡échale un galgo!** you can forget it!

Galicia *n pr* Galicia.

galicismo *sm* gallicism.

galimatías *sm inv* [lenguaje] gibberish *(U)*; [lío] jumble.

gallardía *sf* - **1.** [valentía] bravery - **2.** [elegancia] elegance.

gallardo, da *adj* - **1.** [valiente] brave - **2.** [bien parecido] elegant.

gallear *vi* to strut about, to show off.

gallego, **ga** *adj* & *sm, f* - **1.** Galician - **2.** *C Sur fam* [español] *sometimes pejorative term used to refer to someone or something Spanish.*
➡ **gallego** *sm* [lengua] Galician.

Gallego

Gallego ("Galician") is one of Spain's official languages. It is spoken in the northwestern region of Galicia. Like Spanish and Catalan, it stems from Latin, and it has many similarities to modern Portuguese. For decades Galician was either banned outright or lacked official recognition, and as a consequence it was mainly spoken in rural areas. However, nowadays it is being promoted as the official language for use in education and public administration.

galleta *sf* - **1.** CULIN biscuit *UK*, cookie *US*; **galleta salada** cracker - **2.** *fam* [cachete] slap, smack.

gallina ◇ *sf* [ave] hen; **la gallina ciega** blind man's buff; **acostarse con las gallinas** to go to bed early; **estar como gallina en corral ajeno** to be like a fish out of water; **matar la gallina de los huevos de oro** to kill the goose that lays the golden eggs. ◇ *smf fam* [persona] chicken, coward.

gallináceo, **a** *adj* gallinaceous.

gallinero *sm* - **1.** [corral] henhouse - **2.** *fam* TEATRO gods *sing* - **3.** *fam* [alboroto] madhouse.

gallito *sm fig* cock of the walk.

gallo *sm* - **1.** [ave] cock *UK*, rooster *US*, cockerel; **gallo de pelea** fighting cock; **en menos que canta un gallo** *fam* in no time at all; **otro gallo cantaría** things would be very different - **2.** [al cantar] false note; [al hablar] squeak - **3.** [pez] John Dory - **4.** *fig* [mandón] cock of the walk.

galo, **la** ◇ *adj* HIST Gallic; [francés] French. ◇ *sm, f* [persona] Gaul.

galón *sm* - **1.** [adorno] braid; MIL stripe - **2.** [medida] gallon.

galopada *sf* gallop.

galopante *adj* galloping.

galopar *vi* to gallop.

galope *sm* gallop; **al galope** at a gallop; **a galope tendido** at full gallop.

galpón *sm* Andes, Caribe & R Plata shed.

galvanizar [13] *vt* to galvanize.

gama *sf* [gen] range; MÚS scale.

gamba *sf* prawn.

gamberrada *sf* act of vandalism.

gamberrismo *sm* vandalism; [en fútbol etc] hooliganism.

gamberro, **rra** ◇ *adj* loutish. ◇ *sm, f* vandal; [en fútbol etc] hooligan; **hacer el gamberro** to behave loutishly.

gameto *sm* gamete.

gamín *sm Col* child.

gamo *sm* fallow deer.

gamonal *sm Andes, Amér C & Ven* [cacique] village chief; [caudillo] cacique, local political boss.

gamuza *sf* - **1.** [tejido] chamois (leather); [trapo] duster - **2.** [animal] chamois.

gana *sf* - **1.** [afán]: **gana (de)** desire *o* wish (to); **de buena gana** willingly; **de mala gana** unwillingly; **me da/no me da la gana hacerlo** I damn well feel like/don't damn well feel like doing it - **2.** [apetito] appetite.
➡ **ganas** *sfpl* [deseo]: **tener ganas de algo/hacer algo**, **sentir ganas de algo/hacer algo** to feel like sthg/doing sthg; **no tengo ganas de que me pongan una multa** I don't fancy getting a fine; **morirse de ganas de hacer algo** to be dying to do sthg; **quedarse con ganas de hacer algo** not to manage to do sthg; **tenerle ganas a alguien** to have it in for sb.

ganadería *sf* - **1.** [actividad] livestock farming - **2.** [ganado] livestock - **3.** [lugar] livestock farm.

ganadero, **ra** ◇ *adj* livestock-farming *(antes de s)*; [industria] livestock *(antes de s)*. ◇ *sm, f* livestock farmer.

ganado *sm* livestock, stock; **ganado porcino** pigs *pl*; **ganado vacuno** cattle *pl*.

ganador, **ra** ◇ *adj* winning. ◇ *sm, f* winner.

ganancia *sf* [rendimiento] profit; [ingreso] earnings *pl*; **ganancias y pérdidas** profit and loss; **ganancia líquida** net profit.

ganancial ▷ **bien.**

ganar ◇ *vt* - **1.** [gen] to win; [sueldo, dinero] to earn; [peso, tiempo, terreno] to gain - **2.** [derrotar] to beat; **ganar a alguien a algo** to beat sb at sthg - **3.** [aventajar]: **ganar a alguien en algo** to be better than sb as regards sthg - **4.** [alcanzar - cima etc] to reach, to make it to - **5.** [conquistar - ciudad etc] to take, to capture. ◇ *vi* - **1.** [vencer] to win - **2.** [lograr dinero] to earn money - **3.** [mejorar]: **ganar (con)** to benefit (from); **ganar en algo** to gain in sthg.
➡ **ganarse** *vprnl* - **1.** [conquistar - simpatía, respeto] to earn; [- persona] to win over - **2.** [merecer] to deserve.

ganchillo *sm* [aguja] crochet hook; [labor] crochet; **hacer ganchillo** to crochet.

gancho *sm* - **1.** [gen] hook; [de percha] peg - **2.** Andes, Amér C, Méx & Ven [percha] hanger - **3.** [cómplice - de timador] decoy; [- de vendedor] person who attracts buyers - **4.** *fam* [atractivo] charm, sex appeal; **tener gancho** to have charm *o* sex appeal.

gandul, **la** *fam* ◇ *adj* lazy. ◇ *sm*, *f* lazybones, layabout.

gandulear *vi* to loaf around.

gandulería *sf* idleness.

ganga *sf fam* snip, bargain.

ganglio *sm* ganglion.

gangoso, **sa** *adj* nasal.

gangrena *sf* gangrene.

gangrenado, **da** *adj* gangrenous.

gangrenarse *vprnl* to become gangrenous.

gangrenoso, **sa** *adj* gangrenous.

gángster (*pl* gángsters) *sm* gangster.

gansada *sf fam* silly thing.

ganso, **sa** *sm*, *f* - **1.** [ave - hembra] goose; [- macho] gander - **2.** *fam* [persona] idiot, fool.

ganzúa *sf* picklock.

gañido *sm* yelp.

garabatear *vi* & *vt* to scribble.

garabato *sm* scribble; **hacer garabatos** to scribble.

garaje *sm* garage.

garante *smf* guarantor; **salir garante** to act as guarantor.

garantía *sf* - **1.** [gen] guarantee; **de garantía** reliable, dependable; **ser garantía de algo** to guarantee sthg; **garantías constitucionales** constitutional rights - **2.** [fianza] surety.

garantizado, **da** *adj* guaranteed.

garantizar [13] *vt* - **1.** [gen] to guarantee; **garantizar algo a alguien** to assure sb of sthg - **2.** [avalar] to vouch for.

garbanzo *sm* chickpea; **ser el garbanzo negro de la familia** to be the black sheep of the family.

garbeo *sm fam* stroll; **dar un garbeo** to go for *o* take a stroll.

garbo *sm* [de persona] grace; [de escritura] stylishness, style.

gardenia *sf* gardenia.

garduña *sf* marten.

garete *sm*: **ir** *o* **irse al garete** *fam* to come adrift.

garfio *sm* hook.

gargajo *sm* phlegm.

garganta *sf* - **1.** ANAT throat; **lo tengo atravesado en la garganta** *fig* he/it sticks in my gullet - **2.** [desfiladero] gorge.

gargantilla *sf* choker, necklace.

gárgara (*gen pl*) *sf* gargle, gargling (U); **hacer gárgaras** to gargle; **mandar a alguien a hacer gárgaras** *fam* to send sb packing; **¡vete a hacer gárgaras!** *fam* get lost!

garita *sf* [gen] cabin; [de conserje] porter's lodge; MIL sentry box.

garito *sm despec* [casa de juego] gambling den; [establecimiento] dive.

garra *sf* [de animal] claw; [de ave de rapiña] talon; *despec* [de persona] paw, hand; **caer en las garras de alguien** to fall into sb's clutches; **tener garra** [persona] to have charisma; [novela, canción etc] to be gripping.

garrafa *sf* carafe.

garrafal *adj* monumental, enormous.

garrafón *sm* demijohn.

garrapata *sf* tick.

garrapiñar *vt* [fruta] to candy; [almendras etc] to coat with sugar.

garrocha *sf* pike, lance.

garrotazo *sm* blow with a club *o* stick.

garrote *sm* - **1.** [palo] club, stick - **2.** [torniquete] tourniquet - **3.** [instrumento] garotte.

garúa *sf Andes, R Plata & Ven* drizzle.

garza *sf* heron; **garza real** grey heron.

gas *sm* gas; **con gas** [agua] sparkling, carbonated; [refresco] fizzy, carbonated; **gas ciudad/ natural** town/natural gas; **gas butano** butane (gas); **gas licuado de petróleo** liquified petroleum gas; **gas lacrimógeno** tear gas.
◆ **gases** *smpl* [en el estómago] wind (U).
◆ **a todo gas** *loc adv* flat out, at top speed.

gasa *sf* gauze.

gaseado, **da** *adj* gassed.

gasear *vt* to gas.

gaseoducto *sm* gas pipeline.

gaseoso, **sa** *adj* gaseous; [bebida] fizzy.
◆ **gaseosa** *sf* lemonade UK, soda US.

gasfitería *sf Chile, Ecuad & Perú* plumber's (shop).

gasfitero, **ra** *sm*, *f Chile, Ecuad & Perú* plumber.

gasificación *sf* gasification.

gasificar [10] *vt* to gasify; [bebida] to carbonate.

gasóleo *sm* diesel oil.

gasolina *sf* petrol UK, gas US; **poner gasolina** to fill up (with petrol).

gasolinera *sf* petrol station UK, gas station US.

gastado, **da** *adj* [ropa, pieza etc] worn out; [frase, tema] hackneyed; [persona] broken, burnt out.

gastar ◇ *vt* - **1.** [consumir - dinero, tiempo] to spend; [- gasolina, electricidad] to use (up); [- ropa, zapatos] to wear out - **2.** *fig* [usar - gen] to use; [- ropa] to wear; [- número de zapatos] to take; **gastar una broma (a alguien)** to play a joke (on sb) - **3.** [malgastar] to waste - **4.** *loc*: **gastar-**

las to carry on, to behave. ◇ *vi* - **1.** [despilfarrar] to spend (money) - **2.** [desgastar] to be wearing.

➤ **gastarse** *vprnl* - **1.** [deteriorarse] to wear out - **2.** [terminarse] to run out.

gasto *sm* [acción de gastar] outlay, expenditure; [cosa que pagar] expense; [de energía, gasolina] consumption; [despilfarro] waste; **cubrir gastos** to cover costs, to break even; **no reparar en gastos** to spare no expense; **gasto amortizable** ECON capitalized expense; **gasto deducible** ECON tax-deductible expense; **gasto público** public expenditure; **gastos de envío** postage and packing; **gastos fijos** COM fixed charges O costs; [en una casa] overheads; **gastos generales** overheads; **gastos de mantenimiento** maintenance costs; **gastos de representación** entertainment allowance *sing*.

gástrico, **ca** *adj* gastric.

gastritis *sf inv* gastritis.

gastroenteritis *sf inv* gastroenteritis.

gastrointestinal *adj* gastrointestinal.

gastronomía *sf* gastronomy.

gastronómico, **ca** *adj* gastronomic.

gastrónomo, **ma** *sm, f* gourmet, gastronome.

gatas ➤ **a gatas** *loc adv* on all fours.

gatear *vi* to crawl.

gatera *sf* cat flap O door.

gatillero *sm Amér* hired gunman.

gatillo *sm* trigger; **apretar el gatillo** to press O pull the trigger.

gato, **ta** *sm, f* cat; **gato montés** wildcat; **dar gato por liebre a alguien** to swindle O cheat sb; **buscar tres pies al gato** to overcomplicate matters; **jugar al gato y al ratón** to play cat and mouse; **llevarse el gato al agua** to pull it off; **sólo había cuatro gatos** there was hardly a soul there; **aquí hay gato encerrado** there's something fishy going on here; **el gato escaldado del agua fría huye** *prov* once bitten twice shy.

➤ **gato** *sm* AUTO jack.

GATT (*abrev de* General Agreement on Tariffs and Trade) *sm* GATT.

gatuno, **na** *adj* catlike, feline.

gauchada *sf C Sur* favour; **hacerle una gauchada a alguien** to do sb a favour.

gaucho, **cha** *adj R Dom* helpful, obliging.

➤ **gaucho** *sm* gaucho.

gavilán *sm* sparrowhawk.

gavilla *sf* sheaf.

gaviota *sf* seagull.

gay *adj inv* & *smf* gay (homosexual).

gazapo *sm* - **1.** [animal] young rabbit - **2.** [error] misprint.

gazmoño, **ña** *adj* sanctimonious.

gaznate *sm* gullet.

gazpacho *sm* gazpacho (Andalusian soup made from tomatoes, peppers, cucumbers and bread, served chilled).

GB ◇ *sf* (*abrev de* Gran Bretaña) GB. ◇ *sm* INFORM (*abrev de* **gigabyte**) GB.

géiser (*pl* géiseres), **géyser** (*pl* géyseres) *sm* geyser.

gel *sm* gel.

gelatina *sf* [de carne] gelatine; [de fruta] jelly.

gema *sf* gem.

gemelo, **la** ◇ *adj* twin (antes de s). ◇ *sm, f* [persona] twin.

➤ **gemelo** *sm* [músculo] calf.

➤ **gemelos** *smpl* - **1.** [de camisa] cufflinks - **2.** [prismáticos] binoculars; [para teatro] opera glasses.

gemido *sm* [de persona] moan, groan; [de animal] whine.

Géminis ◇ *sm* [zodiaco] Gemini; **ser Géminis** to be (a) Gemini. ◇ *smf* [persona] Gemini.

gemir [26] *vi* - **1.** [persona] to moan, to groan; [animal] to whine - **2.** [viento] to howl.

gen *sm* gene.

genealogía *sf* genealogy.

genealógico, **ca** *adj* genealogical.

generación *sf* generation; **generación espontánea** spontaneous generation, autogenesis.

generacional *adj* generation (antes de s).

generador, **ra** *adj* generating.

➤ **generador** *sm* generator.

general ◇ *adj* - **1.** [gen] general; **por lo general, en general** in general, generally - **2.** [usual] usual. ◇ *sm* MIL general; **general de brigada** brigadier UK, brigadier general US; **general de división** major general.

generalidad *sf* - **1.** [mayoría] majority - **2.** [vaguedad] generalization.

➤ **generalidades** *sfpl* [principios básicos] basic principles.

generalísimo *sm* supreme commander, generalissimo.

generalista *adj* [médico] general.

Generalitat [xenerali'tat] *sf autonomous government of Catalonia or Valencia*.

generalización *sf* - **1.** [comentario amplio] generalization - **2.** [extensión - de conflicto] escalation, widening; [- de prácticas, enseñanza] spread.

generalizar [13] ◇ *vt* to spread, to make widespread. ◇ *vi* to generalize.

➤ **generalizarse** *vprnl* to become widespread.

generalmente *adv* generally.

generar *vt* [gen] to generate; [engendrar] to create.

genérico, ca *adj* - **1.** [común] generic - **2.** GRAM gender *(antes de s)*.

género *sm* - **1.** [clase] kind, type - **2.** GRAM gender - **3.** LITER genre - **4.** BIOL genus; **el género humano** the human race - **5.** MÚS: **género chico** zarzuela, *Spanish light opera*; **género lírico** opera - **6.** [productos] merchandise, goods *pl* - **7.** [tejido] cloth, material; **géneros de punto** knitwear *(U)*.

generosidad *sf* generosity.

generoso, sa *adj* generous.

génesis *sf inv* genesis.
 Génesis *sm* Genesis.

genético, ca *adj* genetic.
 genética *sf* genetics *(U)*.

genial *adj* - **1.** [autor, compositor etc] of genius - **2.** [estupendo] brilliant, great.

genialidad *sf* - **1.** [capacidad] genius - **2.** [acción] stroke of genius.

genio *sm* - **1.** [talento] genius - **2.** [carácter] nature, disposition - **3.** [personalidad fuerte] spirit; **genio y figura hasta la sepultura** *prov* a true genius - **4.** [mal carácter] bad temper; **estar de/tener mal genio** to be in a mood/bad-tempered - **5.** [ser sobrenatural] genie.

genital *adj* genital.
 genitales *smpl* genitals.

genitivo *sm* genitive.

genocidio *sm* genocide.

genoma *sm* genome; **genoma humano** human genome.

genotipo *sm* genotype.

genovés, esa *adj* & *sm, f* Genoese.

gente *sf* - **1.** [gen] people *pl*; **gente bien** well-to-do people; **gente menuda** kids *pl* - **2.** *fam* [familia] folks *pl*.

gentil <> *adj* [amable] kind, nice. <> *smf* gentile.

gentileza *sf* courtesy, kindness; **¿tendría la gentileza de decirme...?** would you be so kind as to tell me?; **por gentileza de** by courtesy of.

gentilicio *sm* term referring to the natives or inhabitants of a particular place.

gentío *sm* crowd.

gentuza *sf* riffraff.

genuflexión *sf* genuflection; **hacer una genuflexión** to genuflect.

genuino, na *adj* genuine.

GEO (*abrev de* **Grupo Especial de Operaciones**) *sm specially trained police force*, ≃ SAS *UK*, ≃ SWAT *US*.

geofísico, ca <> *adj* geophysical. <> *sm, f* [persona] geophysicist.
 geofísica *sf* [ciencia] geophysics *(U)*.

geografía *sf* geography; *fig*: **varios puntos de la geografía nacional** several parts of the country; **geografía física** physical geography; **geografía política** political geography.

geográfico, ca *adj* geographical.

geógrafo, fa *sm, f* geographer.

geología *sf* geology.

geológico, ca *adj* geological.

geólogo, ga *sm, f* geologist.

geometría *sf* geometry; **geometría del espacio** solid geometry.

geométrico, ca *adj* geometric.

geopolítico, ca *adj* geopolitical.
 geopolítica *sf* geopolitics *(U)*.

georgiano, na *adj* & *sm, f* Georgian.
 georgiano *sm* [lengua] Georgian.

geranio *sm* geranium.

gerencia *sf* - **1.** [gen] management - **2.** [cargo] post of manager - **3.** [oficina] manager's office.

gerente *smf* manager, director.

geriatra *smf* geriatrician.

geriatría *sf* geriatrics *(U)*.

gerifalte *sm* - **1.** ZOOL gerfalcon - **2.** *fig* [persona] bigwig.

germánico, ca <> *adj* [gen] Germanic; [pueblos, carácter] Teutonic. <> *sm, f* [alemán] German; HIST Teuton.
 germánico *sm* [lengua] Germanic.

germano, na <> *adj* [gen] Germanic; [pueblos, carácter] Teutonic. <> *sm, f* [alemán] German; HIST Teuton.

germen *sm lit & fig* germ; **germen de trigo** wheatgerm.

germinación *sf* germination.

germinar *vi lit & fig* to germinate.

gerontología *sf* gerontology.

gerontólogo, ga *sm, f* gerontologist.

gerundio *sm* gerund.

gesta *sf* exploit, feat.

gestación *sf lit & fig* gestation.

gestar *vi* to gestate.
 gestarse *vprnl*: **se estaba gestando un cambio sin precedentes** the seeds of an unprecedented change had been sown.

gesticulación *sf* gesticulation; [de cara] face-pulling.

gesticular *vi* to gesticulate; [con la cara] to pull faces.

gestión *sf* - **1.** [diligencia] step, thing that has to be done; **tengo que hacer unas gestiones** I have a few things to do - **2.** [administración] management; **gestión de cartera** ECON portfolio management; **gestión de datos** INFORM data management; **gestión de ficheros** INFORM file management.

gestionar *vt* - **1.** [tramitar] to negotiate - **2.** [administrar] to manage.

gesto *sm* - **1.** [gen] gesture; **hacer gestos** to gesture, to gesticulate - **2.** [mueca] face, grimace; **torcer el gesto** to pull a face.

gestor, ra <> *adj* managing *(antes de s)*. <> *sm, f person who carries out dealings with public bodies on behalf of private customers or companies, combining the role of solicitor and accountant.*

gestoría *sf office of a 'gestor'.*

gestual *adj* using gestures.

géyser = **géiser.**

ghetto = **gueto.**

giba *sf* - **1.** [de camello] hump - **2.** [de persona] hunchback, hump.

Gibraltar *n pr* Gibraltar.

gibraltareño, ña *adj & sm, f* Gibraltarian.

gigabyte [xiɣa'βait] *sm* INFORM gigabyte.

gigahercio *sm* INFORM gigahertz.

gigante, ta *sm, f* giant.
➡ **gigante** *adj* gigantic.

gigantesco, ca *adj* gigantic.

gigoló [jiyo'lo] *sm* gigolo.

gil, gila *C Sur fam* <> *adj* stupid. <> *sm* jerk, twit UK.

gilipollada, jilipollada *sf fam:* **hacer/decir una gilipollada** to do/say sthg bloody stupid.

gilipollas, jilipollas *fam* <> *adj inv* daft, dumb US. <> *smf inv* pillock, prat.

gilipollez, jilipollez *sf inv fam:* **hacer/decir una gilipollez** to do/say sthg bloody stupid.

gima, gimiera *etc* ⊳ **gemir.**

gimnasia *sf* [deporte] gymnastics *(U)*; [ejercicio] gymnastics *pl*; **gimnasia correctiva** o **médica** o **terapéutica** physiotherapeutic exercises *pl*; **gimnasia deportiva** gymnastics *(U)*; **gimnasia rítmica** rhythmic gymnastics *(U)*; **gimnasia sueca** free exercise, callisthenics *(U)*; **confundir la gimnasia con la magnesia** to get the wrong end of the stick.

gimnasio *sm* gymnasium.

gimnasta *smf* gymnast.

gimnástico, ca *adj* gymnastic.

gimotear *vi* to whine, to whimper.

gimoteo *sm* whining, whimpering.

gin [ʝin] ➡ **gin tonic** *sm* gin and tonic.

gincana, gymkhana [jin'kana] *sf* [de caballos] gymkhana; [de automóviles] rally.

ginebra *sf* gin.

ginecología *sf* gynaecology.

ginecológico, ca *adj* gynaecological.

ginecólogo, ga *sm, f* gynaecologist.

gingivitis *sf inv* gingivitis.

gira *sf* tour.

giralda *sf* weather vane.

girar <> *vi* - **1.** [dar vueltas, torcer] to turn; [rápidamente] to spin - **2.** *fig* [centrarse]: **girar en torno a** o **alrededor de** to be centred around, to centre on - **3.** COM to remit payment. <> *vt* - **1.** [hacer dar vueltas a] to turn; [rápidamente] to spin - **2.** COM to draw - **3.** [dinero - por correo, telégrafo] to transfer, to remit.

girasol *sm* sunflower.

giratorio, ria *adj* revolving; [silla] swivel *(antes de s).*

giro *sm* - **1.** [gen] turn; **giro de 180 grados** *lit & fig* U-turn - **2.** [postal, telegráfico] money order; **giro postal** postal order - **3.** [de letras, órdenes de pago] draft; **giro en descubierto** overdraft - **4.** [expresión] turn of phrase.

gis *sm* Méx chalk.

gitano, na <> *adj* gypsy *(antes de s)*; *fig* wily, crafty. <> *sm, f* gypsy.

glaciación *sf* glaciation.

glacial *adj* glacial; [viento, acogida] icy.

glaciar <> *adj* glacial. <> *sm* glacier.

gladiador *sm* gladiator.

gladiolo, gladíolo *sm* gladiolus.

glande *sm* glans penis.

glándula *sf* gland; **glándula endocrina** endocrine gland; **glándula sebácea** sebaceous gland.

glasé <> *adj* glacé. <> *sm* glacé silk.

glaseado, da *adj* glacé.
➡ **glaseado** *sm* glazing.

glasear *vt* to glaze.

gleba *sf* feudal land.

glicerina *sf* glycerine.

global *adj* global, overall.

globalización *sf* globalization.

globalizar [13] *vt* to globalize.

globo *sm* - **1.** [Tierra] globe, earth; **globo terráqueo** o **terrestre** globe - **2.** [aeróstato, juguete] balloon; **globo sonda** weather balloon - **3.** [lámpara] round glass lampshade - **4.** [esfera] sphere; **globo ocular** eyeball.

globulina *sf* globulin.

glóbulo *sm* MED corpuscle; **glóbulo blanco/ rojo** white/red corpuscle.

gloria *sf* - **1.** [gen] glory - **2.** [celebridad] celebrity, star; **ser una vieja gloria** to be a has-been - **3.** [placer] delight; **estar en la gloria** to be in seventh heaven; **saber a gloria** to taste divine o heavenly.

glorieta *sf* - **1.** [de casa, jardín] arbour - **2.** [plaza - gen] square; [- redonda] circus, roundabout *UK*, traffic circle *US*.

glorificación *sf* glorification.

glorificar [10] *vt* to glorify.

glorioso, sa *adj* - **1.** [importante] glorious - **2.** RELIG Blessed.

glosa *sf* marginal note.

glosar *vt* - **1.** [anotar] to annotate - **2.** [comentar] to comment on.

glosario *sm* glossary.

glotis *sf inv* glottis.

glotón, ona ◇ *adj* gluttonous, greedy. ◇ *sm, f* glutton.

glotonería *sf* gluttony, greed.

glucemia *sf* glycaemia.

glúcido *sm* carbohydrate.

glucosa *sf* glucose.

gluglú *sm* glug-glug.

gluten *sm* gluten.

glúteo, a *adj* gluteal.
◆ **glúteo** *sm* gluteus.

gnomo, nomo *sm* gnome.

gobernabilidad *sf* governability.

gobernable *adj* governable.

gobernación *sf* - **1.** governing - **2.** *Méx*: **Ministerio de la Gobernación** Home Office *UK*, Department of the Interior *US*.

gobernador, ra ◇ *adj* governing *(antes de s)*. ◇ *sm, f* governor.

gobernanta *sf* cleaning and laundry staff manageress.

gobernante ◇ *adj* ruling *(antes de s)*. ◇ *smf* ruler, leader.

gobernar [19] ◇ *vt* - **1.** [gen] to govern, to rule; [casa, negocio] to run, to manage - **2.** [barco] to steer; [avión] to fly. ◇ *vi* NÁUT to steer.

gobierno *sm* - **1.** [gen] government; **gobierno autónomo/central** autonomous/central government; **gobierno militar** military command; **gobierno de transición** caretaker o interim government - **2.** [edificio] government buildings *pl* - **3.** [administración, gestión] running, management - **4.** [control] control.

goce *sm* pleasure; ⊳ **gozar**.

godo, da ◇ *adj* Gothic. ◇ *sm, f* - **1.** HIST Goth - **2.** *despec* [español peninsular] *pejorative term for a mainland Spaniard*.

gol *(pl* **goles)** *sm* goal; **marcar** o **meter un gol** to score a goal; **gol del empate** equalizer; **gol de penalti** penalty goal; **gol en propia meta** own goal; **meter un gol a alguien** to put one over on sb.

goleada *sf* high score, cricket score.

goleador, ra *sm, f* goalscorer.

golear *vt* to score a lot of goals against, to thrash.

goleta *sf* schooner.

golf *sm* golf.

golfa ⊳ **golfo**.

golfante *smf* scoundrel, rascal.

golfear *vi fam* [vaguear] to loaf around.

golfería *sf* - **1.** [golfos] layabouts *pl*, good-for-nothings *pl* - **2.** [granujada] loutish behaviour *(U)*.

golfista *smf* golfer.

golfo, fa ◇ *adj* [gamberro] loutish; [vago] idle. ◇ *sm, f* [gamberro] lout; [vago] layabout.
◆ **golfo** *sm* GEOGR gulf, bay.
◆ **golfa** *sf mfam* [prostituta] tart, whore, hooker *US*.
◆ **Golfo Pérsico** *sm*: **el Golfo Pérsico** the Persian Gulf.

golondrina *sf* - **1.** [ave] swallow - **2.** [barco] motor launch.

golondrino *sm* - **1.** MED boil in the armpit - **2.** ZOOL young swallow.

golosina *sf* [dulce] sweet; [exquisitez] titbit, delicacy.

goloso, sa ◇ *adj* sweet-toothed. ◇ *sm, f* sweet-toothed person.

golpe *sm* - **1.** [gen] blow; [bofetada] smack; [con puño] punch; [en puerta etc] knock; [en tenis, golf] shot; [entre coches] bump, collision; **a golpes** by force; *fig* in fits and starts; **moler a alguien a golpes** to beat sb up; **un golpe bajo** *fig* & DEP a blow below the belt; **golpe de castigo** [en rugby] penalty (kick); **golpe franco** free kick; **golpe de tos** coughing fit; **golpe de viento** gust of wind - **2.** [disgusto] blow - **3.** [atraco] raid, job, heist *US* - **4.** POLÍT: **golpe (de Estado)** coup (d'état) - **5.** [ocurrencia] witticism - **6.** *loc*: **dar el golpe** *fam* to cause a sensation, to be a hit; **errar** o **fallar el golpe** to miss the mark; **no dar** o **pegar golpe** not to lift a finger, not to do a stroke of work.
◆ **de golpe** *loc adv* suddenly.
◆ **de golpe y porrazo** *loc adv* without warning, just like that.
◆ **de un golpe** *loc adv* at one fell swoop, all at once.
◆ **golpe de gracia** *sm* coup de grâce.
◆ **golpe maestro** *sm* masterstroke.

◆ **golpe de suerte** *sm* stroke of luck.

◆ **golpe de vista** *sm* glance; **al primer golpe de vista** at a glance.

golpear *vt & vi* [gen] to hit; [puerta] to bang; [con puño] to punch.

golpeteo *sm* [de dedos, lluvia] drumming; [de puerta, persiana] banging.

golpista ◇ *adj* in favour of military coups. ◇ *smf* person involved in military coup.

golpiza *sf* *Amér* beating.

goma *sf* **- 1.** [sustancia viscosa, pegajosa] gum; **goma arábiga** gum arabic; **goma de mascar** chewing gum; **goma de pegar** glue, gum **- 2.** [tira elástica] rubber band, elastic band *UK*; **goma elástica** elastic **- 3.** [caucho] rubber; **goma espuma** foam rubber; **goma de borrar** rubber *UK*, eraser *US* **- 4.** *Cuba & C Sur* [neumático] tyre *UK*, tire *US* **- 5.** *fam* [preservativo] condom, rubber *US* **- 6.** *Amér C* [fam] [resaca] hangover.

◆ **Goma 2** *sf* plastic explosive.

gomero *sm* *Andes & R Dom* **- 1.** [persona] rubber plantation worker **- 2.** [árbol] rubber tree.

gomina *sf* hair gel.

gomoso, sa *adj* gummy.

gónada *sf* gonad.

góndola *sf* **- 1.** [embarcación] gondola **- 2.** *Chile* [autobús] bus.

gondolero *sm* gondolier.

gong *sm inv* gong.

gonorrea *sf* gonorrhoea.

gordinflón, ona ◇ *adj* chubby, tubby. ◇ *sm, f* fatty.

gordo, da ◇ *adj* **- 1.** [persona] fat; **me cae gordo** I can't stand him **- 2.** [grueso] thick **- 3.** [grande] big **- 4.** [grave] big, serious. ◇ *sm, f* **- 1.** [persona obesa] fat man (*f* fat woman); **armar la gorda** *fig* to kick up a row *o* stink **- 2.** *Amér* [querido] sweetheart, darling **- 3.** *Amér* [como apelativo]: **¿cómo estás, gordo?** hey, how's it going?

◆ **gordo** *sm* [en lotería] first prize, jackpot; **el gordo** *first prize in the Spanish national lottery*.

gordura *sf* fatness.

gorgorito *sm* warble.

gorgoteo *sm* gurgle, gurgling (U).

gorila *sm* **- 1.** ZOOL gorilla **- 2.** [guardaespaldas] bodyguard **- 3.** [en discoteca etc] bouncer.

gorjear *vi* to chirp, to twitter.

gorjeo *sm* chirping, twittering.

gorra *sf* (peaked) cap; **de gorra** for free; **vivir de gorra** to scrounge.

gorrear = **gorronear**.

gorrinada *sf* **- 1.** [guarrada - acción] disgusting behaviour *(U)*; [- lugar] pigsty **- 2.** [mala pasada] dirty trick.

gorrino, na *sm, f* *lit & fig* pig.

gorrión *sm* sparrow.

gorro *sm* [gen] cap; [de niño] bonnet; **gorro de baño** [para ducha] shower cap; [para piscina] swimming cap; **estar hasta el gorro (de)** *fam* to be fed up (with).

gorrón, ona *fam* ◇ *adj* sponging, scrounging. ◇ *sm, f* sponger, scrounger.

gorronear, gorrear *vt & vi* *fam* to sponge, to scrounge.

gorronería *sf* sponging, scrounging.

gota *sf* **- 1.** [de agua, leche, sangre] drop; [de sudor] bead; **caer cuatro gotas** to spit (with rain); **la gota que colma el vaso** the last straw, the straw that breaks the camel's back; **parecerse como dos gotas de agua** to be as like as two peas in a pod; **sudar la gota gorda** to sweat blood, to work very hard **- 2.** [cantidad pequeña]: **una gota de** a (tiny) drop of; **ni gota: no se veía ni gota** you couldn't see a thing; **no tienes ni gota de sentido común** you haven't got an ounce of common sense **- 3.** [enfermedad] gout.

◆ **gotas** *sfpl* [medicamento] drops.

◆ **gota a gota** *sm* MED intravenous drip.

◆ **gota fría** *sf* METEOR *cold front that remains in one place for some time, causing continuous heavy rain*.

gotear ◇ *vi* [líquido] to drip; [techo, depósito etc] to leak; *fig* to trickle through. ◇ *v impers* [chispear] to spit, to drizzle.

goteo *sm* dripping.

gotera *sf* **- 1.** [filtración] leak **- 2.** [mancha] stain *(left by leaking water)*.

gótico, ca *adj* Gothic.

◆ **gótico** *sm* [arte] Gothic.

gourmet = **gurmet**.

goyesco, ca *adj* relating to *o* like Goya.

gozada *sf* *fam*: **es una gozada** it's wonderful.

gozar [13] *vi* to enjoy o.s.; **gozar de algo** to enjoy sthg; **gozar con** to take delight in.

gozne *sm* hinge.

gozo *sm* joy, pleasure; **mi gozo en un pozo** that's just my (bad) luck.

g/p, g.p. (*abrev de* **giro postal**) p.o.

grabación *sf* recording; **grabación digital** digital recording; **grabación en vídeo** video recording.

grabado *sm* **- 1.** [gen] engraving; [en madera] carving **- 2.** [en papel - acción] printing; [- lámina] print.

grabador, **ra** ◇ adj [gen] engraving; [en papel] printing. ◇ sm, f [gen] engraver; [en madera] carver; [en papel] printer.

➤ **grabadora** sf [casete] tape recorder; **grabadora de CD** CD burner; **grabadora de DVD** DVD recorder.

grabar vt - **1.** [gen] to engrave; [en madera] to carve; [en papel] to print; **grabado en su memoria** engraved on his mind - **2.** [sonido, cinta] to record, to tape - **3.** INFORM to save.

➤ **grabarse en** vprnl fig: **grabársele a alguien en la memoria** to become engraved on sb's mind.

gracia sf - **1.** [humor, comicidad] humour; **hacer gracia a alguien** to amuse sb; **no me hizo gracia** I didn't find it funny; **¡maldita la gracia!** it's not a bit funny!; **¡qué gracia!** how funny!; **tener gracia** [ser divertido] to be funny; **tiene gracia** [es curioso] it's funny; **caer en gracia** to be liked - **2.** [arte, habilidad] skill, natural ability - **3.** [encanto] grace, elegance - **4.** [chiste] joke; **hacer una gracia a alguien** to play a prank on sb; **no le rías las gracias** don't laugh when he says something silly - **5.** [favor] favour; [indulto] pardon.

➤ **gracias** sfpl thank you, thanks; **gracias a** thanks to; **gracia a Dios** thank God; **dar las gracias a alguien (por)** to thank sb (for); **muchas gracias** thank you, thanks very much.

grácil adj [gen] graceful; [delicado] delicate.

gracioso, **sa** ◇ adj [divertido] funny, amusing; **¡qué gracioso!** how funny!; **es gracioso que...** it's funny how... ◇ sm, f comedian; **hacerse el gracioso** to try to be funny.

grada sf - **1.** [peldaño] step - **2.** TEATRO row.

➤ **gradas** sfpl DEP terraces.

gradación sf - **1.** [en retórica] climax - **2.** [escalonamiento] scale.

gradería sf = **graderío**.

graderío sm TEATRO rows pl; DEP terraces pl.

grado sm - **1.** [gen] degree; **grado centígrado** degree centigrade - **2.** [fase] stage, level; [índice, nivel] extent, level; **en grado sumo** greatly - **3.** [rango - gen] grade; MIL rank - **4.** EDUC year, class, grade US - **5.** [voluntad]: **hacer algo de buen/mal grado** to do sthg willingly/unwillingly.

graduable adj adjustable.

graduación sf - **1.** [acción] grading; [de la vista] eye-test - **2.** EDUC graduation - **3.** [de bebidas] strength, ≈ proof - **4.** MIL rank.

graduado, **da** ◇ adj - **1.** [termómetro etc] graded - **2.** [universitario] graduate. ◇ sm, f [persona] graduate.

➤ **graduado** sm [título - gen] certificate; [- universitario] degree; **graduado escolar** qualification received on completing primary school.

gradual adj gradual.

graduar [6] vt - **1.** [medir] to gauge, to measure; [regular] to regulate; [vista] to test - **2.** [escalonar] to stagger - **3.** EDUC to confer a degree on - **4.** MIL to confer a rank on, to commission.

➤ **graduarse** vprnl: **graduarse (en)** to graduate (in).

grafía sf written symbol.

gráfico, **ca** adj graphic.

➤ **gráfico** sm [gráfica] graph, chart; [dibujo] diagram; **gráfico de barras** bar chart.

➤ **gráfica** sf graph, chart.

grafismo sm - **1.** [diseño gráfico] graphics (U) - **2.** ARTE graphic art.

grafista smf graphic artist O designer.

grafito sm graphite.

grafología sf graphology.

grafólogo, **ga** sm, f graphologist.

gragea sf - **1.** MED pill, tablet - **2.** [confite] sugar-coated sweet.

grajo sm rook.

gral. (abrev de **general**) gen.

gramática ▷ **gramático**.

gramatical adj grammatical.

gramático, **ca** ◇ adj grammatical. ◇ sm, f [persona] grammarian.

➤ **gramática** sf [disciplina, libro] grammar.

➤ **gramática parda** sf native wit.

gramo sm gram.

gramófono sm gramophone.

gramola sf gramophone.

grampa sf Amér staple.

gran ▷ **grande**.

granada sf - **1.** [fruta] pomegranate - **2.** [proyectil] grenade; **granada de mano** hand grenade.

granar vi to seed.

granate ◇ sm garnet. ◇ adj inv garnet-coloured.

Gran Bretaña sf Great Britain.

grande ◇ adj (antes de s) - **1.** [de tamaño] big, large; [de altura] tall; [de intensidad, importancia] great; **un hombre grande** a big man; **un gran hombre** a great man; **este traje me está grande** this suit is too big for me - **2.** R Dom [fantástico] great - **3.** R Dom [divertido] amusing - **4.** loc: **hacer algo a lo grande** to do sthg in style; **pasarlo en grande** fam to have a great time; **vivir a lo grande** to live in style. ◇ sm [noble] grandee.

➤ **grandes** smpl [adultos] grown-ups, adults.

➤ **a lo grande** loc adv in a big way, in style.

➤ **en grande** loc adv on a large scale.

grandeza *sf* - **1.** [de tamaño] (great) size - **2.** [de sentimientos] generosity, graciousness - **3.** [aristocracia] aristocracy, nobility.

grandilocuencia *sf* grandiloquence.

grandilocuente *adj* grandiloquent.

grandiosidad *sf* grandeur.

grandioso, sa *adj* grand, splendid.

grandullón, ona ◇ *adj* overgrown. ◇ *sm, f* big boy (*f* big girl).

granel ➡ **a granel** *loc adv* - **1.** [sin envase - gen] loose; [- en gran cantidad] in bulk - **2.** [sin orden] any old how, in a rough and ready manner - **3.** [en abundancia] in abundance.

granero *sm* granary.

granito *sm* granite.

granizada *sf* - **1.** METEOR hailstorm - **2.** *fig* [abundancia] hail, shower.

granizado *sm* iced drink.

granizar [13] *v impers* to hail.

granizo *sm* hail.

granja *sf* farm; **granja avícola** chicken *o* poultry farm.

granjearse *vprnl* to gain, to earn.

granjero, ra *sm, f* farmer.

grano *sm* - **1.** [semilla - de cereales] grain; **grano de café** coffee bean; **grano de pimienta** peppercorn - **2.** [partícula] grain - **3.** [en la piel] spot, pimple - **4.** *loc*: **apartar el grano de la paja** to separate the wheat from the chaff; **aportar** *o* **poner uno su grano de arena** to do one's bit; **ir al grano** to get to the point.

granuja *smf* [pillo] rogue, scoundrel; [canalla] trickster, swindler.

granujada *sf* dirty trick.

granulado, da *adj* granulated.

➡ **granulado** *sm* granules *pl*.

granuloso, sa *adj* bumpy.

grapa *sf* - **1.** [para papeles etc] staple; [para heridas] stitch, (wire) suture - **2.** *C Sur* [bebida] grappa.

grapadora *sf* stapler.

grapar *vt* to staple.

grasa *sf* ▷ **graso**.

grasiento, ta *adj* greasy.

graso, sa *adj* [gen] greasy; [con alto contenido en grasas] fatty.

➡ **grasa** *sf* - **1.** [en comestibles] fat; [de cerdo] lard; **grasa animal** animal fat; **grasa saturada** saturated fat; **grasa vegetal** vegetable fat - **2.** [lubricante] grease, oil - **3.** [suciedad] grease.

gratén *sm* gratin; **al gratén** au gratin.

gratificación *sf* - **1.** [moral] reward - **2.** [monetaria] bonus.

gratificante *adj* rewarding.

gratificar [10] *vt* [complacer] to reward; [retribuir] to give a bonus to; [dar propina a] to tip.

gratinado, da *adj* au gratin.

➡ **gratinado** *sm* gratin.

gratinar *vt* to cook au gratin.

gratis *adv* [sin dinero] free, for nothing; [sin esfuerzo] for nothing.

gratitud *sf* gratitude.

grato, ta *adj* pleasant; **nos es grato comunicarle que...** we are pleased to inform you that...

gratuito, ta *adj* - **1.** [sin dinero] free - **2.** [arbitrario] gratuitous; [infundado] unfair, uncalled for.

grava *sf* gravel.

gravamen *sm* - **1.** [impuesto] tax - **2.** [obligación moral] burden.

gravar *vt* - **1.** [con impuestos] to tax - **2.** [agravar] to worsen.

grave *adj* - **1.** [gen] serious; [estilo] formal; **estar grave** to be seriously ill - **2.** [sonido, voz] low, deep - **3.** [GRAM - acento prosódico] *with the stress on the penultimate syllable*; [- tilde] grave.

gravedad *sf* - **1.** [cualidad] seriousness - **2.** FÍS gravity.

gravilla *sf* gravel.

gravitación *sf* gravitation.

gravitar *vi* to gravitate; *fig* [pender]: **gravitar sobre** to hang *o* loom over.

gravoso, sa *adj* burdensome; [costoso] expensive, costly.

graznar *vi* [cuervo] to caw; [ganso] to honk; [pato] to quack; [persona] to squawk.

graznido *sm* [de cuervo] caw, cawing *(U)*; [de ganso] honk, honking *(U)*; [de pato] quack, quacking *(U)*; [de personas] squawk, squawking *(U)*.

Grecia *n pr* Greece.

grecorromano, na *adj* Greco-Roman.

gregario, ria *adj* [animal] gregarious; [persona] incapable of independent thought.

gregoriano, na *adj* Gregorian.

gremial *adj* [gen] (trade) union *(antes de s)*; HIST guild *(antes de s)*.

gremialismo *sm* trade unionism.

gremio *sm* - **1.** [sindicato] (trade) union; [profesión] profession, trade; HIST guild; **ser del gremio** to be in the trade - **2.** *fam* [grupo] league, club.

greña *(gen pl)* *sf* tangle of hair; **andar a la greña (con alguien)** to be at daggers drawn (with sb).

gres *sm* stoneware.

gresca *sf* row.

griego, ga *adj* & *sm, f* Greek.
→ **griego** *sm* [lengua] Greek.

grieta *sf* crack; [entre montañas] crevice; [que deja pasar luz] chink.

grifa *sf fam* marijuana.

grifería *sf* taps *pl*, plumbing.

grifero, ra *sm, f Perú* petrol pump attendant *UK*, gas pump attendant *US*.

grifo *sm* - **1.** [llave] tap *UK*, faucet *US*; **grifo monomando** mixer tap - **2.** *Perú* [gasolinera] petrol station *UK*, gas station *US*.

grillado, da *adj fam* crazy, loopy.

grillete *sm* shackle.

grillo *sm* cricket.

grima *sf* - **1.** [disgusto] annoyance; **dar grima** to get on one's nerves - **2.** [dentera]: **dar grima** to set one's teeth on edge.

gringo, ga ◇ *adj despec Esp* [estadounidense] gringo, Yankee; *Amér* [extranjero] gringo, foreign. ◇ *sm, f Esp* [estadounidense] gringo, Yank; *Amér* [extranjero] gringo, foreigner.

gripa *sf Col & Méx* flu.

gripe *sf* flu.

griposo, sa *adj* fluey.

gris ◇ *adj* [color] grey; [triste] gloomy, miserable. ◇ *sm* grey; **gris marengo** dark grey; **gris perla** pearl grey.

grisáceo, a *adj* greyish.

grisú (*pl* grisúes *o* grisús) *sm* firedamp.

gritar ◇ *vi* [hablar alto] to shout; [chillar] to scream, to yell. ◇ *vt*: **gritar (algo) a alguien** to shout (sthg) at sb.

griterío *sm* screaming, shouting.

grito *sm* [gen] shout; [de dolor, miedo] cry, scream; [de sorpresa, de animal] cry; **dar** *o* **pegar un grito** to shout *o* scream (out); **a grito limpio** *o* **pelado** at the top of one's voice; **pedir algo a gritos** *fig* to be crying out for sthg; **poner el grito en el cielo** to hit the roof; **ser el último grito** to be the latest fashion *o* craze, to be the in thing.

Groenlandia *n pr* Greenland.

grogui *adj lit & fig* groggy.

grosella *sf* redcurrant; **grosella negra** blackcurrant; **grosella silvestre** gooseberry.

grosería *sf* [cualidad] rudeness; [acción] rude thing; [palabrota] swear word.

grosero, ra ◇ *adj* - **1.** [maleducado] rude, crude - **2.** [tosco] coarse, rough. ◇ *sm, f* rude person.

grosor *sm* thickness.

grotesco, ca *adj* grotesque.

grúa *sf* - **1.** *CONSTR* crane - **2.** *AUTO* breakdown truck - **3.** [de la policía] tow truck.

grueso, sa *adj* - **1.** [espeso] thick - **2.** [corpulento] thickset; [obeso] fat - **3.** [grande] large, big - **4.** [mar] stormy.
→ **grueso** *sm* - **1.** [grosor] thickness - **2.** [la mayor parte]: **el grueso de** the bulk of.

grulla *sf* crane.

grumete *sm* cabin boy.

grumo *sm* [gen] lump; [de sangre] clot.

grumoso, sa *adj* lumpy.

gruñido *sm* - **1.** [gen] growl; [de cerdo] grunt; **dar gruñidos** to growl, to grunt - **2.** [de persona] grumble.

gruñir *vi* - **1.** [gen] to growl; [cerdo] to grunt - **2.** [persona] to grumble.

gruñón, ona *fam* ◇ *adj* grumpy. ◇ *sm, f* old grump.

grupa *sf* hindquarters.

grupo *sm* [gen] group; [de árboles] cluster; *TECNOL* unit, set; **en grupo** in a group; **grupo de discusión** *INFORM* forum; **grupo electrógeno** generator; **grupo de empresas** *ECON* (corporate) group; **grupo de noticias** *INFORM* newsgroup; **grupo de presión** pressure group; **grupo de riesgo** risk group.
→ **grupo sanguíneo** *sm* blood group.

grupúsculo *sm* small group; *POLÍT* splinter group.

gruta *sf* grotto.

gta. *abrev de* **glorieta**.

guacal *sm Amér C & Méx* [calabaza] gourd; *Col, Méx & Caribe* [jaula] cage.

guacamol, guacamole *sm* guacamole, avocado dip.

guachada *sf R Dom fam* mean trick.

guachafita *sf Col & Ven fam* racket, uproar.

guachimán *sm Amér* night watchman.

guachinango *sm Méx* [pez] red snapper.

guacho, cha *sm, f Andes & R Dom fam* bastard.

guaco *sm Amér* pottery object found in pre-Columbian Indian tomb.

guadaña *sf* scythe.

guagua *sf Caribe* [autobús] bus; *Andes* [niño] baby.

guajiro, ra *sm, f Cuba* peasant.

guajolote *sm Amér C & Méx* [pavo] turkey; *fig* [tonto] fool, idiot.

guampa *sf Bol & C Sur* horn.

guampudo, da *adj R Dom* horned.

guanajo *sm Caribe* turkey.

guanche *adj* & *smf* Guanche.

guantazo *sm fam* slap.

guante *sm* glove; **guante de boxeo** boxing glove; **arrojar** *o* **tirar el guante** to throw down the gauntlet; **de guante blanco** gentlemanly; **echar el guante a algo** *fam* to get hold of sthg, to get one's hands on sthg; **echar el guante a alguien** *fam* to nab sb; **estar más suave que un guante** *fam* to be as meek as a lamb.

guantera *sf* glove compartment.

guaperas *fam* <> *adj inv*: **es un guaperas** he's a heart-throb. <> *sm inv* **- 1.** [presumido] pretty boy **- 2.** [artista, cantante] heart-throb.

guapo, pa <> *adj* **- 1.** [gen] good-looking; [hombre] handsome; [mujer] pretty **- 2.** *fam* [bonito] cool. <> *sm, f* **- 1.** [valiente]: **a ver quién es el guapo que...** let's see who's brave enough to... **- 2.** *Amér* [fanfarrón] braggart.

guarangada *sf Bol & C Sur* rude remark.

guaraní <> *adj inv* & *smf* Guarani. <> *sm* **- 1.** [lengua] Guarani **- 2.** [moneda] guarani.

Guaraní

Paraguay is the only Latin American country where an indigenous language is used as widely as Spanish. Guaraní was the language spoken by the main indigenous people at the time of the Spanish conquest. The process of racial mixing between Spaniard and Guarani over centuries has resulted in a population that is largely bilingual. In the major urban areas about half the population are able to use both languages freely, while in rural areas Guarani speakers predominate. Spanish is the language of the press and education, but Guarani has had a great influence on the vocabulary of Spanish speakers.

guarda <> *smf* [vigilante] guard, keeper; **guarda forestal** gamekeeper, forest ranger; **guarda jurado** security guard. <> *sf* **- 1.** [tutela] guardianship **- 2.** [de libros] flyleaf.

guardabarrera *smf* level crossing keeper.

guardabarros *sm inv* mudguard *UK*, fender *US*.

guardabosque *smf* forest ranger.

guardacoches *smf inv* parking attendant.

guardacostas *sm inv* [barco] coastguard boat.

guardaespaldas *smf inv* bodyguard.

guardagujas *smf inv* switchman (*f* switchwoman).

guardameta *smf* goalkeeper.

guardamuebles *sm inv* furniture warehouse *(for storage)*.

guardapolvo *sm* overalls *pl*.

guardar *vt* **- 1.** [gen] to keep; [en su sitio] to put away **- 2.** [vigilar] to keep watch over; [proteger] to guard **- 3.** [reservar, ahorrar]: **guardar algo (a** *o* **para alguien)** to save sthg (for sb) **- 4.** [cumplir - ley] to observe; [- secreto, promesa] to keep.

  ◆ **guardarse** *vprnl*: **guardársela a alguien** to have it in for sb.

  ◆ **guardarse de** *vprnl*: **guardarse de hacer algo** [evitar] to avoid doing sthg; [abstenerse de] to be careful not to do sthg.

guardarropa *sm* [gen] wardrobe; [de cine, discoteca etc] cloakroom.

guardarropía *sf* TEATRO wardrobe.

guardavallas *smf inv Amér* goalkeeper.

guardería *sf* nursery; [en el lugar de trabajo] crèche.

guardia <> *sf* **- 1.** [gen] guard; [vigilancia] watch, guard; **en guardia** on guard; **montar (la) guardia** to mount guard; **guardia municipal** urban police; **aflojar** *o* **bajar la guardia** to lower *o* drop one's guard; **la vieja guardia** the old guard **- 2.** [turno] duty; **estar de guardia** to be on duty. <> *sm, f* [policía] policeman (*f* policewoman); **guardia de tráfico** traffic warden.

  ◆ **guardia marina** *sm* sea cadet *in final two years of training*.

  ◆ **Guardia Civil** *sf*: **la Guardia Civil** the Civil Guard.

Guardia Civil

The Guardia Civil is a military-style security force operating under the control of the Spanish Ministry of the Interior and responsible for policing rural areas and highways. They also form the Spanish customs police and are easily recognizable by their traditional black three-cornered hat.

guardián, ana *sm, f* [de persona] guardian; [de cosa] watchman, keeper.

guarecer [30] *vt*: **guarecer (de)** to protect *o* shelter (from).

  ◆ **guarecerse** *vprnl*: **guarecerse (de)** to shelter (from).

guarida *sf* lair; *fig* hideout.

guarismo *sm* figure, number.

guarnecer [30] *vt* **- 1.** [adornar] to decorate; [ropa] to trim; CULIN to garnish **- 2.** [vigilar] to be garrisoned in.

guarnición *sf* **- 1.** CULIN garnish **- 2.** MIL garrison **- 3.** [adorno] decoration; [de ropa] trimming; [de joya] setting.

guarrada *sf fam* [cosa repugnante] filthy thing; [mala pasada] filthy *o* dirty trick.

guarrería *sf* **- 1.** [suciedad] filth, muck **- 2.** [acción] filthy thing **- 3.** [mala pasada] filthy *o* dirty trick.

guarro, **rra** <> adj filthy. <> sm, f - **1.** [animal] pig - **2.** fam [persona] filthy o dirty pig.

guarura sm Méx fam bodyguard.

guasa sf - **1.** fam [gracia] humour; [ironía] irony; **estar de guasa** to be joking - **2.** fam [pesadez]: **tener mucha guasa** to be a pain in the neck.

guasca sf Amér C & Caribe whip.

guasearse vprnl fam: **guasearse (de)** to take the mickey (out of).

guasón, **ona** <> adj fond of teasing. <> sm, f joker, tease.

guata sf - **1.** [de algodón] cotton padding - **2.** Chile fam [barriga] belly.

guateado, **da** adj padded.

Guatemala n pr - **1.** [país] Guatemala - **2.** [ciudad] Guatemala City.

guatemalteco, **ca**, **guatemaltés**, **esa** adj & sm, f Guatemalan.

guateque desus sm private party.

guatón, **ona** adj Chile fam potbellied.

guau sm woof.

guay adj fam cool, neat.

guayabo, **ba** sm, f Amér fam [persona] gorgeous person.
◆ **guayabo** sm - **1.** [árbol] guava tree - **2.** Col fam [resaca] hangover - **3.** Ven fam [nostalgia] homesickness.
◆ **guayaba** sf [fruta] guava.

guayín sm Méx van.

gubernamental adj government (antes de s).

gubernativo, **va** adj government (antes de s).

guepardo sm cheetah.

güero, **ra** adj Méx fam blond (f blonde), fair-haired.

guerra sf war; [referido al tipo de conflicto] warfare; [pugna] struggle, conflict; [de intereses, ideas] conflict; **declarar la guerra** to declare war; **en guerra** at war; **hacer la guerra** to wage war; **guerra sin cuartel** all-out war; **guerra bacteriológica/química** germ/chemical warfare; **guerra civil/mundial** civil/world war; **guerra atómica** o **nuclear** nuclear war; **guerra espacial** o **de las galaxias** star wars; **guerra fría** cold war; **guerra de guerrillas** guerrilla warfare; **guerra a muerte** fight to the death; **guerra de precios** price war; **guerra psicológica** psychological warfare; **guerra santa** Holy War, crusade; **dar guerra** to be a pain, to be annoying.

guerrear vi to (wage) war.

guerrero, **ra** <> adj warlike. <> sm, f [luchador] warrior.
◆ **guerrera** sf [prenda] (military) jacket.

guerrilla sf [grupo] guerrilla group.

guerrillero, **ra** sm, f guerrilla.

gueto, **ghetto** ['geto] sm ghetto.

güevón sm Andes, Arg & Ven vulg prat UK, pillock UK, jerk US.

guía <> smf [persona] guide; **guía turístico** tourist guide. <> sf - **1.** [indicación] guidance - **2.** [libro] guide (book); **guía de carreteras** road atlas; **guía de ferrocarriles** train timetable; **guía telefónica** telephone book o directory - **3.** [de bicicleta] handlebars pl - **4.** [para cortinas] rail.

guiar [9] vt - **1.** [indicar dirección a] to guide, to lead; [aconsejar] to guide, to direct - **2.** AUTO to drive; NÁUT to steer - **3.** [plantas, ramas] to train.
◆ **guiarse** vprnl: **guiarse por algo** to be guided by o to follow sthg.

guija sf pebble.

guijarro sm pebble.

guijarroso, **sa** adj pebbly.

guillado, **da** adj crazy.

guillotina sf guillotine.

guillotinar vt to guillotine.

guinda sf morello cherry.

guindar vt fam: **guindar algo a alguien** to pinch o nick sthg off sb.

guindilla sf chilli (pepper).

guinea sf guinea.

Guinea-Bissau n pr Guinea-Bissau.

Guinea Ecuatorial n pr Equatorial Guinea.

guineano, **na** adj & sm, f Guinean.

guiñapo sm - **1.** [andrajo] rag - **2.** [persona] (physical) wreck.

guiñar vt to wink.
◆ **guiñarse** vprnl to wink at each other.

guiño sm wink.

guiñol sm puppet theatre.

guión sm - **1.** [resumen] framework, outline - **2.** CINE & TV script - **3.** GRAM [signo] hyphen.

guionista smf scriptwriter.

guiri fam despec <> adj foreign. <> smf foreigner.

guirigay sm - **1.** fam [jaleo] racket - **2.** [lenguaje ininteligible] gibberish.

guirlache sm brittle sweet made of roasted almonds or hazelnuts and toffee.

guirnalda sf garland.

guisa sf way, manner; **a guisa de** by way of, as; **de esta guisa** in this way.

guisado sm stew.

guisante sm pea.

guisar vt & vi to cook.
◆ **guisarse** vprnl fig to be cooking, to be going on.

guiso sm dish.

güisqui, **whisky** sm whisky.

guita sf fam dosh.

guitarra ⬦ *sf* guitar; **guitarra acústica** acoustic guitar; **guitarra eléctrica** electric guitar; **chafar la guitarra a alguien** to mess things up for sb. ⬦ *smf* guitarist.

guitarrero, ra *sm, f* guitar maker.

guitarrista *smf* guitarist.

gula *sf* gluttony.

gurí, risa *sm, f* R Dom fam [niño] kid, child; [chico] lad, boy; [chica] lass, girl.

guripa *sm* fam cop.

guru, gurú *sm* guru.

gusanillo *sm* fam: **el gusanillo de la conciencia** conscience; **entrarle a uno el gusanillo de los videojuegos** to be bitten by the videogame bug; **matar el gusanillo** [bebiendo] to have a drink on an empty stomach; [comiendo] to have a snack between meals; **sentir un gusanillo en el estómago** to have butterflies (in one's stomach).

gusano *sm* lit & fig worm; **gusano de luz** glow worm; **gusano de (la) seda** silkworm.

gusarapo, pa *sm, f* creepy-crawly.

gustar ⬦ *vi* [agradar] to be pleasing; **me gusta esa chica/ir al cine** I like that girl/going to the cinema; **me gustan las novelas** I like novels; **gustar de hacer algo** to like o enjoy doing sthg; **como guste** as you wish. ⬦ *vt* to taste, to try.

gustativo, va *adj* taste *(antes de s)*.

gustazo *sm* fam great pleasure; **darse el gustazo de algo/hacer algo** to allow o.s. the pleasure of sthg/doing sthg.

gustillo *sm* aftertaste; **coger el gustillo a algo** to take a liking to sthg.

gusto *sm* - **1.** [gen] taste; [sabor] taste, flavour; **de buen/mal gusto** in good/bad taste; **tener buen/mal gusto** to have good/bad taste; **sobre gustos no hay nada escrito** there's no accounting for taste, each to his own - **2.** [placer] pleasure; **con mucho gusto** gladly, with pleasure; **da gusto estar aquí** it's a real pleasure to be here; **dar gusto a alguien** to please sb; **mucho** o **tanto gusto** pleased to meet you; **tener el gusto de** to have the pleasure of; **tengo el gusto de invitarle** I have the pleasure of inviting you; **tomar gusto a algo** to take a liking to sthg - **3.** [capricho] whim.

➤ **a gusto** *loc adv*: **hacer algo a gusto** [de buena gana] to do sthg willingly o gladly; [cómodamente] to do sthg comfortably; **estar a gusto** to be comfortable o at ease.

gustoso, sa *adj* - **1.** [sabroso] tasty - **2.** [con placer]: **hacer algo gustoso** to do sthg gladly o willingly.

gutural *adj* guttural.

gymkhana = **gincana**.

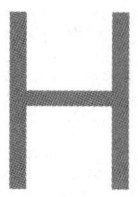

h¹, H *sf* [letra] h, H; **por h o por b** fig for one reason or another.
➤ **H** *(abrev de* **Hermano***)* Br.

h², h. *(abrev de* **hora***)* hr, h.

ha ⬦ ▷ **haber**. ⬦ *(abrev de* **hectárea***)* ha.

haba *sf* broad bean.

habanero, ra *adj* of/relating to Havana.
➤ **habanera** *sf* MÚS habanera.

habano, na *adj* Havanan.
➤ **habano** *sm* Havana cigar.

haber [4] ⬦ *v aux* - **1.** [en tiempos compuestos] to have; **lo he/había hecho** I have/had done it; **los niños ya han comido** the children have already eaten; **en el estreno ha habido mucha gente** there were a lot of people at the premiere - **2.** [expresa reproche]: **haber venido antes** you could have come a bit earlier; **¡haberlo dicho!** why didn't you say so? - **3.** [expresa obligación]: **haber de hacer algo** to have to do sthg; **has de estudiar más** you have to study more. ⬦ *v impers* - **1.** [existir, estar]: **hay** there is/are; **hay mucha gente en la calle** there are a lot of people in the street; **había/ hubo muchos problemas** there were many problems; **habrá dos mil** [expresa futuro] there will be two thousand; [expresa hipótesis] there must be two thousand - **2.** [expresa obligación]: **haber que hacer algo** to have to do sthg; **hay que hacer más ejercicio** one o you should do more exercise; **habrá que soportar su mal humor** we'll have to put up with his bad mood - **3.** *loc*: **algo habrá** there must be something in it; **allá se las haya** that's his/her/your *etc* problem; **habérselas con alguien** to face o confront sb; **¡hay que ver!** well I never!; **lo habido y por haber** everything under the sun; **no hay de qué** don't mention it; **¿qué hay?** fam [saludo] how are you doing? ⬦ *sm* - **1.** [bienes] assets *pl* - **2.** [en cuentas, contabilidad] credit (side).
➤ **haberes** *smpl* [sueldo] remuneration *(U)*.

habichuela *sf* bean.

hábil *adj* - **1.** [diestro] skilful; [inteligente] clever - **2.** [utilizable - lugar] suitable, fit - **3.** DER: **días hábiles** working days.

habilidad *sf* [destreza] skill; [inteligencia] cleverness; **tener habilidad para algo** to be good at sthg.

habiloso, sa *adj* skilful, clever.

habilitación *sf* - **1.** [acondicionamiento] fitting out - **2.** DER [autorización] authorization, right.

habilitado, da ◇ *adj* DER authorized. ◇ *sm, f* paymaster.

habilitar *vt* - **1.** [acondicionar] to fit out, to equip - **2.** [autorizar] to authorize - **3.** [financiar] to finance.

habiloso, sa *adj Chile fam* shrewd, astute.

habitabilidad *sf* habitability.

habitable *adj* habitable, inhabitable.

habitación *sf* [gen] room; [dormitorio] bedroom; **habitación doble** [con cama de matrimonio] double room; [con dos camas] twin room; **habitación individual** *o* **simple** single room; **habitación para invitados** guest room.

habitante *sm* [de ciudad, país] inhabitant; [de barrio] resident.

habitar ◇ *vi* to live. ◇ *vt* to live in, to inhabit.

hábitat (*pl* **hábitats**) *sm* - **1.** [gen] habitat - **2.** [vivienda] housing conditions *pl*.

hábito *sm* habit; **tener el hábito de hacer algo** to be in the habit of doing sthg; **colgar los hábitos** RELIG to leave the priesthood, to give up the cloth; [renunciar] to give it up; **el hábito no hace al monje** clothes don't make the man.

habitual *adj* habitual; [cliente, lector] regular.

habituar [6] *vt*: **habituar a alguien a** to accustom sb to.

◆ **habituarse** *vprnl*: **habituarse a** [gen] to get used *o* accustomed to; [drogas etc] to become addicted to.

habla *sf (el)* - **1.** [idioma] language; [dialecto] dialect; **de habla española** Spanish-speaking - **2.** [facultad] speech; **dejar a alguien sin habla** to leave sb speechless; **quedarse sin habla** to be left speechless - **3.** LING discourse - **4.** [al teléfono]: **estar al habla con alguien** to be on the line to sb.

hablador, ra ◇ *adj* talkative. ◇ *sm, f* chatterbox.

habladurías *sfpl* [rumores] rumours; [chismes] gossip *(U)*.

hablante ◇ *adj* speaking. ◇ *smf* speaker.

hablar ◇ *vi*: **hablar (con)** to talk (to), to speak (to); **hablar por hablar** to talk for the sake of talking; **hablar de** to talk about; **hablar bien/mal de** to speak well/badly of; **hablar en español/inglés** to speak Spanish/English; **hablar en voz alta/baja** to speak loudly/softly; **dar que hablar** to make people talk; **¡mira quién habla!, ¡mira quién fue a hablar!** look

who's talking!; **¡ni hablar!** no way! ◇ *vt* - **1.** [idioma] to speak - **2.** [asunto]: **hablar algo (con)** to discuss sthg (with).

◆ **hablarse** *vprnl* to speak (to each other); **no hablarse** not to be speaking, not to be on speaking terms; **'se habla inglés'** 'English spoken'.

habrá *etc* ▷ **haber**.

hacendado, da *sm, f* landowner.

hacendoso, sa *adj* houseproud.

hacer [60] ◇ *vt* - **1.** [elaborar, crear, cocinar] to make; **hacer un vestido/planes** to make a dress/plans; **hacer un poema/una sinfonía** to write a poem/symphony; **para hacer la carne...** to cook the meat... - **2.** [construir] to build; **han hecho un edificio nuevo** they've put up a new building - **3.** [generar] to produce; **el árbol hace sombra** the tree gives shade; **la carretera hace una curva** there's a bend in the road - **4.** [movimientos, sonidos, gestos] to make; **le hice señas** I signalled to her; **el reloj hace tic-tac** the clock goes tick-tock; **hacer ruido** to make a noise - **5.** [obtener - fotocopia] to make; [- retrato] to paint; [- fotografía] to take - **6.** [realizar - trabajo, estudios] to do; [- viaje] to make; [- comunión] to take; **hoy hace guardia** she's on duty today; **estoy haciendo segundo** I'm in my second year - **7.** [practicar - gen] to do; [- tenis, fútbol] to play; **debes hacer deporte** you should start doing some sport - **8.** [arreglar - casa, colada] to do; [- cama] to make - **9.** [dar aspecto de] to cause to look *o* seem; **este espejo te hace gordo** that mirror makes you look *o* seem fat - **10.** [transformar en]: **hacer a alguien feliz** to make sb happy; **la guerra no le hizo un hombre** the war didn't make him (into) a man; **hizo pedazos el papel** he tore the paper to pieces; **hacer de algo/alguien algo** to make sthg/sb into sthg; **hizo de ella una buena cantante** he made a good singer of her - **11.** [comportarse como]: **hacer el tonto** to act the fool; **hacer el vándalo** to act like a hooligan - **12.** [causar]: **hacer daño a alguien** to hurt sb; **me hizo gracia** I thought it was funny - **13.** CINE & TEATRO to play; **hace el papel de la hija del rey** she plays (the part of) the king's daughter - **14.** [suponer] to think, to reckon; **a estas horas yo te hacía en París** I thought *o* reckoned you'd be in Paris by now - **15.** [ser causa de]: **hacer que alguien haga algo** to make sb do sthg; **me hizo reír** it made me laugh; **has hecho que se enfadara** you've made him angry - **16.** [mandar]: **hacer que se haga algo** to have sthg done; **voy a hacer teñir este traje** I'm going to have the dress dyed. ◇ *vi* - **1.** [intervenir]: **déjame hacer a mí** let me do it - **2.** [actuar]: **hacer de** CINE & TEATRO to play; [trabajar] to act as - **3.** [aparentar]: **hacer como si**

to act as if; **haz como que no te importa** act as if you don't care **- 4.** [procurar, intentar]**: hacer por hacer algo** to try to do sthg; **haré por verle esta noche** I'll try to see him tonight **- 5.** *loc*: **¿hace?** all right? ◇ *v impers* **- 1.** [tiempo meteorológico]**: hace frío/sol/viento** it's cold/sunny/windy; **hace un día precioso** it's a beautiful day **- 2.** [tiempo transcurrido]**: hace diez años** ten years ago; **hace mucho/poco** a long time/not long ago; **hace un mes que llegué** it's a month since I arrived; **no la veo desde hace un año** I haven't seen her for a year.

◆ **hacerse** *vprnl.* **- 1.** [formarse] to form **- 2.** [desarrollarse, crecer] to grow **- 3.** [guisarse, cocerse] to cook **- 4.** [convertirse] to become; **hacerse musulmán** to become a Moslem **- 5.** [resultar] to get; **se hace muy pesado** it gets very tedious **- 6.** [crearse en la mente]**: hacerse ilusiones** to get one's hopes up; **hacerse una idea de algo** to imagine what sthg is like **- 7.** [mostrarse]**: se hace el gracioso/el simpático** he tries to act the comedian/the nice guy; **hacerse el distraído** to pretend to be miles away.

hacha *sf (el)* axe; **enterrar el hacha de guerra** to bury the hatchet; **desenterrar el hacha de guerra** to sharpen one's sword; **ser un hacha** *fam* to be a whizz o an ace.

hachazo *sm* blow of an axe, hack.

hache *sf*: **llamémosle hache** call it what you like; **por hache o por be** for one reason or another.

hachís, hash [xa'ʃis] *sm* hashish.

hacia *prep* **- 1.** [dirección, tendencia, sentimiento] towards; **hacia aquí/allí** this/that way; **hacia abajo** downwards; **hacia arriba** upwards; **hacia atrás** backwards; **hacia adelante** forwards **- 2.** [tiempo] around, about; **hacia las diez** around o about ten o'clock.

hacienda *sf* **- 1.** [finca] country estate o property **- 2.** [bienes] property; **hacienda pública** public purse **- 3.** *R Plata* [ganadería] ranch.

◆ **Hacienda** *sf*: **Ministerio de Hacienda** the Treasury.

hacinamiento *sm* [de personas] overcrowding; [de objetos] heaping, piling.

hacinar *vt* to pile o heap (up).

◆ **hacinarse** *vprnl* [gente] to be crowded together; [cosas] to be piled o heaped (up).

hada *sf (el)* fairy; **hada madrina** fairy godmother.

haga *etc* ⊳ **hacer**.

Haití *n pr* Haiti.

haitiano, na *adj* & *sm, f* Haitian.

hala *interj*: **¡hala!** [para dar ánimo, prisa] come on!; [para expresar incredulidad] no!, you're joking!; [para expresar admiración, sorpresa] wow!

halagador, ra ◇ *adj* flattering. ◇ *sm, f* flatterer.

halagar [16] *vt* to flatter.

halago *sm* flattery.

halague *etc* ⊳ **halagar**.

halagüeño, ña *adj* [prometedor] promising, encouraging.

halcón *sm* **- 1.** ZOOL falcon, hawk **- 2.** *Amér fam* [matón] *government-paid killer*.

halconería *sf* falconry.

hale *interj*: **¡hale!** come on!

hálito *sm* **- 1.** [aliento] breath **- 2.** *fig* [aire] zephyr, gentle breeze.

halitosis *sf inv* bad breath.

hall [xol] (*pl* **halls**) *sm* entrance hall, foyer.

hallar *vt* [gen] to find; [averiguar] to find out.

◆ **hallarse** *vprnl* **- 1.** [en un lugar - persona] to be, to find o.s.; [- casa etc] to be (situated) **- 2.** [en una situación] to be; **hallarse enfermo** to be ill.

hallazgo *sm* **- 1.** [descubrimiento] discovery **- 2.** [objeto] find.

halo *sm* [de astros, santos] halo; [de objetos, personas] aura.

halógeno, na *adj* QUÍM halogenous; [faro] halogen (*antes de s*).

halterofilia *sf* weightlifting.

hamaca *sf* **- 1.** [para colgar] hammock **- 2.** [tumbona - silla] deckchair; [- canapé] sunlounger **- 3.** *R Plata* [columpio] swing **- 4.** *R Plata* [mecedora] rocking chair.

hambre *sf* **- 1.** [apetito] hunger; [inanición] starvation; **hambre canina** ravenous hunger; **tener hambre** to be hungry; **matar de hambre a alguien** to starve sb to death; **matar el hambre** to satisfy one's hunger; **morirse de hambre** to be starving, to be dying of hunger; **pasar hambre** to starve **- 2.** [epidemia] famine **- 3.** *fig* [deseo]**: hambre de** hunger o thirst for **- 4.** *loc*: **a buen hambre no hay pan duro** *prov* beggars can't be choosers; **se juntan el hambre con las ganas de comer** it's one thing on top of another; **ser más listo que el hambre** to be nobody's fool.

hambreador *sm Amér* exploiter.

hambriento, ta ◇ *adj* starving. ◇ *sm, f* starving person; **los hambrientos** the hungry.

hamburguesa *sf* hamburger.

hamburguesería *sf* hamburger joint.

hampa *sf (el)* underworld.

hampón *sm* thug.

hámster ['xamster] (*pl* **hámsters**) *sm* hamster.

hándicap ['xandikap] (*pl* **hándicaps**) *sm* handicap.

hangar *sm* hangar.

hará *etc* ⊳ **hacer**.

haragán, ana ◇ *adj* lazy, idle. ◇ *sm, f* layabout, idler.

haraganear *vi* to laze about, to lounge around.

haraganería *sf* laziness, idleness.

harakiri = **haraquiri**.

harapiento, ta *adj* ragged, tattered.

harapo *sm* rag, tatter.

haraquiri, harakiri *sm* harakiri.

hardware ['xar'wer] *sm* INFORM hardware.

harén *sm* harem.

harina *sf* flour; **estar metido en harina** to be right in the middle of sthg; **ser harina de otro costal** to be a different kettle of fish.

harinoso, sa *adj* floury; [manzana] mealy.

hartar *vt* - **1.** [atiborrar] to stuff (full) - **2.** [fastidiar]: **hartar a alguien** to annoy sb, to get on sb's nerves.

➤ **hartarse** *vprnl* - **1.** [atiborrarse] to stuff *o* gorge o.s. - **2.** [cansarse]: **hartarse (de)** to get fed up (with) - **3.** [no parar]: **hartarse de algo** to do sthg non-stop.

hartazgo, hartón *sm* fill; **darse un hartazgo (de)** to have one's fill (of).

harto, ta *adj* - **1.** [de comida] full - **2.** [cansado]: **harto (de)** tired (of), fed up (with) - **3.** *Andes, Amér C, Caribe & Méx* [mucho] a lot of, lots of; **tiene harto dinero** she has a lot of *o* lots of money; **de este aeropuerto salen hartos aviones** a lot of *o* lots of planes fly from this airport.

➤ **harto** *adv* - **1.** somewhat, rather - **2.** *Andes, Amér C, Caribe & Méx fam* [mucho] a lot, very much; [muy] very, really.

hartón = **hartazgo**.

hash = **hachís**.

hasta ◇ *prep* - **1.** [en el espacio] as far as, up to; **desde aquí hasta allí** from here to there; **¿hasta dónde va este tren?** where does this train go? - **2.** [en el tiempo] until, till; **hasta ahora** (up) until now, so far; **hasta el final** right up until the end; **hasta luego** *o* **pronto** *o* **la vista** see you (later) - **3.** [con cantidades] up to. ◇ *adv* - **1.** [incluso] even - **2.** *Amér C, Col, Ecuad & Méx* [no antes de]: **pintaremos la casa hasta fin de mes** we won't start painting the house until the end of the month.

➤ **hasta que** *loc conj* until, till.

hastiar [9] *vt* [aburrir] to bore; [asquear] to sicken, to disgust.

➤ **hastiarse de** *vprnl* to tire of, to get fed up with.

hastío *sm* [tedio] boredom *(U)*; [repugnancia] disgust.

hatajo *sm* load, bunch; **un hatajo de** [gamberros] a bunch of; [mentiras] a pack of.

hatillo *sm* bundle of clothes.

hato *sm* - **1.** [de ganado] herd; [de ovejas] flock - **2.** [de ropa] bundle.

haya ◇ ⊳ **haber**. ◇ *sf* [árbol] beech (tree); [madera] beech (wood).

hayal *sm* beech grove *o* wood.

haz *sm* - **1.** [de leña] bundle; [de cereales] sheaf - **2.** [de luz] beam; ⊳ **hacer**.

hazaña *sf* feat, exploit.

hazmerreír *sm* laughing stock.

he ⊳ **haber**.

hebilla *sf* buckle.

hebra *sf* - **1.** [de hilo] thread; [de judías, puerros] string; [de tabaco] strand (of tobacco) - **2.** *loc*: **pegar la hebra** *fam* to strike up a conversation; **perder la hebra** to lose the thread.

hebreo, a *adj* & *sm, f* Hebrew.

➤ **hebreo** *sm* [lengua] Hebrew.

hecatombe *sf* carnage *(U)*, disaster.

hechicería *sf* - **1.** [arte] witchcraft, sorcery - **2.** [maleficio] spell.

hechicero, ra ◇ *adj* enchanting, bewitching. ◇ *sm, f* wizard (*f* witch), sorcerer (*f* sorceress).

hechizar [13] *vt* to cast a spell on; *fig* to bewitch, to captivate.

hechizo *sm* - **1.** [maleficio] spell - **2.** *fig* [encanto] magic, charm.

hecho, cha ◇ *pp* ⊳ **hacer**. ◇ *adj* - **1.** [acabado, realizado] done; **bien/mal hecho** well/badly done - **2.** [manufacturado] made: **hecho a mano** handmade; **hecho a máquina** machine-made - **3.** [convertido en]: **estás hecho un artista** you've become quite an artist - **4.** [formado]: **una mujer hecha y derecha** a fully-grown woman - **5.** [carne] done; **quiero el filete muy/poco hecho** I'd like the steak well done/rare.

➤ **hecho** ◇ *sm* - **1.** [obra] action, deed; **a lo hecho, pecho** it's no use crying over spilt milk - **2.** [suceso] event; **hecho consumado** fait accompli - **3.** [realidad, dato] fact. ◇ *interj*: **¡hecho!** it's a deal!, you're on!

➤ **de hecho** *loc adv* in fact, actually.

hechura *sf* - **1.** [de traje] cut - **2.** [forma] shape.

hectárea *sf* hectare.

hectolitro *sm* hectolitre.

hectómetro *sm* hectometre.

heder [20] *vi* - **1.** [apestar] to stink, to reek - **2.** *fig* [fastidiar] to be annoying *o* irritating.

hediondo, da *adj* - **1.** [pestilente] stinking, foul-smelling - **2.** *fig* [insoportable] unbearable.

hedonismo *sm* hedonism.

hedonista ◇ *adj* hedonistic. ◇ *smf* hedonist.

hedor *sm* stink, stench.

hegemonía *sf* [gen] dominance; POLÍT hege‑mony.

hegemónico, ca *adj* [gen] dominant; [clase, partido] ruling.

hégira, héjira *sf* hegira.

helada ⊳ **helado**.

heladería *sf* [tienda] ice-cream parlour; [puesto] ice-cream stall.

heladero, ra *sm, f* ice-cream seller.

helado, da *adj* **- 1.** [hecho hielo - agua] frozen; [- lago] frozen over **- 2.** [muy frío - manos, agua] freezing **- 3.** *fig* [atónito] dumbfounded, speechless.
➤ **helado** *sm* ice-cream.
➤ **helada** *sf* frost.

helar [19] ⟨⟩ *vt* **- 1.** [líquido] to freeze **- 2.** [dejar atónito] to dumbfound. ⟨⟩ *v impers*: **ayer heló** there was a frost last night.
➤ **helarse** *vprnl* to freeze; [plantas] to be frost-bitten.

helecho *sm* fern, bracken.

helénico, ca *adj* Hellenic, Greek.

helenismo *sm* Hellenism.

heleno, na *adj* Hellenic, Greek.

hélice *sf* **- 1.** TECNOL propeller **- 2.** [espiral] spiral.

helicóptero *sm* helicopter.

helio *sm* helium.

helipuerto *sm* heliport.

helvético, ca *adj* & *sm, f* Swiss.

hematíe *sm* red blood cell.

hematología *sf* haematology.

hematológico, ca *adj* haematological.

hematólogo, ga *sm, f* haematologist.

hematoma *sm* bruise; MED haematoma.

hembra *sf* **- 1.** BIOL female; [mujer] woman; [niña] girl **- 2.** [del enchufe] socket.

hemeroteca *sf* newspaper library O archive.

hemiciclo *sm* **- 1.** [semicírculo] semicircle **- 2.** [en el parlamento] floor.

hemiplejia, hemiplejía *sf* hemiplegia.

hemipléjico, ca *adj* & *sm, f* hemiplegic.

hemisférico, ca *adj* hemispheric.

hemisferio *sm* hemisphere.

hemofilia *sf* haemophilia.

hemofílico, ca *adj* & *sm, f* haemophiliac.

hemoglobina *sf* haemoglobin.

hemograma *sm* blood test.

hemopatía *sf* blood disease O disorder.

hemorragia *sf* haemorrhage; **hemorragia nasal** nosebleed.

hemorrágico, ca *adj* haemorrhagic.

hemorroides *sfpl* haemorrhoids, piles.

hender [20], **hendir** [27] *vt* [carne, piel] to carve open, to cleave; [piedra, madera] to crack open; [aire, agua] to cut O slice through.

hendido, da *adj* split (open).

hendidura *sf* [en carne, piel] cut, split; [en piedra, madera] crack.

hendir = **hender**.

heno *sm* hay.

hepático, ca *adj* liver *(antes de s)*, hepatic.

hepatitis *sf inv* hepatitis.

heptagonal *adj* heptagonal.

heptágono *sm* heptagon.

heráldico, ca *adj* heraldic.
➤ **heráldica** *sf* heraldry.

heraldo *sm* herald.

herbario, ria *adj* herbal.
➤ **herbario** *sm* [colección] herbarium.

herbicida *sm* weedkiller.

herbívoro, ra ⟨⟩ *adj* herbivorous. ⟨⟩ *sm, f* herbivore.

herbolario, ria *sm, f* [persona] herbalist.
➤ **herbolario** *sm* [tienda] herbalist's (shop).

herboristería *sf* herbalist's (shop).

hercio, hertz ['erθjo] *sm* hertz.

hercúleo, a *adj* very powerful, incredibly strong.

hércules *sm* ox, very strong man.

heredar *vt*: **heredar (de)** to inherit (from).

heredero, ra *sm, f* heir (*f* heiress); **heredero forzoso** heir apparent; **heredero universal** residuary legatee.

hereditario, ria *adj* hereditary.

hereje *smf* heretic.

herejía *sf* heresy.

herencia *sf* [de bienes] inheritance; [de características] legacy; BIOL heredity.

herético, ca *adj* heretical.

herido, da ⟨⟩ *adj* [gen] injured; [en lucha, atentado] wounded; [sentimentalmente] hurt, wounded. ⟨⟩ *sm, f* [gen] injured person; [en lucha, atentado] wounded person; **no hubo heridos** there were no casualties; **los heridos** the wounded.
➤ **herida** *sf* **- 1.** [lesión] injury; [en lucha, atentado] wound; **herida superficial** flesh wound; **heridas múltiples** multiple injuries **- 2.** [ofensa] injury, offence *(U)*; **hurgar en la herida** to re-open an old wound; **lamerse las heridas** to lick one's wounds; [pena] hurt *(U)*, pain *(U)*.

herir [27] *vt* **- 1.** [físicamente] to injure; [en lucha, atentado] to wound; [vista] to hurt; [oído] to pierce **- 2.** [sentimentalmente] to hurt.

hermafrodita *adj* & *smf* hermaphrodite.

hermanado, da *adj* [gen] united, joined; [ciudades] twinned.

hermanamiento *sm* [gen] union; [de ciudades] twinning.

hermanar *vt* - **1.** [esfuerzos, personas] to unite - **2.** [ciudades] to twin.
→ **hermanarse** *vprnl* [ciudades] to be twinned.

hermanastro, **tra** *sm, f* stepbrother (*f* stepsister).

hermandad *sf* - **1.** [asociación] association; [RELIG - de hombres] brotherhood; [- de mujeres] sisterhood - **2.** [amistad] intimacy, close friendship.

hermano, **na** ◇ *adj* related, connected. ◇ *sm, f* brother (*f* sister); **hermano gemelo** twin brother; **hermano mayor** older brother, big brother; **hermano menor** younger brother, little brother; **hermano de sangre** blood brother; **hermanos siameses** Siamese twins.

hermético, **ca** *adj* - **1.** [al aire] airtight, hermetic; [al agua] watertight, hermetic - **2.** *fig* [persona] inscrutable.

hermetismo *sm* inscrutability.

hermoso, **sa** *adj* [gen] beautiful, lovely; [hombre] handsome; [excelente] wonderful.

hermosura *sf* [gen] beauty; [de hombre] handsomeness.

hernia *sf* hernia, rupture; **hernia discal** slipped disc.

herniado, **da** ◇ *adj* ruptured. ◇ *sm, f* person suffering from a hernia.

herniarse [8] *vprnl* - **1.** MED to rupture o.s. - **2.** *fam* [esforzarse]: **herniarse (a hacer algo)** to bust a gut (doing sthg).

héroe *sm* hero.

heroicidad *sf* - **1.** [cualidad] heroism - **2.** [hecho] heroic deed.

heroico, **ca** *adj* heroic.

heroína *sf* - **1.** [mujer] heroine - **2.** [droga] heroin.

heroinomanía *sf* heroin addiction.

heroinómano, **na** *sm, f* heroin addict.

heroísmo *sm* heroism.

herpes *sm inv* herpes *(U)*.

herradura *sf* horseshoe.

herraje *sm* iron fittings *pl*, ironwork.

herramienta *sf* tool.

herrería *sf* - **1.** [taller] smithy, forge - **2.** [oficio] smithery, blacksmith's trade.

herrero *sm* blacksmith, smith.

herrumbrarse *vprnl* to rust, to go rusty.

herrumbre *sf* - **1.** [óxido] rust - **2.** [sabor] iron taste.

herrumbroso, **sa** *adj* rusty.

hertz = **hercio**.

hervidero *sm* - **1.** [de pasiones, intrigas] hotbed - **2.** [de gente - muchedumbre] swarm, throng; [- sitio] place throbbing o swarming with people.

hervido *sm* stew.

hervir [27] ◇ *vt* to boil. ◇ *vi* - **1.** [líquido] to boil - **2.** *fig* [lugar]: **hervir de** to swarm with - **3.** *fig* [persona]: **hervir en** to be burning with.

hervor *sm* boiling; **dar un hervor a algo** to blanch sthg.

heterodoxia *sf* heterodoxy, unorthodox nature.

heterodoxo, **xa** ◇ *adj* heterodox, unorthodox. ◇ *sm, f* heterodox o unorthodox person.

heterogeneidad *sf* heterogeneity.

heterogéneo, **a** *adj* heterogeneous.

heterosexual *adj* & *smf* heterosexual.

heterosexualidad *sf* heterosexuality.

hexadecimal *adj* INFORM hexadecimal.

hexagonal *adj* hexagonal.

hexágono *sm* hexagon.

hez *sf* *lit & fig* dregs *pl*.
→ **heces** *sfpl* [excrementos] faeces, excrement *sing*.

hg (*abrev de* **hectogramo**) hg.

hiato *sm* hiatus.

hibernación *sf* [de animales] hibernation.

hibernal *adj* winter *(antes de s)*.

hibernar *vi* to hibernate.

híbrido, **da** *adj* *lit & fig* hybrid.
→ **híbrido** *sm* - **1.** [animal, planta] hybrid - **2.** *fig* [mezcla] cross.

hice *etc* ⊳ **hacer**.

hidalgo, **ga** *sm, f* nobleman (*f* noblewoman).

hidratación *sf* [de la piel] moisturizing; [de persona] rehydration; [de sustancia] hydration.

hidratado, **da** *adj* [piel] moist; QUÍM hydrated.

hidratante ◇ *adj* moisturizing. ◇ *sm* moisturizing cream.

hidratar *vt* [piel] to moisturize; QUÍM to hydrate.

hidrato *sm* hydrate; **hidrato de carbono** carbohydrate.

hidráulico, **ca** *adj* hydraulic.
→ **hidráulica** *sf* hydraulics *(U)*.

hídrico, **ca** *adj* hydric.

hidroavión *sm* seaplane.

hidrocarburo *sm* hydrocarbon.

hidrocefalia *sf* water on the brain; MED hydrocephalus.

hidrodinámico, **ca** *adj* hydrodynamic.
→ **hidrodinámica** *sf* hydrodynamics *(U)*.

hidroeléctrico, **ca** *adj* hydroelectric.

hidrófilo, **la** *adj* absorbent; **algodón hidrófilo** cotton wool UK, cotton US.

hidrofobia *sf* hydrophobia.

hidrófobo, ba *adj* hydrophobic, rabid.

hidrófugo, ga *adj* [contra filtraciones] waterproof; [contra humedad] damp-proof.

hidrógeno *sm* hydrogen.

hidrografía *sf* hydrography.

hidrográfico, ca *adj* hydrographic.

hidroplano *sm* - **1.** [barco] hydrofoil - **2.** [avión] seaplane.

hidrosfera *sf* hydrosphere.

hidrosoluble *adj* water-soluble.

hidrostático, ca *adj* hydrostatic.
➡ **hidrostática** *sf* hydrostatics *(U)*.

hidroterapia *sf* hydrotherapy.

hidróxido *sm* hydroxide.

hidruro *sm* hydride.

hieda *etc* ➡ **heder**.

hiedra *sf* ivy.

hiel *sf* - **1.** [bilis] bile; **echar la hiel** to sweat blood - **2.** [mala intención] spleen, bitterness.

hiela *etc* ➡ **helar**.

hielo *sm* ice; **con hielo** [whisky] with ice, on the rocks; **romper el hielo** *fig* to break the ice; **ser más frío que el hielo** to be as cold as ice.

hiena *sf* hyena.

hienda *etc* ➡ **hender, hendir**.

hiera *etc* ➡ **herir**.

hierático, ca *adj* solemn.

hierba, yerba *sf* - **1.** [planta] herb; **mala hierba** weed; **hierba mate** maté; **hierbas medicinales** medicinal herbs - **2.** [césped] grass - **3.** *fam* [droga] grass - **4.** *loc*: **ser mala hierba** to be a nasty piece of work; **mala hierba nunca muere** *prov* ill weeds grow apace *prov*; **y otras hierbas** and so on.

hierbabuena *sf* mint.

hierro *sm* - **1.** [metal] iron; **de hierro** [severo] iron *(antes de s)*; **hierro forjado** wrought iron; **hierro fundido** cast iron; **hierro laminado** sheet metal; **quitar hierro a algo** to play sthg down - **2.** [de puñal] blade; [de flecha] point; **quien a hierro mata a hierro muere** *prov* he who lives by the sword dies by the sword *prov*.

hierva *etc* ➡ **hervir**.

HI-FI *(abrev de* high fidelity*)* *sf* hi-fi.

higadillo *sm*: **higadillos de pollo** chicken livers.

hígado *sm* liver; **echar los hígados** to nearly kill o.s. (with the effort); **tener hígados** to have guts.

higiene *sf* hygiene; **higiene mental** mental health; **higiene personal** personal hygiene.

higiénico, ca *adj* hygienic; **papel higiénico** toilet paper.

higienista *smf* hygienist.

higienización *sf* sterilization.

higienizar [13] *vt* to sterilize.

higo *sm* fig; **higo chumbo** prickly pear; **de higos a brevas** once in a blue moon; **me importa un higo** *fam* I couldn't care less.

higuera *sf* fig tree; **higuera chumba** prickly pear; **estar en la higuera** *fig* to live in a world of one's own.

hijastro, tra *sm, f* stepson *(f* stepdaughter).

hijo, ja *sm, f* - **1.** [descendiente] son *(f* daughter); **hijo adoptivo** adopted child; **hijo de la chingada** *Méx o* **de puta** *vulg* fucking bastard, motherfucker *(f* fucking bitch); **hijo de papá** *fam* daddy's boy; **hijo ilegítimo** *o* **natural** illegitimate child; **hijo no deseado** unwanted child; **hijo pródigo** prodigal son; **hijo único** only child; **cualquier** *o* **todo hijo de vecino** *fam fig* any Tom, Dick or Harry - **2.** [natural] native - **3.** [como forma de dirigirse a alguien]: **¡pues hijo, podrías haber avisado!** you could at least have told me, couldn't you?; **¡hija mía, qué bruta eres!** God, you're stupid!
➡ **hijo** *sm* [hijo o hija] child.
➡ **hijos** *smpl* children.

hilacha *sf* loose thread.

hilada *sf* row.

hilandero, ra *sm, f* spinner.

hilar *vt* [hilo, tela] to spin; [ideas, planes] to think up; **hilar delgado** *o* **muy fino** *fig* to split hairs.

hilarante *adj* hilarious.

hilaridad *sf* hilarity.

hilera *sf* row; **en hilera** in a row.

hilo *sm* - **1.** [fibra, hebra] thread; **colgar** *o* **pender de un hilo** to be hanging by a thread; **mover los hilos** to pull some strings - **2.** [tejido] linen - **3.** [de metal, teléfono] wire; **sin hilos** wireless - **4.** [de agua, sangre] trickle; **apenas le salía un hilo de voz** he was barely able to speak - **5.** [de pensamiento] train; [de discurso, conversación] thread; **perder el hilo** to lose the thread; **seguir el hilo** to follow (the thread).
➡ **hilo dental** *sm* dental floss.
➡ **hilo musical** *sm* piped music.

hilván *sm* - **1.** [costura] tacking *UK*, basting *US* - **2.** [hilo] tacking stitch *UK*, basting stitch *US*.

hilvanado *sm* tacking *UK*, basting *US*.

hilvanar *vt* - **1.** [ropa] to tack *UK*, to baste *US* - **2.** [coordinar - ideas] to piece together - **3.** [improvisar] to throw together.

himen *sm* hymen.

himno *sm* hymn; **himno nacional** national anthem.

hincapié *sm*: **hacer hincapié en** [insistir] to insist on; [subrayar] to emphasize, to stress.

hincar [10] *vt*: **hincar algo en** to stick sthg into.

➣ **hincarse** *vprnl*: **hincarse de rodillas** to fall to one's knees.

hincha ⬦ *smf* [seguidor] fan. ⬦ *sf* [rabia]: **tener hincha a alguien** to have it in for sb.

hinchado, da *adj* - **1.** [rueda, globo] inflated; [cara, tobillo] swollen - **2.** *fig* [persona] bigheaded, conceited; [lenguaje, estilo] bombastic.
➣ **hinchada** *sf* fans *pl*.

hinchar *vt* *lit & fig* to blow up.
➣ **hincharse** *vprnl* - **1.** [pierna, mano] to swell (up) - **2.** *fig* [persona] to become bigheaded - **3.** *fig* [de comida]: **hincharse (a)** to stuff o.s. (with).
➣ **hincharse a** *vprnl* [no parar de]: **hincharse a hacer algo** to do sthg a lot.

hinchazón *sf* swelling.

hinche, hinchiera *etc* ▭ **henchir**.

hindiera *etc* ▭ **hendir**.

hindú (*pl* hindúes *o* hindús) *adj & smf* - **1.** [de la India] Indian - **2.** RELIG Hindu.

hinduismo *sm* Hinduism.

hinojo *sm* fennel.

hinque *etc* ▭ **hincar**.

hip *interj*: ¡**hip hip hurra!** hip, hip, hooray!

hipar *vi* to hiccup, to have hiccups.

híper *sm* *fam* hypermarket.

hiperactividad *sf* hyperactivity.

hiperactivo, va *adj* hyperactive.

hipérbaton (*pl* hipérbatos *o* hiperbatones) *sm* hyperbaton.

hipérbola *sf* hyperbola.

hipérbole *sf* hyperbole.

hiperbólico, ca *adj* GEOM & LITER hyperbolic.

hiperenlace *sm* INFORM hyperlink.

hiperglucemia *sf* hyperglycaemia.

hipermercado *sm* hypermarket.

hipermetropía *sf* long-sightedness.

hiperrealismo *sm artistic movement concerned with almost photographic representation of reality.*

hipersensibilidad *sf* hypersensitivity.

hipersensible *adj* hypersensitive.

hipertensión *sf* high blood pressure.

hipertenso, sa ⬦ *adj* with high blood pressure. ⬦ *sm, f* person with high blood pressure.

hipertexto *sm* INFORM hypertext.

hipertrofia *sf* hypertrophy; *fig* overexpansion.

hípico, ca *adj* [de las carreras] horseracing *(antes de s)*; [de la equitación] showjumping *(antes de s)*.
➣ **hípica** *sf* [carreras de caballos] horseracing; [equitación] showjumping.

hipnosis *sf inv* hypnosis.

hipnótico, ca *adj* hypnotic.

➣ **hipnótico** *sm* hypnotic, narcotic.

hipnotismo *sm* hypnotism.

hipnotización *sf* hypnotization.

hipnotizador, ra ⬦ *adj* hypnotic; *fig* spellbinding, mesmerizing. ⬦ *sm, f* hypnotist.

hipnotizar [13] *vt* to hypnotize; *fig* to mesmerize.

hipo *sm* hiccups *pl*; **tener hipo** to have (the) hiccups; **quitar el hipo a uno** *fig* to take one's breath away.

hipocentro *sm* hypocentre, focus.

hipocondría *sf* hypochondria.

hipocondriaco, ca *adj & sm, f* hypochondriac.

hipocrático, ca *adj*: **juramento hipocrático** Hippocratic oath.

hipocresía *sf* hypocrisy.

hipócrita ⬦ *adj* hypocritical. ⬦ *smf* hypocrite.

hipodérmico, ca *adj* hypodermic.

hipodermis *sf inv* hypodermis.

hipódromo *sm* racecourse, racetrack.

hipófisis *sf inv* pituitary gland.

hipoglucemia *sf* hypoglycaemia.

hipopótamo *sm* hippopotamus.

hipotálamo *sm* hypothalamus.

hipoteca *sf* mortgage; **levantar una hipoteca** to pay off a mortgage.

hipotecable *adj* mortgageable.

hipotecar [10] *vt* - **1.** [bienes] to mortgage - **2.** *fig* [poner en peligro] to compromise, to jeopardize.

hipotecario, ria *adj* mortgage *(antes de s)*.

hipotensión *sf* low blood pressure.

hipotenso, sa ⬦ *adj* with low blood pressure. ⬦ *sm, f* person with low blood pressure.

hipotensor *sm* hypotensive drug.

hipotenusa *sf* hypotenuse.

hipotermia *sf* hypothermia.

hipótesis *sf inv* hypothesis.

hipotético, ca *adj* hypothetic, hypothetical.

hippy, hippie ['xipi] (*pl* hippies) *adj & smf* hippy.

hiriente *adj* [palabras] hurtful, cutting.

hiriera *etc* ▭ **herir**.

hirsuto, ta *adj* [cabello] wiry; [brazo, pecho] hairy.

hirviera *etc* ▭ **hervir**.

hisopo *sm* - **1.** RELIG aspergillum, sprinkler - **2.** BOT hyssop.

hispalense *adj & smf* Sevillian.

hispánico, ca *adj & sm, f* Hispanic, Spanish-speaking.

hispanidad *sf* [cultura] Spanishness; [pueblos] Spanish-speaking world.

hispanista *smf* Hispanist, student of Hispanic culture.

hispano, na ◇ *adj* [español] Spanish; [hispanoamericano] Spanish-American; [en Estados Unidos] Hispanic. ◇ *sm, f* [español] Spaniard; [estadounidense] Hispanic.

hispanoamericano, na ◇ *adj* Spanish-American. ◇ *sm, f* Spanish American.

hispanoárabe ◇ *adj* Hispano-Arabic. ◇ *smf* Spanish Arab.

hispanohablante ◇ *adj* Spanish-speaking. ◇ *smf* Spanish speaker.

histamina *sf* histamine.

histerectomía *sf* hysterectomy.

histeria *sf* fig & MED hysteria.

histérico, ca ◇ *adj* fig & MED hysterical; **ponerse histérico** to get hysterical. ◇ *sm, f* MED hysteric; fig hysterical person.

histerismo *sm* fig & MED hysteria.

histerotomía *sf* hysterotomy.

histología *sf* histology.

historia *sf* - **1.** [gen] history; **historia antigua/universal** ancient/world history; **historia del arte** art history; **hacer historia** to make history; **pasar a la historia** to go down in history - **2.** [narración, chisme] story; **dejarse de historias** to stop beating about the bush.
➤ **historia natural** *sf* natural history.

historiador, ra *sm, f* historian.

historial *sm* [gen] record; [profesional] curriculum vitae, résumé *US*; **historial médico** o **clínico** medical o case history.

historicidad *sf* historicity, historical authenticity.

historicismo *sm* historicism.

histórico, ca *adj* - **1.** [de la historia] historical - **2.** [verídico] factual - **3.** [importante] historic.

historieta *sf* - **1.** [chiste] funny story, anecdote - **2.** [tira cómica] comic strip.

historiografía *sf* historiography.

historiógrafo, fa *sm, f* historiographer.

histriónico, ca *adj* histrionic.

histrionismo *sm* histrionics *pl*.

hit [xit] (*pl* **hits**) *sm* hit.

hitita *adj* & *smf* Hittite.

hitleriano, na [xitle'rjano, ↓na] *adj* & *sm, f* Hitlerite.

hito *sm* lit & fig milestone; **mirar a alguien de hito en hito** to stare at sb.

hizo ▷ **hacer.**

hl (*abrev de* **hectolitro**) hl.

hm (*abrev de* **hectómetro**) hm.

hobby ['xoβi] (*pl* **hobbies**) *sm* hobby.

Hno. (*abrev de* **hermano**) Br.

Hnos. (*abrev de* **hermanos**) Bros.

hocico *sm* - **1.** [de perro] muzzle; [de gato] nose; [de cerdo] snout - **2.** *despec* [de personas - boca] rubber lips *pl*; [- cara] mug; **caer de hocicos** to fall flat on one's face; **meter el hocico en todo** to to stick one's nose into everything.

hockey ['xokei] *sm* hockey; **hockey sobre hielo/patines** ice/roller hockey; **hockey sobre hierba** (field) hockey.

hogar *sm* - **1.** [de chimenea] fireplace; [de horno, cocina] grate - **2.** [domicilio] home; **artículos para el hogar** household goods; **labores del hogar** housework; **hogar, dulce hogar** home, sweet home; **hogar de ancianos** old people's home.

hogareño, ña *adj* [gen] family *(antes de s)*; [amante del hogar] home-loving, homely.

hogaza *sf* large loaf.

hoguera *sf* bonfire; **morir en la hoguera** to be burned at the stake.

hoja *sf* - **1.** [de plantas] leaf; **de hoja caduca** deciduous; **de hoja perenne** evergreen; [de flor] petal; [de hierba] blade - **2.** [de papel] sheet (of paper); [de libro] page; **hoja informativa** newsletter; **hoja de paga** pay slip; **hoja de servicios** record (of service), track record - **3.** [de cuchillo] blade; **hoja de afeitar** razor blade - **4.** [de puertas, ventanas] leaf.
➤ **hoja de cálculo** *sf* INFORM spreadsheet.

hojalata *sf* tinplate.

hojalatería *sf* tinsmith's.

hojalatero *sm* tinsmith.

hojaldre *sm* puff pastry.

hojarasca *sf* - **1.** [hojas secas] (dead) leaves *pl*; [frondosidad] tangle of leaves - **2.** *fig* [paja] rubbish.

hojear *vt* to leaf through.

hola *interj* ¡hola! hello!

Holanda *n pr* Holland.

holandés, esa ◇ *adj* Dutch. ◇ *sm, f* [persona] Dutchman (*f* Dutchwoman).
➤ **holandés** *sm* [lengua] Dutch.
➤ **holandesa** *sf* [papel] *piece of paper measuring 22 x 28 cm.*

holding ['xoldin] (*pl* **holdings**) *sm* holding company.

holgado, da *adj* - **1.** [ropa] baggy, loose-fitting; [habitación, espacio] roomy - **2.** [victoria, situación económica] comfortable.

holganza *sf* leisure.

holgar [39] *vi* [sobrar] to be unnecessary; **huelga decir que...** needless to say...

holgazán, ana ◇ *adj* idle, good-for-nothing. ◇ *sm, f* good-for-nothing.

holgazanear *vi* to laze about.

holgazanería *sf* idleness.

holgué *etc* ⊳ **holgar**.

holgura *sf* - **1.** [anchura - de espacio] room; [- de ropa] bagginess, looseness; [- entre piezas] play, give - **2.** [bienestar] comfort, affluence; **vivir con holgura** to be comfortably off.

hollar [23] *vt* to tread (on).

hollejo *sm* skin *(of grape, olive etc)*.

hollín *sm* soot.

holocausto *sm* holocaust.

holografía *sf* holography.

holograma *sm* hologram.

hombre ◇ *sm* man; **el hombre** [la humanidad] man, mankind; **hombre de acción** man of action; **el hombre de la calle** *o* **de a pie** the man in the street; **hombre de las cavernas** caveman; **hombre de estado** statesman; **hombre de mundo** man of the world; **hombre de negocios** businessman; **hombre de paja** front (man); **hombre de palabra** man of his word; **hombre del saco** *fam* bogeyman; **hombre del tiempo** weatherman; **el abominable hombre de las nieves** the abominable snowman; **un pobre hombre** a nobody; **¡pobre hombre!** poor chap *UK o* guy!; **de hombre a hombre** man to man; **ser muy hombre** to be a (real) man; **ser todo un hombre** to be every bit a man; **ser un hombre hecho y derecho** to be a grown man; **el hombre propone y Dios dispone** *prov* Man proposes, God disposes *prov*; **hombre precavido vale por dos** *prov* forewarned is forearmed *prov*. ◇ *interj*: **¡hombre! ¡qué alegría verte!** (hey,) how nice to see you!

➤ **hombre lobo** (*pl* **hombres lobo**) *sm* werewolf.

➤ **hombre orquesta** (*pl* **hombres orquesta**) *sm* one-man band.

➤ **hombre rana** (*pl* **hombres rana**) *sm* frogman.

hombrera *sf* [de traje, vestido] shoulder pad; [de uniforme] epaulette.

hombría *sf* manliness.

hombro *sm* shoulder; **a hombros** over one's shoulders; **al hombro** across one's shoulder; **hombro con hombro** shoulder to shoulder; **encogerse de hombros** to shrug one's shoulders; **arrimar el hombro** *fig* to lend a hand; **echarse algo al hombro** *fig* to shoulder sthg, to take sthg on; **mirar por encima del hombro a alguien** *fig* to look down one's nose at sb.

hombruno, na *adj* masculine, mannish.

homenaje *sm* [gen] tribute; [al soberano] homage; **partido (de) homenaje** testimonial (match); **en homenaje de** *o* **a** in honour of, as a tribute to; **rendir homenaje a** to pay tribute to.

homenajeado, da ◇ *adj* honoured. ◇ *sm, f* guest of honour.

homenajear *vt* to pay tribute to, to honour.

homeópata *smf* homeopath.

homeopatía *sf* homeopathy.

homeopático, ca *adj* homeopathic.

homérico, ca *adj* - **1.** LITER Homeric - **2.** [épico] epic.

homicida ◇ *adj* [mirada etc] murderous; **arma homicida** murder weapon. ◇ *smf* murderer.

homicidio *sm* homicide, murder; **homicidio frustrado** attempted murder; **homicidio involuntario** manslaughter.

homilía *sf* homily, sermon.

homínido *sm* hominid.

homófono, na *adj* homophonic.

homogeneidad *sf* homogeneity.

homogeneización *sf* homogenization.

homogeneizar [13] *vt* to homogenize.

homogéneo, a *adj* homogenous.

homógrafo, fa *adj* homographic.

➤ **homógrafo** *sm* homograph.

homologable *adj*: **homologable (a)** comparable (to).

homologación *sf* - **1.** [equiparación] bringing into line - **2.** [ratificación - de producto] official authorization; [- de récord] official confirmation.

homologar [16] *vt* - **1.** [equiparar]: **homologar (con)** to bring into line (with), to make comparable (with) - **2.** [dar por válido - producto] to authorize officially; [- récord] to confirm officially.

homólogo, ga ◇ *adj* - **1.** [semejante] equivalent - **2.** GEOM & QUÍM homologous. ◇ *sm, f* counterpart.

homonimia *sf* homonymy.

homónimo, ma ◇ *adj* homonymous. ◇ *sm, f* [tocayo] namesake.

➤ **homónimo** *sm* GRAM homonym.

homosexual *adj & smf* homosexual.

homosexualidad *sf* homosexuality.

hondo, da *adj* - **1.** *lit & fig* [gen] deep; **tiene tres metros de hondo** it's three metres deep; **lo hondo** the depths *pl*; **calar hondo en** to strike a chord with; **en lo más hondo de** in the depths of - **2.** ⊳ **cante**.

➤ **honda** *sf* sling.

hondonada *sf* hollow.

hondura *sf* depth.

Honduras *n pr* Honduras.

hondureño, ña *adj & sm, f* Honduran.

honestamente *adv* [con honradez] honestly; [con decencia] modestly, decently; [con justicia] fairly.

honestidad *sf* [honradez] honesty; [decencia] modesty, decency; [justicia] fairness.

honesto, ta *adj* [honrado] honest; [decente] modest, decent; [justo] fair.

hongo *sm* - **1.** [planta - comestible] mushroom; [- no comestible] toadstool; **crecer como hongos** to spring up like mushrooms - **2.** [enfermedad] fungus - **3.** [sombrero] bowler (hat) *UK*, derby *US*.

honor *sm* honour; **en honor de** in honour of; **hacer honor a** to live up to; **en honor a la verdad** to be (quite) honest; **tener el honor de hacer algo** to have the honour of doing sthg.
  ◆ **honores** *smpl* [ceremonial] honours; **hacer los honores de la casa** *fig* to do the honours, to look after the guests.

honorabilidad *sf* honour.

honorable *adj* honourable.

honorario, ria *adj* honorary.
  ◆ **honorarios** *smpl* fees.

honorífico, ca *adj* honorific.

honra *sf* honour; **es la honra de su país** she's the pride o toast of her country; **tener algo a mucha honra** to be honoured by sthg; **¡y a mucha honra!** and proud of it!
  ◆ **honras fúnebres** *sfpl* funeral *sing*.

honradez *sf* honesty.

honrado, da *adj* honest.

honrar *vt* to honour.
  ◆ **honrarse** *vprnl*: **honrarse (con algo/de hacer algo)** to be honoured (by sthg/to do sthg).

honrilla *sf* pride, concern about what people say.

honroso, sa *adj* - **1.** [que da honra] honorary - **2.** [respetable] honourable, respectable.

hora *sf* - **1.** [del día] hour; **a primera hora** first thing in the morning; **a última hora** [al final del día] at the end of the day; [en el último momento] at the last moment; **dar la hora** to strike the hour; **de última hora** [noticia] latest, up-to-the-minute; [preparativos] last-minute; **'última hora'** 'stop press'; **(pagar) por horas** (to pay) by the hour; **poner el reloj en hora** to set one's watch o clock; **hora de dormir** bedtime; **horas de oficina/trabajo** office/working hours; **hora local/oficial** local/official time; **hora punta** o **pico** *Amér* rush hour; **horas extraordinarias** overtime *(U)*; **horas libres** free time *(U)*; **horas de visita** visiting times; **horas de vuelo** flying time *sing*; **media hora** half an hour - **2.** [momento determinado] time; **¿a qué hora sale?** what time o when does it leave?; **es hora de irse** it's time to go; **es hora de cenar** it's

time for supper; **a la hora** on time; **cada hora** hourly; **en su hora** when the time comes, at the appropriate time; **¿qué hora es?** what time is it?; **hora de cerrar** closing time; **hora H** zero hour - **3.** [cita] appointment; **pedir/dar hora** to ask for/give an appointment; **tener hora en/con** to have an appointment at/with - **4.** [muerte]: **llegó mi hora** my time has come - **5.** *loc*: **a altas horas de la noche** in the small hours; **a buenas horas (mangas verdes)** it's a bit late now; **en mala hora** unluckily; **la hora de la verdad** the moment of truth; **no ver la hora de hacer algo** [no tener tiempo] not to know when one is going to find time to do sthg; [estar ansioso] not to be able to wait to do sthg; **tener las horas contadas** to have one's days numbered; **¡ya era hora!** and about time too!

Hora inglesa

> ♨ In much of Latin America, punctuality is not given the same importance as in the UK or USA. In an ironic recognition of this cultural difference, some people will specify **hora inglesa** (literally "English time") when they mean "punctually" or "on the dot".

horadar *vt* to pierce; [con máquina] to bore through.

horario, ria *adj* time *(antes de s)*.
  ◆ **horario** *sm* timetable; **horario comercial/laboral** opening/working hours *pl*; **horario flexible** flexitime *(U)*; **horario intensivo** *working day without a long break for lunch*; **horario de visitas** visiting hours *pl*.

horca *sf* - **1.** [patíbulo] gallows *pl* - **2.** AGRIC pitchfork.

horcajadas ◆ **a horcajadas** *loc adv* astride.

horchata *sf cold drink made from ground tiger nuts or almonds, milk and sugar*.

horchatería *sf bar where 'horchata' is served*.

horda *sf* horde.

horizontal *adj* horizontal.

horizonte *sm* horizon.

horma *sf* [gen] mould, pattern; [para arreglar zapatos] last; [para conservar zapatos] shoe tree; [de sombrero] hat block; **encontrar alguien la horma de su zapato** *fig* to meet one's match.

hormiga *sf* ant; **ser una hormiga** *fig* to be hard-working and thrifty.

hormigón *sm* concrete; **hormigón armado** reinforced concrete.

hormigonera *sf* concrete mixer.

hormiguear *vi* - **1.** [dar hormigueo]: **me hormiguean las piernas** I've got pins and needles in my legs - **2.** [bullir] to swarm.

hormigueo *sm* pins and needles *pl*.

hormiguero *sm* ants' nest; ⊳ **oso**.

hormiguita *sf fam* hard-working and thrifty person.

hormona *sf* hormone.

hormonal *adj* hormonal.

hornada *sf lit & fig* batch.

hornear *vt* to bake.

hornillo *sm* [para cocinar] camping *o* portable stove; [de laboratorio] small furnace.

horno *sm* CULIN oven; TECNOL furnace; [de cerámica, ladrillos] kiln; **al horno** baked; **alto horno** blast furnace; **altos hornos** [factoría] iron and steelworks; **horno crematorio** crematorium; **horno eléctrico** electric oven; **horno de gas** gas oven; **horno microondas** microwave (oven); **no está el horno para bollos** the time is not right.

horóscopo *sm* - **1.** [signo zodiacal] star sign - **2.** [predicción] horoscope.

horquilla *sf* - **1.** [para el pelo] hairgrip, hairpin, bobby pin *US* - **2.** [de bicicleta etc] fork.

horrendo, da *adj* [gen] horrendous; [muy malo] terrible, awful.

hórreo *sm* raised granary typical of Asturias and Galicia.

horrible *adj* [gen] horrible; [muy malo] terrible, awful.

horripilante *adj* - **1.** [terrorífico] horrifying, spine-chilling - **2.** *fam* [muy malo, feo] dreadful, awful.

horripilar *vt* to terrify, to scare to death.

horror *sm* - **1.** [miedo] terror, horror; **¡qué horror!** how awful!; **tener horror a algo** to have a horror of sthg - **2.** *(gen pl)* [atrocidad] atrocity. ➤ **horrores** *adv fam* terribly, an awful lot.

horrorizado, da *adj* terrified, horrified.

horrorizar [13] *vt* to terrify, to horrify. ➤ **horrorizarse** *vprnl* to be terrified *o* horrified.

horroroso, sa *adj* - **1.** [gen] awful, dreadful - **2.** [muy feo] horrible, hideous - **3.** *fam* [enorme] terrible.

hortaliza *sf* (garden) vegetable.

hortelano, na ◇ *adj* market garden *(antes de s)*. ◇ *sm, f* market gardener.

hortensia *sf* hydrangea.

hortera *fam* ◇ *adj* tasteless, tacky. ◇ *smf* person with no taste.

horterada *sf fam* tacky thing.

hortícola *adj* horticultural.

horticultor, ra *sm, f* horticulturalist.

horticultura *sf* horticulture.

hosco, ca *adj* [persona] sullen, gruff; [lugar] grim, gloomy.

hospedaje *sm* - **1.** [alojamiento] accommodation, lodgings *pl* - **2.** [dinero] (cost of) board and lodging - **3.** INFORM hosting.

hospedar *vt* - **1.** to put up - **2.** INFORM to host. ➤ **hospedarse** *vprnl* to stay.

hospicio *sm* [para niños] orphanage, children's home; [para pobres] poorhouse.

hospital *sm* hospital.

hospitalario, ria *adj* - **1.** [acogedor] hospitable - **2.** [de hospital] hospital *(antes de s)*.

hospitalidad *sf* hospitality.

hospitalización *sf* hospitalization.

hospitalizar [13] *vt* to hospitalize, to take *o* send to hospital.

hostal *sm* guesthouse.

hostelería *sf* catering.

hostelero, ra ◇ *adj* catering *(antes de s)*. ◇ *sm, f* landlord (*f* landlady).

hostería *sf* - **1.** guesthouse - **2.** *C Sur* country hotel.

hostia *sf* - **1.** RELIG host - **2.** *vulg* [bofetada] bash, punch; **dar de hostias a alguien** to beat the shit out of sb - **3.** *vulg* [accidente] smash-up; **darse** *o* **pegarse una hostia** to have a smash-up. ➤ **hostias** *interj vulg*: **¡hostias!** bloody hell!, damn it!

hostiar [9] *vt vulg* to bash.

hostigamiento *sm* harassment.

hostigar [16] *vt* - **1.** [acosar] to pester, to bother - **2.** MIL to harass.

hostil *adj* hostile.

hostilidad *sf* [sentimiento] hostility. ➤ **hostilidades** *sfpl* MIL hostilities.

hostilizar [13] *vt* to harass.

hotel *sm* hotel.

hotelería *sf* hotel industry *o* trade.

hotelero, ra ◇ *adj* hotel *(antes de s)*. ◇ *sm, f* hotel manager (*f* hotel manageress), hotelier.

hoy *adv* - **1.** [en este día] today; **de hoy en adelante** from now on; **hoy mismo** this very day; **por hoy** for now, for the time being - **2.** [en la actualidad] nowadays, today; **hoy día, hoy en día, hoy por hoy** these days, nowadays.

hoyo *sm* - **1.** [gen] hole, pit; [de golf] hole - **2.** *fam* [sepultura] grave.

hoyuelo *sm* dimple.

hoz *sf* sickle; **la hoz y el martillo** the hammer and sickle.

HTML (*abrev de* **hypertext markup language**) *sm* INFORM HTML.

HTTP (*abrev de* **hypertext transfer protocol**) *sm* INFORM HTTP.

huacal *sm Méx* - **1.** [jaula] cage - **2.** [cajón] drawer.

huachafería *sf Perú fam* - **1.** [hecho] tacky thing - **2.** [dicho] naff comment.

huachafo, **fa** *adj Perú fam* tacky.

huacho, **cha** *sm*, *f Amér fam* illegitimate child.

huasca *sf Amér* whip.

huaso, **sa** *sm*, *f Chile fam* farmer, peasant.

hubiera *etc* ⊳ **haber**.

hucha *sf* moneybox.

hueco, **ca** *adj* - **1.** [vacío] hollow - **2.** [sonido] resonant, hollow - **3.** [sin ideas] empty.

➡ **hueco** *sm* - **1.** [cavidad - gen] hole; [- en pared] recess - **2.** [tiempo libre] spare moment - **3.** [espacio libre] space, gap; [de escalera] well; [de ascensor] shaft; **hacer un hueco a alguien** to make space for sb.

huela *etc* ⊳ **oler**.

huelga *sf* strike; **estar/declararse en huelga** to be/to go on strike; **huelga de brazos caídos o cruzados** sit-down (strike); **huelga de celo** work-to-rule; **huelga de hambre** hunger strike; **huelga general** general strike; **huelga indefinida** indefinite strike; **huelga salvaje** wildcat strike; ⊳ **holgar**.

huelguista ⟨⟩ *adj* strike *(antes de s)*. ⟨⟩ *smf* striker.

huella *sf* - **1.** [de persona] footprint; [de animal, rueda] track; **huella digital o dactilar** fingerprint; **seguir las huellas de alguien** to follow in sb's footsteps - **2.** *fig* [vestigio] trace; **sin dejar huella** without (a) trace - **3.** *fig* [impresión profunda] mark; **dejar huella** to leave one's mark; ⊳ **hollar**.

huérfano, **na** *adj* & *sm*, *f* orphan; **es huérfano de madre** his mother is dead, he's lost his mother.

huerta *sf* - **1.** [huerto] market garden *UK*, truck farm *US* - **2.** [tierra de regadío] *irrigated crop-growing region*.

huerto *sm* [de hortalizas] vegetable garden; [de frutales] orchard.

hueso *sm* - **1.** [del cuerpo] bone; **acabar o dar con sus huesos en** to end up in; **estar calado hasta los huesos** to be soaked to the skin; **estar en los huesos** to be all skin and bones; **no poder alguien con sus huesos** to be ready to drop, to be exhausted; **ser un hueso duro de roer** to be a hard nut to crack - **2.** [de fruto] stone *UK*, pit *US* - **3.** *fam* [persona] very strict person; [asignatura] difficult subject - **4.** *Amér & Méx fam* [enchufe] contacts *pl*, influence - **5.** *Méx fam* [trabajo fácil] cushy job.

➡ **hueso de santo** *sm* CULIN *small marzipan roll filled with egg yolk*.

huésped, **da** *sm*, *f* guest.

huestes *sfpl* [gen] army *sing*; [seguidores] followers.

huesudo, **da** *adj* bony.

hueva *sf* roe.

huevada *sf Andes mfam* crap.

huevear *vi Amér fam* to muck about.

huevero, **ra** *sm*, *f* egg seller.

➡ **huevera** *sf* - **1.** [para servir] egg cup - **2.** [para guardar] egg box.

huevo *sm* - **1.** [de animales] egg; **huevo a la copa o tibio** *Andes* soft-boiled egg; **huevo escalfado/frito** poached/fried egg; **huevo pasado por agua/duro** soft-boiled/hard-boiled egg; **huevo de Pascua** Easter egg; **huevos al plato** *eggs cooked in the oven in an earthenware dish*; **huevos revueltos** scrambled eggs; **parecerse como un huevo a una castaña** to be like chalk and cheese - **2.** *(gen pl) vulg* [testículos] balls *pl*; **costar un huevo** [ser caro] to cost a packet o bomb; [ser difícil] to be bloody hard; **saber un huevo** to know a hell of a lot; **tener huevos** to have (a lot of) balls; **¡y un huevo!** bollocks!, like hell!

huevón, **ona** *sm*, *f Andes, Arg & Ven vulg* prat *UK*, pillock *UK*, jerk *US*.

huida *sf* escape, flight.

huidizo, **za** *adj* shy, elusive.

huir [51] ⟨⟩ *vi* - **1.** [escapar]: **huir (de)** [gen] to flee (from); [de cárcel etc] to escape (from); **huir del país** to flee the country - **2.** [evitar]: **huir de algo** to avoid sthg, to keep away from sthg. ⟨⟩ *vt* to avoid.

huiro *sm Chile* seaweed.

hule *sm* oilskin.

hulla *sf* soft coal.

hullero, **ra** *adj* soft coal *(antes de s)*.

humanidad *sf* humanity.

➡ **humanidades** *sfpl* [letras] humanities.

humanismo *sm* humanism.

humanista ⟨⟩ *adj* humanist, humanistic. ⟨⟩ *smf* humanist.

humanístico, **ca** *adj* humanistic.

humanitario, **ria** *adj* humanitarian.

humanitarismo *sm* humanitarianism.

humanización *sf* humanization.

humanizar [13] *vt* to humanize, to make more human.

➡ **humanizarse** *vprnl* to become more human.

humano, **na** *adj* - **1.** [del hombre] human - **2.** [compasivo] humane.

➡ **humano** *sm* human being; **los humanos** mankind *(U)*.

humareda *sf* cloud of smoke.

humeante *adj* [lleno de humo] smoky; [que echa humo] smoking; [que echa vapor] steaming.

humear *vi* [salir humo] to (give off) smoke; [salir vapor] to steam.

humedad *sf* - **1.** [gen] dampness; [en pared, te-cho] damp; [de algo chorreando] wetness; [de piel, ojos etc] moistness - **2.** [de atmósfera etc] humid-ity; **humedad absoluta/relativa** absolute/rel-ative humidity.

humedecer [30] *vt* to moisten.

◆ **humedecerse** *vprnl* to become moist; **hu-medecerse los labios** to moisten one's lips.

humedecimiento *sm* moistening.

húmedo, da *adj* - **1.** [gen] damp; [chorreando] wet; [piel, ojos etc] moist - **2.** [aire, clima, atmós-fera] humid.

húmero *sm* humerus.

humidificador *sm* humidifier.

humidificar [10] *vt* to humidify.

humildad *sf* humility.

humilde *adj* humble.

humillación *sf* humiliation.

humillado, da *adj* humiliated.

humillante *adj* humiliating.

humillar *vt* to humiliate.

◆ **humillarse** *vprnl* to humble o.s.; **humillarse a hacer algo** [rebajarse] to lower o.s. to do sthg, to stoop to doing sthg.

humo *sm* [gen] smoke; [vapor] steam; [de coches etc] fumes *pl*; **echar humo** [gen] to smoke; *fig* to be fuming; **tragarse el humo** [al fumar] to in-hale.

◆ **humos** *smpl fig* [aires] airs; **bajarle a alguien los humos** to take sb down a peg or two; **tener muchos humos** to put on airs.

humor *sm* - **1.** [estado de ánimo] mood; [carácter] temperament; **estar de buen/mal humor** to be in a good/bad mood; **tener un humor de perros** to be in a filthy mood - **2.** [gracia] hu-mour; **un programa de humor** a comedy pro-gramme; **humor negro** black humour - **3.** [ga-nas] mood; **no estoy de humor** I'm not in the mood - **4.** ANAT humour.

humorismo *sm* humour; TEATRO & TV comedy.

humorista *smf* humorist; TEATRO & TV comedi-an (*f* comedienne).

humorístico, ca *adj* humorous.

humus *sm inv* humus.

hundimiento *sm* - **1.** [naufragio] sinking - **2.** [ruina] collapse.

hundir *vt* - **1.** [gen] to sink; **hundir algo en el agua** to put sthg underwater - **2.** [afligir] to devastate, to destroy - **3.** [hacer fracasar] to ruin.

◆ **hundirse** *vprnl* - **1.** [sumergirse] to sink; [in-tencionadamente] to dive - **2.** [derrumbarse] to collapse; [techo] to cave in - **3.** [fracasar] to be ruined.

húngaro, ra *adj* & *sm, f* Hungarian.

◆ **húngaro** *sm* [lengua] Hungarian.

Hungría *n pr* Hungary.

huno, na ⬦ *adj* Hunnish. ⬦ *sm, f* Hun.

huracán *sm* hurricane.

huracanado, da *adj* violent; METEOR hur-ricane-force.

huraño, ña *adj* unsociable.

hurgar [16] *vi*: **hurgar (en)** [gen] to rummage around (in); [con el dedo, un palo] to poke around (in).

◆ **hurgarse** *vprnl*: **hurgarse la nariz** to pick one's nose; **hurgarse los bolsillos** to rummage around in one's pockets.

hurgue *etc* ▷ **hurgar**.

hurón *sm* - **1.** ZOOL ferret - **2.** *fig* [persona] unso-ciable person.

hurra *interj*: **¡hurra!** hurray!

hurtadillas ◆ **a hurtadillas** *loc adv* on the sly, stealthily.

hurtar *vt* to steal.

hurto *sm* theft.

húsar *sm* hussar.

husmear ⬦ *vt* [olfatear] to sniff out, to scent. ⬦ *vi* [curiosear] to nose around.

huso *sm* spindle; [en máquina] bobbin.

◆ **huso horario** *sm* time zone.

huy *interj*: **¡huy!** [dolor] ouch!; [sorpresa] gosh!

huya, huyera *etc* ▷ **huir**.

i (*pl* **íes**), **I** (*pl* **íes**) *sf* [letra] i, I.

I+D (*abrev de* **investigación y desarrollo**) *sf* R & D.

IAE (*abrev de* **impuesto sobre actividades económicas**) *sm Spanish tax paid by profes-sionals and shop owners.*

ib., ibíd. (*abrev de* **ibídem**) ibid.

iba ▷ **ir**.

ibérico, ca *adj* Iberian.

íbero, ra, ibero, ra *adj* & *sm, f* Iberian.

◆ **íbero, ibero** *sm* [lengua] Iberian.

iberoamericano, na *adj* & *sm, f* Latin Amer-ican.

ibídem, ibidem *adv* ibidem, ibid.

ice *etc* ▷ **izar**.

iceberg (*pl* **icebergs**) *sm* iceberg.

icono *sm* icon.

iconoclasta ◇ *adj* iconoclastic. ◇ *smf* iconoclast.

ictericia *sf* jaundice.

ictiología *sf* ichthyology.

id ▷ **ir**.

ida *sf* outward journey; **(billete de) ida y vuelta** return (ticket); **idas y venidas** *fig* comings and goings.

idea *sf* - **1.** [gen] idea; [propósito] intention; **a mala idea** maliciously; **con la idea de** with the idea *o* intention of; **hacerse a la idea de que...** to get used to the idea that...; **hacerse una idea de algo** to get an idea of sthg; **tener idea de hacer algo** to intend to do sthg; **idea fija** obsession; **idea luminosa** brilliant idea, brainwave; **idea preconcebida** preconception; **cuando se le mete una idea en la cabeza...** when he gets an idea into his head...; **¡ni idea!** *fam* search me!, I haven't got a clue!; **no tener ni idea (de)** not to have a clue (about); **tener ideas de bombero** to have wild *o* crazy ideas - **2.** [opinión] impression; **cambiar de idea** to change one's mind.
➡ **ideas** *sfpl* [ideología] ideas.

ideal *adj & sm* ideal; **lo ideal sería hacerlo mañana** ideally, we would do it tomorrow.

idealismo *sm* idealism.

idealista ◇ *adj* idealistic. ◇ *smf* idealist.

idealización *sf* idealization.

idealizar [13] *vt* to idealize.

idear *vt* - **1.** [planear] to think up, to devise - **2.** [inventar] to invent.

ideario *sm* ideology.

ídem *pron* ditto; **ídem de ídem** exactly the same.

idéntico, ca *adj*: **idéntico (a)** identical (to).

identidad *sf* - **1.** [gen] identity - **2.** [igualdad] identical nature.

identificación *sf* identification.

identificar [10] *vt* to identify.
➡ **identificarse** *vprnl*: **identificarse (con)** to identify (with).

ideograma *sm* ideogram, ideograph.

ideología *sf* ideology.

ideológico, ca *adj* ideological.

ideólogo, ga *sm, f* ideologist.

idílico, ca *adj* idyllic.

idilio *sm* love affair.

idioma *sm* language.

idiomático, ca *adj* idiomatic.

idiosincrasia *sf* individual character.

idiosincrásico, ca *adj* characteristic.

idiota ◇ *adj* - **1.** *despec* [tonto] stupid - **2.** [enfermo] mentally deficient. ◇ *smf* idiot.

idiotez *sf* - **1.** [tontería] stupid thing, stupidity (*U*) - **2.** [enfermedad] mental deficiency.

idiotizar [13] *vt* to turn into an idiot, to zombify.

ido, ida *adj* - **1.** [loco] mad, touched - **2.** [distraído]: **estar ido** to be miles away.

idólatra ◇ *adj* *lit & fig* idolatrous. ◇ *smf* idolater (*f* idolatress); *fig* idolizer.

idolatrar *vt* to worship; *fig* to idolize.

idolatría *sf* *lit & fig* idolatry.

ídolo *sm* idol.

idoneidad *sf* suitability.

idóneo, a *adj*: **idóneo (para)** suitable (for).

iglesia *sf* church; **casarse por la iglesia** to get married in church, to have a church wedding; **iglesia parroquial** parish church; **con la iglesia hemos topado** now we're really up against it.

iglú (*pl* **iglúes** *o* **iglús**) *sm* igloo.

ígneo, a *adj* igneous.

ignición *sf* ignition.

ignominia *sf* ignominy.

ignominioso, sa *adj* ignominious.

ignorancia *sf* ignorance; **ignorancia supina** blind ignorance.

ignorante ◇ *adj* ignorant. ◇ *smf* ignoramus.

ignorar *vt* - **1.** [desconocer] not to know, to be ignorant of - **2.** [no tener en cuenta] to ignore.

ignoto, ta *adj* unknown, undiscovered.

igual ◇ *adj* - **1.** [idéntico]: **igual (que)** the same (as); **llevan jerseys iguales** they're wearing the same jumper; **son iguales** they're the same - **2.** [parecido]: **igual (que)** similar (to) - **3.** [equivalente]: **igual (a)** equal (to) - **4.** [liso] even - **5.** [constante - velocidad] constant; [- clima, temperatura] even - **6.** MAT: **A más B es igual a C** A plus B equals C. ◇ *smf* equal; **de igual a igual** as an equal; **no tener igual** to have no equal, to be unrivalled; **sin igual** without equal, unrivalled. ◇ *adv* - **1.** [de la misma manera] the same; **yo pienso igual** I think the same, I think so too; **al igual que** just like; **por igual** equally - **2.** [posiblemente] perhaps; **igual llueve** it could well rain - **3.** DEP: **van iguales** the scores are level - **4.** *loc*: **dar** *o* **ser igual a alguien** to be all the same to sb; **es** *o* **da igual** it doesn't matter, it doesn't make any difference.

igualación *sf* - **1.** [de terreno] levelling; [de superficie] smoothing - **2.** [de cantidades] equalizing.

igualado, da *adj* level.

igualar *vt* - **1.** [gen] to make equal, to equalize; DEP to equalize; **igualar algo a** *o* **con** to equate sthg with - **2.** [persona] to be equal to; **nadie le iguala en generosidad** nobody is as generous as he is - **3.** [terreno] to level; [superficie] to smooth.

 igualarse *vprnl* - **1.** [gen] to be equal, to equal one another; **igualarse a** *o* **con** to be equated with - **2.** [a otra persona]: **igualarse a** *o* **con alguien** to treat sb as an equal.

igualdad *sf* - **1.** [equivalencia] equality; **en igualdad de condiciones** on equal terms; **igualdad de oportunidades** equal opportunities *pl* - **2.** [identidad] sameness.

igualitario, ria *adj* egalitarian.

igualitarismo *sm* egalitarianism.

igualmente *adv* - **1.** [también] also, likewise - **2.** [fórmula de cortesía] the same to you, likewise.

iguana *sf* iguana.

ijada *sf* flank, side.

ijar *sm* = ijada.

ikastola *sf* *primary school in the Basque country where classes are given entirely in Basque.*

ikurriña *sf* Basque national flag.

ilación *sf* cohesion.

ilegal *adj* illegal.

ilegalidad *sf* - **1.** [acción] unlawful act - **2.** [cualidad] illegality.

ilegible *adj* illegible.

ilegitimidad *sf* illegitimacy.

ilegítimo, ma *adj* - **1.** illegitimate - **2.** ⊳ hijo.

ileso, sa *adj* unhurt, unharmed; **salir** *o* **resultar ileso** to escape unharmed.

iletrado, da *adj* & *sm, f* illiterate.

ilícito, ta *adj* illicit.

ilimitado, da *adj* unlimited, limitless.

ilógico, ca *adj* illogical.

iluminación *sf* - **1.** [gen] lighting; [acción] illumination - **2.** RELIG enlightenment.

iluminado, da ⋄ *adj* - **1.** [gen] lit (up) - **2.** RELIG enlightened. ⋄ *sm, f* RELIG enlightened person.

iluminador, ra ⋄ *adj* illuminating. ⋄ *sm, f* lighting technician.

iluminar *vt* - **1.** [gen] to illuminate, to light up - **2.** RELIG to enlighten.

 iluminarse *vprnl* - **1.** to light up - **2.** RELIG to become enlightened.

ilusión *sf* - **1.** [esperanza - gen] hope; [- infundada] delusion, illusion; **hacerse** *o* **forjarse ilusiones** to build up one's hopes; **hacerse la ilusión de** to imagine that; **tener ilusión por** to look forward to - **2.** [emoción] thrill, excite-

ment *(U)*; **¡qué ilusión!** how exciting!; **me hace mucha ilusión** I'm really looking forward to it - **3.** [espejismo] illusion; **ilusión óptica** optical illusion.

ilusionar *vt* - **1.** [esperanzar]: **ilusionar a alguien (con algo)** to build up sb's hopes (about sthg) - **2.** [emocionar] to excite, to thrill.

 ilusionarse *vprnl* - **1.** [esperanzarse]: **ilusionarse (con)** to get one's hopes up (about) - **2.** [emocionarse]: **ilusionarse (con)** to get excited (about).

ilusionismo *sm* conjuring.

ilusionista ⋄ *adj* conjuring *(antes de s)*. ⋄ *smf* illusionist, conjurer.

iluso, sa ⋄ *adj* gullible. ⋄ *sm, f* gullible person.

ilusorio, ria *adj* illusory; [promesa] empty.

ilustración *sf* - **1.** [estampa] illustration - **2.** [cultura] learning.

 Ilustración *sf* HIST: **la Ilustración** the Enlightenment.

ilustrado, da *adj* - **1.** [publicación] illustrated - **2.** [persona] learned - **3.** HIST enlightened.

ilustrador, ra ⋄ *adj* illustrative. ⋄ *sm, f* illustrator.

ilustrar *vt* - **1.** [explicar] to illustrate, to explain - **2.** [publicación] to illustrate - **3.** [educar] to enlighten.

ilustrativo, va *adj* illustrative.

ilustre *adj* - **1.** [gen] illustrious, distinguished - **2.** [título]: **el ilustre señor alcalde** his Worship, the mayor.

ilustrísimo, ma *adj* most illustrious.

 Ilustrísima *sf*: **Su Ilustrísima** Your/His Grace, Your/His Worship.

imagen *sf* [gen] image; TV picture; **a imagen y semejanza de** identical to, exactly the same as; **ser la viva imagen de alguien** to be the spitting image of sb; **una imagen vale más que mil palabras** a picture is worth a thousand words; **imagen borrosa** blur; **imagen congelada** freeze frame; **imagen corporativa** corporate identity.

imaginable *adj* imaginable, conceivable.

imaginación *sf* - **1.** [facultad] imagination; **se deja llevar por la imaginación** he lets his imagination run away with him; **pasar por la imaginación de alguien** to occur to sb, to cross sb's mind; **no me pasó por la imaginación** it never occurred to me - **2.** *(gen pl)* [idea falsa] delusion, imagining; **son imaginaciones tuyas** you're just imagining things, it's all in your mind.

imaginar *vt* - **1.** [gen] to imagine - **2.** [idear] to think up, to invent.

imaginarse *vprnl* to imagine; **¡imagínate!** just think O imagine!; **me imagino que sí** I suppose so.

imaginario, ria *adj* imaginary.

imaginativo, va *adj* imaginative.

imaginería *sf religious image-making.*

imán *sm* - **1.** [para atraer] magnet - **2.** [entre musulmanes] imam.

imanar, imantar *vt* to magnetize.

imbatible *adj* unbeatable.

imbatido, da *adj* unbeaten.

imbebible *adj* undrinkable.

imbécil ◇ *adj* stupid. ◇ *smf* idiot.

imbecilidad *sf* stupidity; **decir/hacer una imbecilidad** to say/do sthg stupid.

imberbe *adj* beardless.

imborrable *adj fig* indelible; [recuerdo] unforgettable.

imbricado, da *adj* overlapping.

imbricar [10] *vt* to overlap.

imbuir [51] *vt*: **imbuir (de)** to imbue (with).

imitación *sf* imitation; [de humorista] impersonation; **a imitación de** in imitation of; **piel de imitación** imitation leather.

imitador, ra *sm, f* imitator; [humorista] impersonator.

imitar *vt* [gen] to imitate, to copy; [a personajes famosos] to impersonate; [producto, material] to simulate.

imitativo, va *adj* imitative.

impaciencia *sf* impatience.

impacientar *vt* to make impatient, to exasperate.

impacientarse *vprnl* to grow impatient.

impaciente *adj* impatient; **impaciente por hacer algo** impatient O anxious to do sthg.

impactante *adj* [imagen] hard-hitting; [belleza] striking.

impactar ◇ *vt* [suj: noticia] to have an impact on. ◇ *vi* [bala] to hit.

impacto *sm* - **1.** [gen] impact; [de bala] hit - **2.** [señal] (impact) mark; **impacto de bala** bullethole; **impacto ambiental** environmental impact.

impagable *adj* invaluable.

impagado, da *adj* unpaid.

impagado *sm* unpaid bill.

impago *sm* non-payment.

impalpable *adj* impalpable.

impar *adj* - **1.** MAT odd - **2.** [sin igual] unequalled.

imparable *adj* unstoppable.

imparcial *adj* impartial.

imparcialidad *sf* impartiality.

impartir *vt* to give.

impase, impasse [im'pas] *sm* impasse.

impasibilidad *sf* impassivity.

impasible *adj* impassive.

impavidez *sf* [valor] fearlessness, courage; [impasibilidad] impassivity.

impávido, da *adj* [valeroso] fearless, courageous; [impasible] impassive.

impecable *adj* impeccable.

impedido, da ◇ *adj* disabled; **estar impedido de un brazo** to have the use of only one arm. ◇ *sm, f* disabled person.

impedimento *sm* [gen] obstacle; [contra un matrimonio] impediment; **no hay ningún impedimento para hacerlo** there's no reason why we shouldn't do it.

impedir [26] *vt* - **1.** [imposibilitar] to prevent; **impedir a alguien hacer algo** to prevent sb from doing sthg - **2.** [dificultar] to hinder, to obstruct.

impeler *vt* - **1.** [hacer avanzar] to propel - **2.** [estimular]: **impeler a alguien a algo/hacer algo** to drive sb to sthg/to do sthg.

impenetrabilidad *sf lit & fig* impenetrability.

impenetrable *adj lit & fig* impenetrable.

impenitente *adj* unrepentant, impenitent; *fig* [incorregible] inveterate.

impensable *adj* unthinkable.

impensado, da *adj* unexpected.

impepinable *adj fam* clear as clear can be, undeniable.

imperante *adj* prevailing.

imperar *vi* to prevail.

imperativo, va *adj* - **1.** [gen & GRAM] imperative - **2.** [autoritario] imperious.

imperativo *sm* [gen & GRAM] imperative.

imperceptible *adj* imperceptible.

imperdible *sm* safety pin.

imperdonable *adj* unforgivable.

imperecedero, ra *adj* non-perishable; *fig* [eterno] immortal, eternal.

imperfección *sf* - **1.** [cualidad] imperfection - **2.** [defecto] flaw, defect.

imperfecto, ta *adj* [gen] imperfect; [defectuoso] faulty, defective.

imperfecto *sm* GRAM imperfect.

imperial *adj* imperial.

imperialismo *sm* imperialism.

imperialista *adj & smf* imperialist.

impericia *sf* lack of skill; [inexperiencia] inexperience.

imperio *sm* - **1.** [territorio] empire - **2.** [dominio] rule; **valer un imperio** to be worth a fortune - **3.** [mandato] emperorship.

imperioso, sa *adj* - **1.** [autoritario] imperious - **2.** [apremiante] urgent, pressing.

impermeabilidad *sf* impermeability.
impermeabilización *sf* waterproofing.
impermeabilizar [13] *vt* to (make) water-proof.
impermeable ◇ *adj* waterproof. ◇ *sm* raincoat, mac *UK*.
impersonal *adj* impersonal.
impertérrito, ta *adj* unperturbed, un-moved; [ante peligros] fearless.
impertinencia *sf* - **1.** [gen] impertinence - **2.** [comentario] impertinent remark.
impertinente ◇ *adj* impertinent. ◇ *smf* [persona] impertinent person.
◆ **impertinentes** *smpl* [anteojos] lor-gnette *sing*.
imperturbable *adj* imperturbable.
ímpetu *sm* - **1.** [brusquedad] force - **2.** [energía] energy - **3.** FÍS impetus.
impetuosidad *sf* [precipitación] impetuosity.
impetuoso, sa ◇ *adj* - **1.** [olas, viento, ata-que] violent - **2.** [persona] impulsive, impetu-ous. ◇ *sm, f* impulsive person.
impida, impidiera *etc* ➡ **impedir**.
impío, a *adj* godless, impious.
implacable *adj* implacable, relentless.
implantación *sf* - **1.** [establecimiento] intro-duction - **2.** BIOL implantation - **3.** MED inser-tion.
implantar *vt* - **1.** [establecer] to introduce - **2.** MED to insert.
◆ **implantarse** *vprnl* - **1.** [establecerse] to be in-troduced - **2.** BIOL to become implanted.
implante *sm* implant; [dental] dental plate.
implementar *vt* to implement.
implemento *sm* implement.
implicación *sf* - **1.** [participación] involvement - **2.** *(gen pl)* [consecuencia] implication.
implicar [10] *vt* - **1.** [involucrar]: **implicar (en)** to involve (in); DER to implicate (in) - **2.** [signifi-car] to mean.
◆ **implicarse** *vprnl* DER to incriminate o.s.; **im-plicarse en** to become involved in.
implícito, ta *adj* implicit.
imploración *sf* entreaty, plea.
implorar *vt* to implore.
impoluto, ta *adj* unpolluted, pure; *fig* un-blemished, untarnished.
imponderable ◇ *adj* [incalculable] invalu-able; [imprevisible] imponderable. ◇ *sm* im-ponderable.
imponente *adj* - **1.** [impresionante] imposing, impressive - **2.** [estupendo] sensational, terrif-ic.
imponer [65] ◇ *vt* - **1.**: **imponer algo (a al-guien)** [gen] to impose sthg (on sb); [respeto] to

command sthg (from sb); **el profesor impuso silencio en la clase** the teacher silenced the class - **2.** [moda] to set; [costumbre] to intro-duce. ◇ *vi* to be imposing.
◆ **imponerse** *vprnl* - **1.** [hacerse respetar] to command respect, to show authority - **2.** [pre-valecer] to prevail - **3.** [asumir - obligación, tarea] to take on - **4.** [ser necesario] to be necessary - **5.** DEP to win, to prevail.
imponible ➡ **base**.
impopular *adj* unpopular.
impopularidad *sf* unpopularity.
importación *sf* [acción] importing; [artículo] import; **de importación** imported.
importador, ra ◇ *adj* importing *(antes de s)*. ◇ *sm, f* importer.
importancia *sf* importance; **dar importan-cia a algo** to attach importance to sthg; **de importancia** important, of importance; **quitar importancia a algo** to play sthg down; **sin im-portancia** unimportant; **darse importancia** to give o.s. airs, to show off.
importante *adj* - **1.** [gen] important; [lesión] serious; **lo importante** the most important thing, the main thing - **2.** [cantidad] consider-able.
importar ◇ *vt* - **1.** [gen & INFORM] to import - **2.** [suj: factura, coste] to amount to, to come to. ◇ *vi* - **1.** [preocupar] to matter; **no me importa** I don't care, it doesn't matter to me; **¿y a ti qué te importa?** what's it got to do with you?; **me importa un bledo** *o* **comino** *o* **pito** *fam* I don't give a damn, I couldn't care less - **2.** [en preguntas] to mind; **¿le importa que me sien-te?** do you mind if I sit down?; **¿te importa-ría acompañarme?** would you mind coming with me? ◇ *v impers* to matter; **no importa** it doesn't matter; **¡qué importa que llueva!** who cares if it's raining.
importe *sm* [gen] price, cost; [de factura] total; **importe total** total cost.
importunar ◇ *vt* to bother, to pester. ◇ *vi* to be tiresome *o* a nuisance.
importuno, na = **inoportuno**.
imposibilidad *sf* impossibility; **su imposibi-lidad para contestar la pregunta** his inabil-ity to answer the question; **imposibilidad físi-ca** physical disability.
imposibilitado, da *adj* disabled; **estar im-posibilitado para hacer algo** to be unable to do sthg.
imposibilitar *vt*: **imposibilitar a alguien pa-ra hacer algo** to make it impossible for sb to do sthg, to prevent sb from doing sthg.
imposible ◇ *adj* - **1.** [irrealizable] impossible - **2.** [insoportable] unbearable, impossible.

◇ *sm*: **pedir imposibles** to ask for the impossible; **hacer lo imposible** to do everything possible and more.

imposición *sf* - **1.** [obligación] imposition - **2.** [impuesto] tax - **3.** BANCA deposit; **hacer** *o* **efectuar una imposición** to make a deposit.

impositivo, va *adj* tax *(antes de s)*.

impostor, ra ◇ *adj* [suplantador] fraudulent. ◇ *sm, f* [suplantador] impostor.

impostura *sf* - **1.** [suplantación] fraud - **2.** [calumnia] slander.

impotencia *sf* impotence.

impotente ◇ *adj* impotent. ◇ *sm* impotent man.

impracticable *adj* - **1.** [irrealizable] impracticable - **2.** [intransitable] impassable.

imprecación *sf* imprecation.

imprecar [10] *vt* to imprecate.

imprecisión *sf* imprecision, vagueness *(U)*.

impreciso, sa *adj* imprecise, vague.

impredecible *adj* unforeseeable; [variable] unpredictable.

impregnar *vt*: **impregnar (de)** to impregnate (with).

◆ **impregnarse** *vprnl*: **impregnarse (de)** to become impregnated (with).

impremeditado, da *adj* unpremeditated.

imprenta *sf* - **1.** [arte] printing - **2.** [máquina] (printing) press - **3.** [establecimiento] printing house.

imprescindible *adj* indispensable, essential; **lo imprescindible** the basics.

impresentable *adj* unpresentable.

impresión *sf* - **1.** [gen] impression; [sensación física] feeling; **cambiar impresiones** to compare notes, to exchange views; **causar (una) buena/mala impresión** to make a good/bad impression; **dar la impresión de** to give the impression of; **tener la impresión de que** to have the impression that - **2.** [huella] imprint; **impresión digital** *o* **dactilar** fingerprint - **3.** [IMPR - acción] printing; [- edición] edition.

impresionable *adj* impressionable.

impresionante *adj* impressive; [error] enormous.

impresionar ◇ *vt* - **1.** [maravillar] to impress - **2.** [conmocionar] to move - **3.** [horrorizar] to shock - **4.** FOTO to expose. ◇ *vi* - **1.** [maravillar] to make an impression - **2.** [conmocionar] to be moving - **3.** [horrorizar] to be shocking.

◆ **impresionarse** *vprnl* - **1.** [maravillarse] to be impressed - **2.** [conmocionarse] to be moved - **3.** [horrorizarse] to be shocked.

impresionismo *sm* impressionism.

impresionista *adj* & *smf* impressionist.

impreso, sa ◇ *pp* ▷ **imprimir**. ◇ *adj* printed.

◆ **impreso** *sm* - **1.** [texto] printed sheet, printed matter *(U)* - **2.** [formulario] form; **impreso de solicitud** application form.

impresor, ra ◇ *adj* printing *(antes de s)*. ◇ *sm, f* [persona] printer.

◆ **impresora** *sf* INFORM printer; **impresora láser/térmica** laser/thermal printer; **impresora de matriz** *o* **de agujas** dot-matrix printer; **impresora de chorro de tinta** ink-jet printer; **impresora de margarita** daisy-wheel printer.

imprevisible *adj* unforeseeable; [variable] unpredictable.

imprevisión *sf* lack of foresight.

imprevisto, ta *adj* unexpected.

◆ **imprevisto** *sm* [hecho] unforeseen circumstance; **salvo imprevistos** barring accidents.

◆ **imprevistos** *smpl* [gastos] unforeseen expenses.

imprimir ◇ *vt* - **1.** [gen] to print; [huella, paso] to leave, to make - **2.** *fig* [transmitir]: **imprimir algo a** to impart *o* bring sthg to. ◇ *vi* to print.

improbabilidad *sf* improbability, unlikelihood.

improbable *adj* improbable, unlikely.

ímprobo, ba *adj culto* Herculean, strenuous.

improcedencia *sf* - **1.** [gen] inappropriateness - **2.** DER inadmissibility.

improcedente *adj* - **1.** [inoportuno] inappropriate - **2.** DER inadmissible; **despido improcedente** unfair dismissal.

improductivo, va *adj* unproductive.

impronta *sf* mark, impression.

impronunciable *adj* unpronounceable.

improperio *sm* insult.

impropiedad *sf* impropriety.

impropio, pia *adj*: **impropio (de)** improper (for), unbecoming (to).

improrrogable *adj* unable to be extended; [plazo] final.

improvisación *sf* improvisation.

improvisado, da *adj* [gen] improvised; [discurso, truco] impromptu; [comentario] ad-lib; [cama etc] makeshift.

improvisar ◇ *vt* [gen] to improvise; [comida] to rustle up; **improvisar una cama** to make (up) a makeshift bed. ◇ *vi* [gen] to improvise; MÚS to extemporize.

improviso ◆ **de improviso** *loc adv* unexpectedly, suddenly; **coger a alguien de improviso** to catch sb unawares.

imprudencia *sf* [en los actos] carelessness *(U)*; [en los comentarios] indiscretion; **imprudencia temeraria** DER criminal negligence.

imprudente ⟷ adj [en los actos] careless, rash; [en los comentarios] indiscreet. ⟷ smf [en los actos] rash person; [en los comentarios] indiscreet person.

impúber ⟷ adj pre-pubescent. ⟷ smf pre-pubescent child.

impúdico, ca adj immodest, indecent.

impuesto, ta pp ⟼ **imponer**.
➡ **impuesto** sm tax; **exento de impuestos** tax-exempt; **impuesto de circulación** road tax; **impuesto al consumo** tax on the consumer; **impuesto ecológico** ecotax, green tax; **impuesto directo/indirecto** direct/indirect tax; **impuesto de lujo** luxury tax; **impuesto municipal** local tax; **impuesto revolucionario** protection money paid by businessmen to terrorists; **impuesto sobre el capital** capital tax; **impuesto sobre el valor añadido** value-added tax; **impuesto sobre la renta** ≃ income tax; **impuesto de sucesión** inheritance tax.

impugnable adj contestable.

impugnación sf contestation, challenge.

impugnar vt to contest, to challenge.

impulsar vt - **1.** [empujar] to propel, to drive - **2.** [incitar]: **impulsar a alguien (a algo/a hacer algo)** to drive sb (to sthg/to do sthg) - **3.** [promocionar] to stimulate.

impulsivo, va ⟷ adj impulsive. ⟷ sm, f impulsive person, hothead.

impulso sm - **1.** [progreso] stimulus, boost - **2.** [fuerza] momentum; **tomar impulso** to take a run-up - **3.** [motivación] impulse, urge.

impulsor, ra ⟷ adj driving (antes de s). ⟷ sm, f dynamic force.

impune adj unpunished; **quedar impune** to go unpunished.

impunemente adv with impunity.

impunidad sf impunity.

impuntualidad sf unpunctuality.

impureza (gen pl) sf impurity.

impuro, ra adj lit & fig impure.

impusiera etc ⟼ **imponer**.

imputable adj: **imputable a** attributable to.

imputación sf accusation.

imputar vt - **1.** [atribuir]: **imputar algo a alguien** [delito] to accuse sb of sthg; [fracaso, error] to attribute sthg to sb - **2.** COM to allocate, to assign.

inabordable adj inaccessible.

inacabable adj interminable, endless.

inacabado, da adj unfinished.

inaccesible adj inaccessible.

inaceptable adj unacceptable.

inactividad sf inactivity.

inactivo, va adj inactive.

inadaptación sf maladjustment.

inadaptado, da ⟷ adj maladjusted. ⟷ sm, f misfit.

inadecuado, da adj [inapropiado] unsuitable, inappropriate.

inadmisible adj inadmissible.

inadvertido, da adj unnoticed; **pasar inadvertido** to go unnoticed.

inagotable adj inexhaustible.

inaguantable adj unbearable.

inalámbrico, ca adj cordless; INFORM wireless.
➡ **inalámbrico** sm cordless telephone.

inalcanzable adj unattainable.

inalienable adj inalienable.

inalterable adj - **1.** [gen] unalterable; [salud] stable; [amistad] undying - **2.** [color] fast - **3.** [rostro, carácter] impassive - **4.** [resultado, marcador] unchanged.

inamovible adj immovable, fixed.

inanición sf starvation.

inanimado, da adj inanimate.

inánime adj lifeless.

inapagable adj unextinguishable.

inapelable adj - **1.** [inevitable] inevitable - **2.** DER not open to appeal.

inapetencia sf lack of appetite.

inapetente adj lacking in appetite.

inaplazable adj [reunión, sesión] that cannot be postponed; [necesidad] urgent, pressing.

inaplicable adj inapplicable, not applicable.

inapreciable adj - **1.** [incalculable] invaluable, inestimable - **2.** [insignificante] imperceptible.

inapropiado, da adj inappropriate.

inarrugable adj crease-resistant.

inasequible adj - **1.** [por el precio] prohibitive - **2.** [inalcanzable - meta, ambición] unattainable; [- persona] unapproachable.

inatacable adj unassailable; fig irrefutable.

inaudible adj inaudible.

inaudito, ta adj unheard-of.

inauguración sf inauguration, opening.

inaugurar vt to inaugurate, to open.

inca adj & smf Inca.

incalculable adj incalculable.

incalificable adj unspeakable, indescribable.

incandescente adj incandescent.

incansable adj untiring, tireless.

incapacidad sf - **1.** [imposibilidad] inability - **2.** [inaptitud] incompetence - **3.** DER incapacity; **incapacidad laboral** industrial disablement o disability.

incapacitado, da ⬦ *adj* [DER - gen] disqualified; [- para testar] incapacitated; [- para traba-
jar] unfit. ⬦ *sm, f* DER disqualified person, person declared unfit.

incapacitar *vt*: **incapacitar (para)** [gen] to disqualify (from); [para trabajar etc] to render unfit
(for).

incapaz *adj* - **1.** [gen]: **incapaz de** incapable of
- **2.** [sin talento]: **incapaz para** incompetent at,
no good at - **3.** DER incompetent; **declarar incapaz a alguien** to declare sb incompetent.

incautación *sf* seizure, confiscation.

incautarse ⬟ **incautarse de** *vprnl* - **1.** DER to
seize, to confiscate - **2.** [apoderarse de] to grab.

incauto, ta ⬦ *adj* gullible. ⬦ *sm, f* gullible
person.

incendiar [8] *vt* to set fire to.
⬟ **incendiarse** *vprnl* to catch fire.

incendiario, ria ⬦ *adj* - **1.** [bomba etc] incendiary - **2.** [artículo, libro etc] inflammatory.
⬦ *sm, f* arsonist, fire-raiser.

incendio *sm* fire; **incendio forestal** forest fire;
incendio provocado arson.

incensario *sm* censer.

incentivar *vt* to motivate.

incentivo *sm* incentive; **incentivo fiscal** tax
incentive.

incertidumbre *sf* uncertainty.

incesante *adj* incessant, ceaseless.

incesto *sm* incest.

incestuoso, sa *adj* incestuous.

incidencia *sf* - **1.** [repercusión] impact, effect
- **2.** [suceso] event.

incidental *adj* incidental, chance *(antes de s)*.

incidente *sm* incident; **incidente diplomático**
diplomatic incident.

incidir ⬟ **incidir en** *vi* - **1.** [incurrir en] to fall
into, to lapse into - **2.** [insistir en] to focus on
- **3.** [influir en] to have an impact on, to affect
- **4.** [suj: rayo] to fall on - **5.** [suj: cirujano] to make
an incision into.

incienso *sm* incense.

incierto, ta *adj* - **1.** [dudoso] uncertain
- **2.** [falso] untrue.

incineración *sf* [de cadáver] cremation; [de ba-
sura] incineration.

incinerador *sm* [para basura] incinerator.

incinerar *vt* [cadáver] to cremate; [basura] to incinerate.

incipiente *adj* incipient; [estado, etapa] early.

incisión *sf* incision.

incisivo, va *adj* - **1.** [instrumento] sharp, cutting - **2.** *fig* [mordaz] incisive - **3.** [diente] incisive.
⬟ **incisivo** *sm* incisor.

inciso, sa *adj* cut.
⬟ **inciso** *sm* passing remark.

incitación *sf* incitement.

incitar *vt*: **incitar a alguien a algo** [violencia,
rebelión etc] to incite sb to sthg; **incitar a alguien a la fuga/venganza** to urge sb to flee/
avenge himself; **incitar a alguien a hacer algo** [rebelarse etc] to incite sb to do sthg; [fugarse,
vengarse] to urge sb to do sthg.

incívico, ca *adj* antisocial.

inclasificable *adj* unclassifiable.

inclemencia *sf* harshness, inclemency.

inclemente *adj* harsh, inclement.

inclinación *sf* - **1.** [desviación] slant, inclination; [de terreno] slope - **2.** *fig* [afición]: **inclinación (a o por)** penchant o propensity (for)
- **3.** [cariño]: **inclinación hacia alguien** fondness towards sb - **4.** [saludo] bow.

inclinar *vt* - **1.** [doblar] to bend; [ladear] to tilt
- **2.** [cabeza] to bow - **3.** [influir] **inclinar a alguien a hacer algo** to persuade sb to do sthg.
⬟ **inclinarse** *vprnl* - **1.** [doblarse] to lean
- **2.** [para saludar]: **inclinarse (ante)** to bow (before).
⬟ **inclinarse a** *vi* [tender a] to be o feel inclined
to.
⬟ **inclinarse por** *vi* [preferir] to favour, to lean
towards.

incluir [51] *vt* [gen] to include; [adjuntar - en car-
tas] to enclose.

inclusión *sf* inclusion.

inclusive *adv* inclusive.

incluso, sa *adj* enclosed.
⬟ **incluso** *adv* & *prep* even.

incógnito, ta *adj* unknown.
⬟ **incógnita** *sf* - **1.** MAT unknown quantity
- **2.** [misterio] mystery.
⬟ **de incógnito** *loc adv* incognito.

incoherencia *sf* - **1.** [cualidad] incoherence
- **2.** [comentario] nonsensical remark.

incoherente *adj* - **1.** [inconexo] incoherent
- **2.** [inconsecuente] inconsistent.

incoloro, ra *adj* *lit & fig* colourless.

incombustible *adj* fire-resistant.

incomestible, incomible *adj* inedible.

incomodar *vt* - **1.** [causar molestia] to bother, to
inconvenience - **2.** [enfadar] to annoy.
⬟ **incomodarse** *vprnl* [enfadarse]: **incomodarse (por)** to get annoyed (about).

incomodidad *sf* - **1.** [de silla etc] uncomfort-
ableness - **2.** [de situación, persona] awkwardness, discomfort - **3.** [molestia - de visita etc] inconvenience.

incómodo, da adj - **1.** [silla etc] uncomfortable - **2.** [situación, persona] awkward, uncomfortable; **sentirse incómodo** to feel awkward o uncomfortable - **3.** [visita] inconvenient.

incomparable adj incomparable.

incomparecencia sf failure to appear (in court).

incompatibilidad sf incompatibility; **incompatibilidad de caracteres** incompatibility.

incompatible adj: **incompatible (con)** incompatible (with).

incompetencia sf incompetence.

incompetente adj incompetent.

incompleto, ta adj - **1.** [gen] incomplete - **2.** [inacabado] unfinished.

incomprendido, da ◇ adj misunderstood. ◇ sm, f misunderstood person.

incomprensible adj incomprehensible.

incomprensión sf lack of understanding.

incompresible adj incompressible.

incomunicación sf - **1.** [gen] lack of communication - **2.** [de detenido] solitary confinement - **3.** [de una localidad] isolation.

incomunicado, da adj - **1.** [gen] isolated - **2.** [por la nieve etc] cut off - **3.** [preso] in solitary confinement.

incomunicar [10] vt [gen] to cut off; [detenido] to place in solitary confinement.

inconcebible adj inconceivable.

inconcluso, sa adj unfinished.

incondicional ◇ adj unconditional; [ayuda] wholehearted; [seguidor] staunch. ◇ smf staunch supporter.

inconexo, xa adj [gen] unconnected; [pensamiento, texto] disjointed.

inconfesable adj shameful.

inconformismo sm nonconformism.

inconformista adj & smf nonconformist.

inconfundible adj unmistakable; [prueba] irrefutable.

incongruencia sf incongruity; **hacer/decir una incongruencia** to do/say sthg incongruous.

incongruente adj incongruous.

inconmensurable adj immeasurable; [espacio] vast.

inconquistable adj unassailable, impregnable.

inconsciencia sf - **1.** [gen] unconsciousness - **2.** fig [falta de juicio] thoughtlessness.

inconsciente ◇ adj - **1.** [gen] unconscious - **2.** fig [irreflexivo] thoughtless. ◇ smf thoughtless person. ◇ sm PSICOL: **el inconsciente** the unconscious.

inconsecuencia sf inconsistency.

inconsecuente ◇ adj inconsistent. ◇ smf inconsistent person.

inconsistencia sf [de tela, pared etc] flimsiness; [de una salsa] runniness; [de argumento, discurso etc] lack of substance.

inconsistente adj [tela, pared etc] flimsy; [salsa] runny; [argumento, discurso etc] lacking in substance.

inconsolable adj disconsolate.

inconstancia sf - **1.** [en el trabajo, la conducta] unreliability - **2.** [de opinión, ideas] changeability.

inconstante adj - **1.** [en el trabajo, la conducta] unreliable - **2.** [de opinión, ideas] changeable.

inconstitucional adj unconstitutional.

inconstitucionalidad sf unconstitutionality.

incontable adj [innumerable] countless.

incontenible adj [alegría] unbounded; [llanto] uncontrollable; [dolor] unbearable.

incontestable adj indisputable, undeniable.

incontinencia sf incontinence.

incontinente adj incontinent.

incontrolable adj uncontrollable.

incontrolado, da adj [velocidad] furious; [situación] out of hand; [comando] maverick, not controlled by the leadership; [aumento de precios etc] spiralling.

inconveniencia sf - **1.** [inoportunidad] inappropriateness - **2.** [comentario] tactless remark; [acto] faux pas, mistake.

inconveniente ◇ adj - **1.** [inoportuno] inappropriate - **2.** [descortés] rude. ◇ sm - **1.** [dificultad] obstacle, problem; **no tener inconveniente en hacer algo** to have no objection to doing sthg - **2.** [desventaja] disadvantage, drawback.

incordiar [8] vt fam to bother, to pester.

incordio sm fam pain, nuisance.

incorporación sf: **incorporación (a)** [gen] incorporation (into); [a un puesto] induction (into).

incorporado, da adj TECNOL built-in.

incorporar vt - **1.** [añadir]: **incorporar (a)** [gen] to incorporate (into); CULIN to mix (into) - **2.** [anexionar]: **incorporar a** to annex as part of - **3.** [levantar] to sit up.

➤ **incorporarse** vprnl - **1.** [empezar]: **incorporarse (a)** [equipo] to join; [trabajo] to start - **2.** [levantarse] to sit up.

incorrección sf - **1.** [inexactitud] incorrectness; [error gramatical] mistake - **2.** [descortesía] lack of courtesy, rudeness (U).

incorrecto, ta adj - **1.** [equivocado] incorrect, wrong - **2.** [descortés] rude, impolite.

incorregible adj incorrigible.

incorruptible *adj* - **1.** [substancia] imperishable - **2.** *fig* [persona] incorruptible.

incorrupto, ta *adj* [cadáver] uncorrupted, not decomposed.

incredulidad *sf* incredulity.

incrédulo, la ◇ *adj* sceptical, incredulous; RELIG unbelieving. ◇ *sm, f* unbeliever.

increíble *adj* - **1.** [difícil de creer] unconvincing, lacking credibility - **2.** *fig* [extraordinario] incredible - **3.** *fig* [inconcebible] unbelievable; **es increíble que pasen cosas así** it's hard to believe that such things can happen.

incrementar *vt* to increase.
➠ **incrementarse** *vprnl* to increase.

incremento *sm* increase; [de temperatura] rise; **incremento salarial** pay increase.

increpar *vt* - **1.** [reprender] to reprimand - **2.** [insultar] to abuse, insult.

incriminación *sf* accusation.

incriminar *vt* to accuse.

incrustación *sf* inlay.

incrustar *vt* - **1.** TECNOL to inlay; [en joyería] to set - **2.** *fam fig* [empotrar]: **incrustar algo en algo** to sink sthg into sthg.
➠ **incrustarse** *vprnl* [cal etc] to become encrusted.

incubación *sf* incubation; **incubación artificial** artificial incubation.

incubadora *sf* incubator.

incubar *vt* - **1.** [huevo] to incubate - **2.** [enfermedad] to be sickening for.

incuestionable *adj* [teoría, razón] irrefutable; [deber] bounden.

inculcar [10] *vt*: **inculcar algo a alguien** to instil sthg into sb.

inculpación *sf* accusation; DER charge.

inculpado, da ◇ *adj* accused; DER charged. ◇ *sm, f* accused.

inculpar *vt*: **inculpar a alguien (de)** [gen] to accuse sb (of); DER to charge sb (with).

inculto, ta ◇ *adj* - **1.** [persona] uneducated - **2.** [tierra] uncultivated. ◇ *sm, f* ignoramus.

incultura *sf* lack of education.

incumbencia *sf*: **es/no es de nuestra incumbencia** it is/isn't a matter for us, it falls/doesn't fall within our area of responsibility; **no es asunto de tu incumbencia** it's none of your business.

incumbir ➠ **incumbir a** *vi*: **incumbir a alguien** to be a matter for sb, to be within sb's area of responsibility; **esto no te incumbe** this is none of your business.

incumplimiento *sm* [de deber] failure to fulfil; [de orden, ley] non-compliance; [de promesa] failure to keep; **incumplimiento de contrato** breach of contract.

incumplir *vt* [deber] to fail to fulfil, to neglect; [orden, ley] to fail to comply with; [promesa] to break; [contrato] to breach.

incunable ◇ *adj* incunabular. ◇ *sm* incunabulum.

incurable *adj* incurable.

incurrir ➠ **incurrir en** *vi* - **1.** [delito, falta] to commit; [error] to make - **2.** [desprecio etc] to incur.

incursión *sf* incursion; **incursión aérea** air raid.

indagación *sf* investigation, inquiry.

indagar [16] ◇ *vt* to investigate, to inquire into. ◇ *vi* to investigate, to inquire.

indebido, da *adj* - **1.** [incorrecto] improper - **2.** [ilegal] unlawful, illegal.

indecencia *sf* - **1.** [cualidad] indecency - **2.** [acción] outrage, crime.

indecente *adj* - **1.** [impúdico] indecent - **2.** [indigno] miserable, wretched.

indecible *adj* [alegría] indescribable; [dolor] unspeakable; **hacer lo indecible para** o **por** to do one's utmost to; **sufrir lo indecible** to suffer indescribable pain.

indecisión *sf* indecisiveness.

indeciso, sa ◇ *adj* - **1.** [persona - inseguro] indecisive; [- que está dudoso] undecided, unsure - **2.** [pregunta, respuesta] hesitant; [resultado] undecided. ◇ *sm, f* undecided voter.

indecoroso, sa *adj* unseemly.

indefectible *adj culto* unfailing.

indefensión *sf* defencelessness.

indefenso, sa *adj* defenceless.

indefinible *adj* indefinable; [edad] uncertain.

indefinido, da *adj* - **1.** [ilimitado] indefinite; [contrato] open-ended - **2.** [impreciso] vague - **3.** GRAM indefinite.

indeleble *adj culto* indelible.

indemne *adj* unhurt, unharmed.

indemnidad *sf culto* indemnity.

indemnización *sf* [gen] compensation; [por despido] severance pay; **indemnización por daños y perjuicios** DER damages *pl*.

indemnizar [13] *vt*: **indemnizar a alguien (por)** to compensate sb (for).

indemostrable *adj* unprovable.

independencia *sf* independence; **con independencia de** independently of.

independentismo *sm* independence movement.

independentista ◇ *adj* advocating independence. ◇ *smf* supporter of independence.

independiente *adj* - **1.** [gen] independent - **2.** [aparte] separate.

independizar [13] *vt* to grant independence to.

➤ **independizarse** *vprnl*: **independizarse (de)** to become independent (of).

indescifrable *adj* [gen] indecipherable; [misterio] inexplicable, impenetrable.

indescriptible *adj* indescribable.

indeseable *adj* undesirable.

indestructible *adj* indestructible.

indeterminación *sf* indecisiveness.

indeterminado, da *adj* **- 1.** [sin determinar] indeterminate; **por, tiempo indeterminado** indefinitely **- 2.** [impreciso] vague **- 3.** GRAM ▭> **artículo**.

indexación *sf* INFORM indexing.

indexar *vt* INFORM to index.

India *n pr*: **(la) India** India.

indiano, na <> *adj* (Latin American) Indian. <> *sm, f* **- 1.** [indígena] (Latin American) Indian **- 2.** [emigrante] *Spanish emigrant to Latin America who returned to Spain having made his fortune.*

indicación *sf* **- 1.** [señal, gesto] sign, signal **- 2.** (*gen pl*) [instrucción] instruction; [para llegar a un sitio] directions *pl* **- 3.** [nota, corrección] note.

indicado, da *adj* suitable, appropriate.

indicador, ra *adj* indicating (*antes de s*).

➤ **indicador** *sm* [gen] indicator; TECNOL gauge, meter; **indicador de carretera** road sign; **indicador económico** economic indicator; **indicador de velocidad** speedometer.

indicar [10] *vt* **- 1.** [señalar] to indicate; [suj: aguja etc] to read **- 2.** [explicar] to tell, to explain to **- 3.** [prescribir] to prescribe.

indicativo, va *adj* indicative.

➤ **indicativo** *sm* GRAM indicative.

índice *sm* **- 1.** [gen] index; [proporción] level, rate; **índice alfabético** alphabetical index; **índice de audiencia** ratings; **índice bursátil** stock market index; **índice del coste de la vida** cost of living index; **índice de materias** *o* **temático** table of contents; **índice de natalidad** birth rate; **índice de precios al consumo** retail price index **- 2.** [señal] sign, indicator; **índice económico** economic indicator **- 3.** [catálogo] catalogue **- 4.** [dedo] index finger.

indicio *sm* sign; [pista] clue; [cantidad pequeña] trace.

Índico *sm*: **el (océano) Índico** the Indian Ocean.

indiferencia *sf* indifference.

indiferente *adj* indifferent; **me es indiferente** [me da igual] I don't mind, it's all the same to me; [no me interesa] I'm not interested in it.

indígena <> *adj* indigenous, native. <> *smf* native.

indigencia *sf culto* destitution, poverty.

indigente <> *adj* destitute, poor. <> *smf* poor person.

indigestarse *vprnl* to get indigestion; **se me ha indigestado esa chica** *fam fig* I can't stomach that girl.

indigestión *sf* indigestion.

indigesto, ta *adj* indigestible; *fam fig* [pesado] stodgy, heavy.

indignación *sf* indignation.

indignante *adj* shocking, outrageous.

indignar *vt* to anger.

➤ **indignarse** *vprnl*: **indignarse (por)** to get angry *o* indignant (about).

indigno, na *adj* **- 1.** [gen]: **indigno (de)** unworthy (of) **- 2.** [impropio] not fitting, wrong **- 3.** [vergonzoso] contemptible, shameful.

indio, dia <> *adj* Indian. <> *sm, f* Indian; **indio americano** Native American; **hacer el indio** to play the fool.

indique *etc* ▭> **indicar**.

indirecto, ta *adj* indirect.

➤ **indirecta** *sf* hint; **lanzar una indirecta a alguien** to drop a hint to sb.

indisciplina *sf* indiscipline.

indisciplinado, da <> *adj* undisciplined. <> *sm, f* undisciplined person.

indiscreción *sf* **- 1.** [cualidad] indiscretion **- 2.** [comentario] indiscreet remark; **si no es indiscreción** if you don't mind my asking.

indiscreto, ta <> *adj* indiscreet. <> *sm, f* indiscreet person.

indiscriminado, da *adj* indiscriminate.

indiscutible *adj* [gen] indisputable; [poder] undisputed.

indisoluble *adj* **- 1.** [substancia] insoluble **- 2.** [unión, ley] indissoluble.

indispensable *adj* indispensable, essential.

indisponer [65] *vt* **- 1.** [enfermar] to make ill, to upset **- 2.** [enemistar] to set at odds.

indisposición *sf* **- 1.** [malestar] indisposition **- 2.** [reticencia] unwillingness.

indispuesto, ta <> *pp* ▭> **indisponer**. <> *adj* indisposed, unwell.

indistinto, ta *adj* **- 1.** [indiferente]: **es indistinto** it doesn't matter, it makes no difference **- 2.** [cuenta, cartilla] joint **- 3.** [perfil, figura] indistinct, blurred.

individual *adj* **- 1.** [gen] individual; [habitación, cama] single; [despacho] personal **- 2.** [prueba, competición] singles (*antes de s*).

➤ **individuales** *smpl* DEP singles.

individualidad *sf* individuality.

individualismo *sm* individualism.

individualista ⟨⟩ *adj* individualistic. ⟨⟩ *smf* individualist.

individualizar [13] *vi* to single people out.

individuo, **dua** *sm, f* person; *despec* individual.

indivisible *adj* indivisible.

indiviso, **sa** *adj* undivided.

indocumentado, **da** ⟨⟩ *adj* - **1.** [sin documentación] without identity papers - **2.** [ignorante] ignorant. ⟨⟩ *sm, f* [ignorante] ignoramus.

indoeuropeo, **a** *adj* Indo-European.
➥ **indoeuropeo** *sm* [lengua] Indo-European.

índole *sf* [naturaleza] nature; [tipo] type, kind.

indolencia *sf* indolence, laziness.

indolente *adj* culto indolent, lazy.

indoloro, **ra** *adj* painless.

indomable *adj* - **1.** [animal] untameable - **2.** [carácter] rebellious; [pueblo] unruly.

indómito, **ta** *adj* - **1.** [animal] untameable - **2.** [carácter] rebellious; [pueblo] unruly.

Indonesia *n pr* Indonesia.

indonesio, **sia** *adj* & *sm, f* Indonesian.
➥ **indonesio** *sm* [lengua] Indonesian.

inducción *sf* - **1.** [gen & FÍS] induction - **2.** [incitación] instigation.

inducir [33] *vt* - **1.** [incitar]: **inducir a alguien a algo/a hacer algo** to lead sb into sthg/into doing sthg; **inducir a error** to mislead - **2.** [deducir] to infer - **3.** FÍS to induce.

inductor, **ra** *adj* instigating.
➥ **inductor** *sm* inductor.

indudable *adj* undoubted; **es indudable que...** there is no doubt that...

indujera *etc* ▷ **inducir**.

indulgencia *sf* indulgence; **indulgencia plenaria** plenary indulgence.

indulgente *adj* indulgent.

indultar *vt* to pardon.

indulto *sm* pardon.

indumentaria *sf* attire.

industria *sf* - **1.** [gen] industry; **industria artesanal** cottage industry; **industria automovilística/pesada/punta** motor/heavy/sunrise industry - **2.** [fábrica] factory.

industrial ⟨⟩ *adj* industrial. ⟨⟩ *smf* industrialist.

industrialismo *sm* industrialism.

industrialización *sf* industrialization.

industrializar [13] *vt* to industrialize.
➥ **industrializarse** *vprnl* to become industrialized.

industrioso, **sa** *adj* industrious.

induzca *etc* ▷ **inducir**.

INE *sm* (*abrev de* **Instituto Nacional de Estadísticas**), *National Institute of Statistics in Bolivia, Chile, Guatemala and Uruguay.*

inédito, **ta** *adj* - **1.** [no publicado] unpublished - **2.** [sorprendente] unheard-of, unprecedented.

inefable *adj* ineffable, inexpressible.

ineficacia *sf* - **1.** [bajo rendimiento] inefficiency - **2.** [baja efectividad] ineffectiveness.

ineficaz *adj* - **1.** [de bajo rendimiento] inefficient - **2.** [de baja efectividad] ineffective.

ineficiencia *sf* - **1.** [bajo rendimiento] inefficiency - **2.** [baja efectividad] ineffectiveness.

ineficiente *adj* - **1.** [de bajo rendimiento] inefficient - **2.** [de baja efectividad] ineffective.

ineludible *adj* unavoidable.

INEM (*abrev de* **Instituto Nacional de Empleo**) *sm Spanish department of employment.*

inenarrable *adj* spectacular.

ineptitud *sf* ineptitude.

inepto, **ta** ⟨⟩ *adj* inept. ⟨⟩ *sm, f* inept person.

inequívoco, **ca** *adj* [apoyo, resultado] unequivocal; [señal, voz] unmistakeable.

inercia *sf* lit & fig inertia.

inerme *adj* [sin armas] unarmed; [sin defensa] defenceless.

inerte *adj* - **1.** [materia] inert - **2.** [cuerpo, cadáver] lifeless.

inescrutable *adj* - **1.** [persona, rostro] inscrutable - **2.** [misterio, verdad] impenetrable.

inesperado, **da** *adj* unexpected.

inestabilidad *sf* instability.

inestable *adj* lit & fig unstable.

inestimable *adj* inestimable, invaluable.

inevitable *adj* inevitable.

inexactitud *sf* inaccuracy.

inexacto, **ta** *adj* - **1.** [impreciso] inaccurate - **2.** [erróneo] incorrect, wrong.

inexcusable *adj* - **1.** [imperdonable] inexcusable - **2.** [ineludible] unavoidable.

inexistencia *sf* nonexistence.

inexistente *adj* nonexistent.

inexorable *adj* - **1.** [inevitable] inexorable - **2.** [inflexible] unyielding.

inexperiencia *sf* inexperience.

inexperto, **ta** ⟨⟩ *adj* - **1.** [falto de experiencia] inexperienced - **2.** [falto de habilidad] unskilful, inexpert. ⟨⟩ *sm, f* person without experience.

inexplicable *adj* inexplicable.

inexpresivo, **va** *adj* expressionless.

inexpugnable *adj* unassailable, impregnable.

inextinguible *adj* [fuego] unquenchable; [sentimiento] undying.

inextricable *adj* intricate.

infalibilidad *sf* infallibility.

infalible *adj* infallible.

infamar *vt culto* to defame.

infame *adj* vile, base.

infamia *sf* - **1.** [deshonra] infamy, disgrace - **2.** [mala acción] vile *o* base deed.

infancia *sf* - **1.** [periodo] childhood - **2.** [todos los niños] children *pl*.

infante, ta *sm, f* - **1.** [niño] infant - **2.** [hijo del rey] infante (*f* infanta), prince (*f* princess).
➡ **infante** *sm* [soldado] infantryman.

infantería *sf* infantry; **infantería de marina** marines *pl*; **infantería ligera** light infantry.

infanticida ◇ *adj* infanticidal. ◇ *smf* infanticide, child-murderer.

infanticidio *sm* infanticide.

infantil *adj* - **1.** [para niños] children's; [de niños] child *(antes de s)* - **2.** *fig* [inmaduro] infantile, childish.

infantilismo *sm* infantilism.

infarto *sm*: **infarto (de miocardio)** heart attack; **infarto cerebral** stroke; **de infarto** *fam* heart-stopping.

infatigable *adj* indefatigable, tireless.

infausto, ta *adj* ill-starred.

infección *sf* infection.

infeccioso, sa *adj* infectious.

infectar *vt* to infect.
➡ **infectarse** *vprnl* to become infected.

infecto, ta *adj* - **1.** [agua, carroña] putrid - **2.** [población, zona] infected - **3.** *fig* [desagradable] foul, terrible.

infelicidad *sf* unhappiness.

infeliz ◇ *adj* - **1.** [desgraciado] unhappy - **2.** *fig* [ingenuo] gullible. ◇ *smf* [ingenuo] gullible person; **un pobre infeliz** a poor wretch.

inferior ◇ *adj*: **inferior (a)** [en espacio, cantidad] lower (than); [en calidad] inferior (to); **una cifra inferior a 100** a figure under *o* below 100. ◇ *smf* inferior.

inferioridad *sf* inferiority; **estar en inferioridad de condiciones** to be at a disadvantage.

inferir [27] *vt* - **1.** [deducir]: **inferir (de)** to deduce (from), to infer (from) - **2.** [ocasionar - herida] to inflict; [- mal] to cause.

infernal *adj lit & fig* infernal.

infestar *vt* to infest; [suj: carteles, propaganda etc] to be plastered across.

infidelidad *sf* [conyugal] infidelity; [a la patria, un amigo] unfaithfulness, disloyalty.

infiel ◇ *adj* - **1.** [desleal - cónyuge] unfaithful; [- amigo] disloyal - **2.** [inexacto] inaccurate, unfaithful. ◇ *smf* RELIG infidel.

infiera *etc* ▭ **inferir**.

infiernillo *sm* portable stove.

infierno *sm lit & fig* hell; **en el quinto infierno** in the middle of nowhere; **¡vete al infierno!** go to hell!

infiltración *sf* - **1.** [de líquido] seeping - **2.** [de persona, ideas] infiltration.

infiltrado, da ◇ *adj* infiltrated. ◇ *sm, f* infiltrator.

infiltrar *vt* - **1.** [inyectar] to inject - **2.** *fig* [ideas] to infiltrate.
➡ **infiltrarse en** *vprnl* to infiltrate.

ínfimo, ma *adj* [calidad, categoría] extremely low; [precio] giveaway; [importancia] knockdown, minimal.

infinidad *sf*: **una infinidad de** an infinite number of; *fig* masses of; **en infinidad de ocasiones** on countless occasions.

infinitesimal *adj* infinitesimal.

infinitivo *sm* infinitive.

infinito, ta *adj lit & fig* infinite; **infinitas veces** hundreds of times.
➡ **infinito** ◇ *sm* infinity. ◇ *adv* [mucho] extremely, infinitely.

infiriera *etc* ▭ **inferir**.

inflación *sf* ECON inflation; **inflación subyacente** underlying inflation.

inflacionario, ria, inflacionista *adj* inflationary.

inflamable *adj* inflammable, flammable.

inflamación *sf* MED inflammation.

inflamar *vt* - **1.** *fig & MED* to inflame - **2.** [encender] to set alight.
➡ **inflamarse** *vprnl* [hincharse] to become inflamed.

inflamatorio, ria *adj* inflammatory.

inflar *vt* - **1.** [soplando] to blow up, to inflate; [con bomba] to pump up - **2.** *fig* [exagerar] to blow up, to exaggerate.
➡ **inflarse** *vprnl*: **inflarse (de)** [hartarse] to stuff o.s. (with).

inflexibilidad *sf lit & fig* inflexibility.

inflexible *adj lit & fig* inflexible.

inflexión *sf* inflection.

infligir [15] *vt* to inflict; [castigo] to impose.

influencia *sf* influence; **bajo la influencia del alcohol** under the influence of alcohol.

influenciable *adj* easily influenced.

influenciar [8] *vt* to influence, to have an influence on.

influir [51] ◇ *vt* to influence. ◇ *vi* to have influence; **influir en** to influence, to have an influence on.

influjo *sm* influence.

influyente *adj* influential.

infografía *sf* computer graphics.

información *sf* **- 1.** [conocimiento] information; **para tu información** for your information; **información confidencial** inside information **- 2.** [PRENSA - noticias] news *(U)*; [- noticia] report, piece of news; [- sección] section, news *(U)*; **información meteorológica** weather report *o* forecast **- 3.** [oficina] information office; [mostrador] information desk **- 4.** TELECOM directory enquiries *pl UK*, directory assistance *US*.

informador, ra ⬦ *adj* informing, reporting. ⬦ *sm, f* reporter.

informal *adj* **- 1.** [desenfadado] informal **- 2.** [irresponsable] unreliable.

informalidad *sf* **- 1.** [desenfado] informality **- 2.** [irresponsabilidad] unreliability.

informante ⬦ *adj* informing. ⬦ *smf* informant, informer.

informar ⬦ *vt*: **informar a alguien (de)** to inform *o* tell sb (about). ⬦ *vi* to inform; PRENSA to report.

➡ **informarse** *vprnl* to find out (details); **informarse de** to find out about.

informático, ca ⬦ *adj* computer *(antes de s)*. ⬦ *sm, f* [persona] computer expert.

➡ **informática** *sf* [ciencia] information technology, computing.

informativo, va *adj* **- 1.** [instructivo, esclarecedor] informative **- 2.** [que da noticias] news *(antes de s)*; [que da información] information *(antes de s)*.

➡ **informativo** *sm* news (bulletin).

informatización *sf* computerization.

informatizar [13] *vt* to computerize.

informe ⬦ *adj* shapeless. ⬦ *sm* **- 1.** [gen] report **- 2.** DER plea.

➡ **informes** *smpl* [gen] information *(U)*; [sobre comportamiento] report *sing*; [para un empleo] references.

infortunado, da ⬦ *adj* unfortunate, unlucky; [encuentro, conversación] ill-fated. ⬦ *sm, f* unfortunate *o* unlucky person.

infortunio *sm* misfortune, bad luck *(U)*.

infracción *sf* infringement; [de circulación] offence.

infractor, ra ⬦ *adj* offending. ⬦ *sm, f* offender.

infraestructura *sf* **- 1.** [de organización] infrastructure **- 2.** [de construcción] foundations *pl*.

in fraganti *loc adv* red-handed, in the act; **coger a alguien in fraganti** to catch sb red-handed *o* in the act.

infrahumano, na *adj* subhuman.

infranqueable *adj* impassable; *fig* insurmountable.

infrarrojo, ja *adj* infrared.

infravalorar *vt* to undervalue, to underestimate.

infrecuente *adj* infrequent.

infringir [15] *vt* [quebrantar] to infringe, to break.

infructuoso, sa *adj* fruitless, unsuccessful.

ínfulas *sfpl* pretensions; **darse** *o* **tener (muchas) ínfulas** to give oneself airs.

infumable *adj* [cigarrillo, tabaco] unsmokable; *fam* [insoportable] unbearable, intolerable.

infundado, da *adj* unfounded.

infundio *sm culto* untruth, lie.

infundir *vt*: **infundir algo a alguien** to fill sb with sthg, to inspire sthg in sb; **infundir miedo** to inspire fear.

infusión *sf* infusion; **infusión de manzanilla** camomile tea.

ingeniar [8] *vt* to invent, to devise.

➡ **ingeniarse** *vprnl*: **ingeniárselas** to manage, to engineer it; **ingeniárselas para hacer algo** to manage *o* contrive to do sthg.

ingeniería *sf* engineering; **ingeniería genética** genetic engineering.

ingeniero, ra *sm, f* engineer; **ingeniero agrónomo** agronomist; **ingeniero de caminos, canales y puertos** civil engineer; **ingeniero industrial/de telecomunicaciones** industrial/telecommunications engineer; **ingeniero de sistemas/sonido** systems/sound engineer.

ingenio *sm* **- 1.** [inteligencia] ingenuity; **aguzar el ingenio** to sharpen one's wits **- 2.** [agudeza] wit, wittiness **- 3.** [máquina] device; **ingenio nuclear** nuclear device.

ingenioso, sa *adj* [inteligente] ingenious, clever; [agudo] witty.

ingente *adj* enormous, huge.

ingenuidad *sf* ingenuousness, naivety.

ingenuo, nua ⬦ *adj* ingenuous, naive. ⬦ *sm, f* ingenuous *o* naive person.

ingerir [27] *vt* to consume, to ingest.

ingestión *sf* consumption.

ingiera, ingiriera ▷ **ingerir**.

Inglaterra *n pr* England.

ingle *sf* groin.

inglés, esa ⬦ *adj* English. ⬦ *sm, f* [persona] Englishman (*f* Englishwoman); **los ingleses** the English.

➡ **inglés** *sm* [lengua] English.

ingobernable *adj* [país] ungovernable; [niño] uncontrollable, unmanageable.

ingratitud *sf* ingratitude, ungratefulness.

ingrato, ta *adj* ungrateful; [trabajo] thankless.

ingrávido, da *adj* weightless.

ingrediente *sm* ingredient.

ingresar ⬦ *vt* BANCA to deposit, to pay in. ⬦ *vi*: **ingresar (en)** [asociación, ejército] to join;

[hospital] to be admitted (to); [convento, universidad] to enter; **ingresar cadáver** to be dead on arrival.

ingreso *sm* - **1.** [gen] entry; [en asociación, ejército] joining; [en hospital, universidad] admission - **2.** BANCA deposit; **hacer un ingreso** to make a deposit.
➡ **ingresos** *smpl* - **1.** [sueldo etc] income *(U)*; **ingresos brutos/netos** gross/net income - **2.** [recaudación] revenue *(U)*.

inhábil *adj* - **1.** [incapacitado - por defecto físico] unfit; [- por la edad] disqualified - **2.** [festivo]: **día inhábil** *weekend day or public holiday.*

inhabilitación *sf* disqualification; [minusvalía] disablement.

inhabilitar *vt* to disqualify.

inhabitable *adj* uninhabitable.

inhabitado, da *adj* uninhabited.

inhalación *sf* inhalation.

inhalador *sm* inhaler.

inhalar *vt* to inhale.

inherente *adj*: **inherente (a)** inherent (in).

inhibición *sf* inhibition.

inhibir *vt* to inhibit.
➡ **inhibirse de** *vprnl* [gen] to keep out of, to stay away from; [responsabilidades] to avoid, to shirk.

inhóspito, ta *adj* inhospitable.

inhumano, na *adj* [despiadado] inhuman; [desconsiderado] inhumane.

inhumar *vt* to inter, to bury.

iniciación *sf* - **1.** [gen] initiation - **2.** [de suceso, curso] start, beginning.

iniciado, da ◇ *adj* initiated. ◇ *sm, f* initiate.

inicial *adj & sf* initial.

inicialización *sf* INFORM initialization.

inicializar [13] *vt* INFORM to initialize.

iniciar [8] *vt* [gen] to start, to initiate; [debate, discusión] to start off; **iniciar a alguien en** to initiate sb into.

iniciativa *sf* initiative; **no tener iniciativa** to lack initiative; **por iniciativa propia** on one's own initiative; **tomar la iniciativa** to take the initiative; **iniciativa de paz** peace initiative; **iniciativa privada** private enterprise.

inicio *sm* start, beginning.

inigualable *adj* unrivalled.

inigualado, da *adj* unequalled.

inimaginable *adj* unimaginable.

inimitable *adj* inimitable.

ininteligible *adj* unintelligible.

ininterrumpido, da *adj* uninterrupted, continuous.

iniquidad *sf* iniquity.

injerencia *sf* interference, meddling.

injerir [27] *vt* to introduce, to insert.
➡ **injerirse** *vprnl* [entrometerse]: **injerirse (en)** to interfere (in), to meddle (in).

injertar *vt* to graft.

injerto *sm* graft.

injiera, injiriera etc *v* ▷ **injerir**.

injuria *sf* [insulto] insult, abuse *(U)*; [agravio] offence; DER slander.

injuriar [8] *vt* [insultar] to insult, to abuse; [agraviar] to offend; DER to slander.

injurioso, sa *adj* insulting, abusive; DER slanderous.

injusticia *sf* injustice; **¡es una injusticia!** that's unfair!; **cometer una injusticia con alguien** to do sb an injustice.

injustificado, da *adj* unjustified.

injusto, ta *adj* unfair, unjust.

inmaculado, da *adj* immaculate.
➡ **Inmaculada** *sf*: **la Inmaculada** the Virgin Mary.

inmadurez *sf* immaturity.

inmaduro, ra *adj* - **1.** [fruta] unripe - **2.** [persona] immature.

inmaterial *adj* immaterial.

inmediaciones *sfpl* [de localidad] surrounding area *sing*; [de lugar, casa] vicinity *sing*.

inmediatamente *adv* immediately, at once.

inmediatez *sf* immediateness, immediacy.

inmediato, ta *adj* - **1.** [gen] immediate; **de inmediato** immediately, at once - **2.** [contiguo] next, adjoining.

inmejorable *adj* unbeatable, that cannot be bettered.

inmemorial *adj* immemorial.

inmensidad *sf* - **1.** [grandeza] immensity - **2.** [multitud] huge amount, sea.

inmenso, sa *adj* - **1.** [gen] immense - **2.** *fig* [profundo] deep.

inmerecido, da *adj* undeserved.

inmersión *sf* immersion; [de submarinista] dive; **inmersión lingüística** language immersion.

inmerso, sa *adj*: **inmerso (en)** immersed (in).

inmigración *sf* immigration.

inmigrante *smf* immigrant.

inmigrar *vi* to immigrate.

inminencia *sf* imminence.

inminente *adj* imminent, impending.

inmiscuirse [51] *vprnl*: **inmiscuirse (en)** to interfere o meddle (in).

inmobiliario, ria *adj* property *(antes de s)*, real estate US *(antes de s)*.

inmobiliaria *sf* - **1.** [agencia] estate agency *UK*, real estate agent *US* - **2.** [constructora] construction company.

inmolación *sf* immolation, sacrifice.

inmolar *vt* to immolate, to sacrifice.

inmoral *adj* immoral.

inmortal *adj* immortal.

inmortalidad *sf* immortality.

inmortalizar [13] *vt* to immortalize.

inmóvil *adj* motionless, still; [coche, tren] stationary.

inmovilidad *sf* immobility.

inmovilismo *sm* defence of the status quo.

inmovilizado, da <> *adj* immobilized; [pierna, brazo] immobile. <> *sm* ECON fixed assets *pl*.

inmovilizar [13] *vt* to immobilize.

inmueble <> *adj*: **bienes inmuebles** real estate *(U)*. <> *sm* [edificio] building.

inmundicia *sf* [suciedad] filth, filthiness; [basura] rubbish.

inmundo, da *adj* filthy, dirty.

inmune *adj* - **1.** MED immune - **2.** [exento] exempt.

inmunidad *sf* immunity; **inmunidad diplomática/parlamentaria** diplomatic/parliamentary immunity.

inmunitario, ria *adj* immune.

inmunizar [13] *vt* to immunize.

inmunodeficiencia *sf* immunodeficiency.

inmunodepresor, ra *adj* immunodepressant.

inmunología *sf* immunology.

inmutable *adj* immutable, unchangeable.

inmutar *vt* to upset, to perturb.
<> **inmutarse** *vprnl* to get upset, to be perturbed; **ni se inmutó** he didn't bat an eyelid.

innato, ta *adj* innate.

innecesario, ria *adj* unnecessary.

innegable *adj* undeniable.

innoble *adj* ignoble.

innombrable *adj* unmentionable.

innovación *sf* innovation.

innovador, ra <> *adj* innovative, innovatory. <> *sm, f* innovator.

innovar *vt* [método, técnica] to improve on.

innumerable *adj* countless, innumerable.

inocencia *sf* innocence.

inocentada *sf* practical joke, trick.

inocente <> *adj* - **1.** [gen & DER] innocent; **declarar inocente a alguien** to find sb innocent *o* not guilty - **2.** [ingenuo - persona] naive, innocent - **3.** [sin maldad - persona] harmless. <> *smf*

- **1.** [persona no culpable] innocent person
- **2.** [persona cándida] innocent; **hacerse el inocente** to play *o* act the innocent.

inocular *vt* to inoculate.

inocuo, cua *adj* innocuous, harmless.

inodoro, ra *adj* odourless.
<> **inodoro** *sm* toilet *UK*, washroom *US*.

inofensivo, va *adj* inoffensive, harmless.

inolvidable *adj* unforgettable.

inoperante *adj* ineffective.

inopia *sf*: **estar en la inopia** to be miles away, to be day-dreaming.

inopinado, da *adj* unexpected.

inoportuno, na, **importuno, na** *adj* - **1.** [en mal momento] inopportune, untimely - **2.** [molesto] inconvenient - **3.** [inadecuado] inappropriate.

inorgánico, ca *adj* inorganic.

inoxidable *adj* rustproof; [acero] stainless.

input ['imput] (*pl* inputs) *sm* input *(U)*.

inquebrantable *adj* unshakeable; [lealtad] unswerving.

inquiera *etc* ▷ **inquirir**.

inquietante *adj* worrying.

inquietar *vt* to worry, to trouble.
<> **inquietarse** *vprnl* to worry, to get anxious.

inquieto, ta *adj* - **1.** [preocupado]: **inquieto (por)** worried *o* anxious (about) - **2.** [agitado, emprendedor] restless.

inquietud *sf* [preocupación] worry, anxiety.
<> **inquietudes** *sfpl* [afán de saber]: **tener inquietudes** to have an inquiring mind.

inquilino, na *sm, f* tenant.

inquina *sf* antipathy, aversion; **tener inquina a** to feel aversion towards.

inquirir [22] *vt* culto to inquire into, to investigate.

inquisición *sf* [indagación] inquiry, investigation.
<> **Inquisición** *sf* [tribunal] Inquisition.

inquisidor, ra *adj* inquisitive, inquiring.
<> **inquisidor** *sm* inquisitor.

inquisitivo, va *adj* inquisitive.

inri *sm*: **para más inri** *fam* to add insult to injury, to crown it all.

insaciable *adj* insatiable.

insalubre *adj* culto insalubrious, unhealthy.

insano, na *adj* [gen] unhealthy; [loco] insane.

insatisfacción *sf* dissatisfaction.

insatisfecho, cha *adj* - **1.** [descontento] dissatisfied - **2.** [no saciado] not full, unsatisfied.

inscribir *vt* - **1.** [grabar]: **inscribir algo (en)** to engrave *o* inscribe sthg (on) - **2.** [apuntar]: **inscribir algo/a alguien (en)** to register sthg/sb (on).

➤ **inscribirse** *vprnl*: **inscribirse (en)** [gen] to enrol (on); [asociación] to enrol (with); [concurso] to enter.

inscripción *sf* - **1.** EDUC registration, enrolment; [en censo, registro] registration; [en partido etc] enrolment; [en concursos etc] entry - **2.** [escrito] inscription.

inscrito, **ta** *pp* ▷ **inscribir**.

insecticida ◇ *adj* insecticidal. ◇ *sm* insecticide.

insectívoro, **ra** *adj* insectivorous.

insecto *sm* insect.

inseguridad *sf* - **1.** [falta de confianza] insecurity - **2.** [duda] uncertainty - **3.** [peligro] lack of safety; **inseguridad ciudadana** lack of law and order.

inseguro, **ra** *adj* - **1.** [sin confianza] insecure - **2.** [dudoso] uncertain - **3.** [peligroso] unsafe.

inseminación *sf* insemination; **inseminación artificial** artificial insemination.

inseminar *vt* to inseminate.

insensatez *sf* foolishness, senselessness; **hacer/decir una insensatez** to do/say sthg foolish.

insensato, **ta** ◇ *adj* foolish, senseless. ◇ *sm, f* foolish o senseless person, fool.

insensibilidad *sf* [emocional] insensitivity; [física] numbness.

insensibilizar *vt* MED to numb.

➤ **insensibilizarse** *vprnl* [emocionalmente] to become desensitized.

insensible *adj* - **1.** [indiferente]: **insensible (a)** insensitive (to) - **2.** [entumecido] numb - **3.** [imperceptible] imperceptible.

inseparable *adj* inseparable.

inserción *sf* insertion; **iniciativas de inserción laboral** employment initiatives.

insertar *vt* [gen & INFORM]: **insertar (en)** to insert (into).

inservible *adj* useless, unserviceable.

insidioso, **sa** *adj* malicious.

insigne *adj* distinguished, illustrious.

insignia *sf* - **1.** [distintivo] badge; MIL insignia - **2.** [bandera] flag, banner.

insignificancia *sf* - **1.** [cualidad] insignificance - **2.** [cosa, hecho] trifle, insignificant thing.

insignificante *adj* insignificant.

insinuación *sf* hint, insinuation.

➤ **insinuaciones** *sfpl* [amorosas] innuendo (U).

insinuante *adj* suggestive, full of innuendo.

insinuar [6] *vt*: **insinuar algo (a)** to hint at o insinuate sthg (to).

➤ **insinuarse** *vprnl* - **1.** [amorosamente]: **insinuarse (a)** to make advances (to) - **2.** [asomar]: **insinuarse detrás de algo** to peep out from behind sthg.

insípido, **da** *adj* lit & fig insipid.

insistencia *sf* insistence.

insistente *adj* insistent.

insistir *vi*: **insistir (en)** to insist (on); **insistir en que** to insist that.

insobornable *adj* incorruptible.

insociable *adj* unsociable.

insolación *sf* - **1.** MED sunstroke (U); **coger una insolación** to get sunstroke - **2.** METEOR sunshine.

insolencia *sf* insolence; **hacer/decir una insolencia** to do/say sthg insolent.

insolente ◇ *adj* [descarado] insolent; [orgulloso] haughty. ◇ *smf* insolent person.

insolidaridad *sf* lack of solidarity.

insolidario, **ria** ◇ *adj* lacking in solidarity. ◇ *sm, f* person lacking in solidarity.

insólito, **ta** *adj* very unusual.

insoluble *adj* insoluble.

insolvencia *sf* insolvency.

insolvente *adj* insolvent.

insomne *adj* sleepless.

insomnio *sm* insomnia, sleeplessness.

insondable *adj* lit & fig unfathomable.

insonorización *sf* soundproofing.

insonorizar [13] *vt* to soundproof.

insoportable *adj* unbearable, intolerable.

insoslayable *adj* inevitable, unavoidable.

insospechable *adj* impossible to tell, unforeseeable.

insospechado, **da** *adj* unexpected, unforeseen.

insostenible *adj* untenable.

inspección *sf* inspection; [policial] search; **inspección de calidad** quality control inspection; **inspección ocular** visual inspection.

inspeccionar *vt* to inspect; [suj: policía] to search.

inspector, **ra** *sm, f* inspector; **inspector de aduanas** customs official; **inspector de Hacienda** tax inspector; **inspector de policía** police inspector.

inspiración *sf* - **1.** [gen] inspiration - **2.** [respiración] inhalation, breath.

inspirado, **da** *adj* inspired.

inspirar *vt* - **1.** [gen] to inspire - **2.** [respirar] to inhale, to breathe in.

➤ **inspirarse** *vprnl*: **inspirarse (en)** to be inspired (by).

instalación *sf* - **1.** [gen] installation; **instalación eléctrica** wiring; **instalación sanitaria** plumbing - **2.** [de gente] settling.

➤ **instalaciones** *sfpl* [deportivas etc] facilities.

instalador, **ra** ◇ *adj* installing, fitting. ◇ *sm, f* fitter.

instalar *vt* - **1.** [montar - antena etc] to instal, to fit; [- local, puesto etc] to set up - **2.** [situar - objeto] to place; [- gente] to settle.

➤ **instalarse** *vprnl* [establecerse]: **instalarse en** to settle (down) in; [nueva casa] to move into.

instancia *sf* - **1.** [solicitud] application (form) - **2.** [ruego] request; **a instancias de** at the request *o* bidding of; **en última instancia** as a last resort - **3.** DER: **juzgado de primera instancia** court of first instance.

instantáneo, a *adj* - **1.** [momentáneo] momentary - **2.** [rápido] instantaneous.

➤ **instantánea** *sf* snapshot, snap.

instante *sm* moment; **a cada instante** all the time, constantly; **al instante** instantly, immediately; **en un instante** in a second.

instar *vt*: **instar a alguien a que haga algo** to urge *o* press sb to do sthg.

instauración *sf* establishment, foundation.

instaurar *vt* to establish, to set up.

instigador, ra <> *adj* instigating. <> *sm, f* instigator.

instigar [16] *vt*: **instigar a alguien (a que haga algo)** to instigate sb (to do sthg); **instigar a algo** to incite to sthg.

instintivo, va *adj* instinctive.

instinto *sm* instinct; **por instinto** instinctively; **instinto maternal** maternal instinct; **instinto de supervivencia** survival instinct.

institución *sf* - **1.** [gen] institution; **institución benéfica** charitable organization; **institución pública** public institution; **ser una institución** *fig* to be an institution - **2.** [de ley, sistema] introduction; [de organismo] establishment; [de premio] foundation.

institucional *adj* institutional.

institucionalizar [13] *vt* to institutionalize.

instituir [51] *vt* - **1.** [fundar - gobierno] to establish; [- premio, sociedad] to found; [- sistema, reglas] to introduce - **2.** [nombrar] to appoint, to name.

instituto *sm* - **1.** [corporación] institute - **2.** EDUC: **instituto (de Enseñanza Secundaria)** state secondary school; **instituto de Formación Profesional** ≃ technical college; **instituto politécnico** polytechnic.

➤ **instituto de belleza** *sm* beauty salon.

institutriz *sf* governess.

instrucción *sf* - **1.** [conocimientos] education; [docencia] instruction; **instrucción militar** military training - **2.** [DER - investigación] preliminary investigation; [- curso del proceso] proceedings *pl*.

➤ **instrucciones** *sfpl* [de uso] instructions.

instructivo, va *adj* [gen] instructive; [juguete, película] educational.

instructor, ra <> *adj* training, instructing. <> *sm, f* [gen] instructor, teacher; DEP coach.

instruido, da *adj* educated.

instruir [51] *vt* - **1.** [enseñar] to instruct - **2.** DER to prepare.

instrumental <> *adj* instrumental. <> *sm* instruments *pl*.

instrumentar *vt* to orchestrate, to score.

instrumentista *smf* - **1.** MÚS instrumentalist - **2.** MED surgeon's assistant.

instrumento *sm* - **1.** *fig* & MÚS instrument; **instrumento de cuerda** string instrument; **instrumento musical** musical instrument; **instrumento de viento** wind instrument - **2.** [herramienta] tool, instrument; **instrumento de precisión** precision tool.

insubordinación *sf* insubordination.

insubordinado, da <> *adj* insubordinate. <> *sm, f* insubordinate (person), rebel.

insubordinar *vt* to stir up, to incite to rebellion.

➤ **insubordinarse** *vprnl* to rebel.

insubstancial = **insustancial**.

insubstituible = **insustituible**.

insuficiencia *sf* - **1.** [escasez] lack, shortage - **2.** MED failure, insufficiency; **insuficiencia cardiaca/renal** heart/kidney failure.

insuficiente <> *adj* insufficient. <> *sm* [nota] fail.

insufrible *adj* intolerable, insufferable.

insular <> *adj* insular, island *(antes de s)*. <> *smf* islander.

insulina *sf* insulin.

insulso, sa *adj* *lit & fig* bland, insipid.

insultante *adj* insulting, offensive.

insultar *vt* to insult.

insulto *sm* insult; **proferir insultos** to hurl insults.

insumisión *sf* rebelliousness.

insumiso, sa <> *adj* rebellious. <> *sm, f* [gen] rebel; MIL *person who refuses to do military or community service*.

insuperable *adj* - **1.** [inmejorable] unsurpassable - **2.** [sin solución] insurmountable, insuperable.

insurrección *sf* insurrection, revolt.

insurrecto, ta *adj* & *sm, f* insurgent, rebel.

insustancial, insubstancial *adj* insubstantial.

insustituible, insubstituible *adj* irreplaceable.

intachable *adj* irreproachable.

intacto, ta *adj* untouched; *fig* intact.

intangible *adj* intangible.

integración *sf* integration; **integración racial** racial integration.

integral ◇ *adj* **- 1.** [total] total, complete **- 2.** [sin refinar - pan, harina, pasta] wholemeal; [- arroz] brown **- 3.** MAT ▭▷ **cálculo**. ◇ *sf* MAT integral.

integrante ◇ *adj* integral, constituent; **estado integrante de la CE** member state of the EC. ◇ *smf* member.

integrar *vt* **- 1.** [gen & MAT] to integrate **- 2.** [componer] to make up.
◆ **integrarse** *vprnl* to integrate; **integrarse en** to become integrated into.

integridad *sf* [gen] integrity; [totalidad] wholeness.

integrismo *sm* **- 1.** RELIG fundamentalism **- 2.** POLÍT reaction, traditionalism.

integrista *adj & smf* **- 1.** RELIG fundamentalist **- 2.** POLÍT reactionary, traditionalist.

íntegro, gra *adj* **- 1.** [completo] whole, entire; [versión etc] unabridged **- 2.** [honrado] upright, honourable.

intelecto *sm* intellect.

intelectual *adj & smf* intellectual.

intelectualizar [13] *vt* to intellectualize.

inteligencia *sf* intelligence; **inteligencia artificial** INFORM artificial intelligence; **inteligencia emocional** emotional intelligence.

inteligente *adj* [gen & INFORM] intelligent.

inteligible *adj* intelligible.

intemperie *sf*: **a la intemperie** in the open air.

intempestivo, va *adj* [clima, comentario] harsh; [hora] ungodly, unearthly; [proposición, visita] inopportune.

intemporal *adj* timeless, independent of time.

intención *sf* intention; **con intención** intentionally; **sin intención** without meaning to; **tener la intención de** to intend to; **tener malas intenciones** to be up to no good; **buena/mala intención** good/bad intentions *pl*; **segunda intención** underhandedness, duplicity; **intención de voto** voting intention; **la intención es lo que cuenta** it's the thought that counts; **de buenas intenciones está el infierno lleno** *prov* the road to hell is paved with good intentions.

intencionado, da *adj* intentional, deliberate; **bien intencionado** [acción] well-meant; [persona] well-meaning; **mal intencionado** [acción] ill-meant, ill-intentioned; [persona] malevolent.

intencional *adj* intentional, deliberate.

intencionalidad *sf* intent.

intendencia *sf* management, administration; **intendencia militar** service corps.

intendente *sm* [militar] quartermaster.

intensidad *sf* [gen] intensity; [de lluvia] heaviness; [de luz, color] brightness; [de amor] passion, strength.

intensificación *sf* intensification.

intensificar [10] *vt* to intensify.
◆ **intensificarse** *vprnl* to intensify.

intensivo, va *adj* intensive.

intenso, sa *adj* [gen] intense; [lluvia] heavy; [luz, color] bright; [amor] passionate, strong.

intentar *vt*: **intentar (hacer algo)** to try (to do sthg).

intento *sm* [tentativa] attempt; [intención] intention; **intento de golpe/robo** attempted coup/robbery; **intento de suicidio** suicide attempt.

intentona *sf*: **intentona (golpista)** POLÍT attempted coup.

interacción *sf* interaction.

interaccionar *vi* to interact.

interactivo, va *adj* INFORM interactive.

intercalar *vt* to insert, to put in.

intercambiable *adj* interchangeable.

intercambiar [8] *vt* to exchange; [lugares, posiciones] to change, to swap.

intercambio *sm* exchange; **hacer un intercambio** to go on an exchange programme; **intercambio comercial** trade.

interceder *vi*: **interceder (por alguien)** to intercede (on sb's behalf).

interceptar *vt* **- 1.** [detener] to intercept **- 2.** [obstruir] to block.

intercesor, ra ◇ *adj* interceding. ◇ *sm, f* interceder, intercessor.

interconexión *sf* interconnection.

intercostal *adj* intercostal, between the ribs.

interés *sm* **- 1.** [gen & FIN] interest; **de interés** interesting; **esperar algo con interés** to await sthg with interest; **tener interés en** *o* **por** to be interested in; **tengo interés en que venga pronto** it's in my interest that he should come soon; **interés acumulado** accrued interest; **interés compuesto** compound interest; **interés interbancario** interbank deposit rate; **interés preferencial** preferential interest rate; **interés simple** simple interest; **intereses creados** vested interests **- 2.** [egoísmo] self-interest, selfishness; **por interés** out of selfishness.

interesado, da ◇ *adj* **- 1.** [gen]: **interesado (en** *o* **por)** interested (in) **- 2.** [egoísta] selfish, self-interested **- 3.** [implicado]: **las partes interesadas** the interested parties. ◇ *sm, f* **- 1.** [deseoso] interested person; **los interesados** those interested **- 2.** [egoísta] selfish *o* self-interested person.

interesante *adj* interesting; **hacerse el/la interesante** to try to draw attention to oneself.

interesar *vi* to interest; **le interesa el arte** she's interested in art.

➤ **interesarse** *vprnl*: **interesarse (en** *o* **por)** to take an interest (in), to be interested (in); **se interesó por tu salud** she asked after your health.

interestatal *adj* interstate.

interfaz *sf* INFORM interface.

interfecto, ta *sm, f* murder victim.

interferencia *sf* interference.

interferir [27] ◇ *vt* - **1.** TELECOM, RADIO & TV to jam - **2.** [interponerse] to interfere with. ◇ *vi*: **interferir (en)** to interfere (in).

interfono *sm* intercom.

interina ▷ interino.

interinidad *sf* - **1.** [cualidad] temporariness - **2.** [tiempo] (period of) temporary employment.

interino, na ◇ *adj* [gen] temporary; [presidente, director etc] acting; [gobierno] interim. ◇ *sm, f* [gen] stand-in; [médico, juez] locum; [profesor] supply teacher.

➤ **interina** *sf* [asistenta] cleaning lady.

interior ◇ *adj* - **1.** [gen] inside, inner; [patio, jardín etc] interior, inside; [habitación, vida] inner - **2.** POLÍT domestic - **3.** GEOGR inland. ◇ *sm* - **1.** [parte de dentro] inside, interior - **2.** GEOGR interior, inland area - **3.** [de una persona] inner self, heart; **en mi interior** deep down.

➤ **interiores** *sfpl* - **1.** CINE interiors - **2.** *Amér* [calzoncillos] underpants *pl*.

interioridad *sf* [carácter] inner self.

➤ **interioridades** *sfpl* [asuntos] private affairs.

interiorismo *sm* interior design.

interiorista *smf* interior designer.

interiorización *sf* internalization; [de sentimientos] bottling-up.

interiorizar [13] *vt* to internalize; [sentimientos] to bottle up.

interjección *sf* interjection.

interlineado *sm* space between the lines.

interlocutor, ra *sm, f* interlocutor, speaker; **su interlocutor** the person she was speaking to.

interludio *sm* [gen & MÚS] interlude.

intermediar [8] *vi* to mediate.

intermediario, ria ◇ *adj* intermediary. ◇ *sm, f* [gen] intermediary; COM middleman; [en disputas] mediator.

intermedio, dia *adj* - **1.** [etapa] intermediate, halfway; [calidad] average; [tamaño] medium - **2.** [tiempo] intervening; [espacio] in between.

➤ **intermedio** *sm* [gen & TEATRO] interval; CINE intermission.

interminable *adj* endless, interminable.

intermitencia *sf* intermittence, intermittency.

intermitente ◇ *adj* intermittent. ◇ *sm* indicator.

internacional *adj* international.

➤ **Internacional** *sf* POLÍT International; **La Internacional** [himno] the Internationale.

internacionalismo *sm* internationalism.

internado, da ◇ *adj* [en manicomio] confined; [en colegio] boarding; POLÍT interned. ◇ *sm, f* [en manicomio] inmate; [en colegio] boarder; POLÍT internee.

➤ **internado** *sm* - **1.** [internamiento - en manicomio] confinement; [- en colegio] boarding - **2.** [colegio] boarding school.

➤ **internada** *sf* DEP break, breakaway.

internamiento *sm* [en manicomio] confinement; [en escuela] boarding; POLÍT internment.

internar *vt*: **internar (en)** [internado] to send to boarding school (at); [manicomio] to commit (to); [campo de concentración] to intern (in).

➤ **internarse** *vprnl*: **internarse (en)** [un lugar] to go *o* penetrate deep (into); [un tema] to become deeply involved (in).

internauta *smf* Internet user.

Internet *sf*: **(la) Internet** the Internet; **en Internet** on the Internet.

internista *adj* & *smf* internist.

interno, na ◇ *adj* - **1.** [gen] internal; POLÍT domestic - **2.** [alumno] boarding - **3.** ▷ medicina. ◇ *sm, f* - **1.** [alumno] boarder - **2.** ▷ médico - **3.** [preso] prisoner, inmate.

interparlamentario, ria *adj* interparliamentary.

interpelación *sf* formal question.

interpelar *vt* to question formally.

interplanetario, ria *adj* interplanetary.

Interpol (*abrev de* **International Criminal Police Organization**) *sf* Interpol.

interpolar *vt* to interpolate, to put in.

interponer [65] *vt* - **1.** [gen] to interpose, to put in - **2.** DER to lodge, to make.

➤ **interponerse** *vprnl* to intervene.

interposición *sf* - **1.** [gen] interposition - **2.** DER lodging (*of an appeal*).

interpretación *sf* - **1.** [explicación] interpretation; **mala interpretación** misinterpretation - **2.** [artística] performance - **3.** [traducción] interpreting.

interpretar *vt* - **1.** [gen] to interpret - **2.** [artísticamente] to perform.

intérprete *smf* - **1.** [traductor & INFORM] interpreter - **2.** [artista] performer - **3.** [comentarista] commentator.

interpuesto, ta *pp* ⊳ **interponer**.

interrelación *sf* interrelation.

interrelacionar *vt* to interrelate.

interrogación *sf* - **1.** [acción] questioning - **2.** [signo] question mark - **3.** [pregunta] question.

interrogador, ra ◇ *adj* questioning. ◇ *sm, f* [gen] questioner; [que usa amenazas etc] interrogator.

interrogante *sm o sf* [incógnita] question mark.

interrogar [16] *vt* [gen] to question; [con amenazas etc] to interrogate.

interrogativo, va *adj* interrogative.

interrogatorio *sm* [gen] questioning; [con amenazas] interrogation.

interrumpir *vt* - **1.** [gen] to interrupt - **2.** [discurso, trabajo] to break off; [viaje, vacaciones] to cut short - **3.** [circulación] to block.
➤ **interrumpirse** *vprnl* to be interrupted; [tráfico] to be blocked.

interrupción *sf* - **1.** [gen] interruption; **interrupción (voluntaria) del embarazo** termination of pregnancy - **2.** [de discurso, trabajo] breaking-off; [de viaje, vacaciones] cutting-short - **3.** [de circulación etc] blocking.

interruptor *sm* switch; **interruptor general** mains switch.

intersección *sf* intersection.

interurbano, na *adj* inter-city; TELECOM long-distance.

intervalo *sm* - **1.** [gen & MÚS] interval; [de espacio] space, gap; **a intervalos** at intervals - **2.** [duración]: **en el intervalo de un mes** in the space of a month.

intervención *sf* - **1.** [gen] intervention - **2.** [discurso] speech; [interpelación] contribution - **3.** COM auditing - **4.** MED operation - **5.** TELECOM tapping.

intervencionismo *sm* interventionism.

intervencionista *adj & smf* interventionist.

intervenir [75] ◇ *vi* - **1.** [participar]: **intervenir (en)** [gen] to take part (in); [pelea] to get involved (in); [discusión etc] to make a contribution (to) - **2.** [dar un discurso] to make a speech - **3.** [interferir]: **intervenir (en)** to intervene (in) - **4.** MED to operate. ◇ *vt* - **1.** MED to operate on - **2.** TELECOM to tap - **3.** [incautar] to seize - **4.** COM to audit.

interventor, ra *sm, f* - **1.** COM auditor - **2.** [en elecciones] scrutineer.

interviú (*pl* interviús) *sf* interview.

intestinal *adj* intestinal.

intestino, na *adj* internecine.
➤ **intestino** *sm* intestine; **intestino delgado/grueso** small/large intestine.

intimar *vi*: **intimar (con)** to become intimate *o* very friendly (with).

intimidación *sf* intimidation.

intimidad *sf* - **1.** [vida privada] private life; [privacidad] privacy; **en la intimidad** in private - **2.** [amistad] intimacy.

intimidar *vt* to intimidate.

íntimo, ma ◇ *adj* - **1.** [vida, fiesta] private; [ambiente, restaurante] intimate - **2.** [relación, amistad] close - **3.** [sentimiento etc] innermost; **en lo (más) íntimo de su corazón/alma** deep down in her heart/soul. ◇ *sm, f* close friend.

intocable *adj* untouchable.
➤ **intocables** *smf pl* [en la India] untouchables.

intolerable *adj* intolerable, unacceptable; [dolor, ruido] unbearable.

intolerancia *sf* - **1.** [actitud] intolerance - **2.** MED allergy.

intolerante ◇ *adj* intolerant. ◇ *smf* intolerant person.

intoxicación *sf* poisoning *(U)*; **intoxicación alimenticia** food poisoning; **intoxicación etílica** alcohol poisoning.

intoxicar [10] *vt* to poison.
➤ **intoxicarse** *vprnl* to poison o.s.

intraducible *adj* untranslatable.

intranquilidad *sf* unease, anxiety.

intranquilizar [13] *vt* to worry, to make uneasy.
➤ **intranquilizarse** *vprnl* to get worried.

intranquilo, la *adj* [preocupado] worried, uneasy; [nervioso] restless.

intransferible *adj* non-transferable, untransferable.

intransigencia *sf* intransigence.

intransigente *adj* intransigent.

intransitable *adj* impassable.

intransitivo, va *adj* intransitive.

intrascendencia *sf* insignificance, unimportance.

intrascendente *adj* insignificant, unimportant.

intratable *adj* unsociable, difficult to get on with.

intrauterino, na *adj* intrauterine.

intravenoso, sa *adj* intravenous.

intrépido, da *adj* intrepid.

intriga *sf* - **1.** [curiosidad] curiosity; **de intriga** suspense *(antes de s)* - **2.** [maquinación] intrigue - **3.** [trama] plot.

intrigado, da *adj* intrigued.

intrigante *adj* intriguing.

intrigar [16] *vt & vi* to intrigue.

intrincado, **da** *adj* - **1.** [bosque etc] thick, dense - **2.** [problema etc] intricate.

intríngulis *sm inv fam*: **tiene su intríngulis** it is quite tricky.

intrínseco, **ca** *adj* intrinsic.

introducción *sf*: **introducción (a)** introduction (to).

introducir [33] *vt* - **1.** [meter - llave, carta etc] to put in, to insert - **2.** [mercancías etc] to bring in, to introduce - **3.** [dar a conocer]: **introducir a alguien en** to introduce sb to; **introducir algo en** to introduce o bring sthg to.

◆ **introducirse** *vprnl*: **introducirse en** to get into.

introductor, **ra** ◇ *adj* introductory; **el país introductor de esta moda** the country that brought in this fashion. ◇ *sm, f* introducer.

introductorio, **ria** *adj* introductory.

intromisión *sf* meddling, interfering.

introspección *sf* introspection.

introspectivo, **va** *adj* introspective.

introvertido, **da** *adj* & *sm, f* introvert.

intrusión *sf* intrusion.

intrusismo *sm* illegal practice of a profession.

intruso, **sa** ◇ *adj* intrusive. ◇ *sm, f* intruder; **intruso informático** hacker.

intubar *vt* to intubate.

intuición *sf* intuition.

intuir [51] *vt* to know by intuition, to sense.

intuitivo, **va** *adj* intuitive.

intuya, **intuyera** etc *v* ▷ **intuir**.

inundación *sf* flood, flooding *(U)*.

inundar *vt* to flood; *fig* to inundate, to swamp.

◆ **inundarse** *vprnl* to flood; **inundarse de** *fig* to be inundated o swamped with.

inusitado, **da** *adj* uncommon, rare.

inusual *adj* unusual.

inútil ◇ *adj* - **1.** [gen] useless; [intento, esfuerzo] unsuccessful, vain - **2.** [inválido] disabled - **3.** [no apto] unfit. ◇ *smf* hopeless case, useless person.

inutilidad *sf* - **1.** [gen] uselessness; [falta de sentido] pointlessness - **2.** [invalidez] disablement.

inutilizar [13] *vt* [gen] to make unusable; [máquinas, dispositivos] to disable, to put out of action.

invadir *vt* to invade; **la invade la tristeza** she's overcome by sadness.

invalidación *sf* invalidation.

invalidar *vt* to invalidate.

invalidez *sf* - **1.** MED disablement, disability; **invalidez permanente/temporal** permanent/temporary disability - **2.** DER invalidity.

inválido, **da** ◇ *adj* - **1.** MED disabled - **2.** DER invalid. ◇ *sm, f* invalid, disabled person; **los inválidos** the disabled.

invariable *adj* invariable.

invasión *sf* invasion.

invasor, **ra** ◇ *adj* invading. ◇ *sm, f* invader.

invencible *adj* invincible; [timidez etc] insurmountable, insuperable.

invención *sf* invention.

invendible *adj* unsaleable.

inventar *vt* [gen] to invent; [narración, falsedades] to make up.

◆ **inventarse** *vprnl* to make up.

inventario *sm* inventory; **hacer el inventario** COM to do the stocktaking.

inventiva *sf* inventiveness.

invento *sm* invention.

inventor, **ra** *sm, f* inventor.

invernadero, **invernáculo** *sm* greenhouse.

invernal *adj* winter *(antes de s)*; [tiempo, paisaje] wintry.

invernar [19] *vi* [pasar el invierno] to (spend the) winter; [hibernar] to hibernate.

inverosímil *adj* unlikely, improbable.

inverosimilitud *sf* unlikeliness, improbability.

inversión *sf* - **1.** [del orden] inversion - **2.** [de dinero, tiempo] investment; **inversiones extranjeras** ECON foreign investments.

inverso, **sa** *adj* opposite, inverse; **inverso a** opposite to; **a la inversa** the other way round; **en orden inverso** in reverse order.

inversor, **ra** ◇ *adj* investing. ◇ *sm, f* COM & FIN investor.

◆ **inversor** *sm* ELECTR inverter.

invertebrado, **da** *adj* invertebrate.

◆ **invertebrado** *sm* invertebrate.

invertido, **da** ◇ *adj* - **1.** [al revés] reversed, inverted; [sentido, dirección] opposite - **2.** [dinero] invested - **3.** [homosexual] homosexual. ◇ *sm, f* homosexual.

invertir [27] *vt* - **1.** [gen] to reverse; [poner boca abajo] to invert, to turn upside down - **2.** [dinero, tiempo, esfuerzo] to invest - **3.** [tardar - tiempo] to spend.

investidura *sf* investiture.

investigación *sf* - **1.** [estudio] research; **investigación y desarrollo** research and development - **2.** [indagación] investigation, inquiry; **investigación judicial** judicial inquiry.

investigador, **ra** ◇ *adj* - **1.** [que estudia] research *(antes de s)* - **2.** [que indaga] investigating. ◇ *sm, f* - **1.** [estudioso] researcher - **2.** [detective] investigator; **investigador privado** private investigator o detective.

investigar [16] ⟨⟩ *vt* - **1.** [estudiar] to research - **2.** [indagar] to investigate. ⟨⟩ *vi* - **1.** [estudiar] to do research - **2.** [indagar] to investigate.

investir [26] *vt:* **investir a alguien con algo** to invest sb with sthg.

inveterado, da *adj* deep-rooted.

inviabilidad *sf* impracticability.

inviable *adj* impractical, unviable.

invicto, ta *adj culto* unconquered, unbeaten.

invidente ⟨⟩ *adj* blind, sightless. ⟨⟩ *smf* blind o sightless person; **los invidentes** the blind.

invierna *etc* ⟿ **invernar**.

invierno *sm* winter; **invierno nuclear** nuclear winter.

invierta *etc* ⟿ **invertir**.

inviolabilidad *sf* inviolability.

inviolable *adj* inviolable.

invirtiera *etc* ⟿ **invertir**.

invisible *adj* invisible.

invista, invistiera *etc* ⟿ **investir**.

invitación *sf* invitation.

invitado, da ⟨⟩ *adj* invited. ⟨⟩ *sm, f* guest.

invitar ⟨⟩ *vt* - **1.** [convidar]: **invitar a alguien (a algo/a hacer algo)** to invite sb (to sthg/to do sthg) - **2.** [pagar]: **os invito** it's my treat, this one's on me; **invitar a alguien a algo** to buy sb sthg *(food, drink)*; **te invito a cenar fuera** I'll take you out for dinner. ⟨⟩ *vi* to pay; **invita la casa** it's on the house.

➤ **invitar a** *vi fig* [incitar]: **invitar a algo** to encourage sthg; **la lluvia invita a quedarse en casa** the rain makes you want to stay at home.

in vitro *loc adv* - **1.** [de probeta] in vitro - **2.** ⟿ **fecundación**.

invocación *sf* invocation.

invocar [10] *vt* to invoke.

involución *sf* regression.

involucionista ⟨⟩ *adj* regressive, reactionary. ⟨⟩ *smf* reactionary.

involucrar *vt:* **involucrar a alguien (en)** to involve sb (in).

➤ **involucrarse** *vprnl:* **involucrarse (en)** to get involved (in).

involuntario, ria *adj* [espontáneo] involuntary; [sin querer] unintentional.

invoque *etc* ⟿ **invocar**.

invulnerabilidad *sf* invulnerability.

invulnerable *adj:* **invulnerable (a)** immune (to), invulnerable (to).

inyección *sf* injection; **poner una inyección** to give an injection.

inyectable ⟨⟩ *adj* injectable. ⟨⟩ *sm* injection.

inyectar *vt* to inject.

➤ **inyectarse** *vprnl* [drogas] to take drugs intravenously; **inyectarse algo** to inject o.s. with sthg.

iodo = **yodo**.

ion *sm* ion.

ionice *etc* ⟿ **ionizar**.

iónico, ca *adj* ionic.

ionizar [13] *vt* to ionize.

ionosfera *sf* ionosphere.

IPC (*abrev de* **índice de precios al consumo**) *sm* Spanish cost of living index, ≃ RPI *UK*.

ipso facto *loc adv* immediately.

ir [61] *vi* - **1.** [gen] to go; **ir hacia el sur/al cine** to go south/to the cinema; **ir en autobús/coche** to go by bus/car; **ir en avión** to fly; **ir en bicicleta** to ride; **ir andando** to go on foot, to walk; **¡vamos!** let's go! - **2.** [expresa duración gradual]: **ir haciendo algo** to be (gradually) doing sthg; **va anocheciendo** it's getting dark; **voy mejorando mi estilo** I'm working on improving my style - **3.** [expresa intención, opinión]: **ir a hacer algo** to be going to do sthg; **voy a decírselo a tu padre** I'm going to tell your father; **te voy a echar de menos** I'm going to miss you - **4.** [cambiar]: **ir a mejor/peor** *etc* to get better/worse *etc* - **5.** [funcionar] to work; **la manivela va floja** the crank is loose; **la televisión no va** the television isn't working - **6.** [desenvolverse] to go; **le va bien en su nuevo trabajo** things are going well for him in his new job; **su negocio va mal** his business is going badly; **¿cómo te va?** how are you doing? - **7.** [vestir]: **ir en/con** to wear; **iba en camisa y con corbata** he was wearing a shirt and tie; **ir de azul/de uniforme** to be dressed in blue/in uniform - **8.** [tener aspecto físico] to look like; **iba hecho un pordiosero** he looked like a beggar - **9.** [vacaciones, tratamiento]: **irle bien a alguien** to do sb good - **10.** [ropa]: **irle (bien) a alguien** to suit sb; **ir con algo** to go with sthg - **11.** [comentario, indirecta]: **ir con** o **por alguien** to be meant for sb, to be aimed at sb - **12.** *loc:* **fue y dijo que...** he went and said that...; **ni me va ni me viene** *fam* I don't care; **¡qué va!** you must be joking!; **ser el no va más** to be the ultimate.

➤ **ir de** *vi* - **1.** [película, novela] to be about - **2.** *fig* [persona] to think o.s.; **va de listo** he thinks he's clever.

➤ **ir por** *vi* - **1.** [buscar]: **ir por algo/alguien** to go and get sthg/sb, to go and fetch sthg/sb - **2.** [alcanzar]: **va por el cuarto vaso de vino** he's already on his fourth glass of wine; **vamos por la mitad de la asignatura** we covered about half the subject.

➤ **irse** *vprnl* - **1.** [marcharse] to go, to leave; **irse a** to go to; **¡vete!** go away! - **2.** [gastarse, desapa-

recer] to go **- 3.** *loc:* **irse abajo** [edificio] to fall down; [negocio] to collapse; [planes] to fall through.
ira *sf* anger, rage.
iracundo, da *adj* angry, irate; [irascible] irascible.
Irán *n pr:* **(el) Irán** Iran.
iraní (*pl* **iraníes** *o* **iranís**) *adj* & *smf* Iranian.
➣ **iraní** *sm* [lengua] Iranian.
Iraq *n pr:* **(el) Iraq** Iraq.
iraquí (*pl* **iraquíes** *o* **iraquís**) *adj* & *smf* Iraqi.
irascible *adj* irascible.
irga, irguiera *etc* ▷ **erguir.**
iris *sm inv* iris.
Irlanda *n pr* Ireland.
irlandés, esa ◇ *adj* Irish. ◇ *sm, f* [persona] Irishman (*f* Irishwoman); **los irlandeses** the Irish.
➣ **irlandés** *sm* [lengua] Irish.
ironía *sf* irony.
irónico, ca *adj* ironic, ironical.
ironizar [13] ◇ *vt* to ridicule. ◇ *vi:* **ironizar (sobre)** to be ironical (about).
IRPF (*abrev de* **impuesto sobre la renta de las personas físicas**) *sm Spanish personal income tax.*
irracional *adj* irrational.
irracionalidad *sf* irrationality.
irradiación *sf* **- 1.** [gen] irradiation **- 2.** [de cultura, ideas] dissemination, spreading.
irradiar [8] *vt lit & fig* to radiate.
irreal *adj* unreal.
irrealidad *sf* unreality.
irrealizable *adj* [sueño, objetivo] unattainable; [plan] impractical.
irrebatible *adj* irrefutable, indisputable.
irreconciliable *adj* irreconcilable.
irreconocible *adj* unrecognizable.
irrecuperable *adj* irretrievable.
irreemplazable *adj* irreplaceable.
irreflexión *sf* rashness.
irreflexivo, va *adj* rash.
irrefrenable *adj* irrepressible, uncontainable.
irrefutable *adj* irrefutable.
irregular *adj* [gen] irregular; [terreno, superficie] uneven.
irregularidad *sf* [gen] irregularity; [de terreno, superficie] unevenness.
irrelevancia *sf* irrelevance.
irrelevante *adj* irrelevant.
irremediable *adj* irremediable.
irreparable *adj* irreparable.
irrepetible *adj* unique, unrepeatable.
irreprimible *adj* irrepressible.

irreprochable *adj* irreproachable.
irresistible *adj* irresistible.
irresoluble *adj* unsolvable.
irresoluto, ta ◇ *adj culto* irresolute. ◇ *sm, f* irresolute person.
irrespetuoso, sa *adj* disrespectful.
irrespirable *adj* unbreathable.
irresponsabilidad *sf* irresponsibility.
irresponsable ◇ *adj* irresponsible. ◇ *smf* irresponsible person.
irreverente *adj* irreverent.
irreversible *adj* irreversible.
irrevocable *adj* irrevocable.
irrigación *sf* irrigation.
irrigar [16] *vt* to irrigate.
irrisorio, ria *adj* **- 1.** [excusa etc] laughable, derisory **- 2.** [precio etc] ridiculously low.
irritabilidad *sf* irritability.
irritable *adj* irritable.
irritación *sf* irritation.
irritante *adj* irritating.
irritar *vt* to irritate.
➣ **irritarse** *vprnl* **- 1.** [enfadarse] to get angry *o* annoyed **- 2.** [suj: piel etc] to become irritated.
irrompible *adj* unbreakable.
irrumpir *vi:* **irrumpir en** to burst into.
irrupción *sf* bursting in.
isabelino, na *adj* [en España] Isabelline; [en Inglaterra] Elizabethan.
ISBN (*abrev de* **international standard book number**) *sm* ISBN.
isla *sf* island; **la isla de Pascua** Easter Island; **isla desierta** desert island.
islam *sm* Islam.
islámico, ca *adj* Islamic.
islamismo *sm* Islam.
islamizar [13] *vt* to Islamize, to convert to Islam.
➣ **islamizarse** *vprnl* to convert to Islam.
islandés, esa ◇ *adj* Icelandic. ◇ *sm, f* [persona] Icelander.
➣ **islandés** *sm* [lengua] Icelandic.
Islandia *n pr* Iceland.
isleño, ña ◇ *adj* island (*antes de s*). ◇ *sm, f* islander.
islote *sm* small, rocky island.
isobara, isóbara *sf* isobar.
isomorfo, fa *adj* isomorphic.
isósceles ◇ *adj inv* isosceles. ◇ *sm inv* isosceles triangle.
isótopo ◇ *adj* isotopic. ◇ *sm* isotope.
Israel *n pr* Israel.
israelí (*pl* **israelíes** *o* **israelís**) *adj* & *smf* Israeli.
israelita *adj* & *smf* Israelite.

ISO (*abrev de* **International Standards Organization**) *sf* ISO.

istmo *sm* isthmus.

Italia *n pr* Italy.

italianismo *sm* Italianism.

italianizar [13] *vt* to Italianize.

italiano, na *adj & sm, f* Italian.
➤ **italiano** *sm* [lengua] Italian.

itálico, ca ⬦ *adj* - **1.** HIST Italic - **2.** ▷ **letra.**
⬦ *sm, f* HIST Italic.

item, ítem *sm* item.

itinerante *adj* itinerant; [embajador] roving.

itinerario *sm* route, itinerary.

ITV (*abrev de* **inspección técnica de vehículos**) *sf* annual technical inspection for motor vehicles of ten years or more, ≃ MOT UK.

IVA (*abrev de* **impuesto sobre el valor añadido**) *sm* VAT.

izar [13] *vt* to raise, to hoist.

izda (*abrev de* izquierda) L, l.

izquierda *sf* ▷ **izquierdo.**

izquierdismo *sm* left-wing views *pl.*

izquierdista ⬦ *adj* left-wing. ⬦ *smf* left-winger.

izquierdo, da *adj* left.
➤ **izquierda** *sf* - **1.** [lado] left; **a la izquierda (de)** on o to the left (of); **girar a la izquierda** to turn left; **por la izquierda** on the left - **2.** [mano] left hand - **3.** POLÍT left (wing); **de izquierdas** left-wing.

izquierdoso, sa *adj fam* leftish.

J

j, J *sf* [letra] j, J.

ja *interj*: **¡ja!** ha!

jabalí (*pl* jabalíes o jabalís) *sm* wild boar.

jabalina *sf* DEP javelin.

jabato, ta *adj* brave.
➤ **jabato** *sm* ZOOL baby wild boar.

jabón *sm* soap; **jabón de afeitar/tocador** shaving/toilet soap; **jabón líquido** liquid soap; **jabón en polvo** soap powder; **dar jabón a alguien** to soft-soap sb.

jabonar *vt* to soap.

jaboncillo *sm* tailor's chalk.

jabonera *sf* soap dish.

jabonoso, sa *adj* soapy.

jaca *sf* [caballo pequeño] pony; [yegua] mare.

jacal *sm* Méx hut.

jacinto *sm* hyacinth.

jaco *sm mfam* junk, heroin.

jacobeo, a *adj* of/relating to St James.

jacobino, na *adj & sm, f* Jacobin.

jactancia *sf* boasting.

jactancioso, sa *adj* boastful.

jactarse *vprnl*: **jactarse (de)** to boast (about o of).

jaculatoria *sf* short prayer.

jade *sm* jade.

jadeante *adj* panting.

jadear *vi* to pant.

jadeo *sm* panting.

jaguar (*pl* jaguars) *sm* jaguar.

jaiba *sf* Andes, Amér C, Caribe & Méx crayfish.

jalar ⬦ *vi mfam* to pig (out), to scoff. ⬦ *vt* Andes, Amér C, Caribe & Méx [tirar] to pull.
➤ **jalarse** *vprnl mfam* to scoff (down).

jalea *sf* jelly; **jalea real** royal jelly.

jalear *vt* to cheer on.

jaleo *sm* - **1.** *fam* [alboroto] row, rumpus; **armar jaleo** to kick up a row o fuss - **2.** *fam* [lío] mess, confusion - **3.** [aplausos, gritos] cheering.

jalón *sm* [palo] marker pole.

jalonar *vt* to stake o mark out; *fig* to mark.

Jamaica *n pr* Jamaica.

jamaicano, na *adj & sm, f* Jamaican.

jamás *adv* never; **no lo he visto jamás** I've never seen him; **la mejor película que jamás se haya hecho** the best film ever made; **jamás de los jamases** never ever.

jamba *sf* jamb, door post.

jamelgo *sm fam* nag.

jamón *sm* ham; **jamón del país** local homemade ham; **jamón (de) York o (en) dulce** boiled ham; **jamón serrano** cured ham, ≃ Parma ham; **¡y un jamón!** *fam* you've got to be joking!, not on your life!

jamona *fam* ⬦ *adj* generously built. ⬦ *sf* generously-built woman.

Japón *n pr*: **(el) Japón** Japan.

japonés, esa *adj & sm, f* Japanese.
➤ **japonés** *sm* [lengua] Japanese.

jaque *sm*: **jaque (al rey)** check; **jaque mate** checkmate; **tener en jaque a alguien** *fig* to keep sb in a state of anxiety.

jaqueca *sf* migraine; **dar jaqueca (a alguien)** *fam* to bother (sb), to pester (sb).

jarabe *sm* syrup; **jarabe para la tos** cough mixture o syrup; **jarabe de palo** beating; **tener mucho jarabe de pico** to have the gift of the gab, to be a smooth talker.

jarana *sf* - **1.** [juerga]: **estar/irse de jarana** to be/go out on the town - **2.** [alboroto] row, rumpus.

jaranero, ra <> *adj* fond of partying. <> *sm, f* party-goer.

jarcia *sf* NÁUT rigging.

jardín *sm* garden, yard US; **jardín botánico** botanical garden; **jardín zoológico** zoological garden, zoo.

➤ **jardín de infancia** *sm* kindergarten, nursery school.

jardinera ▷ jardinero.

jardinería *sf* gardening.

jardinero, ra *sm, f* gardener.

➤ **jardinera** *sf* flowerpot stand; **a la jardinera** CULIN garnished with vegetables.

jarra *sf* - **1.** [para servir] jug - **2.** [para beber] tankard.

➤ **en jarras** *loc adv* [postura] hands on hips.

jarrete *sm* hock.

jarro *sm* jug; **fue como un jarro de agua fría** *fig* it was a bolt from the blue.

jarrón *sm* vase.

jaspe *sm* jasper.

jaspeado, da *adj* mottled, speckled.

➤ **jaspeado** *sm* mottling.

jaspear *vt* to mottle, to speckle.

jauja *sf* fam paradise, heaven on earth; **ser jauja** to be heaven on earth o paradise.

jaula *sf* cage.

jauría *sf* pack of dogs.

Java *n pr* Java.

javanés, esa *adj* & *sm, f* Javanese.

jazmín *sm* jasmine.

jazz [jas] *sm* jazz.

JC (*abrev de* **Jesucristo**) JC.

je *interj*: ¡je! ha!

jeans [jins] *smpl* jeans.

jeep [jip] (*pl* jeeps) *sm* jeep.

jefa ▷ jefe.

jefatura *sf* - **1.** [cargo] leadership - **2.** [organismo] headquarters, head office; **jefatura de policía** police headquarters.

jefazo, za *sm, f* fam big boss.

jefe, fa *sm, f* [gen] boss; [de empresa] manager (*f* manageress); [líder] leader; [de tribu, ejército] chief; [de departamento etc] head; **en jefe** MIL in-chief; **jefe de cocina** chef; **jefe de estación** stationmaster; **jefe de Estado** head of state; **jefe de estudios** deputy head; **jefe de personal** personnel manager; **jefe de producción/ventas** production/sales manager; **jefe de redacción** editor-in-chief.

jején *sm* Amér [insecto] ≃ midge.

jengibre *sm* ginger.

jeque *sm* sheikh.

jerarca *smf* high-ranking person, leader.

jerarquía *sf* - **1.** [organización] hierarchy - **2.** [persona] high-ranking person, leader.

jerárquico, ca *adj* hierarchical.

jerarquizar [13] *vt* to structure in a hierarchical manner.

jerez *sm* sherry; **jerez fino** dry sherry.

jerga *sf* jargon; [argot] slang.

jergón *sm* straw mattress.

jerigonza *sf* [galimatías] gibberish; [jerga] jargon; [argot] slang.

jeringa *sf* syringe.

jeringuilla *sf* syringe; **jeringuilla hipodérmica** hypodermic syringe.

jeroglífico, ca *adj* hieroglyphic.

➤ **jeroglífico** *sm* - **1.** [inscripción] hieroglyphic - **2.** [pasatiempo] rebus.

jerséi (*pl* jerséis), **jersey** (*pl* jerseys) *sm* jumper, pullover.

Jerusalén *n pr* Jerusalem.

Jesucristo *n pr* Jesus Christ.

jesuita *adj* & *sm* Jesuit.

jesús *interj*: ¡jesús! [sorpresa] gosh!, good heavens!; [tras estornudo] bless you!

jet [jet] (*pl* jets) *sm* jet.

jeta *mfam* <> *sf* [cara] mug, face; **romperle la jeta a alguien** to smash sb's face in; **tener (mucha) jeta** to be a cheeky bugger. <> *smf* cheeky bugger.

jet lag ['jetlak] *sm* jet lag.

jet-set ['jetset] *sf* jet set.

jíbaro, ra <> *adj* Jívaro (antes de s). <> *sm, f* Jívaro.

Jibuti *n pr* Djibouti.

jijona *sm* type of nougat made in Jijona.

jilguero *sm* goldfinch.

jilipollada = gilipollada.

jilipollas = gilipollas.

jilipollez = gilipollez.

jinete *smf* rider; [yóquey] jockey.

jiote *sm* Méx rash.

jirafa *sf* - **1.** ZOOL giraffe - **2.** CINE & TV boom.

jirón *sm* - **1.** [andrajo] shred, rag; **hecho jirones** in tatters - **2.** Perú [calle] street.

jitomate *sm* Amér C & Méx tomato.

JJ OO (*abrev de* **juegos olímpicos**) *smpl* Olympic Games.

jo *interj fam*: ¡**jo**! [asombro, admiración] wow!; [enfado, molestia] hell!, Christ!

jockey ['jokei] = **yóquey**.

jocosidad *sf* - **1.** [humor] funniness, humour - **2.** [chiste] quip.

jocoso, sa *adj* jocular.

joder *vulg* ⋄ *vi* - **1.** [copular] to fuck - **2.** [fastidiar] to be a pain in the arse; ¡**no jodas**! [incredulidad] bollocks!, pull the other one! ⋄ *vt* - **1.** [fastidiar] to fuck about o around - **2.** [disgustar] to fuck o piss off - **3.** [estropear] to fuck (up). ⋄ *interj*: ¡**joder**! fuck it!, fucking hell!
➡ **joderse** *vprnl vulg* - **1.** [aguantarse] to fucking well put up with it; ¡**que se joda**! he can fuck off! - **2.** [estropearse] to get fucked (up).

jodido, da *adj vulg* - **1.** [gen] fucked; [anímicamente] fucked up - **2.** [difícil] fucking difficult - **3.** [maldito] fucking.

jodienda *sf vulg* fucking pain (in the arse).

jofaina *sf* wash basin.

jogging ['joɣiŋ] *sm* jogging.

jóker ['joker] (*pl* **jokers**) *sm* joker *(in cards)*.

jolgorio *sm* merrymaking.

jolín, jolines *interj fam*: ¡**jolín**! hell!, Christ!

jondo ⊳ **cante**.

jónico, ca *adj* Ionic.

jornada *sf* - **1.** [de trabajo] working day; **jornada intensiva** *working day from 8 to 3 with only a short lunch break*; **jornada laboral** *working day*; **media jornada** half day; **jornada partida** *typical Spanish working day from 9 to 1 and 4 to 7*; **jornada de reflexión** *day of reflection before elections when campaigning is forbidden* - **2.** [de viaje] day's journey - **3.** DEP round of matches, programme.
➡ **jornadas** *sfpl* [conferencia] conference *sing*.

jornal *sm* day's wage.

jornalero, ra *sm, f* day labourer.

joroba *sf* hump.

jorobado, da ⋄ *adj* - **1.** *fam* [estropeado] knackered; **tengo el estómago jorobado** I've got gut-rot - **2.** [con joroba] hunchbacked. ⋄ *sm, f* hunchback.

jorobar *vt fam* - **1.** [molestar] to cheese off, to annoy - **2.** [estropear] to knacker; **me ha jorobado el estómago** it's given me gut-rot.
➡ **jorobarse** *vprnl fam*: **pues te jorobas** you can like it or lump it.

jorongo *sm Méx* - **1.** [manta] blanket - **2.** [poncho] poncho.

jota *sf* - **1.** [baile] *Aragonese folk song and dance* - **2.** [loc]: **no entender** o **saber ni jota** *fam* not to understand o know a thing; **no ver ni jota** *fam* [por defecto visual] to be as blind as a bat; [por oscuridad etc] not to be able to see a thing.

jotero, ra *sm, f jota dancer*.

joto *sm Méx fam despec* queer *UK*, faggot *US*.

joven ⋄ *adj* young; **de joven** as a young man/woman. ⋄ *smf* young man (*f* young woman); **los jóvenes** young people.

jovenzuelo, la *sm, f* youngster.

jovial *adj* jovial, cheerful.

jovialidad *sf* joviality, cheerfulness.

joya *sf* jewel; *fig* gem; **joyas de fantasía** costume jewellery *(U)*.

joyería *sf* - **1.** [tienda] jeweller's (shop) - **2.** [arte, comercio] jewellery.

joyero, ra *sm, f* [persona] jeweller.
➡ **joyero** *sm* [estuche] jewellery box.

JPI (*abrev de* **juzgado de primera instancia**) *sm* court of first instance.

juanete *sm* bunion.

jubilación *sf* - **1.** [retiro] retirement; **jubilación anticipada** early retirement; **jubilación forzosa** compulsory retirement; **jubilación voluntaria** voluntary retirement - **2.** [dinero] pension.

jubilado, da ⋄ *adj* retired. ⋄ *sm, f* pensioner *UK*, senior citizen.

jubilar *vt*: **jubilar a alguien (de)** to pension sb off o retire sb (from).
➡ **jubilarse** *vprnl* to retire.

jubileo *sm* RELIG jubilee.

júbilo *sm* jubilation, joy.

jubiloso, sa *adj* jubilant, joyous.

judaico, ca *adj* Judaic, Jewish.

judaísmo *sm* Judaism.

judas *sm inv* Judas, traitor.

judeocristiano, na *adj* Judaeo-Christian.

judeoespañol, la ⋄ *adj* Sephardic. ⋄ *sm, f* [persona] Sephardic Jew.
➡ **judeoespañol** *sm* [lengua] Sephardi.

judería *sf* Jewish ghetto o quarter.

judía *sf* bean; **judía blanca/verde** haricot/green bean.

judiada *sf fam* dirty trick.

judicatura *sf* - **1.** [cargo] office of judge - **2.** [institución] judiciary.

judicial *adj* judicial.

judío, a ⟷ *adj* Jewish. ⟷ *sm, f* Jew (*f* Jewess).

judo = yudo.

judoka = yudoca.

juega ⟼ jugar.

juego *sm* - **1.** [gen & DEP] game; [acción] play, playing; [con dinero] gambling; **abrir/cerrar el juego** to begin/finish the game; **estar/poner en juego** to be/put at stake; **¡hagan juego!** place your bets!; **ser un juego de niños** to be child's play; **juego de azar** game of chance; **juego de manos** conjuring trick; **juego de mesa** board game; **juego de palabras** play on words, pun; **juego de prendas** game of forfeit; **juegos malabares** juggling (*U*); *fig* [piruetas] balancing act *sing*; **juego sucio/limpio** foul/clean play; **descubrirle el juego a alguien** to see through sb; **hacerle** *o* **seguirle el juego a alguien** to play along with sb; **doble juego, juego doble** double game, double dealing (*U*); **estar (en) fuera de juego** DEP to be offside; *fig* not to know what's going on - **2.** [mano - de cartas] hand; **me salió un buen juego** I was dealt a good hand - **3.** [conjunto de objetos] set; **juego de herramientas** tool kit; **juego de llaves/sábanas** set of keys/sheets; **juego de té/café** tea/coffee service; **zapatos a juego con el bolso** shoes with matching handbag; **hacer juego (con)** to match.
➤ **juegos florales** *smpl* poetry competition *sing*.
➤ **Juegos Olímpicos** *smpl* Olympic Games.

juegue ⟼ jugar.

juerga *sf fam* rave-up, binge; **irse/estar de juerga** to go/be out on the town; **tomar algo a juerga** to take sthg as a joke.

juerguista *fam* ⟷ *adj* fond of partying. ⟷ *smf* party-goer, reveller.

jueves *sm inv* Thursday; **jueves lardero** Thursday before Shrovetide; **Jueves Santo** Maundy Thursday; **no ser nada del otro jueves** to be nothing out of this world; *ver también* **sábado**.

juez *smf* - **1.** DER judge; **juez de instrucción, juez de primera instancia** examining magistrate; **juez de paz** Justice of the Peace - **2.** [DEP - gen] judge; [- en atletismo] official; **juez de línea** [- fútbol] linesman; [- rugby] touch judge; **juez de salida** starter; **juez de silla** umpire.

jugada *sf* - **1.** DEP period of play; [en tenis, ping-pong] rally; [en fútbol, rugby etc] move; [en ajedrez etc] move; [en billar] shot - **2.** [treta] dirty trick; **hacer una mala jugada a alguien** to play a dirty trick on sb.

jugador, ra ⟷ *adj* [gen] playing; [de juego de azar] gambling. ⟷ *sm, f* [gen] player; [de juego de azar] gambler.

jugar [40] ⟷ *vi* - **1.** [gen] to play; **jugar al ajedrez** to play chess; **jugar en un equipo** to play for a team; **te toca jugar** it's your turn *o* go; **jugar limpio/sucio** to play clean/dirty; **jugar con algo** to play with sthg; **jugar contra alguien** to play (against) sb - **2.** [con dinero]: **jugar (a)** to gamble (on); **jugar (a la Bolsa)** to speculate (on the Stock Exchange) - **3.** [ser desconsiderado]: **jugar con** to play (around) with. ⟷ *vt* - **1.** [gen] to play; [ficha, pieza] to move - **2.** [dinero]: **jugar algo (a algo)** to gamble sthg (on sthg).
➤ **jugarse** *vprnl* - **1.** [apostarse] to bet - **2.** [arriesgar] to risk; **¿qué te juegas a que...?** I bet you... - **3.** *loc*: **jugársela a alguien** to play a dirty trick on sb.

jugarreta *sf fam* dirty trick.

juglar *sm* minstrel.

juglaresco, ca *adj* minstrel *(antes de s)*.

juglaría *sf* minstrelsy.

jugo *sm* - **1.** [gen & ANAT] juice; BOT sap; **jugos gástricos** gastric juices - **2.** [interés] meat, substance; **sacar jugo a algo/alguien** to get the most out of sthg/sb.

jugosidad *sf* juiciness.

jugoso, sa *adj* - **1.** [con jugo] juicy - **2.** *fig* [picante] juicy; [sustancioso] meaty, substantial.

jugué *etc* ⟼ jugar.

juguete *sm lit & fig* toy; **de juguete** toy *(antes de s)*; **juguete bélico** war toy; **juguete educativo** educational toy.

juguetear *vi* to play (around); **juguetear con algo** to toy with sthg.

juguetería *sf* toy shop.

juguetón, ona *adj* playful.

juicio *sm* - **1.** DER trial; **llevar a alguien a juicio** to take sb to court; **juicio civil** civil action; **juicio criminal** criminal trial - **2.** [sensatez] (sound) judgement; [cordura] sanity, reason; **estar/no estar en su (sano) juicio** to be/not to be in one's right mind; **perder el juicio** to lose one's reason, to go mad - **3.** [opinión] opinion; **a mi juicio** in my opinion; **juicio de valor** value judgement.
➤ **Juicio Final** *sm*: **el Juicio Final** the Last Judgement.

juicioso, sa *adj* sensible, wise.

jul. (*abrev de* julio) Jul.

juliana *sf* CULIN *soup made with chopped vegetables and herbs*; **en juliana** julienne.

julio *sm* - **1.** [mes] July - **2.** FÍS joule; *ver también* **septiembre**.

jumbo *sm* jumbo (jet).

jun. (*abrev de* **junio**) Jun.

juncal *sf* bed of rushes.

junco *sm* - **1.** [planta] rush, reed - **2.** [embarcación] junk.

jungla *sf* jungle.

junio *sm* June; *ver también* **septiembre**.

júnior (*pl* **juniors**) ⬦ *adj inv* - **1.** DEP under-21 - **2.** [hijo] junior. ⬦ *sm, f* DEP under-21.

junta *sf* - **1.** [gen] committee; [de empresa, examinadores] board; **junta directiva** board of directors; **junta de gobierno** *government and administrative body in certain autonomous regions*; **junta militar** military junta - **2.** [reunión] meeting; **junta (general) de accionistas** shareholders' meeting - **3.** [juntura] joint; **junta de culata** gasket.

juntamente *adv*: **juntamente con** together with.

juntar *vt* [gen] to put together; [fondos] to raise; [personas] to bring together.
➤ **juntarse** *vprnl* - **1.** [reunirse - personas] to get together; [- ríos, caminos] to meet - **2.** [arrimarse] to draw O move closer - **3.** [convivir] to live together.

junto, ta ⬦ *adj* - **1.** [gen] together - **2.** [próximo] close together. ⬦ *adv*: **todo junto** [ocurrir etc] all at the same time; [escribirse] as one word.
➤ **junto a** *loc prep* - **1.** [al lado de] next to - **2.** [cerca de] right by, near.
➤ **junto con** *loc prep* together with.

juntura *sf* joint.

Júpiter *sm* Jupiter.

jura *sf* [gen] oath; [de un cargo] swearing in; **jura de bandera** oath of allegiance to the flag.

jurado, da *adj* - **1.** [declaración etc] sworn - **2.** ▷ **guarda** - **3.** ▷ **traductor**.
➤ **jurado** *sm* - **1.** [tribunal] jury - **2.** [miembro] member of the jury.

juramentar *vt* to swear in.

juramento *sm* - **1.** [promesa] oath; **bajo juramento** on O under oath; **prestar juramento** to take the oath; **tomar juramento a alguien** to swear sb in; **juramento hipocrático** Hippocratic oath - **2.** [blasfemia] oath, curse.

jurar ⬦ *vt* to swear; [constitución etc] to pledge allegiance to; **te lo juro** I promise, I swear it; **jurar por... que** to swear by... that; **jurar que** to swear that. ⬦ *vi* [blasfemar] to swear; **tenérsela jurada a alguien** to have it in for sb.

jurel *sm* scad, horse mackerel.

jurídico, ca *adj* legal.

jurisconsulto, ta *sm, f* jurist.

jurisdicción *sf* jurisdiction.

jurisdiccional *adj* jurisdictional; [aguas] territorial.

jurisprudencia *sf* [ciencia] jurisprudence; [casos previos] case law; **sentar jurisprudencia** to set a legal precedent.

jurista *smf* jurist.

justa *sf* HIST joust.

justamente *adv* - **1.** [con justicia] justly - **2.** [exactamente] exactly; **justamente, eso es lo que estaba pensando** exactly, that's just what I was thinking.

justicia *sf* - **1.** [gen] justice; [equidad] fairness, justice; **administrar justicia** to administer justice; **en justicia** in (all) fairness; **hacer justicia** to do justice; **justicia social** social justice; **ser de justicia** to be only fair; **tomarse la justicia por su mano** to take the law into one's own hands - **2.** [organización]: **la justicia** the law.

justiciero, ra ⬦ *adj* righteous. ⬦ *sm, f* angel of justice.

justificable *adj* justifiable.

justificación *sf* [gen & IMPR] justification; **justificación automática** automatic justification.

justificado, da *adj* justified.

justificante *sm* written proof (U), documentary evidence (U).

justificar [10] *vt* - **1.** [gen & IMPR] to justify - **2.** [excusar]: **justificar a alguien** to make excuses for sb.
➤ **justificarse** *vprnl* - **1.** [suj: actitud etc] to be justified - **2.** [suj: persona] to justify O excuse o.s.; **justificarse de algo** to excuse o.s. for sthg; **justificarse con alguien** to make one's excuses to sb.

justificativo, va *adj* providing evidence, supporting (*antes de s*).

justiprecio *sm* valuation.

justo, ta *adj* - **1.** [equitativo] fair - **2.** [merecido - recompensa, victoria] deserved; [- castigo] just - **3.** [exacto - medida, hora] exact - **4.** [idóneo] right - **5.** [apretado] tight; **estar** O **venir justo** to be a tight fit - **6.** RELIG righteous.
➤ **justo** ⬦ *sm* RELIG: **los justos** the righteous. ⬦ *adv* just; **justo ahora iba a llamarte** I was just about to ring you; **justo en medio** right in the middle.

juvenil ⬦ *adj* youthful; DEP youth (*antes de s*). ⬦ *smf* (*gen pl*) DEP player in the youth team.

juventud *sf* - **1.** [edad] youth; **¡juventud, divino tesoro!** what it is to be young! - **2.** [conjunto] young people *pl*.

juzgado *sm* - **1.** [tribunal] court; **juzgado municipal** magistrates' court; **juzgado de guardia** *court open during the night or at other times when ordinary courts are shut*; **ser de juzgado de guardia** *fam* to be criminal o a crime - **2.** [jurisdicción] jurisdiction.

juzgar [16] *vt* - **1.** [enjuiciar] to judge; DER to try; **juzgar mal a alguien** to misjudge sb; **a juzgar por (como)** judging by (how) - **2.** [estimar] to consider, to judge.

K

k, K *sf* [letra] k, K.
kafkiano, na *adj* kafkaesque.
kaki = caqui.
kamikaze *sm* - **1.** MIL kamikaze - **2.** *fig* [arriesgado] daredevil.
kárate, cárate *sm* karate.
karateka *smf* karateist.
kart (*pl* **karts**) *sm* go-kart.
katiusca, katiuska *sf* ankle-length rubber boot.
kayac (*pl* **kayacs**) *sm* kayak.
Kazajstán *n pr* Kazakhstan.
Kenia *n pr* Kenya.
keniata *adj & smf* Kenyan.
kepis = quepis.
keroseno = queroseno.
ketchup ['ketʃup] *sm* ketchup.
kg (*abrev de* **kilogramo**) kg.
kibutz [ki'βuθ] (*pl* **kibutzim**) *sm* kibbutz.
kif = quif.
kilo, quilo *sm* - **1.** [peso] kilo - **2.** *fam* [millón] tonne, million.
kilocaloría, quilocaloría *sf* kilocalorie.
kilogramo, quilogramo *sm* kilogram.
kilolitro, quilolitro *sm* kilolitre.
kilometraje, quilometraje *sm* ≃ mileage, distance in kilometres.
kilometrar, quilometrar *vt* to measure in kilometres.

kilométrico, ca, quilométrico, ca *adj* - **1.** [distancia] kilometric - **2.** *fig* [largo] very long.
kilómetro, quilómetro *sm* kilometre; **kilómetro cuadrado** square kilometre; **kilómetros por hora** kilometres per hour.
kilovatio, quilovatio *sm* kilowatt.
kilovoltio, quilovoltio *sm* kilovolt.
kimono = quimono.
kínder *sm* *Andes & Cuba* nursery school UK, kindergarten US.
kiosco = quiosco.
kirsch [kirʃ] *sm* kirsch.
kiwi *sm* [fruto] kiwi (fruit).
km (*abrev de* **kilómetro**) km.
km/h (*abrev de* **kilómetro por hora**) km/h.
knockout [no'kaut] *sm* knockout.
KO (*abrev de* **knockout**) *sm* KO.
kosovar ⬦ *adj* Kosovan. ⬦ *smf* Kosovan, Kosovar.
Kosovo *sm* Kosovo.
Kurdistán *sm* Kurdistan.
kurdo, da ⬦ *adj* Kurdish. ⬦ *sm, f* Kurd.
Kuwait [ku'βait] *n pr* Kuwait.
kuwaití (*pl* **kuwaitíes** o **kuwaitís**) *adj & smf* Kuwaiti.

L

l¹, L *sf* [letra] l, L.
l² (*abrev de* **litro**) l.
L/ *abrev de* **letra**.
la¹ *sm* MÚS A; [en solfeo] lah.
la² ⬦ *art* ▷ **el**. ⬦ *pron* ▷ **lo**.
laberíntico, ca *adj* *lit & fig* labyrinthine.
laberinto *sm* *lit & fig* labyrinth.
labia *sf* *fam* smooth talk; **tener mucha labia** to have the gift of the gab.
labial *adj & sf* labial.
labio *sm* - **1.** ANAT lip; **labio inferior/superior** lower/upper lip; **labio leporino** harelip; **estar pendiente de los labios de alguien** to hang

on sb's every word; **leer los labios** to lip-read; **no despegar los labios** not to utter a word **- 2.** [borde] edge.

labiodental *adj* & *sf* labiodental.

labor *sf* **- 1.** [trabajo] work; [tarea] task; **labor de equipo** teamwork *(U)*; **labores domésticas** household chores; **ser de profesión sus labores** to be a housewife; **no estar por la labor** [distraerse] not to have one's mind on the job; [ser reacio] not to be keen on the idea **- 2.** [de costura] needlework; **labores de punto** knitting.

laborable ▷ **día**.

laboral *adj* labour; [semana, condiciones] working *(antes de s)*.

laboralista ◇ *adj* labour *(antes de s)*. ◇ *smf* labour lawyer.

laboratorio *sm* laboratory; **laboratorio espacial** space laboratory; **laboratorio fotográfico** photographic laboratory; **laboratorio de idiomas** O **lenguas** language laboratory.

laborioso, sa *adj* **- 1.** [difícil] laborious, arduous **- 2.** [trabajador] hard-working.

laborismo *sm* Labour Movement.

laborista ◇ *adj* Labour. ◇ *smf* Labour Party supporter O member; **los laboristas** Labour.

labrador, ra *sm, f* [agricultor] farmer; [trabajador] farm worker.

labranza *sf* farming.

labrar *vt* **- 1.** [campo - cultivar] to cultivate; [- arar] to plough **- 2.** [piedra, metal etc] to work **- 3.** *fig* [desgracia etc] to bring about; [porvenir, fortuna] to carve out.

◆ **labrarse** *vprnl* [porvenir etc] to carve out for o.s.

labriego, ga *sm, f* farmworker.

laburar *vi R Dom fam* [trabajar] to work.

laburo *sm R Dom fam* [trabajo] job.

laca *sf* **- 1.** [gen] lacquer; [para cuadros] lake **- 2.** [para el pelo] hairspray **- 3.** [de uñas] nail varnish.

lacado *sm* lacquering.

lacar [10] *vt* to lacquer.

lacayo *sm* footman; *fig* lackey.

lacerante *adj* [dolor] excruciating, stabbing; [palabras etc] hurtful, cutting; [grito etc] piercing.

lacerar *vt* to lacerate; *fig* to wound.

lacio, cia *adj* **- 1.** [cabello - liso] straight; [- sin fuerza] lank **- 2.** [planta] wilted **- 3.** *fig* [sin fuerza] limp.

lacón *sm* shoulder of pork.

lacónico, ca *adj* laconic.

laconismo *sm* terseness.

lacra *sf* scourge.

lacrar *vt* to seal with sealing wax.

lacre *sm* sealing wax.

lacrimal *adj* lacrimal, tear *(antes de s)*.

lacrimógeno, na *adj* **- 1.** [novela etc] weepy, tear-jerking **- 2.** ▷ **gas**.

lacrimoso, sa *adj* **- 1.** [ojos etc] tearful **- 2.** [historia etc] weepy, tear-jerking.

lactancia *sf* lactation; **lactancia artificial** bottlefeeding; **lactancia materna** breastfeeding.

lactante *smf* breast-fed baby.

lactar *vt* & *vi* to suckle, to breastfeed.

lácteo, a *adj* **- 1.** [gen] milk *(antes de s)*; [industria, productos] dairy **- 2.** *fig* [blanco] milky.

láctico, ca *adj* lactic.

lactosa *sf* lactose.

ladeado, da *adj* tilted, at an angle.

ladear *vt* to tilt.

ladera *sf* slope, mountainside.

ladilla *sf* crab (louse).

ladino, na ◇ *adj* crafty. ◇ *sm, f Amér C, Méx & Ven* [mestizo hispanohablante] *non-white Spanish-speaking person.*

◆ **ladino** *sm* [dialecto] Ladino.

lado *sm* **- 1.** [gen] side; **en el lado de arriba/abajo** on the top/bottom; **a ambos lados** on both sides; **al otro lado de** on the other side of; **estoy de su lado** I'm on her side; **de lado** [torcido] crooked; **dormir de lado** to sleep on one's side; **de lado a lado** from side to side; **echar a un lado** to push aside; **echarse** O **hacerse a un lado** to move aside; **ponerse del lado de alguien** to side with sb; **por un lado** on the one hand; **por otro lado** on the other hand **- 2.** [lugar] place; **debe estar en otro lado** it must be somewhere else; **de un lado para** O **a otro** to and fro; **por todos lados** on all sides, all round **- 3.** *loc:* **dar de lado a alguien** to cold-shoulder sb; **dejar algo de lado** O **a un lado** [prescindir] to leave sthg to one side; **mirar de lado a alguien** [despreciar] to look askance at sb.

◆ **al lado** *loc adv* [cerca] nearby.

◆ **al lado de** *loc prep* [junto a] beside.

◆ **de al lado** *loc adj* next door; **la casa de al lado** the house next door.

ladrador, ra *adj* barking.

ladrar *vi lit & fig* to bark; **estar alguien que ladra** to be in a foul mood.

ladrido *sm lit & fig* bark, barking *(U)*.

ladrillo *sm* **- 1.** CONSTR brick **- 2.** *fam fig* [pesadez] drag, bore.

ladrón, ona ◇ *adj* thieving. ◇ *sm, f* [persona] thief, robber.

◆ **ladrón** *sm* [para varios enchufes] adapter.

lagar *sm* [de vino] winepress; [de aceite] oil press.

lagarta ▷ **lagarto**.

lagartija *sf* (small) lizard.

lagarto, ta *sm, f* ZOOL lizard.

➤ **lagarta** *sf fam fig* [mujer] scheming woman.

lago *sm* lake.

lágrima *sf* tear; **deshacerse en lágrimas** to dissolve into tears; **hacer saltar las lágrimas** to bring tears to the eyes; **llorar a lágrima viva** to cry buckets; **lágrimas de cocodrilo** crocodile tears.

lagrimal ◇ *adj* lacrimal, tear *(antes de s)*. ◇ *sm* corner of the eye.

lagrimear *vi* [suj: persona] to weep; [suj: ojos] to water.

laguna *sf* - **1.** [lago] lagoon - **2.** *fig* [en colección, memoria] gap; [en leyes, reglamento] loophole.

La Habana *n pr* Havana.

laicismo *sm* laicism.

laico, ca ◇ *adj* lay, secular. ◇ *sm, f* layman *(f* laywoman*)*.

laísmo *sm the use of 'la' and 'las' instead of 'le' and 'les' as indirect objects.*

lama *sm* lama.

lambada *sf* lambada.

lamber *vt* Amér fam to lick.

lamé *sm* lamé.

La Meca *n pr* Mecca.

lamentable *adj* - **1.** [triste] terribly sad - **2.** [malo] lamentable, deplorable.

lamentación *sf* moaning *(U)*.

lamentar *vt* to regret, to be sorry about; **lo lamento** I'm very sorry; **lamentamos comunicarle...** we regret to inform you...

➤ **lamentarse** *vprnl*: **lamentarse (de o por)** to complain (about).

lamento *sm* moan, cry of pain.

lamer *vt* to lick.

➤ **lamerse** *vprnl* to lick o.s.

lametón *sm* (big) lick.

lamido, da *adj* skinny.

➤ **lamido** *sm* lick.

lámina *sf* - **1.** [plancha] sheet; [placa] plate - **2.** [rodaja] slice - **3.** [plancha grabada] engraving - **4.** [dibujo] plate.

laminado, da *adj* laminated, rolled.

➤ **laminado** *sm* - **1.** [acción] lamination, rolling - **2.** [material] laminate.

laminador, a *sm, f* rolling mill.

laminar *vt* to laminate, to roll.

lámpara *sf* - **1.** [aparato] lamp; **lámpara de mesa** table lamp; **lámpara de pie** standard lamp; **lámpara de soldar** blowtorch; **lámpara de techo** ceiling lamp - **2.** [bombilla] bulb - **3.** TECNOL valve.

lamparilla *sf* small lamp.

lamparón *sm* grease stain.

lampazo *sm* Amér cloth.

lampiño, ña *adj* [sin barba] beardless, smooth-cheeked; [sin vello] hairless.

lamprea *sf* lamprey.

lana *sf* - **1.** wool; **de lana** woollen; **pura lana virgen** pure new wool; **ir a por lana y volver trasquilado** *prov* to be hoist by one's own petard; **unos cardan la lana y otros llevan la fama** *prov* some do all the work and others get all the credit - **2.** Andes & Cuba fam [dinero] dough, cash.

lanar *adj* wool-bearing.

lance *sm* - **1.** [en juegos, deportes] incident; [acontecimiento] event - **2.** [riña] dispute; ➤ **lanzar**.

lancero *sm* lancer.

lanceta *sf* Andes & Cuba sting.

lancha *sf* - **1.** [embarcación - grande] launch; [- pequeña] boat; **lancha motora** motorboat, motor launch; **lancha neumática** rubber dinghy; **lancha patrullera** patrol boat; **lancha salvavidas** lifeboat - **2.** [piedra] slab.

landa *sf* moor.

landó *sm* landau.

lanero, ra *adj* wool *(antes de s)*.

langosta *sf* - **1.** [crustáceo] lobster - **2.** [insecto] locust.

langostino *sm* king prawn.

languidecer [30] *vi* to languish; [conversación, entusiasmo] to flag.

languidez *sf* [debilidad] listlessness; [falta de ánimo] disinterest.

lánguido, da *adj* [débil] listless; [falto de ánimo] disinterested.

lanilla *sf* - **1.** [pelillo] nap - **2.** [tejido] flannel.

lanolina *sf* lanolin.

lanudo, da *adj* woolly.

lanza *sf* - **1.** [arma - arrojadiza] spear; [- en justas, torneos] lance; **estar lanza en ristre** to be ready for action; **romper una lanza por alguien** to fight for sb - **2.** [de carruaje] shaft.

lanzacohetes *sm inv* rocket launcher.

lanzadera *sf* [de telar] shuttle.

➤ **lanzadera espacial** *sf* space shuttle.

➤ **lanzadera de misiles** *sf* missile launcher.

lanzado, da *adj* - **1.** [atrevido] forward; [valeroso] fearless - **2.** [rápido]: **ir lanzado** to hurtle along.

lanzagranadas *sm inv* grenade launcher.

lanzallamas *sm inv* flamethrower.

lanzamiento *sm* - **1.** [de objeto] throwing; [de cohete] launching - **2.** [DEP - con la mano] throw; [- con el pie] kick; [- en béisbol] pitch; **lanzamiento de disco** discus; **lanzamiento de jaba-**

lina javelin; **lanzamiento de martillo** hammer; **lanzamiento de peso** shot put - **3.** [de producto, artista] launch; [de disco] release.

lanzamisiles *sm inv* rocket launcher.

lanzaplatos *sm inv* DEP (clay pigeon) trap.

lanzar [13] *vt* - **1.** [gen] to throw; [con fuerza] to hurl, to fling; [de una patada] to kick; [bomba] to drop; [flecha, misil] to fire; [cohete] to launch - **2.** [proferir] to let out; [acusación, insulto] to hurl; [suspiro] to heave - **3.** [COM - producto, artista, periódico] to launch; [- disco] to release.

➤ **lanzarse** *vprnl* - **1.** [tirarse] to throw o.s. - **2.** [abalanzarse]: **lanzarse (sobre)** to throw o.s. (upon) - **3.** [empezar]: **lanzarse (a hacer algo)** to get started (doing sthg).

lanzatorpedos *sm inv* torpedo tube.

lapa *sf* - **1.** ZOOL limpet - **2.** *fam fig* [persona] hanger-on, pest; **pegarse como una lapa** to cling like a leech.

La Paz *n pr* La Paz.

lapicera *sf* C Sur ballpoint (pen), Biro®.

lapicero *sm* - **1.** pencil - **2.** Amér C & Perú [bolígrafo] ballpoint pen, Biro®.

lápida *sf* memorial stone; **lápida mortuoria** tombstone.

lapidación *sf* stoning.

lapidar *vt* to stone.

lapidario, ria *adj* solemn.

lapislázuli *sm* lapis lazuli.

lápiz (*pl* lápices) *sm* pencil; **escribir algo a lápiz** to write sthg in pencil; **lápiz de cejas** eyebrow pencil; **lápiz de labios** lipstick; **lápiz de ojos** eyeliner; **lápiz óptico** INFORM light pen.

lapo *sm fam* gob, spit.

lapón, ona *adj & sm, f* Lapp.
➤ **lapón** *sm* [lengua] Lapp.

lapso *sm* space, interval; **lapso de tiempo** space o interval of time.

lapsus *sm inv* lapse, slip.

laque *etc* ▷ **lacar**.

laquear *vt* to lacquer.

lar *sm* - **1.** [lumbre] hearth - **2.** MITOL household god.
➤ **lares** *smpl* [hogar] hearth and home.

lardero ▷ **jueves**.

larga ▷ **largo**.

largar [16] *vt* - **1.** [aflojar] to pay out - **2.** *fam* [dar, decir] to give; **le largué un bofetón** I gave him a smack.
➤ **largarse** *vprnl fam* to clear off.

largavistas *sm inv* Bol & C Sur binoculars *pl*.

largo, ga *adj* - **1.** [en espacio, tiempo] long; **estarle largo a alguien** to be too long for sb - **2.** [alto] tall - **3.** [sobrado]: **media hora larga** a

good half hour - **4.** *fam* [astuto] sly, crafty - **5.** *fam* [generoso]: **largo en hacer algo** generous in doing sthg.

➤ **largo** ◇ *sm* length; **a lo largo** lengthways; **tiene dos metros de largo** it's two metres long; **pasar de largo** to pass by; **vestirse de largo** to dress up, to dress formally; **a lo largo de** [en el espacio] along; [en el tiempo] throughout; **a lo largo y a lo ancho de** right across, throughout; **¡largo de aquí!** go away!, get out of here! ◇ *adv* at length; **largo y tendido** at great length.

➤ **larga** *sf*: **a la larga** in the long run; **dar largas a algo** to put sthg off.

largometraje *sm* feature film.

largue *etc* ▷ **largar**.

larguero *sm* - **1.** CONSTR main beam - **2.** DEP crossbar.

larguirucho, cha *adj fam* lanky.

largura *sf* length.

laringe *sf* larynx.

laringitis *sf inv* laryngitis.

laringología *sf* laryngology.

laringólogo, ga *sm, f* laryngologist.

larva *sf* larva.

larvado, da *adj* latent.

las ◇ *art* ▷ **el**. ◇ *pron* ▷ **lo**.

lasaña *sf* lasagne, lasagna.

lascivia *sf* lasciviousness, lechery.

lascivo, va ◇ *adj* lascivious, lewd. ◇ *sm, f* lascivious o lewd person.

láser ◇ *adj inv* ▷ **rayo**. ◇ *sm inv* laser.

laserterapia *sf* laser therapy.

lasitud *sf* lassitude.

laso, sa *adj* - **1.** [cansado] weary - **2.** [liso] straight.

Las Palmas (de Gran Canaria) *n pr* Las Palmas.

lástima *sf* - **1.** [compasión] pity - **2.** [pena] shame, pity; **dar lástima** to be a crying shame; **da lástima ver gente así** it's sad to see people in that state; **es una lástima que** it's a shame o pity that; **¡qué lástima!** what a shame o pity!; **tener** o **sentir lástima de** to feel sorry for; **quedarse hecho una lástima** to be a sorry o pitiful sight.

lastimar *vt* to hurt.
➤ **lastimarse** *vprnl* to hurt o.s.

lastimoso, sa *adj* pitiful, woeful.

lastrar *vt* to ballast.

lastre *sm* - **1.** [peso] ballast; **soltar lastre** to discharge ballast - **2.** *fig* [estorbo] burden.

lata *sf* - **1.** [envase] can, tin; [de bebidas] can; **en lata** tinned, canned - **2.** *fam* [fastidio] pain; **¡qué lata!** what a pain!; **dar la lata a alguien** to pester sb.

latente *adj* latent.

lateral ⟺ *adj* - **1.** [del lado - gen] lateral; [- puerta, pared] side - **2.** [indirecto] indirect. ⟺ *sm* - **1.** [lado] side - **2.** DEP: **lateral derecho/izquierdo** right/left back.

látex *sm inv* latex.

latido *sm* [del corazón] beat; [en dedo etc] throb, throbbing (U).

latiente *adj* [corazón] beating.

latifundio *sm* large rural estate.

Latifundio

A **latifundio** is a huge estate belonging to a single landowner, of the kind found in southern Spain and in many Latin American countries. Historically, they are associated with backward farming methods and poverty among the workers living on them. This is because most of the rich landowners lived away from their estates and were not over-concerned with productivity. The social problems caused by **latifundios** led to agitation for land reform in many countries. Despite land reform programmes, and more dramatic solutions such as the Mexican and Cuban revolutions, the legacy of the **latifundio** still prevails today in many countries.

latifundismo *sm the system of land tenure characterized by the 'latifundio'.*

latigazo *sm* - **1.** [golpe] lash - **2.** [chasquido] crack (of the whip) - **3.** *fam* [trago] swig.

látigo *sm* whip.

latín *sm* Latin; **latín clásico/vulgar** Classical/Vulgar Latin; **latín de cocina** *o* **macarrónico** dog Latin; **saber (mucho) latín** *fig* to be sharp, to be on the ball.

latinajo *sm fam despec Latin word used in an attempt to sound academic.*

latinismo *sm* Latinism.

latino, na *adj* & *sm, f* Latin.

latinoamericano, na *adj* & *sm, f* Latin American.

latir *vi* - **1.** [suj: corazón] to beat - **2.** [estar latente] to be concealed, to lie.

latitud *sf* GEOGR latitude.

➤ **latitudes** *sfpl* [parajes] region *sing*, area *sing*.

latón *sm* brass.

latoso, sa *fam* ⟺ *adj* tiresome. ⟺ *sm, f* pain (in the neck).

laúd *sm* lute.

laudable *adj* praiseworthy.

láudano *sm* laudanum.

laudatorio, ria *adj* laudatory.

laureado, da *adj* prize-winning.

laurear *vt*: **laurear a alguien (con)** to honour sb (with).

laurel *sm* BOT laurel; CULIN bay leaf.

➤ **laureles** *smpl* [honores] laurels; **dormirse en los laureles** *fig* to rest on one's laurels.

lava *sf* lava.

lavable *adj* washable.

lavabo *sm* - **1.** [objeto] washbasin - **2.** [habitación] lavatory UK, washroom US; **ir al lavabo** to go to the toilet.

lavacoches *smf inv* car washer.

lavadero *sm* [en casa] laundry room; [público] washing place.

lavado *sm* wash, washing (U); **lavado a mano** hand-wash; **lavado de cerebro** brainwashing; **lavado de dinero** money-laundering; **lavado de estómago** stomach pumping; **lavado en seco** dry cleaning.

lavadora *sf* washing machine; **lavadora secadora** washer-drier.

lavamanos *sm inv* washbasin.

lavanda *sf* lavender.

lavandería *sf* laundry; [automática] launderette.

lavandero, ra *sm* laundryman (*f* laundress).

lavaplatos ⟺ *smf inv* [persona] dishwasher, washer-up. ⟺ *sm inv* - **1.** [aparato] dishwasher - **2.** *Chile, Col, Méx & Ven* [fregadero] kitchen sink.

lavar *vt* - **1.** [limpiar] to wash; **lavar a mano** to wash by hand; **lavar en seco** to dry-clean; **lavar y marcar** shampoo and set - **2.** *fig* [honor] to clear; [ofensa] to make up for.

➤ **lavarse** *vprnl* [gen] to wash o.s.; [cara, manos, pelo] to wash; [dientes] to clean.

lavarropas *sm inv R Plata* washing machine.

lavaseco *sm Amér* dry cleaner's.

lavativa *sf* enema.

lavavajillas *sm inv* dishwasher.

laxante ⟺ *adj* laxative. ⟺ *sm* laxative.

laxar *vt* [vientre] to loosen.

laxitud *sf* [de músculo, cable] slackness; *fig* laxity.

laxo, xa *adj* [músculo, cable] slack; *fig* lax.

lazada *sf* bow.

lazarillo *sm* - **1.** [persona] blind person's guide - **2.** ➢ **perro**.

lazo *sm* - **1.** [atadura] bow; **hacer un lazo** to tie a bow - **2.** [trampa] snare; [de vaquero] lasso - **3.** (gen pl) *fig* [vínculo] tie, bond.

Lda. *abrev de* **licenciado.**

Ldo. *abrev de* **licenciado.**

le *pron pers* - **1.** (complemento indirecto) [hombre] (to) him; [mujer] (to) her; [cosa] to it; [usted] to you; **le expliqué el motivo** I explained the reason to him/her; **le tengo miedo** I'm afraid of him/her; **ya le dije lo que pasaría** [a usted] I told you what would happen - **2.** *(complemento directo)* him; [usted] you.

leal <> *adj*: leal (a) loyal (to). <> *smf*: leal (a) loyal supporter (of).

lealtad *sf*: lealtad (a) loyalty (to).

leasing ['lisin] *(pl* **leasings)** *sm system of leasing whereby the lessee has the option of purchasing the property after a certain time.*

lebrel *sm* whippet.

lección *sf* lesson; **aprenderse la lección** to learn one's lesson; **dar a alguien una lección** [como advertencia] to teach sb a lesson; [como ejemplo] to give sb a lesson; **servir de lección** to serve as a lesson.

lechal <> *adj* sucking. <> *sm* sucking lamb.

leche *sf* - **1.** [gen] milk; **leche condensada/en polvo** condensed/powdered milk; **leche de almendras** almond milk; **leche descremada** o **desnatada** skimmed *UK* o skim *US* milk; **leche esterilizada/homogeneizada** sterilized/homogenized milk; **leche merengada** *drink made from milk, egg whites, sugar and cinnamon*; **leche pasterizada** o **pasteurizada** pasteurized milk; **leche semidesnatada** semiskimmed milk - **2.** [de plantas] (milky) sap - **3.** *mfam* [bofetada]: **pegar una leche a alguien** to belt o clobber sb - **4.** *mfam* [accidente] smash-up - **5.** *mfam* [mal humor] bloody awful mood; **estar de mala leche** to be in a bloody awful mood; **tener mala leche** to be a miserable git - **6.** *mfam* [suerte]: **tener mala leche** to have bloody awful luck - **7.** *vulg* [semen] spunk - **8.** *mfam loc*: **ser la leche** [ser raro] to be a nutcase; [ser molesto] to be a pain (in the neck); **¡una leche!** no way!

lechera ⊳ **lechero**.

lechería *sf* dairy.

lechero, ra <> *adj* milk *(antes de s)*, dairy. <> *sm, f* [persona] milkman (*f* milkwoman).
➤ **lechera** *sf* [para transportar] milk churn; [para beber] milk jug.

lecho *sm* - **1.** [gen] bed; **lecho de muerte** deathbed; **ser un lecho de rosas** to be a bed of roses - **2.** [capa] layer.

lechón *sm* sucking pig.

lechoso, sa *adj* milky.

lechuga *sf* lettuce; **lechuga iceberg/romana** iceberg/cos lettuce; **ser más fresco que una lechuga** to be a cheeky devil.

lechuza *sf* (barn) owl.

lectivo, va *adj* school *(antes de s)*.

lector, ra *sm, f* - **1.** [gen] reader - **2.** EDUC language assistant.
➤ **lector** *sm* [de microfilms etc] reader, scanner; **lector óptico** optical scanner.

lectorado *sm* post of language assistant.

lectura *sf* - **1.** [gen] reading; **dar lectura a algo** to read sthg out loud - **2.** [de tesis] viva voce - **3.** [escrito] reading (matter) *(U)* - **4.** [de datos] scanning; **lectura óptica** optical scanning.

leer [50] <> *vt* [gen & INFORM] to read. <> *vi* to read; **leer de corrido** to read fluently; **leer en voz alta/baja** to read aloud/quietly.

legación *sf* legation.

legado *sm* - **1.** [herencia] legacy - **2.** [representante - cargo] legation; [- persona] legate.

legajo *sm* file.

legal *adj* - **1.** [gen] legal; [hora] standard - **2.** [forense] forensic - **3.** *fam* [persona] honest, decent.

legalidad *sf* legality.

legalismo *sm* fine legal point, legalism.

legalista <> *adj* legalistic. <> *smf* legalist.

legalización *sf* - **1.** [gen] legalization - **2.** [certificado] (certificate of) authentication.

legalizar [13] *vt* - **1.** [gen] to legalize - **2.** [certificar] to authenticate.

legañoso, sa *adj* full of sleep.

legar [16] *vt* - **1.** [gen] to bequeath - **2.** [delegar] to delegate.

legendario, ria *adj* legendary.

legible *adj* legible.

legión *sf lit & fig* legion.
➤ **Legión de Honor** *sf* Legion of Honour.

legionario, ria *adj* legionary.
➤ **legionario** *sm* HIST legionary; MIL legionnaire.

legislación *sf* - **1.** [leyes] legislation - **2.** [ciencia] law.

legislador, ra <> *adj* legislative. <> *sm, f* legislator.

legislar *vi* to legislate.

legislativo, va *adj* legislative.

legislatura *sf* - **1.** [periodo] period of office - **2.** [órganos] parliament, legislature.

legitimación *sf* - **1.** [legalización] legitimation - **2.** [certificación] authentication.

legitimar *vt* - **1.** [legalizar] to legitimize - **2.** [certificar] to authenticate.

legitimidad *sf* legitimacy.

legítimo, ma *adj* [gen] legitimate; [auténtico] real, genuine; [oro] pure.

lego, ga <> *adj* - **1.** [gen] lay - **2.** [ignorante] ignorant; **ser lego en** to know nothing about. <> *sm, f* - **1.** [gen] layman (*f* laywoman) - **2.** [ignorante] ignorant person.

legua *sf* league; **legua marina** marine league; **verse a la legua** to stand out a mile.

legue *etc* ⊳ **legar**.

legumbre *(gen pl) sf* pulse, pod vegetable; **le- gumbres secas** dried pulses; **legumbres ver- des** green vegetables.

leguminosas *sfpl* pulses, leguminous veget- ables.

lehendakari = lendakari.

leído, da *adj* - **1.** [obra]: **muy/poco leído** much/little read - **2.** [persona] well-read.
➤ **leída** *sf* reading.

leísmo *sm* GRAM *use of 'le' as direct object in- stead of 'lo'*.

lejanía *sf* distance.

lejano, na *adj* distant; **no está lejano** it's not far (away).

lejía *sf* bleach.

lejos *adv* - **1.** [en el espacio] far (away); **¿está lejos?** is it far?; **a lo lejos** in the distance; **de** *o* **desde lejos** from a distance - **2.** [en el pasa- do] long ago; [en el futuro] far in the future; **eso queda ya lejos** that happened a long time ago - **3.** *loc*: **ir demasiado lejos** to go too far; **llegar lejos** to go far; **sin ir más lejos** indeed.
➤ **lejos de** ◇ *loc conj* far from; **lejos de me- jorar...** far from getting better... ◇ *loc prep* far (away) from.

lelo, la ◇ *adj* stupid, slow; **quedarse lelo** to be stunned. ◇ *sm, f* idiot.

lema *sm* - **1.** [norma] motto; [político, publicitario] slogan - **2.** LING & MAT lemma.

lempira *sm* lempira.

lencería *sf* - **1.** [ropa] linen; **lencería fina** lingerie - **2.** [tienda] draper's.

lendakari, lehendakari [lenda'kari] *sm pres- ident of the autonomous Basque govern- ment.*

lengua *sf* - **1.** [gen] tongue; **sacarle la lengua a alguien** to stick one's tongue out at sb; **con la lengua fuera** out of breath; **lengua de gato** CULIN ≃ chocolate finger (biscuit); **lengua de fuego/tierra** tongue of flame/land; **lengua de víbora** *o* **viperina** malicious tongue; **darle a la lengua** *fam* to chatter; **irse de la lengua** to let the cat out of the bag; **las malas lenguas dicen que...** according to the gossip...; **morderse la lengua** to bite one's tongue; **se le trabó la len- gua** she stumbled over her words; **ser largo de lengua** to be a gossip; **¿te ha comido la lengua el gato?** has the cat got your tongue?, have you lost your tongue?; **tirar a alguien de la lengua** to draw sb out - **2.** [idioma, lenguaje] language; **lengua materna** mother tongue; **lengua muerta** dead language; **lengua oficial** official language.

lenguado *sm* sole.

lenguaje *sm* [gen & INFORM] language; **lengua- je coloquial/comercial** colloquial/business language; **lenguaje cifrado** code; **lenguaje**

corporal body language; **lenguaje gestual** gestures *pl*; **lenguaje máquina** machine lan- guage; **lenguaje de alto nivel/de bajo nivel** high-level/low-level language; **lenguaje de programación** programming language; **len- guaje de los sordomudos** sign language.

lengüeta *sf* [gen & MÚS] tongue.

lengüetazo *sm* lick.

lengüetada *sf* = lengüetazo.

leninismo *sm* Leninism.

leninista *adj* & *smf* Leninist.

lente *sf* lens; **lente de aumento** magnifying glass; **lentes de contacto** contact lenses.
➤ **lentes** *smpl* [gafas] glasses.

lenteja *sf* lentil; **ganarse las lentejas** to earn one's daily bread.

lentejuela *sf* sequin.

lentilla *(gen pl) sf* contact lens.

lentitud *sf* slowness; **con lentitud** slowly.

lento, ta *adj* slow; [veneno] slow-working; [ago- nía, enfermedad] lingering, long drawn out.

leña *sf* - **1.** [madera] firewood; **echar leña al fuego** to add fuel to the flames *o* fire; **llevar leña al monte** to carry coals to Newcastle - **2.** *fam* [golpes] beating; **dar leña a alguien** to beat sb up.

leñador, ra *sm, f* woodcutter.

leñazo *sm* - **1.** *fam* [garrotazo] blow with a stick; [golpe] bang, bash - **2.** [choque] smash-up, crash.

leñe *interj fam*: **¡leñe!** for heaven's sake!

leñera *sf* woodshed.

leño *sm* - **1.** [de madera] log; **dormir como un leño** to sleep like a log - **2.** *fam fig* [persona] blockhead.

leñoso, sa *adj* woody.

Leo ◇ *sm* [zodiaco] Leo; **ser Leo** to be (a) Leo. ◇ *smf* [persona] Leo.

león, ona *sm, f* lion (*f* lioness); *fig* fierce per- son; **no es tan fiero el león como lo pintan** *prov* he/it *etc* is not as bad as he/it *etc* is made out to be.
➤ **león marino** *sm* sea lion.

leonera *sf* - **1.** [jaula] lion's cage - **2.** *fam fig* [cuarto sucio] pigsty.

leonino, na *adj* - **1.** [rostro, aspecto] leonine - **2.** [contrato, condiciones] one-sided, unfair.

leopardo *sm* leopard.

leotardo *sm* - **1.** *(gen pl)* [medias] stockings *pl*, thick tights *pl* - **2.** [de gimnasta etc] leotard.

lépero, ra *adj Amér C & Méx fam* [vulgar] coarse, vulgar; *Cuba fam* [astuto] smart, crafty.

leprosería *sf* leper colony.

leproso, sa ◇ *adj* leprous. ◇ *sm, f* leper.

lerdo, da ◇ *adj* [idiota] dim, slow-witted; [torpe] useless, hopeless. ◇ *sm, f* [idiota] fool, idiot; [torpe] useless idiot.

les *pron pers pl* - **1.** *(complemento indirecto)* (to) them; [ustedes] (to) you; **les expliqué el motivo** I explained the reason to them; **les tengo miedo** I'm afraid of them; **ya les dije lo que pasaría** [a ustedes] I told you what would happen - **2.** *(complemento directo)* them; [ustedes] you.

lesbianismo *sm* lesbianism.

lesbiano, na *adj* lesbian.
➤ **lesbiana** *sf* lesbian.

leseras *sfpl Chile fam* nonsense, rubbish *UK*.

lesión *sf* - **1.** [herida] injury; **lesión cerebral** brain damage - **2.** *fig* [perjuicio] damage, harm - **3.** DER: **lesión grave** grievous bodily harm.

lesionado, da ◇ *adj* injured. ◇ *sm, f* injured person.

lesionar *vt* to injure; *fig* to damage, to harm.
➤ **lesionarse** *vprnl* to injure o.s.

letal *adj* lethal.

letanía *(gen pl) sf lit & fig* litany.

letárgico, ca *adj* - **1.** MED lethargic - **2.** ZOOL hibernating.

letargo *sm* - **1.** MED lethargy - **2.** ZOOL hibernation.

Letonia *n pr* Latvia.

letonio, nia, letón, ona *adj & sm, f* Latvian.
➤ **letonio, letón** *sm* [lengua] Latvian.

letra *sf* - **1.** [signo] letter - **2.** [caligrafía] handwriting - **3.** [estilo] script; IMPR type, typeface; **letra bastardilla** o **cursiva** o **itálica** italic type, italics *pl*; **letra de imprenta** o **molde** IMPR print; [en formularios etc] block capitals *pl*; **letra mayúscula/minúscula** capital/small letter; **letra negrita** o **negrilla** bold (face); **letra versalita** small capital; **la letra con sangre entra** *prov* spare the rod and spoil the child; **leer la letra pequeña** to read the small print; **mandar cuatro letras a alguien** to drop sb a line - **4.** [de canción] lyrics *pl* - **5.** COM: **letra (de cambio)** bill of exchange; **girar una letra** to draw a bill of exchange; **protestar una letra** to protest a bill; **letra avalada** guaranteed bill of exchange; **letra de cambio a la vista** sight bill - **6.** [sentido] literal meaning.
➤ **letras** *sfpl* EDUC arts; **ser de letras** to study an arts subject.

letrado, da ◇ *adj* learned. ◇ *sm, f* lawyer.

letrero *sm* sign; **letrero luminoso** neon sign.

letrina *sf* latrine.

letrista *smf* lyricist.

leucemia *sf* leukaemia.

leucémico, ca ◇ *adj* leukaemia *(antes de s)*. ◇ *sm, f* person suffering from leukaemia.

leucocito *(gen pl) sm* leucocyte.

leva *sf* - **1.** MIL levy - **2.** NÁUT weighing anchor - **3.** MECÁN cam.

levadizo ➞ **puente**.

levadura *sf* yeast, leaven; **levadura de cerveza** brewer's yeast; **levadura en polvo** baking powder.

levantador, ra ◇ *adj* lifting. ◇ *sm, f*: **levantador de pesas** DEP weightlifter.

levantamiento *sm* - **1.** [sublevación] uprising - **2.** [elevación] raising; **levantamiento de pesas** DEP weightlifting - **3.** [supresión] lifting, removal.

levantar *vt* - **1.** [gen] to raise; [peso, capó, trampilla] to lift; **levantar el ánimo** to cheer up; **levantar la vista** o **mirada** to look up - **2.** [separar - pintura, venda, tapa] to remove - **3.** [recoger - campamento] to strike; [- tienda de campaña, puesto] to take down; [- mesa] to clear - **4.** [encender - protestas, polémica] to stir up; **levantar a alguien contra** to stir sb up against - **5.** [suspender - embargo, prohibición] to lift; [- pena, castigo] to suspend; [- sesión] to adjourn - **6.** [redactar - acta, atestado] to draw up.
➤ **levantarse** *vprnl* - **1.** [ponerse de pie] to stand up - **2.** [de la cama] to get up; **levantar tarde** to sleep in - **3.** [elevarse - avión etc] to lift off, to take off; [- niebla] to lift - **4.** [sublevarse] to rise up - **5.** [empezar - viento, oleaje] to get up, to rise; [- tormenta] to gather.

levante *sm* - **1.** [este] east; [región] east coast - **2.** [viento] east wind.
➤ **Levante** *sm* GEOGR *the east coast of Spain between Castellón and Cartagena*.

levar *vt* to weigh.

leve *adj* - **1.** [gen] light; [olor, sabor, temblor] slight - **2.** [pecado, falta, herida] minor - **3.** [enfermedad] mild, slight.

levedad *sf* lightness; [de temblor etc] slightness; [de pecado, falto, herida] minor nature; [de enfermedad] mildness.

levita *sf* frock coat.

levitación *sf* levitation.

levitar *vi* to levitate.

lexema *sm* lexeme.

léxico, ca *adj* lexical.
➤ **léxico** *sm* - **1.** [vocabulario] vocabulary - **2.** [diccionario] lexicon, dictionary.

lexicografía *sf* lexicography.

lexicógrafo, fa *sm, f* lexicographer.

lexicón *sm* lexicon.

ley *sf* - **1.** [gen] law; [parlamentaria] act; **aprobar una ley** to pass a law; **ley de extranjería** Aliens Act; **ley de incompatibilidades** *act regulating which other positions may be held by people holding public office*; **ley marcial** martial law; **ley sálica** Salic law; **ley seca** prohibition law; **hecha la ley, hecha la trampa** laws are made to be broken; **con todas las de la ley** in due form, properly **- 2.** [regla] rule; **ley del embudo** one law for o.s. and another for everyone else; **ley de la ventaja** DEP advantage (law); **ley de la oferta y de la demanda** law of supply and demand; **de buena ley** reliable, sterling **- 3.** [de un metal]: **de ley** [oro] pure; [plata] sterling.

➽ **leyes** *sfpl* [derecho] law *sing*.

leyenda *sf* **- 1.** [narración] legend **- 2.** [inscripción] inscription, legend.

leyera *etc* ▷ **leer.**

liar [9] *vt* **- 1.** [atar] to tie up **- 2.** [envolver - cigarrillo] to roll; **liar algo en** [- papel] to wrap sthg up in; [- toalla etc] to roll sthg up in **- 3.** [involucrar]: **liar a alguien (en)** to get sb mixed up (in) **- 4.** [complicar - asunto etc] to confuse; **¡ya me has liado!** now you've really got me confused!

➽ **liarse** *vprnl* **- 1.** [enredarse] to get muddled up **- 2.** [empezar] to begin, to start; **liarse a hacer algo** to start *o* begin doing sthg **- 3.** *fam* [sexualmente]: **liarse (con)** to get involved (with), to have an affair (with).

libación *sf* libation.

libanés, esa *adj* & *sm, f* Lebanese.

Líbano *sm*: **el Líbano** the Lebanon.

libar *vt* to sip, to suck.

libelo *sm* lampoon.

libélula *sf* dragonfly.

liberación *sf* **- 1.** [gen] liberation; [de preso] release; **liberación de la mujer** women's liberation; **liberación sexual** sexual liberation **- 2.** [de una hipoteca] redemption.

liberado, da *adj* [gen] liberated; [preso] freed.

liberal *adj* & *smf* liberal.

liberalidad *sf* liberality.

liberalismo *sm* liberalism.

liberalización *sf* liberalization; COM deregulation.

liberalizar [13] *vt* to liberalize; COM to deregulate.

liberar *vt* [gen] to liberate; [preso] to free; **liberar de algo a alguien** to free sb from sthg.

➽ **liberarse** *vprnl* to liberate o.s.; **liberarse de algo** to free *o* liberate o.s. from sthg.

Liberia *n pr* Liberia.

libertad *sf* freedom, liberty; **dejar** *o* **poner a alguien en libertad** to set sb free, to release sb; **estar en libertad** to be free; **tener libertad para hacer algo** to be free to do sthg; **tomarse la libertad de hacer algo** to take the liberty of doing sthg; **tomarse libertades** to take liberties; **libertad de circulación de capitales/trabajadores** ECON free movement of capital/

workers; **libertad de conciencia** freedom of conscience; **libertad condicional** probation; **libertad de expresión** freedom of speech; **libertad de imprenta** *o* **prensa** freedom of the press; **libertad provisional (bajo fianza)** bail; **libertad provisional (bajo palabra)** parole.

libertador, ra ⬦ *adj* liberating. ⬦ *sm, f* liberator.

libertar *vt* [gen] to liberate; [preso] to deliver, to set free.

libertario, ria *adj* & *sm, f* libertarian.

libertinaje *sm* licentiousness.

libertino, na ⬦ *adj* licentious. ⬦ *sm, f* libertine.

Libia *n pr* Libya.

libidinoso, sa *adj* libidinous, lewd.

libido *sf* libido.

libio, bia *adj* & *sm, f* Libyan.

libra *sf* [peso, moneda] pound; **libra esterlina** pound sterling.

➽ **Libra** ⬦ *sm* [zodiaco] Libra; **ser Libra** to be (a) Libra. ⬦ *smf* [persona] Libran.

librado, da ⬦ *sm, f* COM drawee. ⬦ *adj*: **salir bien librado** to get off lightly; **salir mal librado** to come off badly.

librador, ra *sm, f* drawer.

libramiento *sm* order of payment.

libranza *sf* = **libramiento.**

librar ⬦ *vt* **- 1.** [eximir]: **librar a alguien (de algo/de hacer algo)** [gen] to free sb (from sthg/from doing sthg); [pagos, impuestos] to exempt sb (from sthg/from doing sthg) **- 2.** [entablar - pelea, lucha] to engage in; [- batalla, combate] to join, to wage **- 3.** COM to draw. ⬦ *vi* [no trabajar] to be off work.

➽ **librarse** *vprnl* **- 1.** [salvarse]: **librarse (de hacer algo)** to escape (from doing sthg); **de buena te libraste** you had a narrow escape **- 2.** [deshacerse]: **librarse de algo/alguien** to get rid of sthg/sb.

libre *adj* **- 1.** [gen] free; [rato, tiempo] spare; [camino, vía] clear; [espacio, piso, lavabo] empty, vacant; **200 metros libres** 200 metres freestyle; **libre de** [gen] free from; [exento] exempt from; **libre de franqueo** post-free; **libre de impuestos** tax-free; **ser libre** *o* **para hacer algo** to be free to do sthg; **ir por libre** to go it alone **- 2.** [alumno] external; **estudiar por libre** to be an external student.

librea *sf* livery.

librecambio *sm* free trade.

librecambismo *sm* (doctrine of) free trade.

librepensador, ra ⬦ *adj* freethinking. ⬦ *sm, f* freethinker.

librería *sf* - **1.** [tienda] bookshop; **librería de ocasión** second-hand bookshop - **2.** [oficio] bookselling - **3.** [mueble] bookcase.

librero, ra ◇ *adj* book *(antes de s)*. ◇ *sm, f* [persona] bookseller. ◇ *sm Amér C, Col & Méx* [mueble] bookcase.

libreta *sf* - **1.** [para escribir] notebook; **libreta de direcciones** address book - **2.** [del banco]: **libreta (de ahorros)** savings book.

libretista *smf Amér* [guionista] screenwriter, scriptwriter.

libreto *sm* - **1.** MÚS libretto - **2.** *Amér* [guión] script.

libro *sm* [gen & COM] book; **llevar los libros** to keep the books; **libro blanco** POLÍT white paper; **libro de bolsillo** paperback; **libro de cabecera/cocina** bedside/cookery book; **libro de caja** cashbook; **libro de comercio** ledger; **libro de consulta/cuentos** reference/story book; **libro de cuentas** o **contabilidad** accounts book; **libro de ejercicios** workbook; **libro de escolaridad** school report; **libro de familia** *document containing personal details of the members of a family*; **libro de reclamaciones** complaints book; **libro de registro (de entradas)** register; **libro sagrado** Book *(in Bible)*; **libro de texto** textbook; **libro de visitas** visitor's book; **colgar los libros** to give up one's studies; **hablar como un libro** to express o.s. very clearly; **ser como un libro abierto** to be an open book.

Lic. *abrev de* **licenciado**.

licántropo, pa ◇ *adj* werewolf *(antes de s)*. ◇ *sm, f* werewolf.

licencia *sf* - **1.** [documento] licence, permit; [autorización] permission; **licencia de armas/caza** gun/hunting licence; **licencia de exportación/importación** export/import licence; **licencia de obras** planning permission; **licencia fiscal** *official authorization to practise a profession*; **licencia poética** poetic licence - **2.** MIL discharge - **3.** [confianza] licence, freedom; **tomarse licencias con alguien** to take liberties with sb.

licenciado, da ◇ *adj* - **1.** EDUC graduate *(antes de s)*; **estar licenciado en derecho** to be a law graduate - **2.** MIL discharged. ◇ *sm, f* - **1.** EDUC graduate; **licenciado en económicas** economics graduate - **2.** MIL discharged soldier.

licenciamiento *sm* MIL discharge.

licenciar [8] *vt* MIL to discharge.

➡ **licenciarse** *vprnl* - **1.** EDUC: **licenciarse (en)** to graduate (in) - **2.** MIL to be discharged.

licenciatura *sf* degree.

licencioso, sa *adj* licentious.

liceo *sm* - **1.** EDUC lycée - **2.** *C Sur & Ven* [instituto] secondary school *UK*, high school *US* - **3.** [de recreo] ≃ social club.

licitación *sf* bid, bidding *(U)*.

licitar *vt* to bid for.

lícito, ta *adj* - **1.** [legal] lawful - **2.** [correcto] right - **3.** [justo] fair.

licor *sm* liquor.

licorera *sf* decanter.

licorería *sf* - **1.** [fábrica] distillery - **2.** [tienda] ≃ off-licence.

licuado *sm Amér* [batido] milk shake.

licuadora *sf* liquidizer, blender.

licuar [6] *vt* - **1.** CULIN to liquidize - **2.** TECNOL to liquefy.

lid *sf* fight; **experto en estas lides** *fig* old hand in these matters.

líder ◇ *adj* leading. ◇ *smf* leader.

liderar *vt* to lead.

liderato, liderazgo *sm* - **1.** [primer puesto] lead; [en liga] first place - **2.** [dirección] leadership.

lidia *sf* - **1.** [arte] bullfighting - **2.** [corrida] bullfight.

lidiar [8] ◇ *vi* [luchar]: **lidiar (con)** to struggle (with). ◇ *vt* TAUROM to fight.

liebre *sf* - **1.** ZOOL hare; **correr como una liebre** to run like a hare; **levantar la liebre** to let the cat out of the bag - **2.** *Chile* [microbús] minibus.

liendre *sf* nit.

lienzo *sm* - **1.** [tela] (coarse) cloth; [paño] piece of cloth - **2.** [para pintar] canvas - **3.** [cuadro] painting.

lifting ['liftin] *(pl* **liftings**) *sm* facelift.

liga *sf* - **1.** [gen] league - **2.** [de medias] suspender.

ligadura *sf* - **1.** MED & MÚS ligature; **ligadura de trompas** MED tubal ligation - **2.** [atadura] bond, tie.

ligamento *sm* ANAT ligament.

ligar [16] ◇ *vt* - **1.** [gen & CULIN] to bind; [atar] to tie (up) - **2.** MED to put a ligature on - **3.** MÚS to slur. ◇ *vi* - **1.** [coincidir]: **ligar (con)** to tally (with) - **2.** *fam* [conquistar]: **ligar (con)** to get off (with).

ligazón *sf* link, connection.

ligereza *sf* - **1.** [levedad] lightness - **2.** [agilidad] agility - **3.** [rapidez] speed - **4.** [irreflexión - cualidad] rashness; [- acto] rash act; **con ligereza** in a superficial manner.

ligero, ra *adj* - **1.** [gen] light; [dolor, rumor, descenso] slight; [traje, tela] thin - **2.** [ágil] agile, nimble - **3.** [rápido] quick, swift - **4.** [irreflexivo] flippant; **hacer algo a la ligera** to do sthg without much thought; **juzgar a alguien a la ligera** to be quick to judge sb; **tomarse algo a la ligera** not to take sthg seriously.

light [lait] *adj inv* [comida] low-calorie; [refresco] diet *(antes de s)*; [cigarrillos] light.

ligón, ona *fam* ⬦ *adj*: **es muy ligón** he's always getting off with sb or other. ⬦ *sm, f* goer, raver.

ligue *sm* *mfam* - **1.** [acción]: **ir de ligue** to go cruising - **2.** [persona] pick-up; ▷ **ligar**.

liguero, ra *adj* DEP league *(antes de s)*.
➤ **liguero** *sm* suspender belt UK, garter belt US.

liguilla *sf* DEP mini-league, round-robin tournament.

lija *sf* - **1.** [papel] sandpaper - **2.** [pez] dog-fish.

lijadora *sf* sander.

lijar *vt* to sand down.

lila ⬦ *sf* [flor] lilac. ⬦ *adj inv* & *sm* [color] lilac.

liliputiense *fam* ⬦ *adj* dwarfish. ⬦ *smf* midget.

lima *sf* - **1.** [utensilio] file; **lima de uñas** nail file; **comer como una lima** to eat like a horse - **2.** BOT lime.

Lima *n pr* Lima.

limadora *sf* polisher.

limar *vt* - **1.** [pulir] to file down - **2.** [perfeccionar] to polish, to add the finishing touches to.

limbo *sm* - **1.** RELIG limbo; **estar en el limbo** *fig* to be miles away - **2.** ASTRON & BOT limb.

limeño, ña ⬦ *adj* of/relating to Lima. ⬦ *sm, f* native/inhabitant of Lima.

limitación *sf* - **1.** [restricción] limitation, limit; **limitación de velocidad** speed limit - **2.** [distrito] boundaries *pl*.

limitado, da *adj* - **1.** [gen] limited - **2.** [poco inteligente] dim-witted.

limitar ⬦ *vt* - **1.** [gen] to limit - **2.** [terreno] to mark out - **3.** [atribuciones, derechos etc] to set out, to define. ⬦ *vi*: **limitar (con)** to border (on).
➤ **limitarse a** *vprnl* to limit o.s. to.

límite ⬦ *adj inv* - **1.** [precio, velocidad, edad] maximum - **2.** [situación] extreme; [caso] borderline. ⬦ *sm* - **1.** [tope] limit; **dentro de un límite** within limits; **su pasión no tiene límite** her passion knows no bounds; **límite de velocidad** speed limit - **2.** [confín] boundary.

limítrofe *adj* [país, territorio] bordering; [terreno, finca] neighbouring.

limón *sm* lemon.

limonada *sf* lemonade.

limonar *sm* lemon grove.

limonero, ra *adj* lemon *(antes de s)*.

➤ **limonero** *sm* lemon tree.

limosna *sf* alms *pl*; **pedir limosna** to beg.

limpia *sf* Amér cleaning.

limpiabotas *smf inv* shoeshine, bootblack UK.

limpiacristales *sm inv* window-cleaning fluid.

limpiador, ra ⬦ *adj* cleaning. ⬦ *sm, f* cleaner.

limpiamente *adv* - **1.** [con destreza] cleanly - **2.** [honradamente] honestly.

limpiaparabrisas *sm inv* windscreen wiper UK, windshield wiper US.

limpiar [8] *vt* - **1.** [gen] to clean; [con trapo] to wipe; [mancha] to wipe away; [zapatos] to polish - **2.** *fig* [desembarazar]: **limpiar algo de algo** to clear sthg of sthg - **3.** *fam* [en el juego] to clean out - **4.** *fam* [robar] to snipe, to pinch.

limpieza *sf* - **1.** [cualidad] cleanliness - **2.** [acción] cleaning; **hacer la limpieza** to do the cleaning; **limpieza de cutis** facial; **limpieza étnica** ethnic cleansing; **limpieza general** spring-cleaning; **limpieza en seco** dry cleaning - **3.** [destreza] skill, cleanness - **4.** [honradez] honesty.

limpio, pia *adj* - **1.** [gen] clean; [pulcro] neat; [cielo, imagen] clear - **2.** [neto - sueldo etc] net - **3.** [honrado] honest; [intenciones] honourable; [juego] clean - **4.** [sin culpa]: **estar limpio** to be in the clear; **limpio de** [sospecha etc] free of - **5.** *fam* [sin dinero] broke, skint - **6.** *fam* [para enfatizar]: **a puñetazo limpio** with bare fists; **a pedrada limpia** with nothing more than stones.

➤ **limpio** *adv* cleanly, fair; **pasar a** *o* **poner en limpio** to make a fair copy of, to write out neatly; **sacar algo en limpio de** to make sthg out from.

limusina *sf* limousine.

linaje *sm* lineage.

linaza *sf* linseed.

lince *sm* lynx; **ser un lince para algo** to be very sharp at sthg.

linchamiento *sm* lynching.

linchar *vt* to lynch.

lindante *adj*: **lindante (con)** [espacios] bordering; [conceptos] bordering (on).

lindar ➤ **lindar con** *vi* - **1.** [terreno] to adjoin, to be next to - **2.** [conceptos, ideas] to border on.

linde *sm o sf* boundary.

lindero, ra *adj* - **1.** [terreno] adjoining, bordering - **2.** [concepto] bordering.
➤ **lindero** *sm* boundary.

lindeza *sf* [belleza] prettiness.
➤ **lindezas** *sfpl* irón [insultos] insults.

lindo, **da** *adj* pretty, lovely; **de lo lindo** a great deal.

línea *sf* - **1.** [gen, DEP & TELECOM] line; **cortar la línea (telefónica)** to cut off the phone; **línea aérea** airline; **línea de banda** sideline, touchline; **línea blanca** white goods *pl*; **línea de conducta** course of action; **línea continua** AUTO solid white line; **línea de crédito/de descubierto** BANCA credit/overdraft limit; **línea divisoria** dividing line; **línea de flotación** waterline; **línea de fuego** MIL firing line; **línea de meta** [en fútbol] goal line; [en carrera] finishing line; **línea de mira** *o* **tiro** line of fire; **línea de puntos** dotted line; **línea recta** straight line; **línea de saque** base line, service line - **2.** [de un coche etc] lines *pl*, shape - **3.** [silueta] figure; **guardar la línea** to watch one's figure - **4.** [estilo] style; **de línea clásica** classical - **5.** [categoría] class, category; **de primera línea** first-rate - **6.** INFORM: **en línea** on-line; **fuera de línea** off-line - **7.** *loc*: **en líneas generales** in broad terms; **en toda la línea** [completamente] all along the line; **leer entre líneas** to read between the lines.

lineal *adj* - **1.** [gen] linear; [dibujo] line - **2.** [aumento] across-the-board.

lineamientos *smpl* *Amér* [generalidades] outline; [directrices] guidelines.

linfa *sf* lymph.

linfático, **ca** *adj* lymphatic.

lingotazo *sm* *fam* swig.

lingote *sm* ingot.

lingüista *smf* linguist.

lingüístico, **ca** *adj* linguistic.
➤ **lingüística** *sf* linguistics.

linier [li'njer] (*pl* **liniers**) *sm* linesman.

linimento *sm* liniment.

lino *sm* - **1.** [planta] flax - **2.** [tejido] linen.

linóleo, **linóleum** (*pl* **linóleum**) *sm* linoleum (U).

linotipia *sf* Linotype®.

linotipista *smf* linotypist.

linterna *sf* - **1.** [farol] lantern, lamp - **2.** [de pilas] torch *UK*, flashlight *US*.
➤ **linterna mágica** *sf* magic lantern.

lío *sm* - **1.** [paquete] bundle - **2.** *fam* [enredo] mess; **hacerse un lío** to get muddled up; **meterse en líos** to get into trouble - **3.** *fam* [jaleo] racket, row; **armar un lío** to kick up a fuss - **4.** *fam* [amorío] affair.

liofilizar [13] *vt* to freeze-dry.

lioso, **sa** *adj* *fam* - **1.** [enredado - asunto] messy; [- explicación] muddled - **2.** [persona] troublemaking.

lípido *sm* lipid.

liposoma *sm* liposome.

liposucción *sf* liposuction.

lipotimia *sf* fainting fit.

liquen *sm* lichen.

liquidación *sf* - **1.** [pago] settlement, payment; **liquidación de bienes** COM liquidation of assets - **2.** [rebaja] clearance sale - **3.** [fin] liquidation.

liquidar *vt* - **1.** [pagar - deuda] to pay; [- cuenta] to settle - **2.** [rebajar] to sell off - **3.** [malgastar] to throw away - **4.** [acabar - asunto] to settle; [- negocio, sociedad] to wind up - **5.** *fam* [matar] to liquidate.

liquidez *sf* ECON & FÍS liquidity.

líquido, **da** *adj* - **1.** [gen] liquid - **2.** ECON [neto] net.
➤ **líquido** *sm* - **1.** [gen] liquid; **líquido de frenos** brake fluid - **2.** ECON liquid assets *pl* - **3.** MED fluid.

lira *sf* - **1.** MÚS lyre - **2.** [moneda] lira.

lírico, **ca** *adj* - **1.** LITER lyric, lyrical - **2.** [musical] musical.
➤ **lírica** *sf* lyric poetry.

lirio *sm* iris; **lirio del valle** lily of the valley.

lirismo *sm* lyricism.

lirón *sm* ZOOL dormouse; **dormir como un lirón** to sleep like a log.

lisboeta *adj* of/relating to Lisbon.

lisiado, **da** ◇ *adj* crippled. ◇ *sm, f* cripple.

lisiar [8] *vt* to maim, to cripple.
➤ **lisiarse** *vprnl* to be maimed *o* crippled.

liso, **sa** ◇ *adj* - **1.** [llano] flat; [sin asperezas] smooth; [pelo] straight; **los 400 metros lisos** the 400 metres; **lisa y llanamente** quite simply; **hablando lisa y llanamente** to put it plainly - **2.** [no estampado] plain. ◇ *sm, f* *Andes, Amér C & Ven* [insolente] cheeky person.

lisonja *sf* flattering remark.

lisonjear *vt* to flatter.

lisonjero, **ra** *adj* flattering; [perspectiva] promising.

lista *sf* - **1.** [enumeración] list; **pasar lista** to call the register; **lista de boda/de espera/de precios** wedding/waiting/price list; **lista de la compra** shopping list; **lista electoral** electoral roll; **lista de éxitos** MÚS hit parade; **lista negra** black list - **2.** [de tela, madera] strip; [de papel] slip; [de color] stripe.
➤ **lista de correos** *sf* poste restante.

listado, **da** *adj* striped.
➤ **listado** *sm* INFORM listing.

listar *vt* INFORM to list.

listín ➤ **listín (de teléfonos)** *sm* (telephone) directory.

listo, **ta** *adj* - **1.** [inteligente, hábil] clever, smart; **dárselas de listo** to make o.s. out to be clever; **pasarse de listo** to be too clever by half; **ser más listo que el hambre** to be nobody's fool - **2.** [preparado] ready; **¿estáis listos?** are you ready?; **estás** *o* **vas listo (si crees que...)** you've got another think coming (if you think that...)

listón *sm* lath; DEP bar; **poner el listón muy alto** *fig* to set very high standards.

lisura *sf* *Arg & Perú* rude remark, bad language *(U)*.

litera *sf* - **1.** [cama] bunk (bed); [de barco] berth; [de tren] couchette - **2.** [vehículo] litter.

literal *adj* literal.

literario, **ria** *adj* literary.

literato, **ta** *sm*, *f* writer.

literatura *sf* literature.

litigante *adj & smf* litigant.

litigar [16] *vi* to go to law.

litigio *sm* DER litigation *(U)*; *fig* dispute; **en litigio** in dispute.

litigue *etc* ⊳ **litigar**.

litio *sm* lithium.

litografía *sf* - **1.** [arte] lithography - **2.** [grabado] lithograph - **3.** [taller] lithographer's (workshop).

litografiar [9] *vt* to lithograph.

litoral ◇ *adj* coastal. ◇ *sm* coast.

litosfera *sf* lithosphere.

litro *sm* litre.

litrona *sf* *mfam* litre bottle of beer.

Lituania *n pr* Lithuania.

lituano, **na** *adj & sm*, *f* Lithuanian.

➤ **lituano** *sm* [lengua] Lithuanian.

liturgia *sf* liturgy.

litúrgico, **ca** *adj* liturgical.

liviano, **na** *adj* - **1.** [ligero - blusa] thin; [- carga] light - **2.** [sin importancia] slight - **3.** [superficial] frivolous.

lividez *sf* [palidez] pallor.

lívido, **da** *adj* - **1.** [pálido] very pale, white as a sheet - **2.** [amoratado] livid.

living ['liβin] *sm* *C Sur* living room.

liza *sf* [lucha] battle; **en liza** in opposition.

ll, **Ll** *sf* [letra] ll, Ll.

llaga *sf* *lit & fig* wound.

llagar [16] *vt* to wound.

➤ **llagarse** *vprnl* to become covered in sores.

llama *sf* - **1.** [de fuego, pasión] flame; **en llamas** ablaze - **2.** ZOOL llama.

llamada *sf* - **1.** [gen] call; [a la puerta] knock; [con timbre] ring; **llamada al orden** call to order; **llamada de socorro** distress signal - **2.** TELECOM telephone call; **devolver una llamada** to phone back; **hacer una llamada** to make a phone call; **llamada urbana/interurbana/a cobro revertido** local/long-distance/reverse-charge call - **3.** [en un libro] reference mark.

llamado, **da** *adj* so-called.

➤ **llamado** *sm* *Amér* [de teléfono] call.

llamamiento *sm* - **1.** [apelación] appeal, call, to call upon sb to do sthg - **2.** MIL call-up.

llamar ◇ *vt* - **1.** [gen] to call; [con gestos] to beckon - **2.** [por teléfono] to phone, to call; **¿quién la llama, por favor?** who is calling, please? - **3.** [convocar] to summon, to call; **llamar (a filas)** MIL to call up - **4.** [atraer] to attract, to call. ◇ *vi* - **1.** [a la puerta etc - con golpes] to knock; [- con timbre] to ring; **están llamando** there's somebody at the door - **2.** [por teléfono] to phone.

➤ **llamarse** *vprnl* [tener por nombre] to be called; **¿cómo te llamas?** what's your name?; **me llamo Pepe** my name's Pepe; **eso es lo que se llama buena suerte** that's what you call good luck.

llamarada *sf* - **1.** [de fuego, ira etc] blaze - **2.** [de rubor] flush.

llamativo, **va** *adj* [color] bright, gaudy; [ropa] showy.

llamear *vi* to burn, to blaze.

llana ⊳ **llano**.

llanero, **ra** ◇ *adj* of the plainspeople. ◇ *sm*, *f* plainsman (*f* plainswoman).

llaneza *sf* naturalness, straightforwardness.

llano, **na** *adj* - **1.** [campo, superficie] flat - **2.** [trato, persona] natural, straightforward - **3.** [pueblo, clase] ordinary - **4.** [lenguaje, expresión] simple, plain - **5.** GRAM paroxytonic.

➤ **llana** *sf* CONSTR trowel.

➤ **llano** *sm* [llanura] plain.

llanta *sf* - **1.** rim - **2.** *Amér* [cubierta] tyre *UK*, tire *US*.

llantera, **llantina** *sf* *fam* blubbing *(U)*.

llanto *sm* tears *pl*, crying.

llanura *sf* plain.

llave *sf* - **1.** [gen] key; **bajo llave** under lock and key; **cerrar con llave** to lock; **echar la llave** to lock up; **llave en mano** [vivienda] ready for immediate occupation; **llave de contacto** ignition key; **llave maestra** master key - **2.** [del agua, gas] tap *UK*, faucet *US*; [de la electricidad] switch; **cerrar la llave de paso** to turn the water/gas off at the mains - **3.** [herramienta] spanner; **llave inglesa** monkey wrench - **4.** [de judo etc] hold, lock - **5.** [signo ortográfico] curly bracket.

llavero *sm* keyring.

llavín *sm* latchkey.

llegada *sf* - **1.** [gen] arrival - **2.** DEP finish.

llegar [16] *vi* - **1.** [a un sitio]: **llegar (de)** to arrive (from); **estar al llegar** [persona] to be on one's way (over); [acontecimiento] to be coming up; **llegar a un hotel/una ciudad** to arrive at a hotel/in a city; **llegaré pronto** I'll be there early - **2.** [un tiempo, la noche etc] to come - **3.** [durar]: **llegar a** o **hasta** to last until - **4.** [alcanzar]: **llegar a** to reach; **no llego al techo** I can't reach the ceiling; **llegar hasta** to reach up to - **5.** [ser suficiente]: **llegar (para)** to be enough (for) - **6.** [lograr]: **llegar a (ser) algo** to get to be sthg, to become sthg; **llegar a hacer algo** to manage to do sthg; **si llego a saberlo** if I get to know of it - **7.** [atreverse]: **llegó a decirme...** he went as far as to say to me...
➤ **llegarse** *vprnl* to go round to.

llenar *vt* - **1.** [ocupar]: **llenar algo (de)** [vaso, hoyo, habitación] to fill sthg (with); [pared, suelo] to cover sthg (with) - **2.** [satisfacer] to satisfy - **3.** [rellenar - impreso] to fill in o out - **4.** [colmar]: **llenar a alguien de** to fill sb with.
➤ **llenarse** *vprnl* - **1.** [ocuparse] to fill up - **2.** [saciarse] to be full - **3.** [cubrirse]: **llenarse de** to become covered in.

llenazo *sm* *fam* full house.

lleno, na *adj* - **1.** [gen] full; [cubierto] covered; **lleno de** [gen] full of; [manchas, pósters] covered in; **lleno hasta los topes** full to bursting, packed out - **2.** *fam* [regordete] chubby.
➤ **lleno** *sm* full house.
➤ **de lleno** *loc adv* full in the face; **acertó de lleno** he was bang on target.

llevadero, ra *adj* bearable.

llevar ◇ *vt* - **1.** [gen] to carry - **2.** [acompañar, coger y depositar] to take; **llevar algo/a alguien a** to take sthg/sb to; **me llevó en coche** he drove me there - **3.** [prenda, objeto personal] to wear; **llevo gafas** I wear glasses; **no llevo dinero** I haven't got any money on me - **4.** [caballo, coche etc] to handle - **5.** [conducir]: **llevar a alguien a algo** to lead sb to sthg; **llevar a alguien a hacer algo** to lead o cause sb to do sthg - **6.** [ocuparse de, dirigir] to be in charge of; [casa, negocio] to look after, to run; **lleva la contabilidad** she keeps the books - **7.** [hacer - de alguna manera]: **lleva muy bien sus estudios** he's doing very well in his studies - **8.** [tener - de alguna manera] to have; **llevar el pelo largo** to have long hair; **llevas las manos sucias** your hands are dirty - **9.** [soportar] to cope with - **10.** [mantener] to keep; **llevar el paso** to keep in step - **11.** [pasarse - tiempo]: **lleva tres semanas sin venir** she hasn't come for three weeks now, it's three weeks since she came last - **12.** [ocupar - tiempo] to take; **me llevó un día hacer este guiso** it took me a day to make this dish - **13.** [sobrepasar en]: **te llevo seis puntos** I'm six points ahead of you; **me lleva dos centímetros** he's two centimetres taller than me - **14.** *loc*: **llevar consigo** [implicar] to lead to, to bring about; **llevar las de perder** to be heading for defeat. ◇ *vi* - **1.** [conducir]: **llevar a** to lead to; **esta carretera lleva al norte** this road leads north - **2.** *(antes de pp)* [haber]: **llevo leída media novela** I'm halfway through the novel; **llevo dicho esto mismo docenas de veces** I've said the same thing time and again - **3.** *(antes de gerundio)* [estar]: **llevar mucho tiempo haciendo algo** to have been doing sthg for a long time.
➤ **llevarse** *vprnl* - **1.** [coger] to take, to steal; **alguien se ha llevado mi sombrero** someone has taken my hat - **2.** [conseguir] to get; **se ha llevado el premio** she has carried off the prize; **yo me llevo siempre las culpas** I always get the blame - **3.** [recibir - susto, sorpresa etc] to get, to receive; **me llevé un disgusto** I was upset - **4.** [entenderse]: **llevarse bien/mal (con alguien)** to get on well/badly (with sb) - **5.** [estar de moda] to be in (fashion); **este año se lleva el verde** green is in this year - **6.** MAT: **me llevo una** carry (the) one.

llorar ◇ *vi* - **1.** [con lágrimas] to cry; **llorar por alguien** to cry over sb - **2.** *fam* [quejarse] to whinge. ◇ *vt*: **llorar la muerte de alguien** to mourn sb's death.

llorera *sf* *fam* crying fit.

llorica *despec* ◇ *adj*: **ser llorica** to be a crybaby. ◇ *smf* crybaby.

lloriquear *vi* to whine, to snivel.

lloriqueo *sm* whining *(U)*, snivelling *(U)*.

lloro *sm* crying *(U)*, tears *pl*.

llorón, ona ◇ *adj* who cries a lot. ◇ *sm, f* crybaby.

lloroso, sa *adj* tearful.

llover [24] ◇ *v impers* to rain; **está lloviendo** it's raining; **llueve sobre mojado** it's one thing after another. ◇ *vi*: **le llueven las ofertas** offers are raining down on him.

llovizna *sf* drizzle.

lloviznar *v impers* to drizzle.

llueva *etc* ▷ **llover**.

lluvia *sf* - **1.** METEOR rain; **bajo la lluvia** in the rain; **lluvia ácida** acid rain; **lluvia radiactiva** (nuclear) fallout; **lluvia torrencial** torrential rain - **2.** [de panfletos, regalos etc] shower; [de preguntas] barrage.

lluvioso, sa *adj* rainy.

lo, la (*mpl* los, *fpl* las) *pron pers (complemento directo)* [cosa] it (*pl* them); [persona] him (*f* her *pl* them); [usted] you.

➤ **lo** ⬦ *pron pers (neutro, predicado)* it; **su hermana es muy guapa pero él no lo es** his sister is very good-looking, but he isn't; **es muy bueno aunque no lo parezca** it's very good, even if it doesn't look it. ⬦ *art det (neutro)*: **lo antiguo me gusta más que lo moderno** I like old things better than modern things; **lo mejor/peor** the best/worst part; **no te imaginas lo grande que era** you can't imagine how big it was.

➤ **lo de** *loc prep*: ¿y lo de la fiesta? what about the party, then?; **siento lo de ayer** I'm sorry about yesterday.

➤ **lo que** *loc conj* what; **acepté lo que me ofrecieron** I accepted what they offered me.

loa *sf* - **1.** [gen] praise - **2.** LITER eulogy.

loable *adj* praiseworthy.

loar *vt* to praise.

lobato, lobezno *sm* wolf cub.

lobby ['loβi] (*pl* lobbies) *sm* lobby, pressure group.

lobezno = lobato.

lobo, ba *sm, f* wolf.

➤ **lobo de mar** *sm* [marinero] sea dog.

lobotomía *sf* lobotomy.

lóbrego, ga *adj* gloomy, murky.

lóbulo *sm* lobe.

local ⬦ *adj* local. ⬦ *sm* - **1.** [edificio] premises *pl* - **2.** [sede] headquarters *pl*.

localidad *sf* - **1.** [población] place, town - **2.** [asiento] seat - **3.** [entrada] ticket; **'no hay localidades'** 'sold out'.

localismo *sm* - **1.** [sentimiento] parochialism - **2.** LING localism.

localista *adj* parochial.

localización *sf* localization, tracking down.

localizar [13] *vt* - **1.** [encontrar] to locate, to track down - **2.** [circunscribir] to localize.

➤ **localizarse en** *vprnl* to become localized in.

locativo *sm* locative.

loción *sf* lotion; **loción capilar** hair lotion; **loción para después del afeitado** aftershave lotion.

loco, ca ⬦ *adj* - **1.** [gen] mad; **estar loco de/por** to be mad with/about; **estar loco de contento** to be wild with joy; **volver loco a alguien** to drive sb mad; **volverse loco por** to be mad about; **loco de atar** *o* remate stark raving mad; **a lo loco** [sin pensar] hastily; [temerariamente] wildly - **2.** [extraordinario - interés, ilusión] tremendous; [- suerte, precio] extraordinary; [- amor, alegría] wild. ⬦ *sm, f* - **1.** *lit & fig* madman (*f* madwoman), lunatic; **cada loco con su tema** everyone has his own axe to grind; **conduce como un loco** he drives like a madman; **hacerse el loco** to play dumb, to pretend not to understand - **2.** *Chile* [molusco] false abalone.

locomoción *sf* transport; [de tren] locomotion.

locomotor, ra *o* **triz** *adj* locomotive.

➤ **locomotora** *sf* engine, locomotive.

locuaz *adj* loquacious, talkative.

locución *sf* phrase.

locura *sf* - **1.** [demencia] madness - **2.** [imprudencia] folly; **hacer locuras** to do crazy things; **ser una locura** to be madness - **3.** [exageración]: **con locura** madly.

locutor, ra *sm, f* [de radio] announcer; [de televisión] presenter.

locutorio *sm* - **1.** [para visitas] visiting room - **2.** TELECOM phone box *o* booth - **3.** RADIO & TV studio.

lodazal *sm* quagmire.

lodo *sm* *lit & fig* mud.

logaritmo *sm* logarithm.

logia *sf* - **1.** [masónica] lodge - **2.** ARQUIT loggia.

lógico, ca ⬦ *adj* logical; **es lógico que se enfade** it stands to reason that he should get angry. ⬦ *sm, f* [persona] logician.

➤ **lógica** *sf* [ciencia] logic.

logístico, ca *adj* logistic.

➤ **logística** *sf* logistics *pl*.

logopeda *smf* speech therapist.

logopedia *sf* speech therapy.

logotipo *sm* logo.

logrado, da *adj* [bien hecho] accomplished.

lograr *vt* [gen] to achieve; [puesto, beca, divorcio] to get, to obtain; [resultado] to obtain, to achieve; [perfección] to attain; [victoria, premio] to win; [deseo, aspiración] to fulfil; **lograr hacer algo** to manage to do sthg; **lograr que alguien haga algo** to manage to get sb to do sthg.

logro *sm* achievement.

LOGSE (*abrev de* Ley de Ordenación General del Sistema Educativo) *sf Spanish Education Act.*

loísmo *sm incorrect use of 'lo' as indirect object instead of 'le'.*

loma *sf* hillock.

lombarda *sf* red cabbage.

lombriz *sf* earthworm, worm; **tener lombrices** to have worms; **lombriz de tierra** earthworm; **lombriz intestinal** tapeworm.

lomo *sm* - **1.** [espalda] back - **2.** [carne] loin - **3.** [de libro] spine - **4.** [de cuchillo] blunt edge.

lona *sf* canvas.

loncha *sf* slice; [de beicon] rasher.

lonche *sm* Perú & Ven - **1.** [merienda] *snack eaten during break time* - **2.** Méx [torta] filled roll.

londinense ◇ *adj* London (antes de s). ◇ *smf* Londoner.

Londres *n pr* London.

longaniza *sf type of spicy, cold pork sausage*.

longevidad *sf* longevity.

longevo, va *adj* long-lived.

longitud *sf* - **1.** [dimensión] length; **tiene medio metro de longitud** it's half a metre long; **longitud de onda** wavelength - **2.** ASTRON & GEOGR longitude.

longitudinal *adj* longitudinal.

long play [lom'plei] (*pl* **long plays**) *sm* LP, album.

longui, longuis *sm* fam: **hacerse el longui** to act dumb, to pretend not to understand.

lonja *sf* - **1.** [loncha] slice - **2.** [edificio] exchange; **lonja de pescado** fish market.

lontananza *sf* background; **en lontananza** in the distance.

loquería *sf* Amér fam mental home.

loquero, ra *sm, f* fam [persona] psychiatric nurse.
➤ **loquero** *sm* Amér [escándalo] row, uproar.

loro *sm* - **1.** [animal] parrot - **2.** fam [charlatán] chatterbox; [mujer fea] fright, ugly old bag - **3.** loc: **estar al loro** vulg to have one's finger on the pulse.

los ◇ *art* ▷ **el**. ◇ *pron* ▷ **lo**.

losa *sf* - **1.** [gen] paving stone, flagstone; [de tumba] tombstone - **2.**: **losa radiante** R Dom underfloor heating.

loseta *sf* floor tile.

lote *sm* - **1.** [parte] share - **2.** [conjunto] batch, lot - **3.** Amér [de tierra] plot (of land) - **4.** fam [mágreo]: **darse** O **pegarse el lote** to kiss and canoodle.

lotería *sf* - **1.** [gen] lottery; **jugar a la lotería** to play the lottery; **le tocó la lotería** she won the lottery; **lotería primitiva** *twice-weekly state-run lottery* - **2.** [tienda] lottery booth - **3.** [juego de mesa] lotto.

lotero, ra *sm, f* seller of lottery tickets.

loto *sf* fam *weekly state-run lottery*.

loza *sf* - **1.** [material] earthenware; [porcelana] china - **2.** [objetos] crockery.

lozanía *sf* - **1.** [de plantas] luxuriance - **2.** [de persona] youthful vigour.

lozano, na *adj* - **1.** [planta] lush, luxuriant - **2.** [persona] youthfully vigorous.

LSD (*abrev de* **Lysergic Acid Diethylamide**) *sm* LSD.

lubina *sf* sea bass.

lubricación *sf* lubrication.

lubricante, lubrificante ◇ *adj* lubricating. ◇ *sm* lubricant.

lubricar [10], **lubrificar** [10] *vt* to lubricate.

lucero *sm* bright star; **lucero del alba/de la tarde** morning/evening star; **como un lucero** as bright as a new pin.

lucha *sf* fight; fig struggle; **abandonar la lucha** to give up the struggle; **lucha armada** armed struggle; **lucha de clases** class struggle O war; **lucha libre** all-in wrestling.

luchador, ra ◇ *adj* fighting. ◇ *sm, f* DEP wrestler; fig fighter.

luchar *vi* to fight; fig to struggle; **luchar contra/por** to fight against/for.

lucidez *sf* lucidity, clarity.

lucido, da *adj* splendid.

lúcido, da *adj* lucid.

luciérnaga *sf* glow-worm.

lucimiento *sm* [de ceremonia etc] sparkle; [de actriz etc] brilliant performance.

lucio *sm* pike.

lucir [32] ◇ *vi* - **1.** [gen] to shine - **2.** [compensar]: **no me lucían tantas horas de trabajo** working so many hours didn't do me much good - **3.** [llevar puesto] to wear - **4.** Amér [parecer] to look - **5.** Amér [tener] to have. ◇ *vt* [gen] to show off; [ropa] to sport.
➤ **lucirse** *vprnl* - **1.** [destacar]: **lucirse (en)** to shine (at) - **2.** fam fig & irón [quedar mal] to really go and do it, to mess things up.

lucrarse *vprnl*: **lucrarse (de)** to profit (from).

lucrativo, va *adj* lucrative; **no lucrativo** non profit-making.

lucro *sm* profit, gain.

lucubrar *vt* to rack one's brains over.

lúdico, ca *adj* [del juego] game (antes de s); [ocioso] of enjoyment, of pleasure.

ludópata *smf* pathological gambling addict.

ludopatía *sf* pathological addiction to gambling.

ludoteca *sf* toy library.

luego ◇ *adv* - **1.** [justo después] then, next; **primero aquí y luego allí** first here and then there; **luego de** immediately after - **2.** [más tarde] later; **¡hasta luego!** see you!, bye!; **hazlo luego** do it later - **3.** Chile, Méx & Ven [pronto] soon. ◇ *conj* - **1.** [así que] so, therefore - **2.**: **luego luego** Méx fam [inmediatamente] immediately, straight away; [de vez en cuando] from time to time.

lugar *sm* **- 1.** [gen] place; [localidad] place, town; [del crimen, accidente etc] scene; [para acampar, merendar etc] spot; **en primer lugar** in the first place, firstly; **en último lugar** lastly, last; **fuera de lugar** out of place; **no hay lugar a duda** there's no room for doubt; **ponte en mi lugar** put yourself in my place; **sin lugar a dudas** without a doubt, undoubtedly; **yo en tu lugar** if I were you; **dejar a alguien en buen/mal lugar** to make sb look good/bad; **poner las cosas en su lugar** to set things straight; **tener lugar** to take place; **lugar de nacimiento** birthplace; **lugar de trabajo** workplace **- 2.** [motivo] cause, reason; **dar lugar a** to bring about, to cause **- 3.** [puesto] position.
➡ **en lugar de** *loc prep* instead of.
➡ **lugar común** *sm* platitude, commonplace.
lugareño, ña ◇ *adj* village *(antes de s)*. ◇ *sm, f* villager.
lugarteniente *sm* deputy.
lúgubre *adj* gloomy, mournful.
lujo *sm* luxury; *fig* profusion; **con todo lujo de detalles** in great detail; **de lujo** luxury *(antes de s)*; **permitirse el lujo de algo/de hacer algo** to be able to afford sthg/to do sthg.
lujoso, sa *adj* luxurious.
lujuria *sf* lust.
lujurioso, sa ◇ *adj* lecherous. ◇ *sm, f* lecher.
lulú ▷ perro.
lumbago *sm* lumbago.
lumbar *adj* lumbar.
lumbre *sf* **- 1.** [fuego] fire; **dar lumbre a alguien** to give sb a light **- 2.** *fig* [resplandor] brightness.
lumbrera *sf fam* leading light.
luminaria *sf* light, lighting *(U)*.
luminosidad *sf* brightness; *fig* brilliance.
luminoso, sa *adj* **- 1.** [gen] bright; [fuente, energía] light *(antes de s)* **- 2.** [idea etc] brilliant.
luminotecnia *sf* lighting.
luna *sf* **- 1.** [astro] moon; **luna creciente** crescent moon *(when waxing)*; **luna llena/nueva** full/new moon; **luna menguante** crescent moon *(when waning)*; **media luna** half moon **- 2.** [cristal] window (pane) **- 3.** [espejo] mirror **- 4.** *loc*: **estar de mala luna** to be in a bad mood; **estar en la luna** to be miles away; **pedir la luna** to ask the impossible.
➡ **luna de miel** *sf* honeymoon.
lunar ◇ *adj* lunar. ◇ *sm* **- 1.** [en la piel] mole, beauty spot **- 2.** [en telas] spot; **a lunares** spotted.
lunático, ca ◇ *adj* crazy. ◇ *sm, f* lunatic.
lunes *sm inv* Monday; *ver también* **sábado**.

luneta *sf* [de coche] windscreen; **luneta trasera** rear windscreen; **luneta térmica** demister.
lupa *sf* magnifying glass.
lúpulo *sm* hops *pl*.
lusitano, na, luso, sa *adj & sm, f* **- 1.** [de Lusitania] Lusitanian **- 2.** [de Portugal] Portuguese.
lustrabotas *sm inv Andes & R Dom* shoeshine, bootblack *UK*.
lustrador *sm Andes & R Plata* shoeshine, bootblack *UK*.
lustrar *vt* to polish.
lustre *sm* **- 1.** [brillo] shine **- 2.** *fig* [gloria] glory.
lustrín *sm Chile* shoeshine box.
lustro *sm* five-year period.
lustroso, sa *adj* shiny.
luteranismo *sm* Lutheranism.
luterano, na *adj & sm, f* Lutheran.
luto *sm* mourning; **de luto** in mourning.
luxación *sf* dislocation.
Luxemburgo *n pr* Luxembourg.
luxemburgués, esa ◇ *adj* Luxembourg *(antes de s)*. ◇ *sm, f* Luxembourger.
luz *sf* [gen] light; [electricidad] electricity; [destello] flash (of light); **apagar la luz** to switch off the light; **a plena luz del día** in broad daylight; **cortar la luz** to cut off the electricity supply; **dar** o **encender la luz** to switch on the light; **pagar (el recibo de) la luz** to pay the electricity (bill); **se ha ido la luz** the lights have gone out; **luz eléctrica** electric light; **luz solar** sunlight; **a la luz de** [una vela, la luna etc] by the light of; [los acontecimientos etc] in the light of; **arrojar luz sobre** to shed light on; **a todas luces** whichever way you look at it; **dar a luz (un niño)** to give birth (to a child); **dar luz verde** to give the green light o the go-ahead; **sacar algo a la luz** [secreto] to bring to light; [obra] to bring out, to publish; **salir a la luz** [descubrirse] to come to light; [publicarse] to come out; **ver la luz** to see the light.
➡ **luces** *sfpl* **- 1.** [cultura] enlightenment *(U)* **- 2.** [inteligencia] intelligence *(U)*; **de pocas luces** dim-witted **- 3.** AUTO lights; **darle las luces a alguien** to flash (one's lights) at sb; **poner las luces de carretera** o **largas** to put (one's headlights) on full beam; **luces de cruce** o **cortas** dipped headlights; **luces de freno** brake lights; **luces de posición** o **situación** sidelights; **luces de tráfico** o **de señalización** traffic lights.
luzca *etc* ▷ **lucir**.
lycra® *sf* Lycra®.

m¹, M *sf* [letra] m, M.

m² (*abrev de* **metro**) m.

m. (*abrev de* **muerto**) d.; **m. 1997** d. 1997.

maca *sf* - **1.** [de fruta] bruise - **2.** [de objetos] flaw.

macabro, bra *adj* macabre.

macana *sf* C Sur, Perú & Ven fam [disparate] stupid thing; [fastidio] pain, drag; [pena] shame.

macanear *vi* C Sur fam [decir tonterías] to talk nonsense; [hacer tonterías] to be stupid.

macarra *sm* fam [de prostitutas] pimp; [rufián] thug.

macarrón *sm* [tubo] sheath (of cable).
➡ **macarrones** *smpl* [pasta] macaroni (U).

macarrónico, ca *adj* fam macaronic.

macedonia *sf* salad; **macedonia de frutas** fruit salad.

maceración *sf* CULIN soaking, maceration.

macerar *vt* CULIN to soak, to macerate.

maceta *sf* - **1.** [tiesto] flowerpot - **2.** [herramienta] mallet.

macetero *sm* flowerpot holder.

machaca *smf* - **1.** fam [pesado] pain - **2.** [trabajador] dogsbody.

machacador, ra *adj* crushing.
➡ **machacadora** *sf* crusher.

machacar [10] <> *vt* - **1.** [triturar] to crush - **2.** fig [insistir] to keep going on about - **3.** fig [empollar] to swot up on. <> *vi* fig: **machacar (sobre)** to go on (about).

machacón, ona <> *adj* tiresome. <> *sm, f* pain.

machaconería *sf* annoying insistence.

machada *sf* act of bravado.

machamartillo ➡ **a machamartillo** *loc adv* very firmly; **creer algo a machamartillo** to be firm in one's belief of sthg.

machete *sm* machete.

machismo *sm* machismo.

machista *adj* & *smf* male chauvinist.

macho <> *adj* - **1.** BIOL male - **2.** fig [hombre] macho. <> *sm* - **1.** BIOL male - **2.** fig [hombre] macho man, he-man - **3.** TECNOL male part; [de enchufe] pin - **4.**: **macho cabrío** billy goat. <> *interj* fam: **¡oye, macho!** oy, mate!

machote, ta *fam* <> *adj* brave; **dárselas de machote** to act like a he-man. <> *sm, f* [niño] big boy (f big girl).
➡ **machote** *sm* Amér [modelo] rough draft.

macizo, za *adj* solid; **estar macizo** *fam* [hombre] to be hunky; [mujer] to be gorgeous.
➡ **macizo** *sm* - **1.** GEOGR massif - **2.** BOT: **macizo de flores** flowerbed.

macramé *sm* macramé.

macro *sf* INFORM macro.

macrobiótico, ca *adj* macrobiotic.
➡ **macrobiótica** *sf* macrobiotics (U).

macroeconomía *sf* macroeconomics (U).

mácula *sf* spot; *fig* blemish.

macuto *sm* backpack, knapsack.

madeja *sf* hank, skein; **enredar la madeja** to complicate matters; **estar hecho una madeja de nervios** to be a bundle of nerves.

madera *sf* - **1.** [gen] wood; CONSTR timber; [tabla] piece of wood; **de madera** wooden; **madera contrachapada** plywood; **tocar madera** to touch wood UK, to knock on wood US - **2.** [disposición]: **tener madera de algo** to have the makings of sthg.

maderaje, maderamen *sm* timbers *pl*.

maderero, ra *adj* timber (antes de s).

madero *sm* - **1.** [tabla] log - **2.** [necio] halfwit - **3.** *mfam* [policía] cop, pig.

madrastra *sf* stepmother.

madre *sf* - **1.** [gen] mother; **es madre de tres niños** she's a mother of three; **madre adoptiva/de alquiler** foster/surrogate mother; **madre biológica** biological mother; **madre de familia** mother; **madre política** mother-in-law; **madre soltera** single mother; **madre superiora** mother superior; **la madre patria** the motherland; **éramos ciento y la madre** *fam* there were hundreds of us there; **me vale madre** Méx *mfam* I couldn't give a damn *O* UK a toss; **ser la madre del cordero** *fig* to be at the very root of the problem - **2.** [poso] dregs *pl* - **3.** [cauce] bed; **salirse de madre** [río] to burst its banks; *fig* [persona] to go too far.
➡ **madre mía** *interj*: **¡madre mía!** Jesus!, Christ!

madreperla *sf* [ostra] pearl oyster; [nácar] mother-of-pearl.

madreselva *sf* honeysuckle.

Madrid *n pr* Madrid.

madrigal *sm* madrigal.

madriguera *sf* lit & fig den; [de conejo] burrow.

madrileño, ña <> *adj* of/relating to Madrid. <> *sm, f* native/inhabitant of Madrid.

madrina *sf* [gen] patroness; [de boda] bridesmaid; [de bautizo] godmother.

madroño *sm* - **1.** [árbol] strawberry tree - **2.** [fruto] strawberry-tree berry.

madrugada *sf* - **1.** [amanecer] dawn; **de madrugada** at daybreak - **2.** [noche] early morning; **las tres de la madrugada** three in the morning - **3.** [madrugón] early rise.

madrugador, ra ◇ *adj* early-rising. ◇ *sm, f* early riser.

madrugar [16] *vi* to get up early; *fig* to be quick off the mark; **a quien madruga Dios le ayuda** *prov* the early bird catches the worm; **no por mucho madrugar amanece más temprano** *prov* time must take its course.

madrugón *sm fam*: **darse un madrugón** to get up very early o at the crack of dawn.

madurar ◇ *vt* - **1.** [gen] to mature; [fruta, mies] to ripen - **2.** [idea, proyecto etc] to think through. ◇ *vi* [gen] to mature; [fruta] to ripen.

madurez *sf* - **1.** [cualidad - gen] maturity; [- de fruta, mies] ripeness - **2.** [edad adulta] adulthood.

maduro, ra *adj* [gen] mature; [fruta, mies] ripe; **de edad madura** middle-aged.

maestra ▷ **maestro**.

maestranza *sf* MIL arsenal.

maestría *sf* - **1.** [habilidad] mastery, skill - **2.** *Amér* [título] master's degree.

maestro, tra ◇ *adj* - **1.** [perfecto] masterly - **2.** [principal] main; [llave] master *(antes de s)*. ◇ *sm, f* - **1.** [profesor] teacher - **2.** [sabio] master - **3.** MÚS maestro - **4.** *Méx* [de universidad] lecturer *UK*, professor *US* - **5.** [director]: **maestro de ceremonias** master of ceremonies; **maestro de cocina** chef; **maestro de obras** foreman; **maestro de orquesta** conductor.

➥ **maestro** *sm* TAUROM matador.

mafia *sf* mafia.

mafioso, sa ◇ *adj* mafia *(antes de s)*. ◇ *sm, f* mafioso.

magdalena *sf* fairy cake.

magenta *adj inv* & *sm* magenta.

magia *sf* magic; **magia blanca/negra** white/ black magic.

mágico, ca *adj* - **1.** [con magia] magic - **2.** [atractivo] magical.

magisterio *sm* - **1.** [título] teaching certificate - **2.** [enseñanza] teaching - **3.** [profesión] teaching profession.

magistrado, da *sm, f* [juez] judge.

➥ **magistrado** *sm Amér* [primer ministro] Prime Minister.

magistral *adj* - **1.** [de maestro] magisterial - **2.** [genial] masterly.

magistratura *sf* - **1.** [oficio] judgeship - **2.** [jueces] magistrature - **3.** [tribunal] tribunal; **magistratura de trabajo** industrial tribunal.

magma *sm* magma.

magnánimo, ma *adj* magnanimous.

magnate *sm* magnate; **magnate del petróleo/de la prensa** oil/press baron.

magnesia *sf* magnesia.

magnesio *sm* magnesium.

magnético, ca *adj lit & fig* magnetic.

magnetismo *sm lit & fig* magnetism.

magnetizar [13] *vt* to magnetize; *fig* to mesmerize.

magnetófono *sm* tape recorder.

magnetoscopio *sm* video recorder.

magnicida *smf* assassin *(of somebody important)*.

magnicidio *sm* assassination *(of somebody important)*.

magnificar [10] *vt* to praise highly.

magnificencia *sf* magnificence.

magnífico, ca *adj* wonderful, magnificent.

magnitud *sf* magnitude.

magno, na *adj* great.

magnolia *sf* magnolia.

mago, ga *sm, f* - **1.** [prestidigitador] magician - **2.** [en cuentos etc] wizard.

magra ▷ **magro**.

magrear *vt mfam* to touch up.

magro, gra *adj* - **1.** [sin grasa] lean - **2.** [pobre] poor.

➥ **magro** *sm* lean meat.

➥ **magra** *sf* slice of ham.

magulladura *sf* bruise.

magullar *vt* to bruise.

maharajá [maraˈxa] *sm* maharajah.

mahometano, na *adj* & *sm, f* Muslim.

mahonesa = **mayonesa**.

maicena® *sf* cornflour *UK*, cornstarch *US*.

maillot [maˈjot] *(pl* **maillots)** *sm* - **1.** [prenda femenina] maillot - **2.** [para ciclistas] jersey; **maillot amarillo** DEP yellow jersey.

maître [ˈmetre] *sm* maître.

maíz *sm* maize *UK*, corn *US*; **maíz dulce** sweetcorn.

maizal *sm* maize field.

maja ▷ **majo**.

majadería *sf* idiocy.

majadero, ra *sm, f* idiot.

majar *vt* [machacar] to crush; [moler] to grind.

majareta *fam* ◇ *adj* nutty. ◇ *smf* nutcase.

majestad *sf* majesty.

➥ **Su Majestad** *sf* His/Her Majesty.

majestuosidad *sf* majesty.

majestuoso, sa *adj* majestic.

majo, ja ◇ *adj* - **1.** [simpático] nice - **2.** [bonito] pretty. ◇ *sm, f* ARTE & HIST Majo *(f* Maja).

majorette [majo'ret] *sf* majorette.

mal ⬦ *adj* ⊳ **malo.** ⬦ *sm* - **1.** [perversión]: **el mal** evil - **2.** [daño] harm, damage - **3.** [enfermedad] illness; **mal de montaña** altitude o mountain sickness; **mal de ojo** evil eye - **4.** [inconveniente] bad thing; **un mal necesario** a necessary evil - **5.** *loc*: **a grandes males, grandes remedios** drastic situations demand drastic action; **del mal, el menos** it's the lesser of two evils; **mal de muchos, consuelo de todos** *prov* at least I'm not the only one; **no hay mal que por bien no venga** *prov* every cloud has a silver lining *prov*. ⬦ *adv* - **1.** [incorrectamente] wrong; **esto está mal hecho** this has been done wrong; **has escrito mal esta palabra** you've spelt that word wrong - **2.** [inadecuadamente] badly; **la fiesta salió mal** the party went off badly; **oigo/veo mal** I can't hear/see very well; **encontrarse mal** [enfermo] to feel ill; [incómodo] to feel uncomfortable; **oler mal** [tener mal olor] to smell bad; *fam* [tener mal cariz] to smell fishy; **saber mal** [tener mal sabor] to taste bad; **me supo mal que no vinieses a mi fiesta** I was none too pleased that you didn't come to my party; **sentar mal a alguien** [ropa] not to suit sb; [comida] to disagree with sb; [comentario, actitud] to upset sb; **tomar algo a mal** to take sthg the wrong way - **3.** [difícilmente] hardly; **mal puede saberlo si no se lo cuentas** he's hardly going to know it if you don't tell him - **4.** *loc*: **estar a mal con alguien** to have fallen out with sb; **ir de mal en peor** to go from bad to worse; **no estaría mal que...** it would be nice if...

➤ **mal que** *loc conj* although, even though; **mal que te pese, las cosas están así** whether you like it or not, that's the way things are.

➤ **mal que bien** *loc adv* somehow or other.

malabar *adj*: **juego malabar** juggling *(U)*.

malabarismo *sm lit & fig* juggling *(U)*; **hacer malabarismos** to juggle.

malabarista *smf* juggler.

malacostumbrado, da *adj* spoiled.

malacostumbrar *vt* to spoil.

malaleche *smf vulg* miserable sod.

malapata *fam* ⬦ *smf* clumsy oaf. ⬦ *sf* tough luck.

malaria *sf* malaria.

Malasia *n pr* Malaysia.

malasio, sia *adj* Malaysian.

malasombra *fam* ⬦ *smf* [persona] pest. ⬦ *sf* [falta de gracia] lack of charm.

malayo, ya *adj & sm, f* Malay, Malayan.

➤ **malayo** *sm* [lengua] Malay, Malayan.

malcomer *vi* to eat poorly.

malcriado, da ⬦ *adj* spoiled. ⬦ *sm, f* spoilt brat.

malcriar [9] *vt* to spoil.

maldad *sf* - **1.** [cualidad] evil - **2.** [acción] evil thing.

maldecir [66] ⬦ *vt* to curse. ⬦ *vi* to curse; **maldecir de** to speak ill of.

maldición *sf* curse.

maldiga, maldijera *etc v* ⊳ **maldecir.**

maldito, ta *adj* - **1.** [embrujado] cursed, damned - **2.** *fam* [para enfatizar] damned; **¡maldita sea!** damn it! - **3.** [marginado - escritor etc] ostracized.

maleable *adj lit & fig* malleable.

maleado, da *adj* corrupt.

maleante ⬦ *adj* wicked. ⬦ *smf* crook.

malear *vt* to corrupt.

malecón *sm* [atracadero] jetty.

maleducado, da ⬦ *adj* rude. ⬦ *sm, f* rude person.

maleficio *sm* curse.

maléfico, ca *adj* evil.

malentendido *sm* misunderstanding.

malestar *sm* - **1.** [dolor] upset, discomfort; **siento un malestar en el estómago** I've got an upset stomach; **sentir malestar general** to feel unwell - **2.** [inquietud] uneasiness, unrest.

maleta *sf* suitcase; **hacer** o **preparar la maleta** to pack (one's bags).

maletera *sf Amér* boot *UK*, trunk *US*.

maletero *sm* boot *UK*, trunk *US*.

maletilla *smf* apprentice bullfighter.

maletín *sm* briefcase.

malévolo, la *adj* malevolent, wicked.

maleza *sf* [arbustos] undergrowth; [malas hierbas] weeds *pl*.

malformación *sf* malformation; **malformación congénita** congenital malformation.

malgastar *vt* [dinero, tiempo] to waste; [salud] to ruin.

malhablado, da ⬦ *adj* foul-mouthed. ⬦ *sm, f* foul-mouthed person.

malhechor, ra *adj & sm, f* criminal.

malherir [27] *vt* to injure seriously.

malhumor *sm* bad mood; **de malhumor** in a bad mood.

malhumorado, da *adj* bad-tempered; [enfadado] in a bad mood.

malicia *sf* - **1.** [maldad] wickedness, evil; [mala intención] malice - **2.** [agudeza] sharpness, alertness.

malicioso, sa *adj* - **1.** [malo] wicked, evil; [malintencionado] malicious - **2.** [avispado] sharp, alert.

maligno, na *adj* malignant.

malintencionado, da ⬦ *adj* ill-intentioned. ⬦ *sm, f* ill-intentioned person.

malla *sf* - **1.** [tejido] mesh; **malla de alambre** wire mesh - **2.** [red] net - **3.** *R Dom* [traje de baño] swimsuit.

🔹 **mallas** *sfpl* - **1.** [de gimnasia] leotard *sing*; [de ballet] tights - **2.** [de portería] net *sing*.

Mallorca *n pr* Majorca.

malnacido, da ◇ *adj* undesirable, nasty. ◇ *sm, f* nasty type.

malnutrido, da *adj* undernourished.

malo, la *(peor es el comparativo y el superlativo de* **malo***; delante de sm sing:* **mal***) adj* - **1.** [gen] bad; [calidad] poor, bad; **lo malo fue que...** the problem was (that)...; **más vale malo conocido que bueno por conocer** *prov* better the devil you know (than the devil you don't) - **2.** [malicioso] wicked - **3.** [enfermo] ill, sick; **estar/ponerse malo** to be/fall ill - **4.** [molesto] unpleasant - **5.** [travieso] naughty.

🔹 **malo, la** *sm, f* [de película etc] villain, baddie.

🔹 **malas** *sfpl*: **estar de malas** to be in a bad mood; **ponerse a (las) malas con** to fall out with; **por las malas** by force.

malogrado, da *adj* - **1.** [desaprovechado] wasted - **2.** [difunto]: **un malogrado poeta** a poet who died before his time.

malograr *vt* - **1.** to waste - **2.** *Andes* [estropear] to make a mess of, to ruin.

🔹 **malograrse** *vprnl* - **1.** [fracasar] to fail - **2.** [morir] to die before one's time - **3.** *Andes* [estropearse - máquina] to break down; [- alimento] to go off, to spoil.

maloliente *adj* smelly.

malparado, da *adj*: **salir malparado de algo** to come out of sthg badly.

malpensado, da ◇ *adj* malicious, evil-minded. ◇ *sm, f* evil-minded person.

malsano, na *adj* unhealthy.

malsonante *adj* rude.

malta *sm* malt.

malteada *sf Amér* [batido] milkshake.

maltés, esa *adj* & *sm, f* Maltese.

maltraer **[73]** *vt* [maltratar] to ill-treat; **llevar** *o* **traer a maltraer** to cause headaches.

maltratar *vt* - **1.** [pegar, insultar] to ill-treat - **2.** [estropear] to damage.

maltrato *sm* ill-treatment.

maltrecho, cha *adj* battered; **dejar maltrecho a alguien** to leave sb in a bad way.

malva ◇ *sf* BOT mallow; **criar malvas** *fam fig* to push up daisies. ◇ *adj inv* mauve. ◇ *sm* [color] mauve.

malvado, da ◇ *adj* evil, wicked. ◇ *sm, f* villain, evil person.

malvender *vt* to sell at a loss.

malversación *sf*: **malversación (de fondos)** embezzlement (of funds).

malversador, ra *sm, f* embezzler.

malversar *vt* to embezzle.

Malvinas *sfpl*: **las (islas) Malvinas** the Falkland Islands, the Falklands.

malvivir *vi* to live badly, to scrape together an existence.

mama *sf* - **1.** [órgano - de mujer] breast; ZOOL udder - **2.** *fam* [madre] mum, mummy.

mamá *sf* - **1.** *fam* mum, mummy - **2.**: **mamá grande** *Col & Méx fam* grandma.

mamadera *sf C Sur & Perú* [biberón] (baby's) bottle.

mamado, da *adj fam* [ebrio] pissed.

🔹 **mamada** *sf* [de bebé] (breast) feed, (breast) feeding *(U)*.

mamar ◇ *vt* - **1.** [suj: bebé] to suckle - **2.** [aprender]: **lo mamó desde pequeño** he was immersed in it as a child - **3.** *mfam fig* [beber] to knock back. ◇ *vi* to suckle; **dar de mamar** to breast-feed.

🔹 **mamarse** *vprnl mfam* [emborracharse] to get plastered.

mamario, ria *adj* mammary.

mamarrachada *sf fam* - **1.** [acción] stupid *o* idiotic thing - **2.** [cuadro etc] rubbish *(U)*.

mamarracho *sm* - **1.** [fantoche] sight, mess - **2.** [imbécil] idiot - **3.** [bodrio] rubbish *(U)*.

mambo *sm* mambo.

mamífero, ra *adj* mammal.

🔹 **mamífero** *sm* mammal.

mamografía *sf* - **1.** MED [técnica] breast scanning, mammography - **2.** MED [resultado] breast scan, mammogram.

mamón, ona *sm, f* - **1.** *vulg* [persona despreciable] bastard, bitch *f*; **¡eres un mamón!** you bastard! - **2.** *vulg* [necio] prat *UK*, jerk *US*.

mamotreto *sm* - **1.** *despec* [libro] hefty tome - **2.** [objeto grande] monstrosity.

mampara *sf* screen.

mamporro *sm fam* punch, clout; [al caer] bump.

mampostería *sf* masonry.

mamut *sm* mammoth.

maná *sm inv* manna.

manada *sf* - **1.** [ZOOL - gen] herd; [- de lobos] pack; [- de ovejas] flock; [- de leones] pride - **2.** *fam* [de gente] crowd, mob.

manager (*pl* **managers**) *sm* manager.

Managua *n pr* Managua.

manantial *sm* spring; *fig* source.

manar *vi lit & fig*: **manar (de)** to flow (from).

manazas ◇ *adj inv* clumsy. ◇ *smf inv* clumsy person.

mancebo, ba *sm, f* young person.

🔹 **manceba** *sf* [concubina] concubine.

mancha *sf* - **1.** [gen] stain, spot; [de tinta] blot; [de color] spot, mark; **extenderse como una mancha de aceite** to spread like wildfire - **2.** ASTRON spot - **3.** [deshonra] blemish; **sin mancha** unblemished.

manchar *vt* - **1.** [ensuciar]**: manchar algo (de** *o* **con)** [gen] to make sthg dirty (with); [con manchas] to stain sthg (with); [emborronar] to smudge sthg (with) - **2.** [deshonrar] to tarnish.
◆ **mancharse** *vprnl* [ensuciarse] to get dirty.

manchego, ga ◇ *adj* of/relating to La Mancha. ◇ *sm, f* native/inhabitant of La Mancha.
◆ **manchego** ▷ **queso**.

manco, ca *adj* [sin una mano] one-handed; [sin manos] handless; [sin un brazo] one-armed; [sin brazos] armless; **no ser manco para** *o* **en** to be a dab hand at.

mancomunar *vt* to pool (together).
◆ **mancomunarse** *vprnl* to join together, to unite.

mancomunidad *sf* association.

mancorna, mancuerna *sf Andes, Amér C, Méx & Ven* cufflink.

mandado, da *sm, f* [subordinado] underling.
◆ **mandado** *sm* [recado] errand.

mandamás (*pl* **mandamases**) *smf* bigwig, boss.

mandamiento *sm* - **1.** [orden - militar] order, command; [- judicial] writ - **2.** RELIG commandment; **los diez mandamientos** the Ten Commandments.

mandanga *sf fam* - **1.** (*gen pl*) [cuento, tontería] story - **2.** [calma] sluggishness, lethargy.

mandar ◇ *vt* - **1.** [dar órdenes a] to order; **mandar a alguien hacer algo** to order sb to do sthg; **mandar hacer algo** to have sthg done - **2.** [enviar] to send - **3.** [dirigir, gobernar] to lead, to be in charge of; [país] to rule. ◇ *vi* - **1.** [gen] to be in charge; [jefe de estado] to rule; **aquí mando yo** I'm in charge here; **mandar en algo** to be in charge of sthg - **2.** *despec* [dar órdenes] to order people around - **3.** *loc:* **¿mande?** *fam* eh?, you what?

mandarín (*pl* **mandarines**) *sm* - **1.** [título] mandarin - **2.** [dialecto] Mandarin.

mandarina *sf* mandarin.

mandarinero *sm* mandarin tree.

mandatario, ria *sm, f* representative, agent; **primer mandatario** [jefe de estado] head of state.

mandato *sm* - **1.** [gen] order, command - **2.** [poderes de representación, disposición] mandate; **mandato judicial** warrant - **3.** POLÍT term of office; [reinado] period of rule.

mandíbula *sf* jaw; **reír a mandíbula batiente** to laugh one's head off.

mandil *sm* [delantal] apron.

mandioca *sf* - **1.** [planta] cassava - **2.** [fécula] tapioca.

mando *sm* - **1.** [poder] command, authority; **al mando de** in charge of; **entregar el mando** to hand over command - **2.** [periodo en poder] term of office - **3.** (*gen pl*) [autoridades] leadership (*U*); MIL command (*U*); **alto mando** MIL high command; **mandos intermedios** middle management *sing* - **4.** [dispositivo] control; **mando automático/a distancia** automatic/remote control.

mandolina *sf* mandolin.

mandón, ona ◇ *adj* bossy. ◇ *sm, f* bossy-boots.

mandrágora *sf* mandrake.

mandril *sm* - **1.** [animal] mandrill - **2.** [pieza] mandrel.

manduca *sf fam* grub, scoff.

manecilla *sf* - **1.** [del reloj] hand - **2.** [cierre] clasp.

manejable *adj* [gen] manageable; [herramienta] easy to use.

manejar ◇ *vt* - **1.** [conocimientos, datos] to use, to marshal - **2.** [máquina, mandos] to operate; [caballo, bicicleta] to handle; [arma] to wield - **3.** [negocio etc] to manage, to run; [gente] to handle - **4.** *fig* [dominar] to boss about - **5.** *Amér* [vehículo] to drive. ◇ *vi Amér* [conducir] to drive.
◆ **manejarse** *vprnl* - **1.** [moverse] to move *o* get about - **2.** [desenvolverse] to manage, to get by.

manejo *sm* - **1.** [de máquina, mandos] operation; [de armas, herramientas] use; **de fácil manejo** user-friendly - **2.** [de conocimientos, datos] marshalling; [de idiomas] command - **3.** [de caballo, bicicleta] handling - **4.** [de negocio etc] management, running - **5.** (*gen pl*) *fig* [intriga] intrigue.

manera *sf* way, manner; **lo haremos a mi manera** we'll do it my way; **a mi manera de ver** the way I see it; **de cualquier manera** [sin cuidado] any old how; [de todos modos] anyway, in any case; **de esta manera** in this way; **de la misma manera** similarly, in the same way; **de mala manera** badly; **de ninguna manera, en manera alguna** [refuerza negación] by no means, under no circumstances; [respuesta exclamativa] no way!, certainly not!; **de todas maneras** anyway; **de una manera** *o* **de otra** one way or another; **en cierta manera** in a way; **manera de ser** way of being, nature; **a la manera de** in the style of, after the fashion of; **de manera que** [para] so (that); **no hay manera** there is no way, it's impossible; **¡qué manera de...!** what a way to...!
◆ **maneras** *sfpl* [modales] manners; **buenas/malas maneras** good/bad manners.

manga *sf* - **1.** [de prenda] sleeve; **en mangas de camisa** in shirtsleeves; **sin mangas** sleeveless; **manga corta/larga** short/long sleeve; **manga raglán** O **ranglán** raglan sleeve; **andar manga por hombro** to be a mess; **sacarse algo de la manga** [improvisar] to make sthg up on the spur of the moment; [idear] to come up with sthg; **ser de manga ancha, tener manga ancha** to be over-indulgent - **2.** [manguera] hosepipe - **3.** [de pastelería] forcing O piping bag - **4.** DEP stage, round.

manganeso *sm* manganese.

mangante *fam* <> *adj* thieving. <> *smf* thief.

mangar [16] *vt fam* to pinch, to nick.

mango *sm* - **1.** [asa] handle - **2.** [árbol] mango tree; [fruta] mango - **3.: no tiene un mango** *R Dom fam* I haven't got a bean, I'm broke.

mangonear *vi fam* - **1.** [entrometerse] to meddle - **2.** [mandar] to push people around, to be bossy - **3.** [manipular] to fiddle about.

mangoneo *sm fam* - **1.** [intromisión] bossing O pushing around - **2.** [manipulación] fiddling.

mangosta *sf* mongoose.

mangue *etc* ⌐> **mangar**.

manguera *sf* hosepipe; [de bombero] fire hose.

mangui *mfam* <> *adj* [persona no fiable] sneaky. <> *smf* - **1.** [ladrón] crook, thief - **2.** [persona no fiable] crook.

manguito *sm* - **1.** [para el frío] muff - **2.** [media manga] protective sleeve, oversleeve.

maní, manises *sm Andes, Caribe & R Plata* peanut.

manía *sf* - **1.** [idea fija] obsession; **manía persecutoria** persecution complex - **2.** [peculiaridad] idiosyncrasy - **3.** [mala costumbre] bad habit - **4.** [afición exagerada] mania, craze - **5.** *fam* [ojeriza] dislike; **coger manía a alguien** to take a dislike to sb; **tener manía a alguien** not to be able to stand sb - **6.** PSICOL mania.

maniaco, ca, maníaco, ca <> *adj* manic. <> *sm, f* maniac; **maniaco sexual** sex maniac.

maniacodepresivo, va *adj* & *sm, f* manic-depressive.

maniatar *vt* to tie the hands of.

maniático, ca <> *adj* fussy. <> *sm, f* fussy person; **es un maniático del fútbol** he's football-crazy.

manicomio *sm* mental O psychiatric hospital *UK*, insane asylum *US*.

manicuro, ra *sm, f* [persona] manicurist.
⌐> **manicura** *sf* [técnica] manicure.

manido, da *adj* [tema etc] hackneyed.

manierismo *sm* ARTE mannerism.

manifestación *sf* - **1.** [de alegría, dolor etc] show, display; [de opinión] declaration, expres-

sion; [indicio] sign - **2.** [por la calle] demonstration; **hacer una manifestación** to hold a demonstration.

manifestante *smf* demonstrator.

manifestar [19] *vt* - **1.** [alegría, dolor etc] to show - **2.** [opinión etc] to express.
⌐> **manifestarse** *vprnl* - **1.** [por la calle] to demonstrate - **2.** [hacerse evidente] to become clear O apparent.

manifiesto, ta *adj* clear, evident; **poner de manifiesto algo** [revelar] to reveal sthg; [hacer patente] to make sthg clear.
⌐> **manifiesto** *sm* manifesto.

manija *sf* handle.

manilla *(gen pl) sf* - **1.** [del reloj] hand - **2.** [grilletes] manacle.

manillar *sm* handlebars *pl*.

maniobra *sf* - **1.** [gen] manoeuvre; **estar de maniobras** MIL to be on manoeuvres; **hacer maniobras** AUTO to manoeuvre - **2.** [treta] trick.

maniobrar *vi* to manoeuvre.

manipulación *sf* - **1.** [gen] handling - **2.** [engaño] manipulation.

manipulador, ra <> *adj* handling. <> *sm, f* handler.

manipular *vt* - **1.** [manejar] to handle - **2.** [mangonear - información, resultados] to manipulate; [- negocios, asuntos] to interfere in.

maniqueo, a <> *adj* Manichean. <> *sm, f* Manichee.

maniquí (*pl* **maniquíes** O **maniquís**) <> *sm* dummy. <> *sm, f* - **1.** [modelo] model - **2.** [persona manipulada] puppet.

manirroto, ta <> *adj* extravagant. <> *sm, f* spendthrift.

manitas <> *adj inv* handy, good with one's hands. <> *smf inv* handy person; **ser un manitas (de plata)** to be (very) good with one's hands; **hacer manitas** to fondle, to touch each other up.

manito *sm Méx fam* pal, mate *UK*, buddy *US*.

manivela *sf* crank.

manjar *sm* delicious food (*U*).

mano <> *sf* - **1.** [gen] hand; **a mano** [cerca] to hand, handy; [sin máquina] by hand; **votación a mano alzada** show of hands; **a mano armada** armed; **dar** O **estrechar la mano a alguien** to shake hands with sb; **darse** O **estrecharse la mano** to shake hands; **echar/tender una mano** to give/offer a hand; **¡manos arriba!, ¡arriba las manos!** hands up!; **mano de obra** [capacidad de trabajo] labour; [trabajadores] workforce; **mano de obra especializada** skilled labour - **2.** [ZOOL - gen] forefoot; [- de perro, gato] (front) paw; [- de cerdo] (front) trotter - **3.** [lado]:

a mano derecha/izquierda on the right/left **- 4.: calle de una sola mano** *R Dom* one-way street; **calle de doble mano** *R Dom* two-way street **- 5.** [de pintura etc] coat **- 6.** [influencia] influence **- 7.** [de mortero] pestle **- 8.** [partida de naipes] game; **ser mano** to (be the) lead **- 9.** [serie, tanda] series **- 10.** *loc*: **alzar la mano contra alguien** to raise one's hand to sb; **bajo mano** secretly; **caer en manos de alguien** to fall into sb's hands; **cargar la mano** to go over the top; **con las manos cruzadas, mano sobre mano** sitting around doing nothing; **coger a alguien con las manos en la masa** to catch sb red-handed *o* in the act; **de primera mano** [coche etc] brand new; [noticias etc] first-hand; **de segunda mano** second-hand; **dejar de la mano** to abandon; **dejar algo en manos de alguien** to leave sthg in sb's hands; **echar mano de algo** to make use of sthg, to resort to sthg; **ensuciarse las manos** to get one's hands dirty; **escaparse de las manos a alguien** [oportunidad etc] to slip through sb's hands; [control, proyecto] to get out of hand for sb; **estar dejado de la mano de Dios** [gen] to be godforsaken; [persona] to be a total failure; **ganar por la mano a alguien** to beat sb to it; **írsele a uno la mano** [perder el control] to lose control; [exagerar] to go too far; **lavarse las manos (de algo)** to wash one's hands (of sthg); **llevarse las manos a la cabeza** [gesticular] to throw one's hands in the air (in horror); *fig* to be horrified; **mano a mano** tête-à-tête; **¡manos a la obra!** let's get down to it!; **meter mano a alguien** [investigar] to get onto sb, to start to investigate sb; [magrear sin consentimiento] to grope sb; [magrear con consentimiento] to touch sb up; **meter mano a algo** [gen] to fiddle about *o* meddle with sthg; [problema, asunto] to tackle sthg; **pedir la mano de una mujer** to ask for a woman's hand (in marriage); **ponerse en manos de alguien** to put o.s. in sb's hands; **ser la mano derecha de alguien** to be sb's right hand man; **tener buena mano para algo** to have a knack for sthg; **tener las manos largas** to be fond of a fight; **tener mano izquierda con la gente** to know how to deal with people; **traerse entre manos algo** to be up to sthg; **venir** *o* **llegar a las manos** to come to blows. ⬦ *sm Andes, Amér C, Caribe & Méx* pal, mate *UK*, buddy *US*.

manojo *sm* bunch; **estar hecho un manojo de nervios** to be a bundle of nerves; **ser un manojo de nervios** to be hyperactive.

manoletina *sf* **- 1.** TAUROM *pass with the cape in bullfighting invented by the Spanish bullfighter, Manolete* **- 2.** [zapato] *type of open, low-heeled shoe, often with a bow; ver también* **tauromaquia**.

manómetro *sm* pressure gauge.

manopla *sf* mitten.

manoseado, da *adj* shabby, worn.

manosear *vt* **- 1.** [gen] to handle roughly; [papel, tela] to rumple **- 2.** [persona] to fondle.

manoseo *sm* fingering, touching.

manotazo *sm* slap.

mansalva ⬦ **a mansalva** *loc adv* [en abundancia] in abundance.

mansedumbre *sf* [gen] calmness, gentleness; [de animal] tameness.

mansión *sf* mansion.

manso, sa *adj* **- 1.** [apacible] calm, gentle **- 2.** [domesticado] tame **- 3.** *Chile* [extraordinario] tremendous.

manta ⬦ *sf* [para abrigarse] blanket; **manta eléctrica** electric blanket; **manta de viaje** travelling rug; **liarse la manta a la cabeza** to take the plunge; **tirar de la manta** to let the cat out of the bag. ⬦ *smf fam* [persona] hopeless *o* useless person; **mi hermano es un manta** my brother's useless.

manteca *sf* fat; [mantequilla] butter; **manteca de cacao** cocoa butter; **manteca de cerdo** lard.

mantecado *sm* **- 1.** [pastel] shortcake **- 2.** [helado] *ice-cream made of milk, eggs and sugar*.

mantecoso, sa *adj* fatty, greasy.

mantel *sm* tablecloth.

mantelería *sf* table linen.

mantener [72] *vt* **- 1.** [sustentar, aguantar] to support **- 2.** [conservar] to keep; [en buen estado] to maintain, to service **- 3.** [tener - relaciones, conversación] to have **- 4.** [defender - opinión] to stick to, to maintain; [- candidatura] to refuse to withdraw.

⬦ **mantenerse** *vprnl* **- 1.** [sustentarse] to subsist, to support o.s. **- 2.** [permanecer, continuar] to remain; [edificio] to remain standing; **mantenerse aparte** [en discusión] to stay out of it.

mantenido, da ⬦ *adj* sustained. ⬦ *sm, f* [hombre] gigolo; [mujer] kept woman.

mantenimiento *sm* **- 1.** [sustento] sustenance **- 2.** [conservación] upkeep, maintenance.

mantequera *sf* butter dish.

mantequería *sf* **- 1.** [fábrica] dairy, butter factory **- 2.** [tienda] grocer's (shop).

mantequilla *sf* butter.

mantiene *etc* ▷ **mantener**.

mantilla *sf* **- 1.** [de mujer] mantilla **- 2.** [de bebé] shawl **- 3.** *loc*: **estar en mantillas** [persona] to be wet behind the ears; [plan] to be in its infancy.

manto *sm* **- 1.** [gen] cloak **- 2.** GEOL mantle.

mantón *sm* shawl; **mantón de Manila** embroidered silk shawl.

mantuviera *etc* ⊳ **mantener**.

manual ⟨⟩ *adj* - **1.** [con las manos] manual - **2.** [manejable] easy-to-use. ⟨⟩ *sm* manual.

manubrio *sm* - **1.** crank - **2.** *Amér* [manillar] handlebars *pl*.

manufacturado, **da** *adj* manufactured.

manufacturar *vt* to manufacture.

manuscrito, **ta** *adj* handwritten.
➤ **manuscrito** *sm* manuscript.

manutención *sf* - **1.** [sustento] support, maintenance - **2.** [alimento] food.

manzana *sf* - **1.** [fruta] apple; **manzana de la discordia** bone of contention - **2.** [grupo de casas] block (of houses).

manzanilla *sf* - **1.** [planta] camomile - **2.** [infusión] camomile tea - **3.** [vino] manzanilla (sherry) - **4.** [aceituna] manzanilla *(type of small olive)*.

manzano *sm* apple tree.

maña *sf* - **1.** [destreza] skill; **tener maña para** to have a knack for; **más vale maña que fuerza** *prov* brain is better than brawn - **2.** [astucia] wits *pl*, guile *(U)*; **darse maña para hacer algo** to contrive to do sthg - **3.** [engaño] ruse, trick.

mañana ⟨⟩ *sf* morning; **a la mañana siguiente** the next morning; **(muy) de mañana** (very) early in the morning; **a las dos de la mañana** at two in the morning; **por la mañana** in the morning. ⟨⟩ *sm*: **el mañana** tomorrow, the future. ⟨⟩ *adv* tomorrow; **a partir de mañana** starting tomorrow, as of tomorrow; **¡hasta mañana!** see you tomorrow!; **mañana por la mañana** tomorrow morning; **pasado mañana** the day after tomorrow.

mañanero, **ra** *adj* - **1.** [madrugador] early rising - **2.** [matutino] morning *(antes de s)*.

mañanitas *sfpl Méx* birthday song *sing*.

maño, **ña** *sm*, *f fam* Aragonese.

mañoso, **sa** *adj* skilful.

mapa *sm* map; **mapa de carreteras** road map; **mapa físico/mudo/político** geographic/blank/political map; **mapa de bits** INFORM bit map; **desaparecer del mapa** *fam* to vanish into thin air.

mapamundi *sm* world map.

maqueta *sf* - **1.** [reproducción a escala] (scale) model - **2.** [de libro] dummy.

maqui = **maquis**.

maquiavélico, **ca** *adj* Machiavellian.

maquila *sf Amér* [de máquinas] assembly; [de ropas] making-up.

maquiladora *sf Amér* assembly plant.

Maquiladora ▬▬▬▬▬▬▬▬▬▬▬

In the 1980s many non-Mexican companies set up assembly plants in areas along the US-Mexican border. They were attracted by the low wages, special tax concessions and the proximity to the US market. They usually assemble parts manufactured elsewhere, and by law they must re-export 80 percent of their production. Today these **maquiladoras** are an important source of income for Mexico and they employ more than a million Mexicans – mostly women. The managers are usually foreigners, whereas the hourly-paid workers, who have little job security and few benefits, are Mexican.

maquillador, **ra** ⟨⟩ *adj* make-up *(antes de s)*. ⟨⟩ *sm*, *f* make-up artist.

maquillaje *sm* - **1.** [producto] make-up - **2.** [acción] making-up.

maquillar *vt* - **1.** [pintar] to make up - **2.** *fig* [disimular] to cover up, to disguise.
➤ **maquillarse** *vprnl* to make o.s. up.

máquina *sf* - **1.** [gen] machine; **a toda máquina** at full pelt; **coser a máquina** to machine-sew; **escribir a máquina** to type; **escrito a máquina** typewritten; **hecho a máquina** machine-made; **máquina de afeitar** electric razor; **máquina de coser** sewing machine; **máquina de escribir** typewriter; **máquina fotográfica** camera; **máquina registradora** cash register; **máquina tragaperras** o **traganíqueles** *Amér* slot machine, fruit machine *UK* - **2.** [locomotora] engine; **máquina de vapor** steam engine - **3.** [mecanismo] mechanism - **4.** *Cuba* [vehículo] car - **5.** [de estado, partido etc] machinery *(U)*.

maquinación *sf* machination.

maquinal *adj* mechanical.

maquinar *vt* to machinate, to plot; **maquinar algo contra alguien** to plot sthg against sb.

maquinaria *sf* - **1.** [gen] machinery - **2.** [de reloj etc] mechanism.

maquinilla *sf*: **maquinilla de afeitar** razor; **maquinilla eléctrica** electric razor.

maquinismo *sm* mechanization.

maquinista *smf* [de tren] engine driver *UK*, engineer *US*; [de barco] engineer.

maquis, **maqui** *smf inv* guerrilla.

mar *sm* o *sf lit & fig* sea; **hacerse a la mar** to set sail, to put (out) to sea; **mar adentro** out to sea; **alta mar** high seas *pl*; **mar de fondo** *lit & fig* groundswell; **mar gruesa** heavy sea; **el mar Egeo** the Aegean Sea; **el mar del Norte** the

North Sea; **el mar Tirreno** the Tyrrhenian Sea; **a mares** a lot; **llover a mares** to rain buckets; **la mar de** [un montón de] loads of, lots of; [muy] really, very; **es la mar de inteligente** she's really intelligent.

mar. (*abrev de* marzo) Mar.

marabunta *sf* - **1.** [de hormigas] plague of ants - **2.** [muchedumbre] crowd.

maraca *sf* maraca.

maracujá *sf Amér* passion fruit.

maraña *sf* - **1.** [maleza] thicket - **2.** *fig* [enredo] tangle.

maratón *sm o sf lit & fig* marathon.

maratoniano, na *adj* marathon.

maravilla *sf* - **1.** [gen] marvel, wonder; **es una maravilla** it's wonderful; **hacer maravillas** to do *o* work wonders; **a las mil maravillas, de maravilla** wonderfully; **venir de maravilla** to be just the thing *o* ticket - **2.** BOT marigold.

maravillar *vt* to amaze.

➤ **maravillarse** *vprnl*: **maravillarse (con)** to be amazed (by).

maravilloso, sa *adj* marvellous, wonderful.

marca *sf* - **1.** [señal] mark; [de rueda, animal] track; [en ganado] brand; [en papel] watermark; **marca de nacimiento** birthmark - **2.** [COM - de tabaco, café etc] brand; [- de coche, ordenador etc] make; **de marca** designer (*antes de s*); **marca de fábrica** trademark; **marca registrada** registered trademark - **3.** [etiqueta] label - **4.** [DEP - gen] performance; [- en carreras] time; [- plusmarca] record - **5.** *loc*: **de marca mayor** [muy grande] enormous; [excelente] outstanding.

marcado, da *adj* - **1.** [gen] marked - **2.** [pelo] set.

➤ **marcado** *sm* - **1.** [señalado] marking - **2.** [peinado] set.

marcador, ra *adj* marking.

➤ **marcador** *sm* - **1.** [tablero] scoreboard; **marcador electrónico** electronic scoreboard - **2.** [DEP - defensor] marker; [- goleador] scorer - **3.** [para libros] bookmark - **4.** *Amér* [rotulador] felt-tip pen; *Méx* [fluorescente] highlighter pen.

marcaje *sm* DEP marking.

marcapasos *sm inv* pacemaker.

marcar [10] <> *vt* - **1.** [gen] to mark - **2.** [poner precio a] to price - **3.** [indicar] to indicate - **4.** [anotar] to note down - **5.** [resaltar] to emphasise - **6.** [número de teléfono] to dial - **7.** [suj: termómetro, contador etc] to read; [suj: reloj] to say - **8.** [DEP - tanto] to score; [- a un jugador] to mark - **9.** [cabello] to set. <> *vi* - **1.** [dejar secuelas] to leave a mark - **2.** DEP [anotar un tanto] to score.

➤ **marcarse** *vprnl fam*: **marcarse un detalle** to do sthg nice *o* kind; **marcarse un tanto** to earn a Brownie point.

marcha *sf* - **1.** [partida] departure - **2.** [ritmo] speed; **a marchas forzadas** [contra reloj] against the clock; **a toda marcha** at top speed; **en marcha** [motor] running; [plan] underway; **poner en marcha** [gen] to start; [dispositivo, alarma] to activate; **ponerse en marcha** [persona] to start off; [máquina] to start; **hacer algo sobre la marcha** to do sthg as one goes along - **3.** AUTO gear; **cambiar de marcha** to change gear; **marcha atrás** reverse; **dar marcha atrás** AUTO to reverse; *fig* to back out - **4.** MIL & POLÍT march; **abrir la marcha** to head the procession; **cerrar la marcha** to bring up the rear - **5.** MÚS march; **marcha fúnebre/nupcial** funeral/wedding march; **Marcha Real** *Spanish national anthem* - **6.** [transcurso] course; [progreso] progress - **7.** DEP walk - **8.** *fam* [animación] liveliness, life; **hay mucha marcha** there's a great atmosphere; **ir de marcha** to go out on the town; **tener (mucha) marcha** to be a (real) raver.

marchante, ta *sm, f* - **1.** dealer - **2.** *Amér C, Méx & Ven* [cliente] customer, patron.

marchar *vi* - **1.** [andar] to walk - **2.** [partir] to leave, to go - **3.** [funcionar] to work - **4.** [desarrollarse] to progress; **el negocio marcha** business is going well.

➤ **marcharse** *vprnl* to leave, to go.

marchitar *vt lit & fig* to wither.

➤ **marchitarse** *vprnl* - **1.** [planta] to fade, to wither - **2.** *fig* [persona] to languish, to fade away.

marchito, ta *adj* - **1.** [planta] faded - **2.** *fig* [persona] worn.

marchoso, sa *fam* <> *adj* lively. <> *sm, f* livewire.

marcial *adj* martial.

marciano, na *adj & sm, f* Martian.

marco *sm* - **1.** [cerco] frame - **2.** *fig* [ambiente, paisaje] setting - **3.** [ámbito] framework - **4.** [moneda] mark - **5.** [portería] goalmouth.

marea *sf* - **1.** [del mar] tide; **marea alta/baja** high/low tide; **marea negra** oil slick - **2.** *fig* [multitud] flood.

mareado, da *adj* - **1.** [con náuseas] sick, queasy; [en coche, avión etc] travelsick - **2.** [aturdido] dizzy - **3.** *fig* [fastidiado] fed up to the back teeth.

marear *vt* - **1.** [provocar náuseas a] to make sick; [en coche, avión etc] to make travelsick; [en barco] to make seasick - **2.** [aturdir] to make dizzy - **3.** *fam* [fastidiar] to annoy.

➤ **marearse** *vprnl* - **1.** [tener náuseas] to feel sick; [en coche, avión etc] to feel travelsick; [en barco] to get seasick - **2.** [estar aturdido] to get dizzy - **3.** [emborracharse] to get drunk.

marejada *sf* - **1.** [mar rizada] heavy sea - **2.** *fig* [agitación] wave of discontent.

marejadilla *sf* slight swell.

maremoto *sm* tidal wave.

marengo ▷ **gris**.

mareo *sm* - **1.** [náuseas] sickness; [en coche, avión etc] travelsickness; [en barco] seasickness - **2.** [aturdimiento] dizziness, giddiness - **3.** *fam fig* [fastidio] drag, pain.

marfil *sm* ivory.

marga *sf* marl.

margarina *sf* margarine.

margarita *sf* - **1.** BOT daisy; **deshojar la margarita** to hum and haw, to shillyshally; **echar margaritas a los cerdos** to cast pearls before swine - **2.** IMPR daisy wheel.

margen *sm o sf* - **1.** (gen f) [de río] bank; [de camino] side - **2.** (gen m) [de página] margin - **3.** (gen m) COM margin; **margen de beneficio** profit margin - **4.** (gen m) [límites] leeway; **al margen de eso, hay otros factores** over and above this, there are other factors; **al margen de la ley** outside the law; **dejar al margen** to exclude; **estar al margen de** to have nothing to do with; **mantenerse al margen de** to keep out of; **margen de error** margin of error; **margen de seguridad** degree of certainty - **5.** (gen m) [ocasión]: **dar margen a alguien para hacer algo** to give sb the chance to do sthg.

marginación *sf* exclusion; **marginación social** exclusion from society.

marginado, da ◇ *adj* excluded. ◇ *sm, f* outcast.

marginal *adj* - **1.** [nota] marginal; [tema] minor - **2.** ARTE & POLÍT fringe.

marginalidad *sf* exclusion.

marginar *vt* - **1.** [excluir] to exclude, to make an outcast; [dar de lado] to give the cold shoulder - **2.** [omitir] to omit.

mariachi *sm* - **1.** [música] mariachi (music) - **2.** [orquesta] mariachi band.

marica *sm* mfam despec queer, poof.

Maricastaña ▷ **tiempo**.

maricón *sm* mfam despec queer, poof.

mariconada *sf* mfam despec [mala jugada] dirty trick.

mariconear *vi* mfam despec to camp it up.

mariconera *sf* fam (man's) clutch bag.

marido *sm* husband.

marihuana *sf* marijuana.

marimacho *sm* fam mannish woman; despec butch woman.

marimorena *sf* row; **armar la marimorena** *fig* to kick up a row.

marina ▷ **marino**.

marinar *vt* to marinate.

marine *sm* MIL marine.

marinería *sf* - **1.** [profesión] sailoring - **2.** [marineros] crew, seamen *pl*.

marinero, ra *adj* [gen] sea *(antes de s)*; [buque] seaworthy; [pueblo] seafaring.
➡ **marinero** *sm* sailor.

marino, na *adj* sea *(antes de s)*, marine.
➡ **marino** *sm* sailor.
➡ **marina** *sf* - **1.** [náutica] seamanship - **2.** MIL: **marino (de guerra)** navy; **marino mercante** merchant navy - **3.** ARTE seascape.

marioneta *sf* [muñeco] marionette, puppet.
➡ **marionetas** *sfpl* [teatro] puppet show *sing*.

mariposa *sf* - **1.** [insecto] butterfly - **2.** [tuerca] wing nut - **3.** [candela, luz] oil lamp - **4.** [en natación] butterfly - **5.** *loc*: **a otra cosa mariposa** let's move on.

mariposear *vi* - **1.** [ser inconstante] to flit about - **2.** [galantear] to flirt.

mariposón *sm* fam flirt, wolf.

mariquita ◇ *sf* [insecto] ladybird UK, ladybug US. ◇ *sm* mfam despec [homosexual] poof, queer.

marisabidilla *sf* know-all.

mariscada *sf* seafood dish.

mariscal *sm* marshal; **mariscal de campo** field marshal.

marisco *sm* seafood *(U)*, shellfish *(U)*.

marisma *sf* salt marsh.

marismeño, ña *adj* marshy.

marisquería *sf* seafood restaurant.

marital *adj* marital.

marítimo, ma *adj* [del mar] maritime; [cercano al mar] seaside *(antes de s)*.

marketing ['marketin] *sm* marketing; **marketing direct** direct marketing.

marmita *sf* pot.

mármol *sm* marble; **de mármol** *fig* cold, insensitive.

marmota *sf* marmot; **dormir como una marmota** to sleep like a log.

mar Muerto *sm*: **el mar Muerto** the Dead Sea.

mar Negro *sm*: **el mar Negro** the Black Sea.

maroma *sf* rope.

maromo *sm* fam bloke, guy.

marque etc ▷ **marcar**.

marqués, esa *sm* marquis (*f* marchioness).

marquesina *sf* glass canopy; [parada de autobús] bus-shelter.

marquetería *sf* marquetry.

marranada *sf fam* **- 1.** [porquería - estado] filthy mess; [- dicho] filthy thing, filth *(U)* **- 2.** [mala jugada] dirty trick.

marrano, na *sm, f* **- 1.** [animal] pig **- 2.** *fam fig* [sucio] (filthy) pig **- 3.** *fam fig* [sin escrúpulos] swine.

marras ➡ **de marras** *loc adj* aforementioned, said.

mar Rojo *sm*: **el mar Rojo** the Red Sea.

marrón *adj* & *sm* brown.

marroquí (*pl* **marroquíes** o **marroquís**) *adj* & *sm, f* Moroccan.

marroquinería *sf* **- 1.** [arte] leatherwork **- 2.** [artículos] leather goods *pl*.

Marruecos *n pr* Morocco.

Marte *sm* Mars.

martes *sm inv* Tuesday; **martes de Carnaval** Shrove Tuesday; **martes y trece** ≃ Friday 13th; *ver también* **sábado**.

martillear, martillar *vt* to hammer.

martillo *sm* **- 1.** hammer; **martillo neumático** pneumatic drill *UK*, jackhammer *US* **- 2.** *Col* [subasta] auction.

martinete *sm* heron.

martín pescador (*pl* **martín pescadores**) *sm* kingfisher.

mártir *smf lit & fig* martyr.

martirio *sm* **- 1.** RELIG martyrdom **- 2.** *fig* [sufrimiento] trial, torment; **ser un martirio chino** to be torture.

martirizar [13] *vt* **- 1.** [torturar] to martyr **- 2.** *fig* [hacer sufrir] to torment, to torture.

maruja *sf fam stereotyped housewife*.

marxismo *sm* Marxism.

marxista *adj* & *smf* Marxist.

marzo *sm* March; *ver también* **septiembre**.

mas *conj* but.

más ◇ *adv* **- 1.** *(compar)* more; **Pepe es más alto/ambicioso** Pepe is taller/more ambitious; **tener más hambre** to be hungrier o more hungry; **más de/que** more than; **más... que...** more... than...; **Juan es más alto que tú** Juan is taller than you; **de más** [de sobra] left over; **hay diez euros de más** there are ten euros left over; **eso está de más** that's not necessary **- 2.** *(superl)*: **el/la/lo más** the most; **el más listo/ambicioso** the cleverest/most ambitious **- 3.** *(en frases negativas)* any more; **no necesito más (trabajo)** I don't need any more (work) **- 4.** *(con pronombres interrogativos e indefinidos)* else; **¿qué/quién más?** what/who else?; **nadie más vino** nobody else came **- 5.** [indica suma] plus; **dos más dos igual a cuatro** two plus two is four **- 6.** [indica intensidad]: **no le aguanto, ¡es más tonto!** I can't stand him, he's so stupid!; **¡qué día más bonito!** what a lovely day! **- 7.** [indica preferencia]: **más vale que nos vayamos a casa** it would be better for us to go home **- 8.** *loc*: **el que más y el que menos** everyone; **es más** indeed, what is more; **más bien** rather; **más o menos** more or less; **¿qué más da?** what difference does it make?; **sin más (ni más)** just like that. ◇ *sm inv* MAT plus (sign); **tiene sus más y sus menos** it has its good points and its bad points.

➡ **a más de** *loc adv* in addition to, as well as.

➡ **por más que** *loc conj* however much; **por más que lo intente no lo conseguirá** however much o hard she tries, she'll never manage it.

masa *sf* **- 1.** [gen] mass; **masa atómica** atomic mass; **masa salarial** total wages bill **- 2.** [multitud] throng; **en masa** en masse **- 3.** CULIN dough **- 4.** ELECTR earth **- 5.** *R Dom* [pastelillo] cake.

➡ **masas** *sfpl*: **las masas** the masses.

masacrar *vt* to massacre.

masacre *sf* massacre.

masaje *sm* massage.

masajista *smf* masseur (*f* masseuse).

mascar [10] *vt* & *vi* to chew.

máscara *sf* **- 1.** [gen] mask; **máscara antigás** gas mask; **máscara de oxígeno** oxygen mask **- 2.** [pretexto] front, pretence; **quitar la máscara a alguien** to unmask sb; **quitarse la máscara** to reveal o.s.

mascarada *sf* **- 1.** [fiesta] masquerade **- 2.** *fig* [farsa] farce.

mascarilla *sf* **- 1.** MED mask **- 2.** [cosmética] face pack.

mascarón *sm* **- 1.** [máscara] large mask **- 2.** ARQUIT grotesque head; **mascarón de proa** figurehead.

mascota *sf* mascot.

masculinidad *sf* masculinity.

masculinizar [13] *vt* to make mannish.

masculino, na *adj* **- 1.** BIOL male **- 2.** [varonil] manly **- 3.** GRAM masculine.

mascullar *vt* to mutter.

masía *sf traditional Catalan or Aragonese farmhouse*.

masificación *sf* overcrowding.

masificar [10] *vt* to cause overcrowding in.

➡ **masificarse** *vprnl* to become overcrowded.

masilla *sf* putty.

masivo, va *adj* mass *(antes de s)*.

masoca *smf fam* masochist.

masón, ona ◇ *adj* masonic. ◇ *sm, f* mason, freemason.

masonería *sf* masonry, freemasonry.

masoquismo *sm* masochism.

masoquista ◇ *adj* masochistic. ◇ *smf* masochist.

masque *etc* ▷ **mascar**.

mass media, mass-media *smpl* mass media.

mastectomía *sf* mastectomy.

máster (*pl* **masters**) *sm* Master's (degree).

masticar [10] *vt* - **1**. [mascar] to chew - **2**. *fig* [pensar] to chew over, to ponder.

mástil *sm* - **1**. NÁUT mast - **2**. [palo] pole - **3**. MÚS neck.

mastín *sm* mastiff.

mastodonte ◇ *sm* mastodon. ◇ *smf fam* giant.

mastuerzo *sm fam* idiot.

masturbación *sf* masturbation.

masturbar *vt* to masturbate.
➡ **masturbarse** *vprnl* to masturbate.

mata *sf* [arbusto] bush, shrub; [matojo] tuft; **matas** scrub.
➡ **mata de pelo** *sf* mop of hair.

matadero *sm* abattoir, slaughterhouse.

matador, ra *fam adj* - **1**. [cansado] killing, exhausting - **2**. [feo] awful, horrendous.
➡ **matador** *sm* matador; *ver también* **tauromaquia**.

matambre *sm Andes & Ven* [carne] flank *o UK* skirt steak; [plato] *flank steak rolled with boiled egg, olives and red pepper, which is cooked and then sliced and served cold.*

matamoscas *sm inv* [pala] flyswat; [espray] flyspray.

matanza *sf* - **1**. [masacre] slaughter - **2**. [del cerdo] pig-killing.

matar *vt* - **1**. [gen] to kill; **estar a matar con alguien** to be at daggers drawn with sb; **matarlas callando** to be up to sthg on the quiet - **2**. [molestar] to drive mad - **3**. [apagar - color] to tone down; [- sed] to slake, to quench; [- hambre] to stay - **4**. [redondear, limar] to round (off).
➡ **matarse** *vprnl* - **1**. [morir] to die - **2**. [suicidarse, esforzarse] to kill o.s.; **matarse a trabajar** to work o.s. to death; **matarse por hacer algo** to kill o.s. in order to do sthg.

matarratas *sm inv* - **1**. [veneno] rat poison - **2**. *fig* [bebida] rotgut.

matasanos *smf inv despec* quack.

matasellos *smf inv* postmark.

matasuegras *sm inv* (party) cracker.

match [matʃ] (*pl* **matches**) *sm* match.
➡ **match ball** ['matʃβol] (*pl* **match balls**) *sm* match ball.

mate ◇ *adj* matt. ◇ *sm* - **1**. [en ajedrez] mate, checkmate - **2**. [en baloncesto] dunk; [en tenis] smash - **3**. BOT [bebida] maté.

Mate

Maté is the national drink in the River Plate region. It is an infusion made using dry maté leaves (**yerba mate**). The drink is made and served in a small hollow gourd, and is drunk through a metal tube called a **bombilla**.

matemático, ca ◇ *adj* mathematical. ◇ *sm, f* [científico] mathematician.
➡ **matemáticas** *sfpl* [ciencia] mathematics (U).

materia *sf* - **1**. [sustancia] matter; **materia grasa** fat; **materia gris** grey matter; **materia orgánica** organic matter - **2**. [material] material; **materia prima, primera materia** raw material - **3**. [tema, asignatura] subject; **en materia de** on the subject of, concerning; **entrar en materia** to get down to business.

material ◇ *adj* - **1**. [gen] physical; [daños, consecuencias] material - **2**. [real] real, actual. ◇ *sm* - **1**. [gen] material; **material de desecho** waste material; **material refractario** heat-resistant material - **2**. [instrumentos] equipment; **material bélico** *o* **de guerra** war material; **material de oficina** office stationery.

materialismo *sm* materialism; **materialismo dialéctico/histórico** dialectical/historical materialism.

materialista ◇ *adj* materialistic. ◇ *smf* materialist.

materializar [13] *vt* - **1**. [idea, proyecto] to realize - **2**. [hacer tangible] to produce.
➡ **materializarse** *vprnl* to materialize.

maternal *adj* motherly, maternal.

maternidad *sf* - **1**. [cualidad] motherhood - **2**. [hospital] maternity hospital.

materno, na *adj* maternal; [lengua] mother (*antes de s*).

matice *etc* ▷ **matizar**.

matinal *adj* morning (*antes de s*).

matiz *sm* - **1**. [variedad - de color, opinión] shade; [- de sentido] nuance, shade of meaning - **2**. [atisbo] trace, hint.

matizar [13] *vt* - **1**. [teñir]: **matizar (de)** to tinge (with) - **2**. *fig* [distinguir - rasgos, aspectos] to distinguish; [- tema] to explain in detail - **3**. *fig* [dar tono especial] to tinge, to colour - **4**. ARTE to blend.

matojo *sm* [mata] tuft; [arbusto] bush, shrub.

matón, ona *sm, f fam* bully.

matorral *sm* thicket.

matraca *sf* [instrumento] rattle; **dar la matraca** *fam fig* to go on, to be a nuisance; **ser una matraca** *fam* to be a pain.

matriarcado *sm* matriarchy.

matrícula *sf* - **1.** [inscripción] registration - **2.** [documento] registration document - **3.** AUTO number plate.

➤ **matrícula de honor** *sf* top marks *pl*.

matriculación *sf* [inscripción] registration.

matricular *vt* to register.

➤ **matricularse** *vprnl* to register.

matrimonial *adj* marital; [vida] married.

matrimonio *sm* - **1.** [gen] marriage; **consumar el matrimonio** to consummate one's marriage; **contraer matrimonio** to get married; **fuera del matrimonio** out of wedlock; **matrimonio civil** civil marriage; **matrimonio de conveniencia** marriage of convenience; **matrimonio religioso** church wedding - **2.** [pareja] married couple.

matriz ◇ *sf* - **1.** ANAT womb - **2.** [de talonario] (cheque) stub - **3.** [molde] mould - **4.** MAT matrix. ◇ *adj* [empresa] parent *(antes de s)*; [casa] head *(antes de s)*; [iglesia] mother *(antes de s)*.

matrona *sf* - **1.** [madre] matron - **2.** [comadrona] midwife - **3.** [en aduanas] *female customs officer responsible for frisking women travellers* - **4.** [en cárceles] female prison warden.

matusalén *sm* very old person; **ser más viejo que matusalén** *fig* to be as old as Methuselah.

matutino, na *adj* morning *(antes de s)*.

maullar *vi* to miaow.

maullido *sm* miaow, miaowing *(U)*.

Mauricio *n pr* Mauritius.

mausoleo *sm* mausoleum.

maxilar ◇ *adj* maxillary, jaw *(antes de s)*. ◇ *sm* jaw.

máxima ▷ **máximo**.

máxime *adv* especially.

máximo, ma ◇ *superl* = **grande**. ◇ *adj* maximum; [galardón, puntuación] highest.

➤ **máximo** *sm* maximum; **al máximo** to the utmost; **llegar al máximo** to reach the limit; **como máximo** [a más tardar] at the latest; [como mucho] at the most.

➤ **máxima** *sf* - **1.** [sentencia, principio] maxim - **2.** [temperatura] high, highest temperature.

maya ◇ *adj* Mayan. ◇ *smf* Maya, Mayan. ◇ *sm* [lengua] Maya.

mayestático, ca *adj* majestic.

mayo *sm* May; *ver también* **septiembre**.

mayonesa, mahonesa *sf* mayonnaise.

mayor ◇ *adj* - **1.** *(compar)*: **mayor (que)** [de tamaño] bigger (than); [de importancia etc] greater (than); [de edad] older (than); [de número] higher (than) - **2.** *(superl)*: **el/la mayor...** [de tamaño]

the biggest...; [de importancia etc] the greatest...; [de edad] the oldest...; [de número] the highest... - **3.** [adulto] grown-up; **hacerse mayor** to grow up; **ser mayor de edad** to be an adult - **4.** [anciano] elderly - **5.** MÚS: **en do mayor** in C major - **6.** *loc*: **al por mayor** COM wholesale. ◇ *smf*: **el/la mayor** [hijo, hermano] the eldest. ◇ *sm* MIL major.

➤ **mayores** *smpl* - **1.** [adultos] grown-ups - **2.** [antepasados] ancestors, forefathers.

mayoral *sm* - **1.** [pastor] chief herdsman - **2.** [capataz] foreman, overseer.

mayorazgo *sm* - **1.** [institución] primogeniture - **2.** [bienes] entailed estate - **3.** [persona] *heir to an entailed estate*; [primogénito] eldest son.

mayordomo *sm* butler.

mayoreo *sm Amér* wholesale; **al mayoreo** wholesale.

mayoría *sf* majority; **son mayoría** they are in the majority; **la mayoría de** most of; **la mayoría de los españoles** most Spaniards; **la mayoría de las veces** usually, most often; **en su mayoría** in the main; **mayoría absoluta/relativa** absolute/relative majority; **mayoría silenciosa** silent majority; **mayoría simple** simple majority.

➤ **mayoría de edad** *sf*: **llegar a la mayoría de edad** to come of age.

mayorista ◇ *adj* wholesale. ◇ *smf* wholesaler.

mayoritario, ria *adj* majority *(antes de s)*.

mayúscula ▷ **letra**.

mayúsculo, la *adj* tremendous, enormous.

maza *sf* mace; [del bombo] drumstick.

mazacote *sm* dry, sticky food.

mazapán *sm* marzipan.

mazazo *sm lit & fig* heavy blow.

mazmorra *sf* dungeon.

mazo *sm* - **1.** [martillo] mallet - **2.** [de mortero] pestle - **3.** [conjunto - de cartas, papeles] bundle; [- de billetes] wad; [- de naipes] balance (of the deck).

mazorca *sf* cob; **mazorca de maíz** corncob.

mazurca *sf* mazurka.

MB *(abrev de **megabyte**) sm* INFORM MB.

MDSMA *sm (abrev de **Ministerio de Desarrollo Sostenible y Medio Ambiente**), Bolivian Department of Sustainable Development and the Environment*.

me *pron pers* - **1.** *(complemento directo)* me; **le gustaría verme** she'd like to see me - **2.** *(complemento indirecto)* (to) me; **me lo dio** he gave it to me; **me tiene miedo** he's afraid of me - **3.** *(reflexivo)* myself.

meada *sf vulg* piss; [mancha] urine stain.

meandro *sm* meander.

mear *vi vulg* to piss.

◆ **mearse** *vprnl vulg* to piss o.s.; **mearse en la cama** to wet one's bed; **mearse (de risa)** to piss o.s. laughing.

MEC *sm* (*abrev de* **Ministerio de Educación y Cultura**), *Uruguayan Department of Education and Culture.*

meca *sf* mecca.

mecachis *interj fam eufem*: **¡mecachis!** sugar! *UK*, shoot! *US*

mecánica ▷ **mecánico**.

mecanicismo *sm* mechanism.

mecánico, ca ◇ *adj* mechanical. ◇ *sm, f* [persona] mechanic; **mecánico dentista** dental technician.

◆ **mecánica** *sf* - **1.** [ciencia] mechanics *(U)* - **2.** [funcionamiento] mechanics *pl*.

mecanismo *sm* - **1.** [estructura] mechanism - **2.** [funcionamiento] way of working, modus operandi; **mecanismos de defensa** PSICOL defence mechanisms.

mecanización *sf* mechanization.

mecanizado, da *adj* mechanized.

mecanizar [13] *vt* to mechanize.

mecano® *sm* Meccano®.

mecanografía *sf* typing; **mecanografía al tacto** touch typing.

mecanografiar [9] *vt* to type.

mecanógrafo, fa *sm, f* typist.

mecapal *sm Amér C & Méx* porter's leather harness.

mecedora *sf* rocking chair.

mecenas *smf inv* patron.

mecenazgo *sm* patronage.

mecer [11] *vt* to rock.

◆ **mecerse** *vprnl* to rock back and forth; [en columpio] to swing.

mecha *sf* - **1.** [de vela] wick - **2.** [de explosivos] fuse; **a toda mecha** *fam* flat out; **aguantar mecha** *fam* to grin and bear it - **3.** [de pelo] streak.

mechero *sm* (cigarette) lighter.

mechón *sm* [de pelo] lock; [de lana] tuft.

medalla *sf* medal; **ponerse medallas** *fig* to show off.

medallero *sm* medals table.

medallista *smf* - **1.** [oficio] maker of medals - **2.** DEP medallist.

medallón *sm* - **1.** [joya] medallion - **2.** [rodaja] médaillon; **medallón de pescado** [empanado] fishcake.

médano *sm* (sand) dune.

media *sf* - **1.** ▷ **medio** - **2.** *Amér* [calcetín] sock.

mediación *sf* mediation; **por mediación de** through.

mediado, da *adj* [medio lleno] half-full; **mediada la película** halfway through the film.

◆ **a mediados de** *loc prep* in the middle of, halfway through.

mediador, ra ◇ *adj* mediating. ◇ *sm, f* mediator.

mediagua *sf R Dom* shack, hut.

medialuna *sf Amér* croissant.

mediana ▷ **mediano**.

medianía *sf* average *o* mediocre person.

mediano, na *adj* - **1.** [intermedio - de tamaño] medium; [- de calidad] average; **de mediana edad** middle-aged; **de mediana estatura** of medium *o* average height - **2.** [mediocre] average, ordinary.

◆ **mediana** *sf* - **1.** GEOM median - **2.** [de carretera] central reservation.

medianoche (*pl* **mediasnoches**) *sf* - **1.** [hora] midnight; **a medianoche** at midnight - **2.** [bollo] *sandwich made with a small bun.*

mediante *prep* by means of.

mediar [8] *vi* - **1.** [llegar a la mitad] to be halfway through; **mediaba julio** it was mid-July - **2.** [estar en medio - tiempo, distancia, espacio]: **mediar entre** to be between; **media un jardín/ un kilómetro entre las dos casas** there is a garden/one kilometre between the two houses; **medió una semana** a week passed by - **3.** [intervenir]: **mediar (en/entre)** to mediate (in/between) - **4.** [interceder]: **mediar (en favor de** *o* **por)** to intercede (on behalf of *o* for) - **5.** [ocurrir] to intervene, to happen; **media la circunstancia de que...** it so happens that...

mediatizar [13] *vt* to determine.

medicación *sf* medication.

medicamento *sm* medicine.

medicar [10] *vt* to give medicine to.

◆ **medicarse** *vprnl* to take medicine.

medicina *sf* medicine; **ejercer la medicina** to practise medicine; **medicina alternativa** alternative medicine; **medicina interna** general medicine *o* practice; **medicina preventiva/ social** preventive/community medicine.

medicinal *adj* medicinal.

medición *sf* measurement.

médico, ca ◇ *adj* medical. ◇ *sm, f* doctor; **ir al médico** to go to the doctor; **médico de cabecera** *o* **familia** family doctor, general practitioner; **médico de guardia** duty doctor; **médico forense** specialist in forensic medicine; **médico interno** houseman *UK*, intern *US*.

medida *sf* - **1.** [gen] measure; [medición] measurement; **a (la) medida** [gen] custom-built; [ropa] made-to-measure; **medida de capacidad** measure (liquid or dry) - **2.** [disposición] measure, step; **tomar medidas** to take measures *o* steps; **medida cautelar** precautionary measure; **medidas represivas** clampdown *sing*; **medidas de seguridad** security measures - **3.** [moderación] moderation; **sin medida** without moderation - **4.** [grado] extent, degree; **en cierta/gran medida** to some/a large extent; **en la medida de lo posible** as far as possible; **en mayor/menor medida** to a greater/lesser extent; **a medida que entraban** as they were coming in.

◆ **medidas** *sfpl* [del cuerpo] measurements; **tomar las medidas a alguien** to take sb's measurements.

medidor *sm Amér* meter.

medieval *adj* medieval.

medievo, medioevo *sm* Middle Ages *pl*.

medina *sf* medina.

medio, dia *adj* - **1.** [gen] half; **a medio camino** [en viaje] halfway there; [en trabajo etc] halfway through; **media docena/hora** half a dozen/an hour; **medio pueblo estaba allí** half the town was there; **a media luz** in the half-light; **hacer algo a medias** to half-do sthg; **pagar a medias** to go halves, to share the cost; **un kilo y medio** one and a half kilos; **son (las dos) y media** it's half past (two) - **2.** [intermedio - estatura, tamaño] medium; [- posición, punto] middle - **3.** [de promedio - temperatura, velocidad] average - **4.** [corriente] ordinary, average.

◆ **medio** ◇ *adv* half; **medio borracho** half drunk; **a medio hacer** half done. ◇ *sm* - **1.** [mitad] half - **2.** [centro] middle, centre; **en medio (de)** in the middle (of); **estar por (en) medio** to be in the way; **equivocarse de medio a medio** to be completely wrong; **meterse o ponerse de por medio** to get in the way; *fig* to interfere; **quitar de en medio a alguien** to get rid of sb, to get sb out of the way - **3.** [sistema, manera] means, method; **por medio de** by means of, through - **4.** [elemento físico] environment; **medio ambiente** environment - **5.** [ambiente social] circle; **en medios bien informados** in well-informed circles - **6.** DEP midfielder.

◆ **medios** *smpl* [recursos] means, resources; **los medios de comunicación** o **información** the media; **medios de producción/transporte** means of production/transport.

◆ **media** *sf* - **1.** [promedio] average; **media aritmética/proporcional** arithmetic/proportional mean; **media horaria** hourly average - **2.** [hora]: **al dar la media** on the half-hour - **3.** (gen pl) [prenda] tights *pl*, stockings *pl* - **4.** DEP midfielders *pl*.

medioambiental *adj* environmental.

mediocampista *smf* midfielder.

mediocre *adj* mediocre, average.

mediocridad *sf* mediocrity.

mediodía (*pl* **mediodías**) *sm* - **1.** [hora] midday, noon; **al mediodía** at noon o midday - **2.** [sur] south.

medioevo = medievo.

mediofondista *smf* middle-distance runner.

mediopensionista *smf child who has lunch at school.*

medique *etc* ⊳ medicar.

medir [26] *vt* - **1.** [gen] to measure; **¿cuánto mides?** how tall are you?; **mido 1,80** ≃ I'm 6 foot (tall); **mide diez metros** it's ten metres long - **2.** [pros, contras etc] to weigh up - **3.** [palabras] to weigh carefully - **4.** [fuerzas] to test out against each other.

◆ **medirse** *vprnl* - **1.** [tomarse medidas] to measure o.s. - **2.** [moderarse] to show restraint - **3.** [enfrentarse]: **medirse con** to meet, to compete against.

meditabundo, da *adj* thoughtful, pensive.

meditación *sf* meditation.

meditar ◇ *vi*: **meditar (sobre)** to meditate (on). ◇ *vt* - **1.** [gen] to meditate, to ponder - **2.** [planear] to plan, to think through.

meditativo, va *adj* pensive.

mediterráneo, a *adj* Mediterranean.

◆ **Mediterráneo** *sm*: **el (mar) Mediterráneo** the Mediterranean (Sea).

médium *smf inv* medium.

medrar *vi* - **1.** [prosperar] to prosper - **2.** [enriquecerse] to get rich - **3.** [crecer] to grow.

medroso, sa ◇ *adj* [miedoso] fearful. ◇ *sm, f* fearful person.

médula *sf* - **1.** ANAT (bone) marrow; **médula espinal** spinal cord; **médula ósea** bone marrow - **2.** [esencia] core; **hasta la médula** to the core.

medusa *sf* jellyfish.

megabyte [megaˈβait] *sm* INFORM megabyte.

megafonía *sf* public-address system; **llamar por megafonía a alguien** to page sb.

megáfono *sm* megaphone.

megalito *sm* megalith.

megalómano, na *adj & sm, f* megalomaniac.

mejicanismo = mexicanismo.

mejicano, na = mexicano.

Méjico *n pr* = México.

mejilla *sf* cheek.

mejillón *sm* mussel; **mejillones a la marinera** *mussels cooked in a tomato, onion and garlic sauce.*

mejor ◇ *adj* - **1.** (compar) better; **no hay nada mejor** there's nothing better, there's nothing to beat it; **mejor (que)** better (than); **es mejor padre que marido** he's a better father than he is a husband **- 2.** *(superl)*: **el/la mejor...** the best...; **su mejor amigo** his best friend; **con la mejor voluntad** with the best will in the world. ◇ *smf*: **el/la mejor (de)** the best (in); **el mejor de todos** the best of all; **lo mejor fue que...** the best thing was that... ◇ *adv* **- 1.** *(compar)*: **mejor (que)** better (than); **ahora veo mejor** I can see better now; **es mejor que no vengas** it would be better if you didn't come; **estar mejor** [no tan malo] to feel better; [recuperado] to be better; **mejor que mejor** so much the better **- 2.** *(superl)* best; **el que la conoce mejor** the one who knows her best.

➡ **a lo mejor** *loc adv* maybe, perhaps.

➡ **mejor dicho** *loc adv* (or) rather.

mejora *sf* **- 1.** [progreso] improvement **- 2.** [aumento] increase.

mejorable *adj* improvable.

mejorar ◇ *vt* **- 1.** [gen] to improve; [enfermo] to make better **- 2.** [aumentar] to increase. ◇ *vi* to improve, to get better.

➡ **mejorarse** *vprnl* to improve, to get better; **¡que te mejores!** get well soon!

mejoría *sf* improvement.

mejunje *sm* *lit & fig* concoction.

melancolía *sf* melancholy.

melancólico, ca ◇ *adj* melancholic. ◇ *sm, f* melancholic person.

melanina *sf* melanin.

melaza *sf* molasses *pl*.

melena *sf* **- 1.** [de persona] long hair *(U)*; **soltarse la melena** to let one's hair down **- 2.** [de león] mane.

➡ **melenas** *sfpl despec* mop *sing* of hair.

melenudo, da *despec* ◇ *adj* with a mop of hair. ◇ *sm, f* person with a mop of hair.

melifluo, flua *adj* honeyed, mellifluous.

melindre *sm* CULIN *fried cake made from honey and sugar.*

➡ **melindres** *smpl* [escrúpulos] affected scrupulousness *(U)*.

melindroso, sa ◇ *adj* affectedly scrupulous. ◇ *sm, f* affectedly scrupulous person.

melisa *sf* lemon balm.

mella *sf* [gen] nick; [en dentadura] gap; **hacer mella en algo** [dañar] to dent sthg; **hacer mella en alguien** to make an impression on sb.

mellado, da *adj* **- 1.** [con hendiduras] nicked **- 2.** [sin dientes] gap-toothed.

mellar *vt* **- 1.** [hacer mellas en] to nick, to chip **- 2.** [menoscabar] to damage.

mellizo, za *adj & sm, f* twin.

melocotón *sm* peach.

melocotonero *sm* peach tree.

melodía *sf* **- 1.** MÚS melody, tune **- 2.** [de teléfono móvil] ring tone.

melódico, ca *adj* melodic.

melodioso, sa *adj* melodious.

melodrama *sm* melodrama.

melodramático, ca *adj* melodramatic.

melomanía *sf* love of music.

melómano, na *sm, f* music lover.

melón *sm* **- 1.** [fruta] melon **- 2.** *fam* [persona] lemon, idiot.

melopea *sf* *fam*: **agarrar una melopea** to get legless.

melosidad *sf* sweetness; [empalago] sickliness.

meloso, sa *adj* **- 1.** [como la miel] honey; *fig* sweet **- 2.** [empalagoso] sickly.

membrana *sf* membrane.

membranoso, sa *adj* membranous.

membresía *sf* *Amér* membership.

membrete *sm* letterhead.

membrillo *sm* **- 1.** [fruto] quince **- 2.** [dulce] quince jelly.

memez *sf* stupidity; [acción, dicho] silly o stupid thing.

memo, ma ◇ *adj* stupid. ◇ *sm, f* idiot, fool.

memorable *adj* memorable.

memorándum *(pl* **memorándum** o **memorandos)** *sm* **- 1.** [cuaderno] notebook **- 2.** [nota diplomática] memorandum.

memoria *sf* **- 1.** [gen & INFORM] memory; **si la memoria no me falla** if my memory serves me right; **¡qué memoria la mía!** what a memory I have!; **de memoria** by heart; **falta de memoria** forgetfulness; **hacer memoria** to try to remember; **tener buena/mala memoria** to have a good/bad memory; **traer a la memoria** to call to mind; **venir a la memoria** to come to mind; **memoria de acceso aleatorio/de sólo lectura** INFORM random-access/read only memory; **memoria expandida/extendida/programable** INFORM expanded/extended/programmable memory; **memoria RAM/ROM** INFORM RAM/ROM **- 2.** [recuerdo] remembrance, remembering; **ser de feliz/ingrata memoria** to be a happy/an unhappy memory **- 3.** [disertación] (academic) paper **- 4.** [informe]: **memoria (anual)** (annual) report **- 5.** [lista] list, record.

➡ **memorias** *sfpl* [biografía] memoirs.

memorial *sm* petition, request.

memorización *sf* memorizing.

memorizar **[13]** *vt* to memorize.

menaje *sm* household goods and furnishings *pl*; **menaje de cocina** kitchenware.

mención *sf* mention; **hacer mención de** to mention; **mención honorífica** honourable mention.

mencionar *vt* to mention.

menda <> *pron fam* [el que habla] yours truly. <> *smf* [uno cualquiera]: **vino un menda y...** this bloke came along and...

mendigar [16] <> *vt* to beg for. <> *vi* to beg.

mendigo, ga *sm, f* beggar.

mendrugo *sm* crust (of bread).

menear *vt* - **1.** [mover - gen] to move; [- cabeza] to shake; [- cola] to wag; [- caderas] to wiggle - **2.** [activar] to get moving.

➤ **menearse** *vprnl* - **1.** [moverse] to move (about); [agitarse] to shake; [oscilar] to sway - **2.** [darse prisa, espabilarse] to get a move on - **3.** *loc*: **un susto de no te menees** *fam* a hell of a scare.

meneo *sm* [gen] movement; [de cabeza] shake; [de cola] wag, wagging *(U)*; [de caderas] wiggling *(U)*; **dar un meneo a algo** *fam* to knock sthg; **dar un meneo a alguien** *fam* to give sb a hiding.

menester *sm* necessity; **haber menester de algo** to be in need of sthg; **ser menester que alguien haga algo** to be necessary for sb to do sthg.

➤ **menesteres** *smpl* [asuntos] business *(U)*, matters *pl*.

menesteroso, sa <> *adj* needy, poor. <> *sm, f* needy o poor person.

menestra *sf* vegetable stew.

mengano, na *sm, f* so-and-so.

mengua *sf* [reducción] reduction; [falta] lack; [descrédito] discredit; **sin mengua de** without detriment to.

menguado, da *adj* reduced, diminished.

menguante *adj* [luna] waning.

menguar [45] <> *vi* - **1.** [disminuir] to decrease, to diminish; [luna] to wane - **2.** [en labor de punto] to decrease. <> *vt* - **1.** [disminuir] to lessen, to diminish - **2.** [en labor de punto] to decrease.

menhir *sm* menhir.

meninge *sf* meninx.

meningitis *sf inv* meningitis.

menisco *sm* meniscus.

menopausia *sf* menopause.

menor <> *adj* - **1.** *(compar)*: **menor (que)** [de tamaño] smaller (than); [de edad] younger (than); [de importancia etc] less o lesser (than); [de número] lower (than) - **2.** *(superl)*: **el/la menor...** [de tamaño] the smallest...; [de edad] the youngest...; [de importancia] the slightest...; [de número] the lowest... - **3.** [de poca importancia] minor; **un problema menor** a minor problem - **4.** [joven]: **ser menor de edad** [para votar, conducir etc] to be under age; DER to be a minor - **5.** MÚS: **en do menor** in C minor - **6.** *loc*: **al por menor** COM retail. <> *smf* - **1.** *(superl)*: **el/la menor** [hijo, hermano] the youngest - **2.** DER [niño] minor.

Menorca *n pr* Minorca.

menos <> *adj inv* - **1.** *(compar)* [cantidad] less; [número] fewer; **menos aire** less air; **menos manzanas** fewer apples; **menos... que...** less/fewer... than...; **tiene menos experiencia que tú** she has less experience than you; **hace menos calor que ayer** it's not as hot as it was yesterday - **2.** *(superl)* [cantidad] the least; [número] the fewest; **el que compró menos acciones** the one who bought the fewest shares; **lo que menos tiempo llevó** the thing that took the least time - **3.** *fam* [peor]: **éste es menos coche que el mío** that car isn't as good as mine. <> *adv* - **1.** *(compar)* less; **menos de/que** less than; **estás menos gordo** you're not as fat - **2.** *(superl)*: **el/la/lo menos** the least; **él es el menos indicado para criticar** he's the last person who should be criticizing; **ella es la menos adecuada para el cargo** she's the least suitable person for the job; **es lo menos que puedo hacer** it's the least I can do - **3.** [expresa resta] minus; **tres menos dos igual a uno** three minus two is one - **4.** [con las horas] to; **son (las dos) menos diez** it's ten to (two) - **5.** *loc*: **es lo de menos** that's the least of it, that's of no importance; **hacer de menos a alguien** to snub sb; **¡menos mal!** just as well!, thank God!; **no es para menos** not without (good) reason; **venir a menos** to go down in the world. <> *sm inv* MAT minus (sign). <> *prep* [excepto] except (for); **todo menos eso** anything but that.

➤ **al menos, por lo menos** *loc adv* at least.

➤ **a menos que** *loc conj* unless; **no iré a menos que me acompañes** I won't go unless you come with me.

➤ **de menos** *loc adj* [que falta] missing; **hay dos euros de menos** there's two euros missing.

menoscabar *vt* [fama, honra etc] to damage; [derechos, intereses, salud] to harm; [belleza, perfección] to diminish.

menoscabo *sm* [de fama, honra etc] damage; [de derechos, intereses, salud] harm; [de belleza, perfección] diminishing; **(ir) en menoscabo de** (to be) to the detriment of.

menospreciar [8] *vt* [despreciar] to scorn, to despise; [infravalorar] to undervalue.

menosprecio *sm* scorn, contempt.

mensaje *sm* [gen & INFORM] message; **mensaje de texto** [en teléfono móvil] text message.

mensajería *sf* - **1.** [de paquetes, cartas] courier service - **2.** [por teléfono] messaging; **mensajería de imágenes** picture messaging.

mensajero, ra <> *adj* message-carrying; *fig* announcing, presaging. <> *sm, f* [gen] messenger; [de mensajería] courier.

menstruación *sf* menstruation.

menstrual *adj* menstrual.

menstruar [6] *vi* to menstruate, to have a period.

mensual *adj* monthly; **1.000 euros mensuales** 1,000 euros a month.

mensualidad *sf* - **1.** [sueldo] monthly salary - **2.** [pago] monthly payment *o* instalment.

menta *sf* mint.

mentado, da *adj* - **1.** [mencionado] above-mentioned, aforementioned - **2.** [famoso] famous.

mental *adj* mental.

mentalidad *sf* mentality; **mentalidad abierta/cerrada** open/closed mind.

mentalización *sf* mental preparation.

mentalizar [13] *vt* to put into a frame of mind.
➤ **mentalizarse** *vprnl* to get into a frame of mind.

mentar [19] *vt* to mention.

mente *sf* - **1.** [gen] mind; **tener en mente algo** to have sthg in mind; **tener en mente hacer algo** to intend to do sthg; **traer a la mente** to bring to mind - **2.** [mentalidad] mentality; **tiene una mente muy abierta** she's very open-minded.

mentecato, ta *sm, f* idiot.

mentir [27] *vi* to lie; **me mintió** she lied to me, she told me a lie; **¡mientes descaradamente!** you're lying shamelessly!, you're a barefaced liar!; **miente como respira** she lies through her teeth.

mentira *sf* lie; [acción] lying; **aunque parezca mentira** strange as it may seem; **de mentira** pretend, false; **parece mentira (que...)** it hardly seems possible (that...), it's scarcely credible (that...); **una mentira como una casa** a whopping great lie; **mentira piadosa** white lie.

mentirijillas ➤ **de mentirijillas** *fam* ◇ *loc adv* [en broma] as a joke, in fun. ◇ *loc adj* [falso] pretend, make-believe.

mentiroso, sa ◇ *adj* lying; [engañoso] deceptive. ◇ *sm, f* liar.

mentís *sm inv* denial; **dar un mentís (a)** to issue a denial (of).

mentol *sm* menthol.

mentolado, da *adj* mentholated.

mentón *sm* chin.

mentor, ra *sm, f* mentor.

menú (*pl* **menús**) *sm* - **1.** [lista] menu; [comida] food; **menú del día** set meal - **2.** INFORM menu; **menú desplegable** pull-down menu.

menudear ◇ *vi* to happen frequently. ◇ *vt* to repeat, to do repeatedly.

menudencia *sf* trifle, insignificant thing.

menudeo *sm* Amér COM retailing.

menudillos *smpl* giblets.

menudo, da *adj* - **1.** [pequeño] small - **2.** [insignificante] trifling, insignificant - **3.** *(antes de s)* [para enfatizar] what!; **¡menudo lío/gol!** what a mess/goal!
➤ **a menudo** *loc adv* often.

meñique ➤ **dedo**.

meollo *sm* core, heart; **llegar al meollo de la cuestión** to come to the heart of the matter.

meón, ona *sm, f fam*: **es una meona** [niña] she's always wetting herself; [mujer] she has a weak bladder.

mequetrefe *smf fam* good-for-nothing.

mercachifle *smf despec* - **1.** [comerciante] pedlar - **2.** [usurero] money-grabber, shark.

mercader *smf* trader.

mercadería *sf* merchandise, goods *pl*.

mercadillo *sm* flea market.

mercado *sm* market; **salir al mercado** to come on to the market; **mercado alcista/bajista** bull/bear market; **mercado bursátil** stock market; **mercado común** Common Market; **mercado de abastos** COM wholesale food market; **mercado de capitales/divisas/valores** capital/currency/securities market; **mercado de futuros** futures market; **mercado de trabajo** labour *o* job market; **mercado interbancario** interbank market; **mercado libre/negro** free/black market; **Mercado Único Europeo** European Single Market.

mercadotecnia *sf* marketing.

mercancía *sf* merchandise *(U)*, goods *pl*.
➤ **mercancías** *sm inv* FERROC goods train, freight train *US*.

mercante *adj* merchant.

mercantil *adj* mercantile, commercial.

mercantilismo *sm* ECON mercantilism; *fig* commercialism.

merced *sf* favour; **merced a** thanks to; **a la merced de algo/alguien** at the mercy of sthg/sb.

mercenario, ria *adj & sm, f* mercenary.

mercería *sf* - **1.** [género] haberdashery *UK*, notions *US* - **2.** [tienda] haberdasher's (shop) *UK*, notions store *US*.

MERCOSUR *sm* (*abrev de* **Mercado Común del Sur**) MERCOSUR.

mercurio *sm* mercury.

Mercurio *sm* Mercury.

merecedor, ra *adj*: **merecedor de** worthy of.

merecer [30] ◇ *vt* to deserve, to be worthy of; **la isla merece una visita** the island is worth a visit; **no merece la pena** it's not worth it. ◇ *vi* to be worthy.

merecido *sm*: **recibir su merecido** to get one's just deserts.

merendar [19] ◇ *vi* to have tea *(as a light afternoon meal).* ◇ *vt* to have for tea.
➤ **merendarse** *vprnl fam*: **merendarse a alguien** to thrash sb.

merendero *sm* open-air café or bar *(in the country or on the beach).*

merendola *sf fam* slap-up tea.

merengue ◇ *sm* **- 1.** CULIN meringue **- 2.** [baile] merengue. ◇ *adj fam* DEP of/relating to Real Madrid Football Club.

merezca *etc* ⊳ **merecer**.

meridiano, na *adj* **- 1.** [hora etc] midday **- 2.** *fig* [claro] crystal-clear.
➤ **meridiano** *sm* meridian.

meridional ◇ *adj* southern. ◇ *smf* southerner.

merienda *sf* tea *(as a light afternoon meal)*; [en el campo] picnic; **merienda de negros** free-for-all; ⊳ **merendar**.

mérito *sm* **- 1.** [cualidad] merit; **hacer méritos para** to do everything possible to **- 2.** [valor] value, worth; **tiene mucho mérito** it's no mean achievement; **de mérito** worthy, deserving.

meritorio, ria ◇ *adj* worthy, deserving. ◇ *sm, f* unpaid trainee O apprentice.

merluza *sf* **- 1.** [pez, pescado] hake **- 2.** *fam* [borrachera]: **agarrar una merluza** to get sozzled.

merma *sf* decrease, reduction.

mermar ◇ *vi* to diminish, to lessen. ◇ *vt* to reduce, to diminish.

mermelada *sf* jam; **mermelada de naranja** marmalade.

mero, ra *adj (antes de s)* mere.
➤ **mero** *sm* grouper.

merodeador, ra *sm, f* prowler, snooper.

merodear *vi*: **merodear (por)** to snoop O prowl (about).

mes *sm* **- 1.** [del año] month **- 2.** [salario] monthly salary **- 3.** [menstruación] period.

mesa *sf* **- 1.** [gen] table; [de oficina, despacho] desk; **bendecir la mesa** to say grace; **poner/quitar la mesa** to set/clear the table; **sentarse a la mesa** to sit down to table; **mesa camilla** *small round table under which a heater is placed*; **mesa de billar** billiard table; **mesa de mezclas** mixing desk; **mesa (de) nido** nest of tables; **mesa de operaciones** operating table; **mesa plegable** folding table **- 2.** [comité] board, committee; [en un debate etc] panel; **mesa directiva** executive board O committee.
➤ **mesa electoral** *sf* polling station.
➤ **mesa redonda** *sf* [coloquio] round table.

mesada *sf* **- 1.** *Amér* [mensualidad] monthly payment, monthly instalment **- 2.** *R Dom* [encimera] worktop.

mesana *sf* **- 1.** [mástil] mizenmast **- 2.** [vela] mizensail.

mescalina *sf* mescalin.

mescolanza = **mezcolanza**.

mesero, ra *sm, f Amér C, Col & Méx* waiter (*f* waitress).

meseta *sf* plateau, tableland.

mesianismo *sm* RELIG messianism; *fig blind faith in one person.*

mesías *sm fig* Messiah.
➤ **Mesías** *sm*: **el Mesías** the Messiah.

mesilla *sf* small table; **mesilla de noche** bedside table.

mesón *sm* **- 1.** HIST inn **- 2.** [bar-restaurante] *old, country-style restaurant and bar.*

mesonero, ra *sm, f* **- 1.** innkeeper **- 2.** *Ven* [camarero] waiter (*f* waitress).

mestizaje *sm* cross-breeding; *fig* mixing.

mestizo, za ◇ *adj* [persona] half-caste; [animal, planta] cross-bred. ◇ *sm, f* half-caste.

mesura *sf* **- 1.** [moderación] moderation, restraint; **con mesura** [moderadamente] in moderation **- 2.** [cortesía] courtesy, politeness **- 3.** [gravedad] dignity, seriousness.

mesurado, da *adj* moderate, restrained.

mesurarse *vprnl* to restrain o.s.

meta *sf* **- 1.** [DEP - llegada] finishing line; [- portería] goal; **meta volante** [en ciclismo] hot spot sprint **- 2.** [objetivo] aim, goal; **fijarse una meta** to set o.s. a target O goal.

metabólico, ca *adj* metabolic.

metabolismo *sm* metabolism.

metadona *sf* methadone.

metafísico, ca ◇ *adj* metaphysical. ◇ *sm, f* [filósofo] metaphysicist.
➤ **metafísica** *sf* [disciplina] metaphysics *(U).*

metáfora *sf* metaphor.

metafórico, ca *adj* metaphorical.

metal *sm* **- 1.** [material] metal; **metal blanco** white metal; **metal pesado** heavy metal; **metales preciosos** precious metals; **el vil metal** filthy lucre **- 2.** MÚS brass.

metálico, ca ◇ *adj* [sonido, color] metallic; [objeto] metal. ◇ *sm*: **pagar en metálico** to pay (in) cash.

metalizado, da *adj* [pintura] metallic.

metalurgia *sf* metallurgy.

metalúrgico, ca ◇ *adj* metallurgical. ◇ *sm, f* metallurgist.

metamorfosis *sf inv lit & fig* metamorphosis.

metano *sm* methane.

metanol *sm* methanol.

metástasis *sf inv* MED metastasis.

metedura ➤ **metedura de pata** *sf* clanger.

meteórico, ca *adj lit & fig* meteoric.

meteorito *sm* meteorite.

meteoro *sm* meteor.

meteorología *sf* meteorology.

meteorológico, ca *adj* meteorological.

meteorólogo, ga *sm, f* meteorologist; RADIO & TV weatherman (*f* weatherwoman).

meter *vt* - **1.** [gen] to put in; **meter algo/a alguien en algo** to put sthg/sb in sthg; **meter la llave en la cerradura** to get the key into the lock; **lo metieron en la cárcel** they put him in prison; **meter dinero en el banco** to put money in the bank; **he metido mis ahorros en esa empresa** I've put all my savings into this venture - **2.** [hacer participar]: **meter a alguien en algo** to get sb into sthg - **3.** [obligar a]: **meter a alguien a hacer algo** to make sb start doing sthg - **4.** [causar]: **meter prisa/miedo a alguien** to rush/scare sb; **meter ruido** to make a noise - **5.** *fam* [asestar] to give; **le metió un puñetazo** he gave him a punch - **6.** *fam* [echar] to give; **meter una bronca a alguien** to tell sb off - **7.** [estrechar - prenda] to take in; **meter el bajo de una falda** to take up a skirt - **8.** *loc*: **a todo meter** as quickly as possible.

➤ **meterse** *vprnl* - **1.** [entrar] to get in; **meterse en** to get into - **2.** *(en frase interrogativa)* [estar] to get to; **¿dónde se ha metido ese chico?** where has that boy got to? - **3.** [dedicarse]: **meterse a** to become; **meterse a torero** to become a bullfighter - **4.** [involucrarse]: **meterse (en)** to get involved (in) - **5.** [entrometerse] to meddle, to interfere; **se mete en todo** he never minds his own business; **meterse por medio** to interfere - **6.** [empezar]: **meterse a hacer algo** to get started on doing sthg.

➤ **meterse con** *vprnl* - **1.** [incordiar] to hassle - **2.** [atacar] to go for.

meterete *smf* C Sur *fam* busybody, nosey-parker UK.

metete *smf* Andes & Amér C *fam* busybody, nosey-parker UK.

meticulosidad *sf* meticulousness.

meticuloso, sa *adj* meticulous.

metido, da *adj* - **1.** [envuelto]: **andar** *o* **estar metido en** to be involved in - **2.** [abundante]: **metido en años** elderly; **metido en carnes** plump.

metódico, ca *adj* methodical.

metodismo *sm* Methodism.

metodista *adj* & *smf* Methodist.

método *sm* - **1.** [sistema] method; **método anticonceptivo** method of contraception, contraceptive method - **2.** EDUC course.

metodología *sf* methodology.

metodológico, ca *adj* methodological.

metomentodo *fam* ◇ *adj inv* meddlesome. ◇ *smf* busybody.

metonimia *sf* metonymy.

metraje *sm* length, running time.

metralla *sf* shrapnel.

metralleta *sf* submachine gun.

métrico, ca *adj* - **1.** [del metro] metric - **2.** LITER metrical.

➤ **métrica** *sf* LITER metrics *(U)*.

metro *sm* - **1.** [gen] metre; **metro cuadrado/cúbico** square/cubic metre; **metros por segundo** metres per second - **2.** [transporte] underground UK, tube UK, subway US - **3.** [cinta métrica] tape measure.

metrópoli *sf* - **1.** [ciudad] metropolis - **2.** [nación] home country.

metrópolis *sf inv* = **metrópoli**.

metropolitano, na *adj* metropolitan.

mexicano, na, mejicano, na *adj* & *sm, f* Mexican.

México, Méjico *n pr* Mexico.

meza *etc* ▷ **mecer**.

mezcla *sf* - **1.** [gen] mixture; [tejido] blend; [de grabación] mix - **2.** [acción] mixing.

mezclador, ra *sm, f* [persona] sound mixer.

➤ **mezclador** *sm* [aparato] mixer; **mezclador de imagen/sonido** vision/sound mixer.

mezclar *vt* - **1.** [gen] to mix; [combinar, armonizar] to blend - **2.** [confundir, desordenar] to mix up - **3.** [implicar]: **mezclar a alguien en** to get sb mixed up in.

➤ **mezclarse** *vprnl* - **1.** [gen]: **mezclarse (con)** to mix (with) - **2.** [esfumarse]: **mezclarse entre** to disappear *o* blend into - **3.** [implicarse]: **mezclarse en** to get mixed up in.

mezcolanza, mescolanza *sf fam* hotchpotch, mishmash.

mezquindad *sf* - **1.** [cualidad] meanness - **2.** [acción] mean action.

mezquino, na *adj* mean, cheap US.

mezquita *sf* mosque.

mg (*abrev de* **miligramo**) mg.

MHz (*abrev de* **megahercio**) MHz.

mi[1] *sm* MÚS E; [en solfeo] mi.

mi[2] (*pl* **mis**) *adj poses* my; **mi casa** my house; **mis libros** my books.

mí *pron pers* (*después de prep*) - **1.** [gen] me; **este trabajo no es para mí** this job isn't for me; **no se fía de mí** he doesn't trust me - **2.** *(reflexivo)* myself - **3.** *loc*: **¡a mí con ésas!** come off it!; **¡a mí qué!** so what?, why should I care?; **para mí** [yo creo] as far as I'm concerned, in my opinion; **por mí** as far as I'm concerned; **por mí, no hay inconveniente** it's fine by me.

mía ▷ **mío**.

miaja *sf* crumb; *fig* tiny bit.

miau *sm* miaow.

mica *sf* mica.

micción *sf* [MED - acción] urination; [- orina] urine.

michelines *smpl fam* spare tyre *sing*.

mico *sm* - **1.** [animal] (long-tailed) monkey - **2.** *fam* [persona] ugly devil; **ser el último mico** to be the lowest of the low; **se volvió mico para abrir la puerta** he had a hell of a job opening the door.

micra *sf* micron.

micrero, ra *sm, f Amér* minibus driver.

micro <> *sm fam* (*abrev de* **micrófono**) mike. <> *sm o sf Chile* [microbús] bus, coach UK.

microbio *sm* germ, microbe.

microbiología *sf* microbiology.

microbús *sm* - **1.** minibus - **2.** *Méx* [taxi] (collective) taxi.

microcirugía *sf* microsurgery.

microclima *sm* microclimate.

microeconomía *sf* microeconomics *(U)*.

microelectrónica *sf* microelectronics *(U)*.

microficha *sf* microfiche.

microfilm (*pl* microfilms), **microfilme** *sm* microfilm.

micrófono *sm* microphone.

microinformática *sf* INFORM microcomputing.

microonda *sf* microwave.

microondas *sm inv* microwave (oven).

microordenador *sm* INFORM microcomputer.

microorganismo *sm* microorganism.

microprocesador *sm* INFORM microprocessor.

microscópico, ca *adj* microscopic.

microscopio *sm* microscope; **microscopio electrónico** electron microscope.

microsurco *sm* microgroove.

mida *etc* ⊳ **medir**.

MIDA *sm* (*abrev de* **Ministerio de Desarrollo Agropecuario**), *Panamanian Department of Agricultural Development*.

midiera *etc* ⊳ **medir**.

miedo *sm* fear; **coger miedo a algo** to develop a fear of sthg; **dar miedo** to be frightening; **me de miedo conducir** I'm afraid O frightened of driving; **meter miedo a** to frighten; **por miedo a** for fear of; **por miedo de que...** for fear that...; **temblar de miedo** to tremble with fear; **tener miedo** to be frightened O scared; **tener miedo a** O **de (hacer algo)** to be afraid of (doing sthg); **miedo cerval** terrible fear, terror ▸▸ **de miedo** *fam*: **esta película está de miedo** this film is brilliant; **lo pasamos de miedo** we

had a whale of a time; **estar cagado de miedo** *vulg* to be shit-scared; **morirse de miedo** to die of fright, to be terrified.

miedoso, sa <> *adj* fearful. <> *sm, f* fearful person.

miel *sf* honey; **dejar a alguien con la miel en los labios** to cut short sb's enjoyment; **miel sobre hojuelas** all the better; **no hay miel sin hiel** every rose has a thorn.

miembro *sm* - **1.** [gen] member - **2.** [extremidad] limb, member; **miembros superiores/inferiores** upper/lower limbs; **miembro (viril)** penis.

miércoles *sm* Wednesday; **miércoles de ceniza** Ash Wednesday; *ver también* **sábado**.

mierda *vulg* <> *sf* - **1.** [excremento] shit - **2.** [suciedad] filth, shit - **3.** [cosa sin valor]: **es una mierda** it's (a load of) crap; **de mierda** shitty, crappy - **4.** *loc*: **irse a la mierda** [proyecto etc] to go down the tubes; **mandar a alguien a la mierda** to tell sb to piss off; **¡vete a la mierda!** go to hell!, piss off! <> *smf vulg* shithead.

mies *sf* [cereal] ripe corn.

➠ **mieses** *sfpl* [campo] cornfields.

miga *sf* [de pan] crumb; **tener miga** *fam* [ser sustancioso] to have a lot to it; [ser complicado] to have more to it than meets the eye.

➠ **migas** *sfpl* CULIN fried breadcrumbs; **hacer buenas/malas migas** *fam* to get on well/badly; **hacerse migas** *fam* [cosa] to be smashed to bits; **hacer migas a alguien** *fam* [desmoralizar] to shatter sb.

migaja *sf* - **1.** [trozo] bit; [de pan] crumb - **2.** *fig* [pizca] scrap.

➠ **migajas** *sfpl* [restos] leftovers.

migra *sf Méx fam despec*: **la migra** *US police border patrol*.

migración *sf* migration.

migraña *sf* migraine.

migrante *smf* migrant.

migrar *vi* to migrate.

migratorio, ria *adj* migratory.

mijo *sm* millet.

mil *num* thousand; **dos mil** two thousand; **mil euros** a thousand euros; **a las mil quinientas** really late; **mil y una/uno** a thousand and one; *ver también* **seis**.

➠ **miles** *smpl* [gran cantidad]: **miles (de)** thousands (of).

milagrero, ra *despec* <> *adj* who believes in miracles. <> *sm, f* person who believes in miracles.

milagro *sm* miracle; **de milagro** miraculously, by a miracle; **hacer milagros** *fig* to work wonders.

milagroso, sa *adj* miraculous; *fig* amazing.

milano *sm* kite.

milenario, ria *adj* ancient.

➤ **milenario** *sm* millennium.

milenio *sm* millennium.

milésimo, ma *num* thousandth; **la milésima parte** a thousandth; **una milésima de segundo** a millisecond.

milhojas *sm inv* CULIN mille feuille.

mili *sf fam* military service; **hacer la mili** to do one's military service.

milicia *sf* - **1.** [profesión] military (profession) - **2.** [grupo armado] militia; **milicias universitarias** *formerly in Spain, military service for students.*

miliciano, na ⬦ *adj* militia *(antes de s)*. ⬦ *sm, f* militiaman (*f* female soldier).

miligramo *sm* milligram.

mililitro *sm* millilitre.

milimetrado ▷ **papel**.

milimétrico, ca *adj* millimetric.

milímetro *sm* millimetre.

militancia *sf* militancy.

militante *adj* & *smf* militant.

militar ⬦ *adj* military. ⬦ *smf* soldier; **los militares** the military. ⬦ *vi*: **militar (en)** to be active (in).

militarismo *sm* militarism.

militarista *adj* & *smf* militarist.

militarización *sf* militarization.

militarizar [13] *vt* to militarize.

milla *sf* mile; **milla (marina)** nautical mile.

millar *sm* thousand; **a millares** by the thousand; **un millar de personas** a thousand people.

millón *num* million; **dos millones** two million; **un millón de personas** a million people; **un millón de cosas que hacer** a million things to do; **un millón de gracias** thanks a million.

➤ **millones** *smpl* [dineral] millions, a fortune *sing*.

millonada *sf fam* fortune, millions *pl*.

millonario, ria ⬦ *adj*: **es millonario** he's a millionaire. ⬦ *sm, f* millionaire (*f* millionairess).

millonésimo, ma *num* millionth; **la millonésima parte** a millionth.

mimado, da *adj* spoilt.

mimar *vt* to spoil, to pamper.

mimbre *sm* wicker; **de mimbre** wickerwork.

mimético, ca *adj* - **1.** [animal, planta] mimetic - **2.** [persona]: **ser mimético** to be a copycat.

mimetismo *sm* - **1.** [de animal, planta] mimetism - **2.** [de persona] mimicry.

mímica *sf* - **1.** [mimo] mime - **2.** [lenguaje] sign language.

mimo *sm* - **1.** [zalamería] mollycoddling - **2.** [cariño] show of affection - **3.** TEATRO mime; **hacer mimo** to perform mime.

mimosa *sf* BOT mimosa.

mimoso, sa *adj* affectionate.

min (*abrev de* **minuto**) min.

mina *sf* - **1.** GEOL & MIL mine; **mina antipersona** anti-personnel mine; **mina de carbón** coalmine; **una mina de información** a mine of information; **ser una mina (de oro)** to be a gold mine - **2.** [de lápiz] lead.

minar *vt* - **1.** MIL to mine - **2.** *fig* [aminorar] to undermine.

mineral ⬦ *adj* mineral. ⬦ *sm* - **1.** GEOL mineral - **2.** [en mineralogía] ore.

mineralizar [13] *vt* to mineralize.

➤ **mineralizarse** *vprnl* to become mineralized.

mineralogía *sf* minerology.

minería *sf* - **1.** [técnica] mining - **2.** [sector] mining industry.

minero, ra ⬦ *adj* mining *(antes de s)*; [producción, riqueza] mineral. ⬦ *sm, f* miner.

miniatura *sf* miniature; **el piso es una miniatura** the flat is tiny; **en miniatura** in miniature.

minicadena *sf* midi system.

mini disk, mini disc *sm inv* mini disc.

minifalda *sf* mini skirt.

minifundio *sm* smallholding.

minigolf (*pl* **minigolfs**) *sm* - **1.** [lugar] crazy golf course - **2.** [juego] crazy golf.

mínima ▷ **mínimo**.

minimalismo *sm* MÚS minimalism.

minimalista *adj* MÚS minimalist.

minimizar [13] *vt* to play down.

mínimo, ma ⬦ *superl* = **pequeño**. ⬦ *adj* - **1.** [lo más bajo posible o necesario] minimum - **2.** [lo más bajo temporalmente] lowest - **3.** [muy pequeño - efecto, importancia etc] minimal, very small; [- protesta, ruido etc] slightest; **no tengo la más mínima idea** I haven't the slightest idea; **como mínimo** at the very least; **en lo más mínimo** in the slightest.

➤ **mínimo** *sm* [límite] minimum; **mínimo común múltiplo** lowest common multiple.

➤ **mínima** *sf* METEOR low, lowest temperature.

minino, na *sm, f fam* pussy (cat).

ministerial *adj* ministerial.

ministerio *sm* - **1.** POLÍT ministry *UK*, department *US* - **2.** RELIG ministry.

➤ **ministerio público, ministerio fiscal** *sm* ≃ Department of Public Prosecution.

➤ **Ministerio de Asuntos Exteriores** *sm* ≃ Foreign Office *UK*, ≃ State Department *US*.

➤ **Ministerio de Economía y Hacienda** *sm* ≃ Treasury *UK*, ≃ Treasury Department *US*.

◆ **Ministerio del Interior** *sm* ≃ Home Office *UK*, ≃ Department of the Interior *US*.

ministro, tra *sm, f* **- 1.** POLÍT minister *UK*, secretary *US*; **ministro sin cartera** minister without portfolio; **primer ministro** prime minister **- 2.** RELIG minister; **ministro de Dios** minister of God.

minoría *sf* minority; **estar en minoría** to be in a o the minority; **minorías étnicas** ethnic minorities.

minorista ◇ *adj* retail. ◇ *smf* retailer.

minoritario, ria *adj* minority *(antes de s)*.

mintiera *etc* ▷ **mentir**.

minucia *sf* trifle, insignificant thing.

minuciosidad *sf* meticulousness, attention to detail.

minucioso, sa *adj* **- 1.** [meticuloso] meticulous **- 2.** [detallado] highly detailed.

minuendo *sm* minuend.

minúsculo, la *adj* **- 1.** [tamaño] tiny, minute **- 2.** [letra] small; IMPR lower-case.

◆ **minúscula** *sf* small letter; IMPR lower-case letter.

minusvalía *sf* **- 1.** ECON depreciation **- 2.** [física] handicap, disability.

minusválido, da ◇ *adj* disabled, handicapped. ◇ *sm, f* disabled o handicapped person.

minusvalorar *vt* to underestimate.

minuta *sf* **- 1.** [factura] fee **- 2.** [menú] menu **- 3.** R Dom [comida] quick meal.

minutero *sm* minute hand.

minuto *sm* minute; **al minuto** a moment later; **guardar un minuto de silencio** to observe a minute's silence.

mío, mía ◇ *adj poses* mine; **este libro es mío** this book is mine; **un amigo mío** a friend of mine; **no es asunto mío** it's none of my business. ◇ *pron poses*: **el mío** mine; **el mío es rojo** mine is red; **esta es la mía** *fam* this is the chance I've been waiting for; **lo mío es el teatro** [lo que me va] theatre is what I should be doing; **los míos** *fam* [mi familia] my folks; [mi bando] my lot, my side.

miocardio *sm* myocardium.

miope ◇ *adj* shortsighted, myopic. ◇ *smf* shortsighted o myopic person.

miopía *sf* shortsightedness, myopia.

MIR (*abrev de* **médico interno residente**) *sm* ≃ houseman *UK*, ≃ intern *US*.

mira ◇ *sf* sight; *fig* intention; **con miras a** with a view to, with the intention of. ◇ *interj*: ¡**mira!** look!

mirado, da *adj* [prudente] careful; **bien mirado** [bien pensado] if you look at it closely.

◆ **mirada** *sf* [gen] look; [rápida] glance; [de cariño, placer, admiración] gaze; **apartar la mirada** to look away; **dirigir** o **lanzar la mirada a** to glance at; **echar una mirada (a algo)** to glance o to have a quick look (at sthg); **fulminar con la mirada a alguien** to look daggers at sb; **hay miradas que matan** if looks could kill; **levantar la mirada** to look up; **mirada asesina** glare; **mirada fija** stare; **mirada furtiva** peek; **mirada perdida** distant look.

mirador *sm* **- 1.** [balcón] enclosed balcony **- 2.** [para ver un paisaje] viewpoint.

miramiento *sm* consideration, circumspection; **andarse con miramientos** to stand on ceremony; **sin miramientos** just like that, without the least consideration.

mirar ◇ *vt* **- 1.** [gen] to look at; [observar] to watch; [fijamente] to stare at; **mirar algo de cerca/lejos** to look at sthg closely/from a distance; **mirar algo por encima** to glance over sthg, to have a quick look at sthg; **mirar a alguien bien/mal** to think highly/poorly of sb; **mirar a alguien de arriba abajo** to look sb up and down; **de mírame y no me toques** very fragile **- 2.** [fijarse] to keep an eye on, to watch **- 3.** [examinar, averiguar] to check, to look through; **le miraron todas las maletas** they searched all her luggage; **mira si ha llegado la carta** go and see if the letter has arrived **- 4.** [considerar] to consider, to take a look at. ◇ *vi* **- 1.** [gen] to look; [observar] to watch; [fijamente] to stare; **mira, yo creo que...** look, I think that... **- 2.** [buscar] to check, to look; **he mirado en todas partes** I've looked everywhere **- 3.** [orientarse]: **mirar a** to face **- 4.** [cuidar]: **mirar por alguien/algo** to look after sb/sthg.

◆ **mirarse** *vprnl* [uno mismo] to look at o.s.; **si bien se mira** *fig* if you really think about it.

mirilla *sf* spyhole.

mirlo *sm* blackbird; **ser un mirlo blanco** to be one in a million.

mirón, ona *fam* ◇ *adj* nosey; [con lascivia] peeping. ◇ *sm, f* **- 1.** [espectador] onlooker **- 2.** [curioso] nosy parker **- 3.** [voyeur] peeping Tom.

mirra *sf* myrrh.

mirto *sm* myrtle.

misa *sf* mass; **cantar/decir/oír misa** to sing/say/hear mass; **ir a misa** [gen] to go to mass o church; *fam fig* to be gospel; **lo que yo digo va a misa** what I say goes; **misa cantada/de campaña** sung/open-air mass; **misa de difuntos** requiem, mass for the dead; **misa del gallo** midnight mass (*on Christmas Eve*); **no saber de la misa la mitad** *fam* not to know half the story.

misal *sm* missal.

misantropía *sf* misanthropy.

misántropo, pa *sm, f* misanthrope, misanthropist.

miscelánea *sf* - **1.** miscellany - **2.** *Méx* [tienda] *small general store.*

miserable ⬦ *adj* - **1.** [pobre] poor; [vivienda] wretched, squalid - **2.** [penoso, insuficiente] miserable - **3.** [vil] contemptible, base - **4.** [tacaño] mean. ⬦ *smf* - **1.** [ruin] wretch, vile person - **2.** [tacaño] mean person, miser.

miseria *sf* - **1.** [pobreza] poverty; **vivir en la miseria** to live in poverty - **2.** [cantidad muy pequeña] pittance - **3.** [desgracia] misfortune - **4.** [tacañería] meanness.

misericordia *sf* compassion; **pedir misericordia** to beg for mercy.

misericordioso, sa ⬦ *adj* compassionate, merciful. ⬦ *sm, f*: **los misericordiosos** the merciful.

mísero, ra *adj* [pobre] wretched; **ni un mísero...** not even a measly O miserable...

misil (*pl* misiles) *sm* missile; **misil de crucero** cruise missile.

misión *sf* - **1.** [gen] mission; [cometido] task - **2.** [expedición científica] expedition.
➡ **misiones** *sfpl* RELIG (overseas) missions.

misionero, ra *adj* & *sm, f* missionary.

misiva *sf* culto missive.

mismo, ma ⬦ *adj* - **1.** [igual] same; **el mismo piso** the same flat; **del mismo color que** the same colour as - **2.** [para enfatizar]: **yo mismo** I myself; **en este mismo cuarto** in this very room; **en su misma calle** right in the street where he lives; **por mí/ti mismo** by myself/yourself; **¡tú mismo!** it's up to you. ⬦ *pron*: **el mismo** the same; **el mismo que vi ayer** the same one I saw yesterday; **lo mismo** the same (thing); **lo mismo que** the same as; **da** O **es lo mismo** it doesn't matter, it doesn't make any difference; **me da lo mismo** I don't care; **por lo mismo** for that (very) reason; **estar en las mismas** to be no further forward.
➡ **mismo** (*después de s*) *adv* - **1.** [para enfatizar]: **lo vi desde mi casa mismo** I saw it from my own house; **ahora/aquí mismo** right now/here; **ayer mismo** only yesterday; **por eso mismo** precisely for that reason - **2.** [por ejemplo]: **escoge uno − cualquiera este mismo** choose any − this one, for instance.

misoginia *sf* misogyny.

misógino, na ⬦ *adj* misogynistic. ⬦ *sm, f* misogynist.

míster (*pl* místers) *sm* DEP ≃ manager.

misterio *sm* mystery.

misterioso, sa *adj* mysterious.

mística ▷ **místico**.

misticismo *sm* mysticism.

místico, ca ⬦ *adj* mystical. ⬦ *sm, f* [persona] mystic.
➡ **mística** *sf* [práctica] mysticism.

mistificar [10], **mixtificar** *vt* to mystify.

mitad *sf* - **1.** [gen] half; **a mitad de precio** at half price; **a mitad de camino** halfway there; **a mitad de película** halfway through the film; **la mitad de** half (of); **la mitad del tiempo no está** half the time she's not in; **mitad y mitad** half and half - **2.** [centro] middle; **en mitad de** in the middle of; **(cortar algo) por la mitad** (to cut sthg) in half.

mítico, ca *adj* mythical.

mitificar [10] *vt* to mythologize.

mitigador, ra *adj* calming.

mitigar [16] *vt* - **1.** [gen] to alleviate, to reduce; [ánimos] to calm; [sed] to slake; [hambre] to take the edge off; [choque, golpe] to soften; [dudas, sospechas] to allay - **2.** [justificar] to mitigate.

mitin (*pl* mítines) *sm* rally, meeting.

mito *sm* - **1.** [gen] myth - **2.** [personaje] mythical figure.

mitología *sf* mythology.

mitológico, ca *adj* mythological.

mitomanía *sf* mythomania.

mitómano, na *adj* & *sm, f* mythomaniac.

mitón *sm* (fingerless) mitten.

mitote *sm* Méx fam [bulla] racket.

mitra *sf* - **1.** [tocado] mitre - **2.** [cargo] office of archbishop/bishop.

mixtificar [10] = mistificar.

mixto, ta *adj* mixed; [comisión] joint.

mixtura *sf* mixture.

mízcalo *sm* milk fungus.

ml (*abrev de* mililitro) ml.

mm (*abrev de* milímetro) mm.

mobiliario *sm* furniture; **mobiliario urbano** street furniture.

mocasín *sm* moccasin.

mocetón, ona *sm, f* fam strapping lad (*f* strapping lass).

moche ▷ **troche**.

mochila *sf* backpack.

mocho, cha *adj* [gen] blunt; [árbol] lopped.
➡ **mocho** *sm* [fregona] mop.

mochuelo *sm* little owl; **cargar con el mochuelo** fam to be landed with it.

moción *sf* motion; **moción de censura** censure motion.

moco *sm* fam snot (U); MED mucus (U); **limpiarse los mocos** to wipe one's nose; **sorberse los mocos** to sniffle, to snuffle; **tener mocos** to have a runny nose; **llorar a moco tendido** fam to cry one's eyes out; **no ser moco de pavo** *fam* to be sthg not to be sneezed at, to be no mean feat.

mocoso, sa ◇ *adj* runny-nosed. ◇ *sm, f fam despec* brat.

moda *sf* [gen] fashion; [furor pasajero] craze; **estar de moda** to be fashionable *o* in fashion; **estar pasado de moda** to be unfashionable *o* out of fashion; **ir a la última moda** to wear the latest fashion; **ponerse de moda** to come into fashion; **moda pasajera** fad.

modal *adj* modal.

➡ **modales** *smpl* manners; **tener buenos/malos modales** to have good/bad manners.

modalidad *sf* form, type; DEP discipline; **modalidad de pago** method of payment.

modelado *sm* modelling.

modelar *vt* to model; *fig* to form, to shape.

modelismo *sm* modelling.

modelo ◇ *adj* model. ◇ *smf* model. ◇ *sm* - **1.** [gen] model; **servir de modelo** to serve as a model; **modelo económico** ECON economic model - **2.** [prenda de vestir] number.

módem ['moðem] (*pl* **modems**) *sm* INFORM modem; **módem fax** fax modem.

moderación *sf* moderation; **con moderación** in moderation.

moderado, da *adj* & *sm, f* moderate.

moderador, ra ◇ *adj* moderating. ◇ *sm, f* chair, chairperson.

moderar *vt* - **1.** [gen] to moderate; [velocidad] to reduce - **2.** [debate] to chair.

➡ **moderarse** *vprnl* to restrain o.s.; **moderarse en algo** to moderate sthg.

modernidad *sf* modernity.

modernismo *sm* - **1.** [gen & LITER] modernism - **2.** [ARQUIT - en España] Modernismo ≃ Art Nouveau.

modernista *adj* & *smf* - **1.** [gen & LITER] modernist - **2.** [ARQUIT - en España] Modernista.

modernización *sf* modernization.

modernizar [13] *vt* to modernize.

➡ **modernizarse** *vprnl* to modernize.

moderno, na ◇ *adj* modern. ◇ *sm, f fam* trendy (person).

modestia *sf* modesty; **falsa modestia** false modesty; **modestia aparte** modesty apart.

modesto, ta ◇ *adj* modest. ◇ *sm, f* modest person.

módico, ca *adj* modest.

modificación *sf* alteration.

modificar [10] *vt* - **1.** [variar] to alter - **2.** GRAM to modify.

modismo *sm* idiom.

modista *sm, f* - **1.** [diseñador] fashion designer - **2.** [que cose] tailor (*f* dressmaker).

modisto *sm* - **1.** [diseñador] fashion designer - **2.** [sastre] tailor.

modo *sm* - **1.** [manera, forma] way; **a modo de** as, by way of; **al modo de** in the style of; **a mi modo** (in) my own way; **de ese modo** in that way; **de ningún modo** in no way; **de todos modos** in any case, anyway; **de un modo u otro** one way or another; **en cierto modo** in some ways; **modo de empleo** instructions *pl* for use; **modo de pensar/ser** way of thinking/being; **modo de vida** way of life; **de modo que** [de manera que] in such a way that; [así que] so - **2.** GRAM mood; **modo adverbial** adverbial phrase.

➡ **modos** *smpl* [modales] manners; **buenos/malos modos** good/bad manners.

modorra *sf fam* drowsiness.

modoso, sa *adj* [recatado] modest; [formal] well-behaved.

modulación *sf* modulation; **modulación de frecuencia** frequency modulation.

modulador, ra *adj* modulating.

➡ **modulador** *sm* modulator.

modular ◇ *adj* modular. ◇ *vt* to modulate.

módulo *sm* - **1.** [gen] module; **módulo lunar** lunar module - **2.** [de muebles] unit.

mofa *sf* mockery; **hacer mofa de** to mock.

mofarse *vprnl* to scoff; **mofarse de** to mock.

moflete *sm* chubby cheek.

mogol, a = mongol.

mogollón *sm mfam* - **1.** [muchos]: **mogollón de** tons *pl* of, loads *pl* of - **2.** [lío] row, commotion; **entraron/salieron a mogollón** everyone rushed in/out at once.

mohín *sm* grimace, face; **hacer un mohín** to make a face.

moho *sm* - **1.** [hongo] mould; **criar moho** to go mouldy - **2.** [herrumbre] rust.

mohoso, sa *adj* - **1.** [con hongo] mouldy - **2.** [oxidado] rusty.

moisés *sm inv* Moses basket.

mojado, da *adj* wet; [húmedo] damp; **llover sobre mojado** to be just too much.

mojama *sf* dried salted tuna.

mojar *vt* [sin querer] to get wet; [a propósito] to wet; [humedecer] to dampen; [comida] to dunk; **no mojes el suelo** don't get the floor wet; **moja el pan en la salsa** dip your bread in the sauce.

➡ **mojarse** *vprnl* - **1.** [con agua] to get wet - **2.** *fam* [comprometerse] to commit o.s.

mojigatería *sf* - **1.** [beatería] prudery - **2.** [falsa humildad] sanctimoniousness.

mojigato, ta ◇ *adj* - **1.** [beato] prudish - **2.** [con falsa humildad] sanctimonious. ◇ *sm, f* - **1.** [beato] prude - **2.** [con falsa humildad] sanctimonious person.

mojón *sm* [piedra] milestone; [poste] milepost.

molar[1] *sm* molar.

molar[2] *fam* ◇ *vt*: ¡cómo me mola esa moto/ ese chico! I think that motorbike/that guy is bloody gorgeous. ◇ *vi* to be bloody gorgeous.

molcajete *sm* *Méx* mortar.

molde *sm* mould.

moldeado *sm* - **1.** [del pelo] soft perm, body-wave - **2.** [de figura, cerámica] moulding.

moldear *vt* - **1.** [gen] to mould - **2.** [modelar] to cast - **3.** [cabello] to give a soft perm to.

moldura *sf* moulding.

mole ◇ *sf* hulk. ◇ *sm* *Méx* [salsa] *thick, cooked chilli sauce*; [guiso] *dish served in 'mole' sauce.*

molécula *sf* molecule.

molecular *adj* molecular.

moler [24] *vt* - **1.** [gen] to grind; [aceitunas] to press; [trigo] to mill - **2.** *fam* [cansar] to wear out.

molestar *vt* - **1.** [perturbar] to annoy; ¿Le molesta que fume? do you mind if I smoke?; perdone que le moleste... I'm sorry to bother you... - **2.** [doler] to hurt - **3.** [ofender] to offend.
➤ **molestarse** *vprnl* - **1.** [incomodarse] to bother; no te molestes, yo lo haré don't bother, I'll do it; molestarse en hacer algo to bother to do sthg; molestarse por alguien/algo to put o.s. out for sb/sthg - **2.** [ofenderse]: molestarse (por algo) to take offence (at sthg).

molestia *sf* - **1.** [incomodidad] nuisance; disculpen las molestias we apologize for any inconvenience; si no es demasiada molestia if it's not too much trouble; tomarse la molestia de hacer algo to take the trouble to do sthg - **2.** [malestar] discomfort; siento una molestia en el estómago my stomach doesn't feel too good.

molesto, ta *adj* - **1.** [incordiante] annoying; [visita] inconvenient - **2.** [irritado]: molesto (con) annoyed (with) - **3.** [con malestar] in discomfort.

molido, da *adj* - **1.** [gen] ground; [trigo] milled - **2.** *fam* [cansado] worn out; estar molido de to be worn out from.

molinero, ra ◇ *adj* milling. ◇ *sm, f* miller.

molinete *sm* - **1.** [ventilador] extractor fan - **2.** [juguete] toy windmill.

molinillo *sm* grinder; **molinillo de café** coffee mill *o* grinder.

molino *sm* mill; **molino de viento** windmill.

molla *sf* - **1.** [parte blanda] flesh - **2.** [gordura] flab.

molleja *sf* gizzard.

mollera *sf* *fam* [juicio] brains *pl*; **ser duro de mollera** [estúpido] to be thick in the head; [testarudo] to be pig-headed.

molusco *sm* mollusc.

momentáneo, a *adj* [de un momento] momentary; [pasajero] temporary.

momento *sm* [gen] moment; [periodo] time; **llegó un momento en que...** there came a time when...; **a cada momento** all the time; **al momento** straightaway; **a partir de este momento** from this moment (on); **de momento, por el momento** for the time being *o* moment; **del momento** [actual] of the day; **de un momento a otro** any minute now; **dentro de un momento** in a moment; **desde el momento (en) que...** [tiempo] from the moment that...; [causa] seeing as...; **en algún momento** sometime; **momentos después** moments later; **por momentos** by the minute; ¡un momento! just a minute!; **momento decisivo** turning point.

momia *sf* mummy.

mona ▷ **mono**.

monacal *adj* monastic.

monada *sf* - **1.** [persona]: su novia es una monada his girlfriend is gorgeous; ¡qué monada de bebé! what a cute baby! - **2.** [cosa] lovely thing; ¡qué monada de falda! what a lovely skirt!
➤ **monadas** *sfpl* [gracias] antics; **hacer monadas** to monkey *o* clown around.

monaguillo *sm* altar boy.

monarca *sm* monarch.

monarquía *sf* monarchy; **monarquía absoluta/constitucional/parlamentaria** absolute/constitutional/parliamentary monarchy.

monárquico, ca ◇ *adj* monarchic. ◇ *sm, f* monarchist.

monasterio *sm* [de monjes] monastery; [de monjas] convent.

monástico, ca *adj* monastic.

Moncloa *sf*: **la Moncloa** *residence of the Spanish premier.*

La Moncloa

This palace in Madrid is the residence of the Spanish premier. It was here that the "Pactos de la Moncloa", economic and social agreements which formed the basis of the transition to democracy, were drawn up and signed by the main Spanish political parties, including the recently legalized Communists and Socialists, in 1977. By extension, **la Moncloa** is used to refer to the Spanish government: "según fuentes de la Moncloa..." according to government sources...

---

monda *sf* [acción] peeling; [piel] peel; **ser la monda** *mfam* [extraordinario] to be amazing; [gracioso] to be a scream.

mondadientes *sm inv* toothpick.

mondadura *sf* - **1.** [acción] peeling - **2.** [piel] peel.

mondar *vt* to peel.

◆ **mondarse** *vprnl*: **mondarse (de risa)** *fam* to laugh one's head off.

mondongo *sm* innards *pl*.

moneda *sf* - **1.** [pieza] coin; **moneda suelta** small change (U); **pagar a alguien con o en la misma moneda** to pay sb back in kind; **ser moneda corriente** to be commonplace - **2.** [divisa] currency; **moneda débil/fuerte** weak/strong currency; **moneda corriente** legal tender; **moneda divisionaria o fraccionaria** minor unit of currency; **moneda única** single currency.

La Moneda

The "Palacio de la Moneda", also known simply as **La Moneda**, is the name of the Chilean Presidential Palace and the seat of the government in the capital, Santiago. Originally built under Spanish colonial rule as the Royal Mint (1805), it became the presidential palace in 1846. It was severely damaged on September 11 1973, when president Salvador Allende attempted to resist the military coup led by General Augusto Pinochet, though the palace was eventually rebuilt, and has now been opened to the public.

monedero *sm* - **1.** [gen] purse - **2.** [tarjeta]: **monedero electrónico** electronic purse.

monegasco, ca *adj* & *sm, f* Monacan, Monegasque.

monería *sf* (*gen pl*) antic; **hacer monerías** to monkey o clown around.

monetario, ria *adj* monetary.

mongol, la, mogol, la ◇ *adj* Mongolian. ◇ *sm, f* [persona] Mongol, Mongolian.
◆ **mongol** *sm* [lengua] Mongol, Mongolian.

mongólico, ca ◇ *adj* MED Down's syndrome (*antes de s*). ◇ *sm, f* MED Down's syndrome person.

mongolismo *sm* Down's syndrome.

monigote *sm* - **1.** [muñeco] rag o paper doll - **2.** [dibujo] doodle - **3.** *fig* [persona] puppet.

monitor, ra *sm, f* [persona] instructor.
◆ **monitor** *sm* INFORM & TECNOL monitor; **monitor en color** colour monitor.

monja *sf* nun.

monje *sm* monk.

mono, na ◇ *adj* - **1.** [bonito] lovely - **2.** *Col* [rubio] blond(e). ◇ *sm, f* - **1.** [animal] monkey; **aunque la mona se vista de seda, mona se queda** *prov* you can't make a silk purse out of a sow's ear *prov*; **mandar a alguien a freír mo-** nas *fam* to tell sb to get lost; **ser el último mono** to be bottom of the heap - **2.** *Col* [rubio] blond(e).

◆ **mono** *sm* - **1.** [prenda - con peto] dungarees *pl*; [- con mangas] overalls *pl* - **2.** *fam* [abstinencia] cold turkey.
◆ **mona** *sf* *fam* [borrachera]: **coger una mona** to get legless; **dormir la mona** to sleep it off.

monocarril *adj* & *sm* monorail.

monocolor *adj* monochrome.

monocorde *adj* - **1.** [monótono] monotonous - **2.** MÚS single-stringed.

monóculo *sm* monocle.

monogamia *sf* monogamy.

monógamo, ma ◇ *adj* monogamous. ◇ *sm, f* monogamous person.

monografía *sf* monograph.

monográfico, ca *adj* monographic.

monolingüe *adj* monolingual.

monolítico, ca *adj* monolithic.

monolito *sm* monolith.

monologar [16] *vi* to give a monologue.

monólogo *sm* monologue; TEATRO soliloquy.

monomanía *sf* obsession.

monomaniaco, ca, monomaníaco, ca *adj* & *sm, f* obsessive.

monopatín *sm* skateboard.

monoplano *adj* & *sm* monoplane.

monoplaza ◇ *adj* single-seat (*antes de s*). ◇ *sm* single-seater.

monopolio *sm* monopoly.

monopolización *sf* monopolization.

monopolizador, ra ◇ *adj* monopolistic. ◇ *sm, f* monopolist.

monopolizar [13] *vt* *lit* & *fig* to monopolize.

monorraíl *adj* & *sm* monorail.

monosilábico, ca *adj* monosyllabic.

monosílabo, ba *adj* monosyllabic.
◆ **monosílabo** *sm* monosyllable.

monoteísmo *sm* monotheism.

monoteísta ◇ *adj* monotheistic. ◇ *smf* monotheist.

monotonía *sf* - **1.** [uniformidad] monotony - **2.** [entonación] monotone.

monótono, na *adj* monotonous.

monovolumen *sm* people carrier.

monóxido *sm* monoxide; **monóxido de carbono** carbon monoxide.

monseñor *sm* Monsignor.

monserga *sf* *fam* drivel (U); **déjate de monsergas, no me vengas con monsergas** don't give me that rubbish.

monstruo ⇔ *adj inv* - **1.** [grande] enormous, monster *(antes de s)* - **2.** [prodigioso] fantastic. ⇔ *sm* - **1.** [gen] monster - **2.** [prodigio] giant, marvel.

monstruosidad *sf* - **1.** [crueldad] monstrosity, atrocity - **2.** [fealdad] hideousness - **3.** [anomalía] freak - **4.** [enormidad] hugeness.

monstruoso, sa *adj* - **1.** [cruel] monstrous - **2.** [feo] hideous - **3.** [enorme] huge, enormous - **4.** [deforme] terribly deformed.

monta *sf* - **1.** [suma] total - **2.** [importancia] importance; **de poca monta** of little importance.

montacargas *sm inv* goods lift *UK*, freight elevator *US*.

montador, ra *sm, f* - **1.** [obrero] fitter - **2.** CINE editor.

montaje *sm* - **1.** [de máquina] assembly - **2.** TEATRO staging - **3.** FOTO montage - **4.** CINE editing - **5.** [farsa] put-up job.

montante *sm* - **1.** [ARQUIT - de armazón] upright; [- de ventana] mullion; [- de puerta] jamb - **2.** [ventanuco] fanlight - **3.** [importe] total; **montantes compensatorios** COM compensating duties - **4.** *loc*: **coger el montante** to go away, to leave.

montaña *sf lit & fig* mountain; **ir de excursión a la montaña** to go on a trip to the mountains; **montaña rusa** roller coaster, big dipper; **hacer una montaña de algo** to make a big thing of sthg; **hacer una montaña de un grano de arena** to make a mountain out of a molehill.

montañero, ra ⇔ *adj* mountaineering. ⇔ *sm, f* mountaineer.

montañés, esa ⇔ *adj* - **1.** [santanderino] of or relating to Santander - **2.** [de la montaña] highland *(antes de s)*, mountain *(antes de s)*. ⇔ *sm, f* - **1.** [santanderino] person from Santander - **2.** [de la montaña] highlander.

montañismo *sm* mountaineering.

montañoso, sa *adj* mountainous.

montar ⇔ *vt* - **1.** [ensamblar - máquina, estantería] to assemble; [- tienda de campaña, tenderete] to put up - **2.** [encajar]: **montar algo en algo** to fit sthg into sthg - **3.** [organizar - negocio, piso] to set up - **4.** [cabalgar] to ride - **5.** [poner encima]: **montar a alguien en** to lift sb onto - **6.** [CULIN - nata] to whip; [- claras, yemas] to beat - **7.** TEATRO to stage - **8.** CINE to cut, to edit. ⇔ *vi* - **1.** [subir] to get on; [en coche] to get in; **montar en** [gen] to get onto; [coche] to get into; [animal] to mount - **2.** [ir montado] to ride; **montar en bicicleta/a caballo** to ride a bicycle/a horse - **3.** [sumar]: **montar a** to come to, to total; **tanto monta** it's all the same.

➡ **montarse** *vprnl* - **1.** [gen] to get on; [en coche] to get in; [en animal] to mount; **montarse en** [gen] to get onto; [coche] to get into; [animal] to mount - **2.** *loc*: **montárselo** *fam* to manage it, to organize things.

monte *sm* [elevación] mountain; [terreno] woodland; **monte bajo** scrub; **echarse** *o* **tirarse al monte** [gen] to take to the hills; *fig* to go to extremes; **no todo el monte es orégano** *prov* life's not a bowl of cherries.

➡ **monte de piedad** *sm* state pawnbroker's.

➡ **monte de Venus** *sm* mons veneris.

montepío *sm* mutual aid society.

montera *sf* bullfighter's hat; *ver también* **tauromaquia**.

montés *adj* wild.

montículo *sm* hillock.

montilla *sm* Montilla *(dry sherry from Montilla near Córdoba)*.

monto *sm* total.

montón *sm* - **1.** [pila] heap, pile; **a** *o* **en montón** everything together *o* at once; **del montón** ordinary, run-of-the-mill - **2.** [muchos] loads; **un montón de** loads of; **a montones** by the bucketload.

montura *sf* - **1.** [cabalgadura] mount - **2.** [arreos] harness; [silla] saddle - **3.** [soporte - de gafas] frame; [- de joyas] mounting.

monumental *adj* - **1.** [ciudad, lugar] famous for its monuments - **2.** [fracaso etc] monumental.

monumento *sm* monument.

monzón *sm* monsoon.

moña ⇔ *sf* - **1.** *fam* [borrachera]: **coger una moña** to get smashed - **2.** [adorno] ribbon. ⇔ *sm mfam* poof.

moño *sm* - **1.** [de pelo] bun *(of hair)*; **agarrarse del moño** [pegarse] to pull each other's hair out; **estar hasta el moño (de)** to be sick to death (of) - **2.** *Amér* [lazo] bow.

moquear *vi* to have a runny nose.

moqueta *sf* fitted carpet.

moquillo *sm* [veterinaria] distemper.

mora *sf* - **1.** [de la zarzamora] blackberry - **2.** [del moral] mulberry.

morada *sf culto* dwelling.

morado, da *adj* purple; **pasarlas moradas** *fam* to have a bad time of it; **ponerse morado** *fam* to stuff o.s.

➡ **morado** *sm* - **1.** [color] purple - **2.** [golpe] bruise.

moral ⇔ *adj* moral. ⇔ *sf* - **1.** [ética] morality - **2.** [ánimo] morale; **estar bajo de moral** to be in poor spirits; **levantar la moral a alguien** to raise sb's morale, to lift sb's spirits. ⇔ *sm* [árbol] mulberry tree.

moraleja *sf* moral.

moralidad *sf* morality.

moralismo *sm* moralism.

moralista *smf* moralist.

moralizar [13] *vi* to moralize.

morapio *sm fam* cheap red wine, plonk.

moratoria *sf* moratorium.

morbo *sm* - **1.** *fam* [placer malsano] morbid pleasure - **2.** MED disease.

morbosidad *sf* morbidity.

morboso, sa *adj* morbid.

morcilla *sf* CULIN ≃ black pudding *UK*, ≃ blood sausage *US*; ¡que te/os den morcilla! *mfam* you can stuff it, then!

morcillo *sm* foreknuckle.

mordacidad *sf* sharpness, mordacity.

mordaz *adj* caustic, biting.

mordaza *sf* gag.

mordedura *sf* bite.

morder [24] ◇ *vt* - **1.** [con los dientes] to bite - **2.** [gastar] to eat into. ◇ *vi* to bite; **estar que muerde** to be hopping mad.
➤ **morderse** *vprnl*: **morderse la lengua/las uñas** to bite one's tongue/nails.

mordida *sf Amér C & Méx fam* [soborno] bribe.

mordisco *sm* bite; **a mordiscos** by biting; **dar un mordisco a algo** to give sthg a bite.

mordisquear *vt* to nibble (at).

moreno, na ◇ *adj* - **1.** [pelo, piel] dark; [por el sol] tanned; **ponerse moreno** to get a tan - **2.** [pan, azúcar] brown. ◇ *sm, f* [de pelo] dark-haired person; [de piel] dark-skinned person.
➤ **morena** *sf* [pez] moray eel.

morera *sf* white mulberry.

moretón *sm* bruise.

morfema *sm* morpheme.

morfina *sf* morphine.

morfología *sf* morphology.

moribundo, da ◇ *adj* dying. ◇ *sm, f* dying person.

morir [25] *vi* - **1.** [gen] to die; **morir de algo** to die of sthg - **2.** [río, calle] to come out - **3.** [fuego] to die down; [luz] to go out; [día] to come to a close.
➤ **morirse** *vprnl* - **1.** [fallecer]: **morirse (de)** to die (of) - **2.** [sentir con fuerza]: **morirse de envidia/ira** to be burning with envy/rage; **me muero de ganas de ir a bailar** I'm dying to go dancing; **me muero de hambre/frío** I'm starving/freezing; **morirse por algo** to be dying for sthg; **morirse por alguien** to be crazy about sb.

morisco, ca ◇ *adj* referring to Moors in Spain baptized after the Reconquest. ◇ *sm, f* baptized Moor.

mormón, ona *adj & sm, f* Mormon.

moro, ra ◇ *adj* - **1.** HIST Moorish - **2.** *fam* [machista] sexist. ◇ *sm, f* - **1.** HIST Moor; **moros y cristianos** *traditional Spanish festival involving mock battle between Moors and Christians* - **2.** [árabe] Arab (*N.B.: the term 'moro' is considered to be racist*); **no hay moros en la costa** the coast is clear.
➤ **moro** *sm fam fig* [machista] sexist (man).

morocho, cha ◇ *adj Andes & R Plata* [persona] dark-haired; *Ven* [mellizo] twin. ◇ *sm, f Andes & R Plata* [moreno] dark-haired person; *Ven* [mellizo] twin.

moroso, sa ◇ *adj* COM defaulting. ◇ *sm, f* COM defaulter, bad debtor.

morralla *sf* - **1.** *despec* [personas] scum; [cosas] junk - **2.** [pescado] small fry - **3.** *Méx* [suelto] loose change.

morrear *mfam vt & vi* to snog.
➤ **morrearse** *vprnl* to snog.

morriña *sf* [por el país de uno] homesickness; [por el pasado] nostalgia.

morro *sm* - **1.** [hocico] snout - **2.** *(gen pl) fam* [labios] (thick) lips *pl*; **beber a morro** to drink straight from the bottle; **estar de morros** to be angry; **por el morro** through sheer cheek o nerve; **romperle los morros a alguien** to smash sb's face in; **¡qué morro tiene!** *fam* he's got a cheek! - **3.** [de coche, avión] nose.

morrocotudo, da *adj fam* tremendous.

morsa *sf* walrus.

morse *sm (en aposición invariable)* Morse (code).

mortadela *sf* Mortadella.

mortaja *sf* shroud.

mortal ◇ *adj* mortal; [caída, enfermedad] fatal; [aburrimiento, susto, enemigo] deadly. ◇ *smf* mortal.

mortalidad *sf* mortality.

mortandad *sf* mortality.

mortecino, na *adj* [luz, brillo] faint; [color, mirada] dull.

mortero *sm* mortar.

mortífero, ra *adj* deadly.

mortificar [10] *vt* to mortify.

moruno, na *adj* Moorish.

mosaico, ca *adj* Mosaic.
➤ **mosaico** *sm* mosaic.

mosca *sf* fly; **mosca tse-tsé** tsetse fly; **aflojar** o **soltar la mosca** to cough up, to fork out; **cazar moscas** to twiddle one's thumbs; **estar con** o **tener la mosca detrás de la oreja** *fam* to be suspicious o distrustful; **estar mosca** *fam* [enfadado] to be in a mood; [con sospechas] to smell a rat; **no se oía ni una mosca** you could have heard a pin drop; **por si las moscas** just in case; **¿qué mosca te ha picado?** what's up with you?

◆ **mosca muerta** *smf* slyboots, hypocrite.
moscardón *sm* - **1.** ZOOL blowfly - **2.** *fam* [persona] pest, creep.
moscatel *sm* Muscatel *(dessert wine made from muscat grapes)*.
moscón *sm* - **1.** ZOOL meatfly, bluebottle - **2.** *fam* [persona] pest, creep.
moscovita *adj* & *smf* Muscovite.
mosqueado, da *adj fam* [enfadado] cross, in a mood.
mosquearse *vprnl fam* [enfadarse] to get cross; [sospechar] to smell a rat.
mosqueo *sm fam* annoyance, anger.
mosquete *sm* musket.
mosquetero *sm* musketeer.
mosquetón *sm* short carbine.
mosquitero *sm* mosquito net.
mosquito *sm* mosquito.
mosso d'Esquadra *sm* *member of the Catalan police force*.
mostacho *sm* moustache.
mostaza *sf* mustard.
mosto *sm* [residuo] must; [zumo de uva] grape juice.
mostrador *sm* [en tienda] counter; [en bar] bar.
mostrar [23] *vt* to show.
◆ **mostrarse** *vprnl* to appear, to show o.s.; **se mostró muy interesado** he expressed great interest.
mota *sf* [de polvo] speck; [en tela] dot.
mote *sm* - **1.** nickname; **poner un mote a alguien** to nickname sb - **2.** *Andes* [maíz] stewed maize UK o corn US.
motel *sm* motel.
motín *sm* [del pueblo] uprising, riot; [de las tropas] mutiny.
motivación *sf* motive, motivation *(U)*.
motivar *vt* - **1.** [causar] to cause; [impulsar] to motivate - **2.** [razonar] to explain, to justify.
motivo *sm* - **1.** [causa] reason, cause; [de crimen] motive; **bajo ningún motivo** under no circumstances; **con motivo de** [por causa de] because of; [para celebrar] on the occasion of; [con el fin de] in order to; **dar motivo a** to give reason to; **sin motivo** for no reason; **tener motivos para** to have reason to - **2.** ARTE, LITER & MÚS motif.
moto *sf* motorbike UK, motorcycle; **ponerse como una moto** *fam* [por nervios] to get worked up; [sexualmente] to get horny; [por drogas] to get high.
motocicleta *sf* motorbike, motorcycle.
motociclismo *sm* motorcycling.
motociclista *smf* motorcyclist.
motonáutico, ca *adj* speedboat *(antes de s).*

◆ **motonáutica** *sf* speedboat racing.
motoneta *sf* Amér (motor) scooter.
motonetista *smf* Amér scooter rider.
motor, motora o **motriz** *adj* motor.
◆ **motor** *sm* - **1.** [aparato] motor, engine; **motor diesel/de gasolina** diesel/fuel engine; **motor de inyección/reacción** fuel-injection/jet engine; **motor de arranque** starter, starting motor; **motor de búsqueda** INFORM search engine; **motor de combustión interna** internal combustion engine; **motor eléctrico** electric motor; **motor de explosión** spark-ignition engine; **motor fuera borda** outboard motor - **2.** [fuerza] dynamic force - **3.** [causa] instigator, cause.
◆ **motora** *sf* motorboat.
motorismo *sm* motorcycling.
motorista *smf* motorcyclist.
motorizado, da *adj* motorized.
motorizar [13] *vt* to motorize.
◆ **motorizarse** *vprnl fam* to get o.s. some wheels.
motosierra *sf* power saw.
motricidad *sf* motivity.
motriz ▷ **motor.**
mousse [mus] *sm inv* CULIN mousse.
movedizo, za *adj* - **1.** [movible] movable, easily moved - **2.** [inestable] unsteady, unstable.
mover [24] *vt* - **1.** [gen & INFORM] to move; [mecánicamente] to drive - **2.** [cabeza - afirmativamente] to nod; [- negativamente] to shake - **3.** [suscitar] to arouse, to provoke - **4.** *fig* [empujar]: **mover a alguien a algo/a hacer algo** to drive sb to sthg/to do sthg.
◆ **mover a** *vi* - **1.** [incitar] to incite to - **2.** [causar] to provoke, to cause.
◆ **moverse** *vprnl* - **1.** [gen] to move; [en la cama] to toss and turn - **2.** [darse prisa] to get a move on - **3.** [hacer gestiones] to make an effort - **4.** [relacionarse]: **moverse en/entre** to move in/among.
movible *adj* movable.
movido, da *adj* - **1.** [debate, torneo] lively; [persona] active, restless; [jornada, viaje] hectic - **2.** FOTO blurred, fuzzy.
◆ **movida** *sf fam* [ambiente] scene; **la movida madrileña** *the Madrid scene of the late 1970s.*
móvil ◇ *adj* mobile, movable. ◇ *sm* - **1.** [motivo] motive - **2.** [juguete] mobile.
movilidad *sf* mobility.
movilización *sf* mobilization.
movilizar [13] *vt* to mobilize.
movimiento *sm* - **1.** [gen & POLÍT] movement; **movimiento obrero/pacifista** working-class/pacifist movement - **2.** FÍS & TECNOL motion; po-

ner en movimiento to put in motion; **movimiento continuo/de rotación** perpetual/rotational motion; **movimiento sísmico** earth tremor **- 3.** [circulación - gen] activity; [- de personal, mercancías] turnover; [- de vehículos] traffic; **movimiento de capital** cash flow **- 4.** [MÚS - parte de la obra] movement; [- velocidad del compás] tempo.

moviola sf editing projector.

moza ⊳ mozo.

mozalbete sm young lad.

mozárabe ◇ adj Mozarabic. ◇ smf [habitante] Mozarab. ◇ sm [lengua] Mozarabic.

mozo, za ◇ adj [joven] young; [soltero] single, unmarried. ◇ sm, f **- 1.** young boy (f young girl), young lad (f young lass) **- 2.** Andes & R Plata [camarero] waiter (f waitress).

➤ **mozo** sm **- 1.** [trabajador] assistant (worker); **mozo de cordel** o **de cuerda** porter; **mozo de estación** (station) porter **- 2.** [recluta] conscript.

➤ **moza** sf [sirvienta] girl, maid.

MP3 (abrev de **MPEG-1 Audio Layer-3**) sm INFORM MP3.

mu sm [mugido] moo; **no decir ni mu** not to say a word.

mucamo, ma sm, f Andes & R Plata [en casa] maid; [en hotel] chamberperson (f chambermaid).

muchachada sf Amér group of youngsters.

muchacho, cha sm, f boy (f girl).

➤ **muchacha** sf [sirvienta] maid.

muchedumbre sf [de gente] crowd, throng; [de cosas] great number, masses pl.

mucho, cha ◇ adj **- 1.** (en sing) [gran cantidad] a lot of; (pl) many, a lot of; (en interrogativas y negativas) much, a lot of; **tengo mucho sueño** I'm very sleepy; **muchos días** several days; **no tengo mucho tiempo** I haven't got much time **- 2.** (en sing) [demasiado]: **hay mucho niño aquí** there are too many kids here. ◇ pron (en sing) a lot; (pl) many, a lot; **tengo mucho que contarte** I have a lot to tell you; **¿queda dinero? - no mucho** is there any money left? - not much o not a lot; **muchos piensan igual** a lot of o many people think the same.

➤ **mucho** adv **- 1.** [gen] a lot; **habla mucho** he talks a lot; **me canso mucho** I get really o very tired; **me gusta mucho** I like it a lot o very much; **no me gusta mucho** I don't like it much; **(no) mucho más tarde** (not) much later **- 2.** [largo tiempo]: **hace mucho que no vienes** I haven't seen you for a long time; **¿dura mucho la obra?** is the play long?; **mucho antes/después** long before/after **- 3.** [frecuentemente]: **¿vienes mucho por aquí?** do you come here often? **- 4.** loc: **como mucho** at the most;

con mucho by far, easily; **ni con mucho** not by a long chalk; **ni mucho menos** far from it, by no means; **no está ni mucho menos decidido** it is by no means decided.

➤ **por mucho que** loc conj no matter how much, however much; **por mucho que insistas** no matter how much o however much you insist.

mucosidad sf mucus.

mucoso, sa adj mucous.

➤ **mucosas** sfpl mucous membranes.

muda sf **- 1.** [de la voz] breaking; [de piel, plumas] moulting **- 2.** [ropa interior] change of underwear.

mudable adj [persona] changeable; [carácter] fickle.

mudanza sf move; **estar de mudanza** to be moving.

mudar ◇ vt **- 1.** [gen] to change; [casa] to move; **cuando mude la voz** when his voice breaks **- 2.** [piel, plumas] to moult. ◇ vi [cambiar]: **mudar de** [opinión, color] to change; [domicilio] to move.

➤ **mudarse** vprnl: **mudarse (de casa)** to move (house); **mudarse (de ropa)** to change.

mudéjar adj & smf Mudejar.

mudo, da ◇ adj **- 1.** [sin habla] dumb **- 2.** [callado] silent, mute; **se quedó mudo** he was left speechless **- 3.** [sin sonido] silent. ◇ sm, f dumb person, mute.

mueble ◇ sm piece of furniture; **los muebles** the furniture (U); **mueble bar** cocktail cabinet; **salvar los muebles** to save face. ◇ adj ⊳ bien.

mueca sf [gen] face, expression; [de dolor] grimace; **hacer muecas** to make faces.

muela sf **- 1.** [diente - gen] tooth; [- molar] molar; **dolor de muelas** toothache; **muela del juicio** wisdom tooth **- 2.** [de molino] millstone; [para afilar] grindstone; ⊳ **moler**.

muelle sm **- 1.** [de colchón, reloj] spring **- 2.** [en el puerto] dock, quay; [en el río] wharf.

muera ⊳ morir.

muerda etc ⊳ morder.

muérdago sm mistletoe.

muere ⊳ morir.

muermo sm fam bore, drag; **tener muermo** to be bored.

muerte sf **- 1.** [gen] death; **a muerte** to the death, to the bitter end; **hasta la muerte** until death; **hasta que la muerte nos separe** till death do us part; **un susto de muerte** a terrible shock; **muerte cerebral** brain death; **muerte natural/violenta** natural/violent death; **muerte súbita** [de bebé] cot death; FÚT sudden death; [en tenis] tiebreak, tiebreaker;

de mala muerte third-rate, lousy; **estar de muerte** *fam* [comida] to be yummy; [persona] to be gorgeous - **2.** [homicidio] murder.

muerto, ta ◇ *pp* ▷ **morir**. ◇ *adj* - **1.** [gen] dead; **caer muerto** to drop dead; **estar muerto (de cansancio)** to be dead tired; **estar muerto de miedo/frío** to be scared/freezing to death; **estar muerto de hambre** to be starving - **2.** [color] dull - **3.** *loc*: **más muerto que vivo** frightened half to death; **medio muerto** [cansado] dead beat; **no tener donde caerse muerto** not to have a penny to one's name. ◇ *sm, f* dead person; [cadáver] corpse; **hubo dos muertos** two people died; **hacerse el muerto** to pretend to be dead, to play dead; **callarse como un muerto** to keep dead quiet; **cargar con el muerto** [trabajo, tarea] to be left holding the baby; [culpa] to get the blame; **el muerto al hoyo y el vivo al bollo** *prov* dead men have no friends *prov*; **hacer el muerto** to float on one's back.

muesca *sf* - **1.** [concavidad] notch, groove - **2.** [corte] nick.

muestra *sf* - **1.** [pequeña cantidad] sample; **muestra gratuita** free sample; **para muestra (basta) un botón** one example is enough - **2.** [señal] sign, show; [prueba] proof; [de cariño, aprecio] token; **dar muestras de** to show signs of - **3.** [modelo] model, pattern - **4.** [exposición] show, exhibition; ▷ **mostrar**.

muestrario *sm* collection of samples.

muestreo *sm* sample; [acción] sampling.

mueva *etc* ▷ **mover**.

mugido *sm* [de vaca] moo, mooing *(U)*; [de toro] bellow, bellowing *(U)*.

mugir [15] *vi* [vaca] to moo; [toro] to bellow.

mugre *sf* filth, muck.

mugriento, ta *adj* filthy.

muja ▷ **mugir**.

mujer *sf* woman; [cónyuge] wife; **ser toda una mujer** to be quite a woman; **mujer de su casa** good housewife; **mujer fatal** femme fatale; **mujer de la limpieza** cleaning lady; **mujer de negocios** businesswoman; **mujer objeto** sex object; **mujer pública** prostitute.

mujeriego, ga *adj* fond of the ladies.
➤ **mujeriego** *sm* womanizer, lady's man.

mujerzuela *sf despec* loose woman.

mulato, ta *adj & sm, f* mulatto.

muleta *sf* - **1.** [para andar] crutch; *fig* prop, support - **2.** TAUROM muleta *(red cape hanging from a stick used to tease the bull)*; *ver también* **tauromaquia**.

muletilla *sf* [frase] pet phrase; [palabra] pet word.

mullido, da *adj* soft, springy.

mullir *vt* to soften; [lana, almohada] to fluff up.

mulo, la *sm, f* - **1.** ZOOL mule; **ser más terco que una mula** to be as stubborn as a mule - **2.** *fam* [persona] brute, beast.

multa *sf* fine; **poner una multa a alguien** to fine sb.

multar *vt* to fine.

multicolor *adj* multicoloured.

multiconfesional *adj* [sociedad, organización] multifaith.

multicopista *sf* duplicator, duplicating machine.

multicultural *adj* multicultural.

multidisciplinar, multidisciplinario, ria *adj* multidisciplinary.

multilateral *adj* multilateral.

multimedia *adj inv* INFORM multimedia.

multimillonario, ria ◇ *adj*: **un negocio multimillonario** a multimillion pound *o* dollar business. ◇ *sm, f* multimillionaire.

multinacional *adj & sf* multinational.

múltiple *adj* [variado] multiple.
➤ **múltiples** *adj pl* [numerosos] many, numerous.

multiplicable *adj* multipliable.

multiplicación *sf* multiplication.

multiplicador, ra *adj* multiplying.
➤ **multiplicador** *sm* MAT multiplier.

multiplicando *sm* multiplicand.

multiplicar [10] *vt & vi* to multiply.
➤ **multiplicarse** *vprnl* - **1.** [persona] to do lots of things at the same time - **2.** BIOL to multiply.

multiplicidad *sf* multiplicity.

múltiplo, pla *adj* multiple.
➤ **múltiplo** *sm* multiple; **mínimo común múltiplo** lowest common multiple.

multipuesto *adj inv* INFORM multi-terminal *(antes de s)*.

multisalas *sm inv* [cine] multiplex cinema.

multitarea *adj inv* INFORM multitasking.

multitud *sf* [de personas] crowd; **una multitud de cosas** loads of *o* countless things.

multitudinario, ria *adj* extremely crowded; [manifestación] mass *(antes de s)*.

multiuso *adj inv* multipurpose.

mundanal *adj* worldly.

mundano, na *adj* - **1.** [del mundo] worldly, of the world - **2.** [de la vida social] (high) society.

mundial ◇ *adj* [política, economía, guerra] world *(antes de s)*; [tratado, organización, fama] worldwide. ◇ *sm* World Championships *pl*; [en fútbol] World Cup.

mundillo *sm* world, circles *pl*; **el mundillo literario** the literary world, literary circles.

mundo *sm* - **1.** [gen] world; **el nuevo mundo** the New World; **el otro mundo** the next world, the hereafter; **irse al otro mundo** to pass away; **el tercer mundo** the Third World; **desde que el mundo es mundo** since the dawn of time; **el mundo anda al revés** the world has been turned on its head; **el mundo es un pañuelo** it's a small world; **medio mundo** half the world, a lot of people; **no es cosa** o **nada del otro mundo** it's nothing special; **ponerse el mundo por montera** not to give a damn what people think; **por nada del mundo** not for (all) the world; **se le cayó el mundo encima** his world fell apart; **todo el mundo** everyone, everybody; **venir al mundo** to come into the world, to be born - **2.** [diferencia]: **hay un mundo entre ellos** they are worlds apart - **3.** [experiencia]: **hombre/mujer de mundo** man/woman of the world; **tener mundo** to be worldly-wise, to know the ways of the world; **ver** o **correr mundo** to see life.

mundología *sf* worldly wisdom, experience of life.

munición *sf* ammunition.

municipal ◇ *adj* town *(antes de s)*, municipal; [elecciones] local; [instalaciones] public. ◇ *smf* ▷ **guardia**.

municipio *sm* - **1.** [corporación] town council - **2.** [edificio] town hall - **3.** [territorio] town, municipality - **4.** [habitantes] inhabitants of a town o municipality.

muñeco, ca *sm, f* [juguete] doll; [marioneta] puppet; **muñeco de peluche** cuddly o soft toy; **muñeco de trapo** rag doll.
➤ **muñeco** *sm fig* puppet.
➤ **muñeca** *sf* - **1.** ANAT wrist - **2.** [mujer] doll - **3.** *Andes & R Dom fam* [enchufe]: **tener muñeco** to have friends in high places.
➤ **muñeco de nieve** *sm* snowman.

muñeira *sf popular Galician dance and music.*

muñequera *sf* wristband.

muñón *sm* stump.

mural ◇ *adj* [pintura] mural; [mapa] wall. ◇ *sm* mural.

muralla *sf* wall.

murciélago *sm* bat.

murga *sf* - **1.** [charanga] band of street musicians - **2.** *fam* [pesadez] drag, pain; **dar la murga** to be a pain.

muriera *etc* ▷ **morir**.

murmullo *sm* [gen] murmur, murmuring *(U)*; [de hojas] rustle, rustling *(U)*; [de insectos] buzz, buzzing *(U)*.

murmuración *sf* backbiting *(U)*, gossip *(U)*.

murmurador, ra ◇ *adj* backbiting, gossiping. ◇ *sm, f* backbiter, gossip.

murmurar ◇ *vt* to murmur. ◇ *vi* - **1.** [susurrar - persona] to murmur, to whisper; [- agua, viento] to murmur, to gurgle; [- hojas] to rustle - **2.** [criticar]: **murmurar (de)** to gossip o backbite (about) - **3.** [rezongar, quejarse] to grumble.

muro *sm lit & fig* wall; **muro de contención** retaining wall; **muro de las lamentaciones** Wailing Wall.
➤ **muro del sonido** *sm* sound barrier.

mus *sm inv card game played in pairs with bidding and in which players communicate by signs.*

musa *sf* - **1.** [inspiración] muse - **2.** MITOL Muse.
➤ **musas** *sfpl* [artes] arts.

musaraña *sf* ZOOL shrew; **mirar a las musarañas** to stare into space o thin air; **pensar en las musarañas** to have one's head in the clouds.

musculación *sf* body-building.

muscular *adj* muscular.

musculatura *sf* muscles *pl*.

músculo *sm* muscle.

musculoso, sa *adj* muscular.

muselina *sf* muslin.

museo *sm* museum; **museo de arte** art gallery.

musgo *sm* moss.

música ▷ **músico**.

musical *adj & sm* musical.

musicalidad *sf* musicality.

músico, ca ◇ *adj* musical. ◇ *sm, f* [persona] musician; **músico callejero** street musician, busker.
➤ **música** *sf* music; **poner música a algo** to set sthg to music; **música clásica/de cámara** classical/chamber music; **música instrumental/vocal** instrumental/choral music; **música ligera/pop** light/pop music; **música ambiental** background music; **música celestial** *irón* hot air, empty words *pl*; **irse con la música a otra parte** to clear off; **mandar a alguien con la música a otra parte** to send sb packing.

musitar *vt* to mutter, to mumble.

muslo *sm* thigh; [de pollo] drumstick.

mustela *sf* - **1.** [comadreja] weasel - **2.** [pez] dogfish.

mustiar [8] *vt* to wither, to wilt.
➤ **mustiarse** *vprnl* to wither, to wilt.

mustio, tia *adj* - **1.** [flor, planta] withered, wilted - **2.** [persona] down, gloomy.

musulmán, ana *adj & sm, f* Muslim, Moslem.

mutable *adj* changeable, mutable.

mutación *sf* [cambio] sudden change; BIOL mutation.

mutante *adj & smf* mutant.

mutar *vt* to mutate.

mutilación *sf* mutilation *(U)*.

mutilado, **da** ▷ *adj* mutilated. ▷ *sm, f* cripple; **mutilado de guerra** disabled veteran.

mutilar *vt* [gen] to mutilate; [estatua] to deface, to spoil.

mutis *sm inv* TEATRO exit; **hacer mutis** [marcharse] to leave, to go away; [callar] to keep quiet, to say nothing; TEATRO to exit.

mutismo *sm* - **1.** [mudez] muteness, dumbness - **2.** [silencio] silence.

mutua ▷ **mutuo**.

mutualidad *sf* - **1.** [asociación] mutual benefit society - **2.** [reciprocidad] mutuality.

mutualista ▷ *adj* mutual benefit society *(antes de s)*. ▷ *smf* member of a mutual benefit society.

mutuo, **tua** *adj* mutual.
◆ **mutua** *sf* mutual benefit society.

muy *adv* - **1.** [mucho] very; **muy bueno/cerca** very good/near; **muy de mañana** very early in the morning; **¡muy bien!** [vale] OK!, all right!; [qué bien] very good!, well done!; **es muy hombre** he's a real man; **eso es muy de ella** that's just like her; **eso es muy de los americanos** that's typically American; **¡el muy idiota!** what an idiot! - **2.** [demasiado] too; **es muy joven para votar** she's too young to vote.

n¹, **N** *sf* [letra] n, N.
◆ **N** *sm* - **1.** (*abrev de* **norte**) N - **2.**: **el 20 N** *20th November, the date of Franco's death*.

n² *sf* MAT: **n euros** n (number of) euros.

nabo *sm* turnip.

nácar *sm* mother-of-pearl.

nacarado, **da** *adj* mother-of-pearl *(antes de s)*.

nacer [29] *vi* - **1.** [venir al mundo - niño, animal] to be born; [- planta] to sprout, to begin to grow; [- pájaro] to hatch (out); **nacer de/en** to be born of/in; **nacer de familia humilde** to be born into a poor family; **nacer para algo** to be born to be sthg; **ha nacido cantante** she's a born singer; **volver a nacer** to have a lucky escape

- **2.** [surgir - pelo] to grow; [- río] to rise, to have its source; [- costumbre, actitud, duda] to have its roots.

nacido, **da** ▷ *adj* born. ▷ *sm, f*: **los nacidos hoy** those born today; **recién nacido** new-born baby; **ser un mal nacido** to be a wicked o vile person.

naciente *adj* - **1.** [día] dawning; [sol] rising - **2.** [gobierno, estado] new, fledgling; [interés] growing.

nacimiento *sm* - **1.** [gen] birth; [de planta] sprouting; **de nacimiento** from birth - **2.** [de río] source - **3.** [origen] origin, beginning - **4.** [belén] Nativity scene.

nación *sf* [gen] nation; [territorio] country.
◆ **Naciones Unidas** *sfpl* United Nations.

nacional ▷ *adj* national; [mercado, vuelo] domestic; [asuntos] home *(antes de s)*. ▷ *smf* HIST Francoist.

nacionalidad *sf* nationality; **doble nacionalidad** dual nationality.

nacionalismo *sm* nationalism.

nacionalista *adj* & *smf* nationalist.

nacionalización *sf* [de educación, bienes] nationalization; [de persona] naturalization.

nacionalizar [13] *vt* - **1.** [banca, bienes] to nationalize - **2.** [persona] to naturalize.
◆ **nacionalizarse** *vprnl* to become naturalized.

nada ▷ *pron* nothing; *(en negativas)* anything; **no he leído nada de este autor** I haven't read anything by this author; **no hay nada como un buen libro** there is nothing like a good book; **nada más** nothing else, nothing more; **no quiero nada más** I don't want anything else; **no dijo nada de nada** he didn't say anything at all; **te he traído un regalito de nada** I've brought you a little something; **de nada** [respuesta a 'gracias'] not at all, you're welcome; **como si nada** as if nothing had happened; **esto no es nada** that's nothing. ▷ *adv* - **1.** [en absoluto] at all; **la película no me ha gustado nada** I didn't like the film at all; **no es nada extraño** it's not at all strange - **2.** [poco] a little, a bit; **no hace nada que salió** he left just a minute ago; **nada menos que** [cosa] no less than; [persona] none other than. ▷ *sf*: **la nada** nothingness, the void; **salir de la nada** to appear out of o from nowhere.
◆ **nada más** *loc conj* no sooner, as soon as; **nada más salir de casa se puso a llover** no sooner had I left the house than it started to rain, as soon as I left the house, it started to rain.

nadador, **ra** ▷ *adj* swimming. ▷ *sm, f* swimmer.

nadar *vi* - **1.** [gen] to swim; [flotar] to float - **2.** [abundar]: **nadar en** [dinero] to be rolling in; [deudas] to be up to one's neck in.

nadería *sf* trifle, little thing.

nadie ⬦ *pron* nobody, no one; **nadie lo sabe** nobody knows; **casi nadie** hardly anybody; **no se lo dije a nadie** I didn't tell anybody; **no ha llamado nadie** nobody phoned. ⬦ *sm*: **un don nadie** a nobody.

nado ➥ **a nado** *loc adv* swimming.

nafta *sf* - **1.** QUÍM naphtha - **2.** *R Dom* [gasolina] petrol *UK*, gas *US*, gasoline *US*.

naftalina *sf* naphthalene, naphthaline.

náhuatl ⬦ *adj* Nahuatl. ⬦ *smf* Nahuatl (indian).

Náhuatl

Although many indigenous languages were (and still are) spoken in what was to become Mexico and Central America at the time of the Spanish conquest, it was Nahuatl, the language of the Aztecs, which the Spaniards adopted as a lingua franca. This has helped to ensure the survival of the language in better health than others, and has also meant that many of its words entered the vocabulary of Spanish, and through it other languages. In English, for example, we find "tomato" and "chocolate". There are still over one and a half million speakers of its various dialects in Mexico today.

naïf [na'if] *adj* naïve, primitivistic.

nailon, nilón, nylon® *sm* nylon.

naipe *sm* (playing) card.
➥ **naipes** *smpl* cards.

nalga *sf* buttock.

nana *sf* - **1.** [canción] lullaby - **2.** *fam* [abuela] grandma, nana - **3.** *Col & Méx* [niñera] nanny.

nanay *interj fam*: ¡**nanay**! no way!, not likely!

nanómetro *sm* nanometre.

napa *sf* nappa (leather).

napalm [na'palm] *sm* napalm.

napia *(gen pl) sf fam* snout, conk.

napoleónico, ca *adj* Napoleonic.

naranja ⬦ *adj inv* orange. ⬦ *sm* [color] orange. ⬦ *sf* [fruto] orange; ¡**naranjas de la china**! no way!
➥ **media naranja** *sf fam* other o better half.

naranjal *sm* orange grove.

naranjo *sm* - **1.** [árbol] orange tree - **2.** [madera] orange (wood).

narcisismo *sm* narcissism.

narcisista *smf* narcissist.

narciso *sm* - **1.** BOT narcissus - **2.** [hombre] narcissist.

narcótico, ca *adj* narcotic.
➥ **narcótico** *sm* narcotic; [droga] drug.

narcotizar [13] *vt* to drug.

narcotraficante *smf* drug trafficker.

narcotráfico *sm* drug trafficking.

nardo *sm* nard, spikenard.

narigudo, da ⬦ *adj* big-nosed. ⬦ *sm, f* big-nosed person.

nariz *sf* - **1.** [órgano] nose; **hablar por la nariz** to talk through one's nose; **sonarse la nariz** to blow one's nose; **tener la nariz tapada** to have a stuffed up o blocked nose; **nariz aguileña/chata/respingona** Roman/snub/turned-up nose - **2.** [orificio] nostril - **3.** [olfato] sense of smell - **4.** *loc*: **me da en la nariz que...** *fam* I've got a feeling that...; **dar a alguien en las narices con algo** *fam* to rub sb's nose in sthg; **darse de narices contra algo** *fam* to bump into sthg, to go flat into sthg; **de narices** *fam* [estupendo] great, brilliant; **estar hasta las narices (de algo)** *fam* to be fed up to the back teeth (with sthg); **hacer algo por narices** *fam* to have no alternative but to do sthg; **me estás hinchando las narices** *fam* you're beginning to get up my nose; **meter las narices en algo** *fam* to poke o stick one's nose into sthg; **no ver uno más allá de sus narices** *fam* not to see past one's nose; **romper las narices a alguien** *fam* to smash sb's face in; **romperse las narices** *fam* to fall flat on one's face; ¡**tiene narices la cosa!** *fam* it's a scandal!

narizotas *smf inv fam* big-nose.

narración *sf* - **1.** [cuento, relato] narrative, story - **2.** [acción] narration.

narrador, ra *sm, f* narrator.

narrar *vt* [contar] to recount, to tell.

narrativo, va *adj* narrative.
➥ **narrativa** *sf* narrative.

NASA (*abrev de* National Aeronautics and Space Administration) *sf* NASA.

nasal *adj* nasal.

nasalizar [13] *vt* to nasalize.

nata *sf* - **1.** *fig* [gen] cream; **nata batida** o **montada** whipped cream - **2.** [de leche hervida] skin.

natación *sf* swimming.

natal *adj* [país] native; [ciudad, pueblo] home (*antes de s*).

natalidad *sf* birth rate.

natillas *sfpl* custard (*U*).

natividad *sf* nativity.
➥ **Natividad** *sf*: **la Natividad** Christmas.

nativo, va *adj* & *sm, f* native.

nato, ta *adj* [gen] born; [cargo, título] ex officio.

natura *sf* nature; **contra natura** against nature, unnatural.

natural ◇ adj - **1.** [gen] natural; [flores, fruta, leche] fresh; **soy rubia natural** I'm a natural blonde; **al natural** [persona] in one's natural state; [fruta] in its own juice; **ser natural en alguien** to be natural o normal for sb - **2.** [nativo] native; **ser natural de** to come from - **3.** [ilegítimo] illegitimate. ◇ smf [nativo] native. ◇ sm [talante] nature, disposition.

naturaleza sf - **1.** [gen] nature; **por naturaleza** by nature; **la madre naturaleza** Mother Nature; **la naturaleza humana** human nature; **naturaleza muerta** still life - **2.** [complexión] constitution.

naturalidad sf naturalness; **con naturalidad** naturally.

naturalismo sm naturalism.

naturalización sf naturalization.

naturalizado, **da** adj naturalized.

naturalizar [13] vt to naturalize.

➤ **naturalizarse** vprnl to become naturalized.

naturismo sm way of life promoting return to nature.

naturista smf person favouring return to nature.

naturópata smf naturopath.

naufragar [16] vi - **1.** [barco] to sink, to be wrecked; [persona] to be shipwrecked - **2.** [fracasar] to fail, to collapse.

naufragio sm - **1.** [de barco] shipwreck - **2.** [fracaso] failure, collapse.

náufrago, **ga** ◇ adj shipwrecked. ◇ sm, f shipwrecked person, castaway.

náusea (gen pl) sf nausea (U), sickness (U); **me da náuseas** it makes me sick; **tener náuseas** to feel nauseated, to feel sick.

nauseabundo, **da** adj nauseating, sickening.

náutico, **ca** adj [gen] nautical; DEP water (antes de s).

➤ **náutica** sf navigation, seamanship.

navaja sf - **1.** [cuchillo - pequeño] penknife; [- más grande] jackknife; **navaja automática** flick knife, switchblade; **navaja de afeitar** razor - **2.** [molusco] razor-shell, razor clam.

navajazo sm stab, slash.

navajero, **ra** sm, f thug who carries a knife.

naval adj naval.

Navarra n pr Navarre.

navarro, **rra** adj & sm, f Navarrese.

nave sf - **1.** [barco] ship; **quemar las naves** to burn one's boats o bridges - **2.** [vehículo] craft; **nave espacial** spaceship, spacecraft; **nave extraterrestre** (extraterrestrial) spaceship - **3.** [de fábrica] shop, plant; [almacén] warehouse - **4.** [de iglesia] nave.

navegable adj navigable.

navegación sf navigation; **navegación aérea/fluvial/marítima** air/river/sea navigation; **navegación de altura** ocean navigation.

navegador sm INFORM browser.

navegante ◇ adj sailing; [pueblo] seafaring. ◇ smf navigator.

navegar [16] ◇ vi [barco] to sail; [avión] to fly; **navegar por Internet** INFORM to surf the Net. ◇ vt [barco] to sail; [avión] to fly.

Navidad sf - **1.** [día] Christmas (Day) - **2.** (gen pl) [periodo] Christmas (time); **felices Navidades** Merry Christmas.

navideño, **ña** adj Christmas (antes de s).

naviero, **ra** adj shipping.

➤ **naviero** sm [armador] shipowner.

➤ **naviera** sf [compañía] shipping company.

navío sm large ship.

nazareno, **na** adj & sm, f Nazarene.

➤ **nazareno** sm penitent in Holy Week processions.

➤ **Nazareno** sm: **el Nazareno** Jesus of Nazareth.

nazca etc ⊳ **nacer**.

nazi adj & smf Nazi.

nazismo sm Nazism.

NB (abrev de nota bene) NB.

neblina sf mist.

nebulosidad sf [de nubes] cloudiness; [de niebla] fogginess.

nebuloso, **sa** adj - **1.** [con nubes] cloudy; [de niebla] foggy - **2.** [idea, mirada] vague.

➤ **nebulosa** sf ASTRON nebula.

necedad sf - **1.** [estupidez] stupidity, foolishness - **2.** [dicho, hecho] stupid o foolish thing; **decir necedades** to talk nonsense.

necesario, **ria** adj necessary; **un mal necesario** a necessary evil; **es necesario hacerlo** it needs to be done; **no es necesario que lo hagas** you don't need to do it; **si fuera necesario** if need be.

neceser sm toilet bag o case.

necesidad sf - **1.** [gen] need; **de (primera) necesidad** essential; **obedecer a la necesidad (de)** to arise from the need (to); **tener necesidad de algo** to need sthg; **hacer de la necesidad virtud** to make a virtue of necessity; **la necesidad aguza el ingenio** prov necessity is the mother of invention prov - **2.** [obligación] necessity; **por necesidad** out of necessity - **3.** [hambre] hunger.

➤ **necesidades** sfpl: **hacer (uno) sus necesidades** eufem to answer the call of nature.

necesitado, **da** ◇ adj needy; **necesitado de** in need of. ◇ sm, f needy o poor person; **los necesitados** the poor.

necesitar *vt* to need; **necesito que me lo digas** I need you to tell me; **'se necesita piso'** 'flat wanted'.
◆ **necesitar de** *vi* to have need of.

necio, cia ◇ *adj* stupid, foolish; *Méx* [fastidioso] boring. ◇ *sm, f* idiot, fool; *Méx* [fastidioso] bore, pain.

nécora *sf* fiddler crab.

necrófago, ga *adj* necrophagous.

necrofilia *sf* necrophilia.

necrología *sf* obituary; [lista de esquelas] obituaries *pl*, obituary column.

necrológico, ca *adj* obituary *(antes de s)*.

necrópolis *sf inv* necropolis.

necrosis *sf inv* necrosis.

néctar *sm* nectar.

nectarina *sf* nectarine.

nefasto, ta *adj* [funesto] ill-fated; [dañino] bad, harmful; [pésimo] terrible, awful.

nefrítico, ca *adj* nephritic.

nefrología *sf* nephrology.

negación *sf* - **1.** [desmentido] denial - **2.** [negativa] refusal - **3.** [lo contrario] antithesis, negation - **4.** GRAM negative.

negado, da ◇ *adj* useless, inept. ◇ *sm, f* useless person, dead loss.

negar [35] *vt* - **1.** [rechazar] to deny - **2.** [denegar] to refuse, to deny; **negarle algo a alguien** to refuse o deny sb sthg.
◆ **negarse** *vprnl*: **negarse (a)** to refuse (to).

negativo, va *adj* - **1.** [gen] negative - **2.** MAT minus *(antes de s)*, negative.
◆ **negativo** *sm* FOTO negative.
◆ **negativa** *sf* - **1.** [rechazo] refusal; **una negativa rotunda** a flat refusal - **2.** [mentís] denial.

negligencia *sf* negligence.

negligente *adj* negligent.

negociable *adj* negotiable.

negociación *sf* negotiation; **negociación colectiva** collective bargaining.

negociado *sm* - **1.** department, section - **2.** *Andes & R Plata* shady deal.

negociador, ra ◇ *adj* negotiating. ◇ *sm, f* negotiator.

negociante *sm, f* [comerciante] businessman (*f* businesswoman); **negociante en vinos** wine merchant.

negociar [8] ◇ *vi* - **1.** [comerciar] to do business; **negociar en** to deal o trade in; **negociar con** to deal o trade with - **2.** [discutir] to negotiate. ◇ *vt* to negotiate.

negocio *sm* - **1.** [gen] business; **el mundo de los negocios** the business world; **negocio familiar** family business - **2.** [transacción] deal,

(business) transaction; **negocio sucio** shady deal, dirty business *(U)* - **3.** [operación ventajosa] good deal, bargain; **hacer negocio** to do well; **negocio redondo** great bargain, excellent deal - **4.** [comercio] trade.

negra *sf* ▷ **negro**.

negrero, ra ◇ *adj* [explotador] tyrannical. ◇ *sm, f* - **1.** HIST slave trader - **2.** [explotador] slave driver.

negrita, negrilla ▷ **letra**.

negro, gra ◇ *adj* - **1.** [gen] black - **2.** [moreno] tanned - **3.** [suerte] awful, rotten; [porvenir] black, gloomy; **pasarlas negras** to have a hard time; **verlo todo negro** to be pessimistic - **4.** [furioso] furious, fuming; **poner negro a alguien** to anger sb; **ponerse negro** to get mad o angry - **5.** CINE: **cine negro** film noir. ◇ *sm, f* black man (*f* black woman); **trabajar como un negro** to work like a slave.
◆ **negro** *sm* [color] black.
◆ **negra** *sf* - **1.** MÚS crotchet - **2.** *loc*: **tener la negra** *fam* to have bad luck.

negroide *adj* negroid.

negrura *sf* blackness.

negruzco, ca *adj* blackish.

negué *etc* ▷ **negar**.

nene, na *sm, f* - **1.** *fam* [niño] baby - **2.** [apelativo cariñoso] dear, darling.

nenúfar *sm* water lily.

neocelandés, esa = **neozelandés**.

neoclasicismo *sm* neoclassicism.

neoclásico, ca ◇ *adj* neoclassical. ◇ *sm, f* neoclassicist.

neofascismo *sm* neofascism.

neofascista *adj* & *smf* neofascist.

neófito, ta *sm, f* - **1.** RELIG neophyte - **2.** [aprendiz] novice.

neogótico, ca *adj* Neo-Gothic.
◆ **neogótico** *sm* Neo-Gothic movement.

neolatino, na *adj* [gen] Neo-Latin; [lengua] Romance.

neolítico, ca *adj* Neolithic.
◆ **neolítico** *sm* Neolithic (period).

neologismo *sm* neologism.

neón *sm* - **1.** QUÍM neon - **2.** [luz] neon light.

neonato, ta *adj* *culto* newborn.

neonazi *adj* & *smf* neo-Nazi.

neorrealismo *sm* neorealism.

neoyorquino, na ◇ *adj* New York *(antes de s)*, of/relating to New York. ◇ *sm, f* New Yorker.

neozelandés, **esa**, **neocelandés**, **esa** <> *adj* New Zealand *(antes de s)*, of/relating to New Zealand. <> *sm, f* New Zealander.

Nepal *n pr*: **el Nepal** Nepal.

nepalés, **esa**, **nepaleses**, **esas**, **nepalí** *(pl* **nepalíes**) *adj* & *sm, f* Nepalese.

◆ **nepalés, nepalí** *sm* [lengua] Nepalese.

nepotismo *sm* nepotism.

Neptuno *n pr* Neptune.

nervio *sm* - **1.** ANAT nerve; **nervio ciático** sciatic nerve; **nervio óptico** optic nerve - **2.** [de carne] sinew - **3.** BOT vein, rib - **4.** [vigor] energy, vigour; **sus niños son puro nervio** her kids never sit still for five minutes - **5.** ARQUIT rib.

◆ **nervios** *smpl* [estado mental] nerves; **está mal de los nervios** he's suffering from a nervous condition; **tener nervios** to be nervous; **poner los nervios de punta a alguien** to get on sb's nerves; **tener los nervios de punta** to be on edge; **tener nervios de acero** to have nerves of steel.

nerviosismo *sm* nervousness, nerves *pl*.

nervioso, **sa** *adj* - **1.** [ANAT - sistema, enfermedad] nervous; [- tejido, célula, centro] nerve *(antes de s)* - **2.** [inquieto] nervous; **ponerse nervioso** to get nervous - **3.** [muy activo] highly-strung - **4.** [irritado] worked-up, uptight; **poner nervioso a alguien** to get on sb's nerves; **ponerse nervioso** to get uptight *o* worked up.

nervudo, **da** *adj* sinewy.

netiqueta *sf* INFORM netiquette.

neto, **ta** *adj* - **1.** [claro] clear, clean; [verdad] simple, plain - **2.** [peso, sueldo] net.

neumático, **ca** *adj* pneumatic.

◆ **neumático** *sm* tyre; **neumático de repuesto** spare tyre.

neumonía *sf* pneumonia.

neuralgia *sf* neuralgia.

neurálgico, **ca** *adj* - **1.** MED neuralgic - **2.** [importante] critical.

neurastenia *sf* nervous exhaustion.

neurasténico, **ca** <> *adj* MED neurasthenic. <> *sm, f* MED neurasthenic person.

neurocirugía *sf* neurosurgery.

neurocirujano, **na** *sm, f* neurosurgeon.

neurología *sf* neurology.

neurológico, **ca** *adj* neurological.

neurólogo, **ga** *sm, f* neurologist.

neurona *sf* neuron, nerve cell.

neuropatía *sf* neuropathy.

neurosis *sf inv* neurosis; **neurosis de guerra** shell shock.

neurótico, **ca** *adj* & *sm, f* neurotic.

neurotransmisor *sm* neurotransmitter.

neutral *adj* & *smf* neutral.

neutralidad *sf* neutrality.

neutralizable *adj* [efecto, consecuencia] remediable.

neutralización *sf* neutralization.

neutralizador, **ra** *adj* neutralizing.

neutralizar [13] *vt* to neutralize.

◆ **neutralizarse** *vprnl* to neutralize each other.

neutro, **tra** *adj* - **1.** [gen] neutral - **2.** BIOL & GRAM neuter.

neutrón *sm* neutron.

nevado, **da** *adj* snowy.

◆ **nevada** *sf* snowfall.

nevar [19] *v impers* to snow.

nevera *sf* fridge *UK*, icebox *US*.

nevería *sf Caribe & Méx* [heladería] ice cream parlour.

nevisca *sf* snow flurry.

neviscar [10] *v impers* to snow lightly.

nexo *sm* link, connection; [relación] relation, connection.

ni <> *conj*: **ni... ni...** neither... nor...; **ni mañana ni pasado** neither tomorrow nor the day after; **ni puedo ni quiero venir** I can't come and I don't want to either, I can't come, nor do I want to; **no... ni...** neither... nor..., not... or... (either); **no es alto ni bajo** he's neither tall nor short, he's not tall or short (either); **no es rojo ni verde ni azul** it's neither red nor green nor blue; **ni un/una...** not a single...; **no me quedaré ni un minuto más** I'm not staying a minute longer; **ni uno/una** not a single one; **no he aprobado ni una** I haven't passed a single one; **ni que** as if; **¡ni que yo fuera tonto!** as if I were that stupid! <> *adv* not even; **anda tan atareado que ni tiene tiempo para comer** he's so busy he doesn't even have time to eat.

Niágara *sm*: **las cataratas del Niágara** the Niagara Falls.

Nicaragua *n pr* Nicaragua.

nicaragüense *adj* & *smf* Nicaraguan.

nicho *sm* niche; **nicho ecológico** ecological niche.

nicotina *sf* nicotine.

nidada *sf* [de crías] brood; [de huevos] clutch.

nidificar [10] *vi* to (build a) nest.

nido *sm* - **1.** [gen] nest; **nido de víboras** *fig* nest of vipers; **caer del nido** to be extremely gullible - **2.** [escondrijo] hiding-place.

niebla *sf* - **1.** [densa] fog; [neblina] mist; **hay niebla** it's foggy - **2.** [confusión] fogginess, cloudiness.

niega *etc* ▷ **negar**.

nieto, **ta** *sm, f* grandson (*f* granddaughter).

nieva *etc* ⊳ **nevar**.

nieve *sf* - **1.** METEOR snow - **2.** CULIN: **a punto de nieve** beaten stiff - **3.** *fam* [cocaína] snow - **4.** *Caribe* & *Méx* [granizado] *drink of flavoured crushed ice.*

➤ **nieves** *sfpl* [nevada] snows, snowfall *sing.*

➤ **nieve carbónica** *sf* carbon dioxide snow.

NIF (*abrev de* **número de identificación fiscal**) *sm* ≃ National Insurance number *UK.*

Níger *sm* Niger.

Nigeria *n pr* Nigeria.

night-club ['naitklub] (*pl* **night-clubs**) *sm* nightclub.

nihilismo *sm* nihilism.

Nilo *sm*: **el Nilo** the (river) Nile.

nilón = **nailon**.

nimbo *sm* - **1.** METEOR nimbus - **2.** [de astro, santo] halo, nimbus.

nimiedad *sf* - **1.** [cualidad] insignificance, triviality - **2.** [dicho, hecho] trifle.

nimio, **mia** *adj* insignificant, trivial.

ninfa *sf* nymph.

ninfómana ⟨⟩ *adj f* nymphomaniac. ⟨⟩ *sf* nymphomaniac.

ninfomanía *sf* nymphomania.

ninguno, **na** ⟨⟩ *adj* (*antes de sm*: **ningún**) no; **no dieron ninguna respuesta** no answer was given; **no tengo ningún interés en hacerlo** I've no interest in doing it, I'm not at all interested in doing it; **no tengo ningún hijo/ninguna buena idea** I don't have any children/good ideas; **no tiene ninguna gracia** it's not funny. ⟨⟩ *pron* [cosa] none, not any; [persona] nobody, no one; **ninguno funciona** none of them works; **no hay ninguno** there aren't any, there are none; **ninguno lo sabrá** no one O nobody will know; **ninguno de** none of; **ninguno de ellos** none of them; **ninguno de los dos** neither of them.

niña ⊳ **niño**.

niñato, **ta** *sm, f* spoiled brat.

niñería *sf* - **1.** [cualidad] childishness *(U)* - **2.** [tontería] silly O childish thing.

niñero, **ra** *adj* fond of children.

➤ **niñera** *sf* nanny.

niñez *sf* childhood.

niño, **ña** ⟨⟩ *adj* young. ⟨⟩ *sm, f* - **1.** [crío] child, boy (*f* girl); [bebé] baby; **los niños** the children; **niño bien** *despec* spoilt brat; **niño probeta** test-tube baby; **niño prodigio** child prodigy; **niño de teta** O **pecho** tiny baby; **estar como un niño con zapatos nuevos** to be as pleased as punch; **es culpa de la crisis - ¡qué crisis ni qué niño muerto!** it's the fault of the

recession - don't talk to me about recessions!; **ser el niño bonito de alguien** to be sb's pet O blue-eyed boy - **2.** [joven] young boy (*f* young girl).

➤ **niña** *sf* [del ojo] pupil; **la niña de los ojos** *fig* the apple of one's eye.

nipón, **ona** *adj* & *sm, f* Japanese.

níquel *sm* nickel.

niquelar *vt* to nickel-plate.

niqui *sm* T-shirt.

nirvana *sm* nirvana.

níspero *sm* medlar.

nitidez *sf* clarity; [de imágenes, colores] sharpness.

nítido, **da** *adj* clear; [imágenes, colores] sharp.

nitrato *sm* nitrate; **nitrato de Chile** Chile saltpetre, nitre.

nítrico, **ca** *adj* nitric.

nitrogenado, **da** *adj* nitrogenous.

nitrógeno *sm* nitrogen.

nitroglicerina *sf* nitroglycerine.

nitroso, **sa** *adj* nitrous.

nivel *sm* - **1.** [gen] level; [altura] height; **al nivel de** level with; **al nivel del mar** at sea level; **nivel del agua** water level - **2.** [grado] level, standard; **tengo un buen nivel de inglés** I'm good at English; **al mismo nivel (que)** on a level O par (with); **a nivel europeo** at a European level; **investigación de alto nivel** high-level research; **nivel mental** level of intelligence; **nivel de vida** standard of living; **niveles de audiencia** ratings - **3.** [herramienta] spirit level.

nivelación *sf* - **1.** [allanamiento] levelling - **2.** [equilibrio] levelling out, evening out.

nivelador, **ra** *adj* levelling.

➤ **niveladora** *sf* bulldozer.

nivelar *vt* - **1.** [allanar] to level - **2.** [equilibrar] to even out; FIN to balance.

no ⟨⟩ *adv* - **1.** [expresa negación - gen] not; [- en respuestas] no; [- con sustantivos] non-; **no sé** I don't know; **no veo nada** I can't see anything; **no es fácil** it's not easy, it isn't easy; **no tiene dinero** he has no money, he hasn't got any money; **todavía no** not yet; **¿no vienes? - no, no creo** aren't you coming? - no, I don't think so; **no fumadores** non-smokers; **no bien** as soon as; **no ya... sino que...** not only... but (also)...; **¡a que no lo haces!** I bet you don't do it!; **¿cómo no?** of course; **pues no, eso sí que no** certainly not; **¡que no!** I said no! - **2.** [expresa duda, extrañeza]: **¿no irás a venir?** you're not coming, are you?; **estamos de acuerdo, ¿no?** we're agreed then, are we?; **es español, ¿no?** he's Spanish, isn't he? ⟨⟩ *sm* no.

n.º (*abrev de* **número**) no.

nobiliario, ria *adj* noble, nobiliary.

noble *adj* & *smf* noble; **los nobles** the nobility.

nobleza *sf* nobility; **nobleza obliga** noblesse oblige.

noche *sf* night; [atardecer] evening; **al caer la noche** at nightfall; **ayer por la noche** last night; **esta noche** tonight; **hacer noche en** to stay the night in; **hacerse de noche** to get dark; **por la noche, de noche** at night; **buenas noches** [despedida] good night; [saludo] good evening; **noche cerrada** dark night; **noche de bodas** wedding night; **noche del estreno** first o opening night; **noche toledana** sleepless night; **de la noche a la mañana** overnight; **pasar la noche en claro** o **vela** to have a sleepless night; **ser la noche y el día** to be as different as night and day.

Nochebuena *sf* Christmas Eve.

nochero *sm* - **1.** C*Sur* night watchman - **2.** *Amér* [mesita] bedside table.

Nochevieja *sf* New Year's Eve.

noción *sf* [concepto] notion; **tener noción (de)** to have an idea (of).
  ↬ **nociones** *sfpl* [conocimiento básico]**: tener nociones de** to have a smattering of.

nocivo, va *adj* [gen] harmful; [gas] noxious.

noctambulismo *sm* being out and about at night.

noctámbulo, la ◇ *adj* active at night; [vida] night *(antes de s)*. ◇ *sm, f* night owl.

nocturno, na *adj* - **1.** [club, tren, vuelo] night *(antes de s)*; [clase] evening *(antes de s)* - **2.** [animales, plantas] nocturnal.
  ↬ **nocturno** *sm* MÚS nocturne.

nodo *sm* node.

nodriza *sf* wet nurse.

nódulo *sm* nodule.

nómada ◇ *adj* nomadic. ◇ *smf* nomad.

nomadismo *sm* nomadism.

nombrado, da *adj* - **1.** [citado] mentioned - **2.** [famoso] famous, well-known.

nombramiento *sm* appointment.

nombrar *vt* - **1.** [citar] to mention - **2.** [designar] to appoint.

nombre *sm* - **1.** [gen] name; **a nombre de** [carta] addressed to; [cheque] made out to; **conocer a alguien de nombre** to know somebody by name; **de nombre Juan** called Juan, Juan by name; **poner nombre a** to name; **sin nombre** nameless; **nombre artístico/comercial** stage name/trade name; **nombre y apellidos** full name; **nombre compuesto** compound name; **nombre de dominio** [inform] domain name; **nombre de pila** first o Christian name; **nombre de soltera** maiden name; **en nombre de** on behalf of; **llamar a las cosas por su nombre** to call a spade a spade; **lo que hizo no tiene nombre** what he did is outrageous - **2.** [fama] reputation; **hacerse un nombre** to make a name for o.s.; **tener mucho nombre** to be renowned o famous - **3.** GRAM noun; **nombre abstracto/colectivo** abstract/collective noun; **nombre común/propio** common/proper noun.

nomenclatura *sf* nomenclature.

nomeolvides *sm inv* - **1.** BOT forget-me-not - **2.** [pulsera] identity bracelet.

nómina *sf* - **1.** [lista de empleados] payroll; **estar en nómina** to be on the staff - **2.** [pago] wage packet, wages *pl* - **3.** [hoja de salario] payslip.

nominación *sf* nomination.

nominado, da *adj* nominated.

nominal *adj* nominal.

nominar *vt* to nominate.

nominativo, va *adj* COM bearing a person's name, nominal.
  ↬ **nominativo** *sm* GRAM nominative.

nomo, gnomo *sm* gnome.

non ◇ *adj* odd, uneven. ◇ *sm* odd number.
  ↬ **nones** *adv* [no] no way, absolutely not.

nonagenario, ria ◇ *adj* ninety-year old. ◇ *sm, f* person in his/her nineties.

nonagésimo, ma *num* ninetieth.

noquear *vt* DEP to knock out.

nordeste = **noreste**.

nórdico, ca ◇ *adj* - **1.** [del norte] northern, northerly - **2.** [escandinavo] Nordic. ◇ *sm, f* Nordic person.

noreste, nordeste ◇ *adj* [posición, parte] northeast, northeastern; [dirección, viento] northeasterly. ◇ *sm* north-east.

noria *sf* - **1.** [para agua] water wheel - **2.** [de feria] big wheel UK, Ferris wheel.

norma *sf* standard; [regla] rule; **es la norma hacerlo así** it's usual to do it this way; **por norma** as a rule; **tener por norma hacer algo** to make it a rule to do sthg; **normas de conducta** [principios] standards (of behaviour) *pl*; **normas de seguridad** safety regulations.

normal *adj* normal; **normal y corriente** run-of-the-mill; **es una persona normal y corriente** he's a perfectly ordinary person.

normalidad *sf* normality.

normalización *sf* - **1.** [vuelta a la normalidad] normalization - **2.** [regularización] standardization.

normalizar [13] *vt* - **1.** [volver normal] to return to normal - **2.** [estandarizar] to standardize.
  ↬ **normalizarse** *vprnl* to return to normal.

normando, da ◇ *adj* - **1.** [de Normandía] Norman - **2.** HIST [nórdico] Norse. ◇ *sm, f* - **1.** [habitante de Normandía] Norman - **2.** HIST [nórdico] Norseman (*f* Norsewoman).

normativo, va *adj* normative.
➡ **normativa** *sf* regulations *pl*.

noroeste ◇ *adj* [posición, parte] northwest, northwestern; [dirección, viento] northwesterly. ◇ *sm* northwest.

norte ◇ *adj* [posición, parte] north, northern; [dirección, viento] northerly. ◇ *sm* - **1.** GEOGR north - **2.** [objetivo] goal, objective; **perder el norte** to lose one's bearings O way.

norteamericano, na *adj* & *sm, f* North American, American.

norteño, ña ◇ *adj* northern. ◇ *sm, f* northerner.

Noruega *n pr* Norway.

noruego, ga *adj* & *sm, f* Norwegian.
➡ **noruego** *sm* [lengua] Norwegian.

nos *pron pers* - **1.** *(complemento directo)* us; **le gustaría vernos** she'd like to see us - **2.** *(complemento indirecto)* (to) us; **nos lo dio** he gave it to us; **nos tiene miedo** he's afraid of us - **3.** *(reflexivo)* ourselves - **4.** *(recíproco)* each other; **nos enamoramos** we fell in love (with each other).

nosocomio *sm* Amér hospital.

nosotros, tras *pron pers* - **1.** *(sujeto)* we - **2.** *(predicado)*: **somos nosotros** it's us - **3.** *(después de prep, complemento)* us; **vente a comer con nosotros** come and eat with us - **4.** *loc*: **entre nosotros** between you and me, just between the two of us.

nostalgia *sf* [del pasado] nostalgia; [de país, amigos] homesickness.

nostálgico, ca ◇ *adj* [del pasado] nostalgic; [de país, amigos] homesick. ◇ *sm, f* nostalgic person.

nota *sf* - **1.** [gen & MÚS] note; **tomar nota de algo** [apuntar] to note sthg down; [fijarse] to take note of sthg; **tomar notas** to take notes; **nota al margen** marginal note; **nota a pie de página** footnote; **nota dominante** prevailing mood; **notas de sociedad** society column *sing* - **2.** EDUC mark; **ir para nota** to go for top marks; **sacar** O **tener buenas notas** to get good marks; **nota de corte** *minimum marks for entry into university* - **3.** [cuenta] bill; **nota de gastos** expenses claim - **4.** *loc*: **dar la nota** to make o.s. conspicuous; **de mala nota** of ill repute; **forzar la nota** to go too far.
➡ **nota bene** *sf* [correspondencia] nota bene, N.B.

notable ◇ *adj* remarkable, outstanding. ◇ *sm* - **1.** EDUC merit, second class - **2.** *(gen pl)* [persona] notable, distinguished person.

notar *vt* - **1.** [advertir] to notice; **te noto cansado** you look tired to me; **hacer notar algo** to point sthg out - **2.** [sentir] to feel; **noto un dolor raro** I can feel a strange pain.
➡ **notarse** *vprnl* to be apparent; **se nota que le gusta** you can tell she likes it; **¡pues no se nota!** you could have fooled me!

notaría *sf* - **1.** [profesión] profession of notary - **2.** [oficina] notary's office.

notariado *sm* [profesión] profession of notary.

notarial *adj* notarial.

notario, ria *sm, f* notary (public).

noticia *sf* news *(U)*; **una noticia** a piece of news; **tener noticias** to have news; **¿tienes noticias suyas?** have you heard from him?; **noticia bomba** *fam* bombshell.
➡ **noticias** *sfpl*: **las noticias** RADIO & TV the news.

noticiario, noticiero *Amér sm* [telediario] television news; CINE newsreel.

notición *sm fam* bombshell.

notificación *sf* notification.

notificar [10] *vt* to notify, to inform.

notoriedad *sf* - **1.** [fama] fame - **2.** [evidencia] obviousness.

notorio, ria *adj* - **1.** [evidente] obvious - **2.** [conocido] widely-known.

nov., novbre. *(abrev de noviembre)* Nov.

novatada *sf* - **1.** [broma] ragging *(U)* - **2.** [error] beginner's mistake; **pagar la novatada** to learn the hard way.

novato, ta ◇ *adj* inexperienced. ◇ *sm, f* novice, beginner.

novecientos, tas *num* nine hundred; *ver también* **seis**.

novedad *sf* - **1.** [cualidad - de nuevo] newness; [- de novedoso] novelty - **2.** [cambio] change - **3.** [noticia] news *(U)*; **sin novedad** without incident; MIL all quiet - **4.** [cosa nueva] new thing; [innovación] innovation.
➡ **novedades** *sfpl* [libros, discos] new releases; [moda] latest fashion *sing*.

novedoso, sa *adj* novel, new.

novel *adj* new, first-time.

novela *sf* novel; **novela de caballerías** tales of chivalry *pl*; **novela por entregas** serial; **novela policíaca** detective story; **novela rosa** romance, romantic novel.

novelar *vt* to fictionalize, to make into a novel.

novelero, ra ◇ *adj* - **1.** [fantasioso] very imaginative - **2.** [aficionado a las novelas] fond of novels. ◇ *sm, f* - **1.** [fantasioso] very imaginative person - **2.** [aficionado a las novelas] person fond of novels.

novelesco, ca *adj* - **1.** [de la novela] fictional - **2.** [fantástico] fantastic, extraordinary.

novelista *smf* novelist.

novelón *sm fam* hefty and badly written novel.

noveno, na *num* ninth; **la novena parte** a ninth.

➤ **novena** *sf* RELIG novena.

noventa *num* ninety; **los (años) noventa** the nineties; *ver también* **seis**.

noviar *vi C Sur & Méx*: **noviar con alguien** to go out with sb, to date sb *US*; **están noviando** they are going out together, they are dating *US*.

noviazgo *sm* engagement.

noviciado *sm* RELIG novitiate.

novicio, cia ◇ *adj fig* & RELIG novice *(antes de s)*. ◇ *sm, f fig* & RELIG novice.

noviembre *sm* November; *ver también* **septiembre**.

novillada *sf* TAUROM *bullfight with young bulls*.

novillero, ra *sm, f* TAUROM apprentice bullfighter.

novillo, lla *sm, f young bull or cow*; **hacer novillos** *fam* to play truant *UK*, to play hooky *US*.

novio, via *sm, f* - **1.** [compañero] boyfriend (*f* girlfriend) - **2.** [prometido] fiancé (*f* fiancée) - **3.** [recién casado] bridegroom (*f* bride); **los novios** the newly-weds.

nubarrón *sm* storm cloud.

nube *sf* - **1.** *fig* [gen] cloud; **nube atómica** mushroom cloud; **nube de tormenta** thundercloud; **nube de verano** [gen] summer shower; *fig* short fit of anger - **2.** [de personas, moscas] swarm - **3.** *loc*: **caído de las nubes** out of the blue; **estar en las nubes** to have one's head in the clouds; **poner algo/a alguien por las nubes** to praise sthg/sb to the skies; **por las nubes** [caro] sky-high, terribly expensive.

nublado, da *adj* - **1.** [encapotado] cloudy, overcast - **2.** *fig* [turbado] clouded, darkened.

nublar *vt lit* & *fig* to cloud.

➤ **nublarse** *vprnl* to cloud over.

nubosidad *sf* cloudiness, clouds *pl*.

nuboso, sa *adj* cloudy.

nuca *sf* nape, back of the neck.

nuclear *adj* nuclear.

nuclearización *sf* nuclearization.

nuclearizar [13] *vt* nuclearize.

núcleo *sm* - **1.** [centro] nucleus; *fig* centre *UK*, center *US*; **núcleo de población** population centre *UK*, population center *US* - **2.** [grupo] core.

nudillo *sm* knuckle.

nudismo *sm* nudism.

nudista *adj* & *smf* nudist.

nudo *sm* - **1.** [gen] knot; **nudo corredizo** slipknot; **se le hizo un nudo en la garganta** she got a lump in her throat - **2.** [cruce] junction; **nudo de comunicaciones** communications centre - **3.** [vínculo] tie, bond - **4.** [punto principal] crux, nub - **5.** [de una planta] node.

nudoso, sa *adj* knotty, gnarled.

nuera *sf* daughter-in-law.

nuestro, tra ◇ *adj poses* our; **nuestro coche** our car; **este libro es nuestro** this book is ours, this is our book; **un amigo nuestro** a friend of ours; **no es asunto nuestro** it's none of our business. ◇ *pron poses*: **el nuestro** ours; **el nuestro es rojo** ours is red; **ésta es la nuestra** *fam* this is the chance we have been waiting for; **lo nuestro es el teatro** [lo que nos va] theatre is what we should be doing; **los nuestros** *fam* [nuestra familia] our folks; [nuestro bando] our lot, our side.

nueva ⟾ **nuevo**.

Nueva York *n pr* New York.

Nueva Zelanda *n pr* New Zealand.

nueve *num* nine; *ver también* **seis**.

nuevo, va ◇ *adj* [gen] new; [patatas, legumbres] new, fresh; [vino] young; **esto es nuevo para mí, no lo sabía** that's news to me, I didn't know it; **ser nuevo en** to be new to; **estar/quedar como nuevo** to be as good as new. ◇ *sm, f* newcomer.

➤ **buena nueva** *sf* good news *(U)*.

➤ **de nuevo** *loc adv* again.

nuez *sf* - **1.** BOT [gen] nut; [de nogal] walnut - **2.** ANAT Adam's apple.

➤ **nuez moscada** *sf* nutmeg.

nulidad *sf* - **1.** [no validez] nullity - **2.** [ineptitud] incompetence - **3.** *fam* [persona] nonentity; **ser una nulidad** to be useless.

nulo, la *adj* - **1.** [sin validez] null and void, invalid - **2.** *fam* [incapacitado]: **nulo (para)** useless (at).

núm. (*abrev de* **número**) No.

numeración *sf* - **1.** [acción] numbering - **2.** [sistema] numerals *pl*, numbers *pl*; **numeración arábiga** o **decimal** Arabic numerals; **numeración binaria** binary numbers *pl*; **numeración romana** Roman numerals.

numerador *sm* MAT numerator.

numeral *adj* numeral.

numerar *vt* to number.

➤ **numerarse** *vprnl* [suj: personas] to number off.

numerario, ria *adj* [profesor, catedrático] tenured, permanent; [miembro] full.

numérico, ca *adj* numerical.

número *sm* - **1.** [gen] number; **sin número** [muchos] countless, innumerable; **número abstracto** abstract number; **número cardinal/ordinal** cardinal/ordinal number; **número complejo/irracional** complex/irrational number; **número complementario** complementary number; **número de matrícula** AUTO registration number; **número de serie** serial number; **número de teléfono** telephone number; **número dígito** digit; **número entero** whole number, integer; **número fraccionario** o **quebrado** fraction; **número par/impar** even/odd number; **número primo** prime number; **número redondo** round number; **número romano** Roman numeral; **en números rojos** in the red; **hacer números** to reckon up; **ser el número uno** to be number one - **2.** [tamaño, talla] size - **3.** [de publicación] issue, number; **número atrasado** back number - **4.** [de lotería] ticket - **5.** MIL member - **6.** [de un espectáculo] turn, number; **montar el número** *fam* to make o cause a scene.
◆ **número atómico** *sm* QUÍM atomic number.

numeroso, sa *adj* numerous; **un grupo numeroso** a large group.

numismático, ca ⬦ *adj* numismatic. ⬦ *sm, f* [persona] numismatist.
◆ **numismática** *sf* [estudio] numismatics *(U)*.

nunca *adv* (en frases afirmativas) never; (en frases negativas) ever; **casi nunca viene** he almost never comes, he hardly ever comes; **¿nunca le has visto?** have you never seen her?, haven't you ever seen her?; **más que nunca** more than ever; **nunca jamás** o **más** never more o again.

nuncio *sm* nuncio.

nupcial *adj* wedding (antes de s).

nupcias *sfpl* wedding *sing*, nuptials; **casarse en segundas nupcias** to remarry, to marry again.

nurse ['nurs] *sf* nurse, nanny.

nutria *sf* otter.

nutrición *sf* nutrition.

nutricionista *smf* Amér dietician.

nutrido, da *adj* - **1.** [alimentado] nourished, fed; **mal nutrido** undernourished - **2.** [numeroso] large.

nutrir *vt* - **1.** [alimentar]: **nutrir (con** o **de)** to nourish o feed (with) - **2.** [fomentar] to feed, to nurture - **3.** [suministrar]: **nutrir (de)** to supply (with).
◆ **nutrirse** *vprnl* - **1.** [gen]: **nutrirse de** o **con** to feed on - **2.** [proveerse]: **nutrirse de** o **con** to supply o provide o.s. with.

nutritivo, va *adj* nutritious.

nylon® ['nailon] = **nailon**.

ñ, Ñ *sf* [letra] ñ, Ñ.

ñato, ta *adj* Andes & R Plata snub-nosed.

ñoñería, ñoñez *sf* inanity, insipidness *(U)*.

ñoño, ña *adj* - **1.** [remilgado] squeamish; [quejica] whining - **2.** [soso] dull, insipid.

ñoqui (gen pl) *sm* CULIN gnocchi *pl*.

ñu *sm* gnu.

ñudo Amér ◆ **al ñudo** *loc adv* in vain.

o¹ (pl oes), **O** (pl Oes) *sf* [letra] o, O.

o² *conj* or; **o... o** either... or; **o sea (que)** in other words.

O *sm* (abrev de **oeste**) W.

o/ *abrev de* **orden**.

oasis *sm inv* lit & fig oasis.

obcecación *sf* blindness, stubbornness.

obcecado, da *adj* - **1.** [tozudo] stubborn - **2.** [obsesionado]: **obcecado por** o **con** blinded by.

obcecar [10] *vt* to blind.
◆ **obcecarse** *vprnl* to become stubborn; **obcecarse en hacer algo** to insist on doing sthg.

obedecer [30] ⬦ *vt*: **obedecer (a alguien)** to obey (sb). ⬦ *vi* - **1.** [acatar] to obey, to do as one is told; **hacerse obedecer** to command obedience - **2.** [someterse]: **obedecer a** to respond to - **3.** [estar motivado]: **obedecer a** to be due to.

obediencia *sf* obedience.

obediente *adj* obedient.

obelisco *sm* obelisk.

obertura *sf* overture.

obesidad *sf* obesity.

obeso, sa ◇ *adj* obese. ◇ *sm, f* obese person.

óbice *sm*: **no ser óbice para** not to be an obstacle to.

obispado *sm* bishopric.

obispo *sm* bishop.

óbito *sm culto* decease, demise.

obituario *sm* obituary.

objeción *sf* objection; **poner objeciones a** to raise objections to; **tener objeciones** to have objections; **objeción de conciencia** conscientious objection.

objetar ◇ *vt* to object to; **no tengo nada que objetar** I have no objection. ◇ *vi* MIL to be a conscientious objector.

objetivar *vt* to treat objectively.

objetividad *sf* objectivity.

objetivo, va *adj* objective.

◆ **objetivo** *sm* - **1.** [finalidad] objective, aim - **2.** MIL target - **3.** FOTO lens.

objeto *sm* - **1.** [gen] object; **ser objeto de** to be the object of; **objeto volante no identificado** unidentified flying object; **objetos de valor** valuables; **objetos perdidos** lost property *(U)* - **2.** [propósito] purpose, object; **sin objeto** [inútilmente] to no purpose, pointlessly; **al** *o* **con objeto de** [para] in order to, with the aim of.

objetor, ra *sm, f* objector; **objetor de conciencia** conscientious objector.

oblicuo, cua *adj* - **1.** [inclinado] oblique, slanting; [mirada] sidelong - **2.** GEOM oblique.

obligación *sf* - **1.** [gen] obligation, duty; **por obligación** out of a sense of duty; **antes es la obligación que la devoción** *prov* business before pleasure - **2.** *(gen pl)* FIN bond, security; **obligación convertible** convertible bond; **obligación del Estado** Treasury bond.

obligado, da *adj* obligatory, compulsory.

obligar [16] *vt*: **obligar a alguien (a hacer algo)** to oblige *o* force sb (to do sthg).

◆ **obligarse** *vprnl*: **obligarse a hacer algo** to undertake to do sthg.

obligatoriedad *sf* obligatory *o* compulsory nature.

obligatorio, ria *adj* obligatory, compulsory.

obligue *etc* ⊳ **obligar.**

oblongo, ga *adj* oblong.

obnubilar *vt* to bewilder, to daze.

oboe ◇ *sm* [instrumento] oboe. ◇ *smf* [persona] oboist.

obra *sf* - **1.** [gen] work *(U)*; **es obra suya** it's his doing; **poner en obra** to put into effect; **obra de caridad** [institución] charity; **obras sociales** community work *(U)*; **por obra (y gracia) de**

thanks to; **obras son amores y no buenas razones** *prov* actions speak louder than words *prov* - **2.** ARTE work (of art); TEATRO play; LITER book; MÚS opus; **obra maestra** masterpiece; **obras completas** complete works - **3.** CONSTR [lugar] building site; [reforma] alteration; **'cerrado por obras'** 'closed for alterations'; **'obras'** [en carretera] 'roadworks'; **obras públicas** public works.

obrador *sm* workshop.

obrar ◇ *vi* - **1.** [actuar] to act - **2.** [causar efecto] to work, to take effect - **3.** [estar en poder]: **obrar en manos de** to be in the possession of. ◇ *vt* to work.

obrero, ra ◇ *adj* [clase] working; [movimiento] labour *(antes de s)*. ◇ *sm, f* [en fábrica] worker; [en obra] workman, labourer; **obrero cualificado** skilled worker.

obscenidad *sf* obscenity.

obsceno, na *adj* obscene.

obscurantismo = oscurantismo.

obscurecer [30] = oscurecer.

obscuridad = oscuridad.

obscuro, ra = oscuro.

obsequiar [8] *vt*: **obsequiar a alguien con algo** to present sb with sthg.

obsequio *sm* gift, present; **obsequio de empresa** complimentary gift.

obsequioso, sa *adj* obliging, attentive.

observación *sf* - **1.** [gen] observation; **en** *o* **bajo observación** under observation - **2.** [comentario] remark, observation; **hacer una observación** to make a remark - **3.** [nota] note - **4.** [cumplimiento] observance.

observador, ra ◇ *adj* observant. ◇ *sm, f* observer.

observancia *sf* observance.

observar *vt* - **1.** [contemplar] to observe, to watch - **2.** [advertir] to notice, to observe - **3.** [acatar - ley, normas] to observe, to respect; [- conducta, costumbre] to follow.

◆ **observarse** *vprnl* to be noticed.

observatorio *sm* observatory.

obsesión *sf* obsession.

obsesionar *vt* to obsess.

◆ **obsesionarse** *vprnl* to be obsessed.

obsesivo, va *adj* obsessive.

obseso, sa ◇ *adj* obsessed. ◇ *sm, f* obsessed *o* obsessive person.

obsoleto, ta *adj culto* obsolete.

obstaculizar [13] *vt* to hinder, to hamper.

obstáculo *sm* obstacle; **un obstáculo para** an obstacle to; **poner obstáculos a algo/alguien** to hinder sthg/sb.

obstante ◆ **no obstante** *loc adv* nevertheless, however.

obstar *vi*: eso no obsta para que vengas si quieres that isn't to say that you can't come if you want to.

obstetricia *sf* obstetrics *(U)*.

obstinación *sf* [persistencia] perseverance; [terquedad] obstinacy, stubbornness.

obstinado, da *adj* [persistente] persistent; [terco] obstinate, stubborn.

obstinarse *vprnl* to refuse to give way; **obstinarse en** to persist in.

obstrucción *sf* lit & fig obstruction.

obstruccionismo *sm* obstructionism, stonewalling.

obstruccionista *adj* & *smf* obstructionist.

obstruir [51] *vt* - **1.** [bloquear] to block, to obstruct - **2.** [obstaculizar] to obstruct, to impede. ◆ **obstruirse** *vprnl* to get blocked (up).

obtención *sf* obtaining.

obtener [72] *vt* [beca, cargo, puntos] to get; [premio, victoria] to win; [ganancias] to make; [satisfacción] to gain.

obturación *sf* blockage, obstruction.

obturador *sm* FOTO shutter.

obturar *vt* to block.

obtuso, sa *adj* - **1.** [sin punta] blunt - **2.** [tonto] obtuse, stupid.

obtuviera *etc* ▷ **obtener**.

obús *(pl* **obuses**) *sm* - **1.** [cañón] howitzer - **2.** [proyectil] shell.

obviar [8] *vt* to avoid, to get round.

obvio, via *adj* obvious.

oca *sf* - **1.** [ave] goose - **2.** [juego] ≈ snakes and ladders.

ocasión *sf* - **1.** [oportunidad] opportunity, chance; **aprovechar una ocasión** to take advantage of an opportunity; **tener ocasión de hacer algo** to have the chance to do sthg; **la ocasión la pintan calva** *fam* this is my/your *etc* big chance - **2.** [momento] moment, time; [vez] occasion; **en dos ocasiones** on two occasions; **en alguna ocasión** sometimes; **en cierta ocasión** once; **en otra ocasión** some other time - **3.** [motivo]: **con ocasión de** on the occasion of; **dar ocasión para algo/hacer algo** to give cause for sthg/to do sthg - **4.** [ganga] bargain; **de ocasión** [precio, artículos etc] bargain *(antes de s)*.

ocasional *adj* - **1.** [accidental] accidental - **2.** [irregular] occasional.

ocasionar *vt* to cause.

ocaso *sm* - **1.** [puesta del sol] sunset - **2.** [decadencia] decline.

occidental ◇ *adj* western. ◇ *smf* westerner.

occidente *sm* west. ◆ **Occidente** *sm* [bloque de países] the West.

occipital *adj* occipital.

OCDE (*abrev de* **Organización para la Cooperación y el Desarrollo Económico**) *sf* OECD.

Oceanía *n pr* Oceania.

oceánico, ca *adj* - **1.** [de un océano] oceanic - **2.** [de Oceanía] Oceanian.

océano *sm* ocean; [inmensidad] sea, host.

oceanografía *sf* oceanography.

oceanográfico, ca *adj* oceanographical.

ochenta *num* eighty; **los (años) ochenta** the eighties; *ver también* **seis**.

ocho *num* eight; **de aquí en ocho días** [en una semana] a week today; *ver también* **seis**.

ochocientos, tas *num* eight hundred; *ver también* **seis**.

ocio *sm* [tiempo libre] leisure; [inactividad] idleness.

ociosidad *sf* idleness.

ocioso, sa *adj* - **1.** [inactivo] idle - **2.** [innecesario] unnecessary; [inútil] pointless.

oclusión *sf* blockage.

oclusivo, va *adj* occlusive. ◆ **oclusiva** *sf* occlusive.

ocre ◇ *sm* ochre. ◇ *adj inv* ochre.

octaedro *sm* octahedron.

octagonal *adj* octagonal.

octágono, na *adj* octagonal. ◆ **octágono** *sm* octagon.

octanaje *sm* octane number.

octano *sm* octane.

octava ▷ **octavo**.

octavilla *sf* - **1.** [de propaganda política] pamphlet, leaflet - **2.** [tamaño] octavo.

octavo, va *num* eighth; **la octava parte** an eighth. ◆ **octavo** *sm* - **1.** [parte] eighth - **2.** DEP: **octavos de final** *round before the quarter final.* ◆ **octava** *sf* MÚS octave.

octeto *sm* - **1.** MÚS octet - **2.** INFORM byte.

octogenario, ria *adj* & *sm, f* octogenarian.

octogésimo, ma *num* eightieth.

octogonal *adj* octagonal.

octubre *sm* October; *ver también* **septiembre**.

OCU (*abrev de* **Organización de Consumidores y Usuarios**) *sf Spanish consumer organization,* ≈ CAB *UK.*

ocular *adj* eye *(antes de s).*

oculista *smf* ophthalmologist.

ocultar *vt* - **1.** [gen] to hide; **ocultar algo a alguien** to hide sthg from sb; **le ocultó la verdad** she hid the truth from him - **2.** [delito] to cover up. ◆ **ocultarse** *vprnl* to hide.

ocultismo *sm* occultism.

ocultista *smf* occultist.

oculto, **ta** *adj* hidden.

ocupación *sf* - **1.** [gen] occupation; **ocupación ilegal de viviendas** squatting - **2.** [empleo] job.

ocupacional *adj* occupational.

ocupado, **da** *adj* - **1.** [persona] busy - **2.** [teléfono, lavabo etc] engaged - **3.** [lugar - gen, por ejército] occupied; [plaza] taken; **tengo las manos ocupadas** I've got my hands full.

ocupante ◇ *adj* occupying. ◇ *smf* occupant; **ocupante ilegal de viviendas** squatter.

ocupar *vt* - **1.** [gen] to occupy - **2.** [superficie, espacio] to take up; [habitación, piso] to live in; [mesa] to sit at; [sillón] to sit in - **3.** [actividad] to take up - **4.** [cargo] to hold - **5.** [dar trabajo a] to find *O* provide work for - **6.** *Amér C & Méx* [usar] to use.

 ocuparse *vprnl* [encargarse]: **ocúpate tú, yo no puedo** you do it, I can't; **ocuparse de** [gen] to deal with; [niños, enfermos, finanzas] to look after; **¡tú ocúpate de lo tuyo!** mind your own business!

ocurrencia *sf* - **1.** [idea] bright idea - **2.** [dicho gracioso] witty remark.

ocurrente *adj* witty.

ocurrir *vi* - **1.** [acontecer] to happen - **2.** [pasar, preocupar]: **¿qué le ocurre a Juan?** what's up with Juan?; **¿te ocurre algo?** is anything the matter?

 ocurrirse *vprnl* [venir a la cabeza]: **no se me ocurre ninguna solución** I can't think of a solution; **¡ni se te ocurra!** don't even think about it!; **se me ocurre que...** it occurs to me that...

oda *sf* ode.

ODECA *sf* (*abrev de* **Organización de Estados Centroamericanos**) OCAS.

odiar [8] *vt* & *vi* to hate.

odio *sm* hatred; **tener odio a algo/alguien** to hate sthg/sb.

odioso, **sa** *adj* hateful, horrible.

odisea *sf* odyssey.

odontología *sf* dentistry.

odontólogo, **ga** *sm*, *f* dentist, dental surgeon.

odre *sm* [de vino] wineskin.

OEA (*abrev de* **Organización de Estados Americanos**) *sf* OAS.

oeste ◇ *adj* [posición, parte] west, western; [dirección, viento] westerly. ◇ *sm* west; **el lejano oeste** the wild west.

ofender ◇ *vt* - **1.** [injuriar] to insult; [palabras] to offend, to hurt - **2.** [a la vista, al oído etc] to offend. ◇ *vi* to cause offence.

 ofenderse *vprnl*: **ofenderse (por)** to take offence (at).

ofendido, **da** ◇ *adj* offended. ◇ *sm*, *f* offended party.

ofensa *sf* - **1.** [acción]: **ofensa (a)** offence (against) - **2.** [injuria] slight, insult.

ofensivo, **va** *adj* offensive.

 ofensiva *sf* offensive; **pasar a la ofensiva** to go on the offensive; **tomar la ofensiva** to take the offensive.

ofensor, **ra** *sm*, *f* offender.

oferta *sf* - **1.** [gen] offer; **oferta en firme** firm offer; **'ofertas de trabajo'** 'situations vacant' - **2.** ECON [suministro] supply; **la oferta y la demanda** supply and demand; **oferta monetaria** money supply - **3.** [rebaja] bargain, special offer; **de oferta** bargain (*antes de s*), on offer - **4.** FIN [proposición] bid, tender; **oferta pública de adquisición** COM takeover bid.

ofertar *vt* to offer.

ofertorio *sm* RELIG offertory.

oficial, **la** *sm*, *f* [obrero] journeyman; [aprendiz] trainee.

 oficial ◇ *adj* official. ◇ *sm* - **1.** MIL officer - **2.** [funcionario] clerk.

oficialidad *sf* official nature.

oficialismo *sm Amér*: **el oficialismo** [gobierno] the Government; [partidarios del gobierno] government supporters.

oficialista *adj Amér* pro-government.

oficializar [13] *vt* to make official.

oficiante *smf* RELIG officiant.

oficiar [8] ◇ *vt* to officiate at. ◇ *vi* - **1.** [sacerdote] to officiate - **2.** [actuar de]: **oficiar de** to act as.

oficina *sf* office; **oficina de correos** post office; **oficina de empleo** job centre; **oficina de turismo** tourist office; **oficina inteligente** INFORM intelligent office.

oficinista *smf* office worker.

oficio *sm* - **1.** [profesión manual] trade; **de oficio** by trade - **2.** [trabajo] job; **no tener oficio ni beneficio** to have no trade - **3.** [experiencia]: **tener mucho oficio** to be very experienced - **4.** RELIG service - **5.** [función] function, role.

 Santo Oficio *sm*: **el Santo Oficio** the Holy Office, the Inquisition.

oficioso, **sa** *adj* unofficial.

ofimática *sf* office automation.

ofrecer [30] *vt* - **1.** [gen] to offer; [fiesta] to give, to throw; **ofrecerle algo a alguien** to offer sb sthg - **2.** [aspecto] to present.

 ofrecerse *vprnl* - **1.** [presentarse] to offer, to volunteer; **ofrecerse a** *O* **para hacer algo** to offer to do sthg - **2.** *loc*: **¿qué se le ofrece?** what can I do for you?

ofrecimiento *sm* offer.

ofrenda *sf* RELIG offering; [por gratitud, amor] gift.

ofrendar *vt* to offer up.

ofrezca *etc* ⊳ ofrecer.

oftalmología *sf* ophthalmology.

oftalmólogo, ga *sm, f* ophthalmologist.

ofuscación *sf* blindness, confusion.

ofuscar [10] *vt* - **1.** [deslumbrar] to dazzle - **2.** [turbar] to blind.

➤ **ofuscarse** *vprnl*: ofuscarse (con) to be blinded (by).

ogro *sm* ogre.

oh *interj*: ¡oh! oh!

ohmio *sm* ohm.

oídas ➤ de oídas *loc adv* by hearsay.

oído *sm* - **1.** [órgano] ear; **decir algo a alguien al oído** to whisper sthg into sb's ear; **oído interno** inner ear; **abrir los oídos** to pay close attention; **de oído** by ear; **toca el piano de oído** she plays the piano by ear; **entrar por un oído y salir por el otro** to go in one ear and out the other; **hacer oídos sordos** to turn a deaf ear; **lastimar los oídos** to offend one's ears; **si llega a oídos de ella...** if she gets to hear about this...; **me zumban los oídos** my ears are burning; **prestar oídos a** to listen carefully to; **regalarle el oído a alguien** to flatter sb; **ser todo oídos** to be all ears - **2.** [sentido] (sense of) hearing; **ser duro de oído** to be hard of hearing; **tener oído, tener buen oído** to have a good ear.

oír [62] ◇ *vt* - **1.** [gen] to hear; **oír hablar de** to hear about; **como quien oye llover** without paying the least attention - **2.** [atender] to listen to; **¡oye bien lo que te digo!** listen to what I'm going to tell you! ◇ *vi* to hear; **oír bien** to hear well; **¡oiga, por favor!** excuse me!; **¡oye!** *fam* hey!; **oír, ver y callar** hear no evil, see no evil, speak no evil.

ojal *sm* buttonhole.

ojalá *interj*: ¡ojalá! if only (that were so)!; ¡ojalá lo haga! I hope she does it!; ¡ojalá fuera ya domingo! I wish it were Sunday!

ojeada *sf* glance, look; **echar una ojeada a algo/alguien** to take a quick glance at sthg/sb, to take a quick look at sthg/sb.

ojear *vt* to have a look at.

ojera *(gen pl) sf* bags *pl* under the eyes.

ojeriza *sf fam* dislike; **tener ojeriza a alguien** to have it in for sb.

ojeroso, sa *adj* with bags under the eyes, haggard.

ojete *sm* - **1.** [bordado] eyelet - **2.** *vulg* [ano] arsehole.

ojiva *sf* - **1.** ARQUIT ogive - **2.** MIL warhead.

ojo ◇ *sm* - **1.** ANAT eye; **poner los ojos en blanco** *lit & fig* to roll one's eyes; **ojo a la funerala** *o* **a la virulé** black eye; **ojos rasgados** almond eyes; **ojos saltones** popping eyes - **2.** [agujero - de aguja] eye; [- de puente] span; **ojo de la cerradura** keyhole; **ojo de la escalera** stairwell - **3.** *loc*: **a ojo** (de buen cubero) roughly, approximately; **a ojos vistas** visibly; **abrir los ojos a alguien** to open sb's eyes; **andar con (mucho) ojo** to be (very) careful; **cerrar los ojos** [morir] to pass away; **cerrar los ojos ante algo** [ignorar] to close one's eyes to sthg; **comerse con los ojos a alguien** *fam* to drool over sb; **con los ojos cerrados** blindly, with one's eyes closed; **costar un ojo de la cara** to cost an arm and a leg; **¡dichosos los ojos que te ven!** *fam* how lovely to see you again!; **echar el ojo a algo** to have one's eye on sthg; **en un abrir y cerrar de ojos** in the twinkling of an eye; **estar ojo alerta** *o* **avizor** to be on the lookout; **mirar algo con buenos/malos ojos** to look favourably/unfavourably on sthg; **no pegar ojo** not to get a wink of sleep; **no quitar los ojos de encima a alguien** not to take one's eyes off sb; **tener ojos de lince** to have eyes like a hawk; **poner los ojos en alguien** to set one's sights on sb; **ser todo ojos** to be all eyes; **tener (buen) ojo** to have a good eye; **tener ojo clínico para algo** to be a good judge of sthg; **ojo por ojo, diente por diente** *prov* an eye for an eye, a tooth for a tooth; **ojos que no ven, corazón que no siente** *prov* what the eye doesn't see, the heart doesn't grieve over. ◇ *interj*: ¡ojo! be careful!, watch out!

➤ **ojo de buey** *sm* [ventana] porthole.

➤ **ojo de gallo** *sm* MED corn.

➤ **ojo de pez** *sm* FOTO fish-eye lens.

okupa *smf mfam* squatter.

ola *sf* wave; **ola de calor** heatwave; **ola de frío** cold spell.

➤ **nueva ola** *sf*: la nueva ola the New Wave.

ole, olé *interj*: ¡ole! bravo!

oleada *sf* - **1.** [del mar] swell - **2.** *fig* [avalancha] wave; **oleadas de refugiados** waves of refugees.

oleaje *sm* swell.

óleo *sm* oil (painting); **al óleo** in oils.

oleoducto *sm* oil pipeline.

oleoso, sa *adj* oily.

oler [49] ◇ *vt* to smell. ◇ *vi* - **1.** [despedir olor]: **oler (a)** to smell (of); **huele fatal** it smells foul - **2.** *fam* [indicando sospecha]: **oler a** to smack of.

➤ **olerse** *vprnl*: olerse algo *fam* to sense sthg.

olfatear *vt* - **1.** [olisquear] to sniff - **2.** [barruntar] to smell, to sense.

➤ **olfatear en** *vi* [indagar] to pry into.

olfativo, va *adj* olfactory.

olfato *sm* - **1.** [sentido] sense of smell - **2.** *fig* [sagacidad] nose, instinct; **tener olfato para algo** to be a good judge of sthg.

oligarca *smf* oligarch.

oligarquía *sf* oligarchy.

oligárquico, ca *adj* oligarchic.

oligofrenia *sf* mental handicap.

oligofrénico, ca ◇ *adj* mentally handicapped. ◇ *sm, f* mentally handicapped person.

olimpiada, olimpíada *sf* Olympiad, Olympic Games *pl*; **las olimpiadas** the Olympics.

olímpicamente *adv fam* blithely.

olímpico, ca *adj* - **1.** DEP olympic - **2.** *fig* [altanero] Olympian, haughty.

olimpismo *sm* Olympic movement.

olisquear *vt* to sniff (at).

oliva *sf* olive.

oliváceo, a *adj* olive.

olivar *sm* olive grove.

olivarero, ra ◇ *adj* olive (antes de s). ◇ *sm, f* olive-grower.

olivera *sf* olive tree.

olivo *sm* olive tree.

olla *sf* pot; **olla exprés** o **a presión** pressure cooker; **olla podrida** CULIN stew; **olla de grillos** bedlam, madhouse.

olmeda *sf* elm grove.

olmo *sm* elm (tree).

olor *sm* smell; **olor a** smell of; **tener olor a** to smell of; **olor corporal** body odour; **en olor de multitud** (considerado incorrecto) enjoying popular acclaim.

oloroso, sa *adj* fragrant.
➡ **oloroso** *sm* oloroso (sherry).

OLP (*abrev de* **Organización para la Liberación de Palestina**) *sf* PLO.

olvidadizo, za *adj* forgetful.

olvidar *vt* - **1.** [gen] to forget - **2.** [dejarse] to leave; **olvidé las llaves en la oficina** I left my keys at the office.
➡ **olvidarse** *vprnl* - **1.** [gen] to forget; **olvidarse de algo/hacer algo** to forget sthg/to do sthg - **2.** [dejarse] to leave.

olvido *sm* - **1.** [de un nombre, hecho etc] forgetting; **caer en el olvido** to fall into oblivion - **2.** [descuido] oversight.

Omán *n pr* Oman.

ombligo *sm* - **1.** ANAT navel - **2.** [centro] centre; **el ombligo del mundo** the centre of the universe - **3.** *loc*: **mirarse el ombligo** *fam* to be wrapped up in o.s.; **se le encogió el ombligo** *fam* she got cold feet.

ombudsman [ˈombuðsman] *sm* ombudsman.

OMG (*abrev de* **organismo modificado genéticamente**) *sm* GMO.

OMC (*abrev de* **Organización Mundial del Comercio**) *sm* WTO.

omisión *sf* omission.

omiso ➩ **caso**.

omitir *vt* to omit.

ómnibus *sm inv* - **1.** omnibus; FERROC local train - **2.** *Cuba & Urug* [urbano] bus; *Andes, Cuba & Urug* [interurbano, internacional] intercity bus.

omnipotencia *sf* omnipotence.

omnipotente *adj* omnipotent.

omnipresente *adj* omnipresent.

omnívoro, ra ◇ *adj* omnivorous. ◇ *sm, f* omnivore.

omoplato, omóplato *sm* shoulder-blade.

OMS (*abrev de* **Organización Mundial de la Salud**) *sf* WHO.

once *num* eleven; *ver también* **seis**.
➡ **onces** *sm Andes* [por la mañana] elevenses; [por la tarde] tea.

ONCE (*abrev de* **Organización Nacional de Ciegos Españoles**) *sf Spanish association for the blind, famous for its national lottery.*

ONCE

Spain's "Organización Nacional de Ciegos Españoles" (National Organization for the Blind) or **ONCE** is a non-profit-making organization which helps those with impaired vision in the fields of education and employment. **ONCE** has been remarkably successful in raising awareness (and funds), making it probably the most famous institution of its kind in Spain. This is mainly due to its two best-known activities: firstly, the lottery it runs, for which its members sell tickets in the streets, and secondly, its sponsorship of the cycling team which bears its name.

onceavo, va *num* eleventh; **la onceava parte** an eleventh.

oncología *sf* oncology.

oncólogo, ga *sm, f* oncologist.

onda *sf* wave; **onda corta/larga/media** short/long/medium wave; **onda eléctrica** o **hertziana** Hertzian wave; **onda expansiva** shock wave; **onda luminosa/sonora** light/sound wave; **estar en la onda** *fam* to be on the ball; **¿que onda?** *Méx & R Plata fam* how's it going?, how are things?

ondeante *adj* rippling.

ondear *vi* to ripple.

ondulación *sf* - **1.** [acción] rippling - **2.** [onda] ripple; [del pelo] wave.

ondulado, da *adj* wavy.

ondulante *adj* undulating.

ondular ⟨⟩ *vi* [agua] to ripple; [terreno] to undulate. ⟨⟩ *vt* to wave.

oneroso, sa *adj* burdensome.

ONG (*abrev de* **organización no gubernamental**) *sf* NGO.

ónice, ónix *smf* onyx.

onírico, ca *adj* dream *(antes de s)*.

ónix = ónice.

onomástico, ca *adj culto* onomastic.

➡ **onomástica** *sf culto* name day.

onomatopeya *sf* onomatopoeia.

ontología *sf* ontology.

ONU (*abrev de* **Organización de las Naciones Unidas**) *sf* UN.

onza *sf* - **1.** [unidad de peso] ounce - **2.** [de chocolate] square.

OPA (*abrev de* **oferta pública de adquisición**) *sf* takeover bid.

opacidad *sf* opacity.

opaco, ca *adj* opaque.

opalino, na *adj* opaline.

➡ **opalina** *sf* opaline.

ópalo *sm* opal.

opción *sf* - **1.** [elección] option; **no hay opción** there is no alternative; **opciones sobre acciones** stock options - **2.** [derecho] right; **dar opción a** to give the right to; **tener opción a** [empleo, cargo] to be eligible for.

opcional *adj* optional.

OPEP (*abrev de* **Organización de Países Exportadores de Petróleo**) *sf* OPEC.

ópera *sf* opera; **ópera bufa** comic opera, opera buffa; **ópera rock** rock opera.

operación *sf* - **1.** [gen] operation; **operación quirúrgica** (surgical) operation - **2.** COM transaction.

Operación Retorno

🏥 At the end of major holiday periods (bank holiday weekends, Easter and the month of August) huge efforts are made to reduce the number of accidents and traffic jams as Spanish holiday-makers head home from the coasts and mountains. Known as **Operación Retorno**, this exercise involves many special measures: for example, road works can be suspended for the weekend, and in congested areas heavy lorries can be kept off the roads, while helicopters are used to observe progress and spot problem areas. The success (or otherwise) of the enterprise is usually front-page news the following Monday.

operacional *adj* operational.

operador, ra *sm, f* - **1.** INFORM & TELECOM operator - **2.** [de la cámara] cameraman; [del proyector] projectionist.

➡ **operador** *sm* MAT operator.

➡ **operador turístico** *sm* tour operator.

operar ⟨⟩ *vt* - **1.** [enfermo]: **operar a alguien (de algo)** [enfermedad] to operate on sb (for sthg); **lo operaron del hígado** they've operated on his liver - **2.** [cambio etc] to bring about, to produce. ⟨⟩ *vi* - **1.** [gen] to operate - **2.** [actuar] to act - **3.** COM & FIN to deal.

➡ **operarse** *vprnl* - **1.** [enfermo] to be operated on, to have an operation; **operarse de algo** to be operated on for sthg; **me voy a operar del hígado** I'm going to have an operation on my liver - **2.** [cambio etc] to occur, to come about.

operario, ria *sm, f* worker.

operatividad *sf* feasibility.

operativo, va *adj* operative.

➡ **operativo** *sm Amér* operation.

opereta *sf* operetta.

opiáceo, a *adj* opiate.

➡ **opiáceo** *sm* opiate.

opinar ⟨⟩ *vt* to believe, to think. ⟨⟩ *vi* to give one's opinion; **opinar de algo/alguien, opinar sobre algo/alguien** to think about sthg/sb; **opinar bien de alguien** to think highly of sb.

opinión *sf* [parecer] opinion; **en mi opinión** in my opinion; **cambiar de opinión** to change one's mind; **expresar** *o* **dar una opinión** to give an opinion; **reservarse la opinión** to reserve judgment; **la opinión pública** public opinion.

opio *sm* opium.

opíparo, ra *adj* sumptuous.

opondrá *etc* ⟹ **oponer**.

oponente *smf* opponent.

oponer [65] *vt* - **1.** [resistencia] to put up - **2.** [argumento, razón] to put forward, to give.

➡ **oponerse** *vprnl* - **1.** [no estar de acuerdo] to be opposed; **oponerse a algo** [desaprobar] to be opposed to sthg, to oppose sthg; [contradecir] to contradict sthg; **me opongo a creerlo** I refuse to believe it - **2.** [obstaculizar]: **oponerse a** to stand in the way of, to impede.

oporto *sm* port (wine).

oportunidad *sf* - **1.** [ocasión] opportunity, chance; **a la primera oportunidad** at the first opportunity; **aprovechar la oportunidad** to seize the opportunity; **darle una/otra oportunidad a alguien** to give sb a/another chance - **2.** [conveniencia] timeliness.

oportunismo *sm* opportunism.

oportunista ⟨⟩ *adj* opportunistic. ⟨⟩ *smf* opportunist.

oportuno, na *adj* - **1.** [pertinente] appropriate - **2.** [propicio] timely; **el momento oportuno** the right time.

oposición *sf* - **1.** [gen] opposition - **2.** [resistencia] resistance - **3.** *(gen pl)* [examen] public entrance examination; **oposición a profesor** public examination to be a teacher; **preparar oposiciones** to be studying for a public entrance examination.

Oposiciones

🔳 These are public examinations held to fill vacancies in the public sector on a national, provincial or local basis. The positions attained through these exams normally imply a job for life (with a working day from 8 a.m. to 3 p.m.), and they are much sought after in a country with a tradition of high unemployment. There are usually far too many candidates for every job advertised, so the requirements listed can be extremely rigorous: if you apply to be a mailman or a clerk you may have to show an in-depth knowledge of the Constitution. This is why many people spend years preparing for these examinations, especially for posts with more responsibility.

opositar *vi*: **opositar (a)** to sit a public entrance examination (for).

opositor, ra *sm, f* - **1.** [a un cargo] *candidate in a public entrance examination* - **2.** [oponente] opponent.

opresión *sf* - **1.** [de un botón] press - **2.** *fig* [represión] oppression - **3.** *fig* [ahogo] difficulty in breathing.

opresivo, va *adj* oppressive.

opresor, ra ⬦ *adj* oppressive. ⬦ *sm, f* oppressor.

oprimir *vt* - **1.** [apretar - botón etc] to press; [- garganta, brazo etc] to squeeze - **2.** [zapatos, cinturón] to pinch, to be too tight for - **3.** *fig* [reprimir] to oppress - **4.** *fig* [angustiar] to weigh down on, to burden.

oprobio *sm* shame, disgrace.

optar *vi* - **1.** [escoger]: **optar (por algo)** to choose (sthg); **optar por hacer algo** to choose to do sthg; **optar entre** to choose between - **2.** [aspirar]: **optar a** to aim for, to go for.

optativo, va *adj* optional.

➡ **optativa** *sf* EDUC option, optional subject.

óptico, ca ⬦ *adj* optic. ⬦ *sm, f* [persona] optician.

➡ **óptica** *sf* - **1.** FÍS optics *(U)* - **2.** [tienda] optician's (shop) - **3.** *fig* [punto de vista] point of view.

optimismo *sm* optimism.

optimista ⬦ *adj* optimistic. ⬦ *smf* optimist.

optimización *sf* optimization.

optimizar *vt* to optimize.

óptimo, ma ⬦ *superl* = **bueno**. ⬦ *adj* optimum.

opuesto, ta ⬦ *pp* ⊳ **oponer**. ⬦ *adj* - **1.** [contrario] conflicting; **opuesto a** opposed *o* contrary to - **2.** [de enfrente] opposite.

opulencia *sf* [riqueza] opulence; [abundancia] abundance; **vivir en la opulencia** to live in luxury; **nadar en la opulencia** to be filthy rich.

opulento, ta *adj* - **1.** [rico] opulent - **2.** [abundante] abundant.

opusiera *etc* ⊳ **oponer**.

ora *conj desus*: **ora... ora...** now... now...

oración *sf* - **1.** [rezo] prayer; **oración fúnebre** memorial speech - **2.** GRAM sentence; **oración principal/subordinada** main/subordinate clause.

oráculo *sm* - **1.** [gen] oracle - **2.** *fig* [persona] fount of wisdom.

orador, ra *sm, f* speaker.

oral ⬦ *adj* oral. ⬦ *sm* ⊳ **examen**.

órale *interj* Méx fam [de acuerdo] right!, sure!; [¡venga!] come on!

orangután *sm* orangutang.

orar *vi* to pray.

oratorio, ria *adj* oratorical.

➡ **oratorio** *sm* - **1.** [lugar] oratory - **2.** MÚS oratorio.

➡ **oratoria** *sf* oratory.

orbe *sm* world, globe.

órbita *sf* - **1.** ASTRON orbit; **entrar/poner en órbita** to go/put into orbit - **2.** [de ojo] eye socket - **3.** *fig* [ámbito] sphere, realm.

orca *sf* killer whale.

órdago *sm all-or-nothing stake in the game of 'mus'*; **de órdago** *fig* magnificent.

orden ⬦ *sm* - **1.** [gen] order; **en orden** [bien colocado] tidy, in its place; [como debe ser] in order; **llamar al orden a alguien** to call sb to order; **poner en orden algo** to tidy sthg up; **por orden** in order; **sin orden ni concierto** in a haphazard way; **las fuerzas del orden** the forces of law and order; **orden de compra** COM purchase order; **orden público** law and order - **2.** [tipo] type, order; **problemas de orden económico** economic problems; **en otro orden de cosas** on the other hand. ⬦ *sf* order; **dar órdenes** to give orders; **por orden de** by order of; **orden de busca y captura** warrant for search and arrest; **orden de caballera** order of knighthood; **orden militar** military order; **orden de pago** payment order; **¡a la orden!** MIL (yes) sir!; **estar a la orden del día** to be the order of the day.

● **del orden de** *loc prep* around, approximately.

● **orden del día** *sm* agenda.

ordenación *sf* - **1.** [organización] ordering, arranging; [disposición] order, arrangement; [de recursos, edificios] planning - **2.** RELIG ordination.

ordenado, da ◇ *adj* [lugar, persona] tidy. ◇ *sm, f* RELIG ordained person.

● **ordenada** *sf* MAT ordinate.

ordenador *sm* INFORM computer; **ordenador central** mainframe computer; **ordenador personal** personal computer; **ordenador portátil** laptop computer.

ordenamiento *sm* legislation, regulations *pl*.

ordenanza ◇ *sm* - **1.** [de oficina] messenger - **2.** MIL orderly. ◇ *sf (gen pl)* ordinance, law; **ordenanzas municipales** by-laws.

ordenar *vt* - **1.** [poner en orden - gen] to arrange, to put in order; [- habitación, armario etc] to tidy (up) - **2.** [mandar] to order - **3.** RELIG to ordain - **4.** *Amér* [solicitar] to order.

● **ordenarse** *vprnl* RELIG to be ordained.

ordeñadora *sf* milking machine.

ordeñar *vt* to milk.

ordeño *sm* milking.

ordinal ◇ *adj* ordinal. ◇ *sm* ▷ **número**.

ordinariez *sf* commonness, coarseness; **decir/hacer una ordinariez** to say/do sthg rude.

ordinario, ria ◇ *adj* - **1.** [común] ordinary, usual; **de ordinario** usually - **2.** [vulgar] common, coarse - **3.** [no selecto] unexceptional - **4.** [no especial - presupuesto, correo] daily; [- tribunal] of first instance. ◇ *sm, f* common o coarse person.

orear *vt* to air.

● **orearse** *vprnl* [ventilarse] to air.

orégano *sm* oregano.

oreja *sf* - **1.** ANAT ear; **calentarle a alguien las orejas** to box sb's ears; **con las orejas gachas** with one's tail between one's legs; **tirar a alguien de las orejas** to give sb a good telling-off; **verle las orejas al lobo** to see what's coming - **2.** [de sillón] wing.

orejera *sf* earflap.

orejudo, da *adj* big-eared.

orfanato, orfelinato *sm* orphanage.

orfandad *sf* orphanhood; *fig* abandonment, neglect.

orfebre *smf* [de plata] silversmith; [de oro] goldsmith.

orfebrería *sf* [obra - de plata] silver work; [- de oro] gold work.

orfelinato = **orfanato**.

orfeón *sm* choral group o society.

organdí (*pl* **organdíes** o **organdís**) *sm* organdie.

orgánico, ca *adj* organic.

organigrama *sm* [gen & INFORM] flowchart.

organillero, ra *sm, f* organ-grinder.

organillo *sm* barrel organ.

organismo *sm* - **1.** BIOL organism - **2.** ANAT body - **3.** *fig* [entidad] organization, body.

organista *smf* organist.

organización *sf* organization; **Organización Mundial del Comercio** COM World Trade Organization.

organizador, ra ◇ *adj* organizing. ◇ *sm, f* organizer.

organizar [13] *vt* to organize.

● **organizarse** *vprnl* - **1.** [persona] to organize o.s. - **2.** [pelea etc] to break out, to happen suddenly.

organizativo, va *adj* organizing.

órgano *sm* organ.

orgasmo *sm* orgasm.

orgía *sf* orgy.

orgiástico, ca *adj* orgiastic.

orgullo *sm* pride.

orgulloso, sa ◇ *adj* proud. ◇ *sm, f* proud person.

orientación *sf* - **1.** [dirección - acción] guiding; [- rumbo] direction - **2.** [posicionamiento - acción] positioning; [- lugar] position - **3.** *fig* [información] guidance; **orientación profesional** careers advice o guidance - **4.** *fig* [tendencia] tendency, leaning.

oriental ◇ *adj* - **1.** [gen] eastern; [del Lejano Oriente] oriental - **2.** *Amér* [de Uruguay] Uruguayan. ◇ *smf* - **1.** oriental - **2.** *Amér* [de Uruguay] Uruguayan.

orientalismo *sm* orientalism.

orientalista *smf* orientalist.

orientar *vt* - **1.** [dirigir] to direct; [casa] to build facing - **2.** *fig* [medidas etc]: **orientar hacia** to direct towards o at - **3.** *fig* [aconsejar] to give advice o guidance to.

● **orientarse** *vprnl* - **1.** [dirigirse - foco etc]: **orientarse a** to point towards o at - **2.** [encontrar el camino] to get one's bearings, to find one's way around - **3.** *fig* [encaminarse]: **orientarse hacia** to be aiming at.

oriente *sm* east.

● **Oriente** *sm*: **el Oriente** the East, the Orient; **Oriente Medio/Próximo** Middle/Near East; **Lejano** o **Extremo Oriente** Far East.

orificio *sm* hole; TECNOL opening.

origen *sm* - **1.** [gen] origin; [ascendencia] origins *pl*, birth; **de origen español** of Spanish origin - **2.** [causa] cause; **dar origen a** to give rise to.

original <> *adj* - **1.** [gen] original - **2.** [raro] eccentric, different. <> *sm* original.

originalidad *sf* - **1.** [gen] originality - **2.** [extravagancia] eccentricity.

originar *vt* to cause.
◆ **originarse** *vprnl* to be caused.

originario, ria *adj* - **1.** [inicial, primitivo] original - **2.** [procedente]: **ser originario de** [costumbres etc] to come from (originally); [persona] to be a native of.

orilla *sf* - **1.** [ribera - de río] bank; [- de mar] shore; **a orillas de** [río] on the banks of; **a orillas del mar** by the sea - **2.** [borde] edge - **3.** [acera] pavement.

orillar *vt* - **1.** [dificultad, obstáculo] to skirt around - **2.** [tela] to edge.

orín *sm* [herrumbre] rust.
◆ **orines** *smpl* [orina] urine *(U)*.

orina *sf* urine.

orinal *sm* chamberpot.

orinar *vi* & *vt* to urinate.
◆ **orinarse** *vprnl* to wet o.s.

Orinoco *sm*: **el Orinoco** the Orinoco.

oriundo, da <> *adj*: **oriundo de** native of. <> *sm, f* DEP *non-Spanish footballer whose mother or father is Spanish.*

orla *sf* - **1.** [adorno] (decorative) trimming - **2.** [fotografía] graduation photograph.

orlar *vt* to decorate with trimmings.

ornamentación *sf* ornamentation.

ornamental *adj* ornamental.

ornamentar *vt* to decorate, to adorn.

ornamento *sm* [objeto] ornament.
◆ **ornamentos** *smpl* RELIG vestments *pl*.

ornar *vt* to decorate, to adorn.

ornato *sm* decoration.

ornitología *sf* ornithology.

ornitólogo, ga *sm, f* ornithologist.

oro *sm* gold; *fig* money, riches *pl*; **de oro** gold; **oro en barras** bullion; **oro en polvo** gold dust; **guardar algo como oro en paño** to treasure sthg; **hacerse de oro** to make one's fortune; **no es oro todo lo que reluce** all that glitters is not gold; **pedir el oro y el moro** to ask the earth.
◆ **oros** *smpl* [naipes] *suit of Spanish cards bearing gold coins.*
◆ **oro negro** *sm* oil.

orogénesis *sf inv* orogenesis.

orografía *sf* - **1.** GEOGR orography - **2.** [relieve] terrain.

orondo, da *adj fam* - **1.** [gordo] plump - **2.** [satisfecho] self-satisfied, smug.

oropel *sm* tinsel.

orquesta *sf* - **1.** [músicos] orchestra; **orquesta de cámara/sinfónica** chamber/symphony orchestra - **2.** [lugar] orchestra pit.

orquestación *sf* orchestration.

orquestar *vt* to orchestrate.

orquestina *sf* dance band.

orquídea *sf* orchid.

ortiga *sf* (stinging) nettle.

ortodoncia *sf* orthodontics *(U)*.

ortodoxia *sf* orthodoxy.

ortodoxo, xa <> *adj* orthodox. <> *sm, f* RELIG member of the Orthodox Church.

ortografía *sf* spelling.

ortográfico, ca *adj* spelling *(antes de s)*.

ortopedia *sf* orthopaedics *(U)*.

ortopédico, ca <> *adj* orthopaedic. <> *sm, f* orthopaedist.

ortopedista *smf* orthopaedist.

oruga *sf* caterpillar.

orujo *sm strong spirit made from grape pressings.*

orzuelo *sm* stye.

os *pron pers* - **1.** *(complemento directo)* you; **me gustaría veros** I'd like to see you - **2.** *(complemento indirecto)* (to) you; **os lo dio** he gave it to you; **os tengo miedo** I'm afraid of you - **3.** *(reflexivo)* yourselves - **4.** *(recíproco)* each other; **os enamorasteis** you fell in love (with each other).

osa ⊳ **oso**.

osadía *sf* - **1.** [valor] boldness, daring - **2.** [descaro] audacity, cheek.

osado, da *adj* - **1.** [valeroso] daring, bold - **2.** [descarado] impudent, cheeky.

osamenta *sf* skeleton.

osar *vi* to dare.

osario *sm* ossuary.

Óscar *sm* CINE Oscar.

oscilación *sf* - **1.** [movimiento] swinging; FÍS oscillation - **2.** [espacio recorrido] swing - **3.** *fig* [variación] fluctuation.

oscilador *sm* oscillator.

oscilar *vi* - **1.** [moverse] to swing; FÍS to oscillate - **2.** *fig* [variar] to fluctuate.

oscilatorio, ria *adj* swinging; FÍS oscillating.

ósculo *sm culto* kiss.

oscurantismo, obscurantismo *sm* obscurantism.

oscurecer [30], obscurecer <> *vt* - **1.** [privar de luz] to darken - **2.** *fig* [mente] to confuse, to cloud - **3.** *fig* [deslucir] to overshadow. <> *v impers* [anochecer] to get dark.
◆ **oscurecerse, obscurecerse** *vprnl* to grow dark.

oscuridad, obscuridad *sf* - **1.** [falta de luz] darkness - **2.** [zona oscura]**: en la oscuridad** in the dark - **3.** *fig* [falta de claridad] obscurity.

oscuro, ra, obscuro, ra *adj* - **1.** [gen] dark; **a oscuras** in the dark - **2.** [nublado] overcast - **3.** *fig* [inusual] obscure - **4.** *fig* [incierto] uncertain, unclear - **5.** *fig* [intenciones, asunto] shady.

óseo, a *adj* bone *(antes de s)*.

osezno *sm* bear cub.

osificarse [10] *vprnl* to ossify.

ósmosis *sf inv* fig & FIS osmosis.

oso, osa *sm, f* bear *(f* she-bear*)*; **oso de felpa** *O* **peluche** teddy bear; **oso hormiguero** anteater; **oso panda** panda; **oso polar** polar bear; **hacer el oso** to act the fool.

➤ **Osa Mayor** *sf* Great Bear.

➤ **Osa Menor** *sf* Little Bear.

ossobuco [oso'buko] *sm* CULIN osso bucco.

ostensible *adj* evident, clear.

ostentación *sf* ostentation, show; **hacer ostentación de algo** to show sthg off, to parade sthg.

ostentador, ra *sm, f* show-off, ostentatious person.

ostentar *vt* - **1.** [poseer] to hold, to have - **2.** [exhibir] to show off, to parade.

ostentoso, sa *adj* ostentatious.

osteópata *smf* osteopath.

osteopatía *sf* [terapia] osteopathy.

ostra *sf* oyster; **aburrirse como una ostra** *fam* to be bored to death.

➤ **ostras** *interj fam:* ¡**ostras!** blimey!

ostracismo *sm* ostracism; **ostracismo político** political wilderness.

OTAN *(abrev de* **Organización del Tratado del Atlántico Norte)** *sf* NATO.

otear *vt* to survey, to scan; *fig* to study.

otero *sm* hillock.

OTI *(abrev de* **Organización de Televisiones Iberoamericanas)** *sf association of all Spanish-speaking television networks.*

otitis *sf inv* inflammation of the ear.

otomano, na *adj & sm, f* Ottoman.

➤ **otomana** *sf* [sofá] ottoman.

otoñal *adj* autumn *UK (antes de s)*, autumnal *UK*, fall *US (antes de s)*.

otoño *sm lit & fig* autumn *UK*, fall *US*.

otorgamiento *sm* granting, conferring; [de un premio] award, presentation; DER execution.

otorgar [16] *vt* to grant; [premio] to award, to present; DER to execute.

otorrino, na *sm, f fam* ear, nose and throat specialist.

otorrinolaringología *sf* ear, nose and throat medicine.

otorrinolaringólogo, ga *sm, f* ear, nose and throat specialist.

otro, tra ⬦ *adj* - **1.** [distinto] another, other; **otro chico** another boy; **el otro chico** the other boy; **(los) otros chicos** (the) other boys; **no hacer otra cosa que llorar** to do nothing but cry; **el otro día** [pasado] the other day - **2.** [nuevo] another; **estamos ante otro Dalí** this is another Dali; **otros tres goles** another three goals. ⬦ *pron (sing)* another (one), *(pl)* others; **dame otro** give me another (one); **el otro** the other one; **(los) otros** (the) others; **yo no lo hice, fue otro** it wasn't me, it was somebody else; **otro habría abandonado, pero no él** anyone else would have given up, but not him; ¡**otra!** [en conciertos] encore!, more!

otrora *adv culto* formerly.

otrosí *adv culto* besides, moreover.

output ['autput] *(pl* **outputs)** *sm* INFORM output *(U)*.

ovación *sf* ovation.

ovacionar *vt* to give an ovation to, to applaud.

oval *adj* oval.

ovalado, da *adj* oval.

óvalo *sm* oval.

ovario *sm* ovary.

oveja *sf* sheep, ewe.

➤ **oveja descarriada** *sf* lost sheep.

➤ **oveja negra** *sf* black sheep.

overbooking [oβer'βukiŋ] *sm* overbooking.

overol, overoles *sm Amér* [ropa - con peto] dungarees *pl UK*, overalls *pl US*; [- para bebé] rompers *pl*.

Oviedo *n pr* Oviedo.

ovillar *vt* to roll *O* wind into a ball.

➤ **ovillarse** *vprnl* to curl up into a ball.

ovillo *sm* ball *(of wool etc)*; **hacerse un ovillo** to curl up into a ball.

ovino, na ⬦ *adj* ovine, sheep *(antes de s)*. ⬦ *sm, f* sheep.

ovíparo, ra *adj* oviparous.

ovni ['ofni] *sm (abrev de* **objeto volador no identificado)** UFO.

ovoide *adj* ovoid.

ovulación *sf* ovulation.

ovular ⬦ *adj* ovular. ⬦ *vi* to ovulate.

óvulo *sm* ovum.

oxidación *sf* rusting.

oxidante ⬦ *adj* oxidizing. ⬦ *sm* oxidizing agent.

oxidar *vt* to rust; QUÍM to oxidize.

➤ **oxidarse** *vprnl* to get rusty.

óxido *sm* - **1.** QUÍM oxide - **2.** [herrumbre] rust.

oxigenación *sf* oxygenation.

oxigenado, da *adj* - **1.** QUÍM oxygenated - **2.** [cabello] peroxided *(antes de s)*, bleached.

oxigenar *vt* QUÍM to oxygenate.
➡ **oxigenarse** *vprnl* - **1.** [airearse] to get a breath of fresh air - **2.** [cabello] to bleach.

oxígeno *sm* oxygen.

oye ▷ oír.

oyente *smf* - **1.** RADIO listener - **2.** [alumno] unregistered student.

oyera *etc* ▷ oír.

ozono *sm* ozone.

ozonosfera *sf* ozonosphere.

P

p, P *sf* [letra] p, P.

p. - **1.** = pág. - **2.** *abrev de* paseo.

pabellón *sm* - **1.** [edificio] pavilion - **2.** [parte de un edificio] block, section - **3.** [en parques, jardines] summerhouse - **4.** [tienda de campaña] bell tent - **5.** [dosel] canopy - **6.** [bandera] flag - **7.**: **pabellón auditivo** outer ear.

pábulo *sm* food, fuel; **dar pábulo a** to feed, to encourage.

PAC *(abrev de* **Política Agrícola Común)** *sf* CAP.

pacato, ta ◇ *adj* - **1.** [mojigato] prudish - **2.** [tímido] shy. ◇ *sm, f* [mojigato] prude.

paceño, ña ◇ *adj* of/relating to La Paz. ◇ *sm, f* native/inhabitant of La Paz.

pacer [29] *vi* to graze.

pachá *(pl* pachás *o* pachaes) *sm* pasha; **vivir como un pachá** *fam* to live like a lord.

Pachamama *sf* Andes Mother Earth.

pachanga *sf fam* rowdy celebration.

pachanguero, ra *adj fam* [música] catchy but mindless.

pacharán *sm liqueur made from anis and sloes.*

pachorra *sf fam* calmness.

pachucho, cha *adj fam* under the weather.

pachulí *(pl* pachulíes *o* pachulís) *sm* patchouli.

paciencia *sf* patience; **armarse de paciencia** to summon up one's patience; **perder la paciencia** to lose one's patience; **tener paciencia** to be patient; **tener más paciencia que un santo** to have the patience of a saint.

paciente *adj* & *smf* patient.

pacificación *sf* pacification.

pacificar [10] *vt* - **1.** [país] to pacify - **2.** [ánimos] to calm.
➡ **pacificarse** *vprnl* [persona] to calm down.

pacífico, ca *adj* [gen] peaceful; [persona] peaceable.

Pacífico *sm*: **el (océano) Pacífico** the Pacific (Ocean).

pacifismo *sm* pacifism.

pacifista *adj* & *smf* pacifist.

paco, ca *sm, f* Andes & Pan *fam* cop.

pacotilla *sf*: **de pacotilla** trashy, third-rate.

pactar ◇ *vt* to agree to. ◇ *vi*: **pactar (con)** to strike a deal (with).

pacto *sm* [gen] agreement, pact; [entre países] treaty; **hacer/romper un pacto** to make/break an agreement; **pacto social** social contract.

padecer [30] ◇ *vt* to suffer, to endure; [enfermedad] to suffer from. ◇ *vi* to suffer; [enfermedad]: **padecer de** to suffer from.

padecimiento *sm* suffering.

pádel ['paðel] *sm ball game for two or four players, played with a small rubber bat on a two-walled court.*

padezca *etc* ▷ padecer.

padrastro *sm* - **1.** [pariente] stepfather - **2.** [pellejo] hangnail.

padrazo *sm fam* adoring father.

padre ◇ *sm* [gen & RELIG] father; **padre de familia** head of the family; **padre espiritual** confessor; **padre soltero** single parent; **de padre y muy señor mío** incredible, tremendous. ◇ *adj inv* - **1.** *Esp fam* [enorme] incredible, tremendous - **2.** *Méx fam* [estupendo] fantastic, great.
➡ **padres** *smpl* - **1.** [padre y madre] parents - **2.** [antepasados] ancestors, forefathers.
➡ **Padres de la Iglesia** *smpl* RELIG Fathers of the Christian Church.
➡ **Santo Padre** *sm* RELIG Holy Father, Pope.

padrenuestro *(pl* padrenuestros) *sm* Lord's Prayer.

padrino *sm* - **1.** [de bautismo] godfather; [de boda] best man - **2.** [en duelos, torneos etc] second - **3.** *fig* [protector] patron.
➡ **padrinos** *smpl* [padrino y madrina] godparents.

padrísimo *adj* Méx *fam* great.

padrón *sm* [censo] census; [para votar] electoral roll O register.

padrote *sm Méx fam* pimp.

paella *sf* paella.

paellera *sf large frying pan or earthenware dish for cooking paella.*

paf *interj* bang!, crash!

pág., p. (*abrev de* **página**) p.

paga *sf* payment; [salario] salary, wages *pl*; [de niño] pocket money; **paga extra** O **extraordinaria** *bonus paid twice a year to Spanish workers.*

Paga extra

This is a bonus, equivalent to one month's wages, which is added to employees' salaries twice a year, in the summer and at Christmas, just in time to help people over these periods of heavy expenditure. It is considered as part of an employee's annual salary.

pagadero, ra *adj* payable; **pagadero a 90 días/a la entrega** payable within 90 days/on delivery.

pagado, da *adj* paid.

pagador, ra <> *adj* paying; **ser buen/mal pagador** to be a reliable/unreliable payer. <> *sm, f* [de obreros etc] paymaster.

paganismo *sm* paganism.

pagano, na *adj & sm, f* pagan, heathen.

pagar [16] <> *vt* [gen] to pay; [deuda] to pay off, to settle; [ronda, gastos, delito] to pay for; [ayuda, favor] to repay; **me las pagarás** *fam* you'll pay for this; **pagar el pato/los platos rotos** *fam* to carry the can; **el que la hace la paga** he/she *etc* will pay for it in the end. <> *vi* to pay; **pagar en efectivo** O **metálico** to pay (in) cash.

pagaré (*pl* **pagarés**) *sm* COM promissory note, IOU; **pagaré del Tesoro** Treasury note.

pagel *sm* pandora.

página *sf* page; **página inicial** O **de inicio** INFORM home page; **página Web** Web page; **las páginas amarillas** the Yellow Pages.

paginación *sf* pagination.

paginar *vt* INFORM to paginate.

pago *sm* payment; *fig* reward, payment; **en pago de** [en recompensa por] as a reward for; [a cambio de] in return for; **pago anticipado/inicial** advance/down payment; **pago por visión** pay-per-view.

➡ **pagos** *smpl* [lugar]: **por estos pagos** around here.

pagoda *sf* pagoda.

pague *etc* ⊳ **pagar**.

pai *sm Amér C & Méx* pie.

paila *sf* - **1.** *Andes, Amér C & Caribe* [sartén] frying pan - **2.** *Chile* [huevos fritos] fried eggs *pl*.

paipai (*pl* **paipais**), **paipay** (*pl* **paipays**) *sm fan made from a palm leaf.*

paisaje *sm* [gen] landscape; [vista panorámica] scenery (*U*), view.

paisajista <> *adj* landscape (*antes de s*). <> *smf* landscape painter.

paisajístico, ca *adj* landscape (*antes de s*).

paisanaje *sm* civilians *pl*.

paisano, na <> *adj* [del mismo país] from the same country. <> *sm, f* [del mismo país] compatriot, fellow countryman (*f* fellow countrywoman).

➡ **paisano** *sm* [civil] civilian; **de paisano** MIL in civilian clothes; **de paisano** [policía] in plain clothes.

Países Bajos *smpl*: **los Países Bajos** the Netherlands.

País Valenciano *sm*: **el País Valenciano** the autonomous region of Valencia.

País Vasco *sm*: **el País Vasco** the Basque Country.

paja *sf* - **1.** [gen] straw - **2.** *fig* [relleno] waffle - **3.** *vulg* [masturbación] wank; **hacerse una paja** to have a wank.

pajar *sm* straw loft.

pájara *sf fig* crafty O sly woman.

pajarera *sf* aviary.

pajarería *sf* pet shop.

pajarita *sf* - **1.** *Esp* [corbata] bow tie - **2.** [de papel] paper bird.

pájaro *sm* - **1.** ZOOL bird; **pájaro bobo** penguin; **pájaro carpintero** woodpecker; **pájaro de mal agüero** bird of ill omen; **más vale pájaro en mano que ciento volando** *prov* a bird in the hand is worth two in the bush; **matar dos pájaros de un tiro** to kill two birds with one stone; **tener pájaros en la cabeza** to be scatterbrained O empty-headed - **2.** *fig* [persona] crafty devil, sly old fox.

pajarraco *sm despec* - **1.** [pájaro] big ugly bird - **2.** [persona] nasty piece of work.

paje *sm* page.

pajilla, pajita *sf* (drinking) straw.

pajizo, za *adj* [de paja] straw (*antes de s*); [color] straw-coloured; [techo] thatched.

pajolero, ra *adj Esp fam* damn, blessed; **no tengo ni pajolera idea** I haven't got the foggiest.

pajuerano, na *R Dom* <> *adj* [de pueblo] countrified. <> *sm, f* [palurdo] bumpkin, hick *US*.

Pakistán = **Paquistán**.

pakistaní (*pl* **pakistaníes** O **pakistanís**) *adj & sm, f* = **paquistaní**.

pala *sf* - **1.** [herramienta] spade; [para recoger] shovel; CULIN slice; **pala mecánica** O **excavado-**

ra excavator, digger **- 2.** [de frontón, ping-pong] bat **- 3.** [de remo, hélice] blade **- 4.** [de diente] upper front tooth.

palabra *sf* **- 1.** [gen] word; **estar bajo palabra** to be under oath; **de palabra** by word of mouth, verbally; **mantener uno su palabra** to keep one's word; **no tener palabra** to go back on one's word; **palabra por palabra** word for word; **sin mediar palabra** without a single word; **tomar** *o* **coger la palabra a alguien** to hold sb to their word; **palabra clave** INFORM key word; **palabra divina** *o* **de Dios** word of God; **palabra de honor** word of honour **- 2.** [habla] speech **- 3.** [derecho de hablar] right to speak; **dar la palabra a alguien** to give the floor to sb **- 4.** *loc*: **dejar a alguien con la palabra en la boca** to cut sb off in mid-sentence; **en cuatro** *o* **dos palabras** in a few words; **en una palabra** in a word; **medir las palabras** to weigh one's words (carefully); **ser palabras mayores** to be an important matter.
◆ **palabras** *sfpl* [discurso] words.

palabrear *vt Amér fam* to agree on.

palabrería *sf fam* hot air.

palabrota *sf* swearword, rude word; **decir palabrotas** to swear.

palacete *sm* mansion, small palace.

palaciego, ga *adj* palace *(antes de s)*, court *(antes de s)*.

palacio *sm* palace; **palacio de congresos** conference centre; **palacio de Justicia** Law Courts *pl*.

palada *sf* **- 1.** [al cavar] spadeful, shovelful **- 2.** [de remo] stroke **- 3.** [de hélice] rotation.

paladar *sm* palate.

paladear *vt* to savour.

paladín *sm* **- 1.** HIST paladin, heroic knight **- 2.** *fig* [adalid] champion, defender.

palanca *sf* **- 1.** [barra, mando] lever; **palanca de cambio** gear lever *o* stick, gearshift *US*; **palanca de mando** joystick **- 2.** [trampolín] diving board.

palangana *sf* [para fregar] washing-up bowl; [para lavarse] wash bowl.

palangre *sm* fishing line with hooks.

palanqueta *sf* jemmy, crowbar.

palatal *adj* palatal.

palatino, na *adj* **- 1.** [de paladar] palatine **- 2.** [de palacio] palace *(antes de s)*, court *(antes de s)*.

palco *sm* box *(at theatre)*; **palco de autoridades** VIP box.

paleocristiano, na *adj* early Christian.

paleografía *sf* paleography.

paleográfico, ca *adj* paleographic.

paleógrafo, fa *sm, f* paleographer.

paleolítico, ca *adj* paleolithic.
◆ **paleolítico** *sm* Paleolithic period.

paleontología *sf* paleontology.

paleontólogo, ga *sm, f* paleontologist.

Palestina *n pr* Palestine.

palestino, na *adj & sm, f* Palestinian.

palestra *sf* arena; **salir** *o* **saltar a la palestra** to enter the fray.

paleta *sf* [gen] small shovel, small spade; [llana] trowel; CULIN slice; ARTE palette; [de ping-pong] bat; *Méx* [helado] ice lolly *UK*, Popsicle® *US*.

paletada *sf* [gen] shovelful, spadeful; [de yeso] trowelful; [de pintura] palette.

paletilla *sf* shoulder blade.

paleto, ta *Esp* ◇ *adj* coarse, uncouth. ◇ *sm, f* country bumpkin, yokel, hick *US*.

paliar [8] *vt* [atenuar] to ease, to relieve.

paliativo, va *adj* palliative.
◆ **paliativo** *sm* **- 1.** MED palliative **- 2.**: **sin paliativos** [derrota, fracaso] resounding.

palidecer [30] *vi* **- 1.** [ponerse pálido] to go *o* turn pale **- 2.** [perder importancia] to pale, to fade.

palidez *sf* paleness.

pálido, da *adj* pale; *fig* dull.

palier [pa'ljer] *sm* AUTO bearing.

palillero *sm* toothpick holder.

palillo *sm* **- 1.** [mondadientes] toothpick **- 2.** [baqueta] drumstick **- 3.** [para comida china] chopstick **- 4.** *fig* [persona delgada] matchstick.

palio *sm* canopy.

palique *sm Esp fam* chat, natter; **estar de palique** to chat, to natter.

palisandro *sm* rosewood.

palito *sm*: **palito (de pescado)** CULIN fish finger.

paliza *sf* **- 1.** [golpes, derrota] beating **- 2.** [esfuerzo] hard grind **- 3.** *fam* [rollo] drag.

palma *sf* **- 1.** [de mano] palm; **conocer algo como la palma de la mano** to know sthg like the back of one's hand **- 2.** [palmera] palm (tree); [hoja de palmera] palm leaf; **llevarse la palma** to be the best; *irón* to take the biscuit.
◆ **palmas** *sfpl* [aplausos] clapping *(U)*, applause *(U)*; **batir palmas** to clap (one's hands).

palmada *sf* **- 1.** [golpe] pat; [más fuerte] slap **- 2.** [aplauso] clap; **palmadas** clapping *(U)*.

palmar[1] ◇ *adj* of the palm *(of the hand)*. ◇ *sm* palm grove.

palmar[2] *fam* ◇ *vi* to kick the bucket, to snuff it. ◇ *vt*: **palmarla** to kick the bucket, to snuff it.

palmarés *sm* - **1.** [historial] record - **2.** [lista] list of winners.

palmear ◇ *vt* - **1.** [aplaudir] to applaud - **2.** [espalda] to slap, to pat. ◇ *vi* to clap, to applaud.

palmera *sf* - **1.** [árbol] palm (tree); [datilera] date palm - **2.** [pastel] flat, butterfly-shaped pastry.

palmeral *sm* palm grove.

palmito *sm* - **1.** [árbol] palmetto, fan palm - **2.** CULIN palm heart - **3.** *Esp fam fig* [buena planta] good looks *pl*; **lucir el palmito** to show off one's good looks.

palmo *sm* handspan; *fig* small amount; **palmo a palmo** bit by bit; **dejar a alguien con un palmo de narices** to let sb down.

palmotear *vi* to clap.

palmoteo *sm* clapping.

palo *sm* - **1.** [gen] stick; [de golf] club; [de portería] post; [de la escoba] handle - **2.** [mástil] mast - **3.** [golpe] blow *(with a stick)*; **moler a alguien a palos** to thrash sb - **4.** *fig* [mala crítica] bad review - **5.** [de baraja] suit - **6.** [madera]: **de palo** wooden - **7.** BOT tree; **palo santo** lignum vitae - **8.** *fig* [pesadez] bind, drag; **dar palo** *fam* to be a bind *o* a drag - **9.** *loc*: **a palo seco** [gen] without anything else; [bebida] neat; **dar palos de ciego** [criticar] to lash out (wildly); [no saber qué hacer] to grope around in the dark; **de tal palo tal astilla** he/she is a chip off the old block.

paloma ▷ palomo.

palomar *sm* dovecote; [grande] pigeon shed.

palomilla *sf* - **1.** [insecto] grain moth - **2.** [tornillo] butterfly nut, wing nut - **3.** [soporte] bracket.

palomino *sm* young dove *o* pigeon.

palomita *sf*: **palomitas** popcorn *(U)*.

palomo, ma *sm, f* dove, pigeon; **paloma mensajera** carrier *o* homing pigeon; **paloma torcaz** ringdove, wood pigeon.

palote *sm* [trazo] downstroke.

palpable *adj* touchable, palpable; *fig* obvious, clear.

palpación *sf* palpation.

palpar ◇ *vt* - **1.** [tocar] to feel, to touch; MED to palpate - **2.** *fig* [percibir] to feel. ◇ *vi* to feel around.

palpitación *sf* beat, beating *(U)*; [con fuerza] throb, throbbing *(U)*.

◆ **palpitaciones** *sfpl* MED palpitations.

palpitante *adj* - **1.** [que palpita] beating; [con fuerza] throbbing - **2.** *fig* [interesante - discusión, competición] lively; [- interés, deseo, cuestión] burning.

palpitar *vi* - **1.** [latir] to beat; [con fuerza] to throb - **2.** *fig* [sentimiento] to be evident.

pálpito *sm* feeling, hunch.

palta *sf Andes & R Dom* avocado.

palúdico, ca *adj* - **1.** MED malarial - **2.** [pantanoso] marshy, swampy.

paludismo *sm* malaria.

palurdo, da ◇ *adj fam* coarse, uncouth. ◇ *sm, f* country bumpkin, yokel, hick US.

pamela *sf* sun hat.

pampa *sf*: **la pampa** the pampas *pl*.

pampero, ra ◇ *adj* of/relating to the pampas. ◇ *sm, f* inhabitant of the pampas.

pamplina *(gen pl) sf fam* trifle, unimportant thing.

pan *sm* - **1.** [alimento] bread; **pan de molde** *o* **inglés** sliced bread; **pan francés** French bread; **pan integral** wholemeal bread; **pan lactal** *Arg* sliced bread; **pan moreno** *o* **negro** [integral] wholemeal bread; [con centeno] black *o* rye bread; **pan rallado** breadcrumbs *pl* - **2.** [hogaza] loaf - **3.** *loc*: **a falta de pan buenas son tortas** you have to make the most of what you've got; **a pan y agua** on bread and water; *fig* on the breadline; **contigo pan y cebolla** I'll go through thick and thin with you; **llamar al pan pan y al vino vino** to call a spade a spade; **ser pan comido** to be a piece of cake, to be as easy as pie; **ser el pan nuestro de cada día** to be a regular occurrence, to be commonplace; **ser más bueno que el pan** to be kindness itself; **no sólo de pan vive el hombre** man cannot live on bread alone.

PAN *sm* - **1.** (*abrev de* **Partido Acción Nacional**), *Mexican political party* - **2.** (*abrev de* **Partido de Avanzada Nacional**), *Guatemalan political party*.

pana *sf* corduroy.

panacea *sf lit & fig* panacea.

panadería *sf* bakery, baker's.

panadero, ra *sm, f* baker.

panal *sm* honeycomb.

panamá (*pl* **panamaes**) *sm* panama (hat).

Panamá *n pr* Panama.

panameño, ña *adj* & *sm, f* Panamanian.

panamericanismo *sm* Pan-Americanism.

Panamericana *sf*: **la Panamericana** the Pan-American Highway.

pancarta *sf* placard, banner.

panceta *sf* bacon.

pancho, cha *adj fam* calm, unruffled; **estar/quedarse tan pancho** to be/remain perfectly calm.

◆ **pancho** *sm R Dom* [comida] hot dog.

páncreas *sm inv* pancreas.

pancreático, ca *adj* pancreatic.
panda <> *sm* ⊳ **oso.** <> *sf Esp* gang.
pandereta *sf* tambourine.
pandero *sm* - **1.** MÚS tambourine - **2.** *Esp fam* [trasero] bum.
pandilla *sf* gang.
pandillero, ra *sm, f* member of a gang.
panecillo *sm Esp* bread roll.
panecito *sm Amér* bread roll.
panegírico, ca *adj* panegyrical, eulogistic.
➡ **panegírico** *sm* panegyric, eulogy.
panel *sm* - **1.** [gen] panel - **2.** [pared, biombo] screen - **3.** [tablero] board; **panel solar** solar panel.
panera *sf* [para servir] bread basket; [para guardar] bread bin.
panero *sm* bread tray.
paneuropeísmo *sm* Europeanism.
pánfilo, la <> *adj* simple, foolish. <> *sm, f* fool, simpleton.
panfletario, ria *adj* propagandist.
panfleto *sm* pamphlet.
pánico *sm* panic; **ser presa del pánico** to be panic-stricken.
panificadora *sf* (large) bakery.
panocha *sf* ear, cob.
panoplia *sf* - **1.** [armadura] panoply - **2.** [armas] collection of arms O weapons.
panorama *sm* - **1.** [vista] panorama - **2.** *fig* [situación] overall state; [perspectiva] outlook.
panorámico, ca *adj* panoramic.
➡ **panorámica** *sf* panorama.
pantagruélico, ca *adj* gargantuan, enormous.
pantaletas *sfpl Amér C, Caribe & Méx* [bragas] panties, knickers *UK*.
pantalla *sf* - **1.** [gen & INFORM] screen; **mostrar en pantalla** to show on the screen; **pantalla acústica** baffle; **pantalla ancha** widescreen; **pantalla de ayuda** help screen; **pantalla de cristal líquido** liquid crystal display; **pantalla de radar** radar screen; **pantalla táctil** touch screen; **la pequeña pantalla** the small screen, television - **2.** [de lámpara] lampshade - **3.** [de chimenea] fireguard - **4.** *fig* [encubridor] front.
pantallazo *sm* screenshot.
pantalón *(gen pl) sm* trousers *pl*, pants *pl US*; **pantalón tejano** O **vaquero** jeans *pl*; **pantalón pitillo** drainpipe trousers *pl*; **bajarse los pantalones** *fig* to give in; **llevar los pantalones** to wear the trousers.
pantano *sm* - **1.** [ciénaga] marsh; [laguna] swamp - **2.** [embalse] reservoir.

pantanoso, sa *adj* - **1.** [cenagoso] marshy, boggy - **2.** *fig* [difícil] tricky.
panteísta <> *adj* pantheistic. <> *smf* pantheist.
panteón *sm* pantheon; [familiar] mausoleum, vault.
pantera *sf* panther; **pantera negra** black panther.
pantimedias *sfpl Méx* tights *UK*, pantyhose *US*.
pantocrátor *sm* Christ Pantocrator.
pantomima *sf* mime; *fig* pantomime *(U)*, acting *(U)*.
pantorrilla *sf* calf.
pantufla *(gen pl) sf* slipper.
panty *(pl pantys) sm* tights *pl*.
panza *sf* belly.
panzada *sf* - **1.** [en el agua] belly flop - **2.** *fam* [hartura]: **darse una panzada de algo** to pig out on sthg.
pañal *sm* nappy *UK*, diaper *US*; **estar en pañales** [en sus inicios] to be in its infancy; [sin conocimientos] not to have a clue; **dejar a alguien en pañales** to leave sb standing O behind.
pañería *sf* [producto] drapery; [tienda] draper's (shop), dry-goods store *US*.
paño *sm* - **1.** [tela] cloth, material - **2.** [trapo] cloth; [para polvo] duster; [de cocina] tea towel - **3.** [lienzo] panel, length - **4.** *loc*: **conocer el paño** to know the score; **ser el paño de lágrimas de alguien** to be a shoulder to cry on for sb.
➡ **paños** *smpl* - **1.** [vestiduras] drapes; **en paños menores** in one's underwear - **2.** *loc*: **paños calientes** half-measures.
pañol *sm* NÁUT storeroom.
pañoleta *sf* shawl, wrap.
pañuelo *sm* [de nariz] handkerchief; [para el cuello] scarf; [para la cabeza] headscarf; **pañuelo de papel** paper handkerchief, tissue.
papa *sf* potato; **no saber ni papa** *fam* not to have a clue.
➡ **Papa** *sm* Pope.
papá *sm fam* dad, daddy, pop *US*; **papá grande** *Méx* grandpa.
➡ **Papá Noel** *sm* Father Christmas.
papachador, ra *adj Méx* comforting.
papachar *vt Méx* to spoil.
papada *sf* [de persona] double chin; [de animal] dewlap.
papado *sm* papacy.
papagayo *sm* - **1.** [pájaro] parrot; **como un papagayo** parrot-fashion - **2.** *Ven* [cometa] kite.
papal *adj* papal.
papalote *sm Amér C, Caribe & Méx* kite.

papamoscas *sm inv* flycatcher.

papanatas *smf inv fam* sucker.

papaya *sf* [fruta] papaya, pawpaw.

papear *vi fam* to eat.

papel *sm* - **1.** [gen] paper; [hoja] sheet of paper; **papel carbón/cuché/secante** carbon/coated/blotting paper; **papel cebolla** onionskin; **papel celofán** Cellophane; **papel confort** *Chile* toilet paper; **papel continuo** INFORM continuous paper; **papel de embalar** *o* **de embalaje** wrapping paper; **papel de estaño** *o* **de aluminio** *o* **de plata** tin *o* aluminium foil; **papel de estraza** brown paper; **papel de fumar** cigarette paper; **papel de lija** sandpaper; **papel higiénico** toilet paper; **papel madera** *R Dom* cardboard; **papel milimetrado** graph paper; **papel pintado** wallpaper; **papel reciclado** recycled paper; **papel sanitario** *Cuba & Méx* toilet paper; **papel sellado** *o* **timbrado** stamp, stamped paper; **papel tapiz** INFORM wallpaper; **papel vegetal** tracing paper; **sobre el papel** on paper; **ser papel mojado** to be worthless - **2.** *fig* & CINE & TEATRO role, part; **desempeñar** *o* **hacer el papel de** to play the role *o* part of; **papel principal/secundario** main/minor part; **hacer buen/mal papel** to do well/badly - **3.** FIN stocks and shares *pl*; **papel de pagos** *special stamps for making certain payments to the State*; **papel del Estado** government bonds *pl*; **papel moneda** paper money, banknotes *pl*.

➡ **papeles** *smpl* [documentos] papers.

papela *sf Esp fam* [documentación] I.D. card.

papeleo *sm* paperwork, red tape.

papelera ➡ **papelero**.

papelería *sf* stationer's (shop).

papelero, ra *adj* paper *(antes de s)*.

➡ **papelera** *sf* - **1.** [cesto - en oficina etc] wastepaper basket *o* bin; [- en la calle] litter bin - **2.** [fábrica] paper mill.

papeleta *sf* - **1.** [boleto] ticket, slip (of paper); [de votación] ballot paper - **2.** EDUC *slip of paper with university exam results* - **3.** *fig* [problema]: **¡menuda papeleta!** that's a nasty one!

papelina *sf fam* wrap.

papelón *sm fam* spectacle; **hacer un papelón** to make a fool of o.s., to be left looking ridiculous.

paperas *sfpl* mumps.

papi *sm fam* daddy, dad.

papila *sf* papilla; **papila gustativa** taste bud.

papilla *sf* - **1.** [para niños] baby food; **echar** *o* **arrojar la primera papilla** *fam* to be as sick as

a dog; **hecho papilla** *fam* [cansado] shattered, exhausted; [cosa] smashed to bits, ruined - **2.** MED barium meal.

papiloma *sm* papilloma.

papiro *sm* papyrus.

papiroflexia *sf* origami.

papista *smf* papist; **ser más papista que el Papa** to be more Catholic than the Pope.

papú *(pl* **papúes** *o* **papús)** *adj* & *sm*, *f* Papuan.

Papúa-Nueva Guinea *n pr* Papua New Guinea.

paquebote *sm* packet boat.

paquete *sm* - **1.** [de libros, regalos etc] parcel; **paquete bomba** parcel bomb; **paquete postal** parcel - **2.** [de cigarrillos, klínex, folios etc] pack, packet; [de azúcar, arroz] bag - **3.** [maleta, bulto etc] bag - **4.** [de medidas] package; **paquete de acciones** block of shares; **paquete turístico** package tour - **5.** *fam* [cosa fastidiosa]: **me ha tocado el paquete de hacer...** I've been lumbered with doing... - **6.** INFORM package; **paquete integrado** integrated package - **7.** *Esp fam* [pañales] nappies - **8.** [en una moto]: **ir de paquete** to ride pillion - **9.** *loc*: **meter un paquete a alguien** *fam* [castigar] to come down on sb like a ton of bricks.

paquidermo *sm* pachyderm.

Paquistán, Pakistán *n pr* Pakistan.

paquistaní *(pl* **paquistaníes** *o* **paquistanís)**, **pakistaní** *(pl* **pakistaníes** *o* **pakistanís)** *adj* & *sm*, *f* Pakistani.

par ⬦ *adj* - **1.** MAT even; **echar algo a pares** *o* **nones** *to decide something between two people by a game involving guessing the number of fingers that another person is holding out behind his/her back* - **2.** [igual] equal. ⬦ *sm* - **1.** [pareja - de zapatos etc] pair - **2.** [dos - veces etc] couple - **3.** [número indeterminado] few, couple; **un par de copas** a couple of *o* a few drinks - **4.** [en golf] par - **5.** [noble] peer.

➡ **a la par** *loc adv* - **1.** [simultáneamente] at the same time - **2.** [a igual nivel] at the same level - **3.** FIN at par.

➡ **de par en par** *loc adj*: **abierto de par en par** wide open.

➡ **sin par** *loc adj* without equal, matchless.

para *prep* - **1.** [finalidad] for; **es para ti** it's for you; **una mesa para el salón** a table for the living room; **esta agua no es buena para beber** this water isn't fit for drinking *o* to drink; **te lo repetiré para que te enteres** I'll repeat it so you understand; **¿para qué?** what for? - **2.** [motivación] (in order) to; **para conseguir sus propósitos** in order to achieve his aims; **lo he hecho para agradarte** I did it to please you

- 3. [dirección] towards; **ir para casa** to head (for) home; **salir para el aeropuerto** to leave for the airport **- 4.** [tiempo] for; **tiene que estar acabado para mañana** it has to be finished by 0 for tomorrow **- 5.** [comparación]: **está muy delgado para lo que come** he's very thin considering how much he eats; **para ser verano hace mucho frío** considering it's summer, it's very cold **- 6.** *(después de adj y antes de infinitivo)* [inminencia, propósito] to; **la comida está lista para servir** the meal is ready to be served; **el atleta está preparado para ganar** the athlete is ready to win.

◆ **para con** *loc prep* towards; **es buena para con los demás** she is kind towards other people.

parabién (*pl* **parabienes**) *sm* congratulations *pl.*

parábola *sf* **- 1.** [alegoría] parable **- 2.** GEOM parabola.

parabólico, ca *adj* parabolic.
◆ **parabólica** *sf* satellite dish.

parabrisas *sm inv* windscreen, windshield *US.*

paracaídas *sm inv* parachute.

paracaidismo *sm* parachuting, parachute jumping.

paracaidista *smf* parachutist; MIL paratrooper.

parachispas *sm inv* fireguard.

parachoques *sm inv* AUTO bumper, fender *US*; FERROC buffer.

parada ⊳ **parado**.

paradero *sm* **- 1.** [de persona] whereabouts *pl* **- 2.** *Chile, Col, Méx & Perú* [parada de autobús] bus stop.

paradigma *sm* paradigm, example.

paradisiaco, ca, paradisíaco, ca *adj* heavenly.

parado, da ⟨⟩ *adj* **- 1.** [inmóvil - coche] stationary, standing; [- persona] still, motionless; [- fábrica, proyecto] at a standstill **- 2.** [pasivo] lacking in initiative **- 3.** *Amér* [de pie] standing **- 4.** *Esp* [sin empleo] unemployed, out of work **- 5.** *loc*: **salir bien/mal parado de algo** to come off well/badly out of sthg. ⟨⟩ *sm, f Esp* [desempleado] unemployed person; **los parados** the unemployed.

◆ **parada** *sf* **- 1.** [detención] stop, stopping *(U)*; **parado de imagen** [de vídeo] freeze-frame function **- 2.** DEP save **- 3.** [de autobús] (bus) stop; [de taxis] taxi rank *UK* 0 stand *US*; [de metro] (underground) station; **parada discrecional** request stop **- 4.** MIL parade.

paradoja *sf* paradox.

paradójico, ca *adj* paradoxical, ironical.

parador *sm* [hotel]: **parador (nacional)** *Esp* state-owned luxury hotel, usually a building of historic or artistic importance.

Parador nacional ▬▬▬▬▬

🏨 There are now over 80 of these luxury hotels which are administered by the Spanish government. **Paradores** are found throughout Spain, both in cities and in the countryside, and their restaurants have a good reputation for serving regional cuisine. Many are in buildings of historical importance, such as castles, mansions and former monasteries, but there are also purpose-built **Paradores**, designed to reflect traditional architectural styles. They are considered to be flagships of the government's policy on tourism.

parafernalia *sf* paraphernalia.

parafina *sf* paraffin.

parafrasear *vt* to paraphrase.

paráfrasis *sf inv* paraphrase.

paraguas *sm inv* umbrella.

Paraguay *n pr*: **(el) Paraguay** Paraguay.

paraguayo, ya *adj & sm, f* Paraguayan.

paragüero *sm* umbrella stand.

paraíso *sm* RELIG Paradise; *fig* paradise; **paraíso fiscal** tax haven; **paraíso terrenal** earthly Paradise.

paraje *sm* spot, place.

paralelismo *sm* **- 1.** GEOM parallelism **- 2.** [semejanza] similarity, parallels *pl.*

paralelo, la *adj*: **paralelo (a)** parallel (to).
◆ **paralelo** *sm* **- 1.** GEOGR parallel **- 2.** [comparación] comparison **- 3.** ELECTR: **estar en paralelo** to be in parallel.
◆ **paralela** *sf* GEOM parallel (line).
◆ **paralelas** *sfpl* DEP parallel bars.

paralelogramo *sm* parallelogram.

parálisis *sf inv* paralysis; **parálisis cerebral** cerebral palsy; **parálisis infantil** polio.

paralítico, ca *adj & sm, f* paralytic.

paralización *sf* paralysis; *fig* halting.

paralizar [13] *vt* to paralyse.
◆ **paralizarse** *vprnl* to become paralysed; [producción etc] to come to a standstill.

paramento *sm* **- 1.** [adorno] adornment **- 2.** CONSTR facing *(of a wall).*

parámetro *sm* parameter.

paramilitar *adj & smf* paramilitary.

páramo *sm* moor, moorland *(U)*; *fig* wilderness.

parangón *sm* paragon; **sin parangón** unparalleled; **tener parangón con** to be comparable with.

paraninfo *sm* assembly hall, auditorium.

paranoia *sf* paranoia.

paranoico, **ca** *adj & sm, f* paranoic.

paranormal *adj* paranormal.

parapente *sm* [deporte] parapenting, paragliding; [paracaídas] parapente.

parapetarse *vprnl lit & fig*: **parapetarse (tras)** to take refuge (behind).

parapeto *sm* [antepecho] parapet; [barandilla] bannister; [barricada] barricade.

parapléjico, **ca** *adj & sm, f* paraplegic.

parapsicología *sf* parapsychology.

parapsicológico, **ca** *adj* parapsychological.

parapsicólogo, **ga** *sm, f* parapsychologist.

parar ⟷ *vi* - **1.** [gen] to stop; **parar de hacer algo** to stop doing sthg; **no para de molestarme** she keeps annoying me; **no para** *fam* he's always on the go; **sin parar** non-stop - **2.** [alojarse] to stay - **3.** [recaer]: **parar en manos de alguien** to come into the possession of sb - **4.** [acabar] to end up; **¿en qué parará este lío?** where will it all end?; **ir a parar a** to end up in. ⟷ *vt* - **1.** [gen] to stop; [golpe] to parry - **2.** [preparar] to prepare, to lay - **3.** *Amér* [levantar] to raise.

➤ **pararse** *vprnl* - **1.** [detenerse] to stop; **pararse a hacer algo** to stop to do sthg - **2.** *Amér* [ponerse de pie] to stand up - **3.** *Méx & Ven* [salir de la cama] to get up.

pararrayos *sm inv* lightning conductor.

parasitario, **ria** *adj* parasitic.

parasitismo *sm* parasitism.

parásito, **ta** *adj* BIOL parasitic.

➤ **parásito** *sm fig & BIOL* parasite.

➤ **parásitos** *smpl* [interferencias] statics *pl*.

parasitología *sf* parasitology.

parasol *sm* parasol.

parcela *sf* - **1.** [de tierra] plot (of land) - **2.** [de saber] area.

parcelación *sf* parcelling out, division into plots.

parcelar *vt* to parcel out, to divide into plots.

parcelario, **ria** *adj* of/relating to plots of land.

parche *sm* - **1.** [gen] patch - **2.** [emplasto] poultice - **3.** [chapuza - mal hecha] botch job; [- para salir del paso] makeshift solution.

parchear *vt fig* to patch up.

parchís *sm inv* ludo.

parcial ⟷ *adj* - **1.** [no total] partial; **a tiempo parcial** part-time - **2.** [no ecuánime] biased. ⟷ *sm* [examen] *end-of-term exam at university*.

parcialidad *sf* [tendenciosidad] bias, partiality.

parco, **ca** *adj* - **1.** [moderado]: **parco (en)** sparing (in) - **2.** [escaso] meagre; [cena] frugal; [explicación] brief, concise.

pardillo, **lla** *Esp* ⟷ *adj* - **1.** [ingenuo] naive - **2.** [palurdo] countrified. ⟷ *sm, f* - **1.** [ingenuo] naive person - **2.** [palurdo] bumpkin, hick *US*.

➤ **pardillo** *sm* ZOOL linnet.

pardo, **da** *adj* greyish-brown, dull brown.

➤ **pardo** *sm* greyish-brown, dull brown.

parear *vt* to pair.

parecer [30] ⟷ *sm* - **1.** [opinión] opinion - **2.** [apariencia]: **de buen parecer** good-looking. ⟷ *vi (antes de s)* to look like; **parece un palacio** it looks like a palace. ⟷ *v cop* to look, to seem; **pareces cansado** you look *o* seem tired. ⟷ *v impers* - **1.** [opinar]: **me parece que...** I think *o* it seems to me that...; **me parece que sí/no** I think/don't think so; **¿qué te parece?** what do you think (of it)? - **2.** [tener aspecto de]: **parece que va a llover** it looks like it's going to rain; **parece que le gusta** it looks as if *o* it seems that she likes it; **eso parece** so it seems; **al parecer** apparently.

➤ **parecerse** *vprnl*: **parecerse (en)** to be alike (in); **parecerse a alguien** [físicamente] to look like sb; [en carácter] to be like sb.

parecido, **da** *adj* similar; **parecido a** similar to, like; **bien parecido** [atractivo] good-looking.

➤ **parecido** *sm*: **parecido (con/entre)** resemblance (to/between).

pared *sf* - **1.** [gen] wall; **pared maestra** main wall; **entre cuatro paredes** cooped-up at home; **las paredes oyen** walls have ears; **si las paredes hablasen...** if the walls could talk...; **subirse por las paredes** to hit the roof, to go up the wall - **2.** [de montaña] side; **pared artificial** climbing wall - **3.** DEP one-two.

paredón *sm* (thick) wall; [de fusilamiento] (execution) wall.

parejo, **ja** *adj*: **parejo (a)** similar (to).

➤ **pareja** *sf* - **1.** [gen] pair; [de novios] couple; **pareja de hecho** *common-law heterosexual or homosexual relationship*; **son una pareja de hecho** they live together as man and wife; **por parejas** in pairs - **2.** [miembro del par - persona] partner; [- guante etc] other one; **la pareja de este calcetín** the other sock of this pair.

parentela *sf fam* relations *pl*, family.

parentesco *sm* relationship.

paréntesis *sm inv* - **1.** [signo] bracket; **entre paréntesis** in brackets, in parentheses - **2.** [intercalación] digression - **3.** [interrupción] break; **hacer un paréntesis** to have a break.

pareo *sm* wraparound skirt.

parezca *etc* ▷ **parecer**.

pargo *sm* porgy.

paria *smf* pariah.

parida *sf fam*: **eso es una parida** that's a load of nonsense; **decir paridas** to talk nonsense.

paridad *sf* - **1.** [semejanza] similarity; [igualdad] equality - **2.** ECON parity; **paridad de cambio** parity of exchange - **3.** INFORM parity.

pariente, ta *sm, f* - **1.** [familiar] relation, relative - **2.** *fam* [cónyuge] old man (*f* missus).

parietal *sm* parietal.

paripé *sm Esp fam*: **hacer el paripé** to put on an act, to pretend.

parir ◇ *vi* to give birth. ◇ *vt* to give birth to.

paritorio *sm* delivery room.

París *n pr* Paris.

parking ['parkin] (*pl* **parkings**) *sm* car park *UK*, parking lot *US*.

párkinson *sm* Parkinson's disease.

parlamentar *vi* to negotiate.

parlamentario, ria ◇ *adj* parliamentary. ◇ *sm, f* member of parliament.

parlamentarismo *sm* parliamentary system.

parlamento *sm* - **1.** POLÍT parliament - **2.** TEATRO speech.

parlanchín, ina *fam* ◇ *adj* chatty. ◇ *sm, f* chatterbox.

parlante *adj* talking.
◆ **parlante** *sm Amér* speaker.

parlotear *vi fam* to chatter.

parloteo *sm fam* chatter.

parmesano, na *adj* & *sm, f* Parmesan.

parnaso *sm culto* parnassus.

paro *sm* - **1.** *Esp* [desempleo] unemployment; **estar en paro** to be unemployed; **paro cíclico/encubierto/estructural** cyclical/hidden/structural unemployment - **2.** *Esp* [subsidio] unemployment benefit; **cobrar el paro** to claim unemployment benefit - **3.** [cesación - acción] shutdown; [- estado] stoppage; **paro cardíaco** cardiac arrest; **paro laboral** industrial action (U) - **4.** *Amér* [huelga] strike.

parodia *sf* parody.

parodiar [8] *vt* to parody.

parón *sm* sudden stoppage.

paroxismo *sm* paroxysm.

parolímpico, ca *adj* Paralympic.

parpadeante *adj* [luz] flickering.

parpadear *vi* - **1.** [pestañear] to blink - **2.** [centellear] to flicker.

parpadeo *sm* - **1.** [pestañeo] blinking - **2.** [centelleo] flickering.

párpado *sm* eyelid.

parque *sm* - **1.** [gen] park; **parque acuático** waterpark; **parque de atracciones** amusement park; **parque comercial** retail park *UK*, shopping mall *US*; **parque eólico** wind farm; **parque nacional** national park; **parque tecnológico** science park; **parque temático** theme park; **(parque) zoológico** zoo - **2.** [vehículos] fleet; **parque de bomberos** *Esp* fire station; **parque móvil** car pool - **3.** [para niños] playpen.

parqué, parquet [par'ke] (*pl* **parquets**) *sm* parquet (floor).

parqueadero *sm Amér* car park, parking lot *US*.

parquear *vt Amér* to park.

parquedad *sf* moderation; **con parquedad** sparingly.

parquet = **parqué**.

parquímetro *sm* parking meter.

parra *sf* grapevine; **subirse a la parra** *fam fig* to hit the roof.

parrafada *sf* earful, dull monologue; **soltar una parrafada sobre el tema** to go on (and on).

párrafo *sm* paragraph.

parral *sm* - **1.** [emparrado] vine arbour - **2.** [terreno] vineyard.

parrampán *sm Amér fam* [tonto] daft.

parranda *sf fam* [juerga]: **irse de parranda** to go out on the town.

parrandear *vi fam* to go out on the town.

parricida *smf* parricide.

parricidio *sm* parricide.

parrilla *sf* - **1.** [utensilio] grill; **a la parrilla** grilled, broiled *US* - **2.** [sala de restaurante] grill-room - **3.** DEP: **parrilla (de salida)** (starting) grid - **4.** *Amér* [baca] roof rack.

parrillada *sf* mixed grill.

párroco *sm* parish priest.

parroquia *sf* - **1.** [iglesia] parish church - **2.** [jurisdicción] parish - **3.** [fieles] parishioners *pl*, parish - **4.** [clientela] clientele.

parroquial *adj* parish (antes de s).

parroquiano, na *sm, f* - **1.** [feligrés] parishioner - **2.** [cliente] customer.

parsimonia *sf* deliberation, calmness; **con parsimonia** unhurriedly.

parsimonioso, sa *adj* unhurried, deliberate.

parte ◇ *sm* report; **dar parte (a alguien de algo)** to report (sthg to sb); **parte facultativo** o **médico** medical report; **parte meteorológico** weather forecast. ◇ *sf* [gen] part; [bando] side; DER party; **la mayor parte de la gente** most people; **la tercera parte de** a third of; **en alguna parte** somewhere; **no lo veo por ninguna parte** I can't find it anywhere; **en parte** to a certain extent, partly; **estar/ponerse de parte de alguien** to be on/to take sb's side; **formar parte de** to be part of; **por mi parte** for my part; **por parte de padre/madre** on one's father's/mother's side; **por partes** bit by bit;

por una parte... por la otra... on the one hand... on the other (hand)...; **tener a alguien de parte de uno** to have sb on one's side; **tomar parte en algo** to take part in sthg; **en todas partes cuecen habas** it's the same the whole world over.

◆ **partes** *sfpl* [genitales] private parts.

◆ **de parte de** *loc prep* on behalf of, for; **¿de parte de (quién)?** TELECOM who is calling, please?

◆ **por otra parte** *loc adv* [además] what is more, besides.

partenaire [parte'ner] *smf* partner.

partera *sf* midwife.

parterre *sm Esp* flowerbed.

partición *sf* - **1.** [reparto] sharing out; [de territorio] partitioning - **2.** MAT division.

participación *sf* - **1.** [colaboración] participation - **2.** [de lotería] share of a lottery ticket - **3.** [comunicación] notice - **4.** ECON: **cuentan con una participación en los beneficios** they are entitled to a share in the profits.

participante ◇ *adj* participating. ◇ *smf* participant.

participar ◇ *vi* - **1.** [colaborar]: **participar (en)** to take part o participate (in); FIN to have a share (in) - **2.** [recibir]: **participar (de)** to receive a share (of) - **3.** [compartir]: **participar de** to share. ◇ *vt*: **participar algo a alguien** to notify sb of sthg.

partícipe ◇ *adj*: **partícipe (de)** involved (in); **hacer partícipe de algo a alguien** [notificar] to notify sb of sthg; [compartir] to share sthg with sb. ◇ *smf* participant.

participio *sm* participle; **participio pasado/presente** past/present participle.

partícula *sf* particle.

particular ◇ *adj* - **1.** [gen] particular; **tiene su sabor particular** it has its own particular taste; **en particular** in particular - **2.** [no público - domicilio, clases etc] private - **3.** [no corriente - habilidad etc] uncommon. ◇ *smf* [persona] member of the public. ◇ *sm* [asunto] matter; **sin otro particular** without further ado.

particularidad *sf* [cualidad] peculiarity; [rasgo] special o distinctive feature.

particularizar [13] ◇ *vt* [caracterizar] to characterize. ◇ *vi* - **1.** [detallar] to go into details - **2.** [personalizar]: **particularizar en alguien** to single sb out.

◆ **particularizarse** *vprnl* [caracterizarse]: **particularizarse por** to be characterized by.

partida *sf* - **1.** [marcha] departure - **2.** [en juego] game; **echar una partida** to have a game - **3.** [documento] certificate; **partida de defun-** ción/matrimonio/nacimiento death/marriage/birth certificate - **4.** [COM - mercancía] consignment; [- entrada] item, entry.

partidario, ria ◇ *adj*: **partidario de** in favour of, for. ◇ *sm, f* supporter.

partidismo *sm* partisanship, bias.

partidista *adj* partisan, biased.

partido *sm* - **1.** POLÍT party - **2.** DEP match; **partido amistoso** friendly (match) - **3.** [futuro cónyuge]: **buen/mal partido** good/bad match - **4.** *loc*: **sacar partido de** to make the most of; **tomar partido por** to side with.

partir ◇ *vt* - **1.** [dividir] to divide, to split - **2.** [repartir] to share out - **3.** [romper] to break open; [cascar] to crack; [tronco, loncha etc] to cut. ◇ *vi* - **1.** [marchar] to leave, to set off - **2.** [basarse]: **partir de** to start from.

◆ **partirse** *vprnl* - **1.** [romperse] to split - **2.** [rajarse] to crack.

◆ **a partir de** *loc prep* starting from; **a partir de aquí** from here on.

partisano, na *adj* & *sm, f* partisan.

partitivo, va *adj* partitive.

◆ **partitivo** *sm* partitive.

partitura *sf* score.

parto *sm* birth; **estar de parto** to be in labour; **parto natural/prematuro** natural/premature birth.

parturienta *sf* woman in labour.

parvulario *sm* nursery school, kindergarten.

párvulo, la *sm, f* infant.

pasa *sf* [fruta] raisin; **pasa de Corinto** currant; **pasa de Esmirna** sultana.

pasable *adj* passable.

pasada ⊳ **pasado**.

pasadizo *sm* passage.

pasado, da *adj* - **1.** [gen] past; **pasado un año** a year later; **lo pasado, pasado está** let bygones be bygones - **2.** [último] last; **el año pasado** last year - **3.** [podrido] off, bad - **4.** [hecho - filete, carne] well done.

◆ **pasado** *sm* [gen] past; GRAM past (tense).

◆ **pasada** *sf* - **1.** [con el trapo] wipe; [con la brocha] coat - **2.** *Esp fam* [barbaridad]: **es una pasada** it's way over the top.

◆ **de pasada** *loc adv* in passing.

◆ **mala pasada** *sf* dirty trick.

pasador *sm* - **1.** [cerrojo] bolt - **2.** [para el pelo] slide - **3.** *Perú* [cordón] shoelace.

pasaje *sm* - **1.** [billete] ticket - **2.** [pasajeros] passengers *pl* - **3.** [calle] passage - **4.** [fragmento] passage.

pasajero, ra ◇ *adj* passing. ◇ *sm, f* passenger.

pasamanos *sm inv* [de escalera interior] bannister; [de escalera exterior] handrail.

pasamontañas *sm inv* balaclava (helmet).

pasante *smf* articled clerk.

pasapalos *smpl Méx & Ven* snacks, appetizers.

pasaporte *sm* passport.

pasapuré *sm* food mill.

pasapurés *sm inv* = pasapuré.

pasar ◇ *vt* - **1.** [gen] to pass; [noticia, aviso] to pass on; ¿me pasas la sal? would you pass me the salt?; **pasar algo por** [filtrar] to pass sthg through - **2.** [cruzar] to cross; **pasar la calle** to cross the road; **pasé el río a nado** I swam across the river - **3.** [traspasar] to pass through - **4.** [trasladar]: **pasar algo a** to move sthg to - **5.** [llevar adentro] to show in; **el criado nos pasó al salón** the butler showed us into the living room - **6.** [contagiar]: **pasar algo a alguien** to give sthg to sb, to infect sb with sthg; **me has pasado la tos** you've given me your cough - **7.** [admitir - instancia etc] to accept - **8.** [consentir]: **pasar algo a alguien** to let sb get away with sthg - **9.** [rebasar - en el espacio] to go through; [- en el tiempo] to have been through; **pasar un semáforo en rojo** to go through a red light - **10.** [emplear - tiempo] to spend; **pasó dos años en Roma** he spent two years in Rome - **11.** [padecer] to go through, to suffer; **pasarlo mal** to have a hard time of it - **12.** [sobrepasar]: **ya ha pasado los veinticinco** he's over twenty-five now; **mi hijo me pasa ya dos centímetros** my son is already two centimetres taller than me - **13.** [adelantar - coche, contrincante etc] to overtake - **14.** CINE to show. ◇ *vi* - **1.** [gen] to pass, to go; **pasó por mi lado** he passed by my side; **el autobús pasa por mi casa** the bus goes past *o* passes in front of my house; **el Manzanares pasa por Madrid** the Manzanares *o* passes through Madrid; **he pasado por tu calle** I went down your street; **pasar de... a...** to go *o* pass from... to...; **pasar de largo** to go by - **2.** [entrar] to go/come in; **¡pase!** come in! - **3.** [poder entrar]: **pasar (por)** to go (through); **por ahí no pasa** it won't go through there - **4.** [ir un momento] to pop in; **pasaré por mi oficina/por tu casa** I'll pop into my office/round to your place - **5.** [suceder] to happen; ¿qué pasa aquí? what's going on here?; ¿qué pasa? what's the matter?; **pase lo que pase** whatever happens, come what may - **6.** [terminarse] to be over; **pasó la Navidad** Christmas is over - **7.** [transcurrir] to go by - **8.** [cambiar - acción]: **pasar a** to move on to; **pasemos a otra cosa** let's move on to something else - **9.** [conformarse]: **pasar (con/sin algo)** to make do (with/without sthg); **tendrá que pasar sin coche** she'll have to make do without a car - **10.** [servir] to be all right, to be usable; **puede pasar** it'll do - **11.** *fam* [prescindir]: **pasar de algo/alguien** to

want nothing to do with sthg/sb; **paso de política** I'm not into politics - **12.** [tolerar]: **pasar por algo** to put up with sthg.

◆ **pasarse** *vprnl* - **1.** [acabarse] to pass; **siéntate hasta que se te pase** sit down until you feel better - **2.** [emplear - tiempo] to spend, to pass; **se pasaron el día hablando** they spent all day talking - **3.** [desaprovechar] to slip by; **se me pasó la oportunidad** I missed my chance - **4.** [estropearse - comida] to go off; [- flores] to fade - **5.** [cambiar de bando]: **pasarse a** to go over to - **6.** [omitir] to miss out; **te has pasado una página** you've missed a page out - **7.** [olvidarse]: **pasársele a alguien** to slip sb's mind; **se me pasó decírtelo** I forgot to mention it to you - **8.** [no fijarse]: **pasársele a alguien** to escape sb's attention; **no se le pasa nada** he never misses a thing - **9.** [excederse]: **pasarse de generoso/bueno** to be far too generous/kind - **10.** *fam* [propasarse] to go too far, to go over the top; **te has pasado diciéndole eso** what you said went too far *o* was over the top - **11.** [divertirse]: ¿qué tal te lo estás pasando? how are you enjoying yourself?; **pasárselo bien/mal** to have a good/bad time.

pasarela *sf* - **1.** [puente] footbridge; [para desembarcar] gangway - **2.** [en un desfile] catwalk.

pasatiempo *sm* [hobby] pastime, hobby.
◆ **pasatiempos** *smpl* PRENSA crossword and puzzles section *sing*.

Pascua *sf* - **1.** [de los judíos] Passover - **2.** [de los cristianos] Easter; **hacer la Pascua a alguien** *fam* [ser pesado] to pester sb; [poner en apuros] to land sb in it.
◆ **Pascuas** *sfpl* [Navidad] Christmas *sing*; **¡felices Pascuas!** Merry Christmas!; **de Pascuas a Ramos** *fam* once in a blue moon.

pascual *adj* Easter *(antes de s)*.

pase *sm* - **1.** [gen, DEP & TAUROM] pass - **2.** *Esp* [proyección] showing, screening - **3.** [desfile] parade; **pase de modelos** fashion parade; *ver también* **tauromaquia**.

paseante *smf* person out for a stroll.

pasear ◇ *vi* to go for a walk. ◇ *vt* to take for a walk; [perro] to walk; *fig* to show off, to parade.
◆ **pasearse** *vprnl* [caminar] to go for a walk.

paseíllo *sm* *parade of bullfighters when they come out into the ring before the bullfight starts*; *ver también* **tauromaquia**.

paseo *sm* - **1.** [acción - a pie] walk; [- en coche] drive; [- a caballo] ride; [- en barca] row; **dar un paseo** [a pie] to go for a walk - **2.** [lugar] avenue; **paseo marítimo** promenade - **3.** *loc*: **mandar** *o* **enviar a alguien a paseo** *fam* to send sb packing.

pasillo *sm* corridor; **pasillo aéreo** air corridor; **pasillo deslizante** travelator; **hacer el pasillo** to form a corridor *(for people to walk down)*.

pasión *sf* passion.
➡ **Pasión** *sf* RELIG: **la pasión** the Passion.

pasional *adj* passionate.

pasionaria *sf* passion flower.

pasividad *sf* passivity.

pasivo, va *adj* - **1.** [gen & GRAM] passive - **2.** [haber] (received) from a pension - **3.** [población etc] inactive.
➡ **pasivo** *sm* COM liabilities *pl*.

pasma *sf* Esp fam: **la pasma** the fuzz *pl*, the cops *pl*.

pasmado, da <> *adj* - **1.** [asombrado] astonished, astounded - **2.** [atontado] stunned. <> *sm, f* halfwit.

pasmar *vt* to astound.
➡ **pasmarse** *vprnl* to be astounded.

pasmarote *smf* fam twit.

pasmo *sm* astonishment.

pasmoso, sa *adj* astonishing.

paso *sm* - **1.** [gen] step; [huella] footprint - **2.** [acción] passing; [cruce] crossing; [camino de acceso] way through, thoroughfare; **abrir paso a alguien** *lit & fig* to make way for sb; **ceder el paso (a alguien)** to let sb past; AUTO to give way (to sb); **'ceda el paso'** 'give way'; **'prohibido el paso'** 'no entry'; **paso elevado** flyover; **paso a nivel** level crossing; **paso peatonal** o **de peatones** pedestrian crossing; **paso subterráneo** subway, underpass US; **paso de cebra** zebra crossing - **3.** [forma de andar] walk; [ritmo] pace; **marcar el paso** to keep time - **4.** [GEOGR - en montaña] pass; [- en el mar] strait - **5.** (gen pl) [gestión] step; [progreso] step forward, advance; **dar los pasos necesarios** to take the necessary steps - **6.** loc: **a cada paso** every other minute; **está a dos** o **cuatro pasos** it's just down the road; **¡a este paso...!** fig at this rate...!; **a paso de tortuga** at a snail's pace; **abrirse paso en la vida** to get on in life; **dar un paso en falso** to make a false move o a mistake; **estar de paso** to be passing through; **paso a paso** step by step; **salir del paso** to get out of trouble.
➡ **de paso** *loc adv* in passing.
➡ **paso del ecuador** *sm* halfway stage in a university course.

pasodoble *sm* paso doble.

pasota Esp fam <> *adj* apathetic. <> *smf* dropout.

pasotismo *sm* Esp fam couldn't-care-less attitude.

pasquín *sm* lampoon.

pasta *sf* - **1.** [masa] paste; [de papel] pulp; **pasta dentífrica** toothpaste - **2.** [CULIN - espagueti etc] pasta; [- de pasteles] pastry; [- de pan] dough; **pastas alimenticias** pasta *(U)* - **3.** [pastelillo] pastry - **4.** Esp fam [dinero] dough - **5.** [encuadernación]: **en pasta** hardback - **6.** loc: **ser de buena pasta** fam to be good-natured.

pastar *vi* to graze.

pastel *sm* - **1.** [CULIN - dulce] cake; [- salado] pie - **2.** ARTE pastel - **3.** fam [chapucería] botch-up - **4.** loc: **descubrir el pastel** to let the cat out of the bag; **repartirse el pastel** to share things out.

pastelería *sf* - **1.** [establecimiento] cake shop, patisserie - **2.** [repostería] pastries *pl*.

pastelero, ra <> *adj* pastry *(antes de s)*. <> *sm, f* [cocinero] pastry cook; [vendedor] owner of a patisserie.

pasteurizado, da [pasteuri'θaðo, da] *adj* pasteurized.

pasteurizar [13] [pasteuri'θar] *vt* to pasteurize.

pastiche *sm* pastiche.

pastilla *sf* - **1.** MED pill, tablet - **2.** [de jabón, chocolate] bar - **3.** [de caldo] cube - **4.** AUTO shoe *(of brakes)* - **5.** ELECTRÓN microchip - **6.** Esp loc: **a toda pastilla** at full pelt.

pastizal *sm* pasture.

pasto *sm* - **1.** [sitio] pasture - **2.** [hierba] fodder - **3.** Amér [hierba] lawn, grass - **4.** loc: **a todo pasto** in abundance; **ser pasto de las llamas** to go up in flames.

pastón *sm* fam: **vale un pastón** it costs a bomb.

pastor, ra *sm, f* [de ganado] shepherd (f shepherdess).
➡ **pastor** *sm* - **1.** [sacerdote] minister; **pastor protestante** Protestant minister - **2.** ➣ **perro**.

pastoral *adj* pastoral.

pastorear *vt* to put out to pasture.

pastoreo *sm* shepherding.

pastoso, sa *adj* - **1.** [blando] pasty; [arroz] sticky - **2.** [seco] dry.

pata <> *sf* - **1.** [pierna] leg - **2.** [pie - gen] foot; [- de perro, gato] paw; [- de vaca, caballo] hoof - **3.** fam [de persona] leg; **a cuatro patas** on all fours; **a pata** on foot; **ir a la pata coja** to hop - **4.** [de mueble] leg; [de gafas] arm - **5.** Chile [etapa] stage - **6.** [ave] duck - **7.** loc: **estirar la pata** to kick the bucket; **meter la pata** to put one's foot in it; **poner/estar patas arriba** to turn/be upside down; **tener mala pata** to be unlucky. <> *sm* Perú [amigo] pal, mate UK, buddy US.
➡ **patas** *sfpl* Chile fam [poca vergüenza] cheek *(U)*.
➡ **pata de gallo** *sf* - **1.** [en la cara] crow's feet *pl* - **2.** [tejido] hound's-tooth check material.
➡ **pata negra** *sm* CULIN type of top-quality cured ham.

patada *sf* kick; [en el suelo] stamp; **dar una patada** a to kick; **dar cien patadas a alguien** to drive sb mad; **dar la patada a alguien** to kick sb out; **sentar como una patada en el estómago** to be like a kick in the teeth; **tratar a alguien a patadas** to treat sb like dirt.

patagón, ona *adj* & *sm, f* Patagonian.

Patagonia *sf*: **la Patagonia** Patagonia.

patalear *vi* to kick about; [en el suelo] to stamp one's feet.

pataleo *sm* kicking *(U)*; [en el suelo] stamping *(U)*.

pataleta *sf* tantrum.

patán <> *adj m* uncivilized, uncouth. <> *sm* bumpkin.

patata *sf* potato; **patatas fritas** [de sartén] chips *UK*, french fries *US*; [de bolsa] crisps *UK*, chips *US*; **patata caliente** *fig* hot potato.

patatero, ra <> *adj* potato *(antes de s)*. <> *sm, f* potato farmer.

patatús *sm fam* funny turn.

paté *sm* paté.

patear <> *vt* [dar un puntapié] to kick; [pisotear] to stamp on. <> *vi* - **1.** [patalear] to stamp one's feet - **2.** *fam fig* [andar] to tramp.
➡ **patearse** *vprnl* [recorrer] to tramp.

patena *sf* paten; **limpio** *o* **blanco como una patena** as clean as a new pin.

patentado, da *adj* patent, patented.

patentar *vt* to patent.

patente <> *adj* obvious; [demostración, prueba] clear. <> *sf* - **1.** [de invento] patent - **2.** [autorización] licence - **3.** *C Sur* [matrícula] number plate *UK*, license plate *US*.

pateo *sm* stamping.

patera *sf* small boat.

paternal *adj* fatherly, paternal.

paternalismo *sm* paternalism.

paternalista *adj* paternalistic.

paternidad *sf* fatherhood; DER paternity.

paterno, na *adj* paternal.

patético, ca *adj* pathetic, moving.

patetismo *sm* pathos *(U)*.

patíbulo *sm* scaffold, gallows *pl*.

patidifuso, sa *adj fam* stunned, floored.

patilla *sf* - **1.** [de pelo] sideboard, sideburn - **2.** [de gafas] arm.

patín *sm* - **1.** [calzado - de cuchilla] ice skate; [- de ruedas] roller skate; [- en línea] roller blade - **2.** [patinete] scooter - **3.** [embarcación] pedal boat.

pátina *sf* patina.

patinador, ra *sm, f* skater.

patinaje *sm* skating; **patinaje artístico** figure skating; **patinaje en línea** in-line skating; **patinaje sobre hielo** ice skating; **patinaje sobre ruedas** roller skating.

patinar *vi* - **1.** [sobre hielo] to skate; [sobre ruedas] to roller-skate - **2.** [resbalar - coche] to skid; [- persona] to slip - **3.** *fam* [meter la pata] to put one's foot in it.

patinazo *sm* - **1.** [de coche] skid; [de persona] slip - **2.** *fam* [planchazo] blunder.

patinete *sm* scooter.

patio *sm* [gen] patio, courtyard; [de escuela] playground; [de cuartel] parade ground; **patio (de butacas)** stalls *pl*; **¡cómo está el patio!** *fam* what a fine state of affairs!

patita *sf*: **poner a alguien de patitas en la calle** *fam* to kick sb out.

patitieso, sa *adj fam* - **1.** [de frío] frozen stiff - **2.** [de sorpresa] aghast, amazed; **dejar patitieso** to astound, to amaze; **quedarse patitieso** to be astounded *o* dumbfounded.

patizambo, ba *adj* knock-kneed.

pato, ta *sm, f* duck; **pagar el pato** to carry the can.

patología *sf* pathology.

patológico, ca *adj* pathological.

patoso, sa *adj fam* clumsy.

patraña *sf fam* fib, lie.

patria ➡ **patrio**.

patriarca *sm* patriarch.

patriarcado *sm* patriarchy.

patriarcal *adj* patriarchal.

patricio, cia *adj* & *sm, f* patrician.

patrimonio *sm* - **1.** [bienes - heredados] inheritance; [- propios] wealth; **patrimonio nacional** [- artístico] national heritage; [- económico] national wealth - **2.** *fig* [de una colectividad] exclusive birthright.

patrio, tria *adj* native.
➡ **patria** *sf* native country, fatherland; **patria chica** home town; **hacer patria** to fly the flag.
➡ **patria potestad** *sf* DER parental authority.

patriota <> *adj* patriotic. <> *smf* patriot.

patriotero, ra *adj despec* jingoistic.

patriótico, ca *adj* patriotic.

patriotismo *sm* patriotism.

patrocinador, ra <> *adj* sponsoring. <> *sm, f* sponsor.

patrocinar *vt* to sponsor.

patrocinio *sm* sponsorship.

patrón, ona *sm, f* - **1.** [de obreros] boss; [de criados] master (*f* mistress) - **2.** [de pensión etc] landlord (*f* landlady) - **3.** [santo] patron saint.

patrón *sm* - **1.** [de barco] skipper - **2.** [medida] standard; **patrón oro** ECON gold standard - **3.** [en costura] pattern; **estar cortados por el mismo patrón** to be cast in the same mould.

patronal ⬦ *adj* - **1.** [empresarial] management *(antes de s)* - **2.** RELIG patron saint *(antes de s)*. ⬦ *sf* - **1.** [de empresa] management - **2.** [de país] employers' organization.

patronato *sm* [gen] board; [con fines benéficos] trust.

patronímico, ca *adj* patronymic.

patrono, na *sm, f* - **1.** [de empresa - encargado] boss; [- empresario] employer - **2.** [santo] patron saint.

patrulla ⬦ *adj* ▷ **coche.** ⬦ *sf* patrol; **estar de patrulla** to be on patrol; **patrulla urbana** vigilante group.

patrullar *vt & vi* to patrol.

patrullero, ra *adj* patrol *(antes de s)*.

patrullero *sm* - **1.** [barco] patrol boat; [avión] patrol plane - **2.** *C Sur* [vehículo] police (patrol) car, cruiser *US*.

paulatino, na *adj* gradual.

pausa *sf* pause, break; MÚS rest; **con pausa** unhurriedly; **hacer una pausa** to pause; **pausa publicitaria** commercial break.

pausado, da *adj* deliberate, slow.

pauta *sf* - **1.** [gen] standard, model; **marcar la pauta** to set the standard; **seguir una pauta** to follow an example - **2.** [en un papel] guideline.

pautado, da *adj* lined, ruled.

pava ▷ **pavo.**

pavero, ra ⬦ *adj* boastful. ⬦ *sm, f* braggart.

pavimentación *sf* [de carretera] road surfacing; [de acera] paving; [de suelo] flooring.

pavimentar *vt* [carretera] to surface; [acera] to pave; [suelo] to floor.

pavimento *sm* [de carretera] road surface; [de acera] paving; [de suelo] flooring.

pavo, va ⬦ *adj fam despec* wet, drippy. ⬦ *sm, f* - **1.** [ave] turkey; **pavo real** peacock (*f* peahen); **se le subió el pavo** she turned as red as a beetroot - **2.** *fam despec* [persona] drip.

pavonearse *vprnl despec*: **pavonearse (de)** to boast o brag (about).

pavoneo *sm despec* showing off, boasting.

pavor *sm* terror.

pavoroso, sa *adj* terrifying.

paya *sf Amér improvised poem accompanied by guitar.*

payasada *sf* clowning *(U)*; **hacer payasadas** to clown around.

payaso, sa ⬦ *adj* clownish. ⬦ *sm, f* clown.

payés, esa *sm, f peasant farmer from Catalonia or the Balearic Islands.*

payo, ya *sm, f* non-gipsy.

paz *sf* peace; [tranquilidad] peacefulness; **dejar a alguien en paz** to leave sb alone o in peace; **estar** o **quedar en paz** to be quits; **firmar la paz** to sign a peace treaty; **hacer las paces** to make (it) up; **poner paz entre** to reconcile, to make peace between; **que en paz descanse, que descanse en paz** may he/she rest in peace.

pazca *etc* ▷ **pacer.**

pazguato, ta *fam despec* ⬦ *adj* simple. ⬦ *sm, f* simpleton.

pazo *sm Galician country mansion.*

PC *sm* - **1.** (*abrev de* **personal computer**) PC - **2.** (*abrev de* **Partido Comunista**) Communist Party.

PD (*abrev de* **posdata**) PS.

pdo. *abrev de* **pasado.**

pe *sf*: **de pe a pa** *fam* from beginning to end.

peaje *sm* toll.

peana *sf* pedestal.

peatón *sm* pedestrian.

peatonal *adj* pedestrian *(antes de s)*.

peca *sf* freckle.

pecado *sm* sin; **estar en pecado** to be in sin; **morir en pecado** to die unrepentant; **pecado mortal** mortal sin; **pecado original** original sin; **pecados capitales** mortal sins; **ser un pecado** to be a sin o crime; **sería un pecado tirar este vestido** it would be a crime to throw out this dress.

pecador, ra ⬦ *adj* sinful. ⬦ *sm, f* sinner.

pecaminoso, sa *adj* sinful.

pecar [10] *vi* - **1.** RELIG to sin - **2.** [pasarse]: **pecar de confiado/generoso** to be overconfident/too generous.

pecera *sf* fish tank; [redonda] fish bowl.

pechera *sf* [de camisa] shirt front; [de blusa, vestido] bust.

pecho *sm* - **1.** [tórax] chest; [de mujer] bosom; **sacar pecho** to stick one's chest out - **2.** [mama] breast; **dar el pecho a** to breastfeed - **3.** *Amér* [en natación] breaststroke; **nadar pecho** to swim the breaststroke - **4.** *loc*: **abrir el pecho a alguien** to open one's heart to sb; **a lo hecho, pecho** it's no use crying over spilt milk; **a pecho descubierto** without protection o any form of defence; **partirse el pecho** to bust a gut, to knock o.s. out; **tomarse algo a pecho** to take sthg to heart.

pechuga *sf* - **1.** [de ave] breast *(meat)* - **2.** *mfam* [de mujer] tits *pl*.

pechugón, ona *adj mfam* big-chested (*f* buxom).

pécora *sf*: **ser una mala pécora** to be a bitch o cow.

pecoso, **sa** *adj* freckly.

pectoral ◇ *adj* - **1.** ANAT pectoral, chest *(antes de s)* - **2.** [en farmacia] cough *(antes de s)*. ◇ *sm* [medicamento] cough mixture o medicine.

pecuario, **ria** *adj* livestock *(antes de s)*.

peculiar *adj* - **1.** [característico] typical, characteristic - **2.** [curioso] peculiar.

peculiaridad *sf* - **1.** [cualidad] uniqueness - **2.** [detalle] particular feature o characteristic.

pecuniario, **ria** *adj* pecuniary.

pedagogía *sf* education, pedagogy.

pedagógico, **ca** *adj* educational.

pedagogo, **ga** *sm*, *f* educator; [profesor] teacher.

pedal *sm* pedal; **pedal de embrague** clutch (pedal); **pedal de freno** brake pedal.

pedalear *vi* to pedal.

pedante ◇ *adj* pompous. ◇ *smf* pompous person.

pedantería *sf* pomposity *(U)*.

pedazo *sm* piece, bit; **a pedazos** in pieces o bits; **caerse a pedazos** to fall to pieces; **hacer pedazos** [gen] to break to bits; *fig* to destroy; **saltar en (mil) pedazos** to be smashed to pieces; **pedazo de alcornoque** o **de animal** o **de bruto** stupid oaf o brute; **ser un pedazo de pan** to be an angel.

pederasta *sm* pederast.

pedestal *sm* pedestal, stand; **poner/tener a alguien en un pedestal** to put sb on a pedestal.

pedestre *adj* on foot.

pediatra *smf* paediatrician.

pediatría *sf* paediatrics *(U)*.

pedicuro, **ra** *sm*, *f* chiropodist UK, podiatrist US.

pedido *sm* COM order; **hacer un pedido** to place an order.

pedigrí, **pedigree** [peðiɣri] *sm* pedigree.

pedigüeño, **ña** ◇ *adj* demanding, clamouring. ◇ *sm*, *f* demanding person.

pedir [26] ◇ *vt* - **1.** [gen] to ask for; [en comercios, restaurantes] to order; **pedir a alguien que haga algo** to ask sb to do sthg; **pedir a alguien (en matrimonio)** to ask for sb's hand (in marriage); **pedir prestado algo a alguien** to borrow sthg from sb - **2.** [exigir] to demand - **3.** [requerir] to call for, to need - **4.** [poner precio]: **pedir (por)** to ask (for); **pide un millón por la moto** he's asking a million for the motorbike. ◇ *vi* [mendigar] to beg.

pedo ◇ *sm* - **1.** *fam* [ventosidad] fart; **tirarse un pedo** to fart - **2.** *mfam* [borrachera]: **cogerse un pedo** to get pissed. ◇ *adj* *mfam*: **estar pedo** to be pissed.

pedofilia *sf* paedophilia.

pedorrear *vi* *vulg* to fart a lot.

pedorreta *sf* *fam* raspberry *(sound)*.

pedrada *sf* - **1.** [acción] throw of a stone - **2.** [golpe] blow o hit with a stone; **a pedradas** by stoning; **matar a alguien a pedradas** to stone sb to death.

pedrea *sf* [en lotería] *group of smaller prizes in the Spanish national lottery*.

pedregal *sm* stony ground.

pedregullo *sm* R Dom gravel.

pedrera *sf* stone quarry.

pedrería *sf* precious stones *pl*.

pedrisco *sm* hail.

pedrusco *sm* rough stone.

pega *sf* - **1.** [pegamento] glue - **2.** [obstáculo] difficulty, hitch; **poner pegas (a)** to find problems (with).
◆ **de pega** *loc adj* false, fake.

pegadizo, **za** *adj* - **1.** [música] catchy - **2.** [contagioso] catching.

pegajoso, **sa** *adj* sticky; *despec* clinging.

pegamento *sm* glue.

pegar [16] ◇ *vt* - **1.** [adherir] to stick; [con pegamento] to glue; [póster, cartel] to fix, to put up; [botón] to sew on - **2.** [arrimar]: **pegar algo a** to put o place sthg against; **pega la silla a la pared** put the chair against the wall - **3.** [golpear] to hit - **4.** [propinar - bofetada, paliza etc] to give; [- golpe] to deal - **5.** [contagiar]: **pegar algo a alguien** to give sb sthg, to pass sthg on to sb - **6.** INFORM to paste. ◇ *vi* - **1.** [adherir] to stick - **2.** [golpear] to hit - **3.** [armonizar] to go together, to match; **pegar con** to go with - **4.** [sol] to beat down.
◆ **pegarse** *vprnl* - **1.** [adherirse] to stick - **2.** [agredirse] to fight, to hit one another - **3.** [golpearse]: **pegarse (un golpe) con algo** to hit o.s. against sthg - **4.** [contagiarse - enfermedad] to be transmitted, to be passed on; [- canción] to be catchy; **se me pegó su acento** I picked up his accent - **5.** *despec* [engancharse]: **pegarse a alguien** to stick to sb - **6.** *loc*: **pegársela a alguien** *fam* to have sb on, to deceive sb; [cónyuge] to cheat on sb.

pegatina *sf* sticker.

pego *sm*: **dar el pego** *fam* to look like the real thing.

pegote *sm* *fam* - **1.** [masa pegajosa] sticky mess - **2.** [chapucería] botch.

pegue *etc* ➞ **pegar**.

peinado *sm* hairdo; [estilo, tipo] hairstyle.

peinar *vt* *lit & fig* to comb.
◆ **peinarse** *vprnl* to comb one's hair.

peine *sm* comb; **pasarse el peine** to comb one's hair; **enterarse de** o **saber lo que vale un peine** *fam* to find out what's what o a thing or two.

peineta *sf* comb worn in the back of the hair.

p.ej. (*abrev de* **por ejemplo**) e.g.

pejiguera *sf fam* drag, pain.

Pekín *n pr* Peking, Beijing.

pela *sf fam* peseta; **no tengo pelas** I'm skint.

peladilla *sf* sugared almond.

pelado, da ◇ *adj* - **1.** [cabeza] shorn - **2.** [piel, cara etc] peeling; [fruta] peeled - **3.** [habitación, monte, árbol] bare - **4.** [número] exact, round; **saqué un aprobado pelado** I passed, but only just - **5.** *fam* [sin dinero] broke, skint. ◇ *sm, f Andes fam* [niño] kid.
➤ **pelado** *sm Esp* haircut.

pelagatos *smf inv fam despec* nobody.

pelaje *sm* [de gato, oso, conejo] fur; [de perro, caballo] coat.

pelambre *sm* mane o mop of hair.

pelambrera *sf* long thick hair (U).

pelandusca *sf fam despec* tart, slut.

pelar *vt* - **1.** [persona] to cut the hair of - **2.** [fruta, patatas] to peel; [guisantes, marisco] to shell - **3.** [aves] to pluck; [conejos etc] to skin - **4.** *fam fig* [dejar sin dinero] to fleece.
➤ **pelarse** *vprnl* - **1.** [cortarse el pelo] to have one's hair cut - **2.** [piel, espalda etc] to peel.

peldaño *sm* step; [de escalera de mano] rung.

pelea *sf* - **1.** [a golpes] fight - **2.** [riña] row, quarrel.

pelear *vi* - **1.** [a golpes] to fight - **2.** [a gritos] to have a row o quarrel - **3.** [esforzarse] to struggle.
➤ **pelearse** *vprnl* - **1.** [a golpes] to fight - **2.** [a gritos] to have a row o quarrel.

pelele *sm* - **1.** *fam despec* [persona] puppet - **2.** [muñeco] guy, straw doll - **3.** [prenda de bebé] rompers *pl*.

peleón, ona *adj* - **1.** [persona] aggressive - **2.** [vino] rough.

peletería *sf* - **1.** [tienda] fur shop, furrier's - **2.** [oficio] furriery - **3.** [pieles] furs *pl*.

peletero, ra *sm, f* furrier.

peliagudo, da *adj* tricky.

pelicano, pelícano *sm* pelican.

película *sf* - **1.** [gen] film; **echar** o **poner una película** to show a film; **película muda/de terror** silent/horror film; **película del Oeste** western; **de película** amazing; **película virgen** FOTO blank film - **2.** *fam* [historia increíble] (tall) story.

peliculero, ra *sm, f fam*: **es muy peliculero** he's always telling tall stories.

peligrar *vi* to be in danger.

peligro *sm* danger; **correr peligro (de)** to be in danger (of); **estar/poner en peligro** to be/put at risk; **en peligro de extinción** [especie, animal] endangered; **fuera de peligro** out of danger; **peligro de incendio** fire hazard; **¡peligro de muerte!** danger!

peligrosidad *sf* danger.

peligroso, sa *adj* dangerous.

pelín *sm fam* mite, tiny bit.

pelirrojo, ja ◇ *adj* ginger, red-headed. ◇ *sm, f* redhead.

pellejo *sm* - **1.** [piel, vida] skin - **2.** [padrastro] hangnail - **3.** *loc*: **arriesgar** o **jugarse el pellejo** to risk one's neck; **estar/ponerse en el pellejo de otro** to be/put o.s. in someone else's shoes; **salvar el pellejo** to save one's skin.

pelliza *sf* fur jacket.

pellizcar [10] *vt* - **1.** [gen] to pinch - **2.** [pan] to pick at.

pellizco *sm* pinch; **dar un pellizco a alguien** to give sb a pinch.

pelma, pelmazo, za *fam despec* ◇ *adj* annoying, tiresome. ◇ *sm, f* bore, pain.

pelo *sm* - **1.** [gen] hair - **2.** [de oso, conejo, gato] fur; [de perro, caballo] coat - **3.** [de melocotón] down - **4.** [de una tela] nap - **5.** *loc*: **con pelos y señales** with all the details; **de medio pelo** second-rate; **montar a caballo a pelo** to ride bareback; **presentarse a un examen a pelo** to enter an exam unprepared; **no tener un pelo de tonto** *fam* to be nobody's fool; **no tener pelos en la lengua** *fam* not to mince one's words; **no verle el pelo a alguien** *fam* not to see hide nor hair of sb; **poner a alguien los pelos de punta** *fam* to make sb's hair stand on end; **por los pelos, por un pelo** by the skin of one's teeth, only just; **ser un hombre de pelo en pecho** to be a real man; **soltarse el pelo** to let one's hair down; **tomar el pelo a alguien** *fam* to pull sb's leg; **venir al pelo a alguien** *fam* to be just right for sb.
➤ **a contra pelo** *loc adv lit & fig* against the grain.

pelota ◇ *sf* - **1.** [gen & DEP] ball; **jugar a la pelota** to play ball; **pelota base** baseball; **pelota vasca** pelota; **devolver la pelota a alguien** to put the ball back into sb's court; **hacer la pelota (a alguien)** *fam* to suck up (to sb); **pasarse la pelota** to pass the buck - **2.** *fam* [cabeza] nut. ◇ *smf* [persona] crawler, creep.
➤ **pelotas** *sfpl vulg* balls; **en pelotas** *mfam* starkers, in the nude.

pelotazo *sm* kick o throw of a ball.

pelotear *vi* to have a kickabout; [en tenis] to knock up.

pelotera *sf fam* scrap, fight.

pelotón *sm* [de soldados] squad; [de gente] crowd; DEP pack; **pelotón de ejecución** firing squad.

pelotudo, da *R Dom fam* ⇔ *adj* stupid. ⇔ *sm, f* jerk.

peluca *sf* wig.

peluche *sm* plush.

peludo, da *adj* hairy.

peluquería *sf* - **1.** [establecimiento] hairdresser's (shop) - **2.** [oficio] hairdressing.

peluquero, ra *sm, f* hairdresser.

peluquín *sm* toupee; **¡ni hablar del peluquín!** *fam* it's out of the question!

pelusa *sf* - **1.** [de tela] fluff - **2.** [vello] down.

pelvis *sf inv* pelvis.

Pemex *smpl* (*abrev de* **Petróleos Mexicanos**) Mexican Oil.

Pemex

▨▨▨ Mexico is one of the world's largest oil producing countries, with estimated oil reserves of 26.9 billion barrels, and oil exports represent about one third of the national income. Petróleos Mexicanos (**Pemex**), the world's sixth largest oil company, was set up following the nationalization of foreign-owned oil companies by President Lázaro Cárdenas in 1938. It has a monopoly, protected by the constitution, and controls virtually all aspects of oil and gas exploitation in Mexico, though some private investment is permitted in petrochemicals. The need for major investment to modernize the industry may, however, lead to a relaxation of these restrictions, though such reforms are likely to prove highly controversial.

pena *sf* - **1.** [lástima] shame, pity; **¡qué pena!** what a shame *o* pity!; **dar pena** to inspire pity; **el pobre me da pena** I feel sorry for the poor chap - **2.** [tristeza] sadness, sorrow - **3.** *(gen pl)* [desgracia] problem, trouble - **4.** *(gen pl)* [dificultad] struggle *(U)*; **a duras penas** with great difficulty - **5.** [castigo] punishment; **so** *o* **bajo pena de** under penalty of; **pena capital** *o* **de muerte** death penalty - **6.** *Amér* [vergüenza] shame, embarrassment; **me da pena** I'm ashamed of it - **7.** *loc:* **(no) valer** *o* **merecer la pena** (not) to be worthwhile *o* worth it; **una película que merece la pena** a film that is worth seeing; **sin pena ni gloria** without distinction.

penacho *sm* - **1.** [de pájaro] crest - **2.** [adorno] plume.

penal ⇔ *adj* criminal. ⇔ *sm* prison.

penalidad *(gen pl)* *sf* suffering *(U)*, hardship.

penalista *smf* [abogado] criminal lawyer.

penalización *sf* - **1.** [acción] penalization - **2.** [sanción] penalty.

penalizar [13] *vt* [gen & DEP] to penalize.

penalti, penalty *sm* DEP penalty; **señalar penalti** to award a penalty; **casarse de penalti** *fam* to have a shotgun wedding.

penar ⇔ *vt* [castigar] to punish. ⇔ *vi* [sufrir] to suffer.

pendejo *sm fam* - **1.** [cobarde] coward - **2.** [tonto] prat, idiot.

➡ **pendejo, ja** *sm, f R Dom fam* [adolescente] kid.

pendenciero, ra ⇔ *adj* who always gets into a fight. ⇔ *sm, f* person who is always getting into fights.

pender *vi* - **1.** [colgar]: **pender (de)** to hang (from) - **2.** [amenaza etc]: **pender sobre** to hang over - **3.** [sentencia etc] to be pending.

pendiente ⇔ *adj* - **1.** [por resolver] pending; [deuda] outstanding; **estar pendiente de** [atento a] to keep an eye on; [a la espera de] to be waiting for - **2.** [asignatura] failed. ⇔ *sm* earring. ⇔ *sf* slope.

pendón, ona *sm, f fam* libertine.

pendonear *vi fam* to hang out.

péndulo *sm* pendulum.

pene *sm* penis.

penene *smf untenured teacher or lecturer.*

penetración *sf* - **1.** [gen] penetration; **penetración de mercado** ECON market penetration - **2.** [sagacidad] astuteness, sharpness.

penetrante *adj* - **1.** [intenso - dolor] acute; [- olor] sharp; [- frío] biting; [- mirada] penetrating; [- voz, sonido etc] piercing - **2.** [sagaz] sharp, penetrating.

penetrar ⇔ *vi:* **penetrar en** [internarse en] to enter; [filtrarse por] to get into, to penetrate; [perforar] to pierce; [llegar a conocer] to get to the bottom of. ⇔ *vt* - **1.** [introducirse en - arma, sonido etc] to pierce, to penetrate; [- humedad, líquido] to permeate; [- emoción, sentimiento] to pierce - **2.** [llegar a conocer - secreto etc] to get to the bottom of - **3.** [sexualmente] to penetrate.

peneuvista ⇔ *adj of/relating to the Basque nationalist party PNV.* ⇔ *smf member/supporter of the Basque nationalist party PNV.*

penicilina *sf* penicillin.

península *sf* peninsula.

peninsular ⇔ *adj* peninsular. ⇔ *smf* peninsular Spaniard.

penique *sm* penny; **peniques** pence.

penitencia *sf* penance; **hacer penitencia** to do penance.

penitenciaría *sf* penitentiary.

penitenciario, ria *adj* prison *(antes de s).*

penitente *smf* penitent.

penoso, sa *adj* - **1.** [trabajoso] laborious - **2.** [lamentable] distressing; [aspecto, espectáculo] sorry - **3.** *Amér C, Caribe, Col & Méx* [vergonzoso] shy.

pensado, da *adj*: **mal pensado** twisted, evil-minded; **en el día/momento menos pensado** when you least expect it; **un mal pensado** a twisted person.

➤ **bien pensado** *loc adv* on reflection.

pensador, ra *sm, f* thinker.

pensamiento *sm* - **1.** [gen] thought; [mente] mind; [idea] idea; **leer el pensamiento a alguien** to read sb's mind o thoughts - **2.** BOT pansy.

pensar [19] <> *vi* to think; **pensar bien/mal de alguien** to think well/ill of sb; **pensar en algo/en alguien/en hacer algo** to think about sthg/about sb/about doing sthg; **piensa en un número/buen regalo** think of a number/good present; **dar que pensar a alguien** to give sb food for thought. <> *vt* - **1.** [reflexionar] to think about o over - **2.** [opinar, creer] to think; **pensar algo de alguien/algo** to think sthg of sb/sthg; **pienso que no vendrá** I don't think she'll come - **3.** [idear] to think up - **4.** [tener la intención de]: **pensar hacer algo** to intend to do sthg.

➤ **pensarse** *vprnl*: **pensarse algo** to think about sthg, to think sthg over.

pensativo, va *adj* pensive, thoughtful.

pensión *sf* - **1.** [dinero] pension; **pensión alimenticia** o **alimentaria** maintenance; **pensión de jubilación/de viudedad** retirement/ widow's pension - **2.** [de huéspedes] ≃ guest house; **media pensión** [en hotel] half board; **estar a media pensión** [en colegio] to have school dinners; **pensión completa** full board.

pensionado *sm* boarding school.

pensionista *smf* - **1.** [jubilado] pensioner - **2.** [en una pensión] guest, lodger - **3.** [en un colegio] boarder.

pentaedro *sm* pentahedron.

pentágono *sm* pentagon.

pentagrama *sm* MÚS stave.

Pentecostés *sm (no se usa el pl)* - **1.** [católico] Whitsun, Whitsuntide - **2.** [judío] Pentecost.

penúltimo, ma *adj & sm, f* penultimate, last but one.

penumbra *sf* semi-darkness, half-light; **en penumbra** in semi-darkness.

penuria *sf* - **1.** [pobreza] penury, poverty - **2.** [escasez] paucity, dearth.

peña *sf* [grupo de amigos] circle, group; [club] club; [quinielística] pool.

peñasco *sm* large crag o rock.

peñón *sm* rock.

➤ **Peñón** *sm*: **el Peñón (de Gibraltar)** the Rock (of Gibraltar).

peón *sm* - **1.** [obrero] unskilled labourer; **peón caminero** navvy - **2.** [en ajedrez] pawn.

peonza *sf* (spinning) top.

peor <> *adj* - **1.** *(compar)*: **peor (que)** worse (than); **peor para él** that's his problem - **2.** *(superl)*: **el/la peor...** the worst... <> *pron*: **el/la peor (de)** the worst (in); **el peor de todos** the worst of all; **lo peor fue que...** the worst thing was that... <> *adv* - **1.** *(compar)*: **peor (que)** worse (than); **ahora veo peor** I see worse now; **estar peor** [enfermo] to get worse; **estoy peor** [de salud] I feel worse; **peor que peor** so much the worse - **2.** *(superl)* worst; **el que lo hizo peor** the one who did it (the) worst.

pepinillo *sm* gherkin.

pepino *sm* BOT cucumber; **me importa un pepino** I couldn't care less.

pepita *sf* - **1.** [de fruta] pip - **2.** [de oro] nugget.

pepito *sm* grilled meat sandwich.

pepona *sf* large cardboard doll.

peppermint = **pipermín**.

peque *etc* ⊏➤ **pecar**.

pequeñez *sf* - **1.** [gen] smallness - **2.** *fig* [insignificancia] trifle; **discutir por pequeñeces** to argue over silly little things.

pequeño, ña <> *adj* small; **me queda pequeño** it's too small for me; [hermano] little; [posibilidad] slight; [ingresos, cifras etc] low. <> *sm, f* [niño] little one; **de pequeño** as a child; **el pequeño, la pequeña** [benjamín] the youngest, the baby.

pequeñoburgués, esa <> *adj* petit bourgeois. <> *sm, f* petit bourgeois (*f* petite bourgeoise).

pequinés <> *adj & smf* Pekinese. <> *sm* [perro] Pekinese.

pera *sf* - **1.** [fruta] pear - **2.** [para ducha etc] (rubber) bulb - **3.** *C Sur* [barbilla] chin - **4.** *loc*: **partir peras** to fall out; **pedir peras al olmo** to ask (for) the impossible; **ser la pera** *fam* to be the limit; **ser una pera en dulce** *fam* to be a gem.

peral *sm* pear tree.

percal *sm* percale; **conocer el percal** to know what one is doing.

percance *sm* mishap.

percatarse *vprnl*: **percatarse (de algo)** to notice (sthg).

percebe *sm* [pez] barnacle.

percepción *sf* [de los sentidos] perception; **percepción extrasensorial** extrasensory perception.

perceptible *adj* [por los sentidos] noticeable, perceptible.

percha *sf* - **1.** [de armario] (coat) hanger - **2.** [de pared] coat rack - **3.** [para pájaros] perch.

perchero *sm* [de pared] coat rack; [de pie] coat stand.

percibir *vt* - **1.** [con los sentidos] to perceive, to notice; [por los oídos] to hear; [ver] to see - **2.** [cobrar] to receive, to get.

percusión *sf* percussion.

percusionista *smf* percussionist.

percutor, percusor *sm* hammer, firing pin.

perdedor, ra ◇ *adj* losing. ◇ *sm, f* loser.

perder [20] ◇ *vt* - **1.** [gen] to lose; **llevas las de perder** you can't hope to win; **salir perdiendo** to come off worst - **2.** [desperdiciar] to waste - **3.** [tren, oportunidad] to miss - **4.** [perjudicar] to be the ruin of. ◇ *vi* - **1.** [salir derrotado] to lose - **2.** [empeorar] to go downhill - **3.** [dejar escapar aire] to deflate, to go down - **4.** *loc*: **echar algo a perder** to spoil sthg; **echarse a perder** [alimento] to go off, to spoil.

→ **perderse** *vprnl* - **1.** [gen] to get lost; **¡piérdete!** *mfam* get lost! - **2.** [desaparecer] to disappear - **3.** [desperdiciarse] to be wasted - **4.** [desaprovechar]: **perderse algo** to miss out on sthg; **¡no te lo pierdas!** don't miss it! - **5.** *fig* [por los vicios] to be beyond salvation - **6.** *fig* [anhelar]: **perderse por** to be mad about.

perdición *sf* ruin, undoing.

pérdida *sf* - **1.** [gen] loss; **no tiene pérdida** you can't miss it - **2.** [de tiempo, dinero] waste - **3.** [escape] leak.

→ **pérdidas** *sfpl* - **1.** FIN & MIL losses; **pérdidas humanas** loss of life - **2.** [daños] damage *(U)* - **3.** [de sangre] haemorrhage *sing*.

perdidamente *adv* hopelessly.

perdido, da ◇ *adj* - **1.** [extraviado] lost; [animal, bala] stray - **2.** [sucio] filthy - **3.** [tiempo] wasted; [ocasión] missed - **4.** *fam* [de remate] complete, utter - **5.** *loc*: **dar algo por perdido** to give sthg up for lost; **estar perdido** to be done for *o* lost. ◇ *sm, f* reprobate.

perdigón *sm* pellet.

perdigonada *sf* - **1.** [tiro] shot - **2.** [herida] gunshot wound.

perdiguero *sm* English setter.

perdiz *sf* partridge; **fueron felices y comieron perdices** they all lived happily ever after.

perdón *sm* pardon, forgiveness; **con perdón** if you'll forgive the expression; **no tener perdón** to be unforgivable; **pedir perdón** to apologize; **¡perdón!** sorry!; **perdón, ¿me deja pasar?** excuse me, could you let me through?

perdonar ◇ *vt* - **1.** [gen] to forgive; **perdonarle algo a alguien** to forgive sb for sthg; **perdone que le moleste** sorry to bother you - **2.** [eximir de - deuda, condena]: **perdonar algo a alguien** to let sb off sthg; **perdonarle la vida a alguien** to spare sb their life - **3.** [desperdiciar]: **no perdonar algo** not to miss sthg. ◇ *vi*: **perdone, ¿cómo ha dicho?** excuse me, what did you say?

perdonavidas *smf inv fam* bully.

perdurar *vi* - **1.** [durar mucho] to endure, to last - **2.** [persistir] to persist.

perecedero, ra *adj* - **1.** [productos] perishable - **2.** [naturaleza] transitory.

perecer [30] *vi* to perish, to die.

peregrina ⇨ **peregrino**.

peregrinación *sf* RELIG pilgrimage.

peregrinaje *sm* RELIG pilgrimage.

peregrinar *vi* RELIG to make a pilgrimage.

peregrino, na ◇ *adj* - **1.** [ave] migratory - **2.** *fig* [extraño] strange. ◇ *sm, f* [persona] pilgrim.

perejil *sm* parsley.

perenne *adj* BOT perennial.

perentorio, ria *adj* urgent, pressing; [gesto, tono] peremptory; **plazo perentorio** fixed time limit.

pereza *sf* idleness; **me da pereza ir a pie** I can't be bothered walking; **sacudirse la pereza** to wake o.s. up.

perezca *etc* ⇨ **perecer**.

perezoso, sa ◇ *adj* [vago] lazy. ◇ *sm, f* [vago] lazy person, idler.

perfección *sf* perfection; **es de una gran perfección** it's exceptionally good; **a la perfección** perfectly, to perfection.

perfeccionamiento *sm* - **1.** [acabado] perfecting - **2.** [mejoramiento] improvement.

perfeccionar *vt* - **1.** [redondear] to perfect - **2.** [mejorar] to improve.

perfeccionismo *sm* perfectionism.

perfeccionista *adj* & *smf* perfectionist.

perfectamente *adv* - **1.** [sobradamente] perfectly - **2.** [muy bien] fine; **¿cómo estas? - estoy perfectamente** how are you? - I'm fine - **3.** [de acuerdo]: **¡perfectamente!** fine!, great!

perfecto, ta *adj* perfect.

perfidia *sf* perfidy, treachery.

pérfido, da ◇ *adj* perfidious, treacherous. ◇ *sm, f* treacherous person.

perfil *sm* - **1.** [contorno] outline, shape - **2.** [de cara, cuerpo] profile; **de perfil** in profile - **3.** *fig* [característica] characteristic - **4.** *fig* [retrato moral] profile - **5.** GEOM cross section.

perfilar *vt* to outline.

➡ **perfilarse** *vprnl* - **1.** [destacarse] to be outlined - **2.** [concretarse] to shape up.

perforación *sf* - **1.** [gen & MED] perforation - **2.** [taladro] bore-hole.

perforador, ra *adj* drilling.

➡ **perforadora** *sf* - **1.** [herramienta] drill - **2.** INFORM card punch.

perforar *vt* [horadar] to perforate; [agujero] to drill; INFORM to punch.

perfumar *vt* to perfume.

➡ **perfumarse** *vprnl* to put perfume on.

perfume *sm* perfume.

perfumería *sf* - **1.** [tienda, arte] perfumery - **2.** [productos] perfumes *pl*.

pergamino *sm* parchment.

pérgola *sf* pergola.

pericia *sf* skill.

pericial *adj* expert.

perico *sm* - **1.** *fam* [pájaro] parakeet - **2.** *mfam* [cocaína] snow - **3.** *Col* [café con leche] white coffee; *loc:* **Perico (el) de los palotes** anybody.

periferia *sf* periphery; [alrededores] outskirts *pl*.

periférico, ca *adj* peripheral; [barrio] outlying.

➡ **periférico** *sm* - **1.** INFORM peripheral - **2.** *Amér C & Méx* [carretera] ring road *UK*, beltway *US*.

perifollos *smpl* *fam* frills (and fripperies).

perífrasis *sf inv:* **perífrasis (verbal)** compound verb.

perifrástico, ca *adj* long-winded.

perilla *sf* goatee; **venir de perilla(s)** to be just the right thing.

perímetro *sm* perimeter.

periodicidad *sf* frequency; TECNOL periodicity.

periódico, ca *adj* [gen] periodic.

➡ **periódico** *sm* newspaper; **periódico dominical** Sunday paper.

periodismo *sm* journalism.

periodista *smf* journalist.

periodístico, ca *adj* journalistic.

periodo, período *sm* period; DEP half; **periodo de prácticas** trial period.

peripatético, ca ◇ *adj* - **1.** FILOS Peripatetic - **2.** *fam* [ridículo] ludicrous. ◇ *sm, f* Peripatetic.

peripecia *sf* incident, adventure.

periplo *sm* journey, voyage.

peripuesto, ta *adj* *fam* dolled-up, tarted-up.

periquete *sm:* **en un periquete** *fam* in a jiffy.

periquito *sm* parakeet.

periscopio *sm* periscope.

perista *smf* *fam* fence, receiver of stolen goods.

peritaje *sm* - **1.** [trabajo] expert work; [informe] expert's report - **2.** [estudios] professional training; **peritaje industrial** industrial studies; **peritaje mercantil** business studies.

peritar *vt* [casa] to value; [coche] to assess the value of, to assess the damage to.

perito *sm* - **1.** [experto] expert; **perito agrónomo** agronomist - **2.** [ingeniero técnico] technician.

perjudicar [10] *vt* to damage, to harm.

perjudicial *adj:* **perjudicial (para)** harmful (to).

perjuicio *sm* harm *(U)*, damage *(U)*; **causar perjuicio a algo/alguien** to do damage to sthg/sb; **ir en perjuicio de** to be detrimental to; **sin perjuicio de** despite.

perjurar *vi* - **1.** [jurar mucho] to swear blind - **2.** [jurar en falso] to commit perjury.

perjurio *sm* perjury.

perjuro, ra ◇ *adj* perjured. ◇ *sm, f* perjuror.

perla *sf* pearl; **perla de cultivo** cultured pearl; *fig* [maravilla] gem, treasure; **de perlas** great, fine; **me viene de perlas** it's just the right thing.

perlado, da *adj* - **1.** [con perlas] pearly; [collar] pearl *(antes de s)* - **2.** [con gotas] beaded.

perlé *sm* beading.

permanecer [30] *vi* - **1.** [en un lugar] to stay - **2.** [en un estado] to remain, to stay.

permanencia *sf* - **1.** [en un lugar] staying, continued stay - **2.** [en un estado] continuation.

permanente ◇ *adj* permanent; [comisión] standing. ◇ *sf* perm; **hacerse la permanente** to have a perm.

permeabilidad *sf* permeability.

permeable *adj* permeable.

permisible *adj* permissible, acceptable.

permisividad *sf* permissiveness.

permisivo, va *adj* permissive.

permiso *sm* - **1.** [autorización] permission; **con permiso** if I may, if you'll excuse me; **dar permiso para hacer algo** to give permission to do sthg; **pedir permiso para hacer algo** to ask permission to do sthg - **2.** [documento] licence, permit; **permiso de armas** gun licence; **permiso de conducir** driving licence *UK*, driver's license *US*; **permiso de residencia** residence

permit; **permiso de trabajo** work permit
- 3. [vacaciones] leave; **estar de permiso** to be
on leave.

permitir *vt* to allow; **permitir a alguien hacer
algo** to allow sb to do sthg; **¿me permite?** may
I?

▸ **permitirse** *vprnl* to allow o.s. (the luxury of);
no puedo permitírmelo I can't afford it.

permuta, permutación *sf* exchange.

permutar *vt* to exchange, to swap.

pernera *sf* trouser leg.

pernicioso, sa *adj* damaging, harmful.

pernil *sm* leg of ham.

perno *sm* bolt.

pernoctar *vi* to stay overnight.

pero <> *conj* but; **la casa es vieja pero céntri-
ca** the house may be old, but it's central; **pero
¿qué es tanto ruido?** what on earth is all this
noise about? <> *sm* snag, fault; **poner peros a
todo** to find fault with everything.

perogrullada *sf fam* truism.

perol *sm* casserole (dish).

peroné *sm* fibula.

perorata *sf* long-winded speech.

peróxido *sm* peroxide.

perpendicular *adj* perpendicular; **ser perpendicular a algo** to be at right angles to sthg.

perpetrar *vt* to perpetrate, to commit.

perpetuar [6] *vt* to perpetuate.

▸ **perpetuarse** *vprnl* to last, to endure.

perpetuidad *sf* perpetuity; **a perpetuidad** in
perpetuity; **presidente a perpetuidad** president for life; **condenado a perpetuidad** condemned to life imprisonment.

perpetuo, tua *adj* **- 1.** [gen] perpetual
- 2. [para toda la vida] lifelong; **DER** life *(antes de s)*.

perplejidad *sf* perplexity, bewilderment.

perplejo, ja *adj* perplexed, bewildered.

perra *sf* **- 1.** [rabieta] tantrum; **coger una perra**
to throw a tantrum **- 2.** [dinero] penny; **estoy
sin una perra** I'm flat broke **- 3.** ▸ **perro**.

perrera ▸ **perrero**.

perrería *sf fam*: **hacer perrerías a alguien** to
play dirty tricks on sb.

perrero, ra *sm, f* [persona] dogcatcher.

▸ **perrera** *sf* **- 1.** [lugar] kennels *pl* **- 2.** [vehícu-
lo] dogcatcher's van.

perro, rra <> *sm, f* **- 1.** [animal] dog (*f* bitch);
perro callejero stray dog; **perro de caza** hunting dog; **perro de compañía** pet dog; **perro
faldero** lapdog; **perro lazarillo** guide dog; **perro lobo** alsatian; **perro lulú** Pomeranian; **perro pastor** sheepdog; **perro policía** police dog;
allí no atan los perros con longaniza money
doesn't grow on trees there; **andar como el
perro y el gato** to fight like cat and dog; **de**
perros [tiempo etc] wretched, lousy; **echar los
perros a alguien** to have a go at sb; **perro ladrador poco mordedor** his bark is worse than
his bite; **ser perro viejo** to be an old hand
- 2. *despec* [persona] swine, dog. <> *adj*
wretched, lousy.

▸ **perro caliente** *sm* hot dog.

perruno, na *adj* canine.

persecución *sf* **- 1.** [seguimiento] pursuit
- 2. [acoso] persecution.

persecutorio, ria *adj* [manía] persecution
(antes de s).

perseguir [43] *vt* **- 1.** [seguir, tratar de obtener]
to pursue **- 2.** [acosar] to persecute **- 3.** [mala
suerte, problema etc] to dog.

perseverancia *sf* perseverance.

perseverante *adj* persistent.

perseverar *vi*: **perseverar (en)** to persevere
(with), to persist (in).

Persia *n pr* Persia.

persiana *sf* blind, shade *US*; **enrollarse como
una persiana** *fam* to go on and on.

persiga ⊳ **perseguir**.

persignarse *vprnl* to cross o.s.

persigo, persiguiera *etc* ⊳ **perseguir**.

persistencia *sf* persistence.

persistente *adj* persistent.

persistir *vi*: **persistir (en)** to persist (in).

persona *sf* **- 1.** [individuo] person; **cien personas** a hundred people; **de persona a persona**
person to person; **en persona** in person; **por
persona** per head; **ser buena persona** to be
nice; **persona mayor** adult, grown-up **- 2.** DER
party; **persona física** private individual; **persona jurídica** legal entity *o* person **- 3.** GRAM
person.

personaje *sm* **- 1.** [persona importante] important person, celebrity; **ser todo un personaje**
fam to be a real big shot **- 2.** [de obra] character.

personal <> *adj* [gen] personal; [teléfono, direc-
ción] private, home *(antes de s)*. <> *sm* **- 1.** [tra-
bajadores] staff, personnel **- 2.** *fam* [gente]
people *pl*. <> *sf* [en baloncesto] personal foul.

personalidad *sf* **- 1.** [características] personality **- 2.** [persona importante] important person,
celebrity.

personalizar [13] *vi* [nombrar] to name names.

personarse *vprnl* to turn up.

personero, ra *sm, f Amér* **- 1.** [representante]
representative **- 2.** [portavoz] spokesperson.

personificación *sf* personification.

personificar *vt* to personify.

perspectiva *sf* **- 1.** [gen] perspective **- 2.** [pai-
saje] view **- 3.** [futuro] prospect; **en perspectiva**
in prospect.

perspicacia *sf* insight, perceptiveness.

perspicaz *adj* sharp, perceptive.

persuadir *vt* to persuade; **persuadir a alguien para que haga algo** to persuade sb to do sthg.

➤ **persuadirse** *vprnl* to convince o.s.; **persuadirse de algo** to become convinced of sthg.

persuasión *sf* persuasion.

persuasivo, va *adj* persuasive.

pertenecer [30] *vi* - **1.** [gen]: **pertenecer a** to belong to - **2.** [corresponder] to be up to, to be a matter for.

perteneciente *adj*: **ser perteneciente a** to belong to.

pertenencia *sf* - **1.** [propiedad] ownership - **2.** [afiliación] membership.

➤ **pertenencias** *sfpl* [enseres] belongings.

pértiga *sf* - **1.** [vara] pole - **2.** DEP pole-vault.

pertinaz *adj* - **1.** [terco] stubborn - **2.** [persistente] persistent.

pertinencia *sf* - **1.** [adecuación] appropriateness - **2.** [relevancia] relevance.

pertinente *adj* - **1.** [adecuado] appropriate - **2.** [relativo] relevant, pertinent.

pertrechar *vt* - **1.** MIL to supply with food and ammunition - **2.** [suministrar] to equip.

➤ **pertrecharse** *vprnl*: **pertrecharse de** to equip o.s. with.

pertrechos *smpl* - **1.** MIL supplies and ammunition - **2.** *fig* [utensilios] gear *(U)*.

perturbación *sf* - **1.** [desconcierto] disquiet, unease - **2.** [disturbio] disturbance; **perturbación del orden público** breach of the peace - **3.** MED mental imbalance - **4.** METEOR unsettled weather *(U)*; **perturbación atmosférica** atmospheric disturbance.

perturbado, da ⬦ *adj* - **1.** MED disturbed, mentally unbalanced - **2.** [desconcertado] perturbed. ⬦ *sm, f* MED mentally unbalanced person.

perturbador, ra ⬦ *adj* unsettling. ⬦ *sm, f* troublemaker.

perturbar *vt* - **1.** [trastornar] to disrupt - **2.** [inquietar] to disturb, to unsettle - **3.** [enloquecer] to perturb.

Perú *n pr*: **(el) Perú** Peru.

peruano, na *adj* & *sm, f* Peruvian.

perversidad *sf* wickedness.

perversión *sf* perversion.

perverso, sa *adj* depraved.

pervertido, da *sm, f* pervert.

pervertidor, ra ⬦ *adj* pernicious, corrupting. ⬦ *sm, f* reprobate, corrupter; **pervertidor de menores** corruptor of minors.

pervertir [27] *vt* to corrupt.

➤ **pervertirse** *vprnl* to become corrupt, to be corrupted.

pervivir *vi* to survive.

pesa *sf* - **1.** [gen] weight - **2.** *(gen pl)* DEP weights *pl*; **alzar pesas** to lift weights.

pesabebés *sm inv* baby-weighing scales *pl*.

pesacartas *sm inv* letter-weighing scales *pl*.

pesada ⮕ **pesado**.

pesadez *sf* - **1.** [peso] weight - **2.** [sensación] heaviness - **3.** [molestia, fastidio] drag, pain - **4.** [aburrimiento] ponderousness.

pesadilla *sf* nightmare.

pesado, da ⬦ *adj* - **1.** [gen] heavy - **2.** [caluroso] sultry - **3.** [lento] ponderous, sluggish - **4.** [duro] difficult, tough - **5.** [aburrido] boring - **6.** [molesto] annoying, tiresome; **¡qué pesado eres!** you're so annoying!; **ponerse pesado** to be a pain. ⬦ *sm, f* bore, pain.

pesadumbre *sf* grief, sorrow.

pésame *sm* sympathy, condolences *pl*; **dar el pésame** to offer one's condolences; **mi más sentido pésame** my deepest sympathies.

pesar ⬦ *sm* - **1.** [tristeza] grief - **2.** [arrepentimiento] remorse - **3.** *loc*: **a pesar mío** against my will. ⬦ *vt* - **1.** [determinar el peso de] to weigh - **2.** [examinar] to weigh up. ⬦ *vi* - **1.** [tener peso] to weigh - **2.** [ser pesado] to be heavy - **3.** [importar] to play an important part - **4.** [molestar]: **me pesa tener que hacerlo** it grieves me to have to do it; **pese a quien pese** in spite of everything - **5.** [entristecer]: **me pesa tener que decirte esto** I'm sorry to have to tell you this.

➤ **pesarse** *vprnl* to weigh o.s.

➤ **a pesar de** *loc prep* despite; **a pesar de todo** in spite of everything.

➤ **a pesar de que** *loc conj* in spite of the fact that.

pesaroso, sa *adj* - **1.** [arrepentido] remorseful - **2.** [afligido] sad.

pesca *sf* - **1.** [acción] fishing; **ir de pesca** to go fishing; **pesca con caña** angling; **pesca con red** net fishing; **pesca de bajura/altura** coastal/deep-sea fishing; **pesca submarina** underwater fishing - **2.** [lo pescado] catch.

pescadería *sf* fishmonger's (shop).

pescadero, ra *sm, f* fishmonger.

pescadilla *sf* whiting.

pescado *sm* fish; **pescado azul/blanco** blue/white fish.

pescador, ra *sm, f* fisherman (*f* fisherwoman).

pescar [10] ⬦ *vt* - **1.** [peces] to catch - **2.** *fig* [enfermedad] to catch - **3.** *fam fig* [conseguir] to get o.s., to land - **4.** *fam fig* [atrapar] to catch - **5.** *fam fig* [entender] to pick up, to understand. ⬦ *vi* to fish, to go fishing.

pescuezo *sm* neck; **retorcer el pescuezo a alguien** *fam* to wring sb's neck.

pese ◂ **pese a** *loc prep* despite; **pese a que** even though.

pesebre *sm* - **1.** [para los animales] manger - **2.** [belén] crib, Nativity scene.

pesero *sm* Amér C & Méx *fixed-rate taxi service.*

peseta *sf* [unidad] peseta.
◂ **pesetas** *sfpl fig* [dinero] money (U).

pesetero, ra ◇ *adj* moneygrubbing. ◇ *sm, f* moneygrubber.

pesimismo *sm* pessimism.

pesimista ◇ *adj* pessimistic. ◇ *smf* pessimist.

pésimo, ma ◇ *superl* = **malo.** ◇ *adj* terrible, awful.

peso *sm* - **1.** [gen] weight; **perder** o **ganar peso** to lose/gain weight; **siento peso en las piernas** my legs feel heavy; **tiene un kilo de peso** it weighs a kilo; **de peso** [razones] weighty, sound; [persona] influential; **peso atómico/molecular** atomic/molecular weight; **peso bruto/neto** gross/net weight; **peso muerto** dead weight; **peso ligero** lightweight; **peso medio** middleweight; **peso mosca** flyweight; **peso pesado** heavyweight; **caer por su propio peso** to be self-evident; **pagar algo a peso de oro** to pay a fortune for sthg; **quitarse un peso de encima** to take a weight off one's mind - **2.** [moneda] peso - **3.** [de atletismo] shot - **4.** [balanza] scales *pl*.

pesque *etc* ▷ **pescar.**

pesquero, ra *adj* fishing.
◂ **pesquero** *sm* fishing boat.

pesquisa *sf* investigation, inquiry.

pestaña *sf* - **1.** [de párpado] eyelash; **pestañas postizas** false eyelashes; **quemarse las pestañas** *fig* to burn the midnight oil - **2.** TECNOL flange.

pestañear *vi* to blink; **sin pestañear** without batting an eyelid.

peste *sf* - **1.** [enfermedad, plaga] plague; **peste bubónica** bubonic plague - **2.** *fam* [mal olor] stink, stench - **3.** [molestia] pest - **4.** *loc:* **decir pestes de alguien** to heap abuse on sb.

pesticida ◇ *adj* pesticidal. ◇ *sm* pesticide.

pestilencia *sf* stench.

pestilente *adj* foul-smelling.

pestillo *sm* [cerrojo] bolt; [mecanismo, en verjas] latch; **correr** o **echar el pestillo** to shoot the bolt.

petaca *sf* - **1.** [para cigarrillos] cigarette case; [para tabaco] tobacco pouch - **2.** [para bebidas] flask - **3.** *Méx* [maleta] suitcase - **4.** *loc:* **hacer la petaca** to make an apple-pie bed.
◂ **petacas** *sfpl Méx fam* buttocks.

pétalo *sm* petal.

petanca *sf* game similar to bowls played in parks, on beach etc.

petardo ◇ *sm* - **1.** [cohete] banger, firecracker - **2.** *fam* [aburrimiento] bore - **3.** *mfam* [porro] joint. ◇ *smf fam* [persona fea] horror, ugly person.

petate *sm* kit bag; **liar el petate** *fam* [marcharse] to pack one's bags and go; [morir] to kick the bucket.

petenera *sf* Andalusian popular song; **salir por peteneras** to go off at a tangent.

petición *sf* - **1.** [acción] request; **a petición de** at the request of - **2.** DER [escrito] petition; **petición de mano** proposal (of marriage).

petimetre, tra *sm, f* fop, dandy.

petirrojo *sm* robin.

petiso, sa, petizo, za ◇ *adj* Andes & R Dom *fam* [person] short. ◇ *sm* Andes & R Dom [caballo] small horse.

peto *sm* - **1.** [de prenda] bib; **pantalón con peto** overalls - **2.** [de armadura] breastplate - **3.** DEP breastguard.

pétreo, a *adj* [de piedra] stone; [como piedra] stony.

petrificar [10] *vt lit & fig* to petrify.

petrodólar *sm* petrodollar.

petróleo *sm* oil, petroleum.

petrolero, ra *adj* oil *(antes de s).*
◂ **petrolero** *sm* oil tanker.

petrolífero, ra *adj* oil *(antes de s).*

petroquímico, ca *adj* petrochemical.
◂ **petroquímica** *sf* petrochemistry.

petulancia *sf* arrogance.

petulante ◇ *adj* opinionated, arrogant. ◇ *smf* opinionated person.

petunia *sf* petunia.

peúco *(gen pl) sm* bootee.

peyorativo, va *adj* pejorative.

pez ◇ *sm* fish; **pez de colores** goldfish; **pez de río** freshwater fish; **pez espada** swordfish; **estar uno como pez en el agua** to be in one's element; **estar pez (en algo)** to have no idea (about sthg). ◇ *sf* pitch, tar.
◂ **pez gordo** *sm fam fig* big shot.

pezón *sm* [de pecho] nipple.

pezuña *sf* hoof.

pH *(abrev de* **potencial de hidrógeno***) sm* pH.

pi *sf* MAT pi.

piadoso, sa *adj* - **1.** [compasivo] kind-hearted - **2.** [religioso] pious.

pianista *smf* pianist.

piano *sm* piano; **piano bar** piano bar; **piano de cola** grand piano; **piano de media cola** baby grand; **como un piano** *fam* huge.

pianola *sf* pianola.

piar [9] *vi* to cheep, to tweet.

piara *sf* herd.

piastra *sf* piastre, piaster.

PIB (*abrev de* **producto interior bruto**) *sm* GDP.

pibe, ba *sm, f R Dom fam* kid.

PIC (*abrev de* **punto de información cultural**) *sm tourist information point.*

pica *sf* - **1.** [naipe] spade - **2.** [lanza] pike; **poner una pica en Flandes** to do the impossible - **3.** TAUROM goad, picador's spear.

picas *sfpl* [palo de baraja] spades.

picada *sf* - **1.** ⊳ **picado** - **2.** *R Dom* snacks *pl*, appetizers *pl*.

picadero *sm* - **1.** [de caballos] riding school - **2.** *fam* [de soltero] bachelor pad.

picadillo *sm* - **1.** [de carne] mince; [de verdura] chopped vegetables *pl*; **hacer picadillo a alguien** *fam* to beat sb to a pulp - **2.** *Chile* [tapas] snacks, appetizers.

picado, da *adj* - **1.** [marcado - piel] pock-marked; [- fruta] bruised - **2.** [agujereado] perforated; **picado de polilla** moth-eaten - **3.** [triturado - alimento] chopped; [- carne] minced; [- tabaco] cut - **4.** [vino] sour - **5.** [diente] decayed - **6.** [mar] choppy - **7.** *fig* [enfadado] annoyed - **8.** AERON: **descender en picado** to dive.

picada *sf* [de mosquito, serpiente] bite; [de avispa, escorpión, ortiga] sting.

picador, ra *sm, f* TAUROM picador; *ver también* **tauromaquia.**

picadora *sf* mincer.

picadura *sf* - **1.** [de mosquito, serpiente] bite; [de avispa, ortiga, escorpión] sting - **2.** [tabaco] (cut) tobacco *(U)*.

picaflor *sm Amér* - **1.** [colibrí] hummingbird - **2.** [galanteador] womanizer.

picante ⟨⟩ *adj* - **1.** [comida etc] spicy, hot - **2.** *fig* [obsceno] saucy. ⟨⟩ *sm* [comida] spicy food; [sabor] spiciness.

picantería *sf Andes* cheap restaurant.

picapleitos *smf inv despec* lawyer.

picaporte *sm* [aldaba] doorknocker; [barrita] latch.

picar [10] ⟨⟩ *vt* - **1.** [suj: mosquito, serpiente] to bite; [suj: avispa, escorpión, ortiga] to sting - **2.** [escocer] to itch; **me pican los ojos** my eyes are stinging - **3.** [triturar - verdura] to chop; [- carne] to mince - **4.** [suj: ave] to peck - **5.** [aperitivo] to pick at - **6.** [tierra, piedra, hielo] to hack at - **7.** *fig* [enojar] to irritate - **8.** *fig* [estimular - persona, caballo] to spur on; [- curiosidad] to prick - **9.** [perforar - billete, ficha] to punch - **10.** [teclear] to type. ⟨⟩ *vi* - **1.** [alimento] to be spicy o hot - **2.** [pez] to bite - **3.** [escocer] to itch

- **4.** [ave] to peck - **5.** [tomar un aperitivo] to nibble - **6.** [sol] to burn - **7.** [dejarse engañar] to take the bait - **8.** *loc*: **picar (muy) alto** to have great ambitions.

picarse *vprnl* - **1.** [vino] to turn sour - **2.** [ropa] to become moth-eaten - **3.** [mar] to get choppy - **4.** [diente] to get a cavity - **5.** [oxidarse] to go rusty - **6.** *fig* [enfadarse] to get annoyed o cross - **7.** *fam* [inyectarse droga] to shoot up.

picardía *sf* - **1.** [astucia] sharpness, craftiness - **2.** [travesura] naughty trick, mischief *(U)*.

picaresco, ca *adj* mischievous, roguish.

picaresca *sf* - **1.** LITER picaresque literature - **2.** [modo de vida] roguery.

pícaro, ra *sm, f* - **1.** [astuto] sly person, rogue - **2.** [travieso] rascal; *ver también* **picaresca.**

picatoste *sm* crouton.

picazón *sf* [en el cuerpo] itch.

picha *sf mfam* dick, knob.

pichi *sm* pinafore (dress).

pichichi *sm* DEP top scorer.

pichincha *sf Bol & R Dom fam* bargain.

pichón *sm* - **1.** ZOOL young pigeon - **2.** *fam fig* [apelativo cariñoso] darling, sweetheart.

pichula *sf Amér vulg* prick, cock.

picnic (*pl* **picnics**) *sm* picnic.

pico *sm* - **1.** [de ave] beak - **2.** [punta, saliente] corner - **3.** [herramienta] pick, pickaxe - **4.** [cumbre] peak - **5.** [cantidad indeterminada]: **cincuenta y pico** fifty-odd, fifty-something; **llegó a las cinco y pico** he got there just after five - **6.** *fam* [boca] gob, mouth; **cerrar el pico** [callar] to shut up; **ser** o **tener un pico de oro** to be a smooth talker, to have the gift of the gab - **7.** *loc*: **andar/irse de picos pardos** to be/go out on the town; **le costó un pico** it cost her a fortune.

picor *sm* [del calor] burning; [que irrita] itch.

picoso, sa *adj Méx* spicy, hot.

picota *sf* - **1.** [de ajusticiados] pillory; **poner a alguien en la picota** *fig* to pillory sb - **2.** [cereza] cherry.

picotazo *sm* peck.

picotear *vt* - **1.** [suj: ave] to peck - **2.** *fig* [comer] to pick at.

pictórico, ca *adj* pictorial.

pida, pidiera *etc* ⊳ **pedir.**

pie *sm* - **1.** [gen & ANAT] foot; **a pie** on foot; **estar de** o **en pie** to be on one's feet o standing; **ponerse de** o **en pie** to stand up; **de pies a cabeza** *fig* from head to toe; **seguir en pie** [vigente] to be still valid; **en pie de igualdad** on an equal footing; **en pie de guerra** at war; **perder/no hacer pie** to go/to be out of one's depth; **pie de atleta** athlete's foot; **pie de foto** caption; **pies de cerdo** (pig's) trotters; **pies**

planos flat feet - **2.** [de micrófono, lámpara etc] stand; [de copa] stem - **3.** TEATRO cue - **4.** *loc*: **al pie de la letra** to the letter, word for word; **al pie del cañón** ready for action; **andar con pies de plomo** to tread carefully; **a pies juntillas** unquestioningly; **a sus pies** at your service; **buscarle (los) tres pies al gato** to split hairs; **cojear del mismo pie** to fall at the same fence; **con buen pie** on the right footing; **dar pie a alguien para que haga algo** to give sb cause to do sthg; **el ciudadano de a pie** the man in the street; **levantarse con el pie izquierdo** to get out of bed on the wrong side; **no dar pie con bola** to get everything wrong; **no tener ni pies ni cabeza** to make no sense at all; **no tenerse de o en pie** [por cansancio] not to be able to stand up a minute longer; *fig* [por ser absurdo] not to stand up; **pararle los pies a alguien** to put sb in their place; **poner pies en polvorosa** to make a run for it; **saber de qué pie cojea alguien** to know sb's weaknesses; **tener un pie en la tumba** to have one foot in the grave.

piedad *sf* - **1.** [compasión] pity; **por piedad** for pity's sake; **tener piedad de** to take pity on - **2.** [religiosidad] piety.
➤ **Piedad** *sf* ARTE Pietà.

piedra *sf* - **1.** [gen] stone; **piedra angular** *lit & fig* cornerstone; **piedra pómez** pumice stone; **piedra preciosa** precious stone; **piedra de toque** touchstone; **poner la primera piedra** [inaugurar] to lay the foundation stone; *fig* to lay the foundations; **no dejar piedra sobre piedra** to leave no stone standing; **no ser de piedra** to be human; **quedarse de piedra** to be thunderstruck; **tirar la piedra y esconder la mano** to play the innocent; **tirar piedras a su propio tejado** to harm oneself - **2.** [de mechero] flint.

piel *sf* - **1.** ANAT skin; **piel roja** redskin *(N.B.: the term 'piel roja' is considered to be racist)*; **piel de gallina** goose bumps; **dejar o jugarse la piel** to risk one's neck; **ser de la piel del diablo** to be a little devil - **2.** [cuero] leather - **3.** [pelo] fur - **4.** [cáscara] skin, peel.

piensa *etc* ➤ **pensar**.

pienso *sm* fodder.

pierda *etc* ➤ **perder**.

pierna *sf* leg; **dormir a pierna suelta** to sleep like a log; **estirar las piernas** to stretch one's legs.

pieza *sf* - **1.** [gen] piece; [de mecanismo] part; **pieza de recambio o repuesto** spare part, extra *US*; **un dos piezas** a two-piece suit; **dejar/quedarse de una pieza** to leave/be thunderstruck - **2.** [presa] specimen - **3.** *irón* [persona]: **ser una buena pieza** to be a fine one o a right one - **4.** [obra dramática] play - **5.** [habitación] room.

pifia *sf* blunder.

pifiar [8] *vt*: **pifiarla** *fam* to put one's foot in it.

pigmentación *sf* pigmentation.

pigmento *sm* pigment.

pigmeo, a *sm, f* pygmy.

pijada *sf* *fam* [dicho] trivial remark; [hecho] trifle.

pijama *sm* pyjamas *pl*.

pijería *sf* *fam* [dicho] trivial remark; [hecho] trifle.

pijo, ja *fam* ◇ *adj* posh. ◇ *sm, f* spoilt rich brat.
➤ **pijo** *sm* *vulg* prick, cock.

pila *sf* - **1.** [generador] battery; **pila atómica** atomic pile; **pila solar** solar cell; **cargar las pilas** *fam* to recharge one's batteries - **2.** [montón] pile; **tiene una pila de deudas** he's up to his neck in debt - **3.** [fregadero] sink; **pila bautismal** (baptismal) font.

pilar *sm* *lit & fig* pillar.

pilastra *sf* pilaster.

píldora *sf* pill; [anticonceptivo]: **la píldora** the pill; **píldora del día siguiente** morning after pill; **dorar la píldora** to sugar the pill.

pileta *sf* *R Dom* [piscina] swimming pool; [en baño] washbasin; [en cocina] sink.

pillaje *sm* pillage.

pillar ◇ *vt* - **1.** [gen] to catch - **2.** [chiste, explicación] to get - **3.** [atropellar] to knock down. ◇ *vi* *fam* [hallarse]: **me pilla lejos** it's out of the way for me; **me pilla de camino** it's on my way; **no me pilla de nuevas** it doesn't surprise me.
➤ **pillarse** *vprnl* [dedos etc] to catch.

pillastre *smf* *fam* rogue, crafty person.

pillo, lla *fam* ◇ *adj* - **1.** [travieso] mischievous - **2.** [astuto] crafty. ◇ *sm, f* - **1.** [pícaro] rascal - **2.** [astuto] crafty person.

pilotar *vt* [avión] to fly, to pilot; [coche] to drive; [barco] to steer.

piloto ◇ *smf* [gen] pilot; [de coche] driver; **piloto automático** automatic pilot; **piloto de pruebas** test pilot. ◇ *sm* - **1.** [luz - de coche] tail light; [- de aparato] pilot lamp - **2.** *C Sur* [impermeable] raincoat. ◇ *adj inv* pilot *(antes de s)*.

piltra *sf* *mfam* pit, bed.

piltrafa *(gen pl)* *sf* scrap; *fam* [persona débil] wreck.

pimentón *sm* - **1.** [dulce] paprika - **2.** [picante] cayenne pepper.

pimienta *sf* pepper; **pimienta blanca/negra** white/black pepper.

pimiento *sm* [fruto] pepper, capsicum; [planta] pimiento, pepper plant; **pimiento morrón** sweet pepper; **me importa un pimiento** *fam* I couldn't care less.

pimpante *adj* - **1.** [satisfecho] well-pleased - **2.** [garboso] swish, smart.

pimpinela *sf* pimpernel.

pimpollo *sm* - **1.** [de rama, planta] shoot; [de flor] bud - **2.** *fam fig* [persona atractiva] gorgeous person.

PIN (*abrev de* **producto interior neto**) *sm* NDP.

pinacoteca *sf* art gallery.

pináculo *sm* - **1.** [gen] pinnacle - **2.** [juego de naipes] pinochle.

pinar *sm* pine wood *o* grove.

pinaza *sf* pine needles *pl*.

pincel *sm* [para pintar] paintbrush; [para maquillar etc] brush.

pincelada *sf* brushstroke; **a grandes pinceladas** *fig* in broad terms.

pinchadiscos *smf inv* disc jockey.

pinchar ◇ *vt* - **1.** [punzar - gen] to prick; [- rueda] to puncture; [- globo, balón] to burst - **2.** [penetrar] to pierce - **3.** *fam* [teléfono] to tap - **4.** *fig* [irritar] to torment - **5.** *fig* [incitar]: **pinchar a alguien para que haga algo** to urge sb to do sthg. ◇ *vi* - **1.** [rueda] to get a puncture - **2.** [barba] to be prickly - **3.** *loc*: **ella ni pincha ni corta** she cuts no ice.

◆ **pincharse** *vprnl* - **1.** [punzarse - persona] to prick o.s.; [- rueda] to get a puncture - **2.** *fig* [irritarse] to get annoyed - **3.** [inyectarse]: **pincharse (algo)** [medicamento] to inject o.s. (with sthg); *fam* [droga] to shoot up (with sthg).

pinchazo *sm* - **1.** [punzada] prick - **2.** [marca] needle mark - **3.** [de neumático, balón etc] puncture, flat *US*.

pinche ◇ *sm, f* kitchen boy (*f* kitchen maid). ◇ *adj Méx fam* lousy, damn.

pinchito *sm* - **1.** CULIN [tapa] aperitif on a stick - **2.** CULIN [pincho moruno] shish kebab.

pincho *sm* - **1.** [punta] (sharp) point - **2.** [espina - de planta] prickle, thorn - **3.** [varilla] pointed stick - **4.** CULIN aperitif on a stick; **pincho moruno** shish kebab.

pindonguear *vi fam* to loaf about.

pineda *sf* pine wood *o* grove.

pinga *sf Andes & Méx vulg* prick, cock.

pingajo *sm fam despec* rag.

pingonear *vi fam* to loaf about.

ping-pong® [pin'pon] *sm* ping-pong, table-tennis.

pingüe *adj* plentiful; **pingües ganancias** fat profit *sing*.

pingüino *sm* penguin.

pinitos *smpl*: **hacer pinitos** *lit & fig* to take one's first steps.

pino *sm* pine; **en el quinto pino** in the middle of nowhere; **hacer el pino** to do a handstand.

Los Pinos

Los Pinos ("The Pine Trees") has been the official home of the Mexican president since 1934, when president Lázaro Cárdenas moved there in preference to the nearby Chapultepec Castle, which he felt was too grand, and which he had turned into a national museum. Recently, **Los Pinos** itself has been opened to public tours for the first time. By extension, "Los Pinos" is used to refer to the Mexican government: según el portavoz de los Pinos... according to the president's spokesperson...

pinta ▷ **pinto**.

pintado, da *adj* - **1.** [coloreado] coloured; **'recién pintado'** 'wet paint' - **2.** [maquillado] made-up - **3.** [moteado] speckled - **4.** *loc*: **el más pintado** the best person around; **venir que ni pintado** to be just the thing.

◆ **pintada** *sf* - **1.** [escrito] graffiti *(U)* - **2.** [ave] guinea fowl.

pintalabios *sm inv* lipstick.

pintar ◇ *vt* - **1.** to paint; **pintar algo de negro** to paint sthg black - **2.** [significar, importar] to count; **aquí no pinto nada** there's no place for me here; **¿qué pinto yo en este asunto?** where do I come in? ◇ *vi* [con pintura] to paint.

◆ **pintarse** *vprnl* - **1.** [maquillarse] to make o.s. up - **2.** [manifestarse] to show, to be evident - **3.** *loc*: **pintárselas uno solo para algo** to be a past master at sthg.

pintarrajear *vt fam despec* to daub.

pinto, ta *adj* speckled, spotted.

◆ **pinta** ◇ *sf* - **1.** [lunar] spot - **2.** *fig* [aspecto] appearance; **tener pinta de algo** to look *o* seem like sthg; **tiene buena pinta** it looks good - **3.** [unidad de medida] pint - **4.** *Méx* [pintada] graffiti *(U)*. ◇ *sm, f fam* [caradura] cheeky so-and-so, shameless person.

pintor, ra *sm, f* painter; **pintor de brocha gorda** painter and decorator; *despec* dauber.

pintoresco, ca *adj* picturesque; *fig* [extravagante] colourful.

pintura *sf* - **1.** ARTE painting; **pintura a la acuarela** watercolour; **pintura al óleo** oil painting; **pintura rupestre** cave painting; **no poder ver a alguien ni en pintura** *fig* not to be able to stand the sight of sb - **2.** [materia] paint.

pinza (*gen pl*) *sf* - **1.** [gen] tweezers *pl*; [de tender ropa] peg, clothespin *US*; **coger algo con pinzas** *fam* to handle sthg with great care - **2.** [de animal] pincer, claw - **3.** [pliegue] fold.

piña *sf* - **1.** [del pino] pine cone - **2.** [ananás] pineapple; **piña colada** piña colada - **3.** *fig* [conjunto de gente] close-knit group; **hacer piña con alguien** to rally around sb - **4.** *fam* [golpe] knock, bash.

piñata *sf* *pot full of sweets which blind-folded children try to break open with sticks at parties*.

piñón *sm* - **1.** [fruto] pine nut; **estar a partir un piñón con alguien** to be hand in glove with sb - **2.** [rueda dentada] pinion; **ser de piñón fijo** to be fixed *o* rigid.

pío, a *adj* pious.

➤ **pío** *sm* cheep, cheeping *(U)*; [de gallina] cluck, clucking *(U)*; **no decir ni pío** *fig* not to make a peep.

piojo *sm* louse; **piojos** lice.

piojoso, sa *adj* lousy, covered in lice; *fig* [sucio] flea-bitten, filthy.

piola ◇ *adj* Arg fam - **1.** [astuto] shrewd - **2.** [estupendo] fabulous. ◇ *sf* Amér [cuerda] cord.

piolín *sm* R Dom cord.

pionero, ra *sm, f* pioneer.

piorrea *sf* pyorrhoea.

pipa *sf* - **1.** [para fumar] pipe; **fumar en pipa** to smoke a pipe - **2.** [pepita] seed, pip; **pipas (de girasol)** *sunflower seeds coated in salt* - **3.** *loc*: **pasarlo** *o* **pasárselo pipa** to have a whale of a time.

pipermín, peppermint [piper'min] *sm* peppermint liqueur.

pipí *sm* *fam* wee-wee; **hacer pipí** to have a wee-wee.

pipón, ona *sm, f* Amér fam nipper, kid.

pipote *sm* Amér rubbish bin UK, garbage can US.

pique ◇ *v* ▷ **picar**. ◇ *sm* - **1.** [enfado] grudge; **tener un pique con alguien** to have a grudge against sb - **2.** [rivalidad] rivalry - **3.** *loc*: **irse a pique** [barco] to sink; [negocio] to go under; [plan] to fail.

piqué *sm* piqué.

piquera *sf* Amér [antro] dive, seedy bar.

piqueta *sf* pickaxe.

piquete *sm* - **1.** [herramienta] peg, stake - **2.** [grupo]: **piquete de ejecución** firing squad; **piquete (de huelga)** picket.

pira *sf* pyre.

pirado, da *adj* *fam* crazy.

piragua *sf* canoe.

piragüismo *sm* canoeing.

piramidal *adj* pyramid-shaped, pyramidal.

pirámide *sf* pyramid.

piraña *sf* piranha.

pirarse *vprnl* *fam* to clear off.

pirata ◇ *adj* pirate *(antes de s)*; [disco] bootleg. ◇ *smf* *lit & fig* pirate; **pirata del aire** hijacker; **pirata informático** hacker.

piratear ◇ *vi* - **1.** [gen] to be involved in piracy - **2.** INFORM to hack. ◇ *vt* INFORM to hack into.

piratería *sf* *lit & fig* piracy; **piratería aérea** hijacking; **piratería informática** hacking; **piratería musical** music piracy.

pirenaico, ca *adj* Pyrenean.

pírex, pyrex® *sm* Pyrex®.

pirindolo *sm* *fam* *fig* thingamabob.

Pirineos *smpl*: **los Pirineos** the Pyrenees.

piripi *adj* *fam* tipsy.

piro *sm* *fam*: **darse el piro** to scarper, to clear off.

piromanía *sf* pyromania.

pirómano, na ◇ *adj* pyromaniacal. ◇ *sm, f* pyromaniac.

piropear *vt* *fam* to make flirtatious comments to, ≃ to wolf-whistle at.

piropo *sm* *fam* flirtatious remark, ≃ wolf whistle.

pirotecnia *sf* pyrotechnics *(U)*.

pirotécnico, ca ◇ *adj* firework *(antes de s)*. ◇ *sm, f* firework specialist.

pirrarse *vprnl* *fam*: **pirrarse por algo/alguien** to be dead keen on sthg/sb.

pírrico, ca *adj* Pyrrhic.

pirueta *sf* pirouette; **hacer piruetas** *fig* [esfuerzo] to perform miracles.

piruleta *sf* lollipop.

pirulí (*pl* pirulís) *sm* lollipop.

pis (*pl* pises) *sm* *fam* pee; **hacer pis** *fam* to have a pee.

pisada *sf* - **1.** [acción] footstep; **seguir las pisadas de alguien** to follow in sb's footsteps - **2.** [huella] footprint.

pisapapeles *sm* *inv* paperweight.

pisar *vt* - **1.** [con el pie] to tread on - **2.** [uvas] to tread - **3.** *fig* [llegar a] to set foot in - **4.** *fig* [despreciar] to trample on - **5.** *fig* [anticiparse]: **pisar un contrato a alguien** to beat sb to a contract; **pisar una idea a alguien** to think of sthg before sb; **pisar fuerte** *fig* to be firing on all cylinders.

piscicultura *sf* fish farming.

piscifactoría *sf* fish farm.

piscina *sf* swimming pool; **piscina al aire libre** open air swimming pool; **piscina climatizada** heated swimming pool.

Piscis ◇ *sm* [zodiaco] Pisces; **ser Piscis** to be (a) Pisces. ◇ *smf* [persona] Pisces.

piscolabis *sm* *inv* *fam* snack.

piso *sm* **- 1.** [vivienda] flat; **piso franco** safe house; **piso piloto** show apartment, show flat *UK* **- 2.** [planta] floor **- 3.** [suelo - de carretera] surface; [- de edificio] floor **- 4.** [capa] layer.

pisotear *vt* **- 1.** [con el pie] to trample on **- 2.** [humillar] to scorn.

pisotón *sm fam* stamp *(of the foot)*.

pista *sf* **- 1.** [gen] track; **pista de aterrizaje** runway; **pista de baile** dance floor; **pista cubierta** indoor track; **pista de esquí** ski slope; **pista de hielo** ice rink; **pista de tenis** tennis court **- 2.** *fig* [indicio] clue; **estar sobre la pista** to be on the right track; **seguir la pista a alguien** to be on sb's trail.

pistacho *sm* pistachio.

pistilo *sm* pistil.

pisto *sm* ≃ ratatouille.

pistola *sf* **- 1.** [arma - con cilindro] gun; [- sin cilindro] pistol; **pistola de agua** water pistol **- 2.** [pulverizador] spraygun; **pintar a pistola** to spray-paint **- 3.** [herramienta] gun.

pistolero, ra *sm, f* [persona] gunman.
➤ **pistolera** *sf* [funda] holster.

pistón *sm* **- 1.** MECÁN piston **- 2.** [MÚS - corneta] cornet; [- llave] key **- 3.** [de arma] percussion cap.

pita *sf* agave.

pitada *sf Amér fam* drag, puff.

pitanza *sf* [ración de comida] daily rations *pl*.

pitar ◇ *vt* **- 1.** [arbitrar - partido] to referee; [- falta] to blow for **- 2.** [abuchear]**: pitar a alguien** to whistle at sb in disapproval **- 3.** *Amér fam* [fumar] to puff (on). ◇ *vi* **- 1.** [tocar el pito] to blow a whistle; [del coche] to toot one's horn **- 2.** [funcionar - cosa] to work; [- persona] to get on **- 3.** *loc*: **salir/irse pitando** to rush out/off; **venir pitando** to come rushing.

pitido *sm* whistle.

pitillera *sf* cigarette case.

pitillo *sm* **- 1.** [cigarrillo] cigarette **- 2.** *Col* [pajita] drinking straw.

pito *sm* **- 1.** [silbato] whistle **- 2.** [claxon] horn **- 3.** *fam* [cigarrillo] fag **- 4.** *fam* [pene] willie **- 5.** *loc*: **(no) me importa un pito** I couldn't give a damn; **por pitos o por flautas** for one reason or another; **tomar a alguien por el pito del sereno** not to take sb seriously.

pitón ◇ *sm* **- 1.** [cuerno] horn **- 2.** [pitorro] spout. ◇ *sf* ▷ **serpiente**.

pitonisa *sf* fortune-teller.

pitorrearse *vprnl fam*: **pitorrearse (de)** to take the mickey (out of).

pitorreo *sm* making fun *(U)*, joking *(U)*; **estar de pitorreo** to be joking.

pitorro *sm* spout.

pituitario, ria *adj* pituitary.

pívot (*pl* **pivots**) *sm, f* DEP pivot.

pivotar *vi* DEP to pivot.

piyama *sm o sf Amér* [pijama] pyjamas; **un piyama** a pair of pyjamas.

pizarra *sf* **- 1.** [roca, material] slate **- 2.** [encerado] blackboard, chalkboard *US*.

pizarrón *sm Amér* blackboard.

pizca *sf fam* **- 1.** [gen] tiny bit; [de sal] pinch; **ni pizca** not one bit **- 2.** *Méx* [cosecha] harvest, crop.

pizpireta *adj f fam* brassy, spirited.

pizza ['pitsa] *sf* pizza.

pizzería [pitse'ria] *sf* pizzeria.

placa *sf* **- 1.** [lámina] plate; [de madera] sheet; **placa solar** solar panel **- 2.** [inscripción] plaque; [de policía] badge **- 3.** [matrícula] number plate **- 4.** [de cocina] ring; **placa de vitrocerámica** glass enamel hob **- 5.** GEOL plate **- 6.** ELECTRÓN board; **placa madre** INFORM motherboard **- 7.**: **placa dental** dental plaque.

placar [10] ◇ *vt* to tackle. ◇ *sm R Dom* built-in cupboard.

placebo *sm* placebo.

placenta *sf* placenta.

placentero, ra *adj* pleasant.

placer *sm* pleasure; **ha sido un placer (conocerle)** it has been a pleasure meeting you.

placidez *sf* [de persona] placidness; [de día, vida, conversación] peacefulness.

plácido, da *adj* [persona] placid; [día, vida, conversación] peaceful.

plafón *sm* ELECTR ceiling rose.

plaga *sf* **- 1.** [gen] plague; AGRIC blight; [animal] pest **- 2.** [epidemia] epidemic.

plagado, da *adj*: **plagado (de)** infested (with).

plagar [16] *vt*: **plagar de** [propaganda etc] to swamp with; [moscas etc] to infest with.

plagiar [8] *vt* **- 1.** [copiar] to plagiarize **- 2.** *Amér* [secuestrar] to kidnap.

plagiario, ria *sm, f Amér* kidnapper.

plagio *sm* **- 1.** [copia] plagiarism **- 2.** *Amér* [secuestro] kidnapping.

plague *etc* ▷ **plagar**.

plaguicida ◇ *adj* pesticidal. ◇ *sm* pesticide.

plan *sm* **- 1.** [proyecto, programa] plan; **hacer planes** to plan; **plan de desarrollo** development plan; **plan de estudios** syllabus; **plan de pensiones** pension plan **- 2.** *fam* [ligue] date **- 3.** *fam* [modo, forma]: **lo dijo en plan serio** he was serious about it; **¡vaya plan de vida!** what a life!; **si te pones en ese plan...** if you're going to be like that about it...; **no es plan** it's just not on.

plana ▷ plano.

plancha *sf* - **1.** [para planchar] iron; **plancha de vapor** steam iron - **2.** [para cocinar] grill; **a la plancha** grilled - **3.** [placa] plate; [de madera] sheet - **4.** *fam* [metedura de pata] boob, blunder - **5.** [en fútbol] diving header - **6.** IMPR plate.

planchado *sm* ironing.

planchar *vt* to iron.

planchazo *sm fam* boob, blunder.

plancton *sm* plankton.

planeador *sm* glider.

planear ⬦ *vt* to plan. ⬦ *vi* - **1.** [hacer planes] to plan - **2.** [en el aire] to glide.

planeta *sm* planet.

planetario, **ria** *adj* - **1.** [de un planeta] planetary - **2.** [mundial] world *(antes de s)*.
▸ **planetario** *sm* planetarium.

planicie *sf* plain.

planificación *sf* planning; **planificación familiar** family planning.

planificar [10] *vt* to plan.

planilla *sf Amér* [formulario] form.

planisferio *sm* planisphere.

planning ['planin] (*pl* **plannings**) *sm* scheduling.

plano, **na** *adj* flat.
▸ **plano** *sm* - **1.** [diseño, mapa] plan - **2.** [nivel, aspecto] level - **3.** CINE shot; **primer plano** close-up; **en segundo plano** *fig* in the background - **4.** GEOM plane - **5.** *loc:* **de plano** [golpear] right, directly; [negar] flatly; **cantar de plano** to make a full confession.
▸ **plana** *sf* - **1.** [página] page; **en primera plana** on the front page - **2.** MIL: **plana mayor** staff - **3.** [loc]: **enmendarle la plana a alguien** to find fault with sb.

planta *sf* - **1.** BOT plant - **2.** [fábrica] plant; **planta depuradora** purification plant; **planta de envase** *o* **envasadora** packaging plant - **3.** [piso] floor; **planta baja** ground floor - **4.** [del pie] sole - **5.** *loc:* **de nueva planta** brand new; **tener buena planta** to be good-looking.

plantación *sf* - **1.** [terreno] plantation - **2.** [acción] planting.

plantado, **da** *adj* standing, planted; **dejar plantado a alguien** *fam* [cortar la relación] to walk out on sb; [no acudir] to stand sb up; **ser bien plantado** to be good-looking.

plantar *vt* - **1.** [sembrar]: **plantar algo (de)** to plant sthg (with) - **2.** [fijar - tienda de campaña] to pitch; [- poste] to put in - **3.** *fam* [asestar] to deal, to land - **4.** *fam* [decir con brusquedad]: **le plantó cuatro frescas** she gave him a piece of her mind - **5.** *fam* [abandonar] to dump, to leave.

▸ **plantarse** *vprnl* - **1.** [gen] to plant o.s. - **2.** [en un sitio con rapidez]: **plantarse en** to get to, to reach - **3.** [en una actitud]: **plantarse en algo** to stick to sthg, to insist on sthg - **4.** [en naipes] to stick.

plante *sm* - **1.** [para protestar] protest - **2.** [plantón]: **dar** *o* **hacer un plante a alguien** to stand sb up.

planteamiento *sm* - **1.** [exposición] raising, posing - **2.** [enfoque] approach.

plantear *vt* - **1.** [exponer - problema] to pose; [- posibilidad, dificultad, duda] to raise - **2.** [enfocar] to approach.

▸ **plantearse** *vprnl*: **plantearse algo** to consider sthg, to think about sthg.

plantel *sm* - **1.** [criadero] nursery bed - **2.** *fig* [conjunto] group.

plantilla *sf* - **1.** [de empresa] staff; **estar en plantilla** to be on the staff - **2.** [suela interior] insole - **3.** [patrón] pattern, template.

plantón *sm*: **dar un plantón a alguien** *fam* to stand sb up.

plañidero, **ra** *adj* plaintive, whining.

plañir ⬦ *vt* to bewail. ⬦ *vi* to moan, to wail.

plaque *etc* ▷ placar.

plaqueta *sf* BIOL platelet.

plasma *sm* plasma.

plasmar *vt* - **1.** *fig* [reflejar] to give shape to - **2.** [modelar] to shape, to mould.

▸ **plasmarse** *vprnl* to emerge, to take shape.

plasta ⬦ *adj mfam*: **ser plasta** to be a pain. ⬦ *smf mfam* [pesado] pain, drag. ⬦ *sf* [cosa blanda] mess.

plástica ▷ plástico.

plasticidad *sf* - **1.** [gen] plasticity - **2.** [expresividad] expressiveness.

plástico, **ca** *adj* - **1.** [gen] plastic - **2.** [expresivo] expressive.
▸ **plástico** *sm* - **1.** [gen] plastic - **2.** *fam* [tarjetas de crédito] plastic (money).
▸ **plástica** *sf* plastic art.

plastificar [10] *vt* to plasticize.

plastilina® *sf* ≃ Plasticine®.

plata *sf* - **1.** [metal] silver; **plata de ley** sterling silver; **hablar en plata** *fam* to speak bluntly - **2.** [objetos de plata] silverware - **3.** *Amér* [dinero] money.

plataforma *sf* - **1.** [gen] platform; **plataforma espacial** space station; **plataforma petrolífera** oil rig - **2.** *fig* [punto de partida] launching pad - **3.** GEOL shelf; **plataforma continental** continental shelf.

platal *sm Amér fam*: **un platal** a fortune, loads of money.

platanal, **platanar** *sm* banana plantation.

platanero *sm* banana tree.

plátano *sm* - **1.** [fruta] banana - **2.** [banano] banana tree; [árbol platanáceo] plane tree.

platea *sf* stalls *pl*.

plateado, da *adj* - **1.** [con plata] silver-plated - **2.** *fig* [color] silvery.

platería *sf* [arte u oficio] silversmithing.

plática *sf Amér C & Méx* talk, chat.

platicar [10] *vi Amér C & Méx* to talk, to chat.

platillo *sm* - **1.** [plato pequeño] small plate; [de taza] saucer - **2.** [de una balanza] pan - **3.** *(gen pl)* MÚS cymbal.

◆ **platillo volante** *sm* flying saucer.

platina *sf* - **1.** [de tocadiscos] turntable - **2.** [de microscopio] slide.

platino *sm* [metal] platinum.

◆ **platinos** *smpl* AUTO & MECÁN contact points.

plato *sm* - **1.** [recipiente] plate, dish; **lavar los platos** to do the washing-up; **plato de postre** dessert plate; **plato hondo** O **sopero** soup dish O plate; **plato llano** plate; **comer en el mismo plato** to be great friends; **pagar los platos rotos** to carry the can; **parecer que alguien no ha roto un plato en su vida** to look as if butter wouldn't melt in one's mouth - **2.** [parte de una comida] course; **primer plato** first course, starter; **de primer plato** for starters; **segundo plato** second course, main course; **plato fuerte** [en una comida] main course; *fig* main part - **3.** [comida] dish; **plato combinado** *single-course meal which usually consists of meat or fish accompanied by chips and vegetables*; **plato principal** main course; **plato preparado** ready-prepared meal - **4.** [de tocadiscos, microondas] turntable - **5.** [de bicicleta] chain wheel.

plató *sm* set.

platónico, ca *adj* Platonic.

platudo, da *adj Amér fam* loaded, rolling in it.

plausibilidad *sf* - **1.** [admisibilidad] acceptability - **2.** [posibilidad] plausibility.

plausible *adj* - **1.** [admisible] acceptable - **2.** [posible] plausible.

playa *sf* - **1.** [en el mar] beach; **ir a la playa de vacaciones** to go on holiday to the seaside - **2.**: **playa de estacionamiento** *Amér* car park *UK*, parking lot *US*.

play-back ['pleiβak] *(pl play-backs) sm*: **hacer play-back** to mime (the lyrics).

play-boy [plei'βoi] *(pl play-boys) sm* playboy.

playero, ra *adj* beach *(antes de s)*.

◆ **playera** *sf Amér C & Méx* [camiseta] T-shirt.

◆ **playeras** *sfpl* - **1.** [de deporte] tennis shoes - **2.** [para la playa] canvas shoes.

plaza *sf* - **1.** [en una población] square; **plaza mayor** main square - **2.** [sitio] place; **tenemos plazas limitadas** there are a limited number of places available - **3.** [asiento] seat; **de dos plazas** two-seater *(antes de s)* - **4.** [puesto de trabajo] position, job; **plaza vacante** vacancy - **5.** [mercado] market, marketplace - **6.** TAUROM: **plaza (de toros)** bullring - **7.** COM [zona] area - **8.** [fortificación]: **plaza fuerte** stronghold.

plazo *sm* - **1.** [de tiempo] period (of time); **en un plazo de un mes** within a month; **mañana termina el plazo de inscripción** the deadline for registration is tomorrow; **a corto/largo plazo** [gen] in the short/long term; ECON short/long term; **a plazo fijo** ECON fixed term; **plazo de entrega** COM delivery time - **2.** [de dinero] instalment; **a plazos** in instalments, on hire purchase.

plazoleta *sf* small square.

pleamar *sf* high tide.

plebe *sf*: **la plebe** *lit & fig* the plebs.

plebeyo, ya *adj* - **1.** HIST plebeian - **2.** [vulgar] common.

plebiscito *sm* plebiscite.

plegable *adj* collapsible, foldaway; [chair] folding.

plegar [35] *vt* to fold; [mesita, hamaca] to fold away.

◆ **plegarse** *vprnl*: **plegarse a algo** to give in O yield to sthg.

plegaria *sf* prayer.

plegue *etc* ⊳ **plegar**.

pleitear *vi* DER to litigate, to conduct a lawsuit.

pleitesía *sf* homage; **rendir pleitesía a alguien** to pay homage to sb.

pleito *sm* - **1.** DER [litigio] legal action *(U)*, lawsuit; [disputa] dispute; **poner un pleito (a alguien)** to take legal action (against sb) - **2.** *Amér* [discusión] argument.

plenario, ria *adj* plenary.

plenilunio *sm* full moon.

plenipotenciario, ria ◇ *adj* plenipotentiary. ◇ *sm, f* envoy.

plenitud *sf* [totalidad] completeness, fullness; **en la plenitud de** at the height of.

pleno, na *adj* full, complete; **en pleno día** in broad daylight; **en plena guerra** in the middle of the war; **le dio en plena cara** she hit him right in the face; **en pleno uso de sus facultades** in full command of his faculties; **la reunión en pleno** the meeting as a whole, everyone at the meeting; **en plena forma** on top form.

◆ **pleno** *sm* - **1.** [reunión] plenary meeting - **2.** [en las quinielas] full claim, ≈ 24 points.

pletórico, ca *adj*: **pletórico de** full of.

pleura *sf* pleural membrane.

pleuresía *sf* pleurisy.

plexiglás® *sm inv* ≃ Perspex®.

pléyade *sf* [conjunto] cluster.

pliega *etc* ⊏⟶ **plegar**.

pliego *sm* - **1.** [hoja] sheet (of paper) - **2.** [carta, documento] *sealed document* o *letter*; **pliego de condiciones** specifications *pl*; **pliego de descargos** list of rebuttals.

pliegue *sm* - **1.** [gen & GEOL] fold - **2.** [en un plisado] pleat.

plisado *sm* pleating.

plisar *vt* to pleat.

plomada *sf* plumb line.

plomería *sf* *Méx, R Plata & Ven* plumber's.

plomero *sm* *Amér C, Caribe, Méx & R Plata* plumber.

plomizo, za *adj* [color] leaden.

plomo *sm* - **1.** [metal] lead; **caer a plomo** to fall o drop like a stone - **2.** [pieza de metal] lead weight - **3.** [fusible] fuse - **4.** *fam* [pelmazo] bore, drag.

pluma ◇ *sf* - **1.** [de ave] feather - **2.** [para escribir] (fountain) pen; **HIST** quill; **pluma estilográfica** fountain pen - **3.** *fig* [estilo de escribir] style - **4.** *Caribe & Méx* [bolígrafo] ballpoint pen - **5.** *Caribe, Col & Méx* [grifo] tap - **6.** *loc:* **tener mucha pluma** to be camp. ◇ *adj inv* DEP featherweight.

plumaje *sm* - **1.** [de ave] plumage - **2.** [adorno] plume.

plumazo *sm* stroke of the pen; **de un plumazo** [al tachar] with a stroke of one's pen; *fig* [al hacer algo] in one fell swoop, at a stroke.

plúmbeo, a *adj fig* tedious, heavy.

plum-cake [pluŋ'keik] (*pl* **plum-cakes**) *sm* fruit cake.

plumero *sm* feather duster; **vérsele a alguien el plumero** *fam* to have sb's number.

plumier (*pl* **plumiers**) *sm* pencil box.

plumilla *sf* nib.

plumín *sm* nib.

plumón *sm* - **1.** [de ave] down - **2.** [anorak] feather-lined anorak - **3.** *Chile & Méx* [rotulador] felt-tip pen.

plural *adj* & *sm* plural.

pluralidad *sf* diversity.

pluralismo *sm* pluralism.

pluralizar [13] *vi* to generalize.

pluriempleado, da *adj:* **estar pluriempleado** to have more than one job.

pluriempleo *sm:* **hacer pluriempleo** to have more than one job.

pluripartidismo *sm* multi-party system.

plurivalente *adj* polyvalent.

plus (*pl* **pluses**) *sm* bonus; **plus de peligrosidad** danger money *(U)*; **plus familiar** family allowance.

pluscuamperfecto *adj* & *sm* pluperfect.

plusmarca *sf* record.

plusvalía *sf* ECON appreciation, added value.

plutocracia *sf* plutocracy.

Plutón *n pr* Pluto.

plutonio *sm* plutonium.

pluvial *adj* rain *(antes de s)*.

pluviómetro *sm* rain gauge.

pluviosidad *sf* rainfall.

p.m. (*abrev de* **post merídiem**) p.m.

PNB (*abrev de* **producto nacional bruto**) *sm* GNP.

PMF (*abrev de* **preguntas más frecuentes**) *sfpl* INFORM FAQ.

PNV (*abrev de* **Partido Nacionalista Vasco**) *sm Basque nationalist party.*

Po *sm:* **el Po** the (River) Po.

población *sf* - **1.** [ciudad] town, city; [pueblo] village - **2.** *Chile* [chabola] shanty town - **3.** [habitantes] population; **población activa** working population; **población flotante** floating population - **4.** [acción de poblar] settlement, populating.

poblado, da *adj* - **1.** [habitado] inhabited; **una zona muy poblada** a densely populated area - **2.** *fig* [lleno] full; **poblado de algo** full of sthg; [barba, cejas] bushy.
◆ **poblado** *sm* settlement.

poblador, ra *sm, f* settler.

poblar [23] *vt* - **1.** [establecerse en] to settle, to colonize - **2.** *fig* [llenar]: **poblar (de)** [plantas, árboles] to plant (with); [peces etc] to stock (with) - **3.** [habitar] to inhabit.
◆ **poblarse** *vprnl* - **1.** [colonizarse] to be settled with - **2.** *fig* [llenarse] to fill up; **poblarse (de)** to fill up (with).

pobre ◇ *adj* poor; ¡**pobre hombre!** poor man!; **pobre en** lacking in; ¡**pobre de mí!** poor me! ◇ *smf* [gen] poor person; **los pobres** the poor, poor people; ¡**el pobre!** poor thing!

pobreza *sf* [escasez] poverty; **pobreza de** lack o scarcity of; **pobreza de espíritu** weakness of character.

pochismo *sm* *Amér fam language mistake caused by English influence.*

pocho, cha *adj* - **1.** [persona] off-colour - **2.** [fruta] over-ripe - **3.** *Méx fam* [americanizado] Americanized.

pocilga *sf* *lit & fig* pigsty.

pocillo *sm* *Amér* small cup.

pócima *sf* - **1.** [poción] potion - **2.** *despec* [bebida de mal sabor] concoction.

poción *sf* potion.

poco, ca ◇ *adj* little (*pl* few), not much (*pl* not many); **poca agua** not much water; **de poca importancia** of little importance; **hay po-**

cos árboles there aren't many trees; **pocas personas lo saben** few o not many people know it; **tenemos poco tiempo** we don't have much time; **hace poco tiempo** not long ago; **dame unos pocos días** give me a few days. ⬦ *pron* little (*pl* few), not much (*pl* not many); **queda poco** there's not much left; **tengo muy pocos** I don't have very many, I have very few; **pocos hay que sepan tanto** not many people know so much; **un poco** a bit; **¿me dejas un poco?** can I have a bit?; **un poco de** a bit of; **un poco de sentido común** a bit of common sense; **unos pocos** a few.

◆ **poco** *adv* - **1.** [escasamente] not much; **este niño come poco** this boy doesn't eat much; **es poco común** it's not very common; **es un poco triste** it's rather sad; **poco más o menos** more or less; **por poco** almost, nearly; **tener en poco a alguien** not to think much of sb - **2.** [brevemente]: **tardaré muy poco** I won't be long; **al poco de...** shortly after...; **dentro de poco** soon, in a short time; **hace poco** a little while ago, not long ago; **poco a poco** [progresivamente] little by little, bit by bit; **¡poco a poco!** [despacio] steady on!, slow down!

poda *sf* - **1.** [acción] pruning - **2.** [tiempo] pruning time.

podadera *sf* pruning knife.

podar *vt* to prune.

podenco *sm* hound.

poder¹ *sm* - **1.** [gen] power; **estar en/hacerse con el poder** to be in/to seize power; **poder adquisitivo** purchasing power; **poder calorífico** calorific value; **tener poder de convocatoria** to be a crowd-puller; **poderes fácticos** *the church, military and press* - **2.** [posesión]: **estar en poder de alguien** to be in sb's hands - **3.** (*gen pl*) [autorización] power, authorization; **dar poderes a alguien para que haga algo** to authorize sb to do sthg; **por poderes** by proxy.

poder² [64] ⬦ *vi* - **1.** [tener facultad] can, to be able to; **no puedo decírtelo** I can't tell you, I'm unable to tell you - **2.** [tener permiso] can, may; **no puedo salir por la noche** I'm not allowed to o I can't go out at night; **¿se puede fumar aquí?** may I smoke here? - **3.** [ser capaz moralmente] can; **no podemos portarnos así con él** we can't treat him like that - **4.** [tener posibilidad, ser posible] may, can; **podías haber cogido el tren** you could have caught the train; **puede estallar la guerra** war could o may break out; **¡hubiera podido invitarnos!** [expresa enfado] she could o might have invited us! - **5.** [ser capaz de dominar - enfermedad, rival]: **poder con** to be able to overcome - **6.** [ser capaz de realizar - tarea]: **poder con** to be able to cope with - **7.** *loc*: **a o hasta más no poder** as much as can be; **es avaro a más no poder** he's as

miserly as can be; **no poder más** [estar cansado] to be too tired to carry on; [estar harto de comer] to be full (up); [estar enfadado] to have had enough; **¿se puede?** may I come in?; **no poder con algo/alguien** [soportar] not to be able to stand sthg/sb; **no puedo con la hipocresía** I can't stand hypocrisy. ⬦ *v impers* [ser posible] may; **puede que llueva** it may o might rain; **¿vendrás mañana? - puede** will you come tomorrow? - I may do; **puede ser** perhaps, maybe. ⬦ *vt* [ser más fuerte que] to be stronger than; **tú eres más alto, pero yo te puedo** you may be taller than me, but I could still beat you up.

poderío *sm* - **1.** [poder] power - **2.** [riqueza] riches *pl*.

poderoso, sa *adj* powerful.

podio, podium *sm* podium.

podología *sf* chiropody.

podólogo, ga *sm, f* chiropodist.

podrá ⬦ *poder*.

podredumbre *sf* - **1.** [putrefacción] putrefaction - **2.** *fig* [inmoralidad] corruption.

podría *v* ⬦ *poder*.

podrido, da ⬦ *pp* ⬦ *pudrir*. ⬦ *adj* - **1.** rotten - **2.** *R Dom* [persona]: **estoy podrido** I'm fed up.

poema *sm* poem; **ser todo un poema** to be heartbreaking.

poesía *sf* - **1.** [género literario] poetry - **2.** [poema] poem.

poeta *smf* poet.

poético, ca *adj* poetic.

◆ **poética** *sf* poetics (U).

poetisa *sf* female poet.

póker = **póquer**.

polaco, ca *adj & sm, f* Polish.

◆ **polaco** *sm* [lengua] Polish.

polaina *sf* leggings *pl*.

polar *adj* polar.

polaridad *sf* polarity.

polarizar [13] *vt* - **1.** *fig* [miradas, atención, esfuerzo] to concentrate - **2.** FÍS to polarize.

◆ **polarizarse** *vprnl* [vida política, opinión pública] to become polarized.

polaroid® *sf inv* Polaroid®.

polca *sf* polka.

polea *sf* pulley.

polémico, ca *adj* controversial.

◆ **polémica** *sf* controversy.

polemizar [13] *vi* to argue, to debate.

polen *sm* pollen.

polenta *sf* cornflour.

poleo *sm* pennyroyal.

poli *fam* ⬦ *smf* cop. ⬦ *sf* cops *pl*.

poliamida *sf* polyamide.

polichinela *sm* - **1.** [personaje] Punchinello - **2.** [títere] puppet, marionette.

policía ⬦ *sm, f* policeman (*f* policewoman). ⬦ *sf*: **la policía** the police; **policía militar/secreta/urbana** military/secret/local police; **policía antidisturbios** riot police; **policía de tráfico** traffic police.

policiaco, ca, policíaco, ca *adj* police (antes de s); [novela, película] detective (antes de s).

policial *adj* police (antes de s).

policlínica *sf* general hospital.

policromo, ma, polícromo, ma *adj* polychromatic.

polideportivo, va *adj* multi-sport; [gimnasio] multi-use.
➤ **polideportivo** *sm* sports centre.

poliedro *sm* polyhedron.

poliéster *sm inv* polyester.

polietileno *sm* polythene *UK*, polyethylene *US*.

polifacético, ca *adj* multifaceted, versatile.

polifónico, ca *adj* polyphonic.

poligamia *sf* polygamy.

polígamo, ma ⬦ *adj* polygamous. ⬦ *sm, f* polygamist.

poligloto, ta, polígloto, ta *adj* & *sm, f* polyglot.

poligonal *adj* polygonal.

polígono *sm* - **1.** GEOM polygon - **2.** [terreno]: **polígono industrial/residencial** industrial/housing estate; **polígono de tiro** firing range.

polilla *sf* moth.

polinización *sf* pollination.

polinomio *sm* polynomial.

polipiel *sf* artificial skin.

pólipo *sm* polyp.

Polisario (abrev de **Frente Popular para la Liberación de Sakiet el Hamra y Río de Oro**) *sm*: **el (Frente) Polisario** the Polisario Front.

polisemia *sf* polysemy.

polisílabo, ba *adj* polysyllabic.
➤ **polisílabo** *sm* polysyllable.

politburó *sm* politburo.

politécnico, ca *adj* polytechnic.
➤ **politécnica** *sf* polytechnic.

politeísta *adj* polytheistic.

política ⬦ **político**.

politicastro *sm despec* bad politician.

político, ca *adj* - **1.** [de gobierno] political - **2.** *fig* [prudente] tactful - **3.** [pariente]: **hermano político** brother-in-law; **familia política** in-laws *pl*.
➤ **político** *sm* politician.

➤ **política** *sf* - **1.** [arte de gobernar] politics (*U*) - **2.** [modo de gobernar, táctica] policy; **política monetaria** monetary policy; **la política de avestruz** burying one's head in the sand.

politiqueo *sm despec* politicking.

politización *sf* politicization.

politizar [13] *vt* to politicize.
➤ **politizarse** *vprnl* to become politicized.

poliuretano *sm* polyurethane.

polivalencia *sf* polyvalency.

polivalente *adj* [vacuna, suero] polyvalent; [edificio, sala] multipurpose.

póliza *sf* - **1.** [de seguro] (insurance) policy - **2.** [sello] *stamp on a document showing that a certain tax has been paid.*

polizón *sm* stowaway.

polla ⬦ **pollo**.

pollera *sf* C Sur skirt.

pollería *sf* poultry shop.

pollito *sm* chick.

pollo, lla *sm, f* - **1.** ZOOL chick - **2.** (gen pl) fig [joven] young kid.
➤ **pollo** *sm* CULIN chicken.
➤ **polla** *sf vulg* cock, prick.
➤ **polla de agua** *sf* [ave] moorhen.

polo *sm* - **1.** [gen] pole; **polo magnético** magnetic pole; **polo norte/sur** North/South Pole; **polo de atracción** o **atención** fig centre of attraction; **ser polos opuestos** fig to be poles apart - **2.** ELECTR terminal; **polo negativo/positivo** negative/positive terminal - **3.** [helado] ice lolly - **4.** [jersey] polo shirt - **5.** DEP polo.

pololear *vi* Chile fam: **pololear con alguien** to go out with sb.

pololeo *sm* Chile fam small job.

pololo, la *sm, f* Chile fam boyfriend (*f* girlfriend).

Polonia *n pr* Poland.

polución *sf* - **1.** [contaminación] pollution - **2.** [eyaculación]: **polución nocturna** wet dream.

polucionar *vt* to pollute.

polvareda *sf* dust cloud; **levantar una gran polvareda** fig to cause a commotion.

polvera *sf* powder compact.

polvo *sm* - **1.** [en el aire] dust; **limpiar** o **quitar el polvo** to do the dusting - **2.** [de un producto] powder; **en polvo** powdered; **polvos de talco** talcum powder; **polvos picapica** itching powder; **estar hecho polvo** fam to be knackered; **hacer polvo algo** to smash sthg; **limpio de polvo y paja** including all charges; **morder el polvo** to be humiliated - **3.** *vulg* [coito] fuck, screw; **echar un polvo** to have a screw.

polvos *smpl* [maquillaje] powder *(U)*; **ponerse polvos** to powder one's face.

pólvora *sf* [sustancia explosiva] gunpowder; **correr como la pólvora** to spread like wildfire; **no ha inventado la pólvora** *fam* he's not the most intelligent person in the world.

polvoriento, ta *adj* [superficie] dusty; [sustancia] powdery.

polvorín *sm* munitions dump.

polvorón *sm* *crumbly sweet made from flour, butter and sugar.*

pomada *sf* ointment.

pomelo *sm* - **1.** [fruto] grapefruit - **2.** [árbol] grapefruit tree.

pómez ⊳ **piedra**.

pomo *sm* knob.

pompa *sf* - **1.** [suntuosidad] pomp - **2.** [ostentación] show, ostentation - **3.:** **pompa (de jabón)** (soap) bubble.

pompas *sfpl* *Méx fam* behind, bottom.

pompas fúnebres *sfpl* - **1.** [servicio] undertaker's *sing* - **2.** [ceremonia] funeral *sing*.

Pompeya *n pr* Pompeii.

pompis *sm inv fam* bottom, backside.

pompón *sm* pompom.

pomposidad *sf* - **1.** [suntuosidad] splendour; [ostentación] showiness - **2.** [en el lenguaje] pomposity.

pomposo, sa *adj* - **1.** [suntuoso] sumptuous; [ostentoso] magnificent, showy - **2.** [lenguaje] pompous.

pómulo *sm* - **1.** [hueso] cheekbone - **2.** [mejilla] cheek.

pon *v* ⊳ **poner**.

ponchar *vt* *Amér C, Caribe & Méx* [rueda] to puncture.

ponchar *vt* *Amér C & Méx* [rueda] to puncture.

poncharse *vprnl* *Amér C & Méx* [rueda] to puncture.

ponche *sm* punch.

ponchera *sf* punch bowl.

poncho *sm* poncho.

ponderación *sf* - **1.** [alabanza] praise - **2.** [moderación] deliberation, considered nature.

ponderado, da *adj* [moderado] considered.

ponderar *vt* - **1.** [alabar] to praise - **2.** [considerar] to consider, to weigh up.

pondrá *etc* ⊳ **poner**.

ponencia *sf* [conferencia] lecture, paper; [informe] report.

ponente *smf* reporter, rapporteur; [en congreso] speaker.

poner [65] ◇ *vt* - **1.** [gen] to put; [colocar] to place, to put - **2.** [vestir]: **poner algo a alguien**

to put sthg on sb - **3.** [contribuir, invertir] to put in; **poner dinero en el negocio** to put money into the business; **poner algo de mi/tu** *etc* **parte** to do my/your *etc* bit - **4.** [hacer estar de cierta manera]: **poner a alguien en un aprieto/de mal humor** to put sb in a difficult position/in a bad mood; **le has puesto colorado** you've made him blush - **5.** [calificar]: **poner a alguien de algo** to call sb sthg - **6.** [oponer]: **poner obstáculos a algo** to hinder sthg; **poner pegas a algo** to raise objections to sthg - **7.** [asignar - precio, medida] to fix, to settle; [- multa, tarea] to give; **le pusieron Mario** they called him Mario - **8.** [TELECOM - telegrama, fax] to send; [- conferencia] to make; **¿me pones con él?** can you put me through to him? - **9.** [conectar - televisión etc] to switch *o* put on; [- despertador] to set; [- instalación, gas] to put in - **10.** CINE, TEATRO & TV to show; **¿qué ponen en la tele?** what's on the telly? - **11.** [montar - negocio] to set up; **ha puesto una tienda** she has opened a shop - **12.** [decorar] to do up; **han puesto su casa con mucho lujo** they've done up their house in real style - **13.** [suponer] to suppose; **pongamos que sucedió así** (let's) suppose that's what happened; **pon que necesitemos cinco días** suppose we need five days; **poniendo que todo salga bien** assuming everything goes according to plan - **14.** [decir] to say; **¿qué pone ahí?** what does it say? - **15.** [huevo] to lay. ◇ *vi* [ave] to lay (eggs).

ponerse ◇ *vprnl* - **1.** [colocarse] to put o.s.; **ponerse de pie** to stand up; **ponte en la ventana** stand by the window - **2.** [ropa, gafas, maquillaje] to put on - **3.** [estar de cierta manera] to go, to become; **se puso rojo de ira** he went red with anger; **se puso colorado** he blushed; **se puso muy guapa** she made herself attractive - **4.** [iniciar]: **ponerse a hacer algo** to start doing sthg - **5.** [de salud]: **ponerse malo** *o* **enfermo** to fall ill; **ponerse bien** to get better - **6.** [llenarse]: **ponerse de algo** to get covered in sthg; **se puso de barro hasta las rodillas** he got covered in mud up to the knees - **7.** [suj: astro] to set - **8.** [llegar]: **ponerse en** to get to. ◇ *v impers* *Amér fam* [parecer]: **se me pone que...** it seems to me that...

pongo ⊳ **poner**.

poniente *sm* [occidente] West; [viento] west wind.

pontificado *sm* papacy.

pontífice *sm* Pope, Pontiff.

pontificio, cia *adj* papal.

ponzoña *sf* [veneno] venom, poison.

ponzoñoso, sa *adj* [venenoso] venomous, poisonous.

pop ◇ *adj* pop. ◇ *sm* ⊳ **música**.

popa *sf* stern.

popelina *sf* poplin.

popelín *sm* = popelina.

popote *sm* Méx drinking straw.

populachero, ra *adj despec* - **1.** [fiesta etc] common, popular - **2.** [discurso etc] populist.

populacho *sm despec* mob, masses *pl*.

popular *adj* - **1.** [del pueblo] of the people; [arte, música] folk - **2.** [famoso] popular.

popularidad *sf* popularity; **gozar de popularidad** to be popular.

popularizar [13] *vt* to popularize.

➡ **popularizarse** *vprnl* to become popular.

populismo *sm* populism.

populista *adj* & *smf* populist.

populoso, sa *adj* populous, crowded.

popurrí *sm* potpourri.

póquer, póker *sm* - **1.** [juego] poker - **2.** [jugada] four of a kind.

por *prep* - **1.** [causa] because of; **se enfadó por tu comportamiento** she got angry because of your behaviour - **2.** *(antes de infinitivo)* [finalidad] (in order) to; *(antes de s, pron)* for; **lo hizo por complacerte** he did it to please you; **lo hice por ella** I did it for her - **3.** [medio, modo, agente] by; **por mensajero/fax** by courier/fax; **por escrito** in writing; **lo cogieron por el brazo** they took him by the arm; **el récord fue batido por el atleta** the record was broken by the athlete - **4.** [tiempo aproximado]: **creo que la boda será por abril** I think the wedding will be some time in April - **5.** [tiempo concreto]: **por la mañana/tarde** in the morning/afternoon; **por la noche** at night; **ayer salimos por la noche** we went out last night; **por unos días** for a few days - **6.** [lugar - aproximadamente en]: **¿por dónde vive?** whereabouts does he live?; **vive por las afueras** he lives somewhere on the outskirts; **había papeles por el suelo** there were papers all over the floor - **7.** [lugar - a través de] through; **iba paseando por el bosque/la calle** she was walking through the forest/along the street; **pasar por la aduana** to go through customs - **8.** [a cambio de, en lugar de] for; **lo ha comprado por poco dinero** she bought it for very little; **cambió el coche por la moto** he exchanged his car for a motorbike; **él lo hará por mí** he'll do it for me - **9.** [distribución] per; **dos euros por unidad** 2 euros each; **20 kms por hora** 20 km an o per hour - **10.** MAT: **dos por dos igual a cuatro** two times two is four - **11.** [en busca de] for; **baja por tabaco** go down to the shops for some cigarettes, go down to get some cigarettes; **a por** for; **vino a por las entradas** she came for the tickets - **12.** [concesión]: **por más** o **mucho que lo intentes no lo conseguirás** however hard you try o try as you might, you'll never

manage it; **no me cae bien, por (muy) simpático que te parezca** you may think he's nice, but I don't like him.

➡ **por qué** *pron* why; **¿por qué lo dijo?** why did she say it?; **¿por qué no vienes?** why don't you come?

porcelana *sf* - **1.** [material] porcelain, china - **2.** [objeto] piece of porcelain o china.

porcentaje *sm* percentage; **trabaja a porcentaje** he works on a commission basis.

porcentual *adj* percentage *(antes de s)*.

porche *sm* [soportal] arcade; [entrada] porch.

porcino, na *adj* pig *(antes de s)*.

porción *sf* portion, piece.

pordiosero, ra *sm, f* beggar.

porfía *sf* [insistencia] persistence; [tozudez] stubbornness.

porfiado, da *adj* persistent; [tozudo] stubborn.

porfiar [9] *vi* [empeñarse]: **porfiar en** to be insistent on.

pormenor *(gen pl) sm* detail; **entrar en pormenores** to go into detail.

pormenorizar [13] ◇ *vt* to describe in detail. ◇ *vi* to go into detail.

porno *adj fam* porno.

pornografía *sf* pornography.

pornográfico, ca *adj* pornographic.

poro *sm* pore.

poroso, sa *adj* porous.

poroto *sm Andes & R Plata* kidney bean.

porque *conj* - **1.** [debido a que] because; **¿por qué lo hiciste? – porque sí** why did you do it? – just because - **2.** [para que] so that, in order that.

porqué *sm* reason; **el porqué de** the reason for.

porquería *sf* - **1.** [suciedad] filth - **2.** [cosa de mala calidad] rubbish *(U)* - **3.** *despec* [golosina] junk food, rubbish *(U)*.

porquero, ra *sm, f* swineherd.

porra ◇ *sf* - **1.** [palo] club; [de policía] truncheon - **2.** CULIN *deep-fried pastry sticks* - **3.** *Méx* DEP [hinchada] supporters - **4.** *loc*: **mandar a alguien a la porra** *fam* to tell sb to go to hell; **¡y una porra!** like hell! ◇ *interj (gen pl) fam*: **¡porras!** hell!, damn it!

porrada *sf fam*: **una porrada (de)** heaps *pl* o tons *pl* (of).

porrazo *sm* [golpe] bang, blow; [caída] bump.

porreta ◇ *smf mfam* [fumador de porros] pothead. ◇ *sf fam* [nariz] hooter.

porrillo ➡ **a porrillo** *loc adv fam* by the bucket.

porro *sm fam* [de droga] joint.

porrón *sm* glass wine jar used for drinking wine from its long spout.

portaaviones, portaviones *sm inv* aircraft carrier.

portabustos *sm inv Amér* bra *sing.*

portada *sf* - **1.** [de libro] title page; [de revista] (front) cover; [de periódico] front page - **2.** [de disco] sleeve.

portador, ra ⬦ *adj* carrying, bearing. ⬦ *sm, f* carrier, bearer; **al portador** COM to the bearer.

portaequipajes *sm inv* - **1.** [maletero] boot UK, trunk US - **2.** [baca] roofrack.

portaestandarte *sm* standard-bearer.

portafolio *sm* = portafolios.

portafolios *sm inv* [carpeta] file; [maletín] attaché case.

portal *sm* - **1.** [entrada] entrance hall; [puerta] main door - **2.** [belén] crib, Nativity scene - **3.** INFORM [página web] portal.

portalámparas *sm inv* socket.

portaligas *sm inv* suspender belt.

portamaletas *sm inv Amér* boot UK, trunk US.

portamonedas *sm inv* purse.

portar *vt* to carry.
➡ **portarse** *vprnl* to behave; **se ha portado bien conmigo** she has treated me well; **portarse mal** to misbehave.

portátil *adj* portable.

portavoz *sm, f* [persona] spokesman (*f* spokeswoman).

portazo *sm*: **dar un portazo** to slam the door.

porte *sm* - **1.** *(gen pl)* [gasto de transporte] carriage, transport costs *pl*; **porte debido/pagado** COM carriage due/paid - **2.** [transporte] carriage, transport - **3.** [aspecto] bearing, demeanour.

porteador, ra ⬦ *adj* bearing, carrying. ⬦ *sm, f* porter.

portento *sm* wonder, marvel.

portentoso, sa *adj* wonderful, amazing.

porteño, ña *adj* from the city of Buenos Aires.

portería *sf* - **1.** [de casa, colegio] caretaker's UK o super(intendant)'s US office o lodge; [de hotel, ministerio] porter's office o lodge - **2.** DEP goal, goalmouth.

portero, ra *sm, f* - **1.** [de casa, colegio] caretaker UK, super(intendant) US; [de hotel, ministerio] porter; **portero automático** o **electrónico** o **eléctrico** entry-phone - **2.** DEP goalkeeper.

pórtico *sm* - **1.** [fachada] portico - **2.** [arcada] arcade.

portón *sm* large door o entrance.

portuario, ria *adj* port *(antes de s)*; [de los muelles] dock *(antes de s)*; **trabajador portuario** docker.

Portugal *n pr* Portugal.

portugués, esa *adj* & *sm, f* Portuguese.
➡ **portugués** *sm* [lengua] Portuguese.

porvenir *sm* future.

pos ➡ **en pos de** *loc prep* - **1.** [detrás de] behind - **2.** [en busca de] after; **correr en pos de alguien** to run after sb.

posada *sf* - **1.** [fonda] inn, guest house - **2.** [hospedaje] lodging, accommodation.

posaderas *sfpl fam* backside *sing*, bottom *sing.*

posadero, ra *sm, f* innkeeper.

posar ⬦ *vt* to put o lay down; [mano, mirada] to rest. ⬦ *vi* to pose.
➡ **posarse** *vprnl* - **1.** [gen] to settle - **2.** [pájaro] to perch; [nave, helicóptero] to come down.

posavasos *sm inv* coaster; [de cartón] beer mat.

posdata, postdata *sf* postscript.

pose *sf* pose; **adoptar una pose** to strike a pose.

poseedor, ra ⬦ *adj* owning, possessing; [de cargo, acciones, récord] holding. ⬦ *sm, f* owner; [de cargo, acciones, récord] holder.

poseer **[50]** *vt* - **1.** [ser dueño de] to own; [estar en poder de] to have, to possess - **2.** [sexualmente] to have.

poseído, da ⬦ *adj*: **poseído por** possessed by. ⬦ *sm, f* possessed person.

posesión *sf* possession; **estar en plena posesión de todas sus facultades** to be in full possession of his/her faculties; **tomar posesión de un cargo** to take up a position o post.

posesivo, va *adj* possessive.
➡ **posesivo** *sm* GRAM possessive.

poseso, sa ⬦ *adj* possessed. ⬦ *sm, f* possessed person.

poseyera *etc* ⊳ poseer.

posgraduado, da, postgraduado, da *adj* & *sm, f* postgraduate.

posguerra, postguerra *sf* post-war period.

posibilidad *sf* possibility, chance; **cabe la posibilidad de que...** there is a chance that...
➡ **posibilidades económicas** *sfpl* financial means o resources.

posibilitar *vt* to make possible.

posible *adj* possible; **es posible que llueva** it could rain; **dentro de lo posible, en lo posible** as far as possible; **de ser posible** if possible; **hacer (todo) lo posible** to do everything possible; **lo antes posible** as soon as possible; **¡no es posible!** surely not!
➡ **posibles** *smpl* (financial) means.

posición *sf* - **1.** [gen] position; **en posición de descanso** standing at ease - **2.** [categoría - social] status *(U)*; **de buena posición** of high social status; [- económica] situation - **3.** DEP position.

posicionarse *vprnl* to take a position *o* stance.

positivar *vt* FOTO to develop.

positivismo *sm* - **1.** [realismo] pragmatism - **2.** FILOS positivism.

positivo, va *adj* [gen & ELECTR] positive.
➡ **positivo** *sm* FOTO print.

posmeridiano, na, postmeridiano, na *adj* afternoon *(antes de s).*

posmodernidad *sf* post-modernism.

posmoderno, na *adj* & *sm, f* postmodernist.

poso *sm* sediment; *fig* trace.

posología *sf* dosage.

posponer [65] *vt* - **1.** [relegar] to put behind, to relegate - **2.** [aplazar] to postpone.

pospuesto, ta *pp* ▷ **posponer**.

pospusiera *etc* ▷ **posponer**.

posta ➡ **a posta** *loc adv* on purpose.

postal ◇ *adj* postal. ◇ *sf* postcard.

postdata = **posdata**.

poste *sm* post, pole; **poste de alta tensión** electricity pylon; DEP post.

póster (*pl* **posters**) *sm* poster.

postergar [16] *vt* - **1.** [retrasar] to postpone - **2.** [relegar] to put behind, to relegate.

posteridad *sf* - **1.** [generación futura] posterity - **2.** [futuro] future.

posterior *adj* - **1.** [en el espacio] rear, back; **posterior a** behind - **2.** [en el tiempo] subsequent, later; **posterior a** subsequent to, after.

posteriori ➡ **a posteriori** *loc adv* later, afterwards.

posterioridad *sf*: **con posterioridad** later, subsequently.

postgraduado = **posgraduado**.

postguerra = **posguerra**.

postigo *sm* - **1.** [contraventana] shutter - **2.** [puerta pequeña] wicket gate.

postín *sm* showiness, boastfulness; **darse postín** to show off; **de postín** posh.

post-it® *sm inv* Post-it®.

postizo, za *adj* - **1.** [falso] false - **2.** [añadido] detachable.
➡ **postizo** *sm* hairpiece.

postmeridiano = **posmeridiano**.

post meridiem *adj* post meridiem.

postoperatorio, ria *adj* post-operative.

postor, ra *sm, f* bidder; **mejor postor** highest bidder.

postración *sf* prostration.

postrar *vt* to weaken, to (make) prostrate.
➡ **postrarse** *vprnl* to prostrate o.s.

postre *sm* dessert, pudding; **de postre** for dessert; **a la postre** *fig* in the end; **para postre** *fig* to cap it all.

postrero, ra *adj (antes de sm sing:* **postrer***) culto* last.

postrimerías *sfpl* final stages.

postulado *sm* postulate.

postulante, ta *sm, f* [para colectas] collector; RELIG postulant.

postular ◇ *vt* [exigir] to call for. ◇ *vi* [para colectas] to collect.

póstumo, ma *adj* posthumous.

postura *sf* - **1.** [posición] position, posture - **2.** [actitud] attitude, stance; **tomar postura** to adopt an attitude.

posventa, postventa *adj inv* after-sales *(antes de s).*

potable *adj* - **1.** [bebible] drinkable; **agua potable** drinking water - **2.** *fam* [aceptable] acceptable, passable.

potaje *sm* [CULIN - guiso] vegetable stew; [- sopa] vegetable soup.

potasio *sm* potassium.

pote *sm* pot.

potencia *sf* - **1.** [gen, MAT & POLÍT] power; **tiene mucha potencia** it's very powerful; **las grandes potencias** the major (world) powers - **2.** [posibilidad]: **en potencia** potentially; **una campeona en potencia** a potential champion.

potencial ◇ *adj* [gen & FÍS] potential. ◇ *sm* - **1.** [fuerza] power - **2.** [posibilidades] potential - **3.** GRAM conditional - **4.** ELECTR (electric) potential.

potenciar [8] *vt* - **1.** [fomentar] to encourage, to promote - **2.** [reforzar] to boost, to strengthen.

potentado, da *sm, f* potentate.

potente *adj* powerful.

potestad *sf* authority, power.

potingue *sm fam* concoction.

potra ▷ **potro**.

potrero *sm Amér* [prado] field, pasture.

potrillo *sm Amér* large glass.

potro, tra *sm, f* ZOOL colt (*f* filly).
➡ **potro** *sm* DEP vaulting horse.
➡ **potra** *sf mfam* [suerte] luck; **tener potra** to be jammy.

pozo *sm* well; [de mina] shaft; **pozo negro** cesspool; **pozo de petróleo** oil well; **ser un pozo de algo** *fig* to be a fountain of sthg; **ser un pozo sin fondo** *fig* to be a bottomless pit.

PP (*abrev de* **Partido Popular**) *sm Spanish political party to the right of the political spectrum.*

ppp (*abrev de* **puntos por pulgada**) INFORM dpi.

práctica ⊏▷ **práctico**.

practicable *adj* **- 1.** [realizable] practicable **- 2.** [transitable] passable.

practicante ◇ *adj* practising. ◇ *smf* **- 1.** [de deporte] practitioner; [de religión] practising member of a church **- 2.** MED medical assistant.

practicar [10] ◇ *vt* **- 1.** [gen] to practise; [deporte] to play **- 2.** [realizar] to carry out, to perform. ◇ *vi* to practise.

práctico, ca *adj* practical.

➤ **práctico** *sm* NÁUT pilot.

➤ **práctica** *sf* **- 1.** [gen] practice; [de un deporte] playing; **llevar algo a la práctica, poner algo en práctica** to put sthg into practice; **en la práctica** in practice; **prácticas de tiro** target practice **- 2.** [clase no teórica] practical.

pradera *sf* large meadow, prairie.

prado *sm* meadow.

➤ **Prado** *sm*: **el (Museo del) Prado** the Prado (Museum).

pragmático, ca ◇ *adj* pragmatic. ◇ *sm, f* [persona] pragmatist.

➤ **pragmática** *sf* LING pragmatics (U).

pragmatismo *sm* pragmatism.

pral. *abrev de* **principal**.

praliné *sm* praline.

praxis *sf inv* practice; FILOS praxis.

PRD *sm* (*abrev de* **Partido de la Revolución Democrática**), *Mexican political party.*

preacuerdo *sm* draft agreement.

preámbulo *sm* **- 1.** [introducción - de libro] foreword, preface; [- de congreso, conferencia] introduction, preamble **- 2.** [rodeo] digression; **sin más preámbulos** without further ado.

preaviso *sm* prior notice.

prebenda *sf* **- 1.** RELIG prebend **- 2.** [favor] special favour.

precalentamiento *sm* DEP warm-up.

precalentar [19] *vt* **- 1.** CULIN to pre-heat **- 2.** DEP to warm up.

precampaña *sf* preliminary campaign.

precariedad *sf* precariousness.

precario, ria *adj* precarious.

precaución *sf* **- 1.** [prudencia] caution, care **- 2.** [medida] precaution; **tomar precauciones** to take precautions.

precaver *vt* to guard against.

➤ **precaverse** *vprnl* to take precautions; **precaverse de** o **contra** to guard (o.s.) against.

precavido, da *adj* **- 1.** [prevenido] prudent; **es muy precavido** he always comes prepared **- 2.** [cauteloso] wary.

precedente ◇ *adj* previous, preceding. ◇ *sm* precedent; **sentar precedente** to set a precedent; **que no sirva de precedente** this is not to become a regular occurrence; **sin precedentes** unprecedented.

preceder *vt* to go before, to precede.

preceptivo, va *adj* obligatory, compulsory.

➤ **preceptiva** *sf* rules *pl*.

precepto *sm* precept; **fiestas de precepto** RELIG days of obligation.

preceptor, ra *sm, f* (private) tutor.

preciado, da *adj* valuable, prized.

preciarse [8] *vprnl* to have self-respect; **preciarse de** to be proud of.

precintado *sm* sealing.

precintadora *sf* sealing machine.

precintar *vt* to seal.

precinto *sm* seal.

precio *sm lit & fig* price; **a cualquier precio** at any price; **poner precio a la cabeza de alguien** to put a price on sb's head; **¿qué precio tiene esto?** how much is this?; **subir/bajar los precios** to raise/lower prices; **al precio de** *fig* at the cost of; **precio de fábrica/de coste** factory/cost price; **precio de compra** purchase price; **precio indicativo** ECON guide price; **precio de mercado** market price; **precio prohibitivo** prohibitively high price; **precio de salida** starting price; **precio de venta (al público)** retail price; **no tener precio** to be priceless.

preciosidad *sf* **- 1.** [valor] value **- 2.** [cosa bonita]: **¡es una preciosidad!** it's lovely o beautiful!

precioso, sa *adj* **- 1.** [valioso] precious **- 2.** [bonito] lovely, beautiful.

precipicio *sm* precipice.

precipitación *sf* **- 1.** [apresuramiento] haste **- 2.** [lluvia] rainfall (U) **- 3.** QUÍM precipitation.

precipitado, da *adj* hasty.

➤ **precipitado** *sm* QUÍM precipitate.

precipitar *vt* **- 1.** [arrojar] to throw o hurl down **- 2.** [acelerar] to hasten, to speed up **- 3.** QUÍM to precipitate.

➤ **precipitarse** *vprnl* **- 1.** [caer] to plunge (down) **- 2.** [acelerarse - acontecimientos etc] to speed up **- 3.** [apresurarse]: **precipitarse (hacia)** to rush (towards) **- 4.** [obrar irreflexivamente] to act rashly.

precisamente *adv* **- 1.** [con precisión] precisely **- 2.** [justamente]: **¡precisamente!** exactly!, precisely!; **precisamente por eso** for that very reason; **precisamente tú lo sugeriste** in fact it was you who suggested it.

precisar *vt* - **1.** [determinar] to fix, to set; [aclarar] to specify exactly - **2.** [necesitar] to need, to require.

precisión *sf* accuracy, precision.

preciso, **sa** *adj* - **1.** [determinado, conciso] precise - **2.** [necesario]: **ser preciso (para algo/hacer algo)** to be necessary (for sthg/to do sthg); **es preciso que vengas** you must come - **3.** [justo] just; **en este preciso momento** at this very moment.

precocidad *sf* precociousness.

precocinado, **da** *adj* pre-cooked.
➡ **precocinado** *sm* pre-cooked dish.

precolombino, **na** *adj* pre-Columbian.

preconcebido, **da** *adj* [idea] preconceived; [plan] drawn up in advance.

preconcebir [26] *vt* to draw up in advance.

preconizar [13] *vt* to recommend, to advise.

precoz *adj* - **1.** [persona] precocious - **2.** [lluvias, frutos etc] early.

precursor, **ra** *sm, f* precursor.

predador, **ra** *adj* predatory.
➡ **predador** *sm* predator.

predatorio, **ria** *adj* [animal, instinto] predatory.

predecesor, **ra** *sm, f* predecessor.

predecir [66] *vt* to predict.

predestinado, **da** *adj*: **predestinado (a)** predestined (to).

predestinar *vt* to predestine.

predeterminar *vt* to predetermine.

predicado *sm* GRAM predicate.

predicador, **ra** *sm, f* preacher.

predicar [10] *vt* & *vi* to preach.

predicción *sf* prediction; [del tiempo] forecast.

predice ⊳ **predecir**.

predicho, **cha** *pp* ⊳ **predecir**.

prediga, **predijera** ⊳ **predecir**.

predilección *sf*: **predilección (por)** preference (for).

predilecto, **ta** *adj* favourite.

predio *sm* - **1.** [finca] estate, property - **2.** *Amér* [edificio] building.

predisponer [65] *vt*: **predisponer (a)** to predispose (to).

predisposición *sf* - **1.** [aptitud]: **predisposición para** aptitude for - **2.** [tendencia]: **predisposición a** predisposition to.

predispuesto, **ta** ⟨⟩ *pp* ⊳ **predisponer**. ⟨⟩ *adj*: **predispuesto (a)** predisposed (to).

predominancia *sf* predominance.

predominante *adj* predominant; [viento, actitudes] prevailing.

predominar *vi*: **predominar (sobre)** to predominate o prevail (over).

predominio *sm* preponderance, predominance (U).

preelectoral *adj* pre-election (antes de s).

preeminencia *sf* preeminence.

preeminente *adj* preeminent.

preescolar ⟨⟩ *adj* nursery (antes de s), preschool. ⟨⟩ *sm* nursery school, kindergarten.

preestreno *sm* preview.

preexistente *adj* pre-existing.

prefabricado, **da** *adj* prefabricated.

prefabricar [10] *vt* to prefabricate.

prefacio *sm* preface.

prefecto *sm* prefect.

prefectura *sf* prefecture; **prefectura de tráfico** traffic division.

preferencia *sf* preference; **con** o **de preferencia** preferably; **dar preferencia (a)** to give priority (to); **tener preferencia** AUTO to have right of way; **tener preferencia por** to have a preference for.

preferente *adj* preferential.

preferentemente *adv* preferably.

preferible *adj*: **preferible (a)** preferable (to).

preferido, **da** *adj* favourite.

preferir [27] *vt*: **preferir algo (a algo)** to prefer sthg (to sthg); **prefiero que vengas** I'd rather you came.

prefigurar *vt* to prefigure.

prefijo *sm* - **1.** GRAM prefix - **2.** TELECOM (telephone) dialling code.

prefiriera *etc* ⊳ **preferir**.

pregón *sm* [discurso] speech; [bando] proclamation, announcement.

pregonar *vt* - **1.** [bando etc] to proclaim, to announce - **2.** *fig* [secreto] to spread about.

pregonero, **ra** *sm, f* - **1.** [de pueblo] town crier - **2.** *despec* [bocazas] blabbermouth.

pregunta *sf* question; **hacer una pregunta** to ask a question; **pregunta capciosa** catch question; **andar a la cuarta** o **última pregunta** to be broke.

preguntar ⟨⟩ *vt* to ask; **preguntar algo a alguien** to ask sb sthg. ⟨⟩ *vi*: **preguntar por** to ask about o after.
➡ **preguntarse** *vprnl*: **preguntarse (si)** to wonder (whether).

prehistoria *sf* prehistory.

prehistórico, **ca** *adj* prehistoric.
prejubilación *sf* early retirement.

Prejubilación

Early retirement ("jubilación anticipada") is for workers aged 61-64. Retirement before 61 falls into the category of prejubilación, and as many as 60-70,000 Spaniards take this option annually, with the result that fewer than 40% of Spaniards aged 55-64 are economically active – some 10% lower than the current EU target for 2010. Prejubilación reduces costs for employers, and enables workers to leave a job on better terms than becoming unemployed, but it places a major burden on the cost of state pension provision.

prejuicio *sm* prejudice.
prejuzgar [16] *vt* & *vi* to prejudge.
prelado *sm* prelate.
preliminar ⬦ *adj* preliminary. ⬦ *sm* (gen pl) preliminary.
➤ **preliminares** *smpl* [de tratado de paz] results of preliminary negotiations.
preludio *sm* [gen & MÚS] prelude.
premamá *adj inv* maternity.
prematrimonial *adj* premarital.
prematuro, **ra** *adj* premature.
premeditación *sf* premeditation; **premeditación y alevosía** malice aforethought.
premeditado, **da** *adj* premeditated.
premeditar *vt* to think out in advance.
premiar [8] *vt* - **1.** [recompensar] to reward - **2.** [dar un premio a] to give a prize to.
premier (*pl* **premiers**) *sm* British prime minister.
premio *sm* - **1.** [en competición] prize; [recompensa] reward; **me tocó un premio** I won a prize; **premio de consolación** consolation prize; **premio gordo** first prize - **2.** [ganador] prize-winner.
premisa *sf* premise.
premolar *adj* & *sm* premolar.
premonición *sf* premonition.
premonitorio, **ria** *adj* warning.
premura *sf* [urgencia] haste.
prenatal *adj* prenatal, antenatal.
prenda *sf* - **1.** [vestido] garment, article of clothing - **2.** [garantía] pledge; **dejar algo en prenda** to leave sthg as a pledge - **3.** [de un juego] forfeit; **jugar a las prendas** to play forfeits - **4.** *loc*: **no soltar prenda** not to say a word.
prendarse *vprnl* to fall in love with.
prendedor *sm* brooch.

prender ⬦ *vt* - **1.** [arrestar] to arrest, to apprehend - **2.** [sujetar] to fasten - **3.** [encender] to light - **4.** [agarrar] to grip. ⬦ *vi* - **1.** [arder] to catch (fire) - **2.** [planta] to take root.
➤ **prenderse** *vprnl* [arder] to catch fire.
prendido, **da** *adj* caught; **quedar prendido de** *fig* to be captivated by.
prensa *sf* - **1.** [gen] press; **prensa amarilla** the gutter press, ≃ the tabloids; **prensa del corazón** romantic magazines *pl*; **tener buena/mala prensa** *fig* to have a good/bad press - **2.** [imprenta] printing press.
prensar *vt* to press.
prenupcial *adj* premarital.
preñado, **da** *adj* - **1.** [mujer] pregnant; **quedarse preñada** to get pregnant - **2.** *fig* [lleno]: **preñado de** full of.
➤ **preñada** *sf* pregnant woman.
preñar *vt* - **1.** [mujer] to make pregnant - **2.** *fig* [llenar]: **preñar de** to fill with.
preñez *sf* pregnancy.
preocupación *sf* concern, worry.
preocupado, **da** *adj*: **preocupado (por)** worried *o* concerned (about).
preocupante *adj* worrying.
preocupar *vt* - **1.** [inquietar] to worry - **2.** [importar] to bother.
➤ **preocuparse** *vprnl* - **1.** [inquietarse]: **preocuparse (por)** to worry (about), to be worried (about) - **2.** [encargarse]: **preocuparse de algo** to take care of sthg; **preocuparse de hacer algo** to see to it that sthg is done; **preocuparse de que...** to make sure that...
preolímpico, **ca** *adj* in the run-up to the Olympics; **torneo preolímpico** Olympic qualifying competition.
preparación *sf* - **1.** [gen] preparation - **2.** [conocimientos] training.
preparado, **da** *adj* - **1.** [dispuesto] ready; [de antemano] prepared; **¡preparados, listos, ya!** ready, steady, go! - **2.** [capacitado]: **preparado (para)** competent *o* talented (in) - **3.** CULIN ready-cooked.
➤ **preparado** *sm* [sustancia] preparation.
preparar *vt* - **1.** [gen] to prepare; [trampa] to set, to lay; [maletas] to pack - **2.** [examen] to prepare for - **3.** DEP to train.
➤ **prepararse** *vprnl*: **prepararse (para algo)** to prepare o.s. *o* get ready (for sthg); **prepararse para hacer algo** to prepare *o* get ready to do sthg.
preparativo, **va** *adj* preparatory, preliminary.
➤ **preparativos** *smpl* preparations.
preparatorio, **ria** *adj* preparatory.

preponderancia *sf* preponderance; **tener preponderancia (sobre)** to predominate (over).

preponderante *adj* prevailing.

preponderar *vi* to prevail.

preposición *sf* preposition.

preposicional *adj* prepositional.

prepotencia *sf* [arrogancia] arrogance.

prepotente *adj* [arrogante] domineering, overbearing.

prepucio *sm* foreskin.

prerrogativa *sf* prerogative.

presa *sf* - **1.** [captura - de cazador] catch; [- de animal] prey; **hacer presa en alguien** to seize *o* grip sb; **ser presa de** to be prey to; **ser presa del pánico** to be panic-stricken - **2.** [dique] dam.

presagiar [8] *vt* [felicidad, futuro] to foretell; [tormenta, problemas] to warn of.

presagio *sm* - **1.** [premonición] premonition - **2.** [señal] omen; **buen/mal presagio** good/bad omen.

presbiterianismo *sm* Presbyterianism.

presbiteriano, **na** *adj & sm, f* Presbyterian.

presbiterio *sm* presbytery.

prescindir ◆ **prescindir de** *vi* - **1.** [renunciar a] to do without - **2.** [omitir] to dispense with - **3.** [no tener en cuenta] to disregard.

prescribir ◇ *vt* to prescribe. ◇ *vi* - **1.** [ordenar] to prescribe - **2.** DER to expire, to lapse.

prescripción *sf* prescription; **prescripción facultativa** medical prescription.

prescrito, **ta** *pp* ▷ **prescribir**.

preselección *sf* short list, shortlisting (U).

preseleccionar *vt* to shortlist; DEP to name in the squad.

presencia *sf* [asistencia, aspecto] presence; **en presencia de** in the presence of; **buena/mala presencia** good/bad looks *pl*; **mucha/poca presencia** great/little presence.

◆ **presencia de ánimo** *sf* presence of mind.

presencial ▷ **testigo**.

presenciar [8] *vt* [asistir] to be present at; [ser testigo de] to witness.

presentable *adj* presentable.

presentación *sf* - **1.** [gen] presentation - **2.** [entre personas] introduction.

presentador, **ra** *sm, f* presenter.

presentar *vt* - **1.** [gen] to present; [dimisión] to tender; [tesis, pruebas, propuesta] to hand in, to submit; [solicitud, recurso, denuncia] to lodge; [moción] to propose; [libro, disco] to launch - **2.** [ofrecer - ventajas, novedades] to offer; [- disculpas, excusas] to make; [- respetos] to pay - **3.** [persona, amigos etc] to introduce; **me pre-**

sentó a sus amigos she introduced me to her friends - **4.** [enseñar] to show - **5.** [tener - aspecto etc] to have, to show; **presenta difícil solución** it's going to be difficult to solve - **6.** [proponer]: **presentar a alguien para** to propose sb for, to put sb forward for.

◆ **presentarse** *vprnl* - **1.** [aparecer] to turn up, to appear - **2.** [en juzgado, comisaría]: **presentarse (en)** to report (to); **presentarse a un examen** to sit an exam - **3.** [darse a conocer] to introduce o.s. - **4.** [para un cargo]: **presentarse (a)** to stand *o* run (for) - **5.** [futuro] to appear, to look - **6.** [problema etc] to arise, to come up.

presente ◇ *adj* - **1.** [gen] present; **aquí presente** here present; **hacer presente algo a alguien** to notify sb of sthg; **hasta el momento presente** up to the present time; **tener presente** [recordar] to remember; [tener en cuenta] to bear in mind; **¡presente!** present! - **2.** [en curso] current; **del presente mes** of this month. ◇ *smf* - **1.** [en un lugar]: **los (aquí) presentes** all those present - **2.** [escrito]: **por la presente le informo...** I hereby inform you... ◇ *sm* - **1.** [gen & GRAM] present; **presente histórico** historical present - **2.** [regalo] gift, present - **3.** [corriente]: **el presente** [mes] the current month; [año] the current year - **4.** *loc*: **mejorando lo presente** without wishing to detract from anyone present.

presentimiento *sm* presentiment, feeling.

presentir [27] *vt* to foresee; **presentir que algo va a pasar** to have a feeling that sthg is going to happen; **presentir lo peor** to fear the worst.

preservación *sf* preservation.

preservar *vt* to protect; **preservar algo/alguien de algo** to protect sthg/sb from sthg.

◆ **preservarse de** *vprnl* to protect o.s. *o* shelter from.

preservativo *sm* condom; **preservativo femenino** female condom.

presidencia *sf* [de nación] presidency; [de asamblea, empresa] chairmanship.

presidenciable *smf* *Amér* potential presidential candidate.

presidencialismo *sm* presidential system.

presidente, **ta** *sm, f* [de nación] president; [de asamblea, empresa] chairman (*f* chairwoman); **presidente (del gobierno)** ≃ prime minister; **presidente de mesa** chief scrutineer.

presidiario, **ria** *sm, f* convict.

presidio *sm* prison.

presidir *vt* - **1.** [ser presidente de] to preside over; [reunión] to chair - **2.** [predominar] to dominate.

presienta, **presintiera** *etc* ▷ **presentir**.

presintonía *sf* [de radio] pre-set station selector.

presión *sf* pressure; **a presión** under pressure; **ejercer presión (sobre)** to pressurize; **altas/bajas presiones** areas of high/low pressure; **presión atmosférica** atmospheric pressure; **presión arterial** *o* **sanguínea** blood pressure; **presión fiscal** ECON tax burden.

presionar *vt* - **1.** [apretar] to press - **2.** *fig* [coaccionar] to pressurize, to put pressure on.

preso, sa ◇ *adj* imprisoned; **meter preso a alguien** to put sb in prison; **preso de conciencia** prisoner of conscience. ◇ *sm, f* prisoner.

prestación *sf* [de servicio - acción] provision; [- resultado] service; **prestación social** social security benefit.

➡ **prestaciones** *sfpl* - **1.** [servicio social] benefits - **2.** [de coche etc] performance features.

prestado, da *adj* on loan; **dar prestado algo** to lend sthg; **pedir/tomar prestado algo** to borrow sthg; **vivir de prestado** to live off other people.

prestamista *smf* moneylender.

préstamo *sm* - **1.** [acción - de prestar] lending; [- de pedir prestado] borrowing - **2.** [cantidad] loan.

prestancia *sf* excellence, distinction.

prestar *vt* - **1.** [dejar - dinero etc] to lend, to loan - **2.** [dar - ayuda etc] to give, to offer; [- servicio] to offer, to provide; [- atención] to pay; [- declaración, juramento] to make - **3.** [transmitir - encanto etc] to lend.

➡ **prestarse a** *vprnl* - **1.** [ofrecerse a] to offer to - **2.** [acceder a] to consent to - **3.** [dar motivo a] to be open to.

presteza *sf* promptness, speed.

prestidigitación *sf* conjuring.

prestidigitador, ra *sm, f* conjurer.

prestigiar [8] *vt* to honour, to give prestige to.

prestigio *sm* prestige.

prestigioso, sa *adj* prestigious.

presto, ta *adj* [dispuesto]: **presto (a)** ready (to).

presumible *adj* probable, likely.

presumido, da ◇ *adj* conceited, vain. ◇ *sm, f* conceited *o* vain person.

presumir ◇ *vt* [suponer] to presume, to assume; **es de presumir que irán** presumably they'll go. ◇ *vi* - **1.** [jactarse] to show off; **presume de guapa** she thinks she's pretty - **2.** [ser vanidoso] to be conceited *o* vain.

presunción *sf* - **1.** [suposición] presumption - **2.** [vanidad] conceit, vanity.

presunto, ta *adj* presumed, supposed; [criminal, robo etc] alleged, suspected.

presuntuoso, sa ◇ *adj* [vanidoso] conceited; [pretencioso] pretentious. ◇ *sm, f* conceited person.

presuponer [65] *vt* to presuppose.

presuposición *sf* assumption.

presupuestar *vt* [gen] to estimate; FIN to budget for.

presupuestario, ria *adj* budgetary, budget *(antes de s)*.

presupuesto, ta *pp* ⊳ **presuponer**.

➡ **presupuesto** *sm* - **1.** [cálculo] budget; [de costo] estimate; **pedir un presupuesto** to ask for an estimate; **presupuestos generales del Estado** ECON *Spanish national budget* - **2.** [suposición] assumption.

presuroso, sa *adj* in a hurry.

prêt-à-porter [pretapor'te] *sm* off-the-peg clothing.

pretencioso, sa ◇ *adj* [persona] pretentious; [cosa] showy. ◇ *sm, f* pretentious person.

pretender *vt* - **1.** [intentar]: **pretender hacer algo** to try to do sthg - **2.** [aspirar a]: **pretender hacer algo** to aspire *o* want to do sthg; **pretender que alguien haga algo** to want sb to do sthg; **¿qué pretendes decir?** what do you mean? - **3.** [afirmar] to claim - **4.** [solicitar] to apply for - **5.** [cortejar] to court.

pretendido, da *adj* supposed.

pretendiente ◇ *smf* - **1.** [aspirante]: **pretendiente (a)** candidate (for) - **2.** [a un trono]: **pretendiente (a)** pretender (to). ◇ *sm* [a una mujer] suitor.

pretensión *sf* - **1.** [intención] aim, intention - **2.** [aspiración] aspiration - **3.** [supuesto derecho]: **pretensión (a** *o* **sobre)** claim (to) - **4.** [afirmación] claim - **5.** *(gen pl)* [exigencia] demand - **6.** *(gen pl)* [presuntuosidad] pretentiousness; **sin pretensiones** unpretentious.

pretérito, ta *adj* past.

➡ **pretérito** *sm* GRAM preterite, past; **pretérito imperfecto** imperfect; **pretérito indefinido** simple past; **pretérito perfecto** (present) perfect; **pretérito pluscuamperfecto** pluperfect.

pretextar *vt* to use as a pretext, to claim.

pretexto *sm* pretext, excuse.

pretil *sm* parapet.

preuniversitario, ria *adj* pre-university.

➡ **preuniversitario** *sm* *in Spain, former one-year course of study, successful completion of which allowed pupils to go to university.*

prevalecer [30] *vi*: **prevalecer (sobre)** to prevail (over).

prevaler [74] *vi*: **prevaler (sobre)** to prevail (over).

➡ **prevalerse de** *vprnl* to take advantage of.

prevaricación sf breach of trust.

prevaricar [10] vi to betray one's trust.

prevención sf - **1.** [acción] prevention; [medida] precaution; **en prevención de** as a precaution against - **2.** [prejuicio] prejudice.

prevenido, da adj - **1.** [previsor]: **ser prevenido** to be cautious - **2.** [avisado, dispuesto]: **estar prevenido** to be prepared.

prevenir [75] vt - **1.** [evitar] to prevent; **más vale prevenir que curar** prov prevention is better than cure prov - **2.** [avisar] to warn - **3.** [prever] to foresee, to anticipate - **4.** [predisponer]: **prevenir a alguien contra algo/alguien** to prejudice sb against sthg/sb.

preventivo, va adj [medicina, prisión] preventive; [medida] precautionary.

prever [76] ◇ vt - **1.** [conjeturar] to foresee, to anticipate - **2.** [planear] to plan - **3.** [predecir] to forecast. ◇ vi: **como era de prever** as was to be expected.

previene etc ⊳ **prevenir**.

previera etc ⊳ **prever**.

previniera etc ⊳ **prevenir**.

previo, via adj prior; **previo pago de multa** on payment of a fine.

previó etc ⊳ **prever**.

previsible adj foreseeable.

previsión sf - **1.** [predicción] forecast - **2.** [visión de futuro] foresight - **3.** [precaución]: **en previsión de** as a precaution against - **4.** Andes & R Plata [social] social security.

previsor, ra adj prudent, farsighted.

previsto, ta ◇ pp ⊳ **prever**. ◇ adj [conjeturado] predicted; [planeado] forecast, expected, planned.

prieto, ta adj - **1.** [ceñido] tight - **2.** Cuba & Méx fam [moreno] dark-skinned.

prima ⊳ **primo**.

primacía sf primacy; **tener primacía sobre algo** to take priority over sthg.

primado sm primate.

primar ◇ vi: **primar (sobre)** to have priority (over). ◇ vt to give a bonus to.

primario, ria adj primary; fig primitive.

primavera sf - **1.** [estación] spring - **2.** fig [juventud] springtime - **3.** fig [año]: **tiene diez primaveras** she is ten years old, she has seen ten summers.

primaveral adj spring (antes de s).

primer, primera ⊳ **primero**.

primerizo, za ◇ adj - **1.** [principiante] novice - **2.** [embarazada] first-time. ◇ sm, f [principiante] beginner.

◆ **primeriza** sf [madre] first-time mother.

primero, ra ◇ num & adj (antes de sm sing: **primer**) - **1.** [para ordenar] first; **el primero de mayo** the first of May - **2.** [en importancia] main, basic; **lo primero** the most important o main thing; **lo primero es lo primero** first things first. ◇ num m y f - **1.** [en orden]: **el primero** the first one; **llegó el primero** he came first; **es el primero de la clase** he's top of the class; **a primeros de mes** at the beginning of the month - **2.** [mencionado antes]: **vinieron Pedro y Juan, el primero con...** Pedro and Juan arrived, the former with...

◆ **primero** ◇ adv - **1.** [en primer lugar] first - **2.** [antes, todo menos]: **primero... que... rather... than...; primero morir que traicionarle** I'd rather die than betray him. ◇ sm - **1.** [piso] first floor - **2.** [curso] first year.

◆ **primera** sf - **1.** AUTO first (gear) - **2.** AERON & FERROC first class - **3.** DEP first division - **4.** loc: **de primera** first-class, excellent.

primicia sf scoop, exclusive.

primitivo, va adj - **1.** [gen] primitive - **2.** [original] original.

primo, ma sm, f - **1.** [pariente] cousin; **primo hermano** first cousin - **2.** fam [tonto] sucker; **hacer el primo** to be taken for a ride.

◆ **prima** sf - **1.** [paga extra] bonus - **2.** [de un seguro] premium; **primo de riesgo** risk premium - **3.** [subvención] subsidy.

◆ **prima dona** sf prima donna.

primogénito, ta adj & sm, f first-born.

primor sm fine thing; **con primor** with skill.

primordial adj fundamental.

primoroso, sa adj - **1.** [delicado] exquisite, fine - **2.** [hábil] skilful.

princesa sf princess.

principado sm principality.

principal ◇ adj main, principal; [puerta] front. ◇ sm [piso] first floor.

príncipe sm prince; **príncipe consorte** prince consort; **príncipe heredero** crown prince.

◆ **príncipe azul** sm Prince Charming.

principesco, ca adj princely.

principiante ◇ adj novice, inexperienced. ◇ smf novice, beginner.

principio sm - **1.** [comienzo] beginning, start; **a principios de** at the beginning of; **a principios de siglo** at the turn of the century; **en un principio** at first; **2.** [fundamento, ley] principle; **en principio** in principle; **por principio** on principle - **3.** [origen] origin, source - **4.** [elemento] element.

◆ **principios** smpl - **1.** [reglas de conducta] principles - **2.** [nociones] rudiments, first principles.

pringar [16] ◇ vt - **1.** [ensuciar] to make greasy - **2.** [mojar] to dip - **3.** fam fig [comprometer] to involve. ◇ vi fam fig to get stuck in.

pringarse *vprnl* - **1.** [ensuciarse] to get covered in grease - **2.** *fam fig* [en asunto sucio] to get one's hands dirty.

pringoso, **sa** *adj* [grasiento] greasy; [pegajoso] sticky.

pringue ⟨⟩ *v* ⟼ **pringar**. ⟨⟩ *sm* [suciedad] muck, dirt; [grasa] grease.

prior, **ra** *sm, f* prior (*f* prioress).

priorato *sm* [vino] *wine from El Priorato in Tarragona.*

priori ⟜ **a priori** *loc adv* in advance, a priori.

prioridad *sf* priority; AUTO right of way.

prioritario, **ria** *adj* priority (*antes de s*).

prisa *sf* haste, hurry; **a** *o* **de prisa** quickly; **a toda prisa** very quickly; **correr prisa** to be urgent; **darse prisa** to hurry (up); **meter prisa a alguien** to hurry *o* rush sb; **tener prisa** to be in a hurry; **de prisa y corriendo** in a slapdash way.

prisión *sf* - **1.** [cárcel] prison - **2.** [encarcelamiento] imprisonment.

prisionero, **ra** *sm, f* prisoner; **hacer prisionero a alguien** to take sb prisoner.

prisma *sm* - **1.** FÍS & GEOM prism - **2.** *fig* [perspectiva] viewpoint, perspective.

prismáticos *smpl* binoculars.

privación *sf* [gen] deprivation; [de libertad] loss; **pasar privaciones** to suffer hardship.

privado, **da** *adj* private; **en privado** in private.

privar ⟨⟩ *vt* [quitar]: **privar a alguien/algo de** to deprive sb/sthg of. ⟨⟩ *vi* - **1.** [gustar]: **le privan los pasteles** he adores cakes - **2.** [estar de moda] to be in (fashion) - **3.** *fam* [beber] to booze.

⟜ **privarse de** *vprnl* to go without.

privativo, **va** *adj* exclusive.

privatizar [13] *vt* to privatize.

privilegiado, **da** ⟨⟩ *adj* - **1.** [favorecido] privileged - **2.** [excepcional] exceptional. ⟨⟩ *sm, f* [afortunado] privileged person.

privilegiar [8] *vt* [persona] to favour.

privilegio *sm* privilege.

pro ⟨⟩ *prep* for, supporting; **una asociación pro derechos humanos** a human rights organization. ⟨⟩ *sm* advantage; **los pros y los contras** the pros and cons.

⟜ **en pro de** *loc prep* for, in support of.

proa *sf* NÁUT prow, bows *pl*; AERON nose.

probabilidad *sf* probability; **con toda probabilidad** in all probability; [oportunidad] likelihood, chance.

probable *adj* probable, likely; **es probable que llueva** it'll probably rain; **es probable que no diga nada** he probably won't say anything.

probador *sm* fitting room.

probar [23] ⟨⟩ *vt* - **1.** [demostrar, indicar] to prove - **2.** [comprobar] to test, to check - **3.** [experimentar] to try - **4.** [degustar] to taste, to try. ⟨⟩ *vi*: **probar a hacer algo** to try to do sthg.

⟜ **probarse** *vprnl* [ropa] to try on.

probeta *sf* test tube.

problema *sm* problem.

problemático, **ca** *adj* problematic.

⟜ **problemática** *sf* problems *pl*.

procacidad *sf* obscenity; [acto] indecent act.

procaz *adj* indecent, obscene.

procedencia *sf* - **1.** [origen] origin - **2.** [punto de partida] point of departure; **con procedencia de** (arriving) from - **3.** [pertinencia] properness, appropriateness.

procedente *adj* - **1.** [originario]: **procedente de** [gen] originating in; AERON & FERROC (arriving) from - **2.** [oportuno] appropriate; DER fitting, right and proper.

proceder ⟨⟩ *sm* conduct, behaviour. ⟨⟩ *vi* - **1.** [originarse]: **proceder de** to come from - **2.** [actuar]: **proceder (con)** to act (with) - **3.** [empezar]: **proceder (a algo/a hacer algo)** to proceed (with sthg/to do sthg) - **4.** [ser oportuno] to be appropriate.

procedimiento *sm* - **1.** [método] procedure, method - **2.** DER proceedings *pl*.

prócer *sm* great person.

procesado, **da** *sm, f* accused, defendant.

procesador *sm* INFORM processor; **procesador Pentium®** Pentium® processor; **procesador de textos** word processor.

procesamiento *sm* - **1.** DER prosecution - **2.** INFORM processing; **procesamiento de textos** word processing.

procesar *vt* - **1.** DER to prosecute - **2.** INFORM to process.

procesión *sf fig* & RELIG procession; **la procesión va por dentro** he/she is putting on a brave face.

procesionaria *sf* processionary moth.

proceso *sm* - **1.** [gen] process - **2.** [desarrollo, intervalo] course - **3.** [DER - juicio] trial; [- causa] lawsuit; **abrir un proceso contra** to bring an action against.

⟜ **proceso de datos** *sm* data processing.

⟜ **proceso de textos** *sm* word processing.

proclama *sf* proclamation.

proclamación *sf* - **1.** [anuncio] notification - **2.** [ceremonia] proclamation.

proclamar *vt* - **1.** [nombrar] to proclaim - **2.** *fig* [aclamar] to acclaim - **3.** [anunciar] to declare.

⟜ **proclamarse** *vprnl* - **1.** [nombrarse] to proclaim o.s. - **2.** [conseguir un título]: **proclamarse campeón** to become champion.

proclive *adj*: **proclive a** prone to.

procreación *sf* procreation.

procrear *vi* to procreate.

procurador, ra *sm, f* DER attorney; **procurador en Cortes** Member of Spanish Parliament.

procurar *vt* - **1.** [intentar]: **procurar hacer algo** to try to do sthg; **procurar que...** to make sure that... - **2.** [proporcionar] to get, to secure.
◆ **procurarse** *vprnl* to get, to obtain (for o.s.)

prodigalidad *sf* - **1.** [derroche] prodigality - **2.** [abundancia] profusion.

prodigar [16] *vt*: **prodigar algo a alguien** to lavish sthg on sb.
◆ **prodigarse** *vprnl* - **1.** [exhibirse] to appear a lot in public - **2.** [excederse]: **prodigarse en** to be lavish with.

prodigio *sm* [suceso] miracle; [persona] wonder, prodigy.

prodigioso, sa *adj* - **1.** [sobrenatural] miraculous - **2.** [extraordinario] wonderful, marvellous.

pródigo, ga *adj* - **1.** [derrochador] extravagant - **2.** [generoso] generous, lavish.

producción *sf* - **1.** [gen & CINE] production; **producción en serie** ECON mass production - **2.** [productos] products *pl*.

producir [33] *vt* - **1.** [gen & CINE] to produce - **2.** [causar] to cause, to give rise to - **3.** [interés, fruto] to yield, to bear.
◆ **producirse** *vprnl* [ocurrir] to take place, to come about.

productividad *sf* productivity.

productivo, va *adj* productive; [que da beneficio] profitable.

producto *sm* - **1.** [gen & MAT] product; AGRIC produce *(U)*; **producto acabado/manufacturado** finished/manufactured product; **producto de belleza** beauty product; **producto interior/nacional bruto** gross domestic/national product; **producto químico** chemical - **2.** [ganancia] profit - **3.** *fig* [resultado] result.

productor, ra <> *adj* producing; **país productor de petróleo** oil-producing country.
<> *sm, f* CINE [persona] producer.
◆ **productora** *sf* CINE [firma] production company.

proeza *sf* exploit, deed.

profanación *sf* desecration.

profanar *vt* to desecrate.

profano, na <> *adj* - **1.** [no sagrado] profane, secular - **2.** [ignorante] ignorant, uninitiated.
<> *sm, f* layman (*f* laywoman), lay person.

profecía *sf* [predicción] prophecy.
◆ **profecías** *sfpl* [libros] Prophets.

proferir [22] *vt* to utter; [insultos] to hurl.

profesar <> *vt* - **1.** [una religión] to follow; [una profesión] to practise - **2.** [admiración etc] to profess. <> *vi* RELIG to take one's vows.

profesión *sf* profession; **de profesión** by profession; **profesión liberal** liberal profession.

profesional *adj* & *smf* professional.

profesionalidad *sf* professionalism.

profesionalismo *sm* = **profesionalidad**.

profesionista *smf Méx* professional.

profeso, sa *adj* professed.
◆ **ex profeso** *loc adv* intentionally, expressly.

profesor, ra *sm, f* [gen] teacher; [de universidad] lecturer; [de autoescuela, esquí etc] instructor; **profesor agregado** lecturer; **profesor asociado** associate lecturer; **profesor ayudante** assistant lecturer; **profesor particular** (private) tutor; **profesor titular** (full) lecturer.

profesorado *sm* - **1.** [plantilla] teaching staff, faculty *US*; [profesión] teachers *pl*, teaching profession - **2.** [cargo] post of teacher; [en la universidad] lectureship.

profeta *sm* prophet.

profético, ca *adj* prophetic.

profetisa *sf* prophetess.

profetizar [13] *vt* to prophesy.

profiera *etc* ▷ **proferir**.

profiláctico, ca *adj* prophylactic.
◆ **profiláctico** *sm* prophylactic, condom.

profilaxis *sf inv* prophylaxis.

prófugo, ga *adj* & *sm, f* fugitive.
◆ **prófugo** *sm* - **1.** DER fugitive - **2.** MIL deserter.

profundidad *sf lit & fig* depth; **en profundidad** in depth; **tiene dos metros de profundidad** it's two metres deep.

profundizar [13] <> *vt fig* to study in depth.
<> *vi* to go into detail; **profundizar en** to study in depth.

profundo, da *adj* - **1.** [gen] deep - **2.** *fig* [respeto, libro, pensamiento] profound, deep; [dolor] intense.

profusión *sf* profusion.

profuso, sa *adj* profuse.

progenie *sf* - **1.** [familia] lineage - **2.** [descendencia] offspring.

progenitor, ra *sm, f* father (*f* mother).
◆ **progenitores** *smpl* parents.

progesterona *sf* progesterone.

programa *sm* - **1.** [gen] programme; **programa espacial** space programme; **programa de intercambio** exchange (programme) - **2.** [de actividades] schedule, programme; [de estudios] syllabus - **3.** INFORM program.

programación *sf* - **1.** INFORM programming - **2.** TV scheduling; **la programación del lunes** Monday's programmes.

programador, ra *sm, f* [persona] programmer.

◆ **programador** *sm* [aparato] programmer.

programar *vt* - **1.** [vacaciones, reforma etc] to plan - **2.** CINE & TV to put on, to show - **3.** TECNOL to programme; INFORM to program.

progre *fam* ◇ *adj* liberal, permissive. ◇ *smf* progressive.

progresar *vi* to progress, to make progress; **progresar en** to make progress in.

progresión *sf* [gen & MAT] progression; [mejora] progress, advance; **progresión aritmética/ geométrica** arithmetic/geometric progression.

progresista *adj* & *smf* progressive.

progresivo, va *adj* progressive.

progreso *sm* progress; **hacer progresos** to make progress.

prohibición *sf* ban, banning *(U)*.

prohibido, da *adj* prohibited, banned; **'prohibido aparcar/fumar'** 'no parking/smoking', 'parking/smoking prohibited'; **'prohibida la entrada'** 'no entry'; **'dirección prohibida'** AUTO 'no entry'.

prohibir *vt* - **1.** [gen] to forbid; **prohibir a alguien hacer algo** to forbid sb to do sthg; **'se prohíbe el paso'** 'no entry' - **2.** [por ley - de antemano] to prohibit; [- a posteriori] to ban.

prohibitivo, va *adj* prohibitive.

prójimo *sm* fellow human being, neighbour.

prole *sf* offspring.

proletariado *sm* proletariat.

proletario, ria *adj* & *sm, f* proletarian.

proliferación *sf* proliferation; **proliferación nuclear** proliferation (of nuclear arms).

proliferar *vi* to proliferate.

prolífico, ca *adj* prolific.

prolijo, ja *adj* - **1.** [extenso] long-winded - **2.** [esmerado] meticulous; [detallado] exhaustive.

prólogo *sm* [de libro] preface, foreword; *fig* prelude.

prolongación *sf* extension.

prolongado, da *adj* long; *fig* [dilatado] lengthy.

prolongar [16] *vt* [gen] to extend; [espera, visita, conversación] to prolong; [cuerda, tubo] to lengthen.

promedio *sm* average; **como promedio** on average.

promesa *sf* - **1.** [compromiso] promise; **hacer una promesa** to make a promise; **romper una promesa** to break a promise - **2.** *fig* [persona] promising talent.

prometedor, ra *adj* promising.

prometer ◇ *vt* to promise. ◇ *vi* [tener futuro] to show promise.

◆ **prometerse** *vprnl* to get engaged.

prometido, da ◇ *sm, f* fiancé (*f* fiancée). ◇ *adj* - **1.** [para casarse] engaged - **2.** [asegurado]: **lo prometido** what has been promised, promise; **cumplir lo prometido** to keep one's promise.

prominencia *sf* - **1.** [abultamiento] protuberance - **2.** [elevación] rise - **3.** [importancia] prominence.

prominente *adj* - **1.** [abultado] protruding - **2.** [elevado, ilustre] prominent.

promiscuidad *sf* promiscuity.

promiscuo, cua *adj* promiscuous.

promoción *sf* - **1.** [gen & DEP] promotion; **promoción de ventas** sales promotion - **2.** [curso] class, year.

promocionar *vt* to promote.

◆ **promocionarse** *vprnl* to put o.s. forward, to promote o.s.

promontorio *sm* promontory.

promotor, ra ◇ *adj* promoting. ◇ *sm, f* promoter; [de una rebelión] instigator; **promotor inmobiliario** COM real estate developer.

promover [24] *vt* - **1.** [iniciar - fundación etc] to set up; [- rebelión] to stir up - **2.** [impulsar] to stimulate - **3.** [ocasionar] to cause - **4.** [ascender]: **promover a alguien a** to promote sb to.

promulgación *sf* [de ley] enactment.

promulgar [16] *vt* [ley] to enact.

pronombre *sm* pronoun; **(pronombre) demostrativo** demonstrative pronoun; **(pronombre) indefinido** indefinite pronoun; **pronombre interrogativo/personal** interrogative/personal pronoun; **(pronombre) posesivo** possessive pronoun; **pronombre relativo** relative pronoun.

pronominal ◇ *adj* pronominal. ◇ *sm* pronominal verb.

pronosticar [10] *vt* to predict, to forecast.

pronóstico *sm* - **1.** [predicción] forecast; **pronóstico del tiempo** weather forecast - **2.** MED prognosis; **de pronóstico leve** suffering from a mild condition; **de pronóstico grave** serious, in a serious condition; **de pronóstico reservado** under observation.

prontitud *sf* promptness.

pronto, ta *adj* quick, fast; [respuesta] prompt, early; [curación, tramitación] speedy.

◆ **pronto** ◇ *adv* - **1.** [rápidamente] quickly; **tan pronto como** as soon as - **2.** [temprano] early; **salimos pronto** we left early - **3.** [dentro de poco] soon; **¡hasta pronto!** see you soon! ◇ *sm fam* sudden impulse.
◆ **al pronto** *loc adv* at first.
◆ **de pronto** *loc adv* suddenly.
◆ **por lo pronto** *loc adv* - **1.** [de momento] for the time being - **2.** [para empezar] to start with.

pronunciación *sf* pronunciation.

pronunciado, da *adj* [facciones] pronounced; [curva] sharp; [pendiente, cuesta] steep; [nariz] prominent.

pronunciamiento *sm* - **1.** [sublevación] uprising - **2.** DER pronouncement.

pronunciar [8] *vt* - **1.** [decir - palabra] to pronounce; [- discurso] to deliver, to make - **2.** [realzar] to accentuate - **3.** DER to pronounce, to pass.
◆ **pronunciarse** *vprnl* - **1.** [definirse]: **pronunciarse (sobre)** to state an opinion (on) - **2.** [sublevarse] to rise up, to revolt.

propagación *sf* - **1.** [gen] spreading *(U)* - **2.** BIOL & FÍS propagation.

propaganda *sf* - **1.** [publicidad] advertising *(U)* - **2.** [prospectos - gen] publicity leaflets *(U)*; [- por correo] junk mail - **3.** [política, religiosa] propaganda.

propagandístico, ca *adj* advertising *(antes de s)*; POLÍT propaganda *(antes de s)*.

propagar [16] *vt* [gen] to spread; [razas, especies] to propagate.
◆ **propagarse** *vprnl* - **1.** [gen] to spread - **2.** BIOL & FÍS to propagate.

propalar *vt* to divulge.

propano *sm* propane.

propasarse *vprnl*: **propasarse (con algo)** to go too far (with sthg); **propasarse con alguien** [sexualmente] to take liberties with sb.

propensión *sf* propensity, tendency.

propenso, sa *adj*: **propenso a algo/a hacer algo** prone to sthg/doing sthg.

propiamente *adv* [adecuadamente] properly; [verdaderamente] really, strictly; **propiamente dicho** strictly speaking; **el pueblo propiamente dicho es sólo esto** strictly speaking, the town is just this area.

propiciar [8] *vt* to be conducive to.

propicio, cia *adj* - **1.** [favorable] propitious, favourable - **2.** [adecuado] suitable, appropriate.

propiedad *sf* - **1.** [derecho] ownership; [bienes] property; **tener algo en propiedad** to own sthg; **propiedad horizontal** joint-ownership *(in a block of flats)*; **propiedad industrial** patent rights *pl*; **propiedad intelectual** copyright; **propiedad privada** private property;

propiedad pública public ownership - **2.** [facultad] property - **3.** [exactitud] accuracy; **usar una palabra con propiedad** to use a word properly.

propietario, ria *sm, f* [de bienes] owner.

propina *sf* tip; **dar de propina** to tip.

propinar *vt* [paliza] to give; [golpe] to deal.

propio, pia *adj* - **1.** [gen] own; **tiene coche propio** she has a car of her own, she has her own car; **por tu propio bien** for your own good - **2.** [peculiar]: **propio de** typical o characteristic of; **no es propio de él** it's not like him - **3.** [apropiado]: **propio (para)** suitable o right (for) - **4.** [en persona] himself *(f* herself)*; **el propio compositor** the composer himself.

proponer [65] *vt* to propose; [candidato] to put forward.
◆ **proponerse** *vprnl*: **proponerse hacer algo** to plan o intend to do sthg.

proporción *sf* - **1.** [gen & MAT] proportion; **en proporción a** in proportion to; **guardar proporción (con)** to be in proportion (to) - **2.** *(gen pl)* [importancia] extent, size.
◆ **proporciones** *sfpl* [tamaño] size *sing*.

proporcionado, da *adj*: **proporcionado (a)** [estatura, sueldo] commensurate (with); [medidas] proportionate (to); **bien proporcionado** well-proportioned.

proporcional *adj* proportional.

proporcionar *vt* - **1.** [facilitar]: **proporcionar algo a alguien** to provide sb with sthg - **2.** *fig* [conferir] to lend, to add.

proposición *sf* - **1.** [propuesta] proposal - **2.** GRAM clause.
◆ **proposiciones** *sfpl* [sugerencias] propositions; **hacer proposiciones a alguien** to proposition sb; **proposiciones deshonestas** improper suggestions.

propósito *sm* - **1.** [intención] intention - **2.** [objetivo] purpose.
◆ **a propósito** ◇ *loc adj* [adecuado] suitable. ◇ *loc adv* - **1.** [adrede] on purpose - **2.** [por cierto] by the way.
◆ **a propósito de** *loc prep* with regard to, concerning.

propuesta *sf* proposal; **a propuesta de** at the suggestion of; [de empleo] offer.

propuesto, ta *pp* ▷ **proponer**.

propugnar *vt* to advocate, to support.

propulsar *vt* - **1.** [impeler] to propel - **2.** *fig* [promover] to promote.

propulsión *sf* propulsion; **propulsión a chorro** jet propulsion.

propulsor, ra ◇ *adj* propulsive. ◇ *sm, f* [persona] promoter.

propulsor *sm* - **1.** [dispositivo] engine - **2.** [combustible] propellent.

propusiera *etc* ⊳ **proponer**.

prorrata *sf* quota, share; **a prorrata** pro rata.

prórroga *sf* - **1.** [gen] extension; [de estudios, servicio militar] deferment - **2.** DEP extra time.

prorrogar [16] *vt* [alargar] to extend; [aplazar] to defer, to postpone.

prorrumpir *vi*: prorrumpir en to burst into.

prosa *sf* LITER prose; **en prosa** in prose.

prosaico, ca *adj* prosaic.

proscribir *vt* - **1.** [prohibir] to ban - **2.** [desterrar] to banish.

proscrito, ta ⬠ *pp* ⊳ **proscribir**. ⬠ *adj* - **1.** [prohibido] banned - **2.** [desterrado] banished. ⬠ *sm, f* [desterrado] exile.

proseguir [43] ⬠ *vt* to continue. ⬠ *vi* to go on, to continue.

proselitismo *sm* proselytism; **hacer proselitismo** to proselytize.

prosélito, ta *sm, f* proselyte.

prosiga *etc* ⊳ **proseguir**.

prosiguiera *etc* ⊳ **proseguir**.

prospección *sf* - **1.** [gen] exploration; [petrolífera, minera] prospecting - **2.** [de clientes]: **prospección (de)** canvassing (for).

prospectivo, va *adj* exploratory.

prospecto *sm* leaflet; COM & EDUC prospectus.

prosperar *vi* - **1.** [mejorar] to prosper, to thrive - **2.** [triunfar] to be successful.

prosperidad *sf* - **1.** [mejora] prosperity - **2.** [éxito] success.

próspero, ra *adj* prosperous, flourishing.

próstata *sf* prostate.

prostíbulo *sm* brothel.

prostitución *sf* - **1.** [gen] prostitution - **2.** *fig* [corrupción] corruption.

prostituir [51] *vt lit & fig* to prostitute.

prostituirse *vprnl* to become a prostitute.

prostituta *sf* prostitute.

protagonismo *sm* leading role; **ganar protagonismo** to become more important.

protagonista *sm, f* - **1.** [gen] main character, hero (*f* heroine); TEATRO lead, leading role - **2.** *fig* [de crimen, hazaña] person responsible.

protagonizar [13] *vt* - **1.** [obra, película] to play the lead in, to star in - **2.** *fig* [crimen] to be one of the main people responsible for; *fig* [hazaña] to play a leading part in.

protección *sf* protection; **bajo la protección de alguien** under the protection of sb; **protección civil** civil defence; **protección de datos** INFORM data protection.

proteccionismo *sm* protectionism.

protector, ra ⬠ *adj* protective. ⬠ *sm, f* [persona] protector.

protector *sm* - **1.** [en boxeo] gumshield - **2.**: **protector labial** lip salve.

protectorado *sm* protectorate.

proteger [14] *vt* - **1.** [gen] to protect; **proteger algo de algo** to protect sthg from sthg - **2.** [apoyar] to support.

protegerse *vprnl* to take cover O refuge.

protegeslip *sm* panty pad O liner.

protegido, da ⬠ *adj* protected. ⬠ *sm, f* protégé (*f* protégée).

proteína *sf* protein; **rico en proteínas** rich in protein.

prótesis *sf inv* - **1.** MED prosthesis; [miembro] artificial limb - **2.** GRAM prothesis.

protesta *sf* protest; DER objection.

protestante *adj & smf* Protestant.

protestantismo *sm* Protestantism.

protestar *vi* - **1.** [quejarse]: **protestar (por/contra)** to protest (about/against); **¡protesto!** DER objection! - **2.** [refunfuñar] to grumble.

protesto *sm* COM: **protesto de letra** noting bill of exchange.

protocolario, ria *adj* formal.

protocolo *sm* - **1.** [gen & INFORM] protocol; **protocolo de comunicación** communications protocol - **2.** [ceremonial] etiquette - **3.** DER *documents handled by a solicitor*.

protón *sm* proton.

prototipo *sm* - **1.** [modelo] archetype - **2.** [primer ejemplar] prototype.

protozoo *sm* protozoan, protozoon.

protuberancia *sf* protuberance, bulge.

provecho *sm* - **1.** [gen] benefit; **buen provecho** enjoy your meal!; **de provecho** [persona] worthy; **hacer provecho** to do good; **sacar provecho de** to make the most of, to take advantage of - **2.** [rendimiento] good effect.

provechoso, sa *adj* - **1.** [ventajoso] beneficial, advantageous - **2.** [lucrativo] profitable.

proveedor, ra *sm, f* supplier; **proveedor de servicios** service provider; **proveedor de acceso a Internet** Internet access provider.

proveer [50] *vt* - **1.** [abastecer] to supply, to provide; **proveer a alguien de algo** to provide sb with sthg - **2.** [puesto, cargo] to fill.

proveerse de *vprnl* - **1.** [ropa, víveres] to stock up on - **2.** [medios, recursos] to arm o.s. with.

proveniente *adj*: **proveniente de** (coming) from.

provenir [75] *vi*: **provenir de** to come from.

proverbial *adj* proverbial.

proverbio *sm* proverb.

providencia *sf* - **1.** [medida] measure, step - **2.** DER ruling.

◆ **Providencia** *sf* Providence.

providencial *adj lit & fig* providential.

proviene *etc* ▷ **provenir**.

provincia *sf* [división administrativa] province.

◆ **provincias** *sfpl* [no la capital] the provinces.

provincial *adj* & *sm* provincial.

provinciano, na *adj* & *sm, f despec* provincial.

proviniera *etc* ▷ **provenir**.

provisión *sf* - **1.** (gen pl) [suministro] supply, provision; [de una plaza] filling (U) - **2.** [disposición] measure; **provisión de fondos** financial reserves *pl*.

provisional *adj* provisional.

provisorio, ria *adj Amér* provisional.

provisto, ta *pp* ▷ **proveer**.

provocación *sf* - **1.** [hostigamiento] provocation - **2.** [ocasionamiento - de incendio] starting; [- de incidente] causing; [- de revuelta] instigation.

provocador, ra ◇ *adj* provocative. ◇ *sm, f* agitator.

provocar [10] *vt* - **1.** [incitar] to incite; **provocar a alguien a hacer algo** [gen] to cause sb to do sthg, to make sb do sthg; [matar, luchar etc] to provoke sb to do sthg - **2.** [irritar] to provoke - **3.** [ocasionar - gen] to cause; [- incendio, rebelión] to start - **4.** [excitar sexualmente] to arouse - **5.:** ¿**te provoca hacerlo?** *Caribe, Col & Méx* [te apetece] would you like to do it?

provocativo, va *adj* provocative.

proxeneta *sm, f* pimp (*f* procuress).

proxenetismo *sm* pimping (U), procuring (U).

próximamente *adv* soon, shortly; CINE coming soon.

proximidad *sf* [cercanía] closeness, proximity.

◆ **proximidades** *sfpl* - **1.** [de ciudad] surrounding area *sing* - **2.** [de lugar] vicinity *sing*.

próximo, ma *adj* - **1.** [cercano] near, close; **próximo a algo** close to sthg; [casa, ciudad] nearby, neighbouring; **en fecha próxima** shortly - **2.** [parecido] similar, close - **3.** [siguiente] next; **el próximo año** next year.

proyección *sf* - **1.** [gen & GEOM] projection - **2.** CINE screening, showing - **3.** *fig* [trascendencia] importance.

proyectar *vt* - **1.** [dirigir - focos etc] to shine, to direct - **2.** [mostrar - película] to project, to screen; [- sombra] to cast; [- diapositivas] to show - **3.** [planear - viaje, operación, edificio] to plan; [- puente, obra] to design - **4.** [arrojar] to throw forwards - **5.** GEOM to project.

proyectil *sm* projectile, missile.

proyectista *smf* designer.

proyecto *sm* - **1.** [intención] project - **2.** [plan] plan; **tener en proyecto hacer algo** to be planning to do sthg - **3.** [diseño - ARQUIT] design; TECNOL plan - **4.** [borrador] draft; **proyecto de ley** bill - **5.** EDUC: **proyecto fin de carrera** *design project forming part of doctoral thesis for architecture students etc*; **proyecto de investigación** [de un grupo] research project; [de una persona] dissertation.

proyector, ra *adj* projecting.

◆ **proyector** *sm* - **1.** [de cine, diapositivas] projector - **2.** [reflector] searchlight; [en el teatro] spotlight.

prudencia *sf* [cuidado] caution, care; [previsión, sensatez] prudence; [moderación] moderation; **con prudencia** in moderation.

prudencial *adj* [sensato] sensible; [moderado] moderate.

prudente *adj* - **1.** [cuidadoso] careful, cautious; [previsor, sensato] sensible - **2.** [razonable] reasonable.

prueba ◇ *v* ▷ **probar**. ◇ *sf* - **1.** [demostración] proof; DER evidence, proof; **no tengo pruebas** I have no proof - **2.** [manifestación] sign, token; **en o como prueba de** in o as proof of - **3.** [trance] ordeal, trial - **4.** EDUC & MED test; **prueba de alcoholemia** Breathalyser®test; **prueba de acceso** entrance examination; **prueba de aptitud** aptitude test; **prueba del embarazo** pregnancy test - **5.** [comprobación] test; **a o de prueba** [trabajador] on trial; [producto comprado] on approval; **es a prueba de agua/balas** it's waterproof/bulletproof; **paciencia a toda prueba** unwavering patience; **poner a prueba** to (put to the) test; **la prueba de fuego** the acid test - **6.** DEP event - **7.** IMPR proof.

prurito *sm* MED itch, itching (U); *fig* urge.

prusiano, na *adj* & *sm, f* Prussian.

PS (*abrev de* post scriptum) PS.

psicoanálisis, sicoanálisis *sm inv* psychoanalysis.

PSC *sf* (*abrev de* **Partido Conservador o Partido Social Conservador**), *Colombian political party*.

PSI (*abrev de* **proveedor de servicio Internet**) *sm* ISP.

psicoanalista, sicoanalista *smf* psychoanalyst.

psicoanalizar [13], **sicoanalizar** [13] *vt* to psychoanalyze.

psicodélico, ca, sicodélico, ca *adj* psychedelic.

psicodrama, sicodrama *sm* psychodrama.

psicología, sicología *sf lit & fig* psychology.

psicológico, ca, sicológico, ca *adj* psychological.

psicólogo, ga, sicólogo, ga *sm, f* psychologist.

psicomotor, ra *adj* psychomotor.

psicomotricidad, sicomotricidad *sf* psychomotricity.

psicópata, sicópata *smf* psychopath.

psicopatía, sicopatía *sf* psychopathy, psychopathic personality.

psicosis, sicosis *sf inv* psychosis; **psicosis maniacodepresiva** manic-depressive psychosis.

psicosomático, ca, sicosomático, ca *adj* psychosomatic.

psicotécnico, ca, sicotécnico, ca *adj* psychotechnical.

➧ **psicotécnico, sicotécnico** *sm* [prueba] psychotechnical test.

psicoterapia, sicoterapia *sf* psychotherapy.

psique *sf* psyche.

psiquiatra, siquiatra *smf* psychiatrist.

psiquiatría, siquiatría *sf* psychiatry.

psiquiátrico, ca, siquiátrico, ca *adj* psychiatric.

➧ **psiquiátrico** *sm* psychiatric O mental hospital.

psíquico, ca, síquico, ca *adj* psychic.

psiquis *sf inv* psyche.

PSOE [pe'soe] (*abrev de* **Partido Socialista Obrero Español**) *sm major Spanish political party to the centre-left of the political spectrum.*

pta. (*abrev de* **peseta**) pta.

púa *sf* - **1.** [de planta] thorn; [de erizo] barb, quill; [de peine] spine, tooth; [de tenedor] prong - **2.** MÚS plectrum.

pub [paβ] (*pl* **pubs**) *sm* bar.

púber, ra *adj* & *sm, f culto* adolescent.

pubertad *sf* puberty.

pubis *sm inv* pubes *pl*.

publicación *sf* publication; **publicación periódica** periodical.

publicar [10] *vt* - **1.** [editar] to publish - **2.** [difundir] to publicize; [ley] to make public, to pass; [aviso] to issue.

publicidad *sf* - **1.** [difusión] publicity; **dar publicidad a algo** to publicize sthg - **2.** COM advertising; TV adverts *pl*, commercials *pl*; **publicidad directa** direct mailing.

publicista *smf* advertising agent.

publicitar *vt* to advertise.

publicitario, ria ⬦ *adj* advertising *(antes de s)*. ⬦ *sm, f* advertising agent.

público, ca *adj* public; **ser público** [conocido] to be common knowledge; **en público** in public; **hacer algo público** to make sthg public.

➧ **público** *sm* - **1.** CINE, TEATRO & TV audience; DEP crowd - **2.** [comunidad] public; **el gran público** the (general) public.

publirreportaje *sm* [anuncio de televisión] promotional film; [en revista] advertising spread.

pucha *interj Andes & R Plata fam* - **1.** [lamento, enojo] sugar! UK, shoot! US - **2.** [expresa sorpresa] wow! - **3.** [expresa enojo] damn!

pucherazo *sm fig* electoral fraud *(U)*.

puchero *sm* - **1.** [perola] cooking pot - **2.** [comida] stew.

➧ **pucheros** *smpl* [gesto] pout *sing*; **hacer pucheros** to pout.

pucho *sm C Sur fam* [colilla] cigarette butt; [cigarillo] cigarette.

pudding = pudin.

pudibundo, da *adj* prudish.

púdico, ca *adj* - **1.** [recatado] modest - **2.** [tímido] bashful.

pudiente ⬦ *adj* wealthy, well-off. ⬦ *smf* wealthy person.

pudiera *etc* ➪ **poder**.

pudin (*pl* **púdines**), **pudding** ['puðin] (*pl* **puddings**) *sm* (plum) pudding.

pudor *sm* - **1.** [recato] (sense of) shame - **2.** [timidez] bashfulness.

pudoroso, sa *adj* - **1.** [recatado] modest - **2.** [tímido] bashful.

pudrir *vt* - **1.** [descomponerse] to rot - **2.** [fastidiar] to be fed up.

➧ **pudrirse** *vprnl* to rot.

puebla *etc* ➪ **poblar**.

pueblerino, na ⬦ *adj* village *(antes de s)*; *despec* rustic, provincial. ⬦ *sm, f* villager; *despec* yokel.

pueblo *sm* - **1.** [población - pequeña] village; [- grande] town - **2.** [nación] people - **3.** [proletariado] (common) people.

pueda *etc* ➪ **poder**.

puente *sm* - **1.** [gen] bridge; **puente colgante** suspension bridge; **puente levadizo** drawbridge; **puente peatonal** footbridge; **tender un puente** to build bridges - **2.** [días festivos]: **hacer puente** *to take an extra day off between two public holidays*.

puente aéreo *sm* [civil] air shuttle; [militar] airlift.

Puente

When a public holiday falls on a Tuesday or a Thursday, Spanish people usually take another day's holiday to make a four day "long weekend". This is called "hacer puente" (literally "making a bridge"). Depending on the employer, this extra day may be regarded as extra to the agreed annual holidays.

puenting *sm* bungee-jumping.

puerco, **ca** ◇ *adj* dirty, filthy. ◇ *sm, f* - **1.** [animal] pig (*f* sow) - **2.** *fam fig* [persona] pig, swine.

puercoespín *sm* porcupine.

puericultor, **ra** *sm, f* nursery nurse.

puericultura *sf* childcare.

pueril *adj fig* childish.

puerilidad *sf fig* childishness.

puerperio *sm* puerperium.

puerro *sm* leek.

puerta *sf* - **1.** [de casa] door; [de jardín, ciudad etc] gate; **de puerta en puerta** from door to door; **llamar a la puerta** to knock on the door; **puerta de embarque** boarding gate; **puerta principal/trasera** front/back door; **puerta corrediza/giratoria** sliding/revolving door; **puerta blindada/vidriera** reinforced/glass door - **2.** *fig* [posibilidad] gateway, opening - **3.** DEP goal, goalmouth - **4.** *loc*: **a las puertas de** on the verge of; **a puerta cerrada** [gen] behind closed doors; [juicio] in camera; **coger la puerta y marcharse** to up and go; **dar a alguien con las puertas en las narices** to slam the door in sb's face; **estar en puertas** to be knocking on the door, to be imminent.

puerto *sm* - **1.** [de mar] port; **llegar a puerto** to come into port; *fig* to make it in the end; **puerto deportivo** marina; **puerto franco** *o* **libre** free port; **puerto pesquero** fishing port - **2.** [de montaña] pass - **3.** INFORM port; **puerto paralelo/serie/USB** parallel/serial/USB port - **4.** *fig* [refugio] haven.

Puerto Rico *n pr* Puerto Rico.

pues *conj* - **1.** [dado que] since, as - **2.** [por lo tanto] therefore, so; **creo, pues, que...** so, I think that... - **3.** [así que] so; **querías verlo, pues ahí está** you wanted to see it, so here it is - **4.** [enfático]: **¡pues ya está!** well, that's it!; **¡pues claro!** but of course!; **¡pues vaya amigo que tienes!** some friend he is!

puesto, **ta** ◇ *pp* ▷ **poner**. ◇ *adj*: **ir muy puesto** to be all dressed up; **iba sólo con lo puesto** all she had with her were the clothes on her back.

puesto *sm* - **1.** [lugar] place - **2.** [empleo] post, position; **puesto de trabajo** job; **escalar puestos** to work one's way up - **3.** [en fila, clasificación etc] place - **4.** [tenderete] stall, stand - **5.** MIL post; **puesto de mando/vigilancia** command/sentry post; **puesto de policía** police station; **puesto de socorro** first-aid post.

puesta *sf* - **1.** [acción]: **puesta a punto** [de una técnica] perfecting; [de un motor] tuning; **puesta al día** updating; **puesta de largo** debut (in society); **puesta en escena** staging, production; **puesta en marcha** [de máquina] starting, start-up; [de acuerdo, proyecto] implementation; **puesta en órbita** putting into orbit; **puesta en práctica** implementation - **2.** [de ave] laying.

puesta de sol *sf* sunset.

puesto que *loc conj* since, as.

puf (*pl* pufs) *sm* pouf, pouffe.

púgil *sm* boxer.

pugilato *sm* boxing.

pugna *sf* fight, battle.

pugnar *vi* - **1.** [luchar] to fight - **2.** *fig* [esforzarse]: **pugnar por** to struggle *o* fight for.

puja *sf* [en subasta - acción] bidding; [- cantidad] bid.

pujante *adj* vigorous.

pujanza *sf* vigour, strength.

pujar ◇ *vi* - **1.** [en subasta] to bid higher - **2.** *fig* [luchar] to struggle. ◇ *vt* to bid.

pulcritud *sf* neatness, tidiness.

pulcro, **cra** *adj* neat, tidy.

pulga *sf* flea; **tener malas pulgas** *fig* to be bad-tempered.

pulgada *sf* inch.

pulgar ▷ **dedo**.

pulgón *sm* plant louse, aphid.

pulido, **da** *adj* polished, clean.

pulido *sm* polish.

pulidor, **ra** *adj* polishing.

pulidora *sf* polisher.

pulimentar *vt* to polish.

pulir *vt* to polish.

pulirse *vprnl* [gastarse] to blow, to throw away.

pulla *sf* gibe.

pulmón *sm* lung; **pulmón de acero** *o* **artificial** iron lung; **a pleno pulmón** [gritar] at the top of one's voice; [respirar] deeply; **tener buenos pulmones** to have a powerful voice.

pulmonar *adj* pulmonary, lung *(antes de s)*.

pulmonía *sf* pneumonia.

pulpa *sf* pulp.

púlpito *sm* pulpit.

pulpo *sm* - **1.** [animal] octopus - **2.** *fam* [hombre]: **es un pulpo** he can't keep his hands off women - **3.** [correa elástica] spider strap.

pulsación *sf* - **1.** [del corazón] beat, beating *(U)* - **2.** [en máquina de escribir] keystroke, tap; [en piano]: **pulsaciones por minuto** keystrokes per minute.

pulsador *sm* button, push button.

pulsar *vt* - **1.** [botón, timbre etc] to press; [teclas de ordenador] to hit, to strike; [teclas de piano] to play; [cuerdas de guitarra] to pluck - **2.** *fig* [opinión pública etc] to sound out.

pulsera *sf* bracelet; **pulsera de tobillo** ankle bracelet.

pulso *sm* - **1.** [latido] pulse; **tomar el pulso a alguien** to take sb's pulse; **tomar el pulso a algo/alguien** *fig* to sound sthg/sb out - **2.** [firmeza]: **tener buen pulso** to have a steady hand; **a pulso** unaided; **echar un pulso (con alguien)** to arm-wrestle (with sb); **ganarse algo a pulso** to deserve sthg.

pulular *vi* to swarm.

pulverización *sf* [de sólido] pulverization; [de líquido] spraying.

pulverizador, ra *adj* spray *(antes de s)*.
➡ **pulverizador** *sm* spray.

pulverizar [13] *vt* - **1.** [líquido] to spray - **2.** [sólido] to reduce to dust; TECNOL to pulverize - **3.** *fig* [aniquilar] to pulverize.

pum *interj*: **¡pum!** bang!

puma *sm* puma.

pumba *interj*: **¡pumba!** wham!, bang!

punce *etc* ➡ **punzar**.

punción *sf* puncture.

pundonor *sm* pride.

punitivo, va *adj* punitive.

punta *sf* - **1.** [extremo - gen] point; [- de pan, pelo] end; [- de dedo, cuerno] tip; **a punta de pistola** at gunpoint; **de punta a punta** from one end to the other; **en punta** pointed; **en la otra punta de algo** at the other end of sthg; **sacar punta a (un lápiz)** to sharpen (a pencil); **a punta (de) pala** by the dozen *o* bucket; **estar de punta con alguien** to be on edge with sb; **ir de punta en blanco** to be dressed up to the nines; **la punta del iceberg** *fig* the tip of the iceberg; **tener algo en la punta de la lengua** *fig* to have sthg on the tip of one's tongue - **2.** [pizca] touch, bit; [de sal] pinch - **3.** [clavo] small nail - **4.** GEOGR point, headland.
➡ **puntas** *sfpl* [del pelo] ends.

puntada *sf* - **1.** [agujero] hole *o* mark left by needle - **2.** [pespunte] stitch.

puntal *sm* [madero] prop; *fig* [apoyo] mainstay.

puntapié *sm* kick; **dar un puntapié a alguien** to kick sb; **echar a alguien a puntapiés** to kick sb out; **tratar a alguien a puntapiés** *fig* to be nasty to sb.

punteado *sm* MÚS plucking.

puntear *vt* to pluck.

puntera ➡ **puntero**.

puntería *sf* - **1.** [destreza] marksmanship; **hacer puntería** to take aim; **tener puntería** to be a good shot - **2.** [orientación] aim.

puntero, ra ◇ *adj* leading. ◇ *sm, f* [líder] leader.
➡ **puntero** *sm* [para señalar] pointer.
➡ **puntera** *sf* [de zapato] toecap.

puntiagudo, da *adj* pointed.

puntilla *sf* point lace; **dar la puntilla** *fig* to give the coup de grâce.
➡ **de puntillas** *loc adv* on tiptoe.

puntillismo *sm* pointillism.

puntilloso, sa *adj* - **1.** [susceptible] touchy - **2.** [meticuloso] punctilious.

punto *sm* - **1.** [gen] point; **punto débil/fuerte** weak/strong point; **punto de ebullición/fusión** boiling/melting point; **punto cardinal** cardinal point; **punto de apoyo** fulcrum; *fig* backup, support; **punto culminante** high point; **puntos a tratar** matters to be discussed; **poner punto final a algo** to bring sthg to a close; **y punto** *fam* and that's that - **2.** [signo ortográfico] dot; **puntocom** [empresa] dotcom; **punto y aparte** full stop, new paragraph; **punto y coma** semi-colon; **punto y seguido** full stop; **puntos suspensivos** dots, suspension points; **dos puntos** colon; **poner los puntos sobre las íes** to dot the i's and cross the t's - **3.** [marca] spot, dot - **4.** [lugar] spot, place; **punto de venta** COM point of sale - **5.** [momento] point, moment; **estar a punto** to be ready; **estar a punto de hacer algo** to be on the point of doing sthg; **llegar a punto (para hacer algo)** to arrive just in time (to do sthg); **al punto** at once, there and then - **6.** [estado] state, condition; **estando las cosas en este punto** things being as they are; **llegar a un punto en que...** to reach the stage where...; **estar a punto de caramelo para** to be ripe for; **estar en su punto** [gen] to be just right; [comida] to be done to a turn; **poner a punto** [gen] to fine-tune; [motor] to tune - **7.** [grado] degree; **hasta tal punto que** to such an extent that - **8.** [cláusula] clause - **9.** [puntada - en costura, cirugía] stitch; **punto de cruz** cross-stitch; **hacer punto** to knit; **un jersey de punto** a knitted jumper **- 10.** [estilo de tejer] knitting; **punto de ganchillo** crochet **- 11.** [pizca, toque] touch **- 12.** [objetivo] end, target.

➤ **en punto** *loc adv* exactly, on the dot.

➤ **hasta cierto punto** *loc adv* to some extent, up to a point.

➤ **punto de partida** *sm* starting point.

➤ **punto de referencia** *sm* point of reference.

➤ **punto de vista** *sm* point of view, viewpoint.

➤ **punto muerto** *sm* **- 1.** AUTO neutral **- 2.** [en un proceso] deadlock; **estar en un punto muerto** to be deadlocked.

puntuable *adj*: **puntuable para** that counts towards.

puntuación *sf* **- 1.** [calificación] mark; [en concursos, competiciones] score **- 2.** [ortográfica] punctuation.

puntual *adj* **- 1.** [en el tiempo] punctual; **ser puntual** to be on time **- 2.** [exacto, detallado] detailed **- 3.** [aislado] isolated, one-off.

puntualidad *sf* [en el tiempo] punctuality.

puntualizar [13] *vt* to specify, to clarify.

puntuar [6] ◇ *vt* **- 1.** [calificar] to mark; DEP to award marks to **- 2.** [escrito] to punctuate. ◇ *vi* **- 1.** [calificar] to mark **- 2.** [entrar en el cómputo]: **puntuar (para)** to count (towards).

punzada *sf* [dolor intenso] stabbing pain *(U)*; *fig* pang, twinge.

punzante *adj* **- 1.** [que pincha] sharp **- 2.** [intenso] sharp, stabbing **- 3.** [mordaz] caustic.

punzón *sm* punch.

puñado *sm* handful; **a puñados** *fig* hand over fist.

puñal *sm* dagger.

puñalada *sf* stab; [herida] stab wound; **coser a puñaladas** *fig* to stab repeatedly; **puñalada trapera** *fig* stab in the back.

puñeta ◇ *sf fam* [tontería]: **hacer la puñeta** to be a pain; **mandar a alguien a hacer puñetas** to tell sb to get lost; **en la quinta puñeta** in the back of beyond. ◇ *interj fam*: **¡puñeta(s)!** damn it!

puñetazo *sm* punch; **lo derribó de un puñetazo** he knocked him to the ground.

puñetería *sf fam* **- 1.** [molestia] bloodymindedness **- 2.** [menudencia] trifle, unimportant thing.

puñetero, ra *fam* ◇ *adj* **- 1.** [persona] damn; **tu puñetero marido** your damn husband **- 2.** [cosa] tricky, awkward. ◇ *sm, f* pain.

puño *sm* **- 1.** [mano cerrada] fist; **son verdades como puños** it's as clear as daylight; **de su puño y letra** in his/her own handwriting; **meter**

o **tener a alguien en un puño** to have sb under one's thumb **- 2.** [de manga] cuff **- 3.** [empuñadura - de espada] hilt; [- de paraguas] handle.

pupa *sf* **- 1.** [erupción] blister **- 2.** *fam* [daño] pain; **hacerse pupa** to hurt o.s.

pupila *sf* pupil.

pupilaje *sm* reserved *o* long-term parking.

pupilo, la *sm, f* **- 1.** [discípulo] pupil **- 2.** [huérfano] ward.

pupitre *sm* desk.

purasangre *sm inv* thoroughbred.

puré *sm* CULIN purée; [sopa] thick soup; **puré de patatas** mashed potatoes *pl*; **estar hecho puré** *fam* to be knackered; **hacer puré a alguien** to beat sb to a pulp.

pureta *fam* ◇ *adj* fogeyish. ◇ *smf* old fogey.

pureza *sf* purity.

purga *sf* **- 1.** MED purgative **- 2.** *fig* [depuración] purge.

purgante *adj* & *sm* purgative.

purgar [16] *vt lit* & *fig* to purge.

➤ **purgarse** *vprnl* to take a purge.

purgatorio *sm* purgatory.

purgue *etc* ▷ **purgar**.

purificación *sf* purification.

purificar [10] *vt* to purify; [mineral, metal] to refine.

purista ◇ *adj* purist *(antes de s).* ◇ *smf* purist.

puritanismo *sm* puritanism.

puritano, na *adj* & *sm, f* puritan.

puro, ra *adj* **- 1.** [gen] pure; [oro] solid **- 2.** [conducta, persona] chaste, innocent **- 3.** [mero] sheer; [verdad] plain; **por pura casualidad** by pure chance.

➤ **puro** *sm* cigar.

púrpura ◇ *adj inv* purple. ◇ *sm* purple.

purpurina *sf* purpurin.

purulento, ta *adj culto* purulent.

pus *sm* pus.

pusiera *etc* ▷ **poner**.

pusilánime *adj* cowardly.

puso ▷ **poner**.

pústula *sf* pimple, spot.

puta ◇ *adj* ▷ **puto**. ◇ *sf vulg* whore; **ir de putas** to go whoring; **de puta madre** fucking brilliant.

putada *sf vulg*: **hacerle una putada a alguien** to be a mean bastard to sb; **¡qué putada!** what a bummer!

putativo, va *adj* putative.

puteado, da *adj vulg* pissed off.

puteo *sm vulg* [con prostitutas]: **ir de puteo** to go whoring.

putero, ra *adj vulg* whoremonger.

puto, ta *adj vulg* - **1.** [maldito] bloody - **2.** [difícil] bloody difficult.

▸ **puto** *sm vulg* male prostitute.

putrefacción *sf* rotting, putrefaction.

putrefacto, ta *adj* rotting.

pútrido, da *adj* putrid.

puzzle ['puθle], **puzle** *sm* jigsaw puzzle.

PVC (*abrev de* cloruro de polivinilo) *sm* PVC.

PVP (*abrev de* precio de venta al público) *sm* ≃ RRP.

PYME (*abrev de* **Pequeña y Mediana Empresa**) *sf* SME.

pyrex® = **pírex**.

pza. (*abrev de* plaza) Sq.

q, Q *sf* [letra] q, Q.

q.e.p.d. (*abrev de* que en paz descanse) RIP.

quántico = **cuántico**.

que ⬥ *pron relat* - **1.** (sujeto) [persona] who, that; [cosa] that, which; **la mujer que me saluda** the woman (who o that is) waving to me; **el que me lo compró** the one who bought it from me; **la moto que me gusta** the motorbike (that) I like - **2.** (complemento directo) [persona] whom, that; [cosa] that, which; **el hombre que conociste ayer** the man (whom o that) you met yesterday; **ese coche es el que me quiero comprar** that car is the one (that o which) I want to buy - **3.** (complemento indirecto): **al/a la que** (to) whom; **ese es el chico al que presté dinero** that's the boy to whom I lent some money - **4.** (complemento circunstancial): **la playa a la que fui** the beach where o to which I went; **la mujer con la que hablas** the woman to whom you are talking; **la mesa sobre la que escribes** the table on which you are writing - **5.** (complemento de tiempo): **(en) que** when; **el día (en) que me fui** the day (when) I left. ⬥ *conj* - **1.** (con oraciones de sujeto) that; **es**

importante que me escuches it's important that you listen to me - **2.** (con oraciones de complemento directo) that; **me ha confesado que me quiere** he has told me that he loves me - **3.** (compar) than; **es más rápido que tú** he's quicker than you; **antes morir que vivir la guerra** I'd rather die than live through a war - **4.** [expresa causa]: **hemos de esperar, que todavía no es la hora** we'll have to wait, as it isn't time yet - **5.** [expresa consecuencia] that; **tanto me lo pidió que se lo di** he asked me for it so insistently that I gave it to him - **6.** [expresa finalidad] so (that); **ven aquí que te vea** come over here so (that) I can see you - **7.** (+ subjuntivo) [expresa deseo] that; **quiero que lo hagas** I want you to do it; **espero que te diviertas** I hope (that) you have fun - **8.** (en oraciones exclamativas): **¡que te diviertas!** have fun!; **¡que te doy un bofetón!** do that again and I'll slap you! - **9.** (en oraciones interrogativas): **¿que quiere venir?** pues que venga so she wants to come? then let her - **10.** [expresa disyunción] or; **quieras que no, harás lo que yo mando** you'll do what I tell you, whether you like it or not - **11.** [expresa hipótesis] if; **que no quieres hacerlo, pues no pasa nada** it doesn't matter if you don't want to do it - **12.** [expresa reiteración] and; **estaban charla que charla** they were talking and talking.

qué ⬥ *adj* [gen] what; [al elegir, al concretar] which; **¿qué hora es?** what's the time?; **¿qué coche prefieres?** which car do you prefer?; **¿a qué distancia?** how far away? ⬥ *pron* (interrogativo) what; **¿qué te dijo?** what did he tell you?; **no sé qué hacer** I don't know what to do; **¿qué?** [¿cómo?] sorry?, pardon? ⬥ *adv* - **1.** [exclamativo] how; **¡qué horror!** how awful!; **¡qué tonto eres!** how stupid you are!, you're so stupid!; **¡qué casa más bonita!** what a lovely house!; **¡y qué!** so what? - **2.** [expresa gran cantidad]: **¡qué de...!** what a lot of...!; **¡qué de gente hay aquí!** what a lot of people there are here!, there are so many people here!

quebrada ⬥ **quebrado.**

quebradero ▸ **quebradero de cabeza** *sm* headache, problem.

quebradizo, za *adj* - **1.** [frágil] fragile, brittle - **2.** [débil] frail - **3.** [voz] weak.

quebrado, da *adj* - **1.** [terreno] rough, uneven; [perfil] rugged - **2.** MAT fractional.

▸ **quebrado** *sm* MAT fraction.

▸ **quebrada** *sf* - **1.** [desfiladero] gorge - **2.** Amér [arroyo] stream.

quebrantado, da *adj* frail.

quebrantahuesos *sm inv* bearded vulture, lammergeier.

quebrantar *vt* - **1.** [incumplir - promesa, ley] to break; [- obligación] to fail in - **2.** [debilitar] to weaken; [moral, resistencia] to break.

◆ **quebrantarse** *vprnl* - **1.** [romperse] to crack - **2.** [debilitarse] to decline, to deteriorate.

quebranto *sm* - **1.** [debilitamiento] weakening, debilitation - **2.** [pena] grief.

quebrar [19] ◇ *vt* [romper] to break. ◇ *vi* FIN to go bankrupt.

◆ **quebrarse** *vprnl* - **1.** [romperse] to break - **2.** [voz] to break, to falter.

quechua ◇ *adj* Quechuan. ◇ *smf* [persona] Quechua. ◇ *sm* [idioma] Quechua.

Quechua ▬▬▬▬▬▬▬

⊞ Quechua, which was the language of the Inca empire, is an Amerindian language still spoken today by more than eight million people in the Andean region. The number of speakers declined dramatically in the centuries following the Spanish conquest, but in more recent years there have been official attempts to promote the language. As with the Aztec language Náhuatl, many Quechua words passed into Spanish, and on to many other languages. For example, in English we find "condor", "jerky" and "quinine".

quedar ◇ *vi* - **1.** [permanecer] to remain, to stay; **el viaje quedó en proyecto** the trip never got beyond the planning stage - **2.** [haber aún, faltar] to be left, to remain; **¿queda azúcar?** is there any sugar left?; **nos quedan 10 euros** we have 10 euros left; **¿cuánto queda para León?** how much further is it to León?; **quedar por hacer** to remain to be done; **queda por fregar el suelo** the floor has still to be cleaned - **3.** [mostrarse]: **quedar como** to come across as; **quedar bien/mal (con alguien)** to make a good/bad impression (on sb) - **4.** [llegar a ser, resultar]: **el trabajo ha quedado perfecto** the job turned out perfectly; **el cuadro queda muy bien ahí** the picture looks great there - **5.** [acabar]: **quedar en** to end in; **quedar en nada** to come to nothing - **6.** [sentar] to look; **te queda un poco corto el traje** your suit is a bit too short; **quedar bien/mal a alguien** to look good/bad on sb; **quedar bien/mal con algo** to go well/badly with sthg - **7.** [citarse]: **quedar (con alguien)** to arrange to meet (sb); **hemos quedado el lunes** we've arranged to meet on Monday - **8.** [acordar]: **quedar en algo/en hacer algo** to agree on sthg/to do sthg; **quedar en que...** to agree that...; **¿en qué quedamos?** what's it to be, then? - **9.** *fam* [estar situado] to be; **queda por las afueras** it's somewhere on the outskirts; **¿por dónde queda?** whereabouts is

it? ◇ *v impers*: **por mí que no quede** don't let me be the one to stop you; **que no quede por falta de dinero** we don't want it to fall through for lack of money.

◆ **quedarse** *vprnl* - **1.** [permanecer - en un lugar] to stay, to remain - **2.** [terminar - en un estado]: **quedarse ciego/sordo** to go blind/deaf; **quedarse triste** to be *o* feel sad; **quedarse sin dinero** to be left penniless; **la pared se ha quedado limpia** the wall is clean now - **3.** [comprar] to take; **me quedo éste** I'll take this one.

◆ **quedarse con** *vprnl* - **1.** [retener, guardarse] to keep - **2.** [preferir] to go for, to prefer - **3.** *mfam* [burlarse de]: **quedarse con alguien** to wind sb up.

quedo, **da** *adj* quiet, soft.

◆ **quedo** *adv* quietly, softly.

quehacer *(gen pl)* *sm* task; **quehaceres domésticos** housework *(U)*.

queimada *sf* flamed punch made from lemon juice, sugar and a type of brandy.

queja *sf* - **1.** [lamento] moan, groan - **2.** [protesta] complaint; **presentar una queja** to lodge *o* make a complaint.

quejarse *vprnl* - **1.** [lamentar] to groan, to cry out; **quejarse de algo/alguien** to bemoan sthg/sb - **2.** [protestar] to complain; **quejarse de** to complain about.

quejica *despec* ◇ *adj* whining, whingeing. ◇ *smf* whinger.

quejido *sm* cry, moan.

quejoso, **sa** *adj*: **quejoso (de)** annoyed *o* upset (with).

quejumbroso, **sa** *adj* whining.

quema *sf* burning.

quemado, **da** *adj* - **1.** [gen] burnt; **oler a quemado** to smell burning; [por agua hirviendo] scalded; [por electricidad] burnt-out; [fusible] blown - **2.** [por sol] sunburnt - **3.** *Amér* [bronceado] tanned - **4.** *loc*: **estar quemado** [agotado] to be burnt-out; [harto] to be fed up.

quemador *sm* burner.

quemadura *sf* [por fuego] burn; **quemadura en tercer grado** third-degree burning; [por agua hirviendo] scald.

quemar ◇ *vt* - **1.** [gen] to burn; [suj: agua hirviendo] to scald; [suj: electricidad] to blow - **2.** [suj: frío] to wither - **3.** *fig* [malgastar] to go through, to fritter away - **4.** *fig* [desgastar] to burn out - **5.** *fig* [hartar] to make fed up. ◇ *vi* - **1.** [estar caliente] to be (scalding) hot - **2.** *fig* [desgastar]: **la política quema** politics burns you out.

◆ **quemarse** *vprnl* - **1.** [por fuego] to burn down; [por agua hirviendo] to get scalded; [por calor] to burn; [por electricidad] to blow - **2.** [por el sol] to get burned - **3.** *fig* [desgastarse] to burn out - **4.** *fig* [hartarse] to get fed up.

quemarropa ➡ **a quemarropa** *loc adv* point-blank.

quemazón *sf* burning; [picor] itch.

quepa *etc* ⊳ caber.

quepis, kepis *sm* kepi.

quepo *etc* ⊳ caber.

queratina *sf* keratin.

querella *sf* - **1.** DER [acusación] charge; **presentar una querella contra alguien** to bring an action against sb - **2.** [discordia] dispute.

querellante *adj* & *smf* DER plaintiff.

querellarse *vprnl* to bring an action.

querencia *sf* homing instinct.

querer [67] ◇ *vt* - **1.** [gen] to want; **quiero una bicicleta** I want a bicycle; **¿quieren ustedes algo más?** would you like anything else?; **querer que alguien haga algo** to want sb to do sthg; **quiero que lo hagas tú** I want you to do it; **querer que pase algo** to want sthg to happen; **queremos que las cosas te vayan bien** we want things to go well for you; **quisiera hacerlo, pero...** I'd like to do it, but... - **2.** [amar] to love - **3.** [en preguntas - con amabilidad]: **¿quiere decirle a su amigo que pase?** could you tell your friend to come in, please? - **4.** [pedir - precio]: **querer algo (por)** to want sthg (for); **¿cuánto quieres por el coche?** how much do you want for the car? - **5.** *fig* & *irón* [dar motivos para]: **tú lo que quieres es que te pegue** you're asking for a smack - **6.** *loc*: **como quien no quiere la cosa** as if it were nothing; **quien bien te quiere te hará llorar** *prov* you have to be cruel to be kind *prov*. ◇ *vi* to want; **ven cuando quieras** come whenever you like *o* want; **no me voy porque no quiero** I'm not going because I don't want to; **queriendo** on purpose; **sin querer** accidentally; **querer decir** to mean; **¿qué quieres decir con eso?** what do you mean by that?; **querer es poder** where there's a will there's a way. ◇ *v impers* [haber atisbos]: **parece que quiere llover** it looks like rain. ◇ *sm* love.

quererse *vprnl* to love each other.

querido, da ◇ *adj* dear. ◇ *sm, f* lover; [apelativo afectuoso] darling.

quermés, quermese *sf* kermiss.

queroseno, keroseno *sm* kerosene.

querrá *etc* ⊳ querer.

querubín *sm* cherub.

quesadilla *sf* *Amér C & Méx filled fried tortilla*.

quesera ⊳ quesero.

quesero, ra ◇ *adj* cheese (*antes de s*). ◇ *sm, f* [persona] cheese maker.

➡ **quesera** *sf* [recipiente] cheese dish.

queso *sm* cheese; **queso gruyère/parmesano/roquefort** Gruyère/Parmesan/Roquefort (cheese); **queso de bola** Dutch cheese; **queso manchego** *hard mild yellow cheese made in La Mancha*; **queso para untar** cheese spread; **queso rallado** grated cheese; **dárselas con queso a alguien** to fool sb.

quetzal [ket'sal] *sm* quetzal.

quevedos *smpl* pince-nez.

quia *interj fam*: **¡quia!** huh!, ha!

quicio *sm* jamb; **estar fuera de quicio** *fig* to be out of kilter; **sacar de quicio a alguien** *fig* to drive sb mad.

quid (*pl* quids) *sm* crux; **el quid de la cuestión** the crux of the matter.

quiebra ◇ *v* ⊳ quebrar. ◇ *sf* - **1.** [ruina] bankruptcy; **ir a la quiebra** to go bankrupt; [en bolsa] crash; **quiebra fraudulenta** DER fraudulent bankruptcy - **2.** *fig* [pérdida] collapse.

quiebro *sm* - **1.** [ademán] swerve - **2.** MÚS trill.

quien *pron* - **1.** (*relativo*) [sujeto] who; [complemento] whom; **fue mi hermano quien me lo explicó** it was my brother who explained it to me; **era Pepe a quien vi/de quien no me fiaba** it was Pepe (whom) I saw/didn't trust - **2.** (*indefinido*): **quienes quieran verlo que se acerquen** whoever wants to see it will have to come closer; **hay quien lo niega** there are those who deny it - **3.** *loc*: **quien más quien menos** everyone.

quién *pron* - **1.** (*interrogativo*) [sujeto] who; [complemento] who, whom; **¿quién es ese hombre?** who's that man?; **no sé quién viene** I don't know who is coming; **¿a quiénes has invitado?** who *o* whom have you invited?; **¿de quién es?** whose is it?; **¿quién es?** [en la puerta] who is it?; [al teléfono] who's calling? - **2.** (*exclamativo*): **¡quién pudiera verlo!** if only I could have seen it!

quienquiera (*pl* quienesquiera) *pron* whoever; **quienquiera que venga** whoever comes.

quiera *etc* ⊳ querer.

quieto, ta *adj* - **1.** [parado] still; **¡estáte quieto!** keep still!; **¡quieto ahí!** don't move! - **2.** *fig* [tranquilo] quiet.

quietud *sf* - **1.** [inmovilidad] stillness - **2.** [tranquilidad] quietness.

quif, kif *sm* hashish.

quijada *sf* jaw.

quijotada *sf* quixotic deed.

quijote *sm* *despec* do-gooder.

quijotesco, ca *adj* quixotic.

quijotismo *sm* quixotism.

quilate *sm* carat.

quilla *sf* NÁUT keel.
quilo *etc* = **kilo**.
quilombo *sm* - **1.** *mfam* [prostíbulo] whorehouse - **2.** *mfam* [lío] mess.
quimera *sf* fantasy.
quimérico, ca *adj* fanciful, unrealistic.
químico, ca <> *adj* chemical. <> *sm, f* [científico] chemist.
◆ **química** *sf* [ciencia] chemistry.
quimioterapia *sf* chemotherapy.
quimono, kimono *sm* kimono.
quina *sf* - **1.** [planta] cinchona - **2.** [bebida] quinine; **ser más malo que la quina** to be truly horrible; **tragar quina** to grin and bear it.
quincalla *sf* trinket.
quincallería *sf* [quincallas] trinkets *pl*.
quince *num* fifteen; **quince días** a fortnight; *ver también* **seis**.
quinceañero, ra <> *adj* teenage. <> *sm, f* teenager.
quinceavo, va *num* fifteenth; **la quinceava parte** a fifteenth.
quincena *sf* fortnight.
quincenal *adj* fortnightly.
quincuagésimo, ma *num* fiftieth.
quiniela *sf* [boleto] pools coupon.
◆ **quinielas** *sfpl* [apuestas] (football) pools; **jugar a las quinielas** to play the pools.
◆ **quiniela hípica** *sf* sweepstake.
quinielista *smf* punter who does the pools.
quinientos, tas *num* five hundred; *ver también* **seis**.
quinina *sf* quinine.
quinqué *sm* oil lamp.
quinquenal *adj* five-year *(antes de s)*.
quinquenio *sm* - **1.** [periodo] five-year period - **2.** [paga] five-yearly increment of salary.
quinqui *smf* *fam* delinquent.
quinta ⊳ **quinto**.
quintaesencia *sf inv* quintessence.
quinteto *sm* quintet.
quintillizo, za *adj & sm, f* quintuplet.
quinto, ta *num* fifth; **la quinta parte** a fifth.
◆ **quinto** *sm* - **1.** [parte] fifth - **2.** MIL recruit, conscript.
◆ **quinta** *sf* - **1.** [finca] country house - **2.** MIL call-up year; **entrar en quintas** to be called up.
quíntuple = **quíntuplo**.
quintuplicar [10] *vt* to increase fivefold.
◆ **quintuplicarse** *vprnl* to increase fivefold.
quíntuplo, pla, quíntuple *adj* quintuple.
◆ **quíntuplo** *sm* quintuple.

quiosco, kiosco *sm* kiosk; [de periódicos] newspaper stand; **quiosco de música** bandstand.
quiosquero, ra *sm, f* owner of a newspaper stand.
quiquiriquí (*pl* **quiquiriquíes**) *sm* cock-a-doodle-do.
quirófano *sm* operating theatre.
quiromancia *sf* palmistry, chiromancy.
quiromántico, ca <> *adj* chiromantic. <> *sm, f* palmist.
quiromasaje *sm* (manual) massage.
quirúrgico, ca *adj* surgical.
quisiera *etc* ⊳ **querer**.
quisque *sm*: **cada** *o* **todo quisque** every man Jack, everyone.
quisquilloso, sa <> *adj* - **1.** [detallista] pernickety - **2.** [susceptible] touchy, over-sensitive. <> *sm, f* - **1.** [detallista] nit picker - **2.** [susceptible] touchy person.
quiste *sm* cyst.
quitaesmalte *sm* nail-polish remover.
quitaipón ◆ **de quitaipón** *loc adj* removable; [capucha] detachable.
quitamanchas *sm inv* stain remover.
quitanieves *sm inv* snow plough.
quitar *vt* - **1.** [gen] to remove; [ropa, zapatos etc] to take off; **quitarle algo a alguien** to take sthg away from sb; **de quita y pon** removable; [capucha] detachable - **2.** [dolor, ansiedad] to take away, to relieve; [sed] to quench - **3.** [tiempo] to take up - **4.** [robar] to take, to steal - **5.** [impedir]: **esto no quita que sea un vago** that doesn't change the fact that he's a layabout - **6.** [exceptuar]: **quitando el queso, me gusta todo** apart from cheese, I'll eat anything - **7.** [desconectar] to switch off.
◆ **quitarse** *vprnl* - **1.** [apartarse] to get out of the way - **2.** [ropa] to take off - **3.** [suj: mancha] to come out - **4.** *loc*: **quitarse a alguien de encima** *o* **de en medio** to get rid of sb.
quitasol *sm* sunshade UK, parasol.
quite *sm* DEP parry; **estar al quite** to be on hand to help.
quiteño, ña *adj* of/relating to Quito.
Quito *n pr* Quito.
quizá, quizás *adv* perhaps; **quizá llueva mañana** it might rain tomorrow; **quizá no lo creas** you may not believe it; **quizá sí** maybe; **quizá no** maybe not.
quórum *sm* quorum.

R

r, R *sf* [letra] r, R.

rabadilla *sf* - **1.** [de persona] coccyx - **2.** [de res] rump.

rábano *sm* radish; **coger el rábano por las hojas** to get the wrong end of the stick; **me importa un rábano** I couldn't care less, I don't give a damn.

rabel *sm* rebec.

rabí *sm* rabbi.

rabia *sf* - **1.** [ira] rage; **me da rabia** it makes me mad; **tenerle rabia a alguien** *fig* not to be able to stand sb - **2.** [enfermedad] rabies.

rabiar [8] *vi* - **1.** [sufrir] to writhe in pain; **rabiar de** o **por** to writhe in - **2.** [enfadarse] to be furious; **estar a rabiar (con alguien)** to be furious (with sb); **hacer rabiar a alguien** to make sb furious - **3.** [desear]: **rabiar por algo/hacer algo** to be dying for sthg/to do sthg; **me gusta a rabiar** I'm crazy about it.

rabieta *sf fam* tantrum; **tener una rabieta** to throw a tantrum.

rabillo *sm* corner; **mirar algo con el rabillo del ojo** to look at sthg out of the corner of one's eye.

rabino *sm* rabbi.

rabiosamente *adv* - **1.** [mucho] terribly - **2.** [con enfado] furiously, in a rage.

rabioso, sa *adj* - **1.** [furioso] furious - **2.** [excesivo] terrible - **3.** [enfermo de rabia] rabid - **4.** [chillón] loud, gaudy.

rabo *sm* - **1.** [de animal] tail; **rabo de buey** oxtail; **irse** o **salir con el rabo entre las piernas** to go off with one's tail between one's legs - **2.** [de hoja, fruto] stem - **3.** *vulg* [pene] prick, cock.

rácano, na *fam* <> *adj* [tacaño] mean, stingy. <> *sm, f* [tacaño] mean devil.

RACE (*abrev de* **Real Automóvil Club de España**) *sm Spanish automobile association*, ≃ AA *UK*, ≃ AAA *US*.

racha *sf* - **1.** [ráfaga] gust (of wind) - **2.** [época] spell; [serie] string; **buena/mala racha** good/bad patch; **a rachas** in fits and starts.

racial *adj* racial.

racimo *sm* - **1.** [de frutos] bunch - **2.** [de flores] raceme.

raciocinio *sm* - **1.** [razón] (power of) reason - **2.** [razonamiento] reasoning (*U*).

ración *sf* - **1.** [porción] portion - **2.** [en bar, restaurante] *large portion of a dish served as a snack*.

racional *adj* rational.

racionalidad *sf* rationality.

racionalismo *sm* rationalism.

racionalización *sf* rationalization.

racionalizar [13] *vt* to rationalize.

racionamiento *sm* rationing.

racionar *vt* to ration.

racismo *sm* racism.

racista *adj* & *smf* racist.

radar (*pl* **radares**) *sm* radar.

radiación *sf* radiation; **radiación solar** solar radiation.

radiactividad *sf* radioactivity.

radiactivo, va, radioactivo, va *adj* radioactive.

radiado, da *adj* - **1.** [por radio - mensaje] radioed; [- programa etc] radio (*antes de s*) - **2.** [radial] radiate.

radiador *sm* radiator.

radial *adj* - **1.** [gen] radial - **2.** *Amér* [emisión, cadena] radio (*antes de s*).

radiante *adj* radiant; **lucía un sol radiante** it was brilliantly sunny.

radiar [9] *vt* - **1.** [irradiar] to radiate - **2.** *FÍS* to irradiate; *MED* to give X-ray treatment to - **3.** [por radio] to broadcast.

radicación *sf* [establecimiento] settling.

radical <> *adj* & *smf* radical. <> *sm* - **1.** *GRAM* & *MAT* root - **2.** *QUÍM* free radical.

radicalismo *sm* - **1.** [intransigencia] severity - **2.** *POLÍT* radicalism.

radicalización *sf* radicalization.

radicalizar [13] *vt* to harden, to make more radical.

➤ **radicalizarse** *vprnl* to become more radical o extreme.

radicar [10] *vi*: **radicar en** [suj: problema etc] to lie in; [suj: población] to be (situated) in.

➤ **radicarse** *vprnl* [establecerse]: **radicarse (en)** to settle (in).

radio <> *sm* - **1.** *ANAT* & *GEOM* radius; **en un radio de** within a radius of; **radio de acción** *TECNOL* range; *fig* sphere of influence - **2.** [de rueda] spoke - **3.** *QUÍM* radium. <> *sf* radio; **oír algo por la radio** to hear sthg on the radio; **oír algo por radio macuto** *fam* to hear sthg on the bush telegraph; **radio digital** digital radio; **radio por Internet** Internet radio; **radio pirata** pirate radio station.

radioactivo = **radiactivo**.

radioaficionado, **da** *sm*, *f* radio ham.

radiocasete *sm* radio cassette (player).

radiocontrol *sm* remote control.

radiodespertador *sm* clock radio.

radiodifusión *sf* broadcasting.

radioemisor, **ra** *adj* radio broadcasting.
➥ **radioemisora** *sf* radio station, radio transmitter.

radioenlace *sm* radio link.

radioescucha *smf inv* listener.

radiofonía *sf* radio (*technology*).

radiofónico, **ca** *adj* radio (*antes de s*).

radiofrecuencia *sf* radio frequency.

radiografía *sf* [fotografía] X-ray; **hacerse una radiografía** to be X-rayed; [ciencia] radiography.

radiografiar [9] *vt* to X-ray.

radiología *sf* radiology.

radiólogo, **ga** *sm*, *f* radiologist.

radionovela *sf* radio soap opera.

radiooperador, **ra** *sm*, *f* radio operator.

radiorreceptor *sm* radio (receiver).

radiorreloj *sm* clock radio.

radiotaxi *sm* taxi (with radio link).

radioteléfono *sm* radiotelephone.

radiotelegrafía *sf* radiotelegraphy.

radiotelegrafista *smf* wireless operator.

radioterapia *sf* radiotherapy.

radiotransmisión *sf* broadcasting.

radiotransmisor *sm* radio transmitter.

radioyente *smf* listener.

radique *etc* ⊳ **radicar**.

RAE (*abrev de* **Real Academia Española**), *institution that sets lexical and syntactic standards for Spanish.*

raer [68] *vt* to scrape (off).

ráfaga *sf* [de aire, viento] gust; [de disparos] burst; [de luces] flash.

rafting *sm* DEP rafting.

raglán ⊳ **manga**.

ragout = **ragú**.

ragtime [rak'taim] *sm* ragtime.

ragú (*pl* **ragúes** O **ragús**), **ragout** [ra'ɣu] (*pl* **ragouts**) *sm* ragout.

raído, **da** *adj* threadbare; [por los bordes] frayed.

raiga *etc* ⊳ **raer**.

raigambre *sf* - **1.** [tradición] tradition - **2.** BOT root system.

raigo *etc* ⊳ **raer**.

raíl, **rail** *sm* rail.

raíz (*pl* **raíces**) *sf* [gen & MAT] root; **raíz cuadrada/cúbica** square/cube root; **a raíz de** as a result of, following; **arrancar algo de raíz** to root sthg out completely; **cortar algo de raíz** to nip sthg in the bud; **echar raíces** to put down roots.

raja *sf* - **1.** [porción] slice - **2.** [grieta] crack.

rajá (*pl* **rajás** O **rajáes**) *sm* rajah.

rajado, **da** *adj* & *sm*, *f fam* chicken.

rajar *vt* - **1.** [partir] to crack; [melón] to slice - **2.** *mfam* [apuñalar] to slash, to cut up.
➥ **rajarse** *vprnl* - **1.** [partirse] to crack - **2.** *fam* [echarse atrás] to chicken out.

rajatabla ➥ **a rajatabla** *loc adv* to the letter, strictly.

ralea *sf despec* breed, ilk.

ralentí *sm* neutral; **al ralentí** AUTO ticking over; CINE in slow motion.

rallado, **da** *adj* grated.

rallador *sm* grater.

ralladura (*gen pl*) *sf* grating; **ralladuras de limón** grated lemon rind.

rallar *vt* to grate.

rally ['rali] (*pl* **rallies**) *sm* rally.

ralo, **la** *adj* [pelo, barba] sparse, thin; [dientes] with gaps between them.

RAM (*abrev de* **random access memory**) *sf* INFORM RAM.

rama *sf* branch; **en rama** raw; **andarse por las ramas** *fam* to beat about the bush; **irse por las ramas** *fam* to go off at a tangent.

ramada *sf Amér* stall.

ramadán *sm* Ramadan.

ramaje *sm* branches *pl*.

ramal *sm* [de carretera, ferrocarril] branch.

ramalazo *sm* - **1.** *fam* [hecho que delata] giveaway sign; **tener un ramalazo** *fam* to be effeminate - **2.** [ataque] fit.

rambla *sf* - **1.** [avenida] avenue, boulevard - **2.** *R Plata* [paseo marítimo] seafront.

ramera *sf* whore, hooker *US*.

ramificación *sf* - **1.** [gen] ramification - **2.** [de carretera, ferrocarril, ciencia] branch.

ramificarse [10] *vprnl* - **1.** [bifurcarse] to branch out - **2.** [subdividirse]: **ramificarse (en)** to subdivide (into).

ramillete *sm* bunch, bouquet.

ramo *sm* - **1.** [de flores] bunch, bouquet - **2.** [rama] branch; **el ramo de la construcción** the building industry.

rampa *sf* - **1.** [para subir y bajar] ramp; **rampa de lanzamiento** launch pad - **2.** [cuesta] steep incline - **3.** [calambre] cramp *(U)*.

ramplón, ona *adj* vulgar, coarse.

rana *sf* frog; **salir rana** *fam* to turn out sadly, to be a disappointment.

ranchero, ra *sm, f* rancher.

➨ **ranchera** *sf* - **1.** MÚS *popular Mexican song* - **2.** AUTO estate car - **3.** *Amér* [furgoneta] van.

rancho *sm* - **1.** [comida] mess - **2.** [granja] ranch - **3.** *loc*: **hacer rancho aparte** to keep to o.s. - **4.** *C Sur & Ven* [choza] shack, shanty; *Ven* [chabola] shanty town.

rancio, cia *adj* - **1.** [pasado] rancid - **2.** [antiguo] ancient - **3.** [añejo - vino] mellow.

ranglán ➢ **manga**.

rango *sm* - **1.** [social] standing - **2.** [jerárquico] rank.

ranking ['raŋkin] (*pl* **rankings**) *sm* ranking.

ranura *sf* groove; [de máquina tragaperras, cabina telefónica] slot.

rapaces ➢ **rapaz**.

rapacidad *sf* rapacity, greed.

rapado, da *adj* shaven.

rapapolvo *sm fam* ticking-off; **dar** *o* **echar un rapapolvo a alguien** to tick sb off.

rapar *vt* [barba, bigote] to shave off; [cabeza] to shave; [persona] to shave the hair of.

➨ **raparse** *vprnl* to shave one's head.

rapaz, za *sm, f fam* lad (*f* lass).

➨ **rapaz** *adj* - **1.** [que roba] rapacious, greedy - **2.** ZOOL ➢ **ave**.

➨ **rapaces** *sfpl* ZOOL birds of prey.

rape *sm* monkfish; **cortar el pelo al rape a alguien** to crop sb's hair.

rapé *sm* (*en aposición invariable*) snuff.

rapero, ra *sm, f* rapper.

rápidamente *adv* quickly.

rapidez *sf* speed; **con rapidez** quickly.

rápido, da *adj* quick, fast; [coche] fast; [beneficio, decisión] quick.

➨ **rápido** ➢ *adv* quickly; **más rápido** quicker; **¡ven, rápido!** come, quick! ➢ *sm* [tren] express train.

➨ **rápidos** *smpl* [de río] rapids.

rapiña *sf* - **1.** [robo] robbery with violence - **2.** ➢ **ave**.

raposa *sf* vixen.

rapsodia *sf* rhapsody.

raptar *vt* to abduct, to kidnap.

rapto *sm* - **1.** [secuestro] abduction, kidnapping - **2.** [ataque] fit.

raptor, ra *sm, f* abductor, kidnapper.

raqueta *sf* - **1.** [para jugar - al tenis] racquet; [- al ping pong] bat - **2.** [para la nieve] snowshoe - **3.** [de croupier] rake.

raquídeo, a *adj* ANAT rachideal.

raquis *sm* vertebral column.

raquítico, ca *adj* - **1.** MED rachitic - **2.** [insuficiente] miserable.

raquitismo *sm* MED rickets *(U)*.

rareza *sf* - **1.** [poco común, extraño] rarity - **2.** [poco frecuente] infrequency - **3.** [extravagancia] idiosyncrasy, eccentricity.

raro, ra *adj* - **1.** [extraño] strange; **¡qué raro!** how odd *o* strange! - **2.** [excepcional] unusual, rare; [visita] infrequent - **3.** [extravagante] odd, eccentric - **4.** [escaso] rare; **rara vez** rarely.

➨ **rara avis** *sm, f* oddity.

ras *sm*: **a ras de** level with; **a ras de tierra** at ground level; **volar a ras de tierra** to fly low.

rasante ➢ *adj* [vuelo] low-level; [tiro] grazing. ➢ *sf* [de carretera] gradient.

rasar *vt* to skim, to graze.

rascacielos *sm inv* skyscraper.

rascar [10] ➢ *vt* - **1.** [con uñas, clavo] to scratch - **2.** [con espátula] to scrape (off); [con cepillo] to scrub - **3.** *despec* [instrumento] to scrape away at. ➢ *vi* to be rough.

➨ **rascarse** *vprnl* to scratch o.s.

rasero *sm* strickle; **medir por el mismo rasero** to treat alike.

rasgado ➢ **ojo**.

rasgar [16] *vt* to tear; [sobre] to tear open.

➨ **rasgarse** *vprnl* to tear.

rasgo *sm* - **1.** [característica] trait, characteristic - **2.** [acto elogiable] act - **3.** [trazo] flourish, stroke.

➨ **rasgos** *smpl* - **1.** [del rostro] features - **2.** [letra] handwriting *(U)*.

➨ **a grandes rasgos** *loc adv* in general terms; **explicar algo a grandes rasgos** to outline sthg.

rasgón *sm* tear.

rasgue *etc* ➢ **rasgar**.

rasguear *vt* to strum.

rasguñar *vt* to scratch.

◆ **rasguñarse** *vprnl* to scratch.

rasguño *sm* scratch; **sin un rasguño** without a scratch.

raso, sa *adj* - **1.** [cucharada etc] level - **2.** [cielo] clear - **3.** [a poca altura] low - **4.** MIL: **soldado raso** private.

◆ **raso** *sm* - **1.** [tela] satin - **2.** *loc*: **al raso** in the open air.

raspa *sf* backbone (of fish).

raspado *sm* - **1.** MED scrape - **2.** [de pieles etc] scraping.

raspador *sm* scraper.

raspadura *sf* (*gen pl*) scraping; [señal] scratch.

raspar ⇔ *vt* - **1.** [rascar] to scrape (off) - **2.** [rasar] to graze, to shave. ⇔ *vi* to be rough.

◆ **rasparse** *vprnl* to scratch o.s.

rasposo, sa *adj* rough.

rasque *etc* ▷ **rascar**.

rastras ◆ **a rastras** *loc adv*: **llevar algo/a alguien a rastras** *lit & fig* to drag sthg/sb along.

rastreador, ra *sm, f* tracker.

rastrear ⇔ *vt* - **1.** [seguir las huellas de] to track - **2.** *fig* [buscar pistas en - suj: persona] to search, to comb; [- suj: reflector, foco] to sweep. ⇔ *vi fig* [indagar] to make enquiries.

rastreo *sm* [de una zona] searching, combing.

rastrero, ra *adj* despicable.

rastrillar *vt* to rake (over).

rastrillo *sm* - **1.** [en jardinería] rake - **2.** [mercado] flea market; [benéfico] jumble sale - **3.** *Méx* [para afeitarse] safety razor.

rastro *sm* - **1.** [pista] trail; **perder el rastro de alguien** to lose track of sb; **sin dejar rastro** without trace; **no hay** o **queda ni rastro de él** there's no sign of him - **2.** [vestigio] trace - **3.** [mercado] flea market.

rastrojo *sm* stubble.

rasurar *vt* to shave.

◆ **rasurarse** *vprnl* to shave.

rata ⇔ *adj fam* stingy, mean. ⇔ *smf fam* stingy person. ⇔ *sf* rat; **rata de sacristía** *fam* fanatical churchgoer; **más pobre que una rata** *fam* as poor as a church mouse.

rataplán *sm* ratatat.

ratear *vi* to pilfer, to steal.

ratería *sf* pilfering, stealing.

ratero, ra *sm, f* petty thief.

raticida *sm* rat poison.

ratificar [10] *vt* to ratify.

◆ **ratificarse en** *vprnl* to stand by, to stick to.

rato *sm* while; **estuvimos hablando mucho rato** we were talking for quite a while; **al poco rato (de)** shortly after; **con esto hay para rato** that should keep us going for a while; **de a ratos** now and again; **dentro de un rato** in a

while; **hace un rato** a while ago; **pasar el rato** to kill time, to pass the time; **pasar un mal rato** to have a hard time of it; **ratos libres** spare time *(U)*; **a ratos** at times; **a ratos perdidos** at odd moments; **un rato (largo)** *fig* really, terribly.

ratón *sm* [gen & INFORM] mouse.

◆ **ratón de biblioteca** *sm* bookworm.

ratonera *sf* - **1.** [para ratas] mousetrap - **2.** *fig* [trampa] trap.

raudal *sm* - **1.** [de agua] torrent - **2.** *fig* [montón] abundance; [de lágrimas] flood; [de desgracias] string; **a raudales** in abundance, by the bucket.

raudo, da *adj* fleet, swift.

ravioli (*gen pl*) *sm* ravioli *(U)*.

raya ⇔ *v* ▷ **raer**. ⇔ *sf* - **1.** [línea] line; [en tejido] stripe; **a rayas** striped - **2.** [del pelo] parting; **hacerse la raya** to part one's hair - **3.** [de pantalón] crease - **4.** *fig* [límite] limit; **pasarse de la raya** to overstep the mark; **mantener** o **tener a raya a alguien** to keep sb in line - **5.** [señal - en disco, pintura etc] scratch - **6.** [pez] ray - **7.** [guión] dash.

rayado, da *adj* - **1.** [a rayas - tela] striped; [- papel] ruled - **2.** [estropeado] scratched.

◆ **rayado** *sm* - **1.** [rayas] stripes *pl* - **2.** [acción] ruling.

rayano, na *adj fig*: **rayano en** bordering on.

rayar ⇔ *vt* - **1.** [marcar] to scratch - **2.** [trazar rayas] to rule lines on. ⇔ *vi* - **1.** [aproximarse]: **rayar en algo** to border on sthg; **raya en los cuarenta** he's pushing forty - **2.** [alba] to break.

◆ **rayarse** *vprnl* to get scratched.

rayera *etc* ▷ **raer**.

rayo *sm* - **1.** [de luz] ray; **rayo solar** sunbeam - **2.** FÍS beam, ray; **rayo láser** laser beam; **rayos infrarrojos/ultravioleta/uva** infrared/ultraviolet/UVA rays; **rayos X** X-rays; **caer como un rayo** *fig* to be a bombshell - **3.** METEOR bolt of lightning; **rayos** lightning *(U)*; **¡que te parta un rayo!** *fam* go to hell! - **4.** [persona]: **ser un rayo** to be like greased lightning; **pasar como un rayo** to flash by - **5.** [de rueda] spoke - **6.** *loc*: **saber/oler a rayos** to taste/smell foul; ▷ **raer**.

rayón *sm* rayon.

rayuela *sf* - **1.** [juego en que se tiran monedas] pitch and toss - **2.** hopscotch.

raza *sf* - **1.** [humana] race; **raza humana** human race - **2.** [animal] breed; **de raza** [caballo] thoroughbred; [perro] pedigree - **3.** *Perú fam* [cara] cheek, nerve.

razón *sf* - **1.** [gen] reason; **atender a razones** to listen to reason; **con razón no vino** no wonder he didn't come; **dar la razón a alguien** to say that sb is right; **en razón de** o **a** in view of; **razón de ser** raison d'être; **hacer entrar en**

razón a alguien to make sb see reason; **perder la razón** to lose one's reason o mind; **tener razón (en hacer algo)** to be right (to do sthg); **no tener razón** to be wrong; **razón de más para hacer algo** all the more reason to do sthg; **y con razón** and quite rightly so - **2.** [información]: **se vende piso: razón aquí** flat for sale: enquire within; **dar razón de** to give an account of - **3.** MAT ratio.

➤ **razón de Estado** sf reasons pl of state.

➤ **razón social** sf COM trade name.

➤ **a razón de** loc adv at a rate of.

razonable adj reasonable.

razonamiento sm reasoning (U).

razonar ◇ vt [argumentar] to reason out. ◇ vi [pensar] to reason.

RDSI (abrev de **Red Digital de Servicios Integrados**) sf INFORM ISDN.

re sm MÚS D; [en solfeo] re.

reacción sf reaction; **reacción en cadena** chain reaction.

reaccionar vi to react; **reaccionar a algo** to react to sthg.

reaccionario, ria adj & sm, f reactionary.

reacio, cia adj stubborn; **reacio a algo** resistant to sthg; **ser reacio a** o **en hacer algo** to be reluctant to do sthg.

reactivación sf revival.

reactivar vt to revive.

reactivo, va adj reactive.

➤ **reactivo** sm QUÍM reagent.

reactor sm - **1.** [propulsor] reactor - **2.** [avión] jet (plane).

readaptación sf readaptation.

readaptar vt to readapt.

➤ **readaptarse** vprnl to readjust.

readmitir vt to accept o take back.

reafirmar vt to confirm; **reafirmar a alguien en algo** to confirm sb in sthg.

➤ **reafirmarse** vprnl to assert o.s.; **reafirmarse en algo** to become confirmed in sthg.

reagrupar vt to regroup, to reorganize.

reajustar vt - **1.** [corregir] to rearrange - **2.** [ECON - precios, impuestos] to make changes to, to raise; [- plantilla] to cut back; [- sector] to streamline; [- salarios] to cut.

reajuste sm - **1.** [cambio] readjustment; **reajuste ministerial** cabinet reshuffle - **2.** [ECON - de precios, impuestos] increase; [- de sector] streamlining; [- de salarios] reduction; **reajuste de plantilla** redundancies pl.

real ◇ adj - **1.** [verdadero] real - **2.** [de monarquía] royal. ◇ sm desus old Spanish coin worth one quarter of a peseta; **no valer un real** to be worthless.

realce ◇ v ▷ **realzar.** ◇ sm - **1.** [esplendor] glamour; **dar realce a algo/alguien** to enhance sthg/sb - **2.** [en pintura] highlight - **3.** [en arquitectura, escultura] relief.

realeza sf - **1.** [monarcas] royalty - **2.** [magnificencia] magnificence.

realidad sf - **1.** [mundo real] reality; **realidad virtual** INFORM virtual reality - **2.** [verdad] truth; **en realidad** actually, in fact.

realismo sm realism.

realista ◇ adj realistic. ◇ smf ARTE realist.

realización sf - **1.** [ejecución] carrying-out; [de proyecto, medidas] implementation; [de sueños, deseos] fulfilment; **realización de beneficios** profit-taking - **2.** [obra] achievement - **3.** CINE production.

realizado, da adj - **1.** [hecho] carried out, performed - **2.** [satisfecho] fulfilled.

realizador, ra sm, f CINE & TV director.

realizar [13] vt - **1.** [ejecutar - esfuerzo, viaje, inversión] to make; [- operación, experimento, trabajo] to perform; [- encargo] to carry out; [- plan, reformas] to implement - **2.** [hacer real] to fulfil, to realize - **3.** CINE to produce.

➤ **realizarse** vprnl - **1.** [en un trabajo] to find fulfilment - **2.** [hacerse real - sueño, predicción, deseo] to come true; [- esperanza, ambición] to be fulfilled - **3.** [ejecutarse] to be carried out.

realmente adv - **1.** [en verdad] in fact, actually - **2.** [muy] really, very.

realquilado, da ◇ adj sublet. ◇ sm, f subtenant.

realquilar vt to sublet.

realzar [13] vt - **1.** [resaltar] to enhance - **2.** [en pintura] to highlight.

reanimación sf - **1.** [física, moral] recovery - **2.** MED resuscitation.

reanimar vt - **1.** [físicamente] to revive - **2.** [moralmente] to cheer up - **3.** MED to resuscitate.

➤ **reanimarse** vprnl to revive.

reanudación sf resumption; [de amistad] renewal.

reanudar vt [conversación, trabajo] to resume; [amistad] to renew.

➤ **reanudarse** vprnl [conversación, trabajo] to resume; [amistad] to be renewed.

reaparecer [30] vi to reappear.

reaparición sf reappearance.

reapertura sf reopening.

rearmar vt to rearm.

rearme sm rearmament.

reavivar vt to revive.

rebaja sf - **1.** [acción] reduction - **2.** [descuento] discount; **hacer una rebaja** to give a discount.

◆ **rebajas** *sfpl* COM sales; **'grandes rebajas'** 'massive reductions'; **estar de rebajas** to have a sale on.

rebajado, da *adj* **- 1.** [precio] reduced **- 2.** [humillado] humiliated.

rebajar *vt* **- 1.** [precio] to reduce; **te rebajo 2 euros** I'll knock 2 euros off for you **- 2.** [persona] to humiliate **- 3.** [intensidad] to tone down **- 4.** [altura] to lower.

◆ **rebajarse** *vprnl* [persona] to humble o.s.; **rebajarse a hacer algo** to lower o.s. o stoop to do sthg; **rebajarse ante alguien** to humble o.s. before sb.

rebanada *sf* slice.

rebanar *vt* [pan] to slice; [dedo etc] to slice off.

rebañar *vt* to scrape clean.

rebaño *sm* flock; [de vacas] herd.

rebasar *vt* to exceed, to surpass; [agua] to overflow; AUTO to overtake.

rebatible *adj* refutable.

rebatir *vt* to refute.

rebato *sm* alarm; **tocar a rebato** to sound the alarm.

rebeca *sf* cardigan.

rebelarse *vprnl* to rebel; **rebelarse contra alguien/algo** to rebel against sb/sthg.

rebelde ◇ *adj* **- 1.** [sublevado] rebel *(antes de s)* **- 2.** [desobediente] rebellious **- 3.** [difícil de dominar - pelo] unmanageable; [- tos] persistent; [- pasiones] unruly **- 4.** DER defaulting. ◇ *smf* **- 1.** [sublevado, desobediente] rebel **- 2.** DER defaulter.

rebeldía *sf* **- 1.** [cualidad] rebelliousness **- 2.** [acción] (act of) rebellion **- 3.** DER default; **declarar a alguien en rebeldía** to declare sb in default.

rebelión *sf* rebellion; **rebelión militar** military uprising.

rebenque *sm* C Sur riding crop.

reblandecer [30] *vt* to soften.

◆ **reblandecerse** *vprnl* to get soft.

rebobinado *sm* rewinding.

rebobinar *vt* to rewind.

reboce *etc* ▷ rebozar.

reborde *sm* edge.

rebosante *adj*: **rebosante (de)** brimming o overflowing (with).

rebosar ◇ *vt* to overflow with, to brim with. ◇ *vi* to overflow; **rebosar de** to be overflowing with; *fig* [persona] to brim with.

rebotar ◇ *vi*: **rebotar (en)** to bounce (off), to rebound (off). ◇ *vt fam* [irritar] to cheese off.

◆ **rebotarse** *vprnl fam* [irritarse] to get cheesed off.

rebote *sm* **- 1.** [bote] bounce, bouncing *(U)* **- 2.** DEP rebound; **de rebote** on the rebound.

rebozado, da *adj* CULIN coated in batter o breadcrumbs.

rebozar [13] *vt* CULIN to coat in batter o breadcrumbs.

rebozo *sm* **- 1.** wrap, muffler **- 2.** *Amér* wrap, shawl.

rebrotar *vi* BOT to sprout; [fenómeno] to reappear.

rebuscado, da *adj* recherché, pretentious.

rebuscamiento *sm* pretentiousness.

rebuscar [10] *vt* to search (around in).

rebuznar *vi* to bray.

rebuzno *sm* bray, braying *(U)*.

recabar *vt* [pedir] to ask for; [conseguir] to obtain.

recadero, ra *sm, f* messenger.

recado *sm* **- 1.** [mensaje] message; **mandar recado de que...** to send word that... **- 2.** [encargo] errand; **hacer recados** to run errands.

recaer [55] *vi* **- 1.** [enfermo] to have a relapse **- 2.** [ir a parar]: **recaer sobre** to fall on **- 3.** [reincidir]: **recaer en** to relapse into.

recaída *sf* relapse.

recaiga *etc* ▷ recaer.

recalar *vi* NÁUT to sight land.

recalcar [10] *vt* to stress, to emphasize.

recalcitrante *adj* recalcitrant.

recalentar [19] *vt* **- 1.** [volver a calentar] to warm up **- 2.** [calentar demasiado] to overheat.

◆ **recalentarse** *vprnl* to overheat.

recámara *sf* **- 1.** [habitación] dressing room **- 2.** [de arma de fuego] chamber **- 3.** *Amér C, Col & Méx* [dormitorio] bedroom.

recamarera *sf Amér C, Col & Méx* chambermaid.

recambiar [8] *vt* to replace.

recambio *sm* spare (part); [para pluma] refill; **de recambio** spare.

recapacitar *vi* to reflect, to think; **recapacitar sobre** to think about.

recapitalización *sf* recapitalization.

recapitulación *sf* recap, recapitulation.

recapitular *vt* to recapitulate, to summarize.

recargable *adj* [batería] rechargeable; [encendedor] refillable.

recargado, da *adj* [estilo etc] overelaborate, affected.

recargar [16] *vt* **- 1.** [volver a cargar - encendedor, recipiente] to refill; [- batería, pila] to recharge; [- fusil, camión] to reload; [- teléfono móvil] to top up **- 2.** [cargar demasiado] to overload **- 3.** [adornar en exceso] to overelaborate **- 4.** [cantidad]: **recargar 20 euros a alguien** to charge sb 20 euros extra **- 5.** [poner en exceso]: **recargar algo de algo** to put too much of sthg in sthg.

recargarse *vprnl Méx* [apoyarse] to lean.

recargo *sm* extra charge, surcharge.

recatado, da *adj* [pudoroso] modest, demure.

recatarse *vprnl*: **recatarse de hacer algo** to shy away from doing sthg; **sin recatarse** openly.

recato *sm* - **1.** [pudor] modesty, demureness - **2.** [reserva]: **sin recato** openly, without reserve - **3.** [cautela] prudence, caution.

recaudación *sf* - **1.** [acción] collection, collecting; **recaudación de impuestos** tax collection - **2.** [cantidad] takings *pl*; DEP gate; [de un cine] box-office takings.

recaudador, ra *sm, f*: **recaudador (de impuestos)** tax collector.

recaudar *vt* to collect.

recaudo ⬤ **a buen recaudo** *loc adv* in safe-keeping; **poner a buen recaudo** to put in a safe place.

recayera *etc* ⊳ **recaer**.

rece *etc* ⊳ **rezar**.

recelar *vi* to be mistrustful; **recelar de** to mistrust.

recelo *sm* mistrust, suspicion.

receloso, sa *adj* mistrustful, suspicious.

recensión *sf* review, write-up.

recepción *sf* - **1.** [gen] reception - **2.** [de carta, paquete] receipt.

recepcionista *smf* receptionist.

receptáculo *sm* receptacle.

receptividad *sf* receptiveness.

receptivo, va *adj* receptive.

receptor, ra ◇ *adj* receiving. ◇ *sm, f* [persona] recipient; **receptor de órgano** organ recipient.

⬤ **receptor** *sm* [aparato] receiver.

recesión *sf* recession.

recesivo, va *adj* - **1.** ECON recessionary - **2.** BIOL recessive.

receta *sf* - **1.** *fig* & CULIN recipe - **2.** MED prescription.

recetar *vt* to prescribe.

recetario *sm* - **1.** MED prescription record - **2.** CULIN recipe book.

rechazar [13] *vt* - **1.** [gen & MED] to reject; [oferta] to turn down - **2.** [repeler - a una persona] to push away; MIL to drive back, to repel.

rechazo *sm* - **1.** [gen & MED] rejection; [hacia una ley, un político] disapproval; **rechazo a hacer algo** refusal to do sthg - **2.** [negación] denial.

rechinar *vi* - **1.** [puerta] to creak; [dientes] to grind; [frenos, ruedas] to screech; [metal] to clank - **2.** [dando dentera] to grate.

rechistar *vi* to answer back; **sin rechistar** without a word of protest.

rechoncho, cha *adj fam* tubby, chubby.

rechupete ⬤ **de rechupete** *loc adv fam* [gen] brilliant, great; [comida] delicious, scrumptious.

recibí *sm*: 'recibí' [en documentos] 'received'.

recibidor *sm* entrance hall.

recibimiento *sm* reception, welcome.

recibir ◇ *vt* - **1.** [gen] to receive; [clase, instrucción] to have - **2.** [dar la bienvenida a] to welcome - **3.** [ir a buscar] to meet. ◇ *vi* [atender visitas] to receive visitors.

⬤ **recibirse** *vprnl Amér*: **recibirse (de)** to graduate, to qualify (as).

recibo *sm* receipt; **acusar recibo de** to acknowledge receipt of; **no ser de recibo** to be unacceptable.

reciclado, da *adj* recycled.

reciclaje *sm* - **1.** [de residuos] recycling - **2.** [de personas] retraining.

reciclar *vt* - **1.** [residuos] to recycle - **2.** [personas] to retrain.

recién *adv* - **1.** recently, newly; **el recién casado** the newly-wed; **los recién llegados** the newcomers; **el recién nacido** the newborn baby - **2.** *Amér* [hace poco] just; **recién llegó** he has just arrived.

reciente *adj* - **1.** [acontecimiento etc] recent - **2.** [pintura, pan etc] fresh.

recientemente *adv* recently.

recinto *sm* [zona cercada] enclosure; [área] place, area; [alrededor de edificios] grounds *pl*; **recinto ferial** fairground *(of trade fair)*.

recio, cia *adj* - **1.** [persona] robust - **2.** [voz] gravelly - **3.** [objeto] solid - **4.** [material, tela] tough, strong - **5.** [lluvia, viento etc] harsh.

recipiente *sm* container, receptacle.

reciprocidad *sf* reciprocity; **en reciprocidad a** in return for.

recíproco, ca *adj* mutual, reciprocal.

recital *sm* - **1.** [de música clásica] recital; [de rock] concert - **2.** [de lectura] reading - **3.** *fig* [exhibición] display, exhibition.

recitar *vt* to recite.

reclamación *sf* - **1.** [petición] claim, demand - **2.** [queja] complaint; **hacer una reclamación** to lodge a complaint.

reclamar ◇ *vt* - **1.** [pedir, exigir] to demand, to ask for - **2.** [necesitar] to demand, to need. ◇ *vi* [protestar]: **reclamar (contra)** to protest (against), to complain (about).

reclamo *sm* - **1.** [para atraer] inducement - **2.** [para cazar] decoy, lure - **3.** [de ave] call - **4.** *Amér* [queja] complaint; *Amér* [reivindicación] claim.

reclinable *adj* reclining.

reclinar *vt*: **reclinar algo (sobre)** to lean sthg (on).

➡ **reclinarse** *vprnl* to lean back; **reclinarse contra algo** to lean against sthg.

reclinatorio *sm* prie-dieu, prayer stool.

recluir [51] *vt* to shut o lock away, to imprison.

➡ **recluirse** *vprnl* to shut o.s. away.

reclusión *sf* - **1.** [encarcelamiento] imprisonment - **2.** *fig* [encierro] seclusion.

recluso, sa *sm, f* [preso] prisoner.

recluta *sm* [obligatorio] conscript; [voluntario] recruit.

reclutamiento *sm* - **1.** [de soldados - obligatorio] conscription; [- voluntario] recruitment - **2.** [de trabajadores] recruitment.

reclutar *vt* - **1.** [soldados - obligatoriamente] conscript; [- voluntariamente] to recruit - **2.** [trabajadores] to recruit. ·

recobrar *vt* [gen] to recover; [conocimiento] to regain; [tiempo perdido] to make up for.

➡ **recobrarse** *vprnl*: **recobrarse (de)** to recover (from).

recochinearse *vprnl fam*: **recochinearse de alguien** to take the mickey out of sb.

recochineo *sm fam* mickey-taking *(U)*.

recodo *sm* bend.

recogedor *sm* dustpan.

recogemigas *sm inv* crumb scoop.

recogepelotas *smf inv* ball boy (*f* ball girl).

recoger [14] *vt* - **1.** [coger] to pick up - **2.** [ordenar, limpiar - mesa] to clear; [- habitación, cosas] to tidy o clear up - **3.** [ir a buscar] to pick up, to fetch - **4.** [albergar] to take in - **5.** [cosechar] to gather, to harvest; [fruta] to pick - **6.** [acortar - prenda] to take up, to shorten.

➡ **recogerse** *vprnl* - **1.** [a dormir, meditar] to retire - **2.** [cabello] to put up.

recogido, da *adj* - **1.** [lugar] withdrawn, secluded - **2.** [cabello] tied back.

➡ **recogida** *sf* - **1.** [gen] collection - **2.** [cosecha] harvest, gathering; [de fruta] picking.

recogimiento *sm* - **1.** [concentración] concentration, absorption - **2.** [retiro] withdrawal, seclusion.

recoja *etc* ⟼ **recoger**.

recolección *sf* - **1.** [cosecha] harvest, gathering - **2.** [recogida] collection.

recolectar *vt* - **1.** [cosechar] to harvest, to gather; [fruta] to pick - **2.** [reunir] to collect.

recolector, ra *sm, f* - **1.** [gen] collector - **2.** [de cosecha] harvester; [de fruta] picker.

recoleto, ta *adj* quiet, secluded.

recomendable *adj* recommendable; **no ser recomendable** not to be a good idea.

recomendación *sf (gen pl)* - **1.** [gen] recommendation - **2.** [referencia] reference.

recomendado, da ◇ *sm, f* protégé (*f* protégée). ◇ *adj Amér* [correspondencia] registered.

recomendar [19] *vt* to recommend; **recomendar a alguien que haga algo** to recommend that sb do sthg.

recompensa *sf* reward; **en recompensa por** in return for.

recompensar *vt* - **1.** [premiar] to reward - **2.** [compensar]: **recompensar a alguien algo** to compensate o reward sb for sthg.

recomponer [65] *vt* to repair, to mend.

recompuesto, ta *pp* ⟼ **recomponer**.

reconcentrar *vt* - **1.** [reunir] to bring together - **2.** [concentrar]: **reconcentrar algo en** to centre o concentrate sthg on - **3.** [hacer denso] to thicken.

➡ **reconcentrarse** *vprnl*: **reconcentrarse (en)** to concentrate (on), to be absorbed (in).

reconciliación *sf* reconciliation.

reconciliar [8] *vt* to reconcile.

➡ **reconciliarse** *vprnl* to be reconciled.

reconcomerse *vprnl*: **reconcomerse (de)** to be consumed (with o by).

reconcomio *sm* grudge, resentment *(U)*.

recóndito, ta *adj* hidden, secret; **en lo más recóndito de mi corazón** in the depths of my heart.

reconducir [33] *vt* to redirect.

reconfortante *adj* - **1.** [anímicamente] comforting - **2.** [físicamente] revitalizing.

reconfortar *vt* - **1.** [anímicamente] to comfort - **2.** [físicamente] to revitalize.

reconocer [31] *vt* - **1.** [gen] to recognize - **2.** MED to examine - **3.** [terreno] to survey.

➡ **reconocerse** *vprnl* - **1.** [identificarse] to cognize each other - **2.** [confesarse]: **reconocerse culpable** to admit one's guilt.

reconocido, da *adj* - **1.** [admitido] recognized, acknowledged - **2.** [agradecido] grateful; **quedo muy reconocido** I am very much obliged to you.

reconocimiento *sm* - **1.** [gen] recognition; **en reconocimiento por** in recognition for; **reconocimiento del habla** INFORM & LING speech recognition - **2.** [agradecimiento] gratitude - **3.** MED examination - **4.** MIL reconnaissance.

reconquista *sf* reconquest, recapture.

➡ **Reconquista** *sf*: **la Reconquista** HIST *the Reconquest of Spain, when the Christian Kings retook the country from the Muslims.*

reconquistar *vt* to recapture, to reconquer; *fig* to regain, to win back.

reconsiderar *vt* to reconsider.

reconstituir [51] *vt* - **1.** [rehacer] to reconstitute - **2.** [reproducir] to reconstruct.

reconstituirse *vprnl* [rehacerse - país] to rebuild.

reconstituyente ◇ *adj* tonic *(antes de s)*. ◇ *sm* tonic.

reconstrucción *sf* - **1.** [de edificios, país etc] rebuilding - **2.** [de sucesos] reconstruction.

reconstruir [51] *vt* - **1.** [edificio, país etc] to rebuild - **2.** [suceso] to reconstruct.

reconvención *sf* reprimand, reproach.

reconvenir [75] *vt* to reprimand, to reproach.

reconversión *sf* restructuring; **reconversión industrial** rationalization of industry.

reconvertir [27] *vt* [gen] to restructure; [industria] to rationalize.

recopilación *sf* - **1.** [acción] collecting, gathering - **2.** [texto - de poemas, artículos] compilation, collection; [- de leyes] code.

recopilar *vt* - **1.** [recoger] to collect, to gather - **2.** [escritos, leyes] to compile.

récord (*pl* **records**) ◇ *sm* record; **batir un récord** to break a record; **establecer un récord** to set a new record; **tener el récord** to hold the record. ◇ *adj inv* record.

recordar [23] ◇ *vt* - **1.** [acordarse de] to remember; **recordar a alguien algo/que haga algo** to remind sb to do sthg - **2.** [traer a la memoria] to remind; **me recuerda a un amigo mío** he reminds me of a friend of mine. ◇ *vi* to remember; **si mal no recuerdo** as far as I can remember.

recordatorio *sm* - **1.** [aviso] reminder - **2.** [estampa] *card given to commemorate sb's first communion, a death etc.*

recordman [re'korman] (*pl* **recordmen** o **recordmans**) *sm* record holder.

recorrer *vt* - **1.** [atravesar - lugar, país] to travel through o across, to cross; [- ciudad] to go round - **2.** [distancia] to cover - **3.** *fig* [con la mirada] to look over.

recorrida *sf* *Amér* [ruta, itinerario] route; [viaje] journey.

recorrido *sm* - **1.** [trayecto] route, path - **2.** [viaje] journey.

recortable *sm* cutout.

recortado, **da** *adj* - **1.** [cortado] cut - **2.** [borde] jagged.

recortar *vt* - **1.** [cortar - lo que sobra] to cut off o away; [- figuras de un papel] to cut out - **2.** [pelo, flequillo] to trim - **3.** *fig* [reducir] to cut.

recortarse *vprnl* [figura etc] to stand out, to be outlined; **recortarse sobre algo** to stand out against sthg.

recorte *sm* - **1.** [pieza cortada] cut, trimming; [de periódico, revista] cutting, clipping - **2.** [reducción] cut, cutback; **recortes presupuestarios** budget cuts - **3.** [cartulina] cutout.

recostar [23] *vt* to lean (back).

recostarse *vprnl* to lie down.

recoveco *sm* - **1.** [rincón] nook, hidden corner - **2.** [curva] bend - **3.** *fig* [complicación]: **sin recovecos** uncomplicated - **4.** *fig* [lo más oculto]: **los recovecos del alma** the innermost recesses of the mind.

recreación *sf* re-creation.

recrear *vt* - **1.** [volver a crear] to recreate - **2.** [entretener] to amuse, to entertain.

recrearse *vprnl* - **1.** [entretenerse] to amuse o.s., to entertain o.s. - **2.** [regodearse] to take delight o pleasure.

recreativo, **va** *adj* recreational.

recreo *sm* - **1.** [entretenimiento] recreation, amusement - **2.** [EDUC - en primaria] playtime *UK*, recess *US*; [- en secundaria] break *UK*, recess *US*.

recriminar *vt* to reproach.

recrudecerse [30] *vprnl* to get worse.

recrudecimiento *sm* worsening, accentuation; [de criminalidad etc] upsurge.

recta ⊳ **recto**.

rectal *adj* rectal.

rectangular *adj* [de forma] rectangular.

rectángulo *sm* rectangle.

rectificación *sf* rectification; [en periódico] correction.

rectificar [10] *vt* - **1.** [error] to rectify, to correct - **2.** [conducta, actitud etc] to improve - **3.** [ajustar] to put right.

rectilíneo, **a** *adj* rectilinear.

rectitud *sf* straightness; *fig* rectitude, uprightness.

recto, **ta** *adj* - **1.** [sin curvas, vertical] straight - **2.** *fig* [íntegro] upright, honourable - **3.** *fig* [literal] literal, true.

recto ◇ *sm* ANAT rectum. ◇ *adv* straight on o ahead.

recta *sf* straight line; **la recta final** *lit* & *fig* the home straight.

rector, **ra** ◇ *adj* governing, guiding. ◇ *sm, f* - **1.** [de universidad] vice-chancellor *UK*, president *US* - **2.** [dirigente] leader, head.

rector *sm* RELIG rector.

rectorado *sm* - **1.** [cargo] vice-chancellorship *UK*, presidency *US* - **2.** [lugar] vice-chancellor's office, rector's office.

rectoría *sf* - **1.** [cargo] rectorate, rectorship - **2.** [casa] rectory.

recuadro *sm* box.

recubierto, **ta** *pp* ⊳ **recubrir**.

recubrimiento *sm* covering, coating.

recubrir *vt* [gen] to cover; [con pintura, barniz] to coat.

recuento *sm* recount.

recuerda *etc* ⊳ **recordar**.

recuerdo *sm* - **1.** [rememoración] memory; **traer recuerdos a alguien de algo** to bring back memories of sthg to sb - **2.** [objeto - de viaje] souvenir; [- de persona] keepsake; **de recuerdo** as a souvenir.

◆ **recuerdos** *smpl* [saludos] regards; **dar recuerdos a alguien (de parte de alguien)** to give one's regards to sb (on sb's behalf); **dale recuerdos de mi parte** give her my regards.

recuesta *etc* ⊏⊐ **recostar**.

recular *vi* - **1.** [retroceder] to go *o* move back - **2.** *fig* [ceder] to back down.

recuperable *adj* [gen] recoverable; [fiestas, horas de trabajo] that can be made up later.

recuperación *sf* - **1.** [de lo perdido, la salud, la economía] recovery; **recuperación de datos** INFORM data recovery - **2.** [fisioterapia] physiotherapy - **3.** EDUC ⊏⊐ **clase**.

recuperar *vt* [lo perdido] to recover; [horas de trabajo] to catch up; [conocimiento] to regain.

◆ **recuperarse** *vprnl* - **1.** [enfermo] to recuperate, to recover - **2.** [de una crisis] to recover; [negocio] to pick up; **recuperarse de algo** to get over sthg.

recurrente ⟨⟩ *adj* - **1.** DER appellant - **2.** [repetido] recurrent. ⟨⟩ *smf* DER appellant.

recurrir *vi* - **1.** [buscar ayuda]: **recurrir a alguien** to turn to sb; **recurrir a algo** to resort to sthg - **2.** DER to appeal; **recurrir contra algo** to appeal against sthg.

recurso *sm* - **1.** [medio] resort; **como último recurso** as a last resort - **2.** DER appeal; **recurso de alzada** appeal (against an official decision); **recurso de apelación** appeal; **recurso de casación** High Court appeal.

◆ **recursos** *smpl* [fondos] resources; **es una mujer llena de recursos** she's a resourceful woman; [financieros] means; **sin recursos** with no means of support; **recursos propios** ECON equities.

recusar *vt* - **1.** DER to challenge - **2.** [rechazar] to reject, to refuse.

red *sf* - **1.** [malla] net; [para cabello] hairnet - **2.** [sistema] network, system; [de electricidad, agua] mains *sing*; **red viaria** road network *o* system - **3.** [organización - de espionaje] ring; [- de tiendas] chain - **4.** INFORM network; **red local/neuronal** local (area)/neural network - **5.** *loc*: **caer en las redes de alguien** to fall into sb's trap.

◆ **Red** *sf*: **la Red** the Net; **navegar por la Red** to surf the Net.

redacción *sf* - **1.** [acción - gen] writing; [- de periódico etc] editing - **2.** [estilo] wording - **3.** [equipo de redactores] editorial team *o* staff - **4.** [oficina] editorial office - **5.** EDUC essay, composition.

redactar *vt* to write (up); [carta] to draft.

redactor, ra *sm, f* [PRENSA - escritor] writer; [- editor] editor; **redactor jefe** editor-in-chief.

redada *sf* [de policía - en un solo lugar] raid; [- en varios lugares] round-up.

redecilla *sf* [de pelo] hairnet.

redención *sf* redemption.

redentor, ra *sm, f* [persona] redeemer.

◆ **Redentor** *sm*: **el Redentor** RELIG the Redeemer.

redicho, cha *adj fam* affected, pretentious.

redil *sm* fold, pen.

redimir *vt* - **1.** [gen] to redeem - **2.** [librar] to free, to exempt.

◆ **redimirse** *vprnl* to redeem o.s.

redireccionar *vt* INFORM to redirect.

redistribuir [51] *vt* to redistribute.

rédito *sm* interest (*U*), yield (*U*).

redoblar ⟨⟩ *vt* to redouble. ⟨⟩ *vi* to roll.

redoble *sm* roll, drumroll.

redomado, da *adj* out-and-out.

redonda ⊏⊐ **redondo**.

redondeado, da *adj* rounded.

redondear *vt* - **1.** [hacer redondo] to round, to make round - **2.** [negocio, acuerdo] to round off - **3.** [cifra, precio] to round up/down.

redondel *sm* - **1.** [gen] circle, ring - **2.** TAUROM bullring.

redondo, da *adj* - **1.** [circular, esférico] round; **a la redonda** around; **caerse redondo** *fig* to collapse in a heap; **girar en redondo** to turn around - **2.** [perfecto] excellent - **3.** [rotundo] categorical; **negar en redondo** to flatly refuse - **4.** [cantidad] round; **mil euros redondos** a round thousand euros.

◆ **redondo** *sm* CULIN topside.

◆ **redonda** *sf* [letra] roman type *o* print.

reducción *sf* - **1.** [gen] reduction; **reducción de gastos** reduction in costs - **2.** [sometimiento] suppression.

reducido, da *adj* - **1.** [pequeño] small - **2.** [limitado] limited - **3.** [estrecho] narrow.

reducir [33] ⟨⟩ *vt* - **1.** [gen] to reduce; **reducir algo a algo** to reduce sthg to sthg - **2.** [someter - país, ciudad] to suppress, to subdue; [- sublevados, atracadores] to bring under control - **3.** MAT [convertir] to convert - **4.** MED to set. ⟨⟩ *vi* AUTO to change down.

◆ **reducirse a** *vprnl* - **1.** [limitarse a] to be reduced to - **2.** [equivaler a] to boil *o* come down to.

reducto *sm* - **1.** [fortificación] redoubt - **2.** *fig* [refugio] stronghold, bastion.

redujera *etc* ⊏⊐ **reducir**.

redundancia *sf* redundancy; **y valga la redundancia** if you'll excuse the repetition.

redundante *adj* redundant, superfluous.

redundar *vi*: **redundar en algo** to have an effect on sthg; **redunda en beneficio nuestro** it is to our advantage.

reduplicar [10] *vt* to redouble.

reduzca *etc* ⊳ **reducir**.

reedición *sf* new edition; [reimpresión] reprint.

reeditar *vt* to bring out a new edition of; [reimprimir] to reprint.

reelección *sf* re-election.

reelegir [42] *vt* to re-elect.

reembolsable *adj* [gastos] reimbursable; [fianza, dinero] refundable; [deuda] repayable.

reembolsar, rembolsar *vt* [gastos] to reimburse; [fianza, dinero] to refund; [deuda] to repay.

reembolso, rembolso *sm* [de gastos] reimbursement; [de fianza, dinero] refund; [de deuda] repayment; **contra reembolso** cash on delivery.

reemplazar [13]**, remplazar** *vt* [gen & INFORM] to replace; **reemplazar algo/alguien por algo/alguien** to replace sthg/sb with sthg/sb.

reemplazo, remplazo *sm* - **1.** [gen & INFORM] replacement - **2.** MIL call-up, draft.

reemprender *vt* to start again.

reencarnación *sf* reincarnation.

reencarnar *vt* to reincarnate.

➡ **reencarnarse en** *vprnl* to be reincarnated as.

reencontrar [23] *vt* to find again.

➡ **reencontrarse** *vprnl* [varias personas] to meet again.

reencuentro *sm* reunion.

reengancharse *vprnl* MIL to re-enlist.

reestrenar *vt* CINE to re-run; TEATRO to revive.

reestreno *sm* CINE rerun; TEATRO revival.

reestructuración *sf* restructuring.

reestructurar *vt* to restructure.

reexpedir [26] *vt* to forward, to send on.

ref. (*abrev de* **referencia**) ref.

refacción *sf* Andes, Amér C, R Plata & Ven repair; Méx [recambio] spare part.

refaccionar *vt* Andes, Amér C & Ven to repair.

refaccionaria *sf* Amér repair workshop.

refectorio *sm* refectory.

referencia *sf* reference; **con referencia a** with reference to; **hacer referencia a** to make reference to, to refer to.

➡ **referencias** *sfpl* [informes] references; **tener buenas referencias** to have good references.

referéndum (*pl* **referendos** *o* **referéndum**) *sm* referendum; **convocar un referéndum** to call a referendum.

referente *adj*: **referente a** concerning, relating to; **en lo referente a** regarding.

referir [27] *vt* - **1.** [narrar] to tell, to recount - **2.** [remitir]: **referir a alguien a** to refer sb to - **3.** [relacionar]: **referir algo a** to relate sthg to.

➡ **referirse a** *vprnl* to refer to; **¿a qué te refieres?** what do you mean?; **por lo que se refiere a...** as far as... is concerned.

refilón ➡ **de refilón** *loc adv* - **1.** [de lado] sideways; **mirar algo de refilón** to look at sthg out of the corner of one's eye - **2.** *fig* [de pasada] briefly.

refinado, da *adj* refined.

➡ **refinado** *sm* refining.

refinamiento *sm* refinement.

refinanciar [8] *vt* to refinance.

refinar *vt* to refine.

refinería *sf* refinery.

refiriera *etc* ⊳ **referir**.

reflector *sm* - **1.** ELECTR spotlight; MIL searchlight - **2.** [telescopio] reflector.

reflejar *vt* lit & fig to reflect.

➡ **reflejarse** *vprnl* lit & fig: **reflejarse (en)** to be reflected (in).

reflejo, ja *adj* - **1.** [onda, rayo] reflected - **2.** [movimiento, dolor] reflex (antes de s).

➡ **reflejo** *sm* - **1.** [gen] reflection - **2.** [destello] glint, gleam - **3.** ANAT reflex; **reflejo condicional** *o* **condicionado** conditioned reflex *o* response.

➡ **reflejos** *smpl* [de peluquería] highlights; **hacerse reflejos** to have highlights put in one's hair.

réflex ◇ *adj inv* reflex. ◇ *sf inv* FOTO [cámara] reflex camera.

reflexión *sf* reflection; **con reflexión** on reflection; **sin previa reflexión** without thinking.

reflexionar *vi* to reflect, to think; **reflexionar sobre algo** to think about sthg.

reflexivo, va *adj* - **1.** [que piensa] reflective, thoughtful - **2.** GRAM reflexive.

refluir [51] *vi* to flow back *o* out.

reflujo *sm* ebb (tide).

reforma *sf* - **1.** [modificación] reform; **reforma agraria** agrarian reform - **2.** [en local, casa etc] alterations *pl*; **hacer reformas** to renovate.

➡ **Reforma** *sf*: **la Reforma** RELIG the Reformation.

reformar *vt* - **1.** [gen & RELIG] to reform - **2.** [local, casa etc] to renovate, to do up.

➡ **reformarse** *vprnl* to mend one's ways.

reformatorio *sm* ≃ youth custody centre UK, ≃ borstal UK, reformatory US; [de menores de 15 años] ≃ remand home.

reformismo *sm* reformism.

reformista *adj* & *smf* reformist.

reformular *vt* to reformulate, to put another way.

reforzado, **da** *adj* reinforced.

reforzar [37] *vt* to reinforce.

refracción *sf* refraction.

refractar *vt* to refract.

refractario, **ria** *adj* - **1.** [material] refractory, heat-resistant - **2.** [opuesto]: **refractario a** averse to - **3.** [inmune]: **refractario a** immune to.

refrán *sm* proverb, saying.

refranero *sm* collection of proverbs o sayings.

refregar [35] *vt* - **1.** [frotar] to scrub - **2.** *fig* [reprochar]: **refregar algo a alguien** to reproach sb for sthg.

refrenar *vt* to curb, to restrain.

➡ **refrenarse** *vprnl* to hold back, to restrain o.s.

refrendar *vt* - **1.** [aprobar] to approve - **2.** [legalizar] to endorse, to countersign.

refrescante *adj* refreshing.

refrescar [10] ◇ *vt* - **1.** [gen] to refresh; [bebidas] to chill - **2.** *fig* [conocimientos] to brush up. ◇ *vi* - **1.** [tiempo] to cool down - **2.** [bebida] to be refreshing.

➡ **refrescarse** *vprnl* - **1.** [tomar aire fresco] to get a breath of fresh air - **2.** [beber algo] to have a drink - **3.** [mojarse con agua fría] to splash o.s. down.

refresco *sm* - **1.** [bebida] soft drink; **refrescos** refreshments - **2.** [relevo]: **de refresco** new, fresh.

refría *etc* ▷ **refreír**.

refriega ◇ *v* ▷ **refregar**. ◇ *sf* scuffle; MIL fracas, skirmish.

refriera *etc* ▷ **refreír**.

refrigeración *sf* - **1.** [aire acondicionado] air-conditioning - **2.** [de alimentos] refrigeration - **3.** [de máquinas] cooling.

refrigerado, **da** *adj* [gen] cooled; [local] air-conditioned; [alimentos] refrigerated.

refrigerador, **ra** *adj* cooling.

➡ **refrigerador** *sm* - **1.** [de alimentos] refrigerator, fridge *UK*, icebox *US* - **2.** [de máquinas] cooling system.

refrigerante *adj* [gen] cooling; [para alimentos] refrigerating.

➡ **refrigerante** *sm* coolant.

refrigerar *vt* - **1.** [alimentos] to refrigerate - **2.** [local] to air-condition - **3.** [máquina] to cool.

refrigerio *sm* snack.

refrito, **ta** *adj* [demasiado frito] over-fried; [frito de nuevo] re-fried.

➡ **refrito** *sm* - **1.** CULIN *sauce made from fried tomato and onion* - **2.** *fig* [cosa rehecha] rehash.

refucilo, **refusilo** *sm* R Dom flash of lightning.

refuerce *etc* ▷ **reforzar**.

refuerzo *sm* reinforcement, strengthening *(U)*.

➡ **refuerzos** *smpl* MIL reinforcements.

refugiado, **da** ◇ *adj* refugee *(antes de s)*. ◇ *sm, f* refugee.

refugiar [8] *vt* to give refuge to.

➡ **refugiarse** *vprnl* to take refuge; **refugiarse de algo** to shelter from sthg.

refugio *sm* - **1.** [lugar] shelter, refuge; **refugio antiaéreo** air-raid shelter; **refugio atómico** nuclear bunker; **refugio subterráneo** bunker, underground shelter - **2.** *fig* [amparo, consuelo] refuge, comfort - **3.** AUTO traffic island.

refulgencia *sf* brilliance.

refulgente *adj* brilliant.

refulgir [15] *vi* to shine brightly.

refundir *vt* - **1.** [material] to re-cast - **2.** LITER to adapt - **3.** *fig* [unir] to bring together.

refunfuñar *vi* to grumble.

refunfuñón, **ona** ◇ *adj* grumpy. ◇ *sm, f* grumbler.

refusilo = **refucilo**.

refutación *sf* refutation.

refutar *vt* to refute.

regadera *sf* - **1.** [para regar] watering can; **estar como una regadera** *fig* to be as mad as a hatter - **2.** Col, Méx & Ven [ducha] shower.

regadío *sm* irrigated land; **de regadío** irrigated, irrigable.

regalado, **da** *adj* - **1.** [muy barato] dirt cheap; **te lo doy regalado** I'm giving it away to you - **2.** [agradable] comfortable, easy.

regalar *vt* - **1.** [dar - de regalo] to give (as a present); [- gratis] to give away - **2.** [agasajar]: **regalar a alguien con algo** to shower sb with sthg.

➡ **regalarse con** *vprnl* to treat o.s. to.

regalía *sf* royal prerogative.

regaliz *sm* liquorice.

regalo *sm* - **1.** [obsequio] present, gift; **un regalo del cielo** a godsend - **2.** [placer] joy, delight.

regalón, **ona** *adj* R Dom & Chile fam spoilt.

regalonear *vt* R Dom & Chile fam to spoil.

regañadientes ➡ **a regañadientes** *loc adv* fam unwillingly, reluctantly.

regañar ◇ *vt* [reprender] to tell off. ◇ *vi* [pelearse] to fall out, to argue.

regañina *sf* - **1.** [reprimenda] ticking off - **2.** [enfado] argument, row.

regaño *sm* telling off.

regar [35] *vt* - **1.** [con agua - planta] to water; [- calle] to hose down - **2.** [suj: río] to flow through - **3.** *fig* [desparramar] to sprinkle, to scatter.

regata *sf* - **1.** NÁUT regatta, boat race - **2.** [reguera] irrigation channel.

regate *sm* - **1.** DEP swerve, sidestep - **2.** *fig* [evasiva] dodge.

regatear <> *vt* - **1.** [escatimar] to be sparing with; **no ha regateado esfuerzos** he has spared no effort - **2.** DEP to beat, to dribble past - **3.** [precio] to haggle over. <> *vi* - **1.** [negociar el precio] to barter, to haggle - **2.** NÁUT to race.

regateo *sm* bartering, haggling.

regazo *sm* lap.

regencia *sf* - **1.** [reinado] regency - **2.** [administración] running, management.

regeneración *sf* regeneration; [moral] reform.

regeneracionismo *sm* political reform movement.

regenerar *vt* to regenerate; [moralmente] to reform.

regenta *sf* wife of the regent.

regentar *vt* [país] to run, to govern; [negocio] to run, to manage; [puesto] to hold.

regente <> *adj* regent. <> *sm, f* - **1.** [de un país] regent - **2.** [administrador - de tienda] manager; [- de colegio] governor - **3.** *Méx* [alcalde] mayor (*f* mayoress).

reggae ['reɣe] *sm* reggae.

regicidio *sm* regicide.

regidor, ra *sm, f* - **1.** [concejal] councillor - **2.** TEATRO stage manager; CINE & TV assistant director.

régimen (*pl* regímenes) *sm* - **1.** [sistema político] regime; **Antiguo régimen** ancien régime; **régimen parlamentario** parliamentary system - **2.** [normativa] rules *pl* - **3.** [dieta] diet; **estar/ponerse a régimen** to be/go on a diet - **4.** [de vida, lluvias etc] pattern, usual routine; **régimen de vida** lifestyle - **5.** LING government.

regimiento *sm* *fig* & MIL regiment.

regio, gia *adj* - **1.** *lit* & *fig* royal - **2.** *Amér fam fig* fantastic.

región *sf* region; MIL district.

regional *adj* regional.

regionalismo *sm* regionalism.

regir [42] <> *vt* - **1.** [reinar en] to rule, to govern - **2.** [administrar] to run, to manage - **3.** LING to govern - **4.** *fig* [determinar] to govern, to determine. <> *vi* - **1.** [ley] to be in force, to apply - **2.** *fig* [persona] to be of sound mind.

➤ **regirse por** *vprnl* to trust in, to be guided by.

registrado, da *adj* - **1.** [grabado] recorded - **2.** [patentado] registered - **3.** *Amér* [correspondencia] registered.

registradora *sf* *Amér* cash register.

registrar <> *vt* - **1.** [inspeccionar - zona, piso] to search; [- persona] to frisk - **2.** [nacimiento, temperatura etc] to register, to record. <> *vi* to search.

➤ **registrarse** *vprnl* - **1.** [suceder] to occur, to happen - **2.** [observarse] to be recorded.

registro *sm* - **1.** [oficina] registry (office); **registro civil** registry (office); **registro de la propiedad** land registry office; **registro mercantil** o **de comercio** business registry office - **2.** [libro] register - **3.** [inspección] search, searching (*U*) - **4.** INFORM record - **5.** LING & MÚS register.

regla *sf* - **1.** [para medir] ruler, rule; **regla de cálculo** slide rule - **2.** [norma] rule; **en regla** in order; **por regla general** as a rule, generally; **salirse de la regla** to overstep the mark o line - **3.** MAT operation; **regla de tres** rule of three - **4.** *fam* [menstruación] period; **tener la regla** to have one's period - **5.** [modelo] example, model.

reglamentación *sf* [acción] regulation; [reglas] rules *pl*, regulations *pl*.

reglamentar *vt* to regulate.

reglamentario, ria *adj* lawful; [arma, balón] within the rules, regulation (*antes de s*); DER statutory.

reglamento *sm* regulations *pl*, rules *pl*; **reglamento de tráfico** traffic regulations *pl*.

regocijar ➤ **regocijarse** *vprnl*: **regocijarse (de** o **con)** to rejoice (in).

regocijo *sm* joy, delight.

regodearse *vprnl*: **regodearse (con)** to take pleasure o delight (in).

regodeo *sm* delight, pleasure; [malicioso] (cruel) delight o pleasure.

regordete *adj* chubby, tubby.

regresar <> *vi* [yendo] to go back, to return; [viniendo] to come back, to return. <> *vt* *Andes, Amér C, Caribe* & *Méx* [devolver] to give back.

➤ **regresarse** *vprnl* *Andes, Amér C, Caribe* & *Méx* [yendo] to go back; [viniendo] to come back, to return.

regresión *sf* - **1.** [de epidemia] regression - **2.** [de exportaciones] drop, decline.

regresivo, va *adj* regressive.

regreso *sm* return; **estar de regreso** to be back.

regué *etc* ▷ **regar**.

reguero *sm* [de sangre, agua] trickle; [de harina etc] dribble, trail; **correr como un reguero de pólvora** to spread like wildfire.

regulación *sf* [gen] regulation; [de nacimientos, tráfico] control; [de mecanismo] adjustment; **regulación de empleo** streamlining, redundancies *pl*.

regulador, ra *adj* regulating, regulatory.

regular <> *adj* **- 1.** [gen] regular; [de tamaño] medium; **de un modo regular** regularly **- 2.** [mediocre] average, fair **- 3.** [normal] normal, usual. <> *sm* MIL regular. <> *adv* all right; [de salud] so-so. <> *vt* [gen] to control, to regulate; [mecanismo] to adjust.

por lo regular *loc adv* as a rule, generally.

regularidad *sf* regularity; **con regularidad** regularly.

regularización *sf* regularization.

regularizar [13] *vt* **- 1.** [volver a la normalidad] to get back to normal **- 2.** [legalizar] to regularize.

regularizarse *vprnl* **- 1.** [volver a la normalidad] to return to normal **- 2.** [legalizarse] to become legitimate.

regurgitar *vt* & *vi* to regurgitate.

regusto *sm* aftertaste; [semejanza, aire] flavour, hint.

rehabilitación *sf* **- 1.** [de personas] rehabilitation; [en un puesto] reinstatement **- 2.** [de local] restoration.

rehabilitar *vt* **- 1.** [personas] to rehabilitate; [en un puesto] to reinstate **- 2.** [local] to restore.

rehacer [60] *vt* **- 1.** [volver a hacer] to redo, to do again **- 2.** [reconstruir] to rebuild **- 3.** INFORM redo.

rehacerse *vprnl* [recuperarse] to recuperate, to recover.

rehecho, cha *pp* ⊳ rehacer.

rehén (*pl* rehenes) *sm* hostage; **tomar como rehén** to take hostage.

rehiciera *etc* ⊳ rehacer.

rehogar [16] *vt* to fry over a low heat.

rehuir [51] *vt* to avoid.

rehusar *vt* & *vi* to refuse.

rehuya *etc* ⊳ rehuir.

rehuyera *etc* ⊳ rehuir.

reimplantar *vt* **- 1.** [reintroducir] to reintroduce **- 2.** MED to implant again.

reimpresión *sf* [tirada] reprint; [acción] reprinting.

reimprimir *vt* to reprint.

reina *sf* **- 1.** [monarca] queen; **reina de belleza** beauty queen; **reina madre** queen mother **- 2.** ⊳ abeja.

reinado *sm* lit & fig reign.

reinante *adj* **- 1.** [monarquía, persona] reigning, ruling **- 2.** [viento] prevailing; [frío, calor] current.

reinar *vi* lit & fig to reign.

reincidencia *sf* relapse; [en un delito] recidivism.

reincidente *adj* & *smf* recidivist.

reincidir *vi*: **reincidir en** [falta, error] to relapse into, to fall back into; [delito] to repeat.

reincorporar *vt* to reincorporate.

reincorporarse *vprnl*: **reincorporarse (a)** to rejoin, to go back to.

reingresar *vi*: **reingresar en** to return to.

reinicializar [13] *vt* INFORM to reset.

reino *sm* BIOL & POLÍT kingdom; fig realm; **el reino de los cielos** the kingdom of Heaven.

Reino Unido *n pr*: **el Reino Unido** the United Kingdom.

reinserción *sf*: **reinserción (social)** (social) rehabilitation o reintegration.

reinsertar *vt* to reintegrate, to rehabilitate.

reinstaurar *vt* to reestablish.

reinstalar *vt* re-install.

reintegración *sf* **- 1.** [a puesto] reinstatement **- 2.** [de dinero] repayment, reimbursement.

reintegrar *vt* **- 1.** [a un puesto] to reinstate **- 2.** [dinero] to repay, to reimburse **- 3.** [timbrar] to stick a fiscal stamp to.

reintegrarse *vprnl*: **reintegrarse (a)** to return (to).

reintegro *sm* **- 1.** [de dinero] repayment, reimbursement; BANCA withdrawal **- 2.** [en lotería] return of one's stake *(in lottery)* **- 3.** [póliza] fiscal stamp.

reír [28] <> *vi* to laugh; **dar que reír** to ask to be laughed at; **echarse a reír** to burst out laughing; **hacer reír a alguien** to make sb laugh. <> *vt* to laugh at.

reírse *vprnl*: **reírse (de)** to laugh (at).

reiterar *vt* to reiterate, to repeat.

reiterarse *vprnl*: **reiterarse en** to reaffirm.

reiterativo, va *adj* repetitive, repetitious.

reivindicación *sf* **- 1.** [de derechos] claim, demand **- 2.** [de atentado] claiming of responsibility.

reivindicar [10] *vt* **- 1.** [derechos, salario etc] to claim, to demand **- 2.** [atentado] to claim responsibility for.

reivindicativo, va *adj*: **plataforma reivindicativa** (set of) demands; **jornada reivindicativa** day of protest.

reja *sf* [gen] bars *pl*; [en el suelo] grating; [celosía] grille; **estar entre rejas** to be behind bars.

rejego, ga *adj* Amér fam [terco] stubborn.

rejilla *sf* **- 1.** [enrejado] grid, grating; [de ventana] grille; [de cocina] grill *(on stove)*; [de horno] gridiron **- 2.** [para sillas, muebles] wickerwork **- 3.** [para equipaje] luggage rack.

rejón *sm* TAUROM type of "banderilla" used by mounted bullfighter.

rejoneador, **ra** *sm*, *f* TAUROM *bullfighter on horseback who uses the "rejón".*

rejuntarse *vprnl fam* to live together.

rejuvenecer [30] *vt* & *vi* to rejuvenate.

→ **rejuvenecerse** *vprnl* to be rejuvenated.

relación *sf* - **1.** [nexo] relation, connection; **con relación a**, **en relación con** in relation to, with regard to; **tener relación con algo** to bear a relation to sthg; **relación precio-calidad** value for money - **2.** [comunicación, trato] relations *pl*, relationship; **estar en buenas/malas relaciones** to be on good/bad terms with sb; **relaciones amorosas** (love) affair *sing*; **relaciones comerciales** [entre individuos] business relationship *sing*; [entre países, empresas] trade (U); **relaciones diplomáticas/públicas** diplomatic/public relations; **relaciones laborales** industrial relations - **3.** [lista] list - **4.** [descripción] account - **5.** [informe] report - **6.** *(gen pl)* [noviazgo] relationship; **llevan cinco años de relaciones** they've been going out together for five years - **7.** MAT ratio; **en una relación de tres a uno** in a ratio of three to one.

→ **relaciones** *sfpl* [contactos] contacts, connections.

relacionar *vt* - **1.** [vincular] to relate, to connect - **2.** [relatar] to tell, to relate.

→ **relacionarse** *vprnl*: **relacionarse (con)** [alternar] to mix (with).

relajación *sf* relaxation.

relajante *adj* relaxing.

relajar *vt* to relax.

→ **relajarse** *vprnl* to relax.

relajo *sm Amér fam* [alboroto] racket, din.

relamer *vt* to lick repeatedly.

→ **relamerse** *vprnl* - **1.** [persona] to lick one's lips - **2.** [animal] to lick its chops.

relamido, **da** *adj* prim and proper.

relámpago *sm* - **1.** [descarga] flash of lightning, lightning (U); [destello] flash - **2.** *fig* [exhalación]: **pasar como un relámpago** to pass by as quick as lightning, to flash past.

relampaguear ⋄ *v impers*: **relampagueó** lightning flashed. ⋄ *vi fig* to flash.

relampagueo *sm* METEOR lightning; [destello] flashing.

relanzamiento *sm* relaunch.

relanzar [13] *vt* to relaunch.

relatar *vt* [suceso] to relate, to recount; [historia] to tell.

relatividad *sf* relativity.

relativismo *sm* relativism.

relativizar [13] *vt* to put into perspective.

relativo, **va** *adj* - **1.** [gen] relative; **en lo relativo a** regarding; **eso es relativo** that depends - **2.** [escaso] limited.

relato *sm* [exposición] account, report; [cuento] tale, story.

relax *sm inv* - **1.** [relajación] relaxation - **2.** [sección de periódico] personal column.

relegar [16] *vt*: **relegar (a)** to relegate (to); **relegar algo al olvido** to banish sthg from one's mind.

relente *sm* (night) dew; **dormir al relente** to sleep out in the open.

relevancia *sf* relevance, importance.

relevante *adj* outstanding, important.

relevar *vt* - **1.** [sustituir] to relieve, to take over from - **2.** [destituir]: **relevar (de)** to dismiss (from), to relieve (of) - **3.** [eximir]: **relevar (de)** to free (from) - **4.** [DEP - en partidos] to substitute; [- en relevos] to take over from.

→ **relevarse** *vprnl* to take turns.

relevo *sm* - **1.** MIL relief, changing - **2.** DEP [acción] relay - **3.** *loc*: **tomar el relevo** to take over.

→ **relevos** *smpl* DEP [carrera] relay (race) *sing*.

releyera *etc* ➪ **releer**.

relicario *sm* RELIG reliquary; [estuche] locket.

relieve *sm* - **1.** [gen, ARTE & GEOGR] relief; **alto relieve** high relief; **bajo relieve** bas-relief - **2.** [importancia] importance; **de relieve** important; **poner de relieve** to underline (the importance of), to highlight.

religión *sf* religion.

religiosamente *adv lit* & *fig* religiously.

religiosidad *sf lit* & *fig* religiousness.

religioso, **sa** ⋄ *adj* religious. ⋄ *sm*, *f* [monje] monk (*f* nun).

relinchar *vi* to neigh, to whinny.

relincho *sm* neigh, neighing (U).

reliquia *sf* relic; [familiar] heirloom.

rellano *sm* - **1.** [de escalera] landing - **2.** [de terreno] shelf.

rellenar *vt* - **1.** [volver a llenar] to refill - **2.** [documento, formulario] to fill in *o* out - **3.** [pollo, cojín etc] to stuff; [tarta, pastel] to fill.

relleno, **na** *adj* [gen] stuffed; [tarta, pastel] filled.

→ **relleno** *sm* [de pollo] stuffing; [de pastel] filling; **de relleno** *fig* as padding, as a filler.

reloj *sm* [de pared] clock; [de pulsera] watch; **reloj analógico/digital** analogue/digital watch; **reloj de arena** hourglass; **reloj de bolsillo** pocket watch; **reloj de cuarzo** quartz watch; **reloj de cuco** cuckoo clock; **reloj despertador** alarm clock; **reloj interno** INFORM internal clock; **reloj de pulsera** watch, wristwatch; **re-**

loj de sol sun dial; **hacer algo contra reloj** to do sthg against the clock; **ser como un reloj** *fig* to be like clockwork.

relojería *sf* - **1.** [tienda] watchmaker's (shop) - **2.** [arte] watchmaking.

relojero, ra *sm, f* watchmaker.

reluciente *adj* shining, gleaming.

relucir [32] *vi lit & fig* to shine; **sacar algo a relucir** to bring sthg up, to mention sthg; **salir a relucir** to come to the surface.

relumbrar *vi* to shine brightly.

reluzca *etc* ⊳ **relucir**.

remachar *vt* - **1.** [machacar] to rivet - **2.** *fig* [recalcar] to drive home, to stress.

remache *sm* - **1.** [acción] riveting - **2.** [clavo] rivet.

remake [ri'meik] (*pl* **remakes**) *sm* remake.

remanente *sm* - **1.** [de géneros] surplus stock; [de productos agrícolas] surplus - **2.** [en cuenta bancaria] balance - **3.** [de beneficios] net profit.

remangar [16], **arremangar** *vt* to roll up.
◆ **remangarse** *vprnl* to roll up one's sleeves.

remanso *sm* still pool; **remanso de paz** oasis of peace.

remar *vi* to row.

remarcar [10] *vt* [recalcar] to underline, to stress.

rematadamente *adv* absolutely, utterly.

rematado, da *adj* utter, complete.

rematar ⇔ *vt* - **1.** [acabar] to finish; **y para rematarla** *fam* to cap it all - **2.** [matar - persona] to finish off; [- animal] to put out of its misery - **3.** DEP to shoot - **4.** [liquidar, vender] to sell off cheaply - **5.** [adjudicar en subasta] to knock down - **6.** *Amér* [subastar] to auction. ⇔ *vi* [en fútbol] to shoot; [de cabeza] to head at goal.

remate *sm* - **1.** [fin, colofón] end; **para remate** [colmo] to cap it all - **2.** ARQUIT top - **3.** [en fútbol] shot; [de cabeza] header at goal - **4.** *Amér* [subasta] auction.
◆ **de remate** *loc adv* totally, completely.

rembolsar = **reembolsar**.

rembolso = **reembolso**.

remecer [11] *vi Méx* to shake.

remedar *vt* to imitate; [por burla] to ape, to mimic.

remediar [8] *vt* [daño] to remedy, to put right; [problema] to solve; [peligro] to avoid, to prevent.

remedio *sm* - **1.** [solución] solution, remedy; **como último remedio** as a last resort; **no hay** o **queda más remedio que...** there's nothing for it but...; **no tener más remedio** to have no alternative o choice; **poner remedio a algo** to do sthg about sthg; **sin remedio** [sin cura, solución] hopeless; [ineludiblemente] inevitably - **2.** [consuelo] comfort, consolation - **3.** [medicamento] remedy, cure; **remedio casero** home remedy.

remedo *sm* imitation; [por burla] parody.

rememorar *vt* to remember, to recall.

remendado, da *adj* patched.

remendar [19] *vt* to mend, to darn.

remendón ⊳ **zapatero**.

remero, ra *sm, f* [persona] rower.
◆ **remera** *sf R Dom* [prenda] T-shirt.

remesa *sf* [de productos] consignment; [de dinero] shipment, remittance.

remeter *vt* to tuck in.

remezón *sm Andes & R Dom* earth tremor.

remienda *etc* ⊳ **remendar**.

remiendo *sm* - **1.** [parche] mend, darn - **2.** *fam* [apaño] patching up, makeshift mending.

remigio *sm* card game where players aim to collect ten particular cards.

remilgado, da *adj* - **1.** [afectado] affected - **2.** [escrupuloso] squeamish; [con comida] fussy, finicky.

remilgo *sm* - **1.** [afectación] affectation - **2.** [escrupulosidad] squeamishness; [con comida] fussiness.

reminiscencia *sf* reminiscence; **tener reminiscencias de** to be reminiscent of.

remisión *sf* - **1.** [envío] sending - **2.** [en texto] cross-reference, reference - **3.** [perdón] remission, forgiveness - **4.** [de dolor] remission.
◆ **sin remisión** *loc adv* without hope of a reprieve.

remiso, sa *adj*: **ser remiso a hacer algo** to be reluctant to do sthg.

remite *sm* sender's name and address.

remitente *smf* sender.

remitir ⇔ *vt* - **1.** [enviar] to send - **2.** [traspasar]: **remitir algo a** to refer sthg to. ⇔ *vi* - **1.** [en texto]: **remitir a** to refer to - **2.** [disminuir] to subside.
◆ **remitirse a** *vprnl* - **1.** [atenerse a] to comply with, to abide by - **2.** [referirse a] to refer to.

remo *sm* - **1.** [pala] oar - **2.** [deporte] rowing.

remodelación *sf* [gen] redesigning; [de gobierno] reshuffle.

remodelar *vt* [gen] to redesing; [gobierno] to reshuffle.

remojar *vt* - **1.** [humedecer] to soak - **2.** *fam* [festejar] to drink to, to celebrate with a drink.

remojo *sm*: **poner en remojo** to leave to soak; **estar en remojo** to be soaking.

remojón *sm fam* [en la piscina, el mar] dip; [bajo la lluvia] soaking, drenching.

remolacha *sf* beetroot *UK*, beet *US*; [azucarera] (sugar) beet.

remolcador, ra *adj* [coche] tow *(antes de s)*; [barco] tug *(antes de s)*.

◆ **remolcador** *sm* [camión] breakdown lorry; [barco] tug, tugboat.

remolcar [10] *vt* [coche] to tow; [barco] to tug.

remolino *sm* - **1.** [de agua] eddy, whirlpool; [de viento] whirlwind; [de humo] cloud, swirl - **2.** [de gente] throng, mass - **3.** [de pelo] cowlick.

remolón, ona ⋄ *adj* lazy. ⋄ *sm, f*: hacerse el remolón to shirk.

remolonear *vi fam* to laze.

remolque *sm* - **1.** [acción] towing; **ir a remolque** *fig* [voluntariamente] to go in tow, to tag along; [obligado] to be dragged along - **2.** [vehículo] trailer.

remontar *vt* [pendiente, río] to go up; [obstáculo] to get over, to overcome.

◆ **remontarse** *vprnl* - **1.** [ave, avión] to soar, to climb high - **2.** [gastos]: **remontarse a** to amount o come to - **3.** *fig* [datar]: **remontarse a** to go o date back to.

rémora *sf* - **1.** [pez] remora - **2.** *fam fig* [obstáculo] drawback, hindrance.

remorder [24] *vt fig*: **remorderle a alguien** to fill sb with remorse.

remordimiento *sm* remorse; **tener remordimientos de conciencia** to suffer pangs of conscience.

remoto, ta *adj* remote; **no tengo ni la más remota idea** I haven't got the faintest idea.

remover [24] *vt* - **1.** [agitar - sopa, café] to stir; [- ensalada] to toss; [- bote, frasco] to shake; [- tierra] to turn over, to dig up - **2.** [reavivar - caso policial] to reopen; [- recuerdos, pasado] to stir up, to rake up - **3.** *Amér* [despedir] to dismiss, to sack.

◆ **removerse** *vprnl* to move about.

remozar *vt* [edificio, fachada] to renovate.

remplazar [13] = reemplazar.

remplazo = reemplazo.

remuerda *etc* ▷ remorder.

remueva *etc* ▷ remover.

remuneración *sf* remuneration.

remunerado, da *adj*: **bien remunerado** well paid; **mal remunerado** badly paid.

remunerar *vt* [pagar] to remunerate.

renacentista *adj* Renaissance *(antes de s)*.

renacer [29] *vi* - **1.** [gen] to be reborn; [flores, hojas] to grow again - **2.** [alegría, esperanza] to return, to revive.

renacimiento *sm* - **1.** [gen] rebirth; [de flores, hojas] budding - **2.** [de alegría, esperanza] revival, return.

◆ **Renacimiento** *sm*: **el Renacimiento** the Renaissance.

renacuajo *sm* tadpole; *fam fig* tiddler.

renal *adj* renal, kidney *(antes de s)*.

renazca *etc* ▷ renacer.

rencilla *sf* quarrel.

rencor *sm* resentment, bitterness; **guardar rencor a** to bear a grudge.

rencoroso, sa ⋄ *adj* resentful, bitter. ⋄ *sm, f* resentful o bitter person.

rendición *sf* surrender.

rendido, da *adj* - **1.** [agotado] exhausted, worn-out; **caer rendido** to collapse - **2.** [sumiso] submissive; [admirador] servile, devoted.

rendija *sf* crack, gap.

rendimiento *sm* - **1.** [de inversión, negocio] yield, return; [de trabajador, fábrica] productivity; [de tierra, cosecha] performance, yield; **a pleno rendimiento** at full capacity - **2.** [de motor] performance.

rendir [26] ⋄ *vt* - **1.** [cansar] to wear out, to tire out - **2.** [rentar] to yield - **3.** [vencer] to defeat, to subdue - **4.** [ofrecer] to give, to present; [pleitesía] to pay. ⋄ *vi* [máquina] to perform well; [negocio] to be profitable; [fábrica, trabajador] to be productive.

◆ **rendirse** *vprnl* - **1.** [entregarse] to give o.s. up, to surrender - **2.** [ceder]: **rendirse a** to submit to, to give in to; **rendirse a la evidencia** to bow to the evidence - **3.** [desanimarse] to give in o up.

renegado, da *adj & sm, f* renegade.

renegar [35] ⋄ *vt* to deny strongly. ⋄ *vi* - **1.** [repudiar]: **renegar de** [ideas] to renounce; [familia] to disown - **2.** *fam* [gruñir] to grumble.

renegociar [8] *vt* to renegotiate.

renegué *etc* ▷ renegar.

Renfe *(abrev de Red Nacional de los Ferrocarriles Españoles)* *sf Spanish state railway network*.

renglón *sm* line; COM item; **a renglón seguido** *fig* in the same breath, straight after.

◆ **renglones** *smpl fam fig* [escrito] lines, words.

reniega *etc* ▷ renegar.

reno *sm* reindeer.

renombrado, da *adj* renowned, famous.

renombrar *vt* INFORM to rename.

renombre *sm* renown, fame; **de renombre** famous.

renovable *adj* renewable.

renovación *sf* [de carné, contrato] renewal; [de mobiliario, local] renovation.

renovar [24] *vt* - **1.** [cambiar - mobiliario, local] to renovate; [- vestuario] to clear out; [- personal, plantilla] to make changes to, to shake out - **2.** [rehacer - carné, contrato, ataques] to renew - **3.** [restaurar] to restore - **4.** [innovar] to rethink, to revolutionize; POLÍT to reform.

renquear *vi* to limp, to hobble.

renta *sf* - **1.** [ingresos] income; **vivir de las rentas** to live off one's (private) income; **renta fija** fixed income; **renta per cápita** *o* **por habitante** per capita income; **renta variable/vitalicia** variable/life annuity - **2.** [alquiler] rent - **3.** [beneficios] return - **4.** [intereses] interest - **5.** [deuda pública] national *o* public debt.

rentabilidad *sf* profitability.

rentabilizar [13] *vt* to make profitable.

rentable *adj* profitable.

rentar ⟺ *vt* - **1.** [rendir] to produce, to yield - **2.** *Méx* [alquilar] to rent. ⟺ *vi* to be profitable.

rentista *smf* person of independent means.

renuencia *sf* reluctance, unwillingness.

renuente *adj*: **renuente a** reluctant to, unwilling to.

renueva *etc* ⟹ **renovar**.

renuncia *sf* [abandono] giving up; [dimisión] resignation; **presentar la renuncia** to resign.

renunciar [8] *vi* - **1.** [abandonar] to give up - **2.** [dimitir] to resign.

◆ **renunciar a** *vi* - **1.** [prescindir de] to give up; [plan, proyecto] to drop; **renunciar al tabaco** to give up *o* stop smoking - **2.** [rechazar]: **renunciar (a hacer algo)** to refuse (to do sthg).

reñido, da *adj* - **1.** [enfadado]: **reñido (con)** on bad terms *o* at odds (with); **están reñidos** they've fallen out - **2.** [disputado] fierce, hard-fought - **3.** [incompatible]: **estar reñido con** to be at odds with, to be incompatible with.

reñir [26] ⟺ *vt* - **1.** [regañar] to tell off - **2.** [disputar] to fight. ⟺ *vi* [enfadarse] to argue, to fall out; **reñir con** to fall out with.

reo, a *sm, f* [culpado] offender, culprit; [acusado] accused, defendant.

reoca *sf* fam: **ser la reoca** [gracioso] to be a scream; [el colmo] to be the limit.

reojo *sm*: **mirar algo de reojo** to look at sthg out of the corner of one's eye.

reordenación *sf* restructuring, reorganization.

reorganización *sf* [gen] reorganization; [del gobierno] reshuffle.

reorganizar [13] *vt* [gen] to reorganize; [gobierno] to reshuffle.

reorientar *vt* to give a new direction to, to refocus.

repanchigarse [16] *vprnl* fam to sprawl out.

repanocha *sf* fam: **ser la repanocha** [gracioso] to be a scream; [el colmo] to be the limit.

repantigarse [16] *vprnl* fam to sprawl out.

reparación *sf* - **1.** [arreglo] repair, repairing (*U*); **en reparación** under repair - **2.** [compensación] reparation, redress.

reparador, ra *adj* [descanso, sueño] refreshing.

reparar ⟺ *vt* [coche etc] to repair, to fix; [error, daño etc] to make amends for; [fuerzas] to make up for, to restore. ⟺ *vi* [advertir]: **reparar en algo** to notice sthg; **no reparar en gastos** to spare no expense.

reparo *sm* - **1.** [objeción] objection; **poner reparos a algo** to raise objections to sthg - **2.** [apuro]: **con reparos** with hesitation *o* reservations; **me da reparo** I feel awkward about it; **no tener reparos en** not to be afraid to; **sin reparos** without reservation, with no holds barred.

repartición *sf* [reparto] sharing out.

repartidor, ra *sm, f* [gen] distributor; [de butano, carbón] deliveryman (f deliverywoman); [de leche] milkman (f milklady); [de periódicos] paperboy (f papergirl).

repartir *vt* - **1.** [dividir - gen] to share out, to divide; [- territorio, nación] to partition - **2.** [distribuir - leche, periódicos, correo] to deliver; [- naipes] to deal (out) - **3.** [esparcir - pintura, mantequilla] to spread - **4.** [asignar - trabajo, órdenes] to give out, to allocate; [- papeles] to assign - **5.** *fig* [administrar] to administer, to dish out.

reparto *sm* - **1.** [división] division, distribution; **reparto de beneficios** ECON profit sharing; **reparto de premios** prizegiving - **2.** [distribución - de leche, periódicos, correo] delivery; [- de naipes] dealing - **3.** [asignación] giving out, allocation; **reparto a domicilio** home delivery - **4.** CINE & TEATRO cast.

repasador *sm R Dom* tea towel.

repasar *vt* - **1.** [revisar] to go over; [lección] to revise UK, to review US - **2.** [zurcir] to darn, to mend - **3.** [volver a pasar - trapo etc] to run over again.

repaso *sm* - **1.** [revisión] revision; [de ropa] darning, mending; **dar un repaso a algo** to look over sthg; **dar un último repaso a algo** to give sthg a final check; **curso de repaso** refresher course - **2.** *fam* [reprimenda] telling off, ticking off.

repatear *vt* fam to bug; **repatear a alguien** to get on sb's wick.

repatriación *sf* repatriation.

repatriar [9] *vt* to repatriate.

◆ **repatriarse** *vprnl* to be repatriated.

repecho *sm* steep slope.

repelencia *sf* repulsion.

repelente *adj* - **1.** [desagradable, repugnante] repulsive - **2.** [ahuyentador] repellent.

repeler *vt* - **1.** [rechazar] to repel - **2.** [repugnar] to repulse, to disgust.

repelús *sm*: **me da repelús** it gives me the shivers.

repeluzno *sm* shiver.

repente *sm* [arrebato] fit.

◆ **de repente** *loc adv* suddenly.

repentinamente *adv* suddenly.

repentino, **na** *adj* sudden.

repera *sf fam*: **ser la repera** to be the limit.

repercusión *sf* - **1.** *fig* [consecuencia] repercussion - **2.** [resonancia] echoes *pl*.

repercutir *vi* - **1.** *fig* [afectar]: **repercutir en** to have repercussions on - **2.** [resonar] to resound, to echo.

repertorio *sm* - **1.** [obras] repertoire - **2.** *fig* [serie] selection.

repesca *sf* - **1.** EDUC resit - **2.** DEP repêchage.

repescar [10] *vt* - **1.** EDUC to allow a resit - **2.** DEP to allow into the repêchage.

repetición *sf* repetition; [de una jugada] action replay.

repetido, **da** *adj* - **1.** [gen] repeated; **repetidas veces** time and time again - **2.** [cromo etc] duplicated.

repetidor, **ra** ◇ *adj* repeating the year. ◇ *sm, f* EDUC student repeating a year.

◆ **repetidor** *sm* ELECTR repeater.

repetir [26] ◇ *vt* to repeat; [ataque] to renew; [en comida] to have seconds of. ◇ *vi* - **1.** [alumno] to repeat a year - **2.** [sabor, alimento]: **repetir (a alguien)** to repeat (on sb) - **3.** [comensal] to have seconds.

◆ **repetirse** *vprnl* - **1.** [fenómeno] to recur - **2.** [persona] to repeat o.s.

repetitivo, **va** *adj* repetitive.

repicar [10] ◇ *vt* [campanas] to ring. ◇ *vi* [campanas] to ring.

repipi *adj fam* - **1.** [cursi] affected - **2.** [sabiondo] know-it-all.

repique ◇ *v* ▷ **repicar**. ◇ *sm* peal, ringing *(U)*.

repiquetear *vi* [campanas] to ring out; [tambor] to beat; [timbre] to ring; [lluvia, dedos] to drum.

repiqueteo *sm* [de campanas] pealing; [de tambor] beating; [de timbre] ringing; [de lluvia, dedos] drumming.

repisa *sf* - **1.** [estante] shelf; [sobre chimenea] mantelpiece - **2.** ARQUIT bracket.

repita *etc* ▷ **repetir**.

repitiera *etc* ▷ **repetir**.

replanteamiento *sm* restatement, reconsideration.

replantear *vt* - **1.** [reenfocar] to reconsider, to restate - **2.** [volver a mencionar] to bring up again.

replay [ri'plei] *(pl* **replays***) sm* replay.

replegar [35] *vt* [ocultar] to retract.

◆ **replegarse** *vprnl* [retirarse] to withdraw, to retreat.

repleto, **ta** *adj*: **repleto (de)** packed (with).

réplica *sf* - **1.** [respuesta] reply - **2.** [copia] replica.

replicar [10] ◇ *vt* [responder] to answer; [objetar] to answer back, to retort. ◇ *vi* [objetar] to answer back.

repliega *etc* ▷ **replegar**.

repliegue *sm* - **1.** [retirada] withdrawal, retreat - **2.** [pliegue] fold.

repoblación *sf* [con gente] repopulation; [con peces] restocking; **repoblación forestal** reafforestation.

repoblar [23] *vt* [con gente] to repopulate; [con peces] to restock; [con árboles] to replant, to reafforest.

◆ **repoblarse** *vprnl*: **repoblarse de** [gente] to be repopulated with; [peces] to be restocked with; [árboles] to be replanted *o* reafforested with.

repollo *sm* cabbage.

reponer [65] *vt* - **1.** [gen] to replace - **2.** CINE & TEATRO to rerun; TV to repeat - **3.** [replicar]: **reponer que** to reply that.

◆ **reponerse** *vprnl*: **reponerse (de)** to recover (from).

reportaje *sm* RADIO & TV report; PRENSA article; **reportaje gráfico** illustrated feature.

reportar *vt* - **1.** [traer] to bring; **no le ha reportado más que problemas** it has caused him nothing but problems - **2.** *Méx* [denunciar] to report; *Andes, Amér C, Méx & Ven* [informar] to report.

◆ **reportarse** *vprnl Amér C, Méx & Ven*: **reportarse (a)** to report (to).

reporte *sm Amér C & Méx* [informe] report; [noticia] news item *o* report.

reportero, **ra**, **repórter** *sm, f* reporter; **reportero gráfico** press photographer.

reposacabezas *sm inv* headrest.

reposado, **da** *adj* relaxed, calm.

reposapiés *sm inv* footrest.

reposar *vi* - **1.** [descansar] to (have a) rest - **2.** [sedimentarse] to stand - **3.** *fig* [yacer] to lie.

reposera *sf R Dom* sun-lounger *UK*, beach recliner *US*.

reposición *sf* - **1.** CINE rerun; TEATRO revival; TV repeat - **2.** [de existencias, pieza etc] replacement.

reposo *sm* [descanso] rest; **en reposo** [cuerpo, persona] at rest; [máquina] not in use; CULIN standing; **guardar reposo** to rest.

repostar ◇ *vi* [coche] to fill up; [avión] to refuel. ◇ *vt* - **1.** [coche] to fill up; [avión] to refuel - **2.** [gasolina] to fill up with - **3.** [provisiones] to stock up on.

repostería *sf* - **1.** [establecimiento] confectioner's (shop) - **2.** [oficio, productos] confectionery.

repostero, **ra** *sm, f* [persona] confectioner.

repostero *sm Andes* [armario] larder, pantry.

reprender *vt* [a niños] to tell off; [a empleados] to reprimand.

reprensible *adj* reprehensible.

reprensión *sf* [a niños] telling-off; [a empleados] reprimand.

represa *sf* dam.

represalia *(gen pl) sf* reprisal; **tomar represalias** to retaliate, to take reprisals.

representación *sf* - **1.** [gen & COM] representation; **en representación de** on behalf of; **tener la representación de** COM to act as a representative for - **2.** TEATRO performance.

representante ◇ *adj* representative. ◇ *smf* - **1.** [gen & COM] representative; **representante de la ley** officer of the law - **2.** [de artista] agent.

representar *vt* - **1.** [gen & COM] to represent - **2.** [aparentar] to look; **representa unos 40 años** she looks about 40 - **3.** [significar] to mean; **representa el 50% del consumo interno** it accounts for 50% of domestic consumption - **4.** [TEATRO - función] to perform; [- papel] to play.

representatividad *sf* representativeness.

representativo, va *adj* - **1.** [simbolizador]: **ser representativo de** to represent - **2.** [característico, relevante]: **representativo (de)** representative (of).

represión *sf* repression.

represivo, va *adj* repressive.

reprimenda *sf* reprimand.

reprimido, da ◇ *adj* repressed. ◇ *sm, f* repressed person.

reprimir *vt* [gen] to suppress; [minorías, disidentes] to repress.

   reprimirse *vprnl*: **reprimirse (de hacer algo)** to restrain o.s. (from doing sthg).

reprís, reprise *(pl reprises) sm* acceleration.

reprobable *adj* reprehensible.

reprobación *sf* reproof, censure.

reprobar [23] *vt* - **1.** to censure, to condemn - **2.** *Amér* [suspender] to fail.

reprochar *vt*: **reprochar algo a alguien** to reproach sb for sthg.

   reprocharse *vprnl*: **reprocharse algo (uno mismo)** to reproach o.s. for sthg.

reproche *sm* reproach; **hacer un reproche a alguien** to reproach sb.

reproducción *sf* reproduction.

reproducir [33] *vt* [gen & ARTE] to reproduce; [gestos] to copy, to imitate.

   reproducirse *vprnl* - **1.** [volver a suceder] to recur - **2.** [procrear] to reproduce.

reproductor, ra ◇ *adj* reproductive. ◇ *sm* player; **reproductor de DVD** DVD player.

reprueba *etc* ⊏➤ reprobar.

reptar *vi* to crawl.

reptil *sm* reptile.

república *sf* republic.

República Checa *sf* Czech Republic.

República Dominicana *sf* Dominican Republic.

republicanismo *sm* republicanism.

republicano, na *adj* & *sm, f* republican.

repudiar [8] *vt* - **1.** [condenar] to repudiate - **2.** [rechazar] to disown.

repudio *sm* disowning.

repuebla *etc* ⊏➤ repoblar.

repuesto, ta ◇ *pp* ⊏➤ reponer. ◇ *adj*: **repuesto (de)** recovered (from).

   repuesto *sm* [gen] reserve; AUTO spare part; **de repuesto** spare, in reserve; **la rueda de repuesto** the spare wheel.

repugnancia *sf* disgust.

repugnante *adj* disgusting.

repugnar ◇ *vi* to be disgusting. ◇ *vt*: **me repugna ese olor/su actitud** I find that smell/her attitude disgusting; **me repugna hacerlo** I'm loath to do it.

repujado, da *adj* embossed.

repujar *vt* to emboss.

repulsa *sf* [censura] condemnation.

repulsión *sf* repulsion.

repulsivo, va *adj* repulsive.

repuntar *vi* Amér [mejorar] to improve.

repusiera *etc* ⊏➤ reponer.

reputación *sf* reputation; **tener mucha reputación** to be very famous.

reputado, da *adj* highly reputed.

requemar *vt* to burn; [planta, tierra] to scorch.

   requemarse *vprnl* to get burnt, to burn.

requerimiento *sm* - **1.** [demanda] entreaty; **a requerimiento de alguien** at sb's request - **2.** [DER - intimación] writ, injunction; [- aviso] summons *sing*.

requerir [27] *vt* - **1.** [necesitar] to require - **2.** [ordenar] to demand - **3.** [pedir]: **requerir a alguien (para) que haga algo** to ask sb to do sthg - **4.** DER to order.

   requerirse *vprnl* [ser necesario] to be required O necessary.

requesón *sm* cottage cheese.

requiebro *sm* flirtatious remark.

réquiem *sm inv* requiem.

requiera *etc* ⊏➤ requerir.

requiriera *etc* ⊏➤ requerir.

requisa *sf* - **1.** [requisición - MIL] requisition; [- en aduana] seizure - **2.** [inspección] inspection.

requisar *vt* MIL to requisition; [en aduana] to seize.

requisito *sm* requirement; **cumplir los requisitos** to fulfil all the requirements; **requisito previo** prerequisite.

res *sf* - **1.** [animal] beast, animal - **2.** *Amér salvo* C *Sur*: **carne de res** beef.

◆ **reses** *smpl Amér* [ganado vacuno] cattle.

resabiado, da *adj fam* know-all *(antes de s)*.

resabio *sm* - **1.** [sabor] nasty aftertaste - **2.** [vicio] persistent bad habit.

resaca *sf* - **1.** *fam* [de borrachera] hangover - **2.** [de las olas] undertow.

resalado, da *adj fam* charming.

resaltar ◇ *vi* - **1.** [destacar] to stand out - **2.** [en edificios - balcón] to stick out; [- decoración] to stand out. ◇ *vt* [destacar] to highlight.

resarcir [12] *vt*: **resarcir a alguien (de)** to compensate sb (for).

◆ **resarcirse** *vprnl* to be compensated; **resarcirse de** [daño, pérdida] to be compensated for; [desengaño, derrota] to make up for.

resbalada *sf Amér fam* slip.

resbaladizo, za *adj lit & fig* slippery.

resbalar *vi* - **1.** [caer]: **resbalar (con** O **sobre)** to slip (on) - **2.** [deslizarse] to slide; **resbalarle a alguien** *fam fig* to leave sb cold - **3.** [estar resbaladizo] to be slippery.

◆ **resbalarse** *vprnl* to slip (over).

resbalón *sm* slip; **dar** O **pegar un resbalón** to slip.

resbaloso, sa *adj* slippery.

rescatar *vt* - **1.** [liberar, salvar] to rescue; [pagando rescate] to ransom - **2.** [recuperar - herencia etc] to recover.

rescate *sm* - **1.** [liberación, salvación] rescue - **2.** [dinero] ransom - **3.** [recuperación] recovery.

rescindir *vt* to rescind.

rescisión *sf* cancellation.

rescoldo *sm* ember; *fig* lingering feeling, flicker.

resecar [10] *vt* - **1.** [piel] to dry out - **2.** [tierra] to parch.

◆ **resecarse** *vprnl* - **1.** [piel] to dry out - **2.** [tierra] to become parched.

reseco, ca *adj* - **1.** [piel, garganta, pan] very dry - **2.** [tierra] parched - **3.** [flaco] emaciated.

resentido, da ◇ *adj* bitter, resentful; **estar resentido con alguien** to be really upset with sb. ◇ *sm, f* bitter O resentful person.

resentimiento *sm* resentment, bitterness.

resentirse [27] *vprnl* - **1.** [debilitarse] to be weakened; [salud] to deteriorate - **2.** [sentir molestias]: **resentirse de** to be suffering from - **3.** [ofenderse] to be offended.

reseña *sf* [de libro, concierto] review; [de partido, conferencia] report.

reseñar *vt* - **1.** [criticar - libro, concierto] to review; [- partido, conferencia] to report on - **2.** [describir] to describe.

reseque *etc* ⊳ **resecar**.

reserva ◇ *sf* - **1.** [de hotel, avión etc] reservation - **2.** [provisión] reserves *pl*; **tener algo de reserva** to keep sthg in reserve; **reservas de divisas/monetarias** ECON foreign currency/ monetary reserves - **3.** [objeción] reservation; **sin reservas** without reservation - **4.** [discreción] discretion - **5.** [de indígenas] reservation - **6.** [de animales] reserve; **reserva natural** nature reserve - **7.** MIL reserve; **pasar a la reserva** to become a reservist. ◇ *smf* DEP reserve, substitute. ◇ *sm* [vino] vintage.

◆ **reservas** *sfpl* - **1.** [energía acumulada] energy reserves - **2.** [recursos] resources.

reservado, da *adj* - **1.** [gen] reserved - **2.** [tema, asunto] confidential.

◆ **reservado** *sm* [en restaurante] private room; FERROC reserved compartment.

reservar *vt* - **1.** [habitación, asiento etc] to reserve, to book - **2.** [guardar - dinero, pasteles etc] to set aside; [- sorpresa] to keep - **3.** [callar - opinión, comentarios] to reserve.

◆ **reservarse** *vprnl* - **1.** [esperar]: **reservarse para** to save o.s. for - **2.** [guardar para sí - secreto] to keep to o.s.; [- dinero, derecho] to retain (for o.s.)

reservista *smf* MIL reservist.

resfriado, da *adj*: **estar resfriado** to have a cold.

◆ **resfriado** *sm* cold; **pescar un resfriado** to catch a cold.

resfriar [9] ◆ **resfriarse** *vprnl* [constiparse] to catch a cold.

resguardar *vt & vi*: **resguardar de** to protect against.

◆ **resguardarse** *vprnl*: **resguardarse de** [en un portal] to shelter from; [con abrigo, paraguas] to protect o.s. against.

resguardo *sm* - **1.** [documento] receipt - **2.** [protección] protection; **al resguardo de** safe from; **ponerse a resguardo de** to take shelter from.

residencia *sf* - **1.** [estancia] stay - **2.** [localidad, domicilio] residence; **segunda residencia** second home; **residencia canina** kennels - **3.** [establecimiento - de estudiantes] hall of residence; [- de ancianos] old people's home; [- de oficiales] residence - **4.** [hotel] boarding house - **5.** [hospital] hospital - **6.** [permiso para extranjeros] residence permit - **7.** [periodo de formación] residency.

residencial *adj* residential.

residente *adj* & *smf* resident.

residir *vi* - **1.** [vivir] to reside - **2.** [radicar]: **residir en** to lie in, to reside in.

residual *(gen pl) adj* residual; **aguas residuales** sewage *(U)*.

residuo *sm (gen pl)* [material inservible] waste, QUÍM residue; **residuos nucleares** nuclear waste *(U)*; **residuos tóxicos** toxic waste *(U)*.

resienta *etc* ▷ **resentirse**.

resignación *sf* resignation.

resignarse *vprnl*: **resignarse (a hacer algo)** to resign o.s. (to doing sthg).

resina *sf* resin.

resinoso, sa *adj* resinous.

resintiera *etc* ▷ **resentirse**.

resistencia *sf* - **1.** [gen, ELECTR & POLÍT] resistance; **ofrecer resistencia** to put up resistance; **resistencia pasiva** passive resistance - **2.** [de puente, cimientos] strength - **3.** [física - para correr etc] stamina.

resistente *adj* [gen] tough, strong; **resistente al calor** heat-resistant.

resistir ◇ *vt* - **1.** [dolor, peso, críticas] to withstand - **2.** [tentación, impulso, deseo] to resist - **3.** [tolerar] to tolerate, to stand; **no lo resisto más, me voy** I can't stand it any longer, I'm off - **4.** [ataque] to resist, to withstand. ◇ *vi* - **1.** [ejército, ciudad etc]: **resistir (a algo/a alguien)** to resist (sthg/sb) - **2.** [corredor etc] to keep going; **resistir a algo** to stand up to sthg, to withstand sthg - **3.** [mesa, dique etc] to take the strain; **resistir a algo** to withstand sthg - **4.** [mostrarse firme - ante tentaciones etc] to resist (it); **resistir a algo** to resist sthg.
◆ **resistirse** *vprnl*: **resistirse (a algo)** to resist (sthg); **resistirse a hacer algo** to refuse to do sthg; **me resisto a creerlo** I refuse to believe it; **no hay hombre que se le resista** no man can resist her; **se le resisten las matemáticas** she just can't get the hang of maths.

resol *sm* (sun's) glare.

resollar [23] *vi* to gasp (for breath); [jadear] to pant.

resolución *sf* - **1.** [solución - de una crisis] resolution; [- de un crimen] solution - **2.** [firmeza] determination - **3.** [decisión] decision; DER ruling; **tomar una resolución** to take a decision - **4.** [de Naciones Unidas etc] resolution.

resoluto, ta *adj* resolute.

resolver [24] *vt* - **1.** [solucionar - duda, crisis] to resolve; [- problema, caso] to solve - **2.** [decidir]: **resolver hacer algo** to decide to do sthg - **3.** [partido, disputa, conflicto] to settle.
◆ **resolverse** *vprnl* - **1.** [solucionarse - duda, crisis] to be resolved; [- problema, caso] to be solved - **2.** [decidirse]: **resolverse a hacer algo** to decide to do sthg - **3.** [en disputa, conflicto]: **resolverse en** to come to nothing more than.

resonancia *sf* - **1.** [gen & FÍS] resonance *(U)*; **resonancia magnética** MED magnetic resonance - **2.** *fig* [importancia] repercussions *pl*.

resonar [23] *vi* to resound, to echo.

resoplar *vi* [de cansancio] to pant; [de enfado] to snort.

resoplido *sm* [por cansancio] pant; [por enfado] snort.

resorte *sm* spring; **saltar como movido por un resorte** to spring up; *fig* means *pl*; **tocar todos los resortes** to pull out all the stops.

respaldar *vt* to back, to support.
◆ **respaldarse** *vprnl* - **1.** [en asiento] to lean back - **2.** *fig* [apoyarse]: **respaldarse en** to fall back on.

respaldo *sm* - **1.** [de asiento] back - **2.** *fig* [apoyo] backing, support.

respectar *v impers*: **por lo que respecta a alguien/a algo, en lo que respecta a alguien/a algo** as far as sb/sthg is concerned.

respectivo, va *adj* respective; **en lo respectivo a** with regard to.

respecto *sm*: **al respecto, a este respecto** in this respect; **no sé nada al respecto** I don't know anything about it; **(con) respecto a, respecto de** regarding.

respetable *adj* - **1.** [venerable] respectable - **2.** [bastante] considerable.

respetar *vt* - **1.** [gen] to respect; [la palabra] to honour; **hacerse respetar** to make o.s. respected - **2.** [acatar] to observe - **3.** [no destruir] to spare; **'respetad las plantas'** 'keep off the flowerbeds'.

respeto *sm*: **respeto (a o por)** respect (for); **es una falta de respeto** it shows a lack of respect; **faltar al respeto a alguien** to be disrespectful to sb; **por respeto a** out of consideration for; **presentar uno sus respetos a alguien** to pay one's respects to sb; **tener respeto a alguien** to have respect for sb.

respetuoso, sa *adj*: **respetuoso (con)** respectful (of).

respingar [16] *vi* [protestar] to make a fuss, to complain.

respingo *sm* [movimiento] start, jump; **dar un respingo** to start.

respingón, ona *adj* snub.

respiración *sf* breathing; MED respiration; **respiración artificial o asistida** artificial respiration; **respiración boca a boca** mouth-to-mouth resuscitation; **contener la respiración** to hold one's breath; **quedarse sin respiración** [asombrado] to be stunned.

respiradero *sm* [hueco] vent; [conducto] ventilation shaft.

respirar ⬦ *vt* - **1.** [aire] to breathe - **2.** *fig* [bondad etc] to exude; **respirar hondo** to take a deep breath. ⬦ *vi* to breathe; *fig* [sentir alivio] to breathe again; **no dejar respirar a alguien** *fig* not to allow sb a moment's peace; **sin respirar** [sin descanso] without a break; [atentamente] with great attention.

respiratorio, ria *adj* respiratory.

respiro *sm* - **1.** [descanso] rest - **2.** [alivio] relief, respite; **dar un respiro a alguien** *fam* to give sb a break.

resplandecer [30] *vi* - **1.** [brillar] to shine - **2.** *fig* [destacar] to shine, to stand out; **resplandecer de algo** to shine with sthg.

resplandeciente *adj* shining; [sonrisa] beaming; [época] glittering; [vestimenta, color] resplendent.

resplandor *sm* - **1.** [luz] brightness; [de fuego] glow - **2.** [brillo] gleam.

responder ⬦ *vt* to answer. ⬦ *vi* - **1.** [contestar]: **responder (a algo)** to answer (sthg) - **2.** [reaccionar]: **responder (a)** to respond (to) - **3.** [responsabilizarse]: **responder de algo/por alguien** to answer for sthg/for sb - **4.** [replicar] to answer back - **5.** [corresponder]: **responder a** to correspond to; **las medidas responden a la crisis** the measures are in keeping with the nature of the crisis.

respondón, ona ⬦ *adj* insolent. ⬦ *sm, f* insolent person.

responsabilidad *sf* responsibility; DER liability; **de responsabilidad** responsible; **exigir responsabilidades a alguien** to hold sb accountable; **tener la responsabilidad de algo** to be responsible for sthg; **responsabilidad civil/penal** DER civil/criminal liability; **responsabilidad limitada** limited liability.

responsabilizar [13] *vt*: **responsabilizar a alguien (de algo)** to hold sb responsible (for sthg).

➡ **responsabilizarse** *vprnl*: **responsabilizarse (de)** to accept responsibility (for).

responsable ⬦ *adj* responsible; **responsable de** responsible for; **hacerse responsable de** [gen] to take responsibility for; [atentado, secuestro] to claim responsibility for. ⬦ *smf* - **1.** [culpable] person responsible - **2.** [encargado] person in charge.

responso *sm* prayer for the dead.

respuesta *sf* - **1.** [gen] answer, reply; [en exámenes] answer; **en respuesta a** in reply to - **2.** *fig* [reacción] response.

resquebrajadura *sf* = resquebrajamiento.

resquebrajamiento *sm* crack.

resquebrajar *vt* to crack.

➡ **resquebrajarse** *vprnl* to crack.

resquemor *sm* resentment, bitterness.

resquicio *sm* - **1.** [abertura] chink; [grieta] crack - **2.** *fig* [pizca] glimmer.

resta *sf* MAT subtraction.

restablecer [30] *vt* to reestablish, to restore.

➡ **restablecerse** *vprnl* - **1.** [curarse]: **restablecerse (de)** to recover (from) - **2.** [reimplantarse] to be reestablished.

restablecimiento *sm* - **1.** [reimplantación] restoration, reestablishment - **2.** [cura] recovery.

restallar *vt* & *vi* [látigo] to crack; [lengua] to click.

restante *adj* remaining; **lo restante** the rest.

restar ⬦ *vt* - **1.** MAT to subtract; **restar una cantidad de otra** to subtract one figure from another - **2.** [disminuir]: **restar importancia a algo/méritos a alguien** to play down the importance of sthg/sb's qualities. ⬦ *vi* [faltar] to be left.

restauración *sf* restoration.

restaurador, ra *sm, f* restorer.

restaurante *sm* restaurant.

restaurar *vt* to restore.

restitución *sf* return.

restituir [51] *vt* - **1.** [devolver - objeto] to return; [- salud] to restore - **2.** [restaurar] to restore.

resto *sm*: **el resto** [gen] the rest; MAT the remainder; **echar el resto** *fig* to do one's utmost.

➡ **restos** *smpl* - **1.** [sobras] leftovers - **2.** [cadáver] remains; **restos mortales** mortal remains - **3.** [ruinas] ruins.

restregar [35] *vt* to rub hard; [para limpiar] to scrub.

➡ **restregarse** *vprnl* [frotarse] to rub.

restricción *sf* restriction.

restrictivo, va *adj* restrictive.

restringir [15] *vt* to limit, to restrict.

resucitar ⬦ *vt* [person] to bring back to life; [costumbre] to resurrect, to revive. ⬦ *vi* [persona] to rise from the dead.

resuella *etc* ▷ **resollar**.

resuello *sm* gasp, gasping (U); [jadeo] pant, panting (U).

resuelto, ta ⬦ *pp* ▷ **resolver**. ⬦ *adj* - **1.** [solucionado] solved - **2.** [decidido] determined; **estar resuelto a hacer algo** to be determined to do sthg.

resuelva *etc* ▷ **resolver**.

resuena *etc* ▷ **resonar**.

resulta *sf*: **de resultas de** as a result of.

resultado *sm* result; **dar resultado** to work (out), to have the desired effect; **dar buen/mal resultado** to be a success/failure.

resultante *adj* & *sf* resultant.

resultar ◇ *vi* - **1.** [acabar siendo]: **resultar (ser)** to turn out (to be); **resultó ileso** he was uninjured; **nuestro equipo resultó vencedor** our team came out on top - **2.** [salir bien] to work (out), to be a success - **3.** [originarse]: **resultar de** to come of, to result from - **4.** [ser] to be; **resulta sorprendente** it's surprising; **me resultó imposible terminar antes** I was unable to finish earlier - **5.** [venir a costar]: **resultar a** to come to, to cost. ◇ *v impers* [suceder]: **resultar que** to turn out that; **ahora resulta que no quiere alquilarlo** now it seems that she doesn't want to rent it.

resultón, ona *adj fam* attractive.

resumen *sm* summary; **en resumen** in short.

resumidero *sm Amér* drain.

resumir *vt* to summarize; [discurso] to sum up.
➡ **resumirse en** *vprnl* - **1.** [sintetizarse en] to be able to be summed up in - **2.** [reducirse a] to boil down to.

resurgimiento *sm* resurgence.

resurgir [15] *vi* to undergo a resurgence, to be revived.

resurrección *sf* resurrection.

retablo *sm* altarpiece.

retaco *sm despec* & *hum* shorty, midget.

retaguardia *sf* [tropa] rearguard; [territorio] rear.

retahíla *sf* string, series.

retal *sm* remnant.

retama *sf* broom.

retar *vt*: **retar (a)** to challenge (to).

retardado, da *adj* delayed.

retardar *vt* [retrasar] to delay; [frenar] to hold up, to slow down.

retazo *sm* remnant; *fig* fragment.

rete *adv Amér fam* very.

retén *sm* - **1.** reserve - **2.** *Amér* [de menores] reformatory, reform school.

retención *sf* - **1.** [en comisaría] detention - **2.** [en el sueldo] deduction - **3.** *(gen pl)* [de tráfico] hold-up - **4.** MED retention.

retener [72] *vt* - **1.** [detener] to hold back; [en comisaría] to detain - **2.** [hacer permanecer] to keep - **3.** [contener - impulso, ira] to hold back, to restrain; [- aliento] to hold - **4.** [conservar] to retain - **5.** [quedarse con] to hold on to, to keep - **6.** [memorizar] to remember - **7.** [deducir del sueldo] to deduct.

reticencia *sf* - **1.** [resistencia] unwillingness - **2.** [insinuación] insinuation, innuendo *(U)*.

reticente *adj* - **1.** [reacio] unwilling, reluctant - **2.** [con insinuaciones] full of insinuation.

reticular *adj* ANAT reticular.

retiene *etc* ▷ **retener**.

retina *sf* retina.

retintín *sm* - **1.** [ironía] sarcastic tone; **con retintín** sarcastically - **2.** [tintineo] ringing.

retirado, da ◇ *adj* - **1.** [jubilado] retired - **2.** [solitario, alejado] isolated, secluded. ◇ *sm, f* [jubilado] retired person.
➡ **retirada** *sf* - **1.** MIL retreat; **batirse en retirada** to beat a retreat; **cubrir la retirada** MIL to cover the retreat; *fig* [tomar precauciones] not to burn one's bridges, to cover o.s. - **2.** [de fondos, moneda, carné] withdrawal - **3.** [de competición, actividad] withdrawal.

retirar *vt* - **1.** [quitar - gen] to remove; [- dinero, moneda, carné] to withdraw; [- nieve] to clear; [- mano] to withdraw - **2.** [jubilar - a deportista] to force to retire; [- a empleado] to retire - **3.** [retractarse de] to take back.
➡ **retirarse** *vprnl* - **1.** [gen] to retire - **2.** [de competición, elecciones] to withdraw; [de reunión] to leave - **3.** [de campo de batalla] to retreat - **4.** [apartarse] to move away.

retiro *sm* - **1.** [jubilación] retirement; [pensión] pension - **2.** [refugio, ejercicio] retreat.

reto *sm* challenge.

retocar [10] *vt* to touch up.

retoce *etc* ▷ **retozar**.

retoño *sm* BOT sprout, shoot; *fig* offspring *(U)*.

retoque ◇ *v* ▷ **retocar**. ◇ *sm* touching-up *(U)*; [de prenda de vestir] alteration; **dar los últimos retoques a** to put the finishing touches to.

retorcer [41] *vt* - **1.** [torcer - brazo, alambre] to twist; [- ropa, cuello] to wring - **2.** *fig* [tergiversar] to twist.
➡ **retorcerse** *vprnl* [contraerse]: **retorcerse (de)** [risa] to double up (with); [dolor] to writhe about (in).

retorcido, da *adj* - **1.** [torcido - brazo, alambre] twisted; [- ropa] wrung out - **2.** *fig* [rebuscado] complicated, involved - **3.** *fig* [malintencionado] twisted, warped.

retórico, ca *adj* rhetorical.
➡ **retórica** *sf lit* & *fig* [discurso] rhetoric.

retornable *adj* returnable; **no retornable** non-returnable.

retornar *vt* & *vi* to return.

retorno *sm* [gen & INFORM] return; **retorno de carro** carriage return.

retortijón *(gen pl) sm* stomach cramp.

retozar [13] *vi* to gambol, to frolic; [amantes] to romp about.

retozón, ona *adj* playful.

retractación *sf* retraction.

retractarse *vprnl* [de una promesa] to go back on one's word; [de una opinión] to take back what one has said; **retractarse de** [lo dicho] to retract, to take back.

retráctil *adj* retractable; [uña] retractile.

retraer [73] *vt* - **1.** [encoger] to retract - **2.** [disuadir]: **retraer a alguien de hacer algo** to persuade sb not to do sthg.
➤ **retraerse** *vprnl* - **1.** [encogerse] to retract - **2.** [retirarse]: **retraerse de** to withdraw from - **3.** [retroceder] to withdraw, to retreat.

retraído, da *adj* withdrawn, retiring.

retraimiento *sm* shyness, reserve.

retransmisión *sf* broadcast; **retransmisión en directo/diferido** live/recorded broadcast.

retransmitir *vt* to broadcast.

retrasado, da ⬦ *adj* - **1.** [país, industria] backward; [reloj] slow; [tren] late, delayed - **2.** [en el pago, los estudios] behind - **3.** MED retarded, backward. ⬦ *sm, f*: **retrasado (mental)** mentally retarded person.

retrasar ⬦ *vt* - **1.** [aplazar] to postpone - **2.** [demorar] to delay, to hold up - **3.** [hacer más lento] to slow down, to hold up - **4.** [en el pago, los estudios] to put back - **5.** [reloj] to put back. ⬦ *vi* [reloj] to be slow.
➤ **retrasarse** *vprnl* - **1.** [llegar tarde] to be late - **2.** [quedarse atrás] to fall behind - **3.** [aplazarse] to be put off - **4.** [reloj] to lose time.

retraso *sm* - **1.** [por llegar tarde] delay; **llegar con (15 minutos de) retraso** to be (15 minutes) late - **2.** [por sobrepasar una fecha] time behind schedule; **llevo en mi trabajo un retraso de 20 páginas** I'm 20 pages behind with my work - **3.** [subdesarrollo] backwardness; **llevar (siglos de) retraso** to be (centuries) behind - **4.** MED mental deficiency.

retratar *vt* - **1.** [fotografiar] to photograph - **2.** [dibujar] to do a portrait of - **3.** *fig* [describir] to portray.
➤ **retratarse** *vprnl fig* [describirse] to describe o.s.

retratista *smf* ARTE portraitist; FOTO (portrait) photographer.

retrato *sm* - **1.** [dibujo] portrait; [fotografía] photograph; **retrato robot** photofit picture; **ser el vivo retrato de alguien** to be the spitting image of sb - **2.** *fig* [reflejo] portrayal.

retreta *sf* retreat.

retrete *sm* toilet.

retribución *sf* [pago] payment; [recompensa] reward.

retribuir [51] *vt* - **1.** [pagar] to pay; [recompensar] to reward - **2.** *Amér* [favor, obsequio] to return.

retro *adj* old-fashioned.

retroactividad *sf* [de ley] retroactivity; [del pago] backdating.

retroactivo, va *adj* [ley] retrospective, retroactive; [pago] backdated.

retroceder *vi* to go back; *fig* to back down; **no retrocederé ante nada** there's no stopping me now.

retroceso *sm* - **1.** [regresión - gen] backward movement; [- en negociaciones] setback; [- en la economía] recession - **2.** [en enfermedad] deterioration.

retrógrado, da *adj & sm, f* reactionary.

retropropulsión *sf* jet propulsion.

retroproyector *sm* overhead projector.

retrospección *sf* retrospection.

retrospectivo, va *adj* retrospective; **echar una mirada retrospectiva a** to look back over.
➤ **retrospectiva** *sf* retrospective.

retrovisor *sm* rear-view mirror.

retuerce *etc* ➱ **retorcer**.

retumbante *adj* resounding.

retumbar *vi* - **1.** [resonar] to resound - **2.** [hacer ruido] to thunder, to boom.

retuviera *etc* ➱ **retener**.

reuma, reúma *sm o sf* rheumatism.

reumático, ca *adj & sm, f* rheumatic.

reumatismo *sm* rheumatism.

reumatología *sf* rheumatology.

reumatólogo, ga *sm, f* rheumatologist.

reunificación *sf* reunification.

reunificar [10] *vt* to reunify.
➤ **reunificarse** *vprnl* to reunify.

reunión *sf* meeting.

reunir *vt* - **1.** [público, accionistas etc] to bring together - **2.** [objetos, textos etc] to collect, to bring together; [fondos] to raise - **3.** [requisitos] to meet; [cualidades] to possess, to combine - **4.** [volver a unir] to put back together.
➤ **reunirse** *vprnl* [congregarse] to meet.

reutilizar [13] *vt* to reuse.

revválida *sf* final exam.

revalidar *vt* - **1.** [ratificar] to confirm - **2.** *Amér* [estudios, diploma] to validate.

revalorización *sf* - **1.** [aumento del valor] appreciation; [de moneda] revaluation - **2.** [restitución del valor] favourable reassessment.

revalorizar [13] *vt* - **1.** [aumentar el valor] to increase the value of; [moneda] to revalue - **2.** [restituir el valor] to reassess in a favourable light.
➤ **revalorizarse** *vprnl* - **1.** [aumentar de valor] to appreciate; [moneda] to be revalued - **2.** [recuperar valor] to be reassessed favourably.

revancha *sf* **- 1.** [venganza] revenge; **tomarse la revancha** to take revenge **- 2.** DEP return match.

revanchismo *sm* vengefulness.

revelación *sf* revelation.

revelado *sm* FOTO developing.

revelador, ra *adj* [aclarador] revealing.
◆ **revelador** *sm* FOTO developer.

revelar *vt* **- 1.** [declarar] to reveal **- 2.** [evidenciar] to show **- 3.** FOTO to develop.
◆ **revelarse** *vprnl*: **revelarse como** to show o.s. to be.

revendedor, ra *sm, f* ticket tout.

revender *vt* to resell; [entradas] to tout.

reventa *sf* resale; [de entradas] touting.

reventado, da *adj fam* shattered, whacked.

reventar [19] ◇ *vt* **- 1.** [explotar] to burst **- 2.** [echar abajo] to break down; [con explosivos] to blow up **- 3.** [hacer fracasar] to ruin, to spoil **- 4.** *fam* [fastidiar] to annoy. ◇ *vi* **- 1.** [explotar] to burst **- 2.** [estar lleno]: **reventar de** to be bursting with **- 3.** [desear mucho]: **reventar por hacer algo** to be bursting to do sthg **- 4.** *fam fig* [perder los nervios]: **reventar (de)** to explode (with).
◆ **reventarse** *vprnl* **- 1.** [explotar] to explode; [rueda] to burst **- 2.** *fam* [cansarse] to get whacked, to tire o.s. to death.

reventón *sm* [pinchazo] blowout, puncture *UK*, flat *US*.

reverberación *sf* [de sonido] reverberation; [de luz, calor] reflection.

reverberar *vi* [sonido] to reverberate; [luz, calor] to reflect.

reverdecer [30] *vi* **- 1.** [campos etc] to become green again **- 2.** *fig* [amor] to revive.

reverencia *sf* **- 1.** [respeto] reverence **- 2.** [saludo - inclinación] bow; [- flexión de piernas] curtsy.

reverenciar [8] *vt* to revere.

reverendo, da *adj* reverend.
◆ **reverendo** *sm* reverend.

reverente *adj* reverent.

reversibilidad *sf* reversibility.

reversible *adj* reversible.

reverso *sm* back, other side; **ser el reverso de la medalla** to be the other side of the coin.

revertir [27] *vi* **- 1.** [volver, devolver] to revert **- 2.** [resultar]: **revertir en** to result in; **revertir en beneficio/perjuicio de** to be to the advantage/detriment of.

revés *sm* **- 1.** [parte opuesta - de papel, mano] back; [- de tela] other o wrong side; **al revés** [- en sentido contrario] the wrong way round; [- en forma opuesta] the other way round; **del revés** [- lo de detrás, delante] the wrong way round, back to front; [- lo de dentro, fuera] inside out; [- lo de arriba, abajo] upside down **- 2.** [bofetada] slap **- 3.** DEP backhand **- 4.** [contratiempo] setback, blow.

revestimiento *sm* covering.

revestir [26] *vt* **- 1.** [recubrir]: **revestir (de)** [gen] to cover (with); [pintura] to coat (with); [forro] to line (with) **- 2.** [poseer - solemnidad, gravedad etc] to take on, to have.
◆ **revestirse** *vprnl*: **revestirse de** [valor, paciencia] to arm o.s. with.

revienta *etc* ▷ **reventar**.

revierta, revirtiera *etc* ▷ **revertir**.

revisar *vt* **- 1.** [repasar] to go over again **- 2.** [inspeccionar] to inspect; [cuentas] to audit **- 3.** [modificar] to revise.

revisión *sf* **- 1.** [repaso] revision **- 2.** [inspección] inspection; **revisión de cuentas** audit; **revisión médica** check-up **- 3.** [modificación] amendment **- 4.** [AUTO - puesta a punto] service; [- anual] ≃ MOT (test).

revisor, ra *sm, f* [en tren] ticket inspector, conductor *US*; [en autobús] (bus) conductor.

revista ◇ *v* ▷ **revistar**. ◇ *sf* **- 1.** [publicación] magazine; **revista del corazón** gossip magazine; **revista de modas** fashion magazine **- 2.** [sección de periódico] section, review **- 3.** [espectáculo teatral] revue **- 4.** [inspección] inspection; **pasar revista a** MIL to inspect, to review; [examinar] to examine.

revistero *sm* [mueble] magazine rack.

revistiera *etc* ▷ **revistir**.

revitalizar [13] *vt* to revitalize.

revival [rri'βaiβal] *sm inv* revival.

revivificar [10] *vt* to revive.

revivir ◇ *vi* to revive. ◇ *vt* [recordar] to revive memories of.

revocable *adj* revocable.

revocación *sf* revocation.

revocar [10] *vt* **- 1.** [gen] to revoke **- 2.** CONSTR to plaster.

revolcar [36] *vt* to throw to the ground, to upend.
◆ **revolcarse** *vprnl* to roll about.

revolcón *sm* tumble, fall; **dar un revolcón a alguien** *fam* to thrash sb; **dar un revolcón con alguien** *fam* to roll in the hay with sb.

revolotear *vi* to flutter (about).

revoloteo *sm* fluttering (about).

revoltijo, revoltillo *sm* jumble.

revoltoso, sa *adj* **- 1.** [travieso] mischievous **- 2.** [sedicioso] rebellious.

revolución *sf* revolution.

revolucionar *vt* **- 1.** [crear conflicto] to cause a stir in **- 2.** [transformar] to revolutionize.

revolucionario, ria *adj* & *sm, f* revolutionary.

revolver [24] *vt* - **1.** [dar vueltas] to turn around; [líquido] to stir - **2.** [mezclar] to mix; [ensalada] to toss - **3.** [desorganizar] to turn upside down, to mess up; [cajones] to turn out - **4.** [irritar] to upset; **me revuelve el estómago** *o* **las tripas** it makes my stomach turn.

◆ **revolver en** *vi* [cajones etc] to rummage around in.

◆ **revolverse** *vprnl* - **1.** [moverse] to move around; [en la cama] to toss and turn - **2.** [volverse] to turn around; **revolverse contra** to turn against.

revólver *sm* revolver.

revoque *etc* ▷ **revocar**.

revuelca ▷ **revolcar**.

revuelo *sm* [agitación] commotion; **armar un gran revuelo** to cause a great stir.

revuelque ▷ **revolcar**.

revuelto, ta ◇ *pp* ▷ **revolver**. ◇ *adj* - **1.** [desordenado] upside down, in a mess - **2.** [alborotado - época etc] troubled, turbulent - **3.** [clima] unsettled - **4.** [aguas] choppy, rough.

◆ **revuelto** *sm* CULIN scrambled eggs *pl*.

◆ **revuelta** *sf* - **1.** [disturbio] riot, revolt - **2.** [curva] bend.

revuelva *etc* ▷ **revolver**.

revulsivo, va *adj fig* stimulating, revitalizing.

◆ **revulsivo** *sm fig* kick-start, stimulus.

rey *sm* king.

◆ **Reyes** *smpl*: **los Reyes** the King and Queen; **(Día de) Reyes** Twelfth Night.

◆ **Reyes Católicos** *smpl*: **los Reyes Católicos** the Spanish Catholic monarchs Ferdinand V and Isabella.

◆ **Reyes Magos** *smpl*: **los Reyes Magos** the Three Kings, the Three Wise Men.

reyerta *sf* fight, brawl.

rezagado, da ◇ *adj*: **ir rezagado** to lag behind. ◇ *sm, f* straggler.

rezagarse [16] *vprnl* to lag *o* fall behind.

rezar [13] ◇ *vt* [oración] to say. ◇ *vi* - **1.** [orar]: **rezar (a)** to pray (to); **rezar por algo/alguien** to pray for sthg/sb - **2.** [decir] to read, to say - **3.** [corresponderse]: **rezar con** to have to do with.

rezo *sm* - **1.** [acción] praying - **2.** [oración] prayer.

rezongar [16] *vi* to grumble, to moan.

rezumar ◇ *vt* - **1.** [transpirar] to ooze - **2.** *fig* [manifestar] to be overflowing with. ◇ *vi* to ooze *o* seep out.

ría ◇ *v* ▷ **reír**. ◇ *sf* estuary.

riachuelo *sm* brook, stream.

riada *sf lit* & *fig* flood.

ribeiro *sm* wine from the province of Orense, Spain.

ribera *sf* [del río] bank; [del mar] shore.

ribereño, ña *adj* [de río] riverside; [de mar] coastal.

ribete *sm* edging (U), trimming (U); *fig* touch, nuance.

ribetear *vt* to edge, to trim.

ribonucleico ▷ **ácido**.

ricamente *adv*: **tan ricamente** quite happily.

rice *etc* ▷ **rizar**.

ricino *sm* [planta] castor oil plant.

rico, ca ◇ *adj* - **1.** [gen] rich - **2.** [abundante]: **rico (en)** rich (in) - **3.** [sabroso] delicious - **4.** [simpático] cute - **5.** *fam* [apelativo]: **¡oye rico!** hey, sunshine! ◇ *sm, f* rich person; **los ricos** the rich; **los nuevos ricos** the nouveaux riches.

rictus *sm inv* - **1.** [de ironía] smirk - **2.** [de desprecio] sneer - **3.** [de dolor] wince.

ricura *sf* [persona] delight, lovely person.

ridiculez *sf* - **1.** [payasada] silly thing, nonsense (U) - **2.** [nimiedad] trifle; **cuesta una ridiculez** it costs next to nothing.

ridiculizar [13] *vt* to ridicule.

ridículo, la *adj* ridiculous; [precio, suma] laughable, derisory.

◆ **ridículo** *sm* ridicule; **hacer el ridículo** to make a fool of o.s.; **poner** *o* **dejar en ridículo a alguien** to make sb look stupid; **quedar en ridículo** to look like a fool.

ríe ▷ **reír**.

riega ▷ **regar**.

riego *sm* [de campo] irrigation; [de jardín] watering; **riego sanguíneo** (blood) circulation.

riegue ▷ **regar**.

riel *sm* - **1.** [de vía] rail - **2.** [de cortina] (curtain) rail.

rienda *sf* - **1.** [de caballería] rein; **dar rienda suelta a** *fig* to give free rein to; **tener a alguien con la rienda corta** *fig* to keep sb on a tight rein - **2.** [moderación] restraint.

◆ **riendas** *sfpl fig* [dirección] reins; **aflojar las riendas** to ease up; **llevar** *o* **tener las riendas** to hold the reins, to be in control.

riera *etc* ▷ **reír**.

riesgo *sm* risk; **a todo riesgo** [seguro, póliza] comprehensive; **correr (el) riesgo de** to run the risk of.

riesgoso, sa *adj Amér* risky.

rifa *sf* raffle.

rifar *vt* to raffle.

◆ **rifarse** *vprnl fig* to fight over, to contest.

rifle *sm* rifle.

rige ▷ **regir**.

rigidez *sf* - **1.** [de un cuerpo, objeto etc] rigidity - **2.** [del rostro] stoniness - **3.** *fig* [severidad] strictness, harshness.

rígido, da *adj* - **1.** [cuerpo, objeto etc] rigid - **2.** [rostro] stony - **3.** [severo - normas etc] harsh; [- carácter] inflexible.

rigiera *etc* ⊳ regir.

rigor *sm* - **1.** [severidad] strictness - **2.** [exactitud] accuracy, rigour; **en rigor** strictly (speaking) - **3.** [inclemencia] harshness.
➧ **de rigor** *loc adj* usual.

rigurosidad *sf* - **1.** [severidad] strictness - **2.** [exactitud] accuracy, rigour - **3.** [inclemencia] harshness.

riguroso, sa *adj* - **1.** [severo] strict - **2.** [exacto] rigorous, disciplined - **3.** [inclemente] harsh.

rija *etc* ⊳ regir.

rima *sf* rhyme.

rimar *vt* & *vi* to rhyme; **rimar con algo** to rhyme with sthg.

rimbombante *adj* - **1.** [estilo, frases] pompous - **2.** [desfile, fiesta etc] ostentatious.

rímel, rimmel® *sm* mascara.

rin *sm* - **1.** *Amér* [ficha telefónica] telephone token - **2.** *Méx* [llanta] wheel rim.

rincón *sm* corner *(inside)*.

rinconera *sf* corner piece.

rinda, rindiera *etc* ⊳ rendir.

ring *(pl* **rings***) sm* (boxing) ring.

rinoceronte *sm* rhinoceros.

riña ◇ *v* ⊳ reñir. ◇ *sf* [disputa] quarrel; [pelea] fight.

riñera *etc* ⊳ reñir.

riñón *sm* kidney; **riñón artificial** kidney machine; **costar un riñón** *fig* to cost a packet; **tener el riñón bien cubierto** *fig* to be well-heeled.
➧ **riñones** *smpl* [región lumbar] lower back *sing*.

riñonada *sf* [región lumbar] lower back; **costar una riñonada** *fig* to cost a packet.

riñonera *sf* [pequeño bolso] bum bag *UK*, fanny pack *US*.

río ◇ *v* ⊳ reír. ◇ *sm* *lit & fig* river; **ir río arriba/abajo** to go upstream/downstream; **a río revuelto, ganancia de pescadores** *prov* it's an ill wind that blows nobody any good *prov*; **cuando el río suena, agua lleva** *prov* there's no smoke without fire *prov*.

Río de Janeiro *sm* Rio de Janeiro.

Río de la Plata *sm* River Plate.

rioja *sm* Rioja (wine).

riojano, na *adj* & *sm, f* Riojan.

rioplatense *adj* of/relating to the River Plate region.

RIP *(abrev de* **requiescat in pace)** RIP.

ripio *sm* LITER *word or phrase included to complete a rhyme.*

riqueza *sf* - **1.** [fortuna] wealth - **2.** [abundancia] richness.

risa *sf* laugh, laughter *(U)*; **me da risa** I find it funny; **¡qué risa!** how funny!; **de risa** funny; **mondarse** *o* **morirse** *o* **partirse de risa** to die of laughter; **se me escapó la risa** I burst out laughing; **tomar algo a risa** to take sthg as a joke.

risco *sm* cliff, crag.

risible *adj* laughable.

risotada *sf* guffaw; **soltar una risotada** to laugh loudly.

ristra *sf* *lit & fig* string.

ristre ➧ **en ristre** *loc adv* at the ready.

risueño, ña *adj* - **1.** [alegre] smiling - **2.** [próspero] sunny, promising.

rítmico, ca *adj* rhythmic.

ritmo *sm* - **1.** [gen] rhythm; **al ritmo de** to the rhythm of; **llevar el ritmo** to keep time; **perder el ritmo** to get out of time; [cardíaco] beat - **2.** [velocidad] pace.

rito *sm* - **1.** RELIG rite - **2.** [costumbre] ritual.

ritual *adj* & *sm* ritual.

rival *adj* & *smf* rival; **sin rival** unrivalled.

rivalidad *sf* rivalry.

rivalizar [13] *vi*: **rivalizar (con)** to compete (with).

rivera *sf* brook, stream.

rizado, da *adj* - **1.** [pelo] curly - **2.** [mar] choppy.
➧ **rizado** *sm* [en peluquería]: **hacerse un rizado** to have one's hair curled.

rizar [13] *vt* - **1.** [pelo] to curl - **2.** [mar] to ripple.
➧ **rizarse** *vprnl* [pelo] to curl.

rizo *sm* - **1.** [de pelo] curl - **2.** [del agua] ripple - **3.** [de avión] loop - **4.** [tela] towelling, terry - **5.** *loc*: **rizar el rizo** to split hairs.

roast-beef = rosbif.

róbalo, robalo *sm* sea bass.

robar *vt* - **1.** [gen] to steal; [casa] to burgle, burglarize *US*; **robar a alguien** to rob sb - **2.** [en naipes] to draw - **3.** [cobrar caro] to rob.

roble *sm* - **1.** BOT oak - **2.** *fig* [persona] strong person; **más fuerte que un roble** as strong as an ox.

robledal, robledo *sm* oak wood *o* grove.

robo *sm* [delito] robbery, theft; [en casa] burglary; **robo a mano armada** armed robbery; **ser un robo** [precios etc] to be daylight robbery.

robot *(pl* **robots***) sm* [gen & INFORM] robot.
➧ **robot de cocina** *sm* food processor.

robótica *sf* robotics *(U)*.

robotización *sf* automation.

robotizar [13] *vt* to automate.

robustecer [30] *vt* to strengthen.
◆ **robustecerse** *vprnl* to get stronger.
robustez *sf* robustness.
robusto, ta *adj* robust.
ROC (*abrev de* reconocimiento óptico de caracteres) *sm* INFORM OCR *(optical character recognition)*.
roca *sf* rock; **firme como una roca** solid as a rock.
rocalla *sf* rubble.
rocambolesco, ca *adj* ludicrous.
roce ◇ *v* ▷ **rozar.** ◇ *sm* - **1.** [rozamiento - gen] rub, rubbing *(U)*; [- suave] brush, brushing *(U)*; FÍS friction - **2.** [desgaste] wear - **3.** [rasguño - en piel] graze; [- en zapato, puerta] scuffmark; [- en metal] scratch - **4.** [trato] close contact - **5.** [desavenencia] brush; **tener un roce con alguien** to have a brush with sb.
rociada *sf* - **1.** [rocío] dew - **2.** [aspersión] sprinkling - **3.** [de insultos, perdigones etc] shower.
rociar [9] *vt* - **1.** [arrojar gotas] to sprinkle; [con espray] to spray - **2.** [arrojar cosas]: **rociar algo (de)** to shower sthg (with) - **3.** [con vino] to wash down.
rocín *sm* nag.
rocío *sm* dew.
rock, rock and roll *sm inv* rock and roll.
rockero, ra = **roquero.**
rococó *adj inv* & *sm* rococo.
rocoso, sa *adj* rocky.
rodaballo *sm* turbot.
rodado, da *adj* - **1.** [piedra] rounded - **2.** [tráfico] road *(antes de s)* - **3.** *loc:* **estar muy rodado** [persona] to be very experienced; **venir rodado para** to be the perfect opportunity to.
◆ **rodada** *sf* tyre track.
rodaja *sf* slice; **en rodajas** sliced.
rodaje *sm* - **1.** [filmación] shooting - **2.** [de motor] running-in - **3.** [experiencia] experience.
Ródano *sm:* **el Ródano** the (River) Rhône.
rodapié *sm* skirting board.
rodar [23] ◇ *vi* - **1.** [deslizar] to roll; **echar algo a rodar** *fig* to set sthg in motion - **2.** [circular] to travel, to go - **3.** [girar] to turn - **4.** [caer]: **rodar (por)** to tumble (down) - **5.** [ir de un lado a otro] to go around - **6.** CINE to shoot. ◇ *vt* - **1.** CINE to shoot - **2.** [automóvil] to run in.
Rodas *n pr* Rhodes.
rodear *vt* - **1.** [gen] to surround; **le rodeó el cuello con los brazos** she put her arms around his neck; **rodear algo de algo** to surround sthg with sthg - **2.** [dar la vuelta a] to go around - **3.** [eludir] to skirt around.
◆ **rodearse** *vprnl:* **rodearse de** to surround o.s. with.

rodeo *sm* - **1.** [camino largo] detour; **dar un rodeo** to make a detour - **2.** *(gen pl)* [evasiva] evasiveness *(U)*; **andar** o **ir con rodeos** to beat about the bush; **hablar sin rodeos** to come straight to the point - **3.** [reunión de ganado] rounding up - **4.** [espectáculo] rodeo.
rodete *sm* round pad.
rodilla *sf* knee; **de rodillas** on one's knees; **doblar** o **hincar la rodilla** [arrodillarse] to go down on one knee; *fig* to bow (down), to humble o.s.; **hincarse de rodillas** to kneel (down).
rodillera *sf* - **1.** [protección] knee pad - **2.** [remiendo] knee patch.
rodillo *sm* [gen] roller; [para repostería] rolling pin.
rododendro *sm* rhododendron.
rodrigón *sm* stake, prop.
rodríguez *sm inv* grass widower; **estar** o **quedarse de rodríguez** to be a grass widower.
roedor, ra *adj* ZOOL rodent *(antes de s).*
◆ **roedor** *sm* rodent.
roedura *sf* - **1.** [acción] gnawing - **2.** [señal] gnaw mark.
roer [69] *vt* - **1.** [con dientes] to gnaw (at) - **2.** *fig* [gastar] to eat away (at) - **3.** *fig* [atormentar] to nag o gnaw (at) - **4.** *loc:* **ser duro de roer** to be a tough nut to crack.
rogar [39] *vt* [implorar] to beg; [pedir] to ask; **rogar a alguien que haga algo** to ask o beg sb to do sthg; **le ruego me perdone** I beg your pardon; **hacerse (de) rogar** to play hard to get; **'se ruega silencio'** 'silence, please'.
rogativa *(gen pl)* *sf* rogation.
rogué *etc* ▷ **rogar.**
roiga *etc* ▷ **roer.**
rojez *sf* - **1.** [cualidad] redness - **2.** [roncha] (red) blotch.
rojizo, za *adj* reddish.
rojo, ja ◇ *adj* red; **ponerse rojo** [gen] to turn red; [ruborizarse] to blush. ◇ *sm, f* POLÍT red.
◆ **rojo** *sm* [color] red; **al rojo vivo** [en incandescencia] red hot; *fig* heated.
rol *(pl* roles*)* *sm* - **1.** [papel] role - **2.** NÁUT muster.
rollizo, za *adj* chubby, plump.
rollo *sm* - **1.** [cilindro] roll; **rollo de primavera** CULIN spring roll - **2.** CINE roll - **3.** *fam* [discurso]: **el rollo de costumbre** the same old story; **soltar el rollo** to go on and on; **tener mucho rollo** to witter on - **4.** *fam* [embuste] tall story - **5.** *fam* [pelmazo, pesadez] bore, drag - **6.** *fam* [tema] stuff; **¿de qué va el rollo?** what's it all about? - **7.** *fam* [relación] relationship; **tener buen/mal rollo (con alguien)** to get on/not to get on with sb - **8.** *fam* [ambiente, tipo de vida] scene; **traerse un mal rollo** to be into a bad scene.

ROM (*abrev de* **read-only memory**) *sf* INFORM ROM.

romance ◇ *adj* Romance. ◇ *sm* - **1.** LING Romance language - **2.** LITER romance - **3.** [idilio] romance.

romancero *sm* LITER collection of romances.

románico, **ca** *adj* - **1.** ARQUIT & ARTE Romanesque - **2.** LING Romance.

◆ **románico** *sm*: **el (estilo) románico** the Romanesque (style).

romanización *sf* Romanization.

romanizar [13] *vt* to Romanize.

romano, **na** ◇ *adj* Roman; RELIG Roman Catholic. ◇ *sm, f* Roman.

romanticismo *sm* - **1.** ARTE & LITER Romanticism - **2.** [sentimentalismo] romanticism.

romántico, **ca** *adj & sm, f* - **1.** ARTE & LITER Romantic - **2.** [sentimental] romantic.

romanza *sf* MÚS ballad.

rombo *sm* GEOM rhombus.

romeo *sm fig person very much in love.*

romería *sf* - **1.** [peregrinación] pilgrimage - **2.** [fiesta] *open-air festivities to celebrate a religious event* - **3.** *fig* [mucha gente] long line.

romero, **ra** *sm, f* [peregrino] pilgrim.

◆ **romero** *sm* BOT rosemary.

romo, **ma** *adj* - **1.** [sin filo] blunt - **2.** [de nariz] snub-nosed.

rompecabezas *sm inv* - **1.** [juego] jigsaw - **2.** *fam* [problema] puzzle.

rompehielos *sm inv* ice-breaker.

rompeolas *sm inv* breakwater.

romper ◇ *vt* - **1.** [gen] to break; [hacer añicos] to smash; [rasgar] to tear - **2.** [interrumpir - monotonía, silencio, hábito] to break; [- hilo del discurso] to break off; [- tradición] to put an end to, to stop - **3.** [terminar - relaciones etc] to break off. ◇ *vi* - **1.** [terminar una relación]: **romper (con alguien)** to break *o* split up (with sb) - **2.** [olas, el día] to break; [hostilidades] to break out; **al romper el alba** *o* **día** at daybreak - **3.** [empezar]: **romper a hacer algo** to suddenly start doing sthg; **romper a llorar** to burst into tears; **romper a reír** to burst out laughing - **4.** *loc*: **de rompe y rasga** [persona] determined.

◆ **romperse** *vprnl* [partirse] to break; [rasgarse] to tear; **se ha roto una pierna** he has broken a leg.

rompevientos *sm Amér* [anorak] anorak; *R Dom* [suéter] polo-neck jersey.

rompiente *sm* reef, shoal.

rompimiento *sm* - **1.** breaking; [de relaciones] breaking-off - **2.** *Amér* [de relaciones, conversaciones] breaking-off; [de pareja] break-up; [de contrato] breach.

ron *sm* rum.

roncar [10] *vi* to snore.

roncha *sf* red blotch.

ronco, **ca** *adj* - **1.** [afónico] hoarse; **se quedó ronco de tanto gritar** he shouted himself hoarse - **2.** [bronco] harsh.

ronda *sf* - **1.** [de vigilancia, visitas] rounds *pl*; **hacer la ronda** to do one's rounds - **2.** [carretera] ring road - **3.** [avenida] avenue - **4.** *fam* [de bebidas, en el juego etc] round - **5.** *C Sur* [corro] circle, ring.

rondalla *sf* group of minstrels.

rondar ◇ *vt* - **1.** [vigilar] to patrol - **2.** [estar próximo]: **me ronda un resfriado** I've got a cold coming on - **3.** [rayar - edad] to be around - **4.** [cortejar] to court. ◇ *vi* [merodear]: **rondar (por)** to wander *o* hang around.

rondín *sm Andes* - **1.** [vigilante] watchman, guard - **2.** [armónica] mouth organ.

ronque *etc* ▷ **roncar**.

ronquera *sf* hoarseness.

ronquido *sm* snore, snoring *(U)*.

ronronear *vi* to purr.

ronroneo *sm* purr, purring *(U)*.

roña ◇ *adj fam* [tacaño] stingy, tight. ◇ *smf fam* [tacaño] stingy person. ◇ *sf* - **1.** [suciedad] filth, dirt - **2.** *fam* [tacañería] stinginess - **3.** [veterinaria] mange.

roñería *sf fam* stinginess.

roñica *fam* ◇ *adj* stingy, tight. ◇ *smf* stingy person.

roñoso, **sa** ◇ *adj* - **1.** [sucio] dirty - **2.** [tacaño] mean. ◇ *sm, f* miser, mean person.

ropa *sf* clothes *pl*; **aligerarse de ropa** [semidesnudo] to strip half-naked; **cambiarse de ropa** to change clothes; **ligero de ropa** scantily clad; **ropa blanca** linen; **ropa de abrigo** warm clothes *pl*; **ropa de cama** bed linen; **ropa hecha** ready-to-wear clothes; **ropa interior** underwear; **ropa sucia** laundry; **lavar la ropa sucia en público** *fig* to wash one's dirty linen in public; **nadar y guardar la ropa** *fig* to cover one's back.

ropaje *sm* robes *pl*.

ropero *sm* - **1.** [armario] wardrobe - **2.** [habitación] walk-in wardrobe; TEATRO cloakroom.

roque *sm* [en ajedrez] castle; **estar/quedarse roque** *fig* to be/fall fast asleep.

roquefort [roke'for] *sm* Roquefort (cheese).

roquero, **ra**, **rockero**, **ra** ◇ *adj* rock *(antes de s)*. ◇ *sm, f* - **1.** [músico] rock musician - **2.** [fan] rock fan.

rorro *sm* baby.

rosa ◇ *sf* [flor] rose; **estar (fresco) como una rosa** to be as fresh as a daisy; **no hay rosa sin espinas** there's no rose without a thorn. ◇ *sm* [color] pink. <> *adj inv* [color] pink; **verlo todo de color (de) rosa** *fig* to see everything through rose-tinted spectacles.

➤ **rosa de los vientos** *sf* NÁUT compass.

rosáceo, a *adj* pinkish.

rosado, da <> *adj* pink. <> *sm* [vino] rosé.

rosal *sm* [arbusto] rose bush.

rosaleda *sf* rose garden.

rosario *sm* - **1.** RELIG rosary; **rezar el rosario** to say one's rosary - **2.** [sarta] string - **3.** *loc*: **acabar como el rosario de la aurora** to finish up badly.

rosbif (*pl* rosbifs), **roast-beef** [ros'ßif] (*pl* roast-beefs) *sm* roast beef.

rosca *sf* - **1.** [de tornillo] thread - **2.** [forma - de anillo] ring; [- espiral] coil - **3.** CULIN ring doughnut - **4.** *loc*: **hacerle la rosca a alguien** to suck up to sb; **pasarse de rosca** [persona] to go over the top.

rosco *sm* ring-shaped bread roll; **no comerse un rosco** *mfam* never to get off with anyone.

roscón *sm* ring-shaped cake; **roscón de reyes** *cake eaten on 6th January*.

roseta *sf* - **1.** ARQUIT rosette - **2.** [de regadera] nozzle.

rosetón *sm* - **1.** [ventana] rose window - **2.** [adorno] ceiling rose.

rosquilla *sf* ring doughnut; **venderse como rosquillas** *fam* to sell like hot cakes.

rosticería *sf* Chile shop selling roast chicken.

rostro *sm* face; **tener (mucho) rostro** *fam fig* to have a real nerve.

rotación *sf* - **1.** [giro] rotation; **rotación de cultivos** crop rotation - **2.** [alternancia] rota; **por rotación** in turn.

rotar *vi* to rotate.

rotativo, va *adj* rotary, revolving.

➤ **rotativo** *sm* newspaper.

➤ **rotativa** *sf* rotary press.

rotatorio, ria *adj* rotary, revolving.

roto, ta <> *pp* ⊳ **romper**. <> *adj* - **1.** [gen] broken; [tela, papel] torn - **2.** *fig* [deshecho - vida etc] destroyed; [- corazón] broken - **3.** *fig* [exhausto] shattered. <> *sm, f* Chile fam despec [trabajador] worker.

➤ **roto** *sm* [en tela] tear, rip.

rotonda *sf* - **1.** [glorieta] roundabout *UK*, traffic circle *US* - **2.** [plaza] circus - **3.** [edificio] rotunda.

rotoso, sa *adj* Andes & R Dom fam ragged, in tatters.

rótula *sf* kneecap.

rotulador *sm* felt-tip pen; [fluorescente] marker pen.

rotular *vt* - **1.** [con rotulador] to highlight - **2.** [calle] to put up a sign on - **3.** [carta, artículo] to head with fancy lettering - **4.** [letrero] to letter.

rótulo *sm* - **1.** [letrero] sign - **2.** [encabezamiento] headline, title.

rotundidad *sf* firmness, categorical nature.

rotundo, da *adj* - **1.** [categórico - negativa, persona] categorical; [- lenguaje, estilo] emphatic, forceful - **2.** [completo] total.

rotura *sf* [gen] break, breaking *(U)*; [de hueso] fracture; [en tela] rip, hole.

roulotte [ru'lot] *sf* caravan *UK*, trailer *US*.

round [raund] (*pl* rounds) *sm* DEP round.

roya ⊳ **roer**.

royalty [ro'jalti] (*pl* royalties) *sm* royalty.

royera, royo *etc* ⊳ **roer**.

rozadura *sf* - **1.** [señal] scratch, scrape - **2.** [herida] graze.

rozamiento *sm* [fricción] rub, rubbing *(U)*; FÍS friction *(U)*.

rozar [13] *vt* - **1.** [gen] to rub; [suavemente] to brush; [suj: zapato] to graze - **2.** [pasar cerca de] to skim, to shave - **3.** *fig* [estar cerca de] to border on; **roza los cuarenta** he's almost forty.

➤ **rozar con** *vi* - **1.** [tocar] to brush against - **2.** *fig* [acercarse a] to verge on.

➤ **rozarse** *vprnl* - **1.** [tocarse] to touch - **2.** [pasar cerca] to brush past each other - **3.** [herirse - rodilla etc] to graze - **4.** *fig* [tener trato]: **rozarse con** to rub shoulders with.

rpm, r.p.m. (*abrev de* **revoluciones por minuto**) rpm.

Rte. *abrev de* **remitente**.

RTVE (*abrev de* **Radiotelevisión Española**) *sf* *Spanish state broadcasting company*.

rúa *sf* street.

ruana *sf* Andes poncho.

rubeola, rubéola *sf* German measles *(U)*.

rubí (*pl* rubíes o rubís) *sm* ruby.

rubia ⊳ **rubio**.

rubicundo, da *adj* ruddy.

rubio, bia <> *adj* - **1.** [pelo, persona] blond (*f* blonde), fair; **teñirse de rubio** to dye one's hair blond; **rubia platino** platinum blonde - **2.** [tabaco] Virginia (*antes de s*) - **3.** [cerveza] lager (*antes de s*). <> *sm, f* [persona] blond (*f* blonde), fair-haired person.

rublo *sm* rouble.

rubor *sm* - **1.** [vergüenza] embarrassment; **causar rubor** to embarrass - **2.** [sonrojo] blush.

ruborizar [13] *vt* [avergonzar] to embarrass.

➤ **ruborizarse** *vprnl* to blush.

ruboroso, sa *adj* blushing.

rúbrica *sf* - **1.** [de firma] flourish - **2.** [título] title - **3.** [conclusión] final flourish; **poner rúbrica a algo** to complete sthg.

rubricar [10] *vt* - **1.** [firmar] to sign with a flourish - **2.** *fig* [confirmar] to confirm - **3.** *fig* [concluir] to complete.

rucio, **cia** adj - **1.** [gris] grey - **2.** Amér fam blond (f blonde).

rudeza sf - **1.** [tosquedad] roughness - **2.** [grosería] coarseness.

rudimentario, **ria** adj rudimentary.

rudimentos smpl rudiments.

rudo, **da** adj - **1.** [tosco] rough - **2.** [brusco] sharp, brusque - **3.** [grosero] rude, coarse.

rueca sf distaff.

rueda ◇ v ▷ **rodar**. ◇ sf - **1.** [pieza] wheel; **rueda delantera/trasera** front/rear wheel; **rueda de repuesto** spare wheel; **la rueda de la fortuna** o **del destino** fig the wheel of fortune; **comulgar con ruedas de molino** fig to be very gullible; **ir sobre ruedas** fig to go smoothly - **2.** [corro] circle.

➡ **rueda de prensa** sf press conference.

➡ **rueda de reconocimiento** sf identification parade.

ruedo sm - **1.** TAUROM bullring - **2.** fig [mundo] sphere, world; **echarse al ruedo** to enter the fray; **ver también tauromaquia**.

ruega etc ▷ **rogar**.

ruego sm request; **ruegos y preguntas** any other business.

rufián sm villain.

rugby sm rugby.

rugido sm [gen] roar; [de persona] bellow.

rugir [15] vi [gen] to roar; [persona] to bellow.

rugosidad sf - **1.** [cualidad] roughness - **2.** [arruga - de persona] wrinkle; [- de tejido] crinkle.

rugoso, **sa** adj - **1.** [áspero - material, terreno] rough - **2.** [con arrugas - rostro etc] wrinkled; [- tejido] crinkled.

ruibarbo sm rhubarb.

ruido sm - **1.** [gen] noise; [sonido] sound; **ruido de fondo** background noise; **mucho ruido y pocas nueces** much ado about nothing - **2.** fig [escándalo] row; **hacer** o **meter ruido** to cause a stir.

ruidoso, **sa** adj [que hace ruido] noisy.

ruin adj - **1.** [vil] low, contemptible - **2.** [avaro] mean.

ruina sf - **1.** [gen] ruin; **amenazar ruina** [edificio] to be about to collapse; **dejar en** o **llevar a la ruina a alguien** to ruin sb; **estar en la ruina** to be ruined; **ser una ruina** to cost a fortune - **2.** [destrucción] destruction - **3.** [fracaso - persona] wreck; **estar hecho una ruina** to be a wreck.

➡ **ruinas** sfpl [históricas] ruins; **en ruinas** in ruins.

ruinoso, **sa** adj - **1.** [poco rentable] ruinous - **2.** [edificio] ramshackle.

ruiseñor sm nightingale.

ruja etc ▷ **rugir**.

ruleta sf roulette.

➡ **ruleta rusa** sf Russian roulette.

ruletear vi Amér C & Méx fam to drive a taxi.

ruletero sm Amér C & Méx fam taxi driver.

rulo sm - **1.** [para el pelo] roller - **2.** [rizo] curl.

ruma sf Andes & Ven heap, pile.

Rumanía, **Rumania** n pr Romania.

rumano, **na** adj & sm, f Romanian.

➡ **rumano** sm [lengua] Romanian.

rumba sf rumba.

rumbo sm - **1.** [dirección] direction, course; **caminar sin rumbo fijo** to walk aimlessly; **ir con rumbo a** to be heading for; **poner rumbo a** to set course for; **perder el rumbo** [barco] to go off course; fig [persona] to lose one's way; **tomar otro rumbo** to take a different tack - **2.** fig [camino] path, direction.

rumboso, **sa** adj fam generous.

rumiante adj & sm ruminant.

rumiar [8] ◇ vt [suj: rumiante] to chew; fig to ruminate, to chew over. ◇ vi [masticar] to ruminate, to chew the cud.

rumor sm - **1.** [ruido sordo] murmur - **2.** [chisme] rumour; **corre el rumor de que** there's a rumour going around that.

rumorearse v impers: **rumorearse que...** to be rumoured that...

runrún sm [ruido confuso] hum, humming (U).

runruneo sm [ruido] hum, humming (U).

rupestre adj cave (antes de s).

rupia sf rupee.

ruptura sf [gen] break; [de relaciones, conversaciones] breaking-off; [de contrato] breach.

rural adj rural.

Rusia n pr Russia.

ruso, **sa** adj & sm, f Russian.

➡ **ruso** sm [lengua] Russian.

rústico, **ca** adj - **1.** [del campo] country (antes de s) - **2.** [tosco] rough, coarse.

➡ **en rústica** loc adj paperback.

ruta sf route; fig way, course.

rutilante adj shining.

rutilar vi to shine brightly.

rutina sf [gen & INFORM] routine; **de rutina** routine; **por rutina** as a matter of course.

rutinario, **ria** adj routine.

Rvda. (abrev de **Reverenda**) Rev. (Mother etc).

Rvdo. (abrev de **Reverendo**) Rev. (Father etc).

S

s¹, s *sf* [letra] s, S.

s.² (*abrev de* **siglo**) c (*century*).

S³ - 1. (*abrev de* **sur**) S **- 2.** (*abrev de* **san**) St.

SA (*abrev de* **sociedad anónima**) *sf* ≃ Ltd, ≃ PLC.

sábado *sm* Saturday; **¿qué día es hoy? - (es) sábado** what day is it (today)? - (it's) Saturday; **cada sábado, todos los sábados** every Saturday; **cada dos sábados, un sábado sí y otro no** every other Saturday; **caer en sábado** to be on a Saturday; **te llamo el sábado** I'll call you on Saturday; **el próximo sábado, el sábado que viene** next Saturday; **el sábado pasado** last Saturday; **el sábado por la mañana/tarde/noche** Saturday morning/afternoon/night; **en sábado** on Saturdays; **nací en sábado** I was born on a Saturday; **este sábado** [pasado] last Saturday; [próximo] this (coming) Saturday; **¿trabajas los sábados?** do you work (on) Saturdays?; **un sábado cualquiera** on any Saturday; **Sábado de Gloria** Easter Saturday.

sabana *sf* savannah.

sábana *sf* sheet; **sábana ajustable** fitted sheet; **sábana bajera/encimera** bottom/top sheet; **se le pegan las sábanas** she's not good at getting up.

sabandija *sf* **- 1.** [animal] creepy-crawly, bug **- 2.** *fig* [persona] worm.

sabañón *sm* chilblain.

sabático, ca *adj* **- 1.** [del sábado] Saturday (*antes de s*) **- 2.** ⊳ **año**.

sabbat ['saβat] *sm* Sabbath.

sabedor, ra *adj*: **ser sabedor de** to be aware of.

sabelotodo *smf inv fam* know-all.

saber [70] ◇ *sm* knowledge. ◇ *vt* **- 1.** [conocer] to know; **ya lo sé** I know; **hacer saber algo a alguien** to inform sb of sthg, to tell sb sthg; **¿se puede saber qué haces?** would you mind telling me what you are doing? **- 2.** [ser capaz de]: **saber hacer algo** to know how to do sthg, to be able to do sthg; **sabe hablar inglés/montar en bici** she can speak English/ride a bike **- 3.** [enterarse] to learn, to find out; **lo supe ayer** I only found out yesterday **- 4.** [entender de] to know about; **sabe mucha física** he knows a lot about physics **- 5.** *loc*: **no saber dónde meterse** not to know where to put o.s. ◇ *vi* **- 1.** [tener sabor]: **saber (a)** to taste (of); **saber bien/mal** to taste good/bad; **saber mal a alguien** *fig* to upset o annoy sb **- 2.** [entender]: **saber de algo** to know about sthg; **ése sí que sabe** he's a canny one **- 3.** [tener noticia]: **saber de alguien** to hear from sb; **saber de algo** to learn of sthg **- 4.** [parecer]: **eso me sabe a disculpa** that sounds like an excuse to me **- 5.** *Andes, Arg & Chile fam* [soler]: **saber hacer algo** to be wont to do sthg **- 6.** *loc*: **no saber uno por dónde se anda** not to have a clue; **que yo sepa** as far as I know; **¡quién sabe!, ¡vete a saber!** who knows!

◆ **saberse** *vprnl*: **saberse algo** to know sthg; **sabérselas todas** *fig* to know all the tricks.

◆ **a saber** *loc adv* [es decir] namely.

sabiduría *sf* **- 1.** [conocimientos] knowledge, learning **- 2.** [prudencia] wisdom; **sabiduría popular** popular wisdom.

sabiendas ◆ **a sabiendas** *loc adv* knowingly; **a sabiendas de que...** knowing that..., quite aware of the fact that...

sabihondo = **sabiondo**.

sabina *sf* [planta] savin.

sabio, bia ◇ *adj* **- 1.** [sensato, inteligente] wise **- 2.** [docto] learned. ◇ *sm, f* [listo] wise person; [docto] learned person.

sabiondo, da, sabihondo, da *adj* & *sm, f* know-all, know-it-all.

sablazo *sm* **- 1.** [golpe] blow with a sabre **- 2.** [herida] sabre wound **- 3.** *fam fig* [de dinero] scrounging (*U*); **dar un sablazo a alguien** to scrounge money off sb.

sable *sm* sabre.

sablear *vi fam* to scrounge money.

sablista *smf fam* scrounger.

sabor *sm* **- 1.** [gusto] taste, flavour; **tener sabor a algo** to taste of sthg; **dejar mal/buen sabor (de boca)** *fig* to leave a nasty taste in one's mouth/a warm feeling **- 2.** *fig* [estilo] flavour.

saborear *vt lit & fig* to savour.

sabotaje *sm* sabotage.

saboteador, ra *sm, f* saboteur.

sabotear *vt* to sabotage.

sabrá *etc* ⊳ **saber**.

sabroso, sa *adj* **- 1.** [gustoso] tasty **- 2.** *fig* [substancioso] tidy, considerable.

sabueso *sm* **- 1.** [perro] bloodhound **- 2.** *fig* [policía] sleuth, detective.

saca *sf* sack.

sacacorchos *sm inv* corkscrew.

sacamuelas *sm inv fam* dentist.

sacapuntas *sm inv* pencil sharpener.

sacar [10] <> *vt* - **1.** [poner fuera, hacer salir] to take out; [lengua] to stick out; **sacar algo de** to take sthg out of; **nos sacaron algo de comer** they gave us something to eat; **sacar a alguien a bailar** to ask sb to dance - **2.** [quitar]: **sacar algo (de)** to remove sthg (from) - **3.** [librar, salvar]: **sacar a alguien de** to get sb out of - **4.** [conseguir]: **no sacas nada mintiéndole** you don't gain anything by lying to him - **5.** [obtener - carné, buenas notas] to get, to obtain; [- premio] to win; [- foto] to take; [- fotocopia] to make; [- dinero del banco] to withdraw - **6.** [sonsacar]: **sacar algo a alguien** to get sthg out of sb - **7.** [extraer - producto]: **sacar algo de** to extract sthg from - **8.** [fabricar] to produce - **9.** [crear - modelo, disco etc] to bring out - **10.** [exteriorizar] to show - **11.** [resolver - crucigrama etc] to do, to finish - **12.** [deducir] to gather, to understand; [conclusión] to come to - **13.** [mostrar] to show; **lo sacaron en televisión** he was on television - **14.** [comprar - entradas etc] to get, to buy - **15.** [prenda - de ancho] to let out; [- de largo] to let down - **16.** [aventajar]: **sacó tres minutos a su rival** he was three minutes ahead of his rival - **17.** [DEP - con la mano] to throw in; [- con la raqueta] to serve. <> *vi* DEP to put the ball into play; [con la raqueta] to serve.
➤ **sacarse** *vprnl* - **1.** [poner fuera]: **sacarse algo (de)** to take sthg out (of) - **2.** [carné etc] to get.
➤ **sacar adelante** *vt* - **1.** [hijos] to bring up - **2.** [negocio] to make a go of.

sacárido *sm* saccharide.

sacarina *sf* saccharine.

sacarosa *sf* sucrose.

sacerdocio *sm* priesthood.

sacerdotal *adj* priestly.

sacerdote, tisa *sm, f* [pagano] priest (*f* priestess).
➤ **sacerdote** *sm* [cristiano] priest.

saciar [8] *vt* - **1.** [satisfacer - sed] to quench; [- hambre] to satisfy, to sate - **2.** *fig* [colmar] to fulfil.
➤ **saciarse** *vprnl* to have had one's fill; *fig* to be satisfied.

saciedad *sf* satiety; **hasta la saciedad** *fig* over and over again.

saco *sm* - **1.** [bolsa] sack, bag; **saco de dormir** sleeping bag - **2.** *fig* [persona]: **ser un saco de mentiras** to be full of lies - **3.** *Amér* [chaqueta] coat - **4.** *loc*: **dar por saco a alguien** *mfam* to screw sb; **entrar a saco en** to sack, to pillage; **mandar a alguien a tomar por saco** *mfam* to tell sb to get stuffed; **no echar algo en saco roto** to take good note of sthg.

sacralizar [13] *vt* to consecrate.

sacramental *adj* sacramental.

sacramentar *vt* to administer the last rites to.

sacramento *sm* sacrament.

sacrificar [10] *vt* - **1.** [gen] to sacrifice; **sacrificar algo a** *lit & fig* to sacrifice sthg to - **2.** [animal - para consumo] to slaughter.
➤ **sacrificarse** *vprnl*: **sacrificarse (para hacer algo)** to make sacrifices (in order to do sthg); **sacrificarse por** to make sacrifices for.

sacrificio *sm lit & fig* sacrifice.

sacrilegio *sm lit & fig* sacrilege.

sacrílego, ga <> *adj* sacrilegious. <> *sm, f* sacrilegious person.

sacristán, ana *sm, f* sacristan, sexton.

sacristía *sf* sacristy.

sacro, cra *adj* - **1.** [sagrado] holy, sacred - **2.** ANAT sacral.
➤ **sacro** *sm* ANAT sacrum.

sacrosanto, ta *adj* sacrosanct.

sacudida *sf* - **1.** [gen] shake; [de la cabeza] toss; [de tren, coche] jolt; **dar sacudidas** to jolt; **sacudida eléctrica** electric shock - **2.** [terremoto] tremor - **3.** *fig* [conmoción] shock.

sacudir *vt* - **1.** [agitar] to shake - **2.** [golpear - alfombra etc] to beat - **3.** [hacer temblar] to shake - **4.** *fig* [conmover] to shake, to shock - **5.** *fam fig* [pegar] to smack, to give a hiding.
➤ **sacudirse** *vprnl* [persona] to get rid of.

sádico, ca <> *adj* sadistic. <> *sm, f* sadist.

sadismo *sm* sadism.

sadomasoquismo *sm* sadomasochism.

sadomasoquista <> *adj* sadomasochistic. <> *smf* sadomasochist.

saeta *sf* - **1.** [flecha] arrow - **2.** [de reloj] hand - **3.** MÚS *flamenco-style song sung on religious occasions*.

safari *sm* - **1.** [expedición] safari; **ir de safari** to go on safari - **2.** [zoológico] safari park.

saga *sf* saga.

sagacidad *sf* astuteness.

sagaz *adj* astute, shrewd.

Sagitario <> *sm* [zodiaco] Sagittarius; **ser Sagitario** to be (a) Sagittarius. <> *smf* [persona] Sagittarian.

sagrado, da *adj* holy, sacred; *fig* sacred.

sagrario *sm* - **1.** [parte del templo] shrine - **2.** [de las hostias] tabernacle.

Sáhara, Sahara *sm*: **el (desierto del) Sáhara** the Sahara (Desert).

sahariana [saxa'rjana] *sf* [prenda] safari jacket.

sahariano, na *adj & sm, f* Saharan.

sainete *sm* - **1.** TEATRO *short, popular comic play* - **2.** [fig] farce.

sajón, ona *adj & sm, f* Saxon.

sal *sf* - **1.** CULIN & QUÍM salt; **sal común** o **de cocina** cooking salt; **sal de fruta** fruit salts; **sal marina** sea salt; **la sal de la vida** *fig* the spark of life - **2.** *fig* [gracia] wit - **3.** *fig* [garbo] charm.
◆ **sales** *sfpl* - **1.** [para reanimar] smelling salts - **2.** [para baño] bath salts.

sala *sf* - **1.** [habitación - gen] room; [- de una casa] lounge, living room; [- de hospital] ward; **sala de embarque** departure lounge; **sala de espera** waiting room; **sala de estar** lounge, living room; **sala de juntas** boardroom; **sala de máquinas** machine room; **sala de operaciones** operating theatre; **sala de partos** delivery room - **2.** [mobiliario] lounge suite - **3.** [local - de conferencias, conciertos] hall; [- de cine, teatro] auditorium; **sala de fiestas** discothèque - **4.** [DER - lugar] court (room); [- magistrados] bench.

saladero *sm* salting room.

salado, da *adj* - **1.** [con sal] salted; [agua] salt *(antes de s)*; [con demasiada sal] salty; **estar salado** to be (too) salty - **2.** *fig* [gracioso] witty - **3.** *Amér C, Caribe & Méx* [desgraciado] unfortunate.

salamandra *sf* - **1.** [animal] salamander - **2.** [estufa] salamander stove.

salami, salame *sm* C Sur salami.

salar *vt* - **1.** [para conservar] to salt - **2.** [para cocinar] to add salt to.

salarial *adj* wage *(antes de s)*.

salario *sm* salary, wages *pl*; [semanal] wage; **salario base** o **básico** basic wage; **salario bruto/neto** gross/net wage; **salario mínimo (interprofesional)** minimum wage.

salaz *adj* salacious.

salazón *sf* [acción] salting.
◆ **salazones** *sfpl* [carne] salted meat *(U)*; [pescado] salted fish *(U)*.

salchicha *sf* sausage.

salchichón *sm* ≃ salami.

saldar *vt* - **1.** [pagar - cuenta] to close; [- deuda] to settle - **2.** *fig* [poner fin a] to settle - **3.** COM to sell off.
◆ **saldarse** *vprnl* [acabar]: **saldarse con** to produce; **la pelea se saldó con 11 heridos** 11 people were injured in the brawl.

saldo *sm* - **1.** [de cuenta] balance; **saldo acreedor/deudor** credit/debit balance; **saldo negativo** overdraft - **2.** [de deudas] settlement - **3.** *(gen pl)* [restos de mercancías] remnant; [rebajas] sale; **de saldo** bargain - **4.** *fig* [resultado] balance.

saldrá *etc* ▷ **salir**.

saledizo, za *adj* projecting.
◆ **saledizo** *sm* overhang.

salero *sm* - **1.** [recipiente] salt cellar UK, salt shaker US - **2.** *fig* [gracia] wit; [donaire] charm.

saleroso, sa *adj* [gracioso] witty; [garboso] charming.

salga *etc* ▷ **salir**.

salida *sf* - **1.** [acción de partir - gen] leaving; [- de tren, avión] departure; **salidas nacionales/internacionales** domestic/international departures - **2.** DEP start; **dar la salida** to start the race; **salida nula** false start - **3.** [lugar] exit, way out; **salida de emergencia/incendios** emergency/fire exit - **4.** [momento]: **quedamos a la salida del trabajo** we agreed to meet after work - **5.** [viaje] trip - **6.** [aparición - de sol, luna] rise; [- de revista, nuevo modelo] appearance - **7.** [COM - posibilidades] market; [- producción] output - **8.** INFORM output - **9.** *fig* [solución] way out; **si no hay otra salida** if there's no alternative - **10.** [pretexto] excuse - **11.** [ocurrencia]: **tener salidas** to be witty; **salida de tono** out-of-place remark - **12.** *fig* [futuro - de carreras etc] opening, opportunity.

salido, da ◇ *adj* - **1.** [saliente] projecting, sticking out; [ojos] bulging - **2.** [animal] on heat - **3.** *mfam* [persona] horny. ◇ *sm, f mfam* [persona] horny bugger.

saliente ◇ *adj* - **1.** [destacable] salient, important - **2.** POLÍT outgoing. ◇ *sm* projection.

salina ▷ **salino**.

salinidad *sf* salinity.

salino, na *adj* saline.
◆ **salina** *sf* - **1.** [en la tierra] salt mine - **2.** *(gen pl)* [en el mar] saltworks *sing*.

salir [71] *vi* - **1.** [ir fuera] to go out; [venir fuera] to come out; **salir de** to go/come out of; **¿salimos al jardín?** shall we go out into the garden?; **¡sal aquí fuera!** come out here! - **2.** [ser novios]: **salir (con alguien)** to go out (with sb) - **3.** [marcharse]: **salir (de/para)** to leave (from/for); **salir corriendo** to go off like a shot - **4.** [desembocar - calle]: **salir a** to open out onto - **5.** [separarse - tapón, anillo etc]: **salir (de)** to come off - **6.** [resultar] to turn out; **ha salido muy estudioso** he has turned out to be very studious; **¿qué salió en la votación?** what was the result of the vote?; **salir elegida actriz del año** to be voted actress of the year; **salir bien/mal** to turn out well/badly; **salir ganando/perdiendo** to come off well/badly - **7.** [proceder]: **salir de** to come from; **el vino sale de la uva** wine comes from grapes - **8.** [surgir - luna, estrellas, planta] to come out; [- sol] to rise; [- dientes] to come through; **le ha salido un sarpullido en la espalda** her back has come out in a rash - **9.** [aparecer - publicación, producto, traumas] to come out; [- moda, ley] to come in; [- en imagen, prensa, televisión] to appear; **¡qué bien sales en la foto!** you look great in the photo!; **ha salido en los periódicos** it's in the papers; **hoy salió por la televisión** he was on television today; **salir de** CINE & TEATRO to appear as - **10.** [en sorteo] to come up - **11.** [presentarse - ocasión, oportunidad] to turn up, to come along; [- problema, contratiempo] to arise; **a lo que salga, salga lo que salga** *fig* whatever happens - **12.** [costar]: **salir (a** o **por)** to work out (at); **salir caro** [de dinero] to be expensive; [por las consecuencias] to be costly - **13.** [decir u obrar inesperadamente]: **nunca se sabe por dónde va a salir** you never know what she's going to do/come out with next - **14.** [parecerse]: **salir a alguien** to turn out like sb, to take after sb - **15.** [en juegos] to lead; **te toca salir a ti** it's your lead - **16.** [quitarse - manchas] to come out - **17.** [librarse]: **salir de** [gen] to get out of; [problema] to get round - **18.** IN-FORM: **salir (de)** to quit, to exit.

◆ **salirse** *vprnl* - **1.** [marcharse - de lugar, asociación etc]: **salirse (de)** to leave - **2.** [filtrarse]: **salirse (por)** [líquido, gas] to leak o escape (through); [humo, aroma] to come out (through) - **3.** [rebosar] to overflow; [leche] to boil over; **el río se salió del cauce** the river broke its banks - **4.** [desviarse]: **salirse (de)** to come off; **el coche se salió de la carretera** the car came off o left the road - **5.** *fig* [escaparse]: **salirse de** [gen] to deviate from; [límites] to go beyond; **salirse del tema** to digress - **6.** *loc*: **salirse con la suya** to get one's own way.

◆ **salir adelante** *vi* - **1.** [persona, empresa] to get by - **2.** [proyecto, propuesta, ley] to be successful.

salitre *sm* saltpetre.

saliva *sf* saliva; **gastar saliva en balde** *fig* to waste one's breath; **tragar saliva** *fig* to bite one's tongue.

salivación *sf* salivation.

salivadera *sf* *Andes* spittoon.

salmo *sm* psalm.

salmodia *sf* singing of psalms; *fig* drone.

salmodiar [8] *vt* to sing in a monotone.

salmón ◇ *sm* [pez] salmon. ◇ *adj* & *sm inv* [color] salmon (pink).

salmonelosis *sf inv* MED salmonella.

salmonete *sm* red mullet.

salmuera *sf* brine.

salobre *adj* salty.

salobridad *sf* saltiness.

salomónico, ca *adj* equitable, even-handed.

salón *sm* - **1.** [habitación - en casa] lounge, sitting room; **salón comedor** living room-dining room; [- en residencia, edificio público] reception hall - **2.** [mobiliario] lounge suite - **3.** [local - de sesiones etc] hall; **salón de actos** assembly hall - **4.** [feria] show, exhibition; **salón de exposiciones** exhibition hall - **5.** [establecimiento] shop; **salón de belleza/masaje** beauty/massage parlour; **salón de té** tea-room.

◆ **de salón** *loc adj* *fig* armchair.

salpicadera *sf* *Méx* mudguard *UK*, fender *US*.

salpicadero *sm* dashboard.

salpicadura *sf* [acción] splashing, spattering; [mancha] spot, spatter.

salpicar [10] *vt* - **1.** [rociar] to splash, to spatter - **2.** *fig* [diseminar]: **salpicar (de)** to pepper (with).

salpicón *sm* CULIN *cold dish of chopped fish, seasoned with pepper, salt, vinegar and onion.*

salpimentar [19] *vt* to season with salt and pepper.

salpullido = sarpullido.

salsa *sf* - **1.** [CULIN - gen] sauce; [- de carne] gravy; **salsa bearnesa/tártara** bearnaise/tartar sauce; **salsa bechamel** o **besamel** bechamel o white sauce; **salsa muselina** *sauce made from egg yolk, butter and whipped cream*; **salsa rosa** thousand island dressing; **salsa de tomate** tomato sauce; **en su propia salsa** *fig* in one's element - **2.** *fig* [interés] spice - **3.** MÚS salsa.

salsera *sf* gravy boat.

saltador, ra ◇ *adj* jumping. ◇ *sm, f* DEP jumper.

saltamontes *sm inv* grasshopper.

saltar ◇ *vt* - **1.** [obstáculo] to jump (over) - **2.** [omitir] to skip, to miss out. ◇ *vi* - **1.** [gen] to jump; **saltar de alegría** to jump for joy; [a la comba] to skip; [al agua] to dive; **saltar sobre alguien** [abalanzarse] to set upon sb; **saltar de un tema a otro** to jump (around) from one subject to another - **2.** [levantarse] to jump up; **saltar de la silla** to jump out of one's seat - **3.** [salir para arriba - objeto] to jump (up); [- champán, aceite] to spurt (out); [- corcho, válvula] to pop out - **4.** [explotar] to explode, to blow up - **5.** [romperse] to break - **6.** [sorprender]: **saltar con** to suddenly come out with - **7.** [reaccionar violentamente] to explode - **8.** [suj: agua, cascada]: **saltar por** to gush down, to pour down - **9.** *loc*: **estar a la que salta** to be always on the lookout.

◆ **saltarse** *vprnl* - **1.** [omitir] to skip, to miss out - **2.** [salir despedido] to pop off - **3.** [no respetar - cola, semáforo] to jump; [- ley, normas] to break.

salteado, da *adj* - **1.** CULIN sautéed - **2.** [espaciado] unevenly spaced.

salteador, ra *sm, f*: **salteador de caminos** highwayman.

saltear *vt* - **1.** [asaltar] to assault - **2.** CULIN to sauté.

saltimbanqui *smf* acrobat.

salto *sm* - **1.** [gen & DEP] jump; **levantarse de un salto** to leap to sb's feet; [grande] leap; [al agua] dive; **dar** o **pegar un salto** to jump; [gran-

de] to leap; **salto de altura/longitud** high/long jump; **salto mortal** somersault; **salto con pértiga** pole vault - **2.** *fig* [diferencia, omisión] gap - **3.** *fig* [progreso] leap forward - **4.** [despeñadero] precipice - **5.** *loc:* **vivir a salto de mata** to live from one day to the next; **dar saltos de alegría** *o* **contento** to jump with joy.
➧ **salto de agua** *sm* waterfall.
➧ **salto de cama** *sm* negligée.

saltón, ona *adj* [ojos] bulging; [dientes] sticking out.

salubre *adj* healthy.

salubridad *sf* - **1.** [cualidad] healthiness - **2.** *culto* [salud pública] public health.

salud ◇ *sf lit & fig* health; **estar bien/mal de salud** to be well/unwell; **rebosar de salud** to glow with health; **beber** *o* **brindar a la salud de alguien** to drink to sb's health; **curarse en salud** to cover one's back. ◇ *interj:* **¡salud!** [para brindar] cheers!; **¡a su salud!** your health!; [después de estornudar] bless you!

saludable *adj* - **1.** [sano] healthy - **2.** *fig* [provechoso] beneficial.

saludar *vt* to greet; **saludar con la mano a alguien** to wave to sb; MIL to salute; **saluda a Ana de mi parte** give my regards to Ana; **le saluda atentamente** yours faithfully.
➧ **saludarse** *vprnl* to greet one another.

saludo *sm* greeting; **retirarle el saludo a alguien** to stop speaking to sb; MIL to salute; **Ana te manda saludos** [en cartas] Ana sends you her regards; [al teléfono] Ana says hello; **un saludo afectuoso** [en cartas] yours sincerely; **saludos** best regards.

salva *sf* MIL salvo; **una salva de aplausos** *fig* a round of applause.

salvación *sf* - **1.** [remedio]: **no tener salvación** to be beyond hope - **2.** [rescate] rescue - **3.** RELIG salvation.

salvado *sm* bran.

salvador, ra ◇ *adj* saving. ◇ *sm, f* [persona] saviour.
➧ **Salvador** *sm* - **1.** RELIG: **el Salvador** the Saviour - **2.** GEOGR: **El Salvador** El Salvador.

salvadoreño, ña *adj & sm, f* Salvadoran.

salvaguarda *sf* INFORM backup.

salvaguardar *vt* to safeguard.

salvaguardia *sf* - **1.** [defensa] safeguard - **2.** [salvoconducto] safe-conduct, pass.

salvajada *sf* atrocity.

salvaje ◇ *adj* - **1.** [gen] wild - **2.** [pueblo, tribu] savage. ◇ *smf* - **1.** [primitivo] savage - **2.** [bruto] maniac.

salvamanteles *sm inv* [llano] table mat; [con pies] trivet.

salvamento *sm* rescue, saving; **equipo de salvamento** rescue team.

salvar *vt* - **1.** [gen & INFORM] to save; **salvar algo/a alguien de algo** to save sthg/sb from sthg - **2.** [rescatar] to rescue - **3.** [superar - moralmente] to overcome; [- físicamente] to go over *o* around - **4.** [recorrer] to cover - **5.** [exceptuar]: **salvando algunos detalles** except for a few details.
➧ **salvarse** *vprnl* - **1.** [librarse] to escape; **sálvese quien pueda** every man for himself - **2.** RELIG to be saved.

salvavidas ◇ *adj inv* life *(antes de s).* ◇ *sm* [chaleco] lifejacket; [flotador] lifebelt.

salve[1] *interj* hail!

salve[2] *sf* prayer dedicated to the Virgin Mary.

salvedad *sf* exception; **con la salvedad de** with the exception of.

salvia *sf* sage.

salvo, va *adj* safe; **estar a salvo** to be safe; **poner algo a salvo** to put sthg in a safe place.
➧ **salvo** *adv* except; **salvo que** unless.

salvoconducto *sm* safe-conduct, pass.

samaritano, na *adj & sm, f* Samaritan.

samba *sf* samba.

sambenito *sm fig* [descrédito] disgrace; **poner** *o* **colgar a alguien el sambenito de borracho** to brand sb a drunk.

samovar *sm* samovar.

samurái *sm* samurai.

san *adj* Saint; **san José** Saint Joseph.

sanar ◇ *vt* [persona] to cure; [herida] to heal. ◇ *vi* [persona] to get better; [herida] to heal.

sanatorio *sm* sanatorium, nursing home.

sanción *sf* - **1.** [castigo] punishment; ECON sanction - **2.** [aprobación] approval.

sancionar *vt* - **1.** [castigar] to punish - **2.** [aprobar] to approve, to sanction.

sandalia *sf* sandal.

sándalo *sm* sandalwood.

sandez *sf* silly thing, nonsense *(U);* **decir sandeces** to talk nonsense.

sandía *sf* watermelon.

sándwich ['sanwitʃ] *(pl* **sándwiches)** *sm* - **1.** [con pan de molde] sandwich - **2.** *Amér* [con pan de barra] filled baguette - **3.** *C Sur* [feriado] *day(s)* taken off between two public holidays.

saneado, da *adj* [FIN - bienes] written off, written down; [- economía] back on a sound footing; [- cuenta] regularized.

saneamiento *sm* - **1.** [higienización - de tierras] drainage; [- de edificio] disinfection - **2.** *fig &* FIN

[- de bienes] write-off, write-down; [- de moneda etc] stabilization; [- de economía] putting back on a sound footing.

sanear *vt* - **1.** [higienizar - tierras] to drain; [- un edificio] to disinfect - **2.** *fig* & FIN [- bienes] to write off *o* down; [- moneda] to stabilize; [- economía] to put back on a sound footing.

sanfermines *smpl festival held in Pamplona when bulls are run through the streets of the town.*

sangrar ⬦ *vi* to bleed. ⬦ *vt* - **1.** [sacar sangre] to bleed - **2.** [vaciar - conducto] to drain off; [- árbol] to tap - **3.** IMPR to indent.

sangre *sf* blood; **donar sangre** to give blood; **de sangre caliente** ZOOL warm-blooded; **de sangre fría** ZOOL cold-blooded; **sangre azul** blue blood; **chuparle a alguien la sangre** to bleed sb dry; **costó sangre, sudor y lágrimas** I sweat blood; **encender** *o* **quemar la sangre a alguien** to make sb's blood boil; **se le heló la sangre** his blood ran cold; **llevar algo en la sangre** to have sthg in one's blood; **no llegó la sangre al río** it didn't get too nasty; **no tiene sangre en las venas** he's got no life in him; **se le subió la sangre a la cabeza** he saw red; **sudar sangre** to sweat blood; **tener mala sangre** to be malicious; **tener sangre de horchata** to be as cool as a cucumber.

➧ **sangre fría** *sf* sangfroid; **a sangre fría** in cold blood.

sangría *sf* - **1.** [bebida] sangria - **2.** MED bloodletting - **3.** *fig* [ruina] drain.

sangriento, ta *adj* - **1.** [ensangrentado, cruento] bloody - **2.** [despiadado, cruel, hiriente] cruel.

sanguijuela *sf lit & fig* leech.

sanguinario, ria *adj* bloodthirsty.

sanguíneo, a *adj* blood *(antes de s)*.

sanguinolento, ta *adj* [que echa sangre] bleeding; [bañado en sangre] bloody; [manchado de sangre] bloodstained; [ojos] bloodshot.

sanidad *sf* - **1.** [salubridad] health, healthiness - **2.** [servicio] public health; [ministerio] health department.

sanitario, ria ⬦ *adj* health *(antes de s)*. ⬦ *sm, f* [persona] health officer.

➧ **sanitarios** *smpl* [instalación] bathroom fittings *pl*.

San José *n pr* San José.

sano, na *adj* - **1.** [saludable] healthy; **sano y salvo** safe and sound - **2.** [positivo - principios, persona etc] sound; [- ambiente, educación] wholesome - **3.** [entero] intact, undamaged - **4.** *loc*: **cortar por lo sano** to make a clean break.

San Salvador *n pr* San Salvador.

sánscrito, ta *adj* Sanskrit.

➧ **sánscrito** *sm* Sanskrit.

sanseacabó *interj fam*: **¡sanseacabó!** that's an end to it!

Santander *n pr* Santander.

santería *sf Amér* [tienda] *shop selling religious mementoes such as statues of saints.*

santero, ra *adj* pious.

Santiago (de Chile) *n pr* Santiago.

Santiago de Compostela *n pr* Santiago de Compostela.

Santiago de Cuba *n pr* Santiago de Cuba.

santiamén ➧ **en un santiamén** *loc adv fam* in a flash.

santidad *sf* saintliness, holiness.

➧ **Santidad** *sf*: **Su Santidad** His Holiness.

santificación *sf* sanctification.

santificar [10] *vt* [consagrar] to sanctify.

santiguar [45] *vt* to make the sign of the cross over.

➧ **santiguarse** *vprnl* [persignarse] to cross o.s.

santo, ta ⬦ *adj* - **1.** [sagrado] holy - **2.** [virtuoso] saintly - **3.** *fam fig* [dichoso] damn; **todo el santo día** all day long. ⬦ *sm, f* RELIG saint.

➧ **santo** *sm* - **1.** [onomástica] saint's day - **2.** [ilustración] illustration - **3.** [estatua] (statue of a) saint - **4.** *loc*: **¿a santo de qué?** why on earth?; **se le fue el santo al cielo** *fam* he/she completely forgot; **llegar y besar el santo** to get sthg at the first attempt; **no ser santo de su devoción** not to be his/her *etc* cup of tea; **¡por todos los santos!** for heaven's sake!; **quedarse para vestir santos** to be left on the shelf.

➧ **santo y seña** *sm* MIL password.

Santo Domingo *n pr* Santo Domingo.

santón *sm* - **1.** RELIG Muslim holy man - **2.** *fig* [persona influyente] guru.

santoral *sm* - **1.** [libro de vidas de santos] *book containing lives of saints* - **2.** [onomásticas] *list of saints' days*.

santuario *sm* shrine; *fig* sanctuary.

santurrón, ona ⬦ *adj* excessively pious. ⬦ *sm, f* excessively pious person.

santurronería *sf* sanctimoniousness.

saña *sf* viciousness, malice.

sapiencia *sf culto* knowledge.

sapo *sm* toad; **echar sapos y culebras** *fig* to rant and rave.

saque ⬦ *v* ▷ **sacar**. ⬦ *sm* - **1.** [en fútbol]: **saque de banda** throw-in; **saque inicial** *o* **de centro** kick-off; **saque de esquina/meta** corner/goal kick - **2.** [en tenis etc] serve; **tener buen saque** to have a good serve; *fig* to have a hearty appetite.

saqueador, ra ⬦ *adj* looting, plundering. ⬦ *sm, f* looter.

saquear *vt* - **1.** [rapiñar - ciudad] to sack; [- tienda etc] to loot - **2.** *fam* [vaciar] to ransack.

saqueo *sm* [de ciudad] sacking; [de tienda etc] looting.

sarao *sm* [fiesta] party.

sarasa *sm fam despec* poof, queer.

sarcasmo *sm* sarcasm.

sarcástico, ca <> *adj* sarcastic. <> *sm, f* sarcastic person.

sarcófago *sm* sarcophagus.

sarcoma *sm* sarcoma.

sardana *sf traditional Catalan dance and music.*

sardina *sf* sardine; **como sardinas en canasta** *o* **en lata** like sardines.

sardinero, ra *adj* sardine *(antes de s)*.

sardo, da *adj & sm, f* Sardinian.
- **sardo** *sm* [lengua] Sardinian.

sardónico, ca *adj* sardonic.

sargento <> *smf* - **1.** MIL ≃ sergeant - **2.** *despec* [mandón] dictator, little Hitler. <> *sm* [herramienta] handscrew.

sari *sm* sari.

sarmiento *sm* vine shoot.

sarna *sf* MED scabies *(U)*; [veterinaria] mange; **sarna con gusto no pica** *prov* some things are a necessary evil.

sarnoso, sa <> *adj* [perro] mangy. <> *sm, f* [persona] scabies sufferer.

sarpullido, salpullido *sm* rash.

sarraceno, na *adj & sm, f* Saracen.

sarro *sm* - **1.** [de dientes] tartar - **2.** [poso] sediment.

sarta *sf lit & fig* string; **una sarta de mentiras** a pack of lies.

sartén *sf* frying pan; **tener la sartén por el mango** to be in control.

sastre, tra *sm, f* tailor.

sastrería *sf* [oficio] tailoring; [taller] tailor's (shop).

Satanás *sm* Satan.

satánico, ca *adj* satanic.

satanismo *sm* Satanism.

satélite <> *sm* satellite; **satélite artificial** satellite; **satélite de comunicaciones** communications satellite. <> *adj fig* satellite *(antes de s)*.

satelización *sf* putting into orbit.

satén *sm* satin; [de algodón] sateen.

satinado, da *adj* glossy.
- **satinado** *sm* gloss.

satinar *vt* to make glossy.

sátira *sf* satire.

satírico, ca <> *adj* satirical. <> *sm, f* satirist.

satirizar [13] *vt* to satirize.

sátiro *sm* - **1.** MITOL satyr - **2.** *fig* [lujurioso] lecher.

satisfacción *sf* satisfaction.

satisfacer [60] *vt* - **1.** [gen] to satisfy; [sed] to quench - **2.** [deuda, pago] to pay, to settle - **3.** [ofensa, daño] to redress - **4.** [duda, pregunta] to answer - **5.** [cumplir - requisitos, exigencias] to meet.
- **satisfacerse** *vprnl* to be satisified.

satisfactorio, ria *adj* satisfactory.

satisfecho, cha <> *pp* ▷ **satisfacer**. <> *adj* satisfied; **satisfecho de sí mismo** self-satisfied; **darse por satisfecho** to be satisfied.

saturación *sf* saturation.

saturado, da *adj*: **saturado (de)** saturated (with).

saturar *vt* to saturate.
- **saturarse** *vprnl*: **saturarse (de)** to become saturated (with).

saturnismo *sm* lead poisoning.

Saturno *n pr* Saturn.

sauce *sm* willow; **sauce llorón** weeping willow.

saudí *(pl* **saudíes** *o* **saudís), saudita** *adj & sm, f* Saudi.

sauna *sf* sauna.

savia *sf* sap; *fig* vitality; **savia nueva** *fig* new blood.

savoir-faire [sa'warfer] *sm* savoir-faire.

saxo <> *sm* [instrumento] sax. <> *smf* [persona] sax player.

saxofón = **saxófono**.

saxofonista *smf* saxophonist.

saxófono, saxofón <> *sm* [instrumento] saxophone. <> *smf* [persona] saxophonist.

sazón *sf* - **1.** [madurez] ripeness; **en sazón** ripe - **2.** [sabor] seasoning, flavouring.
- **a la sazón** *loc adv* then, at that time.

sazonado, da *adj* seasoned.

sazonar *vt* to season.

scanner [es'kaner] = **escáner**.

scooter [es'kuter] = **escúter**.

scotch [es'kotʃ] *(pl* **scotchs)** *sm* scotch (whisky).

scout [es'kaut] *(pl* **scouts)** *sm* scout.

script [es'kript] *(pl* **scripts)** *sm* script.

SCT *sf (abrev de* **Secretaría de Comunicaciones y Transportes),** *Mexican Department of Communication and Transport.*

se *pron pers* - **1.** *(reflexivo)* [de personas] himself *(f* herself *pl* themselves); [usted mismo] yourself *(pl* yourselves); [de cosas, animales] itself *(pl* themselves); **se está lavando, está lavándose** she is washing (herself); **se lavó los dientes** she cleaned her teeth; **espero que se diviertan** I hope you enjoy yourselves; **el perro se**

lame the dog is licking itself; **se lame la herida** it's licking its wound; **se levantaron y se fueron** they got up and left **- 2.** *(reflexivo impersonal)* oneself; **hay que afeitarse todos los días** one has to shave every day, you have to shave every day **- 3.** *(recíproco)* each other, one another; **se aman** they love each other; **se escriben cartas** they write to each other **- 4.** [en construcción pasiva]**: se ha suspendido la reunión** the meeting has been cancelled; **'se prohíbe fumar'** 'no smoking'; **'se habla inglés'** 'English spoken' **- 5.** *(impersonal)*: **en esta sociedad ya no se respeta a los ancianos** in our society old people are no longer respected; **se dice que...** it is said that..., people say that... **- 6.** *(en vez de 'le' o 'les' antes de 'lo', 'la', 'los' o 'las')* *(complemento indirecto)* [gen] to him (*f* to her *pl* to them); [de cosa, animal] to it (*pl* to them); [usted, ustedes) to you; **se lo dio** he gave it to him/her *etc*; **se lo dije, pero no me hizo caso** I told her, but she didn't listen; **si usted quiere, yo se lo arreglo en un minuto** if you like, I'll sort it out for you in a minute.

sé ⊳ **saber.**

sebáceo, a *adj* sebaceous.

SE *sf* (*abrev de* **Secretaría de Economía**), *Mexican Department of Economy.*

sebo *sm* fat; [para jabón, velas] tallow.

seborrea *sf* seborrhoea.

seboso, sa *adj* fatty.

secadero *sm* drying room.

secado *sm* drying.

secador *sm* dryer; **secador de pelo** hair-dryer.

secadora *sf* clothes *o* tumble dryer.

secano *sm* unirrigated *o* dry land.

secante ⟨⟩ *adj* **- 1.** [secador] drying **- 2.** ⊳ **papel - 3.** GEOM secant *(antes de s).* ⟨⟩ *sf* GEOM secant.

secar [10] *vt* **- 1.** [desecar] to dry **- 2.** [enjugar] to wipe away; [con fregona] to mop up.

➤ **secarse** *vprnl* [gen] to dry up; [ropa, vajilla, suelo] to dry.

sección *sf* **- 1.** [gen & GEOM] section **- 2.** [departamento] department.

seccionar *vt* **- 1.** [cortar] to cut; TECNOL to section **- 2.** [dividir] to divide (up).

secesión *sf* secession.

seco, ca *adj* **- 1.** [gen] dry; [plantas, flores] withered; [higos, pasas] dried; **lavar en seco** to dry-clean; **lavado en seco** dry-cleaning **- 2.** [tajante] brusque **- 3.** [flaco] thin, lean **- 4.** [ruido] dull; [tos] dry; [voz] sharp **- 5.** *loc*: **dejar a alguien seco** [matar] to kill sb stone dead; [pasmar] to stun sb; **parar en seco** to stop dead.

➤ **a secas** *loc adv* simply, just; **llámame Juan a secas** just call me Juan.

secreción *sf* secretion.

secretar *vt* to secrete.

secretaría *sf* **- 1.** [cargo] post of secretary **- 2.** [oficina, lugar] secretary's office **- 3.** [organismo] secretariat; **secretaría general** general secretariat.

secretariado *sm* **- 1.** EDUC secretarial skills *pl*; **curso desecretariado** secretarial course **- 2.** [cargo] post of secretary **- 3.** [oficina, lugar] secretary's office **- 4.** [organismo] secretariat.

secretario, ria *sm, f* secretary; **secretario de dirección** secretary to the director; **secretario de Estado** Secretary of State; **secretario general** General Secretary.

secretear *vi* to talk in secret.

secreter *sm* bureau, writing desk.

secreto, ta *adj* [gen] secret; [tono] confidential; **en secreto** in secret.

➤ **secreto** *sm* **- 1.** [gen] secret; **guardar un secreto** to keep a secret; **secreto a voces** open secret; **secreto bancario** banking confidentiality; **secreto de confesión** confessional secret; **secreto de estado** State secret; **secreto profesional** professional secret; **declarar el secreto de sumario** to deny access to information regarding a judicial enquiry **- 2.** [sigilo] secrecy.

secta *sf* sect.

sectario, ria ⟨⟩ *adj* sectarian. ⟨⟩ *sm, f* [miembro de secta] sect member.

sectarismo *sm* sectarianism.

sector *sm* **- 1.** [gen] sector; [grupo] group; **sector primario/secundario** primary/secondary sector; **sector privado/público** private/public sector; **sector terciario** service industries *pl* **- 2.** [zona] area.

sectorial *adj* sectorial.

secuaz *smf despec* minion.

secuela *sf* consequence.

secuencia *sf* sequence.

secuestrador, ra *sm, f* **- 1.** [de persona] kidnapper **- 2.** [de avión] hijacker.

secuestrar *vt* **- 1.** [raptar] to kidnap **- 2.** [avión] to hijack **- 3.** [embargar] to seize.

secuestro *sm* **- 1.** [rapto] kidnapping **- 2.** [de avión, barco] hijack **- 3.** [de bienes etc] seizure, confiscation.

sécula ➤ **sécula seculórum** *loc adv* for ever and ever.

secular ⟨⟩ *adj* **- 1.** [seglar] secular, lay **- 2.** [centenario] age-old. ⟨⟩ *sm* lay person.

secularización *sf* secularization.

secularizar [13] *vt* to secularize.

secundar *vt* to support, to back (up); [propuesta] to second.

secundario, ria *adj* secondary.

secundaria *sf* secondary education.

secuoya *sf* sequoia.

sed ⬦ *v* ▷ **ser**. ⬦ *sf* thirst; **el calor da sed** heat makes you thirsty; **tener sed** to be thirsty; **sed de** *fig* thirst for.

seda *sf* silk; **seda artificial** rayon, artificial silk; **seda cruda/natural** raw/pure silk; **seda dental** dental floss; **estar como una seda** to be as meek as a lamb; **ir como una seda** to go smoothly.

sedal *sm* fishing line.

sedán *sm* sedan.

sedante ⬦ *adj* MED sedative; [música] soothing. ⬦ *sm* sedative.

sedar *vt* MED to sedate; [suj: música] to soothe, to calm.

sedativo, va *adj* MED sedative; [música] soothing.

sede *sf* - **1.** [emplazamiento] headquarters *pl*; [de gobierno] seat; **sede social** head office - **2.** [de campeonato] host - **3.** RELIG see.

⬦ **Santa Sede** *sf*: **la Santa Sede** the Holy See.

sedentario, ria *adj* sedentary.

sedente *adj* seated.

sedición *sf* sedition.

sedicioso, sa ⬦ *adj* seditious. ⬦ *sm, f* rebel.

sediento, ta *adj* - **1.** [de agua] thirsty - **2.** *fig* [deseoso]: **sediento de** hungry for.

sedimentación *sf* sedimentation.

sedimentar *vt* to deposit.

⬦ **sedimentarse** *vprnl* [líquido] to settle.

sedimentario, ria *adj* sedimentary.

sedimento *sm* - **1.** [poso] sediment - **2.** GEOL deposit.

sedoso, sa *adj* silky.

seducción *sf* - **1.** [cualidad] seductiveness - **2.** [acción - gen] attraction, charm; [- sexual] seduction.

seducir [33] *vt* - **1.** [atraer] to attract, to charm; [sexualmente] to seduce - **2.** [persuadir]: **seducir a alguien para que haga algo** to tempt sb to do sthg.

seductor, ra ⬦ *adj* [gen] attractive, charming; [sexualmente] seductive; [persuasivo] tempting. ⬦ *sm, f* seducer.

sedujera, seduzca *etc* ▷ **seducir**.

sefardí (*pl* **sefardíes** o **sefardís**), **sefardita** ⬦ *adj* Sephardic. ⬦ *sm, f* [persona] Sephardi. ⬦ *sm* [lengua] Sephardi.

segador, ra *sm, f* [agricultor] reaper.

⬦ **segadora** *sf* [máquina] reaping machine.

segar [35] *vt* - **1.** AGRIC to reap - **2.** [cortar] to cut off - **3.** *fig* [truncar] to put an end to.

seglar ⬦ *adj* secular, lay. ⬦ *sm* lay person.

segmentación *sf* division.

segmentar *vt* to cut o divide into pieces.

segmento *sm* - **1.** GEOM & ZOOL segment - **2.** [trozo] piece - **3.** [sector] sector.

segregación *sf* - **1.** [separación, discriminación] segregation; **segregación racial** racial segregation - **2.** [secreción] secretion.

segregacionismo *sm* racial segregation.

segregar [16] *vt* - **1.** [separar, discriminar] to segregate - **2.** [secretar] to secrete.

segué *etc* ▷ **segar**.

seguidilla *sf* - **1.** LITER *poem containing four or seven verses used in popular songs* - **2.** (*gen pl*) [baile] *traditional Spanish dance* - **3.** [cante] *mournful flamenco song*.

seguido, da *adj* - **1.** [consecutivo] consecutive; **diez años seguidos** ten years in a row - **2.** [sin interrupción - gen] one after the other; [- línea, pitido etc] continuous.

⬦ **seguido** *adv* - **1.** [inmediatamente después] straight after - **2.** [en línea recta] straight on - **3.** *Amér* [frecuentemente] often.

⬦ **en seguida** *loc adv* straight away, at once; **en seguida nos vamos** we're going in a minute.

seguidor, ra *sm, f* follower.

seguimiento *sm* [de noticia] following; [de clientes] follow-up.

seguir [43] ⬦ *vt* - **1.** [gen] to follow; **seguir de cerca algo** to follow sthg closely; **seguir de cerca a alguien** to tail sb - **2.** [perseguir] to chase - **3.** [reanudar] to continue, to resume - **4.** [cursar]: **sigue un curso de italiano** he's doing an Italian course. ⬦ *vi* - **1.** [sucederse]: **seguir a algo** to follow sthg; **a la tormenta siguió la lluvia** the storm was followed by rain - **2.** [continuar] to continue, to go on; **seguir adelante** to carry on; **¡sigue! ¡no te pares!** go o carry on, don't stop!; **sigo trabajando en la fábrica** I'm still working at the factory; **debes seguir haciéndolo** you should keep on o carry on doing it; **sigo pensando que está mal** I still think it's wrong; **sigue enferma/en el hospital** she's still ill/at the hospital.

⬦ **seguirse** *vprnl* to follow; **seguirse de algo** to follow o be deduced from sthg; **de esto se sigue que estás equivocado** it therefore follows that you are wrong.

según ⬦ *prep* - **1.** [de acuerdo con] according to; **según su opinión, ha sido un éxito** in his opinion o according to him, it was a success; **según yo/tú** *etc* in my/your *etc* opinion - **2.** [dependiendo de] depending on; **según la hora que sea** depending on the time. ⬦ *adv* - **1.** [como] (just) as; **todo permanecía según lo recordaba** everything was just as she remembered it; **actuó según se le recomendó**

he did as he had been advised - **2.** [a medida que] as; **entrarás en forma según vayas entrenando** you'll get fit as you train - **3.** [dependiendo]: **¿te gusta la música?** - **según** do you like music? - it depends; **lo intentaré según esté de tiempo** I'll try to do it, depending on how much time I have.

◆ **según que** *loc adv* depending on whether.

◆ **según qué** *loc adj* certain; **según qué días la clase es muy aburrida** some days the class is really boring.

segunda ▷ **segundo**.

segundero *sm* second hand.

segundo, da ◇ *num* & *adj* second. ◇ *num m y f* - **1.** [en orden]: **el segundo** the second one; **llegó el segundo** he came second - **2.** [mencionado antes]: **vinieron Pedro y Juan, el segundo con...** Pedro and Juan arrived, the latter with... - **3.** [ayudante] number two; **segundo de abordo** NÁUT first mate.

◆ **segundo** *sm* - **1.** [gen] second - **2.** [piso] second floor.

◆ **segunda** *sf* - **1.** AUTO second (gear); **meter la segunda** to go into second (gear) - **2.** AERON & FERROC second class; **viajar en segunda** to travel second class - **3.** DEP second division.

◆ **con segundas** *loc adv* with an ulterior motive.

segundón *sm* second son; *fig* & *despec* failure, second best.

seguramente *adv* probably; **seguramente iré, pero aún no lo sé** the chances are I'll go, but I'm not sure yet.

seguridad *sf* - **1.** [fiabilidad, ausencia de peligro] safety; [protección, estabilidad] security; **de seguridad** [cinturón, cierre] safety *(antes de s)*; [puerta, guardia] security *(antes de s)*; **seguridad ciudadana** public safety; **seguridad vial** road safety - **2.** [certidumbre] certainty; **con seguridad** for sure, definitely - **3.** [confianza] confidence; **seguridad en sí mismo** self-confidence.

◆ **Seguridad Social** *sf* Social Security.

seguro, ra *adj* - **1.** [fiable, sin peligro] safe; [protegido, estable] secure; **sobre seguro** safely, without risk - **2.** [infalible - prueba, negocio etc] reliable - **3.** [confiado] sure; **estar seguro de algo** to be sure about sthg - **4.** [indudable - nombramiento, fecha etc] definite, certain; **tener por seguro que** to be sure that - **5.** [con aplomo] self-confident; **estar seguro de sí mismo** to be self-confident.

◆ **seguro** ◇ *sm* - **1.** [contrato] insurance *(U)*; **seguro a todo riesgo/a terceros** comprehensive/third party insurance; **seguro de incendios/de vida** fire/life insurance; **seguro de paro** o **de desempleo** unemployment benefit; **seguro de cambio** exchange rate hedge; **seguro del coche** car insurance; **seguro de**

invalidez o **incapacidad** disability insurance; **seguro mutuo** joint insurance; **seguro de vida** life insurance - **2.** [seguridad social] *health service office* - **3.** [dispositivo] safety device; [de armas] safety catch - **4.** *Amér C & Méx* [imperdible] safety pin. ◇ *adv* for sure, definitely; **seguro que vendrá** she's bound to come.

seis ◇ *num* & *adj inv* - **1.** [para contar] six; **tiene seis años** she's six (years old) - **2.** [para ordenar] (number) six; **la página seis** page six. ◇ *num m* - **1.** [número] six; **el seis** number six; **doscientos seis** two hundred and six; **treinta y seis** thirty-six - **2.** [en fechas] sixth; **el seis de agosto** the sixth of August - **3.** [en direcciones]: **calle Mayor (número) seis** number six calle Mayor - **4.** [en naipes] six; **el seis de diamantes** the six of diamonds; **echar** o **tirar un seis** to play a six. ◇ *num* & *smpl* - **1.** [referido a grupos]: **invité a diez y sólo vinieron seis** I invited ten and only six came along; **somos seis** there are six of us; **de seis en seis** in sixes; **los seis** the six of them - **2.** [en temperaturas]: **estamos a seis bajo cero** the temperature is six below zero - **3.** [en puntuaciones]: **empatar a seis** to draw six all; **seis a cero** six-nil. ◇ *num f pl* [hora]: **las seis** six o'clock; **son las seis** it's six o'clock.

seiscientos, tas *num* six hundred; *ver también* **seis**.

seísmo *sm* earthquake.

selección *sf* - **1.** [gen] selection; [de personal] recruitment; **selección natural** natural selection - **2.** [equipo] team; **selección nacional** national team.

seleccionador, ra ◇ *adj* - **1.** DEP selecting - **2.** [de personal] recruiting. ◇ *sm, f* - **1.** DEP selector, ≈ manager - **2.** [de personal] recruiter.

seleccionar *vt* to pick, to select.

selectividad *sf* - **1.** [selección] selectivity - **2.** [examen] university entrance examination.

selectivo, va *adj* selective.

selecto, ta *adj* - **1.** [excelente] fine, excellent - **2.** [escogido] exclusive, select.

selector, ra *adj* selecting.

◆ **selector** *sm* selector (button).

selenio *sm* selenium.

selenita ◇ *sf* selenite. ◇ *smf* [habitante] moon dweller.

self-service [selfˈserβis] *sm inv* self-service restaurant.

sellado, da *adj* [documento] sealed; [pasaporte, carta] stamped.

◆ **sellado** *sm* [de documento] sealing; [de pasaporte, carta] stamping.

sellar *vt* - **1.** [timbrar] to stamp - **2.** [lacrar] to seal - **3.** *fig* [pacto, labios] to seal.

sello *sm* - **1.** [gen] stamp - **2.** [tampón] rubber stamp - **3.** [lacre] seal - **4.** [sortija] signet ring - **5.** *Andes & Ven* [de monedas] tails - **6.** *fig* [carácter] hallmark.
➤ **sello discográfico** *sm* record label.

selva *sf* [gen] jungle; [bosque] forest; **selva virgen** virgin forest.

selvático, ca *adj* woodland *(antes de s).*

semáforo *sm* traffic lights *pl.*

semana *sf* week; **entre semana** during the week; **la semana próxima/que viene** next week; **semana laboral** working week.
➤ **Semana Santa** *sf* Easter; RELIG Holy Week.

semanada *sf Amér* (weekly) pocket money.

semanal *adj* weekly.

semanario, ria *adj* weekly.
➤ **semanario** *sm* [publicación semanal] weekly.

semántico, ca *adj* semantic.
➤ **semántica** *sf* semantics *(U).*

semblante *sm* countenance, face.

semblanza *sf* portrait, profile.

sembrado, da *adj* - **1.** [plantado] sown - **2.** *fig* [lleno]: **sembrado de** scattered O plagued with.
➤ **sembrado** *sm* sown field.

sembrador, ra *sm, f* [persona] sower.
➤ **sembradora** *sf* [máquina] seed drill.

sembrar [19] *vt* - **1.** [plantar] to sow; **sembrar algo de algo** to sow sthg with sthg - **2.** *fig* [llenar] to scatter, to strew - **3.** *fig* [confusión, pánico etc] to sow.

semejante <> *adj* - **1.** [parecido]: **semejante (a)** similar (to) - **2.** [tal] such; **jamás aceptaría semejante invitación** I would never accept such an invitation. <> *sm (gen pl)* fellow (human) being.

semejanza *sf* similarity; **a semejanza de** similar to.

semejar *vt* to resemble.
➤ **semejarse** *vprnl* to be alike, to resemble each other; **semejarse a alguien** to resemble sb.

semen *sm* semen.

semental <> *adj* stud *(antes de s).* <> *sm* stud; [caballo] stallion.

semestral *adj* half-yearly, six-monthly.

semestre *sm* period of six months, semester US; **cada semestre** every six months.

semiautomático, ca *adj* semiautomatic.

semicírculo *sm* semicircle.

semiconductor *sm* semiconductor.

semiconsonante *sf* semiconsonant.

semicorchea *sf* semiquaver.

semidirecto *adj* express.

semifinal *sf* semifinal.

semifinalista <> *adj* semifinalist *(antes de s).* <> *smf* semifinalist.

semilla *sf* seed.

semillero *sm* - **1.** [para plantar] seedbed - **2.** [para guardar] seed box - **3.** *fig* [origen] breeding ground.

seminario *sm* - **1.** [escuela para sacerdotes] seminary - **2.** [EDUC - curso, conferencia] seminar; [- departamento] department, school.

seminarista *sm* seminarist.

semioculto, ta *adj* partially hidden.

semiología *sf* LING & MED semiology.

semiólogo, ga *sm, f* LING & MED semiologist.

semiótica *sf* LING & MED semiotics *(U).*

semipesado <> *adj* DEP light heavyweight *(antes de s).* <> *sm* DEP light heavyweight.

semiseco, ca *adj* medium-dry.

semita <> *adj* Semitic. <> *smf* Semite.

semítico, ca *adj* Semitic.

semitismo *sm* Semitism.

semitono *sm* semitone.

semivocal *sf* LING semivowel.

sémola *sf* semolina.

sempiterno, na *adj culto* eternal.

Sena *sm*: **el Sena** the (river) Seine.

senado *sm* senate.

senador, ra *sm, f* senator.

senatorial *adj* - **1.** [del senado] senate *(antes de s)* - **2.** [de senador] senatorial.

sencillez *sf* - **1.** [facilidad] simplicity - **2.** [modestia] unaffectedness, naturalness - **3.** [discreción] plainness.

sencillo, lla *adj* - **1.** [fácil, sin lujo, llano] simple - **2.** [campechano] natural, unaffected - **3.** [billete, unidad etc] single.
➤ **sencillo** *sm* - **1.** [disco] single - **2.** *Andes, Amér C & Méx fam* [cambio] loose change.

senda *sf* = **senda**.

sendero *sm* path.

sendos, das *adj pl* each, respective; **llegaron los dos con sendos paquetes** they arrived each carrying a parcel, they both arrived with their respective parcels.

senectud *sf culto* old age.

Senegal *n pr*: **(el) Senegal** Senegal.

senil *adj* senile.

senilidad *sf* senility.

sénior *(pl* **seniores)** *adj inv & sm* senior.

seno *sm* - **1.** [pecho] breast - **2.** [pechera] bosom; **en el seno de** *fig* within - **3.** [útero]: **seno (materno)** womb - **4.** *fig* [amparo, cobijo] refuge, shelter - **5.** [concavidad] hollow - **6.** MAT sine - **7.** ANAT [de la nariz] sinus.

sensación *sf* - **1.** [percepción] feeling, sensación - **2.** [efecto] sensation; **causar sensación**

to cause a sensation; **causar una gran sensación a alguien** to make a great impression on sb - **3.** [premonición] feeling; **tener la sensación de que** to have a feeling that.

sensacional *adj* sensational.

sensacionalismo *sm* sensationalism.

sensacionalista *adj* sensationalist.

sensatez *sf* wisdom, common sense.

sensato, ta *adj* sensible.

sensibilidad *sf* - **1.** [perceptibilidad] feeling - **2.** [sentimentalismo] sensitivity; **tener la sensibilidad a flor de piel** to be very sensitive - **3.** [don especial] feel - **4.** [de emulsión fotográfica, balanza etc] sensitivity.

sensibilización *sf* - **1.** [concienciación] increased awareness - **2.** FOTO sensitization.

sensibilizar [13] *vt* - **1.** [concienciar] to raise the awareness of - **2.** FOTO to sensitize.

sensible *adj* - **1.** [gen] sensitive - **2.** [evidente] perceptible; [pérdida] significant.

sensiblería *sf despec* mushiness.

sensiblero, ra *adj despec* mushy, sloppy.

sensitivo, va *adj* - **1.** [de los sentidos] sensory - **2.** [receptible] sensitive.

sensor *sm* sensor; **sensor de humo** smoke detector.

sensorial *adj* sensory.

sensual *adj* sensual.

sensualidad *sf* sensuality.

sentado, da *adj* - **1.** [en asiento] seated; **estar sentado** to be sitting down - **2.** [establecido]: **dar algo por sentado** to take sthg for granted; **dejar sentado que...** to make it clear that...

◆ **sentada** *sf* sit-in; **de una sentada** in one go, at one sitting.

sentar [19] *vt* - **1.** [en asiento] to seat, to sit - **2.** [establecer] to establish. ◇ *vi* - **1.** [ropa, color] to suit - **2.** [comida]: **sentar bien/mal a alguien** to agree/disagree with sb - **3.** [vacaciones, medicamento]: **sentar bien a alguien** to do sb good - **4.** [comentario, consejo]: **le sentó mal** it upset her; **le sentó bien** she appreciated it.

◆ **sentarse** *vprnl* to sit down; **sentarse a hacer algo** to sit down and do sthg.

sentencia *sf* - **1.** DER sentence; **dictar sentencia** to pass sentence; **visto para sentencia** ready for judgment - **2.** [proverbio, máxima] maxim.

sentenciar [8] *vt* - **1.** DER: **sentenciar (a alguien a algo)** to sentence (sb to sthg) - **2.** *fig* [condenar, juzgar] to condemn.

sentencioso, sa *adj* sententious.

sentido, da *adj* - **1.** [profundo] heartfelt - **2.** [sensible]: **ser muy sentido** to be very sensitive.

◆ **sentido** *sm* - **1.** [gen] sense; **en cierto sentido** in a sense; **en sentido literal** in a literal sense; **tener sentido** to make sense; **sentido común** common sense; **sentido del humor** sense of humour; **sexto sentido** sixth sense - **2.** [conocimiento] consciousness; **perder/recobrar el sentido** to lose/regain consciousness; **sin sentido** unconscious - **3.** [significado] meaning, sense; **sin sentido** [ilógico] meaningless; [inútil, irrelevante] pointless; **doble sentido** double meaning - **4.** [dirección] direction; **de sentido único** one-way.

◆ **sin sentido** *sm* nonsense (U).

sentimental *adj* sentimental.

sentimentalismo *sm* sentimentality.

sentimentaloide *adj* mushy, sloppy.

sentimiento *sm* - **1.** [gen] feeling; **dejarse llevar por los sentimientos** to get carried away; **herir los sentimientos a alguien** to hurt sb's feelings - **2.** [pena, aflicción]: **le acompaño en el sentimiento** my deepest sympathy.

sentir [27] ◇ *vt* - **1.** [gen] to feel - **2.** [lamentar] to regret, to be sorry about; **siento que no puedas venir** I'm sorry you can't come; **lo siento (mucho)** I'm (really) sorry - **3.** [oír] to hear. ◇ *sm* feelings *pl*, sentiments *pl*.

◆ **sentirse** *vprnl* to feel; **me siento mareada** I feel sick; **se siente superior** she considers herself superior.

seña *sf* [gesto, indicio, contraseña] sign, signal.

◆ **señas** *sfpl* - **1.** [dirección] address *sing*; **señas personales** (personal) description *sing* - **2.** [gesto, indicio] signs; **dar señas de algo** to show signs of sthg; **(hablar) por señas** (to talk) in sign language; **hacer señas (a alguien)** to signal (to sb) - **3.** [detalle] details; **para o por más señas** to be precise.

señal *sf* - **1.** [gen & TELECOM] signal; **señal de alarma/salida** alarm/starting signal; [de teléfono] tone; **señal de ocupado** engaged tone, busy signal *US* - **2.** [indicio, símbolo] sign; **dar señales de vida** to show signs of life; **señal de la Cruz** sign of the Cross; **señal de tráfico** road sign; **en señal de** as a mark o sign of - **3.** [marca, huella] mark; **no quedó ni señal de él** there was no sign of him left; **no dejó ni señal** she didn't leave a trace - **4.** [cicatriz] scar, mark - **5.** [fianza] deposit.

señalado, da *adj* - **1.** [importante - fecha] special; [- personaje] distinguished - **2.** [con cicatrices] scarred, marked.

señalar *vt* - **1.** [marcar, denotar] to mark; [hora, temperatura etc] to indicate, to say - **2.** [indicar - con el dedo, con un comentario] to point out - **3.** [fijar] to set, to fix; **señaló su valor en 1.000 dólares** he set o fixed its value at $1,000.

◆ **señalarse** *vprnl* [perfilarse] to stand out.

señalización *sf* **- 1.** [conjunto de señales] signs *pl*; **señalización vial** roadsigns *pl* **- 2.** [colocación de señales] signposting.

señalizar [13] *vt* to signpost.

señera *sf Catalan flag.*

señor, ra *adj* **- 1.** [refinado] noble, refined **- 2.** *(antes de s) fam* [gran] real.

➤ **señor** *sm* **- 1.** [tratamiento - antes de nombre, cargo] Mr; [- al dirigir la palabra] Sir; **el señor López** Mr López; **¡señor presidente!** Mr President!; **¿qué desea el señor?** what would you like, Sir?; **Muy señor mío** [en cartas] Dear Sir **- 2.** [hombre] man **- 3.** [caballero] gentleman **- 4.** [dueño] owner **- 5.** [amo - de criado] master.

➤ **señora** *sf* **- 1.** [tratamiento - antes de nombre, cargo] Mrs; [- al dirigir la palabra] Madam; **la señora López** Mrs López; **¡señora presidenta!** Madam President!; **¿qué desea la señora?** what would you like, Madam?; **¡señoras y señores!...** Ladies and Gentlemen!...; **Estimada señora** [en cartas] Dear Madam; **¿es usted señora o señorita?** are you Mrs or Miss? **- 2.** [mujer] lady; **señora de compañía** female companion; **señora de la limpieza** cleaning woman **- 3.** [dama] lady **- 4.** [dueña] owner **- 5.** [ama - de criado] mistress **- 6.** [esposa] wife.

➤ **señores** *smpl* [matrimonio]: **los señores Ruiz** Mr & Mrs Ruiz.

➤ **Señor** *sm*: **el Señor** RELIG the Lord.

➤ **Nuestra Señora** *sf* RELIG Our Lady.

señoría *sf* lordship (*f* ladyship); **su señoría** [gen] his lordship; [a un noble] your lordship; [a un parlamentario] the right honourable gentleman/lady; [a un juez] your Honour.

señorial *adj* **- 1.** [majestuoso] stately **- 2.** [del señorío] lordly.

señorío *sm* **- 1.** [dominio] dominion, rule **- 2.** [distinción] nobility.

señorito, ta *adj fam despec* [refinado] lordly.

➤ **señorito** *sm* **- 1.** *desus* [hijo del amo] master **- 2.** *fam despec* [niñato] rich kid.

➤ **señorita** *sf* **- 1.** [soltera, tratamiento] Miss **- 2.** [joven] young lady **- 3.** [maestra]: **la señorita** miss, the teacher **- 4.** *desus* [hija del amo] mistress.

señuelo *sm* **- 1.** [reclamo] decoy **- 2.** *fig* [trampa] bait, lure.

sep., sept. (*abrev de* **septiembre**) Sept.

SEP *sf* (*abrev de* **Secretaría de Educación Pública**), *Mexican Department of Public Education.*

sepa *etc* ▷ **saber**.

sépalo *sm* sepal.

separación *sf* **- 1.** [gen] separation **- 2.** [espacio] space, distance.

➤ **separación de bienes** *sf* DER separate estates (*pl*).

separado, da ◇ *adj* **- 1.** [gen] separate; **está muy separado de la pared** it's too far away from the wall; **por separado** separately **- 2.** [del cónyuge] separated. ◇ *sm, f* separated person.

separar *vt* **- 1.** [gen] to separate; **separar algo de** to separate sthg from **- 2.** [desunir] to take off, to remove **- 3.** [apartar - silla etc] to move away **- 4.** [reservar] to put aside **- 5.** [destituir]: **separar de** to remove o dismiss from.

➤ **separarse** *vprnl* **- 1.** [apartarse] to move apart; **separarse de** to move away from **- 2.** [ir por distinto lugar] to separate, to part company **- 3.** [matrimonio]: **separarse (de alguien)** to separate (from sb) **- 4.** [desprenderse] to come away o off.

separatismo *sm* separatism.

separo *sm Méx* (prison) cell.

sepelio *sm* burial.

sepia *sf* [molusco] cuttlefish.

sept. (*abrev de* **septiembre**), = **sep.**

septentrional *adj* northern.

séptico, ca *adj* septic.

septiembre, setiembre *sm* September; **el 1 de septiembre** the 1st of September; **uno de los septiembres más lluviosos de la última década** one of the rainiest Septembers in the last decade; **a principios/mediados/finales de septiembre** at the beginning/in the middle/at the end of September; **el pasado/próximo (mes de) septiembre** last/next September; **en septiembre** in September; **en pleno septiembre** in mid-September; **este (mes de) septiembre** [pasado] (this) last September; [próximo] next September, this coming September; **para septiembre** by September.

séptimo, ma, sétimo, ma *num* seventh; **la séptima parte** a seventh.

septuagésimo, ma *num* seventieth.

septuplicar [10] *vt* to multiply by seven.

➤ **septuplicarse** *vprnl* to increase sevenfold.

sepulcral *adj* **- 1.** [del sepulcro] tomb *(antes de s)* **- 2.** *fig* [profundo - voz, silencio] lugubrious, gloomy.

sepulcro *sm* tomb.

sepultar *vt* to bury.

sepultura *sf* **- 1.** [enterramiento] burial; **dar sepultura a alguien** to bury sb **- 2.** [fosa] grave.

sepulturero, ra *sm, f* gravedigger.

seque *etc* ▷ **secar**.

sequedad *sf* **- 1.** [falta de humedad] dryness **- 2.** *fig* [antipatía] abruptness, brusqueness.

sequía *sf* drought.

séquito *sm* [comitiva] retinue, entourage.

ser [5] <> *v aux (antes de pp forma la voz pasiva)* to be; **fue visto por un testigo** he was seen by a witness. <> *v cop* - **1.** [gen] to be; **es alto/gracioso** he is tall/funny; **es azul/difícil** it's blue/difficult; **es un amigo/el dueño** he is a friend/the owner - **2.** [empleo, dedicación] to be; **soy abogado/actriz** I'm a lawyer/an actress; **son estudiantes** they're students. <> *vi* - **1.** [gen] to be; **fue aquí** it was here; **lo importante es decidirse** the important thing is to reach a decision; **ser de** [estar hecho de] to be made of; [provenir de] to be from; [ser propiedad de] to belong to; [formar parte de] to be a member of; **¿de dónde eres?** where are you from?; **los juguetes son de mi hijo** the toys are my son's - **2.** [con precios, horas, números] ¿**cuánto es?** how much is it?; **son 30 euros** that'll be 30 euros; ¿**qué (día) es hoy?** what day is it today?, what's today?; **mañana será 15 de julio** tomorrow (it) will be the 15th of July; ¿**qué hora es?** what time is it?, what's the time?; **son las tres (de la tarde)** it's three o'clock (in the afternoon), it's three (pm) - **3.** [servir, ser adecuado]: **ser para** to be for; **este trapo es para (limpiar) las ventanas** this cloth is for (cleaning) the windows; **este libro es para niños** this book is (meant) for children - **4.** *(uso partitivo)*: **ser de los que...** to be one of those (people) who...; **ése es de los que están en huelga** he is one of those on strike. <> *v impers* - **1.** [expresa tiempo] to be; **es muy tarde** it's rather late; **era de noche/de día** it was night/day - **2.** [expresa necesidad, posibilidad]: **es de desear que...** it is to be hoped that...; **es de suponer que aparecerá** presumably, he'll turn up - **3.** [expresa motivo]: **es que no vine porque estaba enfermo** the reason I didn't come is that I was ill - **4.** *loc*: **a no ser que** unless; **como sea** one way or another, somehow or other; **de no ser por** had it not been for; **érase una vez, érase que se era** once upon a time; **no es para menos** not without reason; **o sea** that is (to say), I mean; **por si fuera poco** as if that wasn't enough. <> *sm* [ente] being; **ser humano/vivo** human/living being.

Serbia *n pr* Serbia.

serafín *sm* seraph.

serenar *vt* [calmar] to calm.
◆ **serenarse** *vprnl* [calmarse] to calm down.

serenata *sf* MÚS serenade.

serenidad *sf* - **1.** [tranquilidad] calm - **2.** [quietud] tranquility.

sereno, na *adj* calm.
◆ **sereno** *sm* - **1.** [vigilante] night watchman - **2.** [humedad] night dew.

serial *sm* serial.

serie *sf* - **1.** [gen & TV] series *sing*; [de hechos, sucesos] chain; [de mentiras] string - **2.** [de sellos, monedas] set - **3.** *loc*: **ser un fuera de serie** to be unique.
◆ **de serie** *loc adj* [equipamiento] (fitted) as standard.
◆ **en serie** *loc adv* - **1.** [fabricación]: **fabricar en serie** to mass-produce - **2.** ELECTR in series.

seriedad *sf* - **1.** [gravedad] seriousness - **2.** [responsabilidad] sense of responsibility - **3.** [formalidad - de persona] reliability.

serigrafía *sf* silkscreen printing.

serio, ria *adj* - **1.** [gen] serious; **estar serio** to look serious - **2.** [responsable, formal] responsible - **3.** [sobrio] sober.
◆ **en serio** *loc adv* seriously; **lo digo en serio** I'm serious; **tomar(se) algo/a alguien en serio** to take sthg/sb seriously.

sermón *sm* lit & fig sermon; **echar un sermón por algo** to give a lecture for sthg.

sermoneador, ra *adj* sermonizing.

sermonear *vt* to give a lecture o ticking-off to.

seropositivo, va <> *adj* MED HIV-positive. <> *sm, f* MED HIV-positive person.

serpentear *vi* - **1.** [río, camino] to wind, to snake - **2.** [culebra] to wriggle.

serpentina *sf* streamer.

serpiente *sf* [culebra] snake; LITER serpent; **serpiente de cascabel** rattlesnake; **serpiente pitón** python.

serrallo *sm* seraglio.

serranía *sf* mountainous region.

serrano, na <> *adj* - **1.** [de la sierra] mountain *(antes de s)*, highland *(antes de s)* - **2.** [jamón] cured. <> *sm, f* highlander.

serrar [19] *vt* to saw (up).

serrería *sf* sawmill.

serrín *sm* sawdust.

serrucho *sm* handsaw.

servicial *adj* attentive, helpful.

servicio *sm* - **1.** [gen] service; **fuera de servicio** out of order; **servicio de inteligencia** o **secreto** intelligence o secret service; **servicio de prensa/de urgencias** press/casualty department; **servicio discrecional/público** private/public service; **servicio a domicilio** home delivery service; **servicio de mesa** dinner service; **servicio militar** military service; **servicio de paquetería** parcel service; **servicio posventa** after-sales service; **servicio de té** tea set - **2.** [servidumbre] servants *pl*; **servicio doméstico** domestic help - **3.** [turno] duty; **estar de servicio** to be on duty - **4.** *(gen pl)* [WC] toilet, lavatory, bathroom US - **5.** DEP serve, service - **6.** [cubierto] place setting.

servidor, ra *sm, f* - **1.** [criado] servant - **2.** [en cartas]: **su seguro servidor** yours faithfully - **3.** [yo] yours truly, me; **¿quién es el último? - servidor** who's last? - I am.
➤ **servidor** *sm* INFORM server; **servidor seguro** secure server.

servidumbre *sf* - **1.** [criados] servants *pl* - **2.** [dependencia] servitude.

servil *adj* servile.

servilismo *sm* subservience.

servilleta *sf* serviette, napkin.

servilletero *sm* serviette O napkin ring.

servir [26] ◇ *vt* to serve; **sírvanos dos cervezas** bring us two beers; **¿te sirvo más patatas?** would you like some more potatoes?; **¿en qué puedo servirle?** what can I do for you? ◇ *vi* - **1.** [gen] to serve; **servir en el gobierno** to be a government minister - **2.** [valer, ser útil] to serve, to be useful; **no sirve para estudiar** he's no good at studying; **de nada sirve que se lo digas** it's no use telling him; **servir de algo** to serve as sthg - **3.** [como criado] to be in service.
➤ **servirse** *vprnl* - **1.** [aprovecharse]: **servirse de** to make use of; **sírvase llamar cuando quiera** please call whenever you want - **2.** [comida, bebida] to help o.s.

servoasistido, da *adj* AUTO servo *(antes de s)*.

servodirección *sf* power steering.

servofreno *sm* servo brake.

sésamo *sm* sesame.

sesear *vi* GRAM to pronounce "c" and "z" as "s", as in Andalusian and Latin American dialects.

sesenta *num* sixty; **los (años) sesenta** the sixties; *ver también* **seis**.

seseo *sm* pronunciation of "c" and "z" as an "s".

sesera *sf fam* - **1.** [cabeza] skull, nut - **2.** *fig* [inteligencia] brains *pl*; **estar mal de la sesera** *fam* to be soft in the head.

sesgar [16] *vt* to cut on the bias.

sesgo *sm* - **1.** [oblicuidad] slant; **al sesgo** [gen] on a slant; [costura] on the bias - **2.** *fig* [rumbo] course, path - **3.** [enfoque] bias.

sesgue *etc* ▷ **sesgar**.

sesión *sf* - **1.** [reunión] meeting, session; DER sitting, session; **abrir/levantar la sesión** to open/to adjourn the meeting - **2.** [proyección, representación] show, performance; **sesión continua** continuous showing; **sesión matinal** matinée; **sesión de tarde** afternoon matinée; **sesión de noche** evening showing - **3.** [periodo] session.

seso *(gen pl)* *sm* - **1.** [cerebro] brain - **2.** [sensatez] brains *pl*, sense; **calentarse** O **devanarse los sesos** to rack one's brains; **sorber el seso** O **los sesos a alguien** to brainwash sb.

sestear *vi* to have a nap.

sesudo, da *adj* - **1.** [inteligente] brainy - **2.** [sensato] wise, sensible.

set *(pl* sets*)* *sm* DEP set.

seta *sf* mushroom; **seta venenosa** toadstool.

setecientos, tas *num* seven hundred; *ver también* **seis**.

setenta *num* seventy; **los (años) setenta** the seventies; *ver también* **seis**.

setiembre = **septiembre**.

sétimo = **séptimo**.

seto *sm* fence; **seto vivo** hedge.

setter ['seter] *sm* setter.

seudónimo *sm* pseudonym.

severidad *sf* - **1.** [rigor] severity - **2.** [intransigencia] strictness.

severo, ra *adj* - **1.** [castigo] severe, harsh - **2.** [persona] strict.

Sevilla *n pr* Seville.

sevillano, na *adj* & *sm, f* Sevillian.
➤ **sevillanas** *sfpl* Andalusian dance and song.

sexagenario, ria *adj* & *sm, f* sexagenarian.

sexagésimo, ma *num* sixtieth.

sex-appeal [seksa'pil] *sm inv* sex appeal.

sexismo *sm* sexism.

sexista *adj* & *smf* sexist.

sexo *sm* - **1.** [gen] sex; **bello sexo, sexo débil** fair sex; **sexo tántrico** tantric sex - **2.** [genitales] genitals *pl*.

sexología *sf* sexology.

sexólogo, ga *sm, f* sexologist.

sex-shop [sek'ʃop] *(pl* sex-shops*)* *sm* sex shop.

sextante *sm* sextant.

sexteto *sm* MÚS sextet.

sexto, ta *num* sixth; **la sexta parte** a sixth.

sextuplicar [10] *vt* to multiply by six.
➤ **sextuplicarse** *vprnl* to increase sixfold.

séxtuplo, pla *adj* sixfold.
➤ **séxtuplo** *sm* sextuple.

sexuado, da *adj* sexed.

sexual *adj* [gen] sexual; [educación, vida] sex *(antes de s)*.

sexualidad *sf* sexuality.

sexy = **sexi**.

Seychelles [sei'ʃels] *sfpl*: **las (islas) Seychelles** the Seychelles.

sha [sa, ʃa] *sm* shah.

shakesperiano, na [ʃespi'rjano] *adj* Shakespearian.

sheriff [ˈʃerif] *sm* sheriff.
sherry [ˈʃerri] (*pl* **sherries**) *sm* sherry.
shock = choc.
shorts [ʃorts] *smpl* shorts.
show [ʃou] (*pl* **shows**) *sm* show; **montar un show** *fig* to cause a scene.
si[1] (*pl* **sis**) *sm* MÚS B; [en solfeo] ti.
si[2] *conj* - **1.** *(condicional)* if; **si viene él yo me voy** if he comes, then I'm going; **si hubieses venido te habrías divertido** if you had come, you would have enjoyed yourself - **2.** *(en oraciones interrogativas indirectas)* if, whether; **ignoro si lo sabe** I don't know if o whether she knows - **3.** [expresa protesta] but; **¡si te dije que no lo hicieras!** but I told you not to do it!
sí (*pl* **síes**) ⋄ *adv* - **1.** [afirmación] yes; **¿vendrás? - sí, iré** will you come? - yes, I will; **claro que sí** of course; **creo que sí** I think so; **¿están de acuerdo? - algunos sí** do they agree? - some do - **2.** [uso enfático]: **sí que** really, certainly; **sí que me gusta** I really o certainly like it - **3.** *loc*: **no creo que puedas hacerlo - ¡a que sí!** I don't think you can do it - I bet I can!; **porque sí** [sin razón] because (I/you *etc* felt like it); **van a subir la gasolina - ¡pues sí que...!** petrol prices are going up - what a pain!; **¿sí?** [incredulidad] really? ⋄ *pron pers* - **1.** *(reflexivo)* [de personas] himself (*f* herself *pl* themselves); [usted] yourself (*pl* yourselves); [de cosas, animales] itself (*pl* themselves); **lo quiere todo para sí (misma)** she wants everything for herself; **se acercó la silla hacia sí** he drew the chair nearer (himself); **de (por) sí** [cosa] in itself - **2.** *(reflexivo impersonal)* oneself; **cuando uno piensa en sí mismo** when one thinks about oneself, when you think about yourself. ⋄ *sm* consent; **dar el sí** to give one's consent.
siamés, esa ⋄ *adj* Siamese. ⋄ *sm, f* - **1.** [de Siam] Siamese person, Thai - **2.** [gemelo] Siamese twin.
➤ **siamés** *sm* [gato] Siamese.
sibarita ⋄ *adj* sybaritic. ⋄ *smf* sybarite, epicure.
sibaritismo *sm* sybaritism, epicureanism.
Siberia *n pr*: **(la) Siberia** Siberia.
siberiano, na *adj & sm, f* Siberian.
sibila *sf* MITOL sibyl.
sibilante *adj* sibilant.
sibilino, na *adj* [incomprensible] mysterious, cryptic.
sicario *sm* hired assassin.
Sicilia *n pr* Sicily.
siciliano, na *adj & sm, f* Sicilian.
sicoanálisis = psicoanálisis.
sicoanalista = psicoanalista.
sicoanalizar [13] = psicoanalizar.

sicodélico = psicodélico.
sicodrama = psicodrama.
sicología = psicología.
sicológico = psicológico.
sicólogo, ga = psicólogo.
sicomotricidad = psicomotricidad.
sicópata = psicópata.
sicopatía = psicopatía.
sicosis = psicosis.
sicosomático = psicosomático.
sicotécnico = psicotécnico.
sicoterapia = psicoterapia.
sida (*abrev de* **síndrome de inmunodeficiencia adquirida**) *sm* AIDS.
sidecar (*pl* **sidecares**) *sm* sidecar.
sideral *adj* sidereal.
siderurgia *sf* iron and steel industry.
siderúrgico, ca *adj* iron and steel (*antes de s*).
sidra *sf* cider.
siega ⋄ *v* ▷ **segar**. ⋄ *sf* - **1.** [acción] reaping, harvesting - **2.** [época] harvest (time).
siembra ⋄ *v* ▷ **sembrar**. ⋄ *sf* - **1.** [acción] sowing - **2.** [época] sowing time.
siempre *adv* [gen] always; **como siempre** as usual; **de siempre** usual; **lo de siempre** the usual; **somos amigos de siempre** we've always been friends; **es así desde siempre** it has always been that way; **para siempre, para siempre jamás** for ever and ever; **¿siempre nos vemos mañana?** *Amér* we're still getting together tomorrow, aren't we?
➤ **siempre que** *loc conj* - **1.** [cada vez que] whenever - **2.** [con tal de que] provided that, as long as.
➤ **siempre y cuando** *loc conj* provided that, as long as.
siempreviva *sf* everlasting flower.
sien *sf* temple.
sienta *etc* ▷ **sentar, sentir**.
sierra ⋄ *v* ▷ **serrar**. ⋄ *sf* - **1.** [herramienta] saw; **sierra eléctrica** power saw - **2.** [cordillera] mountain range - **3.** [región montañosa] mountains *pl*.
Sierra Leona *n pr* Sierra Leone.
siervo, va *sm, f* - **1.** [esclavo] serf - **2.** RELIG servant.
siesta *sf* siesta, nap; **dormir** o **echarse la siesta** to have an afternoon nap.
siete ⋄ *num* seven. ⋄ *sf* R Dom *fig*: **de la gran siete** amazing, incredible; **¡la gran siete!** *fam* sugar! *UK*, shoot! *US*; *ver también* **seis**.
➤ **siete y media** *sfpl card game in which players aim to get 7½ points, court cards counting for ½ point.*

sietemesino, na <> *adj* premature. <> *sm, f* premature baby.

sífilis *sf inv* syphilis.

sifilítico, ca *adj* & *sm, f* MED syphilitic.

sifón *sm* - **1.** [agua carbónica] soda (water) - **2.** [de WC] trap, U-bend - **3.** [tubo] siphon.

siga *etc* ▷ **seguir**.

sigilo *sm* [gen] secrecy; [al robar, escapar] stealth.

sigiloso, sa *adj* [discreto] secretive; [al robar, escapar] stealthy.

siglas *sfpl* acronym.

siglo *sm* - **1.** [cien años] century; **el siglo XX** the 20th century; **el siglo III antes de Cristo** the third century before Christ; **el siglo de las Luces** the Age of Enlightenment; **el siglo de Oro** the Golden Age - **2.** *fig* [mucho tiempo]: **hace siglos que no la veo** I haven't seen her for ages; **por los siglos de los siglos** for ever and ever.

signatario, ria *adj* & *sm, f* signatory.

signatura *sf* - **1.** [en biblioteca] catalogue number - **2.** [firma] signature.

significación *sf* - **1.** [importancia] significance - **2.** [significado] meaning.

significado, da *adj* important.
◆ **significado** *sm* - **1.** [sentido] meaning - **2.** LING signifier.

significante *sm* LING signifiant.

significar [10] <> *vt* - **1.** [gen] to mean - **2.** [expresar] to express. <> *vi* [tener importancia]: **no significa nada para mí** it means nothing to me.
◆ **significarse por** *vprnl* to become known for.

significativo, va *adj* significant.

signo *sm* - **1.** [gen] sign; **signo de multiplicar/dividir** multiplication/division sign; **signo del zodiaco** sign of the zodiac - **2.** [en la escritura] mark; **signo de admiración/interrogación** exclamation/question mark - **3.** [símbolo] symbol.

sigo *etc* ▷ **seguir**.

siguiente <> *adj* - **1.** [en el tiempo, espacio] next - **2.** [a continuación] following. <> *smf* - **1.** [el que sigue]: **el siguiente** the next one; **¡el siguiente!** next, please! - **2.** [lo que sigue]: **lo siguiente** the following.

siguiera *etc* v ▷ **seguir**.

sij (*pl* **sijs**) *adj* & *sm, f* Sikh.

sílaba *sf* syllable.

silábico, ca *adj* syllabic.

silbar <> *vt* - **1.** [gen] to whistle - **2.** [abuchear] to hiss, to catcall. <> *vi* - **1.** [gen] to whistle - **2.** [abuchear] to hiss, to catcall - **3.** *fig* [oídos] to ring.

silbato *sm* whistle.

silbido, silbo *sm* - **1.** [gen] whistle - **2.** [para abuchear, de serpiente] hiss, hissing *(U)*.

silenciador *sm* silencer.

silenciar [8] *vt* to hush up, to keep quiet.

silencio *sm* - **1.** [gen] silence; **en silencio** in silence; **guardar silencio (sobre algo)** to keep silent (about sthg); **guardaron un minuto de silencio** they held a minute's silence; **imponer silencio a alguien** to make sb be silent; **reinaba el silencio más absoluto** there was complete silence; **romper el silencio** to break the silence - **2.** MÚS rest.

silencioso, sa *adj* silent, quiet.

sílex *sm inv* flint.

sílfide *sf* sylph.

silicato *sm* silicate.

sílice *sf* silica.

silicio *sm* silicon.

silicona *sf* silicone.

silla *sf* - **1.** [gen] chair; **silla de la reina** *seat made by two people joining hands*; **silla de ruedas** wheelchair; **silla eléctrica** electric chair; **silla de tijera** folding chair - **2.** [de caballo]: **silla (de montar)** saddle.

sillería *sf* set of chairs; [de coro] choir stalls *pl*.

sillín *sm* saddle, seat.

sillón *sm* armchair.

silo *sm* silo.

silogismo *sm* syllogism.

silueta *sf* - **1.** [cuerpo] figure - **2.** [contorno] outline - **3.** [dibujo] silhouette.

silvestre *adj* wild.

sima *sf* chasm.

simbiosis *sf inv* symbiosis.

simbólico, ca *adj* symbolic.

simbolismo *sm* symbolism.

simbolizar [13] *vt* to symbolize.

símbolo *sm* symbol.

simbología *sf* system of symbols.

simetría *sf* symmetry.

simétrico, ca *adj* symmetrical.

simiente *sf culto* seed.

simiesco, ca *adj* simian, apelike.

símil *sm* - **1.** [paralelismo] similarity, resemblance - **2.** LITER simile.

similar *adj*: **similar (a)** similar (to).

similitud *sf* similarity.

simio, mia *sm, f* simian, ape.

simpatía *sf* - **1.** [cordialidad] friendliness - **2.** [cariño] affection; **coger simpatía a alguien** to take a liking to sb; **tener simpatía a, sentir simpatía por** to like - **3.** MED sympathy.

simpático, ca *adj* - **1.** [gen] nice, likeable; [abierto, cordial] friendly; **Juan me cae simpáti-**

co I like Juan **- 2.** [anécdota, comedia etc] amusing, entertaining **- 3.** [reunión, velada etc] pleasant, agreeable **- 4.** ANAT sympathetic.

simpatizante ◇ adj sympathizing. ◇ smf sympathizer.

simpatizar [13] vi: **simpatizar (con)** [persona] to hit it off (with), to get on (with); [cosa] to sympathize (with).

simple ◇ adj **- 1.** [gen] simple **- 2.** [fácil] easy, simple **- 3.** [único, sin componentes] single; **dame una simple razón** give me one single reason **- 4.** [mero] mere; **por simple estupidez** through sheer stupidity **- 5.** MAT prime. ◇ smf [persona] simpleton.

simplemente adv simply.

simpleza sf **- 1.** [de persona] simple-mindedness **- 2.** [tontería] trifle.

simplicidad sf simplicity.

simplificación sf simplification.

simplificar [10] vt to simplify.
◈ **simplificarse** vprnl to be simplified.

simplista ◇ adj simplistic. ◇ smf naïve person.

simplón, ona ◇ adj simple, simpleminded. ◇ sm, f simpleminded person.

simposio, simposium sm symposium.

simulación sf pretence, simulation.

simulacro sm simulation; **simulacro de combate** mock battle; **simulacro de incendio** fire drill.

simulado, da adj **- 1.** [sentimiento, desmayo etc] feigned **- 2.** [combate, salvamento] simulated.

simular vt **- 1.** [sentimiento, desmayo etc] to feign; **simuló que no me había visto** he pretended not to have seen me **- 2.** [enfermedad] to fake **- 3.** [combate, salvamento] to simulate.

simultanear vt to do at the same time.

simultaneidad sf simultaneousness.

simultáneo, nea adj simultaneous.

sin prep without; **sin alcohol** alcohol-free; **estoy sin un euro** I'm penniless; **ha escrito cinco libros sin (contar) las novelas** he has written five books, not counting his novels; **está sin hacer** it hasn't been done yet; **estamos sin vino** we're out of wine; **sin que** (+ subjuntivo) without (+ gerundio); **sin que nadie se enterara** without anyone noticing.
◈ **sin embargo** conj however.

sinagoga sf synagogue.

Sinaí sm: **el Sinaí** Sinai.

sincerarse vprnl: **sincerarse (con alguien)** to open one's heart (to sb).

sinceridad sf sincerity; [llaneza, franqueza] frankness; **con toda sinceridad** in all honesty.

sincero, ra adj sincere; [abierto, directo] frank; **para ser sincero** to be honest.

sincopado, da adj syncopated.

síncope sm blackout; **le dio un síncope** she blacked out.

sincretismo sm synchretism.

sincronía sf [simultaneidad] synchronousness.

sincrónico, ca adj **- 1.** [simultáneo] simultaneous **- 2.** [coordinado] synchronous.

sincronismo sm [simultaneidad] simultaneity.

sincronización sf synchronization.

sincronizar [13] vt [regular] to synchronize.

sindicación sf trade union membership.

sindicado, da adj belonging to a trade union.

sindical adj (trade) union (antes de s).

sindicalismo sm trade unionism.

sindicalista ◇ adj (trade) union (antes de s). ◇ smf trade unionist.

sindicar [10] vt **- 1.** to unionize **- 2.** Andes, R Plata & Ven to accuse.
◈ **sindicarse** vprnl to join a union.

sindicato sm trade union, labor union US; **sindicato amarillo** conservative trade union that leans towards the employers' interests; **sindicato vertical** workers' and employers' union during the Franco period.

síndico sm **- 1.** [representante] community representative **- 2.** [administrador] (official) receiver **- 3.** ECON trustee.

síndrome sm syndrome; **síndrome de abstinencia** withdrawal symptoms pl; **síndrome de clase turista** economy-class syndrome; **síndrome de Down** Down's syndrome; **síndrome de Estocolmo** Stockholm syndrome; **síndrome de inmunodeficiencia adquirida** acquired immune deficiency syndrome; **síndrome premenstrual** premenstrual syndrome; **síndrome tóxico** toxic syndrome caused by ingestion of adulterated rapeseed oil.

sine ◈ **sine die** loc adv indefinitely.

sinergia sf synergy.

sinestesia sf synaesthesia.

sinfín sm vast number; **un sinfín de problemas** no end of problems.

sinfonía sf symphony.

sinfónico, ca adj symphonic.
◈ **sinfónica** sf symphony orchestra.

Singapur n pr Singapore.

singladura sf NÁUT [distancia] day's run; fig [dirección] course.

single ['siŋgel] sm **- 1.** single **- 2.** C Sur [habitación] single room.

singular ⬦ *adj* - **1.** [raro] peculiar, odd - **2.** [único] unique - **3.** GRAM singular. ⬦ *sm* GRAM singular; **en singular** in the singular.

singularidad *sf* - **1.** [rareza, peculiaridad] peculiarity - **2.** [exclusividad] uniqueness.

singularizar [13] *vt* to distinguish, to single out.

➤ **singularizarse** *vprnl* to stand out, to be conspicuous; **singularizarse por algo** to stand out because of sthg.

siniestrado, da ⬦ *adj* [coche, avión etc] crashed, smashed up; [edificio] ruined, destroyed. ⬦ *sm, f* victim.

siniestralidad *sf* accident rate.

siniestro, tra *adj* - **1.** [perverso] sinister - **2.** [desgraciado] disastrous.

➤ **siniestro** *sm* disaster; [accidente de coche] accident, crash; [incendio] fire.

➤ **siniestra** *sf desus* left hand.

sinnúmero *sm*: **un sinnúmero de** countless.

sino¹ *sm* fate, destiny.

sino² *conj* - **1.** [para contraponer] but; **no lo hizo él, sino ella** he didn't do it, she did; **no sólo es listo, sino también trabajador** he's not only clever but also hardworking - **2.** [para exceptuar] except, but; **¿quién sino tú lo haría?** who else but you would do it?; **no quiero sino que se haga justicia** I only want justice to be done.

sínodo *sm* synod.

sinonimia *sf* synonymy.

sinónimo, ma *adj* synonymous; **ser sinónimo de algo** to be synonymous with sthg.

➤ **sinónimo** *sm* synonym.

sinopsis *sf inv* synopsis.

sinóptico, ca *adj* synoptic.

sinovial *adj* synovial.

sinrazón *(gen pl) sf* injustice.

sinsabor *(gen pl) sm* trouble.

sintáctico, ca *adj* syntactic.

sintagma *sm* syntagma.

sintaxis *sf inv* syntax.

síntesis *sf inv* synthesis; **en síntesis** in short; **síntesis del habla** INFORM & LING speech synthesis.

sintético, ca *adj* - **1.** [artificial] synthetic - **2.** [resumido] summarized.

sintetizador, ra *adj* synthesizing.

➤ **sintetizador** *sm* synthesizer.

sintetizar [13] *vt* - **1.** [resumir] to summarize - **2.** [fabricar artificialmente] to synthesize.

sintiera *etc* ⊳ **sentir**.

síntoma *sm* symptom.

sintomático, ca *adj* symptomatic.

sintomatología *sf* symptoms *pl*.

sintonía *sf* - **1.** [música] signature tune - **2.** [conexión] tuning - **3.** *fig* [compenetración] harmony; **en sintonía con** in tune with.

sintonización *sf* - **1.** [conexión] tuning - **2.** *fig* [compenetración] harmonization.

sintonizador *sm* tuner, tuning dial.

sintonizar [13] ⬦ *vt* [conectar] to tune in to. ⬦ *vi* - **1.** [conectar]: **sintonizar (con)** to tune in (to) - **2.** *fig* [compenetrarse]: **sintonizar en algo (con alguien)** to be on the same wavelength (as sb) about sthg.

sinuosidad *sf* bend, wind.

sinuoso, sa *adj* - **1.** [camino] winding - **2.** [movimiento] sinuous - **3.** *fig* [disimulado] devious.

sinusitis *sf inv* sinusitis.

sinvergüenza ⬦ *adj* - **1.** [canalla] shameless - **2.** [fresco, descarado] cheeky. ⬦ *smf* - **1.** [canalla] rogue - **2.** [fresco, descarado] cheeky person.

sionismo *sm* Zionism.

sionista *adj* & *smf* Zionist.

sioux ['siuks] *adj inv* & *smf inv* Sioux.

siquiatra = **psiquiatra**.

siquiatría = **psiquiatría**.

siquiátrico = **psiquiátrico**.

síquico = **psíquico**.

siquiera ⬦ *conj* [aunque] even if; **ven siquiera por pocos días** do come, even if it's only for a few days. ⬦ *adv* [por lo menos] at least; **dime siquiera tu nombre** (you could) at least tell me your name.

➤ **ni (tan) siquiera** *loc conj* not even; **ni (tan) siquiera me hablaron** they didn't even speak to me.

sirena *sf* - **1.** MITOL mermaid, siren - **2.** [señal] siren.

Siria *n pr* Syria.

sirimiri *sm* drizzle.

sirio, ria *adj* & *sm, f* Syrian.

siroco *sm* sirocco.

sirva *etc* ⊳ **servir**.

sirviente, ta *sm, f* servant.

sirviera *etc* ⊳ **servir**.

sisa *sf* - **1.** [de dinero] pilfering - **2.** [en costura] dart; [de manga] armhole.

sisar ⬦ *vt* - **1.** [dinero] to pilfer - **2.** [costura] to take in. ⬦ *vi* to pilfer.

sisear *vt* & *vi* to hiss.

siseo *sm* hiss, hissing *(U)*.

sísmico, ca *adj* seismic.

sismo *sm* earthquake.

sismógrafo *sm* seismograph.

sisón, ona ⬦ *adj* pilfering. ⬦ *sm, f* [ladrón] pilferer, petty thief.

➤ **sisón** *sm* [ave] little bustard.

sistema *sm* - **1.** [gen & INFORM] system; **sistema monetario/nervioso/solar** monetary/nervous/solar system; **sistema experto/operativo** INFORM expert/operating system; **sistema fiscal** *o* **impositivo** tax system; **sistema ABS** AUTO ABS (brake) system; **sistema dual** TV *system enabling dubbed TV programmes to be heard in the original language*; **sistema de gestión de bases de datos** INFORM database management system; **sistema internacional de unidades** SI units *pl*; **sistema métrico (decimal)** metric (decimal) system; **sistema monetario europeo** European Monetary System; **sistema montañoso** mountain chain *o* range; **sistema periódico de los elementos** periodic table of elements - **2.** [método, orden] method.
➤ **por sistema** *loc adv* systematically.

Sistema educativo

The Spanish education system starts with free nursery school from 3 to 6. This is followed by primary school from 6 to 12, and compulsory secondary education from 12 to 16, successful completion of which entitles pupils to a "secondary school diploma". There is then a choice of a general course of study ("bachillerato") or a technical one, both of two years. The bachillerato allows access to university courses: three year diploma courses, or degree courses of four, five or six years. In Latin America, there is great variation in educational provision from country to country. The end of compulsory education ranges from age 11 in Honduras to 16 in Peru, though in most countries it is between 13 and 15. Actual enrolment in primary school is high, even in the poorer countries, but about a third of secondary-school age Latin American children are not actually enrolled. In a poor country such as Guatemala this rises to two-thirds, compared with the high level of secondary enrolment in Argentina, Chile or Cuba.

Sistema Ibérico *sm*: **el Sistema Ibérico** the Iberian mountain chain.

sistemático, ca *adj* systematic.

sistematización *sf* systematization.

sistematizar [13] *vt* to systematize.

sístole *sf* systole.

sitiar [8] *vt* - **1.** [cercar] to besiege - **2.** *fig* [acorralar] to surround.

sitio *sm* - **1.** [lugar] place; **cambiar de sitio (con alguien)** to change places (with sb); **en otro sitio** elsewhere; **poner a alguien en su sitio** to put sb in his/her place - **2.** [espacio] room, space; **hacer sitio a alguien** to make room for sb; **ocupar sitio** to take up space - **3.** [cerco] siege - **4.** INFORM: **sitio Web** Web site - **5.** *Méx* [de taxi] taxi rank *UK o* stand *US*.

sito, ta *adj* located.

situ ➤ **in situ** *loc adv* on the spot.

situación *sf* - **1.** [circunstancias] situation; [legal, social] status; **estar en situación de hacer algo** [gen] to be in a position to do sthg; [suj: enfermo, borracho] to be in a fit state to do sthg; **situación límite** critical situation; **salvar la situación** to save the day - **2.** [condición, estado] state, condition - **3.** [ubicación] location.

situado, da *adj* - **1.** [acomodado] comfortably off; **estar bien situado** to be well off - **2.** [ubicado] located.

situar [6] *vt* - **1.** [colocar] to place, to put; [edificio, ciudad] to site, to locate - **2.** [en clasificación] to place, to rank - **3.** [localizar] to locate, to find.
➤ **situarse** *vprnl* - **1.** [colocarse] to take up position - **2.** [ubicarse] to be located - **3.** [acomodarse, establecerse] to get o.s. established - **4.** [en clasificación] to be placed; **se sitúa entre los mejores** he's (ranked) amongst the best.

siútico, ca *adj Amér fam* naff, tacky.

skai [es'kai] = **escay**.

skateboard [es'keiðβor] (*pl* **skateboards**) *sm* - **1.** [tabla] skateboard - **2.** [deporte] skateboarding.

sketch [es'ketʃ] (*pl* **sketches**) *sm* CINE & TEATRO sketch.

ski [es'ki] = **esquí**.

skin head [es'kinxeð] (*pl* **skin heads**) *sm, f* skinhead.

SL (*abrev de* **sociedad limitada**) *sf* ≃ Ltd.

slalom [es'lalom] = **eslalon**.

slip [es'lip] *sm* briefs *pl*.

slogan [es'loɣan] = **eslogan**.

SM (*abrev de* **Su Majestad**) HM.

smash [es'maʃ] (*pl* **smashes**) *sm* DEP smash.

SMI *sm* - **1.** (*abrev de* **Sistema Monetario Internacional**) IMS - **2.** (*abrev de* **Salario Mínimo Interprofesional**) minimum wage.

SMI

In Spain the government sets a monthly minimum wage to which all workers are entitled. In 2004 this was set at 450 Euros per month. This rate does not apply to those sectors of the economy which have separate agreements between unions and employers, and where the minimum wage tends to be somewhat higher.

smoking [es'mokin] = **esmoquin**.

SMS (*abrev de* **short message service**) *sm* SMS.

s/n (abrev de sin número) abbreviation used in addresses after the street name, where the building has no number.

snob = esnob.

snobismo = esnobismo.

snowboard sm snowboard m.

so ◇ prep under; **so pretexto de** under; **so pena de** under penalty of. ◇ adv: **¡so tonto!** you idiot! ◇ interj: **¡so!** whoa!

sobaco sm armpit.

sobado, da adj - **1.** [cuello, puños etc] worn, shabby; [libro] dog-eared - **2.** fig [argumento, excusa] well-worn, hackneyed.

◆ **sobado** sm CULIN shortcrust pastry.

sobaquera sf armhole.

sobaquina sf fam body odour.

sobar ◇ vt - **1.** [tocar] to finger, to paw - **2.** despec [acariciar, besar] to touch up, to fondle - **3.** [ablandar] to soften. ◇ vi mfam to kip.

soberanía sf sovereignty.

soberano, na ◇ adj - **1.** [independiente] sovereign - **2.** fig [grande] massive; [paliza] thorough; [belleza, calidad] supreme, unrivalled. ◇ sm, f sovereign.

soberbio, bia ◇ adj - **1.** [arrogante] proud, arrogant - **2.** [magnífico] superb - **3.** [grande] huge. ◇ sm, f [persona] arrogant o proud person.

◆ **soberbia** sf - **1.** [arrogancia] pride, arrogance - **2.** [magnificencia] grandeur, splendour.

sobón, ona adj & sm, f fam groper.

sobornar vt to bribe.

soborno sm - **1.** [acción] bribery - **2.** [dinero, regalo] bribe.

sobra sf excess, surplus; **de sobra** [en exceso] more than enough; [de más] superfluous; **aquí estoy de sobra, me voy** I'm off, it's obvious I'm not wanted here; **lo sabemos de sobra** we know it only too well.

◆ **sobras** sfpl - **1.** [de comida] leftovers - **2.** [de tela] remnants.

sobrado, da adj - **1.** [de sobra] more than enough, plenty of - **2.** [de dinero] well off.

sobrante ◇ adj remaining. ◇ sm surplus.

sobrar vi - **1.** [quedar, restar] to be left over, to be spare; **nos sobró comida** we had some food left over - **2.** [haber de más] to be more than enough; **parece que van a sobrar bocadillos** it looks like there are going to be too many sandwiches - **3.** [estar de más] to be superfluous; **lo que dices sobra** that goes without saying.

sobrasada sf Mallorcan spiced sausage.

sobre[1] sm - **1.** [para cartas] envelope - **2.** [para alimentos] sachet, packet - **3.** mfam [cama] sack; **irse al sobre** to hit the sack.

sobre[2] prep - **1.** [encima de] on (top of); **el libro está sobre la mesa** the book is on (top of) the table - **2.** [por encima de] over, above; **el pato vuela sobre el lago** the duck is flying over the lake - **3.** [superioridad] above; **su opinión está sobre las de los demás** his opinion is more important than that of the others - **4.** [acerca de] about, on; **un libro sobre el amor** a book about o on love; **una conferencia sobre el desarme** a conference on disarmament - **5.** [alrededor de] about; **llegarán sobre las diez** they'll arrive at about ten o'clock - **6.** [acumulación] upon; **nos contó mentira sobre mentira** he told us lie upon lie o one lie after another - **7.** [cerca de] upon; **la desgracia estaba ya sobre nosotros** the disaster was already upon us.

sobreabundancia = superabundancia.

sobreabundante = superabundante.

sobrealimentación sf overfeeding.

sobrealimentar vt to overfeed.

sobreañadir vt to add on top of.

sobrecalentar [19] vt to overheat.

sobrecarga sf - **1.** [exceso de carga] excess weight - **2.** [saturación] overload.

sobrecargar [16] vt [gen] to overload; [decoración etc] to overdo.

sobrecargo sm - **1.** NÁUT supercargo - **2.** [de avión] purser.

sobrecogedor, ra adj - **1.** [aterrador] frightening, startling - **2.** [impresionante] moving.

sobrecoger [14] vt - **1.** [asustar] to frighten, to startle - **2.** [impresionar] to move.

◆ **sobrecogerse** vprnl - **1.** [asustarse] to be frightened, to be startled - **2.** [impresionarse] to be moved.

sobrecongelar vt to deep-freeze.

sobrecosto sm extra costs pl.

sobrecubierta sf - **1.** [de libro] (dust) jacket - **2.** [de barco] upper deck.

sobredosis sf inv overdose.

sobreentender = sobrentender.

sobreentendido = sobrentendido.

sobreexcitar, sobrexcitar vt to overexcite.

◆ **sobreexcitarse** vprnl to get overexcited.

sobreexposición sf overexposure.

sobregiro sm COM overdraft.

sobrehumano, na adj superhuman.

sobreimpresión sf superimposing (U).

sobreimprimir vt to superimpose.

sobrellevar vt to bear, to endure.

sobremanera adv exceedingly.

sobremesa sf after-dinner period; **de sobremesa** [programación etc] mid-afternoon (antes de s).

sobrenatural *adj* [extraordinario] supernatural.

sobrenombre *sm* nickname.

sobrentender, sobreentender [20] *vt* to understand, to deduce.

➡ **sobrentenderse** *vprnl* to be inferred o implied.

sobrentendido, da,   sobreentendido, da *adj* implied, implicit.

sobrepasar *vt* - **1.** [exceder] to exceed - **2.** [aventajar]: **sobrepasar a alguien** to overtake sb.

➡ **sobrepasarse** *vprnl* to go too far.

sobrepeso *sm* excess weight.

sobreponer = superponer.

➡ **sobreponerse** *vprnl*: **sobreponerse a algo** to overcome sthg.

sobreposición = superposición.

sobreproducción, superproducción *sf* ECON overproduction *(U)*.

sobreproteger [14] *vt* to overprotect.

sobrepuesto, ta ◇ *adj* = superpuesto. ◇ *pp* ▷ sobreponer.

sobresaliente ◇ *adj* [destacado] outstanding. ◇ *sm* [en escuela] excellent, ≃ A; [en universidad] ≃ first class.

sobresalir [71] *vi* - **1.** [en tamaño] to jut out - **2.** [en importancia] to stand out.

sobresaltar *vt* to startle.

➡ **sobresaltarse** *vprnl* to be startled, to start.

sobresalto *sm* start, fright; **dar un sobresalto a alguien** to make sb start, to give sb a fright.

sobrescribir *vt* to overwrite.

sobrescrito, ta *pp* ▷ sobrescribir.

sobreseer [50] *vt* DER to discontinue, to stay.

sobreseimiento *sm* DER stay.

sobrestimar *vt* to overestimate.

sobresueldo *sm* extra money on the side *(U)*.

sobretasa *sf* surcharge.

sobretodo *sm* Amér overcoat.

sobrevenir [75] *vi* to happen, to ensue; **sobrevino la guerra** the war intervened.

sobreviviente = superviviente.

sobrevivir *vi* to survive; **sobrevivir a alguien** to outlive sb.

sobrevolar [23] *vt* to fly over.

sobrexcitar = sobreexcitar.

sobrexposición *sf* = sobreexposición.

sobriedad *sf* - **1.** [moderación] restraint, moderation - **2.** [no embriaguez] soberness.

sobrino, na *sm, f* nephew (*f* niece).

sobrio, bria *adj* - **1.** [moderado] restrained; **sobrio en** moderate in - **2.** [no excesivo] simple - **3.** [austero, no borracho] sober.

socaire *sm* NÁUT lee; **al socaire de** *fig* under the protection of.

socarrón, ona *adj* sarcastic.

socarronería *sf* sarcasm.

socavar *vt* [excavar por debajo] to dig under; *fig* [debilitar] to undermine.

socavón *sm* [hoyo] hollow; [en la carretera] pothole.

sociabilidad *sf* sociability.

sociable *adj* sociable.

social *adj* - **1.** [gen] social - **2.** COM company *(antes de s)*.

socialdemocracia *sf* social democracy.

socialdemócrata ◇ *adj* social democratic. ◇ *smf* social democrat.

socialismo *sm* socialism.

socialista *adj & smf* socialist.

socialización *sf* ECON nationalization.

socializar [13] *vt* ECON to nationalize.

sociedad *sf* - **1.** [gen] society; **entrar** o **presentarse en sociedad** to come out, to make one's debut; **alta sociedad** high society; **sociedad de consumo** consumer society; **sociedad deportiva** sports club; **sociedad literaria** literary society - **2.** COM [empresa] company; **sociedad anónima** public (limited) company UK, incorporated company US; **sociedad civil** non-profit making company; **sociedad colectiva** general partnership; **sociedad comanditaria** o **en comandita** general and limited partnership; **(sociedad) cooperativa** cooperative; **sociedad de cartera** portfolio company; **sociedad (de responsabilidad) limitada** private limited company; **sociedad industrial** industrial society; **sociedad mixta** joint venture.

socio, cia *sm, f* - **1.** COM partner; **socio accionista** shareholder; **socio capitalista** o **comanditario** sleeping partner UK, silent partner US; **socio fundador** founding partner - **2.** [miembro] member; **socio honorario** honorary member - **3.** *fam* [amigo] mate.

sociocultural *adj* sociocultural.

socioeconomía *sf* socioeconomics *(U)*.

socioeconómico, ca *adj* socioeconomic.

sociolingüístico, ca *adj* sociolinguistic.

➡ **sociolingüística** *sf* sociolinguistics *(U)*.

sociología *sf* sociology.

sociólogo, ga *sm, f* sociologist.

sociopolítico, ca *adj* sociopolitical.

socorrer *vt* to help.

socorrido, da *adj* [útil] useful, handy.

socorrismo *sm* first aid; [en la playa] lifesaving.

socorrista *smf* first aid worker; [en la playa] lifeguard.

socorro ◇ *sm* help, aid. ◇ *interj*: ¡socorro! help!

soda *sf* [bebida] soda water, club soda US.

sódico, ca *adj* sodium *(antes de s)*.

sodio *sm* sodium.

sodomía *sf* sodomy.

sodomita *adj* & *smf* sodomite.

sodomizar [13] *vt* to sodomize.

soez *adj* vulgar, dirty.

sofá *sm* sofa; **sofá cama** o **nido** sofa bed.

sofisma *sm* sophism.

sofisticación *sf* sophistication.

sofisticado, da *adj* sophisticated.

sofocado, da *adj* - **1.** [por cansancio] gasping for breath; [por calor] suffocating - **2.** [por vergüenza] mortified - **3.** [por irritación] hot under the collar.

sofocante *adj* suffocating, stifling.

sofocar [10] *vt* - **1.** [ahogar] to suffocate, to stifle - **2.** [incendio] to put out, to smother - **3.** *fig* [rebelión] to suppress, to quell - **4.** *fig* [avergonzar] to mortify.
◆ **sofocarse** *vprnl* - **1.** [ahogarse] to suffocate - **2.** *fig* [avergonzarse] to go red as a beetroot - **3.** *fig* [irritarse]: **sofocarse (por)** to get hot under the collar (about).

sofoco *sm* - **1.** [ahogo] breathlessness *(U)*; [sonrojo, bochorno] hot flush - **2.** *fig* [vergüenza] mortification - **3.** *fig* [disgusto]: **llevarse un sofoco** to have a fit.

sofocón *sm fam*: **llevarse un sofocón** to get hot under the collar.

sofoque *etc* ▭ **sofocar**.

sofreír [28] *vt* to fry lightly over a low heat.

sofría *etc* ▭ **sofreír**.

sofriera *etc* ▭ **sofreír**.

sofrito, ta *pp* ▭ **sofreír**.
◆ **sofrito** *sm fried tomato and onion sauce.*

sofrología *sf* relaxation therapy.

software ['sofwer] *sm* INFORM software; **software integrado** integrated software.

soga *sf* rope; [para ahorcar] noose; **estar con la soga al cuello** *fig* to be in dire straits; **no hay que mentar la soga en casa del ahorcado** use a little tact.

sois ▭ **ser**.

soja *sf* soya.

sojuzgar [16] *vt* to subjugate.

sol *sm* - **1.** [astro] sun; **a pleno sol** in the sun; **al salir/ponerse el sol** at sunrise/sunset; **hace sol** it's sunny; **sol naciente/poniente** rising/setting sun; **de sol a sol** from dawn to dusk; **no dejar a alguien ni a sol ni a sombra** not to give sb a moment's peace - **2.** [rayos, luz] sunshine, sun; **tomar el sol** to sunbathe - **3.** TAUROM *seats in the sun, the cheapest in the bullring* - **4.** *fig* [angel, ricura] darling, angel - **5.** MÚS G; [en solfeo] so - **6.** [moneda] sol.
◆ **sol y sombra** *sm* [bebida] *mixture of brandy and anisette.*

solace *etc* ▭ **solazar**.

solamente *adv* only, just; **vino solamente él** only he came.

solana *sf* - **1.** [lugar] sunny spot - **2.** [galería] sun lounge.

solano *sm* east wind.

solapa *sf* - **1.** [de prenda] lapel - **2.** [de libro, sobre] flap.

solapado, da *adj* underhand, devious.

solapar *vt* to cover up.

solar ◇ *adj* solar. ◇ *sm* undeveloped plot (of land).

solariego, ga *adj* ancestral.

solárium (*pl* **soláriums**), **solario** *sm* solarium.

solaz *sm* - **1.** [entretenimiento] amusement, entertainment - **2.** [descanso] rest - **3.** [alivio] solace, relief.

solazar [13] *vt* - **1.** to amuse, to entertain - **2.** [aliviar] to solace, to entertain.
◆ **solazarse** *vprnl* to enjoy o.s.

soldada *sf* pay.

soldado *sm* soldier; **soldado de primera** ≃ lance corporal; **soldado raso** private.

soldador, ra *sm, f* [persona] welder.
◆ **soldador** *sm* [aparato] soldering iron.

soldadura *sf* - **1.** [acción] soldering, welding - **2.** [juntura] weld, soldered joint.

soldar [23] *vt* to solder, to weld.

soleado, da *adj* sunny.

solecismo *sm* solecism.

soledad *sf* loneliness; **en soledad** alone; *culto* solitude.

solemne *adj* - **1.** [con pompa] formal - **2.** [grave] solemn - **3.** *fig* [enorme] utter, complete.

solemnidad *sf* [suntuosidad] pomp, solemnity; **de solemnidad** extremely.

soler [81] *vi*: **soler hacer algo** to do sthg usually; **aquí suele llover mucho** it usually rains a lot here; **solíamos ir a la playa cada día** we used to go to the beach every day.

solera *sf* - **1.** [tradición] tradition - **2.** [del vino] sediment; **de solera** vintage - **3.** *C Sur* [vestido] sundress - **4.** *Chile* [de acera] kerb.

solfa *sf* - **1.** MÚS tonic sol-fa - **2.** *fam* [paliza] thrashing - **3.** *loc*: **poner algo en solfa** *fam* to poke fun at sthg.

solfeo *sm* MÚS solfeggio, singing of scales.

solicitante ◇ *adj* applying. ◇ *smf* applicant.

solicitar *vt* - **1.** [pedir] to request; [un empleo] to apply for; **solicitar algo a** o **de alguien** to request sthg of sb - **2.** [persona] to pursue; **estar muy solicitado** to be very popular, to be much sought after.

solícito, ta *adj* solicitous, obliging.

solicitud *sf* - **1.** [petición] request; **presentar una solicitud** to submit a request - **2.** [documento] application - **3.** [atención] care.

solidaridad *sf* solidarity; **en solidaridad con** in solidarity with.

solidario, ria *adj* - **1.** [adherido]: **solidario (con)** sympathetic (to), supporting (of) - **2.** [obligación, compromiso] mutually binding.

solidarizarse [13] *vprnl* to make common cause, to show one's solidarity; **solidarizarse con algo/alguien** to support sthg/sb.

solidez *sf* - **1.** [física] solidity - **2.** [moral] firmness.

solidificación *sf* solidification.

solidificar [10] *vt* to solidify.
➧ **solidificarse** *vprnl* to solidify.

sólido, da *adj* - **1.** [gen] solid; [cimientos, fundamento] firm - **2.** [argumento, conocimiento, idea] sound - **3.** [color] fast.
➧ **sólido** *sm* solid.

soliloquio *sm* soliloquy.

solista ⬦ *adj* solo. ⬦ *smf* soloist.

solitario, ria ⬦ *adj* - **1.** [sin compañía] solitary - **2.** [lugar] lonely, deserted. ⬦ *sm, f* [persona] loner.
➧ **solitario** *sm* - **1.** [diamante] solitaire - **2.** [juego] patience.
➧ **solitaria** *sf* [tenia] tapeworm.

soliviantar *vt* - **1.** [excitar] to stir up - **2.** [indignar] to exasperate.
➧ **soliviantarse** *vprnl* to be infuriated.

sollozar [13] *vi* to sob.

sollozo *sm* sob.

solo, la *adj* - **1.** [sin nadie] alone; **dejar solo a alguien** to leave sb alone; **se quedó solo a temprana edad** he was on his own from an early age; **a solas** alone, by oneself - **2.** [sin nada] on its own; [café] black; [whisky] neat - **3.** [único] single, sole; **ni una sola gota** not a (single) drop; **dame una sola cosa** give me just one thing - **4.** [solitario] lonely.
➧ **solo** *sm* MÚS solo.

sólo *adv* only, just; **no sólo... sino (también)...** not only... but (also)...; **con sólo, sólo con** just by; **sólo que...** only...

solomillo *sm* sirloin.

solsticio *sm* solstice.

soltar [23] *vt* - **1.** [desasir] to let go of - **2.** [desatar - gen] to unfasten; [- nudo] to untie; [- hebilla, cordones] to undo - **3.** [dejar libre] to release - **4.** [desenrollar - cable etc] to let o pay out - **5.** [patada, grito, suspiro etc] to give; **no suelta ni un duro** you can't get a penny out of her - **6.** [decir bruscamente] to come out with.

➧ **soltarse** *vprnl* - **1.** [desasirse] to break free - **2.** [desatarse] to come undone - **3.** [desprenderse] to come off - **4.** *fam* [adquirir habilidad] to get the hang of it; **soltarse en algo** to get the hang of sthg - **5.** [perder timidez] to let go.

soltería *sf* [de hombre] bachelorhood; [de mujer] spinsterhood.

soltero, ra ⬦ *adj* single, unmarried. ⬦ *sm, f* bachelor (*f* single woman).

solterón, ona ⬦ *adj* unmarried. ⬦ *sm, f* old bachelor (*f* spinster, old maid).

soltura *sf* - **1.** [gen] fluency - **2.** [seguridad de sí mismo] assurance.

soluble *adj* - **1.** [que se disuelve] soluble - **2.** [que se soluciona] solvable.

solución *sf* solution.
➧ **solución de continuidad** *sf* interruption; **sin solución de continuidad** uninterrupted.

solucionar *vt* to solve; [disputa] to resolve.

solvencia *sf* - **1.** [económica] solvency - **2.** [capacidad] reliability.

solventar *vt* - **1.** [pagar] to settle - **2.** [resolver] to resolve.

solvente *adj* - **1.** [económicamente] solvent - **2.** *fig* [fuentes etc] reliable.

Somalia *n pr* Somalia.

somático, ca *adj* somatic.

somatizar [13] *vt* MED to convert into physical symptoms.

sombra *sf* - **1.** [proyección - fenómeno] shadow; [- zona] shade; **a la sombra** [- gen] in the shade; *fam* [- en la cárcel] in the slammer; **dar sombra a** to cast a shadow over; **hacer sombra a alguien** to overshadow sb; **ser la sombra de alguien** to be sb's shadow; **tener mala sombra** to be a nasty swine - **2.** [en pintura] shade - **3.** *fig* [anonimato] background; **permanecer en la sombra** to stay out of the limelight - **4.** *fig* [imperfección] stain, blemish - **5.** *fig* [atisbo] trace, touch; **no tener ni sombra de** not to have the slightest bit of - **6.** [mancha] spot - **7.** [suerte]: **buena/mala sombra** good/bad luck - **8.** TAUROM *most expensive seats in bullring, located in the shade.*
➧ **sombra de ojos** *sf* eyeshadow.

sombreado *sm* shading.

sombrerería *sf* - **1.** [fábrica] hat factory - **2.** [tienda] hat shop.

sombrero *sm* - **1.** [prenda] hat; **sombrero de copa** top hat; **sombrero hongo** bowler hat, derby *US*; **quitarse el sombrero** *fig* to take one's hat off - **2.** [de setas] cap.

sombrilla *sf* sunshade, parasol; **me vale sombrilla** *Méx fig* I couldn't care less.

sombrío, bría *adj* - **1.** [oscuro] gloomy, dark - **2.** *fig* [triste] sombre, gloomy.

somero, ra *adj* superficial.

someter *vt* - **1.** [a rebeldes] to subdue - **2.** [presentar]: **someter algo a la aprobación de alguien** to submit sthg for sb's approval; **someter algo a votación** to put sthg to the vote - **3.** [subordinar] to subordinate - **4.** [a operación, interrogatorio etc]: **someter a alguien a algo** to subject sb to sthg.
◆ **someterse** *vprnl* - **1.** [rendirse] to surrender - **2.** [conformarse]: **someterse a algo** to yield o bow to sthg - **3.** [a operación, interrogatorio etc]: **someterse a algo** to undergo sthg.

sometimiento *sm* - **1.** [gen] submission - **2.** [dominio] subjugation.

somier (*pl* **somieres**) *sm* [de muelles] bed springs *pl*; [de tablas] slats (*of bed*).

sommelier = **sumiller**.

somnífero, ra *adj* somniferous.
◆ **somnífero** *sm* sleeping pill.

somnolencia *sf* sleepiness, drowsiness.

somnoliento, ta *adj* drowsy, sleepy.

somos ▷ **ser**.

son *sm* - **1.** [sonido] sound; **bailar al son que le tocan** *fig* to toe the line - **2.** [estilo] way; **en son de** in the manner of; **en son de paz** in peace; ▷ **ser**.

sonado, da *adj* - **1.** [renombrado] famous - **2.** [loco] crazy - **3.** [boxeador] punch drunk.

sonajero *sm* rattle.

sonambulismo *sm* sleepwalking.

sonámbulo, la ◇ *adj* sleepwalking (*antes de s*). ◇ *sm, f* sleepwalker.

sonante ▷ **dinero**.

sonar¹ *sm* sonar.

sonar² [23] *vi* - **1.** [gen] to sound; **suena a falso/chiste** it sounds false/like a joke; **(así o tal) como suena** literally, in so many words - **2.** [timbre] to ring - **3.** [hora]: **sonaron las doce** the clock struck twelve - **4.** [ser conocido, familiar] to be familiar; **me suena** it rings a bell; **no me suena su nombre** I don't remember hearing her name before - **5.** [pronunciarse - letra] to be pronounced - **6.** [rumorearse] to be rumoured.
◆ **sonarse** *vprnl* to blow one's nose.

sonata *sf* sonata.

sonda *sf* - **1.** MED & TECNOL probe; **sonda espacial** space probe - **2.** NÁUT sounding line - **3.** [en una mina] drill, bore.

sondar *vt* - **1.** MED to sound, to probe - **2.** NÁUT to sound - **3.** [terreno] to test; [roca] to drill.

sondear *vt* - **1.** [indagar] to sound out - **2.** [terreno] to test; [roca] to drill.

sondeo *sm* - **1.** [encuesta] (opinion) poll - **2.** [de un terreno] drilling (*U*), boring (*U*) - **3.** NÁUT sounding.

soneto *sm* sonnet.

sónico, ca *adj* sonic, sound (*antes de s*).

sonido *sm* sound.

soniquete *sm* monotonous noise.

sonora ▷ **sonoro**.

sonoridad *sf* - **1.** [gen] sonority - **2.** [acústica] acoustics *pl*.

sonorización *sf* soundtrack recording.

sonorizar [13] *vt* - **1.** [con amplificadores] to fit with a public address system - **2.** CINE [poner sonido] to record the soundtrack for.

sonoro, ra *adj* - **1.** [gen] sound (*antes de s*); [película] talking - **2.** [ruidoso, resonante, vibrante] resonant.

sonreír [28] *vi* - **1.** [reír levemente] to smile - **2.** *fig* [ser favorable] to smile on.
◆ **sonreírse** *vprnl* to smile.

sonriente *adj* smiling.

sonriera *etc* ▷ **sonreír**.

sonrisa *sf* smile.

sonrojar *vt* to cause to blush.
◆ **sonrojarse** *vprnl* to blush.

sonrojo *sm* blush, blushing (*U*).

sonrosado, da *adj* rosy.

sonsacar [10] *vt*: **sonsacar algo a alguien** [conseguir] to wheedle sthg out of sb; [hacer decir] to extract sthg from sb; **sonsacar a alguien** to pump sb for information.

sonso, sa ◇ *adj* *Amér fam* foolish, silly. ◇ *sm, f* fool, idiot.

sonsonete *sm* - **1.** [ruido] tapping (*U*) - **2.** *fig* [entonación] monotonous intonation - **3.** *fig* [cantinela] old tune - **4.** *fig* [sarcasmo] hint of sarcasm.

soñador, ra ◇ *adj* dreamy. ◇ *sm, f* dreamer.

soñar [23] ◇ *vt lit & fig* to dream; **¡ni soñarlo!** not on your life! ◇ *vi lit & fig*: **soñar (con)** to dream (of o about); **soñar con los angelitos** to have sweet dreams; **soñar despierto** to daydream.

soñoliento, ta *adj* sleepy, drowsy.

sopa *sf* - **1.** [guiso] soup; **sopa de ajo** garlic soup; **sopa juliana** o **de verduras** vegetable soup - **2.** [de pan] *piece of soaked bread* - **3.** *loc*: **andar a la sopa boba** to scrounge; **dar sopa con hondas a alguien** to knock the spots off sb; **encontrarse a alguien hasta en la sopa** not to be able to get away from sb; **estar como una sopa** to be sopping wet.

sopapo *sm fam* slap.

sopero, ra *adj* soup (*antes de s*).
◆ **sopera** *sf* [recipiente] soup tureen.

sopesar *vt* to try the weight of; *fig* to weigh up.

sopetón ◆ **de sopetón** *loc adv* suddenly, abruptly.

soplado *sm* [del vidrio] glassblowing.

soplagaitas *fam* ◇ *adj inv* [quisquilloso] fussy. ◇ *smf inv* [quisquilloso] fuss-pot.

soplamocos *sm inv fam* punch on the nose.

soplar ◇ *vt* - **1.** [vela, fuego] to blow out - **2.** [ceniza, polvo] to blow off - **3.** [globo etc] to blow up - **4.** [vidrio] to blow - **5.** *fig* [pregunta, examen] to prompt - **6.** *fig* [denunciar] to squeal - **7.** *fig* [hurtar] to pinch, to nick. ◇ *vi* - **1.** [gen] to blow - **2.** *fam* [beber] to booze.

◆ **soplarse** *vprnl fam* [comer] to gobble up; [beber] to knock back.

soplete *sm* blowlamp.

soplido *sm* blow, puff.

soplo *sm* - **1.** [soplido] blow, puff - **2.** *fig* [instante] breath, moment - **3.** MED murmur - **4.** *fam* [chivatazo] tip-off; **dar el soplo** to squeal, to grass.

soplón, ona *sm, f fam* grass.

soponcio *sm fam* fainting fit; **le dio un soponcio** [desmayo] she passed out; [ataque] she had a fit.

sopor *sm* drowsiness.

soporífero, ra *adj lit & fig* soporific.

soportal *sm* [pórtico] porch.

◆ **soportales** *smpl* [arcadas] arcade *sing*.

soportar *vt* - **1.** [sostener] to support - **2.** [resistir, tolerar] to stand; **¡no le soporto!** I can't stand him! - **3.** [sobrellevar] to endure, to bear.

◆ **soportarse** *vprnl* to stand one another.

soporte *sm* - **1.** [apoyo] support; **soporte publicitario** publicity medium - **2.** INFORM medium; **soporte físico** hardware; **soporte lógico** software.

soprano *smf* soprano.

sor *sf* RELIG sister.

sorber *vt* - **1.** [beber] to sip; [haciendo ruido] to slurp - **2.** [absorber] to soak up, to absorb - **3.** [atraer] to draw o suck in - **4.** *fig* [escuchar atentamente] to drink in.

sorbete *sm* sorbet.

sorbo *sm* - **1.** [acción] gulp, swallow; **beber algo de un sorbo** to drink sthg in one gulp; [pequeño] sip; **beber a sorbos** to sip - **2.** [trago] mouthful; [pequeño] sip - **3.** [cantidad pequeña] drop.

sorda ▷ sordo.

sordera *sf* deafness.

sordidez *sf* - **1.** [miseria] squalor - **2.** [obscenidad, perversión] sordidness.

sórdido, da *adj* - **1.** [miserable] squalid - **2.** [obsceno, perverso] sordid.

sordina *sf* - **1.** MÚS [en instrumentos de viento, cuerda] mute; [en pianos] damper - **2.** [de reloj] muffle.

sordo, da ◇ *adj* - **1.** [que no oye] deaf; **permanecer sordo a** o **ante algo** *fig* to be deaf to sthg; **estar más sordo que una tapia** to be stone deaf; **quedarse sordo** to go deaf - **2.** [pasos] quiet, muffled - **3.** [ruido, dolor] dull. ◇ *sm, f* [persona] deaf person; **los sordos** the deaf; **hacerse el sordo** to turn a deaf ear.

sordomudo, da ◇ *adj* deaf and dumb. ◇ *sm, f* deaf-mute.

soriasis *sf inv* psoriasis.

sorna *sf* sarcasm.

soroche *sm Andes & Arg* altitude sickness.

sorprendente *adj* surprising.

sorprender *vt* - **1.** [asombrar] to surprise - **2.** [atrapar]: **sorprender a alguien (haciendo algo)** to catch sb (doing sthg) - **3.** [coger desprevenido] to catch unawares - **4.** [descubrir] to discover.

◆ **sorprenderse** *vprnl* to be surprised.

sorprendido, da *adj* surprised; **quedarse sorprendido** to be surprised.

sorpresa *sf* surprise; **coger a alguien por sorpresa** to catch sb by surprise; **dar una sorpresa a alguien** to surprise sb; **llevarse una sorpresa** to get a surprise; **de** o **por sorpresa** by surprise.

sorpresivo, va *adj Amér* unexpected.

sortear *vt* - **1.** [rifar] to raffle - **2.** [echar a suertes] to draw lots for - **3.** *fig* [superar] to get round - **4.** *fig* [esquivar] to dodge.

sorteo *sm* - **1.** [lotería] draw - **2.** [rifa] raffle.

sortija *sf* ring.

sortilegio *sm* [hechizo] spell.

SOS (*abrev de* **save our souls**) *sm* SOS.

sosa *sf* soda; **sosa cáustica** caustic soda.

sosegado, da *adj* calm.

sosegar [35] *vt* to calm.

◆ **sosegarse** *vprnl* to calm down.

soseras *smf inv fam* dull person, bore.

sosería *sf* lack of sparkle.

sosias *sm inv* double, lookalike.

sosiega *etc* ▷ sosegar.

sosiego *sm* calm.

soslayar *vt* to avoid.

soslayo ◆ **de soslayo** *loc adv* [oblicuamente] sideways, obliquely; **mirar a alguien de soslayo** to look at sb out of the corner of one's eye.

soso, sa ◇ *adj* - **1.** [sin sal] bland, tasteless - **2.** [sin gracia] dull, insipid. ◇ *sm, f* dull person, bore.

sospecha *sf* suspicion; **despertar sospechas** to arouse suspicion.

sospechar ◇ *vt* [creer, suponer] to suspect; **sospecho que no lo terminará** I doubt whether she'll finish it. ◇ *vi*: **sospechar de** to suspect.

sospechoso, sa ⇔ *adj* suspicious. ⇔ *sm, f* suspect.

sostén *sm* - **1.** [apoyo] support - **2.** [sustento] main support; [alimento] sustenance - **3.** [sujetador] bra, brassiere.

sostener [72] *vt* - **1.** [sujetar] to support, to hold up - **2.** [defender - idea, opinión, tesis] to defend; [- promesa, palabra] to stand by, to keep; **sostener que...** to maintain that... - **3.** [mantener, costear] to support - **4.** [tener - conversación] to hold, to have; [- correspondencia] to keep up.
◆ **sostenerse** *vprnl* to hold o.s. up; [en pie] to stand up; [en el aire] to hang.

sostenido, da *adj* - **1.** [persistente] sustained - **2.** MÚS sharp.
◆ **sostenido** *sm* MÚS sharp.

sostiene, sostuviera *etc v* ⊳ **sostener**.

sota *sf* ≃ jack.

sotana *sf* cassock.

sótano *sm* basement.

sotavento *sm* leeward.

soterrar [19] *vt* [enterrar] to bury; *fig* to hide.

sotto voce [soto'βotʃe] *loc adv* sotto voce.

soufflé [su'fle] *sm* soufflé.

soul *sm* MÚS soul (music).

soviético, ca ⇔ *adj* - **1.** [del soviet] soviet - **2.** [de la URSS] Soviet. ⇔ *sm, f* Soviet.

soy ⊳ ser.

spaghetti [espa'ɣeti] = **espagueti**.

spanglish [es'panglis] *sm* Spanglish.

spaniel [es'panjel] *sm* spaniel.

sparring [es'parrin] (*pl* **sparrings**) *sm* DEP sparring partner.

spot [es'pot], **espot** *sm* advertising spot, commercial.

spray [es'prai] = **espray**.

sprint [es'prin] = **esprint**.

sprinter [es'printer] = **esprínter**.

squash [es'kuaʃ] *sm inv* squash.

squatter [es'kuater] (*pl* **squatters**) *sm* squatter.

Sr. (*abrev de* **señor**) Mr.

Sra. (*abrev de* **señora**) Mrs.

SRE *sf* (*abrev de* **Secretaría de Relaciones Exteriores**), *Mexican Department of Foreign Affairs*.

Sres. (*abrev de* **señores**) Messrs.

Sri Lanka *n pr* Sri Lanka.

Srta. (*abrev de* **señorita**) Miss.

Sta. (*abrev de* **santa**) St.

staff [es'taf] *sm* staff.

stand [es'tan] *sm* stand, stall.

standard [es'tandar] = **estándar**.

standing [es'tandin] *sm* standing, social status.

starter [es'tarter] = **estárter**.

statu quo [es'tatu'kwo] *sm inv* status quo.

status [es'tatus] = **estatus**.

stereo [es'tereo] = **estéreo**.

stick [es'tik] (*pl* **sticks**) *sm* DEP hockey stick.

Sto. (*abrev de* **santo**) St.

stock [es'tok] *sm* stock.

stop, estop [es'top] *sm* - **1.** AUTO stop sign - **2.** [en telegrama] stop.

stress [es'tres] = **estrés**.

strip-tease [es'triptis] *sm inv* striptease.

su (*pl* **sus**) *adj poses* [de él] his; [de ella] her; [de cosa, animal] its; [de uno] one's; [de ellos, ellas] their; [de usted, ustedes] your.

suave *adj* - **1.** [gen] soft - **2.** [liso] smooth - **3.** [sabor, olor, color] delicate - **4.** [apacible - persona, carácter] gentle; [- clima] mild - **5.** [fácil - cuesta, tarea, ritmo] gentle; [- dirección de un coche] smooth.

suavidad *sf* - **1.** [gen] softness - **2.** [lisura] smoothness - **3.** [de sabor, olor, color] delicacy - **4.** [de carácter] gentleness - **5.** [de clima] mildness - **6.** [de cuesta, tarea, ritmo] gentleness; [de la dirección de un coche] smoothness.

suavizante ⇔ *adj* [para ropa, cabello] conditioning; [para piel] moisturizing. ⇔ *sm* conditioner; **suavizante para la ropa** fabric conditioner.

suavizar [13] *vt* - **1.** [gen] to soften; [ropa, cabello] to condition - **2.** [hacer dócil] to temper - **3.** [ascensión, conducción, tarea] to ease; [clima] to make milder - **4.** [sabor, olor, color] to tone down - **5.** [alisar] to smooth.

subacuático, ca *adj* subaquatic.

subafluente *sm* tributary.

subalimentar *vt* to undernourish.

subalquilar *vt* to sublet.

subalterno, **na** <> *adj* [subordinado] auxiliary. <> *sm*, *f* [empleado] subordinate.

➤ **subalterno** *sm* TAUROM *assistant to bullfighter*; *ver también* **tauromaquia**.

subarrendar [19] *vt* to sublet.

subarrendatario, **ria** *sm*, *f* subtenant.

subarriendo *sm* - **1.** [acción] subtenancy - **2.** [contrato] sublease (agreement).

subasta *sf* - **1.** [venta pública] auction; **sacar algo a subasta** to put sthg up for auction - **2.** [contrata pública] tender; **sacar algo a subasta** to put sthg out to tender.

subastador, **ra** <> *adj* auction *(antes de s)*. <> *sm*, *f* auctioneer.

subastar *vt* to auction.

subcampeón, **ona** *sm*, *f* runner-up.

subcampeonato *sm* second place, runner-up's position.

subclase *sf* subclass.

subcomisión *sf* subcommittee.

subconjunto *sm* MAT subset.

subconsciente *adj* & *sm* subconscious.

subcontración *sf* outsourcing.

subcontratar *vt* to outsource.

subcontrato *sm* subcontract.

subcutáneo, **a** *adj* subcutaneous.

subdelegación *sf* subdelegation.

subdelegado, **da** *sm*, *f* subdelegate.

subdesarrollado, **da** *adj* underdeveloped.

subdesarrollo *sm* underdevelopment.

subdirección *sf* [puesto] post of assistant manager.

subdirector, **ra** *sm*, *f* assistant manager.

subdirectorio *sm* INFORM subdirectory.

súbdito, **ta** <> *adj*: **ser súbdito de** to be subject to. <> *sm*, *f* - **1.** [subordinado] subject - **2.** [ciudadano] citizen, national.

subdividir *vt* to subdivide.

➤ **subdividirse** *vprnl* to be subdivided.

subdivisión *sf* subdivision.

subemplear *vt* to underemploy.

subempleo *sm* underemployment.

subespecie *sf* subspecies.

subestimar *vt* to underestimate; [infravalorar] to underrate.

➤ **subestimarse** *vprnl* to underrate o.s.

subgénero *sm* subgenus.

subgrupo *sm* subgroup.

subido, **da** *adj* - **1.** [intenso] strong, intense - **2.** *fam* [en cantidad]: **tiene el guapo subido** he's looking really good today; **está de un im-**bécil **subido** he has been acting like an idiot recently - **3.** *fam* [atrevido] risqué; **subido de tono** [impertinente] impertinent.

➤ **subida** *sf* - **1.** [cuesta] hill - **2.** [ascensión] ascent, climb - **3.** [aumento] increase, rise.

subíndice *sm* subscript.

subinspector, **ra** *sm*, *f* deputy inspector.

subir <> *vi* - **1.** [a piso, azotea] to go/come up; [a montaña, cima] to climb - **2.** [aumentar - precio, temperatura] to go up, to rise; [- cauce, marea] to rise - **3.** [montar - en avión, barco] to get on; [- en coche] to get in; **sube al coche** get into the car - **4.** [cuenta, importe]: **subir a** to come o amount to - **5.** [de categoría] to be promoted - **6.** CULIN [crecer] to rise. <> *vt* - **1.** [ascender - calle, escaleras] to go/come up; [- pendiente, montaña] to climb - **2.** [poner arriba] to lift up; [llevar arriba] to take/bring up - **3.** [aumentar - precio, peso] to put up, to increase; [- volumen de radio etc] to turn up - **4.** [montar]: **subir algo/a alguien a** to lift sthg/sb onto - **5.** [alzar - mano, bandera, voz] to raise; [- persiana] to roll up; [- ventanilla] to wind up - **6.** MÚS to raise the pitch of.

➤ **subirse** *vprnl* - **1.** [ascender]: **subirse a** [árbol] to climb up; [mesa] to climb onto; [piso] to go/come up to - **2.** [montarse]: **subirse a** [tren, avión] to get on, to board; [caballo, bicicleta] to mount; [coche] to get into; **el taxi paró y me subí** the taxi stopped and I got in - **3.** [alzarse - pernera, mangas] to roll up; [- cremallera] to do up; [- pantalones, calcetines] to pull up - **4.** *fam* [emborrachar]: **se le subió a la cabeza** it went to his head.

súbito, **ta** *adj* sudden; **de súbito** suddenly.

subjefe, **fa** *sm*, *f* second-in-command.

subjetividad *sf* subjectivity.

subjetivismo *sm* subjectivism.

subjetivo, **va** *adj* subjective.

sub júdice [suβ'djuðiθe] *adj* DER sub judice.

subjuntivo, **va** *adj* subjunctive.

➤ **subjuntivo** *sm* subjunctive.

sublevación *sf* uprising.

sublevamiento *sm* = **sublevación**.

sublevar *vt* - **1.** [amotinar] to stir up - **2.** [indignar] to infuriate.

➤ **sublevarse** *vprnl* [amotinarse] to rise up, to rebel.

sublimación *sf* - **1.** [exaltación] exaltation - **2.** PSICOL & QUÍM sublimation.

sublimar *vt* - **1.** [exaltar] to exalt - **2.** PSICOL & QUÍM to sublimate.

sublime *adj* sublime.

sublimidad *sf* sublimity.

subliminal *adj* subliminal.

submarinismo *sm* skin-diving.

submarinista <> *adj* skin-diving *(antes de s)*. <> *smf* skin-diver.

submarino, na *adj* underwater.

submarino *sm* submarine.

submúltiplo, pla *adj* submultiple.

submúltiplo *sm* submultiple.

subnormal <> *adj* - **1.** *despec* [minusválido] subnormal - **2.** *fig & despec* [imbécil] moronic. <> *smf* - **1.** *despec* [minusválido] subnormal person - **2.** *fig & despec* [imbécil] moron, cretin.

suboficial *sm* MIL non-commissioned officer.

suborden *sm* BIOL suborder.

subordinación *sf* [gen & GRAM] subordination.

subordinado, da *adj & sm, f* subordinate.

subordinar *vt* [gen & GRAM] to subordinate; **subordinar algo a algo** to subordinate sthg to sthg.

subordinarse *vprnl* to subordinate o.s.

subproducto *sm* by-product.

subrayado, da *adj* underlined.

subrayado *sm* underlining.

subrayar *vt* *lit & fig* to underline.

subrepticio, cia *adj* surreptitious.

subrogación *sf* subrogation.

subrogar [16] *vt* to subrogate.

subsanable *adj* - **1.** [solucionable] solvable - **2.** [corregible] rectifiable.

subsanar *vt* - **1.** [solucionar] to resolve - **2.** [corregir] to correct - **3.** [disculpar] to excuse.

subscribir = suscribir.

subscripción = suscripción.

subscriptor = suscriptor.

subscrito *pp & adj* = suscrito.

subsecretaría *sf* - **1.** [oficina] undersecretary's office - **2.** [cargo] undersecretaryship.

subsecretario, ria *sm, f* - **1.** [de secretario] assistant secretary - **2.** [de ministro] undersecretary.

subsidiar [8] *vt* to subsidize.

subsidiario, ria *adj* - **1.** [de subvención] paid for by the State - **2.** DER ancillary.

subsidio *sm* benefit, allowance; **subsidio de invalidez** disability allowance; **subsidio de paro** unemployment benefit.

subsiguiente *adj* subsequent.

subsistencia *sf* [vida] subsistence.

subsistencias *sfpl* [provisiones] provisions.

subsistente *adj* surviving.

subsistir *vi* - **1.** [vivir] to live, to exist - **2.** [sobrevivir] to survive.

substancia = sustancia.

substancial = sustancial.

substanciar [8] = sustanciar.

substancioso = sustancioso.

substantivación = sustantivación.

substantivar = sustantivar.

substantivo = sustantivo.

substitución = sustitución.

substituible = sustituible.

substituir [51] = sustituir.

substitutivo = sustitutivo.

substituto = sustituto.

substracción = sustracción.

substraer [73] = sustraer.

substrato = sustrato.

subsuelo *sm* subsoil.

subte *sm* R Dom metro, underground UK, subway US.

subteniente *sm* sub-lieutenant.

subterfugio *sm* subterfuge.

subterráneo, a *adj* subterranean, underground.

subterráneo *sm* - **1.** underground tunnel - **2.** Arg [metro] underground.

subtipo *sm* BIOL subtype.

subtitular *vt* [gen & CINE] to subtitle; **versión original subtitulada** original language version with subtitles.

subtítulo *sm* [gen & CINE] subtitle.

subtropical *adj* subtropical.

suburbano, na *adj* suburban.

suburbial *adj*: **barrio suburbial** poor suburb.

suburbio *sm* poor suburb.

subvalorar *vt* to undervalue, to underrate.

subvención *sf* subsidy.

subvencionar *vt* to subsidize.

subversión *sf* subversion.

subversivo, va *adj* subversive.

subvertir [27] *vt* to subvert.

subyacente *adj* underlying.

subyacer *vi* [ocultarse]: **subyacer bajo algo** to underlie sthg.

subyugador, ra *adj* - **1.** [dominador] conquering - **2.** [atrayente] captivating.

subyugar [16] *vt* - **1.** [someter] to subjugate - **2.** *fig* [dominar] to quell, to master - **3.** *fig* [atraer] to captivate.

succión *sf* suction.

succionar *vt* [suj: raíces] to suck up; [suj: bebé] to absorb, to suck.

sucedáneo, a *adj* ersatz, substitute.

sucedáneo *sm* substitute.

suceder <> *v impers* [ocurrir] to happen; **suceda lo que suceda** whatever happens. <> *vt* [sustituir]: **suceder a alguien (en)** to succeed sb (in). <> *vi* [venir después]: **suceder a** to come after, to follow; **a la guerra sucedieron años muy tristes** the war was followed by years of misery.

sucederse *vprnl* to follow.

sucesión *sf* - **1.** [gen] succession - **2.** [descendencia] issue.

sucesivamente *adv* successively; **y así sucesivamente** and so on.

sucesivo, va *adj* - **1.** [consecutivo] successive, consecutive - **2.** [siguiente]**: en días sucesivos les informaremos** we'll let you know over the next few days; **en lo sucesivo** in future.

suceso *sm* - **1.** [acontecimiento] event - **2.** *(gen pl)* [hecho delictivo] crime; [incidente] incident; **sección de sucesos** accident and crime reports.

sucesor, ra ◇ *adj* succeeding. ◇ *sm, f* successor.

sucesorio, ria *adj* succession *(antes de s)*.

suciedad *sf* - **1.** [cualidad] dirtiness *(U)* - **2.** [porquería] dirt, filth *(U)*.

sucinto, ta *adj* - **1.** [conciso] succinct - **2.** [pequeño - biquini etc] skimpy.

sucio, cia *adj* - **1.** [gen] dirty; [al comer, trabajar] messy; **el blanco es un color muy sucio** white is a colour that gets dirty easily; **en sucio** in rough - **2.** [juego] dirty - **3.** [conciencia] bad, guilty.

sucre *sm* [moneda] sucre.

suculento, ta *adj* tasty.

sucumbir *vi* - **1.** [rendirse, ceder]**: sucumbir (a)** to succumb (to) - **2.** [fallecer] to die - **3.** [desaparecer] to fall.

sucursal *sf* branch.

sudaca *adj* & *smf fam racist term referring to a Latin American.*

sudadera *sf* - **1.** [sudor] sweat - **2.** [prenda] sweatshirt.

sudado *sm Amér* stew.

Sudáfrica *n pr* South Africa.

sudafricano, na *adj* & *sm, f* South African.

Sudán *n pr* Sudan.

sudanés, esa *adj* & *sm, f* Sudanese.

sudar ◇ *vi* - **1.** [gen] to sweat - **2.** *fam* [trabajar duro] to sweat blood. ◇ *vt* - **1.** [empapar] to make sweaty - **2.** *fam* [trabajar duro por] to work hard for.

sudario *sm* shroud.

sudeste, sureste ◇ *adj* [posición, parte] southeast, southeastern; [dirección, viento] southeasterly. ◇ *sm* southeast.

sudoeste, suroeste ◇ *adj* [posición, parte] southwest, southwestern; [dirección, viento] southwesterly. ◇ *sm* southwest.

sudor *sm* - **1.** [gen] sweat *(U)*; **con el sudor de su frente** by the sweat of his/her *etc* brow; **sudor frío** cold sweat - **2.** [de botijo etc] condensation.

sudoriento, ta *adj* sweaty.

sudoríparo, ra *adj* sweat *(antes de s)*.

sudoroso, sa *adj* sweaty.

Suecia *n pr* Sweden.

sueco, ca ◇ *adj* Swedish. ◇ *sm, f* [persona] Swede; **hacerse el sueco** *fig* to play dumb, to pretend not to understand.

sueco *sm* [lengua] Swedish.

suegro, gra *sm, f* father-in-law (*f* mother-in-law).

suela *sf* sole; **no llegarle a alguien a la suela del zapato** *fig* not to hold a candle to sb.

suelda *etc* ⊳ **soldar**.

sueldo *sm* salary, wages *pl*; [semanal] wage; **a sueldo** [asesino] hired; [empleado] salaried; **sueldo base** basic salary; **sueldo mínimo** minimum wage; [semanal] basic wage.

suelo *sm* - **1.** [pavimento - en interiores] floor; [- en el exterior] ground; **caerse al suelo** to fall over; **besar el suelo** to fall flat on one's face - **2.** [terreno, territorio] soil; [para edificar] land - **3.** [base] bottom - **4.** *loc*: **arrastrarse por el suelo** to grovel, to humble o.s.; **echar por el suelo un plan** to ruin a project; **estar por los suelos** [persona, precio] to be at rock bottom; [productos] to be dirt cheap; **poner** *o* **tirar por los suelos** to run down, to criticize; ⊳ **soler**.

suelto, ta *adj* - **1.** [gen] loose; [cordones] undone; **¿tienes cinco euros sueltos?** have you got five euros in loose change?; **andar suelto** [en libertad] to be free; [en fuga] to be at large; [con diarrea] to have diarrhoea - **2.** [separado] separate; [desparejado] odd; **no los vendemos sueltos** we don't sell them separately - **3.** [arroz] fluffy - **4.** [lenguaje, estilo] fluent, fluid - **5.** [desenvuelto] comfortable, at ease.

suelto *sm* [calderilla] loose change.

suelta *etc* ⊳ **soltar**.

suena *etc* ⊳ **sonar**.

sueña *etc* ⊳ **soñar**.

sueño *sm* - **1.** [ganas de dormir] sleepiness; [por medicamento etc] drowsiness; **¡qué sueño!** I'm really sleepy!; **tener sueño** to be sleepy - **2.** [estado] sleep; **coger el sueño** to get to sleep; **descabezar un sueño** to have a nap; **no pierdas el sueño por ella** don't lose any sleep over her; **quitarle el sueño a alguien** to keep sb awake; **sueño eterno** *fig* eternal rest; **sueño pesado/ligero** heavy/light sleep - **3.** [imagen mental, objetivo, quimera] dream; **esta casa es un sueño** *fam* this house is a dream; **en sueños** in a dream; **ni en sueños** *fig* no way, under no circumstances.

suero *sm* - **1.** MED serum; **suero artificial** saline solution - **2.** [de la leche] whey.

suerte *sf* - **1.** [azar] chance; **echar** *o* **tirar algo a suertes** to draw lots for sthg; **la suerte está echada** the die is cast - **2.** [fortuna] luck; **des-**

ear suerte a alguien to wish sb luck; **estar de suerte** to be in luck; **por suerte** luckily; **probar suerte** to try one's luck; **¡qué suerte!** that was lucky!; **tener (buena) suerte** to be lucky; **tener mala suerte** to be unlucky - **3.** [destino] fate; **tentar a la suerte** to tempt fate; **tocar** o **caer en suerte a alguien** to fall to sb's lot; **traer mala suerte** to bring bad luck - **4.** [situación] situation, lot - **5.** *culto* [clase]: **toda suerte de** all manner of - **6.** *culto* [manera] manner, fashion; **de suerte que** in such a way that.

suéter (*pl* **suéteres**) *sm* sweater.

suficiencia *sf* - **1.** [capacidad] proficiency - **2.** [idoneidad] suitability - **3.** [presunción] smugness, self-importance.

suficiente ⬦ *adj* - **1.** [bastante] enough; [medidas, esfuerzos] adequate; **no llevo (dinero) suficiente** I don't have enough (money) on me; **no tienes la estatura suficiente** you're not tall enough - **2.** [presuntuoso] smug, full of o.s. ⬦ *sm* [nota] pass.

sufijo *sm* suffix.

sufragar [16] ⬦ *vt* [costes] to defray. ⬦ *vi* *Amér* [votar] to vote.

sufragio *sm* suffrage; **sufragio directo/indirecto** direct/indirect suffrage; **sufragio universal** universal suffrage.

sufragismo *sm* suffragette movement.

sufragista ⬦ *adj* suffragette *(antes de s)*. ⬦ *smf* suffragette.

sufrido, da *adj* - **1.** [resignado] patient, uncomplaining; [durante mucho tiempo] long-suffering - **2.** [resistente - tela] hardwearing; [- color] that does not show the dirt.

sufridor, ra *adj* easily worried.

sufrimiento *sm* suffering.

sufrir ⬦ *vt* - **1.** [gen] to suffer; [accidente] to have - **2.** [soportar] to bear, to stand; **tengo que sufrir sus manías** I have to put up with his idiosyncrasies - **3.** [experimentar - cambios etc] to undergo. ⬦ *vi* [padecer] to suffer; **sufrir de** [enfermedad] to suffer from; **sufrir del estómago** *etc* to have a stomach *etc* complaint.

sugerencia *sf* suggestion; **hacer una sugerencia** to make a suggestion.

sugerente *adj* evocative.

sugerir [27] *vt* - **1.** [proponer] to suggest; **sugerir a alguien que haga algo** to suggest that sb should do sthg - **2.** [evocar] to evoke.

sugestión *sf* suggestion.

sugestionable *adj* impressionable.

sugestionar *vt* to influence.

➤ **sugestionarse** *vprnl* - **1.** [obsesionarse] to become obsessed - **2.** PSICOL to use autosuggestion.

sugestivo, va *adj* - **1.** [atrayente] attractive - **2.** [que sugiere] stimulating, suggesting.

sugiera, sugiriera *etc v* ▷ **sugerir**.

suiche *sm* *Col & Ven* switch.

suicida ⬦ *adj* suicidal. ⬦ *smf* [por naturaleza] suicidal person; [suicidado] person who has committed suicide.

suicidarse *vprnl* to commit suicide.

suicidio *sm* suicide.

sui generis [sui'xeneris] *adj* unusual.

suite [swit] *sf* [gen & MÚS] suite.

Suiza *n pr* Switzerland.

suizo, za *adj* & *sm, f* Swiss.

sujeción *sf* - **1.** [atadura] fastening - **2.** [sometimiento] subjection.

sujetador *sm* bra, brassiere.

sujetapapeles *sm inv* paper clip.

sujetar *vt* - **1.** [agarrar] to hold down - **2.** [aguantar] to fasten; [papeles] to fasten together - **3.** [someter] to subdue; [a niños] to control.

➤ **sujetarse** *vprnl* - **1.** [agarrarse]: **sujetarse a** to hold on to, to cling to - **2.** [aguantarse] to keep in place - **3.** [someterse]: **sujetarse a** to keep o stick to.

sujeto, ta *adj* - **1.** [agarrado - objeto] fastened - **2.** [expuesto]: **sujeto a** subject to.

➤ **sujeto** *sm* - **1.** [gen & GRAM] subject - **2.** [individuo] individual; **sujeto pasivo** ECON taxpayer.

sulfamida *sf* MED sulphonamide.

sulfato *sm* sulphate.

sulfurar *vt* - **1.** [encolerizar] to infuriate - **2.** QUÍM to sulphurate.

➤ **sulfurarse** *vprnl* [encolerizarse] to get mad.

sulfúrico, ca *adj* sulphuric.

sulfuro *sm* sulphide.

sulfuroso, sa *adj* QUÍM sulphurous.

sultán *sm* sultan.

sultana *sf* sultana.

suma *sf* - **1.** [MAT - acción] addition; [- resultado] total - **2.** [conjunto - de conocimientos, datos] total, sum; [- de dinero] sum - **3.** [resumen]: **en suma** in short.

sumamente *adv* extremely.

sumando *sm* addend.

sumar *vt* - **1.** MAT to add together; **sumar algo a algo** to add sthg to sthg; **tres y cinco suman ocho** three and five are o make eight - **2.** [costar] to come to.

➤ **sumarse** *vprnl* - **1.**: **sumarse (a)** [unirse] to join (in) - **2.** [agregarse] to be in addition to.

sumarial *adj* pertaining to an indictment.

sumario, ria *adj* - **1.** [conciso] brief - **2.** DER summary.

sumario *sm* - **1.** DER indictment - **2.** [resumen] summary.

sumarísimo, **ma** *adj* DER swift, expeditious.

sumergible ◇ *adj* waterproof. ◇ *sm* submarine.

sumergir [15] *vt* [hundir] to submerge; [con fuerza] to plunge; [bañar] to dip.

sumergirse *vprnl* - **1.** [hundirse] to submerge; [con fuerza] to plunge - **2.** [abstraerse]: **sumergirse (en)** to immerse o.s. (in).

sumidero *sm* drain.

sumiller (*pl* sumillers), **sommelier** [sumi'jer] (*pl* sommeliers) *sm* sommelier, wine waiter.

suministrador, **ra** ◇ *adj* supply (antes de s). ◇ *sm, f* supplier.

suministrar *vt* to supply; **suministrar algo a alguien** to supply sb with sthg.

suministro *sm* [gen] supply; [acto] supplying.

sumir *vt*: **sumir a alguien en** to plunge sb into.

sumirse en *vprnl* - **1.** [depresión, sueño etc] to sink into - **2.** [estudio, tema] to immerse o.s. in.

sumisión *sf* - **1.** [obediencia - acción] submission; [- cualidad] submissiveness - **2.** [rendición] surrender.

sumiso, **sa** *adj* submissive.

súmmum *sm* height; **el súmmum** the ultimate.

sumo, **ma** *adj* - **1.** [supremo] highest, supreme - **2.** [gran] extreme, great.

a lo sumo *loc adv* at most.

sunnita ◇ *adj* Sunni. ◇ *smf* Sunnite, Sunni Moslem.

suntuosidad *sf* sumptuousness, magnificence.

suntuoso, **sa** *adj* sumptuous, magnificent.

supeditación *sf* subordination.

supeditar *vt*: **supeditar (a)** to subordinate (to); **estar supeditado a** to be dependent on.

supeditarse *vprnl*: **supeditarse a** to submit to.

súper ◇ *adj* fam great, super. ◇ *adv* fam really. ◇ *sm* fam supermarket. ◇ *sf*: **(gasolina) súper** ≃ four-star (petrol).

superable *adj* surmountable.

superabundancia, sobreabundancia *sf* excess.

superabundante, sobreabundante *adj* excessive.

superación *sf* overcoming; **afán de superación** drive to improve.

superar *vt* - **1.** [mejorar] to beat; [récord] to break; **superar algo/a alguien en algo** to beat sthg/sb in sthg - **2.** [ser superior] to exceed, to surpass - **3.** [adelantar - corredor] to overtake, to

pass - **4.** [época, técnica]: **estar superado** to have been superseded - **5.** [vencer - dificultad etc] to overcome.

superarse *vprnl* - **1.** [mejorar] to better o.s. - **2.** [lucirse] to excel o.s.

superávit *sm inv* surplus.

supercarburante *sm* high-grade fuel.

superchería *sf* fraud, hoax.

superdotado, **da** ◇ *adj* extremely gifted. ◇ *sm, f* extremely gifted person.

superestructura *sf* superstructure.

superficial *adj* lit & fig superficial.

superficialidad *sf* superficiality.

superficie *sf* - **1.** [gen] surface; **salir a la superficie** to surface - **2.** [área] area.

superfino, **na** *adj* superfine.

superfluo, **flua** *adj* superfluous; [gasto] unnecessary.

superhombre *sm* superman.

superintendente *smf* superintendent.

superior, **ra** ◇ *adj* RELIG superior. ◇ *sm, f* RELIG superior (*f* mother superior).

superior ◇ *adj* - **1.** [de arriba] top - **2.** [mayor]: **superior (a)** higher (than) - **3.** [mejor]: **superior (a)** superior (to) - **4.** [excelente] excellent - **5.** ANAT & GEOGR upper - **6.** EDUC higher. ◇ *sm (gen pl)* [jefe] superior.

superioridad *sf* lit & fig superiority; **superioridad sobre algo/alguien** superiority over sthg/sb.

superlativo, **va** *adj* - **1.** [belleza etc] exceptional - **2.** GRAM superlative.

superlativo *sm* GRAM superlative.

supermercado *sm* supermarket.

supernova *sf* supernova.

superpoblación *sf* overpopulation.

superpoblado, **da** *adj* overpopulated.

superponer [65], **sobreponer** *vt* - **1.** [poner encima] to put on top - **2.** *fig* [anteponer]: **superponer algo a algo** to put sthg before sthg.

superposición, sobreposición *sf* superimposing.

superpotencia *sf* superpower.

superproducción *sf* - **1.** ECON overproduction (U) - **2.** CINE blockbuster.

superpuesto, ta, sobrepuesto, ta ◇ *adj* superimposed. ◇ *pp* ▷ **superponer**.

supersónico, **ca** *adj* supersonic.

superstición *sf* superstition.

supersticioso, **sa** *adj* superstitious.

supervalorar *vt* to overvalue, to overrate.

supervalorarse *vprnl* to have too high opinion of o.s.

supervisar *vt* to supervise.

supervisión *sf* supervision.

supervisor, ra ⬦ *adj* supervisory. ⬦ *sm, f* supervisor.

supervivencia *sf* survival.

superviviente, sobreviviente ⬦ *adj* surviving. ⬦ *smf* survivor.

supiera *etc* ⊳ **saber**.

supino, na *adj* - **1.** [tendido] supine - **2.** *fig* [excesivo] utter.

suplantación *sf* replacement; **suplantación (de personalidad)** impersonation.

suplantador, ra *sm, f* impostor.

suplantar *vt* to take the place of.

suplementario, ria *adj* supplementary, extra.

suplemento *sm* - **1.** [gen & PRENSA] supplement; **suplemento dominical** Sunday supplement - **2.** [complemento] attachment.

suplencia *sf* EDUC: **hacer suplencias** ≃ to do supply teaching *(U)*.

suplente ⬦ *adj* stand-in *(antes de s)*. ⬦ *smf* - **1.** [gen] stand-in - **2.** TEATRO understudy - **3.** DEP substitute.

supletorio, ria *adj* additional, extra.
➤ **supletorio** *sm* TELECOM extension.

súplica *sf* - **1.** [ruego] plea, entreaty - **2.** DER petition.

suplicar [10] *vt* - **1.** [rogar]: **suplicar algo (a alguien)** to plead for sthg (with sb); **suplicar a alguien que haga algo** to beg sb to do sthg - **2.** DER to appeal to.

suplicio *sm* *lit & fig* torture.

suplique *etc* ⊳ **suplicar**.

suplir *vt* - **1.** [sustituir]: **suplir algo/a alguien (con)** to replace sthg/sb (with) - **2.** [compensar]: **suplir algo (con)** to compensate for sthg (with).

supo ⊳ **saber**.

suponer [65] ⬦ *vt* - **1.** [creer, presuponer] to suppose - **2.** [implicar] to involve, to entail - **3.** [significar] to mean - **4.** [conjeturar] to imagine; **lo suponía** I guessed as much; **te suponía mayor** I thought you were older. ⬦ *vi* to be important. ⬦ *sm*: **ser un suponer** to be conjecture.
➤ **suponerse** *vprnl* to suppose; **se supone que es el mejor** he's supposed to be the best.

suposición *sf* assumption.

supositorio *sm* suppository.

suprarrenal *adj* suprarenal.

supremacía *sf* supremacy.

supremo, ma *adj* *lit & fig* supreme.
➤ **Supremo** *sm* DER: **el Supremo** the High Court *UK*, the Supreme Court *US*.

supresión *sf* - **1.** [de ley, impuesto, derecho] abolition; [de sanciones, restricciones] lifting - **2.** [de palabras, texto] deletion - **3.** [de puestos de trabajo, proyectos] axing.

suprimir *vt* - **1.** [ley, impuesto, derecho] to abolish; [sanciones, restricciones] to lift - **2.** [palabras, texto] to delete - **3.** [puestos de trabajo, proyectos] to axe.

supuesto, ta ⬦ *pp* ⊳ **suponer**. ⬦ *adj* supposed; [culpable, asesino] alleged; [nombre] falso; **dar algo por supuesto** to take sthg for granted; **por supuesto** of course.
➤ **supuesto** *sm* assumption; **en el supuesto de que...** assuming...; **partimos del supuesto de que...** we work on the assumption that...

supuración *sf* suppuration.

supurar *vi* to suppurate, to fester.

supusiera *etc* ⊳ **suponer**.

sur ⬦ *adj* [posición, parte] south, southern; [dirección, viento] southerly. ⬦ *sm* south.

surcar [10] *vt* [tierra] to plough; [aire, agua] to cut o slice through.

surco *sm* - **1.** [zanja] furrow - **2.** [señal - de disco] groove; [- de rueda] rut - **3.** [arruga] line, wrinkle.

sureño, ña ⬦ *adj* southern; [viento] southerly. ⬦ *sm, f* southerner.

sureste = **sudeste**.

surf, surfing *sm* surfing.

surgir [15] *vi* - **1.** [brotar] to spring forth - **2.** [aparecer] to appear - **3.** *fig* [producirse] to arise.

suroeste = **sudoeste**.

surque *etc* ⊳ **surcar**.

surrealismo *sm* surrealism.

surrealista *adj* & *smf* surrealist.

surtido, da *adj* - **1.** [bien aprovisionado] well-stocked - **2.** [variado] assorted.
➤ **surtido** *sm* - **1.** [gama] range - **2.** [caja surtida] assortment.

surtidor *sm* [de gasolina] pump; [de un chorro] spout.

surtir *vt* [proveer]: **surtir a alguien (de)** to supply sb (with).
➤ **surtirse de** *vprnl* [proveerse de] to stock up on.

susceptibilidad *sf* - **1.** [sensibilidad] sensitivity - **2.** [propensión a ofenderse] touchiness.

susceptible *adj* - **1.** [sensible] sensitive - **2.** [propenso a ofenderse] touchy - **3.** [posible]: **susceptible de** liable to.

suscitar *vt* to provoke; [interés, dudas, sospechas] to arouse.

suscribir, subscribir *vt* - **1.** [firmar] to sign - **2.** [ratificar] to endorse - **3.** COM [acciones] to subscribe for.

➤ **suscribirse, subscribirse** *vprnl* - **1.** PRENSA: **suscribirse (a)** to subscribe (to) - **2.** COM: **suscribirse a** to take out an option on.

suscripción, subscripción *sf* subscription.

suscriptor, ra, subscriptor, ra *sm, f* subscriber.

suscrito, ta, subscrito, ta ◇ *pp* ▷ **suscribir**. ◇ *adj*: **estar suscrito a** to subscribe to.

sushi *sm* CULIN sushi.

susodicho, cha *adj* above-mentioned.

suspender *vt* - **1.** [colgar] to hang (up); **suspender algo de algo** to hang sthg from sthg - **2.** EDUC to fail - **3.** [interrumpir] to suspend; [sesión] to adjourn - **4.** [aplazar] to postpone - **5.** [de un cargo] to suspend; **suspender de empleo y sueldo** to suspend without pay.

suspense *sm* suspense.

suspensión *sf* - **1.** [gen & AUTO] suspension; **en suspensión** in suspension; **suspensión de empleo** suspension on full pay; **suspensión de pagos** suspension of payments - **2.** [aplazamiento] postponement; [de reunión, sesión] adjournment.

suspenso, sa *adj* - **1.** [colgado]: **suspenso de** hanging from - **2.** [no aprobado]: **estar suspenso** to have failed - **3.** *fig* [interrumpido]: **en suspenso** pending.

➤ **suspenso** *sm* failure.

suspensores *smpl* *Andes & Arg* braces *UK*, suspenders *US*.

suspicacia *sf* suspicion.

suspicaz *adj* suspicious.

suspirar *vi* - **1.** [dar suspiros] to sigh; **suspirar de** to sigh with - **2.** *fig* [desear]: **suspirar por algo/por hacer algo** to long for sthg/to do sthg.

suspiro *sm* - **1.** [aspiración] sigh; **dar un suspiro** to heave a sigh - **2.** [instante]: **en un suspiro** in no time at all.

sustancia, substancia *sf* - **1.** [gen] substance; **sin sustancia** lacking in substance - **2.** [esencia] essence - **3.** [de alimento] nutritional value.

➤ **sustancia gris** *sf* grey matter.

sustancial, substancial *adj* substantial, significant.

sustanciar [8], substanciar [8] *vt* - **1.** [resumir] to summarize - **2.** DER to substantiate.

sustancioso, sa, substancioso, sa *adj* substantial.

sustantivación, substantivación *sf* nominalization.

sustantivar, substantivar *vi* nominalize.

sustantivo, va, substantivo, va *adj* GRAM noun *(antes de s)*.

➤ **sustantivo, substantivo** *sm* GRAM noun.

sustentar *vt* - **1.** [gen] to support - **2.** *fig* [mantener - la moral] to keep up; [- argumento, teoría] to defend.

sustento *sm* - **1.** [alimento] sustenance; [mantenimiento] livelihood; **ganarse el sustento** to earn one's living - **2.** [apoyo] support.

sustitución, substitución *sf* - **1.** [cambio] replacement; **la sustitución de Elena por Luis** the substitution of Luis for Elena - **2.** DER subrogation.

sustituible, substituible *adj* replaceable.

sustituir [51], substituir [51] *vt*: **sustituir (por)** to replace (with); **sustituir a Elena por Luis** to replace Elena with Luis, to substitute Luis for Elena.

sustitutivo, va, substitutivo, va *adj* substitute.

➤ **sustitutivo, substitutivo** *sm*: **sustitutivo (de)** substitute (for).

sustituto, ta, substituto, ta *sm, f* substitute, replacement.

susto *sm* fright; **dar** o **pegar un susto a alguien** to give sb a fright; **darse** o **pegarse un susto** to get a fright.

sustracción, substracción *sf* - **1.** [robo] theft - **2.** MAT subtraction.

sustraer [73], substraer [73] *vt* - **1.** [robar] to steal - **2.** MAT to subtract.

➤ **sustraerse, substraerse** *vprnl*: **sustraerse a** o **de** [obligación, problema] to avoid.

sustrato, substrato *sm* substratum.

susurrar *vt & vi* to whisper.

susurro *sm* whisper; *fig* murmur.

sutil *adj* [gen] subtle; [velo, tejido] delicate, thin; [brisa] gentle; [hilo, línea] fine.

sutileza *sf* subtlety; [de velo, tejido] delicacy, thinness; [de brisa] gentleness; [de hilo, línea] fineness.

sutura *sf* suture.

suturar *vt* to stitch.

suyo, ya ◇ *adj poses* [de él] his; [de ella] hers; [de uno] one's (own); [de ellos, ellas] theirs; [de usted, ustedes] yours; **este libro es suyo** this book is his/hers *etc*; **un amigo suyo** a friend of his/hers *etc*; **no es asunto suyo** it's none of his/her *etc* business; **es muy suyo** *fam fig* he/she is really selfish. ◇ *pron poses* - **1.**: **el suyo** [de él] his; [de ella] hers; [de cosa, animal] its (own); [de uno] one's own; [de ellos, ellas] theirs; [de usted, ustedes] yours - **2.** *loc*: **de suyo** in itself; **hacer de las suyas** to be up to his/her *etc* usual tricks; **hacer suyo** to make one's own; **lo suyo es el teatro** he/she *etc* should be on the stage; **lo suyo sería volver** the proper thing to do would be to go back; **los suyos** *fam* [su familia] his/her *etc* folks; [su bando] his/her *etc* lot.

swing [swin] *sm* MÚS swing.

t¹, T *sf* [letra] t, T.

t² (*abrev de* **tonelada**) t.

tabacalero, ra *adj* tobacco *(antes de s)*.

tabaco ◇ *sm* **- 1.** [planta] tobacco plant **- 2.** [picadura] tobacco; **tabaco para liar** rolling tobacco; **tabaco de pipa** pipe tobacco; **tabaco negro/rubio** dark/Virginia tobacco **- 3.** [cigarrillos] cigarettes *pl.* ◇ *adj inv* [color] light brown.

tábano *sm* horsefly.

tabaquismo *sm* nicotine poisoning.

tabardo *sm* (coarse) cloak.

tabarra *sf fam*: **dar la tabarra** to be a pest.

tabasco® *sm* Tabasco®.

taberna *sf country-style bar, usually cheap.*

tabernáculo *sm* tabernacle.

tabernario, ria *adj* coarse.

tabernero, ra *sm, f* [propietario] landlord (*f* landlady); [encargado] bartender *US*, barman (*f* barmaid).

tabicar [10] *vt* to wall up.

tabique *sm* **- 1.** [pared] partition (wall) **- 2.** ANAT: **tabique nasal** nasal septum.

tabla *sf* **- 1.** [plancha] plank; **tabla de planchar** ironing board **- 2.** [pliegue] pleat **- 3.** [lista, gráfico] table; **tabla de multiplicación** o **pitagórica** multiplication o Pythagorean table; **tabla periódica** o **de los elementos** periodic table **- 4.** CULIN: **tabla de cocina** chopping board; **tabla de queso** cheeseboard **- 5.** NÁUT [de surf, vela etc] board **- 6.** ARTE panel **- 7.** *loc*: **ser una tabla de salvación** to be a last resort o hope; **hacer tabla rasa** to wipe the slate clean.

➡ **tablas** *sfpl* **- 1.** [en ajedrez]: **quedar en** o **hacer tablas** to end in stalemate **- 2.** TEATRO stage *sing*, boards: **tener tablas** TEATRO to be an experienced actor; *fig* to be an old hand **- 3.** TAUROM *fence surrounding bullring*.

tablado *sm* [de teatro] stage; [de baile] dancefloor; [plataforma] platform.

tablao *sm* flamenco show.

tablero *sm* **- 1.** [gen] board; **tablero de ajedrez** chessboard **- 2.** [en baloncesto] backboard **- 3.**: **tablero (de mandos)** [de avión] instrument panel; [de coche] dashboard.

tableta *sf* **- 1.** MED tablet **- 2.** [de chocolate] bar.

tablilla *sf* MED splint.

tablón *sm* plank; [en el techo] beam; **tablón de anuncios** notice board.

tabú (*pl* **tabúes** o **tabús**) *adj* & *sm* taboo.

tabulación *sf* tabulation.

tabulador, tabuladora *sm, f* tabulator.

tabular *vt* & *vi* to tabulate.

taburete *sm* stool.

tacañería *sf* meanness, miserliness.

tacaño, ña ◇ *adj* mean, miserly. ◇ *sm, f* mean o miserly person.

tacataca, tacatá *sm* babywalker.

tacha *sf* **- 1.** [defecto] flaw, fault; **sin tacha** faultless **- 2.** [clavo] tack.

tachadura *sf* correction, crossing out.

tachar *vt* **- 1.** [lo escrito] to cross out **- 2.** *fig* [acusar]: **tachar a alguien de mentiroso** *etc* to accuse sb of being a liar *etc*.

tacho *sm Andes & R Plata* waste bin.

tachón *sm* **- 1.** [tachadura] correction, crossing out **- 2.** [clavo] stud.

tachonar *vt* **- 1.** [poner clavos] to decorate with studs **- 2.** *fig* [salpicar] to stud; **tachonado de** studded with.

tachuela *sf* tack.

tácito, ta *adj* tacit; [norma, regla] unwritten.

taciturno, na *adj* taciturn.

taco *sm* **- 1.** [tarugo] plug **- 2.** [cuña] wedge **- 3.** *fam fig* [palabrota] swearword; **soltar un taco** to swear **- 4.** *fam fig* [confusión] mess, muddle; **armarse un taco (con algo)** to get into a muddle (over sthg) **- 5.** [de billar] cue **- 6.** [de hojas, billetes de banco] wad; [de billetes de autobús, metro] book **- 7.** [de jamón, queso] hunk **- 8.** *Andes & R Plata* [tacón] heel **- 9.** [tortilla de maíz] taco.

➡ **tacos** *smpl mfam* [años] years (of age).

tacógrafo *sm* tachograph.

tacón *sm* heel; **de tacón alto** high-heeled; **tacón de aguja** stiletto heel.

taconear *vi* **- 1.** [bailarín] to stamp one's feet **- 2.** MIL to click one's heels.

taconeo *sm* [de bailarín] foot-stamping.

táctico, ca *adj* tactical.

➡ **táctica** *sf lit & fig* tactics *pl*.

táctil *adj* tactile.

tacto *sm* **- 1.** [sentido] sense of touch **- 2.** [textura] feel **- 3.** *fig* [delicadeza] tact **- 4.** MED manual examination.

TAE (*abrev de* **tasa anual equivalente**) *sf* Annual Equivalent Rate.

taekwondo [tae'kwondo] *sm* tae kwon do.

tafetán *sm* taffeta.

tahúr, ra *sm, f* cardsharp.

taifa *sf* HIST *independent Muslim kingdom in Iberian peninsula.*

taiga *sf* taiga.

tailandés, **esa** *adj* & *sm, f* Thai.

◆ **tailandés** *sm* [lengua] Thai.

Tailandia *n pr* Thailand.

taimado, **da** ◇ *adj* crafty. ◇ *sm, f* crafty person.

Taiwán [tai'wan] *n pr* Taiwan.

taiwanés, **esa** *adj* & *sm, f* Taiwanese.

tajada *sf* - **1.** [rodaja] slice - **2.** *fig* [parte] share; **sacar tajada de algo** to get sthg out of sthg - **3.** *fam fig* [borrachera]: **agarrarse una tajada** to get plastered *o* legless.

tajante *adj* [categórico] categorical.

tajo *sm* - **1.** [corte] deep cut - **2.** *fam* [trabajo] workplace, work - **3.** [acantilado] precipice.

Tajo *sm*: **el (río) Tajo** the (River) Tagus.

tal ◇ *adj* - **1.** [semejante, tan grande] such; **¡jamás se vio cosa tal!** you've never seen such a thing!; **lo dijo con tal seguridad que...** he said it with such conviction that...; **dijo cosas tales como...** he said such things as... - **2.** [sin especificar] such and such; **a tal hora** at such and such a time - **3.** [desconocido]: **un tal Pérez** a (certain) Mr Pérez. ◇ *pron* - **1.** [alguna cosa] such a thing - **2.** *loc*: **que si tal que si cual** this, that and the other; **ser tal para cual** to be two of a kind; **tal y cual, tal y tal** this and that; **y tal** [etcétera] and so on. ◇ *adv*: **¿qué tal?** how's it going?, how are you doing?; **¿qué tal fue el viaje?** how was the trip?; **déjalo tal cual** leave it just as it is.

◆ **con tal de** *loc prep* as long as, provided; **con tal de volver pronto...** as long as we're back early...

◆ **con tal (de) que** *loc conj* as long as, provided.

◆ **tal (y) como** *loc conj* just as *o* like.

◆ **tal que** *loc prep fam* [como por ejemplo] like.

tala *sf* felling.

taladrador, **ra** *adj* drilling.

◆ **taladradora** *sf* drill.

taladrar *vt* to drill; *fig* [suj: sonido] to pierce.

taladro *sm* - **1.** [taladradora] drill - **2.** [agujero] drill hole.

tálamo *sm* - **1.** *culto* [cama] bed - **2.** ANAT & BOT thalamus.

talante *sm* - **1.** [humor] mood; **estar de buen talante** to be in good humour - **2.** [carácter] character, disposition.

talar *vt* to fell.

talayote *sm megalithic monument found in the Balearic Islands.*

talco *sm* talc, talcum powder.

talego *sm* - **1.** [talega] sack - **2.** *mfam* [cárcel] nick, slammer - **3.** *mfam* [mil pesetas] 1000 peseta note.

talento *sm* - **1.** [don natural] talent; **de talento** talented - **2.** [inteligencia] intelligence.

talentoso, **sa** *adj* talented.

Talgo (*abrev de* **tren articulado ligero Goicoechea Oriol**) *sm Spanish intercity high-speed train.*

talibán ◇ *adj* taliban. ◇ *sm* taliban.

talidomida *sf* thalidomide.

talión *sm*: **la ley del talión** *an eye for an eye and a tooth for a tooth.*

talismán *sm* talisman.

talla *sf* - **1.** [medida] size; **¿qué talla usas?** what size are you? - **2.** [estatura] height - **3.** *fig* [capacidad] stature; **dar la talla** to be up to it - **4.** [ARTE - en madera] carving; [- en piedra] sculpture - **5.** [de piedras preciosas] cutting.

tallado, **da** *adj* [madera] carved; [piedras preciosas] cut.

◆ **tallado** *sm* [de madera, piedra] carving; [de piedras preciosas] cutting.

tallar *vt* [esculpir - madera, piedra] to carve; [- piedra preciosa] to cut.

tallarín (*gen pl*) *sm* noodle.

talle *sm* - **1.** [cintura] waist - **2.** [figura, cuerpo] figure - **3.** [medida] measurement.

taller *sm* - **1.** [gen] workshop - **2.** AUTO garage - **3.** ARTE studio.

tallista *smf* [de madera] wood carver; [de metales] engraver.

tallo *sm* stem; [brote] sprout, shoot.

talludo, **da** *adj* thick-stemmed; *fig* tall.

Talmud *sm*: **el Talmud** the Talmud.

talón *sm* - **1.** [gen & ANAT] heel; **talón de Aquiles** *fig* Achilles' heel; **pisarle a alguien los talones** to be hot on sb's heels - **2.** [cheque] cheque; [matriz] stub; **talón cruzado/devuelto/en blanco** crossed/bounced/blank cheque; **talón bancario** cashier's cheque *UK*, cashier's check *US*; **talón sin fondos** bad cheque.

talonario *sm* [de cheques] cheque book; [de recibos] receipt book.

talonera *sf* heelpiece.

talud *sm* bank, slope.

tamal *sm* *Amér* tamale.

tamaño, **ña** *adj* such; **¡cómo pudo decir tamaña estupidez!** how could he say such a stupid thing!

◆ **tamaño** *sm* size; **de gran tamaño** large; **de tamaño familiar** family-size; **de tamaño natural** life-size.

tamarindo *sm* tamarind.

tambaleante *adj* - **1.** [inestable - silla etc] wobbly, unsteady; [- persona] staggering - **2.** *fig* [gobierno, sistema] unstable.

tambalearse *vprnl* - **1.** [bambolearse - persona] to stagger, to totter; [- mueble] to wobble, to be unsteady; [- tren] to sway - **2.** *fig* [gobierno, sistema] to totter.

tambaleo *sm* [de tren etc] swaying; [de mueble] wobble; [de persona] staggering.

también *adv* also, too; **yo también** me too; **Juan está enfermo - Elena también** Juan is sick - so is Elena; **también a mí me gusta** I like it too, I also like it.

tambor ◇ *sm* - **1.** MÚS & TECNOL drum; [de pistola] cylinder - **2.** ANAT eardrum - **3.** AUTO brake drum. ◇ *smf* [tamborilero] drummer.

tamboril *sm* small drum.

tamborilear *vi* *fig* & MÚS to drum.

tamborileo *sm* drumming.

tamborilero, ra *sm, f* drummer.

Támesis *sm*: **el (río) Támesis** the (River) Thames.

tamice *etc* ⊳ **tamizar**.

tamiz *sm* - **1.** [cedazo] sieve; **pasar algo por el tamiz** to sift sthg - **2.** *fig* [selección] screening procedure.

tamizar [13] *vt* - **1.** [cribar] to sieve - **2.** *fig* [seleccionar] to screen.

tampoco *adv* neither, not... either; **ella no va y tú tampoco** she's not going and neither are you, she's not going and you aren't either; **¿no lo sabías? – yo tampoco** didn't you know? – me neither O neither did I.

tampón *sm* - **1.** [sello] stamp; [almohadilla] ink-pad - **2.** [para la menstruación] tampon; **tampón contraceptivo** contraceptive sponge.

tam-tam *sm* tom tom.

tan *adv* - **1.** [mucho] so; **tan grande/deprisa** so big/quickly; **¡qué película tan larga!** what a long film!; **tan... que...** so... that...; **tan es así que...** so much so that... - **2.** [en comparaciones]: **tan... como...** as... as...
➤ **tan sólo** *loc adv* only.

tanda *sf* - **1.** [grupo, lote] group, batch - **2.** [serie] series; [de inyecciones] course - **3.** [turno de trabajo] shift.

tándem (*pl* **tándemes, tándems** O **tándem**) *sm* - **1.** [bicicleta] tandem - **2.** [pareja] duo, pair.

tanga *sm* tanga, thong *US*.

tangencial *adj* tangential.

tangente ◇ *adj* tangential. ◇ *sf* tangent; **irse** O **salirse por la tangente** to go off at a tangent.

tangible *adj* tangible.

tango *sm* tango.

tanque *sm* - **1.** MIL tank - **2.** [vehículo cisterna] tanker - **3.** [depósito] tank.

tanqueta *sf* armoured car.

tantear ◇ *vt* - **1.** [sopesar - peso, precio, cantidad] to try to guess; [- problema, posibilidades, ventajas] to weigh up - **2.** [probar, sondear] to test (out) - **3.** [toro, contrincante etc] to size up. ◇ *vi* - **1.** [andar a tientas] to feel one's way - **2.** [apuntar los tantos] to (keep) score.

tanteo *sm* - **1.** [prueba, sondeo] testing out; [de posibilidades, ventajas] weighing up; [de contrincante, puntos débiles] sizing up - **2.** [puntuación] score - **3.** DER: **(derecho de) tanteo** first option *(on a purchase)*.

tanto, ta ◇ *adj* - **1.** [gran cantidad] so much (*pl* so many); **tanto dinero** so much money, such a lot of money; **tanta gente** so many people; **tiene tanto entusiasmo/tantos amigos que...** she has so much enthusiasm/so many friends that... - **2.** [cantidad indeterminada] so much (*pl* so many); **nos daban tantos euros al día** they used to give us so many euros per day; **cuarenta y tantos** forty-something, forty-odd; **nos conocimos en el sesenta y tantos** we met sometime in the Sixties - **3.** [en comparaciones]: **tanto... como** as much... as (*pl* as many... as). ◇ *pron* - **1.** [gran cantidad] so much (*pl* so many); **¿cómo puedes tener tantos?** how can you have so many? - **2.** [cantidad indeterminada] so much (*pl* so many); **a tantos de agosto** on such and such a date in August - **3.** [igual cantidad] as much (*pl* so many); **había mucha gente aquí, allí no había tanta** there were a lot of people here, but not as many there; **otro tanto** as much again, the same again; **otro tanto le ocurrió a los demás** the same thing happened to the rest of them - **4.** *loc*: **ser uno de tantos** to be nothing special.
➤ **tanto** ◇ *sm* - **1.** [punto] point; [gol] goal; **marcar un tanto** to score - **2.** *fig* [ventaja] point; **apuntarse un tanto** to earn o.s. a point - **3.** [cantidad indeterminada]: **un tanto** so much, a certain amount; **tanto por ciento** percentage - **4.** *loc*: **estar al tanto (de)** to be on the ball (about). ◇ *adv* - **1.** [mucho]: **tanto (que...)** [cantidad] so much (that...); [tiempo] so long (that...); **no bebas tanto** don't drink so much; **de eso hace tanto que ya no me acordaba** it's been so long since that happened that I don't even remember; **¿tanto te gusta?** do you like it that much?; **tanto mejor/peor** so much the better/worse; **tanto más cuanto que...** all the more so because... - **2.** [en comparaciones]: **tanto como** as much as; **tanto hombres como mujeres** both men and women; **tanto si estoy como si no** whether I'm there or not - **3.** *loc*: **¡y tanto!** most certainly!, you bet!

◆ **tantas** *sfpl fam*: **eran las tantas** it was very late.

◆ **en tanto (que)** *loc conj* while.

◆ **entre tanto** *loc adv* meanwhile.

◆ **por (lo) tanto** *loc conj* therefore, so.

◆ **tanto (es así) que** *loc conj* so much so that.

◆ **un tanto** *loc adv* [un poco] a bit, rather.

Tanzania *n pr* Tanzania.

tanzano, na *adj* & *sm, f* Tanzanian.

tañer ⬦ *vt* [instrumento] to play; [campana] to ring. ⬦ *vi* [campana] to ring.

tañido *sm* [de instumento] sound; [de campana] ringing.

taoísmo *sm* Taoism.

tapa *sf* - **1.** [de caja, baúl, recipiente] lid; **levantarse** O **volarse la tapa de los sesos** *fam* to blow one's brains out - **2.** [aperitivo] snack, tapa; **irse de tapas** to go for some tapas - **3.** [de libro] cover - **4.** [de zapato] heel plate - **5.** [pieza de carne] topside - **6.** *Andes* & *R Dom* [de botella] top; [de frasco] stopper.

tapabarro *sm Andes* mudguard.

tapacubos *sm inv* hubcap.

tapadera *sf* - **1.** [tapa] lid - **2.** [para encubrir] front.

tapadillo ◆ **de tapadillo** *loc adv fam* on the sly.

tapado *sm* - **1.** *R Plata* [abrigo] overcoat - **2.** *Méx fam* [candidato] *undeclared presidential candidate.*

tapar *vt* - **1.** [cerrar - ataúd, cofre] to close (the lid of); [- olla, caja] to put the lid on; [- botella] to put the top on - **2.** [ocultar, cubrir] to cover; [no dejar ver] to block out; [obstruir] to block - **3.** [abrigar - con ropa] to wrap up; [- en la cama] to tuck in - **4.** [encubrir] to cover up - **5.** *Chile* & *Méx* [empaste] to fill.

◆ **taparse** *vprnl* - **1.** [cubrirse] to cover (up) - **2.** [abrigarse - con ropa] to wrap up; [- en la cama] to tuck o.s. in.

taparrabos *sm inv* - **1.** [de hombre primitivo] loincloth - **2.** *fam* [tanga] tanga briefs *pl.*

tapear *vi* to have some tapas.

tapete *sm* - **1.** [paño] runner; [de billar, para cartas] baize; **estar sobre el tapete** *fig* to be up for discussion; **poner algo sobre el tapete** *fig* to put sthg up for discussion - **2.** *Col* & *Méx* [alfombra] rug.

tapia *sf* (stone) wall; **estar sordo como una tapia** *fam* to be (as) deaf as a post.

tapiar [8] *vt* - **1.** [cercar] to wall in - **2.** [enladrillar] to brick up.

tapice *etc* ⊳ **tapizar**.

tapicería *sf* - **1.** [tela] upholstery - **2.** [tienda - para muebles] upholsterer's; [- para cortinas] draper's - **3.** [oficio - de muebles] upholstery; [- de tapices] tapestry making - **4.** [tapices] tapestries *pl.*

tapicero, ra *sm, f* - **1.** [de muebles] upholsterer - **2.** [de tapices] tapestry maker.

tapioca *sf* tapioca.

tapiz *sm* [para la pared] tapestry; *fig* [de nieve, flores] carpet.

tapizado *sm* - **1.** [de mueble] upholstery - **2.** [de pared] tapestries *pl.*

tapizar [13] *vt* [mueble] to upholster; *fig* [campos, calles] to carpet, to cover.

tapón *sm* - **1.** [para tapar - botellas, frascos] stopper; [- de corcho] cork; [- de metal, plástico] cap, top; [- de bañera, lavabo] plug; **tapón de rosca** screw-top - **2.** [en el oído - de cerumen] wax (*U*) in the ear; [- de algodón] earplug - **3.** [atasco] traffic jam - **4.** *fam* [persona] tubby person - **5.** [en baloncesto] block - **6.** *Amér* [fusible] fuse.

taponar *vt* - **1.** [cerrar - lavadero] to put the plug in; [- salida] to block; [- tubería] to stop up - **2.** MED to tampon.

◆ **taponarse** *vprnl* to get blocked; **se le taponaron los oídos** his ears got blocked.

tapujo *sm*: **andarse contapujos** [rodeos] to beat about the bush; **hacer algo sin tapujos** to do sthg openly.

taquería *sf Méx* [quiosco] taco stall; [restaurante] taco restaurant.

taquicardia *sf* tachycardia.

taquigrafía *sf* shorthand, stenography.

taquigrafiar [9] *vt* to write (down) in shorthand.

taquígrafo, fa *sm, f* shorthand writer, stenographer.

taquilla *sf* - **1.** [ventanilla - gen] ticket office, booking office; CINE & TEATRO box office; **en taquilla** at the ticket/box office - **2.** [recaudación] takings *pl* - **3.** [armario] locker - **4.** [casillero] set of pigeonholes.

taquillero, ra ⬦ *adj*: **es un espectáculo taquillero** the show is a box-office hit. ⬦ *sm, f* ticket clerk.

taquimecanografía *sf* shorthand and typing.

taquimecanógrafo, fa *sm, f* shorthand typist.

tara *sf* - **1.** [defecto] defect - **2.** [peso] tare.

tarado, da ⬦ *adj* - **1.** [defectuoso] defective - **2.** *fam despec* [tonto] thick. ⬦ *sm, f fam despec* idiot.

tarántula *sf* tarantula.

tararear *vt* to hum.

tarareo *sm* humming.

tardanza *sf* lateness.

tardar *vi* - **1.** [llevar tiempo] to take; **esto va a tardar** this will take time; **tardó un año en hacerlo** she took a year to do it; **¿cuánto tardarás (en hacerlo)?** how long will you be (doing it)?, how long will it take you (to do it)? - **2.** [retrasarse] to be late; [ser lento] to be slow; **¡no tardéis!** don't be long!; **tardar en hacer algo** to take a long time to do sthg; **no tardaron en hacerlo** they were quick to do it; **a más tardar** at the latest.

tarde ◇ *sf* [hasta las cinco] afternoon; [después de las cinco] evening; **por la tarde** [hasta las cinco] in the afternoon; [después de las cinco] in the evening; **buenas tardes** [hasta las cinco] good afternoon; [después de las cinco] good evening; **de tarde en tarde** from time to time; **muy de tarde en tarde** very occasionally. ◇ *adv* [gen] late; [en exceso] too late; **ya es tarde para eso** it's too late for that now; **llegar tarde** to be late; **se está haciendo tarde** it's getting late; **tarde o temprano** sooner or later; **más vale tarde que nunca** better late than never.

tardío, a *adj* [gen] late; [intento, decisión] belated.

tardo, da *adj* - **1.** [lento] slow - **2.** [torpe] dull; **tardo de oído** hard of hearing.

tardón, ona *sm, f* - **1.** [impuntual] person who is always late - **2.** [lento] slowcoach.

tarea *sf* [gen] task; EDUC homework; **tareas de la casa** housework *(U)*.

tarifa *sf* - **1.** [precio] charge; COM tariff; [en transportes] fare; **tarifa plana** flat rate - **2.** *(gen pl)* [lista] price list.

tarifar ◇ *vt* to price. ◇ *vi fam*: **salir tarifando (con)** to have a row (with).

tarima *sf* - **1.** [estrado] platform - **2.** [suelo] floorboards *pl*.

tarjeta *sf* [gen & INFORM] card; **tarjeta amarilla/roja** DEP yellow/red card; **tarjeta de cliente** store card; **tarjeta de crédito/débito** credit/debit card; **tarjeta de embarque** boarding pass; **tarjeta de felicitación** greetings card; **tarjeta postal** postcard; **tarjeta de recarga** top-up card; **tarjeta de sonido/vídeo** sound/video card; **tarjeta telefónica** postcard; **tarjeta de visita** visiting *o* calling card.

tarot *sm* tarot.

tarrina *sf* tub.

tarro *sm* - **1.** [recipiente] jar - **2.** *mfam* [cabeza] nut, bonce.

tarso *sm* tarsus.

tarta *sf* [gen] cake; [plana, con base de pasta dura] tart; [plana, con base de bizcocho] flan; **tarta de cumpleaños** birthday cake; **tarta helada** ice cream gâteau.

tartajear *vi fam* to stammer, to stutter.

tartaleta *sf* tartlet.

tartamudear *vi* to stammer, to stutter.

tartamudeo *sm* stammer, stammering *(U)*.

tartamudez *sf* stammer, stutter.

tartamudo, da ◇ *adj* stammering, stuttering. ◇ *sm, f* stammerer, stutterer.

tartán *sm* tartan.

tartana *sf* - **1.** [carruaje] trap - **2.** *fam* [coche viejo] banger.

tártaro, ra ◇ *adj* - **1.** [pueblo] Tartar - **2.** ▷ **salsa.** ◇ *sm, f* Tartar.

tartera *sf* [fiambrera] lunch box.

tarugo *sm* - **1.** [de madera] block of wood; [de pan] chunk (of stale bread) - **2.** *fam* [necio] blockhead.

tarumba *adj fam* crazy.

tasa *sf* - **1.** [índice] rate; **tasa de mortalidad/natalidad** death/birth rate; **tasa de paro** *o* **desempleo** (level of) unemployment - **2.** [impuesto] tax; **tasas de aeropuerto** airport tax - **3.** EDUC: **tasas** fees - **4.** [tasación] valuation.

tasación *sf* valuation.

tasador, ra *sm, f* valuer.

tasar *vt* - **1.** [valorar] to value - **2.** [fijar precio] to fix a price for.

tasca *sf* ≃ pub; **ir de tascas** to go on a pub crawl.

tasquear *vi* to go on a pub crawl.

tasqueo *sm* pub crawling.

tata *sm Amér fam* [padre] dad, daddy, pop *US*; ▷ **tato.**

tatarabuelo, la *sm, f* great-great-grandfather (*f* great-great-grandmother).

tataranieto, ta *sm, f* great-great-grandson (*f* great-great-granddaughter).

tate *interj*: **¡tate!** [¡cuidado!] watch out!; [¡ya comprendo!] I see!

tato, ta *fam sm, f* [hermano] big brother (*f* big sister).

◆ **tata** *sf* [niñera] nanny.

tatuaje *sm* - **1.** [dibujo] tattoo - **2.** [acción] tattooing.

tatuar [6] *vt* to tattoo.

◆ **tatuarse** *vprnl* to have a tattoo done.

taurino, na *adj* bullfighting *(antes de s)*.

tauro ◇ *sm* [zodiaco] Taurus; **ser tauro** to be (a) Taurus. ◇ *smf* [persona] Taurean.

tauromaquia *sf* bullfighting.

tautología *sf* tautology.

tautológico, ca *adj* tautological.

taxativo, va *adj* precise, exact.

taxi *sm* taxi.

taxidermia *sf* taxidermy.

taxidermista *smf* taxidermist.

taxímetro *sm* taximeter.

taxista *smf* taxi driver.

taxonomía *sf* taxonomy.

Tayikistán *sm* Tajikistan, Tadjikistan.

taza *sf* - **1.** [para beber] cup; **una taza de té** [recipiente] a teacup; [contenido] a cup of tea - **2.** [de retrete] bowl.

tazón *sm* bowl.

te *pron pers* - **1.** *(complemento directo)* you; **le gustaría verte** she'd like to see you - **2.** *(complemento indirecto)* (to) you; **te lo dio** he gave it to you; **te tiene miedo** he's afraid of you - **3.** *(reflexivo)* yourself - **4.** *(valor impersonal) fam:* **si te dejas pisar, estás perdido** if you let people walk all over you, you've had it.

té *(pl* **tés)** *sm* tea.

tea *sf* [antorcha] torch.

teatral *adj* - **1.** [de teatro - gen] theatre *(antes de s)*; [- grupo] drama *(antes de s)* - **2.** [exagerado] theatrical.

teatralidad *sf* theatrical nature.

teatralizar [13] *vt* to exaggerate.

teatro *sm* - **1.** [gen] theatre; **teatro de la ópera** opera house; **teatro de variedades** music hall *UK*, variety, vaudeville *US*; **teatro lírico** opera and light opera - **2.** *fig* [fingimiento] playacting; **hacer teatro** to playact - **3.** *fig* [escenario] scene.

tebeo® *sm* (children's) comic; **estar más visto que el tebeo** to be old hat.

teca *sf* teak.

techado *sm* roof; **bajo techado** under cover.

techar *vt* to roof.

techo *sm* - **1.** [gen] roof; [dentro de casa] ceiling; **techo solar** AUTO sun roof; **bajo techo** under cover - **2.** *fig* [límite] ceiling.

➡ **sin techo** *smf:* **los sin techo** the homeless.

techumbre *sf* roof.

tecla *sf* [gen, INFORM & MÚS] key; **tecla de borrado/control/función/retorno/suprimir** erase/control/function/return/delete key; **pulsar** *o* **tocar una tecla** to press *o* strike a key; **tocar muchas teclas** [contactar] to pull lots of strings; [abarcar mucho] to have too many things on the go at once.

teclado *sm* [gen & MÚS] keyboard; **teclado expandido** expanded keyboard; **teclado numérico** numeric keypad.

teclear *vt & vi* [en ordenador etc] to type; [en piano] to play.

tecleo *sm* [en piano] playing; [en máquina de escribir] clattering.

teclista *smf* keyboard player.

tecnicismo *sm* - **1.** [cualidad] technical nature - **2.** [término] technical term.

técnico, ca ⬦ *adj* technical. ⬦ *sm, f* - **1.** [mecánico] technician - **2.** [experto] expert - **3.** DEP [entrenador] coach, manager *UK*.

➡ **técnica** *sf* - **1.** [gen] technique - **2.** [tecnología] technology.

tecnicolor *sm* Technicolor®.

tecnificar [10] *vt* to apply technology to.

tecno ⬦ *adj inv* MÚS techno. ⬦ *sm inv* MÚS techno (music).

tecnocracia *sf* technocracy.

tecnócrata ⬦ *adj* technocratic. ⬦ *smf* technocrat.

tecnología *sf* technology; **tecnologías de la información** information technology; **tecnología punta** state-of-the-art technology.

tecnológico, ca *adj* technological.

tecnólogo, ga *sm, f* technologist.

tecolote *sm Amér C & Méx* [búho] owl; [policía] cop *(on night patrol)*.

tectónico, ca *adj* tectonic.

➡ **tectónica** *sf* tectonics *(U)*.

tedéum *sm inv* Te Deum.

tedio *sm* boredom, tedium.

tedioso, sa *adj* tedious.

teflón® *sm* Teflon®.

Tegucigalpa *n pr* Tegucigalpa.

Teherán *n pr* Teheran.

teja *sf* - **1.** [de tejado] tile; **color teja** brick red - **2.** CULIN potato waffle.

tejado *sm* roof.

tejano, na ⬦ *adj* - **1.** [de Texas] Texan - **2.** [tela] denim. ⬦ *sm, f* [persona] Texan.

➡ **tejanos** *smpl* [pantalones] jeans.

tejar ⬦ *sm* brickworks *sing.* ⬦ *vt & vi* to tile.

tejedor, ra ⬦ *adj* weaving. ⬦ *sm, f* weaver.

tejeduría *sf* - **1.** [arte] weaving - **2.** [taller] weaver's shop.

tejemaneje *sm fam* - **1.** [maquinación] intrigue - **2.** [ajetreo] to-do, fuss.

tejer ⬦ *vt* - **1.** [gen] to weave; [labor de punto] to knit - **2.** [telaraña] to spin - **3.** *fig* [labrar - porvenir] to carve out; [- ruina] to bring about. ⬦ *vi* [hacer ganchillo] to crochet; [hacer punto] to knit.

tejido *sm* - **1.** [tela] fabric, material; [en industria] textile - **2.** ANAT tissue.

tejo *sm* - **1.** [juego] hopscotch - **2.** BOT yew - **3.** *loc:* **tirar los tejos a alguien** *fam* to try it on with sb.

tejón *sm* badger.

tel., teléf. *(abrev de* **teléfono)** tel.

tela *sf* - **1.** [tejido] fabric, material; [retal] piece of material; **tela de araña** cobweb; **tela asfáltica** asphalt roofing/flooring; **tela metálica** wire netting - **2.** ARTE [lienzo] canvas - **3.** *fam* [dinero] dough - **4.** *fam* [cosa complicada]: **el examen era tela** the exam was really tricky; **tener (mucha) tela** [ser difícil] to be (very) tricky; **hay tela (para rato)** [trabajo] there's no shortage of

things to do; ¡**tela marinera!** that's too much!
- **5.** *loc:* **poner en tela de juicio** to call into
question.
telar *sm* - **1.** [máquina] loom - **2.** *(gen pl)* [fábrica]
textiles mill - **3.** TEATRO gridiron.
telaraña *sf* spider's web, cobweb; **la telaraña
mundial** INFORM the (World Wide) Web.
tele *sf fam* telly.
teleadicto, ta *sm, f* telly-addict.
telearrastre *sm* ski-tow.
telecabina *sf* cable-car.
telecomedia *sf* television comedy programme.
telecomunicación *sf* [medio] telecommunic-
ation.
➡ **telecomunicaciones** *sfpl* [red] telecommunications.
telediario *sm* television news *(U)*.
teledirigido, da *adj* remote-controlled.
teledirigir [15] *vt* to operate by remote control.
teléf. *(abrev de* **teléfono)** = **tel.**
telefax *sm inv* telefax, fax.
teleférico *sm* cable-car.
telefilme, telefilm *(pl* telefilms) *sm* TV film.
telefonazo *sm fam* ring, buzz; **dar un telefonazo a alguien** to give sb a ring o buzz.
telefonear *vt & vi* to phone.
telefonía *sf* telephony; **telefonía móvil** mobile phones *pl*.
telefónico, ca *adj* telephone *(antes de s)*.
telefonillo *sm fam* [en vivienda] entryphone.
telefonista *smf* telephonist.
teléfono *sm* - **1.** [gen] telephone, phone; **coger el teléfono** to answer the phone; **hablar
por teléfono** to be on the phone; **llamar por
teléfono** to phone; **teléfono fijo/inalámbri-
co/móvil** land line/cordless/mobile UK o cell
US phone; **teléfono público** public phone; **teléfono rojo** hot line; **teléfono WAP** WAP
phone - **2.:** **(número de) teléfono** telephone
number.
telefotografía *sf* telephotography.
telegrafía *sf* telegraphy.
telegrafiar [9] *vt & vi* to telegraph.
telegráfico, ca *adj lit & fig* telegraphic.
telegrafista *smf* telegraphist.
telégrafo *sm* [medio, aparato] telegraph.
➡ **telégrafos** *smpl* [oficina] telegraph office *sing*.
telegrama *sm* telegram.
telele *sm:* **le dio un telele** [desmayo] he had a
fainting fit; [enfado] he had a fit.
telemando *sm* remote control.
telemática *sf* telematics *(U)*.

telémetro *sm* telemeter.
telenovela *sf* television soap opera.
teleobjetivo *sm* telephoto lens.
telepatía *sf* telepathy.
telepático, ca *adj* telepathic.
telequinesia *sf* telekinesis *(U)*.
telescópico, ca *adj* telescopic.
telescopio *sm* telescope.
telesilla *sm* chair lift.
telespectador, ra *sm, f* viewer.
telesquí *sm* ski lift.
teletexto *sm* Teletext®.
teletienda *sf* home shopping programme.
teletipo *sm* - **1.** [aparato] teleprinter - **2.** [texto]
Teletype®.
teletrabajador, ra *sm, f* teleworker.
teletrabajo *sm* teleworking.
televendedor, ra *sm, f* telesales assistant.
televenta *sf* - **1.** [por teléfono] telesales *pl*
- **2.** [por televisión] *TV advertising in which a
phone number is given for clients to contact.*
televidente *smf* viewer.
televisado, da *adj* televised.
televisar *vt* to televise.
televisión *sf* - **1.** [sistema, empresa] television;
salir en o **por (la) televisión** to be on television; **televisión en blanco y negro/en color**
black and white/colour television; **televisión
digital** digital television; **televisión interacti-
va** interactive television; **televisión por ca-
ble/vía satélite** cable/satellite television; **televisión privada/pública** commercial/public
television - **2.** [televisor] television (set).
televisivo, va *adj* television *(antes de s)*.
televisor *sm* television (set); **televisor de
pantalla plana** flatscreen television; **televisor
panorámico** o **de pantalla ancha** widescreen
television.
télex *sm inv* telex; **mandar por télex** to telex.
telón *sm* [de escenario - delante] curtain; [- de-
trás] backcloth; **el telón de acero** HIST the Iron
Curtain; **telón de fondo** *fig* backdrop.
telonero, ra ◇ *adj* support *(antes de s)*.
◇ *sm, f* [cantante] support artist; [grupo] support band.
telúrico, ca *adj* telluric.
tema *sm* - **1.** [asunto] subject; **temas de actualidad** current affairs - **2.** MÚS [de composición,
película] theme; [canción] song - **3.** EDUC [de asignatura, oposiciones] topic; [en libro de texto] unit.
temario *sm* [de asignatura] curriculum; [de opo-
siciones] list of topics.
temático, ca *adj* thematic.
➡ **temática** *sf* subject matter.
tembladera *sf fam* trembling fit.

temblar [19] *vi* - **1.** [tiritar]: **temblar (de)** [gen] to tremble (with); [de frío] to shiver (with); **tiemblo por lo que pueda pasarle** I shudder to think what could happen to him - **2.** [vibrar - suelo, edificio, vehículo] to shudder, to shake; [- voz] to tremble, to shake; **dejar algo temblando** *fam fig* [nevera, botella] to leave sthg almost empty.

tembleque *sm fam* trembling fit; **le dio** *o* **entró un tembleque** he got the shakes.

temblor *sm* shaking *(U)*, trembling *(U)*; **temblor de tierra** earthquake.

tembloroso, sa *adj* trembling, shaky.

temer <> *vt* - **1.** [tener miedo de] to fear, to be afraid of - **2.** [sospechar] to fear. <> *vi* to be afraid; **no temas** don't worry; **temer por** to fear for.

<> **temerse** *vprnl*: **temerse que** to be afraid that, to fear that; **me temo que no vendrá** I'm afraid she won't come; **me temo que sí/no** I'm afraid so/not; **temerse lo peor** to fear the worst.

temerario, ria *adj* rash; [conducción] reckless.

temeridad *sf* - **1.** [cualidad] recklessness - **2.** [acción] folly *(U)*, reckless act.

temeroso, sa *adj* [receloso] fearful.

temible *adj* fearsome.

temor *sm*: **temor (a** *o* **de)** fear (of); **por temor a** *o* **de** for fear of.

témpano *sm*: **témpano (de hielo)** ice floe; **como un témpano** *fig* freezing.

temperado, da *adj* temperate.

temperamental *adj* - **1.** [cambiante] temperamental - **2.** [impulsivo] impulsive.

temperamento *sm* temperament.

temperatura *sf* temperature; **tomar la temperatura a alguien** to take sb's temperature; **temperatura máxima/mínima** highest/lowest temperature; **temperatura ambiente** room temperature.

tempestad *sf* storm.

tempestuoso, sa *adj lit & fig* stormy.

templado, da *adj* - **1.** [tibio - agua, bebida, comida] lukewarm - **2.** GEOGR [clima, zona] temperate - **3.** [nervios] steady; [persona, carácter] calm, composed.

templanza *sf* - **1.** [serenidad] composure - **2.** [moderación] moderation.

templar <> *vt* - **1.** [entibiar - lo frío] to warm (up); [- lo caliente] to cool down - **2.** [calmar - nervios, ánimos] to calm; [- ira] to restrain - **3.** TECNOL [metal etc] to temper - **4.** MÚS to tune. <> *vi* [entibiarse] to get milder.

<> **templarse** *vprnl* [lo frío] to warm up; [lo caliente] to cool down.

templario *sm* Templar.

temple *sm* - **1.** [serenidad] composure - **2.** TECNOL tempering - **3.** ARTE tempera; **al temple** in tempera.

templete *sm* pavilion.

templo *sm lit & fig* temple; **como un templo** *fig* huge.

tempo *sm* tempo.

temporada *sf* - **1.** [periodo concreto] season; [de exámenes] period; **de temporada** [fruta, trabajo] seasonal; **temporada alta/baja** high/low season; **temporada media** mid-season - **2.** [periodo indefinido] (period of) time; **pasé una temporada en el extranjero** I spent some time abroad.

temporal <> *adj* - **1.** [provisional] temporary - **2.** [del tiempo] time *(s)* - **3.** ANAT & RELIG temporal. <> *sm* - **1.** [tormenta] storm; **capear el temporal** *lit & fig* to ride out the storm - **2.** ANAT temporal bone.

temporalidad *sf* temporary nature.

temporario, ria *adj Amér* temporary.

temporero, ra *sm, f* casual labourer.

temporizador *sm* timing device.

tempranero, ra *adj* [persona] early-rising.

temprano, na *adj* early.

<> **temprano** *adv* early.

ten <> tener.

<> **ten con ten** *sm* tact.

tenacidad *sf* tenacity.

tenacillas *sfpl* tongs; [para vello] tweezers; [para rizar el pelo] curling tongs.

tenaz *adj* - **1.** [perseverante] tenacious - **2.** [persistente] stubborn.

tenaza (*gen pl*) *sf* - **1.** [herramienta] pliers *pl* - **2.** [pinzas] tongs *pl* - **3.** ZOOL pincer.

tendedero *sm* - **1.** [cuerda] clothes line; [armazón] clothes horse - **2.** [lugar] drying place.

tendencia *sf* tendency; **tendencia a hacer algo** tendency to do sthg; **tendencia a la depresión** tendency to get depressed; **nuevas tendencias** [en moda, arte] new trends.

tendencioso, sa *adj* tendentious.

tender [20] *vt* - **1.** [colgar - ropa] to hang out - **2.** [tumbar] to lay (out) - **3.** [extender] to stretch (out); [mantel] to spread - **4.** [dar - cosa] to hand; [- mano] to hold out, to offer - **5.** [entre dos puntos - cable, vía] to lay; [- puente] to build; [- cuerda] to stretch - **6.** *fig* [preparar - trampa etc] to lay - **7.** *Amér* [cama] to make; [mesa] to set, to lay.

<> **tender a** *vi* - **1.** [propender]: **tender a hacer algo** to tend to do something; **tender a la depresión** to have a tendency to get depressed - **2.** MAT to approach.

<> **tenderse** *vprnl* to stretch out, to lie down.

tenderete *sm* [puesto] stall.

tendero, ra *sm, f* shopkeeper.

tendido, da *adj* - **1.** [extendido, tumbado] stretched out - **2.** [colgado - ropa] hung out, on the line.

→ **tendido** *sm* - **1.** [instalación - de puente] construction; [- de cable, vía] laying; **tendido eléctrico** electrical installation - **2.** TAUROM front rows *pl*.

tendón *sm* tendon.

tendrá *etc v* ▷ **tener**.

tenebrismo *sm* tenebrism.

tenebroso, sa *adj* dark, gloomy; *fig* shady, sinister.

tenedor¹ *sm* [utensilio] fork.

tenedor², **ra** *sm, f* [poseedor] holder; **tenedor de acciones** shareholder; **tenedor de libros** COM bookkeeper.

teneduría *sf* COM bookkeeping.

tenencia *sf* possession; **tenencia ilícita de armas** illegal possession of arms.

→ **tenencia de alcaldía** *sf* deputy mayor's office.

tener [72] ◇ *v aux* - **1.** *(antes de pp)* [haber]: **teníamos pensado ir al teatro** we had thought of going to the theatre; **te lo tengo dicho** I've told you many times - **2.** *(antes de adj)* [hacer estar]: **me tuvo despierto** it kept me awake; **eso la tiene despistada** that has confused her - **3.** [expresa obligación]: **tener que hacer algo** to have to do sthg; **tiene que ser así** it has to be this way - **4.** [expresa propósito]: **tenemos que ir a cenar un día** we ought to O should go for dinner some time. ◇ *vt* - **1.** [gen] to have; **tengo un hermano** I have O I've got a brother; **tener fiebre** to have a temperature; **tuvieron una pelea** they had a fight; **tener un niño** to have a baby; **¡que tengo buen viaje!** have a good journey!; **hoy tengo clase** I have to go to school today - **2.** [medida, edad, sensación, cualidad] to be; **tiene 3 metros de ancho** it's 3 metres wide; **¿cuántos años tienes?** how old are you?; **tiene diez años** she's ten (years old); **tener hambre/miedo** to be hungry/afraid; **tener mal humor** to be bad-tempered; **le tiene lástima** he feels sorry for her - **3.** [sujetar] to hold; **¿puedes tenerme esto?** could you hold this for me, please?; **tenlo por el asa** hold it by the handle - **4.** [tomar]: **ten el libro que me pediste** here's the book you asked me for; **¡aquí tienes!** here you are! - **5.** [recibir] to get; **tuve un verdadero desengaño** I was really disappointed; **tendrá una sorpresa** he'll get a surprise - **6.** [valorar]: **me tienen por tonto** they think I'm stupid; **tener a alguien en mucho** to think the world of sb - **7.** [guardar, contener] to keep - **8.** *Amér* [llevar]: **tengo tres años aquí** I've been here for three years - **9.** *loc*: **no las tiene todas consigo**

he is not too sure about it; **tener a bien hacer algo** to be kind enough to do sthg; **tener que ver con algo/alguien** [estar relacionado] to have something to do with sthg/sb; [ser equiparable] to be in the same league as sthg/sb.

→ **tenerse** *vprnl* - **1.** [sostenerse]: **tenerse de pie** to stand upright - **2.** [considerarse]: **se tiene por listo** he thinks he's clever.

tengo ▷ **tener**.

tenia *sf* tapeworm.

tenida *sf Chile* suit.

teniente ◇ *sm* lieutenant; **teniente coronel/general** lieutenant colonel/general. ◇ *adj fam* [sordo] deaf (as a post).

→ **teniente (de) alcalde** *smf* deputy mayor.

tenis *sm inv* tennis; **tenis de mesa** table tennis.

tenista *smf* tennis player.

tenístico, ca *adj* tennis *(antes de s)*.

tenor *sm* - **1.** MÚS tenor - **2.** [estilo] tone; **a este tenor** along those lines.

→ **a tenor de** *loc prep* in view of.

tenorio *sm* ladies' man, Casanova.

tensado *sm* tightening.

tensar *vt* [cable, cuerda] to tauten; [arco] to draw.

tensión *sf* - **1.** [gen] tension; **tensión nerviosa** nervous tension - **2.** TECNOL [estiramiento] stress; **en tensión** tensed - **3.** MED: **tensión (arterial)** blood pressure; **tener la tensión alta/baja** to have high/low blood pressure; **tomar la tensión a alguien** to take sb's blood pressure - **4.** ELECTR voltage; **alta tensión** high voltage.

tenso, sa *adj* taut; *fig* tense.

tensor, ra *adj* tightening.

→ **tensor** *sm* - **1.** [dispositivo] turnbuckle - **2.** ANAT tensor.

tentación *sf* temptation; **caer en la tentación** to give in to temptation; **tener la tentación de** to be tempted to; **estos bombones son una tentación** these chocolates are really tempting.

tentáculo *sm* tentacle.

tentador, ra *adj* tempting.

tentar [19] *vt* - **1.** [palpar] to feel - **2.** [atraer, incitar] to tempt.

tentativa *sf* attempt; **tentativa de asesinato** attempted murder; **tentativa de suicidio** suicide attempt.

tentempié *(pl* **tentempiés)** *sm* snack.

tenue *adj* - **1.** [tela, hilo, lluvia] fine - **2.** [luz, sonido, dolor] faint - **3.** [relación] tenuous.

teñido *sm* dyeing.

teñir [26] *vt* - **1.** [ropa, pelo]: **teñir algo (de rojo etc)** to dye sthg (red *etc*) - **2.** *fig* [matizar]: **teñir algo (de)** to tinge sthg (with).

→ **teñirse** *vprnl*: **teñirse (el pelo)** to dye one's hair.

teología *sf* theology; **teología de la liberación** liberation theology.

teológico, **ca** *adj* theological.

teólogo, **ga** *sm, f* theologian.

teorema *sm* theorem.

teoría *sf* theory; **en teoría** in theory; **teoría del conocimiento** epistemology; **teoría de la información** information theory.

teóricamente *adv* theoretically.

teórico, **ca** ◇ *adj* theoretical; **clase teórica** theory class. ◇ *sm, f* [persona] theorist.

teorizar [13] *vi* to theorize.

tequila *sm o sf* tequila.

terapeuta *smf* therapist.

terapéutico, **ca** *adj* therapeutic.
◆ **terapéutica** *sf* therapeutics *(U)*.

terapia *sf* therapy; **terapia ocupacional/de grupo** occupational/group therapy.

tercer ▷ tercero.

tercera ▷ tercero.

tercermundista *adj* third-world *(antes de s)*.

tercero, **ra** *num (antes de sm sing:* **tercer***)* third; **a la tercera va la vencida** third time lucky.
◆ **tercero** *sm* - **1.** [piso] third floor - **2.** [curso] third year - **3.** [mediador, parte interesada] third party; **el tercero en discordia** the third party.
◆ **tercera** *sf* AUTO third (gear).

terceto *sm* - **1.** MÚS trio - **2.** [estrofa] tercet.

terciar [8] ◇ *vt* - **1.** [poner en diagonal - gen] to place diagonally; [- sombrero] to tilt - **2.** [dividir] to divide into three. ◇ *vi* - **1.** [mediar]: **terciar (en)** to mediate (in) - **2.** [participar] to intervene, to take part.
◆ **terciarse** *vprnl* to arise; **si se tercia** if the opportunity arises.

terciario, **ria** *adj* tertiary.
◆ **terciario** *sm* GEOL Tertiary (period).

tercio *sm* - **1.** [tercera parte] third - **2.** MIL ≃ regiment; [de la Guardia Civil] ≃ division - **3.** TAUROM stage *(of bullfight)*; *ver también* **tauromaquia**.

terciopelo *sm* velvet.

terco, **ca** ◇ *adj* stubborn. ◇ *sm, f* stubborn person.

tergal® *sm* Tergal®.

tergiversación *sf* distortion.

tergiversador, **ra** ◇ *adj* distorting. ◇ *sm, f* person who distorts the facts.

tergiversar *vt* to distort, to twist.

termal *adj* thermal.

termas *sfpl* - **1.** [baños] hot baths, spa *sing* - **2.** HIST thermae.

termes *sm inv* = termita.

térmico, **ca** *adj* thermal.

terminación *sf* - **1.** [finalización] completion - **2.** [parte final] end - **3.** GRAM ending.

terminal ◇ *adj* [gen] final; [enfermo] terminal. ◇ *sm* ELECTR & INFORM terminal. ◇ *sf* [de aeropuerto] terminal; [de autobuses] terminus.

terminante *adj* categorical; [prueba] conclusive.

terminar ◇ *vt* to finish. ◇ *vi* - **1.** [acabar] to end; [tren] to stop, to terminate; **terminar en** [objeto] to end in - **2.** [ir a parar]: **terminar (de/en)** to end up (as/in); **terminar por hacer algo** to end up doing sthg - **3.** [reñir] to finish, to split up.
◆ **terminarse** *vprnl* - **1.** [finalizar] to finish - **2.** [agotarse] to run out; **se nos ha terminado la sal** we have run out of salt.

término *sm* - **1.** [fin, extremo] end; **dar término a algo** to bring sthg to a close; **poner término a algo** to put a stop to sthg - **2.** [territorio]: **término (municipal)** district - **3.** [plazo] period; **en el término de un mes** within (the space of) a month - **4.** [lugar, posición] place; **en primer término** ARTE & FOTO in the foreground; **en último término** ARTE & FOTO in the background; *fig* [si es necesario] as a last resort; [en resumidas cuentas] in the final analysis - **5.** [situación, punto] point; **término medio** [media] average; [compromiso] compromise, happy medium; **por término medio** on average - **6.** LING & MAT term; **a mí no me hables en esos términos** don't talk to me like that; **los términos del contrato** the terms of the contract; **en términos generales** generally speaking - **7.** [de transportes] terminus.

terminología *sf* terminology.

terminológico, **ca** *adj* terminological.

termita *sf* termite.

termo *sm* Thermos®(flask).

termoaislante *adj* heat insulating.

termodinámico, **ca** *adj* thermodynamic.
◆ **termodinámica** *sf* thermodynamics *(U)*.

termómetro *sm* thermometer; **poner el termómetro a alguien** to take sb's temperature.

termonuclear *adj* thermonuclear.

termostato *sm* thermostat.

terna *sf* POLÍT *shortlist of three candidates*.

ternario, **ria** *adj* ternary.

ternasco *sf* suckling lamb.

ternero, **ra** *sm, f* [animal] calf.
◆ **ternera** *sf* [carne] veal.

terno *sm* [traje] three-piece suit.

ternura *sf* tenderness.

terquedad *sf* stubbornness.

terracota *sf* terracotta.

terral, tierral *sm Amér* dust cloud.

Terranova *n pr* Newfoundland.

terraplén *sm* embankment.

terráqueo, a *adj* Earth *(antes de s)*, terrestrial.

terrario, terrarium *sm* terrarium.

terrateniente *smf* landowner.

terraza *sf* - **1.** [balcón] balcony - **2.** [de café] terrace, patio - **3.** [azotea] terrace roof - **4.** [bancal] terrace.

terrazo *sm* terrazzo.

terremoto *sm* earthquake.

terrenal *adj* earthly.

terreno, na *adj* earthly.

➡ **terreno** *sm* - **1.** [suelo - gen] land; GEOL terrain; AGRIC soil - **2.** [solar] plot (of land) - **3.** DEP: **terreno (de juego)** field, pitch - **4.** *fig* [ámbito] field - **5.** *loc*: **estar** o **encontrarse en su propio terreno** to be on home ground; **ganar terreno** [imponerse] to gain ground; [progresar] to make up ground; **perder terreno** to lose ground; **preparar el terreno (para)** to pave the way (for); **reconocer** o **tantear el terreno** to see how the land lies; **saber uno el terreno que pisa** to know what one is about; **ser terreno abonado (para algo)** to be fertile ground (for sthg); **sobre el terreno** on the spot.

térreo, a *adj* earthy.

terrestre *adj* - **1.** [del planeta] terrestrial - **2.** [de la tierra] land *(antes de s)*.

terrible *adj* - **1.** [enorme, insoportable] terrible - **2.** [aterrador] terrifying.

terrícola ⇔ *adj* Earth *(antes de s)*. ⇔ *smf* earthling.

terrier *sm* terrier.

territorial *adj* territorial.

territorialidad *sf* territoriality.

territorio *sm* territory; **por todo el territorio nacional** across the country, nationwide.

terrón *sm* - **1.** [de tierra] clod of earth - **2.** [de harina etc] lump; **terrón de azúcar** sugar lump.

terror *sm* [miedo, persona terrible] terror; CINE horror; **película de terror** horror movie; **dar terror** to terrify.

terrorífico, ca *adj* - **1.** [enorme, insoportable] terrible - **2.** [aterrador] terrifying.

terrorismo *sm* terrorism.

terrorista *adj* & *smf* terrorist.

terroso, sa *adj* - **1.** [parecido a la tierra] earthy - **2.** [con tierra] muddy.

terruño *sm* - **1.** [patria] homeland - **2.** [terreno] plot of land.

terso, sa *adj* - **1.** [piel, superficie] smooth - **2.** [aguas, mar] clear - **3.** [estilo, lenguaje] polished.

tersura *sf* - **1.** [de piel, superficie] smoothness - **2.** [de aguas, mar] clarity - **3.** [de estilo, lenguaje] polish.

tertulia *sf regular meeting of people for informal discussion of a particular issue of common interest*; **tertulia literaria** literary circle.

tesina *sf* (undergraduate) dissertation.

tesis *sf inv* [gen & UNIV] thesis.

tesitura *sf* - **1.** [circunstancia] circumstances *pl* - **2.** MÚS tessitura, pitch.

tesón *sm* - **1.** [tenacidad] tenacity, perseverance - **2.** [firmeza] firmness.

tesorería *sf* - **1.** [cargo] treasurership - **2.** [oficina] treasurer's office - **3.** COM liquid capital.

tesorero, ra *sm, f* treasurer.

tesoro *sm* - **1.** [botín] treasure - **2.** [hacienda pública] treasury, exchequer - **3.** *fig* [persona valiosa] gem, treasure - **4.** *fig* [como apelativo] my treasure.

➡ **Tesoro** *sm* ECON: **el Tesoro (Público)** the Treasury.

test (*pl* **tests**) *sm* test; **examen tipo test** multiple choice test; **test de embarazo** pregnancy test.

testa *sf* head.

testado, da *adj* [persona] testate.

testaferro *sm* front man.

testamentaría *sf* - **1.** [documentos] documentation *(of a will)* - **2.** [bienes] estate, inheritance.

testamentario, ria ⇔ *adj* testamentary. ⇔ *sm, f* executor.

testamento *sm* will; *fig* [artístico, intelectual] legacy; **hacer testamento** to write one's will.

➡ **Antiguo Testamento** *sm* Old Testament.

➡ **Nuevo Testamento** *sm* New Testament.

testar ⇔ *vi* [hacer testamento] to make a will. ⇔ *vt* [probar] to test.

testarudez *sf* stubbornness.

testarudo, da ⇔ *adj* stubborn. ⇔ *sm, f* stubborn person.

testear *vt* C Sur to test.

testículo *sm* testicle.

testificar [10] ⇔ *vt* to testify; *fig* to testify to. ⇔ *vi* to testify, to give evidence.

testigo ⇔ *smf* [persona] witness; **poner por testigo a alguien** to cite sb as a witness; **testigo de cargo/descargo** witness for the prosecution/defence; **testigo ocular** o **presencial** eyewitness. ⇔ *sm* - **1.** *fig* [prueba]: **testigo de** proof of - **2.** DEP baton.

➡ **testigo de Jehová** *smf* Jehovah's Witness.

testimonial *adj* - **1.** [documento, prueba etc] testimonial - **2.** *fig* [simbólico] token, symbolic.

testimoniar [8] ⇔ *vt* to testify; *fig* to testify to. ⇔ *vi* to testify, to give evidence.

testimonio *sm* - **1.** [relato] account; DER testimony; **prestar testimonio** to give evidence;

falso testimonio perjury, false evidence - **2.** [prueba] proof; **como testimonio de** as proof of; **dar testimonio de** to prove.

testosterona *sf* testosterone.

testuz *sm o sf* - **1.** [frente] brow - **2.** [nuca] nape.

teta *sf* - **1.** *fam* [de mujer] tit; **dar la teta** to breast-feed; **de teta** nursing - **2.** [de animal] teat.

tétanos *sm inv* tetanus.

tetera *sf* teapot.

tetilla *sf* - **1.** [de hombre, animal] nipple - **2.** [de biberón] teat.

tetina *sf* teat.

tetraedro *sm* tetrahedron.

tetralogía *sf* tetralogy.

tetraplejía *sf* quadriplegia.

tetrapléjico, **ca** *adj* & *sm, f* quadriplegic.

tétrico, **ca** *adj* gloomy.

textil *adj* & *sm* textile.

texto *sm* - **1.** [gen] text; **el Sagrado Texto** the Holy Scripture, the Bible - **2.** [pasaje] passage.

textual *adj* - **1.** [del texto] textual - **2.** [exacto] exact.

textura *sf* texture.

tez *sf* complexion.

ti *pron pers (después de prep)* - **1.** [gen] you; **siempre pienso en ti** I'm always thinking about you; **me acordaré de ti** I'll remember you - **2.** [reflexivo] yourself; **sólo piensas en ti (mismo)** you only think about yourself.

tía ▷ **tío**.

tianguis *sm inv* *Amér C & Méx* open-air market.

tiara *sf* tiara.

tibetano, **na** *adj* & *sm, f* Tibetan.

tibia *sf* shinbone, tibia.

tibieza *sf* - **1.** [calidez] warmth; [falta de calor] lukewarmness - **2.** *fig* [frialdad] lack of enthusiasm.

tibio, **bia** *adj* - **1.** [cálido] warm; [falto de calor] tepid, lukewarm - **2.** *fig* [frío] lukewarm - **3.** *loc*: **poner tibio a alguien** *fam* to speak ill of sb; **ponerse tibio** *fam* [comiendo] to stuff one's face; [ensuciarse] to get filthy.

tiburón *sm* - **1.** [gen] shark - **2.** FIN raider.

tic *sm* tic.

ticket = **tíquet**.

tictac *sm* tick tock.

tiembla *etc* ▷ **temblar**.

tiempo *sm* - **1.** [gen] time; **al poco tiempo** soon afterwards; **a tiempo (de hacer algo)** in time (to do sthg); **al mismo tiempo, a un tiempo** at the same time; **cada cierto tiempo** every so often; **con el tiempo** in time; **no me dio tiempo a terminarlo** I didn't have (enough) time to finish it; **del tiempo** [fruta] of the sea-

son; [bebida] at room temperature; **en mis tiempos** in my day *o* time; **en tiempos** long ago; **estar a** *o* **tener tiempo de** to have time to; **fuera de tiempo** at the wrong moment; **ganar tiempo** to save time; **hacer tiempo** to pass the time; **perder el tiempo** to waste time; **tiempo libre** *o* **de ocio** spare time; **a tiempo parcial** part-time; **tiempo de acceso** INFORM access time; **tiempo de conversación** [de teléfono móvil] talk time; **tiempo muerto** DEP time out; **tiempo real** INFORM real time; **dar tiempo al tiempo** to give things time; **en tiempos de Maricastaña** donkey's years ago; **matar el tiempo** to kill time - **2.** [periodo largo] long time; **con tiempo** in good time; **hace tiempo que** it is a long time since; **hace tiempo que no vive aquí** he hasn't lived here for some time; **tomarse uno su tiempo** to take one's time - **3.** [edad] age; **¿qué tiempo tiene?** how old is he? - **4.** [movimiento] movement; **motor de cuatro tiempos** four-stroke engine - **5.** METEOR weather; **hizo buen/mal tiempo** the weather was good/bad; **si el tiempo lo permite** *o* **no lo impide** weather permitting; **hace un tiempo de perros** it's a foul day; **poner al mal tiempo buena cara** to put a brave face on things - **6.** DEP half - **7.** GRAM tense - **8.** [MÚS - compás] time; [- ritmo] tempo.

tienda ◇ *v* ▷ **tender**. ◇ *sf* - **1.** [establecimiento] shop; **ir de tiendas** to go shopping; **tienda libre de impuestos** duty-free shop; **tienda virtual** online retailer - **2.** [para acampar]: **tienda (de campaña)** tent.

tiene *v* ▷ **tener**.

tienta *sf* TAUROM trial *(of the bulls)*; ▷ **tentar**.

➤ **a tientas** *loc adv* blindly; **andar a tientas** to grope along.

tiento *sm* - **1.** [cuidado] care; [tacto] tact - **2.** *fam* [trago] swig.

tierno, **na** *adj* - **1.** [blando, cariñoso] tender - **2.** [del día] fresh.

tierra *sf* - **1.** [gen] land; **tierra adentro** inland; **tierra de nadie** no-man's-land; **tierra firme** terra firma, dry land; **tierra prometida** *o* **de promisión** Promised Land - **2.** [materia inorgánica] earth, soil; **un camino de tierra** a dirt track; **pista de tierra batida** clay court - **3.** [suelo] ground; **caer a tierra** to fall to the ground; **quedarse en tierra** [pasajero] to miss the plane/boat/train; **tomar tierra** to touch down - **4.** [patria] homeland, native land; **de la tierra** [vino, queso] local - **5.** ELECTR earth *UK*, ground *US*; **conectado a tierra** earthed *UK*, grounded *US* - **6.** *loc*: **echar por tierra algo** to ruin sthg; **echar tierra a un asunto** to hush up an affair; **poner tierra por medio** to make o.s.

scarce; **se lo tragó la tierra** he vanished without trace; **¡trágame tierra!** *fam* I wish the earth would swallow me up!

➤ **Tierra** *sf*: **la Tierra** the Earth.

➤ **Tierra del Fuego** *sf* Tierra del Fuego.

➤ **Tierra Santa** *sf* the Holy Land.

tierral = **terral**.

tieso, sa *adj* - **1.** [rígido] stiff; **quedarse tieso** [de frío] to freeze - **2.** [erguido] erect - **3.** *fam* [muerto] stone dead; **dejar tieso a alguien** to kill sb - **4.** *fam* [sin dinero] broke - **5.** *fig* [engreído] haughty.

tiesto *sm* flowerpot.

tifoideo, a *adj* typhoid *(antes de s)*.

tifón *sm* typhoon.

tifus *sm inv* typhus.

tigre *sm* tiger; **oler a tigre** *fam* to stink.

tigresa *sf* tigress.

TIJ (*abrev de* **Tribunal Internacional de Justicia**) *sm* ICJ (*International Court of Justice*).

tijera *(gen pl)* *sf* scissors *pl*; [de jardinero, esquilador] shears *pl*; **unas tijeras** a pair of scissors/shears; **de tijera** [escalera, silla] folding; **meter la tijera** *lit & fig* to cut.

tijereta *sf* - **1.** [insecto] earwig - **2.** DEP scissors *sing*.

tijeretazo *sm* snip.

tila *sf* [infusión] lime blossom tea.

tildar *vt*: **tildar a alguien de algo** to brand *O* call sb sthg.

tilde *sf* - **1.** [signo ortográfico] tilde - **2.** [acento gráfico] accent.

tiliches *smpl Amér C & Méx* bits and pieces.

tilín *sm* tinkle, tinkling *(U)*; **me hace tilín** *fam* I fancy him.

tilo *sm* [árbol] linden *O* lime tree.

timador, ra *sm, f* confidence trickster, swindler.

timar *vt* - **1.** [estafar]: **timar a alguien** to swindle sb; **timar algo a alguien** to swindle sb out of sthg - **2.** *fig* [engañar] to cheat, to con.

timba *sf* game of cards.

timbal *sm* [MÚS - de orquesta] kettledrum, timbal; [- tamboril] small drum.

timbrado, da *adj* - **1.** [sellado] stamped - **2.** [sonido] clear, true.

timbrazo *sm* loud ring.

timbre *sm* - **1.** [aparato] bell; **tocar el timbre** to ring the bell; **timbre de alarma** alarm (bell) - **2.** [de voz, sonido] tone; TECNOL timbre - **3.** [sello - de documentos] stamp; [- de impuestos] seal; *Amér C & Méx* [- de correos] stamp.

timidez *sf* shyness.

tímido, da ◇ *adj* shy. ◇ *sm, f* shy person.

timo *sm* - **1.** [estafa] swindle; **timo de la estampita** *confidence trick where fake notes are used* - **2.** *fam* [engaño] trick; **¡vaya timo!** what a rip-off! - **3.** ANAT thymus.

timón *sm* - **1.** AERON & NÁUT rudder - **2.** *fig* [gobierno] helm; **llevar el timón de** to be at the helm of - **3.** *Andes & Cuba* [volante] steering wheel.

timonear *vi* to steer.

timonel, timonero *sm* NÁUT helmsman.

timorato, ta *adj* - **1.** [mojigato] prudish - **2.** [tímido] fearful.

tímpano *sm* - **1.** ANAT eardrum - **2.** ARQUIT tympanum.

tina *sf* - **1.** [tinaja] pitcher - **2.** [gran cuba] vat - **3.** *Amér C, Col & Méx* [bañera] bathtub.

tinaja *sf* (large) pitcher.

tinglado *sm* - **1.** [cobertizo] shed - **2.** [armazón] platform - **3.** *fig* [lío] fuss - **4.** *fig* [maquinación] plot.

tinieblas *sfpl* darkness *(U)*; *fig* confusion *(U)*, uncertainty *(U)*; **entre tinieblas** *lit & fig* in the dark.

tino *sm* - **1.** [puntería] good aim - **2.** *fig* [habilidad] skill - **3.** *fig* [juicio] sense, good judgment - **4.** *fig* [moderación] moderation.

tinta *sf* ink; **tinta china** Indian ink; **tinta simpática** invisible ink; **cargar** *O* **recargar las tintas** to exaggerate; **saberlo de buena tinta** to have it on good authority; **sudar tinta** to sweat blood.

➤ **medias tintas** *sfpl*: **andarse con medias tintas** to be wishy-washy.

tintar *vt* to dye.

tinte *sm* - **1.** [sustancia] dye - **2.** [operación] dyeing - **3.** [tintorería] dry cleaner's - **4.** *fig* [tono] shade, tinge.

tintero *sm* [frasco] ink pot; [en la mesa] inkwell; **dejarse algo en el tintero** to leave sthg unsaid.

tintinear *vi* to jingle, to tinkle.

tintineo *sm* tinkle, tinkling *(U)*.

tinto, ta *adj* - **1.** [manchado] stained; **tinto en sangre** bloodstained - **2.** [vino] red.

➤ **tinto** *sm* - **1.** [vino] red wine - **2.** *Col & Ven* [café] black coffee.

tintorera *sf* ZOOL blue shark.

tintorería *sf* dry cleaner's.

tintorero, ra *sm, f* dry cleaner.

tintorro *sm fam* red plonk.

tintura *sf* - **1.** [en farmacia] tincture - **2.** [tinte - sustancia] dye; [- operación] dyeing.

tiña ◇ *v* ▷ **teñir**. ◇ *sf* MED ringworm.

tiñera *etc* ▷ **teñir**.

tiñoso, sa *adj* MED suffering from ringworm.

tío, **a** *sm*, *f* **- 1.** [familiar] uncle (*f* aunt); **tío abuelo** great uncle (*f* great aunt); **tío carnal** blood uncle (*f* blood aunt); **el tío Sam** *fig* Uncle Sam **- 2.** *fam* [individuo] guy (*f* bird) **- 3.** *fam* [como apelativo] mate (*f* darling) **- 4.** *loc:* **no hay tu tía** *fam* there's no way.

tiovivo *sm* merry-go-round *UK*, carousel *US*.

tipazo *sm fam* [de mujer] great figure; [de hombre] good build.

tipear ⬦ *vt Amér* to type. ⬦ *vi* to type.

tipejo, **ja** *sm*, *f despec* individual, character.

típico, **ca** *adj* typical; [traje, restaurante etc] traditional; **típico de** typical of.

tipificación *sf* **- 1.** [gen & DER] classification **- 2.** [normalización] standardization.

tipificar [10] *vt* **- 1.** [gen & DER] to classify **- 2.** [normalizar] to standardize **- 3.** [simbolizar] to typify.

tipismo *sm* local colour.

tiple ⬦ *smf* [cantante] soprano. ⬦ *sm* **- 1.** [voz] soprano **- 2.** [guitarra] treble guitar.

tipo, **pa** *sm*, *f fam* guy (*f* woman).

➡ **tipo** *sm* **- 1.** [clase] type, sort; **no es mi tipo** he is not my type; **todo tipo de** all sorts of **- 2.** [cuerpo - de mujer] figure; [- de hombre] build; **aguantar** o **mantener el tipo** to keep one's calm; **jugarse el tipo** to risk one's neck **- 3.** ECON rate; **tipo de descuento** base rate; **tipo de interés/cambio** interest/exchange rate; **tipo impositivo** tax band **- 4.** IMPR & ZOOL type.

tipografía *sf* [procedimiento] printing.

tipográfico, **ca** *adj* typographical, printing *(antes de s).*

tipógrafo, **fa** *sm*, *f* printer.

tipología *sf* typology.

tíquet *(pl* tiquets*)*, **ticket** ['tiket] *(pl* tickets*) sm* ticket; **tíquet de compra** receipt.

tiquismiquis ⬦ *adj inv fam* [maniático] pernickety. ⬦ *smf inv fam* [maniático] fusspot. ⬦ *smpl* **- 1.** [riñas] squabbles **- 2.** [bagatelas] trifles.

tira *sf* **- 1.** [banda cortada] strip **- 2.** [tirante] strap **- 3.** [de viñetas] comic strip **- 4.** *loc:* **la tira de** *fam* loads *pl* of; **la tira** *Méx fam* [la policía] the cops, the fuzz *UK*.

➡ **tira y afloja** *sm* give and take.

tirabuzón *sm* [rizo] curl.

tirachinas *sm inv* catapult.

tiradero *sm Amér* rubbish dump.

tirado, **da** ⬦ *adj* **- 1.** *fam* [barato] dirt cheap **- 2.** *fam* [fácil] simple, dead easy; **estar tirado** to be a cinch **- 3.** *fam* [débil, cansado] worn-out **- 4.** *fam* [miserable] seedy **- 5.** *loc:* **dejar tirado a alguien** *fam* to leave sb in the lurch. ⬦ *sm*, *f fam* [persona] wretch.

tirada *sf* **- 1.** [lanzamiento] throw **- 2.** [IMPR - número de ejemplares] print run; [- reimpresión] reprint; [- número de lectores] circulation **- 3.** [sucesión] series **- 4.** [distancia]: **hay una tirada hasta allí** it's a fair way o quite a stretch; **de** o **en una tirada** in one go.

tirador, **ra** *sm*, *f* [con arma] marksman.

➡ **tirador** *sm* **- 1.** [mango] handle **- 2.** [de campanilla] bell rope **- 3.** [tirachinas] catapult.

➡ **tiradores** *smpl Bol & R Dom* [tirantes] braces *UK*, suspenders *US*.

tiranía *sf* tyranny.

tiránico, **ca** *adj* tyrannical.

tiranizar [13] *vt* to tyrannize.

tirano, **na** ⬦ *adj* tyrannical. ⬦ *sm*, *f* tyrant.

tirante ⬦ *adj* **- 1.** [estirado] taut **- 2.** *fig* [violento, tenso] tense; **estoy tirante con él** there's tension between us. ⬦ *sm* **- 1.** [de tela] strap **- 2.** ARQUIT brace.

➡ **tirantes** *smpl* [para pantalones] braces *UK*, suspenders *US*.

tirantez *sf fig* tension.

tirar ⬦ *vt* **- 1.** [lanzar] to throw; **tirar algo a alguien/algo** [para hacer daño] to throw sthg at sb/sthg; **tírame una manzana** throw me an apple; **tírale un beso** blow him a kiss **- 2.** [dejar caer] to drop; [derramar] to spill; [volcar] to knock over **- 3.** [desechar, malgastar] to throw away **- 4.** [disparar] to fire; [bomba] to drop; [petardo, cohete] to let off; [foto] to take **- 5.** [derribar] to knock down **- 6.** [jugar - carta] to play; [- dado] to throw **- 7.** [DEP - falta, penalti etc] to take; [- balón] to pass **- 8.** [imprimir] to print **- 9.** *fam* [suspender] to fail. ⬦ *vi* **- 1.** [estirar, arrastrar]: **tirar (de algo)** to pull (sthg); **tira y afloja** give and take **- 2.** [suj: prenda, pernera, manga] to be too tight; **me tira de los lados** it's a bit tight at the sides **- 3.** [disparar] to shoot; **tirar a matar** to shoot to kill **- 4.** *fam* [atraer] to have a pull; **me tira la vida del campo** I feel drawn towards life in the country; **tirar de algo** to attract sthg **- 5.** [cigarrillo, chimenea etc] to draw **- 6.** *fam* [funcionar] to go, to work **- 7.** [dirigirse] to go, to head **- 8.** *fam* [apañárselas] to get by; **ir tirando** to get by; **voy tirando** I'm O.K., I've been worse **- 9.** [durar] to last **- 10.** [parecerse]: **tira a gris** it's greyish; **tira a su abuela** she takes after her grandmother; **tirando a** approaching, not far from **- 11.** [tender]: **tirar para algo** [persona] to have the makings of sthg; **este programa tira a (ser) hortera** this programme is a bit on the tacky side; **el tiempo tira a mejorar** the weather looks as if it's getting better **- 12.** [jugar] to have (one's) go **- 13.** [DEP - con el pie] to kick; [- con la mano] to throw; [- a meta, canasta etc] to shoot.

➡ **tirarse** *vprnl* **- 1.** [lanzarse]: **tirarse (a)** [al agua] to dive (into); [al vacío] to jump (into); **ti-**

rarse sobre alguien to jump on top of sb; **tirarse de** [gen] to jump from; [para bajar] to jump down from; [para matarse] to throw o.s. from **- 2.** [tumbarse] to stretch out **- 3.** [pasar tiempo] to spend **- 4.** *fam* [expeler]: **tirarse un pedo/ eructo** to fart/burp **- 5.** *vulg* [copular]: **tirarse a alguien** to screw sb.

tirita ® *sf* (sticking) plaster *UK*, ≃ Bandaid® *US*.

tirilla ® *sf* ≃ neckband.

tiritar *vi*: **tiritar (de)** to shiver (with).

tiritera, tiritona *sf* shivering.

tiro *sm* **- 1.** [gen] shot; **pegar un tiro a alguien** to shoot sb; **pegarse un tiro** to shoot o.s.; **tiro de gracia** coup de grâce; **tiro libre** [en baloncesto] free throw; **ni a tiros** never in a million years; **me salió el tiro por la culata** it backfired on me; **no van por ahí los tiros** you're a bit wide of the mark there; **sentar como un tiro (a alguien)** *fam* to go down badly (with sb) **- 2.** [acción] shooting; **tiro al blanco** [deporte] target shooting; [lugar] shooting range; **tiro al plato** clay-pigeon shooting; **tiro con arco** archery **- 3.** [huella, marca] bullet mark; [herida] gunshot wound **- 4.** [alcance] range; **a tiro de** within the range of; **a tiro de piedra** a stone's throw away; **ponerse/estar a tiro** [de arma] to come/be within range; *fig* [de persona] to come/ be within one's reach **- 5.** [de chimenea, horno] draw **- 6.** [de pantalón] *distance between crotch and waist*; **vestirse o ponerse de tiros largos** to dress o.s. up to the nines **- 7.** [de caballos] team **- 8.** *fam* [de cocaína] line.

◆ de un tirón *loc adv* in one go.

tirotear ◇ *vt* to fire at. ◇ *vi* to shoot.

tiroteo *sm* [tiros] shooting; [intercambio de disparos] shootout.

tirria *sf fam* dislike; **cogerle o tomarle tirria a alguien** to take a dislike to sb; **tenerle tirria a alguien** to have a grudge against sb.

tisana *sf* herbal tea.

tísico, ca *adj* & *sm, f* MED consumptive.

tisis *sf inv* MED (pulmonary) tuberculosis.

titán *sm fig* giant.

titánico, ca *adj* titanic.

titanio *sm* titanium.

títere *sm lit & fig* puppet; **no dejar títere con cabeza** [destrozar] to destroy everything in sight; [criticar] to spare nobody.

◆ títeres *smpl* [guiñol] puppet show *sing*.

tití *sm* ZOOL marmoset.

titilar *vi* [estrella, luz] to flicker.

titipuchal *sm Amér fam* hubbub.

titiritero, ra *sm, f* **- 1.** [de títeres] puppeteer **- 2.** [acróbata] acrobat.

titubeante *adj* **- 1.** [actitud] hesitant; [voz] stuttering **- 2.** [al andar] tottering.

titubear *vi* **- 1.** [dudar] to hesitate; [al hablar] to stutter **- 2.** [tambalearse] to totter.

titubeo *(gen pl) sm* **- 1.** [duda] hesitation; [al hablar] stutter, stuttering *(U)* **- 2.** [al andar] tottering.

titulación *sf* [académica] qualifications *pl*.

titulado, da ◇ *adj* [diplomado] qualified; [licenciado] graduate *(antes de s)*; **titulado en** with a qualification/degree in. ◇ *sm, f* [diplomado] holder of a qualification; [licenciado] graduate.

titular ◇ *adj* [profesor, médico] official. ◇ *smf* [poseedor] holder. ◇ *sm (gen pl)* PRENSA headline; **con grandes titulares** splashed across the front page. ◇ *vt* [llamar] to title, to call.

◆ titularse *vprnl* **- 1.** [llamarse] to be titled o called **- 2.** [licenciarse]: **titularse (en)** to graduate (in) **- 3.** [diplomarse]: **titularse (en)** to obtain a qualification (in).

título *sm* **- 1.** [gen] title; **título de propiedad** title deed; **títulos de crédito** CINE credits **- 2.** [licenciatura] degree; [diploma] diploma; **tiene muchos títulos** she has a lot of qualifications **- 3.** *fig* [derecho] right; **a título de** as **- 4.** ECON bond, security.

tiza *sf* chalk; **una tiza** a piece of chalk.

tiznadura *sf* [mancha] black mark.

tiznar *vt* to blacken.

◆ tiznarse *vprnl* to be blackened.

tizne *sm o sf* soot.

tizón *sm* burning stick o log.

tlapalería *sf Méx* ironmonger's (shop).

TLC, TLCAN *sm* (*abrev de* **Tratado de Libre Comercio de América del Norte**) NAFTA.

TNT (*abrev de* **trinitrotolueno**) *sm* TNT.

toalla *sf* **- 1.** [para secarse] towel; **toalla de ducha/manos** bath/hand towel; *Amér* **toalla higiénica o sanitaria** sanitary towel *UK* o napkin *US*; **arrojar o tirar la toalla** to throw in the towel **- 2.** [tejido] towelling.

toallero *sm* towel rail.

tobera *sf* nozzle.

tobillera *sf* ankle support.

tobillo *sm* ankle.

tobogán *sm* [rampa] slide; [en parque de atracciones] helter-skelter; [en piscina] chute, flume.

toca *sf* wimple.

tocadiscos *sm inv* record player.

tocado, da *adj* **- 1.** *fam* [chiflado] soft in the head **- 2.** [fruta] bad, rotten **- 3.** [jugador, deportista] slightly injured.

tocado *sm* - **1.** [prenda] headgear *(U)* - **2.** [peinado] hairdo.

tocador *sm* - **1.** [mueble] dressing table - **2.** [habitación - en lugar público] powder room; [- en casa] boudoir.

tocante *adj*: **(en lo) tocante a** regarding.

tocar [10] <> *vt* - **1.** [gen] to touch; [palpar] to feel - **2.** [instrumento, canción] to play; [bombo] to bang; [sirena, alarma] to sound; [campana, timbre] to ring; **el reloj tocó las doce** the clock struck twelve - **3.** [abordar - tema etc] to touch on - **4.** *fig* [conmover] to touch - **5.** *fig* [concernir]: **por lo que a mí me toca/a eso le toca** as far as I'm/that's concerned; **tocar a alguien de cerca** to concern sb closely. <> *vi* - **1.** [entrar en contacto] to touch - **2.** [estar próximo]: **tocar (con)** [gen] to be touching; [país, jardín] to border (on) - **3.** [llamar - a la puerta, ventana] to knock - **4.** [corresponder en reparto]: **tocar a alguien** to be due to sb; **tocamos a mil cada uno** we're due a thousand each; **le tocó la mitad** he got half of it; **te toca a ti hacerlo** [turno] it's your turn to do it; [responsabilidad] it's up to you to do it - **5.** [caer en suerte]: **me ha tocado la lotería** I've won the lottery; **le ha tocado sufrir mucho** he has had to suffer a lot - **6.** [llegar el momento]: **nos toca pagar ahora** it's time (for us) to pay now.

tocarse *vprnl* to touch.

tocata <> *sf* MÚS toccata. <> *sm fam* [tocadiscos] record player.

tocateja ➤ **a tocateja** *loc adv* in cash.

tocayo, **ya** *sm*, *f* namesake.

tocho *sm fam* [libro] massive tome.

tocinería *sf* pork butcher's (shop).

tocinero, **ra** *sm*, *f* pork butcher.

tocineta *sf Amér* bacon.

tocino *sm* [para cocinar] lard; [para comer] fat *(of bacon)*; **tocino entreverado** streaky bacon.

➤ **tocino de cielo** *sm* CULIN *dessert made of syrup and eggs*.

tocología *sf* obstetrics *(U)*.

tocólogo, **ga** *sm*, *f* obstetrician.

tocomocho *sm confidence trick involving the sale of a lottery ticket, claimed to be a certain winner, for a large amount of money*.

todavía *adv* - **1.** [aún] still; [con negativo] yet, still; **todavía no lo he recibido** I still haven't got it, I haven't got it yet; **todavía ayer** as late as yesterday; **todavía no** not yet - **2.** [sin embargo] still - **3.** [incluso] even; **todavía mejor** even better.

todo, **da** <> *adj* - **1.** [gen] all; **todo el mundo** everybody; **todo el libro** the whole book, all (of) the book; **todo el día** all day - **2.** [cada, cualquier]: **todos los días/lunes** every day/ Monday; **todo español** every Spaniard, all

Spaniards - **3.** [para enfatizar]: **es todo un hombre** he's every bit a man; **ya es toda una mujer** she's a big girl now; **fue todo un éxito** it was a great success. <> *pron* - **1.** [todas las cosas] everything, all of them *pl*; **lo vendió todo** he sold everything, he sold it all; **todos están rotos** they're all broken, all of them are broken; **de todo** everything (you can think of); **ante todo** [principalmente] above all; [en primer lugar] first of all; **con todo** despite everything; **después de todo** after all; **de todas todas** without a shadow of a doubt; **sobre todo** above all; **está en todo** he/she always makes sure everything is just so; **todo lo más** at (the) most; **me invitó a cenar y todo** she even asked me to dinner - **2.** [todas las personas]: **todos** everybody; **todas vinieron** everybody o they all came.

➤ **todo** <> *sm* whole; **jugarse el todo por el todo** to stake everything. <> *adv* completely, all.

➤ **del todo** *loc adv*: **no estoy del todo contento** I'm not entirely happy; **no lo hace mal del todo** she doesn't do it at all badly.

todopoderoso, **sa** *adj* almighty.

➤ **Todopoderoso** *sm*: **el Todopoderoso** the Almighty.

todoterreno *sm* all-terrain vehicle.

tofe *sm* coffee-flavoured toffee.

toga *sf* - **1.** [manto] toga - **2.** [traje] gown - **3.** [en el pelo] method of combing one's hair so it becomes straight.

togado, **da** *adj* robed.

toisón ➤ **toisón de oro** *sm* - **1.** [insignia] golden fleece - **2.** [orden] Order of the Golden Fleece.

tojo *sm* gorse.

toldo *sm* [de tienda] awning; [de playa] sunshade.

tolerable *adj* - **1.** [soportable] tolerable - **2.** [perdonable] acceptable.

tolerancia *sf* tolerance.

tolerante <> *adj* tolerant. <> *smf* tolerant person.

tolerar *vt* - **1.** [consentir, aceptar] to tolerate; **tolerar que alguien haga algo** to tolerate sb doing sthg - **2.** [aguantar] to stand.

tolva *sf* hopper.

toma *sf* - **1.** [de biberón, papilla] feed; [de medicamento] dose - **2.** [de sangre] sample - **3.** [de ciudad etc] capture - **4.** [de agua, aire] inlet; **toma de corriente** ELECTR socket; **toma de tierra** ELECTR earth - **5.** CINE [de escena] take.

➤ **toma de conciencia** *sf* realization.

➤ **toma de posesión** *sf* - **1.** [de gobierno, presidente] investiture - **2.** [de cargo] undertaking.

toma y daca *sm*: **ser un toma y daca** to be give and take.

tomadura *sf*: **tomadura de pelo** hoax.

tomar ◇ *vt* - **1.** [gen] to take; [actitud, costumbre] to adopt - **2.** [datos, información] to take down - **3.** [medicina, drogas] to take; [comida, bebida] to have; **¿qué quieres tomar?** what would you like (to drink/eat)? - **4.** [autobús, tren etc] to catch; [taxi] to take - **5.** [contratar] to take on - **6.** [considerar, confundir]: **tomar a alguien por algo/alguien** to take sb for sthg/sb - **7.** *loc*: **tomarla con alguien** *fam* to have it in for sb; **¡toma!** [al dar algo] here you are!; [expresando sorpresa] well I never!; **¡toma (ésa)!** *fam* [expresa venganza] take that! ◇ *vi* - **1.** [encaminarse] to go, to head - **2.** *Amér* [beber alcohol] to drink.

tomarse *vprnl* - **1.** [comida, bebida] to have; [medicina, drogas] to take - **2.** [interpretar] to take; **tomarse algo mal/bien** to take sthg badly/well.

tomate *sm* - **1.** [fruto] tomato; **tomate frito** *unconcentrated puree made by frying peeled tomatoes*; **ponerse como un tomate** to go as red as a beetroot - **2.** [salsa] tomato sauce - **3.** [en calcetín] hole - **4.** *fam* [jaleo] uproar, commotion.

tomatera *sf* tomato plant.

tomavistas *sm inv* cine camera.

tómbola *sf* tombola.

tomillo *sm* thyme.

tomo *sm* - **1.** [volumen] volume - **2.** [libro] tome.

ton ◆ **sin ton ni son** *loc adv* for no apparent reason.

tonada *sf* tune.

tonadilla *sf* ditty.

tonadillero, ra *sm, f* ditty singer/writer.

tonal *adj* tonal.

tonalidad *sf* - **1.** [de color] tone - **2.** MÚS key.

tonel *sm* [recipiente] barrel; **estar/ponerse como un tonel** to be/become (as fat as) a barrel.

tonelada *sf* tonne; **tonelada métrica** metric ton, tonne; **pesar una tonelada** to weigh a ton.

tonelaje *sm* tonnage.

tongo *sm* - **1.** [engaño]: **en la pelea hubo tongo** the fight was fixed - **2.** *Chile fam* [sombrero hongo] bowler hat.

tónico, ca *adj* - **1.** [reconstituyente] revitalizing - **2.** GRAM & MÚS tonic.

◆ **tónico** *sm* - **1.** [reconstituyente] tonic - **2.** [cosmético] skin toner.

◆ **tónica** *sf* - **1.** [bebida] tonic water - **2.** [tendencia] trend - **3.** MÚS tonic.

tonificación *sf* invigoration.

tonificador, ra, tonificante *adj* invigorating.

tonificar [10] *vt* to invigorate.

tonillo *sm despec* [retintín] sarcastic tone of voice.

tono *sm* - **1.** [gen] tone; **estar a tono (con)** to be appropriate (for); **fuera de tono** out of place - **2.** [MÚS - tonalidad] key; [- altura] pitch - **3.** [de color] shade; **tono de piel** complexion - **4.** *loc*: **darse tono** *fam* to give o.s. airs; **ponerse a tono con algo** [emborracharse] to get drunk on sthg; [ponerse al día] to get to grips with sthg; **subido de tono** [chiste, comentario] risqué, obscene; **subir el tono, subir(se) de tono** to get angrier and angrier.

tonsura *sf* tonsure.

tontaina ◇ *adj fam* daft. ◇ *smf fam* daft idiot.

tontear *vi* - **1.** [hacer el tonto] to fool about - **2.** [coquetear]: **tontear (con alguien)** to flirt (with sb).

tontería *sf* - **1.** [estupidez] stupid thing; **decir una tontería** to talk nonsense; **hacer una tontería** to do sthg foolish - **2.** [cosa sin importancia o valor] trifle.

tonto, ta ◇ *adj* stupid; **ponerse tonto** to be difficult; **tonto de capirote** *o* **remate** daft as a brush. ◇ *sm, f* idiot; **hacer el tonto** to play the fool; **hacerse el tonto** to act innocent.

◆ **a lo tonto** *loc adv* [sin notarlo] without realizing it.

◆ **a tontas y a locas** *loc adv* haphazardly.

tontorrón, ona ◇ *adj* daft. ◇ *sm, f* daft idiot.

top (*pl* **tops**) *sm* [prenda] short top.

topacio *sm* topaz.

topadora *sf R Dom* bulldozer.

topar *vi* - **1.** [chocar] to bump into each other - **2.** [encontrarse]: **topar con alguien** to bump into sb; **topar con algo** to come across sthg.

◆ **toparse con** *vprnl* [persona] to bump into; [cosa] to come across.

tope ◇ *adj inv* - **1.** [máximo] top, maximum; [fecha] last - **2.** *mfam* [estupendo] brill, ace. ◇ *adv mfam* [muy] mega, really. ◇ *sm* - **1.** [pieza] block; [para puerta] doorstop - **2.** FERROC buffer - **3.** [límite máximo] limit; [de plazo] deadline - **4.** *Méx* [para velocidad] speed bump - **5.** [freno]: **poner tope a** to rein in, to curtail - **6.** *loc*: **estar hasta los topes** to be bursting at the seams.

◆ **a tope** ◇ *loc adv* [de velocidad, intensidad] flat out. ◇ *loc adj fam* [lleno - lugar] packed.

topera *sf* molehill.

topetazo *sm* bump; **darse un topetazo** [en la cabeza] to bump o.s. on the head.

tópico, ca *adj* - **1.** [manido] clichéd - **2.** MED topical.

◆ **tópico** *sm* cliché.

topless ['toβles] *sm inv* topless bathing; **en topless** topless; **hacer topless** to go topless.

topo *sm* - **1.** *fig* & ZOOL mole - **2.** [lunar] polka dot.

topografía *sf* topography.

topográfico, **ca** *adj* topographical.

topógrafo, **fa** *sm*, *f* topographer.

toponimia *sf* - **1.** [nombres] place names *pl* - **2.** [ciencia] toponymy.

toponímico, **ca** *adj* toponymical.

topónimo *sm* place name.

toque ⟨> *v* ⊳ **tocar**. ⟨> *sm* - **1.** [gen] touch; **dar los últimos toques a algo** to put the finishing touches to sthg - **2.** [aviso] warning; **dar un toque a alguien** [llamar] to call sb; [amonestar] to prod sb, to warn sb; **toque de atención** warning - **3.** [sonido - de campana] chime, chiming *(U)*; [- de tambor] beat, beating *(U)*; [- de sirena etc] blast; **toque de diana** reveille; **toque de difuntos** death knell; **toque de queda** curfew.

toquetear *vt* [manosear - cosa] to fiddle with; [- persona] to fondle.

toqueteo *sm* [de cosa] fiddling; [a persona] fondling.

toquilla *sf* shawl.

torácico, **ca** *adj* thoracic.

tórax *sm inv* thorax.

torbellino *sm* - **1.** [remolino - de aire] whirlwind; [- de agua] whirlpool; [- de polvo] dustcloud - **2.** *fig* [mezcla confusa] spate - **3.** *fig* [persona inquieta] whirlwind.

torcaz ⊳ **paloma**.

torcedura *sf* [esguince] sprain.

torcer [41] ⟨> *vt* - **1.** [gen] to twist; [doblar] to bend - **2.** [girar] to turn - **3.** [desviar] to deflect; *fig* [persona] to corrupt. ⟨> *vi* [girar] to turn.

⬥ **torcerse** *vprnl* - **1.** [retorcerse] to twist; [doblarse] to bend; **me tuerzo al andar/escribir** I can't walk/write in a straight line - **2.** [dislocarse] to sprain - **3.** [ir mal - negocios, día] to go wrong; [- persona] to go astray.

torcido, **da** *adj* [enroscado] twisted; [doblado] bent; [cuadro, corbata] crooked.

tordo, **da** ⟨> *adj* dappled. ⟨> *sm*, *f* [caballo] dapple (horse).

⬥ **tordo** *sm* [pájaro] thrush.

toreador, **ra** *sm*, *f* bullfighter.

torear ⟨> *vt* - **1.** [lidiar] to fight *(bulls)* - **2.** *fig* [eludir] to dodge - **3.** *fig* [burlarse de]: **torear a alguien** to mess sb about. ⟨> *vi* [lidiar] to fight bulls.

toreo *sm* bullfighting.

torero, **ra** ⟨> *adj* bullfighting *(antes de s)*. ⟨> *sm*, *f* [persona] bullfighter; **saltarse algo a la torera** *fig* to flout sthg.

⬥ **torera** *sf* [prenda] bolero (jacket).

toril *sm* bullpen.

tormenta *sf lit* & *fig* storm.

tormento *sm* torment; **ser un tormento** [persona] to be a torment; [cosa] to be torture.

tormentoso, **sa** *adj* stormy; [sueño] troubled.

tornadizo, **za** *adj* fickle.

tornado *sm* tornado.

tornar *culto* ⟨> *vt* - **1.** [convertir]: **tornar algo en (algo)** to turn sthg into (sthg) - **2.** [devolver] to return. ⟨> *vi* - **1.** [regresar] to return - **2.** [volver a hacer]: **tornar a hacer algo** to do sthg again.

⬥ **tornarse** *vprnl* [convertirse]: **tornarse (en)** to turn (into), to become.

tornas *sfpl*: **volver las tornas** to turn the tables.

tornasol *sm* [reflejo] sheen.

tornasolado, **da** *adj* iridescent.

torneado, **da** *adj* - **1.** [cerámica] turned - **2.** [brazos, piernas] shapely.

⬥ **torneado** *sm* turning.

tornear *vt* to turn.

torneo *sm* tournament.

tornero, **ra** *sm*, *f* [con madera] lathe operator.

tornillo *sm* screw; [con tuerca] bolt; **le falta un tornillo** *fam* he has a screw loose.

torniquete *sm* - **1.** MED tourniquet - **2.** [en entrada] turnstile.

torno *sm* - **1.** [de alfarero] (potter's) wheel - **2.** [de carpintero] lathe - **3.** [en entrada] turnstile - **4.** [de dentista] drill - **5.** [para pesos] winch.

⬥ **en torno a** *loc prep* - **1.** [alrededor de] around - **2.** [acerca de] about; **girar en torno a** to be about.

toro *sm* bull; **toro de lidia** fighting bull; **agarrar** *o* **coger el toro por los cuernos** to take the bull by the horns; **ver los toros desde la barrera** to watch from the wings.

⬥ **toros** *smpl* [lidia] bullfight *sing*, bullfighting *(U)*.

toronja *sf* grapefruit.

torpe *adj* - **1.** [gen] clumsy - **2.** [necio] slow, dim-witted.

torpedear *vt* to torpedo.

torpedero *sm* torpedo boat.

torpedo *sm* - **1.** [proyectil] torpedo - **2.** [pez] electric ray.

torpeza *sf* - **1.** [gen] clumsiness; **fue una torpeza hacerlo/decirlo** it was a clumsy thing to do/say - **2.** [falta de inteligencia] slowness.

torrar *vt* to roast.

⬥ **torrarse** *vprnl fam* [de calor] to be roasting.

torre *sf* - **1.** [construcción] tower; ELECTR pylon; **torre (de apartamentos)** tower block; **torre de control** control tower; **torre del homenaje** keep; **torre de marfil** *fig* ivory tower; **torre de perforación** oil derrick - **2.** [en ajedrez] rook, castle - **3.** MIL turret - **4.** [chalé] cottage.

torrefacto, ta *adj* high-roast *(antes de s)*.

torrencial *adj* torrential.

torrente *sm* torrent; **un torrente de** *fig* [gente, palabras etc] a stream O flood of; [dinero, energía] masses of; **un torrente de voz** a powerful voice.

torrentera *sf* watercourse, gully.

torreón *sm* large fortified tower.

torreta *sf* - **1.** MIL turret - **2.** ELECTR pylon.

torrezno *sm* chunk of fried bacon.

tórrido, da *adj* lit & fig torrid.

torrija *sf* French toast *(U)* *(dipped in milk or wine)*.

torsión *sf* - **1.** [del cuerpo, brazo] twist, twisting *(U)* - **2.** MECÁN torsion.

torso *sm* culto torso.

torta *sf* - **1.** CULIN cake; **nos costó la torta un pan** it cost us an arm and a leg - **2.** *Andes, Col, R Plata & Ven* [tarta] cake - **3.** *fam* [bofetada] thump; **dar** O **pegar una torta a alguien** to thump sb - **4.** *fam* [accidente] crash; **darse** O **pegarse una torta** to crash.

➤ **ni torta** *loc adv* *fam* not a thing.

tortazo *sm* - **1.** *fam* [bofetada] thump; **dar** O **pegar un tortazo a alguien** to thump sb; **liarse a tortazos** to come to blows - **2.** *fam* [accidente] crash; **darse** O **pegarse un tortazo** to crash.

tortícolis *sf inv* crick in the neck.

tortilla *sf* - **1.** [de huevo] omelette; **tortilla (a la) española** Spanish O potato omelette; **tortilla (a la) francesa** French O plain omelette; **se dio la vuelta** O **se volvió la tortilla** the tables turned - **2.** [de maíz] tortilla.

tortillera *sf mfam despec* dyke, lesbian.

tortillería *sf* [restaurante] omelette restaurant.

tórtola *sf* turtledove.

tortolito, ta *sm, f (gen pl) fam* [enamorado] lovebird.

tortuga *sf* - **1.** [terrestre] tortoise; [marina] turtle; [fluvial] terrapin - **2.** *fam* [persona o cosa lenta] snail.

tortuosidad *sf* - **1.** [sinuosidad] tortuousness - **2.** *fig* [perversidad] deviousness.

tortuoso, sa *adj* - **1.** [sinuoso] tortuous, winding - **2.** *fig* [perverso] devious.

tortura *sf* torture.

torturador, ra ◇ *adj* torturing. ◇ *sm, f* torturer.

torturar *vt* to torture.

➤ **torturarse** *vprnl* to torture o.s.

torvo, va *adj* fierce.

torzamos ▷ **torcer**.

tos *sf* cough; **tos ferina** whooping cough.

tosco, ca *adj* - **1.** [basto] crude - **2.** *fig* [ignorante] coarse.

toser *vi* to cough.

tosquedad *sf* - **1.** [vulgaridad] crudeness - **2.** *fig* [ignorancia] coarseness.

tostadero *sm* roaster.

tostado, da *adj* - **1.** [pan, almendras] toasted - **2.** [color] brownish - **3.** [piel] tanned.

➤ **tostada** *sf* piece of toast; **café con tostados** coffee and toast.

tostador *sm* toaster.

tostadora *sf* = tostador.

tostar [23] *vt* - **1.** [dorar, calentar - pan, almendras] to toast; [- carne] to brown - **2.** [broncear] to tan - **3.** INFORM to burn.

➤ **tostarse** *vprnl* to get brown; **tostarse (al sol)** to sunbathe.

tostón *sm* - **1.** CULIN crouton - **2.** *fam* [rollo, aburrimiento] bore, drag - **3.** *fam* [persona molesta] pain.

total ◇ *adj* - **1.** [absoluto, completo] total - **2.** *mfam* [estupendo] brill, ace. ◇ *sm* - **1.** [suma] total - **2.** [totalidad, conjunto] whole; **el total del grupo** the whole group; **en total** in all. ◇ *adv* anyway; **total que me marché** so anyway, I left.

totalidad *sf* whole; **en su totalidad** as a whole.

totalitario, ria *adj* totalitarian.

totalitarismo *sm* totalitarianism.

totalizar [13] *vt* to add up to, to amount to.

tótem *(pl* totems O tótemes) *sm* totem.

totémico, ca *adj* totemic.

tour [tur] *(pl* tours) *sm* tour.

➤ **tour de force** *sm* tour de force.

➤ **tour operador** *sm* tour operator.

tournée [tur'ne] *(pl* tournées) *sf* tour; **ir de tournée** to go on tour.

toxicidad *sf* toxicity.

tóxico, ca *adj* toxic, poisonous.

➤ **tóxico** *sm* poison.

toxicología *sf* toxicology.

toxicológico, ca *adj* toxicological.

toxicomanía *sf* drug addiction.

toxicómano, na ◇ *adj* addicted to drugs. ◇ *sm, f* drug addict.

toxina *sf* toxin.

tozudez *sf* stubbornness, obstinacy.

tozudo, da ◇ *adj* stubborn. ◇ *sm, f* stubborn person.

traba *sf fig* [obstáculo] obstacle; **poner trabas (a alguien)** to put obstacles in the way (of sb).

trabado, da *adj* - **1.** [ligado - salsa] smooth; [- discurso] coherent - **2.** [atascado] jammed - **3.** GRAM ending in a consonant.

trabajado, da *adj* - **1.** [obra] carefully worked - **2.** [músculo] developed.

trabajador, ra ◇ *adj* hard-working. ◇ *sm, f* worker; **trabajador por cuenta ajena** employee; **trabajador por cuenta propia** self-employed person.

trabajar ◇ *vi* - **1.** [gen] to work; **trabajar de/en** to work as/in; **trabajar en una empresa** to work for a firm - **2.** CINE & TEATRO to act. ◇ *vt* - **1.** [hierro, barro, tierra] to work; [masa] to knead - **2.** [mejorar] to work on o at - **3.** *fig* [engatusar, convencer]: **trabajar a alguien (para que haga algo)** to work on sb (so that they do sthg).

trabajo *sm* - **1.** [gen] work; **hacer un buen trabajo** to do a good job; **trabajo intelectual/físico** mental/physical effort; **trabajo manual** manual labour; **trabajos forzados** o **forzosos** hard labour *(U)*; **trabajos manuales** [en el colegio] arts and crafts; **ser un trabajo de chinos** to be a finicky job - **2.** [empleo] job; **no tener trabajo** to be out of work - **3.** [estudio escrito] piece of work, essay - **4.** ECON & POLÍT labour - **5.** *fig* [esfuerzo] effort; **costar mucho trabajo** to take a lot of effort.

trabajoso, sa *adj* - **1.** [difícil] hard, difficult - **2.** [molesto] tiresome.

trabalenguas *sm inv* tongue-twister.

trabar *vt* - **1.** [sujetar] to fasten; [con grilletes] to shackle - **2.** [unir] to join - **3.** [iniciar - conversación, amistad] to strike up - **4.** [obstaculizar] to obstruct, to hinder - **5.** CULIN to thicken.
◆ **trabarse** *vprnl* - **1.** [enredarse] to get tangled - **2.** [espesarse] to thicken - **3.** *loc*: **se le trabó la lengua** he got tongue-tied.

trabazón *sf* - **1.** [de piezas, vigas] assembly - **2.** [de ideas, episodios] connection; [de discurso, novela] consistency.

trabilla *sf* [de pantalón] belt loop; [de chaqueta, abrigo] half belt; [de medias, polainas] foot strap.

trabucar *vt* to mix up.
◆ **trabucarse** *vprnl* [al hablar] to get tongue-tied.

trabuco *sm* [arma de fuego] blunderbuss.

traca *sf* string of firecrackers.

tracción *sf* traction; **tracción a las cuatro ruedas** four-wheel drive; **tracción delantera/trasera** front-wheel/rear-wheel drive.

trace *etc* ➪ **trazar**.

tracoma *sm* trachoma.

tractor *sm* tractor.

tractorista *smf* tractor driver.

tradición *sf* tradition.

tradicional *adj* traditional.

tradicionalismo *sm* traditionalism; POLÍT conservatism.

tradicionalista *adj* & *smf* [conservador] traditionalist; POLÍT conservative.

traducción *sf* translation; **traducción automática/simultánea** machine/simultaneous translation; **traducción directa/inversa** translation into/out of one's own language.

traducir [33] ◇ *vt* - **1.** [a otro idioma] to translate - **2.** *fig* [expresar] to express. ◇ *vi*: **traducir (de/a)** to translate (from/into).
◆ **traducirse** *vprnl* [a otro idioma]: **traducirse (por)** to be translated (by o as).
◆ **traducirse en** *vprnl* [ocasionar] to lead to.

traductor, ra ◇ *adj* translating. ◇ *sm, f* translator; **traductor jurado** *translator qualified to work at court and translate legal documents*.

traer [73] *vt* - **1.** [trasladar, provocar] to bring; [consecuencias] to carry, to have; **traer consigo** [implicar] to mean, to lead to - **2.** [llevar] to carry; **¿qué traes ahí?** what have you got there? - **3.** [llevar adjunto, dentro] to have; **trae un artículo interesante** it has an interesting article in it - **4.** [llevar puesto] to wear.
◆ **traerse** *vprnl*: **traérselas** *fam fig* to be a real handful.

tráfago *sm* [de calle, ciudad, oficina] hustle and bustle.

traficante *smf* [de drogas, armas etc] trafficker.

traficar [10] *vi*: **traficar (en/con algo)** to traffic (in sthg).

tráfico *sm* [de vehículos] traffic; [de drogas, armas] trafficking, dealing; **tráfico rodado** road traffic; **tráfico de influencias** political corruption.

tragaderas *sfpl fam*: **tener (buenas) tragaderas** [ser crédulo] to fall for anything; [tener aguante] to be able to stomach anything.

tragaluz *sm* skylight.

tragamonedas *sf inv Amér fam* slot machine.

traganíqueles *sf inv Amér fam* ➪ **máquina**.

tragaperras *sf inv* slot machine.

tragar [16] ◇ *vt* - **1.** [ingerir, creer] to swallow - **2.** [absorber] to swallow up - **3.** *fig* [soportar] to put up with; **no (poder) tragar a alguien** not to be able to stand sb - **4.** *fig* [refrenar] to contain, to keep to o.s.; [lágrimas] to choke back - **5.** *fam* [consumir mucho - suj: persona, coche] to devour, to guzzle. ◇ *vi* - **1.** [ingerir] to swallow - **2.** [aguantar] to grin and bear it; [acceder, ceder] to give in.
◆ **tragarse** *vprnl fig* [soportarse]: **no se tragan** they can't stand each other.

tragedia *sf* tragedy.

trágico, ca *adj* tragic.

tragicomedia *sf* tragicomedy.

tragicómico, ca *adj* tragicomic.

trago *sm* - **1.** [de líquido] mouthful; **dar un trago de algo** to take a swig of sthg; **de un trago** in one gulp - **2.** *fam* [copa] drink; **echar un tra-**

go to have a quick drink **- 3.** *fam* [disgusto]: **ser un trago para alguien** to be tough on sb; **pasar un mal trago** to have a tough time of it.

tragón, **ona** *fam* <> *adj* greedy. <> *sm, f* pig, glutton.

trague *etc* ⊳ **tragar**.

traición *sf* **- 1.** [infidelidad] betrayal; **a traición** treacherously **- 2.** DER treason; **alta traición** high treason.

traicionar *vt* [persona, país, ideales] to betray.

traicionero, **ra** <> *adj* [desleal] treacherous; DER treasonous. <> *sm, f* traitor.

traído, **da** *adj*: **traído y llevado** well-worn, hackneyed.

traidor, **ra** <> *adj* treacherous; DER treasonous. <> *sm, f* traitor.

traiga *etc* ⊳ **traer**.

tráiler ['trailer] (*pl* **trailers**) *sm* **- 1.** CINE trailer **- 2.** AUTO articulated lorry **- 3.** *Méx* [caravana] caravan *UK*, trailer *US*.

trainera *sf* small Basque fishing boat.

traje *sm* **- 1.** [con chaqueta] suit; [de una pieza] dress; **ir de traje** to wear a suit; **traje de baño** swimsuit; **traje de ceremonia** *o* **de gala** dress suit, formal dress *(U)*; **traje de chaqueta** woman's two-piece suit; **traje de etiqueta** evening dress *(U)*; **traje de noche** evening dress; **traje pantalón** trouser suit **- 2.** [regional, de época etc] costume; **traje de luces** matador's outfit **- 3.** [ropa] clothes *pl*; **traje de diario** everyday clothes; **traje de paisano** [de militar] civilian clothes; [de policía] plain clothes; *ver también* **tauromaquia**.

trajeado, **da** *adj* **- 1.** [con chaqueta] wearing a jacket **- 2.** *fam* [arreglado] spruced up.

trajera *etc* ⊳ **traer**.

trajín *sm fam* [ajetreo] bustle.

trajinar *vi fam* to bustle about.

➡ **trajinarse a** *vprnl fam* [ligarse a] to get off with.

trajo ⊳ **traer**.

trama *sf* **- 1.** [de hilos] weft **- 2.** [argumento] plot **- 3.** [conspiración] intrigue.

tramar *vt* [planear] to plot; [complot] to hatch; **estar tramando algo** to be up to something.

tramitación *sf* [acción] processing.

tramitar *vt* **- 1.** [suj: autoridades - pasaporte, permiso] to take the necessary steps to obtain; [- solicitud, dimisión] to process **- 2.** [suj: solicitante]: **tramitar un permiso/visado** to be in the process of applying for a licence/visa.

trámite *sm* [gestión] formal step; **de trámite** routine, formal.

➡ **trámites** *smpl* **- 1.** [proceso] procedure *sing* **- 2.** [papeleo] paperwork *(U)*.

tramo *sm* [espacio] section, stretch; [de escalera] flight (of stairs).

tramontana *sf* north wind.

tramoya *sf* **- 1.** TEATRO stage machinery *(U)* **- 2.** *fig* [enredo] intrigue.

tramoyista *smf* TEATRO stagehand.

trampa *sf* **- 1.** [para cazar] trap; *fig* [engaño] trick; **caer en la trampa** to fall into the trap; **tender una trampa (a alguien)** to set *o* lay a trap (for sb); **hacer trampas** to cheat **- 2.** [trampilla] trapdoor **- 3.** *fam* [deuda] debt.

trampear *vi fam* **- 1.** [estafar] to swindle money **- 2.** [ir tirando] to struggle along.

trampilla *sf* [en el suelo] trapdoor.

trampolín *sm* **- 1.** [de piscina] diving board; [de esquí] ski jump; [en gimnasia] springboard **- 2.** *fig* [medio, impulso] springboard.

tramposo, **sa** <> *adj* [fullero] cheating. <> *sm, f* **- 1.** [fullero] cheat **- 2.** *fam* [moroso] bad debtor.

tranca *sf* **- 1.** [en puerta, ventana] bar **- 2.** [arma] cudgel, stick **- 3.** *fam* [borrachera]: **coger una tranca** to get plastered **- 4.** *loc*: **a trancas y barrancas** with great difficulty.

trancarse *vprnl Amér* [atorarse] to get blocked, to get clogged up.

trancazo *sm* **- 1.** [golpe] blow (with a stick) **- 2.** *fam* [gripe] bout of the flu; [resfriado] cold.

trance *sm* **- 1.** [apuro] difficult situation; **estar en trance de hacer algo** to be about to do sthg; **pasar por un mal trance** to go through a bad patch **- 2.** [estado hipnótico] trance; **estar en trance** to be in a trance.

tranquilidad *sf* peacefulness, calmness; **para mayor tranquilidad** to be on the safe side.

tranquilizador, **ra** *adj* calming.

tranquilizante <> *adj* **- 1.** [música, color etc] soothing **- 2.** MED tranquilizing. <> *sm* MED tranquilizer.

tranquilizar [13] *vt* **- 1.** [calmar] to calm (down) **- 2.** [dar confianza] to reassure.

➡ **tranquilizarse** *vprnl* **- 1.** [calmarse] to calm down **- 2.** [ganar confianza] to feel reassured.

tranquillo *sm Esp fam*: **coger el tranquillo a algo** to get the knack of sthg.

tranquilo, **la** *adj* **- 1.** [sosegado - lugar, música] peaceful; [- persona, tono de voz, mar] calm; **¡(tú) tranquilo!** *fam* don't you worry! **- 2.** [velada, charla, negocio] quiet **- 3.** [mente] untroubled; [conciencia] clear **- 4.** [despreocupado] casual, laid-back; **quedarse tan tranquilo** not to bat an eyelid.

transacción *sf* COM transaction.

transalpino, **na**, **trasalpino**, **na** *adj* transalpine.

transar *vi Amér* [negociar] to come to an arrangement, to reach a compromise; [transigir] to compromise, to give in.

transatlántico, ca, trasatlántico, ca *adj* transatlantic.

━ **transatlántico, trasatlántico** *sm* NÁUT (ocean) liner.

transbordador, trasbordador *sm*
- **1.** NÁUT ferry - **2.** AERON: transbordador (espacial) space shuttle.

transbordar, trasbordar *vi* to change *(trains etc)*.

transbordo, trasbordo *sm*: hacer transbordo to change *(trains etc)*.

transcendencia = trascendencia.

transcendental = trascendental.

transcender [20] = trascender.

transcontinental *adj* transcontinental.

transcribir, trascribir *vt* - **1.** [escribir] to transcribe - **2.** *fig* [expresar] to express in writing.

transcripción, trascripción *sf* transcription.

transcrito, ta, trascrito, ta *adj* transcribed.

transcurrir, trascurrir *vi* - **1.** [tiempo] to pass, to go by - **2.** [ocurrir] to take place, to go off.

transcurso, trascurso *sm* - **1.** [paso de tiempo] passing - **2.** [periodo de tiempo]: en el transcurso de in the course of.

transeúnte *smf* - **1.** [viandante] passer-by - **2.** [residente de paso] temporary resident.

transexual *adj* & *smf* transsexual.

transferencia, trasferencia *sf* transfer; pagar algo mediante transferencia to pay sthg by transfer.

transferir [27], trasferir [27] *vt* to transfer.

transfiguración, trasfiguración *sf* transfiguration.

transfigurarse, trasfigurarse *vprnl* to become transfigured.

transformable, trasformable *adj* convertible *(furniture)*.

transformación, trasformación *sf*
- **1.** [cambio, conversión] transformation - **2.** [en rugby] conversion.

transformador, trasformador *sm* ELECTRÓN transformer.

transformar, trasformar *vt* - **1.** [cambiar radicalmente]: transformar algo/a alguien (en) to transform sthg/sb (into) - **2.** [convertir]: transformar algo (en) to convert sthg (into) - **3.** [en rugby] to convert.

━ **transformarse, trasformarse** *vprnl*
- **1.** [cambiar radicalmente] to be transformed - **2.** [convertirse]: transformarse en algo to be converted into sthg.

transformista, trasformista *smf* [artista] quick-change artist.

tránsfuga, trásfuga *smf* POLÍT defector.

transfuguismo, trasfuguismo *sm* POLÍT defection.

transfusión, trasfusión *sf* transfusion.

transgénico, ca *adj* genetically modified, transgenic.

━ **transgénicos** *smpl* GM foods.

transgredir [78], trasgredir [78] *vt* to transgress.

transgresión, trasgresión *sf* transgression.

transgresor, ra, trasgresor, ra *sm,* *f* transgressor.

transiberiano *sm* Trans-Siberian railway.

transición *sf* transition; periodo de transición transition period; transición democrática transition to democracy.

transido, da *adj*: transido (de) stricken (with); transido de pena grief-stricken.

transigencia *sf* willingness to compromise.

transigente *adj* - **1.** [que cede] compromising - **2.** [tolerante] tolerant.

transigir [15] *vi* - **1.** [ceder] to compromise - **2.** [ser tolerante] to be tolerant.

transistor *sm* transistor.

transitable *adj* [franqueable] passable; [no cerrado al tráfico] open to traffic.

transitar *vi* to go (along).

transitivo, va *adj* transitive.

tránsito *sm* - **1.** [circulación - gen] movement; [- de vehículos] traffic; pasajeros en tránsito a... passengers with connecting flights to...; tránsito rodado road traffic - **2.** [transporte] transit.

transitorio, ria *adj* [gen] transitory; [residencia] temporary; [régimen, medida] transitional, interim.

translúcido, da, traslúcido, da *adj* translucent.

translucirse [32], traslucirse [32] *vprnl* [motivos, sentimientos, cualidades] to show through, to be obvious.

transmediterráneo, a, trasmediterráneo, a *adj* transmediterranean.

transmisible, trasmisible *adj* - **1.** [enfermedad] transmittible - **2.** [título, posesiones] transferrable.

transmisión, trasmisión *sf* - **1.** [gen & AUTO] transmission; de transmisión oral/sexual MED sexually/orally transmitted; transmisión del

pensamiento telepathy - **2.** RADIO & TV broadcast, broadcasting *(U)* - **3.** [de herencia, poderes etc] transference.

transmisor, ra, trasmisor, ra *adj* transmission *(antes de s)*.

➤ **transmisor, trasmisor** *sm* transmitter.

transmitir, transmitir *vt* - **1.** [gen] to transmit; [saludos, noticias] to pass on - **2.** RADIO & TV to broadcast - **3.** [ceder] to transfer.

➤ **transmitirse, trasmitirse** *vprnl* to be transmitted.

transmutación, trasmutación *sf* transmutation.

transmutar, trasmutar *vt* to transmute.

transnacional, trasnacional *adj* transnational.

transparencia, trasparencia *sf* transparency.

transparentarse, trasparentarse *vprnl* - **1.** [tela] to be see-through; [vidrio, líquido] to be transparent - **2.** *fig* [manifestarse] to show through.

transparente, trasparente *adj* [gen] transparent; [tela] see-through.

transpiración, traspiración *sf* perspiration.

transpirar, traspirar *vi* to perspire.

transponer [65], **trasponer** [65] *vt* - **1.** [cambiar] to switch - **2.** [desaparecer detrás de] to disappear behind.

➤ **transponerse, trasponerse** *vprnl* [adormecerse] to doze off.

transportable *adj* portable.

transportador *sm* [para medir ángulos] protractor.

transportar, trasportar *vt* - **1.** [trasladar] to transport - **2.** [embelesar] to captivate.

➤ **transportarse, trasportarse** *vprnl* [embelesarse] to go into raptures.

transporte *sm* transport UK, transportation US; **transporte público** O **colectivo** public transport UK O transportation US.

transportista *smf* carrier.

transposición, trasposición *sf* transposition.

transpuesto, ta = traspuesto.

transvasar, trasvasar *vt* - **1.** [líquido] to decant - **2.** [río] to transfer.

transvase, trasvase *sm* - **1.** [de líquido] decanting - **2.** [de río] transfer.

transversal, trasversal ◇ *adj* transverse. ◇ *sf* GEOM transversal.

tranvía *sm* tram, streetcar US.

trapear *vt* Andes, Amér C & Méx [suelo] to mop.

trapecio *sm* - **1.** [de gimnasia] trapeze - **2.** GEOM trapezium - **3.** ANAT [músculo] trapezius.

trapecista *smf* trapeze artist.

trapero, ra *sm, f* rag-and-bone man (*f* rag-and-bone woman).

trapezoide *sm* ANAT & GEOM trapezoid.

trapichear *vi fam* to be on the fiddle.

trapicheo *sm fam* - **1.** [negocio sucio] fiddle - **2.** [tejemaneje] scheme, scheming *(U)*.

trapío *sm* TAUROM good bearing.

trapisonda *sf fam* - **1.** [riña] row, commotion - **2.** [enredo] scheme.

trapo *sm* - **1.** [trozo de tela] rag - **2.** [gamuza, bayeta] cloth; **pasar el trapo a algo** to wipe sthg with a cloth; **los trapos sucios se lavan en casa** you should not wash your dirty linen in public; **poner a alguien como un trapo** to tear sb to pieces - **3.** TAUROM cape; **entrar al trapo** *fig* to rise to the bait - **4.** *loc*: **a todo trapo** at full pelt.

➤ **trapos** *smpl fam* [ropa] clothes.

tráquea *sf* windpipe; MED trachea.

traqueotomía *sf* tracheotomy.

traqueteo *sm* [ruido] rattling.

tras *prep* - **1.** [detrás de] behind - **2.** [después de, en pos de] after; **uno tras otro** one after the other; **andar tras algo** to be after sthg.

trasalpino, na = transalpino.

trasatlántico, ca = transatlántico.

trasbordador = transbordador.

trasbordar = transbordar.

trasbordo = transbordo.

trascendencia, transcendencia *sf* importance; **tener una gran trascendencia** to be deeply significant.

trascendental, transcendental *adj* - **1.** [importante] momentous - **2.** [meditación] transcendental.

trascendente *adj* momentous.

trascender [20], **transcender** [20] *vi* - **1.** [extenderse]: **trascender (a algo)** to spread (across sthg) - **2.** [filtrarse] to be leaked - **3.** [sobrepasar]: **trascender de** to transcend, to go beyond.

trascribir = transcribir.

trascripción = transcripción.

trascrito, ta = transcrito.

trascurrir = transcurrir.

trascurso = transcurso.

trasegar [35] *vt* - **1.** [desordenar] to rummage about amongst - **2.** [transvasar] to decant.

trasero, ra *adj* back *(antes de s)*, rear *(antes de s)*.

➤ **trasero** *sm fam* backside, butt US.

➤ **trasera** *sf* rear.

trasferencia = transferencia.

trasferir [27] = transferir.

trasfiguración = transfiguración.

trasfigurarse = transfigurarse.

trasfondo *sm* background; [de palabras, intenciones] undertone.

trasformable = transformable.

trasformación = transformación.

trasformador = transformador.

trasformar = transformar.

trasformista = transformista.

trásfuga = tránsfuga.

trasfuguismo = transfuguismo.

trasfusión = transfusión.

trasgredir [78] = transgredir.

trasgresión = transgresión.

trasgresor, ra = transgresor.

trashumancia *sf* seasonal migration (of livestock).

trashumante *adj* seasonally migratory.

trashumar *vi* to migrate seasonally.

trasiega ▷ trasegar.

trasiego *sm* - **1.** [movimiento] comings and goings *pl* - **2.** [transvase] decanting.

trasiegue ▷ trasegar.

traslación *sf* ASTRON passage.

trasladar *vt* - **1.** [desplazar] to move - **2.** [a empleado, funcionario] to transfer - **3.** [reunión, fecha] to postpone, to move back - **4.** [traducir] to translate - **5.** *fig* [expresar]: **trasladar algo al papel** to transfer sthg onto paper.

➤ **trasladarse** *vprnl* - **1.** [desplazarse] to go - **2.** [mudarse] to move; **me traslado de piso** I'm moving flat.

traslado *sm* - **1.** [de casa, empresa, muebles] move, moving (U) - **2.** [de trabajo] transfer - **3.** [de personas] movement.

traslúcido, da = translúcido.

traslucirse [32] = translucirse.

trasluz *sm* reflected light; **al trasluz** against the light.

trasmano ➤ **a trasmano** *loc adv* - **1.** [fuera de alcance] out of reach - **2.** [lejos] out of the way.

trasmediterráneo, a = transmediterráneo.

trasmisible = transmisible.

trasmisión = transmisión.

trasmisor, ra = transmisor.

trasmitir = transmitir.

trasmutación *sf* = transmutación.

trasmutar = transmutar.

trasnacional = transnacional.

trasnochado, da *adj* outdated.

trasnochador, ra ◇ *adj* given to staying up late. ◇ *sm, f* night owl.

trasnochar *vi* to stay up late, to go to bed late.

trasoceánico, ca = transoceánico.

traspapelar *vt* to mislay, to misplace.

➤ **traspapelarse** *vprnl* to get mislaid o misplaced.

trasparencia = transparencia.

trasparentarse = transparentarse.

trasparente = transparente.

traspasar *vt* - **1.** [perforar, atravesar] to go through, to pierce; [suj: líquido] to soak through - **2.** [cruzar] to cross (over); [puerta] to pass through - **3.** [cambiar de sitio] to move - **4.** [vender - jugador] to transfer; [- negocio] to sell (as a going concern) - **5.** *fig* [exceder] to go beyond.

traspaso *sm* - **1.** [venta - de jugador] transfer; [- de negocio] sale (as a going concern) - **2.** [precio - de jugador] transfer fee; [- de negocio] takeover fee.

traspié (*pl* traspiés) *sm* - **1.** [resbalón] trip, stumble; **dar un traspié** to trip up - **2.** *fig* [error] blunder, slip.

traspiración = transpiración.

traspirar = transpirar.

trasplantar *vt* to transplant.

trasplante *sm* transplant, transplanting (U).

trasponer [65] = transponer.

trasportar = transportar.

trasposición *sf* = transposición.

traspuesto, ta, transpuesto, ta *adj* dozing.

trasquilado, da *adj*: **salir trasquilado** *fig* to come off badly.

trasquilar *vt* [esquilar] to shear.

trasquilón *sm*: **hacerle un trasquilón a alguien** to cut sb's hair crooked.

trastabillar *vi* [tambalearse] to stagger; [tropezar] to stumble; [tartamudear] to stutter.

trastada *sf fam* dirty trick; **hacer una trastada a alguien** to play a dirty trick on sb.

trastazo *sm fam* bump, bang; **darse** o **pegarse un trastazo** to bang o bump o.s.

traste *sm* - **1.** MÚS fret - **2.** *C Sur fam* [trasero] bottom - **3.** *Andes, Amér C, Caribe & Méx*: **trastes** utensils - **4.** *loc*: **dar al traste con algo** to ruin sthg; **irse al traste** to fall through.

trastero *sm* junk room.

trastienda *sf* backroom.

trasto *sm* - **1.** [utensilio inútil] piece of junk, junk (U) - **2.** *fam* [persona traviesa] menace, nuisance - **3.** *fam fig* [persona inútil]: **trasto (viejo)** dead loss.

➤ **trastos** *smpl fam* [pertenencias, equipo] things, stuff (U); **tirarse los trastos a la cabeza** to have a flaming row.

trastocar [36] *vt* [cambiar] to turn upside down.

➤ **trastocarse** *vprnl* [enloquecer] to go mad.

trastornado, **da** *adj* disturbed, unbalanced.

trastornar *vt* - **1.** [volver loco] to drive mad - **2.** [inquietar] to worry, to trouble - **3.** [alterar] to turn upside down; [planes] to disrupt, to upset - **4.** [estómago] to upset.
► **trastornarse** *vprnl* [volverse loco] to go mad.

trastorno *sm* - **1.** [mental] disorder; **trastorno bipolar** bipolar disorder; [digestivo] upset - **2.** [alteración - por huelga, nevada] trouble *(U)*, disruption *(U)*; [- por guerra etc] upheaval.

trasvasar = transvasar.

trasvase = transvase.

trasversal = transversal.

trata *sf*: **trata de blancas** white slave trade; **trata de esclavos** slave trade.

tratable *adj* easy-going, friendly.

tratadista *smf* treatise writer, essayist.

tratado *sm* - **1.** [convenio] treaty - **2.** [escrito] treatise.

tratamiento *sm* - **1.** [gen & MED] treatment; **estar en tratamiento** to be receiving treatment; **tratamiento del dolor** pain relief - **2.** [título] title, form of address - **3.** INFORM processing; **tratamiento de datos/textos** data/word processing; **tratamiento por lotes** batch processing.

Tratamiento

In Latin America a lot of importance is attached to forms of address, which is hardly surprising in societies with pronounced differences between social classes. In many countries, higher education is a privilege still largely restricted to the wealthy few and much significance is attached to university degrees and the titles that go with them. Titles such as "licenciado" ("graduate", much used in Mexico), "doctor" (used, for example, in Colombia and Uruguay) and "ingeniero" ("engineer") are used to address people felt to have social standing, sometimes even when they don't actually possess the degree in question. Such titles are also commonly used on business cards and in addresses.

tratante *smf* dealer; [de vinos] merchant.

tratar ◇ *vt* - **1.** [gen & MED] to treat - **2.** [discutir] to discuss - **3.** INFORM to process - **4.** [dirigirse a]: **tratar a alguien de** [usted, tú etc] to address sb as - **5.**: **tratar a alguien de algo** [cretino etc] to call sb sthg. ◇ *vi* - **1.** [intentar]: **tratar de hacer algo** to try to do sthg - **2.** [versar]: **tratar de/sobre** to be about - **3.** [tener relación]: **tratar con alguien** to mix with sb, to have dealings with sb - **4.** [comerciar]: **tratar en** to deal in.

► **tratarse** *vprnl* - **1.** [relacionarse]: **tratarse con** to mix with, to have dealings with - **2.** [versar]: **tratarse de** to be about; **¿de qué se trata?** what's it about?

tratativas *sfpl C Sur* negotiation *sing*.

trato *sm* - **1.** [comportamiento] treatment; **de trato agradable** pleasant; **malos tratos** battering *(U) (of child, wife)* - **2.** [relación] dealings *pl*; **tener trato con alguien** to associate with, to be friendly with - **3.** [acuerdo] deal; **cerrar** o **hacer un trato** to do o make a deal; **¡trato hecho!** it's a deal! - **4.** [tratamiento] title, term of address.

trauma *sm* trauma.

traumático, **ca** *adj* traumatic.

traumatismo *sm* traumatism.

traumatizante *adj* traumatic.

traumatizar [13] *vt* to traumatize.
► **traumatizarse** *vprnl* to be devastated.

traumatología *sf* traumatology.

traumatólogo, **ga** *sm*, *f* traumatologist.

través ► **a través de** *loc prep* - **1.** [de un lado a otro de] across, over - **2.** [por, por medio de] through. ► **de través** *loc adv* [transversalmente] crossways; [de lado] crosswise, sideways.

travesaño *sm* - **1.** ARQUIT crosspiece - **2.** DEP crossbar - **3.** [de escalera] rung.

travesero, **ra** *adj*: **flauta travesera** flute.

travesía *sf* - **1.** [viaje - por mar] voyage, crossing; [- por aire] flight - **2.** [calle] cross-street.

travestido, **da**, **travestí** *(pl* travestís*)* *sm*, *f* transvestite.

travestirse [26] *vprnl* to cross-dress.

travestismo *sm* transvestism.

travesura *sf* [acción] prank, mischief *(U)*; **hacer travesuras** to play pranks, to get up to mischief.

traviesa *sf* - **1.** FERROC sleeper *(on track)* - **2.** CONSTR crossbeam, tie beam.

travieso, **sa** *adj* mischievous.

travista, **travistiera** *etc v* ➤ travestirse.

trayecto *sm* - **1.** [distancia] distance - **2.** [viaje] journey, trip - **3.** [ruta] route; **final de trayecto** end of the line.

trayectoria *sf* - **1.** [recorrido] trajectory - **2.** *fig* [evolución] path.

traza *sf* [aspecto] appearance *(U)*, looks *pl*; **tener trazas de hacer algo** to show signs of doing sthg; **esto no tiene trazas de acabar pronto** this doesn't look as if it's going to finish soon.

trazado *sm* - **1.** [trazo] outline, sketching - **2.** [diseño] plan, design - **3.** [recorrido] route.

trazar [13] *vt* - **1.** [dibujar] to draw, to trace; [ruta] to plot - **2.** [indicar, describir] to outline - **3.** [idear] to draw up.

trazo *sm* **- 1.** [de dibujo, rostro] line **- 2.** [de letra] stroke.

trébol *sm* **- 1.** [planta] clover **- 2.** [naipe] club.
➤ **tréboles** *smpl* [naipes] clubs.

trece *num* thirteen; **mantenerse** *o* **seguir en sus trece** to stick to one's guns; *ver también* **seis**.

treceavo, va *num* thirteenth; **la treceava parte** a thirteenth.

trecho *sm* [espacio] distance; [tiempo] time, while; **de trecho en trecho** every so often.

tregua *sf* truce; *fig* respite.

treinta *num* thirty; **los (años) treinta** the Thirties; *ver también* **seis**.

treintañero, ra *adj* & *sm, f* thirtysomething.

treintena *sf* thirty.

tremebundo, da *adj* terrifying.

tremendo, da *adj* **- 1.** [enorme] tremendous, enormous **- 2.** [travieso] mischievous **- 3.** [atroz, horripilante] horrifying **- 4.** *fam* [gordísimo] really fat **- 5.** *loc*: **tomar** *o* **tomarse algo a la tremenda** to take sthg hard.

trementina *sf* turpentine.

tremolar *vi culto* to wave, to flutter.

tremolina *sf* row, uproar.

trémolo *sm* tremolo.

trémulo, la *adj* [voz] trembling; [luz] flickering.

tren *sm* **- 1.** [ferrocarril] train; **ir en tren** to go by train; **tren de alta velocidad/largo recorrido** high-speed/long-distance train; **tren de cercanías** local train, suburban train; **tren correo** mail train; **tren de mercancías** freight *o* goods train; **estar como (para parar) un tren** to be really gorgeous; **perder el tren** *fig* to miss the boat; **subirse al tren** *fig* to climb on the bandwagon **- 2.** TECNOL line; **tren de aterrizaje** undercarriage, landing gear; **tren de lavado** car wash **- 3.** *fig* [estilo]: **tren de vida** lifestyle; **vivir a todo tren** to live in style.

trena *sf fam* nick, slammer.

trenca *sf* duffle coat.

trence *etc* ⮑ **trenzar**.

trenza *sf* **- 1.** [de pelo] plait **- 2.** [de fibras] braid.

trenzar [13] *vt* **- 1.** [pelo] to plait **- 2.** [fibras] to braid.

trepa *smf fam* social climber.

trepador, ra ◇ *adj*: **planta trepadora** climber, creeper. ◇ *sm, f fam* social climber.

trepanación *sf* trepanation.

trepar ◇ *vt* to climb. ◇ *vi* **- 1.** [subir] to climb **- 2.** *fam* [medrar] to be a social climber.

trepidación *sf* shaking, vibration.

trepidante *adj* **- 1.** [rápido, vivo] frenetic **- 2.** [vibratorio] shaking, vibrating.

trepidar *vi* to shake, to vibrate.

tres *num* three; **de tres al cuarto** cheap, third-rate; **ni a la de tres** for anything in the world, no way; **no ver tres en un burro** to be as blind as a bat; **tres cuartos de lo mismo** the same thing; *ver también* **seis**.
➤ **tres cuartos** *sm inv* [abrigo] three-quarter-length coat.
➤ **tres en raya** *sm* noughts and crosses *(U)* UK, tick-tack-toe US.

trescientos, tas *num* three hundred; *ver también* **seis**.

tresillo *sm* **- 1.** [sofá] three-piece suite **- 2.** [juego de naipes] ombre.

treta *sf* trick.

tríada *sf* triad.

trial *sm* DEP trial; **trial indoor** indoor trial.

triangular *adj* triangular.

triángulo *sm* **- 1.** GEOM & MÚS triangle; **el triángulo de las Bermudas** the Bermuda Triangle; **triángulo equilátero/rectángulo** equilateral/right-angled triangle **- 2.** *fam* [amoroso] ménage à trois.

triates *smpl Amér* triplets.

tribal *adj* tribal.

tribu *sf* tribe; **tribu urbana** *identifiable social group, such as punks or yuppies, made up of young people living in urban areas.*

tribulación *sf* tribulation.

tribuna *sf* **- 1.** [estrado] rostrum, platform; [del jurado] jury box **- 2.** [DEP - localidad] stand; [- graderío] grandstand **- 3.** PRENSA: **tribuna de prensa** press box; **tribuna libre** open forum.

tribunal *sm* **- 1.** [gen] court; **llevar a alguien/acudir a los tribunales** to take sb/go to court; **Tribunal Constitucional** Constitutional Court; **Tribunal Supremo** High Court UK, Supreme Court US; **Tribunal tutelar de menores** Juvenile Court **- 2.** [de examen] board of examiners; [de concurso] panel.

tributación *sf* **- 1.** [impuesto] tax **- 2.** [sistema] taxation.

tributar ◇ *vt* [homenaje] to pay; [respeto, admiración] to have. ◇ *vi* [pagar impuestos] to pay taxes.

tributario, ria ◇ *adj* tax *(antes de s).* ◇ *sm, f* taxpayer.

tributo *sm* **- 1.** [impuesto] tax **- 2.** *fig* [precio] price **- 3.** [homenaje] tribute.

tríceps *sm inv* triceps.

triciclo *sm* tricycle.

tricolor *adj* tricolour, three-coloured.

tricornio *sm* three-cornered hat.

tricotar *vt* & *vi* to knit.

tricotosa *sf* knitting machine.

tridente *sm* trident.

tridimensional *adj* three-dimensional.

trienal *adj* triennial, three-yearly.

trienio *sm* - **1.** [tres años] three years *pl* - **2.** [paga] *three-yearly salary increase.*

trifásico, ca *adj* ELECTR three-phase.

trifulca *sf fam* row, squabble.

trigal *sm* wheat field.

trigésimo, ma *num* thirtieth.

trigo *sm* wheat.

trigonometría *sf* trigonometry.

trigueño, ña *adj* - **1.** [tez] olive; [cabello] corn-coloured - **2.** *Ven* [pelo] dark brown; [persona] olive-skinned.

triguero, ra *adj* [del trigo] wheat *(antes de s)*.

trilateral *adj* trilateral.

trilingüe *adj* trilingual.

trilla *sf* - **1.** [acción] threshing - **2.** [tiempo] threshing time O season.

trillado, da *adj fig* well-worn, trite.

trilladora *sf* [máquina] threshing machine.

trillar *vt* to thresh.

trillizo, za *sm, f* triplet.

trillón *sm* trillion *UK*, quintillion *US*.

trilogía *sf* trilogy.

trimestral *adj* three-monthly, quarterly; [exámenes, notas] end-of-term *(antes de s)*.

trimestre *sm* three months *pl*, quarter; [en escuela, universidad] term.

trimotor ◇ *adj* three-engined. ◇ *sm* three-engined aeroplane.

trinar *vi* to chirp, to warble; **está que trina** *fig* she's fuming.

trincar [10] *fam* ◇ *vt* - **1.** [agarrar] to grab - **2.** [detener] to nick, to arrest. ◇ *vi* [beber] to guzzle.

➡ **trincarse** *vprnl fam* [beberse] to guzzle, to down.

trinchar *vt* to carve.

trinchera *sf* - **1.** MIL trench - **2.** [abrigo] trench coat.

trineo *sm* [pequeño] sledge; [grande] sleigh.

Trinidad *sf*: **la (Santísima) Trinidad** the (Holy) Trinity.

Trinidad y Tobago *n pr* Trinidad and Tobago.

trinitario, ria *adj* & *sm, f* Trinitarian.

trino *sm* [de pájaros] chirp, chirping *(U)*; MÚS trill.

trinque *etc* ⊏➤ **trincar**.

trinquete *sm* NÁUT foremast.

trío *sm* - **1.** [gen] trio - **2.** [de naipes] three of a kind.

tripa *sf* - **1.** [intestino] gut, intestine - **2.** *fam* [barriga] gut, belly; **me duele la tripa** I have belly-ache; **revolverle las tripas a alguien** *fig* to turn sb's stomach.

➡ **tripas** *sfpl fig* [interior] insides; **hacer de tripas corazón** to pluck up one's courage.

tripartito, ta *adj* tripartite.

tripi *sm mfam* tab.

triple ◇ *adj* triple. ◇ *sm* - **1.** [tres veces]: **el triple** three times as much; **el triple de gente** three times as many people - **2.** [en baloncesto] three-pointer.

triplicado *sm* second copy, triplicate; **por triplicado** in triplicate.

triplicar [10] *vt* to triple, to treble.

➡ **triplicarse** *vprnl* to triple, to treble.

trípode *sm* tripod.

tríptico *sm* - **1.** ARTE triptych - **2.** [folleto] three-part document.

triptongo *sm* GRAM triphthong.

tripulación *sf* crew.

tripulante *smf* crew member.

tripular *vt* to man.

triquina *sf* trichina.

triquinosis *sf inv* trichinosis.

triquiñuela *sf (gen pl) fam* trick.

tris *sm*: **estar en un tris de (hacer algo)** to be within a whisker of (doing sthg).

trisílabo, ba *adj* GRAM trisyllabic.

triste *adj* - **1.** [gen] sad; [día, tiempo, paisaje] gloomy, dreary; **es triste que** it's a shame O pity that - **2.** *fig* [color, vestido, luz] pale, faded - **3.** *(antes de s)* [humilde] poor; [sueldo] sorry, miserable; **ni un triste** *fig* not a single.

tristeza *sf* - **1.** [gen] sadness; [de paisaje, día] gloominess, dreariness - **2.** [de color, vestido, luz] paleness.

tristón, ona *adj* rather sad O miserable.

tritón *sm* newt.

trituración *sf* grinding, crushing.

triturador *sm* [de basura] waste-disposal unit; [de papeles] shredder.

trituradora *sf* crushing machine, grinder.

triturar *vt* - **1.** [moler, desmenuzar] to crush, to grind; [papel] to shred - **2.** [masticar] to chew.

triunfador, ra ◇ *adj* winning, victorious. ◇ *sm, f* winner.

triunfal *adj* triumphant.

triunfalismo *sm* triumphalism.

triunfalista *adj* triumphalist.

triunfante *adj* victorious.

triunfar *vi* - **1.** [vencer] to win, to triumph - **2.** [tener éxito] to succeed, to be successful.

triunfo *sm* - **1.** [gen] triumph; [en encuentro, elecciones] victory, win - **2.** [trofeo] trophy - **3.** [en juegos de naipes] trump.

triunvirato *sm* triumvirate.

trivial *adj* trivial.

trivialidad *sf* triviality.

trivializar [13] *vt* to trivialize.

trizas *sfpl*: **hacer trizas algo** [hacer añicos] to smash sthg to pieces; [desgarrar] to tear sthg to shreds; **hacer trizas a alguien** to tear o pull sb to pieces; **estar hecho trizas** [persona] to be shattered.

trocar [36] *vt* - **1.** [transformar]: **trocar algo (en algo)** to change sthg (into sthg) - **2.** [intercambiar] to swap, to exchange.

➡ **trocarse** *vprnl* [transformarse]: **trocarse (en)** to change (into).

trocear *vt* to cut up (into pieces).

trocha *sf* [senda] path; [atajo] shortcut.

troche ➡ **a troche y moche** *loc adv* haphazardly.

trofeo *sm* trophy.

troglodita ◇ *adj* - **1.** [cavernícola] cave dwelling, troglodytic - **2.** *fam* [bárbaro, tosco] rough, brutish. ◇ *smf* - **1.** [cavernícola] cave dweller, troglodyte - **2.** *fam* [bárbaro, tosco] roughneck, brute.

trola *sf fam* fib, lie.

trolebús *sm* trolleybus.

trolero, ra *fam* ◇ *adj* fibbing, lying. ◇ *sm, f* fibber, liar.

tromba *sf* waterspout; **en tromba** [en tropel] in a mad rush, en masse; **tromba de agua** heavy downpour.

trombo *sm* thrombus.

trombón *sm* [instrumento] trombone; [músico] trombonist; **trombón de varas** slide trombone.

trombosis *sf inv* thrombosis.

trompa ◇ *sf* - **1.** [de elefante] trunk; [de oso hormiguero] snout; [de insecto] proboscis - **2.** MÚS horn - **3.** ANAT tube; **trompa de Eustaquio/de Falopio** Eustachian/Fallopian tube - **4.** *fam* [borrachera]: **coger** o **pillar una trompa** to get plastered. ◇ *adj fam* [borracho] plastered.

trompazo *sm fam* bang; **darse** o **pegarse un trompazo con** to bang into.

trompear *vt Amér fam* to punch.

➡ **trompearse** *vprnl Amér fam* to have a fight.

trompeta ◇ *sf* trumpet. ◇ *smf* trumpeter.

trompetilla *sf* ear trumpet.

trompetista *smf* trumpeter.

trompicón *sm* [tropezón] stumble; **a trompicones** in fits and starts.

trompo *sm* - **1.** [juguete] spinning top - **2.** [giro] spin.

tronado, da *adj fam* [loco] nuts, crazy.

tronar ◇ *v impers* & *vi* to thunder. ◇ *vt Méx fam* [fracasar] to fail.

➡ **tronarse** *vprnl Amér fam* to shoot o.s.

tronchante *adj fam* hilarious.

tronchar *vt* [partir] to snap.

➡ **troncharse** *vprnl fam*: **troncharse (de risa)** to split one's sides laughing.

tronco, ca *sm, f mfam* [tipo] guy (bird *f*); [como apelativo] pal, mate.

➡ **tronco** *sm* ANAT & BOT trunk; [talado y sin ramas] log; **dormir como un tronco, estar hecho un tronco** to sleep like a log.

tronera *sf* - **1.** ARQUIT & HIST embrasure - **2.** [en billar] pocket.

trono *sm* throne; **subir al trono** to ascend the throne.

tropa *sf* - **1.** *(gen pl)* MIL troops *pl* - **2.** *fam* [multitud] troop, flock.

tropear *vt Amér* to herd.

tropecientos, tas *adj fam* loads of.

tropel *sm* - **1.** [de personas] mob, crowd; **en tropel** in a mad rush, en masse - **2.** [de cosas] mass, heap.

tropelía *sf* outrage.

tropero *sm R Dom* cowboy.

tropezar [34] *vi* [con el pie]: **tropezar (con)** to trip o stumble (on).

➡ **tropezarse** *vprnl* [encontrarse] to bump into each other, to come across one another; **tropezarse con alguien** to bump into sb.

➡ **tropezar con** *vi* [problema, persona] to run into, to come across.

tropezón *sm* - **1.** [con el pie] trip, stumble; **dar un tropezón** to trip up, to stumble - **2.** *fig* [desacierto] slip-up, blunder.

➡ **tropezones** *smpl* CULIN small chunks.

tropical *adj* tropical.

trópico *sm* tropic.

tropiece *etc* ⊳ **tropezar**.

tropiezo *sm* - **1.** [con el pie] trip, stumble; **dar un tropiezo** to trip up, to stumble - **2.** *fig* [equivocación] blunder, slip-up; [revés] setback - **3.** *fig* [desliz sexual] indiscretion; **tener un tropiezo** to commit an indiscretion.

tropo *sm* figure of speech, trope.

troqué *v* ⊳ **trocar**.

troquel *sm* [molde] mould, die.

troquelado, da *adj* - **1.** [acuñado] [de moneda] minting, mintage; [de medallas] die-casting - **2.** [recorte] cutting.

troquelar *vt* - **1.** [acuñar] [monedas] to mint; [medallas] to cast - **2.** [recortar] to cut.

troquemos ⊳ **trocar**.

trotamundos *smf inv* globe-trotter.

trotar *vi* to trot; *fam fig* [de aquí para allá] to dash *o* run around.

trote *sm* - **1.** [de caballo] trot; **al trote** at a trot - **2.** *fam* [actividad]: **no estar para trotes** not to be up to it.

troupe [trup, 'trupe] (*pl* **troupes**) *sf* troupe.

trova *sf* LITER lyric.

trovador *sm* troubadour.

troyano, na *adj* & *sm, f* Trojan.

trozar *vt* Amér [carne] to cut up; [res, tronco] to butcher, to cut up.

trozo *sm* [gen] piece; [de sendero, camino] stretch; [de obra, película] extract; **cortar algo en trozos** to cut sthg into pieces; **hacer algo a trozos** to do sthg in bits.

trucaje *sm* [gen] trick effect; [fotografía] trick photography.

trucar [10] *vt* to doctor; [motor] to soup up.

trucha *sf* [pez] trout; **trucha a la navarra** *fried trout stuffed with ham*.

truco *sm* - **1.** [trampa, engaño] trick; **truco de magia** magic trick - **2.** [habilidad, técnica] knack; **coger el truco** to get the knack; **truco publicitario** advertising gimmick.

truculencia *sf* horror, terror.

truculento, ta *adj* horrifying, terrifying.

trueca ▷ **trocar**.

truena *etc* ▷ **tronar**.

trueno *sm* - **1.** METEOR clap of thunder, thunder *(U)* - **2.** *fig* [ruido] thunder, boom.

trueque ◇ *v* ▷ **trocar**. ◇ *sm* - **1.** COM & HIST barter - **2.** [intercambio] exchange, swap.

trufa *sf* [hongo, bombón] truffle.

trufar *vt* CULIN to stuff with truffles.

truhán, ana ◇ *adj* crooked. ◇ *sm, f* rogue, crook.

trullo *sm* mfam slammer, nick.

truncado, da *adj* - **1.** [frustrado - vida, carrera] cut short; [- planes, ilusiones] ruined - **2.** GEOM truncated.

truncar [10] *vt* - **1.** [frustrar - vida, carrera] to cut short; [- planes, ilusiones] to spoil, to ruin - **2.** [dejar incompleto - texto, frase] to leave unfinished.

truque *etc* ▷ **trucar**.

trusa *sf* Caribe [traje de baño] swimsuit; R Dom [faja] girdle.

trust [trust] (*pl* **trusts**) *sm* trust, cartel.

tse-tsé ▷ **mosca**.

tu (*pl* **tus**) *adj poses (antes de s)* your.

tú *pron pers* you; **es más alta que tú** she's taller than you; **de tú a tú** [lucha] evenly matched; **hablar** *o* **tratar de tú a alguien** to address sb as 'tú'.

tuareg *adj inv* & *smf inv* Tuareg.

tuba *sf* tuba.

tuberculina *sf* tuberculin.

tubérculo *sm* tuber, root vegetable.

tuberculosis *sf inv* tuberculosis.

tuberculoso, sa ◇ *adj* - **1.** MED tuberculous - **2.** BOT tuberous. ◇ *sm, f* tuberculosis sufferer.

tubería *sf* - **1.** [cañerías] pipes *pl*, pipework - **2.** [tubo] pipe.

tubo *sm* - **1.** [tubería] pipe; **tubo de escape** AUTO exhaust (pipe); **tubo del desagüe** drainpipe - **2.** [recipiente] tube; **tubo de ensayo** test tube - **3.** ANAT tract; **tubo digestivo** digestive tract, alimentary canal - **4.** R Plata & Ven [de teléfono] receiver - **5.** *loc*: **pasar por el tubo** to put up with it.

➡ **por un tubo** *loc adv fam* a hell of a lot.

tubular ◇ *adj* tubular. ◇ *sm* bicycle tyre.

tucán *sm* toucan.

tuerca *sf* nut; **apretar las tuercas a alguien** to tighten the screws on sb.

tuerce ▷ **torcer**.

tuerto, ta ◇ *adj* [sin un ojo] one-eyed; [ciego de un ojo] blind in one eye. ◇ *sm, f* [sin un ojo] one-eyed person; [ciego de un ojo] person who is blind in one eye.

tuerza *etc* ▷ **torcer**.

tuesta *etc* ▷ **tostar**.

tuétano *sm* - **1.** ANAT (bone) marrow - **2.** *fig* [meollo] crux, heart; **hasta el tuétano** *o* **los tuétanos** to the core.

tufarada *sf* waft.

tufillo *sm* whiff.

tufo *sm* - **1.** [mal olor] stench, foul smell - **2.** [emanación] vapour.

tugurio *sm* hovel.

tul *sm* tulle.

tulipa *sf* [de lámpara] tulip-shaped lampshade.

tulipán *sm* tulip.

tullido, da ◇ *adj* paralyzed, crippled. ◇ *sm, f* cripple, disabled person.

tullir *vt* to paralyze, to cripple.

tumba *sf* grave, tomb; **a tumba abierta** at breakneck speed; **ser (como) una tumba** to be as silent as the grave.

tumbar *vt* - **1.** [derribar] to knock over *o* down - **2.** *fam fig* [suspender] to fail - **3.** *fam fig* [suj: noticia] to knock back; [suj: olor] to overpower.

➡ **tumbarse** *vprnl* - **1.** [acostarse] to lie down - **2.** [repantigarse] to lounge, to stretch out.

tumbo *sm* jolt, jerk; **dar tumbos** *o* **un tumbo** [coche etc] to jolt, to jerk; **ir dando tumbos** *fig* [persona] to have a lot of ups and downs.

tumbona *sf* [en la playa] deck chair; [en el jardín] (sun) lounger.

tumefacción *sf* swelling.

tumefacto, ta *adj* swollen.

tumor *sm* tumour.

túmulo *sm* - **1.** [sepulcro] tomb - **2.** [montecillo] burial mound - **3.** [catafalco] catafalque.

tumulto *sm* - **1.** [disturbio] riot, disturbance - **2.** [alboroto] uproar, tumult; **un tumulto de gente** a crowd of people.

tumultuoso, sa *adj* - **1.** [conflictivo] tumultuous, riotous - **2.** [turbulento] rough, stormy.

tuna *sf* - **1.** = **tuno** - **2.** *Amér C & Méx* [fruta] prickly pear.

tunante, ta *sm, f* crook, scoundrel.

tunda *sf fam* [paliza] beating, thrashing.

tundra *sf* tundra.

tunecino, na *adj* & *sm, f* Tunisian.

túnel *sm* tunnel; **salir del túnel** *fig* to turn the corner.

➥ **túnel de lavado** *sm* AUTO car wash.

Túnez *n pr* - **1.** [capital] Tunis - **2.** [país] Tunisia.

tungsteno *sm* tungsten.

túnica *sf* tunic.

Tunicia *n pr* Tunisia.

tuno, na *sm, f* rogue, scoundrel.

➥ **tuno** *sm* student minstrel.

➥ **tuna** *sf* group of student minstrels.

tuntún ➥ **al tuntún** *loc adv* without thinking.

tupé *sm* - **1.** [cabello] quiff - **2.** *fig* [atrevimiento] cheek, nerve.

tupido, da *adj* thick, dense.

tupir *vt* to pack tightly.

turba *sf* - **1.** [combustible] peat, turf - **2.** [muchedumbre] mob.

turbación *sf* - **1.** [desconcierto] upset, disturbance - **2.** [azoramiento] embarrassment.

turbador, ra *adj* - **1.** [desconcertante] disconcerting, troubling - **2.** [emocionante] upsetting, disturbing.

turbante *sm* turban.

turbar *vt* - **1.** [alterar] to disturb - **2.** [emocionar] to upset - **3.** [desconcertar] to trouble, to disconcert.

➥ **turbarse** *vprnl* - **1.** [alterarse] to get upset - **2.** [aturdirse] to get embarrassed.

turbiedad *sf* - **1.** [de agua etc] cloudiness - **2.** *fig* [de negocios etc] shadiness.

turbina *sf* turbine.

turbio, bia *adj* - **1.** [agua etc] cloudy - **2.** [vista] blurred - **3.** *fig* [negocio etc] shady - **4.** *fig* [época etc] turbulent, troubled.

turbopropulsor *sm* turboprop.

turborreactor *sm* turbojet (engine).

turbulencia *sf* - **1.** [de fluido] turbulence - **2.** [alboroto] uproar, clamour.

turbulento, ta *adj* - **1.** [gen] turbulent - **2.** [revoltoso] unruly, rebellious.

turco, ca ⇔ *adj* Turkish. ⇔ *sm, f* [persona] Turk.

➥ **turco** *sm* [lengua] Turkish.

turgente *adj* [formas, muslos] well-rounded.

turismo *sm* - **1.** [gen] tourism; **hacer turismo (por)** to go touring (round); **turismo rural** rural tourism - **2.** AUTO private car.

turista *smf* tourist.

turístico, ca *adj* tourist (antes de s).

turmalina *sf* tourmaline.

túrmix® *sf inv* blender, liquidizer.

turnarse *vprnl*: **turnarse (con alguien)** to take turns (with sb).

turnedó *sm* tournedos.

turno *sm* - **1.** [tanda] turn, go; **le ha llegado el turno de hacerlo** it's his turn to do it - **2.** [de trabajo] shift; **trabajar por turnos** to work shifts; **turno de día/noche** day/night shift.

turón *sm* polecat.

turquesa ⇔ *sf* [mineral] turquoise. ⇔ *adj inv* [color] turquoise. ⇔ *sm* [color] turquoise.

Turquía *n pr* Turkey.

turrón *sm* Christmas sweet similar to marzipan or nougat, made with almonds and honey.

turulato, ta *adj fam* flabbergasted, dumbfounded.

tute *sm* - **1.** [juego] *card game similar to whist* - **2.** *fam fig* [trabajo intenso] hard slog; **darse un tute** to slog away.

tutear *vt* to address as 'tú'.

➥ **tutearse** *vprnl* to address each other as 'tú'.

tutela *sf* - **1.** DER guardianship - **2.** [cargo]: **tutela (de)** responsibility (for); **bajo la tutela de** under the protection of.

tutelaje *sm* DER guardianship.

tutelar ⇔ *adj* - **1.** DER tutelary - **2.** [protector] protecting. ⇔ *vt* to act as guardian to.

tuteo *sm* use of 'tú', familiar form of address.

tutiplén ➥ **a tutiplén** *loc adv fam* to excess, in abundance.

tutor, ra *sm, f* - **1.** DER guardian - **2.** [profesor - privado] tutor; [- de un curso] form teacher.

tutoría *sf* - **1.** DER guardianship - **2.** [de un curso] role of form teacher.

tutti frutti, tuttifrutti *sm* tutti frutti.

tutú *sm* tutu.

tutuma *sf Amér fam variety of nut.*

tuviera *etc* ⊳ **tener**.

tuyo, ya ⇔ *adj poses* yours; **este libro es tuyo** this book is yours; **un amigo tuyo** a friend of yours; **no es asunto tuyo** it's none of your business. ◇ *pron poses:* **el tuyo** yours; **el tuyo es rojo** yours is red; **ésta es la tuya** *fam* this is the chance you've been waiting for; **lo tuyo es el teatro** [lo que haces bien] you should be on the stage; **los tuyos** *fam* [tu familia] your folks; [tu bando] your lot, your side.

TV (*abrev de* **televisión**) *sf* TV.

TVE (*abrev de* **Televisión Española**) *sf Spanish state television network.*

twist [twist] *sm inv* twist *(dance).*

u[1] (*pl* **úes**), **U** (*pl* **Úes**) *sf* [letra] u, U.

u[2] *conj* (*'u' en vez de 'o' antes de palabras que empiezan por 'o' u 'ho')* or; *ver también* **o**.

ubicación *sf* position, location.

ubicar [10] *vt* to place, to position; [edificio etc] to locate.

◆ **ubicarse** *vprnl* [edificio etc] to be situated, to be located.

ubicuidad *sf* ubiquity.

ubicuo, cua *adj* ubiquitous.

ubique *etc* ▷ **ubicar**.

ubre *sf* udder.

UCI (*abrev de* **unidad de cuidados intensivos**) *sf* ICU.

Ucrania *n pr* the Ukraine.

Ud., Vd. *abrev de* **usted**.

UDC (*abrev de* **universal decimal classification**) *sf* UDC.

Uds., Vds. *abrev de* **usted**.

UE (*abrev de* **Unión Europea**) *sf* EU.

UEFA (*abrev de* **Unión de Asociaciones Europeas de Fútbol**) *sf* UEFA.

uf *interj:* **¡uf!** [expresa cansancio, calor] phew!; [expresa fastidio] tut!; [expresa repugnancia] ugh!

ufanarse *vprnl:* **ufanarse de** to boast about.

ufano, na *adj* **- 1.** [satisfecho] proud, pleased **- 2.** [engreído] boastful, conceited.

ufología *sf* ufology.

Uganda *n pr* Uganda.

ugetista ◇ *adj* of or belonging to the 'UGT'. ◇ *smf* member of the 'UGT'.

UGT (*abrev de* **Unión General de los Trabajadores**) *sf* major socialist Spanish trade union.

UHF (*abrev de* **ultra high frequency**) *sf* UHF.

ujier (*pl* **ujieres**) *sm* usher.

újule *interj* Amér: **¡újule!** wow!

ukelele *sm* ukelele.

úlcera *sf* MED ulcer; **úlcera de estómago** stomach ulcer.

ulceración *sf* ulceration.

ulcerar *vt* to ulcerate.

◆ **ulcerarse** *vprnl* MED to ulcerate.

ulterior *adj culto* **- 1.** [en el tiempo] subsequent, ulterior **- 2.** [en el espacio] further.

ulteriormente *adv culto* subsequently.

ultimación *sf* conclusion, completion.

ultimador, ra *sm, f* Amér killer.

últimamente *adv* recently, of late.

ultimar *vt* **- 1.** [gen] to conclude, to complete **- 2.** Amér [matar] to kill.

ultimátum (*pl* **ultimatos** *o* **ultimátum**) *sm* ultimatum.

último, ma ◇ *adj* **- 1.** [gen] last; **por último** lastly, finally; **ser lo último** [lo final] to come last; [el último recurso] to be a last resort; [el colmo] to be the last straw **- 2.** [más reciente] latest, most recent **- 3.** [más remoto] furthest, most remote **- 4.** [más bajo] bottom **- 5.** [más alto] top **- 6.** [de más atrás] back. ◇ *sm, f* **- 1.** [en fila, carrera etc]: **el último** the last (one); **llegar el último** to come last **- 2.** *(en comparaciones, enumeraciones):* **éste último...** the latter...

◆ **última** *sf*: **estar en las últimas** [muriéndose] to be on one's deathbed; [sin dinero] to be down to one's last penny; [sin provisiones] to be down to one's last provisions; **ir a la última** *fam* to wear the latest fashion.

ultra ◇ *adj* POLÍT extreme right-wing. ◇ *smf* POLÍT right-wing extremist.

◆ **non plus ultra** *sm* epitome, height.

ultraderecha *sf* extreme right (wing).

ultraizquierda *sf* extreme left (wing).

ultrajante *adj* insulting, offensive.

ultrajar *vt* to insult, to offend.

ultraje *sm* insult.

ultraligero *sm* microlight.

ultramar *sm* overseas *pl*; **de ultramar** overseas *(antes de s).*

ultramarino, na *adj* overseas *(antes de s).*

◆ **ultramarinos** ◇ *smpl* [comestibles] groceries. ◇ *sm inv* [tienda] grocer's (shop) *sing.*

ultramicroscopio *sm* ultramicroscope.

ultranza ⟶ **a ultranza** *loc adv* - **1.** [con decisión] to the death - **2.** [acérrimamente] out-and-out.

ultrasonido *sm* ultrasound.

ultratumba *sf*: **de ultratumba** from beyond the grave.

ultravioleta *adj inv* ultraviolet.

ulular *vi* - **1.** [viento, lobo] to howl - **2.** [búho] to hoot.

umbilical ⟹ **cordón**.

umbral *sm* - **1.** [gen] threshold - **2.** *fig* [límite] bounds *pl*, realms *pl*.

umbrío, a *adj* shady.

un, una ⟨⟩ *art (antes de sf que empiece por «a» o «ha» tónica:* **un***)* a, an *(ante sonido vocálico);* **un hombre/coche** a man/car; **una mujer/mesa** a woman/table; **un águila/hacha** an eagle/axe; **una hora** an hour. ⟨⟩ *adj* ⟹ **uno**.

unánime *adj* unanimous.

unanimidad *sf* unanimity; **por unanimidad** unanimously.

unción *sf* unction.

uncir [12] *vt* to yoke.

undécimo, ma *num* eleventh.

underground ['anderjraun] *adj inv* underground.

UNED *(abrev de* **Universidad Nacional de Educación a Distancia)** *sf Spanish open university.*

Unesco *(abrev de* **United Nations Educational, Scientific and Cultural Organization)** *sf* UNESCO.

ungimiento *sm* unction.

ungir [15] *vt* to put ointment on; RELIG to anoint.

ungüento *sm* ointment.

únicamente *adv* only, solely.

Unicef *(abrev de* **United Nations Children's Fund)** *sm* UNICEF.

unicelular *adj* single-cell, unicellular.

unicidad *sf* uniqueness.

único, ca *adj* - **1.** [sólo] only; **es lo único que quiero** it's all I want - **2.** [excepcional] unique - **3.** [precio, función, razón] single.

unicornio *sm* unicorn.

unidad *sf* - **1.** [gen, MAT & MIL] unit; **25 euros la unidad** 25 euros each; **unidad de cuidados intensivos** *o* **vigilancia intensiva** intensive care (unit); **unidad central de proceso** INFORM central processing unit; **unidad de combate** combat unit; **unidad de disco** INFORM disk drive; **unidad monetaria** monetary unit; **unidad móvil** TV mobile unit - **2.** [cohesión, acuerdo] unity.

unidireccional *adj* unidirectional, one-way.

unido, da *adj* united; [familia, amigo] close.

unifamiliar *adj* detached; **vivienda unifamiliar** house *(detached or terraced)*.

unificación *sf* - **1.** [unión] unification - **2.** [uniformización] standardization.

unificador, ra *adj* unifying.

unificar [10] *vt* - **1.** [unir] to unite, to join; [países] to unify - **2.** [uniformar] to standardize.

uniformado, da *adj* uniformed.

uniformar *vt* - **1.** [igualar] to standardize - **2.** [poner uniforme] to put into uniform.

uniforme ⟨⟩ *adj* uniform; [superficie] even. ⟨⟩ *sm* uniform.

uniformidad *sf* uniformity; [de superficie] evenness.

uniformización *sf* standardization.

uniformizar [13] *vt* to standardize.

unilateral *adj* unilateral.

unión *sf* - **1.** [gen] union; **en unión de** together with; **Unión Africana** African Union - **2.** [suma, adherimiento] joining together - **3.** TECNOL join, joint.

Unión de hecho

ﬦ Some of Spain's autonomous regions (e.g. Madrid, Andalucía and the Basque Country) have set up a means whereby unmarried couples in a stable relationship can officially register themselves as forming a **unión de hecho** (civil partnership or civil union). This entitles them to many of the same rights as married couples (e.g. when adopting a child, or when applying for public housing), though laws relating to pensions and inheritance are excluded, as they are governed by state law. The Catholic Church has objected to such laws, particularly because they may give the same rights to homosexual as heterosexual couples. Similar recognition has been sought (and has given rise to similar controversy) in some Latin American countries (e.g. Argentina and Chile).

Unión Europea *sf*: **la Unión Europea** the European Union.

unir *vt* - **1.** [pedazos, habitaciones etc] to join - **2.** [empresas, estados, facciones] to unite - **3.** [comunicar - ciudades etc] to link - **4.** [suj: amistad, circunstancias etc] to bind - **5.** [casar] to join, to marry - **6.** [combinar] to combine; **unir algo a algo** to combine sthg with sthg - **7.** [mezclar] to mix *o* blend in.

⟶ **unirse** *vprnl* - **1.** [gen] to join together; **unirse a algo** to join sthg - **2.** [casarse]: **unirse en matrimonio** to be joined in wedlock.

unisexo, unisex *adj inv* unisex.

unisexual *adj* unisexual.

unísono ➾ **al unísono** *loc adv* in unison.

unitario, ria ◇ *adj* - **1.** [de una unidad - estado, nación] single; [- precio] unit *(antes de s)* - **2.** POLÍT unitarian. ◇ *sm, f* POLÍT unitarian.

unitarismo *sm* unitarianism.

universal *adj* - **1.** [gen] universal - **2.** [mundial] world *(antes de s)*.
➾ **universales** *smpl* FILOS universals.

universalidad *sf* universality.

universalismo *sm* universalism.

universalizar [13] *vt* to make widespread.

universidad *sf* university, college *US*, school *US*; **universidad a distancia** ≃ Open University *UK*.

universitario, ria ◇ *adj* university *(antes de s)*. ◇ *sm, f* - **1.** [estudiante] university student - **2.** [licenciado] university graduate.

universo *sm* - **1.** ASTRON universe - **2.** *fig* [mundo] world.

unívoco, ca *adj* univocal, unambiguous.

unja *etc* ⊳ **ungir**.

uno, una ◇ *adj* - **1.** [indefinido] one; **un día volveré** one *o* some day I'll return; **había unos coches mal aparcados** there were some badly parked cars; **había unos 12 muchachos** there were about *o* some 12 boys there - **2.** [numeral] one; **un hombre, un voto** one man, one vote; **la fila uno** row one. ◇ *pron* - **1.** [indefinido] one; **coge uno** take one; **uno de vosotros** one of you; **unos... otros...** some... others...; **una o otro, unos a otros** each other, one another; **uno y otro** both; **unos y otros** all of them - **2.** *fam* [cierta persona] someone, somebody; **hablé con uno que te conoce** I spoke to someone who knows you; **me lo han contado unos** certain people told me so - **3.** [yo] one; **uno ya no está para estos trotes** one isn't really up to this sort of thing any more - **4.** *loc*: **a una** [en armonía, a la vez] together; **de uno en uno, uno a uno, uno por uno** one by one; **juntar varias cosas en una** to combine several things into one; **lo uno por lo otro** it all evens out in the end; **más de uno** many people; **una de dos** it's either one thing or the other; **unos cuantos** a few; **una y no más** once was enough, once bitten, twice shy.
➾ **uno** *sm* [número] (number) one; **el uno** number one; **ver también seis**.
➾ **una** *sf* [hora]: **la una** one o'clock.

untar *vt* - **1.** [pan, tostada]: **untar (con)** to spread (with); [piel, cara etc] to smear (with) - **2.** [máquina, bisagra etc] to grease, to oil - **3.** *fam fig* [sobornar] to grease the palm of, to bribe.
➾ **untarse** *vprnl* - **1.** *fam* [ensuciarse]: **untarse la cara de** *o* **con algo** to smear one's face with sthg - **2.** *fam* [enriquecerse] to line one's pockets.

unto *sm* - **1.** [ungüento] ointment - **2.** [grasa] grease.

untuosidad *sf* greasiness, oiliness.

untuoso, sa *adj* [graso] greasy, oily.

untura *sf* - **1.** [ungüento] ointment - **2.** [grasa] grease.

unza *etc* ⊳ **uncir**.

uña *sf* - **1.** [de mano] fingernail, nail; **hacerse las uñas** to do one's nails; **comerse las uñas** [por preocupación, nerviosismo] to bite one's nails; **dejarse las uñas en algo** to break one's back doing sthg; **ser uña y carne** to be as thick as thieves - **2.** [de pie] toenail - **3.** [garra] claw; **enseñar** *o* **sacar las uñas** to get one's claws out - **4.** [casco] hoof.

uñero *sm* - **1.** [inflamación] whitlow - **2.** [uña encarnada] ingrowing nail - **3.** [de libro] thumb-index.

uperización *sf* U.H.T. treatment.

uperizar [13] *vt* to give U.H.T. treatment.

Ural *sm*: **el Ural** the River Ural.

Urales *smpl*: **los Urales** the Urals.

uralita® *sf* CONSTR *material made of asbestos and cement, usually corrugated and used mainly for roofing*.

uranio *sm* uranium.

Urano *n pr* Uranus.

urbanidad *sf* politeness, courtesy.

urbanismo *sm* town planning.

urbanista *smf* town planner.

urbanístico, ca *adj* town-planning *(antes de s)*.

urbanización *sf* - **1.** [acción] urbanization - **2.** [zona residencial] (housing) estate.

urbanizador, ra ◇ *adj* developing. ◇ *sm, f* developer.

urbanizar [13] *vt* to develop, to urbanize.

urbano, na ◇ *adj* urban, city *(antes de s)*. ◇ *sm, f* traffic policeman (*f* traffic policewoman).

urbe *sf* large city.

urdido *sm* warp.

urdimbre *sf* warp.

urdir *vt* - **1.** [planear] to plot, to forge - **2.** [hilos] to warp.

urea *sf* urea.

uremia *sf* uraemia.

uréter *sm* ureter.

uretra *sf* urethra.

urgencia *sf* - **1.** [cualidad] urgency - **2.** MED emergency; **de urgencia** emergency - **3.** [necesidad] urgent need; **en caso de urgencia** in case of emergency.
➾ **urgencias** *sfpl* MED casualty (department) *sing*; **ingresar por urgencias** to be admitted as an emergency.

urgente *adj* - **1.** [apremiante] urgent - **2.** MED emergency *(s)* - **3.** [correo] express.

urgir [15] *vi* to be urgently necessary; **me urge hacerlo** I urgently need to do it; **urgir a alguien a que haga algo** to urge sb to do sthg.

úrico, ca *adj* uric.

urinario, ria *adj* urinary.
👄 **urinario** *sm* urinal, comfort station *US*.

urja *etc* ⊳ **urgir**.

URL *(abrev de* **uniform resource locator)** *sf* IN-FORM URL.

urna *sf* - **1.** [vasija] urn; **urna cineraria** urn *(for sb's ashes)* - **2.** [caja de cristal] glass case - **3.** [para votar] ballot box; **acudir a las urnas** to go to the polls.

urogallo *sm* capercaillie.

urología *sf* urology.

urólogo, ga *sm, f* urologist.

urraca *sf* magpie.

URSS *(abrev de* **Unión de Repúblicas Socialistas Soviéticas)** *sf* HIST USSR.

ursulina *sf* - **1.** RELIG Ursuline (nun) - **2.** *fig* [mujer recatada] prudish woman.

urticaria *sf* nettle rash.

Uruguay *n pr:* **(el) Uruguay** Uruguay.

uruguayo, ya *adj & sm, f* Uruguayan.

usado, da *adj* - **1.** [utilizado] used; **muy usado** widely used - **2.** [de segunda mano] second-hand - **3.** [gastado] worn-out, worn.

usanza *sf* custom, usage; **a la vieja usanza** in the old way *o* style.

usar ⇔ *vt* - **1.** [gen] to use; **usar algo/a alguien de** *o* **como algo** to use sthg/sb as sthg - **2.** [prenda] to wear. ⇔ *vi:* **usar de** to use, to make use of.
👄 **usarse** *vprnl* - **1.** [emplearse] to be used - **2.** [estar de moda] to be worn.

USB *(abrev de* **universal serial bus)** *sm* INFORM USB.

usina *sf* Amér: **usina eléctrica** power station; **usina nuclear** nuclear power station.

uso *sm* - **1.** [gen] use; **al uso** fashionable; **al uso andaluz** in the Andalusian style; **'de uso externo'** MED 'for external use only'; **en pleno uso de sus facultades mentales** in full possession of his mental faculties; **entrar en uso** to be in service; **fuera de uso** out of use, obsolete; **hacer uso de** [utilizar] to make use of, to use; [de prerrogativa, derecho] to exercise; **tener el uso de la palabra** to have the floor - **2.** *(gen pl)* [costumbre] custom - **3.** LING usage - **4.** [desgaste] wear and tear.
👄 **uso de razón** *sm* age of reason.

usted *pron pers* - **1.** [tratamiento de respeto - sing] you; [- pl]: **ustedes** you *pl*; **contesten ustedes a las preguntas** please answer the questions; **me gustaría hablar con usted** I'd like to talk to you; **¡oiga, usted!** hey, you!; **tratar a alguien de usted** *to address sb using the 'usted' form* - **2.** [tratamiento de respeto - posesivo]: **de usted/ustedes** yours.

usual *adj* usual.

usuario, ria *sm, f* user.

usufructo *sm* DER usufruct, use.

usufructuar [6] *vt* DER to have the usufruct *o* use of.

usufructuario, ria *adj & sm, f* DER usufructuary.

usura *sf* usury.

usurero, ra *sm, f* usurer.

usurpación *sf* usurpation.

usurpador, ra ⇔ *adj* usurping. ⇔ *sm, f* usurper.

usurpar *vt* to usurp.

utensilio *sm* [gen] tool, implement; CULIN utensil; **utensilios de pesca** fishing tackle.

uterino, na *adj* uterine.

útero *sm* womb, uterus.

útil ⇔ *adj* - **1.** [beneficioso, aprovechable] useful - **2.** [eficiente] helpful - **3.** [hábil] working. ⇔ *sm (gen pl)* [herramienta] tool; **útiles de jardinería** gardening tools; AGRIC implement; **útiles de labranza** agricultural implements.

utilería *sf* equipment; CINE & TEATRO props *pl*.

utilidad *sf* - **1.** [cualidad] usefulness - **2.** [beneficio] profit.

utilitario, ria *adj* AUTO run-around, utility.
👄 **utilitario** *sm* AUTO run-around car, utility car, compact *US*.

utilitarismo *sm* utilitarianism.

utilización *sf* use.

utilizar [13] *vt* [gen] to use.

utillaje *sm* tools *pl*.

utopía *sf* utopia.

utópico, ca *adj* utopian.

UV *(abrev de* **ultravioleta)** UV.

uva *sf* grape; **uva de mesa** dessert grape; **uva moscatel** muscatel grape; **uva pasa** raisin; **de uvas a peras** once in a blue moon; **estar de mala uva** to be in a bad mood; **tener mala uva** to be a bad sort, to be a nasty piece of work; **uvas de la suerte** *grapes eaten for good luck as midnight chimes on New Year's Eve*.

úvula *sf* uvula.

uvular *adj* uvular.

uy *interj:* **¡uy!** ahh!, oh!

v, V ['uβe] *sf* [letra] v, V.
➤ **v doble** *sf* W.

v. = vid.

va ▷ **ir.**

vaca *sf* **- 1.** [animal] cow; **vaca lechera/sagrada** dairy/sacred cow; **ponerse como una vaca** to put on a lot of weight **- 2.** [carne] beef.
➤ **vacas flacas** *sfpl fam* lean years.
➤ **vacas gordas** *sfpl fam* years of plenty.

vacaciones *sfpl* holiday *sing*, holidays *UK*, vacation *sing US*; **coger (las) vacaciones** to take one's holidays; **estar/irse de vacaciones** to be/go on holiday.

vacante ◇ *adj* vacant. ◇ *sf* vacancy.

vaciado *sm* **- 1.** [de recipiente] emptying **- 2.** [de estatua] casting, moulding.

vaciar [9] *vt* **- 1.** [gen]: **vaciar algo (de)** to empty sthg (of) **- 2.** [dejar hueco] to hollow (out) **- 3.** ARTE to cast, to mould.

vaciedad *sf* [tontería] trifle.

vacilación *sf* **- 1.** [duda] hesitation; [al elegir] indecision **- 2.** [oscilación] swaying; [de la luz] flickering.

vacilante *adj* **- 1.** [gen] hesitant; [al elegir] indecisive **- 2.** [luz] flickering; [pulso] irregular; [paso] swaying, unsteady.

vacilar ◇ *vi* **- 1.** [dudar] to hesitate; [al elegir] to be indecisive **- 2.** [voz, principios, régimen] to falter **- 3.** [fluctuar - luz] to flicker; [- pulso] to be irregular **- 4.** [tambalearse] to wobble, to sway **- 5.** *fam* [chulear] to swank, to show off **- 6.** *fam* [bromear] to take the mickey. ◇ *vt fam* [tomar el pelo]: **vacilar a alguien** to take the mickey out of sb.

vacilón, ona *fam* ◇ *adj* **- 1.** [chulo] swanky **- 2.** [bromista] jokey, teasing **- 3.** *Amér C, Caribe & Méx* [fiestero] fond of partying. ◇ *sm, f* **- 1.** [chulo] show-off **- 2.** [bromista] tease.
➤ **vacilón** *sm Amér C, Caribe & Méx* [fiesta] party.

vacío, a *adj* empty; **vacío de** [contenido etc] devoid of.
➤ **vacío** *sm* **- 1.** FÍS vacuum; **envasar al vacío** to vacuum-pack; **vacío de poder** power vacuum **- 2.** [abismo, carencia] void **- 3.** [hueco] space, gap **- 4.** *loc*: **caer en el vacío** to fall on

deaf ears; **hacer el vacío a alguien** to send sb to Coventry; **tener un vacío en el estómago** to feel hungry.

vacuidad *sf* [trivialidad] shallowness, vacuity.

vacuna *sf* vaccine; **poner una vacuna a alguien** to vaccinate sb.

vacunación *sf* vaccination.

vacunar *vt* to vaccinate; **vacunar contra algo** to vaccinate against sthg.
➤ **vacunarse** *vprnl* to get vaccinated.

vacuno, na *adj* bovine.

vacuo, cua *adj* [trivial] shallow, vacuous.

vadear *vt* to ford; *fig* to overcome.

vademécum (*pl* **vademecums**) *sm* vade mecum, handbook.

vado *sm* **- 1.** [en acera] lowered kerb; **'vado permanente'** 'keep clear' **- 2.** [de río] ford.

vagabundear *vi* **- 1.** [ser un vagabundo] to lead a vagrant's life **- 2.** [vagar]: **vagabundear (por)** to wander, to roam.

vagabundeo *sm* vagrant's life.

vagabundo, da ◇ *adj* [persona] vagrant; [perro] stray. ◇ *sm, f* tramp, vagrant, bum *US*.

vagamente *adv* vaguely.

vagancia *sf* **- 1.** [holgazanería] laziness, idleness **- 2.** [vagabundeo] vagrancy.

vagar [16] *vi*: **vagar (por)** to wander, to roam.

vagina *sf* vagina.

vaginal *adj* vaginal.

vago, ga ◇ *adj* **- 1.** [perezoso] lazy, idle **- 2.** [impreciso] vague. ◇ *sm, f* lazy person, idler; **hacer el vago** to laze around.

vagón *sm* [de pasajeros] carriage, car *US*; [de mercancías] wagon; **vagón cisterna** tanker, tank wagon; **vagón de mercancías** goods wagon *O* van; **vagón de primera/segunda** first-class/second-class carriage; **vagón restaurante** dining car, restaurant car.

vagoneta *sf* wagon.

vaguada *sf* valley floor.

vague *etc* ▷ **vagar**.

vaguear *vi* to laze around.

vaguedad *sf* **- 1.** [cualidad] vagueness **- 2.** [dicho] vague remark.

vahído *sm* blackout, fainting fit; **me dio un vahído** I fainted.

vaho *sm* **- 1.** [vapor] steam **- 2.** [aliento] breath.
➤ **vahos** *smpl* MED inhalation *sing*.

vaina *sf* **- 1.** [gen] sheath **- 2.** [BOT - envoltura] pod **- 3.** *Amér fam* [engreído] pain in the neck; **¡qué vaina!** *Col, Méx & Ven mfam* what a pain! **- 4.** *Col, Perú & Ven* [problema] pain **- 5.** *Col, Perú & Ven* [cosa] thing.

vainica *sf* hemstitch.

vainilla *sf* vanilla.

vaivén *sm* - **1.** [balanceo - de barco] swaying, rocking; [- de péndulo, columpio] swinging - **2.** [altibajo] ups-and-downs *pl*.

vajilla *sf* crockery; **una vajilla** a dinner service.

valdrá *etc* ▷ **valer**.

vale ◇ *sm* - **1.** [bono] coupon, voucher - **2.** [comprobante] receipt - **3.** [pagaré] I.O.U. - **4.** *Méx & Ven fam* [amigo] pal, mate *UK*, buddy *US*. ◇ *interj* ▷ **valer**.

valedero, **ra** *adj* valid.

valedor, **ra** *sm, f* protector.

valemadrista *adj Amér* - **1.** [apático] apathetic - **2.** [cínico] cynical.

valencia *sf* QUÍM valency.

Valencia *n pr* Valencia.

valenciano, **na** *adj & sm, f* [de Valencia] Valencian.

◆ **valenciana** *sf Amér* [de pantalón] (trouser) turn-up.

valentía *sf* - **1.** [valor] bravery - **2.** [hazaña] act of bravery.

valentón, **ona** *sm, f*: **hacerse el valentón** to boast of one's bravery.

valer [74] ◇ *vt* - **1.** [costar - precio] to cost; [tener un valor de] to be worth; **¿cuánto vale?** [de precio] how much does it cost?, how much is it? - **2.** [ocasionar] to earn - **3.** [merecer] to deserve, to be worth - **4.** [equivaler] to be equivalent *o* equal to. ◇ *vi* - **1.** [merecer aprecio] to be worthy; **hacerse valer** to show one's worth - **2.** [servir]: **valer para algo** to be for sthg; **eso aún vale** you can still use that; **¿para qué vale?** what's it for? - **3.** [ser válido] to be valid; [en juegos] to be allowed - **4.** [ayudar] to help, to be of use - **5.** [tener calidad] to be of worth; **no valer nada** to be worthless *o* useless - **6.** [equivaler]: **valer por** to be worth - **7.** *loc*: **más vale tarde que nunca** better late than never; **más vale que te calles/vayas** it would be better if you shut up/left; **¿vale?** okay?, all right?; **¡vale!** okay!, all right!; **¡vale (ya)!** that's enough! ◇ *sm* worth, value.

◆ **valerse** *vprnl* - **1.** [servirse]: **valerse de algo/alguien** to use sthg/sb - **2.** [desenvolverse]: **valerse (por sí mismo)** to manage on one's own - **3.** *Méx loc*: **¡no se vale!** that's not fair!

valeriana *sf* valerian, allheal.

valeroso, **sa** *adj* brave, courageous.

valga *etc* ▷ **valer**.

valía *sf* value, worth.

validar *vt* to validate.

validez *sf* validity; **dar validez a** to validate.

válido, **da** *adj* valid.

valiente ◇ *adj* - **1.** [valeroso] brave - **2.** *irón* [menudo]: **¡en valiente lío te has metido!** you've got yourself into some mess *o* into a fine mess! ◇ *smf* [valeroso] brave person.

valija *sf* - **1.** [maleta] case, suitcase; **valija diplomática** diplomatic bag - **2.** [de correos] mailbag.

valioso, **sa** *adj* - **1.** [gen] valuable - **2.** [intento, esfuerzo] worthy.

valla *sf* - **1.** [cerca] fence - **2.** DEP hurdle.

◆ **valla publicitaria** *sf* billboard, hoarding.

vallado *sm* fence.

vallar *vt* to put a fence round.

valle *sm* valley.

valor *sm* - **1.** [gen, MAT & MÚS] value; **de valor** valuable; **joyas por valor de...** jewels worth...; **sin valor** worthless; **valor adquisitivo** purchasing power; **valor añadido** ECON added value; **valor nominal** face *o* nominal value; **valor nutritivo** nutritional value - **2.** [importancia] importance; **dar valor a** to give *o* attach importance to; **quitar valor a algo** to take away from sthg, to diminish the importance of sthg - **3.** [valentía] bravery; **armarse de valor** to pluck up one's courage - **4.** [desvergüenza] cheek, nerve - **5.** *fam* [personaje - DEP]: **un joven valor** a young prospect.

◆ **valores** *smpl* - **1.** [principios] values - **2.** FIN securities, bonds; **valores en cartera** investments.

valoración *sf* - **1.** [de precio, pérdidas] valuation - **2.** [de mérito, cualidad, ventajas] evaluation, assessment.

valorar *vt* - **1.** [tasar, apreciar] to value - **2.** [evaluar] to evaluate, to assess.

valorización *sf* - **1.** [de precios, pérdidas] valuation - **2.** [aumento de valor] appreciation.

valorizar [13] *vt* to increase the value of.

◆ **valorizarse** *vprnl* to increase in value.

vals (*pl* **valses**) *sm* waltz.

valva *sf* BOT & ZOOL valve.

válvula *sf* valve; **válvula de seguridad** safety valve.

◆ **válvula de escape** *sf fig* means of letting off steam.

vampiresa *sf fam* vamp, femme fatale.

vampirismo *sm* vampirism.

vampiro *sm* - **1.** [personaje] vampire - **2.** [murciélago] vampire bat.

vanagloriarse [8] *vprnl*: **vanagloriarse (de)** to boast (about), to show off (about).

vandálico, **ca** *adj* [salvaje] vandalistic; **un acto vandálico** an act of vandalism.

vandalismo *sm* vandalism.

vándalo, **la** ◇ *adj* vandal *(antes de s)*. ◇ *sm, f* HIST Vandal.

vándalo *sm fig* [salvaje] vandal.

vanguardia *sf* - **1.** MIL vanguard; **ir a la vanguardia de** *fig* to be at the forefront of - **2.** [cultural] avant-garde, vanguard; **de vanguardia** avant-garde.

vanguardismo *sm* avant-garde.

vanidad *sf* - **1.** [orgullo] vanity - **2.** [inutilidad] futility.

vanidoso, sa ⬦ *adj* vain, conceited. ⬦ *sm, f* vain person.

vano, na *adj* - **1.** [gen] vain; **en vano** in vain - **2.** [vacío, superficial] shallow, superficial.
◆ **vano** *sm* ARQUIT bay.

vapor *sm* - **1.** [emanación] vapour; [de agua] steam; **al vapor** CULIN steamed; **de vapor** [máquina etc] steam *(antes de s)*; **a todo vapor** at full speed; **vapor de agua** FÍS & QUÍM water vapour - **2.** [barco] steamer, steamship.

vaporización *sf* - **1.** FÍS vaporization - **2.** [pulverización] spraying.

vaporizador *sm* - **1.** [pulverizador] spray - **2.** [para evaporar] vaporizer.

vaporizar [13] *vt* - **1.** FÍS to vaporize - **2.** [pulverizar] to spray.
◆ **vaporizarse** *vprnl* FÍS to evaporate, to vaporize.

vaporoso, sa *adj* [fino - tela etc] diaphanous, sheer.

vapulear *vt* to beat, to thrash; *fig* to slate, to tear apart.

vapuleo *sm* beating, thrashing; *fig* slating, tearing apart.

vaquería *sf* dairy.

vaquero, ra ⬦ *adj* cowboy *(antes de s)*. ⬦ *sm, f* [persona] cowboy (*f* cowgirl), cowherd.
◆ **vaqueros** *smpl* [pantalón] jeans.

vaquilla *sf* [vaca] heifer; [toro] young bull.

vara *sf* - **1.** [rama, palo] stick - **2.** [pértiga] pole - **3.** [de metal etc] rod - **4.** [tallo] stem, stalk - **5.** [insignia] staff.

varadero *sm* dry dock.

varado, da *adj* [NÁUT - encallado] aground, stranded; [- en el dique seco] in dry dock.

varar *vi* NÁUT to run aground.

varear *vt* [árboles] to beat (with a pole); [fruta] to knock o beat down.

variabilidad *sf* changeability, variability.

variable ⬦ *adj* changeable, variable. ⬦ *sf* MAT variable.

variación *sf* variation; [del tiempo] change.
◆ **variación magnética** *sf* magnetic declination.

variado, da *adj* varied; [galletas, bombones] assorted.

variante ⬦ *adj* variant. ⬦ *sf* - **1.** [variación] variation; [versión] version - **2.** AUTO by-pass - **3.** [en quiniela] draw or away win.

variar [9] ⬦ *vt* - **1.** [modificar] to alter, to change - **2.** [dar variedad] to vary. ⬦ *vi* - **1.** [cambiar]: **variar (de)** to change; **para variar** *irón* (just) for a change - **2.** [ser diferente]: **variar (de)** to vary o differ (from).

varicela *sf* chickenpox.

varicoso, sa *adj* varicose.

variedad *sf* variety.
◆ **variedades, variétés** *sfpl* TEATRO variety *(U)*, music hall *(U)*.

varilla *sf* - **1.** [barra larga] rod, stick - **2.** [tira larga - de abanico, paraguas] spoke, rib; [- de gafas] arm; [- de corsé] bone, stay.

vario, ria *adj* [variado] varied, different.
◆ **varios, rias** *adj* & *pron pl* several.

variopinto, ta *adj* diverse.

varita *sf* wand; **varita mágica** magic wand.

variz *(gen pl)* *sf* varicose vein.

varón *sm* [hombre] male, man; [chico] boy.

varonil *adj* masculine, male.

vasallo, lla *sm, f* - **1.** [siervo] vassal - **2.** [súbdito] subject.

vasco, ca *adj* & *sm, f* Basque.
◆ **vasco** *sm* [lengua] Basque.

vascuence *sm* [lengua] Basque.

vascular *adj* vascular.

vasectomía *sf* vasectomy.

vaselina® *sf* Vaseline®.

vasija *sf* vessel.

vaso *sm* - **1.** [recipiente, contenido] glass; **un vaso de plástico** a plastic cup; **ahogarse en un vaso de agua** to make a mountain out of a molehill - **2.** ANAT vessel; **vasos capilares** capillaries; **vasos sanguíneos** blood vessels - **3.** BOT vein.

vástago *sm* - **1.** [descendiente] offspring *(U)* - **2.** [brote] shoot - **3.** [varilla] rod.

vasto, ta *adj* vast.

vate *sm culto* bard.

váter *(pl* váteres**), water** *(pl* wateres*) sm* toilet.

vaticano, na *adj* Vatican *(antes de s)*.
◆ **Vaticano** *sm*: **el Vaticano** the Vatican.

vaticinar *vt* to prophesy, to predict.

vaticinio *sm culto* prophecy, prediction.

vatio, watio ['batʃo] *sm* watt.

vaudeville = **vodevil**.

vaya *interj* - **1.** [sorpresa]: **¡vaya!** well! - **2.** [énfasis]: **¡vaya moto!** what a motorbike!; ⊳ **ir**.

VB *abrev de* **visto bueno**.

Vd. *(abrev de* usted*)* = **Ud.**

Vda. *(abrev de* viuda*) abrev de* **viuda**.

Vds. (*abrev de* **ustedes**) = **Uds.**

ve ▷ **ir**.

véase ▷ **ver**.

vecinal *adj* - **1.** [relaciones, trato] neighbourly - **2.** [camino, impuestos] local.

vecindad *sf* - **1.** [vecindario] neighbourhood - **2.** [alrededores] vicinity - **3.** *Méx* [vivienda] tenement house.

vecindario *sm* [de barrio] neighbourhood; [de población] community, inhabitants *pl*.

vecino, na ⋄ *adj* [cercano] neighbouring; **vecino a** next to. ⋄ *sm, f* - **1.** [de la misma casa, calle] neighbour; [de un barrio] resident - **2.** [de una localidad] inhabitant.

vector *sm* vector.

vectorial *adj* vectorial.

veda *sf* - **1.** [prohibición] ban *(on hunting and fishing)*; **levantar la veda** to open the season - **2.** [periodo] close season.

vedado, da *adj* prohibited.

◆ **vedado** *sm* reserve.

vedar *vt* to prohibit.

vedette [be'det] *sf* star.

vega *sf* fertile plain.

vegetación *sf* vegetation.

◆ **vegetaciones** *sfpl* MED adenoids.

vegetal ⋄ *adj* - **1.** BIOL vegetable, plant *(antes de s)* - **2.** [sandwich] salad *(antes de s)*. ⋄ *sm* vegetable.

vegetar *vi* to vegetate.

vegetarianismo *sm* vegetarianism.

vegetariano, na *adj* & *sm, f* vegetarian.

vegetativo, va *adj* vegetative.

vehemencia *sf* [pasión, entusiasmo] vehemence.

vehemente *adj* [apasionado, entusiasta] vehement.

vehículo *sm* [gen] vehicle; [de infección] carrier.

veinte *num* twenty; **los (años) veinte** the twenties; *ver también* **seis**.

veinteañero, ra ⋄ *adj* about twenty years old. ⋄ *sm, f* person about twenty years old.

veinteavo, va *num* twentieth; **la veinteava parte** a twentieth.

veintena *sf* - **1.** [veinte] twenty - **2.** [aproximadamente]: **una veintena (de)** about twenty.

vejación *sf* humiliation.

vejamen *sm* = **vejación**.

vejar *vt* to humiliate.

vejatorio, ria *adj* humiliating.

vejestorio *sm despec* old fogey.

vejez *sf* old age; **¡a la vejez viruelas!** fancy that at his/her age!

vejiga *sf* bladder.

vela *sf* - **1.** [para dar luz] candle; **¿quién le ha dado vela en este entierro?** who asked you to stick your oar in?; **estar a dos velas** not to have two halfpennies to rub together - **2.** [de barco] sail; **a toda vela** under full sail - **3.** DEP sailing; **hacer vela** to go sailing - **4.** [vigilia] vigil; **pasar la noche en vela** [adrede] to stay awake all night; [desvelado] to have a sleepless night.

velada *sf* evening.

velado, da *adj* - **1.** [oculto] veiled, hidden - **2.** FOTO fogged.

velador, ra *adj* watching.

◆ **velador** *sm* - **1.** *Andes & Cuba* [mueble] bedside table - **2.** *Méx & R Plata* [luz] bedside lamp - **3.** *Méx* [centinela] night watchman.

◆ **veladora** *sf* *Amér* [vela] candle.

velamen *sm* sails *pl*.

velar[1] *adj* ANAT & LING velar.

velar[2] ⋄ *vi* - **1.** [cuidar]: **velar por** to look after, to watch over - **2.** [no dormir] to stay awake. ⋄ *vt* - **1.** [de noche - muerto] to keep a vigil over; [- enfermo] to sit up with - **2.** [ocultar] to mask, to veil.

◆ **velarse** *vprnl* FOTO to get fogged.

velatorio *sm* wake, vigil.

veleidad *sf* - **1.** [inconstancia] fickleness, capriciousness - **2.** [antojo, capricho] whim, caprice.

veleidoso, sa *adj* - **1.** [inconstante] fickle - **2.** [caprichoso] capricious.

velero *sm* sailing boat/ship.

veleta ⋄ *sf* weather vane. ⋄ *smf fam* capricious person.

vello *sm* - **1.** [pelusilla] down - **2.** [pelo] hair; **vello púbico** pubic hair.

vellocino *sm* fleece.

vellón *sm* - **1.** [lana] fleece - **2.** [aleación] silver and copper alloy.

velloso, sa *adj* hairy.

velludo, da *adj* hairy.

velo *sm lit & fig* veil; **correr** *o* **echar un (tupido) velo sobre algo** to draw a veil over sthg.

◆ **velo del paladar** *sm* soft palate.

velocidad *sf* - **1.** [gen] speed; **cobrar velocidad** to pick up speed; **perder velocidad** to lose speed; **velocidad máxima** top speed; **velocidad de crucero** cruising speed; **velocidad punta** top speed; **con la velocidad de un rayo** as quick as lightning - **2.** AUTO [marcha] gear; **cambiar de velocidad** to change gear.

velocímetro *sm* speedometer.

velocípedo *sm* velocipede.

velocista *smf* sprinter.

velódromo *sm* cycle track, velodrome.

velomotor *sm* moped.

velorio *sm* wake.

veloz *adj* fast, quick.

ven ⊳ **venir**.

vena *sf* - **1.** [gen, ANAT & GEOL] vein - **2.** [inspiración] inspiration; **tener la vena** to be inspired - **3.** [don] vein, streak; **tener vena de algo** to have a gift for doing sthg - **4.** *loc*: **estar en la vena** to be in the mood; **si se le da la vena** if the mood takes him/her.

venado *sm* ZOOL deer; CULIN venison.

venal *adj* - **1.** [sobornable] venal, corrupt - **2.** [vendible] for sale, saleable.

vencedor, ra ⋄ *adj* winning, victorious. ⋄ *sm, f* winner.

vencer [11] ⋄ *vt* - **1.** [ganar] to beat, to defeat - **2.** [derrotar - suj: sueño, cansancio, emoción] to overcome - **3.** [aventajar]: **vencer a alguien a o en algo** to outdo sb at sthg - **4.** [superar - miedo, obstáculos] to overcome; [- tentación] to resist. ⋄ *vi* - **1.** [ganar] to win, to be victorious - **2.** [caducar - garantía, contrato, plazo] to expire; [- deuda, pago] to fall due, to be payable; [- bono] to mature - **3.** [prevalecer] to prevail.

◆ **vencerse** *vprnl* [estante etc] to give way, to collapse.

vencido, da ⋄ *adj* - **1.** [derrotado] defeated; **darse por vencido** to give up - **2.** [caducado - garantía, contrato, plazo] expired; [- pago, deuda] due, payable; [- bono] mature. ⋄ *sm, f* [en guerra] conquered o defeated person; [en deportes, concursos] loser.

vencimiento *sm* - **1.** [término - de garantía, contrato, plazo] expiry; [- de pago, deuda] falling due; [- de bono] maturing - **2.** [expiración] due date - **3.** [inclinación] giving way, collapse.

venda *sf* bandage; **venda de gasa** gauze bandage; **tener una venda en o delante de los ojos** *fig* to be blind.

vendaje *sm* bandaging; **poner un vendaje** to put on a dressing.

vendar *vt* to bandage; **vendar los ojos a alguien** to blindfold sb.

vendaval *sm* gale.

vendedor, ra ⋄ *adj* selling. ⋄ *sm, f* [gen] seller; [en tienda] shop o sales assistant; [de coches, seguros] salesman (*f* saleswoman); **vendedor ambulante** pedlar, hawker.

vender *vt* lit & *fig* to sell; **vender algo a o por** to sell sthg for.

◆ **venderse** *vprnl* - **1.** [ser vendido] to be sold o on sale; **'se vende'** 'for sale' - **2.** [dejarse sobornar] to sell o.s., to be bribed.

vendido, da *adj* sold; **estar o ir vendido** *fig* not to stand a chance.

vendimia *sf* grape harvest.

vendimiador, ra *sm, f* grape picker.

vendimiar [8] ⋄ *vt* to harvest *(grapes)*. ⋄ *vi* to pick grapes.

vendrá *etc* ⊳ **venir**.

veneno *sm* - **1.** [gen] poison; [de serpiente, insecto] venom - **2.** *fig* [mala intención] venom.

venenoso, sa *adj* - **1.** [gen] poisonous - **2.** *fig* [malintencionado] venomous.

venerable *adj* venerable.

veneración *sf* veneration, worship.

venerar *vt* to venerate, to worship.

venéreo, a *adj* venereal.

venezolano, na *adj* & *sm, f* Venezuelan.

Venezuela *n pr* Venezuela.

venga ⋄ *v* ⊳ **venir**. ⋄ *interj*: ¡**venga!** come on!

vengador, ra ⋄ *adj* avenging. ⋄ *sm, f* avenger.

venganza *sf* vengeance, revenge.

vengar [16] *vt* to avenge.

◆ **vengarse** *vprnl*: **vengarse (de)** to take revenge (on), to avenge o.s. (on).

vengativo, va *adj* vengeful, vindictive.

vengo ⊳ **venir**.

vengue *etc* ⊳ **vengar**.

venia *sf* - **1.** [permiso] permission - **2.** DER [perdón] pardon; **con la venia** [tomando la palabra] by your leave.

venial *adj* petty, venial.

venialidad *sf* veniality, pettiness.

venida *sf* [llegada] arrival.

venidero, ra *adj* coming, future.

venir [75] ⋄ *vi* - **1.** [gen] to come; **venir a/de hacer algo** to come to do sthg/from doing sthg; **venir de algo** [proceder, derivarse] to come from sthg; **venir a alguien con algo** to come to sb with sthg; **no me vengas con exigencias** don't come to me making demands; **venir a por algo** to come to pick up sthg; **el año que viene** next year - **2.** [llegar] to arrive; **vino a las doce** he arrived at twelve o'clock - **3.** [hallarse] to be; **su foto viene en primera página** his photo is o appears on the front page; **el texto viene en inglés** the text is in English - **4.** [acometer, sobrevenir]: **me viene sueño** I'm getting sleepy; **le vinieron ganas de reír** he was seized by a desire to laugh; **le vino una tremenda desgracia** he suffered a great misfortune - **5.** [ropa, calzado]: **venir a alguien** to fit sb; **¿qué tal te viene?** does it fit all right?; **el abrigo le viene pequeño** the coat is too small for her - **6.** [convenir]: **venir bien/mal a alguien** to suit/not to suit sb - **7.** [aproximarse]: **viene a costar un millón** it costs almost a million - **8.** *loc*: **¿a qué viene esto?** what do you mean by that?, what's that in aid of?; **venir a**

menos [negocio] to go downhill; [persona] to go down in the world; **venir a parar en** to end in; **venir a ser** to amount to. ◇ *v aux* - **1.** *(antes de gerundio)* [haber estado]: **venir haciendo algo** to have been doing sthg; **las peleas vienen sucediéndose desde hace tiempo** fighting has been going on for some time - **2.** *(antes de participio)* [estar]: **los cambios vienen motivados por la presión de la oposición** the changes have resulted from pressure on the part of the opposition - **3.** *(antes de infinitivo)* [estar]: **esto viene a costar unos veinte euros** it costs almost twenty euros.

➤ **venirse** *vprnl* - **1.** [volver]: **venirse (de)** to come back *o* return (from) - **2.** *loc*: **venirse abajo** [techo, estante etc] to collapse; [ilusiones] to be dashed.

venoso, sa *adj* venous.

venta *sf* - **1.** [acción] sale, selling; **de venta en...** on sale at...; **estar en venta** to be for sale; **poner a la venta** [casa] to put up for sale; **salir a la venta** to go on sale; [producto] to put on sale; **venta por correo** *o* **por correspondencia** mail-order sale; **venta automatizada** vending-machine sale; **venta al contado** cash sale; **venta a crédito** credit sale; **venta a domicilio** door-to-door selling; **venta a plazos** sale by instalments; **venta pública** public auction; **venta sobre plano** sale of customized goods - **2.** *(gen pl)* [cantidad] sales *pl* - **3.** [posada] country inn.

ventaja *sf* - **1.** [hecho favorable] advantage - **2.** [en competición] lead; **dar ventaja** to give a start; **llevar ventaja a alguien** to have a lead over sb.

ventajista *adj* & *smf* opportunist.

ventajoso, sa *adj* advantageous.

ventana *sf* - **1.** [gen & INFORM] window; **ventana de guillotina** sash window - **2.** [de nariz] nostril.

ventanal *sm* large window.

ventanilla *sf* - **1.** [de vehículo, sobre] window - **2.** [taquilla] counter.

ventear ◇ *v impers* to be very windy. ◇ *vi* to sniff the air.

ventilación *sf* ventilation.

ventilador *sm* ventilator, fan.

ventilar *vt* - **1.** [airear] to air - **2.** [resolver] to clear up - **3.** [discutir] to air - **4.** [difundir] to spread, to make public.

➤ **ventilarse** *vprnl* - **1.** [airearse] to air - **2.** *fam* [terminarse] to knock *o* finish off.

ventisca *sf* blizzard.

ventiscar [10], **ventisquear** *v impers* to blow a blizzard.

ventolera *sf* - **1.** [viento] gust of wind - **2.** [idea extravagante] wild idea; **se le ha dado la ventolera de hacerlo** she has taken it into her head to do it.

ventosa *sf* [gen & ZOOL] sucker.

ventosear *vi* to break wind.

ventosidad *sf* wind, flatulence.

ventoso, sa *adj* windy.

ventrículo *sm* ventricle.

ventrílocuo, cua *sm, f* ventriloquist.

ventriloquía *sf* ventriloquism.

ventura *sf* - **1.** [suerte] luck; **a la (buena) ventura** [al azar] at random, haphazardly; [sin nada previsto] without planning *o* a fixed plan; **por ventura** *fml* luckily; **echar la buena ventura a alguien** to tell sb's fortune - **2.** [casualidad] fate, fortune.

venturoso, sa *adj* happy, fortunate.

Venus *n pr* Venus.

venza *etc* ▷ **vencer.**

ver [76] ◇ *vi* - **1.** [gen] to see - **2.** *loc*: **a ver** [veamos] let's see; **¿a ver?** [mirando con interés] let me see, let's have a look; **¡a ver!** [¡pues claro!] what do you expect?; [al empezar algo] right!; **dejarse ver (por un sitio)** to show one's face (somewhere); **eso está por ver** that remains to be seen; **ni visto ni oído** in the twinkling of an eye; **verás, iba a ir pero...** listen, I was thinking of coming but...; **ya veremos** we'll see. ◇ *vt* - **1.** [gen] to see; [mirar] to look at; [televisión, partido de fútbol] to watch; **¿ves algo?** can you see anything?; **he estado viendo tu trabajo** I've been looking at your work; **ya veo que estás de mal humor** I can see you're in a bad mood; **¿ves lo que quiero decir?** do you see what I mean?; **ir a ver lo que pasa** to go and see what's going on; **es una manera de ver las cosas** that's one way of looking at it; **yo no lo veo tan mal** I don't think it's that bad - **2.** *loc*: **eso habrá que verlo** that remains to be seen; **¡hay que ver qué lista es!** you wouldn't believe how clever she is!; **no puedo verle (ni en pintura)** *fam* I can't stand him; **si no lo veo, no lo creo** you'll never believe it; **si te vi, no me acuerdo** he/she etc doesn't want anything to do with me; **ver venir a alguien** to see what sb is up to. ◇ *sm*: **estar de buen ver** to be good-looking.

➤ **verse** *vprnl* - **1.** [mirarse, imaginarse] to see o.s.; **verse en el espejo** to see o.s. in the mirror; **ya me veo cargando el camión yo solo** I can see myself having to load the lorry on my own - **2.** [percibirse]: **desde aquí se ve el mar** you can see the sea from here - **3.** [encontrarse] to meet, to see each other; **verse con alguien** to see sb; **hace mucho que no nos vemos** we haven't seen each other for a long

time **- 4.** [darse, suceder] to be seen **- 5.** loc: **vérselas venir** fam to see it coming; **vérselas y deseárselas para hacer algo** to have a real struggle doing sthg.
➤ **véase** vprnl [en textos] see.
➤ **por lo visto, por lo que se ve** loc adv apparently.

vera sf **- 1.** [orilla - de río, lago] bank; [- de camino] edge, side **- 2.** fig [lado] side; **a la vera de** next to.

veracidad sf truthfulness.

veranda sf verandah.

veraneante ⟨⟩ adj holiday-making. ⟨⟩ smf holidaymaker, (summer) vacationer US.

veranear vi: **veranear en** to spend one's summer holidays in.

veraneo sm summer holidays pl; **de veraneo** holiday (antes de s).

veraniego, ga adj summer (antes de s).

verano sm summer.

veras sfpl truth (U); **de veras** [verdaderamente] really; [en serio] seriously.

veraz adj truthful.

verbal adj verbal.

verbalizar [13] vt to verbalize.

verbena sf **- 1.** [fiesta] street party (on the eve of certain saints' days) **- 2.** [planta] verbena.

verbenero, ra adj street-party (antes de s).

verbigracia adv culto for example, for instance.

verbo sm **- 1.** GRAM verb **- 2.** [lenguaje] language.

verborrea sf verbal diarrhoea, verbosity.

verbosidad sf verbosity.

verboso, sa adj verbose.

verdad sf **- 1.** [gen] truth; **a decir verdad** to tell the truth; **decir la verdad** to tell the truth; **en verdad** truly, honestly **- 2.** [principio aceptado] fact **- 3.** loc: **no te gusta, ¿verdad?** you don't like it, do you?; **está bueno, ¿verdad?** it's good, isn't it?; **una verdad como un puño** an undeniable fact.
➤ **verdades** sfpl [opinión sincera] true thoughts; **cantar las verdades** fig to speak one's mind; **cantarle** o **decirle a alguien cuatro verdades** fig to tell sb a few home truths.
➤ **de verdad** ⟨⟩ loc adv **- 1.** [en serio] seriously **- 2.** [realmente] really. ⟨⟩ loc adj [auténtico] real.

verdadero, ra adj **- 1.** [cierto, real] true, real; **fue un verdadero lío** it was a real mess **- 2.** [sin falsificar] real **- 3.** [enfático] real.

verde ⟨⟩ adj **- 1.** [gen] green; **verde oliva** olive (green); **estar verde de envidia** to be green with envy; **poner verde a alguien** to criticize sb **- 2.** [fruta] unripe, green **- 3.** [ecologis-

ta] Green, green **- 4.** fig [obsceno] blue, dirty **- 5.** fig [inmaduro - proyecto etc] in its early stages. ⟨⟩ sm [color] green.
➤ **Verdes** smpl [partido]: **los Verdes** the Greens.

verdor sm [color] greenness.

verdoso, sa adj greenish.

verdugo sm **- 1.** [de preso] executioner; [que ahorca] hangman **- 2.** [pasamontañas] balaclava helmet.

verdulería sf greengrocer's (shop).

verdulero, ra sm, f [tendero] greengrocer.
➤ **verdulera** sf fam fig [ordinaria] fishwife.

verdura sf vegetables pl, greens pl.

verdusco, ca adj despec dirty green.

vereda sf **- 1.** [senda] path; **hacer entrar** o **meter a alguien en vereda** to bring sb into line **- 2.** C Sur & Perú [acera] pavement UK, sidewalk US.

veredicto sm verdict.

verga sf **- 1.** ANAT penis **- 2.** NÁUT yard **- 3.** [vara] stick.

vergel sm lush, fertile place.

vergonzante adj shameful.

vergonzoso, sa ⟨⟩ adj **- 1.** [deshonroso] shameful **- 2.** [tímido] bashful. ⟨⟩ sm, f bashful person.

vergüenza sf **- 1.** [turbación] embarrassment; **dar vergüenza** to embarrass; **¡qué vergüenza!** how embarrassing!; **sentir vergüenza** to feel embarrassed; **sentir vergüenza ajena** to feel embarrassed for sb **- 2.** [timidez] bashfulness; **perder la vergüenza** to lose one's inhibitions **- 3.** [remordimiento] shame; **sentir vergüenza** to feel ashamed **- 4.** [deshonra, escándalo] disgrace; **¡es una vergüenza!** it's disgraceful!
➤ **vergüenzas** sfpl [genitales] private parts.

vericueto (gen pl) sm **- 1.** [lugar] rough track **- 2.** [situación] complication.

verídico, ca adj **- 1.** [cierto] true, truthful **- 2.** fig [verosímil] true-to-life, real.

verificación sf check, checking (U).

verificador, ra ⟨⟩ adj [confirmador] checking; [examinador] testing, inspecting. ⟨⟩ sm, f tester, inspector.

verificar [10] vt **- 1.** [comprobar - verdad, autenticidad] to check, to verify **- 2.** [examinar - funcionamiento, buen estado] to check, to test **- 3.** [confirmar - fecha, cita] to confirm **- 4.** [llevar a cabo] to carry out.
➤ **verificarse** vprnl **- 1.** [tener lugar] to take place **- 2.** [resultar cierto - predicción] to come true; [comprobarse] to be verified.

verja *sf* - **1.** [puerta] iron gate; **la verja de Gibraltar** *the border between Spain and Gibraltar* - **2.** [valla] railings *pl* - **3.** [enrejado] grille.

vermú, vermut *(pl* vermuts) *sm* - **1.** [bebida] vermouth - **2.** *Andes & R Plata* [en cine] early-evening showing; *Andes & R Plata* [en teatro] early-evening performance.

vernáculo, la *adj* vernacular.

verónica *sf* - **1.** TAUROM *pass in which matador swings cape away from bull* - **2.** [planta] veronica.

verosímil *adj* - **1.** [creíble] believable, credible - **2.** [probable] likely, probable.

verosimilitud *sf* - **1.** [credibilidad] credibility - **2.** [probabilidad] likeliness.

verruga *sf* wart.

versado, da *adj*: **versado (en)** versed (in).

versallesco, ca *adj fam* [cortés] gallant, chivalrous.

versar *vi*: **versar sobre** to be about, to deal with.

versátil *adj* - **1.** [voluble] changeable, fickle - **2.** *(considerado incorrecto)* [polifacético] versatile.

versatilidad *sf* - **1.** [volubilidad] changeability, fickleness - **2.** [adaptabilidad] versatility.

versículo *sm* verse.

versificación *sf* versification.

versificar [10] ⬦ *vi* to write (in) verse. ⬦ *vt* to put into verse.

versión *sf* - **1.** [gen] version; [en música pop] cover version; **versión original** CINE original (version) - **2.** [traducción] translation, version.

verso *sm* - **1.** [género] verse; **en verso** in verse; **verso blanco/libre** blank/free verse - **2.** [unidad rítmica] line *(of poetry)* - **3.** [poema] poem.

versus *prep culto* versus.

vértebra *sf* vertebra.

vertebrado, da *adj* vertebrate.

➥ **vertebrados** *smpl* ZOOL vertebrates.

vertebral *adj* vertebral.

vertedero *sm* - **1.** [de basuras] rubbish tip *o* dump; [de agua] overflow - **2.** [de pantano] drain, spillway.

verter [20] ⬦ *vt* - **1.** [derramar] to spill - **2.** [vaciar - líquido] to pour (out); [- recipiente] to empty - **3.** [tirar - basura, residuos] to dump - **4.** [traducir]: **verter (a)** to translate (into) - **5.** *fig* [decir] to tell. ⬦ *vi*: **verter a** to flow into.

➥ **verterse** *vprnl* [derramarse] to spill.

vertical ⬦ *adj* GEOM vertical; [derecho] upright. ⬦ *sm* ASTRON vertical circle. ⬦ *sf* GEOM vertical.

verticalidad *sf* verticality, vertical position.

vértice *sm* [gen] vertex; [de cono] apex.

vertido *sm* - **1.** *(gen pl)* [residuo] waste *(U)* - **2.** [acción] dumping.

vertiente *sf* - **1.** [pendiente] slope - **2.** *fig* [aspecto] side, aspect - **3.** *R Dom* [manantial] spring.

vertiginoso, sa *adj* - **1.** [mareante] dizzy - **2.** *fig* [raudo] giddy.

vértigo *sm* - **1.** [enfermedad] vertigo; [mareo] dizziness; **trepar me da vértigo** climbing makes me dizzy - **2.** *fig* [apresuramiento] mad rush, hectic pace - **3.** *fig* [asombro]: **dar vértigo a alguien** to make sb's head spin; **de vértigo** [velocidad, altura] giddy; [cifras] mindboggling.

vesícula *sf*: **vesícula biliar** gall bladder.

vespertino, na *adj* evening *(antes de s)*.

vestal *sf* vestal (virgin).

vestíbulo *sm* [de casa] (entrance) hall; [de hotel, oficina] lobby, foyer.

vestido, da *adj* dressed; **ir vestido** to be dressed; **iba vestido de negro** he was dressed in black.

➥ **vestido** *sm* - **1.** [indumentaria] clothes *pl* - **2.** [prenda femenina] dress; **vestido de noche** evening dress.

vestidor *sm* dressing room.

vestidura *(gen pl)* *sf* clothes *pl*; RELIG vestments *pl*; **rasgarse las vestiduras** to make a fuss.

vestigio *sm* vestige; *fig* sign, trace.

vestimenta *sf* clothes *pl*, wardrobe.

vestir [26] ⬦ *vt* - **1.** [gen] to dress - **2.** [llevar puesto] to wear - **3.** [cubrir] to cover - **4.** *fig* [encubrir]: **vestir algo de** to invest sthg with. ⬦ *vi* - **1.** [ser elegante] to be dressy; **de (mucho) vestir** (very) dressy - **2.** [llevar ropa] to dress - **3.** *fig* [estar bien visto] to be the done thing - **4.** *loc*: **el mismo que viste y calza** the very same, none other; **vísteme despacio que tengo prisa** *prov* more haste, less speed *prov*.

➥ **vestirse** *vprnl* - **1.** [ponerse ropa] to get dressed, to dress; **vestirse de** to wear - **2.** [adquirir ropa]: **vestirse en** to buy one's clothes at - **3.** *fig* [cubrirse]: **vestirse de** to be covered in.

vestuario *sm* - **1.** [vestimenta] clothes *pl*, wardrobe; TEATRO costumes *pl* - **2.** [para cambiarse] changing room; [de actores] dressing room.

veta *sf* - **1.** [filón] vein, seam - **2.** [faja, lista] grain.

vetar *vt* to veto.

veteado, da *adj* grained.

vetear *vt* to grain.

veteranía *sf* seniority, age.

veterano, na *adj* & *sm, f* veteran.

veterinario, ria ⬦ *adj* veterinary. ⬦ *sm, f* [persona] vet, veterinary surgeon.

◆ **veterinaria** *sf* [ciencia] veterinary science O medicine.

veto *sm* veto; **poner veto a algo** to veto sthg.

vetusto, ta *adj culto* ancient, very old.

vez *sf* - **1.** [gen] time; **una vez** once; **dos veces** twice; **tres veces** three times; **¿has estado allí alguna vez?** have you ever been there?; **a mi/tu** *etc* **vez** in my/your *etc* turn; **a la vez (que)** at the same time (as); **cada vez (que)** every time; **cada vez más** more and more; **cada vez menos** less and less; **cada vez la veo más feliz** she seems happier and happier; **de una vez** in one go; **de una vez para siempre** O **por todas** once and for all; **muchas veces** often, a lot; **otra vez** again; **pocas veces, rara vez** rarely, seldom; **por última vez** for the last time; **una o alguna que otra vez** occasionally; **una vez más** once again; **una y otra vez** time and again; **érase una vez** once upon a time - **2.** [turno] turn; **pedir la vez** to ask who is last - **3.** *loc*: **hacer las veces de** to act as.

◆ **a veces, algunas veces** *loc adv* sometimes, at times.

◆ **de vez en cuando** *loc adv* from time to time, now and again.

◆ **en vez de** *loc prep* instead of.

◆ **tal vez** *loc adv* perhaps, maybe.

◆ **una vez que** *loc conj* once, after.

VHF (*abrev de* very high frequency) *sf* VHF.

VHS (*abrev de* video home system) *sm* VHS.

vía ◇ *sf* - **1.** [medio de transporte] route; **por vía aérea** [gen] by air; [correo] (by) airmail; **por vía marítima** by sea; **por vía terrestre** overland, by land; **vía de comunicación** communication route; **vía fluvial** waterway - **2.** [calzada, calle] road; **vía pública** public thoroughfare - **3.** [FERROC - raíl] rails *pl*, track; [- andén] platform; **vía estrecha** narrow gauge; **vía férrea** [ruta] railway line; **vía muerta** siding - **4.** [proceso]: **estar en vías de** to be in the process of; **país en vías de desarrollo** developing country; **una especie en vías de extinción** an endangered species - **5.** ANAT tract; **por vía oral** orally; **por vía venosa** intravenously - **6.** [opción] channel, path; **por vía oficial/judicial** through official channels/the courts - **7.** [camino] way; **dar vía libre** [dejar paso] to give way; [dar libertad de acción] to give a free rein - **8.** DER procedure. ◇ *prep* via.

◆ **Vía Láctea** *sf* Milky Way.

viabilidad *sf* viability.

viable *adj fig* [posible] viable.

viacrucis *sm inv* RELIG Stations *pl* of the Cross, Way of the Cross.

viaducto *sm* viaduct.

viajante *smf* travelling salesperson.

viajar *vi* - **1.** [trasladarse, irse]: **viajar (en)** to travel (by) - **2.** [circular] to run.

viaje *sm* - **1.** [gen] journey, trip; [en barco] voyage; **¡buen viaje!** have a good journey O trip!; **estar/ir de viaje** to be/go away (on a trip); **11 días de viaje** it's an 11-day journey; **viaje de ida/de vuelta** outward/return journey; **viaje de ida y vuelta** return journey O trip; **viaje de negocios** business trip; **viaje de novios** honeymoon; **viaje organizado** package tour; **viaje relámpago** lightning trip O visit - **2.** *fig* [recorrido] trip; **di varios viajes para trasladar los muebles** it took me a good few trips to move all the furniture - **3.** *fam fig* [alucinación] trip - **4.** *fam fig* [golpe] bang, bump.

◆ **viajes** *smpl* [singladuras] travels.

viajero, ra ◇ *adj* [persona] travelling; [ave] migratory. ◇ *sm, f* [gen] traveller; [en transporte público] passenger.

vial ◇ *adj* road (*antes de s*). ◇ *sm* [frasco] phial.

vianda *sf* - **1.** food (*U*) - **2.** *Amér* [recipiente] lunchbox.

viandante *smf* - **1.** [peatón] pedestrian - **2.** [transeúnte] passer-by.

viaraza *sf Amér* - **1.** [enfado] fit of anger - **2.** [ocurrencia] absurd idea.

viario, ria *adj* road (*antes de s*).

viático *sm* - **1.** [dieta] expenses allowance - **2.** RELIG last rites *pl*, viaticum.

víbora *sf* viper.

vibración *sf* vibration.

vibrador, ra *adj* vibrating.

◆ **vibrador** *sm* vibrator.

vibráfono *sm* vibraphone.

vibrante *adj* - **1.** [oscilante] vibrating - **2.** *fig* [emocionante] vibrant - **3.** [trémulo] quivering.

vibrar *vi* - **1.** [oscilar] to vibrate - **2.** *fig* [voz, rodillas etc] to shake - **3.** *fig* [público] to get excited.

vibrátil *adj* vibratile.

vibratorio, ria *adj* vibratory.

vicaría *sf* - **1.** [cargo] vicarship, vicariate; **pasar por la vicaría** to tie the knot - **2.** [residencia] vicarage.

vicario *sm* vicar.

vicealmirante *sm* vice-admiral.

vicecónsul *sm* vice-consul.

vicepresidencia *sf* [de país, asociación] vice-presidency; [de comité, empresa] vice-chairmanship.

vicepresidente, ta *sm, f* [de país, asociación] vice-president; [de comité, empresa] vice-chairman.

vicerrector, ra *sm, f* ≃ vice-rector.

vicesecretario, ria *sm, f* assistant secretary.

viceversa *adv* vice versa.

vichy [bi'tʃi] (*pl* **vichys**) *sm* gingham.

vichysoisse [bitʃi'swas] (*pl* **vichysoisses**) *sf* CU-LIN vichysoisse.

viciado, **da** *adj* [aire] stuffy; [estilo] marred.

viciar [8] *vt* - **1.** [pervertir] to corrupt - **2.** *fig* [falsear] to falsify; [tergiversar] to distort, to twist.
◆ **viciarse** *vprnl* [enviciarse] to take to vice.

vicio *sm* - **1.** [mala costumbre] bad habit, vice; **llorar** *o* **quejarse de vicio** to complain for no (good) reason - **2.** [libertinaje] vice - **3.** [defecto físico, de dicción etc] defect - **4.** *loc*: **de vicio** *fam* [fenomenal] brilliant.

vicioso, sa ◇ *adj* dissolute, depraved. ◇ *sm, f* dissolute person, depraved person.

vicisitud *sf (gen pl)* [avatar] vicissitude; **las vicisitud de la vida** life's ups and downs.

víctima *sf* victim; [en accidente, guerra] casualty; **ser víctima de** to be the victim of; **víctima propiciatoria** scapegoat.

victimar *vt Amér* to kill, to murder.

victoria *sf* victory; **adjudicarse la victoria** to win a victory; **cantar victoria** to claim victory.
◆ **Victoria** *sm*: **el lago Victoria** Lake Victoria.

victoriano, na *adj* Victorian.

victorioso, sa *adj* victorious.

vicuña *sf* vicuña.

vid *sf* vine.

vid., v. (*abrev de* **véase**) v., vid.

vida *sf* life; **amargarse la vida** to make one's life a misery; **buscarse la vida** to try to earn one's own living; **dar la vida por** *fig* to give one's life for; **de toda la vida** [amigo etc] lifelong; **le conozco de toda la vida** I've known him all my life; **de por vida** for life; **en vida de** during the life *o* lifetime of; **en mi/tu** *etc* **vida** never (in my/your *etc*) life; **estar con vida** to be alive; **estar entre la vida y la muerte** to be at death's door; **ganarse la vida** to earn a living; **pasar a mejor vida** to pass away; **pasarse la vida haciendo algo** to spend one's life doing sthg; **perder la vida** to lose one's life; **quitar la vida a alguien** to kill sb; **vida privada/sentimental** private/love life; **vida eterna** eternal life; **la otra vida** the next life; **¡así es la vida!** that's life!, such is life!; **darse** *o* **pegarse la gran vida, darse** *o* **pegarse la vida padre** to live the life of Riley; **enterrarse en vida** to forsake the world; **la vida y milagros de alguien** sb's life story; **llevar una vida de perros** to lead a dog's life; **¡mi vida!, ¡vida mía!** my darling!; **¿qué es de tu vida?** how's life?; **tener la vida pendiente de un hilo** to have one's life hanging by a thread; **tener siete vidas como los gatos** to have nine lives.

vidente *smf* clairvoyant.

vídeo, video ◇ *sm* - **1.** [gen] video; **grabar en vídeo** to videotape, to record on video; **vídeo a la carta** video on demand; **vídeo comu-** nitario *system enabling one video to be shown simultaneously on different television sets in one block of flats*; **vídeo doméstico** home video - **2.** [aparato reproductor] video, VCR *US*. ◇ *adj inv* video *(antes de s)*.

videocámara *sf* camcorder.

videocasete *sm* video, videocassette.

videocinta *sf* video, videotape.

videoclip (*pl* **videoclips**) *sm* (pop) video.

videoclub (*pl* **videoclubes** *o* **videoclubs**) *sm* video club.

videoconferencia *sf* videoconference.

videoedición *sf* video editing.

videojuego *sm* video game.

videoteca *sf* video library.

videoteléfono *sm* videophone.

videoterminal *sm* video terminal.

videotexto *sm* [por señal de televisión] teletext; [por línea telefónica] videotext, viewdata.

videotex *sm inv* = **videotexto**.

vidorra *sf fam* easy life; **pegarse una (gran) vidorra** to live the life of Riley.

vidriado, da *adj* glazed.
◆ **vidriado** *sm* - **1.** [técnica] glazing - **2.** [material] glaze.

vidriero, ra *sm, f* - **1.** [que fabrica cristales] glass merchant *o* manufacturer - **2.** [que coloca cristales] glazier.
◆ **vidriera** *sf* - **1.** [puerta] glass door; [ventana] glass window - **2.** [en catedrales] stained glass window - **3.** *Amér* [escaparate] shop window.

vidrio *sm* - **1.** [material] glass - **2.** [de ventana] window (pane) - **3.** *Amér* [de anteojos] glass - **4.** *Amér* [de vehículo] window; **pagar los vidrios rotos** to carry the can.

vidrioso, sa *adj* - **1.** [quebradizo] brittle - **2.** *fig* [tema, asunto] thorny, delicate - **3.** *fig* [ojos] glazed.

vieira *sf* scallop.

viejo, ja ◇ *adj* old; **hacerse viejo** to get *o* grow old. ◇ *sm, f* - **1.** [anciano] old man (*f* old lady); **los viejos** the elderly; **viejo verde** dirty old man (*f* dirty old woman) - **2.** *fam* [padres] old man (*f* old girl); **mis viejos** my folks - **3.** *Amér fam* [amigo] pal, mate.
◆ **Viejo de Pascua** *sm Chile*: **Viejo de Pascua** *o* **Pascuero** Father Christmas.

viene ▷ **venir**.

vienés, esa *adj* & *sm, f* Viennese.

viento *sm* - **1.** [aire] wind; **hace viento** it's windy; **(viento) alisio** trade wind; **viento de costado** *o* **de lado** crosswind - **2.** MÚS wind - **3.** *loc*: **a los cuatro vientos** from the rooftops; **contra viento y marea** in spite of everything; **despedir** *o* **echar a alguien con viento fresco**

to send sb packing; **mis esperanzas se las lle-vó el viento** my hopes flew out of the window; **viento en popa** splendidly, very nicely.

vientre sm - **1.** ANAT stomach; **hacer de vien-tre** to have a bowel movement; **bajo vientre** lower stomach - **2.** [de vasija etc] belly, rounded part.

viera ⮞ ver.

viernes sm inv Friday; ver también **sábado**.
⮞ **Viernes Santo** sm RELIG Good Friday.

vierta etc ⮞ verter.

viese ⮞ ver.

Vietnam n pr Vietnam.

vietnamita adj & smf Vietnamese.

viga sf [de madera] beam, rafter; [de metal] girder; **viga maestra** main beam.

vigencia sf [de ley etc] validity; [de costumbre] use; **estar/entrar en vigencia** to be in/come into force.

vigente adj [ley etc] in force; [costumbre] in use.

vigésimo, ma num twentieth.

vigía ⬦ sf - **1.** [atalaya] watch tower - **2.** [vigilancia] watch. ⬦ smf lookout.

vigilancia sf - **1.** [cuidado] vigilance, care; **es-tar bajo vigilancia** to be under surveillance - **2.** [vigilantes] guards pl.

vigilante ⬦ adj vigilant. ⬦ smf guard; **vigilante nocturno** night watchman.

vigilar ⬦ vt [enfermo] to watch over; [presos, banco] to guard; [niños, bolso] to keep an eye on; [proceso] to oversee. ⬦ vi to keep watch.

vigilia sf - **1.** [vela] wakefulness; **estar de vigilia** to be awake - **2.** [insomnio] sleeplessness - **3.** [víspera] vigil.

vigor sm - **1.** [gen] vigour - **2.** [vigencia]: **en vigor** in force; **entrar en vigor** to come into force, to take effect.

vigorizador, ra, vigorizante adj [medicamento] fortifying; [actividad] invigorating.

vigorizar [13] vt - **1.** [fortalecer] to fortify - **2.** fig [animar] to animate, to encourage.

vigoroso, sa adj [gen] vigorous, energetic.

VIH (abrev de **virus de la inmunodeficiencia humana**) sm HIV.

vikingo, ga adj & sm, f Viking.

vil adj vile, despicable; [metal] base.

vileza sf - **1.** [acción] vile o despicable act - **2.** [cualidad] vileness.

vilipendiar [8] vt desus - **1.** [despreciar] to despise; [humillar] to humiliate - **2.** [ofender] to vilify, to revile.

villa sf - **1.** [población] small town - **2.** [casa] villa, country house - **3.: villa miseria** Arg & Bol shanty town.

villadiego sm: **coger** o **tomar las de villadie-go** fig to take to one's heels.

villancico sm [navideño] Christmas carol.

villanía sf vile o despicable act, villainy (U).

villano, na ⬦ adj villainous. ⬦ sm, f villain.

villorrio sm despec dump, hole.

vilo ⬥ **en vilo** loc adv - **1.** [suspendido] in the air, suspended - **2.** [inquieto] on tenterhooks; **tener a alguien en vilo** to keep sb in suspense.

vinagre sm vinegar.

vinagrera sf [vasija] vinegar bottle.
⮞ **vinagreras** sfpl CULIN [convoy] cruet sing.

vinagreta sf vinaigrette, French dressing.

vinatero, ra ⬦ adj wine (antes de s). ⬦ sm, f vintner, wine merchant.

vinculación sf link, linking (U).

vinculante adj DER binding; **ser vinculante para algo** to be binding for sthg.

vincular vt - **1.** [enlazar] to link; **vincular algo con algo** to link sthg with o to sthg; [por obligación] to tie, to bind - **2.** DER to entail.
⮞ **vincularse** vprnl [enlazarse] to be linked.

vínculo sm - **1.** [lazo - entre hechos, países] link; [- personal, familiar] tie, bond - **2.** DER entail.

vindicación sf - **1.** [venganza] vengeance, revenge - **2.** [defensa] vindication.

vindicar [10] vt - **1.** [vengar] to avenge, to revenge - **2.** [defender] to vindicate - **3.** [reivindicar] to claim.

vindicativo, va adj [reivindicativo]: **vindicati-vo (de)** in defence (of).

vinícola adj [país, región] wine-producing (antes de s); [industria] wine (antes de s).

vinicultor, ra sm, f wine producer.

vinicultura sf wine producing.

viniera etc ⮞ venir.

vinilo sm vinyl.

vino sm wine; **vino blanco/tinto** white/red wine; **vino dulce/seco** sweet/dry wine; **vino espumoso/generoso** sparkling/full-bodied wine; **vino clarete** light red wine; **vino de mesa** table wine; **vino peleón** plonk, cheap wine; **vino rosado** rosé; ⮞ **venir**.

viña sf vineyard.

viñedo sm (large) vineyard.

viñeta sf - **1.** [de tebeo] (individual) cartoon - **2.** [de libro] vignette.

vio ⮞ ver.

viola ⬦ sf viola. ⬦ smf viola player.

violáceo, a adj violet.
⮞ **violáceo** sm violet.

violación sf - **1.** [de ley, derechos] violation, infringement - **2.** [de persona] rape - **3.: viola-ción de domicilio** unlawful entry.

violador, **ra** adj & sm, f rapist.

violar vt - **1.** [ley, derechos, domicilio] to violate, to infringe - **2.** [persona] to rape.

violencia sf - **1.** [agresividad] violence; **violencia doméstica** domestic violence - **2.** [fuerza - de viento, pasiones] force - **3.** [incomodidad] embarrassment, awkwardness.

violentar vt - **1.** [incomodar] to embarrass, to cause to feel awkward - **2.** [forzar - cerradura] to force; [- domicilio] to break into.
➤ **violentarse** vprnl [incomodarse] to get embarrassed, to feel awkward.

violentismo sm Amér subversiveness.

violentista adj Amér subversive.

violento, **ta** adj - **1.** [gen] violent; [goce] intense - **2.** [incómodo] awkward.

violeta ◇ sf [flor] violet. ◇ adj inv & sm [color] violet.

violetera sf violet seller.

violín ◇ sm violin. ◇ smf violinist.

violinista smf violinist.

violón ◇ sm double bass. ◇ smf double bass player.

violonchelista, **violoncelista** smf cellist.

violonchelo, **violoncelo** ◇ sm cello. ◇ smf cellist.

viperino, **na** adj fig venomous.

viraje sm - **1.** [giro - AUTO] turn; NÁUT tack - **2.** FOTO toning - **3.** fig [cambio] change of direction.

virar ◇ vt - **1.** [girar] to turn (round); NÁUT to tack, to put about - **2.** FOTO to tone. ◇ vi [girar] to turn (round).

virgen ◇ adj [gen] virgin; [cinta] blank; [película] unused. ◇ smf [persona] virgin. ◇ sf ARTE Madonna.
➤ **Virgen** sf: **la Virgen** RELIG the (Blessed) Virgin; **¡Virgen santa!** good heavens!

virginal adj - **1.** [puro] virginal - **2.** RELIG Virgin (antes de s).

virginidad sf virginity.

virgo sm [virginidad] virginity.
➤ **Virgo** ◇ sm [zodiaco] Virgo; **ser Virgo** to be (a) Virgo. ◇ smf [persona] Virgo.

virguería sf fam gem; **hacer virguerías** to do wonders.

vírico, **ca** adj viral.

viril adj virile, manly.

virilidad sf virility.

virreina sf vicereine.

virreinato, **virreino** sm viceroyalty.

virrey sm viceroy.

virtual adj - **1.** [posible] possible, potential - **2.** [casi real] virtual.

virtualidad sf potential.

virtud sf - **1.** [cualidad] virtue; **virtud cardinal/teologal** cardinal/theological virtue - **2.** [poder] power; **tener la virtud de** to have the power o ability to.
➤ **en virtud de** loc prep by virtue of.

virtuosismo sm virtuosity.

virtuoso, **sa** ◇ adj [honrado] virtuous. ◇ sm, f [genio] virtuoso.

viruela sf - **1.** [enfermedad] smallpox - **2.** [pústula] pockmark; **picado de viruelas** pockmarked.

virulé ➤ **a la virulé** loc adj - **1.** [torcido] crooked - **2.** [hinchado]: **un ojo a la virulé** a black eye.

virulencia sf fig & MED virulence.

virulento, **ta** adj fig & MED virulent.

virus sm inv [gen & INFORM] virus; **virus informático** computer virus.

viruta sf shaving.

vis ➤ **vis a vis** loc adv face-to-face. ➤ **vis cómica** sf sense of humour.

visa sf Amér visa.

visado sm visa.

visar vt to endorse.

víscera sf internal organ; **vísceras** entrails.

visceral adj fig & ANAT visceral; **un sentimiento/una reacción visceral** a gut feeling/reaction.

viscosidad sf - **1.** [cualidad] viscosity - **2.** [substancia] slime.

viscoso, **sa** adj [gen] viscous; [baboso] slimy.
➤ **viscosa** sf [tejido] viscose.

visera sf - **1.** [de gorra] peak - **2.** [de casco, suelta] visor - **3.** [de automóvil] sun visor.

visibilidad sf visibility.

visible adj visible; **estar visible** [presentable] to be decent o presentable.

visigodo, **da** ◇ adj Visigothic. ◇ sm, f Visigoth.

visillo (gen pl) sm net/lace curtain.

visión sf - **1.** [sentido, lo que se ve] sight - **2.** [alucinación, lucidez] vision; **ver visiones** to be seeing things - **3.** [punto de vista] (point of) view.

visionar vt to view privately.

visionario, **ria** adj & sm, f visionary.

visir (pl visires) sm vizier.

visita sf - **1.** [gen] visit; [breve] call; **hacer una visita a alguien** to visit sb, to pay sb a visit; **ir de visita** to go visiting; **pasar visita** MED to see one's patients; **visita a domicilio** house call; **visitas médicas** doctor's rounds pl; **visita de cumplido** courtesy visit o call; **visita relámpago** flying visit - **2.** [visitante] visitor; **tener visita** o **visitas** to have visitors - **3.** [a página web] hit.

visitador, ra ⬦ *adj* fond of visiting. ⬦ *sm, f* [de laboratorio] medical sales representative.

visitante ⬦ *adj* DEP visiting, away. ⬦ *smf* visitor.

visitar *vt* [gen] to visit; [suj: médico] to call on.

vislumbrar *vt* - **1.** [entrever] to make out, to discern - **2.** [adivinar] to have an inkling of.

➤ **vislumbrarse** *vprnl* - **1.** [entreverse] to be barely visible - **2.** [adivinarse] to become a little clearer.

vislumbre *sm o sf lit & fig* glimmer.

viso *sm* - **1.** [aspecto]: **tener visos de** to seem; **tiene visos de verdad** it seems pretty true; **tiene visos de hacerse realidad** it could become a reality - **2.** [reflejo - de tejido] sheen; [- de metal] glint.

visón *sm* mink.

visor *sm* - **1.** FOTO viewfinder - **2.** [de arma] sight - **3.** [en fichero] file tab.

víspera *sf* - **1.** [día antes] day before, eve; **en vísperas de** on the eve of; **víspera de festivo** day prior to a public holiday - **2.** *(gen pl)* RELIG evensong *(U)*, vespers *(U)*.

vista ▷ **visto**.

vistazo *sm* glance, quick look; **echar** o **dar un vistazo a** to have a quick look at.

viste ▷ **ver**.

vistiera *etc* ▷ **vestir**.

visto, ta ⬦ *pp* ▷ **ver**. ⬦ *adj*: **estar visto que...** to be clear that...; **estar muy visto** to be old-fashioned; **estar bien/mal visto** to be considered good/frowned upon; **es lo no** o **nunca visto** you've never seen anything like it; **fue visto y no visto** it happened just like that, it was over in a flash.

➤ **vista** ⬦ *v* ▷ **vestir**. ⬦ *sf* - **1.** [sentido] sight, eyesight; [ojos] eyes *pl*; **se le nubló la vista** his eyes clouded over; **perder la vista** to lose one's sight, to go blind; **corto de vista** short-sighted; **vista cansada** eyestrain - **2.** [observación] watching - **3.** [mirada] gaze; **alzar/bajar la vista** to look up/down; **fijar la vista en** to fix one's eyes on, to stare at; **a la vista de** in full view of; **a primera** o **simple vista** [aparentemente] at first sight, on the face of it; **estar a la vista** [visible] to be visible; [muy cerca] to be staring one in the face - **4.** [panorama] view - **5.** DER hearing; **vista oral** hearing - **6.** *loc*: **a vista de pájaro** from a bird's eye view; **conocer a alguien de vista** to know sb by sight; **hacer la vista gorda** to turn a blind eye; **¡hasta la vista!** see you!; **no perder de vista a alguien/algo** [vigilar] not to let sb/sthg out of one's sight; [tener en cuenta] not to lose sight of sb/sthg, not to forget about sb/sthg; **perder de vista** [dejar de ver] to lose sight of; [perder contac-

to] to lose touch with; **saltar a la vista** to be blindingly obvious; **tener vista** to have vision o foresight; **volver la vista atrás** to look back.

➤ **vistas** *sfpl* [panorama] view *sing*; **con vistas al mar** with a sea view.

➤ **visto bueno** *sm*: **el visto bueno** the go-ahead; **dar el visto bueno (a algo)** to give the go-ahead (to sthg); **'visto bueno'** 'approved'.

➤ **a la vista** *loc adv* BANCA at sight.

➤ **con vistas a** *loc prep* with a view to.

➤ **en vista de** *loc prep* in view of, considering.

➤ **en vista de que** *loc conj* since, seeing as.

➤ **por lo visto** *loc adv* apparently.

➤ **visto que** *loc conj* seeing o given that.

vistoso, sa *adj* eye-catching.

visual ⬦ *adj* visual. ⬦ *sf* line of sight.

visualización *sf* - **1.** [gen] visualization - **2.** INFORM display.

visualizar [13] *vt* - **1.** [gen] to visualize - **2.** INFORM to display.

vital *adj* [gen] vital; [ciclo] life *(antes de s)*; [persona] full of life, vivacious.

vitalicio, cia *adj* for life, life *(antes de s)*.

➤ **vitalicio** *sm* - **1.** [pensión] life annuity - **2.** [seguro] life insurance policy.

vitalidad *sf* vitality.

vitalizar [13] *vt* to vitalize.

vitamina *sf* vitamin.

vitaminado, da *adj* with added vitamins, vitamin-enriched.

vitamínico, ca *adj* vitamin *(antes de s)*.

viticultor, ra *sm, f* wine grower, viticulturist.

viticultura *sf* wine growing, viticulture.

vítor *(gen pl)* *sm desus* cheer.

vitorear *vt* to cheer.

vitral *sm* stained-glass window.

vítreo, a *adj* vitreous.

vitrina *sf* - **1.** [en casa] display cabinet; [en tienda] showcase, glass case - **2.** *Andes & Ven* [escaparate] (shop) window.

vitro ➤ **in vitro** *loc adv* in vitro.

vituperar *vt* to criticize harshly, to condemn.

vituperio *sm* harsh criticism, condemnation.

viudedad *sf* - **1.** [viudez - de mujer] widowhood; [- de hombre] widowerhood - **2.**: **(pensión de) viudedad** widow's/widower's pension.

viudo, da ⬦ *adj* widowed; **quedarse viudo** to be widowed. ⬦ *sm, f* widower (f widow).

viva ⬦ *sm* cheer; **dar vivas** to cheer. ⬦ *interj*: **¡viva!** hurrah!; **¡viva el rey!** long live the King!

vivac = **vivaque**.

vivacidad *sf* liveliness.

vivalavirgen *smf inv* happy-go-lucky person.

vivales *smf inv* crafty person.

vivamente *adv* - **1.** [relatar, describir] vividly - **2.** [afectar, emocionar] deeply.

vivaque, vivac *sm* bivouac.

vivaracho, cha *adj* lively, vivacious.

vivaz *adj* - **1.** [color, descripción] vivid - **2.** [persona, discusión, ojos] lively - **3.** [ingenio, inteligencia] alert, sharp - **4.** BOT biennial.

vivencia *(gen pl)* *sf* experience.

víveres *smpl* provisions, supplies.

vivero *sm* - **1.** [de plantas] nursery - **2.** [de peces] fish farm; [de moluscos] bed.

viveza *sf* - **1.** [de colorido, descripción] vividness - **2.** [de persona, discusión, ojos] liveliness; [de ingenio, inteligencia] sharpness.

vívido, da *adj* vivid.

vividor, ra *sm, f despec* parasite, scrounger.

vivienda *sf* - **1.** [alojamiento] housing - **2.** [morada] dwelling; **vivienda de protección oficial** ≃ council house; **vivienda de renta limitada** ≃ council house with fixed maximum rent *o* price.

viviente *adj* living.

vivificante *adj* [que da vida] life-giving; [que reanima] revitalizing.

vivificar **[10]** *vt* [dar vida] to give life to; [reanimar] to revitalize.

vivíparo, ra *adj* viviparous.

vivir ⬦ *vt* [experimentar] to experience, to live through. ⬦ *vi* [gen] to live; [estar vivo] to be alive; **vivir de** to live on *o* off; **vivir para algo/alguien** to live for sthg/sb; **vivir bien** [económicamente] to be well-off; [en armonía] to be happy; **no dejar vivir a alguien** not to give sb any peace; **¿quién vive?** who goes there?; **vivir para ver** who'd have thought it?

vivisección *sf* vivisection.

vivito *adj:* **vivito y coleando** *fam* alive and kicking.

vivo, va *adj* - **1.** [existente - ser, lengua etc] living; **estar vivo** [persona, costumbre, recuerdo] to be alive - **2.** [dolor, deseo, olor] intense; [luz, color, tono] bright - **3.** [gestos, ojos, descripción] lively, vivid - **4.** [activo - ingenio, niño] quick, sharp; [- ciudad] lively - **5.** [pronunciado - ángulo etc] sharp - **6.** [genio] quick, hot.

➤ **vivos** *smpl:* **los vivos** the living.

➤ **en vivo** *loc adv* - **1.** [en directo] live - **2.** [sin anestesia] without anaesthetic.

vizcaíno, na *adj & sm, f* Biscayan; **a la vizcaína** CULIN ⟾ **bacalao**.

Vizcaya *n pr* Vizcaya; **Golfo de Vizcaya** Bay of Biscay.

vizconde, esa *sm, f* viscount (*f* viscountess).

VM (*abrev de* **Vuestra Majestad**) Your Majesty.

VO *sf abrev de* **versión**.

vocablo *sm* word, term.

vocabulario *sm* [riqueza léxica] vocabulary.

vocación *sf* vocation, calling.

vocacional *adj* vocational.

vocal ⬦ *adj* vocal. ⬦ *smf* member. ⬦ *sf* vowel.

vocalista *smf* vocalist.

vocalización *sf* vocalization.

vocalizar **[13]** *vi* to vocalize.

vocativo *sm* vocative.

vocear ⬦ *vt* - **1.** [gritar] to shout *o* call out - **2.** [llamar] to shout *o* call to - **3.** [vitorear] to cheer - **4.** [pregonar - mercancía] to hawk; [- secreto] to publicize. ⬦ *vi* [gritar] to shout.

vocerío *sm* shouting.

vociferante *adj* shouting.

vociferar *vi* to shout.

vodevil, vaudeville [boðe'βil] *sm* vaudeville.

vodka ['boθka] *sm o sf* vodka.

vol. (*abrev de* **volumen**) vol.

volado, da *adj fam* [ido]: **estar volado** to be away with the fairies.

volador, ra *adj* flying.

➤ **volador** *sm* - **1.** [pez] flying fish - **2.** [cohete] rocket.

voladura *sf* [en guerras, atentados] blowing-up; [de edificio en ruinas] demolition *(with explosives)*; [en cantera] blasting.

volandas ➤ **en volandas** *loc adv* in the air, off the ground.

volante ⬦ *adj* flying. ⬦ *sm* - **1.** [para conducir] (steering) wheel; **estar** *o* **ir al volante** to be at the wheel - **2.** [de tela] frill, flounce - **3.** [del médico] (referral) note - **4.** [en bádminton] shuttlecock.

volantín *sm Caribe & Chile* kite.

volar **[23]** ⬦ *vt* [en guerras, atentados] to blow up; [caja fuerte, puerta] to blow open; [edificio en ruinas] to demolish *(with explosives)*; [en cantera] to blast. ⬦ *vi* - **1.** [gen] to fly; [papeles etc] to blow away; **volar a** [una altura] to fly at; [un lugar] to fly to; **echar(se) a volar** to fly away *o* off - **2.** *fam* [desaparecer] to disappear, to vanish - **3.** *fig* [correr] to fly (off), to rush (off); **hacer algo volando** to do sthg at top speed; **me voy volando** I must fly *o* dash - **4.** *fig* [días, años] to fly by.

➤ **volarse** *vprnl* [papeles etc] to be blown away.

volátil *adj fig & QUÍM* volatile.

volatilización *sf* volatilization.

volatilizar **[13]** *vt* to volatilize.

volatilizarse *vprnl* - **1.** FÍS to volatilize, to evaporate - **2.** *fam fig* [persona] to vanish into thin air.

vol-au-vent = **volován**.

volcado *sm* INFORM: **volcado de pantalla** screen dump; **volcado de pantalla en impresora** hard copy.

volcán *sm* volcano.

volcánico, ca *adj* volcanic.

volcar [36] ⋄ *vt* - **1.** [tirar] to knock over; [carretilla] to tip up - **2.** [vaciar] to empty out. ⋄ *vi* [coche, camión] to overturn; [barco] to capsize.

volcarse *vprnl* - **1.** [esforzarse]: **volcarse (con/en)** to bend over backwards (for/in) - **2.** [caerse] to fall over.

volea *sf* volley.

voleibol *sm* volleyball.

voleo *sm* volley; **a** *o* **al voleo** [arbitrariamente] randomly, any old how.

volitivo, va *adj* voluntary.

volován (*pl* volovanes), **vol-au-vent** [bolo'βan] (*pl* vol-au-vents) *sm* vol-au-vent.

volqué *etc* ⊳ **volcar**.

volquete *sm* dumper truck, dump truck *US*.

voltaico, ca *adj* voltaic.

voltaje *sm* voltage.

voltear ⋄ *vt* - **1.** [heno, crepe, torero] to toss; [tortilla - con plato] to turn over; [mesa, silla] to turn upside-down - **2.** *Amér* [derribar] to knock over; *Andes, Amér C, Caribe & Méx* [volver] to turn. ⋄ *vi Méx* [torcer] to turn, to go round.

voltearse *vprnl Andes, Amér C, Caribe & Méx* [volverse] to turn around.

voltereta *sf* [en el suelo] handspring; [en el aire] somersault; **dar una voltereta** to do a somersault; **voltereta lateral** cartwheel.

voltímetro *sm* voltmeter.

voltio *sm* volt.

volubilidad *sf* changeability, fickleness.

voluble *adj* changeable, fickle.

volumen *sm* - **1.** [gen & COM] volume; **a todo volumen** at full blast; **subir/bajar el volumen** [de aparato] to turn up/down the volume; **sube el volumen que no te oímos** speak up, please, we can't hear you; **volumen de contratación** ECON trading volume; **volumen de negocio** *o* **ventas** turnover - **2.** [espacio ocupado] size, bulk.

voluminoso, sa *adj* bulky.

voluntad *sf* - **1.** [determinación] will, willpower; **voluntad de hierro** iron will - **2.** [intención] intention; **buena voluntad** goodwill; **mala voluntad** ill will - **3.** [deseo] wishes *pl*, will; **contra la voluntad de alguien** against sb's will - **4.** [albedrío] free will; **a voluntad** [cuanto se quiere] as much as one likes; **por voluntad propia** of one's own free will - **5.** [cantidad]: **¿qué le debo? – la voluntad** what do I owe you? – whatever you think fit.

voluntariado *sm* voluntary enlistment.

voluntariedad *sf* - **1.** [intencionalidad] volition - **2.** [no obligatoriedad] voluntary nature.

voluntario, ria ⋄ *adj* voluntary. ⋄ *sm, f* volunteer.

voluntarioso, sa *adj* [esforzado] willing.

voluptuosidad *sf* voluptuousness.

voluptuoso, sa *adj* voluptuous.

voluta *sf* spiral.

volver [24] ⋄ *vt* - **1.** [dar la vuelta a] to turn round; [lo de arriba abajo] to turn over - **2.** [poner del revés - boca abajo] to turn upside down; [- lo de dentro fuera] to turn inside out; [- lo de detrás delante] to turn back to front - **3.** [cabeza, ojos etc] to turn - **4.** [convertir en]: **eso le volvió un delincuente** that made him a criminal, that turned him into a criminal. ⋄ *vi* [ir de vuelta] to go back, to return; [venir de vuelta] to come back, to return; **volver de** to come back from; **volver atrás** to turn back; **yo allí no vuelvo** I'm not going back there; **vuelve, no te vayas** come back, don't go; **volver en sí** to come to, to regain consciousness.

volver a *vi* [reanudar] to return to; **volver a hacer algo** [hacer otra vez] to do sthg again.

volverse *vprnl* - **1.** [darse la vuelta, girar la cabeza] to turn round - **2.** [ir de vuelta] to go back, to return; [venir de vuelta] to come back, to return - **3.** [convertirse en] to become; **volverse loco/pálido** to go mad/pale - **4.** *loc*: **volverse atrás** [de una afirmación, promesa] to go back on one's word; [de una decisión] to change one's mind, to back out; **volverse (en) contra (de) alguien** to turn against sb.

vomitar ⋄ *vt* - **1.** [devolver] to vomit, to bring up - **2.** *fig* [expresar] to come out with. ⋄ *vi* to vomit, to be sick.

vomitera *sf* acute vomiting *(U)*.

vomitivo, va *adj* - **1.** MED emetic - **2.** *fig* [asqueroso] sickening, repulsive.

vomitivo *sm* emetic.

vómito *sm* - **1.** [acción] vomiting - **2.** [substancia] vomit *(U)*.

voracidad *sf* voraciousness.

vorágine *sf fig* confusion, whirl.

voraz *adj* - **1.** [persona, apetito] voracious - **2.** *fig* [fuego, enfermedad] raging.

vórtice *sm* - **1.** [de agua] whirlpool, vortex - **2.** [de aire] whirlwind.

vos *pron pers Amér* [tú - sujeto] you; [- objeto] you.

VOSE (*abrev de* **versión original subtitulada en español**) *sf* CINE *original language version subtitled in Spanish.*

voseo *sm practice of using the 'vos' pronoun.*

Voseo

🎴 Voseo means the use of the "vos" form instead of "tú" in the second person singular. This is the norm in the River Plate region, where it is used with a special form of the verb in the present tense (e.g. "vos sabés" instead of "tú sabes"). It is also found in other areas of Latin America. In Chile and areas of Bolivia, Peru and Venezuela, "tú" is also used, indicating slightly less informality. The forms "vos" and "tú" are used alternately in Central America, ranging from mostly "vos" in Costa Rica to mostly "tú" in Panama. In these areas, "vos" may be used with the normal second person singular verb form (e.g. "vos tienes").

vosotros, **tras** *pron pers* you *pl.*

Vosotros

🎴 In Spain, there are two ways to express the second person plural: one implies familiarity with the audience ("vosotros") while the other indicates more courtesy ("ustedes"). "Vosotros" takes the verb in the second person plural, and "ustedes" the third person plural. This double option does not exist in Latin America, where the only form available is "ustedes", except in the religious liturgy, where the "vosotros" is sometimes retained.

votación *sf* vote, voting (*U*); **decidir algo por votación** to put sthg to the vote; **votación a mano alzada** show of hands.

votante *smf* voter.

votar <> *vt* - **1.** [partido, candidato] to vote for; [ley] to vote on - **2.** [aprobar] to pass, to approve *(by vote)*. <> *vi* to vote; **votar por** [emitir un voto por] to vote for; *fig* [estar a favor de] to be in favour of; **votar por que...** to vote (that)...; **votar en blanco** to return a blank ballot paper.

voto *sm* - **1.** [gen] vote; **voto de confianza/censura** vote of confidence/no confidence; **voto por correspondencia** *o* **correo** postal vote; **voto de calidad** casting vote; **voto de castigo** vote against one's own party; **voto secreto** secret ballot - **2.** RELIG vow; **hacer voto de** to vow to; **voto de castidad/pobreza/silencio** vow of chastity/poverty/silence - **3.** [ruego] prayer, plea; **hacer votos por** to pray for; **votos de felicidad** best wishes.

voy ▷ **ir.**

voyeur [bwa'jer] (*pl* **voyeurs**) <> *adj* voyeuristic. <> *sm, f* voyeur.

voyeurismo [bwaje'rismo] *sm* voyeurism.

voz *sf* - **1.** [gen & GRAM] voice; **a media voz** in a low voice, under one's breath; **a voz en cuello** *o* **grito** at the top of one's voice; **aclarar** *o* **aclararse la voz** to clear one's throat; **alzar** *o* **levantar la voz a alguien** to raise one's voice to sb; **en voz alta** aloud; **en voz baja** softly, in a low voice; **mudó la voz** his voice broke; **tener la voz tomada** to be hoarse; **voz activa/pasiva** GRAM active/passive voice; **la voz de la conciencia** the voice of conscience; **voz en off** CINE voice-over; TEATRO voice offstage - **2.** [grito] shout; **a voces** shouting; **dar voces** to shout - **3.** [vocablo] word; **dar la voz de alerta** to raise the alarm; **voz de mando** order, command - **4.** [derecho a expresarse] say, voice; **no tener ni voz ni voto** to have no say in the matter - **5.** *loc*: **correr la voz** to spread the word; **estar pidiendo algo a voces** to be crying out for sthg; **llevar la voz cantante** to be the boss.

vozarrón *sm fam* loud voice.

VPO (*abrev de* **vivienda de protección oficial**) *sf* ≃ council house/flat *UK*, ≃ public housing unit *US*.

vudú (*en aposición invariable*) *sm* voodoo.

vuela ▷ **volar.**

vuelca ▷ **volcar.**

vuelco *sm* upset; **dar un vuelco** [coche] to overturn; [relaciones] to change completely; [empresa] to go to ruin; **me dio un vuelco el corazón** my heart missed *o* skipped a beat.

vuele ▷ **volar.**

vuelo *sm* - **1.** [gen & AERON] flight; **alzar** *o* **emprender** *o* **levantar el vuelo** [despegar] to take flight, to fly off; *fig* [irse de casa] to fly the nest; **coger algo al vuelo** [en el aire] to catch sthg in flight; *fig* [rápido] to catch on to sthg very quickly; **remontar el vuelo** to soar; **vuelo chárter/regular** charter/scheduled flight; **vuelo espacial** space flight; **vuelo libre** hang gliding; **vuelo sin motor** gliding; **vuelos nacionales** domestic flights; **de altos vuelos, de mucho vuelo** of great importance; **no se oía el vuelo de una mosca** you could have heard a pin drop - **2.** [de vestido] fullness; **una falda de vuelo** a full skirt.

vuelque ▷ **volcar.**

vuelta *sf* - **1.** [gen] turn; [acción] turning; **dar una vuelta (a algo)** [recorriéndolo] to go round (sthg); **dar la vuelta al mundo** to go around the world; **darse la vuelta** to turn round; **dar vueltas (a algo)** [girándolo] to turn (sthg) round; **media vuelta** MIL about-turn; AUTO U-turn; **vuelta al ruedo** TAUROM bullfighter's lap of honour - **2.** DEP lap; **vuelta (ciclista)** tour

- 3. [regreso, devolución] return; **billete de ida y vuelta** return ticket; **a la vuelta** [volviendo] on the way back; [al llegar] on one's return; **estar de vuelta** to be back **- 4.** [paseo]: **dar una vuelta** to go for a walk **- 5.** [dinero sobrante] change **- 6.** [ronda, turno] round **- 7.** [parte opuesta] back, other side; **a la vuelta de la esquina** *lit & fig* round the corner; **a la vuelta de la página** over the page **- 8.** [cambio, avatar] change; **dar la** *o* **una vuelta** *fig* to turn around completely **- 9.** [de pantalón] turn-up *UK*, cuff *US*; [de manga] cuff **- 10.** [en labor de punto] row **- 11.** *loc*: **a la vuelta de** [tras] at the end of; **a vuelta de correo** by return of post; **dar la vuelta a la tortilla** *fam* to turn the tables; **darle cien vueltas a alguien** to knock spots off sb; **dar una vuelta/dos** *etc* **vueltas de campana** [coche] to turn over once/twice *etc*; **darle vueltas a algo** to turn sthg over in one's mind; **estar de vuelta de algo** to be blasé about sthg; **estar de vuelta de todo** to be in the know; **la cabeza me da vueltas** my head's spinning; **no tiene vuelta de hoja** there are no two ways about it; **poner a alguien de vuelta y media** [criticar] to call sb all the names under the sun; [regañar] to give sb a good telling-off; **sin vuelta de hoja** irrevocable.

vuelto, ta ⬦ *pp* ⊳ **volver**. ⬦ *adj* turned.
➤ **vuelto** *sm Amér* change.

vuelva *etc* ⊳ **volver**.

vuestro, tra ⬦ *adj poses* your; **vuestro libro/amigo** your book/friend; **este libro es vuestro** this book is yours; **un amigo vuestro** a friend of yours; **no es asunto vuestro** it's none of your business. ⬦ *pron poses*: **el vuestro** yours; **los vuestros están en la mesa** yours are on the table; **lo vuestro es el teatro** [lo que hacéis bien] you should be on the stage; **los vuestros** *fam* [vuestra familia] your folks; [vuestro bando] your lot, your side.

vulcanología *sf* vulcanology.

vulgar *adj* **- 1.** [no refinado] vulgar **- 2.** [corriente, ordinario] ordinary, common; **vulgar y corriente** ordinary **- 3.** [no técnico] non-technical, lay.

vulgaridad *sf* **- 1.** [grosería] vulgarity; **hacer/decir una vulgaridad** to do/say sthg vulgar **- 2.** [banalidad] banality.

vulgarismo *sm* GRAM vulgarism.

vulgarización *sf* popularization.

vulgarizar [13] *vt* to popularize.
➤ **vulgarizarse** *vprnl* to become popular *o* common.

vulgo *sm despec*: **el vulgo** [plebe] the masses *pl*, the common people *pl*; [no expertos] the lay public *(U)*.

vulnerabilidad *sf* vulnerability.

vulnerable *adj* vulnerable.

vulneración *sf* **- 1.** [de prestigio etc] harming, damaging **- 2.** [de ley, pacto etc] violation, infringement.

vulnerar *vt* **- 1.** [prestigio etc] to harm, to damage **- 2.** [ley, pacto etc] to violate, to break.

vulva *sf* vulva.

w, W *sf* [letra] w, W.

wagon-lit [baˈɣonˈlit] *(pl* **wagons-lits***)* *sm* sleeping car.

walkie-talkie [ˈwalkiˈtalki] *(pl* **walkie-talkies***)* *sm* walkie-talkie.

walkman® [ˈwalman] *(pl* **walkmans***)* *sm* Walkman®.

Washington [ˈwaɾiŋton] *n pr* Washington.

water [ˈbater] *(pl* **wateres***)* = **váter**.

waterpolo [waterˈpolo] *sm* water polo.

watio = **vatio**.

WC *(abrev de* **water closet***)* *sm* WC.

web [weβ] *sf*: **la (World Wide) Web** the (World Wide) Web.

western [ˈwester] *(pl* **westerns***)* *sm* CINE western.

whisky [ˈwiski] = **güisqui**.

windsurf [ˈwinsurf], **windsurfing** [ˈwinsurfin] *sm* windsurfing.

WWW *(abrev de* **World Wide Web***)* *sf* WWW.

x, X *sf* [letra] x, X.
➤ **X** *smf*: **la señora X** Mrs X.

xenofobia *sf* xenophobia.

xenófobo, ba ⬦ *adj* xenophobic. ⬦ *sm, f* xenophobe.

xerografía *sf* photocopying, xerography.

xilófon, xilófono *sm* xylophone.

xilografía *sf* **- 1.** [técnica] xylography, wood engraving **- 2.** [impresión] xylograph, wood engraving.

y[1], **Y** *sf* [letra] y, Y.

y[2] *conj* - **1.** [gen] and; **un ordenador y una impresora** a computer and a printer; **horas y horas de espera** hours and hours of waiting - **2.** [pero] and yet; **sabía que no lo conseguiría y seguía intentándolo** she knew she wouldn't manage it and yet she kept on trying - **3.** [en preguntas] what about; **¿y tu mujer?** what about your wife?

ya ◇ *adv* - **1.** [en el pasado] already; **ya me lo habías contado** you had already told me; **ya en 1926** as long ago as 1926 - **2.** [ahora] now; [inmediatamente] at once; **hay que hacer algo ya** something has to be done now/at once; **bueno, yo ya me voy** right, I'm off now; **ya no es así** it's no longer like that - **3.** [en el futuro]: **ya te llamaré** I'll give you a ring some time; **ya hablaremos** we'll talk later; **ya nos habremos ido** we'll already have gone; **ya verás** you'll (soon) see - **4.** [refuerza al verbo]: **ya entiendo/lo sé** I understand/know. ◇ *conj* [distributiva]: **ya (sea) por... ya (sea) por...** whether for... or... ◇ *interj*: **¡ya!** [expresa asentimiento] right!; [expresa comprensión] yes!; **¡ya, ya!** *irón* sure!, yes, of course!

➥ **ya no** *loc adv*: **ya no... sino** not only... but.

➥ **ya que** *loc conj* since; **ya que has venido, ayúdame con esto** since you're here, give me a hand with this.

yacente, yaciente *adj* [gen] lying; ARTE recumbent, reclining.

yacer [77] *vi* to lie.

yaciente = yacente.

yacimiento *sm* - **1.** [minero] bed, deposit; **yacimiento de petróleo** oilfield - **2.** [arqueológico] site.

yaga *etc* ⊳ yacer.

yanqui ◇ *adj* - **1.** HIST Yankee *(antes de s)* - **2.** *fam* [estadounidense] yank. ◇ *smf* - **1.** HIST Yankee - **2.** *fam* [estadounidense] yank.

yantar *desus* ◇ *sm* fare, food. ◇ *vt* to eat.

yarda *sf* yard.

yate *sm* yacht.

yayo, ya *sm, f fam* grandad *(f* grandma).

yazca, yazga *etc* ⊳ yacer.

yegua *sf* mare.

yeísmo *sm* pronunciation of Spanish 'll' as 'y'.

yelmo *sm* helmet.

yema *sf* - **1.** [de huevo] yolk - **2.** [de planta] bud, shoot - **3.** [de dedo] fingertip - **4.** CULIN *sweet made from sugar and egg yolk*.

Yemen *n pr*: (el) Yemen Yemen.

yemenita *adj* & *smf* Yemeni.

yen *(pl* yenes) *sm* yen.

yerba = hierba; **yerba mate** *R Dom* yerba maté.

yerbatero *sm* Andes & Caribe [curandero] healer; [vendedor de hierbas] herbalist.

yerga *etc* ⊳ erguir.

yermo, ma *adj* - **1.** [estéril] barren - **2.** [despoblado] uninhabited.

➥ **yermo** *sm* wasteland.

yerno *sm* son-in-law.

yerra *etc* ⊳ errar.

yerro *sm desus* mistake, error.

yesca *sf* tinder.

yesería *sf* [fábrica] gypsum kiln.

yesero, ra ◇ *adj* plaster *(antes de s)*. ◇ *sm, f* - **1.** [fabricante] plaster manufacturer - **2.** [obrero] plasterer.

yeso *sm* - **1.** GEOL gypsum - **2.** CONSTR plaster - **3.** ARTE gesso.

yesquero *sm* Col & R Plata [encendedor] cigarette lighter.

yeti *sm* yeti.

yeyé *adj* sixties.

yiddish, jiddisch *sm* Yiddish.

yiu-yitsu, jiu-jitsu *sm* jujitsu.

yo ◇ *pron pers* - **1.** *(sujeto)* I; **yo me llamo Luis** I'm called Luis - **2.** *(predicado)*: **soy yo** it's me - **3.** *loc*: **yo que tú/él** *etc* if I were you/him *etc*. ◇ *sm* PSICOL: **el yo** the ego.

yodado, da *adj* iodized.

yodo, iodo *sm* iodine.

yoga *sm* yoga.

yogui *smf* yogi.

yogur *(pl* yogures), **yogurt** *(pl* yogurts) *sm* yoghurt.

yogurtera *sf* yoghurt maker.

yonqui *smf fam* junkie.

yóquey *(pl* yóqueys), **jockey** *(pl* jockeys) *sm* jockey.

yoyó *sm* yoyo.

yuca *sf* - **1.** BOT yucca - **2.** CULIN cassava, manioc.

yudo, judo ['juðo] *sm* judo.

yudoca, judoka [ju'ðoka] *smf* judoist, judoka.

yugo *sm lit & fig* yoke.

Yugoslavia *n pr* HIST Yugoslavia.

yugoslavo, va <> *adj* HIST Yugoslavian. <> *sm, f* Yugoslav.

yugular *adj* & *sf* jugular.

yunque *sm* anvil.

yunta *sf* - **1.** [de bueyes etc] yoke, team - **2.** *Amér* [esposas] cufflink.

yute *sm* jute.

yuxtaponer [65] *vt* to juxtapose.
➤ **yuxtaponerse** *vprnl*: **yuxtaponerse (a)** to be juxtaposed (with).

yuxtaposición *sf* juxtaposition.

yuxtapuesto, ta *pp* ▷ yuxtaponer.

z, Z *sf* [letra] z, Z.

zafacón *sm Caribe* rubbish bin.

zafarrancho *sm* - **1.** NÁUT clearing of the decks; **zafarrancho de combate** MIL call to action stations - **2.** *fig* [destrozo] mess; **se armó un zafarrancho** there as a lot of trouble - **3.** *fig* [riña] row, fracas.

zafarse *vprnl* to get out of it, to escape; **zafarse de** [persona] to get rid of; [obligación] to get out of.

zafiedad *sf* roughness, uncouthness.

zafio, fia *adj* rough, uncouth.

zafiro *sm* sapphire.

zaga *sf* DEP defence; **a la zaga** behind, at the back; **no irle a la zaga a alguien** to be every bit *o* just as good as sb.

zaguán *sm* (entrance) hall.

zaherir *vt* - **1.** [herir] to hurt - **2.** [burlarse de] to mock - **3.** [criticar] to pillory.

zahorí (*pl* zahoríes *o* zahorís) *sm, f* - **1.** [de agua] water diviner - **2.** *fig* [clarividente] mind reader.

zaino, na *adj* - **1.** [caballo] chestnut - **2.** [res] black.

Zaire *n pr* HIST Zaire.

zalamería (*gen pl*) *sf* flattery (*U*); **hacerle zalamerías a alguien** to sweet talk sb.

zalamero, ra <> *adj* flattering; *despec* smooth-talking. <> *sm, f* flatterer; *despec* smooth talker.

zamarra *sf* sheepskin jacket.

Zambia *n pr* Zambia.

zambo, ba <> *adj* [piernas, persona] knock-kneed. <> *sm, f* - **1.** [persona] knock-kneed person - **2.** *Amér* [hijo de persona negra y otra india] *person who has one black and one Indian parent.*

zambomba *sf* MÚS *type of rustic drum.*

zambombazo *sm* bang.

zambullida *sf* dive; **darse una zambullida** [baño] to go for a dip.

zambullir *vt* to dip, to submerge.
➤ **zambullirse** *vprnl*: **zambullirse (en)** [agua] to dive (into); [actividad] to immerse o.s. (in).

zampar *fam vi* to gobble.
➤ **zamparse** *vprnl* to scoff, to wolf down.

zanahoria *sf* carrot.

zanca *sf* [de ave] leg, shank.

zancada *sf* stride.

zancadilla *sf* trip; **poner una** *o* **la zancadilla a alguien** [hacer tropezar] to trip sb up; [engañar] to trick sb.

zancadillear *vt* - **1.** [hacer tropezar] to trip up - **2.** *fig* [engañar] to trick.

zanco *sm* stilt.

zancudo, da *adj* long-legged.
➤ **zancudo** *sm Amér* mosquito.
➤ **zancuda** *sf* wader.

zanganear *vi fam* to laze about.

zángano, na *sm, f fam* [persona] lazy oaf, idler.
➤ **zángano** *sm* [abeja] drone.

zanja *sf* ditch.

zanjar *vt* [poner fin a] to put an end to; [resolver] to settle, to resolve.

zapallo *sm Andes & R Plata* [calabaza] pumpkin.

zapata *sf* - **1.** [cuña] wedge - **2.** [de freno] shoe.

zapateado *sm type of flamenco music and dance.*

zapatear *vi* to stamp one's feet.

zapatería *sf* - **1.** [oficio] shoemaking - **2.** [taller] shoemaker's - **3.** [tienda] shoe shop.

zapatero, ra *sm, f* - **1.** [fabricante] shoemaker - **2.** [reparador]: **zapatero (de viejo** *o* **remendón)** cobbler; **¡zapatero a tus zapatos!** mind your own business! - **3.** [vendedor] shoe seller.

zapatilla *sf* - **1.** [de baile] shoe, pump; [de estar en casa] slipper; [de deporte] sports shoe, trainer - **2.** [de grifo] washer.

zapato *sm* shoe; **zapato de salón** court shoe; **zapato de tacón** high heeled shoe; **saber alguien dónde le aprieta el zapato** to know which side one's bread is buttered.

zapping ['θapin] *sm inv* channel-hopping; **hacer zapping** to channel-hop.

zar, zarina *sm, f* tsar (*f* tsarina), czar (*f* czarina).

zarabanda *sf* - **1.** [danza] saraband - **2.** *fig* [jaleo] commotion, uproar.

Zaragoza *n pr* Saragossa.

zarandear *vt* - **1.** [cosa] to shake - **2.** [persona] to jostle, to knock about.

zarandeo *sm* - **1.** [sacudida] shake, shaking (*U*) - **2.** [empujón] pushing (*U*) o knocking (*U*) about.

zarista *adj* & *smf* Tsarist, Czarist.

zarpa *sf* - **1.** [de animal - uña] claw; [- mano] paw - **2.** *fam* [de persona] paw, hand.

zarpar *vi* to weigh anchor, to set sail; **zarpar rumbo a** to set sail for.

zarpazo *sm* clawing (*U*).

zarrapastroso, sa <> *adj* scruffy, shabby. <> *sm, f* scruff.

zarza *sf* bramble, blackberry bush.

zarzal *sm* bramble patch.

zarzamora *sf* blackberry.

zarzaparrilla *sf* sarsaparilla.

zarzuela *sf* - **1.** MÚS *Spanish light opera* - **2.** CULIN *fish stew in a spicy sauce.*

zas *interj*: **¡zas!** wham!, bang!

zen <> *adj inv* Zen (*antes de s*). <> *sm* Zen.

zenit = **cenit**.

zepelín (*pl* zepelines) *sm* zeppelin.

zigzag (*pl* zigzags o zigzagues) *sm* zigzag; **caminar en zigzag** to walk in a zigzag.

zigzaguear *vi* to zigzag.

Zimbabue *n pr* Zimbabwe.

zinc = **cinc**.

zíngaro, ra = **cíngaro**.

zíper *sm* *Amér C, Méx* & *Ven* zip *UK*, zipper *US*.

zipizape *sm* *fam* squabble, set-to.

zócalo *sm* - **1.** [de pared] skirting board - **2.** [de edificio, pedestal] plinth - **3.** [pedestal] pedestal - **4.** *Méx* [plaza] main square.

zoco *sm* souk, Arabian market.

zodiacal *adj* zodiacal.

zodiaco, zodíaco *sm* zodiac.

zombi, zombie *smf* *lit* & *fig* zombie.

zona *sf* zone, area; **zona azul** AUTO restricted parking zone; **zona catastrófica** disaster area; **zona de exclusión** exclusion zone; **zona eura** EURO euro zone; **zona franca** COM free-trade zone; **zona de urgente reindustrialización** ECON *region given priority status for industrial investment*, ≃ enterprise zone *UK*; **zona verde** [grande] park; [pequeño] lawn.

zoo *sm* zoo.

zoología *sf* zoology.

zoológico, ca *adj* zoological.

➤ **zoológico** *sm* zoo.

zoólogo, ga *sm, f* zoologist.

zoom [θum] (*pl* zooms) *sm* FOTO zoom.

zopenco, ca *fam* <> *adj* idiotic, daft. <> *sm, f* idiot, nitwit.

zoquete <> *adj* stupid. <> *sm* *C Sur* [calcetín] ankle sock. <> *smf* [tonto] blockhead, idiot.

zorro, rra <> *adj* foxy, crafty; **no tener ni zorra idea** I haven't got a bloody clue. <> *sm, f* *lit* & *fig* fox; **zorro azul** blue fox.

➤ **zorro** *sm* [piel] fox (fur).

➤ **zorra** *sf* *mfam* *despec* [ramera] whore, tart, hooker *US*.

➤ **zorros** *smpl* [utensilio] feather duster *sing*; **estar hecho unos zorros** *fam* [cansado, maltrecho] to be whacked, to be done in; [enfurecido] to be fuming.

zozobra *sf* anxiety, worry.

zozobrar *vi* - **1.** [naufragar] to be shipwrecked - **2.** *fig* [fracasar] to fall through.

zueco *sm* clog.

zulo *sm* hideout.

zulú (*pl* zulúes o zulús) *adj* & *sm, f* Zulu.

zumbado, da *fam* <> *adj* crazy. <> *sm, f* crazy person.

zumbador *sm* buzzer.

zumbar <> *vi* [gen] to buzz; [máquinas] to whirr, to hum; **me zumban los oídos** my ears are buzzing. <> *vt* *fam* to bash, to thump; **vino zumbando** he came running.

zumbido *sm* [gen] buzz, buzzing (*U*); [de máquinas] whirr, whirring (*U*).

zumbón, ona *fam* <> *adj* funny, joking. <> *sm, f* joker, tease.

zumo *sm* juice.

zurcido *sm* - **1.** [acción] darning - **2.** [remiendo] darn.

zurcidor, ra *sm, f* darner, mender.

zurcir [12] *vt* to darn; **¡anda y que te zurzan!** *fam* on your bike!, get lost!

zurdo, da <> *adj* [mano etc] left; [persona] left-handed. <> *sm, f* [persona] left-handed person.

➤ **zurda** *sf* - **1.** [mano] left hand - **2.** [pie] left foot.

zurra *sf* beating, hiding; **dar una zurra a alguien** to give sb a hiding.

zurrar *vt* - **1.** [pegar] to beat, to thrash - **2.** [curtir] to tan.

zurza *etc* ▷ **zurcir**.

zutano, na *sm, f* so-and-so, what's-his-name (*f* what's-her-name).

GUÍA PRÁCTICA/PRACTICAL GUIDE

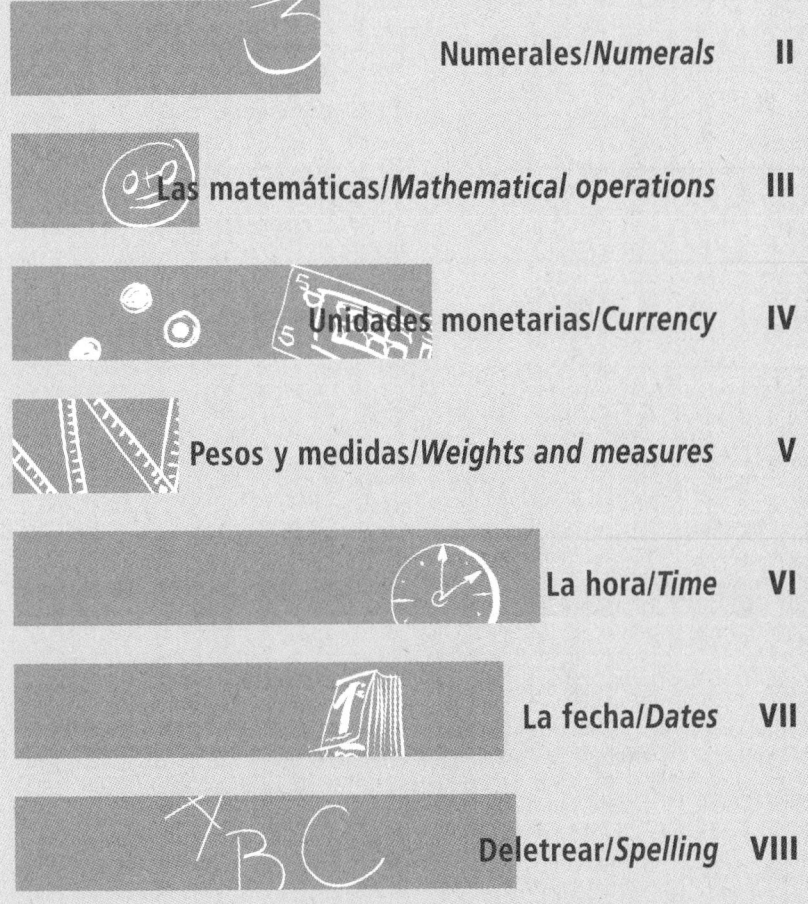

Cardinales — Cardinal numbers

cero	0	zero	veintinueve	29	twenty-nine
uno	1	one	treinta	30	thirty
dos	2	two	treinta y uno	31	thirty-one
tres	3	three	treinta y dos	32	thirty-two
cuatro	4	four	cuarenta	40	forty
cinco	5	five	cincuenta	50	fifty
seis	6	six	sesenta	60	sixty
siete	7	seven	setenta	70	seventy
ocho	8	eight	ochenta	80	eighty
nueve	9	nine	noventa	90	ninety
diez	10	ten	cien	100	one hundred
once	11	eleven	ciento uno	101	one hundred and one
doce	12	twelve	quinientos	500	five hundred
trece	13	thirteen	setecientos	700	seven hundred
catorce	14	fourteen	mil	1000	one thousand
quince	15	fifteen	mil veinte	1020	one thousand and twenty
dieciséis	16	sixteen	mil seiscientos seis	1606	one thousand six hundred and six
diecisiete	17	seventeen	dos mil	2000	two thousand
dieciocho	18	eighteen	un millón	1.000.000	one million
diecinueve	19	nineteen			
veinte	20	twenty			
veintiuno	21	twenty-one			
veintidós	22	twenty-two			
veintitrés	23	twenty-three			
veinticuatro	24	twenty-four			
veinticinco	25	twenty-five			
veintiséis	26	twenty-six			
veintisiete	27	twenty-seven			
veintiocho	28	twenty-eight			

Ordinales — Ordinal numbers

primero	1°	1st	first	decimoquinto	15°	15th	fifteenth
segundo	2°	2nd	second	decimosexto	16°	16th	sixteenth
tercero	3°	3rd	third	decimoséptimo	17°	17th	seventeenth
cuarto	4°	4th	fourth	decimoctavo	18°	18th	eighteenth
quinto	5°	5th	fifth	decimonoveno	19°	19th	nineteenth
sexto	6°	6th	sixth	vigésimo	20°	20th	twentieth
séptimo	7°	7th	seventh	vigésimo primer(o)	21°	21st	twenty-first
octavo	8°	8th	eighth	vigésimo segundo	22°	22nd	twenty-second
noveno	9°	9th	ninth	vigésimo tercero	23°	23nd	twenty-third
décimo	10°	10th	tenth	trigésimo	30°	30th	thirtieth
undécimo	11°	11th	eleventh	centésimo	100°	100th	hundredth
decimosegundo	12°	12th	twelfth	centésimo primero	101°	101st	hundred and first
decimotercero	13°	13th	thirteenth	milésimo	1000°	1000th	thousandth
decimocuarto	14°	14th	fourteenth				

Fracciones y decimales			*Fractions and decimals*
medio	1/2		one half
dos tercios	2/3		two thirds
un décimo/una décima parte	1/10		one tenth
un centésimo/una centésima parte	1/100		one hundredth
cero coma uno	0,1	0.1	(zero) point one
dos coma cinco	2,5	2.5	two point five
seis coma cero tres	6,03	6.03	six point zero three
menos uno	-1		minus one

Las operaciones		*Mathematical operations*
ocho más dos igual a diez	$8 + 2 = 10$	eight plus two equals ten
nueve menos tres igual a seis	$9 - 3 = 6$	nine minus three equals six
siete por tres igual a veintiuno	$7 \times 3 = 21$	seven times three equals twenty-one/ seven multiplied by three equals twenty-one
veinte entre cuatro igual a cinco	$20 \div 4 = 5$	twenty divided by four equals five
la raíz cuadrada de nueve es tres	$\sqrt{9} = 3$	the square root of nine is three
cinco al cuadrado igual a veinticinco	$5^2 = 25$	five squared equals twenty-five

Los porcentajes		*Percentages*
el diez por ciento	10 %	ten percent

El 75% de los estudiantes tiene un ordenador.
75% of students have a computer.

El paro ha aumentado un 0,2%.
The unemployment rate has risen 0.2%.

La moneda británica		British currency
monedas		*coins*
un penique	1p	*one penny*
dos peniques	2p	*two pence*
cinco peniques	5p	*five pence*
diez peniques	10p	*ten pence*
veinte peniques	20p	*twenty pence*
cincuenta peniques	50p	*fifty pence*
una libra/dos libras	£1/£2	*one pound/two pounds*
billetes		*banknotes*
cinco libras	£5	*five pounds*
diez libras	£10	*ten pounds*
veinte libras	£20	*twenty pounds*
cincuenta libras	£50	*fifty pounds*
La moneda estadounidense		**American currency**
monedas		*coins*
un centavo	1c	*one cent*
cinco centavos	5c	*five cents/a nickel*
diez centavos	10c	*ten cents/a dime*
veinticinco centavos	25c	*twenty-five cents/a quarter*
billetes		*banknotes*
un dólar	$1	*one dollar*
cinco dólares	$5	*five dollars*
diez dólares	$10	*ten dollars*
veinte dólares	$20	*twenty dollars*
cincuenta dólares	$50	*fifty dollars*
cien dólares	$100	*one hundred dollars*
La moneda europea		**European currency**
monedas		*coins*
un céntimo	0,01 €	*one cent*
dos céntimos	0,02 €	*two cents*
cinco céntimos	0,05 €	*five cents*
diez céntimos	0,10 €	*ten cents*
veinte céntimos	0,20 €	*twenty cents*
cincuenta céntimos	0,50 €	*fifty cents*
un euro	1,00 €	*one euro*
dos euros	2,00 €	*two euros*
billetes		*banknotes*
cinco euros	5 €	*five euros*
diez euros	10 €	*ten euros*
veinte euros	20 €	*twenty euros*
cincuenta euros	50 €	*fifty euros*
cien euros	100 €	*one hundred euros*
doscientos euros	200 €	*two hundred euros*
quinientos euros	500 €	*five hundred euros*

Longitud		*Length*
milímetro	**mm**	*millimetre**
centímetro	**cm**	*centimetre**
metro	**m**	*metre**
kilómetro	**km**	*kilometre**
pulgada	**in**	*inch*
pie	**ft**	*foot*
yarda	**yd**	*yard*
milla	**mi**	*mile*

* *(US square millimeter, centimeter, meter, kilometer)*

Peso		*Weight*
miligramo	**mg**	*milligram*
gramo	**g**	*gram*
hectogramo	**hg**	*hectogram*
kilo(gramo)	**kg**	*kilo-gram(me)*
tonelada	**t**	*ton*
onza	**1 oz**	*ounce*
libra	**1 lb**	*pound*

Capacidad		*Capacity*
decilitro	**dl**	*decilitre**
litro	**l**	*litre**
onza	**1 oz**	*ounce*
pinta	**1 pt**	*pint*
galón	**gal**	*gallon*

* *(US deciliter, liter)*

Volume		*Volume*
centímetro cúbico	**cm³**	*cubic centimetre**
metro cúbico	**m³**	*cubic metre**
pie cúbico	**ft³**	*cubic foot*
yarda cúbica	**yd³**	*cubic yard*

* *(US cubic centimeter, cubic meter)*

Superficie		*Area*
centímetro cuadrado	**cm²**	*square centimetre**
metro cuadrado	**m²**	*square metre**
kilómetro cuadrado	**km²**	*square kilometre**
hectárea (=10.000m²)	**ha**	*hectare*
pulgada cuadrada	**in²**	*square inch*
pie cuadrado	**ft²**	*square foot*
yarda cuadrada	**yd²**	*square yard*
milla cuadrada	**mi²**	*square mile*

* *(US square centimeter, square meter, square kilometer)*

Temperatura			*Temperature*
grados Celsius/centígrados	**°C**		*degree Celsius*
grados Fahrenheit	**°F**		*degree Fahrenheit*
El agua hierve a 100 grados.	**100°**	**212F**	*Water boils at two hundred and twelve degrees.*
Hoy tenemos 12 grados.	**12°**	**55F**	*Today it's fifty-five degrees.*
Tuve 40 de fiebre.	**40°**	**104F**	*My temperature was one hundred and four.*

Velocidad		*Speed*
metro(s) por segundo	**m/s**	*metres per second*
kilómetro(s) por hora	**km/h**	*kilometres per hour*
milla(s) por hora	**mph**	*miles per hour*

Informática		*IT*
kilobyte	**KB**	*kilobyte*
megabyte	**MB**	*megabyte (= 1024 KB)*
gigabyte	**GB**	*gigabyte (= 1024 MB)*
kilobyte por segundo	**Kbps**	*kilobyte per second*

mañana / *morning*

05:00
las cinco
five o'clock

07:05
las siete y cinco
five past seven

08:10
las ocho y diez
ten past eight

09:15
las nueve y cuarto
a quarter past nine UK/
a quarter after nine US

10:20
las diez y veinte
twenty past ten UK/
twenty after ten US

11:30
las once y media
half past eleven

12:00
las doce del mediodía
noon/twelve a.m./
midday

tarde / *afternoon*

12:30
las doce y media
half past twelve/twelve thirty

13:00
la una
one p.m.

14:00
las dos
two o'clock

15:45
las cuatro menos cuarto
a quarter to four UK/
a quarter of four US/
fifteen forty five

17:23
las cinco y veintitrés
five twenty-three

noche / *night*

24:00
las doce de la noche
twelve p.m./midnight

01:00
la una de la madrugada /
de la mañana
one a.m.

– ¿Qué hora es?
– What time is it?

– Es la una/son las ocho y treinta y cinco.
– It's one o'clock/eight thirty-five.

– ¿A qué hora?
– At what time?

– A/hacia/sobre las once.
– About elevenish.

– Hace media hora.
– Half an hour ago.

– Dentro de tres cuartos de hora.
– In three quarters of an hour.

La fecha/Dates

El calendario		Calendar
el dieciséis de octubre de mil novecientos setenta y cinco	16/10/1975	sixteenth of October nineteen seventy-five
mil cuatrocientos noventa y dos	1492	fourteen ninety-two
dos mil seis	2006	two thousand and six
los años setenta	70 '70	the Seventies
el siglo XVIII	XVIIIᵉ s. XVIII	the eighteenth century
antes/después de Cristo	a. de JC/d. de JC AC/BC	before/after Christ

– ¿Cuál es tu fecha de nacimiento?
– What's your date of birth?

– ¿Cuándo es tu cumpleaños?
– When is your birthday?

– El 30 de julio.
– The thirthieth of July

– ¿En qué mes naciste?
– Which month were you born in?

– ¿En qué año?
– In which year?

– En Mayo del 68.
– In May 1968

– En el siglo XXI.
– In the twenty first Century.

– Nací en marzo.
– I was born in March.

Ayer, hoy, mañana...	Yesterday, today, tomorrow...
hoy	today
mañana	tomorrow
ayer	yesterday
pasado mañana	the day after tomorrow
anteayer	the day before yesterday
el día siguiente	the following day
la víspera	the day before
esta mañana	this morning
esta tarde	this afternoon
mañana por la tarde	tomorrow afternoon
ayer por la noche	yesterday evening
el sábado por la noche	Saturday night
hace dos días	two days ago
la semana pasada	last week
el año que viene	next year
el próximo verano O el verano que viene	next summer
un día sí y uno no	every second day

– ¿Qué día es hoy? O ¿A qué día estamos?
– What day is it today?

– Hoy es 5 de mayo. O Hoy estamos a 5 de mayo.
– Today is the fifth of May.

El alfabeto fonético | Phonetic alphabets

						International	Nato
A	[a]	de Álava		**A**	[eɪ]	Amsterdam	Alpha
B	[be]	de Barcelona		**B**	[bi:]	Benjamin	Bravo
C	[θe]	de Cáceres		**C**	[si:]	Charlie	Charlie
D	[de]	de Dinamarca		**D**	[di:]	David	Delta
E	[e]	de España		**E**	[i:]	Edward	Echo
F	[efe]	de Francia		**F**	[ef]	Frederick	Foxtrot
G	[ge]	de Gerona		**G**	[dʒi]	George	Golf
H	[ache]	de Huelva		**H**	[eitch]	Harry	Hotel
I	[i]	de Italia		**I**	[aɪ]	Isaac	India
J	[jota]	de Jaén		**J**	[dʒaɪ]	Jack	Juliet
K	[ka]	de Kabul		**K**	[keɪ]	King	Kilo
L	[ele]	de Lugo		**L**	[el]	Lucy	Lima
M	[eme]	de Madrid		**M**	[em]	Mary	Mike
N	[ene]	de Navarra		**N**	[en]	Nellie	November
O	[o]	de Oviedo		**O**	[eu]	Oliver	Oscar
P	[pe]	de Pamplona		**P**	[pi:]	Peter	Papa
Q	[ku]	de Quito*		**Q**	[kju:]	Queenie	Quebec
R	[ere]	de Roma		**R**	[ɑ:ʳ]	Robert	Romeo
S	[ese]	de Segovia		**S**	[es]	Sugar	Sierra
T	[te]	de Toledo		**T**	[ti:]	Tommy	Tango
U	[u]	de Uruguay		**U**	[ju:]	Uncle	Uniform
V	[ube]	de Valencia		**V**	[vi:]	Victor	Victor
W	[ube doble]	de Washington		**W**	['dublju:]	William	Whiskey
X	[ekis]	de xilófon		**X**	[eks]	Xmas	X-ray
Y	[i grjega]	de Yucatán		**Y**	[waɪ]	Yellow	Yankee
Z	[θeta]	de Zaragoza		**Z**	[zed]	Zebra	Zulu

– **¿Me lo puede deletrear?**
– How do you spell that?

– **N de Navarra, I de Italia, E de España, T de Toledo , Z de Zaragoza, S de Segovia, C de Cáceres, H de Huelva y E de España.**
– N for November, I for India, E for Echo, T for Tango, Z for Zulu, S for Sierra, C for Charlie, H for Hotel, E for Echo.

– **¿Diga? ¿Es el 05 43 32 36 83? (cero cinco, cuarenta y tres, treinta y dos, treinta y seis, ochenta y tres)**
– Hello? Is this 0543 32 36 83? (oh, five four, three; three, two, three, six, eight three)

– **No, se ha equivocado.**
– No, you've got the wrong number.

ENGLISH–SPANISH
INGLÉS–ESPAÑOL

ENGLISH-SPANISH
INGLÉS-ESPAÑOL

a ¹ (*pl* as OR a's), **A** (*pl* As OR A's) [eɪ] *n* [letter] a *f*, A *f*; **from A to B** de un sitio a otro; **from A to Z** de cabo a rabo, de pe a pa.
► **A** *n* - **1.** MUS la *m* - **2.** SCH [mark] ≃ sobresaliente *m*.

a ² (*stressed* [eɪ], *unstressed* [ə]) (*before vowel or silent 'h'* **an**) *indef art* - **1.** [gen] un (una); **a boy** un chico; **a table** una mesa; **an orange** una naranja; **an eagle** un águila; **a hundred/thousand pounds** cien/mil libras - **2.** [referring to occupation]: **to be a dentist/teacher** ser dentista/maestra - **3.** [to express prices, ratios etc] por; **£10 a person** 10 libras por persona; **50 kilometres an hour** 50 kilómetros por hora; **20p a kilo** 20 peniques el kilo; **twice a week/month** dos veces a la semana/al mes - **4.** [preceding person's name] un(una) tal; **a Mr Jones** un tal señor Jones.

A-1 *adj inf* [excellent] de primera.

A4 *n UK* DIN *m* A4.

AA *n* - **1.** (*abbr of* **Automobile Association**), *asociación británica del automóvil,* ≃ RACE *m* - **2.** (*abbr of* **Associate in Arts**), *titular de una licenciatura de letras en Estados Unidos* - **3.** (*abbr of* **Alcoholics Anonymous**) AA *mpl*.

AAA *n* - **1.** (*abbr of* **Amateur Athletics Association**), *federación británica de atletismo aficionado* - **2.** (*abbr of* **American Automobile Association**), *asociación automovilística estadounidense,* ≃ RACE *m*.

AAUP (*abbr of* **American Association of University Professors**) *n sindicato estadounidense de profesores universitarios.*

aback [ə'bæk] *adv*: **to be taken aback** quedarse desconcertado(da).

abacus ['æbəkəs] (*pl* **-cuses** OR **-ci** [-saɪ]) *n* ábaco *m*.

abandon [ə'bændən] ◇ *vt* [gen] abandonar; [soccer, rugby match] suspender. ◇ *n*: **with abandon** con desenfreno.

abandoned [ə'bændənd] *adj* abandonado(da).

abashed [ə'bæʃt] *adj* avergonzado(da).

abate [ə'beɪt] *vi* [storm] amainar; [noise] disminuir; [fear] apaciguarse.

abattoir ['æbətwɑːr] *n* matadero *m*.

abbess ['æbes] *n* abadesa *f*.

abbey ['æbɪ] *n* abadía *f*.

abbot ['æbət] *n* abad *m*.

abbreviate [ə'briːvɪeɪt] *vt* abreviar.

abbreviation [ə,briːvɪ'eɪʃn] *n* abreviatura *f*.

ABC *n* - **1.** *lit* & *fig* abecé *m* - **2.** (*abbr of* **American Broadcasting Company**) ABC *f*.

abdicate ['æbdɪkeɪt] ◇ *vi* abdicar. ◇ *vt* [responsibility] abdicar de.

abdication [,æbdɪ'keɪʃn] *n* abdicación *f*.

abdomen ['æbdəmen] *n* abdomen *m*.

abdominal [æb'dɒmɪnl] *adj* abdominal.

abduct [əb'dʌkt] *vt* raptar.

abduction [əb'dʌkʃn] *n* rapto *m*.

aberration [,æbə'reɪʃn] *n* aberración *f*, anomalía *f*; **a mental aberration** un despiste.

abet [ə'bet] (*pt* & *pp* **-ted**, *cont* **-ting**) *vt* ▷ **aid**.

abeyance [ə'beɪəns] *n*: **in abeyance** [custom] en desuso; [law] en suspenso.

abhor [əb'hɔːr] (*pt* & *pp* **-red**, *cont* **-ring**) *vt* aborrecer.

abhorrent [əb'hɒrənt] *adj* aborrecible.

abide [ə'baɪd] *vt* soportar, aguantar.

abide by vt insep [law, ruling] acatar; [principles, own decision] atenerse a.

abiding [əˈbaɪdɪŋ] adj [feeling, interest] duradero(ra); **my abiding memory of that day is how excited I was** mi recuerdo más duradero de ese día es lo emocionado que estaba.

ability [əˈbɪlətɪ] (pl -ies) n - **1.** [capability] capacidad f, facultad f; **to do sthg to the best of one's ability** hacer algo lo mejor posible OR lo mejor que uno puede - **2.** [skill] aptitud f.

abject [ˈæbdʒekt] adj - **1.** [poverty] vil, indigente - **2.** [person] sumiso(sa); [apology] humillante.

ablaze [əˈbleɪz] adj - **1.** [on fire] en llamas - **2.** [bright]: **to be ablaze with** resplandecer de.

able [ˈeɪbl] adj - **1.** [capable]: **to be able to do sthg** poder hacer algo; **to feel able to do sthg** sentirse capaz de hacer algo - **2.** [skilful] capaz, competente.

able-bodied [-ˌbɒdɪd] adj (físicamente) sano(na).

ablutions [əˈbluːʃnz] npl fml abluciones fpl.

ably [ˈeɪblɪ] adv competentemente.

ABM (abbr of anti-ballistic missile) n ABM m (misil antibalístico).

abnormal [æbˈnɔːml] adj anormal.

abnormality [ˌæbnɔːˈmælətɪ] (pl -ies) n anormalidad f, anomalía f.

abnormally [æbˈnɔːməlɪ] adv [unusually] anormalmente.

aboard [əˈbɔːd] <> adv a bordo. <> prep [ship, plane] a bordo de; [bus, train] en.

abode [əˈbəʊd] n fml: **of no fixed abode** sin domicilio fijo.

abolish [əˈbɒlɪʃ] vt abolir.

abolition [ˌæbəˈlɪʃn] n abolición f.

A-bomb (abbr of atom bomb) n bomba f A.

abominable [əˈbɒmɪnəbl] adj abominable, deplorable.

abominable snowman n: **the abominable snowman** el abominable hombre de las nieves.

abominably [əˈbɒmɪnəblɪ] adv de forma abominable OR deplorable.

aborigine [ˌæbəˈrɪdʒənɪ] n aborigen mf de Australia.

abort [əˈbɔːt] <> vt - **1.** [pregnancy, plan, project] abortar; [pregnant woman] provocar el aborto a - **2.** COMPUT abortar. <> vi COMPUT abortar.

abortion [əˈbɔːʃn] n aborto m; **to have an abortion** abortar.

abortive [əˈbɔːtɪv] adj frustrado(da), fracasado(da).

abound [əˈbaʊnd] vi - **1.** [be plentiful] abundar - **2.** [be full]: **to abound with** OR **in** abundar en.

about [əˈbaʊt] <> adv - **1.** [approximately] más o menos, como; **there were about fifty/a hundred** había (como) unos cincuenta/cien o así; **at about five o'clock** a eso de las cinco - **2.** [referring to place] por ahí; **to leave things lying about** dejar las cosas por ahí; **to walk about** ir andando por ahí; **to jump about** dar saltos - **3.** [on the point of]: **to be about to do sthg** estar a punto de hacer algo. <> prep - **1.** [relating to, concerning] sobre, acerca de; **a film about Paris** una película sobre París; **what is it about?** ¿de qué trata?; **tell me about your problems** háblame de tus problemas; **there's something odd about that man** hay algo raro en ese hombre - **2.** [referring to place] por; **to wander about the streets** vagar por las calles.

about-turn esp UK, **about-face** esp US n MIL media vuelta f; fig cambio m radical, giro m de 180 grados.

above [əˈbʌv] <> adv - **1.** [on top, higher up] arriba; **the flat above** el piso de arriba; **see above** [in text] véase más arriba - **2.** [more, over]: **children aged five and above** niños de cinco años en adelante. <> prep - **1.** [on top of] encima de - **2.** [higher up than, over] por encima de; **the plane flew above them** el avión pasó por encima de ellos - **3.** [more than, superior to] por encima de; **children above the age of 15** niños mayores de 15 años; **she's not above lying** es muy capaz de mentir.

above all adv sobre todo, por encima de todo.

aboveboard [əˌbʌvˈbɔːd] adj limpio(pia).

abracadabra [ˌæbrəkəˈdæbrə] excl ¡abracadabra!

abrasion [əˈbreɪʒn] n fml [graze] abrasión f.

abrasive [əˈbreɪsɪv] <> adj - **1.** [substance] abrasivo(va) - **2.** [person] cáustico(ca), mordaz. <> n abrasivo m.

abreast [əˈbrest] <> adv: **they were walking four abreast** caminaban en fila de a cuatro. <> prep: **to keep abreast of** mantenerse al día de.

abridged [əˈbrɪdʒd] adj abreviado(da).

abroad [əˈbrɔːd] adv en el extranjero; **to go abroad** ir al extranjero.

abrupt [əˈbrʌpt] adj - **1.** [sudden] repentino(na), súbito(ta) - **2.** [brusque] brusco(ca), seco(ca).

abruptly [əˈbrʌptlɪ] adv - **1.** [suddenly] repentinamente, súbitamente - **2.** [brusquely] secamente, con brusquedad.

ABS (abbr of Antiblockiersystem) n ABS m.

abscess [ˈæbsɪs] n absceso m.

abscond [əbˈskɒnd] vi: **to abscond (with/from)** escaparse OR fugarse (con/de).

abseil ['æbseɪl] *vi*: to abseil (down sthg) descolgarse OR descender haciendo rápel (por algo).

abseiling ['æbseɪŋ] *n* rappel *m*; to go abseiling ir a hacer rappel.

absence ['æbsəns] *n* - **1.** [of person] ausencia *f*; in sb's absence en ausencia de alguien - **2.** [of thing] falta *f*; in the absence of a falta de.

absent ['æbsənt] *adj* - **1.** [not present] ausente; to be absent from faltar a; to be absent without leave MIL ausentarse sin permiso - **2.** [absent-minded] distraído(da).

absentee [,æbsən'ti:] *n* ausente *mf*; absentee ballot US voto *m* por correo.

absenteeism [,æbsən'ti:ɪzm] *n* absentismo *m*.

absent-minded [-'maɪndɪd] *adj* [person] despistado(da); [behaviour] distraído(da).

absent-mindedly [-'maɪndɪdlɪ] *adv* distraídamente.

absinth(e) ['æbsɪnθ] *n* absenta *f*, ajenjo *m*.

absolute ['æbsəlu:t] *adj* absoluto(ta); that's absolute rubbish! ¡menuda tontería es eso!

absolutely ['æbsəlu:tlɪ] ◇ *adv* [completely] absolutamente, completamente; it was absolutely delicious estuvo riquísimo. ◇ *excl* ¡desde luego!, ¡por supuesto!

absolute majority *n* mayoría *f* absoluta.

absolution [,æbsə'lu:ʃn] *n* absolución *f*.

absolve [əb'zɒlv] *vt*: to absolve sb (from) absolver a alguien (de).

absorb [əb'sɔ:b] *vt* - **1.** [gen] absorber; to be absorbed in sthg *fig* estar absorto OR embebido en algo - **2.** *fig* [learn] asimilar.

absorbent [əb'sɔ:bənt] *adj* absorbente; absorbent cotton US algodón *m* hidrófilo.

absorbing [əb'sɔ:bɪŋ] *adj* absorbente.

absorption [əb'sɔ:pʃn] *n* [of liquid] absorción *f*.

abstain [əb'steɪn] *vi* [refrain, not vote]: to abstain (from) abstenerse (de).

abstemious [æb'sti:mjəs] *adj fml* sobrio(bria), moderado(da).

abstention [əb'stenʃn] *n* abstención *f*.

abstinence ['æbstɪnəns] *n*: abstinence (from) abstinencia *f* (de).

abstract ◇ *adj* ['æbstrækt] abstracto(ta). ◇ *n* ['æbstrækt] [summary] resumen *m*, sinopsis *f*. ◇ *vt* [æb'strækt] [summarize] resumir, sintetizar.

abstraction [æb'strækʃn] *n* abstracción *f*.

abstruse [æb'stru:s] *adj* abstruso(sa).

absurd [əb'sɜ:d] *adj* absurdo(da).

absurdity [əb'sɜ:dətɪ] (*pl* **-ies**) *n* irracionalidad *f*.

absurdly [əb'sɜ:dlɪ] *adv* [ridiculously] disparatadamente.

ABTA ['æbtə] (*abbr of* Association of British Travel Agents) *n* asociación británica de agencias de viajes.

abundance [ə'bʌndəns] *n*: (in) abundance (en) abundancia *f*.

abundant [ə'bʌndənt] *adj* abundante.

abundantly [ə'bʌndəntlɪ] *adv* - **1.** [extremely]: it's abundantly clear está clarísimo - **2.** [in large amounts] abundantemente, en abundancia.

abuse ◇ *n* [ə'bju:s] *(U)* - **1.** [offensive remarks] insultos *mpl* - **2.** [misuse, maltreatment] abuso *m*. ◇ *vt* [ə'bju:z] - **1.** [insult] insultar - **2.** [maltreat, misuse] abusar de.

abusive [ə'bju:sɪv] *adj* [person] grosero(ra); [behaviour, language] insultante, ofensivo(va).

abut [ə'bʌt] (*pt & pp* **-ted**, *cont* **-ting**) *vi*: to abut on to lindar con.

abysmal [ə'bɪzml] *adj* pésimo(ma), nefasto(ta).

abysmally [ə'bɪzməlɪ] *adv* pésimamente.

abyss [ə'bɪs] *n* abismo *m*.

a/c (*abbr of* account (current)) c/c.

AC *n* - **1.** UK (*abbr of* athletics club) CA *f* - **2.** (*abbr of* alternating current) CA *f*.

acacia [ə'keɪʃə] *n* acacia *f*.

academic [,ækə'demɪk] ◇ *adj* - **1.** [of college, university] académico(ca) - **2.** [studious] estudioso(sa) - **3.** [hypothetical]: that's completely academic now eso carece por completo de relevancia. ◇ *n* - **1.** [university lecturer] profesor *m* universitario, profesora *f* universitaria - **2.** [intellectual] académico(ca).

academic year *n* año *m* académico.

academy [ə'kædəmɪ] (*pl* **-ies**) *n* academia *f*.

ACAS ['eɪkæs] (*abbr of* Advisory, Conciliation and Arbitration Service) *n* organización británica para el arbitraje en conflictos laborales, ≃ IMAC *m*.

accede [æk'si:d] *vi* - **1.** [agree]: to accede to acceder a - **2.** [monarch]: to accede to the throne subir al trono.

accelerate [ək'seləreɪt] *vi* - **1.** [car, driver] acelerar - **2.** [inflation, growth] acelerarse.

acceleration [ək,selə'reɪʃn] *n* aceleración *f*.

accelerator [ək'seləreɪtər] *n* acelerador *m*.

accelerator board *n* COMPUT placa *f* aceleradora.

accelerator card *n* COMPUT tarjeta *f* aceleradora.

accent ['æksent] *n lit & fig* acento *m*.

accentuate [æk'sentjʊeɪt] *vt* acentuar, poner de relieve.

accept [ək'sept] ◇ *vt* - **1.** [gen] aceptar - **2.** [difficult situation, problem] asimilar - **3.** [defeat, blame, responsibility] asumir, admitir

- **4.** [agree]: **to accept that** admitir que - **5.** [subj: machine - coins, tokens] funcionar con, admitir. ⬦ *vi* aceptar.

acceptable [ək'septəbl] *adj* aceptable.

acceptably [ək'septəblɪ] *adv* [allowably, adequately] aceptablemente.

acceptance [ək'septəns] *n* - **1.** [gen] aceptación *f* - **2.** [of piece of work, article] aprobación *f* - **3.** [of defeat, blame, responsibility] asunción *f*, reconocimiento *m* - **4.** [of person - as part of group etc] admisión *f*.

accepted [ək'septɪd] *adj* [ideas, truth] reconocido(da) por todos.

access ['ækses] ⬦ *n* - **1.** [entry] acceso *m*; **to gain access to** [place] acceder a, conseguir acceso a - **2.** [opportunity to use or see] libre acceso *m*; **to have access to** tener acceso a. ⬦ *vt* COMPUT acceder a.

accessibility [ək,sesə'bɪlətɪ] *n* - **1.** [of place] accesibilidad *f* - **2.** [of service, amenity] facilidad *f* de acceso.

accessible [ək'sesəbl] *adj* - **1.** [place] accesible - **2.** [service, book, film] asequible - **3.** [for the disabled] para discapacitados.

accession [æk'seʃn] *n* - **1.** [of monarch] advenimiento *m* OR subida *f* (al trono) - **2.** [to EU] adhesión *f*.

accessory [ək'sesərɪ] (*pl* -**ies**) *n* - **1.** [of car, vacuum cleaner] accesorio *m* - **2.** LAW cómplice *mf*. ➠ **accessories** *npl* complementos *mpl*.

access road *n* UK vía *f* OR carretera *f* de acceso.

access time *n* COMPUT tiempo *m* de acceso.

accident ['æksɪdənt] *n* accidente *m*; **to have an accident** [gen] tener un accidente; [in car] tener un accidente de coche; **it was an accident** fue sin querer; **by accident** [by chance] por casualidad.

accidental [,æksɪ'dentl] *adj* accidental.

accidentally [,æksɪ'dentəlɪ] *adv* - **1.** [by chance] por casualidad - **2.** [unintentionally] sin querer.

accident-prone *adj* propenso(sa) a los accidentes.

acclaim [ə'kleɪm] ⬦ *n* (U) elogios *mpl*, alabanza *f*. ⬦ *vt* elogiar, alabar.

acclamation [,æklə'meɪʃn] (U) *n* aclamación *f*, vítores *mpl*.

acclimatize, -ise [ə'klaɪmətaɪz], **acclimate** ['æklɪmeɪt] US ⬦ *vt*: **to become acclimatized to sthg** aclimatarse a algo. ⬦ *vi*: **to acclimatize (to)** aclimatarse (a).

accolade ['ækəleɪd] *n* [praise] elogio *m*, halago *m*; [award] galardón *m*.

accommodate [ə'kɒmədeɪt] *vt* - **1.** [provide room for people - subj: person] alojar; [- subj: building, place] albergar - **2.** [provide room for things] acomodar - **3.** [oblige] complacer.

accommodating [ə'kɒmədeɪtɪŋ] *adj* complaciente, servicial.

accommodation UK [ə,kɒmə'deɪʃn] *n* - **1.** [lodging] alojamiento *m* - **2.** [work space] espacio *m*.

accommodations [ə,kɒmə'deɪʃnz] *npl* US = **accommodation**.

accompaniment [ə'kʌmpənɪmənt] *n* MUS acompañamiento *m*.

accompanist [ə'kʌmpənɪst] *n* MUS acompañante *mf*.

accompany [ə'kʌmpənɪ] (*pt* & *pp* -**ied**) *vt* acompañar.

accomplice [ə'kʌmplɪs] *n* cómplice *mf*.

accomplish [ə'kʌmplɪʃ] *vt* [aim, goal] conseguir, alcanzar; [task] realizar.

accomplished [ə'kʌmplɪʃt] *adj* [person] competente, experto(ta); [performance] logrado(da).

accomplishment [ə'kʌmplɪʃmənt] *n* - **1.** [action] realización *f* - **2.** [achievement] logro *m*. ➠ **accomplishments** *npl* dotes *fpl*.

accord [ə'kɔːd] ⬦ *n*: **in accord** de acuerdo; **with one accord** al unísono; **to do sthg of one's own accord** hacer algo por propia voluntad; **the situation improved of its own accord** la situación mejoró por sí sola. ⬦ *vt*: **to accord sthg to sb, to accord sb sthg** conceder algo a alguien. ⬦ *vi*: **to accord with sthg** concordar con algo.

accordance [ə'kɔːdəns] *n*: **in accordance with** de acuerdo con, conforme a.

according [ə'kɔːdɪŋ] ➠ **according to** *prep* - **1.** [as stated or shown by] según; **to go according to plan** ir según lo planeado - **2.** [with regard to] de acuerdo con, conforme a.

accordingly [ə'kɔːdɪŋlɪ] *adv* - **1.** [appropriately] como corresponde - **2.** [consequently] por lo tanto, en consecuencia.

accordion [ə'kɔːdjən] *n* acordeón *m*.

accordionist [ə'kɔːdjənɪst] *n* acordeonista *mf*.

accost [ə'kɒst] *vt* abordar.

account [ə'kaʊnt] *n* - **1.** [with bank, shop etc] cuenta *f* - **2.** [report - spoken] relato *m*; [- written] informe *m* - **3.** [client] cuenta *f*, cliente *m* ▶▶ **to call sb to account** pedir cuentas a alguien; **to give a good account of o.s.** hacer un buen papel; **to take account of sthg, to take sthg into account** tener en cuenta algo; **of no account** sin importancia; **it is of no account to me** me es indiferente; **on no account** bajo ningún pretexto OR concepto. ➠ **accounts** *npl* [of business] cuentas *fpl*.

➠ **by all accounts** adv a decir de todos, según todo el mundo.

➠ **on account of** prep debido a, a causa de.

➠ **account for** vt insep - **1.** [explain] justificar, dar razón de - **2.** [represent] representar.

accountability [ə,kaʊntə'bɪlətɪ] n (U) responsabilidad f.

accountable [ə'kaʊntəbl] adj - **1.** [responsible]: **accountable (for)** responsable (de) - **2.** [answerable]: **accountable to** obligado(da) a rendir cuentas ante.

accountancy [ə'kaʊntənsɪ] n contabilidad f.

accountant [ə'kaʊntənt] n contable mf, contador m, -ra f Amér.

accounting [ə'kaʊntɪŋ] n contabilidad f.

accoutrements UK [ə'ku:trəmənts], **accouterments** US [ə'ku:tərmənts] npl fml impedimenta f, pertrechos mpl.

accredited [ə'kredɪtɪd] adj [ambassador] acreditado(da); [dealer, spokesperson] oficial.

accrue [ə'kru:] vi acumularse.

accumulate [ə'kju:mjʊleɪt] <> vt acumular. <> vi [money, things] acumularse; [problems] amontonarse.

accumulation [ə,kju:mjʊ'leɪʃn] n - **1.** (U) [act of accumulating] acumulación f - **2.** [collection of things] cúmulo m, montón m.

accuracy ['ækjʊrəsɪ] n - **1.** [of description, report] veracidad f - **2.** [of weapon, marksman] precisión f; [of typing, figures] exactitud f, corrección f.

accurate ['ækjʊrət] adj - **1.** [description, report] veraz - **2.** [weapon, marksman, typist] preciso(sa); [figures, estimate] exacto(ta), correcto(ta).

accurately ['ækjʊrətlɪ] adv - **1.** [truthfully] verazmente - **2.** [precisely] con precisión.

accusation [,ækjʊ'zeɪʃn] n - **1.** [charge] acusación f - **2.** LAW denuncia f.

accuse [ə'kju:z] vt: **to accuse sb of sthg/of doing sthg** acusar a alguien de algo/de hacer algo.

accused [ə'kju:zd] (pl **accused**) n LAW: **the accused** el acusado, la acusada.

accusing [ə'kju:zɪŋ] adj acusador(ra).

accusingly [ə'kju:zɪŋlɪ] adv [look at] acusatoriamente; [speak to] en tono acusador.

accustomed [ə'kʌstəmd] adj: **accustomed to** acostumbrado(da) a; **to grow accustomed to** acostumbrarse a.

ace [eɪs] <> adj - **1.: an ace athlete** un as del atletismo - **2.** UK inf [excellent] genial. <> n - **1.** [playing card] as m; **to be within an ace of** fig estar al borde de - **2.** [in tennis] ace m. <> vt US: **to ace an exam** bordar un examen.

acerbic [ə'sɜːbɪk] adj mordaz.

acetate ['æsɪteɪt] n acetato m.

acetic acid [ə'si:tɪk-] n ácido m acético.

acetone ['æsɪtəʊn] n acetona f.

acetylene [ə'setɪli:n] n acetileno m.

ache [eɪk] <> n [pain] dolor m. <> vi - **1.** [hurt] doler; **my back aches** me duele la espalda - **2.** fig [want]: **to be aching for sthg/to do sthg** morirse de ganas de algo/de hacer algo.

achieve [ə'tʃi:v] vt [success, goal, fame] alcanzar, lograr; [ambition] realizar.

achievement [ə'tʃi:vmənt] n - **1.** [accomplishment] logro m, éxito m - **2.** [act of achieving] consecución f, realización f.

Achilles' heel [ə'kɪli:z-] n talón m de Aquiles.

Achilles' tendon [ə'kɪli:z-] n tendón m de Aquiles.

acid ['æsɪd] <> adj - **1.** CHEM ácido(da) - **2.** [sharp-tasting] agrio(agria) - **3.** fig [person, remark] mordaz, corrosivo(va). <> n [chemical, drug] ácido m.

acidic [ə'sɪdɪk] adj ácido(da).

acidity [ə'sɪdətɪ] n - **1.** [of substance, liquid, soil] acidez f - **2.** fig [of person, remark] mordacidad f.

acid house n acid house m.

acid rain n lluvia f ácida.

acid test n fig prueba f de fuego.

acknowledge [ək'nɒlɪdʒ] vt - **1.** [accept] reconocer - **2.** [greet] saludar - **3.** [letter etc]: **to acknowledge receipt of** acusar recibo de - **4.** [recognize]: **to acknowledge sb as** reconocer OR considerar a alguien como.

acknowledg(e)ment [ək'nɒlɪdʒmənt] n - **1.** [acceptance] reconocimiento m - **2.** [confirmation of receipt] acuse m de recibo - **3.** [thanks]: **in acknowledgement of** en señal de agradecimiento por.

➠ **acknowledg(e)ments** npl agradecimientos mpl.

ACLU (abbr of **American Civil Liberties Union**) n asociación estadounidense para la defensa de las libertades civiles.

acme ['ækmɪ] n cenit m, súmmum m.

acne ['æknɪ] n acné m.

acorn ['eɪkɔ:n] n bellota f.

acoustic [ə'ku:stɪk] adj acústico(ca).

➠ **acoustics** npl acústica f.

acoustic guitar n guitarra f acústica.

acquaint [ə'kweɪnt] vt - **1.** [make familiar]: **to acquaint sb with sthg** [information] poner a alguien al corriente de algo; [method, technique] familiarizar a alguien con algo - **2.** [make known]: **to be acquainted with sb** conocer a alguien.

acquaintance [ə'kweɪntəns] n [person] conocido m, -da f; **to make sb's acquaintance** fml conocer a alguien.

acquiesce [ˌækwɪ'es] *vi*: **to acquiesce (to** OR **in sthg)** acceder (a algo).

acquiescence [ˌækwɪ'esns] *n* consentimiento *m*.

acquire [ə'kwaɪəʳ] *vt* **- 1.** [buy, adopt] adquirir **- 2.** [obtain - information, document] hacerse con, procurarse.

acquisition [ˌækwɪ'zɪʃn] *n* adquisición *f*.

acquisitive [ə'kwɪzɪtɪv] *adj* consumista.

acquit [ə'kwɪt] (*pt* & *pp* **-ted**, *cont* **-ting**) *vt* **- 1.** LAW: **to acquit sb of sthg** absolver a alguien de algo **- 2.** [perform]: **to acquit o.s. well/badly** hacer un buen/mal papel.

acquittal [ə'kwɪtl] *n* LAW absolución *f*.

acre ['eɪkəʳ] *n* acre *m*.

acrid ['ækrɪd] *adj* lit & fig acre.

acrimonious [ˌækrɪ'məʊnjəs] *adj* [words] áspero(ra); [dispute] agrio(agria), enconado(da).

acrobat ['ækrəbæt] *n* acróbata *mf*.

acrobatic [ˌækrə'bætɪk] *adj* **- 1.** [somersault, display] acrobático(ca) **- 2.** [person] ágil.

➡ **acrobatics** *npl* acrobacias *fpl*.

acronym ['ækrənɪm] *n* siglas *fpl*.

across [ə'krɒs] <> *adv* **- 1.** [from one side to the other] de un lado a otro; **to walk/run across** cruzar andando/corriendo; **to look across** mirar al otro lado **- 2.** [in measurements]: **the river is 2 km across** el río tiene 2 kms de ancho **- 3.** [in crossword]: **21 across** 21 horizontal

▸▸▸ **to get sthg across (to sb)** hacer entender algo (a alguien). <> *prep* **- 1.** [from one side to the other of] a través de, de un lado a otro de; **to walk/run across the road** cruzar la carretera andando/corriendo; **the bridge across the river** el puente que cruza el río; **he drew a line across the page** trazó una línea a través de la página; **to look across sthg** mirar hacia el otro lado de algo **- 2.** [on the other side of] al otro lado de.

➡ **across from** *prep* enfrente de.

across-the-board *adj* global; [salary rise] lineal.

acrylic [ə'krɪlɪk] <> *adj* acrílico(ca). <> *n* acrílico *m*.

act [ækt] <> *n* **- 1.** [action, deed] acto *m*, acción *f*; **to be in the act of doing sthg** estar haciendo algo; **to catch sb in the act** coger a alguien con las manos en la masa **- 2.** [pretence] farsa *f*, fachada *f* **- 3.** [in parliament] ley *f* **- 4.** [THEAT - part of play] acto *m*; [- routine, turn] número *m*

▸▸▸ **to get in on the act** apuntarse al carro; **to get one's act together** organizarse. <> *vi* **- 1.** [gen] actuar; **to act as** [person] hacer de, fungir de *Méx*; [thing] actuar como **- 2.** [behave]: **to act (as if/like)** comportarse (como si/como) **- 3.** *fig* [pretend] fingir **- 4.** LAW [lawyer, estate agent]: **to act for sb, to act on behalf of sb**

actuar en representación OR nombre de alguien. <> *vt* [part - in play, film] interpretar; **to act the fool** hacer el tonto; **to act the innocent** hacerse el inocente; **act your age!** ¡deja de portarte como un crío!

➡ **act out** *vt sep* **- 1.** [feelings, thoughts] exteriorizar **- 2.** [scene, event] representar.

➡ **act up** *vi* **- 1.** [machine] no ir bien **- 2.** [child] dar guerra.

acting ['æktɪŋ] <> *adj* [interim] en funciones. <> *n* actuación *f*; **I like acting** me gusta actuar.

action ['ækʃn] *n* **- 1.** [gen & MIL] acción *f*; **to take action** tomar medidas; **in action** [person] en acción; [machine] en funcionamiento; **to be killed in action** caer muerto en combate OR en acto de servicio; **to put sthg into action** poner algo en práctica OR marcha; **out of action** [person] fuera de combate; [machine] averiado(da) **- 2.** [deed] acto *m*, acción *f* **- 3.** LAW demanda *f*.

action group *n* grupo *m* de presión.

action replay *n* repetición *f* (de la jugada).

activate ['æktɪveɪt] *vt* [device] activar; [machine] poner en funcionamiento.

active ['æktɪv] *adj* **- 1.** [person, campaigner, encouragement etc] activo(va) **- 2.** [volcano] en actividad; [bomb] activado(da); **on active duty** US MIL en servicio activo.

actively ['æktɪvlɪ] *adv* [encourage, discourage] activamente.

active service *n* MIL servicio *m* activo.

activist ['æktɪvɪst] *n* activista *mf*.

activity [æk'tɪvətɪ] (*pl* **-ies**) *n* **- 1.** [movement, action] actividad *f* **- 2.** [pastime, hobby] afición *f*.

➡ **activities** *npl* [actions] actividades *fpl*.

act of God *n* caso *m* de fuerza mayor.

actor ['æktəʳ] *n* actor *m*.

actress ['æktrɪs] *n* actriz *f*.

actual ['æktʃʊəl] *adj* [emphatic]: **the actual cost is £10** el coste real es de 10 libras; **the actual game starts at three** el partido en sí empieza a las tres; **the actual spot where it happened** el sitio mismo en que ocurrió.

actuality [ˌæktʃʊ'ælətɪ] *n*: **in actuality** en realidad.

actually ['æktʃʊəlɪ] *adv* **- 1.** [really, in truth]: **do you actually like him?** ¿de verdad que te gusta?; **no-one actually saw her** en realidad, nadie la vio; **actually it's not that good** la verdad es que no está tan bien **- 2.** [by the way]: **actually, I was there yesterday** pues yo estuve ayer por allí.

actuary ['æktjʊərɪ] (*pl* **-ies**) *n* actuario *m*, -ria *f* de seguros.

actuate ['æktjʊeɪt] *vt* [mechanism] activar, accionar.

acuity [ə'kju:ətɪ] *n fml* agudeza *f*.

acumen ['ækjʊmen] *n*: **business acumen** vista *f* para los negocios.

acupuncture ['ækjʊpʌŋktʃər] *n* acupuntura *f*.

acute [ə'kju:t] *adj* **- 1.** [illness, pain] agudo(da); [danger] extremo(ma) **- 2.** [perceptive - person] perspicaz **- 3.** [hearing, smell] muy fino(na) **- 4.** LING: **e acute** e *f* acentuada.

acute accent *n* acento *m* agudo.

acutely [ə'kju:tlɪ] *adv* [extremely] extremadamente, profundamente.

ad [æd] (*abbr of* **advertisement**) *n* anuncio *m*.

AD (*abbr of* **Anno Domini**) d. C.

adage ['ædɪdʒ] *n* refrán *m*, adagio *m*.

adamant ['ædəmənt] *adj*: **to be adamant (that)** insistir (en que).

Adam's apple ['ædəmz-] *n* bocado *m* OR nuez *f* de Adán.

adapt [ə'dæpt] ◇ *vt* adaptar. ◇ *vi*: **to adapt (to)** adaptarse (a).

adaptability [ə,dæptə'bɪlətɪ] *n* adaptabilidad *f*.

adaptable [ə'dæptəbl] *adj* [person] adaptable.

adaptation [,ædæp'teɪʃn] *n* adaptación *f*.

adapter, adaptor [ə'dæptər] *n* [ELEC - for several devices] ladrón *m*; [- for different socket] adaptador *m*.

ADC *n* **- 1.** *abbr of* **aide-de-camp - 2.** (*abbr of* **analogue-digital converter**), *convertidor analógico-digital*.

add [æd] *vt* **- 1.** [gen]: **to add sthg (to sthg)** añadir algo (a algo) **- 2.** [numbers] sumar.

◆ **add in** *vt sep* añadir, sumar.

◆ **add on** *vt sep* **- 1.** [to building]: **to add sthg on (to sthg)** añadir algo (a algo) **- 2.** [to bill, total]: **to add sthg on (to sthg)** añadir OR incluir algo (en algo).

◆ **add to** *vt insep* aumentar, acrecentar.

◆ **add up** ◇ *vt sep* [numbers] sumar. ◇ *vi inf* [make sense]: **it doesn't add up** no tiene sentido.

◆ **add up to** *vt insep* venir a ser.

adder ['ædər] *n* víbora *f*.

addict ['ædɪkt] *n* **- 1.** [taking drugs] adicto *m*, -ta *f*; **drug addict** drogadicto *m*, -ta *f*, toxicómano *m*, -na *f*; **heroin addict** heroinómano *m*, -na *f* **- 2.** *fig* [fan] fanático *m*, -ca *f*.

addicted [ə'dɪktɪd] *adj* **- 1.** [to drug]: **addicted (to)** adicto(ta) (a) **- 2.** *fig* [to food, TV]: **to be addicted (to)** ser un fanático (de).

addiction [ə'dɪkʃn] *n* **- 1.** [to drug]: **addiction (to)** adicción *f* (a) **- 2.** *fig* [to food, TV]: **addiction (to)** vicio *m* (por).

addictive [ə'dɪktɪv] *adj lit* & *fig* adictivo(va).

Addis Ababa ['ædɪs 'æbəbə] *n* Addis Abeba.

addition [ə'dɪʃn] *n* **- 1.** MATHS suma *f* **- 2.** [extra thing] adición *f*, añadido *m* **- 3.** [act of adding] incorporación *f*; **in addition** además; **in addition to** además de.

additional [ə'dɪʃənl] *adj* adicional.

additive ['ædɪtɪv] *n* aditivo *m*.

addled ['ædld] *adj* **- 1.** [egg] podrido(da) **- 2.** [brain] hecho(cha) un lío.

add-on ◇ *adj* COMPUT externo(na), complementario(ria). ◇ *n* COMPUT complemento *m*.

address [ə'dres] ◇ *n* **- 1.** [of person, organization] dirección *f*, domicilio *m* **- 2.** COMPUT dirección *f* **- 3.** [speech] discurso *m*, conferencia *f*. ◇ *vt* **- 1.** [letter, parcel, remark]: **to address sthg to** dirigir algo a; **to be addressed to** ir dirigido a **- 2.** [meeting, conference] dirigirse a, hablar ante **- 3.** [issue] abordar; **to address o.s. to sthg** enfrentarse a OR abordar algo.

address book *n* agenda *f* de direcciones.

addressee [,ædre'si:] *n* destinatario *m*, -ria *f*.

adenoids ['ædɪnɔɪdz] *npl* vegetaciones *fpl* (adenoideas).

adept ['ædept] *adj*: **to be adept (at sthg/at doing sthg)** ser experto(ta) (en algo/en hacer algo).

adequacy ['ædɪkwəsɪ] *n* **- 1.** [sufficiency] suficiencia *f* **- 2.** [suitability] idoneidad *f*.

adequate ['ædɪkwət] *adj* **- 1.** [sufficient] suficiente **- 2.** [good enough] aceptable, satisfactorio(ria).

adequately ['ædɪkwətlɪ] *adv* **- 1.** [sufficiently] suficientemente **- 2.** [well enough] aceptablemente, satisfactoriamente.

adhere [əd'hɪər] *vi* **- 1.** [to surface, principle]: **to adhere (to)** adherirse (a) **- 2.** [to rule, decision]: **to adhere to** respetar, observar.

adherence [əd'hɪərəns] *n* **- 1.** [to rule, decision]: **adherence to** observancia *f* OR cumplimiento *m* de **- 2.** [to principle, belief]: **adherence to** adhesión *f* a.

adhesive [əd'hi:sɪv] ◇ *adj* adhesivo(va), adherente. ◇ *n* adhesivo *m*.

adhesive tape *n* cinta *f* adhesiva.

ad hoc [,æd'hɒk] *adj* ad hoc, a propósito.

ad infinitum [,ædɪnfɪ'naɪtəm] *adv* ad infinitum, hasta el infinito.

adjacent [ə'dʒeɪsənt] *adj*: **adjacent (to)** adyacente OR contiguo(gua) (a).

adjective ['ædʒɪktɪv] *n* adjetivo *m*.

adjoin [ə'dʒɔɪn] *vt* [land] lindar con; [room] estar contiguo(gua) a.

adjoining [ə'dʒɔɪnɪŋ] ◇ *adj* [table] adyacente; [room] contiguo(gua). ◇ *prep* junto a.

adjourn [ə'dʒɜːn] ◇ vt [session] levantar; [meeting] interrumpir. ◇ vi: **the court adjourned for an hour** el juicio se interrumpió durante una hora.

adjournment [ə'dʒɜːnmənt] n aplazamiento m.

adjudge [ə'dʒʌdʒ] vt declarar.

adjudicate [ə'dʒuːdɪkeɪt] ◇ vt actuar como juez en. ◇ vi actuar como juez; **to adjudicate on** OR **upon sthg** emitir un fallo OR un veredicto sobre algo.

adjudication [ə,dʒuːdɪ'keɪʃn] n fallo m, decisión f.

adjunct ['ædʒʌŋkt] n complemento m, apéndice m.

adjust [ə'dʒʌst] ◇ vt [machine, setting] ajustar; [clothing] arreglarse. ◇ vi: **to adjust (to)** adaptarse OR amoldarse (a).

adjustable [ə'dʒʌstəbl] adj [machine, chair] regulable.

adjustable spanner n llave f inglesa.

adjusted [ə'dʒʌstɪd] adj: **to be well adjusted** ser una persona equilibrada.

adjustment [ə'dʒʌstmənt] n - **1.** [modification] modificación f, reajuste m; **to make an adjustment to sthg** hacer un reajuste a algo - **2.** (U) [change in attitude]: **adjustment (to)** adaptación f OR amoldamiento m (a).

adjutant ['ædʒutənt] n ayudante m.

ad lib [,æd'lɪb] ◇ adj [improvised] improvisado(da). ◇ n improvisación f. ◇ adv [without preparation] improvisando; [without limit] a voluntad.

◆ **ad-lib** vi (pt & pp -**bed**, cont -**bing**) improvisar.

adman ['ædmæn] (pl **admen** ['ædmen]) n publicista m.

admin ['ædmɪn] (abbr of **administration**) n UK inf papeleo m.

administer [əd'mɪnɪstər] vt [gen] administrar; [punishment] aplicar.

administration [əd,mɪnɪ'streɪʃn] n [gen] administración f; [of punishment] aplicación f.

◆ **Administration** n US: **the Administration** la Administración.

administrative [əd'mɪnɪstrətɪv] adj administrativo(va).

administrator [əd'mɪnɪstreɪtər] n administrador m, -ra f.

admirable ['ædmərəbl] adj admirable.

admirably ['ædmərəblɪ] adv admirablemente.

admiral ['ædmərəl] n almirante m.

Admiralty ['ædmərəltɪ] n UK: **the Admiralty** el Almirantazgo.

admiration [,ædmə'reɪʃn] n admiración f.

admire [əd'maɪər] vt: **to admire sb (for)** admirar a alguien (por).

admirer [əd'maɪrərər] n admirador m, -ra f.

admiring [əd'maɪrɪŋ] adj lleno(na) de admiración.

admiringly [əd'maɪrɪŋlɪ] adv con admiración.

admissible [əd'mɪsəbl] adj LAW admisible.

admission [əd'mɪʃn] n - **1.** [permission to enter] admisión f, ingreso m - **2.** [cost of entrance] entrada f - **3.** [of guilt, mistake] reconocimiento m; **by his/her** etc **own admission** como él mismo/ella misma etc reconoce.

admit [əd'mɪt] (pt & pp -**ted**, cont -**ting**) ◇ vt - **1.** [acknowledge, confess]: **to admit (that)** admitir OR reconocer (que); **to admit doing sthg** reconocer haber hecho algo; **to admit defeat** fig darse por vencido - **2.** [allow to enter or join] admitir; **to be admitted to hospital** UK OR **to the hospital** US ser ingresado en el hospital; **'admits two'** [on ticket] 'válido para dos (personas)'. ◇ vi: **to admit to sthg** [crime] confesar algo.

admittance [əd'mɪtəns] n: **to gain admittance to** conseguir entrar en; **'no admittance'** 'prohibido el paso'.

admittedly [əd'mɪtɪdlɪ] adv sin duda, indudablemente.

admonish [əd'mɒnɪʃ] vt amonestar, apercibir.

ad nauseam [,æd'nɔːzɪæm] adv hasta la saciedad.

ado [ə'duː] n: **without further** OR **more ado** sin más preámbulos, sin mayor dilación.

adolescence [,ædə'lesns] n adolescencia f.

adolescent [,ædə'lesnt] ◇ adj - **1.** [teenage] adolescente - **2.** pej [immature] pueril, infantil. ◇ n [teenager] adolescente mf.

adopt [ə'dɒpt] vt & vi adoptar.

adoption [ə'dɒpʃn] n adopción f.

adoptive [ə'dɒptɪv] adj adoptivo(va).

adorable [ə'dɔːrəbl] adj encantador(ra), adorable.

adoration [,ædə'reɪʃn] n adoración f.

adore [ə'dɔːr] vt - **1.** [love deeply] adorar, querer con locura - **2.** [like very much]: **I adore chocolate** me encanta el chocolate.

adoring [ə'dɔːrɪŋ] adj - **1.** [look] lleno(na) de adoración - **2.** [mother, father] devoto(ta).

adorn [ə'dɔːn] vt adornar.

adornment [ə'dɔːnmənt] n adorno m.

adrenalin [ə'drenəlɪn] n adrenalina f.

Adriatic [,eɪdrɪ'ætɪk] n: **the Adriatic (Sea)** el (mar) Adriático.

adrift [ə'drɪft] ◇ adj [boat] a la deriva. ◇ adv: **to go adrift** fig irse a la deriva.

adroit [ə'drɔɪt] adj diestro(tra).

ADT (*abbr of* **Atlantic Daylight Time**) *n hora de verano de la costa este estadounidense.*

adulation [,ædju'leɪʃn] *n* adulación *f.*

adult ['ædʌlt] <> *adj* - **1.** [fully grown] adulto(ta) - **2.** [mature] maduro(ra) - **3.** [suitable for adults only] para adultos OR mayores. <> *n* adulto *m*, -ta *f.*

adult education *n* educación *f* de adultos.

adulterate [ə'dʌltəreɪt] *vt* adulterar.

adulteration [ə,dʌltə'reɪʃn] *n* adulteración *f.*

adulterer [ə'dʌltərər] *n* adultero *m*, -ra *f.*

adultery [ə'dʌltərɪ] *n* adulterio *m.*

adulthood ['ædʌlthʊd] *n* edad *f* adulta.

advance [əd'vɑːns] <> *n* - **1.** [gen] avance *m* - **2.** [money] adelanto *m*, anticipo *m*. <> *comp:* **advance notice** OR **warning** previo aviso *m*; **advance booking** reserva *f* anticipada; **advance payment** pago *m* anticipado. <> *vt* - **1.** [improve] promover, favorecer - **2.** [bring forward in time] adelantar - **3.** [give in advance]: **to advance sb sthg** adelantarle algo a alguien. <> *vi* avanzar.

◆ **advances** *npl:* **to make advances to sb** [sexual] hacerle proposiciones a alguien, insinuarse a alguien; [business] hacerle una propuesta a alguien.

◆ **in advance** *adv* [pay] por adelantado; [book] con antelación; [know, thank] de antemano; **to arrive half an hour in advance** llegar con media hora de adelanto.

◆ **in advance of** *prep* - **1.** [ahead of] por delante de - **2.** [prior to] con anterioridad a.

advanced [əd'vɑːnst] *adj* - **1.** [developed] avanzado(da); **advanced in years** *euph* entrado(da) en años - **2.** [student, pupil] adelantado(da); [studies] superior.

advancement [əd'vɑːnsmənt] *n* - **1.** [in job] ascenso *m* - **2.** [of cause etc] fomento *m.*

advantage [əd'vɑːntɪdʒ] *n:* **advantage (over)** ventaja *f* (sobre); **to be to one's advantage** ir en beneficio de uno; **to take advantage of sthg** aprovechar algo; **to take advantage of sb** aprovecharse de alguien; **to have** OR **hold the advantage (over sb)** tener OR llevar ventaja (sobre alguien); **advantage Hewitt** [in tennis] ventaja de Hewitt.

advantageous [,ædvən'teɪdʒəs] *adj* ventajoso(sa).

advent ['ædvənt] *n* [arrival] advenimiento *m.*

◆ **Advent** *n* RELIG Adviento *m.*

Advent calendar *n* calendario *m* de Adviento.

adventure [əd'ventʃər] *n* aventura *f.*

adventure holiday *n* vacaciones *fpl* de aventura.

adventure playground *n* UK parque *m* infantil.

adventurer [əd'ventʃərər] *n* - **1.** [adventurous person] aventurero *m*, -ra *f* - **2.** [unscrupulous person] sinvergüenza *mf.*

adventurous [əd'ventʃərəs] *adj* - **1.** [daring] aventurero(ra) - **2.** [dangerous] arriesgado(da).

adverb ['ædvɜːb] *n* adverbio *m.*

adversary ['ædvəsərɪ] (*pl* -**ies**) *n* adversario *m*, -ria *f.*

adverse ['ædvɜːs] *adj* adverso(sa).

adversely ['ædvɜːslɪ] *adv* negativamente.

adversity [əd'vɜːsətɪ] *n* adversidad *f.*

advert ['ædvɜːt] *n* anuncio *m.*

advertise ['ædvətaɪz] <> *vt* anunciar. <> *vi* anunciarse, poner un anuncio; **to advertise for** buscar (*mediante anuncio*).

advertisement [əd'vɜːtɪsmənt] *n* anuncio *m*; **to be a great advertisement for** *fig* hacerle una propaganda excelente a.

advertiser ['ædvətaɪzər] *n* anunciante *mf.*

advertising ['ædvətaɪzɪŋ] *n* publicidad *f.*

advertising agency *n* agencia *f* de publicidad.

advertising campaign *n* campaña *f* publicitaria.

advice [əd'vaɪs] *n* (U) consejos *mpl*; **to take sb's advice** seguir el consejo de alguien; **a piece of advice** un consejo; **to give sb advice** aconsejar a alguien.

advice note *n* aviso *m* de envío.

advisability [əd,vaɪzə'bɪlətɪ] *n* conveniencia *f.*

advisable [əd'vaɪzəbl] *adj* aconsejable.

advise [əd'vaɪz] <> *vt* - **1.** [give advice to]: **to advise sb to do sthg** aconsejar a alguien que haga algo; **to advise sb against sthg/against doing sthg** desaconsejar a alguien algo/que haga algo - **2.** [professionally]: **to advise sb on sthg** asesorar a alguien en algo - **3.** [recommend: caution] recomendar - **4.** *fml* [inform]: **to advise sb (of sthg)** informar a alguien (de algo). <> *vi* - **1.** [give advice]: **to advise against sthg** desaconsejar algo; **to advise against doing sthg** aconsejar no hacer algo - **2.** [professionally]: **to advise on** asesorar en (materia de).

advisedly [əd'vaɪzɪdlɪ] *adv* [deliberately] deliberadamente; [after careful consideration] con conocimiento de causa.

adviser UK, **advisor** US [əd'vaɪzər] *n* [of politician etc] consejero *m*, -ra *f*; [financial, professional] asesor *m*, -ra *f.*

advisory [əd'vaɪzərɪ] *adj* [body] consultivo(va), asesor(ra); **in an advisory capacity** OR **role** en calidad de asesor.

advocacy ['ædvəkəsɪ] *n* apoyo *m*, defensa *f.*

advocate ◇ *n* ['ædvəkət] **- 1.** LAW abogado *m* defensor, abogada *f* defensora **- 2.** [supporter] defensor *m*, -ra *f*, partidario *m*, -ria *f*. ◇ *vt* ['ædvəkeɪt] abogar por.

AEA (*abbr of* **Atomic Energy Authority**) *n organismo británico de energía nuclear,* ≃ CSN *m*.

AEC (*abbr of* **Atomic Energy Commission**) *n organismo estadounidense de energía nuclear,* ≃ CSN *m*.

AEEU (*abbr of* **Amalgamated Engineering and Electrical Union**) *n sindicato británico de ingeniería.*

Aegean [iː'dʒiːən] *n*: **the Aegean (Sea)** el mar Egeo.

aegis ['iːdʒɪs] *n*: **under the aegis of** bajo los auspicios OR la égida de.

aeon *UK,* **eon** *US* ['iːən] *n fig*: **it's been aeons since I saw you** hace siglos que no te veo.

aerial ['eərɪəl] ◇ *adj* aéreo(a). ◇ *n* UK [antenna] antena *f*.

aerobatics [ˌeərəʊ'bætɪks] *n* (U) acrobacia *f* aérea.

aerobics [eə'rəʊbɪks] *n* (U) aerobic *m*.

aerodrome ['eərədrəʊm] *n* aeródromo *m*.

aerodynamic [ˌeərəʊdaɪ'næmɪk] *adj* aerodinámico(ca).
◆ **aerodynamics** ◇ *n* (U) [science] aerodinámica *f*. ◇ *npl* [aerodynamic qualities] aerodinámica *f*.

aerogramme ['eərəgræm] *n* aerograma *m*.

aeronautics [ˌeərə'nɔːtɪks] *n* (U) aeronáutica *f*.

aeroplane ['eərəpleɪn] *n* UK avión *m*.

aerosol ['eərəsɒl] *n* aerosol *m*.

aerospace ['eərəʊspeɪs] *n*: **the aerospace industry** la industria aeroespacial.

aesthete, esthete *US* ['iːsθiːt] *n* esteta *mf*.

aesthetic, esthetic *US* [iːs'θetɪk] *adj* estético(ca).

aesthetically, esthetically *US* [iːs'θetɪklɪ] *adv* estéticamente.

aesthetics, esthetics *US* [iːs'θetɪks] *n* (U) estética *f*.

afar [ə'fɑːʳ] *adv*: **from afar** desde lejos.

affable ['æfəbl] *adj* afable.

affair [ə'feəʳ] *n* **- 1.** [concern, matter] asunto *m* **- 2.** [extra-marital relationship] aventura *f* (amorosa) **- 3.** [event, do] acontecimiento *m*.
◆ **affairs** *npl* asuntos *mpl*.

affect [ə'fekt] *vt* **- 1.** [influence, move emotionally] afectar **- 2.** [put on] fingir, simular.

affectation [ˌæfek'teɪʃn] *n* afectación *f*.

affected [ə'fektɪd] *adj* [insincere] afectado(da).

affection [ə'fekʃn] *n* cariño *m*, afecto *m*.

affectionate [ə'fekʃnət] *adj* cariñoso(sa), afectuoso(sa).

affectionately [ə'fekʃnətlɪ] *adv* cariñosamente, afectuosamente.

affidavit [ˌæfɪ'deɪvɪt] *n* declaración *f* jurada.

affiliate ◇ *n* [ə'fɪlɪət] filial *f*. ◇ *vt* [ə'fɪlɪeɪt]: **to be affiliated to** OR **with** estar afiliado(da) a.

affiliation [əˌfɪlɪ'eɪʃn] *n* afiliación *f*.

affinity [ə'fɪnətɪ] (*pl* **-ies**) *n* **- 1.** [close feeling] afinidad *f*; **to have an affinity with** sentirse afín a **- 2.** [similarity] similitud *f*; **to have an affinity with** tener un parecido con.

affirm [ə'fɜːm] *vt* afirmar.

affirmation [ˌæfə'meɪʃn] *n* **- 1.** [declaration] afirmación *f* **- 2.** [confirmation] confirmación *f*.

affirmative [ə'fɜːmətɪv] ◇ *adj* afirmativo(va). ◇ *n* respuesta *f* afirmativa; **in the affirmative** afirmativamente.

affirmative action *n* discriminación *f* positiva.

Affirmative action

🔳 Designa las medidas concebidas para combatir la discriminación de las minorías étnicas y de las mujeres en los Estados Unidos. Inicialmente fueron introducidas en la década de los sesenta para luchar por la igualdad de oportunidades laborales entre blancos y negros. La noción de "affirmative action" ha llegado a desatar más de una polémica, especialmente en el ámbito racial, donde su detractores han considerado que dispensaba un trato preferencial a los negros y a los hispanos, y continúa siendo objeto de debate.

affix [ə'fɪks] *vt* fijar, pegar.

afflict [ə'flɪkt] *vt* aquejar, afligir; **to be afflicted with sthg** estar aquejido de algo.

affliction [ə'flɪkʃn] *n* aflicción *f*, padecimiento *m*.

affluence ['æfluəns] *n* prosperidad *f*.

affluent ['æfluənt] *adj* pudiente, adinerado(da).

affluent society *n* sociedad *f* próspera.

afford [ə'fɔːd] *vt* **- 1.** [gen]: **to be able to afford** poder permitirse (el lujo de); **we can't afford a car** no nos podemos permitir un coche; **I can't afford the time** no tengo tiempo; **we can't afford to let this happen** no podemos permitirnos el lujo de dejar que esto ocurra **- 2.** *fml* [provide, give] brindar.

affordable [ə'fɔːdəbl] *adj* asequible.

afforestation [æˌfɒrɪ'steɪʃn] *n* repoblación *f* forestal.

affray [ə'freɪ] *n* UK reyerta *f*.

affront [ə'frʌnt] ◇ *n* afrenta *f*. ◇ *vt* afrentar.

Afghan ['æfgæn], **Afghani** [æf'gænɪ] ⟨⟩ *adj* afgano(na). ⟨⟩ *n* afgano *m*, -na *f*.

Afghan hound *n* galgo *m* afgano.

Afghanistan [æf'gænɪstæn] *n* Afganistán.

afield [ə'fiːld] *adv*: **further afield** más lejos.

AFL-CIO (*abbr of* **American Federation of Labor and Congress of Industrial Organizations**) *n* confederación estadounidense de sindicatos de la industria.

afloat [ə'fləʊt] *adj lit* & *fig* a flote.

afoot [ə'fʊt] *adj* [plan] en marcha; **there is a rumour afoot that** corre el rumor de que.

aforementioned [ə,fɔː'menʃənd], **aforesaid** [ə'fɔːsed] *adj* susodicho(cha), arriba mencionado(da).

afraid [ə'freɪd] *adj* - **1.** [gen] asustado(da); **to be afraid of sb** tenerle miedo a alguien; **I'm afraid of them** me dan miedo; **to be afraid of sthg** tener miedo de algo; **to be afraid of doing** OR **to do sthg** tener miedo de hacer algo - **2.** [in apologies]: **to be afraid that** temerse que; **I'm afraid so/not** me temo que sí/no.

afresh [ə'freʃ] *adv* de nuevo.

Africa ['æfrɪkə] *n* África.

African ['æfrɪkən] ⟨⟩ *adj* africano(na). ⟨⟩ *n* africano *m*, -na *f*.

African American *n* afroamericano *m*, -na *f*.

Afrikaans [,æfrɪ'kɑːns] *n* africaans *m*.

Afrikaner [,æfrɪ'kɑːnəʳ] *n* africánder *mf*.

aft [ɑːft] *adv* en popa.

AFT (*abbr of* **American Federation of Teachers**) *n* sindicato estadounidense de profesores.

after ['ɑːftəʳ] ⟨⟩ *prep* - **1.** [gen] después de; **after having...** después de haber...; **after all my efforts** después de todos mis esfuerzos; **after you!** ¡usted primero!; **day after day** día tras día; **the day after tomorrow** pasado mañana; **the week after next** no la semana que viene sino la otra - **2.** *inf* [in search of]: **to be after sthg** buscar algo; **to be after sb** andar detrás de alguien - **3.** [with the name of]: **to be named after sb/sthg** llamarse así por alguien/algo - **4.** [towards retreating person]: **to call after sb** llamar a alguien; **to run after sb** correr tras alguien - **5.** ART: **after Titian** copia de Ticiano - **6.** *US* [telling the time]: **it's twenty after three** son las tres y veinte. ⟨⟩ *adv* más tarde, después. ⟨⟩ *conj* después (de) que; **after you had done it** después de que lo hubieras hecho.

➡ **afters** *npl UK inf* postre *m*.

➡ **after all** *adv* - **1.** [in spite of everything] después de todo - **2.** [it should be remembered] al fin y al cabo.

afterbirth ['ɑːftɜːbɜːθ] *n* placenta *f* (*tras el parto*).

aftercare ['ɑːftəkeəʳ] *n* [on leaving hospital] atención *f* postoperatoria; [on leaving prison] ayuda *f* para la reinserción.

afterlife ['ɑːftəlaɪf] (*pl* **-lives** [-laɪvz]) *n* más allá *m*, vida *f* de ultratumba.

aftermath ['ɑːftəmæθ] *n* [time] periodo *m* posterior; [situation] situación *f* posterior.

afternoon [,ɑːftə'nuːn] *n* tarde *f*; **in the afternoon** por la tarde; **at three in the afternoon** a las tres de la tarde; **good afternoon** buenas tardes.

➡ **afternoons** *adv US* por las tardes.

aftershave ['ɑːftəʃeɪv] *n* loción *f* para después del afeitado.

aftershock ['ɑːftəʃɒk] *n* réplica *f*.

aftertaste ['ɑːftəteɪst] *n* - **1.** [of food, drink] regusto *m*, resabio *m* - **2.** *fig* [of unpleasant experience] mal sabor *m* de boca.

afterthought ['ɑːftəθɔːt] *n* idea *f* a posteriori.

afterward(s) ['ɑːftəwəd(z)] *adv* después, más tarde.

again [ə'gen] *adv* - **1.** [gen] otra vez, de nuevo; **never again** nunca jamás; **he's well again now** ya está bien; **to do sthg again** volver a hacer algo; **to say sthg again** repetir algo; **again and again** una y otra vez; **all over again** otra vez desde el principio; **time and again** una y otra vez - **2.** [asking for repetition]: **what's his name again?** ¿cómo has dicho que se llama?

▶▶ **half as much again** la mitad otra vez; **twice as much again** dos veces lo mismo otra vez; **come again?** *inf* ¿cómo?; **then** OR **there again** por otro lado, por otra parte.

against [ə'genst] ⟨⟩ *prep* contra; **I'm against it** estoy (en) contra (de) ello; **to lean against sthg** apoyarse en algo; **(as) against** a diferencia de, en contraste con. ⟨⟩ *adv* en contra.

age [eɪdʒ] ⟨⟩ *n* - **1.** [gen] edad *f*; **to be of age** *US* ser mayor de edad; **to come of age** alcanzar la mayoría de edad; **to be under age** ser menor (de edad); **what age are you?** ¿qué edad tienes?; **to be forty years of age** tener cuarenta años (de edad); **at the age of thirty** a los treinta años - **2.** [state of being old] vejez *f*. ⟨⟩ *vt* & *vi* (*cont* **ageing** OR **aging**) envejecer.

➡ **ages** *npl* [long time] un montón de tiempo, siglos *mpl*; **ages ago** hace siglos; **I haven't seen her for ages** hace siglos que no la veo.

aged ⟨⟩ *adj* - **1.** [eɪdʒd] [of the stated age]: **children aged between 8 and 15** niños de entre 8 y 15 años de edad - **2.** ['eɪdʒɪd] [very old] anciano(na). ⟨⟩ *npl* ['eɪdʒɪd]: **the aged** los ancianos.

age group *n* (grupo *m* de) edad *f*.

ageing, aging ['eɪdʒɪŋ] ◇ *adj* viejo(ja). ◇ *n* envejecimiento *m*.

ageless ['eɪdʒlɪs] *adj* [person] eternamente joven; [thing] imperecedero(ra).

agency ['eɪdʒənsɪ] (*pl* **-ies**) *n* **- 1.** [business] agencia *f*; **employment/travel agency** agencia de colocaciones/viajes **- 2.** [organization, body] organismo *m*, instituto *m*.

agenda [ə'dʒendə] *n* **- 1.** [of meeting] orden *m* del día; **what's on the agenda?** ¿cuál es el orden del día? **- 2.** [intentions] intenciones *fpl*.

agent ['eɪdʒənt] *n* **- 1.** COMM [of company] representante *mf*, delegado *m*, -da *f*; [of actor] agente *mf* **- 2.** [substance] agente *m* **- 3.** [secret agent] agente *m* (secreto).

age-old *adj* secular.

aggravate ['ægrəveɪt] *vt* **- 1.** [make worse] agravar, empeorar **- 2.** [annoy] irritar.

aggravating ['ægrəveɪtɪŋ] *adj* [annoying] irritante, exasperante.

aggravation [,ægrə'veɪʃn] *n* **- 1.** (*U*) [trouble] irritación *f* **- 2.** [annoying thing] molestia *f*, incomodidad *f*.

aggregate ['ægrɪgət] ◇ *adj* total. ◇ *n* **- 1.** [total] total *m* **- 2.** [material] conglomerado *m*.

aggression [ə'greʃn] *n* agresividad *f*; **act of aggression** agresión *f*.

aggressive [ə'gresɪv] *adj* **- 1.** [belligerent - person] agresivo(va) **- 2.** [forceful - person, campaign] audaz, emprendedor(ra).

aggressively [ə'gresɪvlɪ] *adv* con agresividad.

aggressor [ə'gresər] *n* agresor *m*, -ra *f*.

aggrieved [ə'gri:vd] *adj* ofendido(da), herido(da).

aggro ['ægrəʊ] *n* UK inf camorra *f*, follón *m*.

aghast [ə'gɑːst] *adj*: **aghast (at)** horrorizado(da) (ante).

agile [UK 'ædʒaɪl, US 'ædʒəl] *adj* ágil.

agility [ə'dʒɪlətɪ] *n* agilidad *f*.

aging *adj* & *n* = ageing.

agitate ['ædʒɪteɪt] ◇ *vt* **- 1.** [disturb, worry] inquietar, perturbar **- 2.** [shake about] agitar. ◇ *vi* [campaign]: **to agitate for/against** hacer campaña a favor de/en contra de.

agitated ['ædʒɪteɪtɪd] *adj* inquieto(ta).

agitation [,ædʒɪ'teɪʃn] *n* **- 1.** [anxiety] inquietud *f* **- 2.** POL [campaigning] campaña *f*.

agitator ['ædʒɪteɪtər] *n* [political activist] agitador *m*, -ra *f*.

AGM *n abbr of* **annual general meeting**.

agnostic [æg'nɒstɪk] ◇ *adj* agnóstico(ca). ◇ *n* agnóstico *m*, -ca *f*.

ago [ə'gəʊ] *adv*: **a long time/three days/three years ago** hace mucho tiempo/tres días/tres años.

agog [ə'gɒg] *adj* ansioso(sa), expectante; **agog with excitement** vibrante de emoción.

agonize, -ise ['ægənaɪz] *vi* titubear largamente; **to agonize over** OR **about sthg** atormentarse con algo.

agonized ['ægənaɪzd] *adj* angustioso(sa).

agonizing ['ægənaɪzɪŋ] *adj* angustioso(sa).

agonizingly ['ægənaɪzɪŋlɪ] *adv* angustiosamente; **they came agonizingly close to winning** les faltó poquísimo para ganar.

agony ['ægənɪ] (*pl* **-ies**) *n* **- 1.** [physical pain] dolor *m* muy intenso; **to be in agony** morirse de dolor **- 2.** [mental pain] angustia *f*; **to be in agony** estar angustiado.

agony aunt *n* UK inf consejera *f* sentimental.

agony column *n* UK inf consultorio *m* sentimental.

agoraphobia [,ægərə'fəʊbjə] *n* agorafobia *f*.

agree [ə'griː] ◇ *vi* **- 1.** [be of same opinion]: **to agree (with sb about sthg)** estar de acuerdo (con alguien acerca de algo); **to agree on sthg** [reach agreement] ponerse de acuerdo en algo; **to agree on sthg** [be in agreement] estar de acuerdo en algo **- 2.** [consent]: **to agree (to sthg)** acceder (a algo) **- 3.** [approve]: **to agree with sthg** estar de acuerdo con algo **- 4.** [be consistent] concordar **- 5.** [food]: **to agree with sb** sentarle bien a alguien **- 6.** GRAM: **to agree (with)** concordar (con). ◇ *vt* **- 1.** [fix: date, time] acordar, convenir **- 2.** [be of same opinion]: **to agree that** estar de acuerdo en que **- 3.** [agree, consent]: **to agree to do sthg** acordar hacer algo **- 4.** [concede]: **to agree (that)** reconocer que.

agreeable [ə'griːəbl] *adj* **- 1.** [pleasant] agradable **- 2.** [willing]: **to be agreeable to sthg/doing sthg** estar conforme con algo/hacer algo.

agreeably [ə'griːəblɪ] *adv* agradablemente.

agreed [ə'griːd] ◇ *adj*: **to be agreed on sthg** estar de acuerdo sobre algo; **at the agreed time** a la hora acordada OR convenida. ◇ *adv* **- 1.** [decided] de acuerdo **- 2.** [admittedly] de acuerdo que.

agreement [ə'griːmənt] *n* **- 1.** [accord, settlement, contract] acuerdo *m*; **to be in agreement with** estar de acuerdo con; **to reach an agreement** llegar a un acuerdo **- 2.** [consent] aceptación *f* **- 3.** [consistency] correspondencia *f* **- 4.** GRAM concordancia *f*.

agricultural [,ægrɪ'kʌltʃərəl] *adj* agrícola.

agriculture ['ægrɪkʌltʃər] *n* agricultura *f*.

aground [ə'graʊnd] *adv*: **to run aground** encallar.

ah [ɑː] *excl* ¡ah!

aha [ɑː'hɑː] *excl* ¡ajá!

ahead [ə'hed] *adv* - **1.** [in front] delante; **to go on ahead** ir por delante; **to be sent on ahead** ser enviado por delante - **2.** [forwards] adelante, hacia delante; **go ahead!** ¡por supuesto!; **right** OR **straight ahead** todo recto OR de frente - **3.** [winning]: **to be ahead** [in race] ir en cabeza; [in football, rugby etc] ir ganando; **they went ahead in the fifth minute** a los cinco minutos se pusieron por delante en el marcador - **4.** [in better position] por delante; **to get ahead** [be successful] abrirse camino - **5.** [in time]: **to look** OR **think ahead** mirar hacia el futuro.

◆ **ahead of** *prep* - **1.** [in front of] frente a - **2.** [beating]: **to be two points ahead of** llevar dos puntos de ventaja a - **3.** [in better position than] por delante de - **4.** [in time] antes de, con anterioridad a; **ahead of schedule** por delante de lo previsto.

ahoy [ə'hɔɪ] *excl* NAUT: **land/ship ahoy!** ¡tierra/barco a la vista!

AI *n* - **1.** (*abbr of* **Amnesty International**) AI *f* - **2.** (*abbr of* **artificial intelligence**) IA *f* - **3.** (*abbr of* **artificial insemination**) inseminación *f* artificial.

aid [eɪd] ⬦ *n* ayuda *f*; **medical aid** asistencia *f* médica; **with the aid of** con (la) ayuda de; **to go to the aid of sb** OR **to sb's aid** ir en auxilio de alguien; **in aid of** a beneficio de. ⬦ *vt* - **1.** [help] ayudar - **2.** LAW: **to aid and abet sb** ser cómplice de alguien.

AID *n* - **1.** (*abbr of* **artificial insemination by donor**), *inseminación artificial con semen de donante anónimo* - **2.** (*abbr of* **Agency for International Development**), *organismo estadounidense para el desarrollo internacional.*

aide [eɪd] *n* POL ayudante *mf*.

aide-de-camp [eɪddə'kɒ:] (*pl* **aides-de-camp**) *n* ayudante *m*, -ta *f* de campo.

AIDS, Aids [eɪdz] (*abbr of* **acquired immune deficiency syndrome**) ⬦ *n* SIDA *m*, sida *m*. ⬦ *comp*: **AIDS specialist** especialista de sida; **AIDS patient** sidoso *m*, -sa *f*.

ail [eɪl] ⬦ *vt liter* afligir. ⬦ *vi* estar enfermo(ma).

ailing ['eɪlɪŋ] *adj* - **1.** [ill] enfermo(ma), achacoso(sa) - **2.** *fig* [economy] renqueante.

ailment ['eɪlmənt] *n* achaque *m*, molestia *f*.

aim [eɪm] ⬦ *n* - **1.** [objective] objetivo *m* - **2.** [in firing gun] puntería *f*; **to take aim at** apuntar a. ⬦ *vt* - **1.** [weapon]: **to aim sthg at** apuntar algo a - **2.** [plan, action]: **to be aimed at doing sthg** ir dirigido OR encaminado a hacer algo - **3.** [campaign, publicity, criticism]: **to aim sthg at sb** dirigir algo a alguien. ⬦ *vi* - **1.** [point weapon]: **to aim (at sthg)** apuntar (a algo)

- **2.** [intend]: **to aim at** OR **for sthg** apuntar a OR pretender algo; **to aim to do sthg** pretender hacer algo.

aimless ['eɪmlɪs] *adj* sin un objetivo claro.

aimlessly ['eɪmlɪslɪ] *adv* [wander] sin rumbo fijo.

ain't [eɪnt] *inf* - **1.** (*abbr of* **am not**), ▷ **be** - **2.** (*abbr of* **are not**), ▷ **be** - **3.** (*abbr of* **is not**), ▷ **be** - **4.** (*abbr of* **ave not**), ▷ **have** - **5.** (*abbr of* **has not**), ▷ **have**.

air [eə⁻] ⬦ *n* - **1.** [gen] aire *m*; **into the air** al aire; **by air** en avión; **(up) in the air** *fig* en el aire; **to clear the air** *fig* aclarar las cosas - **2.** [tune] melodía *f* - **3.** RADIO & TV: **on the air** en el aire. ⬦ *comp* aéreo(a). ⬦ *vt* - **1.** [clothes, sheets] airear; [cupboard, room] ventilar - **2.** [views, opinions] expresar - **3.** *US* [broadcast] emitir. ⬦ *vi* [clothes, sheets] airearse; [cupboard, room] ventilarse.

◆ **airs** *npl*: **airs and graces** aires *mpl*; **to give o.s. airs, to put on airs** darse aires.

airbag ['eəbæg] *n* AUT airbag *m*.

airbase ['eəbeɪs] *n* base *f* aérea.

airbed ['eəbed] *n* UK colchón *m* inflable.

airborne ['eəbɔ:n] *adj* - **1.** [troops] aerotransportado(da); [attack] aéreo(a) - **2.** [plane] en el aire, en vuelo.

airbrake ['eəbreɪk] *n* freno *m* neumático.

airbus ['eəbʌs] *n* aerobús *m*.

air-conditioned [-kən'dɪʃnd] *adj* climatizado(da), con aire acondicionado.

air-conditioning [-kən'dɪʃnɪŋ] *n* aire *m* acondicionado.

aircraft ['eəkrɑ:ft] (*pl* **aircraft**) *n* [plane] avión *m*; [any flying machine] aeronave *f*.

aircraft carrier *n* portaaviones *m inv*.

air cushion *n* cojín *m* neumático.

airfield ['eəfi:ld] *n* campo *m* de aviación.

airforce ['eəfɔ:s] ⬦ *n*: **the airforce** las fuerzas aéreas. ⬦ *comp* de las fuerzas aéreas.

air freight *n* transporte *m* por vía aérea.

airgun ['eəgʌn] *n* pistola *f* de aire comprimido.

airhostess ['eə,həʊstɪs] *n* azafata *f*, aeromoza *f Amér*.

airily ['eərəlɪ] *adv* alegremente, despreocupadamente.

airing ['eərɪŋ] *n*: **to give sthg an airing** [clothes, linen] orear OR airear algo; [room] ventilar algo; [opinions] expresar algo.

airing cupboard *n* UK *armario seco y caliente en el que se encuentra la caldera del agua y que se utiliza para guardar la ropa.*

airlane ['eəleɪn] *n* ruta *f* aérea.

airless ['eəlıs] *adj* mal ventilado(da), cargado(da).

airletter ['eəletəʳ] *n* aerograma *m*.

airlift ['eəlıft] <> *n* puente *m* aéreo. <> *vt* aerotransportar, transportar por avión.

airline ['eəlaın] *n* línea *f* aérea.

airliner ['eəlaınəʳ] *n* avión *m* (grande) de pasajeros.

airlock ['eəlɒk] *n* **- 1.** [in tube, pipe] bolsa *f* de aire **- 2.** [airtight chamber] cámara *f* OR esclusa *f* de aire.

airmail ['eəmeıl] *n* correo *m* aéreo; **by airmail** por correo aéreo.

airman ['eəmən] (*pl* -men [-mən]) *n* [aviator] aviador *m*.

air mattress *n* colchón *m* inflable.

airplane ['eəpleın] *n US* avión *m*.

airplay ['eəpleı] *n* tiempo *m* de emisión, cobertura *f* radiofónica.

airpocket ['eəpɒkıt] *n* bolsa *f* de aire.

airport ['eəpɔːt] <> *n* aeropuerto *m*. <> *comp* de aeropuerto.

air raid *n* ataque *m* aéreo.

air-raid shelter *n* refugio *m* antiaéreo.

air rifle *n* fusil *m* de aire comprimido.

airship ['eəʃıp] *n* dirigible *m*.

airsick ['eəsık] *adj*: **to be airsick** marearse *(en el avión)*.

airspace ['eəspeıs] *n* espacio *m* aéreo.

airspeed ['eəspiːd] *n* velocidad *f* de vuelo.

air steward *n* auxiliar *m* de vuelo, aeromozo *m Amér*.

air stewardess *n* auxiliar *f* de vuelo, azafata *f*.

airstrip ['eəstrıp] *n* pista *f* de aterrizaje.

air terminal *n* terminal *f* aérea.

airtight ['eətaıt] *adj* hermético(ca).

airtime ['eətaım] *n* [on radio] espacio *m* radiofónico, cobertura *f* radiofónica.

air-to-air *adj* [missile] aire-aire *(inv)*.

air-traffic control *n* control *m* del tráfico aéreo.

air-traffic controller *n* controlador aéreo *m*, controladora aérea *f*.

air travel *n* (*U*) viajes *mpl* en avión.

airwaves ['eəweıvz] *npl* ondas *fpl*; **on the airwaves** en antena.

airy ['eərı] (*comp* -ier, *superl* -iest) *adj* **- 1.** [room] espacioso(sa) y bien ventilado(da) **- 2.** [fanciful] vano(na), ilusorio(ria) **- 3.** [nonchalant] despreocupado(da).

aisle [aıl] *n* **- 1.** [in church] nave *f* lateral **- 2.** [in plane, theatre, supermarket] pasillo *m*.

ajar [ə'dʒɑːʳ] *adj* entreabierto(ta).

AK *abbr of* Alaska.

aka (*abbr of* also known as) alias.

akin [ə'kın] *adj*: **akin to sthg/to doing sthg** semejante a algo/a hacer algo.

AL *abbr of* Alabama.

Alabama [,ælə'bæmə] *n* Alabama.

alabaster [,ælə'bɑːstəʳ] *n* alabastro *m*.

alacrity [ə'lækrətı] *n* presteza *f*, prontitud *f*.

alarm [ə'lɑːm] <> *n* alarma *f*; **to raise** OR **sound the alarm** dar la (voz de) alarma. <> *vt* alarmar, asustar.

alarm clock *n* despertador *m*.

alarming [ə'lɑːmıŋ] *adj* alarmante.

alarmingly [ə'lɑːmıŋlı] *adv* de manera alarmante.

alarmist [ə'lɑːmıst] *adj* alarmista.

alas [ə'læs] <> *adv* desgraciadamente. <> *excl liter* ¡ay!

Alaska [ə'læskə] *n* Alaska.

Albania [æl'beınjə] *n* Albania.

Albanian [æl'beınjən] <> *adj* albanés(esa). <> *n* **- 1.** [person] albanés *m*, -esa *f* **- 2.** [language] albanés *m*.

albatross ['ælbətrɒs] (*pl* **albatross** OR **-es**) *n* [bird, in golf] albatros *m*.

albeit [ɔːl'biːıt] *conj fml* aunque, si bien.

Alberta [æl'bɜːtə] *n* Alberta.

albino [æl'biːnəʊ] (*pl* **-s**) <> *n* albino *m*, -na *f*. <> *comp* albino(na).

album ['ælbəm] *n* **- 1.** [of stamps, photos] álbum *m* **- 2.** [record] elepé *m*.

alchemy ['ælkəmı] *n* alquimia *f*.

alcohol ['ælkəhɒl] *n* alcohol *m*.

alcoholic [,ælkə'hɒlık] <> *adj* alcohólico(ca). <> *n* alcohólico *m*, -ca *f*.

alcoholism ['ælkəhɒlızm] *n* alcoholismo *m*.

alcopop ['ælkəʊpɒp] *n refresco gaseoso que contiene un cierto porcentaje de alcohol*.

alcove ['ælkəʊv] *n* hueco *m*.

alderman ['ɔːldəmən] (*pl* **-men** [-mən]) *n* ≈ concejal *m*, -la *f*.

ale [eıl] *n tipo de cerveza*.

alert [ə'lɜːt] <> *adj* **- 1.** [vigilant] atento(ta) **- 2.** [perceptive] despierto(ta) **- 3.** [aware]: **to be alert to** ser consciente de. <> *n* [gen & MIL] alerta *f*; **to be on the alert** estar alerta. <> *vt* alertar; **to alert sb to sthg** alertar a alguien de algo.

Aleutian Islands [ə'luːʃjən-] *npl*: **the Aleutian Islands** las islas Aleutianas.

A level (*abbr of* **Advanced level**) *n* UK SCH *nivel escolar necesario para acceder a la universidad.*

A level

> Exámenes de acceso a la universidad en el Reino Unido. Se caracterizan por un alto grado de especialización ya que no se hacen en más de dos o tres asignaturas (excepcionalmente cuatro). Asimismo, las notas son decisivas a la hora de acceder al centro donde se desea cursar estudios.

alfalfa [æl'fælfə] *n* alfalfa *f.*

alfresco [æl'freskəʊ] *adj* & *adv* al aire libre.

algae ['ældʒiː] *npl* algas *fpl.*

algebra ['ældʒɪbrə] *n* álgebra *f.*

Algeria [æl'dʒɪərɪə] *n* Argelia.

Algerian [æl'dʒɪərɪən] <> *adj* argelino(na). <> *n* argelino *m*, -na *f.*

algorithm ['ælgərɪðm] *n* algoritmo *m.*

alias ['eɪlɪəs] <> *adv* alias. <> *n* (*pl* **-es**) alias *m inv.*

alibi ['ælɪbaɪ] *n* coartada *f.*

alien ['eɪljən] <> *adj* **- 1.** [foreign] foráneo(a), extranjero(ra) **- 2.** [from outer space] extraterrestre **- 3.** [unfamiliar] extraño(ña), ajeno(na). <> *n* **- 1.** [from outer space] extraterrestre *mf* **- 2.** LAW [foreigner] extranjero *m*, -ra *f.*

alienate ['eɪljəneɪt] *vt* **- 1.** [make unsympathetic] ganarse la antipatía de **- 2.** [distance emotionally]: **to be alienated from** estar distanciado(da) de.

alienation [,eɪljə'neɪʃn] *n* **- 1.** [separation] separación *f*, alejamiento *m* **- 2.** [not belonging] alienación *f.*

alight [ə'laɪt] <> *adj* [on fire] prendido(da), ardiendo; **to set sthg alight** prender fuego a algo. <> *vi* (*pt* & *pp* **-ed**) *fml* **- 1.** [land] posarse **- 2.** [get off]: **to alight from** apearse de.

align [ə'laɪn] *vt* **- 1.** [line up] alinear, poner en línea **- 2.** [ally]: **to align o.s. with** alinearse con.

alignment [ə'laɪnmənt] *n* **- 1.** [arrangement] alineación *f* **- 2.** [alliance] alineamiento *m.*

alike [ə'laɪk] <> *adj* parecido(da). <> *adv* [treat] de la misma forma, por igual; **to look alike** parecerse; **to think alike** pensar igual.

alimentary canal [,ælɪ'mentərɪ-] *n* tubo *m* digestivo.

alimony ['ælɪmənɪ] *n* pensión *f* alimenticia.

A-line *adj* de vuelo.

alive [ə'laɪv] *adj* **- 1.** [living] vivo(va); **to stay alive** sobrevivir **- 2.** [tradition] con vida **- 3.** [active, lively] lleno(na) de vida; **to come**

alive [story, description] cobrar vida; [person, place] animarse **- 4.** [aware]: **to be alive to** ser consciente de **- 5.** [rats, insects]: **to be alive with** estar infestado(da) de; [rumour, speculation] bullir de.

alkali ['ælkəlaɪ] (*pl* **-s** OR **-ies**) *n* álcali *m.*

alkaline ['ælkəlaɪn] *adj* alcalino(na).

all [ɔːl] <> *adj* **- 1.** (*with sing n*) todo(da); **all the drink** toda la bebida; **all violence is to be condemned** toda forma de violencia es condenable; **all day** todo el día; **all night** toda la noche; **all the time** todo el tiempo OR el rato **- 2.** (*with npl*) todos(das); **all the boxes** todas las cajas; **all men** todos los hombres; **all three died** los tres murieron. <> *pron* **- 1.** (*sing*) [the whole amount] todo *m*, -da *f*; **she drank it all, she drank all of it** se lo bebió todo **- 2.** (*pl*) [everybody, everything] todos *mpl*, -das *f*; **all of them came, they all came** vinieron todos **- 3.** (*with superl*): **he's the cleverest of all** es el más listo de todos; **the most amazing thing of all** lo más impresionante de todo; **best/worst of all...** lo mejor/peor de todo es que... <> *adv* **- 1.** [entirely] completamente; **I'd forgotten all about that** me había olvidado completamente de eso; **it spilled all over the carpet** se derramó por toda la alfombra; **she was dressed all in red** iba vestida toda de rojo; **all alone** completamente solo(la); **that's all very well, but...** sí, eso está muy bien, pero... **- 2.** [in sport, competitions]: **the score is two all** el resultado es de empate a dos; **thirty all** [in tennis] treinta iguales **- 3.** (*with compar*): **the situation was made all the worse by his arrival** la situación se hizo peor si cabe con su llegada; **to run all the faster** correr aun más rápido.

◆ **all but** *adv* casi.

◆ **all in all** *adv* en conjunto.

◆ **all that** *adv* tan; **she's not all that pretty** no es tan guapa.

◆ **for all** <> *prep* a pesar de. <> *conj*: **for all I know** por lo que yo sé; **do it, for all I care!** pues hazlo, ¡a mí qué me importa!

◆ **in all** *adv* en total.

Allah ['ælə] *n* Alá *m.*

all-around US = **all-round.**

allay [ə'leɪ] *vt fml* [suspicions, doubts] despejar; [fears] apaciguar.

all clear *n* **- 1.** [signal] señal *f* de cese de peligro **- 2.** *fig* [go-ahead] luz *f* verde.

allegation [,ælɪ'geɪʃn] *n* acusación *f*; **to make allegations (about)** hacer acusaciones (acerca de).

allege [ə'ledʒ] *vt* alegar; **to allege that** alegar que; **to be alleged to have done/said** ser acusado de haber hecho/dicho.

alleged [ə'ledʒd] *adj* presunto(ta).

allegedly [ə'ledʒɪdlɪ] *adv* presuntamente.

allegiance [ə'li:dʒəns] *n* lealtad *f*.

allegorical [,ælɪ'gɒrɪkl] *adj* alegórico(ca).

allegory ['ælɪgərɪ] (*pl* -ies) *n* alegoría *f*.

alleluia [,ælɪ'lu:jə] *excl* ¡aleluya!

allergic [ə'lɜ:dʒɪk] *adj lit* & *fig*: **allergic (to sthg)** alérgico(ca) (a algo).

allergy ['ælədʒɪ] (*pl* -ies) *n* alergia *f*; **to have an allergy to** tener alergia a.

alleviate [ə'li:vɪeɪt] *vt* aliviar.

alley(way) ['ælɪ(weɪ)] *n* callejuela *f*.

alliance [ə'laɪəns] *n* alianza *f*.

allied ['ælaɪd] *adj* - **1.** [powers, troops] aliado(da) - **2.** [subjects] análogo(ga), afín.

alligator ['ælɪgeɪtər] (*pl* **alligator** OR -**s**) *n* caimán *m*.

all-important *adj* de suma importancia, crucial.

all-in *adj* UK [inclusive] todo incluido.

◆ **all in** ◇ *adj inf* [tired] hecho(cha) polvo. ◇ *adv* [inclusive] todo incluido.

all-in wrestling *n* lucha *f* libre.

alliteration [ə,lɪtə'reɪʃn] *n* aliteración *f*.

all-night *adj* [party etc] que dura toda la noche; [chemist, bar] abierto(ta) toda la noche.

allocate ['æləkeɪt] *vt*: **to allocate sthg to sb** [money, resources] destinar algo a alguien; [task, tickets, seats] asignar algo a alguien.

allocation [,ælə'keɪʃn] *n* - **1.** [sharing out - of money, resources] distribución *f*, reparto *m*; [- of task, tickets, seats] asignación *f* - **2.** [share - of money, resources] distribución *f*, reparto *m*; [- of tickets, seats] asignación *f*.

allot [ə'lɒt] (*pt* & *pp* -**ted**, *cont* -**ting**) *vt* [job, time] asignar; [money, resources] destinar.

allotment [ə'lɒtmənt] *n* - **1.** UK [garden] *parcela municipal arrendada para su cultivo* - **2.** [sharing out - of job, time] asignación *f*; [- of money, resources] distribución *f* - **3.** [share - of money, resources] porción *f*, asignación *f*; [- of time] espacio *m* (de tiempo) concedido.

allow [ə'laʊ] *vt* - **1.** [permit] permitir, dejar; **to allow sb to do sthg** permitir OR dejar a alguien hacer algo; **allow me** permítame - **2.** [set aside - money] apartar, destinar; [- time] dejar - **3.** [officially accept - subj: person] conceder; [- subj: law] admitir, permitir - **4.** [concede]: **to allow that** admitir OR reconocer que.

◆ **allow for** *vt insep* tener en cuenta, contar con.

allowable [ə'laʊəbl] *adj* permisible.

allowance [ə'laʊəns] *n* - **1.** [money received - from government] subsidio *m*; [- from employer] dietas *fpl*; **clothing allowance** asignación *f* para ropa - **2.** US [pocket money] paga *f*, asignación *f* semanal - **3.** FIN desgravación *f* - **4.**: **to**

make allowances for sthg/sb [forgive] disculpar algo/a alguien; [take into account] tener en cuenta algo/a alguien.

alloy ['ælɔɪ] *n* aleación *f*.

all-powerful *adj* todopoderoso(sa), omnipotente.

all right ◇ *adv* - **1.** [gen] bien - **2.** [only just acceptably] (más o menos) bien - **3.** [in answer - yes] vale, bueno - **4.** [certainly] seguro, sin duda; **it's her all right** seguro que es ella - **5.** [do you understand?]: **all right?** ¿vale? - **6.** [now then] bueno, vale; **all right, children, stop talking now!** ¡venga, niños, callaos de una vez! ◇ *adj* - **1.** [gen] bien - **2.** [not bad]: **it's all right, but...** no está mal, pero... - **3.** [allowable]: **is it all right if...?** ¿te importa si...? - **4.** [OK]: **sorry – that's all right** lo siento – no importa.

all-round UK, **all-around** US *adj* - **1.** [multiskilled] completo(ta), polifacético(ca) - **2.** [comprehensive] amplio(plia), extenso(sa).

all-rounder [-'raʊndər] *n* - **1.** [versatile person] persona *f* que hace de todo - **2.** [sportsman, sportswoman] deportista completo *m*, -ta *f*.

all-terrain vehicle *n* todoterreno *m*.

all-time *adj* [favourite] de todos los tiempos; [high, low] histórico(ca).

allude [ə'lu:d] *vi*: **to allude to** aludir a.

allure [ə'ljʊər] *n* encanto *m*, atractivo *m*.

alluring [ə'ljʊərɪŋ] *adj* [person] atrayente; [thing] tentador(ra).

allusion [ə'lu:ʒn] *n* alusión *f*.

ally ◇ *n* ['ælaɪ] (*pl* -ies) aliado *m*, -da *f*. ◇ *vt* [ə'laɪ] (*pt* & *pp* -**ied**): **to ally o.s. with** aliarse con.

◆ **Allies** *npl*: **the Allies** los Aliados.

almanac ['ɔ:lmənæk] *n* [yearbook] anuario *m*; [calendar] almanaque *m*.

almighty [ɔ:l'maɪtɪ] *adj inf* [very big] descomunal.

◆ **Almighty** ◇ *adj* todopoderoso(sa). ◇ *n*: **the Almighty** el Todopoderoso.

almond ['ɑ:mənd] *n* - **1.** [nut] almendra *f* - **2.** [tree] almendro *m*.

almond paste *n* mazapán *m*, pasta *f* de almendras.

almost ['ɔ:lməʊst] *adv* casi.

alms [ɑ:mz] *npl dated* limosna *f*.

aloft [ə'lɒft] *adv* - **1.** [in the air] en lo alto - **2.** NAUT entre el velamen.

alone [ə'ləʊn] ◇ *adj* solo(la); **to be alone with** estar a solas con; **all alone** completamente solo. ◇ *adv* - **1.** [without others] solo(la) - **2.** [only] sólo.

▸▸ **to go it alone** ir por cuenta propia OR por libre; **to leave sthg/sb alone** dejar algo/a alguien en paz.

let alone *conj* no digamos, y mucho menos.

along [ə'lɒŋ] <> *adv* - **1.** [forward] hacia delante; **to go** OR **walk along** avanzar; **she was walking along** iba andando - **2.** [with others or oneself]: **bring it along** tráetelo - **3.** [to this or that place]: **to come along** venir; **to go along** ir. <> *prep* - **1.** [towards one end of, beside] por, a lo largo de - **2.** [in] en; **he lives along Dalry Road** vive en Dalry Road.

all along *adv* todo el rato; **she knew all along** lo sabía desde el principio.

along with *prep* junto con.

alongside [ə,lɒŋ'saɪd] <> *prep* - **1.** [next to] junto a - **2.** [together with] junto con. <> *adv*: **to come alongside** ponerse a la misma altura; **to work alongside** trabajar juntos(tas).

aloof [ə'luːf] <> *adj* frío(a), distante. <> *adv* distante, a distancia; **to remain aloof (from)** mantenerse a distancia (de).

aloud [ə'laʊd] *adv* en alto, en voz alta.

alpaca [æl'pækə] *n* [animal, wool] alpaca *f*.

alphabet ['ælfəbet] *n* alfabeto *m*.

alphabetical [,ælfə'betɪkl] *adj* alfabético(ca); **in alphabetical order** en OR por orden alfabético.

alphabetically [,ælfə'betɪklɪ] *adv* alfabéticamente.

alphabetize, -ise ['ælfəbətaɪz] *vt* ordenar alfabéticamente.

alphanumeric [,ælfənjuː'merɪk] *adj* COMPUT alfanumérico(ca).

alpine ['ælpaɪn] *adj* alpino(na).

Alps [ælps] *npl*: **the Alps** los Alpes.

already [ɔːl'redɪ] *adv* ya.

alright [,ɔːl'raɪt] = **all right**.

Alsace [æl'sæs] *n* Alsacia.

Alsatian [æl'seɪʃn] <> *adj* [of Alsace] alsaciano(na). <> *n* - **1.** [person] alsaciano *m*, -na *f* - **2.** [dog] pastor *m* alemán.

also ['ɔːlsəʊ] *adv* también.

also-ran *n* comparsa *mf*.

Alta. *abbr of* **Alberta**.

altar ['ɔːltəʳ] *n* altar *m*.

alter ['ɔːltəʳ] <> *vt* [modify] alterar, modificar; **to have a dress altered** mandar arreglar un vestido. <> *vi* cambiar.

alteration [,ɔːltə'reɪʃn] *n* - **1.** [gen] alteración *f*; **to make an alteration/alterations to** hacer una modificación/modificaciones en - **2.** [to dress] arreglo *m*.

altercation [,ɔːltə'keɪʃn] *n* altercado *m*.

alter ego (*pl* -s) *n* álter ego *m*.

alternate <> *adj* [UK ɔːl'tɜːnət, US 'ɒːltərnət] - **1.** [by turns] alterno(na) - **2.** [every other]: **on alternate days/weeks** cada dos días/semanas. <> *n* [UK ɔːl'tɜːnət, US 'ɒːltərnət] US sustitu-

to(ta). <> *vt* ['ɔːltərneɪt] alternar. <> *vi* ['ɔːltərneɪt]: **to alternate (with/between)** alternar (con/entre).

alternately [ɔːl'tɜːnətlɪ] *adv* alternativamente.

alternating current ['ɔːltərneɪtɪŋ-] *n* ELEC corriente *f* alterna.

alternation [,ɔːltə'neɪʃn] *n* alternancia *f*.

alternative [ɔːl'tɜːnətɪv] <> *adj* alternativo(va). <> *n* alternativa *f*, opción *f*; **to have no alternative (but to do sthg)** no tener más remedio (que hacer algo).

alternatively [ɔːl'tɜːnətɪvlɪ] *adv* o bien.

alternative medicine *n* medicina *f* alternativa.

alternator ['ɔːltərneɪtər] *n* ELEC alternador *m*.

although [ɔːl'ðəʊ] *conj* aunque.

altitude ['æltɪtjuːd] *n* altitud *f*.

alto ['æltəʊ] (*pl* -s) <> *n* [female singer] contralto *f*; [male singer] contralto *m*. <> *comp* alto.

altogether [,ɔːltə'geðər] *adv* - **1.** [completely] completamente, totalmente; **not altogether** no del todo - **2.** [considering all things] en conjunto, en general - **3.** [in total] en total.

altruism ['æltruɪzm] *n* altruismo *m*.

altruistic [,æltrʊ'ɪstɪk] *adj* altruista.

aluminium UK [,æljʊ'mɪnɪəm], **aluminum** US [ə'luːmɪnəm] <> *n* aluminio *m*. <> *comp* de aluminio.

alumnus [ə'lʌmnəs] (*pl* -ni [-naɪ]) *n* ex-alumno *m*, -na *f*.

always ['ɔːlweɪz] *adv* siempre.

Alzheimer's disease ['æltshaɪməz-] *n* enfermedad *f* de Alzheimer.

am [æm] *vb* |⊃ **be**.

a.m. (*abbr of* **ante meridiem**): **at 3 a.m.** a las tres de la mañana.

AM (*abbr of* **amplitude modulation**) *n* AM *f*.

amalgam [ə'mælgəm] *n fml* & TECH amalgama *f*.

amalgamate [ə'mælgəmeɪt] <> *vt* [ideas] amalgamar; [companies, organizations] fusionar. <> *vi* [of ideas] amalgamarse; [of companies, organizations] fusionarse.

amalgamation [ə,mælgə'meɪʃn] *n* fusión *f*.

amass [ə'mæs] *vt* [fortune, wealth] amasar.

amateur ['æmətər] <> *adj* aficionado(da); *pej* chapucero(ra), poco profesional. <> *n* aficionado *m*, -da *f*; *pej* chapucero *m*, -ra *f*.

amateurish [,æmə'tɜːrɪʃ] *adj* chapucero(ra), poco profesional.

amaze [ə'meɪz] *vt* asombrar.

amazed [ə'meɪzd] *adj* asombrado(da).

amazement [ə'meɪzmənt] *n* asombro *m*; **to my amazement** para gran sorpresa mía.

amazing [ə'meɪzɪŋ] *adj* - **1.** [surprising] asombroso(sa) - **2.** [excellent] genial.

amazingly [ə'meɪzɪŋlɪ] *adv* increíblemente.

Amazon ['æməzn] *n* - **1.** [river]: **the Amazon** el Amazonas - **2.** [region]: **the Amazon (Basin)** la Amazonia, la cuenca amazónica; **the Amazon rainforest** la selva amazónica - **3.** [woman] amazona *f*.

Amazonian [,æmə'zəʊnjən] *adj* amazónico(ca).

ambassador [æm'bæsədər] *n* embajador *m*, -ra *f*.

amber ['æmbər] <> *adj* - **1.** [amber-coloured] de color ámbar, ambarino(na) - **2.** UK [traffic light] ámbar. <> *n* ámbar *m*. <> *comp* [made of amber] de ámbar.

ambiance ['æmbɪəns] = **ambience**.

ambidextrous [,æmbɪ'dekstrəs] *adj* ambidiestro(tra).

ambience, ambiance ['æmbɪəns] *n* ambiente *m*.

ambiguity [,æmbɪ'gjuːətɪ] (*pl* -**ies**) *n* ambigüedad *f*.

ambiguous [æm'bɪgjʊəs] *adj* ambiguo(gua).

ambiguously [æm'bɪgjʊəslɪ] *adv* ambiguamente.

ambition [æm'bɪʃn] *n* ambición *f*.

ambitious [æm'bɪʃəs] *adj* ambicioso(sa).

ambivalence [æm'bɪvələns] *n* ambivalencia *f*.

ambivalent [æm'bɪvələnt] *adj* ambivalente.

amble ['æmbl] *vi* [walk] deambular.

ambulance ['æmbjʊləns] <> *n* ambulancia *f*. <> *comp*: **ambulance man** ambulanciero *m*; **ambulance woman** ambulanciera *f*.

ambush ['æmbʊʃ] <> *n* emboscada *f*. <> *vt* emboscar.

ameba US = **amoeba**.

ameliorate [ə'miːljəreɪt] *vt* & *vi fml* mejorar.

amen [,ɑː'men] *excl* amén.

amenable [ə'miːnəbl] *adj* receptivo(va); **amenable to** favorable a.

amend [ə'mend] *vt* [law] enmendar; [text] corregir; [schedule] modificar.
◆ **amends** *npl*: **to make amends for sthg** reparar algo.

amendment [ə'mendmənt] *n* - **1.** [change - to law] enmienda *f*; [- to text] corrección *f*; [- to schedule] modificación *f* - **2.** [act of changing] enmienda *f*, rectificación *f*.

amenities [ə'miːnətɪz] *npl* [of town] facilidades *fpl*; [of building] comodidades *fpl*.

America [ə'merɪkə] *n* América.
◆ **Americas** *npl*: **the Americas** las Américas.

American [ə'merɪkn] <> *adj* americano(na). <> *n* [person] americano *m*, -na *f*.

American Indian *n* amerindio *m*, -dia *f*.

Americanism [ə'merɪkənɪzm] *n* americanismo *m*.

americanize, -ise [ə'merɪkənaɪz] *vt* americanizar.

amethyst ['æmɪθɪst] *n* amatista *f*.

Amex ['æmeks] *n* - **1.** (*abbr of* **American Stock Exchange**), *segundo mercado bursátil estadounidense* - **2.** (*abbr of* **American Express**) American Express *f*.

amiable ['eɪmjəbl] *adj* amable, agradable.

amiably ['eɪmjəblɪ] *adv* amablemente.

amicable ['æmɪkəbl] *adj* amigable, amistoso(sa).

amicably ['æmɪkəblɪ] *adv* amigablemente, amistosamente.

amid(st) [ə'mɪd(st)] *prep fml* entre, en medio de.

amino acid [ə'miːnəʊ-] *n* aminoácido *m*.

amiss [ə'mɪs] <> *adj*: **something's amiss** algo va mal. <> *adv*: **to take sthg amiss** tomarse algo a mal.

ammo ['æməʊ] *n* (U) *inf* MIL munición *f*.

ammonia [ə'məʊnjə] *n* amoniaco *m*.

ammunition [,æmjʊ'nɪʃn] *n* (U) - **1.** MIL municiones *fpl* - **2.** *fig* [information, argument] argumentos *mpl*.

ammunition dump *n* arsenal *m* OR depósito *m* de municiones.

amnesia [æm'niːzjə] *n* amnesia *f*.

amnesty ['æmnəstɪ] (*pl* -**ies**) *n* amnistía *f*.

Amnesty International *n* Amnistía *f* Internacional.

amoeba UK [ə'miːbə] (*pl* -**bas** OR -**bae** [-biː]), **ameba** US (*pl* -**bas** OR -**bae** [-biː]) *n* ameba *f*.

amok [ə'mɒk], **amuck** *adv*: **to run amok** *enloquecer atacando a gente de forma indiscriminada*.

among(st) [ə'mʌŋ(st)] *prep* entre.

amoral [,eɪ'mɒrəl] *adj* amoral.

amorous ['æmərəs] *adj* apasionado(da).

amorphous [ə'mɔːfəs] *adj* amorfo(fa).

amortize [ə'mɔːtaɪz] *vt* FIN amortizar.

amount [ə'maʊnt] *n* cantidad *f*.
◆ **amount to** *vt insep* - **1.** [total] ascender a - **2.** [be equivalent to] venir a ser.

amp [æmp] *n* - **1.** *abbr of* **ampere** - **2.** *inf* (*abbr of* **amplifier**) ampli *m*.

amperage ['æmpərɪdʒ] *n* ELEC amperaje *m*.

ampere ['æmpeər] *n* amperio *m*.

ampersand ['æmpəsænd] *n* signo " & ".

amphetamine [æm'fetəmiːn] *n* anfetamina *f*.

amphibian [æm'fɪbɪən] *n* anfibio *m*.

amphibious [æm'fɪbɪəs] *adj* [animal, vehicle] anfibio(bia).

amphitheatre UK, **amphitheater** US ['æmfɪ,θɪətər] *n* anfiteatro *m*.

ample ['æmpl] *adj* - **1.** [enough] suficiente; [more than enough] sobrado(da); **to have ample time** tener tiempo de sobra - **2.** [garment, room] amplio(plia); [stomach, bosom] abundante.

amplification [ˌæmplɪfɪ'keɪʃn] *n* - **1.** [of sound] amplificación *f* - **2.** [of idea, statement] desarrollo *m*, explicación *f*.

amplifier ['æmplɪfaɪəʳ] *n* amplificador *m*.

amplify ['æmplɪfaɪ] <> *vt* - **1.** [sound] amplificar - **2.** [idea, statement] desarrollar, ampliar. <> *vi* (*pt & pp* **-ied**)**: to amplify (on sthg)** ampliar (algo).

amply ['æmplɪ] *adv* - **1.** [sufficiently] suficientemente; [more than sufficiently] sobradamente - **2.** [considerably] abundantemente, ampliamente.

ampoule *UK,* **ampule** *US* ['æmpu:l] *n* ampolla *f*.

amputate ['æmpjʊteɪt] *vt & vi* amputar.

amputation [ˌæmpjʊ'teɪʃn] *n* amputación *f*.

Amsterdam [ˌæmstə'dæm] *n* Amsterdam.

Amtrak ['æmtræk] *n organismo que regula y coordina las líneas férreas en Estados Unidos.*

amuck [ə'mʌk] = **amok**.

amulet ['æmjʊlɪt] *n* amuleto *m*.

amuse [ə'mju:z] *vt* - **1.** [make laugh, smile] divertir - **2.** [entertain] distraer; **to amuse o.s. (by doing sthg)** distraerse (haciendo algo).

amused [ə'mju:zd] *adj* - **1.** [person, look] divertido(da); **I was not amused at** OR **by that** no me hizo gracia eso - **2.** [entertained]**: to keep o.s. amused** entretenerse, distraerse.

amusement [ə'mju:zmənt] *n* - **1.** [enjoyment] regocijo *m*, diversión *f* - **2.** [diversion, game] atracción *f*.

amusement arcade *n* salón *m* de juegos.

amusement park *n* parque *m* de atracciones.

amusing [ə'mju:zɪŋ] *adj* divertido(da), gracioso(sa).

an *(stressed* [æn]*, unstressed* [ən]*)* ▷ **a**.

anabolic steroid [ˌænə'bɒlɪk-] *n* esteroide *m* anabolizante.

anachronism [ə'nækrənɪzm] *n* anacronismo *m*.

anachronistic [əˌnækrə'nɪstɪk] *adj* anacrónico(ca).

anaemia *UK,* **anemia** *US* [ə'ni:mjə] *n* anemia *f*.

anaemic *UK,* **anemic** *US* [ə'ni:mɪk] *adj* - **1.** [ill] anémico(ca) - **2.** *fig & pej* [weak, poor] pobre.

anaesthesia *UK,* **anesthesia** *US* [ˌænɪs'θi:zjə] *n* anestesia *f*.

anaesthetic *UK,* **anesthetic** *US* [ˌænɪs'θetɪk] *n* anestesia *f*; **under anaesthetic** bajo los efectos de la anestesia; **local/general anaesthetic** anestesia local/general.

anaesthetist *UK,* **anesthetist** *US* [æ'ni:sθətɪst] *n* anestesista *mf*.

anaesthetize *UK,* **-ise** *UK,* **anesthetize** *US* [æ'ni:sθətaɪz] *vt* anestesiar.

anagram ['ænəgræm] *n* anagrama *m*.

anal ['eɪnl] *adj* anal.

analgesic [ˌænæl'dʒi:sɪk] <> *adj* analgésico(ca). <> *n* analgésico *m*.

analog *US adj & n* = **analogue**.

analogous [ə'næləgəs] *adj fml*: **analogous (to)** análogo(ga) (a).

analogue, analog *US* ['ænəlɒg] <> *adj* [watch, clock] analógico(ca). <> *n fml* equivalente *m*.

analogy [ə'nælədʒɪ] (*pl* **-ies**) *n* analogía *f*; **to draw an analogy with/between** establecer una analogía con/entre; **by analogy** por analogía.

analyse *UK,* **analyze** *US* ['ænəlaɪz] *vt* analizar.

analysis [ə'næləsɪs] (*pl* **analyses** [ə'næləsi:z]) *n* - **1.** [examination] análisis *m inv*; **in the final** OR **last analysis** a fin de cuentas - **2.** [psychoanalysis] psicoanálisis *m inv*; **she is in analysis** se está psicoanalizando.

analyst ['ænəlɪst] *n* - **1.** [gen] analista *mf* - **2.** [psychoanalyst] psicoanalista *mf*.

analytic(al) [ˌænə'lɪtɪk(l)] *adj* analítico(ca).

analyze *US* = **analyse**.

anarchic [æ'nɑ:kɪk] *adj* anárquico(ca).

anarchist ['ænəkɪst] *n* anarquista *mf*.

anarchy ['ænəkɪ] *n* anarquía *f*.

anathema [ə'næθəmə] *n*: **the idea is anathema to me** la idea me parece aberrante.

anatomical [ˌænə'tɒmɪkl] *adj* anatómico(ca).

anatomy [ə'nætəmɪ] (*pl* **-ies**) *n* anatomía *f*.

ANC (*abbr of* **African National Congress**) *n* ANC *m*.

ancestor ['ænsestəʳ] *n lit & fig* antepasado *m*.

ancestry ['ænsestrɪ] (*pl* **-ies**) *n* ascendencia *f*.

anchor ['æŋkəʳ] <> *n* NAUT ancla *f*; **to drop anchor** echar el ancla; **to weigh anchor** levar anclas. <> *vt* - **1.** [secure] sujetar - **2.** *esp US* TV presentar. <> *vi* NAUT anclar.

anchorage ['æŋkərɪdʒ] *n* - **1.** NAUT fondeadero *m* - **2.** [means of securing] sujeción *f*.

anchorman ['æŋkəmæn] (*pl* **-men** [-men]) *n* TV presentador *m*, locutor *m*.

anchorwoman ['æŋkəˌwʊmən] (*pl* **-women** [-ˌwɪmɪn]) *n* presentadora *f*, locutora *f*.

anchovy ['æntʃəvɪ] (*pl* **anchovy** OR **-ies**) *n* [salted] anchoa *f*; [fresh, in vinegar] boquerón *m*.

ancient ['eɪnʃənt] *adj* - **1.** [gen] antiguo(gua) - **2.** *hum* [very old] vetusto(ta).

ancillary [æn'sɪlərɪ] *adj* auxiliar.

and *(strong form* [ænd]*, weak form* [ən]*)* conj - **1.** [gen] y; *(before 'i' or 'hi')* e; **fish and chips**

pescado con patatas fritas; **faster and faster** cada vez más rápido; **it's nice and easy** es sencillito **- 2.** [in numbers]: **one hundred and eighty** ciento ochenta; **one and a half** uno y medio; **2 and 2 is 4** 2 y 2 son 4 **- 3.** [to]: **try and come** intenta venir; **come and see the kids** ven a ver a los niños; **wait and see** espera a ver.

➤ **and so on, and so forth** adv etcétera, y cosas así.

Andalusia [,ændə'lu:ziə] n Andalucía.

Andalusian [,ændə'lu:ziən] <> adj andaluz(za). <> n andaluz m, -za f.

Andes ['ændi:z] npl: **the Andes** los Andes.

Andorra [æn'dɔ:rə] n Andorra.

androgynous [æn'drɒdʒɪnəs] adj andrógino(na).

android ['ændrɔɪd] n androide m.

anecdote ['ænɪkdəʊt] n anécdota f.

anemia US = anaemia.

anemic US = anaemic.

anemone [ə'nemənɪ] n anémona f.

anesthesiologist [,ænɪs,θi:zɪ'ɒlədʒɪst] n anestesista mf.

anesthetic etc US = anaesthetic.

anew [ə'nju:] adv de nuevo, nuevamente.

angel ['eɪndʒəl] n **- 1.** RELIG ángel m **- 2.** inf [delightful person] cielo m, sol m; **angel food cake** US bizcocho ligero elaborado con claras de huevo.

Angeleno [,ændʒə'li:nəʊ] n habitante de Los Ángeles.

angelic [æn'dʒelɪk] adj angelical.

anger ['æŋgə'] <> n ira f, furia f. <> vt enfadar.

angina [æn'dʒaɪnə] n angina f de pecho.

angle ['æŋgl] <> n **- 1.** [gen] ángulo m; **the picture was hanging at an angle** [aslant] el cuadro estaba colgado torcido **- 2.** [point of view] enfoque m. <> vi **- 1.** [fish] pescar (con caña) **- 2.** [manoeuvre]: **to angle for** andar detrás de OR a la caza de.

angler ['æŋglə'] n pescador m, -ra f (con caña).

Anglican ['æŋglɪkən] <> adj anglicano(na). <> n anglicano m, -na f.

anglicism ['æŋglɪsɪzm] n anglicismo m.

angling ['æŋglɪŋ] n pesca f con caña.

Anglo ['æŋgləʊ] prefix anglo-.

Anglo-Saxon [,æŋgləʊ'sæksn] <> adj anglosajón(ona). <> n **- 1.** [person] anglosajón m, -ona f **- 2.** [language] anglosajón m.

Angola [æŋ'gəʊlə] n Angola.

Angolan [æŋ'gəʊlən] <> adj angoleño(ña). <> n angoleño m, -ña f.

angora [æŋ'gɔ:rə] n **- 1.** [goat] cabra f de angora; [rabbit] conejo m de angora **- 2.** [material] angora f.

angrily ['æŋgrəlɪ] adv airadamente.

angry ['æŋgrɪ] (comp -ier, superl -iest) adj [person] enfadado(da); [letter, look, face] furioso(sa), airado(da); **to be angry at** OR **with sb** estar enfadado con alguien; **to get angry with sb** enfadarse con alguien.

angst [æŋst] n angustia f vital.

anguish ['æŋgwɪʃ] n angustia f.

anguished ['æŋgwɪʃt] adj angustiado(da).

angular ['æŋgjʊlə'] adj [face, body] anguloso(sa).

animal ['ænɪml] <> adj [instincts, kingdom] animal; [rights] de los animales. <> n [creature] animal m; pej [person] animal mf.

animate ['ænɪmət] adj animado(da).

animated ['ænɪmeɪtɪd] adj animado(da).

animated cartoon n dibujos mpl animados.

animation [,ænɪ'meɪʃn] n **- 1.** [excitement] emoción f, entusiasmo m **- 2.** [of cartoons] animación f.

animosity [,ænɪ'mɒsətɪ] (pl -ies) n animosidad f, animadversión f.

aniseed ['ænɪsi:d] n anís m.

ankle ['æŋkl] <> n tobillo m. <> comp: **ankle boots** botines mpl; **ankle socks** calcetines mpl cortos.

annals ['ænlz] npl anales mpl.

annex esp US ['æneks] <> n edificio m anejo. <> vt anexionar.

annexation [,ænek'seɪʃn] n anexión f.

annexe esp UK ['æneks] n edificio m anejo.

annihilate [ə'naɪəleɪt] vt [destroy] aniquilar.

annihilation [ə,naɪə'leɪʃn] n [destruction] aniquilación f.

anniversary [,ænɪ'vɜ:sərɪ] (pl -ies) n aniversario m.

annotate ['ænəteɪt] vt fml anotar.

announce [ə'naʊns] vt anunciar.

announcement [ə'naʊnsmənt] n anuncio m.

announcer [ə'naʊnsə'] n: **radio/television announcer** presentador m, -ra f OR locutor m, -ra f de radio/televisión.

annoy [ə'nɔɪ] vt fastidiar, molestar.

annoyance [ə'nɔɪəns] n molestia f.

annoyed [ə'nɔɪd] adj: **to be annoyed at sthg/ with sb** estar molesto(ta) por algo/con alguien; **to get annoyed at sthg/with sb** molestarse por algo/con alguien.

annoying [ə'nɔɪɪŋ] adj fastidioso(sa), irritante.

annual ['ænjʊəl] <> adj anual. <> n **- 1.** [plant] planta f anual **- 2.** [book] anuario m.

annual general meeting n asamblea f general anual.

annually ['ænjʊəlɪ] *adv* anualmente.

annuity [ə'njuːɪtɪ] (*pl* **-ies**) *n* FIN anualidad *f*.

annul [ə'nʌl] (*pt* & *pp* **-led**, *cont* **-ling**) *vt* anular.

annulment [ə'nʌlmənt] *n* anulación *f*.

annum ['ænəm] *n*: **per annum** al año.

Annunciation [ə,nʌnsɪ'eɪʃn] *n*: **the Annunciation** la Anunciación *f*.

anode ['ænəʊd] *n* ánodo *m*.

anoint [ə'nɔɪnt] *vt* ungir.

anomalous [ə'nɒmələs] *adj* anómalo(la).

anomaly [ə'nɒmətlɪ] (*pl* **-ies**) *n* anomalía *f*.

anon. [ə'nɒn] (*abbr of* **anonymous**) anón.

anonymity [,ænə'nɪmətɪ] *n* anonimato *m*.

anonymous [ə'nɒnɪməs] *adj* anónimo(ma).

anonymously [ə'nɒnɪməslɪ] *adv* anónimamente.

anorak ['ænəræk] *n* - **1.** *esp UK* [garment] chubasquero *m*, anorak *m* - **2.** *UK inf* [boring person] petardo *m*, -da *f*.

anorexia (nervosa) [,ænə'reksɪə(nɜː'vəʊsə)] *n* anorexia *f*.

anorexic [,ænə'reksɪk] <> *adj* anoréxico(ca). <> *n* anoréxico *m*, -ca *f*.

another [ə'nʌðə^r] <> *adj* otro(tra); **another one** otro(tra); **in another few minutes** en unos minutos más. <> *pron* otro *m*, -tra *f*; **one after another** uno tras otro, una tras otra; **one another** el uno al otro, la una a la otra; **we love one another** nos queremos; **with one another** el uno con el otro, la una con la otra.

ANSI (*abbr of* **American National Standards Institute**) *n instituto estadounidense de normalización.*

answer ['ɑːnsə^r] <> *n* - **1.** [gen] respuesta *f*; **in answer to** en respuesta a - **2.** [to problem] solución *f*. <> *vt* - **1.** [reply to] responder a, contestar a - **2.** [respond to]: **to answer the door** abrir la puerta; **to answer the phone** coger OR contestar el teléfono. <> *vi* responder, contestar.

🔹 **answer back** *vt sep* & *vi* replicar.

🔹 **answer for** *vt insep* - **1.** [accept responsibility for] responder por; **they have a lot to answer for** tienen mucho que explicar - **2.** [suffer consequences of] responder de.

answerable ['ɑːnsərəbl] *adj*: **answerable (to sb/for sthg)** responsable (ante alguien/de algo).

answering machine ['ɑːnsərɪŋ-] *n* contestador *m* automático.

ant [ænt] *n* hormiga *f*.

antacid [,ænt'æsɪd] *n* antiácido *m*.

antagonism [æn'tægənɪzm] *n* antagonismo *m*.

antagonist [æn'tægənɪst] *n* antagonista *mf*.

antagonistic [æn,tægə'nɪstɪk] *adj* hostil, hostil.

antagonize, -ise [æn'tægənaɪz] *vt* provocar la hostilidad de.

Antarctic [æn'tɑːktɪk] <> *adj* antártico(ca). <> *n*: **the Antarctic** el Antártico.

Antarctica [æn'tɑːktɪkə] *n* (la) Antártida.

Antarctic Circle *n*: **the Antarctic Circle** el Círculo Polar Antártico.

Antarctic Ocean *n*: **the Antarctic Ocean** el océano Antártico.

ante ['æntɪ] *n inf fig*: **to up** OR **raise the ante** subir la apuesta.

anteater ['ænt,iːtə^r] *n* oso *m* hormiguero.

antecedent [,æntɪ'siːdənt] *n fml* [previous event] antecedente *m*.

antediluvian [,æntɪdɪ'luːvjən] *adj hum* antediluviano(na).

antelope ['æntɪləʊp] (*pl* **antelope** OR **-s**) *n* antílope *m*.

antenatal [,æntɪ'neɪtl] *adj* prenatal.

antenatal clinic *n* clínica *f* de preparación al parto.

antenna [æn'tenə] *n* - **1.** (*pl* **-nae** [-niː]) [of insect] antena *f* - **2.** (*pl* **-s**) *US* [aerial] antena *f*.

anteroom ['æntɪrʊm] *n* [antechamber] antesala *f*; [waiting room] sala *f* de espera.

anthem ['ænθəm] *n* himno *m*.

anthill ['ænthɪl] *n* hormiguero *m*.

anthology [æn'θɒlədʒɪ] (*pl* **-ies**) *n* antología *f*.

anthrax ['ænθræks] *n* ántrax *m inv*, carbunco *m*.

anthropologist [,ænθrə'pɒlədʒɪst] *n* antropólogo *m*, -ga *f*.

anthropology [,ænθrə'pɒlədʒɪ] *n* antropología *f*.

anti- ['æntɪ] *prefix* anti-.

antiaircraft [,æntɪ'eəkrɑːft] *adj* antiaéreo(a).

antiballistic missile [,æntɪbə'lɪstɪk-] *n* misil *m* antibalístico.

antibiotic [,æntɪbaɪ'ɒtɪk] *n* antibiótico *m*.

antibody ['æntɪ,bɒdɪ] (*pl* **-ies**) *n* anticuerpo *m*.

anticipate [æn'tɪsɪpeɪt] *vt* - **1.** [expect] prever - **2.** [look forward to] esperar ansiosamente - **3.** [preempt] adelantarse a.

anticipation [æn,tɪsɪ'peɪʃn] *n* [excitement] expectación *f*; **in anticipation** con impaciencia; **in anticipation of** en previsión de.

anticlimax [,æntɪ'klaɪmæks] *n* decepción *f*.

anticlockwise [,æntɪ'klɒkwaɪz] *UK* <> *adj* contrario(ria) al sentido de las agujas del reloj. <> *adv* en sentido contrario al de las agujas del reloj.

antics ['æntɪks] *npl* payasadas *fpl*.

anticyclone [,æntɪ'saɪkləʊn] *n* anticiclón *m*.

antidepressant [,æntɪdɪ'presnt] *n* antidepresivo *m*.

antidote ['æntɪdəʊt] *n lit* & *fig*: antidote (to) antídoto *m* (contra).

antifreeze ['æntɪfriːz] *n* anticongelante *m*.

Antigua [æn'tiːgə] *n* Antigua; **Antigua and Barbuda** Antigua y Barbuda.

antihero ['æntɪ,hɪərəʊ] (*pl* **-es**) *n* antihéroe *m*.

antihistamine [,æntɪ'hɪstəmɪn] *n* antihistamínico *m*.

antipathy [æn'tɪpəθɪ] *n*: antipathy (to OR towards) antipatía *f* (hacia OR por).

antipersonnel ['æntɪ,pɜːsə'nel] *adj* MIL antipersonal.

antiperspirant [,æntɪ'pɜːspərənt] *n* antitranspirante *m*.

antiquarian [,æntɪ'kweərɪən] <> *adj* [bookshop] especializado(da) en libros antiguos. <> *n* anticuario *m*, -ria *f*.

antiquated ['æntɪkweɪtɪd] *adj* anticuado(da).

antique [æn'tiːk] <> *adj* [furniture, object] antiguo(gua). <> *n* antigüedad *f*.

antique dealer *n* anticuario *m*, -ria *f*.

antique shop *n* tienda *f* de antigüedades.

antiquity [æn'tɪkwətɪ] (*pl* **-ies**) *n* antigüedad *f*.

anti-Semitic [-sɪ'mɪtɪk] *adj* antisemita.

anti-Semitism [-'semɪtɪzm] *n* antisemitismo *m*.

antiseptic [,æntɪ'septɪk] <> *adj* antiséptico(ca). <> *n* antiséptico *m*.

antisocial [,æntɪ'səʊʃl] *adj* - **1.** [against society] antisocial - **2.** [unsociable] poco sociable.

antistatic [,æntɪ'stætɪk] *adj* antiestático(ca).

antitank [,æntɪ'tæŋk] *adj* antitanque *(inv)*.

antithesis [æn'tɪθɪsɪs] (*pl* **-theses** [-θɪsiːz]) *n* antítesis *f inv*.

antivirus ['æntɪ'vaɪrəs] *adj* COMPUT antivirus *(inv)*.

antonym ['æntənɪm] *n* antónimo *m*.

Antwerp ['æntwɜːp] *n* Amberes.

anus ['eɪnəs] *n* ano *m*.

anvil ['ænvɪl] *n* yunque *m*.

anxiety [æŋ'zaɪətɪ] (*pl* **-ies**) *n* - **1.** [worry] ansiedad *f*, inquietud *f* - **2.** [cause of worry] preocupación *f* - **3.** [keenness] afán *m*, ansia *f*.

anxious ['æŋkʃəs] *adj* - **1.** [worried] preocupado(da); **to be anxious about** estar preocupado por - **2.** [keen]: **to be anxious that/to do sthg** estar ansioso(sa) por que/por hacer algo.

anxiously ['æŋkʃəslɪ] *adv* con inquietud.

any ['enɪ] <> *adj* - **1.** *(with negative)* ninguno(na); **I haven't read any books** no he leído ningún libro; **I haven't got any money** no tengo nada de dinero - **2.** [some] algún(una); **are there any cakes left?** ¿queda algún pastel?; **is there any milk left?** ¿queda algo de leche?; **can I be of any help?** ¿le puedo ayudar en algo?; **have**

you got any money? ¿tienes dinero? - **3.** [no matter which] cualquier; **any box will do** cualquier caja vale - **4.** □> **case**, **day**, **moment**, **rate**. <> *pron* - **1.** *(with negative)* ninguno *m*, -na *f*; **I didn't get any** a mí no me tocó ninguno - **2.** [some] alguno *m*, -na *f*; **can any of you do it?** ¿sabe alguno de vosotros hacerlo?; **I need some matches, do you have any?** necesito cerillas, ¿tienes?; **few foreign films, if any, are successful here** muy pocas películas extranjeras, por no decir ninguna, tienen éxito aquí - **3.** [no matter which] cualquiera; **take any you like** coge cualquiera que te guste. <> *adv* - **1.** *(with negative)*: **I can't see it any more** ya no lo veo; **he's not feeling any better** no se siente nada mejor; **I can't stand it any longer** no lo aguanto más - **2.** [some, a little]: **do you want any more potatoes?** ¿quieres más patatas?; **is that any better/different?** ¿es así mejor/diferente?

anybody ['enɪ,bɒdɪ] = **anyone**.

anyhow ['enɪhaʊ] *adv* - **1.** [in spite of that] de todos modos - **2.** [carelessly] de cualquier manera - **3.** [in any case] en cualquier caso.

anyone ['enɪwʌn], **anybody** *pron* - **1.** *(in negative sentences)* nadie; **I don't know anyone** no conozco a nadie - **2.** *(in questions)* alguien - **3.** [any person] cualquiera.

anyplace ['enɪpleɪs] US = **anywhere**.

anything ['enɪθɪŋ] *pron* - **1.** *(in negative sentences)* nada; **I don't want anything** no quiero nada - **2.** *(in questions)* algo; **would you like anything else?** ¿quiere algo más? - **3.** [any object, event] cualquier cosa; **it could be anything between two and five** no sé, de dos a cinco.
➤ **anything but** *adv* cualquier cosa menos.

anyway ['enɪweɪ] *adv* - **1.** [in any case] de todas formas OR maneras - **2.** [in conversation] en cualquier caso.

anywhere ['enɪweəʳ], **anyplace** US ['enɪpleɪs] *adv* - **1.** *(in negative sentences)* en ningún sitio; **I didn't go anywhere** no fui a ninguna parte - **2.** *(in questions)* en algún sitio; **did you go anywhere?** ¿fuiste a algún sitio? - **3.** [wherever] cualquier sitio; **anywhere you like** donde quieras - **4.** [any amount, number]: **anywhere between 10 and 100 people** de 10 a 100 personas.

Anzac ['ænzæk] (*abbr of* Australia-New Zealand Army Corps) *n* soldado *australiano o neocelandés*.

AOB, a.o.b. (*abbr of* any other business) *ruegos y preguntas*.

Apache [ə'pætʃɪ] *n* apache *mf*.

apart [ə'pɑːt] *adv* - **1.** [separated] separado(da); **they're not very far apart** están bastante jun-

tos; **we're living apart** vivimos separados
- 2. [in several parts]: **to take sth apart** desmontar algo; **to fall apart** hacerse pedazos
- 3. [aside] aparte; **joking apart** bromas aparte.

➡ **apart from** prep **- 1.** [except for] aparte de,
salvo **- 2.** [as well as] aparte de.

apartheid [ə'pɑːtheɪt] n apartheid m.

apartment [ə'pɑːtmənt] n esp US piso m, apartamento m, departamento m Amér.

apartment building n US bloque m de pisos,
bloque m de departamentos Amér.

apathetic [ˌæpə'θetɪk] adj apático(ca).

apathy ['æpəθɪ] n apatía f.

ape [eɪp] ◇ n simio m. ◇ vt pej copiar, imitar.

Apennines ['æpɪnaɪnz] npl: **the Apennines** los
Apeninos.

aperitif [əperə'tiːf] n aperitivo m.

aperture ['æpə,tjʊəʳ] n abertura f.

apex ['eɪpeks] (pl **-es** OR **apices**) n [top] vértice m.

APEX ['eɪpeks] (abbr of advance purchase excursion) n UK (tarifa f) APEX f.

aphid ['eɪfɪd] n pulgón m.

aphorism ['æfərɪzm] n aforismo m.

aphrodisiac [ˌæfrə'dɪzɪæk] n afrodisíaco m.

apices ['eɪpɪsiːz] pl ⊏⊐ apex.

apiece [ə'piːs] adv cada uno(na).

aplomb [ə'plɒm] n aplomo m.

apocalypse [ə'pɒkəlɪps] n apocalipsis m inv.

apocalyptic [ə,pɒkə'lɪptɪk] adj apocalípti-
co(ca).

apogee ['æpədʒiː] n fig & ASTRON apogeo m.

apolitical [ˌeɪpə'lɪtɪkəl] adj apolítico(ca).

apologetic [ə,pɒlə'dʒetɪk] adj [tone, look] lle-
no(na) de disculpas; **to be very apologetic
(about)** no hacer más que disculparse (por).

apologetically [ə,pɒlə'dʒetɪklɪ] adv pidiendo
disculpas OR perdón.

apologize, -ise [ə'pɒlədʒaɪz] vi: **to apologize
(to sb for sth)** disculparse (ante alguien por
algo); **I apologized to her** le pedí perdón.

apology [ə'pɒlədʒɪ] (pl **-ies**) n disculpa f; **Tom
sends his apologies** [can't come] Tom se excusa por no poder asistir.

apoplectic [ˌæpə'plektɪk] adj **- 1.** MED apopléti-
co(ca) **- 2.** inf [very angry] enfurecido(da).

apoplexy ['æpəpleksɪ] n apoplejía f.

apostle [ə'pɒsl] n RELIG apóstol m.

apostrophe [ə'pɒstrəfɪ] n apóstrofo m.

appal (UK **-led**, cont **-ling**), **appall** US [ə'pɔːl] vt
horrorizar.

Appalachian [ˌæpə'leɪtʃən] ◇ adj apalache.
◇ n: **the Appalachians, the Appalachian
Mountains** los (montes) Apalaches.

appall US = appal.

appalled [ə'pɔːld] adj horrorizado(da).

appalling [ə'pɔːlɪŋ] adj **- 1.** [shocking] horroro-
so(sa) **- 2.** [very bad] pésimo(ma).

appallingly [ə'pɔːlɪŋlɪ] adv **- 1.** [shockingly]
horrorosamente **- 2.** [very badly] pésimamente.

apparatus [ˌæpə'reɪtəs] (pl **apparatus** OR **-es**) n
- 1. [equipment] aparatos mpl; **a piece of apparatus** un aparato **- 2.** POL aparato m.

apparel [ə'pærəl] n US ropa f.

apparent [ə'pærənt] adj **- 1.** [evident] evidente,
patente; **for no apparent reason** sin motivo
aparente **- 2.** [seeming] aparente.

apparently [ə'pærəntlɪ] adv **- 1.** [it seems] al parecer, por lo visto, diz que Amér **- 2.** [seemingly]
aparentemente.

apparition [ˌæpə'rɪʃn] n fml aparición f.

appeal [ə'piːl] ◇ vi **- 1.** [request]: **to appeal (to
sb for sth)** solicitar (de alguien algo) **- 2.** [to
sb's honour, common sense]: **to appeal to** apelar
a **- 3.** LAW: **to appeal (against)** apelar (contra)
- 4. [attract, interest]: **to appeal (to)** atraer (a).
◇ n **- 1.** [request] llamamiento m, súplica f;
[fundraising campaign] campaña f para recaudar fondos **- 2.** LAW apelación f **- 3.** [charm, in-
terest] atractivo m.

appealing [ə'piːlɪŋ] adj **- 1.** [attractive] atracti-
vo(va) **- 2.** [touching] [look, tone] suplicante.

appear [ə'pɪəʳ] vi **- 1.** [gen] aparecer **- 2.** [seem]:
to appear (to be/to do sth) parecer (ser/ha-
cer algo); **it would appear that...** parece
que... **- 3.** [in play, film, on TV]: **to appear on
TV/in a film** salir en televisión/en una película **- 4.** LAW: **to appear (before)** comparecer
(ante).

appearance [ə'pɪərəns] n **- 1.** [gen] aparición f; **to make an appearance** aparecer; **to
put in an appearance** hacer acto de presen-
cia **- 2.** [of sportsman] actuación f **- 3.** [look - of
person, place, object] aspecto m; **by** OR **to all appearances** por lo que parece; **to keep up appearances** guardar las apariencias.

appease [ə'piːz] vt aplacar, apaciguar.

appeasement [ə'piːzmənt] n **- 1.** [placating]
apaciguamiento m **- 2.** POL contemporiza-
ción f.

append [ə'pend] vt fml **- 1.** [add]: **to append
sth (to sth)** agregar algo (a algo) **- 2.** [attach
- document]: **to append sth (to sth)** adjuntar algo (a algo).

appendage [ə'pendɪdʒ] n apéndice m, añadido m.

appendices [ə'pendɪsiːz] npl ⊏⊐ appendix.

appendicitis [ə,pendɪ'saɪtɪs] n (U) apendicitis f
inv.

appendix [ə'pendɪks] (*pl* -dixes OR -dices) *n* [gen & ANAT] apéndice *m*; **to have one's appendix out** OR **removed** operarse de apendicitis.

appetite ['æpɪtaɪt] *n* - **1.** [for food] apetito *m*; **I no longer have any appetite for my food** ya no tengo ganas de comer - **2.** *fig* [enthusiasm]: **appetite for** entusiasmo *m* por.

appetizer, -iser ['æpɪtaɪzəʳ] *n* aperitivo *m*, pasapalos *m inv* Amér.

appetizing, -ising ['æpɪtaɪzɪŋ] *adj* [food] apetitoso(sa).

applaud [ə'plɔːd] *vt* & *vi* *lit* & *fig* aplaudir.

applause [ə'plɔːz] *n* (*U*) aplausos *mpl*.

apple ['æpl] *n* manzana *f*; **she's the apple of my eye** *inf* es la niña de mis ojos.

apple pie *n* pastel *m* de manzana.

apple tree *n* manzano *m*.

appliance [ə'plaɪəns] *n* aparato *m*; **domestic appliance** electrodoméstico *m*.

applicable [ə'plɪkəbl] *adj*: **to be applicable (to)** aplicarse (a).

applicant ['æplɪkənt] *n*: **applicant (for)** solicitante *mf* (de).

application [,æplɪ'keɪʃn] *n* - **1.** [gen] aplicación *f* - **2.** [for job, college, club]: **application (for)** solicitud *f* (para) - **3.** COMPUT aplicación *f*.

application form *n* impreso *m* de solicitud.

applicator ['æplɪkeɪtəʳ] *n* aplicador *m*.

applied [ə'plaɪd] *adj* [science] aplicado(da).

appliqué [ə'pliːkeɪ] *n* SEW aplicación *f*, sobrepuesto *m*.

apply [ə'plaɪ] (*pt* & *pp* -ied) ⬦ *vt* [gen] aplicar; [brakes] echar; **to apply o.s. (to sthg)** aplicarse (en algo). ⬦ *vi* - **1.** [for work, grant] presentar una solicitud; **to apply to sb for sthg** solicitar a alguien algo - **2.** [be relevant] aplicarse; **to apply to** concernir a.

appoint [ə'pɔɪnt] *vt* - **1.** [to job, position]: **to appoint sb (to sthg)** nombrar a alguien (para algo); **to appoint sb as sthg** nombrar a alguien algo - **2.** *fml* [agree]: **at the appointed time** a la hora señalada.

appointment [ə'pɔɪntmənt] *n* - **1.** [to job, position] nombramiento *m*; **'by appointment to Her Majesty the Queen'** 'proveedor de la familia real' - **2.** [job, position] puesto *m*, cargo *m* - **3.** [with businessman, lawyer] cita *f*; [with doctor, hairdresser] hora *f*; **to have an appointment** [with businessman] tener una cita; [with doctor] tener hora; **to make an appointment** concertar una cita; **by appointment** mediante cita.

apportion [ə'pɔːʃn] *vt* [money] repartir; [blame] adjudicar.

apposite ['æpəzɪt] *adj* *fml* oportuno(na).

appraisal [ə'preɪzl] *n* evaluación *f*, valoración *f*.

appraise [ə'preɪz] *vt* *fml* evaluar, valorar.

appreciable [ə'priːʃəbl] *adj* [difference] apreciable, sensible.

appreciably [ə'priːʃəblɪ] *adv* [differ] sensiblemente.

appreciate [ə'priːʃɪeɪt] ⬦ *vt* - **1.** [value, like] apreciar - **2.** [recognize, understand] entender, darse cuenta de - **3.** [be grateful for] agradecer. ⬦ *vi* FIN revalorizarse.

appreciation [ə,priːʃɪ'eɪʃn] *n* - **1.** [liking] aprecio *m* - **2.** [recognition, understanding] entendimiento *m* - **3.** [gratitude] gratitud *f*, agradecimiento *m* - **4.** FIN revalorización *f*, plusvalía *f* - **5.** [of novel, play] crítica *f*.

appreciative [ə'priːʃjətɪv] *adj* [person, remark] agradecido(da); [audience] entendido(da).

apprehend [,æprɪ'hend] *vt* *fml* [arrest] capturar, aprehender.

apprehension [,æprɪ'henʃn] *n* [anxiety] aprensión *f*.

apprehensive [,æprɪ'hensɪv] *adj* aprensivo(va).

apprehensively [,æprɪ'hensɪvlɪ] *adv* con aprensión.

apprentice [ə'prentɪs] ⬦ *n* aprendiz *m*, -za *f*. ⬦ *vt*: **to be apprenticed to sb** estar de aprendiz con alguien.

apprenticeship [ə'prentɪʃɪp] *n* aprendizaje *m*.

approach [ə'prəʊtʃ] ⬦ *n* - **1.** [arrival] llegada *f* - **2.** [way in] acceso *m* - **3.** [method] enfoque *m*, planteamiento *m* - **4.** [to person]: **to make approaches to sb** hacerle propuestas a alguien. ⬦ *vt* - **1.** [come near to] acercarse a - **2.** [ask]: **to approach sb about sthg** dirigirse a alguien acerca de algo - **3.** [problem, situation] abordar - **4.** [level, speed] aproximarse a. ⬦ *vi* aproximarse, acercarse.

approachable [ə'prəʊtʃəbl] *adj* accesible.

approaching [ə'prəʊtʃɪŋ] *adj* próximo(ma), cercano(na).

approbation [,æprə'beɪʃn] *n* *fml* aprobación *f*.

appropriate ⬦ *adj* [ə'prəʊprɪət] apropiado(da), adecuado(da). ⬦ *vt* [ə'prəʊprɪeɪt] - **1.** LAW [take] apropiarse de - **2.** [allocate] destinar.

appropriately [ə'prəʊprɪətlɪ] *adv* de manera apropiada, adecuadamente.

appropriation [ə,prəʊprɪ'eɪʃn] *n* - **1.** [taking] apropiación *f* - **2.** [allocation] asignación *f*.

approval [ə'pruːvl] *n* - **1.** [admiration] aprobación *f* - **2.** [official sanctioning] visto *m* bueno - **3.** COMM: **on approval** a prueba.

approve [ə'pruːv] <> *vi* estar de acuerdo; **to approve of sthg/sb** ver con buenos ojos algo/a alguien. <> *vt* aprobar.

approved [ə'pruːvd] *adj* - **1.** [method] aprobado(da), reconocido(da) - **2.** [supplier] autorizado(da).

approving [ə'pruːvɪŋ] *adj* aprobatorio(ria).

approx. [ə'prɒks] (*abbr of* **approximately**) aprox.

approximate <> *adj* [ə'prɒksɪmət] aproximado(da). <> *vi* [ə'prɒksɪmeɪt]: **to approximate to** aproximarse a.

approximately [ə'prɒksɪmətlɪ] *adv* aproximadamente.

approximation [ə,prɒksɪ'meɪʃn] *n* - **1.** [of number, position] cálculo *m* aproximado - **2.** [similarity]: **approximation (to)** aproximación *f* (a).

Apr. (*abbr of* **April**) abr.

APR *n* - **1.** (*abbr of* **annualized percentage rate**) TAE *mf* - **2.** (*abbr of* **annual purchase rate**), tasa *de* adquisición anual.

après-ski [,æpreɪ'skiː] *n* alterne nocturno en una estación de esquí.

apricot ['eɪprɪkɒt] <> *n* - **1.** [fruit] albaricoque *m*, chabacano *m* Méx, damasco *m* Andes - **2.** [colour] color *m* albaricoque. <> *comp* de albaricoque.

April ['eɪprəl] *n* abril *m*; *see also* **September**.

April Fools' Day *n* primero *m* de abril, ≃ Día *m* de los Santos Inocentes.

apron ['eɪprən] *n* - **1.** [clothing] delantal *m*, mandil *m*; **to be tied to sb's apron strings** *inf* estar pegado a las faldas de alguien - **2.** AERON pista *f* de estacionamiento.

apropos ['æprəpəʊ] <> *adj* oportuno(na). <> *prep*: **apropos (of)** hablando de.

apt [æpt] *adj* - **1.** [pertinent] acertado(da) - **2.** [likely]: **apt to do sthg** propenso(sa) a hacer algo.

Apt. (*abbr of* **apartment**) Apto.

aptitude ['æptɪtjuːd] *n* aptitud *f*; **to have an aptitude for** tener aptitudes para.

aptitude test *n* prueba *f* de aptitud.

aptly ['æptlɪ] *adv* apropiadamente.

aqualung ['ækwəlʌŋ] *n* escafandra *f* autónoma.

aquamarine [,ækwəmə'riːn] *n* [colour] color *m* aguamarina.

aquaplane ['ækwəpleɪn] *vi* UK AUT patinar.

aquarium [ə'kweərɪəm] (*pl* **-riums** OR **-ria** [-rɪə]) *n* acuario *m*.

Aquarius [ə'kweərɪəs] *n* Acuario *m*; **to be (an) Aquarius** ser Acuario.

aquatic [ə'kwætɪk] *adj* acuático(ca).

aqueduct ['ækwɪdʌkt] *n* acueducto *m*.

AR *abbr of* **Arkansas**.

Arab ['ærəb] <> *adj* árabe. <> *n* - **1.** [person] árabe *mf* - **2.** [horse] caballo *m* árabe.

Arabia [ə'reɪbjə] *n* Arabia.

Arabian [ə'reɪbjən] *adj* árabe, arábigo(ga).

Arabian desert *n*: **the Arabian desert** el Desierto de Arabia.

Arabian Sea *n*: **the Arabian Sea** el Mar de Omán.

Arabic ['ærəbɪk] <> *adj* árabe. <> *n* [language] árabe *m*.

Arabic numeral *n* número *m* arábigo.

arable ['ærəbl] *adj* cultivable.

Aragon ['ærəgən] *n* Aragón.

arbiter ['ɑːbɪtər] *n fml* árbitro *m*.

arbitrary ['ɑːbɪtrərɪ] *adj* [random] arbitrario(ria).

arbitrate ['ɑːbɪtreɪt] *vi* arbitrar.

arbitration [,ɑːbɪ'treɪʃn] *n* arbitraje *m*; **the dispute has gone to arbitration** el conflicto ha sido llevado ante un árbitro.

arc [ɑːk] *n* arco *m*.

ARC (*abbr of* **AIDS-related complex**) *n* enfermedad relacionada con el sida.

arcade [ɑː'keɪd] *n* - **1.** [shopping arcade] galería *f* comercial - **2.** [covered passage] arcada *f*, galería *f*.

arcade game *n* videojuego *m*.

arch [ɑːtʃ] <> *adj* travieso(sa), pícaro(ra). <> *n* - **1.** ARCHIT arco *m* - **2.** [of foot] puente *m*. <> *vt* arquear. <> *vi*: **the bridge arches over the river** el puente cruza el río formando un arco.

arch- [ɑːtʃ] *prefix*: **arch-rival** máximo rival.

archaeological,   **archeological** [,ɑːkɪə'lɒdʒɪkl] *adj* arqueológico(ca).

archaeologist, archeologist [,ɑːkɪ'ɒlədʒɪst] *n* arqueólogo *m*, **-ga** *f*.

archaeology, archeology [,ɑːkɪ'ɒlədʒɪ] *n* arqueología *f*.

archaic [ɑː'keɪɪk] *adj* arcaico(ca).

archangel ['ɑːk,eɪndʒəl] *n* arcángel *m*.

archbishop [,ɑːtʃ'bɪʃəp] *n* arzobispo *m*.

archduchess [,ɑːtʃ'dʌtʃɪs] *n* archiduquesa *f*.

archduke [,ɑːtʃ'djuːk] *n* archiduque *m*.

arched [ɑːtʃt] *adj* [gen] arqueado(da); [roof] abovedado(da).

archenemy [,ɑːtʃ'enɪmɪ] (*pl* **-ies**) *n* peor enemigo *m*, enemigo acérrimo.

archeological = **archaeological**.

archeologist = **archaeologist**.

archeology = **archaeology**.

archer ['ɑːtʃər] *n* arquero *m*.

archery ['ɑːtʃərɪ] *n* tiro *m* con arco.

archetypal [,ɑːkɪ'taɪpl] *adj* arquetípico(ca).

archetype ['ɑ:kɪtaɪp] *n* arquetipo *m*.

archipelago [ˌɑ:kɪ'peligəʊ] (*pl* **-es** OR **-s**) *n* archipiélago *m*.

architect ['ɑ:kɪtekt] *n* **- 1.** [of buildings] arquitecto *m*, -ta *f* **- 2.** *fig* [of plan, event] artífice *mf*.

architectural [ˌɑ:kɪ'tektʃərəl] *adj* arquitectónico(ca).

architecture ['ɑ:kɪtektʃə'] *n* [gen & COMPUT] arquitectura *f*.

archive file ['ɑ:kaɪv-] *n* COMPUT fichero *m* archivado.

archives ['ɑ:kaɪvz] *npl* [of documents] archivos *mpl*.

archivist ['ɑ:kɪvɪst] *n* archivero *m*, -ra *f*.

archway ['ɑ:tʃweɪ] *n* [passage] arcada *f*; [entrance] entrada *f* en forma de arco.

Arctic Circle *n*: **the Arctic Circle** el Círculo Polar Ártico.

ardent ['ɑ:dənt] *adj* [supporter, admirer, desire] ardiente, ferviente.

ardour UK, **ardor** US ['ɑ:də'] *n* ardor *m*.

arduous ['ɑ:djʊəs] *adj* arduo(dua).

are (*weak form* [ə'], *strong form* [ɑ:r]) ⊳ **be**.

area ['eərɪə] *n* **- 1.** [region, designated space] zona *f*, área *f*; **in the area** en la zona **- 2.** [of town] zona *f*, barrio *m* **- 3.** *fig* [approximate size, number]: **in the area of** del orden de, alrededor de **- 4.** [surface size] superficie *f*, área *f* **- 5.** [of knowledge, interest] campo *m*.

area code *n* US prefijo *m* (telefónico).

arena [ə'ri:nə] *n* **- 1.** SPORT palacio *m*, pabellón *m* **- 2.** *fig* [area of activity]: **she entered the political arena** saltó al ruedo político.

aren't [ɑ:nt] (*abbr of* are not), ⊳ **be**.

Argentina [ˌɑ:dʒən'ti:nə] *n* (la) Argentina.

Argentine ['ɑ:dʒəntaɪn] ⟨⟩ *adj* argentino(na). ⟨⟩ *n* argentino *m*, -na *f*.

Argentinian [ˌɑ:dʒən'tɪnɪən] ⟨⟩ *adj* argentino(na). ⟨⟩ *n* argentino *m*, -na *f*.

arguable ['ɑ:gjʊəbl] *adj* **- 1.** [questionable] discutible **- 2.** [possible]: **it is arguable that...** se podría afirmar que...

arguably ['ɑ:gjʊəblɪ] *adv* probablemente.

argue ['ɑ:gju:] ⟨⟩ *vi* **- 1.** [quarrel]: **to argue (with sb about sthg)** discutir (con alguien de algo) **- 2.** [reason]: **to argue (for)** abogar (por); **to argue (against)** oponerse (a). ⟨⟩ *vt*: **to argue that** argumentar que.

argument ['ɑ:gjʊmənt] *n* **- 1.** [gen] discusión *f*; **to have an argument (with)** tener una discusión (con) **- 2.** [reason] argumento *m*.

argumentative [ˌɑ:gjʊ'mentətɪv] *adj* propenso(sa) a discutir.

aria ['ɑ:rɪə] *n* aria *f*.

arid ['ærɪd] *adj* *lit* & *fig* árido(da).

Aries ['eəri:z] *n* Aries *m*; **to be (an) Aries** ser Aries.

arise [ə'raɪz] (*pt* **arose**, *pp* **arisen** [ə'rɪzn]) *vi* [appear]: **to arise (from)** surgir (de).

aristocracy [ˌærɪ'stɒkrəsɪ] (*pl* **-ies**) *n* aristocracia *f*.

aristocrat [UK 'ærɪstəkræt, US ə'rɪstəkræt] *n* aristócrata *mf*.

aristocratic [UK ˌærɪstə'krætɪk, US ə,rɪstə'krætɪk] *adj* aristocrático(ca).

arithmetic [ə'rɪθmətɪk] *n* aritmética *f*.

Arizona [ˌærɪ'zəʊnə] *n* Arizona.

ark [ɑ:k] *n* arca *f*.

Arkansas ['ɑ:kənsɔ:] *n* Arkansas.

arm [ɑ:m] ⟨⟩ *n* **- 1.** [of person, chair, record player] brazo *m*; **arm in arm** del brazo; **to chance one's arm** *fig* jugársela; **to keep sb at arm's length** *fig* guardar las distancias con alguien; **to twist sb's arm** *fig* persuadir a alguien **- 2.** [of garment] manga *f* **- 3.** [of organization] rama *f*. ⟨⟩ *vt* armar. ⟨⟩ *vi* armarse.

➡ **arms** *npl* [weapons] armas *fpl*; **to take up arms** tomar las armas; **he's up in arms (about it)** está que se sube por las paredes (por ello).

armada [ɑ:'mɑ:də] *n* armada *f*.

➡ **Armada** *n* HIST: **the Spanish Armada** la Armada Invencible.

armadillo [ˌɑ:mə'dɪləʊ] (*pl* **-s**) *n* armadillo *m*.

Armageddon [ˌɑ:mə'gedn] *n* apocalipsis *f inv*.

armaments ['ɑ:məmənts] *npl* armamento *m*.

armband ['ɑ:mbænd] *n* **- 1.** [indicating mourning, rank] brazalete *m* **- 2.** [for swimming] flotador *m* (en los brazos).

armchair ['ɑ:mtʃeə'] *n* sillón *m*.

armed [ɑ:md] *adj* **- 1.** [police, thieves] armado(da) **- 2.** *fig* [with information]: **armed with** provisto(ta) de.

armed forces *npl* fuerzas *fpl* armadas.

Armenia [ɑ:'mi:njə] *n* Armenia.

Armenian [ɑ:'mi:njən] ⟨⟩ *adj* armenio(nia). ⟨⟩ *n* **- 1.** [person] armenio *m*, -nia *f* **- 2.** [language] armenio *m*.

armhole ['ɑ:mhəʊl] *n* sobaquera *f*, sisa *f*.

armistice ['ɑ:mɪstɪs] *n* armisticio *m*.

armour UK, **armor** US ['ɑ:mə'] *n* **- 1.** [for person] armadura *f* **- 2.** [for military vehicle] blindaje *m*.

armoured UK, **armored** US ['ɑ:məd] *adj* MIL blindado(da).

armoured car [ɑ:məd-] *n* MIL carro *m* blindado.

armour-plated [-'pleɪtɪd] *adj* MIL blindado(da), acorazado(da).

armoury UK (*pl* **-ies**), **armory** US (*pl* **-ies**) ['ɑ:mərɪ] *n* arsenal *m*.

armpit ['ɑ:mpɪt] *n* sobaco *m*, axila *f*.

armrest ['ɑ:mrest] *n* brazo *m*.

arms control [ˈɑːmz-] *n* control *m* armamentístico.

army [ˈɑːmɪ] (*pl* -ies) ⬦ *n lit* & *fig* ejército *m*. ⬦ *comp* del ejército, militar.

aroma [əˈrəʊmə] *n* aroma *m*.

aromatherapy [ərəʊməˈθerəpɪ] *n* aromaterapia *f*.

aromatic [ˌærəˈmætɪk] *adj* aromático(ca).

arose [əˈrəʊz] *pt* ⮕ arise.

around [əˈraʊnd] ⬦ *adv* - **1.** [about, round] por ahí; **to walk/look around** andar/mirar por ahí - **2.** [on all sides] alrededor - **3.** [present, available]: **is John around?** [there] ¿está John por ahí?; [here] ¿está John por aquí? - **4.** [turn, look]: **to turn around** volverse; **to look around** volver la cabeza
▸▸ **to have been around** *inf* haber visto mundo. ⬦ *prep* - **1.** [on all sides of] alrededor de - **2.** [about, round - place] por - **3.** [in the area of] cerca de - **4.** [approximately] alrededor de.

arousal [əˈraʊzl] *n* excitación *f*.

arouse [əˈraʊz] *vt* - **1.** [excite - feeling] despertar; [- person] excitar - **2.** [wake] despertar.

arrange [əˈreɪndʒ] *vt* - **1.** [books, furniture] colocar; [flowers] arreglar - **2.** [event, meeting, party] organizar; **to arrange to do sthg** acordar hacer algo; **we've arranged to meet at nine** hemos quedado a las nueve; **to arrange sthg for sb** organizarle algo a alguien; **to arrange for sb to do sthg** hacer lo necesario para que alguien haga algo - **3.** MUS arreglar.

arranged marriage [əˈreɪndʒd-] *n* matrimonio *m* concertado.

arrangement [əˈreɪndʒmənt] *n* - **1.** [agreement] acuerdo *m*; **to come to an arrangement** llegar a un acuerdo - **2.** [of furniture] disposición *f*, colocación *f*; [of flowers] arreglo *m* - **3.** MUS arreglo *m*.
▸ **arrangements** *npl* preparativos *mpl*; **to make arrangements** hacer los preparativos.

array [əˈreɪ] ⬦ *n* - **1.** [of objects] surtido *m* - **2.** COMPUT matriz *f*. ⬦ *vt* [ornaments etc] disponer.

arrears [əˈrɪəz] *npl* [money owed] atrasos *mpl*; **in arrears** [retrospectively] con retraso; [late] atrasado en el pago.

arrest [əˈrest] ⬦ *n* detención *f*, arresto *m*; **under arrest** detenido(da), bajo arresto. ⬦ *vt* - **1.** [subj: police] detener, arrestar - **2.** [sb's attention] captar, atraer - **3.** *fml* [stop] detener, poner freno a.

arresting [əˈrestɪŋ] *adj* llamativo(va).

arrival [əˈraɪvl] *n* llegada *f*; **late arrival** [of train, bus, mail] retraso *m*; **new arrival** [person] recién llegado *m*, recién llegada *f*; [baby] recién nacido *m*, recién nacida *f*.

arrive [əˈraɪv] *vi* - **1.** [gen] llegar; **to arrive at** [conclusion, decision] llegar a - **2.** [baby] nacer.

arrogance [ˈærəgəns] *n* arrogancia *f*.

arrogant [ˈærəgənt] *adj* arrogante.

arrogantly [ˈærəgəntlɪ] *adv* con arrogancia.

arrow [ˈærəʊ] *n* flecha *f*.

arse UK [ɑːs], **ass** US [æs] *n v inf* [bottom] culo *m*.

arsenal [ˈɑːsənl] *n* arsenal *m*.

arsenic [ˈɑːsnɪk] *n* arsénico *m*.

arson [ˈɑːsn] *n* incendio *m* premeditado.

arsonist [ˈɑːsənɪst] *n* incendiario *m*, -ria *f*.

art [ɑːt] ⬦ *n* arte *m*. ⬦ *comp* [student, college, exhibition] de arte.
▸ **arts** ⬦ *npl* - **1.** SCH & UNIV [humanities] letras *fpl* - **2.** [fine arts]: **the arts** las bellas artes. ⬦ *comp* SCH & UNIV de letras.
▸ **arts and crafts** *npl* artesanía *f*.

art deco [-ˈdekəʊ] *n* art deco *m*.

artefact [ˈɑːtɪfækt] = **artifact**.

arterial [ɑːˈtɪərɪəl] *adj* - **1.** [blood] arterial - **2.** [road] principal.

arteriosclerosis [ɑːˌtɪərɪəʊsklɪˈrəʊsɪs] *n* arteriosclerosis *f inv*.

artery [ˈɑːtərɪ] (*pl* -ies) *n* arteria *f*.

artful [ˈɑːtfʊl] *adj* astuto(ta).

art gallery *n* [public] museo *m* (de arte); [commercial] galería *f* (de arte).

arthritic [ɑːˈθrɪtɪk] *adj* artrítico(ca).

arthritis [ɑːˈθraɪtɪs] *n* artritis *f inv*.

artic [ɑːˈtɪk] (*abbr of* **articulated lorry**) *n* UK *inf* camión *m* articulado.

artichoke [ˈɑːtɪtʃəʊk] *n* alcachofa *f*.

article [ˈɑːtɪkl] *n* artículo *m*; **article of clothing** prenda *f* de vestir.

articled clerk [ˈɑːtɪkld-] *n* UK abogado contratado *m*, abogada contratada *f* en prácticas.

articles of association [ˈɑːtɪklz-] *npl* estatutos *mpl* sociales.

articulate ⬦ *adj* [ɑːˈtɪkjʊlət] [person] elocuente; [speech] claro(ra), bien articulado(da). ⬦ *vt* [ɑːˈtɪkjʊleɪt] [express clearly] expresar.

articulated lorry [ɑːˈtɪkjʊleɪtɪd-] *n* UK camión *m* articulado.

articulation [ɑːˌtɪkjʊˈleɪʃn] *n* - **1.** [speech] articulación *f* - **2.** [of idea, feeling] expresión *f*.

artifact [ˈɑːtɪfækt] *n* artefacto *m*.

artifice [ˈɑːtɪfɪs] *n* - **1.** [trick] artificio *m* - **2.** [trickery] artificiosidad *f*.

artificial [ˌɑːtɪˈfɪʃl] *adj* artificial.

artificial insemination *n* inseminación *f* artificial.

artificial intelligence *n* inteligencia *f* artificial.

artificially [ˌɑːtɪˈfɪʃəlɪ] *adv* artificialmente.

artificial respiration n respiración f artificial.

artillery [ɑ:'tɪlərɪ] n [guns] artillería f.

artisan [ˌɑ:tɪ'zæn] n artesano m, -na f.

artist ['ɑ:tɪst] n artista mf.

artiste [ɑ:'ti:st] n artista mf.

artistic [ɑ:'tɪstɪk] adj - **1.** [gen] artístico(ca) - **2.** [good at art]: **to be artistic** tener sensibilidad artística.

artistically [ɑ:'tɪstɪklɪ] adv artísticamente.

artistry ['ɑ:tɪstrɪ] n maestría f.

artless ['ɑ:tlɪs] adj ingenuo(nua), cándido(da).

art nouveau [ˌɑ:nu:'vəʊ] n art nouveau m.

as (unstressed [əz], stressed [æz]) <> conj - **1.** [referring to time - while] mientras; [- when] cuando; **she told it to me as we walked along** me lo contó mientras paseábamos; **as time goes by** a medida que pasa el tiempo; **she rang (just) as I was leaving** llamó justo cuando iba a salir - **2.** [referring to manner, way] como; **leave it as it is** déjalo como está; **do as I say** haz lo que te digo - **3.** [introducing a statement] como; **as you see,...** como puedes ver,...; **as you know,...** como (ya) sabes,... - **4.** [because] como, ya que ▸▸ **as it is** (ya) de por sí; **things are bad enough as it is** las cosas ya están mal de por sí; **as it turns out...** resulta que...; **as things stand** tal como están las cosas. <> prep como; **I'm speaking as a friend** te hablo como amigo; **she works as a nurse** trabaja de OR como enfermera; **as a boy, I lived in Spain** de niño vivía en España; **she treats it as a game** se lo toma como un juego; **it came as a shock** fue una gran sorpresa. <> adv (in comparisons): **as... as tan... como; as tall as I am** tan alto como yo; **I've lived as long as she has** he vivido durante tanto tiempo como ella; **twice as big** el doble de grande; **it's just as fast** es igual de rápido; **as much as** tanto como; **as many as** tantos(tas) como; **as much wine as you like** tanto vino como quieras.

◆ **as it were** adv por así decirlo.

◆ **as for, as to** prep en cuanto a, por lo que se refiere a.

◆ **as from, as of** prep a partir de.

◆ **as if, as though** conj como si.

◆ **as to** prep UK con respecto a.

AS n (abbr of Associate in Science), titular de una licenciatura de ciencias en Estados Unidos.

ASA (abbr of American Standards Association) n instituto estadounidense de normalización.

a.s.a.p. (abbr of as soon as possible) a la mayor brevedad posible.

asbestos [æs'bestəs] n amianto m, asbesto m.

asbestosis [ˌæsbes'təʊsɪs] n asbestosis f inv.

ascend [ə'send] <> vt subir; **to ascend the throne** subir al trono. <> vi ascender.

ascendancy, ascendency [ə'sendənsɪ] n ascendiente m.

ascendant [ə'sendənt] n: **in the ascendant** en auge.

ascendency [ə'sendənsɪ] = **ascendancy**.

ascending [ə'sendɪŋ] adj ascendiente; **in ascending order** en orden ascendiente.

ascension [ə'senʃn] n [to throne] subida f.
◆ **Ascension** n RELIG Ascensión f.

Ascension Island n Isla de la Ascensión.

ascent [ə'sent] n - **1.** [climb] ascensión f - **2.** [upward slope] subida f, cuesta f - **3.** fig [progress] ascenso m.

ascertain [ˌæsə'teɪn] vt determinar.

ascetic [ə'setɪk] <> adj ascético(ca). <> n asceta mf.

ASCII ['æskɪ] (abbr of American Standard Code for Information Interchange) n ASCII m.

ascorbic acid [ə'skɔ:bɪk-] n ácido m ascórbico.

ascribe [ə'skraɪb] vt: **to ascribe sthg to** atribuir algo a.

aseptic [ˌeɪ'septɪk] adj aséptico(ca).

asexual [ˌeɪ'sekʃʊəl] adj asexual, asexuado(da).

ash [æʃ] n - **1.** [from cigarette, fire] ceniza f - **2.** [tree] fresno m.
◆ **ashes** npl [from cremation] cenizas fpl.

ashamed [ə'ʃeɪmd] adj avergonzado(da), apenado(da) Andes, Amér C & Méx; **I'm ashamed to do it** me da vergüenza hacerlo; **I'm ashamed of...** me da vergüenza...

ashcan ['æʃkæn] n US cubo m de la basura.

ashen-faced ['æʃn,feɪst] adj: **to be ashen-faced** tener la cara pálida.

ashore [ə'ʃɔ:r] adv [swim] hasta la orilla; **to go ashore** desembarcar.

ashtray ['æʃtreɪ] n cenicero m.

Ash Wednesday n miércoles m inv de ceniza.

Asia [UK 'eɪʃə, US 'eɪʒə] n Asia.

Asia Minor n Asia Menor.

Asian [UK 'eɪʃn, US 'eɪʒn] <> adj asiático(ca); **Asian American** americano(na) de origen asiático. <> n asiático m, -ca f.

Asiatic [UK ˌeɪʃɪ'ætɪk, US ˌeɪʒɪ'ætɪk] adj asiático(ca).

aside [ə'saɪd] <> adv - **1.** [to one side] a un lado; **to move aside** apartarse; **to take sb aside** llevar a alguien aparte; **to brush OR sweep sthg aside** dejar algo aparte OR de lado - **2.** [apart]

aparte; **aside from** aparte de. ⬦ *n* - **1.** [in play] aparte *m* - **2.** [remark] inciso *m*, comentario *m* al margen.

ask [ɑːsk] ⬦ *vt* - **1.** [question - person]: **to ask (sb sthg)** preguntar (a alguien algo); **if you ask me...** si quieres que te diga la verdad... - **2.** [put - question]: **to ask a question** hacer una pregunta - **3.** [request, demand] pedir; **to ask sb (to do sthg)** pedir a alguien (que haga algo); **to ask sb for sthg** pedirle algo a alguien - **4.** [invite] invitar. ⬦ *vi* - **1.** [question] preguntar - **2.** [request] pedir.

➥ **ask after** *vt insep* preguntar por.

➥ **ask for** *vt insep* - **1.** [person] preguntar por - **2.** [thing] pedir.

➥ **ask out** *vt sep* [ask to be boyfriend, girlfriend] pedir salir.

askance [əˈskæns] *adv*: **to look askance at sb** mirar a alguien con recelo.

askew [əˈskjuː] *adj* torcido(da).

asking price [ˈɑːskɪŋ-] *n* precio *m* inicial.

asleep [əˈsliːp] *adj* dormido(da); **she's asleep** está dormida OR durmiendo; **to fall asleep** quedarse dormido; **to be fast** OR **sound asleep** estar profundamente dormido.

ASLEF [ˈæzlef] (*abbr of* Associated Society of Locomotive Engineers and Firemen) *n* sindicato británico de ferroviarios.

asparagus [əˈspærəgəs] *n* (*U*) [plant] espárrago *m*; [shoots] espárragos *mpl*.

aspartame [*UK* əˈspɑːteɪm, *US* ˈæspəteɪm] *n* aspartamo *m*.

ASPCA (*abbr of* American Society for the Prevention of Cruelty to Animals) *n sociedad estadounidense protectora de animales*, ≈ SPA *f*.

aspect [ˈæspekt] *n* - **1.** [of subject, plan] aspecto *m* - **2.** [appearance] cariz *m*, aspecto *m* - **3.** [of building] orientación *f*.

aspen [ˈæspən] *n* álamo *m* alpino OR temblón.

aspersions [əˈspɜːʃnz] *npl*: **to cast aspersions on sthg** poner en duda algo.

asphalt [ˈæsfælt] *n* asfalto *m*.

asphyxiate [əsˈfɪksɪeɪt] *vt* asfixiar.

aspic [ˈæspɪk] *n* gelatina *f* de carne.

aspirate [ˈæspərət] *adj* aspirado(da).

aspiration [ˌæspəˈreɪʃn] *n* aspiración *f*.

aspire [əˈspaɪər] *vi*: **to aspire to** aspirar a.

aspirin [ˈæsprɪn] *n* aspirina *f*.

aspiring [əˈspaɪərɪŋ] *adj*: **an aspiring actor** un aspirante a actor.

ass [æs] *n* - **1.** [donkey] asno *m*, -na *f* - **2.** *UK inf* [idiot] burro *m*, -rra *f* - **3.** *US v inf* = **arse**.

assail [əˈseɪl] *vt* - **1.** [attack] atacar, arremeter contra - **2.** *fig* [subj: doubts] asaltar.

assailant [əˈseɪlənt] *n* agresor *m*, -ra *f*.

assassin [əˈsæsɪn] *n* asesino *m*, -na *f*.

assassinate [əˈsæsɪneɪt] *vt* asesinar.

assassination [əˌsæsɪˈneɪʃn] *n* asesinato *m*.

assault [əˈsɔːlt] ⬦ *n* - **1.** MIL: **assault (on)** ataque *m* (contra) - **2.** [physical attack]: **assault (on sb)** agresión *f* (contra alguien); **assault and battery** LAW agresión *f* con resultado de lesiones. ⬦ *vt* [physically] asaltar, agredir; [sexually] abusar de.

assault course *n* pista *f* americana.

assemble [əˈsembl] ⬦ *vt* - **1.** [gather] juntar, reunir - **2.** [fit together] montar. ⬦ *vi* reunirse.

assembly [əˈsemblɪ] (*pl* -ies) *n* - **1.** [meeting, law-making body] asamblea *f* - **2.** [gathering together] reunión *f* - **3.** *UK* [at school] *reunión de todos los profesores y alumnos de un centro al comienzo de cada día escolar* - **4.** [fitting together] montaje *m*.

assembly line *n* cadena *f* de montaje.

assent [əˈsent] ⬦ *n* consentimiento *m*. ⬦ *vi*: **to assent (to)** asentir (a).

assert [əˈsɜːt] *vt* - **1.** [fact, belief] afirmar - **2.** [authority] imponer; **to assert o.s.** imponerse.

assertion [əˈsɜːʃn] *n* afirmación *f*.

assertive [əˈsɜːtɪv] *adj* enérgico(ca).

assess [əˈses] *vt* evaluar.

assessment [əˈsesmənt] *n* - **1.** [evaluation] evaluación *f* - **2.** [calculation] cálculo *m*.

assessor [əˈsesər] *n* tasador *m*, -ra *f*.

asset [ˈæset] *n* - **1.** [valuable quality - of person] cualidad *f* positiva; [- of thing] ventaja *f* - **2.** [valuable person] elemento *m* importante.

➥ **assets** *npl* COMM activo *m*.

asset-stripping [-ˌstrɪpɪŋ] *n adquisición de una empresa para la venta de sus activos y posterior cierre*.

assiduous [əˈsɪdjʊəs] *adj* [gen] dedicado(da); [student] aplicado(da).

assiduously [əˈsɪdjʊəslɪ] *adv* con dedicación.

assign [əˈsaɪn] *vt* - **1.** [gen]: **to assign sthg (to sb)** asignar algo (a alguien); **to assign sb to sthg** asignar a alguien algo; **to assign sb to do sthg** asignar a alguien que haga algo - **2.** [designate for specific use, purpose]: **to assign sthg (to)** destinar algo (a).

assignation [ˌæsɪgˈneɪʃn] *n fml* cita *f* a escondidas.

assignment [əˈsaɪnmənt] *n* - **1.** [task] misión *f*; SCH trabajo *m* - **2.** [act of assigning] asignación *f*.

assimilate [əˈsɪmɪleɪt] *vt* - **1.** [learn] asimilar - **2.** [absorb]: **to assimilate sb (into)** integrar a alguien (en).

assimilation [əˌsɪmɪˈleɪʃn] *n* - **1.** [of ideas, facts] asimilación *f* - **2.** [of people] incorporación *f*.

assist [ə'sɪst] ⬦ *vt*: to assist sb (with sthg/in doing sthg) ayudar a alguien (con algo/a hacer algo). ⬦ *vi* ayudar.

assistance [ə'sɪstəns] *n* ayuda *f*, asistencia *f*; to be of assistance (to) ayudar (a).

assistant [ə'sɪstənt] ⬦ *n* ayudante *mf*; (shop) assistant dependiente *m*, -ta *f*. ⬦ *comp* adjunto(ta); assistant manager director adjunto *m*, directora adjunta *f*; assistant referee árbitro *m*, asistente *f*.

associate ⬦ *adj* [ə'səʊʃɪət] asociado(da). ⬦ *n* [ə'səʊʃɪət] socio *m*, -cia *f*. ⬦ *vt* [ə'səʊʃɪeɪt] asociar; to associate sthg/sb with asociar algo/a alguien con; to be associated with [organization, plan, opinion] estar relacionado con; [people] estar asociado con. ⬦ *vi* [ə'səʊʃɪeɪt]: to associate with sb relacionarse con alguien.

association [ə,səʊsɪ'eɪʃn] *n* - **1.** [organization, act of associating] asociación *f*; in association with en colaboración con - **2.** [in mind] connotación *f*.

assonance ['æsənəns] *n* asonancia *f*.

assorted [ə'sɔːtɪd] *adj* - **1.** [of various types] variado(da) - **2.** [biscuits, sweets] surtido(da).

assortment [ə'sɔːtmənt] *n* surtido *m*.

assuage [ə'sweɪdʒ] *vt fml* [grief] aliviar; [thirst, hunger] saciar.

assume [ə'sjuːm] *vt* - **1.** [suppose] suponer - **2.** [power, responsibility] asumir - **3.** [appearance, attitude] adoptar.

assumed name [ə'sjuːmd-] *n* nombre *m* falso.

assuming [ə'sjuːmɪŋ] *conj* suponiendo que.

assumption [ə'sʌmpʃn] *n* - **1.** [supposition] suposición *f*; on the assumption that suponiendo que - **2.** [of power] asunción *f*.

➡ **Assumption** *n* RELIG: the Assumption la Asunción.

assurance [ə'ʃʊərəns] *n* - **1.** [promise] garantía *f* - **2.** [confidence] seguridad *f* de sí mismo - **3.** [insurance] seguro *m*.

assure [ə'ʃʊə⁽ʳ⁾] *vt* asegurar, garantizar; to assure sb of sthg garantizar a alguien algo; to be assured of sthg tener algo garantizado; rest assured that... ten por seguro que...

assured [ə'ʃʊəd] *adj* [confident] seguro(ra).

AST (*abbr of* **Atlantic Standard Time**) *n hora oficial de la costa este estadounidense.*

asterisk ['æstərɪsk] *n* asterisco *m*.

astern [ə'stɜːn] *adv* NAUT a popa.

asteroid ['æstərɔɪd] *n* asteroide *m*.

asthma ['æsmə] *n* asma *f*.

asthmatic [æs'mætɪk] ⬦ *adj* asmático(ca). ⬦ *n* asmático *m*, -ca *f*.

astigmatism [ə'stɪɡmətɪzm] *n* astigmatismo *m*.

astonish [ə'stɒnɪʃ] *vt* asombrar.

astonishing [ə'stɒnɪʃɪŋ] *adj* asombroso(sa).

astonishment [ə'stɒnɪʃmənt] *n* asombro *m*.

astound [ə'staʊnd] *vt* asombrar, pasmar.

astounding [ə'staʊndɪŋ] *adj* asombroso(sa), pasmoso(sa).

astrakhan [,æstrə'kæn] *n* astracán *m*.

astray [ə'streɪ] *adv*: to go astray [become lost] extraviarse; to lead sb astray [into bad ways] llevar a alguien por el mal camino.

astride [ə'straɪd] ⬦ *adv* a horcajadas. ⬦ *prep* a horcajadas en.

astringent [ə'strɪndʒənt] ⬦ *adj* astringente. ⬦ *n* astringente *m*.

astrologer [ə'strɒlədʒə⁽ʳ⁾] *n* astrólogo *m*, -ga *f*.

astrological [,æstrə'lɒdʒɪkl] *adj* astrológico(ca).

astrologist [ə'strɒlədʒɪst] *n* astrólogo *m*, -ga *f*.

astrology [ə'strɒlədʒɪ] *n* astrología *f*.

astronaut ['æstrənɔːt] *n* astronauta *mf*.

astronomer [ə'strɒnəmə⁽ʳ⁾] *n* astrónomo *m*, -ma *f*.

astronomical [,æstrə'nɒmɪkl] *adj lit* & *fig* astronómico(ca).

astronomy [ə'strɒnəmɪ] *n* astronomía *f*.

astrophysics [,æstrəʊ'fɪzɪks] *n* astrofísica *f*.

astute [ə'stjuːt] *adj* astuto(ta), abusado(da) *Méx*.

asunder [ə'sʌndə⁽ʳ⁾] *adv liter* [apart]: to tear sthg asunder hacer trizas algo.

asylum [ə'saɪləm] *n* - **1.** [mental hospital] manicomio *m* - **2.** [protection] asilo *m*.

asylum seeker [ə'saɪləm'siːkə⁽ʳ⁾] *n* peticionario *m*, -ria *f* de asilo.

asymmetrical [,eɪsɪ'metrɪkl] *adj* asimétrico(ca).

at (*unstressed* [ət],*stressed* [æt]) *prep* - **1.** [indicating place] en; at my father's en casa de mi padre; standing at the window de pie junto a la ventana; at the bottom of the hill al pie de la colina; to arrive at llegar a; at school/work/home en la escuela/el trabajo/casa - **2.** [indicating direction] a; to look at sthg/sb mirar algo/a alguien; she smiled at me me sonrió - **3.** [indicating a particular time]: at a more suitable time en un momento más oportuno; at midnight/noon/eleven o'clock a medianoche/mediodía/las once; at night por la noche; at Christmas/Easter en Navidades/Semana Santa - **4.** [indicating speed, rate, price] a; at 100 mph/high speed a 100 millas por hora/gran velocidad; at £50 (a pair) a 50 libras (el par) - **5.** [indicating particular state, condition]: at peace/war en paz/guerra; she's at lunch está comiendo; to work hard at sthg trabajar duro en algo - **6.** [indicating a particular age] a; at 52/your age a los 52/tu edad - **7.** [indicating tentativeness, noncompletion]: to snatch at sthg intentar agarrar algo; to

nibble at sthg mordisquear algo **- 8.** *(after adjectives)*: **delighted at** encantado con; **experienced at** experimentado en; **puzzled/horrified at** perplejo/horrorizado ante; **he's good/bad at sport** se le dan bien/mal los deportes.

➤ **at all** *adv* **- 1.** *(with negative)*: **not at all** [when thanked] de nada; [when answering a question] en absoluto; **she's not at all happy** no está nada contenta **- 2.** [in the slightest]: **anything at all will do** cualquier cosa valdrá; **do you know her at all?** ¿la conoces (de algo)?

ate [*UK* et, *US* eɪt] *pt* ⊳ **eat**.

atheism ['eɪθɪɪzm] *n* ateísmo *m*.

atheist ['eɪθɪɪst] *n* ateo *m*, -a *f*.

Athenian [ə'θi:njən] ⟨⟩ *adj* ateniense. ⟨⟩ *n* ateniense *mf*.

Athens ['æθɪnz] *n* Atenas.

athlete ['æθli:t] *n* atleta *mf*.

athlete's foot *n* pie *m* de atleta.

athletic [æθ'letɪk] *adj* atlético(ca).

➤ **athletics** *npl* atletismo *m*.

Atlantic [ət'læntɪk] ⟨⟩ *adj* atlántico(ca). ⟨⟩ *n*: **the Atlantic (Ocean)** el (océano) Atlántico.

Atlantis [ət'læntɪs] *n* (la) Atlántida.

atlas ['ætləs] *n* atlas *m inv*.

Atlas ['ætləs] *n*: **the Atlas Mountains** el Atlas.

ATM (*abbr of* **automatic teller machine**) *n* cajero automático.

atmosphere ['ætmə,sfɪər] *n* **- 1.** [of planet] atmósfera *f* **- 2.** [air in room, mood of place] ambiente *m*.

atmospheric [,ætməs'ferɪk] *adj* **- 1.** [pressure, pollution] atmosférico(ca) **- 2.** [attractive, mysterious] sugerente.

atoll ['ætɒl] *n* atolón *m*.

atom ['ætəm] *n* **- 1.** PHYS átomo *m* **- 2.** *fig* [tiny amount] pizca *f*.

atom bomb, atomic bomb *n* bomba *f* atómica.

atomic [ə'tɒmɪk] *adj* atómico(ca).

atomic bomb = **atom bomb**.

atomic energy *n* energía *f* atómica.

atomic number *n* número *m* atómico.

atomizer, -iser ['ætəmaɪzər] *n* atomizador *m*.

atone [ə'təʊn] *vi*: **to atone for** reparar.

atonement [ə'təʊnmənt] *n*: **atonement (for)** reparación *f* (por).

A to Z *n* guía *f* alfabética; [map] callejero *m*.

ATP (*abbr of* **Association of Tennis Professionals**) *n* ATP *f*.

atrocious [ə'trəʊʃəs] *adj* [very bad] atroz.

atrocity [ə'trɒsətɪ] (*pl* **-ies**) *n* [terrible act] atrocidad *f*.

attach [ə'tætʃ] *vt* **- 1.** [with pin, clip]: **to attach sthg (to)** sujetar algo (a); [with string] atar algo (a) **- 2.** [document & COMPUT] adjuntar **- 3.** [importance, blame]: **to attach sthg (to sthg)** atribuir algo (a algo).

attaché [ə'tæʃeɪ] *n* agregado *m*, -da *f*.

attaché case *n* maletín *m*.

attached [ə'tætʃt] *adj* **- 1.** [fastened on]: **attached (to)** adjunto(ta) (a) **- 2.** [for work, job]: **attached to** destinado(da) a **- 3.** [fond]: **to be attached to** tener cariño a.

attachment [ə'tætʃmənt] *n* **- 1.** [device] accesorio *m* **- 2.** COMPUT archivo *m* adjunto **- 3.** [fondness]: **attachment (to)** cariño *m* (por).

attack [ə'tæk] ⟨⟩ *n*: **attack (on)** ataque *m* (contra); **terrorist attack** atentado *m* terrorista; **to be under attack** estar siendo atacado. ⟨⟩ *vt* **- 1.** [gen] atacar **- 2.** [job, problem] acometer. ⟨⟩ *vi* atacar.

attacker [ə'tækər] *n* atacante *mf*.

attain [ə'teɪn] *vt* lograr, alcanzar.

attainment [ə'teɪnmənt] *n* logro *m*.

attempt [ə'tempt] ⟨⟩ *n*: **attempt (at doing sthg)** intento *m* (de hacer algo); **attempt on sb's life** atentado *m* contra la vida de alguien. ⟨⟩ *vt*: **to attempt sthg/to do sthg** intentar algo/hacer algo.

attend [ə'tend] ⟨⟩ *vt* [go to] asistir a. ⟨⟩ *vi* **- 1.** [be present] asistir **- 2.** [pay attention]: **to attend (to)** atender (a).

➤ **attend to** *vt insep* **- 1.** [matter] ocuparse de **- 2.** [customer] atender a; [patient] asistir a.

attendance [ə'tendəns] *n* asistencia *f*; **the attendance for the match was over 10,000** más de 10.000 personas asistieron al partido.

attendant [ə'tendənt] ⟨⟩ *adj* relacionado(da), concomitante. ⟨⟩ *n* [at museum] vigilante *mf*; [at petrol station, in swimming pool] encargado *m*, -da *f*.

attention [ə'tenʃn] ⟨⟩ *n* (U) **- 1.** [gen] atención *f*; **to bring sthg to sb's attention, to draw sb's attention to sthg** llamar la atención de alguien sobre algo; **to attract OR catch sb's attention** atraer OR captar la atención de alguien; **to pay/pay no attention (to)** prestar/no prestar atención (a); **for the attention of** COMM a la atención de; **your attention please!** ¡atención! **- 2.** [care] asistencia *f* **- 3.** MIL: **to stand to attention** ponerse en la posición de firmes, cuadrarse. ⟨⟩ *excl* MIL ¡firmes!

attentive [ə'tentɪv] *adj* atento(ta).

attentively [ə'tentɪvlɪ] *adv* atentamente.

attenuate [ə'tenjʊeɪt] *fml* ⟨⟩ *vt* atenuar. ⟨⟩ *vi* atenuarse.

attest [ə'test] ⟨⟩ *vt* atestiguar. ⟨⟩ *vi*: **to attest to sthg** atestiguar algo.

attic ['ætɪk] n desván m, entretecho m Amér.

attire [ə'taɪəʳ] n (U) atuendo m, atavío m.

attitude ['ætɪtjuːd] n - **1.** [way of thinking, acting]: **attitude (to** OR **towards)** actitud f (hacia) - **2.** [posture] postura f.

attn. (abbr of **for the attention of**) a/a.

attorney [ə'tɜːnɪ] n US abogado m, -da f.

attorney general (pl **attorneys general**) n fiscal m general del estado.

attract [ə'trækt] vt - **1.** [gen] atraer; **to attract sb's attention** llamar la atención de alguien; **to be attracted to** sentirse atraído por - **2.** [support, criticism] suscitar.

attraction [ə'trækʃn] n - **1.** [gen]: **attraction (to sb)** atracción f (hacia OR por alguien) - **2.** [attractiveness - of thing] atractivo m.

attractive [ə'træktɪv] adj atractivo(va).

attractively [ə'træktɪvlɪ] adv de un modo atractivo.

attributable [ə'trɪbjʊtəbl] adj [of thing]: **attributable to** atribuible a.

attribute ◇ vt [ə'trɪbjuːt]: **to attribute sthg to** atribuir algo a. ◇ n ['ætrɪbjuːt] atributo m.

attrition [ə'trɪʃn] n desgaste m; **war of attrition** guerra de desgaste.

attuned [ə'tjuːnd] adj - **1.** [accustomed]: **attuned (to)** acostumbrado(da) (a) - **2.** [ears]: **attuned to** sensible a.

ATV n (abbr of **all terrain vehicle**), todo terreno.

atypical [,eɪ'tɪpɪkl] adj atípico(ca).

atypically [,eɪ'tɪpɪklɪ] adv de manera atípica.

aubergine ['əʊbəʒiːn] n UK berenjena f.

auburn ['ɔːbən] adj castaño rojizo.

auction ['ɔːkʃn] ◇ n subasta f; **at** OR **by auction** mediante subasta; **to put sthg up for auction** sacar algo a subasta. ◇ vt subastar.
→ **auction off** vt sep subastar.

auctioneer [,ɔːkʃə'nɪəʳ] n subastador m, -ra f.

audacious [ɔː'deɪʃəs] adj [daring] audaz; [cheeky] atrevido(da).

audacity [ɔː'dæsətɪ] n - **1.** [daring] audacia f - **2.** [cheek] osadía f, atrevimiento m.

audible ['ɔːdəbl] adj audible.

audience ['ɔːdjəns] n - **1.** [of play, film] público m - **2.** [formal meeting, TV viewers] audiencia f.

audio ['ɔːdɪəʊ] adj de audio.

audio-frequency n audiofrecuencia f.

audiotypist ['ɔːdɪəʊ,taɪpɪst] n mecanógrafo m, -fa f por dictáfono.

audiovisual ['ɔːdɪəʊ-] adj audiovisual.

audit ['ɔːdɪt] ◇ n auditoría f. ◇ vt auditar.

audition [ɔː'dɪʃn] ◇ n prueba f (a un artista). ◇ vi: **to audition for** hacer una prueba para.

auditor ['ɔːdɪtəʳ] n auditor m, -ra f.

auditorium [,ɔːdɪ'tɔːrɪəm] (pl **-riums** OR **-ria** [-rɪə]) n auditorio m.

au fait [,əʊ'feɪ] adj: **au fait with** familiarizado(da) con.

Aug. (abbr of **August**) ago.

augment [ɔːg'ment] vt acrecentar, aumentar.

augur ['ɔːgəʳ] vi: **to augur well/badly** ser un buen/mal augurio.

august [ɔː'gʌst] adj augusto(ta).

August ['ɔːgəst] n agosto m; see also **September**.

Auld Lang Syne [,ɔːldlæŋ'saɪn] n canción escocesa en alabanza de los viejos tiempos que se canta tradicionalmente en Nochevieja.

aunt [ɑːnt] n tía f.

auntie, aunty ['ɑːntɪ] (pl **-ies**) n inf tita f.

au pair [,əʊ'peəʳ] n au pair f.

aura ['ɔːrə] n aura f, halo m.

aural ['ɔːrəl] adj auditivo(va).

aurally ['ɔːrəlɪ] adv: **aurally handicapped** con deficiencia auditiva.

auspices ['ɔːspɪsɪz] npl: **under the auspices of** bajo los auspicios de.

auspicious [ɔː'spɪʃəs] adj prometedor(ra).

Aussie ['ɒzɪ] n inf australiano m, -na f.

austere [ɒ'stɪəʳ] adj austero(ra).

austerity [ɒ'sterətɪ] n austeridad f.

austerity measures npl medidas fpl de austeridad.

Australasia [,ɒstrə'leɪʒə] n Australasia.

Australia [ɒ'streɪljə] n Australia.

Australian [ɒ'streɪljən] ◇ adj australiano(na). ◇ n australiano m, -na f.

Austria ['ɒstrɪə] n Austria.

Austrian ['ɒstrɪən] ◇ adj austriaco(ca). ◇ n austriaco m, -ca f.

AUT (abbr of **Association of University Teachers**) n sindicato británico de profesores universitarios.

authentic [ɔː'θentɪk] adj auténtico(ca).

authenticate [ɔː'θentɪkeɪt] vt autentificar.

authentication [ɔː,θentɪ'keɪʃn] n [gen & COMPUT] autentificación f.

authenticity [,ɔːθen'tɪsətɪ] n autenticidad f.

author ['ɔːθəʳ] n [by profession] escritor m, -ra f; [of particular book, text] autor m, -ra f.

authoritarian [ɔː,θɒrɪ'teərɪən] adj autoritario(ria).

authoritative [ɔː'θɒrɪtətɪv] adj - **1.** [person, voice] autoritario(ria) - **2.** [study] autorizado(da).

authority [ɔːˈθɒrətɪ] (*pl* **-ies**) *n* - **1.** [gen] autoridad *f*; **to be an authority on** ser una autoridad en - **2.** [permission] autorización *f* ▸▸ **to have it on good authority** saberlo de buena tinta.
▸ **authorities** *npl*: **the authorities** las autoridades *fpl*.

authorize, -ise [ˈɔːθəraɪz] *vt*: **to authorize (sb to do sthg)** autorizar (a alguien a hacer algo).

Authorized Version [ˈɔːθəraɪzd-] *n*: **the Authorized Version** *la versión oficial de la Biblia en inglés.*

authorship [ˈɔːθəʃɪp] *n* autoría *f*.

autism [ˈɔːtɪzm] *n* autismo *m*.

autistic [ɔːˈtɪstɪk] *adj* autista.

auto [ˈɔːtəʊ] (*pl* **-s**) *n US* coche *m*.

autobiographical [ˈɔːtəˌbaɪəˈɡræfɪkl] *adj* autobiográfico(ca).

autobiography [ˌɔːtəbaɪˈɒɡrəfɪ] (*pl* **-ies**) *n* autobiografía *f*.

autocrat [ˈɔːtəkræt] *n* autócrata *mf*.

autocratic [ˌɔːtəˈkrætɪk] *adj* autocrático(ca).

autocross [ˈɔːtəʊkrɒs] *n UK* autocross *m*.

Autocue® [ˈɔːtəʊkjuː] *n UK* teleapuntador *m*.

autograph [ˈɔːtəɡrɑːf] ◇ *n* autógrafo *m*. ◇ *vt* autografiar.

automata [ɔːˈtɒmətə] *npl* ▷ **automaton**.

automate [ˈɔːtəmeɪt] *vt* automatizar.

automatic [ˌɔːtəˈmætɪk] ◇ *adj* automático(ca). ◇ *n* - **1.** [car] coche *m* automático - **2.** [gun] arma *f* automática - **3.** [washing machine] lavadora *f* automática.

automatically [ˌɔːtəˈmætɪklɪ] *adv* automáticamente.

automatic pilot *n* - **1.** AERON & NAUT piloto *m* automático - **2.** *fig*: **on automatic pilot** [automatically] con el piloto automático puesto.

automation [ˌɔːtəˈmeɪʃn] *n* automatización *f*.

automaton [ɔːˈtɒmətən] (*pl* **-tons** OR **-ta**) *n* - **1.** [robot] autómata *m* - **2.** *pej* [person] autómata *mf*.

automobile [ˈɔːtəməbiːl] *n US* coche *m*, automóvil *m*.

automotive [ˌɔːtəˈməʊtɪv] *adj* automovilístico(ca).

autonomous [ɔːˈtɒnəməs] *adj* autónomo(ma).

autonomy [ɔːˈtɒnəmɪ] *n* autonomía *f*.

autopilot [ˈɔːtəʊpaɪlət] *n* piloto *m* automático.

autopsy [ˈɔːtɒpsɪ] (*pl* **-ies**) *n* autopsia *f*.

autumn [ˈɔːtəm] ◇ *n* otoño *m*; **in autumn** en otoño. ◇ *comp* otoñal.

autumnal [ɔːˈtʌmnəl] *adj* otoñal.

auxiliary [ɔːɡˈzɪljərɪ] ◇ *adj* auxiliar. ◇ *n* (*pl* **-ies**) - **1.** [medical worker] auxiliar sanitario *m*, auxiliar sanitaria *f* - **2.** [soldier] soldado *m* auxiliar.

Av. (*abbr of* **avenue**) Av.

AV *abbr of* **audiovisual**.

avail [əˈveɪl] ◇ *n*: **to no avail** en vano. ◇ *vt*: **to avail o.s. of sthg** aprovechar algo.

availability [əˌveɪləˈbɪlətɪ] *n* disponibilidad *f*.

available [əˈveɪləbl] *adj* - **1.** [product, service] disponible; **this product is no longer available** ya no comercializamos este producto - **2.** [person] libre, disponible.

avalanche [ˈævəlɑːnʃ] *n lit* & *fig* avalancha *f*, alud *m*.

avant-garde [ˌævɒŋˈɡɑːd] *adj* de vanguardia, vanguardista.

avarice [ˈævərɪs] *n* avaricia *f*.

avaricious [ˌævəˈrɪʃəs] *adj* avaricioso(sa).

Ave. (*abbr of* **avenue**) Avda.

avenge [əˈvendʒ] *vt* vengar.

avenue [ˈævənjuː] *n* - **1.** [wide road] avenida *f* - **2.** *fig* [method, means] camino *m*, vía *f*.

average [ˈævərɪdʒ] ◇ *adj* - **1.** [mean, typical] medio(dia) - **2.** [mediocre] regular. ◇ *n* media *f*, promedio *m*; **on average** de media, por término medio. ◇ *vt* alcanzar un promedio de.
▸ **average out** ◇ *vt sep* sacar la media de. ◇ *vi*: **to average out at** salir a una media de.

averse [əˈvɜːs] *adj*: **not to be averse to sthg/to doing sthg** no hacerle ascos a algo/a hacer algo.

aversion [əˈvɜːʃn] *n* - **1.** [dislike]: **aversion (to)** aversión *f* (a) - **2.** [object of dislike]: **football is my pet aversion** el fútbol es lo que más odio.

avert [əˈvɜːt] *vt* - **1.** [problem, accident] evitar, prevenir - **2.** [eyes, glance] apartar, desviar.

aviary [ˈeɪvjərɪ] (*pl* **-ies**) *n* pajarera *f*.

aviation [ˌeɪvɪˈeɪʃn] *n* aviación *f*.

aviator [ˈeɪvɪeɪtə] *n dated* aviador *m*, -ra *f*.

avid [ˈævɪd] *adj*: **avid (for)** ávido(da) (de).

avocado [ˌævəˈkɑːdəʊ] (*pl* **-s** OR **-es**) *n*: **avocado (pear)** aguacate *m*, palta *f Andes & R Plata*.

avoid [əˈvɔɪd] *vt*: **to avoid (sthg/doing sthg)** evitar(algo/hacer algo); **she's been avoiding me** ha estado esquivándome.

avoidable [əˈvɔɪdəbl] *adj* evitable.

avoidance [əˈvɔɪdəns] ▷ **tax avoidance**.

avowed [əˈvaʊd] *adj* declarado(da).

AWACS [ˈeɪwæks] (*abbr of* **airborne warning and control system**) *n* AWACS *m*.

await [əˈweɪt] *vt* esperar, aguardar.

awake [əˈweɪk] ◇ *adj* - **1.** [not sleeping] despierto(ta); **wide awake** completamente despierto - **2.** *fig* [aware]: **awake to sthg** consciente de algo. ◇ *vt* (*pt* **awoke** OR **awaked**, *pp* **awoken**) *lit* & *fig* despertar. ◇ *vi lit* & *fig* despertarse.

awakening [ə'weɪknɪŋ] *n lit* & *fig* despertar *m*; **a rude awakening** una repentina y desagradable toma de conciencia.

award [ə'wɔːd] <> *n* - **1.** [prize] premio *m*, galardón *m* - **2.** [compensation] indemnización *f*. <> *vt*: **to award sb sthg, to award sthg to sb** [prize] conceder OR otorgar algo a alguien; [compensation] adjudicar algo a alguien.

aware [ə'weəʳ] *adj* - **1.** [conscious]: **aware of** consciente de; **to become aware of** darse cuenta de - **2.** [informed, sensitive] informado(da), al día; **aware of sthg** al día de algo; **to be aware that** estar informado de que.

awareness [ə'weənɪs] *n* conciencia *f*.

awash [ə'wɒʃ] *adj lit* & *fig*: **awash (with)** inundado(da) (de).

away [ə'weɪ] <> *adv* - **1.** [move, walk, drive]: **to walk away (from)** marcharse (de); **to drive away (from)** alejarse (de) *(en coche)*; **to turn** OR **look away** apartar la vista - **2.** [at a distance - in space, time]: **away from** a distancia de; **4 miles away** a 4 millas de distancia; **a long way away** muy lejos; **the exam is two days away** faltan dos días para el examen - **3.** [not at home or office] fuera - **4.** [in safe place]: **to put sthg away** poner algo en su sitio - **5.** [indicating removal or disappearance]: **to fade away** desvanecerse; **to give sthg away** regalar algo; **to take sthg away from sb** quitarle algo a alguien - **6.** [continuously]: **he was working away when...** estaba muy concentrado trabajando cuando... <> *adj* SPORT [team, supporters] visitante; **away game** partido *m* fuera de casa.

awe [ɔː] *n* sobrecogimiento *m*; **to be in awe of sb** sentirse intimidado por alguien.

awesome ['ɔːsəm] *adj* alucinante *Esp*, macanudo(da) *Andes & R Dom*, padrísimo(ma) *Méx*.

awestruck ['ɔːstrʌk] *adj* sobrecogido(da).

awful ['ɔːful] *adj* - **1.** [terrible] terrible, espantoso(sa); **I feel awful** me siento fatal - **2.** *inf* [very great] tremendo(da); **I like it an awful lot** me gusta muchísimo.

awfully ['ɔːflɪ] *adv inf* [very] tremendamente.

awhile [ə'waɪl] *adv liter* un instante, un rato.

awkward ['ɔːkwəd] *adj* - **1.** [clumsy - movement] torpe; [- person] desgarbado(da) - **2.** [embarrassed, embarrassing] incómodo(da) - **3.** [unreasonable] difícil - **4.** [inconvenient - shape, size] poco manejable; [- moment] inoportuno(na).

awkwardly ['ɔːkwədlɪ] *adv* - **1.** [with difficulty] torpemente - **2.** [in an embarrassed way] incómodamente.

awkwardness ['ɔːkwədnɪs] *n* - **1.** [clumsiness] torpeza *f* - **2.** [embarrassment] incomodidad *f* - **3.** [unreasonableness] antipatía *f* - **4.** [inconvenience – of moment] inoportunidad *f*.

awning ['ɔːnɪŋ] *n* toldo *m*.

awoke [ə'wəʊk] *pt* ⊳ **awake**.

awoken [ə'wəʊkn] *pp* ⊳ **awake**.

AWOL ['eɪwɒl] (*abbr of* **absent without leave**) MIL *ausente sin permiso*.

awry [ə'raɪ] <> *adj* torcido(da), ladeado(da). <> *adv*: **to go awry** salir mal.

axe *UK*, **ax** *US* [æks] <> *n* hacha *f*; **to have an axe to grind** tener intereses personales. <> *vt* [project, jobs] suprimir.

axes ['æksiːz] *npl* ⊳ **axis**.

axiom ['æksɪəm] *n* axioma *m*.

axis ['æksɪs] (*pl* **axes**) *n* eje *m*.

axle ['æksl] *n* eje *m*.

ayatollah [ˌaɪə'tɒlə] *n* ayatolá *m*.

aye [aɪ] <> *adv* sí. <> *n* sí *m*.

AZ *abbr of* **Arizona**.

azalea [ə'zeɪljə] *n* azalea *f*.

Azerbaijan [ˌæzəbaɪ'dʒɑːn] *n* Azerbaiyán.

Azerbaijani [ˌæzəbaɪ'dʒɑːnɪ] <> *adj* azerbaiyano(na). <> *n* azerbaiyano *m*, -na *f*.

Azeri [ə'zerɪ] <> *adj* azerí. <> *n* azerí *mf*.

Azores [ə'zɔːz] *npl*: **the Azores** las Azores.

AZT (*abbr of* **azidothymidine**) *n* AZT *m*.

Aztec ['æztek] <> *adj* azteca. <> *n* [person] azteca *mf*.

azure ['æʒəʳ] *adj* azul celeste *(inv)*.

B

b (*pl* **b's** OR **bs**), **B** (*pl* **B's** OR **Bs**) [biː] *n* [letter] b *f*, B *f*.

➡ **B** *n* - **1.** MUS si *m* - **2.** SCH [mark] ≃ bien *m*.

b. (*abbr of* **born**) n.

BA *n* - **1.** (*abbr of* **Bachelor of Arts**), *(titular de una) licenciatura de letras* - **2.** (*abbr of* **British Airways**), *British Airways*.

BAA (*abbr of* **British Airports' Authority**) *n organismo independiente gestor de algunos de los principales aeropuertos británicos*.

babble ['bæbl] <> *n* parloteo *m*. <> *vi* [person] farfullar.

babe [beɪb] *n* - **1.** *liter* [baby] bebé *m* - **2.** *US inf* [term of affection] cariño *m* - **3.** *inf* [attractive person] persona *f* guapa; [attractive man] guaperas *m inv*.

baboon [bə'bu:n] *n* babuino *m*, papión *m*.

baby ['beɪbɪ] (*pl* -ies) <> *n* - **1.** [newborn child] bebé *m*; [infant] niño *m* - **2.** *inf* [term of affection] cariño *m*. <> *comp*: **baby brother** hermanito *m*; **baby sister** hermanita *f*.

baby boomer [-,bu:mə'] *n US niño nacido durante el boom natalicio de los sesenta*.

baby buggy *n* - **1.** *UK* [foldable pushchair] sillita *f* de niño (con ruedas) - **2.** *US* = **baby carriage**.

baby carriage *n US* cochecito *m* de niños.

baby food *n* papilla *f*.

babyish ['beɪbɪɪʃ] *adj pej* infantil.

baby-minder *n UK* niñera *f (durante el día)*.

baby-sit *vi* cuidar a niños.

baby-sitter [-'sɪtə'] *n* canguro *mf*.

bachelor ['bætʃələ'] *n* soltero *m*; **bachelor party** *US* despedida *f* de soltero.

Bachelor of Arts *n* ≃ licenciado *m* en Letras.

Bachelor of Science *n* ≃ licenciado *m* en Ciencias.

bachelor's degree *n* ≃ licenciatura *f*.

back [bæk] <> *adv* - **1.** [in position] atrás; **stand back!** ¡échense para atrás!; **to push back** empujar hacia atrás - **2.** [to former position or state] de vuelta; **to come back** volver; **to go back** volver; **to look back** volver la mirada; **to walk back** volver andando; **to give sthg back** devolver algo; **to be back (in fashion)** estar de vuelta; **he has been there and back** ha estado allí y ha vuelto; **I spent all day going back and forth** pasé todo el día yendo y viniendo - **3.** [in time]: **two weeks back** hace dos semanas; **it dates back to 1960** data de 1960; **back in March** allá en marzo; **to think back (to sthg)** recordar (algo) - **4.** [phone, write] de vuelta; **to pay sb back** [give back money] devolverle el dinero a alguien. <> *n* - **1.** [of person] espalda *f*; [of animal] lomo *m*; **lying on one's back** tumbado de espaldas; **to break the back of** *fig* pasar lo peor *OR* la peor parte de; **behind sb's back** a espaldas de alguien; **to put sb's back up** poner negro a alguien; **to stab sb in the back** *fig* darle a alguien una puñalada por la espalda *OR* trapera; **to turn one's back on sb/sthg** dar la espalda a alguien/algo, volver la espalda a alguien/algo - **2.** [of hand, cheque] dorso *m*; [of coin, page] reverso *m*; [of car, book, head] parte *f* trasera; [of chair] respaldo *m*; [of queue] final *m*; [of room, cupboard] fondo *m*; **the back of beyond** *UK* el quinto pino; **to know somewhere like the back of one's hand** co-

nocer un sitio como la palma de la mano - **3.** SPORT [player] defensa *m*. <> *adj (in compounds)* - **1.** [at the back - door, legs, seat] trasero(ra); [- page] último(ma) - **2.** [overdue - pay, rent] atrasado(da). <> *vt* - **1.** AUT [reverse]: **to back one's car into the garage** meter el coche marcha atrás en el garaje - **2.** [support] respaldar - **3.** [bet on] apostar por - **4.** [strengthen with material] reforzar. <> *vi* [drive backwards] ir marcha atrás; [walk backwards] ir hacia atrás.

🔹 **back to back** *adv* [with backs facing] espalda con espalda.

🔹 **back to front** *adv* al revés.

🔹 **back away** *vi* retroceder.

🔹 **back down** *vi* echarse *OR* volverse atrás.

🔹 **back off** *vi* echarse atrás.

🔹 **back onto** *vt UK* dar *(por la parte de atrás)* a.

🔹 **back out** *vi* echarse *OR* volverse atrás.

🔹 **back up** <> *vt sep* - **1.** [support] apoyar - **2.** [reverse] dar marcha atrás a - **3.** COMPUT hacer una copia de seguridad de. <> *vi* - **1.** [reverse] ir marcha atrás - **2.** COMPUT hacer copias de seguridad.

backache ['bækeɪk] *n* dolor *m* de espalda.

backbencher [,bæk'bentʃə'] *n UK diputado sin cargo en el gabinete del gobierno o la oposición*.

backbiting ['bækbaɪtɪŋ] *n* murmuración *f*, chismorreo *m*.

backbone ['bækbəʊn] *n lit & fig* columna *f* vertebral.

backbreaking ['bæk,breɪkɪŋ] *adj* derrengante.

back burner *n*: **to put sthg on the back burner** aparcar algo.

backchat *UK* ['bæktʃæt], **backtalk** *US n (U) inf* réplicas *fpl*.

backcloth ['bækklɒθ] *UK* = **backdrop**.

backcomb ['bækkəʊm] *vt UK* cardar.

back copy *n* número *m* atrasado.

backdate [,bæk'deɪt] *vt*: **a pay rise backdated to March** un aumento de sueldo con efecto retroactivo desde marzo.

back door *n* puerta *f* trasera; **the team qualified through the back door** *fig* el equipo se clasificó por la puerta trasera.

backdrop ['bækdrɒp], **backcloth** *n lit & fig* telón *m* de fondo.

backer ['bækə'] *n* promotor *m*, -ra *f*, patrocinador *m*, -ra *f*.

backfire [,bæk'faɪə'] *vi* - **1.** [motor vehicle] petardear - **2.** [go wrong]: **it backfired on him** le salió el tiro por la culata.

backgammon ['bæk,gæmən] *n* backgammon *m*.

background ['bækgraʊnd] <> n - **1.** [in picture, view] fondo m; **in the background** [of painting etc] al fondo; [out of the limelight] en la sombra - **2.** [of event, situation] trasfondo m - **3.** [up-bringing] origen m; **family background** ante-cedentes mpl familiares - **4.** [knowledge, exper-ience]: **a background in** conocimientos mpl de. <> comp [music, noise] de fondo; **background information** información sobre el contexto.

backhand ['bækhænd] n revés m.

backhanded ['bækhændɪd] adj fig equívoco(ca).

backhander ['bækhændər] n UK inf: **to give sb a backhander** untarle la mano a alguien, coi-mear a alguien Andes & R Dom, morder a alguien Amér C & Méx.

backing ['bækɪŋ] n - **1.** [support] apoyo m, res-paldo m - **2.** [lining] refuerzo m - **3.** MUS acom-pañamiento m.

back issue = **back number**.

backlash ['bæklæʃ] n reacción f violenta.

backless ['bæklɪs] adj abierto(ta) por la espal-da.

backlog ['bæklɒg] n acumulación f.

back number, back issue n número m atrasado.

backpack ['bækpæk] n mochila f, macuto m.

backpacker ['bækpækər] n mochilero m, -ra f.

backpacking ['bækpækɪŋ] n: **to go backpack-ing** irse de viaje con la mochila.

back passage n euph recto m.

back pay n (U) atrasos mpl.

backpedal [ˌbæk'pedl] (UK **-led**, cont **-ling**) (US **-ed**, cont **-ing**), **backtrack** vi fig: **to back-pedal (on sthg)** dar marcha atrás (con respec-to a algo).

back seat n asiento m trasero OR de atrás; **to take a back seat** fig situarse en segundo pla-no.

back-seat driver n persona que no para de dar consejos al conductor.

backside [ˌbæk'saɪd] n inf trasero m.

backslash ['bækslæʃ] n COMPUT barra f inversa.

backslide [ˌbæk'slaɪd] (pt & pp **-slid** [-'slɪd]) vi reincidir, recaer.

backspace ['bækspeɪs] <> n COMPUT: **backspace (key)** tecla f de retroceso. <> vi retroceder.

backstage [ˌbæk'steɪdʒ] adv entre bastidores.

back street n UK callejuela f de barrio.

backstroke ['bækstrəʊk] n espalda f (en nata-ción); **to do the backstroke** nadar a espalda.

backtalk US = **backchat**.

back-to-back adj [victories, meetings] segui-dos(das).

backtrack ['bæktræk] = **backpedal**.

backup ['bækʌp] <> adj - **1.** [plan] de emergen-cia, alternativo(va); [team] de apoyo - **2.** COM-PUT de seguridad. <> n - **1.** [support] apoyo m - **2.** COMPUT copia f de seguridad.

backward ['bækwəd] <> adj - **1.** [movement, look] hacia atrás - **2.** [country, person] atrasa-do(da). <> adv US = **backwards**.

backward-looking [-ˌlʊkɪŋ] adj pej retrógra-do(da).

backwards ['bækwədz], **backward** US adv - **1.** [move, go] hacia atrás; **backwards and for-wards** [movement] de un lado a otro - **2.** [back to front] al OR del revés.

backwash ['bækwɒʃ] n estela f.

backwater ['bækˌwɔːtər] n fig páramo m, lu-gar m atrasado.

backwoods ['bækwʊdz] npl zona f aislada.

backyard [ˌbæk'jɑːd] n - **1.** UK [yard] patio m - **2.** US [garden] jardín m (trasero).

bacon ['beɪkən] n bacon m, tocino m.

bacteria [bæk'tɪərɪə] npl bacterias fpl.

bacteriology [bækˌtɪərɪ'ɒlədʒɪ] n bacteriolo-gía f.

bad [bæd] (comp **worse**, superl **worst**) adj - **1.** [gen] malo(la); **he's bad at French** se le da mal el francés; **to have a bad back** estar mal de la espalda; **to go bad** [food] echarse a per-der; **to go from bad to worse** ir de mal en peor; **too bad!** ¡mala suerte!; **it's not bad (at all)** no está nada mal; **how are you? – not bad** ¿qué tal? – bien - **2.** [illness] grave - **3.** [guilty]: **to feel bad about sthg** sentirse mal por algo.

bad blood n rencor m, resentimiento m.

bad cheque n cheque m sin fondos.

bad debt n deuda f incobrable.

bade [bæd] pt & pp ⊳ **bid**.

bad feeling n (U) [resentment] rencor m, resen-timiento m.

badge [bædʒ] n - **1.** [for decoration - metal, plastic] chapa f; [- sewn-on] insignia f - **2.** [for identific-ation] distintivo m.

badger ['bædʒər] <> n tejón m. <> vt: **to badger sb (to do sthg)** ponerse pesado(da) con alguien (para que haga algo).

badly ['bædlɪ] (comp **worse**, superl **worst**) adv - **1.** [not well] mal; **to think badly of sb** pensar mal de alguien - **2.** [seriously] gravemente; **I'm badly in need of help** necesito ayuda urgen-temente.

badly-off adj - **1.** [poor] apurado(da) de dine-ro - **2.** [lacking]: **to be badly-off for sthg** estar OR andar mal de algo.

bad-mannered [-'mænəd] adj maleduca-do(da).

badminton ['bædmɪntən] n bádminton m.

bad-mouth vt esp US inf poner verde.

badness ['bædnɪs] n [of behaviour] maldad f.

bad-tempered [-'tempəd] adj - **1.** [by nature]: **to be bad-tempered** tener mal genio - **2.** [in a bad mood]: **to be bad-tempered** estar malhumorado(da).

baffle ['bæfl] vt desconcertar.

baffling ['bæflɪŋ] adj desconcertante.

bag [bæg] ⋄ n - **1.** [container, bagful] bolsa f; **he's nothing but a bag of bones** está en los huesos; **in the bag** inf en el bote; **to pack one's bags** fig hacer las maletas - **2.** [handbag] bolso m, cartera f Andes & R Plata. ⋄ vt (pt & pp **-ged**, cont **-ging**) - **1.** [put into bags] meter en bolsas - **2.** UK inf [reserve] pedirse, reservarse.

◆ **bags** npl - **1.** [under eyes]: **to have bags under one's eyes** inf tener ojeras - **2.** [lots]: **bags of** inf un montón de.

bagel ['beɪgəl] n bollo de pan en forma de rosca.

baggage ['bægɪdʒ] n esp US (U) equipaje m.

baggage car n US furgón m de equipajes.

baggage reclaim n recogida f de equipajes.

baggage room n US consigna f.

baggy ['bægɪ] (comp **-ier**, superl **-iest**) adj holgado(da).

Baghdad [bæg'dæd] n Bagdad.

bag lady n inf vagabunda f.

bagpipes ['bægpaɪps] npl gaita f.

bagsnatcher ['bægsnætʃəʳ] n ladrón que roba dando el tirón.

bah [bɑ:] excl ¡bah!

Bahamas [bə'hɑ:məz] npl: **the Bahamas** las Bahamas.

Bahrain, Bahrein [bɑ:'reɪn] n Bahréin.

Bahraini, Bahreini [bɑ:'reɪnɪ] ⋄ adj bahreiní. ⋄ n bahreiní mf.

Bahrein = Bahrain.

Bahreini = Bahraini.

bail [beɪl] n (U) fianza f; **on bail** bajo fianza.

◆ **bail out** ⋄ vt sep - **1.** [pay bail for] obtener la libertad bajo fianza de - **2.** [rescue] sacar de apuros. ⋄ vi [from plane] tirarse en paracaídas (antes de que se estrelle el avión).

bailiff ['beɪlɪf] n alguacil m.

bait [beɪt] ⋄ n lit & fig cebo m; **to rise to** OR **take the bait** fig picarse, morder el anzuelo. ⋄ vt - **1.** [put bait on] cebar - **2.** [tease, torment] hacer sufrir, cebarse con.

baize [beɪz] n tapete m.

bake [beɪk] ⋄ vt - **1.** [food] cocer al horno - **2.** [bricks, clay] cocer, endurecer. ⋄ vi [food] cocerse al horno.

baked beans [beɪkt-] npl alubias fpl cocidas en salsa de tomate.

baked potato [beɪkt-] n patata f asada OR al horno.

Bakelite® ['beɪkəlaɪt] n baquelita f.

baker ['beɪkəʳ] n panadero m; **baker's (shop)** panadería f.

bakery ['beɪkərɪ] (pl **-ies**) n panadería f, tahona f.

baking ['beɪkɪŋ] ⋄ adj inf: **it's baking hot** hace un calor achicharrante. ⋄ n cocción f.

baking powder n levadura f en polvo.

baking soda n US bicarbonato m en polvo.

baking tin n molde m para cocinar al horno.

balaclava (helmet) [bælə'klɑ:və-] n pasamontañas m inv, verdugo m.

balance ['bæləns] ⋄ n - **1.** [equilibrium] equilibrio m; **to keep/lose one's balance** mantener/perder el equilibrio; **it caught me off balance** me pilló desprevenido(da) - **2.** fig [counterweight] contrapunto m - **3.** [of evidence etc] peso m - **4.** [scales] balanza f; **to be** OR **hang in the balance** estar en el aire - **5.** [of account] saldo m. ⋄ vt - **1.** [keep in balance] poner en equilibrio - **2.** [compare] sopesar - **3.** [in accounting]: **to balance the books/a budget** hacer que cuadren las cuentas/cuadre un presupuesto. ⋄ vi - **1.** [maintain equilibrium] sostenerse en equilibrio - **2.** [in accounting] cuadrar.

◆ **on balance** adv tras pensarlo detenidamente.

balanced ['bælənst] adj [fair] equilibrado(da).

balanced diet n dieta f equilibrada.

balance of payments n balanza f de pagos.

balance of power n equilibrio m de fuerzas.

balance of trade n balanza f comercial.

balance sheet n balance m.

balcony ['bælkənɪ] (pl **-ies**) n - **1.** [on building - big] terraza f; [- small] balcón m - **2.** [in theatre] anfiteatro m, galería f.

bald [bɔ:ld] adj - **1.** [without hair] calvo(va); **to go bald** quedarse calvo(va) - **2.** [tyre] desgastado(da) - **3.** fig [blunt] escueto(ta).

bald eagle n pigargo m cabeciblanco (este pájaro es el símbolo de los Estados Unidos y aparece en todos los emblemas oficiales).

balding ['bɔ:ldɪŋ] adj con calva incipiente.

baldness ['bɔ:ldnɪs] n calvicie f.

bale [beɪl] n bala f.

◆ **bale out** vi UK - **1.** [remove water] achicar agua - **2.** [from plane] tirarse en paracaídas (antes de que se estrelle el avión).

Balearic Islands [bælɪ'ærɪk-], **Balearics** [bælɪ'ærɪks] npl: **the Balearic Islands** las Baleares.

baleful ['beɪlfʊl] adj maligno(na).

Bali ['bɑ:lɪ] n Bali.

balk, baulk [bɔːk] *vi*: to balk (at doing sthg) resistirse (a hacer algo); **I balk at the idea** me repele la idea.

Balkan ['bɔːlkən] *adj* balcánico(ca).

Balkans ['bɔːlkənz], **Balkan States** *npl*: the Balkans los Balcanes.

ball [bɔːl] *n* - **1.** [for tennis, cricket] pelota *f*; [for golf, billiards] bola *f*; [for football, basketball, rugby] balón *m*; **to be on the ball** *fig* estar al tanto de todo; **to play ball with** *fig* colaborar con; **to start/keep the ball rolling** *fig* poner/mantener las cosas en marcha - **2.** [round shape] bola *f* - **3.** [of foot] pulpejo *m* - **4.** [dance] baile *m*; **to have a ball** *fig* pasárselo bomba.

➤ **balls** *v inf* ⬦ *npl* [testicles] pelotas *fpl*. ⬦ *n* *(U)* [nonsense] gilipolleces *fpl*. ⬦ *excl* [expressing disagreement] ¡y un huevo!; [expressing annoyance] ¡leche!

ballad ['bæləd] *n* balada *f*.

ball-and-socket joint *n* ANAT enartrosis *f inv*.

ballast ['bæləst] *n* lastre *m*.

ball bearing *n* cojinete *m* de bolas.

ball boy *n* recogepelotas *m inv*.

ballcock ['bɔːlkɒk] *n* válvula *f* de desagüe.

ballerina [ˌbælə'riːnə] *n* bailarina *f*.

ballet ['bæleɪ] *n* ballet *m*.

ballet dancer *n* bailarín *m*, -ina *f*.

ball game *n* - **1.** *US* [baseball match] partido *m* de béisbol - **2.** *inf* [situation]: **it's a whole new ball game** es una historia totalmente distinta.

ball girl *n* recogepelotas *f inv*.

ballistic [bə'lɪstɪk] *adj* [missile] balístico(ca); **to go ballistic** *inf fig* ponerse hecho(cha) una furia.

ballistics [bə'lɪstɪks] *n* *(U)* balística *f*.

balloon [bə'luːn] ⬦ *n* - **1.** [toy] globo *m* - **2.** [hot-air balloon] globo *m* (aerostático) - **3.** [in cartoon] bocadillo *m*. ⬦ *vi* inflarse.

ballooning [bə'luːnɪŋ] *n* aerostación *f*.

ballot ['bælət] ⬦ *n* - **1.** [voting paper] voto *m*, papeleta *f*, balota *f* *Perú*, boleta *f* electoral *Méx & R Plata* - **2.** [voting process] votación *f*. ⬦ *vt*: **to ballot the members on an issue** someter un asunto a votación entre los afiliados. ⬦ *vi*: **to ballot for sthg** elegir algo por votación.

ballot box *n* [container] urna *f*; **to decide sthg at the ballot box** decidir algo en las urnas.

ballot paper *n* voto *m*, papeleta *f*, balota *f* *Perú*, boleta *f* electoral *Méx & R Plata*.

ball-park figure *n inf* cifra *f* aproximada.

ballpoint (pen) ['bɔːlpɔɪnt-] *n* bolígrafo *m*, pluma *f* atómica *Méx*, esfero *m* *Col*, birome *f* *R Plata*, lápiz *m* de pasta *Chile*.

ballroom ['bɔːlrum] *n* salón *m* de baile.

ballroom dancing *n* *(U)* baile *m* de salón.

balls-up *UK*, **ball-up** *US n v inf* cagada *f*.

balm [bɑːm] *n* bálsamo *m*.

balmy ['bɑːmɪ] (*comp* **-ier**, *superl* **-iest**) *adj* apacible.

baloney [bə'ləʊnɪ] *n* - **1.** *(U)* *inf* bobadas *fpl* - **2.** *US* [sausage] = **bologna**.

balsam ['bɔːlsəm] *n* bálsamo *m*.

balsamic vinegar [bɔːl'sæmɪk-] *n* vinagre *m* (balsámico) de Módena.

balti ['bɔːltɪ] *n* [pan] *cacerola utilizada en la cocina india*; [food] *plato indio sazonado con especias y preparado en un 'balti'*.

Baltic ['bɔːltɪk] ⬦ *adj* báltico(ca). ⬦ *n*: the Baltic (Sea) el (mar) Báltico.

Baltic Republic *n*: the Baltic Republics las repúblicas bálticas.

Baltic State *n*: the Baltic States los países bálticos.

balustrade [ˌbæləs'treɪd] *n* balaustrada *f*.

bamboo [bæm'buː] *n* bambú *m*.

bamboozle [bæm'buːzl] *vt inf* camelar, engatusar.

ban [bæn] ⬦ *n*: ban (on) prohibición *f* (de). ⬦ *vt* (*pt & pp* **-ned**, *cont* **-ning**): **to ban (sb from doing sthg)** prohibir (a alguien hacer algo).

banal [bə'nɑːl] *adj pej* banal, ordinario(ria).

banana [bə'nɑːnə] *n* plátano *m*, banana *f Amér*.

banana republic *n* república *f* bananera.

banana split *n* banana split *m*.

band [bænd] *n* - **1.** [musical group - pop] grupo *m*; [- jazz, military] banda *f* - **2.** [of thieves etc] banda *f* - **3.** [strip] cinta *f*, tira *f* - **4.** [stripe, range] franja *f*.

➤ **band together** *vi* juntarse, agruparse.

bandage ['bændɪdʒ] ⬦ *n* venda *f*. ⬦ *vt* vendar.

Band-Aid® *n US* ≃ tirita® *f Esp*, ≃ curita *f Amér*.

bandan(n)a [bæn'dænə] *n* pañuelo *m* *(para la cabeza)*.

b and b, B and B *n abbr of* bed and breakfast.

bandit ['bændɪt] *n* bandido *m*, -da *f*, bandolero *m*, -ra *f*.

bandmaster ['bændˌmɑːstər] *n* director *m* (de banda musical).

band saw *n* sierra *f* de cinta.

bandsman ['bændzmən] (*pl* **-men** [-mən]) *n* músico *m* (de banda).

bandstand ['bændstænd] *n* quiosco *m* de música.

bandwagon ['bændwægən] *n*: **to jump on the bandwagon** subirse *OR* apuntarse al carro.

bandy ['bændɪ] *adj* (*comp* **-ier**, *superl* **-iest**) [legs] arqueado(da).

◆ **bandy about, bandy around** *vt sep* (*pt & pp* **-ied**) sacar a relucir.

bandy-legged [-,legd] *adj* de piernas arqueadas.

bane [beɪn] *n*: **to be the bane of sb's life** ser la cruz de alguien.

bang [bæŋ] ⬦ *n* - **1.** [blow] golpe *m* - **2.** [loud noise] estampido *m*, estruendo *m*; **to go with a bang** *inf* ser la bomba. ⬦ *vt* - **1.** [hit - drum, desk] golpear; [- knee, head] golpearse - **2.** [door] cerrar de golpe. ⬦ *vi* golpear, dar golpes. ⬦ *adv* - **1.** [exactly]: **bang in the middle of** justo en mitad de; **bang on** [correct] muy acertado(da) - **2.** *inf* [away]: **bang goes** OR **go...** adiós a... ⬦ *excl* ¡pum!
◆ **bangs** *npl* US flequillo *m*.
◆ **bang down** *vt sep* [book, fist] golpear con.

banger ['bæŋər] *n UK* - **1.** *inf* [sausage] salchicha *f* - **2.** *inf* [old car] carraca *f*, cacharro *m* - **3.** [firework] petardo *m*.

Bangkok [bæŋ'kok] *n* Bangkok.

Bangladesh [,bæŋglə'deʃ] *n* Bangladesh.

Bangladeshi [,bæŋglə'deʃi] ⬦ *adj* bangladeshí. ⬦ *n* bangladeshí *mf*.

bangle ['bæŋgl] *n* pulsera *f*, brazalete *m*.

banish ['bænɪʃ] *vt lit* & *fig* desterrar.

banister ['bænɪstər] *n* barandilla *f*, pasamanos *m inv*.

bank [bæŋk] ⬦ *n* - **1.** [gen & FIN] banco *m* - **2.** [by river, lake] ribera *f*, orilla *f* - **3.** [slope] loma *f* - **4.** [of clouds etc] masa *f*. ⬦ *vt* FIN ingresar en el banco. ⬦ *vi* - **1.** FIN: **to bank with** tener una cuenta en - **2.** [plane] ladearse.
◆ **bank on** *vt insep* contar con.

bank account *n* cuenta *f* bancaria.

bank balance *n* saldo *m* bancario.

bankbook ['bæŋkbuk] *n* libreta *f* OR cartilla *f* (del banco).

bank card = **banker's card**.

bank charges *npl* comisiones *fpl* bancarias.

bank details *npl* datos *mpl* bancarios.

bank draft *n* giro *m* bancario.

banker ['bæŋkər] *n* banquero *m*, -ra *f*.

banker's card, bank card *n UK* tarjeta *f* de identificación bancaria.

banker's order *n UK* domiciliación *f* de pago.

bank holiday *n UK* día *m* festivo, fiesta *f* nacional.

banking ['bæŋkɪŋ] *n* banca *f*.

bank loan *n* préstamo *m* OR crédito *m* bancario.

bank manager *n* director *m*, -ra *f* de banco.

bank note *n* billete *m* de banco.

bank rate *n* tipo *m* de interés bancario.

bankrupt ['bæŋkrʌpt] ⬦ *adj* [financially] quebrado(da), en quiebra; **to go bankrupt** quebrar. ⬦ *n* quebrado *m*, -da *f*, insolvente *mf*. ⬦ *vt* llevar a la quiebra.

bankruptcy ['bæŋkrəptsɪ] (*pl* **-ies**) *n* quiebra *f*, bancarrota *f*; *fig* [of ideas] falta *f* total.

bank statement *n* extracto *m* de cuenta.

banner ['bænər] *n* - **1.** [carrying slogan] pancarta *f* - **2.** [comput] banner *m*, pancarta *f* publicitaria.

banoffee [bə'nɒfi:] *n* (*U*) postre hecho con galletas, plátano, mantequilla y leche condensada.

banquet ['bæŋkwɪt] *n* banquete *m*.

bantam ['bæntəm] *n* gallina *f* de Bantam.

bantamweight ['bæntəmweɪt] *n* peso *m* gallo.

banter ['bæntər] ⬦ *n* (*U*) bromas *fpl*. ⬦ *vi* bromear.

bap [bæp] *n UK* bollo *m* de pan, panecillo *m*.

baptism ['bæptɪzm] *n* bautismo *m*; **baptism of fire** bautismo de fuego.

Baptist ['bæptɪst] *n* bautista *mf*.

baptize, -ise [*UK* bæp'taɪz, *US* 'bæptaɪz] *vt* bautizar.

bar [bɑ:r] ⬦ *n* - **1.** [of soap] pastilla *f*; [of gold] lingote *m*; [of wood] barrote *m*; [of metal] barra *f*; [of chocolate] una chocolatina; **to be behind bars** estar entre rejas - **2.** [drinking place] bar *m* - **3.** [counter] barra *f* - **4.** *fig* [obstacle] barrera *f*; [ban] prohibición *f* - **5.** MUS compás *m*. ⬦ *vt* (*pt & pp* **-red**, *cont* -**ring**) - **1.** [close with a bar] atrancar - **2.** [block]: **to bar sb's way** impedir el paso a alguien - **3.** [ban]: **to bar sb (from doing sthg)** prohibir a alguien (hacer algo); **to bar sb from somewhere** prohibir a alguien la entrada en un sitio. ⬦ *prep* [except] menos, salvo; **bar none** sin excepción.
◆ **Bar** *n* LAW: **the Bar** *UK* conjunto de los abogados que ejercen en tribunales superiores; *US* la abogacía.

Barbados [bɑ:'beɪdɒs] *n* Barbados.

barbarian [bɑ:'beəriən] *n lit* & *fig* bárbaro *m*, -ra *f*.

barbaric [bɑ:'bærɪk] *adj* salvaje.

barbarous ['bɑ:bərəs] *adj* bárbaro(ra).

barbecue ['bɑ:bɪkju:] ⬦ *n* barbacoa *f*. ⬦ *vt* asar a la parrilla.

barbed [bɑ:bd] *adj* - **1.** [pointed, spiked] con púa OR púas - **2.** [unkind] envenenado(da), afilado(da).

barbed wire [bɑ:bd-] *n* alambre *m* de espino.

barber ['bɑ:bər] *n* barbero *m*; **barber's** peluquería *f*.

barbershop ['bɑ:bəʃɒp] *n US* barbería *f*.

barbiturate [bɑ:'bɪtjurət] *n* barbitúrico *m*.

Barcelona [ˌbɑːsəˈləʊnə] *n* Barcelona.

bar chart, bar graph *US n* gráfico *m* de barras.

bar code *n* código *m* de barras.

bare [beəʳ] ◇ *adj* **- 1.** [without covering - legs, trees, hills] desnudo(da); [- feet] descalzo(za) **- 2.** [absolute, minimum] esencial; **the bare essentials** lo mínimo indispensable **- 3.** [empty] vacío(a) **- 4.** [mere]: **a bare 10%** tan sólo el 10%. ◇ *vt* descubrir; **to bare one's teeth** enseñar los dientes.

bareback [ˈbeəbæk] *adj* & *adv* a pelo.

barefaced [ˈbeəfeɪst] *adj* descarado(da).

barefoot(ed) [ˌbeəˈfʊt(ɪd)] *adj* & *adv* descalzo(za).

bareheaded [ˌbeəˈhedɪd] *adj* & *adv* descubierto(ta), sin sombrero.

barelegged [ˌbeəˈlegd] *adj* & *adv* con las piernas desnudas.

barely [ˈbeəlɪ] *adv* [scarcely] apenas.

bargain [ˈbɑːgɪn] ◇ *n* **- 1.** [agreement] trato *m*, acuerdo *m*; **into the bargain** además **- 2.** [good buy] ganga *f*, pichincha *f* R Plata. ◇ *vi*: **to bargain (with sb for sthg)** negociar (con alguien para obtener algo).
➡ **bargain for, bargain on** *vt insep* contar con.

bargaining [ˈbɑːgɪnɪŋ] *n* (U) negociación *f*.

bargaining power *n* poder *m* negociador.

barge [bɑːdʒ] ◇ *n* gabarra *f*, barcaza *f*. ◇ *vi* *inf* abrirse paso; **to barge into** [person] chocarse con; [room] irrumpir en.
➡ **barge in** *vi inf*: **to barge in (on)** [conversation etc] entrometerse (en).

barge pole *n inf*: **I wouldn't touch it with a barge pole** no lo quiero ni regalado.

bar graph *US* = **bar chart**.

baritone [ˈbærɪtəʊn] *n* barítono *m*.

barium meal [ˈbeərɪəm-] *n UK* papilla *f* (tomada antes de radiografía).

bark [bɑːk] ◇ *n* **- 1.** [of dog] ladrido *m*; **his bark is worse than his bite** *inf* ≃ perro ladrador, poco mordedor **- 2.** [on tree] corteza *f*. ◇ *vt* gritar. ◇ *vi*: **to bark (at)** ladrar (a).

barking [ˈbɑːkɪŋ] ◇ *adj UK inf* [crazy]: **barking mad** loco(ca) de remate. ◇ *n* (U) ladridos *mpl*.

barley [ˈbɑːlɪ] *n* cebada *f*.

barley sugar *n UK* azúcar *m o f* cande.

barley water *n UK* hordiate *m*.

barmaid [ˈbɑːmeɪd] *n* camarera *f*.

barman [ˈbɑːmən] (*pl* **-men** [-mən]) *n* camarero *m*, barman *m*.

barmy [ˈbɑːmɪ] (*comp* **-ier**, *superl* **-iest**) *adj UK inf* chalado(da), chiflado(da).

barn [bɑːn] *n* granero *m*.

barnacle [ˈbɑːnəkl] *n* percebe *m*.

barn dance *n* baile *m* campestre.

barn owl *n* lechuza *f*.

barometer [bəˈrɒmɪtəʳ] *n* barómetro *m*; *fig* [of public opinion etc] piedra *f* de toque.

baron [ˈbærən] *n* barón *m*; **press/oil baron** *fig* magnate *m* de la prensa/del petróleo.

baroness [ˈbærənɪs] *n* baronesa *f*.

baronet [ˈbærənɪt] *n* baronet *m*.

baroque [bəˈrɒk] *adj* barroco(ca).

barrack [ˈbærək] *vt UK* abroncar, abuchear.
➡ **barracks** *npl* cuartel *m*.

barracking [ˈbærəkɪŋ] *n UK* bronca *f*, abucheo *m*.

barracuda [ˌbærəˈkuːdə] *n* barracuda *f*.

barrage [ˈbærɑːʒ] *n* **- 1.** [of firing] descarga *f*, fuego *m* intenso de artillería **- 2.** [of questions] aluvión *m*, alud *m* **- 3.** *UK* [dam] presa *f*, dique *m*.

barred [bɑːd] *adj* enrejado(da).

barrel [ˈbærəl] *n* **- 1.** [for beer, wine, oil] barril *m* **- 2.** [of gun] cañón *m*.

barrel organ *n* organillo *m*.

barren [ˈbærən] *adj* estéril.

barrette [bəˈret] *n US* pasador *m*.

barricade [ˌbærɪˈkeɪd] ◇ *n* barricada *f*. ◇ *vt* levantar barricadas en; **to barricade o.s. in** atrincherarse *OR* parapetarse en.

barrier [ˈbærɪəʳ] *n lit* & *fig* barrera *f*.

barrier cream *n UK* crema *f* protectora.

barring [ˈbɑːrɪŋ] *prep* salvo; **barring a miracle** a menos que ocurra un milagro.

barrister [ˈbærɪstəʳ] *n UK* abogado *m*, -da *f* (de tribunales superiores).

barroom [ˈbɑːrʊm] *n US* bar *m*.

barrow [ˈbærəʊ] *n* carrito *m*.

bar stool *n* taburete *m* (de bar).

bartender [ˈbɑːtendəʳ] *n esp US* camarero *m*, -ra *f*.

barter [ˈbɑːtəʳ] ◇ *n* trueque *m*. ◇ *vt*: **to barter (sthg for sthg)** trocar (algo por algo). ◇ *vi* trocar.

base [beɪs] ◇ *n* base *f*. ◇ *vt* **- 1.** [place, establish] emplazar; **he's based in Paris** vive en París **- 2.** [use as starting point]: **to base sthg on** *OR* **upon** basar algo en. ◇ *adj pej* bajo(ja), vil.

baseball [ˈbeɪsbɔːl] *n* béisbol *m*.

baseball cap *n* gorra *f* de visera.

base camp *n* campamento *m* base.

Basel, Basle [ˈbɑːzəl] *n* Basilea.

baseless [ˈbeɪslɪs] *adj* infundado(da).

baseline [ˈbeɪslaɪn] *n* [in tennis] línea *f* de fondo.

basement [ˈbeɪsmənt] *n* sótano *m*.

base metal *n* dated metal *m* no precioso.

base rate n tipo m de interés base.

bases ['beɪsiːz] npl ⊳ **basis**.

bash [bæʃ] inf ⟨⟩ n - **1.** [painful blow] porrazo m - **2.** [attempt]: **to have a bash at sthg** intentar algo - **3.** [party] juerga f. ⟨⟩ vt - **1.** [hit - person, thing] darle un porrazo a; [- one's head, knee] darse un porrazo en - **2.** [criticize] arremeter contra.

bashful ['bæʃfʊl] adj [person] vergonzoso(sa); [smile] tímido(da).

basic ['beɪsɪk] adj básico(ca).
➡ **basics** npl - **1.** [rudiments] principios mpl básicos - **2.** [essentials] lo imprescindible.

basically ['beɪsɪklɪ] adv - **1.** [essentially] esencialmente - **2.** [really] en resumen.

basic rate n UK tipo m base.

basic wage n sueldo m base.

basil ['bæzl] n albahaca f.

basin ['beɪsn] n - **1.** UK [bowl] balde m, barreño m - **2.** [wash basin] lavabo m - **3.** GEOG cuenca f.

basis ['beɪsɪs] (pl **bases**) n base f; **on the basis of** de acuerdo con, a partir de; **on a weekly basis** semanalmente; **on a monthly basis** mensualmente.

bask [bɑːsk] vi - **1.** [sunbathe]: **to bask in the sun** tostarse al sol - **2.** fig: **to bask in** [sb's approval, praise] gozar de.

basket ['bɑːskɪt] n - **1.** [container] cesta f - **2.** [in basketball] canasta f.

basketball ['bɑːskɪtbɔːl] ⟨⟩ n baloncesto m. ⟨⟩ comp de baloncesto.

basketwork ['bɑːskɪtwɜːk] n cestería f.

basking shark ['bɑːskɪŋ-] n tiburón m peregrino.

Basle [bɑːl] = **Basel**.

Basque [bɑːsk] ⟨⟩ adj vasco(ca). ⟨⟩ n - **1.** [person] vasco m, -ca f - **2.** [language] vascuence m, euskera m.

basmati (rice) [bæz'mɑːtɪ] n (U) CULIN arroz m basmati.

bass[1] [beɪs] ⟨⟩ adj bajo(ja). ⟨⟩ n - **1.** [singer, bass guitar] bajo m - **2.** [double bass] contrabajo m - **3.** [on hi-fi, amplifier] graves mpl.

bass[2] [bæs] (pl **bass** OR **-es**) n [seawater fish] lubina f.

bass clef [beɪs-] n clave f de fa.

bass drum [beɪs-] n bombo m.

basset (hound) ['bæsɪt-] n basset m.

bass guitar [beɪs-] n bajo m.

bassoon [bə'suːn] n fagot m.

bastard ['bɑːstəd] n - **1.** [illegitimate child] bastardo m, -da f - **2.** v inf pej cabrón m, -ona f, concha f de su madre R Plata.

baste [beɪst] vt regar con grasa.

bastion ['bæstɪən] n bastión m.

bat [bæt] ⟨⟩ n - **1.** [animal] murciélago m - **2.** [for cricket, baseball] bate m - **3.** [for table-tennis] pala f, paleta f
▸▸▮ **I did it off my own bat** lo hice por mi cuenta. ⟨⟩ vt & vi (pt & pp **-ted**, cont **-ting**) batear.

batch [bætʃ] n - **1.** [of bread] hornada f - **2.** [of letters etc] remesa f - **3.** [of work] montón m - **4.** [of products] lote m, partida f - **5.** [of people] grupo m, tanda f.

batch file n COMPUT fichero m por lotes.

batch processing n COMPUT proceso m por lotes.

bated ['beɪtɪd] adj: **with bated breath** con el aliento contenido.

bath [bɑːθ] ⟨⟩ n - **1.** [bathtub] bañera f, bañadera f Arg, tina f Amér - **2.** [act of washing] baño m, bañada f Amér; **to have** OR **take a bath** darse un baño, bañarse. ⟨⟩ vt bañar.
➡ **baths** npl UK [public swimming pool] piscina f municipal, alberca f municipal Méx, pileta f municipal R Plata.

bath chair n silla f de ruedas.

bath cube n cubito con esencias aromáticas para el baño.

bathe [beɪð] ⟨⟩ vt - **1.** [wound] lavar - **2.** [suffuse]: **to be bathed in** OR **with** estar bañado(da) de. ⟨⟩ vi bañarse.

bather ['beɪðə'] n bañista mf.

bathing ['beɪðɪŋ] n (U) baños mpl.

bathing cap n gorro m de baño.

bathing costume, bathing suit n traje m de baño, bañador m, malla f Amér.

bathing trunks npl bañador m.

bath mat n alfombrilla f de baño, tapete m de baño Col & Méx.

bath oil n aceite m de baño.

bathrobe ['bɑːθrəʊb] n - **1.** [made of towelling] albornoz m - **2.** [dressing gown] batín m, bata f.

bathroom ['bɑːθrʊm] n - **1.** UK [room with bath] (cuarto m de) baño m - **2.** [toilet] servicio m.

bath salts npl sales fpl de baño.

bath towel n toalla f de baño.

bathtub ['bɑːθtʌb] n bañera f.

batik [bə'tiːk] n batik m.

baton ['bætən] n - **1.** [of conductor] batuta f - **2.** [in relay race] testigo m - **3.** UK [of policeman] porra f.

baton charge n UK carga f policial (con porras).

batsman ['bætsmən] (pl **-men** [-mən]) n bateador m.

battalion [bə'tæljən] n batallón m.

batten ['bætn] n listón m (de madera).
➡ **batten down** vt insep sujetar con listones.

batter ['bætər] <> *n* pasta *f* para rebozar; *US* [for cakes] mezcla *f* pastelera. <> *vt* - **1.** [child, woman] pegar - **2.** [door, ship] golpear.
➤ **batter down** *vt sep* echar abajo.

battered ['bætəd] *adj* - **1.** [child, woman] maltratado(da) - **2.** [car, hat] abollado(da) - **3.** [fish, vegetables etc] rebozado(da).

battering ['bætərɪŋ] *n* paliza *f*.

battering ram *n* ariete *m*.

battery ['bætərɪ] (*pl* -**ies**) *n* - **1.** [of radio, toy] pila *f*; [of car, guns] batería *f* - **2.** [array, set] serie *f*, conjunto *m*.

battery charger *n* cargador *m* de pilas.

battery hen *n* gallina *f* de granja intensiva.

battle ['bætl] <> *n* - **1.** [in war] batalla *f* - **2.** [struggle]: **battle (for/against/with)** lucha *f* (por/contra/con); **battle of wits** duelo *m* de ingenio; **self-confidence is half the battle** confiar en uno mismo es llevar medio camino andado; **to be fighting a losing battle** luchar por una causa perdida. <> *vi*: **to battle (for/against/with)** luchar (por/contra/con).

battledress ['bætldres] *n* *UK* uniforme *m*.

battlefield ['bætlfi:ld], **battleground** ['bætlgraʊnd] *n* *lit* & *fig* campo *m* de batalla.

battlements ['bætlmənts] *npl* almenas *fpl*.

battleship ['bætlʃɪp] *n* acorazado *m*.

bauble ['bɔ:bl] *n* - **1.** [ornament] baratija *f* - **2.** [for Christmas tree] bola *f* de Navidad.

baulk [bɔ:k] = **balk**.

Bavaria [bə'veərɪə] *n* Baviera.

Bavarian [bə'veərɪən] <> *adj* bávaro(ra). <> *n* bávaro *m*, -ra *f*.

bawdy ['bɔ:dɪ] (*comp* -**ier**, *superl* -**iest**) *adj* verde, picante.

bawl [bɔ:l] <> *vt* gritar. <> *vi* - **1.** [shout] vociferar - **2.** [cry] berrear.

bay [beɪ] <> *n* - **1.** [of coast] bahía *f* - **2.** [for loading] zona *f* de carga y descarga - **3.** [for parking] plaza *f*, estacionamiento *m* - **4.** [horse] caballo *m* bayo
➤ **to keep sthg/sb at bay** mantener algo/a alguien a raya. <> *vi* aullar.

bay leaf *n* (hoja *f* de) laurel *m*.

bayonet ['beɪənɪt] *n* bayoneta *f*.

bay tree *n* laurel *m*.

bay window *n* ventana *f* salediza.

bazaar [bə'zɑ:r] *n* - **1.** [market] bazar *m*, zoco *m* - **2.** *UK* [charity sale] mercadillo *m* benéfico.

bazooka [bə'zu:kə] *n* bazuca *m*.

B & B *abbr of* **bed and breakfast**.

BBC (*abbr of* **British Broadcasting Corporation**) *n* BBC *f*, *compañía estatal británica de radiotelevisión*.

BC - **1.** (*abbr of* **before Christ**) a.C. - **2.** *abbr of* **British Columbia**.

Bcc [,bi:si:'si:] (*abbr of* **blind carbon copy**) *n* Cco.

BCG (*abbr of* **Bacillus Calmette-Guérin**) *n* vacuna de la tuberculosis.

be [bi:] (*pt* was *OR* were, *pp* been) <> *aux vb* - **1.** (*in combination with present participle: to form cont tense*) estar; **what is he doing?** ¿qué hace *OR* está haciendo?; **it's snowing** está nevando; **I'm leaving tomorrow** me voy mañana; **they've been promising it for years** han estado prometiéndolo durante años - **2.** (*in combination with pp: to form passive*) ser; **to be loved** ser amado; **there was no one to be seen** no se veía a nadie; **ten people were killed** murieron diez personas - **3.** (*in question tags*): **you're not going now, are you?** no irás a marcharte ya ¿no?; **the meal was delicious, wasn't it?** la comida fue deliciosa ¿verdad? - **4.** (*followed by 'to' + infinitive*): **I'm to be promoted** me van a ascender; **you're not to tell anyone** no debes decírselo a nadie. <> *cop vb* - **1.** (*with adj, n*) [indicating innate quality, permanent condition] ser; [indicating state, temporary condition] estar; **snow is white** la nieve es blanca; **she's intelligent/tall** es inteligente/alta; **to be a doctor/plumber** ser médico/fontanero; **I'm Welsh** soy galés; **be quiet!** ¡cállate!; **1 and 1 are 2** 1 y 1 son 2; **your hands are cold** tus manos están frías; **I'm tired/angry** estoy cansado/enfadado; **I'm hot** tengo calor; **he's in a difficult position** está en una situación difícil - **2.** [referring to health] estar; **she's ill/better** está enferma/mejor; **how are you?** ¿cómo estás?, ¿qué tal? - **3.** [referring to age]: **how old are you?** ¿qué edad *OR* cuántos años tienes?; **I'm 20 (years old)** tengo 20 años - **4.** [cost] ser, costar; **how much is it?** ¿cuánto es?; **how much was it?** ¿cuánto costó?; **that will be £10, please** son 10 libras; **apples are only 40p a kilo today** hoy las manzanas están a tan sólo 40 peniques el kilo. <> *vi* - **1.** [exist] ser, existir; **the worst prime minister that ever was** el peor primer ministro de todos los tiempos; **be that as it may** aunque así sea; **there is/are** hay; **is there life on Mars?** ¿hay vida en Marte? - **2.** [referring to place] estar; **Valencia is in Spain** Valencia está en España; **he will be here tomorrow** estará aquí mañana - **3.** [referring to movement] estar; **where have you been?** ¿dónde has estado? <> *impers vb* - **1.** [referring to time, dates] ser; **it's two o'clock** son las dos; **it's the 17th of February** estamos a 17 de febrero - **2.** [referring to distance]: **it's 3 km to the next town** hay 3 kms hasta el próximo pueblo **- 3.** [referring to the weather]: **it's hot/cold/windy** hace calor/frío/viento **- 4.** [for emphasis] ser; **it's me** soy yo; **it's the milkman** es el lechero.

beach [biːtʃ] ◇ *n* playa *f*. ◇ *vt* varar.

beach ball *n* pelota *f* de playa.

beach buggy *n* todoterreno *m* para playa.

beachcomber [ˈbiːtʃˌkəʊməʳ] *n* [person] *persona que va buscando objetos de valor en la playa.*

beachhead [ˈbiːtʃhed] *n* MIL cabeza *f* de playa.

beachwear [ˈbiːtʃweəʳ] *n* ropa *f* de playa.

beacon [ˈbiːkən] *n* **- 1.** [warning fire] almenara *f* **- 2.** [lighthouse] faro *m* **- 3.** [radio beacon] radiofaro *m*.

bead [biːd] *n* **- 1.** [of wood, glass] cuenta *f*, abalorio *m* **- 2.** [of sweat] gota *f*.

beading [ˈbiːdɪŋ] *n* (U) [on furniture] moldura *f*; [on walls] astrágalo *m*.

beady [ˈbiːdɪ] (*comp* **-ier**, *superl* **-iest**) *adj*: **beady eyes** ojos pequeños y brillantes.

beagle [ˈbiːgl] *n* beagle *m*.

beak [biːk] *n* pico *m*.

beaker [ˈbiːkəʳ] *n* taza *f* (*sin asa*).

be-all *n*: **money isn't the be-all and end-all** el dinero no lo es todo.

beam [biːm] ◇ *n* **- 1.** [of wood, concrete] viga *f* **- 2.** [of light] rayo *m*. ◇ *vt* transmitir. ◇ *vi* **- 1.** [smile] sonreír resplandeciente **- 2.** [shine] resplandecer, brillar.

beaming [ˈbiːmɪŋ] *adj* radiante.

bean [biːn] *n* CULIN [haricot] judía *f*, habichuela *f*, frijol *m* *Amér*, poroto *m* *Andes*, caraota *f* *Ven*; [of coffee] grano *m*; **to be full of beans** *inf* estar lleno de energía; **to spill the beans** *inf* descubrir el pastel.

beanbag [ˈbiːnbæg] *n* cojín grande relleno de bolitas de polietileno.

beanshoot [ˈbiːnʃuːt], **beansprout** [ˈbiːnsprəʊt] *n* brote *m* de soja.

bear [beəʳ] ◇ *n* **- 1.** [animal] oso *m*, -sa *f* **- 2.** FIN bajista *mf*. ◇ *vt* (*pt* **bore**, *pp* **borne**) **- 1.** [carry] llevar **- 2.** [support] soportar **- 3.** [responsibility] cargar con **- 4.** [marks, signs] llevar **- 5.** [endure] aguantar **- 6.** [fruit, crop] dar **- 7.** [child] dar a luz **- 8.** [feeling] guardar, albergar **- 9.** FIN [interest] devengar. ◇ *vi*: **to bear left** torcer OR doblar a la izquierda; **to bring pressure/influence to bear on** ejercer presión/influencia sobre.

◆ **bear down** *vi*: **to bear down on** echarse encima de.

◆ **bear out** *vt sep* corroborar.

◆ **bear up** *vi* resistir.

◆ **bear with** *vt insep* tener paciencia con; **if you could just bear with me a moment...** si no le importa esperar un momento...

bearable [ˈbeərəbl] *adj* soportable.

beard [bɪəd] *n* barba *f*.

bearer [ˈbeərəʳ] *n* **- 1.** [of stretcher, news, cheque] portador *m*, -ra *f* **- 2.** [of passport] titular *mf* **- 3.** [of name, title] poseedor *m*, -ra *f*.

bear hug *n* *inf* fuerte abrazo *m*.

bearing [ˈbeərɪŋ] *n* **- 1.** [connection]: **bearing (on)** relación *f* (con) **- 2.** [deportment] porte *m* **- 3.** [for shaft] cojinete *m* **- 4.** [on compass] rumbo *m*, orientación *f*; **to get one's bearings** orientarse; **to lose one's bearings** desorientarse.

bear market *n* FIN mercado *m* a la baja.

bearskin [ˈbeəskɪn] *n* **- 1.** [fur] piel *f* de oso **- 2.** [hat] birretina *f*.

beast [biːst] *n* *lit* & *fig* bestia *f*.

beastly [ˈbiːstlɪ] (*comp* **-ier**, *superl* **-iest**) *adj* *dated* atroz.

beat [biːt] ◇ *n* **- 1.** [of drum] golpe *m* **- 2.** [of heart, pulse] latido *m* **- 3.** MUS [rhythm] ritmo *m*; [individual unit of time] golpe *m* (*de compás*) **- 4.** [of wings] batido *m* **- 5.** [of policeman] ronda *f*. ◇ *adj* *inf* hecho(cha) polvo. ◇ *vt* (*pt* **beat**, *pp* **beaten**) **- 1.** [hit - person] pegar; [- thing] golpear; [- carpet] sacudir **- 2.** [wings, eggs, butter] batir **- 3.** MUS [time] marcar **- 4.** [defeat]: **to beat sb (at sthg)** ganar a alguien (a algo); **it beats me** *inf* no me lo explico **- 5.** [reach ahead of]: **to beat sb (to sthg)** adelantarse a alguien (en algo) **- 6.** [be better than] ser mucho mejor que; **beat it!** *inf* ¡largo! ◇ *vi* (*pt* **beat**, *pp* **beaten**) **- 1.** [rain] golpear **- 2.** [heart, pulse] latir; [drums] redoblar.

◆ **beat down** ◇ *vt sep* [seller]: **I managed to beat him down** conseguí que me hiciera una rebaja. ◇ *vi* **- 1.** [sun] pegar fuerte **- 2.** [rain] descargar.

◆ **beat off** *vt sep* [attackers] repeler.

◆ **beat up** *vt sep* *inf* dar una paliza a; **to beat o.s. up (about sth)** castigarse (por algo).

◆ **beat up on** *vt sep* US *inf* dar una paliza a.

beater [ˈbiːtəʳ] *n* **- 1.** [for eggs] batidora *f* **- 2.** [for carpet] sacudidor *m* **- 3.** [of wife, child]: **he's a wife beater** pega a su mujer.

beating [ˈbiːtɪŋ] *n* **- 1.** [hitting] paliza *f*, golpiza *f* *Amér* **- 2.** [defeat] derrota *f*; **to take some beating** *inf* ser difícil de superar.

beatnik [ˈbiːtnɪk] *n* beatnik *mf*.

beat-up *adj* *inf* destartalado(da).

beautician [bjuːˈtɪʃn] *n* esteticista *mf*, esteticienne *f*.

beautiful [ˈbjuːtɪfʊl] *adj* **- 1.** [person] guapo(pa) **- 2.** [thing, animal] precioso(sa) **- 3.** *inf* [very good - shot, weather] espléndido(da).

beautifully [ˈbjuːtəflɪ] *adv* - **1.** [attractively] bellamente - **2.** *inf* [very well] espléndidamente.

beauty [ˈbjuːtɪ] (*pl* -ies) ◇ *n* belleza *f*. ◇ *comp* de belleza.

beauty contest, beauty parade *n* concurso *m* de belleza.

beauty parlour, beauty salon *n* salón *m* de belleza.

beauty queen *n* miss *f*.

beauty salon = beauty parlour.

beauty spot *n* - **1.** [picturesque place] bello paraje *m* - **2.** [on skin] lunar *m*.

beaver [ˈbiːvəʳ] *n* castor *m*.
 beaver away *vi*: to beaver away (at) trabajar con afán (en).

became [bɪˈkeɪm] *pt* ⊳ become.

because [bɪˈkɒz] *conj* porque.
 because of *prep* por, a causa de.

béchamel sauce [ˌbeɪʃəˈmel-] *n* besamel *f*.

beck [bek] *n*: to be at sb's beck and call estar siempre a disposición de alguien.

beckon [ˈbekən] ◇ *vt* [signal to] llamar (con un gesto). ◇ *vi* [signal]: to beckon to sb llamar (con un gesto) a alguien.

become [bɪˈkʌm] (*pt* became, *pp* become) *vi* hacerse; to become happy ponerse contento; to become suspicious volverse receloso; to become angry enfadarse; he became Prime Minister in 1991 en 1991 se convirtió en primer ministro; what has become of...? ¿qué ha sido de...?

becoming [bɪˈkʌmɪŋ] *adj* - **1.** [attractive] favorecedor(ra) - **2.** [appropriate] apropiado(da).

bed [bed] *n* - **1.** [to sleep on] cama *f*; to go to bed irse a la cama; to make the bed hacer la cama; to put sb to bed acostar a alguien; to go to bed with *euph* acostarse con - **2.** [flowerbed] macizo *m*; a bed of roses *fig* un lecho de rosas - **3.** [of sea] fondo *m*; [of river] lecho *m*, cauce *m*.
 bed down *vi* (*pt & pp* -ded, *cont* -ding) acostarse.

bed and breakfast *n* [service] cama *f* y desayuno; [hotel] ≈ pensión *f*.

bed-bath *n* lavado que se hace a alguien que está en cama.

bedbug [ˈbedbʌg] *n* chinche *f*.

bedclothes [ˈbedkləʊðz] *npl* ropa *f* de cama.

bedcover [ˈbedˌkʌvəʳ] *n* colcha *f*.

bedding [ˈbedɪŋ] *n* ropa *f* de cama.

bedding plant *n* planta *f* de jardín.

bedeck [bɪˈdek] *vt*: to bedeck sthg with engalanar algo con.

bedevil [bɪˈdevl] (*UK* -led, *cont* -ling) (*US* -ed, *cont* -ing) *vt*: to be bedevilled with estar plagado(da) de.

bedfellow [ˈbedˌfeləʊ] *n* *fig*: strange bedfellow extraña pareja.

bedlam [ˈbedləm] *n* jaleo *m*, alboroto *m*.

bed linen *n* ropa *f* de cama.

Bedouin, Beduin [ˈbeduɪn] ◇ *adj* beduino(na). ◇ *n* beduino *m*, -na *f*.

bedpan [ˈbedpæn] *n* cuña *f*.

bedraggled [bɪˈdrægld] *adj* mojado y sucio(mojada y sucia).

bedridden [ˈbedˌrɪdn] *adj* postrado(da) en cama.

bedrock [ˈbedrɒk] *n* (U) - **1.** GEOL roca *f* sólida - **2.** *fig* [solid foundation] cimientos *mpl*.

bedroom [ˈbedrʊm] *n* - **1.** [at home] dormitorio *m*, recámara *f* Amér C & Méx - **2.** [in hotel] habitación *f*, recámara *f* Amér C & Méx.

Beds [beds] (*abbr of* Bedfordshire), *condado inglés*.

bedside [ˈbedsaɪd] *n* [side of bed] lado *m* de la cama; [of ill person] lecho *m*; **bedside lamp** lámpara *f* de noche; **bedside table** mesita *f* de noche, nochero *m* Amér, buró *m* Méx.

bedside manner *n* actitud *f* hacia el enfermo.

bedsore [ˈbedsɔːʳ] *n* úlcera *f* por decúbito.

bedspread [ˈbedspred] *n* colcha *f*.

bedtime [ˈbedtaɪm] *n* hora *f* de irse a la cama.

Beduin = Bedouin.

bed-wetting [-ˌwetɪŋ] *n* (U) MED enuresis *f inv*.

bee [biː] *n* abeja *f*; to have a bee in one's bonnet about tener una fijación con.

Beeb [biːb] *n* UK *inf*: the Beeb la BBC.

beef [biːf] *n* carne *f* de vaca, carne *f* de res Amér.
 beef up *vt sep* *inf* reforzar.

beefburger [ˈbiːfˌbɜːgəʳ] *n* hamburguesa *f*.

beeline [ˈbiːlaɪn] *n*: to make a beeline for *inf* irse derechito(ta) hacia.

been [biːn] *pp* ⊳ be.

beep [biːp] *inf* ◇ *n* pitido *m*. ◇ *vi* pitar.

beeper [ˈbiːpəʳ] *n* buscapersonas *m inv*.

beer [bɪəʳ] *n* cerveza *f*.

beer garden *n* terraza *f* interior (de bar).

beeswax [ˈbiːzwæks] *n* cera *f* de abeja.

beet [biːt] *n* - **1.** [sugar beet] remolacha *f* azucarera - **2.** *US* [beetroot] remolacha *f*, betabel *m* Méx, betarraga *f* Chile.

beetle [ˈbiːtl] *n* escarabajo *m*.

beetroot [ˈbiːtruːt] *n* remolacha *f*, betabel *m* Méx, betarraga *f* Chile.

befall [bɪˈfɔːl] (*pt* -fell [-ˈfel], *pp* -fallen [-ˈfɔːlən]) *liter* ◇ *vt* acontecer a. ◇ *vi* acontecer.

befit [bɪˈfɪt] (*pt & pp* -ted, *cont* -ting) *vt fml* corresponder a.

before [bɪˈfɔːʳ] ◇ *adv* antes, endenantes Amér; we went the year before fuimos el año anterior. ◇ *prep* - **1.** [in time] antes de; **they arrived before us** llegaron antes que nosotros - **2.** [in space - facing] ante, delante de. ◇ *conj* antes de; **before it's too late** antes de que sea demasiado tarde.

beforehand [bɪˈfɔːhænd] *adv* con antelación, de antemano.

befriend [bɪˈfrend] *vt* hacer OR entablar amistad con.

befuddled [bɪˈfʌdld] *adj* liado(da), confundido(da).

beg [beg] (*pt* & *pp* **-ged**, *cont* **-ging**) ◇ *vt* - **1.** [money, food] mendigar, pedir - **2.** [favour, forgiveness] suplicar; **to beg sb to do sthg** rogar a alguien que haga algo; **to beg sb for sthg** rogar algo a alguien. ◇ *vi* - **1.** [for money, food]: **to beg (for sthg)** pedir OR mendigar (algo) - **2.** [for favour, forgiveness]: **to beg (for sthg)** suplicar OR rogar (algo).

began [bɪˈgæn] *pt* ⊳ **begin**.

beggar [ˈbegəʳ] *n* [poor person] mendigo *m*, -ga *f*.

begin [bɪˈgɪn] (*pt* **began**, *pp* **begun**, *cont* **-ning**) ◇ *vt*: **to begin (doing** OR **to do sthg)** empezar OR comenzar (a hacer algo). ◇ *vi* empezar, comenzar; **to begin with** para empezar, de entrada.

beginner [bɪˈgɪnəʳ] *n* principiante *mf*.

beginning [bɪˈgɪnɪŋ] *n* comienzo *m*, principio *m*; **at the beginning of the month** a principios de mes; **from beginning to end** de principio a fin.

begonia [bɪˈgəʊnjə] *n* begonia *f*.

begrudge [bɪˈgrʌdʒ] *vt* - **1.** [envy]: **to begrudge sb sthg** envidiar a alguien algo - **2.** [give, do unwillingly]: **to begrudge doing sthg** hacer algo de mala gana OR a regañadientes.

beguile [bɪˈgaɪl] *vt* [charm] seducir.

beguiling [bɪˈgaɪlɪŋ] *adj* seductor(ra).

begun [bɪˈgʌn] *pp* ⊳ **begin**.

behalf [bɪˈhɑːf] *n*: **on behalf of** UK, **in behalf of** US en nombre OR en representación de.

behave [bɪˈheɪv] ◇ *vt*: **to behave o.s.** portarse bien. ◇ *vi* - **1.** [in a particular way] comportarse, portarse - **2.** [in an acceptable way] comportarse OR portarse bien.

behaviour UK, **behavior** US [bɪˈheɪvjəʳ] *n* comportamiento *m*, conducta *f*.

behaviourism UK, **behaviorism** US [bɪˈheɪvjərɪzm] *n* conductismo *m*.

behead [bɪˈhed] *vt* decapitar.

beheld [bɪˈheld] *pt* & *pp* ⊳ **behold**.

behind [bɪˈhaɪnd] ◇ *prep* - **1.** [in space] detrás de - **2.** [causing, responsible for] detrás de - **3.** [in support of] con; **we're behind you** nosotros te apoyamos - **4.** [in time]: **to be behind schedule** ir retrasado(da) - **5.** [less successful than] por de-

trás de. ◇ *adv* - **1.** [in space] detrás - **2.** [in time]: **to be behind (with)** ir atrasado(da) (con) - **3.** [less successful] por detrás. ◇ *n inf* trasero *m*.

behold [bɪˈhəʊld] (*pt* & *pp* **beheld**) *vt liter* contemplar.

beige [beɪʒ] ◇ *adj* beige. ◇ *n* (color *m*) beige *m*.

Beijing [ˌbeɪˈdʒɪŋ] *n* Pekín.

being [ˈbiːɪŋ] *n* - **1.** [creature] ser *m* - **2.** [state of existing]: **it is no longer in being** ya no existe; **to come into being** ver la luz, nacer.

Beirut [ˌbeɪˈruːt] *n* Beirut; **East/West Beirut** Beirut Este/Oeste.

belated [bɪˈleɪtɪd] *adj* tardío(a).

belatedly [bɪˈleɪtɪdlɪ] *adv* tardíamente.

belch [beltʃ] ◇ *n* eructo *m*. ◇ *vt* escupir, arrojar. ◇ *vi* - **1.** [person] eructar - **2.** [smoke, fire] brotar.

beleaguered [bɪˈliːgəd] *adj* - **1.** MIL asediado(da) - **2.** *fig* [harassed] acosado(da).

belfry [ˈbelfrɪ] (*pl* **-ies**) *n* campanario *m*.

Belgian [ˈbeldʒən] ◇ *adj* belga. ◇ *n* belga *mf*.

Belgium [ˈbeldʒəm] *n* Bélgica.

Belgrade [ˌbelˈgreɪd] *n* Belgrado.

belie [bɪˈlaɪ] (*cont* **belying**) *vt* - **1.** [disprove] contradecir, desmentir - **2.** [give false idea of] esconder, encubrir.

belief [bɪˈliːf] *n* - **1.** [faith, principle]: **belief (in)** creencia *f* (en); **to be beyond belief** ser increíble - **2.** [opinion] opinión *f*; **in the belief that** con la idea de que.

believable [bɪˈliːvəbl] *adj* creíble.

believe [bɪˈliːv] ◇ *vt* creer; **believe it or not** lo creas o no. ◇ *vi* - **1.** [be religious] ser creyente - **2.** [know to exist, be good]: **to believe in** creer en.

believer [bɪˈliːvəʳ] *n* - **1.** [religious person] creyente *mf* - **2.** [in idea, action]: **believer in sthg** partidario *m*, -ria *f* de algo.

Belisha beacon [bɪˈliːʃə-] *n* UK *farol intermitente junto a paso de peatones*.

belittle [bɪˈlɪtl] *vt* menospreciar.

Belize [beˈliːz] *n* Belice.

bell [bel] *n* [of church] campana *f*; [handbell] campanilla *f*; [handbell, on door, bike] timbre *m* ▸▸ **the name rings a bell** el nombre me suena.

bell-bottoms *npl* pantalones *mpl* de campana.

belligerence [bɪˈlɪdʒərəns] *n* [aggression] belicosidad *f*.

belligerent [bɪˈlɪdʒərənt] *adj* - **1.** [at war] beligerante - **2.** [aggressive] belicoso(sa).

bellow [ˈbeləʊ] ◇ *vt* gritar. ◇ *vi* - **1.** [person] rugir - **2.** [bull] bramar.

bellows ['beləuz] *npl* fuelle *m*.

bellhop ['belhɒp] *n* US botones *m inv*.

bell-ringer *n* campanero *m*, -ra *f*.

belly ['belɪ] (*pl* -ies) *n* - **1.** [of person] barriga *f*, guata *f* *Chile* - **2.** [of animal] vientre *m*.

bellyache ['belɪeɪk] *inf* ⬦ *n* dolor *m* de barriga. ⬦ *vi* gruñir.

belly button *n inf* ombligo *m*.

belly dancer *n bailarina que practica la danza del vientre*.

belong [bɪ'lɒŋ] *vi* - **1.** [be property]: **to belong to** pertenecer a - **2.** [be member]: **to belong to** ser miembro de - **3.** [be situated in right place]: **where does this book belong?** ¿dónde va este libro?; **he felt he didn't belong there** sintió que no encajaba allí.

belongings [bɪ'lɒŋɪŋz] *npl* pertenencias *fpl*.

Belorussia [,beləʊ'rʌʃə], **Byelorussia** *n* Bielorrusia.

beloved [bɪ'lʌvd] ⬦ *adj* querido(da). ⬦ *n* amado *m*, -da *f*.

below [bɪ'ləʊ] ⬦ *adv* - **1.** [gen] abajo; **the flat below** el piso de abajo - **2.** [in text] más abajo; **see below** véase más abajo - **3.** [with temperatures]: **thirty degrees below** treinta grados bajo cero. ⬦ *prep* - **1.** [lower than in position] (por) debajo de, bajo - **2.** [lower than in rank, number] por debajo de - **3.** [with temperatures]: **thirty degrees below zero** treinta grados bajo cero.

belt [belt] ⬦ *n* - **1.** [for clothing] cinturón *m*, correa *f inf*; **that was below the belt** eso fue un golpe bajo; **to tighten one's belt** apretarse el cinturón; **under one's belt** a las espaldas de uno - **2.** TECH [wide] cinta *f*; [narrow] correa *f* - **3.** [of land, sea] cinturón *m*, franja *f*. ⬦ *vt inf* arrear. ⬦ *vi* UK *inf* ir a toda mecha.
➤ **belt out** *vt sep inf* cantar a voz en grito.
➤ **belt up** *vi* UK *inf* cerrar el pico.

beltway ['belt,weɪ] *n* US carretera *f* de circunvalación.

bemused [bɪ'mjuːzd] *adj* perplejo(ja).

bench [bentʃ] ⬦ *n* - **1.** [seat] banco *m* - **2.** [in lab, workshop] mesa *f* de trabajo - **3.** [in sport] banquillo *m*. ⬦ *vt* SPORT mandar al banquillo.
➤ **benches** *npl* UK [pol] escaños *pl*.

bend [bend] ⬦ *n* curva *f*; **round the bend** *inf* majareta, majara. ⬦ *vt* (*pt & pp* **bent**) doblar. ⬦ *vi* (*pt & pp* **bent**) [person] agacharse; [tree] doblarse; **to bend over backwards for** hacer todo lo humanamente posible por.
➤ **bends** *npl*: **the bends** *la enfermedad de los buzos*.

bendy ['bendɪ] (*comp* -ier, *superl* -iest) *adj* UK flexible.

beneath [bɪ'niːθ] ⬦ *adv* debajo. ⬦ *prep* - **1.** [under] debajo de, bajo - **2.** [unworthy of] indigno(na) de.

benediction [,benɪ'dɪkʃn] *n* bendición *f*.

benefactor ['benɪfæktər] *n* benefactor *m*.

benefactress ['benɪfæktrɪs] *n* benefactora *f*.

beneficial [,benɪ'fɪʃl] *adj*: **beneficial (to)** beneficioso(sa) (para).

beneficiary [,benɪ'fɪʃərɪ] (*pl* -ies) *n* - **1.** LAW [of will] beneficiario *m*, -ria *f* - **2.** [of change in law, new rule] beneficiado *m*, -da *f*.

benefit ['benɪfɪt] ⬦ *n* - **1.** [advantage] ventaja *f*; **for the benefit of** en atención a; **to be to sb's benefit, to be of benefit to sb** ir en beneficio de alguien - **2.** ADMIN [allowance of money] subsidio *m*; **to be on benefit** UK estar cobrando un subsidio estatal. ⬦ *comp* [concert, match] benéfico(ca). ⬦ *vt* beneficiar. ⬦ *vi*: **to benefit from** beneficiarse de.

Benelux ['benɪlʌks] *n* (el) Benelux; **the Benelux countries** los países del Benelux.

benevolent [bɪ'nevələnt] *adj* benevolente.

BEng [,biː'eŋ] (*abbr of* Bachelor of Engineering) *n (titular de un) título de ingeniero*.

Bengal [,beŋ'gɔːl] *n* Bengala; **the Bay of Bengal** el golfo de Bengala.

benign [bɪ'naɪn] *adj* - **1.** [person] bondadoso(sa) - **2.** MED benigno(na).

Benin [be'nɪn] *n* Benín.

bent [bent] ⬦ *pt & pp* ⇨ **bend**. ⬦ *adj* - **1.** [wire, bar] torcido(da) - **2.** [person, body] encorvado(da) - **3.** UK *inf* [dishonest] corrupto(ta) - **4.** [determined]: **to be bent on sthg/on doing sthg** estar empeñado(da) en algo/en hacer algo. ⬦ *n* [natural tendency] inclinación *f*; **bent for** don *m* OR talento *m* para.

bento box *n plato en forma de caja con varios compartimientos típico de la comida japonesa*.

bequeath [bɪ'kwiːð] *vt lit & fig*: **to bequeath sb sthg, to bequeath sthg to sb** legar algo a alguien.

bequest [bɪ'kwest] *n* legado *m*.

berate [bɪ'reɪt] *vt* regañar.

Berber ['bɜːbər] ⬦ *adj* bereber. ⬦ *n* - **1.** [person] bereber *mf* - **2.** [language] bereber *m*.

bereaved [bɪ'riːvd] (*pl* **bereaved**) ⬦ *adj* que llora la muerte de un ser querido; **the bereaved family** la familia del difunto. ⬦ *n*: **the bereaved** la familia del difunto.

bereavement [bɪ'riːvmənt] *n* pérdida *f (de ser querido)*.

bereft [bɪ'reft] *adj liter*: **bereft (of)** ayuno(na) (de).

beret ['bereɪ] *n* boina *f*.

Bering Sea ['berɪŋ-] n: **the Bering Sea** el mar de Bering.

Bering Strait ['berɪŋ-] n: **the Bering Strait** el estrecho de Bering.

berk [bɜːk] n UK inf imbécil mf.

Berks (abbr of **Berkshire**), condado inglés.

Berlin [bɜːˈlɪn] n Berlín; **East/West Berlin** Berlín Este/Oeste; **the Berlin Wall** el muro de Berlín.

Berliner [bɜːˈlɪnəʳ] n berlinés m, -esa f.

berm [bɜːm] n US arcén m.

Bermuda [bəˈmjuːdə] n las Bermudas.

Bermuda shorts npl bermudas mpl.

Bern [bɜːn] n Berna.

berry ['berɪ] (pl -ies) n baya f.

berserk [bəˈzɜːk] adj: **to go berserk** ponerse hecho(cha) una fiera.

berth [bɜːθ] ◇ n - **1.** [in harbour] amarradero m, atracadero m - **2.** [in ship, train] litera f
▸▸ **to give sb a wide berth** mantenerse a distancia de alguien. ◇ vt & vi atracar.

beseech [bɪˈsiːtʃ] (pt & pp besought OR beseeched) vt liter: **to beseech (sb to do sthg)** suplicar (a alguien que haga algo).

beset [bɪˈset] (pt & pp beset, cont -ting) adj: **beset with** OR **by** [subj: person] acosado(da) por; [subj: plan] plagado(da) de.

beside [bɪˈsaɪd] prep - **1.** [next to] al lado de, junto a - **2.** [compared with] comparado(da) con
▸▸ **that's beside the point** eso no importa, eso no viene al caso; **to be beside o.s. with rage** estar fuera de sí; **to be beside o.s. with joy** estar loco(ca) de alegría.

besides [bɪˈsaɪdz] ◇ adv además. ◇ prep aparte de.

besiege [bɪˈsiːdʒ] vt lit & fig asediar; **to be besieged with** verse asediado por.

besotted [bɪˈsɒtɪd] adj: **besotted with** embobado(da) con.

besought [bɪˈsɔːt] pt & pp ▷ **beseech**.

bespectacled [bɪˈspektəkld] adj con gafas.

bespoke [bɪˈspəʊk] adj UK - **1.** [clothes] hecho(cha) a medida - **2.** [tailor] que hace ropa a medida.

best [best] ◇ adj mejor; **best before...** [on packaging] consumir preferentemente antes de... ◇ adv mejor; **which did you like best?** ¿cuál te gustó más? ◇ n: **she's the best** es la mejor; **we're the best** somos los mejores; **to do one's best** hacerlo lo mejor que uno puede; **to make the best of sthg** sacarle el mayor partido posible a algo; **for the best** para bien; **all the best** [ending letter] un abrazo; [saying goodbye] que te vaya bien; **to have the best of both worlds** tenerlo todo.

◂ **at best** adv en el mejor de los casos.

bestial ['bestjəl] adj [disgusting] bestial.

best man n ≃ padrino m de boda.

bestow [bɪˈstəʊ] vt fml: **to bestow sthg on sb** [gift] otorgar OR conceder algo a alguien; [praise] dirigir algo a alguien; [title] conferir algo a alguien.

best-seller n [book] best seller m, éxito m editorial.

best-selling adj de éxito.

bet [bet] ◇ n - **1.** [gen]: **bet (on)** apuesta f (a) - **2.** fig [prediction] predicción f; **it's a safe bet that** seguro que; **to hedge one's bets** cubrirse, guardarse las espaldas. ◇ vt (pt & pp bet OR -ted, cont -ting) apostar. ◇ vi (pt & pp bet OR -ted, cont -ting) - **1.** [gamble]: **to bet (on)** apostar (a) - **2.** [predict]: **to bet on sthg** contar con (que pase) algo; **you bet!** inf ¡ya lo creo!

beta-blocker ['biːtə,blɒkəʳ] n betabloqueante m.

Bethlehem ['beθlɪhem] n Belén.

betray [bɪˈtreɪ] vt - **1.** [person, trust, principles] traicionar - **2.** [secret] revelar - **3.** [feeling] delatar.

betrayal [bɪˈtreɪəl] n - **1.** [of person, trust, principles] traición f - **2.** [of secret] revelación f.

betrothed [bɪˈtrəʊðd] adj dated: **betrothed (to)** prometido(da) (a).

better ['betəʳ] ◇ adj (compar of good) mejor; **to get better** mejorar. ◇ adv (compar of well) - **1.** [in quality] mejor - **2.** [more]: **I like it better** me gusta más; **better known for** más conocido(da) por - **3.** [preferably]: **we had better be going** más vale que nos vayamos ya. ◇ n [best one] mejor mf; **to get the better of sb** poder con alguien. ◇ vt mejorar; **to better o.s.** mejorarse.

better half n inf media naranja f.

better off adj - **1.** [financially] mejor de dinero - **2.** [in better situation]: **you'd be better off going by bus** sería mejor si vas en autobús.
◂ **better-off** n: **the better off** la gente pudiente.

betting ['betɪŋ] n (U) apuestas fpl.

betting shop n UK casa f de apuestas.

between [bɪˈtwiːn] ◇ prep entre; **he sat (in) between Paul and Anne** se sentó entre Paul y Anne; **closed between 1 and 2** cerrado de 1 a 2. ◇ adv: **(in) between** en medio, entremedio.

bevelled UK, **beveled** US ['bevld] adj biselado(da).

beverage ['bevərɪdʒ] n fml bebida f.

bevy ['bevɪ] (pl -ies) n [group, women] panda f.

beware [bɪˈweəʳ] *vi*: **to beware (of)** tener cuidado (con).

bewildered [bɪˈwɪldəd] *adj* desconcertado(da).

bewildering [bɪˈwɪldərɪŋ] *adj* desconcertante.

bewitched [bɪˈwɪtʃt] *adj* hechizado(da).

bewitching [bɪˈwɪtʃɪŋ] *adj* hechizante.

beyond [bɪˈjɒnd] <> *prep* más allá de; **beyond midnight** pasada la medianoche; **beyond my reach/responsibility** fuera de mi alcance/competencia; **it has changed beyond recognition** está irreconocible. <> *adv* más allá.

bi- [baɪ] *prefix* bi-.

biannual [baɪˈænjʊəl] *adj* semestral.

bias [ˈbaɪəs] *n* **- 1.** [prejudice] prejuicio *m* **- 2.** [tendency] tendencia *f*, inclinación *f*.

biased [ˈbaɪəst] *adj* parcial; **to be biased towards/against** tener prejuicios en favor/en contra de.

bib [bɪb] *n* [for baby] babero *m*.

Bible [ˈbaɪbl] *n*: **the Bible** la Biblia.
➡ **bible** *n* biblia *f*.

biblical [ˈbɪblɪkl] *adj* bíblico(ca).

bibliography [ˌbɪblɪˈɒɡrəfɪ] *(pl* **-ies)** *n* bibliografía *f*.

bicarbonate of soda [baɪˈkɑːbənət-] *n* bicarbonato *m* sódico.

bicentenary UK [ˌbaɪsenˈtiːnərɪ] *(pl* **-ies)**, **bicentennial** US [ˌbaɪsenˈtenjəl] *n* bicentenario *m*.

biceps [ˈbaɪseps] *(pl* **biceps)** *n* bíceps *m inv*.

bicker [ˈbɪkəʳ] *vi* reñir.

bickering [ˈbɪkərɪŋ] *n (U)* discusiones *fpl*.

bicycle [ˈbaɪsɪkl] <> *n* bicicleta *f*. <> *comp* de bicicleta.

bicycle path *n* camino *m* para bicicletas.

bicycle pump *n* bomba *f* de bicicleta.

bid [bɪd] <> *n* **- 1.** [attempt]: **bid (for)** intento *m* (de hacerse con) **- 2.** [at auction] puja *f* **- 3.** [financial offer]: **bid (for sthg)** oferta *f* (para adquirir algo). <> *vt (cont* **bidding,** *pt* **bade,** *pp* **bidden** [ˈbɪdn], *cont* **bidding)** **- 1.** *(pt & pp* **bid)** [money] ofrecer; [at auction] pujar **- 2.** *liter* [request]: **to bid sb do sthg** invitar a alguien a hacer algo **- 3.** *fml* [wish]: **to bid sb good morning** dar los buenos días a alguien. <> *vi (pt & pp* **bid,** *cont* **bidding):** **to bid (for)** [at auction] pujar (por); [contract] hacer una oferta(por).

bidder [ˈbɪdəʳ] *n* postor *m*, -ra *f*; **to sell to the highest bidder** vender al mejor postor.

bidding [ˈbɪdɪŋ] *n (U)* [at auction] puja *f*.

bide [baɪd] *vt*: **to bide one's time** esperar el momento oportuno.

bidet [ˈbiːdeɪ] *n* bidé *m*.

biennial [baɪˈenɪəl] <> *adj* bienal. <> *n* [plant] planta *f* bienal.

bier [bɪəʳ] *n* andas *fpl*.

bifocals [ˌbaɪˈfəʊklz] *npl* gafas *fpl* bifocales.

big [bɪɡ] *(comp* **-ger,** *superl* **-gest)** *adj* **- 1.** [large, important] grande, gran *(before singular nouns)*; **a big problem** un gran problema; **big problems** grandes problemas **- 2.** [older] mayor **- 3.** [successful] popular
➡➡ **she's into modern art in a big way** le va mucho el arte moderno.

bigamy [ˈbɪɡəmɪ] *n* bigamia *f*.

Big Apple *n*: **the Big Apple** Nueva York.

big bang *n* ASTRON: **the big bang** el big bang.

Big Ben *n* el Big Ben.

big business *n (U)* [large companies] las grandes compañías.

big cat *n* felino *m* grande.

big deal *inf* <> *n*: **it's no big deal** no tiene (la menor) importancia. <> *excl* ¡y a mí qué!

Big Dipper [-ˈdɪpəʳ] *n* **- 1.** UK [rollercoaster] montaña *f* rusa **- 2.** US ASTRON: **the Big Dipper** la Osa Mayor.

big end *n* cabeza *f* de biela.

big fish *n* inf [person] pez *m* gordo.

big game *n* caza *f* mayor.

big hand *n* **- 1.** [on clock] minutero *m* **- 2.** inf [applause] fuerte aplauso *m*.

bighead [ˈbɪɡhed] *n* inf pej creído *m*, -da *f*.

bigheaded [ˌbɪɡˈhedɪd] *adj* inf pej creído(da).

big-hearted [-ˈhɑːtɪd] *adj* de buen corazón, generoso(sa).

big money *n* inf: **to cost big money** costar mucha pasta OR lana Amér.

big mouth *n* inf bocazas *mf inv*.

big name *n* inf figura *f*.

bigot [ˈbɪɡət] *n* intolerante *mf*.

bigoted [ˈbɪɡətɪd] *adj* intolerante.

bigotry [ˈbɪɡətrɪ] *n* intolerancia *f*.

big screen *n*: **the big screen** la pantalla grande.

big shot *n* inf pez *m* gordo.

big time *n* inf: **the big time** el éxito, la fama.

big toe *n* dedo *m* gordo (del pie).

big top *n* carpa *f*.

big wheel *n* **- 1.** UK [at fairground] noria *f* **- 2.** inf [big shot] pez *m* gordo.

bigwig [ˈbɪɡwɪɡ] *n* inf pej pope *m*, pez *m* gordo.

bike [baɪk] *n* inf [bicycle] bici *f*; [motorcycle] moto *f*.

bikeway [ˈbaɪkweɪ] *n* US [lane] carril-bici *m*.

bikini [bɪˈkiːnɪ] *n* biquini *m*, bikini *m*.

bilateral [ˌbaɪˈlætərəl] *adj* bilateral.

bilberry [ˈbɪlbərɪ] *(pl* **-ies)** *n* arándano *m*.

bile [baɪl] *n* **- 1.** [fluid] bilis *f inv* **- 2.** [anger] hiel *f*.

bilingual [baɪˈlɪŋgwəl] *adj* bilingüe.

bilious [ˈbɪljəs] *adj* - **1.** [sickening] nauseabundo(da) - **2.** [nauseous] bilioso(sa).

bill [bɪl] <> *n* - **1.** [statement of cost]: **bill (for)** [meal] cuenta *f* (de); [electricity, phone] factura *f* (de) - **2.** [in parliament] proyecto *m* de ley - **3.** [of show, concert] programa *m* - **4.** *US* [banknote] billete *m* - **5.** [poster]: **'post** OR **stick no bills'** 'prohibido fijar carteles' - **6.** [beak] pico *m* ▸▸ **a clean bill of health** MED un certificado médico favorable; *fig* el visto bueno. <> *vt* [send a bill]: **to bill sb for** mandar la factura a alguien por.
▸ **Bill** *n* UK inf [police]: **the Bill** la pasma.

billboard [ˈbɪlbɔːd] *n* valla *f* publicitaria, cartelera *f*.

billet [ˈbɪlɪt] <> *n* acantonamiento *m*, alojamiento *m*. <> *vt* acantonar, alojar.

billfold [ˈbɪlfəʊld] *n* US billetera *f*.

billiards [ˈbɪljədz] *n* billar *m*.

billion [ˈbɪljən] *num* - **1.** [thousand million] millar *m* de millones; **three billion** tres mil millones - **2.** UK dated [million million] billón *m*.

billionaire [ˌbɪljəˈneəʳ] *n* multimillonario *m*, -ria *f*.

bill of exchange *n* letra *f* de cambio.

Bill of Rights *n*: **the Bill of Rights** *las diez primeras enmiendas de la Constitución estadounidense.*

bill of sale *n* contrato *m* OR escritura *f* de venta.

billow [ˈbɪləʊ] <> *n* nube *f*. <> *vi* - **1.** [smoke, steam] brotar en nubes - **2.** [sail, skirt] hincharse.

billycan [ˈbɪlɪkæn] *n* cazo *m*.

billy goat [ˈbɪlɪ-] *n* cabrón *m*, macho *m* cabrío.

bimbo [ˈbɪmbəʊ] (*pl* -s OR -es) *n* inf pej niña *f* mona.

bimonthly [ˌbaɪˈmʌnθlɪ] <> *adj* - **1.** [every two months] bimestral - **2.** [twice a month] bimensual. <> *adv* - **1.** [every two months] bimestralmente - **2.** [twice a month] bimensualmente.

bin [bɪn] <> *n* - **1.** UK [for rubbish] cubo *m* de la basura; [for paper] papelera *f* - **2.** [for grain, coal] depósito *m* - **3.** [for bread, flour] caja *f*. <> *vt* inf echar a la basura.

binary [ˈbaɪnərɪ] *adj* binario(ria).

bin bag *n* UK bolsa *f* de basura.

bind [baɪnd] <> *vt* (*pt* & *pp* **bound**) - **1.** [tie up] atar - **2.** [unite - people] unir - **3.** [bandage] vendar - **4.** [book] encuadernar - **5.** [constrain] obligar, comprometer. <> *n* inf - **1.** UK [nuisance] lata *f*, pesadez *f* - **2.** [difficult situation] aprieto *m*.
▸ **bind over** *vt sep* conminar, obligar legalmente.

binder [ˈbaɪndəʳ] *n* - **1.** [cover] carpeta *f* - **2.** [machine] (máquina *f*) encuadernadora *f* - **3.** [person] encuadernador *m*, -ra *f*.

binding [ˈbaɪndɪŋ] <> *adj* obligatorio(ria), vinculante. <> *n* - **1.** [on book] cubierta *f*, tapa *f* - **2.** [on dress, tablecloth] ribete *m*.

binge [bɪndʒ] *inf* <> *n*: **to go on a binge** irse de juerga. <> *vi*: **to binge on sthg** hincharse a algo.

bingo [ˈbɪŋgəʊ] *n* bingo *m*.

bin-liner *n* UK bolsa *f* de basura.

binoculars [bɪˈnɒkjʊləz] *npl* prismáticos *mpl*, gemelos *mpl*.

biochemistry [ˌbaɪəʊˈkemɪstrɪ] *n* bioquímica *f*.

biodegradable [ˌbaɪəʊdɪˈgreɪdəbl] *adj* biodegradable.

biodiversity [ˌbaɪəʊdaɪˈvɜːsətɪ] *n* biodiversidad *f*.

bioethics [ˌbaɪəʊˈeθɪks] *n* (U) bioética *f*.

biographer [baɪˈɒgrəfəʳ] *n* biógrafo *m*, -fa *f*.

biographic(al) [ˌbaɪəˈgræfɪk(l)] *adj* biográfico(ca).

biography [baɪˈɒgrəfɪ] (*pl* **-ies**) *n* biografía *f*.

biological [ˌbaɪəˈlɒdʒɪkl] *adj* biológico(ca).

biological mother *n* madre *f* biológica.

biological weapon *n* arma *f* biológica.

biologist [baɪˈɒlədʒɪst] *n* biólogo *m*, -ga *f*.

biology [baɪˈɒlədʒɪ] *n* biología *f*.

bionic [baɪˈɒnɪk] *adj* biónico(ca).

bionics [baɪˈɒnɪks] *n* (sing) biónica *f*.

biopic [ˈbaɪəʊpɪk] *n* inf película *f* biográfica.

biopsy [ˈbaɪɒpsɪ] (*pl* **-ies**) *n* biopsia *f*.

biotechnology [ˌbaɪəʊtekˈnɒlədʒɪ] *n* biotecnología *f*.

bioterrorism [ˌbaɪəʊˈterərɪzm] *n* bioterrorismo *m*.

biowarfare [ˌbaɪəʊˈwɔːfeəʳ] *n* guerra *f* biológica.

bipartite [ˌbaɪˈpɑːtaɪt] *adj* bipartito(ta).

biplane [ˈbaɪpleɪn] *n* biplano *m*.

bipolar disorder [baɪˈpəʊlədɪsˌɔːdəʳ] *n* MED trastorno *m* bipolar.

birch [bɜːtʃ] *n* - **1.** [tree] abedul *m* - **2.** [stick]: **the birch** la vara.

bird [bɜːd] *n* - **1.** [animal - large] ave *f*; [- small] pájaro *m*; **to kill two birds with one stone** matar dos pájaros de un tiro - **2.** UK inf [woman] tía *f*.

birdcage [ˈbɜːdkeɪdʒ] *n* jaula *f*.

birdie [ˈbɜːdɪ] *n* - **1.** [bird] pajarito *m* - **2.** [in golf] birdie *m*.

bird of paradise *n* ave *f* del paraíso.

bird of prey *n* ave *f* rapaz OR de presa.

birdseed [ˈbɜːdsiːd] *n* alpiste *m*.

bird's-eye view n vista f panorámica.
bird-watcher [-,wɒtʃər] n observador m, -ra f de pájaros.
Biro® ['baɪərəʊ] n bolígrafo m, birome f R Plata, lápiz m de pasta Chile, esfero m Col, pluma f atómica Méx.
birth [bɜ:θ] n [gen] nacimiento m; [delivery] parto m; **by birth** de nacimiento; **to give birth (to)** dar a luz (a).
birth certificate n partida f de nacimiento.
birth control n control m de natalidad.
birthday ['bɜ:θdeɪ] <> n cumpleaños m inv. <> comp [cake, card, present] de cumpleaños.
birthmark ['bɜ:θmɑ:k] n antojo m.
birth mother n madre f biológica.
birthplace ['bɜ:θpleɪs] n lugar m de nacimiento.
birthrate ['bɜ:θreɪt] n índice m de natalidad.
birthright ['bɜ:θraɪt] n derecho m de nacimiento.
Biscay ['bɪskɪ] n: **the Bay of Biscay** el golfo de Vizcaya.
biscuit ['bɪskɪt] n [in UK] galleta f; US [scone] *masa cocida al horno que se suele comer con salsa de carne.*
bisect [baɪ'sekt] vt [gen] dividir en dos; MATHS bisecar.
bisexual [,baɪ'sekʃʊəl] <> adj bisexual. <> n bisexual mf.
bishop ['bɪʃəp] n **- 1.** [in church] obispo m **- 2.** [in chess] alfil m.
bison ['baɪsn] (pl bison OR -s) n bisonte m.
bistro ['bi:strəʊ] (pl -s) n ≃ bar-restaurante m.
bit [bɪt] <> pt ▷ **bite.** <> n **- 1.** [piece] trozo m; **a bit of** un poco de; **a bit of advice** un consejo; **a bit of news** una noticia; **bits and pieces** UK [objects] cosillas fpl, tiliches mpl Amér C & Méx; [possessions] cosas fpl, bártulos mpl; **to fall to bits** [clothes, house] caerse a pedazos; **to take sthg to bits** desmontar algo **- 2.** [amount]: **a bit of** un poco de; **a bit of shopping** algunas compras; **quite a bit of** bastante **- 3.** [short time]: **(for) a bit** un rato **- 4.** [of drill] broca f **- 5.** [of bridle] bocado m, freno m **- 6.** COMPUT bit m
▶▶ **to do one's bit** UK aportar uno su grano de arena; **every bit as... as** igual de... que; **a bit much** demasiado; **not a bit** ni mucho menos, en absoluto.
➡ **a bit** adv un poco; **a bit easier** un poco más fácil.
➡ **bit by bit** adv poco a poco.
bitch [bɪtʃ] <> n **- 1.** [female dog] perra f **- 2.** v inf pej [unpleasant woman] bruja f. <> vi inf **- 1.** [complain] protestar todo el rato **- 2.** [talk unpleasantly]: **to bitch about** poner a parir a.

bitchy ['bɪtʃɪ] (comp -ier, superl -iest) adj inf malicioso(sa).
bite [baɪt] <> n **- 1.** [by dog, person] mordisco m; [by insect, snake] picotazo m **- 2.** inf [food]: **to have a bite (to eat)** comer algo **- 3.** [wound - from dog] mordedura f; [- from insect, snake] picadura f **- 4.** UK [sharp flavour] sabor m fuerte. <> vt (pt bit, pp bitten) **- 1.** [subj: person, animal] morder **- 2.** [subj: insect, snake] picar. <> vi (pt bit, pp bitten) **- 1.** [animal, person]: **to bite (into sthg)** morder (algo); **to bite off sthg** arrancar algo de un mordisco; **to bite off more than one can chew** intentar abarcar demasiado **- 2.** [insect, snake] picar **- 3.** [grip] agarrar **- 4.** [take effect] pegar duro.
biting ['baɪtɪŋ] adj **- 1.** [very cold] gélido(da), cortante **- 2.** [caustic] mordaz.
bit part n papel m secundario.
bitten ['bɪtn] pp ▷ **bite.**
bitter ['bɪtər] <> adj **- 1.** [coffee, chocolate] amargo(ga) **- 2.** [icy] gélido(da) **- 3.** [causing pain] amargo(ga); **to the bitter end** hasta el final **- 4.** [acrimonious] agrio(gria), encona-do(da) **- 5.** [resentful] amargado(da), resenti-do(da). <> n UK [beer] tipo de cerveza amarga.
bitter lemon n bíter m de limón.
bitterly ['bɪtəlɪ] adv: **it's bitterly cold** hace un frío de muerte; **to criticise bitterly** criticar duramente.
bitterness ['bɪtənɪs] n **- 1.** [of taste] amargor m **- 2.** [of wind, weather] gelidez f **- 3.** [resentment] amargura f.
bittersweet ['bɪtəswi:t] adj agridulce.
bitty ['bɪtɪ] (comp -ier, superl -iest) adj UK inf inconexo(xa).
bitumen ['bɪtjʊmɪn] n betún m, chapopote m Méx.
bivouac ['bɪvʊæk] (pt & pp -ked, cont -king) <> n vivaque m. <> vi vivaquear.
biweekly [,baɪ'wi:klɪ] <> adj **- 1.** [every two weeks] quincenal **- 2.** [twice a week] bisemanal. <> adv **- 1.** [every two weeks] quincenalmente **- 2.** [twice a week] dos veces por semana.
bizarre [bɪ'zɑ:r] adj [behaviour, appearance] extravagante; [machine, remark] singular, extraordinario(ria).
blab [blæb] (pt & pp -bed, cont -bing) vi inf irse de la lengua.
black [blæk] <> adj **- 1.** [gen] negro(gra); **black and blue** amoratado(da); **black and white** [films, photos] en blanco y negro; [clear-cut] extremadamente nítido(da) **- 2.** [coffee] solo; [milk] sin leche **- 3.** [angry] furioso(sa). <> n **- 1.** [colour] negro m **- 2.** [person] negro m, -gra f

▸▸ **in black and white** [in writing] por escrito; **to be in the black** tener saldo positivo. ⬦ *vt* UK [boycott] boicotear.

➤ **black out** ⬦ *vt sep* - **1.** [put out lights] dejar sin luz - **2.** [suppress] censurar. ⬦ *vi* desmayarse, perder el conocimiento.

blackball ['blækbɔːl] *vt* votar en contra de.

black belt *n* cinturón *m* negro.

blackberry ['blækbəri] (*pl* -ies) *n* - **1.** [fruit] mora *f* - **2.** [bush] zarzamora *f*.

blackbird ['blækbɜːd] *n* mirlo *m*.

blackboard ['blækbɔːd] *n* pizarra *f*, encerado *m*, pizarrón *m* Amér.

black box *n* [flight recorder] caja *f* negra.

black comedy *n* comedia *f* de humor negro.

blackcurrant [,blæk'kʌrənt] *n* grosella *f* negra, casis *m*.

black economy *n* economía *f* sumergida.

blacken ['blækn] ⬦ *vt* - **1.** [make dark] ennegrecer - **2.** [tarnish] manchar. ⬦ *vi* ennegrecerse.

black eye *n* ojo *m* morado.

blackhead ['blækhed] *n* barrillo *m*.

black hole *n* agujero *m* negro.

black ice *n* *hielo transparente en las carreteras.*

blackjack ['blækdʒæk] *n* - **1.** [card game] veintiuna *f* - **2.** US [weapon] porra *f*, cachiporra *f*.

blackleg ['blækleg] *n* *pej* esquirol *m*.

blacklist ['blæklɪst] ⬦ *n* lista *f* negra. ⬦ *vt* poner en la lista negra.

black magic *n* magia *f* negra.

blackmail ['blækmeɪl] *lit* & *fig* ⬦ *n* chantaje *m*. ⬦ *vt* *lit* & *fig* chantajear.

blackmailer ['blækmeɪlə'] *n* chantajista *mf*.

black mark *n* punto *m* en contra.

black market *n* mercado *m* negro.

blackout ['blækaʊt] *n* - **1.** [in wartime, power cut] apagón *m* - **2.** [of news] censura *f* - **3.** [fainting fit] desmayo *m*.

Black Power *n* el poder negro.

black pudding *n* UK morcilla *f*.

Black Sea *n*: **the Black Sea** el mar Negro.

black sheep *n* oveja *f* negra.

blacksmith ['blæksmɪθ] *n* herrero *m*.

black spot *n* punto *m* negro.

black-tie *adj* de etiqueta.

bladder ['blædə'] *n* ANAT vejiga *f*.

blade [bleɪd] *n* - **1.** [of knife, saw] hoja *f* - **2.** [of propeller] aleta *f*, paleta *f* - **3.** [of grass] brizna *f*, hoja *f*.

blame [bleɪm] ⬦ *n* culpa *f*; **to take the blame for** hacerse responsable de; **to be to blame for** ser el culpable de. ⬦ *vt* echar la culpa a,

culpar; **to blame sthg on sthg/sb, to blame sthg/sb for sthg** culpar algo/a alguien de algo.

blameless ['bleɪmlɪs] *adj* inocente.

blanch [blɑːntʃ] ⬦ *vt* blanquear. ⬦ *vi* palidecer.

blancmange [blə'mɒndʒ] *n* *postre hecho de harina de maíz, leche y azúcar.*

bland [blænd] *adj* soso(sa).

blank [blæŋk] ⬦ *adj* - **1.** [sheet of paper] en blanco; [wall] liso(sa) - **2.** [cassette] virgen - **3.** *fig* [look] vacío(a); **her mind went blank** se le quedó la mente en blanco. ⬦ *n* - **1.** [empty space] espacio *m* en blanco - **2.** MIL [cartridge] cartucho *m* de fogueo

▸▸ **to draw a blank** buscar en vano.

blank cheque *n* cheque *m* en blanco; *fig* carta *f* blanca.

blanket ['blæŋkɪt] ⬦ *adj* [TV coverage] exhaustivo(va); [ban, statement] global, general. ⬦ *n* - **1.** [bed cover] manta *f*, frazada *f* Amér - **2.** [layer] manto *m*. ⬦ *vt* cubrir, tapar.

blanket bath *n* UK baño dado a un enfermo en cama.

blankly ['blæŋklɪ] *adv* [stare] con la mirada vacía.

blare [bleə'] *vi* resonar, sonar.

➤ **blare out** *vi* retumbar, resonar.

blasé [UK 'blɑːzeɪ, US ,blɑː'zeɪ] *adj*: **to be blasé about** estar de vuelta de.

blasphemous ['blæsfəməs] *adj* blasfemo(ma).

blasphemy ['blæsfəmɪ] (*pl* -ies) *n* blasfemia *f*.

blast [blɑːst] ⬦ *n* - **1.** [of bomb] explosión *f* - **2.** [of wind] ráfaga *f*; **we had a blast** US lo pasamos genial. ⬦ *vt* [hole, tunnel] perforar *(con explosivos).* ⬦ *excl* UK *inf* ¡maldita sea!

➤ **(at) full blast** *adv* a todo trapo.

➤ **blast off** *vi* despegar.

blasted ['blɑːstɪd] *adj* *inf* maldito(ta), puñetero(ra).

blast furnace *n* alto horno *m*.

blast-off *n* despegue *m*.

blatant ['bleɪtənt] *adj* descarado(da).

blatantly ['bleɪtəntlɪ] *adv* descaradamente; **blatantly obvious** clarísimo.

blaze [bleɪz] ⬦ *n* - **1.** [fire] incendio *m* - **2.** *fig* [of colour] explosión *f*; [of light] resplandor *m*; **a blaze of publicity** una ola de publicidad. ⬦ *vi* *lit* & *fig* arder.

blazer ['bleɪzə'] *n* *chaqueta de sport generalmente con la insignia de un equipo, colegio etc.*

blazing ['bleɪzɪŋ] *adj* - **1.** [sun, heat] abrasador(ra) - **2.** [row] encendido(da), acalorado(da).

bleach [bliːtʃ] ⬦ *n* lejía *f*. ⬦ *vt* [hair] blanquear; [clothes] desteñir.

bleached [bli:tʃt] *adj* [hair] teñido(da) de rubio; [jeans] desteñido(da).

bleachers ['bli:tʃəz] *npl* US SPORT graderío *m* descubierto.

bleak [bli:k] *adj* - **1.** [future] negro(gra) - **2.** [place, person, face] sombrío(a) - **3.** [weather] desapacible.

bleary ['blɪərɪ] (*comp* -ier, *superl* -iest) *adj* [eyes] nublado(da).

bleary-eyed [ˌblɪərɪ'aɪd] *adj* con los ojos nublados.

bleat [bli:t] <> *n* [of sheep] balido *m*. <> *vi* - **1.** [sheep] balar - **2.** *fig* [person] quejarse.

bleed [bli:d] (*pt & pp* bled) <> *vt* [radiator etc] purgar. <> *vi* sangrar.

bleep [bli:p] <> *n* pitido *m*. <> *vt* llamar con el busca. <> *vi* pitar.

bleeper ['bli:pər] *n* busca *m*, buscapersonas *m inv*.

blemish ['blemɪʃ] <> *n* [mark] señal *f*, marca *f*; *fig* mancha *f*. <> *vt* [reputation] manchar.

blend [blend] <> *n* - **1.** [mix] mezcla *f* - **2.** COMPUT degradado *m*. <> *vt*: **to blend (sthg with sthg)** mezclar (algo con algo). <> *vi*: **to blend (with)** combinarse (con).

◆ **blend in** *vi* armonizar.

◆ **blend into** *vt insep* confundirse con.

blender ['blendər] *n* licuadora *f*, túrmix® *f*.

bless [bles] (*pt & pp* -ed OR blest) *vt* - **1.** RELIG bendecir - **2.** [endow]: **to be blessed with** estar dotado(da) de

▶▶ **bless you!** [after sneezing] ¡jesús!; [thank you] ¡gracias!

blessed ['blesɪd] *adj* - **1.** RELIG bendito(ta) - **2.** [desirable] feliz, maravilloso(sa) - **3.** *inf* [blasted] dichoso(sa).

blessing ['blesɪŋ] *n* - **1.** RELIG bendición *f*; **it was a blessing in disguise** no hay mal que por bien no venga; **to count one's blessings** darse con un canto en los dientes; **it's a mixed blessing** tiene sus pros y sus contras - **2.** *fig* [good wishes] aprobación *f*.

blest [blest] *pt & pp* ▷ **bless**.

blew [blu:] *pt* ▷ **blow**.

blight [blaɪt] <> *n* [plant disease] añublo *m*; *fig* plaga *f*, mal *m*. <> *vt* [hopes, prospects] malograr, arruinar.

blimey ['blaɪmɪ] *excl* UK *inf* ¡ostias!

blind [blaɪnd] <> *adj* - **1.** [unsighted, irrational] ciego(ga); **a blind man** un ciego; **to go blind** quedarse ciego - **2.** *fig* [unaware]: **to be blind to sthg** no ver algo - **3.** UK *inf* [for emphasis]: **it doesn't make a blind bit of difference** no cambia las cosas para nada. <> *adv*: **blind drunk** borracho(cha) como una cuba. <> *n* [for window] persiana *f*. <> *npl*: **the blind** los ciegos. <> *vt* [permanently] dejar ciego(ga); [temporarily] cegar; **to blind sb to sthg** *fig* no dejar a alguien ver algo.

blind alley *n* *lit & fig* callejón *m* sin salida.

blind corner *n* curva *f* sin visibilidad.

blind date *n* cita *f* a ciegas.

blinders ['blaɪndəz] *npl* US anteojeras *fpl*.

blindfold ['blaɪndfəʊld] <> *adv* con los ojos vendados. <> *n* venda *f*. <> *vt* vendar los ojos a.

blinding ['blaɪndɪŋ] *adj* deslumbrante.

blindly ['blaɪndlɪ] *adv* - **1.** [unable to see] a ciegas - **2.** *fig* [guess] a boleo; [accept] ciegamente.

blindness ['blaɪndnɪs] *n* *lit & fig*: **blindness (to)** ceguera *f* (ante).

blind spot *n* - **1.** [when driving] ángulo *m* muerto - **2.** *fig* [inability to understand] punto *m* débil.

blink [blɪŋk] <> *n* [of eyes] parpadeo *m*

▶▶ **in the blink of an eye** en un abrir y cerrar de ojos; **on the blink** *inf* estropeado(da). <> *vt* - **1.** [eyes]: **to blink one's eyes** parpadear - **2.** US AUT: **to blink one's lights** dar las luces (intermitentemente). <> *vi* parpadear.

blinkered ['blɪŋkəd] *adj* - **1.** [horse] con anteojeras - **2.** *fig* [attitude] estrecho(cha) de miras.

blinkers ['blɪŋkəz] *npl* UK anteojeras *fpl*.

blinking ['blɪŋkɪŋ] *adj* UK *inf* condenado(da).

blip [blɪp] *n* - **1.** [sound] pitido *m* - **2.** [image on radar] señal *f* - **3.** *fig* [temporary problem] pequeño bache *m*.

bliss [blɪs] *n* gloria *f*, dicha *f*.

blissful ['blɪsful] *adj* dichoso(sa), feliz.

blissfully ['blɪsfulɪ] *adv* [happy] dichosamente; [smile] felizmente; **to be blissfully unaware of sthg** no tener ni idea de algo.

blister ['blɪstər] <> *n* ampolla *f*. <> *vi* ampollarse.

blistering ['blɪstərɪŋ] *adj* - **1.** [heat] abrasador(ra) - **2.** [attack] feroz.

blister pack *n* blíster *m*.

blithe [blaɪð] *adj* alegre.

blithely ['blaɪðlɪ] *adv* alegremente.

blitz [blɪts] *n* - **1.** MIL bombardeo *m* aéreo - **2.** UK *fig* [attack]: **to have a blitz on the attic** ponerse a limpiar a fondo el ático.

blizzard ['blɪzəd] *n* ventisca *f* (de nieve).

bloated ['bləʊtɪd] *adj* hinchado(da).

blob [blɒb] *n* - **1.** [drop] gota *f* - **2.** [indistinct shape] bulto *m* borroso.

bloc [blɒk] *n* bloque *m*.

block [blɒk] <> *n* - **1.** [gen] bloque *m* - **2.** US [of buildings] manzana *f* - **3.** [obstruction - physical or mental] bloqueo *m* - **4.** TECH: **block and tackle** sistema *m* de poleas. <> *vt* - **1.** [road] cortar;

[pipe] obstruir; [sink, toilet] atascar; **my nose is blocked** tengo la nariz tapada - **2.** [view] tapar - **3.** [prevent] bloquear, obstaculizar - **4.** COMPUT: **to block a stretch of text** seleccionar un bloque de texto.

▰ **block off** *vt sep* bloquear.

▰ **block out** *vt sep* - **1.** [from mind] apartar - **2.** [light] tapar.

▰ **block up** ⟺ *vt sep* obstruir. ⟺ *vi* atascarse, taparse *Amér*.

blockade [blɒ'keɪd] ⟺ *n* bloqueo *m*. ⟺ *vt* bloquear.

blockage ['blɒkɪdʒ] *n* obstrucción *f*.

block booking *n* reserva *f* de grupo.

blockbuster ['blɒkbʌstər] *n inf* [book] (gran) éxito *m* editorial; [film] (gran) éxito de taquilla.

block capitals *npl* mayúsculas *fpl (de imprenta)*.

blockhead ['blɒkhed] *n inf* zoquete *mf*.

block letters *npl* mayúsculas *fpl (de imprenta)*.

block vote *n UK* voto *m* por delegación.

bloke [bləʊk] *n UK* tío *m*, tipo *m*, chavo *m Méx*.

blond [blɒnd] *adj* rubio(bia), catire(ra) *Col & Ven*.

blonde [blɒnd] ⟺ *adj* rubia, catira *Col & Ven*. ⟺ *n* [woman] rubia *f*.

blood [blʌd] *n* sangre *f*; **in cold blood** a sangre fría; **to make one's blood boil** hacer que la sangre se le suba a uno a la cabeza; **to make one's blood run cold** helarle a uno la sangre; **it's in his blood** lo lleva en la sangre; **new OR fresh blood** savia *f* nueva.

blood bank *n* banco *m* de sangre.

bloodbath (['blʌdbɑːθ], *pl* [-bɑːðz]) *n* matanza *f*, carnicería *f*.

blood brother *n* hermano *m* de sangre.

blood cell *n* glóbulo *m*.

blood count *n* recuento *m* de glóbulos.

bloodcurdling ['blʌd,kɜːdlɪŋ] *adj* espeluznante.

blood donor *n* donante *mf* de sangre.

blood group *n* grupo *m* sanguíneo.

bloodhound ['blʌdhaʊnd] *n* sabueso *m*.

bloodless ['blʌdlɪs] *adj* - **1.** [face, lips] macilento(ta), mortecino(na) - **2.** [coup, victory] incruento(ta).

bloodletting ['blʌd,letɪŋ] *n* [killing] derramamiento *m* de sangre.

blood money *n dinero pagado para que se cometa un asesinato*.

blood orange *n* naranja *f* sanguina OR de sangre.

blood poisoning *n* septicemia *f*.

blood pressure *n* presión *f* sanguínea, tensión *f* arterial; **to have high/low blood pressure** tener la tensión alta/baja.

blood relation, blood relative *n* familiar *m* consanguíneo.

bloodshed ['blʌdʃed] *n* derramamiento *m* de sangre.

bloodshot ['blʌdʃɒt] *adj* inyectado(da) (de sangre).

blood sports *npl deportes en que se matan animales*.

bloodstained ['blʌdsteɪnd] *adj* manchado(da) de sangre.

bloodstream ['blʌdstriːm] *n* flujo *m* sanguíneo.

blood test *n* análisis *m inv* de sangre.

bloodthirsty ['blʌd,θɜːstɪ] *adj* sanguinario(ria).

blood transfusion *n* transfusión *f* de sangre.

blood type *n* grupo *m* sanguíneo.

blood vessel *n* vaso *m* sanguíneo.

bloody ['blʌdɪ] ⟺ *adj (comp* -ier, *superl* -iest) - **1.** [war, conflict] sangriento(ta) - **2.** [face, hands] ensangrentado(da) - **3.** *UK v inf* maldito(ta), puñetero(ra), pinche *Méx*; **bloody hell!** ¡hostia! ⟺ *adv UK v inf*: **he's bloody useless** es un puto inútil; **it's bloody brilliant** es de puta madre.

bloody-minded [-'maɪndɪd] *adj UK inf* puñetero(ra).

bloom [bluːm] ⟺ *n* flor *f*; **in bloom** en flor. ⟺ *vi* florecer.

blooming ['bluːmɪŋ] ⟺ *adj* - **1.** *UK inf* [to show annoyance] condenado(da) - **2.** [healthy, attractive] radiante. ⟺ *adv UK inf*: **he's blooming useless** es un inútil del copón.

blossom ['blɒsəm] ⟺ *n* flor *f*; **in blossom** en flor. ⟺ *vi lit & fig* florecer.

blot [blɒt] ⟺ *n* [of ink] borrón *m*; *fig* mancha *f*. ⟺ *vt (pt & pp* -ted, *cont* -ting) - **1.** [paper] emborronar - **2.** [ink] secar.

▰ **blot out** *vt sep* [gen] cubrir, ocultar; [memories] borrar.

blotchy ['blɒtʃɪ] (*comp* -ier, *superl* -iest) *adj* lleno(na) de manchas.

blotting paper ['blɒtɪŋ-] *n (U)* papel *m* secante.

blouse [blaʊz] *n* blusa *f*.

blouson ['bluːzɒn] *n UK* blusón *m*.

blow [bləʊ] ⟺ *vi (pt* blew, *pp* blown) - **1.** [gen] soplar - **2.** [in wind] salir volando, volar - **3.** [fuse] fundirse. ⟺ *vt (pt* blew, *pp* blown) - **1.** [subj: wind] hacer volar - **2.** [whistle, horn] tocar, hacer sonar - **3.** [bubbles] hacer - **4.** [kiss] mandar - **5.** [fuse] fundir - **6.** [clear]: **to blow**

one's nose sonarse la nariz **- 7.** *inf* [money] ventilarse; *inf* [chance] echar a perder. ◇ *n* **- 1.** [hit, shock] golpe *m*; **to come to blows** llegar a las manos; **to soften the blow** ayudar a encajar el golpe **- 2.** [for cause]: **a blow (for)** un empujón OR adelanto (para).
◆ **blow out** ◇ *vt sep* apagar. ◇ *vi* **- 1.** [candle] apagarse **- 2.** [tyre] reventar.
◆ **blow over** *vi* **- 1.** [storm] amainar **- 2.** [scandal] calmarse.
◆ **blow up** ◇ *vt sep* **- 1.** [inflate] inflar **- 2.** [destroy] volar **- 3.** [photograph] ampliar. ◇ *vi* saltar por los aires.

blow-by-blow *adj* [account] con pelos y señales.

blow-dry ◇ *n* secado *m (con secador).* ◇ *vt* secar *(con secador).*

blowfly ['bləʊflaɪ] *(pl* **-flies)** *n* moscardón *m*, moscón *m*.

blowgun US = **blowpipe**.

blowlamp UK ['bləʊlæmp], **blowtorch** *esp* US ['bləʊtɔ:tʃ] *n* soplete *m*.

blown [bləʊn] *pp* ▷ **blow**.

blowout ['bləʊaʊt] *n* **- 1.** [of tyre] pinchazo *m*, reventón *m* **- 2.** *inf* [big meal] comilona *f*.

blowpipe UK ['bləʊpaɪp], **blowgun** US ['bləʊɡʌn] *n* cerbatana *f*.

blowtorch *esp* US = **blowlamp**.

blowzy ['blaʊzɪ] *adj*: **a blowzy woman** una mujer gorda y zarrapastrosa.

BLT *(abbr of* **bacon, lettuce and tomato)** *n* sándwich de tocino, lechuga y tomate.

blubber ['blʌbər] ◇ *n* grasa *f* de ballena. ◇ *vi* *pej* lloriquear.

bludgeon ['blʌdʒən] *vt* apalear.

blue [blu:] ◇ *adj* **- 1.** [colour] azul **- 2.** *inf* [sad] triste **- 3.** [pornographic - film] equis *(inv)*, porno; [- joke] verde. ◇ *n* azul *m*; **in blue** de azul; **out of the blue** en el momento menos pensado.
◆ **blues** *npl*: **the blues** MUS el blues; *inf* [sad feeling] la depre.

blue baby *n* bebé *m* cianótico.

bluebell ['blu:bel] *n* campanilla *f*.

blueberry ['blu:bərɪ] *n* arándano *m*.

bluebird ['blu:bɜ:d] *n* azulejo *m (pájaro).*

blue-black *adj* azul oscuro *(inv)*.

blue-blooded [-'blʌdɪd] *adj* de sangre azul.

bluebottle ['blu:,bɒtl] *n* moscardón *m*, moscón *m*.

blue cheese *n* queso *m* azul.

blue chip *n* acción *f* de rentabilidad segura.
◆ **blue-chip** *comp* [company] de primera.

blue-collar *adj*: **blue-collar worker** obrero *m*, -ra *f*.

blue-eyed boy [-aɪd-] *n* *inf* niño *m* mimado.

blue jeans *npl* US vaqueros *mpl*, tejanos *mpl*.

blue moon *n*: **once in a blue moon** de higos a brevas.

blueprint ['blu:prɪnt] *n* **- 1.** CONSTR cianotipo *m* **- 2.** *fig* [description] proyecto *m*.

bluestocking ['blu:,stɒkɪŋ] *n* *pej* marisabidilla *f*, intelectualoide *f*.

blue tit *n* herrerillo *m*.

bluff [blʌf] ◇ *adj* brusco(ca). ◇ *n* **- 1.** [deception] farol *m*; **to call sb's bluff** desafiar a alguien a que haga lo que dice **- 2.** [cliff] acantilado *m*. ◇ *vt* engañar. ◇ *vi* tirarse un farol.

blunder ['blʌndər] ◇ *n* metedura *f* de pata. ◇ *vi* **- 1.** [make mistake] meter la pata **- 2.** [move clumsily] ir tropezando; **to blunder into sthg** tropezar con algo.

blundering ['blʌndərɪŋ] *adj* estúpido(da).

blunt [blʌnt] ◇ *adj* **- 1.** [knife, pencil] desafilado(da) **- 2.** [point, edge] romo(ma) **- 3.** [forthright] directo(ta), franco(ca). ◇ *vt* **- 1.** [knife] desafilar **- 2.** *fig* [weaken] debilitar, aflojar.

bluntly ['blʌntlɪ] *adv* sin rodeos, con franqueza.

bluntness ['blʌntnɪs] *n* [forthrightness] franqueza *f*.

blur [blɜ:r] ◇ *n* imagen *f* borrosa. ◇ *vt* *(pt & pp* **-red**, *cont* **-ring)* **- 1.** [vision] nublar **- 2.** [distinction] desdibujar, oscurecer.

blurb [blɜ:b] *n* *inf* texto publicitario en la cubierta o solapa de un libro.

blurred [blɜ:d] *adj* **- 1.** [photograph] movido(da) **- 2.** [vision, distinction] borroso(sa).

blurt [blɜ:t] ◆ **blurt out** *vt sep* espetar, decir de repente.

blush [blʌʃ] ◇ *n* rubor *m*. ◇ *vi* ruborizarse.

blusher ['blʌʃər] *n* colorete *m*.

bluster ['blʌstər] ◇ *n* fanfarronería *f*. ◇ *vi* fanfarronear.

blustery ['blʌstərɪ] *adj* borrascoso(sa).

Blvd *(abbr of* **Boulevard)** *bulevar*.

BM *n (abbr of* **Bachelor of Medicine)**, *(titular de una) licenciatura de medicina.*

BMA *(abbr of* **British Medical Association)** *n colegio británico de médicos.*

BMus [,bi:'mju:z] *(abbr of* **Bachelor of Music)** *n (titular de una) licenciatura de música.*

BMX *(abbr of* **bicycle motorcross)** *n* ciclocross *m*.

BO *n (abbr of* **body odour)**, *olor a sudor.*

boa constrictor ['bəʊəkən'strɪktər] *n* boa *f* constrictor.

boar [bɔ:r] *n* **- 1.** [male pig] verraco *m* **- 2.** [wild pig] jabalí *m*.

board [bɔ:d] ◇ *n* **- 1.** [plank] tabla *f* **- 2.** [for notices] tablón *m* **- 3.** [for games] tablero *m* **- 4.** [blackboard] pizarra *f* **- 5.** COMPUT placa *f* **- 6.** [of company]: **board (of directors)** consejo *m* de administración **- 7.** [committee] comité *m*, junta *f* **- 8.** UK [at hotel, guesthouse]: **board and lodging** comida y habitación; **full board** pensión completa; **half board** media pensión **- 9.**: **on board** [ship, plane] a bordo; [bus, train] dentro ▸▸ **above board** en regla; **across the board** lineal, general; **to go by the board** irse al garete; **to sweep the board** arrasar; **to take sthg on board** hacerse cargo de OR aceptar algo. ◇ *vt* **- 1.** [ship, plane] embarcar en; [train, bus] subirse a, embarcarse en *Amér* **- 2.** [in naval battle] abordar. ◇ *vi*: **flight XY879 is now boarding through gate 4** embarque del vuelo XY789 por la puerta 4.

boarder ['bɔːdəʳ] *n* **- 1.** [lodger] huésped *mf* **- 2.** [at school] interno *m*, -na *f*.

board game *n* juego *m* de tablero.

boarding card ['bɔːdɪŋ-] *n* tarjeta *f* de embarque.

boardinghouse (['bɔːdɪŋhaʊs], *pl* [-haʊzɪz]) *n* casa *f* de huéspedes.

boarding school ['bɔːdɪŋ-] *n* internado *m*.

board meeting *n* reunión *f* del consejo de administración.

Board of Trade *n* UK: **the Board of Trade** ≃ el Ministerio de Comercio.

boardroom ['bɔːdrʊm] *n* sala *f* de juntas.

boardwalk ['bɔːdwɔːk] *n* US *paseo marítimo entarimado*.

boast [bəʊst] ◇ *n* alarde *m*. ◇ *vt* disfrutar de, presumir de tener. ◇ *vi*: **to boast (about)** alardear OR jactarse (de), compadrear (de) *Amér*.

boastful ['bəʊstfʊl] *adj* fanfarrón(ona).

boat [bəʊt] *n* [large] barco *m*; [small] barca *f*; **by boat** en barco; **to rock the boat** complicar las cosas; **to be in the same boat** estar en el mismo barco OR en la misma situación.

boater ['bəʊtəʳ] *n* [hat] canotié *m*, sombrero *m* de paja.

boating ['bəʊtɪŋ] *n* paseo *m* en barco; **to go boating** dar un paseo en barco.

boatswain ['bəʊsn], **bosun** *n* NAUT contramaestre *m*.

boat train *n* tren *que enlaza con un puerto*.

bob [bɒb] ◇ *n* **- 1.** [hairstyle] corte *m* de chico **- 2.** UK *inf* *dated* [shilling] chelín *m* **- 3.** = **bobsleigh**. ◇ *vi* (*pt* & *pp* -**bed**, *cont* -**bing**) [boat] balancearse.

bobbin ['bɒbɪn] *n* bobina *f*.

bobble ['bɒbl] *n* pompón *m*.

bobby ['bɒbɪ] (*pl* -**ies**) *n* UK *inf* poli *m*.

bobby pin *n* US horquilla *f*.

bobby socks, bobby sox *npl* US calcetines *mpl* cortos de colegiala.

bobsleigh ['bɒbsleɪ], **bob** *n* bobsleigh *m*.

bode [bəʊd] *vi liter*: **to bode ill/well for** traer malos/buenos presagios para.

bodice ['bɒdɪs] *n* **- 1.** [of dress] cuerpo *m* **- 2.** [undergarment] corpiño *m*.

bodily ['bɒdɪlɪ] ◇ *adj* corporal, físico(ca). ◇ *adv*: **to lift/move sb bodily** levantar/mover a alguien por la fuerza.

body ['bɒdɪ] (*pl* -**ies**) *n* **- 1.** [gen] cuerpo *m*; **(to earn enough) to keep body and soul together** (ganar lo justo para) seguir tirando **- 2.** [corpse] cadáver *m*; **over my dead body** por encima de mi cadáver **- 3.** [organization] entidad *f*; **a body of thought/opinion** una corriente de pensamiento/opinión **- 4.** [of car] carrocería *f*; [of plane] fuselaje *m* **- 5.** [item of clothing] body *m*.

body building *n* culturismo *m*.

bodyguard ['bɒdɪgɑːd] *n* guardaespaldas *mf inv*, guarura *m* *Méx*.

body language *n* lenguaje *m* corporal.

body odour *n* olor *m* corporal.

body piercing *n* piercing *m*.

body search *n* cacheo *m*.

body shop *n* [garage] taller *m* de carrocería.

body stocking *n* [woman's undergarment] body *m*; [dancer's garment] malla *f*.

bodywork ['bɒdɪwɜːk] *n* carrocería *f*.

boffin ['bɒfɪn] *n* UK *inf* lumbrera *f*.

bog [bɒg] *n* **- 1.** [marsh] cenagal *m*, lodazal *m* **- 2.** UK *v inf* [toilet] baño *m*.

bogey ['bəʊgɪ] *n* **- 1.** [in golf] bogey *m* **- 2.** UK *inf* [piece of mucus] moco *m*.

bogged down [ˌbɒgd-] *adj* **- 1.** [in details, work]: **bogged down (in)** empantanado(da) (en) **- 2.** [in mud, snow]: **bogged down in** atascado(da) en.

boggle ['bɒgl] *vi*: **the mind boggles!** ¡es increíble!

boggy ['bɒgɪ] *adj* cenagoso(sa), pantanoso(sa).

Bogotá [ˌbɒgəˈtɑː] *n* Bogotá.

bogus ['bəʊgəs] *adj* falso(sa).

Bohemia [bəʊˈhiːmjə] *n* Bohemia.

bohemian [bəʊˈhiːmɪən] ◇ *adj* bohemio(mia). ◇ *n* bohemio *m*, -mia *f*. ✦ **Bohemian** ◇ *adj* bohemio(mia). ◇ *n* bohemio *m*, -mia *f*.

boil [bɔɪl] ◇ *n* **- 1.** MED pústula *f* **- 2.** [boiling point]: **to bring sthg to the boil** hacer que algo hierva; **to come to the boil** romper a hervir. ◇ *vt* **- 1.** [water] hervir; **to boil the kettle** poner el agua a hervir **- 2.** [food] cocer. ◇ *vi* hervir. ✦ **boil away** *vi* [evaporate] (hervir hasta) consumirse. ✦ **boil down to** *vt insep* reducirse a.

◆ **boil over** *vi* - **1.** [liquid] rebosar - **2.** *fig* [feelings] desbordarse.

boiled [bɔɪld] *adj* cocido(da); **boiled egg** [hard-boiled] huevo *m* duro; [soft-boiled] huevo *m* pasado por agua; **boiled sweets** *UK* caramelos *mpl* (duros).

boiler ['bɔɪlər] *n* caldera *f*.

boiler room *n* sala *f* de calderas.

boiler suit *n UK* mono *m*.

boiling ['bɔɪlɪŋ] *adj* - **1.** [liquid] hirviendo - **2.** *inf* [hot]: **I'm boiling** estoy asado(da) de calor; **it's boiling** hace un calor de muerte - **3.** [angry]: **boiling with rage** ciego(ga) de ira.

boiling point *n* punto *m* de ebullición.

boisterous ['bɔɪstərəs] *adj* ruidoso(sa), alborotador(ra).

bold [bəʊld] *adj* - **1.** [brave, daring] audaz - **2.** [lines, design] marcado(da) - **3.** [colour] vivo(va) - **4.** TYPO: **bold type** OR **print** negrita *f*.

boldly ['bəʊldlɪ] *adv* [bravely] con audacia, audazmente.

Bolivia [bə'lɪvɪə] *n* Bolivia.

Bolivian [bə'lɪvɪən] ⬦ *adj* boliviano(na). ⬦ *n* boliviano *m*, -na *f*.

bollard ['bɒlɑːd] *n* [on road] poste *m*.

bollocks ['bɒləks] *UK* v *inf* ⬦ *npl* cojones *mpl*. ⬦ *excl* ¡un cojón!, ¡qué cojones!

Bolshevik ['bɒlʃɪvɪk] ⬦ *adj* bolchevique. ⬦ *n* bolchevique *mf*.

bolster ['bəʊlstər] ⬦ *n* cabezal *m*. ⬦ *vt* fortalecer, reforzar.

◆ **bolster up** *vt insep* reforzar.

bolt [bəʊlt] ⬦ *n* - **1.** [on door, window] cerrojo *m* - **2.** [type of screw] perno *m*. ⬦ *adv*: **bolt upright** muy derecho(cha). ⬦ *vt* - **1.** [fasten together] atornillar - **2.** [door, window] echar el cerrojo a - **3.** [food] tragarse. ⬦ *vi* salir disparado(da).

bomb [bɒm] ⬦ *n* - **1.** bomba *f* - **2.** *US inf* [failure] desastre *m*. ⬦ *vt* bombardear. ⬦ *vi US inf* [fail] fracasar estrepitosamente.

bombard [bɒm'bɑːd] *vt fig & MIL*: **to bombard (with)** bombardear (a).

bombardment [bɒm'bɑːdmənt] *n* bombardeo *m*.

bombastic [bɒm'bæstɪk] *adj* grandilocuente, rimbombante.

bomb disposal squad *n* equipo *m* de artificieros.

bomber ['bɒmər] *n* - **1.** [plane] bombardero *m* - **2.** [person] terrorista *mf* que pone bombas.

bomber jacket *n* cazadora *f* (de aviador).

bombing ['bɒmɪŋ] *n* bombardeo *m*.

bombshell ['bɒmʃel] *n fig* bombazo *m*; **a blonde bombshell** *inf* una rubia explosiva.

bona fide ['bəʊnə'faɪdɪ] *adj* auténtico(ca).

bonanza [bə'nænzə] *n* mina *f*.

bond [bɒnd] ⬦ *n* - **1.** [between people] lazo *m*, vínculo *m* - **2.** [binding promise] compromiso *m* - **3.** FIN bono *m*. ⬦ *vt* [glue] adherir; *fig* [people] unir; **to bond sthg to** adherir algo a. ⬦ *vi* [stick together]: **to bond (together)** adherirse; *fig* [people] unirse.

bonded warehouse ['bɒndɪd-] *n* depósito *m* franco.

bone [bəʊn] ⬦ *n* [gen] hueso *m*; [of fish] raspa *f*, espina *f*; **bone of contention** manzana *f* de la discordia; **to feel** OR **know sthg in one's bones** tener el presentimiento de algo; **to make no bones about sthg** no andarse con rodeos acerca de algo; **to make no bones about doing sthg** no tener ningún reparo en hacer algo. ⬦ *vt* [fish] quitar las espinas a; [meat] deshuesar.

bone china *n* porcelana *f* fina.

bone-dry *adj* completamente seco(ca).

bone-idle *adj* haragán(ana), gandul(la).

boneless ['bəʊnlɪs] *adj* [meat] deshuesado(da); [fish] sin raspa.

bone marrow *n* tuétano *m*.

bonfire ['bɒn,faɪər] *n* hoguera *f*.

bongo ['bɒŋgəʊ] (*pl* **-s** OR **-es**) *n*: **bongo (drum)** bongó *m*.

Bonn [bɒn] *n* Bonn.

bonnet ['bɒnɪt] *n* - **1.** *UK* [of car] capó *m* - **2.** [hat] toca *f*.

bonny ['bɒnɪ] (*comp* **-ier**, *superl* **-iest**) *adj Scotland* majo(ja).

bonus ['bəʊnəs] (*pl* **-es**) *n* [extra money] prima *f*; [for increased productivity] plus *m*; *fig* beneficio *m* adicional.

bonus issue *n UK* FIN emisión *f* gratuita de acciones.

bony ['bəʊnɪ] (*comp* **-ier**, *superl* **-iest**) *adj* - **1.** [person, hand] huesudo(da) - **2.** [meat] lleno(na) de huesos; [fish] espinoso(sa).

boo [buː] ⬦ *excl* ¡bu! ⬦ *n* (*pl* **-s**) abucheo *m*. ⬦ *vt & vi* abuchear.

boob [buːb] *n inf* [mistake] metedura *f* de pata.

◆ **boobs** *npl UK* v *inf* [woman's breasts] tetas *fpl*.

boob tube *n* - **1.** *UK* [garment] top *m* sin mangas ni tirantes - **2.** *US inf* [television] caja *f* tonta.

booby prize ['buːbɪ-] *n* premio otorgado al último o al peor (en broma).

booby trap ['buːbɪ-] *n* - **1.** [bomb] bomba *f* camuflada - **2.** [type of prank] trampa *f* (broma).

◆ **booby-trap** *vt* poner una trampa explosiva en.

boogie ['buːgɪ] *inf* ⬦ *n* baile *m*. ⬦ *vi* menear el esqueleto.

book [bʊk] ◇ *n* - **1.** [for reading] libro *m*; **to do sthg by the book** hacer algo como mandan los cánones; **to throw the book at sb** castigar duramente a alguien - **2.** [of stamps] librillo *m*; [of tickets, cheques] talonario *m*; [of matches] caja *f* (*de solapa*). ◇ *vt* - **1.** [reserve] reservar; **to be fully booked** estar completo - **2.** *inf* [subj: police] multar - **3.** *UK* FTBL mostrar una tarjeta amarilla a. ◇ *vi* hacer reserva.

◆ **books** *npl* COMM libros *mpl*; **to do the books** hacer las cuentas; **to be in sb's good/bad books** estar a bien/a mal con alguien.

◆ **book in** *UK* ◇ *vt sep* hacer una reserva a. ◇ *vi* registrarse.

◆ **book up** *vt sep*: **to be booked up** estar completo.

bookable ['bʊkəbl] *adj UK* - **1.** [seats, tickets] reservable con antelación - **2.** FTBL sancionable con tarjeta.

bookbinding ['bʊk,baɪndɪŋ] *n* encuadernación *f*.

bookcase ['bʊkkeɪs] *n* estantería *f*.

book club *n* ≈ círculo *m* de lectores.

bookend ['bʊkend] *n* sujetalibros *m inv*.

bookie ['bʊkɪ] *n inf* corredor *m*, -ra *f* de apuestas.

booking ['bʊkɪŋ] *n* - **1.** *esp UK* [reservation] reserva *f* - **2.** *UK* FTBL tarjeta *f* amarilla.

booking clerk *n esp UK* taquillero *m*, -ra *f*.

booking office *n esp UK* taquilla *f*.

bookish ['bʊkɪʃ] *adj* aficionado(da) a la lectura seria.

bookkeeper ['bʊk,ki:pər] *n* contable *mf*.

bookkeeping ['bʊk,ki:pɪŋ] *n* contabilidad *f*.

booklet ['bʊklɪt] *n* folleto *m*.

bookmaker ['bʊk,meɪkər] *n* corredor *m*, -ra *f* de apuestas.

bookmark ['bʊkmɑ:k] *n* - **1.** separador *m* - **2.** COMPUT marcador *m*.

bookseller ['bʊk,selər] *n* librero *m*, -ra *f*.

bookshelf ['bʊkʃelf] (*pl* **-shelves** [-ʃelvz]) *n* [shelf] estante *m*; [bookcase] estantería *f*, librero *m* Chile & Méx.

bookshop *UK* ['bʊkʃɒp], **bookstore** *US* ['bʊkstɔ:r] *n* librería *f*.

bookstall ['bʊkstɔ:l] *n UK* puesto *m* de libros.

bookstore *esp US* = **bookshop**.

book token *n esp UK* vale *m* para comprar libros.

bookworm ['bʊkwɜ:m] *n* ratón *m* de biblioteca.

boom [bu:m] ◇ *n* - **1.** [loud noise] estampido *m*, estruendo *m* - **2.** [increase] auge *m*, boom *m* - **3.** NAUT botavara *f* - **4.** [for TV camera, microphone] jirafa *f*. ◇ *vi* - **1.** [make noise] tronar - **2.** ECON estar en auge.

boomerang ['bu:məræŋ] *n* bumerán *m*.

boon [bu:n] *n* gran ayuda *f*.

boor [bʊər] *n* patán *m*.

boorish ['bʊərɪʃ] *adj* basto(ta).

boost [bu:st] ◇ *n* - **1.** [in profits, production] incremento *m* - **2.** [to popularity, spirits] empujón *m*, estímulo *m*. ◇ *vt* - **1.** [increase] incrementar - **2.** [improve] levantar.

booster ['bu:stər] *n* MED inyección *f* de refuerzo.

boot [bu:t] ◇ *n* - **1.** [item of footwear] bota *f*; [ankle boot] botín *m* - **2.** *UK* [of car] maletero *m*, cajuela *f* Méx, baúl *m* Col & R Plata, maletera *f* Perú. ◇ *vt* - **1.** *inf* [kick] dar una patada a - **2.** COMPUT arrancar.

◆ **to boot** *adv* además.

◆ **boot out** *vt sep inf* echar, poner (de patitas) en la calle.

◆ **boot up** *vt sep* COMPUT arrancar.

booth [bu:ð] *n* - **1.** [at fair] puesto *m* - **2.** [for phoning, voting] cabina *f*.

bootleg ['bu:tleg] *adj* [recording] pirata; [whisky] de contrabando.

bootlegger ['bu:t,legər] *n* contrabandista *mf*.

booty ['bu:tɪ] *n* - **1.** botín *m* - **2.** *US inf* [sexual intercourse]: **to get some booty** mojar el churro *Esp* OR bizcocho *R Plata*, echarse un caldito *Méx*.

booze [bu:z] *inf* ◇ *n* (U) priva *f*. ◇ *vi* privar, empinar el codo.

boozer ['bu:zər] *n inf* - **1.** [person] borrachuzo *m*, -za *f*, curda *mf* Amér - **2.** *UK* [pub] ≈ bareto *m*.

bop [bɒp] *inf* ◇ *n* - **1.** [hit] golpecito *m* - **2.** [disco] disco *f* - **3.** [dance] baile *m*. ◇ *vt* (*pt & pp* **-ped**, *cont* **-ping**) dar un golpecito a. ◇ *vi* (*pt & pp* **-ped**, *cont* **-ping**) bailar.

border ['bɔ:dər] ◇ *n* - **1.** [between countries] frontera *f* - **2.** [edge] borde *m* - **3.** [in garden] parterre *m*, arriate *m*. ◇ *vt* - **1.** [country] limitar con - **2.** [edge] bordear.

◆ **border on** *vt insep* rayar en.

borderline ['bɔ:dəlaɪn] ◇ *adj*: **a borderline case** un caso dudoso. ◇ *n fig* frontera *f*, límite *m*.

bore [bɔ:r] ◇ *pt* ▷ **bear**. ◇ *n* - **1.** *pej* [person] pelmazo *m*, -za *f*, pesado *m*, -da *f*; [situation, event] rollo *m*, lata *f* - **2.** [of gun] calibre *m*. ◇ *vt* - **1.** [not interest] aburrir; **to bore sb stiff** OR **to tears** OR **to death** aburrir a alguien un montón - **2.** [drill] taladrar, horadar.

bored [bɔ:d] *adj* aburrido(da); **to be bored with sthg** estar harto de algo; **to be bored stiff** OR **to tears** OR **to death** aburrirse como una ostra.

boredom ['bɔ:dəm] *n* aburrimiento *m*.

boring ['bɔ:rɪŋ] *adj* aburrido(da), cansador(ra) *R Plata*.

born [bɔ:n] *adj* - **1.** [given life] nacido(da); **to be born** nacer; **born and bred** nacido y criado - **2.** [natural] nato(ta).

born-again Christian *n cristiano convertido a una secta evangélica.*

borne [bɔ:n] *pp* ⊳ **bear.**

Borneo [ˈbɔ:nɪəʊ] *n* Borneo.

borough [ˈbʌrə] *n* [area of town] distrito *m*; [town] municipio *m*.

borrow [ˈbɒrəʊ] *vt*: **to borrow sthg from sb** coger OR tomar algo prestado a alguien; **can I borrow your bike?** ¿me prestas tu bici?

borrower [ˈbɒrəʊəʳ] *n* - **1.** [of money] prestatario *m*, -ria *f* - **2.** [library user] usuario *m*, -ria *f*.

borrowing [ˈbɒrəʊɪŋ] *n* (U) préstamos *mpl*.

Bosnia [ˈbɒznɪə] *n* Bosnia.

Bosnia-Herzegovina [-,hɜːtsəgəˈviːnə] *n* Bosnia-Hercegovina.

Bosnian [ˈbɒznɪən] ◇ *adj* bosnio(nia). ◇ *n* bosnio *m*, -nia *f*.

bosom [ˈbʊzəm] *n* - **1.** [of woman] busto *m*, pecho *m* - **2.** *fig* [centre of emotions] seno *m*; **bosom friend** amigo *m*, -ga *f* del alma.

Bosporus [ˈbɒspərəs], **Bosphorus** [ˈbɒsfərəs] *n*: **the Bosporus** el Bósforo.

boss [bɒs] ◇ *n* jefe *m*, -fa *f*; **to be one's own boss** trabajar por cuenta propia. ◇ *vt pej* mangonear, dar órdenes a.

⏺ **boss about, boss around** *vt sep pej* mangonear, dar órdenes a.

bossy [ˈbɒsɪ] (*comp* **-ier,** *superl* **-iest**) *adj* mandón(ona).

bosun [ˈbəʊsn] = **boatswain.**

botanic(al) [bəˈtænɪk(l)] *adj* botánico(ca).

botanical garden *n* jardín *m* botánico.

botanist [ˈbɒtənɪst] *n* botánico *m*, -ca *f*.

botany [ˈbɒtənɪ] *n* botánica *f*.

botch [bɒtʃ] ⏺ **botch up** *vt sep inf* estropear, hacer chapuceramente.

both [bəʊθ] ◇ *adj* los dos, las dos, ambos(bas). ◇ *pron*: **both (of them)** los dos, las dos *f*, ambos *mpl*, -bas *fpl*; **both of us are coming** vamos los dos. ◇ *adv*: **she is both pretty and intelligent** es guapa e inteligente.

bother [ˈbɒðəʳ] ◇ *vt* - **1.** [worry] preocupar; [irritate] fastidiar, fregar *Amér*; **I/she can't be bothered to do it** no tengo/tiene ganas de hacerlo - **2.** [pester] molestar. ◇ *vi*: **to bother (doing** OR **to do sthg)** molestarse (en hacer algo); **to bother about** preocuparse por. ◇ *n* (U) - **1.** [inconvenience] problemas *mpl* - **2.** [pest, nuisance] molestia *f*.

bothered [ˈbɒðəd] *adj* preocupado(da).

Botswana [bɒˈtswɑːnə] *n* Botsuana.

bottle [ˈbɒtl] ◇ *n* - **1.** [gen] botella *f* - **2.** [of shampoo, medicine - plastic] bote *m*; [- glass] frasco *m* - **3.** [for baby] biberón *m* - **4.** (U) *UK inf* [courage] agallas *fpl*. ◇ *vt* - **1.** [wine] embotellar - **2.** [fruit] envasar.

⏺ **bottle out** *vi UK inf* achantarse, arrugarse.

⏺ **bottle up** *vt sep* reprimir.

bottle bank *n* contenedor *m* de vidrio.

bottled [ˈbɒtld] *adj* embotellado(da).

bottle-feed *vt* criar con biberón.

bottleneck [ˈbɒtlnek] *n* - **1.** [in traffic] embotellamiento *m* - **2.** [in production] atasco *m*.

bottle-opener *n* abridor *m*, abrebotellas *m inv*.

bottle party *n fiesta a la que los invitados traen bebida.*

bottom [ˈbɒtəm] ◇ *adj* - **1.** [lowest] más bajo(ja), de abajo del todo - **2.** [least successful] peor. ◇ *n* - **1.** [lowest part - of glass, bottle] culo *m*; [- of bag, mine, sea] fondo *m*; [- of ladder, hill] pie *m*; [- of page, list] final *m* - **2.** [farthest point] final *m*, fondo *m* - **3.** [of class etc] parte *f* más baja - **4.** [buttocks] culo *m*, trasero *m*, traste *m Amér* - **5.** [root]: **at the bottom of** detrás de; **to get to the bottom of** llegar al fondo de.

⏺ **bottom out** *vi* tocar fondo.

bottomless [ˈbɒtəmlɪs] *adj* - **1.** [very deep] sin fondo, insondable - **2.** [endless] inagotable.

bottom line *n fig*: **the bottom line is...** a fin de cuentas...

bough [baʊ] *n* rama *f*.

bought [bɔ:t] *pt* & *pp* ⊳ **buy.**

boulder [ˈbəʊldəʳ] *n* roca *f* grande y de forma redonda.

boulevard [ˈbuːləvɑːd] *n* bulevar *m*.

bounce [baʊns] ◇ *vi* - **1.** [gen] rebotar - **2.** [light] reflejarse - **3.** [person]: **to bounce into the room** irrumpir en el cuarto; **to bounce (on sthg)** dar botes (en algo) - **4.** [cheque] ser rechazado(da) por el banco. ◇ *vt* botar. ◇ *n* bote *m*.

⏺ **bounce back** *vi* recuperarse.

bouncer [ˈbaʊnsəʳ] *n inf* matón *m*, gorila *m* (de un local).

bouncy [ˈbaʊnsɪ] (*comp* **-ier,** *superl* **-iest**) *adj* - **1.** [lively] animado(da), dinámico(ca) - **2.** [springy] elástico(ca).

bound [baʊnd] ◇ *pt* & *pp* ⊳ **bind.** ◇ *adj* - **1.** [certain]: **it's bound to happen** seguro que va a pasar - **2.** [obliged]: **bound (by sthg/to do sthg)** obligado(da) (por algo/a hacer algo); **I'm bound to say** OR **admit** tengo que decir OR admitir - **3.** [for place]: **to be bound for** ir rumbo a. ◇ *n* salto *m*. ◇ *vt*: **to be bounded by** estar rodeado(da) de. ◇ *vi* ir dando saltos.

⏺ **bounds** *npl* [limits] límites *mpl*; **out of bounds** (en) zona prohibida.

boundary ['baʊndərɪ] (*pl* -ies) *n* [gen] límite *m*; [between countries] frontera *f*.

boundless ['baʊndlɪs] *adj* ilimitado(da).

bountiful ['baʊntɪfʊl] *adj liter* [ample] generoso(sa), opulento(ta).

bounty ['baʊntɪ] *n liter* [generosity] magnificencia *f*, generosidad *f*.

bouquet [bəʊ'keɪ] *n* [of flowers] ramo *m*.

bourbon ['bɜ:bən] *n* bourbon *m*, whisky *m* americano.

bourgeois ['bɔːʒwɑ:] *adj* burgués(esa).

bout [baʊt] *n* - **1.** [attack] ataque *m*, acceso *m* - **2.** [session] racha *f* - **3.** [boxing match] combate *m*.

boutique [bu:'ti:k] *n* boutique *f*.

bow[1] [baʊ] ⟨⟩ *n* - **1.** [act of bowing] reverencia *f* - **2.** [of ship] proa *f*. ⟨⟩ *vt* inclinar. ⟨⟩ *vi* - **1.** [make a bow] inclinarse - **2.** [defer]: **to bow to sthg** ceder OR doblegarse ante algo.
◆ **bow down** *vi* doblegarse.
◆ **bow out** *vi* retirarse.

bow[2] [bəʊ] *n* - **1.** [weapon, for musical instrument] arco *m* - **2.** [knot] lazo *m*.

bowels ['baʊəlz] *npl lit* & *fig* entrañas *fpl*.

bowl [bəʊl] ⟨⟩ *n* - **1.** [gen] cuenco *m*, bol *m*; [for soup] plato *m*; [for washing clothes] barreño *m*, balde *m* - **2.** [of toilet] taza *f*; [of pipe] cazoleta *f*. ⟨⟩ *vt* lanzar. ⟨⟩ *vi* lanzar la bola.
◆ **bowls** *n (U) juego similar a la petanca que se juega sobre césped*.
◆ **bowl over** *vt sep* - **1.** [knock over] atropellar - **2.** *fig* [surprise, impress] dejar atónito(ta).

bow-legged [,bəʊ'legɪd] *adj* de piernas arqueadas, estevado(da).

bowler ['bəʊlə'] *n* - **1.** CRICKET lanzador *m* - **2.**: **bowler (hat)** bombín *m*, sombrero *m* hongo, tongo *m* Chile.

bowling ['bəʊlɪŋ] *n (U)* bolos *mpl*.

bowling alley *n* - **1.** [building] bolera *f* - **2.** [alley] calle *f*.

bowling green *n campo de césped para jugar a los 'bowls'*.

bow tie [bəʊ-] *n* pajarita *f*.

bow window [bəʊ-] *n* mirador *m*.

box [bɒks] ⟨⟩ *n* - **1.** [container, boxful] caja *f*; [for jewels] estuche *m* - **2.** THEAT palco *m* - **3.** *UK inf* [television]: **the box** la tele - **4.** [in printed questionnaire etc] casilla *f*. ⟨⟩ *vt* - **1.** [in boxing] boxear con - **2.** [put in boxes] encajonar. ⟨⟩ *vi* boxear.
◆ **box in** *vt sep* - **1.** [cut off] encerrar, encajonar - **2.** [build a box around] proteger con una caja.

boxed [bɒkst] *adj* presentado(da) en una caja.

boxer ['bɒksə'] *n* - **1.** [fighter] boxeador *m*, púgil *m* - **2.** [dog] boxer *m*.

boxer shorts *npl* calzoncillos *mpl*, boxers *mpl*.

boxing ['bɒksɪŋ] *n* boxeo *m*, box *m Amér C & Méx*.

Boxing Day *n fiesta nacional en Inglaterra y Gales el 26 de diciembre (salvo domingos) en que tradicionalmente se da el aguinaldo.*

boxing glove *n* guante *m* de boxeo, guante *m* de box *Amér C & Méx*.

boxing ring *n* ring *m*, cuadrilátero *m*.

box junction *n UK* cruce *m* con parilla.

box number *n* apartado *m* de correos.

box office *n* taquilla *f*, boletería *f Amér*.

boxroom ['bɒksrʊm] *n UK* trastero *m*.

boy [bɔɪ] ⟨⟩ *n* - **1.** [male child] chico *m*, niño *m*, pibe *m R Plata* - **2.** *inf* [young man] chaval *m*. ⟨⟩ *excl*: **(oh) boy!** *US inf* ¡jolín!, ¡vaya, vaya!

boycott ['bɔɪkɒt] ⟨⟩ *n* boicot *m*. ⟨⟩ *vt* boicotear.

boyfriend ['bɔɪfrend] *n* novio *m*, pololo *m Chile*.

boyish ['bɔɪɪʃ] *adj* - **1.** [man] juvenil - **2.** [woman, figure] masculino(na).

boy scout *n* (boy) scout *m*.

Br, Bro (*abbr of* **brother**) [preceding name of monk] Hno.

bra [brɑ:] *n* sujetador *m*, sostén *m*, ajustadores *mpl Cuba*, brasier *m Col & Méx*, corpiño *m Arg*.

brace [breɪs] ⟨⟩ *n* - **1.** [on teeth] aparato *m* corrector - **2.** [on leg] soporte *m* para la pierna - **3.** [pair] par *m*. ⟨⟩ *vt* [steady] tensar; **to brace o.s. (for)** *lit* & *fig* prepararse (para).
◆ **braces** *npl UK* tirantes *mpl*, tiradores *mpl Bol & R Plata*.

bracelet ['breɪslɪt] *n* brazalete *m*, pulsera *f*.

bracing ['breɪsɪŋ] *adj* tonificante.

bracken ['brækn] *n* helechos *mpl*.

bracket ['brækɪt] ⟨⟩ *n* - **1.** [support] soporte *m*, palomilla *f* - **2.** [parenthesis - round] paréntesis *m inv*; [- square] corchete *m*; **in brackets** entre paréntesis - **3.** [group] sector *m*, banda *f*. ⟨⟩ *vt* - **1.** [enclose in brackets] poner entre paréntesis - **2.** [group]: **to bracket sthg/sb (together) with** agrupar algo/a alguien (junto) con.

brackish ['brækɪʃ] *adj* salobre.

brag [bræg] (*pt & pp* -**ged**, *cont* -**ging**) *vi* fanfarronear, jactarse, compadrear *Amér*.

braid [breɪd] ⟨⟩ *n* - **1.** [on uniform] galón *m* - **2.** [hairstyle] trenza *f*. ⟨⟩ *vt* trenzar.

braille [breɪl] *n* braille *m*.

brain [breɪn] *n lit* & *fig* cerebro *m*; **to have sthg on the brain** tener algo metido en la cabeza.
◆ **brains** *npl* cerebro *m*, seso *m*; **to pick sb's brains** recurrir a los conocimientos de alguien.

brainchild ['breɪntʃaɪld] *n inf* invención *f*, idea *f*.

brain death n muerte f cerebral.

brain drain n fuga f de cerebros.

brainless ['breɪnlɪs] adj estúpido(da).

brainstorm ['breɪnstɔ:m] n - **1.** UK [moment of aberration] momento m de atontamiento OR estupidez - **2.** US [brilliant idea] idea f genial, genialidad f.

brainstorming ['breɪn,stɔ:mɪŋ] n: **brainstorming session** tormenta de ideas.

brainteaser ['breɪn,ti:zə] n rompecabezas m inv.

brainwash ['breɪnwɒʃ] vt lavar el cerebro a.

brainwave ['breɪnweɪv] n idea f genial.

brainy ['breɪnɪ] (comp -ier, superl -iest) adj inf listo(ta).

braise [breɪz] vt estofar, cocer a fuego lento.

brake [breɪk] <> n lit & fig freno m. <> vi frenar.

brake light n luz f de freno.

brake lining n forro m del freno.

brake pedal n pedal m del freno.

brake shoe n zapata f del freno.

bramble ['bræmbl] n [bush] zarza f, zarzamora f; [fruit] mora f.

bran [bræn] n salvado m.

branch [brɑːntʃ] <> n - **1.** [of tree, subject] rama f - **2.** [of river] afluente m; [of railway] ramal m - **3.** [of company, bank] sucursal f. <> vi bifurcarse.

➤ **branch off** vi desviarse.

➤ **branch out** vi [person] ampliar horizontes; [firm] expandirse, diversificarse.

branch line n ramal m.

brand [brænd] <> n - **1.** [of product] marca f - **2.** fig [type] tipo m, estilo m - **3.** [mark] hierro m. <> vt - **1.** [cattle] marcar (con hierro) - **2.** fig [classify]: **to brand sb (as sthg)** tildar a alguien (de algo).

brandish ['brændɪʃ] vt [weapon] blandir; [letter etc] agitar.

brand leader n marca f líder OR puntera.

brand name n marca f.

brand-new adj flamante.

brandy ['brændɪ] (pl -ies) n coñac m, brandy m.

brash [bræʃ] adj pej enérgico e insolente.

Brasilia [brə'zɪljə] n Brasilia.

brass [brɑːs] n - **1.** [metal] latón m - **2.** MUS: **the brass** el metal.

brass band n banda f de metal.

brasserie ['bræsərɪ] n restaurante m.

brassiere [UK 'bræsɪə, US brə'zɪr] n sostén m, sujetador m.

brass tacks npl inf: **to get down to brass tacks** ir al grano.

brat [bræt] n inf pej mocoso m, -sa f.

bravado [brə'vɑːdəʊ] n bravuconería f.

brave [breɪv] <> adj valiente. <> n guerrero m indio. <> vt [weather, storm] desafiar; [sb's anger] hacer frente a.

bravely ['breɪvlɪ] adv valientemente.

bravery ['breɪvərɪ] n valentía f.

bravo [,brɑː'vəʊ] excl ¡bravo!

brawl [brɔːl] n gresca f, reyerta f.

brawn [brɔːn] n (U) - **1.** [muscle] musculatura f, fuerza f física - **2.** UK [meat] carne de cerdo en gelatina.

brawny ['brɔːnɪ] (comp -ier, superl -iest) adj musculoso(sa).

bray [breɪ] vi [donkey] rebuznar.

brazen ['breɪzn] adj [person] descarado(da); [lie] burdo(da).

➤ **brazen out** vt sep: **to brazen it out** echarle cara.

brazier ['breɪzjə] n brasero m.

Brazil [brə'zɪl] n (el) Brasil.

Brazilian [brə'zɪljən] <> adj brasileño(ña), brasilero(ra) Amér. <> n brasileño m, -ña f, brasilero m, -ra f Amér.

brazil nut n nuez f de Pará.

breach [briːtʃ] <> n - **1.** [act of disobedience] incumplimiento m; **breach of confidence** abuso m de confianza; **to be in breach of sthg** incumplir algo; **breach of contract** incumplimiento de contrato - **2.** [opening, gap] brecha f; **to step into the breach** echar una mano - **3.** fig [in friendship, marriage] ruptura f. <> vt - **1.** [disobey] incumplir - **2.** [make hole in] abrir (una) brecha en.

breach of the peace n alteración f del orden público.

bread [bred] n - **1.** [food] pan m; **bread and butter** [buttered bread] pan con mantequilla; fig [main income] sustento m diario - **2.** inf [money] pasta f.

bread bin UK, **bread box** US n panera f.

breadboard ['bredbɔːd] n tabla f (de cortar el pan).

bread box US = **bread bin**.

breadcrumbs ['bredkrʌmz] npl migas fpl (de pan); CULIN pan m rallado.

breaded ['bredɪd] adj empanado(da).

breadline ['bredlaɪn] n: **to be on the breadline** vivir en la miseria.

breadth [bretθ] n - **1.** [in measurements] anchura f - **2.** fig [scope] amplitud f.

breadwinner ['bred,wɪnə] n: **he's the breadwinner** es el que mantiene a la familia.

break [breɪk] <> n - **1.** [gap - in clouds] claro m; [- in line] espacio m en blanco; [- in transmission] corte m - **2.** [fracture] rotura f, fractura f - **3.** [rupture]: **break (with)** ruptura f (con) - **4.** [pause]: **break (from)** descanso m (de); **to**

have OR **take a break** tomarse un descanso **- 5.** [holiday] vacaciones *fpl* **- 6.** [playtime] recreo *m* **- 7.** *inf* [chance] oportunidad *f*; **a lucky break** un golpe de suerte **- 8.** *liter*: **at break of day** al alba **- 9.** COMPUT: **break (key)** tecla *f* de interrupción. ◇ *vt* (*pt* **broke**, *pp* **broken**) **- 1.** [gen] romper; [arm, leg etc] romperse; **the river broke its banks** el río se desbordó; **to break sb's hold** escaparse OR liberarse de alguien **- 2.** [machine] estropear **- 3.** [journey, contact] interrumpir **- 4.** [habit, health] acabar con; [strike] reventar **- 5.** [law, rule] violar; [appointment, word] faltar a **- 6.** [record] batir **- 7.** [in tennis - service] romper **- 8.** [tell]: **to break the news (of sthg to sb)** dar la noticia (de algo a alguien). ◇ *vi* (*pt* **broke**, *pp* **broken**) **- 1.** [come to pieces] romperse **- 2.** [stop working] estropearse **- 3.** [pause] parar; [weather] cambiar **- 4.** [start - day] romper; [- storm] estallar, desencadenarse **- 5.** [wave] romper **- 6.** [escape]: **to break loose** OR **free** escaparse **- 7.** [voice] cambiar **- 8.** [news] divulgarse ▶▶ **to break even** salir sin pérdidas ni beneficios.

◆ **break away** *vi* escaparse; **to break away (from)** [end connection] separarse (de); POL escindirse (de).

◆ **break down** ◇ *vt sep* **- 1.** [destroy - gen] derribar, echar abajo; [- resistance] vencer **- 2.** [analyse] descomponer **- 3.** [cause to decompose] descomponer. ◇ *vi* **- 1.** [collapse, disintegrate, fail] venirse abajo **- 2.** [stop working] estropearse **- 3.** [lose emotional control] perder el control **- 4.** [decompose] descomponerse.

◆ **break in** ◇ *vi* **- 1.** [enter by force] entrar por la fuerza **- 2.** [interrupt]: **to break in (on sthg/sb)** interrumpir (algo/a alguien). ◇ *vt sep* **- 1.** [horse, shoes] domar **- 2.** [person] amoldar.

◆ **break into** *vt insep* **- 1.** [house, shop] entrar (por la fuerza) en, allanar; [box, safe] forzar **- 2.** [begin suddenly]: **to break into song/a run** echarse a cantar/correr **- 3.** [become involved in] introducirse OR adentrarse en.

◆ **break off** ◇ *vt sep* **- 1.** [detach] partir **- 2.** [end] romper; [holiday] interrumpir. ◇ *vi* **- 1.** [become detached] partirse **- 2.** [stop talking] interrumpirse **- 3.** [stop working] parar (de trabajar).

◆ **break out** *vi* **- 1.** [fire, fighting, panic] desencadenarse; [war] estallar **- 2.** [become covered]: **he broke out in spots** se le salieron granos **- 3.** [escape]: **to break out (of)** escapar (de).

◆ **break through** ◇ *vt insep* abrirse paso a través de. ◇ *vi* abrirse paso.

◆ **break up** ◇ *vt sep* **- 1.** [ice] hacer pedazos; [car] desguazar **- 2.** [relationship] romper; [talks] poner fin a; [fight] poner fin a; [crowd] disolver. ◇ *vi* **- 1.** [into smaller pieces] hacerse pedazos

- 2. [relationship] deshacerse; [conference] concluir; [school, pupils] terminar; **to break up with sb** romper con alguien **- 3.** [crowd] disolverse.

◆ **break with** *vt insep* romper con.

breakable ['breɪkəbl] *adj* frágil.

breakage ['breɪkɪdʒ] *n* rotura *f*.

breakaway ['breɪkəweɪ] *adj* disidente.

break dancing *n* break (dance) *m*.

breakdown ['breɪkdaʊn] *n* **- 1.** [of car, train] avería *f*; [of talks, in communications] ruptura *f*; [of law and order] colapso *m*; **nervous breakdown** crisis *f* (nerviosa) **- 2.** [analysis] desglose *m*.

breaker ['breɪkər] *n* [wave] ola *f* grande.

breakfast ['brekfəst] ◇ *n* desayuno *m*; **to have breakfast** desayunar. ◇ *vi fml*: **to breakfast (on sthg)** desayunar (algo).

breakfast cereal *n* cereales *mpl (para desayuno)*.

breakfast television *n* UK programación *f* matinal de televisión.

break-in *n* robo *m (con allanamiento de morada)*.

breaking ['breɪkɪŋ] *n*: **breaking and entering** LAW allanamiento *m* de morada.

breaking point *n*: **to be at breaking point** estar al límite.

breakneck ['breɪknek] *adj*: **at breakneck speed** a (una) velocidad de vértigo.

breakthrough ['breɪkθruː] *n* avance *m*.

breakup ['breɪkʌp] *n* ruptura *f*.

breakup value *n* COMM valor *m* en liquidación.

bream [briːm] (*pl* **bream** OR **-s**) *n* [sea bream] besugo *m*; [freshwater] brema *f*.

breast [brest] *n* **- 1.** [of woman] pecho *m*, seno *m*; [of man] pecho *m* **- 2.** [meat of bird] pechuga *f* **- 3.** *liter* [seat of emotions] corazón *m*; **to make a clean breast of it** confesarlo abiertamente.

breast-feed *vt* & *vi* amamantar, dar de mamar.

breast milk *n (U)* leche *f* materna.

breast pocket *n* bolsillo *m* del pecho OR de arriba.

breaststroke ['breststrəʊk] *n* braza *f*.

breath [breθ] *n* **- 1.** [act of breathing] respiración *f*; **to take a deep breath** respirar hondo; **to be a breath of fresh air** *fig* [person, experience] ser un soplo de aire fresco; **to get one's breath back** recuperar el aliento; **to go for a breath of (fresh) air** salir a tomar un poco de aire; **to hold one's breath** [stop breathing] aguantar la respiración; [wait anxiously] contener el aliento; **to say sthg under one's breath** decir algo en voz baja; **to take one's breath**

away dejar a uno sin habla OR respiración; **to waste/save one's breath** gastar/no gastar saliva **- 2.** [air from mouth] aliento m; **out of breath** sin aliento.

breathable ['briːðəbl] adj respirable.

breathalyse UK, **-yze** US ['breθəlaɪz] vt hacer la prueba del alcohol a.

Breathalyser® UK, **-yzer®** US ['breθəlaɪzər] n alcoholímetro m.

breathe [briːð] <> vi respirar; **to breathe more easily** fig respirar (más) tranquilo. <> vt **- 1.** [inhale] respirar, aspirar **- 2.** [exhale] despedir.

➡ **breathe in** vt sep & vi aspirar.

➡ **breathe out** vi espirar.

breather ['briːðər] n inf respiro m, descanso m.

breathing ['briːðɪŋ] n respiración f.

breathing space n (periodo m de) respiro m.

breathless ['breθlɪs] adj **- 1.** [out of breath] ahogado(da), jadeante **- 2.** [with excitement] sin aliento (por la emoción).

breathtaking ['breθ,teɪkɪŋ] adj sobrecogedor(ra), impresionante.

breath test n prueba f del alcohol.

breed [briːd] <> n **- 1.** [of animal] raza f **- 2.** fig [sort] especie f. <> vt (pt & pp bred [bred]) **- 1.** [animals] criar; [plants] cultivar **- 2.** fig [suspicion] alimentar; [contempt, hatred] concitar. <> vi (pt & pp bred [bred]) procrear, reproducirse.

breeder ['briːdər] n [of animals] criador m, -ra f.

breeder reactor n reactor m reproductor.

breeding ['briːdɪŋ] n **- 1.** [of animals] cría f; [of plants] cultivo m **- 2.** [manners] educación f.

breeding-ground n [of ideas, activity] campo m de cultivo.

breeze [briːz] <> n brisa f. <> vi: **to breeze in/out** entrar/salir como si tal cosa.

breezeblock ['briːzblɒk] n UK bloque de cemento y cenizas de coque.

breezy ['briːzɪ] (comp **-ier**, superl **-iest**) adj **- 1.** [windy]: **it's breezy** hace aire **- 2.** [cheerful] jovial, despreocupado(da).

brevity ['brevɪtɪ] n brevedad f.

brew [bruː] <> vt [beer] elaborar; [tea, coffee] preparar. <> vi **- 1.** [tea] reposar **- 2.** [trouble] fraguarse.

brewer ['bruːər] n cervecero m, -ra f.

brewery ['brʊərɪ] (pl **-ies**) n fábrica f de cerveza.

briar ['braɪər] n brezo m.

bribe [braɪb] <> n soborno m, coima f Andes & R Plata, mordida f Méx. <> vt: **to bribe (sb to do sthg)** sobornar (a alguien para que haga algo),

coimear (a alguien para que haga algo) Andes & R Dom, mordar (a alguien para que haga algo) Méx.

bribery ['braɪbərɪ] n soborno m.

brick [brɪk] n ladrillo m.

➡ **brick up** vt sep enladrillar, tapiar (con ladrillos).

bricklayer ['brɪk,leɪər] n albañil m.

brickwork ['brɪkwɜːk] n enladrillado m, ladrillos mpl.

bridal ['braɪdl] adj nupcial; **bridal dress** traje m de novia.

bride [braɪd] n novia f; **the bride and groom** los novios.

bridegroom ['braɪdɡrʊm] n novio m.

bridesmaid ['braɪdzmeɪd] n dama f de honor.

bridge [brɪdʒ] <> n **- 1.** [gen] puente m; **I'll cross that bridge when I come to it** ya me preocuparé de eso cuando llegue el momento **- 2.** [on ship] puente m de mando **- 3.** [of nose] caballete m **- 4.** [card game] bridge m. <> vt fig [gap] llenar.

bridging loan ['brɪdʒɪŋ-] n UK préstamo m puente.

bridle ['braɪdl] <> n brida f. <> vt embridar. <> vi: **to bridle (at)** indignarse (por OR ante).

bridle path n camino m de herradura.

brief [briːf] <> adj **- 1.** [short, to the point] breve; **in brief** en resumen **- 2.** [clothes] corto(ta). <> n **- 1.** LAW [statement] sumario m, resumen m **- 2.** UK [instructions] instrucciones fpl. <> vt: **to brief sb (on)** informar a alguien (acerca de).

➡ **briefs** npl [underpants] calzoncillos mpl; [knickers] bragas fpl.

briefcase ['briːfkeɪs] n maletín m, portafolios m inv.

briefing ['briːfɪŋ] n [meeting] reunión f informativa; [instructions] instrucciones fpl.

briefly ['briːflɪ] adv **- 1.** [for a short time] brevemente **- 2.** [concisely] en pocas palabras.

brigade [brɪ'ɡeɪd] n brigada f.

brigadier [,brɪɡə'dɪər] n brigadier m, general m de brigada.

bright [braɪt] adj **- 1.** [light] brillante; [day, room] luminoso(sa); [weather] despejado(da) **- 2.** [colour] vivo(va) **- 3.** [lively - eyes] brillante; [- smile] radiante **- 4.** [intelligent - person] listo(ta); [- idea] genial **- 5.** [hopeful] prometedor(ra).

➡ **brights** npl US inf faros mpl.

➡ **bright and early** adv muy temprano.

brighten ['braɪtn] vi **- 1.** [become lighter] clarear, despejarse **- 2.** [become more cheerful] alegrarse.

brighten up <> *vt sep* animar, alegrar. <> *vi* - **1.** [become more cheerful] animarse - **2.** [weather] clarear, despejarse.

brightly ['braɪtlɪ] *adv* - **1.** [shine] de forma resplandeciente - **2.** [coloured] vivamente - **3.** [cheerfully] alegremente.

brightness ['braɪtnɪs] *n* - **1.** [of light] luminosidad *f*, brillo *m* - **2.** [of colour] viveza *f*.

brilliance ['brɪljəns] *n* - **1.** [cleverness] brillantez *f* - **2.** [of colour, light] brillo *m*.

brilliant ['brɪljənt] *adj* - **1.** [clever] genial - **2.** [colour] vivo(va) - **3.** [light, career, future] brillante - **4.** *inf* [wonderful] fenomenal, genial.

brilliantly ['brɪljəntlɪ] *adv* - **1.** [cleverly] de manera genial - **2.** [coloured] vivamente - **3.** [shine] brillantemente.

Brillo pad® ['brɪləʊ-] *n* estropajo *m* (jabonoso) de aluminio.

brim [brɪm] <> *n* - **1.** [edge] borde *m* - **2.** [of hat] ala *f*. <> *vi* (*pt & pp* -**med**, *cont* -**ming**) *lit & fig*: **to brim with** rebosar de.

brim over *vi lit & fig*: **to brim over (with)** rebosar (de).

brine [braɪn] *n* - **1.** [for food] salmuera *f* - **2.** [sea water] agua *f* de mar.

bring [brɪŋ] (*pt & pp* **brought**) *vt* - **1.** [gen] traer; **to bring sthg to an end** poner fin a algo - **2.** LAW: **to bring charges against** presentar una denuncia contra; **to bring sb to trial** llevar a alguien a juicio ▸▸ **I/he** *etc* **couldn't bring myself/himself** *etc* **to do it** yo/él *etc* era incapaz de hacerlo.

bring about *vt sep* producir.

bring along *vt sep* traer.

bring around, bring round, bring to *vt sep* [make conscious] reanimar, hacer recuperar el conocimiento.

bring back *vt sep* - **1.** [books etc] devolver; [person] traer de vuelta - **2.** [shopping] traer - **3.** [memories] traer (a la memoria) - **4.** [practice, hanging] volver a introducir; [fashion] recuperar.

bring down *vt sep* - **1.** [from upstairs] bajar - **2.** [plane, bird] derribar; [government, tyrant] derrocar - **3.** [prices] reducir.

bring forward *vt sep* - **1.** [meeting, elections etc] adelantar - **2.** [in bookkeeping] sumar a la siguiente columna.

bring in *vt sep* - **1.** [introduce - law] implantar; [- bill] presentar - **2.** [earn] ganar, ingresar - **3.** LAW [verdict] pronunciar.

bring off *vt sep* [plan] sacar adelante; [deal] cerrar.

bring on *vt sep* producir, ocasionar; **you brought it on yourself** tú (solo) te lo buscaste.

bring out *vt sep* - **1.** [new product, book] sacar - **2.** [the worst *etc* in sb] revelar, despertar.

bring round, bring to *vt sep* = **bring around**.

bring up *vt sep* - **1.** [raise - children] criar - **2.** [mention] sacar a relucir - **3.** [vomit] devolver.

brink [brɪŋk] *n*: **on the brink of** al borde de.

brisk [brɪsk] *adj* - **1.** [quick] rápido(da) - **2.** [trade, business] boyante, activo(va) - **3.** [efficient, confident - manner] enérgico(ca); [- person] eficaz - **4.** [weather] fresco(ca).

brisket ['brɪskɪt] *n* carne *f* de pecho.

briskly ['brɪsklɪ] *adv* - **1.** [quickly] rápidamente - **2.** [efficiently, confidently] con soltura y eficacia.

bristle ['brɪsl] <> *n* [gen] cerda *f*; [of person] pelillo *m*. <> *vi* - **1.** [stand up] erizarse, ponerse de punta - **2.** [react angrily]: **to bristle (at)** enfadarse (por).

bristle with *vt insep* estar sembrado(da) de.

bristly ['brɪslɪ] (*comp* -**ier**, *superl* -**iest**) *adj* [chin, face] con barba áspera OR de tres días; [moustache] erizado(da), pinchudo(da).

Brit [brɪt] *n inf* británico *m*, -ca *f*.

Britain ['brɪtn] *n* Gran Bretaña.

British ['brɪtɪʃ] <> *adj* británico(ca). <> *npl*: **the British** los británicos.

British Columbia *n* (la) Columbia Británica.

British Isles *npl*: **the British Isles** las Islas Británicas.

British Summer Time *n hora oficial británica entre finales de marzo y de octubre.*

Briton ['brɪtn] *n* británico *m*, -ca *f*.

Britpop ['brɪtpɒp] *n* el Britpop.

brittle ['brɪtl] *adj* quebradizo(za), frágil.

Bro = **Br**.

broach [brəʊtʃ] *vt* abordar, sacar a colación.

B road *n UK* ≃ carretera *f* comarcal.

broad [brɔːd] <> *adj* - **1.** [shoulders, river, street] ancho(cha); [grin] amplio(plia) - **2.** [range, interests] amplio(plia) - **3.** [description, outline] general, a grandes rasgos - **4.** [hint] claro(ra) - **5.** [accent] cerrado(da), marcado(da) ▸▸ **in broad daylight** a plena luz del día. <> *n US inf* tía *f*, tipa *f*.

broadband ['brɔːdbænd] <> *adj* COMPUT de banda ancha. <> *n* COMPUT banda *f* ancha.

broad bean *n* haba *f*.

broadcast ['brɔːdkɑːst] <> *n* emisión *f*. <> *vt* (*pt & pp* **broadcast**) emitir.

broadcaster ['brɔːdkɑːstə'] *n* locutor *m*, -ra *f*.

broadcasting ['brɔːdkɑːstɪŋ] *n (U)* TV emisión *f* (televisiva); RADIO radiodifusión *f*.

broaden ['brɔːdn] <> *vt* - **1.** [road, pavement] ensanchar - **2.** [scope, appeal] ampliar. <> *vi* [river, road] ensancharse; [smile] hacerse más amplia.

broaden out ◇ *vt sep* ampliar. ◇ *vi* ampliarse.

broadly ['brɔːdlɪ] *adv* - **1.** [gen] en general; **broadly speaking** en líneas generales - **2.** [smile] abiertamente.

broadly-based [-'beɪst] *adj* [party] de amplia base; [course] muy completo(ta), que abarca muchos temas.

broadsheet ['brɔːdʃiːt] *n* periódico de calidad *(con hojas de gran tamaño)*.

brocade [brə'keɪd] *n* brocado *m*.

broccoli ['brɒkəlɪ] *n* brécol *m*.

brochure ['brəʊʃər] *n* folleto *m*.

brogues [brəʊgz] *npl* zapatos gruesos de cuero con dibujo calado y estilo clásico.

broil [brɔɪl] *vt US* asar a la parrilla.

broiler ['brɔɪlər] *n* - **1.** [young chicken] pollo *m* - **2.** *US* [grill] parrilla *f*.

broke [brəʊk] ◇ *pt* ⊳ **break**. ◇ *adj inf* sin blanca, sin un duro, bruja *Méx*; **to go broke** ir a la ruina; **to go for broke** jugárselo todo.

broken ['brəʊkn] ◇ *pp* ⊳ **break**. ◇ *adj* - **1.** [gen] roto(ta); **broken home** hogar *m* OR familia *f* de padres separados - **2.** [not working] estropeado(da) - **3.** [interrupted - sleep] entrecortado(da); [- journey] discontinuo(nua) - **4.** [hesitant, inaccurate]: **she speaks broken French** chapurrea el francés.

broken-down *adj* - **1.** [car, machine] averiado(da) - **2.** [building] destartalado(da).

broker ['brəʊkər] *n* [of stock] corredor *m*; [of insurance] agente *mf*.

brokerage ['brəʊkərɪdʒ] *n* corretaje *m*.

brolly ['brɒlɪ] *(pl* -**ies***) n UK inf* paraguas *m inv*.

bronchitis [brɒŋ'kaɪtɪs] *n* (U) bronquitis *f inv*.

bronze [brɒnz] ◇ *n* - **1.** [metal, sculpture] bronce *m* - **2.** = **bronze medal**. ◇ *comp* de bronce.

bronze medal, bronze *n* medalla *f* de bronce.

brooch [brəʊtʃ] *n* broche *m*, alfiler *m*.

brood [bruːd] ◇ *n* - **1.** [of birds] nidada *f* - **2.** *inf* [of children] prole *f*. ◇ *vi*: **to brood (over** OR **about)** dar vueltas (a).

broody ['bruːdɪ] *(comp* -**ier***, superl* -**iest***) adj* - **1.** [sad] apesadumbrado(da) - **2.** [bird] clueco(ca).

brook [brʊk] ◇ *n* arroyo *m*. ◇ *vt fml* tolerar.

broom [bruːm] *n* - **1.** [brush] escoba *f* - **2.** [plant] retama *f*.

broomstick ['bruːmstɪk] *n* palo *m* de escoba.

Bros., bros. *(abbr of* **brothers***)* Hnos.

broth [brɒθ] *n* caldo *m*.

brothel ['brɒθl] *n* burdel *m*.

brother ['brʌðər] ◇ *n* - **1.** [relative, monk] hermano *m* - **2.** *fig* [comrade] camarada *m*. ◇ *excl US inf* ¡dios mío!

brotherhood ['brʌðəhʊd] *n* - **1.** [companionship] fraternidad *f* - **2.** [religious organization] cofradía *f*, hermandad *f*; [professional association] gremio *m*, colegio *m*.

brother-in-law *(pl* **brothers-in-law***) n* cuñado *m*.

brotherly ['brʌðəlɪ] *adj* fraternal, fraterno(na).

brought [brɔːt] *pt* & *pp* ⊳ **bring**.

brow [braʊ] *n* - **1.** [forehead] frente *f* - **2.** [eyebrow] ceja *f*; **to knit one's brows** fruncir el ceño OR entrecejo - **3.** [of hill] cima *f*, cresta *f*.

browbeat ['braʊbiːt] *(pt* -**beat**, *pp* -**beaten***) vt* intimidar, amedrentar.

browbeaten ['braʊbiːtn] *adj* intimidado(da), amedrentado(da).

brown [braʊn] ◇ *adj* - **1.** [gen] marrón; [hair, eyes] castaño(ña) - **2.** [tanned] moreno(na). ◇ *n* marrón *m*; **in brown** de marrón. ◇ *vt* [food] dorar.

brown bread *n* pan *m* integral.

brownie ['braʊnɪ] *n US* bizcocho de chocolate y nueces.

Brownie point *n*: **to gain Brownie points** *fig* apuntarse tantos.

brown paper *n* (U) papel *m* de embalar.

brown rice *n* arroz *m* integral.

brown sugar *n* azúcar *m* moreno, azúcar *f* morena.

browse [braʊz] ◇ *vi* - **1.** [person] echar un ojo, mirar; **to browse through** hojear - **2.** [animal] pacer - **3.** COMPUT navegar. ◇ *vt* COMPUT navegar por.

browser ['braʊzər] *n* COMPUT navegador *m*.

bruise [bruːz] ◇ *n* magulladura *f*, cardenal *m*. ◇ *vt* - **1.** [person, arm] magullar, contusionar; [fruit] magullar - **2.** *fig* [feelings] herir. ◇ *vi* [person] magullarse, contusionarse; [fruit] magullarse.

bruised [bruːzd] *adj* - **1.** [arm, knee, fruit] magullado(da) - **2.** *fig* [person] dolido(da); [feelings] herido(da).

Brummie, Brummy ['brʌmɪ] *n UK inf* natural o habitante de Birmingham.

brunch [brʌntʃ] *n* brunch *m (combinación de desayuno y almuerzo que se toma tarde por la mañana).*

Brunei ['bruːnaɪ] *n* Brunei.

brunette [bruː'net] *n* morena *f*.

brunt [brʌnt] *n*: **to bear** OR **take the brunt of** aguantar lo peor de.

brush [brʌʃ] ◇ *n* - **1.** [for hair, teeth] cepillo *m*; [for shaving, decorating] brocha *f*; [of artist] pincel *m*; [broom] escoba *f* - **2.** [encounter] roce *m*.

◇ *vt* - **1.** [clean with brush] cepillar; **to brush one's hair** cepillarse el pelo - **2.** [move with hand] quitar, apartar - **3.** [touch lightly] rozar.

➤ **brush aside** *vt sep* [dismiss] hacer caso omiso de.

➤ **brush off** *vt sep* [dismiss] hacer caso omiso de.

➤ **brush up** ◇ *vt sep fig* [revise] repasar. ◇ *vi*: **to brush up on** repasar.

brushed [brʌʃt] *adj* [steel, chrome] cepillado(da); [cotton, nylon] afelpado(da).

brush-off *n inf*: **to give sb the brush-off** mandar a alguien a paseo.

brush-up *n inf*: **to have a wash and brush-up** lavarse y peinarse, arreglarse.

brushwood ['brʌʃwʊd] *n* leña *f*, ramojo *m*.

brushwork ['brʌʃwɜ:k] *n* (estilo *m* de) pincelada *f*.

brusque [bru:sk] *adj* brusco(ca).

Brussels ['brʌslz] *n* Bruselas.

brussels sprout *n* col *f* de Bruselas.

brutal ['bru:tl] *adj* brutal.

brutality [bru:'tælətɪ] (*pl* **-ies**) *n* brutalidad *f*.

brutalize, -ise ['bru:təlaɪz] *vt* - **1.** [make cruel] embrutecer - **2.** [treat brutally] tratar brutalmente.

brute [bru:t] ◇ *adj* bruto(ta). ◇ *n* - **1.** [large animal] bestia *f*, bruto *m* - **2.** [bully] bestia *mf*.

BS *US* (*abbr of* **Bachelor of Science**) *n* (*titular de una*) *licenciatura de ciencias*.

BSc (*abbr of* **Bachelor of Science**) *n* (*titular de una*) *licenciatura de ciencias*.

BSE (*abbr of* **bovine spongiform encephalopathy**) *n* EEB *f* (*encefalopatía espongiforme bovina*).

BSI (*abbr of* **British Standards Institution**) *n* *instituto británico de normalización*.

B-side *n* cara *f* dos *OR* B.

BST - **1.** *abbr of* **British Summer Time** - **2.** (*abbr of* **British Standard Time**), *hora oficial británica*.

BT *n* British Telecom, *compañía telefónica británica*.

BTW (*abbr of* **by the way**) *adv* por cierto.

bubble ['bʌbl] ◇ *n* [gen] burbuja *f*; [of soap] pompa *f*. ◇ *vi* - **1.** [produce bubbles] burbujear - **2.** [make a bubbling sound] borbotar - **3.** [be full]: **to bubble with** rebosar de.

bubble bath *n* espuma *f* de baño.

bubble gum *n* chicle *m* (de globo).

bubblejet printer ['bʌbldʒet-] *n* COMPUT impresora *f* de inyección.

bubbly ['bʌblɪ] ◇ *adj* (*comp* **-ier**, *superl* **-iest**) - **1.** [full of bubbles] con burbujas - **2.** [lively] alegre, vivo(va). ◇ *n inf* champán *m*.

buck [bʌk] ◇ *n* (*pl* **buck** *OR* **-s**) - **1.** [male animal] macho *m* - **2.** *esp US inf* [dollar] dólar *m*; **to make a fast buck** hacer pasta rápidamente - **3.** *inf* [responsibility]: **the buck stops with me** a mí me toca lidiar con eso; **to pass the buck to sb** echarle el muerto a alguien. ◇ *vt inf* [oppose] oponerse a, ir en contra de. ◇ *vi* corcovear, encabritarse.

➤ **buck up** *inf* ◇ *vt sep* - **1.** [improve] mejorar; **buck your ideas up** más vale que espabiles - **2.** [cheer up] animar. ◇ *vi* - **1.** [hurry up] darse prisa - **2.** [cheer up] animarse.

bucket ['bʌkɪt] *n* - **1.** [container, bucketful] cubo *m* - **2.** *inf* [large quantity]: **buckets of** un montón de.

buckle ['bʌkl] ◇ *n* hebilla *f*. ◇ *vt* - **1.** [fasten] abrochar con hebilla - **2.** [bend] combar. ◇ *vi* [wheel] combarse; [knees] doblarse.

➤ **buckle down** *vi*: **to buckle down (to)** dedicarse seriamente (a).

➤ **buckle up** *vi US* abrocharse el cinturón.

Bucks [bʌks] (*abbr of* **Buckinghamshire**), *condado inglés*.

buckshot ['bʌkʃɒt] *n* perdigones *mpl*.

buckskin ['bʌkskɪn] *n* ante *m*.

buckteeth [bʌk'ti:θ] *npl* dientes *mpl* salientes.

buckwheat ['bʌkwi:t] *n* alforfón *m*.

bud [bʌd] ◇ *n* [shoot] brote *m*; [flower] capullo *m*; **to nip sthg in the bud** *fig* cortar algo de raíz. ◇ *vi* (*pt & pp* **-ded**, *cont* **-ding**) brotar, echar brotes.

Buddha ['bʊdə] *n* Buda *m*.

Buddhism ['bʊdɪzm] *n* budismo *m*.

Buddhist ['bʊdɪst] ◇ *adj* budista. ◇ *n* budista *mf*.

budding ['bʌdɪŋ] *adj* en ciernes.

buddy ['bʌdɪ] (*pl* **-ies**) *n esp US inf* [friend] amiguete *m*, -ta *f*, colega *mf*, compa *m* Amér.

budge [bʌdʒ] ◇ *vt* mover. ◇ *vi* [move] moverse; [give in] ceder.

budgerigar ['bʌdʒərɪgɑ:ʳ] *n* periquito *m*.

budget ['bʌdʒɪt] ◇ *adj* económico(ca). ◇ *n* presupuesto *m*; **the Budget** *UK* el presupuesto nacional *OR* del estado. ◇ *vt* [money] presupuestar; [time] planificar. ◇ *vi* presupuestar.

➤ **budget for** *vt insep* contar con.

budget account *n UK* [with a shop] cuenta *f*; [with a bank] cuenta para domiciliaciones.

budgetary ['bʌdʒɪtrɪ] *adj* presupuestario(ria).

budgie ['bʌdʒɪ] *n inf* periquito *m*.

Buenos Aires [ˌbwenəs'aɪrɪz] *n* Buenos Aires.

buff [bʌf] ◇ *adj* color de ante. ◇ *n inf* [expert] aficionado *m*, -da *f*.

buffalo ['bʌfələʊ] (*pl* **buffalo, -s** *OR* **-es**) *n* búfalo *m*.

buffer ['bʌfəʳ] *n* - **1.** *UK* [for trains] tope *m* - **2.** *US* [of car] parachoques *m inv* - **3.** [protection] defensa *f*, salvaguarda *f* - **4.** COMPUT búfer *m*.

buffer state *n* estado *m* tapón.

buffet[1] [*UK* 'bʊfeɪ, *US* bə'feɪ] *n* - **1.** [meal] bufé *m* - **2.** [cafeteria] cafetería *f*.

buffet[2] ['bʌfɪt] *vt* [physically] golpear.

buffet car ['bʊfeɪ-] *n* coche *m* restaurante.

buffoon [bə'fuːn] *n* bufón *m*.

bug [bʌg] <> *n* - **1.** *esp US* [small insect] bicho *m* - **2.** *inf* [illness] virus *m*; **stomach bug** virus del estómago - **3.** *inf* [listening device] micrófono *m* oculto - **4.** COMPUT error *m* - **5.** [enthusiasm] manía *f*. <> *vt* (*pt & pp* **-ged**, *cont* **-ging**) - **1.** *inf* [spy on - room] poner un micrófono oculto en; [- phone] pinchar, intervenir - **2.** *esp US inf* [annoy] fastidiar, jorobar.

bugbear ['bʌgbeəʳ] *n* fastidio *m*, pesadilla *f*.

bugger ['bʌgəʳ] *UK v inf* <> *n* - **1.** [unpleasant person] cabrón *m*, -ona *f*; **the lucky bugger!** ¡qué suerte tiene el cabrón/la cabrona! - **2.** [difficult, annoying task] coñazo *m*. <> *excl* ¡mierda! <> *vt*: **bugger it!** ¡mierda!
➤ **bugger off** *vi v inf*: **bugger off!** ¡vete a tomar por culo!

buggy ['bʌgɪ] (*pl* **-ies**) *n* - **1.** [carriage] calesa *f* - **2.** [pushchair] sillita *f* de ruedas; *US* [pram] cochecito *m* de niño.

bugle ['bjuːgl] *n* corneta *f*, clarín *m*.

build [bɪld] <> *vt* (*pt & pp* **built**) - **1.** [construct] construir - **2.** *fig* [form, create] crear. <> *n* complexión *f*, constitución *f*.
➤ **build into** *vt sep* - **1.** [construct as part of] empotrar - **2.** [include in] incorporar.
➤ **build (up)on** <> *vt insep* [further] desarrollar. <> *vt sep* [base on] fundar en.
➤ **build up** <> *vt sep* - **1.** [business - establish] poner en pie; [- promote] fomentar - **2.** [person] fortalecer; **to build up one's reputation** labrarse una reputación. <> *vi* acumularse.

builder ['bɪldəʳ] *n* constructor *m*, -ra *f*.

building ['bɪldɪŋ] *n* - **1.** [structure] edificio *m* - **2.** [profession] construcción *f*.

building and loan association *n US* ≃ caja *f* de ahorros.

building block *n* [toy] bloque *m* de construcción; *fig* [element] componente *m* esencial.

building contractor *n* contratista *mf* de obras.

building site *n* obra *f*.

building society *n UK* ≃ caja *f* de ahorros.

buildup ['bɪldʌp] *n* [increase] acumulación *f*, incremento *m* gradual; [of troops] concentración *f*.

built [bɪlt] <> *pt & pp* ⊳ **build**. <> *adj*: heavily/slightly built de complexión fuerte/débil; **to be built for** dar el tipo para.

built-in *adj* - **1.** [physically integrated] empotrado(da) - **2.** [inherent] incorporado(da).

built-up *adj* urbanizado(da).

bulb [bʌlb] *n* - **1.** [for lamp] bombilla *f* - **2.** [of plant] bulbo *m* - **3.** [bulb-shaped part] parte *f* redondeada.

bulbous ['bʌlbəs] *adj* bulboso(sa).

Bulgaria [bʌl'geərɪə] *n* Bulgaria.

Bulgarian [bʌl'geərɪən] <> *adj* búlgaro(ra). <> *n* - **1.** [person] búlgaro *m*, -ra *f* - **2.** [language] búlgaro *m*.

bulge [bʌldʒ] <> *n* - **1.** [lump] protuberancia *f*, bulto *m* - **2.** [sudden increase] alza *f*. <> *vi*: **to bulge (with)** rebosar (de), estar atestado(da) (de).

bulging ['bʌldʒɪŋ] *adj* [muscles] fornido(da); [pocket] abultado(da).

bulimia (nervosa) [bjʊ'lɪmɪə-] *n* bulimia *f* (nerviosa).

bulk [bʌlk] <> *n* - **1.** [mass] bulto *m*, volumen *m* - **2.** [large body] mole *f* - **3.** [large quantity]: **in bulk** a granel - **4.** [majority, most of]: **the bulk of** la mayor parte de. <> *adj* a granel.

bulk buying [-'baɪɪŋ] *n* compra *f* al por mayor.

bulkhead ['bʌlkhed] *n* mamparo *m*.

bulky ['bʌlkɪ] (*comp* **-ier**, *superl* **-iest**) *adj* voluminoso(sa).

bull [bʊl] *n* - **1.** [male cow] toro *m* - **2.** [male animal] macho *m* - **3.** FIN alcista *mf* - **4.** (*U*) *esp US v inf* [nonsense] gilipolleces *fpl*.

bulldog ['bʊldɒg] *n* buldog *m*.

bulldog clip *n* pinza *f* sujetapapeles.

bulldoze ['bʊldəʊz] *vt* [ground] nivelar; [building] derribar; *fig* [force] forzar; **to bulldoze sb into doing sthg** *fig* forzar a alguien a hacer algo.

bulldozer ['bʊldəʊzəʳ] *n* bulldozer *m*.

bullet ['bʊlɪt] *n* - **1.** [of gun] bala *f* - **2.** [typo] topo *m*.

bulletin ['bʊlətɪn] *n* - **1.** [news] boletín *m*; [medical report] parte *m* - **2.** [regular publication] boletín *m*, gaceta *f*.

bulletin board *n esp US* tablón *m* de anuncios.

bullfight ['bʊlfaɪt] *n* corrida *f* (de toros).

bullfighter ['bʊl,faɪtəʳ] *n* torero *m*, -ra *f*.

bullfighting ['bʊl,faɪtɪŋ] *n* toreo *m*.

bullfinch ['bʊlfɪntʃ] *n* camachuelo *m*.

bullion ['bʊljən] *n* (*U*) lingotes *mpl*.

bullish ['bʊlɪʃ] *adj* FIN alcista.

bull market *n* mercado *m* en alza OR alcista.

bullock ['bʊlək] *n* buey *m*, toro *m* castrado.

bullring ['bʊlrɪŋ] *n* - **1.** [stadium] plaza *f* (de toros) - **2.** [arena] ruedo *m*.

bullrush [ˈbʊlrʌʃ] = bulrush.

bull's-eye n diana f.

bullshit [ˈbʊlʃɪt] vulg ⋄ n (U) gilipolleces fpl. ⋄ vi (pt & pp **-ted**, cont **-ting**) decir gilipolleces.

bull terrier n bulterrier m.

bully [ˈbʊlɪ] ⋄ n (pl **-ies**) abusón m, matón m. ⋄ vt (pt & pp **-ied**) intimidar; **to bully sb into doing sthg** obligar a alguien con amenazas a hacer algo.

bullying [ˈbʊlɪɪŋ] n intimidación f.

bulrush, bullrush [ˈbʊlrʌʃ] n anea f.

bum [bʌm] n - **1.** esp UK v inf [bottom] cola f Amér, poto m Chile & Perú, traste m - **2.** US inf pej [tramp] vagabundo m, -da f - **3.** US inf pej [idler] holgazán m, -ana f, vago m, -ga f, flojo m, -ja f Amér.
➤ **bum around** esp US vi (pt & pp **-med**, cont **-ming**) US inf - **1.** [waste time] haraganear, flojear Amér - **2.** [travel aimlessly] vagabundear.

bumblebee [ˈbʌmblbiː] n abejorro m.

bumbling [ˈbʌmblɪŋ] adj inútil.

bumf, bumph [bʌmf] n (U) UK inf papelotes mpl, papeleo m.

bump [bʌmp] ⋄ n - **1.** [lump - on head] chichón m; [- on road] bache m - **2.** [knock, blow, noise] golpe m. ⋄ vt [car] chocar con OR contra; [head, knee] golpearse en; **I bumped my head on the door** me di con la cabeza en la puerta.
➤ **bump into** vt insep [meet by chance] toparse con, encontrarse con.
➤ **bump off** vt sep inf cargarse a.
➤ **bump up** vt sep inf aumentar, subir.

bumper [ˈbʌmpər] ⋄ adj abundante; **bumper edition** edición especial. ⋄ n - **1.** AUT parachoques m inv - **2.** US RAIL tope m.

bumper-to-bumper adj: **the cars were bumper-to-bumper** había una caravana (de coches).

bumph [bʌmf] = bumf.

bumptious [ˈbʌmpʃəs] adj pej engreído(da).

bumpy [ˈbʌmpɪ] (comp **-ier**, superl **-iest**) adj - **1.** [road] lleno(na) de baches - **2.** [ride, journey] con muchas sacudidas.

bun [bʌn] n - **1.** [cake, bread roll] bollo m - **2.** [hairstyle] moño m, chongo m Amér.
➤ **buns** npl US inf trasero m, culo m.

bunch [bʌntʃ] ⋄ n [of people] grupo m; [of flowers] ramo m; [of fruit] racimo m; [of keys] manojo m. ⋄ vt agrupar. ⋄ vi agruparse.
➤ **bunches** npl [hairstyle] coletas fpl.

bundle [ˈbʌndl] ⋄ n - **1.** [of clothes] lío m, bulto m; [of notes, papers] fajo m; [of wood] haz m; **to be a bundle of nerves** fig ser un manojo de nervios - **2.** COMPUT paquete m. ⋄ vt [clothes] empaquetar de cualquier manera; [person] empujar.

➤ **bundle off** vt sep despachar.

➤ **bundle up** vt sep [put into bundles] liar.

bundled software [ˈbʌndld-] n COMPUT software m incluido.

bung [bʌŋ] ⋄ n tapón m. ⋄ vt UK inf - **1.** [throw] echar, tirar - **2.** [pass] pasar, alcanzar.

bungalow [ˈbʌŋgələʊ] n bungalow m.

bunged up [bʌŋd-] adj [drain] atascado(da), obstruido(da); [nose] taponado(da).

bungee-jumping [ˈbʌndʒɪ-] n puenting m.

bungle [ˈbʌŋgl] vt chapucear.

bunion [ˈbʌnjən] n juanete m.

bunk [bʌŋk] n - **1.** [bed] litera f - **2.** (U) inf [nonsense] tonterías fpl.
➤➤ **to do a bunk** inf poner pies en polvorosa.

bunk bed n litera f.

bunker [ˈbʌŋkər] n - **1.** [shelter, in golf] bunker m - **2.** [for coal] carbonera f.

bunny [ˈbʌnɪ] (pl **-ies**) n: **bunny (rabbit)** conejito m, -ta f.

Bunsen burner [ˈbʌnsn-] n mechero m Bunsen.

bunting [ˈbʌntɪŋ] n (U) [flags] banderitas fpl.

buoy [UK bɔɪ, US ˈbuːɪ] n boya f.
➤ **buoy up** vt sep [encourage] alentar, animar.

buoyancy [ˈbɔɪənsɪ] n - **1.** [ability to float] flotabilidad f - **2.** [optimism] optimismo m.

buoyant [ˈbɔɪənt] adj - **1.** [able to float] boyante, capaz de flotar - **2.** [optimistic - gen] optimista; [- market] con tendencia alcista.

burden [ˈbɜːdn] ⋄ n - **1.** [heavy load] carga f - **2.** fig [heavy responsibility]: **burden on** carga f para. ⋄ vt: **to burden sb with** cargar a alguien con.

bureau [ˈbjʊərəʊ] (pl **-x**) n - **1.** [government department] departamento m, oficina f - **2.** [office] oficina f - **3.** UK [desk] secreter m; US [chest of drawers] cómoda f.

bureaucracy [bjʊəˈrɒkrəsɪ] (pl **-ies**) n burocracia f.

bureaucrat [ˈbjʊərəkræt] n pej burócrata mf.

bureaucratic [ˌbjʊərəˈkrætɪk] adj pej burocrático(ca).

bureaux [ˈbjʊərəʊz] npl ⊳ bureau.

burger [ˈbɜːgər] n hamburguesa f.

burglar [ˈbɜːglər] n ladrón m, -ona f.

burglar alarm n alarma f antirrobo.

burglarize US = burgle.

burglary [ˈbɜːglərɪ] (pl **-ies**) n robo m (de una casa).

burgle [ˈbɜːgl], **burglarize** [ˈbɜːgləraɪz] US vt robar, desvalijar (una casa).

burial [ˈberɪəl] n entierro m.

burial ground n cementerio m.

burk [bɜːk] *n UK inf* tonto *m*, -ta *f*.

Burkina Faso [bɜːˌkiːnəˈfæsəʊ] *n* Burkina Faso.

burly [ˈbɜːlɪ] (*comp* **-ier**, *superl* **-iest**) *adj* fornido(da).

Burma [ˈbɜːmə] *n* Birmania.

Burmese [ˌbɜːˈmiːz] <> *adj* birmano(na). <> *n* - **1.** [person] birmano *m*, -na *f* - **2.** [language] birmano *m*.

burn [bɜːn] <> *vt* (*pt & pp* **burnt** OR **-ed**) - **1.** [gen] quemar - **2.** [injure - by heat, fire] quemarse - **3.** COMPUT tostar, grabar. <> *vi* (*pt & pp* **burnt** OR **-ed**) - **1.** [gen] arder; **to burn with passion/hatred** arder de pasión/odio - **2.** [be alight] estar encendido(da) - **3.** [food] quemarse - **4.** [cause burning sensation] escocer - **5.** [become sunburnt] quemarse. <> *n* quemadura *f*.

burn down <> *vt sep* incendiar. <> *vi* - **1.** [be destroyed by fire] incendiarse - **2.** [burn less brightly] apagarse.

burn out <> *vt sep* [exhaust]: **to burn o.s. out** quemarse. <> *vi* apagarse, consumirse.

burn up <> *vt sep* quemar. <> *vi* quemarse.

burner [ˈbɜːnər] *n* quemador *m*.

burning [ˈbɜːnɪŋ] *adj* - **1.** [on fire] en llamas - **2.** [heat, passion, interest] ardiente; **it was burning hot** hacía un calor abrasador - **3.** [cheeks, face] colorado(da) - **4.** [controversial]: **burning question** pregunta *f* candente.

burnish [ˈbɜːnɪʃ] *vt* bruñir.

Burns' Night *n fiesta celebrada en Escocia el 25 de enero en honor del poeta escocés Robert Burns.*

burnt [bɜːnt] *pt & pp* ⊳ **burn**.

burnt-out *adj lit & fig* quemado(da).

burp [bɜːp] *inf* <> *n* eructo *m*. <> *vi* eructar.

burqa [ˈbɜːkə] *n* burqa *m*.

burrow [ˈbʌrəʊ] <> *n* madriguera *f*. <> *vi* - **1.** [dig] escarbar (un agujero) - **2.** *fig* [in order to search] hurgar.

bursar [ˈbɜːsər] *n* tesorero *m*, -ra *f*, administrador *m*, -ra *f*.

bursary [ˈbɜːsərɪ] (*pl* **-ies**) *n UK* beca *f*.

burst [bɜːst] <> *vi* (*pt & pp* **burst**) - **1.** [gen] reventarse; [bag] romperse; [tyre] pincharse - **2.** [explode] estallar - **3.** [door, lid]: **to burst open** abrirse de golpe - **4.** [go suddenly]: **to burst into** irrumpir en; **to burst through** abrirse paso a través de. <> *vt* (*pt & pp* **burst**) [gen] reventar; [tyre] pinchar. <> *n* [of gunfire, enthusiasm] estallido *m*.

burst in on *vt insep* interrumpir.

burst into *vt insep* - **1.** [tears, song]: **to burst into tears/song** romper a llorar/cantar - **2.** [flames] estallar en - **3.** [subj: plants]: **to burst into flower** florecer.

burst out <> *vt insep* [say suddenly] exclamar. <> *vi* [begin suddenly]: **to burst out laughing/crying** echarse a reír/llorar.

bursting [ˈbɜːstɪŋ] *adj* - **1.** [full] lleno(na) a estallar - **2.** [with emotion]: **bursting with** rebosando de - **3.** [eager]: **to be bursting to do sthg** estar deseando hacer algo.

Burundi [bʊˈrʊndɪ] *n* Burundi.

bury [ˈberɪ] (*pt & pp* **-ied**) *vt* - **1.** [in ground] enterrar - **2.** [hide - face, memory] ocultar - **3.** *fig* [immerse]: **to bury o.s. in sthg** enfrascarse en algo.

bus [bʌs] <> *n* autobús *m*, micro *m Chile*, camión *m Amér C & Méx*, colectivo *m Arg & Bol*, carrito *m* por puesto *Ven*, omnibús *m Perú & Urug*, guagua *f Cuba*; **by bus** en autobús. <> *vt US*: **to bus tables** [in restaurant] recoger mesas.

bus conductor *n* cobrador *m*, -ra *f*.

bus driver *n* conductor *m*, -ra *f* de autobús, chofer *mf Amér*.

bush [bʊʃ] *n* - **1.** [plant] arbusto *m* - **2.** [open country]: **the bush** el campo abierto, el monte ▶▶ **to beat about the bush** andarse por las ramas.

bushel [ˈbʊʃl] *n UK = 36,37 litros; US = 35,24 litros*.

bushy [ˈbʊʃɪ] (*comp* **-ier**, *superl* **-iest**) *adj* poblado(da), espeso(sa).

business [ˈbɪznɪs] <> *n* - **1.** (*U*) [commerce, amount of trade] negocios *mpl*; **to be away on business** estar en viaje de negocios; **to mean business** *inf* ir en serio; **to go out of business** quebrar - **2.** [company] negocio *m*, empresa *f* - **3.** [concern, duty] oficio *m*, ocupación *f*; **to have no business doing** OR **to do sthg** no tener derecho a hacer algo; **mind your own business!** *inf* ¡no te metas donde no te llaman!; **that's none of your business** eso no es asunto tuyo - **4.** (*U*) [affair, matter] asunto *m*. <> *comp*: **business interests** intereses *mpl* comerciales; **business hours** horas *fpl* de oficina; **business English** inglés *m* comercial.

business address *n* dirección *f* comercial.

business card *n* tarjeta *f* de visita.

business class *n* clase *f* preferente.

businesslike [ˈbɪznɪslaɪk] *adj* formal y eficiente.

businessman [ˈbɪznɪsmæn] (*pl* **-men** [-men]) *n* empresario *m*, hombre *m* de negocios.

business school *n* escuela *f* OR academia *f* comercial.

business studies *npl* empresariales *mpl*.

business trip *n* viaje *m* de negocios.

businesswoman [ˈbɪznɪsˌwʊmən] (*pl* **-women** [-ˌwɪmɪn]) *n* empresaria *f*, mujer *f* de negocios.

busker ['bʌskər] n UK músico m ambulante OR callejero.

bus lane n carril m bus, pista f sólo bus Chile.

bus-shelter n marquesina f (de parada de autobús).

bus station n estación f OR terminal f de autobuses.

bus stop n parada f de autobús, paradero m Amér C, Andes & Méx.

bust [bʌst] (pt & pp **-ed** OR **bust**) <> adj inf - **1.** [broken] fastidiado(da), roto(ta) - **2.** [bankrupt]: **to go bust** quebrar. <> n - **1.** [bosom, statue] busto m - **2.** inf [raid] redada f. <> vt - **1.** inf [break] fastidiar, estropear - **2.** [arrest] pillar, empapelar; [raid] hacer una redada en.

bustle ['bʌsl] <> n bullicio m. <> vi apresurarse.

bustling ['bʌslɪŋ] adj bullicioso(sa).

bust-up n inf - **1.** [quarrel] trifulca f, camorra f - **2.** [breakup] ruptura f.

busy ['bɪzɪ] <> adj (comp **-ier**, superl **-iest**) - **1.** [occupied] ocupado(da); **to be busy doing sthg** estar ocupado haciendo algo - **2.** [hectic - life, week] ajetreado(da); [- town, office] concurrido(da), animado(da); [- road] con mucho tráfico - **3.** [active] activo(va) - **4.** esp US TELEC [engaged] comunicando. <> vt: **to busy o.s. (doing sthg)** ocuparse (haciendo algo).

busybody ['bɪzɪ,bɒdɪ] (pl **-ies**) n pej entrometido m, -da f.

busy signal n US TELEC señal f de comunicando.

but [bʌt] <> conj pero; **we were poor but happy** éramos pobres pero felices; **she owns not one but two houses** tiene no una sino dos casas; **but now let's talk about you** pero ahora hablemos de ti. <> prep menos, excepto; **everyone but Jane was there** todos estaban allí, menos Jane; **we've had nothing but bad weather** no hemos tenido más que mal tiempo; **he has no one but himself to blame** la culpa no es de otro más que él OR sino de él. <> adv fml: **had I but known** de haberlo sabido; **we can but try** por intentarlo que no quede; **she has but recently joined the firm** hace tan sólo un tiempo que entró en la empresa.

◆ **but for** conj de no ser por; **but for her I'd have died** de no ser por ella, hubiera muerto.

◆ **but then** adv: **I really liked the book, but then it is by my favourite author** me gustó mucho el libro, pero claro, es de mi escritor favorito.

butane ['bju:teɪn] n butano m.

butch [bʊtʃ] adj UK inf [woman] marimacho; [man] muy macho.

butcher ['bʊtʃər] <> n - **1.** [occupation] carnicero m, -ra f; **butcher's (shop)** carnicería f - **2.** [indiscriminate killer] carnicero m, -ra f, asesino m, -na f. <> vt [animal - for meat] matar; fig [kill indiscriminately] hacer una carnicería con.

butchery ['bʊtʃərɪ] n fig [indiscriminate killing] matanza f, carnicería f.

butler ['bʌtlər] n mayordomo m.

butt [bʌt] <> n - **1.** [of cigarette, cigar] colilla f - **2.** [of rifle] culata f - **3.** [for water] tina f - **4.** [of joke, remark] blanco m - **5.** US inf [bottom] trasero m, culo m. <> vt topetar.

◆ **butt in** vi [interrupt]: **to butt in on sb** cortar a alguien; **to butt in on sthg** entrometerse en algo.

◆ **butt out** vi US dejar de entrometerse.

butter ['bʌtər] <> n mantequilla f; **butter wouldn't melt in her mouth** inf parece una mosquita muerta. <> vt untar con mantequilla.

◆ **butter up** vt sep inf dar coba a.

butter bean n judía f blanca, frijol m blanco Amér, poroto m blanco, poroto m de manteca R Plata, caraota f Ven.

buttercup ['bʌtəkʌp] n ranúnculo m.

butter dish n mantequera f.

buttered ['bʌtəd] adj con mantequilla.

butterfingers ['bʌtə,fɪŋgəz] (pl **butterfingers**) n inf manazas mf inv.

butterfly ['bʌtəflaɪ] (pl **-ies**) n - **1.** [insect] mariposa f; **to have butterflies in one's stomach** inf estar hecho un manojo de nervios - **2.** [swimming style] (estilo m) mariposa f.

buttermilk ['bʌtəmɪlk] n suero m de leche.

butterscotch ['bʌtəskɒtʃ] n dulce hecho hirviendo azúcar y mantequilla.

buttocks ['bʌtəks] npl nalgas fpl.

button ['bʌtn] <> n - **1.** [gen & COMPUT] botón m - **2.** US [badge] chapa f. <> vt = **button up**.

◆ **button up** vt sep abotonar, abrochar.

buttonhole ['bʌtnhəʊl] <> n - **1.** [hole] ojal m - **2.** UK [flower] flor f para el ojal. <> vt inf enganchar, coger por banda.

button mushroom n champiñón m pequeño.

buttress ['bʌtrɪs] n contrafuerte m.

buxom ['bʌksəm] adj [woman] maciza, pechugona.

buy [baɪ] <> vt (pt & pp **bought**) lit & fig comprar; **to buy sthg from sb** comprar algo a alguien; **to buy sb sthg** comprar algo a alguien, comprar algo para alguien. <> n compra f.

◆ **buy in** vt sep UK aprovisionarse de.

◆ **buy into** vt insep [company] comprar acciones en.

◆ **buy off** vt sep sobornar, comprar.

➤ **buy out** *vt sep* - **1.** [in business] comprar la parte de - **2.** [from army]: **to buy o.s. out** *pagar dinero para salirse del ejército*.

➤ **buy up** *vt sep* acaparar.

buyer ['baɪə'] *n* - **1.** [purchaser] comprador *m*, -ra *f* - **2.** [profession] jefe *m*, -fa *f* de compras.

buyer's market *n* mercado *m* de compradores.

buyout ['baɪaʊt] *n adquisición de la mayoría de las acciones de una empresa*.

buzz [bʌz] ⟨⟩ *n* [of insect, machinery] zumbido *m*; [of conversation] rumor *m*; **to give sb a buzz** *inf* [on phone] dar un toque *OR* llamar a alguien. ⟨⟩ *vi* - **1.** [make noise] zumbar - **2.** *fig* [be active]: **to buzz (with)** bullir (de). ⟨⟩ *vt* [on intercom] llamar.

➤ **buzz off** *vi UK inf*: **buzz off!** ¡lárgate!

buzzard ['bʌzəd] *n* - **1.** *UK* [hawk] águila *f* ratonera - **2.** *US* [vulture] buitre *m*.

buzzer ['bʌzə'] *n* timbre *m*.

buzzing ['bʌzɪŋ] *n* zumbido *m*.

buzzword ['bʌzwɜːd] *n inf* palabra *f* de moda.

by [baɪ] *prep* - **1.** [indicating cause, agent] por; **caused/written by** causado/escrito por; **a book by Joyce** un libro de Joyce - **2.** [indicating means, method, manner]: **to travel by bus/train/plane/ship** viajar en autobús/tren/avión/barco; **to pay by cheque** pagar con cheque; **to take sb by the hand** coger a alguien de la mano; **by candlelight** a la luz de las velas; **he got rich by buying land** se hizo rico comprando terrenos; **by nature** por naturaleza; **by profession/trade** de profesión/oficio - **3.** [beside, close to] junto a; **by the sea** junto al mar - **4.** [past] por delante de; **to walk by sb/sthg** pasear por delante de alguien/algo; **we drove by the castle** pasamos por el castillo (conduciendo) - **5.** [via, through] por; **we entered by the back door** entramos por la puerta trasera - **6.** [with time - at or before, during] para; **I'll be there by eight** estaré allí para las ocho; **by 1916 it was all over** en 1916 ya todo estaba decidido; **by now** ya; **by day/night** por el día/la noche, de día/noche - **7.** [according to] según; **by law/my standards** según la ley/mis criterios - **8.** [in division] entre; [in multiplication, measurements] por; **to divide 20 by 2** dividir 20 entre 2; **to multiply 20 by 2** multiplicar 20 por 2; **twelve feet by ten** doce pies por diez - **9.** [in quantities, amounts] por; **by the thousand** *OR* **thousands** por miles; **by the metre** por metros; **by the day/hour** por día/horas; **prices were cut by 50%** los precios fueron rebajados (en) un 50% - **10.** [indicating gradual change]: **day by day** día a día; **one by one** uno a uno - **11.** [to explain a word or expression] con, por; **what do you mean by 'all**

right'? ¿qué quieres decir con 'bien'?; **what do you understand by the word 'subsidiarity'?** ¿qué entiendes por 'subsidiariedad'? ▶▶ **(all) by oneself** solo(la); **did you do it all by yourself?** ¿lo hiciste tú solo?

bye(-bye) [baɪ(baɪ)] *excl inf* ¡hasta luego!

bye-election = **by-election**.

byelaw ['baɪlɔː] = **bylaw**.

by-election, bye-election *n* elección *f* parcial.

Byelorussia [bɪ,eləʊ'rʌʃə] = **Belorussia**.

bygone ['baɪɡɒn] *adj* pasado(da).

➤ **bygones** *npl*: **let bygones be bygones** lo pasado, pasado está.

bylaw, byelaw ['baɪlɔː] *n* reglamento *m OR* estatuto *m* local.

by-line *n* [in article] pie *m* de autor.

bypass ['baɪpɑːs] ⟨⟩ *n* - **1.** [road] carretera *f* de circunvalación - **2.** *MED*: **bypass (operation)** (operación *f* de) by-pass *m*. ⟨⟩ *vt* evitar.

by-product *n* - **1.** [product] subproducto *m* - **2.** [consequence] consecuencia *f*.

bystander ['baɪ,stændə'] *n* espectador *m*, -ra *f*.

byte [baɪt] *n COMPUT* byte *m*.

byword ['baɪwɜːd] *n*: **to be a byword (for)** ser sinónimo de.

c[1] (*pl* **c's** *OR* **cs**), **C** (*pl* **C's** *OR* **Cs**) [siː] *n* [letter] c *f*, C *f*.

➤ **C** *n* - **1.** *MUS* do *m* - **2.** (*abbr of* **celsius, centigrade**) C.

c[2] - **1.** (*abbr of* **century**) s. - **2.** (*abbr of* **cent(s)**) cént.

c. (*abbr of* **circa**) h.

ca. (*abbr of* **circa**) h.

c/a - **1.** *abbr of* **credit account** - **2.** (*abbr of* **current account**) c/c.

CA *abbr of* **Central America**. *abbr of* **California**.

CAA *n* - **1.** (*abbr of* **Civil Aviation Authority**), *organismo independiente regulador de la* *aviación civil en Gran Bretaña* - **2.** (*abbr of* **Civil Aeronautics Authority**), *dirección estadounidense de aviación civil.*

cab [kæb] *n* - **1.** [taxi] taxi *m* - **2.** [of lorry] cabina *f.*

CAB (*abbr of* **Citizens' Advice Bureau**) *n* oficina británica de información y asistencia al ciudadano.

cabaret ['kæbəreɪ] *n* cabaret *m.*

cabbage ['kæbɪdʒ] *n* col *f*, repollo *m.*

cabbie, cabby ['kæbɪ] *n inf* taxista *mf.*

caber ['keɪbər] *n Scotland*: **tossing the caber** prueba de lanzamiento de una pesada pértiga en los 'Highland Games'.

cabin ['kæbɪn] *n* - **1.** [on ship] camarote *m* - **2.** [in aircraft] cabina *f* - **3.** [house] cabaña *f.*

cabin cruiser *n* yate *m* de motor.

cabinet ['kæbɪnɪt] *n* - **1.** [cupboard] armario *m*; [with glass pane] vitrina *f* - **2.** POL consejo *m* de ministros, gabinete *m.*

cabinet-maker *n* ebanista *mf.*

cabinet minister *n* ministro *m*, -tra *f* (*en el gabinete*).

cable ['keɪbl] ◇ *n* - **1.** [rope, wire] cable *m* - **2.** [telegram] cablegrama *m.* ◇ *vt* cablegrafiar.

cable car *n* teleférico *m.*

cable railway *n* funicular *m* aéreo.

cable television, cable TV *n* televisión *f* por cable.

caboodle [kə'bu:dl] *n inf*: **the whole caboodle** todo el rollo.

cache [kæʃ] ◇ *n* - **1.** [store] alijo *m* - **2.** COMPUT caché *f.* ◇ *vt* COMPUT poner en la memoria caché.

cache memory *n* COMPUT memoria *f* caché.

cachet ['kæʃeɪ] *n fml* caché *m.*

cackle ['kækl] ◇ *n* - **1.** [of hen] cacareo *m* - **2.** [of person] risotada *f.* ◇ *vi* - **1.** [hen] cacarear - **2.** [person] reírse.

cacophony [kæ'kɒfənɪ] *n* cacofonía *f.*

cactus ['kæktəs] (*pl* **-tuses** OR **-ti** [-taɪ]) *n* cactus *m inv.*

CAD (*abbr of* **computer-aided design**) *n* CAD *m.*

caddie ['kædɪ] ◇ *n* cadi *mf.* ◇ *vi*: **to caddie (for)** hacer de cadi (para).

caddy ['kædɪ] (*pl* **-ies**) *n* cajita *f* para el té.

cadence ['keɪdəns] *n* [of voice] cadencia *f*, ritmo *m.*

cadet [kə'det] *n* cadete *m.*

cadge [kædʒ] *UK inf* ◇ *vt*: **to cadge sthg (off** OR **from sb)** gorronear algo (a alguien). ◇ *vi*: **to cadge off** OR **from sb** gorronear a alguien.

Cadiz [kə'dɪz] *n* Cádiz.

caesarean (section) *UK*, **cesarean (section)** *US* [sɪ'zeərɪən-] *n* cesárea *f.*

CAF (*abbr of* **cost and freight**) C y F.

cafe, café ['kæfeɪ] *n* café *m*, cafetería *f.*

cafeteria [,kæfɪ'tɪərɪə] *n* (restaurante *m*) autoservicio *m*, cantina *f.*

caffeine ['kæfi:n] *n* cafeína *f.*

cage [keɪdʒ] *n* jaula *f.*

caged [keɪdʒd] *adj* enjaulado(da).

cagey ['keɪdʒɪ] (*comp* **-ier**, *superl* **-iest**) *adj inf* reservado(da).

cagoule [kə'gu:l] *n UK* chubasquero *m*, canguro *m.*

cahoots [kə'hu:ts] *n*: **in cahoots (with)** *inf* confabulado(da) (con).

CAI (*abbr of* **computer-aided instruction**) *n* EAO *f.*

Cairo ['kaɪərəʊ] *n* El Cairo.

cajole [kə'dʒəʊl] *vt*: **to cajole sb (into doing sthg)** engatusar a alguien (para que haga algo).

cake [keɪk] *n* - **1.** [sweet food] pastel *m*, tarta *f*, torta *f Amér*; **to be a piece of cake** *inf fig* ser pan comido; **to sell like hot cakes** *inf* venderse como rosquillas, venderse como pan caliente *Amér*; **you can't have your cake and eat it** *inf* no se puede estar en misa y repicando - **2.** [of fish, potato] medallón *m* empanado - **3.** [of soap] pastilla *f.*

caked [keɪkt] *adj*: **caked with mud** cubierto(ta) de barro seco.

cake tin *UK*, **cake pan** *US n* molde *m.*

cal. [kæl] (*abbr of* **calorie**) cal.

CAL (*abbr of* **computer assisted learning**) & (*abbr of* **computer aided learning**) *n* enseñanza *f* asistida por ordenador.

calamine lotion [kæləmaɪn-] *n* loción *f* de calamina.

calamitous [kə'læmɪtəs] *adj fml* calamitoso(sa).

calamity [kə'læmɪtɪ] (*pl* **-ies**) *n fml* calamidad *f.*

calcium ['kælsɪʊm] *n* calcio *m.*

calculate ['kælkjʊleɪt] *vt* - **1.** [work out] calcular - **2.** [plan]: **to be calculated to do sthg** estar pensado(da) para hacer algo.

➧ **calculate on** *vi*: **to calculate on sthg** contar con algo; **you can't calculate on them accepting** no puedes contar con que acepten.

calculated ['kælkjʊleɪtɪd] *adj* [murder, deception] premeditado(da); [risk] calculado(da), medido(da).

calculating ['kælkjʊleɪtɪŋ] *adj pej* calculador(ra).

calculation [,kælkjʊ'leɪʃn] *n* cálculo *m.*

calculator ['kælkjʊleɪtər] *n* calculadora *f.*

calculus [,kælkjʊləs] *n* cálculo *m.*

calendar [ˈkælɪndəʳ] n calendario m.

calendar month n mes m civil.

calendar year n año m civil.

calf [kɑːf] (pl **calves**) n - **1.** [young animal - of cow] ternero m, -ra f, becerro m, -rra f; [- of whale] ballenato m; [- of other animals] cría f - **2.** [leather] piel f de becerro - **3.** [of leg] pantorrilla f.

caliber US = **calibre**.

calibrate [ˈkælɪbreɪt] vt calibrar.

calibre, caliber US [ˈkælɪbəʳ] n - **1.** [quality] nivel m - **2.** [size] calibre m.

calico [ˈkælɪkəʊ] n percal m, calicó m.

California [ˌkælɪˈfɔːnjə] n California.

Californian [ˌkælɪˈfɔːnjən] <> adj californiano(na). <> n californiano m, -na f.

calipers US = **callipers**.

call [kɔːl] <> n - **1.** [cry, attraction, vocation] llamada f, llamado m Amér; [cry of bird] reclamo m - **2.** TELEC llamada f, llamado m Amér; **to give sb a call** llamar a alguien - **3.** [visit] visita f; **to pay a call on sb** hacerle una visita a alguien - **4.** [demand]: **call for** llamamiento m - **5.** [summons]: **on call** de guardia. <> vt - **1.** [gen & TELEC] llamar; **I'm called Joan** me llamo Joan; **what is it called?** ¿cómo se llama?; **he called my name** me llamó por el nombre; **we'll call it £10** dejémoslo en 10 libras - **2.** [announce - flight] anunciar; [- strike, meeting, election] convocar. <> vi - **1.** [gen & TELEC] llamar; **who's calling?** ¿quién es? - **2.** [visit] pasar.

◆ **call at** vt insep [subj: train] efectuar parada en.

◆ **call back** <> vt sep - **1.** [on phone] volver a llamar - **2.** [ask to return] hacer volver. <> vi - **1.** [on phone] volver a llamar - **2.** [visit again] volver a pasarse.

◆ **call by** vi inf pasarse.

◆ **call for** vt insep - **1.** [collect] ir a buscar - **2.** [demand] pedir; **this calls for a drink** esto merece un trago.

◆ **call in** <> vt sep - **1.** [send for] llamar - **2.** [recall - product, banknotes] retirar; [- loan] exigir pago de. <> vi: **to call in (at)** pasarse (por).

◆ **call off** vt sep - **1.** [meeting, party] suspender; [strike] desconvocar - **2.** [dog etc] llamar (para deje de atacar).

◆ **call on** vt insep - **1.** [visit] visitar - **2.** [ask]: **to call on sb to do sthg** pedir a alguien que haga algo.

◆ **call out** <> vt sep - **1.** [order to help - troops] movilizar; [- police, firemen] hacer intervenir - **2.** [order to strike] llamar a la huelga a, llamar al paro a Amér - **3.** [cry out] gritar. <> vi gritar.

◆ **call round** vi pasarse.

◆ **call up** vt sep - **1.** MIL llamar a filas - **2.** esp US [on telephone] llamar (por teléfono) - **3.** COMPUT visualizar.

CALL (abbr of **computer assisted (or aided) language learning**) n enseñanza f de idiomas asistida por ordenador.

call box n UK cabina f telefónica.

call centre n centro m de atención telefónica.

caller [ˈkɔːləʳ] n - **1.** [visitor] visita f - **2.** [on telephone] persona f que llama.

caller (ID) display n [on telephone] identificador m de llamada.

call girl n prostituta f (que concierta sus citas por teléfono).

calligraphy [kəˈlɪgrəfɪ] n caligrafía f.

call-in n US RADIO & TV programa m a micrófono abierto.

calling [ˈkɔːlɪŋ] n - **1.** [profession] profesión f - **2.** [vocation] vocación f.

calling card n US tarjeta f de visita.

callipers UK, **calipers** US [ˈkælɪpəz] npl - **1.** MED aparato m ortopédico - **2.** [for measuring] calibrador m.

callous [ˈkæləs] adj despiadado(da), cruel.

callously [ˈkæləslɪ] adv despiadadamente, cruelmente.

callousness [ˈkæləsnɪs] n crueldad f.

call-up n UK llamamiento m a filas, reclutamiento m.

callus [ˈkæləs] (pl **-es**) n callo m.

calm [kɑːm] <> adj - **1.** [not worried or excited] tranquilo(la) - **2.** [evening, weather] apacible - **3.** [sea] en calma. <> n calma f. <> vt calmar.

◆ **calm down** <> vt sep calmar. <> vi calmarse.

calmly [ˈkɑːmlɪ] adv tranquilamente, con calma.

calmness [ˈkɑːmnɪs] n calma f.

Calor gas® [ˈkæləʳ-] n UK (gas m) butano m.

calorie [ˈkælərɪ] n caloría f.

calorific [ˌkæləˈrɪfɪk] adj [fattening] que engorda.

calve [kɑːv] vi parir (un becerro).

calves [kɑːvz] npl ⊏> **calf**.

cam [kæm] n leva f.

CAM (abbr of **computer aided manufacture**) n FAO f.

camaraderie [ˌkæməˈrɑːdərɪ] n camaradería f.

camber [ˈkæmbəʳ] n [of road] peralte m.

Cambodia [kæmˈbəʊdjə] n Camboya.

Cambodian [kæmˈbəʊdjən] <> adj camboyano(na). <> n camboyano m, -na f.

Cambs (abbr of **Cambridgeshire**), condado inglés.

camcorder ['kæm,kɔːdəʳ] n camcorder m, videocámara f.

came [keɪm] pt ▷ **come**.

camel ['kæml] n camello m.

camellia [kəˈmiːljə] n camelia f.

cameo ['kæmɪəʊ] (pl -s) n - **1.** [jewellery] camafeo m - **2.** [in acting] actuación f breve y memorable; [in writing] excelente descripción f.

camera ['kæmərə] n cámara f.

◆ **in camera** adv fml a puerta cerrada.

cameraman ['kæmərəmæn] (pl -men [-men]) n cámara m.

Cameroon [,kæməˈruːn] n (el) Camerún.

Cameroonian [,kæməˈruːnɪən] <> adj camerunés(esa). <> n camerunés m, -esa f.

camisole ['kæmɪsəʊl] n combinación f, picardías m inv.

camomile ['kæməmaɪl] <> n manzanilla f. <> comp: camomile tea manzanilla f.

camouflage ['kæməflɑːʒ] <> n camuflaje m. <> vt camuflar.

camp [kæmp] <> n - **1.** [gen & MIL] campamento m - **2.** [temporary mass accommodation] campo m; **prison camp** campo de prisioneros; **(summer) camp** US colonia f, campamento m de verano - **3.** [faction] bando m. <> vi acampar. <> adj inf amanerado(da).

◆ **camp out** vi acampar (al aire libre).

campaign [kæmˈpeɪn] <> n campaña f. <> vi: **to campaign (for/against)** hacer campaña (a favor de/en contra de).

campaigner [kæmˈpeɪnəʳ] n - **1.** [supporter of cause] defensor m, -ra f - **2.** [experienced person]: **an experienced campaigner** un veterano.

camp bed n cama f plegable.

camper ['kæmpəʳ] n - **1.** [person] campista mf - **2.**: **camper (van)** autocaravana f.

campground ['kæmpgraʊnd] n US camping m.

camphor ['kæmfəʳ] n alcanfor m.

camping ['kæmpɪŋ] n camping m, acampada f; **to go camping** ir de acampada.

camping site, campsite ['kæmpsaɪt] n camping m.

campus ['kæmpəs] (pl -es) n campus m inv, ciudad f universitaria.

camshaft ['kæmʃɑːft] n árbol m de levas.

can¹ [kæn] <> n [for drink, food] lata f, bote m; [for oil, paint] lata f; US [for garbage] cubo m. <> vt (pt & pp -ned, cont -ning) enlatar.

can² (weak form [kən], strong form [kæn], conditional and preterite form **could**; negative form **cannot** and **can't**) modal vb - **1.** [be able to] poder; **can you come to lunch?** ¿puedes venir a comer?; **she couldn't come** no pudo venir; **I can't** OR **cannot afford it** no me lo puedo permitir; **can**

you see/hear something? ¿ves/oyes algo? - **2.** [know how to] saber; **I can speak French** hablo francés, sé hablar francés; **I can play the piano** sé tocar el piano; **can you drive/cook?** ¿sabes conducir/cocinar? - **3.** [indicating permission, in polite requests] poder; **you can use my car if you like** puedes utilizar mi coche si quieres; **we can't wear jeans to work** no nos dejan llevar vaqueros en el trabajo; **can I speak to John, please?** ¿puedo hablar con John, por favor? - **4.** [indicating disbelief, puzzlement]: **you can't be serious** estás de broma ¿no?; **what can she have done with it?** ¿qué puede haber hecho con ello?; **we can't just leave him here** no podemos dejarlo aquí de esta forma - **5.** [indicating possibility] poder; **you could have done it** podrías haberlo hecho; **I could see you tomorrow** podríamos vernos mañana - **6.** [indicating usual state or behaviour] poder; **she can be a bit stubborn sometimes** a veces puede ser un poco terca; **this city can be very chilly** esta ciudad puede llegar a ser muy fría.

Canada ['kænədə] n (el) Canadá.

Canadian [kəˈneɪdjən] <> adj canadiense. <> n [person] canadiense mf.

canal [kəˈnæl] n canal m.

canary [kəˈneərɪ] (pl -ies) n canario m.

Canary Islands, Canaries [kəˈneərɪz] npl: **the Canary Islands** las (islas) Canarias.

cancan ['kænkæn] n cancán m.

cancel ['kænsl] (UK -led, cont -ling) (US -ed, cont -ing) vt - **1.** [call off] cancelar, suspender - **2.** [invalidate - cheque, debt] cancelar; [- order] anular; [- stamp] matar.

◆ **cancel out** vt sep anular.

cancellation [,kænsəˈleɪʃn] n suspensión f.

cancer ['kænsəʳ] <> n [disease] cáncer m. <> comp de cáncer; **cancer patient** enfermo m, -ma f de cáncer; **cancer research** investigación f sobre el cáncer.

◆ **Cancer** n Cáncer m; **to be (a) cancer** ser Cáncer.

cancerous ['kænsərəs] adj canceroso(sa).

candelabra [,kændɪˈlɑːbrə] n candelabro m.

C and F (abbr of cost and freight) C y F.

candid ['kændɪd] adj franco(ca), sincero(ra).

candidacy ['kændɪdəsɪ] n candidatura f.

candidate ['kændɪdət] n: **candidate (for)** candidato m, -ta f (a).

candidature ['kændɪdətʃəʳ] n candidatura f.

candidly ['kændɪdlɪ] adv con franqueza OR sinceridad.

candidness ['kændɪdnɪs] n franqueza f, sinceridad f.

candied ['kændɪd] adj confitado(da).

candle ['kændl] *n* vela *f*, esperma *f* *Amér*; **to burn the candle at both ends** *inf* no descansar en todo el día.

candlelight ['kændllaɪt] *n*: **by candlelight** a la luz de una vela.

candlelit ['kændllɪt] *adj* [dinner] a la luz de las velas.

candlestick ['kændlstɪk] *n* candelero *m*.

candour *UK*, **candor** ['kændər] *US n* franqueza *f*, sinceridad *f*.

candy ['kændɪ] (*pl* -ies) *n esp US* - **1.** *(U)* [confectionery] golosinas *fpl*; **candy bar** chocolatina *f* - **2.** [sweet] caramelo *m*.

candyfloss *UK* ['kændɪflɒs], **cotton candy** *US n* azúcar *m* hilado, algodón *m*.

cane [keɪn] ◇ *n* - **1.** *(U)* [for making furniture, supporting plant] caña *f*, mimbre *m* - **2.** [walking stick] bastón *m* - **3.** [for punishment]: **the cane** la vara. ◇ *comp* de caña OR mimbre. ◇ *vt* azotar *(con la vara)*.

cane sugar *n* azúcar *m* o *f* de caña.

canine ['keɪnaɪn] ◇ *adj* canino(na). ◇ *n*: **canine (tooth)** [diente *m*] canino *m*, colmillo *m*.

canister ['kænɪstər] *n* [for tea] bote *m*; [for film] lata *f*; [for gas] bombona *f*; **smoke canister** bote de humo.

cannabis ['kænəbɪs] *n* cannabis *m*.

canned [kænd] *adj* - **1.** [food, drink] enlatado(da), en lata - **2.** *inf fig* [applause, music, laughter] grabado(da).

cannelloni [,kænɪ'ləʊnɪ] *n (U)* canelones *mpl*.

cannibal ['kænɪbl] *n* caníbal *mf*.

cannibalize, -ise ['kænɪbəlaɪz] *vt* desmontar para aprovechar algunas piezas.

cannon ['kænən] *n* (*pl* **cannon** OR -s) cañón *m*.
◆ **cannon into** *vt insep UK* chocar de lleno con.

cannonball ['kænənbɔːl] *n* bala *f* de cañón.

cannot ['kænɒt] *fml* (*abbr of* **can not**), ⊳ **can**.

canny ['kænɪ] (*comp* -ier, *superl* -iest) *adj* [shrewd] astuto(ta).

canoe [kə'nuː] ◇ *n* [gen] canoa *f*; SPORT piragua *f*. ◇ *vi* (*cont* **canoeing**) ir en canoa.

canoeing [kə'nuːɪŋ] *n* piragüismo *m*.

canon ['kænən] *n* - **1.** [clergyman] canónigo *m* - **2.** [general principle] canon *m* - **3.** [of mass]: **the Canon** el canon.

canonize, -ise ['kænənaɪz] *vt* canonizar.

canoodle [kə'nuːdl] *vi UK inf* hacerse arrumacos.

can opener *n esp US* abrelatas *m inv*.

canopy ['kænəpɪ] (*pl* -ies) *n* - **1.** [over bed, seat] dosel *m* - **2.** [of trees] copas *fpl*.

cant [kænt] *n (U) pej* [insincere talk] hipocresías *fpl*.

can't [kɑːnt] (*abbr of* **can not**), ⊳ **can**.

Cantabrian Mountains [kæn'teɪbrɪən-] *npl*: **the Cantabrian Mountains** la cordillera Cantábrica.

cantaloup *UK*, **cantaloupe** ['kæntəluːp] *US n* melón *m* cantalupo.

cantankerous [kæn'tæŋkərəs] *adj* [person] refunfuñón(ona), cascarrabias *(inv)*.

canteen [kæn'tiːn] *n* - **1.** [restaurant] cantina *f* - **2.** [set of cutlery] (juego *m* de) cubertería *f*.

canter ['kæntər] ◇ *n* medio galope *m*. ◇ *vi* ir a medio galope.

cantilever ['kæntɪliːvər] *n* voladizo *m*.

Canton [kæn'tɒn] *n* Cantón.

Cantonese [,kæntə'niːz] ◇ *adj* cantonés(esa). ◇ *n* - **1.** [person] cantonés *m*, -esa *f* - **2.** [language] cantonés *m*.

canvas ['kænvəs] *n* - **1.** [cloth] lona *f*; **under canvas** [in a tent] en una tienda (de campaña) - **2.** [for painting on, finished painting] lienzo *m*.

canvass ['kænvəs] ◇ *vt* - **1.** POL [person] solicitar el voto a - **2.** [opinion] pulsar. ◇ *vi* solicitar votos yendo de puerta en puerta.

canvasser ['kænvəsər] *n* - **1.** [for political support] persona que solicita votos yendo de puerta en puerta - **2.** [for poll] encuestador *m*, -ra *f*.

canvassing ['kænvəsɪŋ] *n* - **1.** *(U)* [for political support]: **to go canvassing** ir a solicitar votos - **2.** [for poll] sondeos *mpl*.

canyon ['kænjən] *n* cañón *m*.

cap [kæp] ◇ *n* - **1.** [hat - peaked] gorra *f*; [- with no peak] gorro *m*; **to go cap in hand to sb** acudir a alguien en actitud humilde - **2.** [on bottle] tapón *m*; [on jar] tapa *f*; [on pen] capuchón *m* - **3.** [limit] tope *m* - **4.** *UK* [contraceptive device] diafragma *m*. ◇ *vt* (*pt* & *pp* **-ped**, *cont* **-ping**) - **1.** [top]: **to be capped with** estar coronado(da) de - **2.** [outdo]: **to cap it all** para colmo.

CAP [kæp, ,si:eɪ'pi:] (*abbr of* **Common Agricultural Policy**) *n* PAC *f*.

capability [,keɪpə'bɪlətɪ] (*pl* -ies) *n* capacidad *f*.

capable ['keɪpəbl] *adj* - **1.** [able]: **to be capable of sthg/of doing sthg** ser capaz de algo/de hacer algo - **2.** [competent] competente.

capably ['keɪpəblɪ] *adv* competentemente.

capacious [kə'peɪʃəs] *adj fml* espacioso(sa).

capacitor [kə'pæsɪtər] *n* condensador *m* eléctrico.

capacity [kə'pæsɪtɪ] (*pl* -ies) ◇ *n* - **1.** [gen]: **capacity (for)** capacidad *f* (de); **seating capacity** aforo *m*; **to capacity** al completo; **capacity for doing** OR **to do sthg** capacidad de hacer algo; **within one's capacity** dentro de las posibilidades de uno **- 2.** [position] calidad *f*; **in my capacity as...** en calidad de... <> *comp*: **capacity audience** lleno *m* absoluto OR total.

cape [keɪp] *n* **- 1.** GEOG cabo *m* **- 2.** [cloak] capa *f*.

Cape of Good Hope *n*: **the Cape of Good Hope** el Cabo de Buena Esperanza.

caper ['keɪpə'] <> *n* **- 1.** [food] alcaparra *f* **- 2.** *inf* [escapade] treta *f*. <> *vi* retozar.

Cape Town *n* Ciudad del Cabo.

Cape Verde [-vɜ:d] *n*: **the Cape Verde Islands** las islas de Cabo Verde.

capillary [kə'pɪlərɪ] *(pl* **-ies)** *n* capilar *m*.

capita ⊳ **per capita.**

capital ['kæpɪtl] <> *adj* **- 1.** [letter] mayúscula **- 2.** [punishable by death] capital. <> *n* **- 1.** [of country, main centre] capital *f* **- 2.**: **capital (letter)** mayúscula *f*; **in capitals** en mayúsculas **- 3.** [money] capital *m*; **to make capital (out) of** *fig* sacar partido de.

capital allowance *n* desgravación *f* por inversiones.

capital assets *npl* bienes *mpl* de capital, activo *m* fijo.

capital expenditure *n (U)* inversión *f* de capital.

capital gains tax *n* impuesto *m* sobre plusvalías.

capital goods *npl* bienes *mpl* de capital.

capital-intensive *adj* que utiliza gran volumen de capital.

capitalism ['kæpɪtəlɪzm] *n* capitalismo *m*.

capitalist ['kæpɪtəlɪst] <> *adj* capitalista. <> *n* capitalista *mf*.

capitalize, -ise ['kæpɪtəlaɪz] *vi*: **to capitalize on sthg** aprovechar algo, capitalizar algo.

capital punishment *n (U)* pena *f* capital.

capital stock *n* capital *m* social.

Capitol ['kæpɪtl] *n*: **the Capitol** el Capitolio.

Capitol Hill ['kæpɪtl-] *n* el Capitolio.

capitulate [kə'pɪtjuleɪt] *vi*: **to capitulate (to)** capitular (ante).

capitulation [kə,pɪtju'leɪʃn] *n* capitulación *f*.

cappuccino [,kæpu'tʃi:nəu] *(pl* **-s)** *n* capuchino *m*.

capricious [kə'prɪʃəs] *adj* [person] caprichoso(sa); [behaviour] inconstante; [weather] variable.

Capricorn ['kæprɪkɔ:n] *n* Capricornio *m*; **to be (a) Capricorn** ser Capricornio.

caps [kæps] *(abbr of* **capital letters)** mayúsc.

capsicum ['kæpsɪkəm] *n* pimiento *m*.

capsize [kæp'saɪz] <> *vt* hacer volcar OR zozobrar. <> *vi* volcar, zozobrar.

capsule ['kæpsju:l] *n* cápsula *f*.

Capt. *(abbr of* **captain)** Capt.

captain ['kæptɪn] <> *n* [gen] capitán *m*, -ana *f*; [of aircraft] comandante *mf*. <> *vt* capitanear.

caption ['kæpʃn] *n* [under picture etc] pie *m*, leyenda *f*; [heading] encabezamiento *m*.

captivate ['kæptɪveɪt] *vt* cautivar.

captivating ['kæptɪveɪtɪŋ] *adj* cautivador(ra).

captive ['kæptɪv] <> *adj* **- 1.** [imprisoned] en cautividad, en cautiverio **- 2.** *fig* [market] asegurado(da); **captive audience** *público forzado a ver o escuchar algo.* <> *n* cautivo *m*, -va *f*.

captivity [kæp'tɪvətɪ] *n*: **in captivity** en cautividad, en cautiverio.

captor ['kæptə'] *n* apresador *m*, -ra *f*.

capture ['kæptʃə'] <> *vt* **- 1.** [gen] capturar **- 2.** [audience, share of market] hacerse con; [city] tomar **- 3.** [scene, mood, attention] captar **- 4.** [comput] introducir. <> *n* [of person] captura *f*; [of city] toma *f*.

car [kɑ:'] <> *n* **- 1.** [motorcar] coche *m*, automóvil *m*, carro *m* *Amér*, auto *m*; **by car** en coche **- 2.** [on train] vagón *m*, coche *m*. <> *comp* [door, tyre etc] del coche, INDUST del automóvil; [accident] de automóvil.

Caracas [kə'rækəs] *n* Caracas.

carafe [kə'ræf] *n* garrafa *f*.

car alarm *n* alarma *f* de coche.

caramel ['kærəmel] *n* **- 1.** [burnt sugar] caramelo *m* (líquido), azúcar *m* quemado **- 2.** [sweet] tofe *m*.

caramelize, -ise ['kærəməlaɪz] *vt* poner a punto de caramelo, caramelizar.

carat ['kærət] *n UK* quilate *m*; **24-carat gold** oro de 24 quilates.

caravan ['kærəvæn] <> *n* caravana *f*, roulotte *f*. <> *comp* [holiday] en caravana OR roulotte; [park] para caravanas OR roulottes.

caravanning ['kærəvænɪŋ] *n UK*: **to go caravanning** ir de caravaning.

caravan site *n UK* camping *m* para caravanas OR roulottes.

caraway seed ['kærəweɪ-] *n* carvi *m*.

carbohydrate [,kɑ:bəʊ'haɪdreɪt] *n* CHEM hidrato *m* de carbono.

➡ **carbohydrates** *npl* [in food] féculas *fpl*.

carbon ['kɑ:bən] *n* **- 1.** [element] carbono *m* **- 2.** copia en papel carbón **- 3.** = **carbon paper.**

carbonated ['kɑ:bəneɪtɪd] *adj* con gas, carbónico(ca).

carbon copy *n* [document] copia *f* en papel carbón; *fig* [exact copy] calco *m*.

carbon dating [-'deɪtɪŋ] *n* datación *f* por carbono 14.

carbon dioxide [-daɪ'ɒksaɪd] *n* bióxido *m* OR dióxido *m* de carbono.

carbon fibre n UK fibra f de carbono.

carbon monoxide [-mɒ'nɒksaɪd] n monóxido m de carbono.

carbon paper, carbon n (U) papel m carbón.

car-boot sale n venta de objetos usados colocados en el portaequipajes del coche.

carburettor UK, **carburetor** US [ˌkɑːbə'retər] n carburador m.

carcass ['kɑːkəs] n [gen] cadáver m (de animal); [of bird] carcasa f; [at butcher's] canal m.

carcinogenic [ˌkɑː'sɪnə'dʒenɪk] adj cancerígeno(na).

card [kɑːd] ⇔ n - 1. [playing card] carta f, naipe m; **to play one's cards right** hacer las cosas bien; **to put** OR **lay one's cards on the table** poner las cartas boca arriba OR sobre la mesa - 2. [for information, greetings, computers] tarjeta f; [for identification] carné m - 3. [postcard] postal f - 4. [cardboard] cartulina f. ⇔ vt US [ask for ID] pedir el carné a.

➡ **cards** npl las cartas, los naipes; **to play cards** jugar a las cartas.

➡ **on the cards** UK, **in the cards** US adv inf más que probable.

cardamom ['kɑːdəməm] n cardamomo m.

cardboard ['kɑːdbɔːd] ⇔ n (U) cartón m. ⇔ comp de cartón.

cardboard box n caja f de cartón.

card-carrying [-'kærɪŋ] adj: **to be a card-carrying member of the party** ser miembro del partido.

cardiac ['kɑːdɪæk] adj cardíaco(ca).

cardiac arrest n paro m cardíaco.

cardigan ['kɑːdɪgən] n rebeca f, cárdigan m.

cardinal ['kɑːdɪnl] ⇔ adj capital. ⇔ n RELIG cardenal m.

cardinal number, cardinal numeral n número m cardinal.

card index n UK fichero m.

cardiograph ['kɑːdɪəgrɑːf] n cardiógrafo m.

cardiology [ˌkɑːdɪ'ɒlədʒɪ] n cardiología f.

cardphone ['kɑːdfəʊn] n tarjeta f telefónica.

cardiovascular [ˌkɑːdɪəʊ'væskjʊlər] adj cardiovascular.

card table n mesita f plegable (para jugar a cartas).

card vote n UK voto m por delegación.

care [keər] ⇔ n - 1. [gen] cuidado m; **medical care** asistencia f médica; **in sb's care** al cargo OR cuidado de alguien; **to be in/be taken into care** estar/ser internado en un centro de protección de menores; **to take care of** [person] cuidar de; [animal, machine] cuidar; [deal with] encargarse de; **take care!** [goodbye] ¡nos vemos!, ¡cuídate!; **to take care (to do sthg)** tener cuidado (de hacer algo) - 2. [cause of worry] preocupación f, problema m. ⇔ vi - 1. [be concerned]: **to care (about)** preocuparse (de OR por) - 2. [mind]: **I don't care** no me importa; **I couldn't care less** inf me importa un pito.

➡ **care of** prep al cuidado de, en casa de.

➡ **care for** vt insep dated [like]: **I don't care for cheese** no me gusta el queso; **he still cares for her** todavía la quiere.

CARE [keər] (abbr of **Cooperative for American Relief Everywhere**) n organización humanitaria estadounidense.

career [kə'rɪər] ⇔ n carrera f. ⇔ comp de carrera. ⇔ vi ir a toda velocidad.

careerist [kə'rɪərɪst] n pej arribista mf.

careers [kə'rɪəz] comp vocacional, profesional.

careers adviser n asesor m, -ra f de orientación profesional.

career woman n mujer f de carrera.

carefree ['keəfriː] adj despreocupado(da).

careful ['keəfʊl] adj [gen] cuidadoso(sa); [driver] prudente; [work] esmerado(da); **be careful!** ¡ten cuidado!; **to be careful with money** ser mirado OR cuidadoso con el dinero; **to be careful to do sthg** tener cuidado de hacer algo.

carefully ['keəflɪ] adv - 1. [cautiously] cuidadosamente, con cuidado; [drive] con cuidado - 2. [thoroughly] detenidamente.

careless ['keəlɪs] adj - 1. [inattentive] descuidado(da) - 2. [unconcerned] despreocupado(da).

carelessly ['keəlɪslɪ] adv - 1. [inattentively - gen] descuidadamente; [- drive] con poco cuidado - 2. [unconcernedly] despreocupadamente.

carelessness ['keəlɪsnɪs] n - 1. [inattention] descuido m - 2. [lack of concern] despreocupación f.

carer ['keərər] n persona que cuida de un familiar impedido o enfermo.

caress [kə'res] ⇔ n caricia f, apapacho m Méx. ⇔ vt acariciar.

caretaker ['keəˌteɪkər] n UK conserje mf.

caretaker government n gobierno m provisional.

car ferry n transbordador m OR ferry m de coches.

cargo ['kɑːgəʊ] (pl **-es** OR **-s**) ⇔ n carga f, cargamento m. ⇔ comp de carga.

car hire n UK alquiler m OR renta f Méx de coches, arrendamiento m de autos.

Carib ['kærɪb] n [language] caribe m.

Caribbean [UK kærɪ'bɪən, US kə'rɪbɪən] ⇔ adj caribe. ⇔ n: **the Caribbean (Sea)** el (mar) Caribe.

caribou ['kærɪbuː] (pl **caribou** OR **-s**) n caribú m.

caricature ['kærɪkə,tjʊəʳ] <> n lit & fig caricatura f. <> vt caricaturizar.

caries ['keəri:z] n caries f inv.

caring ['keərɪŋ] adj solícito(ta), dedicado(da).

caring professions npl: the caring professions las profesiones relacionadas con la asistencia social.

carnage ['kɑ:nɪdʒ] n carnicería f, matanza f.

carnal ['kɑ:nl] adj liter carnal.

carnation [kɑ:'neɪʃn] n clavel m.

carnival ['kɑ:nɪvl] n carnaval m.

carnivore ['kɑ:nɪvɔ:ʳ] n carnívoro m, -ra f.

carnivorous [kɑ:'nɪvərəs] adj carnívoro(ra).

carol ['kærəl] n villancico m.

carouse [kə'raʊz] vi andar de parranda.

carousel [,kærə'sel] n - 1. esp US [at fair] tiovivo m - 2. [at airport] cinta f transportadora.

carp [kɑ:p] <> n (pl carp OR -s) carpa f. <> vi: to carp (about) refunfuñar OR renegar (de).

car park n UK aparcamiento m, parqueadero m Col & Pan, estacionamiento m Amér.

carpenter ['kɑ:pəntəʳ] n carpintero m, -ra f.

carpentry ['kɑ:pəntrɪ] n carpintería f.

carpet ['kɑ:pɪt] <> n lit & fig alfombra f; fitted carpet moqueta f; to sweep sthg under the carpet fig echar tierra a algo. <> vt - 1. [fit with carpet] enmoquetar - 2. fig [cover] cubrir.

carpet slipper n zapatilla f.

carpet sweeper [-'swi:pəʳ] n cepillo m mecánico (de alfombras).

car pool n - 1. UK [of company] parque m móvil - 2. [car-sharing scheme] acuerdo para ir al trabajo compartiendo un vehículo.

carport ['kɑ:,pɔ:t] n US cochera f.

car rental n US alquiler m OR renta f Méx de coches, arrendamiento m de autos.

carriage ['kærɪdʒ] n - 1. [horsedrawn vehicle] carruaje m - 2. UK [railway coach] vagón m - 3. [transport of goods] transporte m; carriage paid OR free UK porte pagado; carriage forward UK porte a cuenta del destinatario - 4. [on typewriter] carro m - 5. liter [bearing] porte m.

carriage clock n reloj grande con asa.

carriage return n retorno m de carro.

carriageway ['kærɪdʒweɪ] n UK calzada f.

carrier ['kærɪəʳ] n - 1. COMM transportista mf - 2. [airline] aerolínea f - 3. [of disease] portador m, -ra f - 4. MIL: (aircraft)carrier portaaviones m inv - 5. [on bicycle] portaequipajes m inv - 6. = carrier bag.

carrier bag n bolsa f (de papel o plástico).

carrier pigeon n paloma f mensajera.

carrion ['kærɪən] n carroña f.

carrot ['kærət] n - 1. [vegetable] zanahoria f - 2. inf [incentive] señuelo m, aliciente m.

carry ['kærɪ] (pt & pp -ied) <> vt - 1. [transport] llevar - 2. [have about one's person] llevar encima - 3. [disease] ser portador de - 4. [involve] acarrear, conllevar - 5. [motion, proposal] aprobar - 6. [be pregnant with] estar embarazada de - 7. MATHS llevarse. <> vi [sound] oírse.

◆ **carry away** vt insep: to get carried away exaltarse.

◆ **carry forward, carry over** vt sep llevar a la página siguiente; carried forward suma y sigue.

◆ **carry off** vt sep - 1. [make a success of] llevar a cabo - 2. [win] llevarse.

◆ **carry on** <> vt insep - 1. [continue] continuar, seguir; to carry on doing sthg continuar OR seguir haciendo algo - 2. [conversation] mantener. <> vi - 1. [continue]: to carry on (with) continuar OR seguir (con) - 2. inf [make a fuss] exagerar la nota - 3. inf dated [have a love affair]: to carry on with tener un lío con.

◆ **carry out** vt insep - 1. [perform] llevar a cabo - 2. [fulfil] cumplir.

◆ **carry over** vt sep = carry forward.

◆ **carry through** vt sep [accomplish] llevar a cabo.

carryall ['kærɪɔ:l] n US bolsa f de viaje.

carrycot ['kærɪkɒt] n esp UK moisés m, capazo m.

carry-on n UK inf lío m, follón m.

carry-out n US & Scotland comida f para llevar.

carsick ['kɑ:,sɪk] adj mareado(da) (al ir en coche).

cart [kɑ:t] <> n - 1. [for horse] carro m, carreta f - 2. US [trolley] carrito m. <> vt inf acarrear.

carte blanche ['kɑːtblɑ̃ʃ] n carta f blanca.

cartel [kɑ:'tel] n pej cártel m.

cartilage ['kɑ:tɪlɪdʒ] n cartílago m.

carton ['kɑ:tn] n - 1. [strong cardboard box] caja f de cartón - 2. [for liquids] cartón m, envase m.

cartoon [kɑ:'tu:n] n - 1. [satirical drawing] chiste m (en viñeta) - 2. [comic strip] tira f cómica - 3. [film] dibujos mpl animados.

cartoonist [kɑ:'tu:nɪst] n dibujante mf de chistes.

cartridge ['kɑ:trɪdʒ] n - 1. [for gun, camera & COMPUT] cartucho m - 2. [for pen] recambio m - 3. [for record player] portaagujas m inv.

cartridge paper n papel m de dibujo.

cartwheel ['kɑ:twi:l] n voltereta f lateral.

carve [kɑ:v] <> vt - 1. [wood] tallar; [stone] esculpir - 2. [meat] trinchar - 3. [name, message] grabar. <> vi trinchar.

◆ **carve out** vt sep [niche, place] conquistar; to carve out a future for o.s. labrarse un porvenir.

carve up vt sep repartir.

carving ['kɑːvɪŋ] n - **1.** [art, work - wooden] tallado m; [- stone] labrado m, cincelado m - **2.** [object - wooden, stone] talla f.

carving knife n cuchillo m de trinchar.

car wash n lavado m de coches.

cascade [kæ'skeɪd] <> n cascada f. <> vi caer en cascada.

case [keɪs] n - **1.** [gen & GRAM] caso m; **to be the case** ser el caso; **a case in point** un ejemplo claro; **in that/which case** en ese/cuyo caso; **as OR whatever the case may be** según sea el caso; **in case of** en caso de - **2.** [argument] argumentos mpl; **the case for/against (sthg)** los argumentos a favor/en contra (de algo) - **3.** LAW [trial, inquiry] pleito m, causa f - **4.** [container - of leather] funda f; [- of hard material] estuche m - **5.** UK [suitcase] maleta f, petaca f Méx, valija f R Plata.

in any case adv en cualquier caso, de todas formas.

in case conj & adv por si acaso; **in case she doesn't come** por si no viene.

case history n historial m (clínico), historia f clínica Amér.

case study n estudio m de casos prácticos.

cash [kæʃ] <> n - **1.** [notes and coins] (dinero m) efectivo m, metálico m; **to pay (in) cash** pagar al contado OR en efectivo - **2.** inf [money] dinero m, plata f Amér - **3.** [payment]: **cash in advance** pago m al contado por adelantado; **cash on delivery** entrega f contra reembolso. <> vt cobrar, hacer efectivo.

cash in vi: **to cash in on** inf sacar partido de.

cash and carry n almacén de venta al por mayor.

cashbook ['kæʃbʊk] n libro m de caja.

cash box n caja f con cerradura (para el dinero).

cash card n esp US tarjeta f de cajero automático.

cash crop n cultivo m para comercialización.

cash desk n UK caja f.

cash discount n descuento m por pronto pago.

cash dispenser [-dɪ'spensə'], **cash point** n esp US cajero m automático.

cashew (nut) ['kæʃuː-] n (nuez f de) anacardo m.

cash flow n flujo m de fondos, cash-flow m.

cashier [kæ'ʃɪə'] n cajero m, -ra f.

cashless ['kæʃlɪs] adj sin dinero en efectivo.

cash machine = cash dispenser.

cashmere [kæʃ'mɪə'] <> n cachemir m, cachemira f. <> comp de cachemir OR cachemira.

cash payment n pago m en efectivo OR al contado.

cash point ['kæʃpɔɪnt] = cash dispenser.

cash price n precio m al contado.

cash register n caja f (registradora).

cash sale n venta f al contado.

casing ['keɪsɪŋ] n [of tyre, machine] cubierta f; [of electric cable] revestimiento m.

casino [kə'siːnəʊ] (pl -s) n casino m.

cask [kɑːsk] n tonel m, barril m.

casket ['kɑːskɪt] n - **1.** [for jewels] estuche m - **2.** US [coffin] ataúd m.

Caspian Sea ['kæspɪən-] n: **the Caspian Sea** el mar Caspio.

casserole ['kæsərəʊl] n - **1.** [stew] guiso m - **2.** [pan] cazuela f, cacerola f.

cassette [kæ'set] n cinta f, casete f.

cassette deck n platina f, pletina f.

cassette player n casete m, magnetófono m.

cassette recorder n casete m, magnetófono m.

cassock ['kæsək] n sotana f.

cast [kɑːst] <> n [of play, film] reparto m. <> vt (pt & pp cast) - **1.** [look] echar, lanzar; **to cast doubt on sthg** poner algo en duda; **to cast a spell on** embrujar OR hechizar a - **2.** [light] irradiar; [shadow] proyectar - **3.** [throw] arrojar, lanzar - **4.** [choose for play]: **to cast sb as** asignar a alguien el papel de - **5.** [vote] emitir - **6.** [metal, statue] fundir - **7.** [shed - skin] mudar.

cast about, cast around vi: **to cast about for sthg** buscar algo.

cast aside vt sep [person] abandonar; [idea] rechazar.

cast off <> vt sep desechar, abandonar. <> vi NAUT soltar amarras.

castanets [ˌkæstə'nets] npl castañuelas fpl.

castaway ['kɑːstəweɪ] n náufrago m, -ga f.

caste [kɑːst] n casta f.

caster, castor ['kɑːstə'] n [wheel] ruedecilla f.

caster sugar, castor sugar n UK azúcar m extrafino.

castigate ['kæstɪgeɪt] vt fml [behaviour, report] censurar.

casting ['kɑːstɪŋ] n [for film, play] reparto m.

casting vote n voto m de calidad.

cast iron n hierro m fundido.

cast-iron adj - **1.** [made of cast iron] de hierro fundido - **2.** [alibi, excuse] irrebatible, indiscutible; [will] férreo(a), de hierro.

castle ['kɑːsl] n - **1.** [building] castillo m - **2.** [in chess] torre f.

castor ['kɑːstə'] = caster.

castor oil n aceite m de ricino.

castor sugar = caster sugar.

castrate [kæ'streɪt] *vt* castrar.

castration [kæ'streɪʃn] *n* castración *f*.

casual ['kæʒʊəl] *adj* - **1.** [relaxed, indifferent] despreocupado(da) - **2.** *pej* [offhand] descuidado(da), informal - **3.** [chance - visitor] ocasional; [- remark] casual - **4.** [informal – clothes] de sport, informal - **5.** [irregular - labourer etc] eventual.

casually ['kæʒʊəlɪ] *adv* - **1.** [in a relaxed manner, indifferently] con aire despreocupado - **2.** [informally] informalmente.

casualty ['kæʒjʊəltɪ] (*pl* **-ies**) *n* - **1.** [gen] víctima *f*; MIL baja *f* - **2.** (*U*) [ward] urgencias *fpl*.

casualty department *n* unidad *f* de urgencias.

cat [kæt] *n* - **1.** [domestic] gato *m*, -ta *f*; **to let the cat out of the bag** descubrir el pastel; **to be like a cat on hot bricks** UK OR **on a hot tin roof** US estar en ascuas; **to put the cat among the pigeons** UK meter el lobo en el redil; **to rain cats and dogs** llover a cántaros; **to think that one is the cat's whiskers** UK creerse que uno es el oro y el moro - **2.** [wild] felino *m*.

cataclysmic [,kætə'klɪzmɪk] *adj* catastrófico(ca).

catacombs ['kætəku:mz] *npl* catacumbas *fpl*.

Catalan ['kætə,læn] <> *adj* catalán(ana). <> *n* - **1.** [person] catalán *m*, -ana *f* - **2.** [language] catalán *m*.

catalogue UK**, catolog** US ['kætəlɒg] <> *n* - **1.** [of items] catálogo *m* - **2.** *fig* [series] serie *f*. <> *vt* - **1.** [make official list of] catalogar - **2.** *fig* [list] enumerar.

Catalonia [,kætə'ləʊnɪə] *n* Cataluña.

Catalonian [,kætə'ləʊnɪən] <> *adj* catalán(ana). <> *n* [person] catalán *m*, -ana *f*.

catalyst ['kætəlɪst] *n* *lit* & *fig* catalizador *m*.

catalytic convertor [,kætə'lɪtɪk kən'vɜ:tər] *n* catalizador *m*.

catamaran [,kætəmə'ræn] *n* catamarán *m*.

catapult ['kætəpʌlt] UK <> *n* - **1.** HIST [hand-held] tirachinas *m inv* - **2.** HIST [machine] catapulta *f*. <> *vt* - **1.** [hurl] lanzar - **2.** *fig* [propel] catapultar.

cataract ['kætərækt] *n* [waterfall, in eye] catarata *f*.

catarrh [kə'tɑ:r] *n* (*U*) catarro *m*.

catastrophe [kə'tæstrəfɪ] *n* catástrofe *f*.

catastrophic [,kætə'strɒfɪk] *adj* catastrófico(ca).

cat burglar *n* UK ladrón *que entra trepando*.

catcall ['kætkɔ:l] *n* silbido *m*, pitido *m*.

catch [kætʃ] <> *vt* (*pt* & *pp* **caught**) - **1.** [gen] coger, agarrar *Amér*; [ball] atrapar - **2.** [fish] pescar; [stop - person] parar - **3.** [be in time for]: **I've got a train to catch** tengo que coger un

tren; **to catch the (last) post** UK llegar a la (última) recogida del correo - **4.** [hear clearly] entender, llegar a oír - **5.** [interest, imagination] despertar - **6.** [see]: **to catch sight** OR **a glimpse of** alcanzar a ver - **7.** [hook - shirt etc] engancharse; [shut in door - finger] pillarse - **8.** [light] reflejar - **9.** [strike] golpear. <> *vi* (*pt* & *pp* **caught**) - **1.** [become hooked, get stuck] engancharse - **2.** [start to burn] prenderse, encenderse. <> *n* - **1.** [of ball etc] parada *f* - **2.** [of fish] pesca *f*, captura *f* - **3.** [fastener - on door] pestillo *m*; [- on necklace] cierre *m* - **4.** [snag] trampa *f*.

◆ **catch at** *vt insep* intentar agarrar.

◆ **catch on** *vi* - **1.** [become popular] hacerse popular - **2.** *inf* [understand]: **to catch on (to)** caer en la cuenta (de).

◆ **catch out** *vt sep* [trick] pillar.

◆ **catch up** <> *vt sep* alcanzar. <> *vi*: **we'll soon catch up** pronto nos pondremos a la misma altura; **to catch up on** [sleep] recuperar; [work, reading] ponerse al día con.

◆ **catch up with** *vt insep* - **1.** [group etc] alcanzar - **2.** [criminal] pillar, descubrir.

catch-22 *n* callejón *m* sin salida.

catch-all *adj* general.

catching ['kætʃɪŋ] *adj* contagioso(sa).

catchment area ['kætʃmənt-] *n* UK zona *f* de captación.

catchphrase ['kætʃfreɪz] *n* muletilla *f*.

catchword ['kætʃwɜ:d] *n* eslogan *m*, lema *m*.

catchy ['kætʃɪ] (*comp* **-ier**, *superl* **-iest**) *adj* pegadizo(za).

catechism ['kætɪkɪzm] *n* catecismo *m*.

categorical [,kætɪ'gɒrɪkl] *adj* [statement] categórico(ca); [denial] rotundo(da).

categorically [,kætɪ'gɒrɪklɪ] *adv* [state] categóricamente; [deny] rotundamente.

categorize, -ise ['kætəgəraɪz] *vt*: **to categorize sb (as)** clasificar OR catalogar a alguien (de).

category ['kætəgərɪ] (*pl* **-ies**) *n* categoría *f*.

cater ['keɪtər] <> *vi* proveer comida. <> *vt* US [party, event] dar el servicio de comida y bebida de.

◆ **cater for** *vt insep* UK [tastes, needs] atender a; [social group] estar destinado(da) a; **I hadn't catered for that** no había contado con eso.

◆ **cater to** *vt insep* complacer.

caterer ['keɪtərər] *n* [firm] empresa *f* de hostelería.

catering ['keɪtərɪŋ] *n* [at wedding etc] servicio *m* de banquetes; [trade] hostelería *f*.

caterpillar ['kætəpɪlər] *n* oruga *f*.

caterpillar tracks *npl* (rodado *m* de) oruga *f*.

cat flap *n* UK gatera *f*.

catharsis [kə'θɑːsɪs] (*pl* **catharses** [kə'θɑːsiːz]) *n fml* catarsis *f inv*.

cathedral [kə'θiːdrəl] *n* catedral *f*.

catheter ['kæθɪtər] *n* catéter *m*.

cathode ray tube ['kæθəud-] *n* tubo *m* de rayos catódicos.

Catholic ['kæθlɪk] <> *adj* católico(ca). <> *n* católico *m*, -ca *f*.

catholic *adj* diverso(sa), variado(da).

Catholicism [kə'θɒlɪsɪzm] *n* catolicismo *m*.

catkin ['kætkɪn] *n* candelilla *f*, amento *m*.

Catseyes® ['kætsaɪz] *npl UK* catafaros *mpl*.

catsuit ['kætsuːt] *n UK* malla de manga larga hasta el tobillo.

catsup ['kætsəp] *n US* ketchup *m*.

cattle ['kætl] *npl* ganado *m* (vacuno).

cattle grid *n UK* reja de tubos metálicos en la calzada para impedir el paso al ganado.

catty ['kætɪ] (*comp* **-ier**, *superl* **-iest**) *adj inf pej* [spiteful] malintencionado(da).

catwalk ['kætwɔːk] *n* pasarela *f*.

Caucasian [kɔː'keɪzjən] <> *adj* **- 1.** GEOG caucásico(ca) - **2.** [white] de raza blanca. <> *n* - **1.** GEOG caucásico *m*, -ca *f* - **2.** [white person] persona *f* de raza blanca.

caucus ['kɔːkəs] *n* [political group] comité *m*.
Caucus *n US* congreso de los principales partidos estadounidenses.

caught [kɔːt] *pt* & *pp* ⊳ **catch**.

cauliflower ['kɒlɪ,flauər] *n* coliflor *f*.

causal ['kɔːzl] *adj* causal.

cause [kɔːz] <> *n* - **1.** [gen] causa *f* - **2.** [grounds]: **cause (for)** motivo *m* (para); **cause for complaint** motivo de queja; **cause to do sthg** motivo para hacer algo. <> *vt* causar; **to cause sb to do sthg** hacer que alguien haga algo.

causeway ['kɔːzweɪ] *n* [road] carretera *f* elevada.

caustic ['kɔːstɪk] *adj* - **1.** CHEM cáustico(ca) - **2.** [comment] mordaz, hiriente.

caustic soda *n* sosa *f* cáustica.

cauterize, -ise ['kɔːtəraɪz] *vt* cauterizar.

caution ['kɔːʃn] <> *n* - **1.** (*U*) [care] precaución *f*, cautela *f* - **2.** [warning] advertencia *f*, amonestación *f*. <> *vt* - **1.** [warn - against danger] prevenir; [- against behaving rudely etc] advertir, avisar - **2.** *UK* [subj: policeman]: **to caution sb (for)** amonestar a alguien (por).

cautionary ['kɔːʃənərɪ] *adj* instructivo(va), con moraleja.

cautious ['kɔːʃəs] *adj* prudente, cauto(ta).

cautiously ['kɔːʃəslɪ] *adv* prudentemente, cautelosamente.

cautiousness ['kɔːʃəsnɪs] *n* cautela *f*, precaución *f*.

cavalier [,kævə'lɪər] *adj* arrogante, desdeñoso(sa).

cavalry ['kævlrɪ] *n* caballería *f*.

cave [keɪv] *n* cueva *f*.
cave in *vi* - **1.** [roof, ceiling] hundirse, derrumbarse - **2.** [yield]: **to cave in (to)** ceder OR transigir (ante).

caveman ['keɪvmæn] (*pl* **-men** [-men]) *n* cavernícola *mf*, hombre *m* de las cavernas.

cavern ['kævən] *n* caverna *f*.

cavernous ['kævənəs] *adj* cavernoso(sa), grande y profundo(da).

caviar(e) ['kævɪɑːr] *n* caviar *m*.

caving ['keɪvɪŋ] *n UK* espeleología *f*.

cavity ['kævətɪ] (*pl* **-ies**) *n* - **1.** [in object, structure] cavidad *f* - **2.** [in tooth] caries *f inv* - **3.** [in body]: **nasal cavity** fosa *f* nasal.

cavity wall insulation *n UK* aislamiento *m* de doble pared.

cavort [kə'vɔːt] *vi* retozar, brincar.

cayenne (pepper) [keɪ'en-] *n* [powder] (pimienta *f* de) cayena *f*; [pepper] guindilla *f*.

CB *n abbr of* **citizens' band**.

CBC (*abbr of* **Canadian Broadcasting Corporation**) *n* cadena canadiense de radiotelevisión.

CBE (*abbr of* **Commander of (the Order of) the British Empire**) *n (titular de) distinción honorífica británica*.

CBI *abbr of* **Confederation of British Industry**.

CBS (*abbr of* **Columbia Broadcasting System**) *n* ≃ CBS *f (cadena estadounidense de televisión)*.

cc *n* - **1.** (*abbr of* **cubic centimetre**) cc - **2.** (*abbr of* **carbon copy**) cc.

CCTV (*abbr of* **closed-circuit television**) *n* circuito cerrado de televisión.

CD *n* - **1.** (*abbr of* **compact disc**) CD *m* - **2.** (*abbr of* **Corps Diplomatique**) CD.

CD burner *n* grabadora *f* de CD.

CDI (*abbr of* **compact disc interactive**) *n* COMPUT CDI *m*.

CD player *n* reproductor *m* de CD.

CD-R (*abbr of* **compact disc recordable**) *n* CD-R *m*.

CD-R drive *n* grabadora *f* de CD-R.

CD-ROM burner *n* estampadora *f* de CD.

CD-RW (*abbr of* **compact disc rewritable**) *n* CD-RW *m*.

CDT (*abbr of* **Central Daylight Time**) *hora de verano del centro de Estados Unidos*.

CD tower *n* torre *f* de almacenamiento de CDs.

CDW *n abbr of* **collision damage waiver.**

CE *abbr of* **Church of England.**

cease [si:s] *fml* ◇ *vt* cesar; **to cease doing** OR **to do sthg** dejar de hacer algo; **cease fire!** ¡alto el fuego! ◇ *vi* cesar.

cease-fire *n* alto *m* el fuego.

ceaseless ['si:slɪs] *adj fml* incesante.

ceaselessly ['si:slɪslɪ] *adv fml* incesantemente.

cedar (tree) ['si:dər-] *n* cedro *m*.

cede [si:d] *vt*: **to cede sthg (to)** ceder algo (a).

CEEB (*abbr of* **College Entry Examination Board**) *n* organismo encargado del acceso a la enseñanza superior en Estados Unidos.

Ceefax® ['si:fæks] *n UK servicio de teletexto de la BBC.*

ceilidh ['keɪlɪ] *n en Escocia e Irlanda, fiesta en la que se baila y se canta música regional.*

ceiling ['si:lɪŋ] *n* - **1.** [of room] techo *m* - **2.** [limit] tope *m*, límite *m*.

celebrate ['selɪbreɪt] *vt* & *vi* celebrar.

celebrated ['selɪbreɪtɪd] *adj* célebre, famoso(sa).

celebration [ˌselɪ'breɪʃn] *n* - **1.** *(U)* [activity, feeling] celebración *f* - **2.** [event] fiesta *f*, festejo *m*.

celebrity [sɪ'lebrətɪ] *(pl* -**ies)** *n* celebridad *f*.

celeriac [sɪ'lerɪæk] *n* apio *m* nabo.

celery ['selərɪ] *n* apio *m*.

celestial [sɪ'lestjəl] *adj* celestial.

celibacy ['selɪbəsɪ] *n* celibato *m*.

celibate ['selɪbət] *adj* célibe.

cell [sel] *n* - **1.** BIOL & POL célula *f* - **2.** COMPUT celda *f* - **3.** [prisoner's, nun's or monk's room] celda *f*, separo *m* Amér - **4.** ELEC pila *f*.

cellar ['selər] *n* - **1.** [basement] sótano *m* - **2.** [stock of wine] bodega *f*.

cellist ['tʃelɪst] *n* violoncelista *mf*.

cello ['tʃeləʊ] *(pl* -**s)** *n* violoncelo *m*.

Cellophane® ['seləfeɪn] *n* celofán® *m*.

cellphone ['selfəʊn], **cellular phone** ['seljʊlər-] *n US* teléfono *m* móvil, celular *m* Amér.

cellulite ['seljʊlaɪt] *n* celulitis *f inv*.

Celluloid® ['seljʊlɔɪd] *n* celuloide *m*.

cellulose ['seljʊləʊs] *n* celulosa *f*.

Celsius ['selsɪəs] *adj* centígrado(da); **20 degrees Celsius** 20 grados centígrados.

Celt [kelt] *n* celta *mf*.

Celtic ['keltɪk] ◇ *adj* celta, céltico(ca). ◇ *n* celta *m*.

cement [sɪ'ment] ◇ *n* - **1.** [for concrete] cemento *m* - **2.** [glue] cola *f*, pegamento *m*. ◇ *vt* - **1.** [cover with cement] cubrir con cemento - **2.** [glue] pegar, encolar - **3.** [agreement, relationship] cimentar, fortalecer.

cement mixer *n* hormigonera *f*.

cemetery ['semɪtrɪ] *(pl* -**ies)** *n* cementerio *m*.

cenotaph ['senətɑ:f] *n* cenotafio *m*.

censor ['sensər] ◇ *n* censor *m*, -ra *f*. ◇ *vt* censurar.

censorship ['sensəʃɪp] *n* censura *f*.

censure ['senʃər] ◇ *n* censura *f*. ◇ *vt* censurar.

census ['sensəs] *(pl* -**uses)** *n* censo *m*.

cent [sent] *n* centavo *m*.

centenary UK [sen'ti:nərɪ] *(pl* -**ies)**, **centennial** US [sen'tenjəl] *n* centenario *m*.

center US = **centre.**

centigrade ['sentɪgreɪd] *adj* centígrado(da); **20 degrees centigrade** 20 grados centígrados.

centigram(me) ['sentɪgræm] *n* centigramo *m*.

centilitre UK, **centiliter** US ['sentɪˌli:tər] *n* centilitro *m*.

centimetre UK, **centimeter** US ['sentɪˌmi:tər] *n* centímetro *m*.

centipede ['sentɪpi:d] *n* ciempiés *m inv*.

central ['sentrəl] *adj* - **1.** [gen] central; **in central Spain** en el centro de España; **to be central to** ser el eje OR la pieza clave de - **2.** [easily reached] céntrico(ca).

Central African ◇ *adj* centroafricano(na). ◇ *n* centroafricano *m*, -na *f*.

Central African Republic *n*: **the Central African Republic** la república Centroafricana.

Central America *n* Centroamérica.

Central American ◇ *adj* centroamericano(na). ◇ *n* centroamericano *m*, -na *f*.

Central Asia *n* Asia Central.

Central Europe *n* Europa Central.

central government *n* gobierno *m* central.

central heating *n* calefacción *f* central.

centralization [ˌsentrəlar'zeɪʃn] *n* centralización *f*.

centralize, -ise ['sentrəlaɪz] *vt* centralizar.

centralized ['sentrəlaɪzd] *adj* centralizado(da).

central locking [-'lɒkɪŋ] *n* cierre *m* centralizado.

centrally ['sentrəlɪ] *adv*: **centrally situated** OR **located** céntrico(ca).

centrally heated *adj* con calefacción central.

central nervous system *n* sistema *m* nervioso central.

central processing unit *n* unidad *f* central de proceso.

central reservation *n UK* mediana *f*.

centre UK**, center** US ['sentər] <> n centro m; **centre of attention/gravity** centro de atención/gravedad; **the centre** POL el centro. <> adj **- 1.** [middle] central **- 2.** POL centrista. <> vt centrar.

◆ **centre around, centre on** vt insep centrarse en.

centre back, centre half n defensa mf central.

centre-fold n póster m central.

centre forward n delantero m, -ra f centro (inv).

centre half = centre back.

centrepiece UK**, centerpiece** US ['sentəpi:s] n **- 1.** [decoration] centro m de mesa **- 2.** [principal element] punto m central.

centre-spread n póster m central.

centrifugal force [sentrɪ'fju:gl-] n fuerza f centrífuga.

century ['sentʃʊrɪ] (pl **-ies**) n siglo m; **the 20th century** el siglo XX.

CEO (abbr of chief executive officer) n presidente m, -ta f.

ceramic [sɪ'ræmɪk] adj de cerámica, cerámico(ca).

◆ **ceramics** <> n cerámica f. <> npl [objects] piezas fpl de cerámica.

cereal ['sɪərɪəl] n **- 1.** [crop] cereal m **- 2.** [breakfast food] cereales mpl.

cerebral ['serɪbrəl] adj cerebral.

cerebral palsy n parálisis f inv cerebral.

ceremonial [,serɪ'məʊnjəl] <> adj ceremonial. <> n ceremonial m.

ceremonious [,serɪ'məʊnjəs] adj ceremonioso(sa).

ceremony ['serɪmənɪ] (pl **-ies**) n ceremonia f; **without ceremony** sin miramientos; **to stand on ceremony** andarse con cumplidos OR ceremonias.

cert [sɜːt] n UK inf cosa f segura.

certain ['sɜːtn] adj **- 1.** [gen] seguro(ra); **he's certain to be late** (es) seguro que llega tarde; **to be certain (of)** estar seguro (de); **to make certain (of)** asegurarse (de); **for certain** con toda seguridad **- 2.** [particular, some] cierto(ta); **to a certain extent** hasta cierto punto **- 3.** [named person]: **a certain...** un(una) tal...

certainly ['sɜːtnlɪ] adv desde luego; **certainly not!** ¡claro que no!

certainty ['sɜːtntɪ] (pl **-ies**) n seguridad f; **it's a certainty that...** es seguro que...

CertEd [,sɜːt'ed] (abbr of Certificate in Education) n diploma universitario de pedagogía.

certifiable [,sɜːtɪ'faɪəbl] adj [mad]: **she's certifiable** está para que la encierren.

certificate [sə'tɪfɪkət] n [gen] certificado m; SCH & UNIV diploma m, título m; [of birth, death] partida f.

certification [,sɜːtɪfɪ'keɪʃn] n certificación f.

certified ['sɜːtɪfaɪd] adj [document] certificado(da); [person] diplomado(da).

certified mail n US correo m certificado.

certified public accountant n US contable diplomado m, contable diplomada f, contador público m, contadora pública f Amér.

certify ['sɜːtɪfaɪ] (pt & pp **-ied**) vt **- 1.** [declare true] certificar **- 2.** [declare officially]: **to certify sb dead** dar constancia de la muerte de alguien **- 3.** [declare insane] declarar demente.

cervical [sə'vaɪkl] adj cervical.

cervical smear n citología f, frotis f cervical.

cervix ['sɜːvɪks] (pl **-ices** [-ɪsi:z]) n [of womb] cuello m del útero.

cesarean (section) = caesarean (section).

cessation [se'seɪʃn] n fml cese m.

cesspit ['sespɪt]**, cesspool** ['sespu:l] n pozo m negro.

CET (abbr of Central European Time) hora de Europa Central.

cf. (abbr of confer) cf., cfr.

c/f (abbr of carried forward) suma y sigue.

c & f (abbr of cost and freight) c y f.

CFC (abbr of chlorofluorocarbon) n CFC m.

cg (abbr of centigram) cg m.

C & G (abbr of City and Guilds) n diploma británico de formación profesional.

CGA (abbr of colour graphics adapter) n CGA m.

ch (abbr of central heating) cal. cent.

ch. (abbr of chapter) cap.

Chad [tʃæd] n el Chad.

chafe [tʃeɪf] <> vt [rub] rozar. <> vi **- 1.** [skin] irritarse **- 2.** [person]: **to chafe at** irritarse por.

chaff [tʃɑːf] n barcia f.

chaffinch ['tʃæfɪntʃ] n pinzón m.

chain [tʃeɪn] <> n cadena f; **chain of mountains** cordillera f, cadena f montañosa; **chain of office** ≃ collar m de mando; **chain of events** serie f OR cadena f de acontecimientos. <> vt [person, object] encadenar.

chain letter n carta que se hace circular en cadena para obtener algún beneficio.

chain reaction n reacción f en cadena.

chain saw n motosierra f, sierra f mecánica.

chain-smoke vi fumar un cigarrillo tras otro.

chain-smoker n fumador empedernido m, fumadora empedernida f.

chain store n tienda f (de una cadena).

chair [tʃeəʳ] <> *n* - **1.** [gen] silla *f*; [armchair] sillón *m* - **2.** [university post] cátedra *f* - **3.** [of meeting] presidencia *f*; **to take the chair** presidir, tomar la presidencia. <> *vt* presidir.

chair lift *n* telesilla *m*.

chairman ['tʃeəmən] (*pl* **-men** [-mən]) *n* presidente *m*.

chairmanship ['tʃeəmənʃɪp] *n* presidencia *f*.

chairperson ['tʃeə,pɜːsn] (*pl* **-s**) *n* presidente *m*, -ta *f*.

chairwoman ['tʃeə,wumən] (*pl* **-women** [,wɪmɪn]) *n* presidenta *f*.

chaise longue [ʃeɪz'lɒŋ] (*pl* **chaises longues** [ʃeɪz'lɒŋ]) *n* tumbona *f*, chaise-longue *f*.

chalet ['ʃæleɪ] *n* chalé *m*, chalet *m*.

chalice ['tʃælɪs] *n* cáliz *m*.

chalk [tʃɔːk] *n* - **1.** [for drawing] tiza *f*, gis *m Méx* - **2.** [type of rock] creta *f*.
◆ **by a long chalk** *adv* con diferencia, con mucho.
◆ **not by a long chalk** *adv* ni mucho menos, de ninguna manera.
◆ **chalk up** *vt sep* [attain] apuntarse, anotarse *Amér*.

chalkboard ['tʃɔːkbɔːd] *n US* pizarra *f*, encerado *m*.

challenge ['tʃælɪndʒ] <> *n* desafío *m*, reto *m*. <> *vt* - **1.** [to fight, competition]: **to challenge sb (to sthg/to do sthg)** desafiar a alguien (a algo/a que haga algo) - **2.** [question] poner en tela de juicio.

challenger ['tʃælɪndʒəʳ] *n* [for title, leadership] aspirante *mf*; [opponent] contrincante *mf*.

challenging ['tʃælɪndʒɪŋ] *adj* - **1.** [task, job] estimulante, que supone un reto - **2.** [look, tone of voice] desafiante.

chamber ['tʃeɪmbəʳ] *n* [room] cámara *f*.
◆ **chambers** *npl* despacho *m*.

chambermaid ['tʃeɪmbəmeɪd] *n* [at hotel] camarera *f*.

chamber music *n* música *f* de cámara.

chamber of commerce *n* cámara *f* de comercio.

chamber orchestra *n* orquesta *f* de cámara.

chameleon [kə'miːljən] *n* camaleón *m*.

chamois[1] ['ʃæmwɑː] (*pl* **chamois**) *n* [animal] gamuza *f*.

chamois[2] ['ʃæmɪ] *n*: **chamois (leather)** gamuza *f*.

champ [tʃæmp] <> *n inf* campeón *m*, -ona *f*. <> *vi* mordisquear.

champagne [,ʃæm'peɪn] *n* champán *m*.

champion ['tʃæmpjən] <> *n* - **1.** [of competition] campeón *m*, -ona *f* - **2.** [of cause] defensor *m*, -ra *f*. <> *vt* defender.

championship ['tʃæmpjənʃɪp] *n* campeonato *m*.

chance [tʃɑːns] <> *n* - **1.** [luck] azar *m*, suerte *f*; **by chance** por casualidad - **2.** [likelihood] posibilidad *f*; **not to stand a chance (of)** no tener ninguna posibilidad (de); **by any chance** por casualidad, acaso; **on the off chance** por si acaso - **3.** [opportunity] oportunidad *f* - **4.** [risk] riesgo *m*; **to take a chance (on)** correr un riesgo *OR* arriesgarse (con). <> *adj* fortuito(ta), casual. <> *vt* arriesgar; **to chance it** arriesgarse. <> *vi liter* [happen]: **to chance to do sthg** hacer algo por casualidad.

chancellor ['tʃɑːnsələʳ] *n* - **1.** [chief minister] canciller *m* - **2.** *US UNIV* ≃ rector *m*.

Chancellor of the Exchequer *n UK* Ministro *m*, -tra *f* de Economía y Hacienda.

chancy ['tʃɑːnsɪ] (*comp* **-ier**, *superl* **-iest**) *adj inf* arriesgado(da).

chandelier [,ʃændə'lɪəʳ] *n* (lámpara *f* de) araña *f*, candil *m Méx*.

change [tʃeɪndʒ] <> *n* - **1.** [gen] cambio *m*; **change of clothes** muda *f*; **it makes a change** es un cambio; **for a change** para variar - **2.** [from payment] vuelta *f*, cambio *m*, vuelto *m Amér* - **3.** [coins] suelto *m*, calderilla *f*, sencillo *m Andes*, feria *f Méx*, menudo *m Col* - **4.** [money in exchange]: **have you got change for £5?** ¿tienes cambio de 5 libras? <> *vt* - **1.** [gen] cambiar; **to change sthg into** transformar algo en; **to change pounds into francs** cambiar libras en *Esp OR* a francos; **to change direction** cambiar de rumbo; **to change one's mind** cambiar de idea *OR* opinión - **2.** [goods in shop] cambiar - **3.** [switch - job, gear, train] cambiar de; **to change hands** *COMM* cambiar de mano; **to change one's shirt** cambiarse de camisa; **to get changed** cambiarse de ropa. <> *vi* - **1.** [alter] cambiar; **to change into sthg** transformarse en algo - **2.** [change clothes] cambiarse - **3.** [change trains, buses] hacer transbordo.
◆ **change over** *vi* [convert]: **to change over to** cambiar a.

changeable ['tʃeɪndʒəbl] *adj* variable.

changed [tʃeɪndʒd] *adj*: **he's a changed man** es otro, es un hombre nuevo.

change machine *n* máquina *f* de cambio.

change of life *n*: **the change of life** la menopausia.

changeover ['tʃeɪndʒ,əʊvəʳ] *n*: **changeover (to)** cambio *m* (a).

change purse *n US* portamonedas *m inv*, monedero *m*, chauchera *f Chile*.

changing ['tʃeɪndʒɪŋ] *adj* cambiante.

changing room *n* - **1.** *SPORT* vestuario *m* - **2.** [in clothes shop] probador *m*.

channel ['tʃænl] ◇ *n* canal *m.* ◇ *vt* (*UK* -**led**, *cont* -**ling**, *US* -**ed**, *cont* -**ing**) *lit* & *fig* canalizar.
◆ **Channel** *n*: **the (English) Channel** el Canal de la Mancha.
◆ **channels** *npl* [procedure] conductos *mpl*, medios *mpl*.

Channel Islands *npl*: **the Channel Islands** las islas del Canal de la Mancha.

Channel tunnel *n*: **the Channel tunnel** el túnel del Canal de la Mancha.

chant [tʃɑːnt] ◇ *n* - **1.** RELIG canto *m* - **2.** [of demonstrators] consigna *f*; [at sports match] cántico *m.* ◇ *vt* - **1.** RELIG cantar - **2.** [words] corear. ◇ *vi* - **1.** RELIG salmodiar - **2.** [repeat words] corear.

chaos ['keɪɒs] *n* caos *m inv.*

chaotic [keɪ'ɒtɪk] *adj* caótico(ca).

chap [tʃæp] *n UK inf* tipo *m*, tío *m.*

chapat(t)i [tʃə'pætɪ] *n* chapati *m.*

chapel ['tʃæpl] *n* capilla *f.*

chaperon(e) ['ʃæpərəʊn] ◇ *n* carabina *f*, acompañanta *f.* ◇ *vt* acompañar.

chaplain ['tʃæplɪn] *n* capellán *m.*

chapped [tʃæpt] *adj* agrietado(da).

chapter ['tʃæptər] *n lit* & *fig* capítulo *m.*

char [tʃɑːr] ◇ *n UK* [cleaner] mujer *f* de la limpieza. ◇ *vt* (*pt* & *pp* -**red**, *cont* -**ring**) [burn] carbonizar, calcinar. ◇ *vi* (*pt* & *pp* -**red**, *cont* -**ring**) [work as cleaner] trabajar de mujer de la limpieza.

character ['kærəktər] *n* - **1.** [nature, quality, letter] carácter *m*; **to be out of/in character (for)** no ser/ser típico (de) - **2.** [in film, book, play] personaje *m* - **3.** *inf* [person of stated kind] tipo *m* - **4.** *inf* [person with strong personality]: **to be a character** ser todo un carácter.

characteristic [,kærəktə'rɪstɪk] ◇ *adj* característico(ca). ◇ *n* característica *f.*

characteristically [,kærəktə'rɪstɪklɪ] *adv* típicamente.

characterization [,kærəktəraɪ'zeɪʃn] *n* caracterización *f.*

characterize, -ise ['kærəktəraɪz] *vt* - **1.** [typify] caracterizar - **2.** [portray]: **to characterize sthg as** definir algo como.

charade [ʃə'rɑːd] *n* farsa *f.*
◆ **charades** *n (U)* charadas *fpl.*

charcoal ['tʃɑːkəʊl] *n* [for barbecue etc] carbón *m* (vegetal); [for drawing] carboncillo *m.*

chard [tʃɑːd] *n* acelga *f.*

charge [tʃɑːdʒ] ◇ *n* - **1.** [cost] precio *m*; **admission charge** entrada *f*; **free of charge** gratis; **will that be cash or charge?** *US* ¿pagará en efectivo o con tarjeta? - **2.** LAW cargo *m*, acusación *f* - **3.** [responsibility]: **to have charge of sthg** tener algo al cargo de uno; **to take**

charge (of) hacerse cargo (de); **to be in charge** ser el encargado(la encargada); **in charge of** encargado(da) de - **4.** ELEC carga *f* - **5.** MIL [of cavalry] carga *f.* ◇ *vt* - **1.** [customer, sum] cobrar; **to charge sthg to sb** cargar algo en la cuenta de alguien - **2.** [suspect, criminal]: **to charge sb (with)** acusar a alguien (de) - **3.** [attack] cargar contra - **4.** [battery] cargar. ◇ *vi* - **1.** [ask in payment]: **to charge (for)** cobrar (por) - **2.** [rush] cargar; **to charge in/out** entrar/salir en tromba.

chargeable ['tʃɑːdʒəbl] *adj* - **1.** [costs] cobrable, cobradero(ra) - **2.** [offence] punible.

charge account *n* cuenta *f* de crédito.

charge card *n* tarjeta *f* de compra.

charged [tʃɑːdʒd] *adj* cargado(da).

charge hand *n UK* ayudante *mf* de capataz.

charge nurse *n UK* enfermero *m*, -ra *f* jefe.

charger ['tʃɑːdʒər] *n* - **1.** [for batteries] cargador *m* - **2.** *liter* [horse] caballo *m* de batalla.

charge sheet *n UK* atestado *m* policial.

chariot ['tʃærɪət] *n* carro *m*, cuadriga *f.*

charisma [kə'rɪzmə] *n* carisma *m.*

charismatic [,kærɪz'mætɪk] *adj* carismático(ca).

charitable ['tʃærətəbl] *adj* - **1.** [person, remark] caritativo(va) - **2.** [organization] benéfico(ca).

charity ['tʃærɪtɪ] (*pl* -**ies**) *n* - **1.** [kindness, money] caridad *f* - **2.** [organization] institución *f* benéfica.

charity shop *n UK tienda de una entidad benéfica en la que se venden productos de segunda mano donados por simpatizantes.*

charlatan ['ʃɑːlətən] *n* charlatán *m*, -ana *f.*

charm [tʃɑːm] ◇ *n* - **1.** [appeal, attractiveness] encanto *m* - **2.** [spell] encantamiento *m*, hechizo *m* - **3.** [on bracelet] dije *m*, amuleto *m.* ◇ *vt* dejar encantado(da).

charm bracelet *n* pulsera *f* con dijes.

charmer ['tʃɑːmər] *n*: **he's a real charmer** es muy cumplido.

charming ['tʃɑːmɪŋ] *adj* encantador(ra).

charmingly ['tʃɑːmɪŋlɪ] *adv* [attractive, naïve] encantadoramente; [smile, dress] de un modo encantador.

charred [tʃɑːd] *adj* carbonizado(da), calcinado(da).

chart [tʃɑːt] ◇ *n* - **1.** [diagram] gráfico *m*; **weather chart** mapa *m* del tiempo - **2.** [map] carta *f.* ◇ *vt* - **1.** [plot, map] representar en un mapa - **2.** *fig* [describe] trazar.
◆ **charts** *npl*: **the charts** la lista de éxitos.

charter ['tʃɑːtər] ◇ *n* [document] carta *f.* ◇ *comp* chárter (*inv*), alquilado(da). ◇ *vt* [plane, boat] fletar.

chartered accountant [ˈtʃɑːtəd-] *n UK* contable colegiado *m*, contable colegiada *f*, contador colegiado *m*, contadora colegiada *f Amér.*

charter flight *n* vuelo *m* chárter.

chart-topping *adj UK* número uno en la lista de éxitos.

chary [ˈtʃeərɪ] (*comp* -ier, *superl* -iest) *adj*: to be chary of doing sthg ser reacio(cia) a la hora de hacer algo.

chase [tʃeɪs] ⬦ *n* [pursuit] persecución *f*; to give chase emprender la persecución. ⬦ *vt* - **1.** [pursue] perseguir - **2.** [drive away] ahuyentar - **3.** [money, jobs] ir detrás de, ir a la caza de. ⬦ *vi*: to chase after sthg/sb perseguir algo/a alguien.

➤ **chase up** *vt sep UK* [person] localizar; [information] buscar, intentar hacerse con; to chase sb up about sthg ponerse en contacto con alguien para recordarle algo.

chaser [ˈtʃeɪsər] *n* copa de licor tomada después de una cerveza.

chasm [ˈkæzm] *n* [deep crack] sima *f*; *fig* [divide] abismo *m*.

chassis [ˈʃæsɪ] (*pl* chassis) *n* [of vehicle] chasis *m inv*.

chaste [tʃeɪst] *adj* casto(ta).

chasten [ˈtʃeɪsn] *vt* escarmentar.

chastise [tʃæˈstaɪz] *vt fml* [scold] reprender.

chastity [ˈtʃæstətɪ] *n* castidad *f*.

chat [tʃæt] ⬦ *n* [gen & COMPUT] charla *f*, conversación *f Amér*, plática *f Amér C & Méx.* ⬦ *vi* (*pt & pp* -ted, *cont* -ting) [gen & COMPUT] charlar.

➤ **chat up** *vt sep UK inf* intentar ligar con, tirarse un lance con.

chat line *n* línea *f* compartida.

chat room *n* COMPUT sala *f* de conversación.

chatter [ˈtʃætər] ⬦ *n* - **1.** [of person] cháchara *f*, parloteo *m* - **2.** [of bird] gorjeo *m*; [of monkey] chillidos *mpl.* ⬦ *vi* - **1.** [person] parlotear - **2.** [bird] gorjear; [monkey] chillar - **3.** [teeth] castañetear.

chatterbox [ˈtʃætəbɒks] *n inf* parlanchín *m*, -ina *f*.

chatty [ˈtʃætɪ] (*comp* -ier, *superl* -iest) *adj* - **1.** [person] dicharachero(ra) - **2.** [letter] informal.

chauffeur [ˈʃəʊfər] ⬦ *n* chófer *mf.* ⬦ *vt* hacer de chófer para; we were chauffeured to our hotel un chófer nos llevó al hotel.

chauvinist [ˈʃəʊvɪnɪst] *n* - **1.** [sexist] sexista *mf*; male chauvinist machista *m* - **2.** [nationalist] chovinista *mf*.

chauvinistic [ˌʃəʊvɪˈnɪstɪk] *adj* - **1.** [sexist] sexista - **2.** [nationalistic] chovinista.

cheap [tʃiːp] ⬦ *adj* - **1.** [inexpensive] barato(ta) - **2.** [low - quality] de mala calidad - **3.** [vulgar - joke etc] de mal gusto - **4.** *US* [stingy] mezquino(na). ⬦ *adv* barato. ⬦ *n*: on the cheap en plan barato.

cheapen [ˈtʃiːpn] *vt* [degrade] rebajar, degradar.

cheaply [ˈtʃiːplɪ] *adv* barato.

cheapness [ˈtʃiːpnɪs] *n* - **1.** [low cost] lo barato, baratura *f* - **2.** [low quality] baja calidad *f* - **3.** [vulgarity - of joke etc] mal gusto *m*.

cheapskate [ˈtʃiːpskeɪt] *n inf pej* agarrado *m*, -da *f*.

cheat [tʃiːt] ⬦ *n* tramposo *m*, -sa *f*. ⬦ *vt* engañar, estafar; to cheat sb out of sthg estafar algo a alguien; to feel cheated sentirse engañado. ⬦ *vi* - **1.** [in exam] copiar; [at cards] hacer trampas - **2.** *inf* [be unfaithful]: to cheat on sb pegársela a alguien.

cheating [ˈtʃiːtɪŋ] *n* [in games] trampas *fpl*; [in business] fraude *m*.

check [tʃek] ⬦ *n* - **1.** [inspection, test]: check (on) inspección *f OR* control *m* (de); to keep a check on controlar - **2.** [restraint]: check (on) restricción *f* (en); to put a check on sthg controlar *OR* restringir algo; in check bajo control - **3.** *US* [cheque] cheque *m* - **4.** *US* [bill] cuenta *f*, nota *f* - **5.** *US* [tick] señal *f* de visto bueno - **6.** [pattern] cuadros *mpl* - **7.** [in chess] jaque *m*. ⬦ *vt* - **1.** [test, verify] comprobar - **2.** [inspect - machine, product] inspeccionar; [- ticket, passport] revisar, controlar - **3.** [restrain, stop] refrenar, contener; to check o.s. detenerse. ⬦ *vi* comprobar; to check (for/on sthg) comprobar (algo).

➤ **check in** ⬦ *vt sep* [luggage, coat] facturar, despachar *Amér.* ⬦ *vi* - **1.** [at hotel] inscribirse, registrarse - **2.** [at airport] facturar.

➤ **check off** *vt sep* ir comprobando (en una lista).

➤ **check out** ⬦ *vt sep* - **1.** [luggage, coat] recoger - **2.** [investigate] comprobar - **3.** *inf* [look at] mirar. ⬦ *vi* [from hotel] dejar el hotel.

➤ **check up** *vi*: to check up (on sthg) informarse (acerca de algo); to check up on sb hacer averiguaciones sobre alguien.

checkbook *US* = chequebook.

checked [tʃekt] *adj* a cuadros.

checkered *US* = chequered.

checkers [ˈtʃekəz] *n* (*U*) *US* damas *fpl*.

check guarantee card *n US* tarjeta *f* de identificación bancaria.

check-in *n* facturación *f*.

check-in desk *n* mostrador *m* de facturación.

checking account [ˈtʃekɪŋ-] *n US* cuenta *f* corriente.

checklist [ˈtʃeklɪst] *n* lista *f* (de cosas por hacer).

checkmate ['tʃekmeɪt] *n* jaque *m* mate.

checkout ['tʃekaʊt] *n* caja *f.*

checkpoint ['tʃekpɔɪnt] *n* control *m.*

checkup ['tʃekʌp] *n* chequeo *m*, revisión *f.*

Cheddar (cheese) ['tʃedər-] *n* (queso *m*) cheddar *m.*

cheek [tʃi:k] <> *n* - **1.** [of face] mejilla *f* - **2.** *inf* [impudence] cara *f*, descaro *m*. <> *vt inf* ser descarado(da) con.

cheekbone ['tʃi:kbəʊn] *n* pómulo *m.*

cheekily ['tʃi:kɪlɪ] *adv* con descaro.

cheekiness ['tʃi:kɪnɪs] *n* descaro *m.*

cheeky ['tʃi:kɪ] (*comp* -ier, *superl* -iest) *adj* descarado(da).

cheer [tʃɪər] <> *n* [shout] aclamación *f*, grito *m* de entusiasmo; **cheers** vítores *mpl*. <> *vt* - **1.** [shout approval, encouragement at] aclamar, vitorear - **2.** [gladden] animar. <> *vi* gritar con entusiasmo.
◆ **cheers** *excl* [when drinking] ¡salud!; *UK inf* [thank you] ¡gracias!; *inf* [goodbye] ¡hasta luego!
◆ **cheer on** *vt sep* animar con gritos de aliento.
◆ **cheer up** <> *vt sep* animar. <> *vi* animarse.

cheerful ['tʃɪəfʊl] *adj* - **1.** [gen] alegre - **2.** [attitude, agreement] entusiasta.

cheerfully ['tʃɪəfʊlɪ] *adv* - **1.** [joyfully - smile, sing] alegremente - [- dress, decorate] con colores vivos - **2.** [willingly] con entusiasmo.

cheerfulness ['tʃɪəfʊlnɪs] *n* [of person] buen humor *m*; [of dress, song] alegría *f.*

cheering ['tʃɪərɪŋ] <> *adj* [gladdening] alentador(ra). <> *n* (*U*) vítores *mpl*, aclamaciones *fpl.*

cheerio [,tʃɪərɪ'əʊ] *excl UK inf* ¡hasta otra!, ¡hasta luego!

cheerleader ['tʃɪə,li:dər] *n* animadora *f* (*de un equipo*).

cheerless ['tʃɪəlɪs] *adj* triste, deprimente.

cheery ['tʃɪərɪ] (*comp* -ier, *superl* -iest) *adj* animado(da), alegre.

cheese [tʃi:z] *n* queso *m.*

cheeseboard ['tʃi:zbɔ:d] *n* tabla *f* de quesos.

cheeseburger ['tʃi:z,bɜ:gər] *n* hamburguesa *f* con queso.

cheesecake ['tʃi:zkeɪk] *n* pastel *m* OR tarta *f* de queso.

cheesy ['tʃi:zɪ] (*comp* -ier, *superl* -iest) *adj* - **1.** [tasting of cheese] con sabor a queso - **2.** [smell] a queso.

cheetah ['tʃi:tə] *n* guepardo *m*, onza *f.*

chef [ʃef] *n* chef *m*, jefe *m* de cocina.

chemical ['kemɪkl] <> *adj* químico(ca). <> *n* sustancia *f* química.

chemically ['kemɪklɪ] *adv* químicamente.

chemical weapons *npl* armas *fpl* químicas.

chemist ['kemɪst] *n* - **1.** *UK* [pharmacist] farmacéutico *m*, -ca *f*; **chemist's (shop)** farmacia *f* - **2.** [scientist] químico *m*, -ca *f.*

chemistry ['kemɪstrɪ] *n* - **1.** [science] química *f* - **2.** [composition, characteristics] composición *f* (química).

chemotherapy [,ki:məʊ'θerəpɪ] *n* quimioterapia *f.*

cheque *UK,* **check** *US* [tʃek] *n* cheque *m*, talón *m*; **to pay by cheque** pagar con cheque.

cheque account *n* cuenta *f* corriente.

chequebook *UK,* **checkbook** *US* ['tʃekbʊk] *n* talonario *m* de cheques, chequera *f Amér.*

cheque card *n UK* tarjeta *f* de identificación bancaria.

chequered *UK* ['tʃekəd], **checkered** *US* ['tʃekerd] *adj* - **1.** [patterned] a cuadros - **2.** [varied] lleno(na) de altibajos.

Chequers ['tʃekəz] *n segunda residencia oficial del primer ministro británico.*

cherish ['tʃerɪʃ] *vt* - **1.** [hope, memory] abrigar, albergar - **2.** [privilege, right] apreciar - **3.** [person, thing] tener mucho cariño a.

cherished ['tʃerɪʃt] *adj* [memory] querido(da); [hope] anhelado(da).

cherry ['tʃerɪ] (*pl* -ies) *n* [fruit] cereza *f*; **cherry (tree)** cerezo *m.*

cherub ['tʃerəb] (*pl* -s OR -im [-ɪm]) *n* - **1.** [angel] querubín *m* - **2.** [child] ricura *f*, angelito *m.*

chervil ['tʃɜ:vɪl] *n* perifollo *m*, cerafolio *m.*

Ches. (*abbr of* Cheshire), *condado inglés.*

chess [tʃes] *n* ajedrez *m.*

chessboard ['tʃesbɔ:d] *n* tablero *m* de ajedrez.

chest [tʃest] *n* - **1.** ANAT pecho *m*; **to get sthg off one's chest** *inf* contar algo para desahogarse - **2.** [box, trunk - gen] arca *f*, cofre *m*; [- for tools] caja *f.*

chestnut ['tʃesnʌt] <> *adj* [colour] castaño(ña). <> *n* [nut] castaña *f*; **chestnut (tree)** castaño *m.*

chest of drawers (*pl* chests of drawers) *n* cómoda *f.*

chesty ['tʃestɪ] (*comp* -ier, *superl* -iest) *adj* [cough] de pecho.

chevron ['ʃevrən] *n* [on uniform] galón *m.*

chew [tʃu:] <> *n* [sweet] gominola *f*. <> *vt* - **1.** [food] masticar - **2.** [nails] morderse; [carpet] morder.
◆ **chew over** *vt sep fig* rumiar.
◆ **chew up** *vt sep* [food] masticar; [slippers] mordisquear; [tape] destrozar.

chewing gum ['tʃu:ɪŋ-] *n* chicle *m*, goma *f* de mascar.

chewy [tʃu:ɪ] (*comp* -ier, *superl* -iest) *adj* [meat, pasta] correoso(sa); [toffee, sweets] gomoso(sa).

chic [ʃiːk] ◇ *adj* chic *(inv)*, elegante. ◇ *n* estilo *m*, elegancia *f*.

chicanery [ʃɪˈkeɪnərɪ] *n (U)* supercherías *fpl*, engaños *mpl*.

chick [tʃɪk] *n* - **1.** [baby bird] polluelo *m* - **2.** *inf* [woman] nena *f*.

chicken [ˈtʃɪkɪn] ◇ *adj inf* [cowardly] gallina. ◇ *n* - **1.** [bird] gallina *f*; **it's a chicken and egg situation** es como lo del huevo y la gallina - **2.** [food] pollo *m* - **3.** *inf* [coward] gallina *mf*.

◆ **chicken out** *vi inf*: **to chicken out (of sthg/ of doing sthg)** rajarse (a la hora de algo/de hacer algo).

chickenfeed [ˈtʃɪkɪnfiːd] *n (U) fig* miseria *f*.

chickenpox [ˈtʃɪkɪnpɒks] *n* varicela *f*.

chicken wire *n* tela *f* metálica *(con agujeros hexagonales)*.

chickpea [ˈtʃɪkpiː] *n* garbanzo *m*.

chicory [ˈtʃɪkərɪ] *n* achicoria *f*.

chide [tʃaɪd] *(pt* chided OR chid [tʃɪd], *pp* chid OR chidden [ˈtʃɪdn]) *vt liter:* **to chide sb for** reprender a alguien por.

chief [tʃiːf] ◇ *adj* principal. ◇ *n* jefe *m*, -fa *f*.

chief constable *n UK* ≃ jefe *m* superior de policía.

Chief Executive *n US* [US president] presidente *m*, -ta *f*.

chief executive officer *n US* [head of company] director *m*, -ra *f* general.

◆ **Chief Executive** *n US* [US president] presidente *m*, -ta *f*.

chief justice *n* presidente *m*, -ta *f* del tribunal supremo.

chiefly [ˈtʃiːflɪ] *adv* - **1.** [mainly] principalmente - **2.** [especially, above all] por encima de todo.

chief of staff *n* jefe *m*, -fa *f* del estado mayor.

chief superintendent *n* inspector *m*, -ra *f* jefe.

chieftain [ˈtʃiːftən] *n* jefe *m*, -fa *f*, cacique *m*.

chiffon [ˈʃɪfɒn] *n* gasa *f*.

chihuahua [tʃɪˈwaːwə] *n* chihuahua *mf*.

chilblain [ˈtʃɪlbleɪn] *n* sabañón *m*.

child [tʃaɪld] *(pl* children) *n* - **1.** [boy, girl] niño *m*, -ña *f* - **2.** [son, daughter] hijo *m*, -ta *f*.

childbearing [ˈtʃaɪld,beərɪŋ] *n*: **of childbearing age** en edad de tener hijos.

child benefit *n (U) UK* subsidio pagado a todas las familias por cada hijo.

childbirth [ˈtʃaɪldbɜːθ] *n (U)* parto *m*.

childcare [ˈtʃaɪldkeər] *n* cuidado *m* de los niños.

childhood [ˈtʃaɪldhʊd] *n* infancia *f*, niñez *f*.

childish [ˈtʃaɪldɪʃ] *adj pej* infantil.

childishly [ˈtʃaɪldɪʃlɪ] *adv pej* de manera infantil.

childless [ˈtʃaɪldlɪs] *adj* sin hijos.

childlike [ˈtʃaɪldlaɪk] *adj* [person] como un niño; [smile, trust] de niño.

childminder [ˈtʃaɪld,maɪndər] *n UK* niñera *f (durante el día)*.

child prodigy *n* niño *m*, -ña *f* prodigio.

childproof [ˈtʃaɪldpruːf] *adj* a prueba de niños.

children [ˈtʃɪldrən] *npl* ⊳ **child**.

children's home *n* hogar *m* infantil.

Chile [ˈtʃɪlɪ] *n* Chile.

Chilean [ˈtʃɪlɪən] ◇ *adj* chileno(na). ◇ *n* chileno *m*, -na *f*.

chili [ˈtʃɪlɪ] = **chilli**.

chill [tʃɪl] ◇ *adj* frío(a). ◇ *n* - **1.** [illness] resfriado *m* - **2.** [in temperature]: **there's a chill in the air** hace un poco de fresco - **3.** [feeling of fear] escalofrío *m*. ◇ *vt* - **1.** [drink, food] (dejar) enfriar - **2.** [person - with cold] enfriar; [- with fear] hacer sentir escalofríos. ◇ *vi* - **1.** enfriarse - **2.** *inf* [relax] relajarse.

◆ **chill out** *vi inf* relajarse.

chilli [ˈtʃɪlɪ] *(pl* -ies), **chili** *n* guindilla *f*, chile *m*, ají *m Andes & R Plata*.

chilling [ˈtʃɪlɪŋ] *adj* [frightening] escalofriante.

chilli powder *n* guindilla *f* en polvo.

chilly [ˈtʃɪlɪ] *(comp* -ier, *superl* -iest) *adj* frío(a).

chime [tʃaɪm] ◇ *n* [of clock] campanada *f*; [of bells] repique *m*. ◇ *vt* [time] dar. ◇ *vi* [bell] repicar; [clock] sonar.

chimney [ˈtʃɪmnɪ] *n* chimenea *f*.

chimneypot [ˈtʃɪmnɪpɒt] *n* cañón *m* de chimenea.

chimneysweep [ˈtʃɪmnɪswiːp] *n* deshollinador *m*, -ra *f*.

chimp [tʃɪmp], **chimpanzee** [,tʃɪmpənˈziː] *n* chimpancé *mf*.

chin [tʃɪn] *n* barbilla *f*.

china [ˈtʃaɪnə] ◇ *n* porcelana *f*. ◇ *comp* de porcelana.

China [ˈtʃaɪnə] *n* la China; **the People's Republic of China** la República Popular China.

china clay *n* caolín *m*.

China Sea *n*: **the China Sea** el mar de China.

Chinatown [ˈtʃaɪnətaʊn] *n* barrio *m* chino *(de la comunidad oriental)*.

chinchilla [tʃɪnˈtʃɪlə] *n* chinchilla *f*.

Chinese [,tʃaɪˈniːz] ◇ *adj* chino(na). ◇ *n* - **1.** [person] chino *m*, -na *f* - **2.** [language] chino *m*. ◇ *npl*: **the Chinese** los chinos.

Chinese cabbage *n* (hojas *fpl* de) col *f* china.

Chinese lantern *n* farolillo *m* chino.

Chinese leaves *npl UK* (hojas *fpl* de) col *f* china.

chink [tʃɪŋk] ◇ *n* - **1.** [narrow opening] grieta *f*; [of light] resquicio *m* - **2.** [sound] tintineo *m*. ◇ *vi* tintinear.

chinos ['tʃiːnəʊz] *npl* pantalones *mpl* de algodón.

chintz [tʃɪnts] ◇ *n* zaraza *f*. ◇ *comp* de zaraza.

chinwag ['tʃɪnwæg] *n inf* charla *f*.

chip [tʃɪp] ◇ *n* **- 1.** *UK* [fried potato chip] patata *f* frita; *US* [potato crisp] patata *f* frita *(de bolsa o de churrería)* **- 2.** [fragment - gen] pedacito *m*; [- of wood] viruta *f*; [- of stone] lasca *f* **- 3.** [flaw - in cup, glass] mella *f*, desportilladura *f* **- 4.** COMPUT chip *m* **- 5.** [token] ficha *f* ▸▸▸ **when the chips are down** cuando llega la hora de la verdad; **to have a chip on one's shoulder** estar resentido, tener uno un poco de complejo. ◇ *vt (pt & pp* **-ped**, *cont* **-ping)** [damage] mellar, desportillar.

◆ **chip in** ◇ *vt insep inf* [pay money] poner. ◇ *vi (pt & pp* **-ped**, *cont* **-ping) - 1.** [pay money] poner dinero **- 2.** [in conversation] intervenir.

◆ **chip off** *vt sep* desconchar.

chipboard ['tʃɪpbɔːd] *n* aglomerado *m*.

chipmunk ['tʃɪpmʌŋk] *n* ardilla *f* listada.

chipolata [ˌtʃɪpə'lɑːtə] *n* salchicha *f* pequeña.

chipped ['tʃɪpt] *adj* [flawed] mellado(da), desconchado(da).

chippings ['tʃɪpɪŋz] *npl esp US* [of stone] gravilla *f*; [of wood] virutas *fpl*; **'loose chippings'** 'gravilla suelta'.

chip shop *n UK* tienda en la que se vende pescado y patatas fritas.

chiropodist [kɪ'rɒpədɪst] *n* podólogo *m*, -ga *f*, pedicuro *m*, -ra *f*.

chiropody [kɪ'rɒpədɪ] *n* podología *f*.

chirp [tʃɜːp] *vi* [bird] piar; [insect] chirriar.

chirpy ['tʃɜːpɪ] *(comp* **-ier**, *superl* **-iest) adj esp UK inf* alegre.

chisel ['tʃɪzl] ◇ *n* [for wood] formón *m*, escoplo *m*; [for stone] cincel *m*. ◇ *vt (UK* **-led**, *cont* **-ling**, *US* **-ed**, *cont* **-ing)** [wood] escoplear; [stone] cincelar.

chit [tʃɪt] *n* [note] nota *f*.

chitchat ['tʃɪttʃæt] *n (U) inf* cháchara *f*.

chivalrous ['ʃɪvlrəs] *adj* caballeroso(sa).

chivalry ['ʃɪvlrɪ] *n* **- 1.** *liter* [of knights] caballería *f* **- 2.** [good manners] caballerosidad *f*.

chives [tʃaɪvz] *npl* cebollana *f*, cebollino *m*.

chloride ['klɔːraɪd] *n* cloruro *m*.

chlorinated ['klɔːrɪneɪtɪd] *adj* clorado(da).

chlorine ['klɔːriːn] *n* cloro *m*.

chlorofluorocarbon ['klɔːrəʊˌfluərəʊ'kɑːbən] *n* clorofluorocarbono *m*.

chloroform ['klɒrəfɔːm] *n* cloroformo *m*.

choc-ice ['tʃɒkaɪs] *n UK* bombón *m* helado.

chock [tʃɒk] *n* cuña *f*, calzo *m*.

chock-a-block, chock-full *adj inf*: **chock-a-block (with)** hasta los topes (de).

chocolate ['tʃɒkələt] ◇ *n* **- 1.** [food, drink] chocolate *m* **- 2.** [sweet] bombón *m*. ◇ *comp* de chocolate.

choice [tʃɔɪs] ◇ *n* **- 1.** [gen] elección *f*; **to do sthg by** OR **from choice** elegir hacer algo; **to have no choice but to do sthg** no tener más remedio que hacer algo **- 2.** [person chosen] preferido *m*, -da *f*; [thing chosen] alternativa *f* preferida **- 3.** [variety, selection] surtido *m*. ◇ *adj* de primera calidad.

choir ['kwaɪər] *n* coro *m*.

choirboy ['kwaɪəbɔɪ] *n* niño *m* de coro.

choke [tʃəʊk] ◇ *n* AUT estárter *m*. ◇ *vt* **- 1.** [subj: person] estrangular, ahogar **- 2.** [subj: fumes] asfixiar, ahogar; [subj: fishbone etc] hacer atragantarse **- 3.** [block - pipes, gutter] atascar. ◇ *vi* [on fishbone etc] atragantarse; [to death] asfixiarse.

◆ **choke back** *vt insep* contener, reprimir.

cholera ['kɒlərə] *n* cólera *m*.

cholesterol [kə'lestərɒl] *n* colesterol *m*.

choose [tʃuːz] *(pt* **chose**, *pp* **chosen**) ◇ *vt* **- 1.** [select] elegir, escoger; **there's little** OR **not much to choose between them** no se sabe cuál es mejor **- 2.** [decide]: **to choose to do sthg** decidir hacer algo; **do whatever you choose** haz lo que quieras. ◇ *vi* elegir, escoger.

choos(e)y ['tʃuːzɪ] *(comp* **-ier**, *superl* **-iest) adj* [gen] quisquilloso(sa); [about food] exigente, remilgado(da).

chop [tʃɒp] ◇ *n* **- 1.** CULIN chuleta *f* **- 2.** [blow - with axe] hachazo *m*; [- with hand] golpe *m*, tajo *m*; **I'm for the chop** *fig* mi puesto es uno de los que se van a cargar. ◇ *vt (pt & pp* **-ped**, *cont* **-ping)** **- 1.** [vegetables, meat] picar; [wood] cortar **- 2.** *inf* [funding, budget] recortar. ◇ *vi (pt & pp* **-ped**, *cont* **-ping)**: **to chop and change** cambiar cada dos por tres.

◆ **chops** *npl inf* morros *mpl*, jeta *f*.

◆ **chop down** *vt sep* talar.

◆ **chop up** *vt sep* [vegetables, meat] picar; [wood] cortar.

chopper ['tʃɒpər] *n* **- 1.** [for wood] hacha *f*; [for meat] cuchillo *m* de carnicero **- 2.** *inf* [helicopter] helicóptero *m*.

chopping board ['tʃɒpɪŋ-] *n* tajo *m* OR tabla *f* de cocina.

choppy ['tʃɒpɪ] *(comp* **-ier**, *superl* **-iest) adj* picado(da).

chopsticks ['tʃɒpstɪks] *npl* palillos *mpl*.

choral ['kɔːrəl] *adj* coral.

chord [kɔːd] *n* MUS acorde *m*; **to strike a chord (with)** calar hondo (en).

chore [tʃɔːʳ] *n* - **1.** [task] tarea *f*, faena *f* - **2.** *inf* [boring thing] lata *f*.

choreographer [ˌkɒrɪˈɒɡrəfəʳ] *n* coreógrafo *m*, -fa *f*.

choreography [ˌkɒrɪˈɒɡrəfɪ] *n* coreografía *f*.

chortle [ˈtʃɔːtl] *vi* reírse con satisfacción.

chorus [ˈkɔːrəs] ⟨⟩ *n* - **1.** [part of song, refrain] estribillo *m* - **2.** [choir, group of singers or dancers] coro *m*. ⟨⟩ *vt* corear todos a una.

chose [tʃəʊz] *pt* ⤳ choose.

chosen [ˈtʃəʊzn] *pp* ⤳ choose.

choux pastry [ʃuː-] *n* pasta *f* brisa.

chow [tʃaʊ] *n inf* [food] manduca *f*.

chowder [ˈtʃaʊdəʳ] *n sopa espesa de pescado o mariscos.*

Christ [kraɪst] ⟨⟩ *n* Cristo *m*. ⟨⟩ *excl* ¡vaya por Dios!

christen [ˈkrɪsn] *vt* bautizar.

christening [ˈkrɪsnɪŋ] ⟨⟩ *n* bautizo *m*. ⟨⟩ *comp* de bautizo.

Christian [ˈkrɪstʃən] ⟨⟩ *adj* cristiano(na). ⟨⟩ *n* cristiano *m*, -na *f*.

Christianity [ˌkrɪstɪˈænətɪ] *n* cristianismo *m*.

Christian name *n* nombre *m* de pila.

Christmas [ˈkrɪsməs] ⟨⟩ *n* Navidad *f*; **happy** OR **merry Christmas!** ¡Feliz Navidad! ⟨⟩ *comp* navideño(ña).

Christmas cake *n UK pastel de Navidad con frutas cubierto de mazapán y glaseado por encima.*

Christmas card *n* crismas *m inv*, christmas *m inv*.

Christmas carol *n* villancico *m*.

Christmas cracker *n UK cilindro de papel que produce un estallido al abrirlo y que tiene dentro un regalito de Navidad.*

Christmas Day *n* día *m* de Navidad.

Christmas Eve *n* Nochebuena *f*.

Christmas pudding *n UK pudín de frutas que se come caliente el día de Navidad.*

Christmas stocking *n* calcetín largo en el que se meten regalos por Nochebuena.

Christmastime [ˈkrɪsməstaɪm] *n* (U) Navidad *f*, Navidades *fpl*.

Christmas tree *n* árbol *m* de Navidad.

chrome [krəʊm], **chromium** [ˈkrəʊmɪəm] ⟨⟩ *n* cromo *m*. ⟨⟩ *comp* cromado(da).

chromosome [ˈkrəʊməsəʊm] *n* cromosoma *m*.

chronic [ˈkrɒnɪk] *adj* - **1.** [illness, unemployment] crónico(ca) - **2.** [liar, alcoholic] empedernido(da).

chronically [ˈkrɒnɪklɪ] *adv* crónicamente.

chronicle [ˈkrɒnɪkl] ⟨⟩ *n* crónica *f*. ⟨⟩ *vt* narrar cronológicamente.

chronological [ˌkrɒnəˈlɒdʒɪkl] *adj* cronológico(ca).

chronologically [ˌkrɒnəˈlɒdʒɪklɪ] *adv* cronológicamente.

chronology [krəˈnɒlədʒɪ] *n* [sequence] cronología *f*.

chrysalis [ˈkrɪsəlɪs] (*pl* **-lises** [-lɪsiːz]) *n* crisálida *f*.

chrysanthemum [krɪˈsænθəməm] (*pl* **-s**) *n* crisantemo *m*.

chubby [ˈtʃʌbɪ] (*comp* **-bier**, *superl* **-biest**) *adj* [person, hands] rechoncho(cha); **to have chubby cheeks** ser mofletudo(da).

chuck [tʃʌk] *vt inf* - **1.** [throw] tirar, arrojar, aventar *Amér*; **to chuck sb out** echar a alguien - **2.** [job, girlfriend] mandar a paseo, dejar.

➤ **chuck away, chuck out** *vt sep inf* tirar.

chuckle [ˈtʃʌkl] ⟨⟩ *n* risita *f*. ⟨⟩ *vi* reírse entre dientes.

chuffed [tʃʌft] *adj UK inf*: **to be chuffed (with sthg/to do sthg)** estar como unas castañuelas (con algo/al hacer algo).

chug [tʃʌɡ] (*pt & pp* **-ged**, *cont* **-ging**) *vi* [train] traquetear; [car] resoplar.

chum [tʃʌm] *n inf* [gen] amiguete *m*, -ta *f*, manito *m Méx*; [at school] compañero *m*, -ra *f*.

chummy [ˈtʃʌmɪ] (*comp* **-mier**, *superl* **-miest**) *adj inf*: **to be chummy (with)** ser muy amiguete(ta) (de).

chump [tʃʌmp] *n inf* tontín *m*, -ina *f*.

chunk [tʃʌŋk] *n* - **1.** [piece] trozo *m* - **2.** *inf* [large amount] tajada *f*.

chunky [ˈtʃʌŋkɪ] (*comp* **-ier**, *superl* **-iest**) *adj* - **1.** [person] cuadrado(da), fornido(da) - **2.** [furniture] macizo(za); [jumper] grueso(sa).

church [tʃɜːtʃ] *n* iglesia *f*; **to go to church** ir a misa.

Church

> La anglicana "Church of England" es la Iglesia oficial de Inglaterra. Su líder laico es el soberano y su cabeza espiritual, el arzobispo de Canterbury. La rama irlandesa de la "Church of England" se llama "Church of Ireland" y la rama escocesa se denomina "Episcopal Church". En Escocia, la "Church of Scotland" es presbiteriana, de tendencia calvinista. Los miembros de su clero se llaman "ministers" y no hay obispos dentro de esta jerarquía. En EE. UU. el estado no es confesional ya que lo prohibe la primera enmienda de su constitución, si bien los telepredicadores ("televangelists") tienen mucha influencia, sobre todo en los estados del sur.

churchgoer [ˈtʃɜːtʃˌɡəʊəʳ] *n* practicante *mf*.

churchman ['tʃɜ:tʃmən] (*pl* -men [-mən]) *n* clérigo *m*.

Church of England *n*: the Church of England la Iglesia Anglicana.

Church of Scotland *n*: the Church of Scotland la Iglesia de Escocia.

churchyard ['tʃɜ:tʃjɑ:d] *n* cementerio *m*, camposanto *m*.

churlish ['tʃɜ:lɪʃ] *adj* descortés, maleducado(da).

churn [tʃɜ:n] <> *n* - **1.** [for making butter] mantequera *f* - **2.** [for transporting milk] lechera *f*. <> *vt* [stir up] agitar. <> *vi*: **my stomach churned** se me revolvió el estómago.

◆ **churn out** *vt sep inf* hacer como churros OR en cantidades industriales.

◆ **churn up** *vt sep* agitar.

chute [ʃu:t] *n* [for water] vertedor *m*, conducto *m*; [slide] tobogán *m*; [for waste] rampa *f*.

chutney ['tʃʌtnɪ] *n salsa agridulce y picante de fruta y semillas.*

CI *abbr of* **Channel Islands**.

CIA (*abbr of* **Central Intelligence Agency**) *n* CIA *f*.

cicada [sɪ'kɑ:də] *n* cigarra *f*.

CID (*abbr of* **Criminal Investigation Department**) *n* UK ≃ Brigada *f* de Policía Judicial.

cider ['saɪdər] *n* - **1.** sidra *f* - **2.** US [non-alcoholic] zumo *m* Esp OR jugo *m* Amér de manzana.

cigar [sɪ'gɑ:r] *n* puro *m*.

cigarette [ˌsɪgə'ret] *n* cigarrillo *m*.

cigarette butt *n* colilla *f*.

cigarette end UK = **cigarette butt**.

cigarette holder *n* boquilla *f*.

cigarette lighter *n* mechero *m*, encendedor *m*.

cigarette paper *n* papel *m* de fumar.

C-in-C *abbr of* **commander-in-chief**.

cinch [sɪntʃ] *n inf*: **it's a cinch** está tirado, es pan comido.

cinder ['sɪndər] *n* ceniza *f*.

cinderblock ['sɪndəblɒk] *n* US *ladrillo grande de cemento y cenizas de coque.*

Cinderella [ˌsɪndə'relə] *n* Cenicienta *f*.

cine-camera ['sɪnɪ-] *n* cámara *f* cinematográfica.

cine-film ['sɪnɪ-] *n* película *f* cinematográfica.

cinema ['sɪnəmə] *n* cine *m*.

cinematic [ˌsɪnɪ'mætɪk] *adj* cinematográfico(ca).

cinnamon ['sɪnəmən] *n* canela *f*.

cipher, cypher ['saɪfər] *n* [secret writing system] código *m*, cifra *f*.

circa ['sɜ:kə] *prep* hacia.

circle ['sɜ:kl] <> *n* - **1.** [gen] círculo *m*; **to come full circle** volver al punto de partida; **to go round in circles** darle (mil) vueltas al mismo tema - **2.** [in theatre] anfiteatro *m*; [in cinema] entresuelo *m*. <> *vt* - **1.** [draw a circle round] rodear con un círculo - **2.** [move round] describir círculos alrededor de. <> *vi* dar vueltas.

circuit ['sɜ:kɪt] *n* - **1.** [gen] circuito *m* - **2.** [of track] vuelta *f*.

circuit board *n* tarjeta *f* de circuito impreso.

circuit breaker *n* cortacircuitos *m inv*.

circuitous [sə'kju:ɪtəs] *adj* tortuoso(sa).

circular ['sɜ:kjʊlər] <> *adj* - **1.** [gen] circular - **2.** [argument, discussion] que no lleva a ninguna parte. <> *n* circular *f*.

circulate ['sɜ:kjʊleɪt] <> *vi* - **1.** [gen] circular - **2.** [socialize] alternar. <> *vt* [rumour, document] hacer circular.

circulation [ˌsɜ:kjʊ'leɪʃn] *n* - **1.** [of blood, money] circulación *f*; **in circulation** en circulación - **2.** [of magazine, newspaper] tirada *f*.

circumcise ['sɜ:kəmsaɪz] *vt* circuncidar.

circumcision [ˌsɜ:kəm'sɪʒn] *n* circuncisión *f*; **female circumcision** circuncisión femenina.

circumference [sə'kʌmfərəns] *n* circunferencia *f*.

circumflex ['sɜ:kəmfleks] *n*: **circumflex (accent)** (acento *m*) circunflejo *m*.

circumnavigate [ˌsɜ:kəm'nævɪgeɪt] *vt* circunnavegar.

circumscribe ['sɜ:kəmskraɪb] *vt fml* circunscribir.

circumspect ['sɜ:kəmspekt] *adj* circunspecto(ta).

circumstance ['sɜ:kəmstəns] *n* circunstancia *f*; **circumstances** circunstancias *fpl*; **under** OR **in no circumstances** bajo ningún concepto; **in** OR **under the circumstances** dadas las circunstancias.

circumstantial [ˌsɜ:kəm'stænʃl] *adj fml*: **circumstantial evidence** pruebas *fpl* indiciarias.

circumvent [ˌsɜ:kəm'vent] *vt fml* burlar, evadir.

circus ['sɜ:kəs] *n* - **1.** [for entertainment] circo *m* - **2.** [in place names] glorieta *f*.

cirrhosis [sɪ'rəʊsɪs] *n* cirrosis *f inv*.

CIS (*abbr of* **Commonwealth of Independent States**) *n* CEI *f*.

cissy ['sɪsɪ] (*pl* -**ies**) *n* UK *inf* - **1.** [cowardly male] cobardica *m* - **2.** [effeminate male] mariquita *m*.

cistern ['sɪstən] *n* - **1.** UK [in roof] depósito *m* de agua - **2.** [in toilet] cisterna *f*.

citation [saɪ'teɪʃn] *n* - **1.** [official praise]: **citation (for)** mención *f* (por) - **2.** [quotation] cita *f*.

cite [saɪt] *vt* citar.

citizen ['sɪtɪzn] *n* ciudadano *m*, -na *f*.

Citizens' Advice Bureau *n oficina britá-nica de información y asistencia al ciuda-dano.*

Citizens' Band *n banda de radio reservada para radioaficionados y conductores.*

citizenship ['sɪtɪznʃɪp] *n* ciudadanía *f.*

citric acid ['sɪtrɪk-] *n* ácido *m* cítrico.

citrus fruit ['sɪtrəs-] *n* cítrico *m.*

city ['sɪtɪ] *(pl* -ies) *n* ciudad *f.*
➤ **City** *n UK*: **the City** la City *(barrio financiero de Londres).*

city centre *n* centro *m* de la ciudad.

city hall *n US* ayuntamiento *m.*

city technology college *n UK centro de formación profesional financiado por la industria.*

civic ['sɪvɪk] *adj* - **1.** [duty, pride] cívico(ca) - **2.** [leader, event] público(ca).

civic centre *n UK zona de la ciudad donde se encuentran los edificios públicos.*

civics ['sɪvɪks] *n (U)* **SCH** educación *f* cívica.

civil ['sɪvl] *adj* - **1.** [involving ordinary citizens] civil - **2.** [polite] cortés, correcto(ta).

civil defence *n* protección *f* civil.

civil disobedience *n* desobediencia *f* civil.

civil engineer *n* ingeniero *m*, -ra *f* civil.

civil engineering *n* ingeniería *f* civil.

civilian [sɪ'vɪljən] *<> n* civil *mf. <> comp* [organization] civil; [clothes] de paisano.

civility [sɪ'vɪlətɪ] *n* urbanidad *f*, cortesía *f.*

civilization [ˌsɪvɪlaɪ'zeɪʃn] *n* civilización *f.*

civilize, -ise ['sɪvɪlaɪz] *vt* civilizar.

civilized ['sɪvɪlaɪzd] *adj* civilizado(da).

civil law *n* derecho *m* civil.

civil liberties *npl* libertades *fpl* civiles.

civil list *n UK presupuesto de la familia real votado cada año en el Parlamento.*

civil rights *npl* derechos *mpl* civiles.

civil servant *n* funcionario *m*, -ria *f* público, -ca *f.*

civil service *n* administración *f* pública.

civil war *n* guerra *f* civil.

CJD *(abbr of* Creutzfeldt-Jakob disease) *n* enfermedad *f* de Creutzfeldt-Jakob.

cl *(abbr of* centilitre) cl.

clad [klæd] *adj liter*: **clad in** vestido(da) de.

cladding ['klædɪŋ] *n UK* revestimiento *m.*

claim [kleɪm] *<> n* - **1.** [for pay, insurance, expenses] reclamación *f*; **pay claim** reivindicación *f* salarial - **2.** [of right] reivindicación *f*, demanda *f*; **to have a claim on sb** tener un derecho sobre alguien; **to lay claim to sthg** reclamar algo - **3.** [assertion] afirmación *f. <> vt* - **1.** [allowance, expenses, lost property] reclamar - **2.** [responsibility, credit] atribuirse - **3.** [main-

tain]: **to claim (that)** mantener que. *<> vi*: **to claim on one's insurance** reclamar al seguro; **to claim for sthg** reclamar algo.

claimant ['kleɪmənt] *n* [to throne] pretendiente *mf*; [of unemployment benefit] solicitante *mf*; **LAW** demandante *mf.*

claim form *n* impreso *m* de solicitud, formulario *m* de solicitud, forma *f* de solicitud *Méx.*

clairvoyant [kleə'vɔɪənt] *<> adj* clarividente. *<> n* clarividente *mf.*

clam [klæm] *n* almeja *f.*
➤ **clam up** *vi (pt & pp* -med, *cont* -ming) *inf* cerrar la boca *OR* el pico.

clamber ['klæmbər] *vi* trepar; **to clamber down a tree** bajar por un árbol.

clammy ['klæmɪ] *(comp* -mier, *superl* -miest) *adj* [hands] húmedo(da), pegajoso(sa); [weather] bochornoso(sa).

clamor *US* = **clamour.**

clamorous ['klæmərəs] *adj* clamoroso(sa).

clamour *UK,* **clamor** *US* ['klæmər] *<> n (U)* - **1.** [noise] clamor *m* - **2.** [demand]: **clamour (for)** demandas *fpl* (de). *<> vi*: **to clamour for sthg** exigir a voces algo.

clamp [klæmp] *<> n* [gen] abrazadera *f*; [for car wheel] cepo *m. <> vt* - **1.** [with clamp] sujetar (con una abrazadera) - **2.** [with wheel clamp] poner un cepo a.
➤ **clamp down** *vi*: **to clamp down on** poner freno a.

clampdown ['klæmpdaun] *n*: **a clampdown on speeding** medidas *fpl* contundentes contra los excesos de velocidad.

clan [klæn] *n* clan *m.*

clandestine [klæn'destɪn] *adj* clandestino(na).

clang [klæŋ] *<> n* ruido *m* metálico. *<> vi* hacer un ruido metálico.

clanger ['klæŋər] *n UK inf* metedura *f* de pata; **to drop a clanger** meter la pata.

clank [klæŋk] *<> n* ruido *m* seco y metálico. *<> vi* hacer un ruido seco y metálico.

clap [klæp] *<> n* - **1.** [on back] palmada *f* - **2.** [sound]: **a clap of thunder** un trueno. *<> vt (pt & pp* -ped, *cont* -ping) - **1.**: **to clap one's hands** dar palmadas - **2.** *inf* [place]: **he clapped the book onto the table** golpeó el libro en la mesa; **to clap eyes on** *inf* ver. *<> vi (pt & pp* -ped, *cont* -ping) aplaudir.

clapboard ['klæpbɔːd] *n US* tablilla *f.*

clapped-out [klæpt-] *adj UK inf* [car] destartalado(da).

clapperboard ['klæpəbɔːd] *n* claqueta *f.*

clapping ['klæpɪŋ] *n (U)* aplausos *mpl.*

claptrap ['klæptræp] *n (U) inf* chorradas *fpl.*

claret ['klærət] *n* burdeos *m inv.*

clarification [ˌklærɪfɪ'keɪʃn] *n* aclaración *f.*

clarify ['klærɪfaɪ] (*pt* & *pp* **-ied**) *vt* aclarar.
clarinet [ˌklærə'net] *n* clarinete *m*.
clarity ['klærətɪ] *n* claridad *f*.
clash [klæʃ] ◇ *n* - **1.** [difference - of interests] conflicto *m*; [- of personalities] choque *m* - **2.** [fight, disagreement]: **clash (with)** conflicto *m* (con) - **3.** [noise] estruendo *m*, estrépito *m*. ◇ *vi* - **1.** [fight, disagree]: **to clash (with)** enfrentarse (con) - **2.** [opinions, policies] estar en desacuerdo - **3.** [date, event]: **to clash (with)** coincidir (con) - **4.** [colour]: **to clash (with)** desentonar (con) - **5.** [cymbals] sonar.
clasp [klɑ:sp] ◇ *n* [on necklace, bracelet] broche *m*; [on belt] cierre *m*, hebilla *f*. ◇ *vt* [person] abrazar; [thing] agarrar.
class [klɑ:s] ◇ *n* - **1.** [gen] clase *f* - **2.** [category] clase *f*, tipo *m*; **to be in a class of one's own** ser incomparable. ◇ *comp* [struggle] de clases. ◇ *vt*: **to class sb (as)** clasificar a alguien (de).
class-conscious *adj pej* clasista.
classic ['klæsɪk] ◇ *adj* [typical] clásico(ca). ◇ *n* clásico *m*.
◆ **classics** *npl* (lenguas *fpl*) clásicas *fpl*.
classical ['klæsɪkl] *adj* clásico(ca).
classical music *n* música *f* clásica.
classification [ˌklæsɪfɪ'keɪʃn] *n* clasificación *f*.
classified ['klæsɪfaɪd] *adj* [secret] reservado(da), secreto(ta).
classified ad *n* anuncio *m* por palabras.
classify ['klæsɪfaɪ] (*pt* & *pp* **-ied**) *vt* clasificar.
classless ['klɑ:slɪs] *adj* sin clases.
classmate ['klɑ:smeɪt] *n* compañero *m*, -ra *f* de clase.
classroom ['klɑ:srom] *n* aula *f*, clase *f*.
classroom assistant *n* SCH ayudante *mf* del profesor.
classy ['klɑ:sɪ] (*comp* **-ier**, *superl* **-iest**) *adj inf* con clase.
clatter ['klætər] ◇ *n* [gen] estrépito *m*; [of pots, pans, dishes] ruido *m* (de cacharros); [of hooves] chacoloteo *m*. ◇ *vi* [hooves] chacolotear; [person, car etc]: **to clatter down/into sthg** armar un gran estrépito al caer por/chocar con algo.
clause [klɔ:z] *n* - **1.** [in legal document] cláusula *f* - **2.** GRAM oración *f*.
claustrophobia [ˌklɔ:strə'fəobjə] *n* claustrofobia *f*.
claustrophobic [ˌklɔ:strə'fəobɪk] *adj* claustrofóbico(ca).
claw [klɔ:] ◇ *n* - **1.** [of animal, bird] garra *f*; [of cat] uña *f* - **2.** [of crab, lobster] pinza *f*. ◇ *vt* arañar. ◇ *vi*: **to claw at sthg** [cat] arañar algo; [person] intentar agarrarse a algo.
◆ **claw back** *vt sep* UK lograr recuperar.
clay [kleɪ] *n* arcilla *f*.

clay pigeon shooting *n* tiro *m* al plato.
clean [kli:n] ◇ *adj* - **1.** [gen] limpio(pia) - **2.** [page] en blanco - **3.** [environmentally-friendly] no contaminante - **4.** [record, reputation] impecable, irreprochable; [driving licence] sin multas; **to come clean about sthg** confesar algo - **5.** [joke] inocente - **6.** [outline] neto(ta), nítido(da). ◇ *adv* totalmente. ◇ *vt* & *vi* limpiar; **to clean one's teeth** limpiarse los dientes. ◇ *n* limpieza *f*; **to give sthg a clean** limpiar algo.
◆ **clean out** *vt sep* - **1.** [clear out] limpiar el interior de - **2.** *inf* [take money from] desplumar - **3.** *inf* [take everything from]: **the burglars cleaned us out** (los ladrones) nos limpiaron la casa.
◆ **clean up** ◇ *vt sep* [clear up] ordenar, limpiar; **to clean o.s. up** asearse. ◇ *vi inf* [win money, prizes] arrasar.
cleaner ['kli:nər] *n* - **1.** [person] limpiador *m*, -ra *f* - **2.** [substance] producto *m* de limpieza - **3.** [shop]: **cleaner's** tintorería *f*.
cleaning ['kli:nɪŋ] *n* limpieza *f*.
cleaning lady *n* mujer *f* OR señora *f* de la limpieza.
cleanliness ['klenlɪnɪs] *n* limpieza *f*.
cleanly ['kli:nlɪ] *adv* limpiamente.
cleanness ['kli:nnɪs] *n* limpieza *f*.
cleanse [klenz] *vt* [gen] limpiar; [soul] purificar; **to cleanse sthg/sb of sthg** limpiar algo/a alguien de algo.
cleanser ['klenzər] *n* crema *f* OR loción *f* limpiadora.
clean-shaven [-'ʃeɪvn] *adj* [never growing a beard] barbilampiño(ña); [recently shaved] bien afeitado(da).
cleanup ['kli:nʌp] *n* limpieza *f*.
clear [klɪər] ◇ *adj* - **1.** [gen] claro(ra); [day, road, view] despejado(da); **to make sthg clear (to)** dejar algo claro (a); **it's clear that...** está claro que...; **are you clear about it?** ¿lo entiendes?; **to make o.s. clear** explicarse con claridad - **2.** [transparent] transparente - **3.** [well-defined] [sound, picture] nítido(da) - **4.** [free of blemishes - skin] terso(sa) - **5.** [free - time] libre - **6.** [not touching]: **to be clear of the ground** no tocar el suelo - **7.** [conscience] tranquilo(la), limpio(pia) - **8.** [complete - day, week] entero(ra); [- profit] limpio(pia), neto(ta). ◇ *adv* [out of the way]: **stand clear!** ¡aléjense!; **to jump/step clear** saltar/dar un paso para hacerse a un lado. ◇ *n*: **in the clear** [out of danger] fuera de peligro; [free from suspicion] fuera de (toda) sospecha. ◇ *vt* - **1.** [remove objects, obstacles from] despejar; [forest] talar; [pipe] desatascar; **they cleared the area of mines** limpiaron el área de minas; **to clear a**

space hacer sitio; **to clear the table** quitar la mesa; **to clear one's throat** aclararse la garganta - **2.** [remove] quitar - **3.** [jump] saltar - **4.** [pay] liquidar - **5.** [authorize] aprobar - **6.** [prove not guilty] declarar inocente; **to be cleared of sthg** salir absuelto de algo - **7.** [cheque] conformar, dar por bueno - **8.** [not touch]: **it must clear the ground** no debe tocar el suelo. ◇ *vi* despejarse.

◆ **clear away** *vt sep* poner en su sitio.
◆ **clear off** *vi UK inf* largarse.
◆ **clear out** ◇ *vt sep* limpiar a fondo. ◇ *vi inf* largarse.
◆ **clear up** ◇ *vt sep* - **1.** [room, mess] limpiar; [toys, books] recoger - **2.** [disagreement] aclarar; [mystery] resolver. ◇ *vi* - **1.** [weather] despejarse; [infection] desaparecer - **2.** [tidy up] ordenar, recoger.

clearance ['klɪərəns] *n* - **1.** [removal - of rubbish, litter] despeje *m*, limpieza *f*; [of slums, houses] eliminación *f* - **2.** [permission] autorización *f*, permiso *m* - **3.** [free space] distancia *f* libre.

clearance sale *n* (venta *f* de) liquidación *f*.

clear-cut *adj* [issue, plan] bien definido(da); [division] nítido(da).

clear-headed [-'hedɪd] *adj* lúcido(da).

clearing ['klɪərɪŋ] *n* claro *m*.

clearing bank *n UK* banco *m* de compensación.

clearing house *n* - **1.** [bank] cámara *f* de compensación - **2.** [organization] centro *m* de intercambio de información.

clearing up *n* limpieza *f*.

clearly ['klɪəlɪ] *adv* - **1.** [gen] claramente - **2.** [plainly] obviamente.

clearout ['klɪəraʊt] *n esp UK inf* limpieza *f*; **to have a clearout** ordenar y tirar lo que no sirva.

clear-sighted [-'saɪtɪd] *adj* perspicaz.

clearway ['klɪəweɪ] *n UK carretera donde no se puede parar.*

cleavage ['kli:vɪdʒ] *n* [between breasts] escote *m*.

cleaver ['kli:vər] *n* cuchillo *m* OR cuchilla *f* de carnicero.

clef [klef] *n* clave *f*.

cleft [kleft] *n* grieta *f*.

cleft palate *n* fisura *f* de paladar.

clematis ['klemətɪs] *n* clemátide *f*.

clemency ['klemənsɪ] *n fml* [mercy] clemencia *f*.

clementine ['kleməntaɪn] *n* clementina *f*.

clench [klentʃ] *vt* apretar.

clergy ['klɜ:dʒɪ] *npl*: **the clergy** el clero.

clergyman ['klɜ:dʒɪmən] (*pl* **-men** [-mən]) *n* clérigo *m*.

cleric ['klerɪk] *n* clérigo *m*.

clerical ['klerɪkl] *adj* - **1.** [work] de oficina; [worker] administrativo(va) - **2.** [in church] clerical.

clerk [*UK* klɑːk, *US* klɜːrk] *n* - **1.** [in office] oficinista *mf* - **2.** [in court] secretario *m*, escribano *m* - **3.** *US* [shop assistant] dependiente *m*, -ta *f*.

clever ['klevər] *adj* - **1.** [intelligent] listo(ta), inteligente - **2.** [idea, invention] ingenioso(sa); [with hands] hábil.

cleverly ['klevəlɪ] *adv* - **1.** [intelligently] inteligentemente - **2.** [skilfully] ingeniosamente.

cleverness ['klevənɪs] *n* [intelligence] inteligencia *f*.

cliché ['kli:ʃeɪ] *n* cliché *m*.

click [klɪk] ◇ *n* [of tongue, fingers] chasquido *m*; [of camera, door & COMPUT] clic *m*. ◇ *vt* [fingers, tongue] chasquear. ◇ *vi* - **1.** [heels] sonar con un taconazo; [camera] dar un chasquido, hacer clic - **2.** *inf* [fall into place]: **suddenly, it clicked** de pronto, caí en la cuenta - **3.** COMPUT hacer clic; **to click on sthg** hacer clic en algo.

client ['klaɪənt] *n* cliente *m*, -ta *f*.

clientele [,kli:ən'tel] *n* clientela *f*.

cliff [klɪf] *n* [on coast] acantilado *m*; [inland] precipicio *m*.

cliffhanger ['klɪf,hæŋər] *n* [film, story] historia *f* de suspense.

climactic [klaɪ'mæktɪk] *adj* culminante.

climate ['klaɪmɪt] *n* [weather] clima *m*; *fig* [atmosphere] ambiente *m*.

climatic [klaɪ'mætɪk] *adj* climático(ca).

climax ['klaɪmæks] *n* [culmination] clímax *m*, culminación *f*.

climb [klaɪm] ◇ *n* [gen] subida *f*; [up mountain] escalada *f*. ◇ *vt* [stairs, ladder] subir; [tree] trepar a; [mountain] escalar. ◇ *vi* - **1.** [to climb over sthg** trepar por algo; **to climb into sthg** meterse en algo - **2.** [plant] trepar; [road, plane] subir - **3.** [increase] subir.

◆ **climb down** *vi* apearse del burro.

climb-down *n* vuelta *f* atrás.

climber ['klaɪmər] *n* - **1.** [mountaineer] alpinista *mf*, andinista *mf Amér*; [rock climber] escalador *m*, -ra *f* - **2.** [plant] enredadera *f*.

climbing ['klaɪmɪŋ] *n* montañismo *m*, alpinismo *m*, andinismo *m Amér*.

climbing frame *n UK barras de metal para que trepen los niños.*

climes [klaɪmz] *npl liter* parajes *mpl*.

clinch [klɪntʃ] *vt* [deal] cerrar.

cling [klɪŋ] (*pt & pp* **clung**) *vi* - **1.** [hold tightly]: **to cling (to)** agarrarse (a) - **2.** [clothes, person]: **to cling (to)** pegarse (a) - **3.** [to ideas, principles]: **to cling to** aferrarse a.

clingfilm ['klɪŋfɪlm] *n UK* film *m* de plástico adherente.

clinging ['klɪŋɪŋ] *adj* - **1.** [person, child] pegajoso(sa) - **2.** [clothes] ajustado(da), ceñido(da).

clinic ['klɪnɪk] *n* clínica *f*.

clinical ['klɪnɪkl] *adj* - **1.** MED clínico(ca) - **2.** [cold] frío(a).

clinically ['klɪnɪklɪ] *adv* - **1.** MED clínicamente - **2.** [coldly] fríamente.

clink [klɪŋk] ⟨> *n* tintineo *m*. ⟨> *vi* tintinear.

clip [klɪp] (*pt* & *pp* -**ped**, *cont* -**ping**) ⟨> *n* - **1.** [for paper] clip *m*; [for hair] horquilla *f*; [on earring] cierre *m* - **2.** [of film] fragmento *m*, secuencias *fpl* - **3.** [cut]: **to give sb's hair a clip** cortarle el pelo a alguien. ⟨> *vt* - **1.** [fasten] sujetar - **2.** [cut - lawn, newspaper cutting] recortar; [punch - tickets] picar - **3.** *inf* [hit] dar un golpecito en.

clipboard ['klɪpbɔːd] *n* - **1.** [for writing] tabloncillo *m* con pinza sujetapapeles - **2.** COMPUT portapapeles *m inv*.

clip-on *adj* [gen] de enganche; [earrings] de clip.

clipped [klɪpt] *adj* [staccato] entrecortado(da).

clippers ['klɪpəz] *npl* [for nails] cortaúñas *m inv*; [for hair] maquinilla *f* para cortar el pelo; [for hedges, grass] tijeras *fpl* de podar.

clipping ['klɪpɪŋ] *n* - **1.** [from newspaper] recorte *m* - **2.** [of nails] pedazo *m*.

clique [kliːk] *n pej* camarilla *f*.

cloak [kləʊk] ⟨> *n* - **1.** [garment] capa *f* - **2.** [of secrecy] manto *m*. ⟨> *vt*: **to be cloaked in** estar rodeado(da) de.

cloak-and-dagger *adj* de intriga.

cloakroom ['kləʊkrʊm] *n* - **1.** [for clothes] guardarropa *m* - **2.** *UK* [toilets] servicios *mpl*.

clobber ['klɒbə'] *inf* ⟨> *n (U) UK* - **1.** [things] bártulos *mpl*, trastos *mpl* - **2.** [clothes] indumentaria *f*, trapos *mpl*. ⟨> *vt* atizar.

clock [klɒk] *n* - **1.** [timepiece] reloj *m*; **round the clock** día y noche, las 24 horas; **to put the clock back** *liter* atrasar el reloj OR la hora; *fig* retroceder en el tiempo; **to put the clock forward** adelantar el reloj OR la hora - **2.** [mileometer] cuentakilómetros *m inv*.

● **clock in, clock on** *vi UK* fichar (a la entrada).

● **clock off, clock out** *vi UK* fichar (a la salida).

● **clock up** *vt insep* [miles etc] recorrer.

clockwise ['klɒkwaɪz] *adj* & *adv* en el sentido de las agujas del reloj.

clockwork ['klɒkwɜːk] ⟨> *n*: **to go like clockwork** ir sobre ruedas. ⟨> *comp* de cuerda.

clod [klɒd] *n* terrón *m*.

clog [klɒg] *vt* (*pt* & *pp* -**ged**, *cont* -**ging**) atascar, obstruir.

● **clogs** *npl* zuecos *mpl*.

● **clog up** ⟨> *vt sep* [drain, pipe] atascar; [eyes, nose] congestionar. ⟨> *vi* atascarse.

clogged [klɒgd] *adj* [drains, roads] atascado(da); [pores] obstruido(da).

cloister ['klɔɪstə'] *n* claustro *m*.

clone [kləʊn] ⟨> *n* [gen & COMPUT] clon *m*. ⟨> *vt* clonar.

cloning ['kləʊnɪŋ] *n* clonación *f*.

close¹ [kləʊs] ⟨> *adj* - **1.** [near] cercano(na); **close to** cerca de; **close to tears/laughter** a punto de llorar/reír; **close up, close to** de cerca; **close by, close at hand** muy cerca; **we arrived on time, but it was a close shave** OR **thing** llegamos a tiempo, pero por los pelos - **2.** [relationship, friend] íntimo(ma); **to be close to sb** estar muy unido(da) a alguien - **3.** [relative, family] cercano(na), próximo(ma); [resemblance]: **to bear a close resemblance to sb** parecerse mucho a alguien; [link, tie, cooperation] estrecho(cha) - **4.** [questioning] minucioso(sa); [examination] detallado(da); [look] de cerca; **to keep a close watch on** vigilar de cerca - **5.** [room, air] cargado(da); [weather] bochornoso(sa) - **6.** [contest, race] reñido(da); [result] apretado(da). ⟨> *adv* cerca; **close to** cerca de. ⟨> *n* [in street names] callejón *m*.

● **close on, close to** *prep* [almost] cerca de.

close² [kləʊz] ⟨> *vt* - **1.** [gen] cerrar - **2.** [meeting, conference] clausurar; [discussion, speech] acabar, terminar - **3.** [gap] reducir - **4.** COMPUT [window, application] cerrar. ⟨> *vi* - **1.** [gen] cerrarse - **2.** [shop] cerrar - **3.** [meeting, film, day] terminar. ⟨> *n* final *m*; **to bring sthg to a close** dar por terminado algo; **to draw to a close** tocar a su fin.

● **close down** ⟨> *vt sep* cerrar (definitivamente). ⟨> *vi* [factory etc] cerrarse (definitivamente).

● **close in** *vi* acercarse; **to close in on sthg/sb** rodear OR cercar algo/a alguien.

● **close off** *vt insep* [road] cortar; [room] cerrar.

close-cropped [ˌkləʊs-] *adj* al rape.

closed [kləʊzd] *adj* cerrado(da).

closed circuit television *n* televisión *f* por circuito cerrado.

closedown ['kləʊzdaʊn] *n* cierre *m*.

closed shop *n* empresa donde sólo se contrata a afiliados de un determinado sindicato.

close-fitting [ˌkləʊs-] *adj* ajustado(da), ceñido(da).

close-knit [ˌkləʊs-] *adj* muy unido(da).

closely ['kləʊslɪ] *adv* - **1.** [of connection, relation etc] estrechamente; **to be closely involved in sthg** estar muy metido en algo; [resemble] mucho - **2.** [carefully] atentamente.

closeness ['kləʊsnɪs] *n* - **1.** [nearness] proximidad *f* - **2.** [intimacy] intimidad *f*.

closeout ['kləʊzaʊt] *n US* liquidación *f*.

close quarters [ˌkləʊs-] *npl*: **at close quarters** de cerca.

close season [ˈkləʊs-] *n UK* (temporada *f* de) veda *f*.

closet [ˈklɒzɪt] ⬦ *adj inf* en secreto. ⬦ *n US* armario *m*

▸▸ **to come out of the closet** salir del armario. ⬦ *vt*: **to be closeted with** estar encerrado(da) con.

close-up [ˈkləʊs-] *n* primer plano *m*.

closing [ˈkləʊzɪŋ] *adj* final, último(ma).

closing price *n* precio *m* OR cotización *f* de cierre.

closing time *n* hora *f* de cierre.

closure [ˈkləʊʒəʳ] *n* cierre *m*.

clot [klɒt] ⬦ *n* - **1.** [in blood] coágulo *m* - **2.** *UK inf* [fool] bobo *m*, -ba *f*. ⬦ *vi* (*pt & pp* -**ted**, *cont* -**ting**) [blood] coagularse.

cloth [klɒθ] *n* - **1.** *(U)* [fabric] tela *f* - **2.** [piece of cloth] trapo *m*.

clothe [kləʊð] *vt fml* vestir; **clothed in** vestido(da) de.

clothes [kləʊðz] *npl* ropa *f*; **to put one's clothes on** ponerse la ropa, vestirse; **to take one's clothes off** quitarse la ropa, desvestirse.

clothes basket *n* cesta *f* de la ropa sucia.

clothes brush *n* cepillo *m* para la ropa.

clotheshorse [ˈkləʊðzhɔːs] *n* tendedero *m* (plegable).

clothesline [ˈkləʊðzlaɪn] *n* cuerda *f* para tender la ropa.

clothes peg *UK,* **clothespin** *US* [ˈkləʊðzpɪn] *n* pinza *f* (para la ropa).

clothing [ˈkləʊðɪŋ] *n* ropa *f*.

clotted cream [ˌklɒtɪd-] *n* nata muy espesa típica de Cornualles.

cloud [klaʊd] ⬦ *n* nube *f*; **to be under a cloud** ser mirado con malos ojos; **every cloud has a silver lining** no hay mal que por bien no venga. ⬦ *vt* - **1.** [mirror, window] empañar - **2.** [memory, happiness] oscurecer - **3.** [mind] obnubilar; [issue] complicar.

▸▸ **cloud over** *vi lit & fig* nublarse.

cloudburst [ˈklaʊdbɜːst] *n* chaparrón *m*.

cloudless [ˈklaʊdlɪs] *adj* despejado(da), sin nubes.

cloudy [ˈklaʊdɪ] (*comp* -**ier**, *superl* -**iest**) *adj* - **1.** [overcast] nublado(da) - **2.** [murky] turbio(bia) - **3.** [confused - idea etc] vago(ga), impreciso(sa).

clout [klaʊt] *inf* ⬦ *n* - **1.** [blow] bofetón *m*, tortazo *m* - **2.** *(U)* [influence] influencia *f*. ⬦ *vt* dar un tortazo a.

clove [kləʊv] *n*: **a clove of garlic** un diente de ajo.

cloves *npl* [spice] clavos *mpl*.

clover [ˈkləʊvəʳ] *n* trébol *m*.

cloverleaf [ˈkləʊvəliːf] (*pl* -**leaves** [-liːvz]) *n* [plant] hoja *f* de trébol.

clown [klaʊn] *n* - **1.** [performer] payaso *m* - **2.** [fool] payaso *m*, -sa *f*.

▸▸ **clown around** *vi* hacer payasadas.

cloying [ˈklɔɪɪŋ] *adj* empalagoso(sa).

club [klʌb] ⬦ *n* - **1.** [organization, place] club *m* - **2.** [nightclub] discoteca *f* - **3.** [weapon] porra *f*, garrote *m* - **4.**: (golf) **club** palo *m* de golf. ⬦ *comp* del club. ⬦ *vt* (*pt & pp* -**bed**, *cont* -**bing**) apalear, aporrear.

▸▸ **clubs** *npl* [cards] tréboles *mpl*.

▸▸ **club together** *vi UK* recolectar dinero.

club car *n US* RAIL vagón *m* OR coche *m* club.

clubhouse [ˈklʌbhaʊs, *pl* [-haʊzɪz]) *n* [for golfers] (edificio *m* del) club *m*.

cluck [klʌk] *vi* - **1.** [hen] cloquear - **2.** [person] chasquear la lengua.

clue [kluː] *n* - **1.** [in crime] pista *f*; **not to have a clue (about)** no tener ni idea (de) - **2.** [explanation] clave *f* - **3.** [in crossword] pregunta *f*, clave *f*.

clued-up [kluːd-] *adj UK inf* bien informado(da), al tanto.

clueless [ˈkluːlɪs] *adj UK inf*: **to be clueless (about)** no tener ni idea (de).

clump [klʌmp] ⬦ *n* - **1.** [of bushes] mata *f*; [of trees, flowers] grupo *m* - **2.** [sound] ruido *m* de pisadas. ⬦ *vi*: **to clump about** andar pesadamente.

clumsily [ˈklʌmzɪlɪ] *adv* - **1.** [ungracefully] torpemente - **2.** [awkwardly, unskillfully] toscamente, rudimentariamente - **3.** [tactlessly] torpemente, sin tacto.

clumsy [ˈklʌmzɪ] (*comp* -**ier**, *superl* -**iest**) *adj* - **1.** [ungraceful] torpe - **2.** [unwieldy] difícil de manejar - **3.** [tactless] torpe, sin tacto.

clung [klʌŋ] *pt & pt* ▷ **cling**.

cluster [ˈklʌstəʳ] ⬦ *n* [group] grupo *m*; [of grapes] racimo *m*. ⬦ *vi* agruparse.

clutch [klʌtʃ] ⬦ *n* AUT embrague *m*. ⬦ *vt* [hand] estrechar; [arm, baby] agarrar. ⬦ *vi*: **to clutch at sthg** tratar de agarrarse a algo.

▸▸ **clutches** *npl*: **in the clutch of** en las garras de.

clutch bag *n* bolso *m* de mano *(sin asas)*.

clutter [ˈklʌtəʳ] ⬦ *n* desorden *m*. ⬦ *vt* cubrir desordenadamente.

cm (*abbr of* centimetre) cm.

CND (*abbr of* Campaign for Nuclear Disarmament) *n* organización británica contra el armamento nuclear.

CNG (*abbr of* compressed natural gas) *n* GNC *m*, gas *m* natural comprimido.

co- [kəʊ] *prefix* co-.

c/o (*abbr of* care of) c/d.

Co. - 1. (*abbr of* Company) Cía. **- 2.** *abbr of* County.

CO ⬦ *n* (*abbr of* commanding officer), *rango militar*, ≃ Cte. *mf* ⬦ *abbr of* Colorado.

coach [kəʊtʃ] ⬦ *n* **- 1.** [bus] autocar *m* **- 2.** RAIL vagón *m* **- 3.** [horsedrawn] carruaje *m* **- 4.** SPORT entrenador *m*, -ra *f* **- 5.** [tutor] profesor *m*, -ra *f* particular **- 6.: coach (class)** US clase *f* turista. ⬦ *vt* **- 1.** SPORT entrenar **- 2.** [tutor] dar clases particulares a.

coaching [ˈkəʊtʃɪŋ] *n* (*U*) **- 1.** SPORT entrenamiento *m* **- 2.** [tutoring] clases *fpl* particulares.

coach trip *n* UK excursión *f* en autocar.

coagulate [kəʊˈægjʊleɪt] *vi* coagularse.

coal [kəʊl] *n* carbón *m*.

coalesce [ˌkəʊəˈles] *vi fml* fundirse.

coalface [ˈkəʊlfeɪs] *n* frente *m* de una mina de carbón.

coalfield [ˈkəʊlfiːld] *n* yacimiento *m* de carbón.

coalition [ˌkəʊəˈlɪʃn] *n* coalición *f*.

coalman [ˈkəʊlmæn] (*pl* -men [-men]) *n* UK carbonero *m*.

coalmine [ˈkəʊlmaɪn] *n* mina *f* de carbón.

coalminer [ˈkəʊlˌmaɪnər] *n* minero *m* (de carbón).

coalmining [ˈkəʊlˌmaɪnɪŋ] *n* minería *f* del carbón.

coarse [kɔːs] *adj* **- 1.** [skin, hair, sandpaper] áspero(ra); [fabric] basto(ta) **- 2.** [person, joke] ordinario(ria), guarango(ga) *Chile & R Plata*.

coarse fishing *n* UK pesca de río exceptuando a los salmónidos.

coarsen [ˈkɔːsn] ⬦ *vt* **- 1.** [person, manners] embrutecer **- 2.** [make rough] curtir. ⬦ *vi* **- 1.** [become vulgar] embrutecerse **- 2.** [become rough] curtirse.

coast [kəʊst] ⬦ *n* costa *f*. ⬦ *vi* **- 1.** [in car] ir en punto muerto **- 2.** [progress easily]: **they coasted into the semifinals** se metieron en las semifinales sin ningún esfuerzo.

coastal [ˈkəʊstl] *adj* costero(ra).

coaster [ˈkəʊstər] *n* [small mat] posavasos *m inv*.

coastguard [ˈkəʊstɡɑːd] *n* **- 1.** [person] guardacostas *mf inv* **- 2.** [organization]: **the coastguard** los guardacostas (*pl*).

coastline [ˈkəʊstlaɪn] *n* litoral *m*.

coat [kəʊt] ⬦ *n* **- 1.** [overcoat] abrigo *m*, sobretodo *m R Plata*; [for women] tapado *m R Plata*; [jacket] chaqueta *f* **- 2.** [of animal] pelo *m*, pelaje *m* **- 3.** [layer] capa *f*. ⬦ *vt*: **to coat sthg (with)** cubrir algo (de).

coat hanger *n* percha *f*, gancho *m Amér C, Andes & Méx*.

coating [ˈkəʊtɪŋ] *n* [of dust etc] capa *f*; [of chocolate, silver] baño *m*.

coat of arms (*pl* coats of arms) *n* escudo *m* de armas.

coauthor [kəʊˈɔːθər] *n* coautor *m*, -ra *f*.

coax [kəʊks] *vt*: **to coax sb (to do** OR **into doing sthg)** engatusar a alguien (para que haga algo).

coaxial cable [kəʊˈæksɪəl-] *n* COMPUT cable *m* coaxial.

cob [kɒb] ⬢ corn.

cobalt [ˈkəʊbɔːlt] *n* **- 1.** CHEM cobalto *m* **- 2.** [colour] azul *m* cobalto.

cobble [ˈkɒbl] ⬤ cobble together *vt sep* pergeñar (de cualquier manera).

cobbled [ˈkɒbld] *adj* adoquinado(da).

cobbler [ˈkɒblər] *n* zapatero (remendón) *m*, zapatera (remendona) *f*.

cobbles [ˈkɒblz], **cobblestones** [ˈkɒblstəʊnz] *npl* adoquines *mpl*.

Cobol [ˈkəʊbɒl] (*abbr of* Common Business Orientated Language) *n* COMPUT Cobol *m*.

cobra [ˈkəʊbrə] *n* cobra *f*.

cobweb [ˈkɒbweb] *n* telaraña *f* (*abandonada*).

Coca-Cola® [ˌkəʊkəˈkəʊlə] *n* Coca-Cola® *f*.

cocaine [kəʊˈkeɪn] *n* cocaína *f*.

cock [kɒk] ⬦ *n* **- 1.** [male chicken] gallo *m* **- 2.** [male bird] macho *m* **- 3.** *vulg* [penis] polla *f*. ⬦ *vt* **- 1.** [gun] montar, amartillar **- 2.** [head] ladear. ⬤ **cock up** *vt sep* UK *v inf* jorobar, fastidiar.

cock-a-hoop *adj inf* [delighted]: **to be cock-a-hoop** estar como unas castañuelas.

cockatoo [ˌkɒkəˈtuː] (*pl* -s) *n* cacatúa *f*.

cockerel [ˈkɒkrəl] *n* gallo *m* joven.

cocker spaniel [ˌkɒkə-] *n* cocker *m*.

cockeyed [ˈkɒkaɪd] *adj inf* **- 1.** [lopsided] torcido(da) **- 2.** [foolish] disparatado(da).

cockfight [ˈkɒkfaɪt] *n* pelea *f* de gallos.

cockle [ˈkɒkl] *n* berberecho *m*.

Cockney [ˈkɒknɪ] (*pl* Cockneys) ⬦ *n* **- 1.** [person] *persona procedente del este de Londres* **- 2.** [dialect, accent] *dialecto del este de Londres*. ⬦ *comp del este de Londres*.

cockpit [ˈkɒkpɪt] *n* [in civil aviation] cabina *f*; MIL carlinga *f*.

cockroach [ˈkɒkrəʊtʃ] *n* cucaracha *f*.

cocksure [ˌkɒkˈʃʊər] *adj* presuntuoso(sa).

cocktail [ˈkɒkteɪl] *n* cóctel *m*.

cocktail dress *n* vestido *m* de fiesta.

cocktail shaker [-ˌʃeɪkər] *n* coctelera *f*.

cocktail stick *n* palillo *m*.

cock-up *n v inf* pifia *f*.

cocky [ˈkɒkɪ] (*comp* -ier, *superl* -iest) *adj inf* chulo(la).

cocoa [ˈkəʊkəʊ] n - **1.** [powder] cacao m - **2.** [drink] chocolate m.

coconut [ˈkəʊkənʌt] n coco m.

cocoon [kəˈkuːn] ⟨⟩ n - **1.** ZOOL capullo m - **2.** fig [protective environment]: **to live in a cocoon** vivir entre algodones. ⟨⟩ vt fig arropar.

cod [kɒd] (pl **cod** OR **-s**) n bacalao m.

COD (abbr of **cash on delivery**) entrega contra reembolso.

code [kəʊd] ⟨⟩ n - **1.** [gen] código m - **2.** [for telephone] prefijo m. ⟨⟩ vt - **1.** [encode] codificar, cifrar - **2.** [give identifier to] clasificar.

coded [ˈkəʊdɪd] adj codificado(da).

codeine [ˈkəʊdiːn] n codeína f.

code name n nombre m en clave.

code of practice n código m (de ética) profesional.

cod-liver oil n aceite m de hígado de bacalao.

codswallop [ˈkɒdzˌwɒləp] n (U) UK inf bobadas fpl.

coed [ˌkəʊˈed] ⟨⟩ adj (abbr of **coeducational**) mixto(ta). ⟨⟩ n - **1.** US (abbr of **coeducational student**), estudiante de un colegio mixto - **2.** UK (abbr of **coeducational school**), colegio mixto.

coeducational [ˌkəʊedjuːˈkeɪʃənl] adj mixto(ta).

coefficient [ˌkəʊɪˈfɪʃnt] n coeficiente m.

coerce [kəʊˈɜːs] vt: **to coerce sb (into doing sthg)** coaccionar a alguien (para que haga algo).

coercion [kəʊˈɜːʃn] n coacción f.

coexist [ˌkəʊɪgˈzɪst] vi coexistir.

coexistence [ˌkəʊɪgˈzɪstəns] n coexistencia f.

C of E (abbr of **Church of England**) n UK iglesia anglicana; **she's C of E** es anglicana.

coffee [ˈkɒfɪ] n café m.

coffee bar n UK cafetería f.

coffee break n descanso m para el café.

coffee cup n taza f de café.

coffee mill n molinillo m de café.

coffee morning n UK reunión matinal, generalmente benéfica, en la que se sirve café.

coffeepot [ˈkɒfɪpɒt] n cafetera f (para servir).

coffee shop n - **1.** UK [shop] cafetería f - **2.** US [restaurant] café m.

coffee table n mesita f baja (de salón).

coffee-table book n libro grande con fotografías o ilustraciones que se coloca a la vista, generalmente sobre la mesita del salón.

coffers [ˈkɒfəz] npl arcas fpl.

coffin [ˈkɒfɪn] n ataúd m.

cog [kɒg] n [tooth on wheel] diente m; [wheel] rueda f dentada; **a cog in the machine** una pieza insignificante del engranaje.

cogent [ˈkəʊdʒənt] adj contundente, convincente.

cogitate [ˈkɒdʒɪteɪt] vi fml meditar.

cognac [ˈkɒnjæk] n coñac m.

cognitive [ˈkɒgnɪtɪv] adj cognitivo(va), cognoscitivo(va).

cogwheel [ˈkɒgwiːl] n rueda f dentada.

cohabit [ˌkəʊˈhæbɪt] vi fml: **to cohabit (with)** cohabitar (con).

coherent [kəʊˈhɪərənt] adj coherente.

coherently [kəʊˈhɪərəntlɪ] adv coherentemente.

cohesion [kəʊˈhiːʒn] n cohesión f.

cohesive [kəʊˈhiːsɪv] adj [group] unido(da).

cohort [ˈkəʊhɔːt] n pej acólito m, -ta f, secuaz mf.

COI (abbr of **Central Office of Information**) n oficina gubernamental británica de información al público.

coil [kɔɪl] ⟨⟩ n - **1.** [of rope, wire] rollo m; [of hair] tirabuzón m; [of smoke] espiral f - **2.** ELEC bobina f - **3.** UK [contraceptive device] DIU m, espiral f. ⟨⟩ vi enrollarse, enroscarse. ⟨⟩ vt enrollar, enroscar.

◆ **coil up** vt sep enrollar.

coiled [kɔɪld] adj [rope etc] enrollado(da); [spring] en espiral.

coin [kɔɪn] ⟨⟩ n moneda f. ⟨⟩ vt [invent] acuñar; **to coin a phrase...** como se suele decir...

coinage [ˈkɔɪnɪdʒ] n - **1.** [currency] moneda f - **2.** [invention] palabra f de nuevo cuño.

coin-box n depósito m de monedas.

coincide [ˌkəʊɪnˈsaɪd] vi: **to coincide (with)** coincidir (con).

coincidence [kəʊˈɪnsɪdəns] n coincidencia f.

coincidental [kəʊˌɪnsɪˈdentl] adj fortuito(ta).

coincidentally [kəʊˌɪnsɪˈdentəlɪ] adv: **coincidentally his name was the same as mine** dio la coincidencia de que tenía el mismo nombre que yo.

coin-operated [ˈɒpəˌreɪtɪd] adj que funciona con monedas.

coitus [ˈkəʊɪtəs] n fml coito m.

coke [kəʊk] n - **1.** [fuel] coque m - **2.** drug sl coca f.

Coke® [kəʊk] n Coca-Cola® f.

Col. (abbr of **colonel**) Col.

cola [ˈkəʊlə] n (bebida f de) cola f.

colander [ˈkʌləndər] n colador m, escurridor m.

cold [kəʊld] ⟨⟩ adj frío(a); **it's cold** hace frío; **my hands are cold** tengo las manos frías; **I'm**

cold tengo frío; **to get cold** enfriarse. <> *n* - **1.** [illness] resfriado *m*, constipado *m*; **to catch (a) cold** resfriarse, coger un resfriado - **2.** [low temperature] frío *m*.

cold-blooded [-'blʌdɪd] *adj* - **1.** [animal] de sangre fría - **2.** [person] despiadado(da); [killing] a sangre fría.

cold cream *n* crema *f* limpiadora.

cold cuts *npl esp US* embutidos *mpl*, fiambres *mpl*.

cold feet *npl*: **he got cold feet** *inf* se echó atrás.

cold-hearted [-'hɑːtɪd] *adj* [person] duro(ra) de corazón; [action] despiadado(da).

coldly ['kəʊldlɪ] *adv* con frialdad.

coldness ['kəʊldnɪs] *n* frialdad *f*.

cold shoulder *n*: **to give sb the cold shoulder** *inf* dar de lado a alguien *Esp*, hacer el vacío a alguien.

cold sore *n* calentura *f*.

cold storage *n* [of food] conservación *f* en frío.

cold sweat *n* sudor *m* frío.

cold war *n*: **the cold war** la guerra fría.

coleslaw ['kəʊlslɔː] *n* ensalada de col, zanahoria, cebolla y mayonesa.

colic ['kɒlɪk] *n* cólico *m*.

collaborate [kə'læbəreɪt] *vi*: **to collaborate (with)** colaborar (con).

collaboration [kə,læbə'reɪʃn] *n* - **1.** [teamwork]: **collaboration (with)** colaboración *f* (con) - **2.** *pej* [with enemy]: **collaboration (with)** colaboracionismo *m* (con).

collaborative [kə'læbərətɪv] *adj* de colaboración.

collaborator [kə'læbəreɪtəʳ] *n* - **1.** [colleague] colaborador *m*, -ra *f* - **2.** *pej* [traitor] colaboracionista *mf*.

collage ['kɒlɑːʒ] *n* collage *m*.

collagen ['kɒlədʒən] *n* colágeno *m*.

collapse [kə'læps] <> *n* - **1.** [of building] derrumbamiento *m*, desplome *m*; [of roof] hundimiento *m* - **2.** [of marriage, system] fracaso *m*; [of government, currency] caída *f*; [of empire] derrumbamiento *m* - **3.** MED colapso *m*. <> *vi* - **1.** [building, person] derrumbarse, desplomarse; [roof, prices] hundirse; **to collapse with laughter** partirse de risa - **2.** [plan, business] venirse abajo - **3.** MED sufrir un colapso - **4.** [fold up] plegarse.

collapsible [kə'læpsəbl] *adj* plegable.

collar ['kɒləʳ] <> *n* - **1.** [on clothes] cuello *m* - **2.** [for dog] collar *m* - **3.** TECH collar *m*. <> *vt inf* [subj: police] pescar, cazar; [subj: boss etc] pillar, parar.

collarbone ['kɒləbəʊn] *n* clavícula *f*.

collate [kə'leɪt] *vt* - **1.** [compare] cotejar - **2.** [put in order] poner en orden.

collateral [kɒ'lætərəl] *n* garantía *f* subsidiaria, seguridad *f* colateral.

collation [kə'leɪʃn] *n* - **1.** [comparison] cotejo *m* - **2.** [ordering] ordenación *f*.

colleague ['kɒliːg] *n* colega *mf*.

collect [kə'lekt] <> *vt* - **1.** [gather together] reunir, juntar; **to collect o.s.** concentrarse - **2.** [as a hobby] coleccionar - **3.** [go to get - person, parcel] recoger - **4.** [money, taxes] recaudar. <> *vi* - **1.** [gather] congregarse, reunirse - **2.** [accumulate] acumularse - **3.** [for charity, gift] hacer una colecta. <> *adv US* TELEC: **to call (sb) collect** llamar (a alguien) a cobro revertido.
◆ **collect up** *vt sep* recoger.

collectable [kə'lektəbl] <> *adj* interesante para un coleccionista. <> *n* pieza *f* interesante para un coleccionista.

collected [kə'lektɪd] *adj* - **1.** [calm] sosegado(da) - **2.** LIT: **collected works** obras *fpl* completas.

collecting [kə'lektɪŋ] *n* [hobby] coleccionismo *m*.

collection [kə'lekʃn] *n* - **1.** [of stamps, art etc] colección *f* - **2.** [of poems, stories etc] recopilación *f* - **3.** [of rubbish, mail] recogida *f*; [of taxes] recaudación *f* - **4.** [of money] colecta *f*.

collective [kə'lektɪv] <> *adj* colectivo(va). <> *n* colectivo *m*.

collective bargaining *n* negociación *f* colectiva.

collectively [kə'lektɪvlɪ] *adv* colectivamente.

collective ownership *n* propiedad *f* colectiva.

collector [kə'lektəʳ] *n* - **1.** [as a hobby] coleccionista *mf* - **2.** [of taxes] recaudador *m*, -ra *f* - **3.** [of debts, rent] cobrador *m*, -ra *f*.

collector's item *n* pieza *f* de coleccionista.

college ['kɒlɪdʒ] <> *n* - **1.** [for further education] instituto *m*, escuela *f* - **2.** *US* [university] universidad *f* - **3.** *UK* [of university] *colegio universitario que forma parte de ciertas universidades* - **4.** [organized body] colegio *m*. <> *comp* universitario(ria).

college of education *n UK escuela f de formación de profesores de enseñanza primaria y secundaria.*

collide [kə'laɪd] *vi*: **to collide (with)** [gen] chocar (con); [vehicles] colisionar OR chocar (con).

collie ['kɒlɪ] *n* collie *m*.

colliery ['kɒljərɪ] (*pl* -ies) *n* mina *f* de carbón.

collision [kə'lıʒn] n lit & fig: **collision (with/ between)** choque m (con/entre), colisión f (con/entre); **to be on a collision course (with)** fig estar al borde del enfrentamiento (con).

collision damage waiver n franquicia f.

colloquial [kə'ləʊkwıəl] adj coloquial.

collude [kə'lu:d] vi: **to collude with** estar en connivencia con.

collusion [kə'lu:ʒn] n: **in collusion with** en connivencia con.

cologne [kə'ləʊn] n colonia f.

Colombia [kə'lɒmbıə] n Colombia.

Colombian [kə'lɒmbıən] <> adj colombiano(na). <> n colombiano m, -na f.

colon ['kəʊlən] n - **1.** ANAT colon m - **2.** [punctuation mark] dos puntos mpl.

colonel ['kɜ:nl] n coronel mf.

colonial [kə'ləʊnjəl] adj colonial.

colonialism [kə'ləʊnjəlızm] n colonialismo m.

colonist ['kɒlənıst] n colono m.

colonize, -ise ['kɒlənaız] vt colonizar.

colonnade [ˌkɒlə'neıd] n columnata f.

colony ['kɒlənı] n (pl -ies) n colonia f.

color US = **colour**.

Colorado [ˌkɒlə'rɑ:dəʊ] n Colorado.

colorado beetle n escarabajo m de la patata.

colossal [kə'lɒsl] adj colosal.

colostomy [kə'lɒstəmı] (pl -ies) n colostomía f.

colour UK, **color** US ['kʌlər] <> n color m; **what colour is it?** ¿de qué color es?; **in colour** [magazine] a color; [film] en color; **to change colour** cambiar de color. <> adj en color. <> vt - **1.** [give colour to] dar color a; [with pen, crayon] colorear - **2.** [dye] teñir - **3.** [affect] influenciar. <> vi [blush] ruborizarse.

⬥ **colours** npl colores mpl.

⬥ **colour in** vt sep colorear.

colour bar n discriminación f racial.

colour-blind adj daltónico(ca).

colour-coded adj identificado(da) por color.

coloured UK, **colored** US ['kʌləd] adj - **1.** [pens, sheets etc] de colores - **2.** [with stated colour]: **maroon-coloured** de color granate; **brightly-coloured** de vivos colores - **3.** [person - black] de color.

colourfast UK, **colorfast** US ['kʌləfɑ:st] adj que no destiñe.

colourful UK, **colorful** US ['kʌləfʊl] adj - **1.** [brightly coloured] de vivos colores - **2.** [story] animado(da) - **3.** [person] pintoresco(ca) - **4.** [language] expresivo(va).

colouring UK, **coloring** US ['kʌlərıŋ] n - **1.** [in food] colorante m - **2.** [complexion, hair] tez f - **3.** [of animal's skin] color m, coloración f.

colourless UK, **colorless** US ['kʌləlıs] adj - **1.** [not coloured] incoloro(ra) - **2.** fig [uninteresting] soso(sa), anodino(na).

colour scheme n combinación f de colores.

colour supplement n UK suplemento m en color.

colt [kəʊlt] n potro m.

column ['kɒləm] n - **1.** [gen] columna f - **2.** [of people, vehicles] hilera f.

columnist ['kɒləmnıst] n columnista mf.

coma ['kəʊmə] n coma m.

comatose ['kəʊmətəʊs] adj MED comatoso(sa).

comb [kəʊm] <> n peine m. <> vt lit & fig peinar.

combat ['kɒmbæt] <> n combate m. <> vt combatir.

combative ['kɒmbətıv] adj combativo(va).

combination [ˌkɒmbı'neıʃn] n combinación f.

combination lock n cerradura f de combinación.

combine <> vt [kəm'baın]: **to combine sthg (with)** combinar algo (con). <> vi [kəm'baın] combinarse, unirse. <> n ['kɒmbaın] - **1.** [group] grupo m - **2.** = **combine harvester**.

combine harvester [-'hɑ:vıstər], **combine** n cosechadora f.

combustible [kəm'bʌstəbl] adj combustible.

combustion [kəm'bʌstʃn] n combustión f.

come [kʌm] vi (pt **came**, pp **come**) - **1.** [move] venir; [arrive] llegar; **coming!** ¡ahora voy!; **the news came as a shock** la noticia constituyó un duro golpe; **the time has come** ha llegado la hora; **he doesn't know whether he's coming or going** fig no sabe si va o viene - **2.** [reach]: **to come up/down to** llegar hasta; **the water came up to her thighs** el agua le llegaba hasta los muslos - **3.** [happen] pasar; **come what may** pase lo que pase; **how did you come to fail your exam?** ¿cómo es que suspendiste el examen? - **4.** [become]: **to come true** hacerse realidad; **to come unstuck** despegarse; **my shoelaces have come undone** se me han desatado los cordones - **5.** [begin gradually]: **to come to do sthg** llegar a hacer algo - **6.** [be placed in order]: **to come first/last in a race** llegar el primero/el último en una carrera; **she came second in the exam** quedó segunda en el examen; **P comes before Q** la P viene antes de la Q - **7.** v inf [sexually] correrse.

▸▸ **come to think of it** ahora que lo pienso.

⬥ **to come** adv: **in (the) days/years to come** en días/años venideros.

◆ **come about** *vi* [happen] pasar, ocurrir.

◆ **come across** ◇ *vt insep* [find] encontrar. ◇ *vi* [speaker, message]: **to come across well/badly** causar buena/mala impresión; **to come across as sthg** resultar ser algo.

◆ **come along** *vi* - **1.** [arrive by chance - opportunity] surgir; [- bus] aparecer, llegar - **2.** [progress] ir; **the project is coming along nicely** el proyecto va muy bien

▶▶**come along!** [expressing encouragement] ¡venga!; [hurry up] ¡date prisa!

◆ **come apart** *vi* deshacerse.

◆ **come at** *vt insep* [attack] atacar.

◆ **come back** *vi* - **1.** [return] volver - **2.** [in talk, writing]: **to come back to sthg** volver a algo - **3.** [memory]: **to come back to sb** volverle a la memoria a alguien - **4.** [become fashionable again] volver a estar de moda.

◆ **come by** *vt insep* - **1.** [get, obtain] conseguir - **2.** [visit, drop in on]: **they came by our house** se pasaron por nuestra casa.

◆ **come down** *vi* - **1.** [from upstairs] bajar - **2.** [decrease] bajar - **3.** [descend - plane, parachutist] aterrizar; [- rain] caer.

◆ **come down to** *vt insep* reducirse a.

◆ **come down with** *vt insep* coger, agarrar *(enfermedad)*.

◆ **come forward** *vi* presentarse.

◆ **come from** *vt insep* [noise etc] venir de; [person] ser de.

◆ **come in** *vi* - **1.** [enter] entrar, pasar; **come in!** ¡pase! - **2.** [arrive - train, letters, donations] llegar - **3.** [be involved] entrar; **it's a good plan, but where do I come in?** el plan está bien pero ¿dónde encajo yo? - **4.** [be introduced] entrar en vigor.

◆ **come in for** *vt insep* [criticism etc] recibir, llevarse.

◆ **come into** *vt insep* - **1.** [inherit] heredar - **2.** [begin to be]: **to come into being** nacer, ver la luz; **to come into force** entrar en vigor; **to come into sight** vislumbrarse.

◆ **come of** *vt insep* [result from] resultar de; **what came of your plans?** ¿qué fue de tus planes?

◆ **come off** ◇ *vi* - **1.** [button] descoserse; [label] despegarse; [lid] soltarse; [stain] quitarse - **2.** [plan, joke] salir bien, dar resultado - **3.** [person]: **to come off well/badly** salir bien/mal parado. ◇ *vt insep* [medicine] dejar de tomar

▶▶**come off it!** *inf* ¡venga ya!

◆ **come on** *vi* - **1.** [start] empezar; **I think I have a cold coming on** creo que me estoy constipando - **2.** [start working - lights, heating] encenderse - **3.** [progress] ir; **it's coming on nicely** va muy bien

▶▶**come on!** [expressing encouragement, urging haste] ¡vamos!; [expressing disbelief] ¡venga ya!

◆ **come out** *vi* - **1.** [screw, tooth] caerse - **2.** [stain] quitarse - **3.** [become known] salir a la luz - **4.** [appear - product, book, sun] salir; [- film] estrenarse - **5.** [in exam, race etc] terminar, acabar; **who came out on top?** ¿quién acabó ganando? - **6.** [go on strike] ponerse en huelga - **7.** [declare publicly]: **to come out for/against sthg** declararse a favor/en contra de algo - **8.** [as homosexual] declararse homosexual - **9.** [photograph] salir.

◆ **come out in** *vt insep*: **she has come out in spots** le han salido unos granos.

◆ **come out with** *vt insep* [remark] decir.

◆ **come over** ◇ *vt insep* [subj: feeling] sobrevenir; **I don't know what has come over her** no sé qué le pasa. ◇ *vi* [to visit] pasarse.

◆ **come round** *vi* - **1.** [to visit] pasarse - **2.** [change opinion]: **to come round (to sthg)** terminar por aceptar (algo) - **3.** [regain consciousness] volver en sí - **4.** [happen] venir.

◆ **come through** ◇ *vt insep* [difficult situation, period] pasar por, atravesar; [operation, war] sobrevivir a. ◇ *vi* - **1.** [arrive] llegar - **2.** [survive] sobrevivir.

◆ **come to** ◇ *vt insep* - **1.** [reach]: **to come to an end** tocar a su fin; **to come to power** subir al poder; **to come to a decision** alcanzar una decisión - **2.** [amount to] ascender a; **the plan came to nothing** el plan se quedó en nada - **3.** [subj: memory, thought]: **the idea suddenly came to me** se me ocurrió la idea de pronto. ◇ *vi* [regain consciousness] volver en sí.

◆ **come under** *vt insep* - **1.** [be governed by] estar bajo - **2.** [heading in book etc] venir en, ir bajo - **3.** [suffer]: **to come under attack** ser atacado.

◆ **come up** *vi* - **1.** [name, topic, opportunity] surgir - **2.** [be imminent] estar al llegar - **3.** [sun, moon] salir.

◆ **come up against** *vt insep* tropezarse OR toparse con.

◆ **come upon** *vt insep* [find] cruzarse con, encontrar.

◆ **come up to** *vt insep* - **1.** [approach - in space] acercarse a; [- in time]: **it's coming up to Christmas/six o'clock** nos acercamos a la Navidad/a las seis de la tarde - **2.** [expectations] estar a la altura de.

◆ **come up with** *vt insep* [idea] salir con; [solution] encontrar.

comeback ['kʌmbæk] *n* [return] reaparición *f*; **to make a comeback** [fashion] volver (a ponerse de moda); [actor] hacer una reaparición; [in match] recuperarse.

Comecon ['kɒmɪkɒn] (*abbr of* **Council for Mutual Economic Aid**) *n* CAME *m*.

comedian [kə'miːdjən] *n* cómico *m*, humorista *m*.

comedienne [kə,mi:dɪ'en] *n* cómica *f*, humorista *f*.

comedown ['kʌmdaʊn] *n inf* degradación *f*.

comedy ['kɒmədɪ] (*pl* **-ies**) *n* - **1**. [film, play] comedia *f*; [on television] serie *f* de humor - **2**. [humorous entertainment] humorismo *m* - **3**. [amusing nature] comicidad *f*.

comely ['kʌmlɪ] *adj liter* hermoso(sa), bello(lla).

come-on *n*: **to give sb the come-on** *inf* insinuarse a alguien.

comet ['kɒmɪt] *n* cometa *m*.

come-uppance [,kʌm'ʌpəns] *n*: **to get one's come-uppance** *inf* llevarse uno su merecido.

comfort ['kʌmfət] <> *n* - **1**. [gen] comodidad *f*; **we managed it, but it was a bit too close for comfort** lo conseguimos, pero por poco - **2**. [solace] consuelo *m*. <> *vt* consolar, confortar.

comfortable ['kʌmftəbl] *adj* - **1**. [gen] cómodo(da) - **2**. [financially secure] acomodado(da) - **3**. [after operation, accident] en estado satisfactorio - **4**. [victory, job, belief] fácil; [lead, majority] amplio(plia); **it's a comfortable hour's walk away** está a una buena hora de camino.

comfortably ['kʌmftəblɪ] *adv* - **1**. [sit, sleep] cómodamente - **2**. [without financial difficulty] sin aprietos; **comfortably off** acomodado(da) - **3**. [easily] fácilmente.

comforter ['kʌmfətəˌ] *n* - **1**. [for baby] chupete *m* - **2**. *US* [quilt] edredón *m*.

comforting ['kʌmfətɪŋ] *adj* reconfortante.

comfort station *n US euph* aseos *mpl*.

comfy ['kʌmfɪ] (*comp* **-ier**, *superl* **-iest**) *adj inf* cómodo(da).

comic ['kɒmɪk] <> *adj* cómico(ca). <> *n* - **1**. [comedian] cómico *m*, -ca *f*, humorista *mf* - **2**. [magazine - for children] tebeo *m*; [- for adults] cómic *m*.

➡ **comics** *npl US* [in newspaper] sección *f* de tiras cómicas.

comical ['kɒmɪkl] *adj* cómico(ca).

comic strip *n* tira *f* cómica.

coming ['kʌmɪŋ] <> *adj* [future] próximo(ma). <> *n*: **comings and goings** idas *fpl* y venidas.

comma ['kɒmə] *n* coma *f*.

command [kə'mɑːnd] <> *n* - **1**. [order] orden *f* - **2**. (*U*) [control] mando *m*; **to be in command of** [of people, tasks, operations] estar al mando de; [of senses] tener pleno dominio de - **3**. [of language, skill] dominio *m*; **to have sthg at one's command** dominar algo - **4**. COMPUT comando *m*. <> *vt* - **1**. [order]: **to command sb (to do sthg)** ordenar OR mandar a alguien (que haga algo) - **2**. MIL [control] comandar - **3**. [deserve - respect, attention] hacerse acreedor(ra) de; [- high price] alcanzar.

commandant [,kɒmən'dænt] *n* comandante *mf*.

commandeer [,kɒmən'dɪəˌ] *vt* requisar.

commander [kə'mɑːndəˌ] *n* - **1**. [in army] comandante *mf* - **2**. [in navy] capitán *m*, -ana *f* de fragata.

commander-in-chief (*pl* **commanders-in-chief**) *n* comandante *mf* en jefe.

commanding [kə'mɑːndɪŋ] *adj* - **1**. [lead, position, height] dominante - **2**. [voice, manner] autoritario(ria).

commanding officer *n* oficial *mf* al mando.

commandment [kə'mɑːndmənt] *n* RELIG mandamiento *m*.

command module *n* módulo *m* de mando.

commando [kə'mɑːndəʊ] (*pl* **-s** OR **-es**) *n* comando *m*.

command performance *n* obra teatral representada a petición del jefe de estado o rey.

commemorate [kə'meməreɪt] *vt* conmemorar.

commemoration [kə,memə'reɪʃn] *n* conmemoración *f*.

commemorative [kə'memərətɪv] *adj* conmemorativo(va).

commence [kə'mens] *fml* <> *vt*: **to commence (doing sthg)** comenzar OR empezar (a hacer algo). <> *vi* comenzar, empezar.

commencement [kə'mensmənt] *n fml* inicio *m*, comienzo *m*.

commend [kə'mend] *vt* - **1**. [praise] alabar - **2**. [recommend]: **to commend sthg (to)** recomendar algo (a).

commendable [kə'mendəbl] *adj* admirable, loable.

commendation [,kɒmen'deɪʃn] *n* [special award] distinción *f*, mención *f*.

commensurate [kə'menʃərət] *adj fml*: **commensurate with** acorde OR en proporción con.

comment ['kɒment] <> *n* comentario *m*; **no comment** sin comentarios. <> *vt*: **to comment that** comentar que. <> *vi* comentar; **to comment on** hacer comentarios sobre.

commentary ['kɒməntrɪ] (*pl* **-ies**) *n* - **1**. [on match, event] comentarios *mpl* - **2**. [analysis] comentario *m*.

commentate ['kɒmənteɪt] *vi* RADIO & TV: **to commentate (on sthg)** hacer de comentarista (de algo).

commentator ['kɒmənteɪtəˌ] *n* comentarista *mf*.

commerce ['kɒmɜːs] *n* (*U*) comercio *m*.

commercial [kə'mɜːʃl] <> *adj* comercial. <> *n* anuncio *m* (*televisivo o radiofónico*).

commercial bank *n* banco *m* comercial.

commercial break n pausa f publicitaria.

commercialism [kə'mɜːʃəlɪzm] n comercialismo m.

commercialize, -ise [kə'mɜːʃəlaɪz] vt comercializar.

commercialized [kə'mɜːʃəlaɪzd] adj comercializado(da).

commercially [kə'mɜːʃəlɪ] adv comercialmente.

commercial television n UK televisión f comercial.

commercial traveller n UK dated viajante mf de comercio.

commercial vehicle n UK vehículo m de transporte de mercancías.

commiserate [kə'mɪzəreɪt] vi: I commiserated with her le dije cuánto lo sentía.

commiseration [kə,mɪzə'reɪʃn] n conmiseración f; my commiserations cuánto lo siento.

commission [kə'mɪʃn] ◇ n - 1. [money, investigative body] comisión f - 2. [piece of work] encargo m. ◇ vt encargar; to commission sb (to do sthg) encargar a alguien (que haga algo).

commissionaire [kə,mɪʃə'neəʳ] n UK portero m (uniformado).

commissioned officer [kə'mɪʃnd-] n oficial o suboficial (salvo sargentos) del ejército.

commissioner [kə'mɪʃnəʳ] n comisario m, -ria f.

commit [kə'mɪt] (pt & pp -ted, cont -ting) vt - 1. [crime, sin etc] cometer - 2. [pledge - money, resources] destinar; to commit o.s. (to) comprometerse (a) - 3. [consign - to mental hospital] ingresar; to commit sb to prison encarcelar a alguien; to commit sthg to memory aprender algo de memoria.

commitment [kə'mɪtmənt] n compromiso m.

committed [kə'mɪtɪd] adj comprometido(da); committed to the cause entregado(da) a la causa.

committee [kə'mɪtɪ] n comisión f, comité m.

commode [kə'məud] n [with chamber pot] silla f con orinal incorporado.

commodity [kə'mɒdətɪ] (pl -ies) n producto m básico.

common ['kɒmən] ◇ adj - 1. [gen]: common (to) común (a) - 2. [ordinary - man, woman] corriente, de la calle - 3. UK pej [vulgar] vulgar, ordinario(ria). ◇ n campo m común.
◆ in common adv en común.

commoner ['kɒmənəʳ] n plebeyo m, -ya f.

common good n: for the common good para el bien común.

common ground n puntos mpl en común.

common knowledge n: it's common knowledge es de todos sabido, es del dominio público.

common law n derecho m consuetudinario.
◆ common-law adj [wife, husband] de hecho.

commonly ['kɒmənlɪ] adv generalmente, comúnmente.

Common Market n: the Common Market el Mercado Común.

commonplace ['kɒmənpleɪs] adj corriente, común.

common room n [for pupils] sala f de estudiantes; [for teachers] sala f de profesores.

Commons ['kɒmənz] npl UK: the Commons la Cámara de los Comunes.

common sense n sentido m común.

Commonwealth ['kɒmənwelθ] n: the Commonwealth la Commonwealth.

Commonwealth

La Commonwealth se compone de 54 estados soberanos que, en algún momento, formaron parte del Imperio Británico. El estatuto de la Commonwealth --fundado sobre principios de autonomía, igualdad y lealtad a la corona por parte de las colonias y dependencias británicas-- fue adoptado en 1931. A pesar del desmoronamiento del Imperio, el monarca británico continúa a la cabeza de la Commonwealth y los dirigentes de todos los estados miembros se reúnen bienalmente para celebrar una "Commonwealth Conference". Los juegos de la Commonwealth permiten a los estados miembros competir en la mayoría de las disciplinas olímpicas y tienen lugar cada cuatro años en un país diferente.

Commonwealth of Independent States n: the Commonwealth of Independent States la Comunidad de Estados Independientes.

commotion [kə'məuʃn] n alboroto m.

communal ['kɒmjunl] adj comunal.

commune ◇ n ['kɒmjuːn] comuna f. ◇ vi [kə'mjuːn]: to commune with estar en comunión OR comulgar con.

communicate [kə'mjuːnɪkeɪt] ◇ vt transmitir, comunicar. ◇ vi: to communicate (with) comunicarse (con).

communicating [kə'mjuːnɪkeɪtɪŋ] adj [door] que comunica.

communication [kə,mjuːnɪ'keɪʃn] n - 1. [contact] comunicación f - 2. [letter, phone call] comunicado m.
◆ communications npl comunicaciones fpl.

communication cord n UK alarma f (de un tren o metro).

communications satellite, comsat *n* satélite *m* de comunicaciones.

communicative [kə'mjuːnɪkətɪv] *adj* comunicativo(va).

communicator [kə'mjuːnɪkeɪtəʳ] *n*: **a good/ bad communicator** una persona con/sin dotes para comunicar ideas.

communion [kə'mjuːnjən] *n* [communication] comunión *f*.

➧ **Communion** *n (U)* RELIG comunión *f*.

communiqué [kə'mjuːnɪkeɪ] *n* comunicado *m*.

Communism ['kɒmjunɪzm] *n* comunismo *m*.

Communist ['kɒmjunɪst] <> *adj* comunista. <> *n* comunista *mf*.

community [kə'mjuːnətɪ] (*pl* -ies) *n* comunidad *f*.

community centre *n* centro *m* social.

community home *n* UK centro *m* docente para delincuentes menores de edad.

community policing *n fomento de las buenas relaciones entre policía y vecindario.*

community service *n (U)* servicios *mpl* a la comunidad.

community spirit *n* civismo *m*.

commutable [kə'mjuːtəbl] *adj* [sentence] conmutable.

commutation ticket [,kɒmjuː'teɪʃn-] *n* US abono *m*, boleto *m* de abono *Amér*.

commute [kə'mjuːt] <> *vt* LAW conmutar. <> *vi* [to work] *viajar diariamente al lugar de trabajo.*

commuter [kə'mjuːtəʳ] *n persona que viaja diariamente al lugar de trabajo.*

compact <> *adj* [kəm'pækt] [small and neat] compacto(ta). <> *n* ['kɒmpækt] - **1.** [for face powder] polvera *f* - **2.** US [car] utilitario *m*. <> *vt* [kəm'pækt] comprimir.

compact disc *n* disco *m* compacto, compact disc *m*.

compact disc player *n* compact *m* (disc), reproductor *m* de discos compactos.

companion [kəm'pænjən] *n* compañero *m*, -ra *f*.

companionable [kəm'pænjənəbl] *adj* [person] sociable; [evening, silence] agradable.

companionship [kəm'pænjənʃɪp] *n* [friendly relationship] compañerismo *m*.

company ['kʌmpənɪ] (*pl* -ies) *n* [gen] compañía *f*; [business] empresa *f*, compañía *f*; **to keep sb company** hacer compañía a alguien; **to part company (with)** separarse (de).

company car *n* coche *m* de la empresa, carro *m* de la compañía *Amér*, auto *m* de la compañía.

company director *n* gerente *mf* OR director *m*, -ra *f* de la empresa.

company secretary *n secretario del consejo de administración.*

comparable ['kɒmprəbl] *adj*: **comparable (to** OR **with)** comparable (a).

comparative [kəm'pærətɪv] <> *adj* - **1.** [relative] relativo(va) - **2.** [study] comparado(da) - **3.** GRAM comparativo(va). <> *n* GRAM comparativo *m*.

comparatively [kəm'pærətɪvlɪ] *adv* relativamente.

compare [kəm'peəʳ] <> *vt*: **to compare sthg/ sb (with), to compare sthg/sb (to)** comparar algo/a alguien (con); **compared with** OR **to** [as opposed to] comparado con; [in comparison with] en comparación con. <> *vi*: **to compare (with)** compararse (con); **to compare favourably/unfavourably with** ser mejor/peor que.

comparison [kəm'pærɪsn] *n* comparación *f*; **in comparison (with** OR **to)** en comparación (con).

compartment [kəm'pɑːtmənt] *n* - **1.** [container] compartimento *m*, compartimiento *m* - **2.** RAIL departamento *m*, compartimiento *m*.

compartmentalize, -ise [,kɒmpɑː't'mentəlaɪz] *vt* compartimentar.

compass ['kʌmpəs] *n* - **1.** [magnetic] brújula *f* - **2.** *fml* [scope] alcance *m*.

➧ **compasses** *npl* compás *m*.

compassion [kəm'pæʃn] *n* compasión *f*.

compassionate [kəm'pæʃənət] *adj* compasivo(va).

compatibility [kəm,pætə'bɪlətɪ] *n*: **compatibility (with)** compatibilidad *f* (con).

compatible [kəm'pætəbl] *adj*: **compatible (with)** compatible (con).

compatriot [kəm'pætrɪət] *n* compatriota *mf*.

compel [kəm'pel] (*pt* & *pp* -led, *cont* -ling) *vt* - **1.** [force] obligar; **to compel sb to do sthg** forzar OR obligar a alguien a hacer algo - **2.** [cause - feeling] despertar.

compelling [kəm'pelɪŋ] *adj* - **1.** [argument, reason] convincente - **2.** [book, film] absorbente.

compendium [kəm'pendɪəm] (*pl* -diums OR -dia [-dɪə]) *n* [book] compendio *m*.

compensate ['kɒmpenseɪt] <> *vt*: **to compensate sb for sthg** [financially] compensar OR indemnizar a alguien por algo. <> *vi*: **to compensate for sthg** compensar algo.

compensation [,kɒmpen'seɪʃn] *n* - **1.** [money]: **compensation (for)** indemnización *f* (por) - **2.** [way of compensating]: **compensation (for)** compensación *f* (por).

compere ['kɒmpeəʳ] UK <> *n* presentador *m*, -ra *f*. <> *vt* presentar.

compete [kəm'pi:t] *vi* - **1.** [gen]**: to compete (for/in)** competir (por/en); **to compete (with** OR **against)** competir (con) - **2.** [be in conflict] rivalizar.

competence ['kɒmpɪtəns] *n* [proficiency] competencia *f*.

competent ['kɒmpɪtənt] *adj* competente, capaz.

competently ['kɒmpɪtəntlɪ] *adv* competentemente.

competing [kəm'pi:tɪŋ] *adj* [conflicting] contrapuesto(ta).

competition [ˌkɒmpɪ'tɪʃn] *n* - **1.** [rivalry] competencia *f* - **2.** [competitors, rivals]**: the competition** la competencia - **3.** [race, sporting event] competición *f* - **4.** [contest] concurso *m*.

competitive [kəm'petətɪv] *adj* - **1.** [match, exam, prices] competitivo(va) - **2.** [person, spirit] competidor(ra).

competitively [kəm'petətɪvlɪ] *adv* - **1.** [play] competitivamente - **2.** COMM [price, market] de forma competitiva.

competitor [kəm'petɪtər] *n* competidor *m*, -ra *f*.

compilation [ˌkɒmpɪ'leɪʃn] *n* recopilación *f*, compilación *f*.

compile [kəm'paɪl] *vt* recopilar, compilar.

complacency [kəm'pleɪsnsɪ] *n* autocomplacencia *f*.

complacent [kəm'pleɪsnt] *adj* autocomplaciente.

complacently [kəm'pleɪsntlɪ] *adv* con autosatisfacción.

complain [kəm'pleɪn] *vi* - **1.** [moan]**: to complain (about)** quejarse (de) - **2.** MED: **to complain of sthg** sufrir algo.

complaining [kəm'pleɪnɪŋ] *adj* protestón(ona).

complaint [kəm'pleɪnt] *n* - **1.** [gen] queja *f* - **2.** MED problema *m*, dolencia *f*.

complement ◇ *n* ['kɒmplɪmənt] - **1.** [gen & GRAM] complemento *m* - **2.** [number]**: we offer a full complement of services** ofrecemos una gama completa de servicios. ◇ *vt* ['kɒmplɪˌment] complementar.

complementary [ˌkɒmplɪ'mentərɪ] *adj* - **1.** [gen] complementario(ria) - **2.** [medicine] alternativo(va).

complete [kəm'pli:t] ◇ *adj* - **1.** [total] total; **a complete idiot** un auténtico idiota - **2.** [lacking nothing] completo(ta); **bathroom complete with shower** baño con ducha - **3.** [finished] terminado(da). ◇ *vt* - **1.** [finish] terminar, acabar - **2.** [form] rellenar - **3.** [make whole - collection] completar; [- disappointment, amazement] colmar, rematar.

completely [kəm'pli:tlɪ] *adv* completamente.

completion [kəm'pli:ʃn] *n* finalización *f*, terminación *f*.

complex ['kɒmpleks] ◇ *adj* complejo(ja). ◇ *n* complejo *m*.

complexion [kəm'plekʃn] *n* - **1.** [of face] tez *f*, cutis *m inv* - **2.** [nature] naturaleza *f*, carácter *m*.

complexity [kəm'pleksətɪ] *(pl -ies)* *n* complejidad *f*.

compliance [kəm'plaɪəns] *n* [obedience]**: compliance (with)** cumplimiento *m* (de), acatamiento *m* (de).

compliant [kəm'plaɪənt] *adj* dócil, sumiso(sa).

complicate ['kɒmplɪkeɪt] *vt* complicar.

complicated ['kɒmplɪkeɪtɪd] *adj* complicado(da).

complication [ˌkɒmplɪ'keɪʃn] *n* complicación *f*.

complicity [kəm'plɪsətɪ] *n*: **complicity (in)** complicidad *f* (en).

compliment ◇ *n* ['kɒmplɪmənt] cumplido *m*; **my compliments to the cook** felicitaciones a la cocinera. ◇ *vt* ['kɒmplɪment]**: to compliment sb (on)** felicitar a alguien (por).
➤ **compliments** *npl fml* saludos *mpl*.

complimentary [ˌkɒmplɪ'mentərɪ] *adj* - **1.** [remark] elogioso(sa); [person] halagador(ra) - **2.** [drink, seats] gratis *(inv)*.

complimentary ticket *n* entrada *f* gratuita.

compliments slip *n* nota *f* de cortesía.

comply [kəm'plaɪ] *(pt & pp -ied)* *vi*: **to comply with sthg** [standards] cumplir (con) algo; [request] acceder a algo; [law] acatar algo.

component [kəm'pəʊnənt] *n* TECH pieza *f*; [element] elemento *m*, parte *f* integrante.

compose [kəm'pəʊz] *vt* - **1.** [constitute] componer; **to be composed of** estar compuesto OR componerse de - **2.** [music, poem, letter] componer - **3.** [calm]**: to compose o.s.** calmarse, tranquilizarse.

composed [kəm'pəʊzd] *adj* tranquilo(la).

composer [kəm'pəʊzər] *n* compositor *m*, -ra *f*.

composite ['kɒmpəzɪt] ◇ *adj* compuesto(ta). ◇ *n* combinación *f*, conjunto *m*.

composition [ˌkɒmpə'zɪʃn] *n* - **1.** [gen] composición *f* - **2.** [essay] redacción *f*.

compost [UK 'kɒmpɒst, US 'kɒmpəʊst] *n* compost *m*, abono *m*.

composure [kəm'pəʊʒər] *n* compostura *f*, calma *f*.

compound ◇ *adj* ['kɒmpaʊnd] compuesto(ta). ◇ *n* ['kɒmpaʊnd] - **1.** [gen & CHEM] compuesto *m* - **2.** [enclosed area] recinto *m*. ◇ *vt* [kəm'paʊnd] [exacerbate] agravar.

compound fracture *n* fractura *f* complicada.

compound interest *n* interés *m* compuesto.

comprehend [,kɒmprɪ'hend] *vt* comprender.

comprehension [,kɒmprɪ'henʃn] *n* comprensión *f*.

comprehensive [,kɒmprɪ'hensɪv] ⬦ *adj* **- 1.** [wide-ranging] completo(ta) **- 2.** [defeat, victory] rotundo(da) **- 3.** [insurance] a todo riesgo. ⬦ *n UK* = **comprehensive school**.

comprehensively [,kɒmprɪ'hensɪvlɪ] *adv* [cover] extensamente; [study] minuciosamente; [beat] abrumadoramente.

comprehensive school, comprehensive *n instituto de enseñanza media no selectiva en Gran Bretaña*.

compress [kəm'pres] *vt* **- 1.** [squeeze, press & COMPUT] comprimir **- 2.** [shorten] reducir.

compression [kəm'preʃn] *n* **- 1.** [of air & COMPUT] compresión *f* **- 2.** [of text] reducción *f*.

comprise [kəm'praɪz] *vt* **- 1.** [consist of] comprender **- 2.** [form] constituir.

compromise ['kɒmprəmaɪz] ⬦ *n* arreglo *m*, término *m* medio. ⬦ *vt* comprometer; **to compromise o.s.** comprometerse. ⬦ *vi* llegar a un arreglo, transigir.

compromising ['kɒmprəmaɪzɪŋ] *adj* comprometedor(ra).

compulsion [kəm'pʌlʃn] *n* **- 1.** [strong desire] ganas *fpl* irrefrenables **- 2.** *(U)* [force] obligación *f*.

compulsive [kəm'pʌlsɪv] *adj* **- 1.** [gambler] empedernido(da); [liar] compulsivo(va) **- 2.** [fascinating, compelling] absorbente.

compulsory [kəm'pʌlsərɪ] *adj* [gen] obligatorio(ria); [redundancy, retirement] forzoso(sa).

compulsory purchase *n UK* expropiación *f*.

compunction [kəm'pʌŋkʃn] *n* (U) escrúpulos *mpl*, reparos *mpl*.

computation [,kɒmpju:'teɪʃn] *n* cálculo *m*.

compute [kəm'pju:t] *vt* computar, calcular.

computer [kəm'pju:təʳ] ⬦ *n* ordenador *m*, computadora *f Amér*. ⬦ *comp* de ordenadores, de computadoras *Amér*.

computer dating [-'deɪtɪŋ] *n citas organizadas por una agencia matrimonial a través de ordenador*.

computer game *n* juego *m* de ordenador.

computer-generated [kəm,pju:tə'dʒenəreɪtɪd] *adj* generado(da) por ordenador.

computer graphics *npl* infografía *f*.

computerization [kəm,pju:təraɪ'zeɪʃn] *n* informatización *f*.

computerize, -ise [kəm'pju:təraɪz] *vt* informatizar.

computerized [kəm'pju:təraɪzd] *adj* informatizado(da), computerizado(da).

computer language *n* lenguaje *m* de ordenador.

computer-literate *adj* con conocimientos de informática.

computer program *n* programa *m* informático.

computing [kəm'pju:tɪŋ], **computer science** *n* informática *f*.

comrade ['kɒmreɪd] *n* camarada *mf*.

comradeship ['kɒmreɪdʃɪp] *n* camaradería *f*.

comsat ['kɒmsæt] = **communications satellite**.

con [kɒn] *inf* ⬦ *n* **- 1.** [trick] timo *m*, estafa *f* **- 2.** *prison sl* presidiario *m*, -ria *f*. ⬦ *vt* (*pt* & *pp* **-ned**, *cont* **-ning**) timar, estafar; **to con sb out of sthg** timarle algo a alguien; **to con sb into doing sthg** engañar a alguien para que haga algo.

concave [,kɒn'keɪv] *adj* cóncavo(va).

conceal [kən'si:l] *vt* [object, substance, information] ocultar; [feelings] disimular; **to conceal sthg from sb** ocultarle algo a alguien.

concede [kən'si:d] ⬦ *vt* **- 1.** [defeat, a point] admitir, reconocer **- 2.** [goal] encajar. ⬦ *vi* [gen] ceder; [in sports, chess] rendirse.

conceit [kən'si:t] *n* engreimiento *m*, vanidad *f*.

conceited [kən'si:tɪd] *adj* engreído(da), vanidoso(sa).

conceivable [kən'si:vəbl] *adj* concebible, imaginable.

conceivably [kən'si:vəblɪ] *adv* posiblemente; **I can't conceivably do that** no puedo hacer eso por nada del mundo.

conceive [kən'si:v] ⬦ *vt* concebir. ⬦ *vi* **- 1.** MED concebir **- 2.** [imagine]: **to conceive of sthg** imaginarse algo.

concentrate ['kɒnsəntreɪt] ⬦ *vt* concentrar. ⬦ *vi*: **to concentrate (on)** concentrarse (en).

concentrated ['kɒnsəntreɪtɪd] *adj* **- 1.** [fruit juice, washing powder] concentrado(da) **- 2.** [effort] decidido(da), intenso(sa).

concentration [,kɒnsən'treɪʃn] *n* concentración *f*.

concentration camp *n* campo *m* de concentración.

concentric [kən'sentrɪk] *adj* concéntrico(ca).

concept ['kɒnsept] *n* concepto *m*.

conception [kən'sepʃn] *n* **- 1.** [gen] concepción *f* **- 2.** [idea] concepto *m*, idea *f*.

conceptualize, -ise [kən'septjuəlaɪz] *vt* formarse un concepto de, conceptualizar.

concern [kən'sɜ:n] ⬦ *n* **- 1.** [worry, anxiety] preocupación *f* **- 2.** [matter of interest] asunto *m*; **it's no concern of yours** no es asunto tuyo **- 3.** [company] negocio *m*, empresa *f*. ⬦ *vt* **- 1.** [worry] preocupar; **to be concerned about** preocuparse por **- 2.** [involve] concernir; **those concerned** los interesados; **to be concerned**

with [subj: person] ocuparse de; **to concern o.s. with sthg** preocuparse de OR por algo; **as far as... is concerned** por lo que a... respecta **- 3.** [book, film etc] tratar de; **it concerns your parents** tiene que ver con tus padres.

concerned [kən'sɜːnd] *adj* [person] preocupado(da); [expression] de preocupación.

concerning [kən'sɜːnɪŋ] *prep* en relación con.

concert ['kɒnsət] *n* concierto *m*.
➤ **in concert** *adv* **- 1.** MUS en directo, en concierto **- 2.** *fml* [acting as one] conjuntamente.

concerted [kən'sɜːtɪd] *adj* conjunto(ta).

concert hall *n* sala *f* de conciertos.

concertina [,kɒnsə'tiːnə] <> *n* concertina *f*. <> *vi* (*pt* & *pp* **-ed**, *cont* **-ing**) quedarse hecho(cha) un acordeón.

concerto [kən'tʃeətəʊ] (*pl* **-s**) *n* concierto *m*.

concession [kən'seʃn] *n* **- 1.** [allowance, franchise] concesión *f* **- 2.** UK [special price] descuento *m*, rebaja *f* **- 3.** UK [reduced ticket - for cinema, theatre] entrada *f* con descuento; [- for public transport] billete *m* con descuento.

concessionary [kən'seʃnərɪ] *adj* de descuento, especial.

concierge [,kɒnsɪ'ɛəʒ] *n* US [in hotel] conserje *mf*.

conciliation [kən,sɪlɪ'eɪʃn] *n* conciliación *f*.

conciliatory [kən'sɪlɪətrɪ] *adj* conciliador(ra).

concise [kən'saɪs] *adj* conciso(sa).

concisely [kən'saɪslɪ] *adv* de manera concisa.

conclave ['kɒŋkleɪv] *n* cónclave *m*.

conclude [kən'kluːd] <> *vt* **- 1.** [bring to an end] concluir, terminar **- 2.** [deduce]: **to conclude (that)** concluir que **- 3.** [agreement] llegar a; [business deal] cerrar; [treaty] firmar. <> *vi* terminar, concluir.

conclusion [kən'kluːʒn] *n* **- 1.** [decision] conclusión *f*; **to jump to the wrong conclusion** sacar precipitadamente una conclusión errónea **- 2.** [ending] conclusión *f*, final *m*; **a foregone conclusion** un resultado inevitable **- 3.** [of business deal] cierre *m*; [of treaty, agreement] firma *f*.

conclusive [kən'kluːsɪv] *adj* concluyente.

concoct [kən'kɒkt] *vt* **- 1.** [excuse, story] ingeniar **- 2.** [food] confeccionar; [drink] preparar.

concoction [kən'kɒkʃn] *n* [drink] brebaje *m*; [food] mezcla *f*.

concord ['kɒŋkɔːd] *n* concordia *f*.

concourse ['kɒŋkɔːs] *n* [of station etc] vestíbulo *m*.

concrete ['kɒŋkriːt] <> *adj* [definite, real] concreto(ta). <> *n* hormigón *m*, concreto *m* Amér. <> *comp* [made of concrete] de hormigón. <> *vt* cubrir con hormigón.

concrete mixer *n* hormigonera *f*.

concubine ['kɒŋkjʊbaɪn] *n* concubina *f*.

concur [kən'kɜː] (*pt* & *pp* **-red**, *cont* **-ring**) *vi* [agree]: **to concur (with)** estar de acuerdo OR coincidir (con).

concurrently [kən'kʌrəntlɪ] *adv* simultáneamente, al mismo tiempo.

concussed [kən'kʌst] *adj*: **to be concusseded** haber sufrido una conmoción cerebral.

concussion [kən'kʌʃn] *n* conmoción *f* cerebral.

condemn [kən'dem] *vt* **- 1.** [gen]: **to condemn sb (for/to)** condenar a alguien (por/a) **- 2.** [building] declarar en ruinas.

condemnation [,kɒndem'neɪʃn] *n* condena *f*.

condemned [kən'demd] *adj* **- 1.** LAW [condemned to death] condenado(da) a muerte **- 2.** [building] declarado(da) en ruinas.

condensation [,kɒnden'seɪʃn] *n* [on walls] condensación *f*; [on glass] vaho *m*.

condense [kən'dens] <> *vt* condensar. <> *vi* condensarse.

condensed milk [kən'denst-] *n* leche *f* condensada.

condescend [,kɒndɪ'send] *vi* **- 1.** [talk down]: **to condescend to sb** hablar a alguien con tono de superioridad **- 2.** [deign]: **to condescend to do sthg** condescender OR rebajarse a hacer algo.

condescending [,kɒndɪ'sendɪŋ] *adj* altivo(va), condescendiente.

condiment ['kɒndɪmənt] *n* condimento *m*.

condition [kən'dɪʃn] <> *n* **- 1.** [state] estado *m*; **in good/bad condition** en buen/mal estado; **to be out of condition** no estar en forma **- 2.** MED [disease, complaint] afección *f* **- 3.** [provision] condición *f*; **on condition that** a condición de que; **on one condition** con una condición. <> *vt* **- 1.** [gen] condicionar **- 2.** [hair] acondicionar.
➤ **conditions** *npl* condiciones *fpl*; **weather conditions** estado del tiempo.

conditional [kən'dɪʃənl] <> *adj* condicional; **to be conditional on** OR **upon** depender de. <> *n*: **the conditional** el condicional.

conditionally [kən'dɪʃnəlɪ] *adv* condicionalmente.

conditioner [kən'dɪʃnər] *n* suavizante *m*.

conditioning [kən'dɪʃnɪŋ] *n* **- 1.** [psychological] condicionamiento *m* **- 2.** [physical] preparación *f*.

condo ['kɒndəʊ] *n* US *inf abbr of* **condominium**.

condolences [kən'dəʊlənsɪz] *npl* pésame *m*; **to offer one's condolences** dar el pésame.

condom ['kɒndəm] *n* preservativo *m*, condón *m*.

condominium [ˌkɒndə'mɪnɪəm] *n* US - **1.** [apartment] piso *m*, apartamento *m* - **2.** [apartment block] bloque *m* de pisos OR apartamentos.

condone [kən'dəʊn] *vt* perdonar, tolerar.

condor ['kɒndɔːr] *n* cóndor *m*.

conducive [kən'djuːsɪv] *adj*: **conducive to** favorable para.

conduct ◇ *n* ['kɒndʌkt] - **1.** [behaviour] conducta *f* - **2.** [carrying out] dirección *f*. ◇ *vt* [kən'dʌkt] - **1.** [carry out] dirigir, llevar a cabo - **2.** [behave]: **to conduct o.s. well/badly** comportarse bien/mal - **3.** MUS dirigir - **4.** PHYS conducir. ◇ *vi* [kən'dʌkt] [lead orchestra, choir] dirigir.

conducted tour [kən'dʌktɪd-] *n* visita *f* con guía.

conductor [kən'dʌktər] *n* - **1.** [of orchestra, choir] director *m*, -ra *f* - **2.** [on bus] cobrador *m* - **3.** US [on train] revisor *m*, -ra *f*.

conductress [kən'dʌktrɪs] *n* [on bus] cobradora *f*.

conduit ['kɒndɪt] *n* conducto *m*.

cone [kəʊn] *n* - **1.** [shape] cono *m* - **2.** [for ice cream] cucurucho *m* - **3.** [from tree] piña *f*.

◆ **cone off** *vt sep UK cortar temporalmente (un carril o carretera) con conos.*

confectioner [kən'fekʃnər] *n* confitero *m*, -ra *f*; **confectioner's (shop)** confitería *f*.

confectionery [kən'fekʃnərɪ] *n (U)* dulces *mpl*, golosinas *fpl*.

confederation [kənˌfedə'reɪʃn] *n* confederación *f*.

confer [kən'fɜːr] ◇ *vt (pt & pp* -**red**, *cont* -**ring**) *fml*: **to confer sthg (on)** otorgar OR conferir algo (a). ◇ *vi (pt & pp* -**red**, *cont* -**ring**): **to confer (with)** consultar (con).

conference ['kɒnfərəns] *n* congreso *m*, conferencia *f*; **in conference** reunido.

conference call *n* multiconferencia *f*, llamada *f* OR llamado *m* Amér en conferencia.

conference centre *n* - **1.** [purpose-built building] palacio *m* de congresos - **2.** [in hotel etc] centro *m* de congresos.

conference hall *n* sala *f* de conferencias OR congresos.

conferencing ['kɒnfərənsɪŋ] *n* multiconferencias *fpl*.

confess [kən'fes] ◇ *vt* confesar; **to confess (that)** admitir OR confesar que. ◇ *vi* - **1.** [to crime & RELIG] confesarse; **to confess to sthg** confesar algo - **2.** [admit]: **to confess to sthg** admitir algo.

confession [kən'feʃn] *n* confesión *f*.

confessional [kən'feʃənl] *n* confesionario *m*.

confetti [kən'fetɪ] *n* confeti *m*.

confidant [ˌkɒnfɪ'dænt] *n* confidente *m*.

confidante [ˌkɒnfɪ'dænt] *n* confidente *f*.

confide [kən'faɪd] ◇ *vt* confiar. ◇ *vi*: **to confide (in)** confiarse (a).

confidence ['kɒnfɪdəns] *n* - **1.** [self-assurance] confianza *f* OR seguridad *f* (en sí mismo/misma) - **2.** [trust] confianza *f*; **to have confidence in sb** tener confianza en alguien - **3.** [secrecy]: **in confidence** en secreto - **4.** [secret] intimidad *f*, secreto *m*.

confidence trick *n* timo *m*, estafa *f*.

confident ['kɒnfɪdənt] *adj* - **1.** [self-assured - person] seguro de sí mismo(segura de sí misma); [- smile, attitude] confiado(da) - **2.** [sure]: **confident (of)** seguro(ra) (de).

confidential [ˌkɒnfɪ'denʃl] *adj* [gen] confidencial; [secretary, clerk] de confianza.

confidentiality ['kɒnfɪˌdenʃɪ'ælətɪ] *n* confidencialidad *f*.

confidentially [ˌkɒnfɪ'denʃəlɪ] *adv* - **1.** [secretly] en confianza - **2.** [secretively] confidencialmente.

confidently ['kɒnfɪdəntlɪ] *adv* - **1.** [with self-assurance] con seguridad - **2.** [trustingly] con toda confianza.

configuration [kənˌfɪɡə'reɪʃn] *n* [gen & COMPUT] configuración *f*.

confine [kən'faɪn] *vt* - **1.** [limit, restrict] limitar, restringir; **to be confined to** limitarse a; **to confine o.s. to** limitarse a - **2.** [shut up] recluir, encerrar.

confined [kən'faɪnd] *adj* [space] reducido(da), limitado(da).

confinement [kən'faɪnmənt] *n* - **1.** [imprisonment] reclusión *f* - **2.** dated & MED parto *m*.

confines ['kɒnfaɪnz] *npl* confines *mpl*, límites *mpl*.

confirm [kən'fɜːm] *vt* confirmar.

confirmation [ˌkɒnfə'meɪʃn] *n* confirmación *f*.

confirmed [kən'fɜːmd] *adj* [non-smoker] inveterado(da); [bachelor] empedernido(da).

confiscate ['kɒnfɪskeɪt] *vt* confiscar.

confiscation [ˌkɒnfɪ'skeɪʃn] *n* confiscación *f*, incautación *f*.

conflagration [ˌkɒnflə'ɡreɪʃn] *n fml* conflagración *f*.

conflict ◇ *n* [ˈkɒnflɪkt] conflicto *m*; **conflict of interests** conflicto de intereses. ◇ *vi* [kənˈflɪkt]: **to conflict (with)** estar en desacuerdo (con).

conflicting [kənˈflɪktɪŋ] *adj* contrapuesto(ta).

conform [kənˈfɔːm] *vi* **- 1.** [behave as expected] amoldarse a las normas sociales **- 2.** [be in accordance]: **to conform (to** OR **with)** [expectations] corresponder (a); [rules] ajustarse (a).

conformist [kənˈfɔːmɪst] ◇ *adj* conformista. ◇ *n* conformista *mf*.

conformity [kənˈfɔːmətɪ] *n*: **conformity (to** OR **with)** conformidad *f* (con).

confound [kənˈfaʊnd] *vt* [confuse, defeat] confundir, desconcertar.

confounded [kənˈfaʊndɪd] *adj inf* maldito(ta).

confront [kənˈfrʌnt] *vt* **- 1.** [problem, task] afrontar, hacer frente a **- 2.** [subj: problem, task] presentarse a **- 3.** [enemy etc] enfrentarse con **- 4.** [challenge]: **to confront sb (with)** poner a alguien cara a cara (con).

confrontation [ˌkɒnfrʌnˈteɪʃn] *n* enfrentamiento *m*, confrontación *f*.

confuse [kənˈfjuːz] *vt* **- 1.** [bewilder] desconcertar, confundir **- 2.** [mix up]: **to confuse (with)** confundir (con) **- 3.** [complicate, make less clear] complicar.

confused [kənˈfjuːzd] *adj* **- 1.** [person] confundido(da), desconcertado(da) **- 2.** [reasoning, situation] confuso(sa).

confusing [kənˈfjuːzɪŋ] *adj* confuso(sa).

confusion [kənˈfjuːʒn] *n* **- 1.** [gen] confusión *f* **- 2.** [of person] desconcierto *m*.

conga [ˈkɒŋɡə] *n*: **the conga** la conga.

congeal [kənˈdʒiːl] *vi* [fat] solidificarse; [blood] coagularse.

congenial [kənˈdʒiːnjəl] *adj* ameno(na), agradable.

congenital [kənˈdʒenɪtl] *adj* MED congénito(ta).

conger eel [ˈkɒŋɡə-] *n* congrio *m*.

congested [kənˈdʒestɪd] *adj* **- 1.** [road] congestionado(da); [area] superpoblado(da) **- 2.** MED congestionado(da).

congestion [kənˈdʒestʃn] *n* [of traffic & MED] congestión *f*.

conglomerate [kənˈɡlɒmərət] *n* COMM conglomerado *m*.

conglomeration [kənˌɡlɒməˈreɪʃn] *n fml* conglomerado *m*.

Congo [ˈkɒŋɡəʊ] *n* [country, river]: **the Congo** el Congo.

Congolese [ˌkɒŋɡəˈliːz] ◇ *adj* congoleño(ña). ◇ *n* congoleño *m*, -ña *f*.

congratulate [kənˈɡrætʃʊleɪt] *vt*: **to congratulate sb (on)** felicitar a alguien (por); **to congratulate o.s. (on)** sentirse satisfecho(cha) (con).

congratulations [kənˌɡrætʃʊˈleɪʃənz] ◇ *npl* felicitaciones *fpl*. ◇ *excl* ¡enhorabuena!

congratulatory [kənˈɡrætʃʊlətrɪ] *adj* de felicitación.

congregate [ˈkɒŋɡrɪɡeɪt] *vi* [people] congregarse; [animals] juntarse.

congregation [ˌkɒŋɡrɪˈɡeɪʃn] *n* RELIG feligreses *mpl*.

congress [ˈkɒŋɡres] *n* congreso *m*.
◆ **Congress** *n* [in US]: **(the) Congress** el Congreso.

Congress

> Por el artículo primero de la constitución estadounidense de 1789 se constituye el Congreso de EE. UU. ese mismo año, el cual está formado por dos instituciones: el Senado ("Senate") o cámara alta y la Cámara de Representantes ("House of Representatives") o cámara baja. Cada estado está representado por dos senadores, mientras que el número de diputados de la Cámara de Representantes varía según la población (hay un total de 435 diputados). El Senado debe ratificar todos los tratados con dos tercios de los votos. Los proyectos de ley son propuestos por la Cámara de Representantes pero han de ser aprobados por ambas cámaras (que tienen el mismo poder legislativo).

congressional [kənˈɡreʃənl] *adj* US POL del Congreso.

congressman [ˈkɒŋɡresmən] (*pl* **-men** [-mən]) *n* US congresista *m*.

congresswoman [ˈkɒŋɡresˌwʊmən] (*pl* **-women** [-ˌwɪmɪn]) *n* US congresista *f*.

conical [ˈkɒnɪkl] *adj* cónico(ca).

conifer [ˈkɒnɪfə] *n* conífera *f*.

coniferous [kəˈnɪfərəs] *adj* conífero(ra).

conjecture [kənˈdʒektʃə] ◇ *n* conjetura *f*. ◇ *vt*: **to conjecture (that)** conjeturar que. ◇ *vi* hacer conjeturas.

conjugal [ˈkɒndʒʊɡl] *adj* conyugal.

conjugate [ˈkɒndʒʊɡeɪt] *vt* conjugar.

conjugation [ˌkɒndʒʊˈɡeɪʃn] *n* conjugación *f*.

conjunction [kənˈdʒʌŋkʃn] *n* **- 1.** GRAM conjunción *f* **- 2.** [combination]: **in conjunction with** juntamente con.

conjunctivitis [kənˌdʒʌŋktɪˈvaɪtɪs] *n* conjuntivitis *f inv*.

conjure [ˈkʌndʒə] ◇ *vt* hacer aparecer. ◇ *vi* hacer juegos de manos.
◆ **conjure up** *vt sep* [evoke] evocar.

conjurer, conjuror ['kʌndʒərəʳ] *n* prestidigitador *m*, -ra *f*.

conjuring trick ['kʌndʒərɪŋ-] *n* juego *m* de manos.

conjuror ['kʌndʒərəʳ] = **conjurer**.

conk [kɒŋk] *n inf* [nose] napia *f*.

➤ **conk out** *vi inf* - **1.** [break down] escacharrarse - **2.** [fall asleep] quedarse roque.

conker ['kɒŋkəʳ] *n* UK castaña *f* (del castaño de Indias).

conman ['kɒnmæn] (*pl* -**men** [-men]) *n* estafador *m*, timador *m*.

connect [kə'nekt] <> *vt* - **1.** [join]: **to connect sthg (to)** conectar algo (a); **to get connected** conectarse - **2.** [on telephone]: **I'll connect you now** ahora le paso OR pongo - **3.** [associate]: **to connect sthg/sb (with)** asociar algo/a alguien (con) - **4.** ELEC: **to connect sthg to** conectar algo a. <> *vi* [train, plane, bus]: **to connect (with)** enlazar (con).

connected [kə'nektɪd] *adj* [related]: **connected (with)** relacionado(da) (con).

Connecticut [kə'netɪkət] *n* Connecticut.

connecting [kə'nektɪŋ] *adj* - **1.** [service, flight] de enlace - **2.** [door] que comunica.

connection, connexion [kə'nekʃn] *n* - **1.** [gen, ELEC & COMPUT]: **connection (between/with)** conexión *f* (entre/con); **in connection with** con relación OR respecto a - **2.** [plane, train, bus] enlace *m* - **3.** [professional acquaintance] contacto *m*; **to have good connections** tener mucho enchufe.

connective tissue [kə'nektɪv-] *n* tejido *m* conjuntivo.

connexion [kə'nekʃn] UK = **connection**.

connive [kə'naɪv] *vi* - **1.** [plot]: **to connive (with)** confabularse (con) - **2.** [allow to happen]: **to connive at sthg** hacer la vista gorda con algo.

conniving [kə'naɪvɪŋ] *adj* intrigante.

connoisseur [ˌkɒnə'sɜːʳ] *n* entendido *m*, -da *f*.

connotation [ˌkɒnə'teɪʃn] *n* connotación *f*.

conquer ['kɒŋkəʳ] *vt* - **1.** [take by force] conquistar - **2.** [gain control of, overcome] vencer.

conqueror ['kɒŋkərəʳ] *n* conquistador *m*, -ra *f*.

conquest ['kɒŋkwest] *n* conquista *f*.

cons [kɒnz] *npl* - **1.** UK *inf*: **all mod cons** con todas las comodidades - **2.** ➪ **pro**.

Cons. *abbr of* **Conservative**.

conscience ['kɒnʃəns] *n* conciencia *f*; **in all conscience** en conciencia.

conscientious [ˌkɒnʃɪ'enʃəs] *adj* concienzudo(da).

conscientiously [ˌkɒnʃɪ'enʃəslɪ] *adv* a conciencia.

conscientious objector *n* objetor *m*, -ra *f* de conciencia.

conscious ['kɒnʃəs] *adj* - **1.** [gen] consciente; **to be conscious of** ser consciente de; **to become conscious of** darse cuenta de - **2.** [intentional] deliberado(da).

consciously ['kɒnʃəslɪ] *adv* deliberadamente.

consciousness ['kɒnʃəsnɪs] *n* - **1.** [gen] conciencia *f* - **2.** [state of being awake] conocimiento *m*; **to lose/regain consciousness** perder/recobrar el conocimiento.

conscript <> *n* ['kɒnskrɪpt] recluta *mf*. <> *vt* [kən'skrɪpt] reclutar.

conscription [kən'skrɪpʃn] *n* servicio *m* militar obligatorio.

consecrate ['kɒnsɪkreɪt] *vt fig* & RELIG consagrar.

consecration [ˌkɒnsɪ'kreɪʃn] *n* RELIG consagración *f*.

consecutive [kən'sekjʊtɪv] *adj* consecutivo(va); **on three consecutive days** tres días seguidos.

consecutively [kən'sekjʊtɪvlɪ] *adv* consecutivamente.

consensus [kən'sensəs] *n* consenso *m*.

consent [kən'sent] <> *n (U)* - **1.** [permission] consentimiento *m* - **2.** [agreement]: **by general** OR **common consent** de común acuerdo. <> *vi*: **to consent (to)** consentir (en).

consenting [kən'sentɪŋ] *adj*: **consenting adults** *adultos que aceptan mutuamente tener relaciones sexuales.*

consequence ['kɒnsɪkwəns] *n* - **1.** [result] consecuencia *f*; **in consequence** por consiguiente - **2.** [importance] importancia *f*.

consequent ['kɒnsɪkwənt] *adj* consiguiente.

consequently ['kɒnsɪkwəntlɪ] *adv* por consiguiente.

conservation [ˌkɒnsə'veɪʃn] *n* [gen] conservación *f*; [environmental protection] protección *f* del medio ambiente.

conservation area *n* zona *f* protegida.

conservationist [ˌkɒnsə'veɪʃənɪst] *n* ecologista *mf*.

conservatism [kən'sɜːvətɪzm] *n* conservadurismo *m*.

➤ **Conservatism** *n* POL conservadurismo *m*.

conservative [kən'sɜːvətɪv] <> *adj* - **1.** [not modern] conservador(ra) - **2.** [estimate, guess] moderado(da). <> *n* conservador *m*, -ra *f*.

➤ **Conservative** <> *adj* POL conservador(ra). <> *n* POL conservador *m*, -ra *f*.

Conservative Party *n*: **the Conservative Party** el Partido Conservador.

conservatory [kən'sɜːvətrɪ] (*pl* -**ies**) *n pequeña habitación acristalada adosada a una casa.*

conserve ◇ n ['kɒnsɜːv] compota f. ◇ vt [kən'sɜːv] [energy, supplies] ahorrar; [nature, wildlife] conservar, preservar.

consider [kən'sɪdəʳ] vt - **1.** [gen] considerar; **to consider doing sthg** considerar hacer algo; **to consider whether to do sthg** pensarse si hacer algo; **to consider o.s. lucky** considerarse afortunado(da) - **2.** [take into account] tener en cuenta; **all things considered** teniéndolo todo en cuenta.

considerable [kən'sɪdrəbl] adj considerable.

considerably [kən'sɪdrəblɪ] adv considerablemente, sustancialmente.

considerate [kən'sɪdərət] adj considerado(da).

consideration [kən,sɪdə'reɪʃn] n - **1.** [gen] consideración f; **to take sthg into consideration** tomar OR tener algo en cuenta; **several options are under consideration** se están considerando varias posibilidades - **2.** [factor] factor m - **3.** [amount of money] retribución f.

considered [kən'sɪdəd] adj: **it is my considered opinion that...** tras pensarlo detenidamente creo que...

considering [kən'sɪdərɪŋ] ◇ prep habida cuenta de, teniendo en cuenta. ◇ conj después de todo.

consign [kən'saɪn] vt: **to consign sthg/sb to** relegar algo/a alguien a.

consignee [ˌkɒnsaɪ'niː] n consignatario m, -ria f.

consignment [ˌkən'saɪnmənt] n remesa f.

consignment note n talón m de expedición.

consignor [kən'saɪnəʳ] n consignador m, -ra f.

consist [kən'sɪst] ➡ **consist in** vt insep consistir en. ➡ **consist of** vt insep constar de.

consistency [kən'sɪstənsɪ] (pl -ies) n - **1.** [coherence - of behaviour, policy] consecuencia f, coherencia f; [of work, performances] regularidad f - **2.** [texture] consistencia f.

consistent [kən'sɪstənt] adj - **1.** [regular] constante - **2.** [coherent]: **consistent (with)** consecuente (con).

consistently [kən'sɪstəntlɪ] adv - **1.** [without exception] constantemente - **2.** [argue, reason] consecuentemente.

consolation [ˌkɒnsə'leɪʃn] n consuelo m.

consolation prize n premio m de consolación.

console ◇ n ['kɒnsəʊl] consola f. ◇ vt [kən'səʊl] consolar; **to console o.s. with the thought that...** consolarse pensando que...

consolidate [kən'sɒlɪdeɪt] ◇ vt - **1.** [strengthen] consolidar - **2.** [merge] fusionar. ◇ vi [merge] fusionarse.

consolidation [kən,sɒlɪ'deɪʃn] (U) n - **1.** [strengthening] consolidación f - **2.** [merging] fusión f.

consommé [UK kən'sɒmeɪ, US ,kɒnsə'meɪ] n consomé m.

consonant ['kɒnsənənt] n consonante f.

consort ◇ vi [kən'sɔːt] fml: **to consort with sb** asociarse con OR frecuentar a alguien. ◇ n ['kɒnsɔːt] consorte mf.

consortium [kən'sɔːtjəm] (pl -tiums OR -tia [-tjə]) n consorcio m.

conspicuous [kən'spɪkjʊəs] adj [building] visible; [colour] llamativo(va); **he felt conspicuous** le pareció que llamaba mucho la atención; **to be conspicuous by its absence** brillar por su ausencia.

conspicuously [kən'spɪkjʊəslɪ] adv [behave] ostentosamente; **they have conspicuously failed to solve the problem** han tenido un fracaso estrepitoso en su intento de resolver el problema.

conspiracy [kən'spɪrəsɪ] (pl -ies) n conspiración f.

conspirator [kən'spɪrətəʳ] n conspirador m, -ra f.

conspiratorial [kən,spɪrə'tɔːrɪəl] adj cómplice.

conspire [kən'spaɪəʳ] ◇ vt: **to conspire to do sthg** conspirar para hacer algo. ◇ vi - **1.** [plan secretly]: **to conspire (against/with)** conspirar (contra/con) - **2.** [combine] confabularse.

constable ['kʌnstəbl] n policía mf, agente mf.

constabulary [kən'stæbjʊlərɪ] (pl -ies) n policía f (de una zona determinada).

constancy ['kɒnstənsɪ] n - **1.** [of purpose] constancia f - **2.** liter [faithfulness] fidelidad f.

constant ['kɒnstənt] ◇ adj - **1.** [gen] constante - **2.** liter [faithful] fiel. ◇ n constante f.

constantly ['kɒnstəntlɪ] adv [forever] constantemente.

constellation [ˌkɒnstə'leɪʃn] n constelación f.

consternation [ˌkɒnstə'neɪʃn] n consternación f.

constipated ['kɒnstɪpeɪtɪd] adj estreñido(da).

constipation [ˌkɒnstɪ'peɪʃn] n estreñimiento m.

constituency [kən'stɪtjʊənsɪ] (pl -ies) n [area] distrito m electoral, circunscripción f.

constituency party n UK delegación f local de un partido.

constituent [kən'stɪtjʊənt] ◇ adj integrante, constituyente. ◇ n - **1.** [element] componente m o f - **2.** [voter] votante mf, elector m, -ra f.

constitute ['kɒnstɪtjuːt] vt constituir.

constitution [ˌkɒnstɪ'tjuːʃn] n constitución f.

Constitution *n*: **the Constitution** [in US] la Constitución.

Constitution

La constitución estadounidense fue redactada tras la independencia, durante una convención extraordiaria celebrada en Filadelfia en 1787 y entró en vigor al año siguiente. Junto con la Declaración de Independencia y la Carta de Derechos, constituyó los cimientos de lo que puede considerarse el primer estado moderno. Por su parte, la Constitución británica no es un documento escrito propiamente hablando, sino que las leyes se han ido creando a lo largo de los años siguiendo el principio de jurisprudencia.

constitutional [ˌkɒnstɪˈtjuːʃənl] *adj* constitucional.

constrain [kənˈstreɪn] *vt* - **1.** [coerce]: **to constrain sb to do sthg** forzar a alguien a hacer algo - **2.** [restrict] coartar, constreñir.

constrained [kənˈstreɪnd] *adj* [smile] forzado(daː); [manner] inhibido(da).

constraint [kənˈstreɪnt] *n* - **1.** [restriction]: **constraint (on)** limitación *f* (de) - **2.** [coercion] coacción *f*.

constrict [kənˈstrɪkt] *vt* - **1.** [compress] apretar - **2.** [limit] limitar.

constricting [kənˈstrɪktɪŋ] *adj* - **1.** [clothing] que aprieta - **2.** [circumstances, lifestyle] opresivo(va).

construct ◇ *vt* [kənˈstrʌkt] *lit* & *fig* construir. ◇ *n* [ˈkɒnstrʌkt] *fml* concepto *m*.

construction [kənˈstrʌkʃn] ◇ *n* construcción *f*; **under construction** en construcción. ◇ *comp* de la construcción; **construction site** obra *f*.

construction industry *n* (industria *f* de la) construcción *f*.

constructive [kənˈstrʌktɪv] *adj* constructivo(va).

constructively [kənˈstrʌktɪvlɪ] *adv* de forma constructiva.

construe [kənˈstruː] *vt* *fml*: **to construe sthg as** interpretar algo como.

consul [ˈkɒnsəl] *n* cónsul *mf*.

consular [ˈkɒnsjʊləʳ] *adj* consular.

consulate [ˈkɒnsjʊlət] *n* consulado *m*.

consult [kənˈsʌlt] ◇ *vt* consultar. ◇ *vi*: **to consult with sb** consultar a *OR* con alguien.

consultancy [kənˈsʌltənsɪ] (*pl* **-ies**) *n* - **1.** [company] consultoría *f* - **2.** *UK* [med] puesto *m* de especialista.

consultancy fee *n* honorarios *mpl* de consultoría.

consultant [kənˈsʌltənt] *n* - **1.** [expert] asesor *m*, -ra *f* - **2.** *UK* [hospital doctor] (médico) especialista *m*, (médica) especialista *f*.

consultation [ˌkɒnsəlˈteɪʃn] *n* - **1.** [gen] consulta *f* - **2.** [discussion] discusión *f*.

consulting room [kənˈsʌltɪŋ-] *n* consultorio *m*, consulta *f*.

consume [kənˈsjuːm] *vt* *lit* & *fig* consumir.

consumer [kənˈsjuːməʳ] ◇ *n* consumidor *m*, -ra *f*. ◇ *comp* [protection, rights] del consumidor; [advice] al consumidor.

consumer credit *n* (*U*) crédito *m* al consumidor.

consumer durables *npl* bienes *mpl* de consumo duraderos.

consumer goods *npl* bienes *mpl* de consumo.

consumerism [kənˈsjuːmərɪzm] *n* *pej* [theory] consumismo *m*.

consumer society *n* sociedad *f* de consumo.

consumer spending *n* consumo *m* privado, gastos *mpl* de consumo personal.

consummate ◇ *adj* [kənˈsʌmət] - **1.** [skill, ease] absoluto(ta) - **2.** [liar, politician, snob] consumado(da). ◇ *vt* [ˈkɒnsəmeɪt] - **1.** [marriage] consumar - **2.** [deal] cerrar; [achievement] completar, redondear.

consummation [ˌkɒnsəˈmeɪʃn] *n* - **1.** [of marriage] consumación *f* - **2.** [culmination] culminación *f*.

consumption [kənˈsʌmpʃn] *n* - **1.** [use] consumo *m* - **2.** *dated* [tuberculosis] tisis *f inv*.

cont. (*abbr of* **continued**); **'cont. page 30'** 'sigue en la página 30'.

contact [ˈkɒntækt] ◇ *n* contacto *m*; **in contact (with)** en contacto (con); **to lose contact with** perder (el) contacto con; **to make contact with** ponerse en contacto con. ◇ *vt* ponerse en contacto con.

contacts *npl* *inf* [contact lenses] lentillas *fpl*, lentes *fpl* de contacto.

contact lens *n* lentilla *f*, lente *f* de contacto.

contact number *n* número *m* de contacto.

contagious [kənˈteɪdʒəs] *adj* contagioso(sa).

contain [kənˈteɪn] *vt* contener; **to contain o.s.** contenerse.

contained [kənˈteɪnd] *adj* [unemotional] mesurado(da).

container [kənˈteɪnəʳ] *n* - **1.** [box, bottle etc] recipiente *m*, envase *m* - **2.** [for transporting goods] contenedor *m*.

containerize, -ise [kənˈteɪnəraɪz] *vt* COMM [goods] poner en contenedores.

container ship *n* barco *m* *OR* buque *m* de transporte de contenedores.

containment [kənˈteɪnmənt] *n* contención *f*.

contaminate 112

contaminate [kənˈtæmɪneɪt] *vt* contaminar.

contaminated [kənˈtæmɪneɪtɪd] *adj* contaminado(da).

contamination [kən,tæmɪˈneɪʃn] *n* contaminación *f*.

cont'd (*abbr of* continued); 'cont'd page 30' 'sigue en la página 30'.

contemplate [ˈkɒntempleɪt] ⋄ *vt* - **1.** [consider] considerar, pensar en; **to contemplate doing sthg** contemplar la posibilidad de hacer algo - **2.** *fml* [look at] contemplar. ⋄ *vi* reflexionar.

contemplation [,kɒntemˈpleɪʃn] *n* - **1.** [thought] reflexión *f* - **2.** *fml* [act of looking quietly] contemplación *f*.

contemplative [kənˈtemplətɪv] *adj* contemplativo(va).

contemporary [kənˈtempərərɪ] (*pl* -ies) ⋄ *adj* contemporáneo(a). ⋄ *n* contemporáneo *m*, -a *f*.

contempt [kənˈtempt] *n* - **1.** [scorn]: **contempt (for)** desprecio *m* OR desdén *m* (por); **to hold sb in contempt** despreciar a alguien - **2.** LAW desacato *m*.

contemptible [kənˈtemptəbl] *adj* despreciable.

contemptuous [kənˈtemptʃʊəs] *adj* despreciativo(va); **to be contemptuous of sthg** despreciar algo.

contend [kənˈtend] ⋄ *vi* - **1.** [deal]: **to contend with** enfrentarse a; **I've got enough to contend with** ya tengo suficientes problemas que afrontar - **2.** [compete]: **to contend for/against** competir por/contra. ⋄ *vt fml*: **to contend that** sostener OR afirmar que.

contender [kənˈtendər] *n* [gen] contendiente *mf*; [for title] aspirante *mf*.

content ⋄ *adj* [kənˈtent]: **content (with)** contento(ta) OR satisfecho(cha) (con); **to be content to do sthg** contentarse con hacer algo; **I'd be quite content to go** iría de buena gana. ⋄ *n* [ˈkɒntent] contenido *m*. ⋄ *vt* [kənˈtent]: **to content o.s. with sthg/with doing sthg** contentarse con algo/con hacer algo.

➤ **contents** *npl* - **1.** [of container, letter etc] contenido *m* - **2.** [heading in book] índice *m*.

contented [kənˈtentɪd] *adj* satisfecho(cha), contento(ta).

contentedly [kənˈtentɪdlɪ] *adv* con satisfacción.

contention [kənˈtenʃn] *n fml* - **1.** [argument, assertion] argumento *m*; **it is my contention that...** en mi opinión... - **2.** (*U*) [disagreement] disputas *fpl* - **3.** [competition]: **to be in contention for sthg** tener posibilidades de ganar algo.

contentious [kənˈtenʃəs] *adj fml* controvertido(da), polémico(ca).

contentment [kənˈtentmənt] *n* satisfacción *f*.

contest ⋄ *n* [ˈkɒntest] - **1.** [competition] concurso *m*; [in boxing] combate *m* - **2.** [for power, control] lucha *f*, contienda *f*. ⋄ *vt* [kənˈtest] - **1.** [seat, election] presentarse como candidato(ta) a - **2.** [dispute - statement] disputar; [- decision] impugnar.

contestant [kənˈtestənt] *n* [in quiz show] concursante *mf*; [in race] participante *mf*; [in boxing match] contrincante *mf*.

context [ˈkɒntekst] *n* contexto *m*; **out of context** fuera de contexto.

continent [ˈkɒntɪnənt] *n* continente *m*.

➤ **Continent** *n UK*: **the Continent** Europa continental.

continental [,kɒntɪˈnentl] ⋄ *adj* - **1.** GEOG continental - **2.** *UK* [European] de Europa continental. ⋄ *n UK inf* europeo *m* (a) (*de Europa continental*).

continental breakfast *n* desayuno *m* continental.

continental quilt *n UK* edredón *m*.

contingency [kənˈtɪndʒənsɪ] (*pl* -ies) *n* contingencia *f*.

contingency plan *n* plan *m* de emergencia.

contingent [kənˈtɪndʒənt] ⋄ *adj fml*: **contingent on** OR **upon** supeditado(da) a. ⋄ *n* - **1.** MIL contingente *m* - **2.** [group] representación *f*.

continual [kənˈtɪnjʊəl] *adj* continuo(nua), constante.

continually [kənˈtɪnjʊəlɪ] *adv* continuamente, constantemente.

continuation [kən,tɪnjʊˈeɪʃn] *n* continuación *f*.

continue [kənˈtɪnjuː] ⋄ *vt*: **to continue (doing** OR **to do sthg)** continuar (haciendo algo); '**to be continued**' 'continuará'. ⋄ *vi*: **to continue (with sthg)** continuar (con algo).

continuity [,kɒntɪˈnjuːətɪ] *n* - **1.** [coherence] continuidad *f*; **continuity announcer** locutor *m*, -ra *f* de continuidad - **2.** CIN: **continuity girl** script *f*, anotadora *f*.

continuous [kənˈtɪnjʊəs] *adj* continuo(nua).

continuous assessment *n* evaluación *f* continua.

continuously [kənˈtɪnjʊəslɪ] *adv* continuamente, ininterrumpidamente.

contort [kənˈtɔːt] ⋄ *vt* retorcer. ⋄ *vi* retorcerse.

contortion [kənˈtɔːʃn] *n* contorsión *f*.

contour [ˈkɒn,tʊər] ⋄ *n* - **1.** [outline] contorno *m* - **2.** [on map] curva *f* de nivel. ⋄ *comp*: **contour map** mapa *m* topográfico; **contour line** curva *f* de nivel.

contraband ['kɒntrəbænd] ◇ adj de contrabando. ◇ n contrabando m.

contraception [,kɒntrə'sepʃn] n anticoncepción f.

contraceptive [,kɒntrə'septɪv] ◇ adj anticonceptivo(va). ◇ n anticonceptivo m.

contraceptive pill n píldora f anticonceptiva.

contract ◇ n ['kɒntrækt] contrato m. ◇ vt [kən'trækt] **- 1.** [through legal agreement]: **to contract sb (to do sthg)** contratar a alguien (para hacer algo); **to contract to do sthg** comprometerse (por contrato) a hacer algo **- 2.** fml [illness, disease] contraer **- 3.** [muscle, word, debt] contraer. ◇ vi [kən'trækt] [decrease in size, length] contraerse.

⇒ **contract in** vi esp UK acceder formalmente a participar.

⇒ **contract out** ◇ vt sep: **they've contracted out refuse collection to a private firm** han contratado a una empresa privada para que se encargue de la recogida de la basura. ◇ vi esp UK: **to contract out (of)** optar formalmente por no participar (en).

contraction [kən'trækʃn] n contracción f.

contractor [kən'træktər] n contratista mf.

contractual [kən'træktʃuəl] adj contractual.

contradict [,kɒntrə'dɪkt] vt contradecir.

contradiction [,kɒntrə'dɪkʃn] n contradicción f; **contradiction in terms** contradicción f en sí misma.

contradictory [,kɒntrə'dɪktərɪ] adj contradictorio(ria).

contraflow ['kɒntrəfləʊ] n habilitación del carril contrario.

contralto [kən'træltəʊ] (pl -s) n contralto mf.

contraption [kən'træpʃn] n chisme m, artilugio m.

contrary ['kɒntrərɪ] ◇ adj **- 1.** [opposite] contrario(ria); **contrary to** en contra de **- 2.** [kən'treərɪ] [awkward] puñetero(ra), que lleva la contraria siempre. ◇ n: **the contrary** lo contrario; **on the contrary** al contrario; **to the contrary** en contra; **unless I hear to the contrary** a menos que me digan lo contrario OR otra cosa.

⇒ **contrary to** prep en contra de.

contrast ◇ n ['kɒntrɑːst]: **contrast (between)** contraste m (entre); **by** OR **in contrast** en cambio; **in contrast with** OR **to** a diferencia de; **to be a contrast (to** OR **with)** contrastar (con). ◇ vt [kən'trɑːst]: **to contrast sthg with** contrastar algo con. ◇ vi [kən'trɑːst]: **to contrast (with)** contrastar (con).

contrasting [kən'trɑːstɪŋ] adj [personalities, views] opuesto(ta); [colours] que contrastan.

contravene [,kɒntrə'viːn] vt contravenir.

contravention [,kɒntrə'venʃn] n contravención f.

contribute [kən'trɪbjuːt] ◇ vt **- 1.** [give] contribuir, aportar **- 2.** [to magazine, newspaper]: **to contribute (to)** escribir (para). ◇ vi **- 1.** [gen]: **to contribute (to)** contribuir (a) **- 2.** [write material]: **to contribute to** colaborar con.

contributing [kən'trɪbjuːtɪŋ] adj contribuyente.

contribution [,kɒntrɪ'bjuːʃn] n **- 1.** [gen]: **contribution (to)** contribución f (a) **- 2.** [article] colaboración f **- 3.** [to social security] cotización f.

contributor [kən'trɪbjʊtər] n **- 1.** [of money] contribuyente mf **- 2.** [to magazine, newspaper] colaborador m, -ra f.

contributory [kən'trɪbjʊtərɪ] adj [factor] contribuyente.

contributory pension scheme n plan m de pensiones contributivo.

contrite ['kɒntraɪt] adj arrepentido(da).

contrition [kən'trɪʃn] n arrepentimiento m.

contrivance [kən'traɪvns] n **- 1.** [contraption] artilugio m **- 2.** [ploy] estratagema f, treta f.

contrive [kən'traɪv] fml vt **- 1.** [engineer] maquinar, idear **- 2.** [manage]: **to contrive to do sthg** lograr hacer algo.

contrived [kən'traɪvd] adj inverosímil.

control [kən'trəʊl] ◇ n **- 1.** [gen & COMPUT] control m; [on spending] restricción f; **beyond** OR **outside one's control** fuera del control de uno; **in control of** al mando de; **to be in control of o.s.** tener el control de sí mismo; **to be in control of the situation** dominar la situación; **out of/under control** fuera de/bajo control; **to gain control (of)** hacerse con el control (de); **to take control (of)** tomar el control (de) **- 2.** [of emotions] dominio m, control m; **to lose control** perder el dominio. ◇ vt (pt & pp **-led**, cont **-ling**) **- 1.** [gen] controlar; **to control o.s.** dominarse, controlarse **- 2.** [operate - machine, plane] manejar; [- central heating] regular. ◇ comp de control.

⇒ **controls** npl [of machine, vehicle] mandos mpl.

control group n grupo m de control.

control key n COMPUT tecla f de control.

controlled [kən'trəʊld] adj **- 1.** [person] controlado(da) **- 2.** ECON dirigido(da).

controller [kən'trəʊlər] n FIN interventor m, -ra f; RADIO & TV director m, -ra f.

controlling interest n participación f mayoritaria.

control panel n tablero m de instrumentos OR de mandos.

control tower n torre f de control.

controversial [ˌkɒntrəˈvɜːʃl] *adj* polémico(ca), controvertido(da).

controversy [ˈkɒntrəvɜːsɪ, *UK* kənˈtrɒvəsɪ] (*pl* -ies) *n* polémica *f*, controversia *f*.

conundrum [kəˈnʌndrəm] (*pl* -s) *n fml* [problem] enigma *m*.

conurbation [ˌkɒnɜːˈbeɪʃn] *n* conurbación *f*.

convalesce [ˌkɒnvəˈles] *vi* convalecer.

convalescence [ˌkɒnvəˈlesns] *n* convalecencia *f*.

convalescent [ˌkɒnvəˈlesnt] <> *adj* [patient] convaleciente. <> *n* convaleciente *mf*.

convection [kənˈvekʃn] *n* convección *f*.

convector [kənˈvektəʳ] *n* calentador *m* de convección, convector *m*.

convene [kənˈviːn] <> *vt* convocar. <> *vi* reunirse.

convener [kənˈviːnəʳ] *n UK* [trade union official] *sindicalista que supervisa a los delegados sindicales de una empresa.*

convenience [kənˈviːnjəns] *n* comodidad *f*, conveniencia *f*; **do it at your convenience** hágalo cuando le venga bien; **at your earliest convenience** en cuanto le sea posible.

convenience food *n* comida *f* preparada.

convenience store *n* tienda *f* de ultramarinos *(que abre hasta tarde)*.

convenient [kənˈviːnjənt] *adj* - **1.** [suitable] conveniente; **is Monday convenient?** ¿te viene bien el lunes? - **2.** [handy - size] práctico(ca); [- position] adecuado(da); **convenient for** [well-situated] bien situado(da) para.

conveniently [kənˈviːnjəntlɪ] *adv* convenientemente; **conveniently located** bien situado(da).

convent [ˈkɒnvənt] *n* convento *m*.

convention [kənˈvenʃn] *n* convención *f*.

conventional [kənˈvenʃənl] *adj* convencional.

conventionally [kənˈvenʃnəlɪ] *adv* de manera convencional.

convent school *n* colegio *m* de monjas.

converge [kənˈvɜːdʒ] *vi lit* & *fig*: **to converge (on)** converger (en); **the protesters converged on the palace** los manifestantes se dieron cita ante el palacio.

conversant [kənˈvɜːsənt] *adj fml*: **conversant with** familiarizado(da) con.

conversation [ˌkɒnvəˈseɪʃn] *n* conversación *f*; **to make conversation (with)** dar conversación (a).

conversational [ˌkɒnvəˈseɪʃənl] *adj* coloquial; **conversational style** estilo familiar.

conversationalist [ˌkɒnvəˈseɪʃnəlɪst] *n* conversador *m*, -ra *f*.

converse <> *adj* [ˈkɒnvɜːs] *fml* contrario(ria), opuesto(ta). <> *n* [ˈkɒnvɜːs]: **the converse** lo contrario OR opuesto. <> *vi* [kənˈvɜːs] *fml*: **to converse (with)** conversar (con).

conversely [kənˈvɜːslɪ] *adv fml* a la inversa.

conversion [kənˈvɜːʃn] *n* - **1.** [gen, COMPUT & RELIG] conversión *f* - **2.** [in building] reforma *f* - **3.** [in rugby] transformación *f*.

conversion table *n* tabla *f* de conversión OR de equivalencias.

convert <> *vt* [kənˈvɜːt] - **1.** [gen & COMPUT]: **to convert sthg (to OR into)** convertir algo (en) - **2.** [change belief of]: **to convert sb (to)** convertir a alguien (a) - **3.** [in rugby] transformar. <> *vi* [kənˈvɜːt] - **1.** [change]: **to convert from sthg to** pasarse de algo a - **2.** RELIG: **to convert to sthg** convertirse a algo - **3.** [in rugby] hacer una transformación. <> *n* [ˈkɒnvɜːt] converso *m*, -sa *f*.

converted [kənˈvɜːtɪd] *adj* - **1.** [building, ship] acondicionado(da) - **2.** RELIG converso(sa).

convertible [kənˈvɜːtəbl] <> *adj* - **1.** [sofa]: **convertible sofa** sofá-cama *m* - **2.** [currency] convertible - **3.** [car] descapotable. <> *n* (coche *m*) descapotable *m*.

convex [kɒnˈveks] *adj* convexo(xa).

convey [kənˈveɪ] *vt* - **1.** *fml* [transport] transportar, llevar - **2.** [express]: **to convey sthg (to)** transmitir algo (a).

conveyancing [kənˈveɪənsɪŋ] *n (U)* redacción *f* de escrituras de traspaso.

convict <> *n* [ˈkɒnvɪkt] presidiario *m*, -ria *f*. <> *vt* [kənˈvɪkt]: **to convict sb of** condenar a alguien por, declarar a alguien culpable de.

convicted [kənˈvɪktɪd] *adj* convicto(ta).

conviction [kənˈvɪkʃn] *n* - **1.** [belief, fervour] convicción *f* - **2.** LAW condena *f*.

convince [kənˈvɪns] *vt*: **to convince sb (of sthg/to do sthg)** convencer a alguien (de algo/para que haga algo).

convinced [kənˈvɪnst] *adj*: **convinced (of)** convencido(da) (de).

convincing [kənˈvɪnsɪŋ] *adj* convincente.

convivial [kənˈvɪvɪəl] *adj* [gathering, atmosphere] agradable; [group] alegre.

convoluted [ˈkɒnvəluːtɪd] *adj* [tortuous] enrevesado(da).

convoy [ˈkɒnvɔɪ] *n* convoy *m*; **in convoy** en convoy.

convulse [kənˈvʌls] *vt*: **to be convulsed with** [pain] retorcerse de; [laughter] troncharse de.

convulsion [kənˈvʌlʃn] *n* MED convulsión *f*.

convulsive [kənˈvʌlsɪv] *adj* convulsivo(va).

coo [kuː] *vi* arrullar.

cook [kʊk] <> *n* cocinero *m*, -ra *f*. <> *vt* - **1.** [gen] cocinar, guisar; [prepare] preparar, hacer **- 2.** *inf* [falsify] falsificar. ◇ *vi* **- 1.** [prepare food] cocinar, guisar **- 2.** [subj: food] cocerse, hacerse.

◆ **cook up** *vt sep* [plan, deal] tramar, urdir; [excuse] inventarse.

cookbook ['kʊk,bʊk] = **cookery book**.

cooked [kʊkt] *adj* cocido(da).

cooker ['kʊkəʳ] *n esp UK* cocina *f (aparato)*.

cookery ['kʊkərɪ] *n* cocina *f (arte)*.

cookery book, cookbook *n* libro *m* de cocina.

cookie ['kʊkɪ] *n* **- 1.** *US* [biscuit] galleta *f* **- 2.** COMPUT cookie *m*.

cooking ['kʊkɪŋ] ◇ *n* **- 1.** [activity]: **do you like cooking?** ¿te gusta cocinar? **- 2.** [food] cocina *f*. ◇ *comp* [utensils, salt] de cocina; [oil, sherry] para cocinar OR guisar.

cooking apple *n* manzana *f* para asar.

cookout ['kʊkaʊt] *n US* barbacoa *f* al aire libre.

cool [kuːl] ◇ *adj* **- 1.** [not warm] fresco(ca); [lukewarm] tibio(bia); **it's cool** hace fresco **- 2.** [calm] tranquilo(la) **- 3.** [unfriendly] frío(a) **- 4.** *inf* [hip] guay, chachi. ◇ *vt* refrescar. ◇ *vi* **- 1.** [become less warm] enfriarse **- 2.** [abate] calmarse, aplacarse. ◇ *n*: **to keep/lose one's cool** mantener/perder la calma.

◆ **cool down** ◇ *vt sep* **- 1.** [make less warm] refrescar **- 2.** [make less angry] calmar. ◇ *vi* **- 1.** [become less warm] enfriarse **- 2.** [become less angry] calmarse.

◆ **cool off** *vi* **- 1.** [become less warm] refrescarse **- 2.** [become less angry] calmarse.

coolant ['kuːlənt] *n* refrigerante *m*.

cool box *n* nevera *f* portátil.

cool-headed [-'hedɪd] *adj* [person] sereno(na); [reaction] calmado(da).

cooling-off period ['kuːlɪŋ-] *n* tiempo en el que los sindicatos y la patronal pueden intentar llegar a un acuerdo antes de que se declare una huelga.

cooling tower ['kuːlɪŋ-] *n* torre *f* de refrigeración.

coolly ['kuːlɪ] *adv* **- 1.** [calmly] con tranquilidad **- 2.** [coldly] con frialdad.

coolness ['kuːlnɪs] *n* **- 1.** [in temperature] frescor *m* **- 2.** [unfriendliness] frialdad *f* **- 3.** [calmness] serenidad *f*.

coop [kuːp] *n* gallinero *m*.

◆ **coop up** *vt sep inf* encerrar.

cooperate [kəʊ'ɒpəreɪt] *vi*: **to cooperate (with)** cooperar (con).

cooperation [kəʊ,ɒpə'reɪʃn] *n* cooperación *f*.

cooperative [kəʊ'ɒpərətɪv] ◇ *adj* **- 1.** [helpful] servicial, dispuesto(ta) a ayudar **- 2.** [collective] cooperativo(va). ◇ *n* cooperativa *f*.

co-opt *vt*: **to co-opt sb onto sthg** nombrar a alguien miembro de algo.

coordinate ◇ *n* [kəʊ'ɔːdɪnət] coordenada *f*. ◇ *vt* [kəʊ'ɔːdɪneɪt] coordinar.

◆ **coordinates** *npl* [clothes] conjuntos *mpl*.

coordination [kəʊ,ɔːdɪ'neɪʃn] *n* coordinación *f*.

co-ownership *n* copropiedad *f*.

cop [kɒp] *n inf* poli *mf*; **the cops** la poli.

◆ **cop out** *vi* (*pt & pp* **-ped**, *cont* **-ping**) *inf*: **to cop out (of)** escaquearse (de).

cope [kəʊp] *vi* arreglárselas; **to cope with** [work] poder con; [problem, situation] hacer frente a.

copier ['kɒpɪəʳ] *n* copiadora *f*, fotocopiadora *f*.

copilot ['kəʊ,paɪlət] *n* copiloto *mf*.

copious ['kəʊpjəs] *adj* copioso(sa), abundante.

cop-out *n inf* escaqueo *m*.

copper ['kɒpəʳ] *n* **- 1.** [metal] cobre *m* **- 2.** *UK inf* [policeman] poli *mf*, paco *m*, -ca *f Andes*.

◆ **coppers** *npl UK* calderilla *f (sólo de monedas de uno y dos peniques)*.

coppice ['kɒpɪs], **copse** [kɒps] *n* bosquecillo *m*.

copulate ['kɒpjʊleɪt] *vi*: **to copulate (with)** copular (con).

copulation [,kɒpjʊ'leɪʃn] *n* cópula *f*.

copy ['kɒpɪ] ◇ *n* **- 1.** [imitation, duplicate] copia *f* **- 2.** [of book, magazine] ejemplar *m*. ◇ *vt* (*pt & pp* **-ied**) **- 1.** [imitate & COMPUT] copiar **- 2.** [photocopy] fotocopiar. ◇ *vi* (*pt & pp* **-ied**) copiar.

◆ **copy down** *vt sep* copiar (por escrito).

◆ **copy in** *vt sep*: **to copy sb in (on sth)** mandar una copia a alguien (de algo).

◆ **copy out** *vt sep* copiar, pasar a limpio.

copycat ['kɒpɪkæt] ◇ *n inf* copión *m*, -ona *f*. ◇ *comp* [crime] calcado de otro(calcada de otra).

copy protect *vt* COMPUT proteger contra copia.

copyright ['kɒpɪraɪt] *n (U)* derechos *mpl* de autor.

copy typist *n UK* mecanógrafo *m*, -fa *f*.

copywriter ['kɒpɪ,raɪtəʳ] *n* redactor *m*, -ra *f* de textos publicitarios.

coral ['kɒrəl] ◇ *n* coral *m*. ◇ *comp* de coral.

coral reef *n* arrecife *m* de coral.

Coral Sea *n*: **the Coral Sea** el mar del Coral.

cord [kɔːd] ◇ *n* **- 1.** [string] cuerda *f*; [for tying clothes] cordón *m* **- 2.** [cable] cable *m*, cordón *m* **- 3.** [fabric] pana *f*. ◇ *comp* de pana.

◆ **cords** *npl* pantalones *mpl* de pana.

cordial ['kɔːdjəl] ◇ *adj* cordial. ◇ *n* refresco *m (hecho a base de concentrado de fruta)*.

cordially ['kɔːdɪəlɪ] *adv* cordialmente.

Cordoba ['kɔːdəbə] *n* Córdoba.

cordon [ˈkɔːdn] n cordón m.
← cordon off vt sep acordonar.
cordon bleu [-ˈblɜː] adj de primera clase.
corduroy [ˈkɔːdərɔɪ] <> n pana f. <> comp de pana.
core [kɔːr] <> n - **1.** [of fruit] corazón m - **2.** [of Earth, nuclear reactor, group] núcleo m - **3.** [of issue, matter] meollo m; **to the core** hasta la médula. <> vt quitar el corazón de.
corer [ˈkɔːrər] n sacacorazones m inv.
core time n UK en un sistema de horario flexible, periodo en el que todos deben estar trabajando.
Corfu [kɔːˈfuː] n Corfú.
corgi [ˈkɔːgɪ] (pl -s) n corgi mf.
coriander [ˌkɒrɪˈændər] n cilantro m.
cork [kɔːk] n corcho m.
corkage [ˈkɔːkɪdʒ] n recargo que se paga en un restaurante por haber consumido bebidas traídas de fuera.
corked [kɔːkt] adj con sabor a corcho.
corkscrew [ˈkɔːkskruː] n sacacorchos m inv.
cormorant [ˈkɔːmərənt] n cormorán m.
corn [kɔːn] <> n - **1.** UK [wheat, barley, oats] cereal m - **2.** US [maize] maíz m, choclo m Andes & R Plata; **corn on the cob** mazorca f - **3.** [callus] callo m. <> comp US de maíz.
Corn abbr of **Cornwall**.
cornea [ˈkɔːnɪə] (pl -s) n córnea f.
corned beef [kɔːnd-] n fiambre de carne de vaca cocinada y enlatada.
corner [ˈkɔːnər] <> n - **1.** [angle - of street, page, screen] esquina f; [- of room, cupboard] rincón m; [- of mouth] comisura f; **to cut corners** economizar esfuerzos, atajar; **just around the corner** a la vuelta de la esquina - **2.** [bend - in street, road] curva f - **3.** [faraway place] rincón m - **4.** [in football] saque m de esquina, córner m. <> vt - **1.** [trap] arrinconar - **2.** [monopolize] acaparar.
corner flag n banderín m de córner.
corner kick n FTBL saque m de esquina, córner m.
corner shop n pequeña tienda de barrio que vende comida, artículos de limpieza etc.
cornerstone [ˈkɔːnəstəun] n fig piedra f angular.
cornet [ˈkɔːnɪt] n - **1.** [instrument] corneta f - **2.** UK [ice-cream cone] cucurucho m.
cornfield [ˈkɔːnfiːld] n - **1.** UK campo m de cereal - **2.** US maizal m.
cornflakes [ˈkɔːnfleɪks] npl copos mpl de maíz, cornflakes mpl.
cornflour UK [ˈkɔːnflauər], **cornstarch** US [ˈkɔːnstɑːtʃ] n harina f de maíz, maicena® f.

cornice [ˈkɔːnɪs] n cornisa f.
Cornish [ˈkɔːnɪʃ] <> adj de Cornualles. <> n [language] córnico m. <> npl: **the Cornish** los córnicos.
cornstarch US = **cornflour**.
cornucopia [ˌkɔːnjuˈkəupjə] n liter cornucopia f.
Cornwall [ˈkɔːnwɔːl] n Cornualles.
corny [ˈkɔːnɪ] (comp -ier, superl -iest) adj inf trillado(da).
corollary [kəˈrɒlərɪ] (pl -ies) n corolario m.
coronary [ˈkɒrənrɪ] (pl -ies), **coronary thrombosis** [-θrɒmˈbəusɪs] (pl coronary thromboses [-θrɒmˈbəusiːz]) n trombosis f inv coronaria, infarto m.
coronation [ˌkɒrəˈneɪʃn] n coronación f.
coroner [ˈkɒrənər] n juez de instrucción que investiga los casos de muerte sospechosa.
Corp. (abbr of corporation) Corp.
corpora [ˈkɔːpərə] npl ⊳ **corpus**.
corporal [ˈkɔːpərəl] n cabo mf.
corporal punishment n castigo m corporal.
corporate [ˈkɔːpərət] adj - **1.** [business] corporativo(va); [strategy, culture] empresarial - **2.** [collective] colectivo(va).
corporate hospitality n (U) atenciones fpl de la compañía.
corporate identity, corporate image n imagen f corporativa.
corporation [ˌkɔːpəˈreɪʃn] n - **1.** [company] ≈ sociedad f anónima - **2.** UK [council] ayuntamiento m.
corporation tax n UK impuesto m de sociedades.
corps [kɔːr] (pl corps) n cuerpo m; **the press corps** los periodistas acreditados.
corpse [kɔːps] n cadáver m.
corpulent [ˈkɔːpjulənt] adj obeso(sa).
corpus [ˈkɔːpəs] (pl -pora OR -puses) n corpus m inv.
corpuscle [ˈkɔːpʌsl] n glóbulo m.
corral [kɒˈrɑːl] n corral m.
correct [kəˈrekt] <> adj - **1.** [accurate - time, amount, forecast] exacto(ta); [- answer, spelling, information] correcto(ta); **you're correct** tienes razón - **2.** [socially acceptable] correcto(ta) - **3.** [appropriate, required] apropiado(da). <> vt corregir.
correction [kəˈrekʃn] n corrección f.
correctly [kəˈrektlɪ] adv - **1.** [gen] correctamente; **I don't think I can have heard you correctly** no estoy segura de haberte oído bien - **2.** [appropriately, as required] apropiadamente.
correlate [ˈkɒrəleɪt] <> vt relacionar, vincular. <> vi: **to correlate (with)** guardar correspondencia (con).

correlation [ˌkɒrə'leɪʃn] *n*: **correlation (between)** correlación *f* (entre).

correspond [ˌkɒrɪ'spɒnd] *vi* - **1.** [correlate]: **to correspond (with OR to)** corresponder (con OR a) - **2.** [match]: **to correspond (with OR to)** coincidir (con) - **3.** [write letters]: **to correspond (with)** cartearse (con).

correspondence [ˌkɒrɪ'spɒndəns] *n*: **correspondence (with/between)** correspondencia *f* (con/entre).

correspondence course *n* curso *m* por correspondencia.

correspondent [ˌkɒrɪ'spɒndənt] *n* [reporter] corresponsal *mf*.

corresponding [ˌkɒrɪ'spɒndɪŋ] *adj* correspondiente.

corridor ['kɒrɪdɔːʳ] *n* pasillo *m*, corredor *m*.

corroborate [kə'rɒbəreɪt] *vt* corroborar.

corroboration [kəˌrɒbə'reɪʃn] *n* corroboración *f*.

corrode [kə'rəʊd] ⬦ *vt* corroer. ⬦ *vi* corroerse.

corrosion [kə'rəʊʒn] *n* corrosión *f*.

corrosive [kə'rəʊsɪv] *adj* [poison, substance] corrosivo(va).

corrugated ['kɒrəgeɪtɪd] *adj* ondulado(da).

corrugated iron *n* chapa *f* ondulada.

corrupt [kə'rʌpt] ⬦ *adj* [gen & COMPUT] corrupto(ta). ⬦ *vt* [gen & COMPUT] corromper; **to corrupt a minor** pervertir a un menor.

corruption [kə'rʌpʃn] *n* corrupción *f*.

corsage [kɔː'sɑːʒ] *n* ramillete *m*.

corset ['kɔːsɪt] *n* corsé *m*.

Corsica ['kɔːsɪkə] *n* Córcega *f*.

Corsican ['kɔːsɪkən] ⬦ *adj* corso(sa). ⬦ *n* - **1.** [person] corso *m*, -sa *f* - **2.** [language] corso *m*.

cortege, cortège [kɔː'teɪʒ] *n* cortejo *m*.

cortisone ['kɔːtɪzəʊn] *n* cortisona *f*.

cos[1] [kɒz] *UK inf abbr of* **because**.

cos[2] [kɒs] = **cos lettuce**.

cosh [kɒʃ] ⬦ *n* porra *f*. ⬦ *vt* aporrear.

cosignatory [ˌkəʊ'sɪgnətrɪ] (*pl* -**ies**) *n* cosignatario *m*, -ria *f*.

cosine ['kəʊsaɪn] *n* coseno *m*.

cos lettuce [kɒs-'letɪs], **cos** *n UK* lechuga *f* romana.

cosmetic [kɒz'metɪk] ⬦ *n* cosmético *m*. ⬦ *adj* *fig* superficial.

cosmetic surgery *n* cirugía *f* estética.

cosmic ['kɒzmɪk] *adj* cósmico(ca).

cosmonaut ['kɒzmənɔːt] *n* cosmonauta *mf*.

cosmopolitan [kɒzmə'pɒlɪtn] *adj* cosmopolita.

cosmos ['kɒzmɒs] *n*: **the cosmos** el cosmos.

cosset ['kɒsɪt] *vt* mimar.

cost [kɒst] ⬦ *n* coste *m*, costo *m*; **at cost** [comm] a precio de coste; **at no extra cost** sin costo adicional; **at the cost of** a costa de; **at all costs** a toda costa. ⬦ *vt* (*pt* & *pp* **cost** OR -**ed**) - **1.** [gen] costar; **it cost us £20/a lot of effort** nos costó 20 libras/mucho esfuerzo; **how much does it cost?** ¿cuánto cuesta OR vale? - **2.** [estimate] presupuestar, preparar un presupuesto de.

➤ **costs** *npl* LAW litisexpensas *fpl*, costas *fpl* (judiciales).

co-star ['kəʊ-] ⬦ *n* coprotagonista *mf*. ⬦ *vt*: **the film co-stars...** la película está coprotagonizada por... ⬦ *vi*: **to co-star in a film** coprotagonizar una película.

Costa Rica [ˌkɒstə'riːkə] *n* Costa Rica.

Costa Rican [ˌkɒstə'riːkən] ⬦ *adj* costarricense. ⬦ *n* costarricense *mf*.

cost-effective *adj* rentable.

cost-effectiveness *n* rentabilidad *f*.

costing ['kɒstɪŋ] *n* cálculo *m* del coste.

costly ['kɒstlɪ] (*comp* -**ier**, *superl* -**iest**) *adj* costoso(sa).

cost of living *n*: **the cost of living** el coste de la vida.

costume ['kɒstjuːm] *n* - **1.** [gen] traje *m* - **2.** [swimming costume] traje *m* de baño.

costume jewellery *n* (*U*) joyas *fpl* de fantasía, bisutería *f*.

cosy *UK*, **cozy** *US* ['kəʊzɪ] ⬦ *adj* (*comp* -**ier**, *superl* -**iest**) - **1.** [warm and comfortable - room] acogedor(ra); [- clothes] cómodo(da) - **2.** [intimate] agradable, amigable. ⬦ *n* (*pl* -**ies**) funda *f* para tetera.

cot [kɒt] *n* - **1.** *UK* [for child] cuna *f* - **2.** *US* [folding bed] cama *f* plegable, catre *m*.

cot death *n* muerte *f* súbita infantil.

cottage ['kɒtɪdʒ] *n* casa *f* de campo, chalé *m*.

cottage cheese *n* queso *m* fresco.

cottage hospital *n UK* hospital pequeño en el campo.

cottage industry *n* industria *f* casera.

cottage pie *n UK* pastel de carne picada con una capa de puré de patatas.

cotton ['kɒtn] ⬦ *n* - **1.** [fabric, plant] algodón *m* - **2.** [thread] hilo *m* (de algodón). ⬦ *comp* [dress, shirt, mill] de algodón; INDUST algodonero(ra).

➤ **cotton on** *vi inf*: **to cotton on (to)** caer en la cuenta (de).

cotton bud *UK*, **cotton swab** *US n* bastoncillo *m* (de algodón).

cotton candy *n US* azúcar *m* hilado, algodón *m*.

cotton swab *US* = **cotton bud**.

cotton wool *n* algodón *m* (hidrófilo).

couch [kaʊtʃ] ⟨⟩ n - **1.** [sofa] sofá m - **2.** [in doctor's surgery] diván m. ⟨⟩ vt: **to couch sthg in** formular algo en.

couchette [kuːˈʃet] n UK litera f.

couch potato n inf persona perezosa que pasa mucho tiempo en el sofá viendo la televisión.

cougar [ˈkuːgə] (pl cougar OR -s) n puma m.

cough [kɒf] ⟨⟩ n tos f; **to have a cough** tener tos. ⟨⟩ vi toser. ⟨⟩ vt escupir.
◆ **cough up** vt sep - **1.** [bring up] escupir - **2.** v inf [pay up] soltar.

coughing [ˈkɒfɪŋ] n (U) tos f.

cough mixture, cough syrup n UK jarabe m para la tos.

cough sweet n UK caramelo m para la tos.

cough syrup = cough mixture.

could [kʊd] pt ▷ can.

couldn't [ˈkʊdnt] (abbr of = could not), = can.

could've [ˈkʊdəv] (abbr of = could have), = can.

council [ˈkaʊnsl] ⟨⟩ n - **1.** [of a town] ayuntamiento m; [of a county] ≃ diputación f - **2.** [group, organization] consejo m - **3.** [meeting] junta f, consejo m. ⟨⟩ comp [meeting, leader] del ayuntamiento; [tenant] de una vivienda protegida.

council estate n urbanización de viviendas de protección oficial.

council house n UK ≃ casa f de protección oficial.

councillor [ˈkaʊnsələ] n concejal m, -la f.

Council of Europe n Consejo m de Europa.

council tax n UK impuesto municipal basado en el valor de la propiedad, ≃ contribución f urbana.

counsel [ˈkaʊnsəl] ⟨⟩ n - **1.** (U) fml [advice] consejo m; **to keep one's own counsel** reservarse su opinión - **2.** [lawyer] abogado m, -da f. ⟨⟩ vt (UK -led, cont -ling, US -ed, cont -ing) aconsejar; **to counsel sb to do sthg** fig aconsejar a alguien hacer algo.

counselling UK, **counseling** US [ˈkaʊnsəlɪŋ] n (U) ayuda f psicológica.

counsellor UK, **counselor** US [ˈkaʊnsələ] n - **1.** [gen] consejero m, -ra f - **2.** [therapist] psicólogo m, -ga f - **3.** US [lawyer] abogado m, -da f.

count [kaʊnt] ⟨⟩ n - **1.** [total] total m; [of votes] recuento m; **to keep/lose count of** llevar/perder la cuenta de - **2.** [point] punto m - **3.** LAW [charge] cargo m - **4.** [aristocrat] conde m. ⟨⟩ vt - **1.** [add up] contar; [total, cost] calcular - **2.** [consider]: **to count sb as** considerar a alguien como - **3.** [include] incluir, contar. ⟨⟩ vi

contar; **to count (up) to** contar hasta; **to count for nothing** no contar para nada; **to count as** contar como.
◆ **count against** vt insep perjudicar.
◆ **count in** vt sep inf contar con.
◆ **count (up)on** vt insep contar con.
◆ **count out** vt sep - **1.** [money] ir contando - **2.** [leave out] no contar con.
◆ **count up** vt insep contar.

countdown [ˈkaʊntdaʊn] n cuenta f atrás.

countenance [ˈkaʊntənəns] ⟨⟩ n liter [face] semblante m. ⟨⟩ vt aceptar.

counter [ˈkaʊntə] ⟨⟩ n - **1.** [in shop] mostrador m; **over the counter** sin receta médica; [in bank] ventanilla f - **2.** [in board game] ficha f. ⟨⟩ vt: **to counter sthg with** responder a algo mediante; **to counter sthg by doing sthg** contrarrestar algo haciendo algo. ⟨⟩ vi: **to counter with sthg/by doing sthg** contestar con algo/haciendo algo.
◆ **counter to** adv contrario a, en contra de; **to run counter to** ir en contra de.

counteract [ˌkaʊntəˈrækt] vt contrarrestar.

counterattack [ˌkaʊntərəˈtæk] ⟨⟩ n contraataque m. ⟨⟩ vt & vi contraatacar.

counterbalance [ˌkaʊntəˈbæləns] vt fig contrapesar, compensar.

counterclaim [ˈkaʊntəkleɪm] n contrarréplica f.

counterclockwise [ˌkaʊntəˈklɒkwaɪz] adv US en sentido opuesto a las agujas del reloj.

counterespionage [ˌkaʊntərˈespɪənɑːʒ] n contraespionaje m.

counterfeit [ˈkaʊntəfɪt] ⟨⟩ adj falsificado(da). ⟨⟩ vt falsificar.

counterfoil [ˈkaʊntəfɔɪl] n matriz f.

counterintelligence [ˌkaʊntərɪnˈtelɪdʒəns] n contraespionaje m.

countermand [ˌkaʊntəˈmɑːnd] vt revocar.

countermeasure [ˈkaʊntəˌmeʒə] n medida f en contra, contramedida f.

counteroffensive [ˌkaʊntərəˈfensɪv] n contraofensiva f.

counterpart [ˈkaʊntəpɑːt] n homólogo m, -ga f.

counterpoint [ˈkaʊntəpɔɪnt] n MUS contrapunto m.

counterproductive [ˌkaʊntəprəˈdʌktɪv] adj contraproducente.

counter-revolution n contrarrevolución f.

countersank [ˈkaʊntəsæŋk] pt ▷ countersink.

countersign [ˈkaʊntəsaɪn] vt refrendar, ratificar.

countersink [ˈkaʊntəsɪŋk] (pt -sank, pp -sunk [-sʌŋk]) vt avellanar.

countess [ˈkaʊntɪs] n condesa f.

countless ['kaʊntlɪs] *adj* innumerables.

countrified ['kʌntrɪfaɪd] *adj pej* [person] pueble-rino(na); [area] provinciano(na).

country ['kʌntrɪ] (*pl* -**ies**) ◇ *n* - **1.** [nation] pa-ís *m* - **2.** [population]: **the country** el pueblo - **3.** [countryside]: **the country** el campo - **4.** [terrain] terreno *m*. ◇ *comp* campestre.

country and western ◇ *n* música *f* country. ◇ *comp* [music] country *(inv)*; [fan] del country.

country club *n* club *m* de campo.

country dancing *n* (*U*) baile *m* tradicional.

country house *n* casa *f* solariega.

countryman ['kʌntrɪmən] (*pl* -**men** [-mən]) *n* [from same country] compatriota *m*.

country music = country and western.

country park *n* UK *parque natural abierto al público.*

countryside ['kʌntrɪsaɪd] *n* [land] campo *m*; [landscape] paisaje *m*.

countrywoman ['kʌntrɪ,wʊmən] (*pl* -**women** [-,wɪmɪn]) *n* [from same country] compatriota *f*.

county ['kaʊntɪ] (*pl* -**ies**) *n* condado *m*.

county council *n* UK *organismo que gobier-na un condado,* ≃ diputación *f* provincial.

county court *n* UK *tribunal de justicia de un condado,* ≃ audiencia *f* provincial.

county town UK, **county seat** US *n* capital *f* de condado.

coup [ku:] *n* - **1.** [rebellion]: **coup (d'état)** gol-pe *m* (de estado) - **2.** [masterstroke] éxito *m*.

coupé ['ku:peɪ] *n* cupé *m*.

couple ['kʌpl] ◇ *n* - **1.** [two people in relation-ship] pareja *f* - **2.** [two objects, people]: **a couple (of)** un par (de) - **3.** [a few - objects, people]: **a couple (of)** un par (de), unos (unas). ◇ *vt* - **1.** [join]: **to couple sthg (to)** enganchar algo (con) - **2.** *fig* [associate]: **to couple sthg with** asociar algo con; **coupled with** unido(da) a, junto con.

couplet ['kʌplɪt] *n* pareado *m*.

coupling ['kʌplɪŋ] *n* RAIL enganche *m*.

coupon ['ku:pɒn] *n* [gen] vale *m*, cupón *m*; [for pools] boleto *m*.

courage ['kʌrɪdʒ] *n* valor *m*; **to take courage (from)** animarse (con); **she didn't have the courage of her convictions** no tuvo valor para defender sus principios.

courageous [kə'reɪdʒəs] *adj* valiente.

courageously [kə'reɪdʒəslɪ] *adv* valientemen-te.

courgette [kɔ:'ʒet] *n* UK calabacín *m*, calabaci-ta *f* Méx, zapallito *m* (italiano).

courier ['kʊrɪəʳ] *n* - **1.** [on holiday] guía *mf* - **2.** [to deliver letters, packages] mensajero *m*, -ra *f*.

course [kɔ:s] ◇ *n* - **1.** [gen] curso *m*; [of lectures] ciclo *m*; UNIV carrera *f*; **course of treatment** MED tratamiento *m*; **to change course** cam-biar de rumbo; **to be on course for** [ship, plane] ir rumbo a; *fig* [on target] ir camino de; **to run** OR **take its course** seguir su curso; **off course** fuera de su rumbo; **course (of action)** cami-no *m* (a seguir); **in the course of** a lo largo de - **2.** [of meal] plato *m* - **3.** SPORT [for golf] cam-po *m*; [for race] circuito *m*. ◇ *vi liter* [flow] co-rrer.

➤ **of course** *adv* - **1.** [inevitably, not surprisingly] naturalmente - **2.** [certainly] claro, por supues-to; **of course not** claro que no, desde luego que no.

coursebook ['kɔ:sbʊk] *n* libro *m* de texto.

coursework ['kɔ:swɜ:k] *n* (*U*) trabajo *m* realiza-do durante el curso.

court [kɔ:t] ◇ *n* - **1.** [place of trial, judge, jury etc] tribunal *m*; **to appear in court** comparecer ante el juez; **to go to court** ir a juicio; **to take sb to court** llevar a alguien a juicio - **2.** SPORT cancha *f*, pista *f*; **on court** en la can-cha OR pista - **3.** [of king, queen etc] corte *f* - **4.** [courtyard] patio *m*. ◇ *vt* [danger] exponer-se a; [favour] solicitar. ◇ *vi dated* [go out togeth-er] cortejarse.

courteous ['kɜ:tjəs] *adj* cortés.

courtesan [,kɔ:tɪ'zæn] *n* cortesana *f*.

courtesy ['kɜ:tɪsɪ] ◇ *n* cortesía *f*. ◇ *comp* de cortesía.

➤ **(by) courtesy of** *prep* [the author] con per-miso de; [a company] por cortesía OR gentileza de.

courtesy bus *n* [at airport] *autobús gratuito para llevar huéspedes al hotel.*

courtesy car *n* coche *m* de cortesía, carro *m* de cortesía Amér, auto *m* de cortesía.

courthouse (['kɔ:thaʊs], *pl* [-haʊzɪz]) *n* US pala-cio *m* de justicia.

courtier ['kɔ:tjəʳ] *n* cortesano *m*.

court-martial ◇ *n* (*pl* court-martials OR courts-martial) consejo *m* de guerra. ◇ *vt* (*UK* -led, *cont* -ling, *US* -ed, *cont* -ing) juzgar en consejo de guerra.

court of appeal UK, **court of appeals** US *n* tribunal *m* de apelación.

court of inquiry *n* comisión *f* de investiga-ción.

court of law *n* tribunal *m* (de justicia).

courtroom ['kɔ:trʊm] *n* sala *f* del tribunal.

courtship ['kɔ:tʃɪp] *n* - **1.** [of people] noviazgo *m* - **2.** [of animals] cortejo *m*.

court shoe *n* zapato *m* de salón *(con tacón bajo)*.

courtyard ['kɔ:tjɑ:d] *n* patio *m*.

cousin ['kʌzn] *n* primo *m*, -ma *f*.

couture [kuːˈtʊər] *n* alta costura *f*.

cove [kəʊv] *n* cala *f*, ensenada *f*.

coven [ˈkʌvən] *n* aquelarre *m*.

covenant [ˈkʌvənənt] *n* - **1.** [of money] *compromiso escrito para el pago regular de una contribución especialmente con fines caritativos* - **2.** [agreement] convenio *m*.

Coventry [ˈkɒvəntrɪ] *n*: **to send sb to Coventry** hacer el vacío a alguien.

cover [ˈkʌvər] <> *n* - **1.** [covering] cubierta *f*; [lid] tapa *f*; [for seat, typewriter] funda *f* - **2.** [blanket] manta *f*; **under the covers** debajo de las sábanas - **3.** [of book] tapa *f*, cubierta *f*; [of magazine - at the front] portada *f*; [- at the back] contraportada *f* - **4.** [protection, shelter] refugio *m*, cobijo *m*; **air cover** apoyo *m* aéreo, cobertura *f* aérea; **to take cover** [from weather, gunfire] ponerse a cubierto, refugiarse; **under cover** [from weather] a cubierto, bajo techo - **5.** [concealment] tapadera *f*; **under cover of** al amparo *OR* abrigo de; **to break cover** salir al descubierto - **6.** [insurance] cobertura *f*. <> *vt* - **1.** [gen]: **to cover sthg (with)** cubrir algo (de); [with lid] tapar algo (con) - **2.** [insure]: **to cover sb (against)** cubrir *OR* asegurar a alguien (contra) - **3.** [include] abarcar - **4.** [report on] informar sobre, cubrir - **5.** [discuss, deal with] abarcar, cubrir.

⬥ **cover up** *vt sep* - **1.** [place sthg over] tapar - **2.** [conceal] encubrir.

coverage [ˈkʌvərɪdʒ] *n* [of news] cobertura *f* informativa.

coveralls [ˈkʌvərɔːlz] *npl US* mono *m*.

cover charge *n* cubierto *m*.

cover girl *n* modelo *f OR* chica *f* de portada.

covering [ˈkʌvərɪŋ] *n* - **1.** [for floor etc] cubierta *f* - **2.** [of snow, dust] capa *f*.

covering letter *UK*, **cover letter** *US n* [with CV] carta *f* de presentación; [with parcel, letter] nota *f* aclaratoria.

cover note *n UK* póliza *f* provisional.

cover price *n* [of magazine] precio *m* *(de una revista)*.

covert [ˈkʌvət] *adj* [operation] encubierto(ta), secreto(ta); [glance] furtivo(va).

cover-up *n* encubrimiento *m*.

cover version *n* versión *f*.

covet [ˈkʌvɪt] *vt* codiciar.

cow [kaʊ] <> *n* - **1.** [female type of cattle] vaca *f* - **2.** [female elephant, whale, seal] hembra *f* - **3.** *UK inf pej* [woman] bruja *f*. <> *vt* acobardar, intimidar.

coward [ˈkaʊəd] *n* cobarde *mf*.

cowardice [ˈkaʊədɪs] *n* cobardía *f*.

cowardly [ˈkaʊədlɪ] *adj* cobarde.

cowboy [ˈkaʊbɔɪ] <> *n* - **1.** [cattlehand] vaquero *m*, tropero *m R Plata* - **2.** *UK inf* [dishonest workman] chorizo *m*. <> *comp* de vaqueros; **cowboy boots** botas *fpl* camperas.

cower [ˈkaʊər] *vi* encogerse.

cowhide [ˈkaʊhaɪd] *n* cuero *m*.

co-worker *n US* compañero *m*, -ra *f* de trabajo.

cowpat [ˈkaʊpæt] *n* boñiga *f*.

cowshed [ˈkaʊʃed] *n* establo *m*.

cox [kɒks], **coxswain** [ˈkɒksən] *n* timonel *mf*.

coy [kɔɪ] *adj* tímido(da).

coyly [ˈkɔɪlɪ] *adv* con timidez afectada.

coyote [kɔɪˈəʊtɪ] *n* coyote *m*.

cozy *US* = **cosy**.

c/p (*abbr of* **carriage paid**) pp.

CPA *n US abbr of* **certified public accountant**.

CPI (*abbr of* **Consumer Price Index**) *n* IPC *m*.

Cpl. *abbr of* **corporal**.

c.p.s. (*abbr of* **characters per second**) c.p.s.

CPS (*abbr of* **Crown Prosecution Service**) *acusación popular*.

CPU (*abbr of* **central processing unit**) *n* COMPUT CPU *f*.

crab [kræb] *n* cangrejo *m*.

crab apple *n* manzana *f* silvestre.

crack [kræk] <> *n* - **1.** [split - in wood, ground] grieta *f*; [- in glass, pottery] raja *f* - **2.** [gap] rendija *f*; **at the crack of dawn** al romper el alba - **3.** [sharp noise - of whip] chasquido *m*; [- of twigs] crujido *m* - **4.** [joke] chiste *m* - **5.** *inf* [attempt]: **to have a crack at sthg** intentar algo - **6.** [cocaine] crack *m*. <> *adj* de primera. <> *vt* - **1.** [cause to split] romper, partir - **2.** [egg, nut] cascar - **3.** [whip etc] chasquear - **4.** [bang]: **to crack one's head** golpearse la cabeza - **5.** *inf* [open - bottle] abrir; [- safe] forzar - **6.** [code] dar con la clave de, descifrar; [problem] resolver - **7.** *inf* [tell - joke] contar. <> *vi* - **1.** [split - skin, wood, ground] agrietarse; [- pottery, glass] partirse, rajarse - **2.** [break down] hundirse, venirse abajo - **3.** [make sharp noise - whip] chasquear; [- twigs] crujir - **4.** *UK inf* [act quickly]: **to get cracking** ponerse manos a la obra.

⬥ **crack down** *vi*: **to crack down (on)** tomar medidas severas (contra).

⬥ **crack up** *vi* - **1.** [under pressure] venirse abajo - **2.** *inf* [laugh] partirse de risa.

crackdown [ˈkrækdaʊn] *n*: **crackdown (on)** ofensiva *f* (contra).

cracked [ˈkrækt] *adj* - **1.** [damaged - wall] agrietado(da); [- vase] rajado(da) - **2.** [voice] ronco(ca) - **3.** *inf* [mad] majareta.

cracker [ˈkrækər] *n* - **1.** [biscuit] galleta *f* (salada) - **2.** *UK* [for Christmas] *cilindro de papel que produce un estallido al abrirlo y que tiene dentro un regalito de Navidad*.

crackers ['krækəz] *adj UK inf* majareta.

cracking ['krækɪŋ] *adj inf* - **1.** [fast]: **a cracking pace** un ritmo tremendo - **2.** [excellent] genial.

crackle ['krækl] <> *n* [of fire, cooking] crujido *m*, chasquido *m*; [on phone, radio] interferencias *fpl*. <> *vi* [fire] crujir, chasquear; [radio] sonar con interferencias.

crackling ['kræklɪŋ] *n (U)* - **1.** [of fire, dry leaves] crujido *m*; [on phone, radio] interferencias *fpl* - **2.** [pork skin] cortezas *fpl*.

crackpot ['krækpɒt] *inf* <> *adj* descabellado(da). <> *n* chiflado *m*, -da *f*.

cradle ['kreɪdl] <> *n* - **1.** [baby's bed, birthplace] cuna *f* - **2.** [hoist] andamio *m* colgante. <> *vt* acunar, mecer.

craft [krɑːft] *n* - **1.** [trade] oficio *m*; [skill] arte *m* - **2.** (*pl* **craft**) [boat] embarcación *f*.
◆ **crafts** *npl* artesanía *f*.

craftsman ['krɑːftsmən] (*pl* **-men** [-mən]) *n* artesano *m*.

craftsmanship ['krɑːftsmənʃɪp] *n (U)* - **1.** [skill] destreza *f*, habilidad *f* - **2.** [skilled work] artesanía *f*.

craftsmen *npl* ▻ **craftsman**.

crafty ['krɑːftɪ] (*comp* **-ier**, *superl* **-iest**) *adj* astuto(ta).

crag [kræg] *n* peñasco *m*.

craggy ['krægɪ] (*comp* **-ier**, *superl* **-iest**) *adj* - **1.** [rock] escarpado(da) - **2.** [face] anguloso(sa), de facciones pronunciadas.

Crakow, Krakow ['krækaʊ] *n* Cracovia.

cram [kræm] (*pt & pp* **-med**, *cont* **-ming**) <> *vt* - **1.** [push - books, clothes] embutir; [people] apiñar - **2.** [overfill]: **to cram sthg with** atiborrar *OR* atestar algo de; **to be crammed (with)** estar repleto(ta) (de). <> *vi* [study] empollar.

cramming ['kræmɪŋ] *n* [studying] empolladura *f*, empollada *f*.

cramp [kræmp] <> *n* calambre *m*; **stomach cramps** retortijones *mpl* de vientre. <> *vt* [restrict, hinder] coartar, limitar.

cramped [kræmpt] *adj* [flat, conditions] estrecho(cha).

crampon ['kræmpən] *n* crampón *m*.

cranberry ['krænbərɪ] (*pl* **-ies**) *n* arándano *m* (agrio).

crane [kreɪn] <> *n* - **1.** [machine] grúa *f* - **2.** [bird] grulla *f*. <> *vt* estirar. <> *vi* estirarse.

cranium ['kreɪnjəm] (*pl* **-niums** *OR* **-nia** [-njə]) *n* cráneo *m*.

crank [kræŋk] <> *n* - **1.** [handle] manivela *f* - **2.** *inf* [eccentric] majareta *mf*. <> *vt* - **1.** [wind] girar - **2.** AUT poner en marcha con la manivela.

crankshaft ['kræŋkʃɑːft] *n* cigüeñal *m*.

cranky ['kræŋkɪ] (*comp* **-ier**, *superl* **-iest**) *adj inf* - **1.** [odd] extravagante, estrambótico(ca) - **2.** *US* [bad-tempered] refunfuñón(ona).

cranny ['krænɪ] ▻ **nook**.

crap [kræp] *v inf* <> *n (U)* - **1.** [gen] mierda *f* - **2.** [nonsense]: **to talk crap** decir gilipolleces. <> *adj UK* de mierda, muy chungo(ga).

crappy ['kræpɪ] (*comp* **-ier**, *superl* **-iest**) *adj v inf* de mierda, muy chungo(ga).

crash [kræʃ] <> *n* - **1.** [accident] colisión *f*, choque *m*, estrellón *m Amér*; **train crash** accidente *m* de tren - **2.** [loud noise] estruendo *m* - **3.** FIN crac *m*, quiebra *f*. <> *vt* [plane] estrellar; **to crash the car** tener un accidente con el coche. <> *vi* - **1.** [collide - two vehicles] chocar, colisionar; [one vehicle - into wall etc] estrellarse; **to crash into sthg** chocar *OR* estrellarse contra algo - **2.** [make crashing noise] armar estruendo; **to crash to the ground** caerse y hacerse añicos - **3.** FIN quebrar - **4.** COMPUT colgarse, bloquearse.
◆ **crash out** *vi* dormir.

crash barrier *n* valla *f* protectora.

crash course *n* curso *m* acelerado, cursillo *m* intensivo de introducción.

crash diet *n* régimen *m* drástico.

crash-dive *vi sumergirse a gran profundidad y con gran rapidez.*

crash helmet *n* casco *m* protector.

crash-land <> *vt* hacer un aterrizaje forzoso con. <> *vi* realizar un aterrizaje forzoso.

crash landing *n* aterrizaje *m* forzoso.

crass [kræs] *adj* burdo(da); **a crass error** un craso error.

crate [kreɪt] *n* caja *f (para embalaje o transporte)*.

crater ['kreɪtər] *n* cráter *m*.

cravat [krə'væt] *n* pañuelo *m (de hombre)*.

crave [kreɪv] <> *vt* ansiar. <> *vi*: **to crave for sthg** ansiar algo.

craving ['kreɪvɪŋ] *n* [gen]: **craving (for sthg/to do sthg)** anhelo *m* (de algo/de hacer algo); [of pregnant woman]: **craving (for sthg)** antojo *m* (de algo).

crawl [krɔːl] <> *vi* - **1.** [baby] andar a gatas, gatear - **2.** [insect, person] arrastrarse - **3.** [move slowly, with difficulty] avanzar lentamente, ir a paso de tortuga - **4.** *inf* [be covered]: **to be crawling with sthg** estar infestado(da) de algo - **5.** *inf* [grovel]: **to crawl (to)** arrastrarse (ante). <> *n* - **1.** [slow pace]: **at a crawl** a paso de tortuga - **2.** [swimming stroke]: **the crawl** el crol.

crawler lane ['krɔːlər-] *n UK* carril *m* para tráfico lento.

crayon ['kreɪɒn] *n* (barra *f* de) cera *f*.

craze [kreɪz] *n* moda *f*.

crazed [kreɪzd] *adj* enloquecido(da); **crazed with** loco(ca) de.

crazy ['kreɪzɪ] (*comp* -ier, *superl* -iest) *adj inf* - **1.** [mad - person] loco(ca); [- idea] disparatado(da); **like crazy** como un loco - **2.** [enthusiastic]: **to be crazy about** estar loco(ca) por.

crazy paving *n UK* enlosado *m* irregular.

creak [kri:k] <> *n* [of floorboard, bed] crujido *m*; [of door, hinge] chirrido *m*. <> *vi* [floorboard, bed] crujir; [door, hinge] chirriar.

creaky ['kri:kɪ] (*comp* -ier, *superl* -iest) *adj* [floorboard, bed] que cruje; [door, hinge] chirriante.

cream [kri:m] <> *adj* [in colour] (color) crema (inv). <> *n* - **1.** [food] nata *f* - **2.** [cosmetic, mixture for food] crema *f*; **cream of tomato soup** crema de tomate - **3.** [colour] (color *m*) crema *m* - **4.** [elite]: **the cream** la flor y nata, la crema. <> *vt* CULIN batir; **creamed potatoes** puré *m* de patatas.

◆ **cream off** *vt sep* seleccionar, separar.

cream cake *n UK* pastel *m* de nata, pastel *m* de crema *Amér*, masa *f* de crema *R Plata*.

cream cheese *n* queso *m* cremoso *OR* blanco.

cream cracker *n UK* galleta *f* sin azúcar (que generalmente se come con queso).

cream of tartar *n* crémor *m* tártaro.

cream tea *n UK* merienda a base de de té con bollos con nata y mermelada.

creamy ['kri:mɪ] (*comp* -ier, *superl* -iest) *adj* - **1.** [taste, texture] cremoso(sa) - **2.** [colour] (color) crema (inv).

crease [kri:s] <> *n* [deliberate - in shirt] pliegue *m*; [- in trousers] raya *f*; [accidental] arruga *f*. <> *vt* arrugar. <> *vi* [gen] arrugarse; [forehead] fruncirse.

creased [kri:st] *adj* arrugado(da).

crease-resistant *adj* inarrugable.

create [kri:'eɪt] *vt* [gen] crear; [interest] producir.

creation [kri:'eɪʃn] *n* creación *f*.

creative [kri:'eɪtɪv] *adj* [gen] creativo(va); [energy] creador(ra); **creative writing** creación *f* literaria.

creativity [,kri:eɪ'tɪvətɪ] *n* creatividad *f*.

creator [kri:'eɪtər] *n* creador *m*, -ra *f*.

creature ['kri:tʃər] *n* criatura *f*; **a creature of habit** un animal de costumbres.

crèche [kreʃ] *n UK* guardería *f* (infantil).

credence ['kri:dns] *n*: **to give** *OR* **lend credence to** dar crédito a.

credentials [krɪ'denʃlz] *npl* credenciales *fpl*.

credibility [,kredə'bɪlətɪ] *n* credibilidad *f*.

credible ['kredəbl] *adj* creíble, digno(na) de crédito.

credit ['kredɪt] <> *n* - **1.** [financial aid] crédito *m*; **to be in credit** tener saldo acreedor *OR* positivo; **on credit** a crédito - **2.** (U) [praise] reconocimiento *m*; **to have sthg to one's credit** [successfully completed] tener uno algo en su haber; **to be to sb's credit** [in sb's favour] ir en favor de alguien; **to do sb credit** decir mucho en favor de alguien; **to give sbcredit for** reconocer a alguien el mérito de - **3.** [towards qualification, degree] crédito *m* - **4.** [money credited] saldo *m* acreedor *OR* positivo. <> *vt* - **1.** FIN [add] abonar; **we'll credit your account** lo abonaremos en su cuenta - **2.** [believe] creer - **3.** [give credit to]: **to credit sb with** atribuir a alguien el mérito de.

◆ **credits** *npl* [on film] títulos *mpl*.

creditable ['kredɪtəbl] *adj fml* meritorio(ria), encomiable.

credit account *n UK* cuenta *f* de crédito.

credit card *n* tarjeta *f* de crédito.

credit control *n* control *m* de crédito.

credit facilities *npl* facilidades *fpl* de crédito.

credit limit *UK,* **credit line** *US n* límite *m* de crédito.

credit note *n* [from shop] vale *m* de compra.

creditor ['kredɪtər] *n* acreedor *m*, -ra *f*.

credit rating *n* calificación *f* de solvencia.

credit squeeze *n* restricción *f* de créditos.

credit transfer *n* transferencia *f* bancaria.

creditworthy ['kredɪt,wɜ:ðɪ] *adj* solvente.

credulity [krɪ'dju:lətɪ] *n fml* credulidad *f*.

credulous ['kredjʊləs] *adj* crédulo(la).

creed [kri:d] *n* credo *m*.

creek [kri:k] *n* - **1.** [inlet] cala *f* - **2.** *US* [stream] riachuelo *m*.

creep [kri:p] <> *vi* (*pt & pp* crept) - **1.** [person] deslizarse, andar con sigilo - **2.** [insect] arrastrarse; [traffic etc] avanzar lentamente - **3.** *inf* [grovel]: **to creep (to sb)** hacer la pelota (a alguien). <> *n inf* - **1.** [unctuous person] pelotillero *m*, -ra *f*, pelota *mf* - **2.** [horrible person] asqueroso *m*, -sa *f*.

◆ **creeps** *npl*: **to give sb the creeps** *inf* ponerle a alguien la piel de gallina.

◆ **creep in** *vi* [mistake] introducirse.

◆ **creep up on** *vt* - **1.** [subj: person, animal] acercarse sigilosamente a - **2.** [subj: old age, deadline] aproximarse a.

creeper ['kri:pər] *n* enredadera *f*, bejuco *m* *Amér*.

creepy ['kri:pɪ] (*comp* -ier, *superl* -iest) *adj inf* horripilante, espeluznante.

creepy-crawly [-'krɔ:lɪ] (*pl* -ies) *n inf* bicho *m*.

cremate [krɪ'meɪt] *vt* incinerar.

cremation [krɪ'meɪʃn] *n* incineración *f*.

crematorium [ˌkremə'tɔːrɪəm] (*pl* **-riums** OR **-ria** [-rɪə]) *UK*, **crematory** ['kremətrɪ] (*pl* **-ies**) *US* *n* crematorio *m*.

creosote ['krɪəsəʊt] ⬦ *n* creosota *f*. ⬦ *vt* aplicar creosota a.

crepe [kreɪp] *n* - **1.** [cloth] crespón *m* - **2.** [rubber] crepé *m* - **3.** [thin pancake] crep *f*.

crepe bandage *n UK* venda *f* de gasa.

crepe paper *n (U)* papel *m* crespón.

crepe-soled shoes [-səʊld-] *npl UK* zapatos *mpl* de suela de crepé.

crept [krept] *pt* & *pp* ▷ **creep**.

Cres. *abbr of* Crescent.

crescendo [krɪ'ʃendəʊ] (*pl* **-s**) *n* crescendo *m*.

crescent ['kresnt] ⬦ *adj* creciente. ⬦ *n* - **1.** [shape] medialuna *f* - **2.** [street] *calle en forma de medialuna*.

cress [kres] *n* berro *m*.

crest [krest] *n* - **1.** [on bird's head, of wave] cresta *f* - **2.** [of hill] cima *f*, cumbre *f* - **3.** [on coat of arms] blasón *m*.

crestfallen ['krest,fɔːln] *adj* alicaído(da).

Crete [kriːt] *n* Creta *f*.

cretin ['kretɪn] *n inf* [idiot] cretino *m*, -na *f*.

Creutzfeldt-Jakob disease [ˌkrɔɪtsfelt'jækɒb-] *n* enfermedad *f* de Creutzfeldt-Jakob.

crevasse [krɪ'væs] *n* grieta *f*, fisura *f*.

crevice ['krevɪs] *n* grieta *f*, hendidura *f*.

crew [kruː] *n* - **1.** [of ship, plane] tripulación *f* - **2.** [on film set etc] equipo *m*.

crew cut *n* rapado *m*, corte *m* al cero.

crewman ['kruːmæn] (*pl* **-men** [-men]) *n* [of ship, plane] tripulante *m*; [on film set etc] miembro *m* del equipo.

crew-neck(ed) [-nek(t)] *adj* con cuello redondo.

crib [krɪb] ⬦ *n* - **1.** [cot] cuna *f* - **2.** *US inf* [place] casa *f*, cantón *f* Méx. ⬦ *vt* (*pt* & *pp* **-bed**, *cont* **-bing**) *inf*: **to crib sthg off** OR **from sb** copiar algo de alguien.

cribbage ['krɪbɪdʒ] *n juego de cartas en que la puntuación se anota colocando clavijas en un tablero*.

crick [krɪk] ⬦ *n* [in neck] tortícolis *f inv*; **to have a crick in one's neck** tener tortícolis. ⬦ *vt* torcerse.

cricket ['krɪkɪt] ⬦ *n* - **1.** [game] cricket *m* - **2.** [insect] grillo *m*. ⬦ *comp* de cricket.

cricketer ['krɪkɪtər] *n* jugador *m*, -ra *f* de cricket.

crikey ['kraɪkɪ] *excl UK inf* ¡caramba!

crime [kraɪm] ⬦ *n* - **1.** [serious offence] crimen *m*; [less serious offence] delito *m* - **2.** [criminal behaviour - serious] criminalidad *f*; [- less serious] delincuencia *f* - **3.** [immoral act] crimen *m*. ⬦ *comp*: **crime novel** novela *f* policíaca; **crime squad** brigada *f* de investigación criminal; **crimes against humanity** crímenes contra la humanidad.

crime wave *n* ola *f* de delincuencia.

criminal ['krɪmɪnl] ⬦ *adj* - **1.** LAW [act, behaviour] criminal, delictivo(va); [law] penal; [lawyer] criminalista; **criminal offence** delito *m* (penal) - **2.** [shameful]: **it's criminal** es un crimen. ⬦ *n* [serious] criminal *mf*; [less serious] delincuente *mf*.

criminalize, -ise ['krɪmɪnəlaɪz] *vt* [person] criminalizar.

criminal record *n* antecedentes *mpl* penales.

criminology [ˌkrɪmɪ'nɒlədʒɪ] *n* criminología *f*.

crimp [krɪmp] *vt* ondular, rizar.

crimson ['krɪmzn] ⬦ *adj* - **1.** [in colour] carmesí - **2.** [with embarrassment] colorado(da). ⬦ *n* carmesí *m*.

cringe [krɪndʒ] *vi* - **1.** [out of fear] encogerse - **2.** *inf* [with embarrassment] sentir vergüenza ajena.

crinkle ['krɪŋkl] ⬦ *n* arruga *f*. ⬦ *vt* arrugar. ⬦ *vi* arrugarse.

cripple ['krɪpl] ⬦ *n dated* & *offens* tullido *m*, -da *f*, lisiado *m*, -da *f*. ⬦ *vt* - **1.** MED dejar inválido(da) - **2.** [country, industry] paralizar, inmovilizar; [ship, plane] inutilizar.

crippling ['krɪplɪŋ] *adj* - **1.** MED postrador(ra) - **2.** [severe] abrumador(ra).

crisis ['kraɪsɪs] (*pl* **crises** ['kraɪsiːz]) *n* crisis *f inv*.

crisp [krɪsp] *adj* - **1.** [pastry, bacon, snow] crujiente; [banknote, vegetables, weather] fresco(ca) - **2.** [brisk] directo(ta), categórico(ca).

➤ **crisps** *npl UK* patatas *fpl* fritas *(de bolsa)*.

crispbread ['krɪspbred] *n galleta salada y alargada de centeno o trigo*.

crispy ['krɪspɪ] (*comp* **-ier**, *superl* **-iest**) *adj* crujiente.

crisscross ['krɪskrɒs] ⬦ *adj* entrecruzado(da). ⬦ *vt* entrecruzar. ⬦ *vi* entrecruzarse.

criterion [kraɪ'tɪərɪən] (*pl* **-ria** [-rɪə] OR **-rions**) *n* criterio *m*.

critic ['krɪtɪk] *n* crítico *m*, -ca *f*.

critical ['krɪtɪkl] *adj* [gen] crítico(ca); [illness] grave; **to be critical of** criticar; **critical acclaim** la aclamación de la crítica.

critically ['krɪtɪklɪ] *adv* [gen] críticamente; **critically important** de vital importancia; **critically acclaimed** aclamado(da) por la crítica; [ill] gravemente.

criticism ['krɪtɪsɪzm] *n* crítica *f*.

criticize, -ise ['krɪtɪsaɪz] *vt* & *vi* criticar.

critique [krɪ'tiːk] *n* crítica *f*.

croak [krəʊk] <> n - **1.** [of frog] croar m, canto m; [of raven] graznido m - **2.** [hoarse voice] ronquido m, estertor m. <> vi - **1.** [frog] croar; [raven] graznar - **2.** [person] ronquear.

Croat ['krəʊæt], **Croatian** [krəʊ'eɪʃn] <> adj croata. <> n - **1.** [person] croata mf - **2.** [language] croata m.

Croatia [krəʊ'eɪʃə] n Croacia.

Croatian = **Croat**.

crochet ['krəʊʃeɪ] <> n ganchillo m. <> vt hacer a ganchillo.

crockery ['krɒkərɪ] n loza f, vajilla f.

crocodile ['krɒkədaɪl] (pl **crocodile** OR -s) n cocodrilo m.

crocus ['krəʊkəs] (pl -es) n azafrán m (planta).

croft [krɒft] n UK pequeña granja que proporciona sustento a la familia propietaria.

croissant ['krwæsɒ] n cruasán m, medialuna f R Plata, cachito m Ven.

crony ['krəʊnɪ] (pl -ies) n inf amiguete m.

crook [krʊk] <> n - **1.** [criminal] ratero m, -ra f, delincuente mf - **2.** inf [dishonest person] ladrón m, -ona f, sinvergüenza mf - **3.** [of arm, elbow] pliegue m - **4.** [shepherd's staff] cayado m. <> vt doblar.

crooked ['krʊkɪd] adj - **1.** [teeth, tie] torcido(da) - **2.** [back] encorvado(da); [path] sinuoso(sa) - **3.** inf [dishonest - person, policeman] corrupto(ta); [- deal] sucio(cia).

croon [kruːn] vt & vi canturrear.

crop [krɒp] <> n - **1.** [kind of plant] cultivo m - **2.** [harvested produce] cosecha f, pizca f Méx - **3.** inf [group - of people] hornada f; [- of books, films etc] cosecha f - **4.** [whip] fusta f. <> vt (pt & pp -ped, cont -ping) - **1.** [cut short] cortar (muy corto) - **2.** [subj: cows, sheep] pacer.
➤ **crop up** vi surgir.

cropper ['krɒpə] n inf: **to come a cropper** [fall] darse un batacazo; [slip up] pegar un patinazo; [business] irse a la porra.

crop spraying [-,spreɪɪŋ] n fumigación f.

croquet ['krəʊkeɪ] n croquet m.

croquette [krɒ'ket] n croqueta f.

cross [krɒs] <> adj enfadado(da); **to get cross (with)** enfadarse (con). <> n - **1.** [gen] cruz f - **2.** [hybrid] cruce m, cruza f Amér; **a cross between** [combination] una mezcla de - **3.** SPORT centro m. <> vt - **1.** [gen & FIN] cruzar - **2.** [face - subj: expression] reflejarse en - **3.** SPORT centrar - **4.** [oppose] contrariar - **5.** RELIG: **to cross o.s.** santiguarse. <> vi - **1.** [intersect] cruzarse - **2.** [boat, ship] hacer una travesía.
➤ **cross off, cross out** vt sep tachar.

crossbar ['krɒsbɑːr] n - **1.** [on goal] larguero m, travesaño m - **2.** [on bicycle] barra f.

crossbow ['krɒsbəʊ] n ballesta f.

crossbreed ['krɒsbriːd] n híbrido m.

cross-Channel adj [ferry] que hace la travesía del Canal de la Mancha; [route] a través del Canal de la Mancha.

cross-check n verificación f (con otro método).
➤ **crosscheck** vt verificar (con otro método).

cross-country <> adj & adv a campo traviesa. <> n cross m.

cross-cultural adj intercultural.

cross-dressing n travestismo m.

crossed line [krɒst-] n TELEC cruce m de líneas.

cross-examination n interrogatorio m (para comprobar veracidad).

cross-examine vt interrogar (para comprobar veracidad).

cross-eyed ['krɒsaɪd] adj bizco(ca).

cross-fertilize vt [plants] fecundar por fertilización cruzada.

crossfire ['krɒs,faɪər] n fuego m cruzado.

crosshead ['krɒs,hed] adj: **crosshead screw** tornillo m de cabeza en cruz; **crosshead screwdriver** destornillador m de cabeza en cruz.

crossing ['krɒsɪŋ] n - **1.** [on road] cruce m, paso m de peatones; [on railway line] paso a nivel - **2.** [sea journey] travesía f.

crossing guard n - **1.** US persona encargada de ayudar a cruzar la calle a los colegiales; [on railway line] paso a nivel - **2.** [sea journey] travesía f.

cross-legged ['krɒslegd] adv con las piernas cruzadas.

crossly ['krɒslɪ] adv con enfado.

crossply ['krɒsplaɪ] <> adj de carcasa diagonal. <> n (pl -ies) neumático m de carcasa diagonal.

cross-purposes npl: **I think we're at cross-purposes** creo que estamos hablando de cosas distintas.

cross-question vt interrogar (para comprobar veracidad).

cross-refer vt remitir.

cross-reference n remisión f, referencia f.

crossroads ['krɒsrəʊdz] (pl **crossroads**) n cruce m; **to be at a crossroads** fig estar en una encrucijada.

cross-section n - **1.** [drawing] sección f transversal - **2.** [sample] muestra f representativa.

crosswalk ['krɒswɔːk] n US paso m de peatones.

crossways ['krɒsweɪz] = **crosswise**.

crosswind ['krɒswɪnd] n viento m de costado.

crosswise ['krɒswaɪz], **crossways** adv en diagonal, transversalmente.

crossword (puzzle) ['krɒswɜːd-] *n* crucigrama *m*.

crotch [krɒtʃ] *n* entrepierna *f*.

crotchet ['krɒtʃɪt] *n* negra *f*.

crotchety ['krɒtʃɪtɪ] *adj UK inf* refunfuñón(ona).

crouch [krautʃ] *vi* [gen] agacharse; [ready to spring] agazaparse.

croup [kruːp] *n* - **1.** [illness] crup *m* - **2.** [of horse] grupa *f*.

croupier ['kruːpɪər] *n* crupier *mf*.

crouton ['kruːtɒn] *n* cuscurro *m*, picatoste *m*.

crow [krəu] <> *n* corneja *f*; **as the crow flies** en línea recta. <> *vi* - **1.** [cock] cantar - **2.** *inf* [gloat] darse pisto, vanagloriarse.

crowbar ['krəubaːr] *n* palanca *f*.

crowd [kraud] <> *n* - **1.** [mass of people] multitud *f*, muchedumbre *f*; [at football match etc] público *m* - **2.** [particular group] gente *f*. <> *vi* agolparse, apiñarse; **to crowd in/out** entrar/salir en tropel. <> *vt* - **1.** [room, theatre etc] llenar - **2.** [people] meter, apiñar.

crowded ['kraudɪd] *adj*: **crowded (with)** repleto(ta) *OR* abarrotado(da) (de).

crown [kraun] <> *n* - **1.** [of royalty, on tooth] corona *f* - **2.** [of hat] copa *f*; [of head] coronilla *f*; [of hill] cumbre *f*, cima *f*. <> *vt* - **1.** [gen] coronar; **to crown it all** para colmo - **2.** [tooth] poner una corona a.

Crown <> *n*: **the Crown** [monarchy] la Corona. <> *comp* de la Corona.

crown court *n* ≃ tribunal *m* superior de lo penal.

crowning ['kraunɪŋ] *adj* supremo(ma).

crown jewels *npl* joyas *fpl* de la corona.

crown prince *n* príncipe *m* heredero.

crow's feet *npl* patas *fpl* de gallo.

crow's nest *n* cofa *f*.

crucial ['kruːʃl] *adj* crucial.

crucially ['kruːʃlɪ] *adv* de manera crucial; **crucially important** de importancia crucial.

crucible ['kruːsɪbl] *n* crisol *m*.

crucifix ['kruːsɪfɪks] *n* crucifijo *m*.

Crucifixion [ˌkruːsɪˈfɪkʃn] *n*: **the Crucifixion** la Crucifixión.

crucify ['kruːsɪfaɪ] (*pt & pp* -ied) *vt lit & fig* crucificar.

crude [kruːd] <> *adj* - **1.** [rubber, oil, joke] crudo(da) - **2.** [person, behaviour] basto(ta), vulgar - **3.** [drawing, sketch] tosco(ca). <> *n* crudo *m*.

crudely ['kruːdlɪ] *adv* - **1.** [say, remark] vulgarmente - **2.** [sketch, write] toscamente.

crude oil *n* crudo *m*.

cruel [kruəl] (*comp* -ler, *superl* -lest) *adj* [gen] cruel; [blow] duro(ra); [winter] crudo(da).

cruelly ['kruəlɪ] *adv* - **1.** [sadistically] cruelmente - **2.** [painfully, harshly] dolorosamente.

cruelty ['kruəltɪ] *n* (*U*) crueldad *f*.

cruet ['kruːɪt] *n* vinagreras *fpl*, convoy *m*.

cruise [kruːz] <> *n* crucero *m*. <> *vi* - **1.** [sail] hacer un crucero - **2.** [drive, fly] ir a velocidad de crucero.

cruise missile *n* misil *m* de crucero.

cruiser ['kruːzər] *n* - **1.** [warship] crucero *m* - **2.** [cabin cruiser] yate *m* (*para cruceros*).

crumb [krʌm] *n* - **1.** [of food] miga *f*, migaja *f* - **2.** [of information] migaja *f*, pizca *f*.

crumble ['krʌmbl] <> *n* postre a base de compota de fruta con masa quebrada dulce por encima. <> *vt* desmigajar. <> *vi* - **1.** [building, cliff] desmoronarse; [plaster] caerse - **2.** *fig* [relationship, hopes] derrumbarse, venirse abajo.

crumbly ['krʌmblɪ] (*comp* -ier, *superl* -iest) *adj* que se desmigaja con facilidad.

crummy ['krʌmɪ] (*comp* -mier, *superl* -miest) *adj inf* [bad] chungo(ga).

crumpet ['krʌmpɪt] *n* - **1.** [food] bollo que se come tostado - **2.** (*U*) *inf* [women] tías *fpl*.

crumple ['krʌmpl] <> *vt* [dress, suit] arrugar; [letter] estrujar. <> *vi* - **1.** [dress, suit, face] arrugarse; [car] quedarse hecho(cha) un acordeón - **2.** [body] desplomarse; [army, government] sucumbir.

crumple up *vt sep* estrujar.

crunch [krʌntʃ] <> *n* crujido *m*; **when it comes to the crunch** *inf* a la hora de la verdad. <> *vt* [with teeth] ronzar. <> *vi* crujir.

crunchy ['krʌntʃɪ] (*comp* -ier, *superl* -iest) *adj* crujiente.

crusade [kruːˈseɪd] <> *n lit & fig* cruzada *f*. <> *vi*: **to crusade for/against** hacer una cruzada en pro/en contra de.

crusader [kruːˈseɪdər] *n* - **1.** HIST cruzado *m* - **2.** [campaigner] paladín *m*, defensor *m*, -ra *f*.

crush [krʌʃ] <> *n* - **1.** [crowd] gentío *m*, aglomeración *f* - **2.** *inf* [infatuation]: **to have a crush on sb** estar colado(da) *OR* loco(ca) por alguien - **3.** *UK* [drink] zumo *m* (*al que se ha añadido agua*). <> *vt* - **1.** [squash] aplastar - **2.** [grind - garlic, grain] triturar; [- ice] picar; [- grapes] exprimir - **3.** [destroy] demoler.

crush barrier *n UK* valla *f* de contención.

crushing ['krʌʃɪŋ] *adj* - **1.** [defeat, blow] aplastante, abrumador(ra) - **2.** [remark] demoledor(ra).

crust [krʌst] *n* - **1.** [on bread, of snow, earth] corteza *f* - **2.** [on pie] parte *f* dura.

crustacean [krʌˈsteɪʃn] *n* crustáceo *m*.

crusty ['krʌstɪ] (*comp* -ier, *superl* -iest) *adj* - **1.** [food] crujiente - **2.** [person] brusco(ca).

crutch [krʌtʃ] *n* - **1.** [stick] muleta *f*; *fig* [support] apoyo *m*, soporte *m* - **2.** [crotch] entrepierna *f*.

crux [krʌks] *n*: **the crux of the matter** el quid de la cuestión.

cry [kraɪ] <> *n* (*pl* **cries**) - **1.** [weep] llanto *m*, llorera *f* - **2.** [shout] grito *m*; **to be a far cry from** no parecerse en nada a - **3.** [of bird] chillido *m*. <> *vt* (*pt* & *pp* **cried**): **to cry o.s. to sleep** llorar hasta dormirse. <> *vi* (*pt* & *pp* **cried**) - **1.** [weep] llorar - **2.** [shout] gritar; **to cry for help** gritar pidiendo ayuda.

➡ **cry off** *vi* volverse atrás.

➡ **cry out** <> *vt* gritar. <> *vi* [call out] gritar.

➡ **cry out for** *vt insep* pedir a voces.

crybaby ['kraɪˌbeɪbɪ] (*pl* **-ies**) *n inf pej* llorón *m*, -ona *f*.

crying ['kraɪɪŋ] <> *adj*: **a crying shame** una verdadera vergüenza; **a crying need for sthg** una necesidad imperiosa de algo. <> *n* (*U*) llanto *m*.

cryogenics [ˌkraɪəˈdʒenɪks] *n* (*sing*) criogenia *f*.

crypt [krɪpt] *n* cripta *f*.

cryptic ['krɪptɪk] *adj* críptico(ca).

crystal ['krɪstl] <> *n* cristal *m*. <> *comp* de cristal.

crystal ball *n* bola *f* de cristal.

crystal clear *adj* - **1.** [transparent] cristalino(na) - **2.** [clearly stated] claro(ra) como el agua.

crystallize, -ise ['krɪstəlaɪz] <> *vi lit* & *fig* cristalizar. <> *vt* - **1.** [make clear] cristalizar - **2.** [preserve in sugar] confitar, escarchar.

CS gas *n* gas *m* lacrimógeno.

CST (*abbr of* **Central Standard Time**) *hora oficial en el centro de los EE.UU.*

ct (*abbr of* **carat**) quil.

CT *abbr of* **Connecticut**.

CTC *n abbr of* **city technology college**.

cu. (*abbr of* **cubic**) c.

cub [kʌb] *n* - **1.** [young animal] cachorro *m* - **2.** [boy scout] lobato *m*, boy scout de entre 8 y 11 años.

Cuba ['kju:bə] *n* Cuba.

Cuban ['kju:bən] <> *adj* cubano(na). <> *n* [person] cubano *m*, -na *f*.

cubbyhole ['kʌbɪhəʊl] *n* [room] cuchitril *m*; [cupboard] armario *m*.

cube [kju:b] <> *n* [gen] cubo *m*; [of sugar] terrón *m*. <> *vt* - **1.** MATHS elevar al cubo - **2.** [cut up] cortar en dados.

cube root *n* raíz *f* cúbica.

cubic ['kju:bɪk] *adj* cúbico(ca).

cubicle ['kju:bɪkl] *n* [at swimming pool] caseta *f*; [in shop] probador *m*; [in toilets] cubículo *m*.

cubism ['kju:bɪzm] *n* cubismo *m*.

cubist ['kju:bɪst] *n* cubista *mf*.

Cub Scout *n* lobato *m*, boy scout de entre 8 y 11 años.

cuckoo ['kʊku:] *n* cuco *m*, cuclillo *m*.

cuckoo clock *n* reloj *m* de cuco.

cucumber ['kju:kʌmbər] *n* pepino *m*.

cud [kʌd] *n*: **to chew the cud** *lit* & *fig* rumiar.

cuddle ['kʌdl] <> *n* abrazo *m*. <> *vt* abrazar, apapachar *Méx*. <> *vi* abrazarse.

➡ **cuddle up** *vi*: **to cuddle up (to)** arrimarse (a).

cuddly ['kʌdlɪ] (*comp* **-ier**, *superl* **-iest**) *adj* [person, child] mimoso(sa).

cuddly toy ['kʌdlɪ-] *n* muñeco *m* de peluche.

cudgel ['kʌdʒəl] <> *n* porra *f*; **to take up the cudgels for** salir en defensa de. <> *vt* (*UK* **-led**, *cont* **-ling**, *US* **-ed**, *cont* **-ing**) aporrear; **to cudgel one's brains** *US* devanarse los sesos.

cue [kju:] *n* - **1.** RADIO, THEAT & TV entrada *f*; **on cue** justo en aquel instante; **to take one's cue from** guiarse por - **2.** *fig* [stimulus, signal] señal *f* - **3.** [in snooker, pool] taco *m*.

cuff [kʌf] <> *n* - **1.** [of sleeve] puño *m*; **off the cuff** [speech, remarks] improvisado(da), sacado(da) de la manga - **2.** *US* [of trouser leg] vuelta *f* - **3.** [blow] cachete *m*. <> *vt* dar un cachete a.

cuff link *n* gemelo *m*, collera *f Andes*.

cuisine [kwɪˈzi:n] *n* cocina *f*.

cul-de-sac ['kʌldəsæk] *n* callejón *m* sin salida.

culinary ['kʌlɪnərɪ] *adj* culinario(ria).

cull [kʌl] <> *n* sacrificio *m* (*selectivo*). <> *vt* - **1.** [animals] sacrificar (*selectivamente*) - **2.** *fml* [information, facts] recoger.

culminate ['kʌlmɪneɪt] *vi*: **to culminate in** culminar en.

culmination [ˌkʌlmɪˈneɪʃn] *n* culminación *f*.

culottes [kju:ˈlɒts] *npl* falda *f* pantalón.

culpable ['kʌlpəbl] *adj fml*: **culpable (of)** culpable (de); **culpable homicide** homicidio *m* involuntario.

culprit ['kʌlprɪt] *n* culpable *mf*.

cult [kʌlt] <> *n* - **1.** RELIG culto *m* - **2.** [person, activity, object] objeto *m* de culto. <> *comp* [series, movie] de culto.

cultivate ['kʌltɪveɪt] *vt* - **1.** [gen] cultivar - **2.** [get to know - person] hacer amistad con.

cultivated ['kʌltɪveɪtɪd] *adj* - **1.** [cultured] culto(ta) - **2.** [land] cultivado(da).

cultivation [ˌkʌltɪˈveɪʃn] *n* (*U*) cultivo *m*.

cultural ['kʌltʃərəl] *adj* cultural.

culture ['kʌltʃər] *n* - **1.** [gen] cultura *f* - **2.** [of bacteria] cultivo *m*.

cultured ['kʌltʃəd] *adj* culto(ta).

cultured pearl *n* perla *f* cultivada.

culture shock *n* choque *m* cultural.

culture vulture *n inf hum* devorador insaciable de cultura.

culvert ['kʌlvət] *n* alcantarilla *f*, desagüe *m*.

cumbersome ['kʌmbəsəm] *adj* - **1.** [package] abultado(da), voluminoso(sa); [machinery] aparatoso(sa) - **2.** [system] torpe.

cumin ['kʌmɪn] *n* comino *m*.

cumulative ['kju:mjʊlətɪv] *adj* acumulativo(va).

cunning ['kʌnɪŋ] <> *adj* [gen] astuto(ta); [device, idea] ingenioso(sa). <> *n* (U) astucia *f*.

cup [kʌp] <> *n* - **1.** [gen] taza *f* - **2.** [prize, of bra] copa *f*. <> *vt* (*pt & pp* -**ped**, *cont* -**ping**) ahuecar.

cupboard ['kʌbəd] *n* armario *m*.

cupcake ['kʌpkeɪk] *n US* magdalena *f*.

cup holder *n* [team, person] (actual) campeón *m* de copa.

cupid ['kju:pɪd] *n* [figure] cupido *m*.

cupola ['kju:pələ] (*pl* -**s**) *n* cúpula *f*.

cup tie *n UK* partido *m* de copa.

curable ['kjʊərəbl] *adj* curable.

curate ['kjʊərət] *n* coadjutor *m*, -ra *f*, auxiliar *mf*.

curator [ˌkjʊə'reɪtəʳ] *n* conservador *m*, -ra *f*.

curb [kɜ:b] <> *n* - **1.** [control]: **curb (on)** control *m OR* restricción *f* (de); **to put a curb on sthg** poner freno a algo - **2.** *US* [in road] bordillo *m*, bordo *m* de la banqueta *Méx*, cordón *m* de la vereda *R Plata*, cuneta *f Chile*, sardinel *m Col*. <> *vt* controlar, contener.

curd cheese [kɜ:d-] *n UK* requesón *m*.

curdle ['kɜ:dl] *vi* [milk] cuajarse; *fig* [blood] helarse.

cure [kjʊəʳ] <> *n* - **1.** MED: **cure (for)** cura *f* (para) - **2.** [solution]: **cure (for)** remedio *m* (a). <> *vt* - **1.** MED curar - **2.** [problem, inflation] remediar - **3.** [rid]: **to cure sb of sthg** hacer a alguien abandonar algo - **4.** [food, tobacco] curar; [leather] curtir.

cure-all *n* panacea *f*.

curfew ['kɜ:fju:] *n* toque *m* de queda.

curio ['kjʊərɪəʊ] (*pl* -**s**) *n* curiosidad *f*, rareza *f*.

curiosity [ˌkjʊərɪ'ɒsətɪ] *n* curiosidad *f*.

curious ['kjʊərɪəs] *adj* curioso(sa); **to be curious about** sentir curiosidad por; **I'm curious to know...** tengo ganas de saber...

curiously ['kjʊərɪəslɪ] *adv* - **1.** [inquisitively] con curiosidad - **2.** [oddly] curiosamente.

curl [kɜ:l] <> *n* - **1.** [of hair] rizo *m* - **2.** [of smoke] voluta *f*. <> *vt* - **1.** [hair] rizar - **2.** [twist] enroscar. <> *vi* - **1.** [hair] rizarse - **2.** [paper] abarquillarse, curvarse; **to curl into a ball** acurrucarse, hacerse un ovillo.

➤ **curl up** *vi* [person, animal] acurrucarse, hacerse un ovillo; [leaf, paper] abarquillarse, curvarse.

curler ['kɜ:ləʳ] *n* rulo *m*.

curling ['kɜ:lɪŋ] *n* curling *m*, deporte que consiste en hacer deslizar piedras planas sobre el hielo.

curling tongs *npl* tenacillas *fpl* de rizar.

curly ['kɜ:lɪ] (*comp* -**ier**, *superl* -**iest**) *adj* [hair] rizado(da); [pig's tail] enroscado(da).

currant ['kʌrənt] *n* pasa *f* de Corinto.

currency ['kʌrənsɪ] (*pl* -**ies**) *n* - **1.** FIN moneda *f*; **foreign currency** divisa *f* - **2.** *fml* [acceptability]: **to gain currency** ganar aceptación.

current ['kʌrənt] <> *adj* [price, method, girlfriend] actual; [year] presente, en curso; [issue] último(ma); [ideas, expressions, customs] común, corriente; **in current use** de uso común. <> *n* corriente *f*.

current account *n UK* cuenta *f* corriente.

current affairs *npl* temas *mpl* de actualidad.

current assets *npl* activo *m* circulante.

current liabilities *npl* pasivo *m* circulante.

currently ['kʌrəntlɪ] *adv* actualmente.

curriculum [kə'rɪkjələm] (*pl* -**lums** OR -**la** [-lə]) *n* [course of study] plan *m* de estudios, temario *m*.

curriculum vitae [-'vi:taɪ] (*pl* **curricula vitae**) *n UK* currículum *m* (vitae).

curried ['kʌrɪd] *adj* al curry.

curry ['kʌrɪ] (*pl* -**ies**) *n* curry *m*.

curry powder *n* curry *m* en polvo.

curse [kɜ:s] <> *n* - **1.** [evil charm] maldición *f*; **to put a curse on** echar una maldición a - **2.** [swearword] taco *m*, palabrota *f* - **3.** [source of problems] azote *m*. <> *vt* maldecir. <> *vi* [swear] maldecir, soltar tacos.

cursor ['kɜ:səʳ] *n* COMPUT cursor *m*.

cursory ['kɜ:sərɪ] *adj* superficial, por encima.

curt [kɜ:t] *adj* brusco(ca), seco(ca).

curtail [kɜ:'teɪl] *vt* - **1.** [visit] acortar - **2.** [expenditure] reducir; [rights] restringir.

curtailment [kɜ:'teɪlmənt] *n fml* [of expenditure] reducción *f*; [of rights] restricción *f*.

curtain ['kɜ:tn] *n* - **1.** [gen] cortina *f* - **2.** [in theatre] telón *m*.

➤ **curtain off** *vt sep* separar con una cortina.

curtain call *n* salida *f* a escena para saludar.

curtain raiser *n fig* preludio *m*, preámbulo *m*.

curts(e)y ['kɜ:tsɪ] <> *n* reverencia *f* (de mujer). <> *vi* (*pt & pp* **curtsied**) hacer una reverencia (una mujer).

curvaceous [kɜ:'veɪʃəs] *adj inf* escultural.

curvature ['kɜ:vətʃəʳ] (U) *n* - **1.** [of Earth] curvatura *f* - **2.** MED [of spine] desviación *f*.

curve [kɜːv] ◇ *n* curva *f*. ◇ *vi* [river] torcer, hacer una curva; [surface] curvarse, arquearse.

curved [kɜːvd] *adj* curvo(va).

curvy ['kɜːvɪ] (*comp* -ier, *superl* -iest) *adj* - **1.** [line] sinuoso(sa) - **2.** *inf* [figure] escultural.

cushion ['kʊʃn] ◇ *n* - **1.** [for sitting on] cojín *m*, almohadón *m* - **2.** [protective layer] colchón *m*. ◇ *vt lit & fig* amortiguar; **to be cushioned against** estar protegido(da) contra.

cushy ['kʊʃɪ] (*comp* -ier, *superl* -iest) *adj inf* cómodo(da); **a cushy job** OR **number** un chollo (de trabajo).

custard ['kʌstəd] *n* (*U*) natillas *fpl*.

custard pie *n* tarta *f* de crema.

custard powder *n* (*U*) polvos *mpl* para hacer natillas.

custodian [kʌ'stəʊdjən] *n* - **1.** [of building, museum] conservador *m*, -ra *f* - **2.** [of tradition, values] guardián *m*, -ana *f*.

custody ['kʌstədɪ] *n* custodia *f*; **to take sb into custody** detener a alguien; **in custody** bajo custodia.

custom ['kʌstəm] ◇ *n* - **1.** [tradition, habit] costumbre *f* - **2.** (*U*) *fml* [trade] clientela *f*. ◇ *adj* hecho(cha) de encargo.

◆ **customs** *n* [place] aduana *f*; **to go through customs** pasar por la aduana.

customary ['kʌstəmrɪ] *adj* acostumbrado(da), habitual.

custom-built *adj* hecho(cha) de encargo.

customer ['kʌstəmər] *n* - **1.** [client] cliente *mf* - **2.** *inf* [person] tipo *m*, individuo *m*.

customer services *npl* servicio *m* de atención al cliente.

customize, -ise ['kʌstəmaɪz] *vt* [gen & COMPUT] personalizar.

custom-made *adj* [shoes, suit] hecho(cha) a la medida; [car] hecho(cha) de encargo.

Customs and Excise *n* (*U*) *UK* oficina del gobierno encargada de la recaudación de derechos arancelarios.

customs duty *n* (*U*) derechos *mpl* de aduana, aranceles *mpl*.

customs officer *n* agente *mf* de aduanas.

cut [kʌt] ◇ *n* - **1.** [gen] corte *m* - **2.** [reduction]: **cut (in)** reducción *f* (de); **wage cut** recorte *m* salarial - **3.** *inf* [share] parte *f*
▸▸ **to be a cut above the rest** *inf* ser superior al resto. ◇ *vt* (*pt & pp* cut, *cont* -ting) - **1.** [gen & COMPUT] cortar; **to cut sb's hair** cortarle el pelo a alguien; **to cut a hole** hacer un agujero; **to cut class** *US* faltar a clase; [one's finger etc] cortarse; **to cut o.s.** cortarse - **2.** [spending, staff etc] reducir, recortar; [text]

acortar - **3.** [tooth] echar - **4.** *inf* [lecture] fumarse. ◇ *vi* (*pt & pp* cut, *cont* -ting) [gen & COMPUT] cortar.

◆ **cut across** *vt insep* - **1.** [take short cut] atajar OR cortar por - **2.** [go beyond] rebasar, trascender.

◆ **cut back** ◇ *vt sep* - **1.** [plant] podar - **2.** [expenditure, budget] reducir. ◇ *vi*: **to cut back (on sth)** reducir OR recortar (algo).

◆ **cut down** ◇ *vt sep* - **1.** [chop down] cortar, talar - **2.** [reduce] reducir. ◇ *vi*: **to cut down on smoking** OR **cigarettes** fumar menos.

◆ **cut in** *vi* - **1.** [interrupt]: **to cut in (on sb)** cortar OR interrumpir (a alguien) - **2.** [in car] colarse.

◆ **cut off** *vt sep* - **1.** [gen] cortar - **2.** [interrupt] interrumpir - **3.** [separate]: **to be cut off (from)** [person] estar aislado(da) (de); [town, village] quedarse incomunicado(da) (de).

◆ **cut out** ◇ *vt sep* - **1.** [remove] recortar - **2.** [dress, pattern etc] cortar; **to be cut out for sthg** *fig* [person] estar hecho(cha) para algo - **3.** [stop]: **to cut out smoking** OR **cigarettes** dejar de fumar; **cut it out!** *inf* ¡basta ya! - **4.** [exclude - light etc] eliminar; **to cut sb out of one's will** desheredar a alguien. ◇ *vi* [stall] calarse, pararse.

◆ **cut through** *vt insep* - **1.** [object, liquid] cortar - **2.** [take short cut through] atajar OR cortar por.

◆ **cut up** *vt sep* [chop up] cortar, desmenuzar.

cut-and-dried *adj* [issue, result] claro(ra); [formula, answer] preestablecido(da).

cut and paste *vt & vi* COMPUT cortar y pegar.

cutback ['kʌtbæk] *n*: **cutback (in)** recorte *m* OR reducción *f* (en).

cute [kjuːt] *adj* [appealing] mono(na), lindo(da).

cut glass ◇ *n* cristal *m* tallado. ◇ *comp* de cristal tallado.

cuticle ['kjuːtɪkl] *n* cutícula *f*.

cutlery ['kʌtlərɪ] *n* (*U*) cubertería *f*, cubiertos *mpl*.

cutlet ['kʌtlɪt] *n* chuleta *f*.

cutoff point *n* [limit] límite *m*.

cutout ['kʌtaʊt] *n* - **1.** [on machine] cortacircuitos *m inv* - **2.** [shape] recorte *m*.

cut-price, cut-rate *US adj* de oferta, rebajado(da); **cut-price offers** ofertas *fpl*.

cutter ['kʌtər] *n* [tool]: **wire cutters** cortaalambres *m inv*; **glass cutter** diamante *m*.

cutthroat ['kʌtθrəʊt] *adj* [ruthless] encarnizado(da).

cutting ['kʌtɪŋ] ◇ *adj* [sarcastic] cortante, hiriente. ◇ *n* - **1.** [of plant] esqueje *m* - **2.** [from newspaper] recorte *m* - **3.** *UK* [for road, railway] desmonte *m*, paso *m* estrecho.

cuttlefish ['kʌtlfɪʃ] (*pl* **cuttlefish**) *n* jibia *f*, sepia *f*.

cut-up *adj* UK *inf* [upset] disgustado(da).

CV (*abbr of* **curriculum vitae**) *n* UK CV *m*.

cwo (*abbr of* **cash with order**) *pago al contado*.

cwt. *abbr of* **hundredweight**.

cyanide ['saɪənaɪd] *n* cianuro *m*.

cybercafe ['saɪbə,kæfeɪ] *n* cibercafé *m*.

cybercrime ['saɪbəkraɪm] *n* ciberdelito *m*.

cybernetics [,saɪbə'netɪks] *n* (U) cibernética *f*.

cyberspace ['saɪbəspeɪs] *n* ciberespacio *m*.

cyclamen ['sɪkləmən] (*pl* **cyclamen**) *n* ciclamen *m*.

cycle ['saɪkl] <> *n* - **1.** [series of events, poems, songs] ciclo *m* - **2.** [bicycle] bicicleta *f*. <> *comp*: **cycle lane** carril *m* bici; **cycle path** carril *m* bici; **cycle race** carrera *f* ciclista. <> *vi* ir en bicicleta.

cyclic(al) ['saɪklɪk(l)] *adj* cíclico(ca).

cycling ['saɪklɪŋ] *n* ciclismo *m*; **to go cycling** ir en bicicleta.

cyclist ['saɪklɪst] *n* ciclista *mf*.

cyclone ['saɪkləʊn] *n* ciclón *m*.

cygnet ['sɪgnɪt] *n* pollo *m* de cisne.

cylinder ['sɪlɪndəʳ] *n* - **1.** [shape, engine component] cilindro *m* - **2.** [container - for gas] bombona *f*.

cylinder head *n* culata *f* del cilindro.

cylinder-head gasket *n* junta *f* de la culata.

cylindrical [sɪ'lɪndrɪkl] *adj* cilíndrico(ca).

cynic ['sɪnɪk] *n* cínico *m*, -ca *f*.

cynical ['sɪnɪkl] *adj* cínico(ca).

cynically ['sɪnɪklɪ] *adv* cínicamente.

cynicism ['sɪnɪsɪzm] *n* cinismo *m*.

cypher ['saɪfəʳ] = **cipher**.

cypress ['saɪprəs] *n* ciprés *m*.

Cypriot ['sɪprɪət] <> *adj* chipriota. <> *n* chipriota *mf*; **Greek Cypriot** grecochipriota *mf*; **Turkish Cypriot** turcochipriota *mf*.

Cyprus ['saɪprəs] *n* Chipre.

cyst [sɪst] *n* quiste *m*.

cystic fibrosis [,sɪstɪkfaɪ'brəʊsɪs] *n* (U) fibrosis *f inv* quística (del páncreas).

cystitis [sɪs'taɪtɪs] *n* cistitis *f inv*.

cytology [saɪ'tɒlədʒɪ] *n* citología *f*.

czar [zɑːʳ] *n* zar *m*; **the government drugs czar** UK jefe *m*, -fa *f* de la lucha contra el narcotráfico.

Czech [tʃek] <> *adj* checo(ca). <> *n* - **1.** [person] checo *m*, -ca *f* - **2.** [language] checo *m*.

Czech Republic *n*: **the Czech Republic** la República Checa.

d [di:] (*pl* **d's** OR **ds**), **D** [di:] (*pl* **D's** OR **Ds**) *n* [letter] d *f*, D *f*.

◆ **D** *n* - **1.** MUS re *m* - **2.** SCH ≃ suspenso *m* - **3.** US *abbr of* **Democrat**, **Democratic**.

d² [di:] (*abbr of* **penny**) *antiguamente penique*.

d. (*abbr of* **died**) m.; **d. 1913** m. 1913.

D.A. *n* US *abbr of* **district attorney**.

dab [dæb] <> *n* [small amount] toque *m*, pizca *f*; [of powder] pizca *f*. <> *vt* (*pt & pp* **-bed**, *cont* **-bing**) - **1.** [skin, wound] dar ligeros toques en - **2.** [cream, ointment]: **to dab sthg on** OR **onto** aplicar algo sobre. <> *vi* (*pt & pp* **-bed**, *cont* **-bing**): **to dab at** dar ligeros toques en.

dabble ['dæbl] *vi*: **to dabble (in)** pasar el tiempo OR entretenerse (con).

dab hand *n* UK: **to be a dab hand (at sthg)** ser un fenómeno OR un hacha (en algo OR haciendo algo).

dachshund ['dækshʊnd] *n* perro *m* salchicha.

dad [dæd], **daddy** ['dædɪ] (*pl* **-ies**) *n inf* papá *m*.

daddy longlegs [-'lɒŋlegz] (*pl* **daddy longlegs**) *n* típula *f*.

daffodil ['dæfədɪl] *n* narciso *m*.

daft [dɑːft] *adj* UK *inf* tonto(ta), baboso(sa) *Amér*.

dagger ['dægəʳ] *n* daga *f*, puñal *m*.

dahlia ['deɪljə] *n* dalia *f*.

daily ['deɪlɪ] <> *adj* diario(ria); **on a daily basis** día a día, cada día. <> *adv* diariamente; **twice daily** dos veces al día. <> *n* (*pl* **-ies**) [newspaper] diario *m*.

daintily ['deɪntɪlɪ] *adv* delicadamente, finamente.

dainty ['deɪntɪ] (*comp* **-ier**, *superl* **-iest**) *adj* delicado(da), fino(na).

dairy ['deərɪ] (*pl* **-ies**) *n* - **1.** [on farm] vaquería *f* - **2.** [shop] lechería *f* - **3.** [factory] central *f* lechera.

dairy cattle *npl* vacas *fpl* lecheras.

dairy farm *n* vaquería *f*.

dairy products *npl* productos *mpl* lácteos.

dais ['deɪɪs] *n* tarima *f*, estrado *m*.

daisy ['deɪzɪ] (*pl* **-ies**) *n* margarita *f* (flor).

daisy wheel *n* margarita *f* (de máquina de escribir).

Dakota [də'kəʊtə] *n* Dakota.

dal [dɑːl] = **dhal**.

dale [deɪl] *n* valle *m*.

dalmatian [dæl'meɪʃn] *n* [dog] dálmata *m*.

dam [dæm] (*pt & pp* **-med**, *cont* **-ming**) ◇ *n* [across river] presa *f*. ◇ *vt* represar.

◆ **dam up** *vt sep* [feelings] reprimir.

damage ['dæmɪdʒ] ◇ *n* **- 1.** [physical harm]: **damage (to)** daño *m* (a); **to cause damage to sthg** ocasionar daños a algo **- 2.** [harmful effect]: **damage (to)** perjuicio *m* (a). ◇ *vt* dañar.

◆ **damages** *npl* LAW daños *mpl* y perjuicios.

damaging ['dæmɪdʒɪŋ] *adj*: **damaging (to)** perjudicial (para).

Damascus [də'mæskəs] *n* Damasco.

Dame [deɪm] *n* UK *título honorífico concedido a una mujer.*

damn [dæm] ◇ *adj inf* maldito(ta), pinche *Méx*. ◇ *adv inf* tela de, muy; **don't be so damn stupid** no seas tan rematadamente estúpido. ◇ *n inf*: **I don't give** OR **care a damn (about it)** me importa un bledo. ◇ *vt* **- 1.** [gen & RELIG] condenar **- 2.** *v inf* [curse]: **damn it!** ¡maldita sea! ◇ *excl v inf* ¡maldita sea!

damnable ['dæmnəbl] *adj dated* [appalling] terrible, detestable.

damnation [dæm'neɪʃn] ◇ *n* RELIG condenación *f*. ◇ *excl v inf* ¡maldición!

damned [dæmd] *inf* ◇ *adj* maldito(ta), pinche *Méx*; **I'm damned if I know why she did it** que me maten si sé por qué lo hizo; **well I'll be** OR **I'm damned!** ¡ostras! ◇ *adv* tela de, muy.

damning ['dæmɪŋ] *adj* condenatorio(ria).

damp [dæmp] ◇ *adj* húmedo(da). ◇ *n* humedad *f*. ◇ *vt* [make wet] humedecer.

◆ **damp down** *vt sep* **- 1.** [fire] sofocar **- 2.** [enthusiasm] apagar.

damp course *n* UK (aislante *m*) hidrófugo *m*.

dampen ['dæmpən] *vt* **- 1.** [make wet] humedecer **- 2.** *fig* [emotion] apagar.

damper ['dæmpər] *n* **- 1.** MUS apagador *m*, sordina *f* **- 2.** [for fire] regulador *m* de tiro

▸▸ **to put a damper on sthg** aguar OR estropear algo.

dampness ['dæmpnɪs] *n* humedad *f*.

damson ['dæmzn] *n* (ciruela *f*) damascena *f*.

dance [dɑːns] ◇ *n* baile *m*. ◇ *vt* bailar. ◇ *vi* **- 1.** [to music] bailar **- 2.** [move quickly and lightly] agitarse, moverse.

dance floor *n* pista *f* de baile.

dancer ['dɑːnsər] *n* bailarín *m*, -ina *f*.

dancing ['dɑːnsɪŋ] *n* (*U*) baile *m*.

D and C (*abbr of* **dilation and curettage**) *n* legrado *m*, raspado *m*.

dandelion ['dændɪlaɪən] *n* diente *m* de león.

dandruff ['dændrʌf] *n* caspa *f*.

dandy ['dændɪ] (*pl* **-ies**) *n* dandi *m*.

Dane [deɪn] *n* danés *m*, -esa *f*.

danger ['deɪndʒər] *n*: **danger (to)** peligro *m* (para); **in/out of danger** en/fuera de peligro; **to be in danger of doing sthg** correr el riesgo de hacer algo.

danger list *n* UK: **to be on the danger list** [species, institution] estar en vías de desaparición; [person] estar en estado crítico.

danger money *n* (*U*) UK plus *m* OR prima *f* de peligrosidad.

dangerous ['deɪndʒərəs] *adj* peligroso(sa).

dangerous driving *n* LAW conducción *f* temeraria.

dangerously ['deɪndʒərəslɪ] *adv* **- 1.** [riskily] peligrosamente **- 2.** MED: **to be dangerously ill** estar grave OR en estado crítico.

danger zone *n* zona *f* de peligro.

dangle ['dæŋgl] ◇ *vt* colgar; *fig*: **to dangle sthg before sb** tentar a alguien con algo. ◇ *vi* colgar, pender.

Danish ['deɪnɪʃ] ◇ *adj* danés(esa). ◇ *n* **- 1.** [language] danés *m* **- 2.** US = **Danish pastry**. ◇ *npl* [people]: **the Danish** los daneses.

Danish blue *n* queso *m* azul danés.

Danish pastry, Danish *n* pastel de hojaldre con crema o manzana o almendras etc.

dank [dæŋk] *adj* húmedo(da) e insalubre.

Danube ['dænjuːb] *n*: **the Danube** el Danubio.

dapper ['dæpər] *adj* pulcro(cra), atildado(da).

dappled ['dæpld] *adj* **- 1.** [light] moteado(da) **- 2.** [horse] rodado(da).

dare [deər] ◇ *vt* **- 1.** [be brave enough]: **to dare to do sthg** atreverse a hacer algo, osar hacer algo **- 2.** [challenge]: **to dare sb to do sthg** desafiar a alguien a hacer algo

▸▸ **I dare say (...)** supongo OR me imagino (que...) ◇ *vi* atreverse, osar; **how dare you!** ¿cómo te atreves? ◇ *n* desafío *m*, reto *m*.

daredevil ['deə,devl] *n* temerario *m*, -ria *f*.

daren't [deənt] (*abbr of* = **dare not**) = **dare**.

Dar es-Salaam [,dɑːressə'lɑːm] *n* Dar es Salam.

daring ['deərɪŋ] ◇ *adj* atrevido(da), audaz. ◇ *n* audacia *f*.

dark [dɑːk] ◇ *adj* **- 1.** [night, colour, hair] oscuro(ra); **it's getting dark** está oscureciendo; **it was already dark** ya era de noche **- 2.** [person, skin] moreno(na), cambujo(ja) *Amér* **- 3.** [thoughts, days, mood] sombrío(a), triste **- 4.** [look, comment, side of character etc] siniestro(tra). ◇ *n* **- 1.** [darkness]: **the dark** la oscuridad; **to be in the dark about sthg** estar a oscuras sobre algo **- 2.** [night]: **before/after dark** antes/después del anochecer.

Dark Ages *npl*: **the Dark Ages** la Alta Edad Media *(antes del año mil).*

darken ['dɑːkn] ⬦ *vt* oscurecer. ⬦ *vi* - **1.** [become darker] oscurecerse - **2.** [look angry] ensombrecerse.

dark glasses *npl* gafas *fpl* oscuras, anteojos *mpl* OR lentes *mpl* oscuros *Amér.*

dark horse *n* - **1.** [person who does sthg unexpected] figura *f* OR persona *f* enigmática - **2.** [in competition] competidor *m*, -ra *f* sorpresa.

darkness ['dɑːknɪs] *n* oscuridad *f.*

darkroom ['dɑːkrʊm] *n* PHOT cuarto *m* oscuro.

darling ['dɑːlɪŋ] ⬦ *adj* - **1.** [dear] querido(da) - **2.** *inf* [cute] adorable, encantador(ra). ⬦ *n* - **1.** [loved person] encanto *m* - **2.** *inf* [addressing any woman] maja *f* - **3.** [idol] preferido *m*, -da *f*, niño bonito *m*, niña bonita *f.*

darn [dɑːn] ⬦ *adj inf* maldito(ta), condenado(da). ⬦ *adv inf* tela de, muy; **don't be so darn stupid** no seas tan rematadamente estúpido. ⬦ *n* zurcido *m.* ⬦ *vt* zurcir. ⬦ *excl inf* ¡maldita sea!

darning ['dɑːnɪŋ] *n (U)* [things] ropa *f* para zurcir; [task] zurcido *m.*

darning needle *n* aguja *f* de zurcir.

dart [dɑːt] ⬦ *n* - **1.** [arrow] dardo *m* - **2.** SEW pinza *f.* ⬦ *vt* [look, glance] lanzar. ⬦ *vi* precipitarse.

⬩ **darts** *n (U)* [game] dardos *mpl.*

dartboard ['dɑːtbɔːd] *n* blanco *m*, diana *f.*

dash [dæʃ] ⬦ *n* - **1.** [of liquid] gotas *fpl*, chorrito *m*; [of colour] toque *m* - **2.** [in punctuation] guión *m* - **3.** *esp US* AUT salpicadero *m* - **4.** [rush]: **to make a dash for sthg** salir disparado(da) hacia algo. ⬦ *vt* - **1.** *liter* [throw] arrojar - **2.** [hopes] frustrar, malograr. ⬦ *vi* ir de prisa; **I must dash!** ¡me voy pitando!

⬩ **dash off** *vt sep* [write quickly] escribir de prisa.

dashboard ['dæʃbɔːd] *n* salpicadero *m.*

dashing ['dæʃɪŋ] *adj* gallardo(da), apuesto(ta).

dastardly ['dæstədlɪ] *adj dated* ruin, malvado(da).

DAT [dæt] (*abbr of* digital audio tape) *n* DAT *f.*

data ['deɪtə] *n (U)* datos *mpl.*

databank ['deɪtəbæŋk] *n* banco *m* de datos.

database ['deɪtəbeɪs] *n* COMPUT base *f* de datos.

data capture *n* introducción *f* de datos.

data management *n* COMPUT gestión *f* de datos.

data processing *n* proceso *m* de datos.

data protection *n* COMPUT protección *f* de datos.

date [deɪt] ⬦ *n* - **1.** [in time] fecha *f*; **to date** hasta la fecha - **2.** [appointment] cita *f* - **3.** *US* [person] pareja *f (con la que se sale)* - **4.** [per-

formance] actuación *f* - **5.** [fruit] dátil *m.* ⬦ *vt* - **1.** [establish the date of] datar - **2.** [mark with the date] fechar - **3.** *US* [go out with] salir con. ⬦ *vi* [go out of fashion] pasar de moda, quedarse anticuado.

⬤ **date back to, date from** *vt insep* [object, building] datar de; [custom] remontarse a.

dated ['deɪtɪd] *adj* anticuado(da).

date line *n* meridiano *m* de cambio de fecha.

date of birth *n* fecha *f* de nacimiento.

date stamp *n* - **1.** [device] fechador *m* - **2.** [mark] sello *m* de fecha.

daub [dɔːb] *vt*: **to daub sthg with** embadurnar algo con.

daughter ['dɔːtər] *n* hija *f.*

daughter-in-law (*pl* **daughters-in-law**) *n* nuera *f.*

daunt [dɔːnt] *vt* intimidar, acobardar.

daunting ['dɔːntɪŋ] *adj* amedrantador(ra).

dawdle ['dɔːdl] *vi* remolonear, entretenerse.

dawn [dɔːn] ⬦ *n* - **1.** [of day] amanecer *m*, alba *f*; **at dawn** al amanecer; **from dawn to dusk** de sol a sol - **2.** [of era, period] albores *mpl*, amanecer *m.* ⬦ *vi* - **1.** [day] amanecer - **2.** [era, period] nacer.

⬤ **dawn (up)on** *vt insep*: **it dawned on me that...** caí en la cuenta de que...

dawn chorus *n* canto *m* de los pájaros al amanecer.

day [deɪ] *n* - **1.** [gen] día *m*; **I work an eight-hour day** trabajo una jornada de ocho horas; **the day before/after** el día anterior/siguiente; **the day before yesterday** anteayer; **the day after tomorrow** pasado mañana; **any day now** cualquier día de estos; **from day to day** de un día para otro; **one** OR **some day, one of these days** un día de estos; **day and night** día y noche; **to call it a day** dejarlo por hoy; **to make sb's day** dar un alegrón a alguien; **to save sthg for a rainy day** guardar algo para cuando haga verdadera falta; **his days are numbered** tiene los días contados; **it's early days yet** es aún pronto para hablar, sería prematuro aventurar nada - **2.** [period in history]: **in my/your** *etc* **day** en mis/tus *etc* tiempos; **in the days of...** en tiempos de...; **in those days** en aquellos tiempos, **in this day and age** en nuestros días; **these days** hoy día.

⬩ **days** *adv* de día.

daybreak ['deɪbreɪk] *n* amanecer *m*, alba *f*; **at daybreak** al amanecer.

day-care centre *n* guardería *f* (infantil).

daydream ['deɪdriːm] ⬦ *n* sueño *m*, ilusión *f.* ⬦ *vi* soñar despierto(ta).

daygirl ['deɪgɜːl] *n UK* SCH (alumna *f*) externa *f.*

Day-Glo® ['deɪgləʊ] *adj* fluorescente.

daylight ['deɪlaɪt] n - **1.** [light] luz f del día; **in broad daylight** a plena luz del día; **it was still daylight** todavía era de día - **2.** [dawn] amanecer m - **3.** inf phr: **to scare the (living) daylights out of sb** dar un susto de muerte a alguien.

daylight robbery n (U) inf: **that's daylight robbery!** ¡es un auténtico timo OR robo!

daylight saving time n horario m oficial de verano.

day nursery n guardería f (infantil).

day off (pl days off) n día m libre.

day pupil n UK SCH externo m, -na f.

day release n (U) sistema en que los trabajadores dedican un día de trabajo a la formación profesional en un centro de enseñanza.

day return n UK billete m de ida y vuelta (en el día).

dayroom ['deɪru:m] n sala f de estar (en hospital, asilo etc).

day school n colegio m sin internado.

day shift n turno m de día.

daytime ['deɪtaɪm] <> n (U) día m. <> comp de día, diurno(na).

day-to-day adj cotidiano(na), diario(ria).

daytrader ['deɪtreɪdə'] n [St Ex] operador m, -ra f de posiciones diarias.

day trip n excursión f (de un día).

day-tripper n UK excursionista mf.

daze [deɪz] <> n: **in a daze** aturdido(da). <> vt lit & fig aturdir.

dazed [deɪzd] adj lit & fig aturdido(da).

dazzle ['dæzl] <> n (U) - **1.** [of light] resplandor m - **2.** [impressiveness] hechizo m, fascinación f. <> vt lit & fig deslumbrar.

dazzling ['dæzlɪŋ] adj lit & fig deslumbrante.

DC n - **1.** (abbr of direct current) CC f - **2.** abbr of District of Columbia.

D/D abbr of direct debit.

D-day ['di:deɪ] n el día D.

DDT (abbr of dichlorodiphenyltrichloroethane) n DDT m.

DE (abbr of Delaware) abbr of Delaware.

DEA (abbr of Drug Enforcement Administration) n organismo estadounidense para la lucha contra la droga.

deacon ['di:kn] n diácono m.

deaconess [,di:kə'nes] n diaconisa f.

deactivate [,di:'æktɪveɪt] vt desactivar.

dead [ded] <> adj - **1.** [person, animal, plant] muerto(ta); **a dead body** un cadáver; **to be dead on arrival** ingresar cadáver; **to shoot sb dead** matar a alguien a tiros; **he wouldn't be seen dead doing that** no haría eso por nada del mundo - **2.** [numb - leg, arm] dormido(da), entumecido(da); **my arm has gone dead** se me ha dormido el brazo - **3.** [telephone] cortado(da); [car battery] descargado(da) - **4.** [silence] absoluto(ta), completo(ta) - **5.** [lifeless - town, party] sin vida. <> adv - **1.** [directly, precisely] justo - **2.** [completely] totalmente, completamente; **to be dead set against sthg** estar totalmente en contra de algo; **to be dead set on sthg** estar decidido a hacer algo; **'dead slow'** 'al paso' - **3.** inf [very] la mar de, muy - **4.** [suddenly]: **to stop dead** parar en seco. <> n [middle, depth]: **at dead of night** en medio de la noche. <> npl: **the dead** los muertos.

deadbeat ['dedbi:t] n US inf holgazán m, -ana f.

dead centre n: **in the dead centre** en pleno centro.

dead duck n inf: **it's a dead duck** está condenado al fracaso.

deaden ['dedn] vt atenuar.

dead end n lit & fig callejón m sin salida.

dead-end job n trabajo m sin futuro.

deadhead ['dedhed] vt quitar las flores marchitas a.

dead heat n empate m.

deadline ['dedlaɪn] n [period] plazo m; [date] fecha f tope.

deadlock ['dedlɒk] n punto m muerto.

deadlocked ['dedlɒkt] adj paralizado(da).

dead loss n inf - **1.** [person] inútil mf - **2.** [thing] inutilidad f.

deadly ['dedlɪ] <> adj (comp -ier, superl -iest) - **1.** [gen] mortal - **2.** [accuracy] absoluto(ta). <> adv [boring] mortalmente, terriblemente; [serious] totalmente.

deadly nightshade [-'naɪtʃeɪd] n (U) belladona f.

deadpan ['dedpæn] adj [expression] inexpresivo(va), serio(ria); [humour] socarrón(ona).

Dead Sea n: **the Dead Sea** el mar Muerto.

dead wood UK, **deadwood** US ['dedwud] n (U) fig [people] gente f que sobra; [in text] paja f.

deaf [def] <> adj - **1.** [unable to hear] sordo(da) - **2.** [unwilling to hear]: **to be deaf to sthg** hacer oídos sordos a algo. <> npl: **the deaf** los sordos.

deaf-and-dumb adj sordomudo(da).

deafen ['defn] vt ensordecer.

deafening ['defnɪŋ] adj ensordecedor(ra).

deaf-mute <> adj sordomudo(da). <> n sordomudo m, -da f.

deafness ['defnɪs] n sordera f.

deal [di:l] (pt & pp dealt) <> n - **1.** [quantity]: **a good OR great deal (of)** mucho - **2.** [agreement] acuerdo m; [business agreement] trato m; **to do OR strike a deal with sb** hacer un trato con alguien; **it's a deal!** ¡trato hecho! **- 3.** *inf* [treatment] trato *m*; **big deal!** ¡vaya cosa! **- 4.** [price]: **to get a good deal on sthg** conseguir algo a un precio barato. <> *vt* **- 1.** [strike]: **to deal sb/sthg a blow, to deal a blow to sb/sthg** *lit* & *fig* asestar un golpe a alguien/algo **- 2.** [cards] repartir, dar. <> *vi* **- 1.** [in cards] repartir, dar **- 2.** [in drugs] traficar con droga.

◆ **deal in** *vt insep* COMM comerciar en, vender.

◆ **deal out** *vt sep* repartir.

◆ **deal with** *vt insep* **- 1.** [handle - situation, problem] hacer frente a, resolver; [- customer] tratar con **- 2.** [be about] tratar de **- 3.** [be faced with] enfrentarse a.

dealer ['diːlə*r*] *n* **- 1.** [trader] comerciante *mf* **- 2.** [in drugs, arms] traficante *mf* **- 3.** [in cards] repartidor *m*, -ra *f*.

dealership ['diːləʃɪp] *n* concesionario *m*.

dealing ['diːlɪŋ] *n* comercio *m*.

◆ **dealings** *npl* [personal] trato *m*; [in business] tratos *mpl*.

dealt [delt] *pt* & *pp* ⊳ **deal**.

dean [diːn] *n* **- 1.** [of university] ≈ decano *m* **- 2.** [of church] deán *m*.

dear [dɪə*r*] <> *adj* **- 1.** [loved] querido(da); **dear to sb** preciado(da) para alguien **- 2.** [expensive] caro(ra) **- 3.** [in letter]: **Dear Sir** Estimado señor, Muy señor mío; **Dear Madam** Estimada señora; **Dear Daniela** Querida Daniela. <> *n*: **my dear** cariño *m*, -ña *f*. <> *excl*: **oh dear!** ¡vaya por Dios!

dearly ['dɪəlɪ] *adv* **- 1.** [very much]: **I love you dearly** te quiero muchísimo; **I would dearly love to...** me encantaría... **- 2.** [severely]: **to pay dearly for sthg** pagar algo caro.

dearth [dɜːθ] *n* carencia *f*, escasez *f*.

death [deθ] *n* muerte *f*; **to be put to death** ser ejecutado(da); **to frighten sb to death** dar un susto de muerte a alguien; **to be sick to death of sthg/of doing sthg** estar hasta las narices de algo/de hacer algo; **to starve to death** morir de hambre; **to be at death's door** estar a las puertas de la muerte.

deathbed ['deθbed] *n* lecho *m* de muerte.

death certificate *n* partida *f* OR certificado *m* de defunción.

death duty *UK*, **death tax** *US n* impuesto *m* de sucesiones.

deathly ['deθlɪ] <> *adj* (*comp* -ier, *superl* -iest) [silence] sepulcral. <> *adv*: **he was deathly pale** estaba pálido como un muerto; **her hands were deathly cold** tenía las manos frías como las de un muerto.

death penalty *n* pena *f* de muerte.

death rate *n* índice *m* OR tasa *f* de mortalidad.

death row *n* US corredor *m* de la muerte.

death sentence *n* pena *f* de muerte.

death squad *n* escuadrón *m* de la muerte.

death tax *US* = **death duty**.

death toll *n* número *m* de víctimas mortales.

death trap *n* inf trampa *f* mortal, sitio *m* muy peligroso.

Death Valley *n* la Valle de la Muerte.

deathwatch beetle ['deθwɒtʃ-] *n* carcoma *f*.

death wish *n* ganas *fpl* de morir.

deb [deb] *UK inf* = **debutante**.

débâcle [de'bɑːkl] *n* debacle *f*.

debar [diː'bɑːr] (*pt* & *pp* -**red**, *cont* -**ring**) *vt*: **to debar sb from** [place] prohibir a alguien la entrada en; **to debar sb from doing sthg** prohibir a alguien hacer algo.

debase [dɪ'beɪs] *vt* degradar; **to debase o.s.** rebajarse.

debasement [dɪ'beɪsmənt] *n* degradación *f*.

debatable [dɪ'beɪtəbl] *adj* discutible.

debate [dɪ'beɪt] <> *n* debate *m*; **that's open to debate** eso es discutible. <> *vt* **- 1.** [issue] discutir, debatir **- 2.** [what to do]: **to debate (whether to do sthg)** pensarse (si hacer algo). <> *vi* discutir, debatir.

debating society [dɪ'beɪtɪŋ-] *n asociación que organiza debates en una universidad.*

debauched [dɪ'bɔːtʃt] *adj* depravado(da).

debauchery [dɪ'bɔːtʃərɪ] *n* depravación *f*, libertinaje *m*.

debenture [dɪ'bentʃə*r*] *n* obligación *f*.

debenture stock *n* (U) *UK* obligaciones *fpl*.

debilitate [dɪ'bɪlɪteɪt] *vt* debilitar.

debilitating [dɪ'bɪlɪteɪtɪŋ] *adj* debilitador(ra), debilitante.

debility [dɪ'bɪlətɪ] *n* debilidad *f*.

debit ['debɪt] <> *n* debe *m*, débito *m*. <> *vt*: **to debit sb OR sb's account with an amount, to debit an amount to sb** adeudar OR cargar una cantidad en la cuenta de alguien.

debit card *n* tarjeta *f* de débito.

debit note *n* nota *f* de cargo.

debonair [ˌdebə'neə*r*] *adj* apuesto(ta).

debrief [ˌdiː'briːf] *vt* pedir un informe completo a *(tras una misión)*.

debriefing [ˌdiː'briːfɪŋ] *n* sesión *f* informativa (tras una misión).

debris ['deɪbriː] *n* (U) [of building] escombros *mpl*; [of aircraft] restos *mpl*.

debt [det] *n* deuda *f*; **to be in debt (to sb)** tener una deuda (con alguien); **to get into debt** endeudarse; **to be in sb's debt** *fig* estar en deuda con alguien.

debt collector *n* cobrador *m*, -ra *f* de morosos.

debtor ['detə*r*] *n* deudor *m*, -ra *f*.

debug [ˌdiːˈbʌg] (*pt & pp* **-ged**, *cont* **-ging**) *vt* - **1.** [room] quitar micrófonos ocultos de - **2.** COMPUT depurar.

debunk [ˌdiːˈbʌŋk] *vt* desmentir, desacreditar.

debut [ˈdeɪbjuː] *n* debut *m*.

debutante [ˈdebjʊtɑːnt], **deb** *n* debutante *f*.

Dec. (*abbr of* **December**) dic.

decade [ˈdekeɪd] *n* década *f*.

decadence [ˈdekədəns] *n* decadencia *f*.

decadent [ˈdekədənt] *adj* decadente.

decaff [ˈdiːkæf] *n inf* descafeinado *m*.

decaffeinated [dɪˈkæfɪneɪtɪd] *adj* descafeinado(da).

decal [ˈdiːkæl] *n US* calcomanía *f*.

decamp [dɪˈkæmp] *vi inf* escabullirse, esfumarse.

decant [dɪˈkænt] *vt* decantar.

decanter [dɪˈkæntər] *n* licorera *f*.

decapitate [dɪˈkæpɪteɪt] *vt* decapitar.

decathlete [dɪˈkæθliːt] *n* decatleta *mf*.

decathlon [dɪˈkæθlɒn] *n* decatlón *m*.

decay [dɪˈkeɪ] <> *n* (*U*) - **1.** [of tooth] caries *f inv*; [of body, plant] descomposición *f* - **2.** *fig* [of building] deterioro *m*; [of society] corrupción *f*, degradación *f*. <> *vi* - **1.** [tooth] picarse; [body, plant] pudrirse, descomponerse - **2.** *fig* [building] deteriorarse; [society] corromperse, degradarse.

deceased [dɪˈsiːst] *fml* <> *adj* difunto(ta), fallecido(da). <> *n* (*pl* **deceased**): **the deceased** el difunto(la difunta).

deceit [dɪˈsiːt] *n* engaño *m*.

deceitful [dɪˈsiːtfʊl] *adj* [person, smile] embustero(ra); [behaviour] falso(sa).

deceive [dɪˈsiːv] *vt* engañar; **to deceive o.s.** engañarse (a uno mismo/una misma).

decelerate [ˌdiːˈseləreɪt] *vi* desacelerar.

December [dɪˈsembər] *n* diciembre *m*; *see also* **September**.

decency [ˈdiːsnsɪ] *n* - **1.** [respectability] decencia *f* - **2.** [consideration]: **to have the decency to do sthg** tener la delicadeza de hacer algo.

decent [ˈdiːsnt] *adj* - **1.** [gen] decente - **2.** [considerate]: **that's very decent of you** es muy amable de tu parte.

decently [ˈdiːsntlɪ] *adv* [behave, dress] decentemente.

decentralization [diːˌsentrəlaɪˈzeɪʃn] *n* descentralización *f*.

decentralize, -ise [ˌdiːˈsentrəlaɪz] *vt* descentralizar.

deception [dɪˈsepʃn] *n* engaño *m*.

deceptive [dɪˈseptɪv] *adj* engañoso(sa).

deceptively [dɪˈseptɪvlɪ] *adv* engañosamente.

decibel [ˈdesɪbel] *n* decibelio *m*.

decide [dɪˈsaɪd] <> *vt* - **1.** [gen]: **to decide (to do sthg)** decidir (hacer algo); **to decide (that)** decidir que - **2.** [person] hacer decidirse - **3.** [issue, case] resolver. <> *vi* decidir; **I couldn't decide** no me decidía; **I decided against doing it** decidí no hacerlo.

➡ **decide (up)on** *vt insep* decidirse por.

decided [dɪˈsaɪdɪd] *adj* - **1.** [advantage, improvement] indudable - **2.** [person] decidido(da); [opinion] categórico(ca).

decidedly [dɪˈsaɪdɪdlɪ] *adv* - **1.** [clearly] decididamente, indudablemente - **2.** [resolutely] con decisión.

deciding [dɪˈsaɪdɪŋ] *adj*: **deciding vote** voto *m* decisivo.

deciduous [dɪˈsɪdjʊəs] *adj* de hoja caduca.

decimal [ˈdesɪml] <> *adj* decimal. <> *n* (número *m*) decimal *m*.

decimal currency *n* moneda *f* de sistema decimal.

decimalize, -ise [ˈdesɪmǝlaɪz] *vt UK* convertir al sistema decimal.

decimal place *n* cifra *f OR* posición *f* decimal.

decimal point *n* coma *f* decimal.

decimate [ˈdesɪmeɪt] *vt* diezmar.

decimation [ˌdesɪˈmeɪʃn] *n* destrucción *f*.

decipher [dɪˈsaɪfər] *vt* descifrar.

decision [dɪˈsɪʒn] *n* decisión *f*; **to make a decision** tomar una decisión.

decision-making *n* toma *f* de decisiones.

decisive [dɪˈsaɪsɪv] *adj* - **1.** [person] decidido(da) - **2.** [factor, event] decisivo(va).

decisively [dɪˈsaɪsɪvlɪ] *adv* - **1.** [act, speak] con decisión, decididamente - **2.** [beaten, superior] claramente.

decisiveness [dɪˈsaɪsɪvnɪs] *n* decisión *f*.

deck [dek] <> *n* - **1.** [of ship] cubierta *f*; [of bus] piso *m* - **2.** [of cards] baraja *f* - **3.** *US* [of house] entarimado *m* (*junto a una casa*). <> *vt*: **to deck sthg with** engalanar algo con.

➡ **deck out** *vt sep* [place, object] engalanar, adornar; [person] ataviar.

deckchair [ˈdektʃeər] *n* tumbona *f*.

deckhand [ˈdekhænd] *n* marinero *m*.

declaration [ˌdekləˈreɪʃn] *n* declaración *f*.

Declaration of Independence *n*: **the Declaration of Independence** *la declaración de independencia estadounidense de 1776*.

declare [dɪˈkleər] *vt* declarar.

declared [dɪˈkleəd] *adj* declarado(da).

declassify [ˌdiːˈklæsɪfaɪ] (*pt & pp* **-ied**) *vt* [information] levantar el secreto oficial a.

decline [dɪˈklaɪn] <> *n* declive *m*; **in decline** en decadencia; **on the decline** en declive. <> *vt* [offer] declinar; [request] denegar; **to decline to do sthg** rehusar hacer algo. <> *vi* - **1.** [number, importance] decrecer, disminuir - **2.** [standards, quality] decaer; [health] deteriorarse - **3.** [refuse] rehusar, negarse.

declutch [dɪ'klʌtʃ] *vi* AUT desembragar, quitar el embrague.

decode [,di:'kəʊd] *vt* descodificar.

decoder [,di:'kəʊdəʳ] *n* descodificador *m*.

decommission [,di:kə'mɪʃn] *vt* - **1.** [nuclear power station] desmantelar - **2.** [arms] entregar.

decompose [,di:kəm'pəʊz] *vi* descomponerse.

decomposition [,di:kɒmpə'zɪʃn] *n* descomposición *f*.

decompression chamber [,di:kəm'preʃn-] *n* cámara *f* de descompresión.

decompression sickness [,di:kəm'preʃn-] *n* aeroembolismo *m*.

decongestant [,di:kən'dʒestənt] *n* descongestionante *m*.

decontaminate [,di:kən'tæmɪneɪt] *vt* descontaminar.

décor ['deɪkɔːʳ] *n* decoración *f*.

decorate ['dekəreɪt] *vt* - **1.** [make pretty]: **to decorate sthg (with)** decorar algo (de) - **2.** [with paint] pintar; [with wallpaper] empapelar - **3.** [with medal] condecorar.

decoration [,dekə'reɪʃn] *n* - **1.** [gen] decoración *f* - **2.** [ornament] adorno *m* - **3.** [medal] condecoración *f*.

decorative ['dekərətɪv] *adj* decorativo(va).

decorator ['dekəreɪtəʳ] *n* [painter] pintor *m*, -ra *f*; [paperhanger] empapelador *m*, -ra *f*.

decorous ['dekərəs] *adj fml* decoroso(sa).

decorum [dɪ'kɔːrəm] *n* decoro *m*.

decoy <> *n* ['di:kɔɪ] señuelo *m*. <> *vt* [dɪ'kɔɪ] atraer *(mediante un señuelo)*.

decrease <> *n* ['di:kri:s]: **decrease (in)** disminución *f* (de), reducción *f* (de). <> *vt & vi* [dɪ'kri:s] disminuir.

decreasing [di:'kri:sɪŋ] *adj* decreciente.

decree [dɪ'kri:] <> *n* - **1.** [order, decision] decreto *m* - **2.** US [judgment] sentencia *f*, fallo *m*. <> *vt* decretar.

decree absolute *(pl* **decrees absolute)** *n* UK LAW sentencia *f* definitiva de divorcio.

decree nisi [-'naɪsaɪ] *(pl* **decrees nisi)** *n* UK LAW sentencia *f* provisional de divorcio.

decrepit [dɪ'krepɪt] *adj* - **1.** [person] decrépito(ta) - **2.** [thing] deteriorado(da).

decriminalize [,di:'krɪmɪnəlaɪz] *vt* despenalizar.

decry [dɪ'kraɪ] *(pt & pp* **-ied)** *vt fml* censurar, deplorar.

dedicate ['dedɪkeɪt] *vt* - **1.** dedicar; **to dedicate o.s. to sthg** consagrarse OR dedicarse a algo - **2.** US [open for public use] inaugurar.

dedicated ['dedɪkeɪtɪd] *adj* [person & COMPUT] dedicado(da).

dedication [,dedɪ'keɪʃn] *n* - **1.** [commitment] dedicación *f* - **2.** [in book] dedicatoria *f*.

deduce [dɪ'dju:s] *vt*: **to deduce (sthg from sthg)** deducir (algo de algo).

deduct [dɪ'dʌkt] *vt*: **to deduct (from)** deducir (de), descontar (de).

deduction [dɪ'dʌkʃn] *n* deducción *f*.

deed [di:d] *n* - **1.** [action] acción *f*, obra *f* - **2.** LAW escritura *f*.

deed poll *(pl* **deed polls** OR **deeds poll)** *n* UK: **to change one's name by deed poll** cambiarse oficialmente de nombre.

deem [di:m] *vt fml* estimar; **to deem it wise to do sthg** estimar prudente hacer algo.

deep [di:p] <> *adj* - **1.** [gen] profundo(da); **to be 10 feet deep** tener 10 pies de profundidad - **2.** [sigh, breath, bowl] hondo(da); **to take a deep breath** respirar hondo - **3.** [colour] intenso(sa) - **4.** [sound, voice] grave. <> *adv* [dig, cut] hondo; **to advance deep into enemy territory** adentrarse en territorio enemigo; **deep down** OR **inside** por dentro; **to be deep in thought** estar sumido(da) en sus pensamientos; **to go** OR **run deep** estar muy arraigado(da).

deepen ['di:pn] <> *vt* [hole, channel] ahondar, hacer más profundo(da). <> *vi* - **1.** [river, sea] ahondarse, hacerse más profundo(da) - **2.** [crisis, recession] agudizarse; [emotion, darkness] hacerse más intenso(sa).

deepening ['di:pnɪŋ] *adj* [crisis, recession] cada vez más agudo(da).

deep freeze *n* congelador *m*.
➠ **deep-freeze** *vt* congelar.

deeply ['di:plɪ] *adv* [gen] profundamente; [dig, breathe, sigh] hondo.

deep-rooted *adj* profundamente arraigado(da).

deep-sea *adj*: **deep-sea diving** buceo *m* de profundidad; **deep-sea fishing** pesca *f* de altura.

deep-seated *adj* profundamente arraigado(da).

deep-set *adj* [eyes] hundido(da).

deer [dɪəʳ] *(pl* **deer)** *n* ciervo *m*.

deerstalker ['dɪə,stɔːkəʳ] *n especie de gorro con orejeras.*

de-escalate [,di:'eskəleɪt] <> *vt* suavizar, paliar. <> *vi* suavizarse.

deface [dɪ'feɪs] *vt* pintarrajear.

defamation [,defə'meɪʃn] *n fml* difamación *f*.

defamatory [dɪ'fæmətrɪ] *adj fml* difamatorio(ria).

default [dɪ'fɔːlt] <> n - 1. [on payment, agreement] incumplimiento m; [failure to attend] incomparecencia f (del contrario); **by default** [win] por incomparecencia - 2. COMPUT: **default (setting)** configuración f por defecto. <> vi incumplir un compromiso; **to default on sthg** incumplir algo.

defaulter [dɪ'fɔːltə'] n [on payment] moroso m, -sa f.

defeat [dɪ'fiːt] <> n derrota f; **to admit defeat** darse por vencido(da). <> vt [team, opponent] derrotar; [motion] rechazar; [plans] frustrar.

defeatism [dɪ'fiːtɪzm] n derrotismo m.

defeatist [dɪ'fiːtɪst] <> adj derrotista. <> n derrotista mf.

defecate ['defəkeɪt] vi fml defecar.

defect <> n ['diːfekt] [fault] defecto m. <> vi [dɪ'fekt] POL desertar; **to defect to the other side** pasarse al otro bando.

defection [dɪ'fekʃn] n [to another country] deserción f; [to another party] cambio m de bando.

defective [dɪ'fektɪv] adj defectuoso(sa).

defector [dɪ'fektə'] n [to another country] desertor m, -ra f; [to another party] tránsfuga mf.

defence UK, **defense** US [dɪ'fens] n defensa f; **in defence of** en defensa de.
➤ **defences** npl [of country] defensas fpl.

defenceless UK, **defenseless** US [dɪ'fenslɪs] adj indefenso(sa).

defend [dɪ'fend] <> vt defender; **to defend o.s.** defenderse. <> vi SPORT defender.

defendant [dɪ'fendənt] n acusado m, -da f.

defender [dɪ'fendə'] n - 1. [gen] defensor m, -ra f - 2. SPORT defensa mf.

defense US = defence.

defenseless US = defenceless.

defensive [dɪ'fensɪv] <> adj - 1. [weapons, tactics] defensivo(va) - 2. [person]: **to be defensive** ponerse a la defensiva. <> n: **on the defensive** a la defensiva.

defer [dɪ'fɜː'] (pt & pp -red, cont -ring) <> vt aplazar. <> vi: **to defer to sb** deferir con OR a alguien.

deference ['defərəns] n deferencia f.

deferential [ˌdefə'renʃl] adj deferente, respetuoso(sa).

defiance [dɪ'faɪəns] n desafío m; **in defiance of** en desafío de, a despecho de.

defiant [dɪ'faɪənt] adj desafiante.

defiantly [dɪ'faɪəntlɪ] adv de manera desafiante.

deficiency [dɪ'fɪʃnsɪ] (pl -ies) n - 1. [lack] escasez f, insuficiencia f - 2. [inadequacy] deficiencia f.

deficient [dɪ'fɪʃnt] adj - 1. [lacking]: **to be deficient in** ser deficitario(ria) en, estar falto(ta) de - 2. [inadequate] deficiente.

deficit ['defɪsɪt] n déficit m.

defile [dɪ'faɪl] vt [desecrate] profanar; fig [mind, purity] corromper.

define [dɪ'faɪn] vt definir.

definite ['defɪnɪt] adj - 1. [plan, date, answer] definitivo(va) - 2. [improvement, difference] indudable, claro(ra) - 3. [sure - person] seguro(ra); **I am quite definite (about it)** estoy bastante seguro (de ello) - 4. [categorical] tajante, concluyente.

definitely ['defɪnɪtlɪ] adv - 1. [without doubt] sin duda - 2. [for emphasis] desde luego, con (toda) seguridad; **definitely not** desde luego que no.

definition [defɪ'nɪʃn] n - 1. [gen] definición f; **by definition** por definición - 2. [clarity] nitidez f.

definitive [dɪ'fɪnɪtɪv] adj definitivo(va).

deflate [dɪ'fleɪt] <> vt - 1. [balloon] desinflar; fig [person] bajar los humos a - 2. ECON producir una deflación. <> vi desinflarse.

deflation [dɪ'fleɪʃn] n ECON deflación f.

deflationary [dɪ'fleɪʃnərɪ] adj ECON deflacionario(ria), deflacionista.

deflect [dɪ'flekt] vt [gen] desviar; [criticism] soslayar.

deflection [dɪ'flekʃn] n desviación f.

defog [ˌdiː'fɒg] vt US AUT desempañar.

defogger [ˌdiː'fɒgə'] n US AUT dispositivo m antivaho, luneta f térmica.

deforest [ˌdiː'fɒrɪst] vt deforestar.

deforestation [diːˌfɒrɪ'steɪʃn] n deforestación f.

deform [diː'fɔːm] vt deformar.

deformed [dɪ'fɔːmd] adj deforme.

deformity [dɪ'fɔːmətɪ] (pl -ies) n [in foetus, baby] malformación f (congénita); [in adult] deformidad f.

defragment [ˌdiː'frægment] vt COMPUT desfragmentar.

defraud [dɪ'frɔːd] vt defraudar, estafar.

defray [dɪ'freɪ] vt sufragar, correr con.

defibrillator [diː'fɪbrɪleɪtə'] n MED desfibrilador m.

defrost [ˌdiː'frɒst] <> vt - 1. [gen] descongelar - 2. US AUT [demist] desempañar. <> vi descongelarse.

deft [deft] adj habilidoso(sa), diestro(tra).

deftly ['deftlɪ] adv con destreza.

defunct [dɪ'fʌŋkt] adj [body, organization] desaparecido(da); [plan] desechado(da).

defuse [ˌdiː'fjuːz] vt UK - 1. [bomb] desactivar - 2. [situation] distender.

defy [dɪ'faɪ] (*pt* & *pp* **-ied**) *vt* **- 1.** [disobey - person, authority] desobedecer; [law, rule] violar **- 2.** [challenge]: **to defy sb to do sthg** retar OR desafiar a alguien a hacer algo **- 3.** [attempts, efforts] hacer inútil; **to defy description** ser indescriptible; **to defy explanation** ser inexplicable.

degenerate ◇ *adj* [dɪ'dʒenərət] degenerado(da). ◇ *n* [dɪ'dʒenərət] degenerado *m*, -da *f*. ◇ *vi* [dɪ'dʒenəreɪt]: **to degenerate (into)** degenerar (en).

degradation [ˌdegrə'deɪʃn] *n* degradación *f*.

degrade [dɪ'greɪd] *vt* degradar; **to degrade o.s.** rebajarse.

degrading [dɪ'greɪdɪŋ] *adj* denigrante, degradante.

degree [dɪ'griː] *n* **- 1.** [unit of measurement, amount] grado *m*; **a degree of risk** un cierto riesgo; **by degrees** paulatinamente, poco a poco **- 2.** [qualification] título *m* universitario, ≃ licenciatura *f*; **to have/take a degree (in sthg)** tener/hacer una licenciatura (en algo) **- 3.** [course] ≃ carrera *f*.

dehumanize, -ise [diː'hjuːmənaɪz] *vt* deshumanizar.

dehydrated [ˌdiːhaɪ'dreɪtɪd] *adj* deshidratado(da).

dehydration [ˌdiːhaɪ'dreɪʃn] *n* deshidratación *f*.

de-ice [diː'aɪs] *vt* quitar el hielo de.

de-icer [diː'aɪsər] *n* (producto *m*) descongelante *m*.

deign [deɪn] *vt*: **to deign to do sthg** dignarse a hacer algo.

deity [diː'ɪtɪ] (*pl* **-ies**) *n* deidad *f*, divinidad *f*.

déjà vu [ˌdeʒɑː'vjuː] *n* (sensación *f* de) déjà vu *m*.

dejected [dɪ'dʒektɪd] *adj* abatido(da).

dejection [dɪ'dʒekʃn] *n* abatimiento *m*.

del (*abbr of* **delete**) [on keyboard] supr.

Del. *abbr of* **Delaware**.

Delaware ['deləweər] *n* Delaware.

delay [dɪ'leɪ] ◇ *n* retraso *m*; **without delay** sin demora. ◇ *vt* retrasar; **to delay starting sthg** retrasar el comienzo de algo. ◇ *vi*: **to delay (in doing sthg)** retrasarse (en hacer algo).

delayed [dɪ'leɪd] *adj*: **to be delayed** [person] retrasarse; [train, flight] llevar retraso.

delayed-action [dɪ'leɪd-] *adj* de efecto retardado; **delayed-action shutter** PHOT (disparador *m*) automático *m*.

delectable [dɪ'lektəbl] *adj* **- 1.** [food] deleitable **- 2.** [person] apetecible.

delegate ◇ *n* ['delɪgət] delegado *m*, -da *f*. ◇ *vt* ['delɪgeɪt]: **to delegate sthg (to sb)** delegar algo (en alguien); **to delegate sb to do sthg** delegar a alguien para hacer algo. ◇ *vi* ['delɪgeɪt] delegar responsabilidades.

delegation [ˌdelɪ'geɪʃn] *n* delegación *f*.

delete [dɪ'liːt] *vt* [gen & COMPUT] borrar, suprimir; [cross out] tachar.

delete key *n* COMPUT tecla *f* de borrado.

deletion [dɪ'liːʃn] *n* supresión *f*.

deli ['delɪ] *n inf abbr of* **delicatessen**.

deliberate ◇ *adj* [dɪ'lɪbərət] **- 1.** [intentional] deliberado(da) **- 2.** [slow] pausado(da). ◇ *vi* [dɪ'lɪbəreɪt] *fml* deliberar.

deliberately [dɪ'lɪbərətlɪ] *adv* **- 1.** [on purpose] adrede, deliberadamente **- 2.** [slowly] pausadamente.

deliberation [dɪˌlɪbə'reɪʃn] *n* **- 1.** [careful consideration] deliberación *f* **- 2.** [slowness] pausa *f*. ◆ **deliberations** *npl* deliberaciones *fpl*.

delicacy ['delɪkəsɪ] (*pl* **-ies**) *n* **- 1.** [gracefulness, tact] delicadeza *f* **- 2.** [food] exquisitez *f*, manjar *m*.

delicate ['delɪkət] *adj* **- 1.** [gen] delicado(da) **- 2.** [subtle - colour, taste] suave, sutil **- 3.** [tactful] delicado(da), prudente; [instrument] sensible.

delicately ['delɪkətlɪ] *adv* **- 1.** [gracefully, tactfully] con delicadeza **- 2.** [subtly] suavemente, sutilmente.

delicatessen [ˌdelɪkə'tesn] *n* ≃ charcutería *f*, ≃ (tienda *f* de) ultramarinos *m inv*.

delicious [dɪ'lɪʃəs] *adj* delicioso(sa).

delight [dɪ'laɪt] ◇ *n* **- 1.** [great pleasure] gozo *m*, regocijo *m*; **to our delight** para gran alegría nuestra; **to take delight in doing sthg** disfrutar haciendo algo **- 2.** [thing, person] delicia *f*, placer *m*. ◇ *vt* encantar. ◇ *vi*: **to delight in sthg/in doing sthg** disfrutar con algo/haciendo algo.

delighted [dɪ'laɪtɪd] *adj* encantado(da), muy contento(ta); **delighted by** OR **with** encantado con; **to be delighted to do sthg/that** estar encantado de hacer algo/de que; **I'd be delighted (to come)** me encantaría (ir).

delightful [dɪ'laɪtfʊl] *adj* [gen] encantador(ra); [meal] delicioso(sa); [view] muy agradable.

delightfully [dɪ'laɪtfʊlɪ] *adv* maravillosamente.

delimit [diː'lɪmɪt] *vt fml* delimitar.

delineate [dɪ'lɪnɪeɪt] *vt fml* concretar, precisar.

delinquency [dɪ'lɪŋkwənsɪ] *n* delincuencia *f*.

delinquent [dɪ'lɪŋkwənt] ◇ *adj* [behaviour] delictivo(va); [child] delincuente. ◇ *n* delincuente *mf*.

delirious [dɪ'lɪrɪəs] *adj* [with fever] delirante; *fig* [ecstatic] enfervorizado(da).

delirium [dɪ'lɪrɪəm] *n* delirio *m*, desvarío *m*.

deliver [dɪˈlɪvər] ◇ *vt* - **1.** [hand over] entregar; [distribute] repartir; **to deliver sthg to sb** entregar algo a alguien - **2.** [give - speech, verdict, lecture] pronunciar; [- message, warning, ultimatum] transmitir; [- blow, kick] asestar - **3.** [service] prestar - **4.** [baby] traer al mundo - **5.** *fml* [free] liberar, libertar - **6.** *US* POL [votes] captar. ◇ *vi* - **1.** [take to home, office] hacer reparto - **2.** [fulfil promise] cumplir (lo prometido).

deliverance [dɪˈlɪvərəns] *n* *fml* liberación *f*.

delivery [dɪˈlɪvərɪ] (*pl* -ies) *n* - **1.** [handing over] entrega *f*; [distribution] reparto *m* - **2.** [goods delivered] partida *f* - **3.** [way of speaking] (estilo *m* de) discurso *m* - **4.** [birth] parto *m*.

delivery note *n* albarán *m*.

delivery van *UK*, **delivery truck** *US* *n* furgoneta *f* de reparto.

delphinium [delˈfɪnɪəm] (*pl* -s) *n* espuela *f* de caballero.

delta [ˈdeltə] (*pl* -s) *n* [of river] delta *m*.

delude [dɪˈluːd] *vt* engañar; **to delude o.s.** engañarse (a uno mismo/una misma).

deluge [ˈdeljuːdʒ] ◇ *n* [flood] diluvio *m*, aluvión *m*; *fig* [huge number] aluvión *m*. ◇ *vt*: **to be deluged with** verse inundado(da) por.

delusion [dɪˈluːʒn] *n* espejismo *m*, engaño *m*; **delusions of grandeur** delirios *mpl* de grandeza.

de luxe [dəˈlʌks] *adj* de lujo.

delve [delv] *vi*: **to delve (into)** [bag, cupboard] hurgar (en); *fig* [mystery] ahondar (en), profundizar (en).

Dem. *abbr of* Democrat. *abbr of* Democratic.

demagogue [ˈdeməgɒg] *n* demagogo *m*, -ga *f*.

demand [dɪˈmɑːnd] ◇ *n* - **1.** [claim, firm request] exigencia *f*, reclamación *f*; **on demand** a petición; **wage demand** demanda *f* OR reivindicación salarial - **2.** [need & ECON]: **demand for** demanda *f* de; **in demand** solicitado(da). ◇ *vt* [gen] exigir; [pay rise] reivindicar, demandar; **to demand to do sthg** exigir hacer algo.

demanding [dɪˈmɑːndɪŋ] *adj* - **1.** [exhausting] que exige mucho esfuerzo - **2.** [not easily satisfied] exigente.

demarcation [ˌdiːmɑːˈkeɪʃn] *n* demarcación *f*.

demarcation dispute *n* *conflicto entre sindicatos y la patronal sobre la delimitación de las tareas que sus miembros deben realizar en el trabajo.*

dematerialize, -ise [diːməˈtɪərɪəlaɪz] *vi* desvanecerse (en el aire).

demean [dɪˈmiːn] *vt* humillar, degradar; **to demean o.s.** humillarse, rebajarse.

demeaning [dɪˈmiːnɪŋ] *adj* humillante, denigrante.

demeanour *UK*, **demeanor** *US* [dɪˈmiːnər] *n (U)* *fml* comportamiento *m*.

demented [dɪˈmentɪd] *adj* demente.

dementia [dɪˈmenʃə] *n* demencia *f*.

demerara sugar [ˌdeməˈreərə-] *n* *UK* azúcar *m* moreno.

demigod [ˈdemɪgɒd] *n* semidiós *m*.

demijohn [ˈdemɪdʒɒn] *n* damajuana *f*.

demilitarized zone, demilitarised zone [ˌdiːˈmɪlɪtəraɪzd-] *n* zona *f* desmilitarizada.

demise [dɪˈmaɪz] *n* *fml* - **1.** [death] defunción *f*, fallecimiento *m* - **2.** [end] desaparición *f*.

demist [ˌdiːˈmɪst] *vt* *UK* desempañar.

demister [ˌdiːˈmɪstər] *n* *UK* AUT dispositivo *m* antivaho, luneta *f* térmica.

demo [ˈdeməʊ] (*abbr of* demonstration) *n* *inf* - **1.** mani *f* - **2.** MUS maqueta *f*.

demobilize, -ise [ˌdiːˈməʊbɪlaɪz] *vt* desmovilizar.

democracy [dɪˈmɒkrəsɪ] (*pl* -ies) *n* democracia *f*.

democrat [ˈdeməkræt] *n* demócrata *mf*.
➤ **Democrat** *n* *US* demócrata *mf*.

democratic [deməˈkrætɪk] *adj* democrático(ca).
➤ **Democratic** *adj* *US* demócrata.

democratically [ˌdeməˈkrætɪklɪ] *adv* democráticamente.

Democratic Party *n* *US* Partido *m* Demócrata.

democratize, -ise [dɪˈmɒkrətaɪz] *vt* democratizar.

demographic [ˌdeməˈgræfɪk] *adj* demográfico(ca).

demolish [dɪˈmɒlɪʃ] *vt* - **1.** [building] demoler; [argument, myth] destrozar - **2.** [defeat] aplastar - **3.** *inf* [eat] zamparse.

demolition [ˌdeməˈlɪʃn] *n* [of building] demolición *f*; [of argument, myth] destrucción *f*.

demon [ˈdiːmən] ◇ *n* demonio *m*. ◇ *comp inf* fenomenal.

demonstrable [dɪˈmɒnstrəbl] *adj* demostrable.

demonstrably [dɪˈmɒnstrəblɪ] *adv* [better, different] manifiestamente.

demonstrate [ˈdemənstreɪt] ◇ *vt* - **1.** [prove] demostrar - **2.** [show] hacer una demostración de. ◇ *vi* manifestarse; **to demonstrate for/against sthg** manifestarse a favor/en contra de algo.

demonstration [demənˈstreɪʃn] *n* - **1.** [of machine, product] demostración *f* - **2.** [public meeting] manifestación *f*.

demonstrative [dɪˈmɒnstrətɪv] *adj* efusivo(va), expresivo(va).

demonstrator ['demənstreɪtəʳ] n - **1.** [in march] manifestante mf - **2.** [of machine, product] demostrador m, -ra f comercial.

demoralize, -ise [dɪ'mɒrəlaɪz] vt desmoralizar.

demoralized [dɪ'mɒrəlaɪzd] adj desmoraliza-do(da).

demote [ˌdiː'məʊt] vt descender de categoría.

demotion [ˌdiː'məʊʃn] n descenso m de categoría.

demotivate [ˌdiː'məʊtɪveɪt] vt desmotivar.

demure [dɪ'mjʊəʳ] adj recatado(da).

demystify [ˌdiː'mɪstɪfaɪ] (pt & pp -ied) vt arrojar luz sobre.

den [den] n [lair] guarida f.

denationalization ['diːˌnæʃnəlaɪ'zeɪʃn] n privatización f, desnacionalización f.

denationalize, -ise [ˌdiː'næʃnəlaɪz] vt privatizar, desnacionalizar.

denial [dɪ'naɪəl] n - **1.** [refutation] negación f, rechazo m; **she's in denial about her drink problem** se niega a aceptar que tiene un problema con la bebida - **2.** [of rumour] desmenti-do m - **3.** [refusal] denegación f.

denier ['denɪəʳ] n denier m.

denigrate ['denɪgreɪt] vt fml desacreditar.

denim ['denɪm] n tela f vaquera.

☞ **denims** npl (pantalones mpl) vaqueros mpl.

denim jacket n cazadora f vaquera.

denizen ['denɪzn] n liter & hum morador m, -ra f.

Denmark ['denmɑːk] n Dinamarca.

denomination [dɪˌnɒmɪ'neɪʃn] n - **1.** [religious group] confesión f - **2.** [of money] valor m.

denominator [dɪ'nɒmɪneɪtəʳ] n denomina-dor m.

denote [dɪ'nəʊt] vt fml denotar.

denounce [dɪ'naʊns] vt denunciar.

dense [dens] adj - **1.** [gen] denso(sa); [trees] tupido(da) - **2.** inf [stupid] bruto(ta).

densely ['densli] adv densamente; **densely packed** muy apretado(da).

density ['densətɪ] (pl -ies) n densidad f.

dent [dent] ◇ n [on car] abolladura f. ◇ vt [car] abollar.

dental ['dentl] adj dental; **dental surgery** clíni-ca f OR consultorio m dental.

dental floss n hilo m OR seda f dental.

dental plate n [dentures] dentadura f postiza.

dental surgeon n odontólogo m, -ga f.

dental treatment n tratamiento f dental.

dented ['dentɪd] adj [car] abollado(da).

dentist ['dentɪst] n dentista mf; **to go to the dentist's** ir al dentista.

dentistry ['dentɪstrɪ] n odontología f.

dentures ['dentʃəz] npl dentadura f postiza.

denunciation [dɪˌnʌnsɪ'eɪʃn] n denuncia f, condena f.

deny [dɪ'naɪ] (pt & pp -ied) vt - **1.** [refute] ne-gar, rechazar; **to deny doing sthg** negar ha-ber hecho algo - **2.** [rumour] desmentir - **3.** fml [refuse]: **to deny sb sthg** denegar algo a al-guien.

deodorant [diː'əʊdərənt] n desodorante m.

depart [dɪ'pɑːt] vi fml - **1.** [leave]: **to depart (from)** salir (de); **this train will depart from Platform 2** este tren efectuará su salida por la vía 2 - **2.** [differ]: **to depart from sthg** apartar-se de algo.

department [dɪ'pɑːtmənt] n - **1.** [gen] departa-mento m - **2.** [in government] ministerio m.

departmental [ˌdiːpɑːt'mentl] adj [gen] depar-tamental; [head, secretary] del departamento.

department store n grandes almace-nes mpl.

departure [dɪ'pɑːtʃəʳ] n - **1.** [of train, plane] sali-da f; [of person] marcha f, partida f - **2.** [change]: **departure (from)** abandono m (de); **a new de-parture** un nuevo enfoque.

departure lounge n [in airport] sala f de em-barque; [in coach station] vestíbulo m de salidas.

depend [dɪ'pend] vi: **to depend on** depender de; **you can depend on me** puedes confiar en mí; **it depends** depende; **depending on** se-gún, dependiendo de.

dependable [dɪ'pendəbl] adj fiable.

dependant [dɪ'pendənt] n: **my dependants** las personas a mi cargo.

dependence [dɪ'pendəns] n: **dependence (on)** dependencia f (de); **drug dependence** drogo-dependencia f.

dependent [dɪ'pendənt] adj - **1.** [gen]: **to be de-pendent (on)** depender (de) - **2.** [addicted] adicto(ta).

depict [dɪ'pɪkt] vt - **1.** [in picture] representar, retratar - **2.** [describe]: **to depict sthg/sb as sthg** describir algo/a alguien como algo.

depilatory [dɪ'pɪlətrɪ] adj depilador(ra), depi-latorio(ria).

deplete [dɪ'pliːt] vt mermar, reducir.

depletion [dɪ'pliːʃn] n [gen] merma f, reduc-ción f; [of ozone layer] degradación f.

deplorable [dɪ'plɔːrəbl] adj deplorable.

deplore [dɪ'plɔːʳ] vt deplorar.

deploy [dɪ'plɔɪ] vt desplegar.

deployment [dɪ'plɔɪmənt] n despliegue m.

depopulated [ˌdiː'pɒpjʊleɪtɪd] adj despobla-do(da).

depopulation [diːˌpɒpjʊ'leɪʃn] n despobla-ción f.

deport [dɪ'pɔːt] vt deportar.

deportation [ˌdiːpɔː'teɪʃn] n deportación f.

deportation order *n* orden *f* de deportación.

depose [dɪ'pəuz] *vt* deponer.

deposit [dɪ'pɒzɪt] <> *n* - **1.** GEOL yacimiento *m* - **2.** [sediment] poso *m*, sedimento *m* - **3.** [payment into bank] ingreso *m*, imposición *f*; **to make a deposit** hacer un ingreso - **4.** [down payment - on house, car] entrada *f*; [- on hotel room] señal *f*, adelanto *m*; [- on hired goods] fianza *f*, enganche *m* *Méx*; [- on bottle] dinero *m* del envase OR casco. <> *vt* - **1.** [put down] depositar - **2.** [in bank] ingresar.

deposit account *n* UK cuenta *f* de ahorro a plazo fijo.

depositor [də'pɒzɪtər] *n* impositor *m*, -ra *f*, depositante *mf*.

depot ['depəu] *n* - **1.** [storage facility] almacén *m*; [for weapons] depósito *m* - **2.** [for buses] cochera *f* - **3.** US [bus or train terminus] terminal *f*, estación *f*.

depraved [dɪ'preɪvd] *adj* depravado(da).

depravity [dɪ'prævətɪ] *n* depravación *f*.

deprecate ['deprɪkeɪt] *vt* *fml* censurar.

deprecating ['deprɪkeɪtɪŋ] *adj* desaprobatorio(ria).

depreciate [dɪ'priːʃɪeɪt] *vi* depreciarse.

depreciation [dɪ,priːʃɪ'eɪʃn] *n* depreciación *f*.

depress [dɪ'pres] *vt* - **1.** [person] deprimir - **2.** [economy] desactivar - **3.** [price, share value] reducir.

depressant [dɪ'presənt] *n* depresor *m*.

depressed [dɪ'prest] *adj* deprimido(da).

depressing [dɪ'presɪŋ] *adj* deprimente.

depression [dɪ'preʃn] *n* - **1.** [gen & ECON] depresión *f*; **to suffer from depression** sufrir depresiones - **2.** *fml* [in pillow] hueco *m*.
➡ **Depression** *n* HIST: **the (Great) Depression** la Gran Depresión.

depressive [dɪ'presɪv] *adj* depresivo(va).

deprivation [,deprɪ'veɪʃn] *n* - **1.** [poverty] miseria *f* - **2.** [lack] privación *f*.

deprive [dɪ'praɪv] *vt*: **to deprive sb of sthg** privar a alguien de algo.

deprived [dɪ'praɪvd] *adj* [children, childhood] necesitado(da); [area] desfavorecido(da).

dept. *abbr of* **department**.

depth [depθ] *n* profundidad *f*; **in depth** a fondo; **to be out of one's depth** [in water] no hacer pie; **he was out of his depth with that job** ese trabajo le venía grande.
➡ **depths** *npl*: **the depths** [of the sea] las profundidades; **in the depths of winter** en pleno invierno; **to be in the depths of despair** estar en un abismo de desesperación.

depth charge *n* carga *f* de profundidad.

deputation [,depjʊ'teɪʃn] *n* delegación *f*.

deputize, -ise ['depjʊtaɪz] *vi*: **to deputize (for)** actuar en representación (de).

deputy ['depjʊtɪ] <> *adj*: **deputy head** subdirector *m*, -ra *f*; **deputy prime minister** vicepresidente *m*, -ta *f* del gobierno. <> *n* (*pl* -ies) - **1.** [second-in-command] asistente *mf*, suplente *mf* - **2.** POL diputado *m*, -da *f* - **3.** US [deputy sheriff] ayudante *mf* del sheriff.

derail [dɪ'reɪl] *vt* & *vi* [train] descarrilar.

derailment [dɪ'reɪlmənt] *n* descarrilamiento *m*.

deranged [dɪ'reɪndʒd] *adj* perturbado(da), trastornado(da).

derby [UK 'dɑːbɪ, US 'dɜːbɪ] (*pl* -ies) *n* - **1.** [sports event] derby *m* (local) - **2.** US [hat] bombín *m*, sombrero *m* hongo.

deregulate [,diː'regjʊleɪt] *vt* liberalizar.

deregulation [,diːregjʊ'leɪʃn] *n* liberalización *f*.

derelict ['derəlɪkt] *adj* abandonado(da), en ruinas.

deride [dɪ'raɪd] *vt* mofarse de.

derision [dɪ'rɪʒn] *n* mofa *f*, burla *f*.

derisive [dɪ'raɪsɪv] *adj* burlón(ona).

derisory [də'raɪzərɪ] *adj* - **1.** [puny, trivial] irrisorio(ria) - **2.** [derisive] burlón(ona).

derivation [,derɪ'veɪʃn] *n* [of word] origen *m*.

derivative [dɪ'rɪvətɪv] <> *adj* *pej* carente de originalidad. <> *n* derivado *m*.

derive [dɪ'raɪv] <> *vt* - **1.** [draw, gain]: **to derive sthg from sthg** encontrar algo en algo - **2.** [come]: **to be derived from** derivar de. <> *vi*: **to derive from** derivar de.

dermatitis [,dɜːmə'taɪtɪs] *n* dermatitis *f* *inv*.

dermatologist [,dɜːmə'tɒlədʒɪst] *n* dermatólogo *m*, -ga *f*.

dermatology [,dɜːmə'tɒlədʒɪ] *n* dermatología *f*.

derogatory [dɪ'rɒgətrɪ] *adj* despectivo(va).

derrick ['derɪk] *n* - **1.** [crane] grúa *f* - **2.** [over oil well] torre *f* de perforación.

derv [dɜːv] *n* UK gasóleo *m*, gasoil *m*.

desalination [diː,sælɪ'neɪʃn] *n* desalinización *f*.

descant ['deskænt] *n* contrapunto *m*.

descend [dɪ'send] <> *vt* *fml* [go down] descender por. <> *vi* - **1.** *fml* [go down] descender - **2.** [subj: silence, gloom]: **to descend (on sthg/sb)** invadir (algo/a alguien) - **3.** [arrive]: **to descend on sb** presentarse en casa de alguien - **4.** [stoop]: **to descend to sthg/to doing sthg** rebajarse a algo/a hacer algo.

descendant [dɪ'sendənt] *n* descendiente *mf*.

descended [dɪ'sendɪd] *adj*: **to be descended from** ser descendiente de, descender de.

descending [dɪ'sendɪŋ] *adj*: in descending order en orden descendente OR decreciente.

descent [dɪ'sent] *n* - **1.** [downwards movement] descenso *m*, bajada *f* - **2.** [origin] ascendencia *f*.

describe [dɪ'skraɪb] *vt* describir; to describe o.s. as definirse como.

description [dɪ'skrɪpʃn] *n* - **1.** [account] descripción *f* - **2.** [type]: of all descriptions de todo tipo.

descriptive [dɪ'skrɪptɪv] *adj* descriptivo(va).

desecrate ['desɪkreɪt] *vt* profanar.

desecration [,desɪ'kreɪʃn] *n* profanación *f*.

desegregate [,di:'segrɪgeɪt] *vt* abolir la segregación racial en.

deselect [,di:sɪ'lekt] *vt UK* no reelegir como candidato.

desert ⬦ *n* ['dezət] - **1.** GEOG desierto *m* - **2.** [boring place]: **(cultural) desert** páramo *m* cultural. ⬦ *vt* [dɪ'zɜ:t] abandonar. ⬦ *vi* MIL desertar.

➡ **deserts** *npl* [dɪ'zɜ:t]: he got his just deserts se llevó su merecido.

deserted [dɪ'zɜ:tɪd] *adj* [place] desierto(ta).

deserter [dɪ'zɜ:tər] *n* desertor *m*, -ra *f*.

desertion [dɪ'zɜ:ʃn] *n* - **1.** [gen] abandono *m* - **2.** MIL deserción *f*.

desert island ['dezət-] *n* isla *f* desierta.

deserve [dɪ'zɜ:v] *vt* merecer, ameritar *Amér*; to deserve to do sthg merecer hacer algo; they got what they deserved se llevaron su merecido.

deserved [dɪ'zɜ:vd] *adj* merecido(da).

deservedly [dɪ'zɜ:vɪdlɪ] *adv* merecidamente.

deserving [dɪ'zɜ:vɪŋ] *adj* meritorio(ria), encomiable; **deserving of** *fml* merecedor(ra) de.

desiccated ['desɪkeɪtɪd] *adj* desecado(da); **desiccated coconut** coco seco y rallado.

design [dɪ'zaɪn] ⬦ *n* - **1.** [gen] diseño *m*; [of garment] corte *m* - **2.** [pattern] dibujo *m* - **3.** *fml* [intention] designio *m*, intención *f*; by design adrede; to have designs on tener las miras puestas en. ⬦ *vt* - **1.** [gen] diseñar - **2.** [conceive, intend] concebir.

designate ⬦ *adj* ['dezɪgnət] designado(da). ⬦ *vt* ['dezɪgneɪt] designar, nombrar; to designate sb as sthg/to do sthg designar a alguien algo/para hacer algo.

designation [,dezɪg'neɪʃn] *n fml* [name] denominación *f*.

designer [dɪ'zaɪnər] ⬦ *adj* [clothes, drugs] de diseño; [glasses] de marca. ⬦ *n* [gen] diseñador *m*, -ra *f*; THEAT escenógrafo *m*, -fa *f*.

desirable [dɪ'zaɪərəbl] *adj* - **1.** *fml* [appropriate] deseable, conveniente - **2.** [attractive] atractivo(va), apetecible.

desire [dɪ'zaɪər] ⬦ *n*: desire (for sthg/to do sthg) deseo *m* (de algo/de hacer algo). ⬦ *vt* desear; it leaves a lot to be desired deja mucho que desear.

desirous [dɪ'zaɪərəs] *adj fml*: desirous of sthg/of doing sthg deseoso(sa) de algo/de hacer algo.

desist [dɪ'zɪst] *vi fml*: to desist (from doing sthg) desistir (de hacer algo).

desk [desk] *n* - **1.** [gen] mesa *f*, escritorio *m*; [in school] pupitre *m*; **cash desk** caja *f* - **2.** [service area]: **cash desk** caja *f*; **information desk** (mostrador *m* de) información *f*.

desk lamp *n* flexo *m*, lámpara *f* de mesa.

desktop ['desk,tɒp] *adj* COMPUT: **desktop (computer)** ordenador *m* de sobremesa.

desktop publishing *n* COMPUT autoedición *f*.

desolate ['desələt] *adj* [place, person] desolado(da); [feeling] desolador(ra).

desolation [,desə'leɪʃn] *n* desolación *f*.

despair [dɪ'speər] ⬦ *n* desesperación *f*; to do sthg in despair hacer algo desesperadamente. ⬦ *vi* desesperarse; to despair of sb desesperarse con alguien; to despair of sthg/doing sthg perder la esperanza de algo/hacer algo.

despairing [dɪ'speərɪŋ] *adj* [attempt] desesperado(da); [look, cry] de desesperación.

despairingly [dɪ'speərɪŋlɪ] *adv* con desesperación.

despatch [dɪ'spætʃ] = **dispatch**.

desperate ['desprət] *adj* desesperado(da); to be desperate for sthg necesitar algo desesperadamente.

desperately ['desprətlɪ] *adv* - **1.** [want, fight, love] desesperadamente - **2.** [ill] gravemente; [poor, unhappy, shy] tremendamente.

desperation [,despə'reɪʃn] *n* desesperación *f*; in desperation con desesperación.

despicable [dɪ'spɪkəbl] *adj* despreciable.

despise [dɪ'spaɪz] *vt* despreciar.

despite [dɪ'spaɪt] *prep* a pesar de, pese a.

despondent [dɪ'spɒndənt] *adj* descorazonado(da).

despot ['despɒt] *n* déspota *mf*.

despotic [de'spɒtɪk] *adj* despótico(ca).

dessert [dɪ'zɜ:t] *n* postre *m*.

dessertspoon [dɪ'zɜ:tspu:n] *n* - **1.** [spoon] cuchara *f* de postre - **2.** [spoonful] cucharada *f* (de las de postre).

dessert wine *n* vino *m* dulce.

destabilize, -ise [,di:'steɪbɪlaɪz] *vt* desestabilizar.

destination [,destɪ'neɪʃn] *n* destino *m*.

destined ['destɪnd] *adj* - **1.** [fated, intended]: **destined for sthg/to do sthg** destinado(da) a algo/a hacer algo - **2.** [bound]: **destined for** con destino a.

destiny ['destɪnɪ] (*pl* -ies) *n* destino *m*.

destitute ['destɪtjuːt] *adj* indigente, en la miseria.

de-stress [diː'stres] *vi* desestresarse.

destroy [dɪ'strɔɪ] *vt* - **1.** [ruin] destruir - **2.** [defeat] aplastar - **3.** [put down] matar, sacrificar.

destroyer [dɪ'strɔɪər] *n* - **1.** [ship] destructor *m* - **2.** [person or thing] destructor *m*, -ra *f*.

destruction [dɪ'strʌkʃn] *n* destrucción *f*.

destructive [dɪ'strʌktɪv] *adj* [gen] destructivo(va); [influence] pernicioso(sa).

destructively [dɪ'strʌktɪvlɪ] *adv* destructivamente.

desultory ['desəltrɪ] *adj fml* [conversation] sin interés; [attempt] sin convicción.

Det. *abbr of* **Detective**.

detach [dɪ'tætʃ] *vt* - **1.** [pull off]: **to detach sthg (from)** quitar OR separar algo (de) - **2.** [disassociate]: **to detach o.s. from sthg** distanciarse de algo.

detachable [dɪ'tætʃəbl] *adj* [handle etc] de quita y pon; [collar] postizo(za).

detached [dɪ'tætʃt] *adj* [objective] objetivo(va); [aloof] distante.

detached house *n* casa *f* OR chalé *m* individual.

detachment [dɪ'tætʃmənt] *n* - **1.** [objectivity] objetividad *f*; [aloofness] distanciamiento *m* - **2.** MIL destacamento *m*.

detail ['diːteɪl] <> *n* - **1.** [small point] detalle *m* - **2.** (*U*) [facts, points] detalles *mpl*; **to go into detail** entrar en detalles; **in detail** detalladamente, con detalle - **3.** MIL destacamento *m*. <> *vt* [list] detallar.

➡ **details** *npl* [information] información *f*; [personal] datos *mpl*.

detailed ['diːteɪld] *adj* detallado(da).

detain [dɪ'teɪn] *vt* [gen] retener; [in police station] detener.

detainee [ˌdiːteɪ'niː] *n* [gen] detenido *m*, -da *f*; [political] preso político *m*, presa política *f*.

detect [dɪ'tekt] *vt* [gen] detectar; [difference] notar, percibir.

detection [dɪ'tekʃn] (*U*) *n* - **1.** [gen] detección *f* - **2.** [of crime] investigación *f*; [of drugs] descubrimiento *m*.

detective [dɪ'tektɪv] *n* [private] detective *mf*; [policeman] agente *mf*.

detective novel *n* novela *f* policíaca.

detector [dɪ'tektər] *n* detector *m*.

détente [deɪ'tɒnt] *n* POL distensión *f*.

detention [dɪ'tenʃn] *n* - **1.** [of suspect, criminal] detención *f*, arresto *m*; **in detention** bajo arresto - **2.** [at school] *castigo consistente en tener que quedarse en la escuela después de clase.*

detention centre *n* UK - **1.** [for juvenile delinquents] centro *m* de internamiento de delincuentes juveniles - **2.** [for asylum seekers] centro *m* de internamiento de inmigrantes (*que esperan recibir asilo político*).

deter [dɪ'tɜːr] (*pt & pp* -red, *cont* -ring) *vt*: **to deter sb (from doing sthg)** disuadir a alguien (de hacer algo).

detergent [dɪ'tɜːdʒənt] *n* detergente *m*.

deteriorate [dɪ'tɪərɪəreɪt] *vi* [health, economy] deteriorarse; [weather] empeorar.

deterioration [dɪˌtɪərɪə'reɪʃn] *n* [of health, economy] deterioro *m*; [of weather] empeoramiento *m*.

determination [dɪˌtɜːmɪ'neɪʃn] *n* determinación *f*.

determine [dɪ'tɜːmɪn] *vt* determinar; **to determine to do sthg** *fml* decidir OR resolver hacer algo.

determined [dɪ'tɜːmɪnd] *adj* decidido(da); **determined to do sthg** decidido(da) OR resuelto(ta) a hacer algo.

deterrent [dɪ'terənt] <> *adj* disuasorio(ria). <> *n* elemento *m* de disuasión; **to serve as a deterrent** tener un efecto disuasorio; **nuclear deterrent** armas *fpl* nucleares disuasorias.

detest [dɪ'test] *vt* detestar.

detestable [dɪ'testəbl] *adj* detestable.

dethrone [dɪ'θrəʊn] *vt* destronar.

detonate ['detəneɪt] <> *vt* hacer detonar. <> *vi* detonar.

detonator ['detəneɪtər] *n* detonador *m*.

detour ['diːˌtʊər] *n* desvío *m*; **to make a detour** dar un rodeo.

detox ['diːtɒks] *n* desintoxicación *f*.

detract [dɪ'trækt] *vi*: **to detract from sthg** [gen] mermar algo, aminorar algo; [achievement] restar importancia a algo.

detractor [dɪ'træktər] *n* detractor *m*, -ra *f*.

detriment ['detrɪmənt] *n*: **to the detriment of** en detrimento de.

detrimental [ˌdetrɪ'mentl] *adj* perjudicial.

detritus [dɪ'traɪtəs] *n* (*U*) desperdicios *mpl*; GEOL detrito *m*, detritus *m inv*.

deuce [djuːs] *n* (*U*) TENNIS deuce *m*, cuarenta *f*.

Deutschmark ['dɔɪtʃˌmɑːk] *n* marco *m* alemán.

devaluation [ˌdiːvæljʊ'eɪʃn] *n* devaluación *f*.

devalue [ˌdiː'væljuː] *vt* - **1.** FIN devaluar - **2.** [person, achievement] menospreciar.

devastate ['devəsteɪt] *vt* [area, city] devastar, asolar; *fig* [person] desolar.

devastated ['devəsteɪtɪd] *adj* [area, city] devastado(da), asolado(da); *fig* [person] desolado(da).

devastating ['devəsteɪtɪŋ] *adj* - **1.** [destructive - hurricane etc] devastador(ra) - **2.** [effective - remark, argument] abrumador(ra) - **3.** [upsetting - news, experience] desolador(ra) - **4.** [attractive] imponente, irresistible.

devastation [ˌdevə'steɪʃn] *n* [destruction] devastación *f*.

develop [dɪ'veləp] <> *vt* - **1.** [idea, argument, product, method] desarrollar - **2.** [land] urbanizar; [region] desarrollar - **3.** [illness] contraer; [habit] adquirir; **to develop a fault** estropearse - **4.** PHOT revelar. <> *vi* - **1.** [grow] desarrollarse; **to develop into sthg** transformarse en algo - **2.** [appear] presentarse.

developed [dɪ'veləpt] *adj* [country, region] desarrollado(da).

developer [dɪ'veləpəʳ] *n* - **1.** [of land] promotor *m*, -ra *f* - **2.** [person]: **early/late developer** niño *m*, -ña *f* con desarrollo precoz/tardío - **3.** PHOT [chemical] líquido *m* de revelado, revelador *m*.

developing country [dɪ'veləpɪŋ-] *n* país *m* en vías de desarrollo.

development [dɪ'veləpmənt] *(U)* *n* - **1.** [growth] desarrollo *m* - **2.** [of design] elaboración *f*; [of product] desarrollo *m* - **3.** [developed land] urbanización *f* - **4.** [new event] (nuevo) acontecimiento *m*; **recent developments** la evolución reciente - **5.** [advance - in science etc] avance *m* - **6.** [of illness] contracción *f*; [of fault] aparición *f*.

deviant ['di:vjənt] <> *adj* irregular, anómalo(la); [sexually] pervertido(da). <> *n* pervertido *m*, -da *f*.

deviate ['di:vɪeɪt] *vi*: **to deviate from sthg** apartarse OR desviarse de algo.

deviation [ˌdi:vɪ'eɪʃn] *n* desviación *f*.

device [dɪ'vaɪs] *n* - **1.** [gen] dispositivo *m*; **to leave sb to their own devices** [with nothing to do] dejar a alguien a su aire; [without help] dejar a alguien que se las componga solo - **2.** COMPUT dispositivo *m* periférico.

devil ['devl] *n* diablo *m*, demonio *m*; **little devil** diablillo *m*; **poor devil** pobre diablo; **you lucky devil!** ¡vaya suerte que tienes!; **who/where/why the devil...?** ¿quién/dónde/por qué demonios...?

➤ **Devil** *n* [Satan]: **the Devil** el Diablo, el Demonio.

devilish ['devlɪʃ] *adj* diabólico(ca).

devil-may-care *adj* irresponsable.

devil's advocate *n* abogado *m* del diablo.

devious ['di:vjəs] *adj* - **1.** [person, scheme] retorcido(da); [means] enrevesado(da) - **2.** [route] sinuoso(sa), tortuoso(sa).

devise [dɪ'vaɪz] *vt* [instrument, system] diseñar; [plan] concebir.

devoid [dɪ'vɔɪd] *adj fml*: **devoid of** desprovisto(ta) de.

devolution [ˌdi:və'lu:ʃn] *n* POL ≃ autonomía *f*, ≃ traspaso *m* de competencias.

Devolution

Este término hace referencia en el Reino Unido al proyecto de descentralización del parlamento británico llevado a cabo tras las elecciones de 1997, en las que obtuvo la mayoría el partido laborista. El nuevo gobierno organizó sendos referendos y tras ellos se crearon parlamentos regionales en Edimburgo ("Scottish Parliament") y Cardiff ("Welsh Assembly") por primera vez en 300 y 500 años respectivamente. Estos parlamentos tienen distintos niveles de autonomía, pero carecen de competencias en materia de defensa o política exterior, por ejemplo.

devolve [dɪ'vɒlv] <> *vt* transferir. <> *vi fml*: **to devolve on** OR **upon** recaer en.

devote [dɪ'vəʊt] *vt*: **to devote sthg to** dedicar OR consagrar algo a; **to devote o.s. to** dedicarse OR consagrarse a.

devoted [dɪ'vəʊtɪd] *adj* [lovers] unido(da); [follower, admirer] ferviente; **to be devoted to sb** tenerle mucho cariño a alguien.

devotee [ˌdevə'ti:] *n* [fan] devoto *m*, -ta *f*, admirador *m*, -ra *f*.

devotion [dɪ'vəʊʃn] *(U)* *n* - **1.** [commitment]: **devotion (to)** dedicación *f* (a) - **2.** [to family, lover & RELIG] devoción *f*.

devour [dɪ'vaʊəʳ] *vt lit* & *fig* devorar.

devout [dɪ'vaʊt] *adj* RELIG devoto(ta), piadoso(sa).

dew [dju:] *n* rocío *m*.

dexterity [dek'sterətɪ] *n* destreza *f*, habilidad *f*.

dexterous, dextrous ['dekstrəs] *adj* diestro(tra).

dextrose ['dekstrəʊs] *n* dextrosa *f*.

dextrous ['dekstrəs] = **dexterous**.

DFE (*abbr of* **Department for Education**) *n* ministerio británico de educación.

dhal, dal [dɑ:l] *n* potaje de legumbres típico de la comida india muy especiado.

DHSS (*abbr of* **Department of Health and Social Security**) *n* antiguo ministerio británico de la seguridad social.

diabetes [ˌdaɪə'bi:ti:z] *n* diabetes *f inv*.

diabetic [ˌdaɪə'betɪk] <> *adj* - **1.** [person] diabético(ca) - **2.** [jam, chocolate] para diabéticos. <> *n* diabético *m*, -ca *f*.

diabolic(al) [ˌdaɪəˈbɒlɪk(l)] adj - **1.** [evil] diabólico(ca) - **2.** inf [very bad] pésimo(ma).

diaeresis UK (pl **-eses** [-ɪsiːz]), **dieresis** US [daɪˈerɪsɪs] (pl **-eses**) n diéresis f inv.

diagnose [ˈdaɪəgnəʊz] vt MED diagnosticar; **she was diagnosed as having cancer** le diagnosticaron cáncer.

diagnosis [ˌdaɪəgˈnəʊsɪs] (pl **-oses** [-əʊsiːz]) n MED [verdict] diagnóstico m; [science, activity] diagnosis f inv.

diagnostic [ˌdaɪəgˈnɒstɪk] adj MED diagnóstico(ca).

diagonal [daɪˈægənl] <> adj diagonal. <> n diagonal f.

diagonally [daɪˈægənəlɪ] adv diagonalmente, en diagonal.

diagram [ˈdaɪəgræm] n diagrama m.

diagrammatic [ˌdaɪəgrəˈmætɪk] adj gráfico(ca), esquemático(ca).

dial [ˈdaɪəl] <> n - **1.** [of watch, clock] esfera f - **2.** [of meter] cuadrante m - **3.** [of telephone] disco m; [of radio] dial m. <> vt (UK **-led**, cont **-ling**, US **-ed**, cont **-ing**) [number] marcar.

dialect [ˈdaɪəlekt] n dialecto m.

dialling code [ˈdaɪəlɪŋ-] n UK prefijo m (telefónico).

dialling tone UK [ˈdaɪəlɪŋ-], **dial tone** US n señal f de llamada.

dialogue UK, **dialog** US [ˈdaɪəlɒg] n diálogo m.

dial tone US = dialling tone.

dialysis [daɪˈælɪsɪs] n diálisis f inv.

diameter [daɪˈæmɪtər] n diámetro m.

diametrically [ˌdaɪəˈmetrɪklɪ] adv: **diametrically opposed** diametralmente opuesto(ta).

diamond [ˈdaɪəmənd] n - **1.** [gem, playing card, in baseball] diamante m - **2.** [shape] rombo m.
→ **diamonds** npl diamantes mpl.

diamond wedding n bodas fpl de diamante.

diaper [ˈdaɪpər] n US pañal m.

diaphanous [daɪˈæfənəs] adj diáfano(na).

diaphragm [ˈdaɪəfræm] n diafragma m.

diarrh(o)ea [ˌdaɪəˈrɪə] n diarrea f.

diary [ˈdaɪərɪ] (pl **-ies**) n - **1.** [appointment book] agenda f - **2.** [journal] diario m.

diatribe [ˈdaɪətraɪb] n diatriba f.

dice [daɪs] <> n (pl **dice**) dado m. <> npl: to **play dice** jugar a los dados; **no dice!** US inf ¡qué va! <> vt cortar en cuadraditos.

dicey [ˈdaɪsɪ] (comp **-ier**, superl **-iest**) adj esp UK inf arriesgado(da).

dichotomy [daɪˈkɒtəmɪ] (pl **-ies**) n dicotomía f.

Dictaphone® [ˈdɪktəfəʊn] n dictáfono m.

dictate <> vt [dɪkˈteɪt]: to **dictate sthg (to sb)** dictar algo (a alguien). <> vi [dɪkˈteɪt] - **1.** [read

out]: to **dictate (to sb)** dictar (a alguien) - **2.** [make demands]: to **dictate to sb** dar órdenes a alguien. <> n [ˈdɪkteɪt] [of one's conscience] dictado m.

dictation [dɪkˈteɪʃn] n dictado m; to **take** OR **do dictation** escribir al dictado.

dictator [dɪkˈteɪtər] n dictador m, -ra f.

dictatorship [dɪkˈteɪtəʃɪp] n dictadura f.

diction [ˈdɪkʃn] n dicción f.

dictionary [ˈdɪkʃənrɪ] (pl **-ies**) n diccionario m; **Japanese dictionary** diccionario de japonés.

did [dɪd] pt ⊳ **do**.

didactic [dɪˈdæktɪk] adj didáctico(ca).

diddle [ˈdɪdl] vt inf timar.

didn't [ˈdɪdnt] (abbr of = did not), = **do**.

die [daɪ] <> vi (pt & pp **died**, cont **dying**) - **1.** [gen] morir; to **be dying** estar muriéndose; to **be dying for sthg/to do sthg** morirse por algo/por hacer algo - **2.** liter [feeling, fire] extinguirse. <> n - **1.** [for stamping metal] cuño m, troquel m; [for casting metal] troquel m - **2.** (pl **dice**) esp US [dice] dado m.
→ **die away** vi desvanecerse.
→ **die down** vi [wind] amainar; [sound] apaciguarse; [fire] remitir; [excitement, fuss] calmarse.
→ **die out** vi extinguirse.

diehard [ˈdaɪhɑːd] n intransigente mf.

dieresis US = diaeresis.

diesel [ˈdiːzl] n - **1.** [fuel] gasóleo m, gasoil m - **2.** [vehicle] vehículo m diésel.

diesel engine n AUT motor m diésel; RAIL locomotora f diésel.

diesel fuel, diesel oil n gasóleo m, gasoil m.

diet [ˈdaɪət] <> n - **1.** [eating pattern] dieta f - **2.** [to lose weight] régimen m; to **be on a diet** estar a régimen. <> comp [low-calorie] light (inv), bajo(ja) en calorías. <> vi estar a régimen.

dietary [ˈdaɪətrɪ] adj dietético(ca), alimenticio(cia).

dietary fibre n (U) fibra f (alimenticia).

dieter [ˈdaɪətər] n persona f a régimen.

dietician [ˌdaɪəˈtɪʃn] n especialista mf en dietética.

differ [ˈdɪfər] vi - **1.** [be different] ser diferente; to **differ from sthg** distinguirse OR diferir de algo - **2.** [disagree]: to **differ with sb (about sthg)** disentir OR discrepar de alguien (en algo).

difference [ˈdɪfrəns] n diferencia f; **it didn't make any difference** [changed nothing] no cambió nada; **it doesn't make any difference** [it's all the same] da lo mismo; to **make all the**

difference suponer una gran diferencia; **they settled their differences** resolvieron sus diferencias.

different ['dɪfrənt] *adj*: **different (from)** diferente OR distinto(ta) (de); **she's a different person** es otra.

differential [ˌdɪfə'renʃl] ◇ *adj* diferencial. ◇ *n* - **1.** [between pay scales] diferencia *f* salarial - **2.** TECH diferencial *m*.

differentiate [ˌdɪfə'renʃɪeɪt] ◇ *vt*: **to differentiate (sthg from sthg)** diferenciar OR distinguir (algo de algo). ◇ *vi*: **to differentiate between** diferenciar OR distinguir entre.

differently ['dɪfrəntlɪ] *adv* de forma diferente, de otra forma; **differently abled** discapacitado(da).

difficult ['dɪfɪkəlt] *adj* difícil.

difficulty ['dɪfɪkəltɪ] (*pl* **-ies**) *n* dificultad *f*; **to have difficulty in doing sthg** tener dificultad en OR para hacer algo.

diffidence ['dɪfɪdəns] *n* retraimiento *m*.

diffident ['dɪfɪdənt] *adj* retraído(da).

diffuse ◇ *adj* [dɪ'fju:s] - **1.** [gen] difuso(sa) - **2.** [city, company] extenso(sa). ◇ *vt* [dɪ'fju:z] difundir. ◇ *vi* [dɪ'fju:z] difundirse.

diffusion [dɪ'fju:ʒn] *n* difusión *f*.

dig [dɪg] ◇ *vt* (*pt* & *pp* **dug**, *cont* **digging**) - **1.** [hole - with spade] cavar; [- with hands, paws] escarbar - **2.** [garden] cavar en; [mine] excavar - **3.** [press]: **to dig sthg into** clavar OR hundir algo en. ◇ *vi* (*pt* & *pp* **dug**, *cont* **digging**) - **1.** [with spade] cavar; [with hands, paws] escarbar - **2.** [press]: **to dig into** clavarse OR hundirse en. ◇ *n* - **1.** [unkind remark] pulla *f* - **2.** ARCHAEOL excavación *f*.

◆ **dig out** *vt sep* - **1.** [rescue] desenterrar, sacar - **2.** *inf* [find - letter, object] rescatar, desempolvar; [- information] encontrar.

◆ **dig up** *vt sep* [body, treasure, information] desenterrar; [plant, tree] arrancar.

digest ◇ *n* ['daɪdʒest] compendio *m*. ◇ *vt* [dɪ'dʒest] *lit* & *fig* digerir.

digestible [dɪ'dʒestəbl] *adj* digerible.

digestion [dɪ'dʒestʃn] *n* digestión *f*.

digestive [dɪ'dʒestɪv] *adj* digestivo(va); **digestive system** aparato *m* digestivo.

digestive biscuit [dɪ'dʒestɪv-] *n* UK galleta *f* integral.

digit ['dɪdʒɪt] *n* - **1.** [figure] dígito *m* - **2.** [finger, toe] dedo *m*.

digital ['dɪdʒɪtl] *adj* digital.

digital camera *n* cámara *f* digital.

digital radio *n* radio *f* digital.

digital recording *n* grabación *f* digital.

digital television, digital TV *n* televisión *f* digital.

digital watch *n* reloj *m* digital.

digitize, -ise ['dɪdʒɪtaɪz] *vt* digitalizar.

dignified ['dɪgnɪfaɪd] *adj* [gen] digno(na); [ceremonious] ceremonioso(sa).

dignify ['dɪgnɪfaɪ] (*pt* & *pp* **-ied**) *vt* dignificar.

dignitary ['dɪgnɪtrɪ] (*pl* **-ies**) *n* dignatario *m*, -ria *f*.

dignity ['dɪgnətɪ] *n* dignidad *f*.

digress [daɪ'gres] *vi* apartarse del tema; **to digress from** apartarse OR desviarse de.

digression [daɪ'greʃn] *n* digresión *f*.

digs [dɪgz] *npl* UK *inf* alojamiento *m*; **to live in digs** vivir en un cuarto de alquiler.

dike [daɪk] *n* - **1.** [wall, bank] dique *m* - **2.** *inf pej* [lesbian] tortillera *f*.

dilapidated [dɪ'læpɪdeɪtɪd] *adj* [building] derruido(da); [car] destartalado(da).

dilate [daɪ'leɪt] ◇ *vt* dilatar. ◇ *vi* dilatarse.

dilated [daɪ'leɪtɪd] *adj* dilatado(da).

dilemma [dɪ'lemə] *n* dilema *m*.

dilettante [ˌdɪlɪ'tæntɪ] (*pl* **-tes** OR **-ti** [-tɪ]) *n* diletante *mf*.

diligence ['dɪlɪdʒəns] *n* [hard work] diligencia *f*.

diligent ['dɪlɪdʒənt] *adj* diligente.

dill [dɪl] *n* eneldo *m*.

dillydally ['dɪlɪdælɪ] (*pt* & *pp* **-ied**) *vi* *inf* andar perdiendo el tiempo.

dilute [daɪ'lu:t] ◇ *adj* diluido(da). ◇ *vt* diluir.

dilution [daɪ'lu:ʃn] *n* dilución *f*.

dim [dɪm] ◇ *adj* (*comp* **-mer**, *superl* **-mest**) - **1.** [light] tenue; [room] sombrío(bría) - **2.** [outline, figure] borroso(sa) - **3.** [eyesight] débil - **4.** [memory] vago(ga) - **5.** *inf* [stupid] tonto(ta), torpe. ◇ *vt* (*pt* & *pp* **-med**, *cont* **-ming**) atenuar. ◇ *vi* (*pt* & *pp* **-med**, *cont* **-ming**) [light] atenuarse.

dime [daɪm] *n* US *moneda de diez centavos*; **they're a dime a dozen** [common] los hay a porrillo OR mansalva.

dimension [dɪ'menʃn] *n* dimensión *f*.

◆ **dimensions** *npl* dimensiones *fpl*.

-dimensional [dɪ'menʃənl] *suffix*: **one-dimensional** unidimensional; **two-dimensional** bidimensional.

diminish [dɪ'mɪnɪʃ] *vt* & *vi* disminuir.

diminished [dɪ'mɪnɪʃt] *adj* reducido(da).

diminished responsibility *n* LAW responsabilidad *f* atenuada *(por enajenación mental)*.

diminutive [dɪ'mɪnjʊtɪv] *fml* ◇ *adj* diminuto(ta). ◇ *n* GRAM diminutivo *m*.

dimly ['dɪmlɪ] *adv* - **1.** [see] indistintamente; [remember] vagamente - **2.**: **a dimly lit room** una habitación con luz tenue.

dimmers ['dɪməz] *npl* US [dipped headlights] luces *fpl* cortas OR de cruce; [parking lights] luces *fpl* de posición OR situación.

dimmer switch = dimmer.

dimple ['dɪmpl] *n* hoyuelo *m*.

dimwit ['dɪmwɪt] *n inf* bobo *m*, -ba *f*.

dim-witted [-'wɪtɪd] *adj inf* estúpido(da), bobo(ba).

din [dɪn] *n inf* estrépito *m*, relajo *m* Amér.

dine [daɪn] *vi fml* cenar.

◆ **dine out** *vi* cenar fuera.

diner ['daɪnər] *n* - **1.** [person] comensal *mf* - **2.** US [restaurant - cheap] restaurante *m* barato; [- on the road] ≃ restaurante *m* OR parador *m* de carretera.

dingdong [,dɪŋ'dɒŋ] <> *adj inf* [battle, argument] reñido(da). <> *n* [of bell] din don *m*.

dinghy ['dɪŋgɪ] (*pl* -ies) *n* [sailing boat] bote *m*; [made of rubber] lancha *f* neumática.

dingo ['dɪŋgəʊ] (*pl* -es) *n* dingo *m*.

dingy ['dɪndʒɪ] (*comp* -ier, *superl* -iest) *adj* [room, street] lóbrego(ga); [clothes, carpet] deslustrado(da).

dining car ['daɪnɪŋ-] *n* vagón *m* restaurante, coche *m* comedor Amér.

dining room ['daɪnɪŋ-] *n* comedor *m*.

dining table ['daɪnɪŋ-] *n* mesa *f* de comedor.

dinner ['dɪnər] *n* - **1.** [evening meal] cena *f*; [midday meal] comida *f*, almuerzo *m*; **to have dinner** [in the evening] cenar; [at lunchtime] comer, almorzar - **2.** [formal event] cena *f* de gala, banquete *m*.

dinner dance *n* cena *f* con baile.

dinner jacket *n* esmoquin *m*.

dinner party *n* cena *f* (en casa con amigos).

dinner service *n* vajilla *f*.

dinner table *n* mesa *f*.

dinnertime ['dɪnətaɪm] *n* [in the evening] la hora de la cena; [at midday] la hora del almuerzo OR de la comida.

dinosaur ['daɪnəsɔːr] *n* [reptile] dinosaurio *m*.

dint [dɪnt] *n fml*: **by dint of** a base de.

diocese ['daɪəsɪs] *n* diócesis *f inv*.

diode ['daɪəʊd] *n* diodo *m*.

dioxin [daɪ'ɒksɪn] *n* dioxina *f*.

dip [dɪp] <> *n* - **1.** [in road, ground] pendiente *f* - **2.** [sauce] salsa *f* - **3.** [swim] chapuzón *m*; **to go for/take a dip** ir a darse/darse un chapuzón. <> *vt* (*pt & pp* -**ped**, *cont* -**ping**) - **1.** [into liquid]: **to dip sthg in** OR **into sthg** mojar algo en algo - **2.** UK [headlights]: **to dip one's lights** poner las luces de cruce. <> *vi* (*pt & pp* -**ped**, *cont* -**ping**) descender suavemente.

Dip. UK *abbr of* diploma.

diphtheria [dɪf'θɪərɪə] *n* difteria *f*.

diphthong ['dɪfθɒŋ] *n* diptongo *m*.

diploma [dɪ'pləʊmə] (*pl* -s) *n* diploma *m*.

diplomacy [dɪ'pləʊməsɪ] *n* diplomacia *f*.

diplomat ['dɪpləmæt] *n* - **1.** [official] diplomático *m*, -ca *f* - **2.** [tactful person] persona *f* diplomática.

diplomatic [,dɪplə'mætɪk] *adj* diplomático(ca).

diplomatic bag *n* valija *f* diplomática.

diplomatic corps *n* cuerpo *m* diplomático.

diplomatic immunity *n* inmunidad *f* diplomática.

diplomatic relations *npl* relaciones *fpl* diplomáticas.

dipsomaniac [,dɪpsə'meɪnɪæk] *n* dipsomaníaco *m*, -ca *f*.

dipstick ['dɪpstɪk] *n* AUT varilla *f* del aceite (para medir el nivel).

dipswitch ['dɪpswɪtʃ] *n* UK AUT interruptor *m* de luces de cruce.

dire ['daɪər] *adj* - **1.** [consequences] grave; [warning] serio(ria); [need, poverty] extremo(ma) - **2.** UK *inf* [terrible] fatal.

direct [dɪ'rekt] <> *adj* directo(ta). <> *vt* - **1.** [gen]: **to direct sthg at sb** dirigir algo a alguien - **2.** [person to place]: **to direct sb (to)** indicar a alguien el camino (a) - **3.** [order]: **to direct sb to do sthg** mandar a alguien hacer algo. <> *adv* directamente.

direct action *n* acción *f* directa.

direct current *n* corriente *f* continua.

direct debit *n* UK domiciliación *f* (de pago).

direct dialling [-'daɪəlɪŋ] *n* llamada *f* directa.

direct hit *n*: **to score a direct hit** dar en el blanco.

direction [dɪ'rekʃn] *n* dirección *f*; **in all directions** en todas direcciones; **sense of direction** sentido *m* de la orientación; **under the direction of** bajo la dirección de.

◆ **directions** *npl* - **1.** [instructions to place] señas *fpl*, indicaciones *fpl* - **2.** [instructions for use] instrucciones *fpl* (de uso), modo *m* de empleo.

directive [dɪ'rektɪv] *n* directiva *f*.

directly [dɪ'rektlɪ] *adv* - **1.** [gen] directamente - **2.** [immediately] inmediatamente - **3.** [very soon] pronto, en breve.

direct mail *n* propaganda *f* por correo.

director [dɪ'rektər] *n* director *m*, -ra *f*.

directorate [dɪ'rektərət] *n* [board of directors] dirección *f*, (junta *f*) directiva *f*.

director-general (*pl* **directors-general** OR **director-generals**) *n* director general *m*, directora general *f*.

Director of Public Prosecutions *n* UK ≃ fiscal general *mf* del Estado.

directorship [dɪ'rektəʃɪp] *n* dirección *f*.

directory [dɪˈrektərɪ] (pl -ies) n - **1.** [gen] guía f (alfabética) - **2.** COMPUT directorio m.
directory assistance n US (servicio m de) información f telefónica.
directory enquiries n UK (servicio m de) información f telefónica.
direct rule n gobierno m directo.
direct selling n (U) venta f directa.
direct speech n estilo m directo.
direct taxation n (U) impuestos mpl directos.
dirge [dɜːdʒ] n canto m fúnebre.
dirt [dɜːt] n (U) - **1.** [mud, dust] suciedad f - **2.** [earth] tierra f.
dirt track n camino m de tierra.
dirty [ˈdɜːtɪ] <> adj (comp -ier, superl -iest) - **1.** [gen] sucio(cia); **to get dirty** ensuciarse - **2.** [joke] verde; [film] pornográfico(ca); [book, language] obsceno(na); **dirty word** palabrota f. <> vt (pt & pp -ied) ensuciar.
disability [ˌdɪsəˈbɪlətɪ] (pl -ies) n discapacidad f, minusvalía f; **people with disabilities** los discapacitados, los minusválidos.
disable [dɪsˈeɪbl] vt - **1.** [person] discapacitar, incapacitar - **2.** [tank, machinery] inutilizar.
disabled [dɪsˈeɪbld] <> adj [person] discapacitado(da), minusválido(da); **disabled toilet** servicio m para discapacitados OR minusválidos. <> npl: **the disabled** los minusválidos, los discapacitados.
disablement [dɪsˈeɪblmənt] n discapacidad f, minusvalía f.
disabuse [ˌdɪsəˈbjuːz] vt fml: **to disabuse sb (of sthg)** desengañar a alguien (de algo).
disadvantage [ˌdɪsədˈvɑːntɪdʒ] n desventaja f; **to be at a disadvantage** estar en desventaja; **to be to one's disadvantage** ir en perjuicio de uno.
disadvantaged [ˌdɪsədˈvɑːntɪdʒd] adj desfavorecido(da).
disadvantageous [ˌdɪsædvɑːnˈteɪdʒəs] adj desventajoso(sa), desfavorable.
disaffected [ˌdɪsəˈfektɪd] adj desafecto(ta).
disaffection [ˌdɪsəˈfekʃn] n desafección f.
disagree [ˌdɪsəˈgriː] vi - **1.** [have different opinions]: **to disagree (with)** no estar de acuerdo (con) - **2.** [conflict] contradecirse, no concordar - **3.** [subj: food, drink]: **to disagree with sb** sentar mal a alguien.
disagreeable [ˌdɪsəˈgriːəbl] adj desagradable.
disagreement [ˌdɪsəˈgriːmənt] n - **1.** [fact of disagreeing] desacuerdo m - **2.** [argument] discusión f - **3.** [dissimilarity] discrepancia f.
disallow [ˌdɪsəˈlaʊ] vt - **1.** fml [appeal, claim] rechazar - **2.** [goal] anular.
disappear [ˌdɪsəˈpɪə] vi desaparecer.

disappearance [ˌdɪsəˈpɪərəns] n desaparición f.
disappoint [ˌdɪsəˈpɔɪnt] vt [person] decepcionar, desilusionar; [expectations, hopes] defraudar.
disappointed [ˌdɪsəˈpɔɪntɪd] adj - **1.** [person]: **disappointed (in OR with sthg)** decepcionado(da) (con algo) - **2.** [expectations, hopes] defraudado(da).
disappointing [ˌdɪsəˈpɔɪntɪŋ] adj decepcionante.
disappointment [ˌdɪsəˈpɔɪntmənt] n decepción f, desilusión f; **to be a disappointment** ser decepcionante.
disapproval [ˌdɪsəˈpruːvl] n desaprobación f.
disapprove [ˌdɪsəˈpruːv] vi estar en contra; **to disapprove of sthg** desaprobar algo;: **to disapprove of sb** no ver con buenos ojos a alguien.
disapproving [ˌdɪsəˈpruːvɪŋ] adj desaprobatorio(ria).
disarm [dɪsˈɑːm] <> vt lit & fig desarmar. <> vi desarmarse.
disarmament [dɪsˈɑːməmənt] n desarme m.
disarming [dɪsˈɑːmɪŋ] adj arrebatador(ra).
disarray [ˌdɪsəˈreɪ] n: **in disarray** [clothes, hair] en desorden; [army, political party] sumido(da) en el desconcierto.
disassociate [ˌdɪsəˈsəʊʃɪeɪt] vt: **to disassociate o.s. from** desasociarse OR disociarse de.
disaster [dɪˈzɑːstə] n [gen] desastre m; [earthquake, eruption] catástrofe f.
disaster area n [after natural disaster] zona f catastrófica.
disastrous [dɪˈzɑːstrəs] adj desastroso(sa).
disastrously [dɪˈzɑːstrəslɪ] adv desastrosamente.
disband [dɪsˈbænd] <> vt disolver, disgregar. <> vi disolverse, disgregarse.
disbelief [ˌdɪsbɪˈliːf] n: **in OR with disbelief** con incredulidad.
disbelieve [ˌdɪsbɪˈliːv] vt dudar de, no creer.
disc UK, **disk** US [dɪsk] n disco m.
discard [dɪˈskɑːd] vt [old clothes etc] desechar; [possibility] descartar.
discarded [dɪˈskɑːdɪd] adj desechado(da).
disc brake n freno m de disco.
discern [dɪˈsɜːn] vt - **1.** [gen] discernir; [improvement] percibir - **2.** [figure, outline] distinguir.
discernible [dɪˈsɜːnəbl] adj - **1.** [visible] distinguible - **2.** [noticeable] apreciable.
discerning [dɪˈsɜːnɪŋ] adj refinado(da); [audience] entendido(da).

discharge ◇ n ['dɪstʃɑːdʒ] - **1.** [of patient] alta f; [of prisoner, defendant] puesta f en libertad; [of soldier] licencia f - **2.** fml [of duty etc] cumplimiento m - **3.** [of gas, smoke] emisión f; [of sewage] vertido m - **4.** [of debt] liquidación f - **5.** [MED - from nose] mucosidad f; [- from wound] supuración f - **6.** ELEC descarga f. ◇ vt [dɪs'tʃɑːdʒ] - **1.** [patient] dar de alta; [prisoner, defendant] poner en libertad; [soldier] licenciar - **2.** fml [duty etc] cumplir - **3.** [gas, smoke] emitir, despedir; [sewage] verter; [cargo] descargar - **4.** [debt] liquidar.

discharged bankrupt [dɪs'tʃɑːdʒd-] n quebrado m rehabilitado.

disciple [dɪ'saɪpl] n [follower & RELIG] discípulo m, -la f.

disciplinarian [ˌdɪsɪplɪ'neərɪən] n amante mf de la disciplina severa.

disciplinary ['dɪsɪplɪnərɪ] adj disciplinario(ria); **disciplinary action** fpl disciplinarias.

discipline ['dɪsɪplɪn] ◇ n disciplina f. ◇ vt - **1.** [control] disciplinar - **2.** [punish] castigar.

disciplined ['dɪsɪplɪnd] adj disciplinado(da).

disc jockey n pinchadiscos mf inv.

disclaim [dɪs'kleɪm] vt fml negar.

disclaimer [dɪs'kleɪməʳ] n descargo m de responsabilidad.

disclose [dɪs'kləʊz] vt revelar.

disclosure [dɪs'kləʊʒəʳ] n revelación f.

disco ['dɪskəʊ] (pl -s) (abbr of discotheque) n - **1.** [place] discoteca f; [event] baile m - **2.** [type of music] música f disco.

discoloration [dɪsˌkʌlə'reɪʃn] n [fading, staining] descoloramiento m; [stain] mancha f descolorida.

discolour UK, **discolor** US [dɪs'kʌləʳ] ◇ vt descolorir. ◇ vi descolorirse.

discoloured UK, **discolored** US [dɪs'kʌləd] adj descolorido(da).

discomfort [dɪs'kʌmfət] n - **1.** [uncomfortableness] incomodidad f - **2.** [pain] molestia f.

disconcert [ˌdɪskən'sɜːt] vt desconcertar.

disconcerting [ˌdɪskən'sɜːtɪŋ] adj [worrying] desconcertante; [embarrassing] enojoso(sa).

disconnect [ˌdɪskə'nekt] ◇ vt - **1.** [detach] quitar, separar - **2.** [from gas, electricity - appliance] desconectar; [- house, subscriber] cortar el suministro a; [- supply] cortar - **3.** [on phone - person] cortar la línea a; [- phone] cortar. ◇ vi [from Internet] desconectarse.

disconnected [ˌdɪskə'nektɪd] adj inconexo(xa).

disconsolate [dɪs'kɒnsələt] adj desconsolado(da).

discontent [ˌdɪskən'tent] n: **discontent (with)** descontento m (ta) (con).

discontented [ˌdɪskən'tentɪd] adj descontento(ta).

discontentment [ˌdɪskən'tentmənt] n: **discontentment (with)** descontento m (ta) (con).

discontinue [ˌdɪskən'tɪnjuː] vt interrumpir.

discontinued line [ˌdɪskən'tɪnjuːd-] n COMM producto m OR modelo m que ya no se fabrica.

discord ['dɪskɔːd] n - **1.** [disagreement] discordia f - **2.** MUS disonancia f.

discordant [dɪ'skɔːdənt] adj - **1.** [unpleasant] discordante - **2.** MUS disonante.

discotheque ['dɪskəʊtek] n discoteca f.

discount ◇ n ['dɪskaʊnt] descuento m; **at a discount** con descuento. ◇ vt [UK dɪs'kaʊnt, US 'dɪskaʊnt] [report, claim] descartar.

discount rate n tipo m OR tarifa f de descuento.

discount store n tienda f de saldos.

discourage [dɪ'skʌrɪdʒ] vt - **1.** [dispirit] desanimar - **2.** [crime, behaviour] impedir; [thieves, tourists] ahuyentar; **to discourage sb from doing sthg** disuadir a alguien de hacer algo.

discouraging [dɪ'skʌrɪdʒɪŋ] adj desalentador(ra).

discourse ['dɪskɔːs] n fml: **discourse (on)** discurso m (sobre).

discourteous [dɪs'kɜːtjəs] adj fml descortés.

discourtesy [dɪs'kɜːtɪsɪ] n descortesía f.

discover [dɪ'skʌvəʳ] vt descubrir.

discoverer [dɪ'skʌvərəʳ] n descubridor m, -ra f.

discovery [dɪ'skʌvərɪ] (pl -ies) n descubrimiento m.

discredit [dɪs'kredɪt] ◇ n descrédito m, desprestigio m. ◇ vt - **1.** [person, organization] desacreditar, desprestigiar - **2.** [idea, report] refutar.

discredited [dɪskredɪtɪd] adj desacreditado(da), desprestigiado(da).

discreet [dɪ'skriːt] adj discreto(ta).

discreetly [dɪ'skriːtlɪ] adv discretamente, con discreción.

discrepancy [dɪ'skrepənsɪ] (pl -ies) n: **discrepancy (in/between)** discrepancia f (en/entre).

discrete [dɪs'kriːt] adj fml diferente, independiente.

discretion [dɪ'skreʃn] (U) n - **1.** [tact] discreción f - **2.** [judgment] criterio m; **at the discretion of** a voluntad de.

discretionary [dɪ'skreʃənərɪ] adj discrecional.

discriminate [dɪ'skrɪmɪneɪt] vi - **1.** [distinguish]: **to discriminate (between)** discriminar OR distinguir (entre) - **2.** [treat unfairly]: **to discriminate against sb** discriminar a alguien.

discriminating [dɪ'skrɪmɪneɪtɪŋ] adj refinado(da); [audience] entendido(da).

discrimination [dɪˌskrɪmɪ'neɪʃn] *n* - **1.** [prejudice]: **discrimination (against)** discriminación *f* (hacia) - **2.** [judgment] (buen) gusto *m*.

discus ['dɪskəs] (*pl* -**es**) *n* [object] disco *m* (*en atletismo*); **the discus** [competition] el lanzamiento de disco.

discuss [dɪ'skʌs] *vt* - **1.** [gen]: **to discuss sthg (with sb)** hablar de algo (con alguien) - **2.** [subj: book, lecture] tratar de.

discussion [dɪ'skʌʃn] *n* discusión *f*; **it's under discussion** está siendo discutido.

disdain [dɪs'deɪn] *fml* <> *n*: **disdain (for)** desdén *m OR* desprecio *m* (hacia). <> *vt* desdeñar, despreciar. <> *vi*: **to disdain to do sthg** no dignarse (a) hacer algo.

disdainful [dɪs'deɪnfʊl] *adj* desdeñoso(sa).

disease [dɪ'ziːz] *n* lit & fig enfermedad *f*.

diseased [dɪ'ziːzd] *adj* lit & fig enfermo(ma).

disembark [ˌdɪsɪm'bɑːk] *vi* desembarcar.

disembarkation [ˌdɪsembɑː'keɪʃn] *n* [of people] desembarco *m*; [of goods] desembarque *m*.

disembodied [ˌdɪsɪm'bɒdɪd] *adj* incorpóreo(a).

disembowel [ˌdɪsɪm'baʊəl] (*UK* -**led**, *cont* -**ling**) (*US* -**ed**, *cont* -**ing**) *vt* destripar, achurar *R Plata*.

disenchanted [ˌdɪsɪn'tʃɑːntɪd] *adj*: **disenchanted (with)** desencantado(da) (con).

disenchantment [ˌdɪsɪn'tʃɑːntmənt] *n* desencanto *m*.

disenfranchise [ˌdɪsɪn'fræntʃaɪz] = **disfranchise**.

disengage [ˌdɪsɪn'geɪdʒ] *vt* - **1.** [release]: **to disengage sthg (from)** soltar *OR* desenganchar algo (de); **to disengage o.s. (from)** soltarse *OR* desengancharse (de) - **2.** TECH [gears] quitar; [clutch] soltar; [mechanism] liberar.

disentangle [ˌdɪsɪn'tæŋgl] *vt*: **to disentangle sthg (from)** desenredar algo (de); **to disentangle o.s. from** [barbed wire etc] desenredarse de; *fig* [relationship] zafarse de, desembarazarse de.

disfavour *UK*, **disfavor** *US* [dɪs'feɪvəʳ] *n* - **1.** [disapproval] desaprobación *f* - **2.** [state of being disapproved of] desgracia *f*; **to be in disfavour (with)** no ser visto, -ta *f* con buenos ojos (por).

disfigure [dɪs'fɪgəʳ] *vt* desfigurar.

disfranchise [ˌdɪs'fræntʃaɪz], **disenfranchise** *vt* privar del derecho al voto.

disgorge [dɪs'gɔːdʒ] *vt* expulsar.

disgrace [dɪs'greɪs] <> *n* vergüenza *f*; **he's a disgrace to his family** es una deshonra para su familia; **to be in disgrace** [minister, official] estar desprestigiado(da); [child, pet] estar castigado(da). <> *vt* deshonrar; **to disgrace o.s.** desprestigiarse.

disgraceful [dɪs'greɪsfʊl] *adj* vergonzoso(sa); **it's disgraceful** es una vergüenza.

disgruntled [dɪs'grʌntld] *adj* disgustado(da).

disguise [dɪs'gaɪz] <> *n* disfraz *m*; **in disguise** [policeman, famous person] de incógnito. <> *vt* disfrazar; **to disguise o.s. as** disfrazarse de.

disgust [dɪs'gʌst] <> *n*: **disgust (at)** [physical] asco *m* (hacia); [moral] indignación *f* (ante); **in disgust** [physical] lleno de asco; [moral] lleno de indignación. <> *vt* [physically] repugnar; [morally] indignar; **the smell disgusts me** el olor me da asco.

disgusting [dɪs'gʌstɪŋ] *adj* [physically] asqueroso(sa); [morally] indignante.

dish [dɪʃ] *n* - **1.** [container] fuente *f* - **2.** *US* [plate] plato *m* - **3.** [course] plato *m*.
◆ **dishes** *npl* platos *mpl*; **to do OR wash the dishes** fregar (los platos).
◆ **dish out** *vt sep inf* repartir.
◆ **dish up** *vt sep inf* servir.

dish aerial *UK*, **dish antenna** *US n* (antena *f*) parabólica *f*.

disharmony [ˌdɪs'hɑːmənɪ] *n* discordia *f*.

dishcloth ['dɪʃklɒθ] *n* [for washing, wiping] bayeta *f*; [for drying] paño *m* (de cocina).

disheartened [dɪs'hɑːtnd] *adj* descorazonado(da).

disheartening [dɪs'hɑːtnɪŋ] *adj* descorazonador(ra).

dishevelled *UK*, **disheveled** *US* [dɪ'ʃevəld] *adj* desaliñado(da); [hair] despeinado(da).

dishonest [dɪs'ɒnɪst] *adj* deshonesto(ta), nada honrado(da).

dishonesty [dɪs'ɒnɪstɪ] *n* falta *f* de honradez.

dishonor *US* = **dishonour**.

dishonour *UK*, **dishonor** *US* [dɪs'ɒnəʳ] *fml* <> *n* deshonra *f*, deshonor *m*. <> *vt* deshonrar.

dishonourable *UK*, **dishonorable** *US* [dɪs'ɒnərəbl] *adj* deshonroso(sa).

dish soap *n US* lavavajillas *m inv* (detergente).

dish towel *n US* paño *m* (de cocina).

dishwasher ['dɪʃˌwɒʃəʳ] *n* - **1.** [machine] lavavajillas *m inv* (electrodoméstico) - **2.** [person] lavaplatos *mf inv*.

dishwashing liquid *n US* lavavajillas *m inv* (detergente).

dishy ['dɪʃɪ] (*comp* -**ier**, *superl* -**iest**) *adj UK inf*: **to be dishy** estar buenísimo(ma).

disillusioned [ˌdɪsɪ'luːʒnd] *adj* desilusionado(da); **to become disillusioned (with)** desilusionarse (con).

disillusionment [ˌdɪsɪ'luːʒnmənt] *n*: **disillusionment (with)** desilusión *f* (con).

disincentive [ˌdɪsɪn'sentɪv] *n* traba *f*.

disinclined [ˌdɪsɪnˈklaɪnd] *adj*: **to be disinclined to do sthg** no tener ganas de hacer algo.

disinfect [ˌdɪsɪnˈfekt] *vt* desinfectar.

disinfectant [ˌdɪsɪnˈfektənt] *n* desinfectante *m*.

disinformation [ˌdɪsɪnfəˈmeɪʃn] *n* desinformación *f*.

disingenuous [ˌdɪsɪnˈdʒenjʊəs] *adj* falso(sa), poco honrado(da).

disinherit [ˌdɪsɪnˈherɪt] *vt* desheredar.

disintegrate [dɪsˈɪntɪgreɪt] *vi lit* & *fig* desintegrarse.

disintegration [dɪsˌɪntɪˈgreɪʃn] *n* desintegración *f*.

disinterested [ˌdɪsˈɪntrəstɪd] *adj* - **1.** [objective] desinteresado(da) - **2.** *inf* [uninterested]: **disinterested (in)** indiferente (a).

disinvestment [ˌdɪsɪnˈvestmənt] *n* desinversión *f*.

disjointed [dɪsˈdʒɔɪntɪd] *adj* deslabazado(da).

disk [dɪsk] *n* - **1.** COMPUT disco *m*; [diskette] disquete *m* - **2.** *US* = **disc**.

disk drive *n* COMPUT disquetera *f*, unidad *f* de disco.

diskette [dɪskˈet] *n* disquete *m*.

disk operating system [-ɒpəreɪtɪŋ-] *n* COMPUT sistema *m* operativo de disco.

dislike [dɪsˈlaɪk] ⟨⟩ *n* - **1.** [feeling]: **dislike (for)** [things] aversión *f* (a); [people] antipatía *f* (por); **to take a dislike to** cogerle manía a - **2.** [thing not liked]: **her likes and dislikes** las cosas que le gustan y las que no le gustan. ⟨⟩ *vt*: **I dislike her** no me gusta,: **I dislike them** no me gustan.

dislocate [ˈdɪsləkeɪt] *vt* - **1.** MED dislocar; **to dislocate one's shoulder** dislocarse el hombro - **2.** [disrupt] trastocar.

dislodge [dɪsˈlɒdʒ] *vt*: **to dislodge sthg/sb (from)** sacar algo/a alguien (de).

disloyal [ˌdɪsˈlɔɪəl] *adj*: **disloyal (to)** desleal (a).

dismal [ˈdɪzml] *adj* - **1.** [weather, future] oscuro(ra), sombrío(a); [place, atmosphere] deprimente - **2.** [attempt, failure] penoso(sa), lamentable.

dismantle [dɪsˈmæntl] *vt* [machine] desmontar; [organization] desmantelar.

dismay [dɪsˈmeɪ] ⟨⟩ *n* (*U*) consternación *f*; **to my/his** *etc* **dismay** para mi/su *etc* consternación. ⟨⟩ *vt* consternar.

dismember [dɪsˈmembər] *vt* desmembrar.

dismiss [dɪsˈmɪs] *vt* - **1.** [refuse to take seriously] desechar - **2.** [from job]: **to dismiss sb (from)** despedir a alguien (de) - **3.** [allow to leave]: **to dismiss sb** dar a alguien permiso para irse.

dismissal [dɪsˈmɪsl] *n* - **1.** [from job] despido *m*, remoción *f Amér* - **2.** [refusal to take seriously] rechazo *m*.

dismissive [dɪsˈmɪsɪv] *adj*: **dismissive (of)** despreciativo(va) (hacia).

dismount [ˌdɪsˈmaʊnt] *vi*: **to dismount (from sthg)** desmontar (de algo).

disobedience [ˌdɪsəˈbiːdjəns] *n* desobediencia *f*.

disobedient [ˌdɪsəˈbiːdjənt] *adj*: **disobedient (to)** desobediente (con).

disobey [ˌdɪsəˈbeɪ] *vt* & *vi* desobedecer.

disorder [dɪsˈɔːdər] *n* - **1.** [disarray]: **in disorder** en desorden - **2.** (*U*) [rioting] disturbios *mpl* - **3.** MED [physical] afección *f*, dolencia *f*; [mental] trastorno *m*, perturbación *f*.

disordered [dɪsˈɔːdəd] *adj* - **1.** [in disarray] desordenado(da) - **2.** MED: **mentally disordered** perturbado(da), con trastornos mentales.

disorderly [dɪsˈɔːdəlɪ] *adj* - **1.** [untidy] desordenado(da) - **2.** [unruly - behaviour] incontrolado(da); [- person] alborotador(ra).

disorderly conduct *n* LAW conducta *f* escandalosa.

disorganized, -ised [dɪsˈɔːgənaɪzd] *adj* desorganizado(da).

disorientated *UK* [dɪsˈɔːrɪənteɪtɪd], **disoriented** *US* [dɪsˈɔːrɪəntɪd] *adj* desorientado(da).

disown [dɪsˈəʊn] *vt* [gen] renegar de; [statement] no reconocer como propio(pia).

disparage [dɪˈspærɪdʒ] *vt* menospreciar.

disparaging [dɪˈspærɪdʒɪŋ] *adj* menospreciativo(va).

disparate [ˈdɪspərət] *adj fml* dispar.

disparity [dɪˈspærətɪ] (*pl* -ies) *n*: **disparity (between/in)** disparidad *f* (entre/en).

dispassionate [dɪˈspæʃnət] *adj* desapasionado(da).

dispatch, despatch [dɪˈspætʃ] ⟨⟩ *n* - **1.** [message] despacho *m* - **2.** [sending] envío *m*. ⟨⟩ *vt* [goods, parcel] expedir; [message, messenger, troops] enviar.

dispatch box *n UK* POL zona de la Cámara de los Comunes donde los parlamentarios más importantes pronuncian sus discursos.

dispatch rider *n* MIL correo *m*; [courier] mensajero *m* (ra).

dispel [dɪˈspel] (*pt* & *pp* -led, *cont* -ling) *vt* disipar.

dispensable [dɪˈspensəbl] *adj* prescindible.

dispensary [dɪˈspensərɪ] (*pl* -ies) *n* dispensario *m*.

dispensation [ˌdɪspenˈseɪʃn] *n* [permission] dispensa *f*.

dispense [dɪˈspens] *vt* - **1.** [advice] ofrecer; [justice] administrar - **2.** [drugs, medicine] despachar.

➤ **dispense with** *vt insep* prescindir de.

dispenser [dɪ'spensə'] *n* [machine, container] máquina *f* expendedora.

dispersal [dɪ'spɜːsl] *n* dispersión *f*.

disperse [dɪ'spɜːs] <> *vt* dispersar. <> *vi* dispersarse.

dispirited [dɪ'spɪrɪtɪd] *adj* desanimado(da).

dispiriting [dɪ'spɪrɪtɪŋ] *adj* descorazonador(ra).

displace [dɪs'pleɪs] *vt* [supplant] reemplazar, sustituir.

displaced person [dɪs'pleɪst-] *n* desplazado *m*, -da *f*.

displacement [dɪs'pleɪsmənt] *n* [of people] desplazamiento *m*.

display [dɪ'spleɪ] <> *n* - **1.** [arrangement - in shop window] escaparate *m*; [- in museum] exposición *f*; [- on stall, pavement] muestrario *m*; **on display** expuesto(ta) - **2.** [demonstration, public event] demostración *f* - **3.** [sporting] exhibición *f* - **4.** COMPUT pantalla *f*. <> *vt* - **1.** [arrange] exponer - **2.** [show] demostrar - **3.** [on screen] mostrar.

display advertising *n* publicidad *f* a gran escala.

displease [dɪs'pliːz] *vt* [annoy] disgustar; [anger] enfadar.

displeasure [dɪs'pleʒə'] *n* [annoyance] disgusto *m*; [anger] enfado *m*.

disposable [dɪ'spəʊzəbl] *adj* desechable; **disposable income** poder *m* adquisitivo.

disposal [dɪ'spəʊzl] *n* - **1.** [removal] eliminación *f* - **2.** US trituradora *f* de basuras - **3.** [availability]: **to have sthg at one's disposal** disponer de algo.

dispose [dɪ'spəʊz] *►* **dispose of** *vt insep* [rubbish] deshacerse de; [problem] quitarse de encima OR de en medio.

disposed [dɪ'spəʊzd] *adj* - **1.** [willing]: **to be disposed to do sthg** estar dispuesto(ta) a hacer algo - **2.** [friendly]: **to be well disposed to** OR **towards sb** tener buena disposición hacia alguien.

disposition [ˌdɪspə'zɪʃn] *n* - **1.** [temperament] carácter *m* - **2.** [willingness, tendency]: **disposition to do sthg** predisposición *f* a hacer algo.

dispossess [ˌdɪspə'zes] *vt fml*: **to dispossess sb of sthg** desposeer a alguien de algo.

disproportion [ˌdɪsprə'pɔːʃn] *n* desproporción *f*.

disproportionate [ˌdɪsprə'pɔːʃnət] *adj*: **disproportionate (to)** desproporcionado(da) (a).

disprove [ˌdɪs'pruːv] *vt* refutar.

dispute [dɪ'spjuːt] <> *n* - **1.** [quarrel] disputa *f* - **2.** (U) [disagreement] conflicto *m*, desacuer-

do *m*; **in dispute** [people] en desacuerdo; [matter] en litigio, en entredicho - **3.** INDUST conflicto *m* laboral. <> *vt* cuestionar.

disqualification [dɪs,kwɒlɪfɪ'keɪʃn] *n* descalificación *f*.

disqualify [ˌdɪs'kwɒlɪfaɪ] (*pt & pp* -**ied**) *vt* - **1.** [subj: authority, illness etc]: **to disqualify sb (from doing sthg)** incapacitar a alguien (para hacer algo) - **2.** SPORT descalificar - **3.** UK [from driving] retirar el permiso de conducir a.

disquiet [dɪs'kwaɪət] *n* inquietud *f*, desasosiego *m*.

disregard [ˌdɪsrɪ'gɑːd] <> *n*: **disregard (for)** indiferencia *f* (a), despreocupación *f* (por). <> *vt* hacer caso omiso de.

disrepair [ˌdɪsrɪ'peə'] *n*: **in a state of disrepair** deteriorado(da).

disreputable [dɪs'repjʊtəbl] *adj* [person, company] de mala fama; [behaviour] vergonzante.

disrepute [ˌdɪsrɪ'pjuːt] *n*: **to bring sthg into disrepute** desprestigiar OR desacreditar algo; **to fall into disrepute** desprestigiarse, desacreditarse.

disrespectful [ˌdɪsrɪ'spektfʊl] *adj* irrespetuoso(sa).

disrupt [dɪs'rʌpt] *vt* [meeting] interrumpir; [transport system] trastornar, perturbar; [class] revolucionar, enredar en.

disruption [dɪs'rʌpʃn] *n* [of meeting] interrupción *f*; [of transport system] trastorno *m*.

disruptive [dɪs'rʌptɪv] *adj* [effect] perjudicial; [child, behaviour] revoltoso(sa).

dissatisfaction ['dɪs,sætɪs'fækʃn] *n* descontento *m*.

dissatisfied [ˌdɪs'sætɪsfaɪd] *adj*: **dissatisfied (with)** insatisfecho(cha) OR descontento(ta) (con).

dissect [dɪ'sekt] *vt* MED disecar; *fig* [study] analizar minuciosamente.

dissection [dɪ'sekʃn] *n* MED disección *f*; *fig* [study] análisis *m inv* minucioso.

disseminate [dɪ'semɪneɪt] *vt* difundir, divulgar.

dissemination [dɪ,semɪ'neɪʃn] *n* difusión *f*, divulgación *f*.

dissension [dɪ'senʃn] *n* disensión *f*.

dissent [dɪ'sent] <> *n* [gen] disconformidad *f*, disentimiento *m*; SPORT: **he was booked for dissent** lo amonestaron por protestar. <> *vi*: **to dissent (from)** disentir (de).

dissenter [dɪ'sentə'] *n* disidente *mf*.

dissenting [dɪ'sentɪŋ] *adj* discrepante.

dissertation [ˌdɪsə'teɪʃn] *n* - **1.** US [doctoral] tesis *f inv* - **2.** UK [lower degree] tesina *f*.

disservice [ˌdɪs'sɜːvɪs] *n*: **to do sb a disservice** hacer un flaco servicio a alguien.

dissident ['dɪsɪdənt] *n* disidente *mf*.

dissimilar [ˌdɪ'sɪmɪləʳ] *adj*: **dissimilar (to)** distinto(ta) (de).

dissipate ['dɪsɪpeɪt] ⟨⟩ *vt* - **1.** [heat, fears] disipar - **2.** [efforts, money] desperdiciar, derrochar. ⟨⟩ *vi* disiparse.

dissipated ['dɪsɪpeɪtɪd] *adj* disoluto(ta).

dissociate [dɪ'səʊʃɪeɪt] *vt* disociar, separar; **to dissociate o.s. from** desvincularse de.

dissolute ['dɪsəluːt] *adj* disoluto(ta).

dissolution [ˌdɪsə'luːʃn] *n* disolución *f*.

dissolve [dɪ'zɒlv] ⟨⟩ *vt* disolver. ⟨⟩ *vi* - **1.** [substance] disolverse - **2.** *fig* [disappear] desvanecerse, desaparecer.

➧ **dissolve in(to)** *vt insep* [tears] deshacerse en.

dissuade [dɪ'sweɪd] *vt*: **to dissuade sb (from doing sthg)** disuadir a alguien (de hacer algo).

distance ['dɪstəns] ⟨⟩ *n* distancia *f*; **at a distance** a distancia; **from a distance** desde lejos; **in the distance** a lo lejos. ⟨⟩ *vt*: **to distance o.s. from** distanciarse de.

distance learning *n* enseñanza *f* a distancia.

distant ['dɪstənt] *adj* - **1.** [place, time, relative] lejano(na); **distant from** distante de - **2.** [person, manner] frío(a), distante.

distaste [dɪs'teɪst] *n*: **distaste (for)** desagrado *m* (por).

distasteful [dɪs'teɪstfʊl] *adj* desagradable.

Dist. Atty *abbr of* **district attorney**.

distemper [dɪ'stempəʳ] *n* - **1.** [paint] (pintura *f* al) temple *m* - **2.** [disease] moquillo *m*.

distended [dɪ'stendɪd] *adj* dilatado(da).

distil *UK* (*pt* & *pp* -**led**, *cont* -**ling**), **distill** *US* [dɪ'stɪl] *vt* - **1.** [liquid] destilar - **2.** [information] extraer.

distiller [dɪ'stɪləʳ] *n* destilador *m*, -ra *f*.

distillery [dɪ'stɪlərɪ] (*pl* -**ies**) *n* destilería *f*.

distinct [dɪ'stɪŋkt] *adj* - **1.** [different]: **distinct (from)** distinto(ta) (de); **as distinct from** a diferencia de - **2.** [clear - improvement] notable, visible; [- possibility] claro(ra).

distinction [dɪ'stɪŋkʃn] *n* - **1.** [difference, excellence] distinción *f*; **to draw** OR **make a distinction between** hacer una distinción entre - **2.** [in exam result] sobresaliente *m*.

distinctive [dɪ'stɪŋktɪv] *adj* característico(ca), particular.

distinctly [dɪ'stɪŋktlɪ] *adv* - **1.** [see, remember] claramente - **2.** [improve] notablemente - **3.** [very]: **it is distinctly possible that...** es muy posible que...

distinguish [dɪ'stɪŋgwɪʃ] *vt* - **1.** [gen]: **to distinguish sthg (from)** distinguir algo (de) - **2.** [perform well]: **to distinguish o.s.** distinguirse.

distinguished [dɪ'stɪŋgwɪʃt] *adj* distinguido(da).

distinguishing [dɪ'stɪŋgwɪʃɪŋ] *adj* distintivo(va).

distort [dɪ'stɔːt] *vt* - **1.** [shape, face] deformar; [sound] distorsionar - **2.** [truth, facts] tergiversar.

distorted [dɪ'stɔːtɪd] *adj* - **1.** [shape, face] deformado(da); [sound] distorsionado(da) - **2.** [account, report] tergiversado(da).

distortion [dɪ'stɔːʃn] *n* - **1.** [of shape, face] deformación *f*; [of sound] distorsión *f* - **2.** [of truth, facts] tergiversación *f*.

distract [dɪ'strækt] *vt* [person, attention]: **to distract sb (from)** distraer a alguien (de).

distracted [dɪ'stræktɪd] *adj* ausente.

distraction [dɪ'strækʃn] *n* - **1.** [interruption, diversion] distracción *f* - **2.** [state of mind] confusión *f*; **to drive sb to distraction** volver loco a alguien.

distraught [dɪ'strɔːt] *adj* consternado(da).

distress [dɪ'stres] ⟨⟩ *n* - **1.** [anxiety] angustia *f*; [pain] dolor *m* - **2.** [danger, difficulty] peligro *m*. ⟨⟩ *vt* afligir, apenar.

distressed [dɪ'strest] *adj* angustiado(da), afligido(da).

distressing [dɪ'stresɪŋ] *adj* angustioso(sa).

distress signal *n* señal *f* de socorro.

distribute [dɪ'strɪbjuːt] *vt* distribuir, repartir.

distribution [ˌdɪstrɪ'bjuːʃn] *n* distribución *f*.

distributor [dɪ'strɪbjʊtəʳ] *n* - **1.** COMM distribuidor *m*, -ra *f* - **2.** AUT delco® *m*, distribuidor *m*.

district ['dɪstrɪkt] *n* - **1.** [area - of country] zona *f*, región *f*; [- of town] barrio *m* - **2.** [administrative area] distrito *m*.

district attorney *n* US fiscal *mf* (del distrito).

district council *n* UK ADMIN ≃ municipio *m*.

district nurse *n* UK enfermera encargada de atender a domicilio a los pacientes de una zona.

District of Columbia *n* distrito *m* de Columbia.

distrust [dɪs'trʌst] ⟨⟩ *n* desconfianza *f*. ⟨⟩ *vt* desconfiar de.

distrustful [dɪs'trʌstfʊl] *adj* desconfiado(da).

disturb [dɪ'stɜːb] *vt* - **1.** [interrupt - person] molestar; [- concentration, sleep] perturbar - **2.** [upset, worry] inquietar - **3.** [alter - surface, arrangement] alterar; [- papers] desordenar.

disturbance [dɪ'stɜːbəns] *n* - **1.** [fight] tumulto *m*, alboroto *m*; **there were a number of minor disturbances throughout the night** se produjeron algunos disturbios durante la noche - **2.** LAW: **disturbance of the peace** alteración *f* del orden público - **3.** [interruption] interrupción *f* - **4.** [of mind, emotions] trastorno *m*.

disturbed [dɪ'stɜːbd] *adj* - **1.** [upset, ill] trastornado(da) - **2.** [worried] inquieto(ta).

disturbing [dɪ'stɜːbɪŋ] *adj* inquietante, preocupante.

disuse [ˌdɪs'juːs] *n*: **to fall into disuse** [regulation] caer en desuso; [building, mine] verse paulatinamente abandonado(da).

disused [ˌdɪs'juːzd] *adj* abandonado(da).

ditch [dɪtʃ] <> *n* [gen] zanja *f*; [by road] cuneta *f*. <> *vt inf* - **1.** [end relationship with] romper con - **2.** [get rid of] deshacerse de.

dither ['dɪðəʳ] *vi* vacilar.

ditto ['dɪtəʊ] *adv* ídem.

diuretic [ˌdaɪjʊ'retɪk] *n* diurético *m*.

diva ['diːvə] (*pl* -**s**) *n* diva *f*.

divan [dɪ'væn] *n* diván *m*.

divan bed *n* cama *f* turca.

dive [daɪv] <> *vi* (*UK* -**d**, *US* -**d** OR **dove**, *pp* -**d**) - **1.** [into water - person] zambullirse, tirarse al agua; [- submarine, bird, fish] sumergirse - **2.** [with breathing apparatus] bucear, clavarse *Amér* - **3.** [through air - person] lanzarse; [- plane] caer en picado - **4.** [into bag, cupboard]: **to dive into** meter la mano en. <> *n* - **1.** [of person - into water] zambullida *f* - **2.** [of submarine] inmersión *f* - **3.** [of person - through air] salto *m*; SPORT [- by goalkeeper] estirada *f*; **it was a dive** se ha tirado - **4.** [of plane] picado *m* - **5.** *inf pej* [bar, restaurant] garito *m*, antro *m*.

dive-bomb *vt* bombardear (cayendo en picado).

diver ['daɪvəʳ] *n* [underwater] buceador *m*, -ra *f*; [professional] buzo *m*; [from diving board] saltador *m*, -ra *f* (de trampolín).

diverge [daɪ'vɜːdʒ] *vi* - **1.** [gen]: **to diverge (from)** divergir (de) - **2.** [disagree] discrepar.

divergence [daɪ'vɜːdʒəns] *n* divergencia *f*.

divergent [daɪ'vɜːdʒənt] *adj* divergente.

diverse [daɪ'vɜːs] *adj* diverso(sa).

diversification [daɪˌvɜːsɪfɪ'keɪʃn] *n* diversificación *f*.

diversify [daɪ'vɜːsɪfaɪ] (*pt* & *pp* -**ied**) <> *vt* diversificar. <> *vi* diversificarse.

diversion [daɪ'vɜːʃn] *n* - **1.** [of traffic, river, funds] desvío *m* - **2.** [distraction] distracción *f*.

diversionary [daɪ'vɜːʃnrɪ] *adj* hecho(cha) para distraer la atención.

diversity [daɪ'vɜːsətɪ] *n* diversidad *f*.

divert [daɪ'vɜːt] *vt* - **1.** [traffic, river, funds] desviar - **2.** [person, attention] distraer.

divide [dɪ'vaɪd] <> *vt*: **to divide sthg (between** OR **among)** dividir algo (entre); **to divide sthg into** dividir algo en; **to divide sthg by** dividir algo entre OR por; **divide 3 into 89** divide 89 entre 3. <> *vi* - **1.** [river, road, wall] bifurcarse - **2.** [group] dividirse. <> *n* [difference] división *f*.

➭ **divide up** *vt sep* - **1.** [split up] dividir - **2.** [share out] repartir.

divided [dɪ'vaɪdɪd] *adj* dividido(da).

dividend ['dɪvɪdend] *n* FIN dividendo *m*; [profit] beneficio *m*; **to pay dividends** proporcionar beneficios.

dividers [dɪ'vaɪdəz] *npl* compás *m* de puntas.

dividing line [dɪ'vaɪdɪŋ-] *n* línea *f* divisoria.

divine [dɪ'vaɪn] <> *adj* divino(na). <> *vt* [guess] adivinar.

diving ['daɪvɪŋ] *(U)* *n* - **1.** [into water] salto *m* - **2.** [with breathing apparatus] buceo *m*; **to go diving** hacer submarinismo.

divingboard ['daɪvɪŋbɔːd] *n* trampolín *m*.

diving suit *n* traje *m* de buceo, escafandra *f*.

divinity [dɪ'vɪnətɪ] (*pl* -**ies**) *n* - **1.** [godliness, deity] divinidad *f* - **2.** [study] teología *f*.

divisible [dɪ'vɪzəbl] *adj*: **divisible (by)** divisible (por).

division [dɪ'vɪʒn] *n* - **1.** [gen] división *f* - **2.** [of labour, responsibility] reparto *m*.

division sign *n* signo *m* de división.

divisive [dɪ'vaɪsɪv] *adj* divisivo(va).

divorce [dɪ'vɔːs] <> *n* divorcio *m*. <> *vt* - **1.** [husband, wife] divorciarse de - **2.** [separate]: **to divorce sthg from** separar algo de. <> *vi* divorciarse.

divorced [dɪ'vɔːst] *adj* divorciado(da).

divorcee [dɪvɔː'siː] *n* divorciado *m*, -da *f*.

divulge [daɪ'vʌldʒ] *vt* divulgar, revelar.

DIY *abbr of* do-it-yourself.

dizziness ['dɪzɪnɪs] *n* [because of heights] vértigo *m*; [because of illness etc] mareo *m*.

dizzy ['dɪzɪ] (*comp* -**ier**, *superl* -**iest**) *adj* - **1.** [because of illness etc] mareado(da) - **2.** [because of heights]: **to feel dizzy** sentir vértigo - **3.** *fig* [heights] inimaginable, de vértigo.

DJ *n abbr of* disc jockey. *abbr of* dinner jacket.

Djakarta [dʒə'kɑːtə] = Jakarta.

Djibouti [dʒɪˈbuːtɪ] n Yibuti.

dl (abbr of **decilitre**) dl.

DLit(t) [ˌdiːˈlɪt] (abbr of **Doctor of Letters**), titular de un doctorado de letras.

dm (abbr of **decimetre**) dm.

DMus [ˌdiːˈmjuːz] (abbr of **Doctor of Music**) titular de un doctorado de música.

DNA (abbr of **deoxyribonucleic acid**) n ADN m.

DNS (abbr of **Domain Name System**) n COMPUT DNS m.

do [duː] ◇ aux vb (pt **did**) - **1.** (in negatives): **don't leave it there** no lo dejes ahí; **I didn't want to see him** no quería verlo - **2.** (in questions): **what did he want?** ¿qué quería?; **do you think she'll come?** ¿crees que vendrá? - **3.** (referring back to previous vb): **do you think so? – yes, I do** ¿tú crees? – sí; **she reads more than I do** lee más que yo; **so do I/they** yo/ellos también - **4.** (in question tags): **you know her, don't you?** la conoces, ¿no?; **I annoyed you, didn't I?** te molesté, ¿verdad?; **so you think you can dance, do you?** así que te crees que sabes bailar, ¿no? - **5.** (for emphasis): **I did tell you but you've forgotten** sí que te lo dije, pero te has olvidado; **do come in** ¡pase, por favor! ◇ vt (pt **did**, pp **done**) - **1.** [gen] hacer; **she does aerobics/gymnastics** hace aerobic/gimnasia; **to do the cooking/cleaning** hacer la comida/limpieza; **to do one's hair** peinarse; **to do one's teeth** lavarse los dientes; **he did his duty** cumplió con su deber; **what can I do for you?** ¿en qué puedo servirle?; **they do cheap meals for students** dan OR hacen comidas baratas para estudiantes; **what can we do?** ¿qué le vamos a hacer?; **we'll have to do something about that tree** tendremos que hacer algo con ese árbol - **2.** [have particular effect] causar, hacer; **to do more harm than good** hacer más mal que bien - **3.** [referring to job]: **what do you do?** ¿a qué te dedicas? - **4.** [study] hacer; **I did physics at school** hice física en la escuela - **5.** [travel at a particular speed] ir a; **the car can do 110 mph** el coche alcanza las 110 millas por hora - **6.** [be good enough for]: **will that do you?** ¿te vale eso?; **that'll do me nicely** eso me viene estupendamente. ◇ vi (pt **did**, pp **done**) - **1.** [gen] hacer; **do as she says** haz lo que te dice; **they're doing really well** les va muy bien; **he could do better** lo podría hacer mejor; **how did you do in the exam?** ¿qué tal te salió el examen?; **you would do well to reconsider** harías bien en volverlo a pensar - **2.** [be good enough, sufficient] servir, valer; **this kind of behaviour won't do** ese tipo de comportamiento no es aceptable; **that will do (nicely)** con eso vale; **that will do!** [showing annoyance] ¡basta ya!

how do you do? [greeting] ¿cómo está usted?; [answer] mucho gusto. ◇ n [party] fiesta f.

dos npl (pl **dos** OR **do's**): **dos and don'ts** normas fpl básicas.

do away with vt insep [disease, poverty] acabar con; [law, reforms] suprimir.

do down vt sep inf: **to do sb down** menospreciar a alguien; **to do o.s. down** menospreciarse.

do for vt insep inf: **these kids will do for me** estos críos van a terminar conmigo; **I thought I was done for** creí que me moría.

do in vt sep inf [kill] cargarse, cepillarse; [beat up] inflar a palos.

do out of vt sep: **to do sb out of sthg** estafar algo a alguien.

do over vt sep US volver a hacer.

do up vt sep - **1.** [fasten - shoelaces, tie] atar; [- coat, buttons] abrochar; **do your shoes up** átate los zapatos; **do your coat up** abróchate el abrigo - **2.** [decorate] renovar, redecorar; **to do o.s. up** arreglarse - **3.** [wrap up] envolver.

do with vt insep - **1.** [need]: **I could do with a drink/new car** no me vendría mal una copa/un coche nuevo - **2.** [have connection with]: **that has nothing to do with it** eso no tiene nada que ver (con ello); **it's something to do with the way he speaks** tiene que ver con su forma de hablar.

do without ◇ vt insep pasar sin; **I can do without your sarcasm** podrías ahorrarte tu sarcasmo. ◇ vi apañárselas.

DOA (abbr of **dead on arrival**) adj: **she was DOA** ingresó cadáver.

doable [ˈduːəbl] adj inf realizable, factible.

dob abbr of **date of birth**.

Doberman [ˈdəʊbəmən] (pl **-s**) n: **Doberman (pinscher)** dóberman m.

docile [UK ˈdəʊsaɪl, US ˈdɒsəl] adj dócil.

dock [dɒk] ◇ n - **1.** [in harbour] dársena f, muelle m - **2.** [in court] banquillo m (de los acusados). ◇ vt [wages] recortar; [money from wages] descontar. ◇ vi [ship] atracar; [spacecraft] acoplarse.

docker [ˈdɒkər], **dockworker** n estibador m.

docket [ˈdɒkɪt] n - **1.** UK marbete m - **2.** US LAW orden m del día.

docklands [ˈdɒkləndz] npl UK barrio m portuario.

dockworker [ˈdɒkwɜːkər] n = **docker**.

dockyard [ˈdɒkjɑːd] n astillero m.

doctor [ˈdɒktər] ◇ n - **1.** [of medicine] médico m, -ca f; **to go to the doctor's** ir al médico - **2.** [holder of PhD] doctor m, -ra f. ◇ vt - **1.** [results, text] amañar - **2.** UK [cat] castrar - **3.** [food, drink] adulterar.

doctorate [ˈdɒktərət], **doctor's degree** n doctorado m.

doctrinaire [ˌdɒktrɪˈneəʳ] adj doctrinario(ria).

doctrine [ˈdɒktrɪn] n doctrina f.

docudrama [ˌdɒkjʊˈdrɑːmə] (pl -s) n TV docudrama m.

document ⬦ n [ˈdɒkjʊmənt] [gen & COMPUT] documento m. ⬦ vt [dɒkjʊment] documentar.

documentary [ˌdɒkjʊˈmentərɪ] ⬦ adj documental. ⬦ n (pl -ies) documental m.

documentation [ˌdɒkjʊmenˈteɪʃn] n documentación f.

doddering [ˈdɒdərɪŋ], **doddery** [ˈdɒdərɪ] adj inf renqueante.

doddle [ˈdɒdl] n UK inf: **it's a doddle** está tirado(da) OR chupado(da).

Dodecanese [ˌdəʊdɪkəˈniːz] npl: **the Dodecanese** el Dodecaneso.

dodge [dɒdʒ] ⬦ n inf [fraud] artimaña f, truco m; **a tax dodge** un truco para pagar menos impuestos. ⬦ vt esquivar. ⬦ vi echarse a un lado, apartarse bruscamente.

Dodgems® [ˈdɒdʒəmz] npl UK autos mpl de choque.

dodgy [ˈdɒdʒɪ] adj UK inf [business, plan] arriesgado(da); [brakes, weather, situation] chungo(ga).

doe [dəʊ] n **- 1.** [female deer] gama f **- 2.** [female rabbit] coneja f.

DOE n **- 1.** UK (abbr of **Department of the Environment**), ministerio del medio ambiente **- 2.** US (abbr of **Department of Energy**), ministerio de energía.

doer [ˈduːəʳ] n inf emprendedor m, -ra f, persona f práctica.

does (weak form [dəz], strong form [dʌz]) vb ⊳ **do.**

doesn't [ˈdʌznt] (abbr of = does not), = **do.**

dog [dɒg] ⬦ n **- 1.** [animal] perro m; **it's a dog's life** es una vida de perros; **to go to the dogs** inf echarse a perder, irse al garete **- 2.** US [hot dog] perrito m caliente. ⬦ vt (pt & pp **-ged**, cont **-ging**) **- 1.** [subj: person] seguir **- 2.** [subj: problems, bad luck] perseguir.

dog biscuit n galleta f de perro.

dog collar n **- 1.** [of dog] collar m de perro **- 2.** [of priest] alzacuello m.

dog-eared [-ɪəd] adj manoseado(da), sobado(da).

dog-end n inf colilla f.

dogfight [ˈdɒgfaɪt] n **- 1.** [between dogs] pelea f de perros **- 2.** [between aircraft] combate m aéreo.

dog food n comida f para perros.

dogged [ˈdɒgɪd] adj tenaz, obstinado(da).

doggy [ˈdɒgɪ] (pl -ies) n perrito m.

doggy bag n bolsa que da el restaurante para llevarse las sobras a casa.

dogma [ˈdɒgmə] n dogma m.

dogmatic [dɒgˈmætɪk] adj dogmático(ca).

do-gooder [-ˈgʊdəʳ] n pej persona bien intencionada que sin querer resulta entrometida.

dog paddle n: **to do the dog paddle** nadar como los perros.

dogsbody [ˈdɒgz,bɒdɪ] (pl -ies) n UK inf último mono m, burro m de carga.

dog tag n placa f de identificación (de un soldado).

doing [ˈduːɪŋ] n: **this is all your doing** es de tu entera responsabilidad.
➡ **doings** npl actividades fpl.

do-it-yourself n bricolaje m.

doldrums [ˈdɒldrəmz] npl fig: **to be in the doldrums** [trade] estar estancado(da); [person] estar abatido(da).

dole [dəʊl] n (subsidio m de) paro m; **to be on the dole** estar parado(da).
➡ **dole out** vt sep distribuir, repartir.

doleful [ˈdəʊlfʊl] adj triste, lastimero(ra).

doll [dɒl] n [toy] muñeca f.

dollar [ˈdɒləʳ] n dólar m.

dolled up [dɒld-] adj inf [woman] emperifollada.

dollhouse US = **doll's house.**

dollop [ˈdɒləp] n inf cucharada f.

doll's house UK, **dollhouse** US [ˈdɒlhaʊs] n casa f de muñecas.

dolly [ˈdɒlɪ] (pl -ies) n **- 1.** [doll] muñequita f **- 2.** TECH [for TV or film camera] travelín m, plataforma f móvil.

Dolomites [ˈdɒləmaɪts] npl: **the Dolomites** los Dolomitas.

dolphin [ˈdɒlfɪn] n delfín m.

domain [dəˈmeɪn] n **- 1.** [sphere of interest] campo m, ámbito m **- 2.** [land] dominios mpl **- 3.** COMPUT dominio m.

dome [dəʊm] n [roof] cúpula f; [ceiling] bóveda f.

domestic [dəˈmestɪk] ⬦ adj **- 1.** [internal - policy, flight] nacional **- 2.** [chores, water supply, animal] doméstico(ca) **- 3.** [home-loving] hogareño(ña), casero(ra). ⬦ n **- 1.** [servant] doméstico m, -ca f, criado m, -da f **- 2.** inf [row] riña f.

domestic appliance n electrodoméstico m.

domesticated [dəˈmestɪkeɪtɪd] adj **- 1.** [animal] domesticado(da) **- 2.** hum [person] bien enseñado(da).

domesticity [ˌdəʊmeˈstɪsətɪ] n (U) vida f hogareña.

domicile [ˈdɒmɪsaɪl] n fml domicilio m.

dominance [ˈdɒmɪnəns] n (U) **- 1.** [control, power] dominación f, control m **- 2.** [importance] predominancia f.

dominant [ˈdɒmɪnənt] *adj* dominante.

dominate [ˈdɒmɪneɪt] *vt* dominar.

dominating [ˈdɒmɪneɪtɪŋ] *adj* dominante.

domination [ˌdɒmɪˈneɪʃn] *n* - **1.** [control, power] dominación *f* - **2.** [importance] predominancia *f*.

domineering [ˌdɒmɪˈnɪərɪŋ] *adj* dominante.

Dominica [dəˈmɪnɪkə] *n* Dominica.

Dominican Republic [dəˈmɪnɪkən-] *n*: **the Dominican Republic** la República Dominicana.

dominion [dəˈmɪnjən] *n* - **1.** (*U*) [power] dominio *m* - **2.** [land] dominios *mpl*.

domino [ˈdɒmɪnəʊ] (*pl* -es) *n* dominó *m*.
➡ **dominoes** *npl* dominó *m*.

domino effect *n* efecto *m* dominó.

don [dɒn] ◇ *n* UK UNIV profesor *m*, -ra *f* de universidad. ◇ *vt* (*pt & pp* -ned, *cont* -ning) ponerse.

donate [dəˈneɪt] *vt* donar.

donation [dəˈneɪʃn] *n* - **1.** [act of donating] donación *f* - **2.** [sum] donativo *m*.

done [dʌn] ◇ *pp* ➡ **do**. ◇ *adj* - **1.** [finished] listo(ta) - **2.** [cooked] hecho(cha); **well-done** muy hecho - **3.** [socially acceptable]: **it's not the done thing** no se hace, está mal visto. ◇ *adv* [to conclude deal]: **done!** ¡(trato) hecho!

donkey [ˈdɒŋkɪ] (*pl* donkeys) *n* burro *m*.

donkey jacket *n* chaqueta gruesa que suelen llevar los obreros.

donkeywork [ˈdɒŋkɪwɜːk] *n* UK inf parte *f* más pesada del trabajo.

donor [ˈdəʊnəʳ] *n* donante *mf*.

donor card *n* carné *m* de donante.

don't [dəʊnt] (*abbr of* = **do not**), = **do**.

donut [ˈdəʊnʌt] *n* US [with hole] donut® *m*.

doodle [ˈduːdl] ◇ *n* garabato *m*. ◇ *vi* garabatear.

doom [duːm] *n* perdición *f*, fatalidad *f*.

doomed [duːmd] *adj* [plan, mission] condenado(da) al fracaso; **to be doomed to sthg/to do sthg** estar condenado a algo/a hacer algo.

door [dɔːʳ] *n* - **1.** [gen] puerta *f*; **to open the door to** fig abrir la puerta a - **2.** [doorway] entrada *f*.

doorbell [ˈdɔːbel] *n* timbre *m* (*de la puerta*).

doorhandle [ˈdɔːhændl] *n* [gen] tirador *m* (*de la puerta*); [of car] manija *f*.

doorknob [ˈdɔːnɒb] *n* pomo *m*.

doorknocker [ˈdɔːˌnɒkəʳ] *n* aldaba *f*.

doorman [ˈdɔːmən] (*pl* -men [-mən]) *n* portero *m*.

doormat [ˈdɔːmæt] *n* - **1.** [mat] felpudo *m* - **2.** fig [person]: **he's a doormat** se deja pisotear por todo el mundo.

doorstep [ˈdɔːstep] *n* peldaño *m* de la puerta; **to turn up on sb's doorstep** aparecer en la puerta de alguien.

doorstop [ˈdɔːstɒp] *n* tope *m* (*de la puerta*).

door-to-door *adj* a domicilio.

doorway [ˈdɔːweɪ] *n* entrada *f*.

dope [dəʊp] ◇ *n* inf - **1.** [cannabis] maría *f* - **2.** [for athlete, horse] estimulante *m* - **3.** [fool] bobo *m*, -ba *f*, tonto *m*, -ta *f*. ◇ *vt* drogar, dopar.

dope test *n* inf control *m* OR prueba *f* antidoping.

dopey [ˈdəʊpɪ] (*comp* -ier, *superl* -iest) *adj* inf - **1.** [groggy] atontado(da), grogui - **2.** [stupid] bobo(ba).

dormant [ˈdɔːmənt] *adj* - **1.** [volcano] inactivo(va) - **2.** [idea, law] (en estado) latente.

dormer (window) [ˈdɔːməʳ-] *n* claraboya *f*, buhardilla *f*.

dormice [ˈdɔːmaɪs] *npl* ➡ **dormouse**.

dormitory [ˈdɔːmətrɪ] (*pl* -ies) *n* dormitorio *m* (*colectivo*).

Dormobile® [ˈdɔːməˌbiːl] *n* combi *m*.

dormouse [ˈdɔːmaʊs] (*pl* -mice) *n* lirón *m*.

Dors (*abbr of* **Dorset**), *condado inglés*.

DOS [dɒs] (*abbr of* **disk operating system**) *n* DOS *m*.

dosage [ˈdəʊsɪdʒ] *n* dosis *f* inv.

dose [dəʊs] ◇ *n* lit & fig dosis *f* inv; **a dose of flu** un ataque de gripe. ◇ *vt*: **to dose sb (with)** medicar a alguien (con).

doss [dɒs] ➡ **doss down** *vi* UK inf echarse a dormir.

dosser [ˈdɒsəʳ] *n* UK inf gandul *m*, -la *f*, vago *m*, -ga *f*.

dosshouse [ˈdɒshaʊs], *pl* [-haʊzɪz]) *n* UK inf pensión *f* de mala muerte.

dossier [ˈdɒsɪeɪ] *n* expediente *m*, dosier *m*.

dot [dɒt] ◇ *n* punto *m*; **on the dot** en punto. ◇ *vt* (*pt & pp* -ted, *cont* -ting) salpicar.

DOT (*abbr of* **Department of Transportation**) *n* ministerio estadounidense de transporte.

dotage [ˈdəʊtɪdʒ] *n*: **to be in one's dotage** chochear.

dotcom [ˈdɒtkɒm] *adj* puntocom.

dote [dəʊt] ➡ **dote (up)on** *vt insep* adorar.

doting [ˈdəʊtɪŋ] *adj* complaciente.

dot-matrix printer *n* COMPUT impresora *f* matricial.

dotted line [ˈdɒtɪd-] *n* línea *f* de puntos; **to sign on the dotted line** firmar.

dotty [ˈdɒtɪ] (*comp* -ier, *superl* -iest) *adj* inf chiflado(da).

double [ˈdʌbl] ◇ *adj* - **1.** [gen] doble - **2.** [repeated] repetido(da); **it's double the price**

cuesta el doble; **double three eight two** treinta y tres, ochenta y dos; **written with a double "t"** con dos tes. ◇ *adv* - **1.** [twice] el doble; **to cost double** costar el doble; **to see double** ver doble - **2.** [in two - fold] en dos; **to bend double** doblarse, agacharse. ◇ *n* - **1.** [twice as much] el doble - **2.** [drink] doble *m* - **3.** [lookalike] doble *mf*. ◇ *vt* doblar. ◇ *vi* - **1.** [increase twofold] doblarse, duplicarse - **2.** [have second purpose]: **to double as** hacer las veces de.

➤ **doubles** *npl* TENNIS dobles *mpl*; **doubles match** partido *m* de dobles.

➤ **double up** ◇ *vt sep*: **to be doubled up** doblarse; **to be doubled up with laughter** troncharse de risa. ◇ *vi* [bend over] doblarse.

double act *n* pareja *f* de humoristas.

double agent *n* agente *mf* doble.

double-barrelled *UK*, **double-barreled** *US* [-'bærəld] *adj* - **1.** [shotgun] de dos cañones - **2.** [name] *con dos apellidos unidos con guión.*

double bass [-beɪs] *n* contrabajo *m*.

double bed *n* cama *f* de matrimonio.

double-breasted [-'brestɪd] *adj* cruzado(da).

double-check *vt* & *vi* verificar dos veces.

double chin *n* papada *f*.

double-click ◇ *n* COMPUT doble clic *m*. ◇ *vt* COMPUT hacer doble clic en. ◇ *vi* COMPUT hacer doble clic.

double cream *n* nata *f* enriquecida.

double-cross *vt* traicionar.

double-dealer *n* traicionero *m*, -ra *f*.

double-decker [-'dekə˞] *n* autobús *m* de dos pisos.

double-density *adj* COMPUT de doble densidad.

double-dutch *n* *UK hum*: **to talk double-dutch** hablar en chino; **it's double-dutch to me** me suena a chino.

double-edged *adj* *lit* & *fig* de doble filo.

double entendre [ˌduːblɑːˈtɑːndr] *n* frase *f* ambigua, equívoco *m*.

double figures *npl* números *mpl* de dos cifras.

double-glazing [-'gleɪzɪŋ] *n* doble acristalamiento *m*.

double-jointed [-'dʒɔɪntɪd] *adj* con articulaciones muy flexibles.

double-park *vi* aparcar en doble fila.

double-quick *inf* ◇ *adj* rapidísimo(ma). ◇ *adv* rapidísimamente.

double room *n* habitación *f* doble.

double-sided *adj* COMPUT [disk] de dos caras.

double take *n*: **to do a double take** quedarse atónito(ta) OR con la boca abierta.

double-talk *n* (*U*) embustes *mpl*, engañifas *fpl*.

double time *n* paga *f* doble.

double vision *n* visión *f* doble.

double whammy [-'wæmɪ] *n* mazazo *m* por partida doble.

doubly ['dʌblɪ] *adv* doblemente.

doubt [daʊt] ◇ *n* duda *f*; **there is no doubt that** no hay OR cabe duda de que; **without (a) doubt** sin duda (alguna); **beyond all doubt** fuera de toda duda; **to be in doubt about sthg** estar dudando acerca de algo; **to cast doubt on** poner en duda; **no doubt** sin duda. ◇ *vt* - **1.** [not trust] dudar de - **2.** [consider unlikely] dudar; **I doubt it** lo dudo; **to doubt whether** OR **if** dudar que.

doubtful ['daʊtfʊl] *adj* - **1.** [gen] dudoso(sa) - **2.** [unsure] incierto(ta); **to be doubtful about** OR **of** tener dudas acerca de.

doubtless ['daʊtlɪs] *adv* sin duda.

dough [dəʊ] *n* (*U*) - **1.** [for baking] masa *f*, pasta *f* - **2.** *v inf* [money] pasta *f*, lana *f* *Méx*.

doughnut ['dəʊnʌt] *n* [without hole] buñuelo *m*; [with hole] donut® *m*.

dour [dʊə˞] *adj* adusto(ta).

douse [daʊs] *vt* - **1.** [put out] apagar - **2.** [drench] mojar, empapar.

dove¹ [dʌv] *n* paloma *f*.

dove² [dəʊv] *US pt* ➭ **dive**.

dovecot(e) ['dʌvkɒt] *n* palomar *m*.

dovetail ['dʌvteɪl] *vt* & *vi* encajar.

dovetail joint *n* cola *f* de milano.

dowager ['daʊədʒə˞] *n* *liter* viuda *f* rica.

dowdy ['daʊdɪ] (*comp* -ier, *superl* -iest) *adj* poco elegante.

Dow-Jones average [ˌdaʊˈdʒəʊnz-] *n* índice *m* Dow-Jones.

down [daʊn] ◇ *adv* - **1.** [downwards] (hacia) abajo; **to fall down** caer; **to bend down** agacharse; **down here/there** aquí/allí abajo - **2.** [along]: **I'm going down the pub** voy a acercarme al pub - **3.** [southwards] hacia el sur; **we're going down to Brighton** vamos a bajar a Brighton - **4.** [lower in amount]: **you must keep your weight down** debes intentar no engordar; **prices are coming down** los precios van bajando - **5.** [including]: **down to the last detail** hasta el último detalle - **6.** [as deposit]: **to pay £5 down** pagar 5 libras ahora (y el resto después) - **7.** [in written form]: **to write sthg down** apuntar algo. ◇ *prep* - **1.** [downwards]: **they ran down the hill** corrieron cuesta abajo; **he walked down the stairs** bajó la escalera; **rain poured down the window** la lluvia resbalaba por la ventana - **2.** [along]: **she was walking down the street** iba andando por la calle. ⬦ *adj* - **1.** [depressed] deprimido(da) - **2.** [behind]: **he's a minute down on the leader** va un minuto por detrás del líder; **we're three goals down** nos sacan tres goles - **3.** [written] por escrito - **4.** [not in operation]: **the computer is down again** el ordenador se ha estropeado otra vez - **5.** [lower in amount]: **prices are down** los precios han bajado - **6.** [ill]: **to be down with the flu** estar con gripe. ⬦ *n* [feathers] plumón *m*; [hair] pelusa *f*, vello *m*; *US* [in American football] *cada uno de los cuatro intentos de avance que tiene el equipo atacante.* ⬦ *vt* - **1.** [knock over] derribar - **2.** [swallow] beberse de un trago

▶▶ to down tools [go on strike] declararse en huelga.

⬥ downs *npl UK montes, especialmente los del sur de Inglaterra.*

⬥ down with *excl*: **down with the King!** ¡abajo el rey!

down-and-out ⬦ *adj* vagabundo(da). ⬦ *n* vagabundo *m*, -da *f*.

down-at-heel *adj esp UK* desastrado(da).

downbeat ['daʊnbiːt] *adj inf* pesimista.

downcast ['daʊnkɑːst] *adj fml* - **1.** [sad] alicaído(da), triste - **2.** [looking downwards] mirando al suelo.

downer ['daʊnər] *n inf* - **1.** [drug] tranquilizante *m* - **2.** [depressing event or person]: **it's a real downer** es muy deprimente; **to be on a downer** estar con la depre.

downfall ['daʊnfɔːl] *n* [of person] ruina *f*; [of regime] caída *f*.

downgrade ['daʊngreɪd] *vt* degradar.

downhearted [,daʊn'hɑːtɪd] *adj* desanimado(da).

downhill [,daʊn'hɪl] ⬦ *adj* cuesta abajo. ⬦ *adv* - **1.** [downwards] cuesta abajo - **2.** [worse]: **to be going downhill** ir cuesta abajo. ⬦ *n* [skiing] descenso *m*.

Downing Street ['daʊnɪŋ-] *n calle londinense donde se encuentran las residencias del Primer Ministro y del ministro de Finanzas; por extensión designa al gobierno británico.*

Downing Street ▬▬▬▬▬▬▬

▦ En los números 10 y 11 de esta calle londinense se encuentran las residencias oficiales del primer ministro británico y del ministro de Hacienda respectivamente. El término **Downing Street** se emplea a menudo para designar al gobierno, como por ejemplo en la frase: "there has been no statement from Downing Street" ("Downing Street no ha hecho declaraciones").

download [,daʊn'ləʊd] ⬦ *n* COMPUT descarga *f*. ⬦ *vt* COMPUT descargar, bajar.

down-market *adj* barato(ta).

down payment *n* entrada *f*.

downplay ['daʊnpleɪ] *vt* minimizar.

downpour ['daʊnpɔːr] *n* chaparrón *m*, aguacero *m*.

downright ['daʊnraɪt] ⬦ *adj* patente, manifiesto(ta). ⬦ *adv* completamente.

downside ['daʊnsaɪd] *n* desventaja *f*, inconveniente *m*.

Down's syndrome *n* síndrome *m* de Down.

downstairs [,daʊn'steəz] ⬦ *adj* de abajo. ⬦ *adv* abajo; **to come/go downstairs** bajar (la escalera).

downstream [,daʊn'striːm] *adv* río OR aguas abajo.

downtime ['daʊntaɪm] *n* tiempo *m* de inactividad, paro *m* técnico.

down-to-earth *adj* realista, práctico(ca).

downtown [,daʊn'taʊn] *US* ⬦ *adj* del centro (de la ciudad). ⬦ *n* centro *m* (urbano). ⬦ *adv* [live] en el centro; [go] al centro; **he gave me a lift downtown** me llevó OR me dio *Amér C, Méx & Perú* un aventón al centro.

downtrodden ['daʊn,trɒdn] *adj* oprimido(da).

downturn ['daʊntɜːn] *n* bajón *m*.

down under *adv en/a Australia o Nueva Zelanda.*

downward ['daʊnwəd] ⬦ *adj* - **1.** [towards the ground] hacia abajo - **2.** [decreasing] descendente. ⬦ *adv US* = **downwards**.

downwards ['daʊnwədz], **downward** *adv* - **1.** [gen] hacia abajo; **face downwards** boca abajo - **2.** [in hierarchy]: **everyone, from the president downwards** todos, empezando por el presidente.

downwind [,daʊn'wɪnd] *adv* a favor del viento.

dowry ['daʊərɪ] (*pl* -ies) *n* dote *f*.

doz. (*abbr of* **dozen**) doc.

doze [dəʊz] ⬦ *n* sueñecito *m*; **to have a doze** echar una cabezada. ⬦ *vi* dormitar.

⬥ doze off *vi* dormirse, quedarse adormilado(da).

dozen ['dʌzn] ⬦ *num adj*: **a dozen eggs** una docena de huevos. ⬦ *n* docena *f*; **50p a dozen** 50 peniques la docena.

⬥ dozens *npl inf*: **dozens of** montones *mpl* de.

dozy ['dəʊzɪ] (*comp* -ier, *superl* -iest) *adj* - **1.** [sleepy] soñoliento(ta), amodorrado(da) - **2.** *UK inf* [stupid] tonto(ta).

DPh, DPhil [,diː'fɪl] (*abbr of* **Doctor of Philosophy**) *n titular de un doctorado en filosofía.*

DPP *n abbr of* **Director of Public Prosecutions**.

Dr. - 1. (*abbr of* **Doctor**) Dr **- 2.** (*abbr of* **Drive**) ≃ c/.

drab [dræb] (*comp* **-ber,** *superl* **-best**) *adj* [colour] apagado(da); [building, clothes] soso(sa); [lives] monótono(na).

draconian [drə'kəʊnjən] *adj fml* draconiano(na).

draft [drɑ:ft] ⇔ *n* **- 1.** [early version] borrador *m* **- 2.** [money order] letra *f* de cambio, giro *m* **- 3.** *US* MIL: **the draft** la llamada a filas **- 4.** *US* = **draught.** ⇔ *vt* **- 1.** [write] redactar, hacer un borrador de **- 2.** *US* MIL llamar a filas **- 3.** [transfer - staff etc] transferir.

draft dodger [-dɒdʒər] *n US persona que se libra de alistarse en el ejército mediante subterfugios.*

draftee [ˌdrɑ:f'ti:] *n US* recluta *m*.

draftsman *US* = **draughtsman.**

draftsmanship *US* = **draughtsmanship.**

drafty *US* = **draughty.**

drag [dræg] ⇔ *vt* (*pt & pp* **-ged,** *cont* **-ging**) **- 1.** [gen & COMPUT] arrastrar; **to drag and drop sthg** arrastrar y soltar algo **- 2.** [lake, river] dragar, rastrear. ⇔ *vi* (*pt & pp* **-ged,** *cont* **-ging**) **- 1.** [dress, coat] arrastrarse **- 2.** [time, play] ir muy despacio. ⇔ *n inf* **- 1.** [bore - thing] lata *f*, rollo *m*; [- person] pesado *m*, -da *f* **- 2.** [on cigarette] calada *f*, chupada *f*, pitada *f* *Amér* **- 3.** [cross-dressing]: **in drag** vestido de mujer **- 4.** [air resistance] resistencia *f* aerodinámica.

◆ **drag down** *vt sep* hundir, deprimir.

◆ **drag into** *vt sep* [person] meter OR involucrar en.

◆ **drag on** *vi* ser interminable.

◆ **drag out** *vt sep* **- 1.** [protract] prolongar **- 2.** [extract - fact, information] sacar.

dragnet ['drægnet] *n* **- 1.** [net] red *f* barredera **- 2.** *fig* [to catch criminal] emboscada *f*.

dragon ['drægən] *n* **- 1.** [beast] dragón *m* **- 2.** *inf* [woman] bruja *f*.

dragonfly ['drægnflaɪ] (*pl* **-ies**) *n* libélula *f*.

dragoon [drə'gu:n] ⇔ *n* dragón *m*. ⇔ *vt*: **to dragoon sb into** forzar a alguien a.

drag racing *n* (*U*) carreras *fpl* de coches trucados OR modificados.

dragster ['drægstər] *n* coche *m* trucado OR modificado.

drain [dreɪn] ⇔ *n* **- 1.** [for water] desagüe *m*; [for sewage] alcantarilla *f*; [grating] sumidero *m*; **to go down the drain** echarse a perder **- 2.** [depletion]: **it's a drain on my energy** agota todas mis energías. ⇔ *vt* **- 1.** [marsh, field] drenar; [vegetables] escurrir **- 2.** [energy, resources] agotar **- 3.** [drink, glass] apurar. ⇔ *vi* **- 1.** [dishes] escurrirse **- 2.** [colour, blood, tension] desaparecer poco a poco.

drainage ['dreɪnɪdʒ] *n* **- 1.** [pipes, ditches] alcantarillado *m* **- 2.** [of land] drenaje *m*.

draining board *UK* ['dreɪnɪŋ-], **drainboard** *US* ['dreɪnbɔ:rd] *n* escurridero *m*.

drainpipe ['dreɪnpaɪp] *n* tubo *m* de desagüe.

drainpipes, drainpipe trousers *npl UK* pantalón *m* de pitillo.

drake [dreɪk] *n* pato *m*.

dram [dræm] *n* chupito *m*.

drama ['drɑ:mə] ⇔ *n* **- 1.** [gen] drama *m* **- 2.** [subject] teatro *m* **- 3.** [excitement] dramatismo *m*. ⇔ *comp* de arte dramático.

dramatic [drə'mætɪk] *adj* **- 1.** [concerned with theatre] dramático(ca) **- 2.** [gesture, escape, improvement] espectacular.

dramatically [drə'mætɪklɪ] *adv* **- 1.** [noticeably] espectacularmente **- 2.** [theatrically] dramáticamente.

dramatist ['dræmətɪst] *n* dramaturgo *m*, -ga *f*.

dramatization [ˌdræmətaɪ'zeɪʃn] *n* dramatización *f*.

dramatize, -ise ['dræmətaɪz] *vt* **- 1.** [rewrite as play] adaptar **- 2.** *pej* [make exciting] dramatizar.

drank [dræŋk] *pt* ▷ **drink.**

drape [dreɪp] *vt*: **to drape sthg over sthg** cubrir algo con algo; **draped with** OR **in** cubierto con.

◆ **drapes** *npl US* cortinas *fpl*.

draper ['dreɪpər] *n* pañero *m*, -ra *f*.

drastic ['dræstɪk] *adj* [extreme, urgent, noticeable] drástico(ca).

drastically ['dræstɪklɪ] *adv* [change, decline] drásticamente.

draught *UK*, **draft** *US* [drɑ:ft] *n* **- 1.** [air current] corriente *f* de aire **- 2.** [gulp] trago *m* **- 3.** [beer]: **on draught** de barril.

◆ **draughts** *n UK* (*U*) damas *fpl*.

draught beer *n UK* cerveza *f* de barril.

draughtboard ['drɑ:ftbɔ:d] *n UK* tablero *m* de damas.

draughtsman *UK*, **draftsman** *US* ['drɑ:ftsmən] (*pl* **-men** [-mən]) *n* delineante *mf*.

draughtsmanship *UK*, **draftsmanship** *US* ['drɑ:ftsmənʃɪp] *n* **- 1.** [technique] dibujo *m* lineal **- 2.** [skill] ejecución *f* de un dibujo lineal.

draughty *UK* (*comp* **-ier,** *superl* **-iest**), **drafty** *US* ['drɑ:ftɪ] (*comp* **-ier,** *superl* **-iest**) *adj* que tiene corrientes de aire; **it's draughty** hay corriente.

draw [drɔ:] ⇔ *vt* (*pt* **drew,** *pp* **drawn**) **- 1.** [sketch] dibujar; [line, circle] trazar; [a picture] hacer **- 2.** [pull - cart etc] tirar de; **she drew the comb through her hair** se pasó el peine por el pelo; **he drew her towards him** la atrajo hacia él, tomándola en sus brazos **- 3.** [curtains - open] descorrer; [- close] correr **- 4.** [breathe]: **to draw breath** respirar **- 5.** [gun, sword] sacar

- 6. [pension, benefit] percibir **- 7.** [cheque] librar **- 8.** [conclusion] sacar, llegar a **- 9.** [distinction, comparison] establecer **- 10.** [attract - criticism, praise, person] atraer; **to draw sb's attention to sthg** llamar la atención de alguien hacia algo; **to be** OR **feel drawn to** sentirse atraído(da) a OR por. ⬦ vi (pt **drew**, pp **drawn**) **- 1.** [sketch] dibujar **- 2.** [move] moverse; **to draw away** alejarse; **to draw closer** acercarse; **to draw to an end** OR **a close** llegar a su fin **- 3.** SPORT: **to draw (with)** empatar (con). ⬦ n **- 1.** SPORT empate m **- 2.** [lottery] sorteo m **- 3.** [attraction] atracción f.

⬥ **draw in** vi [days] acortarse.

⬥ **draw into** vt sep: **to draw sb into sthg** involucrar a alguien en algo.

⬥ **draw on** vt insep **- 1.** [reserves, experience] recurrir a; [statistics, facts] barajar **- 2.** [cigarette] dar una calada a.

⬥ **draw out** vt sep **- 1.** [encourage to talk] hacer hablar **- 2.** [prolong] prolongar **- 3.** [money] sacar.

⬥ **draw up** ⬦ vt sep [draft] preparar, redactar. ⬦ vi [stop] pararse.

⬥ **draw upon** vt insep [reserves, experience] recurrir a; [statistics, facts] barajar.

drawback ['drɔ:bæk] n inconveniente m, desventaja f.

drawbridge ['drɔ:brɪdʒ] n puente m levadizo.

drawer [drɔ:ʳ] n [in desk, chest] cajón m.

drawing ['drɔ:ɪŋ] n dibujo m.

drawing board n tablero m de delineante; **back to the drawing board!** inf ¡hay que volver a empezar desde el principio!

drawing pin n UK chincheta f.

drawing room n cuarto m de estar, salón m.

drawl [drɔ:l] ⬦ n manera lenta y poco clara de hablar, alargando las vocales. ⬦ vt hablar de manera lenta y poco clara, alargando las vocales.

drawn [drɔ:n] ⬦ pp ▷ **draw**. ⬦ adj **- 1.** [curtain, blind] corrido(da), cerrado(da) **- 2.** [tired, ill] cansado(da), ojeroso(sa).

drawn-out adj interminable.

drawstring ['drɔ:strɪŋ] n cordón m.

dread [dred] ⬦ n terror m, pavor m. ⬦ vt: **to dread (doing sthg)** temer (hacer algo); **I dread to think** me horroriza (el) pensarlo.

dreaded ['dredɪd] adj terrible.

dreadful ['dredful] adj **- 1.** [very unpleasant - pain, weather] terrible, espantoso(sa) **- 2.** [poor - play, English] horrible, fatal **- 3.** [for emphasis - waste, bore] espantoso(sa).

dreadfully ['dredfulɪ] adv terriblemente.

dreadlocks ['dredlɒks] npl pelo m al estilo rastafari.

dream [dri:m] ⬦ n lit & fig sueño m; **bad dream** pesadilla f. ⬦ adj ideal. ⬦ vt (pt & pp -ed OR **dreamt**): **to dream (that)** soñar que; **I never dreamt this would happen** jamás creí OR imaginé que esto pudiera suceder. ⬦ vi (pt & pp -ed OR **dreamt**) lit & fig: **to dream of doing sthg** soñar con hacer algo; **to dream (of** OR **about)** soñar (con); **I wouldn't dream of it** ¡ni hablar!, ¡de ninguna manera!

⬥ **dream up** vt sep inventar, idear.

dreamer ['dri:məʳ] n soñador m, -ra f.

dreamily ['dri:mɪlɪ] adv distraídamente.

dreamlike ['dri:mlaɪk] adj de ensueño.

dreamt [dremt] pp ▷ **dream**.

dream world n mundo m de ensueño.

dreamy ['dri:mɪ] (comp **-ier**, superl **-iest**) adj **- 1.** [distracted] soñador(ra) **- 2.** [peaceful, dreamlike] de ensueño.

dreary ['drɪərɪ] (comp **-ier**, superl **-iest**) adj **- 1.** [weather, day] triste **- 2.** [job, life] monótono(na); [persona] gris.

dredge [dredʒ] vt dragar.

⬥ **dredge up** vt sep **- 1.** [with dredger] sacar del agua (al dragar) **- 2.** fig [from past] sacar a relucir.

dredger ['dredʒəʳ] n NAUT draga f.

dregs [dregz] npl **- 1.** [of liquid] posos mpl **- 2.** fig [of society] escoria f.

drench [drentʃ] vt empapar; **drenched to the skin** calado(da) hasta los huesos; **to be drenched in** OR **with** estar empapado(da) en.

dress [dres] ⬦ n **- 1.** [woman's garment] vestido m **- 2.** (U) [clothing] traje m. ⬦ vt **- 1.** [clothe] vestir; **to be dressed in** ir vestido(da) de; **to be dressed** estar vestido(da); **to get dressed** vestirse **- 2.** [bandage] vendar **- 3.** CULIN aliñar, aderezar. ⬦ vi **- 1.** [put on clothing] vestirse **- 2.** [wear clothes] vestir; **to dress well/badly** vestir bien/mal.

⬥ **dress up** ⬦ vt sep disfrazar. ⬦ vi **- 1.** [in costume] disfrazarse **- 2.** [in best clothes] engalanarse.

dressage ['dresɑ:ʒ] n doma f de caballos.

dress circle n palco m de platea.

dresser ['dresəʳ] n **- 1.** [for dishes] aparador m **- 2.** US [chest of drawers] cómoda f **- 3.** [person]: **he's a smart/sloppy dresser** es elegante/descuidado en el vestir.

dressing ['dresɪŋ] n **- 1.** [bandage] vendaje m **- 2.** [for salad] aliño m **- 3.** US [for turkey etc] relleno m.

dressing gown n bata f.

dressing room n THEAT camerino m; SPORT vestuario m.

dressing table n tocador m.

dressmaker ['dres,meɪkəʳ] *n* costurero *m*, -ra *f*, modisto *m*, -ta *f*.

dressmaking ['dres,meɪkɪŋ] *n* costura *f*.

dress rehearsal *n* ensayo *m* general.

dress shirt *n* camisa *f* de vestir.

dressy ['dresɪ] (*comp* -ier, *superl* -iest) *adj* elegante.

drew [dru:] *pt* ⊳ draw.

dribble ['drɪbl] ◇ *n* - **1.** [saliva] baba *f* - **2.** [trickle] hilo *m*. ◇ *vt* - **1.** SPORT [ball] regatear - **2.** [liquid]: **to dribble saliva** babear. ◇ *vi* - **1.** [drool] babear - **2.** [spill] gotear, caer gota a gota.

dribs [drɪbz] *npl*: **in dribs and drabs** poco a poco.

dried [draɪd] ◇ *pp* & *pt* ⊳ dry. ◇ *adj* [gen] seco(ca); [milk, eggs] en polvo.

dried-up *adj* seco(ca).

drier ['draɪəʳ] = dryer.

drift [drɪft] ◇ *n* - **1.** [trend, movement] movimiento *m*, tendencia *f*; [of current] flujo *m* - **2.** [meaning] sentido *m*; **I get your drift** entiendo la idea - **3.** [mass - of snow] ventisquero *m*; [- of sand, leaves] montículo *m*. ◇ *vi* - **1.** [boat] ir a la deriva - **2.** [snow, sand, leaves] amontonarse - **3.** [person] ir sin rumbo; **to drift into** [job, marriage] dejarse llevar a; **to drift apart** tener cada vez menos en común.

◆ **drift off** *vi* [person] dormirse, quedarse dormido(da).

drifter ['drɪftəʳ] *n* [person] *persona que no permanece por mucho tiempo en un sitio o empleo.*

driftwood ['drɪftwʊd] *n* madera *f* de deriva.

drill [drɪl] ◇ *n* - **1.** [tool - gen] taladro *m*; [- bit] broca *f*; [- dentist's] fresa *f*; [- in mine, oilfield] perforadora *f* - **2.** [exercise - for fire, battle] simulacro *m*. ◇ *vt* - **1.** [tooth, wood, oil well] perforar - **2.** [instruct - people, pupils] adiestrar, entrenar; [- soldiers] instruir; **to drill sthg into sb** inculcar algo en alguien. ◇ *vi*: **to drill into/ for** perforar en/en busca de.

drily ['draɪlɪ] = dryly.

drink [drɪŋk] ◇ *n* - **1.** [gen] bebida *f*; **a drink of water** un trago de agua - **2.** [alcoholic beverage] copa *f*; **would you like a drink?** ¿quieres tomar algo (de beber)?; **to have a drink** tomar algo, tomar una copa. ◇ *vt* (*pt* **drank**, *pp* **drunk**) beber. ◇ *vi* (*pt* **drank**, *pp* **drunk**) beber; **to drink to sb/sb's success** beber a la salud de alguien/por el éxito de alguien.

drinkable ['drɪŋkəbl] *adj* - **1.** [suitable for drinking] potable - **2.** [palatable]: **this wine is very drinkable** este vino no está nada mal.

drink-driving *UK*, **drunk-driving** *US n* conducción *f* en estado de embriaguez.

drinker ['drɪŋkəʳ] *n* - **1.** [of alcohol] bebedor *m*, -ra *f* - **2.** [of tea, coffee]: **tea/coffee drinker** persona que bebe té/café.

drinking ['drɪŋkɪŋ] *n* (*U*) bebida *f*.

drinking fountain *n* fuente *f* (de agua potable).

drinking water ['drɪŋkɪŋ-] *n* agua *f* potable.

drip [drɪp] ◇ *n* - **1.** [drop] gota *f*; [drops] goteo *m* - **2.** MED gota a gota *m inv* - **3.** *inf* [wimp] soso *m*, -sa *f*. ◇ *vt* (*pt* & *pp* **-ped**, *cont* **-ping**) [sweat, blood] chorrear. ◇ *vi* (*pt* & *pp* **-ped**, *cont* **-ping**) - **1.** [liquid, tap, nose] gotear - **2.** [person]: **to be dripping with sthg** [sweat, blood] estar chorreando algo; [diamonds, furs] estar cubierto(ta) de algo.

drip-dry *adj* de lava y pon.

drip-feed ◇ *n* gota a gota *m inv*. ◇ *vt* alimentar gota a gota.

dripping ['drɪpɪŋ] ◇ *adj*: **dripping (wet)** chorreando, empapado(da). ◇ *n* grasa *f* (*de carne*), pringue *m* o *f*.

drive [draɪv] ◇ *n* - **1.** [outing] paseo *m* (en coche); **to go for a drive** ir a dar una vuelta en coche - **2.** [journey] viaje *m* (en coche); **it's a two-hour drive (away)** está a dos horas en coche - **3.** [urge] instinto *m* - **4.** [campaign] campaña *f* - **5.** [energy] vigor *m*, energía *f* - **6.** [road to house] camino *m* (de entrada) - **7.** [street] calle *f* - **8.** [in golf, tennis] drive *m* - **9.** COMPUT unidad *f* de disco. ◇ *vt* (*pt* **drove**, *pp* **driven**) - **1.** [vehicle] conducir, manejar *Amér* - **2.** [passenger] llevar (en coche) - **3.** [fuel, power] impulsar - **4.** [force to move - gen] arrastrar; [- cattle] arrear; **it drove people from their homes** obligó a la gente a abandonar sus hogares - **5.** [motivate] motivar - **6.** [force]: **to drive sb to do sthg** conducir OR llevar a alguien a hacer algo; **to drive sb to despair** hacer desesperar a alguien; **to drive sb mad** OR **crazy** volver loco a alguien - **7.** [hammer] clavar - **8.** SPORT [hit hard] golpear con fuerza. ◇ *vi* (*pt* **drove**, *pp* **driven**) AUT conducir, manejar *Amér*; **I don't drive** no sé conducir; **I drove there** fui en coche.

◆ **drive at** *vt insep* insinuar, querer decir.

drive-by *n* (*pl* **drive-bys**) tiroteo OR asesinato *desde un vehículo.*

drive-in *US* ◇ *n* - **1.** [restaurant] *restaurante de comida rápida donde se sirve a la clientela en su coche* - **2.** CIN autocine *m*. ◇ *adj*: **drive-in bank** *banco en el que se puede realizar transacciones desde el coche.*

drivel ['drɪvl] *n* (*U*) *inf* tonterías *fpl*.

driven ['drɪvn] *pp* ⊳ drive.

driver ['draɪvəʳ] *n* - **1.** [gen] conductor *m*, -ra *f*; RAIL maquinista *mf*; [of racing car] piloto *mf* - **2.** COMPUT controlador *m*.

driver's license *US* = driving licence.

drive shaft *n* (eje *m* de) transmisión *f*.

driveway ['draɪvweɪ] *n* camino *m* (de entrada).

driving ['draɪvɪŋ] <> *adj* [rain] torrencial; [wind] huracanado(da). <> *n* (*U*) conducción *f*, el conducir.

driving force *n* fuerza *f* motriz.

driving instructor *n* profesor *m*, -ra *f* de autoescuela.

driving lesson *n* clase *f* de conducir OR conducción.

driving licence *UK*, **driver's license** *US n* carné *m* OR permiso *m* de conducir.

driving mirror *n* retrovisor *m*.

driving school *n* autoescuela *f*.

driving test *n* examen *m* de conducir.

drizzle ['drɪzl] <> *n* llovizna *f*, garúa *f Andes & R Plata*. <> *impers vb* lloviznar.

drizzly ['drɪzlɪ] (*comp* -ier, *superl* -iest) *adj* llovíznoso(sa).

droll [drəʊl] *adj* gracioso(sa).

dromedary ['drɒmədrɪ] (*pl* -ies) *n* dromedario *m*.

drone [drəʊn] <> *n* - **1.** [hum] zumbido *m* - **2.** [bee] zángano *m*. <> *vi* zumbar.

drone on *vi*: **to drone on (about)** soltar una perorata (sobre).

drool [druːl] *vi* - **1.** [dribble] babear - **2.** *fig* [admire]: **he was drooling over her** se le caía la baba con ella.

droop [druːp] *vi* - **1.** [shoulders] encorvarse; [eyelids] cerrarse; [head] inclinarse; [flower] marchitarse - **2.** [person]: **their spirits drooped** se desanimaron.

drop [drɒp] <> *n* - **1.** [of liquid, milk, whisky] gota *f* - **2.** [sweet] pastilla *f* - **3.** [decrease]: **drop (in)** [price] caída *f* (de); [temperature] descenso *m* (de); [demand, income] disminución *f* (en) - **4.** [distance down] caída *f*. <> *vt* (*pt & pp* -ped, *cont* -ping) - **1.** [let fall - gen] dejar caer; [- bomb] lanzar; **I dropped the book** se me cayó el libro; **she dropped a stitch** se le escapó un punto - **2.** [decrease] reducir - **3.** [voice] bajar - **4.** [abandon - subject, course] dejar; [- charges] retirar; [- person, lover] abandonar; [- player] excluir, no seleccionar - **5.** [utter - hint, remark] lanzar, soltar; **he's always dropping names** siempre se las está dando de conocer a gente importante - **6.** SPORT [game, set] perder - **7.** [write]: **to drop sb a line** mandar unas líneas a alguien - **8.** [let out of car] dejar. <> *vi* (*pt & pp* -ped, *cont* -ping) - **1.** [fall down] caer; **it dropped onto the ground** se cayó al suelo; **to drop to one's knees** arrodillarse; **drop dead!** ¡vete a la porra!; **we walked until we dropped** estuvimos andando hasta no poder más - **2.** [fall away - ground] ceder - **3.** [decrease - temperature, price, voice] bajar; [- attendance, demand, unemployment] disminuir; [- wind] calmarse, amainar.

drops *npl* MED gotas *fpl*.

drop by *vi inf*: **to drop by (at)** pasarse (por).

drop in *vi inf*: **to drop in on** pasarse por casa de.

drop off <> *vt sep* [person, letter] dejar. <> *vi* - **1.** [fall asleep] quedarse dormido(da), dormirse - **2.** [grow less] disminuir, bajar.

drop out *vi*: **to drop out (of** OR **from)** [school, college] dejar de asistir (a); [competition] retirarse (de).

drop-in centre *n centro patrocinado por los servicios sociales, iglesias etc, a donde la gente puede ir a pasar un rato.*

droplet ['drɒplɪt] *n* gotita *f*.

dropout ['drɒpaʊt] *n* [from society] marginado *m*, -da *f*; [from university] persona *f* que ha dejado los estudios.

dropper ['drɒpə'] *n* cuentagotas *m inv*.

droppings ['drɒpɪŋz] *npl* excrementos *mpl* (*de animal*).

drop shot *n* dejada *f*.

dross [drɒs] *n inf* [rubbish] basura *f*.

drought [draʊt] *n* sequía *f*.

drove [drəʊv] <> *pt* ▷ **drive**. <> *n* [of people] multitud *f*.

drown [draʊn] <> *vt* - **1.** [kill] ahogar - **2.** [sound]: **to drown sb/sthg (out)** ahogar a alguien/algo. <> *vi* ahogarse.

drowsy ['draʊzɪ] (*comp* -ier, *superl* -iest) *adj* [person] somnoliento(ta).

drudge [drʌdʒ] *n* esclavo *m*, -va *f* del trabajo.

drudgery ['drʌdʒərɪ] *n trabajo pesado y monótono.*

drug [drʌg] <> *n* - **1.** [medicine] medicamento *m* - **2.** [narcotic] droga *f*; **to be on** OR **take drugs** drogarse. <> *vt* (*pt & pp* -ged, *cont* -ging) - **1.** [person] drogar - **2.** [food, drink] echar droga a.

drug abuse *n* consumo *m* de drogas.

drug addict *n* drogadicto *m*, -ta *f*, toxicómano *m*, -na *f*.

drug addiction *n* drogadicción *f*, toxicomanía *f*.

drug dealer *n* narcotraficante *mf*.

drugs test *n* prueba *f* antidoping.

drugstore ['drʌgstɔː'] *n US* farmacia *f* (*que también vende productos de perfumería, cosméticos, periódicos etc*).

druid ['druːɪd] *n* druida *m*.

drum [drʌm] <> *n* - **1.** [instrument, of machine] tambor *m*; **drums** batería *f* - **2.** [container, cylinder] bidón *m*. ⇔ *vt* (*pt & pp* -med, *cont* -ming) [fingers] tamborilear con. ⇔ *vi* (*pt & pp* -med, *cont* -ming) [rain, hoofs] golpetear.

◆ **drum into** *vt sep*: **to drum sthg into sb** inculcar algo a alguien.

◆ **drum up** *vt sep* intentar conseguir.

drumbeat ['drʌmbiːt] *n* toque *m* de tambor.

drum brake *n* freno *m* de tambor.

drummer ['drʌməʳ] *n* [in orchestra] tambor *mf*; [in pop group] batería *mf*.

drumming ['drʌmɪŋ] *n* - **1.** [of fingers, rain] tamborileo *m* - **2.** [playing drum] el tocar el tambor; **the drumming on the album is fantastic** la batería en el disco es sensacional.

drum roll *n* redoble *m* de tambor.

drumstick ['drʌmstɪk] *n* - **1.** [for drum] palillo *m* - **2.** [food] muslo *m*.

drunk [drʌŋk] ⇔ *pp* ▷ drink. ⇔ *adj* - **1.** [on alcohol] borracho(cha); **to get drunk** emborracharse; **to be drunk** estar borracho(cha); **drunk and disorderly** borracho(cha) y escandaloso(sa) - **2.** *fig* [excited, carried away]: **to be drunk with** OR **on** estar ebrio(ebria) de. ⇔ *n* borracho *m*, -cha *f*.

drunkard ['drʌŋkəd] *n* borracho *m*, -cha *f*.

drunk-driving US = drink-driving.

drunken ['drʌŋkn] *adj* - **1.** [person] borracho(cha) - **2.** [talk, steps, stupor] de borracho(cha).

drunken driving = drink-driving.

drunkenness ['drʌŋkənnɪs] *n* embriaguez *f*.

dry [draɪ] ⇔ *adj* (*comp* -ier, *superl* -iest) - **1.** [gen] seco(ca) - **2.** [day] sin lluvia - **3.** [earth, soil] árido(da) - **4.** [thirsty] sediento(ta); **to feel** OR **be dry** tener sed - **5.** [dull] aburrido(da) - **6.** [humour] lacónico(ca). ⇔ *vt* (*pt & pp* **dried**) [gen] secar; [hands, hair] secarse; **to dry o.s.** secarse; **to dry one's eyes** secarse las lágrimas. ⇔ *vi* (*pt & pp* **dried**) secarse.

◆ **dry out** ⇔ *vt sep* secar. ⇔ *vi* secarse.

◆ **dry up** ⇔ *vt sep* secar. ⇔ *vi* - **1.** [river, well] secarse - **2.** [stop - supply] agotarse - **3.** [stop speaking] quedarse en blanco - **4.** [dry dishes] secar.

dry battery *n* pila *f* (seca).

dry-clean *vt* limpiar en seco.

dry cleaner *n*: **dry cleaner's (shop)** tintorería *f*.

dry-cleaning *n* limpieza *f* en seco.

dry dock *n* dique *m* seco.

dryer ['draɪəʳ] *n* [for clothes] secadora *f*.

dry goods *npl* - **1.** UK [tobacco, coffee etc] alimentos *mpl* no perecederos - **2.** US [cloth products] artículos *mpl* de mercería.

dry ice *n* nieve *f* carbónica.

dry land *n* tierra *f* firme.

dryly, drily ['draɪlɪ] *adv* [wryly] secamente.

dryness ['draɪnɪs] *n* - **1.** [gen] sequedad *f* - **2.** [of ground, lecture] aridez *f* - **3.** [of comment, humour] laconismo *m*.

dry rot *n* putrefacción *f* de la madera.

dry run *n* ensayo *m*.

dry ski slope *n* pista *f* de esquí artificial.

dry-stone wall *n* muro construido con piedras amontonadas y sin mortero.

drysuit ['draɪsuːt] *n* traje *m* de neopreno.

DSS (*abbr of* **Department of Social Security**) *n* ministerio británico de la seguridad social.

DST (*abbr of* **daylight saving time**) *hora de verano*.

DT *abbr of* **data transmission**.

DTI (*abbr of* **Department of Trade and Industry**) *n* ministerio británico de comercio e industria.

DTP (*abbr of* **desktop publishing**) *n* autoed. *f*.

DT's [ˌdiː'tiːz] (*abbr of* **delirium tremens**) *npl inf*: **to have the DT's** tener un delírium trémens.

dual ['djuːəl] *adj* doble.

dual carriageway *n* UK carretera de dos sentidos y doble vía separados, ≃ autovía *f*.

dual control *n* doble mando *m*.

dual nationality *n* doble nacionalidad *f*.

dual-purpose *adj* de doble uso.

dubbed [dʌbd] *adj* - **1.** CIN doblado(da) - **2.** [nicknamed] apodado(da).

dubious ['djuːbjəs] *adj* - **1.** [questionable - person, deal, reasons] sospechoso(sa); [- honour, distinction] paradójico(ca) - **2.** [uncertain, undecided] dudoso(sa); **to feel** OR **be dubious (about)** tener dudas (sobre).

Dublin ['dʌblɪn] *n* Dublín.

Dubliner ['dʌblɪnəʳ] *n* dublinés *m*, -esa *f*.

duchess ['dʌtʃɪs] *n* duquesa *f*.

duchy ['dʌtʃɪ] (*pl* -ies) *n* ducado *m*.

duck [dʌk] ⇔ *n* - **1.** [bird] pato *m*, -ta *f*; **to take to sthg like a duck to water** encontrarse en seguida en su salsa con algo - **2.** [food] pato *m*. ⇔ *vt* - **1.** [lower] agachar, bajar - **2.** [try to avoid - duty] eludir, esquivar - **3.** [submerge] sumergir. ⇔ *vi* - **1.** [lower head] agacharse - **2.** [dive]: **to duck behind/into sthg** esconderse detrás de/en algo.

◆ **duck out** *vi*: **to duck out (of sthg/of doing sthg)** zafarse (de algo/de hacer algo).

duckling ['dʌklɪŋ] *n* patito *m*.

duct [dʌkt] *n* conducto *m*.

dud [dʌd] ⇔ *adj* [gen] falso(sa); [mine] que no estalla; [cheque] sin fondos. ⇔ *n* persona o cosa inútil.

dude [dju:d] *n US inf* [man] tipo *m*, tío *m Esp*; [term of address] colega *m Esp*, tío *m Esp*, mano *m Andes, Amér C & Méx*, flaco *m R Plata*.

dude ranch *n US* rancho *m* para turistas.

due [dju:] ⟨⟩ *adj* **- 1.** [expected] esperado(da); **it's due out in May** saldrá en mayo; **she's due back soon** volverá dentro de poco; **the train's due in half an hour** el tren debe llegar dentro de media hora **- 2.** [appropriate] debido(da); **with all due respect** sin ganas de ofender; **in due course** [at appropriate time] a su debido tiempo; [eventually] al final **- 3.** [owed, owing] pagadero(ra); **I'm due a bit of luck** ya sería hora que tuviera un poco de suerte; **how much are you due?** ¿cuánto te deben?; **to be due to** deberse a. ⟨⟩ *n* [deserts]: **to give sb their due** hacer justicia a alguien. ⟨⟩ *adv*: **due north/south** derecho hacia el norte/sur.
➤ **dues** *npl* cuota *f*.
➤ **due to** *prep* debido a.

due date *n* (fecha *f* de) vencimiento *m*.

duel ['dju:əl] ⟨⟩ *n* duelo *m*. ⟨⟩ *vi* (*UK* **-led**, *cont* **-ling**, *US* **-ed**, *cont* **-ing**) batirse en duelo.

duet [dju:'et] *n* dúo *m*.

duff [dʌf] *adj UK inf* inútil.
➤ **duff up** *vt sep UK inf* dar una paliza a.

duffel bag, duffle bag ['dʌfl-] *n* morral *m*.

duffel coat ['dʌfl-] *n* trenca *f*.

duffle bag ['dʌfl-] = **duffel bag**.

duffle coat ['dʌfl-] = **duffel coat**.

dug [dʌg] *pt & pp* ⟳ **dig**.

dugout ['dʌgaʊt] *n* **- 1.** [canoe] *canoa hecha con un tronco ahuecado* **- 2.** SPORT foso *m*, banquillo *m*.

duke [dju:k] *n* duque *m*.

dull [dʌl] ⟨⟩ *adj* **- 1.** [boring] aburrido(da) **- 2.** [listless] torpe **- 3.** [dim] apagado(da) **- 4.** [cloudy] gris, triste **- 5.** [thud, boom, pain] sordo(da). ⟨⟩ *vt* **- 1.** [senses] embotar, entorpecer; [pain] aliviar; [pleasure, memory] enturbiar **- 2.** [make less bright] deslustrar.

duly ['dju:lɪ] *adv* **- 1.** [properly] debidamente **- 2.** [as expected] como era de esperar.

dumb [dʌm] *adj* **- 1.** [unable to speak] mudo(da); **to be struck dumb** quedarse de una pieza **- 2.** *esp US inf* [stupid] estúpido(da).

dumbbell ['dʌmbel] *n* [weight] pesa *f*.

dumbstruck ['dʌmstrʌk] *adj* mudo(da) de asombro.

dumbwaiter [,dʌm'weɪtər] *n* [lift] montaplatos *m inv*.

dummy ['dʌmɪ] ⟨⟩ *adj* falso(sa). ⟨⟩ *n* (*pl* **-ies**) **- 1.** [of ventriloquist] muñeco *m*; [in shop window] maniquí *m* **- 2.** [copy] imitación *f* **- 3.** *UK* [for baby] chupete *m*, chupón *m Méx* **- 4.** SPORT amago *m* **- 5.** *inf* [idiot] imbécil *mf*. ⟨⟩ *vt* SPORT amagar.

dummy run *n* ensayo *m*, prueba *f*.

dump [dʌmp] ⟨⟩ *n* **- 1.** [for rubbish] basurero *m*, vertedero *m* **- 2.** [for ammunition] depósito *m* **- 3.** COMPUT volcado *m* de memoria **- 4.** *inf* [ugly place - house] casucha *f*; [- hotel] hotelucho *m*. ⟨⟩ *vt* **- 1.** [put down - sand, load] descargar; [- bags, washing] dejar **- 2.** [dispose of] deshacerse de **- 3.** COMPUT volcar **- 4.** *inf* [jilt] deshacerse de. ⟨⟩ *vi vulgar* jiñar.
➤ **dumps** *npl*: **to be (down) in the dumps** tener murria, estar por los suelos.

dumper (truck) *UK* ['dʌmpər-], **dump truck** *US n* volquete *m*.

dumping ['dʌmpɪŋ] *n* [of rubbish] vertido *m*; **'no dumping'** 'prohibido verter basura'.

dumping ground *n* vertedero *m*.

dumpling ['dʌmplɪŋ] *n bola de masa que se guisa al vapor con carne y verduras*.

dump truck *US* = **dumper (truck)**.

dumpy ['dʌmpɪ] (*comp* **-ier**, *superl* **-iest**) *adj inf* bajito y regordete (bajita y regordeta).

dunce [dʌns] *n* zoquete *mf*, burro *m*, -rra *f*.

dune [dju:n] *n* duna *f*.

dung [dʌŋ] *n* [of animal] excremento *m*; [used as manure] estiércol *m*.

dungarees [,dʌŋgə'ri:z] *npl* **- 1.** *UK* [for work] mono *m*, overol *m Amér*; [fashion garment] pantalones *mpl* de peto, mameluco *m* **- 2.** *US* [heavy jeans] *vaqueros de tela gruesa utilizados para trabajar*.

dungeon ['dʌndʒən] *n* mazmorra *f*, calabozo *m*.

dunk [dʌŋk] *vt* mojar.

duo ['dju:əʊ] *n* dúo *m*.

dupe [dju:p] ⟨⟩ *n* primo *m*, -ma *f*, inocente *mf*. ⟨⟩ *vt*: **to dupe sb (into doing sthg)** embaucar a alguien (para que haga algo).

duplex ['dju:pleks] *n US* **- 1.** [apartment] dúplex *m* **- 2.** [house] casa *f* adosada.

duplicate ⟨⟩ *adj* ['dju:plɪkət] duplicado(da). ⟨⟩ *n* ['dju:plɪkət] copia *f*, duplicado *m*; **in duplicate** por duplicado. ⟨⟩ *vt* ['dju:plɪkeɪt] **- 1.** [copy] duplicar, hacer una copia de **- 2.** [double, repeat] repetir.

duplication [,dju:plɪ'keɪʃn] (*U*) *n* **- 1.** [copying] duplicación *f* **- 2.** [doubling, repetition] repetición *f*.

duplicity [dju:'plɪsətɪ] *n fml* doblez *f*, duplicidad *f*.

Dur (*abbr of* **Durham**) *condado inglés*.

durability [,djʊərə'bɪlətɪ] *n* durabilidad *f*.

durable ['djʊərəbl] *adj* duradero(ra).

duration [djʊ'reɪʃn] *n* duración *f*; **for the duration of** durante.

duress [djʊ'res] *n*: **under duress** bajo coacción.

Durex® ['djʊəreks] *n* [condom] preservativo *m*, condón *m*.

during ['djʊərɪŋ] *prep* durante.

dusk [dʌsk] *n* crepúsculo *m*, anochecer *m*.

dusky ['dʌskɪ] (*comp* -ier, *superl* -iest) *adj liter* moreno(na).

dust [dʌst] ◇ *n* polvo *m*; **coal dust** cisco *m*; **to gather dust** [get dusty] cubrirse de polvo; *fig* [be ignored] quedar arrinconado(da). ◇ *vt* - **1.** [clean] quitar el polvo a, limpiar - **2.** [cover with powder]: **to dust sthg (with)** espolvorear algo (con). ◇ *vi* quitar el polvo.
➡ **dust off** *vt sep lit* & *fig* desempolvar.

dustbin ['dʌstbɪn] *n UK* cubo *m* de la basura.

dustcart ['dʌstkɑ:t] *n UK* camión *m* de la basura.

dustcloth ['dʌstklɒθ] *n US* trapo *m* del polvo.

dust cover = **dust jacket**.

duster ['dʌstə'] *n* - **1.** [cloth] bayeta *f*, trapo *m* (del polvo) - **2.** *US* [overall] guardapolvo *m*.

dust jacket, dust cover *n* sobrecubierta *f*.

dustman ['dʌstmən] (*pl* -men [-mən]) *n UK* basurero *m*.

dustpan ['dʌstpæn] *n* recogedor *m*.

dustsheet ['dʌstʃi:t] *n UK* guardapolvo *m* (para muebles).

dust storm *n* vendaval *m* de polvo.

dustup ['dʌstʌp] *n inf* reyerta *f*, riña *f*.

dusty ['dʌstɪ] (*comp* -ier, *superl* -iest) *adj* [covered in dust] polvoriento(ta).

Dutch [dʌtʃ] ◇ *adj* holandés(esa). ◇ *n* [language] holandés *m*. ◇ *npl*: **the Dutch** los holandeses.

Dutch auction *n UK subasta en la que se va reduciendo el precio de venta hasta encontrar comprador.*

Dutch cap *n UK* diafragma *m*.

Dutch courage *n* valentía *f* causada por la embriaguez.

Dutch elm disease *n hongo que ataca los olmos.*

Dutchman ['dʌtʃmən] (*pl* -men [-mən]) *n* holandés *m*.

Dutchwoman ['dʌtʃ,wʊmən] (*pl* -women [-,wɪmɪn]) *n* holandesa *f*.

dutiable ['dju:tjəbl] *adj* sujeto(ta) a derechos de aduana.

dutiful ['dju:tɪfʊl] *adj* obediente, sumiso(sa).

duty ['dju:tɪ] (*pl* -ies) *n* - **1.** *(U)* [moral, legal responsibility] deber *m*; **to do one's duty** cumplir con su deber - **2.** [work] servicio *m*; **to be on/**

off duty estar/no estar de servicio - **3.** [tax] impuesto *m*; **customs duty** derechos *mpl* arancelarios.
➡ **duties** *npl* tareas *fpl*.

duty bound *adj*: **to be duty bound (to do sthg)** estar obligado(da) (a hacer algo).

duty-free ◇ *adj* libre de impuestos. ◇ *n (U) inf* artículos *mpl* libres de impuestos.

duty-free shop *n* tienda *f* libre de impuestos.

duty officer *n* oficial *mf* de guardia.

duvet ['du:veɪ] *n UK* edredón *m*.

duvet cover *n UK* funda *f* del edredón.

DVD (*abbr of* **Digital Versatile Disk**) *n* DVD *m*.

DVD player *n* reproductor *m* de DVD.

DVD recorder *n* grabador *m* de DVD.

DVD ROM (*abbr of* **Digital Versatile Disk read only memory**) *n* DVD ROM *m*.

dwarf [dwɔ:f] ◇ *adj* enano(na). ◇ *n* (*pl* -s OR dwarves [dwɔ:vz]) enano *m*, -na *f*. ◇ *vt* achicar, empequeñecer.

dwell [dwel] *vi* (*pt* & *pp* -ed OR dwelt) *liter* morar, habitar.
➡ **dwell on** *vt insep* darle vueltas a.

-dweller ['dwelə'] *suffix*: **cave-dweller** habitante *mf* de las cavernas; **city-dweller** habitante *mf* de la ciudad.

dwelling ['dwelɪŋ] *n liter* morada *f*.

dwelt [dwelt] *pt* & *pp* ▷ **dwell**.

dwindle ['dwɪndl] *vi* ir disminuyendo.

dwindling ['dwɪndlɪŋ] *adj* decreciente.

dye [daɪ] ◇ *n* tinte *m*, colorante *m*. ◇ *vt* teñir; **to dye one's hair** teñirse el pelo.

dyed [daɪd] *adj* teñido(da).

dying ['daɪɪŋ] ◇ *cont* ▷ **die**. ◇ *adj* - **1.** [person, animal] moribundo(da) - **2.** [activity, practice] en vías de desaparición. ◇ *npl*: **the dying** los moribundos.

dyke [daɪk] = **dike**.

dynamic [daɪ'næmɪk] *adj* dinámico(ca).
➡ **dynamics** *npl* dinámica *f*.

dynamism ['daɪnəmɪzm] *n* dinamismo *m*.

dynamite ['daɪnəmaɪt] ◇ *n lit* & *fig* dinamita *f*. ◇ *vt* dinamitar.

dynamo ['daɪnəməʊ] (*pl* -s) *n* dinamo *f*.

dynasty [*UK* 'dɪnəstɪ, *US* 'daɪnəstɪ] (*pl* -ies) *n* dinastía *f*.

dysentery ['dɪsntrɪ] *n* disentería *f*.

dysfunctional [dɪs'fʌŋkʃənəl] *adj* disfuncional.

dyslexia [dɪs'leksɪə] *n* dislexia *f*.

dyslexic [dɪs'leksɪk] *adj* disléxico(ca).

dyspepsia [dɪs'pepsɪə] *n* dispepsia *f*.

dystrophy ['dɪstrəfɪ] ▷ **muscular dystrophy**.

E

e (*pl* **e's** OR **es**), **E** (*pl* **E's** OR **Es**) [i:] *n* [letter] e *f*, E *f*.

◆ **E** *n* **- 1.** MUS mi *m* **- 2.** SCH [mark] ≃ suspenso *m* **- 3.** (*abbr of* **east**) E *m* **- 4.** *inf* [drug] (*abbr of* **ecstasy**) extasis *m inv*.

ea. (*abbr of* **each**) c/u; **£3.00 ea.** 3 libras cada uno.

each [i:tʃ] ◇ *adj* cada. ◇ *pron* cada uno *m*, una *f*; **one each** uno cada uno; **each of us/the boys** cada uno de nosotros/los niños; **two of each** dos de cada (uno); **each other** el uno al otro; **they kissed each other** se besaron; **we know each other** nos conocemos.

e-account *n* cuenta *f* electrónica.

eager ['i:gəʳ] *adj* [pupil] entusiasta; [smile, expression] de entusiasmo; **to be eager for sthg/to do sthg** estar ansioso(sa) por algo/por hacer algo.

eagerly ['i:gəlı] *adv* con entusiasmo; **eagerly awaited** largamente esperado(da).

eagle ['i:gl] *n* águila *f*.

eagle-eyed [-'aɪd] *adj* con ojos de lince.

eaglet ['i:glɪt] *n* aguilucho *m*.

ear [ɪəʳ] *n* **- 1.** [outer part] oreja *f*; [inner part] oído *m*; **to go in one ear and out the other** *inf* entrar por un oído y salir por el otro; **to have** OR **keep one's ear to the ground** *inf* mantenerse al corriente **- 2.** *fig* [attention] atención *f* **- 3.** *fig* [talent]: **to have an ear for** tener oído para **- 4.** [of corn] espiga *f* **- 5.** MUS: **by ear** de oído; **to play it by ear** *fig* improvisar sobre la marcha.

earache ['ɪəreɪk] *n* dolor *m* de oídos.

eardrum ['ɪədrʌm] *n* tímpano *m*.

earl [ɜ:l] *n* conde *m*.

earlier ['ɜ:lɪəʳ] ◇ *adj* anterior. ◇ *adv* antes; **earlier on** antes.

earliest ['ɜ:lɪəst] ◇ *adj* primero(ra). ◇ *n*: **at the earliest** como muy pronto.

earlobe ['ɪələub] *n* lóbulo *m* (de la oreja).

early ['ɜ:lɪ] ◇ *adj* (*comp* **-ier**, *superl* **-iest**) **- 1.** [before expected time, in day] temprano(na); **she was early** llegó temprano; **I'll take an early lunch** almorzaré pronto OR temprano; **to get up early** madrugar **- 2.** [at beginning]: **early morning** la madrugada; **the early**

chapters los primeros capítulos; **her early life** los primeros años de su vida; **in the early 1950s** a principios de los años 50. ◇ *adv* **- 1.** [before expected time] temprano, pronto; **we got up early** nos levantamos temprano; **it arrived ten minutes early** llegó con diez minutos de adelanto **- 2.** [at beginning]: **as early as 1920** ya en 1920; **early this morning** esta mañana temprano; **early in the year** a principios de año; **early in the book** al comienzo del libro; **early on** temprano.

early retirement *n* prejubilación *f*, jubilación *f* anticipada.

early warning system *n* MIL sistema *m* de alerta precoz.

earmark ['ɪəmɑ:k] *vt*: **to be earmarked for** estar destinado(da) a.

earn [ɜ:n] *vt* **- 1.** [be paid] ganar **- 2.** [generate - subj: business, product] generar **- 3.** *fig* [gain - respect, praise] ganarse.

earned income [ɜ:nd-] *n* rentas *fpl* del trabajo.

earner ['ɜ:nəʳ] *n* fuente *f* de ingresos.

earnest ['ɜ:nɪst] *adj* [gen] serio(ria); [wish] sincero(ra).

◆ **in earnest** ◇ *adj* serio(ria). ◇ *adv* [seriously] en serio.

earnestly ['ɜ:nɪstlɪ] *adv* [talk] seriamente; [wish] sinceramente.

earnings ['ɜ:nɪŋz] *npl* [of person] ingresos *mpl*; [of company] ganancias *fpl*.

earnings-related *adj* proporcional a los ingresos.

ear, nose and throat specialist *n* otorrinolaringólogo *m*, -ga *f*.

earphones ['ɪəfəunz] *npl* auriculares *mpl*.

earplugs ['ɪəplʌgz] *npl* tapones *mpl* para los oídos.

earring ['ɪərɪŋ] *n* pendiente *m*, arete *m* Amér.

earshot ['ɪəʃɒt] *n*: **within/out of earshot** al alcance/fuera del alcance del oído.

ear-splitting *adj* ensordecedor(ra).

earth [ɜ:θ] ◇ *n* **- 1.** [gen] tierra *f*; **how/what/where/why on earth...?** ¿cómo/qué/dónde/por qué demonios...?; **to cost the earth** UK costar un dineral **- 2.** [in electric plug, appliance] toma *f* de tierra. ◇ *vt* UK: **to be earthed** estar conectado(da) a tierra.

earthenware ['ɜ:θnweəʳ] ◇ *adj* de loza, de barro. ◇ *n* loza *f*.

earthling ['ɜ:θlɪŋ] *n* terrícola *mf*.

earthly ['ɜ:θlɪ] *adj* **- 1.** [of material world] terrenal **- 2.** *inf* [possible] posible; **what earthly reason could she have for doing it?** ¿a cuento de qué haría lo que hizo?

earthquake ['ɜ:θkweɪk] *n* terremoto *m*.

earthshattering ['ɜ:θ,ʃætərɪŋ] adj UK inf extra-ordinario(ria).

earth tremor n temblor m de tierra.

earthward(s) ['ɜ:θwəd(z)] adv hacia la tierra.

earthworks ['ɜ:θwɜ:ks] npl ARCHAEOL terra-plén m.

earthworm ['ɜ:θwɜ:m] n lombriz f (de tierra).

earthy ['ɜ:θɪ] (comp **-ier**, superl **-iest**) adj - **1.** [rather crude] natural, desinhibido(da) - **2.** [of, like earth] terroso(sa).

earwax ['ɪəwæks] n cerumen m.

earwig ['ɪəwɪg] n tijereta f.

ease [i:z] <> n (U) - **1.** [lack of difficulty] facili-dad f; **with ease** con facilidad - **2.** [comfort] comodidad f; **at ease** cómodo(da); **ill at ease** incómodo(da). <> vt - **1.** [pain, grief] calmar, aliviar; [problems, tension] atenuar - **2.** [move carefully]: **to ease sthg open** abrir algo con cui-dado; **to ease o.s. out of sthg** levantarse des-pacio de algo. <> vi [problem] atenuarse; [pain] calmarse; [rain, wind] amainar; [grip] relajarse, aflojarse.

✏ **ease off** vi [problem] atenuarse; [pain] cal-marse; [rain, wind] amainar.

✏ **ease up** vi - **1.** inf [treat less severely]: **to ease up on sb** no ser tan duro(ra) con alguien - **2.** [rain, wind] aflojar, amainar - **3.** [relax - per-son] tomarse las cosas con más calma.

easel ['i:zl] n caballete m.

easily ['i:zɪlɪ] adv - **1.** [without difficulty] fácil-mente - **2.** [without doubt] sin lugar a dudas - **3.** [in a relaxed manner] tranquilamente, rela-jadamente.

easiness ['i:zɪnɪs] n [lack of difficulty] facilidad f.

east [i:st] <> n - **1.** [direction] este m - **2.** [region]: **the east** el este. <> adj oriental; [wind] del es-te. <> adv: **east (of)** al este (de).

✏ **East** n: **the East** POL el Este; [Asia] el Oriente.

eastbound ['i:stbaʊnd] adj con dirección este.

East End n: **the East End** el este de Londres.

Easter ['i:stər] n - **1.** [period] Semana f Santa - **2.** [festival] Pascua f.

Easter egg n huevo m de Pascua.

Easter Island n la isla de Pascua.

easterly ['i:stəlɪ] adj del este; **in an easterly direction** hacia el este.

eastern ['i:stən] adj del este, oriental.

✏ **Eastern** adj [gen & POL] del Este; [from Asia] oriental.

Easter Sunday n Domingo m de Resurrec-ción.

East German <> adj de Alemania Oriental. <> n [person] alemán m, -ana f oriental.

East Germany n: **(the former) East Ger-many** (la antigua) Alemania Oriental.

eastward ['i:stwəd] <> adj hacia el este. <> adv = **eastwards**.

eastwards ['i:stwədz], **eastward** adv hacia el este.

easy ['i:zɪ] <> adj (comp **-ier**, superl **-iest**) - **1.** [not difficult] fácil - **2.** [life, time] cómodo(da) - **3.** [manner] natural, relajado(da). <> adv: **to go easy on sb** inf no ser muy duro(ra) con al-guien; **to go easy on sthg** inf no pasarse con algo; **to take it OR things easy** tomarse las co-sas con calma.

easy-care adj UK no delicado(da).

easy chair n [armchair] sillón m, butaca f.

easygoing [,i:zɪ'gəʊɪŋ] adj [person] tolerante, tranquilo(la); [manner] relajado(da).

easy-peasy n inf hum chupado(da).

eat [i:t] (pt ate, pp eaten) vt & vi comer.

✏ **eat away, eat into** vt sep - **1.** [corrode] co-rroer - **2.** [deplete] mermar.

✏ **eat out** vi comer fuera.

✏ **eat up** vt sep - **1.** [food] comerse - **2.** [money, time] consumir un montón de.

eatable ['i:təbl] adj comible, comestible.

eaten ['i:tn] pp ⊳ **eat**.

eater ['i:tər] n: **I'm not a great fruit eater** no como mucha fruta.

eatery ['i:tərɪ] n US restaurante m.

eating apple ['i:tɪŋ-] n manzana f (para co-mer).

eau de cologne [,əʊdəkə'ləʊn] n (agua f de) co-lonia f.

eaves ['i:vz] npl alero m.

eavesdrop ['i:vzdrop] (pt & pp **-ped**, cont **-ping**) vi: **to eavesdrop (on)** escuchar secretamente (a).

e-banking n banca f electrónica.

ebb [eb] <> n reflujo m; **the ebb and flow of** fig los altibajos de; **at a low ebb** fig de capa caída. <> vi - **1.** [tide, sea] bajar - **2.** liter [strength, pain, feeling]: **to ebb (away)** decrecer, disminuir.

ebb tide n marea f baja, bajamar f.

ebony ['ebənɪ] <> adj liter [colour] de color éba-no. <> n ébano m.

ebullient [ɪ'bʊljənt] adj [person] entusiasta; [wit, manner] exuberante.

e-business n - **1.** [company] empresa f elec-trónica - **2.** [electronic commerce] comercio m electrónico.

EC (abbr of European Community) n CE f.

e-cash n dinero m electrónico.

eccentric [ɪk'sentrɪk] <> adj excéntrico(ca). <> n excéntrico m, -ca f.

eccentricity [,eksen'trɪsətɪ] (pl **-ies**) n excentri-cidad f.

ecclesiastic(al) [ɪ,kliːzɪˈæstɪk(l)] *adj* eclesiásti-co(ca).

ECG (*abbr of* **electrocardiogram**) *n* ECG *m*.

ECH UK (*abbr of* **electric central heating**) cal. cent. eléc.

echelon [ˈeʃəlɒn] *n fml* [level in organization] esfe-ra *f*, rango *m*.

echo [ˈekəʊ] ⬦ *n* (*pl* **-es**) *lit* & *fig* eco *m*. ⬦ *vt* (*pt* & *pp* **-ed**, *cont* **-ing**) [words] repetir; [opin-ion] hacerse eco de. ⬦ *vi* (*pt* & *pp* **-ed**, *cont* **-ing**) resonar.

éclair [eɪˈkleəʳ] *n pastelillo relleno de nata*.

eclectic [ɪˈklektɪk] *adj* ecléctico(ca).

eclipse [ɪˈklɪps] ⬦ *n lit* & *fig* eclipse *m*; **a total/partial eclipse** un eclipse total/parcial. ⬦ *vt fig* eclipsar.

eco- [ˈiːkəʊ] (*abbr of* **ecology** *or* **ecological**) *pre-fix* eco-.

eco-friendly [ˈiːkəʊˈfrendlɪ] *adj* ecológico(ca).

ecological [,iːkəˈlɒdʒɪkl] *adj* **- 1.** [pattern, bal-ance, impact] ecológico(ca) **- 2.** [group, move-ment, person] ecologista.

ecologically [,iːkəˈlɒdʒɪklɪ] *adv* ecológicamen-te.

ecologist [ɪˈkɒlədʒɪst] *n* **- 1.** [scientist] ecólo-go *m*, -ga *f* **- 2.** [conservationist] ecologista *mf*.

ecology [ɪˈkɒlədʒɪ] *n* ecología *f*.

e-commerce *n* comercio *m* electrónico.

economic [,iːkəˈnɒmɪk] *adj* **- 1.** [of money, in-dustry] económico(ca) **- 2.** [profitable] rentable.

Economic and Monetary Union *n* Unión *f* Económica y Monetaria.

economical [,iːkəˈnɒmɪkl] *adj* económico(ca); **to be economical with the truth** no decir to-da la verdad.

economics [,iːkəˈnɒmɪks] ⬦ *n* (*U*) economía *f*. ⬦ *npl* [of plan, business] aspecto *m* económico.

economist [ɪˈkɒnəmɪst] *n* economista *mf*.

economize, -ise [ɪˈkɒnəmaɪz] *vi*: **to economize (on)** economizar (en).

economy [ɪˈkɒnəmɪ] (*pl* **-ies**) *n* economía *f*; **eco-nomies of scale** economías *fpl* de escala.

economy class *n* clase *f* turista.

economy-class syndrome *n* síndrome *m* de la clase turista.

economy drive *n* campaña *f* de ahorro.

economy-size(d) *adj* de tamaño económico.

ecosystem [ˈiːkəʊˌsɪstəm] *n* ecosistema *m*.

ecotax [ˈiːkəʊtæks] *n* ecotasa *f*.

ecotourism [,iːkəʊˈtʊərɪzm] *n* ecoturismo *m*.

ECSC (*abbr of* **European Coal & Steel Com-munity**) *n* CECA *f*.

ecstasy [ˈekstəsɪ] (*pl* **-ies**) *n* **- 1.** [great happiness] éxtasis *m inv*; **to go into ecstasies about** ex-tasiarse ante **- 2.** [drug] éxtasis *m inv*.

ecstatic [ek'stætɪk] *adj* extático(ca).

ecstatically [ek'stætɪklɪ] *adv* eufóricamente.

ECT (*abbr of* **electroconvulsive therapy**) *n* te-rapia de electrochoque.

ectoplasm [ˈektəplæzm] *n* ectoplasma *m*.

Ecuador [ˈekwədɔːʳ] *n* (el) Ecuador.

Ecuadoran [,ekwəˈdɔːrən], **Ecuadorian** [,ekwəˈdɔːrɪən] ⬦ *adj* ecuatoriano(na). ⬦ *n* ecuatoriano *m*, -na *f*.

ecumenical [iːkjʊˈmenɪkl] *adj* ecuménico(ca).

eczema [ˈeksɪmə] *n* eccema *m*, eczema *m*.

ed. - 1. (*abbr of* **edition**) ed. **- 2.** (*abbr of* **edit-or**) ed.

eddy [ˈedɪ] ⬦ *n* (*pl* **-ies**) remolino *m*. ⬦ *vi* (*pt* & *pp* **-ied**) arremolinarse.

Eden [ˈiːdn] *n*: **(the Garden of) Eden** (el jardín del) Edén *m*.

edge [edʒ] ⬦ *n* **- 1.** [of cliff, table, garden] bor-de *m*; **to be on the edge of** estar al borde de **- 2.** [of coin] canto *m*; [of knife] filo *m* **- 3.** [ad-vantage]: **to have an edge over** OR **the edge on** llevar ventaja a **- 4.** *fig* [sharpness - of voice] nota *f* de enfado, aspereza *f*. ⬦ *vi*: **to edge towards** ir poco a poco hacia; **to edge away/closer** ir alejándose/acercándose poco a po-co.
◆ **on edge** *adj* con los nervios de punta.

edged [edʒd] *adj*: **edged with** [trees] bordea-do(da) de; [lace, gold] ribeteado(da) de.

edgeways [ˈedʒweɪz], **edgewise** [ˈedʒwaɪz] *adv* de lado.

edging [ˈedʒɪŋ] *n* ribete *m*, orla *f*.

edgy [ˈedʒɪ] (*comp* **-ier**, *superl* **-iest**) *adj* ner-vioso(sa).

edible [ˈedɪbl] *adj* comestible.

edict [ˈiːdɪkt] *n* edicto *m*.

edifice [ˈedɪfɪs] *n fml* edificio *m* imponente.

edify [ˈedɪfaɪ] (*pt* & *pp* **-ied**) *vt fml* edificar.

edifying [ˈedɪfaɪɪŋ] *adj fml* edificante.

Edinburgh [ˈedɪnbrə] *n* Edimburgo.

edit [ˈedɪt] *vt* **- 1.** [correct - text] corregir, revisar **- 2.** COMPUT editar **- 3.** [select material for - book] editar **- 4.** CIN, RADIO & TV montar **- 5.** [run - news-paper, magazine] dirigir.
◆ **edit out** *vt sep* eliminar.

edition [ɪˈdɪʃn] *n* edición *f*.

editor [ˈedɪtəʳ] *n* **- 1.** [of newspaper, magazine] di-rector *m*, -ra *f* **- 2.** [of section of newspaper, pro-gramme, text] redactor *m*, -ra *f* **- 3.** [compiler - of book] editor *m*, -ra *f* **- 4.** CIN, RADIO & TV monta-dor *m*, -ra *f* **- 5.** COMPUT editor *m*.

editorial [,edɪˈtɔːrɪəl] ⬦ *adj* editorial; **editorial staff** redacción *f*. ⬦ *n* editorial *m*.

EDT (*abbr of* **Eastern Daylight Time**) *n hora de verano de Nueva York*.

educate ['edʒukeɪt] *vt* - **1.** [at school, college] educar - **2.** [inform] informar.

educated ['edʒukeɪtɪd] *adj* - **1.** [person] culto(ta) - **2.** [guess] bien fundado(da).

education [,edʒu'keɪʃn] *n (U)* - **1.** [activity, sector] enseñanza *f* - **2.** [process or result of teaching] educación *f*.

educational [,edʒu'keɪʃənl] *adj* educativo(va); [establishment] docente.

educationalist [,edʒu'keɪʃnəlɪst] *n* pedagogo *m*, -ga *f*.

educative ['edʒukətɪv] *adj fml* educativo(va).

educator ['edʒukeɪtər] *n esp US fml* educador *m*, -ra *f*.

edutainment [edʒ'teɪnmənt] *n* juegos *mpl* educativos.

Edwardian [ed'wɔːdɪən] *adj* eduardiano(na).

EEC (*abbr of* **European Economic Community**) *n* CEE *f*.

EEG (*abbr of* **electroencephalogram**) *n* EEG *m*.

eel [iːl] *n* anguila *f*.

EENT (*abbr of* **eye, ear, nose and throat**) *n* otorrinolaringología y ojos.

EET (*abbr of* **Eastern European Time**) *n* hora de Europa oriental.

efface [ɪ'feɪs] *vt* borrar.

effect [ɪ'fekt] <> *n* efecto *m*; **to have an effect on** tener OR surtir efecto en; **to do sthg for effect** hacer algo para causar efecto; **to take effect** [law, rule] entrar en vigor; [drug] hacer efecto; **to put sthg into effect** poner algo en práctica; **to the effect that** en el sentido de que; **to that effect** a tal efecto; **words to that effect** palabras por el estilo. <> *vt* efectuar, llevar a cabo.

◆ **effects** *npl*: **(special) effects** efectos *mpl* especiales.

effective [ɪ'fektɪv] *adj* - **1.** [successful] eficaz - **2.** [actual, real] efectivo(va) - **3.** [law, ceasefire] operativo(va).

effectively [ɪ'fektɪvlɪ] *adv* - **1.** [well, successfully] eficazmente - **2.** [in fact] de hecho.

effectiveness [ɪ'fektɪvnɪs] *n* eficacia *f*.

effeminate [ɪ'femɪnət] *adj pej* afeminado(da).

effervesce [,efə'ves] *vi* estar en efervescencia.

effervescent [,efə'vesənt] *adj* efervescente.

effete [ɪ'fiːt] *adj pej* [weak, effeminate] afeminado(da).

efficacious [efɪ'keɪʃəs] *adj fml* eficaz.

efficacy ['efɪkəsɪ] *n* eficacia *f*.

efficiency [ɪ'fɪʃənsɪ] *n* [gen] eficiencia *f*; [of machine] rendimiento *m*.

efficient [ɪ'fɪʃənt] *adj* [gen] eficiente; [machine] de buen rendimiento.

efficiently [ɪ'fɪʃəntlɪ] *adv* [competently] con eficiencia, eficientemente.

effigy ['efɪdʒɪ] (*pl* **-ies**) *n* efigie *f*.

effluent ['efluənt] *n* aguas *fpl* residuales.

effort ['efət] *n* - **1.** [gen] esfuerzo *m*; **to be worth the effort** merecer la pena; **with effort** con esfuerzo; **to make the effort to do sthg** hacer el esfuerzo de hacer algo; **to make an/no effort to do sthg** hacer un esfuerzo/no hacer ningún esfuerzo por hacer algo - **2.** *inf* [result of trying] tentativa *f*.

effortless ['efətlɪs] *adj* fácil, sin gran esfuerzo.

effortlessly ['efətlɪslɪ] *adv* sin esfuerzo alguno, fácilmente.

effrontery [ɪ'frʌntərɪ] *n* descaro *m*.

effusive [ɪ'fjuːsɪv] *adj* efusivo(va).

effusively [ɪ'fjuːsɪvlɪ] *adv* efusivamente.

EFL ['efəl, ,iːef'el] (*abbr of* **English as a foreign language**) *n* inglés para extranjeros.

EFTA ['eftə] (*abbr of* **European Free Trade Association**) *n* EFTA *f*.

e.g. (*abbr of* **exempli gratia**) *adv* p. ej.

egalitarian [ɪ,gælɪ'teərɪən] *adj* igualitario(ria).

egg [eg] *n* - **1.** [gen] huevo *m*, blanquillo *m Amér C & Méx* - **2.** [ovum] óvulo *m*.

◆ **egg on** *vt sep* incitar.

eggcup ['egkʌp] *n* huevera *f*.

eggplant ['egplɑːnt] *n US* berenjena *f*.

eggshell ['egʃel] *n* cáscara *f* de huevo.

egg timer *n* reloj *m* de arena.

egg whisk *n* batidor *m* (de huevos), varilla *f*.

egg white *n* clara *f* (de huevo).

egg yolk [-jəuk] *n* yema *f* (de huevo).

ego ['iːgəu] (*pl* **-s**) *n* - **1.** [opinion of self] amor *m* propio - **2.** [psych] ego *m*.

egocentric [,iːgəu'sentrɪk] *adj* egocéntrico(ca).

egoism ['iːgəuɪzm] *n* egoísmo *m*.

egoist ['iːgəuɪst] *n* egoísta *mf*.

egoistic [,iːgəu'ɪstɪk] *adj* egoísta.

egotism ['iːgətɪzm] *n* egotismo *m*.

egotist ['iːgətɪst] *n* egotista *mf*.

egotistic(al) [,iːgə'tɪstɪk(l)] *adj* egotista.

ego trip *n inf*: **to be on an ego trip** estar haciendo algo que hace creerse a uno el ombligo del mundo.

Egypt ['iːdʒɪpt] *n* Egipto.

Egyptian [ɪ'dʒɪpʃn] <> *adj* egipcio(cia). <> *n* [person] egipcio *m*, -cia *f*.

eh [eɪ] *excl UK inf* - **1.** [inviting reply, agreement] ¿no?, ¿verdad? - **2.** [asking for repeat] ¿cómo?, ¿qué?

eiderdown ['aɪdədaun] *n esp UK* edredón *m*.

eight [eɪt] *num* ocho; *see also* **six**.

eighteen [,eɪ'tiːn] *num* dieciocho; *see also* **six**.

eighteenth [ˌeɪˈtiːnθ] *num* decimoctavo(va); *see also* **sixth**.

eighth [eɪtθ] *num* octavo(va); *see also* **sixth**.

eightieth [ˈeɪtɪɪθ] *num* octogésimo(ma); *see also* **sixth**.

eighty [ˈeɪtɪ] (*pl* **-ies**) *num* ochenta; *see also* **sixty**.

Eire [ˈeərə] *n* Eire.

either [ˈaɪðəʳ ˈiːðəʳ] <> *adj* - **1.** [one or the other] cualquiera de los dos; **she couldn't find either jumper** no podía encontrar ninguno de los dos jerseys; **you can do it either way** lo puedes hacer como quieras; **I don't care either way** me da igual - **2.** [each] cada; **on either side** a ambos lados. <> *pron*: **either (of them)** cualquiera de ellos(ellas); **I don't like either (of them)** no me gusta ninguno de ellos (ninguna de ellas). <> *adv* (in negatives) tampoco; **she can't and I can't either** ella no puede y yo tampoco. <> *conj*: **either... or...** o... o; **either you or me** o tú o yo; **I don't like either him or his wife** no me gusta ni él ni su mujer.

ejaculate [ɪˈdʒækjʊleɪt] <> *vt* [exclaim] exclamar. <> *vi* [have orgasm] eyacular.

eject [ɪˈdʒekt] *vt* - **1.** [object] expulsar - **2.** [person]: **to eject sb (from)** expulsar a alguien (de).

ejector seat *UK* [ɪˈdʒektəʳ-], **ejection seat** *US* [ɪˈdʒekʃn-] *n* asiento *m* eyectable.

eke [iːk] ◆ **eke out** <> *vt sep* [money, supply] estirar. <> *vt insep*: **to eke out a living** ganarse la vida a duras penas.

EKG (*abbr of* **electrocardiogram**) *n US* ECG *m*.

elaborate <> *adj* [ɪˈlæbrət] [ceremony] complicado(da); [carving] trabajado(da); [explanation, plan] detallado(da). <> *vi* [ɪˈlæbəreɪt]: **to elaborate on sthg** ampliar algo, explicar algo con más detalle.

elaborately [ɪˈlæbərətlɪ] *adv* [decorate] laboriosamente, profusamente; [plan] detalladamente.

elapse [ɪˈlæps] *vi* transcurrir.

elastic [ɪˈlæstɪk] <> *adj* - **1.** [gen] elástico(ca) - **2.** *fig* [flexible] flexible. <> *n* elástico *m*.

elasticated [ɪˈlæstɪkeɪtɪd] *adj* elástico(ca).

elastic band *n UK* gomita *f*, goma *f* (elástica).

elasticity [ˌelæˈstɪsətɪ] *n* [stretchiness] elasticidad *f*.

elated [ɪˈleɪtɪd] *adj* eufórico(ca).

elation [ɪˈleɪʃn] *n* euforia *f*, regocijo *m*.

elbow [ˈelbəʊ] <> *n* codo *m*. <> *vt*: **to elbow sb aside** apartar a alguien a codazos.

elbow grease *n inf*: he put a lot of elbow grease into polishing the silver se empleó a fondo limpiando la plata.

elbowroom [ˈelbəʊrʊm] *n inf* espacio *m* (libre), sitio *m*.

elder [ˈeldəʳ] <> *adj* mayor. <> *n* - **1.** [older person] mayor *mf* - **2.** [of tribe, church] anciano *m* - **3.**: **elder (tree)** saúco *m*.

elderberry [ˈeldəˌberɪ] (*pl* **-ies**) *n* baya *f* de saúco.

elderly [ˈeldəlɪ] <> *adj* mayor, anciano(na). <> *npl*: **the elderly** los ancianos.

elder statesman *n* antiguo mandatario *m*.

eldest [ˈeldɪst] *adj* mayor.

elect [ɪˈlekt] <> *adj* electo(ta); **the president elect** el presidente electo. <> *vt* - **1.** [by voting] elegir; **to elect sb (as) sthg** elegir a alguien (como) algo - **2.** *fml* [choose]: **to elect to do sthg** optar por *OR* decidir hacer algo.

elected [ɪˈlektɪd] *adj* elegido(da).

election [ɪˈlekʃn] *n* elección *f*; **to have** *OR* **hold an election** celebrar (unas) elecciones; **local elections** elecciones *fpl* municipales.

election campaign *n* campaña *f* electoral.

electioneering [ɪˌlekʃəˈnɪərɪŋ] *n pej* electoralismo *m*.

elective [ɪˈlektɪv] *n US & Scotland* SCH & UNIV materia *f* optativa.

elector [ɪˈlektəʳ] *n* elector *m*, -ra *f*.

electoral [ɪˈlektərəl] *adj* electoral.

electoral college *n cuerpo de compromisarios de un colegio electoral*.

electoral register, electoral roll *n*: **the electoral register** el censo electoral.

electorate [ɪˈlektərət] *n*: **the electorate** el electorado.

electric [ɪˈlektrɪk] *adj* - **1.** [gen] eléctrico(ca) - **2.** *fig* [exciting] electrizante. ◆ **electrics** *npl UK inf* sistema *m* eléctrico.

electrical [ɪˈlektrɪkl] *adj* eléctrico(ca).

electrical engineer *n* ingeniero *m*, -ra *f* en electrónica.

electrical engineering *n* ingeniería *f* eléctrica, electrotecnia *f*.

electrically [ɪˈlektrɪklɪ] *adv* por electricidad.

electrical shock *US* = **electric shock**.

electric blanket *n* manta *f* eléctrica, frazada *f* eléctrica *Amér*, cobija *f* eléctrica *Amér*.

electric chair *n*: **the electric chair** la silla eléctrica.

electric cooker *n* cocina *f* eléctrica.

electric current *n* corriente *f* eléctrica.

electric fire *n* estufa *f* eléctrica.

electric guitar *n* guitarra *f* eléctrica.

electrician [ˌɪlekˈtrɪʃn] *n* electricista *mf*.

electricity [ˌɪlekˈtrɪsətɪ] *n* electricidad *f*.

electric light *n* luz *f* eléctrica.

electric shock UK**, electrical shock** US n descarga f eléctrica.

electric shock therapy n terapia f de electrochoque.

electric storm n tormenta f eléctrica.

electrify [ɪ'lektrɪfaɪ] (pt & pp -ied) vt **- 1.** [rail line] electrificar **- 2.** fig [excite] electrizar.

electrifying [ɪ'lektrɪfaɪŋ] adj electrizante.

electro- [ɪ'lektrəʊ] prefix electro-.

electrocardiograph [ɪ,lektrəʊ'kɑːdɪəgrɑːf] n electrocardiógrafo m.

electrocute [ɪ'lektrəkjuːt] vt electrocutar; **to electrocute o.s., to be electrocuted** electrocutarse.

electrode [ɪ'lektrəʊd] n electrodo m.

electrolysis [,ɪlek'trɒləsɪs] n electrólisis f inv.

electromagnetic [ɪ,lektrəʊmæg'netɪk] adj electromagnético(ca).

electron [ɪ'lektrɒn] n electrón m.

electronic [,ɪlek'trɒnɪk] adj electrónico(ca).
◆ **electronics** ◇ n (U) [technology] electrónica f. ◇ npl [equipment] sistema m electrónico.

electronic banking n banca f electrónica.

electronic data processing n proceso m electrónico de datos.

electronic mail n correo m electrónico.

electronic mailbox n buzón m electrónico.

electronic tag n brazalete m electrónico (que permite conocer la localización de presos en libertad condicional).

electronic tagging n sistema electrónico que permite conocer la localización de presos en libertad condicional gracias al brazalete electrónico que están obligados a llevar.

electroplated [ɪ'lektrəʊ,pleɪtɪd] adj galvanizado(da).

elegance ['elɪgəns] n elegancia f.

elegant ['elɪgənt] adj elegante, elegantoso(sa) Amér.

elegantly ['elɪgəntlɪ] adv elegantemente, con elegancia.

elegy ['elɪdʒɪ] (pl -ies) n elegía f.

element ['elɪmənt] n **- 1.** [gen] elemento m **- 2.** [amount, proportion] toque m, matiz m **- 3.** [in heater, kettle] resistencia f
▸▸ **to be in one's element** estar en su elemento.
◆ **elements** npl **- 1.** [basics] elementos mpl **- 2.** [weather]: **the elements** los elementos.

elementary [,elɪ'mentərɪ] adj elemental; **elementary education** enseñanza f primaria.

elementary school n US escuela f primaria.

elephant ['elɪfənt] (pl **elephant** OR **-s**) n elefante m.

elevate ['elɪveɪt] vt: **to elevate sthg/sb (to** OR **into)** elevar algo/a alguien (a la categoría de).

elevated ['elɪveɪtɪd] adj fml elevado(da).

elevation [,elɪ'veɪʃn] n fml **- 1.** [promotion] elevación f **- 2.** [height] altura f, altitud f.

elevator ['elɪveɪtər] n US ascensor m, elevador m Méx.

eleven [ɪ'levn] num once m; see also **six**.

elevenses [ɪ'levnzɪz] n (U) UK tentempié m (que se toma sobre las once de la mañana).

eleventh [ɪ'levnθ] num undécimo(ma); see also **sixth**.

eleventh hour n fig: **at the eleventh hour** en el último momento.

elf [elf] (pl **elves**) n duende m, elfo m.

elicit [ɪ'lɪsɪt] vt fml **- 1.** [response, reaction]: **to elicit sthg (from sb)** provocar algo (en alguien) **- 2.** [information]: **to elicit sthg (from sb)** sacar algo (a alguien).

eligibility [,elɪdʒə'bɪlətɪ] n **- 1.** [suitability] elegibilidad f **- 2.** dated [of bachelor] idoneidad f.

eligible ['elɪdʒəbl] adj **- 1.** [suitable, qualified] elegible; **to be eligible for sthg/to do sthg** reunir los requisitos para algo/para hacer algo **- 2.** dated [marriageable]: **to be eligible** ser un buen partido.

eliminate [ɪ'lɪmɪneɪt] vt eliminar; **to be eliminated from sthg** ser eliminado(da) de algo.

elimination [ɪ,lɪmɪ'neɪʃn] n eliminación f.

elite [ɪ'liːt] ◇ adj selecto(ta). ◇ n élite f.

elitism [ɪ'liːtɪzm] n pej elitismo m.

elitist [ɪ'liːtɪst] pej ◇ adj elitista. ◇ n elitista mf.

elixir [ɪ'lɪksər] n liter lit & fig elixir m.

Elizabethan [ɪ,lɪzə'biːθn] ◇ adj isabelino(na). ◇ n isabelino m, -na f.

elk [elk] (pl **elk** OR **-s**) n **- 1.** [in Europe] alce m **- 2.** [in North America] ciervo m canadiense.

ellipse [ɪ'lɪps] n elipse f.

elliptical [ɪ'lɪptɪkl] adj elíptico(ca).

elm [elm] n: **elm (tree)** olmo m.

elocution [,elə'kjuːʃn] n dicción f.

elongated ['iːlɒŋgeɪtɪd] adj alargado(da).

elope [ɪ'ləʊp] vi: **to elope (with)** fugarse (con).

elopement [ɪ'ləʊpmənt] n fuga f.

eloquence ['eləkwəns] n elocuencia f.

eloquent ['eləkwənt] adj elocuente.

eloquently ['eləkwəntlɪ] adv elocuentemente.

El Salvador [,el'sælvədɔːr] n El Salvador.

else [els] adv: **anything else?** ¿algo más?; **I don't need anything else** no necesito nada más; **everyone else** todos los demás(todas las demás); **everywhere else** en OR a cualquier otra parte; **little else** poco más; **nothing/nobody else** nada/nadie más; **someone/**

something else otra persona/cosa; **somewhere else** en OR a otro sitio; **who else?** ¿quién si no?; **who else came?** ¿quién más vino?; **what else?** ¿qué más?; **where else?** ¿en OR a qué otro sitio?

or else conj - **1.** [or if not] si no, de lo contrario - **2.** [as threat]: **you had better watch it, or else** ándate con cuidado, o verás.

elsewhere [els'weəʳ] adv a OR en otro sitio.

ELT (abbr of English language teaching) n enseñanza del inglés.

elucidate [ɪ'luːsɪdeɪt] fml <> vt elucidar. <> vi aclararlo.

elude [ɪ'luːd] vt [gen] escaparse de, eludir a; [blow] esquivar; **his name eludes me** no consigo recordar su nombre.

elusive [ɪ'luːsɪv] adj [person, success] esquivo(va); [quality] difícil de encontrar.

elves [elvz] ▷ elf.

'em [əm] pron inf abbr of them.

emaciated [ɪ'meɪʃɪeɪtɪd] adj demacrado(da).

e-mail (abbr of electronic mail) <> n COMPUT correo m electrónico; **e-mail account** cuenta f de correo electrónico; **e-mail address** dirección f electrónica; **e-mail phone** teléfono m con correo electrónico. <> vt - **1.** COMPUT [document] enviar por correo electrónico - **2.** COMPUT [person] enviar un correo electrónico a.

emanate ['eməneɪt] fml <> vt emanar. <> vi: to **emanate from** emanar de.

emancipate [ɪ'mænsɪpeɪt] vt: to **emancipate sb (from)** emancipar a alguien (de).

emancipation [ɪ,mænsɪ'peɪʃn] n: **emancipation (from)** emancipación f (de).

emasculate [ɪ'mæskjʊleɪt] vt fml [weaken] debilitar, minar.

emasculation [ɪ,mæskjʊ'leɪʃn] n fml [weakening] debilitación f.

embalm [ɪm'baːm] vt embalsamar.

embankment [ɪm'bæŋkmənt] n - **1.** RAIL terraplén m - **2.** [of river] dique m.

embargo [em'baːgəʊ] <> n (pl -es): **embargo (on)** embargo m OR prohibición f (de). <> vt (pt & pp -ed, cont -ing) prohibir.

embark [ɪm'baːk] vi embarcar; to **embark on** fig embarcarse en.

embarkation [,embaː'keɪʃn] n [gen] embarque m; [of troops] embarco m.

embarkation card n UK tarjeta f de embarque.

embarrass [ɪm'bærəs] vt - **1.** [gen] avergonzar; **it embarrasses me** me da vergüenza - **2.** [financially] poner en un aprieto.

embarrassed [ɪm'bærəst] adj [ashamed] avergonzado(da); [uneasy] violento(ta).

embarrassing [ɪm'bærəsɪŋ] adj embarazoso(sa), violento(ta); **how embarrassing!** ¡qué vergüenza!

embarrassment [ɪm'bærəsmənt] n - **1.** [feeling] vergüenza f, pena f Andes, Amér C & Méx - **2.** [embarrassing person or thing]: to **be an embarrassment to sb** ser motivo de vergüenza para alguien.

embassy ['embəsɪ] (pl -ies) n embajada f.

embattled [ɪm'bætld] adj [troubled] asediado(da), acosado(da).

embedded [ɪm'bedɪd] adj - **1.** [buried & COMPUT]: **embedded (in)** incrustado(da) (en) - **2.** [ingrained]: **embedded (in)** arraigado(da) (en).

embellish [ɪm'belɪʃ] vt: to **embellish sthg (with)** adornar algo (con).

embers ['embəz] npl brasas fpl, rescoldos mpl.

embezzle [ɪm'bezl] vt malversar.

embezzlement [ɪm'bezlmənt] n malversación f.

embezzler [ɪm'bezləʳ] n malversador m, -ra f.

embittered [ɪm'bɪtəd] adj amargado(da), resentido(da).

emblazoned [ɪm'bleɪznd] adj - **1.** [in heraldry]: **emblazoned (on/with)** blasonado(da) (en/con) - **2.** [shown prominently]: **emblazoned across** estampado(da) en.

emblem ['embləm] n emblema m.

embodiment [ɪm'bɒdɪmənt] n personificación f, encarnación f.

embody [ɪm'bɒdɪ] (pt & pp -ied) vt personificar, encarnar; to **be embodied in sthg** estar plasmado en algo.

embolism ['embəlɪzm] n embolia f.

embossed [ɪm'bɒst] adj - **1.** [heading, design]: **embossed (on)** [paper] estampado(da) (en); [leather, metal] repujado(da) (en) - **2.** [paper]: **embossed (with)** estampado(da) (con) - **3.** [leather, metal]: **embossed (with)** repujado(da) (con).

embrace [ɪm'breɪs] <> n abrazo m. <> vt - **1.** [hug] abrazar, dar un abrazo a - **2.** fml [convert to] convertirse a, abrazar - **3.** fml [include] abarcar. <> vi abrazarse.

embrocation [,embrə'keɪʃn] n fml linimento m.

embroider [ɪm'brɔɪdəʳ] <> vt - **1.** SEW bordar - **2.** pej [embellish] adornar. <> vi SEW bordar.

embroidered [ɪm'brɔɪdəd] adj SEW bordado(da).

embroidery [ɪm'brɔɪdərɪ] n (U) bordado m.

embroil [ɪm'brɔɪl] vt: to **get/be embroiled (in)** enredarse/estar enredado(da) (en).

embryo ['embrɪəʊ] (pl -s) n embrión m; **in embryo** fig en estado embrionario.

embryonic [,embrɪ'ɒnɪk] adj fig en estado embrionario.

emcee [ˌemˈsiː] (*abbr of* master of ceremonies) *n inf* presentador *m*, -ra *f*.

emend [ɪˈmend] *vt* enmendar, corregir.

emerald [ˈemərəld] <> *adj* [colour] esmeralda *m inv*; **emerald green** verde *m* esmeralda; **the Emerald Isle** Irlanda. <> *n* [stone] esmeralda *f*.

emerge [ɪˈmɜːdʒ] <> *vi* - **1.** [gen]: **to emerge (from)** salir (de) - **2.** [come into existence, become known] surgir, emerger. <> *vt*: **it emerged that...** resultó que...

emergence [ɪˈmɜːdʒəns] *n* surgimiento *m*, aparición *f*.

emergency [ɪˈmɜːdʒənsɪ] <> *adj* [case, exit] de emergencia; [ward, services] de urgencia; [supplies] de reserva; [meeting] extraordinario(ria). <> *n* (*pl* **-ies**) emergencia *f*.

emergency exit *n* salida *f* de emergencia.

emergency landing *n* aterrizaje *m* forzoso.

emergency room *n US* (sala *f* de) urgencias *fpl*.

emergency services *npl* servicios *mpl* de urgencia.

emergency stop *n* parada *f* en seco.

emergent [ɪˈmɜːdʒənt] *adj* pujante, emergente.

emery board [ˈemərɪ-] *n* lima *f* de uñas.

emetic [ɪˈmetɪk] <> *adj* emético(ca). <> *n* emético *m*.

emigrant [ˈemɪɡrənt] *n* emigrante *mf*.

emigrate [ˈemɪɡreɪt] *vi*: **to emigrate (to/from)** emigrar (a/de).

emigration [ˌemɪˈɡreɪʃn] *n* emigración *f*.

émigré [ˈemɪɡreɪ] *n fml* emigrado político *m*, emigrada política *f*.

eminence [ˈemɪnəns] *n (U)* [prominence] eminencia *f*.

eminent [ˈemɪnənt] *adj* eminente.

eminently [ˈemɪnəntlɪ] *adv fml* eminentemente, sumamente.

emir [eˈmɪəʳ] *n* emir *m*.

emirate [ˈemərət] *n* emirato *m*.

emissary [ˈemɪsərɪ] (*pl* **-ies**) *n fml* emisario *m*, -ria *f*.

emission [ɪˈmɪʃn] *n* emisión *f*.

emit [ɪˈmɪt] (*pt* & *pp* **-ted**, *cont* **-ting**) *vt* [gen] emitir; [smell, smoke] despedir.

emollient [ɪˈmɒlɪənt] *n* MED emoliente *m*.

emolument [ɪˈmɒljʊmənt] *n fml* emolumento *m*.

emoticon [ɪˈməʊtɪkɒn] *n* COMPUT emoticono *m*.

emotion [ɪˈməʊʃn] *n* emoción *f*.

emotional [ɪˈməʊʃənl] *adj* - **1.** [gen] emotivo(va) - **2.** [needs, problems] emocional; **to get emotional** emocionarse.

emotionally [ɪˈməʊʃnəlɪ] *adv* - **1.** [with strong feeling] emotivamente - **2.** [psychologically] emocionalmente.

emotionless [ɪˈməʊʃnlɪs] *adj* desapasionado(da).

emotive [ɪˈməʊtɪv] *adj* emotivo(va); [issue] que despierta pasiones.

empathize, -ise [ˈempəθaɪz] *vi*: **to empathize (with)** identificarse (con).

empathy [ˈempəθɪ] *n*: **empathy (with)** empatía *f* (con).

emperor [ˈempərəʳ] *n* emperador *m*.

emphasis [ˈemfəsɪs] (*pl* **-ases** [-əsiːz]) *n*: **emphasis (on)** énfasis *m inv* (en); **to lay** OR **place emphasis on** poner énfasis en, hacer hincapié en.

emphasize, -ise [ˈemfəsaɪz] *vt* [word, syllable] acentuar; [point, fact, feature] subrayar, hacer hincapié en; **to emphasize that...** subrayar que...

emphatic [ɪmˈfætɪk] *adj* [denial] rotundo(da), categórico(ca); [victory] convincente.

emphatically [ɪmˈfætɪklɪ] *adv* - **1.** [deny] rotundamente, enfáticamente; [win] convincentemente - **2.** [certainly] ciertamente.

emphysema [ˌemfɪˈsiːmə] *n* enfisema *m*.

empire [ˈempaɪəʳ] *n* imperio *m*.

empirical [ɪmˈpɪrɪkl] *adj* empírico(ca).

empiricism [ɪmˈpɪrɪsɪzm] *n* empirismo *m*.

employ [ɪmˈplɔɪ] *vt* - **1.** [give work to] emplear; **to be employed as** estar empleado(da) de - **2.** *fml* [use] utilizar, emplear; **to employ sthg as sthg/to do sthg** utilizar algo de algo/para hacer algo.

employable [ɪmˈplɔɪəbl] *adj* empleable.

employee [ɪmˈplɔɪiː] *n* empleado *m*, -da *f*.

employer [ɪmˈplɔɪəʳ] *n* - **1.** [individual] patrono *m*, -na *f*, empresario *m*, -ria *f* - **2.** [company]: **one of the country's biggest employers** una de las empresas que más trabajadores tiene en el país.

employment [ɪmˈplɔɪmənt] *n* empleo *m*; **to be in employment** tener trabajo.

employment agency *n* agencia *f* de trabajo.

empower [ɪmˈpaʊəʳ] *vt fml*: **to be empowered to do sthg** estar autorizado(da) a OR para hacer algo.

empress [ˈemprɪs] *n* emperatriz *f*.

emptiness [ˈemptɪnɪs] *(U) n* - **1.** [of place] soledad *f*, vacuidad *f* - **2.** [feeling] vacío *m*.

empty [ˈemptɪ] (*pl* **-ies**) <> *adj* (*comp* **-ier**, *superl* **-iest**) - **1.** [gen] vacío(a); [town] desierto(ta) - **2.** *pej* [words, threat, promise] vano(na). <> *vt* (*pt* & *pp* **-ied**) vaciar; **to empty sthg into sthg**

vaciar algo en algo; **to empty the water out of the bottle** vaciar de agua la botella. ◇ *vi* (*pt & pp* **-ied**) vaciarse. ◇ *n inf* casco *m*.

empty-handed [-'hændɪd] *adv* con las manos vacías.

empty-headed [-'hedɪd] *adj pej* bobo(ba).

EMS (*abbr of* **European Monetary System**) *n* SME *m*.

EMU (*abbr of* **Economic and Monetary Union**) *n* UEM *f*.

emu ['iːmjuː] (*pl* **emu** OR **-s**) *n* [bird] emú *m*.

emulate ['emjʊleɪt] *vt* emular.

emulsion [ɪ'mʌlʃn] *n* - **1.**: **emulsion (paint)** pintura *f* al agua - **2.** PHOT emulsión *f*.

enable [ɪ'neɪbl] *vt* - **1.** [allow]: **to enable sb to do sthg** permitir a alguien hacer algo - **2.** COMPUT ejecutar.

enact [ɪ'nækt] *vt* - **1.** LAW promulgar - **2.** [act] representar.

enactment [ɪ'næktmənt] *n* LAW promulgación *f*.

enamel [ɪ'næml] *n* - **1.** [gen] esmalte *m* - **2.** [paint] pintura *f* de esmalte.

enamelled UK**, enameled** US [ɪ'næmld] *adj* esmaltado(da).

enamel paint *n* pintura *f* de esmalte.

enamoured UK**, enamored** US [ɪ'næməd] *adj*: **enamoured of** [thing] entusiasmado(da) con; [person] enamorado(da) de.

en bloc [ɑ:'blɒk] *adv fml* en bloque.

enc. (*abbr of* **enclosure** OR **enclosed**) *adj*.

encampment [ɪn'kæmpmənt] *n* campamento *m*.

encapsulate [ɪn'kæpsjʊleɪt] *vt*: **to encapsulate sthg (in)** sintetizar algo (en).

encase [ɪn'keɪs] *vt*: **encased in** revestido(da) de.

encash [ɪn'kæʃ] *vt* UK fml cobrar, hacer efectivo.

enchanted [ɪn'tʃɑ:ntɪd] *adj*: **enchanted (by** OR **with)** encantado(da) (con).

enchanting [ɪn'tʃɑ:ntɪŋ] *adj* encantador(ra).

encircle [ɪn'sɜ:kl] *vt* rodear.

enclave ['enkleɪv] *n* enclave *m*.

enclose [ɪn'kləʊz] *vt* - **1.** [surround, contain] rodear; **enclosed by** OR **with** rodeado de; **an enclosed space** un espacio cerrado - **2.** [put in envelope] adjuntar; **'please find enclosed...'** 'envío adjunto...'

enclosure [ɪn'kləʊʒər] *n* - **1.** [place] recinto *m* (vallado) - **2.** [in letter] anexo *m*, documento *m* adjunto.

encompass [ɪn'kʌmpəs] *vt fml* - **1.** [include] abarcar - **2.** [surround] rodear.

encore ['ɒŋkɔːr] ◇ *n* bis *m*. ◇ *excl* ¡otra!

encounter [ɪn'kaʊntər] ◇ *n* encuentro *m*. ◇ *vt fml* encontrarse con.

encourage [ɪn'kʌrɪdʒ] *vt* - **1.** [give confidence to]: **to encourage sb (to do sthg)** animar a alguien (a hacer algo) - **2.** [foster] fomentar.

encouragement [ɪn'kʌrɪdʒmənt] *n* [confidence boosting] ánimo *m*, aliento *m*; [fostering] fomento *m*.

encouraging [ɪn'kʌrɪdʒɪŋ] *adj* alentador(ra), esperanzador(ra).

encroach [ɪn'krəʊtʃ] *vi*: **to encroach on** OR **upon** [rights, territory] usurpar; [privacy, time] invadir.

encrusted [ɪn'krʌstɪd] *adj*: **encrusted with** incrustado(da) de.

encrypt [ɪn'krɪpt] *vt* COMPUT encriptar.

encumber [ɪn'kʌmbər] *vt fml*: **to be encumbered with** tener que cargar con.

encyclop(a)edia [ɪn,saɪklə'pi:djə] *n* enciclopedia *f*.

encyclop(a)edic [ɪn,saɪkləʊ'pi:dɪk] *adj* enciclopédico(ca).

end [end] ◇ *n* - **1.** [last part, finish] fin *m*, final *m*; **at the end of May/2002** a finales de mayo/ 2002; **at the end of the week** al final de la semana; **my patience is at an end** se me está agotando la paciencia; **to be at the end of one's tether** UK OR **rope** US estar hasta la coronilla; **to bring sthg to an end** poner fin a algo; **to come to an end** llegar a su fin; **'the end'** [in films] 'FIN'; **to put an end to sthg** poner fin a algo; **at the end of the day** *fig* a fin de cuentas, al fin y al cabo; **in the end** al final - **2.** [of two-ended thing] extremo *m*; [of pointed thing] punta *f*; [of stadium] fondo *m*; [of phone line] lado *m*; **end to end** extremo con extremo; **to turn sthg on its end** poner algo boca abajo; **cigarette end** colilla *f* - **3.** *fml* [purpose] fin *m*, objetivo *m*; **an end in itself** fin en sí mismo - **4.** *liter* [death] final *m*. ◇ *vt* terminar; **to end sthg (with)** terminar algo (con). ◇ *vi* [finish] acabarse, terminarse; **to end in/with** acabar en/con, terminar en/con.

◆ **no end** *adv inf*: **it cheered me up no end** me alegró un montón.

◆ **no end of** *prep inf* la mar de.

◆ **on end** *adv* - **1.** [upright - hair] de punta; [- object] de pie - **2.** [continuously]: **for days on end** durante días y días.

◆ **end up** *vi* acabar, terminar; **to end up doing sthg** acabar OR terminar por hacer algo/haciendo algo; **to end up in** ir a parar a.

endanger [ɪn'deɪndʒər] *vt* poner en peligro.

endangered species [ɪn'deɪndʒəd-] *n* especie *f* en peligro de extinción.

endear [ɪn'dɪər] *vt*: **to endear sb to sb** hacer que alguien congenie con alguien; **to endear o.s. to sb** hacerse querer por alguien.

endearing [ɪnˈdɪərɪŋ] adj atrayente, simpático(ca).

endearment [ɪnˈdɪəmənt] n: term of endearment palabra f tierna OR cariñosa.

endeavour UK, **endeavor** US [ɪnˈdevər] fml ◇ n esfuerzo m. ◇ vt: to endeavour to do sthg procurar hacer algo.

endemic [enˈdemɪk] adj lit & fig endémico(ca).

ending [ˈendɪŋ] n final m, desenlace m.

endive [ˈendaɪv] n - 1. [curly lettuce] escarola f - 2. [chicory] endibia f, achicoria f.

endless [ˈendlɪs] adj [gen] interminable; [patience, resources] inagotable.

endlessly [ˈendlɪslɪ] adv interminablemente; [patient, kind] infinitamente.

endorse [ɪnˈdɔːs] vt - 1. [approve] apoyar, respaldar - 2. [cheque] endosar - 3. UK AUT: to endorse sb's driving licence hacer constar una sanción en el carné de conducir de alguien.

endorsement [ɪnˈdɔːsmənt] n - 1. [approval] apoyo m, respaldo m - 2. [of cheque] endoso m - 3. UK [on driving licence] nota de sanción que consta en el carné de conducir.

endoscope [ˈendəskəʊp] n MED endoscopio m.

endow [ɪnˈdaʊ] vt - 1. fml [equip]: to be endowed with estar dotado(da) de - 2. [donate money to] donar fondos a.

endowment [ɪnˈdaʊmənt] n - 1. fml [ability] dote f - 2. [gift of money] donación f.

endowment insurance n seguro m de vida mixto.

endowment mortgage n hipoteca-inversión f, hipoteca mixta en la que se pagan los plazos a un seguro de vida y los intereses al acreedor.

end product n producto m final.

end result n resultado m final.

endurable [ɪnˈdjʊərəbl] adj tolerable.

endurance [ɪnˈdjʊərəns] n resistencia f.

endurance test n prueba f de resistencia.

endure [ɪnˈdjʊər] ◇ vt soportar, aguantar. ◇ vi fml perdurar.

enduring [ɪnˈdjʊərɪŋ] adj fml perdurable.

end user n COMPUT usuario m final.

endways [ˈendweɪz] adv - 1. [not sideways] de frente - 2. [with ends touching] extremo con extremo.

enema [ˈenɪmə] n enema m.

enemy [ˈenɪmɪ] (pl -ies) ◇ n enemigo m, -ga f. ◇ comp enemigo(ga).

energetic [ˌenəˈdʒetɪk] adj - 1. [lively, physically taxing] enérgico(ca) - 2. [enthusiastic] activo(va), vigoroso(sa).

energy [ˈenədʒɪ] (pl -ies) n energía f.

energy-saving adj ahorrador(ra) de energía.

enervate [ˈenəveɪt] vt fml enervar, debilitar.

enervating [ˈenəveɪtɪŋ] adj fml enervante.

enfold [ɪnˈfəʊld] vt liter: to enfold sthg/sb (in) envolver algo/a alguien (en).

enforce [ɪnˈfɔːs] vt [law] hacer cumplir, aplicar; [standards] imponer.

enforceable [ɪnˈfɔːsəbl] adj aplicable.

enforced [ɪnˈfɔːst] adj forzoso(sa).

enforcement [ɪnˈfɔːsmənt] n aplicación f.

enfranchise [ɪnˈfræntʃaɪz] vt - 1. [give vote to] conceder el derecho de voto a - 2. [set free] manumitir.

engage [ɪnˈgeɪdʒ] ◇ vt - 1. [attract] atraer; to engage sb in conversation entablar conversación con alguien - 2. [TECH - clutch] pisar; [- gear] meter - 3. fml [employ] contratar; to be engaged in OR on dedicarse a, estar ocupado(da) en. ◇ vi [be involved]: to engage in [gen] dedicarse a; [conversation] entablar.

engaged [ɪnˈgeɪdʒd] adj - 1. [to be married]: engaged (to) prometido(da) (con); to get engaged prometerse - 2. [busy, in use] ocupado(da); engaged in sthg ocupado en algo - 3. TELEC comunicando.

engaged tone n UK señal f de comunicando.

engagement [ɪnˈgeɪdʒmənt] n - 1. [to be married] compromiso m; [period] noviazgo m - 2. [appointment] cita f, compromiso m.

engagement ring n anillo m de compromiso.

engaging [ɪnˈgeɪdʒɪŋ] adj atractivo(va).

engender [ɪnˈdʒendər] vt fml engendrar.

engine [ˈendʒɪn] n - 1. [of vehicle] motor m - 2. RAIL locomotora f, máquina f.

engine driver n UK maquinista mf.

engineer [ˌendʒɪˈnɪər] ◇ n - 1. [gen] ingeniero m, -ra f - 2. US [engine driver] maquinista mf. ◇ vt - 1. [construct] construir - 2. [contrive] tramar.

engineering [ˌendʒɪˈnɪərɪŋ] n ingeniería f.

England [ˈɪŋglənd] n Inglaterra.

English [ˈɪŋglɪʃ] ◇ adj inglés(esa). ◇ n [language] inglés m. ◇ npl [people]: the English los ingleses.

English breakfast n desayuno m inglés.

English Channel n: the English Channel el canal de la Mancha.

Englishman [ˈɪŋglɪʃmən] (pl -men [-mən]) n inglés m.

English muffin n US ≃ bollo m.

Englishwoman [ˈɪŋglɪʃˌwʊmən] (pl -women [-ˌwɪmɪn]) n inglesa f.

engrave [ɪnˈgreɪv] vt lit & fig: to engrave sthg (on) grabar algo (en).

engraver [ɪnˈgreɪvər] n grabador m, -ra f.

engraving [ɪnˈgreɪvɪŋ] *n* grabado *m*.

engrossed [ɪnˈgrəʊst] *adj*: **to be engrossed (in)** estar absorto(ta) (en).

engrossing [ɪnˈgrəʊsɪŋ] *adj* absorbente.

engulf [ɪnˈgʌlf] *vt*: **to be engulfed in** [flames etc] verse devorado(da) por; [fear, despair] verse sumido(da) en.

enhance [ɪnˈhɑːns] *vt* [gen] aumentar, acrecentar; [status, position] elevar; [beauty] realzar.

enhancement [ɪnˈhɑːnsmənt] *n* [gen] aumento *m*; [of status, position] elevación *f*; [of beauty] realce *m*.

enigma [ɪˈnɪgmə] *n* enigma *m*.

enigmatic [ˌenɪgˈmætɪk] *adj* enigmático(ca).

enjoy [ɪnˈdʒɔɪ] <> *vt* - **1.** [like] disfrutar de; **did you enjoy the film/book?** ¿te gustó la película/el libro?; **she enjoys reading** le gusta leer; **enjoy your meal!** ¡que aproveche!, ¡buen provecho!; **to enjoy o.s.** pasarlo bien, divertirse - **2.** *fml* [possess] gozar OR disfrutar de. <> *vi US*: **enjoy!** [enjoy yourself] ¡que lo pases bien!; [before meal] ¡que aproveche!

enjoyable [ɪnˈdʒɔɪəbl] *adj* agradable.

enjoyment [ɪnˈdʒɔɪmənt] *n* - **1.** [pleasure] placer *m* - **2.** [possession] disfrute *m*, posesión *f*.

enlarge [ɪnˈlɑːdʒ] *vt* [gen, PHOT & POL] ampliar.

➠ **enlarge (up)on** *vt insep* ampliar, explicar con detalle.

enlargement [ɪnˈlɑːdʒmənt] *n* [gen, PHOT & POL] ampliación *f*.

enlighten [ɪnˈlaɪtn] *vt fml* aclarar, iluminar.

enlightened [ɪnˈlaɪtnd] *adj* amplio(plia) de miras.

enlightening [ɪnˈlaɪtnɪŋ] *adj* instructivo(va), informativo(va).

enlightenment [ɪnˈlaɪtnmənt] *n (U)* aclaración *f*.

➠ **Enlightenment** *n*: **the Enlightenment** la Ilustración.

enlist [ɪnˈlɪst] <> *vt* - **1.** [person] alistar, reclutar - **2.** [support] obtener. <> *vi MIL*: **to enlist (in)** alistarse (en).

enlisted man [ɪnˈlɪstɪd-] *n US* recluta *m*.

enliven [ɪnˈlaɪvn] *vt* avivar, animar.

en masse [ˌɒnˈmæs] *adv* en masa.

enmeshed [ɪnˈmeʃt] *adj*: **to be enmeshed in** estar enredado(da) en.

enmity [ˈenmətɪ] *(pl* -**ies***) n* enemistad *f*.

ennoble [ɪˈnəʊbl] *vt* ennoblecer.

enormity [ɪˈnɔːmətɪ] *n* [extent] enormidad *f*.

enormous [ɪˈnɔːməs] *adj* enorme.

enormously [ɪˈnɔːməslɪ] *adv* enormemente.

enough [ɪˈnʌf] <> *adj* bastante, suficiente; **do you have enough glasses?** ¿tienes suficientes vasos? <> *pron* bastante; **is this enough?** ¿basta con eso?; **more than enough** más que suficiente; **that's enough** [sufficient] ya está bien; **enough is enough** ya basta, ya está bien; **that's enough (of that)!** ¡basta ya!; **to have had enough (of)** [expressing annoyance] estar harto(ta) (de). <> *adv* bastante, suficientemente; **I was stupid enough to believe her** fui lo bastante tonto como para creerla; **he was good enough to lend me his car** *fml* tuvo la bondad de dejarme su coche; **strangely enough** curiosamente.

enquire [ɪnˈkwaɪə^r] *vi* [ask for information] informarse, pedir información; **to enquire about sthg** informarse de algo; **to enquire when/how/whether...** preguntar cuándo/cómo/si...

➠ **enquire after** *vt insep* preguntar por.

➠ **enquire into** *vt insep* investigar.

enquiry [ɪnˈkwaɪrɪ] *(pl* -**ies***) n* - **1.** [question] pregunta *f*; **'Enquiries'** 'Información' - **2.** [investigation] investigación *f*.

enraged [ɪnˈreɪdʒd] *adj* enfurecido(da).

enrich [ɪnˈrɪtʃ] *vt* enriquecer; [soil] fertilizar.

enrol *UK (pt & pp* -**led**, *cont* -**ling)**, **enroll** *US* [ɪnˈrəʊl] <> *vt* matricular. <> *vi*: **to enrol (on)** matricularse (en).

enrolment *UK*, **enrollment** *US* [ɪnˈrəʊlmənt] *n (U)* matrícula *f*, inscripción *f*.

en route [ˌɒnˈruːt] *adv*: **en route (from/to)** en el camino (de/a).

ensconced [ɪnˈskɒnst] *adj fml*: **ensconced (in)** repantigado(da) OR arrellanado(da) (en).

enshrine [ɪnˈʃraɪn] *vt*: **to be enshrined in sthg** estar amparado(da) OR salvaguardado(da) por algo.

ensign [ˈensaɪn] *n* - **1.** [flag] bandera *f*, enseña *f* - **2.** *US* [sailor] ≃ alférez *m* de fragata.

enslave [ɪnˈsleɪv] *vt* esclavizar.

ensue [ɪnˈsjuː] *vi fml* seguir; [war] sobrevenir.

ensuing [ɪnˈsjuːɪŋ] *adj fml* subsiguiente.

en suite [ɑ̃ˈswiːt] *adj*: **with an en suite bathroom** con cuarto de baño privado.

ensure [ɪnˈʃʊə^r] *vt*: **to ensure (that)** asegurar que.

ENT *(abbr of* **Ear, Nose & Throat***) n* otorrinolaringología *f*.

entail [ɪnˈteɪl] *vt* [involve] conllevar, suponer.

entangled [ɪnˈtæŋgld] *adj* - **1.** [gen]: **to be entangled (in)** estar enredado(da) (en) - **2.** [emotionally]: **to be entangled with sb** tener un lío con alguien.

entanglement [ɪnˈtæŋglmənt] *n* [emotional] lío *m*.

enter [ˈentə^r] <> *vt* - **1.** [gen] entrar en - **2.** [join - profession, parliament] ingresar en; [- university] matricularse en; [- army, navy] alistarse en - **3.** [become involved in - politics etc] meterse en; [- race, examination etc] inscribirse en - **4.** [register]: **to enter sthg/sb for sthg** inscribir algo/a alguien en algo - **5.** [write down] anotar, apuntar - **6.** [appear in] presentarse *OR* aparecer en - **7.** COMPUT introducir. <> *vi* - **1.** [come or go in] entrar - **2.** [participate]: **to enter (for sthg)** inscribirse (en algo).

➤ **enter into** *vt insep* entrar en; [agreement] comprometerse a; [conversation, negotiations] entablar.

enteritis [,entə'raɪtɪs] *n* enteritis *f inv*.

enter key *n* COMPUT tecla *f* enter.

enterprise ['entəpraɪz] *n* - **1.** [project, company] empresa *f* - **2.** [initiative] iniciativa *f*.

enterprise culture *n* cultura *f* empresarial.

enterprise zone *n zona del Reino Unido donde se fomenta la actividad industrial y empresarial.*

enterprising ['entəpraɪzɪŋ] *adj* emprendedor(ra).

entertain [,entə'teɪn] <> *vt* - **1.** [amuse] divertir, entretener - **2.** [invite] recibir (en casa) - **3.** *fml* [idea, proposal] considerar - **4.** *fml* [hopes, ambitions] abrigar. <> *vi* - **1.** [amuse] divertir, entretener - **2.** [have guests] recibir.

entertainer [,entə'teɪnə˚] *n* artista *mf*.

entertaining [,entə'teɪnɪŋ] <> *adj* divertido(da), entretenido(da). <> *n* (U): **she does a lot of entertaining** siempre tiene invitados en casa.

entertainment [,entə'teɪnmənt] <> *n* - **1.** (U) [amusement] diversión *f*, entretenimiento *m*, entretención *f* *Amér* - **2.** [show] espectáculo *m*. <> *comp* del espectáculo.

entertainment allowance *n* gastos *mpl* de representación.

enthral (*pt & pp* **-led**, *cont* **-ling**) *UK*, **enthrall** *US* [ɪn'θrɔ:l] *vt* cautivar, embelesar.

enthralling [ɪn'θrɔ:lɪŋ] *adj* cautivador(ra).

enthrone [ɪn'θrəʊn] *vt fml* entronizar.

enthuse [ɪn'θju:z] *vi*: **to enthuse (about)** entusiasmarse (por).

enthusiasm [ɪn'θju:zɪæzm] *n* - **1.** [passion, eagerness]: **enthusiasm (for)** entusiasmo *m* (por) - **2.** [interest] pasión *f*, interés *m*.

enthusiast [ɪn'θju:zɪæst] *n* entusiasta *mf*.

enthusiastic [ɪn,θju:zɪ'æstɪk] *adj* [person] entusiasta; [cry, response] entusiástico(ca).

enthusiastically [ɪn,θju:zɪ'æstɪklɪ] *adv* con entusiasmo.

entice [ɪn'taɪs] *vt* seducir, atraer; **nothing could entice me to do that** no haría eso de ninguna manera.

enticing [ɪn'taɪsɪŋ] *adj* tentador(ra), atractivo(va).

entire [ɪn'taɪə˚] *adj* entero(ra); **the entire evening** toda la noche.

entirely [ɪn'taɪəlɪ] *adv* completamente; **I'm not entirely sure** no estoy del todo seguro.

entirety [ɪn'taɪrətɪ] *n fml*: **in its entirety** en su totalidad.

entitle [ɪn'taɪtl] *vt* [allow]: **to entitle sb to sthg** dar a alguien derecho a algo; **to entitle sb to do sthg** autorizar a alguien a hacer algo.

entitled [ɪn'taɪtld] *adj* - **1.** [allowed]: **to be entitled to sthg/to do sthg** tener derecho a algo/a hacer algo - **2.** [book, song, film] titulado(da).

entitlement [ɪn'taɪtlmənt] *n* derecho *m*.

entity ['entətɪ] (*pl* **-ies**) *n* entidad *f*.

entomology [,entə'mɒlədʒɪ] *n* entomología *f*.

entourage [,ɒntʊ'rɑ:ʒ] *n* séquito *m*.

entrails ['entreɪlz] *npl* entrañas *fpl*.

entrance <> *n* ['entrəns]: **entrance (to)** entrada *f* (a *OR* de); **to gain entrance to** *fml* [building] lograr acceso a; [society, university] lograr el ingreso en. <> *vt* [ɪn'trɑ:ns] encantar, hechizar.

entrance examination *n* examen *m* de ingreso.

entrance fee *n* [for museum] (precio *m* de) entrada *f*.

entrancing [ɪn'trɑ:nsɪŋ] *adj* encantador(ra), cautivador(ra).

entrant ['entrənt] *n* participante *mf*.

entreat [ɪn'tri:t] *vt*: **to entreat sb (to do sthg)** suplicar *OR* rogar a alguien (que haga algo).

entreaty [ɪn'tri:tɪ] (*pl* **-ies**) *n* ruego *m*, súplica *f*.

entrepreneur [,ɒntrəprə'nɜ:r] *n* empresario *m*, -ria *f*.

entrepreneurial [,ɒntrəprə'nɜ:rɪəl] *adj* empresarial.

entrust [ɪn'trʌst] *vt*: **to entrust sthg to sb, to entrust sb with sthg** confiar algo a alguien.

entry ['entrɪ] (*pl* **-ies**) *n* - **1.** [gen]: **entry (into)** entrada *f* (en); **'no entry'** 'se prohibe la entrada', 'prohibido el paso' - **2.** *fig* [joining - of group, society] ingreso *m* - **3.** [in competition] participante *mf* - **4.** [in diary] anotación *f*; [in ledger] partida *f*.

entry fee *n* [for competition] cuota *f* de inscripción.

entry form *n* boleto *m* *OR* impreso *m* de inscripción.

entryway ['entrɪ,weɪ] *n US* camino *m* (de entrada).

entwine [ɪn'twaɪn] <> *vt* entrelazar. <> *vi* entrelazarse.

E number *n* número *m* E.

enumerate [ɪ'nju:məreɪt] *vt* enumerar.

enunciate [ɪ'nʌnsɪeɪt] <> vt - **1.** [word] pronunciar - **2.** [idea, plan] enunciar. <> vi vocalizar.

envelop [ɪn'veləp] vt: to envelop sthg/sb in envolver algo/a alguien en.

envelope ['envələʊp] n sobre m.

enviable ['envɪəbl] adj envidiable.

envious ['envɪəs] adj [person] envidioso(sa); [look] de envidia; **to be envious of** tener envidia de.

enviously ['envɪəslɪ] adv con envidia.

environment [ɪn'vaɪərənmənt] n - **1.** [natural world]: **the environment** el medio ambiente; **Department of the Environment** UK ministerio m del medio ambiente - **2.** [surroundings] entorno m - **3.** [atmosphere] ambiente m - **4.** COMPUT entorno m.

environmental [ɪn,vaɪərən'mentl] adj - **1.** [gen] medioambiental, ambiental; **environmental pollution** contaminación f del medio ambiente - **2.** [group, campaigner] ecologista.

environmentalist [ɪn,vaɪərən'mentəlɪst] n ecologista mf.

environmentally [ɪn,vaɪərən'mentəlɪ] adv ecológicamente; **environmentally friendly** ecológico(ca), que no daña al medio ambiente.

Environmental Protection Agency n US agencia gubernamental de protección medioambiental.

environs [ɪn'vaɪərənz] npl alrededores mpl.

envisage [ɪn'vɪzɪdʒ], **envision** US [ɪn'vɪʒn] vt prever.

envoy ['envɔɪ] n enviado m, -da f.

envy ['envɪ] <> n envidia f; **to be the envy of** ser la envidia de; **to be green with envy** estar muerto(ta) de envidia. <> vt (pt & pp -ied): **to envy (sb sthg)** envidiar (algo a alguien).

enzyme ['enzaɪm] n enzima f.

eon US = aeon.

epaulet(te) ['epə'let] n charretera f.

ephemeral [ɪ'femərəl] adj efímero(ra).

epic ['epɪk] <> adj épico(ca). <> n [poem, work] epopeya f; [film] película f épica.

epicentre UK, **epicenter** US ['episentər] n epicentro m.

epidemic [,epɪ'demɪk] n epidemia f.

epidural [,epɪ'djʊərəl] n epidural f.

epigram ['epɪgræm] n epigrama m.

epilepsy ['epɪlepsɪ] n epilepsia f.

epileptic [,epɪ'leptɪk] <> adj epiléptico(ca). <> n epiléptico m, -ca f.

Epiphany [ɪ'pɪfənɪ] n Epifanía f.

episcopal [ɪ'pɪskəpl] adj [of bishop] episcopal.

episode ['epɪsəʊd] n - **1.** [event] episodio m - **2.** [of story, TV series] capítulo m.

episodic [,epɪ'sɒdɪk] adj episódico(ca).

epistle [ɪ'pɪsl] n epístola f.

epitaph ['epɪtɑːf] n epitafio m.

epithet ['epɪθet] n epíteto m.

epitome [ɪ'pɪtəmɪ] n: **the epitome of** [person] la personificación de; [thing] el vivo ejemplo de.

epitomize, -ise [ɪ'pɪtəmaɪz] vt [subj: person] personificar; [subj: thing] representar el paradigma de.

epoch ['iːpɒk] n época f.

epoch-making adj histórico(ca), que hace época.

eponymous [ɪ'pɒnɪməs] adj epónimo(ma).

EPOS ['iːpɒs] (abbr of electronic point of sale) n punto de venta electrónica.

equable ['ekwəbl] adj [calm, reasonable] ecuánime.

equal ['iːkwəl] <> adj igual; **equal to** [sum] igual a; **equal rights** igualdad de derechos; **on equal terms** en igualdad de condiciones; **to be equal to** [task etc] estar a la altura de. <> n igual mf; **to treat sb as an equal** tratar a alguien de igual a igual. <> vt (UK -**led**, cont -**ling**, US -**ed**, cont -**ing**) - **1.** MATHS ser igual a - **2.** [person, quality] igualar.

equality [iː'kwɒlətɪ] n igualdad f.

equalize, -ise ['iːkwəlaɪz] <> vt igualar. <> vi SPORT empatar.

equalizer ['iːkwəlaɪzər] n SPORT gol m del empate.

equally ['iːkwəlɪ] adv - **1.** [gen] igualmente; **equally important** de igual importancia - **2.** [share, divide] a partes iguales, por igual - **3.** [just as likely] de igual modo.

equal opportunities npl igualdad f de oportunidades.

Equal Opportunities Commission n organismo gubernamental británico contra la discriminación sexual.

equal(s) sign n signo m de igualdad.

equanimity [,ekwə'nɪmətɪ] n ecuanimidad f.

equate [ɪ'kweɪt] vt: **to equate sthg with** equiparar algo con.

equation [ɪ'kweɪʒn] n ecuación f.

equator [ɪ'kweɪtər] n: **the Equator** el Ecuador.

equatorial [,ekwə'tɔːrɪəl] adj ecuatorial.

Equatorial Guinea n Guinea Ecuatorial f.

equestrian [ɪ'kwestrɪən] adj ecuestre.

equidistant [,iːkwɪ'dɪstənt] adj: **equidistant (from)** equidistante (de).

equilateral triangle [,iːkwɪ'lætərəl-] n triángulo m equilátero.

equilibrium [,iːkwɪ'lɪbrɪəm] n equilibrio m.

equine ['ekwaɪn] adj equino(na).

equinox ['iːkwɪnɒks] n equinoccio m.

equip [ɪ'kwɪp] (pt & pp **-ped,** cont **-ping**) vt
- 1. [provide with equipment]: **to equip sthg
(with)** equipar algo (con); **to equip sb (with)**
proveer a alguien (de) **- 2.** [prepare]: **to be
equipped for** estar preparado(da) para.

equipment [ɪ'kwɪpmənt] n (U) equipo m.

equitable ['ekwɪtəbl] adj equitativo(va).

equity ['ekwɪtɪ] n (U) FIN [of company] capital m
social; [of shareholders] fondos mpl propios.

◆ **equities** npl FIN acciones fpl ordinarias.

equivalent [ɪ'kwɪvələnt] ◇ adj equivalente;
to be equivalent to equivaler a. ◇ n equivalente m.

equivocal [ɪ'kwɪvəkl] adj equívoco(ca).

equivocate [ɪ'kwɪvəkeɪt] vi andarse con ambi-
güedades.

er [ɜːr] excl ¡ejem!

ER ◇ n US (abbr of **Emergency Room**) (sala f
de) urgencias fpl. ◇ (abbr of **Elizabeth Re-
gina**), emblema de la reina Isabel.

era ['ɪərə] (pl **-s**) n era f, época f.

eradicate [ɪ'rædɪkeɪt] vt erradicar.

eradication [ɪ,rædɪ'keɪʃn] n erradicación f.

erase [ɪ'reɪz] vt lit & fig borrar.

eraser [ɪ'reɪzər] n esp US goma f de borrar.

erect [ɪ'rekt] ◇ adj **- 1.** [person, posture] ergui-
do(da) **- 2.** [penis] erecto(ta). ◇ vt **- 1.** [building,
statue] erigir, levantar **- 2.** [tent] montar.

erection [ɪ'rekʃn] n **- 1.** (U) [of building, statue]
construcción f **- 2.** [erect penis] erección f.

ergonomic [,ɜːgə'nɒmɪk] adj ergonómico(ca).

ergonomics [,ɜːgə'nɒmɪks] n ergonomía f.

Eritrea [,erɪ'treɪə] n Eritrea.

Eritrean [,erɪ'treɪən] ◇ adj eritreo(a). ◇ n eri-
treo m, -a f.

ERM (abbr of **Exchange Rate Mechanism**) n
mecanismo de tipos de cambio del SME.

ermine ['ɜːmɪn] n armiño m.

erode [ɪ'rəʊd] ◇ vt **- 1.** [rock, soil] erosionar;
[metal] desgastar **- 2.** [confidence, rights] mermar. ◇ vi **- 1.** [rock, soil] erosionarse; [metal]
desgastarse **- 2.** [confidence, rights] mermarse.

erogenous zone [ɪ'rɒdʒɪnəs-] n zona f eróge-
na.

erosion [ɪ'rəʊʒn] n **- 1.** [of rock, soil] erosión f;
[of metal] desgaste m **- 2.** [of confidence, rights]
merma f.

erotic [ɪ'rɒtɪk] adj erótico(ca).

eroticism [ɪ'rɒtɪsɪzm] n erotismo m.

err [ɜːr] vi equivocarse, errar; **to err is human**
errar es humano; **to err on the side of caution** pecar de prudente.

errand ['erənd] n recado m, mandado m; **to go
on** OR **run an errand** hacer un recado.

erratic [ɪ'rætɪk] adj irregular.

erroneous [ɪ'rəʊnjəs] adj fml erróneo(a).

error ['erər] n error m; **to make an error** cometer un error; **spelling error** falta f de ortografía; **error of judgment** error de cálculo; **in er-
ror** por equivocación.

error message n COMPUT mensaje m de error.

erstwhile ['ɜːstwaɪl] adj liter antiguo(gua).

erudite ['eruːdaɪt] adj erudito(ta).

erupt [ɪ'rʌpt] vi [volcano] entrar en erupción; fig
[violence, war] estallar.

eruption [ɪ'rʌpʃn] n **- 1.** [of volcano] erupción f
- 2. [of violence, war] estallido m, explosión f.

ESA (abbr of **European Space Agency**) n
ESA f.

escalate ['eskəleɪt] vi **- 1.** [conflict] intensificarse **- 2.** [costs] ascender, incrementarse.

escalation [,eskə'leɪʃn] n **- 1.** [of conflict, viol-
ence] intensificación f, escalada f **- 2.** [of costs]
ascenso m, incremento m.

escalator ['eskəleɪtər] n escalera f mecánica.

escapade [,eskə'peɪd] n aventura f.

escape [ɪ'skeɪp] ◇ n **- 1.** [gen] fuga f **- 2.** [leak-
age - of gas, water] escape m. ◇ vt **- 1.** [avoid]
escapar a, eludir; **to escape notice** pasar
inadvertido(da) **- 2.** [subj: fact, name]: **her name
escapes me right now** ahora mismo no me sale su nombre. ◇ vi **- 1.** [gen]: **to escape (from)**
escaparse (de) **- 2.** [survive] escapar.

escape clause n cláusula f de escape.

escape key n COMPUT tecla f de escape.

escape route n **- 1.** [from prison] vía f de escape **- 2.** [from fire] salida f de emergencia.

escapism [ɪ'skeɪpɪzm] n (U) escapismo m, evasión f.

escapist [ɪ'skeɪpɪst] adj de evasión.

escapologist [,eskə'pɒlədʒɪst] n escapista mf.

escarpment [ɪ'skɑːpmənt] n escarpa f.

eschew [ɪs'tʃuː] vt fml evitar.

escort ◇ n ['eskɔːt] **- 1.** [guard] escolta f; **under
escort** bajo escolta **- 2.** [companion] acompañante mf. ◇ vt [ɪ'skɔːt] escoltar; **to escort sb
home** acompañar a alguien a casa.

escort agency n agencia f de acompañantes.

ESF [iːes'ef] (abbr of **European Social Fund**) n
FSE m.

Eskimo ['eskɪməʊ] ◇ adj esquimal. ◇ n (pl **-s**)
- 1. [person] esquimal mf **- 2.** [language] esquimal m.

ESL (abbr of **English as a Second Language**) n
inglés como segunda lengua.

esophagus US n = oesophagus.

esoteric [,esə'terɪk] adj esotérico(ca).

esp. (abbr of **especially**) esp.

ESP *n* - **1.** (*abbr of* **extrasensory perception**) percepción *f* extrasensorial - **2.** (*abbr of* **English for special purposes**), *inglés especializado.*

espadrille [ˌespə'drɪl] *n* alpargata *f.*

especially [ɪ'speʃəlɪ] *adv* - **1.** [more than usually, specifically] especialmente - **2.** [in particular] sobre todo.

Esperanto [ˌespə'ræntəʊ] *n* esperanto *m.*

espionage ['espɪə,nɑːʒ] *n* espionaje *m.*

esplanade [ˌesplə'neɪd] *n* paseo *m* marítimo.

espouse [ɪ'spaʊz] *vt* apoyar.

espresso [e'spresəʊ] (*pl* -**s**) *n* café *m* exprés.

Esq. (*abbr of* **esquire**) D.; **James Roberts, Esq.** D. James Roberts.

Esquire [ɪ'skwaɪə] *n* Sr. Don; **B. Jones Esquire** Sr. Don B. Jones.

essay ['eseɪ] *n* - **1.** SCH redacción *f*, composición *f*; UNIV trabajo *m* - **2.** LIT ensayo *m.*

essayist ['eseɪɪst] *n* ensayista *mf.*

essence ['esns] *n* esencia *f*; **in essence** esencialmente.

essential [ɪ'senʃl] *adj* - **1.** [absolutely necessary]: **essential (to** OR **for)** esencial OR indispensable (para) - **2.** [basic] fundamental, esencial.

➡ **essentials** *npl* - **1.** [basic commodities]: **the essentials** lo indispensable - **2.** [most important elements] los elementos esenciales.

essentially [ɪ'senʃəlɪ] *adv* [basically] esencialmente.

est. *abbr of* **established**. *abbr of* **estimated**.

EST (*abbr of* **Eastern Standard Time**) *n* hora oficial de la costa este de los EE UU.

establish [ɪ'stæblɪʃ] *vt* - **1.** [gen] establecer; **to establish contact with** establecer contacto con; **to establish o.s. (as)** establecerse (como) - **2.** [facts, cause] verificar.

established [ɪ'stæblɪʃt] *adj* - **1.** [custom] arraigado(da) - **2.** [company] establecido(da), consolidado(da).

establishment [ɪ'stæblɪʃmənt] *n* establecimiento *m.*

➡ **Establishment** *n*: **the Establishment** el sistema.

estate [ɪ'steɪt] *n* - **1.** [land, property] finca *f* - **2.**: **(housing) estate** urbanización *f* - **3.**: **(industrial) estate** polígono *m* industrial - **4.** LAW [inheritance] herencia *f.*

estate agency *n* UK agencia *f* inmobiliaria.

estate agent *n* UK agente inmobiliario *m*, agente inmobiliaria *f.*

estate car *n* UK ranchera *f*, coche *m* familiar.

estd., est'd. *abbr of* **established**.

esteem [ɪ'stiːm] ⬦ *n* estima *f*; **to hold sthg/sb in high esteem** tener en mucha estima algo/a alguien. ⬦ *vt* estimar, apreciar.

esthetic US = **aesthetic**.

estimate ⬦ *n* ['estɪmət] - **1.** [calculation, judgment] cálculo *m*, estimación *f* - **2.** [written quote] presupuesto *m*. ⬦ *vt* ['estɪmeɪt] estimar.

estimated ['estɪmeɪtɪd] *adj* estimado(da), calculado(da).

estimation [ˌestɪ'meɪʃn] *n* - **1.** [opinion] juicio *m*; **in my estimation** a mi juicio - **2.** [calculation] cálculo *m.*

Estonia [e'stəʊnɪə] *n* Estonia.

Estonian [e'stəʊnɪən] ⬦ *adj* estonio(nia). ⬦ *n* - **1.** [person] estonio *m*, -nia *f* - **2.** [language] estonio *m.*

estranged [ɪ'streɪndʒd] *adj* [from husband, wife] separado(da); **his estranged son** su hijo, con el que no se habla.

estrogen US = **oestrogen**.

estuary ['estjʊərɪ] (*pl* -**ies**) *n* estuario *m.*

ETA (*abbr of* **estimated time of arrival**) *n* hora prevista de llegada.

e-tailer ['iːteɪlə] *n* tienda *f* electrónica.

et al. [ˌet'æl] (*abbr of* **et alii**) et al.

etc. (*abbr of* **etcetera**) etc.

etcetera [ɪt'setərə] *adv* etcétera.

etch [etʃ] *vt* [engrave] grabar al aguafuerte; *fig* [imprint]: **to be etched on sb's memory** estar grabado(da) en la memoria de alguien.

etching ['etʃɪŋ] *n* aguafuerte *m o f.*

eternal [ɪ'tɜːnl] *adj* [gen] eterno(na); *fig* [complaints, whining] perpetuo(tua), continuo(nua).

eternally [ɪ'tɜːnəlɪ] *adv* [gen] eternamente; [complain, whine] continuamente.

eternity [ɪ'tɜːnətɪ] *n* eternidad *f.*

eternity ring *n* UK alianza *f* del amor eterno.

ether ['iːθə] *n* éter *m.*

ethereal [ɪ'θɪərɪəl] *adj* etéreo(a).

ethic ['eθɪk] *n* ética *f.*

➡ **ethics** ⬦ *n* (*U*) [study] ética *f.* ⬦ *npl* [morals] moralidad *f.*

ethical ['eθɪkl] *adj* ético(ca).

Ethiopia [ˌiːθɪ'əʊpɪə] *n* Etiopía.

Ethiopian [ˌiːθɪ'əʊpɪən] ⬦ *adj* etíope. ⬦ *n* etíope *mf.*

ethnic ['eθnɪk] *adj* - **1.** [traditions, groups, conflict] étnico(ca) - **2.** [food] *típico de una cultura distinta a la occidental*; **ethnic music** música étnica.

ethnic cleansing [-'klensɪŋ] *n* limpieza *f* étnica.

ethnic minority *n* minoría *f* étnica.

ethnology [eθ'nɒlədʒɪ] *n* etnología *f.*

ethos ['iːθɒs] *n* ética *f*, código *m* de valores.

etiquette ['etɪket] *n* etiqueta *f.*

e-trade *n* (*U*) comercio *m* electrónico.

etymology [,etɪ'mɒlədʒɪ] (pl -ies) n etimología f.

EU (abbr of **European Union**) n UE f.

eucalyptus [,ju:kə'lɪptəs] n eucalipto m.

eulogize, -ise ['ju:lədʒaɪz] vt elogiar.

eulogy ['ju:lədʒɪ] (pl -ies) n elogio m.

eunuch ['ju:nək] n eunuco m.

euphemism ['ju:fəmɪzm] n eufemismo m.

euphemistic [,ju:fə'mɪstɪk] adj eufemístico(ca).

euphoria [ju:'fɔ:rɪə] n euforia f.

euphoric [ju:'fɒrɪk] adj eufórico(ca).

eureka [juə'ri:kə] excl ¡eureka!

euro ['juərəu] n [currency] euro m.

Euro- ['juərəu] prefix euro-.

Eurocheque ['juərəu,tʃek] n eurocheque m.

Europe ['juərəp] n Europa f.

European [,juərə'pi:ən] <> adj europeo(a). <> n europeo m, -a f.

European Central Bank n: the European Central Bank el Banco Central Europeo.

European Commission n: the European Commission la Comisión Europea.

European Community n: the European Community la Comunidad Europea.

Europeanism [,juərə'pi:ənɪzm] n europeísmo m.

Europeanize, -ise [,juərə'pi:ənaɪz] vt europeizar.

European Monetary System n: the European Monetary System el Sistema Monetario Europeo.

European Union n: the European Union la Unión Europea.

Eurosceptic ['uərəu,skeptɪk] <> adj euroescéptico(ca). <> n euroescéptico m, -ca f.

Eurostar ['uərəustɑ:r] n Eurostar m.

euro zone n FIN zona f euro.

euthanasia [,ju:θə'neɪzjə] n eutanasia f.

evacuate [ɪ'vækjueɪt] vt evacuar.

evacuation [ɪ,vækju'eɪʃn] n evacuación f.

evacuee [ɪ,vækju'i:] n evacuado m, -da f.

evade [ɪ'veɪd] vt [gen] eludir; [taxes] evadir.

evaluate [ɪ'væljueɪt] vt evaluar.

evaluation [ɪ,vælju'eɪʃn] n evaluación f.

evangelical [,i:væn'dʒelɪkl] adj evangélico(ca).

evangelism [ɪ'vændʒəlɪzm] n evangelismo m.

evangelist [ɪ'vændʒəlɪst] n evangelista mf.

evangelize, -ise [ɪ'vændʒəlaɪz] vt evangelizar.

evaporate [ɪ'væpəreɪt] vi [liquid] evaporarse; fig [feeling] desvanecerse.

evaporated milk [ɪ'væpəreɪtɪd-] n leche f evaporada.

evaporation [ɪ,væpə'reɪʃn] n evaporación f.

evasion [ɪ'veɪʒn] n - 1. [of responsibility, payment etc] evasión f - 2. [lie] evasiva f.

evasive [ɪ'veɪsɪv] adj evasivo(va); **to take evasive action** quitarse de en medio.

evasiveness [ɪ'veɪsɪvnɪs] n actitud f evasiva.

eve [i:v] n: **on the eve of** en la víspera de.

even ['i:vn] <> adj - 1. [regular] uniforme, constante - 2. [calm] sosegado(da) - 3. [flat, level] llano(na), liso(sa) - 4. [equal - contest, teams] igualado(da); [- chance] igual; **to get even with** ajustarle las cuentas a - 5. [number] par. <> adv - 1. [gen] incluso, hasta; **even now/then** incluso ahora/entonces; **not even** ni siquiera - 2. [in comparisons] aun; **even more** aun más.

➡ **even as** conj incluso mientras.

➡ **even if** conj aunque, aun cuando, así Amér.

➡ **even so** conj aun así.

➡ **even though** conj aunque.

➡ **even out** <> vt sep igualar. <> vi igualarse.

even-handed [-'hændɪd] adj imparcial.

evening ['i:vnɪŋ] n - 1. [end of day - early part] tarde f; [- later part] noche f; **in the evening** por la tarde/noche - 2. [event, entertainment] velada f.

➡ **evenings** adv [early] por la tarde; [late] por la noche.

evening class n clase f nocturna.

evening dress n - 1. [worn by man] traje m de etiqueta - 2. [worn by woman] traje m de noche.

evening star n: the evening star el lucero de la tarde.

evenly ['i:vnlɪ] adv - 1. [regularly] de modo uniforme - 2. [equally] igualmente, equitativamente; **evenly matched** muy igualados(das) - 3. [calmly] sosegadamente.

evenness ['i:vnnɪs] n - 1. [regularity] uniformidad f - 2. [equality] igualdad f.

evensong ['i:vnsɒŋ] n (U) vísperas fpl.

event [ɪ'vent] n - 1. [happening] acontecimiento m, suceso m; **in the event of** en caso de; **in the event that it rains** (en) caso de que llueva - 2. SPORT prueba f.

➡ **in any event** adv en todo caso.

➡ **in the event** adv UK al final, llegada la hora.

even-tempered [-'tempəd] adj apacible, ecuánime.

eventful [ɪ'ventfʊl] adj accidentado(da).

eventide home ['i:vntaɪd-] n UK euph residencia f de ancianos.

eventing [ɪ'ventɪŋ] n UK SPORT: **(three-day) eventing** concurso hípico de tres días.

eventual [ɪ'ventʃʊəl] adj final.

eventuality [ɪ,ventʃʊ'ælətɪ] (pl -ies) n eventualidad f.

eventually [ɪ'ventʃʊəlɪ] adv finalmente.

ever ['evə^r] *adv* - **1.** [at any time] alguna vez; **have you ever done it?** ¿lo has hecho alguna vez?; **the best ever** el mejor de todos los tiempos; **hardly ever** casi nunca; **if ever** si acaso - **2.** [all the time] siempre; **all he ever does is complain** no hace más que quejarse; **as ever** como siempre; **for ever** para siempre - **3.** [for emphasis]: **ever so big** muy grande; **ever such a mess** un lío tan grande; **we had ever such a good time** lo pasamos verdaderamente en grande; **why/how ever did you do it?** ¿por qué/cómo diablos lo hiciste?; **what ever can it be?** ¿qué diablos puede ser?
➡ **ever since** <> *adv* desde entonces. <> *conj* desde que. <> *prep* desde.

Everest ['evərɪst] *n* Everest.

evergreen ['evəgri:n] <> *adj* de hoja perenne. <> *n* árbol *m* de hoja perenne.

everlasting [,evə'lɑ:stɪŋ] *adj* eterno(na).

every ['evrɪ] *adj* cada; **every day** cada día, todos los días; **every week** todas las semanas; **there's every chance he'll win** tiene bastantes posibilidades de ganar.
➡ **every now and then, every so often** *adv* de vez en cuando.
➡ **every other** *adj*: **every other day** un día sí y otro no, cada dos días.
➡ **every which way** *adv US* en todas direcciones, sin orden ni concierto.

everybody ['evrɪ,bɒdɪ] = **everyone**.

everyday ['evrɪdeɪ] *adj* diario(ria), cotidiano(na).

everyone ['evrɪwʌn], **everybody** *pron* todo el mundo, todos(das).

everyplace *US* = **everywhere**.

everything ['evrɪθɪŋ] *pron* todo; **money isn't everything** el dinero no lo es todo.

everywhere ['evrɪweə^r], **everyplace** *US* ['evrɪ,pleɪs] *adv* en OR por todas partes; [with verbs of motion] a todas partes; **everywhere you go** dondequiera que vayas.

evict [ɪ'vɪkt] *vt*: **to evict sb from** desahuciar a alguien de.

eviction [ɪ'vɪkʃn] *n* desahucio *m*.

eviction notice *n* notificación *f* de desahucio.

evidence ['evɪdəns] *(U) n* - **1.** [proof] pruebas *fpl* - **2.** LAW [of witness] declaración *f*, testimonio *m*; **to give evidence** dar testimonio, prestar declaración.
➡ **in evidence** *adj* [noticeable]: **to be in evidence** hacerse notar.

evident ['evɪdənt] *adj* evidente, manifiesto(ta).

evidently ['evɪdəntlɪ] *adv* - **1.** [seemingly] por lo visto, al parecer - **2.** [obviously] evidentemente.

evil ['i:vl] <> *adj* [person] malo(la), malvado(da); [torture, practice] perverso(sa), vil. <> *n* - **1.** [evil quality] maldad *f* - **2.** [evil thing] mal *m*.

evil-minded [-'maɪndɪd] *adj* malintencionado(da).

evince [ɪ'vɪns] *vt fml* mostrar.

evocation [,evəʊ'keɪʃn] *n* evocación *f*.

evocative [ɪ'vɒkətɪv] *adj* evocador(ra), sugerente.

evoke [ɪ'vəʊk] *vt* - **1.** [memory, emotion] evocar - **2.** [response] producir.

evolution [,i:və'lu:ʃn] *n* - **1.** BIOL evolución *f* - **2.** [development] desarrollo *m*.

evolve [ɪ'vɒlv] <> *vt* desarrollar. <> *vi* - **1.** BIOL: **to evolve (into/from)** evolucionar (en/de) - **2.** [develop] desarrollarse.

ewe [ju:] *n* oveja *f*.

ex [eks] *n inf* [former spouse, lover etc] ex *mf*.

ex- [eks] *prefix* ex-.

exacerbate [ɪg'zæsəbeɪt] *vt* exacerbar.

exact [ɪg'zækt] <> *adj* exacto(ta); **to be exact** para ser exactos. <> *vt*: **to exact sthg (from)** arrancar algo (a).

exacting [ɪg'zæktɪŋ] *adj* - **1.** [job, work] arduo(dua) - **2.** [standards] severo(ra); [person] exigente.

exactitude [ɪg'zæktɪtju:d] *n fml* exactitud *f*.

exactly [ɪg'zæktlɪ] <> *adv* [precisely] exactamente; **it's exactly ten o'clock** son las diez en punto; **not exactly** [not really] no precisamente; [as reply] no exactamente. <> *excl* ¡exacto!, ¡exactamente!

exaggerate [ɪg'zædʒəreɪt] *vt & vi* exagerar.

exaggerated [ɪg'zædʒəreɪtɪd] *adj* exagerado(da).

exaggeration [ɪg,zædʒə'reɪʃn] *n* exageración *f*.

exalted [ɪg'zɔ:ltɪd] *adj* [person, position] elevado(da).

exam [ɪg'zæm] (*abbr of* **examination**) *n* examen *m*; **to take** OR **sit an exam** hacer un examen.

examination [ɪg,zæmɪ'neɪʃn] *n* - **1.** = **exam** - **2.** [inspection] inspección *f*, examen *m* - **3.** MED reconocimiento *m* - **4.** [consideration] estudio *m*.

examination board *n* tribunal *m* examinador.

examine [ɪg'zæmɪn] *vt* - **1.** [gen] examinar - **2.** MED reconocer - **3.** [consider - idea, proposal] estudiar - **4.** LAW interrogar.

examiner [ɪg'zæmɪnə^r] *n* examinador *m*, -ra *f*; **internal examiner** *examinador perteneciente al centro*; **external examiner** *examinador independiente o externo*.

example [ɪgˈzɑːmpl] *n* ejemplo *m*; **for example** por ejemplo; **to follow sb's example** seguir el ejemplo de alguien; **to make an example of sb** imponer un castigo ejemplar a alguien.

exasperate [ɪgˈzæspəreɪt] *vt* exasperar, sacar de quicio.

exasperating [ɪgˈzæspəreɪtɪŋ] *adj* exasperante.

exasperation [ɪg,zæspəˈreɪʃn] *n* exasperación *f*.

excavate [ˈekskəveɪt] *vt* excavar.

excavation [,ekskəˈveɪʃn] *n* excavación *f*.

excavator [ˈekskə,veɪtər] *n* UK [machine] excavadora *f*.

exceed [ɪkˈsiːd] *vt* - **1.** [amount, number] exceder, sobrepasar - **2.** [limit, expectations] rebasar.

exceedingly [ɪkˈsiːdɪŋlɪ] *adv* extremadamente.

excel [ɪkˈsel] (*pt & pp* -led, *cont* -ling) ◇ *vi*: to excel (in OR at) sobresalir (en). ◇ *vt*: to excel o.s. UK lucirse.

excellence [ˈeksələns] *n* excelencia *f*.

Excellency [ˈeksələnsɪ] (*pl* -ies) *n*: Your/His Excellency Su Excelencia.

excellent [ˈeksələnt] *adj* excelente.

except [ɪkˈsept] ◇ *prep & conj*: except (for) excepto, salvo. ◇ *vt*: to except sb (from) exceptuar OR excluir a alguien (de).

excepted [ɪkˈseptɪd] *adj* exceptuando a, excepto.

excepting [ɪkˈseptɪŋ] *prep* excepto, salvo.

exception [ɪkˈsepʃn] *n* - **1.** [exclusion]: exception (to) excepción *f* (a); with the exception of a excepción de; without exception sin excepción - **2.** [offence]: to take exception to ofenderse por.

exceptional [ɪkˈsepʃənl] *adj* excepcional.

exceptionally [ɪkˈsepʃnəlɪ] *adv* excepcionalmente.

excerpt [ˈeksɜːpt] *n*: excerpt (from) extracto *m* (de).

excess ◇ *adj* [ɪkˈses] excedente. ◇ *n* [ˈekses] exceso *m*; in excess of más de, por encima de; to excess en exceso.

➡ **excesses** *npl* excesos *mpl*.

excess baggage, excess luggage *n* exceso *m* de equipaje.

excess fare *n* UK suplemento *m*.

excessive [ɪkˈsesɪv] *adj* excesivo(va).

excess luggage = excess baggage.

exchange [ɪksˈtʃeɪndʒ] ◇ *n* - **1.** [gen] intercambio *m*; in exchange (for) a cambio (de) - **2.** FIN cambio *m* - **3.** TELEC: (telephone) exchange central *f* telefónica - **4.** *fml* [conversation]: a heated exchange una acalorada discusión.

◇ *vt* [swap] intercambiar; [goods in shop] cambiar; to exchange sthg for sthg cambiar algo por algo; to exchange sthg with sb intercambiar algo con alguien.

exchange rate *n* FIN tipo *m* de cambio.

Exchequer [ɪksˈtʃekər] *n* UK: the Exchequer ≈ Hacienda.

excise [ˈeksaɪz] ◇ *n* (U) impuestos *mpl* sobre el consumo interior. ◇ *vt* *fml* extirpar.

excise duties *npl* derechos *mpl* arancelarios.

excitable [ɪkˈsaɪtəbl] *adj* excitable.

excite [ɪkˈsaɪt] *vt* - **1.** [person] emocionar; [sexually] excitar - **2.** [suspicion, interest] despertar, suscitar.

excited [ɪkˈsaɪtɪd] *adj* emocionado(da), entusiasmado(da).

excitement [ɪkˈsaɪtmənt] *n* emoción *f*.

exciting [ɪkˈsaɪtɪŋ] *adj* emocionante, apasionante.

excl. (*abbr of* excluding) *sin incluir*; excl. taxes sin incluir impuestos.

exclaim [ɪkˈskleɪm] ◇ *vt* exclamar. ◇ *vi*: to exclaim (at) exclamar (ante).

exclamation [,ekskləˈmeɪʃn] *n* exclamación *f*.

exclamation mark *UK*, **exclamation point** *US n* signo *m* de admiración.

exclude [ɪkˈskluːd] *vt*: to exclude sthg/sb (from) excluir algo/a alguien (de).

excluding [ɪkˈskluːdɪŋ] *prep* sin incluir, con excepción de.

exclusion [ɪkˈskluːʒn] *n*: exclusion (from) exclusión *f* (de); to the exclusion of haciendo caso omiso de.

exclusion clause *n* cláusula *f* de exclusión.

exclusive [ɪkˈskluːsɪv] ◇ *adj* - **1.** [sole] exclusivo(va) - **2.** [high-class] selecto(ta). ◇ *n* [news story] exclusiva *f*.

➡ **exclusive of** *prep* excluyendo.

exclusively [ɪkˈskluːsɪvlɪ] *adv* exclusivamente.

excommunicate [,ekskəˈmjuːnɪkeɪt] *vt* excomulgar.

excommunication [ˈekskə,mjuːnɪˈkeɪʃn] *n* excomunión *f*.

excrement [ˈekskrɪmənt] *n* excremento *m*.

excrete [ɪkˈskriːt] *vt* *fml* excretar.

excruciating [ɪkˈskruːʃɪeɪtɪŋ] *adj* insoportable.

excursion [ɪkˈskɜːʃn] *n* excursión *f*.

excusable [ɪkˈskjuːzəbl] *adj* perdonable.

excuse ◇ *n* [ɪkˈskjuːs] excusa *f*; to make an excuse dar una excusa, excusarse. ◇ *vt* [ɪkˈskjuːz] - **1.** [gen]: to excuse sb (for sthg/for doing sthg) perdonar a alguien (por algo/por haber hecho algo); to excuse o.s. (for doing

sthg) excusarse OR disculparse (por haber hecho algo) - **2.** [let off]: **to excuse sb (from)** dispensar a alguien (de)
▶▶ **excuse me** [to attract attention] oiga (por favor); [when coming past] con permiso; [apologizing] perdone; US [pardon me?] ¿perdón?, ¿cómo?

ex-directory *adj* UK *que no figura en la guía telefónica.*

exec [ɪgˈzek] *abbr of* **executive**.

execrable [ˈeksɪkrəbl] *adj fml* execrable.

execute [ˈeksɪkjuːt] *vt* [gen & COMPUT] ejecutar.

execution [ˌeksɪˈkjuːʃn] *n* ejecución *f*.

executioner [ˌeksɪˈkjuːʃnər] *n* verdugo *m*.

executive [ɪgˈzekjutɪv] ⬦ *adj* - **1.** [decision-making] ejecutivo(va) - **2.** [for company executives] para OR de ejecutivos. ⬦ *n* - **1.** [person] ejecutivo *m*, -va *f* - **2.** [committee] ejecutiva *f*, órgano *m* ejecutivo.

executive director *n* director ejecutivo *m*, directora ejecutiva *f*.

executive toy *n* juego *m* de concentración *(para la oficina).*

executor [ɪgˈzekjutər] *n* albacea *m*.

exemplary [ɪgˈzempləri] *adj* [perfect] ejemplar.

exemplify [ɪgˈzemplɪfaɪ] *(pt & pp* -**ied**) *vt* ejemplificar.

exempt [ɪgˈzempt] ⬦ *adj*: **exempt (from)** exento(ta) (de). ⬦ *vt*: **to exempt sthg/sb (from)** eximir algo/a alguien (de).

exemption [ɪgˈzempʃn] *n* exención *f*.

exercise [ˈeksəsaɪz] ⬦ *n* - **1.** [gen] ejercicio *m*; **an exercise in** un ejercicio de; **to take exercise** hacer ejercicio - **2.** MIL maniobra *f*. ⬦ *vt* - **1.** [dog] llevar de paseo; [horse] entrenar - **2.** *fml* [power, right] ejercer; [caution, restraint] mostrar - **3.** [trouble]: **to exercise sb's mind** preocupar a alguien. ⬦ *vi* hacer ejercicio.

exercise bike *n* bicicleta *f* estática.

exercise book *n* cuaderno *m* de ejercicios.

exert [ɪgˈzɜːt] *vt* ejercer; **to exert o.s.** esforzarse.

exertion [ɪgˈzɜːʃn] *n* esfuerzo *m*.

ex gratia [eksˈɡreɪʃə] *adj* UK ex gratia.

exhale [eksˈheɪl] ⬦ *vt* exhalar, despedir. ⬦ *vi* espirar.

exhaust [ɪgˈzɔːst] ⬦ *n (U)* [fumes] gases *mpl* de combustión; **exhaust (pipe)** tubo *m* de escape. ⬦ *vt* agotar.

exhausted [ɪgˈzɔːstɪd] *adj* [person] agotado(da).

exhausting [ɪgˈzɔːstɪŋ] *adj* agotador(ra).

exhaustion [ɪgˈzɔːstʃn] *n* agotamiento *m*.

exhaustive [ɪgˈzɔːstɪv] *adj* exhaustivo(va).

exhibit [ɪgˈzɪbɪt] ⬦ *n* - **1.** ART objeto *m* expuesto; US [exhibition] exposición *f* - **2.** LAW prueba *f*

(instrumental). ⬦ *vt* - **1.** *fml* [feeling] mostrar, manifestar - **2.** ART exponer. ⬦ *vi* ART exponer.

exhibition [ˌeksɪˈbɪʃn] *n* - **1.** ART exposición *f* - **2.** [of feeling] manifestación *f*, demostración *f* ▶▶ **to make an exhibition of o.s.** UK ponerse en evidencia, hacer el ridículo.

exhibitionist [ˌeksɪˈbɪʃnɪst] *n* exhibicionista *mf*.

exhibitor [ɪgˈzɪbɪtər] *n* expositor *m*, -ra *f*.

exhort [ɪgˈzɔːt] *vt fml*: **to exhort sb to do sthg** exhortar a alguien a hacer algo.

exhume [eksˈhjuːm] *vt fml* exhumar.

exile [ˈeksaɪl] ⬦ *n* - **1.** [condition] exilio *m*; **in exile** en el exilio - **2.** [person] exiliado *m*, -da *f*. ⬦ *vt*: **to exile sb (from/to)** exiliar a alguien (de/a).

exiled [ˈeksaɪld] *adj* exiliado(da).

exist [ɪgˈzɪst] *vi* existir.

existence [ɪgˈzɪstəns] *n* existencia *f*; **to be in existence** existir; **to come into existence** nacer.

existentialism [ˌegzɪˈstenʃəlɪzm] *n* existencialismo *m*.

existentialist [ˌegzɪˈstenʃəlɪst] ⬦ *adj* existencialista. ⬦ *n* existencialista *mf*.

existing [ɪgˈzɪstɪŋ] *adj* existente, actual.

exit [ˈeksɪt] ⬦ *n* salida *f*. ⬦ *vi* [gen & COMPUT] salir; THEAT hacer mutis.

exit poll *n* UK sondeo *m* electoral *(a la salida de los colegios electorales).*

exit visa *n* visado *m* OR visa *f* Amér de salida.

exodus [ˈeksədəs] *n* éxodo *m*.

ex officio [ˌeksəˈfɪʃɪəʊ] *adj & adv fml* en virtud del cargo.

exonerate [ɪgˈzɒnəreɪt] *vt*: **to exonerate sb (from)** exonerar a alguien (de).

exorbitant [ɪgˈzɔːbɪtənt] *adj* [cost] excesivo(va); [demand, price] exorbitante.

exorcist [ˈeksɔːsɪst] *n* exorcista *mf*.

exorcize, -ise [ˈeksɔːsaɪz] *vt* exorcizar.

exotic [ɪgˈzɒtɪk] *adj* exótico(ca).

expand [ɪkˈspænd] ⬦ *vt* ampliar. ⬦ *vi* extenderse, ampliarse; [materials, fluids] expandirse, dilatarse.
➡ **expand (up)on** *vt insep* desarrollar.

expanse [ɪkˈspæns] *n* extensión *f*.

expansion [ɪkˈspænʃn] *n* expansión *f*.

expansion card *n* COMPUT tarjeta *f* de expansión.

expansionist [ɪkˈspænʃənɪst] *adj* expansionista.

expansion slot *n* COMPUT ranura *f* de expansión.

expansive [ɪk'spænsɪv] *adj* [relaxed, talkative] expansivo(va).

expat ['ekspæt] *n* UK *inf* emigrado *m*, -da *f*.

expatriate [eks'pætrɪət] <> *adj* expatriado(da). <> *n* expatriado *m*, -da *f*.

expect [ɪk'spekt] <> *vt* - **1.** [gen] esperar; **to expect sb to do sthg** esperar que alguien haga algo; **to expect sthg (from sb)** esperar algo (de alguien); **to expect the worst** esperarse lo peor; **as expected** como era de esperar - **2.** [suppose] imaginarse, suponer; **I expect so** supongo que sí. <> *vi* - **1.** [anticipate]: **to expect to do sthg** esperar hacer algo - **2.** [be pregnant]: **to be expecting** estar embarazada OR en estado.

expectancy ⊳ **life expectancy**.

expectant [ɪk'spektənt] *adj* expectante.

expectantly [ɪk'spektəntlɪ] *adv* con expectación.

expectant mother *n* futura madre *f*, mujer *f* embarazada.

expectation [,ekspek'teɪʃn] *n* esperanza *f*; **against all expectation** OR **expectations**, **contrary to all expectation** OR **expectations** contrariamente a lo que se esperaba; **to live up to/fall short of expectations** estar/no estar a la altura de lo esperado.

expectorant [ɪk'spektərənt] *n* expectorante *m*.

expedient [ɪk'spi:djənt] *fml* <> *adj* conveniente, oportuno(na). <> *n* recurso *m*.

expedite ['ekspɪdaɪt] *vt* *fml* acelerar.

expedition [,ekspɪ'dɪʃn] *n* - **1.** [journey] expedición *f* - **2.** [outing] salida *f*.

expeditionary force [,ekspɪ'dɪʃnərɪ-] *n* cuerpo *m* expedicionario.

expel [ɪk'spel] (*pt* & *pp* **-led**, *cont* **-ling**) *vt* - **1.** [person]: **to expel sb (from)** expulsar a alguien (de) - **2.** [gas, liquid]: **to expel sthg (from)** expeler algo (de).

expend [ɪk'spend] *vt*: **to expend sthg (on)** emplear algo (en).

expendable [ɪk'spendəbl] *adj* reemplazable.

expenditure [ɪk'spendɪtʃər] *n* (U) gasto *m*.

expense [ɪk'spens] *n* (U) gasto *m*; **to go to great expense (to do sthg)** incurrir en grandes gastos (para hacer algo); **at the expense of** [sacrificing] a costa de; **at sb's expense** *lit* & *fig* a costa de alguien; **to spare no expense** no repararse en gastos.

◆ **expenses** *npl* COMM gastos *mpl*; **on expenses** a cargo de la empresa.

expense account *n* cuenta *f* de gastos.

expensive [ɪk'spensɪv] *adj* caro(ra).

experience [ɪk'spɪərɪəns] <> *n* experiencia *f*. <> *vt* experimentar.

experienced [ɪk'spɪərɪənst] *adj*: **experienced (at** OR **in)** experimentado(da) (en).

experiment [ɪk'sperɪmənt] <> *n* experimento *m*; **to carry out an experiment** llevar a cabo un experimento. <> *vi*: **to experiment (with/on)** experimentar (con), hacer experimentos (con).

experimental [ɪk,sperɪ'mentl] *adj* experimental.

expert ['eksp3:t] <> *adj*: **expert (at sthg/at doing sthg)** experto(ta) (en algo/en hacer algo); **expert advice** la opinión de un experto. <> *n* experto *m*, -ta *f*.

expertise [,eksp3:'ti:z] *n* (U) pericia *f*.

expire [ɪk'spaɪər] *vi* [licence, membership] caducar; [lease, deadline] vencer.

expiry [ɪk'spaɪərɪ] *n* [of licence, membership] caducación *f*; [of lease, deadline] vencimiento *m*.

expiry date *n* fecha *f* de caducidad.

explain [ɪk'spleɪn] <> *vt*: **to explain sthg (to sb)** explicar algo (a alguien). <> *vi* explicar; **to explain to sb about sthg** explicarle a alguien.

◆ **explain away** *vt sep* justificar.

explanation [,eksplə'neɪʃn] *n*: **explanation (for)** explicación *f* (de).

explanatory [ɪk'splænətrɪ] *adj* explicativo(va), aclaratorio(ria).

expletive [ɪk'spli:tɪv] *n* *fml* palabrota *f*.

explicit [ɪk'splɪsɪt] *adj* explícito(ta).

explode [ɪk'spləʊd] <> *vt* [bomb] hacer explotar; [building etc] volar; *fig* [theory] reventar. <> *vi* *lit* & *fig* estallar, explotar.

exploit <> *n* ['eksplɔɪt] proeza *f*, hazaña *f*. <> *vt* [ɪk'splɔɪt] explotar.

exploitation [,eksplɔɪ'teɪʃn] *n* (U) explotación *f*.

exploration [,eksplə'reɪʃn] *n* exploración *f*.

exploratory [ɪk'splɒrətrɪ] *adj* [operation, examination] exploratorio(ria); [talks] preparatorio(ria).

explore [ɪk'splɔ:r] *vt* & *vi* *lit* & *fig* explorar.

explorer [ɪk'splɔ:rər] *n* explorador *m*, -ra *f*.

explosion [ɪk'spləʊʒn] *n* explosión *f*.

explosive [ɪk'spləʊsɪv] <> *adj* explosivo(va). <> *n* explosivo *m*.

explosive device *n* artefacto *m* explosivo.

exponent [ɪk'spəʊnənt] *n* - **1.** [supporter] partidario *m*, -ria *f* - **2.** [expert] experto *m*, -ta *f*.

exponential [,ekspə'nenʃl] *adj* *fml* [growth] vertiginoso(sa).

export <> *n* ['ekspɔ:t] - **1.** [act] exportación *f* - **2.** [exported product] artículo *m* de exportación. <> *comp* de exportación. <> *vt* [ɪk'spɔ:t] COMM & COMPUT exportar.

◆ **exports** *npl* exportaciones *fpl*.

exportable [ɪk'spɔ:təbl] *adj* exportable.

exportation [,ekspɔ:'teɪʃn] *n* exportación *f*.

exporter [ek'spɔ:tər] *n* exportador *m*, -ra *f*.

export licence n UK licencia f de exportación.

expose [ɪk'spəʊz] vt - **1.** [to sunlight, danger etc & PHOT] exponer; **to be exposed to sthg** estar OR verse expuesto a algo - **2.** [reveal, uncover] descubrir.

exposé [eks'pəʊzeɪ] n revelación f.

exposed [ɪk'spəʊzd] adj [land, house, position] expuesto(ta), al descubierto.

exposition [ˌekspə'zɪʃn] n - **1.** fml [explanation] explicación f - **2.** [exhibition] feria f.

exposure [ɪk'spəʊʒəʳ] n - **1.** [to light, radiation] exposición f - **2.** MED hipotermia f - **3.** [unmasking - of person] desenmascaramiento m; [- of corruption] revelación f - **4.** PHOT [time] (tiempo m de) exposición f; [photograph] fotografía f - **5.** [publicity] publicidad f.

exposure meter n fotómetro m.

expound [ɪk'spaʊnd] fml ◇ vt exponer. ◇ vi: **to expound on sthg** hablar sobre algo.

express [ɪk'spres] ◇ adj - **1.** UK [letter, delivery] urgente - **2.** [train, coach] expreso(sa), rápido(da) - **3.** fml [specific] expreso(sa). ◇ adv urgente. ◇ n [train] expreso m. ◇ vt expresar; **to express o.s.** expresarse.

expression [ɪk'spreʃn] n expresión f.

expressionism [ɪk'spreʃənɪzm] n expresionismo m.

expressionist [ɪk'spreʃənɪst] ◇ adj expresionista. ◇ n expresionista mf.

expressionless [ɪk'spreʃənlɪs] adj inexpresivo(va).

expressive [ɪk'spresɪv] adj [full of feeling] expresivo(va).

expressively [ɪk'spresɪvlɪ] adv de manera expresiva.

expressly [ɪk'spreslɪ] adv [specifically] expresamente.

expressway [ɪk'spresweɪ] n US autopista f.

expropriate [eks'prəʊprɪeɪt] vt fml expropiar.

expropriation [eksˌprəʊprɪ'eɪʃn] n fml expropiación f.

expulsion [ɪk'spʌlʃn] n: **expulsion (from)** expulsión f (de).

exquisite [ɪk'skwɪzɪt] adj exquisito(ta).

exquisitely [ɪk'skwɪzɪtlɪ] adv [beautifully] de forma exquisita.

ex-serviceman n UK excombatiente m.

ex-servicewoman n UK excombatiente f.

ext., extn. (abbr of extension) ext., extn.; **ext. 4174** ext. 4174.

extant [ek'stænt] adj existente.

extemporize, -ise [ɪk'stempəraɪz] vi fml improvisar.

extend [ɪk'stend] ◇ vt - **1.** [gen] extender; [house] ampliar; [road, railway] prolongar; [visa, deadline] prorrogar - **2.** [offer - welcome, help] brindar; [- credit] conceder. ◇ vi - **1.** [become longer] extenderse - **2.** [include]: **to extend to sthg** incluir algo - **3.** [from surface, object] sobresalir.

extendable [ɪk'stendəbl] adj - **1.** [deadline, visa] prorrogable - **2.** [ladder] extensible.

extended-play [ɪk'stendɪd-] adj [record] EP (inv).

extension [ɪk'stenʃn] n - **1.** [gen & TELEC] extensión f - **2.** [to building] ampliación f - **3.** [of visit] prolongación f; [of deadline, visa] prórroga f - **4.** COMPUT: **filename extension** extensión f del nombre de fichero - **5.** ELEC: **extension (lead)** alargador m.

extension cable n alargador m.

extensive [ɪk'stensɪv] adj [gen] extenso(sa); [changes] profundo(da); [negotiations] amplio(plia); **to make extensive use of** hacer (un) gran uso de.

extensively [ɪk'stensɪvlɪ] adv [gen] extensamente; [change] profundamente; **to use sthg extensively** hacer (un) gran uso de algo.

extent [ɪk'stent] n - **1.** [size] extensión f - **2.** [of problem, damage] alcance m - **3.** [degree]: **to what extent...?** ¿hasta qué punto...?; **to the extent that** [in that, in so far as] en la medida en que; [to the point where] hasta tal punto que; **to some/a certain extent** hasta cierto punto; **to a large** OR **great extent** en gran medida.

extenuating circumstances [ɪk'stenjʊeɪtɪŋ-] npl circunstancias fpl atenuantes.

exterior [ɪk'stɪərɪəʳ] ◇ adj exterior. ◇ n exterior m.

exterminate [ɪk'stɜːmɪneɪt] vt exterminar.

extermination [ɪkˌstɜːmɪ'neɪʃn] n exterminio m.

external [ɪk'stɜːnl] adj externo(na).
➡ **externals** npl aspecto m exterior.

externally [ɪk'stɜːnəlɪ] adv por fuera; **'to be applied externally'** 'de uso tópico'.

extinct [ɪk'stɪŋkt] adj extinto(ta).

extinction [ɪk'stɪŋkʃn] n [of species] extinción f.

extinguish [ɪk'stɪŋgwɪʃ] vt fml [gen] extinguir; [cigarette] apagar.

extinguisher [ɪk'stɪŋgwɪʃəʳ] n extintor m.

extn. = **ext.**

extol (pt & pp **-led**, cont **-ling**) UK, **extoll** US [ɪk'stəʊl] vt [merits, values] ensalzar.

extort [ɪk'stɔːt] vt: **to extort sthg from sb** [confession, promise] arrancar algo a alguien; [money] sacar algo a alguien.

extortion [ɪk'stɔːʃn] n extorsión f.

extortionate [ɪk'stɔːʃnət] adj desorbitado(da), exorbitante.

extra ['ekstrə] ◇ adj [additional] adicional; [spare] de más, de sobra; **take extra care** pon sumo cuidado. ◇ n - **1.** [addition] extra m - **2.** [additional charge] suplemento m - **3.** CIN & THEAT extra mf. ◇ adv extra; **to pay/charge extra** pagar/cobrar un suplemento; **be extra careful** pon sumo cuidado.

extra- ['ekstrə] prefix extra-.

extract ◇ n ['ekstrækt] - **1.** [from book, piece of music] fragmento m - **2.** CHEM extracto m. ◇ vt [ɪk'strækt]: **to extract sthg (from)** [gen] extraer algo (de); [confession] arrancar algo (de).

extraction [ɪk'strækʃn] n extracción f.

extracurricular [ˌekstrəkə'rɪkjʊlər] adj SCH extraescolar.

extradite ['ekstrədaɪt] vt: **to extradite sb (from/to)** extraditar a alguien (de/a).

extradition [ˌekstrə'dɪʃn] ◇ n extradición f. ◇ comp de extradición.

extramarital [ˌekstrə'mærɪtl] adj extramatrimonial.

extramural [ˌekstrə'mjʊərəl] adj UNIV fuera de la universidad pero organizado por ella.

extraneous [ɪk'streɪnjəs] adj - **1.** [irrelevant] ajeno(na) - **2.** [outside] externo(na).

extraordinary [ɪk'strɔːdnrɪ] adj extraordinario(ria).

extraordinary general meeting n junta f (general) extraordinaria.

extrapolate [ɪk'stræpəleɪt] ◇ vt - **1.** MATHS: **to extrapolate sthg (from)** extrapolar algo (a partir de) - **2.** [deduce]: **to extrapolate sthg (from)** deducir algo (a partir de). ◇ vi - **1.** MATHS: **to extrapolate from** extrapolar a partir de - **2.** [deduce]: **to extrapolate from** deducir a partir de.

extrasensory perception [ˌekstrə'sensərɪ-] n percepción f extrasensorial.

extraterrestrial [ˌekstrətə'restrɪəl] ◇ adj extraterrestre. ◇ n extraterrestre mf.

extra time n UK FTBL prórroga f.

extravagance [ɪk'strævəgəns] n - **1.** (U) [excessive spending] derroche m, despilfarro m - **2.** [luxury] extravagancia f.

extravagant [ɪk'strævəgənt] adj - **1.** [wasteful] derrochador(ra) - **2.** [expensive] caro(ra) - **3.** [exaggerated] extravagante.

extravaganza [ɪkˌstrævə'gænzə] n fastos mpl, espectáculo público de enorme fastuosidad.

extreme [ɪk'striːm] ◇ adj extremo(ma). ◇ n [furthest limit] extremo m; **to go to extremes** tener que recurrir a medidas extremas; **in the extreme** en grado sumo, en extremo.

extremely [ɪk'striːmlɪ] adv [very] sumamente, extremadamente.

extremism [ɪk'striːmɪzm] n extremismo m.

extremist [ɪk'striːmɪst] ◇ adj extremista. ◇ n extremista mf.

extremity [ɪk'stremətɪ] (pl -ies) n - **1.** fml [extreme adversity] suma gravedad f - **2.** [extremeness] extremosidad f - **3.** fml [end] extremo m.

➡ **extremities** npl [of body] extremidades fpl.

extricate ['ekstrɪkeɪt] vt: **to extricate sthg from** lograr sacar algo de; **to extricate o.s. from** lograr salirse de.

extrovert ['ekstrəvɜːt] ◇ adj extrovertido(da). ◇ n extrovertido m, -da f.

extruded [ɪk'struːdɪd] adj [metal, plastic] extrudido(da).

exuberance [ɪg'zjuːbərəns] n euforia f.

exuberant [ɪg'zjuːbərənt] adj eufórico(ca).

exude [ɪg'zjuːd] vt lit & fig rezumar.

exult [ɪg'zʌlt] vi: **to exult (at** OR **in)** regocijarse (por).

exultant [ɪg'zʌltənt] adj [person] jubiloso(sa); [cry] de júbilo.

eye [aɪ] ◇ n ojo m; **all eyes will be on her** será el centro de todas las miradas; **before my** etc **(very) eyes** ante mis etc propios ojos; **to cast** OR **run one's eye over sthg** echar un ojo OR un vistazo a algo; **to catch one's/sb's eye** llamar la atención de uno/alguien; **to clap** OR **lay** OR **set eyes on sb** echar el ojo a alguien; **to cry one's eyes out** llorar a lágrima viva; **to feast one's eyes on sthg** regalarse la vista con algo; **to have an eye for sthg** tener buen ojo para algo; **to have one's eye on sthg** tener el ojo echado a algo; **in my** etc **eyes** a mi etc entender; **in the eyes of the law** a (los) ojos de la ley; **to keep one's eyes open for, to keep an eye out for** estar atento(ta) a; **to keep an eye on sthg** vigilar algo; **there is more to this than meets the eye** esto es más complicado de lo que parece; **to open sb's eyes (to sthg)** abrirle los ojos a alguien (sobre algo); **not to see eye to eye with sb** no ver las cosas de la misma forma que alguien; **to close** OR **shut one's eyes to sthg** cerrar los ojos a algo; **to turn a blind eye (to sthg)** hacer la vista gorda (a algo); **to be up to one's eyes in work** UK estar hasta el cuello de trabajo. ◇ vt (cont eye**ing** OR eying) mirar.

➡ **eye up** vt sep UK comerse con los ojos.

eyeball ['aɪbɔːl] ◇ n globo m ocular. ◇ vt inf clavar los ojos en.

eyebath ['aɪbɑːθ] n lavaojos m inv, baño m ocular.

eyebrow ['aɪbraʊ] n ceja f; **to raise one's eyebrows** fig arquear las cejas.

eyebrow pencil n delineador m de cejas.

eye candy n (U) inf hum & pej persona o cosa atractiva superficialmente pero sin mucho contenido.

eye-catching adj llamativo(va).

eye contact n contacto m visual.

eyedrops ['aɪdrɒps] npl colirio m.

eyeglasses ['aɪglɑsɪz] n US [spectacles] gafas fpl Esp, lentes mpl Amér.

eyelash ['aɪlæʃ] n pestaña f.

eyelet ['aɪlɪt] n ojete m.

eye level n: at eye level a la altura de los ojos.

eyelid ['aɪlɪd] n párpado m; she didn't bat an eyelid ni siquiera parpadeó.

eyeliner ['aɪˌlaɪnər] n lápiz m de ojos.

eye-opener n inf [revelation] revelación f; [surprise] sorpresa f.

eyepatch ['aɪpætʃ] n parche m (en el ojo).

eye shadow n sombra f de ojos.

eyesight ['aɪsaɪt] n vista f; to have good eyesight tener buena vista.

eyesore ['aɪsɔːr] n horror m, monstruosidad f.

eyestrain ['aɪstreɪn] n vista f cansada.

eye test n revisión f ocular.

eyetooth ['aɪtuːθ] (pl -teeth) n: to give one's eyeteeth for sthg/to do sthg dar lo que fuera por algo/por hacer algo.

eyewash ['aɪwɒʃ] n (U) inf [nonsense] disparates mpl, tonterías fpl.

eyewitness [ˌaɪˈwɪtnɪs] n testigo mf ocular.

eyrie ['ɪərɪ] n aguilera f.

e-zine ['iːziːn] n fanzine m electrónico.

f (pl f's OR fs), **F** (pl F's OR Fs) [ef] n [letter] f f, F f.
F ◇ n - **1.** MUS fa m - **2.** SCH ≃ muy deficiente m. ◇ adj (abbr of Fahrenheit) F.

FA (abbr of Football Association) n federación inglesa de fútbol.

FAA (abbr of Federal Aviation Administration) n dirección federal estadounidense de aviación civil.

fab [fæb] adj inf genial.

fable ['feɪbl] n [traditional story] fábula f.

fabled ['feɪbld] adj legendario(ria).

fabric ['fæbrɪk] n - **1.** [cloth] tela f, tejido m - **2.** [of building, society] estructura f.

fabricate ['fæbrɪkeɪt] vt - **1.** [invent - story] inventar; [- evidence] falsear - **2.** [manufacture] fabricar.

fabrication [ˌfæbrɪˈkeɪʃn] n - **1.** [lying, lie] invención f - **2.** [manufacture] fabricación f.

fabulous ['fæbjʊləs] adj inf [excellent] fabuloso(sa).

fabulously ['fæbjʊləslɪ] adv fabulosamente, increíblemente.

facade [fəˈsɑːd] n fachada f.

face [feɪs] ◇ n - **1.** [of person] cara f, rostro m; face to face cara a cara; to fly in the face of sthg oponerse a algo; to look sb in the face mirar a alguien a la cara; to lose face quedar mal; to save face salvar las apariencias; to say sthg to sb's face decir algo a alguien en la cara; to show one's face dejarse ver; face time US [meeting] tiempo m de contacto personal; in your face inf atrevido(da) - **2.** [expression] semblante m, cara f; to make OR pull a face hacer muecas; her face fell puso cara larga - **3.** [person] cara f; new faces caras nuevas - **4.** [of cliff, mountain, coin] cara f; [of building] fachada f - **5.** [of clock, watch] esfera f - **6.** [appearance, nature] aspecto m - **7.** [surface] superficie f; the face of the earth la faz de la tierra; on the face of it a primera vista. ◇ vt - **1.** [point towards] mirar a - **2.** [confront, accept, deal with] hacer frente a, enfrentarse a; let's face it no nos engañemos - **3.** inf [cope with] aguantar, soportar. ◇ vi: to face forwards/south mirar hacia delante/al sur.
➤ **face down** adv boca abajo.
➤ **face up** adv boca arriba.
➤ **in the face of** prep [in spite of] ante.
➤ **face up to** vt insep hacer frente a, enfrentarse a.

facecloth ['feɪsklɒθ] n UK toallita f (para lavarse).

face cream n crema f facial.

faceless ['feɪslɪs] adj anónimo(ma), sin rostro.

face-lift n [on face] lifting m, estiramiento m de piel; to have a face-lift hacerse un lifting; fig [on building etc] lavado m de cara.

face pack n mascarilla f facial.

face powder n (U) polvos mpl (para la cara).

face-saving [-ˈseɪvɪŋ] adj para salvar las apariencias.

facet ['fæsɪt] n faceta f.

facetious [fəˈsiːʃəs] adj guasón(ona).

face-to-face adj cara a cara.

face value n [of coin, stamp] valor m nominal; to take sthg at face value tomarse algo literalmente.

facial ['feɪʃl] ◇ adj facial; [expression] de la cara. ◇ n limpieza f de cutis.

facile [UK 'fæsaɪl, US 'fæsl] adj fml & pej [remark, analysis] superficial; [reply, solution] facilón(ona).

facilitate [fə'sɪlɪteɪt] vt fml facilitar.

facility [fə'sɪlətɪ] (pl -ies) n - **1.** [ability]: **to have a facility for sthg** tener facilidad para algo - **2.** [feature] prestación f.

➼ **facilities** npl [amenities] instalaciones fpl; [services] servicios mpl.

facing ['feɪsɪŋ] adj opuesto(ta).

facsimile [fæk'sɪmɪlɪ] n facsímil m.

facsimile machine fml = **fax machine**.

fact [fækt] n - **1.** [piece of information] dato m; [established truth] hecho m; **the fact is** el hecho es que; **the fact remains that...** no obstante...; **to know sthg for a fact** saber algo a ciencia cierta - **2.** [truth] realidad f.

➼ **in fact** conj & adv de hecho, en realidad.

fact-finding [-'faɪndɪŋ] adj de investigación.

faction ['fækʃn] n [group] facción f.

factional ['fækʃənl] adj [dispute] entre facciones.

fact of life n: **it's a fact of life** es un hecho indiscutible.

➼ **facts of life** npl euph: **to tell sb (about) the facts of life** contar a alguien cómo nacen los niños.

factor ['fæktər] n factor m.

factory ['fæktərɪ] (pl -ies) n fábrica f.

factory farming n cría f intensiva de animales de granja.

factory ship n buque m factoría.

factotum [fæk'təʊtəm] (pl -s) n factótum m.

fact sheet n UK hoja f informativa.

factual ['fæktʃʊəl] adj basado(da) en hechos reales.

faculty ['fækltɪ] (pl -ies) n - **1.** [gen] facultad f - **2.** US [in college]: **the faculty** el profesorado.

FA Cup n ≃ Copa f del Rey.

fad [fæd] n [of society] moda f pasajera; [of person] capricho m.

faddy ['fædɪ] (comp **-ier**, superl **-iest**) adj inf pej tiquismiquis (inv).

fade [feɪd] ◇ vt descolorar, desteñir. ◇ vi - **1.** [jeans, curtains, paint] descolorarse, desteñirse; [flower] marchitarse - **2.** [light, sound, smile] irse apagando - **3.** [memory, feeling, interest] desvanecerse.

➼ **fade away** vi desvanecerse.

➼ **fade out** ◇ vt CIN fundir en negro. ◇ vi CIN fundirse en negro; MUS apagarse.

faded ['feɪdɪd] adj descolorido(da), desteñido(da).

faeces UK, **feces** US ['fiːsiːz] npl heces fpl.

Faeroe, Faroe ['feərəʊ] n: **the Faeroe Islands, the Faeroes** las islas Faroe.

faff [fæf] ➼ **faff about, faff around** vi UK inf enredar, perder el tiempo.

fag [fæg] n inf - **1.** UK [cigarette] pitillo m - **2.** US pej [homosexual] marica m, maricón m, joto m Méx.

fagged out [fægd-] adj UK inf molido(da), hecho(cha) polvo.

Fahrenheit ['færənhaɪt] adj Fahrenheit (inv).

fail [feɪl] ◇ vt - **1.** [exam, test, candidate] suspender - **2.** [not succeed]: **to fail to do sthg** no lograr hacer algo - **3.** [neglect]: **to fail to do sthg** no hacer algo - **4.** [let down] fallar. ◇ vi - **1.** [not succeed] fracasar; **if all else fails** en último extremo - **2.** [not pass exam] suspender - **3.** [stop functioning] fallar - **4.** [weaken] debilitarse.

failed [feɪld] adj fracasado(da).

failing ['feɪlɪŋ] ◇ n [weakness] fallo m. ◇ prep a falta de; **failing that** en su defecto.

fail-safe adj [device] protegido(da) en caso de fallos.

failure ['feɪljər] n - **1.** [lack of success, unsuccessful thing] fracaso m - **2.** [person] fracasado m, -da f - **3.** [in exam] suspenso m - **4.** [act of neglecting]: **her failure to do it** el que no lo hiciera - **5.** [breakdown, malfunction] avería f, fallo m - **6.** [of nerve, courage etc] pérdida f.

faint [feɪnt] ◇ adj - **1.** [weak, vague] débil, tenue; [outline] impreciso(sa); [memory, longing] vago(ga); [trace, hint, smell] ligero(ra), leve - **2.** [chance] reducido(da), remoto(ta) - **3.** [dizzy] mareado(da). ◇ vi desmayarse.

faint-hearted [-'hɑːtɪd] adj pusilánime.

faintly ['feɪntlɪ] adv - **1.** [smile, shine] débilmente; [recall] vagamente - **2.** [ludicrous, pathetic] ligeramente.

faintness ['feɪntnɪs] n (U) - **1.** [dizziness] mareos mpl - **2.** [of image] imprecisión f - **3.** [of memory] vaguedad f; [of smell, sound] levedad f.

fair [feər] ◇ adj - **1.** [just] justo(ta); **it's not fair!** ¡no hay derecho!; **to be fair...** para ser justos... - **2.** [quite large] considerable - **3.** [quite good] bastante bueno(na); **'fair'** SCH 'regular' - **4.** [hair] rubio(bia) - **5.** [skin, complexion] claro(ra) - **6.** [weather] bueno(na) - **7.** liter [beautiful] hermoso(sa). ◇ n - **1.** UK [unfair] feria f - **2.** [trade fair] feria f. ◇ adv [fairly] limpio.

➼ **fair enough** adv UK inf está bien, vale.

fair copy n copia f en limpio.

fair game n: **to be fair game (for)** ser un blanco m legítimo (para).

fairground ['feəɡraʊnd] n feria f.

fair-haired [-'heəd] adj rubio(bia).

fairly ['feəlɪ] *adv* - **1.** [moderately] bastante - **2.** [justly] justamente, equitativamente.

fair-minded [-'maɪndɪd] *adj* justo(ta), equitativo(va).

fairness ['feənɪs] *n* [justness] justicia *f*; **in fairness (to)** para ser justos (con).

fair play *n* juego *m* limpio.

fairway ['feəweɪ] *n* calle *f* (*en golf*).

fairy ['feərɪ] (*pl* **-ies**) *n* hada *f*.

fairy lights *npl* UK bombillas *fpl* OR luces *fpl* de colores.

fairy tale *n* cuento *m* de hadas.

fait accompli [,feɪtə'kɒmplɪ] (*pl* **faits accomplis** [,feɪtə'kɒmplɪ]) *n* hecho *m* consumado.

faith [feɪθ] *n* fe *f*; **in good/bad faith** de buena/mala fe.

faithful ['feɪθfʊl] <> *adj* fiel. <> *npl* RELIG: **the faithful** los fieles.

faithfully ['feɪθfʊlɪ] *adv* fielmente; **'Yours faithfully'** UK [in letter] 'le saluda atentamente'.

faithfulness ['feɪθfʊlnɪs] *n* fidelidad *f*.

faith healer *n persona que pretende curar enfermedades mediante la fe religiosa.*

faithless ['feɪθlɪs] *adj* [disloyal] desleal.

fake [feɪk] <> *adj* falso(sa). <> *n* - **1.** [object, painting] falsificación *f* - **2.** [person] impostor *m*, -ra *f*. <> *vt* - **1.** [results, signature] falsificar - **2.** [illness, emotions] fingir. <> *vi* [pretend] fingir.

falcon ['fɔːlkən] *n* halcón *m*.

Falkland Islands ['fɔːklənd-], **Falklands** ['fɔːkləndz] *npl*: **the Falkland Islands** las (islas) Malvinas.

fall [fɔːl] <> *vi* (*pt* **fell**, *pp* **fallen**) - **1.** [gen] caer; **he fell off the chair** se cayó de la silla; **she fell backwards** se cayó hacia atrás; **to fall to bits** OR **pieces** hacerse pedazos; **to fall flat** *fig* no causar el efecto deseado - **2.** [decrease] bajar, disminuir - **3.** [become]: **to fall asleep** dormirse; **to fall ill** ponerse enfermo(ma); **to fall silent** quedarse en silencio; **to fall vacant** quedar libre; **to fall in love** enamorarse, encamotarse *Andes & Amér C*; **to fall open** caer abierto(ta) - **4.** [belong, be classed]: **to fall into/under** pertenecer a - **5.** [MIL - city]: **to fall (to)** caer (en manos de) - **6.** UK POL [constituency]: **to fall to sb/sthg** ir a parar a alguien/algo - **7.** [cover]: **to fall on** OR **across** [light] iluminar; [shadow] oscurecer. <> *n* - **1.** [gen] caída *f* - **2.** [meteor]: **a fall of snow** una nevada - **3.** [MIL - of city] caída *f* - **4.** [decrease]: **fall (in)** descenso *m* (de) - **5.** US [autumn] otoño *m*.

◆ **falls** *npl* cataratas *fpl*.

◆ **fall about** *vi* UK *inf*: **to fall about (laughing)** partirse (de risa), troncharse.

◆ **fall apart** *vi* [book, chair] caerse a trozos, romperse; *fig* [country, person] desmoronarse.

◆ **fall away** *vi* - **1.** [land] descender - **2.** [plaster] desprenderse.

◆ **fall back** *vi* [person, crowd] echarse atrás, retroceder.

◆ **fall back on** *vt insep* [resort to] recurrir a.

◆ **fall behind** *vi* - **1.** [in race] quedarse atrás - **2.** [with rent, work] retrasarse.

◆ **fall down** *vi* - **1.** [to ground] caerse - **2.** [fail] fallar.

◆ **fall for** *vt insep* - **1.** *inf* [fall in love with] enamorarse de - **2.** [trick, lie] tragarse.

◆ **fall in** *vi* - **1.** [roof, ceiling] desplomarse, hundirse - **2.** MIL formar filas.

◆ **fall in with** *vt insep* [plan] aceptar; [crowd] juntarse con.

◆ **fall off** *vi* - **1.** [branch, handle] desprenderse - **2.** [demand, numbers] disminuir.

◆ **fall on** *vt insep* - **1.** [subj: eyes, gaze] posarse en - **2.** [attack] caer OR lanzarse sobre.

◆ **fall out** *vi* - **1.** [hair, tooth]: **his hair is falling out** se le está cayendo el pelo - **2.** [argue] pelearse, discutir - **3.** MIL romper filas.

◆ **fall over** <> *vt insep* tropezar con; **to be falling over o.s. to do sthg** *inf* desvivirse por hacer algo. <> *vi* [person, chair etc] caerse.

◆ **fall through** *vi* [plan, deal] fracasar.

◆ **fall to** *vt insep*: **it fell to me to do it** me tocó a mí hacerlo.

fallacious [fə'leɪʃəs] *adj fml* erróneo(a), falso(sa).

fallacy ['fæləsɪ] (*pl* **-ies**) *n* concepto *m* erróneo, falacia *f*.

fallen ['fɔːln] *pp* ⊳ **fall**.

fall guy *n* US *inf* [scapegoat] cabeza *m* de turco.

fallible ['fæləbl] *adj* falible.

falling ['fɔːlɪŋ] *adj* [decreasing] descendente, en descenso.

fallopian tube [fə'ləʊpɪən-] *n* trompa *f* de Falopio.

fallout ['fɔːlaʊt] *n* (*U*) - **1.** [radiation] lluvia *f* radiactiva - **2.** [consequences] secuelas *fpl*.

fallout shelter *n* refugio *m* atómico.

fallow ['fæləʊ] *adj* en barbecho; **to lie fallow** quedar en barbecho.

false [fɔːls] *adj* [gen] falso(sa); [eyelashes, nose] postizo(za).

false alarm *n* falsa alarma *f*.

falsehood ['fɔːlshʊd] *n fml* falsedad *f*.

falsely ['fɔːlslɪ] *adv* falsamente.

false start *n* [in race] salida *f* nula; *fig* comienzo *m* en falso.

false teeth *npl* dentadura *f* postiza.

falsetto [fɔːl'setəʊ] <> *n* (*pl* **-s**) falsete *m*. <> *adv* con falsete.

falsify ['fɔːlsɪfaɪ] (*pt* & *pp* **-ied**) *vt* [facts, accounts] falsificar.

falter ['fɔːltər] *vi* vacilar.

faltering ['fɔːltərɪŋ] *adj* [steps, voice] vacilante, titubeante.

fame [feɪm] *n* fama *f*.

familiar [fə'mɪljər] *adj* **- 1.** [known] familiar, conocido(da); **to be familiar to sb** serle familiar a alguien **- 2.** [conversant]: **familiar with** familiarizado(da) con; **to be on familiar terms with sb** tener trato informal con alguien **- 3.** *pej* [too informal - person] que se toma muchas confianzas; [- tone, manner] demasiado amistoso(sa).

familiarity [fə,mɪlɪ'ærətɪ] *n* (*U*) **- 1.** [knowledge]: **familiarity with** conocimiento *m* de **- 2.** [normality] familiaridad *f* **- 3.** *pej* [excessive informality] familiaridades *fpl*, confianzas *fpl*.

familiarize, -ise [fə'mɪljəraɪz] *vt*: **to familiarize o.s./sb with sthg** familiarizarse/familiarizar a alguien con algo.

family ['fæmlɪ] (*pl* **-ies**) ⬦ *n* familia *f*. ⬦ *comp* **- 1.** [belonging to family] familiar **- 2.** [suitable for all ages] para toda la familia.

family business *n* negocio *m* familiar.

family credit *n* (*U*) *UK* ≃ prestación *f* OR ayuda *f* familiar.

family doctor *n* médico *m* de cabecera.

family life *n* vida *f* familiar.

family planning *n* planificación *f* familiar.

family tree *n* árbol *m* genealógico.

famine ['fæmɪn] *n* hambruna *f*.

famished ['fæmɪʃt] *adj* *inf* [very hungry] muerto(ta) de hambre, famélico(ca).

famous ['feɪməs] *adj*: **famous (for)** famoso(sa) (por).

famously ['feɪməslɪ] *adv* *dated*: **to get on** OR **along famously (with sb)** llevarse de maravilla (con alguien).

fan [fæn] ⬦ *n* **- 1.** [of paper, silk] abanico *m* **- 2.** [electric or mechanical] ventilador *m* **- 3.** [of musician, fan etc] fan *mf*, admirador *m*, -ra *f*; [of music, art etc] aficionado *m*, -da *f*; FTBL hincha *mf*. ⬦ *vt* (*pt* & *pp* **-ned**, *cont* **-ning**) **- 1.** [cool] abanicar; **to fan o.s.** abanicarse **- 2.** [stimulate - fire, feelings] avivar.
➤ **fan out** *vi* (*pt* & *pp* **-ned**, *cont* **-ning**) desplegarse en abanico.

fanatic [fə'nætɪk] *n* fanático *m*, -ca *f*.

fanatical [fə'nætɪkl] *adj* fanático(ca).

fanaticism [fə'nætɪsɪzm] *n* fanatismo *m*.

fan belt *n* correa *f* del ventilador.

fanciful ['fænsɪfʊl] *adj* **- 1.** [odd] rocambolesco(ca) **- 2.** [elaborate] extravagante.

fan club *n* club *m* de fans.

fancy ['fænsɪ] ⬦ *vt* (*pt* & *pp* **-ied**) **- 1.** *inf* [feel like]: **I fancy a cup of tea/going to the cinema** me apetece una taza de té/ir al cine **- 2.** *inf* [desire]: **do you fancy her?** ¿te gusta?; **to fancy o.s.** tenérselo creído; **to fancy o.s. as sthg** dárselas de algo **- 3.** [imagine]: **fancy meeting you here!** ¡qué casualidad encontrarte por aquí!; **fancy that!** ¡imagínate!, ¡mira por donde! **- 4.** *dated* [think] creer. ⬦ *n* (*pl* **-ies**) **- 1.** [desire, liking] capricho *m*; **to take a fancy to** encapricharse con **- 2.** [fantasy] fantasía *f*. ⬦ *adj* (*comp* **-ier**, *superl* **-iest**) **- 1.** [elaborate] elaborado(da) **- 2.** [expensive] de lujo, caro(ra); [prices] exorbitante.

fancy dress *n* (*U*) disfraz *m*.

fancy-dress party *n* fiesta *f* de disfraces.

fancy goods *npl* artículos *mpl* de regalo.

fanfare ['fænfeər] *n* fanfarria *f*.

fang [fæŋ] *n* colmillo *m*.

fan heater *n* convector *m*, estufa *f* de aire.

fan mail *n* (*U*) cartas *fpl* de fans.

fanny ['fænɪ] *n* US *inf* [buttocks] culo *m*.

fanny pack *n* US riñonera *f*, banano *m* Chile.

fantasize, -ise ['fæntəsaɪz] *vi* fantasear; **to fantasize about sthg/about doing sthg** soñar con algo/con hacer algo.

fantastic [fæn'tæstɪk] *adj* **- 1.** [gen] fantástico(ca), chévere *Andes* **- 2.** [exotic] exótico(ca).

fantastically [fæn'tæstɪklɪ] *adv* **- 1.** [extremely] enormemente **- 2.** [exotically] de manera exótica.

fantasy ['fæntəsɪ] (*pl* **-ies**) ⬦ *n* fantasía *f*. ⬦ *comp* de ensueño.

fantasy football *n* (*U*) ≃ la liga fantástica®.

fanzine ['fænziːn] *n* fanzine *m*.

fao (*abbr of* **for the attention of**) a/a.

FAO (*abbr of* **Food and Agriculture Organization**) *n* FAO *f*.

FAQ ⬦ (*abbr of* **free alongside quay**), *muelle franco*. ⬦ *n* COMPUT (*abbr of* **frequently asked questions**) PMF *fpl*.

far [fɑːr] ⬦ *adv* **- 1.** [in distance, time] lejos; **is it far?** ¿está lejos?; **how far is it?** ¿a qué distancia está?; **how far is it to Prague?** ¿cuánto hay de aquí a Praga?; **far away** OR **off** [a long way away, a long time away] lejos; **as far back as 1900** ya en 1900; **so far** por ahora, hasta ahora; **far and wide** por todas partes; **from far and wide** de todas partes; **as far as** hasta **- 2.** [in degree or extent]: **far more/better/ stronger** mucho más/mejor/más fuerte; **I wouldn't trust him very far** no me fiaría mucho de él; **how far have you got?** ¿hasta dónde has llegado?; **he's not far wrong** OR **out** OR **off** no anda del todo descaminado; **as far as I**

know que yo sepa; **as far as I'm concerned** por OR en lo que a mí respecta; **as far as possible** en (la medida de) lo posible; **it's all right as far as it goes** para lo que es, no está mal; **far and away, by far** con mucho; **far from it** en absoluto, todo lo contrario; **so far** [until now] hasta el momento; [to a certain extent] hasta un cierto punto; **so far so good** por OR hasta ahora todo va bien; **to go so far as to do sthg** llegar incluso a hacer algo; **to go too far** ir demasiado lejos. <> adj (comp **farther** OR **further**, superl **farthest** OR **furthest**) **- 1.** [extreme] extremo(ma) **- 2.** liter [remote] lejano(na).

faraway ['fɑːrəweɪ] adj **- 1.** [land etc] lejano(na) **- 2.** [look, expression] ausente.

farce [fɑːs] n lit & fig farsa f.

farcical ['fɑːsɪkl] adj absurdo(da), grotesco(ca).

fare [feəʳ] <> n **- 1.** [payment] (precio m del) billete m; [in taxi] tarifa f; [passenger] pasajero m, -ra f (de taxi) **- 2.** (U) fml [food] comida f. <> vi [manage]: **she fared well/badly** le fue bien/mal.

Far East n: **the Far East** el Extremo Oriente.

fare stage n UK [of bus] zona f tarifaria.

farewell [ˌfeəˈwel] <> n despedida f. <> excl liter ¡vaya con Dios!

farfetched [ˌfɑːˈfetʃt] adj traído(da) por los pelos, inverosímil.

farm [fɑːm] <> n [smaller] granja f, chacra f Amér; [larger] hacienda f. <> vt [land] cultivar; [livestock] criar. <> vi [grow crops] cultivar la tierra; [raise livestock] criar ganado.

➠ **farm out** vt sep subcontratar.

farmer ['fɑːməʳ] n [on smaller farm] granjero m, -ra f, chacarero m, -ra f Amér; [on larger farm] agricultor m, -ra f.

farmhand ['fɑːmhænd], **farm labourer, farm worker** n peón m, labriego m, -ga f.

farmhouse ['fɑːmhaʊs, pl -haʊzɪz] n granja f, caserío m.

farming ['fɑːmɪŋ] (U) n **- 1.** AGRIC & INDUST agricultura f **- 2.** [act - of crops] cultivo m; [- of animals] cría f, crianza f.

farm labourer = farmhand.

farmland ['fɑːmlænd] n (U) tierras fpl de labranza.

farmstead ['fɑːmsted] n US granja f.

farm worker = farmhand.

farmyard ['fɑːmjɑːd] n corral m.

Faroe = Faeroe.

far-off adj lejano(na), remoto(ta).

far-reaching [-ˈriːtʃɪŋ] adj trascendental, de amplio alcance.

farrier ['færɪəʳ] n herrero m, -ra f.

farsighted [ˌfɑːˈsaɪtɪd] adj **- 1.** [gen] con visión de futuro **- 2.** US [long-sighted] présbita.

fart [fɑːt] v inf <> n **- 1.** [flatulence] pedo m **- 2.** [person] gilipuertas mf inv. <> vi tirarse un pedo.

farther ['fɑːðəʳ] compar ▭➤ **far**.

farthest ['fɑːðəst] superl ▭➤ **far**.

fascia ['feɪʃə] n **- 1.** [on shop] rótulo m **- 2.** AUT salpicadero m **- 3.** [for mobile phone] carcasa f.

fascinate ['fæsɪneɪt] vt fascinar.

fascinating ['fæsɪneɪtɪŋ] adj fascinante.

fascination [ˌfæsɪˈneɪʃn] n fascinación f.

fascism ['fæʃɪzm] n fascismo m.

fascist ['fæʃɪst] <> adj fascista. <> n fascista mf.

fashion ['fæʃn] <> n **- 1.** [clothing, style, vogue] moda f; **in/out of fashion** de/pasado de moda **- 2.** [manner] manera f; **after a fashion** más o menos. <> vt fml **- 1.** [make] elaborar **- 2.** fig [mould] forjar.

fashionable ['fæʃnəbl] adj de moda.

fashion-conscious adj que sigue la moda.

fashion designer n diseñador m, -ra f de modas.

fashion show n pase m OR desfile m de modelos.

fast [fɑːst] <> adj **- 1.** [rapid] rápido(da) **- 2.** [clock, watch]: **her watch is two minutes fast** su reloj va dos minutos adelantado **- 3.** [dye, colour] sólido(da), que no destiñe. <> adv **- 1.** [rapidly] rápido, rápidamente; **how fast were they going?** ¿a qué velocidad conducían? **- 2.** [firmly]: **stuck fast** bien pegado(da); **to hold fast to sthg** [person, object] agarrarse fuerte a algo; [principles] mantenerse fiel a algo; **fast asleep** profundamente dormido. <> n ayuno m. <> vi ayunar.

fast breeder reactor n reactor m (reproductor) rápido.

fasten ['fɑːsn] <> vt **- 1.** [gen] sujetar; [clothes, belt] abrochar; **he fastened his coat** se abrochó el abrigo **- 2.** [attach]: **to fasten sthg to sthg** fijar algo a algo **- 3.** [hands, teeth] apretar. <> vi: **to fasten on to sb/sthg** aferrarse a alguien/algo.

fastener ['fɑːsnəʳ] n cierre m; [zip] cremallera f.

fastening ['fɑːsnɪŋ] n [of door, window] cerrojo m, pestillo m.

fast food n (U) comida f rápida.

fast-forward <> n avance m rápido. <> vt & vi correr hacia adelante.

fastidious [fəˈstɪdɪəs] adj [fussy] quisquilloso(sa).

fast lane *n* [on motorway] carril *m* rápido; **to live life in the fast lane** *fig* llevar un tren de vida frenético.

fat [fæt] <> *adj* (*comp* **-ter**, *superl* **-test**) **- 1.** [gen] gordo(da); **to get fat** engordar **- 2.** [meat] con mucha grasa **- 3.** [book, package] grueso(sa) **- 4.** [profit, fee, cheque] jugoso(sa) **- 5.** *iro* [small]: **a fat lot of good** OR **use that was!** ¡pues sí que sirvió de mucho eso! <> *n* **- 1.** [gen] grasa *f* **- 2.** [for cooking] manteca *f*.

fatal ['feɪtl] *adj* **- 1.** [mortal] mortal **- 2.** [serious] fatal, funesto(ta).

fatalism ['feɪtəlɪzm] *n* fatalismo *m*.

fatalistic [,feɪtə'lɪstɪk] *adj* fatalista.

fatality [fə'tælətɪ] (*pl* **-ies**) *n* **- 1.** [accident victim] víctima *f* mortal **- 2.** [predestination] fatalidad *f*.

fatally ['feɪtəlɪ] *adv* **- 1.** [mortally] mortalmente **- 2.** [seriously] gravemente.

fate [feɪt] *n* **- 1.** [destiny] destino *m*; **to tempt fate** tentar a la suerte **- 2.** [result, end] suerte *f*, final *m*.

fated ['feɪtɪd] *adj* predestinado(da); **to be fated to do sthg** estar predestinado a hacer algo.

fateful ['feɪtfʊl] *adj* fatídico(ca).

fat-free *adj* sin grasas.

father ['fɑːðər] <> *n lit & fig* padre *m*. <> *vt* engendrar.

➡ **Father** *n* **- 1.** [priest] padre *m* **- 2.** [God] Padre *m*.

Father Christmas *n* UK Papá *m* Noel.

fatherhood ['fɑːðəhʊd] *n* paternidad *f*.

father-in-law (*pl* **father-in-laws** OR **fathers-in-law**) *n* suegro *m*.

fatherly ['fɑːðəlɪ] *adj* paternal.

Father's Day *n* día *m* del padre.

fathom ['fæðəm] <> *n* braza *f*. <> *vt*: **to fathom sthg/sb (out)** llegar a comprender algo/a alguien.

fatigue [fə'tiːg] <> *n* fatiga *f*. <> *vt* fatigar.

➡ **fatigues** *npl* traje *m* de faena.

fatness ['fætnɪs] *n* [of person] gordura *f*.

fatten ['fætn] *vt* engordar.

➡ **fatten up** *vt sep* engordar, cebar.

fattening ['fætnɪŋ] *adj* que engorda.

fatty ['fætɪ] <> *adj* (*comp* **-ier**, *superl* **-iest**) graso(sa). <> *n* (*pl* **-ies**) *inf pej* gordinflón *m*, -ona *f*.

fatuous ['fætjʊəs] *adj* necio(cia).

faucet ['fɔːsɪt] *n* US grifo *m*, llave *f* *Amér*, canilla *f* *R Plata*, paja *f* *Amér C*, caño *m* *Perú*.

fault [fɔːlt] <> *n* **- 1.** [responsibility] culpa *f*; **it's my fault** es culpa mía; **through no fault of my own** sin que la culpa sea mía; **to be at** fault tener la culpa **- 2.** [mistake, imperfection] defecto *m*; **to find fault with** encontrar defectos a **- 3.** GEOL falla *f* **- 4.** [in tennis] falta *f*. <> *vt*: **to fault sb (on sthg)** criticar a alguien (en OR por algo).

faultless ['fɔːltlɪs] *adj* perfecto(ta), impecable.

faulty ['fɔːltɪ] (*comp* **-ier**, *superl* **-iest**) *adj* [machine, system] defectuoso(sa); [reasoning, logic] imperfecto(ta).

fauna ['fɔːnə] *n* fauna *f*.

faux pas [,fəʊ'pɑː] (*pl* **faux pas**) *n* plancha *f*, metedura *f* de pata.

favour UK, **favor** US ['feɪvər] <> *n* **- 1.** [gen] favor *m*; **in sb's favour** a favor de alguien; **to be in/out of favour (with)** ser/dejar de ser popular (con); **to do sb a favour** hacerle un favor a alguien; **to curry favour with sb** tratar de congraciarse con alguien; **to rule in sb's favour** fallar a favor de alguien **- 2.** [favouritism] favoritismo *m*. <> *vt* **- 1.** [prefer] decantarse por, preferir **- 2.** [treat better, help] favorecer **- 3.** *iro* [honour]: **to favour sb with sthg** honrar a alguien con algo.

➡ **in favour** *adv* [in agreement] a favor.

➡ **in favour of** *prep* **- 1.** [in preference to] en favor de **- 2.** [in agreement with]: **to be in favour of sthg/of doing sthg** estar a favor de algo/de hacer algo.

favourable UK, **favorable** US ['feɪvrəbl] *adj* [positive] favorable.

favourably UK, **favorably** US ['feɪvrəblɪ] *adv* favorablemente.

favoured UK, **favored** US ['feɪvəd] *adj* [with special advantages] privilegiado(da), favorecido(da).

favourite UK, **favorite** US ['feɪvrɪt] <> *adj* favorito(ta). <> *n* favorito *m*, -ta *f*.

➡ **favorites** *npl* COMPUT favoritos *mpl*.

favouritism UK, **favoritism** US ['feɪvrɪtɪzm] *n* favoritismo *m*.

fawn [fɔːn] <> *adj* beige (*inv*). <> *n* [animal] cervato *m*, cervatillo *m*. <> *vi*: **to fawn on sb** adular a alguien.

fax [fæks] <> *n* fax *m*. <> *vt* **- 1.** [send fax to] mandar un fax a **- 2.** [send by fax] enviar por fax.

fax machine, facsimile machine *n* fax *m*.

fax number *n* número *m* de fax.

faze [feɪz] *vt esp* US *inf* desconcertar.

FBI (*abbr of* **Federal Bureau of Investigation**) *n* FBI *m*.

FD (*abbr of* **Fire Department**) *n* cuerpo de bomberos en *Estados Unidos*.

FDA (*abbr of* **Food and Drug Administration**) *n organismo estadounidense para el control de medicamentos y productos alimentarios*.

FE n abbr of **Further Education**.

fear [fɪəʳ] <> n - **1.** [gen] miedo m, temor m; **for fear of** por miedo a - **2.** [risk] peligro m. <> vt - **1.** [be afraid of] temer - **2.** [anticipate] temerse; **to fear (that)...** temerse que... <> vi [be afraid]: **to fear for sb/sthg** temer por alguien/algo.

fearful ['fɪəfʊl] adj - **1.** fml [frightened] temeroso(sa) - **2.** [frightening] terrible, pavoroso(sa).

fearless ['fɪəlɪs] adj valiente, intrépido(da).

fearlessly ['fɪəlɪslɪ] adv sin miedo.

fearsome ['fɪəsəm] adj terrible, espantoso(sa).

feasibility [,fiːzə'bɪlətɪ] n viabilidad f.

feasibility study n estudio m de viabilidad.

feasible ['fiːzəbl] adj factible, viable.

feast [fiːst] <> n [meal] banquete m, festín m. <> vi: **to feast on** OR **off sthg** darse un banquete a base de algo.

feat [fiːt] n hazaña f.

feather ['feðəʳ] n pluma f.

feather bed n colchón m de plumas.

featherbrained ['feðəbreɪnd] adj [person] atontolinado(da); [idea, scheme] disparatado(da).

featherweight ['feðəweɪt] n [boxer] peso m pluma.

feature ['fiːtʃəʳ] <> n - **1.** [characteristic] característica f - **2.** [of face] rasgo m - **3.** GEOG accidente m geográfico - **4.** [article] artículo m de fondo - **5.** RADIO & TV [programme] programa m especial - **6.** CIN = **feature film**. <> vt [subj: film] tener como protagonista a; [subj: exhibition] tener como atracción principal a. <> vi: **to feature (in)** aparecer OR figurar (en).

feature film n largometraje m.

featureless ['fiːtʃəlɪs] adj anodino(na).

Feb. [feb] (abbr of **February**) feb.

February ['februərɪ] n febrero m; see also **September**.

feces US = **faeces**.

feckless ['feklɪs] adj irresponsable.

fed [fed] pt & pp ⊳ **feed**.

Fed [fed] <> n inf - **1.** (abbr of **Federal Reserve Board**), órgano de control del banco central estadounidense - **2.** US [FBI agent] agente mf del FBI. <> n - **1.** abbr of **federal** - **2.** abbr of **federation**.

federal ['fedrəl] adj federal.

Federal Bureau of Investigation n FBI m.

federalism ['fedrəlɪzm] n federalismo m.

federation [,fedə'reɪʃn] n federación f.

fed up adj: **fed up (with)** harto(ta) (de).

fee [fiː] n [to lawyer, doctor etc] honorarios mpl; **membership fee** cuota f de socio; **entrance fee** entrada f; **school fees** (precio m de) matrícula f.

feeble ['fiːbl] adj - **1.** [weak] débil - **2.** [poor, silly] pobre, flojo(ja).

feebleminded [,fiːbl'maɪndɪd] adj corto(ta) de entendederas.

feebleness ['fiːblnɪs] n (U) - **1.** [weakness] debilidad f - **2.** [of excuse, joke] flojedad f.

feebly ['fiːblɪ] adv - **1.** [weakly] débilmente - **2.** [ineffectively] de modo poco convincente.

feed [fiːd] <> vt (pt & pp **fed**) - **1.** [gen] alimentar; [animal] dar de comer a - **2.** [put, insert]: **to feed sthg into sthg** introducir algo en algo. <> vi comer; **to feed on** OR **off sthg** lit & fig alimentarse de algo. <> n - **1.** [of baby] toma f - **2.** [animal food] pienso m.

feedback ['fiːdbæk] n (U) - **1.** [reaction] respuesta f, reacciones fpl - **2.** COMPUT & ELEC realimentación f; [on guitar etc] feedback m.

feedbag ['fiːdbæg] n US morral m.

feeder ['fiːdəʳ] <> n [baby]: **he's a messy feeder** se ensucia mucho cuando come. <> comp: **feeder road** carretera f secundaria.

feeding bottle ['fiːdɪŋ-] n UK biberón m.

feel [fiːl] <> vt (pt & pp **felt**) - **1.** [touch] tocar - **2.** [sense, notice, experience] sentir; **I felt myself blushing** noté que me ponía colorado(da) - **3.** [believe] creer; **to feel (that)** creer OR pensar que

⯈⯈ **not to feel o.s.** no encontrarse bien. <> vi (pt & pp **felt**) - **1.** [have sensation]: **to feel hot/cold/sleepy** tener calor/frío/sueño; **how do you feel?** ¿cómo te encuentras? - **2.** [have emotion]: **to feel safe/happy** sentirse seguro/feliz - **3.** [seem] parecer (al tacto) - **4.** [by touch]: **to feel for sthg** buscar algo a tientas - **5.** [be in mood]: **do you feel like a drink/eating out?** ¿te apetece OR te provoca Andes & Méx beber algo/comer fuera? <> n - **1.** [sensation, touch] tacto m, sensación f - **2.** [atmosphere] atmósfera f

⯈⯈ **to have a feel for sthg** tener un don especial para algo.

feeler ['fiːləʳ] n antena f.

feeling ['fiːlɪŋ] n - **1.** [emotion] sentimiento m; **bad feeling** resentimiento m - **2.** [sensation] sensación f - **3.** [intuition] presentimiento m; **I have a** OR **get the feeling (that)...** me da la sensación de que... - **4.** [opinion] opinión f - **5.** [understanding] apreciación f, entendimiento m; **to have a feeling for sthg** saber apreciar algo.

⯈ **feelings** npl sentimientos mpl; **to hurt sb's feelings** herir los sentimientos de alguien; **no hard feelings?** ¿todo olvidado?, ¿sin rencores?

fee-paying [-'peɪɪŋ] adj UK de pago.

feet [fiːt] npl ⊳ **foot**.

feign [feɪn] *vt fml* fingir, aparentar.
feint [feɪnt] <> *n* finta *f*. <> *vi* fintar.
feisty ['faɪstɪ] (*comp* **-ier,** *superl* **-iest**) *adj esp US inf* combativo(va).
felicitous [fɪ'lɪsɪtəs] *adj fml* afortunado(da).
feline ['fi:laɪn] <> *adj* felino(na). <> *n fml* felino *m*.
fell [fel] <> *pt* ▷ **fall.** <> *vt* **- 1.** [tree] talar **- 2.** [person] derribar.
▶ **fells** *npl* GEOG monte *m*.
fellow ['feləʊ] <> *adj:* **fellow students/prisoners** compañeros de clase/celda; **fellow citizens** conciudadanos. <> *n* **- 1.** *dated* [man] tipo *m* **- 2.** [comrade, peer] camarada *mf*, compañero *m*, -ra *f* **- 3.** [of a society] miembro *m* **- 4.** [of college] miembro *m* del claustro de profesores.
fellowship ['feləʊʃɪp] *n* **- 1.** [comradeship] camaradería *f* **- 2.** [society] asociación *f* **- 3.** [grant] beca *f* de investigación.
felony ['felənɪ] (*pl* **-ies**) *n US* LAW crimen *m*, delito *m* grave.
felt [felt] <> *pt* & *pp* ▷ **feel.** <> *n (U)* fieltro *m*.
felt-tip pen *n* rotulador *m*.
female ['fi:meɪl] <> *adj* [animal, plant, connector] hembra; [figure, sex] femenino(na). <> *n* **- 1.** [female animal] hembra *f* **- 2.** [woman] mujer *f*.
feminine ['femɪnɪn] <> *adj* femenino(na). <> *n* GRAM femenino *m*.
femininity [femɪ'nɪnətɪ] *n* femineidad *f*.
feminism ['femɪnɪzm] *n* feminismo *m*.
feminist ['femɪnɪst] *n* feminista *mf*.
fence [fens] <> *n* valla *f*; **to sit on the fence** *fig* nadar entre dos aguas. <> *vt* [surround] vallar, cercar.
▶ **fence off** *vt sep* cerrar con una valla OR cerca.
fencing ['fensɪŋ] *n* **- 1.** SPORT esgrima *f* **- 2.** [material] material *m* para cercas.
fend [fend] *vi:* **to fend for o.s.** valerse por sí mismo(ma).
▶ **fend off** *vt sep* [blows] defenderse de, desviar; [questions, reporters] eludir.
fender ['fendər] *n* **- 1.** [round fireplace] pantalla *f*, guardafuego *m* **- 2.** [on boat] defensa *f* **- 3.** *US* [on car] guardabarros *m inv*.
fennel ['fenl] *n* hinojo *m*.
fens [fenz] *npl UK* pantanal *m*, zona *f* pantanosa.
feral ['fɪərəl] *adj* asilvestrado(da).
ferment <> *n* ['fɜ:ment] [unrest] agitación *f*; **in ferment** en estado de agitación. <> *vi* [fə'ment] fermentar.
fermentation [ˌfɜ:mən'teɪʃn] *n* fermentación *f*.

fermented [fə'mentɪd] *adj* fermentado(da).
fern [fɜ:n] *n* helecho *m*.
ferocious [fə'rəʊʃəs] *adj* feroz.
ferociously [fə'rəʊʃəslɪ] *adv* ferozmente.
ferocity [fə'rɒsətɪ] *n* ferocidad *f*.
ferret ['ferɪt] *n* hurón *m*.
▶ **ferret about, ferret around** *vi inf* rebuscar.
▶ **ferret out** *vt sep inf* conseguir descubrir.
ferris wheel ['ferɪs-] *n esp US* noria *f*.
ferry ['ferɪ] <> *n* [large, for cars] transbordador *m*, ferry *m*; [small] barca *f*. <> *vt* llevar, transportar.
ferryboat ['ferɪbəʊt] *n* transbordador *m*, ferry *m*.
ferryman ['ferɪmən] (*pl* **-men** [-mən]) *n* barquero *m*.
fertile ['fɜ:taɪl] *adj* fértil.
fertility [fə'tɪlətɪ] *n* fertilidad *f*.
fertility drug *n* medicamento *m* fertilizante.
fertilization [ˌfɜ:tɪlaɪ'zeɪʃn] *n* **- 1.** AGRIC fertilización *f*, abono *m* **- 2.** BIOL fecundación *f*.
fertilize, -ise ['fɜ:tɪlaɪz] *vt* **- 1.** AGRIC fertilizar, abonar **- 2.** BIOL fecundar.
fertilizer ['fɜ:tɪlaɪzər] *n* fertilizante *m*, abono *m*.
fervent ['fɜ:vənt] *adj* ferviente.
fervour *UK,* **fervor** *US* ['fɜ:vər] *n* fervor *m*.
fester ['festər] *vi lit* & *fig* enconarse.
festival ['festəvl] *n* **- 1.** [event, celebration] festival *m* **- 2.** [holiday] día *m* festivo.
festive ['festɪv] *adj* festivo(va).
festive season *n:* **the festive season** las Navidades.
festivities [fes'tɪvətɪz] *npl* festividades *fpl*.
festoon [fe'stu:n] *vt* engalanar.
fetal ['fi:tl] *US* = **foetal.**
fetch [fetʃ] *vt* **- 1.** [go and get] ir a buscar, traer **- 2.** *inf* [raise - money] venderse por, alcanzar.
fetching ['fetʃɪŋ] *adj* atractivo(va).
fete, fête [feɪt] <> *n* fiesta *f* benéfica. <> *vt* festejar, agasajar.
fetid ['fetɪd] *adj* fétido(da).
fetish ['fetɪʃ] *n* **- 1.** [object of sexual obsession] fetiche *m* **- 2.** [mania] obsesión *f*, manía *f*.
fetishism ['fetɪʃɪzm] *n* fetichismo *m*.
fetlock ['fetlɒk] *n* espolón *m*.
fetter ['fetər] *vt* encadenar, atar.
▶ **fetters** *npl* grilletes *mpl*.
fettle ['fetl] *n:* **in fine fettle** en plena forma.
fetus ['fi:təs] *US* = **foetus.**
feud [fju:d] <> *n* disputa *f*, enfrentamiento *m* duradero. <> *vi* pelearse.
feudal ['fju:dl] *adj* feudal.
fever ['fi:vər] *n lit* & *fig* fiebre *f*; **to have a fever** tener fiebre.

fevered ['fiːvəd] *adj lit & fig* febril.

feverish ['fiːvərɪʃ] *adj lit & fig* febril.

fever pitch *n*: excitement was at fever pitch los ánimos estaban muy exaltados.

few [fjuː] <> *adj* pocos(cas); **the next few weeks** las próximas semanas; **a few** algunos(nas); **a few more potatoes** algunas patatas más; **quite a few, a good few** bastantes; **few and far between** escasos, contados. <> *pron* pocos *mpl*, -cas *f*; **a few (of them)** algunos *mpl*, -nas *f*; **quite a few** bastantes *mpl* & *fpl*.

fewer ['fjuːər] <> *adj* menos; **no fewer than** nada menos que. <> *pron* menos.

fewest ['fjuːəst] *adj* menos; **I made the fewest mistakes** fui el que cometió menos errores.

FHA (*abbr of* **Federal Housing Administration**) *n organismo estadounidense para la gestión de viviendas sociales.*

fiancé [fɪ'ɒnseɪ] *n* prometido *m*.

fiancée [fɪ'ɒnseɪ] *n* prometida *f*.

fiasco [fɪ'æskəʊ] (*UK* **-s**, *US* **-es**) *n* fiasco *m*.

fib [fɪb] *inf* <> *n* bola *f*, trola *f*. <> *vi* (*pt & pp* **-bed**, *cont* **-bing**) decir bolas *OR* trolas.

fibber ['fɪbər] *n inf* bolero *m*, -ra *f*, trolero *m*, -ra *f*.

fibre *UK*, **fiber** *US* ['faɪbər] *n* fibra *f*.

fibreboard *UK*, **fiberboard** *US* ['faɪbəbɔːd] *n* (*U*) tablero *m* de fibras.

fibreglass *UK*, **fiberglass** *US* ['faɪbəglɑːs] <> *n* (*U*) fibra *f* de vidrio. <> *comp* de fibra de vidrio.

fibre-optic *adj* de fibra óptica.

fibre optics *n* (*U*) fibra *f* óptica.

fibroid ['faɪbrɔɪd] *n* fibroma *m*.

fibrositis [ˌfaɪbrə'saɪtɪs] *n* fibrositis *f inv*.

fickle ['fɪkl] *adj* voluble.

fiction ['fɪkʃn] *n* **- 1.** [stories] (literatura *f* de) ficción *f* **- 2.** [fabrication] ficción *f*.

fictional ['fɪkʃənl] *adj* **- 1.** [literary] novelesco(ca) **- 2.** [invented] ficticio(cia).

fictionalize, -ise ['fɪkʃənəlaɪz] *vt* novelar.

fictitious [fɪk'tɪʃəs] *adj* [false] ficticio(cia).

fiddle ['fɪdl] <> *n* **- 1.** [violin] violín *m*; **(as) fit as a fiddle** sano(na) como una manzana; **to play second fiddle (to)** estar relegado(da) a un segundo plano (respecto a) **- 2.** *UK inf* [fraud] timo *m*. <> *vt UK inf* amañar. <> *vi* [play around]: **to fiddle (with sthg)** juguetear (con algo).

◆ **fiddle about, fiddle around** *vi* [play around]: **to fiddle about (with sthg)** juguetear (con algo).

fiddler ['fɪdlər] *n* violinista *mf*.

fiddly ['fɪdlɪ] (*comp* **-ier**, *superl* **-iest**) *adj UK* [job] delicado(da); [gadget] intrincado(da).

fidelity [fɪ'delətɪ] *n* fidelidad *f*.

fidget ['fɪdʒɪt] *vi* moverse sin parar, no estarse quieto(ta).

fidgety ['fɪdʒɪtɪ] *adj inf* nervioso(sa), inquieto(ta).

fiduciary [fɪ'djuːʃjərɪ] <> *adj* fiduciario(ria). <> *n* (*pl* **-ies**) fiduciario *m*, -ria *f*.

field [fiːld] <> *n* [gen & COMPUT] campo *m*; **in the field** sobre el terreno; **field of vision** campo visual. <> *vt* **- 1.** [team] alinear; [candidate] presentar **- 2.** [ball] parar y devolver.

field day *n*: **to have a field day** disfrutar de lo lindo.

fielder ['fiːldər] *n* jardinero *m*, -ra *f*.

field event *sn* pruebas *fpl* atléticas de salto y lanzamiento.

field glasses *npl* prismáticos *mpl*, gemelos *mpl*.

field marshal *n* mariscal *m* de campo.

field mouse *n* ratón *m* de campo.

field trip *n* salida *f* para realizar trabajo de campo.

fieldwork ['fiːldwɜːk] *n* (*U*) trabajo *m* de campo.

fieldworker ['fiːldwɜːkər] *n* investigador *m*, -ra *f* que realiza trabajo de campo.

fiend [fiːnd] *n* **- 1.** [cruel person] malvado *m*, -da *f* **- 2.** *inf* [fanatic] fanático *m*, -ca *f*.

fiendish ['fiːndɪʃ] *adj* **- 1.** [evil] malévolo(la), diabólico(ca) **- 2.** *inf* [very difficult] endiablado(da).

fierce [fɪəs] *adj* [gen] feroz; [temper] endiablado(da); [loyalty] ferviente; [heat] asfixiante.

fiercely ['fɪəslɪ] *adv* **- 1.** [aggressively, ferociously] ferozmente **- 2.** [wildly] furiosamente **- 3.** [intensely] encarnizadamente, intensamente.

fiery ['faɪərɪ] (*comp* **-ier**, *superl* **-iest**) *adj* **- 1.** [burning] ardiente **- 2.** [volatile - temper] endiablado(da); [- speech] encendido(da), fogoso(sa); [- person] apasionado(da) **- 3.** [bright red] encendido(da).

FIFA ['fiːfə] (*abbr of* **Fédération Internationale de Football Association**) *n* FIFA *f*.

fifteen [fɪf'tiːn] *num* quince; *see also* **six**.

fifteenth [ˌfɪf'tiːnθ] *num* decimoquinto(ta); *see also* **sixth**.

fifth [fɪfθ] *num* quinto(ta); *see also* **sixth**.

Fifth Amendment *n*: **the Fifth Amendment** *la quinta enmienda de la Constitución* *de los Estados Unidos que garantiza los derechos de las personas inculpadas por un delito.*

Fifth Amendment

La quinta enmienda a la Constitución estadounidense, recogida en la "Bill of Rights" o carta de derechos, establece que ningún ciudadano está obligado a facilitar información ante un tribunal de justicia que pueda ser empleada en su contra y que no podrá ser encarcelado ni sufrir el embargo de sus bienes a menos que haya tenido un juicio justo. Esta enmienda también dispone que un ciudadano no podrá ser juzgado dos veces por el mismo delito. Ante un tribunal, se emplea la expresión "to plead the Fifth" ("acogerse a la Quinta") para recurrir a este derecho; la misma expresión es utilizada en tono jocoso cuando en lenguaje cotidiano se quiere dar a entender que no se tiene la intención de responder a una pregunta.

fiftieth ['fɪftɪəθ] *num* quincuagésimo(ma); *see also* **sixth**.

fifty ['fɪftɪ] *num* cincuenta; *see also* **sixty**.

fifty-fifty <> *adj* al cincuenta por ciento; **a fifty-fifty chance** unas posibilidades del cincuenta por ciento. <> *adv*: **to go fifty-fifty** ir a medias.

fig [fɪg] *n* higo *m*.

fight [faɪt] <> *n* [physical, verbal] pelea *f*; *fig* [struggle] lucha *f*; **to have a fight (with)** pelearse (con); **to put up a fight** oponer resistencia. <> *vt* (*pt & pp* **fought**) [gen] luchar contra; [in punch-up] pelearse con; [battle, campaign] librar; [war] luchar en. <> *vi* (*pt & pp* **fought**) - **1.** [in punch-up] pelearse; [in war] luchar - **2.** *fig* [battle, struggle]: **to fight (for/against)** luchar (por/contra) - **3.** [argue]: **to fight (about OR over)** pelearse OR discutir (por).
◆ **fight back** <> *vt insep* [tears, feelings] reprimir, contener. <> *vi* defenderse.
◆ **fight off** *vt sep* - **1.** [deter] rechazar - **2.** [overcome] ahuyentar, sobreponerse a.
◆ **fight out** *vt sep*: **they are left fighting it out for second place** van a tener que disputarse el segundo puesto.

fighter ['faɪtər] *n* - **1.** [plane] caza *m* - **2.** [soldier] combatiente *mf* - **3.** [boxer] púgil *mf* - **4.** [combative person] luchador *m*, -ra *f*.

fighting ['faɪtɪŋ] *n* (*U*) [on streets, terraces] peleas *fpl*; [in war] combates *mpl*.

fighting chance *n*: **to have a fighting chance (of doing sthg)** tener posibilidades (de hacer algo).

figment ['fɪgmənt] *n*: **to be a figment of sb's imagination** ser producto de la imaginación de alguien.

figurative ['fɪgərətɪv] *adj* figurado(da).

figuratively ['fɪgərətɪvlɪ] *adv* figuradamente.

figure [*UK* 'fɪgər, *US* 'fɪgjər] <> *n* - **1.** [statistic, number] cifra *f*; **to put a figure on sthg** dar un número exacto de algo; **to be in single/double figures** no sobrepasar/sobrepasar la decena - **2.** [shape of person, personality] figura *f* - **3.** [diagram] figura *f*. <> *vt esp US* [suppose] figurarse, suponer. <> *vi* - **1.** [feature] figurar - **2.** *inf* [be logical]: **that figures** es lógico.
◆ **figure out** *vt sep* [reason, motives] figurarse; [problem etc] resolver; [amount, quantity] calcular; **to figure out how to do sthg** dar con la manera de hacer algo.

figurehead ['fɪgəhed] *n* - **1.** [on ship] mascarón *m* de proa - **2.** [leader without real power] testaferro *m*.

figure of eight *UK*, **figure eight** *US n* forma *f* de ocho.

figure of speech *n* forma *f* de hablar.

figure skating *n* patinaje *m* artístico.

figurine [*UK* 'fɪgəri:n, *US* ,fɪgjə'ri:n] *n* estatuilla *f*.

Fiji ['fi:dʒi:] *n* Fiji.

Fijian [,fi:'dʒi:ən] <> *adj* fijiano(na). <> *n* fijiano *m*, -na *f*.

filament ['fɪləmənt] *n* [in lightbulb] filamento *m*.

filch [fɪltʃ] *vt inf* birlar, mangar.

file [faɪl] <> *n* - **1.** [folder] carpeta *f*; [box] archivador *m* - **2.** [report] expediente *m*, dossier *m*; **on file, on the files** archivado - **3.** COMPUT archivo *m* - **4.** [tool] lima *f* - **5.** [line]: **in single file** en fila india. <> *vt* - **1.** [put in file] archivar - **2.** LAW presentar - **3.** [shape, smooth] limar. <> *vi* - **1.** [walk in single file] ir en fila - **2.** LAW: **to file for divorce** presentar una demanda de divorcio.

filename ['faɪl,neɪm] *n* COMPUT nombre *m* de archivo.

filet *US* = **fillet**.

filibuster ['fɪlɪbʌstər] *vi esp US* POL pronunciar discursos obstruccionistas.

filigree ['fɪlɪgriː] <> *adj* de filigrana. <> *n* (*U*) filigrana *f*.

filing cabinet ['faɪlɪŋ-] *n* archivador *m*.

filing clerk ['faɪlɪŋ-] *n UK* archivero *m*, -ra *f* (de oficina).

Filipino [,fɪlɪ'pi:nəʊ] <> *adj* filipino(na). <> *n* (*pl* **-s**) filipino *m*, -na *f*.

fill [fɪl] <> *vt* - **1.** [gen]: **to fill sthg (with)** llenar algo (de) - **2.** [gap, hole, crack] rellenar; [tooth] empastar, calzar *Col* - **3.** [need, vacancy etc] cubrir; [time] ocupar. ⋄ *n*: **to eat one's fill** comer hasta hartarse; **to have had one's fill of sthg** estar hasta la coronilla de algo.

● **fill in** ⋄ *vt sep* - **1.** [complete] rellenar - **2.** [inform]: **to fill sb in (on)** poner a alguien al corriente (de). ⋄ *vt insep*: **to be filling in time** estar matando el tiempo. ⋄ *vi* [substitute]: **to fill in (for sb)** sustituir (a alguien).

● **fill out** ⋄ *vt sep* [complete] rellenar. ⋄ *vi* [get fatter] engordar.

● **fill up** ⋄ *vt sep* llenar (hasta arriba). ⋄ *vi* - **1.** [gen] llenarse - **2.** [buy petrol] repostar.

filled [fɪld] *adj* - **1.** [roll] relleno(na) - **2.** [with emotion]: **filled with** lleno(na) de.

filler ['fɪləʳ] *n* [for cracks] masilla *f*.

filler cap *n* UK tapón *m* del depósito de gasolina.

fillet UK, **filet** US ['fɪlɪt] ⋄ *n* filete *m*. ⋄ *vt* cortar en filetes.

fillet steak *n* filete *m*, bife *m* de lomo *R Plata*.

fill-in *n* inf [person] sustituto *m*, -ta *f*; [thing] sustitutivo *m*.

filling ['fɪlɪŋ] ⋄ *adj* [satisfying] que llena mucho. ⋄ *n* - **1.** [in tooth] empaste *m* Esp, calza *f* Col, tapadura *f Chile & Méx*, emplomadura *f R Plata* - **2.** [in cake, sandwich] relleno *m*.

filling station *n* estación *f* de servicio OR de nafta *R Plata*, gasolinera *f*, bomba *f Chile, Col, Ecuad & Ven*, grifo *m Perú*.

filly ['fɪlɪ] (*pl* **-ies**) *n* potranca *f*.

film [fɪlm] ⋄ *n* - **1.** [gen] película *f* - **2.** (U) [art of cinema] cine *m*; **the film industry** la industria cinematográfica. ⋄ *vt & vi* filmar, rodar.

filming ['fɪlmɪŋ] *n* (U) rodaje *m*, filmación *f*.

film noir *n* CIN cine *m* negro.

film star *n* estrella *f* de cine.

filmstrip ['fɪlm.strɪp] *n* serie *f* de diapositivas *f*.

film studio *n* estudio *m* cinematográfico.

Filofax® ['faɪləʊfæks] *n* agenda *f* de anillas.

filter ['fɪltəʳ] ⋄ *n* filtro *m*. ⋄ *vt* [purify] filtrar. ⋄ *vi* [people]: **to filter in/out** ir entrando/saliendo.

● **filter out** *vt sep* [remove by filtering] filtrar.

● **filter through** *vi* filtrarse.

filter coffee *n* café *m* de filtro.

filter lane *n* UK carril *m* de giro.

filter paper *n* (papel *m* de) filtro *m*.

filter-tipped [-'tɪpt] *adj* con filtro.

filth [fɪlθ] *n* (U) - **1.** [dirt] suciedad *f*, porquería *f* - **2.** [obscenity] obscenidades *fpl*.

filthy ['fɪlθɪ] (*comp* **-ier**, *superl* **-iest**) *adj* - **1.** [very dirty] mugriento(ta), sucísimo(ma) - **2.** [obscene] obsceno(na).

filtration plant [fɪl'treɪʃn-] *n* estación *f* depuradora.

fin [fɪn] *n* - **1.** [on fish] aleta *f* - **2.** US [on swimmer] aleta *f*.

final ['faɪnl] ⋄ *adj* - **1.** [last] último(ma) - **2.** [at end] final - **3.** [definitive] definitivo(va). ⋄ *n* final *f*.

● **finals** *npl* UNIV exámenes *mpl* finales.

final demand *n* último aviso *m*.

finale [fɪ'nɑːlɪ] *n* final *m*.

finalist ['faɪnəlɪst] *n* finalista *mf*.

finalize, -ise ['faɪnəlaɪz] *vt* ultimar.

finally ['faɪnəlɪ] *adv* - **1.** [at last] por fin, finalmente - **2.** [lastly] finalmente, por último.

finance ⋄ *n* ['faɪnæns] (U) - **1.** [money management] finanzas *fpl* - **2.** [money] fondos *mpl*. ⋄ *vt* [faɪ'næns] financiar.

● **finances** *npl* finanzas *fpl*.

financial [fɪ'nænʃl] *adj* financiero(ra).

financial adviser *n* asesor financiero *m*, asesora financiera *f*.

financially [fɪ'nænʃəlɪ] *adv* económicamente; **to be financially independent** tener independencia económica.

financial services *npl* servicios *mpl* financieros.

financial year UK, **fiscal year** US *n* [for budgets] ejercicio *m*; [for tax purposes] año *m* fiscal.

financier [fɪ'nænsɪəʳ] *n* UK financiero *m*, -ra *f*, financista *mf* Amér.

finch [fɪntʃ] *n* pinzón *m*.

find [faɪnd] ⋄ *vt* (*pt & pp* **found**) - **1.** [gen] encontrar; **to find one's way** encontrar el camino; **a species not found in Britain** una especie que no se encuentra en Gran Bretaña; **I found it easy** me resultó fácil; **how did you find the film?** ¿qué te pareció la película? - **2.** [realize - fact] darse cuenta de, descubrir - **3.** LAW: **to be found guilty/not guilty (of)** ser declarado(da) culpable/inocente (de). ⋄ *n* hallazgo *m*, descubrimiento *m*.

● **find out** ⋄ *vi* - **1.** [become aware] enterarse - **2.** [obtain information] informarse. ⋄ *vt insep* [truth] descubrir; [fact] averiguar. ⋄ *vt sep* [person] descubrir.

findings ['faɪndɪŋz] *npl* resultados *mpl*, conclusiones *fpl*.

fine [faɪn] ⋄ *adj* - **1.** [excellent] magnífico(ca), excelente - **2.** [perfectly satisfactory]: **it's/that's fine** está bien; **how are you? – fine thanks** ¿qué tal? – muy bien - **3.** [weather] bueno(na); **it will be fine tomorrow** mañana hará buen día - **4.** [thin, smooth, delicate] fino(na) - **5.** [minute - detail, distinction] sutil; [- adjustment, tuning] milimétrico(ca). ⋄ *adv* [well] bien; [very well] muy bien. ⋄ *n* multa *f*. ⋄ *vt* multar.

fine arts *npl* bellas artes *fpl*.

finely ['faɪnlɪ] *adv* **- 1.** [chopped] muy fino(na), en trocitos **- 2.** [accurately] con precisión.

fineness ['faɪnnɪs] *n* **- 1.** [quality] excelencia *f* **- 2.** [thinness, smoothness, delicateness] finura *f* **- 3.** [subtlety] sutileza *f*.

finery ['faɪnərɪ] *n (U)* galas *fpl*.

finesse [fɪ'nes] *n* finura *f*, delicadeza *f*.

fine-tooth comb ['faɪntu:θ-] *n*: **to go over sthg with a fine-tooth comb** examinar algo minuciosamente.

fine-tune ['faɪntjuːn] *vt* poner a punto.

finger ['fɪŋgər] *<> n* dedo *m*; **she didn't lay a finger on him** no le tocó un pelo de la ropa; **he didn't lift a finger to help** no movió un dedo para ayudar; **to keep one's fingers crossed** cruzar los dedos; **to point a OR the finger at sb** señalar a alguien con el dedo; **to put one's finger on sthg** acertar a identificar algo; **to twist sb round one's little finger** tener a alguien en el bote. *<> vt* acariciar con los dedos.

fingermark ['fɪŋgəmɑːk] *n* huella *f* (de dedo), dedada *f*.

fingernail ['fɪŋgəneɪl] *n* uña *f (de las manos)*.

fingerprint ['fɪŋgəprɪnt] *n* huella *f* dactilar OR digital; **to take sb's fingerprints** tomar las huellas dactilares OR digitales a alguien.

fingertip ['fɪŋgətɪp] *n* punta *f* del dedo; **at one's fingertips** al alcance de la mano; **to have a subject at one's fingertips** saber un tema al dedillo.

finicky ['fɪnɪkɪ] *adj pej* [person] melindroso(sa); [task] minucioso(sa), delicado(da).

finish ['fɪnɪʃ] *<> n* **- 1.** [end] final *m*; [in race] meta *f* **- 2.** [surface texture] acabado *m*. *<> vt*: **to finish sthg/doing sthg** acabar OR terminar algo/de hacer algo. *<> vi* terminar; **to finish second** terminar en segundo lugar.

➡ **finish off** *vt sep* [food, task] acabar OR terminar del todo.

➡ **finish up** *vi* acabar, terminar.

➡ **finish with** *vt insep* [boyfriend etc] romper con.

finished ['fɪnɪʃt] *adj* **- 1.** [ready, over] acabado(da), terminado(da) **- 2.** [no longer interested]: **to be finished with sthg** no querer tener nada que ver con algo **- 3.** *inf* [done for] acabado(da).

finishing line ['fɪnɪʃɪŋ-] *n* línea *f* de meta.

finishing school ['fɪnɪʃɪŋ-] *n* colegio privado donde se prepara a las alumnas de clase alta para entrar en sociedad.

finite ['faɪnaɪt] *adj* **- 1.** [limited] finito(ta) **- 2.** GRAM conjugado(da).

Finland ['fɪnlənd] *n* Finlandia *f*.

Finn [fɪn] *n* [person] finlandés *m*, -esa *f*.

Finnish ['fɪnɪʃ] *<> adj* finlandés(esa). *<> n* [language] finlandés *m*.

fiord [fjɔːd] = **fjord**.

fir [fɜːr], **fir tree** *n* abeto *m*.

fire ['faɪər] *<> n* **- 1.** [gen] fuego *m*; **on fire** en llamas; **to catch fire** prender; **to open fire (on sb)** abrir fuego (contra alguien); **to set fire to** prender fuego a **- 2.** [blaze] incendio *m* **- 3.** *UK* [heater]: **(electric/gas) fire** estufa *f* (eléctrica/de gas). *<> vt* **- 1.** [shoot] disparar; **to fire a shot** disparar **- 2.** [rap out]: **to fire questions at sb** acribillar a alguien a preguntas **- 3.** *esp US* [dismiss] despedir. *<> vi*: **to fire (on OR at)** disparar (contra).

fire alarm *n* alarma *f* antiincendios.

firearm ['faɪərɑːm] *n* arma *f* de fuego.

fireball ['faɪəbɔːl] *n* bola *f* de fuego.

firebomb ['faɪəbɒm] *<> n* bomba *f* incendiaria. *<> vt* lanzar bombas incendiarias a.

firebreak ['faɪəbreɪk] *n* cortafuego *m*.

fire brigade *UK*, **fire department** *US n* cuerpo *m* de bomberos.

fire chief *US n* = **fire master**.

firecracker ['faɪə,krækər] *n* petardo *m*.

fire department *US* = **fire brigade**.

fire door *n* puerta *f* cortafuegos.

fire drill *n* simulacro *m* de incendio.

fire-eater *n* [performer] tragafuegos *mf inv*.

fire engine *n* coche *m* de bomberos.

fire escape *n* escalera *f* de incendios.

fire exit *n* salida *f* de incendios.

fire extinguisher *n* extintor *m*.

fire fighter *n* bombero *m*, -ra *f*.

fireguard ['faɪəgɑːd] *n* pantalla *f (de chimenea)*.

fire hazard *n* objeto *m* que supone peligro de incendio.

firehouse ['faɪəhaʊs] *n US* cuartel *m* de bomberos.

fire hydrant [-'haɪdrənt], **fireplug** ['faɪəplʌg] *n* boca *f* de incendio.

firelight ['faɪəlaɪt] *n* luz *f* del fuego.

firelighter ['faɪəlaɪtər] *n* pastilla *f* para encender el fuego.

fireman ['faɪəmən] *(pl* **-men** [-mən]*) n* bombero *m*.

fire master *UK*, **fire chief** *US n* jefe *m*, -fa *f* del cuerpo de bomberos.

fireplace ['faɪəpleɪs] *n* chimenea *f*.

fireplug *n US* = **fire hydrant**.

firepower ['faɪə,paʊər] *n* potencia *f* de fuego.

fireproof ['faɪəpruːf] *adj* ignífugo(ga), resistente al fuego.

fire-raiser [-,reɪzər] *n UK* pirómano *m*, -na *f*, incendiario *m*, -ria *f*.

fire regulations *npl* normativa *f* sobre incendios.

fire service *n* UK cuerpo *m* de bomberos.

fireside ['faɪəsaɪd] *n*: **by the fireside** al calor de la chimenea.

fire station *n* parque *m* de bomberos.

firewall ['faɪəwɔːl] *n* COMPUT cortafuego *m*.

firewood ['faɪəwʊd] *n* leña *f*.

firework ['faɪəwɜːk] *n* fuego *m* de artificio.
◆ **fireworks** *npl* fuegos *mpl* artificiales.

firework display *n* espectáculo *m* pirotécnico.

firing ['faɪərɪŋ] *n* (U) MIL disparos *mpl*.

firing squad *n* pelotón *m* de ejecución OR fusilamiento.

firm [fɜːm] *<> adj* - **1.** [gen] firme; **to stand firm** mantenerse firme - **2.** FIN [steady] estable. *<> n* empresa *f*.
◆ **firm up** *<> vt sep* [arrangements] concretar. *<> vi* [prices] afianzarse.

firmly ['fɜːmlɪ] *adv* firmemente.

firmness ['fɜːmnɪs] *n* firmeza *f*.

first [fɜːst] *<> adj* primero(ra); **the first day** el primer día; **for the first time** por primera vez; **first thing (in the morning)** a primera hora (de la mañana); **first things first** lo primero es lo primero; **I don't know the first thing about it** no tengo ni la más remota idea del asunto. *<> adv* - **1.** [gen] primero; **to come first** quedar primero(ra); **first of all** en primer lugar - **2.** [for the first time] por primera vez. *<> n* - **1.** [person] primero *m*, -ra *f* - **2.** [unprecedented event] acontecimiento *m* sin precedentes - **3.** UK UNIV ≃ sobresaliente *m*.
◆ **at first** *adv* al principio.
◆ **at first hand** *adv* de primera mano.

first aid *n* (U) [treatment] primeros auxilios *mpl*; [technique] socorrismo *m*.

first-aider [-'eɪdə'] *n* socorrista *mf*.

first-aid kit *n* botiquín *m* de primeros auxilios.

first-class *<> adj* - **1.** [excellent] de primera, clase *Amér* - **2.** UK UNIV: **first-class degree** ≃ sobresaliente *m* - **3.** [letter, ticket] de primera clase. *<> adv* [travel] en primera clase.

first-class mail *n* servicio *m* de correo más caro y rápido que el de segunda clase.

first cousin *n* primo *m*, -ma *f* carnal.

first day cover *n* sobre timbrado en el primer día de emisión de sus sellos.

first-degree *adj* - **1.** MED: **first-degree burn** quemadura *f* de primer grado - **2.** US LAW: **first-degree murder** homicidio *m* en primer grado.

first floor *n* - **1.** UK [above ground level] primer piso *m* - **2.** US [at ground level] planta *f* baja.

firsthand [,fɜːst'hænd] *<> adj* de primera mano. *<> adv* directamente.

first lady *n* primera dama *f*.

first language *n* lengua *f* materna.

first lieutenant *n* ≃ teniente *mf*.

firstly ['fɜːstlɪ] *adv* en primer lugar.

first mate, first officer *n* segundo *m* de a bordo.

first name *n* nombre *m* de pila.
◆ **first-name** *adj*: **to be on first-name terms (with)** ≃ tutearse (con).

first night *n* noche *f* del estreno.

first offender *n* delincuente *mf* sin antecedentes penales.

first officer = first mate.

first-rate *adj* de primera.

first refusal *n* primera opción *f* de compra.

First World War *n*: **the First World War** la Primera Guerra Mundial.

firtree ['fɜːtriː] = fir.

fiscal ['fɪskl] *adj* fiscal.

fiscal year *n* US año *m* fiscal.

fish [fɪʃ] *<> n* (*pl* fish) - **1.** [animal] pez *m* - **2.** (U) [food] pescado *m*. *<> vt* pescar en. *<> vi* - **1.** [for fish]: **to fish (for sthg)** pescar (algo) - **2.** [for compliments etc]: **to fish for sthg** buscar algo.
◆ **fish out** *vt sep inf* [bring out] sacar.

fish and chips *npl* pescado *m* frito con patatas fritas.

fish and chip shop *n* UK tienda *f* de pescado frito con patatas fritas.

fishbowl ['fɪʃbəʊl] *n* pecera *f*.

fishcake ['fɪʃkeɪk] *n* pastelillo *m* de pescado.

fisherman ['fɪʃəmən] (*pl* **-men** [-mən]) *n* pescador *m*.

fishery ['fɪʃərɪ] (*pl* **-ies**) *n* caladero *m*.

fish-eye lens *n* objetivo *m* de ojo de pez.

fish factory *n* fábrica *f* de pescado.

fish farm *n* piscifactoría *f*.

fish fingers UK, **fish sticks** US *npl* palitos *mpl* de pescado.

fishhook ['fɪʃhʊk] *n* anzuelo *m*.

fishing ['fɪʃɪŋ] *n* pesca *f*; **to go fishing** ir de pesca.

fishing boat *n* barco *m* pesquero.

fishing line *n* sedal *m*.

fishing net *n* red *f* de pesca.

fishing rod *n* caña *f* de pescar.

fishmonger ['fɪʃ,mʌŋgə'] *n esp* UK pescadero *m*, -ra *f*; **fishmonger's (shop)** pescadería *f*.

fishnet ['fɪʃnet] *n*: **fishnet tights** medias *fpl* de malla.

fish slice *n* UK paleta *f*, espátula *f*.

fish sticks *US* = **fish fingers**.

fishwife ['fɪʃwaɪf] (*pl* **-wives** [-waɪvz]) *n pej* verdulera *f*.

fishy ['fɪʃɪ] (*comp* **-ier**, *superl* **-iest**) *adj* **- 1.** [smell, taste] a pescado **- 2.** *inf* [suspicious] sospechoso(sa).

fission ['fɪʃn] *n* fisión *f*.

fissure ['fɪʃər] *n* fisura *f*.

fist [fɪst] *n* puño *m*.

fit [fɪt] ◇ *adj* **- 1.** [suitable]: **fit (for sthg/to do sthg)** apto(ta) (para algo/para hacer algo); **to see** *OR* **think fit to do sthg** creer conveniente hacer algo; **do as you think fit** haz lo que te parezca conveniente **- 2.** [healthy] en forma; **to keep fit** mantenerse en forma. ◇ *n* **- 1.** [of clothes, shoes etc]: **it's a good fit** le/te *etc* sienta *OR* va bien; **it's a tight fit** le/te *etc* va justo(ta) **- 2.** [bout, seizure] ataque *m*; **he had a fit** *lit & fig* le dio un ataque; **in fits and starts** a trompicones. ◇ *vt* (*pt & pp* **-ted**, *cont* **-ting**) **- 1.** [be correct size for] sentar bien a, ir bien a **- 2.** [place]: **to fit sthg into** encajar algo en **- 3.** [provide]: **to fit sthg with** equipar algo con; **to have an alarm fitted** poner una alarma **- 4.** [be suitable for] adecuarse a, corresponder a **- 5.** [for clothes]: **she was fitted for her dress** le tomaron las medidas para el vestido. ◇ *vi* (*pt & pp* **-ted**, *cont* **-ting**) **- 1.** [clothes, shoes] estar bien de talla **- 2.** [part - when assembling etc]: **this bit fits in here** esta pieza encaja aquí **- 3.** [have enough room] caber.

➤ **fit in** ◇ *vt sep* [accommodate] hacer un hueco a. ◇ *vi* **- 1.** [subj: person]: **to fit in (with)** adaptarse (a) **- 2.** [be compatible]: **it doesn't fit in with our plans** no encaja con nuestros planes.

fitful ['fɪtfʊl] *adj* irregular, intermitente.

fitment ['fɪtmənt] *n* accesorio *m*.

fitness ['fɪtnɪs] (*U*) *n* **- 1.** [health] buen estado *m* físico **- 2.** [suitability]: **fitness (for)** idoneidad *f* (para).

fitted ['fɪtəd] *adj* **- 1.** [suited]: **fitted (for** *OR* **to)** idóneo(a) (para); **to be fitted to do sthg** ser idóneo para hacer algo **- 2.** [tailored] a medida **- 3.** *UK* [built-in] empotrado(da).

fitted carpet ['fɪtəd-] *n* moqueta *f*.

fitted kitchen ['fɪtəd-] *n UK* cocina *f* amueblada a medida.

fitter ['fɪtər] *n* [mechanic] (mecánico *m*) ajustador *m*.

fitting ['fɪtɪŋ] ◇ *adj fml* adecuado(da). ◇ *n* **- 1.** [part] accesorio *m* **- 2.** [for clothing] prueba *f*.

➤ **fittings** *npl* accesorios *mpl*.

fitting room *n* probador *m*.

five [faɪv] *num* cinco; *see also* **six**.

five-day week *n* semana *f* inglesa.

fiver ['faɪvər] *n UK inf (billete de) cinco libras*.

five-star *adj* [hotel] de cinco estrellas; [treatment] de primera.

fix [fɪks] ◇ *vt* **- 1.** [attach, decide on] fijar; **to fix sthg (to)** fijar algo (a) **- 2.** [repair] arreglar, refaccionar *Amér* **- 3.** *inf* [rig] amañar **- 4.** *esp US* [prepare - food, drink] preparar. ◇ *n* **- 1.** *inf* [difficult situation]: **to be in a fix** estar en un aprieto **- 2.** *drug sl* dosis *f inv*.

➤ **fix up** *vt sep* **- 1.** [provide]: **to fix sb up with** proveer a alguien de **- 2.** [arrange] organizar, preparar.

fixation [fɪkˈseɪʃn] *n*: **fixation (on** *OR* **about)** fijación *f* (con).

fixed [fɪkst] *adj* fijo(ja).

fixed assets *npl* activo *m* inmovilizado.

fixture ['fɪkstʃər] *n* **- 1.** [furniture] instalación *f* fija **- 2.** [permanent feature] rasgo *m* característico **- 3.** [sports event] encuentro *m*.

fizz [fɪz] ◇ *vi* burbujear. ◇ *n* [sound] burbujeo *m*.

fizzle ['fɪzl] ➤ **fizzle out** *vi* [firework, fire] apagarse; [enthusiasm] disiparse.

fizzy ['fɪzɪ] (*comp* **-ier**, *superl* **-iest**) *adj* [gen] gaseoso(sa); [water, soft drink] con gas.

fjord, fiord [fjɔːd] *n* fiordo *m*.

FL *abbr of* **Florida**.

flab [flæb] *n* (*U*) grasa *f*, michelines *mpl*.

flabbergasted ['flæbəgɑːstɪd] *adj* pasmado(da).

flabby ['flæbɪ] (*comp* **-ier**, *superl* **-iest**) *adj* fofo(fa).

flaccid ['flæsɪd] *adj* fláccido(da).

flag [flæg] ◇ *n* [banner] bandera *f*. ◇ *vi* (*pt & pp* **-ged**, *cont* **-ging**) decaer.

➤ **flag down** *vt sep* [taxi] parar; **to flag sb down** hacer señales a alguien para que se detenga.

Flag Day *n* [in the US] *14 de junio, día de la bandera en Estados Unidos*.

flag of convenience *n* pabellón *m* de conveniencia.

flagon ['flægən] *n* **- 1.** [bottle] botellón *m* **- 2.** [jug] jarro *m*.

flagpole ['flægpəʊl] *n* asta *f (de bandera)*.

flagrant ['fleɪgrənt] *adj* flagrante.

flagship ['flægʃɪp] *n* **- 1.** [ship] buque *m* insignia **- 2.** [model] estandarte *m*.

flagstone ['flægstəʊn] *n* losa *f*.

flail [fleɪl] ◇ *vt* sacudir, agitar con violencia. ◇ *vi* agitarse con violencia.

flair [fleər] *n* **- 1.** [ability] don *m*; **to have a flair for sthg** tener un don para algo **- 2.** [style] estilo *m*.

flak [flæk] *n* (*U*) **- 1.** [gunfire] fuego *m* antiaéreo **- 2.** *inf* [criticism] críticas *fpl*.

flake [fleɪk] ◇ *n* [of skin] escama *f*; [of snow] copo *m*; [of paint] desconchón *m*. ◇ *vi* [skin] descamarse; [paint, plaster] desconcharse.
➤ **flake out** *vi inf* caer rendido(da).

flaky [ˈfleɪkɪ] (*comp* -**ier**, *superl* -**iest**) *adj* - **1.** [skin] con escamas; [paintwork] desconchado(da) - **2.** *US inf* [person] raro(ra).

flaky pastry *n* hojaldre *m*.

flambé [ˈflɑːmbeɪ] ◇ *adj* flameado(da). ◇ *vt* (*pt & pp* -**ed**, *cont* -**ing**) flamear.

flamboyant [flæmˈbɔɪənt] *adj* - **1.** [person, behaviour] extravagante - **2.** [clothes, design] vistoso(sa), llamativo(va).

flame [fleɪm] ◇ *n* llama *f*; **in flames** en llamas; **to burst into flames** incendiarse; **an old flame** un antiguo amor. ◇ *vt* COMPUT lanzar llamaradas a. ◇ *vi* [be on fire] llamear.

flameproof [ˈfleɪmpruːf] *adj* ignífugo(ga), resistente al fuego.

flame-retardant [-rɪˈtɑːdənt] *adj* de combustión lenta.

flame-thrower [-ˈθrəʊər] *n* lanzallamas *m inv*.

flaming [ˈfleɪmɪŋ] *adj* - **1.** [fire-coloured] llameante - **2.** *UK* [row, argument] acalorado(da) - **3.** *UK inf* [expressing annoyance] maldito(ta).

flamingo [fləˈmɪŋɡəʊ] (*pl* -**s** OR -**es**) *n* flamenco *m*.

flammable [ˈflæməbl] *adj* inflamable.

flan [flæn] *n* tarta *f* (*de fruta etc*).

Flanders [ˈflɑːndəz] *n* Flandes.

flange [flændʒ] *n* pestaña *f*, reborde *m*.

flank [flæŋk] ◇ *n* - **1.** [of animal] costado *m*, ijada *f* - **2.** [of army] flanco *m*. ◇ *vt*: **to be flanked by** estar flanqueado(da) por.

flannel [ˈflænl] *n* - **1.** [fabric] franela *f* - **2.** *UK* [facecloth] toallita *f* (*de baño para lavarse*).
➤ **flannels** *npl* pantalones *mpl* de franela.

flannelette [ˌflænəˈlet] *n* muletón *m*.

flap [flæp] ◇ *n* - **1.** [of pocket, book, envelope] solapa *f*; [of skin] colgajo *m* - **2.** *inf* [panic]: **to be in a flap** estar histérico(ca). ◇ *vt* (*pt & pp* -**ped**, *cont* -**ping**) agitar; [wings] batir. ◇ *vi* (*pt & pp* -**ped**, *cont* -**ping**) [flag, skirt] ondear; [wings] aletear.

flapjack [ˈflæpdʒæk] *n* - **1.** *UK* [biscuit] galleta *f* de avena - **2.** *US* [pancake] torta *f*, crepe *f*.

flare [fleər] ◇ *n* [signal] bengala *f*. ◇ *vi* - **1.** [burn brightly]: **to flare (up)** llamear - **2.** [intensify]: **to flare (up)** estallar - **3.** [widen] acampanarse.
➤ **flares** *npl UK* pantalones *mpl* de campana.

flared [fleəd] *adj* acampanado(da).

flash [flæʃ] ◇ *adj* - **1.** [photography] con flash - **2.** *inf* [expensive-looking] chulo(la); *pej* ostentoso(sa). ◇ *n* - **1.** [of light] destello *m*; **a flash of lightning** un relámpago, un refucilo *R Plata*

- **2.** PHOT flash *m* - **3.** [of genius, inspiration etc] momento *m*; [of anger] acceso *m*; **in a flash** en un instante; **quick as a flash** como un rayo. ◇ *vt* - **1.** [shine in specified direction] dirigir; [switch on briefly] encender intermitentemente - **2.** [a smile, look] lanzar - **3.** [show - picture, image] mostrar; [- information, news] emitir. ◇ *vi* - **1.** [light] destellar - **2.** [eyes] brillar - **3.** [rush]: **to flash by** OR **past** pasar como un rayo - **4.** [appear] aparecer; **it flashed across his mind that...** de pronto se le ocurrió que...

flashback [ˈflæʃbæk] *n* escena *f* retrospectiva, flashback *m*.

flashbulb [ˈflæʃbʌlb] *n* flash *m*.

flash card *n* tarjeta en la que aparece una palabra o dibujo y que se emplea como material didáctico.

flashcube [ˈflæʃkjuːb] *n* flash *m* (en forma de) cubo.

flasher [ˈflæʃər] *n* - **1.** [light] indicador *m* - **2.** *UK inf* [man] exhibicionista *m*.

flash flood *n* riada *f*.

flashgun [ˈflæʃɡʌn] *n* disparador *m* de flash.

flashlight [ˈflæʃlaɪt] *n US* [torch] linterna *f*.

flash point *n* - **1.** [moment] punto *m* álgido - **2.** [place] punto *m* conflictivo.

flashy [ˈflæʃɪ] (*comp* -**ier**, *superl* -**iest**) *adj inf* chulo(la); *pej* ostentoso(sa).

flask [flɑːsk] *n* - **1.** [thermos flask] termo® *m* - **2.** [used in chemistry] matraz *m* - **3.** [hip flask] petaca *f*.

flat [flæt] ◇ *adj* (*comp* -**ter**, *superl* -**test**) - **1.** [surface, ground] llano(na); [feet] plano(na) - **2.** [shoes] bajo(ja), de piso *Méx* - **3.** [tyre] desinflado(da), ponchado(da) *Méx* - **4.** [refusal, denial] rotundo(da) - **5.** [business, trade] flojo(ja); [voice, tone] monótono(na); [colour] soso(sa); [performance, writing] desangelado(da) - **6.** MUS [lower than correct note] desafinado(da); [lower than stated note] bemol (*inv*) - **7.** [fare, price] único(ca) - **8.** [beer, lemonade] muerto(ta), sin fuerza - **9.** [battery] descargado(da). ◇ *adv* - **1.** [level]: **to lie flat** estar totalmente extendido(da); **to fall flat on one's face** [person] caerse de bruces - **2.** [absolutely]: **flat broke** sin blanca, quebrado, sin un centavo *Amér* - **3.** [of time]: **in five minutes flat** en cinco minutos justos - **4.** MUS: **to sing/play flat** desafinar. ◇ *n* - **1.** *UK* [apartment] piso *m*, apartamento *m*, departamento *m Amér* - **2.** *US* [tyre] pinchazo *m* - **3.** MUS bemol *m*.
➤ **flat out** *adv* a toda velocidad.

flat cap *n UK* gorra *f* de tela.

flat-chested [-ˈtʃestɪd] *adj* de poco pecho, liso(sa).

flatfish [ˈflætfɪʃ] (*pl* **flatfish**) *n* pez *m* plano (*lenguado etc*).

flat-footed [-'futɪd] *adj* [with flat feet] de pies planos.

flatly ['flætlɪ] *adv* - **1.** [refuse, deny] de plano, rotundamente - **2.** [speak, perform] monótonamente.

flatmate ['flætmeɪt] *n UK* compañero *m*, -ra *f* de piso.

flat racing *n (U)* carreras *fpl* de caballos sin obstáculos.

flat rate *n* tarifa *f* plana.

flatten ['flætn] *vt* - **1.** [surface, paper, bumps] allanar, aplanar; [paper] alisar; **to flatten o.s. against sthg** pegarse a algo - **2.** [building, city] arrasar - **3.** *inf* [person, boxer] tumbar.
➤ **flatten out** ◇ *vi* allanarse, nivelarse. ◇ *vt sep* allanar.

flatter ['flætər] *vt* - **1.** [subj: person, report] adular, halagar; **to flatter o.s. (that)** congratularse *OR* felicitarse de que - **2.** [subj: clothes, colour, photograph] favorecer.

flatterer ['flætərə] *n* adulador *m*, -ra *f*.

flattering ['flætərɪŋ] *adj* - **1.** [remark, interest] halagador(ra) - **2.** [clothes, colour, photograph] favorecedor(ra).

flattery ['flætərɪ] *n (U)* halagos *mpl*, adulación *f*.

flatulence ['flætjʊləns] *n* flatulencia *f*.

flatware ['flætweə'] *n (U) US* cubiertos *mpl*.

flaunt [flɔːnt] *vt* ostentar, hacer gala de.

flautist *UK* ['flɔːtɪst], **flutist** *US* ['fluːtɪst] *n* flautista *mf*.

flavour *UK*, **flavor** *US* ['fleɪvər] ◇ *n* - **1.** [taste] sabor *m* - **2.** *fig* [atmosphere] aire *m*, sabor *m*. ◇ *vt* condimentar.

flavouring *UK*, **flavoring** *US* ['fleɪvərɪŋ] *n (U)* condimento *m*; **artificial flavouring** aromatizante *m* artificial.

flaw [flɔː] *n* [fault] desperfecto *m*, imperfección *f*.

flawed [flɔːd] *adj* imperfecto(ta), defectuoso(sa).

flawless ['flɔːlɪs] *adj* impecable.

flax [flæks] *n* lino *m*.

flay [fleɪ] *vt lit* & *fig* desollar.

flea [fliː] *n* pulga *f*; **to send sb away with a flea in his/her ear** echar una buena reprimenda a alguien.

flea market *n* rastro *m*.

fleck [flek] ◇ *n* mota *f*. ◇ *vt*: **flecked with** salpicado(da) de.

fled [fled] *pt* & *pp* ▷ **flee**.

fledg(e)ling ['fledʒlɪŋ] ◇ *adj* [person] novato(ta); [state] joven. ◇ *n* polluelo *m*.

flee [fliː] (*pt* & *pp* **fled**) ◇ *vt* huir de. ◇ *vi*: **to flee (from/to)** huir (de/a).

fleece [fliːs] ◇ *n* - **1.** vellón *m* - **2.** [garment] forro *m* polar. ◇ *vt inf* [cheat] desplumar.

fleet [fliːt] *n* - **1.** [of ships] flota *f* - **2.** [of cars, buses] parque *m* (móvil).

fleeting ['fliːtɪŋ] *adj* fugaz.

Fleet Street *n calle londinense que antiguamente era el centro de la prensa británica y cuyo nombre todavía se utiliza para referirse a ésta.*

Flemish ['flemɪʃ] ◇ *adj* flamenco(ca). ◇ *n* [language] flamenco *m*. ◇ *npl*: **the Flemish** los flamencos.

flesh [fleʃ] *n* - **1.** [of body] carne *f*; **to be one's (own) flesh and blood** [family] ser de la misma sangre que uno; **in the flesh** en persona - **2.** [of fruit, vegetable] pulpa *f*.
➤ **flesh out** *vt sep* desarrollar.

flesh wound *n* herida *f* superficial.

fleshy ['fleʃɪ] (*comp* -**ier**, *superl* -**iest**) *adj* [fat] gordo(da).

flew [fluː] *pt* ▷ **fly**.

flex [fleks] ◇ *n* ELEC cable *m*, cordón *m*. ◇ *vt* flexionar.

flexibility [,fleksə'bɪlətɪ] *n* flexibilidad *f*.

flexible ['fleksəbl] *adj* flexible.

flexitime ['fleksɪtaɪm] *n (U)* horario *m* flexible.

flick [flɪk] ◇ *n* - **1.** [of whip, towel] golpe *m* rápido - **2.** [with finger] toba *f*. ◇ *vt* - **1.** [whip, towel] dar un golpe rápido con - **2.** [with finger] dar una toba - **3.** [switch] apretar, pulsar.
➤ **flicks** *npl inf*: **the flicks** el cine.
➤ **flick through** *vt insep* hojear.

flicker ['flɪkə'] ◇ *n* parpadeo *m*; *fig*: **a flicker of hope** un rayo de esperanza; **a flicker of interest** un atisbo de interés. ◇ *vi* [eyes, flame] parpadear.

flick knife *n UK* navaja *f* automática.

flier ['flaɪə'] *n* - **1.** [pilot] aviador *m*, -ra *f* - **2.** *esp US* [advertising leaflet] folleto *m* publicitario.

flight [flaɪt] *n* - **1.** [gen] vuelo *m*; **flight of fancy** *OR* **of the imagination** vuelo de la imaginación - **2.** [of stairs, stairs] tramo *m* - **3.** [of birds] bandada *f* - **4.** [escape] huida *f*, fuga *f*.

flight attendant *n* auxiliar *mf* de vuelo.

flight crew *n* tripulación *f* de vuelo.

flight deck *n* **- 1.** [of plane] cabina *f* del piloto **- 2.** [of aircraft carrier] cubierta *f* de vuelo.

flight path *n* ruta *f* de vuelo.

flight recorder *n* caja *f* negra.

flighty ['flaɪtɪ] (*comp* **-ier**, *superl* **-iest**) *adj* frívolo(la), veleidoso(sa).

flimsy ['flɪmzɪ] (*comp* **-ier**, *superl* **-iest**) *adj* **- 1.** [dress, material] muy ligero(ra) **- 2.** [structure] débil, poco sólido(da) **- 3.** [excuse] flojo(ja).

flinch [flɪntʃ] *vi* **- 1.** [shudder] estremecerse; **without flinching** sin pestañear **- 2.** [be reluctant]: **to flinch (from sthg/from doing sthg)** retroceder (ante algo/ante hacer algo); **without flinching** sin inmutarse.

fling [flɪŋ] ⬦ *n* **- 1.** [affair] aventura *f* (amorosa) **- 2.** [irresponsible adventure]: **to have a fling** echar una cana al aire. ⬦ *vt* (*pt* & *pp* **flung**) arrojar; **he flung himself to the ground** se arrojó al suelo.

flint [flɪnt] *n* **- 1.** [rock] sílex *m* **- 2.** [in lighter] piedra *f*.

flip [flɪp] ⬦ *vt* (*pt* & *pp* **-ped**, *cont* **-ping**) **- 1.** [turn] dar la vuelta a; **to flip sthg open** abrir algo de golpe **- 2.** [switch] pulsar **- 3.** [coin] lanzar al aire. ⬦ *vi* (*pt* & *pp* **-ped**, *cont* **-ping**) *inf* **- 1.** [become angry] ponerse hecho(cha) una furia **- 2.** [go mad] volverse majareta. ⬦ *n* [of coin] lanzamiento *m* al aire.
➭ **flip through** *vt insep* hojear.

flip-flop *n* [shoe] chancleta *f*.

flippant ['flɪpənt] *adj* frívolo(la).

flippantly ['flɪpəntlɪ] *adv* frívolamente.

flipper ['flɪpər] *n* aleta *f*.

flipping ['flɪpɪŋ] *UK inf* ⬦ *adj* condenado(da), maldito(ta). ⬦ *adv* condenadamente.

flip side *n* [of record] cara *f* B; [of situation] otra cara *f* de la moneda.

flirt [flɜːt] ⬦ *n* coqueto *m*, -ta *f*. ⬦ *vi* **- 1.** [with person]: **to flirt (with)** flirtear *OR* coquetear (con) **- 2.** [with idea]: **to flirt with** acariciar, contemplar.

flirtation [flɜːˈteɪʃn] *n* **- 1.** [flirting] flirteo *m*, coqueteo *m* **- 2.** [love affair] amorío *m*, aventura *f* **- 3.** [brief interest]: **I had a brief flirtation with the idea of going abroad** me pasó por la cabeza la idea de ir al extranjero.

flirtatious [flɜːˈteɪʃəs] *adj* coqueto(ta).

flit [flɪt] (*pt* & *pp* **-ted**, *cont* **-ting**) *vi* **- 1.** [bird] revolotear **- 2.** [expression, idea]: **to flit through** pasar rápidamente por, cruzar.

float [fləʊt] ⬦ *n* **- 1.** [for fishing line] corcho *m* **- 2.** [for swimming] flotador *m* **- 3.** [in procession] carroza *f* **- 4.** [supply of change] cambio *m*. ⬦ *vt*

- 1. [on water] hacer flotar **- 2.** [idea, project] plantear, lanzar **- 3.** [company] lanzar a bolsa. ⬦ *vi* flotar.

floating ['fləʊtɪŋ] *adj* flotante.

floating voter *n* *UK* votante indeciso *m*, votante indecisa *f*.

flock [flɒk] ⬦ *n* **- 1.** [of sheep] rebaño *m*; [of birds] bandada *f* **- 2.** *fig* [of people] multitud *f*, tropel *m* **- 3.** RELIG grey *f*. ⬦ *vi*: **to flock to** acudir en masa *OR* tropel a.

floe [fləʊ] *n* témpano *m*.

flog [flɒg] (*pt* & *pp* **-ged**, *cont* **-ging**) *vt* **- 1.** [whip] azotar **- 2.** *UK inf* [sell] vender.

flood [flʌd] ⬦ *n* **- 1.** [of water] inundación *f* **- 2.** [of letters, people] aluvión *m*, riada *f*. ⬦ *vt* *lit* & *fig*: **to flood sthg (with)** inundar algo (de). ⬦ *vi* **- 1.** [river] desbordarse **- 2.** [street, land] inundarse, anegarse **- 3.** [arrive in masses]: **to flood in** [letters etc] llegar a montones; [people] entrar a raudales; **the memories came flooding back** los recuerdos lo asaltaron de repente.
➭ **floods** *npl fig*: **to be in floods of tears** llorar a mares.

floodgates ['flʌdgeɪts] *npl*: **to open the floodgates to** abrir paso a.

flooding ['flʌdɪŋ] *n* (U) inundación *f*.

floodlight ['flʌdlaɪt] *n* foco *m*.

floodlit ['flʌdlɪt] *adj* iluminado(da) con focos.

flood tide *n* pleamar *f*, marea *f* alta.

floor [flɔːr] ⬦ *n* **- 1.** [of room, forest] suelo *m*; [of club, disco] pista *f* **- 2.** [of sea, valley] fondo *m* **- 3.** [of building] piso *m*, planta *f* **- 4.** [at meeting, debate]: **to give/have the floor** dar/tener la palabra **- 5.** [of stock exchange] patio *m*, parqué *m*. ⬦ *vt* **- 1.** [knock down] derribar **- 2.** [baffle] desconcertar, dejar perplejo(ja).

floorboard ['flɔːbɔːd] *n* tabla *f* (del suelo).

floor cloth *n* *UK* trapo *m* del suelo.

flooring ['flɔːrɪŋ] *n* solería *f*, suelo *m*.

floor lamp *n* *US* lámpara *f* de pie.

floor show *n* espectáculo *m* de cabaré.

floorwalker ['flɔːˌwɔːkər] *n* *esp US* jefe *m*, -fa *f* de sección (*en tiendas*).

floozy ['fluːzɪ] (*pl* **-ies**) *n* *dated* & *pej* pelandusca *f*.

flop [flɒp] *inf* ⬦ *n* [failure] fracaso *m*. ⬦ *vi* (*pt* & *pp* **-ped**, *cont* **-ping**) **- 1.** [fail] fracasar **- 2.** [fall] desplomarse.

floppy ['flɒpɪ] (*comp* **-ier**, *superl* **-iest**) *adj* caído(da), flojo(ja).

floppy (disk) *n* disco *m* flexible, disquete *m*.

flora ['flɔːrə] *n* flora *f*; **flora and fauna** flora y fauna.

floral ['flɔːrəl] *adj* **- 1.** [made of flowers] floral **- 2.** [patterned with flowers] de flores.

floret ['flɒrɪt] *n* [of broccoli] cogollo *m*.

florid ['flɒrɪd] *adj* - **1.** [extravagant] florido(da) - **2.** [red] rojizo(za).

Florida ['flɒrɪdə] *n* Florida.

florist ['flɒrɪst] *n* florista *mf*; **florist's (shop)** floristería *f*.

floss [flɒs] <> *n* (*U*) [dental floss] hilo *m* OR seda *f* dental. <> *vt*: **to floss one's teeth** limpiarse los dientes con hilo dental.

flotation [fləʊ'teɪʃn] *n* COMM [of shares] emisión *f*; [of company] salida *f* a bolsa.

flotilla [flə'tɪlə] *n* flotilla *f*.

flotsam ['flɒtsəm] *n* (*U*): **flotsam and jetsam** restos *mpl* de un naufragio; *fig* desechos *mpl* de la humanidad.

flounce [flaʊns] <> *n* - **1.** [movement] desplante *m*, bufido *m* - **2.** SEW volante *m*. <> *vi* moverse con aire de indignación; **to flounce out** salir airadamente.

flounder ['flaʊndər] <> *n* (*pl* **flounder** OR -**s**) platija *f*. <> *vi* - **1.** [move with difficulty] debatirse, forcejear - **2.** [when speaking] titubear.

flour ['flaʊər] *n* harina *f*.

flourish ['flʌrɪʃ] <> *vi* florecer. <> *vt* agitar. <> *n*: **to do sthg with a flourish** hacer algo exageradamente.

flourishing ['flʌrɪʃɪŋ] *adj* floreciente.

flout [flaʊt] *vt* desobedecer.

flow [fləʊ] <> *n* flujo *m*; **traffic flow** circulación *f*. <> *vi* - **1.** [gen] fluir, correr - **2.** [tide] subir, crecer - **3.** [hair, clothes] ondear - **4.** [result]: **to flow from** emanar de.

flow chart, flow diagram *n* organigrama *m*, cuadro *m* sinóptico.

flower ['flaʊər] <> *n* lit & fig flor *f*. <> *comp* de flores. <> *vi* lit & fig florecer.

flowerbed ['flaʊəbed] *n* arriate *m*, parterre *m*, cantero *m* Cuba & R Plata.

flowering ['flaʊərɪŋ] <> *adj* floreciente. <> *n* florecimiento *m*.

flowerpot ['flaʊəpɒt] *n* maceta *f*, tiesto *m*.

flowery ['flaʊəri] (*comp* -**ier**, *superl* -**iest**) *adj* - **1.** [patterned] de flores, floreado(da) - **2.** *pej* [elaborate] florido(da).

flowing ['fləʊɪŋ] *adj* [movement, writing, style] fluido(da); [water] corriente; [hair, clothes] suelto(ta).

flown [fləʊn] *pp* ▷ **fly**.

fl. oz. *abbr of* **fluid ounce**.

flu [fluː] *n* gripe *f*, gripa *f* Amér; **to have flu** tener la gripe.

fluctuate ['flʌktʃʊeɪt] *vi* fluctuar.

fluctuation [ˌflʌktʃʊ'eɪʃn] *n* fluctuación *f*.

flue [fluː] *n* [of chimney] tiro *m*.

fluency ['fluːənsɪ] *n* soltura *f*, fluidez *f*; **fluency in French** dominio *m* del francés.

fluent ['fluːənt] *adj* - **1.** [in foreign language]: **to be fluent in French, to speak fluent French** dominar el francés - **2.** [style] fluido(da).

fluently ['fluːəntlɪ] *adv* con soltura; **to speak French fluently** dominar el francés.

fluff [flʌf] <> *n* pelusa *f*. <> *vt* *inf* [action, task] hacer mal; [words, lines] decir mal.

➥ **fluff up** *vt sep* [cushion] mullir; [feathers] ahuecar.

fluffy ['flʌfɪ] (*comp* -**ier**, *superl* -**iest**) *adj* [jumper] de pelusa; [toy] de peluche.

fluid ['fluːɪd] <> *n* fluido *m*, líquido *m*. <> *adj* - **1.** [flowing] fluido(da) - **2.** [situation, opinion] incierto(ta).

fluid ounce *n* onza *f* líquida (*unos 30 ml*).

fluke [fluːk] *n* *inf* chiripa *f*; **by a fluke** por OR de chiripa.

flummox ['flʌməks] *vt* UK *inf* desconcertar.

flung [flʌŋ] *pt* & *pp* ▷ **fling**.

flunk [flʌŋk] *vt* & *vi* esp US *inf* catear.

➥ **flunk out** *vi* US *inf* ser expulsado(da).

fluorescent [fluə'resnt] *adj* fluorescente.

fluorescent light *n* luz *f* fluorescente.

fluoride ['fluəraɪd] *n* fluoruro *m*.

fluorine ['fluəriːn] *n* flúor *m*.

flurry ['flʌrɪ] (*pl* -**ies**) *n* - **1.** [shower] ráfaga *f* - **2.** [burst] torbellino *m*.

flush [flʌʃ] <> *adj* - **1.** [level]: **flush with** nivelado(da) con - **2.** *inf* [with plenty of money]: **to be flush** andar bien de dinero. <> *n* - **1.** [lavatory mechanism] cadena *f*; **give the toilet a flush** tira de la cadena - **2.** [blush] rubor *m* - **3.** [sudden feeling] arrebato *m*; **in the first flush of youth** *liter* en la primera juventud. <> *vt* - **1.** [toilet]: **to flush the toilet** tirar de la cadena - **2.** [down toilet]: **to flush sthg away** tirar algo al váter - **3.** [force out of hiding]: **to flush sb out** hacer salir a alguien. <> *vi* [blush] ruborizarse.

flushed [flʌʃt] *adj* - **1.** [red-faced] encendido(da) - **2.** [excited]: **flushed (with)** enardecido(da) (por).

fluster ['flʌstər] <> *n*: **to get in a fluster** aturullarse. <> *vt* aturullar.

flustered ['flʌstəd] *adj* aturullado(da).

flute [fluːt] *n* MUS flauta *f*.

fluted ['fluːtɪd] *adj* acanalado(da).

flutist US = **flautist**.

flutter ['flʌtər] <> *n* - **1.** [of wings] aleteo *m*; [of eyelashes] pestañeo *m* - **2.** [of heart] palpitación *f* - **3.** *inf* [of excitement] arranque *m*. <> *vt* agitar; **to flutter one's eyelashes** parpadear. <> *vi* - **1.** [bird] aletear - **2.** [flag, dress] ondear - **3.** [heart] palpitar.

flux [flʌks] *n* [change]: **to be in a state of flux** cambiar constantemente.

fly [flaɪ] ⬦ *n* (*pl* **flies**) **- 1.** [insect] mosca *f*; **a fly in the ointment** una pega **- 2.** [of trousers] bragueta *f*. ⬦ *vt* (*pt* **flew**, *pp* **flown**) **- 1.** [plane] pilotar; [kite, model aircraft] hacer volar **- 2.** [passengers, supplies] transportar en avión **- 3.** [flag] ondear. ⬦ *vi* (*pt* **flew**, *pp* **flown**) **- 1.** [bird, plane] volar; **time flies** el tiempo vuela; **I must fly!** ¡me voy volando!; **to go flying** *inf* [fall over] caer aparatosamente; **to send sthg/sb flying, to knock sthg/sb flying** *inf* mandar algo/a alguien por los aires **- 2.** [travel by plane] ir en avión **- 3.** [pilot a plane] pilotar **- 4.** [rumours, stories] abundar **- 5.** [attack]: **to fly at sb** arremeter contra alguien **- 6.** [flag] ondear.
◆ **fly away** *vi* irse volando.
◆ **fly in** ⬦ *vt sep* traer *(en avión)*. ⬦ *vi* [person] llegar *(en avión)*; [plane] aterrizar.
◆ **fly into** *vt insep*: **to fly into a rage** *OR* **a temper** montar en cólera.
◆ **fly out** ⬦ *vt sep* llevarse *(en avión)*. ⬦ *vi* irse *(en avión)*.

flyby *US* = **flypast**.

fly-fishing *n* pesca *f* con mosca.

fly half *n UK* (medio *m*) apertura *m*.

flying ['flaɪɪŋ] ⬦ *adj* **- 1.** [able to fly] volador(ra), volante **- 2.** [running]: **a flying leap** *OR* **jump** un salto con carrerilla. ⬦ *n*: **I hate/love flying** odio/me encanta ir en avión; **her hobby is flying** es aficionada a la aviación.

flying colours *npl*: **to pass (sthg) with flying colours** salir airoso(sa) (de algo).

flying doctor *n* médico que utiliza el avión para visitar a sus pacientes en zonas muy alejadas.

flying officer *n UK* ≃ teniente *mf* de aviación.

flying picket *n* piquete *m* volante.

flying saucer *n* platillo *m* volante.

flying squad *n* brigada *f* volante.

flying start *n*: **to get off to a flying start** empezar con muy buen pie.

flying visit *n* visita *f* relámpago.

flyleaf ['flaɪliːf] (*pl* **-leaves**) *n* (hoja *f* de) guarda *f*.

flyover ['flaɪ‚əʊvəʳ] *n UK* paso *m* elevado.

flypast *UK* ['flaɪ‚pɑːst], **flyby** *US* ['flaɪ‚baɪ] *n* desfile *m* aéreo.

flysheet ['flaɪʃiːt] *n* doble techo *m*.

fly spray *n* matamoscas *m inv* *(en aerosol)*.

flyweight ['flaɪweɪt] *n* peso *m* mosca.

flywheel ['flaɪwiːl] *n* volante *m* *(de motor)*.

FM (*abbr of* **frequency modulation**) FM *f*.

FMCS (*abbr of* **Federal Mediation and Conciliation Services**) *n* organismo estadounidense de arbitraje en conflictos laborales, ≃ IMAC *m*.

FO *n abbr of* **Foreign Office**.

foal [fəʊl] *n* potro *m*.

foam [fəʊm] ⬦ *n* **- 1.** [bubbles] espuma *f* **- 2.**: **foam (rubber)** gomaespuma *f*. ⬦ *vi* hacer espuma; **to foam at the mouth** echar espuma por la boca.

foamy ['fəʊmɪ] (*comp* **-ier**, *superl* **-iest**) *adj* espumoso(sa).

fob [fɒb] (*pt & pp* **-bed**, *cont* **-bing**) ◆ **fob off** *vt sep*: **to fob sb off (with sthg)** quitarse a alguien de encima (con algo); **to fob sthg off on sb** endosar a alguien algo.

FOB, f.o.b. (*abbr of* **free on board**) f.a.b.

fob watch *n* reloj *m* de bolsillo.

focal ['fəʊkl] *adj* [important] clave *(inv)*.

focal point ['fəʊkl-] *n* punto *m* focal *OR* central.

focus ['fəʊkəs] ⬦ *n* (*pl* **-cuses** *OR* **-ci** [-saɪ]) [gen] foco *m*; **in focus** enfocado; **out of focus** desenfocado; **focus of attention** centro *m* de atención. ⬦ *vt* **- 1.** [eyes, lens, rays] enfocar **- 2.** [attention] fijar, centrar. ⬦ *vi* **- 1.** [eyes, lens]: **to focus (on sthg)** enfocar (algo) **- 2.** [attention]: **to focus on sthg** centrarse en algo.

fodder ['fɒdəʳ] *n* forraje *m*.

foe [fəʊ] *n liter* enemigo *m*, -ga *f*.

FOE *n* **- 1.** (*abbr of* **Friends of the Earth**) AT *mpl* **- 2.** (*abbr of* **Fraternal Order of Eagles**) organización benéfica estadounidense.

foetal, fetal ['fiːtl] *adj* fetal.

foetus, fetus ['fiːtəs] *n* feto *m*.

fog [fɒg] *n* niebla *f*.

fogbound ['fɒgbaʊnd] *adj* inmovilizado(da) por la niebla.

fogey ['fəʊgɪ] = **fogy**.

foggiest ['fɒgɪəst] *n inf*: **I haven't the foggiest** no tengo la menor idea.

foggy ['fɒgɪ] (*comp* **-ier**, *superl* **-iest**) *adj* [day] de niebla; **it's foggy** hay niebla.

foghorn ['fɒghɔːn] *n* sirena *f* *(de niebla)*.

fog lamp *n* faro *m* antiniebla.

fogy, fogey ['fəʊgɪ] (*pl* **-ies**) *n inf* carroza *mf*, carca *mf*.

foible ['fɔɪbl] *n* manía *f*.

foil [fɔɪl] ⬦ *n* **- 1.** (*U*) [metal sheet] papel *m* de aluminio *OR* de plata **- 2.** [contrast]: **to be a foil to** *OR* **for** complementar. ⬦ *vt* frustrar.

foist [fɔɪst] *vt*: **to foist sthg on sb** endosar algo a alguien.

fold [fəʊld] ⬦ *vt* [sheet, blanket] doblar; [chair, pram] plegar; **to fold one's arms** cruzar los brazos. <> *vi* - **1.** [table, chair etc] plegarse - **2.** *inf* [collapse] venirse abajo. <> *n* - **1.** [in material, paper] pliegue *m* - **2.** [for animals] redil *m* - **3.** *fig* [spiritual home]: **the fold** el redil.

◆ **fold up** <> *vt sep* - **1.** [bend] doblar - **2.** [close up] plegar. <> *vi* - **1.** [bend] doblarse - **2.** [close up] plegarse - **3.** [collapse] venirse abajo.

foldaway ['fəʊldə,weɪ] *adj* plegable.

folder ['fəʊldəʳ] *n* [gen & COMPUT] carpeta *f*.

folding ['fəʊldɪŋ] *adj* plegable; [ladder] de tijera.

foliage ['fəʊlɪɪdʒ] *n* follaje *m*.

folk [fəʊk] <> *adj* popular. <> *npl* [people] gente *f*. <> *n* = **folk music**.

◆ **folks** *npl inf* - **1.** [parents] padres *mpl* - **2.** [everyone] chicos *mpl*, -cas *f*.

folklore ['fəʊklɔːʳ] *n* folclore *m*.

folk music *n* - **1.** [traditional] música *f* folclórica OR popular - **2.** [contemporary] música *f* folk.

folk singer *n* - **1.** [traditional] cantante *mf* de música popular - **2.** [contemporary] cantante *mf* folk.

folk song *n* - **1.** [traditional] canción *f* popular - **2.** [contemporary] canción *f* folk.

folksy ['fəʊksɪ] (*comp* -ier, *superl* -iest) *adj* US *inf* [friendly] campechano(na).

follicle ['fɒlɪkl] *n* folículo *m*.

follow ['fɒləʊ] <> *vt* - **1.** [gen] seguir - **2.** [understand] comprender. <> *vi* - **1.** [gen] seguir; **the numbers are as follows** los números son los siguientes - **2.** [be logical] ser lógico(ca); **it follows that** se deduce que - **3.** [understand] comprender.

◆ **follow up** *vt sep* - **1.** [monitor] hacer un seguimiento de - **2.** [continue]: **to follow sthg up with** proseguir algo con.

follower ['fɒləʊəʳ] *n* partidario *m*, -ria *f*, seguidor *m*, -ra *f*.

following ['fɒləʊɪŋ] <> *adj* siguiente. <> *n* partidarios *mpl*; [of team] afición *f*. <> *prep* tras.

follow-up <> *adj* de seguimiento. <> *n* - **1.** [service] seguimiento *m* - **2.** [continuation] continuación *f*.

folly ['fɒlɪ] *n* (U) [foolishness] locura *f*.

foment [fəʊ'ment] *vt fml* fomentar.

fond [fɒnd] *adj* - **1.** [affectionate] afectuoso(sa), cariñoso(sa) - **2.** [having a liking]: **to be fond of sb** tener cariño a alguien; **to be fond of sthg/of doing sthg** ser aficionado(da) a algo/a hacer algo - **3.** *fml* [naive, unrealistic] inocente.

fondle ['fɒndl] *vt* acariciar.

fondly ['fɒndlɪ] *adv* - **1.** [affectionately] afectuosamente, con cariño - **2.** [naively] inocentemente.

fondness ['fɒndnɪs] *n* - **1.** [affection]: **fondness (for)** cariño *m* (a) - **2.** [liking]: **fondness for** afición *f* a.

fondue ['fɒndjuː] *n* fondue *f*.

font [fɒnt] *n* - **1.** [in church] pila *f* bautismal - **2.** COMPUT fuente *f*.

food [fuːd] *n* comida *f*; **food for thought** materia *f* de reflexión.

food chain *n* cadena *f* alimentaria.

food mixer *n* batidora *f* eléctrica.

food poisoning [-ˌpɔɪznɪŋ] *n* intoxicación *f* alimenticia.

food processor [-ˌprəʊsesəʳ] *n* robot *m* de cocina.

food stamp *n* US cupón estatal canjeable por comida.

foodstuffs ['fuːdstʌfs] *npl* comestibles *mpl*.

fool [fuːl] <> *n* - **1.** [idiot] idiota *mf*, imbécil *mf*; **to make a fool of sb/of o.s.** poner a alguien/ponerse en ridículo; **to act OR play the fool** hacer el tonto - **2.** UK [dessert] *mousse de fruta con nata*. <> *vt* [deceive] engañar; **to fool sb into doing sthg** embaucar a alguien para que haga algo. <> *vi* bromear.

◆ **fool about, fool around** *vi* - **1.** [behave foolishly]: **to fool about (with sthg)** hacer el tonto (con algo) - **2.** [be unfaithful]: **to fool about (with sb)** tontear (con alguien).

foolhardy ['fuːlˌhɑːdɪ] *adj* temerario(ria).

foolish ['fuːlɪʃ] *adj* tonto(ta), estúpido(da).

foolishly ['fuːlɪʃlɪ] *adv* tontamente, estúpidamente.

foolishness ['fuːlɪʃnɪs] *n* (U) necedad *f*.

foolproof ['fuːlpruːf] *adj* infalible.

foolscap ['fuːlzkæp] *n* (U) ≃ pliego *m*.

foot [fʊt] <> *n* - **1.** (*pl* feet) [gen] pie *m*; [of bird, animal] pata *f*; **to be on one's feet** estar de pie; **to get to one's feet** levantarse; **on foot** a pie, andando; **to be back on one's feet** haberse recuperado; **to be rushed off one's feet** andar muy atareado(da); **to have itchy feet** tener ganas de viajar; **to put one's foot down** [be firm] ponerse firme; [accelerate] pisar fuerte; **to put one's foot in it** meter la pata; **to put one's feet up** descansar; **to set foot in** poner los pies en; **to stand on one's own two feet** valerse por sí mismo(ma) - **2.** (*pl* feet) [unit of measurement] = 30,48 *cm* pie *m*. <> *vt inf*: **to foot the bill (for sthg)** pagar la cuenta (de algo).

footage ['fʊtɪdʒ] *n* (U) secuencias *fpl*.

foot-and-mouth disease *n* fiebre *f* aftosa.

football ['fʊtbɔːl] *n* - **1.** [game - soccer] fútbol *m*; [- American football] fútbol *m* americano - **2.** [ball] balón *m*.

football club *n* UK club *m* de fútbol.

footballer ['fʊtbɔːləʳ], **football player** n UK futbolista mf.

football field n US campo m de fútbol americano.

football game n US partido m de fútbol americano.

football ground n UK estadio m de fútbol.

football match n UK partido m de fútbol.

football pitch n UK campo m de fútbol.

football player = footballer.

football pools npl UK quinielas fpl.

football supporter n UK hincha mf.

football team n UK equipo m de fútbol.

footbrake ['fʊtbreɪk] n freno m de pedal.

footbridge ['fʊtbrɪdʒ] n puente m peatonal, pasarela f.

foothills ['fʊthɪlz] npl estribaciones fpl.

foothold ['fʊthəʊld] n punto m de apoyo para el pie; **to get a foothold** [on mountain, rockface] encontrar un punto de apoyo; [in organization, company] afianzarse.

footing ['fʊtɪŋ] n - **1.** [foothold] equilibrio m; **to lose one's footing** perder el equilibrio - **2.** [basis] base f; **on an equal footing (with)** en pie de igualdad (con).

footlights ['fʊtlaɪts] npl candilejas fpl.

footman ['fʊtmən] (pl -men [-mən]) n lacayo m.

footmark ['fʊtmɑːk] n pisada f.

footnote ['fʊtnəʊt] n nota f a pie de página.

footpath ['fʊtpɑːθ, pl -pɑːðz] n senda f, camino m.

footprint ['fʊtprɪnt] n huella f, pisada f.

footsore ['fʊtsɔːʳ] adj con los pies doloridos.

footstep ['fʊtstep] n - **1.** [sound] paso m - **2.** [footprint] pisada f; **to follow in sb's footsteps** seguir los pasos de alguien.

footwear ['fʊtweəʳ] n calzado m.

footwork ['fʊtwɜːk] n (U) juego m de piernas.

for [fɔːʳ] <> prep - **1.** [indicating intention, destination, purpose] para; **this is for you** esto es para ti; **I'm going for the paper** voy (a) por el periódico; **the plane for Paris** el avión para OR de París; **it's time for bed** es hora de irse a la cama; **we did it for a laugh** OR **for fun** lo hicimos de broma OR para divertirnos; **to wait for the bus** esperar el autobús; **to go for a walk** ir a dar un paseo; **what's it for?** ¿para qué es OR sirve? - **2.** [representing, on behalf of] por; **the MP for Barnsley** el diputado por Barnsley; **let me do it for you** deja que lo haga por ti; **he plays for England** juega en la selección inglesa; **to work for** trabajar para - **3.** [because of] por; **for various reasons** por varias razones; **a prize for bravery** un premio a la valentía; **to jump for joy** dar saltos de alegría; **for fear of failing** por miedo al fracaso

- **4.** [with regard to] para; **to be ready for sthg** estar listo(ta) para algo; **it's not for me to say** no me toca a mí decidir; **he looks young for his age** parece más joven de lo que es; **to feel sorry/glad for sb** sentirlo/alegrarse por alguien - **5.** [indicating amount of time, space] para; **there's no time/room for it** no hay tiempo/sitio para eso - **6.** [indicating period of time - during] durante; [- by, in time for] para; **she cried for two hours** estuvo llorando durante dos horas; **I've lived here for three years** llevo tres años viviendo aquí, he vivido aquí (durante) tres años; **I've worked here for years** trabajo aquí desde hace años; **I'll do it for tomorrow** lo tendré hecho para mañana - **7.** [indicating distance] en; **there were roadworks for 50 miles** había obras en 50 millas; **we walked for miles** andamos millas y millas - **8.** [indicating particular occasion] para; **I got it for my birthday** me lo regalaron para OR por mi cumpleaños; **it's scheduled for the 30th** está programado para el día 30; **for the first time** por vez primera - **9.** [indicating amount of money, price] por; **I bought/sold it for £10** lo compré/vendí por 10 libras; **they're 50p for ten** son 50 peniques los diez - **10.** [in favour of, in support of] a favor de; **is she for or against it?** ¿está a favor o en contra?; **to vote for sthg/sb** votar por algo/a alguien; **to be all for sthg** estar completamente a favor de algo - **11.** [in ratios] por - **12.** [indicating meaning]: **green is for go** el verde quiere decir adelante; **P for Peter** P de Pedro; **what's the Greek for 'mother'?** ¿cómo se dice 'madre' en griego? <> conj fml [as, since] ya que.

for all <> prep - **1.** [in spite of] a pesar de, pese a; **for all your moaning** a pesar de lo mucho que te quejas - **2.** [considering how little] para; **for all the good it has done me** para lo que me ha servido. <> conj: **for all he promised to do it, he never actually did** con todo lo que prometió que lo haría, al final nada; **for all I care, she could be dead** por mí, como si se muere; **for all I know** por lo que yo sé, que yo sepa.

forage ['fɒrɪdʒ] vi [search]: **to forage (for sthg)** buscar (algo).

foray ['fɒreɪ] n lit & fig: **foray (into)** incursión f (en).

forbad [fə'bæd], **forbade** [fə'beɪd] pt ⊳ forbid.

forbearing [fɔː'beərɪŋ] adj tolerante.

forbid [fə'bɪd] (pt -bade OR -bad, pp forbid OR -bidden, cont -bidding) vt: **to forbid sb (to do sthg)** prohibir a alguien (hacer algo); **God OR Heaven forbid!** ¡no quiera Dios!

forbidden [fə'bɪdn] adj prohibido(da).

forbidding [fə'bɪdɪŋ] *adj* [building, landscape] inhóspito(ta); [person, expression] severo(ra), austero(ra).

force [fɔːs] ◇ *n* fuerza *f*; **a force to be reckoned with** alguien/algo a tener en cuenta; **a force for change** una fuerza impulsora del cambio; **force of habit** la fuerza de la costumbre; **sales force** personal *m* de ventas; **security forces** fuerzas *fpl* de seguridad; **by force** a la fuerza; **to be in/come into force** estar/entrar en vigor; **in force** [in large numbers] en masa, en gran número. ◇ *vt* forzar; **to force sb to do sthg** [gen] forzar a alguien a hacer algo; [subj: event, circumstances] obligar a alguien a hacer algo; **to force sthg on sb** imponer algo a alguien; **to force sthg open** forzar algo, abrir algo a la fuerza; **to force one's way through/into** abrirse paso a la fuerza a través de/para entrar en.
◆ **forces** *npl*: **the forces** las fuerzas armadas; **to join forces (with)** unirse (con).
◆ **by force of** *prep* a fuerza de.
◆ **force back** *vt sep* [crowd, enemy] hacer retroceder; [emotion, tears] contener, reprimir.
◆ **force down** *vt sep* - **1.** [food, drink] tragar a la fuerza - **2.** [aircraft] obligar a aterrizar.

forced [fɔːst] *adj* forzado(da).

forced landing *n* aterrizaje *m* forzoso.

force-feed *vt* alimentar a la fuerza.

forceful ['fɔːsfʊl] *adj* [person, impression] fuerte; [support, recommendation] enérgico(ca); [speech, idea, argument] contundente.

forcefully ['fɔːsfʊlɪ] *adv* enérgicamente.

forcemeat ['fɔːsmiːt] *n esp UK* (picadillo *m* de) relleno *m*.

forceps ['fɔːseps] *npl* fórceps *m inv*.

forcible ['fɔːsəbl] *adj* - **1.** [using physical force] por la fuerza - **2.** [reminder, example, argument] contundente.

forcibly ['fɔːsəblɪ] *adv* - **1.** [using physical force] por la fuerza - **2.** [remind] vivamente; [express, argue] convincentemente.

ford [fɔːd] ◇ *n* vado *m*. ◇ *vt* vadear.

fore [fɔːʳ] ◇ *adj* NAUT de proa. ◇ *n*: **to come to the fore** emerger, empezar a destacar.

forearm ['fɔːrɑːm] *n* antebrazo *m*.

forebears ['fɔːbeəz], **forefathers** *npl fml* antepasados *mpl*.

foreboding [fɔː'bəʊdɪŋ] *n* - **1.** [presentiment] presagio *m* - **2.** [apprehension] desasosiego *m*.

forecast ['fɔːkɑːst] ◇ *n* [prediction] predicción *f*, previsión *f*; [of weather] pronóstico *m*. ◇ *vt* (*pt & pp* forecast *OR* -**ed**) [predict] predecir; [weather] pronosticar.

forecaster ['fɔːkɑːstəʳ] *n* [economic, political] analista *mf*; [of weather] meteorólogo *m*, -ga *f*.

foreclose [fɔː'kləʊz] ◇ *vi*: **to foreclose on sb** privar a alguien del derecho a redimir su hipoteca. ◇ *vt* ejecutar.

foreclosure [fɔː'kləʊʒəʳ] *n* ejecución *f*.

forecourt ['fɔːkɔːt] *n* patio *m*.

forefathers ['fɔːˌfɑːðəz] *npl* = **forebears**.

forefinger ['fɔːˌfɪŋgəʳ] *n* (dedo *m*) índice *m*.

forefront ['fɔːfrʌnt] *n*: **in** *OR* **at the forefront of** en *OR* a la vanguardia de.

forego [fɔː'gəʊ] = **forgo**.

foregoing [fɔː'gəʊɪŋ] ◇ *adj* anterior, precedente. ◇ *n fml*: **the foregoing** lo anteriormente dicho.

foregone conclusion ['fɔːgɒn-] *n*: **it's a foregone conclusion** es un resultado conocido de antemano.

foreground ['fɔːgraʊnd] *n* primer plano *m*; **in the foreground** en primer plano.

forehand ['fɔːhænd] *n* [stroke] golpe *m* natural, drive *m*.

forehead ['fɔːhed] *n* frente *f*.

foreign ['fɒrən] *adj* - **1.** [from abroad] extranjero(ra) - **2.** [external - policy, trade] exterior; [- correspondent, holiday] en el extranjero - **3.** [unwanted, harmful] extraño(ña) - **4.** [alien, untypical]: **foreign (to sb/sthg)** ajeno(na) (a alguien/algo).

foreign affairs *npl* asuntos *mpl* exteriores.

foreign aid *n* [received] ayuda *f* extranjera; [granted] ayuda *f* al exterior.

foreign body *n* cuerpo *m* extraño.

foreign currency *n* (*U*) divisa *f*.

foreigner ['fɒrənəʳ] *n* extranjero *m*, -ra *f*.

foreign exchange (*U*) *n* divisas *fpl*; **foreign exchange markets/rates** mercados *mpl*/cambio *m* de divisas.

foreign investment *n* (*U*) inversión *f* extranjera.

foreign minister *n* ministro *m*, -tra *f* de asuntos exteriores.

Foreign Office *n* UK: **the Foreign Office** el Ministerio de Asuntos Exteriores británico.

Foreign Secretary *n* UK Ministro *m*, -tra *f* de Asuntos Exteriores.

foreleg ['fɔːleg] *n* pata *f* delantera.

foreman ['fɔːmən] (*pl* -**men** [-mən]) *n* - **1.** [of workers] encargado *m* - **2.** [of jury] presidente *m*.

foremost ['fɔːməʊst] ◇ *adj* primero(ra). ◇ *adv*: **first and foremost** ante todo, por encima de todo.

forename ['fɔːneɪm] *n* nombre *m* (de pila).

forensic [fə'rensɪk] *adj* forense.

forensic medicine *n* medicina *f* forense.

forerunner ['fɔ:,rʌnəʳ] n [precursor] precursor m, -ra f.

foresee [fɔ:'si:] (pt -saw [-'sɔ:], pp -seen) vt prever.

foreseeable [fɔ:'si:əbl] adj previsible; **for** OR **in the foreseeable future** en un futuro próximo.

foreseen [fɔ:'si:n] pp ▷ foresee.

foreshadow [fɔ:'ʃædəʊ] vt presagiar.

foreshortened [fɔ:'ʃɔ:tnd] adj escorzado(da).

foresight ['fɔ:saɪt] n (U) previsión f.

foreskin ['fɔ:skɪn] n prepucio m.

forest ['fɒrɪst] n bosque m.

forestall [fɔ:'stɔ:l] vt anticiparse a.

forestry ['fɒrɪstrɪ] n silvicultura f.

foretaste ['fɔ:teɪst] n anticipo m, adelanto m.

foretell [fɔ:'tel] (pt & pp -told) vt predecir.

forethought ['fɔ:θɔ:t] n previsión f.

foretold [fɔ:'təʊld] pt & pp ▷ foretell.

forever [fə'revəʳ] adv - **1.** [eternally] para siempre - **2.** inf [incessantly] siempre, continuamente - **3.** inf [a long time]: **it took (us) forever** nos llevó una eternidad.

forewarn [fɔ:'wɔ:n] vt prevenir, advertir.

foreword ['fɔ:wɜ:d] n prefacio m.

forfeit ['fɔ:fɪt] ◇ n [penalty] precio m; [in game] prenda f. ◇ vt renunciar a, perder.

forgave [fə'geɪv] pt ▷ forgive.

forge [fɔ:dʒ] ◇ n fragua f, forja f. ◇ vt - **1.** [gen] forjar, fraguar - **2.** [falsify] falsificar.
◆ **forge ahead** vi hacer grandes progresos.

forger ['fɔ:dʒəʳ] n falsificador m, -ra f.

forgery ['fɔ:dʒərɪ] (pl -ies) n falsificación f.

forget [fə'get] (pt -got, pp -gotten, cont -getting) ◇ vt: **to forget (to do sthg)** olvidar (hacer algo); **I've forgotten it** se me ha olvidado; **forget it!** [no way] ¡ni hablar!; **to forget o.s.** dejarse llevar por un impulso. ◇ vi: **to forget (about sthg)** olvidarse (de algo).

forgetful [fə'getfʊl] adj olvidadizo(za), desmemoriado(da).

forgetfulness [fə'getfʊlnɪs] n mala memoria f.

forget-me-not n nomeolvides m inv.

forgive [fə'gɪv] (pt -gave, pp -given) vt: **to forgive sb (for sthg/for doing sthg)** perdonar a alguien (algo/por haber hecho algo).

forgiveness [fə'gɪvnɪs] n perdón m.

forgiving [fə'gɪvɪŋ] adj indulgente.

forgo, forego [fɔ:'gəʊ] (pt -went, pp -gone [-'gɒn]) vt sacrificar, renunciar a.

forgot [fə'gɒt] pt ▷ forget.

forgotten [fə'gɒtn] pp ▷ forget.

fork [fɔ:k] ◇ n - **1.** [for food] tenedor m - **2.** [for gardening] horca f - **3.** [in road etc] bifurcación f.
◇ vi bifurcarse.

◆ **fork out** inf ◇ vt insep: **to fork out money on** OR **for sthg** soltar pelas para algo. ◇ vi: **to fork out for sthg** soltar pelas para algo.

forklift truck ['fɔ:klɪft-] n carretilla f elevadora.

forlorn [fə'lɔ:n] adj - **1.** [person, expression] consternado(da) - **2.** [place, landscape] desolado(da) - **3.** [hope, attempt] desesperado(da).

form [fɔ:m] ◇ n - **1.** [shape, type] forma f; **in the form of** en forma de; **to take the form of** consistir en - **2.** [fitness]: **on form** UK, **in form** US en forma; **off form** en baja forma - **3.** [document] impreso m, formulario m, planilla f Amér - **4.** [figure - of person] figura f - **5.** UK [class] clase f - **6.** [usual behaviour]: **true to form** como era de esperar. ◇ vt formar; [plan] concebir; [impression, idea] formarse. ◇ vi formarse.

formal ['fɔ:ml] adj - **1.** [gen] formal; [education] convencional - **2.** [clothes, wedding, party] de etiqueta.

formality [fɔ:'mælətɪ] (pl -ies) n formalidad f.

formalize, -ise ['fɔ:məlaɪz] vt formalizar.

formally ['fɔ:məlɪ] adv formalmente; [dressed] de etiqueta.

format ['fɔ:mæt] ◇ n [gen & COMPUT] formato m; [of meeting] plan m. ◇ vt (pt & pp -ted, cont -ting) COMPUT formatear.

formation [fɔ:'meɪʃn] n formación f.

formative ['fɔ:mətɪv] adj formativo(va).

former ['fɔ:məʳ] ◇ adj - **1.** [previous] antiguo(gua); **in former times** antiguamente - **2.** [first of two] primero(ra). ◇ n: **the former** el primero(la primera)/los primeros(las primeras).

formerly ['fɔ:məlɪ] adv antes, antiguamente.

form feed n avance m de página.

Formica® [fɔ:'maɪkə] n formica® f.

formidable ['fɔ:mɪdəbl] adj - **1.** [frightening] imponente, temible - **2.** [impressive] formidable.

formless ['fɔ:mlɪs] adj sin forma, informe.

formula ['fɔ:mjʊlə] (pl -as OR -ae [-i:]) n - **1.** [gen] fórmula f - **2.** [baby milk] leche f maternizada.

formulate ['fɔ:mjʊleɪt] vt formular.

formulation [,fɔ:mjʊ'leɪʃn] n formulación f.

fornicate ['fɔ:nɪkeɪt] vi fml fornicar.

forsake [fə'seɪk] (pt forsook, pp forsaken) vt liter abandonar.

forsaken [fə'seɪkn] adj abandonado(da).

forsook [fə'sʊk] pt ▷ forsake.

forsythia [fɔ:'saɪθjə] n forsitia f.

fort [fɔːt] *n* fuerte *m*, fortaleza *f*; **to hold the fort (for sb)** quedarse al cargo (en lugar de alguien).

forte [ˈfɔːtɪ] *n* fuerte *m*.

forth [fɔːθ] *adv liter* - **1.** [outwards, onwards] hacia adelante; **to go forth** partir - **2.** [into future]: **from that day forth** desde aquel día en adelante.

forthcoming [fɔːθˈkʌmɪŋ] *adj* - **1.** [election, events] próximo(ma); [book] de próxima aparición - **2.** [help, information, answer] disponible; **no reply was forthcoming** no hubo respuesta - **3.** [person] abierto(ta).

forthright [ˈfɔːθraɪt] *adj* [person, manner, opinions] directo(ta), franco(ca); [opposition] rotundo(da).

forthwith [ˌfɔːθˈwɪθ] *adv fml* inmediatamente.

fortieth [ˈfɔːtɪɪθ] <> *num adj* cuadragésimo(ma). <> *num n* - **1.** [in order] cuadragésimo *m*, -ma *f* - **2.** [fraction] cuarentavo *m*; *see also* **sixth**.

fortification [ˌfɔːtɪfɪˈkeɪʃn] *n* fortificación *f*.

fortified wine [ˈfɔːtɪfaɪd-] *n* vino *m* licoroso.

fortify [ˈfɔːtɪfaɪ] (*pt & pp* -**ied**) *vt* - **1.** MIL fortificar - **2.** [person, resolve] fortalecer.

fortitude [ˈfɔːtɪtjuːd] *n* fortaleza *f*, valor *m*.

fortnight [ˈfɔːtnaɪt] *n* quincena *f*; **in a fortnight** en quince días.

fortnightly [ˈfɔːtˌnaɪtlɪ] <> *adj* quincenal. <> *adv* quincenalmente.

fortress [ˈfɔːtrɪs] *n* fortaleza *f*.

fortuitous [fɔːˈtjuːɪtəs] *adj fml* fortuito(ta), casual.

fortunate [ˈfɔːtʃnət] *adj* afortunado(da).

fortunately [ˈfɔːtʃnətlɪ] *adv* afortunadamente.

fortune [ˈfɔːtʃuːn] *n* - **1.** [money, luck] fortuna *f* - **2.** [future]: **to tell sb's fortune** decir a alguien la buenaventura.

➡ **fortunes** *npl* [vicissitudes] vicisitudes *fpl*; [luck] suerte *f*.

fortune-teller [-ˌtelər] *n* adivino *m*, -na *f*.

forty [ˈfɔːtɪ] *num* cuarenta; *see also* **sixty**.

forum [ˈfɔːrəm] (*pl* -**s**) *n lit & fig* foro *m*.

forward [ˈfɔːwəd] <> *adj* - **1.** [towards front - movement] hacia adelante; [near front - position etc] delantero(ra) - **2.** [towards future]: **forward planning** planificación *f* (de futuro) - **3.** [advanced]: **we're no further forward** no hemos adelantado (nada) - **4.** [impudent] atrevido(da). <> *adv* - **1.** [ahead] hacia adelante; **to go** OR **move forward** avanzar - **2.** [in time]: **to bring sthg forward** adelantar algo; **to put a clock forward (by 30 minutes)** adelantar un reloj (30 minutos). <> *n* SPORT delantero *m*, -ra *f*. <> *vt* - **1.** [letter, e-mail] remitir; **'please forward'** 'remítase al destinatario' - **2.** *fml* [further] promover.

forwarding address [ˈfɔːwədɪŋ-] *n* nueva dirección *f* (*para reenvío de correo*).

forward-looking [-ˈlʊkɪŋ] *adj* progresista.

forwardness [ˈfɔːwədnɪs] *n* [boldness] atrevimiento *m*.

forwards [ˈfɔːwədz] = **forward**.

forward slash *n* TYPO barra *f* inclinada.

forwent [fɔːˈwent] *pt* ▷ **forgo**.

fossil [ˈfɒsl] *n* fósil *m*.

fossil fuel *n* combustible *m* fósil.

fossilized, -ised [ˈfɒsɪlaɪzd] *adj* fosilizado(da).

foster [ˈfɒstər] <> *adj* [home] de acogida. <> *vt* - **1.** [child] acoger - **2.** [idea, arts, relations] promover. <> *vi* acoger a un niño en la familia de uno.

foster child *n* menor *mf* en régimen de acogida.

foster parents *npl* familia *f* de acogida.

fought [fɔːt] *pt & pp* ▷ **fight**.

foul [faʊl] <> *adj* - **1.** [unclean - smell] fétido(da); [- taste] asqueroso(sa); [- water, language] sucio(cia) - **2.** [very unpleasant] horrible; **to fall foul of sb** ponerse a mal con alguien. <> *n* falta *f*. <> *vt* - **1.** [make dirty] ensuciar - **2.** SPORT cometer una falta contra - **3.** [obstruct] enmarañarse en.

➡ **foul up** *vt sep inf* fastidiar, echar a perder.

foul-mouthed [-ˈmaʊðd] *adj pej* malhablado(da).

foul play *n* (U) - **1.** SPORT juego *m* sucio - **2.** [criminal acts] actos *mpl* criminales.

found [faʊnd] <> *pt & pp* ▷ **find**. <> *vt*: **to found sthg (on)** fundar algo (en).

foundation [faʊnˈdeɪʃn] *n* - **1.** [organization, act of establishing] fundación *f* - **2.** [basis] fundamento *m*, base *f* - **3.** [make-up]: **foundation (cream)** crema *f* base.

➡ **foundations** *npl fig &* CONSTR cimientos *mpl*.

foundation stone *n* primera piedra *f*.

founder [ˈfaʊndər] <> *n* fundador *m*, -ra *f*. <> *vi lit & fig* hundirse, irse a pique.

founder member n miembro fundador m, miembro fundadora f.

founding ['faʊndɪŋ] n fundación f.

founding father n fundador m.

foundry ['faʊndrɪ] (pl -ies) n fundición f.

fount [faʊnt] n [origin] fuente f.

fountain ['faʊntɪn] n - **1.** [structure] fuente f - **2.** [jet] chorro m.

fountain pen n (pluma f) estilográfica f.

four [fɔːr] num cuatro; **on all fours** a gatas; see also **six**.

four-leaved clover [-liːvd-] n trébol m de cuatro hojas.

four-letter word n palabrota f, taco m.

four-poster (bed) n cama f de columnas.

foursome ['fɔːsəm] n grupo m de cuatro personas.

four-star adj [hotel] de cuatro estrellas.

fourteen [,fɔː'tiːn] num catorce; see also **six**.

fourteenth [,fɔː'tiːnθ] <> num adj decimocuarto(ta). <> num n - **1.** [in order] decimocuarto m, -ta f - **2.** [fraction] catorceavo m; see also **sixth**.

fourth [fɔːθ] num cuarto(ta); see also **sixth**.

Fourth of July n: the Fourth of July el cuatro de julio, día de la independencia de los Estados Unidos.

Fourth of July

El cuatro de julio, o Día de la Independencia, se celebra la fiesta nacional de EE. UU. Se trata del aniversario de la firma de la Declaración de Independencia estadounidense en 1776. Aquel histórico acontecimiento, que marcó el nacimiento de la nación, se conmemora en todo el territorio estadounidense con fuegos artificiales, discursos y desfiles.

four-way stop n US cruce m (de cuatro stops).

four-wheel drive n [system] tracción f a las cuatro ruedas; [car] todoterreno m.

fowl [faʊl] (pl **fowl** OR -s) n ave f de corral.

fox [fɒks] <> n zorro m. <> vt [perplex] dejar perplejo(ja).

foxglove ['fɒksglʌv] n digital f, dedalera f.

foxhole ['fɒkshəʊl] n hoyo m para atrincherarse.

foxhound ['fɒkshaʊnd] n perro m raposero OR zorrero.

foxhunt ['fɒkshʌnt] n cacería f de zorros.

foxhunting ['fɒks,hʌntɪŋ] n caza f de zorros.

foxy ['fɒksɪ] adj inf [sexy] cañón (inv), sexy.

foyer ['fɔɪeɪ] n vestíbulo m.

FP n (abbr of former pupil) AA mf.

Fr. (abbr of father) P.

fracas [UK 'frækɑː, US 'freɪkəs] (pl UK **fracas**, US **fracases**) n fml riña f, gresca f.

fraction ['frækʃn] n - **1.** MATHS quebrado m, fracción f - **2.** [small part] fracción f; **can you lift it up a fraction?** ¿puedes levantarlo un poquitín?

fractionally ['frækʃnəlɪ] adv ligeramente.

fractious ['frækʃəs] adj desapacible, irritable.

fracture ['fræktʃər] <> n fractura f. <> vt fracturar.

fragile ['frædʒaɪl] adj frágil.

fragility [frə'dʒɪlətɪ] n fragilidad f.

fragment <> n ['frægmənt] [of glass, text] fragmento m; [of paper, plastic] trozo m. <> vi ['frægment] fragmentarse.

fragmentary ['frægməntrɪ] adj fragmentario(ria).

fragmented [fræg'mentɪd] adj fragmentado(da).

fragrance ['freɪgrəns] n fragancia f.

fragrant ['freɪgrənt] adj fragante.

frail [freɪl] adj frágil.

frailty ['freɪltɪ] (pl -ies) n - **1.** fragilidad f - **2.** [imperfection] flaqueza f.

frame [freɪm] <> n - **1.** [of picture, door] marco m; [of glasses] montura f; [of chair, bed] armadura f; [of bicycle] cuadro m; [of boat] armazón m o f - **2.** [physique] cuerpo m. <> vt - **1.** [put in a frame] enmarcar - **2.** [express] formular, expresar - **3.** inf [set up] tender una trampa a, amañar la culpabilidad de.

frame of mind n estado m de ánimo, humor m.

framework ['freɪmwɜːk] n - **1.** [physical structure] armazón m o f, esqueleto m - **2.** [basis] marco m.

France [frɑːns] n Francia.

franchise ['fræntʃaɪz] n - **1.** POL sufragio m, derecho m de voto - **2.** COMM concesión f, licencia f exclusiva.

franchisee [,fræntʃaɪ'ziː] n concesionario m, -ria f.

frank [fræŋk] <> adj franco(ca). <> vt franquear.

frankfurter ['fræŋkfɜːtər] n salchicha f de Fráncfort.

frankincense ['fræŋkɪnsens] n incienso m.

franking machine ['fræŋkɪŋ-] n máquina f de franquear.

frankly ['fræŋklɪ] adv francamente.

frankness ['fræŋknɪs] n franqueza f.

frantic ['fræntɪk] adj frenético(ca).

frantically [ˈfræntɪklɪ] *adv* frenéticamente.

fraternal [frəˈtɜːnl] *adj* fraternal, fraterno(na).

fraternity [frəˈtɜːnətɪ] *(pl* **-ies)** *n* **- 1.** *fml* [community] gremio *m*, cofradía *f* **- 2.** *US* [in university] *asociación de estudiantes que suele funcionar como club social* **- 3.** *(U)* *fml* [friendship] fraternidad *f*.

fraternize, -ise [ˈfrætənaɪz] *vi*: **to fraternize (with)** fraternizar (con).

fraud [frɔːd] *n* **- 1.** *(U)* [deceit] fraude *m* **- 2.** *pej* [impostor] farsante *mf*.

fraudulent [ˈfrɔːdjʊlənt] *adj* fraudulento(ta).

fraught [frɔːt] *adj* **- 1.** [full]: **fraught with** lleno(na) *OR* cargado(da) de **- 2.** *UK* [frantic] tenso(sa).

fray [freɪ] <> *vt fig* [nerves] crispar, poner de punta. <> *vi* **- 1.** [sleeve, cuff] deshilacharse **- 2.** *fig* [temper, nerves] crisparse. <> *n liter*: **to enter the fray** saltar a la palestra.

frayed [freɪd] *adj* [sleeve, cuff] deshilachado(da).

frazzled [ˈfræzld] *adj inf* rendido(da).

FRB *(abbr of* **Federal Reserve Board)** *n órgano de control del banco central estadounidense.*

FRCP *(abbr of* **Fellow of the Royal College of Physicians)** *miembro del colegio británico de médicos.*

FRCS *(abbr of* **Fellow of the Royal College of Surgeons)** *miembro del colegio británico de cirujanos.*

freak [friːk] <> *adj* imprevisible, inesperado(da). <> *n* **- 1.** [strange creature - in appearance] fenómeno *m*, monstruo *m*; [- in behaviour] estrafalario *m*, -ria *f* **- 2.** [unusual event] anormalidad *f*, caso *m* insólito **- 3.** *inf* [fanatic]: **film/fitness freak** fanático *m*, -ca *f* del cine/ejercicio.
◆ **freak out** *inf* <> *vi* flipar, alucinar. <> *vt sep* flipar, alucinar.

freakish [ˈfriːkɪʃ] *adj* anormal, extraño(ña).

freckle [ˈfrekl] *n* peca *f*.

free [friː] <> *adj* *(comp* **freer,** *superl* **freest)** **- 1.** [gen]: **free (from** *OR* **of)** libre (de); **to be free to do sthg** ser libre de hacer algo; **feel free!** ¡adelante!, ¡cómo no!; **to set free** liberar **- 2.** [not paid for] gratis *(inv)*, gratuito(ta); **free of charge** gratis *(inv)* **- 3.** [unattached] suelto(ta) **- 4.** [generous]: **to be free with sthg** no regatear algo. <> *adv* **- 1.** [without payment]: **(for) free** gratis **- 2.** [run] libremente **- 3.** [loose]: **to pull/cut sthg free** soltar algo tirando/cortando. <> *vt (pt & pp* **freed) - 1.** [release] liberar, libertar; **to free sb of sthg** librar a alguien de algo **- 2.** [make available] dejar libre **- 3.** [extricate - person] rescatar; [- one's arm, oneself] soltar.

◆ **free up** *vt sep* [space, funds] liberar; [time, person] dejar libre.

-free [friː] *suffix*: **lead-free** sin plomo.

freebie [ˈfriːbɪ] *n inf* regalito *m*.

freedom [ˈfriːdəm] *n* libertad *f*; **freedom from** indemnidad *f* ante *OR* de.

freedom fighter *n* persona *f* que lucha por la libertad.

free enterprise *n* libre empresa *f*.

free-fall *n (U)* caída *f* libre.

Freefone®, freephone [ˈfriːfəʊn] *n (U) UK* teléfono *m* *OR* número *m* gratuito.

free-for-all *n* refriega *f*.

free gift *n* obsequio *m*.

freehand [ˈfriːhænd] *adj* & *adv* a pulso.

freehold [ˈfriːhəʊld] <> *adv* en propiedad absoluta. <> *n* propiedad *f* absoluta.

freeholder [ˈfriːhəʊldər] *n* propietario absoluto *m*, propietaria absoluta *f*.

free house *n pub no controlado por una compañía cervecera.*

free kick *n* tiro *m* libre.

freelance [ˈfriːlɑːns] <> *adj* free-lance. <> *adv* como free-lance. <> *n* free-lance *mf*. <> *vi* trabajar como free-lance.

freelancer [ˈfriːlɑːnsər] *n* free-lance *mf*.

freeloader [ˈfriːləʊdər] *n inf* gorrón *m*, -ona *f*.

freely [ˈfriːlɪ] *adv* **- 1.** [readily - admit, confess] sin reparos; [- available] fácilmente **- 2.** [openly] abiertamente, francamente **- 3.** [without restrictions] libremente **- 4.** [generously] liberalmente.

free-market economy *n* economía *f* de libre mercado.

Freemason [ˈfriːˌmeɪsn] *n* francmasón *m*, masón *m*.

freephone [ˈfriːfəʊn] = **freefone**.

Freepost® [ˈfriːpəʊst] *n* franqueo *m* pagado.

free-range *adj* de granja.

free sample *n* muestra *f* (gratuita).

freesia [ˈfriːzjə] *n* fresia *f*.

free speech *n* libertad *f* de expresión.

freestanding [ˌfriːˈstændɪŋ] *adj* independiente.

freestyle [ˈfriːstaɪl] *n* [in swimming] estilo *m* libre.

freethinker [ˌfriːˈθɪŋkər] *n* librepensador *m*, -ra *f*.

free trade *n* libre cambio *m*.

freeway [ˈfriːweɪ] *n US* autopista *f*.

freewheel [ˌfriːˈwiːl] *vi* [on bicycle] andar sin pedalear; [in car] ir en punto muerto.

freewheeling [ˌfriːˈwiːlɪŋ] *adj inf* informal.

free will n libre albedrío m; **to do sthg of one's own free will** hacer algo por voluntad propia.

free world n: **the free world** el mundo libre.

freeze [fri:z] <> vt (pt **froze**, pp **frozen**) - **1.** [gen] helar - **2.** [food, wages, prices] congelar - **3.** [assets] bloquear. <> vi (pt **froze**, pp **frozen**) - **1.** [gen] helarse - **2.** [food, wages, prices] congelarse - **3.** COMPUT bloquearse. <> impers vb METEOR helar. <> n - **1.** [cold weather] helada f - **2.** [of wages, prices] congelación f.
freeze over vi helarse.
freeze up vi - **1.** [gen] helarse - **2.** COMPUT bloquearse.

freeze-dried [-'draɪd] adj liofilizado(da).

freeze frame n - **1.** [photograph] fotograma m - **2.** [on video] imagen f congelada.

freezer ['fri:zəʳ] n congelador m.

freezing ['fri:zɪŋ] <> adj - **1.** [gen] helado(da) - **2.** [weather] muy frío(a); **it's freezing in here** hace un frío espantoso aquí. <> n = **freezing point**.

freezing point n punto m de congelación.

freight [freɪt] n (U) - **1.** [goods] mercancías fpl, flete m - **2.** [transport] transporte m.

freight train n (tren m de) mercancías m inv.

French [frentʃ] <> adj francés(esa). <> n [language] francés m. <> npl: **the French** los franceses.

French bean n judía f verde, ejote m Amér C & Méx, chaucha f R Plata, poroto m verde Chile, habichuela f Col, vainita f Ven.

French bread n (U) pan m de barra.

French Canadian <> adj francocanadiense. <> n francocanadiense mf.

French chalk n (U) jaboncillo m, jabón m de sastre.

French dressing n [vinaigrette] vinagreta f.

French fries, fries npl esp US patatas fpl fritas (de sartén).

Frenchman ['frentʃmən] (pl -men [-mən]) n francés m.

French polish n laca f.

French Riviera n: **the French Riviera** la Riviera francesa.

French stick n UK barra f de pan.

French toast n esp US torrija f.

French windows npl puertaventanas fpl.

Frenchwoman ['frentʃ,wʊmən] (pl -women [-,wɪmɪn]) n francesa f.

frenetic [frə'netɪk] adj frenético(ca).

frenzied ['frenzɪd] adj [haste, activity] frenético(ca).

frenzy ['frenzɪ] (pl -ies) n frenesí m; **a frenzy of activity** una actividad frenética OR febril.

frequency ['fri:kwənsɪ] (pl -ies) n frecuencia f.

frequency modulation n RADIO frecuencia f modulada.

frequent <> adj ['fri:kwənt] frecuente. <> vt [frɪ'kwent] frecuentar.

frequently ['fri:kwəntlɪ] adv a menudo, con frecuencia.

fresco ['freskəʊ] (pl -es OR -s) n fresco m.

fresh [freʃ] <> adj - **1.** [gen] fresco(ca); [flavour, taste] refrescante; **fresh from** recién salido(da) de - **2.** [bread] del día - **3.** [not canned] natural - **4.** [water] dulce - **5.** [pot of tea, fighting] nuevo(va); **to make a fresh start** empezar de nuevo. <> adv - **1.** recién; **to be fresh out of sthg** inf haberse quedado sin algo - **2.** [original] original.

freshen ['freʃn] <> vt [air] refrescar. <> vi [wind] soplar más fuerte.
freshen up <> vt sep - **1.** [wash]: **to freshen o.s. up** refrescarse - **2.** [smarten up] arreglar. <> vi [person] refrescarse.

fresher ['freʃəʳ] n UK estudiante mf de primer año.

freshly ['freʃlɪ] adv recién.

freshman ['freʃmən] (pl -men [-mən]) n estudiante mf de primer año.

freshness ['freʃnɪs] n (U) - **1.** [of food] frescura f - **2.** [originality] novedad f, originalidad f - **3.** [brightness] pulcritud f - **4.** [refreshing quality] frescor m.

freshwater ['freʃ,wɔ:təʳ] adj de agua dulce.

fret [fret] (pt & pp -ted, cont -ting) vi preocuparse.

fretful ['fretfʊl] adj [baby] quejoso(sa); [night, sleep] agitado(da), inquieto(ta).

fretsaw ['fretsɔ:] n [manual] segueta f; [electrical] sierra f de calar.

Freudian slip ['frɔɪdɪən-] n lapsus m inv.

Fri. (abbr of **Friday**) viern.

friar ['fraɪəʳ] n fraile m.

friction ['frɪkʃn] n fricción f.

Friday ['fraɪdɪ] n viernes m inv; see also **Saturday**.

fridge [frɪdʒ] n esp UK nevera f, refrigerador m Amér, heladera f R Plata, refrigeradora f Col & Perú.

fridge-freezer n UK combi m, nevera f congeladora.

fried [fraɪd] adj frito(ta).

friend [frend] n - **1.** [close acquaintance] amigo m, -ga f, cuate mf inv Amér C & Méx; **to be friends** ser amigos; **to be friends with sb** ser amigo de alguien; **to make friends (with)** ha-

cerse amigo (de), trabar amistad (con)
- 2. [supporter - of cause] partidario *m*, -ria *f*;
[- of country] aliado *m*, -da *f*.

friendless ['frendlıs] *adj* sin amigos.

friendly ['frendlı] <> *adj* (*comp* **-ier**, *superl* **-iest**) **- 1.** [person] amable, simpático(ca);
[attitude, manner, welcome] amistoso(sa); **to be friendly with sb** llevarse bien con alguien
- 2. [nation] amigo(ga), aliado(da) **- 3.** [argument, game] amistoso(sa). <> *n* (*pl* **-ies**) *esp UK* partido *m* amistoso.

friendly society *n UK* mutua *f*, mutualidad *f*.

friendship ['frendʃıp] *n* amistad *f*.

fries [fraız] = **French fries**.

Friesian (cow) ['fri:zjən-] *n* vaca *f* frisona.

frieze [fri:z] *n* friso *m*.

frigate ['frıgət] *n* fragata *f*.

fright [fraıt] *n* **- 1.** [fear] miedo *m*; **to take fright** espantarse, asustarse **- 2.** [shock] susto *m*; **to give sb a fright** dar un susto a alguien.

frighten ['fraıtn] *vt* asustar; **to frighten sb into doing sthg** atemorizar a alguien para que haga algo.

◆ **frighten away, frighten off** *vt sep* espantar, ahuyentar.

frightened ['fraıtnd] *adj* asustado(da); **to be frightened of sthg/of doing sthg** tener miedo a algo/a hacer algo.

frightening ['fraıtnıŋ] *adj* aterrador(ra), espantoso(sa).

frightful ['fraıtful] *adj dated* terrible, espantoso(sa).

frigid ['frıdʒıd] *adj* [sexually] frígido(da).

frill [frıl] *n* **- 1.** [decoration] volante *m* **- 2.** *inf* [extra] adorno *m*.

frilly ['frılı] (*comp* **-ier**, *superl* **-iest**) *adj* con volantes.

fringe [frındʒ] <> *n* **- 1.** [decoration] flecos *mpl*
- 2. *UK* [of hair] flequillo *m*, cerquillo *m Amér*
- 3. [edge] periferia *f* **- 4.** [extreme] margen *m*.
<> *vt* (*cont* **fringeing**) [edge] bordear.

fringe benefit *n* beneficio *m* complementario.

fringe group *n* grupo *m* marginal.

fringe theatre *n UK* teatro *m* experimental.

Frisbee® ['frızbı] *n* frisbee® *m*, plato *m* volador.

Frisian Islands ['frıʒən-] *npl*: **the Frisian Islands** las islas Frisias.

frisk [frısk] <> *vt* cachear, registrar. <> *vi* retozar, brincar.

frisky ['frıskı] (*comp* **-ier**, *superl* **-iest**) *adj inf* retozón(ona), juguetón(ona).

fritter ['frıtər] *n* buñuelo *m*.

◆ **fritter away** *vt sep*: **to fritter money/time away on sthg** malgastar dinero/tiempo en algo.

frivolity [frı'vɒlətı] (*pl* **-ies**) *n* frivolidad *f*.

frivolous ['frıvələs] *adj* frívolo(la).

frizzy ['frızı] (*comp* **-ier**, *superl* **-iest**) *adj* crespo(pa), ensortijado(da).

fro [frəʊ] ⊳ **to**.

frock [frɒk] *n dated* vestido *m*.

frog [frɒg] *n* [animal] rana *f*; **to have a frog in one's throat** tener carraspera.

frogman ['frɒgmən] (*pl* **-men**) *n* hombre *m* rana.

frogmarch ['frɒgmɑ:tʃ] *vt* llevar por la fuerza.

frogmen ['frɒgmən] *npl* ⊳ **frogman**.

frogspawn ['frɒgspɔ:n] *n* (*U*) huevos *mpl* de rana.

frolic ['frɒlık] <> *n* juego *m* alegre. <> *vi*
(*pt & pp* **-ked**, *cont* **-king**) retozar, triscar.

from (*weak form* [frəm], *strong form* [frɒm]) *prep*
- 1. [indicating source, origin, removal] de; **where are you from?** ¿de dónde eres?; **I got a letter from her today** hoy me ha llegado una carta suya; **a flight from Paris** un vuelo de París; **to translate from Spanish into English** traducir del español al inglés; **he took a notebook from his pocket** sacó un cuaderno del bolsillo; **he's not back from work yet** aún no ha vuelto del trabajo; **to take sthg away from sb** quitar algo a alguien **- 2.** [indicating a deduction]: **take 15 (away) from 19** quita 15 a 19; **to deduct sthg from sthg** deducir *OR* descontar algo de algo **- 3.** [indicating escape, separation] de; **he ran away from home** huyó de casa **- 4.** [indicating position] desde; **seen from above/below** visto desde arriba/abajo; **a light bulb hung from the ceiling** una bombilla colgaba del techo
- 5. [indicating distance] de; **it's 60 km from here** está a 60 kms de aquí; **how far is London from here?** ¿a qué distancia está Londres de aquí?
- 6. [indicating material object is made out of] de; **it's made from wood/plastic** está hecho(cha) de madera/plástico **- 7.** [starting at a particular time] desde; **closed from 1 pm to 2 pm** cerrado de 13h a 14h; **from birth** desde el nacimiento; **from now on** de ahora en adelante; **from the moment I saw him** desde el momento en que lo vi **- 8.** [indicating difference, change] de; **to be different from** ser diferente de; **from... to** de... a; **the price went up from £100 to £150** el precio subió de 100 a 150 libras **- 9.** [because of, as a result of] de; **to die from cold** morir de frío; **to suffer from cold/hunger** padecer frío/hambre **- 10.** [on the evidence of] por; **to speak from personal experience** hablar por propia experiencia; **I could see from her**

face she was angry por la cara que tenía vi que estaba enfadada **- 11.** [indicating lowest amount]: **prices range from £5 to £500** los precios oscilan entre 5 y 500 libras; **prices start from £50** hay a partir de 50 libras; **it could take anything from 15 to 20 weeks** podría llevar de 15 a 20 semanas.

frond [frɒnd] *n* fronda *f*.

front [frʌnt] <> *n* **- 1.** [gen] parte *f* delantera; [of building] fachada *f*; [of queue] principio *m*; [of dress, shirt] parte *f* de delante **- 2.** METEOR, MIL & POL frente *m* **- 3.** [issue, area] terreno *m*; **on the domestic/employment front** a nivel nacional/de empleo **- 4.** [on coast]: **(sea) front** paseo *m* marítimo **- 5.** [outward appearance] fachada *f*; **to put on a front** ponerse una máscara. <> *adj* [gen] delantero(ra); [page] primero(ra). <> *vt* [lead] dirigir; [rock band] liderar.
◆ **in front** *adv* **- 1.** [further forward] delante **- 2.** [winning] ganando.
◆ **in front of** *prep* delante de.
◆ **front onto** *vt insep* [be opposite] dar a.

frontage ['frʌntɪdʒ] *n* fachada *f*.

frontal ['frʌntl] *adj* frontal.

front bench [ˌfrʌnt'bentʃ] *n* UK *en la Cámara de los Comunes, cada una de las dos filas de escaños ocupadas respectivamente por los ministros del gobierno y los principales líderes de la oposición mayoritaria.*

front desk *n* recepción *f*.

front door *n* puerta *f* principal.

frontier [UK 'frʌn,tɪər, US frʌn'tɪər] *n lit & fig* frontera *f*.

frontispiece ['frʌntɪspiːs] *n* frontispicio *m*.

front line *n*: **the front line** la primera línea.

front man *n* **- 1.** [of group] portavoz *mf* **- 2.** [of programme] presentador *m* **- 3.** [of rock band] líder *m*.

front-page *adj* de primera página OR plana.

front room *n* sala *f* de estar.

front-runner *n* favorito *m*, -ta *f*.

front-wheel drive *n* [vehicle] vehículo *m* de tracción delantera.

frost [frɒst] <> *n* **- 1.** [layer of ice] escarcha *f* **- 2.** [weather] helada *f*. <> *vi*: **to frost over** OR **up** cubrirse de escarcha.

frostbite ['frɒstbaɪt] *n (U)* MED congelación *f*.

frostbitten ['frɒst,bɪtn] *adj* MED congelado(da).

frosted ['frɒstɪd] *adj* **- 1.** [glass] esmerilado(da) **- 2.** US CULIN escarchado(da).

frosting ['frɒstɪŋ] *n* US glaseado *m*, betún *m Méx.*

frosty ['frɒstɪ] (*comp* -ier, *superl* -iest) *adj* **- 1.** [very cold] de helada **- 2.** [covered with frost] escarchado(da) **- 3.** *fig* [unfriendly] glacial.

froth [frɒθ] <> *n* espuma *f*. <> *vi* hacer espuma.

frothy ['frɒθɪ] (*comp* -ier, *superl* -iest) *adj* espumoso(sa).

frown [fraʊn] <> *n*: **to give a frown** fruncir el ceño. <> *vi* fruncir el ceño.
◆ **frown (up)on** *vt insep* desaprobar.

froze [frəʊz] *pt* ⊳ **freeze**.

frozen [frəʊzn] <> *pp* ⊳ **freeze**. <> *adj* **- 1.** [gen] helado(da) **- 2.** [foodstuffs] congelado(da) **- 3.** *fig* [rigid]: **frozen (with)** tieso(sa) (de).

FRS *n* **- 1.** (*abbr of* **Fellow of the Royal Society**), *miembro de la Royal Society, organización británica para la investigación científica* **- 2.** (*abbr of* **Federal Reserve System**), *banco central estadounidense.*

frugal ['fruːgl] *adj* frugal.

fruit [fruːt] <> *n* (*pl* **fruit** OR **fruits**) **- 1.** [food] fruta *f* **- 2.** [result] fruto *m*; **to bear fruit** dar fruto. <> *comp* [made with fruit] de frutas; [producing fruit] frutal; **fruit bowl** frutero *m*. <> *vi* dar fruto.

fruitcake ['fruːtkeɪk] *n* pastel *m* de frutas.

fruiterer ['fruːtərər] *n* UK frutero *m*, -ra *f*; **fruiterer's (shop)** frutería *f*.

fruitful ['fruːtfʊl] *adj* [successful] fructífero(ra).

fruition [fruː'ɪʃn] *n*: **to come to fruition** [plan] realizarse; [hope] cumplirse.

fruit juice *n* zumo *m* de fruta.

fruitless ['fruːtlɪs] *adj* infructuoso(sa).

fruit machine *n* UK máquina *f* tragaperras.

fruit salad *n* macedonia *f* (de frutas).

frumpy ['frʌmpɪ] (*comp* -ier, *superl* -iest) *adj* anticuado(da) en la manera de vestir.

frustrate [frʌ'streɪt] *vt* frustrar.

frustrated [frʌ'streɪtɪd] *adj* frustrado(da).

frustrating [frʌ'streɪtɪŋ] *adj* frustrante.

frustration [frʌ'streɪʃn] *n* frustración *f*.

fry [fraɪ] (*pt & pp* **fried**) <> *vt* [food] freír. <> *vi* [food] freírse.

frying pan ['fraɪɪŋ-] *n* sartén *f*, paila *f Andes & Amér C*; **to jump out of the frying pan into the fire** salir de Guatemala y meterse en Guatepeor.

FSA [ˌefes'eɪ] (*abbr of* **food standards agency**) *n* UK *agencia gubernamental encargada de la seguridad alimentaria.*

ft. *abbr of* **foot**.

FT (*abbr of* **Financial Times**) *n diario británico de información económica*; **the FT index** *el índice bursátil del Financial Times.*

FTC (abbr of **Federal Trade Commission**) n organismo estadounidense encargado de hacer respetar la legislación sobre monopolios.

FTP (abbr of **File Transfer Protocol**) n COMPUT FTP m.

fuchsia ['fjuːʃə] n fucsia f.

fuck [fʌk] vulg ◇ vt & vi joder, follar, chingar Méx. ◇ excl ¡joder!
➤ **fuck off** vi vulg: **fuck off!** ¡vete a tomar por culo!

fucking ['fʌkɪŋ] adj vulg - **1.** [to show anger]: **you fucking idiot!** ¡idiota de los cojones! - **2.** [for emphasis]: **where are my fucking keys?** ¿dónde coño están mis llaves?; **you must be fucking stupid** hay que ser gilipollas.

fuddled ['fʌdld] adj aturdido(da).

fuddy-duddy ['fʌdɪˌdʌdɪ] (pl **fuddy-duddies**) n inf carcamal mf.

fudge [fʌdʒ] ◇ n (U) [sweet] dulce de azúcar, leche y mantequilla. ◇ vt inf esquivar, eludir.

fuel [fjʊəl] ◇ n combustible m; **to add fuel to the fire** OR **the flames** echar leña al fuego. ◇ vt (UK **-led**, cont **-ling**, US **-ed**, cont **-ing**) - **1.** [supply with fuel] abastecer de combustible, alimentar - **2.** [increase] exacerbar, agravar.

fuel pump n bomba f de combustible.

fuel tank n depósito m de gasolina.

fugitive ['fjuːdʒətɪv] n fugitivo m, -va f.

fugue [fjuːg] n fuga f.

fulcrum ['fʊlkrəm] (pl **-crums** OR **-cra** [-krə]) n fulcro m, punto m de apoyo.

fulfil (pt & pp **-led**, cont **-ling**), **fulfill** US [fʊl'fɪl] vt [promise, duty, threat] cumplir; [hope, ambition] realizar; [obligation] cumplir con; [role] desempeñar; [requirement] satisfacer; **to fulfil o.s.** realizarse.

fulfilling [fʊl'fɪlɪŋ] adj gratificante.

fulfilment, fulfillment US [fʊl'fɪlmənt] n - **1.** [satisfaction] satisfacción f, realización f (de uno mismo) - **2.** [of promise, duty, threat] cumplimiento m; [of hope, ambition] realización f; [of role] desempeño m; [of requirement] satisfacción f.

full [fʊl] ◇ adj - **1.** [filled]: **full (of)** lleno(na) (de); **I'm full!** [after meal] ¡no puedo más! - **2.** [schedule] completo(ta) - **3.** [complete - recovery, employment, control] pleno(na); [- name, price, fare] completo(ta); [- explanation, information] detallado(da); [- member, professor] numerario(ria); **three full weeks** tres semanas enteras - **4.** [maximum - volume, power etc] máximo(ma); **at full speed** a toda velocidad - **5.** [flavour, sound] rico(ca) - **6.** [plump] grueso(sa) - **7.** [wide] holgado(da), amplio(plia). ◇ adv - **1.** [directly] justo, de lleno - **2.** [very]: **to**

know sthg full well saber algo perfectamente - **3.** [at maximum] al máximo. ◇ n: **to pay in full** pagar el total; **write your name in full** escriba su nombre y apellidos; **to the full** al máximo, completamente; **to live life to the full** disfrutar de la vida al máximo.

fullback ['fʊlbæk] n (defensa mf) lateral mf.

full-blooded [-'blʌdɪd] adj - **1.** [pure-blooded] de pura raza - **2.** [strong, complete] vigoroso(sa).

full-blown [-'bləʊn] adj [gen] auténtico(ca); [AIDS]: **to have full-blown AIDS** haber desarrollado el SIDA por completo.

full board n pensión f completa.

full-bodied [-'bɒdɪd] adj de mucho cuerpo.

full dress n (U) [of soldiers etc] uniforme m de gala.

full-fledged US = **fully-fledged**.

full-frontal adj: **a full-frontal picture** un desnudo frontal.

full-grown [-'grəʊn] adj adulto(ta).

full house n - **1.** [at show, event] lleno m - **2.** [in bingo] cartón m completo - **3.** [at cards] full m.

full-length ◇ adj - **1.** [portrait, mirror] de cuerpo entero - **2.** [dress] largo(ga) - **3.** [novel] extenso(sa); [film] de largo metraje. ◇ adv [stretched out] a lo largo, completamente.

full moon n luna f llena.

fullness, fulness ['fʊlnɪs] n [of voice] riqueza f; [of life] plenitud f; **in the fullness of time** a su debido tiempo.

full-page adj a toda plana.

full-scale adj - **1.** [life-size] de tamaño natural - **2.** [complete] a gran escala.

full-size(d) adj - **1.** [life-size] de tamaño natural - **2.** [adult] adulto(ta) - **3.** US AUT: **full-sized car** turismo m.

full stop ◇ n punto m. ◇ adv UK [and that's that] y punto.

full time n UK SPORT final m del (tiempo reglamentario del) partido.
➤ **full-time** adj & adv a tiempo completa.

full up adj lleno(na).

fully ['fʊlɪ] adv - **1.** [completely] completamente - **2.** [thoroughly] detalladamente.

fully-fashioned UK, **full-fashioned** US [-'fæʃnd] adj ajustado(da).

fully-fledged UK, **full-fledged** US [-'fledʒd] adj fig hecho(cha) y derecho(cha); [member] de pleno derecho.

fulness ['fʊlnɪs] = **fullness**.

fulsome ['fʊlsəm] adj exagerado(da), excesivo(va); **to be fulsome in one's praise (of sthg/ sb)** colmar de elogios (algo/a alguien).

fumble

fumble ['fʌmbl] <> vt perder, no agarrar bien. <> vi hurgar; **to fumble for sthg** [for key, light switch] buscar algo a tientas; [for words] buscar algo titubeando.

fume [fju:m] vi [with anger] echar humo, rabiar. ➡ **fumes** npl humo m.

fumigate ['fju:mɪgeɪt] vt fumigar.

fun [fʌn] <> n (U) **- 1.** [pleasure, amusement] diversión f; **my uncle/parachuting is great fun** mi tío/el paracaidismo es muy divertido; **to have fun** divertirse; **have fun!** ¡que te diviertas!; **for fun, for the fun of it** por diversión **- 2.** [playfulness]: **he's full of fun** le encanta todo lo que sea diversión **- 3.** [at sb else's expense]: **to make fun of sb, to poke fun at sb** reírse OR burlarse de alguien. <> adj inf divertido(da).

function ['fʌŋkʃn] <> n **- 1.** [gen & MATHS] función f; **function key** COMPUT tecla f de función **- 2.** [formal social event] acto m. <> vi funcionar; **to function as** hacer de.

functional ['fʌŋkʃnəl] adj **- 1.** [practical] funcional **- 2.** [operational] en funcionamiento.

functionary ['fʌŋkʃnərɪ] (pl **-ies**) n funcionario m, -ria f.

function key n COMPUT tecla f de función.

fund [fʌnd] <> n fondo m. <> vt financiar. ➡ **funds** npl fondos mpl.

fundamental [,fʌndə'mentl] adj: **fundamental (to)** fundamental (para). ➡ **fundamentals** npl fundamentos mpl.

fundamentalism [,fʌndə'mentəlɪzm] n integrismo m, fundamentalismo m.

fundamentalist [,fʌndə'mentəlɪst] n integrista mf, fundamentalista mf.

fundamentally [,fʌndə'mentəlɪ] adv fundamentalmente.

funding ['fʌndɪŋ] n **- 1.** [financing] financiación f **- 2.** [funds] fondos mpl.

fund-raising [-,reɪzɪŋ] <> n recaudación f de fondos. <> comp de OR para recaudación de fondos.

funeral ['fju:nərəl] n funeral m.

funeral director n director m de funeraria.

funeral parlour n funeraria f.

funeral service n honras fpl fúnebres, exequias fpl.

funereal [fju:'nɪərɪəl] adj fúnebre.

funfair ['fʌnfeər] n feria f.

fungus ['fʌŋgəs] (pl **-gi** [-gaɪ] OR **-guses**) n hongo m.

funk [fʌŋk] n (U) **- 1.** MUS (música f) funky m **- 2.** dated [fear] canguis m inv, mieditis f inv.

funky ['fʌŋkɪ] (comp **-ier**, superl **-iest**) adj MUS funky (inv).

funnel ['fʌnl] <> n **- 1.** [for pouring] embudo m **- 2.** [on ship] chimenea f. <> vt (UK **-led**, cont **-ling**, US **-ed**, cont **-ing**) [liquid] pasar por un embudo; [money, food] canalizar. <> vi pasar.

funnily ['fʌnɪlɪ] adv [strangely] de manera rara; **funnily enough** curiosamente.

funny ['fʌnɪ] (comp **-ier**, superl **-iest**) adj **- 1.** [amusing] divertido(da); **I don't think that's funny** no me hace gracia **- 2.** [odd] raro(ra) **- 3.** [ill] pachucho(cha).

funny bone n hueso m de la risa.

funny farm n US inf hum casa f de los locos.

fun run n carrera atlética de fondo con fines benéficos.

fur [fɜːr] n **- 1.** [on animal] pelaje m, pelo m **- 2.** [garment] (prenda f de) piel f.

fur coat n abrigo m de piel OR pieles.

furious ['fjʊərɪəs] adj **- 1.** [very angry] furioso(sa) **- 2.** [frantic] frenético(ca).

furiously ['fjʊərɪəslɪ] adv **- 1.** [angrily] con furia **- 2.** [frantically] frenéticamente.

furled [fɜːld] adj plegado(da).

furlong ['fɜːlɒŋ] n 201,17 metros.

furnace ['fɜːnɪs] n horno m.

furnish ['fɜːnɪʃ] vt **- 1.** [fit out] amueblar **- 2.** fml [provide - goods, explanation] proveer, suministrar; [- proof] aducir; **to furnish sb with sthg** proporcionar algo a alguien.

furnished ['fɜːnɪʃt] adj amueblado(da).

furnishings ['fɜːnɪʃɪŋz] npl mobiliario m.

furniture ['fɜːnɪtʃər] n (U) muebles mpl, mobiliario m; **a piece of furniture** un mueble.

furniture polish n cera f para muebles.

furore UK [fjʊ'rɔːrɪ], **furor** US ['fjʊrɔːr] n escándalo m.

furrier ['fʌrɪər] n peletero m, -ra f.

furrow ['fʌrəʊ] n lit & fig surco m.

furrowed ['fʌrəʊd] adj **- 1.** [field, land] arado(da) **- 2.** [brow] arrugado(da).

furry ['fɜːrɪ] (comp **-ier**, superl **-iest**) adj **- 1.** [animal] peludo(da) **- 2.** [toy] de peluche.

further ['fɜːðər] <> compar > **far**. <> adv **- 1.** [in distance] más lejos; **how much further is it?** ¿cuánto queda?; **further on** más adelante **- 2.** [to a more advanced point]: **they decided not to take the matter any further** decidieron no seguir adelante con el asunto; **this mustn't go any further** esto debe quedar entre nosotros **- 3.** [in degree, extent, time] más; **further on/back** más adelante/atrás **- 4.** [in addition] además. <> adj [additional]: **until further notice** hasta nuevo aviso; **nothing further** nada más. <> vt promover, fomentar. ➡ **further to** prep fml con relación a.

further education *n* UK estudios postescolares no universitarios.

furthermore [,fɜ:ðə'mɔ:ʳ] *adv* lo que es más.

furthermost ['fɜ:ðəməʊst] *adj* más lejano(na).

furthest ['fɜ:ðɪst] <> *superl* ▷ **far**. <> *adj*
- **1.** [in distance] más lejano(na) - **2.** [greatest - in degree, extent] extremo(ma). <> *adv* - **1.** [in distance] más lejos - **2.** [to greatest degree, extent] más.

furtive ['fɜ:tɪv] *adj* furtivo(va).

furtively ['fɜ:tɪvlɪ] *adv* furtivamente.

fury ['fjʊərɪ] *n* furia *f*; **in a fury** furioso(sa).

fuse *esp* UK, **fuze** US [fju:z] <> *n* - **1.** ELEC fusible *m* - **2.** [of bomb] espoleta *f*; [of firework] mecha *f*. <> *vt* fundir. <> *vi* - **1.** [gen & ELEC] fundirse - **2.** [companies] fusionarse.

fuse-box *n* caja *f* de fusibles.

fused [fju:zd] *adj* [fitted with a fuse] con fusible.

fuselage ['fju:zəlɑ:ʒ] *n* fuselaje *m*.

fuse wire *n* alambre *m* de fusibles.

fusillade [,fju:zə'leɪd] *n* descarga *f* de fusilería.

fusion ['fju:ʒn] *n* fusión *f*.

fuss [fʌs] <> *n* (U) - **1.** [excitement, anxiety] jaleo *m*, alboroto *m*; **to make a fuss** armar un escándalo - **2.** [complaints] protestas *fpl*
▸▸ **to make a fuss of sb** UK mimar a alguien. <> *vi* apurarse, angustiarse.
◆ **fuss over** *vt insep* mimar.

fusspot ['fʌspɒt] *n* inf quisquilloso *m*, -sa *f*.

fussy ['fʌsɪ] (*comp* **-ier**, *superl* **-iest**) *adj*
- **1.** [fastidious] quisquilloso(sa); **I'm not fussy** me da lo mismo - **2.** [over-decorated] recargado(da), aparatoso(sa).

fusty ['fʌstɪ] (*comp* **-ier**, *superl* **-iest**) *adj*
- **1.** [not fresh] con olor a cerrado - **2.** [old-fashioned] anticuado(da), rancio(cia).

futile ['fju:taɪl] *adj* inútil, vano(na).

futility [fju:'tɪlətɪ] *n* inutilidad *f*.

futon ['fu:tɒn] *n* futón *m*.

future ['fju:tʃəʳ] <> *n* futuro *m*; **in future** de ahora en adelante; **in the future** en el futuro; **in the not too distant future** en un futuro próximo; **future (tense)** futuro *m*. <> *adj* futuro(ra).
◆ **futures** *npl* FIN futuros *mpl*.

futuristic [,fju:tʃə'rɪstɪk] *adj* futurista.

fuzz [fʌz] *n* - **1.** [hair] vello *m* - **2.** *inf* [police]: **the fuzz** la poli.

fuzzy ['fʌzɪ] (*comp* **-ier**, *superl* **-iest**) *adj*
- **1.** [hair] crespo(pa) - **2.** [photo, image] borroso(sa) - **3.** [thoughts, mind] confuso(sa).

fwd. *abbr of* **forward**.

FYI *abbr of* **for your information**.

g^1 (*pl* **g's** OR **gs**), **G** (*pl* **G's** OR **Gs**) [dʒi:] *n* [letter] g *f*, G *f*.
◆ **G** *n* - **1.** MUS sol *m* - **2.** (*abbr of* **good**) B. - **3.** US CIN (*abbr of* **general (audience)**) para todos los públicos.

g^2 *n* - **1.** (*abbr of* **gram**) g. *m* - **2.** (*abbr of* **gravity**) g. *f*

GA *abbr of* **Georgia**.

gab [gæb] ▷ **gift**.

gabardine [,gæbə'di:n] *n* gabardina *f*.

gabble ['gæbl] <> *vt* & *vi* farfullar, balbucir. <> *n* farfulleo *m*.

gable ['geɪbl] *n* aguilón *m*.

Gabon [gæ'bɒn] *n* (el) Gabón.

Gabonese [,gæbə'ni:z] <> *adj* gabonés(esa). <> *n* gabonés *m*, -esa *f*. <> *npl*: **the Gabonese** los gaboneses.

gad [gæd] (*pt* & *pp* **-ded**, *cont* **-ding**) ◆ **gad about** *vi* inf andar por ahí holgazaneando.

gadget ['gædʒɪt] *n* artilugio *m*, chisme *m*.

gadgetry ['gædʒɪtrɪ] *n* (U) artilugios *mpl*.

Gaelic ['geɪlɪk] <> *adj* gaélico(ca). <> *n* [language] gaélico *m*.

gaffe [gæf] *n* metedura *f* de pata, patinazo *m*.

gaffer ['gæfəʳ] *n* UK inf [boss] mandamás *m*.

gag [gæg] <> *n* - **1.** [for mouth] mordaza *f* - **2.** inf [joke] chiste *m*. <> *vt* (*pt* & *pp* **-ged**, *cont* **-ging**) amordazar. <> *vi* (*pt* & *pp* **-ged**, *cont* **-ging**) [retch] tener arcadas.

gaiety ['geɪətɪ] *n* alegría *f*, regocijo *m*.

gaily ['geɪlɪ] *adv* alegremente.

gain [geɪn] <> *n* - **1.** [profit] beneficio *m*, ganancia *f* - **2.** [improvement] mejora *f* - **3.** [increase] aumento *m*. <> *vt* - **1.** [gen] ganar - **2.** [speed] cobrar - **3.** [access] lograr - **4.** [subj: watch, clock] adelantar. <> *vi* - **1.** [advance]: **to gain in sthg** ganar algo - **2.** [benefit]: **to gain (from** OR **by)** beneficiarse (de) - **3.** [watch, clock] adelantarse.
◆ **gain on** *vt insep* ganar terreno a.

gainful ['geɪnfʊl] *adj* fml: **gainful employment** trabajo *m* remunerado.

gainfully ['geɪnfʊlɪ] *adv* fml provechosamente.

gainsay [,geɪn'seɪ] (*pt* & *pp* **-said**) *vt* fml negar, contradecir.

gait [geɪt] *n* andares *mpl*, forma *f* de andar.

gaiters ['geɪtəz] *npl* polainas *fpl*.

gal. *abbr of* **gallon**.

gala ['gɑːlə] <> *n* [celebration] fiesta *f*. <> *comp* de gala.

Galapagos Islands [gə'læpəgəs-] *npl*: **the Galapagos Islands** las islas Galápagos.

galaxy ['gæləksɪ] (*pl* **-ies**) *n* galaxia *f*.

gale [geɪl] *n* vendaval *m*.

Galicia [gə'lɪʃɪə] *n* Galicia *f*.

gall [gɔːl] <> *n* [nerve]: **to have the gall to do sthg** tener el descaro de hacer algo. <> *vt* indignar.

gall. *abbr of* **gallon**.

gallant *adj* - **1.** ['gælənt] [courageous] valiente, valeroso(sa) - **2.** [gə'lænt 'gælənt] [polite to women] galante.

gallantry ['gæləntrɪ] *n* - **1.** [courage] valentía *f*, heroísmo *m* - **2.** [politeness to women] galantería *f*.

gall bladder *n* vesícula *f* biliar.

galleon ['gælɪən] *n* galeón *m*.

gallery ['gælərɪ] (*pl* **-ies**) *n* - **1.** [for exhibiting art] museo *m*; [for selling art] galería *f* - **2.** [in courtroom, parliament] tribuna *f* - **3.** [in theatre] gallinero *m*, paraíso *m*.

galley ['gælɪ] (*pl* **galleys**) *n* - **1.** [ship] galera *f* - **2.** [kitchen] cocina *f*.

Gallic ['gælɪk] *adj* galo(la).

galling ['gɔːlɪŋ] *adj* indignante.

gallivant [ˌgælɪ'vænt] *vi inf* andar por ahí holgazaneando.

gallon ['gælən] *n* [in UK] = *4,546 litros* galón *m*; [in US] = *3,785 litros* galón *m*.

gallop ['gæləp] <> *n* galope *m*. <> *vi lit & fig* galopar.

galloping ['gæləpɪŋ] *adj* [soaring] galopante.

gallows ['gæləʊz] (*pl* **gallows**) *n* horca *f*, patíbulo *m*.

gallstone ['gɔːlstəʊn] *n* cálculo *m* biliar.

Gallup poll ['gæləp-] *n UK* sondeo *m* de opinión.

galore [gə'lɔːr] *adj* en abundancia.

galoshes [gə'lɒʃɪz] *npl* chanclos *mpl*.

galvanize, -ise ['gælvənaɪz] *vt* - **1.** TECH galvanizar - **2.** [impel]: **to galvanize sb into action** impulsar a alguien a la acción.

Gambia ['gæmbɪə] *n*: (**the**) **Gambia** Gambia.

Gambian ['gæmbɪən] <> *adj* gambiano(na). <> *n* gambiano *m*, -na *f*.

gambit ['gæmbɪt] *n* táctica *f*.

gamble ['gæmbl] <> *n* [calculated risk] riesgo *m*; **to take a gamble** arriesgarse. <> *vi* - **1.** [bet] jugar; **to gamble on** [race etc] apostar a; [stock exchange] jugar a - **2.** [take risk]: **to gamble on** contar de antemano con que.

gambler ['gæmblər] *n* jugador *m*, -ra *f*.

gambling ['gæmblɪŋ] *n* (*U*) juego *m*.

gambol ['gæmbl] (*UK* **-led**, *cont* **-ling**) (*US* **-ed**, *cont* **-ing**) *vi* triscar, retozar.

game [geɪm] <> *n* - **1.** [gen] juego *m* - **2.** [of football, rugby etc] partido *m*; [of snooker, chess, cards] partida *f* - **3.** [hunted animals] caza *f*
▶▶ **to beat sb at their own game** ganar a alguien la partida en su propio terreno; **the game's up** se acabó el juego; **to give the game away** desvelar el secreto. <> *adj* - **1.** [brave] valiente - **2.** [willing]: **game (for sthg/to do sthg)** dispuesto(ta) (a algo/a hacer algo).

◆ **games** <> *n* (*U*) [at school] deportes *mpl*. <> *npl* [sporting contest] juegos *mpl*.

gamekeeper ['geɪmˌkiːpər] *n* guarda *mf* de caza.

gamely ['geɪmlɪ] *adv* - **1.** [bravely] con determinación - **2.** [willingly] de buena gana.

game reserve *n* coto *m* de caza.

games console *n* consola *f* de juegos.

gamesmanship ['geɪmzmənʃɪp] *n* falta *f* de deportividad.

gaming ['geɪmɪŋ] *n* (*U*) juegos *mpl*.

gamma rays ['gæmə-] *npl* rayos *mpl* gamma.

gammon ['gæmən] *n* jamón *m*; **gammon steak** loncha *f* de jamón a la plancha.

gammy ['gæmɪ] (*comp* **-ier**, *superl* **-iest**) *adj UK inf* fastidiado(da).

gamut ['gæmət] *n* gama *f*; **to run the gamut of sthg** recorrer toda la gama de algo.

gander ['gændər] *n* [male goose] ganso *m*.

gang [gæŋ] *n* - **1.** [of criminals] banda *f* - **2.** [of young people] pandilla *f*.

◆ **gang up** *vi inf*: **to gang up (on sb)** confabularse (contra alguien).

Ganges ['gændʒiːz] *n*: **the (River) Ganges** el (río) Ganges.

gangland ['gæŋlænd] *n* (*U*) mundo *m* del hampa.

gangling ['gæŋglɪŋ], **gangly** ['gæŋglɪ] (*comp* **-ier**, *superl* **-iest**) *adj* larguirucho(cha), desgarbado(da).

gangplank ['gæŋplæŋk], **gangway** *n* pasarela *f*, plancha *f*.

gangrene ['gæŋgriːn] *n* gangrena *f*.

gangrenous ['gæŋgrɪnəs] *adj* gangrenoso(sa).

gangster ['gæŋstər] *n* gángster *m*.

gangway ['gæŋweɪ] *n* - **1.** *UK* [aisle] pasillo *m* - **2.** = **gangplank**.

gannet ['gænɪt] (*pl* **gannet** OR **-s**) *n* [bird] alcatraz *m*.

gantry ['gæntrɪ] (*pl* **-ies**) *n* pórtico *m* *(para grúas)*.

gaol [dʒeɪl] *UK* = **jail**.

gap [gæp] *n* **- 1.** [empty space, in market] hueco *m*; [in traffic, trees, clouds] claro *m*; [in text] espacio *m* en blanco **- 2.** [interval] intervalo *m* **- 3.** *fig* [in knowledge, report] laguna *f* **- 4.** *fig* [great difference] desfase *m*.

gape [geɪp] *vi* [person] mirar boquiabierto(ta).

gaping ['geɪpɪŋ] *adj* **- 1.** [open-mouthed] boquiabierto(ta) **- 2.** [wound] abierto(ta); [hole] enorme.

garage [*UK* 'gæra:ʒ, 'gærɪdʒ, *US* gə'ra:ʒ] *n* **- 1.** [for keeping car] garaje *m* **- 2.** *UK* [for fuel] gasolinera *f* **- 3.** [for car repair] taller *m* **- 4.** *UK* [for selling cars] concesionario *m* de automóviles.

garb [gɑ:b] *n* *fml* atuendo *m*.

garbage ['gɑ:bɪdʒ] *n* (U) *esp US* **- 1.** [refuse] basura *f* **- 2.** *inf* [nonsense] chorradas *fpl*, tonterías *fpl*.

garbage can *n* *US* cubo *m* de la basura.

garbage collector *n* *US* basurero *m*, -ra *f*.

garbage truck *n* *US* camión *m* de la basura.

garbled ['gɑ:bld] *adj* confuso(sa).

garden ['gɑ:dn] <> *n* jardín *m*. <> *comp* de jardín. <> *vi* trabajar en el jardín.
gardens *npl* jardines *mpl*.

garden centre *n* centro *m* de jardinería.

garden city *n* *UK* ciudad *f* jardín.

gardener ['gɑ:dnər] *n* jardinero *m*, -ra *f*.

gardenia [gɑ:'di:njə] *n* gardenia *f*.

gardening ['gɑ:dnɪŋ] <> *n* jardinería *f*; **to do some gardening** trabajar en el jardín. <> *comp* de jardinería.

garden party *n* recepción *f* al aire libre.

gargantuan [gɑ:'gæntjʊən] *adj* descomunal.

gargle ['gɑ:gl] *vi* hacer gárgaras.

gargoyle ['gɑ:gɔɪl] *n* gárgola *f*.

garish ['geərɪʃ] *adj* chillón(ona), llamativo(va).

garland ['gɑ:lənd] *n* guirnalda *f*.

garlic ['gɑ:lɪk] *n* ajo *m*.

garlic bread *n* pan *m* de ajo.

garlicky ['gɑ:lɪkɪ] *adj* *inf* [food] con mucho ajo; [breath] con olor a ajo.

garment ['gɑ:mənt] *n* prenda *f* (de vestir).

garner ['gɑ:nər] *vt* *fml* hacer acopio de.

garnet ['gɑ:nɪt] *n* granate *m*.

garnish ['gɑ:nɪʃ] <> *n* guarnición *f*. <> *vt* guarnecer.

garret ['gærət] *n* desván *m*, buhardilla *f*.

garrison ['gærɪsn] <> *n* guarnición *f*. <> *vt* **- 1.** [town, fort] guarnecer, proteger **- 2.** [troops] acuartelar.

garrulous ['gærələs] *adj* parlanchín(ina), gárrulo(la).

garter ['gɑ:tər] *n* **- 1.** [band round leg] liga *f* **- 2.** *US* [suspender] portaligas *m* *inv*, liguero *m*.

gas [gæs] <> *n* (*pl* **-es** OR **-ses**) **- 1.** [gen] gas *m* **- 2.** *US* [petrol] gasolina *f*, bencina *f* Chile, nafta *f* R Plata. <> *vt* (*pt* & *pp* **-sed**, *cont* **-sing**) asfixiar con gas.

gas chamber *n* cámara *f* de gas.

gas cooker, gas stove *n* *UK* cocina *f* de gas, estufa *f* de gas Amér C, Col & Méx.

gas cylinder *n* bombona *f* de gas, garrafa *f* de gas R Plata, balón *m* de gas Chile.

gas fire *n* *UK* estufa *f* de gas.

gas fitter *n* técnico *m*, -ca *f* (de la compañía de gas).

gas gauge *n* *US* indicador *m* del nivel de gasolina OR bencina Chile OR nafta R Plata.

gash [gæʃ] <> *n* raja *f*. <> *vt* rajar.

gasket ['gæskɪt] *n* junta *f*.

gasman ['gæsmæn] (*pl* **-men** [-men]) *n* hombre *m* del gas.

gas mask *n* máscara *f* antigás.

gas meter *n* contador *m* OR medidor *m* Amér del gas.

gasoline ['gæsəli:n] *n* *US* gasolina *f*.

gasometer [gæ'sɒmɪtər] *n* gasómetro *m*.

gas oven *n* **- 1.** [for cooking] horno *m* de gas **- 2.** [gas chamber] cámara *f* de gas.

gasp [gɑ:sp] <> *n* **- 1.** [pant] resuello *m*, jadeo *m* **- 2.** [of shock, surprise] grito *m* ahogado. <> *vi* **- 1.** [breathe quickly] resollar, jadear **- 2.** [in shock, surprise] ahogar un grito.

gas pedal *n* *US* acelerador *m*.

gasping ['gɑ:spɪŋ] *adj* *UK* *inf*: **to be gasping (for a drink)** estar muerto(ta) de sed.

gas station *n* *US* gasolinera *f*, grifo *m* Perú, bomba *f* Chile, Col & Ven, estación *f* de nafta R Plata.

gas stove *n* = **gas cooker**.

gassy ['gæsɪ] (*comp* **-ier**, *superl* **-iest**) *adj* *pej* con mucho gas.

gas tank *n* *US* depósito *m* de gasolina, tanque *m* de gasolina Perú OR de bencina Chile OR de nafta R Plata.

gas tap *n* llave *f* del gas.

gastric ['gæstrɪk] *adj* gástrico(ca).

gastritis [gæs'traɪtɪs] *n* gastritis *f inv*.

gastroenteritis ['gæstrəʊ,entə'raɪtɪs] *n* (U) gastroenteritis *f inv*.

gastronomic [,gæstrə'nɒmɪk] *adj* gastronómico(ca).

gastronomy [gæs'trɒnəmɪ] *n* gastronomía *f*.

gasworks ['gæswɜ:ks] (*pl* **gasworks**) *n* fábrica *f* de gas.

gate [geɪt] *n* - **1.** [gen] puerta *f*; [metal] verja *f* - **2.** SPORT [takings] taquilla *f*; [attendance] entrada *f*.

-gate

El escándalo del Watergate, que sacudió a los Estados Unidos en 1972, tuvo un gran efecto no sólo sobre la política americana, sino también sobre la lengua inglesa. De hecho, el término "Watergate" ha generado toda una serie de derivados donde el sufijo "-gate" se asocia a un nombre o incidente sinónimo de escándalo público. Así, "Irangate" hace referencia a la venta ilegal de armas al gobierno iraní por parte del gobierno de Reagan a mediados de los ochenta, y "Contragate" al financiamiento de la campaña terrorista llevada a cabo contra el Estado nicaragüense gracias al dinero así obtenido. "Monicagate" evoca el proceso judicial del presidente Clinton en 1998 como consecuencia de su relación con la joven becaria Monica Lewinsky. No cabe duda de que futuros escándalos continuarán dando lugar a expresiones de nuevo cuño con este sufijo.

gatecrash ['geɪtkræʃ] *inf* ⬦ *vt* colarse en. ⬦ *vi* colarse.

gatecrasher ['geɪt,kræʃər] *n inf* intruso *m*, -sa *f*.

gatehouse ['geɪthaus, *pl* -haʊzɪz] *n* - **1.** [of park, castle] casa *f* del guarda - **2.** [of house] casa *f* del portero.

gatekeeper ['geɪt,ki:pər] *n* portero *m*, -ra *f*.

gateway ['geɪtweɪ] *n* - **1.** [entrance] puerta *f*, pórtico *m* - **2.** [means of access]: **the Pyrenees, gateway to the Iberian Peninsula** los Pirineos, antesala de la Península Ibérica - **3.** COMPUT pasarela *f*.

gather ['gæðər] ⬦ *vt* - **1.** [collect] recoger; **to gather together** reunir - **2.** [dust] llenarse de - **3.** [increase - speed, strength] ganar, cobrar - **4.** [understand]: **to gather (that)** deducir que - **5.** [cloth] fruncir. ⬦ *vi* [people, animals] reunirse; [clouds] acumularse.

◆ **gather up** *vt sep* recoger.

gathering ['gæðərɪŋ] *n* [meeting] reunión *f*.

gauche [gəʊʃ] *adj* torpe.

gaudy ['gɔ:dɪ] (*comp* **-ier**, *superl* **-iest**) *adj* chillón(ona), llamativo(va).

gauge, gage US [geɪdʒ] ⬦ *n* - **1.** [for fuel, temperature] indicador *m*; [for width of tube, wire] calibrador *m* - **2.** [calibre] calibre *m* - **3.** RAIL ancho *m* de vía. ⬦ *vt lit & fig* calibrar.

Gaul [gɔ:l] *n* - **1.** [country] la Galia - **2.** [person] galo *m*, -la *f*.

gaunt [gɔ:nt] *adj* - **1.** [person, face] demacrado(da) - **2.** [building, landscape] adusto(ta).

gauntlet ['gɔ:ntlɪt] *n* guante *m*; **to run the gauntlet of sthg** exponerse a algo; **to throw down the gauntlet (to sb)** arrojar el guante (a alguien).

gauze [gɔ:z] *n* gasa *f*.

gave [geɪv] *pt* ⬥ **give**.

gawky ['gɔ:kɪ] (*comp* **-ier**, *superl* **-iest**) *adj* desgarbado(da).

gawp [gɔ:p] *vi*: **to gawp (at sthg/sb)** mirar boquiabierto(ta) (algo/a alguien).

gay [geɪ] ⬦ *adj* - **1.** [homosexual] gay, homosexual - **2.** [cheerful, lively, bright] alegre. ⬦ *n* gay *mf*.

Gaza Strip ['gɑ:zə-] *n*: **the Gaza Strip** la franja de Gaza.

gaze [geɪz] ⬦ *n* mirada *f* fija. ⬦ *vi*: **to gaze (at sthg/sb)** mirar fijamente (algo/a alguien).

gazebo [gə'zi:bəʊ] (*pl* **-s**) *n* belvedere *m*.

gazelle [gə'zel] (*pl* **gazelle** OR **-s**) *n* gacela *f*.

gazette [gə'zet] *n* [newspaper] gaceta *f*.

gazetteer [,gæzɪ'tɪər] *n* índice *m* geográfico.

gazump [gə'zʌmp] *vt* UK *inf*: **to gazump sb** *acordar vender una casa a alguien y luego vendérsela a otro a un precio más alto*.

GB *n* - **1.** (*abbr of* **Great Britain**) GB *f* - **2.** COMPUT (*abbr of* **gigabyte**) GB *m*.

GBH *n abbr of* **grievous bodily harm**.

GC (*abbr of* **George Cross**) *n* (*titular de la*) *segunda condecoración británica en importancia*.

GCH UK (*abbr of* **gas central heating**) cal. cent. por gas.

GCHQ (*abbr of* **Government Communications Headquarters**) *n centro de recogida de información de los servicios secretos británicos*.

GCSE (*abbr of* **General Certificate of Secondary Education**) *n examen final de enseñanza secundaria en Gran Bretaña*.

Gdns. *abbr of* **Gardens**.

GDP (*abbr of* **gross domestic product**) *n* PIB *m*.

gear [gɪər] ⬦ *n* - **1.** [mechanism] engranaje *m* - **2.** [speed - of car, bicycle] marcha *f*; **in gear** con una marcha metida; **out of gear** en punto muerto; **to change gear** cambiar de marcha - **3.** (U) [equipment, clothes] equipo *m* - **4.** (U) *inf* [stuff, possessions] bártulos *mpl*. ⬦ *vt*: **to gear sthg to** orientar OR encaminar algo hacia.

◆ **gear up** *vi*: **to gear up for sthg/to do sthg** hacer preparativos para algo/para hacer algo.

gearbox ['gɪəbɒks] *n* caja *f* de cambios.

gear lever, gear stick *UK*, **gear shift** *US n* palanca *f* de cambios.

gear wheel *n* rueda *f* dentada.

gee [dʒi:] *excl* - **1.** [to horse]: **gee up!** ¡arre! - **2.** *US inf* [expressing surprise, excitement]: **gee (whiz)!** ¡caramba!, ¡jolines!

geek [gi:k] *n esp US inf* lelo *m*, -la *f*, tontaina *mf*; **a computer geek** un monstruo de la informática.

geese [gi:s] *npl* ⊳ **goose**.

Geiger counter ['gaɪgər-] *n* contador *m* Geiger.

geisha (girl) ['geɪʃə-] *n* geisha *f*.

gel [dʒel] ◇ *n* [for shower] gel *m*; [for hair] gomina *f*. ◇ *vi* (*pt & pp* **-led**, *cont* **-ling**) - **1.** [thicken] aglutinarse - **2.** [plan] cuajar; [idea, thought] tomar forma.

gelatin ['dʒelətɪn], **gelatine** [ˌdʒelə'ti:n] *n* gelatina *f*.

gelding ['geldɪŋ] *n* caballo *m* castrado.

gelignite ['dʒelɪgnaɪt] *n* gelignita *f*.

gem [dʒem] *n* [precious stone] gema *f*; [jewel, special person, thing] joya *f*.

Gemini ['dʒemɪnaɪ] *n* Géminis *m inv*; **to be (a) Gemini** ser Géminis.

gemstone ['dʒemstəʊn] *n* piedra *f* preciosa.

gen [dʒen] *n UK inf (U)* información *f*, detalles *mpl*.
➤ **gen up** *vi* (*pt & pp* **-ned**, *cont* **-ning**) *UK inf*: **to gen up (on sthg)** informarse (sobre algo).

gen. - **1.** (*abbr of* **general**) gral - **2.** (*abbr of* **generally**) grlte.

Gen. (*abbr of* **General**) ≃ Gen (*rango militar*).

gender ['dʒendər] *n* - **1.** GRAM género *m* - **2.** [sex] sexo *m*.

gene [dʒi:n] *n* gen *m*.

genealogist [ˌdʒi:nɪ'ælədʒɪst] *n* genealogista *mf*.

genealogy [ˌdʒi:nɪ'ælədʒɪ] (*pl* **-ies**) *n* genealogía *f*.

genera ['dʒenərə] *npl* ⊳ **genus**.

general ['dʒenərəl] ◇ *adj* general. ◇ *n* general *m*.
➤ **in general** *adv* - **1.** [as a whole] en general - **2.** [usually] por lo general.

general anaesthetic *n* anestesia *f* general.

general delivery *n US* lista *f* de correos.

general election *n* elecciones *fpl* generales.

generality [ˌdʒenə'rælətɪ] (*pl* **-ies**) *n* generalidad *f*.

generalization [ˌdʒenərəlaɪ'zeɪʃn] *n* generalización *f*.

generalize, -ise ['dʒenərəlaɪz] *vi*: **to generalize (about)** generalizar (sobre).

general knowledge *n* cultura *f* general.

generally ['dʒenərəlɪ] *adv* en general.

general manager *n* director *m*, -ra *f* general.

general practice *n* - **1.** [work] medicina *f* general - **2.** [clinic] consulta *f*.

general practitioner *n* médico *m*, -ca *f* de cabecera.

general public *n*: **the general public** el gran público.

general-purpose *adj* de uso general.

general strike *n* huelga *f* general.

generate ['dʒenəreɪt] *vt* generar.

generation [ˌdʒenə'reɪʃn] *n* generación *f*; **first/ second generation** de primera/segunda generación.

generation gap *n* brecha *f* generacional.

generator ['dʒenəreɪtər] *n* generador *m*.

generic [dʒɪ'nerɪk] *adj* genérico(ca).

generosity [ˌdʒenə'rɒsətɪ] *n* generosidad *f*.

generous ['dʒenərəs] *adj* generoso(sa); [cut of clothes] amplio(plia).

generously ['dʒenərəslɪ] *adv* generosamente.

genesis ['dʒenəsɪs] (*pl* **-eses** [-əsi:z]) *n* génesis *f inv*.

genetic [dʒɪ'netɪk] *adj* genético(ca).
➤ **genetics** *n* (*U*) genética *f*.

genetically modified [dʒɪ'netɪkəlɪ'mɒdɪfaɪd] *adj* modificado(da) genéticamente, transgénico(ca).

genetic engineering *n* ingeniería *f* genética.

genetic fingerprinting [-'fɪŋgəprɪntɪŋ] *n* identificación *f* genética.

genial ['dʒi:njəl] *adj* cordial, afable.

genie ['dʒi:nɪ] (*pl* **genies** OR **genii** ['dʒi:nɪaɪ]) *n* genio *m*, duende *m*.

genitals ['dʒenɪtlz] *npl* genitales *mpl*.

genius ['dʒi:njəs] (*pl* **-es**) *n* genio *m*; **genius for sthg/for doing sthg** don *m* para algo/para hacer algo.

genocide ['dʒenəsaɪd] *n* genocidio *m*.

genome ['dʒi:nəʊm] *n* genoma *m*.

genre ['ʒrə] *n* género *m*.

gent [dʒent] *n inf* caballero *m*.
➤ **gents** *n UK* [toilets] servicio *m* de caballeros.

genteel [dʒen'ti:l] *adj* fino(na), refinado(da).

gentile ['dʒentaɪl] ◇ *adj* gentil, no judío(a). ◇ *n* gentil *mf*.

gentle ['dʒentl] *adj* - **1.** [kind] tierno(na), dulce - **2.** [breeze, movement, slope] suave - **3.** [scolding] ligero(ra); [hint] sutil.

gentleman ['dʒentlmən] (pl -men [-mən]) n
- **1.** [well-behaved man] caballero m; **gentleman's agreement** pacto m de caballeros
- **2.** [man] señor m, caballero m.

gentlemanly ['dʒentlmənlɪ] adj caballeroso(sa).

gentleness ['dʒentlnɪs] n - **1.** [kindness] ternura f, dulzura f - **2.** [softness] suavidad f.

gently ['dʒentlɪ] adv - **1.** [kindly] tiernamente, dulcemente - **2.** [softly, smoothly] suavemente
- **3.** [carefully] con cuidado.

gentry ['dʒentrɪ] n alta burguesía f.

genuflect ['dʒenjuːflekt] vi fml hacer una genuflexión.

genuine ['dʒenjuɪn] adj - **1.** [real] auténtico(ca), genuino(na) - **2.** [sincere] sincero(ra).

genuinely ['dʒenjuɪnlɪ] adv - **1.** [really] auténticamente - **2.** [sincerely] sinceramente.

genus ['dʒiːnəs] (pl genera) n género m.

geographer [dʒɪ'ɒgrəfər] n geógrafo m, -fa f.

geographical [,dʒɪə'græfɪkl] adj geográfico(ca).

geography [dʒɪ'ɒgrəfɪ] n geografía f.

geological [,dʒɪə'lɒdʒɪkl] adj geológico(ca).

geologist [dʒɪ'ɒlədʒɪst] n geólogo m, -ga f.

geology [dʒɪ'ɒlədʒɪ] n geología f.

geometric(al) [,dʒɪə'metrɪk(l)] adj geométrico(ca).

geometry [dʒɪ'ɒmətrɪ] n geometría f.

geophysics [,dʒiː'əʊfɪzɪks] n (U) geofísica f.

Geordie ['dʒɔːdɪ] <> adj de o relativo a Tyneside. <> n [person] natural o habitante de Tyneside.

George Cross ['dʒɔːdʒ-] n UK ≃ medalla f al mérito civil.

Georgia ['dʒɔːdʒə] n [in US, in Europe] Georgia.

Georgian ['dʒɔːdʒən] <> adj GEOG & HIST georgiano(na). <> n - **1.** [person] georgiano m, -na f
- **2.** [language] georgiano m.

geranium [dʒɪ'reɪnjəm] (pl -s) n geranio m.

gerbil ['dʒɜːbɪl] n jerbo m, gerbo m.

geriatric [,dʒerɪ'ætrɪk] <> adj [of old people] geriátrico(ca). <> n - **1.** MED anciano m, -na f
- **2.** inf [very old person] vejestorio m.

germ [dʒɜːm] n fig & BIOL germen m; MED microbio m.

German ['dʒɜːmən] <> adj alemán(ana). <> n
- **1.** [person] alemán m, -ana f - **2.** [language] alemán m.

Germanic [dʒɜː'mænɪk] adj germánico(ca).

German measles n rubéola f.

German shepherd (dog) n pastor m alemán.

Germany ['dʒɜːmənɪ] (pl -ies) n Alemania.

germicide ['dʒɜːmɪsaɪd] n germicida m.

germinate ['dʒɜːmɪneɪt] vt & vi lit & fig germinar.

germination [,dʒɜːmɪ'neɪʃn] n lit & fig germinación f.

germ warfare n guerra f bacteriológica.

Gerona [dʒə'rəʊnə] n Gerona.

gerrymandering ['dʒerɪmændərɪŋ] n división de una zona electoral de forma que se da ventaja a un partido frente a otros.

gerund ['dʒerənd] n gerundio m.

gestation [dʒe'steɪʃn] n gestación f.

gestation period n lit & fig periodo m de gestación.

gesticulate [dʒes'tɪkjʊleɪt] vi gesticular.

gesticulation [dʒe,stɪkjʊ'leɪʃn] n gesticulación f.

gesture ['dʒestʃər] <> n gesto m. <> vi: **to gesture to** o **towards sb** hacer gestos a alguien.

get [get] (UK got, cont -ting) (US got, pp gotten, cont -ting) <> vt - **1.** [bring, fetch] traer; **can I get you something to eat/drink?** ¿te traigo algo de comer/beber?; **I'll get my coat** voy a por el abrigo; **could you get me the boss, please?** [when phoning] póngame con el jefe - **2.** [door, phone] contestar a - **3.** [obtain] conseguir; **she got top marks** sacó las mejores notas - **4.** [buy] comprar - **5.** [receive] recibir; **when did you get the news?** ¿cuándo recibiste la noticia?; **what did you get for your birthday?** ¿qué te regalaron para tu cumpleaños?; **she gets a good salary** gana un buen sueldo; **we don't get much rain** no llueve mucho - **6.** [catch - bus, criminal, illness] coger, agarrar Amér; **I've got a cold** estoy resfriado; **he got cancer** contrajo cáncer - **7.** [cause to do]: **to get sb to do sthg** hacer que alguien haga algo; **I'll get my sister to help** le pediré a mi hermana que ayude - **8.** [cause to be done]: **to get sthg done** mandar hacer algo; **have you got the car fixed yet?** ¿te han arreglado ya el coche? - **9.** [cause to become]: **to get sthg ready** preparar algo; **to get sthg dirty** ensuciar algo; **to get sb pregnant** dejar a alguien preñada; **to get things going** poner las cosas en marcha - **10.** [cause to move]: **can you get it through the gap?** ¿puedes meterlo por el hueco?; **to get sthg/sb out of sthg** conseguir sacar algo/a alguien de algo - **11.** [experience - a sensation]: **do you get the feeling he doesn't like us?** ¿no te da la sensación de que no le gustamos?; **I got the impression she was unhappy** me dio la impresión de que era feliz; **I get a thrill out of driving fast** disfruto con la velocidad al volante - **12.** [understand] entender; **I don't get it** inf no me aclaro, no lo entiendo; **he didn't seem to get the point** no pareció captar el sentido **- 13.** *inf* [annoy] poner negro(gra); **what really gets me is his smugness** lo que me pone negro es lo engreído que es **- 14.** [find]: **you get a lot of artists here** hay mucho artista por aquí. ◇ *vi* **- 1.** [become] ponerse; **to get angry/pale** ponerse furioso/pálido; **to get ready** prepararse; **I'm getting cold/bored** me estoy enfriando/aburriendo; **it's getting late** se está haciendo tarde **- 2.** [arrive] llegar; **how do I get there?** ¿cómo se llega (allí)?; **to get home** llegar a casa; **I only got back yesterday** regresé justo ayer **- 3.** [eventually succeed]: **to get to do sthg** llegar a hacer algo; **I never got to know him/visit Moscow** nunca llegué a conocerle/visitar Moscú; **she got to enjoy the classes** llegaron a gustarle las clases; **did you get to see him?** ¿conseguiste verlo? **- 4.** [progress] llegar; **how far have you got?** ¿cuánto llevas?, ¿hasta dónde has llegado?; **we only got as far as buying the paint** no llegamos más que a comprar la pintura; **I got to the point where I didn't care any more** llegó un punto en el que ya nada me importaba; **now we're getting somewhere** ahora sí que vamos por buen camino; **we're getting nowhere** así no llegamos a ninguna parte. ◇ *aux vb*: **to get excited** emocionarse; **someone could get hurt** alguien podría resultar herido; **I got beaten up** me zurraron; **let's get going** OR **moving** pongámonos en marcha.

● **get about** *vi* **- 1.** [move from place to place] salir a menudo **- 2.** [circulate - news etc] difundirse; = **get around**.

● **get across** *vt sep*: **to get sthg across to sb** hacerle comprender algo a alguien; **to get a message across** transmitir un mensaje.

● **get ahead** *vi* [in life] abrirse camino.

● **get along** *vi* **- 1.** [manage] arreglárselas, apañárselas **- 2.** [progress]: **how are you getting along?** ¿cómo te va? **- 3.** [have a good relationship]: **to get along (with sb)** llevarse bien (con alguien).

● **get around, get round** ◇ *vt insep* [overcome - problem] evitar; [- obstacle] sortear. ◇ *vi* **- 1.** [circulate - news etc] difundirse **- 2.** [eventually do]: **to get around to (doing) sthg** sacar tiempo para (hacer) algo; = **get about**.

● **get at** *vt insep* **- 1.** [reach] llegar a, alcanzar; **he's determined to get at the truth** está decidido a descubrir la verdad **- 2.** [imply] referirse a; **what are you getting at?** ¿qué quieres decir con eso? **- 3.** *inf* [criticize]: **stop getting at me!** ¡deja ya de meterte conmigo!

● **get away** *vi* **- 1.** [leave] salir, irse **- 2.** [go on holiday]: **I really need to get away** necesito unas buenas vacaciones; **to get away from it all** escaparse de todo **- 3.** [escape] escaparse.

● **get away with** *vt insep* salir impune de; **she lets him get away with everything** ella se lo consiente todo.

● **get back** ◇ *vt sep* [recover, regain] recuperar; **they got their money back** les devolvieron el dinero. ◇ *vi* **- 1.** [move away] echarse atrás, apartarse **- 2.** [return] volver.

● **get back to** *vt insep* **- 1.** [return to previous state, activity] volver a; **to get back to sleep/normal** volver a dormirse/a la normalidad; **to get back to work** volver a trabajar OR al trabajo **- 2.** *esp US inf* [phone back]: **I'll get back to you later** te llamo de vuelta más tarde.

● **get by** *vi* apañárselas.

● **get down** *vt sep* **- 1.** [depress] deprimir **- 2.** [fetch from higher level] bajar **- 3.** [write down] anotar.

● **get down to** *vt insep*: **to get down to doing sthg** ponerse a hacer algo; **to get down to work** ponerse manos a la obra.

● **get in** ◇ *vi* **- 1.** [enter] entrar **- 2.** [arrive] llegar **- 3.** [be elected] salir elegido(da). ◇ *vt sep* **- 1.** [bring in - washing] meter dentro; [- harvest] recoger; [- provisions] aprovisionarse de **- 2.** [interject]: **to get a word in** decir algo.

● **get in on** *vt insep* apuntarse a.

● **get into** *vt insep* **- 1.** [car] subir a **- 2.** [become involved in] meterse en; **to get into an argument (with)** meterse en una discusión (con) **- 3.** [enter into a particular situation, state]: **to get into a panic** OR **state** ponerse nerviosísimo(ma); **to get into trouble** meterse en líos; **to get into the habit of doing sthg** adquirir el hábito OR coger la costumbre de hacer algo **- 4.** [be accepted as a student at]: **she managed to get into Oxford** consiguió entrar en Oxford **- 5.** *inf* [affect]: **what's got into you?** ¿qué mosca te ha picado?

● **get off** ◇ *vt sep* **- 1.** [remove] quitar **- 2.** [prevent from being punished] librar. ◇ *vt insep* **- 1.** [go away from] irse OR salirse de; **get off my land!** ¡fuera de mis tierras! **- 2.** [train, bus, table] bajarse de. ◇ *vi* **- 1.** [leave bus, train] bajarse, desembarcarse *Amér* **- 2.** [escape punishment] escaparse; **he got off lightly** salió bien librado **- 3.** [depart] irse, salir.

● **get off with** *vt insep* UK *inf* ligar con.

● **get on** ◇ *vt sep* [put on] ponerse. ◇ *vt insep* [bus, train, horse] subirse a. ◇ *vi* **- 1.** [enter bus, train] subirse, montarse **- 2.** [have a good relationship] llevarse bien **- 3.** [progress]: **how are you getting on?** ¿cómo te va? **- 4.** [proceed]: **to get on with sthg** seguir OR continuar con algo **- 5.** [be successful professionally] triunfar **- 6.** [grow old]: **he's getting on a bit** se está haciendo mayor.

● **get on for** *vt insep inf* [be approximately]: **it's getting on for five o'clock** son casi las cinco; **she's getting on for 65** ronda los 65.

get on to *vt insep* - **1.** [begin talking about] ponerse a hablar de - **2.** [contact] ponerse en contacto con.

get out ◇ *vt sep* [remove - object, prisoner] sacar; [- stain etc] quitar; **she got a pen out of her bag** sacó un bolígrafo del bolso. ◇ *vi* - **1.** [leave] salir; **get out!** ¡vete de aquí! - **2.** [leave car, bus, train] bajarse - **3.** [become known - news] difundirse, filtrarse.

get out of ◇ *vt insep* - **1.** [car, bus, train] bajar de; [bed] levantarse de - **2.** [escape from] escapar OR huir de - **3.** [avoid] librarse de, eludir; **to get out of (doing) sthg** librarse de (hacer) algo. ◇ *vt sep* [cause to escape from]: **to get sb out of jail** ayudar a alguien a escapar de la cárcel.

get over ◇ *vt insep* - **1.** [recover from] recuperarse de; **you'll get over it** ya se te pasará - **2.** [overcome] superar. ◇ *vt sep* [communicate] hacer comprender.

get over with *vt sep*: **to get sthg over with** terminar con algo.

get round *vt insep* = **get around**.

get through ◇ *vt insep* - **1.** [job, task] terminar, acabar - **2.** [exam] aprobar - **3.** [food, drink] consumir - **4.** [unpleasant situation] sobrevivir a, aguantar. ◇ *vi* - **1.** [make oneself understood]: **to get through (to sb)** hacerse comprender (por alguien) - **2.** TELEC conseguir comunicar.

get to ◇ *vt insep inf* [annoy] fastidiar, molestar. ◇ *vi* [end up] ir a parar.

get together ◇ *vt sep* [organize - project, demonstration] organizar, montar; [- team] juntar; [- report] preparar. ◇ *vi* juntarse, reunirse.

get up ◇ *vi* levantarse. ◇ *vt insep* [organize - petition etc] preparar, organizar.

get up to *vt insep inf* hacer, montar; **I wonder what they're getting up to** me pregunto qué demonios estarán haciendo.

getaway ['getəweɪ] *n* fuga *f*, huida *f*; **to make one's getaway** darse a la fuga.

getaway car *n* vehículo *m* utilizado en la fuga.

get-together *n inf* reunión *f*.

getup ['getʌp] *n inf* indumentaria *f*, atuendo *m*.

get-up-and-go *n inf* dinamismo *m*.

get-well card *n* tarjeta que se envía a una persona enferma deseándole que se mejore pronto.

geyser ['giːzər] *n* - **1.** [hot spring] géiser *m* - **2.** UK [water heater] calentador *m* de agua.

Ghana ['gɑːnə] *n* Ghana.

Ghanaian [gɑːˈneɪən] ◇ *adj* ghanés(esa). ◇ *n* ghanés *m*, -esa *f*.

ghastly ['gɑːstlɪ] (*comp* -ier, *superl* -iest) *adj* - **1.** *inf* [very bad, unpleasant] horrible, espantoso(sa) - **2.** [horrifying] horripilante - **3.** [ill] fatal.

gherkin ['gɜːkɪn] *n* pepinillo *m*.

ghetto ['getəʊ] (*pl* -s OR -es) *n* gueto *m*.

ghetto blaster [-ˈblɑːstər] *n inf* radiocasete portátil de gran tamaño y potencia.

ghost [gəʊst] *n* [spirit] fantasma *m*; **he doesn't have a ghost of a chance** no tiene ni la más remota posibilidad.

ghostly ['gəʊstlɪ] (*comp* -ier, *superl* -iest) *adj* fantasmal.

ghost town *n* pueblo *m* fantasma.

ghostwrite ['gəʊstraɪt] (*pt* -wrote, *pp* -written) *vt* escribir anónimamente para otras personas.

ghostwriter ['gəʊstˌraɪtər] *n* escritor anónimo que escribe un libro en lugar de su autor oficial.

ghostwritten ['gəʊstˌrɪtn] *pp* ⊳ **ghostwrite**.

ghostwrote ['gəʊstrəʊt] *pp* ⊳ **ghostwrite**.

ghoul [guːl] *n* - **1.** [spirit] espíritu *m* del mal - **2.** *pej* [ghoulish person] persona *f* macabra.

ghoulish ['guːlɪʃ] *adj* macabro(bra).

GHQ (*abbr of* **general headquarters**) *n* cuartel general.

giant ['dʒaɪənt] ◇ *adj* gigantesco(ca). ◇ *n* gigante *m*.

giant-size(d) *adj* de tamaño gigante.

gibber ['dʒɪbər] *vi* farfullar.

gibberish ['dʒɪbərɪʃ] *n* galimatías *m inv*.

gibbon ['gɪbən] *n* gibón *m*.

gibe [dʒaɪb] ◇ *n* pulla *f*. ◇ *vi*: **to gibe (at)** mofarse (de).

giblets ['dʒɪblɪts] *npl* menudillos *mpl*.

Gibraltar [dʒɪˈbrɔːltər] *n* Gibraltar; **the Rock of Gibraltar** el Peñón.

giddy ['gɪdɪ] (*comp* -ier, *superl* -iest) *adj* mareado(da); **to be giddy** [have vertigo] tener vértigo.

gift [gɪft] *n* - **1.** [present] regalo *m*, obsequio *m* - **2.** [talent] don *m*; **to have a gift for sthg/for doing sthg** tener un don especial para algo/para hacer algo; **to have the gift of the gab** tener un pico de oro.

gift certificate US = **gift token**.

gifted ['gɪftɪd] *adj* - **1.** [talented] dotado(da), de talento - **2.** [extremely intelligent] superdotado(da).

gift token, gift certificate, gift voucher *n* UK vale *m* OR cupón *m* para regalo.

gift-wrapped [-ræpt] *adj* envuelto(ta) para regalo.

gig [gɪg] n inf [concert] actuación f, concierto m.

gigabyte ['gaɪgəbaɪt] n COMPUT gigabyte m.

gigantic [dʒaɪ'gæntɪk] adj gigantesco(ca).

giggle ['gɪgl] <> n - **1.** [laugh] risita f, risa f tonta - **2.** UK inf [fun]: **it's a real giggle** es la mar de divertido; **to do sthg for a giggle** hacer algo por puro cachondeo. <> vi [laugh] soltar risitas.

giggly ['gɪglɪ] (comp -ier, superl -iest) adj con la risa tonta.

GIGO ['gaɪgəʊ] (abbr of garbage in, garbage out) información errónea genera resultados erróneos.

gigolo ['ʒɪgələʊ] (pl -s) n pej gigoló m.

gigot ['ʒiːgəʊ] n pierna f de cordero.

gilded ['gɪldɪd] = **gilt**.

gill [dʒɪl] n [unit of measurement] = 0,142 litros.

gills [gɪlz] npl [of fish] agallas fpl.

gilt [gɪlt], **gilded** <> adj dorado(da). <> n dorado m.

~ **gilts** npl FIN valores mpl de máxima garantía.

gilt-edged adj FIN de máxima garantía.

gimme ['gɪmɪ] inf (abbr of give me) ⊳ **give**.

gimmick ['gɪmɪk] n pej artilugio m innecesario; **advertising gimmick** reclamo m publicitario.

gin [dʒɪn] n ginebra f; **gin and tonic** gin-tonic m.

ginger ['dʒɪndʒəʳ] <> adj UK [hair] bermejo(ja); **to have ginger hair** ser pelirrojo(ja); [cat] de color bermejo. <> n jengibre m.

ginger ale n [mixer] ginger-ale m.

ginger beer n [slightly alcoholic] refresco m de jengibre.

gingerbread ['dʒɪndʒəbred] n - **1.** [cake] pan m de jengibre - **2.** [biscuit] galleta f de jengibre.

ginger-haired [-'heəd] adj pelirrojo(ja).

gingerly ['dʒɪndʒəlɪ] adv con mucho tiento.

gingham ['gɪŋəm] n guinga f.

gingivitis [,dʒɪndʒɪ'vaɪtɪs] n gingivitis f inv.

ginseng ['dʒɪnseŋ] n ginseng m.

gipsy, gypsy ['dʒɪpsɪ] <> adj gitano(na). <> n (pl -ies) UK gitano m, -na f.

giraffe [dʒɪ'rɑːf] (pl giraffe OR -s) n jirafa f.

gird [gɜːd] ⊳ **loin**.

girder ['gɜːdəʳ] n viga f.

girdle ['gɜːdl] n [corset] faja f.

girl [gɜːl] n - **1.** [child] niña f - **2.** [young woman] chica f - **3.** [daughter] niña f, chica f - **4.** inf [female friend]: **the girls** las amigas, las chicas.

girl Friday n secretaria f.

girlfriend ['gɜːlfrend] n - **1.** [female lover] novia f - **2.** [female friend] amiga f.

girl guide UK, **girl scout** US n [individual] exploradora f.

~ **Girl Guides** n [organization]: **the Girl Guides** las exploradoras.

girlie magazine ['gɜːlɪ-] n inf revista f porno.

girlish ['gɜːlɪʃ] adj de niña.

girl scout US n = **girl guide**.

giro ['dʒaɪrəʊ] (pl -s) n UK - **1.** (U) [system] giro m - **2.**: **giro (cheque)** cheque m para giro bancario.

girth [gɜːθ] n - **1.** [circumference] circunferencia f - **2.** [of horse] cincha f.

gist [dʒɪst] n: **the gist of** lo esencial de; **to get the gist (of sthg)** entender el sentido (de algo).

give [gɪv] <> vt (pt gave, pp given) - **1.** [gen] dar; [time, effort] dedicar; [attention] prestar; **to give sb/sthg sthg, to give sthg to sb/sthg** dar algo a alguien/algo; **he was given twenty years** [sentenced to] le cayeron veinte años; **to give a shrug** encogerse de hombros; **to give sb a look** lanzar una mirada a alguien - **2.** [as present]: **to give sb sthg, to give sthg to sb** regalar algo a alguien - **3.** [hand over]: **to give sb sthg, to give sthg to sb** entregar OR dar algo a alguien - **4.** inf [pay]: **to give sthg (for sthg)** dar OR pagar algo (por algo)

▶▶▶ **I am given to believe** OR **understand that...** fml tengo entendido que...; **I'd give anything** OR **my right arm to do that** daría cualquier cosa por hacer eso. <> vi (pt gave, pp given) [collapse, break] romperse, ceder; [stretch] dar de sí. <> n [elasticity] elasticidad f.

~ **give or take** prep más o menos; **in half an hour give or take five minutes** dentro de media hora, cinco minutos más o cinco minutos menos.

~ **give away** vt sep - **1.** [as present] regalar - **2.** [reveal] revelar, descubrir - **3.** [bride] llevar al altar.

~ **give back** vt sep [return] devolver, regresar Méx.

~ **give in** vi - **1.** [admit defeat] rendirse, darse por vencido(da), transar Amér - **2.** [agree unwillingly]: **to give in to sthg** ceder ante algo.

~ **give off** vt insep [produce, emit] despedir.

~ **give out** <> vt sep [distribute] repartir, distribuir. <> vi [supply, strength] agotarse, acabarse; [legs, machine] fallar.

~ **give over** <> vt sep [dedicate]: **to be given over to sthg** dedicarse a algo. <> vi UK inf [stop]: **give over!** ¡basta OR vale ya!

~ **give up** <> vt sep - **1.** [stop] abandonar; **to give up chocolate** dejar de comer chocolate

- 2. [job] dejar **- 3.** [surrender]: **to give o.s. up (to sb)** entregarse (a alguien). ⬦ *vi* rendirse, darse por vencido(da).

◆ **give up on** *vt insep* [abandon] dejar por imposible.

give-and-take *n* toma y daca *m*.

giveaway ['gɪvə,weɪ] ⬦ *adj* **- 1.** [tell-tale] revelador(ra) **- 2.** [very cheap] de regalo. ⬦ *n* [telltale sign] indicio *m*, signo *m* revelador.

given ['gɪvn] ⬦ *pp* ⊳ **give.** ⬦ *adj* **- 1.** [set, fixed] dado(da); **at any given time** en cualquier momento **- 2.** [prone]: **to be given to sthg/to doing sthg** ser dado(da) a algo/a hacer algo. ⬦ *prep* [taking into account] dado(da); **given that** dado que.

given name *n esp US* nombre *m* de pila.

giver ['gɪvəʳ] *n* donante *mf.*

glacial ['gleɪsjəl] *adj lit* & *fig* glacial.

glacier ['glæsjəʳ] *n* glaciar *m.*

glad [glæd] (*comp* **-der,** *superl* **-dest**) *adj* **- 1.** [happy, pleased] alegre, contento(ta); **to be glad about/that** alegrarse de/de que **- 2.** [willing]: **to be glad to do sthg** tener gusto en hacer algo **- 3.** [grateful]: **to be glad of sthg** agradecer algo.

gladden ['glædn] *vt liter* regocijar, llenar de gozo.

glade [gleɪd] *n liter* claro *m.*

glad-hand ['glædhænd] *vt inf pej* dar la mano efusivamente a.

gladiator ['glædɪeɪtəʳ] *n* gladiador *m.*

gladly ['glædlɪ] *adv* **- 1.** [happily, eagerly] alegremente **- 2.** [willingly] con mucho gusto.

glamor *US* = **glamour.**

glamorize, -ise ['glæməraɪz] *vt* hacer más atractivo(va).

glamorous ['glæmərəs] *adj* atractivo(va), lleno(na) de encanto.

glamour *UK,* **glamor** *US* ['glæməʳ] *n* encanto *m*, atractivo *m*, sofisticación *f.*

glance [glɑːns] ⬦ *n* [quick look] mirada *f*, vistazo *m*; **to cast** OR **take a glance at sthg** echar un vistazo a algo; **at a glance** de un vistazo; **at first glance** a primera vista. ⬦ *vi* [look quickly]: **to glance at sb** lanzar una mirada a alguien; **to glance at sthg** echar una ojeada OR un vistazo a algo; **to glance at** OR **through sthg** hojear algo.

◆ **glance off** *vt insep* rebotar en.

glancing ['glɑːnsɪŋ] *adj* de refilón.

gland [glænd] *n* glándula *f.*

glandular fever ['glændjʊləʳ-] *n* mononucleosis *f inv* infecciosa.

glare [gleəʳ] ⬦ *n* **- 1.** [scowl] mirada *f* asesina **- 2.** [blaze, dazzle] resplandor *m*, deslumbramiento *m* **- 3.** (*U*) *fig* [of publicity] foco *m.* ⬦ *vi* **- 1.** [scowl]: **to glare (at sthg/sb)** mirar con furia (algo/a alguien) **- 2.** [blaze, dazzle] brillar.

glaring ['gleərɪŋ] *adj* **- 1.** [very obvious] flagrante **- 2.** [blazing, dazzling] deslumbrante.

glasnost ['glæznɒst] *n* glasnost *f.*

glass [glɑːs] ⬦ *n* **- 1.** [material] vidrio *m*, cristal *m* **- 2.** [drinking vessel, glassful] vaso *m*; [with stem] copa *f* **- 3.** (*U*) [glassware] cristalería *f.* ⬦ *comp* de vidrio OR cristal.

◆ **glasses** *npl* [spectacles] gafas *fpl.*

glassblowing ['glɑːs,bləʊɪŋ] *n* soplado *m* de vidrio.

glass fibre *n* (*U*) *UK* fibra *f* de vidrio.

glasshouse ['glɑːshaʊs, *pl* -haʊzɪz] *n UK* [greenhouse] invernadero *m.*

glassware ['glɑːsweəʳ] *n* (*U*) cristalería *f.*

glassy ['glɑːsɪ] (*comp* **-ier,** *superl* **-iest**) *adj* **- 1.** [smooth, shiny] cristalino(na) **- 2.** [blank, lifeless] vidrioso(sa).

Glaswegian [glæz'wiːdʒən] ⬦ *adj de o relativo a Glasgow.* ⬦ *n* [person] *natural o habitante de Glasgow.*

glaucoma [glɔː'kəʊmə] *n* glaucoma *m.*

glaze [gleɪz] ⬦ *n* [on pottery] vidriado *m*; [on food] glaseado *m.* ⬦ *vt* **- 1.** [pottery] vidriar; [food] glasear **- 2.** [window] acristalar.

◆ **glaze over** *vi* [eyes] velarse.

glazed [gleɪzd] *adj* **- 1.** [dull, bored] vidrioso(sa) **- 2.** [pottery] vidriado(da); [food] glaseado(da) **- 3.** [door, window] acristalado(da).

glazier ['gleɪzjəʳ] *n* vidriero *m*, -ra *f.*

gleam [gliːm] ⬦ *n* destello *m*; [of hope] rayo *m.* ⬦ *vi* relucir.

gleaming ['gliːmɪŋ] *adj* reluciente.

glean [gliːn] *vt* [gather] recoger; [information] extraer.

glee [gliː] *n* (*U*) [joy, delight] alegría *f*, regocijo *m.*

gleeful ['gliːfʊl] *adj* alegre, jubiloso(sa).

glen [glen] *n Scotland* cañada *f.*

glib [glɪb] (*comp* **-ber,** *superl* **-best**) *adj pej* de mucha labia.

glibly ['glɪblɪ] *adv pej* con mucha labia.

glide [glaɪd] *vi* **- 1.** [move smoothly] deslizarse **- 2.** [fly] planear.

glider ['glaɪdəʳ] *n* [plane] planeador *m.*

gliding ['glaɪdɪŋ] *n* [sport] vuelo *m* sin motor.

glimmer ['glɪməʳ] ⬦ *n* **- 1.** [faint light] luz *f* tenue **- 2.** *fig* [trace, sign] atisbo *m*; [of hope] rayo *m.* ⬦ *vi* brillar tenuemente.

glimpse [glɪmps] <> n - **1.** [look, sight] vislumbre f; **to catch a glimpse of sthg/sb** entrever algo/a alguien - **2.** [idea, perception] asomo m, atisbo m. <> vt entrever, vislumbrar.

glint [glɪnt] <> n - **1.** [flash] destello m - **2.** [in eyes] brillo m. <> vi destellar.

glisten ['glɪsn] vi relucir, brillar.

glitch [glɪtʃ] n inf pequeño fallo m técnico.

glitter ['glɪtər] <> n - **1.** [shine] brillo m - **2.** [for decoration] purpurina f. <> vi relucir, brillar.

glittering ['glɪtərɪŋ] adj brillante, reluciente.

glitzy ['glɪtsɪ] (comp -ier, superl -iest) adj inf [glamorous] deslumbrante.

gloat [gləʊt] vi: **to gloat (over sthg)** regodearse (con algo).

global ['gləʊbl] adj [worldwide] mundial, global; **the global village** la aldea global.

globalization [ˌgləʊbəlaɪˈzeɪʃn] n globalización f.

globally ['gləʊbəlɪ] adv - **1.** [overall] en términos globales - **2.** [worldwide] mundialmente.

global warming [-ˈwɔːmɪŋ] n calentamiento m global, cambio m climático.

globe [gləʊb] n - **1.** [gen] globo m - **2.** [spherical map] globo m (terráqueo).

globetrotter ['gləʊbˌtrɒtər] n inf trotamundos mf inv.

globule ['glɒbjuːl] n gota f.

gloom [gluːm] n (U) - **1.** [darkness] penumbra f - **2.** [unhappiness] pesimismo m, melancolía f.

gloomy ['gluːmɪ] (comp -ier, superl -iest) adj - **1.** [dark, cloudy] oscuro(ra) - **2.** [unhappy] triste, melancólico(ca) - **3.** [without hope - report, forecast] pesimista; [- situation, prospects] desalentador(ra).

glorification [ˌglɔːrɪfɪˈkeɪʃn] n glorificación f.

glorified ['glɔːrɪfaɪd] adj pej [jumped-up] con pretensiones.

glorify ['glɔːrɪfaɪ] (pt & pp -ied) vt [overpraise] ensalzar.

glorious ['glɔːrɪəs] adj magnífico(ca), espléndido(da).

glory ['glɔːrɪ] n (pl -ies) - **1.** [gen] gloria f - **2.** [beauty, splendour] esplendor m.
➤ **glories** npl [triumphs] éxitos mpl, triunfos mpl.
➤ **glory in** vt insep [relish] disfrutar de, regocijarse con.

Glos (abbr of Gloucestershire) condado inglés.

gloss [glɒs] n - **1.** [shine] lustre m, brillo m - **2.**: **gloss (paint)** pintura f esmalte.
➤ **gloss over** vt insep tocar muy por encima.

glossary ['glɒsərɪ] (pl -ies) n glosario m.

glossy ['glɒsɪ] (comp -ier, superl -iest) adj - **1.** [smooth, shiny] brillante, lustroso(sa) - **2.** [on shiny paper] de papel satinado.

glossy magazine n revista f lujosa a todo color.

glove [glʌv] n guante m.

glove compartment n guantera f.

glove puppet n UK guiñol m (marioneta).

glow [gləʊ] <> n - **1.** [light] brillo m, fulgor m - **2.** [flush] rubor m - **3.** [feeling] calor m, ardor m. <> vi - **1.** [gen] brillar - **2.** [flush]: **to glow (with)** [embarrassment] sonrojarse (de); [happiness, pleasure etc] estar rebosante (de).

glower ['glaʊər] vi: **to glower (at sthg/sb)** mirar con furia (algo/a alguien).

glowing ['gləʊɪŋ] adj [very favourable] entusiasta.

glow-worm n luciérnaga f.

glucose ['gluːkəʊs] n glucosa f.

glue [gluː] <> n [paste] pegamento m; [for glueing wood, metal etc] cola f. <> vt (cont glueing OR gluing) [paste] pegar (con pegamento); [wood, metal etc] encolar; **to be glued to sthg** [absorbed by] estar pegado(da) a algo.

glue-sniffing [-ˌsnɪfɪŋ] n inhalación f de pegamento.

glum [glʌm] (comp -mer, superl -mest) adj [unhappy] sombrío(a).

glut [glʌt] n exceso m, superabundancia f.

gluten ['gluːtən] n gluten m.

glutinous ['gluːtɪnəs] adj pegajoso(sa), glutinoso(sa).

glutton ['glʌtn] n [greedy person] glotón m, -ona f; **to be a glutton for punishment** ser un masoquista.

gluttony ['glʌtənɪ] n glotonería f, gula f.

glycerin ['glɪsərɪn], **glycerine** ['glɪsəriːn] n glicerina f.

gm (abbr of gram) gr.

GM [dʒiːˈem] adj transgénico(ca), modificado(da) genéticamente; **GM foods** alimentos transgénicos; **GM products** productos modificados genéticamente.

GMB n importante sindicato de obreros británicos.

GM foods npl alimentos mpl transgénicos.

GMO (abbr of genetically modified organism) n OMG m.

GMT (abbr of Greenwich Mean Time) hora GMT del meridiano de Greenwich.

gnarled [nɑːld] adj nudoso(sa).

gnash [næʃ] vt: **to gnash one's teeth** hacer rechinar los dientes.

gnat [næt] *n* mosquito *m*.

gnaw [nɔ:] *vt* [chew] roer; **to gnaw (away) at sb** corroer a alguien.

gnome [nəʊm] *n* gnomo *m*.

GNP (*abbr of* **gross national product**) *n* PNB *m*.

gnu [nu:] (*pl* **gnu** OR **-s**) *n* ñu *m*.

GNVQ (*abbr of* **General National Vocational Qualification**) *n* SCH *curso de formación profesional de dos años de duración para los mayores de 16 años en Inglaterra y Gales.*

go [gəʊ] ⇔ *vi* (*pt* **went**, *pp* **gone**) - **1.** [move, travel, attend] ir; **where are you going?** ¿adónde vas?; **he's gone to Portugal** se ha ido a Portugal; **we went by bus/train** fuimos en autobús/tren; **to go and do sthg** ir a hacer algo; **where does this path go?** ¿adónde lleva este camino?; **to go right/left** girar a la derecha/izquierda; **to go swimming/shopping** ir a nadar/de compras; **to go for a walk/run** ir a dar un paseo/a correr; **to go to church/school** ir a misa/la escuela; **to go to work** ir a trabajar; **where do we go from here?** ¿y ahora qué? - **2.** [depart - person] irse, marcharse; [- bus] irse, salir; **I must go, I have to go** tengo que irme; **what time does the bus go?** ¿a qué hora sale OR se va el autobús?; **it's time we went** es hora de irse OR marcharse; **let's go!** ¡vámonos! - **3.** [pass - time] pasar; **the time went slowly/quickly** el tiempo pasaba lentamente/rápido - **4.** [progress] ir; **to go well/badly** ir bien/mal; **how's it going?** *inf* [how are you?] ¿qué tal? - **5.** [belong, fit] ir; **the plates go in the cupboard** los platos van en el armario; **it won't go into the suitcase** no cabe en la maleta - **6.** [become] ponerse; **to go grey** ponerse gris; **to go mad** volverse loco(c a); **to go blind** quedarse ciego(ga) - **7.** [be or remain in a particular state]: **to go naked** andar desnudo(da); **to go hungry** pasar hambre; **we went in fear of our lives** temíamos por nuestras vidas; **to go unpunished** salir impune - **8.** [indicating intention, certainty, expectation]: **to be going to do sthg** ir a hacer algo; **what are you going to do now?** ¿qué vas a hacer ahora?; **he said he was going to be late** dijo que llegaría tarde; **it's going to rain/snow** va a llover/nevar; **I feel like I'm going to be sick** me parece que voy a devolver; **she's going to have a baby** va a tener un niño - **9.** [match, be compatible]: **to go (with)** ir bien (con); **this blouse goes well with the skirt** esta blusa va muy bien OR hace juego con la falda; **those colours don't really go** la verdad es que esos colores no combinan bien - **10.** [function, work] funcionar; **is the tape recorder still going?** [still in working order] ¿funciona todavía el casete?; [still on] ¿está to-

davía encendido el casete? - **11.** [bell, alarm] sonar - **12.** [start] empezar; **ready to go** listo(ta) para empezar - **13.** [when referring to saying, story or song] decir; **as the saying goes** como dice el refrán; **how does that song go?** ¿cómo es OR dice esa canción? - **14.** [stop working] estropearse; **the fuse must have gone** se ha debido de fundir el fusible - **15.** [deteriorate]: **her sight/hearing is going** está perdiendo la vista/el oído - **16.** [be spent]: **to go on** ir a parar a, gastarse en; **all my money goes on food and rent** todo el dinero se me va en comida y alquiler - **17.** [be given]: **the prize/contract went to B. Jones** el premio/contrato le fue concedido a B. Jones - **18.** [be disposed of]: **he'll have to go** habrá que despedirlo; **everything must go!** ¡gran liquidación! - **19.** *inf* [with negative - in giving advice]: **now, don't go catching cold** y cuidado no cojas frío ¿eh? - **20.** *inf* [expressing irritation, surprise]: **now what's he gone and done?** ¿qué leches ha hecho ahora?; **she's gone and bought a new car!** ¡ha ido y se ha comprado un coche nuevo!; **you've gone and done it now!** ¡ya la has liado! - **21.** [in division]: **three into two won't go** tres no es divisible por dos

▸▸▸ **it just goes to show (that)...** eso demuestra OR prueba que... ⇔ *vt* (*pt* **went**, *pp* **gone**) - **1.** [make noise of] hacer; **the dog went 'woof'** el perro hizo '¡guau!' - **2.** *inf* [say] decir. ⇔ *n* (*pl* **goes**) - **1.** [turn] turno *m*; **it's my go** me toca a mí - **2.** *inf* [attempt]: **to have a go at sthg** intentar OR probar algo; **have a go!** ¡prueba!, ¡inténtalo! - **3.** *inf* [success]: **to make a go of sthg** tener éxito con OR en algo

▸▸▸ **to have a go at sb** *inf* echar una bronca a alguien; **to be on the go** *inf* no parar, estar muy liado(da).

◆ **to go** *adv* - **1.** [remaining]: **there are only three days to go** sólo quedan tres días - **2.** [to take away] para llevar.

◆ **go about** ⇔ *vt insep* - **1.** [perform] hacer, realizar; **to go about one's business** ocuparse uno de sus asuntos - **2.** [tackle]: **to go about doing sthg** apañárselas para hacer algo; **how do you intend going about it?** ¿cómo piensas hacerlo? ⇔ *vi* = **go around**.

◆ **go after** *vt insep* ir a por OR detrás de.

◆ **go against** *vt insep* - **1.** [conflict with, be unfavourable to] ir en contra de - **2.** [act contrary to] actuar en contra de.

◆ **go ahead** *vi* - **1.** [begin]: **to go ahead (with sthg)** seguir adelante (con algo); **go ahead!** ¡adelante! - **2.** [take place] celebrarse - **3.** [in match, contest] ponerse por delante.

◆ **go along** *vi* [proceed]: **as you go along** a medida que lo vayas haciendo; **he made it up as he went along** se lo inventaba sobre la marcha.

go along with vt insep estar de acuerdo con; **he agreed to go along with our ideas** aceptó nuestras ideas sin demasiado entusiasmo.

go around, go round, go about vi - **1.** inf [behave in a certain way]: **to go around doing sthg** ir por ahí haciendo algo - **2.** [associate]: **to go around with sb** juntarse con alguien - **3.** [joke, illness, story] correr (por ahí); **there's a rumour going around about her** corren rumores acerca de ella.

go away vi - **1.** [person, animal] irse; **go away!** ¡vete! - **2.** [pain] desaparecer.

go back vi - **1.** [return] volver - **2.** [clocks] atrasarse.

go back on vt insep [one's word, promise] faltar a.

go back to vt insep - **1.** [return to activity] continuar OR seguir con; **to go back to sleep** volver a dormir - **2.** [return to previous topic] volver a - **3.** [date from] datar de, remontarse a.

go before vi [precede] preceder; **we wanted to forget what had gone before** queríamos olvidar lo ocurrido.

go by ◇ vi [time, people, vehicles] pasar. ◇ vt insep - **1.** [be guided by] guiarse por - **2.** [judge from]: **going by her accent, I'd say she was French** a juzgar por su acento yo diría que es francesa.

go down ◇ vi - **1.** [descend] bajar - **2.** [get lower - prices, temperature, swelling] bajar - **3.** [be accepted]: **to go down well/badly** tener una buena/mala acogida - **4.** [sun] ponerse - **5.** [tyre, balloon] deshincharse - **6.** [be relegated] descender. ◇ vt insep bajar.

go down with vt insep inf [illness] coger, pillar, agarrar Amér.

go for vt insep - **1.** [choose] decidirse por, escoger - **2.** [be attracted to]: **I don't really go for men like him** no me gustan mucho los hombres como él - **3.** [attack] lanzarse sobre, atacar - **4.** [try to obtain - record, job] ir a por - **5.** [be valid] valer para; **does that go for me too?** ¿eso va por mí también?

go forward vi [clocks] adelantarse.

go in vi entrar.

go in for vt insep - **1.** [competition, exam] presentarse a - **2.** [take up as a profession] dedicarse a - **3.** inf [enjoy]: **he goes in for sports in a big way** hace un montón de deporte; **I don't really go in for classical music** no me va la música clásica.

go into vt insep - **1.** [enter] entrar en - **2.** [discuss, describe in detail] entrar en; **to go into detail** entrar en detalles - **3.** [investigate] investigar - **4.** [take up as a profession] dedicarse a - **5.** [be put into - subj: effort, money] invertirse; [- subj: work]: **a lot of hard work went into that book** hay mucho trabajo invertido en ese

libro - **6.** [begin]: **to go into a rage** ponerse frenético(ca); **to go into a dive** empezar a caer en picado.

go off ◇ vi - **1.** [leave] irse - **2.** [explode - bomb] estallar; [- gun] dispararse - **3.** [alarm] saltar, sonar - **4.** [go bad - food] echarse a perder, estropearse; [- milk] cortarse - **5.** [lights, heating] apagarse - **6.** [happen]: **to go off (well/badly)** salir (bien/mal). ◇ vt insep inf [lose interest in] perder el gusto a OR el interés en OR por.

go off with vt insep inf: **he went off with his best friend's wife** se largó con la mujer de su mejor amigo.

go on ◇ vi - **1.** [take place] pasar, ocurrir - **2.** [continue]: **to go on (doing sthg)** seguir (haciendo algo); **I can't go on!** ¡no puedo más!; **shall I tell you? – go on** ¿te lo cuento? – vale - **3.** [proceed to further activity]: **to go on to sthg/to do sthg** pasar a algo/a hacer algo - **4.** [proceed to another place]: **we went on to a nightclub afterwards** después nos fuimos a una discoteca - **5.** [pass - time] pasar - **6.** [go in advance]: **you go on, I'll wait here** tú continúa, yo te espero aquí - **7.** [heating etc] encenderse - **8.** [talk for too long]: **to go on (about)** no parar de hablar (de); **don't go on about it** déjalo ya, no sigas con eso. ◇ vt insep - **1.** [be guided by] guiarse por - **2.** [start]: **to go on a diet** ponerse a régimen. ◇ excl ¡venga!, ¡vamos!; **go on, treat yourself** ¡venga, hombre! ¡date el gusto!

go on at vt insep [nag] dar la lata a.

go out vi - **1.** [leave house] salir; **to go out for a meal** cenar fuera - **2.** [as friends or lovers]: **to go out (with sb)** salir (con alguien), pololear (con alguien) Chile - **3.** [tide] bajar - **4.** [light, fire, cigarette] apagarse - **5.** [stop being fashionable] pasarse de moda.

go over vt insep - **1.** [examine] repasar - **2.** [repeat] repetir.

go over to vt insep - **1.** [change to] cambiar OR pasar a - **2.** [change sides to] pasarse a; **to go over to the other side** pasarse al otro bando - **3.** RADIO & TV conectar con.

go round vi - **1.** [be enough for everyone]: **there's just enough to go round** hay lo justo para que alcance para todos - **2.** [revolve] girar, dar vueltas, = **go around**.

go through ◇ vt insep - **1.** [penetrate] atravesar - **2.** [experience] pasar por, experimentar - **3.** [spend] gastarse - **4.** [study, search through] registrar; **she went through his pockets** le miró en los bolsillos - **5.** [read] examinar leyendo; [say out loud] enumerar, decir en alto; **I'll go through it again** lo voy a repetir. ◇ vi - **1.** [enter] pasar - **2.** [in competition] clasificarse - **3.** [bill, divorce etc] aprobarse.

go through with vt insep llevar a cabo.

◆ **go towards** *vt insep* contribuir a.

◆ **go under** *vi lit* & *fig* hundirse.

◆ **go up** ◇ *vi* - **1.** [rise - person, prices, temperature, balloon] subir - **2.** [be built] levantarse, construirse - **3.** [be promoted] subir - **4.** [explode] explotar, saltar por los aires - **5.** [burst into flames]: **to go up (in flames)** ser pasto de las llamas - **6.** [be uttered]: **a shout went up from amongst the crowd** unos gritos surgieron de entre la multitud. ◇ *vt insep* subir; **we went up the Eiffel Tower** subimos a la torre Eiffel.

◆ **go up to** *vt insep* [approach] acercarse a.

◆ **go with** *vt insep* [be included with] ir con.

◆ **go without** ◇ *vt insep* prescindir de. ◇ *vi* apañárselas.

goad [gəʊd] *vt* [provoke] aguijonear, incitar; **to goad sb into doing sthg** incitar a alguien a hacer algo.

go-ahead ◇ *adj* [dynamic] emprendedor(ra), dinámico(ca). ◇ *n (U)* [permission] luz *f* verde; **to give sb the go-ahead (for)** darle a alguien luz verde (para).

goal [gəʊl] *n* - **1.** SPORT [point scored] gol *m*; [area between goalposts] portería *f*, meta *f*, arco *m* *Amér*; **to score a goal** marcar un gol - **2.** [aim] objetivo *m*, meta *f*.

goalie ['gəʊlɪ] *n inf* portero *m*, -ra *f*, guardameta *mf*, arquero *m*, -ra *f Amér*.

goalkeeper ['gəʊl,kiːpə'] *n* portero *m*, -ra *f*, guardameta *mf*, arquero *m*, -ra *f Amér*.

goalless ['gəʊllɪs] *adj*: **goalless draw** empate *m* a cero.

goalmouth ['gəʊlmaʊθ, *pl* ɪmaʊðz] *n* portería *f*, meta *f*, arco *m Amér*.

goalpost ['gəʊlpəʊst] *n* poste *m* (de la portería).

goat [gəʊt] *n* [animal] cabra *f*.

goatee [gəʊˈtiː] *n* perilla *f*.

gob [gɒb] *v inf* ◇ *n UK* [mouth] pico *m*. ◇ *vi* (*pt* & *pp* -bed, *cont* -bing) [spit] escupir.

gobble ['gɒbl] *vt* [food] engullir, tragar.

◆ **gobble down, gobble up** *vt sep* engullir, tragar.

gobbledygook ['gɒbldɪguːk] *n (U)* - **1.** [incomprehensible language] jerga *f* incomprensible, jerigonza *f* - **2.** *inf* [nonsense] tonterías *fpl*.

go-between *n* intermediario *m*, -ria *f*.

Gobi ['gəʊbɪ] *n*: **the Gobi Desert** el desierto de Gobi.

goblet ['gɒblɪt] *n* copa *f*.

goblin ['gɒblɪn] *n* duende *m*.

gobsmacked ['gɒbsmækt] *adj UK inf* alucinado(da), flipado(da).

go-cart = **go-kart**.

god [gɒd] *n* dios *m*.

◆ **God** ◇ *n* Dios *m*; **God knows** sabe Dios; **for God's sake** ¡por el amor de Dios!; **thank God** ¡gracias a Dios! ◇ *excl*: **(my) God!** ¡Dios (mío)!

◆ **gods** *npl UK inf*: **the gods** THEAT el gallinero.

godchild ['gɒdtʃaɪld] (*pl* -children [-,tʃɪldrən]) *n* ahijado *m*, -da *f*.

goddam(n) ['gɒdæm] *esp US* ◇ *adj* maldito(ta). ◇ *excl* ¡maldita sea!

goddaughter ['gɒd,dɔːtə'] *n* ahijada *f*.

goddess ['gɒdɪs] *n* diosa *f*.

godfather ['gɒd,fɑːðə'] *n* padrino *m*.

godforsaken ['gɒdfə,seɪkn] *adj* dejado(da) de la mano de Dios.

godmother ['gɒd,mʌðə'] *n* madrina *f*.

godparents ['gɒd,peərənts] *npl* padrinos *mpl*.

godsend ['gɒdsend] *n*: **to be a godsend** venir como agua de mayo.

godson ['gɒdsʌn] *n* ahijado *m*.

goes [gəʊz] ⊳ **go**.

gofer ['gəʊfə'] *n US inf* recadero *m*, -ra *f*.

go-getter [-'getə'] *n* persona *f* emprendedora y ambiciosa.

goggle ['gɒgl] *vi*: **to goggle (at sthg/sb)** mirar con ojos desorbitados (algo/a alguien).

goggles ['gɒglz] *npl* [for swimming] gafas *fpl* submarinas; [for skiing] gafas de esquí; [for welding] gafas de protección.

go-go dancer *n* gogó *mf*.

going ['gəʊɪŋ] ◇ *adj* - **1.** *UK* [available] disponible; **is there any beer going?** ¿no habrá una cervecita para mí?; **you have a lot going for you** *inf* tienes mucho futuro - **2.** [rate] actual. ◇ *n (U)* - **1.** [rate of advance] marcha *f* OR **that was good going** ¡qué rápido! - **2.** [conditions] condiciones *fpl*; **to be rough** OR **heavy going** hacerse pesado; **to be easy going** ser fácil.

going concern *n* empresa *f* rentable y en marcha.

goings-on *npl inf* tejemanejes *mpl*.

go-kart, go-cart [-kɑːt] *n* kart *m*.

gold [gəʊld] ◇ *adj* [gold-coloured] dorado(da). ◇ *n* - **1.** [gen] oro *m*; **to be as good as gold** ser más bueno que el pan - **2.** [medal] medalla *f* de oro. ◇ *comp* [made of gold] de oro.

golden ['gəʊldən] *adj* - **1.** [made of gold] de oro - **2.** [gold-coloured] dorado(da).

golden age *n* edad *f* de oro.

◆ **Golden Age** *n* [in Spanish history] Siglo *m* de Oro.

golden eagle *n* águila *f* real.

golden handshake *n gratificación cuantiosa al jubilarse*.

golden opportunity *n* ocasión *f* de oro.

golden retriever *n* golden retriever *m*.

golden rule *n* regla *f* de oro.

golden wedding *n* bodas *fpl* de oro.

goldfish ['gəʊldfɪʃ] (*pl* **goldfish**) *n* pez *m* de colores.

goldfish bowl *n* pecera *f*.

gold leaf *n* pan *m* de oro.

gold medal *n* medalla *f* de oro.

goldmine ['gəʊldmaɪn] *n* lit & fig mina *f* de oro.

gold-plated [-'pleɪtɪd] *adj* chapado(da) en oro.

goldsmith ['gəʊldsmɪθ] *n* orfebre *mf*.

gold standard *n*: the gold standard el patrón oro.

golf [gɒlf] *n* golf *m*.

golf ball *n* [for golf] pelota *f* de golf.

golf club *n* - **1.** [society, place] club *m* de golf - **2.** [stick] palo *m* de golf.

golf course *n* campo *m* de golf.

golfer ['gɒlfər] *n* golfista *mf*.

golly ['gɒlɪ] *excl* inf dated ¡caray!, ¡cáspita!

gondola ['gɒndələ] *n* [boat] góndola *f*.

gondolier [ˌgɒndə'lɪər] *n* gondolero *m*, -ra *f*.

gone [gɒn] <> *pp* ▷ **go**. <> *adj*: those days are gone esos tiempos ya pasaron. <> *prep* [past]: **it was gone six already** ya eran las seis pasadas.

gong [gɒŋ] *n* gong *m*.

gonna ['gɒnə] *inf* (*abbr of* going to) ▷ **go**.

gonorrh(o)ea [ˌgɒnə'rɪə] *n* gonorrea *f*.

goo [gu:] *n* inf pringue *m*.

good [gʊd] <> *adj* (*comp* **better**, *superl* **best**) - **1.** [gen] bueno(na); **it's good to see you** me alegro de verte; **she's good at it** se le da bien; **he's a very good singer** canta muy bien; **to be good with** saber manejárselas con; **she's good with her hands** es muy mañosa; **it's good for you** es bueno, es beneficioso; **to feel good** sentirse fenomenal; **that feels good!** ¡qué gusto!; **it's good that...** está bien que...; **to look good** [attractive] estar muy guapo(pa); [appetizing, promising] tener buena pinta; **it looks good on you** te queda bien; **good looks** atractivo *m*; **be good!** ¡sé bueno!, ¡pórtate bien!; **good!** ¡muy bien!, ¡estupendo! - **2.** [kind] amable; **to be good to sb** ser amable con alguien; **to be good enough to do sthg** ser tan amable de hacer algo; **that was very good of him** fue muy amable de su parte ▶ **it's a good job** OR **thing (that)...** menos mal que...; **good for you!** ¡muy bien!, ¡bien hecho!; **to give as good as one gets** devolver todos los golpes; **to make sthg good** reparar OR enmendar algo. <> *n* - **1.** *(U)* [benefit] bien *m*; **for the good of** por el bien de; **for your own good** por tu propio bien; **it will do him good**

le hará bien - **2.** [use] beneficio *m*, provecho *m*; **what's the good of...?** ¿de OR para qué sirve...?; **it's no good** no sirve para nada; **will this be any good?** ¿servirá esto para algo? - **3.** [morally correct behaviour] el bien; **to be up to no good** estar tramando algo malo. <> *adv* - **1.** [expresses approval] estupendo - **2.** *inf* [well] bien.

◆ **goods** *npl* - **1.** [COMM - for sale] productos *mpl*, artículos *mpl*; [- when transported] mercancías *fpl*; **to come up with** OR **deliver the goods** UK inf cumplir (lo prometido) - **2.** ECON bienes *mpl*.

◆ **as good as** *adv* casi, prácticamente; **it's as good as new** está como nuevo.

◆ **for good** *adv* [forever] para siempre.

◆ **good afternoon** *excl* ¡buenas tardes!

◆ **good day** *excl* Australia dated ¡buenas!, ¡buenos días!

◆ **good evening** *excl* [in the evening] ¡buenas tardes!; [at night] ¡buenas noches!

◆ **good morning** *excl* ¡buenos días!, ¡buen día! Amér

◆ **good night** *excl* ¡buenas noches!

goodbye [ˌgʊd'baɪ] <> *excl* ¡adiós!; **to say goodbye** despedirse. <> *n* adiós *m*.

good-for-nothing <> *adj* inútil. <> *n* inútil *mf*.

Good Friday *n* Viernes *m* Santo.

good-humoured [-'hju:məd] *adj* jovial.

good-looking [-'lʊkɪŋ] *adj* [person] guapo(pa).

good-natured [-'neɪtʃəd] *adj* bondadoso(sa).

goodness ['gʊdnɪs] <> *n* *(U)* - **1.** [kindness] bondad *f* - **2.** [nutritive quality] alimento *m*. <> *excl*: **(my) goodness!** ¡Dios mío!; **for goodness' sake!** ¡por Dios!; **thank goodness** ¡gracias a Dios!

goods train [gʊdz-] *n* UK mercancías *m* inv.

good-tempered [-'tempəd] *adj* afable.

good turn *n*: **to do sb a good turn** hacer un favor a alguien.

goodwill [ˌgʊd'wɪl] *n* - **1.** [kind feelings] buena voluntad *f* - **2.** COMM fondo *m* de comercio.

goody ['gʊdɪ] *inf* <> *n* (*pl* **-ies**) [person] bueno *m*, -na *f*. <> *excl* ¡qué chupi!

◆ **goodies** *npl* inf - **1.** [delicious food] golosinas *fpl* - **2.** [desirable objects] cosas *fpl* apetecibles.

gooey ['gu:ɪ] (*comp* **gooier**, *superl* **gooiest**) *adj* inf [sticky] pegajoso(sa); [cake, dessert, film] empalagoso(sa).

goof [gu:f] US inf <> *n* [mistake] metedura *f* de pata. <> *vi* meter la pata.

◆ **goof off** *vi* US inf escaquearse.

goofy ['gu:fɪ] (*comp* **-ier**, *superl* **-iest**) *adj* inf [silly] bobo(ba), tonto(ta).

goose [gu:s] (*pl* **geese**) *n* [bird] ganso *m*, oca *f*.

gooseberry ['guzbərɪ] (*pl* **-ies**) *n* - **1.** [fruit] grosella *f* silvestre, uva *f* espina - **2.** *esp UK inf* [third person]: **to play gooseberry** hacer de carabina.

goosebumps *US* ['gu:sbʌmps] *inf npl* = **gooseflesh**.

gooseflesh ['gu:sfleʃ] *n* carne *f* de gallina.

gopher ['gəʊfər] *n* taltuza *f*.

gore [gɔ:r] <> *n liter* [blood] sangre *f* (derramada). <> *vt* dar una cornada a, cornear.

gorge [gɔ:dʒ] <> *n* cañón *m*, garganta *f*. <> *vt*: **to gorge o.s. on** *OR* **with** atracarse de. <> *vi* hartarse, saciarse.

gorgeous ['gɔ:dʒəs] *adj* - **1.** [lovely] magnífico(ca), espléndido(da) - **2.** *inf* [good-looking]: **to be gorgeous** estar como un tren.

gorilla [gə'rɪlə] *n* gorila *mf*.

gormless ['gɔ:mlɪs] *adj UK inf* memo(ma), lerdo(da).

gorse [gɔ:s] *n* (*U*) tojo *m*.

gory ['gɔ:rɪ] (*comp* **-ier**, *superl* **-iest**) *adj* [death, scene] sangriento(ta); [details, film] escabroso(sa).

gosh [gɒʃ] *excl inf* ¡joroba!, ¡caray!

go-slow *n UK* huelga *f* de celo.

gospel ['gɒspl] <> *n* - **1.** [doctrine] evangelio *m* - **2.**: **gospel (truth)** la pura verdad. <> *comp* MUS espiritual negro, gospel (*inv*).
♦ **Gospel** *n* [in Bible] Evangelio *m*.

gossamer ['gɒsəmər] *n* (*U*) - **1.** [spider's thread] telaraña *f* - **2.** [material] gasa *f*.

gossip ['gɒsɪp] <> *n* - **1.** [conversation] cotilleo *m* - **2.** [person] cotilla *mf*, chismoso *m*, -sa *f*. <> *vi* cotillear.

gossip column *n* ecos *mpl* de sociedad.

got [gɒt] *pt* & *pp* ▷ **get**.

Gothic ['gɒθɪk] *adj* gótico(ca).

gotta ['gɒtə] *inf* (*abbr of* **got to**) ▷ **get**.

gotten ['gɒtn] *pp US* ▷ **get**.

gouge [gaʊdʒ] ♦ **gouge out** *vt sep* [hole] excavar; [eyes] arrancar.

goulash ['gu:læʃ] *n* gulasch *m*.

gourd [gʊəd] *n* calabaza *f*.

gourmet ['gʊəmeɪ] <> *n* gastrónomo *m*, -ma *f*, gourmet *mf*. <> *comp* para *OR* de gastrónomos.

gout [gaʊt] *n* gota *f*.

govern ['gʌvən] <> *vt* - **1.** POL gobernar - **2.** [control] dictar, guiar. <> *vi* POL gobernar.

governess ['gʌvənɪs] *n* institutriz *f*.

governing ['gʌvənɪŋ] *adj* gobernante.

governing body *n* organismo *m* rector.

government ['gʌvnmənt] <> *n* gobierno *m*. <> *comp* gubernamental.

governmental [,gʌvn'mentl] *adj* gubernamental.

governor ['gʌvənər] *n* - **1.** *US* POL gobernador *m*, -ra *f* - **2.** [of school, bank, prison] director *m*, -ra *f*.

governor-general (*pl* **governor-generals** *OR* **governors-general**) *n* gobernador *m*, -ra *f* general.

govt (*abbr of* **government**) gob.

gown [gaʊn] *n* - **1.** [dress] vestido *m*, traje *m* - **2.** [of judge etc] toga *f*.

GP (*abbr of* **general practitioner**) *n* médico *m*, -ca *f* de cabecera.

GPO (*abbr of* **General Post Office**) *n* - **1.** [in UK] *antiguo servicio de correos británico* - **2.** [in US] *servicio de correos estadounidense*.

gr. *abbr of* **gross**.

grab [græb] <> *vt* (*pt* & *pp* **-bed**, *cont* **-bing**) - **1.** [snatch away] arrebatar; **to grab sthg off sb** arrebatar algo a alguien; [grip] agarrar, asir - **2.** *inf* [sandwich, lunch] pillar, coger - **3.** *inf* [appeal to] seducir. <> *vi* (*pt* & *pp* **-bed**, *cont* **-bing**): **to grab at sthg** intentar agarrar algo. <> *n*: **to make a grab at** *OR* **for sthg** intentar arrebatar/agarrar algo.

grace [greɪs] <> *n* - **1.** (*U*) [elegance] elegancia *f*, gracia *f* - **2.** [graciousness]: **to do sthg with good grace** hacer algo de buena gana; **to have the grace to do sthg** tener la delicadeza de hacer algo - **3.** (*U*) [delay] prórroga *f* - **4.** [prayer] bendición *f* de la mesa; **to say grace** bendecir la mesa. <> *vt fml* - **1.** [honour] honrar - **2.** [decorate] adornar, embellecer.

graceful ['greɪsfʊl] *adj* - **1.** [beautiful] elegante - **2.** [gracious] cortés.

graceless ['greɪslɪs] *adj* - **1.** [ugly] desagradable, feo(a) - **2.** [ill-mannered] descortés.

gracious ['greɪʃəs] <> *adj* - **1.** [polite] cortés - **2.** [elegant] elegante. <> *excl*: **(good) gracious!** ¡Dios mío!

graciously ['greɪʃəslɪ] *adv* - **1.** [politely] cortésmente - **2.** [elegantly] elegantemente.

gradation [grə'deɪʃn] *n* gradación *f*.

grade [greɪd] <> *n* - **1.** [level, quality] clase *f*, calidad *f*; **to make the grade** dar la talla - **2.** *US* [class] curso *m*, clase *f* - **3.** [mark] nota *f*. <> *vt* - **1.** [classify] clasificar - **2.** [mark, assess] calificar.

grade crossing *n US* paso *m* a nivel.

grade school *n US* escuela *f* primaria.

gradient ['greɪdjənt] *n* pendiente *f*.

grad school *n US* escuela *f* de posgrado.

gradual ['grædʒʊəl] *adj* gradual.

gradually ['grædʒʊəlɪ] *adv* gradualmente.

graduate <> *n* ['grædʒʊət] - **1.** [person with a degree] licenciado *m*, -da *f*, egresado *m*, -da *f Amér* - **2.** *US* [of high school] ≃ bachiller *mf*. <> *comp US* [postgraduate] de posgrado. <> *vi* ['grædʒʊeɪt] - **1.** [with a degree]: **to graduate (from)** licenciarse (por), licensirse (en) *Amér*, egresar (de) *Amér* - **2.** *US* [from high school]: **to graduate (from)** ≃ obtener el título de bachiller (en) - **3.** [progress]: **to graduate from sthg (to)** pasar de algo (a).

graduated ['grædjʊeɪtɪd] *adj* graduado(da).

graduate school *n US* departamento *f* de posgraduados.

graduation [,grædʒʊ'eɪʃn] *n* graduación *f*, egreso *m Amér*.

graffiti [grə'fi:tɪ] *n (U)* pintada *f*.

graft [grɑ:ft] <> *n* - **1.** MED & BOT injerto *m* - **2.** *UK inf* [hard work] curro *m* muy duro - **3.** *US inf* [corruption] chanchullos *mpl*, corruptelas *fpl*. <> *vt* - **1.** MED & BOT: **to graft sthg (onto sthg)** injertar algo (en algo) - **2.** [idea, system]: **to graft sthg (onto sthg)** implantar algo (en algo).

grain [greɪn] *n* - **1.** [seed, granule] grano *m* - **2.** *(U)* [crop] cereales *mpl* - **3.** *fig* [small amount] pizca *f* - **4.** [pattern] veta *f*; **to go against the grain** ir contra natura.

gram, gramme [græm] *n* gramo *m*.

grammar ['græmə'] *n* gramática *f*.

grammar checker *n* COMPUT corrector *m* de gramática.

grammar school *n* [in UK] *colegio subvencionado para mayores de once años con un programa de asignaturas tradicional*; [in US] escuela *f* primaria.

grammatical [grə'mætɪkl] *adj* - **1.** [of grammar] gramatical - **2.** [correct] (gramaticalmente) correcto(ta).

gramme [græm] *UK* = **gram**.

gramophone ['græməfəʊn] *dated* <> *n* gramófono *m*. <> *comp* de gramófono.

gran [græn] *n UK inf* abuelita *f*, yaya *f*, mamá *f* grande *Méx*.

Granada [grə'nɑ:də] *n* Granada.

granary ['grænərɪ] *(pl* -ies) *n* granero *m*.

grand [grænd] <> *adj* - **1.** [impressive] grandioso(sa) - **2.** [ambitious] ambicioso(sa) - **3.** [important] distinguido(da) - **4.** *inf dated* [excellent] fenomenal. <> *n inf* [thousand pounds or dollars]: **a grand** mil libras/dólares; **five grand** cinco mil libras/dólares.

Grand Canyon *n*: the **Grand Canyon** el Gran Cañón.

grandchild ['grænt∫aɪld] *(pl* -children [-,t∫ɪldrən]) *n* nieto *m*, -ta *f*.

grand(d)ad ['grændæd] *n inf* abuelito *m*, yayo *m*, papá *m* grande *Méx*.

granddaughter ['græn,dɔ:tə'] *n* nieta *f*.

grand duke *n* gran duque *m*.

grandeur ['grændʒə'] *n* - **1.** [splendour] grandiosidad *f* - **2.** [status] grandeza *f*.

grandfather ['grænd,fɑ:ðə'] *n* abuelo *m*.

grandfather clock *n* reloj *m* de caja OR de pie.

grandiose ['grændɪəʊz] *adj pej* [building, design] fastuoso(sa), ostentoso(sa); [plan] ambicioso(sa).

grand jury *n US* jurado *m* de acusación.

grandma ['grænmɑ:] *n inf* abuelita *f*, yaya *f*, mamá *f* grande *Méx*.

grand master *n* gran maestro *m*.

grandmother ['græn,mʌðə'] *n* abuela *f*.

Grand National *n*: the **Grand National** *importante carrera anual de caballos que se celebra en Aintree*.

grandpa ['grænpɑ:] *n inf* abuelito *m*, yayo *m*, papá *m* grande *Méx*.

grandparents ['græn,peərənts] *npl* abuelos *mpl*.

grand piano *n* piano *m* de cola.

grand prix [,grɒn'pri:] *(pl* **grands prix** [,grɒn'pri:]) *n* gran premio *m*, grand prix *m*.

grand slam *n* SPORT [in tennis] gran slam *m*; [in rugby] gran slam *m*.

grandson ['grænsʌn] *n* nieto *m*.

grandstand ['grændstænd] *n* tribuna *f*.

grand total *n* [total number] cantidad *f* total; [total sum, cost] importe *m* total.

granite ['grænɪt] *n* granito *m*.

granny ['grænɪ] *(pl* -ies) *n inf* abuelita *f*, yaya *f*, mamá *f* grande *Méx*.

granny flat *n UK alojamiento independiente que forma parte de una vivienda (concebido para un familiar anciano)*.

granola [grə'nəʊlə] *n US* muesli *m* de avena.

grant [grɑ:nt] <> *n* subvención *f*; [for study] beca *f*. <> *vt fml* - **1.** [gen] conceder; **to take sthg/sb for granted** no apreciar algo/a alguien en lo que vale; **it is taken for granted that...** se da por sentado que... - **2.** [admit - truth, logic] admitir, aceptar; **I grant (that)...** admito que...

granulated sugar ['grænjʊleɪtɪd-] *n* azúcar *m* granulado.

granule ['grænju:l] *n* gránulo *m*.

grape [greɪp] *n* uva *f*; **a bunch of grapes** un racimo de uvas.

grapefruit ['greɪpfru:t] *(pl* **grapefruit** OR -s) *n* pomelo *m*, toronja *f Amér*.

grape picking [-'pɪkɪŋ] *n (U)* vendimia *f*.

grapevine ['greɪpvaɪn] *n* - **1.** [plant] vid *f*; [against wall] parra *f* - **2.** [information channel]: **I heard on the grapevine that...** me ha dicho un pajarito que...

graph [grɑːf] *n* gráfico *m*, gráfica *f*.

graphic ['græfɪk] *adj lit & fig* gráfico(ca).
➤ **graphics** *npl* - **1.** [pictures] ilustraciones *fpl* - **2.** COMPUT gráficos *mpl*.

graphic design *n* diseño *m* gráfico.

graphic designer *n* grafista *mf*, diseñador gráfico *m*, diseñadora gráfica *f*.

graphic equalizer *n* ecualizador *m* gráfico.

graphics card *n* COMPUT tarjeta *f* gráfica.

graphite ['græfaɪt] *n* grafito *m*.

graphology [græ'fɒlədʒɪ] *n* grafología *f*.

graph paper *n* (U) papel *m* cuadriculado.

grapple ['græpl] ➤ **grapple with** *vt insep* - **1.** [person] forcejear con - **2.** [problem] esforzarse por resolver.

grappling iron ['græplɪŋ-] *n* rezón *m*.

grasp [grɑːsp] ⬦ *n* - **1.** [grip] agarre *m*, asimiento *m* - **2.** [power to achieve]: **in OR within sb's grasp** al alcance de alguien - **3.** [understanding] comprensión *f*; **to have a good grasp of sthg** dominar algo. ⬦ *vt* - **1.** [grip, seize] agarrar, asir - **2.** [understand] comprender - **3.** [opportunity] aprovechar.

grasping ['grɑːspɪŋ] *adj pej* avaro(ra), codicioso(sa).

grass [grɑːs] ⬦ *n* - **1.** [plant] hierba *f*, pasto *m* *Amér*, zacate *f* *Méx*; [lawn] césped *m*; [pasture] pasto *m*, pasto *m* *Amér*, grama *f* *Amér C & Ven*; **'keep off the grass'** 'prohibido pisar el césped' - **2.** *inf* [marijuana] hierba *f*, maría *f*. ⬦ *vi* *UK inf*: **to grass (on sb)** chivarse (de alguien) *Esp*, delatar (a alguien) *Amér*.

grasshopper ['grɑːs,hɒpəʳ] *n* saltamontes *m inv*.

grassland ['grɑːslænd] *n* pastos *mpl*, pastizal *m*.

grass roots ⬦ *npl* bases *fpl*. ⬦ *comp* de base.

grass snake *n* culebra *f*.

grassy ['grɑːsɪ] (*comp* **-ier**, *superl* **-iest**) *adj* cubierto(ta) de hierba.

grate [greɪt] ⬦ *n* parrilla *f*, rejilla *f*. ⬦ *vt* rallar. ⬦ *vi* rechinar, chirriar; **to grate on sb's nerves** poner a alguien los nervios de punta.

grateful ['greɪtfʊl] *adj* [gen] agradecido(da); [smile, letter] de agradecimiento; **to be grateful to sb (for sthg)** estar agradecido a alguien (por algo); **I'm very grateful to you** te lo agradezco mucho; **I'd be grateful if you could do it by tomorrow** te agradecería que lo hicieras para mañana.

gratefully ['greɪtfʊlɪ] *adv* con agradecimiento.

grater ['greɪtəʳ] *n* rallador *m*.

gratification [,grætɪfɪ'keɪʃn] *n* satisfacción *f*.

gratify ['grætɪfaɪ] (*pt & pp* **-ied**) *vt* - **1.** [please - person]: **to be gratified** estar satisfecho(cha) - **2.** [satisfy - wish] satisfacer.

gratifying ['grætɪfaɪɪŋ] *adj* satisfactorio(ria), gratificante.

grating ['greɪtɪŋ] ⬦ *adj* chirriante. ⬦ *n* [grille] reja *f*, enrejado *m*.

gratitude ['grætɪtjuːd] *n* (U): **gratitude (to sb for)** agradecimiento *m* OR gratitud *f* (a alguien por).

gratuitous [grə'tjuːɪtəs] *adj fml* gratuito(ta).

gratuity [grə'tjuːɪtɪ] (*pl* **-ies**) *n fml* [tip] propina *f*.

grave [greɪv] ⬦ *adj* grave. ⬦ *n* sepultura *f*, tumba *f*; **he must be turning in his grave!** ¡si levantara la cabeza!

grave accent [grɑːv-] *n* acento *m* grave.

gravedigger ['greɪv,dɪgəʳ] *n* sepulturero *m*, -ra *f*.

gravel ['grævl] ⬦ *n* grava *f*, gravilla *f*. ⬦ *comp* de grava OR gravilla.

gravelled *UK*, **graveled** *US* ['grævld] *adj* cubierto(ta) de grava OR gravilla.

gravestone ['greɪvstəʊn] *n* lápida *f* (sepulcral).

graveyard ['greɪvjɑːd] *n* cementerio *m*.

gravitate ['grævɪteɪt] *vi*: **to gravitate towards** [be attracted] verse atraído(da) por.

gravity ['grævɪtɪ] *n* gravedad *f*.

gravy ['greɪvɪ] *n* - **1.** (U) [meat juice] salsa *f* OR jugo *m* de carne - **2.** *US v inf* [easy money] pasta *f* fácil.

gravy boat *n* salsera *f*.

gravy train *n inf*: **the gravy train** el chollo del siglo.

gray *US* = **grey**.

graze [greɪz] ⬦ *vt* - **1.** [feed on] pacer OR pastar en - **2.** [cause to feed] apacentar - **3.** [skin, knee etc] rasguñar - **4.** [touch lightly] rozar. ⬦ *vi* pacer, pastar. ⬦ *n* rasguño *m*.

grease [griːs] ⬦ *n* grasa *f*. ⬦ *vt* engrasar.

grease gun *n* pistola *f* engrasadora.

greasepaint ['griːspeɪnt] *n* maquillaje *m* (de teatro).

greaseproof paper [,griː'spruːf-] *n* (U) *UK* papel *m* de cera *(para envolver)*.

greasy ['griːzɪ] (*comp* **-ier**, *superl* **-iest**) *adj* grasiento(ta); [inherently] graso(sa).

great [greɪt] ⬦ *adj* - **1.** [gen] grande; [heat] intenso(sa); **with great care** con mucho cuidado; **a great deal of...** un montón de... - **2.** *inf* [splendid] estupendo(da), fenomenal, chévere *Andes*; **we had a great time** lo pasamos en grande; **great!** ¡estupendo! ⬦ *adv*: **great big** enorme; **you great big coward!** ¡pero qué cobardica eres! ⬦ *n* grande *mf*.

Great Barrier Reef *n*: the Great Barrier Reef la Gran Barrera de Coral.

Great Bear *n*: the Great Bear la Osa Mayor.

Great Britain *n* Gran Bretaña.

greatcoat ['greɪtkəʊt] *n* gabán *m*.

Great Dane *n* gran danés *m*.

Greater ['greɪtəʳ] *adj*: **Greater London/ Manchester** el área metropolitana de Londres/Manchester.

great-grandchild *n* bisnieto *m*, -ta *f*.

great-grandfather *n* bisabuelo *m*.

great-grandmother *n* bisabuela *f*.

Great Lakes *npl*: the Great Lakes los Grandes Lagos.

greatly ['greɪtlɪ] *adv* enormemente.

greatness ['greɪtnɪs] *n* grandeza *f*.

Great Wall of China *n*: the Great Wall of China la Gran Muralla China.

Great War *n*: the Great War HIST la Gran Guerra, la Primera Guerra Mundial.

Grecian ['griːʃn] *adj* griego(ga).

Greece [griːs] *n* Grecia.

greed [griːd] *n (U)*: **greed (for)** [food] glotonería *f* (con); [money] codicia *f* (de); [power] ambición *f* (de).

greedily ['griːdɪlɪ] *adv* con avidez.

greedy ['griːdɪ] (*comp* **-ier,** *superl* **-iest**) *adj* - **1.** [for food] glotón(ona) - **2.** [for money, power]: **greedy for** codicioso(sa) OR ávido(da) de.

Greek [griːk] ⬦ *adj* griego(ga); **the Greek Islands** las islas griegas. ⬦ *n* - **1.** [person] griego *m*, -ga *f* - **2.** [language] griego *m*.

green [griːn] ⬦ *adj* - **1.** [gen] verde - **2.** [environmentalist] verde, ecologista - **3.** *inf* [inexperienced] novato(ta) - **4.** *inf* [jealous]: **green (with envy)** muerto(ta) de envidia - **5.** *inf* [ill, pale] pálido(da). ⬦ *n* - **1.** [colour] verde *m*; **in green** de verde - **2.** [in village] parque *m* comunal - **3.** [in golf] green *m*.

⬦ **Green** *n* POL verde *mf*, ecologista *mf*; **the Greens** los verdes.

⬦ **greens** *npl* [vegetables] verdura *f*.

greenback ['griːnbæk] *n* US *inf* billete *m* (*dólar estadounidense*).

green bean *n* judía *f* verde, ejote *m* Amér C & Méx, chaucha *f* R Plata, vainita *f* Ven, poroto *m* verde Chile, habichuela *f* Col.

green belt *n* UK cinturón *m* verde.

Green Beret *n* US *inf*: the Green Berets los boinas verdes.

green card *n* - **1.** UK [for vehicle] *seguro que cubre a los conductores en el extranjero* - **2.** US [work permit] permiso *m* de trabajo.

Green Card

Para vivir y trabajar en Estados Unidos, todo ciudadano extranjero necesita el documento llamado **Green Card** ("tarjeta verde"), si bien en la actualidad ya no es de dicho color. El proceso para obtener este permiso de residencia permanente es largo y complicado. Se puede conceder a familiares directos de ciudadanos estadounidenses (como por ejemplo, esposos), a refugiados o asilados políticos que lo hayan sido desde hace al menos un año y a trabajadores con un contrato indefinido (o patrocinados por su empresa). Asimismo, existe el sistema llamado informalmente "Green Card Lottery", que, mediante un programa informático aleatorio, concede 50.000 permisos a ciudadanos de países con un nivel bajo de inmigración a EE UU.

greenery ['griːnərɪ] *n* follaje *m*, vegetación *f*.

green fingers *npl* UK: **to have green fingers** tener dotes para la jardinería.

greenfly ['griːnflaɪ] (*pl* greenfly OR **-ies**) *n* pulgón *m*.

greengrocer ['griːnˌgrəʊsəʳ] *n* verdulero *m*, -ra *f*; **greengrocer's (shop)** verdulería *f*.

greenhorn ['griːnhɔːn] *n* US - **1.** [newcomer] recién llegado *m*, -da *f* - **2.** [novice] novato *m*, -ta *f*.

greenhouse ['griːnhaʊs, *pl* -haʊzɪz] *n* invernadero *m*.

greenhouse effect *n*: the greenhouse effect el efecto invernadero.

greenhouse gas *n* gas *m* invernadero.

greenish ['griːnɪʃ] *adj* verdoso(sa).

greenkeeper ['griːnˌkiːpəʳ] *n persona encargada del cuidado de un campo de golf*.

Greenland ['griːnlənd] *n* Groenlandia.

Greenlander ['griːnləndəʳ] *n* groenlandés *m*, -esa *f*.

green light *n fig*: **to give sb the green light** dar luz verde a alguien.

green paper *n* POL libro *m* verde.

Green Party *n*: the Green Party los verdes.

green salad *n* ensalada *f* verde.

green thumb *n* US: **to have a green thumb** tener dotes para la jardinería.

greet [griːt] *vt* - **1.** [say hello to] saludar - **2.** [receive] recibir - **3.** [subj: sight, smell]: **he was greeted by total chaos** se encontró con un auténtico caos.

greeting ['griːtɪŋ] *n* saludo *m*.

greetings *npl*: Christmas/birthday greetings! ¡feliz navidad/cumpleaños!; **greetings from...** recuerdos de...

greetings card *UK* ['gri:tıŋz-], **greeting card** *US* n tarjeta f de felicitación.

gregarious [grı'geərıəs] *adj* [person] sociable; [animal] gregario(ria).

gremlin ['gremlın] n *inf* duende m.

Grenada [grə'neıdə] n Granada.

grenade [grə'neıd] n: **(hand) grenade** granada f (de mano).

Grenadian [grə'neıdjən] <> *adj* granadino(na). <> n granadino m, -na f.

grenadier [,grenə'dıə'] n granadero m.

grenadine ['grenədi:n] n granadina f.

grew [gru:] *pt* ⊳ **grow**.

grey *UK*, **gray** *US* [greı] <> *adj lit & fig* gris; **a grey hair** una cana; **he is going grey** [greyhaired] le están saliendo canas. <> n gris m; **in grey** de gris.

grey area n tema m oscuro, área f difusa.

grey-haired [-'heəd] *adj* canoso(sa).

greyhound ['greıhaʊnd] n galgo m.

greying *UK*, **graying** *US* ['greııŋ] *adj* canoso(sa).

grey matter n *(U)* - **1.** MED materia f gris - **2.** *inf* [brain power] cerebro m.

grey squirrel n ardilla f gris.

grid [grıd] n - **1.** [grating] reja f, enrejado m - **2.** [system of squares] cuadrícula f.

griddle ['grıdl] n plancha f.

gridiron ['grıd,aıən] n - **1.** [in cooking] parrilla f - **2.** *US* [game] fútbol m americano; [field] *campo de fútbol americano*.

gridlock ['grıdlɒk] n *US* embotellamiento m, atasco m.

grief [gri:f] n *(U)* - **1.** [sorrow] dolor m, pesar m - **2.** *inf* [trouble] problemas mpl

▸▸ **to come to grief** [person] sufrir un percance; [plans] irse al traste; **good grief!** ¡madre mía!

grief-stricken *adj* desconsolado(da), apesadumbrado(da).

grievance ['gri:vns] n (motivo m de) queja f.

grieve [gri:v] <> *vt*: **it grieves me to say it** *fml* me apena decirlo. <> *vi*: **to grieve (for)** llorar (por).

grieving ['gri:vıŋ] n *(U)* aflicción f.

grievous ['gri:vəs] *adj fml* grave.

grievous bodily harm n *(U)* lesiones fpl graves.

grievously ['gri:vəslı] *adv fml* gravemente.

grill [grıl] <> n - **1.** [on cooker] grill m; [for barbecue] parrilla f - **2.** [food] parrillada f. <> *vt*

- **1.** [on cooker] asar al grill; [on barbecue] asar a la parrilla - **2.** *inf* [interrogate] someter a un duro interrogatorio.

grille [grıl] n [on radiator, machine] rejilla f; [on window, door] reja f.

grim [grım] (*comp* **-mer**, *superl* **-mest**) *adj*

- **1.** [expression] adusto(ta); [determination] inexorable - **2.** [place, facts, prospect] desolador(ra).

grimace [grı'meıs] <> n mueca f. <> *vi* hacer una mueca.

grime [graım] n mugre f.

grimly ['grımlı] *adv* - **1.** [resolutely] con determinación - **2.** [mirthlessly] lúgubremente.

grimy ['graımı] (*comp* **-ier**, *superl* **-iest**) *adj* mugriento(ta).

grin [grın] <> n sonrisa f (abierta). <> *vi* (*pt & pp* **-ned**, *cont* **-ning**): **to grin (at)** sonreír (a); **to grin and bear it** poner al mal tiempo buena cara.

grind [graınd] <> *vt* (*pt & pp* **ground**)

- **1.** [crush] moler - **2.** [press]: **to grind sthg into sthg** aplastar algo contra algo. <> *vi* (*pt & pp* **ground**) [scrape] rechinar, chirriar. <> n - **1.** [hard, boring work] rutina f; **what a grind!** ¡qué lata! - **2.** *US inf* [hard worker] currante mf.

▸ **grind down** *vt sep* [oppress] oprimir, acogotar.

▸ **grind up** *vt sep* pulverizar, hacer polvo.

grinder ['graındə'] n molinillo m.

grinding ['graındıŋ] *adj* - **1.** [unbearable] insoportable - **2.** [poverty] absoluto(ta).

grip [grıp] <> n - **1.** [grasp, hold]: **to have a grip (on sthg/sb)** tener (algo/a alguien) bien agarrado - **2.** [control, domination]: **grip on** control m de, dominio m de; **in the grip of sthg** en las garras de algo, dominado(da) por algo; **to get to grips with** llegar a controlar; **to get a grip on o.s.** calmarse, controlarse; **to lose one's grip** *fig* perder el control - **3.** [adhesion] sujeción f, adherencia f - **4.** [handle] asidero m - **5.** [bag] bolsa f de viaje. <> *vt* (*pt & pp* **-ped**, *cont* **-ping**) - **1.** [grasp] agarrar, asir; [hand] apretar; [weapon] empuñar - **2.** [seize] apoderarse de. <> *vi* (*pt & pp* **-ped**, *cont* **-ping**) adherirse.

gripe [graıp] *inf* <> n [complaint] queja f. <> *vi*: **to gripe (about)** quejarse (de).

gripping ['grıpıŋ] *adj* apasionante.

grisly ['grızlı] (*comp* **-ier**, *superl* **-iest**) *adj* [horrible, macabre] espeluznante, horripilante.

grist [grıst] n: **it's all grist to the mill** todo vale *OR* sirve.

gristle ['grısl] n cartílago m, ternilla f.

gristly ['grıslı] (*comp* **-ier**, *superl* **-iest**) *adj* cartilaginoso(sa).

grit [grɪt] ◇ *n* - **1.** [stones] grava *f*; [sand, dust] arena *f* - **2.** *inf* [courage] valor *m*. ◇ *vt* (*pt & pp* **-ted**, *cont* **-ting**) echar arena en (*las calles*).

➡ **grits** *npl* *US* granos *mpl* de maíz molidos.

gritter ['grɪtər] *n* vehículo que esparce arena o gravilla por las carreteras en tiempos de heladas.

gritty ['grɪtɪ] (*comp* **-ier**, *superl* **-iest**) *adj* - **1.** [stony] arenoso(sa) - **2.** *inf* [brave] valiente.

grizzled ['grɪzld] *adj* canoso(sa).

grizzly ['grɪzlɪ] (*pl* **-ies**) *n*: **grizzly (bear)** oso *m* pardo.

groan [grəʊn] ◇ *n* gemido *m*, quejido *m*. ◇ *vi* - **1.** [moan] gemir - **2.** [creak] crujir.

grocer ['grəʊsər] *n* tendero *m*, -ra *f*, abarrotero *m*, -ra *f* *Amér*; **grocer's (shop)** tienda *f* de comestibles *OR* ultramarinos, supermercado *m*, abarrotería *f* *Amér C*.

groceries ['grəʊsərɪz] *npl* [foods] comestibles *mpl*, abarrotes *mpl* *Amér*.

grocery ['grəʊsərɪ] (*pl* **-ies**) *n* *US* [shop] tienda *f* de comestibles *OR* ultramarinos, supermercado *m*, abarrotería *f* *Amér*.

groggy ['grɒgɪ] (*comp* **-ier**, *superl* **-iest**) *adj* atontado(da).

groin [grɔɪn] *n* ingle *f*.

groom [gru:m] ◇ *n* - **1.** [of horses] mozo *m* de cuadra - **2.** [bridegroom] novio *m*. ◇ *vt* - **1.** [brush] cepillar, almohazar - **2.** [prepare]: **to groom sb (for sthg)** preparar a alguien (para algo).

groove [gru:v] *n* [deep line] ranura *f*; [in record] surco *m*.

grope [grəʊp] ◇ *vt* - **1.** [try to find]: **to grope one's way** andar a tientas - **2.** [fondle] toquetear, meter mano a. ◇ *vi*: **to grope (about) for sthg** [object] buscar algo a tientas; [solution, remedy] buscar algo a ciegas.

gross [grəʊs] ◇ *adj* - **1.** [total] bruto(ta) - **2.** *fml* [serious, inexcusable] grave, intolerable - **3.** [coarse, vulgar] basto(ta), vulgar - **4.** *inf* [obese] obeso(sa) - **5.** *inf* [revolting] asqueroso(sa). ◇ *n* (*pl* **gross** *OR* **-es**) gruesa *f*. ◇ *vt* ganar en bruto.

gross domestic product *n* producto *m* interior bruto.

grossly ['grəʊslɪ] *adv* [seriously] enormemente.

gross national product *n* producto *m* nacional bruto.

gross profit *n* beneficio *m* bruto.

grotesque [grəʊ'tesk] *adj* grotesco(ca).

grotto ['grɒtəʊ] (*pl* **-es** *OR* **-s**) *n* gruta *f*.

grotty ['grɒtɪ] (*comp* **-ier**, *superl* **-iest**) *adj* *UK* *inf* asqueroso(sa), cochambroso(sa).

grouchy ['graʊtʃɪ] (*comp* **-ier**, *superl* **-iest**) *adj* *inf* refunfuñón(ona).

ground [graʊnd] ◇ *pt & pp* ⊳ **grind**. ◇ *n* - **1.** [surface of earth] suelo *m*; [soil] tierra *f*; **above/below ground** sobre/bajo tierra; **on the ground** en el suelo; **to be thin on the ground** ser escaso(sa); **to get sthg off the ground** *fig* poner algo en marcha - **2.** [area of land] terreno *m*; *SPORT* campo *m* - **3.** [subject area] terreno *m*; **to be on familiar ground** pisar terreno conocido; **to break fresh** *OR* **new ground** abrir nuevas fronteras - **4.** [advantage]: **to gain/lose ground** ganar/perder terreno

▸▸▸ **to cut the ground from under sb's feet** tomar la delantera a alguien; **to go to ground** esconderse, refugiarse; **to run sthg/sb to ground** encontrar (finalmente) algo/a alguien; **to stand one's ground** mantenerse firme. ◇ *vt* - **1.** [base]: **to be grounded on** *OR* **in sthg** basarse en algo - **2.** [aircraft, pilot] hacer permanecer en tierra - **3.** *US* *inf* [child] castigar sin salir - **4.** *US ELEC*: **to be grounded** estar conectado(da) a tierra.

➡ **grounds** *npl* - **1.** [reason]: **grounds (for sthg/for doing sthg)** motivos *mpl* (para algo/para hacer algo); **on the grounds of** por motivos; **on the grounds that** aduciendo que, debido a que - **2.** [around house] jardines *mpl*; [of public building] terrenos *mpl* - **3.** [of coffee] posos *mpl* - **4.** [area] zona *f*.

ground beef *n* *US* carne *f* picada.

groundbreaking ['graʊnd,breɪkɪŋ] *adj* pionero(ra).

ground control *n* control *m* de tierra.

ground cover *n* maleza *f*.

ground crew, ground staff *n* personal *m* de tierra.

ground floor *n* planta *f* baja; **ground floor flat** (piso *m*) bajo *m*.

grounding ['graʊndɪŋ] *n*: **grounding (in)** base *f* (de), conocimientos *mpl* básicos (de).

groundless ['graʊndlɪs] *adj* infundado(da), sin fundamento.

ground level *n*: **at ground level** a nivel del suelo.

groundnut ['graʊndnʌt] *n* cacahuete *m*.

ground plan *n* [of building] planta *f*.

ground rent *n* alquiler pagado al propietario de un terreno durante largo tiempo con el fin de edificar.

ground rules *npl* reglas *fpl* básicas.

groundsheet ['graʊndʃi:t] *n* lona *f* impermeable (*para camping etc*).

groundskeeper ['graʊnzki:pər] *n* *SPORT* jardinero *m*, -ra *f*.

groundsman ['graʊndzmən] (*pl* **-men** [-mən]) *n* *UK* cuidador *m* del campo *OR* terreno de juego.

ground staff n - **1.** [at sports ground] personal m al cargo de las instalaciones - **2.** UK = **ground crew**.

groundswell ['graundswel] n [of opinion etc] oleada f, ola f.

groundwork ['graundwɜːk] n (U) trabajo m preliminar.

group [gruːp] ⬦ n grupo m. ⬦ vt agrupar. ⬦ vi: **to group (together)** agruparse.

groupie ['gruːpɪ] n inf groupie mf.

group practice n gabinete m médico.

group therapy n terapia f de grupo.

grouse [graus] ⬦ n (pl grouse OR -s) - **1.** [bird] urogallo m - **2.** inf [complaint] queja f. ⬦ vi inf quejarse.

grove [grəuv] n [of trees] arboleda f; **lemon grove** limonar m.

➤ **Grove** n [in street names] nombre de ciertas calles británicas.

grovel ['grɒvl] (UK, pt & pp -led, cont -ling) (US, pt & pp -ed, cont -ing) vi lit & fig: **to grovel (to)** arrastrarse (ante).

grow [grəu] ⬦ vi (pt grew, pp grown) - **1.** [gen] crecer - **2.** [become] volverse, ponerse; **to grow dark** oscurecer; **to grow old** envejecer - **3.** [come]: **to grow to do sthg** llegar a hacer algo. ⬦ vt (pt grew, pp grown) - **1.** [plants] cultivar - **2.** [hair, beard] dejarse crecer.

➤ **grow apart** vi distanciarse.

➤ **grow into** vt insep - **1.** [clothes, shoes] crecer lo suficiente para poder llevar - **2.** [become, turn into] convertirse en.

➤ **grow on** vt insep inf: **it's growing on me** me gusta cada vez más.

➤ **grow out** vi [perm, dye] irse, desaparecer.

➤ **grow out of** vt insep - **1.** [become too big for]: **he has grown out of his clothes** se le ha quedado pequeña la ropa - **2.** [lose - habit] perder; **he'll grow out of it** ya se le pasará.

➤ **grow up** vi crecer; **when I grow up** cuando sea mayor; **I grew up in Ireland** me crié en Irlanda; **grow up!** ¡no seas niño!

grower ['grəuə'] n cultivador m, -ra f.

growl [graul] ⬦ n [of dog, person] gruñido m; [of engine] rugido m. ⬦ vi [dog, person] gruñir; [engine] rugir.

grown [grəun] ⬦ pp ⮑ **grow**. ⬦ adj adulto(ta).

grown-up ⬦ adj [mature] maduro(ra). ⬦ n persona f mayor.

growth [grəuθ] n - **1.** [gen]: **growth (of OR in)** crecimiento m (de) - **2.** MED tumor m.

growth rate n tasa f de crecimiento.

grub [grʌb] n - **1.** [insect] larva f, gusano m - **2.** inf [food] manduca f, papeo m.

grubby ['grʌbɪ] (comp -ier, superl -iest) adj sucio(cia), mugriento(ta).

grudge [grʌdʒ] ⬦ n rencor m; **to bear sb a grudge, to bear a grudge against sb** guardar rencor a alguien. ⬦ vt: **to grudge sb sthg** conceder algo a alguien a regañadientes; **to grudge doing sthg** hacer algo a regañadientes.

grudging ['grʌdʒɪŋ] adj concedido(da) a regañadientes.

grudgingly ['grʌdʒɪŋlɪ] adv a regañadientes, de mala gana.

gruelling UK, **grueling** US ['gruəlɪŋ] adj agotador(ra).

gruesome ['gruːsəm] adj espantoso(sa), horripilante.

gruff [grʌf] adj - **1.** [hoarse] bronco(ca) - **2.** [rough, unfriendly] hosco(ca), brusco(ca).

grumble ['grʌmbl] ⬦ n - **1.** [complaint] queja f - **2.** [of stomach] gruñido m (de tripas). ⬦ vi - **1.** [complain] quejarse, refunfuñar; **to grumble about sthg** quejarse de algo, refunfuñar por algo - **2.** [stomach] gruñir, hacer ruido.

grumbling ['grʌmblɪŋ] n (U) - **1.** [complaining] refunfuñeo m, quejas fpl - **2.** [of stomach] gruñidos mpl (de las tripas).

grumpy ['grʌmpɪ] (comp -ier, superl -iest) adj inf gruñón(ona).

grunge [grʌndʒ] n MUS grunge m.

grunt [grʌnt] ⬦ n gruñido m. ⬦ vi gruñir.

G-string n taparrabos m inv, tanga m.

Guadeloupe [ˌgwaːdəˈluːp] n Guadalupe.

guarantee [ˌgærənˈtiː] ⬦ n garantía f; **under guarantee** en periodo de garantía. ⬦ vt garantizar.

guarantor [ˌgærənˈtɔːr] n garante mf.

guard [gaːd] ⬦ n - **1.** [person] guardia mf; [in prison] carcelero m, -ra f - **2.** [group of guards, operation] guardia f; **to be on/stand guard** estar de/hacer guardia; **to be on (one's) guard (against)** estar en guardia OR alerta (contra); **to catch sb off guard** coger a alguien desprevenido - **3.** UK RAIL jefe m de tren - **4.** [protective device - for body] protector m; [- for machine] cubierta f protectora. ⬦ vt - **1.** [protect, hide] guardar - **2.** [prevent from escaping] vigilar.

➤ **guard against** vt insep evitar.

guard dog n perro m guardián.

guarded ['gaːdɪd] adj cauteloso(sa).

guardian ['gaːdjən] n - **1.** [of child] tutor m, -ra f - **2.** [protector] guardián m, -ana f, protector m, -ra f.

guardian angel n ángel m custodio OR de la guarda.

guardianship ['gaːdjənʃɪp] n tutela f.

guardrail ['gaːdreɪl] n US [on road] barrera f de protección.

guardsman ['gɑːdzmən] (*pl* **-men** [-mən]) *n* [in UK] guardia *m* (de la Guardia Real).

guard's van *n* UK furgón *m* de cola.

Guatemala [ˌgwɑːtə'mɑːlə] *n* Guatemala.

Guatemalan [ˌgwɑːtə'mɑːlən] ⟨> *adj* guatemalteco(ca). ⟨> *n* guatemalteco *m*, -ca *f*.

guava ['gwɑːvə] *n* guayaba *f*.

guerilla [gə'rɪlə] = **guerrilla**.

Guernsey ['gɜːnzɪ] *n* - **1.** [place] Guernsey - **2.** [sweater] jersey *m* grueso de lana - **3.** [cow] vaca *f* de Guernsey.

guerrilla, guerilla [gə'rɪlə] *n* guerrillero *m*, -ra *f*; **urban guerrilla** guerrillero urbano.

guerrilla warfare *n* (U) guerra *f* de guerrillas.

guess [ges] ⟨> *n* suposición *f*, conjetura *f*; **to take a guess** intentar adivinar; **it's anybody's guess** vete a saber, ¿quién sabe? ⟨> *vt* adivinar; **guess what?** ¿sabes qué? ⟨> *vi* - **1.** [conjecture] adivinar; **to guess at sthg** tratar de adivinar algo; **to guess right** acertar; **to guess wrong** equivocarse; **to keep sb guessing** tener a alguien en la incertidumbre - **2.** [suppose]: **I guess (so)** supongo OR me imagino que sí.

guesstimate ['gestɪmət] *n inf* cálculo *m* a bulto.

guesswork ['ges' wɜːk] *n* (U) conjeturas *fpl*, suposiciones *fpl*.

guest [gest] *n* - **1.** [at home, on programme] invitado *m*, -da *f* - **2.** [at hotel] huésped *mf* ▸▸▸ **be my guest!** ¡pues claro!

guesthouse ['gesthaʊs, *pl* -haʊzɪz] *n* casa *f* de huéspedes.

guest of honour *n* invitado *m*, -da *f* de honor.

guestroom ['gestrʊm] *n* cuarto *m* de los invitados.

guest star *n* estrella *f* invitada.

guffaw [gʌ'fɔː] ⟨> *n* risotada *f*, carcajada *f*. ⟨> *vi* reírse a carcajadas.

Guiana [gaɪ'ænə] *n* (la) Guayana.

guidance ['gaɪdəns] *n* (U) - **1.** [help] orientación *f*, consejos *mpl* - **2.** [leadership] dirección *f*; **under the guidance of** bajo la dirección de.

guide [gaɪd] ⟨> *n* - **1.** [person] guía *mf* - **2.** [book] guía *f*. ⟨> *vt* - **1.** [show by leading] guiar - **2.** [control] conducir, dirigir - **3.** [influence]: **to be guided by** guiarse por.
▸▸ **Guides** *n* = **Girl Guides**.

guide book *n* guía *f*.

guided missile ['gaɪdɪd-] *n* misil *m* teledirigido.

guide dog *n* perro *m* lazarillo.

guidelines ['gaɪdlaɪnz] *npl* directrices *fpl*.

guiding ['gaɪdɪŋ] *adj* [principle] rector(ra).

guild [gɪld] *n* - **1.** HIST gremio *m* - **2.** [association] corporación *f*.

guildhall ['gɪldhɔːl] *n* sede de un gremio.

guile [gaɪl] *n* (U) astucia *f*.

guileless ['gaɪllɪs] *adj liter* inocente, candoroso(sa).

guillemot ['gɪlɪmɒt] *n* arao *m* común.

guillotine ['gɪlə,tiːn] ⟨> *n* - **1.** [gen] guillotina *f* - **2.** UK POL estipulación de un tiempo determinado para debatir un proyecto de ley. ⟨> *vt* guillotinar.

guilt [gɪlt] *n* - **1.** [remorse] culpa *f* - **2.** LAW culpabilidad *f*.

guiltily ['gɪltɪlɪ] *adv* con aire de culpabilidad.

guilty ['gɪltɪ] (*comp* **-ier**, *superl* **-iest**) *adj* - **1.** [gen]: **guilty (of)** culpable (de); **to be found guilty/not guilty** ser declarado(da) culpable/inocente; **to have a guilty conscience** tener remordimientos de conciencia - **2.** [secret, thought] que causa remordimiento.

guinea ['gɪnɪ] *n* guinea *f*.

Guinea ['gɪnɪ] *n* Guinea.

Guinea-Bissau [-bɪ'saʊ] *n* Guinea-Bissau.

guinea fowl *n* gallina *f* de Guinea.

guinea pig ['gɪnɪ-] *n lit & fig* conejillo *m* de Indias.

guise [gaɪz] *n fml* apariencia *f*.

guitar [gɪ'tɑːr] *n* guitarra *f*.

guitarist [gɪ'tɑːrɪst] *n* guitarrista *mf*.

gulch [gʌltʃ] *n* US barranco *m*.

gulf [gʌlf] *n* - **1.** [sea] golfo *m* - **2.** [chasm] sima *f*, abismo *m* - **3.** [big difference]: **gulf (between)** abismo *m* (entre).
▸▸ **Gulf** *n*: **the Gulf** el Golfo.

Gulf Stream *n*: **the Gulf Stream** la corriente del Golfo.

gull [gʌl] *n* gaviota *f*.

gullet ['gʌlɪt] *n* esófago *m*.

gullible ['gʌləbl] *adj* crédulo(la).

gully ['gʌlɪ] (*pl* **-ies**) *n* barranco *m*.

gulp [gʌlp] ⟨> *n* trago *m*. ⟨> *vt* [liquid] tragarse; [food] engullir. ⟨> *vi* tragar saliva.
▸▸ **gulp down** *vt sep* [liquid] tragarse; [food] engullir.

gum [gʌm] ⟨> *n* - **1.** [chewing gum] chicle *m* - **2.** [adhesive] pegamento *m* - **3.** ANAT encía *f*. ⟨> *vt* (*pt & pp* **-med**, *cont* **-ming**) pegar, engomar.

gumboil ['gʌmbɔɪl] *n* flemón *m*.

gumboots ['gʌmbuːts] *npl* UK botas *fpl* de agua OR de goma.

gumption ['gʌmpʃn] *n* (U) *inf* - **1.** [common sense] seso *m*, sentido *m* común - **2.** [determination] agallas *fpl*, coraje *m*.

gumshoe ['gʌmʃuː] *n* US *crime sl* sabueso *m*, polizonte *mf*.

gun [gʌn] *n* - **1.** [pistol] pistola *f*; [rifle] escopeta *f*, fusil *m*; [artillery] cañón *m*; **to stick to one's**

guns mantenerse en sus trece; **to jump the gun** adelantarse a los acontecimientos **- 2.** [tool] pistola *f*.

◆ **gun down** *vt sep* (*pt & pp* **-ned**, *cont* **-ning**) abatir (a tiros).

gunboat ['gʌnbəʊt] *n* lancha *f* cañonera, cañonero *m*.

gundog ['gʌndɒg] *n* perro *m* de caza.

gunfire ['gʌnfaɪəʳ] *n* (U) disparos *mpl*, tiroteo *m*.

gunge [gʌndʒ] *n* (U) UK *inf* porquería *f*.

gung-ho [,gʌŋ'həʊ] *adj* UK *inf* **- 1.** [overenthusiastic] demasiado entusiasta **- 2.** [jingoistic] belicoso(sa).

gunk [gʌŋk] *n inf* porquería *f*.

gunman ['gʌnmən] (*pl* **-men** [-mən]) *n* pistolero *m*.

gunner ['gʌnəʳ] *n* artillero *m*.

gunpoint ['gʌnpɔɪnt] *n*: **at gunpoint** a punta de pistola.

gunpowder ['gʌn,paʊdəʳ] *n* pólvora *f*.

gunrunning ['gʌn,rʌnɪŋ] *n* tráfico *m* de armas.

gunshot ['gʌnʃɒt] *n* tiro *m*, disparo *m*.

gunsmith ['gʌnsmɪθ] *n* armero *m*.

gurgle ['gɜːgl] ⟨⟩ *vi* **- 1.** [water] gorgotear **- 2.** [baby] gorjear. ⟨⟩ *n* **- 1.** [of water] gorgoteo *m* **- 2.** [of baby] gorjeo *m*.

guru ['gʊruː] *n lit & fig* gurú *m*.

gush [gʌʃ] ⟨⟩ *n* chorro *m*. ⟨⟩ *vt* chorrear. ⟨⟩ *vi* **- 1.** [flow out] chorrear, manar **- 2.** *pej* [enthuse] ser muy efusivo(va).

gushing ['gʌʃɪŋ] *adj pej* efusivo(va).

gusset ['gʌsɪt] *n* escudete *m*.

gust [gʌst] ⟨⟩ *n* ráfaga *f*, racha *f*. ⟨⟩ *vi* [wind] soplar racheado(da).

gusto ['gʌstəʊ] *n*: **with gusto** con deleite.

gut [gʌt] ⟨⟩ *n* **- 1.** MED intestino *m* **- 2.** [strong thread] sedal *m*. ⟨⟩ *vt* (*pt & pp* **-ted**, *cont* **-ting**) **- 1.** [animal] destripar; [fish] limpiar **- 2.** [subj: fire] destruir el interior de.

◆ **guts** *npl inf* **- 1.** [intestines] tripas *fpl*; **to hate sb's guts** odiar a alguien a muerte **- 2.** [courage] agallas *fpl*.

gut reaction *n* primer impulso *m*.

gutsy ['gʌtsɪ] *adj* con agallas.

gutter ['gʌtəʳ] *n* **- 1.** [ditch] cuneta *f* **- 2.** [on roof] canalón *m*.

guttering ['gʌtərɪŋ] *n* (U) canalones *mpl*.

gutter press *n pej* prensa *f* amarilla OR sensacionalista.

guttural ['gʌtərəl] *adj* gutural.

guv [gʌv] *n* UK *inf* jefe *m*.

guy [gaɪ] *n* **- 1.** *inf* [man] tipo *m*, tío *m*, chavo *m* Méx **- 2.** UK [dummy] *muñeco que se quema la noche de Guy Fawkes*.

Guyana [gaɪ'ænə] *n* Guyana.

Guy Fawkes' Night *n* UK *fiesta que se celebra el 5 de noviembre en que se encienden hogueras y se lanzan fuegos artificiales*.

guy rope *n* viento *m*, cuerda *f* (de tienda de campaña).

guzzle ['gʌzl] ⟨⟩ *vt* zamparse. ⟨⟩ *vi* zampar.

gym [dʒɪm] *n inf* **- 1.** [gymnasium] gimnasio *m* **- 2.** [exercises] gimnasia *f*.

gymkhana [dʒɪm'kɑːnə] *n* gincana *f*.

gymnasium [dʒɪm'neɪzjəm] (*pl* **-siums** OR **-sia** [-zjə]) *n* gimnasio *m*.

gymnast ['dʒɪmnæst] *n* gimnasta *mf*.

gymnastics [dʒɪm'næstɪks] *n* (U) gimnasia *f*.

gym shoes *npl* zapatillas *fpl* de gimnasia.

gymslip ['dʒɪm,slɪp] *n* UK bata *f* de colegio.

gynaecological UK, **gynecological** US [,gaɪnəkə'lɒdʒɪkl] *adj* ginecológico(ca).

gynaecologist UK, **gynecologist** US [,gaɪnə'kɒlədʒɪst] *n* ginecólogo *m*, -ga *f*.

gynaecology UK, **gynecology** US [,gaɪnə'kɒlədʒɪ] *n* ginecología *f*.

gyp [dʒɪp] ⟨⟩ *vt* US timar, estafar. ⟨⟩ *n* UK: **my knee has been giving me gyp** tengo la rodilla fastidiada.

gypsy ['dʒɪpsɪ] (*pl* **-ies**) = **gipsy**.

gyrate [dʒaɪ'reɪt] *vi* girar.

gyration [dʒaɪ'reɪʃn] *n* giro *m*, rotación *f*.

gyroscope ['dʒaɪrəskəʊp] *n* giroscopio *m*.

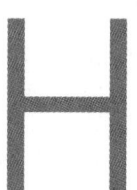

h (*pl* **h's** OR **hs**), **H** (*pl* **H's** OR **Hs**) [eɪtʃ] *n* [letter] h *f*, H *f*.

ha [hɑː] *excl* ¡ah!

habeas corpus [,heɪbjəs'kɔːpəs] *n* hábeas corpus *m*.

haberdashery ['hæbədæʃərɪ] (*pl* **-ies**) *n* **- 1.** UK [selling sewing materials] mercería *f* **- 2.** US [selling men's clothing] tienda *f* de ropa para caballeros.

habit ['hæbɪt] *n* **- 1.** [custom] costumbre *f*, hábito *m*; **to be in the habit of doing sthg** tener la costumbre de hacer algo; **to make a habit of sthg** tomar algo por costumbre; **to make a**

habit of doing sthg tener por costumbre hacer algo; **to have a drug habit** ser drogadicto(ta) **- 2.** [garment] hábito *m*.

habitable ['hæbɪtəbl] *adj* habitable.

habitat ['hæbɪtæt] *n* hábitat *m*.

habitation [hæbɪ'teɪʃn] *n* **- 1.** [occupation] ocupación *f*, habitación *f* **- 2.** [house] morada *f*.

habit-forming [-,fɔ:mɪŋ] *adj* que crea hábito.

habitual [hə'bɪtʃʊəl] *adj* **- 1.** [usual] habitual, acostumbrado(da) **- 2.** [smoker, gambler] empedernido(da).

habitually [hə'bɪtʃʊəlɪ] *adv* por costumbre, habitualmente.

hack [hæk] <> *n* **- 1.** *pej* [writer] escritorzuelo *m*, -la *f*; [journalist] gacetillero *m*, -ra *f* **- 2.** *US inf* [taxi] taxi *m*. <> *vt* **- 1.** [cut] cortar en tajos, acuchillar **- 2.** COMPUT piratear. <> *vi* [cut] dar tajos OR hachazos.

◆ **hack into** *vt insep* piratear.

◆ **hack through** *vt insep* [cut]: **to hack (one's way) through sthg** abrirse paso por OR a través de algo a hachazos.

hacker ['hækər] *n*: **(computer) hacker** pirata *mf* informático.

hacking ['hækɪŋ] *n* COMPUT piratería *f (informática)*.

hacking cough *n* tos *f* seca.

hackles ['hæklz] *npl* pelo o plumas del cuello de un animal; **to make sb's hackles rise** poner negro a alguien.

hackney cab, hackney carriage ['hæknɪ-] *n fml* [taxi] taxi *m*.

hackneyed ['hæknɪd] *adj pej* trillado(da), gastado(da).

hacksaw ['hæksɔ:] *n* sierra *f* para metales.

had *(weak form* [həd]*, strong form* [hæd]*) pt* & *pp* ⊳ **have**.

haddock ['hædək] *(pl* **haddock***) n* eglefino *m*.

hadn't ['hædnt] = **had not** ⊳ **have**.

haematology [,hi:mə'tɒlədʒɪ] = **hematology**.

haemoglobin [,hi:mə'gləʊbɪn] = **hemoglobin**.

haemophilia [,hi:mə'fɪlɪə] = **hemophilia**.

haemophiliac [,hi:mə'fɪlɪæk] = **hemophiliac**.

haemorrhage ['hemərɪdʒ] = **hemorrhage**.

haemorrhoids ['hemərɔɪdz] = **hemorrhoids**.

hag [hæg] *n pej* bruja *f*, arpía *f*.

haggard ['hægəd] *adj* ojeroso(sa).

haggis ['hægɪs] *n* plato típico escocés hecho con las asaduras del cordero.

haggle ['hægl] *vi*: **to haggle (with sb over** OR **about sthg)** regatear (algo con alguien).

Hague [heɪg] *n*: **The Hague** La Haya.

hail [heɪl] <> *n* **- 1.** METEOR granizo *m*, pedrisco *m* **- 2.** *fig* [large number] lluvia *f*. <> *vt* **- 1.** [call] llamar; [taxi] parar **- 2.** [acclaim]: **to**

hail sb as sthg aclamar a alguien algo; **to hail sthg as sthg** ensalzar algo catalogándolo de algo. <> *impers vb*: **it's hailing** está granizando.

hailstone ['heɪlstəʊn] *n* granizo *m*, piedra *f*.

hair [heər] *n* **- 1.** (U) [gen] pelo *m*; **to have short hair** tener el pelo corto; **to do one's hair** arreglarse el pelo; **to let one's hair down** [fig] soltarse el pelo; **to make sb's hair stand on end** ponerle a alguien los pelos de punta; **to split hairs** hilar muy fino, rizar el rizo **- 2.** [on person's skin] vello *m*.

hairbrush ['heəbrʌʃ] *n* cepillo *m* (para el pelo).

haircut ['heəkʌt] *n* corte *m* de pelo; **to have a haircut** cortarse el pelo.

hairdo ['heədu:] *(pl* **-s***) n inf* peinado *m*.

hairdresser ['heə,dresər] *n* peluquero *m*, -ra *f*; **hairdresser's (salon)** peluquería *f*.

hairdressing ['heə,dresɪŋ] <> *n* peluquería *f*. <> *comp* de peluquería.

hairdryer ['heə,draɪər] *n* secador *m* (de pelo).

hair gel *n* gomina *f*.

hairgrip ['heəgrɪp] *n* UK horquilla *f*.

hairline ['heəlaɪn] *n* nacimiento *m* del pelo.

hairline fracture *n* fractura *f* muy fina.

hairnet ['heənet] *n* redecilla *f*.

hairpiece ['heəpi:s] *n* peluquín *m*, postizo *m*.

hairpin ['heəpɪn] *n* horquilla *f* de moño.

hairpin bend *n* curva *f* muy cerrada.

hair-raising [-,reɪzɪŋ] *adj* espeluznante.

hair remover [-rɪ,mu:vər] *n* crema *f* depilatoria, depilatorio *m*.

hair-restorer *n* crecepelo *m*, loción *f* capilar.

hair's breadth *n*: **by a hair's breadth** por un pelo; **within a hair's breadth of** al borde de.

hair slide *n* UK pasador *m*.

hair-splitting *n* (U) *pej* sutilezas *fpl*.

hairspray ['heəspreɪ] *n* laca *f* (para el pelo).

hairstyle ['heəstaɪl] *n* peinado *m*.

hairstylist ['heə,staɪlɪst] *n* peluquero *m*, -ra *f*.

hairy ['heərɪ] *(comp* **-ier***, superl* **-iest***) adj* **- 1.** [covered in hair] peludo(da) **- 2.** *inf* [scary] espeluznante, espantoso(sa).

Haiti ['heɪtɪ] *n* Haití.

Haitian ['heɪʃn] <> *adj* haitiano(na). <> *n* haitiano *m*, -na *f*.

hake [heɪk] *(pl* **hake** OR **-s***) n* merluza *f*.

halal [hə'lɑ:l] <> *adj* [meat] *que ha sido matado de acuerdo con la ley musulmana*. <> *n car- ne de animal matado de acuerdo con la ley musulmana*.

hale [heɪl] *adj*: **hale and hearty** sano(na) y fuerte.

half [UK hɑ:f, US hæf] <> *adj* medio(dia); **half a dozen/mile** media docena/milla; **half an**

hour media hora. ⬦ *adv* - **1.** [gen]: **half na-ked/Spanish** medio desnudo/español; **half full/open** medio lleno/abierto; **half and half** mitad y mitad; **not half!** *UK inf* ¡y cómo! - **2.** [by half]: **half as big (as)** la mitad de grande (que) - **3.** [in telling the time]: **half past nine, half after nine** *US* las nueve y media; **it's half past** son y media. ⬦ *n* - **1.** (*pl* **halves**) [one of two parts] mitad *f*; **one half of the group** una mitad del grupo; **a pound/mile and a half** una libra/milla y media; **by half** en un cincuenta por ciento; **in half** por la mitad, en dos; **he doesn't do things by halves** no hace las cosas a medias; **to be too clever by half** pasarse de listo(ta); **to go halves (with sb)** ir a medias (con alguien) - **2.** (*pl* **halfs**) [fraction, halfback, child's ticket] medio *m* - **3.** (*pl* **halves**) [of sports match] tiempo *m*, mitad *f* - **4.** (*pl* **halfs**) [of beer] media pinta *f*. ⬦ *pron* la mitad; **half of it/them** la mitad.

halfback ['hɑːfbæk] *n* [in rugby] medio *m*.

half-baked [-'beɪkt] *adj* descabalado(da).

half board *n* media pensión *f*.

half-breed ⬦ *adj* mestizo(za). ⬦ *n* mestizo *m*, -za *f* (*atención: el término 'half-breed' se considera racista*).

half-brother *n* hermanastro *m*.

half-caste [-kɑːst] ⬦ *adj* mestizo(za). ⬦ *n* mestizo *m*, -za *f* (*atención: el término 'half-caste' se considera racista*).

half cock *n*: **to go off (at) half cock** fracasar por falta de preparación.

half-day *n* media jornada *f*.

half-hearted [-'hɑːtɪd] *adj* poco entusiasta.

half-heartedly [ˌ'hɑːtɪdlɪ] *adv* sin entusiasmo.

half hour *n* media hora *f*.

half-light *n* media luz *f*.

half-mast *n*: **at half-mast** [flag] a media asta.

half moon *n* media luna *f*.

half note *n* *US* MUS blanca *f*.

halfpenny ['heɪpnɪ] (*pl* **-pennies** OR **-pence**) *n* medio penique *m*.

half-price *adj* a mitad de precio.

➡ **half price** *adv* a mitad de precio.

half-sister *n* hermanastra *f*.

half term *n* *UK* cortas vacaciones escolares a mitad de trimestre.

half time *n* (U) descanso *m*.

half tone *n* *US* MUS semitono *m*.

half-truth *n* verdad *f* a medias.

halfway [hɑːf'weɪ] ⬦ *adj* intermedio(dia). ⬦ *adv* - **1.** [in space]: **I was halfway down the street** llevaba la mitad de la calle andada - **2.** [in time]: **the film was halfway through** la película iba por la mitad

➠ **to meet sb halfway** llegar a una solución de compromiso con alguien (*cediendo ambas partes*).

half-wit *n* imbécil *mf*.

half-yearly *adj* semestral.

➡ **half yearly** *adv* semestralmente.

halibut ['hælɪbət] (*pl* **halibut** OR **-s**) *n* fletán *m*.

halitosis [ˌhælɪ'təʊsɪs] *n* halitosis *f inv*.

hall [hɔːl] *n* - **1.** [entrance to house] vestíbulo *m*; [corridor] pasillo *m* - **2.** [public building, large room] sala *f* - **3.** *UK* UNIV residencia *f* universitaria, colegio *m* mayor; **to live in halls** vivir en una residencia universitaria - **4.** [country house] mansión *f*, casa *f* solariega.

halleluja [ˌhælɪ'luːjə] *excl* ¡aleluya!

hallmark ['hɔːlmɑːk] *n* - **1.** [typical feature] sello *m* distintivo - **2.** [on metal] contraste *m*.

hallo [həˈləʊ] = **hello**.

hall of residence (*pl* **halls of residence**) *n* *UK* residencia *f* universitaria, colegio *m* mayor.

hallowed ['hæləʊd] *adj* [respected] santificado(da), sagrado(da).

Hallowe'en [ˌhæləʊ'iːn] *n* fiesta celebrada la noche del 31 de octubre.

hallucinate [hə'luːsɪneɪt] *vi* alucinar.

hallucination [ˌhəluːsɪ'neɪʃn] *n* alucinación *f*.

hallucinogenic [hə,luːsɪnə'dʒenɪk] *adj* alucinógeno(na).

hallway ['hɔːlweɪ] *n* [entrance to house] vestíbulo *m*; [corridor] pasillo *m*.

halo ['heɪləʊ] (*pl* **-es** OR **-s**) *n* halo *m*, aureola *f*.

halogen ['hælədʒen] ⬦ *n* halógeno *m*. ⬦ *comp* halógeno(na).

halt [hɔːlt] ⬦ *n* [stop]: **to come to a halt** [vehicle] pararse; [activity] interrumpirse; **to grind to a halt** [vehicle] ir parando lentamente; [process] paralizarse; **to call a halt to** poner fin a. ⬦ *vt* [person] parar, detener; [development, activity] interrumpir. ⬦ *vi* [person, train] pararse, detenerse; [development, activity] interrumpirse.

halter ['hɔːltə'] *n* [for horse] ronzal *m*, cabestro *m*, bozal *m* Amér.

halterneck ['hɔːltənek] *adj* escotado(da) por detrás.

halting ['hɔːltɪŋ] *adj* vacilante.

halve [*UK* hɑːv, *US* hæv] *vt* - **1.** [reduce by half] reducir a la mitad - **2.** [divide] partir en dos, partir por la mitad.

halves [*UK* hɑːvz, *US* hævz] *pl* ➟ **half**.

ham [hæm] ⬦ *n* - **1.** [meat] jamón *m* - **2.** *pej* [actor] histrión *m*, comicastro *m* - **3.** [radio fanatic]: **(radio) ham** radioaficionado *m*, -da *f*. ⬦ *comp* de jamón. ⬦ *vt* (*pt & pp* **-med**, *cont* **-ming**): **to ham it up** sobreactuar.

hamburger ['hæmbɜːgər] *n* - **1.** [burger] hamburguesa *f* - **2.** (U) *US* [mince] carne *f* picada.

ham-fisted [-'fɪstɪd] *adj* torpe, desmañado(da).

hamlet ['hæmlɪt] *n* aldea *f*.

hammer ['hæməʳ] ⬦ *n* [gen & SPORT] martillo *m*. ⬦ *vt* - **1.** [with tool] martillear - **2.** [with fist] aporrear - **3.** *inf* [defeat] dar una paliza a. ⬦ *vi* - **1.** [with tool] martillear - **2.** [with fist]: **to hammer (on sthg)** aporrear (algo)
▸▸▸ **to hammer away at sthg** [task] trabajar con ahínco en algo; [demand, subject] machacar algo.
◆ **hammer in** *vt sep*: **to hammer sthg into sb** meter algo en la cabeza a alguien.
◆ **hammer out** ⬦ *vt insep* [solution, agreement] alcanzar con esfuerzo. ⬦ *vt sep* [dent] quitar a martillo.

hammock ['hæmək] *n* hamaca *f*, chinchorro *m* *Méx*.

hammy ['hæmɪ] (*comp* -ier, *superl* -iest) *adj inf* histriónico(ca), exagerado(da).

hamper ['hæmpəʳ] ⬦ *n* - **1.** [for food] cesta *f*, canasta *f* - **2.** *US* [for laundry] cesto *m* de la ropa sucia. ⬦ *vt* obstaculizar.

hamster ['hæmstəʳ] *n* hámster *m*.

hamstring ['hæmstrɪŋ] ⬦ *n* tendón *m* de la corva. ⬦ *vt* (*pt & pp* -strung [-strʌŋ]) paralizar.

hand [hænd] ⬦ *n* - **1.** [gen] mano *f*; **hands up!** ¡manos arriba!; **to hold hands** ir cogidos de la mano; **hand in hand** [people] (cogidos) de la mano; **by hand** a mano; **at the hands of** a manos de; **in hand** [problem, situation] bajo control; **to have two games in hand** haber jugado dos partidos menos; **in the hands of** en manos de; **to have sthg on one's hands** tener algo en sus manos; **to change hands** cambiar de manos *OR* de dueño; **to force sb's hand** apretar las tuercas a alguien; **to get** *OR* **lay one's hands on sthg** hacerse con algo; **to get** *OR* **lay one's hands on sb** pillar a alguien; **to get out of hand** [situation] hacerse incontrolable; [person] desmandarse; **to give sb a free hand** dar carta blanca a alguien; **to give** *OR* **lend sb a hand (with)** echar una mano a alguien (con); **to go hand in hand** [things] ir de la mano; **to have one's hands full** estar muy ocupado(da); **to have time in hand** tener tiempo de sobra; **to overplay one's hand** *fig* extralimitarse; **to take sb in hand** hacerse cargo *OR* ocuparse de alguien; **to try one's hand at sthg** intentar hacer algo; **to wait on sb hand and foot** traérselo todo en bandeja a alguien; **to wash one's hands of sthg** lavarse las manos con respecto a algo; **with his bare hands** con sus propias manos - **2.** [influence] intervención *f*, influencia *f*; **to have a hand in sthg/in doing sthg** intervenir en algo/al hacer algo - **3.** [worker - on farm] bracero *m*, peón *m*; [- on

ship] tripulante *mf* - **4.** [of clock, watch] manecilla *f*, aguja *f* - **5.** [handwriting] letra *f* - **6.** [applause]: **a big hand** un gran aplauso. ⬦ *vt*: **to hand sthg to sb, to hand sb sthg** dar *OR* entregar algo a alguien.
◆ **(close) at hand** *adv* cerca.
◆ **on hand** *adv* al alcance de la mano.
◆ **on the other hand** *conj* por otra parte.
◆ **out of hand** *adv* [completely] terminantemente.
◆ **to hand** *adv* a mano.
◆ **hand back** *vt sep* devolver.
◆ **hand down** *vt sep* [heirloom] dejar en herencia; [knowledge] transmitir.
◆ **hand in** *vt sep* [essay, application] entregar; [resignation] presentar.
◆ **hand on** *vt sep* pasar, hacer circular.
◆ **hand out** *vt sep* repartir, distribuir.
◆ **hand over** ⬦ *vt sep* - **1.** [baton, money] entregar - **2.** [responsibility, power] ceder. ⬦ *vi*: **to hand over (to)** dar paso (a).

handbag ['hændbæg] *n* bolso *m*, bolsa *f Méx*, cartera *f Andes*.

handball ['hændbɔːl] *n* balonmano *m*.

handbill ['hændbɪl] *n* panfleto *m*.

handbook ['hændbʊk] *n* manual *m*.

handbrake ['hændbreɪk] *n* freno *m* de mano.

handclap ['hændklæp] *n*: **slow handclap** aplauso lento y rítmico de protesta.

handcrafted ['hænd,krɑːftɪd] *adj* hecho(cha) a mano, de artesanía.

handcuff ['hændkʌf] *vt* esposar.

handcuffs ['hændkʌfs] *npl* esposas *fpl*.

handful ['hændfʊl] *n* - **1.** [gen] puñado *m* - **2.** *inf* [uncontrollable person]: **to be a handful** ser un demonio.

handgun ['hændgʌn] *n* pistola *f*.

handheld PC ['hændheld-] *n* ordenador *m* de bolsillo, asistente *m* personal.

handicap ['hændɪkæp] ⬦ *n* - **1.** [disability] discapacidad *f*, minusvalía *f* - **2.** [disadvantage] desventaja *f*, obstáculo *m* - **3.** SPORT hándicap *m*. ⬦ *vt* (*pt & pp* -ped, *cont* -ping) estorbar, obstaculizar.

handicapped ['hændɪkæpt] ⬦ *adj* discapacitado(da), minusválido(da). ⬦ *npl*: **the handicapped** los discapacitados, los minusválidos.

handicraft ['hændɪkrɑːft] *n* [skill] artesanía *f*.

handiwork ['hændɪwɜːk] *n* (*U*) [doing, work] obra *f*.

handkerchief ['hæŋkətʃɪf] (*pl* -chiefs *OR* -chieves [-tʃiːvz]) *n* pañuelo *m*.

handle ['hændl] ⬦ *n* [of tool, broom, knife] mango *m*; [of door, window] manilla *f*; [of suitcase, cup, jug] asa *f*; [of racket] empuñadura *f*; **to fly off the handle** perder los estribos. ⬦ *vt* [gen] manejar; [order, complaint, application] encargarse de; [negotiations, takeover] conducir; [people] tratar.

handlebars [ˈhændlbɑːz] *npl* manillar *m*, manubrio *m* *Amér*.

handler [ˈhændlər] *n* - **1.** [of animal] adiestrador *m*, -ra *f* - **2.** [at airport]: **(baggage) handler** mozo *m* de equipajes.

handling charges [ˈhændlɪŋ-] *npl* [at bank] gastos *mpl* de tramitación.

hand lotion *n* loción *f* para las manos.

hand luggage *n* *UK* equipaje *m* de mano.

handmade [ˌhændˈmeɪd] *adj* hecho(cha) a mano.

hand-me-down *n* *inf* prenda *f* heredada.

handout [ˈhændaʊt] *n* - **1.** [gift] donativo *m* - **2.** [leaflet] hoja *f* (informativa); [in class] notas *fpl*.

handover [ˈhændəʊvər] *n* [of power] cesión *f*, transferencia *f*; [of prisoners, baton] entrega *f*.

handpicked [ˌhændˈpɪkt] *adj* cuidadosamente escogido(da).

handrail [ˈhændreɪl] *n* pasamano *m*, barandilla *f*.

handset [ˈhændset] *n* auricular *m* *(de teléfono)*; **to lift/replace the handset** descolgar/colgar (el teléfono).

hands free kit *n* kit *m* manos libres.

handshake [ˈhændʃeɪk] *n* apretón *m* de manos.

hands-off *adj* de no intervención.

handsome [ˈhænsəm] *adj* - **1.** [man] guapo, atractivo - **2.** [literary] [woman] bella - **3.** [reward, profit] considerable.

handsomely [ˈhænsəmlɪ] *adv* [generously] generosamente.

hands-on *adj* práctico(ca).

handstand [ˈhændstænd] *n* pino *m*.

hand-to-mouth *adj* precario(ria).

◆ **hand to mouth** *adv* precariamente.

handwriting [ˈhændˌraɪtɪŋ] *n* letra *f*, caligrafía *f*.

handwritten [ˈhændˌrɪtn] *adj* escrito(ta) a mano.

handy [ˈhændɪ] (*comp* **-ier**, *superl* **-iest**) *adj inf* - **1.** [useful] práctico(ca); **to come in handy** venir bien - **2.** [skilful] mañoso(sa) - **3.** [near] a mano, cerca; **to keep sthg handy** tener algo a mano.

handyman [ˈhændɪmæn] (*pl* **-men** [-men]) *n*: **a good handyman un** manitas.

hang [hæŋ] ◇ *vt* - **1.** (*pt & pp* **hung**) [fasten] colgar; [washing] tender; [wallpaper] poner - **2.** (*pt & pp* **hung** OR **hanged**) [execute] ahorcar; **to hang o.s.** ahorcarse. ◇ *vi* - **1.** (*pt & pp* **hung**) [be fastened] colgar, pender

- **2.** (*pt & pp* **hung** OR **hanged**) [be executed] ser ahorcado(da) - **3.** (*pt & pp* **hung**) *US inf*: **I'm going to hang with my friends tonight** voy a ir por ahí esta noche con los amigos - **4.** COMPUT colgarse. ◇ *n*: **to get the hang of sthg** *inf* coger el tranquillo a algo.

◆ **hang about, hang around, hang round** *vi* - **1.** [pass time] pasar el rato; **they didn't hang about** se pusieron en marcha sin perder un minuto - **2.** [wait] esperar; **hang about!** ¡un momento!

◆ **hang on** ◇ *vt insep* [depend on] depender de. ◇ *vi* - **1.** [keep hold]: **to hang on (to)** agarrarse (a) - **2.** *inf* [continue waiting] esperar, aguardar - **3.** [persevere] resistir.

◆ **hang onto** *vt insep* - **1.** [keep hold of] agarrarse a - **2.** [keep] quedarse con; [power] aferrarse a.

◆ **hang out** ◇ *vt sep* [washing] tender. ◇ *vi inf* [spend time] pasar el rato.

◆ **hang round** = **hang about**.

◆ **hang together** *vi* [alibi, argument] sostenerse, tenerse en pie.

◆ **hang up** ◇ *vt sep* colgar. ◇ *vi* colgar.

◆ **hang up on** *vt insep*: **to hang up on sb** colgarle a alguien.

hangar [ˈhæŋər] *n* hangar *m*.

hangdog [ˈhæŋdɒg] *adj* avergonzado(da).

hanger [ˈhæŋər] *n* percha *f*.

hanger-on (*pl* **hangers-on**) *n* lapa *f*, parásito *m*.

hang glider *n* [apparatus] ala *f* delta.

hang gliding *n* vuelo *m* con ala delta.

hanging [ˈhæŋɪŋ] *n* - **1.** *(U)* [form of punishment] la horca - **2.** [execution] ahorcamiento *m* - **3.** [drapery] colgadura *f*.

hangman [ˈhæŋmən] (*pl* **-men** [-mən]) *n* verdugo *m*.

hangover [ˈhæŋˌəʊvər] *n* - **1.** [from drinking] resaca *f* - **2.** [from past]: **hangover (from)** vestigio *m* (de).

hang-up *n* *inf* complejo *m*.

hanker [ˈhæŋkər] ◆ **hanker after, hanker for** *vt insep* anhelar.

hankering [ˈhæŋkərɪŋ] *n*: **hankering after** OR **for** anhelo *m* de.

hankie, hanky [ˈhæŋkɪ] (*pl* **-ies**) (*abbr of* **handkerchief**) *n* *inf* pañuelo *m*.

Hants [hænts] (*abbr of* **Hampshire**) *condado inglés*.

haphazard [ˌhæpˈhæzəd] *adj* [arrangement] desordenado(da), caótico(ca); [decision] arbitrario(ria).

haphazardly [ˌhæpˈhæzədlɪ] *adv* [arranged] desordenadamente, de cualquier manera.

hapless [ˈhæplɪs] *adj liter* desventurado(da).

happen ['hæpən] *vi* - **1.** [occur] pasar, ocurrir; **to happen to sb** pasarle *OR* sucederle a alguien - **2.** [chance]: **I happened to be looking out of the window...** dio la casualidad de que estaba mirando por la ventana...; **do you happen to have a pen on you?** ¿no tendrás un boli por casualidad?; **as it happens...** da la casualidad de que...

happening ['hæpənɪŋ] *n* suceso *m*, acontecimiento *m*.

happily ['hæpɪlɪ] *adv* - **1.** [with pleasure] alegremente, felizmente - **2.** [willingly] con mucho gusto - **3.** [fortunately] afortunadamente.

happiness ['hæpɪnɪs] *n* [state] felicidad *f*; [feeling] alegría *f*.

happy ['hæpɪ] (*comp* **-ier**, *superl* **-iest**) *adj* - **1.** [gen contented] feliz; [pleased] contento(ta); [cheerful] alegre; **happy Christmas/birthday!** ¡feliz navidad/cumpleaños!; **to be happy with/about sthg** estar contento con algo - **2.** [causing contentment] feliz, alegre - **3.** [fortunate] feliz, oportuno(na) - **4.** [willing]: **to be happy to do sthg** estar más que dispuesto(ta) a hacer algo; **I'd be happy to do it** yo lo haría con gusto.

happy-go-lucky *adj* despreocupado(da).

happy hour *n inf* espacio de tiempo durante el cual en un bar las bebidas se venden a precio reducido.

happy medium *n* término *m* medio.

harangue [hə'ræŋ] <> *n* arenga *f*. <> *vt* arengar.

harass ['hærəs] *vt* acosar.

harassed ['hærəst] *adj* agobiado(da).

harassment ['hærəsmənt] *n* acoso *m*.

harbinger ['hɑːbɪndʒər] *n liter* precursor *m*, heraldo *m*.

harbour *UK*, **harbor** *US* ['hɑːbər] <> *n* puerto *m*. <> *vt* - **1.** [feeling] abrigar - **2.** [person] dar refugio a, encubrir.

harbour master *n* capitán *m* de puerto.

hard [hɑːd] <> *adj* - **1.** [gen] duro(ra); [frost] fuerte; **to go hard** endurecerse; **to be hard on sb/sthg** [subj: person] ser duro con alguien/algo; [subj: work, strain] perjudicar a alguien/algo; [subj: result] ser inmerecido(da) para alguien/algo - **2.** [difficult] difícil; **hard of hearing** duro de oído - **3.** [forceful - push, kick etc] fuerte - **4.** [fact, news] concreto(ta) - **5.** *UK* [extreme]: **hard left/right** extrema izquierda/derecha. <> *adv* - **1.** [try, rain] mucho; [work] duro; [listen] atentamente; [think] detenidamente - **2.** [push, kick] fuerte, con fuerza ▶▶ **to be hard pushed** *OR* **put** *OR* **pressed to do sthg** vérselas y deseárselas para hacer algo; **to feel hard done by** sentirse tratado injustamente.

hardback ['hɑːdbæk] <> *adj* de pasta dura. <> *n* edición *f* en pasta dura.

hardball ['hɑːdbɔːl] *n US* béisbol *m*; **to play hardball (with sb)** ponerse duro(ra) (con alguien), adoptar una línea dura (con alguien).

hard-bitten *adj* duro(ra), curtido(da).

hardboard ['hɑːdbɔːd] *n* madera *f* conglomerada.

hard-boiled *adj lit & fig* duro(ra).

hard cash *n* dinero *m* contante y sonante.

hard cider *n US* sidra *f*.

hard copy *n* COMPUT copia *f* impresa.

hard-core *adj* - **1.** [support] acérrimo(ma) - **2.** [pornography] duro(ra).
▸ **hard core** *n* [of group] núcleo *m*.

hard court *n* pista *f* de cemento, pista de superficie dura.

hard currency *n* divisa *f* fuerte.

hard disk *n* COMPUT disco *m* duro.

hard drive *n* COMPUT unidad *f* de disco duro.

hard drugs *npl* drogas *fpl* duras.

harden ['hɑːdn] <> *vt* - **1.** [gen] endurecer - **2.** [resolve, opinion] reforzar. <> *vi* - **1.** [gen] endurecerse - **2.** [resolve, opinion] reforzarse.

hardened ['hɑːdnd] *adj* [criminal] habitual.

hardening ['hɑːdnɪŋ] *n* endurecimiento *m*.

hard hat *n* casco *m* (de protección).

hard-headed [-'hedɪd] *adj* práctico(ca), realista.

hard-hearted [-'hɑːtɪd] *adj* insensible, sin corazón.

hard-hitting [-'hɪtɪŋ] *adj* impactante.

hard labour *n (U)* trabajos *mpl* forzados.

hard line *n*: **to take a hard line on sthg** seguir una tendencia de mano dura con algo.
▸ **hard-line** *adj* de línea dura.
▸ **hard lines** *npl UK*: **hard lines!** ¡mala suerte!

hard-liner *n* partidario *m*, -ria *f* de la línea dura.

hardly ['hɑːdlɪ] *adv* apenas; **hardly ever/anything** casi nunca/nada; **that's hardly fair** eso no es justo; **I'm hardly a communist, am I?** ¡pues sí que tengo yo mucho que ver con el comunismo!

hardness ['hɑːdnɪs] *n* - **1.** [firmness] dureza *f* - **2.** [difficulty] dificultad *f*.

hard-nosed [-'nəʊzd] *adj* contundente, decidido(da).

hard sell *n* venta *f* agresiva.

hardship ['hɑːdʃɪp] *n* - **1.** *(U)* [difficult conditions] privaciones *fpl*, penurias *fpl* - **2.** [difficult circumstance] infortunio *m*.

hard shoulder *n* UK AUT arcén *m*, acotamiento *m* Méx, berma *f* Andes, banquina *f* R Plata, hombrillo *m* Ven.

hard up *adj inf*: **to be hard up** andar mal de dinero; **to be hard up for sthg** andar escaso(sa) de algo.

hardware ['hɑːdweəʳ] *(U) n* - **1.** [tools, equipment] artículos *mpl* de ferretería - **2.** COMPUT hardware *m*, soporte *m* físico.

hardware store *n* US ferretería *f*.

hardwearing [,hɑːd'weərɪŋ] *adj* UK resistente.

hardwood ['hɑːdwʊd] *n* madera *f* noble.

hardworking [,hɑːd'wɜːkɪŋ] *adj* trabajador(ra).

hardy ['hɑːdɪ] (*comp* **-ier**, *superl* **-iest**) *adj* - **1.** [person, animal] fuerte, robusto(ta) - **2.** [plant] resistente.

hare [heəʳ] ⟨⟩ *n* liebre *f*. ⟨⟩ *vi* UK *inf*: **to hare off** echar a correr a toda pastilla.

harebrained ['heə,breɪnd] *adj inf* atolondrado(da).

harelip [,heə'lɪp] *n* labio *m* leporino.

harem [UK hɑː'riːm, US 'hærəm] *n* harén *m*.

haricot (bean) ['hærɪkəʊ-] *n* judía *f*, alubia *f*, frijol *m* Amér, poroto *m* Andes, caraota *f* Ven.

hark [hɑːk] ⟐ **hark back** *vi* [subj: person]: **to hark back to sthg** volver a OR rememorar algo.

harlequin ['hɑːləkwɪn] *n* arlequín *m*.

Harley Street ['hɑːlɪ-] *n* calle londinense famosa por sus médicos especialistas.

harm [hɑːm] ⟨⟩ *n* daño *m*; **to do harm to sthg/sb, to do sthg/sb harm** [physically] hacer daño a algo/alguien; *fig* perjudicar algo/a alguien; **to mean no harm (by sthg)** no tener mala intención (al hacer algo); **there's no harm in it** no hay nada malo en ello; **there's no harm in trying/asking** no se pierde nada por intentarlo/preguntar; **to be out of harm's way** estar a salvo; **to come to no harm** [person] salir sano y salvo; [thing] no dañarse. ⟨⟩ *vt* [gen] hacer daño a, dañar; [reputation, chances, interests] dañar.

harmful ['hɑːmfʊl] *adj*: **harmful (to)** perjudicial OR dañino(na) (para); [substance] nocivo(va) (para).

harmless ['hɑːmlɪs] *adj* inofensivo(va).

harmlessly ['hɑːmlɪslɪ] *adv* sin causar daño.

harmonic [hɑː'mɒnɪk] *adj* armónico(ca).

harmonica [hɑː'mɒnɪkə] *n* armónica *f*.

harmonious [hɑː'məʊnjəs] *adj* armonioso(sa).

harmonium [hɑː'məʊnjəm] (*pl* **-s**) *n* armonio *m*.

harmonize, -ise ['hɑːmənaɪz] ⟨⟩ *vi*: **to harmonize (with)** armonizar (con). ⟨⟩ *vt* armonizar.

harmony ['hɑːmənɪ] (*pl* **-ies**) *n* armonía *f*; **in harmony with** en armonía con.

harness ['hɑːnɪs] ⟨⟩ *n* - **1.** [for horse] arreos *mpl*, guarniciones *fpl* - **2.** [for child] andadores *mpl*; [for climbing etc] correaje *m*. ⟨⟩ *vt* - **1.** [horse] enjaezar, poner los arreos a - **2.** [use] aprovechar.

harp [hɑːp] *n* arpa *f*.
⟐ **harp on** *vi*: **to harp on (about sthg)** dar la matraca (con algo).

harpist ['hɑːpɪst] *n* arpista *mf*.

harpoon [hɑː'puːn] ⟨⟩ *n* arpón *m*. ⟨⟩ *vt* arponear.

harpsichord ['hɑːpsɪkɔːd] *n* clavicémbalo *m*.

harrowing ['hærəʊɪŋ] *adj* horroroso(sa), pavoroso(sa).

harry ['hærɪ] (*pt & pp* **-ied**) *vt* - **1.** [badger]: **to harry sb (for sthg)** acosar a alguien (para obtener algo) - **2.** MIL hostigar.

harsh [hɑːʃ] *adj* - **1.** [life, conditions, winter] duro(ra) - **2.** [punishment, decision, person] severo(ra) - **3.** [texture, taste, voice] áspero(ra); [light, sound] violento(ta).

harshly ['hɑːʃlɪ] *adv* - **1.** [punish, criticize, treat] severamente, duramente - **2.** [grate] ásperamente; [shine] violentamente.

harshness ['hɑːʃnɪs] *n* - **1.** [of life, conditions, winter] dureza *f* - **2.** [of punishment, decision, person] severidad *f* - **3.** [of texture, taste, voice] aspereza *f*; [of light, sound] violencia *f*.

harvest ['hɑːvɪst] ⟨⟩ *n* [gen] cosecha *f*, pizca *f* Méx; [of grapes] vendimia *f*. ⟨⟩ *vt* cosechar.

harvest festival *n* festividad religiosa para celebrar la recogida de la cosecha.

has (*weak form* [həz], *strong form* [hæz]) (*3rd person sing*) ⟶ **have**.

has-been *n inf pej* vieja gloria *f*.

hash [hæʃ] *n* - **1.** [meat] picadillo *m* (*de carne*) - **2.** *inf* [mess]: **to make a hash of sthg** hacer algo fatal - **3.** *inf* [hashish] hachís *m*, chocolate *m*.
⟐ **hash up** *vt sep* UK *inf* [make a mess of] fastidiar.

hash browns *npl* US patatas cortadas en cuadraditos, fritas y servidas en forma de croqueta.

hashish ['hæʃiːʃ] *n* hachís *m*.

hasn't ['hæznt] = **has not** ⟶ **have**.

hassle ['hæsl] *inf* ⟨⟩ *n* (U) [annoyance] rollo *m*, lío *m*; **it's a real hassle** es una lata. ⟨⟩ *vt* dar la lata a.

haste [heɪst] *n* prisa *f*; **to do sthg in haste** hacer algo de prisa y corriendo; **to make haste** *dated* darse prisa, apresurarse.

hasten ['heɪsn] *fml* ⟨⟩ *vt* acelerar. ⟨⟩ *vi*: **to hasten (to do sthg)** apresurarse (a hacer algo).

hastily ['heɪstɪlɪ] *adv* **- 1.** [quickly] de prisa, precipitadamente **- 2.** [rashly] a la ligera, sin reflexionar.

hasty ['heɪstɪ] (*comp* -ier, *superl* -iest) *adj* **- 1.** [quick] apresurado(da), precipitado(da) **- 2.** [rash] irreflexivo(va).

hat [hæt] *n* sombrero *m*; **keep it under your hat** de esto ni palabra a nadie; **to be talking through one's hat** no decir más que pamplinas; **that's old hat** eso está más visto que el tebeo.

hatbox ['hæt,bɒks] *n* sombrerera *f.*

hatch [hætʃ] ⟨⟩ *vi* [chick] romper el cascarón, salir del huevo; **when the eggs hatch** cuando los polluelos rompen el cascarón. ⟨⟩ *vt* **- 1.** [chick, egg] empollar, incubar **- 2.** *fig* [scheme, plot] tramar. ⟨⟩ *n* [for serving food] ventanilla *f.*

hatchback ['hætʃ,bæk] *n* coche *m* con puerta trasera; **a four-door hatchback** un cinco puertas.

hatchet ['hætʃɪt] *n* hacha *f*; **to bury the hatchet** hacer las paces.

hatchet job *n inf*: **to do a hatchet job on sb** despellejar a alguien.

hatchway ['hætʃ,weɪ] *n* escotilla *f.*

hate [heɪt] ⟨⟩ *n* odio *m.* ⟨⟩ *vt* odiar; **to hate doing sthg** odiar hacer algo; **I hate to admit it** me cuesta admitirlo; **I hate to seem pernickety, but...** no es que quiera ser quisquillosa, pero...

hateful ['heɪtfʊl] *adj* odioso(sa).

hatred ['heɪtrɪd] *n* odio *m.*

hat trick *n* SPORT *tres tantos marcados por un jugador en el mismo partido.*

haughty ['hɔːtɪ] (*comp* -ier, *superl* -iest) *adj* altanero(ra), altivo(va).

haul [hɔːl] ⟨⟩ *n* **- 1.** [of stolen goods] botín *m*; [of drugs] alijo *m* **- 2.** [distance]: **long haul** largo camino *m*, largo trayecto *m.* ⟨⟩ *vt* **- 1.** [pull] tirar, arrastrar **- 2.** [by lorry] transportar.

haulage ['hɔːlɪdʒ] *n* transporte *m.*

haulage contractor *n* transportista *mf*, contratista *mf* de transportes.

haulier UK ['hɔːlɪəʳ], **hauler** US ['hɔːlər] *n* transportista *mf*, contratista *mf* de transportes.

haunch [hɔːntʃ] *n* **- 1.** [of person] asentaderas *fpl*; **to squat on one's haunches** ponerse en cuclillas **- 2.** [of animal] pernil *m.*

haunt [hɔːnt] ⟨⟩ *n* sitio *m* favorito, lugar *m* predilecto. ⟨⟩ *vt* **- 1.** [subj: ghost - house] aparecer en; [- person] aparecerse a **- 2.** [subj: memory, fear, problem] atormentar, obsesionar.

haunted ['hɔːntɪd] *adj* **- 1.** [house, castle] encantado(da) **- 2.** [look] atormentado(da).

haunting ['hɔːntɪŋ] *adj* fascinante e inquietante.

Havana [hə'vænə] *n* La Habana.

have [hæv] ⟨⟩ *aux vb* (*pt & pp* had) *(to form perfect tenses)* haber; **I have eaten** he comido; **I've been on holiday** he estado de vacaciones; **we've never met before** no nos conocemos; **he hasn't gone yet, has he?** no se habrá ido ya ¿no?; **I've finished** – ¿ah sí?; **no, he hasn't (done it)** no, no lo ha hecho; **yes, he has (done it)** sí, lo ha hecho; **I was out of breath, having run all the way** estaba sin aliento después de haber corrido todo el camino. ⟨⟩ *vt* (*pt & pp* had) **- 1.** [possess, receive]: **to have (got)** tener; **I have no money, I haven't got any money** no tengo dinero; **he has big hands** tiene las manos grandes; **I've got things to do** tengo cosas que hacer; **I had a letter from her** tuve carta de ella; **she's got loads of imagination** tiene mucha imaginación; **do you have a car?/have you got a car?** ¿tienes coche? **- 2.** [experience, suffer] tener; **I had an accident** tuve un accidente; **I had a nasty surprise** me llevé una desagradable sorpresa; **to have a cold** tener un resfriado; **to have a good time** pasarlo bien **- 3.** *(referring to an action, instead of another vb):* **it will have no effect** no tendrá ningún efecto; **to have a look** mirar, echar una mirada; **to have a walk** dar un paseo; **to have a swim** darse un baño, nadar; **to have breakfast** desayunar; **to have lunch** comer; **to have dinner** cenar; **to have a cigarette** fumarse un cigarrillo; **to have an operation** operarse **- 4.** [give birth to]: **to have a baby** tener un niño **- 5.** [cause to be done]: **to have sb do sthg** hacer que alguien haga algo; **she had me clean my teeth again** me hizo lavarme los dientes otra vez; **to have sthg done** hacer que se haga algo; **I'm having the house decorated** voy a contratar a alguien para que me decore la casa; **to have one's hair cut** (ir a) cortarse el pelo **- 6.** [be treated in a certain way]: **I had my car stolen** me robaron el coche **- 7.** *inf* [cheat]: **you've been had** te han timado

▸▸▸ **to have it in for sb** tenerla tomada con alguien; **to have had it** [car, machine] estar para el arrastre; **these clothes have had it** esta ropa está para tirarla; **I've had it!** [expressing exhaustion] ¡no puedo más! ⟨⟩ *modal vb* (*pt & pp* had) [be obliged]: **to have (got) to do sthg** tener que hacer algo; **do you have to go?/have you got to go?** ¿tienes que irte?; **I've got to go to work** tengo que ir a trabajar.

◆ **haves** *npl*: **the haves and have nots** los ricos y los pobres.

◆ **have off** *vt sep* [as holiday] tener libre.

◆ **have on** *vt sep* **- 1.** [be wearing] llevar (puesto); **to have nothing on** no llevar nada encima

OR puesto **- 2.** [tease] vacilar, tomar el pelo a **- 3.** [have to do]**: to have (got) a lot on** tener mucho que hacer; **have you got anything on Friday?** ¿estás libre *OR* haces algo el viernes?

◆ **have out** *vt sep* **- 1.** [have removed]**: to have one's tonsils out** operarse de las amígdalas; **she had a tooth out** le sacaron una muela **- 2.** [discuss frankly]**: to have it out with sb** poner las cuentas claras con alguien.

◆ **have up** *vt sep UK inf***: to have sb up for sthg** llevar a alguien al juzgado por algo.

haven ['heɪvn] *n fig* refugio *m*, asilo *m*.

haven't ['hævnt] **= have not** ⊳ **have.**

haversack ['hævəsæk] *n* mochila *f*, zurrón *m*.

havoc ['hævək] *n (U)* estragos *mpl*; **to play havoc with sthg** causar estragos en algo.

Hawaii [hə'waɪi:] *n* Hawai.

Hawaiian [hə'waɪjən] ⋄ *adj* hawaiano(na). ⋄ *n* hawaiano *m*, -na *f*.

hawk [hɔːk] ⋄ *n lit & fig* halcón *m*; **to watch sb like a hawk** observar a alguien con ojos de lince. ⋄ *vt* vender por las calles.

hawker ['hɔːkəʳ] *n* vendedor *m*, -ra *f* ambulante, abonero *m*, -ra *f Méx*.

hawthorn ['hɔːθɔːn] *n* majuelo *m*, espino *m*.

hay [heɪ] *n* heno *m*.

hay fever *n (U)* fiebre *f* del heno.

haystack ['heɪˌstæk] *n* almiar *m*.

haywire ['heɪˌwaɪəʳ] *adj inf***: to go haywire** [person] volverse majareta; [plan] liarse, embrollarse; [computer, TV etc] changarse.

hazard ['hæzəd] ⋄ *n* riesgo *m*, peligro *m*. ⋄ *vt* [guess, suggestion] aventurar, atreverse a hacer.

hazardous ['hæzədəs] *adj* peligroso(sa).

hazard warning lights *npl UK* luces *fpl* de emergencia.

haze [heɪz] *n* neblina *f*.

hazel ['heɪzl] ⋄ *adj* color avellana *(inv)*. ⋄ *n* [tree] avellano *m*.

hazelnut ['heɪzlˌnʌt] *n* avellana *f*.

hazy ['heɪzɪ] *(comp* -ier, *superl* -iest) *adj* **- 1.** [misty] neblinoso(sa) **- 2.** [vague] vago(ga), confuso(sa).

H-bomb *n* bomba *f* H.

h & c *(abbr of* **hot and cold (water))** c & f.

he [hiː] ⋄ *pers pron* él; **he's tall/happy** es alto/feliz; **he loves fish** le encanta el pescado; **he can't do it él** no puede hacerlo; **there he is** allí está; **he who** *fml* aquel que, el que. ⋄ *n inf***:** **it's a he** [animal] es macho; [baby] es (un) niño. ⋄ *comp***: he-goat** macho cabrío *m*; **he-bear** oso *m* macho.

HE *(abbr of* **His/Her Excellency)** S. Exc., S.E.

head [hed] ⋄ *n* **- 1.** ANAT & COMPUT cabeza *f*; **a** *OR* **per head** por persona, por cabeza; **it never entered my head** nunca se me pasó por la cabeza; **off the top of one's head** así de repente; **I couldn't make head nor tail of it** aquello no tenía ni pies ni cabeza; **on your own head be it** tú veras lo que haces, es responsabilidad tuya; **to be banging one's head against a brick wall** predicar en el desierto; **to be soft in the head** estar mal de la sesera; **to bite** *OR* **snap sb's head off** soltar un bufido a alguien sin motivo; **to be off one's head** *UK*, **to be out of one's head** *US* estar como una cabra; **it was over my head** no me enteré de nada; **we put our heads together** tratamos de resolverlo juntos; **it went to her head** se le subió a la cabeza; **to keep/lose one's head** no perder/perder la cabeza; **to laugh one's head off** reír a mandíbula batiente; **to sing/shout one's head off** cantar/gritar a todo pulmón **- 2.** [mind, brain] talento *m*, aptitud *f*; **she has a head for figures** se le dan bien las cuentas **- 3.** [top - gen] cabeza *f*; [- of bed] cabecera *f* **- 4.** [of flower] cabezuela *f*; [of cabbage] cogollo *m* **- 5.** [on beer] espuma *f* **- 6.** [leader] jefe *m*, -fa *f* **- 7.** [head teacher] director *m*, -ra *f* (de colegio)

▸▸▸ **to come to a head** llegar a un punto crítico. ⋄ *vt* **- 1.** [procession, convoy, list, page] encabezar **- 2.** [organization, delegation] dirigir **- 3.** FTBL cabecear. ⋄ *vi***: to head north/for home** dirigirse hacia el norte/a casa.

◆ **heads** *npl* [on coin] cara *f*; **heads or tails?** ¿cara o cruz?

◆ **head for** *vt insep* **- 1.** [place] dirigirse a **- 2.** *fig* [trouble, disaster] ir camino de.

◆ **head off** ⋄ *vt sep* **- 1.** [intercept] interceptar **- 2.** *fig* [forestall] anticiparse a. ⋄ *vi* [go] marcharse.

headache ['hedeɪk] *n* **- 1.** MED dolor *m* de cabeza; **I have a headache** me duele la cabeza **- 2.** *fig* [problem] quebradero *m* de cabeza.

headband ['hedbænd] *n* cinta *f*, banda *f (para el pelo)*.

headboard ['hedˌbɔːd] *n* cabecero *m*.

head boy *n UK* [at school] *alumno delegado principal que suele representar a sus condiscípulos en actos escolares.*

head cold *n* resfriado que provoca dolor de cabeza pero no tos.

head count *n* recuento *m* (de los asistentes).

headdress ['hedˌdres] *n* tocado *m*.

header ['hedəʳ] *n* **- 1.** FTBL cabezazo *m* **- 2.** TYPO encabezamiento *m*.

headfirst [ˌhed'fɜːst] *adv* de cabeza.

headgear ['hedˌgɪəʳ] *n (U)* tocado *m*.

head girl *n UK* [in school] *alumna delegada principal que suele representar a sus condiscípulas en actos escolares.*

headhunt ['hedhʌnt] *vt* contratar *(nuevos talentos).*

headhunter ['hed,hʌntəʳ] *n* cazatalentos *mf inv.*

heading ['hedɪŋ] *n* encabezamiento *m.*

headlamp ['hedlæmp] *n UK* faro *m.*

headland ['hedlənd] *n* cabo *m*, promontorio *m.*

headlight ['hedlaɪt] *n* faro *m.*

headline ['hedlaɪn] *n* titular *m.*

headlong ['hedlɒŋ] <> *adv* **- 1.** [headfirst] de cabeza **- 2.** [quickly, unthinkingly] precipitadamente. <> *adj* [unthinking] precipitado(da).

headmaster [,hed'mɑːstəʳ] *n* director *m* (de colegio).

headmistress [,hed'mɪstrɪs] *n* directora *f* (de colegio).

head office *n* oficina *f* central.

head of state *n* jefe *m* de Estado.

head-on <> *adj* de frente, frontal. <> *adv* de frente.

headphones ['hedfəʊnz] *npl* auriculares *mpl.*

headquarter [hed'kwɔːtəʳ] *vt*: **to be headquartered in** tener la sede en.

headquarters [,hed'kwɔːtəz] *npl* (oficina *f*) central *f*, sede *f*; MIL cuartel *m* general.

headrest ['hedrest] *n* reposacabezas *m inv.*

headroom ['hedrʊm] *n (U)* [in car] espacio *m* entre la cabeza y el techo; [below bridge] altura *f* libre, gálibo *m.*

headscarf ['hedskɑːf] *(pl* **-scarves** [-skɑːvz] OR **-scarfs)** *n* pañuelo *m (para la cabeza).*

headset ['hedset] *n* auriculares *mpl* con micrófono.

headship ['hedʃɪp] *n* SCH dirección *f* (de colegio).

headstand ['hedstænd] *n*: **to do a headstand** hacer el pino *(con la cabeza tocando el suelo).*

head start *n*: **head start (on** OR **over)** ventaja *f* (con respecto a).

headstone ['hedstəʊn] *n* lápida *f* mortuoria.

headstrong ['hedstrɒŋ] *adj* obstinado(da).

head teacher *n* director *m*, -ra *f* (de colegio).

head waiter *n* maître *m*, capitán *m* de meseros *Méx.*

headway ['hedweɪ] *n*: **to make headway** avanzar, hacer progresos.

headwind ['hedwɪnd] *n* viento *m* de proa.

heady ['hedɪ] *(comp* **-ier**, *superl* **-iest)** *adj* **- 1.** [exciting] excitante, emocionante **- 2.** [causing giddiness] embriagador(ra).

heal [hiːl] <> *vt* **- 1.** [person] curar; [wound] cicatrizar **- 2.** *fig* [troubles, discord] remediar. <> *vi* [wound] cicatrizar.

➡ **heal up** *vi* cicatrizarse.

healing ['hiːlɪŋ] <> *adj* curativo(va). <> *n* curación *f.*

health [helθ] *n* **- 1.** [gen] salud *f*; **to be in good/ poor health** estar bien/mal de salud; **to drink (to) sb's health** brindar por alguien **- 2.** *fig* [of country, organization] buen estado *m.*

health care *n* asistencia *f* sanitaria.

health centre *n* ambulatorio *m*, centro *m* sanitario.

health-conscious *adj* consciente de los problemas relacionados con la salud.

health farm *n* clínica *f* de adelgazamiento.

health food *n* comida *f* dietética.

health food shop *n* tienda *f* de dietética.

health hazard *n* peligro *m* para la salud.

health service *n* servicio *m* sanitario de la Seguridad Social, ≃ INGS *m.*

health visitor *n UK* enfermero *m*, -ra *f* visitante.

healthy ['helθɪ] *(comp* **-ier**, *superl* **-iest)** *adj* **- 1.** [gen] sano(na), saludable **- 2.** [profit] pingüe **- 3.** [attitude, respect] natural, sano(na).

heap [hiːp] <> *n* montón *m*, pila *f*, ruma *f Amér*; **in a heap** amontonado. <> *vt* **- 1.** [pile up]: **to heap sthg (on** OR **onto sthg)** amontonar algo (sobre algo) **- 2.** [give]: **to heap sthg on sb** colmar a alguien de algo.

➡ **heaps** *npl inf* montones *fpl*, mogollón *m.*

hear [hɪəʳ] *(pt & pp* **heard** [hɜːd]) <> *vt* **- 1.** [gen] oír; **I hear (that...)** me dicen que... **- 2.** LAW ver. <> *vi* [gen] oír; **did you hear about her husband?** ¿te enteraste de lo de su marido?; **have you heard about that job yet?** ¿sabes algo del trabajo ese?; **to hear from sb** tener noticias de alguien

▸▸ **to have heard of** haber oído hablar de; **I won't hear of it!** ¡de eso ni hablar!

➡ **hear out** *vt sep* escuchar (sin interrumpir).

hearing ['hɪərɪŋ] *n* **- 1.** [sense] oído *m*; **in** OR **within sb's hearing** al alcance del oído de alguien; **hard of hearing** duro de oído **- 2.** LAW vista *f*; **to give sb a fair hearing** *fig* dar a alguien la oportunidad de que se exprese.

hearing aid *n* audífono *m.*

hearsay ['hɪəseɪ] *n (U)* habladurías *fpl.*

hearse [hɜːs] *n* coche *m* fúnebre.

heart [hɑːt] *n* **- 1.** [gen] corazón *m*; **from the heart** con toda sinceridad; **my heart leapt** me dio un vuelco el corazón; **my heart sank** se me cayó el alma a los pies; **it's a subject close to my heart** es un tema que me apasiona; **from**

the bottom of my heart de (todo) corazón; **his heart isn't in it** no pone el corazón en ello; **in my heart of hearts** en lo más profundo de mi corazón; **to do sthg to one's heart's content** hacer algo cuanto uno quiera; **to break sb's heart** romper OR partir el corazón a alguien; **to set one's heart on sthg/on doing sthg** estar muy ilusionado(da) con algo/con hacer algo; **to take sthg to heart** tomarse algo a pecho; **to have a heart of gold** tener un corazón de oro - **2.** [courage]: **I didn't have the heart to tell her** no tuve valor para decírselo; **to lose heart** descorazonarse - **3.** [centre - of issue, problem] quid m; [- of city etc] centro m; [- of lettuce] cogollo m.

◆ **hearts** npl corazones mpl; **the six of hearts** el seis de corazones.

◆ **at heart** adv en el fondo.

◆ **by heart** adv de memoria.

heartache ['hɑːteɪk] n dolor m.

heart attack n infarto m.

heartbeat ['hɑːtbiːt] n latido m.

heartbreaking ['hɑːt,breɪkɪŋ] adj desolador(ra).

heartbroken ['hɑːt,brəʊkn] adj desolado(da), abatido(da).

heartburn ['hɑːtbɜːn] n ardor m de estómago.

heart disease n enfermedades fpl cardíacas OR del corazón.

heartening ['hɑːtnɪŋ] adj alentador(ra).

heart failure n paro m cardíaco.

heartfelt ['hɑːtfelt] adj sincero(ra), de todo corazón.

hearth [hɑːθ] n hogar m.

heartland ['hɑːtlænd] n fig núcleo m, corazón m.

heartless ['hɑːtlɪs] adj cruel, inhumano(na).

heartrending ['hɑːt,rendɪŋ] adj desgarrador(ra).

heart-searching n (U) examen m de conciencia.

heartthrob ['hɑːtθrɒb] n ídolo m.

heart-to-heart ◇ n charla f íntima. ◇ adj íntimo(ma).

heart transplant n transplante m de corazón.

heartwarming ['hɑːt,wɔːmɪŋ] adj gratificante, grato(ta).

hearty ['hɑːtɪ] (comp **-ier**, superl **-iest**) adj - **1.** [laughter] bonachón(ona); [welcome, congratulations, thanks] cordial; [person] fuertote(ta) - **2.** [meal] abundante; [appetite] bueno(na) - **3.** [dislike, distrust] profundo(da).

heat [hiːt] ◇ n - **1.** [gen] calor m - **2.** [specific temperature] temperatura f - **3.** fig [pressure] tensión f; **in the heat of the moment** en el calor del momento - **4.** [eliminating round] serie f, prueba f eliminatoria - **5.** ZOOL: **on** UK OR **in heat** en celo. ◇ vt calentar.

◆ **heat up** ◇ vt sep calentar. ◇ vi calentarse.

heated ['hiːtɪd] adj - **1.** [swimming pool] climatizado(da) - **2.** [debate, argument] acalorado(da).

heater ['hiːtəʳ] n calentador m, estufa f.

heath [hiːθ] n [place] brezal m.

heathen ['hiːðn] ◇ adj pagano(na). ◇ n pagano m, -na f.

heather ['heðəʳ] n brezo m.

heating ['hiːtɪŋ] n calefacción f.

heat rash n sarpullido m (por el calor).

heat-resistant adj refractario(ria), resistente al calor.

heat-seeking [-,siːkɪŋ] adj termodirigido(da).

heatstroke ['hiːtstrəʊk] n (U) insolación f.

heat wave n ola f de calor.

heave [hiːv] ◇ vt - **1.** [pull] tirar de, arrastrar; [push] empujar - **2.** inf [throw] tirar, lanzar. ◇ vi - **1.** [pull] tirar - **2.** [rise and fall - waves] ondular; [- chest] palpitar - **3.** [retch]: **my stomach heaved** tuve náuseas. ◇ n [pull] tirón m; [push] empujón m.

heaven ['hevn] n [Paradise] cielo m; **heaven (alone) knows!** ¡sabe Dios!; **for heaven's sake!** ¡por el amor de Dios!; **thank heaven!** ¡gracias a Dios!; **it was heaven** [delightful] fue divino.

◆ **heavens** npl: **the heavens** liter los cielos; **(good) heavens!** ¡cielos!

heavenly ['hevnlɪ] adj - **1.** inf dated [delightful] divino(na) - **2.** liter [of the skies] celestial.

heavily ['hevɪlɪ] adv - **1.** [smoke, drink] mucho; [rain] con fuerza; **heavily in debt** con muchas deudas - **2.** [solidly]: **heavily built** corpulento(ta) - **3.** [breathe, sigh] profundamente - **4.** [sit, move, fall] pesadamente - **5.** [speak] pesarosamente.

heaviness ['hevɪnɪs] n - **1.** [of fighting, traffic] intensidad f; [of casualties] gran número m - **2.** [of soil, mixture] densidad f - **3.** [of movement, breathing] pesadez f; [of blow] dureza f.

heavy ['hevɪ] (comp **-ier**, superl **-iest**) adj - **1.** [gen] pesado(da); [solid] sólido(da); **how heavy is it?** ¿cuánto pesa?; **heavy build** corpulencia f - **2.** [traffic, rain, fighting] intenso(sa); **a heavy cold** un fuerte resfriado; **to be a heavy sleeper** tener el sueño muy profundo; **to be a heavy smoker/drinker** ser un fumador/bebedor empedernido - **3.** [losses, responsibility] grande **- 4.** [soil, mixture] denso(sa) **- 5.** [blow] duro(ra); [fine, defeat] duro(ra) **- 6.** [busy - schedule, day] apretado(da) **- 7.** [work] duro(ra) **- 8.** [weather, air, day] cargado(da) **- 9.** [sad]: **with a heavy heart** con pesar **- 10.** [laden]: **heavy with** *liter* cargado(da) de.

heavy cream *n* *US* nata *f* para montar.

heavy-duty *adj* [materials] resistente; [machinery] sólido(da), para grandes cargas.

heavy goods vehicle *n* *UK* vehículo *m* (de transporte) pesado.

heavy-handed [-'hændɪd] *adj* torpe, poco sutil.

heavy industry *n* industria *f* pesada.

heavy metal *n* MUS música *f* heavy, heavy metal *m*.

heavyweight ['hevɪweɪt] <> *adj* SPORT de los pesos pesados. <> *n* SPORT peso *m* pesado.

Hebrew ['hi:bru:] <> *adj* hebreo(a). <> *n* **- 1.** [person] hebreo *m*, -a *f* **- 2.** [language] hebreo *m*.

Hebrides ['hebrɪdi:z] *npl*: **the Hebrides** las Hébridas.

heck [hek] *excl*: **what/where/why the heck...?** ¿qué/dónde/por qué demonios...?; **a heck of a lot of** la mar de.

heckle ['hekl] *vt* & *vi* interrumpir con exabruptos.

heckler ['heklər] *n* espectador molesto *m*, espectadora molesta *f* (*que interrumpe un espectáculo*).

hectare ['hekteər] *n* hectárea *f*.

hectic ['hektɪk] *adj* muy agitado(da), ajetreado(da).

hector ['hektər] *vt* intimidar.

he'd [hi:d] **- 1.** = he had ⊳ **have - 2.** = he would ⊳ **would**.

hedge [hedʒ] <> *n* seto *m*. <> *vi* [prevaricate] contestar con evasivas.

hedgehog ['hedʒhɒg] *n* erizo *m*.

hedgerow ['hedʒrəʊ] *n* seto *m* (*en el campo*).

hedonism ['hi:dənɪzm] *n* hedonismo *m*.

hedonist ['hi:dənɪst] *n* hedonista *mf*.

heed [hi:d] <> *n*: **to pay heed to sb** hacer caso a alguien; **to take heed of sthg** tener algo en cuenta. <> *vt* *fml* tener en cuenta.

heedless ['hi:dlɪs] *adj*: **to be heedless of sthg** no hacer caso de algo.

heel [hi:l] *n* **- 1.** [of foot] talón *m*; **to dig one's heels in** plantarse, mantenerse en sus trece; **to follow hard on the heels (of)** ir inmediatamente a continuación (de); **to take to one's**

heels poner pies en polvorosa; **to turn on one's heel** dar media vuelta **- 2.** [of shoe] tacón *m*, taco *m* *Amér*.

hefty ['heftɪ] (*comp* **-ier**, *superl* **-iest**) *adj inf* **- 1.** [person] fornido(da) **- 2.** [salary, fee, fine] considerable, importante.

heifer ['hefər] *n* vaquilla *f*.

height [haɪt] *n* **- 1.** [gen] altura *f*; [of person] estatura *f*; **5 metres in height** 5 metros de altura; **what height is it/are you?** ¿cuánto mide/mides? **- 2.** [zenith]: **the height of** [gen] el punto álgido de; [ignorance, bad taste] el colmo de.

➤ **heights** *npl* [high places] alturas *fpl*; **to be afraid of heights** tener vértigo.

heighten ['haɪtn] <> *vt* intensificar, aumentar. <> *vi* intensificarse, aumentar.

heinous ['heɪnəs] *adj fml* execrable, atroz.

heir [eər] *n* heredero *m*.

heir apparent (*pl* **heirs apparent**) *n* heredero *m* forzoso.

heiress ['eərɪs] *n* heredera *f*.

heirloom ['eəlu:m] *n* reliquia *f* de familia.

heist [haɪst] *n* *inf* golpe *m*, robo *m*.

held [held] *pt* & *pp* ⊳ **hold**.

helices ['helɪsi:z] *npl* ⊳ **helix**.

helicopter ['helɪkɒptər] *n* helicóptero *m*.

heliport ['helɪpɔ:t] *n* helipuerto *m*.

helium ['hi:lɪəm] *n* helio *m*.

helix ['hi:lɪks] (*pl* **-es** OR **helices**) *n* [spiral] hélice *f*.

hell [hel] <> *n* infierno *m*; **what/where/why the hell...?** *inf* ¿qué/dónde/por qué demonios...?; **one** OR **a hell of a lot** *inf* muchísimo; **one** OR **a hell of a mess** *inf* un lío de mil demonios; **one** OR **a hell of a nice guy** *inf* un tipo estupendo; **like hell** [a lot] una barbaridad; [not at all so] ¡qué va!; **it was hell** *inf* fue un infierno; **to run like hell** *inf* correr como un loco; **to get the hell out (of)** *inf* salir echando leches (de); **all hell broke loose** *inf* se armó la gorda; **to do sthg for the hell of it** *inf* hacer algo porque sí; **to give sb hell** *inf* hacérselas pasar canutas a alguien; **go to hell!** *v inf* ¡vete al infierno!; **to play hell with sthg** *inf* causar estragos en algo; **to hell with...** *inf* ¡a la porra (con)...!; **neighbours from hell** *inf* vecinos infernales; **boyfriend from hell** *inf* novio infernal. <> *excl inf* ¡hostias!

he'll [hi:l] **- 1.** = he will ⊳ **will - 2.** = he shall ⊳ **shall**.

hell-bent *adj*: **to be hell-bent on sthg/on doing sthg** estar totalmente decidido(da) a hacer algo.

hellish ['helɪʃ] *adj inf* diabólico(ca), infernal.

hello [hə'ləʊ], **hallo, hullo** *excl* **- 1.** [as greeting] ¡hola!; [on phone - when answering] ¡diga!, ¡bueno! *Méx*, ¡holá! *R Plata*, ¡aló! *Andes*; [- when calling] ¡oiga!, ¡holá! *R Plata*, ¡aló! *Andes*; **to say hello to sb** saludar a alguien **- 2.** [to attract attention] ¡oiga!

helm [helm] *n lit* & *fig* timón *m*; **at the helm** al timón.

helmet ['helmɪt] *n* casco *m*.

helmsman ['helmzmən] (*pl* **-men** [-mən]) *n* NAUT timonel *m*.

help [help] ◇ *n* **- 1.** [gen & COMPUT] ayuda *f*; **with the help of** con la ayuda de; **to be a help** ser una ayuda; **to be of help** ayudar **- 2.** (*U*) [emergency aid] socorro *m*, ayuda *f*. ◇ *vt* **- 1.** [assist]: **to help sb (to) do sthg/with sthg** ayudar a alguien (a hacer algo/con algo); **can I help you?** [in shop, bank] ¿en qué puedo servirle? **- 2.** [avoid]: **I can't help it/feeling sad** no puedo evitarlo/evitar que me dé pena; **it can't be helped** ¿qué se le va a hacer? **- 3.** [with food, drink]: **to help o.s. (to sthg)** servirse (algo). ◇ *vi*: **to help (with)** ayudar (con). ◇ *excl* ¡socorro!, ¡auxilio!
➤ **help out** ◇ *vt sep* echar una mano a. ◇ *vi* echar una mano.

helper ['helpər] *n* **- 1.** [gen] ayudante *mf* **- 2.** *US* [to do housework] mujer *f* OR señora *f* de la limpieza.

helpful ['helpfʊl] *adj* **- 1.** [willing to help] servicial, atento(ta) **- 2.** [providing assistance] útil.

helping ['helpɪŋ] *n* ración *f*; **would you like a second helping?** ¿quiere repetir?

helping hand *n*: **to lend a helping hand** ayudar.

helpless ['helplɪs] *adj* [child] indefenso(sa); [look, gesture] impotente.

helplessly ['helplɪslɪ] *adv* **- 1.** [unable to stop] sin poder parar **- 2.** [in a helpless manner] impotentemente.

helpline ['helplaɪn] *n* servicio *m* de asistencia telefónica.

help menu *n* COMPUT menú *m* de ayuda.

Helsinki ['helsɪŋkɪ] *n* Helsinki.

helter-skelter [,heltə'skeltər] *UK* ◇ *n* tobogán *m* gigante. ◇ *adv* atropelladamente.

hem [hem] ◇ *n* dobladillo *m*. ◇ *vt* (*pt* & *pp* **-med**, *cont* **-ming**) hacerle el dobladillo a.
➤ **hem in** *vt sep* rodear, cercar.

he-man *n inf hum* tiarrón *m*.

hematology, haematology [,hi:mə'tɒlədʒɪ] *n* hematología *f*.

hemisphere ['hemɪˌsfɪər] *n* [of earth & ANAT] hemisferio *m*.

hemline ['hemlaɪn] *n* bajo *m* (*de falda etc*).

hemoglobin, haemoglobin [,hi:mə'gləʊbɪn] *n* hemoglobina *f*.

hemophilia, haemophilia [,hi:mə'fɪlɪə] *n* hemofilia *f*.

hemophiliac, haemophiliac [,hi:mə'fɪlɪæk] *n* hemofílico *m*, -ca *f*.

hemorrhage, haemorrhage ['hemərɪdʒ] ◇ *n* hemorragia *f*. ◇ *vi* tener una hemorragia.

hemorrhoids, haemorrhoids ['hemərɔɪdz] *npl* hemorroides *fpl*.

hemp [hemp] *n* cáñamo *m*.

hen [hen] *n* **- 1.** [female chicken] gallina *f* **- 2.** [female bird] hembra *f*.

hence [hens] *adv fml* **- 1.** [therefore] por lo tanto, así pues **- 2.** [from now]: **five years hence** de aquí a cinco años.

henceforth [,hens'fɔːθ] *adv fml* de ahora en adelante, en lo sucesivo.

henchman ['hentʃmən] (*pl* **-men** [-mən]) *n pej* esbirro *m*.

henna ['henə] ◇ *n* henna *f*. ◇ *vt* teñir con henna.

hen party, hen night *n inf* despedida *f* de soltera.

henpecked ['henpekt] *adj pej*: **a henpecked husband** un calzonazos.

hepatitis [,hepə'taɪtɪs] *n* hepatitis *f inv*.

her [hɜːr] ◇ *pers pron* **- 1.** (direct - unstressed) la; (- stressed) ella; [referring to ship, car etc] lo; **I know her** la conozco; **I like her** me gusta; **it's her** es ella; **if I were** OR **was her** si (yo) fuera ella; **you can't expect her to do it** no esperarás que ella lo haga; **fill her up!** AUT ¡llénemelo!, ¡lleno, por favor! **- 2.** (indirect - used with other 3rd person pronouns) se; **he sent her a letter** le mandó una carta; **we spoke to her** hablamos con ella; **I gave it to her** se lo di **- 3.** (after prep, in comparisons etc) ella; **I'm shorter than her** yo soy más bajo que ella. ◇ *poss adj* su, sus (pl); **her coat** su abrigo; **her children** sus niños; **her name is Sarah** se llama Sarah; **it wasn't her fault** no fue culpa suya OR su culpa; **she washed her hair** se lavó el pelo.

herald ['herəld] ◇ *vt fml* **- 1.** [signify, usher in] anunciar **- 2.** [proclaim] proclamar. ◇ *n* **- 1.** [messenger] heraldo *m* **- 2.** [sign] anuncio *m*.

heraldry ['herəldrɪ] *n* heráldica *f*.

herb [*UK* hɜːb, *US* ɜːrb] *n* hierba *f* (aromática o medicinal).

herbaceous [hɜːˈbeɪʃəs] *adj* herbáceo(a).

herbal [*UK* 'hɜːbl, *US* ɜːrbl] *adj* [remedy, medicine] a base de hierbas.

herbal tea *n* infusión *f*.

herbivore ['hɜːbɪvɔːʳ] *n* herbívoro *m*, -ra *f*.

herd [hɜːd] ◇ *n* [of cattle, goats] rebaño *m*; [of elephants] manada *f*. ◇ *vt* - **1.** [drive] llevar en rebaño - **2.** *fig* [push] conducir (en grupo) bruscamente.

herdsman ['hɜːdzmən] (*pl* -**men** [-mən]) *n* [of cattle] vaquero *m*.

here [hɪəʳ] *adv* aquí; **here he is/they are** aquí está/están; **here it is** aquí está; **here is the book** aquí tienes el libro; **here are the keys** aquí tienes las llaves; **here you are** [when giving] aquí tienes; **here and there** aquí y allá; **here's to** [in toast] brindemos por.

hereabouts UK ['hɪərə,baʊts], **hereabout** US [,hɪərə'baʊt] *adv* por aquí.

hereafter [,hɪərˈɑːftəʳ] ◇ *adv fml* [from now on] a partir de ahora, de ahora en adelante; [later on] más tarde. ◇ *n*: **the hereafter** el más allá, la otra vida.

hereby [,hɪəˈbaɪ] *adv fml* - **1.** [in documents] por la presente - **2.** [when speaking]: **I hereby declare you the winner** desde este momento te declaro vencedor.

hereditary [hɪˈredɪtrɪ] *adj* hereditario(ria).

heredity [hɪˈredətɪ] *n* herencia *f*.

heresy ['herəsɪ] (*pl* -**ies**) *n fig* & RELIG herejía *f*.

heretic ['herətɪk] *n* RELIG hereje *mf*.

herewith [,hɪəˈwɪð] *adv fml* [with letter]: '**please find herewith...**' 'le mando adjunto...'.

heritage ['herɪtɪdʒ] *n* patrimonio *m*.

heritage centre *n* edificio o museo en un lugar de interés histórico.

hermaphrodite [hɜːˈmæfrədaɪt] ◇ *adj* ZOOL hermafrodita. ◇ *n* ZOOL hermafrodita *mf*.

hermetically [hɜːˈmetɪklɪ] *adv*: **hermetically sealed** cerrado(da) herméticamente.

hermit ['hɜːmɪt] *n* ermitaño *m*, -ña *f*.

hernia ['hɜːnjə] *n* hernia *f*.

hero ['hɪərəʊ] (*pl* -**es**) *n* - **1.** [gen] héroe *m* - **2.** [idol] ídolo *m* - **3.** US [sandwich] bocadillo hecho con una barra de pan larga y estrecha, relleno de varios ingredientes.

heroic [hɪˈrəʊɪk] *adj* heroico(ca).

heroin ['herəʊɪn] *n* heroína *f (droga)*; **heroin addict** heroinómano *m*, -na *f*.

heroine ['herəʊɪn] *n* heroína *f*.

heroism ['herəʊɪzm] *n* heroísmo *m*.

heron ['herən] (*pl* **heron** OR -**s**) *n* garza *f* real.

hero worship *n* veneración *f*.

herpes ['hɜːpiːz] *n* herpes *m inv*.

herring ['herɪŋ] (*pl* **herring** OR -**s**) *n* arenque *m*.

herringbone ['herɪŋbəʊn] *n* [pattern] espiga *f*, espiguilla *f*.

hers [hɜːz] *poss pron* suyo(suya); **that money is hers** ese dinero es suyo; **those keys are hers** esas llaves son suyas; **it wasn't his fault, it was hers** no fue culpa de él sino de ella; **a friend of hers** un amigo suyo, un amigo de ella; **mine is good, but hers is bad** el mío es bueno pero el suyo es malo.

herself [hɜːˈself] *pron* - **1.** *(reflexive)* se; *(after prep)* sí misma; **with herself** consigo misma - **2.** *(for emphasis)* ella misma; **she did it herself** lo hizo ella sola.

Herts. [hɑːts] (*abbr of* **Hertfordshire**), condado inglés.

he's [hiːz] - **1.** = **he is** ▷ **be** - **2.** = **he has** ▷ **have**.

hesitant ['hezɪtənt] *adj* - **1.** [unsure of oneself] indeciso(sa), inseguro(ra) - **2.** [faltering, slow to appear] vacilante.

hesitate ['hezɪteɪt] *vi* vacilar, dudar; **to hesitate to do sthg** dudar en hacer algo.

hesitation [,hezɪˈteɪʃn] *n* vacilación *f*; **without hesitation** sin vacilar; **to have no hesitation in doing sthg** no dudar en hacer algo.

hessian ['hesɪən] *n* UK arpillera *f*.

heterogeneous [,hetərəˈdʒiːnjəs] *adj fml* heterogéneo(a).

heterosexual [,hetərəʊˈsekʃʊəl] ◇ *adj* heterosexual. ◇ *n* heterosexual *mf*.

hew [hjuː] (*pt* -**ed**, *pp* -**ed** OR -**n**) *vt liter* [tree, branch] tallar; [figure, statue] tallar.

hex [heks] *n* [curse] maleficio *m*, maldición *f*.

hexagon ['heksəgən] *n* hexágono *m*.

hexagonal [hek'sægənl] *adj* hexagonal.

hey [heɪ] *excl* ¡eh!, ¡oye!, ¡che! Amér

heyday ['heɪdeɪ] *n* apogeo *m*, auge *m*.

HGV (*abbr of* **heavy goods vehicle**) *n*: **an HGV licence** un carné de vehículo de gran tonelaje.

hi [haɪ] *excl inf* [hello] ¡hola!

HI *abbr of* **Hawaii**.

hiatus [haɪˈeɪtəs] (*pl* -**es**) *n fml* [pause] interrupción *f*.

hiatus hernia *n* hernia *f* de hiato.

hibernate ['haɪbəneɪt] *vi* hibernar.

hibernation [,haɪbəˈneɪʃn] *n* hibernación *f*.

hiccough, hiccup ['hɪkʌp] ◇ *n* - **1.** [caused by wind] hipo *m*; **to have (the) hiccoughs** tener hipo - **2.** *fig* [difficulty] contratiempo *m*. ◇ *vi* (*pt* & *pp* -**ped**, *cont* -**ping**) hipar.

hick [hɪk] *n esp US inf pej* paleto *m*, -ta *f*, palurdo *m*, -da *f*.

hickey [hɪkɪ] *n esp US inf* [lovebite] marca *f* de un beso, chupetón *m*.

hid [hɪd] *pt* ▷ **hide**.

hidden ['hɪdn] <> pp ▷ hide. <> adj oculto(ta).

hide [haɪd] <> vt (pt hid, pp hidden) - **1.** [conceal] esconder, ocultar; **to hide sthg (from sb)** esconder OR ocultar algo (a alguien) - **2.** [cover] tapar, ocultar. <> vi (pt hid, pp hidden) esconderse. <> n - **1.** [animal skin] piel f - **2.** [for watching birds, animals] puesto m.

hide-and-seek n escondite m.

hideaway ['haɪdəweɪ] n inf escondite m.

hidebound ['haɪdbaʊnd] adj pej de miras estrechas.

hideous ['hɪdɪəs] adj horrible, espantoso(sa).

hideout ['haɪdaʊt] n guarida f, escondrijo m.

hiding ['haɪdɪŋ] n - **1.** [concealment]: **in hiding** escondido(da) - **2.** inf [beating]: **to give sb/get a (good) hiding** darle a alguien/recibir una (buena) paliza.

hiding place n escondite m.

hierarchical [ˌhaɪə'rɑːkɪkl] adj jerárquico(ca).

hierarchy ['haɪərɑːkɪ] (pl -ies) n jerarquía f.

hieroglyphics [ˌhaɪərə'glɪfɪks] npl jeroglíficos mpl.

hi-fi ['haɪfaɪ] <> adj de alta fidelidad. <> n equipo m de alta fidelidad.

higgledy-piggledy [ˌhɪgldɪ'pɪgldɪ] inf <> adj desordenado(da). <> adv de cualquier manera, a la buena de Dios.

high [haɪ] <> adj - **1.** [gen] alto(ta); [altitude] grande; **it's 6 metres high** tiene 6 metros de alto OR altura; **how high is it?** ¿cuánto mide?; **temperatures in the high 20s** temperaturas cercanas a los 30 grados; **at high speed** a gran velocidad; **to have a high opinion of** tener muy buen concepto de - **2.** [wind] fuerte - **3.** [risk, quality] grande - **4.** [ideals, principles, tone] elevado(da) - **5.** [high-pitched] agudo(da) - **6.** inf colocado(da). <> adv alto; **he threw the ball high in the air** lanzó la pelota muy alto. <> n - **1.** [highest point] punto m álgido; **to reach a new high** alcanzar un nuevo récord - **2.** [weather front] anticiclón m; [top temperature] máxima f.

highball ['haɪbɔːl] n US highball m.

highbrow ['haɪbraʊ] adj culto(ta), intelectual.

high chair n trona f.

high-class adj [superior] de (alta) categoría.

high command n alto mando m.

high commissioner n alto comisario m, alta comisaria f.

High Court n UK tribunal m supremo.

high-density adj COMPUT de alta densidad.

higher ['haɪər] adj [exam, qualification] superior.

◆ **Higher** n: **Higher (Grade)** en Escocia, examen realizado al final de la enseñanza secundaria.

higher education n enseñanza f superior.

high-fidelity adj de alta fidelidad.

high-flier n persona ambiciosa y con un prometedor futuro.

high-flying adj [ambitious] ambicioso y prometedor (ambiciosa y prometedora).

high-handed [-'hændɪd] adj despótico(ca).

high-heeled [-'hiːld] adj de tacón alto.

high horse n inf: **to get on one's high horse** echar un sermón.

high jump n salto m de altura; **you're** OR **you'll be for the high jump** UK inf te la vas a cargar.

Highlands ['haɪləndz] npl: **the Highlands** [of Scotland] las Tierras Altas de Escocia.

high-level adj de alto nivel.

high life n: **the high life** la buena vida.

highlight ['haɪlaɪt] <> n [of event, occasion] punto m culminante. <> vt - **1.** [visually] resaltar, marcar - **2.** [emphasize] destacar, resaltar.

◆ **highlights** npl - **1.** [in hair] reflejos mpl - **2.** [of match] mejores momentos mpl.

highlighter (pen) ['haɪlaɪtə-] n rotulador m, marcador m.

highly ['haɪlɪ] adv - **1.** [very, extremely] muy; **highly paid** bien pagado(da) - **2.** [favourably]: **to speak highly of sb** hablar muy bien de alguien; **to think highly of sb** tener a alguien en mucha estima.

highly-strung adj muy nervioso(sa).

high mass n misa f mayor.

Highness ['haɪnɪs] n: **His/Her/Your (Royal) Highness** Su Alteza f (Real); **their (Royal) Highnesses** Sus Altezas (Reales).

high-octane adj de alto octanaje.

high-pitched [-'pɪtʃt] adj agudo(da).

high point n [of occasion] momento m OR punto m culminante.

high-powered [-'paʊəd] adj - **1.** [powerful] de gran potencia - **2.** [prestigious - activity, place] prestigioso(sa); [- person] de altos vuelos.

high-pressure adj - **1.** [cylinder, gas etc] a alta presión - **2.** METEOR [zone, area] de altas presiones - **3.** [tactics, approach] agresivo(va).

high priest n RELIG sumo sacerdote m.

high-ranking [-'ræŋkɪŋ] adj [in army etc] de alta graduación; [in government]: **high-ranking official** alto cargo m.

high resolution adj COMPUT de alta resolución.

high-rise adj: **high-rise building** torre f.

high-risk *adj* de alto riesgo.

high school *n* ≃ instituto *m* de bachillerato.

high seas *npl*: **the high seas** alta mar *f*.

high season *n* temporada *f* alta.

high-speed *adj* de alta velocidad.

high-spirited *adj* [person] animado(da).

high spot *n* punto *m* culminante.

high street ◇ *adj* UK [bank] comercial. ◇ *n* calle *f* mayor OR principal.

hightail ['haɪteɪl] *vt esp US inf*: **to hightail it** pirárselas.

high tea *n* UK merienda-cena *f*.

high tech, hi-tech [-'tek] *adj* de alta tecnología.

high-tension *adj* de alta tensión.

high tide *n* [of sea] marea *f* alta.

high treason *n* alta traición *f*.

high water *n* (*U*) marea *f* alta.

highway ['haɪweɪ] *n* - **1.** US [main road between cities] autopista *f* - **2.** UK [any main road] carretera *f*.

Highway Code *n* UK: **the Highway Code** el código de la circulación.

high wire *n* alambre *m*, cuerda *f* floja.

hijack ['haɪdʒæk] ◇ *n* [of aircraft] secuestro *m* aéreo. ◇ *vt* [aircraft] secuestrar.

hijacker ['haɪdʒækər] *n* secuestrador *m*, -ra *f* (*de un avión*).

hike [haɪk] ◇ *n* - **1.** [long walk] excursión *f*, caminata *f*; **to go for** OR **on a hike** ir de excursión - **2.** [increase] subida *f*. ◇ *vi* [go for walk] ir de excursión.

hiker ['haɪkər] *n* excursionista *mf*.

hiking ['haɪkɪŋ] *n* excursionismo *m*; **to go hiking** ir de excursión.

hilarious [hɪ'leərɪəs] *adj* desternillante.

hilarity [hɪ'lærətɪ] *n fml* hilaridad *f*.

hill [hɪl] *n* - **1.** [mound] colina *f* - **2.** [slope] cuesta *f*.

hillbilly ['hɪl,bɪlɪ] (*pl* -ies) *n* US *pej* palurdo *m*, -da *f* de las montañas.

hillside ['hɪlsaɪd] *n* ladera *f*.

hill start *n* AUT arranque *m* en una cuesta.

hilltop ['hɪltɒp] *n* cumbre *f* de una colina.

hilly ['hɪlɪ] (*comp* -ier, *superl* -iest) *adj* montañoso(sa).

hilt [hɪlt] *n* puño *m*, empuñadura *f*; **to support/ defend sb to the hilt** apoyar/defender a alguien sin reservas; **to be mortgaged to the hilt** tener una hipoteca enorme.

him [hɪm] *pers pron* - **1.** (*direct - unstressed*) lo, le; (*- stressed*) él; **I know him** lo OR le conozco; **I like him** me gusta; **it's him** es él; **if I were** OR **was**

him si (yo) fuera él; **you can't expect him to do it** no esperarás que él lo haga - **2.** (*indirect - gen*) le; (*- with other 3rd person pronouns*) se; **she sent him a letter** le mandó una carta; **we spoke to him** hablamos con él; **I gave it to him** se lo di - **3.** (*after prep, in comparisons etc*) él; **I'm shorter than him** yo soy más bajo que él.

Himalayan [,hɪmə'leɪən] *adj* himalayo(ya).

Himalayas [,hɪmə'leɪəz] *npl*: **the Himalayas** el Himalaya.

himself [hɪm'self] *pron* - **1.** (*reflexive*) se; (*after prep*) sí mismo; **with himself** consigo mismo - **2.** (*for emphasis*) él mismo; **he did it himself** lo hizo él solo.

hind [haɪnd] ◇ *adj* trasero(ra). ◇ *n* (*pl* hind OR -s) cierva *f*.

hinder ['hɪndər] *vt* [gen] estorbar; [progress, talks, attempts] entorpecer, dificultar.

Hindi ['hɪndɪ] *n* [language] hindi *m*.

hindmost ['haɪndməʊst] *adj* postrero(ra).

hindquarters ['haɪndkwɔːtəz] *npl* cuartos *mpl* traseros.

hindrance ['hɪndrəns] *n* [obstacle] obstáculo *m*, impedimento *m*; [person] estorbo *m*.

hindsight ['haɪndsaɪt] *n*: **with the benefit of hindsight** ahora que se sabe lo que pasó.

Hindu ['hɪnduː] ◇ *adj* hindú. ◇ *n* (*pl* -s) hindú *mf*.

Hinduism ['hɪnduːɪzm] *n* hinduismo *m*.

hinge [hɪndʒ] *n* [on door, window] bisagra *f*.
➡ **hinge (up)on** *vt insep* (*cont* hingeing) [depend on] depender de.

hint [hɪnt] ◇ *n* - **1.** [indication] indirecta *f*; **to drop a hint** lanzar una indirecta; **to take the hint** darse por aludido(da) - **2.** [piece of advice] consejo *m* - **3.** [small amount, suggestion] atisbo *m*, asomo *m*; [of colour] pizca *f*. ◇ *vi*: **to hint at sthg** insinuar algo. ◇ *vt*: **to hint that** insinuar que.

hinterland ['hɪntəlænd] *n* [area around coast, river] interior *m*.

hip [hɪp] ◇ *n* ANAT cadera *f*. ◇ *adj inf* moderno(na).

hipbath ['hɪpbɑːθ] *n* baño *m* de asiento.

hipbone ['hɪpbəʊn] *n* hueso *m* de la cadera.

hip flask *n* petaca *f*.

hip-hop *n* MUS hip hop *m*.

hippie, hippy ['hɪpɪ] *n* hippy *mf*.

hippo ['hɪpəʊ] (*pl* -s) *n inf* hipopótamo *m*.

hippopotamus [,hɪpə'pɒtəməs] (*pl* -muses OR -mi [-maɪ]) *n* hipopótamo *m*.

hippy ['hɪpɪ] (*pl* -ies) = hippie.

hire ['haɪə'] ⋄ n (U) [of car, equipment] alquiler m; **for hire** [taxi] libre; **'boats for hire'** 'se
alquilan barcos'; **on hire** de alquiler. ⋄ vt
- **1.** [rent] alquilar - **2.** [employ] contratar.
◆ **hire out** vt sep [car, equipment] alquilar;
[one's services] ofrecer.

hire car n UK coche m de alquiler.

hire purchase n (U) UK compra f a plazos; **to
buy sthg on hire purchase** comprar algo a
plazos.

his [hɪz] ⋄ poss adj su, sus (pl); **his house** su
casa; **his children** sus niños; **his name is Joe**
se llama Joe; **it wasn't his fault** no fue culpa
suya OR su culpa; **he washed his hair** se lavó
el pelo. ⋄ poss pron suyo(suya); **that money
is his** ese dinero es suyo; **those keys are his**
esas llaves son suyas; **it wasn't her fault, it
was his** no fue culpa de ella sino de él; **a friend
of his** un amigo suyo, un amigo de él; **mine is
good, but his is bad** el mío es bueno pero el
suyo es malo.

Hispanic [hɪ'spænɪk] ⋄ adj hispánico(ca). ⋄ n
esp US hispano m, -na f.

hiss [hɪs] ⋄ n - **1.** [of person] bisbiseo m, siseo m - **2.** [of steam, gas, snake] silbido m. ⋄ vt
[performance] silbar, abuchear. ⋄ vi - **1.** [per-
son] bisbisear, sisear; [to express disapproval] silbar, abuchear - **2.** [steam, gas, snake] silbar.

histogram ['hɪstəgræm] n histograma m.

historian [hɪ'stɔːrɪən] n historiador m, -ra f.

historic [hɪ'stɒrɪk] adj [significant] histórico(ca).

historical [hɪ'stɒrɪkəl] adj histórico(ca).

history ['hɪstərɪ] (pl -ies) ⋄ n - **1.** [gen] historia f; **to go down in history** pasar a la historia; **to make history** hacer historia - **2.** [past
record & COMPUT] historial m. ⋄ comp [book,
teacher, programme] de historia.

histrionics [hɪstrɪ'ɒnɪks] npl pej teatro m, teatralidad f.

hit [hɪt] ⋄ n - **1.** [blow] golpe m - **2.** [successful
strike] impacto m; **to score a direct hit** dar de
lleno en el blanco - **3.** [success, record] éxito m
- **4.** COMPUT visita f. ⋄ comp de éxito. ⋄ vt
(pt & pp hit, cont -ting) - **1.** [subj: person] pegar, golpear - **2.** [crash into] chocar contra OR
con - **3.** [reach] alcanzar; [bull's-eye] dar en
- **4.** [affect badly] afectar - **5.** [occur to]: **the solution hit me** se me ocurrió la solución
▸▸ **to hit it off (with sb)** hacer buenas migas
(con alguien).
◆ **hit back** vi: **to hit back (at sb)** devolver la
pelota (a alguien); **to hit back (at sthg)** responder (a algo).
◆ **hit on** vt insep - **1.** = hit upon - **2.** US inf
[chat up] ligar con.
◆ **hit out** vi: **to hit out at** [physically] tratar de
golpear; [criticize] condenar.

◆ **hit upon, hit on** vt insep [think of] dar con.

hit-and-miss = hit-or-miss.

hit-and-run adj [driver] que se da a la fuga después de causar un accidente; [accident] en que
el conductor se da a la fuga.

hitch [hɪtʃ] ⋄ n [problem, snag] problema m, pega f. ⋄ vt - **1.** [catch]: **to hitch a lift** conseguir
que le lleven a uno en coche - **2.** [fasten]: **to
hitch sthg on** OR **onto sthg** enganchar algo a
algo. ⋄ vi [hitchhike] hacer autostop.
◆ **hitch up** vt sep [clothes] subirse.

hitchhike ['hɪtʃhaɪk] vi hacer autostop.

hitchhiker ['hɪtʃhaɪkə'] n autoestopista mf.

hi-tech [,haɪ'tek] = high tech.

hitherto [,hɪðə'tuː] adv fml hasta ahora.

hit list n lista f negra, lista f de futuras víctimas.

hit man n asesino m a sueldo.

hit-or-miss, hit-and-miss adj azaroso(sa),
a la buena de Dios.

hit parade n dated lista f de éxitos.

HIV (abbr of **human immunodeficiency virus**)
n VIH m; **to be HIV-positive** ser seroposíti-
vo(va).

hive [haɪv] n [for bees] colmena f; **a hive of
activity** un enjambre, un centro de actividad.
◆ **hive off** vt sep [separate] transferir.

HM (abbr of **His (or Her) Majesty**) SM.

HMG (abbr of **His (or Her) Majesty's Government**) expresión utilizada en documentos
oficiales en Gran Bretaña.

HMI (abbr of **His (or Her) Majesty's Inspector**)
n inspector de enseñanza en Gran Bretaña.

HMO (abbr of **health maintenance organization**) n US organización para el mantenimiento de la salud.

HMS (abbr of **His (or Her) Majesty's Ship**) buque de guerra británico.

HMSO (abbr of **His (or Her) Majesty's Stationery Office**) n servicio oficial de publicaciones en Gran Bretaña, ≃ Imprenta f Nacional.

HNC (abbr of **Higher National Certificate**) n
diploma técnico en Gran Bretaña.

HND (abbr of **Higher National Diploma**) n diploma técnico superior en Gran Bretaña.

hoard [hɔːd] ⋄ n [store] acumulación f, acopio m. ⋄ vt [collect, save] acumular; [food] acaparar.

hoarding ['hɔːdɪŋ] n UK [for advertisements,
posters] valla f publicitaria.

hoarfrost ['hɔːfrɒst] n escarcha f.

hoarse [hɔːs] adj - **1.** [voice] ronco(ca) - **2.** [per-
son] afónico(ca).

hoax [həʊks] *n* engaño *m*; **hoax call** falsa alarma telefónica.

hoaxer ['həʊksər] *n* bromista *mf*.

hob [hɒb] *n* UK [on cooker] encimera *f*.

hobble ['hɒbl] *vi* [limp] cojear.

hobby ['hɒbɪ] (*pl* **-ies**) *n* [leisure activity] hobby *m*, afición *f*.

hobbyhorse ['hɒbɪhɔːs] *n* **- 1.** [toy] caballo *m* de juguete **- 2.** [favourite topic] caballo *m* de batalla, tema *m* favorito.

hobnob ['hɒbnɒb] (*pt* & *pp* **-bed**, *cont* **-bing**) *vi*: **to hobnob with sb** codearse con alguien.

hobo ['həʊbəʊ] (*pl* **-es** OR **-s**) *n* US [tramp] vagabundo *m*, -da *f*.

Ho Chi Minh City [,həʊ,tʃiː'mɪn-] *n* Ho Chi Minh.

hock [hɒk] *n* [wine] vino *m* blanco del Rin.

hockey ['hɒkɪ] *n* **- 1.** [on grass] hockey *m* sobre hierba **- 2.** US [ice hockey] hockey *m* sobre hielo.

hocus-pocus [,həʊkəs'pəʊkəs] *n (U)* [trickery] camelo *m*, engaño *m*.

hod [hɒd] *n* [for bricks] artesa *f*, gaveta *f*.

hodgepodge US = **hotchpotch**.

hoe [həʊ] <> *n* azada *f*, azadón *m*. <> *vt* remover con la azada.

hog [hɒg] <> *n* US [pig] cerdo *m*, puerco *m*; **to go the whole hog** *fig* tirar la casa por la ventana. <> *vt* (*pt* & *pp* **-ged**, *cont* **-ging**) *inf* [monopolize] acaparar.

Hogmanay ['hɒgməneɪ] *n denominación escocesa de la Nochevieja.*

hoist [hɔɪst] <> *n* [pulley, crane] grúa *f*; [lift] montacargas *m inv*. <> *vt* izar.

hokum ['həʊkəm] *n* US *inf* palabrería *f*.

hold [həʊld] <> *vt* (*pt* & *pp* **held**) **- 1.** [have hold of] tener cogido(da) **- 2.** [keep in position] sujetar **- 3.** [sustain, support] sostener, aguantar **- 4.** [embrace] abrazar **- 5.** [as prisoner] detener; **to hold sb prisoner/hostage** tener a alguien como prisionero/rehén **- 6.** [keep] guardar **- 7.** [maintain - interest etc] mantener **- 8.** [have, possess] poseer **- 9.** [contain - gen] contener; [- number of people] tener cabida para; [- fears, promise etc] guardar **- 10.** [conduct, stage - event] celebrar; [- conversation] mantener; [- inquiry] realizar **- 11.** *fml* [consider] considerar; **to hold (that)** mantener OR sostener que; **to hold sb responsible for sthg** considerar a alguien responsable de algo; **to hold sthg dear** apreciar mucho algo **- 12.** [on telephone]: **please hold the line** no cuelgue por favor **- 13.** MIL ocupar, tener
▶▶ **hold it** OR **everything!** ¡para!, ¡espera!; **to hold one's own** defenderse. <> *vi* (*pt* & *pp* **held**) **- 1.** [luck, weather] continuar así; [promise, offer] seguir en pie; **to hold still** OR

steady estarse quieto **- 2.** [on phone] esperar. <> *n* **- 1.** [grasp, grip]: **to have a firm hold on sthg** tener algo bien agarrado; **to take** OR **lay hold of sthg** agarrar algo; **to get hold of sthg** [obtain] hacerse con algo; **to get hold of sb** [find] localizar a alguien **- 2.** [of ship, aircraft] bodega *f* **- 3.** [control, influence] dominio *m*, control *m*; **to take hold** [fire] extenderse.
▶ **on hold** *adv*: **to put sthg on hold** suspender algo temporalmente; **to put sb on hold** [on phone] poner a alguien a la espera.
▶ **hold against** *vt sep*: **to hold sthg against sb** *fig* tener algo contra alguien.
▶ **hold back** <> *vi* [hesitate] vacilar; **to hold back from doing sthg** abstenerse de hacer algo. <> *vt sep* **- 1.** [tears, anger] contener, reprimir **- 2.** [secret] ocultar, no revelar **- 3.** [person]: **to hold sb back from doing sthg** impedir a alguien hacer algo.
▶ **hold down** *vt sep* [job] conservar.
▶ **hold off** <> *vt sep* [fend off] rechazar. <> *vi* no producirse; **the rain held off** no llovió.
▶ **hold on** *vi* **- 1.** [wait] esperar; [on phone] no colgar **- 2.** [grip]: **to hold on (to sthg)** agarrarse (a algo).
▶ **hold onto** *vt insep* [keep] retener.
▶ **hold out** <> *vt sep* [hand] tender; [arms] extender. <> *vi* **- 1.** [last] durar **- 2.** [resist]: **to hold out (against sthg/sb)** resistir (ante algo/a alguien).
▶ **hold out for** *vt insep* insistir en.
▶ **hold up** <> *vt sep* **- 1.** [raise] levantar, alzar **- 2.** [delay] retrasar **- 3.** *inf* [rob] atracar, asaltar. <> *vi* [theory, facts] tenerse en pie.
▶ **hold with** *vt insep* [approve of] estar de acuerdo con.

holdall ['həʊldɔːl] *n* UK bolsa *f* de viaje.

holder ['həʊldər] *n* **- 1.** [container] soporte *m*; [for candle] candelero *m*; [for cigarette] boquilla *f* **- 2.** [owner] titular *mf*; [of ticket, record, title] poseedor *m*, -ra *f*.

holding ['həʊldɪŋ] <> *n* **- 1.** [investment] participación *f* **- 2.** [farm] propiedad *f*, terreno *m* de cultivo. <> *adj* [action, operation] de mantenimiento.

holdup ['həʊldʌp] *n* **- 1.** [delay] retraso *m* **- 2.** [robbery] atraco *m* a mano armada.

hole [həʊl] *n* **- 1.** [gen] agujero *m*; [in ground, road etc] hoyo *m*; [of animal] madriguera *f*; **to pick holes in sthg** [criticize] encontrar defectos en algo **- 2.** [in golf] hoyo *m*; **hole in one** hoyo en uno **- 3.** [horrible place] cuchitril *m* **- 4.** *inf* [predicament] apuro *m*, aprieto *m*.
▶ **hole up** *vi* [hide, take shelter] esconderse, refugiarse.

holiday ['hɒlɪdeɪ] *n* **- 1.** [vacation] vacaciones *fpl*; **to be/go on holiday** estar/ir de vacaciones **- 2.** [public holiday] fiesta *f*, día *m* festivo.

◆ **holidays** *n* *US*: **the holidays** las fiestas *OR* vacaciones (de Navidad); **happy holidays!** ¡felices fiestas!

Holidays

En el Reino Unido las celebraciones religiosas no suelen ser día festivo a nivel nacional, a excepción del Viernes Santo y del día de Navidad. Otros tres días de fiesta coinciden con estas fechas: "Easter Monday" (lunes de Pascua), "Boxing Day" (26 de diciembre) y "New Year's Day" (1 de enero). Hay dos fiestas más en mayo: "May Day" (primer lunes) y "Spring Bank Holiday" (último lunes), y otra en agosto: "Summer bank Holiday" (último lunes de agosto). Escocia e Irlanda del Norte tienen algunas fiestas distintas. En Estados Unidos cada estado tiene sus propios días festivos, además de las fiestas nacionales. Estas son "Christmas Day", "New Year's Day", "Labor Day" (primer lunes de septiembre), "Columbus Day" (segundo lunes de octubre) y "Thanksgiving" (cuarto jueves de noviembre). En otras días se commemoran aniversarios de líderes importantes: "Martin Luther King Day" (tercer lunes de enero) y "Presidents' Day" (tercer lunes de febrero, aniversario de los presidentes Lincoln y Washington). Por último, también se celebran eventos relacionados con distintas guerras: "Memorial Day" (en memoria de las víctimas de guerra, último lunes de mayo), "Independence Day" (4 de julio) y "Veteran's Day" (11 de noviembre).

holiday camp *n* *UK* colonia *f* veraniega.

holiday home *n* *UK* casa *f* para las vacaciones.

holidaymaker ['hɒlɪdeɪ,meɪkə'] *n* *UK* turista *mf*.

holiness ['həʊlɪnɪs] *n* santidad *f*.

◆ **Holiness** *n* [in titles]: **His/Your Holiness** Su Santidad.

holistic [həʊ'lɪstɪk] *adj* holístico(ca).

Holland ['hɒlənd] *n* Holanda.

holler ['hɒlə'] *vt* & *vi* *esp US* *inf* gritar.

hollow ['hɒləʊ] ◇ *adj* **- 1.** [not solid] hueco(ca) **- 2.** [cheeks, eyes] hundido(da) **- 3.** [resonant] sonoro(ra), resonante **- 4.** [false, meaningless] vano(na); [laugh] falso(sa). ◇ *n* hueco *m*; [in ground] depresión *f*, hondonada *f*.

◆ **hollow out** *vt sep* **- 1.** [make hollow] dejar hueco(ca) **- 2.** [make by hollowing] hacer ahuecando.

holly ['hɒlɪ] *n* acebo *m*.

holocaust ['hɒləkɔːst] *n* holocausto *m*.

◆ **Holocaust** *n*: **the Holocaust** el Holocausto.

hologram ['hɒləgræm] *n* holograma *m*.

hols [hɒlz] (*abbr of* **holidays**) *npl* *UK* *inf* vacas *fpl*, vacaciones *fpl*.

holster ['həʊlstə'] *n* pistolera *f*, funda *f* (de pistola).

holy ['həʊlɪ] (*comp* **-ier**, *superl* **-iest**) *adj* **- 1.** [sacred] sagrado(da); [water] bendito(ta) **- 2.** [pure and good] santo(ta).

Holy Communion *n* Sagrada Comunión *f*.

Holy Ghost *n*: **the Holy Ghost** el Espíritu Santo.

Holy Land *n*: **the Holy Land** Tierra Santa.

holy orders *npl* sagradas órdenes *fpl*; **to take holy orders** ordenarse (sacerdote).

Holy Spirit *n*: **the Holy Spirit** el Espíritu Santo.

homage ['hɒmɪdʒ] *n* *(U)* *fml* homenaje *m*; **to pay homage to** rendir homenaje a.

home [həʊm] ◇ *n* **- 1.** [house, flat] casa *f*; **away from home** [not in & SPORT] fuera de casa; **to make one's home somewhere** establecerse en algún sitio; **to work from home** *UK* trabajar desde casa; **it's a home from home** *UK* *OR* **home away from home** *US* me siento como en mi propia casa **- 2.** [own country] tierra *f*; [own city] ciudad *f* natal **- 3.** [family] hogar *m*; **to leave home** independizarse, irse de casa **- 4.** [place of origin] cuna *f* **- 5.** [institution] residencia *f*. ◇ *adj* **- 1.** [not foreign] nacional **- 2.** [in one's own home - cooking] casero(ra); [- life] familiar; [- improvements] en la casa; [- delivery] a domicilio **- 3.** SPORT de casa. ◇ *adv* [to one's house] a casa; [at one's house] en casa.

▸▸▸ **to bring sthg home to sb** hacer que alguien se dé cuenta de algo; **to drive** *OR* **hammer sthg home to sb** hacer que alguien se dé perfecta cuenta de algo.

◆ **at home** *adv* **- 1.** [in one's house, flat] en casa **- 2.** [comfortable]: **at home (with)** a gusto (con); **to make o.s. at home** acomodarse; **make yourself at home** estás en tu casa **- 3.** [in one's own country] en mi país **- 4.** SPORT: **to play at home** jugar en casa.

◆ **home in** *vi*: **to home in on sthg** dirigirse hacia algo; *fig* centrarse en algo.

home address *n* domicilio *m* particular.

home banking *n* *(U)* telebanco *m*.

home brew *n* [beer] cerveza *f* casera.

homecoming ['həʊm,kʌmɪŋ] *n* **- 1.** [return] regreso *m* a casa **- 2.** *US* SCH & UNIV recepción *f* para antiguos alumnos.

home computer *n* ordenador *m* doméstico.

home economics *n* *(U)* economía *f* doméstica.

home ground n - **1.** [familiar place]: **to be on home ground** estar en territorio conocido - **2.** [familiar subject]: **to be on home ground** estar en su terreno - **3. SPORT** campo m propio.

homegrown [,həum'grəun] adj [grown in one's garden] de cosecha propia; [not imported] de la tierra, local.

home help n UK asistente empleado por el ayuntamiento para ayudar en las tareas domésticas a enfermos y ancianos.

homeland ['həumlænd] n - **1.** [country of birth] tierra f natal, patria f - **2.** [in South Africa] homeland m, territorio donde se confinaba a la población negra.

homeless ['həumlıs] <> adj sin hogar. <> npl: **the homeless** las personas sin hogar.

homelessness ['həumlısnəs] n (fenómeno m de la) carencia f de hogar.

home loan n crédito m hipotecario, hipoteca f.

homely ['həumlı] adj - **1.** [simple] sencillo(lla) - **2.** [unattractive] feúcho(cha).

homemade [,həum'meıd] adj [food] casero(ra); [clothes] de fabricación casera.

home movie n película f casera.

Home Office n UK: **the Home Office** el Ministerio del Interior británico.

homeopathic [,həumıəu'pæθık] adj homeopático(ca).

homeopathy [,həumı'ɒpəθı] n homeopatía f.

homeowner ['həum,əunə'] n propietario m, -ria f de vivienda.

home page n [on Internet] página f inicial OR de inicio.

home rule n autonomía f.

home run n US inf trayecto m final.

home school vt US educar en casa.

Home Secretary n UK: **the Home Secretary** el Ministro del Interior británico.

homesick ['həumsık] adj nostálgico(ca); **to be homesick** tener morriña.

homesickness ['həum,sıknıs] n morriña f.

homestead ['həumsted] n granja f.

home straight n: **the home straight** la recta final.

hometown ['həumtaun] n pueblo m/ciudad f natal.

home truth n: **to tell sb a few home truths** soltarle a alguien cuatro verdades.

homeward ['həumwəd] <> adj de regreso OR vuelta (a casa). <> adv = **homewards**.

homewards ['həumwədz], **homeward** adv hacia casa.

homework ['həumwз:k] n (U) lit & fig deberes mpl.

homey, homy ['həumı] US <> adj confortable, agradable. <> n inf [friend] amiguete m, -ta f.

homicidal ['hɒmısaıdl] adj homicida.

homicide ['hɒmısaıd] n homicidio m.

homily ['hɒmılı] (pl -ies) n [lecture] sermón m.

homing ['həumıŋ] adj: **homing instinct** querencia f; **homing device** [on missile] sistema m de guiado pasivo.

homing pigeon n paloma f mensajera.

homogeneous [,hɒmə'dʒi:njəs] adj homogéneo(a).

homogenize, -ise [hə'mɒdʒənaız] vt UK homogeneizar.

homosexual [,hɒmə'sekʃuəl] <> adj homosexual. <> n homosexual mf.

homosexuality [,hɒmə,sekʃu'ælətı] n homosexualidad f.

homy = **homey.**

Hon. abbr of **Honourable.** abbr of **Honorary.**

Honduran [hɒn'djuərən] <> adj hondureño(ña). <> n hondureño m, -ña f.

Honduras [hɒn'djuərəs] n Honduras.

hone [həun] vt - **1.** [sharpen] afilar - **2.** [develop, refine] afinar.

honest ['ɒnıst] adj - **1.** [trustworthy, legal] honrado(da) - **2.** [frank] franco(ca), sincero(ra); **to be honest...** si he de serte franco...

honestly ['ɒnıstlı] <> adv - **1.** [truthfully] honradamente - **2.** [expressing sincerity] de verdad, en serio. <> excl [expressing impatience, disapproval] ¡será posible!

honesty ['ɒnıstı] n - **1.** [trustworthiness] honradez f - **2.** [frankness] sinceridad f; **in all honesty...** si he de serte franco...

honey ['hʌnı] n - **1.** [food] miel f - **2.** esp US [form of address] cielo m, mi vida f.

honeybee ['hʌnıbi:] n abeja f (obrera).

honeycomb ['hʌnıkəum] n panal m.

honeymoon ['hʌnımu:n] <> n luna f de miel; fig periodo m idílico. <> vi pasar la luna de miel.

honeysuckle ['hʌnı,sʌkl] n madreselva f.

Hong Kong [,hɒŋ'kɒŋ] n Hong Kong.

honk [hɒŋk] <> vi - **1.** [motorist] tocar el claxon - **2.** [goose] graznar. <> vt tocar. <> n - **1.** [of horn] bocinazo m - **2.** [of goose] graznido m.

honor US = **honour.**

honorary [UK 'ɒnərərı, US ɒnə'reərı] adj - **1.** [given as an honour] honorario(ria) - **2.** [unpaid] honorífico(ca).

honor roll n US lista f de honor.

honour UK, **honor** US ['ɒnə'] <> n - **1.** [gen] honor m, honra f; **in honour of** en honor de - **2.** [source of pride - person] honra f. <> vt

- **1.** [promise, agreement] cumplir; [debt] satisfacer; [cheque] pagar, aceptar - **2.** *fml* [bring honour to] honrar.

◆ **Honour** *n* [in titles]: **His/Her/Your Honour** Su Señoría.

◆ **honours** *npl* - **1.** [tokens of respect] honores *mpl* - **2.** UK UNIV: **honours degree** *licenciatura de cuatro años necesaria para acceder a un máster*. ▸▸ **to do the honours** hacer los honores de la casa.

honourable UK, **honorable** US ['ɒnrəbl] *adj* - **1.** [proper] honroso(sa) - **2.** [morally upright] honorable.

◆ **Honourable** *adj* [in titles] Honorable; **the Honourable gentleman/lady** Su Señoría el señor diputado/la señora diputada.

honourably UK, **honorably** US ['ɒnərəblɪ] *adv* [properly] honrosamente.

honour bound *adj*: **to be honour bound to do sthg** estar moralmente obligado(da) a hacer algo.

honours list *n* UK *lista de personas que reciben un título nobiliario de manos de la corona británica*.

Hons. *abbr of* **honours degree**.

hooch [hu:tʃ] *n* US *inf* alcohol *m* (*destilado clandestinamente*).

hood [hʊd] *n* - **1.** [on cloak, jacket] capucha *f* - **2.** [of pram, convertible car] capota *f*; [of cooker] campana *f* - **3.** US [car bonnet] capó *m*.

hooded ['hʊdɪd] *adj* - **1.** [wearing a hood] encapuchado(da) - **2.** [eyes] de grandes párpados.

hoodlum ['hu:dləm] *n* US *inf* matón *m*.

hoodwink ['hʊdwɪŋk] *vt* engañar.

hoof [hu:f, hʊf] (*pl* -**s** OR **hooves**) *n* [of horse] casco *m*; [of cow etc] pezuña *f*.

hook [hʊk] ⬦ *n* - **1.** [gen] gancho *m*; **off the hook** [phone] descolgado(da) - **2.** [for catching fish] anzuelo *m* - **3.** [fastener] corchete *m* ▸▸ **to get sb off the hook** sacar a alguien del apuro. ⬦ *vt* - **1.** [attach with hook] enganchar - **2.** [fish] pescar, coger - **3.** [arm, leg]: **he hooked his leg around the chair** enganchó la silla con el pie.

◆ **hook up** *vt sep*: **to hook sthg up to sthg** conectar algo a algo; **to hook with sb** reunirse OR juntarse con alguien, ligar con alguien.

hook and eye (*pl* **hooks and eyes**) *n* corchete *m*.

hooked [hʊkt] *adj* - **1.** [nose] aguileño(ña), ganchudo(da) - **2.** *inf* [addicted]: **to be hooked (on)** estar enganchado(da) (a).

hooker ['hʊkər] *n* US *inf* puta *f*.

hook(e)y ['hʊkɪ] *n* US *inf*: **to play hookey** hacer novillos.

hooligan ['hu:lɪgən] *n* gamberro *m*.

hooliganism ['hu:lɪgənɪzm] *n* gamberrismo *m*.

hoop [hu:p] *n* aro *m*.

hoop-la ['hu:plɑ:] *n* (*U*) [game] *juego de feria consistente en colar aros en los premios*.

hooray [hʊ'reɪ] = **hurray**.

hoot [hu:t] ⬦ *n* - **1.** [of owl] grito *m*, ululato *m*; [of horn] bocinazo *m*; **a hoot of laughter** una carcajada - **2.** UK *inf* [amusing thing or person]: **she's/it was a hoot** es/fue la monda. ⬦ *vi* [owl] ulular; [horn] sonar; **to hoot with laughter** reírse a carcajadas. ⬦ *vt* tocar.

hooter ['hu:tər] *n* - **1.** [horn] claxon® *m*, bocina *f* - **2.** UK *inf* [nose] napias *fpl*.

Hoover® ['hu:vər] *n* UK aspiradora *f*.

◆ **hoover** ⬦ *vt* pasar la aspiradora por. ⬦ *vi* pasar la aspiradora.

hooves [hu:vz] *npl* ▭ **hoof**.

hop [hɒp] ⬦ *n* - **1.** [of person] salto *m* a la pata coja - **2.** [of bird etc] saltito *m* - **3.** *inf* [air trip] vuelo *m* corto. ⬦ *vi* (*pt & pp* -**ped**, *cont* -**ping**) - **1.** [person] saltar a la pata coja - **2.** [bird etc] dar saltitos - **3.** [move nimbly] ponerse de un brinco. ⬦ *vt* (*pt & pp* -**ped**, *cont* -**ping**) US *inf* [bus, train] subirse a.

◆ **hops** *npl* lúpulo *m*.

hope [həʊp] ⬦ *vi*: **to hope (for sthg)** esperar (algo); **I hope so/not** espero que sí/no; **to hope for the best** esperar que todo vaya bien. ⬦ *vt*: **to hope (that)** esperar que; **to hope to do sthg** esperar hacer algo. ⬦ *n* esperanza *f*; **to be beyond hope** ser un caso desesperado; **in the hope of** con la esperanza de; **to pin one's hopes on sthg** poner uno todas sus esperanzas en algo; **I don't hold out much hope** no tengo muchas esperanzas; **to raise sb's hopes** dar esperanzas a alguien.

hope chest *n* US ajuar *m*.

hopeful ['həʊpfʊl] <> *adj* **- 1.** [optimistic] optimista; **to be hopeful of sthg/of doing sthg** tener esperanzas de algo/hacer algo **- 2.** [promising] prometedor(ra), esperanzador(ra). <> *n* aspirante *mf*.

hopefully ['həʊpfəlɪ] *adv* **- 1.** [in a hopeful way] esperanzadamente **- 2.** [with luck] con suerte; **hopefully not** espero que no.

hopeless ['həʊplɪs] *adj* **- 1.** [despairing] desesperado(da) **- 2.** [impossible] imposible **- 3.** *inf* [useless] inútil.

hopelessly ['həʊplɪslɪ] *adv* **- 1.** [despairingly] desesperadamente **- 2.** [completely] totalmente.

hopper ['hɒpəʳ] *n* [funnel] tolva *f*.

hopping ['hɒpɪŋ] *adv*: **to be hopping mad** estar echando chispas.

hopscotch ['hɒpskɒtʃ] *n* tejo *m*, rayuela *f Amér*.

horde [hɔːd] *n* horda *f*.
<> **hordes** *npl fig* una multitud.

horizon [hə'raɪzn] *n* [of sky] horizonte *m*; **on the horizon** en el horizonte; *fig* a la vuelta de la esquina.
<> **horizons** *npl* horizontes *mpl*.

horizontal [ˌhɒrɪ'zɒntl] <> *adj* horizontal. <> *n*: **the horizontal** la horizontal.

hormone ['hɔːməʊn] *n* hormona *f*.

hormone replacement therapy *n* terapia *f* de sustitución hormonal.

horn [hɔːn] *n* **- 1.** [of animal] cuerno *m*, cacho *m Amér* **- 2.** MUS [instrument] trompa *f* **- 3.** [on car] claxon® *m*, bocina *f*; [on ship] sirena *f* **- 4.** *US inf* [telephone] teléfono *m*.

hornet ['hɔːnɪt] *n* avispón *m*.

horn-rimmed [-'rɪmd] *adj* con montura de concha.

horny ['hɔːnɪ] (*comp* **-ier**, *superl* **-iest**) *adj* **- 1.** [scale, body, armour] córneo(a); [hand] calloso(sa) **- 2.** *v inf* [sexually excited] cachondo(da), caliente.

horoscope ['hɒrəskəʊp] *n* horóscopo *m*.

horrendous [hɒ'rendəs] *adj* horrendo(da).

horrible ['hɒrəbl] *adj* **- 1.** [gen] horrible **- 2.** [nasty, mean] malo(la).

horribly ['hɒrəblɪ] *adv* **- 1.** [horrifically] horriblemente **- 2.** *inf* [very] terriblemente, tremendamente.

horrid ['hɒrɪd] *adj esp UK* [person] antipático(ca); [idea, place] horroroso(sa).

horrific [hɒ'rɪfɪk] *adj* horrendo(da).

horrify ['hɒrɪfaɪ] (*pt & pp* **-ied**) *vt* horrorizar.

horrifying ['hɒrɪfaɪɪŋ] *adj* horroroso(sa), horripilante.

horror ['hɒrəʳ] *n* horror *m*; **to my/his horror** para mi/su horror; **to have a horror of sthg** tener horror a algo.

horror film *n* película *f* de terror OR de miedo.

horror-struck *adj* horrorizado(da).

hors d'oeuvre [ɔː'dɜːvr] (*pl* **hors d'oeuvres** [ɔː'dɜːvr]) *n* entremeses *mpl*.

horse [hɔːs] *n* [animal] caballo *m*.

horseback ['hɔːsbæk] <> *adj*: **horseback riding** equitación *f*. <> *n*: **on horseback** a caballo.

horsebox *UK* ['hɔːsbɒks], **horsecar** *US* ['hɔːskɑːʳ] *n* remolque *m* para el transporte de caballos.

horse chestnut *n* [nut] castaña *f* de Indias; **horse chestnut (tree)** castaño *m* de Indias.

horse-drawn *adj* tirado(da) por caballos.

horsefly ['hɔːsflaɪ] (*pl* **-flies**) *n* tábano *m*.

horsehair ['hɔːsheəʳ] *n* crin *f*.

horseman ['hɔːsmən] (*pl* **-men** [-mən]) *n* jinete *m*.

horseplay ['hɔːspleɪ] *n (U)* pelea *f* en broma.

horsepower ['hɔːsˌpaʊəʳ] *n (U)* caballos *mpl* de vapor.

horse racing *n (U)* carreras *fpl* de caballos.

horseradish ['hɔːsˌrædɪʃ] *n* rábano *m* silvestre.

horserider ['hɔːsraɪdəʳ] *n esp US* jinete *m*, amazona *f*.

horse riding *n* equitación *f*; **to go horse riding** montar a caballo.

horseshoe ['hɔːsʃuː] *n* herradura *f*.

horse show *n* concurso *m* hípico.

horse-trading *n fig & pej* regateo *m*.

horse trials *npl* concurso *m* hípico.

horsewhip ['hɔːswɪp] (*pt & pp* **-ped**, *cont* **-ping**) *vt* azotar.

horsewoman ['hɔːsˌwʊmən] (*pl* **-women** [-ˌwɪmɪn]) *n* amazona *f*.

horticultural [ˌhɔːtɪ'kʌltʃərəl] *adj* hortícola.

horticulture ['hɔːtɪkʌltʃəʳ] *n* horticultura *f*.

hose [həʊz] <> *n* [hosepipe] manguera *f*. <> *vt* [irrigate] regar con manguera; [wash] limpiar con manguera.
<> **hose down** *vt sep* limpiar con manguera.

hosepipe ['həʊzpaɪp] *n* manguera *f*.

hosiery ['həʊzɪərɪ] *n (U)* medias *fpl* y calcetines.

hospice ['hɒspɪs] *n* hospital *m* para enfermos terminales.

hospitable [hɒ'spɪtəbl] *adj* hospitalario(ria).

hospital ['hɒspɪtl] *n* hospital *m*, nosocomio *m Amér*.

hospitality [ˌhɒspɪ'tælətɪ] *n* hospitalidad *f*.

hospitality suite *n* bar *m* con barra libre (*en conferencias etc*).

hospitalize, -ise ['hɒspɪtəlaɪz] *vt* hospitalizar.

host [həʊst] <> *n* **- 1.** [person, place, organization] anfitrión *m*, -ona *f*; **host country** país *m* anfitrión OR organizador **- 2.** [compere] presentador *m*, -ra *f* - **3.** *liter* [large number]: **a host of** una multitud de - **4.** RELIG hostia *f* - **5.** COMPUT host *m*, anfitrión *m*. ◇ *vt* - **1.** [show] presentar; [event] ser el anfitrión de - **2.** COMPUT albergar, hospedar.

hostage ['hɒstɪdʒ] *n* rehén *m*; **to be taken/held hostage** ser cogido(da)/mantenido(da) como rehén.

hostel ['hɒstl] *n* albergue *m*.

hostelry ['hɒstəlrɪ] *(pl* -ries) *n hum* [pub] bar *m*.

hostess ['həʊstes] *n* - **1.** [at party] anfitriona *f* - **2.** [in club etc] chica *f* de alterne.

host family *n* familia *f* de acogida.

hostile [UK 'hɒstaɪl, US 'hɒstl] *adj* - **1.** [antagonistic, enemy]: **hostile (to)** hostil (hacia) - **2.** [unfavourable] adverso(sa), desfavorable.

hostility [hɒ'stɪlətɪ] *n* [antagonism] hostilidad *f*.
◆ **hostilities** *npl* hostilidades *fpl*.

hot [hɒt] *adj* (*comp* -ter, *superl* -test) - **1.** [gen] caliente; **I'm hot** tengo calor - **2.** [weather, climate] caluroso(sa); **it's (very) hot** hace (mucho) calor - **3.** [spicy] picante, picoso(sa) *Méx* - **4.** *inf* [expert]: **hot on** OR **at** experto(ta) en - **5.** [recent] caliente, último(ma) - **6.** [temper] vivo(va).
◆ **hot up** *vi* (*pt & pp* -ted, *cont* -ting) *inf* animarse, calentarse.

hot-air balloon *n* aeróstato *m*, globo *m*.

hotbed ['hɒtbed] *n* semillero *m*.

hotchpotch UK ['hɒtʃpɒtʃ], **hodgepodge** US ['hɒdʒpɒdʒ] *n inf* revoltijo *m*, batiburrillo *m*.

hot-cross bun *n bollo a base de especias y pasas con una cruz dibujada en una cara que se come en Semana Santa*.

hot dog *n* perrito *m* caliente.

hotel [həʊ'tel] ◇ *n* hotel *m*. ◇ *comp* [gen] de hotel; INDUST hotelero(ra).

hotelier [həʊ'telɪə'] *n* hotelero *m*, -ra *f*.

hot flush *UK*, **hot flash** *US n* sofoco *m*.

hotheaded [,hɒt'hedɪd] *adj* irreflexivo(va).

hothouse ['hɒthaʊs, *pl* -haʊzɪz] () ◇ *n* [greenhouse] invernadero *m*. ◇ *comp* de invernadero.

hot line *n* - **1.** [for information, help etc] línea *f* directa - **2.** [for politician] teléfono *m* rojo.

hotly ['hɒtlɪ] *adv* - **1.** [passionately] acaloradamente - **2.** [closely]: **we were hotly pursued** nos pisaban los talones.

hotplate ['hɒtpleɪt] *n* - **1.** [for cooking] placa *f* - **2.** [for keeping food warm] calientaplatos *m inv*.

hotpot ['hɒtpɒt] *n UK estofado de cabrito típico de Lancashire*.

hot potato *n inf fig* tema *m* espinoso.

hot rod *n* AUT coche *m* trucado.

hot seat *n inf*: **to be in the hot seat** ser quien tiene que sacar las castañas del fuego.

hot spot *n* - **1.** [exciting place] lugar *m* de moda - **2.** POL zona *f* conflictiva, polvorín *m*.

hot-tempered *adj* iracundo(da).

hot water *n fig*: **to get into/be in hot water** meterse/estar en un berenjenal.

hot-water bottle *n* bolsa *f* de agua caliente.

hot-wire *vt inf*: **to hot-wire a car** poner un coche en marcha haciendo un puente.

hound [haʊnd] ◇ *n* [dog] perro *m* de caza, sabueso *m*. ◇ *vt* - **1.** [persecute] acosar - **2.** [drive]: **to hound sb out (of somewhere)** conseguir echar a alguien (de algún sitio) acosándolo.

hour ['aʊə'] *n* - **1.** [gen] hora *f*; **half an hour** media hora; **70 miles per** OR **an hour** 70 millas por hora; **to pay by the hour** pagar por horas; **on the hour** a la hora en punto cada hora; **in the small hours** a altas horas de la madrugada - **2.** *liter* [important time] momento *m*.
◆ **hours** *npl* - **1.** [of business] horas *fpl*; **after hours** fuera de horas - **2.** [of person - routine]: **to keep late hours** acostarse muy tarde.

hourly ['aʊəlɪ] *adj & adv* - **1.** [every hour] cada hora - **2.** [per hour] por hora.

house ◇ *n* [haʊs, *pl* 'haʊzɪz] - **1.** [gen] casa *f*; **it's on the house** la casa invita, es cortesía de la casa; **to put** OR **set one's house in order** poner las cosas en orden - **2.** POL cámara *f* - **3.** [in theatre] audiencia *f*; **to bring the house down** *inf* ser un exitazo, ser muy aplaudido(da). ◇ *vt* [haʊz] [person, family] alojar; [department, library, office] albergar. ◇ *adj* - **1.** [within business] de la empresa - **2.** [wine] de la casa.

house arrest *n*: **under house arrest** bajo arresto domiciliario.

houseboat ['haʊsbəʊt] *n* casa *f* flotante.

housebound ['haʊsbaʊnd] *adj* confinado(da) en casa.

housebreaking ['haʊs,breɪkɪŋ] *n* allanamiento *m* de morada.

housebroken ['haʊs,brəʊkn] *adj US* [pet] bien enseñado(da).

housecoat ['haʊskəʊt] *n* bata *f*.

household ['haʊshəʊld] ◇ *adj* - **1.** [domestic] doméstico(ca), de la casa - **2.** [word, name] conocido(da) por todos. ◇ *n* hogar *m*.

householder ['haʊs,həʊldə'] *n* [owner] dueño *m*, -ña *f*; [tenant] inquilino *m*, -na *f*.

househunting ['haʊs,hʌntɪŋ] *n* búsqueda *f* de vivienda.

house husband *n* amo *m* de casa *(encargado de las tareas domésticas)*.

housekeeper ['haʊs,kiːpə'] *n* ama *f* de llaves.

housekeeping ['haʊs̩ki:pɪŋ] *n* (*U*) - **1.** [work] quehaceres *mpl* domésticos, tareas *fpl* domésticas - **2.**: **housekeeping (money)** dinero *m* para los gastos de la casa.

houseman ['haʊsmən] (*pl* **-men** [-mən]) *n UK* interno *m*, -na *f*.

house music *n* música *f* house.

House of Commons *n UK*: **the House of Commons** la Cámara de los Comunes.

House of Lords *n UK*: **the House of Lords** la Cámara de los Lores.

House of Representatives *n US*: **the House of Representatives** la Cámara de los Representantes.

house-owner *n* propietario *m*, -ria *f* (de una vivienda).

houseplant ['haʊspla:nt] *n* planta *f* interior.

house-proud *adj* muy ama de su casa.

Houses of Parliament *n*: **the Houses of Parliament** el Parlamento británico.

house-to-house *adj* de casa en casa.

house-train *vt UK* enseñar dónde hacer sus necesidades a (*perro, gato*).

housewarming (party) ['haʊs,wɔ:mɪŋ-] *n* fiesta *f* de inauguración de una casa.

housewife ['haʊswaɪf] (*pl* **-wives** [-waɪvz]) *n* ama *f* de casa.

housework ['haʊswɜ:k] *n* (*U*) quehaceres *mpl* domésticos.

housing ['haʊzɪŋ] ◇ *n* - **1.** [houses] vivienda *f*; [act of accommodating] alojamiento *m* - **2.** [covering] cubierta *f* protectora; AUT cárter *m*. ◇ *comp* de la vivienda.

housing association *n UK* cooperativa *f* de viviendas.

housing benefit *n* (*U*) *subsidio estatal para ayudar al pago del alquiler y de otros gastos.*

housing development *n* urbanización *f*.

housing estate *UK*, **housing project** *US n* *urbanización generalmente de protección oficial,* ≃ fraccionamiento *m Méx*.

hovel ['hɒvl] *n* casucha *f*, tugurio *m*.

hover ['hɒvər] *vi* - **1.** [fly] cernerse - **2.** [linger] merodear - **3.** [hesitate] debatirse.

hovercraft ['hɒvəkrɑːft] (*pl* **hovercraft** OR **-s**) *n* aerodeslizador *m*.

hoverport ['hɒvəpɔːt] *n* puerto *m* para aerodeslizadores.

how [haʊ] *adv* - **1.** [gen] cómo; **how do you do it?** ¿cómo se hace?; **I found out how he did it** averigüé cómo lo hizo; **how are you?** ¿cómo estás?; **how do you do?** mucho gusto - **2.** [referring to degree, amount]: **how high is it?** ¿cuánto mide de alto OR de altura?; **he asked how high it was** preguntó cuánto medía de alto; **how expensive is it?** ¿qué precio tiene?, ¿es muy caro?; **how far is it to Paris?** ¿a qué distancia está París de aquí?; **how long have you been waiting?** ¿cuánto llevas esperando?; **how many people came?** ¿cuánta gente vino?; **how old are you?** ¿qué edad OR cuántos años tienes? - **3.** [in exclamations] qué; **how nice/awful!** ¡qué bonito/horrible!; **how I hate doing it!** ¡cómo OR cuánto odio tener que hacerlo!; **how can you say that?** ¿cómo puedes decir eso?

◆ **how about** *adv*: **how about a drink?** ¿qué tal una copa?; **how about you?** ¿qué te parece?, ¿y tú?

◆ **how much** ◇ *pron* cuánto(ta); **how much does it cost?** ¿cuánto cuesta? ◇ *adj* cuánto(ta); **how much bread?** ¿cuánto pan?

howdy ['haʊdɪ] *excl US inf* ¡hola!

however [haʊ'evər] ◇ *adv* - **1.** [nevertheless] sin embargo, no obstante - **2.** [no matter how]: **however difficult it may be** por (muy) difícil que sea; **however many times** OR **much I told her** por mucho que se lo dijera - **3.** [how] cómo; **however did you know?** ¿cómo lo sabías? ◇ *conj* comoquiera que; **however you want** como quieras.

howl [haʊl] ◇ *n* - **1.** [of animal] aullido *m* - **2.** [of person - in pain, anger] alarido *m*, grito *m*; **a howl of laughter** una carcajada. ◇ *vi*

- 1. [animal] aullar **- 2.** [person - in pain, anger] gritar; **to howl with laughter** reírse a carcajadas **- 3.** [wind] bramar.

howler ['haʊlə'] *n inf* error *m* garrafal.

howling ['haʊlɪŋ] *adj inf* [success] clamoroso(sa).

hp (*abbr of* **horsepower**) CV *m*, cv *m*.

HP (*abbr of* **hire purchase**) *n* **- 1.** *UK*: **to buy sthg on HP** comprar algo a plazos **- 2.** = **hp**.

HQ *n abbr of* **headquarters**.

hr (*abbr of* **hour**) h.

HRH (*abbr of* **His/Her Royal Highness**) S.A.R. *mf*

HRT *n abbr of* **hormone replacement therapy**.

HS (*abbr of* **high school**) Inst. *m*

HST (*abbr of* **Hawaiian Standard Time**) *hora oficial de Hawai*.

ht *abbr of* **height**.

HT (*abbr of* **high tension**) AT *f*.

HTML (*abbr of* **hypertext markup language**) *n* COMPUT HTML *m*.

hub [hʌb] *n* **- 1.** [of wheel] cubo *m* **- 2.** [of activity] centro *m*, eje *m*.

hub airport *n US* aeropuerto *m* principal.

hubbub ['hʌbʌb] *n* alboroto *m*, barullo *m*.

hubcap ['hʌbkæp] *n* tapacubos *m inv*.

huddle ['hʌdl] <> *vi* **- 1.** [crouch, curl up] acurrucarse **- 2.** [cluster] apretarse unos contra otros, apiñarse. <> *n* piña *f*, grupo *m*.

hue [hju:] *n* **- 1.** [shade] tono *m*, matiz *m* **- 2.** [colour] color *m*.

huff [hʌf] <> *n*: **in a huff** mosqueado(da). <> *vi*: **to huff and puff** bufar, resoplar.

huffy ['hʌfɪ] (*comp* **-ier**, *superl* **-iest**) *adj inf* **- 1.** [offended] mosqueado(da) **- 2.** [touchy] susceptible, enfadadizo(za).

hug [hʌg] <> *n* abrazo *m*; **to give sb a hug** abrazar a alguien, dar un abrazo a alguien. <> *vt* (*pt & pp* **-ged**, *cont* **-ging**) **- 1.** [embrace, hold] abrazar; **to hug sthg to o.s.** abrazar algo fuertemente **- 2.** [stay close to] ceñirse OR ir pegado a.

huge [hju:dʒ] *adj* enorme.

hulk [hʌlk] *n* **- 1.** [of ship] casco *m* abandonado **- 2.** [person] tiarrón *m*, -ona *f*.

hulking ['hʌlkɪŋ] *adj* gigantesco(ca).

hull [hʌl] *n* casco *m*.

hullabaloo [,hʌləbə'lu:] *n inf* conmoción *f*, alboroto *m*.

hullo [hə'ləʊ] = **hello**.

hum [hʌm] <> *vi* (*pt & pp* **-med**, *cont* **-ming**) **- 1.** [buzz] zumbar **- 2.** [sing] canturrear, tararear **- 3.** [be busy] bullir, hervir

to hum and haw titubear, vacilar. <> *vt* (*pt & pp* **-med**, *cont* **-ming**) tararear, canturrear. <> *n* (*U*) zumbido *m*; [of conversation] murmullo *m*.

human ['hju:mən] <> *adj* humano(na). <> *n*: **human (being)** (ser *m*) humano *m*.

humane [hju:'meɪn] *adj* humano(na).

humanely [hju:'meɪnlɪ] *adv* humanamente.

human error *n* error *m* humano.

humanist ['hju:mənɪst] *n* humanista *mf*.

humanitarian [hju:,mænɪ'teərɪən] <> *adj* humanitario(ria). <> *n* persona *f* que lucha por la justicia social.

humanity [hju:'mænətɪ] *n* humanidad *f*.

humanities *npl*: **the humanities** las humanidades.

humanly ['hju:mənlɪ] *adv*: **humanly possible** humanamente posible.

human nature *n* la naturaleza humana.

human race *n*: **the human race** la raza humana.

human resources *npl* recursos *mpl* humanos.

human rights *npl* derechos *mpl* humanos.

humble ['hʌmbl] <> *adj* humilde. <> *vt fml* humillar; **to humble o.s.** humillarse.

humbly ['hʌmblɪ] *adv* humildemente.

humbug ['hʌmbʌg] *n* **- 1.** (*U*) *dated* [hypocrisy] farsa *f*, hipocresía *f* **- 2.** *UK* [sweet] caramelo *m* de menta.

humdrum ['hʌmdrʌm] *adj* rutinario(ria), aburrido(da).

humid ['hju:mɪd] *adj* húmedo(da).

humidity [hju:'mɪdətɪ] *n* humedad *f*.

humiliate [hju:'mɪlɪeɪt] *vt* humillar.

humiliating [hju:'mɪlɪeɪtɪŋ] *adj* humillante.

humiliation [hju:,mɪlɪ'eɪʃn] *n* humillación *f*.

humility [hju:'mɪlətɪ] *n* humildad *f*.

hummingbird ['hʌmɪŋbɜ:d] *n* colibrí *m*.

humor *US* = **humour**.

humorist ['hju:mərɪst] *n* humorista *mf*.

humorous ['hju:mərəs] *adj* **- 1.** [remark, situation] gracioso(sa) **- 2.** [play, publication] humorístico(ca).

humour *UK*, **humor** *US* ['hju:mə'] <> *n* **- 1.** [sense of fun, mood] humor *m*; **in good/bad humour** *fml* de buen/mal humor **- 2.** [funny side] gracia *f*. <> *vt* complacer, seguir la corriente a.

hump [hʌmp] <> *n* **- 1.** [hill] montículo *m* **- 2.** [on back] joroba *f*, giba *f*, curca *f Amér*. <> *vt inf* [carry] acarrear, cargar con.

humpbacked bridge ['hʌmpbækt-] *n* puente *m* peraltado.

humus ['hju:məs] *n* humus *m inv*.

hunch [hʌntʃ] <> n inf presentimiento m, corazonada f. <> vt encorvar. <> vi encorvarse.

hunchback ['hʌntʃbæk] n jorobado m, -da f.

hunched [hʌntʃt] adj encorvado(da).

hundred ['hʌndrəd] num cien; a OR one hundred cien; a OR one hundred and eighty ciento ochenta; **three hundred** trescientos; **five hundred** quinientos; see also **six**.

◆ **hundreds** npl cientos mpl, centenares mpl.

hundredth ['hʌndrətθ] <> num adj centésimo(ma). <> num n [fraction] centésimo m; a hundredth of a second una centésima; see also **sixth**.

hundredweight ['hʌndrədweɪt] n [in UK] = 50,8 kg; [in US] = 45,3 kg.

hung [hʌŋ] <> pt & pp ▷ **hang**. <> adj POL sin mayoría.

Hungarian [hʌŋ'geərɪən] <> adj húngaro(ra). <> n - **1.** [person] húngaro m, -ra f - **2.** [language] húngaro m.

Hungary ['hʌŋgərɪ] n Hungría.

hunger ['hʌŋgər] n - **1.** [for food] hambre f - **2.** liter [for change, knowledge etc] sed f.

◆ **hunger after, hunger for** vt insep liter anhelar, ansiar.

hunger strike n huelga f de hambre.

hung over adj inf: **to be hung over** tener resaca.

hungry ['hʌŋgrɪ] (comp -ier, superl -iest) adj - **1.** [for food] hambriento(ta); **to be/go hungry** tener/pasar hambre - **2.** [eager]: **to be hungry for** tener ansias de.

hung up adj inf acomplejado(da).

hunk [hʌŋk] n - **1.** [large piece] pedazo m, trozo m - **2.** inf [attractive man] tío m bueno, macizo m.

hunt [hʌnt] <> n - **1.** [of animals, birds] caza f; UK [foxhunting party] partida f de caza - **2.** [for person, clue etc] busca f, búsqueda f. <> vi - **1.** [for animals, birds] cazar - **2.** [for person, clue etc]: **to hunt (for sthg)** buscar (algo). <> vt - **1.** [animals, birds] cazar - **2.** [person] perseguir.

◆ **hunt down** vt sep atrapar.

hunter ['hʌntər] n - **1.** [of animals, birds] cazador m, -ra f - **2.** [of things]: **bargain/autograph hunter** persona que anda a la caza de gangas/autógrafos.

hunting ['hʌntɪŋ] <> n - **1.** [of animals] caza f; **to go hunting** ir de caza OR cacería - **2.** UK [of foxes] caza f del zorro. <> comp de caza.

hurdle ['hɜːdl] <> n - **1.** [in race] valla f - **2.** [obstacle] obstáculo m. <> vt saltar.

hurl [hɜːl] vt - **1.** [throw] lanzar, arrojar - **2.** [shout] proferir, soltar.

hurray, hooray [hʊ'reɪ] excl ¡hurra!

hurricane ['hʌrɪkən] n huracán m.

hurried ['hʌrɪd] adj [hasty] apresurado(da).

hurriedly ['hʌrɪdlɪ] adv apresuradamente.

hurry ['hʌrɪ] <> n prisa f; **to be in a hurry** tener prisa; **to do sthg in a hurry** hacer algo de prisa OR apresuradamente; **to be in no hurry to do sthg** [unwilling] no tener ningunas ganas de hacer algo. <> vt (pt & pp -ied) [person] meter prisa a; [work, speech] apresurar. <> vi (pt & pp -ied): **to hurry (to do sthg)** apresurarse (a hacer algo), darse prisa (en hacer algo).

◆ **hurry up** <> vi darse prisa. <> vt sep meter prisa a.

hurt [hɜːt] <> vt (pt & pp hurt) - **1.** [physically - person] hacer daño a; [- one's leg, arm] hacerse daño en; **nobody was hurt** nadie resultó herido; **to hurt o.s.** hacerse daño - **2.** [emotionally] herir - **3.** [harm] perjudicar. <> vi (pt & pp hurt) - **1.** [gen] doler; **my head hurts** me duele la cabeza - **2.** [cause physical pain, do harm] hacer daño. <> adj - **1.** [injured] herido(da) - **2.** [offended] dolido(da), ofendido(da); [feelings] herido(da). <> n (U) [emotional pain] dolor m.

hurtful ['hɜːtfʊl] adj hiriente.

hurtle ['hɜːtl] vi: **to hurtle past** pasar como un rayo; **to hurtle over** precipitarse por.

husband ['hʌzbənd] n marido m.

hush [hʌʃ] <> n silencio m. <> excl ¡silencio!, ¡a callar!

◆ **hush up** vt sep echar tierra a.

hush money n (U) inf soborno m (para pagar el silencio de alguien), coima f (para pagar el silencio de alguien) Andes & R Dom.

husk [hʌsk] n [of seed, grain] cáscara f, cascarilla f.

husky ['hʌskɪ] <> adj (comp -ier, superl -iest) [hoarse] ronco(ca). <> n husky m, perro m esquimal.

hustings ['hʌstɪŋz] npl UK campaña f electoral.

hustle ['hʌsl] <> vt - **1.** [hurry] meter prisa a - **2.** US [persuade]: **to hustle sb into doing sthg** presionar a alguien para que haga algo. <> n: **hustle (and bustle)** bullicio m, ajetreo m.

hut [hʌt] n - **1.** [rough house] cabaña f, choza f, jacal m Guat, Méx & Ven - **2.** [shed] cobertizo m.

hutch [hʌtʃ] n conejera f.

hyacinth ['haɪəsɪnθ] n jacinto m.

hybrid ['haɪbrɪd] <> adj híbrido(da). <> n híbrido m.

hydrangea [haɪ'dreɪndʒə] n hortensia f.

hydrant ['haɪdrənt] n boca f de riego; [for fire] boca f de incendio.

hydraulic [haɪ'drɔːlɪk] adj hidráulico(ca).

◆ **hydraulics** n (U) hidráulica f.

hydrocarbon [ˌhaɪdrəˈkɑːbən] *n* hidrocarburo *m*.

hydrochloric acid [ˌhaɪdrəˈklɔːrɪk-] *n* ácido *m* clorhídrico.

hydroelectric [ˌhaɪdrəʊɪˈlektrɪk] *adj* hidroeléctrico(ca).

hydroelectricity [ˌhaɪdrəʊɪlekˈtrɪsətɪ] *n* hidroelectricidad *f*.

hydrofoil [ˈhaɪdrəfɔɪl] *n* embarcación *f* con hidroala.

hydrogen [ˈhaɪdrədʒən] *n* hidrógeno *m*.

hydrogen bomb *n* bomba *f* de hidrógeno.

hydrophobia [ˌhaɪdrəˈfəʊbjə] *n* fml [rabies] hidrofobia *f*.

hydroplane [ˈhaɪdrəpleɪn] *n* - **1.** [speedboat] hidroplano *m* - **2.** [hydrofoil] embarcación *f* con hidroala.

hyena [haɪˈiːnə] *n* hiena *f*.

hygiene [ˈhaɪdʒiːn] *n* higiene *f*.

hygienic [haɪˈdʒiːnɪk] *adj* higiénico(ca).

hygienist [haɪˈdʒiːnɪst] *n* higienista *mf* dental.

hymn [hɪm] *n* himno *m*.

hymn book *n* himnario *m*.

hype [haɪp] *inf* <> *n* bombo *m*, publicidad *f* exagerada. <> *vt* dar mucho bombo a.

hyped up [haɪpd-] *adj* inf [nervous] hecho(cha) un manojo de nervios.

hyper [ˈhaɪpə] *adj* inf nervioso(sa), excitable.

hyperactive [ˌhaɪpərˈæktɪv] *adj* hiperactivo(va).

hyperbole [haɪˈpɜːbəlɪ] *n* hipérbole *f*.

hyperlink [ˈhaɪpəˌlɪŋk] *n* COMPUT hiperenlace *m*.

hypermarket [ˈhaɪpəˌmɑːkɪt] *n* hipermercado *m*.

hypersensitive [ˌhaɪpəˈsensɪtɪv] *adj* hipersensible.

hypertension [ˌhaɪpəˈtenʃn] *n* MED hipertensión *f*.

hypertext [ˈhaɪpətekst] <> *n* COMPUT hipertexto *m*. <> *comp* COMPUT: **hypertext link** enlace *m* hipertextual OR de hipertexto.

hyperventilate [ˌhaɪpəˈventɪleɪt] *vi* hiperventilar.

hyphen [ˈhaɪfn] *n* guión *m*.

hyphenate [ˈhaɪfəneɪt] *vt* escribir con guión.

hypnosis [hɪpˈnəʊsɪs] *n* hipnosis *f* inv; **under hypnosis** hipnotizado(da).

hypnotic [hɪpˈnɒtɪk] *adj* hipnótico(ca).

hypnotism [ˈhɪpnətɪzm] *n* hipnotismo *m*.

hypnotist [ˈhɪpnətɪst] *n* hipnotizador *m*, -ra *f*.

hypnotize, -ise [ˈhɪpnətaɪz] *vt* hipnotizar.

hypoallergenic [ˈhaɪpəʊˌælɪˈdʒenɪk] *adj* hipoalergénico(ca).

hypochondriac [ˌhaɪpəˈkɒndriæk] *n* hipocondríaco *m*, -ca *f*.

hypocrisy [hɪˈpɒkrəsɪ] *n* hipocresía *f*.

hypocrite [ˈhɪpəkrɪt] *n* hipócrita *mf*.

hypocritical [ˌhɪpəˈkrɪtɪkl] *adj* hipócrita.

hypodermic needle [ˌhaɪpəˈdɜːmɪk-] *n* aguja *f* hipodérmica.

hypodermic syringe [ˌhaɪpəˈdɜːmɪk-] *n* jeringuilla *f* hipodérmica.

hypothermia [ˌhaɪpəʊˈθɜːmɪə] *n* hipotermia *f*.

hypothesis [haɪˈpɒθɪsɪs] (*pl* **-theses** [-θɪsiːz]) *n* hipótesis *f* inv.

hypothesize, -ise [haɪˈpɒθɪsaɪz] <> *vt* plantear como hipótesis. <> *vi* hacer hipótesis.

hypothetical [ˌhaɪpəˈθetɪkl] *adj* hipotético(ca).

hysterectomy [ˌhɪstəˈrektəmɪ] (*pl* **-ies**) *n* histerectomía *f*.

hysteria [hɪsˈtɪərɪə] *n* histeria *f*.

hysterical [hɪsˈterɪkl] *adj* - **1.** [frantic] histérico(ca) - **2.** inf [very funny] tronchante, desternillante.

hysterics [hɪsˈterɪks] *npl* - **1.** [panic, excitement] histeria *f*, histerismo *m* - **2.** inf [fits of laughter]: **to be in hysterics** troncharse OR partirse de risa.

Hz (*abbr of* **hertz**) Hz.

i (*pl* **i's** OR **is**), **I** (*pl* **I's** OR **Is**) [aɪ] *n* [letter] i *f*, I *f*.

I[1] [aɪ] *pers pron* yo; **I'm happy** soy feliz; **I'm leaving** me voy; **she and I were at college together** ella y yo fuimos juntos a la universidad; **it is I** fml soy yo; **I can't do that** yo no puedo hacer eso.

I[2] *abbr of* **Island**, **Isle**.

IA *abbr of* **Iowa**.

Iberian [aɪˈbɪərɪən] <> *adj* ibérico(ca). <> *n* ibero *m*, -ra *f*.

Iberian peninsula *n*: **the Iberian peninsula** la Península Ibérica.

ice [aɪs] <> *n* - **1.** [frozen water] hielo *m*; **to break the ice** fig romper el hielo - **2.** UK [ice cream] helado *m*. <> *vt* CULIN glasear, alcorzar.
◆ **ice over, ice up** *vi* helarse.

ice age *n* era *f* glaciar.

iceberg [ˈaɪsbɜːg] n iceberg m.

iceberg lettuce n lechuga f iceberg.

icebox [ˈaɪsbɒks] n - **1.** UK [in refrigerator] congelador m - **2.** US [refrigerator] refrigerador m.

icebreaker [ˈaɪsˌbreɪkəʳ] n [ship] rompehielos m inv.

ice bucket n cubo m del hielo.

ice cap n casquete m polar.

ice-cold adj helado(da).

ice cream n helado m.

ice cream van n UK furgoneta de venta de helados.

ice cube n cubito m de hielo.

iced [aɪst] adj - **1.** [cooled with ice] con hielo - **2.** [covered in icing] glaseado(da).

ice floe n témpano m de hielo.

ice hockey n hockey m sobre hielo.

Iceland [ˈaɪslənd] n Islandia.

Icelander [ˈaɪsləndəʳ] n islandés m, -esa f.

Icelandic [aɪsˈlændɪk] <> adj islandés(esa). <> n [language] islandés m.

ice lolly n UK polo m.

ice pick n pico m para el hielo.

ice rink n pista f de (patinaje sobre) hielo.

ice skate n patín m de cuchilla.

<> **ice-skate** vi patinar sobre hielo.

ice-skater n patinador m, -ra f sobre hielo.

ice-skating n patinaje m sobre hielo.

icicle [ˈaɪsɪkl] n carámbano m.

icily [ˈaɪsɪlɪ] adv [in unfriendly way] glacialmente, con mucha frialdad.

icing [ˈaɪsɪŋ] n glaseado m; **the icing on the cake** fig la guinda.

icing sugar n UK azúcar m glas.

ICJ (abbr of International Court of Justice) n TIJ m.

icon, ikon [ˈaɪkɒn] n COMPUT & RELIG icono m.

iconoclast [aɪˈkɒnəklæst] n iconoclasta mf.

ICU (abbr of intensive care unit) n UCI f.

icy [ˈaɪsɪ] (comp **-ier**, superl **-iest**) adj - **1.** [gen] helado(da) - **2.** fig [unfriendly] glacial.

id [ɪd] n ello m, id m.

I'd [aɪd] - **1.** = I had ⊳ have - **2.** = I would ⊳ would.

ID <> n abbr of identification. <> abbr of Idaho.

Idaho [ˈaɪdəˌhəʊ] n Idaho.

ID card = identity card.

IDD (abbr of international direct dialling) sistema de llamadas telefónicas internacionales directas.

idea [aɪˈdɪə] n - **1.** [gen] idea f; **to have an idea of sthg** tener (alguna) idea de algo; **to have no idea** no tener ni idea; **to get the idea** inf captar la idea, hacerse una idea; **to get the idea (that)...** tener la impresión de que...; **the idea is to...** la idea es... - **2.** [intuition, feeling] sensación f, impresión f; **to have an idea (that)...** tener la sensación de que...

ideal [aɪˈdɪəl] <> adj: **ideal (for)** ideal (para). <> n ideal m.

idealism [aɪˈdɪəlɪzm] n idealismo m.

idealist [aɪˈdɪəlɪst] n idealista mf.

idealize, -ise [aɪˈdɪəlaɪz] vt idealizar.

ideally [aɪˈdɪəlɪ] adv - **1.** [perfectly] idealmente; [suited] perfectamente - **2.** [preferably] preferiblemente, a ser posible.

identical [aɪˈdentɪkl] adj idéntico(ca).

identical twins npl gemelos mpl idénticos.

identifiable [aɪˈdentɪfaɪəbl] adj identificable.

identification [aɪˌdentɪfɪˈkeɪʃn] n - **1.** [gen]: **identification (with)** identificación f (con) - **2.** [documentation] documentación f.

identify [aɪˈdentɪfaɪ] (pt & pp **-ied**) <> vt identificar; **to identify sb with sthg** relacionar a alguien con algo. <> vi: **to identify with sb/ sthg** identificarse con alguien/algo.

Identikit picture® [aɪˈdentɪkɪt-] n fotorrobot f.

identity [aɪˈdentətɪ] (pl **-ies**) n identidad f.

identity card, ID card n carné m OR documento m de identidad, cédula f de identidad Amér.

ideological [ˌaɪdɪəˈlɒdʒɪkl] adj ideológico(ca).

ideology [ˌaɪdɪˈɒlədʒɪ] (pl **-ies**) n ideología f.

idiom [ˈɪdɪəm] n - **1.** [phrase] locución f, modismo m - **2.** fml [style] lenguaje m.

idiomatic [ˌɪdɪəˈmætɪk] adj natural.

idiosyncrasy [ˌɪdɪəˈsɪŋkrəsɪ] (pl **-ies**) n rareza f, manía f.

idiot [ˈɪdɪət] n [fool] idiota mf.

idiotic [ˌɪdɪˈɒtɪk] adj idiota.

idle [ˈaɪdl] <> adj - **1.** [lazy] perezoso(sa), vago(ga) - **2.** [not working - machine, factory] parado(da); [- person] desocupado(da), sin trabajo - **3.** [rumour] infundado(da); [threat, boast] vano(na); [curiosity] que no viene a cuento. <> vi estar en punto muerto.

<> **idle away** vt sep perder, desperdiciar.

idleness [ˈaɪdlnɪs] n [laziness] pereza f, holgazanería f.

idler [ˈaɪdləʳ] n vago m, -ga f, holgazán m, -ana f.

idly [ˈaɪdlɪ] adv - **1.** [lazily] sin hacer nada, haciendo el vago - **2.** [without purpose] distraídamente.

idol [ˈaɪdl] n ídolo m.

idolize, -ise [ˈaɪdəlaɪz] vt idolatrar.

idyll(l) [ˈɪdɪl] n idilio m.

idyllic [ɪˈdɪlɪk] adj idílico(ca).

i.e. (abbr of id est) i.e., es decir.

if [ɪf] <> *conj* - **1.** [gen] si; **if I were you** yo que tú, yo en tu lugar - **2.** [though] aunque; **he's clever, if a little arrogant** es listo, aunque algo arrogante. <> *n*: **ifs and buts** peros *mpl*, pegas *fpl*.

➤ **if not** *conj* - **1.** [otherwise] si no, de lo contrario - **2.** [not to say] por no decir; **it was cheeky, if not downright rude of him** fue mucha cara-dura de su parte, por no decir grosería.

➤ **if only** <> *conj* - **1.** [naming a reason] aunque sólo sea; **at least he got me a present, if only a little one** por lo menos me han comprado un regalo, aunque sea pequeño - **2.** [expressing regret] si; **if only I'd been quicker!** ¡ojalá hubiera sido más rápido! <> *excl* ¡ojalá!

iffy [ˈɪfɪ] (*comp* -**ier**, *superl* -**iest**) *adj inf* dudo-so(sa).

igloo [ˈɪɡluː] (*pl* -**s**) *n* iglú *m*.

ignite [ɪɡˈnaɪt] <> *vt* encender. <> *vi* encen-derse.

ignition [ɪɡˈnɪʃn] *n* - **1.** [act of igniting] ignición *f* - **2.** [in car] encendido *m*; **to switch on the ig-nition** arrancar (el motor).

ignition key *n* llave *f* de contacto.

ignoble [ɪɡˈnəʊbl] *adj fml* innoble.

ignominious [ˌɪɡnəˈmɪnɪəs] *adj fml* ignominio-so(sa).

ignominy [ˈɪɡnəmɪnɪ] *n* (*U*) *fml* ignominia *f*.

ignoramus [ˌɪɡnəˈreɪməs] (*pl* -**es**) *n* ignoran-te *mf*.

ignorance [ˈɪɡnərəns] *n* ignorancia *f*.

ignorant [ˈɪɡnərənt] *adj* - **1.** [uneducated, rude] ignorante - **2.** *fml* [unaware]: **to be ignorant of sthg** ignorar algo.

ignore [ɪɡˈnɔːr] *vt* [thing] no hacer caso de, igno-rar; [person] no hacer caso a, ignorar.

iguana [ɪˈɡwɑːnə] (*pl* **iguana** OR -**s**) *n* iguana *f*.

ikon [ˈaɪkɒn] = **icon**.

IL *abbr of* **Illinois**.

ileum [ˈɪlɪəm] (*pl* **ilea** [ˈɪlɪə]) *n* íleon *m*.

ilk [ɪlk] *n*: **of that ilk** [of that sort] de ese tipo.

ill [ɪl] <> *adj* - **1.** [unwell] enfermo(ma); **to feel ill** encontrarse mal; **to be taken** OR **to fall ill** caer OR ponerse enfermo(ma) - **2.** [bad] ma-lo(la). <> *adv* - **1.** [badly] mal - **2.** *fml* [unfavour-ably]: **to speak/think ill of sb** hablar/pensar mal de alguien.

➤ **ills** *npl* desgracias *fpl*, infortunios *mpl*.

ill. *abbr of* **illustration**.

I'll [aɪl] = **I will** ⊳ **will**; = **I shall** ⊳ **shall**.

ill-advised [-ədˈvaɪzd] *adj* [action] poco aconse-jable; [person] imprudente; **you would be ill-advised to do that** harías mal en hacer eso.

ill at ease *adj* incómodo(da).

ill-bred *adj* maleducado(da).

ill-considered *adj* poco meditado(da).

ill-disposed *adj*: **to be ill-disposed towards** tener mala disposición hacia.

illegal [ɪˈliːgl] *adj* ilegal.

illegally [ɪˈliːgəlɪ] *adv* ilegalmente.

illegible [ɪˈledʒəbl] *adj* ilegible.

illegitimate [ˌɪlɪˈdʒɪtɪmət] *adj* ilegítimo(ma).

ill-equipped [-ɪˈkwɪpt] *adj*: **to be ill-equipped to do sthg** estar mal preparado(da) para ha-cer algo.

ill-fated [-ˈfeɪtɪd] *adj* infausto(ta).

ill feeling *n* resentimiento *m*.

ill-founded [-ˈfaʊndɪd] *adj* sin fundamento, in-fundado(da).

ill-gotten gains [-ˈɡɒtən-] *npl fml* ganan-cias *fpl* ilícitas.

ill health *n* mala salud *f*.

illicit [ɪˈlɪsɪt] *adj* ilícito(ta).

illicitly [ɪˈlɪsɪtlɪ] *adv* de manera ilícita.

ill-informed *adj* mal informado(da).

Illinois *n* Illinois.

illiteracy [ɪˈlɪtərəsɪ] *n* analfabetismo *m*.

illiterate [ɪˈlɪtərət] <> *adj* analfabeto(ta). <> *n* analfabeto *m*, -ta *f*.

ill-mannered *adj* grosero(ra), descortés.

illness [ˈɪlnɪs] *n* enfermedad *f*.

illogical [ɪˈlɒdʒɪkl] *adj* ilógico(ca).

ill-suited *adj*: **ill-suited (for)** poco adecua-do(da) (para).

ill-tempered *adj* malhumorado(da).

ill-timed [-ˈtaɪmd] *adj* inoportuno(na).

ill-treat *vt* maltratar.

ill-treatment *n* (*U*) malos tratos *mpl*.

illuminate [ɪˈluːmɪneɪt] *vt* - **1.** [light up] ilumi-nar - **2.** [explain] ilustrar, aclarar.

illuminated [ɪˈluːmɪneɪtɪd] *adj* iluminado(da).

illuminating [ɪˈluːmɪneɪtɪŋ] *adj* esclarece-dor(ra).

illumination [ɪˌluːmɪˈneɪʃn] *n* [lighting] alum-brado *m*, iluminación *f*.

➤ **illuminations** *npl* UK iluminaciones *fpl*, alumbrado *m* decorativo.

illusion [ɪˈluːʒn] *n* - **1.** [gen] ilusión *f*; **to have no illusions about** no hacerse ilusiones sobre; **to be under the illusion that** creer equivoca-damente que - **2.** [magic trick] truco *m* de ilu-sionismo.

illusionist [ɪˈluːʒənɪst] *n* ilusionista *mf*.

illusory [ɪˈluːsərɪ] *adj fml* ilusorio(ria).

illustrate [ˈɪləstreɪt] *vt* ilustrar.

illustration [ˌɪləˈstreɪʃn] *n* ilustración *f*.

illustrator [ˈɪləstreɪtər] *n* ilustrador *m*, -ra *f*.

illustrious [ɪˈlʌstrɪəs] *adj fml* ilustre.

ill will n rencor m, animadversión f; **to bear sb ill will** guardar rencor a alguien.

ill wind [-wɪnd] n: **it's an ill wind (that blows nobody any good)** prov no hay mal que por bien no venga.

I'm [aɪm] = **I am** ⊏▷ **be**.

image ['ɪmɪdʒ] n imagen f; **to be the image of sb** [exactly like] ser el vivo retrato de alguien.

imagery ['ɪmɪdʒrɪ] n (U) imágenes fpl.

imaginable [ɪ'mædʒɪnəbl] adj imaginable.

imaginary [ɪ'mædʒɪnrɪ] adj imaginario(ria).

imagination [ɪ,mædʒɪ'neɪʃn] n imaginación f; **use your imagination!** ¡imagínatelo!

imaginative [ɪ'mædʒɪnətɪv] adj imaginativo(va).

imagine [ɪ'mædʒɪn] vt - **1.** [gen] imaginar; **imagine never having to work!** ¡imagina que nunca tuvieras que trabajar!; **imagine (that)!** ¡imagínate!; **I can't imagine what he means** no tengo ni idea de qué quiere decir - **2.** [suppose]: **to imagine (that)** imaginarse que.

imaginings [ɪ'mædʒɪnɪŋz] npl imaginaciones fpl.

imbalance [ˌɪm'bæləns] n desequilibrio m.

imbecile ['ɪmbɪsiːl] n imbécil mf.

imbue [ɪm'bjuː] vt: **to be imbued with** estar imbuido(da) de.

IMF (abbr of **International Monetary Fund**) n FMI m.

IMHO (abbr of **in my humble opinion**) adv inf en mi humilde opinión.

imitate ['ɪmɪteɪt] vt imitar.

imitation [ˌɪmɪ'teɪʃn] ◇ n imitación f. ◇ adj de imitación; **imitation jewellery** bisutería f.

imitator ['ɪmɪteɪtəʳ] n imitador m, -ra f.

immaculate [ɪ'mækjʊlət] adj - **1.** [clean and tidy] inmaculado(da); [taste] exquisito(ta) - **2.** [performance, timing] impecable, perfecto(ta).

immaculately [ɪ'mækjʊlətlɪ] adv - **1.** [cleanly, tidily] de manera inmaculada - **2.** [performed, timed] impecablemente, a la perfección.

immaterial [ˌɪmə'tɪərɪəl] adj [irrelevant, unimportant] irrelevante.

immature [ˌɪmə'tjʊəʳ] adj inmaduro(ra); [animal] joven.

immaturity [ˌɪmə'tjʊərətɪ] n - **1.** [lack of judgment] inmadurez f - **2.** [youth] juventud f.

immeasurable [ɪ'meʒrəbl] adj inmenso(sa), inconmensurable.

immediacy [ɪ'miːdjəsɪ] n inmediatez f.

immediate [ɪ'miːdjət] adj - **1.** [gen] inmediato(ta); **in the immediate future** en un futuro inmediato; **in the immediate vicinity** en las inmediaciones - **2.** [family] más cercano(na).

immediately [ɪ'miːdjətlɪ] ◇ adv - **1.** [at once] inmediatamente - **2.** [directly] directamente. ◇ conj en cuanto, tan pronto como.

immemorial [ˌɪmɪ'mɔːrɪəl] adj inmemorial; **from time immemorial** desde tiempos inmemoriales.

immense [ɪ'mens] adj inmenso(sa).

immensely [ɪ'menslɪ] adv [gen] inmensamente; [enjoyable, difficult] enormemente.

immensity [ɪ'mensətɪ] n inmensidad f.

immerse [ɪ'mɜːs] vt - **1.** [plunge]: **to immerse sthg in sthg** sumergir algo en algo - **2.** [involve]: **to immerse o.s. in sthg** enfrascarse en algo.

immersion heater [ɪ'mɜːʃn-] n calentador m de inmersión.

immigrant ['ɪmɪgrənt] ◇ n inmigrante mf. ◇ comp inmigrante.

immigration [ˌɪmɪ'greɪʃn] ◇ n inmigración f. ◇ comp de inmigración.

imminence ['ɪmɪnəns] n inminencia f.

imminent ['ɪmɪnənt] adj inminente.

immobile [ɪ'məʊbaɪl] adj inmóvil.

immobilization [ɪ,məʊbɪlaɪ'zeɪʃn] n inmovilización f.

immobilize, -ise [ɪ'məʊbɪlaɪz] vt inmovilizar.

immobilizer [ɪ'məʊbɪlaɪzəʳ] n AUTO inmovilizador m.

immodest [ɪ'mɒdɪst] adj - **1.** [vain] vanidoso(sa), inmodesto(ta) - **2.** [indecent] indecente, indecoroso(sa).

immoral [ɪ'mɒrəl] adj inmoral.

immorality [ˌɪmə'rælətɪ] n inmoralidad f.

immortal [ɪ'mɔːtl] ◇ adj inmortal. ◇ n - **1.** [god] dios m OR divinidad f inmortal - **2.** [hero] inmortal mf.

immortality [ˌɪmɔː'tælətɪ] n inmortalidad f.

immortalize, -ise [ɪ'mɔːtəlaɪz] vt inmortalizar.

immune [ɪ'mjuːn] adj - **1.** [gen & MED]: **immune (to)** inmune (a) - **2.** [exempt]: **immune (from)** exento(ta) (de).

immune system n sistema m inmunológico.

immunity [ɪ'mjuːnətɪ] n - **1.** [gen & MED]: **immunity (to)** inmunidad f (a) - **2.** [exemption]: **immunity (from)** exención f (de).

immunization [ˌɪmjuːnaɪ'zeɪʃn] n inmunización f.

immunize, -ise ['ɪmjuːnaɪz] vt: **to immunize sb (against sthg)** inmunizar a alguien (contra algo).

immunodeficiency [ˌɪmjuːnəʊdɪ'fɪʃənsɪ] n inmunodeficiencia f.

immunology [ˌɪmjuːn'ɒlədʒɪ] n inmunología f.

immutable [ɪ'mjuːtəbl] adj fml inmutable.

imp [ɪmp] *n* **- 1.** [creature] duendecillo *m* **- 2.** [naughty child] diablillo *m*.

impact ◇ *n* ['ɪmpækt] impacto *m*; **on impact** en el momento del impacto; **to make an impact on** OR **upon** causar impacto en. ◇ *vt* [ɪm'pækt] **- 1.** [collide with] chocar con **- 2.** [influence] influenciar.

impair [ɪm'peər] *vt* [sight, hearing] dañar, debilitar; [movement] entorpecer; [ability, efficiency] mermar; [prospects] perjudicar.

impaired [ɪm'peəd] *adj* defectuoso(sa).

impale [ɪm'peɪl] *vt*: **to be impaled on sthg** quedar atravesado(da) en algo.

impart [ɪm'pɑ:t] *vt fml* **- 1.** [information]: **to impart sthg (to sb)** comunicar algo (a alguien) **- 2.** [feeling, quality]: **to impart sthg (to sthg)** conferir algo (a algo).

impartial [ɪm'pɑ:ʃl] *adj* imparcial.

impartiality [ɪm,pɑ:ʃɪ'ælətɪ] *n* imparcialidad *f*.

impassable [ɪm'pɑ:səbl] *adj* intransitable, impracticable.

impasse [æm'pɑ:s] *n* impasse *m*, callejón *m* sin salida.

impassioned [ɪm'pæʃnd] *adj* apasionado(da).

impassive [ɪm'pæsɪv] *adj* impasible.

impatience [ɪm'peɪʃns] *n* impaciencia *f*.

impatient [ɪm'peɪʃnt] *adj* impaciente; **to be impatient to do sthg** estar impaciente por hacer algo; **to be impatient for sthg** esperar algo con impaciencia; **to get impatient** impacientarse.

impatiently [ɪm'peɪʃntlɪ] *adv* impacientemente, con impaciencia.

impeach [ɪm'pi:tʃ] *vt* [president, official] iniciar un proceso de destitución contra.

impeachment [ɪm'pi:tʃmənt] *n US* [of president, official] proceso *m* de destitución.

impeccable [ɪm'pekəbl] *adj* impecable.

impeccably [ɪm'pekəblɪ] *adv* impecablemente.

impede [ɪm'pi:d] *vt* dificultar, entorpecer.

impediment [ɪm'pedɪmənt] *n* **- 1.** [obstacle] impedimento *m*, obstáculo *m* **- 2.** [disability] defecto *m*.

impel [ɪm'pel] (*pt & pp* **-led**, *cont* **-ling**) *vt*: **to impel sb to do sthg** impulsar a alguien a hacer algo.

impending [ɪm'pendɪŋ] *adj* inminente.

impenetrable [ɪm'penɪtrəbl] *adj* **- 1.** [impossible to penetrate] impenetrable **- 2.** [impossible to understand] incomprensible.

imperative [ɪm'perətɪv] ◇ *adj* [need] apremiante, imperativo(va); **it is imperative that...** es imprescindible que... ◇ *n* imperativo *m*.

imperceptible [,ɪmpə'septəbl] *adj* imperceptible.

imperfect [ɪm'pɜ:fɪkt] ◇ *adj* [not perfect] imperfecto(ta). ◇ *n* GRAM: **imperfect (tense)** (pretérito *m*) imperfecto *m*.

imperfection [,ɪmpə'fekʃn] *n* imperfección *f*.

imperial [ɪm'pɪərɪəl] *adj* **- 1.** [of an empire or emperor] imperial **- 2.** [system of measurement]: **imperial system** sistema anglosajón de medidas.

imperialism [ɪm'pɪərɪəlɪzm] *n* imperialismo *m*.

imperialist [ɪm'pɪərɪəlɪst] ◇ *adj* imperialista. ◇ *n* imperialista *mf*.

imperil [ɪm'perɪl] (*UK* **-led**, *cont* **-ling**) (*US* **-ed**, *cont* **-ing**) *vt fml* poner en peligro.

imperious [ɪm'pɪərɪəs] *adj* imperioso(sa).

impersonal [ɪm'pɜ:snl] *adj* impersonal.

impersonate [ɪm'pɜ:səneɪt] *vt* [try to pass as] hacerse pasar por; [do impression of] imitar.

impersonation [ɪm,pɜ:sə'neɪʃn] *n* **- 1.** [pretending to be]: **charged with impersonation of a policeman** acusado de hacerse pasar por policía **- 2.** [impression] imitación *f*; **to do impersonations (of)** imitar (a), hacer imitaciones (de).

impersonator [ɪm'pɜ:səneɪtər] *n* imitador *m*, -ra *f*.

impertinence [ɪm'pɜ:tɪnəns] *n (U)* impertinencia *f*, insolencia *f*.

impertinent [ɪm'pɜ:tɪnənt] *adj* impertinente, insolente.

imperturbable [,ɪmpə'tɜ:bəbl] *adj* imperturbable.

impervious [ɪm'pɜ:vjəs] *adj* [not influenced]: **impervious to** insensible a.

impetuous [ɪm'petʃʊəs] *adj* impetuoso(sa).

impetus ['ɪmpɪtəs] *n (U)* **- 1.** [momentum] ímpetu *m* **- 2.** [stimulus] impulso *m*.

impinge [ɪm'pɪndʒ] *vi*: **to impinge on sthg/sb** afectar algo/a alguien.

impish ['ɪmpɪʃ] *adj* travieso(sa).

implacable [ɪm'plækəbl] *adj* implacable.

implant ◇ *n* ['ɪmplɑ:nt] implante *m*. ◇ *vt* [ɪm'plɑ:nt] **- 1.** [fix - idea etc]: **to implant sthg in** OR **into** inculcar algo en **- 2.** MED: **to implant sthg in** OR **into** implantar algo en.

implausible [ɪm'plɔ:zəbl] *adj* inverosímil.

implement ◇ *n* ['ɪmplɪmənt] herramienta *f*. ◇ *vt* ['ɪmplɪment] llevar a cabo, poner en práctica.

implementation [,ɪmplɪmen'teɪʃn] *n* puesta *f* en práctica.

implicate ['ɪmplɪkeɪt] *vt*: **to implicate sb in** implicar OR involucrar a alguien en.

implication [,ɪmplɪ'keɪʃn] *n* **- 1.** [involvement] implicación *f*, complicidad *f* **- 2.** [inference] consecuencia *f*; **by implication** de forma indirecta.

implicit [ɪm'plɪsɪt] *adj* **- 1.** [gen]: **implicit (in)** implícito(ta) (en) **- 2.** [complete - belief] absoluto(ta); [- faith] incondicional.

implicitly [ɪm'plɪsɪtlɪ] *adv* **- 1.** [by inference] implícitamente **- 2.** [completely] incondicionalmente, ciegamente.

implied [ɪm'plaɪd] *adj* implícito(ta).

implode [ɪm'pləʊd] *vi* **- 1.** [star, building] implosionar **- 2.** [government, organization] estallar.

implore [ɪm'plɔ:ʳ] *vt*: **to implore sb (to do sthg)** suplicar a alguien (que haga algo).

imply [ɪm'plaɪ] (*pt & pp* **-ied**) *vt* **- 1.** [suggest] insinuar, dar a entender **- 2.** [involve] implicar, suponer.

impolite [,ɪmpə'laɪt] *adj* maleducado(da), descortés.

imponderable [ɪm'pɒndrəbl] *adj* imponderable, inestimable.

➡ **imponderables** *npl* imponderables *mpl*.

import ◇ *n* [ɪm'pɔ:t] **- 1.** [act of importing, product] importación *f* **- 2.** *fml* [meaning] sentido *m*, significado *m* **- 3.** *fml* [importance] trascendencia *f*, importancia *f*. ◇ *vt* [ɪm'pɔ:t] [gen & COMPUT] importar.

importance [ɪm'pɔ:tns] *n* importancia *f*.

important [ɪm'pɔ:tnt] *adj*: **important (to)** importante (para); **it's not important** no importa.

importantly [ɪm'pɔ:tntlɪ] *adv*: **more importantly** lo que es aún más importante.

importation [,ɪmpɔ:'teɪʃn] *n* importación *f*.

imported [ɪm'pɔ:tɪd] *adj* importado(da), de importación.

importer [ɪm'pɔ:təʳ] *n* importador *m*, -ra *f*.

impose [ɪm'pəʊz] ◇ *vt*: **to impose sthg (on)** imponer algo (a). ◇ *vi*: **to impose (on)** abusar (de), molestar (a).

imposing [ɪm'pəʊzɪŋ] *adj* imponente, impresionante.

imposition [,ɪmpə'zɪʃn] *n* **- 1.** [enforcement] imposición *f* **- 2.** [cause of trouble] molestia *f*.

impossibility [ɪm,pɒsə'bɪlətɪ] (*pl* **-ies**) *n* imposibilidad *f*.

impossible [ɪm'pɒsəbl] ◇ *adj* **- 1.** [gen] imposible **- 2.** [person, behaviour] inaguantable, insufrible. ◇ *n*: **to do the impossible** hacer lo imposible.

impostor, imposter US [ɪm'pɒstəʳ] *n* impostor *m*, -ra *f*.

impotence ['ɪmpətəns] *n* impotencia *f*.

impotent ['ɪmpətənt] *adj* impotente.

impound [ɪm'paʊnd] *vt* confiscar, incautarse.

impoverished [ɪm'pɒvərɪʃt] *adj* [country, people, imagination] empobrecido(da).

impracticable [ɪm'præktɪkəbl] *adj* impracticable, irrealizable.

impractical [ɪm'præktɪkl] *adj* poco práctico(ca).

imprecation [,ɪmprɪ'keɪʃn] *n* *fml* imprecación *f*.

imprecise [ɪmprɪ'saɪs] *adj* impreciso(sa).

impregnable [ɪm'pregnəbl] *adj* *lit & fig* incontestable.

impregnate ['ɪmpregneɪt] *vt* **- 1.** [introduce substance into]: **to impregnate sthg (with)** impregnar OR empapar algo (de) **- 2.** *fml* [fertilize] fecundar.

impresario [,ɪmprɪ'sɑ:rɪəʊ] (*pl* **-s**) *n* empresario *m*, -ria *f* de espectáculos.

impress [ɪm'pres] ◇ *vt* **- 1.** [produce admiration in] impresionar; **I was favourably impressed** me causó buena impresión **- 2.** [stress]: **to impress sthg on sb** hacer comprender a alguien la importancia de algo. ◇ *vi* [create good impression] causar buena impresión; [show off] impresionar.

impression [ɪm'preʃn] *n* **- 1.** [gen] impresión *f*; **to make an impression** impresionar; **to make a good/bad impression** causar una buena/mala impresión; **to be under the impression that** tener la impresión de que **- 2.** [imitation] imitación *f*.

impressionable [ɪm'preʃnəbl] *adj* impresionable.

impressionism [ɪm'preʃənɪzm] *n* impresionismo *m*.

impressionist [ɪm'preʃənɪst] ◇ *adj* ART impresionista. ◇ *n* **- 1.** [imitator] imitador *m*, -ra *f* **- 2.** ART impresionista *mf*.

impressive [ɪm'presɪv] *adj* impresionante.

imprint ['ɪmprɪnt] *n* **- 1.** [mark] huella *f*, impresión *f* **- 2.** [publisher's name] pie *m* de imprenta.

imprinted [ɪm'prɪntɪd] *adj* **- 1.** [marked] marcado(da) **- 2.** *fig* [on mind, memory]: **imprinted on** impreso(sa) OR grabado(da) en.

imprison [ɪm'prɪzn] *vt* encarcelar.

imprisonment [ɪm'prɪznmənt] *n* encarcelamiento *m*.

improbable [ɪm'prɒbəbl] *adj* [event] improbable; [story, excuse] inverosímil; [clothes, hat] estrafalario(ria); [contraption] extraño(ña).

impromptu [ɪm'prɒmptju:] *adj* improvisado(da).

improper [ɪm'prɒpəʳ] *adj* **- 1.** [unsuitable] impropio(pia) **- 2.** [incorrect, illegal] indebido(da) **- 3.** [rude] indecente, indecoroso(sa).

impropriety [ɪmprə'praɪətɪ] *n* **- 1.** [unsuitability] impropiedad *f* **- 2.** [rudeness] indecencia *f*.

improve [ɪm'pru:v] ◇ *vi* mejorar; **to improve on OR upon sthg** mejorar algo. ◇ *vt* mejorar.

improved [ɪm'pru:vd] *adj* mejorado(da).

improvement [ɪm'pru:vmənt] *n* **- 1.** [gen]: **improvement (in/on)** mejora *f* (en/con respecto a); **to be an improvement on sthg** ser mejor que algo **- 2.** [in health] mejoría *f* **- 3.** [to home] reforma *f*.

improvisation [ˌɪmprəvaɪˈzeɪʃn] *n* improvisación *f*.

improvise [ˈɪmprəvaɪz] *vt* & *vi* improvisar.

imprudent [ɪmˈpruːdənt] *adj* imprudente.

impudent [ˈɪmpjʊdənt] *adj* insolente, descarado(da).

impugn [ɪmˈpjuːn] *vt fml* impugnar.

impulse [ˈɪmpʌls] *n* impulso *m*; **on impulse** sin pensar.

impulse buying [-ˈbaɪɪŋ] *n (U)* compra *f* impulsiva.

impulsive [ɪmˈpʌlsɪv] *adj* impulsivo(va).

impunity [ɪmˈpjuːnətɪ] *n*: **with impunity** impunemente.

impure [ɪmˈpjʊəʳ] *adj lit* & *fig* impuro(ra).

impurity [ɪmˈpjʊərətɪ] *(pl* -ies) *n* impureza *f*.

IMRO [ˈɪmrəʊ] (*abbr of* **Investment Management Regulatory Organization**) *n organismo regulador de inversiones.*

in [ɪn] <> *prep* **- 1.** [indicating place, position] en; **in a box/the garden/the lake** en una caja/el jardín/el lago; **in Paris/Belgium/the country** en París/Bélgica/el campo; **that coat in the window** el abrigo del escaparate; **to be in hospital/prison** estar en el hospital/la cárcel; **in here/there** aquí/allí dentro **- 2.** [wearing]: **she was still in her nightclothes** todavía llevaba su ropa de dormir; **he was dressed in a suit** llevaba un traje; **the woman in the skirt** la mujer de la falda **- 3.** [appearing in, included in] en; **there's a mistake in this paragraph** hay un error en este párrafo; **she's in today's paper** sale en el periódico de hoy **- 4.** [at a particular time]: **at four o'clock in the morning/afternoon** a las cuatro de la mañana/tarde; **in the morning/afternoon** por la mañana/tarde; **in 2006/May/the spring** en 2006/mayo/primavera **- 5.** [within] en; **he learned to type in two weeks** aprendió a escribir a máquina en dos semanas; **I'll be ready in five minutes** estoy listo en cinco minutos **- 6.** [during] desde hace; **it's my first decent meal in weeks** es lo primero decente que como desde hace *OR* en semanas **- 7.** [indicating situation, circumstances]: **in these circumstances** en estas circunstancias; **to live/die in poverty** vivir/morir en la pobreza; **in danger/difficulty** en peligro/dificultades; **in the sun** al sol; **in the rain** bajo la lluvia; **don't go out in this weather** no salgas con este tiempo; **a rise in prices** un aumento de los precios **- 8.** [indicating manner, condition] en; **in a loud/soft voice** en voz alta/baja; **in pencil/ink** a lápiz/bolígrafo; **in this way** de este modo **- 9.** [indicating emotional state] con; **in**

anger/joy con enfado/alegría; **in my excitement I forgot the keys** con la emoción se me olvidaron las llaves **- 10.** [specifying area of activity]: **advances in medicine** avances en la medicina; **he's in computers** se dedica a informática **- 11.** [with numbers - showing quantity, age]: **in large/small quantities** en grandes/pequeñas cantidades; **in (their) thousands** *OR* por millares; **she's in her sixties** anda por los sesenta **- 12.** [describing arrangement]: **in a line/circle** en línea/círculo; **to stand in twos** estar en pares *OR* parejas **- 13.** [as regards] en; **in these matters** en estos temas; **two metres in length/width** dos metros de largo/ancho; **a change in direction** un cambio de dirección **- 14.** [in ratios]: **one in ten** uno de cada diez; **five pence in the pound** cinco peniques por libra **- 15.** *(after superl)* de; **the best in the world** el mejor del mundo **- 16.** *(+ present participle)*: **in doing sthg** al hacer algo ▸▸ **there's nothing in it for us** no tiene ninguna ventaja para nosotros. <> *adv* **- 1.** [inside] dentro; **put the clothes in** mete la ropa (dentro); **to jump in** saltar adentro; **do come in** pasa por favor **- 2.** [at home, work]: **is Judith in?** ¿está Judith?; **I'm staying in tonight** esta noche no salgo **- 3.** [of train, boat, plane]: **is the train in yet?** ¿ha llegado el tren? **- 4.** [of tide]: **the tide's in** la marea está alta ▸▸ **you're in for a surprise** te vas a llevar una sorpresa; **we're in for some bad weather** nos espera mal tiempo; **you're in for it** *inf* te vas a enterar de lo que vale un peine; **to be in on it** estar en el ajo; **to have it in for sb** tenerla tomada con alguien. <> *adj inf* de moda; **short skirts are in this year** este año se llevan las faldas cortas.

◆ **ins** *npl*: **the ins and outs** los detalles, los pormenores.

◆ **in that** *conj* en el sentido de que.

in. *abbr of* **inch**.

IN *abbr of* **Indiana**.

inability [ˌɪnəˈbɪlətɪ] *n*: **inability (to do sthg)** incapacidad *f* (de hacer algo).

inaccessible [ˌɪnəkˈsesəbl] *adj* inaccesible.

inaccuracy [ɪnˈækjʊrəsɪ] *(pl* -ies) *n* **- 1.** *(U)* [quality of being inaccurate] inexactitud *f* **- 2.** [imprecise statement] incorrección *f*, error *m*.

inaccurate [ɪnˈækjʊrət] *adj* inexacto(ta).

inaction [ɪnˈækʃn] *n* pasividad *f*, inacción *f*.

inactive [ɪnˈæktɪv] *adj* inactivo(va).

inactivity [ˌɪnækˈtɪvɪtɪ] *n* inactividad *f*.

inadequacy [ɪnˈædɪkwəsɪ] *(pl* -ies) *n* [of thing, system] insuficiencia *f*; [of person] incapacidad *f*.

inadequate [ɪnˈædɪkwət] *adj* **- 1.** [insufficient] insuficiente **- 2.** [person] incapaz.

inadmissible [,ınəd'mısəbl] *adj* inadmisible.

inadvertent [,ınəd'vɜ:tnt] *adj* accidental, fortuito(ta).

inadvertently [,ınəd'vɜ:tntlı] *adv* sin querer, accidentalmente.

inadvisable [,ınəd'vaızəbl] *adj* desaconsejable, poco aconsejable.

inalienable [ın'eıljənəbl] *adj fml* inalienable.

inane [ı'neın] *adj* necio(cia).

inanely [ı'neınlı] *adv* neciamente.

inanimate [ın'ænımət] *adj* inanimado(da).

inanity [ı'nænətı] *n* necedad *f*.

inapplicable [,ınə'plıkəbl] *adj* inaplicable.

inappropriate [,ınə'prəuprıət] *adj* [remark, clothing] impropio(pia); [time] inoportuno(na).

inarticulate [,ına:'tıkjulət] *adj* [person] que no se expresa bien; [speech] mal pronunciado(da) OR expresado(da).

inasmuch [,ınəz'mʌtʃ] ➧ **inasmuch as** *conj* en la medida en que.

inattention [,ınə'tenʃn] *n*: **inattention (to)** falta *f* de atención (a).

inattentive [,ınə'tentıv] *adj*: **inattentive (to)** desatento(ta) (a).

inaudible [ı'nɔ:dıbl] *adj* inaudible.

inaugural [ı'nɔ:gjurəl] *adj* [gen] inaugural; [ceremony] de investidura.

inaugurate [ı'nɔ:gjureıt] *vt* - **1.** [leader, president] investir - **2.** [building, system] inaugurar.

inauguration [ı,nɔ:gju'reıʃn] *n* - **1.** [of leader, president] investidura *f* - **2.** [of building, system] inauguración *f*.

inauspicious [,ınɔ:'spıʃəs] *adj* [circumstances] desfavorable; [beginning, time] poco propicio(cia).

in-between *adj* intermedio(dia).

inborn [,ın'bɔ:n] *adj* innato(ta).

inbound ['ınbaund] *adj* de llegada.

in-box *n* [for e-mail] buzón *m* de entrada.

inbred [,ın'bred] *adj* - **1.** [closely related] consanguíneo(a), endogámico(ca) - **2.** [inborn] innato(ta).

inbreeding ['ın,bri:dıŋ] *n* endogamia *f*.

inbuilt [,ın'bılt] *adj* [in person] innato(ta); [in thing] inherente.

inc. (*abbr of* **inclusive**) inclus.; **12th-15th April inc.** 12-15 de abril inclus.

Inc. [ıŋk] (*abbr of* **incorporated**) *US* ≃ S.A.

Inca ['ıŋkə] *n* inca *mf*.

incalculable [ın'kælkjuləbl] *adj* [very great] incalculable.

incandescent [,ınkæn'desnt] *adj* incandescente.

incantation [,ınkæn'teıʃn] *n* conjuro *m*, ensalmo *m*.

incapable [ın'keıpəbl] *adj* - **1.** [unable]: **to be incapable of sthg/of doing sthg** ser incapaz de algo/de hacer algo - **2.** [useless] incompetente.

incapacitate [,ınkə'pæsıteıt] *vt* incapacitar.

incapacitated [,ınkə'pæsıteıtıd] *adj* incapacitado(da).

incapacity [,ınkə'pæsətı] *n*: **incapacity (for)** incapacidad *f* (para).

incarcerate [ın'kɑ:səreıt] *vt fml* encarcelar.

incarceration [ın,kɑ:sə'reıʃn] *n fml* encarcelamiento *m*.

incarnate [ın'kɑ:neıt] *adj*: **she's generosity incarnate** es la generosidad personificada.

incarnation [,ınkɑ:'neıʃn] *n* - **1.** [personification] personificación *f* - **2.** [existence] encarnación *f*.

incendiary device [ın'sendjərı-] *n* artefacto *m* incendiario.

incense ◇ *n* ['ınsens] incienso *m*. ◇ *vt* [ın'sens] enfurecer, indignar.

incentive [ın'sentıv] *n* incentivo *m*.

incentive scheme *n* plan *m* de incentivos.

incentivize [ın'sentıvaız] *vt* incentivar.

inception [ın'sepʃn] *n fml* inicio *m*, origen *m*.

incessant [ın'sesnt] *adj* incesante, constante.

incessantly [ın'sesntlı] *adv* incesantemente, constantemente.

incest ['ınsest] *n* incesto *m*.

incestuous [ın'sestjuəs] *adj* - **1.** [sexually] incestuoso(sa) - **2.** *fig* [too close] cerrado en sí mismo, cerrada en sí misma.

inch [ıntʃ] ◇ *n* = 2,54 *cm* pulgada *f*; **to be within an inch of doing sthg** estar en un tris de hacer algo. ◇ *vi*: **to inch forward** avanzar poco a poco.

incidence ['ınsıdəns] *n* [of disease, theft] índice *m*.

incident ['ınsıdənt] *n* incidente *m*, suceso *m*.

incidental [,ınsı'dentl] *adj* accesorio(ria), secundario(ria).

incidentally [,ınsı'dentəlı] *adv* por cierto, a propósito.

incidental music *n* música *f* de acompañamiento.

incinerate [ın'sınəreıt] *vt* incinerar, quemar.

incinerator [ın'sınəreıtər] *n* incinerador *m*.

incipient [ın'sıpıənt] *adj fml* incipiente.

incision [ın'sıʒn] *n* incisión *f*.

incisive [ın'saısıv] *adj* [comment, person] incisivo(va); [mind] penetrante.

incisor [ın'saızər] *n* incisivo *m*.

incite [ın'saıt] *vt* incitar; **to incite sb to do sthg** incitar a alguien a que haga algo.

incitement [ın'saıtmənt] *n* (U): **incitement (to sthg/to do sthg)** instigación *f* (a algo/a hacer algo).

incl. *abbr of* **including, inclusive**.

inclement [ɪn'klemənt] *adj fml* inclemente.

inclination [ˌɪnklɪ'neɪʃn] *n* **- 1.** *(U)* [liking, preference] inclinación *f*, propensión *f* **- 2.** [tendency]: **inclination to do sthg** tendencia *f* a hacer algo.

incline ◇ *n* ['ɪnklaɪn] pendiente *f*, cuesta *f*. ◇ *vt* [ɪn'klaɪn] [head] inclinar, ladear.

inclined [ɪn'klaɪnd] *adj* **- 1.** [tending]: **to be inclined to sthg** ser propenso(sa) OR tener tendencia a algo; **to be inclined to do sthg** tener tendencia a hacer algo; **I'm inclined to agree** creo que estoy de acuerdo **- 2.** *fml* [wanting]: **to be inclined to do sthg** estar dispuesto(ta) a hacer algo **- 3.** [sloping] inclinado(da).

include [ɪn'kluːd] *vt* **- 1.** [gen] incluir **- 2.** [with letter] adjuntar.

included [ɪn'kluːdɪd] *adj* incluido(da).

including [ɪn'kluːdɪŋ] *prep* incluyendo; **six died, including a child** murieron seis personas, incluyendo a un niño.

inclusion [ɪn'kluːʒn] *n* inclusión *f*.

inclusive [ɪn'kluːsɪv] *adj* **- 1.** [including everything] inclusivo(va); **one to nine inclusive** uno a nueve inclusive **- 2.** [including all costs]: **inclusive of VAT** con el IVA incluido; **£150 inclusive** 150 libras todo incluido.

inclusivity [ˌɪnkluː'sɪvɪtɪ] *n* política *f* de inclusión.

incognito [ˌɪnkɒg'niːtəʊ] *adv* de incógnito.

incoherent [ˌɪnkəʊ'hɪərənt] *adj* incoherente.

income ['ɪŋkʌm] *n* *(U)* [gen] ingresos *mpl*; [from property] renta *f*; [from investment] réditos *mpl*.

incomes policy *n UK* política *f* de rentas.

income support *n* *(U) UK subsidio para personas con muy bajos ingresos o desempleados sin derecho a subsidio de paro*, ≃ salario *m* social.

income tax *n* impuesto *m* sobre la renta.

incoming ['ɪnˌkʌmɪŋ] *adj* **- 1.** [tide] ascendente **- 2.** [flight] de llegada **- 3.** [government, president] entrante **- 4.** [mail, report] recibido(da); **incoming phone call** llamada de fuera OR del exterior.

incommunicado [ˌɪnkəmjuː'nɪ'kɑːdəʊ] *adv* en aislamiento, incomunicado(da).

incomparable [ɪn'kɒmpərəbl] *adj* incomparable, sin par.

incompatible [ˌɪnkəm'pætɪbl] *adj* [gen & COMPUT]: **incompatible (with)** incompatible (con).

incompetence [ɪn'kɒmpɪtəns] *n* incompetencia *f*, incapacidad *f*.

incompetent [ɪn'kɒmpɪtənt] *adj* incompetente, incapaz.

incomplete [ˌɪnkəm'pliːt] *adj* incompleto(ta).

incomprehensible [ɪnˌkɒmprɪ'hensəbl] *adj* incomprensible.

inconceivable [ˌɪnkən'siːvəbl] *adj* inconcebible.

inconclusive [ˌɪnkən'kluːsɪv] *adj* [evidence, argument] poco convincente; [meeting, outcome] sin conclusión clara.

incongruous [ɪn'kɒŋgrʊəs] *adj* incongruente.

inconsequential [ˌɪnkɒnsɪ'kwenʃl] *adj* intrascendente, de poca importancia.

inconsiderable [ˌɪnkən'sɪdərəbl] *adj*: **not inconsiderable** nada insignificante OR despreciable.

inconsiderate [ˌɪnkən'sɪdərət] *adj* desconsiderado(da).

inconsistency [ˌɪnkən'sɪstənsɪ] (*pl* **-ies**) *n* **- 1.** [between theory and practice] inconsecuencia *f*; [between statements etc] falta *f* de correspondencia **- 2.** [contradictory point] contradicción *f*.

inconsistent [ˌɪnkən'sɪstənt] *adj* **- 1.** [translation, statement]: **inconsistent (with)** incoherente OR incongruente (con) **- 2.** [group, government, person] inconsecuente **- 3.** [erratic] irregular, desigual.

inconsolable [ˌɪnkən'səʊləbl] *adj* inconsolable.

inconspicuous [ˌɪnkən'spɪkjʊəs] *adj* discreto(ta).

incontinence [ɪn'kɒntɪnəns] *n* incontinencia *f*.

incontinent [ɪn'kɒntɪnənt] *adj* incontinente.

incontrovertible [ˌɪnkɒntrə'vɜːtəbl] *adj* incontrovertible.

inconvenience [ˌɪnkən'viːnjəns] ◇ *n* **- 1.** [difficulty, discomfort] molestia *f*, incomodidad *f*; **we apologize for any inconvenience caused** disculpen las molestias **- 2.** [inconvenient thing] inconveniente *m*. ◇ *vt* incomodar, causar molestias a.

inconvenient [ˌɪnkən'viːnjənt] *adj* [time] inoportuno(na); [location] incómodo(da); **that date is inconvenient** esa fecha no me viene bien.

incorporate [ɪn'kɔːpəreɪt] *vt* **- 1.** [integrate]: **to incorporate sthg/sb (in** OR **into)** incorporar algo/a alguien (en) **- 2.** [include] incluir, comprender.

incorporated [ɪn'kɔːpəreɪtɪd] *adj* COMM: **incorporated company** sociedad *f* anónima.

incorporation [ɪnˌkɔːpə'reɪʃn] *n* **- 1.** [integration] incorporación *f* **- 2.** COMM [of company] constitución *f* en sociedad anónima.

incorrect [ˌɪnkə'rekt] *adj* incorrecto(ta), erróneo(a).

incorrigible [ɪn'kɒrɪdʒəbl] *adj* incorregible.

incorruptible [ˌɪnkə'rʌptəbl] *adj* incorruptible.

increase ◇ *n* [ˈɪnkriːs]: **increase (in)** [gen] aumento *m* (de); [in price, temperature] subida *f* (de); **to be on the increase** ir en aumento. ◇ *vt* [ɪnˈkriːs] **- 1.** [gen] aumentar, incrementar **- 2.** [price] subir. ◇ *vi* [ɪnˈkriːs] [gen] aumentar; [price, temperature] subir.

increased [ɪnˈkriːst] *adj* mayor.

increasing [ɪnˈkriːsɪŋ] *adj* creciente.

increasingly [ɪnˈkriːsɪŋlɪ] *adv* cada vez más.

incredible [ɪnˈkredəbl] *adj* increíble.

incredibly [ɪnˈkredəblɪ] *adv* increíblemente.

incredulous [ɪnˈkredjʊləs] *adj* incrédulo(la).

increment [ˈɪnkrɪmənt] *n* incremento *m*.

incriminate [ɪnˈkrɪmɪneɪt] *vt* incriminar; **to incriminate o.s.** incriminarse a sí mismo.

incriminating [ɪnˈkrɪmɪneɪtɪŋ] *adj* comprometedor(ra).

incubate [ˈɪnkjʊbeɪt] ◇ *vt* [egg] incubar, empollar. ◇ *vi* **- 1.** [egg] incubarse **- 2.** [infection] incubar.

incubation [ˌɪnkjʊˈbeɪʃn] *n* incubación *f*.

incubator [ˈɪnkjʊbeɪtə˞] *n* [for baby] incubadora *f*.

inculcate [ˈɪnkʌlkeɪt] *vt fml*: **to inculcate sthg in** OR **into** inculcar algo en.

incumbent [ɪnˈkʌmbənt] *fml* ◇ *adj*: **to be incumbent on** OR **upon sb to do sthg** incumbir a alguien hacer algo. ◇ *n* titular *mf*.

incur [ɪnˈkɜːr] (*pt* & *pp* **-red**, *cont* **-ring**) *vt* [wrath, criticism] incurrir en, atraerse; [debt] contraer; [expenses] incurrir en.

incurable [ɪnˈkjʊərəbl] *adj lit* & *fig* incurable.

incursion [*UK* ɪnˈkɜːʃn, *US* ɪnˈkɜːrʒn] *n* incursión *f*.

indebted [ɪnˈdetɪd] *adj* **- 1.** [grateful]: **indebted (to)** en deuda (con) **- 2.** [owing money]: **indebted (to)** endeudado(da) (con).

indecency [ɪnˈdiːsnsɪ] *n* indecencia *f*.

indecent [ɪnˈdiːsnt] *adj* **- 1.** [improper] indecente **- 2.** [unreasonable, excessive] desmedido(da).

indecent assault *n* abusos *mpl* deshonestos.

indecent exposure *n* exhibicionismo *m*.

indecipherable [ˌɪndɪˈsaɪfərəbl] *adj* indescifrable.

indecision [ˌɪndɪˈsɪʒn] *n* indecisión *f*.

indecisive [ˌɪndɪˈsaɪsɪv] *adj* **- 1.** [person] indeciso(sa) **- 2.** [result] no decisivo(va).

indeed [ɪnˈdiːd] *adv* **- 1.** [certainly] ciertamente; **are you coming?** – **indeed I am** ¿vienes tú? – por supuesto que sí **- 2.** [in fact] de hecho **- 3.** [for emphasis] realmente; **very big indeed** grandísimo(ma); **very few indeed** poquísimos(mas) **- 4.** [to express surprise, disbelief]: **indeed?** ¿ah sí? **- 5.** [what is more] es más.

indefatigable [ˌɪndɪˈfætɪgəbl] *adj* infatigable, incansable.

indefensible [ˌɪndɪˈfensəbl] *adj* [position, view] insostenible, indefendible; [behaviour] inexcusable.

indefinable [ˌɪndɪˈfaɪnəbl] *adj* indefinible.

indefinite [ɪnˈdefɪnɪt] *adj* **- 1.** [time, number] indefinido(da) **- 2.** [answer, opinion] impreciso(sa) **- 3.** GRAM indeterminado(da), indefinido(da).

indefinitely [ɪnˈdefɪnətlɪ] *adv* **- 1.** [for unfixed period] indefinidamente **- 2.** [imprecisely] de forma imprecisa.

indelible [ɪnˈdeləbl] *adj* indeleble.

indelicate [ɪnˈdelɪkət] *adj* poco delicado(da).

indemnify [ɪnˈdemnɪfaɪ] (*pt* & *pp* **-ied**) *vt*: **to indemnify sb for** indemnizar a alguien por; **to indemnify sb against** asegurar a alguien contra.

indemnity [ɪnˈdemnətɪ] *n* **- 1.** [insurance] indemnidad *f* **- 2.** [compensation] indemnización *f*.

indent [ɪnˈdent] ◇ *n* [in text] sangrado *m*. ◇ *vt* **- 1.** [dent] mellar **- 2.** [text] sangrar.

indentation [ˌɪndenˈteɪʃn] *n* **- 1.** [dent] mella *f*, muesca *f* **- 2.** [in text] sangrado *m*.

indenture [ɪnˈdentʃə˞] *n* contrato *m* de aprendizaje.

independence [ˌɪndɪˈpendəns] *n* independencia *f*; **to gain independence** independizarse.

Independence Day *n* el Día de la Independencia.

independent [ˌɪndɪˈpendənt] *adj*: **independent (of)** independiente (de).

independently [ˌɪndɪˈpendəntlɪ] *adv* independientemente; **independently of** aparte de.

independent school *n UK* colegio *m* privado.

in-depth *adj* a fondo, exhaustivo(va).

indescribable [ˌɪndɪˈskraɪbəbl] *adj* indescriptible.

indestructible [ˌɪndɪˈstrʌktəbl] *adj* indestructible.

indeterminate [ˌɪndɪˈtɜːmɪnət] *adj* indeterminado(da).

index [ˈɪndeks] ◇ *n* (*pl* **-es** OR **indices**) índice *m*. ◇ *vt* [book] poner un índice a.

index card *n* ficha *f*.

index finger *n* (dedo *m*) índice *m*.

index-linked [-lɪŋkt] *adj* indexado(da).

India [ˈɪndjə] *n* (la) India.

India ink *US* = **Indian ink.**

Indian [ˈɪndjən] ◇ *adj* **- 1.** [from India] indio(dia), hindú **- 2.** [from the Americas] indio(dia). ◇ *n* **- 1.** [from India] indio *m*, -dia *f*, hindú *mf* **- 2.** [from the Americas] indio *m*, -dia *f*.

Indiana [ˌɪndɪˈænə] *n* Indiana.

Indian ink *UK*, **India ink** *US n* tinta *f* china.

Indian Ocean *n*: the Indian Ocean el océano Índico.

Indian summer *n* veranillo *m* de San Martín.

india rubber *n* [material] caucho *m*; [eraser] goma *f* de borrar.

indicate ['ɪndɪkeɪt] <> *vt* indicar. <> *vi* [when driving]: **to indicate left/right** indicar a la izquierda/derecha.

indication [,ɪndɪ'keɪʃn] *n* - **1.** [suggestion, idea] indicación *f* - **2.** [sign] indicio *m*, señal *f*.

indicative [ɪn'dɪkətɪv] <> *adj*: **indicative of sthg** indicativo(va) de algo. <> *n* GRAM indicativo *m*.

indicator ['ɪndɪkeɪtər] *n* - **1.** [sign, criterion] indicador *m* - **2.** [on car] intermitente *m*.

indices ['ɪndɪsi:z] *npl* ⊳ **index**.

indict [ɪn'daɪt] *vt*: **to indict sb (for)** acusar a alguien (de).

indictable [ɪn'daɪtəbl] *adj* procesable.

indictment [ɪn'daɪtmənt] *n* - **1.** LAW acusación *f* - **2.** [criticism] crítica *f* severa.

indie ['ɪndɪ] *adj* UK inf independiente.

indifference [ɪn'dɪfrəns] *n* indiferencia *f*.

indifferent [ɪn'dɪfrənt] *adj* - **1.** [uninterested]: **indifferent (to)** indiferente (a) - **2.** [mediocre] mediocre.

indigenous [ɪn'dɪdʒɪnəs] *adj* indígena.

indigestible [,ɪndɪ'dʒestəbl] *adj* lit & fig indigesto(ta).

indigestion [,ɪndɪ'dʒestʃn] *n* (U) indigestión *f*.

indignant [ɪn'dɪgnənt] *adj*: **indignant (at)** indignado(da) (por).

indignantly [ɪn'dɪgnəntlɪ] *adv* con indignación.

indignation [,ɪndɪg'neɪʃn] *n* indignación *f*.

indignity [ɪn'dɪgnətɪ] (*pl* -**ies**) *n* indignidad *f*.

indigo ['ɪndɪgəʊ] <> *adj* (color) añil. <> *n* añil *m*.

indirect [,ɪndɪ'rekt] *adj* indirecto(ta).

indirect costs *npl* gastos *mpl* indirectos.

indirect lighting *n* iluminación *f* indirecta.

indirectly [,ɪndɪ'rektlɪ] *adv* indirectamente.

indirect speech *n* estilo *m* indirecto.

indiscreet [,ɪndɪ'skri:t] *adj* indiscreto(ta).

indiscretion [,ɪndɪ'skreʃn] *n* indiscreción *f*.

indiscriminate [,ɪndɪ'skrɪmɪnət] *adj* indiscriminado(da).

indiscriminately [,ɪndɪ'skrɪmɪnətlɪ] *adv* indiscriminadamente.

indispensable [,ɪndɪ'spensəbl] *adj* indispensable, imprescindible.

indisposed [,ɪndɪ'spəʊzd] *adj* fml [unwell] indispuesto(ta).

indisputable [,ɪndɪ'spju:təbl] *adj* incuestionable.

indistinct [,ɪndɪ'stɪŋkt] *adj* [memory] confuso(sa); [words] imperceptible, indistinto(ta); [picture, marking] borroso(sa), indistinto(ta).

indistinguishable [,ɪndɪ'stɪŋgwɪʃəbl] *adj*: **indistinguishable (from)** indistinguible (de).

individual [,ɪndɪ'vɪdʒʊəl] <> *adj* - **1.** [gen] individual - **2.** [tuition] particular - **3.** [approach, style] personal. <> *n* individuo *m*.

individualist [,ɪndɪ'vɪdʒʊəlɪst] *n* individualista *mf*.

individualistic ['ɪndɪ,vɪdʒʊə'lɪstɪk] *adj* individualista.

individuality ['ɪndɪ,vɪdʒʊ'ælətɪ] *n* individualidad *f*.

individually [,ɪndɪ'vɪdʒʊəlɪ] *adv* [separately] individualmente, por separado.

indivisible [,ɪndɪ'vɪzəbl] *adj* indivisible.

Indochina [,ɪndəʊ'tʃaɪnə] *n* Indochina.

indoctrinate [ɪn'dɒktrɪneɪt] *vt* adoctrinar.

indoctrination [ɪn,dɒktrɪ'neɪʃn] *n* adoctrinamiento *m*.

indolent ['ɪndələnt] *adj* indolente.

indomitable [ɪn'dɒmɪtəbl] *adj* indómito(ta), indomable.

Indonesia [,ɪndə'ni:zjə] *n* Indonesia.

Indonesian [,ɪndə'ni:zjən] <> *adj* indonesio(sia). <> *n* - **1.** [person] indonesio *m*, -sia *f* - **2.** [language] indonesio *m*.

indoor ['ɪndɔːr] *adj* [gen] interior; [shoes] de andar por casa; [plant] de interior; [sports] en pista cubierta; **indoor swimming pool** piscina *f* cubierta.

indoors [,ɪn'dɔːz] *adv* [gen] dentro; [at home] en casa.

indubitably [ɪn'dju:bɪtəblɪ] *adv* fml indudablemente, sin duda.

induce [ɪn'dju:s] *vt* - **1.** [persuade]: **to induce sb to do sthg** inducir OR persuadir a alguien a que haga algo - **2.** [labour, sleep, anger] provocar.

inducement [ɪn'dju:smənt] *n* [incentive] incentivo *m*, aliciente *m*.

induction [ɪn'dʌkʃn] *n* - **1.** [into official position]: **induction into** introducción *f* OR inducción *f* a - **2.** ELEC & MED inducción *f* - **3.** [introduction to job] introducción *f*.

induction course *n* cursillo *m* introductorio, curso *m* de iniciación.

indulge [ɪn'dʌldʒ] <> *vt* - **1.** [whim, passion] satisfacer - **2.** [child, person] consentir; **to indulge o.s.** darse un gusto, permitirse un lujo. <> *vi*: **to indulge in sthg** permitirse algo.

indulgence [ɪn'dʌldʒəns] *n* - **1.** [act of indulging] indulgencia *f* - **2.** [special treat] capricho *m*.

indulgent [ɪn'dʌldʒənt] *adj* indulgente.

industrial [ɪn'dʌstrɪəl] *adj* industrial.

industrial action *n* huelga *f*; **to take industrial action** declararse en huelga.

industrial estate *UK*, **industrial park** *US n* polígono *m* industrial.

industrial injury *n* lesión *f* laboral.

industrialist [ɪn'dʌstrɪəlɪst] *n* industrial *mf*.

industrialization [ɪn,dʌstrɪəlaɪ'zeɪʃn] *n* industrialización *f*.

industrialize, -ise [ɪn'dʌstrɪəlaɪz] <> *vt* industrializar. <> *vi* industrializarse.

industrial park *US* = **industrial estate**.

industrial relations *npl* relaciones *fpl* laborales.

industrial revolution *n* revolución *f* industrial.

industrial tribunal *n* tribunal *m* laboral.

industrious [ɪn'dʌstrɪəs] *adj* diligente, trabajador(ra).

industry ['ɪndəstrɪ] (*pl* -ies) *n* - **1.** [gen] industria *f*; **the tourist industry** el sector turístico - **2.** *fml* [hard work] laboriosidad *f*.

inebriated [ɪ'ni:brɪeɪtɪd] *adj fml* ebrio(ebria).

inedible [ɪn'edɪbl] *adj* - **1.** [that cannot be eaten] no comestible - **2.** [bad-tasting] incomible.

ineffective [,ɪnɪ'fektɪv] *adj* ineficaz, inútil.

ineffectual [,ɪnɪ'fektʃʊəl] *adj* inútil.

inefficiency [,ɪnɪ'fɪʃnsɪ] *n* ineficiencia *f*.

inefficient [,ɪnɪ'fɪʃnt] *adj* ineficiente.

inelegant [ɪn'elɪgənt] *adj* poco elegante.

ineligible [ɪn'elɪdʒəbl] *adj* inelegible; **to be ineligible for** no tener derecho a.

inept [ɪ'nept] *adj* inepto(ta); **inept at** incapaz para.

ineptitude [ɪ'neptɪtju:d] *n* ineptitud *f*.

inequality [,ɪnɪ'kwɒlətɪ] (*pl* -ies) *n* desigualdad *f*.

inequitable [ɪn'ekwɪtəbl] *adj fml* injusto(ta).

inert [ɪ'nɜ:t] *adj* inerte.

inertia [ɪ'nɜ:ʃə] *n* inercia *f*.

inescapable [,ɪnɪ'skeɪpəbl] *adj* ineludible.

inessential [,ɪnɪ'senʃl] *adj*: **inessential (to)** innecesario(ria) (para).

inevitable [ɪn'evɪtəbl] <> *adj* inevitable. <> *n*: **the inevitable** lo inevitable.

inevitably [ɪn'evɪtəblɪ] *adv* inevitablemente.

inexact [,ɪnɪg'zækt] *adj* inexacto(ta).

inexcusable [,ɪnɪk'skju:zəbl] *adj* inexcusable, imperdonable.

inexpensive [,ɪnɪk'spensɪv] *adj* barato(ta), económico(ca).

inexperience [,ɪnɪk'spɪərɪəns] *n* inexperiencia *f*.

inexperienced [,ɪnɪk'spɪərɪənst] *adj* inexperto(ta); **to be inexperienced at sthg** no tener experiencia en algo.

inexpert [ɪn'ekspɜ:t] *adj* inexperto(ta).

inexplicable [,ɪnɪk'splɪkəbl] *adj* inexplicable.

inexplicably [,ɪnɪk'splɪkəblɪ] *adv* inexplicablemente.

inextricably [,ɪnɪk'strɪkəblɪ] *adv* indisolublemente, inseparablemente.

infallible [ɪn'fæləbl] *adj* infalible.

infamous ['ɪnfəməs] *adj* infame.

infancy ['ɪnfənsɪ] *n* primera infancia *f*; **to be in its infancy** *fig* dar sus primeros pasos.

infant ['ɪnfənt] *n* - **1.** [baby] bebé *m* - **2.** [young child] niño pequeño *m*, niña pequeña *f*.

infantile ['ɪnfəntaɪl] *adj* infantil.

infant mortality *n* mortalidad *f* infantil.

infantry ['ɪnfəntrɪ] *n* infantería *f*.

infantryman ['ɪnfəntrɪmən] (*pl* -men [-mən]) *n* soldado *m* de infantería.

infant school *n UK* colegio *m* preescolar *(para niños de entre 4 y 7 años)*.

infatuated [ɪn'fætjʊeɪtɪd] *adj*: **infatuated (with)** encaprichado(da) (con).

infatuation [ɪn,fætjʊ'eɪʃn] *n*: **infatuation (with)** encaprichamiento *m* (con).

infect [ɪn'fekt] *vt* - **1.** [wound] infectar; [person]: **to infect sb (with sthg)** contagiar (algo) a alguien - **2.** *fig* [spread to] contagiar.

infected [ɪn'fektɪd] *adj*: **infected (with)** [wound] infectado(da) (de); [patient] contagiado(da) (de).

infection [ɪn'fekʃn] *n* - **1.** [disease] infección *f* - **2.** [spreading of germs] contagio *m*.

infectious [ɪn'fekʃəs] *adj* - **1.** [disease] infeccioso(sa) - **2.** [laugh, attitude] contagioso(sa).

infer [ɪn'fɜ:r] (*pt & pp* -**red**, *cont* -**ring**) *vt* - **1.** [deduce]: **to infer (that)** deducir OR inferir que; **to infer sthg (from sthg)** deducir OR inferir algo (de algo) - **2.** *inf* [imply] insinuar.

inference ['ɪnfrəns] *n* - **1.** [conclusion] conclusión *f* - **2.** [deduction]: **by inference** por deducción.

inferior [ɪn'fɪərɪər] <> *adj*: **inferior (to)** inferior (a). <> *n* [in status] inferior *mf*.

inferiority [ɪn,fɪərɪ'ɒrətɪ] *n* inferioridad *f*.

inferiority complex *n* complejo *m* de inferioridad.

inferno [ɪn'fɜ:nəʊ] (*pl* -s) *n* [hell] infierno *m*; **the building was an inferno** el edificio sufría un pavoroso incendio.

infertile [ɪn'fɜ:taɪl] *adj* estéril.

infertility [,ɪnfə'tɪlətɪ] *n* esterilidad *f*.

infestation [,ɪnfe'steɪʃn] *n* plaga *f*.

infested [ɪn'festɪd] *adj*: **infested with** infestado(da) de.

infidelity [,ɪnfɪ'delətɪ] *n* [of partner] infidelidad *f*.

infighting ['ɪn,faɪtɪŋ] n (U) disputas fpl internas.

infiltrate ['ɪnfɪltreɪt] ◇ vt infiltrar. ◇ vi: to infiltrate into sthg infiltrarse en algo.

infinite ['ɪnfɪnət] adj infinito(ta).

infinitely ['ɪnfɪnətlɪ] adv infinitamente.

infinitesimal [,ɪnfɪnɪ'tesɪml] adj infinitesimal.

infinitive [ɪn'fɪnɪtɪv] n infinitivo m; in the infinitive en infinitivo.

infinity [ɪn'fɪnətɪ] n - **1.** MATHS infinito m - **2.** [incalculable number]: an infinity (of) infinidad f (de).

infirm [ɪn'fɜːm] ◇ adj achacoso(sa). ◇ npl: the infirm los enfermos.

infirmary [ɪn'fɜːmərɪ] (pl -ies) n - **1.** [hospital] hospital m - **2.** [room] enfermería f.

infirmity [ɪn'fɜːmətɪ] (pl -ies) n - **1.** [illness] dolencia f - **2.** [state] enfermedad f.

inflamed [ɪn'fleɪmd] adj MED inflamado(da).

inflammable [ɪn'flæməbl] adj [burning easily] inflamable.

inflammation [,ɪnflə'meɪʃn] n MED inflamación f.

inflammatory [ɪn'flæmətrɪ] adj incendiario(ria).

inflatable [ɪn'fleɪtəbl] adj inflable, hinchable.

inflate [ɪn'fleɪt] ◇ vt - **1.** [gen] inflar, hinchar - **2.** [prices] inflar, aumentar. ◇ vi inflarse, hincharse.

inflated [ɪn'fleɪtɪd] adj - **1.** [gen] inflado(da), hinchado(da) - **2.** [prices] desorbitado(da).

inflation [ɪn'fleɪʃn] n ECON inflación f.

inflationary [ɪn'fleɪʃnrɪ] adj ECON inflacionista.

inflation-proof adj protegido(da) contra la inflación.

inflexible [ɪn'fleksəbl] adj - **1.** [material, person, attitude] inflexible - **2.** [decision, arrangement] fijo(ja).

inflict [ɪn'flɪkt] vt: to inflict sthg on sb infligir algo a alguien.

in-flight adj durante el vuelo.

influence ['ɪnfluəns] ◇ n: influence (on OR over sb) influencia f (sobre alguien); influence (on sthg) influencia (en algo); to be a bad influence on sb tener mala influencia en alguien; under the influence of [person, group] bajo la influencia de; [alcohol, drugs] bajo los efectos de. ◇ vt influenciar.

influential [,ɪnflʊ'enʃl] adj influyente.

influenza [,ɪnflʊ'enzə] n fml gripe f.

influx ['ɪnflʌks] n afluencia f.

info ['ɪnfəʊ] n (U) inf información f.

inform [ɪn'fɔːm] vt: to inform sb (of/about sthg) informar a alguien (de/sobre algo).
➤ **inform on** vt insep delatar.

informal [ɪn'fɔːml] adj informal; [language] familiar.

informally [ɪn'fɔːməlɪ] adv de manera informal.

informant [ɪn'fɔːmənt] n - **1.** [informer] confidente mf, delator m, -ra f - **2.** [of researcher] informante mf.

information [,ɪnfə'meɪʃn] n (U): information (on OR about) información f OR datos mpl (sobre); a piece of information un dato; for your information para tu información.

information desk n (mostrador m de) información f.

information technology n informática f.

informative [ɪn'fɔːmətɪv] adj informativo(va).

informed [ɪn'fɔːmd] adj informado(da); informed guess conjetura f bien fundada.

informer [ɪn'fɔːmər] n confidente mf, delator m, -ra f.

infrared [,ɪnfrə'red] adj infrarrojo(ja).

infrastructure ['ɪnfrə,strʌktʃər] n infraestructura f.

infrequent [ɪn'friːkwənt] adj infrecuente.

infringe [ɪn'frɪndʒ] ◇ vt (cont infringing) - **1.** [rule] infringir - **2.** [right] vulnerar. ◇ vi (cont infringing): to infringe on sthg vulnerar algo.

infringement [ɪn'frɪndʒmənt] n - **1.** [of rule] infracción f - **2.** [of right] violación f.

infuriate [ɪn'fjʊərɪeɪt] vt enfurecer, exasperar.

infuriating [ɪn'fjʊərɪeɪtɪŋ] adj exasperante.

infuse [ɪn'fjuːz] ◇ vt: to infuse sb with sthg infundir algo a alguien. ◇ vi reposar (una infusión).

infusion [ɪn'fjuːʒn] n infusión f.

ingenious [ɪn'dʒiːnjəs] adj ingenioso(sa).

ingenuity [,ɪndʒɪ'njuːətɪ] n ingenio m, inventiva f.

ingenuous [ɪn'dʒenjʊəs] adj fml ingenuo(nua).

ingest [ɪn'dʒest] vt fml ingerir.

ingot ['ɪŋgət] n lingote m.

ingrained [ɪn'greɪnd] adj - **1.** [ground in] incrustado(da) - **2.** [deeply rooted] arraigado(da).

ingratiate [ɪn'greɪʃɪeɪt] vt: to ingratiate o.s. with sb congraciarse con alguien.

ingratiating [ɪn'greɪʃɪeɪtɪŋ] adj obsequioso(sa), lisonjero(ra).

ingratitude [ɪn'grætɪtjuːd] n ingratitud f.

ingredient [ɪn'griːdjənt] n ingrediente m.

ingrowing ['ɪn,grəʊɪŋ], **ingrown** ['ɪn,grəʊn] adj encarnado(da).

inhabit [ɪn'hæbɪt] vt habitar.

inhabitant [ɪn'hæbɪtənt] n habitante mf.

inhalation [,ɪnhə'leɪʃn] n inhalación f.

inhale [ɪn'heɪl] ◇ *vt* inhalar. ◇ *vi* [gen] inspirar; [smoker] tragarse el humo.

inhaler [ɪn'heɪlə'] *n* MED inhalador *m*.

inherent [ɪn'hɪərənt, ɪn'herənt] *adj*: **inherent (in)** inherente (a).

inherently [ɪn'hɪərəntlɪ, ɪn'herəntlɪ] *adv* intrínsecamente.

inherit [ɪn'herɪt] *vt*: **to inherit sthg (from sb)** heredar algo (de alguien).

inheritance [ɪn'herɪtəns] *n* herencia *f*.

inhibit [ɪn'hɪbɪt] *vt* - **1.** [restrict] impedir - **2.** [person] cohibir.

inhibited [ɪn'hɪbɪtɪd] *adj* [repressed, reserved] cohibido(da), inhibido(da).

inhibition [,ɪnhɪ'bɪʃn] *n* inhibición *f*.

inhospitable [,ɪnhɒ'spɪtəbl] *adj* - **1.** [unwelcoming] inhospitalario(ria) - **2.** [harsh] inhóspito(ta).

in-house ◇ *adj* [journal, report] de circulación interna; [worker] de plantilla; [training] en el lugar de trabajo. ◇ *adv* en la misma empresa.

inhuman [ɪn'hju:mən] *adj* - **1.** [cruel] inhumano(na) - **2.** [not human] infrahumano(na).

inhumane [,ɪnhju:'meɪn] *adj* inhumano(na).

inimitable [ɪ'nɪmɪtəbl] *adj* inimitable.

iniquity [ɪ'nɪkwətɪ] (*pl* **-ies**) *n* iniquidad *f*.

initial [ɪ'nɪʃl] ◇ *adj* inicial. ◇ *vt* (*UK*, *pt & pp* **-led**, *cont* **-ling**, *US*, *pt & pp* **-ed**, *cont* **-ing**) poner las iniciales a.
➤ **initials** *npl* [of person] iniciales *fpl*.

initialize, -ise [ɪ'nɪʃəlaɪz] *vt* COMPUT inicializar.

initially [ɪ'nɪʃəlɪ] *adv* inicialmente.

initiate [ɪ'nɪʃɪeɪt] ◇ *vt* iniciar; **to initiate sb into sthg** iniciar a alguien en algo. ◇ *n* iniciado *m*, -da *f*.

initiation [ɪ,nɪʃɪ'eɪʃn] *n* iniciación *f*.

initiative [ɪ'nɪʃətɪv] *n* iniciativa *f*; **to have/take the initiative** llevar/tomar la iniciativa; **to use one's initiative** hacer uso de su propia iniciativa; **on one's own initiative** por iniciativa propia.

inject [ɪn'dʒekt] *vt* - **1.** MED: **to inject sb with sthg, to inject sthg into sb** inyectarle algo a alguien - **2.** [life, excitement etc]: **to inject sthg into sthg** infundir algo a algo - **3.** [funds, capital]: **to inject sthg into sthg** inyectar algo en *OR* a algo.

injection [ɪn'dʒekʃn] *n* inyección *f*.

injunction [ɪn'dʒʌŋkʃn] *n* interdicto *m*, requerimiento *m* judicial.

injure [ˈɪndʒə'] *vt* [gen] herir; SPORT lesionar; [reputation] dañar; [chances] perjudicar; **to injure o.s.** lesionarse, hacerse daño.

injured [ˈɪndʒəd] ◇ *adj* [gen] herido(da); SPORT lesionado(da); [reputation] dañado(da). ◇ *npl*: **the injured** los heridos.

injurious [ɪn'dʒʊərɪəs] *adj* *fml*: **injurious (to)** pernicioso(sa) (para).

injury [ˈɪndʒərɪ] (*pl* **-ies**) *n* - **1.** [wound] herida *f*; [to muscle, broken bone] lesión *f*; **to do o.s. an injury** hacerse daño - **2.** (*U*) [physical harm] lesiones *fpl*.

injury time *n* (tiempo *m* de) descuento *m*.

injustice [ɪn'dʒʌstɪs] *n* injusticia *f*; **to do sb an injustice** ser injusto(ta) con alguien.

ink [ɪŋk] ◇ *n* tinta *f*. ◇ *comp* de tinta.
➤ **ink in** *vt sep* repasar con tinta.

ink-jet printer *n* COMPUT impresora *f* de chorro de tinta.

inkling [ˈɪŋklɪŋ] *n*: **to have an inkling of sthg** tener una vaga idea de algo; **to have an inkling that** tener la vaga idea de que.

inkpad [ˈɪŋkpæd] *n* tampón *m*, almohadilla *f*.

inkwell [ˈɪŋkwel] *n* tintero *m*.

inlaid [,ɪn'leɪd] *adj* incrustado(da); **inlaid with** [jewels] con incrustaciones de.

inland ◇ *adj* [ˈɪnlənd] interior. ◇ *adv* [ɪn'lænd] [go] hacia el interior; [remain] en el interior.

Inland Revenue *n* UK: **the Inland Revenue** ≃ Hacienda *f*.

in-laws *npl* suegros *mpl*.

inlet [ˈɪnlet] *n* - **1.** [stretch of water] entrante *m* - **2.** [way in] entrada *f*, admisión *f*.

in-line skating *n* SPORT patinaje *m* en línea.

inmate [ˈɪnmeɪt] *n* [of prison] preso *m*, -sa *f*; [of mental hospital] interno *m*, -na *f*.

inmost [ˈɪnməʊst], **innermost** *adj* *liter* [deepest] más íntimo(ma), más profundo(da).

inn [ɪn] *n* fonda *f*; [pub] *pub decorado a la vieja usanza*.

innards [ˈɪnədz] *npl* tripas *fpl*.

innate [,ɪ'neɪt] *adj* innato(ta).

inner [ˈɪnə'] *adj* - **1.** [gen] interior - **2.** [feelings] íntimo(ma); [fears, doubts, meaning] interno(na).

inner city ◇ *n* núcleo *m* urbano deprimido. ◇ *comp* de los núcleos urbanos deprimidos.

innermost [ˈɪnəməʊst] = **inmost**.

inner tube *n* cámara *f* (de aire).

inning [ˈɪnɪŋ] *n* [in baseball] entrada *f*, inning *m*.

innings [ˈɪnɪŋz] (*pl* **innings**) *n* [in cricket] entrada *f*, turno *m*; **to have had a good innings** *fig* haber tenido una vida larga y provechosa.

innocence [ˈɪnəsəns] *n* inocencia *f*.

innocent [ˈɪnəsənt] ◇ *adj*: **innocent (of)** inocente (de). ◇ *n* [naive person] inocente *mf*.

innocuous [ɪ'nɒkjʊəs] *adj* inocuo(cua), inofensivo(va).

innovation [,ɪnə'veɪʃn] *n* innovación *f*.

innovative [ˈɪnəvətɪv] *adj* innovador(ra).

innovator [ˈɪnəveɪtə'] *n* innovador *m*, -ra *f*.

innuendo [,ɪnjuː'endəʊ] (*pl* **-es** *OR* **-s**) *n* **- 1.** [individual remark] insinuación *f*, indirecta *f* **- 2.** (*U*) [style of speaking] insinuaciones *fpl*, indirectas *fpl*; **sexual innuendo** juegos *mpl* de palabras *(sobre sexo)*.

innumerable [ɪ'njuːmərəbl] *adj* innumerable.

inoculate [ɪ'nɒkjuleɪt] *vt*: **to inoculate sb (against sthg)** inocular a alguien (contra algo); **to inoculate sb with sthg** inocular algo a alguien.

inoculation [ɪ,nɒkjʊ'leɪʃn] *n* inoculación *f*.

inoffensive [,ɪnə'fensɪv] *adj* inofensivo(va).

inoperable [ɪn'ɒprəbl] *adj* **- 1.** MED inoperable **- 2.** *fml* [unworkable] impracticable.

inoperative [ɪn'ɒprətɪv] *adj* **- 1.** [rule, tax etc] en suspenso **- 2.** [machine]: **to be inoperative** no funcionar.

inopportune [ɪn'ɒpətjuːn] *adj* *fml* inoportuno(na).

inordinate [ɪ'nɔːdɪnət] *adj* *fml* desmesurado(da).

inorganic [,ɪnɔː'gænɪk] *adj* inorgánico(ca).

in-patient *n* paciente interno *m*, paciente interna *f*.

input ['ɪnpʊt] ◇ *n* **- 1.** [contribution] aportación *f*, contribución *f* **- 2.** COMPUT & ELEC entrada *f*. ◇ *vt* (*pt & pp* input *OR* **-ted**, *cont* **-ting**) COMPUT introducir.

inquest ['ɪnkwest] *n* investigación *f* judicial.

inquire [ɪn'kwaɪəʳ] ◇ *vi* [ask for information] informarse, preguntar; **to inquire about sthg** informarse de algo. ◇ *vt*: **to inquire when/ if/how...** preguntar cuándo/si/cómo...

➤ **inquire after** *vt insep* preguntar por.
➤ **inquire into** *vt insep* investigar.

inquiring [ɪn'kwaɪərɪŋ] *adj* **- 1.** [mind] inquieto(ta), lleno(na) de curiosidad **- 2.** [look, tone] inquisitivo(va).

inquiry [ɪn'kwaɪərɪ] (*pl* **-ies**) *n* **- 1.** [question] consulta *f*, pregunta *f*; **'Inquiries'** 'Información' **- 2.** [investigation] investigación *f*; **to hold an inquiry (into)** emprender una investigación (sobre).

inquiry desk *n* (mostrador *m* de) información *f*.

inquisition [,ɪnkwɪ'zɪʃn] *n* interrogatorio *m*.

➤ **Inquisition** *n*: **the Inquisition** la Inquisición.

inquisitive [ɪn'kwɪzətɪv] *adj* curioso(sa).

inroads ['ɪnrəʊdz] *npl*: **to make inroads into** [savings, supplies] mermar; [market, enemy territory] abrirse paso en.

insane [ɪn'seɪn] ◇ *adj* [mad] demente; *fig* [jealousy, person] loco(ca); **to drive sb insane** volver loco a alguien. ◇ *npl*: **the insane** los enfermos mentales.

insanitary [ɪn'sænɪtrɪ] *adj* antihigiénico(ca).

insanity [ɪn'sænətɪ] *n* MED demencia *f*; [craziness] locura *f*.

insatiable [ɪn'seɪʃəbl] *adj* insaciable.

inscribe [ɪn'skraɪb] *vt* **- 1.** [engrave]: **to inscribe sthg (on sthg)** inscribir algo (en algo) **- 2.** [write]: **to inscribe sthg in sthg** escribir algo en algo a modo de dedicatoria.

inscription [ɪn'skrɪpʃn] *n* **- 1.** [engraved] inscripción *f* **- 2.** [written] dedicatoria *f*.

inscrutable [ɪn'skruːtəbl] *adj* inescrutable.

insect ['ɪnsekt] *n* insecto *m*.

insect bite *n* picadura *f* de insecto.

insecticide [ɪn'sektɪsaɪd] *n* insecticida *m*.

insect repellent *n* loción *f* antiinsectos.

insecure [,ɪnsɪ'kjʊəʳ] *adj* **- 1.** [not confident] inseguro(ra) **- 2.** [not safe] poco seguro(ra).

insecurity [,ɪnsɪ'kjʊərətɪ] *n* inseguridad *f*.

insensible [ɪn'sensəbl] *adj* *fml* **- 1.** [unconscious] inconsciente **- 2.** [unaware]: **to be insensible of sthg** no ser consciente de algo **- 3.** [unable to feel]: **to be insensible to sthg** ser insensible a algo.

insensitive [ɪn'sensətɪv] *adj*: **insensitive (to)** insensible (a).

insensitivity [ɪn,sensə'tɪvətɪ] *n*: **insensitivity (to)** insensibilidad *f* (a).

inseparable [ɪn'seprəbl] *adj*: **inseparable (from)** inseparable (de).

insert ◇ *vt* [ɪn'sɜːt]: **to insert sthg (in** *OR* **into)** [hole] introducir algo (en); [text] insertar algo (en). ◇ *n* ['ɪnsɜːt] PRESS encarte *m*.

insertion [ɪn'sɜːʃn] *n* inserción *f*.

inset ['ɪnset] *n* recuadro *m* *(insertado en la esquina de otro de mayor tamaño)*.

inshore ◇ *adj* ['ɪnʃɔːʳ] costero(ra). ◇ *adv* [ɪn'ʃɔːʳ] hacia la orilla *OR* la costa.

inside [ɪn'saɪd] ◇ *prep* dentro de; **inside three months** en menos de tres meses. ◇ *adv* **- 1.** [be, remain] dentro; [go, move, look] adentro; **come inside!** ¡metéos dentro! **- 2.** *fig* [feel, hurt etc] por dentro **- 3.** *inf* [in prison] en chirona. ◇ *adj* interior; **inside leg measurement** medida *f* de la entrepierna. ◇ *n* interior *m*; **from the inside** desde dentro; **to overtake on the inside** [of road] adelantar por dentro; **inside out** [wrong way] al revés; **to turn sthg inside out** [clothing] dar la vuelta a algo; **to know sthg inside out** conocer algo de arriba abajo *OR* al dedillo.

➤ **insides** *npl* *inf* tripas *fpl*.
➤ **inside of** *prep* US [building, object] dentro de.

inside information *n* (*U*) información *f* confidencial.

inside job *n inf robo cometido con la ayuda de un empleado de la empresa o local allanados.*

inside lane *n* AUT carril *m* de dentro; SPORT calle *f* de dentro.

insider [ˌɪnˈsaɪdər] *n* persona *f* con información confidencial *(dentro de una organización).*

insider dealing, insider trading *n* (U) *en bolsa, uso indebido de información privilegiada.*

inside story *n* historia *f* real.

insidious [ɪnˈsɪdɪəs] *adj* insidioso(sa).

insight [ˈɪnsaɪt] *n* - **1.** (U) [power of understanding] perspicacia *f*, capacidad *f* de penetración - **2.** [understanding] idea *f*.

insignia [ɪnˈsɪgnɪə] (*pl* **insignia**) *n* insignias *fpl*.

insignificance [ˌɪnsɪgˈnɪfɪkəns] *n* insignificancia *f*.

insignificant [ˌɪnsɪgˈnɪfɪkənt] *adj* insignificante.

insincere [ˌɪnsɪnˈsɪər] *adj* insincero(ra).

insincerity [ˌɪnsɪnˈserətɪ] *n* insinceridad *f*.

insinuate [ɪnˈsɪnjʊeɪt] *vt pej*: **to insinuate (that)** insinuar (que).

insinuation [ɪnˌsɪnjʊˈeɪʃn] *n pej* insinuación *f*.

insipid [ɪnˈsɪpɪd] *adj pej* soso(sa), insípido(da).

insist [ɪnˈsɪst] <> *vt*: **to insist that** insistir en que. <> *vi*: **to insist on sthg** exigir algo; **to insist (on doing sthg)** insistir (en hacer algo).

insistence [ɪnˈsɪstəns] *n* insistencia *f*; **insistence on sthg/on doing sthg** empeño *m* en algo/en hacer algo.

insistent [ɪnˈsɪstənt] *adj* - **1.** [determined] insistente; **to be insistent on sthg** insistir en algo - **2.** [continual] persistente.

in situ [ˌɪnˈsɪtjuː] *adv* in situ.

insofar [ˌɪnsəʊˈfɑːr] ➧ **insofar as** *conj* en la medida en que.

insole [ˈɪnsəʊl] *n* plantilla *f*.

insolence [ˈɪnsələns] *n* insolencia *f*.

insolent [ˈɪnsələnt] *adj* insolente.

insoluble UK [ɪnˈsɒljʊbl], **insolvable** US [ɪnˈsɒlvəbl] *adj* insoluble.

insolvency [ɪnˈsɒlvənsɪ] *n* insolvencia *f*.

insolvent [ɪnˈsɒlvənt] *adj* insolvente.

insomnia [ɪnˈsɒmnɪə] *n* insomnio *m*.

insomniac [ɪnˈsɒmnɪæk] *n* insomne *mf*.

insomuch [ˌɪnsəʊˈmʌtʃ] ➧ **insomuch as** *conj* en la medida en que.

inspect [ɪnˈspekt] *vt* inspeccionar; [troops] pasar revista a.

inspection [ɪnˈspekʃn] *n* inspección *f*; [of troops] revista *f*; **on closer inspection** tras un examen más detallado.

inspector [ɪnˈspektər] *n* inspector *m*, -ra *f*; [on bus, train] revisor *m*, -ra *f*.

inspiration [ˌɪnspəˈreɪʃn] *n* - **1.** [gen] inspiración *f* - **2.** [source of inspiration]: **inspiration (for)** fuente *f* de inspiración (para).

inspirational [ˌɪnspəˈreɪʃnl] *adj* inspirador(ra).

inspire [ɪnˈspaɪər] *vt* - **1.** [stimulate, encourage]: **to inspire sb (to do sthg)** alentar OR animar a alguien (a hacer algo) - **2.** [fill]: **to inspire sb with sthg, to inspire sthg in sb** inspirar algo a alguien.

inspired [ɪnˈspaɪəd] *adj* inspirado(da).

inspiring [ɪnˈspaɪərɪŋ] *adj* [stimulating, exciting] inspirador(ra).

instability [ˌɪnstəˈbɪlətɪ] *n* inestabilidad *f*.

install UK, **instal** US [ɪnˈstɔːl] *vt* - **1.** [gen & COMPUT] instalar - **2.** [appoint]: **to install sb (as)** investir a alguien (con el cargo de) - **3.** [settle]: **to install o.s. in front of the fire** instalarse frente al fuego.

installation [ˌɪnstəˈleɪʃn] *n* [gen & COMPUT] instalación *f*.

installment US = **instalment**.

installment plan *n* US compra *f* a plazos.

instalment UK, **installment** US [ɪnˈstɔːlmənt] *n* - **1.** [payment] plazo *m*, abono *m* Méx; **in instalments** a plazos - **2.** TV & RADIO episodio *m*; [of novel] entrega *f*.

instance [ˈɪnstəns] *n* [example, case] ejemplo *m*; **for instance** por ejemplo; **in the first instance** *fml* en primer lugar; **in this instance** en este caso.

instant [ˈɪnstənt] <> *adj* instantáneo(a). <> *n* [moment] instante *m*; **at that** OR **the same instant** en aquel mismo instante; **the instant (that)...** en cuanto...; **this instant** ahora mismo.

instantaneous [ˌɪnstənˈteɪnjəs] *adj* instantáneo(a).

instantly [ˈɪnstəntlɪ] *adv* en el acto.

instead [ɪnˈsted] *adv* en cambio; **I came instead** yo vine en su lugar; **if you haven't got any sugar, you can use honey instead** si no tiene azúcar, utilice miel en su lugar.
➧ **instead of** *prep* en lugar de, en vez de; **I came instead of her** yo vine en su lugar.

instep [ˈɪnstep] *n* [of foot] empeine *m*.

instigate [ˈɪnstɪgeɪt] *vt* iniciar; **to instigate sb to do sthg** instigar a alguien a hacer algo.

instigation [ˌɪnstɪˈgeɪʃn] *n*: **at the instigation of** a instancias de.

instigator [ˈɪnstɪgeɪtər] *n* instigador *m*, -ra *f*.

instil UK (*pt* & *pp* **-led**, *cont* **-ling**), **instill** US (*pt* & *pp* **-ed**, *cont* **-ing**) [ɪnˈstɪl] *vt*: **to instil sthg in** OR **into sb** inculcar algo a alguien.

instinct ['ɪnstɪŋkt] *n* instinto *m*; **my first instinct was...** mi primer impulso fue...

instinctive [ɪn'stɪŋktɪv] *adj* instintivo(va).

instinctively [ɪn'stɪŋktɪvlɪ] *adv* instintivamente.

institute ['ɪnstɪtjuːt] <> *n* instituto *m*. <> *vt* [proceedings] iniciar, entablar; [system] instituir.

institution [ˌɪnstɪ'tjuːʃn] *n* - **1.** [gen] institución *f* - **2.** [home - for children, old people] asilo *m*; [- for mentally-handicapped] hospital *m* psiquiátrico.

institutional [ˌɪnstɪ'tjuːʃənl] *adj* - **1.** [of organization] institucional - **2.** [food, life etc] *típico de un hospital, una cárcel etc.*

institutionalized, -ised [ˌɪnstɪ'tjuːʃnə,laɪzd] *adj* - **1.** *pej* [influenced by institutional life] *acostumbrado a la vida hospitalaria carcelaria etc* - **2.** [established] institucionalizado(da).

institutional racism, institutionalized racism *n* racismo *m* institucional.

instruct [ɪn'strʌkt] *vt* - **1.** [tell, order]: **to instruct sb to do sthg** ordenar a alguien que haga algo - **2.** [teach]: **to instruct sb (in sthg)** instruir a alguien (en algo).

instruction [ɪn'strʌkʃn] *n* [gen & COMPUT] instrucción *f*.

➠ **instructions** *npl* [for use] instrucciones *fpl*.

instruction manual *n* manual *m* de instrucciones.

instructive [ɪn'strʌktɪv] *adj* instructivo(va).

instructor [ɪn'strʌktər] *n* - **1.** [gen] instructor *m* - **2.** [in skiing] monitor *m* - **3.** [in driving] profesor *m* - **4.** *US* [at college] profesor *m*, -ra *f*.

instructress [ɪn'strʌktrɪs] *n* instructora *f*; [in skiing] monitora *f*; [in driving] profesora *f*.

instrument ['ɪnstrʊmənt] *n* instrumento *m*.

instrumental [ˌɪnstrʊ'mentl] <> *adj* - **1.** [important, helpful]: **to be instrumental in sthg** jugar un papel fundamental en algo - **2.** MUS instrumental. <> *n* pieza *f* instrumental.

instrumentalist [ˌɪnstrʊ'mentəlɪst] *n* instrumentista *mf*.

instrument panel *n* tablero *m* de instrumentos.

insubordinate [ˌɪnsə'bɔːdɪnət] *adj* insubordinado(da).

insubordination ['ɪnsə,bɔːdɪ'neɪʃn] *n* insubordinación *f*.

insubstantial [ˌɪnsəb'stænʃl] *adj* [frame, structure] endeble; [meal] poco sustancioso(sa).

insufferable [ɪn'sʌfərəbl] *adj* insufrible.

insufficient [ˌɪnsə'fɪʃnt] *adj*: **insufficient (for)** insuficiente (para).

insular ['ɪnsjʊlər] *adj* [narrow-minded] estrecho(cha) de miras.

insulate ['ɪnsjʊleɪt] *vt* aislar; **to insulate sb against** OR **from sthg** aislar a alguien de algo.

insulating tape ['ɪnsjʊleɪtɪŋ-] *n* UK cinta *f* aislante.

insulation [ˌɪnsjʊ'leɪʃn] *n* [electrical] aislamiento *m*; [against the cold] aislamiento *m* térmico.

insulin ['ɪnsjʊlɪn] *n* insulina *f*.

insult <> *vt* [ɪn'sʌlt] [with words] insultar; [with actions] ofender. <> *n* ['ɪnsʌlt] [remark] insulto *m*; [action] ofensa *f*; **to add insult to injury** para colmo, para más inri.

insulting [ɪn'sʌltɪŋ] *adj* [remark] insultante; [behaviour] ofensivo(va), insultante.

insuperable [ɪn'suːprəbl] *adj fml* insalvable, insuperable.

insurance [ɪn'ʃʊərəns] <> *n* - **1.** [against fire, accident, theft]: **insurance (against)** seguro *m* (contra) - **2.** *fig* [safeguard, protection]: **insurance (against)** prevención *f* (contra). <> *comp* de seguros; **insurance company** compañía *f* de seguros.

insurance broker *n* agente *mf* de seguros.

insurance policy *n* póliza *f* de seguros.

insurance premium *n* prima *f* (del seguro).

insure [ɪn'ʃʊər] <> *vt* - **1.** [against fire, accident, theft]: **to insure sthg/sb (against)** asegurar algo/a alguien (contra) - **2.** *US* [make certain] asegurar. <> *vi* [prevent]: **to insure (against)** prevenir OR prevenirse (contra).

insured [ɪn'ʃɔːd] <> *adj* - **1.** [against fire, accident, theft]: **insured (against** OR **for)** asegurado(da) (contra) - **2.** *US* [certain] asegurado(da). <> *n*: **the insured** el asegurado(la asegurada).

insurer [ɪn'ʃʊərər] *n* asegurador *m*, -ra *f*.

insurgent [ɪn'sɜːdʒənt] *n* insurgente *mf*.

insurmountable [ˌɪnsə'maʊntəbl] *adj fml* infranqueable, insuperable.

insurrection [ˌɪnsə'rekʃn] *n* insurrección *f*.

intact [ɪn'tækt] *adj* intacto(ta).

intake ['ɪnteɪk] *n* - **1.** [of food, drink] ingestión *f*; [of air] inspiración *f* - **2.** [in army] reclutamiento *m*; [in organization] número *m* de ingresos - **3.** TECH [inlet] toma *f*.

intangible [ɪn'tændʒəbl] *adj* intangible; **intangible assets** bienes *mpl* inmateriales.

integral ['ɪntɪgrəl] *adj* integrante, intrínseco(ca); **to be integral to** ser parte integrante de.

integrate ['ɪntɪgreɪt] <> *vi*: **to integrate (with** OR **into)** integrarse (en). <> *vt*: **to integrate sthg/sb with sthg, to integrate sthg/sb into sthg** integrar algo/a alguien en algo.

integrated ['ɪntɪgreɪtɪd] *adj* [gen & COMPUT] integrado(da).

integrated circuit *n* circuito *m* integrado.

integration [ˌɪntɪˈgreɪʃn] n: integration (with OR into) integración f (en).

integrity [ɪnˈtegrətɪ] n integridad f.

intellect [ˈɪntəlekt] n [mind, cleverness] intelecto m, inteligencia f.

intellectual [ˌɪntəˈlektjʊəl] ◇ adj intelectual. ◇ n intelectual mf.

intellectualize, -ise [ˌɪntəˈlektjʊəlaɪz] vt intelectualizar, dar tono intelectual a.

intelligence [ɪnˈtelɪdʒəns] n (U) - **1.** [ability to think] inteligencia f - **2.** [information] información f secreta - **3.** [information service] servicio m secreto OR de espionaje.

intelligence quotient n coeficiente m de inteligencia.

intelligence test n test m de inteligencia.

intelligent [ɪnˈtelɪdʒənt] adj [gen & COMPUT] inteligente.

intelligently [ɪnˈtelɪdʒəntlɪ] adv inteligentemente.

intelligentsia [ɪnˌtelɪˈdʒentsɪə] n: the intelligentsia la intelectualidad.

intelligible [ɪnˈtelɪdʒəbl] adj inteligible.

intemperate [ɪnˈtempərət] adj fml [remarks, climate] destemplado(da); [behaviour] inmoderado(da).

intend [ɪnˈtend] vt pretender; to intend doing OR to do sthg tener la intención de hacer algo; what do you intend to do? ¿qué piensas hacer?; later than I had intended más tarde de lo que había pensado; to be intended for/as sthg [project, book] estar pensado para/como algo; the flowers were intended for you las flores eran para ti.

intended [ɪnˈtendɪd] adj [effect, result] pretendido(da).

intense [ɪnˈtens] adj - **1.** [extreme, profound] intenso(sa) - **2.** [serious - person] muy serio(ria).

intensely [ɪnˈtenslɪ] adv - **1.** [very - boring, irritating] enormemente - **2.** [very much - suffer] intensamente; [- dislike] profundamente.

intensify [ɪnˈtensɪfaɪ] ◇ vt (pt & pp -ied) intensificar. ◇ vi intensificarse.

intensity [ɪnˈtensətɪ] n intensidad f.

intensive [ɪnˈtensɪv] adj [concentrated] intensivo(va).

intensive care n (U): (in) intensive care (bajo) cuidados mpl intensivos.

intensive care unit n unidad f de cuidados intensivos OR de vigilancia intensiva.

intent [ɪnˈtent] ◇ adj - **1.** [absorbed] atento(ta) - **2.** [determined]: to be intent on OR upon doing sthg estar empeñado(da) en hacer algo. ◇ n fml intención f; to all intents and purposes para todos los efectos.

intention [ɪnˈtenʃn] n intención f; to have no intention of no tener la menor intención de.

intentional [ɪnˈtenʃənl] adj deliberado(da), intencionado(da); it wasn't intentional fue sin querer.

intentionally [ɪnˈtenʃənəlɪ] adv deliberadamente, intencionadamente.

intently [ɪnˈtentlɪ] adv atentamente.

inter [ɪnˈtɜːr] (pt & pp -red, cont -ring) vt fml sepultar.

interact [ˌɪntərˈækt] vi - **1.** [communicate, work together]: to interact (with sb) relacionarse (con alguien) - **2.** [react]: to interact (with sthg) interaccionar (con algo).

interaction [ˌɪntərˈækʃn] n interacción f.

interactive [ˌɪntərˈæktɪv] adj COMPUT interactivo(va).

interactivity [ˌɪntərækˈtɪvɪtɪ] n interactividad f.

intercede [ˌɪntəˈsiːd] vi fml: to intercede (with/for) interceder (ante/por).

intercept [ˌɪntəˈsept] vt interceptar.

interception [ˌɪntəˈsepʃn] n interceptación f.

interchange ◇ n [ˈɪntətʃeɪndʒ] - **1.** [exchange] intercambio m - **2.** [on motorway] enlace m. ◇ vt [ˌɪntəˈtʃeɪndʒ] intercambiar.

interchangeable [ˌɪntəˈtʃeɪndʒəbl] adj: interchangeable (with) intercambiable (con).

intercity [ˌɪntəˈsɪtɪ] ◇ adj UK interurbano(na), intercity. ◇ n [train] tren m interurbano.

intercom [ˈɪntəkɒm] n [for block of flats] portero m automático; [within a building] interfono m.

interconnect [ˌɪntəkəˈnekt] ◇ vt interconectar. ◇ vi: to interconnect (with) relacionarse (con).

intercontinental [ˈɪntəˌkɒntɪˈnentl] adj intercontinental.

intercontinental ballistic missile n misil m balístico intercontinental.

intercourse [ˈɪntəkɔːs] n (U): sexual intercourse relaciones fpl sexuales, coito m.

interdenominational [ˈɪntədɪˌnɒmɪˈneɪʃənl] adj interconfesional.

interdepartmental [ˈɪntəˌdiːpɑːtˈmentl] adj interdepartamental.

interdependent [ˌɪntədɪˈpendənt] adj interdependiente.

interdict [ˈɪntədɪkt] n LAW & RELIG interdicto m.

interest [ˈɪntrəst] ◇ n - **1.** [gen]: interest (in) interés m (en OR por); that's of no interest eso no tiene interés; in the interest OR interests of [in order to benefit] en interés de; [in order to achieve] en pro de; to take an interest in sthg interesarse por algo - **2.** FIN interés m; to pay the interest on a loan pagar los intereses de un préstamo - **3.** [hobby] afición *f*. ⋄ *vt* interesar; **to interest sb in sthg/in doing sthg** interesar a alguien en algo/en hacer algo.

interested ['ɪntrəstɪd] *adj* interesado(da); **I'm not interested** no me interesa; **to be interested in sthg/in doing sthg** estar interesado en algo/en hacer algo; **I'm interested in that subject** me interesa el tema.

interest-free *adj* sin interés.

interesting ['ɪntrəstɪŋ] *adj* interesante.

interest rate *n* tipo *m* de interés.

interface ⋄ *n* ['ɪntəfeɪs] - **1.** COMPUT interfaz *f*, interface *m* - **2.** [junction, boundary] zona *f* de interacción. ⋄ *vt* [ɪntə'feɪs] COMPUT conectar mediante interfaz.

interfere [,ɪntə'fɪəʳ] *vi* - **1.** [meddle]: **to interfere (with OR in sthg)** entrometerse OR interferir (en algo) - **2.** [damage] interferir; **to interfere with sthg** [career, routine] interferir en algo; [work, performance] interrumpir algo.

interference [,ɪntə'fɪərəns] *n* (U) - **1.** [meddling]: **interference (with OR in)** intromisión *f* OR interferencia *f* (en) - **2.** [on radio, TV, telephone] interferencia *f*.

interfering [,ɪntə'fɪərɪŋ] *adj pej* entrometido(da).

interim ['ɪntərɪm] ⋄ *adj* [report] parcial; [measure] provisional; [government] interino(na). ⋄ *n*: **in the interim** entre tanto.

interior [ɪn'tɪərɪəʳ] ⋄ *adj* - **1.** [inner] interior - **2.** POL [minister, department] del Interior. ⋄ *n* interior *m*.

interior decorator, interior designer *n* interiorista *mf*.

interject [,ɪntə'dʒekt] *vt fml* interponer.

interjection [,ɪntə'dʒekʃn] *n* - **1.** [remark] exclamación *f* - **2.** GRAM interjección *f*.

interleave [,ɪntə'liːv] *vt*: **to interleave sthg (with)** interfoliar algo (con).

interlock [,ɪntə'lɒk] ⋄ *vi* [fingers] entrelazarse; [cogs] engranar. ⋄ *vt*: **to interlock sthg (with)** [fingers] entrelazar algo (con); [cogs] engranar algo (con).

interloper ['ɪntələʊpəʳ] *n* intruso *m*, -sa *f*.

interlude ['ɪntəluːd] *n* - **1.** [pause] intervalo *m* - **2.** [interval] descanso *m*, intermedio *m*.

intermarry [,ɪntə'mærɪ] (*pt & pp* -**ied**) *vi*: **to intermarry (with)** casarse (con) (*parientes o personas de distinta raza, religión etc*).

intermediary [,ɪntə'miːdjərɪ] (*pl* -**ies**) *n* intermediario *m*, -ria *f*, mediador *m*, -ra *f*.

intermediate [,ɪntə'miːdjət] *adj* intermedio(dia).

interminable [ɪn'tɜːmɪnəbl] *adj* interminable.

intermingle [,ɪntə'mɪŋgl] *vi*: **to intermingle (with)** entremezclarse (con).

intermission [,ɪntə'mɪʃn] *n* [of film] descanso *m*; [of play, opera, ballet] entreacto *m*.

intermittent [,ɪntə'mɪtənt] *adj* intermitente.

intern ⋄ *vt* [ɪn'tɜːn] recluir, internar. ⋄ *n* ['ɪntɜːn] *esp US* médico *m* interno residente.

internal [ɪn'tɜːnl] *adj* - **1.** [gen] interno(na) - **2.** [within a country] interior, nacional; **internal flight** vuelo *m* nacional.

internal combustion engine *n* motor *m* de combustión interna.

internally [ɪn'tɜːnəlɪ] *adv* - **1.** [gen] internamente - **2.** [within a country] a nivel nacional.

Internal Revenue Service *n US*: **the Internal Revenue Service** ≃ la Agencia Tribuaria *Esp*, ≃ la Dirección General Impositiva *Amér*.

international [,ɪntə'næʃənl] ⋄ *adj* internacional. ⋄ *n UK* - **1.** SPORT [match] encuentro *m* internacional - **2.** SPORT [player] internacional *mf*.

international date line *n*: **the international date line** la línea de cambio de fecha.

internationally [,ɪntə'næʃnəlɪ] *adv* internacionalmente.

International Monetary Fund *n*: **the International Monetary Fund** el Fondo Monetario Internacional.

international relations *npl* relaciones *fpl* internacionales.

internecine [*UK* ,ɪntə'niːsaɪn, *US* ,ɪntər'niːsn] *adj fml* intestino(na).

internee [,ɪntɜː'niː] *n* recluso *m*, -sa *f*, internado *m*, -da *f*.

Internet ['ɪntənet] *n*: **the Internet** Internet *f*; **on the Internet** en Internet.

Internet access *n* acceso *m* a Internet.

Internet access provider *n* proveedor *m* de acceso a Internet.

Internet café *n* cibercafé *m*.

Internet connection *n* conexión *f* a Internet.

Internet radio *n* radio *f* por Internet.

Internet Service Provider *n* proveedor *m* de servicios Internet.

Internet start-up company *n* empresa *f* electrónica aparecida con Internet.

Internet television, Internet TV *n* televisión *f* por Internet.

internment [ɪn'tɜːnmənt] *n* reclusión *f*, internamiento *m*.

interpersonal [,ɪntə'pɜːsənl] *adj* interpersonal.

interplay ['ɪntəpleɪ] *n* (U): **interplay (of/between)** interacción *f* (de/entre).

Interpol ['ɪntəpɒl] *n* Interpol *f*.

interpolate [ɪn'tɜːpəleɪt] *vt fml*: **to interpolate sthg (into)** interpolar algo (en).

interpose [ˌɪntə'pəʊz] vt fml interponer; **to interpose o.s.** interponerse.

interpret [ɪn'tɜːprɪt] ⟷ vt interpretar. ⟷ vi hacer de intérprete.

interpretation [ɪn,tɜːprɪ'teɪʃn] n interpretación f.

interpreter [ɪn'tɜːprɪtər] n [person] intérprete mf.

interpreting [ɪn'tɜːprɪtɪŋ] n [occupation] interpretación f.

interracial [ˌɪntə'reɪʃl] adj interracial.

interrelate [ˌɪntərɪ'leɪt] ⟷ vt interrelacionar. ⟷ vi: **to interrelate (with)** interrelacionarse (con).

interrogate [ɪn'terəgeɪt] vt [gen & COMPUT] interrogar.

interrogation [ɪn,terə'geɪʃn] n interrogatorio m.

interrogation mark n US signo m de interrogación.

interrogative [ˌɪntə'rɒgətɪv] ⟷ adj GRAM interrogativo(va). ⟷ n - **1.** GRAM [form]: **the interrogative** la forma interrogativa - **2.** GRAM [word] interrogativo m.

interrogator [ɪn'terəgeɪtər] n interrogador m, -ra f.

interrupt [ˌɪntə'rʌpt] vt & vi interrumpir.

interruption [ˌɪntə'rʌpʃn] n interrupción f.

intersect [ˌɪntə'sekt] ⟷ vi cruzarse. ⟷ vt cruzar.

intersection [ˌɪntə'sekʃn] n US [of roads] cruce m, intersección f.

intersperse [ˌɪntə'spɜːs] vt: **to be interspersed with** OR **by** estar entremezclado con.

interstate ['ɪntəsteɪt] n US autopista f interestatal.

interval ['ɪntəvl] n - **1.** [gen & MUS]: **interval (between)** intervalo m (entre); **at intervals** [now and again] a ratos; **at regular intervals** a intervalos regulares; **at monthly/yearly intervals** a intervalos de un mes/un año - **2.** UK [at play, concert] intermedio m, descanso m.

intervene [ˌɪntə'viːn] vi - **1.** [gen]: **to intervene (in)** intervenir (en) - **2.** [prevent thing from happening] interponerse; **the war intervened** sobrevino la guerra - **3.** [pass] transcurrir.

intervening [ˌɪntə'viːnɪŋ] adj [time] transcurrido(da); [space] intermedio(dia); **the intervening period** el ínterin.

intervention [ˌɪntə'venʃn] n intervención f.

interventionist [ˌɪntə'venʃənɪst] ⟷ adj intervencionista. ⟷ n intervencionista mf.

interview ['ɪntəvjuː] ⟷ n [gen] entrevista f; [with police] interrogatorio m. ⟷ vt [gen] entrevistar; [subj: policeman] interrogar.

interviewee [ˌɪntəvjuː'iː] n entrevistado m, -da f.

interviewer ['ɪntəvjuːər] n entrevistador m, -ra f.

interweave [ˌɪntə'wiːv] fig ⟷ vt (pt **-wove**, pp **-woven**) entretejer. ⟷ vi entretejerse.

intestate [ɪn'testeɪt] adj: **to die intestate** morir intestado(da).

intestine [ɪn'testɪn] n intestino m.
➤ **intestines** npl intestinos mpl.

intimacy ['ɪntɪməsɪ] (pl **-ies**) n: **intimacy (between/with)** intimidad f (entre/con).

intimate ⟷ adj ['ɪntɪmət] - **1.** [gen] íntimo(ma) - **2.** fml [sexually]: **to be intimate with sb** tener relaciones íntimas con alguien - **3.** [knowledge] profundo(da). ⟷ n ['ɪntɪmət] fml amigo íntimo m, amiga íntima f. ⟷ vt ['ɪntɪmeɪt] fml: **to intimate (that)** dar a entender (que).

intimately ['ɪntɪmətlɪ] adv - **1.** [very closely] íntimamente - **2.** [acquainted] en la intimidad - **3.** [in detail] a fondo.

intimation [ˌɪntɪ'meɪʃn] n fml señal f, indicio m.

intimidate [ɪn'tɪmɪdeɪt] vt intimidar.

intimidation [ɪn,tɪmɪ'deɪʃn] n intimidación f.

into ['ɪntʊ] prep - **1.** [inside] en; **to go into a room** entrar en una habitación; **to put sthg into sthg** meter algo en algo; **to get into a car** subir a un coche - **2.** [against] con; **to bump/crash into** tropezar/chocar con - **3.** [referring to change in condition etc]: **to turn** OR **develop into** convertirse en; **to translate sthg into Spanish** traducir algo al español - **4.** [concerning] en relación con; **research into electronics** investigación en torno a la electrónica - **5.** [in expressions of time]: **fifteen minutes into the game** a los quince minutos de empezar el partido; **well into the spring** hasta bien entrada la primavera - **6.** MATHS: **to divide 4 into 8** dividir 8 entre 4 - **7.** inf [interested in]: **I'm into classical music** me va OR me mola la música clásica.

intolerable [ɪn'tɒlrəbl] adj fml [position, conditions] intolerable; [boredom, pain] inaguantable.

intolerance [ɪn'tɒlərəns] n intolerancia f.

intolerant [ɪn'tɒlərənt] adj intolerante; **to be intolerant of** ser intolerante con.

intonation [ˌɪntə'neɪʃn] n entonación f.

intoxicated [ɪn'tɒksɪkeɪtɪd] adj - **1.** [drunk] embriagado(da), ebrio(ebria) - **2.** fig [excited]: **intoxicated (by** OR **with)** ebrio(ebria) (de).

intoxicating [ɪn'tɒksɪkeɪtɪŋ] adj embriagador(ra); **intoxicating liquor** bebida f alcohólica.

intoxication [ɪn,tɒksɪ'keɪʃn] n embriaguez f.

intractable [ɪn'træktəbl] *adj fml* - **1.** [stubborn] intratable - **2.** [insoluble] inextricable, insoluble.

intranet ['ɪntrənet] *n* COMPUT intranet *f*.

intransigent [ɪn'trænzɪdʒənt] *adj* intransigente.

intransitive [ɪn'trænzətɪv] *adj* intransitivo(va).

intrauterine device [ˌɪntrə'juːtəraɪn-] *n* dispositivo *m* intrauterino.

intravenous [ˌɪntrə'viːnəs] *adj* intravenoso(sa).

in-tray *n* bandeja *f* de entrada.

intrepid [ɪn'trepɪd] *adj liter* intrépido(da).

intricacy ['ɪntrɪkəsɪ] (*pl* **-ies**) *n* - **1.** [complexity] complejidad *f* - **2.** [detail] entresijo *m*.

intricate ['ɪntrɪkət] *adj* intrincado(da), enrevesado(da).

intrigue [ɪn'triːg] <> *n* intriga *f*. <> *vt* intrigar. <> *vi*: **to intrigue (against sb)** intrigar (contra alguien).

intriguing [ɪn'triːgɪŋ] *adj* intrigante.

intrinsic [ɪn'trɪnsɪk] *adj* intrínseco(ca).

intro ['ɪntrəʊ] (*pl* **-s**) *n inf* [of song] entrada *f*.

introduce [ˌɪntrə'djuːs] *vt* - **1.** [present - person, programme] presentar; **to introduce sb (to sb)** presentar a alguien (a alguien); **to introduce o.s.** presentarse - **2.** [bring in]: **to introduce sthg (to OR into)** introducir algo (en) - **3.** [show for first time]: **to introduce sb to sthg** iniciar a alguien en algo - **4.** [signal beginning of] preludiar.

introduction [ˌɪntrə'dʌkʃn] *n* - **1.** [gen]: **introduction (to sthg)** introducción *f* (a algo) - **2.** [of people]: **introduction (to sb)** presentación *f* (a alguien).

introductory [ˌɪntrə'dʌktrɪ] *adj* [chapter] introductorio(ria); [remarks] preliminar; [price, offer] de lanzamiento.

introspective [ˌɪntrə'spektɪv] *adj* introspectivo(va).

introvert ['ɪntrəvɜːt] *n* introvertido *m*, -da *f*.

introverted ['ɪntrəvɜːtɪd] *adj* introvertido(da).

intrude [ɪn'truːd] *vi* [interfere]: **to intrude (on OR upon sb)** inmiscuirse (en los asuntos de alguien); **to intrude (on OR upon sthg)** inmiscuirse (en algo); [disturb] molestar.

intruder [ɪn'truːdər] *n* intruso *m*, -sa *f*.

intrusion [ɪn'truːʒn] *n* [into sb's business] intromisión *f*; [into a place] intrusión *f*.

intrusive [ɪn'truːsɪv] *adj* [interfering] entrometido(da); [unwanted] indeseado(da).

intuition [ˌɪntjuː'ɪʃn] *n* intuición *f*.

intuitive [ɪn'tjuːɪtɪv] *adj* intuitivo(va).

Inuit ['ɪnʊɪt] <> *adj* inuit *(inv)*. <> *n* inuit *mf inv*.

inundate ['ɪnʌndeɪt] *vt* - **1.** *fml* [flood] inundar - **2.** [overwhelm] desbordar; **to be inundated with** verse desbordado por.

inured [ɪ'njʊəd] *adj fml*: **to be/become inured to sthg** estar habituado(da)/habituarse a algo.

invade [ɪn'veɪd] *vt* invadir.

invader [ɪn'veɪdər] *n* invasor *m*, -ra *f*.

invalid <> *adj* [ɪn'vælɪd] - **1.** [marriage, vote, ticket] nulo(la) - **2.** [argument, result] que no es válido(da). <> *n* ['ɪnvəlɪd] inválido *m*, -da *f*.

➤ **invalid out** *vt sep*: **to be invalided out (of)** ser licenciado(da) por invalidez (de).

invalidate [ɪn'vælɪdeɪt] *vt* [theory] refutar; [rule] invalidar; [marriage, election] anular, invalidar.

invaluable [ɪn'væljʊəbl] *adj*: **invaluable (to)** [information, advice] inestimable (para); [person] valiosísimo(ma) (para).

invariable [ɪn'veərɪəbl] *adj* invariable.

invariably [ɪn'veərɪəblɪ] *adv* siempre, invariablemente.

invasion [ɪn'veɪʒn] *n* invasión *f*.

invective [ɪn'vektɪv] *n (U) fml* invectivas *fpl*.

inveigle [ɪn'veɪgl] *vt*: **to inveigle sb into doing sthg** embaucar a alguien para que haga algo.

invent [ɪn'vent] *vt* inventar.

invention [ɪn'venʃn] *n* - **1.** [gen] invención *f* - **2.** [ability to invent] inventiva *f*.

inventive [ɪn'ventɪv] *adj* [person, mind] inventivo(va); [solution] ingenioso(sa).

inventor [ɪn'ventər] *n* inventor *m*, -ra *f*.

inventory ['ɪnvəntrɪ] (*pl* **-ies**) *n* - **1.** [list] inventario *m* - **2.** [goods] existencias *fpl*.

inventory control *n* control *m* de inventario.

inverse [ɪn'vɜːs] <> *adj* [proportion, relation] inverso(sa). <> *n fml*: **the inverse** lo contrario.

invert [ɪn'vɜːt] *vt* invertir.

invertebrate [ɪn'vɜːtɪbreɪt] *n* invertebrado *m*.

inverted commas [ɪn'vɜːtɪd-] *npl UK* comillas *fpl*; **in inverted commas** entre comillas.

inverted snob [ɪn'vɜːtɪd-] *n persona que finge que no le gustan las cosas caras o de buena calidad.*

invest [ɪn'vest] <> *vt* - **1.** [money, time, energy]: **to invest sthg (in)** invertir algo (en) - **2.** *fml* [endow]: **to invest sb with** investir a alguien de. <> *vi lit & fig*: **to invest (in)** invertir (en).

investigate [ɪn'vestɪgeɪt] *vt & vi* investigar.

investigation [ɪnˌvestɪ'geɪʃn] *n* [enquiry, examination]: **investigation (into)** investigación *f* (en).

investigative [ɪn'vestɪgətɪv] *adj* de investigación.

investigator [ɪn'vestɪgeɪtəʳ] n investigador m, -ra f.

investiture [ɪn'vestɪtʃəʳ] n investidura f.

investment [ɪn'vestmənt] n inversión f.

investment analyst n analista financiero m, analista financiera f.

investment trust n fondo m de inversiones.

investor [ɪn'vestəʳ] n inversor m, -ra f.

inveterate [ɪn'vetərət] adj [liar] incorregible; [reader, smoker] empedernido(da).

invidious [ɪn'vɪdɪəs] adj [task, role] desagradable; [comparison] odioso(sa).

invigilate [ɪn'vɪdʒɪleɪt] vt & vi UK vigilar (en un examen).

invigilator [ɪn'vɪdʒɪleɪtəʳ] n UK vigilante mf (en un examen).

invigorating [ɪn'vɪgəreɪtɪŋ] adj [bath, walk] vigorizante; [experience] estimulante.

invincible [ɪn'vɪnsɪbl] adj **- 1.** [unbeatable] invencible **- 2.** [determination] inalterable, inamovible.

invisible [ɪn'vɪzɪbl] adj invisible.

invisible assets npl activo m inmaterial.

invisible earnings npl ingresos mpl invisibles.

invisible ink n tinta f simpática.

invitation [ˌɪnvɪ'teɪʃn] n invitación f; **an invitation to sthg/to do sthg** una invitación a algo/a hacer algo.

invite [ɪn'vaɪt] vt **- 1.** [gen]: **to invite sb (to sthg/to do sthg)** invitar a alguien (a algo/a hacer algo) **- 2.** [ask for, provoke] buscarse.

inviting [ɪn'vaɪtɪŋ] adj tentador(ra).

in vitro fertilization [ˌɪn'viːtrəʊ-] n fertilización f in vitro.

invoice ['ɪnvɔɪs] <> n factura f. <> vt **- 1.** [send invoice to] mandar la factura a **- 2.** [prepare invoice for] facturar.

invoke [ɪn'vəʊk] vt **- 1.** fml [quote as justification] invocar, acogerse a **- 2.** [cause] suscitar.

involuntary [ɪn'vɒləntrɪ] adj involuntario(ria).

involve [ɪn'vɒlv] vt **- 1.** [entail, require]: **to involve sthg/doing sthg** conllevar algo/hacer algo; **it involves working weekends** supone OR implica trabajar los fines de semana **- 2.** [concern, affect] afectar a; **to be involved in sthg** [accident, crash] verse envuelto en algo **- 3.** [make part of sthg]: **to involve sb (in)** involucrar a alguien (en); **to involve o.s. in** meterse en.

involved [ɪn'vɒlvd] adj **- 1.** [complex] enrevesado(da), complicado(da) **- 2.** [participating]: **to be involved in** estar metido(da) en; **he didn't want to get involved** no quería tener nada

que ver **- 3.** [in a relationship]: **to be/get involved with sb** estar liado(da)/liarse con alguien.

involvement [ɪn'vɒlvmənt] n **- 1.:** **involvement (in)** [crime] implicación f (en); [running sthg] participación f (en) **- 2.** [concern, enthusiasm]: **involvement (in)** compromiso m (con) **- 3.** (U) [relationship] relación f sentimental.

invulnerable [ɪn'vʌlnərəbl] adj: **to be invulnerable (to)** ser invulnerable (a).

inward ['ɪnwəd] <> adj **- 1.** [inner] interno(na) **- 2.** [towards the inside] hacia el interior. <> adv US = **inwards**.

inwardly ['ɪnwədlɪ] adv por dentro.

inwards, inward ['ɪnwədz] adv hacia dentro.

in-your-face adj inf impactante.

IOC (abbr of **International Olympic Committee**) n COI m.

iodine [UK 'aɪədiːn, US 'aɪədaɪn] n yodo m.

IOM abbr of **Isle of Man**.

ion ['aɪən] n ión m.

Ionian Sea [aɪ'əʊnjən-] n: **the Ionian Sea** el mar Jónico.

iota [aɪ'əʊtə] n pizca f, ápice m.

IOU (abbr of **I owe you**) n pagaré.

IOW abbr of **Isle of Wight**.

Iowa ['aɪəʊə] n Iowa.

IPA (abbr of **International Phonetic Alphabet**) n AFI m.

IQ (abbr of **intelligence quotient**) n C.I. m

IRA <> n (abbr of **Irish Republican Army**) IRA m. <> n US (abbr of **Individual Retirement Account**) cuenta f de retiro OR jubilación individual.

Iran [ɪ'rɑːn] n (el) Irán.

Iranian [ɪ'reɪnjən] <> adj iraní. <> n [person] iraní mf.

Iraq [ɪ'rɑːk] n (el) Irak.

Iraqi [ɪ'rɑːkɪ] <> adj iraquí. <> n [person] iraquí mf.

irascible [ɪ'ræsəbl] adj irascible.

irate [aɪ'reɪt] adj iracundo(da), airado(da).

Ireland ['aɪələnd] n Irlanda; **the Republic of Ireland** la República de Irlanda.

iridescent [ˌɪrɪ'desənt] adj iridiscente.

iris ['aɪərɪs] (pl -es) n **- 1.** [flower] lirio m **- 2.** [of eye] iris m inv.

Irish ['aɪrɪʃ] <> adj irlandés(esa). <> n [language] irlandés m. <> npl [people]: **the Irish** los irlandeses.

Irish coffee n café m irlandés.

Irishman ['aɪrɪʃmən] (pl -men [-mən]) n irlandés m.

Irish Sea n: **the Irish Sea** el mar de Irlanda.

Irish stew n estofado de carne, patatas y verdura.

Irishwoman ['aɪrɪʃ,wʊmən] (pl **-women** [-,wɪmɪn]) n irlandesa f.

irk [ɜːk] vt fastidiar.

irksome ['ɜːksəm] adj fastidioso(sa).

IRN (abbr of **Independent Radio News**) n agencia británica de noticias para emisoras de radio privadas.

iron ['aɪən] <> adj lit & fig de hierro. <> n - **1.** [metal, nutrient] hierro m - **2.** [for clothes] plancha f - **3.** [golf club] hierro m. <> vt & vi planchar.

➡ **iron out** vt sep fig [overcome] resolver.

Iron Age <> n: the Iron Age la Edad del Hierro. <> comp de la Edad del Hierro.

Iron Curtain n: the Iron Curtain el telón de acero.

ironic(al) [aɪ'rɒnɪk(l)] adj irónico(ca); **how ironical(al)!** ¡qué ironía!

ironically [aɪ'rɒnɪklɪ] adv irónicamente.

ironing ['aɪənɪŋ] n - **1.** [work] planchado m; **to do the ironing** planchar la ropa - **2.** [clothes to be ironed] ropa f para planchar.

ironing board n tabla f de planchar.

iron lung n pulmón m de acero OR artificial.

ironmonger ['aɪən,mʌŋgər] n UK ferretero m, -ra f; **ironmonger's (shop)** ferretería f, tlapalería f Méx.

ironworks ['aɪənwɜːks] (pl **ironworks**) n [where iron is smelted] fundición f; [where iron is cast] herrería f.

irony ['aɪrənɪ] (pl **-ies**) n ironía f; **the irony of it is that...** lo curioso del caso es que...

irradiate [ɪ'reɪdɪeɪt] vt irradiar.

irrational [ɪ'ræʃənl] adj irracional.

irreconcilable [ɪ,rekən'saɪləbl] adj [completely different] irreconciliable.

irredeemable [,ɪrɪ'diːməbl] adj fml - **1.** [hopeless] irreparable, insalvable - **2.** FIN no amortizable.

irrefutable [,ɪrɪ'fjuːtəbl] adj fml irrefutable.

irregular [ɪ'regjʊlər] adj [gen & GRAM] irregular.

irregularity [ɪ,regjʊ'lærətɪ] (pl **-ies**) n irregularidad f.

irregularly [ɪ'regjʊlərlɪ] adv [at uneven intervals] de forma irregular.

irrelevance [ɪ'reləvəns], **irrelevancy** [ɪ'reləvənsɪ] (pl **-ies**) n - **1.** [state of being irrelevant] irrelevancia f, falta f de pertinencia - **2.** [something irrelevant]: **to be an irrelevance** ser algo sin importancia.

irrelevant [ɪ'reləvənt] adj irrelevante, que no viene al caso; **that's irrelevant** eso no viene al caso.

irreligious [,ɪrɪ'lɪdʒəs] adj irreligioso(sa).

irremediable [,ɪrɪ'miːdjəbl] adj fml irremediable, irreparable.

irreparable [ɪ'repərəbl] adj irreparable, irremediable.

irreplaceable [,ɪrɪ'pleɪsəbl] adj irreemplazable, insustituible.

irrepressible [,ɪrɪ'presəbl] adj [enthusiasm] irreprimible; [person] imparable.

irreproachable [,ɪrɪ'prəʊtʃəbl] adj irreprochable.

irresistible [,ɪrɪ'zɪstəbl] adj irresistible.

irresolute [ɪ'rezəluːt] adj fml irresoluto(ta).

irrespective [,ɪrɪ'spektɪv] ➡ **irrespective of** prep independientemente de.

irresponsible [,ɪrɪ'spɒnsəbl] adj irresponsable.

irretrievable [,ɪrɪ'triːvəbl] adj - **1.** [damage, situation] irreparable - **2.** [lost thing] irrecuperable.

irreverent [ɪ'revərənt] adj irreverente, irrespetuoso(sa).

irreversible [,ɪrɪ'vɜːsəbl] adj [judgment] irrevocable; [change] irreversible.

irrevocable [ɪ'revəkəbl] adj irrevocable.

irrigate ['ɪrɪgeɪt] vt regar, irrigar.

irrigation [,ɪrɪ'geɪʃn] <> n riego m, irrigación f. <> comp de riego; **irrigation channel** acequia f.

irritable ['ɪrɪtəbl] adj [person] irritable; [answer, tone] irritado(da).

irritant ['ɪrɪtənt] n - **1.** [irritating situation] motivo m de irritación - **2.** [substance] sustancia f irritante.

irritate ['ɪrɪteɪt] vt irritar.

irritating ['ɪrɪteɪtɪŋ] adj irritante.

irritation [,ɪrɪ'teɪʃn] n - **1.** [anger, soreness] irritación f - **2.** [cause of anger] motivo m de irritación.

IRS (abbr of **Internal Revenue Service**) n US: the IRS ≈ Hacienda f.

is [ɪz] vb ⊳ be.

ISBN (abbr of **International Standard Book Number**) n ISBN m.

ISDN (abbr of **Integrated Services Delivery Network**) n COMPUT RDSI f.

Islam ['ɪzlɑːm] n [religion] islam m, islamismo m.

Islamabad [ɪz'lɑːməbæd] n Islamabad.

Islamic fundamentalist n fundamentalista mf islámico, -ca f.

Islamist ['ɪzləmɪst] adj & n islamista mf.

island ['aɪlənd] n - **1.** [in water] isla f - **2.** [in traffic] isleta f, refugio m.

islander ['aɪləndər] n isleño m, -ña f.

isle [aɪl] n [as part of name] isla f; liter [island] ínsula f.

Isle of Man n: the Isle of Man la isla de Man.

Isle of Wight [-waɪt] *n*: **the Isle of Wight** la isla de Wight.

isn't [ˈɪznt] (*abbr of* = **is not**), ▷ **be**.

isobar [ˈaɪsəbɑːr] *n* isobara *f*.

isolate [ˈaɪsəleɪt] *vt* - **1.**: **to isolate sb (from)** [physically] aislar a alguien (de); [socially] marginar a alguien (de) - **2.** MED: **to isolate sb** poner a alguien en cuarentena - **3.** CHEM & ELEC: **to isolate sthg (from)** aislar algo (de).

isolated [ˈaɪsəleɪtɪd] *adj* aislado(da).

isolation [ˌaɪsəˈleɪʃn] *n* [solitariness] aislamiento *m*; **in isolation** [alone] en soledad; [separately] aisladamente.

isolationism [ˌaɪsəˈleɪʃənɪzm] *n* aislacionismo *m*.

isosceles triangle [aɪˈsɒsɪliːz-] *n* triángulo *m* isósceles.

isotope [ˈaɪsətəʊp] *n* isótopo *m*.

ISP (*abbr of* **Internet Service Provider**) *n* PSI *m*.

Israel [ˈɪzreɪəl] *n* Israel.

Israeli [ɪzˈreɪlɪ] ⬦ *adj* israelí. ⬦ *n* israelí *mf*.

Israelite [ˈɪzrəlaɪt] ⬦ *adj* israelita. ⬦ *n* israelita *mf*.

issue [ˈɪʃuː] ⬦ *n* - **1.** [important subject] cuestión *f*, tema *m*; **at issue** en cuestión; **to avoid the issue** evitar el tema; **to make an issue of sthg** darle demasiada importancia a algo - **2.** [of newspaper, magazine] número *m* - **3.** [of stamps, shares, banknotes] emisión *f*. ⬦ *vt* - **1.** [statement, warning] hacer público(ca); [decree] promulgar - **2.** [stamps, shares, banknotes] emitir, poner en circulación - **3.** [give]: **to issue sthg to sb, to issue sb with sthg** [passport, document] expedir algo a alguien; [ticket] proporcionar algo a alguien. ⬦ *vi fml*: **to issue (from)** surgir (de).

isthmus [ˈɪsməs] *n* istmo *m*.

it [ɪt] *pron* - **1.** [referring to specific thing or person - subj] él *m*, ella *f*; [- direct object] lo *m*, la *f*; [- indirect object] le; **it is in my hand** está en mi mano; **it broke** se rompió; **did you find it?** ¿lo encontraste?; **give it to me** dámelo; **I like it** me gusta; **he gave it a kick** le dio una patada - **2.** *(with prepositions)* él *m*, ella *f*; [meaning 'this matter' etc] ello; **as if his life depended on it** como si le fuera la vida en ello; **in it** dentro; **give this bone to it** dale este hueso; **have you been to it before?** ¿has estado antes?; **he's good at it** se le da bien; **on it** encima; **to talk about it** hablar de él/ella/ello; **under/beneath it** debajo; **beside it** al lado; **from/of it** de él/ella/ello; **over it** por encima - **3.** *(impersonal use)*: **it was raining** llovía; **it is cold today** hace frío hoy; **it's two o'clock** son las dos; **who is it? - it's Mary/me** ¿quién es? - soy Mary/yo;

what day is it? ¿a qué (día) estamos hoy?; **it's Monday** es lunes; **it says here that...** aquí dice que...; **it's the children who worry me most** son los niños lo que más me preocupa.

IT *n abbr of* **information technology**.

Italian [ɪˈtæljən] ⬦ *adj* italiano(na). ⬦ *n* - **1.** [person] italiano *m*, -na *f* - **2.** [language] italiano *m*.

italic [ɪˈtælɪk] *adj* cursiva.
➡ **italics** *npl* cursiva *f*.

Italy [ˈɪtəlɪ] *n* Italia.

itch [ɪtʃ] ⬦ *n* picor *m*, picazón *f*. ⬦ *vi* - **1.** [be itchy - person] tener picazón; [- arm, leg etc] picar; **my arm is itching** me pica el brazo - **2.** *fig* [be impatient]: **to be itching to do sthg** estar deseando hacer algo.

itchy [ˈɪtʃɪ] (*comp* **-ier**, *superl* **-iest**) *adj* [garment, material] que pica; **I've got an itchy arm** me pica el brazo.

it'd [ˈɪtəd] - **1.** (*abbr of* = **it had**), ▷ **have** - **2.** (*abbr of* = **it would**), ▷ **would**.

item [ˈaɪtəm] *n* - **1.** [in collection] artículo *m*; [on list, agenda] punto *m* - **2.** [article in newspaper] artículo *m*; **news item** noticia *f*.

itemize, -ise [ˈaɪtəmaɪz] *vt* detallar.

itemized bill [ˈaɪtəmaɪzd-] *n* factura *f* detallada.

itinerant [ɪˈtɪnərənt] *adj* itinerante, ambulante.

itinerary [aɪˈtɪnərərɪ] (*pl* **-ies**) *n* itinerario *m*.

it'll [ɪtl] - **1.** (*abbr of* = **it will**), ▷ **will** - **2.** (*abbr of* = **it shall**), ▷ **shall**.

its [ɪts] *poss adj* su, sus *(pl)*; **the dog broke its leg** el perro se rompió la pata.

it's [ɪts] - **1.** (*abbr of* = **it is**), ▷ **be** - **2.** (*abbr of* = **it has**), ▷ **have**.

itself [ɪtˈself] *pron* - **1.** *(reflexive)* se; *(after prep)* sí mismo(ma); **with itself** consigo mismo(ma) - **2.** *(for emphasis)*: **the town itself is lovely** el pueblo en sí es muy bonito; **in itself** en sí; **it's simplicity itself** es la sencillez misma.

IUCD (*abbr of* **intrauterine contraceptive device**) *n* DIU *m*.

IUD (*abbr of* **intrauterine device**) *n* DIU *m*.

I've [aɪv] (*abbr of* = **I have**), ▷ **have**.

IVF (*abbr of* **in vitro fertilization**) *n* fertilización *in vitro*.

ivory [ˈaɪvərɪ] ⬦ *adj* [ivory-coloured] de color marfil, marfileño(ña). ⬦ *n* marfil *m*. ⬦ *comp* de marfil.

Ivory Coast *n*: **the Ivory Coast** la Costa de Marfil.

ivory tower *n* torre *f* de marfil.

ivy [ˈaɪvɪ] *n* hiedra *f*.

Ivy League *n US grupo de ocho prestigiosas universidades del este de los EE.UU.*

Ivy League

Así se denomina a un grupo de ocho universidades del nordeste de los Estados Unidos: Brown, Columbia, Cornell, Dartmouth, Harvard, la Universidad de Pensilvania, Princeton y Yale. Estas ocho universidades se encuentran entre las más prestigiosas del país. Aunque originalmente el cometido de la Ivy League era el de promover encuentros deportivos entre las universidades que la componen, ha acabado por convertirse en sinónimo de una educación de prestigio, altamente competitiva y reservada a una élite.

J

j (*pl* **j's** OR **js**), **J** (*pl* **J's** OR **Js**) [dʒeɪ] *n* [letter] j *f*, J *f*.

jab [dʒæb] <> *n* - **1.** [with elbow] codazo *m*; [in boxing] golpe *m* corto - **2.** UK inf [injection] pinchazo *m*. <> *vt* (*pt & pp* -bed, *cont* -bing): **to jab sthg into** clavar algo en; **to jab sthg at** apuntarle algo a. <> *vi* (*pt & pp* -bed, *cont* -bing): **to jab at sthg/sb** intentar golpear algo/a alguien.

jabber ['dʒæbər] <> *vt* farfullar. <> *vi* charlotear.

jack [dʒæk] *n* - **1.** [device] gato *m* - **2.** ELEC [plug] clavija *f*; [socket] clavijero *m* - **3.** [French deck playing card] ≃ jota *f*; [Spanish deck playing card] ≃ sota *f*.

➤ **jack in** *vt sep* UK inf mandar a paseo, dejar.

➤ **jack up** *vt sep* - **1.** [lift with a jack] levantar con gato - **2.** [force up] subir.

jackal ['dʒækəl] *n* chacal *m*.

jackdaw ['dʒækdɔ:] *n* grajilla *f*.

jacket ['dʒækɪt] *n* - **1.** [garment] chaqueta *f*, americana *f*, saco *m* Amér - **2.** [potato skin] piel *f* - **3.** [book cover] sobrecubierta *f* - **4.** US [of record] cubierta *f*.

jacket potato *n* patata *f* asada con piel.

jackhammer ['dʒæk,hæmər] *n* US martillo *m* neumático.

jack-in-the-box *n* caja *f* sorpresa.

jack knife *n* navaja *f*.

➤ **jack-knife** *vi*: **the lorry jack-knifed** derrapó la parte delantera del camión.

jack-of-all-trades (*pl* jacks-of-all-trades) *n persona que sabe un poco de todo.*

jack plug *n* clavija *f*.

jackpot ['dʒækpɒt] *n* (premio *m*) gordo *m*.

Jacobean [,dʒækə'bɪən] *adj* de la época de Jacobo I.

Jacobite ['dʒækəbaɪt] <> *adj* jacobita. <> *n* jacobita *mf*.

Jacuzzi® [dʒə'ku:zɪ] *n* jacuzzi® *m*.

jade [dʒeɪd] <> *adj* [jade-coloured] jade (*inv*). <> *comp* de jade. <> *n* - **1.** [stone] jade *m* - **2.** [colour] color *m* jade.

jaded ['dʒeɪdɪd] *adj* [tired] agotado(da); [bored] hastiado(da).

jagged ['dʒægɪd] *adj* dentado(da).

jaguar ['dʒægjʊər] *n* jaguar *m*.

jail, gaol [dʒeɪl] <> *n* cárcel *f*; **in jail** en la cárcel. <> *vt* encarcelar.

jailbird ['dʒeɪlbɜ:d] *n* inf preso *m*, -sa *f* reincidente.

jailbreak ['dʒeɪlbreɪk] *n* fuga *f*, evasión *f*.

jailer ['dʒeɪlər] *n* carcelero *m*, -ra *f*.

jam [dʒæm] <> *n* - **1.** [preserve] mermelada *f* - **2.** [of traffic] embotellamiento *m*, atasco *m* - **3.** MUS *sesión improvisada de jazz o rock* - **4.** inf [difficult situation]: **to get into/be in a jam** meterse/estar en un apuro. <> *vt* (*pt & pp* -med, *cont* -ming) - **1.** [place roughly] meter a la fuerza - **2.** [fix] sujetar; **jam the door shut** atranca la puerta - **3.** [pack tightly] apiñar - **4.** [fill] abarrotar, atestar - **5.** TELEC bloquear - **6.** [cause to stick] atascar; **it's jammed** se ha atascado - **7.** RADIO interferir. <> *vi* (*pt & pp* -med, *cont* -ming) - **1.** [stick] atascarse - **2.** MUS improvisar.

Jamaica [dʒə'meɪkə] *n* Jamaica.

Jamaican [dʒə'meɪkn] <> *adj* jamaicano(na). <> *n* jamaicano *m*, -na *f*.

jamb [dʒæm] *n* jamba *f*.

jamboree [,dʒæmbə'ri:] *n* - **1.** [celebration] juerga *f* - **2.** [gathering of scouts] reunión *f* de niños exploradores.

jam jar *n* tarro *m* de mermelada.

jamming ['dʒæmɪŋ] *n* RADIO interferencia *f*.

jam-packed [-'pækt] *adj* inf a tope, atestado(da).

jam session *n* jam session *f*, *sesión improvisada de jazz o rock.*

jam tart *n pastel de confitura relleno de mermelada de fresa o frambuesa.*

Jan. [dʒæn] (*abbr of* January) ene. *m*

jangle ['dʒæŋgl] <> *n* tintineo *m*. <> *vt* hacer tintinear. <> *vi* tintinear.

janitor ['dʒænɪtəʳ] *n US & Scotland* conserje *m*, portero *m*.

January ['dʒænjʊərɪ] *n* enero *m*; *see also* **September**.

Japan [dʒə'pæn] *n* (el) Japón.

Japanese [,dʒæpə'niːz] <> *adj* japonés(esa). <> *n* (*pl* **Japanese**) [language] japonés *m*. <> *npl*: **the Japanese** los japoneses.

jape [dʒeɪp] *n dated* broma *f*.

jar [dʒɑːʳ] <> *n* tarro *m*. <> *vt* (*pt & pp* **-red**, *cont* **-ring**) [shake] sacudir. <> *vi* (*pt & pp* **-red**, *cont* **-ring**) **- 1.** [upset]: **to jar (on sb)** poner los nervios de punta a (alguien) **- 2.** [clash - opinions] discordar; [- colours] desentonar.

jargon ['dʒɑːgən] *n* jerga *f*.

jarring ['dʒɑːrɪŋ] *adj* **- 1.** [upsetting] crispante **- 2.** [blow] contundente **- 3.** [clashing - opinions] discordante; [- colours] que desentonan.

jasmine ['dʒæzmɪn] *n* jazmín *m*.

jaundice ['dʒɔːndɪs] *n* ictericia *f*.

jaundiced ['dʒɔːndɪst] *adj fig* [attitude, view] desencantado(da).

jaunt [dʒɔːnt] *n* excursión *f*.

jaunty ['dʒɔːntɪ] (*comp* **-ier**, *superl* **-iest**) *adj* [hat, wave] airoso(sa); [person] vivaz, desenvuelto(ta).

Java ['dʒɑːvə] *n* **- 1.** Java **- 2.** *US inf* [coffee] café *m*.

javelin ['dʒævlɪn] *n* jabalina *f*.

jaw [dʒɔː] <> *n* [of person, animal] mandíbula *f*. <> *vi inf* cotorrear.

jawbone ['dʒɔːbəʊn] *n* [of person, animal] mandíbula *f*, maxilar *m*.

jay [dʒeɪ] *n* arrendajo *m*.

jaywalk ['dʒeɪwɔːk] *vi* cruzar la calle descuidadamente.

jaywalker ['dʒeɪwɔːkəʳ] *n* peatón *m* imprudente.

jazz [dʒæz] *n* **- 1.** MUS jazz *m* **- 2.** *inf* [insincere talk] palabrería *f*; **and all that jazz** y todo el rollo.
➡ **jazz up** *vt sep inf* alegrar, avivar.

jazz band *n* conjunto *m* OR banda *f* de jazz.

jazz singer *n* cantante *mf* de jazz.

jazzy ['dʒæzɪ] (*comp* **-ier**, *superl* **-iest**) *adj* [bright] llamativo(va).

JD (*abbr of* **Justice Department**) *n ministerio de justicia estadounidense*.

jealous ['dʒeləs] *adj* **- 1.** [envious]: **to be jealous (of)** tener celos OR estar celoso(sa) (de) **- 2.** [possessive]: **to be jealous (of)** ser celoso(sa) (de).

jealously ['dʒeləslɪ] *adv* celosamente.

jealousy ['dʒeləsɪ] *n* (U) celos *mpl*.

jeans [dʒiːnz] *npl* vaqueros *mpl*, bluyínes *mpl* Amér.

jeep [dʒiːp] *n* jeep *m*, campero *m* Amér.

jeer [dʒɪəʳ] <> *vt* [boo] abuchear; [mock] mofarse de. <> *vi*: **to jeer (at sb)** [boo] abuchear (a alguien); [mock] mofarse (de alguien).
➡ **jeers** *npl* [booing] abucheo *m*; [mocking] burlas *fpl*.

jeering ['dʒɪərɪŋ] *adj* burlón(ona).

Jehovah's Witness [dʒɪ'həʊvəz-] *n* testigo *mf* de Jehová.

Jell-O® ['dʒeləʊ] *n US* jalea *f*, gelatina *f*.

jelly ['dʒelɪ] (*pl* **-ies**) *n* **- 1.** [dessert] jalea *f*, gelatina *f* **- 2.** [jam] mermelada *f*.

jelly baby *n UK* gominola *m* en forma de muñeco.

jelly bean *n* gominola *f*, caramelo *m* de goma Amér, gomita *f* Chile.

jellyfish ['dʒelɪfɪʃ] (*pl* **jellyfish** OR **-es**) *n* medusa *f*.

jelly roll *n US* brazo *m* de gitano.

jemmy *UK* ['dʒemɪ], **jimmy** *US* ['dʒɪmɪ] (*pl* **-ies**) *n* palanqueta *f*.

jeopardize, -ise ['dʒepədaɪz] *vt* poner en peligro, arriesgar.

jeopardy ['dʒepədɪ] *n*: **in jeopardy** en peligro.

jerk [dʒɜːk] <> *n* **- 1.** [of head] movimiento *m* brusco; [of arm] tirón *m*; [of vehicle] sacudida *f* **- 2.** *v inf* [fool] idiota *mf*, majadero *m*, -ra *f*. <> *vt* tirar bruscamente de; **he jerked his head round** giró la cabeza bruscamente. <> *vi* [person] saltar; [vehicle] dar sacudidas.

jerkily ['dʒɜːkɪlɪ] *adv* [person] a trompicones; [vehicle] a tirones, a sacudidas.

jerkin ['dʒɜːkɪn] *n* **- 1.** HIST jubón *m* **- 2.** [modern garment] chaqueta *f* sin mangas.

jerky ['dʒɜːkɪ] <> *adj* (*comp* **-ier**, *superl* **-iest**) brusco(ca), espasmódico(ca). <> *n US* tasajo *m*, cecina *f*.

jerry-built ['dʒerɪ-] *adj* mal construido(da).

jersey ['dʒɜːzɪ] (*pl* **jerseys**) *n* **- 1.** [sweater] jersey *m* **- 2.** [in cycling] maillot *m* **- 3.** [cloth] tejido *m* de punto.

Jersey ['dʒɜːzɪ] *n* Jersey.

jest [dʒest] *n*: **in jest** en broma.

jester ['dʒestəʳ] *n* bufón *m*.

Jesuit ['dʒezjʊɪt] <> *adj* jesuita. <> *n* jesuita *m*.

Jesus (Christ) ['dʒiːzəs-] <> *n* Jesús *m*, Jesucristo *m*. <> *excl inf* ¡Santo Dios!

jet [dʒet] <> *n* **- 1.** [aircraft] reactor *m* **- 2.** [stream] chorro *m* **- 3.** [nozzle, outlet] boca *f*, boquilla *f*. <> *vi* (*pt & pp* **-ted**, *cont* **-ting**) [travel by plane] viajar en avión.

jet-black *adj* negro(gra) azabache.

jet engine *n* reactor *m*.

jetfoil ['dʒetfɔɪl] n hidroplano m.

jet lag n desfase m horario.

jet-propelled [-prə'peld] adj a reacción.

jetsam ['dʒetsəm] ⊳ **flotsam**.

jet set n: **the jet set** la jet-set.

jet ski n moto f acuática.

jettison ['dʒetɪsən] vt [cargo] deshacerse de; fig [ideas] desechar.

jetty ['dʒetɪ] (pl -ies) n embarcadero m, malecón m.

Jew [dʒu:] n judío m, -a f.

jewel ['dʒu:əl] n - **1.** [gemstone] piedra f preciosa - **2.** [jewellery] joya f - **3.** [in watch] rubí m.

jewel case n US caja f (de CD).

jeweller UK, **jeweler** US ['dʒu:ələˠ] n joyero m, -ra f; **jeweller's (shop)** joyería f.

jewellery UK, **jewelry** US ['dʒu:əlrɪ] n (U) joyas fpl, alhajas fpl.

Jewess ['dʒu:ɪs] n judía f.

Jewish ['dʒu:ɪʃ] adj judío(a).

jib [dʒɪb] ⊳ n - **1.** [beam] aguilón m - **2.** [sail] foque m. ⊳ vi (pt & pp -bed, cont -bing): **to jib at doing sthg** vacilar en hacer algo.

jibe [dʒaɪb] n pulla f, burla f.

jiffy ['dʒɪfɪ] n inf: **in a jiffy** en un segundo.

Jiffy bag® n sobre m acolchado.

jig [dʒɪg] ⊳ n giga f. ⊳ vi (pt & pp -ged, cont -ging) danzar dando brincos.

jiggle ['dʒɪgl] vt menear.

jigsaw (puzzle) ['dʒɪgsɔ:-] n rompecabezas m inv, puzzle m.

jihad [dʒɪ'hɑ:d] n yihad f, guerra f santa.

jilt [dʒɪlt] vt dejar plantado(da).

jimmy US = **jemmy**.

jingle ['dʒɪŋgl] ⊳ n - **1.** [sound] tintineo m - **2.** [song] sintonía f (de anuncio publicitario). ⊳ vi tintinear.

jingoism ['dʒɪŋgəʊɪzm] n patriotería f.

jinx [dʒɪŋks] n gafe m.

jinxed ['dʒɪŋkst] adj gafado(da).

jitters ['dʒɪtəz] npl inf: **to have the jitters** estar como un flan.

jittery ['dʒɪtərɪ] adj inf: **to be jittery** estar como un flan.

jive [dʒaɪv] ⊳ n - **1.** [dance] swing m - **2.** US inf [glib talk] palabrería f. ⊳ vi bailar el swing.

job [dʒɒb] n - **1.** [paid employment] trabajo m, empleo m; **out of a job** sin trabajo; **to learn on the job** aprender con la práctica - **2.** [task & COMPUT] tarea f; **to do a good job** hacerlo bien; **to make a good job of sthg** hacer un buen trabajo con algo - **3.** [difficult task]: **we had a job doing it** nos costó mucho hacerlo - **4.** [function] cometido m, deber m - **5.** inf [plastic surgery]: **she's had a nose job** se ha he-

cho la cirugía en la nariz - **6.** UK phr: **it's a good job that...** inf menos mal que...; **that's just the job** inf eso me viene de perilla.

jobbing ['dʒɒbɪŋ] adj UK (que trabaja) a destajo.

Jobcentre n UK oficina f de empleo.

job description n descripción f de trabajo.

jobless ['dʒɒblɪs] ⊳ adj desempleado(da). ⊳ npl: **the jobless** los desempleados.

job lot n lote m de saldos.

job satisfaction n satisfacción f en el trabajo.

job security n seguridad f en el trabajo.

job seeker n demandante mf de empleo.

Job Seekers Allowance n UK subsidio m de desempleo.

jobsharing ['dʒɒbʃeərɪŋ] n (U) empleo m compartido.

jockey ['dʒɒkɪ] ⊳ n (pl -s) jockey m, jinete m. ⊳ vi: **to jockey for position** competir por colocarse en mejor posición.

jockstrap ['dʒɒkstræp] n suspensorio m.

jocular ['dʒɒkjʊləˠ] adj - **1.** [cheerful] bromista - **2.** [funny] jocoso(sa).

jodhpurs ['dʒɒdpəz] npl pantalón m de montar.

Joe Public [dʒəʊ-] n UK el hombre de la calle.

jog [dʒɒg] ⊳ n trote m; **to go for a jog** hacer footing. ⊳ vt (pt & pp -ged, cont -ging) golpear ligeramente; **to jog sb's memory** refrescar la memoria a alguien. ⊳ vi (pt & pp -ged, cont -ging) hacer footing.

jogger ['dʒɒgəˠ] n persona f que hace footing.

jogging ['dʒɒgɪŋ] n footing m.

joggle ['dʒɒgl] vt menear.

john [dʒɒn] n US inf [toilet] wáter m.

John Hancock [-'hænkɒk] n US inf [signature] firma f.

join [dʒɔɪn] ⊳ n juntura f. ⊳ vt - **1.** [unite] unir, juntar, empatar Amér - **2.** [get together with] reunirse con; **I'll join you for lunch** os acompaño a almorzar; **may I join you?** ¿te importa si me siento aquí? - **3.** [become a member of - political party, trade union] afiliarse a; [- club] hacerse socio de; [- army] alistarse en - **4.** [take part in] unirse a; **to join the queue** UK, **to join the line** US meterse en la cola. ⊳ vi - **1.** [rivers] confluir; [edges, pieces] unirse, juntarse - **2.** [become a member - of political party, trade union] afiliarse; [- of club] hacerse socio; [- of army] alistarse.

➤ **join in** ⊳ vt insep participar en, tomar parte en. ⊳ vi participar, tomar parte.

➤ **join up** vi MIL alistarse.

joiner ['dʒɔɪnəˠ] n carpintero m.

joinery ['dʒɔɪnərɪ] n carpintería f.

joint [dʒɔɪnt] ⊳ adj [responsibility] compartido(da); [effort] conjunto(ta); **joint owner** copropietario m, -ria f. ◇ n - **1.** ANAT articulación f - **2.** [place where things are joined] juntura f, junta f, empate m Amér - **3.** UK [of meat - uncooked] corte m para asar; [- cooked] asado m - **4.** inf pej [place] antro m, garito m - **5.** inf [cannabis cigarette] porro m.

joint account n cuenta f conjunta.

jointed ['dʒɔɪntɪd] adj articulado(da).

jointly ['dʒɔɪntlɪ] adv conjuntamente.

joint ownership n copropiedad f.

joint-stock company n ≈ sociedad f anónima.

joint venture n empresa f conjunta.

joist [dʒɔɪst] n vigueta f.

jojoba [hə'həʊbə] n jojoba f.

joke [dʒəʊk] ◇ n [funny story] chiste m; [funny action] broma f; **to do sthg for a joke** hacer algo en broma; **to go beyond a joke** pasarse de castaño oscuro; **to play a joke on sb** gastarle una broma a alguien; **to be a joke** [person] ser un inútil; [situation] ser una tomadura de pelo; **it's no joke** [not easy] no es (nada) fácil. ◇ vi bromear; **you're joking** estás de broma; **I'm not joking** hablo en serio; **to joke about sthg/with sb** bromear acerca de algo/con alguien.

joker ['dʒəʊkə'] n - **1.** [funny person] bromista mf - **2.** [useless person] inútil mf - **3.** [playing card] comodín m.

jollity ['dʒɒlətɪ] n alegría f.

jolly ['dʒɒlɪ] ◇ adj (comp -ier, superl -iest) [person, laugh] alegre; [time] divertido(da). ◇ adv UK inf muy; **jolly good!** ¡genial!

jolt [dʒəʊlt] ◇ n - **1.** liter sacudida f - **2.** fig susto m. ◇ vt - **1.** [jerk] sacudir, zarandear - **2.** [shock] sacudir; **to jolt sb into doing sthg** acabar convenciendo a alguien de hacer algo. ◇ vi traquetear.

Joneses ['dʒəʊnzɪz] npl: **to keep up with the Joneses** no ser menos que el vecino.

Jordan ['dʒɔːdn] n Jordania; **the (River) Jordan** el (río) Jordán.

Jordanian [dʒɔː'deɪnjən] ◇ adj jordano(na). ◇ n jordano m, -na f.

joss stick [dʒɒs-] n varita f de incienso.

jostle ['dʒɒsl] ◇ vt empujar, dar empujones a. ◇ vi empujar, dar empujones.

jot [dʒɒt] n pizca f; **I don't care a jot** no me importa en lo más mínimo.

➡ **jot down** vt sep (pt & pp -ted, cont -ting) apuntar, anotar.

jotter ['dʒɒtə'] n bloc m.

jottings ['dʒɒtɪŋz] npl apuntes mpl, notas fpl.

journal ['dʒɜːnl] n - **1.** [magazine] revista f, boletín m - **2.** [diary] diario m.

journalese [ˌdʒɜːnə'liːz] n pej jerga f periodística.

journalism ['dʒɜːnəlɪzm] n periodismo m.

journalist ['dʒɜːnəlɪst] n periodista mf.

journey ['dʒɜːnɪ] ◇ n (pl -s) viaje m. ◇ vi viajar.

joust [dʒaʊst] vi justar.

jovial ['dʒəʊvjəl] adj jovial.

jowls [dʒaʊlz] npl carrillos mpl.

joy [dʒɔɪ] n - **1.** [happiness] alegría f, regocijo m - **2.** [cause of joy] placer m, deleite m.

joyful ['dʒɔɪfʊl] adj alegre.

joyfully ['dʒɔɪfʊlɪ] adv alegremente.

joyous ['dʒɔɪəs] adj jubiloso(sa).

joyously ['dʒɔɪəslɪ] adv jubilosamente.

joyride ['dʒɔɪraɪd] ◇ n vuelta f en un coche robado. ◇ vi (pt -rode, pp -ridden) darse una vuelta en un coche robado.

joyrider ['dʒɔɪraɪdə'] n persona que se da una vuelta en un coche robado.

joystick ['dʒɔɪstɪk] n [of aircraft] palanca f de mando; [for video games, computers] joystick m.

JP n abbr of **Justice of the Peace.**

Jr. US (abbr of **Junior**) jr; **Mark Andrews Jr.** Mark Andrews, hijo.

jubilant ['dʒuːbɪlənt] adj [person] jubiloso(sa); [shout] alborozado(da).

jubilation [ˌdʒuːbɪ'leɪʃn] n júbilo m, alborozo m.

jubilee ['dʒuːbɪliː] n aniversario m.

Judaism ['dʒuːdeɪɪzm] n judaísmo m.

judder ['dʒʌdə'] vi UK vibrar; **to judder to a halt** pararse con una sacudida.

judge [dʒʌdʒ] ◇ n [gen & LAW] juez mf; **to be a good judge of character** tener buen ojo para la gente. ◇ vt - **1.** [gen & LAW] juzgar - **2.** [age, distance] calcular. ◇ vi juzgar; **to judge from** OR **by, judging from** OR **by** a juzgar por.

judg(e)ment ['dʒʌdʒmənt] n - **1.** LAW fallo m, sentencia f; **to pass judgement (on sb)** pronunciar sentencia (sobre alguien) - **2.** [opinion] juicio m; **to pass judgement (on sb/sthg)** pronunciarse (sobre alguien/algo); **to reserve judgement** reservarse la opinión - **3.** [ability to form opinion] juicio m; **against my better judgement** en contra de lo que me dicta el juicio - **4.** [punishment] castigo m.

judg(e)mental [dʒʌdʒ'mentl] adj pej: **to be judgemental** emitir juicios.

judicial [dʒuː'dɪʃl] adj judicial.

judiciary [dʒuː'dɪʃərɪ] n: **the judiciary** [part of government] el poder judicial; [judges] la judicatura.

judicious [dʒuː'dɪʃəs] adj juicioso(sa).

judo ['dʒuːdəʊ] n judo m.

jug [dʒʌg] n jarra f.

juggernaut ['dʒʌɡənɔːt] n camión m grande.

juggle ['dʒʌɡl] <> vt - **1.** [throw] hacer juegos malabares con - **2.** [rearrange] jugar con. <> vi hacer juegos malabares.

juggler ['dʒʌɡlər] n malabarista mf.

jugular (vein) ['dʒʌɡjʊlər-] n yugular f.

juice [dʒuːs] n - **1.** [from fruit, vegetables] zumo m - **2.** [from meat] jugo m.

juicer ['dʒuːsər] n exprimidor m.

juicy ['dʒuːsɪ] (comp -ier, superl -iest) adj - **1.** [gen] jugoso(sa) - **2.** inf [scandalous] sabroso(sa), picante.

jujitsu [dʒuː'dʒɪtsuː] n jiu-jitsu m.

jukebox ['dʒuːkbɒks] n máquina f de discos.

Jul. (abbr of July) jul.

July [dʒuː'laɪ] n julio m; see also **September**.

jumble ['dʒʌmbl] <> n [mixture] revoltijo m. <> vt: **to jumble (up)** revolver.

jumble sale n UK rastrillo m benéfico.

jumbo jet ['dʒʌmbəʊ-] n jumbo m.

jumbo-sized ['dʒʌmbəʊsaɪzd] adj gigante, de tamaño familiar.

jump [dʒʌmp] <> n - **1.** [act of jumping] salto m - **2.** [start, surprised movement] sobresalto m - **3.** [fence in horsejumping] obstáculo m - **4.** [rapid increase] incremento m, salto m
▶▶ to keep one jump ahead of sb mantener la delantera con respecto a alguien. <> vt - **1.** [cross by jumping] saltar - **2.** [attack] asaltar - **3.** [miss out] saltarse - **4.** US [train, bus] colarse en. <> vi - **1.** [spring] saltar; **to jump across sthg** cruzar algo de un salto; **to jump out of the window** tirarse por la ventana - **2.** [make a sudden movement] sobresaltarse; **his heart jumped** le dio un vuelco el corazón - **3.** [increase rapidly] dar un salto, aumentar de golpe.
◆ jump at vt insep no dejar escapar.

jumped-up ['dʒʌmpt-] adj UK inf pej creído(da), presuntuoso(sa).

jumper ['dʒʌmpər] n - **1.** UK [pullover] jersey m, chomba f R Plata, chompa f Andes - **2.** US [dress] pichi m.

jumper cables npl US cables mpl de empalme (de batería).

jump jet n avión m de despegue vertical.

jump leads npl cables mpl de empalme (de batería).

jump-start vt [by pushing] arrancar empujando; [using jump leads] arrancar haciendo un puente.

jumpsuit ['dʒʌmpsuːt] n mono m.

jumpy ['dʒʌmpɪ] (comp -ier, superl -iest) adj inquieto(ta).

Jun, Jun. abbr of **June**.

Jun., Junr US (abbr of **Junior**) jr.

junction ['dʒʌŋkʃn] n [of roads] cruce m; UK [on motorway] salida f; [of railway lines] empalme m.

junction box n caja f de empalmes.

juncture ['dʒʌŋktʃər] n fml: **at this juncture** en esta coyuntura.

June [dʒuːn] n junio m; see also **September**.

jungle ['dʒʌŋɡl] n lit & fig selva f.

jungle gym n US barras de metal para que trepen los niños.

junior ['dʒuːnjər] <> adj - **1.** [partner, member] de menor antigüedad, júnior (inv); [officer] subalterno(na) - **2.** [after name]: **Mark Andrews junior** Mark Andrews, hijo. <> n - **1.** [person of lower rank] subalterno m, -na f - **2.** [younger person]: **he's my junior** soy mayor que él - **3.** US SCH & UNIV alumno de penúltimo año.

junior college n US colegio universitario para los primeros años.

junior doctor n médico que lleva poco ejerciendo.

junior high school n US ≃ instituto m de bachillerato (13-15 años).

junior minister n UK subsecretario m, -ria f.

junior school n UK ≃ escuela f primaria.

juniper ['dʒuːnɪpər] n enebro m.

junk [dʒʌŋk] inf <> n (U) [unwanted things] trastos mpl. <> vt inf tirar a la basura.

junket ['dʒʌŋkɪt] n - **1.** [pudding] dulce m de leche cuajada - **2.** inf pej [trip] viaje lujoso pagado con dinero del estado.

junk food n pej comida f basura.

junkie ['dʒʌŋkɪ] n inf yonqui mf.

junk mail n (U) pej propaganda f (por correo).

junk shop n tienda f de objetos usados, cambalache m R Plata.

junta [UK 'dʒʌntə, US 'hʊntə] n junta f militar.

Jupiter ['dʒuːpɪtər] n Júpiter m.

jurisdiction [ˌdʒʊərɪs'dɪkʃn] n jurisdicción f.

jurisprudence [ˌdʒʊərɪs'pruːdəns] n jurisprudencia f.

juror ['dʒʊərər] n jurado m.

jury ['dʒʊərɪ] (pl -ies) n jurado m; **the jury is still out on that** eso está por ver.

jury box n tribuna f del jurado.

jury service n servicio realizado como miembro de un jurado.

just [dʒʌst] <> adv - **1.** [recently]: **he has just left/moved** acaba de salir/mudarse - **2.** [at that moment]: **we were just leaving when...** justo íbamos a salir cuando...; **I'm just about to do it** voy a hacerlo ahora; **I couldn't do it just then** no lo podía hacer en aquel momento; **just as I was leaving** justo en el momento en que salía; **just recently** hace muy poco; **just**

yesterday ayer mismo **- 3.** [only, simply] sólo, solamente; **he's just a child** no es más que un niño; **'just add water'** 'simplemente añada un poco de agua'; **if you need help, just ask** si necesitas ayuda, no tienes más que pedirla; **just a minute** OR **moment** OR **second** un momento **- 4.** [almost not] apenas; **I (only) just did it** conseguí hacerlo por muy poco **- 5.** [for emphasis]: **I just know it!** ¡estoy seguro!; **just imagine!** ¡imagínate!; **just look what you've done!** ¡mira lo que has hecho! **- 6.** [exactly, precisely] exactamente, precisamente; **just what I need** justo lo que necesito; **just here/there** aquí/allí mismo **- 7.** [in requests]: **could you just open your mouth?** ¿podrías abrir la boca un momento, por favor? <> *adj* justo(ta).

➤ **just about** *adv* **- 1.** [nearly] casi **- 2.** [more or less] más o menos.

➤ **just as** *adv*: **just as... as** tan... como, igual de... que.

➤ **just now** *adv* **- 1.** [a short time ago] hace un momento **- 2.** [at this moment] justo ahora, ahora mismo.

justice ['dʒʌstɪs] *n* justicia *f*; **to bring sb to justice** llevar a alguien ante los tribunales; **to do justice to sthg** [to a job] estar a la altura de algo; [to a meal] hacerle los honores a algo.

Justice of the Peace (*pl* **Justices of the Peace**) *n* juez *mf* de paz.

justifiable ['dʒʌstɪfaɪəbl] *adj* justificable.

justifiable homicide *n* ≃ homocidio *m* con eximente de defensa propia.

justifiably ['dʒʌstɪfaɪəblɪ] *adv* justificadamente.

justification [,dʒʌstɪfɪ'keɪʃn] *n* justificación *f*.

justify ['dʒʌstɪfaɪ] (*pt & pp* **-ied**) *vt* **- 1.** [explain]: **to justify (sthg/doing sthg)** justifica (algo/el haber hecho algo) **- 2.** TYPO justificar.

justly ['dʒʌstlɪ] *adv* justamente.

jut [dʒʌt] (*pt & pp* **-ted**, *cont* **-ting**) *vi*: **to jut (out)** sobresalir.

jute [dʒuːt] *n* yute *m*.

juvenile ['dʒuːvənaɪl] <> *adj* **- 1.** LAW juvenil **- 2.** *pej* [childish] infantil. <> *n* LAW menor *mf* (de edad).

juvenile court *n* tribunal *m* (tutelar) de menores.

juvenile delinquent *n* delincuente *mf* juvenil.

juxtapose [,dʒʌkstə'pəʊz] *vt*: **to juxtapose sthg (with)** yuxtaponer algo (a).

juxtaposition [,dʒʌkstəpə'zɪʃn] *n* yuxtaposición *f*.

k (*pl* **k's** OR **ks**), **K** (*pl* **K's** OR **Ks**) [keɪ] *n* [letter] k *f*, K *f*.

➤ **K** *n* **- 1.** (*abbr of* kilobyte(s)) K **- 2.** *abbr of* Knight **- 3.** *abbr of* thousand.

kaftan ['kæftæn] *n* caftán *m*.

Kalahari Desert [,kælə'hɑːrɪ-] *n*: **the Kalahari Desert** el desierto de Kalahari.

kale [keɪl] *n* col *f* rizada.

kaleidoscope [kə'laɪdəskəʊp] *n* lit & fig caleidoscopio *m*, calidoscopio *m*.

kamikaze [,kæmɪ'kɑːzɪ] *n* kamikaze *m*.

Kampuchea [,kæmpu'tʃɪə] *n* Kampuchea.

kangaroo [,kæŋgə'ruː] *n* canguro *m*.

Kansas ['kænzəs] *n* Kansas.

kaolin ['keɪəlɪn] *n* caolín *m*.

kaput [kə'pʊt] *adj* inf escacharrado(da).

karaoke [kɑːrɑː'əʊkɪ] *n* karaoke *m*.

karat ['kærət] *n* US quilate *m*.

karate [kə'rɑːtɪ] *n* kárate *m*.

Kashmir [kæʃ'mɪə] *n* Cachemira.

Katar = **Qatar**.

Katmandu [,kætmæn'duː] *n* Katmandú.

kayak ['kaɪæk] *n* kayac *m*.

Kazakhstan [,kæzæk'stɑːn] *n* (el) Kazajstán.

Kb *n* [comput] Kb.

KC (*abbr of* King's Counsel) *abogado del Estado*.

kcal (*abbr of* kilocalorie) kcal.

kebab [kɪ'bæb] *n* pincho *m* moruno, brocheta *f*.

kedgeree ['kedʒəriː] *n* (U) UK plato de arroz, pescado y huevo duro.

keel [kiːl] *n* quilla *f*; **on an even keel** en equilibrio estable.

➤ **keel over** *vi* [ship] zozobrar; [person] desplomarse.

keen [kiːn] *adj* **- 1.** [enthusiastic] entusiasta; **to be keen on sthg** ser aficionado(da) a algo; **she is keen on you** tú le gustas; **I'm not keen on the idea** no me entusiasma la idea; **to be keen to do** OR **on doing sthg** tener ganas de hacer algo **- 2.** [intense - interest, desire] profundo(da); [- competition] reñido(da) **- 3.** [sharp - sense of smell, hearing, vision] agudo(da); [- eye, ear] fino(na); [- mind] agudo, penetrante.

keenly ['ki:nlɪ] adv - **1.** [intensely - interested] vivamente; [- contested] reñidamente - **2.** [intently] atentamente.

keenness ['ki:nnɪs] n - **1.** [enthusiasm] entusiasmo m - **2.** [of interest] intensidad f, viveza f; [of competition] ferocidad f - **3.** [sharpness] agudeza f.

keep [ki:p] ◇ vt (pt & pp **kept**) - **1.** [maintain in a particular place or state or position] mantener; **to keep sb waiting/awake** tener a alguien esperando/despierto; **to keep sb talking** darle conversación a alguien - **2.** [retain] quedarse con; **keep the change** quédese con la vuelta - **3.** [put aside, store] guardar; **to keep sthg for sb** guardar algo para alguien - **4.** [prevent]: **to keep sb/sthg from doing sthg** impedir a alguien/algo hacer algo - **5.** [detain] detener; **what kept you?** ¿por qué llegas tan tarde? - **6.** [fulfil, observe - appointment] acudir a; [- promise, vow] cumplir - **7.** [not disclose]: **to keep sthg from sb** ocultar algo a alguien; **to keep sthg to o.s.** no contarle algo a nadie - **8.** [in writing - record, account] llevar; [- diary] escribir; [- note] tomar - **9.** [own - animals, shop] tener

▸▸ **they keep themselves to themselves** no tienen mucho trato con nadie. ◇ vi (pt & pp **kept**) - **1.** [remain] mantenerse; **to keep quiet** callarse; **to keep still** estarse quieto - **2.** [continue]: **to keep doing sthg** [repeatedly] no dejar de hacer algo; [without stopping] continuar OR seguir haciendo algo; **to keep going** seguir adelante - **3.** [continue in a particular direction] continuar, seguir; **to keep left/right** circular por la izquierda/derecha; **to keep north/south** seguir hacia el norte/el sur - **4.** [food] conservar - **5.** UK [be in a particular state of health] estar, andar; **how are you keeping?** ¿qué tal estás? ◇ n - **1.** [food, board etc] manutención f, sustento m; **to earn one's keep** ganarse el pan - **2.** [of castle] torre f del homenaje.

◆ **keeps** n: **for keeps** para siempre.
◆ **keep at** vt insep: **to keep at it** perseverar.
◆ **keep back** ◇ vt sep [information] ocultar; [money, salary] retener. ◇ vi no acercarse.
◆ **keep down** vt sep - **1.** [repress] contener - **2.** [food]: **she can't keep anything down** lo vomita todo.
◆ **keep off** vt insep [subject] 'evitar'; **'keep off the grass'** 'no pisar la hierba'.
◆ **keep on** ◇ vi - **1.** [continue]: **to keep on doing sthg** [continue to do] continuar OR seguir haciendo algo; [do repeatedly] no dejar de hacer algo - **2.** [talk incessantly]: **to keep on (about)** seguir dale que te pego (con). ◇ vt sep [not sack] mantener en el puesto.
◆ **keep on at** vt insep UK dar la lata a.

◆ **keep out** ◇ vt sep no dejar pasar. ◇ vi: **'keep out'** 'prohibida la entrada'.
◆ **keep to** ◇ vt insep - **1.** [follow] ceñirse a - **2.** [fulfil, meet] cumplir. ◇ vt sep [limit] limitar
◆ **keep up** ◇ vt sep mantener; **to keep up appearances** guardar las apariencias; **keep up the good work!** ¡sigue así! ◇ vi - **1.** [maintain pace, level etc] mantener el ritmo; **to keep up with sb/sthg** seguir el ritmo de alguien/algo - **2.** [stay in contact]: **to keep up with sb** mantener contacto con alguien

keeper ['ki:pə'] n - **1.** [of park, zoo] guarda mf - **2.** UK [goalkeeper] guardameta m.

keep-fit UK ◇ n (U) ejercicios mpl de mantenimiento. ◇ comp [class, exercises] de mantenimiento; [enthusiast] de ejercicios de mantenimiento.

keeping ['ki:pɪŋ] n - **1.** [care]: **in sb's keeping** al cuidado de alguien; **in safe keeping** en lugar seguro - **2.** [conformity, harmony]: **in/out of keeping (with)** de acuerdo/en desacuerdo (con).

keepsake ['ki:pseɪk] n recuerdo m.

keg [keg] n barrilete m.

kelp [kelp] n varec m, alga f marina.

ken [ken] n: **to be beyond one's ken** resultar del todo incomprensible para uno.

kennel ['kenl] n - **1.** [for dog] caseta f del perro - **2.** US = **kennels**.
◆ **kennels** npl UK residencia f para perros.

Kentucky [ken'tʌkɪ] n Kentucky.

Kenya ['kenjə] n Kenia.

Kenyan ['kenjən] ◇ adj keniano(na). ◇ n keniano m, -na f.

kept [kept] pt & pp ▷ **keep**.

kerb [kɜ:b] n UK bordillo m, cordón m de la vereda R Plata, cuneta f Chile, bordo m de la banqueta Méx, sardinel m Col.

kerb crawler [-,krɔ:lə'] n UK conductor que busca prostitutas desde el coche.

kerbstone ['kɜ:bstəʊn] n UK piedra f de bordillo.

kerfuffle [kə'fʌfl] n UK inf follón m.

kernel ['kɜ:nl] n [of nut, fruit] pepita f.

kerosene ['kerəsi:n] n queroseno m.

kestrel ['kestrəl] n cernícalo m.

ketchup ['ketʃəp] n ketchup m, catsup m.

kettle ['ketl] n tetera f para hervir, hervidor m; **to put the kettle on** poner el agua a hervir.

kettledrum ['ketldrʌm] n timbal m.

key [ki:] ◇ n - **1.** [for lock] llave f - **2.** [of typewriter, computer, piano] tecla f - **3.** [explanatory list] clave *f* - **4.** [solution, answer]: **the key (to)** la clave (de) - **5.** MUS [scale of notes] tono *m*; **off key** desafinado(da). ⬦ *adj* clave *(inv).*

➤ **key in** *vt sep* teclear.

keyboard ['ki:bɔːd] *n* teclado *m*.

keyboarder ['ki:bɔːdəʳ] *n* teclista *mf*.

keyboard shortcut *n* atajo *m* de teclado.

key card *n* tarjeta *f* de acceso.

keyed up [ki:d-] *adj* nervioso(sa).

keyhole ['ki:həʊl] *n* ojo *m* de la cerradura.

keyhole surgery *n* cirugía *f* endoscópica.

keynote ['ki:nəʊt] ⬦ *n* núcleo *m* fundamental. ⬦ *comp*: **keynote speech** discurso *m* principal.

keypad ['ki:pæd] *n* teclado *m* numérico.

keypunch ['ki:pʌntʃ] *n* perforadora *f*.

key ring *n* llavero *m*.

keystone ['ki:stəʊn] *n* - **1.** [stone] clave *f* - **2.** [essential idea] piedra *f* angular.

keystroke ['ki:strəʊk] *n* pulsación *f (de tecla).*

kg (*abbr of* **kilogram**) kg *m*.

KGB *n* KGB *m*.

khaki ['kɑːki] ⬦ *adj* caqui. ⬦ *n* caqui *m*.

➤ **khakis** *npl* US pantalones *mpl* de soldado.

Khmer [kə'meəʳ] ⬦ *adj* jemer. ⬦ *n* - **1.** [person] jemer *mf*; **the Khmer Rouge** los Jemeres Rojos - **2.** [language] jemer *m*.

kibbutz [kɪ'bʊts] (*pl* **kibbutzim** [ˌkɪbʊt'siːm] OR **-es**) *n* kibutz *m*.

kick [kɪk] ⬦ *n* - **1.** [from person] patada *f*, puntapié *m*; [from animal] coz *f* - **2.** *inf* [excitement]: **to do sthg for kicks** hacer algo para divertirse; **to get a kick from sthg** disfrutar con algo - **3.** *inf* [of drink]: **to have a kick** estar cantidad de fuerte. ⬦ *vt* - **1.** [hit once with foot] dar una patada OR un puntapié a; [hit repeatedly with foot] dar patadas OR puntapiés a; **he kicked the ball back to them** les devolvió la pelota de un puntapié - **2.** *fig* [be angry with]: **I could have kicked myself** estaba que me tiraba de los pelos - **3.** *inf* [give up] dejar. ⬦ *vi* [person] dar patadas; [animal] dar coces, cocear.

➤ **kick about, kick around** *vi* UK *inf* andar rondando por ahí.

➤ **kick back** *vi* US [relax] relajarse.

➤ **kick in** *vi* - **1.** [drug] surtir efecto - **2.** [start] empezar.

➤ **kick off** *vi* - **1.** [football] hacer el saque inicial - **2.** *inf* [start activity] empezar.

➤ **kick out** *vt sep inf* echar, poner de patitas en la calle.

➤ **kick up** *vt insep inf* [a fuss, racket] armar.

kickoff ['kɪkɒf] *n* saque *m* inicial.

kick-start *vt* [bike] arrancar *(dando una patada al pedal)*; [economy] reactivar.

kid [kɪd] ⬦ *n* - **1.** *inf* [child] crío *m*, -a *f*, chavalín *m*, -ina *f* - **2.** *inf* [young person] chico *m*, -ca *f*, chaval *m*, -la *f*, pibe *m*, -ba *f* Amér - **3.** [young goat] cabrito *m* - **4.** [leather] cabritilla *f*. ⬦ *comp* *inf* [brother, sister] menor, pequeño(ña). ⬦ *vt* (*pt* & *pp* **-ded**, *cont* **-ding**) *inf* - **1.** [tease] tomar el pelo a - **2.** [delude]: **to kid o.s.** hacerse ilusiones. ⬦ *vi* (*pt* & *pp* **-ded**, *cont* **-ding**) *inf*: **to be kidding** estar de broma; **no kidding!** [honestly] ¡en serio!; [really] ¡no me digas!

kiddie, kiddy ['kɪdɪ] (*pl* **-ies**) *n* *inf* crío *m*, -a *f*.

kid gloves *npl*: **to treat** OR **handle sb with kid gloves** tratar a alguien con mucho tacto.

kidnap ['kɪdnæp] (UK **-ped**, *cont* **-ping**) (US **-ed**, *cont* **-ing**) *vt* secuestrar, raptar, plagiar Amér.

kidnapping UK, **kidnaping** US ['kɪdnæpɪŋ] *n* secuestro *m*, rapto *m*, plagio *m* Amér.

kidney ['kɪdnɪ] (*pl* **kidneys**) *n* ANAT & CULIN riñón *m*.

kidney bean *n* judía *f* pinta, frijol *m* Amér OR poroto *m* Andes rojo *(con forma de riñón)*, caraota *f* roja *(con forma de riñón)* Ven.

kidney machine *n* riñón *m* artificial.

Kilimanjaro [ˌkɪlɪmən'dʒɑːrəʊ] *n* Kilimanjaro.

kill [kɪl] ⬦ *vt* - **1.** [gen] matar; **he was killed in an accident** murió en un accidente; **my feet are killing me!** ¡cómo me duelen los pies! - **2.** *fig* [cause to end, fail] poner fin a - **3.** [occupy]: **to kill time** matar el tiempo. ⬦ *vi* matar. ⬦ *n* - **1.** [killing]: **we watched the wolves move in for the kill** vimos cómo los lobos se preparaban para caer sobre su presa - **2.** [dead animal] presa *f*.

➤ **kill off** *vt sep* - **1.** [cause death of] acabar con - **2.** *fig* [cause to end] poner fin a.

killer ['kɪləʳ] *n* - **1.** [person, animal] asesino *m*, -na *f* - **2.** [disease] enfermedad *f* mortal.

killer whale *n* orca *f*.

killing ['kɪlɪŋ] ⬦ *adj inf* [very funny] desternillante. ⬦ *n* asesinato *m*; **to make a killing** *inf* hacer tu agosto, forrarse.

killjoy ['kɪldʒɔɪ] *n* aguafiestas *mf inv*.

kiln [kɪln] *n* horno *m*.

kilo ['kiːləʊ] (*pl* **-s**) (*abbr of* **kilogram**) *n* kilo *m*.

kilo- [kɪlə] *prefix* kilo-.

kilobyte ['kɪləbaɪt] *n* kilobyte *m*.

kilocalorie ['kɪləˌkælərɪ] *n* kilocaloría *f*.

kilogram(me) ['kɪləgræm] *n* kilogramo *m*.

kilohertz ['kɪləhɜːtz] (*pl* **kilohertz**) *n* kilohercio *m*.

kilojoule ['kɪlədʒuːl] *n* kilojulio *m*.

kilometre UK ['kɪləˌmiːtəʳ], **kilometer** US [kɪ'lɒmɪtəʳ] *n* kilómetro *m*.

kilowatt ['kɪləwɒt] *n* kilovatio *m*.

kilt [kɪlt] *n* falda *f* escocesa.

kimono [kɪ'məʊnəʊ] (*pl* **-s**) *n* kimono *m*.

kin [kɪn] ⊏▷ **kith**.

kind [kaɪnd] ◇ *adj* [person, gesture] amable; [thought] considerado(da); **to be kind to sb** ser amable con alguien; **would you be so kind as to...?** ¿sería usted tan amable de...? ◇ *n* tipo *m*, clase *f*; **a kind of** una especie de; **all kinds of** todo tipo de; **kind of** *esp US inf* bastante; **nothing of the kind** nada por el estilo; **coffee of a kind** una especie de café; **they're two of a kind** son tal para cual; **in kind** [payment] en especie.

kindergarten ['kɪndə,gɑ:tn] *n* jardín *m* de infancia.

kind-hearted [-'hɑ:tɪd] *adj* bondadoso(sa).

kindle ['kɪndl] *vt* **- 1.** [fire] encender **- 2.** *fig* [idea, feeling] despertar.

kindling ['kɪndlɪŋ] *n* (*U*) leña *f* menuda, astillas *fpl*.

kindly ['kaɪndlɪ] ◇ *adj* (*comp* **-ier**, *superl* **-iest**) amable, bondadoso(sa). ◇ *adv* **- 1.** [gently, favourably] amablemente; **to look kindly on sthg/sb** mirar algo/a alguien con buenos ojos **- 2.** [please]: **will you kindly...?** ¿sería tan amable de...? ▸▸ **not to take kindly to sthg** no tomarse algo bien.

kindness ['kaɪndnɪs] *n* **- 1.** [gentleness] amabilidad *f* **- 2.** [helpful act] favor *m*.

kindred ['kɪndrɪd] *adj* [similar] afín; **kindred spirit** alma *f* gemela.

kinetic [kɪ'netɪk] *adj* cinético(ca).

kinfolk(s) ['kɪnfəʊk(s)] *US* = **kinsfolk**.

king [kɪŋ] *n* rey *m*.

kingdom ['kɪŋdəm] *n* reino *m*.

kingfisher ['kɪŋ,fɪʃər] *n* martín *m* pescador.

kingpin ['kɪŋpɪn] *n* *fig* [person] persona *f* clave.

king-size(d) [-saɪz(d)] *adj* [cigarette] extralargo; [pack] gigante; [bed] extragrande.

kink [kɪŋk] *n* [in rope] retorcimiento *m*; [in hair] rizo *m*.

kinky ['kɪŋkɪ] (*comp* **-ier**, *superl* **-iest**) *adj inf* morboso(sa), pervertido(da).

kinship ['kɪnʃɪp] *n* **- 1.** [family relationship] parentesco *m* **- 2.** [closeness] afinidad *f*.

kiosk ['ki:ɒsk] *n* **- 1.** [small shop] quiosco *m* **- 2.** *UK* [telephone box] cabina *f* telefónica.

kip [kɪp] *UK inf* ◇ *n* cabezadita *f*, sueñecito *m*. ◇ *vi* (*pt* & *pp* **-ped**, *cont* **-ping**) sobar, dormir.

kipper ['kɪpər] *n* arenque *m* ahumado.

Kirk [kɜ:k] *n Scotland*: **the Kirk** la Iglesia de Escocia.

kirsch [kɪəʃ] *n* kirsch *m*.

kiss [kɪs] ◇ *n* beso *m*. ◇ *vt* besar; **to kiss sb goodbye** dar un beso de despedida a alguien. ◇ *vi* besarse.

kiss curl *n UK* caracol *m* (*rizo*).

kiss of life *n* [to resuscitate sb]: **the kiss of life** la respiración boca a boca.

kit [kɪt] *n* **- 1.** [set of implements] equipo *m* **- 2.** *UK* [clothes] equipo *m* **- 3.** [to be assembled] modelo *m* para armar, kit *m*. ▸ **kit out** *vt sep* (*pt* & *pp* **-ted**, *cont* **-ting**) *UK* equipar.

kit bag *n* macuto *m*, petate *m*.

kitchen ['kɪtʃɪn] *n* cocina *f*.

kitchenette [,kɪtʃɪ'net] *n* cocina *f* pequeña.

kitchen garden *n* huerto *m*.

kitchen sink *n* fregadero *m*.

kitchen unit *n* módulo *m* de cocina.

kitchenware ['kɪtʃɪnweər] *n* (*U*) artículos *mpl* de cocina.

kite [kaɪt] *n* **- 1.** [toy] cometa *f*, papalote *m* *Amér C & Méx*, volantín *m* *Chile*, barrilete *m* *R Plata*, papagayo *m* *Ven* **- 2.** [bird] milano *m*.

Kite mark *n UK* marchamo oficial de calidad.

kitesurfing ['kaɪtsɜ:fɪŋ] *n* kitesurf *m*.

kith [kɪθ] *n*: **kith and kin** parientes *mpl* y amigos.

kitsch [kɪtʃ] *n* kitsch *m*.

kitten ['kɪtn] *n* gatito *m*.

kitty ['kɪtɪ] (*pl* **-ies**) *n* [for bills, drinks] fondo *m* común; [in card games] bote *m*, puesta *f*.

kiwi ['ki:wi:] *n* **- 1.** [bird] kiwi *m* **- 2.** *inf* [New Zealander] neocelandés *m*, -esa *f*.

kiwi (fruit) *n* kiwi *m*.

KKK *abbr of* Ku Klux Klan.

klaxon ['klæksn] *n* bocina *f*, claxon *m*.

Kleenex® ['kli:neks] *n* kleenex® *m*, pañuelo *m* de papel.

kleptomaniac [,kleptə'meɪnɪæk] *n* cleptómano *m*, -na *f*.

km (*abbr of* **kilometre**) km.

km/h (*abbr of* **kilometres per hour**) km/h.

knack [næk] *n*: **it's easy once you've got the knack** es fácil cuando le coges el tranquillo; **he has the knack of appearing at the right moment** tiene el don de aparecer en el momento adecuado.

knacker ['nækər] *UK* ◇ *n* [horse slaughterer] matarife *m*. ◇ *vt inf* **- 1.** [exhaust] dejar hecho(cha) polvo a **- 2.** [break] cascar.

knackered ['nækəd] *adj UK inf* **- 1.** [exhausted] hecho(cha) polvo **- 2.** [broken] cascado(da).

knapsack ['næpsæk] *n* mochila *f*.

knave [neɪv] *n* [playing card - in British pack] jota *f*; [- in Spanish pack] sota *f*.

knead [niːd] *vt* amasar.

knee [niː] <> *n* rodilla *f*; **to be on one's knees** [kneeling] estar de rodillas; **to bring sb to their knees** *fig* hacer hincar la rodilla a alguien. <> *vt* dar un rodillazo a.

kneecap ['niːkæp] *n* rótula *f*.

knee-deep *adj* [snow, water]: **the snow was knee-deep** la nieve llegaba hasta las rodillas; [person]: **knee-deep in water** con el agua hasta las rodillas.

knee-high *adj* que llega hasta las rodillas.

kneel [niːl] *vi* (*UK* **knelt**, *US* **-ed** OR **knelt**) [go down on knees] arrodillarse; [be on knees] estar de rodillas.

◆ **kneel down** *vi* arrodillarse.

knee-length *adj* hasta las rodillas.

knees-up *n UK inf* jolgorio *m*, juerga *f*.

knell [nel] *n* toque *m* de difuntos.

knelt [nelt] *pt* & *pp* ⊳ **kneel**.

knew [njuː] *pt* ⊳ **know**.

knickers ['nɪkəz] *npl* - **1.** *UK* [underwear] bragas *fpl*, calzones *mpl Amér*, pantaletas *fpl Amér C* & *Méx*, bombacha *f R Plata*, blúmer *m Amér C* - **2.** *US* [knickerbockers] bombachos *mpl*.

knick-knack ['nɪknæk] *n* chuchería *f*, baratija *f*.

knife [naɪf] <> *n* (*pl* **knives**) cuchillo *m*. <> *vt* acuchillar.

knight [naɪt] <> *n* - **1.** HIST caballero *m* - **2.** [knighted man] hombre con el título de 'Sir' - **3.** [in chess] caballo *m*. <> *vt* conceder el título de 'Sir' a.

knighthood ['naɪthʊd] *n* - **1.** [present-day title] título *m* de 'Sir' - **2.** HIST título *m* de caballero.

knit [nɪt] <> *adj*: **closely** OR **tightly knit** muy unido(da). <> *vt* (*pt* & *pp* **knit** OR **-ted**, *cont* **-ting**) [make with wool] tejer, tricotar. <> *vi* (*pt* & *pp* **knit** OR **-ted**, *cont* **-ting**) - **1.** [with wool] hacer punto - **2.** [join] soldarse.

knitted ['nɪtɪd] *adj* de punto.

knitting ['nɪtɪŋ] *n* (*U*) - **1.** [activity] labor *f* de punto - **2.** [work produced] punto *m*, calceta *f*.

knitting machine *n* máquina *f* de tricotar, tricotosa *f*.

knitting needle *n* aguja *f* de hacer punto.

knitwear ['nɪtweəʳ] *n* (*U*) género *m* OR ropa *f* de punto.

knives [naɪvz] *npl* ⊳ **knife**.

knob [nɒb] *n* - **1.** [on door, drawer, bedstead] pomo *m* - **2.** [on TV, radio etc] botón *m*.

knobbly *UK* ['nɒblɪ] (*comp* **-ier**, *superl* **-iest**), **knobby** *US* ['nɒbɪ] (*comp* **-ier**, *superl* **-iest**) *adj* [gen] nudoso(sa); [knees] huesudo(da).

knock [nɒk] <> *n* - **1.** [hit] golpe *m* - **2.** *inf* [piece of bad luck] revés *m*. <> *vt* - **1.** [hit hard] golpear; **to knock a nail into a wall** clavar un clavo en una pared; **to knock one's head** darse en la cabeza; **to knock sb over** [gen] hacer caer a alguien; AUT atropellar a alguien; **to knock sthg over** tirar OR volcar algo, voltear algo *Amér* - **2.** [make by hitting] hacer, abrir; **to knock a hole in a wall** abrir un agujero en una pared - **3.** *inf* [criticize] cargarse, poner por los suelos. <> *vi* - **1.** [on door]: **to knock (at** OR **on)** llamar (a) - **2.** [car engine] golpetear.

◆ **knock about, knock around** *inf* <> *vt sep* [beat up] pegar. <> *vi* - **1.** [travel a lot] rodar - **2.** [spend time]: **to knock about with sb** andar con alguien.

◆ **knock back** *vt sep inf* pimplarse.

◆ **knock down** *vt sep* - **1.** [subj: car, driver] atropellar - **2.** [building] derribar - **3.** [price] rebajar.

◆ **knock off** <> *vt sep* - **1.** [lower price by]: **I'll knock £5 off it** lo rebajaré en cinco libras - **2.** *inf* [do quickly] despachar. <> *vi inf* [stop working] parar de currar.

◆ **knock out** *vt sep* - **1.** [subj: person, punch] dejar sin conocimiento; [subj: boxer] dejar fuera de combate; [subj: drug] dejar dormido a - **2.** [eliminate from competition] eliminar.

◆ **knock up** <> *vt sep* [make hurriedly] hacer de prisa. <> *vi* TENNIS pelotear.

knocker ['nɒkəʳ] *n* [on door] aldaba *f*.

knocking ['nɒkɪŋ] *n* - **1.** (*U*) [on door etc] golpes *mpl* - **2.** *inf* [criticism] palos *mpl*, críticas *fpl*.

knock-kneed [-'niːd] *adj* patizambo(ba).

knock-on effect *n UK* reacción *f* en cadena; **to have a knock-on effect on sthg** repercutir en algo.

knockout ['nɒkaʊt] *n* K.O. *m*

knockout competition *n UK* competición *f* por el sistema de eliminación.

knock-up *n* TENNIS peloteo *m*.

knot [nɒt] <> *n* - **1.** [gen] nudo *m*; **to tie/untie a knot** hacer/deshacer un nudo; **to tie the knot** *inf* [marry] casarse - **2.** [of people] corrillo *m*. <> *vt* (*pt* & *pp* **-ted**, *cont* **-ting**) anudar.

knotty ['nɒtɪ] (*comp* **-ier**, *superl* **-iest**) *adj* intrincado(da).

know [nəʊ] <> *vt* (*pt* **knew**, *pp* **known**) - **1.** [gen]: **to know (that)** saber (que); [language] saber hablar; **to know how to do sthg** saber hacer algo; **to know sthg backwards** saberse algo al dedillo; **to get to know sthg** enterarse de algo; **to let sb know (about)** avisar a alguien (de) - **2.** [be familiar with - person,

place] conocer; **to get to know sb** llegar a conocer a alguien. ◇ *vi* (*pt* **knew**, *pp* **known**)
- 1. [have knowledge] saber; **to know of** OR **about sthg** saber algo, estar enterado(da) de algo; **he's not her brother – I know** no es su hermano – ya lo sé; **I don't know** no lo sé; **you know** [to emphasize] ¿sabes?; [to remind] ¡ya sabes!, ¡sí hombre!; **as far as I know** que yo sepa; **God** OR **Heaven knows!** ¡sabe Dios!; **there is no knowing...** no hay modo de saber...; **I know better** a mí no me engaña **- 2.** [be knowledgeable]: **to know about sthg** saber de algo. ◇ *n*: **to be in the know** estar enterado(da).

know-all, know-it-all *n* UK sabelotodo *mf*, sabihondo *m*, -da *f*.

know-how *n* conocimientos *mpl*, know-how *m*.

knowing ['nəʊɪŋ] *adj* cómplice.

knowingly ['nəʊɪŋlɪ] *adv* **- 1.** [in knowing manner] con complicidad **- 2.** [intentionally] a sabiendas.

know-it-all = **know-all**.

knowledge ['nɒlɪdʒ] *n* (U) **- 1.** [awareness] conocimiento *m*; **it's common knowledge that** es de dominio común que; **to my knowledge** que yo sepa, según tengo entendido; **to the best of my knowledge** por lo que yo sé **- 2.** [facts known by individual] conocimientos *mpl*.

knowledgeable ['nɒlɪdʒəbl] *adj* entendido(da).

known [nəʊn] ◇ *pp* ▷ **know**. ◇ *adj* conocido(da).

knuckle ['nʌkl] *n* **- 1.** [on hand] nudillo *m* **- 2.** [of pork] codillo *m*.

◆ **knuckle down** *vi* ponerse seriamente a trabajar; **to knuckle down to sthg/to doing sthg** dedicarse seriamente a algo/a hacer algo.

◆ **knuckle under** *vi* pasar por el aro.

KO (*abbr of* **knock-out**) K.O. *m*

koala (bear) [kəʊ'ɑːlə-] *n* koala *m*.

kook [kuːk] *n* US inf majara *mf*, majareta *mf*.

kooky ['kuːkɪ] (*comp* -**ier**, *superl* -**iest**) *adj* US inf majara, majareta.

Koran [kɒ'rɑːn] *n*: **the Koran** el Corán.

Korea [kə'rɪə] *n* Corea.

Korean [kə'rɪən] ◇ *adj* coreano(na). ◇ *n* **- 1.** [person] coreano *m*, -na *f* **- 2.** [language] coreano *m*.

kosher ['kəʊʃəʳ] *adj* **- 1.** [meat] kosher, permitido(da) por la religión judía **- 2.** inf [reputable] limpio(pia), legal.

Kosovo ['kɒsəvəʊ] *n* Kosovo *m*.

kowtow [ˌkaʊ'taʊ] *vi*: **to kowtow (to)** arrastrarse OR rebajarse (ante).

Kremlin ['kremlɪn] *n*: **the Kremlin** el Kremlin.

KS *abbr of* **Kansas**.

KT *abbr of* **Knight**.

Kuala Lumpur [ˌkwɑːlə'lʊmpəʳ] *n* Kuala Lumpur.

kudos ['kjuːdɒs] *n* prestigio *m*.

Ku Klux Klan [kuːklʌks'klæn] *n*: **the Ku Klux Klan** el Ku-Klux-Klan.

kumquat ['kʌmkwɒt] *n* naranjita *f* china.

kung fu [ˌkʌŋ'fuː] *n* kung-fu *m*.

Kurd [kɜːd] *n* kurdo *m*, -da *f*.

Kurdish ['kɜːdɪʃ] *adj* kurdo(da).

Kurdistan [kɜːdɪ'stɑːn] *n* (el) Kurdistán.

Kuwait [kjuː'weɪt] *n* Kuwait.

Kuwaiti [kjuː'weɪtɪ] ◇ *adj* kuwaití. ◇ *n* kuwaití *mf*.

kW (*abbr of* **kilowatt**) kW.

KY *abbr of* **Kentucky**.

l [pl **l's** OR **ls**), **L** (*pl* **L's** OR **Ls**) [el] *n* [letter] l *f*, L *f*.
◆ **L** *n* **- 1.** *abbr of* **lake** **- 2.** (*abbr of* **large**) G **- 3.** (*abbr of* **left**) izq. **- 4.** (*abbr of* **learner**) L.

l (*abbr of* **litre**) l.

la [lɑː] *n* MUS la *m*.

LA *n* **- 1.** (*abbr of* **Los Angeles**) Los Ángeles **- 2.** (*abbr of* **Louisiana**) Luisiana.

lab [læb] inf = **laboratory**.

label ['leɪbl] ◇ *n* **- 1.** [identification] etiqueta *f* **- 2.** [of record] sello *m* discográfico, casa *f* discográfica. ◇ *vt* (UK -**led**, *cont* -**ling**, US -**ed**, *cont* -**ing**) **- 1.** [fix label to] etiquetar **- 2.** pej [describe]: **to label sb (as)** calificar OR etiquetar a alguien (de).

labor US = **labour**.

laboratory [UK lə'bɒrətrɪ, US 'læbrə,tɔːrɪ] (*pl* -**ies**), **lab** ◇ *n* laboratorio *m*. ◇ *comp* de laboratorio.

Labor Day *n* US Día *m* del Trabajador *(el primer lunes de septiembre)*.

laborious [lə'bɔːrɪəs] *adj* laborioso(sa).
labor union *n* US sindicato *m*.
labour *UK*, **labor** *US* ['leɪbər] ◇ *n* - **1.** [work] trabajo *m* - **2.** [piece of work] esfuerzo *m* - **3.** [workers] mano *f* de obra - **4.** [giving birth] parto *m*; **in labour** de parto. ◇ *vt* insistir sobre. ◇ *vi* - **1.** [work] trabajar - **2.** [work with difficulty]: **to labour at** OR **over** trabajar afanosamente en - **3.** [persist]: **to labour under a delusion** ser víctima de una ilusión.
◆ **Labour** ◇ *adj* POL laborista. ◇ *n* (U) UK POL los laboristas.
labour camp *n* campo *m* de trabajo.
labour costs *npl* coste *m* de mano de obra.
laboured *UK*, **labored** *US* ['leɪbəd] *adj* [style] trabajoso(sa); [gait, breathing] penoso(sa), fatigoso(sa).
labourer *UK*, **laborer** *US* ['leɪbərər] *n* obrero *m*, -ra *f*.
labour force *n* mano *f* de obra.
labour-intensive *adj* que emplea mucha mano de obra.
labour market *n* mercado *m* de trabajo.
labour of love *n* trabajo *m* hecho por amor al arte.
labour pains *npl* dolores *mpl* del parto.
Labour Party *n* UK: **the Labour Party** el partido Laborista.
labour relations *npl* relaciones *fpl* laborales.
laboursaving *UK*, **laborsaving** *US* ['leɪbəseɪvɪŋ] *adj* que ahorra trabajo.
Labrador ['læbrədɔːr] *n* - **1.** [dog] labrador *m* - **2.** GEOG Labrador.

labyrinth ['læbərɪnθ] *n* laberinto *m*.
lace [leɪs] ◇ *n* - **1.** [fabric] encaje *m* - **2.** [shoelace] cordón *m*. ◇ *comp* de encaje. ◇ *vt* - **1.** [shoe, boot] atar - **2.** [drink, food]: **coffee laced with brandy** café con unas gotas de coñac.
◆ **lace up** *vt sep* atar.
lacemaking ['leɪs,meɪkɪŋ] *n* labor *f* de encaje.
laceration [,læsə'reɪʃn] *n fml* laceración *f*.
lace-up ◇ *adj* de cordón. ◇ *n* UK zapato *m* de cordón.
lack [læk] ◇ *n* falta *f*, carencia *f*; **for** OR **through lack of** por falta de; **there was no lack of excitement** no faltó emoción. ◇ *vt* carecer de. ◇ *vi*: **to be lacking in** carecer de; **to be lacking** faltar.
lackadaisical [,lækə'deɪzɪkl] *adj pej* apático(ca).
lackey ['lækɪ] (*pl* **lackeys**) *n pej* lacayo *m*.
lacklustre *UK*, **lackluster** *US* ['læk,lʌstər] *adj pej* soso(sa), apagado(da).
laconic [lə'kɒnɪk] *adj* lacónico(ca).
lacquer ['lækər] ◇ *n* laca *f*. ◇ *vt* - **1.** [wood, metal] laquear - **2.** [hair] poner laca en.
lacrosse [lə'krɒs] *n* lacrosse *m*.
lactic acid ['læktɪk-] *n* ácido *m* láctico.
lacy ['leɪsɪ] (*comp* **-ier**, *superl* **-iest**) *adj* de encaje.
lad [læd] *n inf* [boy] chaval *m*, chavalo *m* Amér; **come on lads!** ¡vamos chicos!
ladder ['lædər] ◇ *n* - **1.** [for climbing] escalera *f* - **2.** UK [in tights] carrera *f*. ◇ *vt* UK [tights] hacerse una carrera en. ◇ *vi* UK [tights] hacerse una carrera.
laden ['leɪdn] *adj*: **laden (with)** cargado(da) (de).
la-di-da, lah-di-dah [,lɑːdɪ'dɑː] *adj inf pej* cursi, afectado(da).
ladies *UK* ['leɪdɪz], **ladies' room** *US n* lavabo *m* de señoras.
ladle ['leɪdl] ◇ *n* cucharón *m*. ◇ *vt* servir con cucharón.
lady ['leɪdɪ] (*pl* **-ies**) ◇ *n* - **1.** [woman] señora *f* - **2.** [woman of high status] dama *f* - **3.** US inf [to address woman] señora *f*. ◇ *comp* mujer; **lady doctor** doctora *f*.
◆ **Lady** *n* - **1.** [woman of noble rank] lady *f* - **2.** RELIG: **Our Lady** Nuestra Señora *f*.
ladybird *UK* ['leɪdɪbɜːd], **ladybug** *US* ['leɪdɪbʌg] *n* mariquita *f*.
lady-in-waiting [-'weɪtɪŋ] (*pl* **ladies-in-waiting**) *n* dama *f* de honor.
lady-killer *n inf* tenorio *m*, castigador *m*.
ladylike ['leɪdɪlaɪk] *adj* elegante, propio(pia) de una señora.
lag [læg] ◇ *vi* (*pt & pp* **-ged**, *cont* **-ging**) - **1.** [move more slowly]: **to lag (behind)** reza-

garse **- 2.** [develop more slowly]: **to lag (behind)** andar a la zaga. ⬦ *vt* (*pt* & *pp* **-ged**, *cont* **-ging**) [pipes] revestir. ⬦ *n* [delay] retraso *m*, demora *f*.

lager [ˈlɑːɡəʳ] *n* cerveza *f* rubia.

lager lout *n UK* ≃ gamberro *m* de litrona.

lagging [ˈlæɡɪŋ] *n* revestimiento *m*.

lagoon [ləˈɡuːn] *n* laguna *f*.

lah-di-dah [ˌlɑːdɪˈdɑː] = **la-di-da**.

laid [leɪd] *pt* & *pp* ▷ **lay**.

laid-back *adj inf* relajado(da), cachazudo(da).

lain [leɪn] *pp* ▷ **lie**.

lair [leəʳ] *n* guarida *f*.

laissez-faire [ˌleɪseɪˈfeəʳ] ⬦ *adj* no intervencionista. ⬦ *n* política *f* económica de no intervencionismo.

laity [ˈleɪətɪ] *n RELIG:* **the laity** los seglares, los legos.

lake [leɪk] *n* lago *m*.

Lake District *n:* **the Lake District** *el Distrito de los Lagos al noroeste de Inglaterra.*

Lake Geneva *n* lago *m* Leman.

lakeside [ˈleɪksaɪd] *adj* a orillas del lago.

lamb [læm] *n* cordero *m*.

lambast [læmˈbæst], **lambaste** [læmˈbeɪst] *vt* vapulear.

lamb chop *n* chuleta *f* de cordero.

lambing [ˈlæmɪŋ] *n* época *f* del parto de las ovejas.

lambskin [ˈlæmskɪn] *n* piel *f* de cordero.

lambswool [ˈlæmzwʊl] ⬦ *n* lana *f* de cordero. ⬦ *comp* de lana de cordero.

lame [leɪm] *adj* **- 1.** [person, horse] cojo(ja) **- 2.** [excuse, argument] pobre.

lamé [ˈlɑːmeɪ] *n* lamé *m*.

lame duck *n* **- 1.** *fig* [person] inútil *mf*; [business] fracaso *m* **- 2.** *US* [President] presidente *m* saliente.

lamely [ˈleɪmlɪ] *adv* poco convincentemente.

lament [ləˈment] ⬦ *n* lamento *m*. ⬦ *vt* lamentar.

lamentable [ˈlæməntəbl] *adj* lamentable.

laminated [ˈlæmɪneɪtɪd] *adj* **- 1.** [gen] laminado(da) **- 2.** [ID card] plastificado(da).

lamp [læmp] *n* lámpara *f*.

lamplight [ˈlæmplaɪt] *n* luz *f* de la lámpara.

lampoon [læmˈpuːn] ⬦ *n* pasquín *m*, sátira *f*. ⬦ *vt* satirizar.

lamppost [ˈlæmppəʊst] *n* farola *f*, farol *m*.

lampshade [ˈlæmpʃeɪd] *n* pantalla *f* (*de lámpara*).

lance [lɑːns] ⬦ *n* lanza *f*. ⬦ *vt* abrir con lanceta.

lance corporal *n* soldado *m* de primera.

lancet [ˈlɑːnsɪt] *n* lanceta *f*.

Lancs. (*abbr of* **Lancashire**) *condado inglés.*

land [lænd] ⬦ *n* **- 1.** [gen] tierra *f* **- 2.** [property] tierras *fpl*, finca *f*. ⬦ *vt* **- 1.** [unload] desembarcar **- 2.** [plane] hacer aterrizar **- 3.** [catch - fish] pescar **- 4.** *inf* [obtain] conseguir, pillar **- 5.** *inf* [place]: **to land sb in sthg** meter a alguien en algo; **to land sb with sb/sthg** cargar a alguien con alguien/algo. ⬦ *vi* **- 1.** [by plane] aterrizar, tomar tierra **- 2.** [from ship] desembarcar **- 3.** [fall] caer **- 4.** [end up] ir a parar.

◆ **land up** *vi inf:* **to land up (in)** ir a parar (a).

landed gentry [ˈlændɪd-] *npl:* **the landed gentry** la aristocracia terrateniente.

landfill site [ˈlændfɪl-] *n* vertedero *m* de basuras.

landing [ˈlændɪŋ] *n* **- 1.** [of stairs] rellano *m*, descansillo *m* **- 2.** [of aeroplane] aterrizaje *m* **- 3.** [of person] desembarque *m*, desembarco *m*.

landing card *n* tarjeta *f* de desembarque.

landing craft *n* lancha *f* de desembarco.

landing gear *n* (*U*) tren *m* de aterrizaje.

landing stage *n* desembarcadero *m*.

landing strip *n* pista *f* de aterrizaje.

landlady [ˈlændˌleɪdɪ] (*pl* **-ies**) *n* **- 1.** [of rented room or building] casera *f* **- 2.** [of hotel, pub] patrona *f*.

landlocked [ˈlændlɒkt] *adj* sin acceso al mar.

landlord [ˈlændlɔːd] *n* **- 1.** [of rented room or building] dueño *m*, casero *m* **- 2.** [of pub] patrón *m*.

landmark [ˈlændmɑːk] *n* **- 1.** [prominent feature] punto *m* de referencia **- 2.** *fig* [in history] hito *m*.

landmine [ˈlændmaɪn] *n* mina *f* de tierra.

landowner [ˈlændˌəʊnəʳ] *n* terrateniente *mf*.

landscape [ˈlændskeɪp] ⬦ *n* paisaje *m*. ⬦ *vt* ajardinar.

landscape gardener *n* (jardinero *m*) paisajista *m*, (jardinera *f*) paisajista.

landslide [ˈlændslaɪd] *n* **- 1.** [of earth, rocks] desprendimiento *m* de tierras **- 2.** *POL* victoria *f* arrolladora *OR* aplastante.

landslip [ˈlændslɪp] *n* pequeño desprendimiento *m* de tierras.

lane [leɪn] *n* **- 1.** [road in country] camino *m* **- 2.** [road in town] callejuela *f*, callejón *m* **- 3.** [for traffic] carril *m*; **'keep in lane'** *cartel que prohíbe el cambio de carril* **- 4.** [in swimming pool, race track] calle *f* **- 5.** [for shipping, aircraft] ruta *f*.

language [ˈlæŋɡwɪdʒ] *n* **- 1.** [gen] idioma *m*, lengua *f* **- 2.** [faculty or style of communication & *COMPUT*] lenguaje *m*.

language laboratory *n* laboratorio *m* de idiomas.

languid ['læŋgwɪd] *adj* lánguido(da).
languish ['læŋgwɪʃ] *vi* [in misery] languidecer; [in prison] pudrirse.
languorous ['læŋgərəs] *adj liter* lánguido(da).
lank [læŋk] *adj* lacio(cia).
lanky ['læŋkɪ] (*comp* -ier, *superl* -iest) *adj* larguirucho(cha).
lanolin(e) ['lænəlɪn] *n* lanolina *f*.
lantern ['læntən] *n* farol *m*.
Laos [laus] *n* Laos.
Laotian ['lauʃən] <> *adj* laosiano(na). <> *n* - **1.** [person] laosiano *m*, -na *f* - **2.** [language] laosiano *m*.
lap [læp] <> *n* - **1.** [of person] regazo *m* - **2.** [of race] vuelta *f*. <> *vt* (*pt & pp* -ped, *cont* -ping) - **1.** [subj: animal] beber a lengüetadas - **2.** [overtake in race] doblar. <> *vi* (*pt & pp* -ped, *cont* -ping) [water, waves] romper con suavidad.
➤ **lap up** *vt sep* - **1.** [drink] beber a lengüetadas - **2.** *fig* [compliments, lies] tragarse; [information] asimilar con avidez.
laparoscopy [ˌlæpəˈrɒskəpɪ] (*pl* -ies) *n* laparoscopia *f*.
La Paz [læˈpæz] *n* La Paz.
lapdog ['læpdɒg] *n* [dog] perro *m* faldero.
lapel [ləˈpel] *n* solapa *f*.
Lapland ['læplænd] *n* Laponia.
Lapp [læp] <> *adj* lapón(ona). <> *n* - **1.** [person] lapón *m*, -ona *f* - **2.** [language] lapón *m*.
lapse [læps] <> *n* - **1.** [slip-up] fallo *m*, lapsus *m inv* - **2.** [in behaviour] desliz *m* - **3.** [of time] lapso *m*, periodo *m*. <> *vi* - **1.** [membership] caducar; [treatment, agreement] cumplir, expirar - **2.** [standards, quality] bajar momentáneamente; [tradition] extinguirse, desaparecer - **3.** [subj: person]: **to lapse into** terminar cayendo en.
lapsed [læpst] *adj* no practicante.
lap-top (computer) *n* COMPUT ordenador *m* portátil.
larceny ['lɑːsənɪ] *n* (*U*) hurto *m*, latrocinio *m*.
larch [lɑːtʃ] *n* alerce *m*.
lard [lɑːd] *n* manteca *f* de cerdo.
larder ['lɑːdər] *n* despensa *f*.
large [lɑːdʒ] *adj* [gen] grande; [family] numeroso(sa); [sum] importante.
➤ **at large** *adv* - **1.** [as a whole] en general - **2.** [escaped prisoner, animal] suelto(ta).
➤ **by and large** *adv* en general.
largely ['lɑːdʒlɪ] *adv* [mostly] en gran parte; [chiefly] principalmente.
larger-than-life ['lɑːdʒə-] *adj* exageradamente arquetípico(ca).
large-scale *adj* a gran escala.

largesse, largess US [lɑːˈdʒes] *n* generosidad *f*.
lark [lɑːk] *n* - **1.** [bird] alondra *f* - **2.** *inf* [joke] broma *f*; **for a lark** para divertirse.
➤ **lark about** *vi* hacer el tonto.
larva ['lɑːvə] (*pl* -vae [-viː]) *n* larva *f*.
laryngitis [ˌlærɪnˈdʒaɪtɪs] *n* (*U*) laringitis *f inv*.
larynx ['lærɪŋks] *n* laringe *f*.
lasagna, lasagne [ləˈzænjə] *n* (*U*) lasaña *f*.
lascivious [ləˈsɪvɪəs] *adj* lascivo(va), lujurioso(sa).
laser ['leɪzər] *n* láser *m*.
laser beam *n* rayo *m* láser.
laser printer *n* COMPUT impresora *f* láser.
laser show *n* juego *m* de luces láser.
lash [læʃ] <> *n* - **1.** [eyelash] pestaña *f* - **2.** [blow with whip] latigazo *m*. <> *vt* - **1.** *lit & fig* [whip] azotar - **2.** [tie]: **to lash sthg (to)** amarrar algo (a).
➤ **lash out** *vi* - **1.** [attack]: **to lash out at sb** [physically] soltar un golpe a alguien; [verbally] arremeter contra alguien - **2.** *UK inf* [spend money]: **to lash out (on sthg)** tirar la casa por la ventana (con algo).
lass [læs] *n* chavala *f*, muchacha *f*.
lasso [læˈsuː] <> *n* (*pl* -s) lazo *m*. <> *vt* (*pt & pp* -ed, *cont* -ing) coger con lazo, lazar.
last [lɑːst] <> *adj* último(ma); **last month/Tuesday** el mes/martes pasado; **last March** en marzo del año pasado; **last but one** penúltimo(ma); **last but two** antepenúltimo(ma); **last night** anoche; **down to the last detail** hasta el último detalle. <> *adv* - **1.** [most recently] por última vez; **when I last called him** la última vez que lo llamé - **2.** [finally, in final position] en último lugar; **he arrived last** llegó el último; **last but not least** por último, pero no por ello menos importante. <> *pron*: **the year/Saturday before last** no el año/sábado pasado, sino el anterior; **the last but one** el penúltimo (la penúltima); **the night before last** anteanoche; **the time before last** la vez anterior a la pasada; **to leave sthg till last** dejar algo para el final. <> *n*: **the last I saw/heard of him** la última vez que lo vi/que oí de él. <> *vi* durar; [food] conservarse.
➤ **at (long) last** *adv* por fin.
last-ditch *adj* último(ma), desesperado(da).
lasting ['lɑːstɪŋ] *adj* [peace, effect] duradero(ra).
lastly ['lɑːstlɪ] *adv* - **1.** [to conclude] por último - **2.** [at the end] al final.
last-minute *adj* de última hora.
last name *n* apellido *m*.
last post *n UK* - **1.** [postal collection] última recogida *f* - **2.** MIL [toque *m* de] retreta *f*.
last rites *npl* últimos sacramentos *mpl*.

last straw *n*: **it was the last straw** fue la gota que colmó el vaso.

Last Supper *n*: **the Last Supper** la Última Cena.

last word *n*: **to have the last word** tener la última palabra.

latch [lætʃ] *n* pestillo *m*; **the door is on the latch** la puerta sólo tiene el pestillo echado.

◆ **latch onto** *vt insep inf* [person] pegarse OR engancharse a; [idea] pillar.

latchkey ['lætʃkiː] (*pl* **latchkeys**) *n* llave *f* (*de la casa*).

late [leɪt] ◇ *adj* - **1.** [not on time] con retraso; **to be late (for)** llegar tarde (a); **the flight is twenty minutes late** el vuelo lleva veinte minutos de retraso; **the bus was an hour late** el autobús llegó con una hora de retraso - **2.** [near end of]: **in the late afternoon** al final de la tarde; **in late December** a finales de diciembre; **it's getting late** se está haciendo tarde - **3.** [later than normal] tardío(a); **we had a late breakfast** desayunamos tarde - **4.** [former]: **the late president** el ex-presidente - **5.** [dead] difunto(ta). ◇ *adv* - **1.** [gen] tarde; **they are open late** abren hasta tarde - **2.** [near end of period]: **late in the day** al final del día; **late in August** a finales de agosto.

◆ **of late** *adv* últimamente, recientemente.

latecomer ['leɪt,kʌmə*] *n* persona *f* que llega tarde.

lately ['leɪtlɪ] *adv* últimamente, recientemente.

lateness ['leɪtnɪs] *n* (*U*) retraso *m*.

late-night *adj* [late evening] nocturno(na), de noche; [after midnight] de madrugada; **late-night chemist's** farmacia *f* de guardia.

latent ['leɪtənt] *adj* latente.

later ['leɪtə*] ◇ *adj* - **1.** [date, edition] posterior - **2.** [near end of]: **in later life** en la madurez; **in the later 15th century** a finales del siglo XV. ◇ *adv* [at a later time]: **later (on)** más tarde; **no later than Friday** el viernes como muy tarde.

lateral ['lætərəl] *adj* lateral.

latest ['leɪtɪst] ◇ *adj* [most recent] último(ma). ◇ *n*: **at the latest** a más tardar, como muy tarde.

latex ['leɪteks] ◇ *n* látex *m*. ◇ *comp* de látex.

lath [lɑːθ] *n* listón *m*.

lathe [leɪð] *n* torno *m*.

lather ['lɑːðə*] ◇ *n* espuma *f* (de jabón). ◇ *vt* enjabonar.

Latin ['lætɪn] ◇ *adj* - **1.** [temperament, blood] latino(na) - **2.** [studies] de latín. ◇ *n* [language] latín *m*.

Latin America *n* Latinoamérica *f*, América *f* Latina.

Latin American ◇ *adj* latinoamericano(na). ◇ *n* [person] latinoamericano *m*, -na *f*.

latitude ['lætɪtjuːd] *n* - **1.** GEOG latitud *f* - **2.** *fml* [freedom] libertad *f*.

latrine [lə'triːn] *n* letrina *f*.

latter ['lætə*] ◇ *adj* - **1.** [near to end] último(ma) - **2.** [second] segundo(da). ◇ *n*: **the latter** éste *m*, -ta *f*.

latter-day *adj* moderno(na).

latterly ['lætəlɪ] *adv* últimamente, recientemente.

lattice ['lætɪs] *n* enrejado *m*, celosía *f*.

lattice window *n* ventana *f* de celosía.

Latvia ['lætvɪə] *n* Letonia.

Latvian ['lætvɪən] ◇ *adj* letón(ona). ◇ *n* - **1.** [person] letón *m*, -ona *f* - **2.** [language] letón *m*.

laudable ['lɔːdəbl] *adj* loable.

laugh [lɑːf] ◇ *n* - **1.** [sound] risa *f*; **to have the last laugh** ser el último en reírse - **2.** *inf* [fun, joke]: **to have a laugh** divertirse; **he's a good laugh** es un cachondo; **to do sthg for laughs** OR **a laugh** hacer algo para divertirse OR en cachondeo. ◇ *vi* reírse.

◆ **laugh at** *vt insep* [mock] reírse de.

◆ **laugh off** *vt sep* [dismiss] tomarse a risa.

laughable ['lɑːfəbl] *adj pej* [absurd] ridículo(la), risible.

laughing gas ['lɑːfɪŋ-] *n* gas *m* hilarante.

laughing stock ['lɑːfɪŋ-] *n* hazmerreír *m*.

laughter ['lɑːftə*] *n* (*U*) risa *f*.

launch [lɔːntʃ] ◇ *n* - **1.** [of boat, ship] botadura *f* - **2.** [of rocket, missile, product] lanzamiento *m* - **3.** [boat] lancha *f*. ◇ *vt* - **1.** [boat, ship] botar - **2.** [missile, attack, product & COMPUT] lanzar - **3.** [company] fundar.

◆ **launch into** *vt insep* [attack] emprender; [lecture, explanation] enfrascarse en.

launching ['lɔːntʃɪŋ] *n* - **1.** [of boat, ship] botadura *f* - **2.** [of rocket, missile, product] lanzamiento *m*.

launch(ing) pad ['lɔːntʃ(ɪŋ)-] *n* plataforma *f* de lanzamiento.

launder ['lɔːndə*] *vt* - **1.** [wash] lavar - **2.** *inf* [money] blanquear.

laund(e)rette [lɔːn'dret], **Laundromat**® *US* ['lɔːndrəmæt] *n* lavandería *f* (automática).

laundry ['lɔːndrɪ] (*pl* **-ies**) *n* - **1.** [clothes - about to be washed] colada *f*, ropa *f* sucia; [- newly washed] ropa *f* limpia; **to do the laundry** hacer la colada - **2.** [business, room] lavandería *f*.

laundry basket *n* cesto *m* de la ropa sucia.

laureate ['lɔːrɪət] ▷ **poet laureate**.

laurels ['lɒrəlz] *npl*: **to rest on one's laurels** dormirse en los laureles.

lava ['lɑːvə] *n* lava *f*.

lavatory ['lævətrɪ] (*pl* -ies) *n* - **1.** [receptacle] wáter *m* - **2.** [room] servicio *m*; **to go to the lavatory** ir al baño.

lavatory paper *n* UK papel *m* higiénico.

lavender ['lævəndəʳ] ◇ *adj* [colour] de color lavanda. ◇ *n* - **1.** [plant] lavanda *f*, espliego *m* - **2.** [colour] color *m* lavanda.

lavish ['lævɪʃ] ◇ *adj* - **1.** [person] pródigo(ga); [gifts, portions] muy generoso(sa); **to be lavish with** [praise, attention] ser pródigo en; [money] ser desprendido(da) con - **2.** [sumptuous] espléndido(da), suntuoso(sa). ◇ *vt*: **to lavish sthg on** [praise, care] prodigar algo a; [time, money] gastar algo en.

lavishly ['lævɪʃlɪ] *adv* - **1.** [generously] generosamente - **2.** [sumptuously] suntuosamente.

law [lɔ:] ◇ *n* - **1.** [gen] ley *f*; **against the law** ilegal; **to break the law** infringir *OR* violar la ley; **law and order** el orden público; **the law of the jungle** la ley de la selva - **2.** [set of rules, study, profession] derecho *m* - **3.** *inf* [police]: **the law** la poli ◇ *comp* [degree] en derecho; [student] de derecho; [firm] jurídico(ca).

▸▸ **to lay down the law** imponer *OR* dictar la ley. ◇ *comp* [degree] en derecho; [student] de derecho; [firm] jurídico(ca).

law-abiding [-ə,baɪdɪŋ] *adj* observante de la ley.

law-breaker *n* infractor *m*, -ra *f* de la ley.

law court *n* tribunal *m* de justicia.

law enforcement officer *n* agente *mf* de policía.

law firm *n* bufete de abogados.

lawful ['lɔ:fʊl] *adj* fml legal, lícito(ta).

lawfully ['lɔ:fʊlɪ] *adv* fml legalmente, lícitamente.

lawless ['lɔ:lɪs] *adj* [without laws] anárquico(ca).

Law Lords *npl* UK LAW: **the Law Lords** *los miembros de la Cámara de los Lores que forman el Tribunal Supremo.*

lawmaker ['lɔ:,meɪkəʳ] *n* legislador *m*, -ra *f*.

lawn [lɔ:n] *n* [grass] césped *m*, pasto *m* Amér, grama *f* Amér C & Ven.

lawnmower ['lɔ:n,məʊəʳ] *n* cortacésped *mf*.

lawn party *n* US recepción *f* al aire libre.

lawn tennis *n* tenis *m* sobre hierba.

law school *n* facultad *f* de derecho; **he went to law school** estudió derecho.

lawsuit ['lɔ:su:t] *n* pleito *m*.

lawyer ['lɔ:jəʳ] *n* abogado *m*, -da *f*.

lax [læks] *adj* [discipline, morals] relajado(da); [person] negligente; [security] poco riguroso(sa).

laxative ['læksətɪv] *n* laxante *m*.

laxity ['læksətɪ], **laxness** ['læksnɪs] *n* [of discipline] relajamiento *m*, relajación *f*; [of person] negligencia *f*; [of security] falta *f* de rigor.

lay [leɪ] ◇ *pt* ▷ **lie.** ◇ *vt* (*pt & pp* laid) - **1.** [put, place] colocar, poner; **to lay o.s. open to sthg** exponerse a algo - **2.** [prepare - plans] hacer - **3.** [put in position - bricks] poner; [- cable, trap] tender; [- foundations] echar; **to lay the table** poner la mesa - **4.** [egg] poner - **5.** [blame, curse]: **to lay sthg on sb** echar algo a alguien. ◇ *adj* - **1.** [not clerical] laico(ca) - **2.** [untrained, unqualified] profano(na), lego(ga).

▸ **lay aside** *vt sep* - **1.** [store for future - food] guardar; [- money] ahorrar - **2.** [prejudices, reservations] dejar a un lado.

▸ **lay before** *vt sep* [present] exponer, presentar.

▸ **lay down** *vt sep* - **1.** [set out] imponer, establecer - **2.** [put down - arms] deponer, entregar; [- tools] dejar.

▸ **lay into** *vt insep* inf arremeter contra.

▸ **lay off** ◇ *vt sep* [make redundant] despedir. ◇ *vt insep* inf [stop, give up]: **to lay off (doing sthg)** dejar (de hacer algo). ◇ *vi* inf: **lay off!** ¡déjame en paz!

▸ **lay on** *vt sep* [transport, entertainment] organizar; [food] preparar.

▸ **lay out** *vt sep* - **1.** [arrange, spread out] disponer - **2.** [plan, design] diseñar el trazado de.

▸ **lay over** *vi* US hacer noche.

layabout ['leɪəbaʊt] *n* UK inf holgazán *m*, -ana *f*, gandul *m*, -la *f*, atorrante *mf* Amér.

lay-by (*pl* lay-bys) *n* UK área *f* de descanso.

layer ['leɪəʳ] ◇ *n* - **1.** [of substance, material] capa *f* - **2.** fig [level] nivel *m*. ◇ *vt* [hair] cortar a capas.

layette [leɪ'et] *n* ajuar *m* (del bebé).

layman ['leɪmən] (*pl* -men [-mən]) *n* - **1.** [untrained, unqualified person] profano *m*, -na *f*, lego *m*, -ga *f* - **2.** RELIG laico *m*, -ca *f*.

lay-off *n* [redundancy] despido *m*.

layout ['leɪaʊt] *n* [of building, garden] trazado *m*, diseño *m*; [of text] presentación *f*, composición *f*; [of page & COMPUT] diseño *m*.

layover ['leɪəʊvəʳ] *n* US [gen] parada *f*; [of plane] escala *f*.

laze [leɪz] *vi*: **to laze (about OR around)** gandulear, holgazanear.

lazily ['leɪzɪlɪ] *adv* perezosamente.

laziness ['leɪzɪnɪs] *n* [idleness] pereza *f*.

lazy ['leɪzɪ] (*comp* -ier, *superl* -iest) *adj* - **1.** [person] perezoso(sa), vago(ga), atorrante *R Plata* - **2.** [stroll, gesture] lento(ta); [afternoon] ocioso(sa).

lazybones ['leɪzɪbəʊnz] (*pl* lazybones) *n* inf gandul *m*, -la *f*, holgazán *m*, -ana *f*.

lb (*abbr of* pound) lb.

LB *abbr of* **Labrador**.

lbw (*abbr of* **leg before wicket**) *protección ilegal de los palos con la pierna en cricket.*

lc (*abbr of* **lower case**) cb.

LC (*abbr of* **Library of Congress**) *n biblioteca del Congreso de Estados Unidos.*

L/C *abbr of* **letter of credit**.

LCD *n abbr of* **liquid crystal display**.

Ld *abbr of* **Lord**.

L-driver *n UK conductor que lleva la L.*

LEA (*abbr of* **local education authority**) *n organismo responsable de educación en un área determinada de Gran Bretaña.*

lead[1] [li:d] <> *n* - **1.** [winning position] delantera *f*; **to be in** OR **have the lead** llevar la delantera, ir en cabeza; **to take the lead** ponerse a la cabeza - **2.** [amount ahead]: **to have a lead of...** llevar una ventaja de... - **3.** [initiative, example] ejemplo *m*; **to take the lead** [do sthg first] tomar la delantera - **4.** THEAT: **(to play) the lead** (hacer) el papel principal - **5.** [clue] pista *f* - **6.** [for dog] correa *f* - **7.** [wire, cable] cable *m*. <> *adj* [singer, actor] principal; [guitar, guitarist] solista; [story in newspaper] más destacado(da). <> *vt* (*pt & pp* **led**) - **1.** [be in front of] encabezar; **to lead sb by ten minutes** llevar a alguien diez minutos de ventaja; **they are leading France three-nil** van ganando a Francia por tres goles a cero - **2.** [take, guide, direct] conducir; **to lead the way** enseñar el camino - **3.** [be in charge of, take the lead in] dirigir; [debate] moderar - **4.** [life] llevar - **5.** [cause]: **to lead sb to do sthg** llevar a alguien a hacer algo; **we were led to believe that...** nos dieron a entender que... <> *vi* (*pt & pp* **led**) - **1.** [go]: **to lead (to)** conducir OR llevar (a) - **2.** [give access to]: **to lead (to** OR **into)** dar (a) - **3.** [be winning] ir en cabeza - **4.** [result in]: **to lead to** conducir a - **5.** [in cards] salir.

lead away *vt sep*: **to lead sb away** llevarse a alguien.

lead off *vi* [road, corridor]: **to lead off (from)** salir (de); [in card game, discussion] empezar.

lead on *vt sep* [pretend to be attracted to] dar esperanzas a.

lead up to *vt insep* - **1.** [build up to] conducir a, preceder - **2.** [plan to introduce] apuntar a.

lead[2] [led] <> *n* - **1.** [metal] plomo *m* - **2.** [in pencil] mina *f*. <> *comp* [made of or with lead] de plomo.

leaded ['ledɪd] *adj* - **1.** [petrol] con plomo - **2.** [window] emplomado(da).

leaden ['ledn] *adj liter* - **1.** [dark grey] plomizo(za) - **2.** [heavy] pesado(da).

leader ['li:də'] *n* - **1.** [of party etc, in competition] líder *mf* - **2.** UK [in newspaper] editorial *m*, artículo *m* de fondo.

leadership ['li:dəʃɪp] *n* (*U*) - **1.** [people in charge]: **the leadership** los líderes, los dirigentes - **2.** [position of leader] liderazgo *m* - **3.** [qualities of leader] autoridad *f*, dotes *fpl* de mando.

lead-free [led-] *adj* sin plomo.

lead guitar *n* guitarra *f* solista.

leading ['li:dɪŋ] *adj* - **1.** [major - athlete, writer] destacado(da); [- company] principal - **2.** [main - role, part] principal - **3.** [at front] que va en cabeza.

leading article *n UK* editorial *m*, artículo *m* de fondo.

leading lady *n* primera actriz *f*.

leading light *n* figura *f* destacada.

leading man *n* primer actor *m*.

leading question *n pregunta formulada de tal manera que sugiere una respuesta determinada.*

lead pencil [led-] *n* lápiz *m* de mina.

lead poisoning [led-] *n* saturnismo *m*.

lead time [li:d-] *n* COMM tiempo *m* de entrega.

leaf [li:f] *n* (*pl* **leaves**) - **1.** [of tree, book] hoja *f* - **2.** [of table] hoja *f* abatible.

leaf through *vt insep* hojear.

leaflet ['li:flɪt] <> *n* [small brochure] folleto *m*; [piece of paper] octavilla *f*. <> *vt* repartir folletos en.

leafy ['li:fɪ] (*comp* **-ier**, *superl* **-iest**) *adj* frondoso(sa).

league [li:g] *n* [gen & SPORT] liga *f*; **to be in league with** [work with] estar confabulado con.

league table *n* clasificación *f*.

leak [li:k] <> *n* - **1.** [hole - in tank, bucket] agujero *m*; [- in roof] gotera *f* - **2.** [escape] escape *m*, fuga *f* - **3.** [of information] filtración *f*. <> *vt* [information] filtrar. <> *vi* - **1.** [bucket] tener un agujero; [roof] tener goteras; [boot] calar - **2.** [water, gas] salirse, escaparse; **to leak (out) from** salirse de.

leak out *vi* - **1.** [liquid] salirse, escaparse - **2.** [secret, information] filtrarse.

leakage ['li:kɪdʒ] *n* fuga *f*, escape *m*.

leaky ['li:kɪ] (*comp* **-ier**, *superl* **-iest**) *adj* [tank, bucket] con agujeros; [roof] con goteras; [tap] que gotea.

lean [li:n] <> *adj* - **1.** [person] delgado(da) - **2.** [meat] magro(gra) - **3.** [winter, year] de escasez. <> *vt* (*pt & pp* **leant** OR **-ed**) [support, prop]: **to lean sthg against** apoyar algo contra. <> *vi* (*pt & pp* **leant** OR **-ed**) - **1.** [bend, slope] inclinarse; **to lean out of the window** asomarse a la ventana - **2.** [rest]: **to lean on/against** apoyarse en/contra.

leaning ['li:nɪŋ] *n*: **leaning (towards)** inclinación *f* (hacia OR por).

leant [lent] *pt & pp* ⊳ **lean**.

lean-to (*pl* **lean-tos**) *n* cobertizo *m*.

leap [li:p] ◇ *n* salto *m*. ◇ *vi* (*pt & pp* **leapt** OR **-ed**) [gen] saltar; [prices] dispararse.

◆ **leap at** *vt insep* [opportunity] no dejar escapar.

leapfrog ['li:pfrɒg] ◇ *n* pídola *f*, rango *m* R *Plata*. ◇ *vt* (*pt & pp* **-ged**, *cont* **-ging**) saltar.

leapt [lept] *pt & pp* ▷ **leap**.

leap year *n* año *m* bisiesto.

learn [lɜ:n] (*pt & pp* **-ed** OR **learnt**) ◇ *vt* **- 1.** [acquire knowledge of, memorize] aprender; **to learn (how) to do sthg** aprender a hacer algo **- 2.** [hear]: **to learn (that)** enterarse de (que). ◇ *vi* **- 1.** [acquire knowledge] aprender **- 2.** [hear]: **to learn (of** OR **about)** enterarse (de).

learned ['lɜ:nɪd] *adj* erudito(ta).

learner ['lɜ:nər] *n* [beginner] principiante *mf*; [student] estudiante *mf*.

learner (driver) *n* conductor *m* principiante OR en prácticas.

learner's permit *n* US carné *m* de conducir provisional.

learning ['lɜ:nɪŋ] *n* saber *m*, erudición *f*.

learning curve *n* ritmo *m* de aprendizaje.

learning disability *n* discapacidad *f* para el aprendizaje.

learnt [lɜ:nt] *pt & pp* ▷ **learn**.

lease [li:s] ◇ *n* LAW contrato *m* de arrendamiento, arriendo *m*; **to give sb a new lease of life** UK OR **on life** US darle nueva vida a alguien. ◇ *vt* arrendar; **to lease sthg from/to sb** arrendar algo de/a alguien.

leaseback ['li:sbæk] *n* retroarriendo *m*.

leasehold ['li:shəʊld] ◇ *adj* arrendado(da). ◇ *adv* en arriendo.

leaseholder ['li:s,həʊldər] *n* arrendatario *m*, -ria *f*.

leash [li:ʃ] *n* [for dog] correa *f*.

least [li:st] (*superl of* **little**) ◇ *adj* [smallest in amount, degree] menor; **he earns the least money** es el que menos dinero gana. ◇ *pron* [smallest amount]: **the least** lo menos; **it's the least (that) he can do** es lo menos que puede hacer; **not in the least** en absoluto; **to say the least** por no decir otra cosa. ◇ *adv* [to the smallest amount, degree] menos.

◆ **at least** *adv* por lo menos, al menos.

◆ **least of all** *adv* y menos (todavía).

◆ **not least** *adv* sobre todo.

leather ['leðər] ◇ *n* piel *f*, cuero *m*. ◇ *comp* [jacket, trousers] de cuero; [shoes, bag] de piel.

leatherette [,leðə'ret] *n* polipiel *f*, skay *m*.

leave [li:v] ◇ *vt* (*pt & pp* **left**) **- 1.** [gen] dejar; **he left it to her to decide** dejó que ella deci-

diera; **to leave sb alone** dejar a alguien en paz; **it leaves me cold** me da igual, me trae al fresco **- 2.** [go away from - place] irse de; [- house, room, work] salir de; [- wife] abandonar; **to leave home** irse de casa **- 3.** [do not take, forget] dejarse **- 4.** [bequeath]: **to leave sb sthg, to leave sthg to sb** dejarle algo a alguien. ◇ *vi* (*pt & pp* **left**) [bus, train, plane] salir; [person] irse, marcharse. ◇ *n* [time off, permission] permiso *m*; **to be on leave** estar de permiso.

◆ **leave behind** *vt sep* **- 1.** [abandon] dejar **- 2.** [forget] dejarse **- 3.** [walking, in race]: **to get left behind** quedarse atrás.

◆ **leave off** ◇ *vt sep* [omit] no incluir en. ◇ *vt insep* [stop]: **to leave off (doing sthg)** dejar (de hacer algo). ◇ *vi*: **to carry on from where one left off** continuar desde donde uno lo había dejado.

◆ **leave out** *vt sep* **- 1.** [omit] omitir **- 2.** [exclude] excluir; **to feel left out** sentirse excluido(da).

◆ **leave over** *vt sep*: **to be left over** sobrar.

leave of absence *n* excedencia *f*.

leaves [li:vz] *npl* ▷ **leaf**.

Lebanese [,lebə'ni:z] ◇ *adj* libanés(esa). ◇ *n* (*pl* **Lebanese**) [person] libanés *m*, -esa *f*.

Lebanon ['lebənən] *n*: **(the) Lebanon** (el) Líbano.

lecherous ['letʃərəs] *adj* lascivo(va), lujurioso(sa).

lechery ['letʃərɪ] *n* lascivia *f*, lujuria *f*.

lectern ['lektən] *n* atril *m*.

lecture ['lektʃər] ◇ *n* **- 1.** [talk - at university] clase *f*; [- at conference] conferencia *f*; **to give a lecture (on)** [- at university] dar una clase (sobre); [- at conference] dar una conferencia (sobre) **- 2.** [criticism, reprimand] sermón *m*. ◇ *vt* [scold] echar un sermón a. ◇ *vi* [give talk]: **to lecture (on/in)** [at university] dar clases (de/en); [at conference] dar una conferencia (sobre/en).

lecture hall *n* [at university] aula *f*; [in conference centre] sala *f* de conferencias.

lecturer ['lektʃərər] *n* [at university] profesor *m*, -ra *f* de universidad.

lecture theatre *n* [at university] aula *f*; [in conference centre] sala *f* de conferencias.

led [led] *pt & pp* ▷ **lead¹** .

LED (*abbr of* **light-emitting diode**) *n* LED *m*.

ledge [ledʒ] *n* **- 1.** [of window] alféizar *m*, antepecho *m* **- 2.** [of mountain] saliente *m*.

ledger ['ledʒər] *n* libro *m* mayor.

lee [li:] *n* [shelter]: **in the lee of** al abrigo de.

leech [li:tʃ] *n lit & fig* sanguijuela *f*.

leek [li:k] *n* puerro *m*.

leer [lɪəʳ] ◇ n mirada f lasciva. ◇ vi: **to leer at sb** mirar lascivamente a alguien.

Leeward Islands ['li:wəd-] npl: **the Leeward Islands** las islas de Sotavento.

leeway ['li:weɪ] n [room to manoeuvre] libertad f (de acción OR movimientos).

left [left] ◇ adj - **1.** [remaining]: **to be left** quedar; **there's no wine left** no queda vino - **2.** [not right] izquierdo(da). ◇ adv a la izquierda. ◇ n izquierda f; **on** OR **to the left** a la izquierda; **keep to the left!** [on road signs] ¡circulen por la izquierda!

➤ **Left** n POL: **the Left** la izquierda.

left-hand adj de la izquierda, izquierdo(da); **the left-hand side** el lado izquierdo, la izquierda.

left-hand drive n vehículo m que tiene el volante a la izquierda.

left-handed [-'hændɪd] ◇ adj - **1.** [person] zurdo(da) - **2.** [implement] para zurdos - **3.** US [compliment] con doble sentido. ◇ adv con la (mano) izquierda.

left-hander [-'hændəʳ] n zurdo m, -da f.

Leftist ['leftɪst] ◇ adj POL izquierdista, de izquierdas. ◇ n POL izquierdista mf.

left luggage (office) n UK consigna f.

leftover ['leftəʊvəʳ] adj sobrante.

➤ **leftovers** npl sobras fpl.

left wing n POL izquierda f.

➤ **left-wing** adj de izquierdas, izquierdista.

left-winger n POL izquierdista mf.

lefty ['leftɪ] (pl **-ies**) n - **1.** UK inf pej & POL izquierdoso m, -sa f - **2.** US [left-handed person] zurdo m, -da f.

leg [leg] n - **1.** [of person] pierna f; **to be on one's last legs** estar en las últimas; **you don't have a leg to stand on** no tienes en qué basarte; **to pull sb's leg** tomarle el pelo a alguien - **2.** [of animal] pata f - **3.** [of trousers] pernera f, pierna f - **4.** CULIN [of lamb, pork] pierna f; [of chicken] muslo m - **5.** [of furniture] pata f - **6.** [of journey] etapa f; [of cup tie] partido m.

legacy ['legəsɪ] (pl **-ies**) n lit & fig legado m.

legal ['li:gl] adj - **1.** [lawful] legal - **2.** [concerning the law] jurídico(ca), legal.

legal action n pleito m, demanda f; **to take legal action against sb** presentar una demanda contra alguien.

legal aid n asistencia f de un abogado de oficio.

legality [li:'gælətɪ] n legalidad f.

legalize, -ise ['li:gəlaɪz] vt legalizar.

legally ['li:gəlɪ] adv legalmente; **legally responsible** responsable ante la ley; **legally binding** con fuerza de ley.

legal tender n moneda f de curso legal.

legation [lɪ'geɪʃn] n legación f.

legend ['ledʒənd] n lit & fig leyenda f.

legendary ['ledʒəndrɪ] adj legendario(ria).

leggings ['legɪŋz] npl mallas fpl.

leggy ['legɪ] (comp **-ier**, superl **-iest**) adj de largas y bonitas piernas.

legible ['ledʒəbl] adj legible.

legibly ['ledʒəblɪ] adv de manera legible.

legion ['li:dʒən] ◇ n lit & fig legión f. ◇ adj fml: **to be legion** ser innumerables.

legionnaire's disease [,li:dʒə'neəz-] n legionella f.

legislate ['ledʒɪsleɪt] vi legislar; **to legislate for/against** dictar una ley a favor de/en contra de.

legislation [,ledʒɪs'leɪʃn] n legislación f.

legislative ['ledʒɪslətɪv] adj legislativo(va).

legislator ['ledʒɪsleɪtəʳ] n legislador m, -ra f.

legislature ['ledʒɪsleɪtʃəʳ] n asamblea f legislativa.

legitimacy [lɪ'dʒɪtɪməsɪ] n legitimidad f.

legitimate [lɪ'dʒɪtɪmət] adj legítimo(ma).

legitimately [lɪ'dʒɪtɪmətlɪ] adv legítimamente.

legitimize, -ise [lɪ'dʒɪtəmaɪz] vt legitimar.

legless ['legləs] adj UK inf [drunk] trompa, como una cuba.

legroom ['legrʊm] n (U) espacio m para las piernas.

leg-warmers [-,wɔ:məz] npl calentadores mpl.

legwork ['legwɜ:k] n (U): **to do the legwork** encargarse del trabajo de campo.

Leics (abbr of **Leicestershire**) condado inglés.

leisure [UK 'leʒəʳ, US 'li:ʒəʳ] n ocio m; **do it at your leisure** hazlo cuando tengas tiempo.

leisure centre n centro m deportivo y cultural.

leisurely [UK 'leʒəlɪ, US 'li:ʒərlɪ] adj lento(ta).

leisure time n tiempo m libre.

lemming ['lemɪŋ] n [animal] lemming m.

lemon ['lemən] n [fruit] limón m.

lemonade [,lemə'neɪd] n - **1.** UK [fizzy drink] gaseosa f - **2.** [made with fresh lemons] limonada f.

lemon curd n UK crema f OR cuajada f de limón.

lemongrass ['leməngrɑ:s] n (U) hierba f limonera.

lemon juice n zumo m de limón.

lemon sole n mendo m limón.

lemon squash n UK refresco m de limón.

lemon squeezer [-'skwi:zəʳ] n exprimidor m, exprimelimones m inv.

lemon tea n té m con limón.

lend [lend] (*pt* & *pp* **lent**) *vt* - **1.** [loan] prestar, dejar; **to lend sb sthg, to lend sthg to sb** prestarle algo a alguien - **2.** [offer]: **to lend sthg (to sb)** prestar algo (a alguien); **to lend sb a hand** echar una mano a alguien; **to lend itself to sthg** prestarse a algo - **3.** [add]: **to lend sthg to** prestar algo a.

lender ['lendər] *n* prestamista *mf*.

lending library ['lendɪŋ-] *n* biblioteca *f* pública.

lending rate ['lendɪŋ-] *n* tipo *m* de interés (en un crédito).

length [leŋθ] *n* - **1.** [measurement] longitud *f*, largo *m*; **what length is it?** ¿cuánto mide de largo?; **it's a metre in length** tiene un metro de largo - **2.** [whole distance, size] extensión *f*; **throughout the length and breadth of** a lo largo y ancho de - **3.** [duration] duración *f* - **4.** [of swimming pool] largo *m* - **5.** [piece - of string, wood] trozo *m*; [- of cloth] largo *m*
▸▸ **to go to great lengths to do sthg** hacer todo lo posible para hacer algo.
◂ **at length** *adv* - **1.** [eventually] por fin - **2.** [in detail - speak] largo y tendido; [- discuss] con detenimiento.

lengthen ['leŋθən] ◇ *vt* alargar. ◇ *vi* alargarse.

lengthways ['leŋθweɪz] *adv* a lo largo.

lengthy ['leŋθɪ] (*comp* -**ier**, *superl* -**iest**) *adj* [stay, visit] extenso(sa); [discussions, speech] prolijo(ja), prolongado(da).

leniency ['liːnjənsɪ] *n* indulgencia *f*.

lenient ['liːnjənt] *adj* indulgente.

lens [lenz] *n* - **1.** [in glasses] lente *f*; [in camera] objetivo *m* - **2.** [contact lens] lentilla *f*, lente *f* de contacto.

lent [lent] *pt* & *pp* ▷ **lend**.

Lent [lent] *n* Cuaresma *f*.

lentil ['lentɪl] *n* lenteja *f*.

Leo ['liːəʊ] *n* Leo *m*; **to be (a) Leo** ser Leo.

leopard ['lepəd] *n* leopardo *m*.

leopardess ['lepədɪs] *n* leopardo *m* hembra.

leotard ['liːətɑːd] *n* malla *f*.

leper ['lepər] *n* leproso *m*, -sa *f*.

leprechaun ['leprəkɔːn] *n* duende *m* de las leyendas irlandesas.

leprosy ['leprəsɪ] *n* lepra *f*.

lesbian ['lezbɪən] ◇ *adj* lesbiano(na). ◇ *n* lesbiana *f*.

lesbianism ['lezbɪənɪzm] *n* lesbianismo *m*.

lesion ['liːʒn] *n* lesión *f*.

less [les] (*compar of* **little**) ◇ *adj* menos; **less... than** menos... que; **less and less...** cada vez menos... ◇ *pron* menos; **the less you work, the less you earn** cuanto menos trabajas, menos ganas; **it costs less than you think** cuesta

menos de lo que piensas; **no less than** nada menos que. ◇ *adv* menos; **less than five** menos de cinco; **less often** menos; **less and less** cada vez menos. ◇ *prep* [minus] menos.

lessee [le'siː] *n* *fml* [of land, business premises] arrendatario *m*, -ria *f*; [of house, flat] inquilino *m*, -na *f*.

lessen ['lesn] ◇ *vt* aminorar, reducir. ◇ *vi* aminorarse, reducirse.

lesser ['lesər] *adj* menor; **to a lesser extent** OR **degree** en menor grado.

lesson ['lesn] *n* - **1.** [class] clase *f*; **to give/take lessons (in)** dar/recibir clases (de) - **2.** [warning experience] lección *f*; **to teach sb a lesson** darle una buena lección a alguien.

lessor [le'sɔːr] *n* *fml* arrendador *m*, -ra *f*.

lest [lest] *conj* *fml* para que no; **lest we forget** no sea que nos olvidemos.

let [let] *vt* (*pt* & *pp* **let**, *cont* -**ting**) - **1.** [allow]: **to let sb do sthg** dejar a alguien hacer algo; **to let sthg happen** dejar que algo ocurra; **she let her hair grow** se dejó crecer el pelo; **to let sb know sthg** avisar a alguien de algo; **to let go of sthg/sb** soltar algo/a alguien; **to let sthg/sb go** [release] liberar a algo/alguien, soltar a algo/alguien; **to let o.s. go** [relax] soltarse el pelo; [become slovenly] abandonarse - **2.** [in verb forms]: **let's go!** ¡vamos!; **let's see** veamos; **let him wait!** ¡déjale que espere! - **3.** [rent out - house, room] alquilar; [- land] arrendar; **'to let'** 'se alquila'.
◂ **let alone** *adv* ni mucho menos.
◂ **let down** *vt sep* - **1.** [deflate] desinflar - **2.** [disappoint] fallar, defraudar.
◂ **let in** *vt sep* - **1.** [admit] dejar entrar; **he let himself in** entró con su llave - **2.** [leak] dejar pasar.
◂ **let in for** *vt sep*: **to let o.s. in for sthg** meterse en algo.
◂ **let in on** *vt sep*: **to let sb in on sthg** confiar OR revelar a alguien algo.
◂ **let off** *vt sep* - **1.** [excuse]: **to let sb off sthg** eximir a alguien de algo - **2.** [not punish] perdonar - **3.** [cause to explode - bomb] hacer estallar; [- gun] disparar - **4.** [gas] despedir.
◂ **let on** *vi*: **don't let on!** ¡no cuentes nada!
◂ **let out** *vt sep* - **1.** [allow to go out] dejar salir - **2.** [emit - sound] soltar.
◂ **let up** *vi* - **1.** [heat, rain] amainar - **2.** [person] parar.

letdown ['letdaʊn] *n inf* chasco *m*, decepción *f*.

lethal ['liːθl] *adj* letal, mortífero(ra).

lethargic [lə'θɑːdʒɪk] *adj* - **1.** [mood] letárgico(ca); [person] aletargado(da) - **2.** [apathetic] apático(ca).

lethargy ['leθədʒɪ] *n* - **1.** [drowsiness] letargo *m* - **2.** [apathy] apatía *f*.

let's [lets] (*abbr of* = **let us**), ▷ **let**.

letter ['letər] *n* - **1.** [written message] carta *f* - **2.** [of alphabet] letra *f*; **to the letter** *fig* al pie de la letra.

letter bomb *n* carta *f* bomba.

letterbox ['letəbɒks] *n* UK buzón *m*.

letter carrier *n* US [postman] cartero *m*, -ra *f*.

letterhead ['letəhed] *n* membrete *m*.

lettering ['letərɪŋ] *n (U)* [writing] letra *f*.

letter of credit *n* carta *f* de crédito.

letter opener *n* abrecartas *m inv*.

letter-perfect *adj* US impecable.

letters patent *npl* patente *f*.

lettuce ['letɪs] *n* lechuga *f*.

letup ['letʌp] *n* tregua *f*, respiro *m*.

leuk(a)emia [lu:'ki:mɪə] *n* leucemia *f*.

levee ['levɪ] *n* US [embankment] dique *m*.

level ['levl] ◇ *adj* - **1.** [equal in speed, score] igualado(da); **they are level** van igualados; [equal in height] nivelado(da); **to be level (with sthg)** estar al mismo nivel (que algo) - **2.** [flat - floor, surface] liso(sa), llano(na); [- spoonful] raso(sa). ◇ *adv*: **level (with)** al mismo nivel OR altura (que); **to fly level with the ground** volar a ras de suelo; **to draw level with sb** llegar a la altura de alguien. ◇ *n* - **1.** [gen] nivel *m*; **to be on a level (with)** estar al mismo nivel (que); **to be on the level** *inf* ser de fiar - **2.** [storey] piso *m* - **3.** US [spirit level] nivel *m* de burbuja de aire. ◇ *vt* (UK -**led**, *cont* -**ling**, US -**ed**, *cont* -**ing**) - **1.** [make flat] allanar - **2.** [demolish - building] derribar; [- forest] arrasar - **3.** [weapon]: **to level sthg at** apuntar (con) algo a - **4.** [accusation, criticism]: **to level sthg at** OR **against sb** dirigir algo a alguien.
◆ **level off, level out** *vi* - **1.** [stabilize, slow down] estabilizarse - **2.** [ground] nivelarse; [plane] enderezarse.
◆ **level with** *vt insep inf* ser sincero(ra) con.

level crossing *n* UK paso *m* a nivel.

level-headed [-'hedɪd] *adj* sensato(ta), equilibrado(da).

level pegging [-'pegɪŋ] *adj* UK: **to be level pegging** estar igualado(da).

lever [UK 'li:vər, US 'levər] *n* - **1.** [handle, bar] palanca *f* - **2.** *fig* [tactic] resorte *m*.

leverage [UK 'li:vərɪdʒ, US 'levərɪdʒ] *n (U)* - **1.** [force] fuerza *f* de apalanque - **2.** *fig* [influence] influencia *f*.

leviathan [lɪ'vaɪəθn] *n* [huge thing or person] gigante *m*.

levitation [ˌlevɪ'teɪʃn] *n* levitación *f*.

levity ['levətɪ] *n* ligereza *f*.

levy ['levɪ] ◇ *n*: **levy (on)** [financial contribution] contribución *f* (a OR para); [tax] tasa *f* OR impuesto *m* (sobre). ◇ *vt* (*pt & pp* -**ied**) - **1.** [impose] imponer - **2.** [collect] recaudar.

lewd [lju:d] *adj* [person, look] lascivo(va); [behaviour, song] obsceno(na); [joke] verde.

lexical ['leksɪkl] *adj* léxico(ca).

LI *abbr of* **Long Island**.

liability [ˌlaɪə'bɪlətɪ] (*pl* -**ies**) *n* - **1.** [legal responsibility]: **liability (for)** responsabilidad *f* (de OR por) - **2.** [hindrance] estorbo *m*.
◆ **liabilities** *npl* FIN pasivo *m*, deudas *fpl*.

liable ['laɪəbl] *adj* - **1.** [likely]: **that's liable to happen** eso pueda que ocurra - **2.** [prone]: **to be liable to** ser propenso(sa) a - **3.** [legally responsible]: **to be liable (for)** ser responsable (de).

liaise [lɪ'eɪz] *vi*: **to liaise (with)** estar en contacto (con); **to liaise (between)** servir de enlace (entre).

liaison [lɪ'eɪzɒn] *n* - **1.** [contact, co-operation]: **liaison (with/between)** coordinación *f* (con/entre), enlace *m* (con/entre) - **2.** [affair, relationship]: **liaison (with/between)** amorío *m* (con/entre).

liar ['laɪər] *n* mentiroso *m*, -sa *f*.

Lib. *abbr of* **Liberal**.

libel ['laɪbl] ◇ *n* libelo *m*. ◇ *vt* (UK -**led**, *cont* -**ling**, US -**ed**, *cont* -**ing**) calumniar.

libellous UK, **libelous** US ['laɪbələs] *adj* difamatorio(ria).

liberal ['lɪbərəl] ◇ *adj* - **1.** [tolerant] liberal - **2.** [generous, abundant] generoso(sa). ◇ *n* liberal *mf*.
◆ **Liberal** ◇ *adj* POL liberal. ◇ *n* POL liberal *mf*.

liberal arts *npl esp* US letras *fpl*.

Liberal Democrat UK ◇ *adj* demócrata liberal. ◇ *n* demócrata liberal *mf*.

liberalize, -ise ['lɪbərəlaɪz] *vt* liberalizar.

liberal-minded [-'maɪndɪd] *adj* liberal.

liberate ['lɪbəreɪt] *vt* liberar.

liberation [ˌlɪbə'reɪʃn] *n* liberación *f*.

liberator ['lɪbəreɪtər] *n* libertador *m*, -ra *f*.

Liberia [laɪ'bɪərɪə] *n* Liberia.

Liberian [laɪ'bɪərɪən] ◇ *adj* liberiano(na). ◇ *n* liberiano *m*, -na *f*.

libertine ['lɪbəti:n] *n* libertino *m*, -na *f*.

liberty ['lɪbətɪ] (*pl* -**ies**) *n* libertad *f*; **at liberty** en libertad; **to be at liberty to do sthg** ser libre de hacer algo; **to take liberties (with sb)** tomarse demasiadas libertades (con alguien).

libido [lɪ'bi:dəʊ] (*pl* -**s**) *n* libido *f*.

Libra ['li:brə] *n* Libra *f*; **to be (a) Libra** ser Libra.

librarian [laɪ'breərɪən] *n* bibliotecario *m*, -ria *f*.

librarianship [laɪ'breərɪənʃɪp] *n* biblioteconomía *f.*

library ['laɪbrərɪ] (*pl* **-ies**) *n* **- 1.** [public institution] biblioteca *f* **- 2.** [private collection] colección *f.*

library book *n* libro *m* de biblioteca.

libretto [lɪ'bretəʊ] (*pl* **-s**) *n* libreto *m.*

Libya ['lɪbɪə] *n* Libia.

Libyan ['lɪbɪən] ◇ *adj* libio(bia). ◇ *n* libio *m*, -bia *f.*

lice [laɪs] *npl* ▷ **louse**.

licence, license[1] *US* ◇ *n* **- 1.** [gen] permiso *m*, licencia *f*; **under license** con autorización *OR* permiso oficial **- 2.** AUT carné *m OR* permiso *m* de conducir. ◇ *vt US* = **license**.

licence ['laɪsəns] = **license**.

licence fee *n UK* TV *impuesto anual que tienen que pagar todos los hogares con un televisor y que se usa para financiar la televisión pública.*

licence number *n* AUT matrícula *f.*

license *US*, **licence** ['laɪsəns] ◇ *vt* [person, organization] dar licencia a; [activity] autorizar. ◇ *n US* = **licence**.

licensed ['laɪsənst] *adj* **- 1.** [person]: **to be licensed to do sthg** estar autorizado(da) para hacer algo **- 2.** [object] registrado(da), con licencia **- 3.** *UK* [premises] autorizado(da) a vender alcohol.

licensee [,laɪsən'si:] *n* concesionario *m*, -ria *f.*

license plate *n US* (placa *f* de) matrícula *f.*

licensing hours ['laɪsənsɪŋ-] *npl UK horas en que un pub está autorizado a servir alcohol.*

Licensing hours

Tradicionalmente, la legislación que regula los horarios de los pubs británicos ha sido muy estricta, aunque se suavizó ligeramente en 1988. Desde entonces, en lugar de abrir únicamente de 11:30 a 14:30 y de 18:00 a 22:30, los pubs en Inglaterra pueden permanecer abiertos desde las 11:00 hasta las 23:00. En Escocia, en cambio, la reglamentación es menos estricta y los pubs que así lo solicitan pueden abrir hasta la una de la madrugada los fines de semana. En la actualidad, el gobierno británico está estudiando una mayor liberalización de horarios en Inglaterra y Gales.

licensing laws ['laɪsənsɪŋ-] *npl UK leyes que controlan la venta de bebidas alcohólicas.*

licentious [laɪ'senʃəs] *adj fml & pej* licencioso(sa).

lichen ['laɪkən] *n* liquen *m.*

lick [lɪk] ◇ *n* **- 1.** [act of licking] lametón *m*, lametada *f* **- 2.** *inf* [small amount]: **a lick of paint** una mano de pintura. ◇ *vt* **- 1.** *lit & fig* lamer, lamber *Amér*; **to lick one's lips** relamerse (los labios) **- 2.** *inf* [defeat] dar una paliza a.

licorice ['lɪkərɪs] = **liquorice**.

lid [lɪd] *n* **- 1.** [cover] tapa *f* **- 2.** [eyelid] párpado *m.*

lido ['li:dəʊ] (*pl* **-es**) *n* **- 1.** *UK* [swimming pool] piscina *f* (al aire libre) **- 2.** [resort] balneario *m.*

lie [laɪ] ◇ *n* mentira *f*; **to tell lies** contar mentiras, mentir. ◇ *vi* **- 1.** (*pt* **lied**, *pp* **lied**, *cont* **lying**) [tell lie] mentir; **to lie to sb** mentirle a alguien **- 2.** (*pt* **lay**, *pp* **lain**, *cont* **lying**) [lie down] tumbarse, echarse; [be buried] yacer; **to be lying** estar tumbado(da) **- 3.** (*pt* **lay**, *pp* **lain**, *cont* **lying**) [be situated] hallarse; **there is snow lying on the ground** hay nieve en el suelo; **he is lying in fourth place** se encuentra en cuarto lugar **- 4.** (*pt* **lay**, *pp* **lain**, *cont* **lying**) [be - solution, attraction] hallarse, encontrarse **- 5.** (*pt* **lay**, *pp* **lain**, *cont* **lying**): **to lie low** permanecer escondido(da).

◆ **lie about, lie around** *vi* estar *OR* andar tirado(da).

◆ **lie down** *vi* tumbarse, echarse; **not to take sthg lying down** no quedarse cruzado de brazos ante algo.

◆ **lie in** *vi UK* quedarse en la cama hasta tarde.

Liechtenstein ['lɪktən,staɪn] *n* Liechtenstein.

lie detector *n* detector *m* de mentiras.

lie-down *n UK*: **to have a lie-down** echarse un rato.

lie-in *n UK*: **to have a lie-in** quedarse en la cama hasta tarde.

lieu [lju:, lu:] ◆ **in lieu** *adv* a cambio; **in lieu of** en lugar de.

Lieut. (*abbr of* **lieutenant**) ≃ Tte.

lieutenant [*UK* lef'tenənt, *US* lu:'tenənt] *n* **- 1.** MIL teniente *m* **- 2.** [deputy] lugarteniente *mf* **- 3.** *US* [police officer] oficial *mf* de policía.

lieutenant colonel *n* teniente *m* coronel.

life [laɪf] (*pl* **lives**) ◇ *n* **- 1.** [gen] vida *f*; **that's life!** ¡así es la vida!; **for life** de por vida, para toda la vida; **for the life of me** *inf* por mucho que lo intento; **not on your life!** *inf* ¡ni en broma!; **to breathe life into sthg** infundir una nueva vida a algo; **to come to life** [thing] cobrar vida; [person] reanimarse de pronto; **how's life?** *inf* ¿qué tal?; **to lay down one's life** dar (uno) su vida; **to risk life and limb** jugarse el pellejo; **to scare the life out of sb** pegarle a alguien un susto de muerte; **to take sb's life** acabar con la vida de alguien; **to take one's own life** quitarse la vida **- 2.** *inf* [life imprisonment] cadena *f* perpetua. ◇ *comp* [member etc] vitalicio(cia).

life-and-death *adj* [situation] de vida o muerte; [struggle] a vida o muerte.

life annuity *n* renta *f* OR pensión *f* anual vitalicia.

life assurance = **life insurance**.

life belt *n* flotador *m*, salvavidas *m inv*.

lifeblood ['laɪfblʌd] *n* [source of strength] alma *f*, sustento *m*.

lifeboat ['laɪfbəʊt] *n* [on a ship] bote *m* salvavidas; [on shore] lancha *f* de salvamento.

life buoy *n* flotador *m*, salvavidas *m inv*.

life cycle *n* ciclo *m* vital.

life expectancy *n* expectativa *f* de vida.

lifeguard ['laɪfgɑːd] *n* socorrista *mf*.

life imprisonment [-ɪmˈprɪznmənt] *n* cadena *f* perpetua.

life insurance, life assurance *n (U)* seguro *m* de vida.

life jacket *n* chaleco *m* salvavidas.

lifeless ['laɪflɪs] *adj* - **1.** [dead] sin vida - **2.** [listless] insulso(sa).

lifelike ['laɪflaɪk] *adj* realista, natural.

lifeline ['laɪflaɪn] *n* - **1.** [rope] cuerda *f* OR cable *m* (de salvamento) - **2.** [something vital for survival] cordón *m* umbilical.

lifelong ['laɪflɒŋ] *adj* de toda la vida.

life peer *n* UK noble británico con título no hereditario.

life preserver [-prɪˌzɜːvəʳ] *n* US - **1.** [life jacket] chaleco *m* salvavidas - **2.** [life belt] flotador *m*, salvavidas *m inv*.

life raft *n* balsa *f* salvavidas.

lifesaver ['laɪfˌseɪvəʳ] *n* - **1.** [person] socorrista *mf* - **2.** *fig* [relief, help]: **it was a real lifesaver** me salvó la vida, me sacó de un gran apuro.

life sentence *n* (condena *f* a) cadena *f* perpetua.

life-size(d) [-saɪz(d)] *adj* (de) tamaño natural.

lifespan ['laɪfspæn] *n* vida *f*.

lifestyle ['laɪfstaɪl] *n* estilo *m* OR modo *m* de vida.

life-support system *n* aparato *m* de respiración artificial.

lifetime ['laɪftaɪm] *n* vida *f*.

lift [lɪft] ◇ *n* - **1.** [ride - in car etc]: **to give sb a lift (somewhere)** acercar OR llevar a alguien (a algún sitio), dar (un) aventón a alguien (a algún sitio) Col & Méx - **2.** UK [elevator] ascensor *m*, elevador *m Méx*. ◇ *vt* - **1.** [gen] levantar; **to lift sthg down** bajar algo; **to lift sthg out of sthg** sacar algo de algo - **2.** [plagiarize] copiar. ◇ *vi* - **1.** [rise] levantarse, alzarse - **2.** [disappear - mist] disiparse.

lift-off *n* despegue *m*.

ligament ['lɪgəmənt] *n* ligamento *m*.

light [laɪt] ◇ *adj* - **1.** [gen] ligero(ra); [rain] fino(na); [traffic] ligero(ra) - **2.** [not strenuous - du-

ties, responsibilities] simple; [- work] suave; [- punishment] leve - **3.** [low-calorie, low-alcohol] light - **4.** [bright] luminoso(sa), lleno(na) de luz; **it's growing light** se hace de día - **5.** [pale - colour] claro(ra). ◇ *n* - **1.** [brightness, source of light] luz *f* - **2.** [for cigarette, pipe] fuego *m*, lumbre *f*; **have you got a light?** ¿tienes fuego? - **3.** [perspective]: **in the light of** UK, **in light of** US a la luz de; **to see sthg/sb in a different light** ver algo/a alguien de otra manera distinta - **4.** *liter* [look in eyes] brillo *m*

▶▶ **to bring sthg to light** sacar algo a la luz; **to come to light** salir a la luz (pública); **to set light to** prender fuego a; **to see the light** verlo claro; **to throw** OR **cast** OR **shed light on** arrojar luz sobre. ◇ *vt (pt & pp* **lit** OR **-ed)** - **1.** [ignite] encender - **2.** [illuminate] iluminar. ◇ *vi* prenderse. ◇ *adv* [travel] con poco equipaje.

➤ **light up** ◇ *vt sep (pt & pp* **lit** OR **-ed)** - **1.** [illuminate] iluminar - **2.** [start smoking] encender. ◇ *vi* - **1.** [look happy] iluminarse, encenderse - **2.** *inf* [start smoking] encender un cigarrillo.

light aircraft (*pl* **light aircraft**) *n* avioneta *f*.

light ale *n* UK tipo suave de cerveza rubia.

light bulb *n* bombilla *f*, foco *m Méx*, bombillo *m Amér C & Col*, bombita *f R Plata*, bujía *f Amér C*, ampolleta *f Chile*.

light cream *n* US nata *f* líquida.

lighted ['laɪtɪd] *adj* [illuminated] iluminado(da).

light-emitting diode [-ɪˈmɪtɪŋ-] *n* diodo *m* emisor de luz.

lighten ['laɪtn] ◇ *vt* - **1.** [make brighter - room] iluminar; [- hair] aclarar - **2.** [make less heavy] aligerar. ◇ *vi* - **1.** [brighten] aclararse - **2.** [become happier, more relaxed] alegrarse.

lighter ['laɪtəʳ] *n* [cigarette lighter] encendedor *m*, mechero *m*.

light-fingered [-ˈfɪŋgəd] *adj* *inf* largo(ga) de uñas.

light-headed [-ˈhedɪd] *adj* [dizzy] mareado(da); [emotionally] exaltado(da).

light-hearted [-ˈhɑːtɪd] *adj* - **1.** [cheerful] alegre - **2.** [amusing] frívolo(la).

lighthouse ['laɪthaʊs] (*pl* [-haʊzɪz]) *n* faro *m*.

light industry *n* industria *f* ligera.

lighting ['laɪtɪŋ] *n* iluminación *f*; **street lighting** alumbrado *m* público.

lighting-up time *n* hora *f* de encendida del alumbrado público.

lightly ['laɪtlɪ] *adv* - **1.** [gently] suavemente - **2.** [slightly] ligeramente - **3.** [frivolously] a la ligera.

light meter *n* fotómetro *m*.

lightning ['laɪtnɪŋ] *n (U)*: **a flash of lightning** un relámpago; **a bolt of lightning** un rayo; **it was struck by lightning** lo alcanzó un rayo.

lightning conductor *UK*, **lightning rod** *US* n pararrayos m inv.

lightning strike n UK huelga f salvaje.

light opera n opereta f.

light pen n lápiz m óptico.

lights-out n hora en que se apagan las luces.

lightweight ['laɪtweɪt] ◇ adj - **1.** [object] ligero(ra) - **2.** fig [person] de poca monta. ◇ n - **1.** [boxer] peso m ligero - **2.** fig [person] figura f menor.

light year n año m luz.

likable, likeable ['laɪkəbl] adj simpático(ca).

like [laɪk] ◇ prep - **1.** [gen] como; *(in questions or indirect questions)* cómo; **what did it taste like?** ¿a qué sabía?; **what did it look like?** ¿cómo era?; **tell me what it's like** dime cómo es; **something like £100** algo así como cien libras; **something like that** algo así, algo por el estilo - **2.** [in the same way as] como, igual que; **like this/that** así - **3.** [typical of] propio(pia) OR típico(ca) de; **it's not like them** no es su estilo. ◇ vt - **1.** [find pleasant, approve of]: **I like cheese** me gusta el queso; **I like it/them** me gusta/gustan; **I don't like it/them** no me gusta/gustan; **he likes doing** OR **to do sthg** (a él) le gusta hacer algo - **2.** [want] querer; **would you like some more?** ¿quieres un poco más?; **I'd like to come tomorrow** querría OR me gustaría venir mañana; **I'd like you to come to dinner** me gustaría que vinieras a cenar; **whenever you like** cuando quieras; **I don't like to bother her** no quiero molestarla; [in shops, restaurants]: **I'd like a kilo of apples/the soup** póngame un kilo de manzanas/la sopa. ◇ vi querer; **if you like** si quieres. ◇ adj [similar] semejante; [the same] igual. ◇ n: **and the like** de sb/sthg alguien/algo del estilo; **and the like** y similares, y cosas por el estilo; **I've never seen the like (of it)** nunca he visto nada igual.

➤ **likes** npl [things one likes] gustos mpl, preferencias fpl.

likeable ['laɪkəbl] = **likable**.

likelihood ['laɪklɪhʊd] n probabilidad f; **in all likelihood** con toda probabilidad.

likely ['laɪklɪ] ◇ adj - **1.** [probable] probable; **rain is likely** es probable que llueva; **he's likely to come** es probable que venga; **a likely story!** iro ¡puro cuento! - **2.** [suitable] indicado(da). ◇ adv: **most likely** muy probablemente.

like-minded [-'maɪndɪd] adj de ideas afines.

liken ['laɪkn] vt: **to liken sthg/sb to** comparar algo/a alguien con.

likeness ['laɪknɪs] n - **1.** [resemblance]: **likeness (to)** parecido m (con) - **2.** [portrait] retrato m.

likewise ['laɪkwaɪz] adv [similarly] de la misma forma; **to do likewise** hacer lo mismo.

liking ['laɪkɪŋ] n: **to have a liking for sthg** tener afición f por OR a algo; **to take a liking to sb** tomar OR coger cariño m a alguien; **to be to sb's liking** ser del gusto de alguien; **for my/his liking** etc para mi/su gusto etc.

lilac ['laɪlək] ◇ adj [colour] lila. ◇ n - **1.** [tree, flower] lila f - **2.** [colour] lila m.

Lilo® ['laɪləʊ] (pl -s) n UK colchoneta f, colchón m hinchable.

lilt [lɪlt] n entonación f, deje m.

lilting ['lɪltɪŋ] adj melodioso(sa).

lily ['lɪlɪ] (pl -ies) n lirio m, azucena f.

lily of the valley (pl lilies of the valley) n lirio m de los valles.

Lima ['liːmə] n Lima.

limb [lɪm] n - **1.** [of body] miembro m - **2.** [of tree] rama f

➤➤ **to be out on a limb** estar aislado(da).

limber ['lɪmbər] ➤ **limber up** vi calentar, desentumecerse.

limbo ['lɪmbəʊ] (pl -s) n - **1.** (U) [uncertain state]: **to be in limbo** estar en un estado de incertidumbre - **2.** [dance]: **the limbo** el limbo.

lime [laɪm] n - **1.** [fruit] lima f - **2.** [drink]: **lime (juice)** lima f - **3.** [linden tree] tilo m - **4.** CHEM cal f

lime cordial n refresco m de lima.

lime-green adj (de color) verde lima.

limelight ['laɪmlaɪt] n: **in the limelight** en (el) candelero.

limerick ['lɪmərɪk] n copla humorística de cinco versos.

limestone ['laɪmstəʊn] n (U) (piedra f) caliza f.

limey ['laɪmɪ] (pl limeys) n US inf término peyorativo que designa a un inglés.

limit ['lɪmɪt] ◇ n - **1.** [gen] límite m - **2.** [test of patience]: **you're the limit!** inf ¡eres el colmo!

➤➤ **off limits** en zona prohibida; **within limits** dentro de un límite. ◇ vt limitar; **to limit o.s. to** limitarse a.

limitation [ˌlɪmɪ'teɪʃn] n limitación f.

limited ['lɪmɪtɪd] adj [restricted] limitado(da); **to be limited to** estar limitado a.

limited edition n edición f limitada.

limited (liability) company n sociedad f limitada.

limitless ['lɪmɪtlɪs] adj ilimitado(da).

limo ['lɪməʊ] n inf abbr of **limousine**.

limousine ['lɪməziːn] n limusina f.

limp [lɪmp] ◇ adj flojo(ja). ◇ n cojera f; **to have a limp** cojear. ◇ vi cojear.

limpet ['lɪmpɪt] n lapa f.

limply ['lɪmplɪ] *adv* lánguidamente.

linchpin ['lɪntʃpɪn] *n fig* eje *m*.

Lincs. [lɪŋks] (*abbr of* **Lincolnshire**) *condado inglés.*

linctus ['lɪŋktəs] *n UK* jarabe *m* para la tos.

line [laɪn] <> *n* - **1.** [gen & MIL] línea *f* - **2.** [row] fila *f*; **in a line** en fila - **3.** *esp US* [queue] cola *f*; **to stand** OR **wait in line** hacer cola - **4.** [course - direction] línea *f*; [- of action] camino *m*; **to walk in a straight line** andar en línea recta; **what's his line of business?** ¿a qué negocios se dedica?; **to follow the party line** seguir las directrices del partido; **along the same lines** por el estilo - **5.** [length - of rope, for washing] cuerda *f*; [- for fishing] sedal *m*; [- of wire] hilo *m*, cable *m* - **6.** TELEC: **(telephone) line** línea *f* (telefónica); **hold the line, please** no cuelgue, por favor; **the line is busy** está comunicando; **it's a bad line** hay interferencias; **your wife is on the line for you** su mujer al teléfono - **7.** [on page] línea *f*, renglón *m*; [of poem, song] verso *m*; [letter]: **to drop sb a line** *inf* mandar unas letras a alguien - **8.** [system of transport]: **(railway) line** [track] vía *f* (férrea); [route] línea *f* (férrea); **shipping line** [company] compañía *f* naviera; [route] ruta *f* marítima - **9.** [wrinkle] arruga *f* - **10.** [alignment]: **in line** alineado(da); **to be in line for promotion** estar camino de un ascenso - **11.** [succession of kings etc] línea *f*; **a long line of mistakes** una larga serie de errores - **12.** [borderline] límite *m*, frontera *f* - **13.** COMM línea *f*; **line of credit** línea *f* de crédito

▸▸ **to be on the right lines** estar en el buen camino; **along similar lines** de manera parecida; **to draw the line at sthg** no pasar por algo, negarse a algo; **to read between the lines** leer entre líneas; **to step out of line** saltarse las reglas. <> *vt* - **1.** [form rows along] alinearse a lo largo de; **crowds lined the street** la gente se apiñaba a los lados de la calle - **2.** [coat, curtains] forrar; [drawer] cubrir el interior de.

▸ **lines** *npl* - **1.** SCH *castigo consistente en escribir la misma frase gran número de veces* - **2.** THEAT papel *m*.

▸ **on the line** *adv*: **to be on the line** estar en juego.

▸ **out of line** *adv*: **to be out of line** estar fuera de lugar.

▸ **line up** <> *vt sep* - **1.** [make into a row or queue] alinear - **2.** [arrange] programar, organizar. <> *vi* [form a queue] alinearse, ponerse en fila.

lineage ['lɪnɪɪdʒ] *n fml* linaje *m*.

linear ['lɪnɪəʳ] *adj* lineal.

lined [laɪnd] *adj* - **1.** [of paper] reglado(da), de rayas - **2.** [wrinkled] arrugado(da).

line dancing *n* baile en el que los participantes se colocan en fila y se mueven al mismo tiempo que los otros.

line drawing *n* dibujo *m* lineal.

line feed *n* avance *m* de línea.

linen ['lɪnɪn] <> *n* - **1.** [cloth] lino *m* - **2.** [tablecloths, sheets] ropa *f* blanca OR de hilo; **bed linen** ropa *f* de cama. <> *comp* - **1.** [suit, napkins] de hilo - **2.** [cupboard, drawer] de la ropa.

linen basket *n* cesta *f* de la ropa (sucia).

line printer *n* impresora *f* de línea.

liner ['laɪnəʳ] *n* [ship] transatlántico *m*.

linesman ['laɪnzmən] (*pl* **-men** [-mən]) *n* juez *m* de línea.

lineup ['laɪnʌp] *n* - **1.** [of players, competitors] alineación *f* - **2.** *US* [identification parade] rueda *f* de identificación.

linger ['lɪŋgəʳ] *vi* - **1.** [remain - over activity] entretenerse; [- in a place] rezagarse - **2.** [persist] persistir.

lingerie ['lænʒərɪ] *n* ropa *f* interior femenina.

lingering ['lɪŋgərɪŋ] *adj* [illness, hopes] persistente; [death] lento(ta); [kiss] largo(ga).

lingo ['lɪŋgəʊ] (*pl* **-es**) *n inf* [foreign language] idioma *m*; [jargon] jerga *f*.

linguist ['lɪŋgwɪst] *n* - **1.** [someone good at languages]: **he's a good linguist** tiene facilidad para las lenguas - **2.** [student or teacher of linguistics] lingüista *mf*.

linguistic [lɪŋ'gwɪstɪk] *adj* lingüístico(ca).

linguistics [lɪŋ'gwɪstɪks] *n* (U) lingüística *f*.

liniment ['lɪnɪmənt] *n* linimento *m*.

lining ['laɪnɪŋ] *n* - **1.** [gen & AUT] forro *m* - **2.** [of stomach, nose] paredes *fpl* interiores.

link [lɪŋk] <> *n* - **1.** [of chain] eslabón *m*; **the weakest link** el punto más débil - **2.** [connection] conexión *f*, enlace *m*; **rail link** enlace ferroviario; **telephone link** conexión OR línea *f* telefónica; **links (between/with)** lazos *mpl* (entre/con), vínculos *mpl* (entre/con). <> *vt* - **1.** [connect - cities] comunicar, enlazar; [- computers] conectar; [- facts] relacionar, asociar; **to link sthg with** OR **to** relacionar OR asociar algo con - **2.** [join - arms] enlazar. <> *vi* COMPUT: **to link to sth** enlazar con algo.

▸ **link up** *vt sep*: **to link sthg up (with)** conectar algo (con).

linkage ['lɪŋkɪdʒ] *n* (U) [relationships] conexión *f*.

linked [lɪŋkt] *n* - **1.** [connected - cities] unido(da); [- computers] conectado(da); [- facts] relacionado(da) - **2.** [joined - arms] enlazado(da).

links [lɪŋks] (*pl* **links**) *n* campo *m* de golf (*cerca del mar*).

linkup ['lɪŋkʌp] *n* [of TV channels] conexión *f*; [of spaceships] acoplamiento *m*.

lino ['laɪnəʊ], **linoleum** [lɪ'nəʊljəm] *n* linóleo *m*.

linseed oil ['lɪnsiːd-] n aceite m de linaza.
lint [lɪnt] n (U) - **1.** [dressing] hilas fpl - **2.** US [fluff] pelusa f.
lintel ['lɪntl] n dintel m.
lion ['laɪən] n león m.
lion cub n cachorro m de león.
lioness ['laɪənes] n leona f.
lionize, -ise ['laɪənaɪz] vt encumbrar.
lip [lɪp] n - **1.** [of mouth] labio m; **my lips are sealed** soy una tumba; **to keep a stiff upper lip** mantener el tipo - **2.** [of cup] borde m; [of jug] pico m.
liposuction ['lɪpəʊˌsʌkʃən] n liposucción f.
lip-read vi leer los labios.
lip-reading n lectura f de labios.
lip salve [-sælv] n UK vaselina® f, cacao m.
lip service n: **to pay lip service to sthg** hablar en favor de algo sin hacer nada al respeto.
lipstick ['lɪpstɪk] n - **1.** [container] lápiz m OR barra f de labios - **2.** [substance] carmín m.
liquefy ['lɪkwɪfaɪ] (pt & pp -ied) <> vt licuar. <> vi licuarse.
liqueur [lɪˈkjʊəʳ] n licor m.
liquid ['lɪkwɪd] <> adj líquido(da). <> n líquido m.
liquid assets npl activo m disponible.
liquidate ['lɪkwɪdeɪt] vt liquidar.
liquidation [ˌlɪkwɪˈdeɪʃn] n liquidación f; **to go into liquidation** ir a la quiebra.
liquidator ['lɪkwɪdeɪtəʳ] n liquidador m, -ra f.
liquid crystal display n pantalla f de cristal líquido.
liquidity [lɪˈkwɪdətɪ] n [having money] liquidez f.
liquidize, -ise ['lɪkwɪdaɪz] vt UK licuar.
liquidizer ['lɪkwɪdaɪzəʳ] n UK licuadora f.
liquor ['lɪkəʳ] n (U) esp US alcohol m, bebida f alcohólica.
liquorice, licorice ['lɪkərɪʃ, 'lɪkərɪs] n (U) regaliz m.
liquor store n US tienda donde se venden bebidas alcohólicas para llevar.
lira ['lɪərə] n lira f.
lisp [lɪsp] <> n ceceo m. <> vi cecear.
list [lɪst] <> n lista f. <> vt - **1.** [in writing] hacer una lista de - **2.** [in speech] enumerar. <> vi NAUT escorar.
listed building [ˌlɪstɪd-] n UK edificio declarado de interés histórico y artístico.
listed company [ˌlɪstɪd-] n UK sociedad f que se cotiza en bolsa.
listen ['lɪsn] vi - **1.** [give attention]: **to listen (to sthg/sb)** escuchar (algo/a alguien); **to listen for** estar atento a - **2.** [heed advice]: **to listen (to sb/sthg)** hacer caso (a alguien/de algo); **to listen to reason** atender a razones.

listen in vi - **1.** RADIO: **to listen in (to a programme)** escuchar OR sintonizar (un programa en) una emisora - **2.** [eavesdrop]: **to listen in (on sthg)** escuchar (algo) a hurtadillas.
listen up vi US inf escuchar.
listener ['lɪsnəʳ] n - **1.** [person listening]: **she's a good listener** sabe escuchar - **2.** [to radio] radioyente mf.
listeria [lɪsˈtiːəriə] n - **1.** [illness] listeriosis f inv - **2.** [bacteria] listeria f.
listing ['lɪstɪŋ] n listado m.
listings npl cartelera f.
listless ['lɪstlɪs] adj apático(ca).
list price n precio m de catálogo.
lit [lɪt] pt & pp ▷ light.
litany ['lɪtənɪ] (pl -ies) n lit & fig letanía f.
liter US = litre.
literacy ['lɪtərəsɪ] n alfabetización f.
literal ['lɪtərəl] adj literal.
literally ['lɪtərəlɪ] adv literalmente; **to take sthg literally** tomarse algo al pie de la letra.
literary ['lɪtərərɪ] adj [gen] literario(ria).
literate ['lɪtərət] adj - **1.** [able to read and write] alfabetizado(da) - **2.** [well-read] culto(ta), instruido(da).
literature ['lɪtrətʃəʳ] n - **1.** [novels, plays, poetry] literatura f - **2.** [books on a particular subject] publicaciones fpl, bibliografía f - **3.** [printed information] documentación f.
lithe [laɪð] adj ágil.
lithograph ['lɪθəgrɑːf] n litografía f.
Lithuania [ˌlɪθjʊˈeɪniə] n Lituania.
Lithuanian [ˌlɪθjʊˈeɪnjən] <> adj lituano(na). <> n - **1.** [person] lituano m, -na f - **2.** [language] lituano m.
litigant ['lɪtɪgənt] n fml litigante mf, pleiteante mf.
litigate ['lɪtɪgeɪt] vi fml litigar, pleitear.
litigation [ˌlɪtɪˈgeɪʃn] n fml litigio m, pleito m.
litmus paper ['lɪtməs-] n papel m de tornasol.
litre UK, **liter** US ['liːtəʳ] n litro m.
litter ['lɪtəʳ] <> n - **1.** [waste material] basura f - **2.** [newborn animals] camada f. <> vt: **to litter sthg (with)** ensuciar algo (de); **papers littered the floor** había papeles esparcidos por el suelo.
litterbin ['lɪtəˌbɪn] n UK papelera f.
litterlout UK ['lɪtəlaʊt], **litterbug** ['lɪtəbʌg] n persona que ensucia la vía pública.
litter tray n bandeja para la arena del gato.
little ['lɪtl] <> adj - **1.** [small in size, younger] pequeño(ña); **a little dog** un perrito; **you poor little thing!** ¡pobrecillo! - **2.** [short in length] corto(ta); **a little while** un ratito - **3.** (comp less, superl least) [not much] po-

co(ca); **a little bit** un poco; **he speaks little English** habla poco inglés; **he speaks a little English** habla un poco de inglés. <> *pron:* **I understood very little** entendí muy poco; **a little** un poco; **a little under half** algo menos de la mitad. <> *adv* poco; **little by little** poco a poco.

little finger *n* dedo *m* meñique.

little-known *adj* poco conocido(da).

liturgy ['lɪtədʒɪ] (*pl* -ies) *n* [form of worship] liturgia *f*.

live [lɪv] <> *vi* - **1.** [gen] vivir; **the greatest that ever lived** el mejor de todos los tiempos - **2.** [continue to be alive] seguir viviendo, vivir; **long live the Queen!** ¡viva la reina! <> *vt* vivir; **to live a quiet life** llevar una vida tranquila; **to live it up** *inf* pegarse la gran vida.
◆ **live down** *vt sep* lograr hacer olvidar.
◆ **live for** *vt insep* vivir para.
◆ **live in** *vi* [student] ser interno(na); [servant, nanny] residir OR vivir en la casa.
◆ **live off** *vt insep* [savings, land] vivir de; [people] vivir a costa de.
◆ **live on** <> *vt insep* - **1.** [survive on] vivir con OR de; **it wasn't enough to live on** no daba para vivir - **2.** [eat] vivir de, alimentarse de. <> *vi* [memory, feeling] permanecer, perdurar.
◆ **live out** *vt insep* - **1.** [life] acabar; **he won't live out the month** no va a vivir hasta finales de mes - **2.** [dream, fantasy] realizar.
◆ **live together** *vi* vivir juntos.
◆ **live up to** *vt insep* estar a la altura de.
◆ **live with** *vt insep* - **1.** [live in same house as] vivir con - **2.** [accept - situation, problem] aceptar.

live [laɪv] <> *adj* - **1.** [living] vivo(va) - **2.** [coals] encendido(da) - **3.** [bomb] sin explotar; [ammunition] real - **4.** ELEC cargado(da) - **5.** [broadcast, performance] en directo. <> *adv* [broadcast, perform] en directo, en vivo.

live-in [lɪv-] *adj inf* [housekeeper] residente; **Jane's live-in lover** el amante de Jane instalado en su casa.

livelihood ['laɪvlɪhʊd] *n* sustento *m*, medio *m* de vida.

liveliness ['laɪvlɪnɪs] *n* [of person] vivacidad *f*, viveza *f*; [of mind] sagacidad *f*, agudeza *f*; [of debate] animación *f*.

lively ['laɪvlɪ] (*comp* -ier, *superl* -iest) *adj* - **1.** [person, debate, time] animado(da) - **2.** [mind] agudo(da), perspicaz - **3.** [colours] vivo(va).

liven ['laɪvn] ◆ **liven up** <> *vt sep* animar. <> *vi* animarse.

liver ['lɪvə'] *n* hígado *m*.

Liverpudlian [ˌlɪvə'pʌdlɪən] <> *adj* de o relativo a Liverpool. <> *n* natural o habitante de Liverpool.

liver sausage *UK*, **liverwurst** *US* ['lɪvəwɜːst] *n* paté *m* de hígado en embutido.

livery ['lɪvərɪ] (*pl* -ies) *n* [of servant] librea *f*; [of company] uniforme *m*.

lives [laɪvz] *npl* ⊳ **life**.

livestock ['laɪvstɒk] *n* ganado *m*.

live wire [laɪv-] *n* - **1.** [wire] cable *m* cargado OR con corriente - **2.** *inf* [person] persona *f* llena de vida.

livid ['lɪvɪd] *adj* - **1.** [angry] furioso(sa) - **2.** [blue-grey] lívido(da).

living ['lɪvɪŋ] <> *adj* [relatives, language] vivo(va); [artist etc] contemporáneo(a). <> *n* - **1.** [means of earning money] medio *m* de vida; **what do you do for a living?** ¿cómo te ganas la vida?; **to earn a living** ganarse la vida - **2.** [lifestyle] vida *f*.

living conditions *npl* condiciones *fpl* de vida.

living expenses *npl* gastos *mpl* de mantenimiento.

living room *n* sala *f* de estar, salón *m*.

living standards *npl* nivel *m* de vida.

lizard ['lɪzəd] *n* [small] lagartija *f*; [big] lagarto *m*.

llama ['lɑːmə] (*pl* **llama** OR -s) *n* llama *f*.

lo [ləʊ] *excl*: **lo and behold** ¡he aquí!

load [ləʊd] <> *n* - **1.** [thing carried] carga *f* - **2.** [amount of work]: **a heavy/light load** mucho/poco trabajo - **3.** [large amount]: **loads/a load of** *inf* montones o un montón de; **it was a load of rubbish** *inf* fue una porquería. <> *vt* - **1.** [gen & COMPUT]: **to load sthg/sb (with)** cargar algo/a alguien (de) - **2.** [camera, video recorder]: **he loaded the camera with a film** cargó la cámara con una película.
◆ **load up** *vt sep & vi* cargar.

loaded ['ləʊdɪd] *adj* - **1.** [dice] trucado(da); [question, statement] con doble sentido OR intención - **2.** *inf* [rich] forrado(da).

loading bay ['ləʊdɪŋ-] *n* zona *f* de carga y descarga.

loaf [ləʊf] (*pl* **loaves**) *n* [of bread] pan *m*; **a loaf of bread** un pan.

loafer ['ləʊfə'] *n* [shoe] mocasín *m*.

loam [ləʊm] *n* marga *f*.

loan [ləʊn] <> *n* préstamo *m*; **on loan** prestado(da). <> *vt* prestar; **to loan sthg to sb, to loan sb sthg** prestar algo a alguien.

loan account *n* cuenta *f* de crédito.

loan capital *n* capital *m* en préstamo.

loan shark *n* *inf pej* usurero *m*, -ra *f*.

loath, loth [ləʊθ] *adj*: **to be loath to do sthg** ser reacio(cia) a hacer algo.

loathe [ləʊð] *vt*: **to loathe (doing sthg)** aborrecer OR detestar (hacer algo).

loathing [ˈləʊðɪŋ] *n* aborrecimiento *m*, odio *m*.

loathsome [ˈləʊðsəm] *adj* [person, behaviour] odioso(sa), detestable; [smell] repugnante.

loaves [ləʊvz] *npl* ▷ **loaf**.

lob [lɒb] ◇ *n* TENNIS lob *m*. ◇ *vt* (*pt & pp* -**bed**, *cont* -**bing**) - **1.** [throw] lanzar - **2.** TENNIS [ball] hacer un lob con, bombear; [opponent] hacer un lob a.

lobby [ˈlɒbɪ] ◇ *n* (*pl* -**ies**) - **1.** [hall] vestíbulo *m* - **2.** [pressure group] grupo *m* de presión, lobby *m*. ◇ *vt* (*pt & pp* -**ied**) ejercer presión (política) sobre.

lobbyist [ˈlɒbɪɪst] *n* miembro *mf* de un lobby.

lobe [ləʊb] *n* lóbulo *m*.

lobelia [ləˈbiːljə] *n* lobelia *f*.

lobotomy [ləˈbɒtəmɪ] (*pl* -**ies**) *n* lobotomía *f*.

lobster [ˈlɒbstər] *n* langosta *f*.

local [ˈləʊkl] ◇ *adj* local. ◇ *n inf* - **1.** [person]: **the locals** [in village] los lugareños; [in town] los vecinos del lugar - **2.** UK [pub] bar *m* del barrio - **3.** US [bus, train] omnibús *m*.

local anaesthetic *n* anestesia *f* local.

local area network *n* COMPUT red *f* de área local.

local authority *n* UK autoridad *f* local.

local call *n* llamada *f* local.

local colour *n* ambientación *f*.

local derby *n* UK partido *m* entre dos equipos locales.

locale [ləʊˈkɑːl] *n fml* lugar *m*, emplazamiento *m*.

local government *n* gobierno *m* municipal.

locality [ləʊˈkælətɪ] (*pl* -**ies**) *n* localidad *f*.

localized, -ised [ˈləʊkəlaɪzd] *adj* localizado(da).

locally [ˈləʊkəlɪ] *adv* - **1.** [on local basis] localmente, en el lugar - **2.** [nearby] cerca, por la zona.

local time *n* hora *f* local.

locate [UK ləʊˈkeɪt, US ˈləʊkeɪt] ◇ *vt* - **1.** [find] localizar - **2.** [situate] ubicar. ◇ *vi* US [settle] establecerse.

location [ləʊˈkeɪʃn] *n* - **1.** [place] ubicación *f*, situación *f* - **2.** [finding] localización *f* - **3.** CIN: **on location** en exteriores.

loc. cit. (*abbr of* **loco citato**) loc. cit.

loch [lɒk, lɒx] *n Scotland* lago *m*.

lock [lɒk] ◇ *n* - **1.** [of door] cerradura *f*, chapa *f* *Amér*; [of bicycle] candado *m*; **under lock & key** bajo siete llaves - **2.** [on canal] esclusa *f* - **3.** AUT [steering lock] ángulo *m* de giro - **4.** *liter* [of hair] mechón *m*

▶▶ **lock, stock and barrel** por completo. ◇ *vt* - **1.** [with key] cerrar con llave; [with padlock] cerrar con candado - **2.** [keep safely] poner bajo llave - **3.** [immobilize] bloquear - **4.** [hold firmly]: **to be locked in an embrace** estar abrazados(das) fuertemente; **to be locked in combat** estar enzarzados(das) en una lucha. ◇ *vi* - **1.** [with key, padlock] cerrarse - **2.** [become immobilized] bloquearse.

◆ **locks** *npl liter* [hair] cabellos *mpl*.

◆ **lock in** *vt sep* encerrar.

◆ **lock out** *vt sep* - **1.** [accidentally] dejar fuera al cerrar accidentalmente la puerta; **to lock o.s. out** quedarse fuera (*por olvidarse de la llave dentro*) - **2.** [deliberately] dejar fuera a.

◆ **lock up** ◇ *vt sep* - **1.** [person - in prison] encerrar; [- in asylum] internar - **2.** [house] cerrar (con llave) - **3.** [valuables] guardar bajo llave. ◇ *vi* cerrar (con llave).

lockable [ˈlɒkəbl] *adj* bloqueable.

locker [ˈlɒkər] *n* taquilla *f*, armario *m*.

locker room *n* US vestuario *m* con taquillas.

locket [ˈlɒkɪt] *n* guardapelo *m*.

lockout [ˈlɒkaʊt] *n* cierre *m* patronal.

locksmith [ˈlɒksmɪθ] *n* cerrajero *m*, -ra *f*.

lockup [ˈlɒkʌp] *n* - **1.** [prison] calabozo *m*, prisión *f* - **2.** UK [garage] garaje *m*.

loco [ˈləʊkəʊ] *inf* ◇ *adj* US loco(ca). ◇ *n* (*pl* -**s**) UK [locomotive] locomotora *f*.

locomotive [ˈləʊkə,məʊtɪv] *n* locomotora *f*.

locum [ˈləʊkəm] (*pl* -**s**) *n* interino *m*, -na *f*.

locust [ˈləʊkəst] *n* langosta *f* (*insecto*).

lodge [lɒdʒ] ◇ *n* - **1.** [caretaker's *etc* room] portería *f* - **2.** [of manor house] casa *f* del guarda - **3.** [for hunting] refugio *m* - **4.** [of freemasons] logia *f*. ◇ *vi* - **1.** [stay]: **to lodge (with sb)** alojarse (con alguien) - **2.** [become stuck] alojarse - **3.** *fig* [in mind] grabarse. ◇ *vt fml* [appeal, complaint] presentar.

lodger [ˈlɒdʒər] *n* huésped *mf*.

lodging [ˈlɒdʒɪŋ] *n* ▷ **board**.

◆ **lodgings** *npl* habitación *f* (alquilada).

loft [lɒft] *n* [in house] desván *m*, entretecho *m* *Chile & Col*; [for hay] pajar *m*; US [warehouse apartment] *almacén reformado y convertido en apartamento*.

lofty [ˈlɒftɪ] (*comp* -**ier**, *superl* -**iest**) *adj* - **1.** [noble] noble, elevado(da) - **2.** *pej* [haughty] arrogante, altanero(ra) - **3.** *liter* [high] elevado(da), alto(ta).

log [lɒg] ◇ *n* - **1.** [of wood] tronco *m*; [for fire] leño *m* - **2.** [written record - of ship] diario *m* de a bordo; COMPUT registro *m*. ◇ *vt* (*pt & pp* -**ged**, *cont* -**ging**) registrar.

◆ **log in** *vi* COMPUT entrar.

◆ **log off** *vi* COMPUT salir.

◆ **log on** *vi* COMPUT entrar.

➤ **log out** *vi* COMPUT salir.

loganberry ['lɔʊɡənbərɪ] (*pl* **-ies**) *n* zarza *f* frambuesa.

logarithm ['lɒɡərɪðm] *n* logaritmo *m*.

logbook ['lɒɡbʊk] *n* - **1.** [of ship] diario *m* de a bordo; [of plane] diario *m* de vuelo - **2.** [of car] documentación *f*.

log cabin *n* cabaña *f*.

log fire *n* fuego *m* (de leña).

loggerheads ['lɒɡəhedz] *n*: **to be at logger-heads** estar a matar.

logic ['lɒdʒɪk] *n* lógica *f*.

logical ['lɒdʒɪkl] *adj* lógico(ca).

logically ['lɒdʒɪklɪ] *adv* - **1.** [gen] lógicamente - **2.** [reasonably, sensibly] razonablemente, sensatamente.

logistical [lə'dʒɪstɪkl] *adj* logístico(ca).

logistics [lə'dʒɪstɪks] <> *n* (U) logística *f*. <> *npl* logística *f*.

logjam ['lɒɡdʒæm] *n* atolladero *m*.

logo ['ləʊɡəʊ] (*pl* **-s**) *n* logo *m*, logotipo *m*.

logrolling ['lɒɡrəʊlɪŋ] *n* (U) US acción de alabar o respaldar el trabajo de alguien para recibir después el mismo trato.

loin [lɔɪn] *n* lomo *m*.

➤ **loins** *npl* ijada *f*; **to gird one's loins** prepararse para la batalla.

loincloth ['lɔɪnklɒθ] *n* taparrabos *m inv*.

loiter ['lɔɪtə'] *vi* [for bad purpose] merodear; [hang around] vagar.

loll [lɒl] *vi* - **1.** [sit, lie about] repantigarse - **2.** [hang down] colgar; **his head was lolling** cabeceaba.

lollipop ['lɒlɪpɒp] *n* pirulí *m*.

lollipop lady *n* UK mujer encargada de parar el tráfico en un paso de cebra para que crucen los niños.

lollipop man *n* UK hombre encargado de parar el tráfico en un paso de cebra para que crucen los niños.

lolly ['lɒlɪ] (*pl* **-ies**) *n inf* - **1.** [lollipop] pirulí *m* - **2.** UK [ice lolly] polo *m* - **3.** UK [money] pasta *f*.

London ['lʌndən] *n* Londres.

Londoner ['lʌndənə'] *n* londinense *mf*.

lone [ləʊn] *adj* solitario(ria).

loneliness ['ləʊnlɪnɪs] *n* soledad *f*.

lonely ['ləʊnlɪ] (*comp* **-ier**, *superl* **-iest**) *adj* - **1.** [person] solo(la) - **2.** [time, childhood, place] solitario(ria).

lone parent *n* UK [man] padre *m* soltero; [woman] madre *f* soltera.

loner ['ləʊnə'] *n* solitario *m*, -ria *f*.

lonesome ['ləʊnsəm] *adj* US inf - **1.** [person] solo(la) - **2.** [place] solitario(ria).

long [lɒŋ] <> *adj* largo(ga); **the table is 5m long** la mesa mide OR tiene 5m de largo; **two days long** de dos días de duración; **the journey is 50km long** el viaje es de 50 km; **the book is 500 pages long** el libro tiene 500 páginas; **a long time** mucho tiempo; **a long way from** muy lejos de. <> *adv* mucho tiempo; **how long will it take?** ¿cuánto se tarda?; **how long will you be?** ¿cuánto tardarás?; **how long have you been waiting?** ¿cuánto tiempo llevas esperando?; **how long have you known them?** ¿cuánto hace que los conoces?; **how long is the journey?** ¿cuánto hay de viaje?; **I'm no longer young** ya no soy joven; **I can't wait any longer** no puedo esperar más; **as long as a week** hasta una semana; **so long** *inf* hasta luego OR pronto; **before long** pronto; **for long** mucho tiempo. <> *n*: **the long and the short of it is that...** en pocas palabras lo que pasa es que... <> *vt*: **to long to do sthg** desear ardientemente hacer algo.

➤ **as long as, so long as** *conj* mientras; **as long as you do it, so will I** siempre y cuando tú lo hagas, yo también lo haré.

➤ **long for** *vt insep* desear ardientemente.

long. (*abbr of* **longitude**) long.

long-awaited [-ə'weɪtɪd] *adj* tan esperado (tan esperada).

long-distance *adj* [runner] de fondo; [lorry driver] para distancias grandes.

long-distance call *n* conferencia *f* (telefónica) Esp, llamada *f* de larga distancia.

long division *n* división *f* no abreviada.

long-drawn-out *adj* interminable.

long drink *n* [without alcohol] refresco *m*; [with alcohol] combinado *m*.

longevity [lɒn'dʒevətɪ] *n* longevidad *f*.

longhaired [ˌlɒŋ'heəd] *adj* de pelo largo.

longhand ['lɒŋhænd] *n* escritura *f* a mano.

long-haul *adj* de larga distancia.

longing ['lɒŋɪŋ] <> *adj* anhelante. <> *n* - **1.** [desire] anhelo *m*, deseo *m*; [nostalgia] nostalgia *f*, añoranza *f* - **2.** [strong wish]: **(a) longing (for)** (un) ansia *f* (de).

longingly ['lɒŋɪŋlɪ] *adv* de manera anhelante.

longitude ['lɒndʒɪtjuːd] *n* longitud *f*.

long johns *npl* calzones *mpl* largos.

long jump *n* salto *m* de longitud.

long-lasting *adj* duradero(ra).

long-life *adj* de larga duración.

longlist ['lɒŋlɪst] *n* selección *f* inicial.

long-lost *adj* desaparecido(da) hace tiempo.

long-playing record [-'pleɪɪŋ-] *n* elepé *m*.

long-range *adj* - **1.** [missile, bomber] de largo alcance - **2.** [plan, forecast] a largo plazo.

long-running adj [TV programme] en antena mucho tiempo; [play] en cartelera mucho tiempo; [dispute] que dura desde tiempo inmemorial.

longshoreman ['lɒŋʃɔːmən] (pl -men [-mən]) n US estibador m.

long shot n posibilidad f remota.

longsighted [ˌlɒŋ'saɪtɪd] adj présbita.

long-standing adj antiguo(gua).

longsuffering [ˌlɒŋ'sʌfərɪŋ] adj sufrido(da).

long term n: in the long term a largo plazo.
➡ **long-term** adj [gen] a largo plazo; [unemployed] de larga duración.

long vacation n UK vacaciones fpl de verano.

long wave n (U) onda f larga.

longways ['lɒŋweɪz] adv a lo largo, longitudinalmente.

longwearing [ˌlɒŋ'weərɪŋ] adj US resistente.

long weekend n fin m de semana largo, puente m.

longwinded [ˌlɒŋ'wɪndɪd] adj prolijo(ja).

loo [luː] (pl -s) n UK inf retrete m, wáter m.

loofa(h) ['luːfə] n esponja f vegetal.

look [lʊk] ◇ n - **1.** [with eyes] mirada f; to give sb a look mirar a alguien; to take OR have a look (at sthg) mirar algo; let her have a look déjale ver; to have a look through sthg ojear algo - **2.** [search]: to have a look (for sthg) buscar (algo) - **3.** [appearance] aspecto m; his new look su nuevo look; I don't like the look of it no me gusta nada; by the look OR looks of it, it has been here for ages parece que hace años que está aquí. ◇ vi - **1.** [with eyes]: to look (at sthg/sb) mirar (algo/a alguien) - **2.** [search]: to look (for sthg/sb) buscar (algo/a alguien) - **3.** [building, window]: to look (out) onto dar a - **4.** [have stated appearance] verse; [seem] parecer;: what does it look like? ¿cómo es?; it looks good on you te queda bien; he looks as if he hasn't slept tiene pinta de no haber dormido; it looks like rain OR as if it will rain parece que va a llover; she looks like her mother se parece a su madre. ◇ vt - **1.** [look at] mirar - **2.** [appear]: to look one's age representar la edad que se tiene; to look one's best vestir elegantemente. ◇ excl: look!, look here! ¡mira!

➡ **looks** npl belleza f.
➡ **look after** vt insep - **1.** [take care of] cuidar - **2.** [be responsible for] encargarse de.
➡ **look at** vt insep - **1.** [see, glance at] mirar, aguaitar Amér; [examine] examinar; [check over] echar un vistazo a - **2.** [judge, evaluate] ver.
➡ **look back** vi [reminisce]: to look back on sthg recordar algo; she's never looked back no ha dejado de prosperar.

➡ **look down on** vt insep [condescend to] despreciar.
➡ **look for** vt insep buscar.
➡ **look forward to** vt insep esperar (con ilusión); I'm looking forward to the trip creo que la excursión va a ser buenísima; to be looking forward to doing sthg estar deseando hacer algo.
➡ **look into** vt insep [problem, possibility] estudiar; [issue] investigar.
➡ **look on** ◇ vt insep = look upon. ◇ vi mirar, observar.
➡ **look out** vi [be careful] tener cuidado; look out! ¡cuidado!
➡ **look out for** vt insep estar atento(ta) a.
➡ **look over** vt sep mirar por encima.
➡ **look round** ◇ vt insep [shop] echar un vistazo a; [castle, town] visitar. ◇ vi - **1.** [turn head] volver la cabeza - **2.** [in shop] mirar.
➡ **look through** vt insep - **1.** [look at briefly - book, paper] hojear; [- collection, pile] echar un vistazo a - **2.** [check] revisar.
➡ **look to** vt insep - **1.** [turn to] recurrir a - **2.** [think about] pensar en.
➡ **look up** ◇ vt sep - **1.** [in book] buscar - **2.** [visit - person] ir a ver OR visitar. ◇ vi [improve] mejorar.
➡ **look upon** vt insep: to look upon sthg/sb as considerar algo/a alguien como.
➡ **look up to** vt insep respetar, admirar.

look-alike n sosia m.

look-in n UK inf: to get a look-in [chance to win] tener la posibilidad (de ganar); [chance to participate] tener la oportunidad (de participar).

lookout ['lʊkaʊt] n - **1.** [place] puesto m de observación, atalaya f - **2.** [person] guardia mf, centinela mf - **3.** [search]: to be on the lookout for estar al acecho de.

loom [luːm] ◇ n telar m. ◇ vi - **1.** [rise up] surgir OR aparecer amenazante - **2.** fig [be imminent] cernerse; to loom large [be worrying] ser agobiante.
➡ **loom up** vi divisarse sombríamente.

LOOM (abbr of Loyal Order of the Moose) n organización benéfica estadounidense.

looming ['luːmɪŋ] adj inminente.

loony ['luːnɪ] inf ◇ adj (comp -ier, superl -iest) majara, chiflado(da). ◇ n (pl -ies) majara mf, chiflado m, -da f.

loop [luːp] ◇ n - **1.** [shape] lazo m - **2.** COMPUT bucle m - **3.** [contraceptive] esterilete m - **4.**: to be out of the loop US no estar al corriente. ◇ vt: to loop sthg round sthg pasar algo alrededor de algo. ◇ vi hacer un lazo.

loophole ['luːphəʊl] n laguna f.

loo roll n UK inf rollo m de papel higiénico.

loose [luːs] ◇ *adj* - **1.** [not firmly fixed] flojo(ja); **to come loose** aflojarse - **2.** [unattached - paper, sweets, hair, knot] suelto(ta) - **3.** [clothes, fit] holgado(da) - **4.** *dated* [promiscuous] promiscuo(cua) - **5.** [inexact - translation] poco exacto (poco exacta), impreciso(sa) - **6.** [association] no muy estrecho (no muy estrecha) - **7.** *US inf* [relaxed]: **to stay loose** estar tranqui. ◇ *n (U)*: **to be on the loose** andar suelto(ta).

loose change *n* (dinero *m*) suelto *m*, sencillo *m Andes*, feria *f Méx*, menudo *m Col*.

loose end *n* cabo *m* suelto; **to be at a loose end** *UK*, **to be at loose ends** *US* no tener nada que hacer.

loose-fitting *adj* amplio(plia), holgado(da).

loose-leaf binder *n* carpeta *f* de hojas sueltas.

loosely ['luːslɪ] *adv* - **1.** [not firmly] holgadamente, sin apretar - **2.** [inexactly] vagamente.

loosen ['luːsn] ◇ *vt* aflojar. ◇ *vi* aflojarse.

◆ **loosen up** *vi* - **1.** [before game, race] desentumecerse - **2.** *inf* [relax] relajarse.

loot [luːt] ◇ *n* botín *m*. ◇ *vt* saquear.

looter ['luːtər] *n* saqueador *m*, -ra *f*.

looting ['luːtɪŋ] *n* saqueo *m*.

lop [lɒp] (*pt & pp* -**ped**, *cont* -**ping**) *vt* podar.

◆ **lop off** *vt sep* cortar.

lope [ləʊp] *vi* andar con paso largo y ligero.

lop-sided [-'saɪdɪd] *adj* - **1.** [uneven] ladeado(da), torcido(da) - **2.** *fig* [biased] desequilibrado(da).

lord [lɔːd] *n UK* [man of noble rank] noble *m*.

◆ **Lord** *n* - **1.** RELIG: **the Lord** [God] el Señor; **good Lord!** *UK* ¡Dios mío! - **2.** [in titles] lord *m*; [as form of address]: **my Lord** [bishop] su Ilustrísima; [judge] su Señoría.

◆ **Lords** *npl UK* POL: **the Lords** la Cámara de los Lores.

Lord Chancellor *n UK presidente de la Cámara de los Lores y responsable de Justicia en Inglaterra y Gales*.

lordly ['lɔːdlɪ] (*comp* -**ier**, *superl* -**iest**) *adj* - **1.** [noble] señorial, noble - **2.** *pej* [arrogant] arrogante, altivo(va).

Lord Mayor *n UK* alcalde *m*.

Lordship ['lɔːdʃɪp] *n*: **your/his Lordship** su Señoría *f*.

Lord's Prayer *n*: **the Lord's Prayer** el Padrenuestro.

lore [lɔːr] *n (U)* saber *m* OR tradición *f* popular.

lorry ['lɒrɪ] (*pl* -**ies**) *n UK* camión *m*.

lorry driver *n UK* camionero *m*, -ra *f*.

lose [luːz] (*pt & pp* **lost**) ◇ *vt* perder; **to lose one's way** perderse; **my watch has lost ten minutes** mi reloj se ha atrasado diez minutos; **to lose o.s. in sthg** *fig* quedarse absorto(ta) en

algo; **to lose sight of sthg/sb** *lit & fig* perder de vista algo/a alguien. ◇ *vi* - **1.** [fail to win] perder - **2.** [clock, watch] atrasarse.

◆ **lose out** *vi* salir perdiendo; **to lose out on sthg** salir perdiendo en algo.

loser ['luːzər] *n* - **1.** [of competition] perdedor *m*, -ra *f*; **to be a good/bad loser** saber/no saber perder - **2.** *inf pej* [unsuccessful person] desgraciado *m*, -da *f*.

losing ['luːzɪŋ] *adj* vencido(da), derrotado(da).

loss [lɒs] *n* - **1.** [gen] pérdida *f*; **loss of life** muertes *fpl*; **to make a loss** sufrir pérdidas - **2.** [failure to win] derrota *f* - **3.**: **a dead loss** *inf* una birria

◆ **to be at a loss to explain sthg** no saber cómo explicar algo; **to cut one's losses** ahorrarse problemas cortando por lo sano.

loss adjuster [-ə'dʒʌstər] *n* perito *m* tasador de seguros.

loss leader *n* COMM artículo *m* de reclamo.

lost [lɒst] ◇ *pt & pp* ▷ **lose**. ◇ *adj* - **1.** [unable to find way] perdido(da); **to get lost** perderse; **get lost!** *inf* ¡vete a la porra! - **2.** [that cannot be found] extraviado(da), perdido(da) - **3.** [ineffective]: **to be lost on sb** no surtir efecto en alguien - **4.** [opportunity] desaprovechado(da).

lost-and-found office *n US* oficina *f* de objetos perdidos.

lost cause *n* causa *f* perdida.

lost property *n (U)* objetos *mpl* perdidos.

lost property office *n UK* oficina *f* de objetos perdidos.

lot [lɒt] *n* - **1.** [large amount]: **a lot of, lots of** mucho(cha); **a lot of people** mucha gente, muchas personas; **a lot of problems** muchos problemas; **the lot** todo - **2.** [group, set] lote *m* - **3.** *inf* [group of people] panda *f*, pandilla *f* - **4.** [destiny] destino *m*, suerte *f* - **5.** *US* [of land] terreno *m*; [car park] aparcamiento *m* - **6.** [at auction] partida *f*, lote *m*

◆ **to draw lots** echar a suerte.

◆ **a lot** *adv* mucho; **quite a lot** bastante; **such a lot** tanto.

loth [ləʊθ] = **loath**.

lotion ['ləʊʃn] *n* loción *f*.

lottery ['lɒtərɪ] (*pl* -**ies**) *n* lotería *f*.

lottery ticket *n* billete *m* de lotería.

lotus position ['ləʊtəs-] *n* posición *f* de loto.

loud [laʊd] ◇ *adj* - **1.** [voice, music] alto(ta); [bang, noise] fuerte; [person] ruidoso(sa) - **2.** [emphatic]: **to be loud in one's criticism of** ser enérgico(ca) en la crítica de - **3.** [too bright] chillón(ona), llamativo(va). ◇ *adv* alto, fuerte; **loud and clear** alto y claro; **out loud** en voz alta.

loudhailer [ˌlaʊd'heɪlər] *n UK* megáfono *m*.

loudly ['laʊdlɪ] *adv* - **1.** [shout] a voz en grito; [talk] en voz alta - **2.** [gaudily] con colores chillones OR llamativos.

loudmouth ['laʊdmaʊθ] *(pl* [-maʊðz]*) n inf* bocazas *m* & *f inv*.

loudness ['laʊdnɪs] *n* fuerza *f*, intensidad *f*.

loudspeaker [,laʊd'spiːkəʳ] *n* altavoz *m*, altoparlante *m* Amér.

Louisiana [luː,iːzɪ'ænə] *n* Luisiana.

lounge [laʊndʒ] *n* - **1.** [in house] salón *m* - **2.** [in airport] sala *f* de espera - **3.** UK [lounge bar] salón-bar *m*. ⟨⟩ *vi (cont* **lounging**) repantigarse.

◆ **lounge about, lounge around** *vi* holgazanear.

lounge bar *n* UK salón-bar *m*.

lounge suit *n* UK traje *m*.

louse [laʊs] *n* - **1.** *(pl* **lice**) [insect] piojo *m* - **2.** *(pl* **-s**) *inf pej* [person] canalla *mf*.

◆ **louse up** US *vt sep v inf* jorobar, fastidiar.

lousy ['laʊzɪ] *(comp* **-ier**, *superl* **-iest**) *adj inf* - **1.** [poor quality] fatal, pésimo(ma) - **2.** [ill]: **to feel lousy** sentirse fatal.

lout [laʊt] *n* gamberro *m*.

louvre UK, **louver** US ['luːvəʳ] *n* persiana *f*.

lovable ['lʌvəbl] *adj* encantador(ra), adorable.

love [lʌv] ⟨⟩ *n* - **1.** [gen] amor *m*; **give her my love** dale un abrazo de mi parte; **she sends her love** te manda recuerdos; **love from** [at end of letter] un abrazo de; **a love-hate relationship** una relación de amor y odio; **to be in love (with)** estar enamorado(da) (de); **to fall in love with sb** enamorarse de alguien; **to make love** hacer el amor - **2.** [liking, interest] pasión *f*; **a love of** OR **for** una pasión por - **3.** *inf* [form of address] cariño *m* - **4.** TENNIS: **30 love** 30 a nada. ⟨⟩ *vt* - **1.** [sexually, sentimentally] amar, querer - **2.** [son, daughter, parents, friend] querer - **3.** [like]: **I love football** me encanta el fútbol; **I love going to** OR **to go to the theatre** me encanta ir al teatro.

love affair *n* aventura *f* amorosa.

lovebite ['lʌvbaɪt] *n* chupetón *m*.

loveless ['lʌvlɪs] *adj* sin amor.

love letter *n* carta *f* de amor.

love life *n* vida *f* amorosa.

lovely ['lʌvlɪ] *(comp* **-ier**, *superl* **-iest**) *adj* - **1.** [beautiful - person] encantador(ra); [- dress, place] precioso(sa) - **2.** [pleasant] estupendo(da).

lovemaking ['lʌv,meɪkɪŋ] *n (U)* relaciones *fpl* sexuales.

lover ['lʌvəʳ] *n* - **1.** [sexual partner] amante *mf* - **2.** [enthusiast] amante *mf*, aficionado *m*, -da *f*.

lovesick ['lʌvsɪk] *adj* enfermo(ma) de amor (no correspondido).

love song *n* canción *f* de amor.

love story *n* historia *f* de amor.

loving ['lʌvɪŋ] *adj* cariñoso(sa), afectuoso(sa).

lovingly ['lʌvɪŋlɪ] *adv* cariñosamente, afectuosamente.

low [ləʊ] ⟨⟩ *adj* - **1.** [gen] bajo(ja); **cook on a low heat** cocinar a fuego lento; **in the low twenties** 20 y algo; **a low trick** una mala jugada - **2.** [little remaining] escaso(sa); **to be low on sthg** andar escaso de algo; **the batteries are low** se me están acabando las pilas - **3.** [unfavourable - opinion] malo(la); [- esteem] poco(ca) - **4.** [dim] tenue - **5.** [dress, neckline] escotado(da) - **6.** [depressed] deprimido(da). ⟨⟩ *adv* - **1.** [gen] bajo; **the batteries are running low** las pilas están acabándose; **morale is running very low** la moral está por los suelos; **low paid** mal pagado - **2.** [speak] en voz baja. ⟨⟩ *n* - **1.** [low point] punto *m* más bajo - **2.** METEOR [low pressure area] área *f* de bajas presiones; [lowest temperature] mínima *f*.

low-alcohol *adj* bajo(ja) en alcohol.

lowbrow ['ləʊbraʊ] *adj* PRESS & TV para las masas.

low-calorie *adj* light *(inv)*, bajo(ja) en calorías.

Low Countries *npl*: **the Low Countries** los Países Bajos.

low-cut *adj* escotado(da).

low-down *inf* ⟨⟩ *adj* bajo(ja), sucio(cia). ⟨⟩ *n*: **to give sb the low-down (on sthg)** dar los detalles concretos (sobre algo) a alguien.

lower[1] ['ləʊəʳ] ⟨⟩ *adj* inferior. ⟨⟩ *vt* - **1.** [gen] bajar; [flag] arriar; **to lower o.s. to do sthg** rebajarse a hacer algo; **to lower one's eyes** bajar la mirada - **2.** [reduce] reducir.

lower[2] ['laʊəʳ] *vi* - **1.** [be dark] estar oscuro(ra) - **2.** [frown]: **to lower at sb** fruncir el ceño a alguien.

Lower Chamber [,ləʊəʳ-] *n* POL Cámara *f* Baja.

lower class [,ləʊəʳ-] *n*: **the lower class** OR **lower classes** las clases bajas.

◆ **lower-class** *adj* de clase baja.

Lower House [,ləʊəʳ-] *n* Cámara *f* Baja.

lowest common denominator ['ləʊɪst-] *n* mínimo común denominador *m*.

low-fat *adj* bajo(ja) en grasas.

low-flying *adj* de vuelo bajo OR rasante.

low frequency *n* baja frecuencia *f*.

low gear *n*: **in low gear** en primera o segunda.

low-key *adj* discreto(ta).

Lowlands ['ləʊləndz] *npl*: **the Lowlands** [of Scotland] las Tierras Bajas (de Escocia).

lowly ['ləʊlɪ] *(comp* **-ier**, *superl* **-iest**) *adj* humilde.

low-lying *adj* bajo(ja).

Low Mass *n* misa *f* hablada.
low-necked [-'nekt] *adj* escotado(da).
low-paid *adj* mal pagado (mal pagada).
low-rise *adj* bajo(ja), de poca altura.
low season *n* temporada *f* baja.
low-tech [-'tek] *adj* [industry] de baja tecnología; [solution] rudimentario(ria).
low tide *n* marea *f* baja.
loyal ['lɔɪəl] *adj* leal, fiel.
loyalist ['lɔɪəlɪst] *n* [gen] leal *mf*; [in Northern Ireland] lealista *mf*.
loyalty ['lɔɪəltɪ] (*pl* **-ies**) *n* lealtad *f*, fidelidad *f*.
lozenge ['lɒzɪndʒ] *n* - **1.** [tablet] pastilla *f* - **2.** [shape] rombo *m*.
LP (*abbr of* **long-playing record**) *n* LP *m*.
LPG [,elpi:'dʒi:] (*abbr of* **liquified petroleum gas**) *n* GLP *m*.
L-plate *n* UK placa *f* L (de prácticas).
LSD (*abbr of* **lysergic acid diethylamide**) *n* LSD *m*.
LSE (*abbr of* **London School of Economics**) *n* escuela londinense de ciencias políticas y económicas.
Lt. (*abbr of* **lieutenant**) ≃ Tte.
LT (*abbr of* **low tension**) *n* BT.
Ltd, ltd (*abbr of* **limited**) S.L.
lubricant ['lu:brɪkənt] *n* lubricante *m*.
lubricate ['lu:brɪkeɪt] *vt* lubricar.
lubrication [,lu:brɪ'keɪʃn] *n* lubricación *f*.
lucid ['lu:sɪd] *adj* - **1.** [clear] claro(ra) - **2.** [not confused] lúcido(da).
lucidly ['lu:sɪdlɪ] *adv* claramente, lúcidamente.
luck [lʌk] *n* suerte *f*; **good/bad luck** [good, bad fortune] buena/mala suerte; **good luck!** [said to express best wishes] ¡suerte!; **bad OR hard luck!** ¡mala suerte!; **to be in luck** estar de suerte; **to try one's luck at sthg** probar suerte a OR con algo; **with (any) luck** con un poco de suerte.
➤ **luck out** *vi* US *inf* tener potra.
luckily ['lʌkɪlɪ] *adv* afortunadamente.
luckless ['lʌklɪs] *adj* desafortunado(da).
lucky ['lʌkɪ] (*comp* **-ier**, *superl* **-iest**) *adj* - **1.** [fortunate - person] afortunado(da); [- event] oportuno(na); **to be lucky** [person] tener suerte; **it's lucky he came** fue una suerte que llegara - **2.** [bringing good luck] que trae buena suerte; **lucky number** número *m* de la suerte.
lucky dip *n* UK caja *f* de las sorpresas.
lucrative ['lu:krətɪv] *adj* lucrativo(va).
ludicrous ['lu:dɪkrəs] *adj* absurdo(da), ridículo(la).
ludo ['lu:dəʊ] *n* UK parchís *m*.
lug [lʌg] (*pt* & *pp* **-ged**, *cont* **-ging**) *vt inf* arrastrar.
luggage ['lʌgɪdʒ] *n* UK equipaje *m*.

luggage rack *n* UK [of car] baca *f*; [in train] portaequipajes *m inv*.
luggage van *n* UK furgón *m* de equipajes.
lugubrious [lu:'gu:brɪəs] *adj fml* lúgubre.
lukewarm ['lu:kwɔ:m] *adj* - **1.** [tepid] tibio(bia), templado(da) - **2.** [unenthusiastic] indiferente.
lull [lʌl] <> *n*: **lull (in)** [activity] respiro *m* (en); [conversation] pausa *f* (en); [fighting] tregua *f* (en); **the lull before the storm** *fig* la calma antes de la tormenta. <> *vt*: **to lull sb into a false sense of security** infundir una sensación de falsa seguridad a alguien; **to lull sb to sleep** adormecer OR hacer dormir a alguien.
lullaby ['lʌləbaɪ] (*pl* **-ies**) *n* nana *f*, canción *f* de cuna.
lumbago [lʌm'beɪgəʊ] *n* (U) lumbago *m*.
lumber ['lʌmbər] <> *n* (U) - **1.** US [timber] maderos *mpl* - **2.** UK [bric-a-brac] trastos *mpl*. <> *vi* moverse pesadamente.
➤ **lumber with** *vt sep* UK *inf*: **to lumber sb with sthg** cargar a alguien con algo.
lumbering ['lʌmbərɪŋ] *adj* torpe, pesado(da).
lumberjack ['lʌmbədʒæk] *n* leñador *m*, -ra *f*.
lumbermill ['lʌmbə,mɪl] *n* US aserradero *m*, serrería *f*.
lumber-room *n* UK cuarto *m* trastero.
lumberyard ['lʌmbəjɑ:d] *n* almacén *m* de madera.
luminous ['lu:mɪnəs] *adj* luminoso(sa).
lump [lʌmp] <> *n* - **1.** [of coal, earth] trozo *m*; [of sugar] terrón *m*; [in sauce] grumo *m* - **2.** [on body] bulto *m* - **3.** *fig* [in throat] nudo *m*. <> *vt*: **to lump sthg together** [things] amontonar algo; [people, beliefs] agrupar OR juntar algo; **you can lump it!** *inf* ¡te aguantas!
lumpectomy [,lʌm'pektəmɪ] (*pl* **-ies**) *n* extirpación *f* de un tumor de pecho.
lump sum *n* suma *f* OR cantidad *f* global.
lumpy ['lʌmpɪ] (*comp* **-ier**, *superl* **-iest**) *adj* [sauce] grumoso(sa); [mattress] lleno(na) de bultos.
lunacy ['lu:nəsɪ] *n* locura *f*.
lunar ['lu:nər] *adj* lunar.
lunatic ['lu:nətɪk] <> *adj pej* demencial. <> *n* - **1.** *pej* [fool] idiota *mf* - **2.** [insane person] loco *m*, -ca *f*.
lunatic asylum *n* manicomio *m*.
lunatic fringe *n* sector *m* extremista.
lunch [lʌntʃ] <> *n* comida *f*, almuerzo *m*; **to have lunch** almorzar, comer; **why don't we do lunch some time?** ¿por qué no almorzamos juntos algún día de estos? <> *vi* almorzar, comer.
luncheon ['lʌntʃən] *n* comida *f*, almuerzo *m*.
luncheon meat *n* carne de cerdo en lata troceada.

luncheon voucher *n UK* vale *m* del almuerzo.

lunch hour *n* hora *f* del almuerzo.

lunchtime ['lʌntʃtaɪm] *n* hora *f* del almuerzo.

lung [lʌŋ] *n* pulmón *m*.

lung cancer *n* cáncer *m* de pulmón.

lunge [lʌndʒ] (*cont* **lunging**) *vi* lanzarse; **to lunge at sb** arremeter contra alguien.

lupin *UK* ['lu:pɪn], **lupine** *US* ['lu:paɪn] *n* altramuz *m*, lupino *m*.

lurch [lɜ:tʃ] ⟨> *n* [of boat] bandazo *m*; [of person] tumbo *m*; **to leave sb in the lurch** dejar a alguien en la estacada. ⟨> *vi* [boat] dar bandazos; [person] tambalearse.

lure [ljʊəʳ] ⟨> *n* fascinación *f*, atracción *f*. ⟨> *vt* atraer.

lurid ['ljʊərɪd] *adj* - **1.** [brightly coloured] chillón(ona) - **2.** [shockingly unpleasant] espeluznante - **3.** [sensational] escabroso(sa).

lurk [lɜ:k] *vi* - **1.** [person] estar al acecho - **2.** [memory, danger, fear] ocultarse.

lurking ['lɜ:kɪŋ] *adj* [suspicion] que sigue rondando.

luscious ['lʌʃəs] *adj lit & fig* apetitoso(sa).

lush [lʌʃ] ⟨> *adj* - **1.** [luxuriant] exuberante - **2.** *inf* [rich] lujoso(sa). ⟨> *n US inf* [drunkard] borracho *m*, -cha *f*.

lust [lʌst] *n* - **1.** [sexual desire] lujuria *f* - **2.** [strong desire]: **lust for sthg** ansia *f* de algo.
◆ **lust after, lust for** *vt insep* - **1.** [desire - wealth, success] codiciar - **2.** [desire sexually] desear.

luster *US* = **lustre**.

lustful ['lʌstfʊl] *adj* lascivo(va).

lustre *UK*, **luster** *US* ['lʌstəʳ] *n* [brightness] lustre *m*.

lusty ['lʌstɪ] (*comp* **-ier**, *superl* **-iest**) *adj* vigoroso(sa).

lute [lu:t] *n* laúd *m*.

luv [lʌv] *n UK inf* rey *m*, reina *f*; **what do you want, luv?** ¿qué quieres, rey?

luvvie ['lʌvɪ] *n inf* actor *m*, -triz *f* pedante.

Luxembourg ['lʌksəm,bɜ:g] *n* Luxemburgo.

luxuriant [lʌg'ʒʊərɪənt] *adj* exuberante, abundante.

luxuriate [lʌg'ʒʊərɪeɪt] *vi*: **to luxuriate (in)** deleitarse (con).

luxurious [lʌg'ʒʊərɪəs] *adj* [gen] lujoso(sa); [lifestyle] de lujo.

luxury ['lʌkʃərɪ] (*pl* **-ies**) ⟨> *n* lujo *m*. ⟨> *comp* de lujo.

luxury goods *npl* artículos *mpl* de lujo.

LV *abbr of* **luncheon voucher**.

LW (*abbr of* **long wave**) *n* OL *f*.

lychee [,laɪ'tʃi:] *n* lichi *m*.

Lycra® ['laɪkrə] ⟨> *n* lycra® *f*. ⟨> *comp* de lycra®.

lying ['laɪɪŋ] ⟨> *adj* mentiroso(sa). ⟨> *n (U)* mentiras *fpl*.

lymph gland [lɪmf-] *n* glándula *f* linfática.

lynch [lɪntʃ] *vt* linchar.

lynx [lɪŋks] (*pl* **lynx** *OR* **-es**) *n* lince *m*.

lyre ['laɪəʳ] *n* lira *f*.

lyric ['lɪrɪk] *adj* lírico(ca).

lyrical ['lɪrɪkl] *adj* - **1.** [poetic] lírico(ca) - **2.** [enthusiastic] entusiasmado(da).

lyrics ['lɪrɪks] *npl* letra *f*.

m[1] (*pl* **m's** *OR* **ms**), **M** (*pl* **M's** *OR* **Ms**) [em] *n* [letter] m *f*, M *f*.
◆ **M** - **1.** *abbr of* **motorway** - **2.** (*abbr of* **medium**) M.

m[2] - **1.** (*abbr of* **metre**) m - **2.** (*abbr of* **million**) m - **3.** *abbr of* **mile**.

ma [mɑ:] *n esp US inf* mamá *f*.

MA ⟨> *n abbr of* **Master of Arts**. ⟨> *abbr of* **Massachusetts**.

ma'am [mæm] *n* señora *f*.

mac [mæk] (*abbr of* **mackintosh**) *n UK inf* [coat] impermeable *m*.

macabre [mə'kɑ:brə] *adj* macabro(bra).

Macao [mə'kaʊ] *n* Macao.

macaroni [,mækə'rəʊnɪ] *n (U)* macarrones *mpl*.

macaroni cheese *n (U)* macarrones *mpl* al gratén.

macaroon [,mækə'ru:n] *n* mostachón *m*, macarrón *m*.

mace [meɪs] *n* - **1.** [ornamental rod] maza *f* - **2.** [spice] macis *f inv*.

Macedonia [,mæsɪ'dəʊnɪə] *n* Macedonia.

Macedonian [,mæsɪ'dəʊnɪən] ⟨> *adj* macedonio(nia). ⟨> *n* - **1.** [person] macedonio *m*, -nia *f* - **2.** [language] macedonio *m*.

machete [mə'ʃetɪ] *n* machete *m*.

Machiavellian [,mækɪə'velɪən] *adj* maquiavélico(ca).

machinations [ˌmækɪ'neɪʃnz] *npl* maquinaciones *fpl*.

machine [mə'ʃiːn] <> *n* **- 1.** [power-driven device] máquina *f* **- 2.** [organization] aparato *m*. <> *vt* **- 1.** SEW coser a máquina **- 2.** TECH producir a máquina.

machine code *n* COMPUT código *m* máquina.

machinegun [mə'ʃiːngʌn] <> *n* [with tripod] ametralladora *f*; [hand-held] metralleta *f*. <> *vt* (*pt* & *pp* **-ned**, *cont* **-ning**) ametrallar.

machine language *n* COMPUT lenguaje *m* máquina.

machine-readable *adj* COMPUT legible para el ordenador.

machinery [mə'ʃiːnərɪ] *n lit* & *fig* maquinaria *f*.

machine shop *n* taller *m* de máquinas.

machine tool *n* máquina *f* herramienta.

machine-washable *adj* lavable a máquina.

machinist [mə'ʃiːnɪst] *n* operario *m*, -ria *f* (de máquina).

machismo [mə'tʃɪzməʊ] *n* machismo *m*.

macho ['mætʃəʊ] *adj inf* macho.

mackerel ['mækrəl] (*pl* **mackerel** OR **-s**) *n* caballa *f*.

mackintosh ['mækɪntɒʃ] *n UK* impermeable *m*.

macramé [mə'krɑːmɪ] *n* macramé *m*.

macro ['mækrəʊ] (*abbr of* **macroinstruction**) *n* COMPUT macro *f*.

macrobiotic [ˌmækrəʊbaɪ'ɒtɪk] *adj* macrobiótico(ca).

macrocosm ['mækrəʊkɒzm] *n* macrocosmo *m*.

macroeconomics ['mækrəʊˌiːkə'nɒmɪks] *n* (*U*) macroeconomía *f*.

mad [mæd] (*comp* **-der**, *superl* **-dest**) *adj* **- 1.** [gen] loco(ca); [attempt, idea] disparatado(da), descabellado(da); **to be mad about sb/sthg** estar loco(ca) por alguien/algo; **to go mad** volverse loco **- 2.** [furious] furioso(sa) **- 3.** [hectic] desenfrenado(da); **like mad** como loco.

Madagascan [ˌmædə'gæskən] <> *adj* malgache. <> *n* **- 1.** [person] malgache *mf* **- 2.** [language] malgache *m*.

Madagascar [ˌmædə'gæskəʳ] *n* Madagascar.

madam ['mædəm] *n* **- 1.** [woman] señora *f* **- 2.** [in brothel] madam *f*.

madcap ['mædkæp] *adj* descabellado(da), disparatado(da).

mad cow disease *n* el mal de las vacas locas.

madden ['mædn] *vt* volver loco(ca), exasperar.

maddening ['mædnɪŋ] *adj* enloquecedor(ra).

made [meɪd] *pt* & *pp* ⊳ **make**.

-made [məɪd] *suffix*: **French-made** fabricado(da) en Francia.

Madeira [mə'dɪərə] *n* **- 1.** [wine] madeira *m*, madera *m* **- 2.** GEOG Madeira.

made-to-measure *adj* hecho(cha) a la medida.

made-up *adj* **- 1.** [with make-up - face, person] maquillado(da); [- lips, eyes] pintado(da) **- 2.** [prepared] (ya) preparado(da) **- 3.** [invented] inventado(da).

madhouse ['mædhaʊs] (*pl* **-həʊzɪz**) *n* manicomio *m*.

madly ['mædlɪ] *adv* [frantically] enloquecidamente; **madly in love** locamente enamorado.

madman ['mædmən] (*pl* **-men** [-mən]) *n* loco *m*.

madness ['mædnɪs] *n* locura *f*; **it's madness** es una locura.

Madonna [mə'dɒnə] *n* **- 1.** RELIG: **the Madonna** la Virgen **- 2.** ART madona *f*.

Madrid [mə'drɪd] *n* Madrid.

madrigal ['mædrɪgl] *n* madrigal *m*.

madwoman ['mædˌwʊmən] (*pl* **-women** [-ˌwɪmɪn]) *n* loca *f*.

maestro ['maɪstrəʊ] (*pl* **-tros** OR **-tri** [-trɪ]) *n* maestro *m*.

Mafia ['mæfɪə] *n*: **the Mafia** la mafia.

mag [mæg] (*abbr of* **magazine**) *n inf* revista *f*.

magazine [ˌmægə'ziːn] *n* **- 1.** [periodical] revista *f* **- 2.** [news programme] magazín *m* **- 3.** [on a gun] recámara *f*.

magenta [mə'dʒentə] <> *adj* magenta. <> *n* magenta *m*.

maggot ['mægət] *n* gusano *m*, larva *f*.

Maghreb ['mʌgreb] *n*: **the Maghreb** el Magreb.

magic ['mædʒɪk] <> *adj* **- 1.** [gen] mágico(ca); **magic spell** hechizo *m* **- 2.** [referring to conjuring] de magia **- 3.** *inf* [very good] genial. <> *n* magia *f*; **as if by magic** como por arte de magia.

magical ['mædʒɪkl] *adj lit* & *fig* mágico(ca).

magic carpet *n* alfombra *f* mágica.

magic eye *n UK* célula *f* fotoeléctrica.

magician [mə'dʒɪʃn] *n* **- 1.** [conjuror] mago *m*, -ga *f*, prestidigitador *m*, -ra *f* **- 2.** [wizard] mago *m*.

magic wand *n* varita *f* mágica.

magisterial [ˌmædʒɪ'stɪərɪəl] *adj fml* [authoritative] magistral.

magistrate ['mædʒɪstreɪt] *n* juez *mf* de primera instancia.

magistrates' court *n UK* juzgado *m* de primera instancia.

Magna Carta [ˌmægnə'kɑːtə] *n*: **the Magna Carta** la Carta Magna.

magnanimous [mæg'nænɪməs] *adj* magnánimo(ma).

magnate [ˈmægneɪt] n magnate mf.

magnesium [mægˈniːzɪəm] n magnesio m.

magnet [ˈmægnɪt] n imán m.

magnetic [mægˈnetɪk] adj - **1.** [attracting iron] magnético(ca) - **2.** fig [appealingly forceful] carismático(ca).

magnetic disk n disco m magnético.

magnetic field n campo m magnético.

magnetic tape n cinta f magnética.

magnetism [ˈmægnɪtɪzm] n lit & fig magnetismo m.

magnification [ˌmægnɪfɪˈkeɪʃn] n - **1.** [process] ampliación f - **2.** [degree of enlargement] aumento m.

magnificence [mægˈnɪfɪsəns] n grandiosidad f, esplendor m.

magnificent [mægˈnɪfɪsənt] adj [building, splendour] grandioso(sa); [idea, book, game] magnífico(ca).

magnify [ˈmægnɪfaɪ] (pt & pp -ied) vt - **1.** [in vision] aumentar, ampliar - **2.** [in the mind] exagerar.

magnifying glass [ˈmægnɪfaɪɪŋ-] n lupa f, lente f de aumento.

magnitude [ˈmægnɪtjuːd] n magnitud f.

magnolia [mægˈnəʊljə] n - **1.** [tree] magnolio m - **2.** [flower] magnolia f.

magnum [ˈmægnəm] (pl -s) n botella de champán o vino de 1,5 litros de capacidad.

magpie [ˈmægpaɪ] n urraca f.

maharaja(h) [ˌmɑːhəˈrɑːdʒə] n maharajá m.

mahogany [məˈhɒgənɪ] n - **1.** [wood] caoba f - **2.** [colour] caoba m.

maid [meɪd] n [in hotel] camarera f, recamarera f Amér C & Méx; [domestic] criada f, china f Amér.

maiden [ˈmeɪdn] ◇ adj inaugural. ◇ n liter doncella f.

maiden aunt n tía f soltera.

maiden name n nombre m de soltera.

maiden speech n POL primer discurso m como parlamentario.

mail [meɪl] ◇ n - **1.** [system] correo m; by mail por correo - **2.** [letters, parcels received] correspondencia f. ◇ vt esp US [send] mandar por correo; [put in mail box] echar al buzón.

mailbag [ˈmeɪlbæg] n saca f de correspondencia.

mailbox [ˈmeɪlbɒks] n - **1.** US [letterbox] buzón m - **2.** COMPUT buzón m.

mailing list [ˈmeɪlɪŋ-] n [for mailshots] lista f de distribución de publicidad OR información; COMPUT lista f de correo.

mailman [ˈmeɪlmən] (pl -men [-mən]) n US cartero m.

mail order n venta f por correo.

mailshot [ˈmeɪlʃɒt] n folleto m de publicidad (por correo).

mail train n tren m correo.

mail van n UK - **1.** AUT furgoneta f postal - **2.** RAIL vagón m postal.

maim [meɪm] vt mutilar.

main [meɪn] ◇ adj principal. ◇ n [pipe] tubería f principal; [wire] cable m principal.
◆ **mains** npl: **the mains** [gas, water] la tubería principal; [electricity] la red eléctrica.
◆ **in the main** adv por lo general.

main course n plato m fuerte.

mainframe (computer) [ˈmeɪnfreɪm-] n unidad f central, procesador m central.

mainland [ˈmeɪnlənd] ◇ adj continental; **mainland Spain** la Península. ◇ n: **on the mainland** en tierra firme.

main line n RAIL línea f principal.
◆ **mainline** ◇ adj [station] de una línea principal. ◇ vt & vi drug sl chutarse.

mainly [ˈmeɪnlɪ] adv principalmente.

main road n carretera f principal.

mainsail [ˈmeɪnseɪl, ˈmeɪnsəl] n vela f mayor.

mainstay [ˈmeɪnsteɪ] n fundamento m, base f.

mainstream [ˈmeɪnstriːm] ◇ adj [gen] predominante; [taste] corriente; [political party] convencional. ◇ n: **the mainstream** la tendencia general.

maintain [meɪnˈteɪn] vt - **1.** [gen] mantener - **2.** [support, provide for] sostener, sustentar - **3.** [assert]: **to maintain (that)** sostener que.

maintenance [ˈmeɪntənəns] n - **1.** [gen] mantenimiento m - **2.** [money] pensión f alimenticia.

maintenance order n UK LAW orden m de pensión alimenticia.

maisonette [ˌmeɪzəˈnet] n US dúplex m inv.

maize [meɪz] n maíz m.

Maj. (abbr of **Major**) ≃ Cte.

majestic [məˈdʒestɪk] adj majestuoso(sa).

majestically [məˈdʒestɪklɪ] adv majestuosamente.

majesty [ˈmædʒəstɪ] (pl -ies) n [grandeur] majestad f.
◆ **Majesty** n: **His/Her/Your Majesty** Su Majestad.

major [ˈmeɪdʒər] ◇ adj - **1.** [important] importante; [main] principal; **of major importance** de gran importancia - **2.** MUS mayor. ◇ n MIL comandante m; US [subject] especialidad f. ◇ vi: **to major in** US [subject] especializarse en.

Majorca [məˈjɔːkə, məˈdʒɔːkə] n Mallorca.

Majorcan [mə'jɔːkən, mə'dʒɔːkən] ◇ *adj* mallorquín(ina). ◇ *n* mallorquín *m*, -ina *f*.

majorette [ˌmeɪdʒə'ret] *n* majorette *f*.

major general *n* general *m* de división.

majority [mə'dʒɒrətɪ] (*pl* -ies) *n* mayoría *f*; **in a** OR **the majority** en una OR la mayoría.

majority shareholder *n* accionista *mf* principal.

make [meɪk] ◇ *vt* (*pt* & *pp* **made**) - **1.** [produce] hacer; **it made a lot of noise** hizo mucho ruido; **she makes her own clothes** se hace su propia ropa - **2.** [perform - action] hacer; **to make a speech** pronunciar OR dar un discurso; **to make a decision** tomar una decisión; **to make a mistake** cometer un error; **to make a payment** efectuar un pago - **3.** [cause to be, cause to do] hacer; **it makes me seem fatter** me hace parecer más gordo; **it makes me sick** me pone enfermo; **it makes me want to...** me da ganas de...; **it made him angry** hizo que se enfadara; **you make me jump!** ¡vaya susto que me has dado!; **we were made to wait in the hall** nos hicieron esperar en el vestíbulo; **to make sb happy** hacer a alguien feliz; **to make sb sad** entristecer a alguien; **to make sb nervous** poner nervioso a alguien; **to make o.s. heard** hacerse oír; **don't make me laugh!** ¡no me hagas reír! - **4.** [force]: **to make sb do sthg** hacer que alguien haga algo, obligar a alguien a hacer algo; **they made the hostages lie on the ground** hicieron tumbarse en el suelo a los rehenes - **5.** [construct]: **to be made of sthg** estar hecho(cha) de algo; **it's made of wood/metal** está hecho de madera/metal; **made in Spain** fabricado en España; **what's it made of?** ¿de qué está hecho? - **6.** [add up to] hacer, ser; **2 and 2 make 4** 2 y 2 hacen OR son 4 - **7.** [calculate] calcular; **I make it 50/six o'clock** calculo que serán 50/las seis; **what time do you make it?** ¿qué hora tienes? - **8.** [earn] ganar; **she makes £20,000 a year** gana 20.000 libras al año; **to make a profit** obtener beneficios; **to make a loss** sufrir pérdidas - **9.** [have the right qualities for] ser; **she'd make a good doctor** seguro que sería una buena doctora; **books make excellent presents** los libros son un regalo excelente - **10.** [reach] llegar a - **11.** [cause to be a success]: **she really makes the play** ella es la que de verdad levanta la obra - **12.** [gain - friend, enemy] hacer; **to make friends with sb** hacerse amigo de alguien

▸▸ **to make it** [arrive in time] conseguir llegar a tiempo; [be a success] alcanzar el éxito; [be able to attend] venir-ir; [survive] vivir; **to have it made** tenerlo hecho, tener el éxito asegurado; **to make do with sthg** apañarse OR arreglarse con algo; **make a right/left** US da vuelta

a la derecha/izquierda. ◇ *n* - **1.** [brand] marca *f*; **what make is your car?** ¿de qué marca es tu coche? - **2.** *v inf pej*: **to be on the make** [act dishonestly, selfishly] barrer siempre para dentro.

◆ **make for** *vt insep* - **1.** [move towards] dirigirse a OR hacia - **2.** [contribute to] posibilitar, contribuir a.

◆ **make into** *vt sep*: **to make sthg into sthg** convertir algo en algo.

◆ **make of** *vt sep* - **1.** [understand] entender; **what do you make of this word?** ¿qué entiendes tú por esta palabra? - **2.** [have opinion of] opinar de.

◆ **make off** *vi* darse a la fuga.

◆ **make off with** *vt insep inf* largarse con.

◆ **make out** ◇ *vt sep* - **1.** [see] distinguir; [hear] entender, oír - **2.** *inf* [understand - word, number] descifrar; [- person, attitude] comprender - **3.** [fill out - form] rellenar, cumplimentar; [- cheque, receipt] extender; [- list] hacer - **4.** US *inf* [sexually] darse el lote, fajar *Méx* - **5.** *inf* [pretend]: **to make o.s. out to be sthg** dárselas de algo. ◇ *vt insep inf* [pretend] fingir, pretender; **she makes out she's tough** se las da de dura.

◆ **make up** ◇ *vt sep* - **1.** [compose, constitute] componer, constituir - **2.** [invent] inventar - **3.** [apply cosmetics to] maquillar; **to make o.s. up** maquillarse - **4.** [prepare - parcel, prescription, bed] preparar, hacer - **5.** [make complete - amount] completar; [- difference] cubrir; [- deficit, lost time] recuperar - **6.** [resolve - quarrel]: **to make it up (with sb)** hacer las paces (con alguien). ◇ *vi* [become friends again]: **to make up (with sb)** hacer las paces (con alguien). ◇ *n* US [test] *examen que se realiza más tarde si no se pude hacer en su día.*

◆ **make up for** *vt insep* compensar; **to make up for lost time** recuperar el tiempo perdido.

◆ **make up to** *vt sep*: **to make it up to sb (for sthg)** recompensar a alguien (por algo).

make-believe *n* (U) fantasías *fpl*.

makeover ['meɪkəʊvə*] *n* [of person] cambio *m* de imagen; [of home, garden] reforma *f* completa.

maker ['meɪkə*] *n* [of film, programme] creador *m*, -ra *f*; [of product] fabricante *mf*.

makeshift ['meɪkʃɪft] *adj* [temporary] provisional; [improvized] improvisado(da).

make-up *n* - **1.** [cosmetics] maquillaje *m*; **make-up bag** neceser *m*; **make-up remover** loción *f* OR leche *f* desmaquilladora - **2.** [person's character] carácter *m* - **3.** [structure] estructura *f*; [of team] composición *f*.

making ['meɪkɪŋ] *n* [of product] fabricación *f*; [of film] rodaje *m*; [of decision] toma *f*; **this is history in the making** esto pasará a la historia; **your problems are of your own making** tus problemas te los has buscado tú mismo; **to be the making of sb/sthg** ser la causa del éxito de alguien/algo; **to have the makings of** tener madera de.

maladjusted [ˌmælə'dʒʌstɪd] *adj* inadaptado(da).

malaise [mə'leɪz] *n fml* malestar *m*.

malaria [mə'leərɪə] *n* malaria *f*.

Malawi [mə'lɑːwɪ] *n* Malaui.

Malawian [mə'lɑːwɪən] <> *adj* malauita. <> *n* malauita *mf*.

Malay [mə'leɪ] <> *adj* malayo(ya). <> *n* **- 1.** [person] malayo *m*, -ya *f* **- 2.** [language] malayo *m*.

Malaya [mə'leɪə] *n* Malaya.

Malayan [mə'leɪən] <> *adj* malayo(ya). <> *n* malayo *m*, -ya *f*.

Malaysia [mə'leɪzɪə] *n* Malaisia.

Malaysian [mə'leɪzɪən] <> *adj* malaisio(sia). <> *n* malaisio *m*, -sia *f*.

Maldives ['mɔːldɪːvz] *npl*: **the Maldives** las Maldivas.

male [meɪl] <> *adj* **- 1.** [animal] macho **- 2.** [human] masculino(na), varón **- 3.** [concerning men] masculino(na), del hombre. <> *n* **- 1.** [animal] macho *m* **- 2.** [human] varón *m*.

male nurse *n* enfermero *m*.

malevolent [mə'levələnt] *adj* malévolo(la).

malformed [mæl'fɔːmd] *adj* malformado(da).

malfunction [mæl'fʌŋkʃn] <> *n* fallo *m*. <> *vi* averiarse.

Mali ['mɑːlɪ] *n* Malí.

malice ['mælɪs] *n* malicia *f*.

malicious [mə'lɪʃəs] *adj* malicioso(sa).

malign [mə'laɪn] <> *adj* maligno(na), perjudicial. <> *vt fml* difamar.

malignant [mə'lɪgnənt] *adj* **- 1.** MED maligno(na) **- 2.** *fml* [full of hate] malvado(da).

malinger [mə'lɪŋgəʳ] *vi pej* fingirse enfermo(ma).

malingerer [mə'lɪŋgərəʳ] *n pej* enfermo fingido *m*, enferma fingida *f*.

mall [mɔːl] *n esp US*: **(shopping) mall** centro *m* comercial peatonal.

malleable ['mælɪəbl] *adj lit* & *fig* maleable.

mallet ['mælɪt] *n* mazo *m*.

malnourished [ˌmæl'nʌrɪʃt] *adj* malnutrido(da).

malnutrition [ˌmælnjuː'trɪʃn] *n* malnutrición *f*.

malpractice [ˌmæl'præktɪs] *n (U)* LAW negligencia *f*.

malt [mɔːlt] *n* **- 1.** [grain] malta *f* **- 2.** [whisky] whisky *m* de malta **- 3.** *US leche malteada con helado*.

Malta ['mɔːltə] *n* Malta.

Maltese [ˌmɔː'tiːz] <> *adj* maltés(esa). <> *n* (*pl* **Maltese**) **- 1.** [person] maltés *m*, -esa *f* **- 2.** [language] maltés *m*.

maltreat [ˌmæl'triːt] *vt* maltratar.

maltreatment [ˌmæl'triːtmənt] *n* malos tratos *mpl*.

malt whisky *n* whisky *m* de malta.

mammal ['mæml] *n* mamífero *m*.

mammogram ['mæməgræm] *n* MED mamografía *f*.

mammoth ['mæməθ] <> *adj* descomunal, gigante. <> *n* mamut *m*.

man [mæn] <> *n* (*pl* **men**) **- 1.** [gen] hombre *m*; **the man in the street** el hombre de la calle, el ciudadano de a pie; **to talk man to man** hablar de hombre a hombre; **to be man enough to do sthg** ser lo suficientemente hombre para hacer algo **- 2.** [humankind] el hombre. <> *vt* (*pt* & *pp* **-ned**, *cont* **-ning**) [gen] manejar; [ship, plane] tripular; **manned 24 hours a day** [telephone] en servicio las 24 horas del día.

manacles ['mænəklz] *npl* esposas *fpl*, grilletes *mpl*.

manage ['mænɪdʒ] <> *vi* **- 1.** [cope] poder **- 2.** [survive] apañárselas. <> *vt* **- 1.** [succeed]: **to manage to do sthg** conseguir hacer algo **- 2.** [company] dirigir, llevar; [money] administrar, manejar; [pop star] representar; [time] organizar **- 3.** [be available for]: **I can only manage an hour tonight** sólo dispongo de una hora esta noche **- 4.** [cope with] poder con; **can you manage that box?** ¿puedes con la caja?

manageable ['mænɪdʒəbl] *adj* [task] factible, posible; [children] dominable; [inflation, rate] controlable.

management ['mænɪdʒmənt] *n* **- 1.** [control, running] gestión *f* **- 2.** [people in control] dirección *f*.

management consultant *n* asesor *m*, -ra *f* en gestión de empresas.

manager ['mænɪdʒəʳ] *n* **- 1.** [of company] director *m*, -ra *f*; [of shop] jefe *m*, -fa *f*; [of pop star] manager *mf* **- 2.** SPORT ≃ entrenador *m*.

manageress [ˌmænɪdʒə'res] *n UK* [of company] directora *f*; [of shop] jefa *f*.

managerial [ˌmænɪ'dʒɪərɪəl] *adj* directivo(va).

managing director ['mænɪdʒɪŋ-] *n* director *m*, -ra *f* gerente.

Mancunian [mæŋ'kjuːnjən] <> *adj* de o relativo a Manchester. <> *n* natural o habitante de Manchester.

mandarin ['mændərɪn] *n* **- 1.** [fruit] mandarina *f* **- 2.** [civil servant] mandarín *m*, -ina *f*, alto burócrata *m*.

mandate ['mændeɪt] n - **1.** [elected right or authority] mandato m; **to have a mandate to do sthg** tener autoridad para hacer algo - **2.** [task] misión f.

mandatory ['mændətrɪ] adj obligatorio(ria).

mandolin [mændə'lɪn] n mandolina f.

mane [meɪn] n [of horse] crin f; [of lion] melena f.

man-eating [-,i:tɪŋ] adj que come carne humana.

maneuver US = **manoeuvre.**

manfully ['mænfʊlɪ] adv valientemente.

mange [meɪndʒ] n sarna f.

manger ['meɪndʒər] n pesebre m.

mangetout (pea) [,mɑ:ʒ'tu:-] n UK guisante m mollar, tirabeque m, arveja f china Andes, Col & Ven, chícharo m chino Amér C & Méx.

mangle ['mæŋgl] vt [crush] aplastar; [tear to pieces] despedazar.

mango ['mæŋgəʊ] (pl **-es** OR **-s**) n mango m.

mangrove ['mæŋgrəʊv] n mangle m; **mangrove swamp** manglar m.

mangy ['meɪndʒɪ] (comp **-ier,** superl **-iest**) adj sarnoso(sa).

manhandle ['mæn,hændl] vt [person]: **they manhandled her into the van** la metieron en el camión a empujones.

manhole ['mænhəʊl] n boca f (del alcantarillado).

manhood ['mænhʊd] n - **1.** [state] virilidad f - **2.** [time] edad f adulta.

manhour ['mæn,aʊər] n hora f hombre.

manhunt ['mænhʌnt] n búsqueda f (de un delincuente).

mania ['meɪnjə] n - **1.** [excessive liking]: **mania (for)** pasión f (por) - **2.** PSYCHOL manía f.

maniac ['meɪnɪæk] n - **1.** [madman] maníaco m, -ca f - **2.** [fanatic] fanático m, -ca f.

manic ['mænɪk] adj maníaco(ca).

manic-depressive <> adj maníacodepresivo(va). <> n maníacodepresivo m, -va f.

manicure ['mænɪ,kjʊər] <> n manicura f. <> vt: **to manicure sb** hacerle la manicura a alguien; **to manicure one's nails** arreglarse las uñas.

manifest ['mænɪfest] fml <> adj manifiesto(ta), evidente. <> vt manifestar.

manifestation [,mænɪfes'teɪʃn] n fml manifestación f.

manifestly ['mænɪfestlɪ] adv fml evidentemente.

manifesto [,mænɪ'festəʊ] (pl **-s** OR **-es**) n manifiesto m.

manifold ['mænɪfəʊld] <> adj liter múltiple. <> n AUT colector m.

manil(l)a [mə'nɪlə] adj manila (inv).

Manila [mə'nɪlə] n Manila.

manipulate [mə'nɪpjʊleɪt] vt - **1.** [control for personal benefit] manipular - **2.** [controls, lever] manejar.

manipulation [mə,nɪpjʊ'leɪʃn] n - **1.** [control for personal benefit] manipulación f - **2.** [of controls, lever] manejo m.

manipulative [mə'nɪpjʊlətɪv] adj manipulador(ra).

Manitoba [,mænɪ'təʊbə] n Manitoba.

mankind [mæn'kaɪnd] n la humanidad.

manly ['mænlɪ] (comp **-ier,** superl **-iest**) adj varonil, viril.

man-made adj [environment, problem, disaster] producido(da) por el hombre; [fibre, lake, goods] artificial.

manna ['mænə] n maná m.

manned [mænd] adj tripulado(da).

mannequin ['mænɪkɪn] n dated maniquí mf.

manner ['mænər] n - **1.** [method] manera f, forma f; **in a manner of speaking** por así decirlo - **2.** [bearing, attitude] actitud f - **3.** liter [type, sort] tipo m, clase f; **all manner of** toda clase OR todo tipo de.

➡ **manners** npl modales mpl; **it's good/bad manners to do sthg** es de buena/mala educación hacer algo.

mannered ['mænəd] adj fml afectado(da), amanerado(da).

mannerism ['mænərɪzm] n costumbre f (típica de uno).

mannish ['mænɪʃ] adj [woman] hombruno(na).

manoeuvrable UK, **maneuverable** US [mə'nu:vrəbl] adj manejable.

manoeuvre UK, **maneuver** US [mə'nu:vər] <> n lit & fig maniobra f. <> vt maniobrar, manejar. <> vi maniobrar.

➡ **manoeuvres** npl MIL maniobras fpl.

manor ['mænər] n [house] casa f solariega.

manpower ['mæn,paʊər] n [manual workers] mano f de obra; [white-collar workers] personal m.

manservant ['mænsɜ:vənt] (pl **menservants**) n dated criado m, sirviente m, mucamo m Amér.

mansion ['mænʃn] n [manor] casa f solariega; [big house] casa grande.

man-size(d) adj de tamaño extralargo.

manslaughter ['mæn,slɔ:tər] n homicidio m involuntario.

mantelpiece ['mæntlpi:s] n repisa f (de la chimenea).

mantle ['mæntl] n - **1.** [layer, covering] capa f - **2.** [of leadership, high office] manto m.

man-to-man adj de hombre a hombre.

manual ['mænjʊəl] <> adj manual. <> n manual m.

manually ['mænjʊəlɪ] adv manualmente, a mano.

manual worker n obrero m, -ra f.

manufacture [ˌmænjʊˈfæktʃəʳ] ⟨> n manufactura f, fabricación f. ⟨> vt **- 1.** [make] manufacturar, fabricar **- 2.** [invent] inventar.

manufacturer [ˌmænjʊˈfæktʃərəʳ] n fabricante mf.

manufacturing [ˌmænjʊˈfæktʃərɪŋ] n manufactura f, fabricación f.

manufacturing industries npl industrias fpl manufactureras.

manure [məˈnjʊəʳ] n estiércol m, abono m.

manuscript [ˈmænjʊskrɪpt] n **- 1.** [gen] manuscrito m **- 2.** [in exam] hoja f de examen.

Manx [mæŋks] ⟨> adj de o relativo a la Isla de Man. ⟨> n [language] lengua de la Isla de Man.

many [ˈmenɪ] ⟨> adj (comp **more**, superl **most**) muchos(chas); **many people** muchas personas, mucha gente; **how many?** ¿cuántos(tas)?; **I wonder how many people went** me pregunto cuánta gente fue; **too many** demasiados(das); **there weren't too many students** no había muchos estudiantes; **as many... as** tantos(tas)... como; **they have three times as many soldiers as us** tienen el triple de soldados que nosotros; **so many** tantos(tas); **I've never seen so many people** nunca había visto tanta gente; **a good** OR **great many** muchísimos(mas). ⟨> pron muchos(chas); **twice as many** el doble; **four times as many** cuatro veces esa cantidad.

Maori [ˈmaʊrɪ] ⟨> adj maorí. ⟨> n maorí mf.

map n mapa m.
➡ **map out** vt sep [mæp] (pt & pp -ped, cont -ping) planear, planificar.

maple [ˈmeɪpl] n arce m.

maple leaf n hoja f de arce.

maple syrup n jarabe m de arce.

mar [mɑːʳ] (pt & pp -red, cont -ring) vt deslucir.

Mar. (abbr of **March**) mar.

marathon [ˈmærəθən] ⟨> adj maratoniano(na). ⟨> n maratón m.

marathon runner n corredor m, -ra f de maratón.

marauder [məˈrɔːdəʳ] n merodeador m, -ra f.

marauding [məˈrɔːdɪŋ] adj **- 1.** [human] merodeador(ra) **- 2.** [animal] en busca de su presa.

marble [ˈmɑːbl] n **- 1.** [stone] mármol m **- 2.** [for game] canica f.
➡ **marbles** n (U) [game] canicas fpl, bolitas fpl R Plata.

march [mɑːtʃ] ⟨> n **- 1.** MIL marcha f **- 2.** [of demonstrators] marcha f (de protesta) **- 3.** [steady progress] avance m. ⟨> vi **- 1.** [in formation, in protest] marchar **- 2.** [speedily]: **to**

march out salir enfadado(da); **to march up to sb** abordar a alguien decididamente. ⟨> vt llevar por la fuerza.

March [mɑːtʃ] n marzo m; see also **September**.

marcher [ˈmɑːtʃəʳ] n [protester] manifestante mf.

marching orders [ˈmɑːtʃɪŋ-] npl: **to give sb his/her marching orders** expulsar a alguien.

marchioness [ˈmɑːʃənes] n marquesa f.

march-past n desfile m.

Mardi Gras [ˌmɑːdɪˈɡrɑː] n martes m inv de Carnaval.

mare [meəʳ] n yegua f.

margarine [ˌmɑːdʒəˈriːn, ˌmɑːɡəˈriːn] n margarina f.

marge [mɑːdʒ] n inf margarina f.

margin [ˈmɑːdʒɪn] n **- 1.** [gen] margen m **- 2.** [of desert, forest] límite m, lindero m.

marginal [ˈmɑːdʒɪnl] adj **- 1.** [unimportant] marginal **- 2.** UK POL: **marginal seat** OR **constituency** escaño vulnerable a ser perdido en las elecciones por tener una mayoría escasa.

marginally [ˈmɑːdʒɪnəlɪ] adv ligeramente.

marigold [ˈmærɪɡəʊld] n caléndula f.

marihuana, marijuana [ˌmærɪˈwɑːnə] n marihuana f.

marina [məˈriːnə] n puerto m deportivo.

marinade [ˌmærɪˈneɪd] ⟨> n [of fish] marinada f; [of meat] adobo m. ⟨> vt & vi [fish] marinar.

marinate [ˈmærɪneɪt] vt & vi [fish] marinar; [meat] adobar.

marine [məˈriːn] ⟨> adj marino(na). ⟨> n soldado m de infantería de marina.

marionette [ˌmærɪəˈnet] n marioneta f, títere m.

marital [ˈmærɪtl] adj marital, matrimonial.

marital status n estado m civil.

maritime [ˈmærɪtaɪm] adj marítimo(ma).

Maritime Provinces, Maritimes npl: **the Maritime Provinces** las Provincias Marítimas.

marjoram [ˈmɑːdʒərəm] n mejorana f.

mark [mɑːk] ⟨> n **- 1.** [stain] mancha f; [scratch] marca f **- 2.** [written symbol - on paper] marca f; [- in the sand] señal f **- 3.** [in exam] nota f; [point] punto m; **to get good marks** sacar buenas notas **- 4.** [stage, level]: **once past the halfway mark** una vez llegado a medio camino; **above the billion mark** por encima del billón **- 5.** [sign - of respect] señal f; [- of illness, old age] huella f **- 6.** SPORT: **on your marks, get set, go!** preparados, listos, ¡ya! **- 7.** [currency] marco m
➡➡ **to make one's mark** dejar huella, distinguirse; **to be quick/slow off the mark** reaccionar rápido/tarde; **wide of the mark** lejos de la verdad. ⟨> vt **- 1.** [stain] manchar; [scratch] marcar **- 2.** [label - with initials etc] señalar **- 3.** [exam, essay] puntuar, calificar

- 4. [identify - place] señalar; [- beginning, end] marcar **- 5.** [commemorate] conmemorar **- 6.** [characterize] caracterizar **- 7.** SPORT marcar.

➤ **mark down** vt sep **- 1.** COMM [price] rebajar; [goods] bajar el precio de **- 2.** [downgrade] bajar la nota a.

➤ **mark off** vt sep [cross off] poner una marca en.

➤ **mark up** vt sep **- 1.** COMM [price] subir; [goods] subir el precio de **- 2.** [give higher grade] subir la nota a.

marked [mɑːkt] adj [improvement] notable; [difference] marcado(da), acusado(da).

markedly ['mɑːkɪdlɪ] adv [better] sensiblemente; [worse] acusadamente; [different] marcadamente.

marker ['mɑːkəʳ] n **- 1.** [sign] señal f **- 2.** SPORT marcador m, -ora f.

marker pen n rotulador m.

market ['mɑːkɪt] <> n mercado m; on the market a la venta. <> vt comercializar.

marketable ['mɑːkɪtəbl] adj vendible, comercializable.

market day n (día m de) mercado m.

market forces npl fuerzas fpl del mercado.

market garden n esp UK [small] huerto m; [large] huerta f.

marketing ['mɑːkɪtɪŋ] n [subject] marketing m; [selling] comercialización f.

marketplace ['mɑːkɪtpleɪs] n lit & fig mercado m.

market price n precio m de mercado.

market research n estudio m de mercados.

market town n población f con mercado.

market value n valor m actual OR en venta.

marking ['mɑːkɪŋ] n **- 1.** [of exams etc] corrección f **- 2.** SPORT marcaje m.

➤ **markings** npl [of flower, animal] pintas fpl, manchas fpl; [on road] señales fpl.

marksman ['mɑːksmən] (pl -men [-mən]) n tirador m.

marksmanship ['mɑːksmənʃɪp] n puntería f.

markup ['mɑːkʌp] n recargo m.

marmalade ['mɑːməleɪd] n mermelada f (de cítricos).

maroon [mə'ruːn] adj granate.

marooned [mə'ruːnd] adj incomunicado(da), aislado(da).

marquee [mɑː'kiː] n carpa f, toldo m grande; US [of building] marquesina f.

marquess ['mɑːkwɪs] n marquesa f.

marquis ['mɑːkwɪs] n marqués m.

marriage ['mærɪdʒ] n **- 1.** [act] boda f **- 2.** [state, institution] matrimonio m.

marriage bureau n UK agencia f matrimonial.

marriage certificate n certificado m de matrimonio.

marriage guidance n asesoría f matrimonial.

marriage guidance counsellor n consejero m, -ra f matrimonial.

married ['mærɪd] adj **- 1.** [person] casado(da); a married couple un matrimonio **- 2.** [life] matrimonial, de casado(da).

marrow ['mærəʊ] n **- 1.** UK [vegetable] calabacín m grande **- 2.** [in bones] médula f.

marry ['mærɪ] (pt & pp -ied) <> vt **- 1.** [take as husband or wife] casarse con; to get married casarse **- 2.** [sanction marriage of] casar. <> vi casarse.

Mars [mɑːz] n Marte m.

marsh [mɑːʃ] n **- 1.** [area of land] zona f pantanosa **- 2.** [type of land] pantano m.

marshal ['mɑːʃl] <> n **- 1.** MIL mariscal m **- 2.** [steward] oficial mf, miembro mf del servicio de orden **- 3.** US [officer] jefe m, -fa f de policía. <> vt (UK -led, cont -ling, US -ed, cont -ing) [people] dirigir, conducir; [thoughts] ordenar.

marshalling yard ['mɑːʃlɪŋ-] n estación f de clasificación de trenes.

marshland ['mɑːʃlænd] n tierra f pantanosa.

marshmallow [UK ,mɑːʃ'mæləʊ, US 'mɑːrʃ,meləʊ] n **- 1.** [sweet] esponja f (golosina de merengue blando) **- 2.** [substance] malvavisco m.

marshy ['mɑːʃɪ] (comp -ier, superl -iest) adj pantanoso(sa).

marsupial [mɑː'suːpjəl] n marsupial m.

martial ['mɑːʃl] adj [music, discipline] militar.

martial arts [,mɑːʃl-] npl artes fpl marciales.

martial law [,mɑːʃl-] n ley f marcial.

Martian ['mɑːʃn] <> adj marciano(na). <> n marciano m, -na f.

martin ['mɑːtɪn] n avión m.

martini [mɑː'tiːnɪ] n martini m.

Martinique [,mɑːtɪ'niːk] n (la) Martinica.

martyr ['mɑːtəʳ] n mártir mf.

martyrdom ['mɑːtədəm] n martirio m.

martyred ['mɑːtəd] adj [expression] de mártir.

marvel ['mɑːvl] <> n maravilla f; it's a marvel he managed es un milagro que haya podido. <> vi (UK -led, cont -ling, US -ed, cont -ing): to marvel (at) maravillarse OR asombrarse (ante).

marvellous UK, **marvelous** US ['mɑːvələs] adj maravilloso(sa).

Marxism ['mɑːksɪzm] n marxismo m.

Marxist [ˈmɑːksɪst] <> *adj* marxista. <> *n* marxista *mf*.

Maryland [ˈmeərɪlænd] *n* Maryland.

marzipan [ˈmɑːzɪpæn] *n* mazapán *m*.

mascara [mæsˈkɑːrə] *n* rímel *m*.

mascot [ˈmæskət] *n* mascota *f*.

masculine [ˈmæskjʊlɪn] *adj* [gen] masculino(na); [woman, appearance] hombruno(na).

masculinity [ˌmæskjʊˈlɪnətɪ] *n* masculinidad *f*.

mash [mæʃ] <> *n inf* puré *m* de patatas. <> *vt* hacer puré.

MASH [mæʃ] (*abbr of* **mobile army surgical hospital**) *n hospital militar estadounidense de campaña*.

mask [mɑːsk] <> *n lit* & *fig* máscara *f*. <> *vt* - **1.** [to hide] enmascarar - **2.** [cover up] ocultar, disfrazar.

masked [mɑːskt] *adj* enmascarado(da).

masking tape [ˈmɑːskɪŋ-] *n* cinta *f* adhesiva de pintor.

masochism [ˈmæsəkɪzm] *n* masoquismo *m*.

masochist [ˈmæsəkɪst] *n* masoquista *mf*.

masochistic [ˌmæsəˈkɪstɪk] *adj* masoquista.

mason [ˈmeɪsn] *n* - **1.** [stonemason] cantero *m* - **2.** [freemason] masón *m*.

masonic [məˈsɒnɪk] *adj* masónico(ca).

masonry [ˈmeɪsnrɪ] *n* [stones] albañilería *f*.

masquerade [ˌmæskəˈreɪd] *vi*: **to masquerade as** hacerse pasar por; **he masqueraded under the name of...** se identificó bajo el nombre de...

mass [mæs] <> *n* - **1.** [gen] masa *f* - **2.** [large amount] montón *m* - **3.** [religious ceremony] misa *f*. <> *adj* [unemployment] masivo(va); [communication] de masas. <> *vt* agrupar, concentrar. <> *vi* agruparse, concentrarse.

    ↪ **masses** *npl* - **1.** *inf* [lots] montones *mpl* - **2.** [workers]: **the masses** las masas.

Massachusetts [ˌmæsəˈtʃuːsɪts] *n* Massachusetts.

massacre [ˈmæsəkəʳ] <> *n* matanza *f*, masacre *f*. <> *vt* masacrar.

massage [*UK* ˈmæsɑːʒ, *US* məˈsɑːʒ] <> *n* masaje *m*. <> *vt* dar un masaje a.

massage parlour *n* - **1.** [for massage] salón *m* de masajes - **2.** *euph* [brothel] burdel *m*.

masseur [mæˈsɜːr] *n* masajista *m*.

masseuse [mæˈsɜːz] *n* masajista *f*.

massive [ˈmæsɪv] *adj* [gen] enorme; [majority] aplastante.

massively [ˈmæsɪvlɪ] *adv* enormemente.

mass-market *adj* para un mercado masivo.

mass media *n* & *npl*: **the mass media** los medios de comunicación de masas.

mass-produce *vt* producir OR fabricar en serie.

mass production *n* producción *f* OR fabricación *f* en serie.

mast [mɑːst] *n* - **1.** [on boat] mástil *m* - **2.** RADIO & TV poste *m*, torre *f*.

master [ˈmɑːstəʳ] <> *n* - **1.** [of people, animals] amo *m*, dueño *m*; [of house] señor *m* - **2.** *fig* [of situation] dueño *m*, -ña *f* - **3.** *UK* [teacher – primary school] maestro *m*; [- secondary school] profesor *m* - **4.** [of recording] original *m*. <> *adj* maestro(tra). <> *vt* - **1.** [situation] dominar, controlar; [difficulty] vencer, superar - **2.** [technique etc] dominar.

master bedroom *n* dormitorio *m* principal.

master disk *n* COMPUT disco *m* maestro.

masterful [ˈmɑːstəfʊl] *adj* autoritario(ria).

master key *n* llave *f* maestra.

masterly [ˈmɑːstəlɪ] *adj* magistral.

mastermind [ˈmɑːstəmaɪnd] <> *n* cerebro *m*. <> *vt* ser el cerebro de, dirigir.

Master of Arts (*pl* **Masters of Arts**) *n* - **1.** [degree] máster *m* en Letras - **2.** [person] licenciado *m*, -da *f* con máster en Letras.

master of ceremonies (*pl* **masters of ceremonies**) *n* maestro *m* de ceremonias.

Master of Science (*pl* **Masters of Science**) *n* - **1.** [degree] máster *m* en Ciencias - **2.** [person] licenciado *m*, -da *f* con máster en Ciencias.

masterpiece [ˈmɑːstəpiːs] *n lit* & *fig* obra *f* maestra.

master plan *n* plan *m* maestro.

master's degree *n* máster *m*.

masterstroke [ˈmɑːstəstrəʊk] *n* golpe *m* maestro.

master switch *n* interruptor *m* general.

masterwork [ˈmɑːstəwɜːk] *n* obra *f* maestra.

mastery [ˈmɑːstərɪ] *n* dominio *m*.

mastic [ˈmæstɪk] *n* masilla *f*.

masticate [ˈmæstɪkeɪt] *vt* & *vi fml* masticar.

mastiff [ˈmæstɪf] *n* mastín *m*.

masturbate [ˈmæstəbeɪt] *vi* masturbarse.

masturbation [ˌmæstəˈbeɪʃn] *n* masturbación *f*.

mat [mæt] *n* - **1.** [rug] alfombrilla *f*; [beer mat] posavasos *m inv*; [tablemat] salvamanteles *m inv* - **2.** [doormat] felpudo *m*.

match [mætʃ] <> *n* - **1.** [game] partido *m* - **2.** [for lighting] cerilla *f*, cerillo *m* *Amér C & Méx*, fósforo *m Amér* - **3.** [equal]: **to be a match for** estar a la altura de; **to be no match for** no poder competir con. <> *vt* - **1.** [be the same as] coincidir con - **2.** [pair off]: **to match sthg (to)** emparejar algo (con) - **3.** [be equal with] competir con, llegar a la altura de - **4**. [go well with] hacer juego con. <> *vi* - **1**. [be the same] coincidir - **2**. [go together well] hacer juego, combinar.

matchbox ['mætʃbɒks] *n* caja *f* de cerillas.

matched [mætʃt] *adj*: **to be well matched** [well suited] hacer buena pareja; [equal in strength] estar igualados(das).

matching ['mætʃɪŋ] *adj* a juego.

matchless ['mætʃlɪs] *adj liter* sin par.

matchmaker ['mætʃˌmeɪkəʳ] *n* casamentero *m*, -ra *f*, celestina *f*.

match play *n* GOLF matchplay *m* (*juego por hoyos*).

match point *n* TENNIS pelota *f* OR punto *m* de partido.

matchstick ['mætʃstɪk] *n* cerilla *f*, cerillo *m* Andes & Méx.

mate [meɪt] <> *n* - **1**. *inf* [friend] amigo *m*, -ga *f*, compañero *m*, -ra *f*, compa *mf* Amér - **2**. US [spouse] esposo *m*, -sa *f* - **3**. UK *inf* [term of address] colega *m* - **4**. [of animal] macho *m*, hembra *f* - **5**. NAUT: **(first) mate** (primer) oficial *m*. <> *vi* [animals]: **to mate (with)** aparearse (con).

material [mə'tɪərɪəl] <> *adj* - **1**. [physical] material - **2**. [important] sustancial. <> *n* - **1**. [substance] material *m* - **2**. [type of substance] materia *f* - **3**. [fabric] tela *f*, tejido *m* - **4**. [type of fabric] tejido *m* - **5**. (*U*) [ideas, information] información *f*, documentación *f*.

➤ **materials** *npl*: **building materials** materiales *mpl* de construcción; **writing materials** objetos *mpl* de escritorio; **cleaning materials** productos *mpl* de limpieza.

materialism [mə'tɪərɪəlɪzm] *n* materialismo *m*.

materialist [mə'tɪərɪəlɪst] *n* materialista *mf*.

materialistic [mə,tɪərɪə'lɪstɪk] *adj* materialista.

materialize, -ise [mə'tɪərɪəlaɪz] *vi* - **1**. [happen] materializarse, producirse - **2**. [appear] aparecer.

materially [mə'tɪərɪəlɪ] *adv* - **1**. [physically] materialmente - **2**. [significantly, importantly] sustancialmente.

maternal [mə'tɜːnl] *adj* [gen] maternal; [grandparent] materno(na).

maternity [mə'tɜːnətɪ] *n* maternidad *f*.

maternity dress *n* vestido *m* premamá.

maternity hospital *n* hospital *m* de maternidad.

maternity leave *n* baja *f* por maternidad.

math US = **maths**.

mathematical [,mæθə'mætɪkl] *adj* matemático(ca).

mathematician [,mæθəmə'tɪʃn] *n* matemático *m*, -ca *f*.

mathematics [,mæθə'mætɪks] *n* (*U*) matemáticas *fpl*.

maths UK [mæθs], **math** US [mæθ] (*abbr of* **mathematics**) *inf* <> *n* (*U*) mates *fpl*. <> *comp* de matemáticas.

maths coprocessor [-,kəʊ'prəʊsesəʳ] *n* COMPUT coprocesador *m* matemático.

matinée ['mætɪneɪ] *n* [at cinema] primera sesión *f*; [at theatre] función *f* de tarde, vermú *f* Amér.

mating call ['meɪtɪŋ-] *n* llamada *f* nupcial.

mating season ['meɪtɪŋ-] *n* época *f* de celo.

matriarch ['meɪtrɪɑːk] *n* matriarca *f*.

matrices ['meɪtrɪsiːz] *npl* ⊳ **matrix**.

matriculate [mə'trɪkjʊleɪt] *vi* matricularse.

matriculation [mə,trɪkjʊ'leɪʃn] *n* matrícula *f*.

matrimonial [,mætrɪ'məʊnjəl] *adj* matrimonial.

matrimony ['mætrɪmənɪ] *n* (*U*) matrimonio *m*.

matrix ['meɪtrɪks] (*pl* **matrices** OR **-es**) *n* matriz *f*.

matron ['meɪtrən] *n* - **1**. UK [in hospital] enfermera *f* jefa - **2**. [in school] *mujer a cargo de la enfermería* - **3**. US [in prison] funcionaria *f* de prisiones, carcelera *f*.

matronly ['meɪtrənlɪ] *adj euph* [figure] corpulenta y de edad madura.

matt UK, **matte** US [mæt] *adj* mate.

matted ['mætɪd] *adj* enmarañado(da).

matter ['mætəʳ] <> *n* - **1**. [question, situation] asunto *m*; **a matter of life and death** un asunto de vida o muerte; **the fact** OR **truth of the matter is (that)...** la verdad es que...; **that's another** OR **a different matter** es otra cuestión OR cosa; **as a matter of course** automáticamente; **to make matters worse** para colmo de desgracias; **as a matter of principle** por principio; **within a matter of hours** en cuestión de horas; **a matter of opinion** una cuestión de opiniones; **it's a matter of time** es cuestión de tiempo - **2**. [trouble, cause of pain]: **what's the matter (with it/her)?** ¿qué (le) pasa?; **is anything the matter?** ¿pasa algo?; **something's the matter with my car** algo le pasa a mi coche - **3**. PHYS materia *f* - **4**. (*U*) [material] material *m*; **printed matter** impresos *mpl*. <> *vi* [be important] importar; **it doesn't matter** no importa.

➤ **as a matter of fact** *adv* en realidad.

➤ **for that matter** *adv* de hecho.

➤ **no matter** *adv*: **no matter how hard I try** por mucho que lo intente; **no matter what he does** haga lo que haga; **we must win, no matter what** tenemos que ganar como sea.

Matterhorn ['mætə,hɔːn] *n*: **the Matterhorn** el monte Cervino.

matter-of-fact *adj* pragmático(ca).

matting ['mætɪŋ] *n* estera *f*.

mattress ['mætrɪs] *n* colchón *m*.

mature [mə'tjʊəʳ] <> *adj* [person, wine] maduro(ra); [cheese] curado(da). <> *vi* **- 1.** [gen] madurar **- 2.** [wine] envejecer.

mature student *n* UK UNIV estudiante *mf* adulto, -ta *f*.

maturity [mə'tjʊərətɪ] *n* **- 1.** [gen] madurez *f* **- 2.** FIN vencimiento *m*.

maudlin ['mɔːdlɪn] *adj* [tearful] llorón(ona); [sentimental] sensiblero(ra).

maul [mɔːl] *vt* [savage] herir gravemente.

Mauritian [mə'rɪʃən] <> *adj* mauriciano(na). <> *n* mauriciano *m*, -na *f*.

Mauritius [mə'rɪʃəs] *n* (la) isla Mauricio.

mausoleum [ˌmɔːsə'lɪəm] (*pl* -s) *n* mausoleo *m*.

mauve [məʊv] <> *adj* malva. <> *n* malva *m*.

maverick ['mævərɪk] *n* inconformista *mf*.

mawkish ['mɔːkɪʃ] *adj* sensiblero(ra).

max. [mæks] (*abbr of* **maximum**) máx.

maxim ['mæksɪm] (*pl* -s) *n* máxima *f*.

maxima ['mæksɪmə] *pl* ⊏▷ **maximum**.

maximize, -ise ['mæksɪmaɪz] *vt* maximizar.

maximum ['mæksɪməm] <> *adj* máximo(ma). <> *n* (*pl* **maxima** OR **-s**) máximo *m*; **at the maximum** como máximo.

may [meɪ] *modal vb* poder; **the coast may be seen** se puede ver la costa; **you may like it** puede OR es posible que te guste; **I may come, I may not** puede que venga, puede que no; **will you do it? – I may do** ¿lo harás? – puede que sí; **it may be done in two different ways** puede hacerse de dos maneras (distintas); **may I come in?** ¿se puede (pasar)?; **may I?** ¿me permite?; **if I may** si me permite; **it may be cheap, but it's good** puede que sea barato, pero es bueno; **may all your dreams come true!** ¡que todos tus sueños se hagan realidad!; **be that as it may** aunque así sea; **come what may** pase lo que pase.

May [meɪ] *n* mayo *m*; *see also* **September**.

Maya ['maɪə] *n*: **the Maya** los mayas.

Mayan ['maɪən] *adj* maya.

maybe ['meɪbiː] *adv* **- 1.** [perhaps] quizás, tal vez; **maybe she'll come** tal vez venga **- 2.** [approximately] más o menos.

mayday ['meɪdeɪ] *n* s.o.s. *m*, señal *f* de socorro.

May Day *n* Primero *m* de Mayo.

mayfly ['meɪflaɪ] (*pl* -flies) *n* cachipolla *f*, efímera *f*.

mayhem ['meɪhem] *n* alboroto *m*, jaleo *m*.

mayonnaise [ˌmeɪə'neɪz] *n* mayonesa *f*.

mayor [meəʳ] *n* alcalde *m*, -esa *f*.

mayoress ['meərɪs] *n* alcaldesa *f*.

maypole ['meɪpəʊl] *n* mayo *m*.

maze [meɪz] *n* lit & fig laberinto *m*.

MB - 1. (*abbr of* **megabyte**) MB *m* **- 2.** *abbr of* **Manitoba**.

MBA (*abbr of* **Master of Business Administration**) *n* (titular de un) título postuniversitario de empresariales de unos dos años de duración.

MBE (*abbr of* **Member of the Order of the British Empire**) *n* (titular de) distinción honorífica británica.

MC *n abbr of* **master of ceremonies**.

MCAT (*abbr of* **Medical College Admissions Test**) *n* examen de acceso a los estudios de medicina en Estados Unidos.

McCoy [mə'kɔɪ] *n inf*: **it's the real McCoy** es auténtico(ca).

MCP *n inf abbr of* **male chauvinist pig**.

MD <> *n* **- 1.** *abbr of* **Doctor of Medicine** **- 2.** *abbr of* **managing director**. <> *abbr of* **Maryland**.

MDT (*abbr of* **Mountain Daylight Time**) hora de verano de los Estados de las montañas Rocosas.

me [miː] *pers pron* **- 1.** *(direct, indirect)* me; **can you see/hear me?** ¿me ves/oyes?; **it's me** soy yo; **they spoke to me** hablaron conmigo; **she gave it to me** me lo dio; **give it to me!** ¡dámelo! **- 2.** *(stressed)*: **you can't expect me to do it** no esperarás que yo lo haga **- 3.** *(after prep)* mí; **they went with/without me** fueron conmigo/sin mí **- 4.** *(in comparisons)* yo; **she's shorter than me** (ella) es más baja que yo.

ME <> *n* **- 1.** (*abbr of* **myalgic encephalomyelitis**), encefalomielitis miálgica **- 2.** (*abbr of* **medical examiner**), médico forense. <> *abbr of* **Maine**.

meadow ['medəʊ] *n* prado *m*, pradera *f*.

meagre UK**, meager** US ['miːgəʳ] *adj* miserable, escaso(sa).

meal [miːl] *n* comida *f*; **to make a meal of sthg** UK fig & pej recrearse en algo.

meals on wheels *npl* UK servicio domiciliario de comidas preparadas para ancianos y necesitados.

mealtime ['miːltaɪm] *n* hora *f* de la comida; **at mealtimes** en la hora de la comida.

mealy-mouthed [ˌmiːlɪ'maʊðd] *adj pej* evasivo(va).

mean [miːn] <> *vt* (*pt & pp* **meant**) **- 1.** [signify] significar, querer decir; **what does that word mean?** ¿qué quiere decir esa palabra?; **it means nothing to me** no significa nada para mí **- 2.** [have in mind] querer decir, referirse a; **what do you mean?** ¿qué quieres decir?;

do you know what I mean? ¿sabes?; **to mean to do sthg** tener la intención de OR querer hacer algo; **I meant to phone you earlier** iba a llamarte antes; **to be meant for** estar destinado(da) a; **they were meant for each other** estaban hechos el uno para el otro; **to be meant to do sthg** deber hacer algo; **that's not meant to be there** eso no debería estar allí; **it was meant to be a surprise** se suponía que era una sorpresa; **it was meant to be a joke** era solamente una broma; **to mean well** tener buenas intenciones **- 3.** [be serious about]: **I mean it** hablo OR lo digo en serio **- 4.** [be important, matter] significar; **it means a lot to us** significa mucho para nosotros **- 5.** [entail] suponer, implicar

▸▸**I mean** quiero decir, o sea. ◇ *adj* **- 1.** [miserly] tacaño(ña), amarrete *(inv)* Chile & R Plata; **to be mean with** ser tacaño con **- 2.** [unkind] mezquino(na), malo(la); **to be mean to sb** ser malo con alguien **- 3.** [average] medio(dia) **- 4.**: **he's no mean singer** [excellent] es un cantante de primera; **it's no mean task** [difficult, challenging] es una tarea muy difícil. ◇ *n* [average] promedio *m*, media *f*.

meander [mɪˈændəʳ] *vi* **- 1.** [river, road] serpentear **- 2.** [walk aimlessly] vagar; [write, speak aimlessly] divagar.

meaning [ˈmiːnɪŋ] *n* **- 1.** [sense - of a word etc] significado *m* **- 2.** [significance] intención *f*, sentido *m* **- 3.** [purpose, point] propósito *m*, razón *f* de ser.

meaningful [ˈmiːnɪŋfʊl] *adj* **- 1.** [expressive] significativo(va) **- 2.** [profound] profundo(da).

meaningless [ˈmiːnɪŋlɪs] *adj* **- 1.** [without meaning, purpose] sin sentido **- 2.** [irrelevant, unimportant] irrelevante.

meanness [ˈmiːnnɪs] *n* **- 1.** [stinginess] tacañería *f* **- 2.** [unkindness] mezquindad *f*.

means [miːnz] ◇ *n* [method, way] medio *m*; **we have no means of doing it** no tenemos manera de hacerlo; **a means to an end** un medio para alcanzar un objetivo; **by means of** por medio de; **by legal means** legalmente. ◇ *npl* [money] recursos *mpl*, medios *mpl*.

◆ **by all means** *adv* por supuesto.

◆ **by no means** *adv* en absoluto, de ningún modo.

means test *n esp* UK evaluación *f* sobre los ingresos económicos.

meant [ment] *pt* & *pp* ▷ **mean**.

meantime [ˈmiːnˌtaɪm] *n*: **in the meantime** mientras tanto.

meanwhile [ˈmiːnˌwaɪl] *adv* mientras tanto.

measles [ˈmiːzlz] *n*: **(the) measles** sarampión *m*.

measly [ˈmiːzlɪ] *(comp* **-ier,** *superl* **-iest)** *adj inf* raquítico(ca).

measurable [ˈmeʒərəbl] *adj* [significant] notable, sensible.

measurably [ˈmeʒərəblɪ] *adv* notablemente, sensiblemente.

measure [ˈmeʒəʳ] ◇ *n* **- 1.** [step, action] medida *f* **- 2.** [degree]: **a measure of** cierto grado de; **and for good measure** y encima, y además **- 3.** [of alcohol] medida *f* **- 4.** [indication, sign]: **a measure of** una muestra de **- 5.** US MUS compás *m*. ◇ *vt* [object] medir; [damage, impact etc] determinar, evaluar. ◇ *vi* medir.

◆ **measure up** *vi* dar la talla; **to measure up to** estar a la altura de.

measured [ˈmeʒəd] *adj* [tone] moderado(da); [step] pausado(da).

measurement [ˈmeʒəmənt] *n* medida *f*.

measuring jug [ˈmeʒərɪŋ-] *n* jarra *f* graduada.

measuring tape [ˈmeʒərɪŋ-] *n* cinta *f* métrica.

meat [miːt] *n* **- 1.** [foodstuff] carne *f*; **cold meat** fiambre *m* **- 2.** [substance, content] sustancia *f*.

meatball [ˈmiːtbɔːl] *n* albóndiga *f*.

meat pie *n* UK empanada *f* de carne.

meaty [ˈmiːtɪ] *(comp* **-ier,** *superl* **-iest)** *adj fig* sustancioso(sa).

Mecca [ˈmekə] *n* GEOG La Meca; *fig* meca *f*.

mechanic [mɪˈkænɪk] *n* mecánico *m*, -ca *f*.

◆ **mechanics** ◇ *n* (U) [study] mecánica *f*. ◇ *npl fig* mecanismos *mpl*.

mechanical [mɪˈkænɪkl] *adj* [worked by machinery, routine] mecánico(ca).

mechanical engineering *n* ingeniería *f* mecánica, mecánica *f* industrial.

mechanism [ˈmekənɪzm] *n lit* & *fig* mecanismo *m*.

mechanize, -ise [ˈmekənaɪz] *vt* mecanizar.

MEd [ˌemˈed] *(abbr of Master of Education)* *n (titular de un) título postuniversitario de pedagogía de unos dos años de duración.*

medal [ˈmedl] *n* medalla *f*.

medallion [mɪˈdæljən] *n* medallón *m*.

medallist UK, **medalist** US [ˈmedəlɪst] *n* ganador *m*, -ra *f* de una medalla.

meddle [ˈmedl] *vi*: **to meddle (in)** entrometerse (en); **to meddle with sthg** manosear algo.

meddlesome [ˈmedlsəm] *adj* entrometido(da), meterete *R Plata.*

media [ˈmiːdjə] ◇ *pl* ▷ **medium.** ◇ *n* & *npl*: **the media** los medios de comunicación.

mediaeval [ˌmedrˈiːvl] = **medieval.**

media event *n montaje de los medios de difusión.*

median [ˈmiːdjən] ◇ *adj* mediano(na). ◇ *n* US [of road] mediana *f*.

media studies *npl* ciencias *fpl* de la información.

mediate ['mi:dɪeɪt] ⬦ *vt* negociar. ⬦ *vi*: **to mediate (for/between)** mediar (por/entre).

mediation [ˌmi:dɪ'eɪʃn] *n* mediación *f*.

mediator ['mi:dɪeɪtə'] *n* mediador *m*, -ra *f*.

medic ['medɪk] *n inf* - **1.** [medical student] estudiante *mf* de medicina - **2.** [doctor] médico *m*, -ca *f*.

Medicaid ['medɪkeɪd] *n US sistema estatal de ayuda médica.*

Medicaid/Medicare

En 1965 se establecieron en Estados Unidos dos programas de atención sanitaria: Medicare y Medicaid. El primero, dirigido a mayores de 65 años, se financia por medio de contribuciones a la seguridad social y una prima mensual individual. Además hay que pagar un pequeño suplemento cada vez que se utiliza un servicio médico. El número de beneficiarios de Medicare está en continuo aumento, por lo que el programa se enfrenta a problemas financieros y tendrá que ser renovado para satisfacer la demanda. Por su parte, Medicaid, que también debe afrontar problemas presupuestarios, está dirigido a personas con ingresos bajos o alguna discapacidad y se financia a través del gobierno federal y los distintos gobiernos estatales.

medical ['medɪkl] ⬦ *adj* médico(ca). ⬦ *n* reconocimiento *m* médico, chequeo *m*.

medical certificate *n* - **1.** [result of medical exam] certificado *m* médico - **2.** [for sickness] parte *m OR* notificación *f* de baja médica.

medical examiner *n US* forense *mf*.

medical student *n* estudiante *mf* de medicina.

Medicare ['medɪkeə'] *n US ayuda médica estatal para ancianos.*

medicated ['medɪkeɪtɪd] *adj* medicinal.

medication [ˌmedɪ'keɪʃn] *n* medicación *f*; **to be on medication** tomar medicación.

medicinal [me'dɪsɪnl] *adj* medicinal.

medicine ['medsɪn] *n* - **1.** [treatment of illness] medicina *f*; **Doctor of Medicine** UNIV doctor *m*, -ra *f* en medicina - **2.** [substance] medicina *f*, medicamento *m*.

medicine man *n* chamán *m*, hechicero *m*.

medieval, mediaeval [ˌmedɪ'i:vl] *adj* medieval.

mediocre [ˌmi:dɪ'əʊkə'] *adj* mediocre.

mediocrity [ˌmi:dɪ'ɒkrətɪ] *n* mediocridad *f*.

meditate ['medɪteɪt] *vi*: **to meditate (on OR upon)** meditar (sobre).

meditation [ˌmedɪ'teɪʃn] *n* meditación *f*.

Mediterranean [ˌmedɪtə'reɪnjən] ⬦ *n* - **1.** [sea]: **the Mediterranean (Sea)** el (mar) Mediterráneo - **2.** [person] mediterráneo *m*, -a *f*. ⬦ *adj* mediterráneo(a).

medium ['mi:djəm] ⬦ *adj* mediano(na). ⬦ *n* - **1.** (*pl* **media**) [way of communicating] medio *m* - **2.** (*pl* **mediums**) [spiritualist] médium *mf*.

medium-dry *adj* semiseco(ca).

medium-sized [-saɪzd] *adj* de tamaño mediano.

medium wave *n* onda *f* media.

medley ['medlɪ] (*pl* **medleys**) *n* - **1.** [mixture] mezcla *f*, amalgama *f* - **2.** [selection of music] popurrí *m*.

meek [mi:k] *adj* sumiso(sa), dócil.

meekly ['mi:klɪ] *adv* sumisamente, dócilmente.

meet [mi:t] ⬦ *vt* (*pt & pp* **met**) - **1.** [by chance] encontrarse con; [for first time, come across] conocer; [by arrangement, for a purpose] reunirse con - **2.** [go to meet - person] ir/venir a buscar; [- train, bus]: **I met the eight o'clock train to pick up my son** fui a buscar a mi hijo en el tren de las ocho - **3.** [need, demand, condition] satisfacer; [target] cumplir con; [deadline] cumplir - **4.** [deal with - problem, challenge] hacer frente a - **5.** [costs, debts] pagar - **6.** [experience - problem, situation] encontrarse con - **7.** [hit, touch] darse OR chocar contra - **8.** [face]: **her eyes met his** sus ojos se encontraron con los de él - **9.** [join] juntarse OR unirse con - **10.** [play against] enfrentarse con. ⬦ *vi* (*pt & pp* **met**) - **1.** [by chance] encontrarse; [by arrangement, for a purpose] verse; [for a purpose] reunirse - **2.** [get to know sb] conocerse; **shall we meet at eight?** ¿quedamos a las ocho? - **3.** [hit in collision] chocar; [touch] tocar - **4.** [eyes]: **their eyes met** sus miradas se cruzaron - **5.** [join - roads etc] juntarse - **6.** [play each other] enfrentarse. ⬦ *n US* [meeting] encuentro *m*.

➤ **meet up** *vi*: **to meet up (with sb)** quedar (con alguien); **we're meeting up for lunch** hemos quedado para comer.

➤ **meet with** *vt insep* - **1.** [problems, resistance]: **meet with refusal** ser rechazado(da); **to meet with success** tener éxito; **to meet with failure** fracasar - **2.** *US* [by arrangement] reunirse con.

meeting ['mi:tɪŋ] *n* - **1.** [for discussions, business] reunión *f* - **2.** [by chance, in sport] encuentro *m*; [by arrangement] cita *f*; [formal] entrevista *f* - **3.** [people at meeting]: **the meeting** la asamblea.

meeting place *n* lugar *m* de encuentro.

mega- [megə] *prefix* - **1.** [in measurements] mega- - **2.** *inf* [very big] super-.

megabyte ['megəbaɪt] *n* COMPUT megabyte *m*, mega *m*.

megahertz ['megəhɜ:ts] n megahercio m.

megalomania [ˌmegələ'meɪnjə] n megalomanía f.

megalomaniac [ˌmegələ'meɪnɪæk] n megalómano m, -na f.

megaphone ['megəfəʊn] n megáfono m.

megaton ['megətʌn] n megatón m.

megawatt ['megəwɒt] n megavatio m.

melamine ['meləmi:n] n melamina f.

melancholy ['melənkəlɪ] <> adj melancólico(ca). <> n melancolía f.

mellow ['meləʊ] <> adj - 1. [sound, colour, light] suave; [wine] añejo(ja) - 2. [fruit] maduro(ra). <> vt: **to be mellowed by** [age] estar apaciguado(da) por; [alcohol] sentirse relajado(da) por. <> vi [sound, light] suavizarse; [person] ablandarse.

melodic [mɪ'lɒdɪk] adj melódico(ca).

melodious [mɪ'ləʊdjəs] adj melodioso(sa).

melodrama ['melədrɑ:mə] n melodrama m.

melodramatic [ˌmelədrə'mætɪk] adj melodramático(ca).

melody ['melədɪ] (pl -ies) n melodía f.

melon ['melən] n melón m.

melt [melt] <> vt - 1. [make liquid] derretir - 2. fig [soften] ablandar. <> vi - 1. [become liquid] derretirse - 2. fig [soften] ablandarse - 3. [disappear]: **to melt into the crowd** desaparecer entre la multitud; **to melt away** [savings] esfumarse; [anger] desvanecerse.
◆ **melt down** vt sep fundir.

meltdown ['meltdaʊn] n - 1. [act of melting] fusión f - 2. [incident] fuga f radiactiva.

melting point ['meltɪŋ-] n punto m de fusión.

melting pot ['meltɪŋ-] n fig crisol m.

member ['membər] <> n - 1. [of social group] miembro mf - 2. [of party, union] afiliado m, -da f; [of organization, club] socio m, -cia f - 3. [limb, penis] miembro m. <> comp miembro.

Member of Congress (pl **Members of Congress**) n miembro mf del Congreso (de los Estados Unidos).

Member of Parliament (pl **Members of Parliament**) n UK diputado m, -da f (del parlamento británico).

membership ['membəʃɪp] n - 1. [of party, union] afiliación f; [of club] calidad f de socio - 2. [number of members - of party, union] número m de afiliados; [- of club] número m socios - 3. [people themselves]: **the membership** [of organization] los miembros; [of party, union] los afiliados; [of club] los socios.

membership card n [of party, union] carnet m de afiliado, -da f; [of club] carnet m de socio, -cia f.

membrane ['membreɪn] n membrana f.

memento [mɪ'mentəʊ] (pl -s) n recuerdo m.

memo ['meməʊ] (pl -s) n memorándum m.

memoirs ['memwɑ:z] npl memorias fpl.

memo pad n bloc m de notas.

memorabilia [ˌmemərə'bɪlɪə] npl objetos personales de una celebridad.

memorable ['memərəbl] adj memorable.

memorandum [ˌmemə'rændəm] (pl -da [-də] OR -dums) n fml memorándum m.

memorial [mɪ'mɔ:rɪəl] <> adj conmemorativo(va). <> n monumento m conmemorativo.

memorize, -ise ['meməraɪz] vt memorizar, aprender de memoria.

memory ['memərɪ] (pl -ies) n - 1. [faculty, of computer] memoria f - 2. [thing or things remembered] recuerdo m; **from memory** de memoria; **within living memory** que se recuerda; **to have no memory of sthg** no recordar algo; **to lose one's memory** perder la memoria; **to keep sb's memory alive** mantener vivo el recuerdo de alguien; **to search one's memory** intentar recordar; **in memory of** en memoria de.

memory card n COMPUT tarjeta f de expansión de memoria.

men [men] npl ⊏> **man**.

menace ['menəs] <> n - 1. [threat] amenaza f; [danger] peligro m - 2. [threatening quality]: **with menace** de modo amenazador - 3. inf [nuisance, pest] pesadez f, lata f. <> vt amenazar.

menacing ['menəsɪŋ] adj amenazador(ra).

menacingly ['menəsɪŋlɪ] adv amenazadoramente.

menagerie [mɪ'nædʒərɪ] n colección f particular de animales.

mend [mend] <> n inf: **to be on the mend** ir recuperándose. <> vt [shoes, toy] arreglar; [socks] zurcir; [clothes] remendar; **to mend one's ways** enmendarse.

mending ['mendɪŋ] n: **to do the mending** zurcir OR remendar la ropa.

menfolk ['menfəʊk] npl hombres mpl.

menial ['mi:njəl] adj servil, de baja categoría.

meningitis [ˌmenɪn'dʒaɪtɪs] n (U) meningitis f inv.

menopause ['menəpɔ:z] n: **the menopause** la menopausia.

menservants ['mensɜ:vənts] npl ⊏> **manservant**.

men's room n US: **the men's room** los servicios de caballeros.

menstrual ['menstrʊəl] adj menstrual.

menstruate ['menstrʊeɪt] vi menstruar, tener la menstruación.

menstruation [ˌmenstrʊ'eɪʃn] *n* menstruación *f*.

menswear ['menzweəʳ] *n* ropa *f* de caballeros.

mental ['mentl] *adj* mental.

mental age *n* edad *f* mental.

mental block *n*: **to have a mental block about** tener bloqueo mental respecto a.

mental hospital *n* hospital *m* psiquiátrico.

mentality [men'tælətɪ] *n* mentalidad *f*.

mentally ['mentəlɪ] *adv* mentalmente; **to be mentally ill/retarded** ser un enfermo/retrasado mental.

mentally handicapped ['mentəlɪ-] *npl*: **the mentally handicapped** los disminuidos psíquicos.

➤ **mentally-handicapped** *adj* disminuido psíquico (disminuida psíquica).

mental note *n*: **to make a mental note to do sthg** tomar nota mentalmente de hacer algo.

menthol ['menθɒl] *n* mentol *m*.

mentholated ['menθəleɪtɪd] *adj* mentolado(da).

mention ['menʃn] <> *vt*: **to mention sthg (to)** mencionar algo (a); **not to mention** sin mencionar, además de; **don't mention it!** ¡de nada!, ¡no hay de qué! <> *n* mención *f*.

mentor ['mentɔːʳ] *n fml* mentor *m*, -ra *f*.

menu ['menjuː] *n* - **1.** [in restaurant] carta *f* - **2.** COMPUT menú *m*.

menu bar *n* COMPUT barra *f* de menú.

menu-driven *adj* COMPUT a base de menús.

meow *US* = **miaow**.

MEP (*abbr of* **Member of the European Parliament**) *n* eurodiputado *m*, -da *f*.

mercantile ['mɜːkəntaɪl] *adj* mercantil.

mercenary ['mɜːsɪnrɪ] <> *adj* mercenario(ria). <> *n* (*pl* **-ies**) mercenario *m*, -ria *f*.

merchandise ['mɜːtʃəndaɪz] *n* (*U*) mercancías *fpl*, géneros *mpl*.

merchant ['mɜːtʃənt] <> *adj* [seaman, ship] mercante. <> *n* comerciante *mf*.

merchant bank *n UK* banco *m* mercantil.

merchant navy *UK*, **merchant marine** *US n* marina *f* mercante.

merciful ['mɜːsɪfʊl] *adj* - **1.** [showing mercy] compasivo(va) - **2.** [fortunate] afortunado(da).

mercifully ['mɜːsɪfʊlɪ] *adv* [fortunately] afortunadamente.

merciless ['mɜːsɪlɪs] *adj* implacable, despiadado(da).

mercilessly ['mɜːsɪlɪslɪ] *adv* implacablemente, despiadadamente.

mercurial [mɜː'kjʊərɪəl] *adj* voluble.

mercury ['mɜːkjʊrɪ] *n* mercurio *m*.

Mercury ['mɜːkjʊrɪ] *n* Mercurio *m*.

mercy ['mɜːsɪ] (*pl* **-ies**) *n* - **1.** [kindness, pity] compasión *f*; **to have mercy on** apiadarse de; **to beg for mercy** pedir clemencia; **at the mercy of** *fig* a merced de - **2.** [blessing] suerte *f*.

mercy killing *n* eutanasia *f*.

mere [mɪəʳ] *adj* simple, mero(ra); **she's a mere child** no es más que una niña.

merely ['mɪəlɪ] *adv* simplemente, sólo.

merge [mɜːdʒ] <> *vt* - **1.** [gen] mezclar - **2.** COMM & COMPUT fusionar. <> *vi* - **1.** [join, combine]: **to merge (with)** [company] fusionarse (con); [roads, branches] unirse OR convergir (con) - **2.** [blend - colours] fundirse, mezclarse; **to merge into** confundirse con. <> *n* COMPUT fusión *f*.

merger ['mɜːdʒəʳ] *n* COMM fusión *f*.

meridian [mə'rɪdɪən] *n* meridiano *m*.

meringue [mə'ræŋ] *n* merengue *m*.

merino [mə'riːnəʊ] *adj* [wool] merino(na); [jumper, scarf] de lana merina.

merit ['merɪt] <> *n* mérito *m*. <> *vt* merecer, ser digno(na) de.

➤ **merits** *npl* ventajas *fpl*; **to consider the merits of** sopesar las ventajas de; **to judge sthg on its merits** evaluar OR juzgar algo según sus méritos.

meritocracy [ˌmerɪ'tɒkrəsɪ] (*pl* **-ies**) *n* meritocracia *f*.

mermaid ['mɜːmeɪd] *n* sirena *f*.

merrily ['merɪlɪ] *adv* - **1.** [gen] alegremente - **2.** [burn, sparkle] resplandeciente.

merriment ['merɪmənt] *n liter* alegría *f*, diversión *f*.

merry ['merɪ] (*comp* **-ier**, *superl* **-iest**) *adj* - **1.** [gen] alegre - **2.** [party] animado(da); **Merry Christmas!** ¡feliz Navidad! - **3.** *inf* [tipsy] alegre, achispado(da).

merry-go-round *n* tiovivo *m*, calesitas *fpl R Plata*.

merrymaking ['merɪˌmeɪkɪŋ] *n* (*U*) *liter* diversión *f*, juerga *f*.

mesh [meʃ] <> *n* malla *f*. <> *vi fig* encajar.

mesmerize, -ise ['mezməraɪz] *vt*: **to be mesmerized (by)** estar fascinado(da) (por).

mess [mes] *n* - **1.** [untidy state] desorden *m*, entrevero *m R Plata*; **to be a mess** estar revuelto(ta); **to make a mess of sthg** hacer algo muy mal - **2.** [muddle, problematic situation] lío *m* - **3.** MIL [room] comedor *m*; [food] rancho *m*.

➤ **mess about, mess around** *inf* <> *vt sep* vacilar. <> *vi* - **1.** [waste time] pasar el rato; [fool around] hacer el tonto - **2.** [interfere]: **to mess about with sthg** manosear algo.

➤ **mess up** *vt sep inf* - **1.** [clothes] ensuciar; [room] desordenar - **2.** [plan, evening] echar a perder.

━━ **mess with** vt insep inf meterse con.

message ['mesɪdʒ] n - **1.** [piece of information] mensaje m, recado m - **2.** [of book etc] mensaje m
▸▸ **to get the message** inf entender.

message board n [gen & COMPUT] tablón m de anuncios.

messenger ['mesɪndʒəʳ] n mensajero m, -ra f; **by messenger** por mensajero.

Messiah [mɪ'saɪə] n: **the Messiah** el Mesías.

Messrs, Messrs. ['mesəz] (abbr of **messieurs**) Sres.

messy ['mesɪ] (comp **-ier**, superl **-iest**) adj - **1.** [dirty] sucio(cia); [untidy] desordenado(da) - **2.** inf [complicated, confused] complicado(da), enredado(da).

met [met] pt & pp ▷ **meet**.

Met [met] n - **1.** (abbr of **Metropolitan Opera**); **the Met** el (teatro de la ópera) Metropolitan de Nueva York - **2.** UK (abbr of **Metropolitan Police**); **the Met** la policía de Londres.

metabolism [mə'tæbəlɪzm] n metabolismo m.

metal ['metl] ⟨⟩ n metal m. ⟨⟩ comp de metal, metálico(ca).

metallic [mɪ'tælɪk] adj - **1.** [gen] metálico(ca) - **2.** [paint, finish] metalizado(da).

metallurgy [mə'tælədʒɪ] n metalurgia f.

metalwork ['metlwɜ:k] n [craft] metalistería f.

metalworker ['metl,wɜ:kəʳ] n metalista m.

metamorphose [,metə'mɔ:fəʊz] vi fml: **to metamorphose (into)** transformarse (en).

metamorphosis [,metə'mɔ:fəsɪs, ,metəmɔ:'fəʊsɪs] (pl **-phoses** [-si:z]) n lit & fig metamorfosis f inv.

metaphor ['metəfəʳ] n metáfora f.

metaphorical [,metə'fɒrɪkl] adj metafórico(ca).

metaphysical [,metə'fɪzɪkl] adj metafísico(ca).

metaphysics [,metə'fɪzɪks] n metafísica f.

mete [mi:t] ━━ **mete out** vt sep: **to mete sthg out to sb** imponer algo a alguien.

meteor ['mi:tɪəʳ] n bólido m.

meteoric [mi:tɪ'ɒrɪk] adj fig meteórico(ca), vertiginoso(sa).

meteorite ['mi:tjəraɪt] n meteorito m.

meteorological [,mi:tjərə'lɒdʒɪkl] adj meteorológico(ca).

meteorologist [,mi:tjə'rɒlədʒɪst] n meteorólogo(ga).

meteorology [,mi:tjə'rɒlədʒɪ] n meteorología f.

meter ['mi:təʳ] ⟨⟩ n - **1.** [device] contador m - **2.** US = **metre**. ⟨⟩ vt [measure] medir.

methadone ['meθədəʊn] n metadona f.

methane ['mi:θeɪn] n metano m.

method ['meθəd] n método m.

methodical [mɪ'θɒdɪkl] adj metódico(ca).

methodically [mɪ'θɒdɪklɪ] adv metódicamente.

Methodist ['meθədɪst] ⟨⟩ adj metodista. ⟨⟩ n metodista mf.

methodology [,meθə'dɒlədʒɪ] (pl **-ies**) n metodología f.

meths [meθs] n UK inf alcohol m metilado OR desnaturalizado.

methylated spirits ['meθɪleɪtɪd-] n alcohol m metilado OR desnaturalizado.

meticulous [mɪ'tɪkjʊləs] adj meticuloso(sa), minucioso(sa).

meticulously [mɪ'tɪkjʊləslɪ] adv meticulosamente, minuciosamente.

Met Office (abbr of **Meteorological Office**) n instituto británico de meteorología.

metre UK, **meter** US ['mi:təʳ] n metro m.

metric ['metrɪk] adj métrico(ca).

metrication [,metrɪ'keɪʃn] n UK adopción f del sistema métrico decimal.

metric system n: **the metric system** el sistema métrico.

metric ton n tonelada f métrica.

metro ['metrəʊ] (pl **-s**) n metro m.

metronome ['metrənəʊm] n metrónomo m.

metropolis [mɪ'trɒpəlɪs] (pl **-es**) n metrópoli f.

metropolitan [,metrə'pɒlɪtn] adj [of a metropolis] metropolitano(na).

mettle ['metl] n: **to be on one's mettle** estar dispuesto(ta) a hacer lo mejor posible; **he showed** OR **proved his mettle** mostró su valor.

mew [mju:] = **miaow**.

mews [mju:z] (pl **mews**) n UK callejuela de antiguas caballerizas convertidas en viviendas de lujo.

Mexican ['meksɪkn] ⟨⟩ adj mexicano(na), mejicano(na). ⟨⟩ n mexicano m, -na f, mejicano m, -na f.

Mexico ['meksɪkəʊ] n México, Méjico.

Mexico City n México DF, Ciudad f de México.

mezzanine ['metsəni:n] n - **1.** [floor] entresuelo m - **2.** US [in theatre] primer palco m OR piso m.

mg (abbr of **milligram**) mg m.

Mgr - 1. (abbr of **Monseigneur, Monsignor**) Mons - **2.** abbr of **manager**.

MHR n (abbr of **Member of the House of Representatives**) miembro de la Cámara de los Representantes m.

MHz (abbr of **megahertz**) MHz.

MI5 (*abbr of* **Military Intelligence 5**) *n orga-nismo británico de contraespionaje.*

MI6 (*abbr of* **Military Intelligence 6**) *n orga-nismo británico de espionaje.*

MIA (*abbr of* **missing in action**) *desaparecido en combate.*

miaow *UK* [miː'aʊ], **meow** *US* [mɪ'aʊ] ◇ *n* maullido *m.* ◇ *vi* maullar.

mice [maɪs] *npl* ⊳ **mouse.**

Mich. *abbr of* **Michigan.**

Michigan ['mɪʃɪɡən] *n* Michigan.

mickey ['mɪkɪ] *n UK inf*: **to take the mickey out of sb** tomar el pelo a alguien; **to take the mickey out of sthg** burlarse de algo.

micro ['maɪkrəʊ] (*pl* **-s**) *n* microordenador *m,* microcomputadora *f Amér.*

micro- ['maɪkrəʊ] *prefix* micro-.

microbe ['maɪkrəʊb] *n* microbio *m.*

microbiologist [ˌmaɪkrəʊbaɪ'ɒlədʒɪst] *n* micro-biólogo *m,* -ga *f.*

microbiology [ˌmaɪkrəʊbaɪ'ɒlədʒɪ] *n* microbio-logía *f.*

microchip ['maɪkrəʊtʃɪp] *n* COMPUT microchip *m.*

microcircuit ['maɪkrəʊˌsɜːkɪt] *n* microcircui-to *m.*

microcomputer [ˌmaɪkrəʊkəm'pjuːtəʳ] *n* micro-ordenador *m,* microcomputadora *f Amér.*

microcosm ['maɪkrəkɒzm] *n* microcosmos *m inv.*

microfiche ['maɪkrəʊfiːʃ] (*pl* **microfiche** OR **-s**) *n* microficha *f.*

microfilm ['maɪkrəʊfɪlm] *n* microfilm *m.*

microlight ['maɪkrəlaɪt] *n* ultraligero *m.*

micromesh ['maɪkrəʊmeʃ] *n* malla *f* extrafina (para medias).

micron ['maɪkrɒn] *n* micra *f,* micrón *m.*

microorganism [ˌmaɪkrəʊ'ɔːɡənɪzm] *n* micro-organismo *m.*

microphone ['maɪkrəfəʊn] *n* micrófono *m.*

microprocessor ['maɪkrəʊˌprəʊsesəʳ] *n* COMPUT microprocesador *m.*

micro scooter *n* patinete *m.*

microscope ['maɪkrəskəʊp] *n* microscopio *m.*

microscopic [ˌmaɪkrə'skɒpɪk] *adj* lit & fig mi-croscópico(ca).

microsurgery [ˌmaɪkrə'sɜːdʒərɪ] *n* microciru-gía *f.*

microwave ['maɪkrəweɪv] ◇ *n*: **microwave (oven)** microondas *m inv.* ◇ *vt* cocinar en el microondas.

mid- [mɪd] *prefix* medio(dia); **(in) mid-morning** a media mañana; **(in) mid-August** a mediados de agosto; **(in) mid-winter** en pleno invierno; **she's in her mid-twenties** tiene unos 25 años.

midair [mɪd'eəʳ] ◇ *adj* en el aire. ◇ *n*: **in midair** en el aire.

midday ['mɪddeɪ] *n* mediodía *m.*

middle ['mɪdl] ◇ *adj* - **1.** [gen] del medio - **2.** [in time]: **she's in her middle twenties** tie-ne unos 25 años. ◇ *n* - **1.** [of room, town etc] medio *m,* centro *m*; **in the middle (of)** en el medio OR centro (de); **the one in the middle** el del medio; **in the middle of the month/the 19th century** a mediados del mes/del si-glo XIX; **in the middle of the week** a mitad de semana; **to be in the middle of doing sthg** es-tar haciendo algo; **in the middle of the night** en plena noche; **in the middle of nowhere** en el quinto pino - **2.** [waist] cintura *f.*

middle age *n* madurez *f.*

middle-aged *adj* de mediana edad.

Middle Ages *npl*: **the Middle Ages** la Edad Media.

middle-class *adj* de clase media.

middle classes *npl*: **the middle classes** la clase media.

middle distance *n*: **in the middle distance** en segundo plano OR término.

➤ **middle-distance** *adj* [race] de medio fondo.

Middle East *n*: **the Middle East** el Oriente Medio.

Middle Eastern *adj* del Oriente Medio.

middleman ['mɪdlmæn] (*pl* **-men** [-men]) *n* in-termediario *m.*

middle management *n (U)* cuadros *mpl* OR mandos *mpl* intermedios.

middle name *n* segundo nombre *m (en un nombre compuesto).*

middle-of-the-road *adj* - **1.** [music] conven-cional - **2.** POL moderado(da).

middle school *n UK* escuela para niños de 8 a 12 años.

middleweight ['mɪdlweɪt] *n* peso *m* medio.

middling ['mɪdlɪŋ] *adj* regular.

Middx (*abbr of* **Middlesex**), *antiguo condado inglés.*

midfield [ˌmɪd'fiːld] *n* FTBL centro *m* del campo.

midge [mɪdʒ] *n* (tipo *m* de) mosquito *m.*

midget ['mɪdʒɪt] *n* enano *m,* -na *f.*

midi system ['mɪdɪ-] *n* minicadena *f.*

Midlands ['mɪdləndz] *npl*: **the Midlands** la re-gión central de Inglaterra.

midnight ['mɪdnaɪt] ◇ *n* medianoche *f.* ◇ *comp* de medianoche.

midriff ['mɪdrɪf] *n* diafragma *m.*

midst [mɪdst] *n*: **in the midst of** en medio de; **in our midst** entre nosotros.

midstream [mɪd'striːm] *n* - **1.** [of river]: **in midstream** en medio de la corriente - **2.** *fig* [when talking]: **in midstream** en medio de la conversación.

midsummer ['mɪd,sʌmər] *n* pleno verano *m*.

midway [,mɪd'weɪ] *adv* - **1.** [in space]: **midway (between)** a medio camino (entre) - **2.** [in time]: **midway (through)** a la mitad (de).

midweek ◇ *adj* [mɪd'wiːk] de entre semana. ◇ *adv* ['mɪdwiːk] entre semana.

Midwest [,mɪd'west] *n*: **the Midwest** *la llanura central de los Estados Unidos.*

Midwestern [,mɪd'westən] *adj de o relativo a la llanura central de los Estados Unidos.*

midwife ['mɪdwaɪf] (*pl* -**wives** [-waɪvz]) *n* comadrona *f*.

midwifery ['mɪd,wɪfərɪ] *n* obstetricia *f*.

miffed [mɪft] *adj inf* mosqueado(da), fastidiado(da).

might [maɪt] ◇ *modal vb* - **1.** [expressing possibility]: **he might be armed** podría estar armado; **I might do it** puede que OR quizás lo haga; **I might come, I might not** puede que venga, puede que no; **will you do it? – I might do** ¿lo harás? – puede que sí; **we might have been killed, had we not been careful** si no hubiéramos tenido cuidado, podríamos haber muerto; **will you tell them? – I might as well** ¿se lo dirás? – ¿por qué no? - **2.** [expressing suggestion]: **you might have told me!** ¡podrías habérmelo dicho!; **it might be better to wait** quizás sea mejor esperar - **3.** *fml* [asking permission]: **he asked if he might leave the room** pidió permiso para salir - **4.** [expressing concession]: **you might well be right, but...** puede que tengas razón, pero... ▸▸ **I might have known** OR **guessed** podría haberlo sospechado. ◇ *n* (U) fuerza *f*, poder *m*.

mightn't ['maɪtənt] (*abbr of* = **might not**), ⊳ **might**.

might've ['maɪtəv] (*abbr of* = **might have**), ⊳ **might**.

mighty ['maɪtɪ] ◇ *adj* (*comp* -**ier**, *superl* -**iest**) - **1.** [strong] fuerte; [powerful] poderoso(sa) - **2.** [very large] enorme. ◇ *adv esp US* muy.

migraine ['miːgreɪn, 'maɪgreɪn] *n* jaqueca *f*, migraña *f*.

migrant ['maɪgrənt] ◇ *adj* - **1.** [bird, animal] migratorio(ria) - **2.** [workers] inmigrante. ◇ *n* - **1.** [bird] ave *f* migratoria - **2.** [person] emigrante *mf*.

migrate [UK maɪ'greɪt, US 'maɪgreɪt] *vi* emigrar.

migration [maɪ'greɪʃn] *n* emigración *f*.

migratory ['maɪgrətrɪ] *adj* migratorio(ria).

mike [maɪk] (*abbr of* **microphone**) *n inf* micro *m*.

mild [maɪld] ◇ *adj* - **1.** [taste, disinfectant, wind] suave; [effect, surprise, illness, punishment] leve - **2.** [person, nature] apacible; [tone of voice] sosegado(da), sereno(na) - **3.** [climate] templado(da). ◇ *n tipo de cerveza ligera.*

mildew ['mɪldjuː] *n* [gen] moho *m*; [on plants] añublo *m*.

mildly ['maɪldlɪ] *adv* - **1.** [gen] ligeramente, levemente; **to put it mildly** por no decir más - **2.** [talk] suavemente.

mild-mannered *adj* apacible, sosegado(da).

mildness ['maɪldnɪs] *n* [of voice, manner, person] suavidad *f*, serenidad *f*; [of reproach, illness, punishment] levedad *f*.

mile [maɪl] *n* milla *f*; **we could see for miles** la vista nos alcanzaba a ver mucho; **we had walked for miles** habíamos andado muchísimo; **this is miles better** esto es muchísimo mejor; **it's miles away** [place] está muy lejos; **to be miles away** *fig* estar en la luna.

mileage ['maɪlɪdʒ] *n* distancia *f* en millas.

mileage allowance *n* pago *m* por millas recorridas, ≃ kilometraje *m*.

mileometer, milometer [maɪ'lɒmɪtər] *n* cuentamillas *m inv*, ≃ cuentakilómetros *m inv*.

milestone ['maɪlstəʊn] *n* - **1.** [marker stone] mojón *m*, hito *m* - **2.** *fig* [event] hito *m*.

milieu [, UK 'miːljɜː, US miː'ljuː] (*pl* -**s** OR -**x**) *n* entorno *m*, (medio) ambiente *m*.

militant ['mɪlɪtənt] ◇ *adj* militante. ◇ *n* militante *mf*.

militarism ['mɪlɪtərɪzm] *n* militarismo *m*.

militarist ['mɪlɪtərɪst] *n* militarista *mf*.

militarized zone, militarised zone ['mɪlɪtəraɪzd-] *n* zona *f* militar.

military ['mɪlɪtrɪ] ◇ *adj* militar. ◇ *n*: **the military** los militares, las fuerzas armadas.

military police *n* policía *f* militar.

military service *n* servicio *m* militar.

militate ['mɪlɪteɪt] *vi fml*: **to militate against sthg** militar en contra de algo.

militia [mɪ'lɪʃə] *n* milicia *f*.

milk [mɪlk] ◇ *n* leche *f*. ◇ *vt* - **1.** [cow etc] ordeñar - **2.** [use to own ends] sacar todo el jugo a; **they milked him for every penny he had** le chuparon hasta el último centavo.

milk chocolate ◇ *n* chocolate *m* con leche. ◇ *comp* de chocolate con leche.

milk float *UK*, **milk truck** *US n vehículo eléctrico distribuidor de leche.*

milking ['mɪlkɪŋ] *n* ordeño *m*.
milkman ['mɪlkmən] (*pl* **-men** [-mən]) *n* lechero *m*.
milk round *n UK* [by milkman] recorrido *m* del lechero.
milk shake *n* batido *m*.
milk tooth *n* diente *m* de leche.
milk truck *n US* = **milk float**.
milky ['mɪlkɪ] (*comp* **-ier**, *superl* **-iest**) *adj* - **1.** *UK* [with milk] con mucha leche - **2.** [pale white] lechoso(sa), pálido(da).
Milky Way *n*: **the Milky Way** la Vía Láctea.
mill [mɪl] ◇ *n* - **1.** [flour-mill] molino *m* - **2.** [factory] fábrica *f* - **3.** [grinder] molinillo *m*. ◇ *vt* moler.
◆ **mill about, mill around** *vi* arremolinarse.
millennium [mɪ'leniəm] (*pl* **-nnia** [-nɪə]) *n* milenio *m*.
miller ['mɪlər] *n* molinero *m*, -ra *f*.
millet ['mɪlɪt] *n* mijo *m*.
milli- ['mɪlɪ] *prefix* mili-.
millibar ['mɪlɪbɑ:r] *n* milibar *m*.
milligram(me) ['mɪlɪɡræm] *n* miligramo *m*.
millilitre *UK*, **milliliter** *US* ['mɪlɪ,li:tər] *n* mililitro *m*.
millimetre *UK*, **millimeter** *US* ['mɪlɪ,mi:tər] *n* milímetro *m*.
millinery ['mɪlɪnrɪ] *n* sombrerería *f* (de señoras).
million ['mɪljən] *n* millón *m*; **four million dollars** cuatro millones de dólares; **a million, millions of** *fig* millones de.
millionaire [,mɪljə'neər] *n* millonario *m*.
millionairess [,mɪljə'neərɪs] *n* millonaria *f*.
millipede ['mɪlɪpi:d] *n* milpiés *m inv*.
millisecond ['mɪlɪ,sekənd] *n* milésima *f* de segundo.
millstone ['mɪlstəʊn] *n* piedra *f* de molino, muela *f*; **a millstone round one's neck** una cruz.
millwheel ['mɪlwi:l] *n* rueda *f* de molino.
milometer [maɪ'lɒmɪtər] = **mileometer**.
mime [maɪm] ◇ *n* - **1.** [acting] mímica *f*, pantomima *f* - **2.** [act] imitación *f* a base de gestos. ◇ *vt* describir con gestos. ◇ *vi* hacer mímica.
mimic ['mɪmɪk] ◇ *n* imitador *m*, -ra *f*. ◇ *vt* (*pt* & *pp* **-ked**, *cont* **-king**) imitar.
mimicry ['mɪmɪkrɪ] *n* imitación *f*.
mimosa [mɪ'məʊzə] *n* mimosa *f*.
min. [mɪn] - **1.** (*abbr of* **minute**) min - **2.** (*abbr of* **minimum**) mín.
Min. *abbr of* **ministry**.

mince [mɪns] ◇ *n UK* carne *f* picada. ◇ *vt* picar. ◇ *vi* andar con afectación.
mincemeat ['mɪnsmi:t] *n* [fruit] *mezcla de fruta confitada y especias*.
mince pie *n* [sweet cake] *pastelillo navideño de fruta confitada y frutos secos*.
mincer ['mɪnsər] *n* máquina *f* de picar carne.
mind [maɪnd] ◇ *n* - **1.** [gen] mente *f*; **state of mind** estado *m* de ánimo; **to calculate sthg in one's mind** calcular algo mentalmente; **to come into OR to cross sb's mind** pasársele a alguien por la cabeza; **the first thing that came into my mind** lo primero que me vino a la mente; **to have sthg on one's mind** estar preocupado por algo; **to keep an open mind** tener una actitud abierta; **to put OR set sb's mind at rest** tranquilizar a alguien; **it slipped my mind** se me olvidó; **to take sb's mind off sthg** hacer olvidar algo a alguien; **that was a load OR weight off my mind** me quité un peso de encima; **are you out of your mind?** ¿estás loco?; **great minds think alike!** ¡ves! ahí estamos de acuerdo; **to broaden one's mind** ampliar los horizontes de uno; **to make one's mind up** decidirse - **2.** [attention] atención *f*; **to concentrate one's mind** hacer que uno se concentre; **to put one's mind to sthg** poner empeño en algo - **3.** [opinion]: **to change one's mind** cambiar de opinión; **to my mind** en mi opinión; **to be in two minds about sthg** no estar seguro(ra) de algo; **to speak one's mind** hablar sin rodeos - **4.** [memory] memoria *f*; **to bear sthg in mind** tener presente algo; **to call sthg to mind** recordar algo; **to cast one's mind back** echar la mente *OR* mirada atrás - **5.** [intention]: **to have sthg in mind** tener algo en mente; **to have a mind to do sthg** estar pensando en hacer algo; **nothing could be further from my mind** nada más lejos de mis intenciones. ◇ *vi* - **1.** [be bothered]: **do you mind?** ¿te importa?; **I don't mind...** no me importa...; **which do you want? – I don't mind** ¿cuál prefieres? – me da igual; **never mind** [don't worry] no te preocupes; [it's not important] no importa - **2.** [be careful]: **mind out!** *UK* ¡cuidado! ◇ *vt* - **1.** [be bothered about, dislike]: **do you mind if I leave?** ¿te molesta si me voy?; **I don't mind waiting** no me importa esperar; **I wouldn't mind a...** no me vendría mal un... - **2.** [pay attention to] tener cuidado con; **mind you don't fall** ten cuidado no te vayas a caer - **3.** [take care of] cuidar - **4.** [concentrate on]: **mind your own business!** ¡métete en tus asuntos!
◆ **mind you** *adv*: **he's a bit deaf; mind you, he is old** está un poco sordo; te advierto que es ya mayor.

minder ['maɪndəʳ] *n UK inf* [bodyguard] guardaespaldas *m* & *f inv*.

mindful ['maɪndfʊl] *adj*: **mindful of** consciente de.

mindless ['maɪndlɪs] *adj* - **1.** [stupid] absurdo(da), sin sentido - **2.** [not requiring thought] aburrido(da).

mind reader *n* adivinador *m*, -ora *f* del pensamiento.

mindset ['maɪndset] *n* mentalidad *f*.

mind's eye *n*: **in one's mind's eye** en la mente (de uno).

mine¹ [maɪn] *poss pron* mío (mía); **that money is mine** ese dinero es mío; **his car hit mine** su coche chocó contra el mío; **it wasn't your fault, it was mine** la culpa no fue tuya sino mía; **a friend of mine** un amigo mío.

mine² [maɪn] ◇ *n* mina *f*; **a mine of information** una mina de información. ◇ *vt* - **1.** [excavate - coal] extraer - **2.** [lay mines in] minar.

mine detector *n* detector *m* de minas.

minefield ['maɪnfiːld] *n lit* & *fig* campo *m* de minas.

minelayer ['maɪn,leɪəʳ] *n* minador *m*.

miner ['maɪnəʳ] *n* minero *m*, -ra *f*.

mineral ['mɪnərəl] ◇ *adj* mineral. ◇ *n* mineral *m*.

mineralogy [,mɪnə'rælədʒɪ] *n* mineralogía *f*.

mineral water *n* agua *f* mineral.

minestrone [,mɪnɪ'strəʊnɪ] *n* (sopa *f*) minestrone *f*.

minesweeper ['maɪn,swiːpəʳ] *n* dragaminas *m inv*.

mingle ['mɪŋgl] ◇ *vt*: **to mingle sthg with** mezclar algo con. ◇ *vi* - **1.** [combine]: **to mingle (with)** mezclarse (con) - **2.** [socially]: **to mingle (with)** alternar (con).

mini ['mɪnɪ] *n* minifalda *f*.

miniature ['mɪnətʃəʳ] ◇ *adj* en miniatura. ◇ *n* - **1.** [painting] miniatura *f* - **2.** [of alcohol] botellín *f* de licor en miniatura - **3.** [small scale]: **in miniature** en miniatura.

minibus ['mɪnɪbʌs] (*pl* -**es**) *n* microbús *m*, micro *m*, buseta *f Col, C Rica, Ecuad & Ven*, pesero *m Méx*, liebre *f Chile*.

minicab ['mɪnɪkæb] *n UK taxi que se puede pedir por teléfono, pero no se puede parar en la calle.*

minicomputer [,mɪnɪkəm'pjuːtəʳ] *n* miniordenador *m*, minicomputadora *f Amér*.

minidish ['mɪnɪdɪʃ] *n* miniparabólica *f*.

minima ['mɪnɪmə] *pl* ⊳ **minimum**.

minimal ['mɪnɪml] *adj* mínimo(ma).

minimize, -ise ['mɪnɪ,maɪz] *vt* minimizar.

minimum ['mɪnɪməm] ◇ *adj* mínimo(ma). ◇ *n* (*pl* -**mums** OR -**ma**) mínimo *m*.

minimum lending rate [-'lendɪŋ-] *n* tipo *m* de descuento oficial.

minimum wage *n* salario *m* mínimo.

Minimum wage

El salario mínimo se introdujo en el Reino Unido en abril de 1999 y define la tarifa mínima por hora a nivel nacional que debe pagar un empresario a sus trabajadores. Esta tarifa, establecida por un comité llamado "Low Pay Comission", varía según la edad del trabajador (es más baja para los menores de 22 años e inferior aún para los menores de 18). Ciertos grupos, como por ejemplo los au pairs, están exentos. A pesar de que su introducción fue muy polémica, en la actualidad las empresas reconocen que no ha elevado sustancialmente sus costes.

mining ['maɪnɪŋ] ◇ *n* minería *f*. ◇ *adj* minero(ra); **mining engineer** ingeniero *m*, -ra *f* de minas.

minion ['mɪnjən] *n hum* & *pej* lacayo *m*.

miniseries ['mɪnɪsɪəriːz] (*pl* miniseries) *n* miniserie *f*.

miniskirt ['mɪnɪskɜːt] *n* minifalda *f*.

minister ['mɪnɪstəʳ] *n* - **1.** POL: **minister (for)** ministro *m*, -tra *f* (de) - **2.** RELIG pastor *m*, -ra *f*. ⚫ **minister to** *vt insep* [needs] atender a.

ministerial [,mɪnɪ'stɪərɪəl] *adj* ministerial.

minister of state *n*: **minister of state (for)** secretario *m*, -ria *f* de estado (para).

ministry ['mɪnɪstrɪ] (*pl* -**ies**) *n* - **1.** POL ministerio *m*; **Ministry of Defence** Ministerio de Defensa - **2.** RELIG: **the ministry** el clero, el sacerdocio.

mink [mɪŋk] (*pl* mink) *n* visón *m*.

mink coat *n* abrigo *m* de visón.

Minnesota [,mɪnɪ'səʊtə] *n* Minnesota.

minnow ['mɪnəʊ] *n* - **1.** [fish] pececillo *m* (de agua dulce) - **2.** [team] comparsa *f*.

minor ['maɪnəʳ] ◇ *adj* [gen] menor; [injury] leve; **of minor importance** de poca importancia. ◇ *n* menor *mf* (de edad); US [subject] subespecialidad *f*. ◇ *vi* US [subject] estudiar una subespecialidad.

minority [maɪ'nɒrətɪ] (*pl* -**ies**) *n* minoría *f*; **to be in a** OR **the minority** estar en la minoría, ser minoría.

minority government *n* gobierno *m* minoritario.

minster ['mɪnstəʳ] *n* catedral *f*.

minstrel ['mɪnstrəl] *n* juglar *m*.

mint [mɪnt] <> n - **1.** [herb] menta f, hierbabuena f - **2.** [peppermint] pastilla f de menta - **3.** [for coins]: **the mint** la Casa de la Moneda; **in mint condition** en perfecto estado, como nuevo(va). <> vt acuñar.

mint sauce n salsa f de menta.

minuet [ˌmɪnjʊˈet] n minué m.

minus ['maɪnəs] <> prep - **1.** MATHS [less]: **4 minus 2 is 2** 4 menos 2 es 2 - **2.** [in temperatures]: **it's minus 5°C** estamos a 5 grados bajo cero. <> adj MATHS [less than zero] negativo(va). <> n (pl -es) - **1.** MATHS signo m (de) menos - **2.** [disadvantage] desventaja f.

minuscule ['mɪnəskjuːl] adj minúsculo(la).

minus sign n signo m (de) menos.

minute[1] ['mɪnɪt] n minuto m; **at any minute** en cualquier momento; **at the minute** en este momento; **at the last minute** en el último momento; **just a minute** un momento; **this minute** ahora mismo; **up to the minute** [news] de última hora; [technology] punta (inv); **wait a minute** espera un momento.

➡ **minutes** npl acta f; **to take (the) minutes** levantar OR tomar acta.

minute[2] [maɪˈnjuːt] adj [very small] diminuto(ta).

minutiae [maɪˈnjuːʃɪaɪ] npl minucias fpl.

miracle ['mɪrəkl] n lit & fig milagro m.

miraculous [mɪˈrækjʊləs] adj milagroso(sa).

miraculously [mɪˈrækjʊləslɪ] adv milagrosamente.

mirage [mɪˈrɑːʒ] n lit & fig espejismo m.

mire [maɪəʳ] n fango m, lodo m.

mirror ['mɪrəʳ] <> n espejo m. <> vt reflejar.

mirror image n reflejo m a la inversa.

mirth [mɜːθ] n risa f.

misadventure [ˌmɪsədˈventʃəʳ] n desgracia f, desventura f; **death by misadventure** LAW muerte f accidental.

misanthropist [mɪsˈænθrəpɪst] n misántropo m, -pa f.

misapprehension ['mɪsˌæprɪˈhenʃn] n - **1.** [misunderstanding] malentendido m - **2.** [mistaken belief] creencia f errónea.

misappropriate [ˌmɪsəˈprəʊprɪeɪt] vt malversar.

misappropriation ['mɪsəˌprəʊprɪˈeɪʃn] n: **misappropriation (of)** malversación f (de).

misbehave [ˌmɪsbɪˈheɪv] vi portarse mal.

misc abbr of **miscellaneous**.

miscalculate [ˌmɪsˈkælkjʊleɪt] vt & vi calcular mal.

miscalculation [ˌmɪskælkjʊˈleɪʃn] n - **1.** (U) [poor judgment] cálculos mpl erróneos - **2.** [mistake] error m de cálculo.

miscarriage [ˌmɪsˈkærɪdʒ] n [at birth] aborto m (natural).

miscarriage of justice n error m judicial.

miscarry [ˌmɪsˈkærɪ] (pt & pp -ied) vi - **1.** [woman] tener un aborto (natural) - **2.** [plan] fracasar.

miscellaneous [ˌmɪsəˈleɪnjəs] adj diverso(sa).

miscellany [UK mɪˈselənɪ, US ˈmɪsəleɪnɪ] (pl -ies) n miscelánea f.

mischance [ˌmɪsˈtʃɑːns] n - **1.** [piece of bad luck] infortunio m, desgracia f - **2.** [bad luck] mala suerte f; **by mischance** por desgracia.

mischief ['mɪstʃɪf] n (U) - **1.** [playfulness] picardía f - **2.** [naughty behaviour] travesuras fpl, diabluras fpl - **3.** [harm] daño m.

mischievous ['mɪstʃɪvəs] adj - **1.** [playful] lleno(na) de picardía - **2.** [naughty] travieso(sa).

misconceived [ˌmɪskənˈsiːvd] adj mal concebido(da).

misconception [ˌmɪskənˈsepʃn] n concepto m erróneo, idea f falsa.

misconduct [ˌmɪsˈkɒndʌkt] n mala conducta f.

misconstrue [ˌmɪskənˈstruː] vt fml malinterpretar.

miscount [ˌmɪsˈkaʊnt] vt & vi contar mal.

misdeed [ˌmɪsˈdiːd] n liter fechoría f.

misdemeanour UK, **misdemeanor** US [ˌmɪsdɪˈmiːnəʳ] n fml delito m menor, falta f.

misdirected [ˌmɪsdɪˈrektɪd] adj [efforts] mal encaminado(da); [letter] con la dirección equivocada.

miser ['maɪzəʳ] n avaro m, -ra f.

miserable ['mɪzrəbl] adj - **1.** [unhappy] infeliz, triste - **2.** [wretched, poor] miserable - **3.** [weather] horrible - **4.** [pathetic] lamentable.

miserably ['mɪzrəblɪ] adv - **1.** [unhappily] tristemente - **2.** [wretchedly, poorly] miserablemente - **3.** [pathetically] lamentablemente.

miserly ['maɪzəlɪ] adj miserable, mezquino(na).

misery ['mɪzərɪ] (pl -ies) n - **1.** [unhappiness] desdicha f, tristeza f - **2.** [suffering] sufrimiento m.

misfire [ˌmɪsˈfaɪəʳ] vi - **1.** [gun] encasquillarse - **2.** [car engine] no arrancar - **3.** [plan] fracasar.

misfit ['mɪsfɪt] n inadaptado m, -da f.

misfortune [mɪsˈfɔːtʃuːn] n - **1.** [bad luck] mala suerte f - **2.** [piece of bad luck] desgracia f.

misgivings [mɪsˈgɪvɪŋz] npl recelo m, recelos mpl.

misguided [ˌmɪsˈgaɪdɪd] adj [person] descaminado(da); [attempt] equivocado(da).

mishandle [ˌmɪsˈhændl] vt - **1.** [person, animal] maltratar - **2.** [affair] llevar mal.

mishap ['mɪshæp] n percance m, contratiempo m; **without mishap** sin problemas.

mishear [ˌmɪsˈhɪəʳ] (pt & pp -heard [-ˈhɜːd]) vt & vi oír mal.

mishmash ['mɪʃmæʃ] *n inf* batiburrillo *m*.

misinform [ˌmɪsɪn'fɔ:m] *vt* informar mal.

misinformation [ˌmɪsɪnfə'meɪʃn] *n* información *f* errónea.

misinterpret [ˌmɪsɪn'tɜ:prɪt] *vt* malinterpretar.

misjudge [ˌmɪs'dʒʌdʒ] *vt* - **1.** [guess wrongly] calcular mal - **2.** [appraise wrongly] juzgar mal.

misjudg(e)ment [ˌmɪs'dʒʌdʒmənt] *n* - **1.** [poor judgment] estimación *f* equivocada - **2.** [error of judgment] error *m* de juicio.

mislay [ˌmɪs'leɪ] (*pt & pp* -**laid**) *vt* extraviar, perder.

mislead [ˌmɪs'li:d] (*pt & pp* -**led**) *vt* engañar.

misleading [ˌmɪs'li:dɪŋ] *adj* engañoso(sa).

misled [ˌmɪs'led] *pt & pp* ▷ **mislead**.

mismanage [ˌmɪs'mænɪdʒ] *vt* [company] gestionar mal; [situation] llevar mal.

mismanagement [ˌmɪs'mænɪdʒmənt] *n* mala administración *f*.

mismatch [ˌmɪs'mætʃ] *vt*: **to be mismatched** emparejar mal.

misnomer [ˌmɪs'nəʊmər] *n* término *m* equivocado.

misogynist [mɪ'sɒdʒɪnɪst] *n* misógino *m*.

misplace [ˌmɪs'pleɪs] *vt* extraviar, perder.

misplaced [ˌmɪs'pleɪst] *adj* [trust] mal encaminado(da), fuera de lugar.

misprint ['mɪsprɪnt] *n* errata *f*, error *m* de imprenta.

mispronounce [ˌmɪsprə'naʊns] *vt* pronunciar mal.

misquote [ˌmɪs'kwəʊt] *vt* citar incorrectamente.

misread [ˌmɪs'ri:d] (*pt & pp* -**read**) *vt* - **1.** [read wrongly] leer mal - **2.** [misinterpret] malinterpretar.

misrepresent ['mɪsˌreprɪ'zent] *vt* [person] dar una imagen equivocada de; [words] tergiversar.

misrepresentation ['mɪsˌreprɪzen'teɪʃn] *n* - **1.** *(U)* [wrong interpretation] mala interpretación *f* - **2.** [false account] tergiversación *f*.

misrule [ˌmɪs'ru:l] *n* mal gobierno *m*.

miss [mɪs] ◇ *vt* - **1.** [fail to see - TV programme, film] perderse; [- error, person in crowd] no ver - **2.** [fail to hear] no oír - **3.** [omit] saltarse - **4.** [shot] fallar; [ball] no dar a; **to miss the target** no dar en el blanco - **5.** [feel absence of] echar de menos OR en falta; **I miss you** te echo de menos - **6.** [opportunity] perder, dejar pasar; [turning] pasarse - **7.** [train, bus] perder - **8.** [appointment] faltar a, no asistir a; [deadline] no cumplir - **9.** [avoid] evitar; **I just missed being run over** no me atropellaron por muy poco. ◇ *vi* fallar. ◇ *n* fallo *m*; **to give sthg a miss** *inf* pasar de algo.

◆ **miss out** ◇ *vt sep* pasar por alto. ◇ *vi*: **to miss out (on sthg)** perderse (algo).

Miss [mɪs] *n* señorita *f*; **Miss Brown** la señorita Brown.

misshapen [ˌmɪs'ʃeɪpn] *adj* deforme.

missile [*UK* 'mɪsaɪl, *US* 'mɪsəl] *n* - **1.** [weapon] misil *m* - **2.** [thrown object] proyectil *m*.

missile launcher [-ˌlɔ:ntʃər] *n* lanzamisiles *m inv*.

missing ['mɪsɪŋ] *adj* - **1.** [lost] perdido(da), extraviado(da) - **2.** [not present] ausente; **to be missing** faltar.

missing link *n* eslabón *m* perdido.

missing person *n* desaparecido *m*, -da *f*.

mission ['mɪʃn] *n* misión *f*.

missionary ['mɪʃənrɪ] (*pl* -**ies**) *n* misionero *m*, -ra *f*.

Mississippi [ˌmɪsɪ'sɪpɪ] *n* - **1.** [river]: **the Mississippi (River)** el (río) Misisipí - **2.** [state] Misisipí.

missive ['mɪsɪv] *n fml* misiva *f*.

Missouri [mɪ'zʊərɪ] *n* Misuri.

misspell [ˌmɪs'spel] (*pt & pp* -**spelt** OR -**spelled**) *vt* escribir mal.

misspelling [ˌmɪs'spelɪŋ] *n* falta *f* de ortografía.

misspelt [ˌmɪs'spelt] *pt & pp* ▷ **misspell**.

mist [mɪst] *n* [gen] neblina *f*; [at sea] bruma *f*.

◆ **mist over, mist up** *vi* [windows, spectacles] empañarse; [eyes] llenarse de lágrimas.

mistake [mɪ'steɪk] ◇ *n* error *m*; **to make a mistake** equivocarse, cometer un error; **by mistake** por error. ◇ *vt* (*pt* -**took**, *pp* -**taken**) - **1.** [misunderstand] entender mal - **2.** [fail to recognize]: **to mistake sthg/sb for** confundir algo/a alguien con; **there's no mistaking it** es inconfundible.

mistaken [mɪ'steɪkn] ◇ *pp* ▷ **mistake**. ◇ *adj* equivocado(da); **to be mistaken about sb/sthg** estar equivocado respecto a alguien/algo.

mistaken identity *n*: **a case of mistaken identity** un caso de identificación errónea.

mistakenly [mɪs'teɪknlɪ] *adv* equivocadamente.

mister ['mɪstər] *n inf* amigo *m*.

◆ **Mister** *n* señor *m*; **mister Brown** el señor Brown.

mistime [ˌmɪs'taɪm] *vt* hacer a destiempo, calcular mal.

mistletoe ['mɪsltəʊ] *n* muérdago *m*.

mistook [mɪ'stʊk] *pt* ▷ **mistake**.

mistranslation [ˌmɪstræns'leɪʃn] *n* traducción *f* equivocada.

mistreat [ˌmɪs'tri:t] *vt* maltratar.

mistreatment [ˌmɪsˈtriːtmənt] n (U) malos tratos mpl.

mistress [ˈmɪstrɪs] n - **1.** [female lover] amante f, querida f - **2.** UK [school teacher - primary] maestra f, señorita f; [- secondary] profesora f - **3.** [woman in control] señora f; **mistress of the situation** dueña f de la situación.

mistrial [ˈmɪstraɪəl] n juicio m nulo.

mistrust [ˌmɪsˈtrʌst] <> n desconfianza f, recelo m. <> vt desconfiar de.

mistrustful [ˌmɪsˈtrʌstfʊl] adj desconfiado(da), receloso(sa); **to be mistrustful of** desconfiar de.

misty [ˈmɪstɪ] (comp -ier, superl -iest) adj [gen] neblinoso(sa); [at sea] brumoso(sa).

misunderstand [ˌmɪsʌndəˈstænd] (pt & pp -stood) vt & vi entender mal.

misunderstanding [ˌmɪsʌndəˈstændɪŋ] n malentendido m.

misunderstood [ˌmɪsʌndəˈstʊd] pt & pp ▷ **misunderstand**.

misuse <> n [ˌmɪsˈjuːs] uso m indebido. <> vt [ˌmɪsˈjuːz] hacer uso indebido de.

MIT (abbr of Massachusetts Institute of Technology) n principal instituto de investigación tecnológica en Estados Unidos.

mite [maɪt] n - **1.** [insect] ácaro m, insecto m diminuto - **2.** inf [small amount]: **a mite** un pelín, una pizca - **3.** [small child] criatura f.

miter US = **mitre**.

mitigate [ˈmɪtɪgeɪt] vt fml mitigar, atenuar.

mitigating [ˈmɪtɪgeɪtɪŋ] adj fml: **mitigating circumstances** circunstancias fpl atenuantes.

mitigation [ˌmɪtɪˈgeɪʃn] n fml [circumstance] descargo m, atenuante m.

mitre UK, **miter** US [ˈmaɪtər] n - **1.** [hat] mitra f - **2.** [joint] inglete m.

mitt [mɪt] n manopla f; US [for baseball] guante m.

mitten [ˈmɪtn] n manopla f.

mix [mɪks] <> vt: **to mix sthg (with)** mezclar algo (con). <> vi - **1.** [substances] mezclarse; [activities] ir bien juntos(tas) - **2.** [socially]: **to mix with** alternar con. <> n mezcla f.
◆ **mix up** vt sep - **1.** [confuse] confundir - **2.** [disorder] mezclar.

mixed [mɪkst] adj - **1.** [of different kinds] surtido(da), variado(da); **to have mixed feelings about** tener sentimientos encontrados acerca de; **mixed salad** ensalada f mixta - **2.** [of different sexes] mixto(ta).

mixed-ability adj UK [class, group] con alumnos de varios niveles.

mixed blessing n: it is a mixed blessing tiene su lado bueno y su lado malo.

mixed doubles n (U) dobles mpl mixtos.

mixed economy n economía f mixta.

mixed grill n parrillada f mixta.

mixed marriage n matrimonio m mixto.

mixed up adj - **1.** [confused] confuso(sa); **to get mixed up** confundirse - **2.** [involved]: **mixed up in** [fight, crime] involucrado(da) en.

mixer [ˈmɪksər] n - **1.** [for food] batidora f; [for cement] hormigonera f - **2.** [for music] mesa f de mezclas - **3.** [non-alcoholic drink] bebida no alcohólica para mezclar con bebidas alcohólicas.

mixer tap n UK monomando m, grifo OR caño m Perú único OR llave f Amér OR paja f Amér C OR canilla f R Plata única (para agua fría y caliente), caño m único (para agua fría y caliente) Perú.

mixing bowl [ˈmɪksɪŋ-] n cuenco m (para mezclar).

mixture [ˈmɪkstʃər] n [gen] mezcla f; [of sweets] surtido m.

mix-up n inf confusión f.

MK, mk abbr of **mark**.

ml (abbr of **millilitre**) ml.

MLitt [ˌemˈlɪt] (abbr of **Master of Literature, Master of Letters**) n (titular de un) título postuniversitario de unos dos años de duración en el campo de las humanidades.

MLR n abbr of **minimum lending rate**.

mm (abbr of **millimetre**) mm.

MMR [ˌememˈɑːr] (abbr of **measles, mumps & rubella**) n MED sarampión, paperas y rubeola.

MN abbr of **Minnesota**.

mnemonic [nɪˈmɒnɪk] n frase f mnemotécnica.

m.o. abbr of **money order**.

MO <> n - **1.** (abbr of **medical officer**), oficial médico - **2.** (abbr of **modus operandi**), modus operandi. <> abbr of **Missouri**.

moan [məʊn] <> n - **1.** [of pain, sadness] gemido m - **2.** inf [complaint] queja f. <> vi - **1.** [in pain, sadness] gemir - **2.** inf [complain]: **to moan (about)** quejarse (de).

moaning [ˈməʊnɪŋ] n (U) [complaining] quejas fpl.

moat [məʊt] n foso m.

mob [mɒb] <> n muchedumbre f, turba f. <> vt (pt & pp -bed, cont -bing) agolparse en torno de, asediar.

mobile [ˈməʊbaɪl] <> adj - **1.** [able to move] móvil - **2.** [able to travel]: **to be mobile** poder viajar. <> n móvil m.

mobile home n caravana f.

mobile library n bibliobús m.

mobile phone n teléfono m móvil.

mobility [məˈbɪlətɪ] n movilidad f.

mobility allowance n UK ayuda económica que reciben los minusválidos para poder viajar.

mobilization [ˌməʊbɪlaɪˈzeɪʃn] n movilización f.

mobilize, -ise [ˈməʊbɪlaɪz] <> vt movilizar. <> vi movilizarse.

moccasin [ˈmɒkəsɪn] n mocasín m.

mock [mɒk] <> adj fingido(da); **mock (exam)** simulacro m de examen. <> vt burlarse de. <> vi burlarse.

mockery [ˈmɒkərɪ] n burlas fpl; **to make a mockery of sthg** poner en ridículo algo.

mocking [ˈmɒkɪŋ] adj burlón(ona).

mockingbird [ˈmɒkɪŋbɜːd] n sinsonte m.

mock-up n maqueta f de tamaño natural.

mod [mɒd] n UK mod mf, aficionado a la música soul inglesa de los años 60.

MOD n abbr of Ministry of Defence.

mod cons [ˌmɒd-] (abbr of modern conveniences) npl UK inf: **all mod cons** con todas las comodidades.

mode [məʊd] n modo m.

model [ˈmɒdl] <> n - **1.** [gen] modelo m - **2.** [small copy] maqueta f - **3.** [for painter, in fashion] modelo mf. <> adj - **1.** [exemplary] modelo (inv) - **2.** [reduced-scale] en miniatura. <> vt (UK -led, cont -ling, US -ed, cont -ing) - **1.** [shape] modelar - **2.** [wear] lucir (en pase de modelos) - **3.** [copy]: **to model o.s. on sb** tener a alguien como modelo - **4.** COMPUT simular por ordenador. <> vi (UK -led, cont -ling, US -ed, cont -ing) trabajar de modelo.

modem [ˈməʊdem] n COMPUT módem m.

moderate <> adj [ˈmɒdərət] moderado(da). <> n [ˈmɒdərət] POL moderado m, -da f. <> vt [ˈmɒdəreɪt] moderar. <> vi [ˈmɒdəreɪt] [in debate] hacer de moderador.

moderately [ˈmɒdərətlɪ] adv moderadamente.

moderation [ˌmɒdəˈreɪʃn] n moderación f; **in moderation** con moderación.

moderator [ˈmɒdəreɪtər] n [of exam] moderador m, -ra f.

modern [ˈmɒdən] adj moderno(na).

modern-day adj de nuestros días.

modernism [ˈmɒdənɪzm] n modernismo m.

modernization [ˌmɒdənaɪˈzeɪʃn] n modernización f.

modernize, -ise [ˈmɒdənaɪz] <> vt modernizar. <> vi modernizarse.

modern languages npl lenguas fpl modernas.

modest [ˈmɒdɪst] adj - **1.** [gen] modesto(ta) - **2.** [improvement] ligero(ra); [price] módico(ca).

modestly [ˈmɒdɪstlɪ] adv [gen] modestamente; [improve] ligeramente.

modesty [ˈmɒdɪstɪ] n modestia f.

modicum [ˈmɒdɪkəm] n fml: **a modicum of** un mínimo de.

modification [ˌmɒdɪfɪˈkeɪʃn] n modificación f.

modify [ˈmɒdɪfaɪ] (pt & pp -ied) vt modificar.

modular [ˈmɒdjʊlər] adj modular.

modulated [ˈmɒdjʊleɪtɪd] adj modulado(da).

modulation [ˌmɒdjʊˈleɪʃn] n modulación f.

module [ˈmɒdjuːl] n módulo m.

moggy [ˈmɒgɪ] (pl -ies) n UK inf minino m.

mogul [ˈməʊgl] n magnate mf.

mohair [ˈməʊheər] <> n mohair m. <> comp de mohair.

Mohican [məʊˈhiːkən] n - **1.** [person] mohicano m, -na f - **2.** [hairstyle] cresta f.

moist [mɔɪst] adj húmedo(da).

moisten [ˈmɔɪsn] vt humedecer.

moisture [ˈmɔɪstʃər] n humedad f.

moisturize, -ise [ˈmɔɪstʃəraɪz] vt hidratar.

moisturizer [ˈmɔɪstʃəraɪzər] n (crema f) hidratante m.

molar [ˈməʊlər] n muela f.

molasses [məˈlæsɪz] n (U) melaza f.

mold US = mould.

Moldavia [mɒlˈdeɪvɪə] n Moldavia.

mole [məʊl] n - **1.** [animal, spy] topo m - **2.** [spot] lunar m.

molecular [məˈlekjʊlər] adj molecular.

molecule [ˈmɒlɪkjuːl] n molécula f.

molehill [ˈməʊlhɪl] n topera f.

molest [məˈlest] vt - **1.** [sexually] abusar sexualmente de - **2.** [annoy] molestar.

molester [məˈlestər] n: **child molester** pervertidor m, -ra f de menores.

mollify [ˈmɒlɪfaɪ] (pt & pp -ied) vt fml apaciguar.

mollusc, mollusk US [ˈmɒləsk] n molusco m.

mollycoddle [ˈmɒlɪˌkɒdl] vt inf mimar.

Molotov cocktail [ˈmɒlətɒf-] n cóctel m molotov.

molt US = moult.

molten [ˈməʊltn] adj fundido(da).

mom [mɒm] n US inf mamá f.

moment [ˈməʊmənt] n momento m; **moment of truth** momento de la verdad; **at any moment** de un momento a otro; **at the moment** en este momento; **at the last moment** en el último momento; **for the moment** de momento; **for one moment** por un momento; **in a moment** enseguida; **just a moment** un momento.

momentarily [ˈməʊməntərɪlɪ] adv - **1.** [for a short time] momentáneamente - **2.** US [soon] pronto, de un momento a otro.

momentary ['məʊməntrɪ] *adj* momentáneo(a).

momentous [mə'mentəs] *adj* trascendental.

momentum [mə'mentəm] *n (U)* - **1.** PHYS momento *m* - **2.** *fig* [speed, force] ímpetu *m*, impulso *m*; **to gather momentum** cobrar intensidad.

momma ['mɒmə], **mommy** ['mɒmɪ] *n US* mamá *f*.

Mon. (*abbr of* Monday) lun.

Monaco ['mɒnəkəʊ] *n* Mónaco.

monarch ['mɒnək] *n* monarca *mf*.

monarchist ['mɒnəkɪst] *n* monárquico *m*, -ca *f*.

monarchy ['mɒnəkɪ] (*pl* -ies) *n* - **1.** [gen] monarquía *f* - **2.** [royal family]: **the monarchy** la familia real.

monastery ['mɒnəstrɪ] (*pl* -ies) *n* monasterio *m*.

monastic [mə'næstɪk] *adj* monástico(ca).

Monday ['mʌndɪ] *n* lunes *m inv*; *see also* **Saturday**.

monetarism ['mʌnɪtərɪzm] *n* monetarismo *m*.

monetarist ['mʌnɪtərɪst] *n* monetarista *mf*.

monetary ['mʌnɪtrɪ] *adj* monetario(ria).

money ['mʌnɪ] *n* dinero *m*, plata *f Andes, Col & Ven*; **to make money** hacer dinero; **we got our money's worth** sacamos provecho a nuestro dinero; **for my money** en mi opinión.

money belt *n* cinturón *m* monedero.

moneybox ['mʌnɪbɒks] *n* hucha *f*.

money laundering *n* blanqueo *m* de dinero.

moneylender ['mʌnɪˌlendə'] *n* prestamista *mf*.

moneymaker ['mʌnɪˌmeɪkə'] *n* mina *f* (de dinero).

moneymaking ['mʌnɪˌmeɪkɪŋ] *adj* [scheme] para hacer dinero.

money market *n* mercado *m* monetario.

money order *n* giro *m* postal.

money-spinner [-ˌspɪnə'] *n esp UK inf* mina *f* (de dinero).

money supply *n* oferta *f* monetaria.

mongol ['mɒŋgəl] *dated & offens* <> *adj* mongólico(ca). <> *n* mongólico *m*, -ca *f*.

➡ **Mongol = Mongolian.**

Mongolia [mɒŋ'gəʊlɪə] *n* Mongolia.

Mongolian [mɒŋ'gəʊlɪən], **Mongol** <> *adj* mongol(la). <> *n* - **1.** [person] mongol *m*, -la *f* - **2.** [language] mongol *m*.

mongoose ['mɒŋguːs] (*pl* -s) *n* mangosta *f*.

mongrel ['mʌŋgrəl] *n* perro *m* cruzado.

monitor ['mɒnɪtə'] <> *n* [gen & COMPUT] monitor *m*. <> *vt* - **1.** [check] controlar, hacer un seguimiento de - **2.** [listen to] escuchar.

monk [mʌŋk] *n* monje *m*.

monkey ['mʌŋkɪ] (*pl* **monkeys**) *n* mono *m*.

monkey nut *n* cacahuete *m*.

monkey wrench *n* llave *f* inglesa.

mono ['mɒnəʊ] <> *adj* monoaural, mono (*inv*). <> *n* - **1.** *inf* [sound]: **in mono** en mono - **2.** *US inf* [glandular fever] mononucleosis *f inv* infecciosa.

monochrome ['mɒnəkrəʊm] *adj* monocromo(ma).

monocle ['mɒnəkl] *n* monóculo *m*.

monogamous [mɒ'nɒgəməs] *adj* monógamo(ma).

monogamy [mɒ'nɒgəmɪ] *n* monogamia *f*.

monogrammed ['mɒnəgræmd] *adj* bordado(da) con iniciales.

monolingual [ˌmɒnə'lɪŋgwəl] *adj* monolingüe.

monolithic [ˌmɒnə'lɪθɪk] *adj* monolítico(ca).

monologue, monolog *US* ['mɒnəlɒg] *n* monólogo *m*.

mononucleosis ['mɒnəʊˌnjuːklɪ'əʊsɪs] *n US* mononucleosis *f inv* infecciosa.

monoplane ['mɒnəpleɪn] *n* monoplano *m*.

monopolize, -ise [mə'nɒpəlaɪz] *vt* monopolizar.

monopoly [mə'nɒpəlɪ] (*pl* -ies) *n*: **monopoly (on** OR **of)** monopolio *m* (de); **Monopolies and Mergers Commission** *comisión antimonopolios británica*.

monorail ['mɒnəreɪl] *n* monorraíl *m*.

monosodium   glutamate [ˌmɒnə'səʊdjəm'gluː'təmeɪt] *n* glutamato *m* monosódico.

monosyllabic [ˌmɒnəsɪ'læbɪk] *adj* [word] monosilábico(ca).

monosyllable ['mɒnəˌsɪləbl] *n* monosílabo *m*.

monotone ['mɒnətəʊn] *n*: **in a monotone** con voz monótona.

monotonous [mə'nɒtənəs] *adj* monótono(na).

monotonously [mə'nɒtənəslɪ] *adv* de forma monótona.

monotony [mə'nɒtənɪ] *n* monotonía *f*.

monoxide [mɒ'nɒksaɪd] *n* monóxido *m*.

Monsignor [ˌmɒn'siːɲə'] *n* monseñor *m*.

monsoon [mɒn'suːn] *n* monzón *m*.

monster ['mɒnstə'] <> *n* - **1.** [imaginary creature, cruel person] monstruo *m* - **2.** [very large thing] mastodonte *m*. <> *adj* gigantesco(ca), enorme.

monstrosity [mɒn'strɒsətɪ] (*pl* -ies) *n* monstruosidad *f*.

monstrous ['mɒnstrəs] *adj* - **1.** [very unfair, frightening, ugly] monstruoso(sa) - **2.** [very large] gigantesco(ca).

montage ['mɒntɑːʒ] *n* montaje *m*.

Montana [mɒn'tænə] *n* Montana.

Montenegro [ˌmɒntɪ'niːgrəʊ] *n* Montenegro.

Montevideo [ˌmɒntɪvɪ'deɪəʊ] *n* Montevideo.

month [mʌnθ] *n* mes *m*.

monthly ['mʌnθlɪ] <> *adj* mensual. <> *adv* mensualmente. <> *n* (*pl* **-ies**) revista *f* mensual.

Montreal [mɒntrɪ'ɔːl] *n* Montreal.

monument ['mɒnjʊmənt] *n* monumento *m*.

monumental [,mɒnju'mentl] *adj* **- 1.** [gen] monumental **- 2.** [error] descomunal.

moo [muː] <> *n* (*pl* **-s**) mugido *m*. <> *vi* mugir.

mooch [muːtʃ] **➤ mooch about, mooch around** *vi inf* deambular.

mood [muːd] *n* [of individual] humor *m*; [of public, voters] disposición *f*; **in a (bad) mood** de mal humor; **in a good mood** de buen humor; **not to be in the mood for sthg** no estar de humor para algo.

moody ['muːdɪ] (*comp* **-ier**, *superl* **-iest**) *adj pej* **- 1.** [changeable] de humor variable **- 2.** [bad-tempered] malhumorado(da), irritable.

moon [muːn] *n* luna *f*; **to be over the moon** *inf* estar dando saltos de alegría.

moonbeam ['muːnbiːm] *n* rayo *m* de luna.

moonlight ['muːnlaɪt] <> *n* luz *f* de la luna; **by moonlight** a la luz de la luna. <> *vi* (*pt* & *pp* **-ed**) *inf* estar pluriempleado(da).

moonlighting ['muːnlaɪtɪŋ] *n* pluriempleo *m*.

moonlit ['muːnlɪt] *adj* [night] de luna; [landscape] iluminado(da) por la luna.

moonscape ['muːnskeɪp] *n* paisaje *m* lunar.

moonstruck ['muːnstrʌk] *adj inf* chiflado(da), chalado(da).

moor [mɔːr] <> *n esp UK* páramo *m*, brezal *m*. <> *vt* amarrar. <> *vi* echar las amarras.

Moor [mɔːr] *n* moro *m*, -ra *f*.

moorings ['mɔːrɪŋz] *npl* [ropes, chains] amarras *fpl*; [place] amarradero *m*.

Moorish ['mɔːrɪʃ] *adj* moro(ra), morisco(ca).

moorland ['mɔːlənd] *n esp UK* páramo *m*, brezal *m*.

moose [muːs] (*pl* **moose**) *n* [North American] alce *m*.

moot [muːt] *vt* proponer.

moot point *n*: **it's a moot point** es discutible.

mop [mɒp] <> *n* **- 1.** [for cleaning] fregona *f* **- 2.** *inf* [of hair] pelambrera *f*, chasca *f Andes*. <> *vt* (*pt* & *pp* **-ped**, *cont* **-ping**) **- 1.** [clean with mop] fregar, pasar la fregona por **- 2.** [dry with cloth - sweat] enjugar.

➤ mop up *vt sep* [clean up] limpiar.

mope [məʊp] *vi pej* estar deprimido(da).

➤ mope about, mope around *vi pej* vagar como un alma en pena.

moped ['məʊped] *n* ciclomotor *m*, motoneta *f Amér*.

moral ['mɒrəl] <> *adj* moral; **moral support** apoyo *m* moral. <> *n* [lesson] moraleja *f*.

➤ morals *npl* [principles] moral *f*.

morale [mə'rɑːl] *n (U)* moral *f*.

moralistic [,mɒrə'lɪstɪk] *adj pej* moralista.

morality [mə'rælətɪ] (*pl* **-ies**) *n* **- 1.** [gen] moralidad *f* **- 2.** [system of principles] moral *f*.

moralize, -ise ['mɒrəlaɪz] *vi pej*: **to moralize (about** OR **on)** moralizar (sobre).

morally ['mɒrəlɪ] *adv* moralmente.

Moral Majority *n* grupo de presión ultra-conservador apoyado por las iglesias fundamentalistas en Estados Unidos.

morass [mə'ræs] *n* cenagal *m*.

moratorium [,mɒrə'tɔːrɪəm] (*pl* **-ria** [-rɪə]) *n fml*: **moratorium (on)** moratoria *f* (para).

morbid ['mɔːbɪd] *adj* morboso(sa).

more [mɔːr] <> *adv* **- 1.** (with adj and adverbs) más; **more important (than)** más importante (que); **more quickly/often (than)** más rápido/a menudo (que) **- 2.** [to a greater degree] más; **she's more like a mother to me than a sister** para mí ella es más una madre que una hermana; **we were more hurt than angry** más que enfadados estábamos heridos; **I couldn't agree more** estoy completamente de acuerdo **- 3.** [another time]: **once/twice more** una vez/dos veces más. <> *adj* más; **there are more trains in the morning** hay más trenes por la mañana; **more food than drink** más comida que bebida; **more than 70 people died** más de 70 personas murieron; **have some more tea** toma un poco más de té; **I finished two more chapters today** acabé otros dos capítulos hoy. <> *pron* más; **more than five** más de cinco; **he's got more than I have** él tiene más que yo; **there's more if you want it** hay más si quieres; **I don't want any more** no quiero más; **there's no more (left)** no queda nada (más); **what more do you want?** ¿qué más quieres?; **(and) what's more** (y lo que) es más.

➤ any more *adv*: **not... any more** ya no...; **she doesn't live here any more** ya no vive aquí.

➤ more and more *adv, adj* & *pron* cada vez más.

➤ more or less *adv* más o menos; **she more or less suggested I had stolen it** lo que vino a decir es que yo lo había robado.

moreover [mɔː'rəʊvər] *adv fml* además, es más.

morgue [mɔːg] *n* depósito *m* de cadáveres.

MORI ['mɔːrɪ] (*abbr of* **Market** & **Opinion Research Institute**) *n* empresa británica especializada en encuestas de opinión.

moribund ['mɒrɪbʌnd] *adj fml* agonizante *fig*.

Mormon ['mɔːmən] *n* mormón *m*, -ona *f*.

morning ['mɔːnɪŋ] *n* **- 1.** [first part of day] mañana *f*; **in the morning** por la mañana; **six**

o'clock in the morning las seis de la mañana; **on Monday morning** el lunes por la mañana **- 2.** [between midnight and dawn] madrugada *f* **- 3.** [tomorrow morning]: **in the morning** mañana por la mañana.

◆ **mornings** *adv US* por la mañana.

morning-after pill *n* píldora *f* del día siguiente.

morning dress *n esp UK* traje *m* de etiqueta.

morning sickness *n (U)* náuseas *fpl* del embarazo.

Moroccan [mə'rɒkən] ◇ *adj* marroquí. ◇ *n* marroquí *mf*.

Morocco [mə'rɒkəʊ] *n* Marruecos.

moron ['mɔ:rɒn] *n inf* imbécil *mf*.

moronic [mə'rɒnɪk] *adj* imbécil.

morose [mə'rəʊs] *adj* malhumorado(da).

morphine ['mɔ:fi:n] *n* morfina *f*.

morris dancing ['mɒrɪs-] *n (U)* baile regional inglés cuyos bailarines llevan campanillas cosidas a la ropa.

Morse (code) [mɔ:s-] *n* (código *m*) morse *m*.

morsel ['mɔ:sl] *n* bocado *m*.

mortal ['mɔ:tl] ◇ *adj* **- 1.** [gen] mortal **- 2.** [fear] espantoso(sa). ◇ *n* mortal *mf*.

mortality [mɔ:'tælətɪ] *n* mortalidad *f*.

mortality rate *n* tasa *f* de mortalidad.

mortally ['mɔ:təlɪ] *adv* **- 1.** [wounded] mortalmente, de muerte **- 2.** [offended] profundamente.

mortar ['mɔ:təʳ] *n* **- 1.** [cement mixture] argamasa *f* **- 2.** [gun, bowl] mortero *m*.

mortarboard ['mɔ:təbɔ:d] *n* sombrero en forma de cuadrado negro del cual cuelga una borla, típico de las graduaciones.

mortgage ['mɔ:gɪdʒ] ◇ *n* hipoteca *f*. ◇ *vt* hipotecar.

mortgagee [,mɔ:gɪ'dʒi:] *n* acreedor hipotecario *m*, acreedora hipotecaria *f*.

mortgagor [,mɔ:gɪ'dʒɔ:ʳ] *n* deudor hipotecario *m*, deudora hipotecaria *f*.

mortician [mɔ:'tɪʃn] *n US* director *m*, -ra *f* de funeraria.

mortified ['mɔ:tɪfaɪd] *adj* muerto(ta) de vergüenza.

mortise lock ['mɔ:tɪs-] *n* cerradura *f* embutida.

mortuary ['mɔ:tʃʊərɪ] *(pl* **-ies)** *n* depósito *m* de cadáveres, tanatorio *m*.

mosaic [mə'zeɪɪk] *n* mosaico *m*.

Moslem ['mɒzləm] = **Muslim**.

mosque [mɒsk] *n* mezquita *f*.

mosquito [mə'ski:təʊ] *(pl* **-es** OR **-s)** *n* mosquito *m*, zancudo *m Amér.*

mosquito net *n* mosquitera *f*.

moss [mɒs] *n* musgo *m*.

mossy ['mɒsɪ] *(comp* **-ier***, superl* **-iest)** *adj* cubierto(ta) de musgo.

most [məʊst] *(superl of* **many)** ◇ *adj* **- 1.** [the majority of] la mayoría de; **most people** la mayoría de la gente **- 2.** [largest amount of]: **(the) most** más; **who has got (the) most money?** ¿quién es el que tiene más dinero? ◇ *pron* **- 1.** [the majority]: **most (of)** la mayoría (de); **most are women** la mayoría son mujeres; **most of the time** la mayor parte del tiempo **- 2.** [largest amount]: **I earn (the) most** soy el que más dinero gana; **the most I've ever won** lo máximo que he ganado; **most of the time** la mayor parte del tiempo; **at most** como mucho

▸▸ **to make the most of sthg** sacarle el mayor partido a algo. ◇ *adv* **- 1.** [to the greatest extent]: **(the) most** el/la/lo más; **the most handsome man** el hombre más guapo; **what I like most** lo que más me gusta; **most often** más a menudo **- 2.** *fml* [very] muy; **most certainly** con toda seguridad **- 3.** *US* [almost] casi.

mostly ['məʊstlɪ] *adv* [in the main part] principalmente; [usually] normalmente.

MOT *(abbr of* **Ministry of Transport test)** *n* ≃ ITV *f*; **to have one's car MOT'd** ≃ pasar la ITV.

motel [məʊ'tel] *n* motel *m*.

moth [mɒθ] *n* polilla *f*.

mothball ['mɒθbɔ:l] *n* bola *f* de naftalina.

moth-eaten *adj* apolillado(da).

mother ['mʌðəʳ] ◇ *n* madre *f*. ◇ *vt pej* [spoil] mimar.

motherboard ['mʌðə,bɔ:d] *n* COMPUT placa *f* madre.

motherhood ['mʌðəhʊd] *n* maternidad *f*.

Mothering Sunday ['mʌðərɪŋ-] *n* el día de la madre.

mother-in-law *(pl* **mothers-in-law** OR **mother-in-laws)** *n* suegra *f*.

motherland ['mʌðəlænd] *n* madre *f* patria.

motherless ['mʌðəlɪs] *adj* sin madre, huérfano(na) de madre.

motherly ['mʌðəlɪ] *adj* maternal.

Mother Nature *n* la madre naturaleza.

mother-of-pearl ◇ *n* nácar *m*. ◇ *comp* de nácar.

Mother's Day *n* el día de la madre.

mother superior *n* madre *f* superiora.

mother-to-be *(pl* **mothers-to-be)** *n* futura madre *f*.

mother tongue *n* lengua *f* materna.

motif [məʊ'ti:f] *n* ART & MUS motivo *m*.

motion ['məʊʃn] ◇ *n* **- 1.** [gen] movimiento *m*; **to set sthg in motion** poner algo en marcha;

to go through the motions (of doing sthg) (hacer algo para) cubrir el expediente **- 2.** [proposal] moción f. ⋄ vt: **to motion sb to do sthg** indicar a alguien con un gesto que haga algo. ⋄ vi: **to motion to sb** hacer una señal (con la mano) a alguien.

motionless ['məʊʃənlɪs] adj inmóvil.

motion picture n US película f.

motivate ['məʊtɪveɪt] vt motivar.

motivated ['məʊtɪveɪtɪd] adj motivado(da).

motivation [,məʊtɪ'veɪʃn] n motivación f.

motive ['məʊtɪv] n [gen] motivo m; [for crime] móvil m.

motley ['mɒtlɪ] adj pej variopinto(ta), abigarrado(da).

motocross ['məʊtəkrɒs] n motocross m.

motor ['məʊtə'] ⋄ adj UK [industry, accident] automovilístico(ca); [mechanic] de automóviles. ⋄ n - **1.** [engine] motor m - **2.** UK inf [car] coche m. ⋄ vi inf [go fast] ir a toda pastilla.

Motorail® ['məʊtəreɪl] n UK servicio m ferroviario de transporte de coches.

motorbike ['məʊtəbaɪk] n moto f.

motorboat ['məʊtəbəʊt] n lancha f motora.

motorcade ['məʊtəkeɪd] n caravana f de coches.

motorcar ['məʊtəkɑː'] n automóvil m.

motorcycle ['məʊtə,saɪkl] n motocicleta f.

motorcyclist ['məʊtə,saɪklɪst] n motociclista mf.

motoring ['məʊtərɪŋ] ⋄ adj UK automovilístico(ca); **motoring offence** infracción f de tráfico. ⋄ n automovilismo m.

motorist ['məʊtərɪst] n automovilista mf, conductor m, -ra f.

motorize, -ise ['məʊtəraɪz] vt motorizar.

motor lodge n US motel m.

motor racing n (U) carreras fpl de coches, automovilismo m deportivo.

motor scooter n Vespa® f, escúter m.

motorsport ['məʊtəspɔːt] n carreras fpl de coches.

motor vehicle n vehículo m de motor.

motorway ['məʊtəweɪ] UK ⋄ n autopista f. ⋄ comp de autopista.

mottled ['mɒtld] adj con manchas, moteado(da).

motto ['mɒtəʊ] (pl -s OR -es) n lema m.

mould, mold US [məʊld] ⋄ n - **1.** [growth] moho m - **2.** [shape] molde m. ⋄ vt lit & fig moldear.

moulding, molding US ['məʊldɪŋ] n [decoration] moldura f.

mouldy, moldy US (comp -ier, superl -iest), **moldy** US (comp -ier, superl -iest) ['məʊldɪ] adj mohoso(sa).

moult UK, **molt** US [məʊlt] ⋄ vt mudar. ⋄ vi [bird] mudar la pluma; [dog] mudar el pelo.

mound [maʊnd] n - **1.** [small hill] montículo m - **2.** [untidy pile] montón m.

mount [maʊnt] ⋄ n - **1.** [gen] montura f; [for photograph] marco m; [for jewel] engaste m - **2.** [mountain] monte m. ⋄ vt - **1.** [horse, bike] subirse a, montar en - **2.** fml [hill, steps] subir - **3.** [attack] lanzar; **to mount guard over sthg/sb** montar guardia para vigilar algo/a alguien - **4.** [exhibition] montar - **5.** [jewel] engastar; [photograph] enmarcar. ⋄ vi - **1.** [increase] aumentar - **2.** [climb on horse] montar.

mountain ['maʊntɪn] n lit & fig montaña f; **to make a mountain out of a molehill** hacer una montaña de un grano de arena.

mountain bike n bicicleta f de montaña.

mountain climbing n montañismo m, andinismo m Amér.

mountaineer [,maʊntɪ'nɪə'] n montañero m, -ra f, andinista mf Amér.

mountaineering [,maʊntɪ'nɪərɪŋ] n montañismo m, andinismo m Amér.

mountainous ['maʊntɪnəs] adj montañoso(sa).

mountain range n cordillera f, cadena f montañosa.

mountain rescue n rescate m de montaña.

mounted ['maʊntɪd] adj montado(da).

Mountie ['maʊntɪ] n inf agente de la policía montada del Canadá.

mourn [mɔːn] ⋄ vt [person] llorar por; [thing] lamentar de. ⋄ vi: **to mourn for sb** llorar la muerte de alguien.

mourner ['mɔːnə'] n doliente mf.

mournful ['mɔːnfʊl] adj [face, voice] afligido(da), lúgubre; [sound] lastimero(ra).

mourning ['mɔːnɪŋ] n luto m; **in mourning** de luto.

mouse [maʊs] (pl mice) n ZOOL & COMPUT ratón m.

mouse mat n COMPUT alfombrilla f.

mousetrap ['maʊstræp] n ratonera f.

moussaka [muː'sɑːkə] n musaka f.

mousse [muːs] n - **1.** [food] mousse m - **2.** [for hair] espuma f.

moustache UK [mə'stɑːʃ], **mustache** US ['mʌstæʃ] n bigote m.

mouth ⋄ n [maʊθ] [gen] boca f; [of river] desembocadura f; **to keep one's mouth shut** inf callarse, no abrir la boca. ⋄ vt [maʊð] articular con los labios (sin hablar).

mouthful ['maʊθfʊl] *n* - **1.** [of food] bocado *m*; [of drink] trago *m* - **2.** *inf* [difficult word] trabalenguas *m inv*.

mouthorgan ['maʊθ,ɔːgən] *n* armónica *f*, rondín *m Amér*.

mouthpiece ['maʊθpiːs] *n* - **1.** [of telephone] micrófono *m* - **2.** [of musical instrument] boquilla *f* - **3.** [spokesperson] portavoz *mf*.

mouth-to-mouth *adj*: **mouth-to-mouth resuscitation** (respiración *f*) boca a boca *m*.

mouthwash ['maʊθwɒʃ] *n* elixir *m* bucal.

mouth-watering [-,wɔːtərɪŋ] *adj* muy apetitoso(sa).

movable ['muːvəbl] *adj* movible.

move [muːv] ◇ *n* - **1.** [movement] movimiento *m*; **a move towards** un paso hacia; **a move away from** un alejamiento de; **on the move** [travelling around] viajando; [beginning to move] en marcha; **to get a move on** *inf* espabilarse, darse prisa - **2.** [change - of house] mudanza *f*; [- of job] cambio *m* - **3.** [in board game] jugada *f*; **it's your move** mueves tú - **4.** [course of action] medida *f*. ◇ *vt* - **1.** [shift] mover; **to move sthg closer** acercar algo - **2.** [change - house] mudarse de; [- job] cambiar de - **3.** [transfer, postpone] trasladar - **4.** [affect] conmover - **5.** [in debate - motion] proponer - **6.** [cause]: **to move sb to do sthg** mover OR llevar a alguien a hacer algo. ◇ *vi* - **1.** [gen] moverse; [events] cambiar; **move closer** acércate - **2.** [change house] mudarse; [change job] cambiar de trabajo.

◆ **move about, move around** *vi* - **1.** [fidget] ir de aquí para allá - **2.** [travel] viajar.

◆ **move along** ◇ *vt sep* dispersar. ◇ *vi* - **1.** [move towards front or back] hacerse a un lado, correrse - **2.** [move away - crowd, car] circular.

◆ **move around** *vi* = move about.

◆ **move away** *vi* - **1.** [walk away] apartarse - **2.** [go to live elsewhere] marcharse.

◆ **move in** ◇ *vt sep* [troops] mandar. ◇ *vi* - **1.** [to new house] instalarse; **to move in with sb** irse a vivir con alguien - **2.** [take control, attack] intervenir.

◆ **move off** *vi* [vehicle, procession] ponerse en marcha.

◆ **move on** ◇ *vt sep* dispersar. ◇ *vi* - **1.** [go away] marcharse - **2.** [progress] avanzar, cambiar; **to move on (to a different subject)** pasar a otro tema.

◆ **move out** ◇ *vt sep* [troops] retirar. ◇ *vi* mudarse; **my girlfriend moved out yesterday** mi novia se fue a vivir a otra casa ayer.

◆ **move over** *vi* hacer sitio, correrse.

◆ **move up** *vi* [on bench etc] hacer sitio, correrse.

moveable = movable.

movement ['muːvmənt] *n* [gen] movimiento *m*; **the free movement of goods** la libre circulación de mercancías.

movie ['muːvɪ] *n esp US* película *f*; **to go to the movies** ir al cine.

movie camera *n* cámara *f* cinematográfica.

moviegoer ['muːvɪ,gəʊəʳ] *n US* persona *f* que va mucho al cine.

movie star *n US* estrella *f* de cine.

movie theater *n US* cine *m*.

moving ['muːvɪŋ] *adj* - **1.** [touching] conmovedor(ra) - **2.** [not fixed] móvil.

moving staircase *n* escalera *f* mecánica.

mow [məʊ] *vt* (*pt* -ed, *pp* -ed OR **mown**) [grass, lawn] cortar; [corn] segar.

◆ **mow down** *vt sep* acribillar.

mower ['məʊəʳ] *n* cortacésped *mf*.

mown [məʊn] *pp* ▷ mow.

Mozambican [,məʊzəm'biːkən] ◇ *adj* mozambiqueño(ña). ◇ *n* mozambiqueño *m*, -ña *f*.

Mozambique [,məʊzəm'biːk] *n* Mozambique.

MP *n* - **1.** (*abbr of* **Military Police**) PM *f* - **2.** *UK* *abbr of* **Member of Parliament** - **3.** (*abbr of* **Mounted Police**), *la policía montada del Canadá*.

MPEG (*abbr of* **Moving Pictures Expert Group**) *n* [comput] MPEG *m*.

mpg (*abbr of* **miles per gallon**) millas/galón; **it does 35 mpg** consume 35 millas/galón.

mph (*abbr of* **miles per hour**) mph.

MPhil [,em'fil] (*abbr of* **Master of Philosophy**) *n (titular de un) título postuniversitario de unos dos años de duración en el campo de las humanidades.*

Mr ['mɪstəʳ] *n* Sr.; **Mr Jones** el Sr. Jones.

MRC (*abbr of* **Medical Research Council**) *n principal organismo gubernamental para la investigación en el campo de la medicina.*

MRI (*abbr of* **magnetic resonance imaging**) *n* RM *f*.

Mrs ['mɪsɪz] *n* Sra.; **Mrs Jones** la Sra. Jones.

MRSA [,emaːres'eɪ] (*abbr of* **methicillin resistant Staphylococcus aureus**) *n* MED estafilococo *m* áureo resistente a la meticilina.

Ms [mɪz] *n abreviatura utilizada delante de un apellido de mujer cuando no se quiere especificar si está casada o no.*

MS¹ ◇ *n* - **1.** (*abbr of* **manuscript**) ms. - **2.** (*abbr of* **Master of Science**), *(titular de un) título postuniversitario de unos dos años de duración en el campo de las ciencias.* ◇ *abbr of* **Mississippi**.

MS², **ms** *n abbr of* **multiple sclerosis**.

MSc (*abbr of* **Master of Science**) *n* (titular *mf* de un) máster *m* en Ciencias.

MSF (*abbr of* **Manufacturing, Science and Finance Union**) *n antiguo sindicato británico*.

msg [emes'dʒi:] (*abbr of* **message**) *n* msj.

MSG *n abbr of* **monosodium glutamate**.

Msgr (*abbr of* **Monsignor**) Msr.

MST (*abbr of* **Mountain Standard Time**) *hora oficial de los Estados de las montañas Rocosas*.

Mt (*abbr of* **mount**) mte.

MT *abbr of* **Montana**.

much [mʌtʃ] ⟨⟩ *adj* (*comp* **more**, *superl* **most**) mucho(cha); **there isn't much rice left** no queda mucho arroz; **after much thought** tras mucho reflexionar; **as much time as...** tanto tiempo como...; **twice as much flour** el doble de harina; **how much...?** ¿cuánto(ta)...?; **how much time?** ¿cuánto tiempo?; **so much** tanto(ta); **too much** demasiado(da). ⟨⟩ *pron* mucho; **have you got much?** ¿tienes mucho?; **I don't see much of him** no lo veo mucho; **much of the time** una buena parte del tiempo; **I don't think much of it** no me parece gran cosa; **this isn't much of a party** esta fiesta no es nada del otro mundo; **as much as** tanto como; **twice as much** el doble; **I thought as much** ya me lo imaginaba; **how much?** ¿cuánto?; **so much for** tanto con; **too much** demasiado; **it's not up to much** *inf* no es precisamente una maravilla. ⟨⟩ *adv* mucho; **I don't go out much** no salgo mucho; **much too cold** demasiado frío; **they are much the same** son muy parecidos; **thank you very much** muchas gracias; **as much as** tanto como; **so much tanto**; **he is not so much stupid as lazy** más que tonto es vago; **without so much as...** sin siquiera...; **too much** demasiado.

⬧ **much as** *conj*: **much as (I like him)** por mucho OR más que (me guste).

muchness ['mʌtʃnɪs] *n*: **to be much of a muchness** venir a ser lo mismo.

muck [mʌk] *inf n* (*U*) - **1.** [dirt] mugre *f*, porquería *f* - **2.** [manure] estiércol *m*.

⬧ **muck about, muck around** UK *inf* ⟨⟩ *vt sep* hacer perder el tiempo. ⟨⟩ *vi* hacer el indio OR tonto.

⬧ **muck in** *vi* UK *inf* arrimar el hombro.

⬧ **muck out** *vt sep* limpiar.

⬧ **muck up** *vt sep* UK *inf* fastidiar.

muckraking ['mʌkreɪkɪŋ] *fig n* sensacionalismo *m*, periodismo *m* del cotilleo.

mucky ['mʌkɪ] (*comp* **-ier**, *superl* **-iest**) *adj* mugriento(ta).

mucus ['mju:kəs] *n* mucosidad *f*.

mud [mʌd] *n* barro *m*, lodo *m*.

muddle ['mʌdl] ⟨⟩ *n* - **1.** [disorder] desorden *m*; **to be in a muddle** estar en desorden - **2.** [confusion] lío *m*, confusión *f*; **to be in a muddle** estar hecho un lío; **to get into a muddle** hacerse un lío. ⟨⟩ *vt* - **1.** [put into disorder] desordenar - **2.** [confuse] liar, confundir.

⬧ **muddle along** *vi* apañárselas más o menos.

⬧ **muddle through** *vi* arreglárselas.

⬧ **muddle up** *vt sep* [put into disorder] desordenar; [confuse] liar, confundir.

muddle-headed [-,hedɪd] *adj* [plan] confuso(sa); [person] incapaz de pensar con claridad.

muddy ['mʌdɪ] ⟨⟩ *adj* (*comp* **-ier**, *superl* **-iest**) - **1.** [gen] embarrado(da), lleno(na) de barro; [river] cenagoso(sa) - **2.** [in colour] marrón. ⟨⟩ *vt* (*pt & pp* **-ied**) *fig* embrollar.

mudflap ['mʌdflæp] *n* alfombra *f* salpicadero.

mudflat ['mʌdflæt] *n* marisma *f*.

mudguard ['mʌdgɑːd] *n* guardabarros *m inv*, tapabarro *m Andes*.

mudpack ['mʌdpæk] *n* mascarilla *f* facial (de barro).

mudslinging ['mʌd,slɪŋɪŋ] *n* (*U*) *fig* insultos *mpl*, improperios *mpl*.

muesli ['mju:zlɪ] *n* UK muesli *m*.

muff [mʌf] ⟨⟩ *n* manguito *m*. ⟨⟩ *vt inf* [catch] fallar; [chance] dejar escapar.

muffin ['mʌfɪn] *n* - **1.** UK [eaten with butter] *especie de bollo de pan que se come caliente* - **2.** US [cake] *especie de magdalena que se come caliente*.

muffle ['mʌfl] *vt* [sound] amortiguar.

muffled ['mʌfld] *adj* - **1.** [sound] apagado(da) - **2.** [wrapped up warmly]: **muffled (up)** abrigado(da), tapado(da).

muffler ['mʌflər] *n* US [for car] silenciador *m*.

mug [mʌg] ⟨⟩ *n* - **1.** [cup] taza *f* (alta) - **2.** *inf* [fool] primo *m*, -ma *f* - **3.** *inf* [face] jeta *f*. ⟨⟩ *vt* (*pt & pp* **-ged**, *cont* **-ging**) asaltar, atracar.

mugger ['mʌgər] *n* atracador *m*, -ra *f*.

mugging ['mʌgɪŋ] *n* [attack] atraco *m*.

muggy ['mʌgɪ] (*comp* **-ier**, *superl* **-iest**) *adj* bochornoso(sa).

mugshot ['mʌgʃɒt] *n inf* foto *f* (hecha por la policía).

mujaheddin [,mu:dʒəhe'di:n] *npl* muyahidín *mpl*.

mulatto [mju:'lætəʊ] (*pl* **-s** OR **-es**) *n* mulato *m*, -ta *f*.

mulberry ['mʌlbərɪ] (*pl* **-ies**) *n* - **1.** [tree] morera *f*, moral *m* - **2.** [fruit] mora *f*.

mule [mju:l] *n* mula *f*.

mull [mʌl] ⬧ **mull over** *vt sep* reflexionar sobre.

mullah ['mʌlə] *n* mulá *m*.

mulled [mʌld] *adj*: **mulled wine** *vino caliente con azúcar y especias*.

mullet ['mʌlɪt] (*pl* **mullet** OR **-s**) *n*: **grey mullet** mújol *m*; **red mullet** salmonete *m*.

mulligatawny [ˌmʌlɪgəˈtɔːnɪ] *n sopa de carne con especias*.

multi- [ˈmʌltɪ] *prefix* multi-.

multicoloured *UK*, **multicolored** *US* [ˌmʌltɪˈkʌləd] *adj* multicolor.

multicultural [ˌmʌltɪˈkʌltʃərəl] *adj* multicultural.

multifaith [ˈmʌltɪfeɪθ] *adj* [society, organization] multiconfesional.

multifarious [ˌmʌltɪˈfeərɪəs] *adj* múltiple.

multigym [mʌltɪˈdʒɪm] *n* multiestación *f* (de musculación).

multilateral [ˌmʌltɪˈlætərəl] *adj* multilateral.

multimedia [ˌmʌltɪˈmiːdjə] *adj* COMPUT multimedia *(inv)*.

multimillionaire [ˈmʌltɪˌmɪljəˈneəʳ] *n* multimillonario *m*, -ria *f*.

multinational [ˌmʌltɪˈnæʃənl] <> *adj* multinacional. <> *n* multinacional *f*.

multiple [ˈmʌltɪpl] <> *adj* múltiple. <> *n* múltiplo *m*.

multiple-choice *adj* tipo test *(inv)*.

multiple crash *n* colisión *f* múltiple OR en cadena.

multiple injuries *npl* heridas *fpl* múltiples.

multiple sclerosis [-sklɪˈrəʊsɪs] *n* esclerosis *f inv* múltiple.

multiplex cinema [ˈmʌltɪpleks-] *n* (cine *m*) multisalas *m inv*.

multiplication [ˌmʌltɪplɪˈkeɪʃn] *n* multiplicación *f*.

multiplication sign *n* signo *m* de multiplicación.

multiplication table *n* tabla *f* de multiplicar.

multiplicity [ˌmʌltɪˈplɪsətɪ] *n* multiplicidad *f*.

multiply [ˈmʌltɪplaɪ] <> *vt* (*pt & pp* -ied) multiplicar. <> *vi* (*pt & pp* -ied) - **1.** MATHS multiplicar - **2.** [increase, breed] multiplicarse.

multipurpose [ˌmʌltɪˈpɜːpəs] *adj* multiuso *(inv)*.

multiracial [ˌmʌltɪˈreɪʃl] *adj* multirracial.

multistorey *UK*, **multistory** *US* [ˌmʌltɪˈstɔːrɪ] <> *adj* de varias plantas. <> *n* aparcamiento *m* de varias plantas.

multitude [ˈmʌltɪtjuːd] *n* multitud *f*.

multi-user *adj* COMPUT multiusuario.

mum [mʌm] *UK inf* <> *n* mamá *f*. <> *adj*: **to keep mum** no decir ni pío, mantener la boca cerrada.

mumble [ˈmʌmbl] <> *vt* mascullar, decir entre dientes. <> *vi* musitar, hablar entre dientes.

mumbo jumbo [ˈmʌmbəʊˈdʒʌmbəʊ] *n pej* galimatías *m inv*.

mummify [ˈmʌmɪfaɪ] (*pt & pp* -ied) *vt* momificar.

mummy [ˈmʌmɪ] (*pl* -ies) *n* - **1.** *UK inf* [mother] mamá *f* - **2.** [preserved body] momia *f*.

mumps [mʌmps] *n (U)* paperas *fpl*.

munch [mʌntʃ] *vt & vi* masticar.

mundane [mʌnˈdeɪn] *adj* prosaico(ca).

mung bean [mʌŋ-] *n* tipo de legumbre procedente de Asia.

municipal [mjuːˈnɪsɪpl] *adj* municipal.

municipality [mjuːˌnɪsɪˈpælətɪ] (*pl* -ies) *n* municipio *m*.

munificent [mjuːˈnɪfɪsənt] *adj fml* munífico(ca), dadivoso(sa).

munitions [mjuːˈnɪʃnz] *npl* municiones *fpl*.

mural [ˈmjuːərəl] *n* mural *m*.

murder [ˈmɜːdəʳ] <> *n* asesinato *m*; **to get away with murder** hacer lo que a uno le viene en gana. <> *vt* - **1.** [kill] asesinar - **2.** *inf* [defeat] dar una paliza a.

murderer [ˈmɜːdərəʳ] *n* asesino *m*.

murderess [ˈmɜːdərɪs] *n* asesina *f*.

murderous [ˈmɜːdərəs] *adj* asesino(na), homicida.

murky [ˈmɜːkɪ] (*comp* -ier, *superl* -iest) *adj* - **1.** [water, past] turbio(bia) - **2.** [night, street] sombrío(a), lúgubre.

murmur [ˈmɜːməʳ] <> *n* - **1.** [low sound] murmullo *m* - **2.** MED [of heart] soplo *m*. <> *vt & vi* murmurar.

muscle [ˈmʌsl] *n* - **1.** MED músculo *m* - **2.** *fig* [power] poder *m*.
◆ **muscle in** *vi* entrometerse.

muscleman [ˈmʌslmən] (*pl* -men [-mən]) *n* forzudo *m*.

Muscovite [ˈmʌskəvaɪt] <> *adj* moscovita. <> *n* moscovita *mf*.

muscular [ˈmʌskjʊləʳ] *adj* - **1.** [of muscles] muscular - **2.** [strong] musculoso(sa).

muscular dystrophy [-ˈdɪstrəfɪ] *n* distrofia *f* muscular.

muse [mjuːz] <> *n* musa *f*. <> *vi* meditar, reflexionar.

museum [mjuːˈziːəm] *n* museo *m*.

mush [mʌʃ] *n (U) inf* - **1.** [gunge] pasta *f*, masa *f* blandengue - **2.** [drivel] sensiblerías *fpl*.

mushroom [ˈmʌʃrʊm] <> *n* [button] champiñón *m*; [field] seta *f*; BOT hongo *m*, callampa *f* *Chile*. <> *vi* extenderse rápidamente.

mushroom cloud *n* hongo *m* nuclear.

mushy [ˈmʌʃɪ] (*comp* -ier, *superl* -iest) *adj* - **1.** [very soft] blandengue - **2.** [over-sentimental] sensiblero(ra).

music [ˈmjuːzɪk] *n* música *f*.

musical ['mju:zɪkl] <> adj - 1. [gen] musical - 2. [talented in music] con talento para la música. <> n musical m.

musical box UK, **music box** US n caja f de música.

musical chairs n (U) el juego de las sillas.

musical instrument n instrumento m musical.

music box US n = musical box.

music centre n cadena f (musical), equipo m (de música).

music hall n UK [building] teatro m de variedades OR de revista; [genre] music-hall m.

musician [mju:'zɪʃn] n músico m, -ca f.

music stand n atril m.

musk [mʌsk] n almizcle m.

musket ['mʌskɪt] n mosquete m.

muskrat ['mʌskræt] n rata f almizclada.

Muslim, Moslem ['muzlɪm] <> adj musulmán(ana). <> n musulmán m, -ana f.

muslin ['mʌzlɪn] n muselina f.

musquash ['mʌskwɒʃ] n - 1. [animal] rata f almizclada - 2. [fur] piel f de rata almizclada.

muss [mʌs] vt US: **to muss sthg (up)** [hair] despeinar; [clothes] arrugar.

mussel ['mʌsl] n mejillón m, choro m Andes.

must [mʌst] <> aux vb - 1. [have to, intend to] deber, tener que; **I must go** tengo que OR debo irme; **if I must** si no hay más remedio - 2. [as suggestion] tener que; **you must come and see us** tienes que venir a vernos - 3. [to express likelihood] deber (de); **it must be true** debe (de) ser verdad; **they must have known** deben de haberlo sabido. <> n inf: binoculars are a **must** unos prismáticos son imprescindibles; **the film is a must** no puedes perderte esta película.

mustache US = moustache.

mustard ['mʌstəd] n mostaza f; **mustard and cress** UK brotes mpl de mostaza y berro.

mustard gas n gas m mostaza.

muster ['mʌstər] <> vt reunir; **to muster the courage to do sthg** armarse de valor para hacer algo. <> vi reunirse.
➧ **muster up** vt insep [strength, support] reunir; [courage] armarse de.

must've ['mʌstəv] (abbr of = must have), [⟳] must.

musty ['mʌstɪ] (comp -ier, superl -iest) adj [room] que huele a cerrado; [book] que huele a viejo.

mutant ['mju:tənt] <> adj mutante. <> n mutante mf.

mutate [mju:'teɪt] vi: **to mutate (into)** mutarse (en).

mutation [mju:'teɪʃn] n mutación f.

mute [mju:t] <> adj mudo(da). <> n [person] mudo m, -da f. <> vt amortiguar.

muted ['mju:tɪd] adj - 1. [not bright] apagado(da) - 2. [subdued] contenido(da).

mutilate ['mju:tɪleɪt] vt mutilar.

mutilation [,mju:tɪ'leɪʃn] n mutilación f.

mutineer [,mju:tɪ'nɪər] n amotinado m, -da f.

mutinous ['mju:tɪnəs] adj rebelde.

mutiny ['mju:tɪnɪ] <> n (pl -ies) motín m. <> vi (pt & pp -ied) amotinarse.

mutt [mʌt] n inf - 1. [fool] bobo m, -ba f - 2. esp US [dog] chucho m.

mutter ['mʌtər] <> vt musitar, mascullar. <> vi murmurar; **to mutter to sb** gruñirle a alguien; **to mutter to o.s.** refunfuñar.

muttering ['mʌtərɪŋ] n (U) murmullos mpl.

mutton ['mʌtn] n (carne f de) carnero m; **mutton dressed as lamb** UK lobo m con piel de cordero (mujer madura vestida de jovencita),.

mutual ['mju:tʃuəl] adj - 1. [reciprocal] mutuo(tua) - 2. [common] común.

mutual fund n US fondo m de inversión colectiva.

mutually ['mju:tʃuəlɪ] adv mutuamente; **mutually exclusive** que se excluyen mutuamente.

Muzak® ['mju:zæk] n ≈ hilo m musical®.

muzzle ['mʌzl] <> n - 1. [animal's nose and jaws] hocico m, morro m - 2. [wire guard] bozal m - 3. [of gun] boca f. <> vt - 1. [put muzzle on] poner bozal a - 2. fig [silence] amordazar, silenciar.

MVP (abbr of most valuable player) jugador más valioso.

MW (abbr of medium wave) OM f.

my [maɪ] poss adj - 1. [gen] mi, mis (pl); **my house/sister** mi casa/hermana; **my children** mis hijos; **my name is Sarah** me llamo Sarah; **it wasn't my fault** no fue culpa mía OR mi culpa; **I washed my hair** me lavé el pelo - 2. [in titles]: **my Lord** milord; **my Lady** milady.

myopic [maɪ'ɒpɪk] adj - 1. MED miope - 2. [attitude, policy] corto(ta) de miras.

myriad ['mɪrɪəd] liter <> adj innumerables. <> n miríada f.

myrrh [mɜ:r] n mirra f.

myrtle ['mɜ:tl] n mirto m, arrayán m.

myself [maɪ'self] pron - 1. (reflexive) me; (after prep) mí mismo(ma); **with myself** conmigo mismo - 2. (for emphasis) yo mismo(ma); **I did it myself** lo hice yo solo(la).

mysterious [mɪ'stɪərɪəs] adj misterioso(sa); **to be mysterious about sthg** andarse con misterios sobre algo.

mysteriously [mɪˈstɪəriəslɪ] *adv* misteriosamente.

mystery [ˈmɪstərɪ] ⟨⟩ *adj* sorpresa. ⟨⟩ *n* (*pl* -ies) misterio *m*.

mystery shopping *n* compra *f* oculta.

mystery story *n* novela *f* de intriga.

mystery tour *n* viaje *m* sorpresa.

mystic [ˈmɪstɪk] ⟨⟩ *adj* místico(ca). ⟨⟩ *n* místico *m*, -ca *f*.

mystical [ˈmɪstɪkl] *adj* místico(ca).

mysticism [ˈmɪstɪsɪzm] *n* misticismo *m*.

mystified [ˈmɪstɪfaɪd] *adj* desconcertado(da), perplejo(ja).

mystifying [ˈmɪstɪfaɪɪŋ] *adj* desconcertante.

mystique [mɪˈstiːk] *n* misterio *m*.

myth [mɪθ] *n* mito *m*.

mythic [ˈmɪθɪk] *adj* [like a myth] mítico(ca).

mythical [ˈmɪθɪkl] *adj* - **1.** [imaginary] mítico(ca) - **2.** [untrue] falso(sa).

mythological [ˌmɪθəˈlɒdʒɪkl] *adj* mitológico(ca).

mythology [mɪˈθɒlədʒɪ] (*pl* -ies) *n* - **1.** [collection of myths] mitología *f* - **2.** [set of false beliefs] mito *m*.

myxomatosis [ˌmɪksəməˈtəʊsɪs] *n* mixomatosis *f inv*.

n (*pl* n's OR ns), **N** (*pl* N's OR Ns) [en] *n* [letter] n *f*, N *f*.

➡ **N** (*abbr of* **north**) N.

n/a, N/A (*abbr of* **not applicable**) no corresponde.

NA (*abbr of* **Narcotics Anonymous**) *n* organización estadounidense de ayuda a los toxicómanos.

NAACP (*abbr of* **National Association for the Advancement of Colored People**) *n* organización estadounidense de ayuda a la gente de color.

NAAFI [ˈnæfɪ] (*abbr of* **Navy, Army** & **Air Force Institute**) *n* organización gubernamental encargada del aprovisionamiento de las fuerzas armadas británicas.

nab [næb] (*pt* & *pp* -**bed**, *cont* -**bing**) *vt inf* - **1.** [arrest] pillar - **2.** [get quickly] coger.

nadir [ˈneɪˌdɪəʳ] *n* - **1.** ASTRON nadir *m* - **2.** *fig* [low point] punto *m* más bajo.

naff [næf] *adj UK inf* [film, story] hortera; [behaviour] de mal gusto.

NAFTA (*abbr of* **North American Free Trade Agreement**) *n* NAFTA *f*, TLC *m*.

nag [næg] ⟨⟩ *vt* (*pt* & *pp* -**ged**, *cont* -**ging**) [subj: person] dar la lata a. ⟨⟩ *vi* (*pt* & *pp* -**ged**, *cont* -**ging**) - **1.** [person]: **to nag (at sb)** dar la lata (a alguien) - **2.** [thought, doubt]: **to nag at sb** consumir OR corroer a alguien. ⟨⟩ *n inf* - **1.** [person] pesado *m*, -da *f* - **2.** [horse] jamelgo *m*, rocín *m*.

nagging [ˈnægɪŋ] *adj* - **1.** [thought, doubt] persistente - **2.** [person] gruñón(ona).

nail [neɪl] ⟨⟩ *n* - **1.** [for fastening] clavo *m*; **to hit the nail on the head** dar en el clavo - **2.** [of finger, toe] uña *f*. ⟨⟩ *vt*: **to nail sthg to sthg** clavar algo en OR a algo.

➡ **nail down** *vt sep* - **1.** [fasten] clavar - **2.** [person]: **I couldn't nail him down** no pude hacerle concretar.

nail-biting *adj* emocionantísimo(ma), lleno(na) de suspense.

nailbrush [ˈneɪlbrʌʃ] *n* cepillo *m* de uñas.

nail file *n* lima *f* de uñas.

nail polish *n* esmalte *m* para las uñas.

nail scissors *npl* tijeras *fpl* para las uñas.

nail varnish *n* esmalte *m* para las uñas.

nail varnish remover [-rɪˈmuːvəʳ] *n* quitaesmaltes *m inv*.

naive, naïve [naɪˈiːv] *adj* ingenuo(nua).

naivety, naïvety [naɪˈiːvtɪ] *n* ingenuidad *f*.

naked [ˈneɪkɪd] *adj* - **1.** [gen] desnudo(da); **naked flame** llama *f* sin protección - **2.** [blatant - hostility, greed] abierto(ta); [- facts] sin tapujos - **3.** [unaided]: **with the naked eye** a simple vista.

NALGO [ˈnælgəʊ] (*abbr of* **National and Local Government Officers' Association**) *n* antiguo sindicato de funcionarios británicos.

Nam [næm] (*abbr of* **Vietnam**) *n US inf* Vietnam *m*.

NAM (*abbr of* **National Association of Manufacturers**) *n* organización de empresarios estadounidenses.

name [neɪm] ⟨⟩ *n* [gen] nombre *m*; [surname] apellido *m*; **what's your name?** ¿cómo te llamas?; **my name is John** me llamo John; **by**

name por el nombre; **is there anyone by the name of...?** ¿hay alguien que se llame...?; **it's in my wife's name** estáa nombre de mi mujer; **in the name of** en nombre de; **in name only** sólo de nombre; **to call sb names** llamar de todo a alguien; **to have a good name** tener buena fama; **to make a name for o.s.** hacerse un nombre. <> *vt -* **1.** [christen] poner nombre a; **we named him Jim** le llamamos Jim; **to name sb after sb** *UK*, **to name sb for sb** *US* poner a alguien el nombre de alguien - **2.** [identify] nombrar - **3.** [date, price] poner, decir - **4.** [appoint] nombrar.

namedropping ['neɪmdrɒpɪŋ] *n:* **he loves namedropping** le encanta alardear mencionando nombres de gente que conoce o a la que ha leído.

nameless ['neɪmlɪs] *adj -* **1.** [unknown - person, author] anónimo(ma) - **2.** [indescribable] indescriptible.

namely ['neɪmlɪ] *adv* a saber.

nameplate ['neɪmpleɪt] *n* placa *f* con el nombre.

namesake ['neɪmseɪk] *n* tocayo *m*, -ya *f*.

Namibia [nɑːˈmɪbɪə] *n* Namibia.

Namibian [nɑːˈmɪbɪən] <> *adj* namibio(bia). <> *n* namibio *m*, -bia *f*.

nan(a) [næn(ə)] *n inf UK* yaya *f*, abuelita *f*.

nan bread [næn-] *n (U) pan indio sin levadura*.

nanny ['nænɪ] *(pl -ies) n* niñera *f*.

nanny goat *n* cabra *f*.

nanometre ['nænəʊ,miːtə'], **nanometer** *US n* nanómetro *m*.

nap [næp] <> *n* siesta *f*; **to take** *OR* **have a nap** echar una siesta. <> *vi (pt & pp -ped, cont -ping)* echar una siesta; **we were caught napping** *inf* nos pillaron desprevenidos.

napalm ['neɪpɑːm] *n* napalm *m*.

nape [neɪp] *n:* **nape of the neck** nuca *f*.

napkin ['næpkɪn] *n* servilleta *f*.

nappy ['næpɪ] *(pl -ies) n UK* pañal *m*.

nappy liner *n parte desechable de un pañal de gasa*.

narcissi [nɑːˈsɪsaɪ] *npl* ▷ **narcissus**.

narcissism ['nɑːsɪsɪzm] *n* narcisismo *m*.

narcissistic [,nɑːsɪˈsɪstɪk] *adj* narcisista.

narcissus [nɑːˈsɪsəs] *(pl -cissuses OR -cissi) n* narciso *m*.

narcotic [nɑːˈkɒtɪk] <> *adj* narcótico(ca). <> *n* narcótico *m*.

nark [nɑːk] *UK inf* <> *n* [police informer] soplón *m*, -ona *f*. <> *vt* cabrear.

narky ['nɑːkɪ] *(comp -ier, superl -iest) adj UK inf* de mala uva.

narrate [UK nəˈreɪt, US ˈnæreɪt] *vt* narrar.

narration [UK nəˈreɪʃn, US næˈreɪʃn] *n* narración *f*.

narrative ['nærətɪv] <> *adj* narrativo(va). <> *n* - **1.** [account] narración *f* - **2.** [art of narrating] narrativa *f*.

narrator [UK nəˈreɪtəʳ, US ˈnæreɪtər] *n* narrador *m*, -ra *f*.

narrow ['nærəʊ] <> *adj -* **1.** [not wide] estrecho(cha) - **2.** [limited] estrecho(cha) de miras - **3.** [victory, defeat] por un estrecho margen; [majority] escaso(sa); [escape, miss] por muy poco, por los pelos. <> *vt -* **1.** [eyes] entornar - **2.** [gap, choice] reducir. <> *vi -* **1.** [become less wide] estrecharse - **2.** [eyes] entornarse - **3.** [gap] acortarse, reducirse.

◆ **narrow down** *vt sep* reducir.

narrow-gauge *adj* RAIL de vía estrecha.

narrowly ['nærəʊlɪ] *adv* [barely] por muy poco.

narrow-minded [-ˈmaɪndɪd] *adj* estrecho(cha) de miras.

NASA ['næsə] *(abbr of National Aeronautics and Space Administration) n* la NASA.

nasal ['neɪzl] *adj* nasal.

nascent ['neɪsənt] *adj fml* naciente.

nastily ['nɑːstɪlɪ] *adv -* **1.** [unkindly] con mala intención - **2.** [painfully]: **he fell nastily** tuvo una caída muy mala.

nastiness ['nɑːstɪnɪs] *n* [unkindness] mala intención *f*.

nasturtium [nəsˈtɜːʃəm] *(pl -s) n* capuchina *f*.

nasty ['nɑːstɪ] *(comp -ier, superl -iest) adj -* **1.** [unkind] malintencionado(da); **to be nasty to sb** ser malo(la) con alguien - **2.** [smell, taste, feeling] desagradable; [weather] horrible; **cheap and nasty** barato(ta) y de mal gusto - **3.** [problem, decision] peliagudo(da) - **4.** [injury, disease] doloroso(sa); [accident] grave; [fall] malo(la).

NAS/UWT *(abbr of National Association of Schoolmasters/Union of Women Teachers) n sindicato británico de profesores*.

nation ['neɪʃn] *n* nación *f*.

national ['næʃənl] <> *adj* nacional. <> *n* súbdito *m*, -ta *f*.

national anthem *n* himno *m* nacional.

national debt *n* deuda *f* pública.

national dress *n* traje *m* típico (de un país).

national grid *n UK* red eléctrica nacional.

National Guard *n US:* **the National Guard** la Guardia Nacional estadounidense.

National Health Service *n UK:* **the National Health Service** *organismo gestor de la salud pública*, ≈ INGS.

National Insurance *n UK* ≃ Seguridad *f* Social.

nationalism ['næʃnəlɪzm] *n* nacionalismo *m*.

nationalist ['næʃnəlɪst] ◇ *adj* nacionalista. ◇ *n* nacionalista *mf*.

nationality [ˌnæʃə'næləti] (*pl* **-ies**) *n* nacionalidad *f*.

nationalization [ˌnæʃnəlaɪ'zeɪʃn] *n* nacionalización *f*.

nationalize, -ise ['næʃnəlaɪz] *vt* nacionalizar.

nationalized ['næʃnəlaɪzd] *adj* nacionalizado(da).

national park *n* parque *m* nacional.

national service *n UK* MIL servicio *m* militar.

National Trust *n UK*: **the National Trust** *organización británica encargada de la preservación de edificios históricos y lugares de interés*, ≃ el Patrimonio Nacional.

nationwide ['neɪʃənwaɪd] ◇ *adj* de ámbito nacional. ◇ *adv* [travel] por todo el país; [be broadcast] a todo el país.

native ['neɪtɪv] ◇ *adj* - **1.** [country, area] natal - **2.** [speaker] nativo(va); **native language** lengua *f* materna - **3.** [plant, animal]: **native (to)** originario(ria) (de). ◇ *n* [of country, area] natural *mf*, nativo *m*, -va *f*.

Native American *n* indio americano *m*, india americana *f*.

Nativity [nə'tɪvəti] *n*: **the Nativity** la Natividad.

nativity play *n* obra teatral sobre la Natividad.

NATO ['neɪtəʊ] (*abbr of* **North Atlantic Treaty Organization**) *n* la OTAN.

natter ['nætər] *UK inf* ◇ *n*: **to have a natter** charlar. ◇ *vi* charlar.

natty ['næti] (*comp* **-ier**, *superl* **-iest**) *adj inf* [smart] chulo(la), elegante.

natural ['nætʃrəl] ◇ *adj* - **1.** [gen] natural - **2.** [comedian, musician] nato(ta); **to die of natural causes** morir por causas naturales. ◇ *n*: **to be a natural** tener talento natural.

natural childbirth *n* parto *m* natural.

natural disaster *n* desastre *m* natural.

natural gas *n* gas *m* natural.

natural history *n* historia *f* natural.

naturalist ['nætʃrəlɪst] *n* naturalista *mf*.

naturalize, -ise ['nætʃrəlaɪz] *vt* naturalizar; **to be naturalized** naturalizarse.

naturally ['nætʃrəli] *adv* - **1.** [as expected, understandably] naturalmente - **2.** [unaffectedly] con naturalidad - **3.** [instinctively] por naturaleza; **to come naturally to sb** ser innato en alguien - **4.** [in nature] de forma natural, en la naturaleza.

naturalness ['nætʃrəlnɪs] *n* naturalidad *f*.

natural resources *npl* recursos *mpl* naturales.

natural science *n* ciencias *fpl* naturales.

natural wastage *n* (U) reducción de plantilla por jubilación escalonada.

nature ['neɪtʃər] *n* - **1.** [gen] naturaleza *f*; **matters of this nature** asuntos de esta índole - **2.** [disposition] modo *m* de ser, carácter *m*; **by nature** por naturaleza.

nature reserve *n* reserva *f* natural.

nature trail *n* sendero *m* natural.

naturist ['neɪtʃərɪst] *n* naturista *mf*.

naughty ['nɔːti] (*comp* **-ier**, *superl* **-iest**) *adj* - **1.** [badly behaved] travieso(sa), malo(la) - **2.** [rude] verde, atrevido(da).

nausea ['nɔːsjə] *n* náuseas *fpl*.

nauseam ['nɔːzɪæm] ⊏▷ **ad nauseam**.

nauseate ['nɔːsɪeɪt] *vt lit & fig* dar náuseas a.

nauseating ['nɔːsɪeɪtɪŋ] *adj lit & fig* nauseabundo(da).

nauseous ['nɔːsjəs] *adj* - **1.** [sick]: **to feel nauseous** sentir náuseas - **2.** *fig* [revolting] nauseabundo(da).

nautical ['nɔːtɪkl] *adj* náutico(ca), marítimo(ma).

nautical mile *n* milla *f* marina.

naval ['neɪvl] *adj* naval.

naval officer *n* oficial *mf* de marina.

nave [neɪv] *n* nave *f*.

navel ['neɪvl] *n* ombligo *m*.

navigable ['nævɪgəbl] *adj* navegable.

navigate ['nævɪgeɪt] ◇ *vt* - **1.** [steer] pilotar, gobernar - **2.** [travel safely across] surcar, navegar por. ◇ *vi* [in plane, ship] dirigir, gobernar; [in car] dar direcciones.

navigation [ˌnævɪ'geɪʃn] *n* navegación *f*.

navigator ['nævɪgeɪtər] *n* oficial *mf* de navegación, navegante *mf*.

navvy ['nævi] (*pl* **-ies**) *n UK inf* peón *m* caminero.

navy ['neɪvi] ◇ *n* (*pl* **-ies**) armada *f*. ◇ *adj* [in colour] azul marino (inv).

navy blue ◇ *adj* azul marino *(inv)*. ◇ *n* azul *m* marino.

Nazi ['nɑ:tsɪ] ◇ *adj* nazi. ◇ *n* (*pl* **-s**) nazi *mf*.

NB - 1. (*abbr of* **nota bene**) N.B. - **2.** *abbr of* **New Brunswick**.

NBA *n* - **1.** (*abbr of* **National Basketball Association**) NBA *f* - **2.** (*abbr of* **National Boxing Association**), *federación de boxeo estadounidense*.

NBC (*abbr of* **National Broadcasting Company**) *n* NBC *f*.

NC - 1. (*abbr of* **no charge**) gratis - **2.** *abbr of* **North Carolina**.

NCC (*abbr of* **Nature Conservancy Council**) *n* instituto británico para la conservación de la naturaleza, ≃ Icona *m*.

NCCL (*abbr of* **National Council for Civil Liberties**) *n* organización independiente británica para la defensa de los derechos del ciudadano.

NCO *n abbr of* **noncommissioned officer**.

ND *abbr of* **North Dakota**.

NE - 1. *abbr of* **Nebraska** - **2.** *abbr of* **New England** - **3.** (*abbr of* **north-east**) NE.

Neanderthal [nɪ'ændətɑ:l] ◇ *adj* de Neanderthal. ◇ *n* (hombre *m* de) Neanderthal *m*.

neap tide [ni:p-] *n* marea *f* muerta.

near [nɪər] ◇ *adj* - **1.** [close in distance, time] cercano(na); **the near side** el lado más cercano; **in the near future** en un futuro próximo - **2.** [related] cercano(na), próximo(ma); **the nearest thing to...** lo más parecido a... - **3.** [almost happened]: **it was near chaos** faltó poco para el caos; **it was a near thing** poco le faltó. ◇ *adv* - **1.** [close in distance, time] cerca; **nowhere near** ni de lejos, ni mucho menos; **to draw** OR **come near** acercarse - **2.** [almost] casi. ◇ *prep* - **1.** [close in position]: **near (to)** cerca de; **to go near sthg** acercarse a algo - **2.** [close in time]: **it's getting near (to)** Christmas ya estamos casi en Navidades; **near the end** casi al final; **nearer the time** cuando se acerque la fecha - **3.** [on the point of]: **near (to)** al borde de - **4.** [similar to]: **near (to)** cerca de; **it's near (to) the truth** se acerca a la verdad. ◇ *vt* acercarse OR aproximarse a. ◇ *vi* acercarse, aproximarse.

nearby [nɪə'baɪ] ◇ *adj* cercano(na). ◇ *adv* cerca.

Near East *n*: **the Near East** el Oriente Próximo.

nearly ['nɪəlɪ] *adv* casi; **I nearly fell** por poco me caigo; **not nearly** ni con mucho, ni mucho menos.

near miss *n* - **1.** [nearly a hit]: **it was a near miss** falló por poco - **2.** [nearly a collision] incidente *m* aéreo (sin colisión).

nearness ['nɪənɪs] *n* proximidad *f*, cercanía *f*.

nearside ['nɪəsaɪd] ◇ *adj* [right-hand drive] del lado izquierdo; [left-hand drive] del lado derecho. ◇ *n* [right-hand drive] lado *m* izquierdo; [left-hand drive] lado derecho.

nearsighted [,nɪə'saɪtɪd] *adj* US miope, corto(ta) de vista.

neat [ni:t] *adj* - **1.** [tidy, precise - gen] pulcro(cra); [- room, house] arreglado(da); [- handwriting] esmerado(da) - **2.** [smart] arreglado(da), pulcro(cra) - **3.** [skilful] hábil - **4.** [undiluted] solo(la) - **5.** US inf [very good] guay.

neatly ['ni:tlɪ] *adv* - **1.** [tidily, smartly] con pulcritud; [write] con esmero - **2.** [skilfully] hábilmente.

neatness ['ni:tnɪs] *n* [gen] pulcritud *f*; [of handwriting] esmero *m*; [skilfulness] habilidad *f*.

Nebraska [nɪ'bræskə] *n* Nebraska.

nebulous ['nebjʊləs] *adj fml* nebuloso(sa).

NEC (*abbr of* **National Exhibition Centre**) *n* gran complejo para ferias y exposiciones de Birmingham, Gran Bretaña.

necessarily [UK 'nesəsrəlɪ, ,nesə'serəlɪ] *adv* necesariamente, por fuerza; **not necessarily** no necesariamente.

necessary ['nesəsrɪ] *adj* - **1.** [required] necesario(ria) - **2.** [inevitable] inevitable.

necessitate [nɪ'sesɪteɪt] *vt fml* requerir, exigir.

necessity [nɪ'sesətɪ] *n* (*pl* **-ies**) necesidad *f*; **of necessity** por fuerza, por necesidad.

➤ **necessities** *npl* artículos *mpl* de primera necesidad.

neck [nek] ◇ *n* [of person, bottle, dress] cuello *m*; [of animal] pescuezo *m*, cuello; **to be up to one's neck (in sthg)** estar hasta el cuello (de algo); **to breathe down sb's neck** estar encima de alguien; **to stick one's neck out** arriesgarse. ◇ *vi inf* pegarse el lote.

neckerchief ['nekətʃɪf] (*pl* **-chiefs** OR **-chieves** [-tʃiːvz]) *n* pañuelo *m* de cuello.

necklace ['neklɪs] *n* collar *m*.

neckline ['neklaɪn] *n* escote *m*.

necktie ['nektaɪ] *n* US corbata *f*.

nectar ['nektər] *n* néctar *m*.

nectarine ['nektərɪn] *n* nectarina *f*.

née [neɪ] *adj* de soltera.

need [ni:d] ◇ *n*: **need (for sthg/to do sthg)** necesidad *f* (de algo/de hacer algo); **to be in** OR **to have need of sthg** necesitar algo; **he was in need of rest** le hacía falta descansar; **to have no need of** no necesitar; **there's no need for you to cry** no hace falta que llores; **if need be** si hace falta; **in need** necesitado(da). ◇ *vt* - **1.** [require] necesitar; **I need a haircut** me hace falta un corte de pelo; **the**

floor needs cleaning hay que limpiar el suelo; **that's all we need!** ¡sólo nos faltaba eso! **- 2.** [be obliged]: **to need to do sthg** tener que hacer algo. ◇ *modal vb:* **to need to do sthg** necesitar hacer algo; **need we go?** ¿tenemos que irnos?; **it need not happen** no tiene por qué ser así.

◆ **needs** *adv:* **if needs must** si es menester.

needle ['ni:dl] ◇ *n* aguja *f*; **it's like looking for a needle in a haystack** es como buscar una aguja en un pajar. ◇ *vt inf* pinchar.

needlecord ['ni:dlkɔ:d] *n* pana *f* fina.

needlepoint ['ni:dlpɔɪnt] *n* bordado *m*.

needless ['ni:dlɪs] *adj* innecesario(ria); **needless to say...** está de más decir que...

needlessly ['ni:dlɪslɪ] *adv* innecesariamente.

needlework ['ni:dlwɜ:k] *n* **- 1.** [embroidery] bordado *m* **- 2.** *(U)* [activity] costura *f*.

needn't ['ni:dnt]   *(abbr   of   =   need not),* ▷ **need**.

needy ['ni:dɪ] ◇ *adj (comp* **-ier,** *superl* **-iest)** necesitado(da). ◇ *npl:* **the needy** los necesitados.

nefarious [nɪ'feərɪəs] *adj fml* execrable, infame.

negate [nɪ'geɪt] *vt fml* anular, invalidar.

negation [nɪ'geɪʃn] *n fml* invalidación *f*, anulación *f*.

negative ['negətɪv] ◇ *adj* negativo(va). ◇ *n* **- 1.** PHOT negativo *m* **- 2.** LING partícula *f* negativa, negación *f*; **to answer in the negative** decir que no.

negative equity *n depreciación del valor de mercado de una vivienda por debajo de su valor hipotecado.*

neglect [nɪ'glekt] ◇ *n* [of garden, work] descuido *m*, desatención *f*; [of duty] incumplimiento *m*; **a state of neglect** un estado de abandono. ◇ *vt* **- 1.** [ignore] desatender **- 2.** [duty, work] no cumplir con; **to neglect to do sthg** dejar de hacer algo.

neglected [nɪ'glektɪd] *adj* desatendido(da).

neglectful [nɪ'glektfʊl] *adj* descuidado(da), negligente; **to be neglectful of sthg/sb** desatender algo/a alguien.

negligee ['neglɪʒeɪ] *n* salto *m* de cama.

negligence ['neglɪdʒəns] *n* negligencia *f*.

negligent ['neglɪdʒənt] *adj* negligente.

negligently ['neglɪdʒəntlɪ] *adv* con negligencia.

negligible ['neglɪdʒəbl] *adj* insignificante.

negotiable [nɪ'gəʊʃjəbl] *adj* negociable.

negotiate [nɪ'gəʊʃɪeɪt] ◇ *vt* **- 1.** [obtain through negotiation] negociar **- 2.** [obstacle] salvar, franquear; [bend] remontar, tomar. ◇ *vi:* **to negotiate (with sb for sthg)** negociar (con alguien algo).

negotiation [nɪ,gəʊʃɪ'eɪʃn] *n* negociación *f*.

◆ **negotiations** *npl* negociaciones *fpl*.

negotiator [nɪ'gəʊʃɪeɪtəʳ] *n* negociador *m*, -ra *f*.

Negress ['ni:grɪs] *n* negra *f*.

Negro ['ni:grəʊ] ◇ *adj* negro(gra). ◇ *n (pl* **-es)** negro *m*, -gra *f*.

neigh [neɪ] *vi* relinchar.

neighbour *UK,* **neighbor** *US* ['neɪbəʳ] *n* vecino *m*, -na *f*.

neighbourhood *UK,* **neighborhood** *US* ['neɪbəhʊd] *n* **- 1.** [of town] barrio *m*, vecindad *f*; **in the neighbourhood (of)** en la zona (de) **- 2.** [approximate figure]: **in the neighbourhood of** alrededor de.

neighbourhood watch *n UK* vigilancia *f* de vecinos.

neighbouring *UK,* **neighboring** *US* ['neɪbərɪŋ] *adj* vecino(na).

neighbourly *UK,* **neighborly** *US* ['neɪbəlɪ] *adj* [advice] de buen vecino; **to be neighbourly** ser un buen vecino.

neither ['naɪðəʳ, 'ni:ðəʳ] ◇ *adv:* **I don't drink - me neither** no bebo - yo tampoco; **the food was neither good nor bad** la comida no era ni buena ni mala; **to be neither here nor there** no tener nada que ver. ◇ *pron* ninguno(na); **neither of us/them** ninguno de nosotros/ellos. ◇ *adj:* **neither cup is blue** ninguna de las dos tazas es azul. ◇ *conj:* **neither... nor...** ni... ni...; **she could neither eat nor sleep** no podía ni comer ni dormir.

neo- ['ni:əʊ] *prefix* neo-.

neoclassical [,ni:əʊ'klæsɪkl] *adj* neoclásico(ca).

neolithic [,ni:əʊ'lɪθɪk] *adj* neolítico(ca).

neologism [ni:'ɒlədʒɪzm] *n* neologismo *m*.

neon ['ni:ɒn] *n* neón *m*.

neon light *n* luz *f* de neón.

neon sign *n* letrero *m* de neón.

Nepal [nɪ'pɔ:l] *n* (el) Nepal.

Nepalese [,nepə'li:z] ◇ *adj* nepalés(esa). ◇ *n (pl* **Nepalese)** [person] nepalés *m*, -esa *f*.

Nepali [nɪ'pɔ:lɪ] *n* [language] nepalés *m*, nepalí *m*.

nephew ['nefju:] *n* sobrino *m*.

nepotism ['nepətɪzm] *n* nepotismo *m*.

Neptune ['neptju:n] *n* Neptuno *m*.

nerve [nɜ:v] *n* **- 1.** ANAT nervio *m* **- 2.** [courage] valor *m*; **to keep one's nerve** mantener la calma, no perder los nervios; **to lose one's nerve** echarse atrás, perder el valor **- 3.** [cheek] cara *f*; **to have the nerve to do sthg** tener la cara de hacer algo.

◆ **nerves** *npl* nervios *mpl*; **to get on sb's nerves** sacar de quicio a alguien.

nerve centre *n fig* [headquarters] punto *m* OR centro *m* neurálgico.

nerve gas *n* gas *m* nervioso.

nerve-racking [-ˌrækɪŋ] *adj* crispante, angustioso(sa).

nervous [ˈnɜːvəs] *adj* **- 1.** ANAT & PSYCHOL nervioso(sa) **- 2.** [apprehensive] inquieto(ta), aprensivo(va); **to be nervous of sthg/of doing sthg** tener miedo a algo/a hacer algo; **to be nervous about sthg** estar inquieto por algo.

nervous breakdown *n* crisis *f inv* nerviosa.

nervously [ˈnɜːvəslɪ] *adv* con nerviosismo, nerviosamente.

nervousness [ˈnɜːvəsnɪs] *n* nerviosismo *m*.

nervous system *n* sistema *m* nervioso.

nervous wreck *n* manojo *m* de nervios.

nervy [ˈnɜːvɪ] (*comp* **-ier**, *superl* **-iest**) *adj* **- 1.** *inf* [nervous] nervioso(sa) **- 2.** US [cheeky] descarado(da).

nest [nest] <> *n* nido *m*; **ant's nest** hormiguero *m*; **wasps' nest** avispero *m*; **nest of tables** mesas *fpl* nido. <> *vi* anidar.

nest egg *n* ahorros *mpl*.

nestle [ˈnesl] *vi* **- 1.** [settle snugly - in chair] arrellanarse; [- in bed] acurrucarse **- 2.** [be situated] estar situado(da) OR emplazado(da).

nestling [ˈneslɪŋ] *n* polluelo *m*.

net [net] <> *adj* **- 1.** [weight, price, loss] neto(ta) **- 2.** [result, effect] final. <> *n* red *f*. <> *vt* (*pt & pp* **-ted**, *cont* **-ting**) **- 1.** [catch] coger con red **- 2.** [acquire] embolsarse **- 3.** [gain as profit - subj: person] obtener un beneficio neto de; [- subj: deal] reportar un beneficio neto de.

Net [net] *n* COMPUT: **the Net** la Red; **to surf the Net** navegar por la Red.

netball [ˈnetbɔːl] *n deporte parecido al baloncesto femenino*.

net curtains *npl* visillos *mpl*.

Netherlands [ˈneðələndz] *npl*: **the Netherlands** los Países Bajos.

netiquette [ˈnetɪket] *n* COMPUT netiqueta *f*.

net profit *n* beneficio *m* neto.

net revenue *n* US facturación *f*.

netting [ˈnetɪŋ] *n* red *f*, malla *f*.

nettle [ˈnetl] <> *n* ortiga *f*. <> *vt* irritar, molestar.

network [ˈnetwɜːk] <> *n* **- 1.** [gen & COMPUT] red *f* **- 2.** RADIO & TV [station] cadena *f*. <> *vt* **- 1.** RADIO & TV [broadcast] emitir en toda la cadena **- 2.** COMPUT conectar a la red.

neuralgia [njʊəˈrældʒə] *n* neuralgia *f*.

neurological [ˌnjʊərəˈlɒdʒɪkl] *adj* neurológico(ca).

neurologist [ˌnjʊəˈrɒlədʒɪst] *n* neurólogo *m*, -ga *f*.

neurology [ˌnjʊəˈrɒlədʒɪ] *n* neurología *f*.

neurosis [ˌnjʊəˈrəʊsɪs] (*pl* **-ses** [-siːz]) *n* neurosis *f inv*.

neurosurgery [ˌnjʊərəʊˈsɜːdʒərɪ] *n* neurocirugía *f*.

neurotic [ˌnjʊəˈrɒtɪk] <> *adj* neurótico(ca). <> *n* neurótico *m*, -ca *f*.

neuter [ˈnjuːtər] <> *adj* neutro(tra). <> *vt* castrar.

neutral [ˈnjuːtrəl] <> *adj* **- 1.** [gen] neutro(tra) **- 2.** [non-allied] neutral **- 3.** [unexpressive] inexpresivo(va) **- 4.** [shoe cream] incoloro(ra). <> *n* **- 1.** AUT punto *m* muerto **- 2.** [country] país *m* neutral; [person] persona *f* neutral.

neutrality [njuːˈtrælətɪ] *n* neutralidad *f*.

neutralize, -ise [ˈnjuːtrəlaɪz] *vt* neutralizar.

neutron [ˈnjuːtrɒn] *n* neutrón *m*.

neutron bomb *n* bomba *f* de neutrones.

Nevada [nɪˈvɑːdə] *n* Nevada.

never [ˈnevər] *adv* **- 1.** [at no time] nunca, jamás; **I've never done it** no lo he hecho nunca; **never again** nunca más; **never ever** nunca jamás, nunca en la vida; **well I never!** ¡vaya!, ¡caramba! **- 2.** *inf* [as negative] no; **I never knew** no lo sabía; **you never did!** ¡no (me digas)!

never-ending *adj* interminable, inacabable.

never-never *n* UK *inf*: **on the never-never** a plazos *mpl*.

nevertheless [ˌnevəðəˈles] *adv* sin embargo, no obstante.

new [njuː] *adj* nuevo(va); [baby] recién nacido (recién nacida); **we'll have to buy a new one** tendremos que comprar otro; **to be new to sthg** ser nuevo(va) en algo; **as good as new** como nuevo.

news *n* (U) noticias *fpl*; **a piece of news** una noticia; **the news** [gen] las noticias; [on TV] el telediario; **that's news to me** me coge de nuevas; **to break the news to sb** dar la noticia a alguien.

New Age *n* new age *m*, *movimiento que gira en torno a las ciencias ocultas, medicinas alternativas, religiones orientales etc.*

new blood *n fig* sangre *f* OR savia *f* nueva.

newborn [ˈnjuːbɔːn] *adj* recién nacido (recién nacida).

New Brunswick [-ˈbrʌnzwɪk] *n* New Brunswick.

New Caledonia [-ˌkælɪˈdəʊnjə] *n* Nueva Caledonia.

New Caledonian [-ˌkælɪˈdəʊnjən] <> *adj* neocaledonio(nia). <> *n* neocaledonio *m*, -nia *f*.

newcomer [ˈnjuːˌkʌmər] *n*: **newcomer (to)** recién llegado *m*, recién llegada *f* (a).

New Delhi *n* Nueva Delhi.

New England *n* Nueva Inglaterra.

newfangled [,nju:'fæŋgld] *adj inf pej* moderno(na).

new-found *adj* [gen] recién descubierto (recién descubierta); [friend] reciente.

Newfoundland ['nju:fəndlənd] *n* Terranova.

New Guinea *n* Nueva Guinea.

New Hampshire [-'hæmpʃəʳ] *n* New Hampshire.

New Hebrides *npl*: the New Hebrides las Nuevas Hébridas.

New Jersey *n* Nueva Jersey.

newly ['nju:lɪ] *adv* recién.

newlyweds ['nju:lɪwedz] *npl* recién casados *mpl*.

New Mexico *n* Nuevo Méjico.

new moon *n* luna *f* nueva.

New Orleans [-'ɔ:lɪənz] *n* Nueva Orleans.

news agency *n* agencia *f* de noticias.

newsagent *UK* ['nju:zeɪdʒənt], **newsdealer** *US* ['nju:zdi:lər] *n* [person] vendedor *m*, -ra *f* de periódicos; **newsagent's (shop)** *tienda en la que se vende prensa así como tabaco y chucherías*.

news bulletin *n* boletín *m* de noticias.

newscast ['nju:zkɑ:st] *n* TV telediario *m*; RADIO noticiario *m*.

newscaster ['nju:zkɑ:stəʳ] *n* presentador *m*, -ra *f*, locutor *m*, -ra *f*.

news conference *n* rueda *f* de prensa.

New South Wales *n* Nueva Gales del Sur.

newsdealer *US* = newsagent.

newsflash ['nju:zflæʃ] *n* noticia *f* de última hora.

newsgroup ['nju:zgru:p] *n* COMPUT grupo *m* (de noticias).

newshound ['nju:zhaʊnd] *n* sabueso *m* de la prensa.

newsletter ['nju:z,letəʳ] *n* boletín *m*.

newsman ['nju:zmæn] (*pl* -men [-men]) *n* periodista *m*, reportero *m*.

newspaper ['nju:z,peɪpəʳ] *n* - **1.** [publication, company] periódico *m*; [daily] diario *m* - **2.** [paper] papel *m* de periódico.

newspaperman ['nju:z,peɪpəmæn] (*pl* -men [-men]) *n* periodista *mf*.

newsprint ['nju:zprɪnt] *n* papel *m* de periódico.

newsreader ['nju:z,ri:dəʳ] *n* presentador *m*, -ra *f*, locutor *m*, -ra *f*.

newsreel ['nju:zri:l] *n* noticiario *m* cinematográfico.

newsroom ['nju:zrʊm] *n* (sala *f* de) redacción *f*.

newssheet ['nju:z,ʃi:t] *n* hoja *f* informativa.

newsstand ['nju:zstænd] *n US* quiosco *m* de periódicos.

newsworthy ['nju:z,wɜ:ðɪ] *adj* de interés periodístico.

newt [nju:t] *n* tritón *m*.

new technology *n* nueva tecnología *f*.

New Testament *n*: the New Testament el Nuevo Testamento.

new town *n UK ciudad nueva construida por el gobierno*.

new wave *n* nueva ola *f*.

New World *n*: the New World el Nuevo Mundo.

New Year *n* Año *m* Nuevo; **Happy New Year!** ¡Feliz Año Nuevo!

New Year's Day *n* el día de Año Nuevo.

New Year's Eve *n* Nochevieja *f*.

New York [-'jɔ:k] *n* - **1.** [city]: **New York (City)** Nueva York - **2.** [state]: **New York (State)** (el estado de) Nueva York.

New Yorker [-'jɔ:kəʳ] *n* neoyorquino *m*, -na *f*.

New Zealand [-'zi:lənd] *n* Nueva Zelanda.

New Zealander [-'zi:ləndəʳ] *n* neozelandés *m*, -esa *f*.

next [nekst] <> *adj* - **1.** [in time] próximo(ma); **the next day** el día siguiente; **next Tuesday/year** el martes/el año que viene; **next week** la semana próxima *OR* que viene; **the next week** los próximos siete días - **2.** [in space - page etc] siguiente; [- room, house] de al lado. <> *pron* el siguiente (la siguiente); **who's next?** ¿quién es el siguiente?; **next, please!** ¡el siguiente, por favor!; **the day after next** pasado mañana; **the week after next** la semana que viene no, la otra. <> *adv* - **1.** [afterwards] después; **what should I do next?** ¿qué hago ahora?; **it's my go next** ahora me toca a mí - **2.** [again] de nuevo; **when do they next play?** ¿cuándo vuelven a jugar? - **3.** [with superlatives]: **next best/biggest** *etc* el segundo mejor/más grande *etc*. <> *prep US* al lado de, junto a.

➤ **next to** *prep* al lado de, junto a; **next to nothing** casi nada; **in next to no time** en un abrir y cerrar de ojos.

next door *adv* (en la casa de) al lado.

➤ **next-door** *adj*: **next-door neighbour** vecino *m*, -na *f* de al lado.

next of kin *n* pariente más cercano *m*, pariente más cercana *f*.

NF <> *n abbr of* National Front. <> *abbr of* Newfoundland.

NFL (*abbr of* National Football League) *n federación estadounidense de fútbol americano*.

NFU (*abbr of* National Farmers' Union) *n asociación británica de agricultores*.

NG *abbr of* National Guard.

NGO (*abbr of* **non-governmental organiza-tion**) *n* ONG *f*.

NH *abbr of* **New Hampshire**.

NHL (*abbr of* **National Hockey League**) *n federación estadounidense de hockey sobre hielo*.

NHS (*abbr of* **National Health Service**) *n*: **the National Health Service** *organismo gestor de la salud pública*, ≃ INGS.

NHS

El **National Health Service** o **NHS** fue creado por el gobierno laborista británico en 1948 para permitir que todos los británicos tengan acceso a la asistencia médica gratuita. El gasto en sanidad es una de las partidas más abultadas de los presupuestos del Estado, y a pesar de los controvertidos recortes y los cierres de hospitales durante el gobierno de Margaret Thatcher en la década de los 80, nunca ha dejado de crecer. Sin embargo, hoy en día los políticos ya no se atreven a proclamar que el NHS es "la envidia del planeta", ya que dicha institución se encuentra en situación de crisis casi permanente debido a la escasez de fondos. Por consiguiente, hay pacientes que no tienen acceso a ciertos tratamientos considerados demasiado costosos, falta espacio en los hospitales, el personal médico es insuficiente y los pacientes a menudo deben esperar meses para ser operados. Esta situación ha provocado una gradual pérdida de fe en la capacidad del NHS para atender las necesidades sanitarias de los británicos, cosa que ha animado a muchos a suscribir seguros de salud privados. Últimamente el gobierno ha admitido que se necesita aumentar radicalmente el gasto en sanidad para procurar que el Reino Unido alcance la media europea. En consecuencia, el incremento impositivo que sufrirán los contribuyentes británicos será probablemente uno de los asuntos políticos más controvertidos en los próximos años.

NI ⬦ *n abbr of* **National Insurance**. ⬦ *abbr of* **Northern Ireland**.

Niagara [naɪˈægrə] *n*: **Niagara Falls** las cataratas del Niágara.

nib [nɪb] *n* plumilla *f*.

nibble [ˈnɪbl] ⬦ *n* mordisquito *m*. ⬦ *vt* mordisquear. ⬦ *vi*: **to nibble at sthg** mordisquear algo.

Nicaragua [ˌnɪkəˈrægjʊə] *n* Nicaragua.

Nicaraguan [ˌnɪkəˈrægjʊən] ⬦ *adj* nicaragüense. ⬦ *n* nicaragüense *mf*.

nice [naɪs] *adj* **- 1.** [attractive] bonito(ta); **you look nice** estás guapa; [good] bueno(na); **it smells nice** huele bien **- 2.** [kind] amable;

[friendly] agradable, simpático(ca), dije *Amér*; **that was nice of you** fue muy amable de tu parte; **to be nice to sb** ser bueno con alguien **- 3.** [pleasant] agradable; **to have a nice time** pasarlo bien.

nice-looking [-ˈlʊkɪŋ] *adj* [person] atractivo(va), guapo(pa); [car, room] bonito(ta).

nicely [ˈnaɪslɪ] *adv* **- 1.** [well, attractively] bien **- 2.** [politely] educadamente, con educación **- 3.** [satisfactorily] bien; **that will do nicely** esto irá de perlas.

nicety [ˈnaɪsətɪ] (*pl* **-ies**) *n* detalle *m*.

niche [niːʃ] *n* **- 1.** [in wall] nicho *m*, hornacina *f* **- 2.** [in life] hueco *m* **- 3.** COMM nicho *m*.

nick [nɪk] ⬦ *n* **- 1.** [cut] cortecito *m*; [notch] muesca *f* **- 2.** *UK inf* [jail]: **the nick** el trullo, la trena **- 3.** [condition]: **in good/bad nick** *UK inf* en buenas/malas condiciones
▶ **in the nick of time** justo a tiempo. ⬦ *vt* **- 1.** [cut] cortar; [make notch in] mellar **- 2.** *UK inf* [steal] birlar, mangar **- 3.** *UK inf* [arrest] trincar, pillar.

nickel [ˈnɪkl] *n* **- 1.** [metal] níquel *m* **- 2.** *US* [coin] moneda *f* de cinco centavos.

nickname [ˈnɪkneɪm] ⬦ *n* apodo *m*. ⬦ *vt* apodar.

nicotine [ˈnɪkətiːn] *n* nicotina *f*.

niece [niːs] *n* sobrina *f*.

nifty [ˈnɪftɪ] (*comp* **-ier**, *superl* **-iest**) *adj inf* [clever] apañado(da).

Niger [ˈnaɪdʒər] *n* **- 1.** [country] Níger **- 2.** [river]: **the (River) Niger** el (río) Níger.

Nigeria [naɪˈdʒɪərɪə] *n* Nigeria.

Nigerian [naɪˈdʒɪərɪən] ⬦ *adj* nigeriano(na). ⬦ *n* nigeriano *m*, -na *f*.

Nigerien [naɪˈdʒɪərɪən] ⬦ *adj* nigerino(na). ⬦ *n* nigerino *m*, -na *f*.

niggardly [ˈnɪɡədlɪ] *adj* [person] avaro(ra), tacaño(ña); [gift, amount] miserable.

niggle [ˈnɪɡl] ⬦ *n* [worry] duda *f* (insignificante). ⬦ *vt UK* **- 1.** [worry] inquietar **- 2.** [criticize] meterse con. ⬦ *vi* **- 1.** [worry]: **it niggled at me all day** le di vueltas todo el día **- 2.** [criticize] criticar, quejarse.

nigh [naɪ] *adv liter* [near] cerca; **well nigh** [almost] casi.

night [naɪt] ⬦ *adj* nocturno(na). ⬦ *n* noche *f*; [evening] tarde *f*; **last night** anoche, ayer por la noche; **tomorrow night** mañana por la noche; **on Monday night** el lunes por la noche; **at night** por la noche, de noche; **night and day, day and night** noche y día, día y noche; **to have an early/a late night** irse a dormir pronto/tarde.

➤ **nights** *adv* **- 1.** *US* [at night] por las noches **- 2.** *UK* [nightshift]: **to work nights** hacer el turno de noche.

nightcap ['naɪtkæp] n - **1.** [drink] *bebida que se toma antes de ir a dormir* - **2.** [hat] gorro m de dormir.

nightclothes ['naɪtkləʊðz] npl ropa f de dormir.

nightclub ['naɪtklʌb] n club m nocturno.

nightdress ['naɪtdres] n camisón m, dormilona f Ven.

nightfall ['naɪtfɔːl] n anochecer m.

nightgown ['naɪtgaʊn] n camisón m, dormilona f Amér.

nightie ['naɪtɪ] n inf camisón m.

nightingale ['naɪtɪŋgeɪl] n ruiseñor m.

nightlife ['naɪtlaɪf] n vida f nocturna.

nightlight ['naɪtlaɪt] n lucecita f (que se deja encendida durante la noche).

nightly ['naɪtlɪ] <> adj nocturno(na), de cada noche. <> adv cada noche, todas las noches.

nightmare ['naɪtmeəʳ] n lit & fig pesadilla f.

nightmarish ['naɪtmeərɪʃ] adj de pesadilla.

night owl n fig noctámbulo m, -la f.

night porter n recepcionista mf del turno de noche.

night safe n cajero m nocturno.

night school n (U) escuela f nocturna.

night shift n turno m de noche.

nightshirt ['naɪtʃɜːt] n camisa f de dormir (masculina).

nightspot ['naɪtspɒt] n club m nocturno.

nightstick ['naɪtstɪk] n US porra f.

nighttime ['naɪttaɪm] n noche f.

night watchman n vigilante m nocturno, nochero m Chile & Urug.

nihilism ['naɪəlɪzm] n nihilismo m.

nil [nɪl] n - **1.** [nothing] nada f - **2.** UK SPORT cero m; **five nil** cinco a cero.

Nile [naɪl] n: **the Nile** el Nilo.

nimble ['nɪmbl] adj - **1.** [person, fingers] ágil - **2.** [mind] rápido(da).

nimbly ['nɪmblɪ] adv con agilidad.

nine [naɪn] num nueve; see also **six**.

nineteen [ˌnaɪn'tiːn] num diecinueve; see also **six**.

nineteenth [ˌnaɪn'tiːnθ] num decimonoveno(na).

ninetieth ['naɪntɪəθ] <> num adj nonagésimo(ma). <> num n [fraction] noventa m; see also **sixth**.

ninety ['naɪntɪ] num noventa; see also **sixty**.

ninth [naɪnθ] num noveno(na); see also **sixth**.

nip [nɪp] <> n - **1.** [pinch] pellizco m; [bite] mordisco m - **2.** [of drink] trago m. <> vt (pt & pp -ped, cont -ping) [pinch] pellizcar;

[bite] mordisquear. <> vi (pt & pp -ped, cont -ping) inf [dash]: **to nip out** salir un momento.

nipper ['nɪpəʳ] n UK inf chiquillo m, chaval m, chigüín m Amér C.

nipple ['nɪpl] n - **1.** [of woman] pezón m - **2.** [of baby's bottle, man] tetilla f.

nippy ['nɪpɪ] (comp -ier, superl -iest) adj - **1.** [cold] fresco(ca); **it's a bit nippy this morning** hace fresquito esta mañana - **2.** [quick] rápido(da).

nit [nɪt] n - **1.** [in hair] liendre f - **2.** UK inf [idiot] imbécil mf.

nitpicking ['nɪtpɪkɪŋ] inf <> adj puñetero(ra). <> n (U): **that's just nitpicking** no son más que nimiedades.

nitrate ['naɪtreɪt] n nitrato m.

nitric acid ['naɪtrɪk-] n ácido m nítrico.

nitrogen ['naɪtrədʒən] n nitrógeno m.

nitroglycerin(e) [ˌnaɪtrəʊ'glɪsəriːn] n nitroglicerina f.

nitty-gritty [ˌnɪtɪ'grɪtɪ] n inf: **to get down to the nitty-gritty** ir al grano.

nitwit ['nɪtwɪt] n inf imbécil mf.

nix [nɪks] US <> n [nothing] nada f. <> adv no. <> vt [say no to] decir (que) no a.

NJ abbr of **New Jersey**.

NLQ (abbr of near letter quality) de calidad correspondencia.

NLRB (abbr of National Labor Relations Board) n organismo estadounidense para arbitraje laboral, ≃ IMAC m.

NM abbr of **New Mexico**.

no [nəʊ] <> adv [gen] no; **to say no** decir que no; **you're no better than me** tú no eres mejor que yo. <> adj no; **I have no time** no tengo tiempo; **there are no taxis** no hay taxis; **a woman with no money** una mujer sin dinero; **that's no excuse** esa no es excusa que valga; **he's no fool** no es ningún tonto; **she's no friend of mine** no es amiga mía; **'no smoking/parking/cameras'** 'prohibido fumar/aparcar/hacer fotos'. <> n (pl -es) no m; **he/she won't take no for an answer** no acepta una respuesta negativa.

No., no. (abbr of number) n.º

Noah's ark ['nəʊəz-] n el arca f de Noé.

nobble ['nɒbl] vt UK inf - **1.** [racehorse] drogar - **2.** [bribe] sobornar - **3.** [detain - person] coger por banda y dar la lata a.

Nobel prize [nəʊ'bel-] n premio m Nobel; **Nobel prize winner** premio mf Nobel.

nobility [nə'bɪlətɪ] n nobleza f.

noble ['nəʊbl] <> adj noble. <> n noble mf.

nobleman ['nəʊblmən] (pl -men [-mən]) n noble m.

noblewoman ['nəʊbl,wʊmən] (*pl* **-women** [-,wɪmɪn]) *n* noble *f*.

nobly ['nəʊblɪ] *adv* noblemente, con generosidad.

nobody ['nəʊbədɪ], **no one** <> *pron* nadie. <> *n* (*pl* **-ies**) *pej* don nadie *m*.

no-brainer ['nəʊ'breɪnə'] *n* US *inf*: it's a no-brainer es pan comido.

no-claims bonus *n* bonificación *f* por ausencia de siniestralidad.

nocturnal [nɒk'tɜ:nl] *adj* nocturno(na).

nod [nɒd] <> *n* inclinación *f* de cabeza. <> *vt* (*pt* & *pp* **-ded**, *cont* **-ding**): **to nod one's head** [in agreement] asentir con la cabeza; [to indicate sthg] indicar con la cabeza; [as greeting] saludar con la cabeza. <> *vi* (*pt* & *pp* **-ded**, *cont* **-ding**) **- 1.** [in agreement] asentir con la cabeza **- 2.** [to indicate sthg] indicar con la cabeza **- 3.** [as greeting] saludar con la cabeza.

◆ **nod off** *vi* quedarse dormido(da).

node [nəʊd] *n* nodo *m*.

nodule ['nɒdju:l] *n* nódulo *m*.

no-frills ['nəʊ,frɪlz] *adj* sencillo(lla).

no-go area *n* UK zona *f* (de entrada) prohibida.

noise [nɔɪz] *n* ruido *m*; **to make a noise** hacer ruido.

noiseless ['nɔɪzlɪs] *adj* silencioso(sa).

noiselessly ['nɔɪzlɪslɪ] *adv* silenciosamente.

noisily ['nɔɪzɪlɪ] *adv* ruidosamente.

noisy ['nɔɪzɪ] (*comp* **-ier**, *superl* **-iest**) *adj* ruidoso(sa); **it was very noisy** había mucho ruido.

nomad ['nəʊmæd] *n* nómada *mf*.

nomadic [nə'mædɪk] *adj* nómada.

no-man's-land *n* tierra *f* de nadie.

nominal ['nɒmɪnl] *adj* nominal.

nominally ['nɒmɪnəlɪ] *adv* nominalmente.

nominate ['nɒmɪneɪt] *vt* **- 1.** [propose]: **to nominate sb (for** OR **as)** proponer a alguien (por OR como) **- 2.** [appoint]: **to nominate sb (to sthg)** nombrar a alguien (algo).

nomination [,nɒmɪ'neɪʃn] *n* **- 1.** [proposal] nominación *f* **- 2.** [appointment]: **nomination (to sthg)** nombramiento *m* (a algo).

nominee [,nɒmɪ'ni:] *n* candidato *m*, -ta *f*.

non- [nɒn] *prefix* no.

nonaddictive [,nɒnə'dɪktɪv] *adj* que no crea adicción.

nonaggression [,nɒnə'greʃn] *n* no agresión *f*.

nonalcoholic [,nɒnælkə'hɒlɪk] *adj* sin alcohol.

nonaligned [,nɒnə'laɪnd] *adj* no alineado(da).

nonbeliever [,nɒnbɪ'li:və'] *n* no creyente *mf*.

nonchalant [UK 'nɒnʃələnt, US ,nɒnʃə'lɑ:nt] *adj* despreocupado(da).

nonchalantly [UK 'nɒnʃələntlɪ, US ,nɒnʃə'lɑ:ntlɪ] *adv* con despreocupación.

noncombatant [UK ,nɒn'kɒmbətənt, US ,nɒnkəm'bætənt] *n* no combatiente *mf*.

noncommissioned officer [,nɒnkə'mɪʃənd-] *n* suboficial *mf*.

noncommittal [,nɒnkə'mɪtl] *adj* evasivo(va).

noncompetitive [,nɒnkəm'petɪtɪv] *adj* no competitivo(va).

non compos mentis [-,kɒmpəs'mentɪs] *adj* que no está en posesión de sus facultades mentales.

nonconformist [,nɒnkən'fɔ:mɪst] <> *adj* inconformista. <> *n* inconformista *mf*.

noncontributory [,nɒnkən'trɪbjʊtərɪ] *adj* no contributivo (no contributiva).

noncooperation ['nɒnkəʊ,ɒpə'reɪʃn] *n* no cooperación *f*.

nondescript [UK 'nɒndɪskrɪpt, US ,nɒndɪ'skrɪpt] *adj* anodino(na), soso(sa).

nondrinker [,nɒn'drɪŋkə'] *n* persona *f* que no bebe (alcohol).

nondrip [,nɒn'drɪp] *adj* que no gotea.

nondriver [,nɒn'draɪvə'] *n* persona *f* que no sabe conducir.

none [nʌn] <> *pron* **- 1.** [not any] nada; **there is none left** no queda nada; **it's none of your business** no es asunto tuyo; **I'll have none of your nonsense** no voy a aguantar tus tonterías **- 2.** [not one - object, person] ninguno(na); **none of us/the books** ninguno de nosotros/de los libros; **I had none** no tenía ninguno. <> *adv*: **I'm none the worse/better** no me ha perjudicado/ayudado en nada; **I'm none the wiser** no me ha aclarado nada.

◆ **none too** *adv* no demasiado; **none too soon** justo a tiempo.

nonentity [nɒ'nentətɪ] (*pl* **-ies**) *n* cero *m* a la izquierda.

nonessential [,nɒnɪ'senʃl] *adj* no esencial.

nonetheless [,nʌnðə'les] *adv* sin embargo, no obstante.

non-event *n* chasco *m*.

nonexecutive director [,nɒn'ɪgsekjətɪv-] *n* director no ejecutivo *m*, directora no ejecutiva *f*.

nonexistent [,nɒnɪg'zɪstənt] *adj* inexistente.

nonfiction [,nɒn'fɪkʃn] *n* no ficción *f*.

nonflammable [,nɒn'flæməbl] *adj* ininflamable.

noninfectious [,nɒnɪn'fekʃəs] *adj* no infeccioso(sa).

noninflammable [,nɒnɪn'flæməbl] *adj* ininflamable.

noninterference [ˌnɒnɪntəˈfɪərəns], **nonintervention** [ˌnɒnɪntəˈvenʃn] *n* no intervención *f*.

non-invasive *adj* no invasivo (no invasiva).

non-iron *adj* que no necesita plancha.

nonmalignant [ˌnɒnməˈlɪgnənt] *adj* no maligno (no maligna).

non-member *n* no socio *m*.

non-negotiable *adj* no negociable.

no-no *n inf*: it's a no-no eso no se hace.

no-nonsense *adj* práctico(ca).

nonparticipation [ˌnɒnpɑːtɪsəˈpeɪʃən] *n* no participación *f*.

nonpayment [ˌnɒnˈpeɪmənt] *n* impago *m*.

nonplussed, nonplused US [ˌnɒnˈplʌst] *adj* perplejo(ja).

non-profit-making UK, **non-profit** US *adj* sin fines lucrativos.

nonproliferation [ˈnɒnprəˌlɪfəˈreɪʃn] *n* no proliferación *f*.

nonrenewable [ˌnɒnrɪˈnjuːəbl] *adj* [natural resources] no renovable; [contract] no prorrogable.

nonresident [ˌnɒnˈrezɪdənt] *n* - **1.** [of country] no residente *mf* - **2.** [of hotel]: **open to non-residents** abierto al público.

nonreturnable [ˌnɒnrɪˈtɜːnəbl] *adj* no retornable, sin retorno.

nonsense [ˈnɒnsəns] ◇ *n* (U) - **1.** [gen] tonterías *fpl*; **it is nonsense to suggest that...** es absurdo sugerir que...; **stop this nonsense at once!** ¡dejaros de tonterías ahora mismo!; **to make (a) nonsense of sthg** dar al traste con algo - **2.** [incomprehensible words] galimatías *m inv*; **it's nonsense to me** me es incomprensible. ◇ *excl* ¡tonterías!

nonsensical [nɒnˈsensɪkl] *adj* disparatado(da), absurdo(da).

non sequitur [-ˈsekwɪtər] *n* incoherencia *f*, incongruencia *f*.

nonshrink [ˌnɒnˈʃrɪŋk] *adj* que no encoge.

nonslip [ˌnɒnˈslɪp] *adj* antideslizante.

nonsmoker [ˌnɒnˈsməʊkər] *n* no fumador *m*, no fumadora *f*.

nonstarter [ˌnɒnˈstɑːtər] *n* UK - **1.** [plan]: **to be a nonstarter** *inf* estar condenado(da) al fracaso - **2.** [in race] *caballo participante en una carrera que no toma la salida*.

nonstick [ˌnɒnˈstɪk] *adj* antiadherente.

nonstop [ˌnɒnˈstɒp] ◇ *adj* [activity, rain] continuo(nua), incesante; [flight] sin escalas. ◇ *adv* sin parar.

nontoxic [ˌnɒnˈtɒksɪk] *adj* no tóxico(ca).

nontransferable [ˌnɒntrænzˈfɜːrəbl] *adj* intransferible.

nonviolence [ˌnɒnˈvaɪələns] *n* no violencia *f*.

nonvoter [ˌnɒnˈvəʊtər] *n* persona *f* que no vota.

nonvoting [ˌnɒnˈvəʊtɪŋ] *adj* - **1.** [person] sin voto - **2.** FIN [shares] sin derecho a voto.

nonwhite [ˌnɒnˈwaɪt] ◇ *adj* que no es de raza blanca. ◇ *n* persona *f* que no es de raza blanca.

noodles [ˈnuːdlz] *npl* tallarines *mpl* chinos.

nook [nʊk] *n* [of room] rincón *m*, recoveco *m*; **every nook and cranny** todos los recovecos.

noon [nuːn] *n* mediodía *m*.

noonday [ˈnuːndeɪ] *comp* de mediodía.

no one *pron* = **nobody**.

noose [nuːs] *n* [loop] nudo *m* corredizo; [for hanging] soga *f*.

no-place US = **nowhere**.

nor [nɔːr] *conj* - **1.** ⊳ **neither** - **2.** [and not] ni; **I don't smoke – nor do I** no fumo – yo tampoco; **I don't know, nor do I care** ni lo sé, ni me importa.

Nordic [ˈnɔːdɪk] *adj* nórdico(ca).

Norf (*abbr of* **Norfolk**), *condado inglés*.

norm [nɔːm] *n* norma *f*; **the norm** lo normal.

normal [ˈnɔːml] ◇ *adj* normal. ◇ *n*: **above normal** por encima de lo normal; **to return to normal** volver a la normalidad.

normality [nɔːˈmælɪtɪ], **normalcy** US [ˈnɔːmlsɪ] *n* normalidad *f*.

normalize, -ise [ˈnɔːməlaɪz] ◇ *vt* normalizar. ◇ *vi* normalizarse.

normally [ˈnɔːməlɪ] *adv* normalmente.

Normandy [ˈnɔːməndɪ] *n* Normandía.

Norse [nɔːs] *adj* nórdico(ca).

north [nɔːθ] ◇ *n* - **1.** [direction] norte *m* - **2.** [region]: **the North** el norte. ◇ *adj* del norte; **North London** el norte de Londres. ◇ *adv*: **north (of)** al norte (de).

North-South divide

> Se refiere a la división entre el opulento sur, en especial Londres y los condados del sudeste, y el norte de Inglaterra. El norte había sido tradicionalmente el corazón industrial del país pero muchas de sus áreas geográficas han ido sufriendo una decadencia económica y social como consecuencia del declive de la industria manufacturera en Gran Bretaña. La disparidad entre las dos regiones queda reflejada en el hecho de que los precios y los alquileres de las viviendas en el sur son mucho más elevados que en el norte, y en que la tasa de desempleo es mucho menor en las zonas meridionales.

North Africa *n* África del Norte.

North America *n* Norteamérica.

North American <> *adj* norteamericano(na). <> *n* norteamericano *m*, -na *f*.

Northants [nɔː'θænts] (*abbr of* **Northamptonshire**), *condado inglés.*

northbound ['nɔːθbaʊnd] *adj* (con) dirección (al) norte.

North Carolina [-,kærə'laɪnə] *n* Carolina del Norte.

Northd (*abbr of* **Northumberland**), *condado inglés.*

North Dakota [-də'kəʊtə] *n* Dakota del Norte.

northeast [,nɔːθ'iːst] <> *n* - **1.** [direction] nordeste *m* - **2.** [region]: **the Northeast** el nordeste. <> *adj* del nordeste. <> *adv*: **northeast (of)** al nordeste (de).

northeasterly [,nɔːθ'iːstəlɪ] *adj* del nordeste; **in a northeasterly direction** hacia el nordeste.

northerly ['nɔːðəlɪ] *adj* del norte; **in a northerly direction** hacia el norte.

northern ['nɔːðən] *adj* del norte, norteño(ña); **northern France** el norte de Francia.

Northerner ['nɔːðənər] *n* norteño *m*, -ña *f*.

Northern Ireland *n* Irlanda del Norte.

Northern Lights *npl*: **the Northern Lights** la aurora boreal.

northernmost ['nɔːðənməʊst] *adj* más septentrional OR al norte.

Northern Territory *n* (el) Territorio del Norte.

North Korea *n* Corea del Norte.

North Korean <> *adj* norcoreano(na). <> *n* norcoreano *m*, -na *f*.

North Pole *n*: **the North Pole** el Polo Norte.

North Sea <> *n*: **the North Sea** el Mar del Norte. <> *comp* [fishing] en el Mar del Norte; [oil, oilrig] del Mar del Norte.

North Star *n*: **the North Star** la estrella Polar.

North Vietnam *n* Vietnam del Norte.

North Vietnamese <> *adj* norvietnamita. <> *n* norvietnamita *mf*.

northward ['nɔːθwəd] <> *adj* hacia el norte. <> *adv* = **northwards**.

northwards ['nɔːθwədz], **northward** *adv* hacia el norte.

northwest [,nɔːθ'west] <> *n* - **1.** [direction] noroeste *m* - **2.** [region]: **the Northwest** el noroeste. <> *adj* del noroeste. <> *adv*: **northwest (of)** al noroeste (de).

northwesterly [,nɔːθ'westəlɪ] *adj* del noroeste; **in a northwesterly direction** hacia el noroeste.

Northwest Territories *npl* Canada: **the Northwest Territories** los territorios del Noroeste.

Norway ['nɔːweɪ] *n* Noruega.

Norwegian [nɔː'wiːdʒən] <> *adj* noruego(ga). <> *n* - **1.** [person] noruego *m*, -ga *f* - **2.** [language] noruego *m*.

Nos., nos. (*abbr of* **numbers**) n.ᵒˢ.

nose [nəʊz] *n* [of person] nariz *f*; [of animal] hocico *m*; [of plane, car] morro *m*; **under one's nose** delante de las narices de uno; **to cut off one's nose to spite one's face** salir uno perjudicado al intentar perjudicar a otro; **to have a nose for sthg** tener olfato para algo; **he gets up my nose** *inf* me saca de quicio; **to keep one's nose out of sthg** no meter las narices en algo; **to look down one's nose at sb/sthg** mirar por encima del hombro a alguien/algo; **to pay through the nose** pagar un dineral; **to poke** OR **stick one's nose in** *inf* meter las narices; **to turn up one's nose at sthg** hacerle ascos a algo.

⬥ **nose about, nose around** *vi* curiosear.

nosebag ['nəʊzbæg] *n* morral *m*.

nosebleed ['nəʊzbliːd] *n* hemorragia *f* nasal.

nosecone ['nəʊzkəʊn] *n* morro *m*.

nosedive ['nəʊzdaɪv] <> *n* [of plane] picado *m*. <> *vi lit & fig* bajar en picado.

nosey ['nəʊzɪ] = **nosy**.

nosh [nɒʃ] *n* UK *inf* papeo *m*.

nosh-up *n* UK *inf* comilona *f*.

no-smoking *adj* [area, carriage] para no fumadores; [flight] de no fumadores.

nostalgia [nɒ'stældʒə] *n*: **nostalgia (for)** nostalgia *f* (de).

nostalgic [nɒ'stældʒɪk] *adj* nostálgico(ca).

nostril ['nɒstrəl] *n* ventana *f* de la nariz.

nosy ['nəʊzɪ] (*comp* **-ier**, *superl* **-iest**), **nosey** *adj* fisgón(ona), entrometido(da).

not [nɒt] *adv* no; **this is not the first time** no es la primera vez; **it's green, isn't it?** es verde, ¿no?; **not me** yo no; **I hope/think not** espero/creo que no; **not a chance** de ninguna manera; **not even a...** ni siquiera un(una)...; **not all** OR **every** no todos(das); **not always** no siempre; **not that...** no es que...; **not at all** [no] en absoluto; [to acknowledge thanks] de nada.

notable ['nəʊtəbl] <> *adj* notable; **to be notable for sthg** destacar por algo. <> *n* notable *mf*, personaje *m*.

notably ['nəʊtəblɪ] *adv* - **1.** [in particular] especialmente - **2.** [noticeably] notablemente, marcadamente.

notary ['nəʊtərɪ] (*pl* **-ies**) *n*: **notary (public)** notario *m*, -ria *f*.

notation [nəʊ'teɪʃn] *n* notación *f*.

notch [nɒtʃ] *n* - **1.** [cut] muesca *f* - **2.** *fig* [on scale] punto *m*.

⬥ **notch up** *vt insep* apuntarse.

note [nəʊt] <> n - **1.** [gen] nota f; **to make a note of sthg** tomar nota de algo; **to take note of sthg** tener algo presente; **to compare notes** cambiar impresiones - **2.** [paper money] billete m - **3.** [tone] tono m - **4.** [importance]: **of note** de importancia, notable. <> vt - **1.** [observe] notar; **please note that...** tenga en cuenta que... - **2.** [mention] mencionar.

◆ **notes** npl [written record] apuntes mpl; **to take notes** tomar apuntes; [in book] notas fpl.

◆ **note down** vt sep anotar, apuntar.

notebook ['nəʊtbʊk] n - **1.** [for taking notes] libreta f, cuaderno m - **2.** COMPUT: **notebook (computer)** ordenador m portátil.

noted ['nəʊtɪd] adj destacado(da); **to be noted for** distinguirse por.

notepad ['nəʊtpæd] n bloc m de notas.

notepaper ['nəʊtpeɪpəʳ] n papel m de escribir OR de cartas.

noteworthy ['nəʊt,wɜːðɪ] (comp -ier, superl -iest) adj digno(na) de mención, significativo(va).

nothing ['nʌθɪŋ] <> pron nada; **I've got nothing to do** no tengo nada que hacer; **there's nothing complicated about it** no tiene nada de complicado; **there's nothing in it** [it's untrue] es falso; **there's nothing to it** es facilísimo; **for nothing** [free] gratis; [for no purpose] en vano, en balde; **he's nothing if not generous** otra cosa no será pero desde luego generoso sí que es; **nothing but** tan sólo; **there's nothing for it (but to do sthg)** UK no hay más remedio (que hacer algo); **nothing much** no mucho. <> adv: **to be nothing like sb/sthg** no parecerse en nada a alguien/algo; **I'm nothing like finished** no he terminado ni mucho menos.

nothingness ['nʌθɪŋnɪs] n nada f.

notice ['nəʊtɪs] <> n - **1.** [on wall, door] cartel m; [in newspaper] anuncio m - **2.** [attention] atención f; **to come to one's notice** llegar al conocimiento de uno; **to escape one's notice** pasarle inadvertido OR escapársele a uno; **to take notice (of)** hacer caso (de), prestar atención (a); **to take no notice (of)** no hacer caso (de); **he/she didn't take a blind bit of notice** no hizo ni el más mínimo caso - **3.** [warning] aviso m; **at short notice** casi sin previo aviso; **until further notice** hasta nuevo aviso; **without notice** sin previo aviso - **4.** [at work]: **to be given one's notice** ser despedido(da); **to hand in one's notice** presentar la dimisión. <> vt - **1.** [sense, smell] notar; [see] fijarse en, ver; **to notice sb doing sthg** fijarse en alguien que está haciendo algo - **2.** [realize] darse cuenta de. <> vi darse cuenta.

noticeable ['nəʊtɪsəbl] adj notable.

noticeably ['nəʊtɪsəblɪ] adv notablemente.

notice board n tablón m de anuncios.

notification [,nəʊtɪfɪ'keɪʃn] n notificación f.

notify ['nəʊtɪfaɪ] (pt & pp -ied) vt: **to notify sb (of sthg)** notificar OR comunicar (algo) a alguien.

notion ['nəʊʃn] n noción f.

◆ **notions** npl US artículos mpl de mercería.

notional ['nəʊʃənl] adj hipotético(ca).

notoriety [,nəʊtə'raɪətɪ] n mala fama f.

notorious [nəʊ'tɔːrɪəs] adj famoso(sa), célebre; **to be notorious for sthg** ser muy conocido(da) por algo.

notoriously [nəʊ'tɔːrɪəslɪ] adv: **it is notoriously difficult** es conocido por lo difícil que es.

Notts [nɒts] (abbr of **Nottinghamshire**), condado inglés.

notwithstanding [,nɒtwɪθ'stændɪŋ] fml <> prep a pesar de. <> adv sin embargo, no obstante.

nougat ['nuːgɑː] n dulce hecho a base de nueces y frutas.

nought [nɔːt] num cero; **noughts and crosses** tres m en raya.

noun [naʊn] n nombre m, sustantivo m.

nourish ['nʌrɪʃ] vt - **1.** [feed] nutrir, alimentar - **2.** [entertain] alimentar, albergar.

nourishing ['nʌrɪʃɪŋ] adj nutritivo(va), rico(ca).

nourishment ['nʌrɪʃmənt] n alimento m, sustento m.

Nov. (abbr of **November**) nov.

Nova Scotia [,nəʊvə'skəʊʃə] n Nueva Escocia.

Nova Scotian [,nəʊvə'skəʊʃn] <> adj neoescocés(esa). <> n neoescocés m, -esa f.

novel ['nɒvl] <> adj original. <> n novela f.

novelist ['nɒvəlɪst] n novelista mf.

novelty ['nɒvltɪ] (pl -ies) n - **1.** [gen] novedad f - **2.** [cheap object] baratija f (poco útil).

November [nə'vembəʳ] n noviembre m; see also **September**.

novice ['nɒvɪs] n - **1.** [inexperienced person] principiante mf - **2.** RELIG novicio m, -cia f.

Novocaine® ['nəʊvəkeɪn] n novocaína® f.

now [naʊ] <> adv - **1.** [at this time, at once] ahora; **do it now** hazlo ahora; **he's been away for two weeks now** lleva dos semanas fuera; **any day now** cualquier día de éstos; **any time now** en cualquier momento; **for now** por ahora, por el momento; **now and then** OR **again** de vez en cuando - **2.** [nowadays] hoy día - **3.** [at a particular time in the past] entonces - **4.** [to introduce statement] vamos a ver. <> conj: **now (that)** ahora que, ya que. <> n ahora; **five days from now** de aquí a cinco días; **from now on** a partir de ahora; **they should be here by now** ya deberían estar aquí; **up until now** hasta ahora.

NOW [naʊ] (*abbr of* **National Organization for Women**) *n principal organización estadounidense contra la discriminación sexual.*

nowadays ['naʊədeɪz] *adv* hoy en día, actualmente.

nowhere *UK* ['nəʊweəʳ], **no-place** *US* ◇ *adv* [be] en ninguna parte; [go] a ninguna parte; **nowhere else** en ninguna otra parte; **to appear out of** OR **from nowhere** salir de la nada; **to be getting nowhere** no estar avanzando nada, no ir a ninguna parte; **(to be) nowhere near (as... as...)** (no ser) ni mucho menos (tan... como...); **this is getting us nowhere** esto no nos lleva a nada. ◇ *n*: **we have nowhere to hide** no tenemos dónde escondernos.

no-win situation *n situación en la que se haga lo que se haga se sale perdiendo.*

noxious ['nɒkʃəs] *adj* nocivo(va).

nozzle ['nɒzl] *n* boquilla *f*.

NP *n abbr of* **notary public**.

NS *abbr of* **Nova Scotia**.

NSC (*abbr of* **National Security Council**) *n consejo federal estadounidense para la coordinación de la política exterior y de defensa.*

NSPCC (*abbr of* **National Society for the Prevention of Cruelty to Children**) *n organización benéfica británica para la prevención de malos tratos a los niños.*

NSW *n abbr of* **New South Wales**.

NT *n* - **1.** (*abbr of* **New Testament**) N.T. *m* - **2.** *abbr of* **National Trust**.

nth [enθ] *adj inf*: **to the nth degree** al máximo; **for the nth time** por enésima vez.

nuance [nju:'ɑ:ns] *n* matiz *m*.

nub [nʌb] *n*: **the nub** el quid.

nubile [*UK* 'nju:baɪl, *US* 'nu:bəl] *adj fml* & *hum* núbil.

nuclear ['nju:klɪəʳ] *adj* nuclear.

nuclear bomb *n* bomba *f* atómica.

nuclear disarmament *n* desarme *m* nuclear.

nuclear energy *n* energía *f* nuclear.

nuclear family *n* familia *f* nuclear.

nuclear fission *n* fisión *f* nuclear.

nuclear-free zone *n* zona *f* desnuclearizada.

nuclear fusion *n* fusión *f* nuclear.

nuclear physics *n* física *f* nuclear.

nuclear power *n* energía *f* nuclear.

nuclear power station *n* central *f* nuclear.

nuclear reactor *n* reactor *m* nuclear.

nuclear winter *n* invierno *m* nuclear.

nucleus ['nju:klɪəs] (*pl* **-lei** [-lɪaɪ]) *n lit* & *fig* núcleo *m*.

nude [nju:d] ◇ *adj* desnudo(da). ◇ *n* ART desnudo *m*; **in the nude** desnudo(da).

nudge [nʌdʒ] ◇ *n* - **1.** [with elbow] codazo *m* - **2.** *fig* [to encourage] empujón *m*. ◇ *vt* - **1.** [with elbow] dar un codazo a - **2.** *fig* [to encourage] empujar.

nudist ['nju:dɪst] ◇ *adj* nudista. ◇ *n* nudista *mf*.

nudity ['nju:dətɪ] *n* desnudez *f*.

nugget ['nʌgɪt] *n* - **1.** [of gold] pepita *f* - **2.** *fig* [valuable piece]: **nuggets of wisdom** gotas *fpl* de sabiduría.

nuisance ['nju:sns] *n* [thing] fastidio *m*, molestia *f*; [person] pesado *m*; **to make a nuisance of o.s.** dar la lata.

NUJ (*abbr of* **National Union of Journalists**) *n sindicato británico de periodistas.*

nuke [nju:k] *inf* ◇ *n* bomba *f* atómica. ◇ *vt* - **1.** MIL atacar con arma nuclear - **2.** [cook in microwave] cocinar en el microondas.

null [nʌl] *adj*: **null and void** nulo(la) y sin efecto.

nullify ['nʌlɪfaɪ] (*pt* & *pp* **-ied**) *vt* anular.

NUM (*abbr of* **National Union of Mineworkers**) *n sindicato británico de mineros.*

numb [nʌm] ◇ *adj* entumecido(da); **to be numb with cold** estar helado(da) de frío; **to be numb with fear** estar paralizado(da) de miedo. ◇ *vt* entumecer.

number ['nʌmbəʳ] ◇ *n* - **1.** [gen] número *m*; **a number of** varios(rias); **a large number of** gran número de; **large numbers of** grandes cantidades de; **any number of** la mar de - **2.** [of car] matrícula *f*. ◇ *vt* - **1.** [amount to] ascender a - **2.** [give a number to] numerar - **3.** [include]: **to be numbered among** figurar entre.

number-crunching [-,krʌntʃɪŋ] *n inf* cálculo *m* a gran escala.

numberless ['nʌmbəlɪs] *adj* incontables, innumerables.

number one ◇ *adj* principal, número uno. ◇ *n inf* [oneself] uno mismo (una misma).

numberplate ['nʌmbəpleɪt] *n* matrícula *f* (de vehículo).

Number Ten *n* el número 10 de Downing Street, residencia oficial del primer ministro británico.

numbness ['nʌmnɪs] *n* - **1.** [with cold] entumecimiento *m* - **2.** *fig* [with shock, fear] parálisis *f inv*.

numbskull ['nʌmskʌl] *n* = **numskull**.

numeracy ['nju:mərəsɪ] *n* UK conocimiento *m* básico de aritmética.

numeral ['nju:mərəl] *n* número *m*, cifra *f*.

numerate ['nju:mərət] *adj* UK competente en aritmética.

numerical [nju:'merɪkl] *adj* numérico(ca).

numerous ['nju:mərəs] *adj* numeroso(sa).

numskull, numbskull ['nʌmskʌl] *n inf* imbécil *mf*, mentecato *m*, -ta *f*.

nun [nʌn] *n* monja *f*.

nuptial ['nʌpʃl] *adj fml* nupcial.

nurse [nɜ:s] ◇ *n* MED enfermero *m*, -ra *f*; [nanny] niñera *f*. ◇ *vt* - **1.** [care for] cuidar, atender - **2.** [try to cure - a cold] curarse - **3.** *fig* [nourish] abrigar - **4.** [subj: mother] criar, amamantar.

nursemaid ['nɜ:smeɪd] *n* niñera *f*.

nursery ['nɜ:sərɪ] ◇ *adj* [education] pre-escolar. ◇ *n* (*pl* -ies) - **1.** [at home] cuarto *m* de los niños; [away from home] guardería *f* - **2.** [for plants] semillero *m*, vivero *m*.

nursery nurse *n* UK [at school] niñera *f*; [in hospital] enfermera *f* puericultora.

nursery rhyme *n* poema *m* OR canción *f* infantil.

nursery school *n* parvulario *m*, escuela *f* de párvulos.

nursery slopes *npl* pista *f* para principiantes.

nursing ['nɜ:sɪŋ] *n* [profession] profesión *f* de enfermera; [of patient] asistencia *f*, cuidado *m*.

nursing home *n* [for old people] clínica *f* de reposo (privada); [for childbirth] clínica *f* (privada) de maternidad.

nurture ['nɜ:tʃər] *vt* - **1.** [child, plant] criar - **2.** [plan, feelings] alimentar.

NUS (*abbr of* **National Union of Students**) *n* sindicato nacional de estudiantes en Gran Bretaña.

nut [nʌt] *n* - **1.** [to eat] nuez *f* - **2.** [of metal] tuerca *f*; **the nuts and bolts** *fig* lo esencial, lo básico - **3.** *inf* [mad person] chiflado *m*, -da *f* - **4.** *inf* [enthusiast] maniático *m*, -ca *f* - **5.** *inf* [head]: **she's off her nut** UK está mal del coco.

➡ **nuts** *inf* ◇ *adj*: **to be nuts** estar chalado(da). ◇ *excl* US ¡maldita sea!

NUT (*abbr of* **National Union of Teachers**) *n* sindicato británico de profesores.

nutcase ['nʌtkeɪs] *n inf* pirado *m*, -da *f*.

nutcrackers ['nʌt,krækəz] *npl* cascanueces *m inv*.

nutmeg ['nʌtmeg] *n* nuez *f* moscada.

nutrient ['nju:trɪənt] *n* sustancia *f* nutritiva.

nutrition [nju:'trɪʃn] *n* nutrición *f*, alimentación *f*.

nutritional [nju:'trɪʃənl] *adj* nutritivo(va).

nutritionist [nju:'trɪʃənɪst] *n* dietista *mf*.

nutritious [nju:'trɪʃəs] *adj* nutritivo(va).

nutshell ['nʌtʃel] *n*: **in a nutshell** en una palabra.

nutter ['nʌtər] *n* UK *inf* chiflado *m*, -da *f*.

nuzzle ['nʌzl] ◇ *vt* rozar con el hocico. ◇ *vi*: **to nuzzle (up) against** arrimarse a.

NV *abbr of* **Nevada**.

NVQ (*abbr of* **National Vocational Qualification**) *n* título de formación profesional en Inglaterra y Gales.

NW (*abbr of* **north-west**) NO.

NWT *abbr of* **Northwest Territories**.

NY *abbr of* **New York**.

NYC *abbr of* **New York City**.

nylon ['naɪlɒn] ◇ *n* nylon *m*. ◇ *comp* de nylon.

➡ **nylons** *npl dated* medias *fpl* de nylon.

nymph [nɪmf] *n* ninfa *f*.

nymphomaniac [,nɪmfə'meɪnɪæk] *n* ninfómana *f*.

NYSE (*abbr of* **New York Stock Exchange**) *n* la Bolsa de Nueva York.

NZ *abbr of* **New Zealand**.

o (*pl* **o's** OR **os**), **O** (*pl* **O's** OR **Os**) [əʊ] *n* - **1.** [letter] o *f*, O *f* - **2.** [zero] cero *m*.

oaf [əʊf] *n* zoquete *mf*, lerdo *m*, -da *f*.

oak [əʊk] ◇ *n* roble *m*. ◇ *comp* de roble.

OAP *n abbr of* **old age pensioner**.

oar [ɔ:r] *n* remo *m*; **to put** OR **stick one's oar in** entrometerse.

oarlock ['ɔ:lɒk] *n* US [rowlock] escálamo *m*, tolete *m*.

oarsman ['ɔ:zmən] (*pl* -**men** [-mən]) *n* remero *m*.

oarswoman ['ɔ:z,wʊmən] (*pl* -**women** [-,wɪmɪn]) *n* remera *f*.

OAS (*abbr of* **Organization of American States**) *n* OEA *f*.

oasis [əʊ'eɪsɪs] (*pl* **oases** [əʊ'eɪsi:z]) *n lit* & *fig* oasis *m inv*.

oatcake ['əʊtkeɪk] *n* galleta *f* de avena.

oath [əʊθ] *n* - **1.** [promise] juramento *m*; **on** OR **under oath** bajo juramento - **2.** [swearword] palabrota *f*.

oatmeal ['əʊtmiːl] US <> *n* [flakes] copos *mpl* de avena; [porridge] avena *f*. <> *comp* de avena.

oats [əʊts] *npl* [grain] avena *f*.

OAU (*abbr of* **Organization of African Unity**) *n* OUA *f*.

obdurate ['ɒbdjʊrət] *adj fml* obstinado(da).

OBE (*abbr of* **Order of the British Empire**) *n* (*titular de*) *distinción honorífica británica*.

obedience [ə'biːdjəns] *n*: **obedience (to sb)** obediencia *f* (a alguien).

obedient [ə'biːdjənt] *adj* obediente.

obediently [ə'biːdjəntlɪ] *adv* obedientemente.

obelisk ['ɒbəlɪsk] *n* obelisco *m*.

obese [əʊ'biːs] *adj fml* obeso(sa).

obesity [əʊ'biːsətɪ] *n* obesidad *f*.

obey [ə'beɪ] *vt* & *vi* obedecer.

obfuscate ['ɒbfʌskeɪt] *vt fml* oscurecer.

obituary [ə'bɪtʃʊərɪ] (*pl* **-ies**) *n* nota *f* necrológica, necrología *f*.

object <> *n* ['ɒbdʒɪkt] - **1.** [gen & COMPUT] objeto *m* - **2.** [aim] objeto *m*, propósito *m* - **3.** GRAM complemento *m*. <> *vt* [ɒb'dʒekt] objetar. <> *vi*: **to object (to sthg/to doing sthg)** oponerse (a algo/a hacer algo); **I object to that comment** me parece muy mal ese comentario.

objection [əb'dʒekʃn] *n* objeción *f*, reparo *m*; **to have no objection (to sthg/to doing sthg)** no tener inconveniente (en algo/en hacer algo).

objectionable [əb'dʒekʃənəbl] *adj* [person] desagradable; [behaviour] censurable.

objective [əb'dʒektɪv] <> *adj* objetivo(va). <> *n* objetivo *m*.

objectively [əb'dʒektɪvlɪ] *adv* objetivamente.

objectivity [,ɒbdʒek'tɪvətɪ] *n* objetividad *f*.

object lesson ['ɒbdʒɪkt-] *n*: **an object lesson in sthg** un perfecto ejemplo de algo.

objector [əb'dʒektər] *n* oponente *mf*.

obligate ['ɒblɪɡeɪt] *vt fml*: **to obligate sb to do sthg** obligar a alguien a hacer algo.

obligation [,ɒblɪ'ɡeɪʃn] *n* - **1.** [compulsion] obligación *f*; **to be under an obligation to do sthg** tener la obligación de hacer algo - **2.** [duty] deber *m*.

obligatory [ə'blɪɡətrɪ] *adj* obligatorio(ria).

oblige [ə'blaɪdʒ] <> *vt* - **1.** [force]: **to oblige sb to do sthg** obligar a alguien a hacer algo - **2.** *fml* [do a favour to] hacer un favor a; **I would be much obliged if...** le estaría muy agradecido si... <> *vi* hacer el favor.

obliging [ə'blaɪdʒɪŋ] *adj* servicial, atento(ta).

oblique [ə'bliːk] <> *adj* - **1.** [indirect - reference] indirecto(ta) - **2.** [slanting] oblicuo(cua). <> *n* TYPO barra *f*.

obliquely [ə'bliːklɪ] *adv* [indirectly] indirectamente.

obliterate [ə'blɪtəreɪt] *vt* arrasar.

obliteration [ə,blɪtə'reɪʃn] *n* arrasamiento *m*.

oblivion [ə'blɪvɪən] *n* olvido *m*.

oblivious [ə'blɪvɪəs] *adj* inconsciente; **to be oblivious to** OR **of sthg** no ser consciente de algo.

oblong ['ɒblɒŋ] <> *adj* rectangular, oblongo(ga). <> *n* rectángulo *m*.

obnoxious [əb'nɒkʃəs] *adj* repugnante, detestable.

oboe ['əʊbəʊ] *n* oboe *m*.

oboist ['əʊbəʊɪst] *n* oboe *mf*, oboísta *mf*.

obscene [əb'siːn] *adj* obsceno(na), indecente.

obscenity [əb'senətɪ] (*pl* **-ies**) *n* obscenidad *f*.

obscure [əb'skjʊər] <> *adj lit* & *fig* oscuro(ra). <> *vt* - **1.** [make difficult to understand] oscurecer - **2.** [hide] esconder.

obscurity [əb'skjʊərətɪ] *n lit* & *fig* oscuridad *f*.

obsequious [əb'siːkwɪəs] *adj fml* & *pej* servil.

observable [əb'zɜːvəbl] *adj* visible, observable.

observably [əb'zɜːvəblɪ] *adv* visiblemente.

observance [əb'zɜːvns] *n* observancia *f*, cumplimiento *m*.

observant [əb'zɜːvnt] *adj* observador(ra).

observation [,ɒbzə'veɪʃn] *n* - **1.** [by police] vigilancia *f*; [by doctor] observación *f* - **2.** [comment] observación *f*, comentario *m*.

observation post *n* puesto *m* de observación.

observatory [əb'zɜːvətrɪ] (*pl* **-ies**) *n* observatorio *m*.

observe [əb'zɜːv] *vt* - **1.** [gen] observar - **2.** [obey] cumplir con, observar.

observer [əb'zɜːvər] *n* observador *m*, -ra *f*.

obsess [əb'ses] *vt* obsesionar; **to be obsessed by** OR **with** estar obsesionado con.

obsession [əb'seʃn] *n* obsesión *f*.

obsessional [əb'seʃənl] *adj* obsesivo(va).

obsessive [əb'sesɪv] *adj* obsesivo(va).

obsolescence [,ɒbsə'lesns] *n* obsolescencia *f*.

obsolescent [,ɒbsə'lesnt] *adj* obsolescente, que está cayendo en desuso.

obsolete ['ɒbsəliːt] *adj* obsoleto(ta).

obstacle ['ɒbstəkl] *n* - **1.** [object] obstáculo *m* - **2.** [difficulty] estorbo *m*, impedimento *m*.

obstacle race *n* carrera *f* de obstáculos.

obstetrician [,ɒbstə'trɪʃn] *n* tocólogo *m*, -ga *f*, obstetra *mf*.

obstetrics [ɒb'stetrɪks] n obstetricia f.

obstinacy ['ɒbstɪnəsɪ] n terquedad f, obstinación f.

obstinate ['ɒbstənət] adj - **1.** [stubborn] obstinado(da), terco(ca) - **2.** [persistent] tenaz.

obstinately ['ɒbstənətlɪ] adv obstinadamente, tercamente.

obstreperous [əb'strepərəs] adj fml & hum [unruly] desmandado(da).

obstruct [əb'strʌkt] vt - **1.** [block] obstruir, bloquear - **2.** [hinder] estorbar, entorpecer.

obstruction [əb'strʌkʃn] n [gen & SPORT] obstrucción f; [blockage] atasco m.

obstructive [əb'strʌktɪv] adj obstructor(ra).

obtain [əb'teɪn] vt obtener, conseguir.

obtainable [əb'teɪnəbl] adj que se puede conseguir, disponible.

obtrusive [əb'truːsɪv] adj [smell] penetrante; [colour] chillón(ona); [person] entrometido(da).

obtrusively [əb'truːsɪvlɪ] adv indiscretamente.

obtuse [əb'tjuːs] adj lit & fig obtuso(sa).

obverse ['ɒbvɜːs] n - **1.** [front side] anverso m - **2.** [opposite]: **the obverse of** la otra cara de.

obviate ['ɒbvɪeɪt] vt fml evitar, obviar.

obvious ['ɒbvɪəs] <> adj obvio(via), evidente. <> n: **to state the obvious** afirmar lo obvio OR lo evidente.

obviously ['ɒbvɪəslɪ] adv - **1.** [of course] evidentemente, obviamente; **obviously not** claro que no - **2.** [clearly] claramente, obviamente; **he's obviously lying** está claro que miente.

obviousness ['ɒbvɪəsnɪs] n obviedad f, lo evidente.

OCAS (abbr of Organization of Central American States) n ODECA f.

occasion [ə'keɪʒn] <> n - **1.** [time] vez f, ocasión f; **on one occasion** una vez, en una ocasión; **on several occasions** varias veces, en varias ocasiones; **on occasion** fml de vez en cuando - **2.** [important event] acontecimiento m; **to rise to the occasion** ponerse a la altura de las circunstancias - **3.** fml [opportunity] ocasión f. <> vt fml [cause] ocasionar, causar.

occasional [ə'keɪʒənl] adj [trip, drink] esporádico(ca); [showers] ocasional.

occasionally [ə'keɪʒnəlɪ] adv de vez en cuando.

occasional table n mesita f (auxiliar).

occult [ɒ'kʌlt] <> adj oculto(ta). <> n: **the occult** lo oculto.

occupancy ['ɒkjʊpənsɪ] n ocupación f.

occupant ['ɒkjʊpənt] n - **1.** [of building, room] inquilino m, -na f - **2.** [of chair, vehicle] ocupante mf.

occupation [,ɒkjʊ'peɪʃn] n - **1.** [job] empleo m, ocupación f - **2.** [pastime] pasatiempo m - **3.** MIL [of country, building] ocupación f.

occupational [,ɒkjuː'peɪʃənl] adj laboral, profesional.

occupational hazard n: occupational hazards gajes mpl del oficio.

occupational therapist n terapeuta mf ocupacional.

occupational therapy n terapia f ocupacional.

occupied ['ɒkjʊpaɪd] adj ocupado(da).

occupier ['ɒkjʊpaɪər] n inquilino m, -na f.

occupy ['ɒkjʊpaɪ] (pt & pp -ied) vt - **1.** [gen] ocupar - **2.** [live in] habitar - **3.** [entertain]: **to occupy o.s.** entretenerse.

occur [ə'kɜːr] (pt & pp -red, cont -ring) vi - **1.** [happen] ocurrir, suceder - **2.** [be present] encontrarse - **3.** [thought, idea]: **to occur to sb** ocurrírsele a alguien; **it occurs to me that...** se me ocurre que...

occurrence [ə'kʌrəns] n - **1.** [event] acontecimiento m - **2.** [coming about] aparición f.

ocean ['əʊʃn] n océano m.

oceangoing ['əʊʃn,gəʊɪŋ] adj marítimo(ma).

Oceania [,əʊʃɪ'ɑːnɪə] n Oceanía.

Oceanian [,əʊʃɪ'ɑːnɪən] <> adj oceánico(ca). <> n oceánico m, -ca f.

ochre UK**, ocher** US ['əʊkər] adj ocre.

o'clock [ə'klɒk] adv: **it's one o'clock** es la una; **it's two/three o'clock** son las dos/las tres; **at one/two o'clock** a la una/las dos.

OCR n - **1.** COMPUT (abbr of optical character reader) LOC m - **2.** COMPUT (abbr of optical character recognition) ROC m.

Oct. (abbr of October) oct.

octagon ['ɒktəgən] n octágono m.

octagonal [ɒk'tægənl] adj octagonal.

octane ['ɒkteɪn] n octano m.

octane number, octane rating n octanaje m.

octave ['ɒktɪv] n octava f.

octet [ɒk'tet] n octeto m.

October [ɒk'təʊbər] n octubre m; see also **September**.

octogenarian [,ɒktəʊdʒɪ'neərɪən] n octogenario m, -ria f.

octopus ['ɒktəpəs] (pl -pi OR -puses [-paɪ]) n pulpo m.

OD abbr of **overdose**. abbr of **overdrawn**.

odd [ɒd] adj - **1.** [strange] raro(ra), extraño(ña) - **2.** [not part of pair] sin pareja, suelto(ta) - **3.** [number] impar - **4.** inf [leftover] sobrante

- 5. inf [occasional]: **I play the odd game** juego alguna que otra vez **- 6.** inf [approximately]: **30 odd years** 30 y tantos OR y pico años.

◆ **odds** npl **- 1.**: **the odds** [probability] las probabilidades; [in betting] las apuestas; **the odds are that...** lo más probable es que...; **against all odds** contra viento y marea; **against the odds** contra (todo) pronóstico **- 2.** [bits]: **odds and ends** chismes mpl, cosillas fpl
▶▶ **to be at odds with sthg** no concordar con algo; **to be at odds with sb** estar reñido con alguien.

oddball ['ɒdbɔːl] n inf excéntrico m, -ca f.

oddity ['ɒdɪtɪ] (pl **-ies**) n rareza f.

odd-job man UK, **odd jobber** US n hombre m que hace chapuzas.

odd jobs npl chapuzas fpl.

oddly ['ɒdlɪ] adv extrañamente; **oddly enough** aunque parezca mentira.

oddments ['ɒdmənts] npl retales mpl.

odds-on ['ɒdz-] adj inf: **the odds-on favourite** el favorito indiscutible; **it's odds-on that...** fijo que...

ode [əʊd] n oda f.

odious ['əʊdjəs] adj odioso(sa), detestable.

odometer [əʊ'dɒmɪtər] n US cuentakilómetros m inv.

odorless US adj = odourless.

odour UK, **odor** US ['əʊdər] n [gen] olor m; [of perfume] fragancia f.

odourless UK, **odorless** US ['əʊdəlɪs] adj inodoro(ra).

odyssey ['ɒdɪsɪ] (pl **odysseys**) n liter odisea f.

OECD (abbr of Organization for Economic Cooperation and Development) n OCDE f.

oesophagus UK, **esophagus** US [ɪ'sɒfəgəs] n esófago m.

oestrogen UK, **estrogen** US [iː'strədʒən] n estrógeno m.

of (unstressed [əv], stressed [ɒv]) prep **- 1.** [gen] de; **the cover of a book** la portada de un libro; **the King of England** el rey de Inglaterra; **a cousin of mine** un primo mío; **both of us** nosotros dos, los dos; **the worst of them** el peor de ellos; **to die of sthg** morir de algo **- 2.** [expressing quantity, referring to container] de; **thousands of people** miles de personas; **there are three of us** somos tres; **a litre of petrol** un litro de gasolina; **a cup of coffee** un café, una taza de café **- 3.** [indicating amount, age, time] de; **a child of five** un niño de cinco (años); **at the age of five** a los cinco años; **an increase of 6%** un incremento del 6%; **the 12th of February** el 12 de febrero; **the night of the disaster** la noche del desastre **- 4.** [made from] de; **a dress of silk** un vestido de seda; **to be made of sthg** estar hecho de algo **- 5.** [with emotions,

opinions]: **fear of ghosts** miedo a los fantasmas; **love of good food** amor por la buena mesa; **it was very kind of you** fue muy amable de OR por tu parte.

off [ɒf] ◇ adv **- 1.** [away]: **to drive off** alejarse conduciendo; **to turn off** salir de la carretera; **I'm off!** ¡me voy! **- 2.** [at a distance - in time]: **it's two days off** quedan dos días; **that's a long time off** aún queda mucho para eso; [- in space]: **it's ten miles off** está a diez millas; **far off** lejos **- 3.** [so as to remove]: **to take sthg off** [gen] quitar algo; [one's clothes] quitarse algo; **to cut sthg off** cortar algo; **could you help me off with my coat?** ¿me ayudas a quitarme el abrigo? **- 4.** [so as to complete]: **to finish off** terminar, acabar; **to kill off** rematar **- 5.** [not at work] libre; **a day off** un día libre; **time off** tiempo m libre **- 6.** [so as to separate]: **to fence off** vallar; **to wall off** tapiar **- 7.** [so as to stop working]: **to turn off** [light, radio] apagar; [water, tap] cerrar **- 8.** [discounted]: **£10 off** 10 libras de descuento **- 9.** [having money]: **to be well/badly off** andar bien/mal de dinero. ◇ prep **- 1.** [away from]: **to get off sthg** bajarse de algo; **to keep off sthg** mantenerse alejado de algo; **'keep off the grass'** 'prohibido pisar el césped' **- 2.** [close to]: **just off the coast** muy cerca de la costa; **it's off Oxford Street** está al lado de Oxford Street **- 3.** [removed from]: **to cut a slice off sthg** cortar un pedazo de algo; **take your hands off me!** ¡quítame las manos de encima! **- 4.** [not attending]: **to be off work/duty** no estar trabajando/de servicio; **a day off work** un día de vacaciones **- 5.** inf [no longer liking]: **she's off coffee/her food** no le apetece café/comer **- 6.** [deducted from]: **there's 10% off the price** hay un 10% de rebaja sobre el precio **- 7.** inf [from]: **I bought it off him** se lo compré a él. ◇ adj **- 1.** [gone bad - meat, cheese] pasado(da), estropeado(da); [- milk] cortado(da) **- 2.** [light, radio, device] apagado(da); [water, electricity] desconectado(da); [tap] cerrado(da) **- 3.** [cancelled] suspendido(da); **the wedding's off** se ha cancelado la boda **- 4.** [not being served]: **the ice cream's off today** no hay helado hoy **- 5.** inf [offhand] brusco(ca), descortés.

offal ['ɒfl] n (U) asaduras fpl.

off-balance adv **- 1.** [not standing firmly] en equilibrio precario; **to throw** OR **push sb off-balance** hacer perder el equilibrio a alguien **- 2.** [unprepared] desprevenido(da).

offbeat ['ɒfbiːt] adj inf original, poco convencional.

off-centre ◇ adj descentrado(da). ◇ adv a un lado.

off-chance n: **on the off-chance** por si acaso.

off colour adj indispuesto(ta).

offcut ['ɒfkʌt] *n* [of fabric] retazo *m*; [of wood] trozo *m* suelto.

off-day *n* mal día *m*.

off duty *adj* [policeman] fuera de servicio; [soldier] de permiso.

offence *UK*, **offense** *US* [ə'fens] *n* - **1.** [crime] delito *m* - **2.** [cause of upset] ofensa *f*; **to cause sb offence** ofender a alguien; **to take offence** ofenderse.

offend [ə'fend] <> *vt* ofender. <> *vi* - **1.** [contravene]: **to offend against sthg** infringir algo - **2.** [commit a crime] cometer un delito.

offended [ə'fendɪd] *adj* ofendido(da).

offender [ə'fendər] *n* - **1.** [criminal] delincuente *mf* - **2.** [culprit] culpable *mf*.

offending [ə'fendɪŋ] *adj* [object] enojoso(sa); [word, statement] ofensivo(va).

offense *US n* - **1.** = **offence** - **2.** ['ɒfens] *SPORT* ataque *m*.

offensive [ə'fensɪv] <> *adj* - **1.** [remark, behaviour] ofensivo(va); [smell] repugnante - **2.** [aggressive] atacante. <> *n* - **1.** *MIL* ofensiva *f* - **2.** *fig* [attack]: **to go on** OR **take the offensive** tomar la ofensiva.

offensiveness [ə'fensɪvnɪs] *n*: **the offensiveness of** lo ofensivo de.

offer ['ɒfər] <> *n* oferta *f*; **on offer** [available] disponible; [at a special price] en oferta. <> *vt* ofrecer; **to offer sthg to sb, to offer sb sthg** ofrecer algo a alguien; [be willing]: **to offer to do sthg** ofrecerse a hacer algo. <> *vi* [volunteer] ofrecerse.

offering ['ɒfərɪŋ] *n* - **1.** [thing offered] ofrecimiento *m*; [gift] regalo *m* - **2.** [sacrifice] ofrenda *f*.

off-guard *adj* desprevenido(da).

offhand [,ɒf'hænd] <> *adj* frío(a), indiferente. <> *adv* de improviso.

office ['ɒfɪs] *n* - **1.** [gen] oficina *f* - **2.** [room] despacho *m*, oficina *f* - **3.** *US* [of doctor, dentist] consulta *f*, consultorio *m* - **4.** [position of authority] cargo *m*; **in office** [political party] en el poder; [person] en el cargo; **to take office** [political party] subir al poder; [person] asumir el cargo.

office automation *n* ofimática *f*.

office block *n* bloque *m* de oficinas.

office boy *n* chico *m* de los recados.

officeholder ['ɒfɪs,həʊldər] *n* alto cargo *m* gubernamental.

office hours *npl* horas *fpl* de oficina.

office junior *n* *UK* subalterno *m*, -na *f*, cadete *m* *R Plata*.

Office of Fair Trading *n* organismo gubernamental regulador de la competencia en Gran Bretaña.

officer ['ɒfɪsər] *n* - **1.** *MIL* oficial *mf* - **2.** [in organization, trade union] delegado *m*, -da *f* - **3.** [in police force] agente *mf*.

office work *n* trabajo *m* de oficina.

office worker *n* oficinista *mf*.

official [ə'fɪʃl] <> *adj* oficial. <> *n* [of government] funcionario *m*, -ria *f*; [of trade union] representante *mf*.

officialdom [ə'fɪʃəldəm] *n* burocracia *f*.

officially [ə'fɪʃəlɪ] *adv* oficialmente.

official receiver *n* síndico *m*, depositario *m*, -ria *f* judicial.

officiate [ə'fɪʃɪeɪt] *vi*: **to officiate (at)** oficiar (en).

officious [ə'fɪʃəs] *adj* pej que se excede en cumplir su deber.

offing ['ɒfɪŋ] *n*: **to be in the offing** estar al caer OR a la vista.

off-key <> *adj* desafinado(da). <> *adv* desafinadamente.

off-licence *n* *UK* tienda donde se venden bebidas alcohólicas para llevar.

off limits *adj* esp *US* prohibido(da).

off-line <> *adj* - **1.** [printer] desconectado(da) - **2.** [operation] fuera de línea. <> *adv*: **to go off-line** desconectarse.

offload [ɒf'ləʊd] *vt inf*: **to offload sthg onto sb** echarle a alguien algo encima.

off-peak <> *adj* [electricity, phone call, travel] de tarifa reducida; [period] económico(ca). <> *adv* en las horas de tarifa reducida.

off-putting [-,pʊtɪŋ] *adj* - **1.** [unpleasant] repelente, chocante - **2.** [distracting]: **it's very off-putting** me distrae mucho.

off-ramp *n* *US* carril *m* de deceleración OR de salida.

off sales *npl* *UK* venta de bebidas alcohólicas para llevar.

off season *n*: **the off season** la temporada baja.

➝ **off-season** *adj* de temporada baja.

offset ['ɒfset] (*pt* & *pp* **offset**, *cont* **-ting**) *vt* compensar, contrarrestar.

offshoot ['ɒfʃuːt] *n* vástago *m*, retoño *m*.

offshore ['ɒfʃɔːr] <> *adj* [wind] costero(ra); [fishing] de bajura; [oil rig] marítimo(ma); [banking] en bancos extranjeros. <> *adv* mar adentro, cerca de la costa; **two miles offshore** a dos millas de la costa.

offside <> *adj* [,ɒf'saɪd] - **1.** [part of vehicle - right-hand drive] izquierdo(da); [- left-hand drive] derecho(cha) - **2.** *SPORT* fuera de juego. <> *adv* [,ɒf'saɪd] *SPORT* fuera de juego. <> *n* ['ɒfsaɪd] [of vehicle - right-hand drive] lado *m* izquierdo; [- left-hand drive] lado *m* derecho.

offspring ['ɒfsprɪŋ] (*pl* **offspring**) *n* - **1.** [of people *fml* & *hum* [- child] descendiente *mf*; [- children] descendencia *f*, prole *f* - **2.** [of animals] crías *fpl*.

offstage [,ɒf'steɪdʒ] *adj* & *adv* entre bastidores.

off-the-peg *adj UK* confeccionado(da).

off-the-record <> *adj* extraoficial, oficioso(sa). <> *adv* extraoficialmente, oficiosamente.

off-the-wall *adj* descabellado(da), extravagante.

off-white *adj* blancuzco(ca).

OFGAS ['ɒfgæs] (*abbr of* Office of Gas Supply) *n organismo británico regulador del suministro de gas.*

OFLOT ['ɒflɒt] (*abbr of* Office of the National Lottery) *n organismo británico regulador de la lotería nacional.*

OFT *n abbr of* Office of Fair Trading.

OFTEL ['ɒftel] (*abbr of* Office of Telecommunications) *n organismo gubernamental británico para la supervisión de los servicios de telecomunicaciones.*

often ['ɒfn, 'ɒftn] *adv* [many times] a menudo; **how often do you go?** ¿cada cuánto OR con qué frecuencia vas?; **I don't often see him** no lo veo mucho; **I don't do it as often as I used to** no lo hago tanto como antes.
➡ **all too often** *adv* con demasiada frecuencia.
➡ **as often as not** *adv* con frecuencia, muchas veces.
➡ **every so often** *adv* cada cierto tiempo.
➡ **more often than not** *adv* la mayoría de las veces.

OFWAT ['ɒfwɒt] (*abbr of* Office of Water Supply) *n organismo gubernamental británico para la supervisión del suministro de agua.*

ogle ['əʊgl] *vt pej* comerse con los ojos.

ogre ['əʊgə] *n* [in fairy tales] ogro *m*.

oh [əʊ] *excl* - **1.** [to introduce comment] ¡ah!; **oh really?** ¿de verdad? - **2.** [expressing hesitation] mmm... - **3.** [expressing joy, surprise, fear] ¡oh!; **oh no!** ¡no!

OH *abbr of* Ohio.

Ohio [əʊ'haɪəʊ] *n* Ohio.

ohm [əʊm] *n* ohmio *m*.

OHMS (*abbr of* On His/Her Majesty's Service) *expresión que indica el carácter oficial de un documento en Gran Bretaña.*

oil [ɔɪl] <> *n* - **1.** [gen] aceite *m* - **2.** [petroleum] petróleo *m*. <> *vt* engrasar, lubricar.
➡ **oils** *npl* ART: **to paint in oils** pintar al óleo.

oilcan ['ɔɪlkæn] *n* aceitera *f*.

oil change *n* cambio *m* de aceite.

oilcloth ['ɔɪlklɒθ] *n* hule *m*.

oilfield ['ɔɪfiːld] *n* yacimiento *m* petrolífero.

oil filter *n* filtro *m* del aceite.

oil-fired [-,faɪəd] *adj* de fuel-oil.

oil industry *n*: **the oil industry** la industria petrolífera.

oilman ['ɔɪlmən] (*pl* **-men** [-mən]) *n* [businessman] magnate *m* del petróleo; [worker] trabajador *m* (del sector) petrolero.

oil paint *n* pintura *f* al óleo.

oil painting *n* (pintura *f* al) óleo *m*.

oilrig ['ɔɪlrɪg] *n* plataforma *f* petrolífera.

oilskins ['ɔɪlskɪnz] *npl* [coat] impermeable *m*, chubasquero *m*.

oil slick *n* marea *f* negra.

oil tanker *n* - **1.** [ship] petrolero *m* - **2.** [lorry] camión *m* cisterna.

oil well *n* pozo *m* petrolífero OR de petróleo.

oily ['ɔɪlɪ] (*comp* **-ier**, *superl* **-iest**) *adj* - **1.** [food] aceitoso(sa); [rag, cloth] grasiento(ta); [skin, hair] graso(sa) - **2.** *pej* [smarmy] empalagoso(sa).

ointment ['ɔɪntmənt] *n* pomada *f*, ungüento *m*.

OK[1]**, okay** [,əʊ'keɪ] *inf* <> *adj*: **I'm OK** estoy bien; **the food was OK** la comida no estuvo mal; **is it OK with you?** ¿te parece bien? <> *n* (*pl* **OKs**): **to give (sb) the OK** dar el visto bueno (a alguien). <> *adv* bastante bien. <> *excl* - **1.** [gen] vale, de acuerdo - **2.** [to introduce new topic] bien, vale. <> *vt* (*pt* & *pp* **OKed**, *cont* **OKing**) aprobar, dar el visto bueno a.

OK[2] *abbr of* Oklahoma.

Oklahoma [,əʊklə'həʊmə] *n* Oklahoma.

okra ['əʊkrə] *n* quingombó *m*.

old [əʊld] <> *adj* - **1.** [gen] viejo(ja); **how old are you?** ¿cuántos años tienes?, ¿qué edad tienes?; **I'm 20 years old** tengo 20 años; **an old woman** una vieja; **old people** las personas mayores; **when I'm older** cuando sea mayor - **2.** [former] antiguo(gua); **in the old days** antiguamente, en el pasado - **3.** *inf* [as intensifier]: **any old thing** cualquier cosa. <> *npl*: **the old** los ancianos.

old age *n* la vejez.

old age pension *n UK* jubilación *f*, pensión *f*.

old age pensioner *n UK* pensionista *mf*, jubilado *m*, -da *f*.

Old Bailey [-'beɪlɪ] *n*: **the Old Bailey** *el juzgado criminal central de Inglaterra.*

olden ['əʊldn] *adj*: **in the olden days** antaño.

old-fashioned [-'fæʃnd] *adj* - **1.** [outmoded] pasado(da) de moda, anticuado(da) - **2.** [traditional] antiguo(gua), tradicional.

old flame *n* antiguo amor *m*.

old hat *adj inf pej*: **to be old hat** estar muy visto(ta).

old maid n pej [spinster] vieja solterona f.

old master n - **1.** [painter] antiguo maestro m de la pintura - **2.** [painting] antigua obra f maestra de la pintura.

old people's home n residencia f OR hogar m de ancianos.

Old Testament n: the Old Testament el Antiguo Testamento.

old-time adj de antaño, antiguo(gua).

old-timer n - **1.** [veteran] veterano m, -na f - **2.** esp US [old man] viejo m, -ja f.

old wives' tale n cuento m de viejas.

Old World n: the Old World el Viejo Mundo.

O level n UK examen y calificación sobre una asignatura concreta que se pasaba a los 16 años.

oligarchy ['ɒlɪgɑːkɪ] (pl **-ies**) n oligarquía f.

olive ['ɒlɪv] <> adj: olive (green) verde oliva. <> n [fruit] aceituna f, oliva f; **olive (tree)** olivo m.

olive oil n aceite m de oliva.

Olympic [ə'lɪmpɪk] adj olímpico(ca).
◆ **Olympics** npl: the Olympics los Juegos Olímpicos.

Olympic Games npl: the Olympic Games los Juegos Olímpicos.

OM (abbr of Order of Merit) n (titular de) distinción honorífica británica.

Oman [əʊ'mɑːn] n Omán.

OMB (abbr of Office of Management and Budget) n organismo estadounidense de asesoramiento al presidente en materia presupuestaria.

ombudsman ['ɒmbʊdzmən] (pl **-men** [-mən]) n ≃ defensor m del pueblo.

omelet(te) ['ɒmlɪt] n tortilla f.

omen ['əʊmen] n presagio m.

ominous ['ɒmɪnəs] adj siniestro(tra), de mal agüero.

ominously ['ɒmɪnəslɪ] adv siniestramente, amenazadoramente.

omission [ə'mɪʃn] n omisión f.

omit [ə'mɪt] (pt & pp **-ted**, cont **-ting**) vt omitir; [name - from list] pasar por alto; **to omit to do sthg** no hacer algo.

omnibus ['ɒmnɪbəs] n - **1.** [book] antología f - **2.** UK RADIO & TV programa que emite todos los capítulos de la semana seguidos.

omnipotence [ɒm'nɪpətəns] n fml omnipotencia f.

omnipotent [ɒm'nɪpətənt] adj fml omnipotente.

omnipresent [,ɒmnɪ'prezənt] adj fml omnipresente.

omniscient [ɒm'nɪsɪənt] adj fml omnisciente.

omnivorous [ɒm'nɪvərəs] adj omnívoro(ra).

on [ɒn] <> prep - **1.** [indicating position - gen] en; [- on top of] sobre, en; **on a chair** en OR sobre una silla; **on the wall/ground** en la pared/el suelo; **to stand on one leg** ponerse a la pata coja; **he was lying on his side/back** estaba tumbado de costado/de espaldas; **she had a strange look on her face** su rostro tenía un extraño aspecto; **on the left/right** a la izquierda/derecha; **I haven't got any money on me** no llevo nada de dinero encima - **2.** [indicating means]: **it runs on diesel** funciona con diesel; **on TV/the radio** en la tele/la radio; **she's on the telephone** está al teléfono; **he lives on fruit** vive (a base) de fruta; **to hurt o.s. on sthg** hacerse daño con algo - **3.** [indicating mode of transport]: **to travel on a bus/train/ship** viajar en autobús/tren/barco; **I was on the bus** iba en el autobús; **to get on a bus/train/ship** subirse a un autobús/tren/barco; **on foot** a pie; **on horseback** a caballo - **4.** [indicating time, activity]: **on Thursday** el jueves; **on Thursdays** los jueves; **on my birthday** el día de mi cumpleaños; **on the 10th of February** el 10 de febrero; **on the 10th** el día 10; **on my return, on returning** al volver; **on business/holiday** de negocios/vacaciones - **5.** [concerning] sobre, acerca; **a book on astronomy** un libro acerca de OR sobre astronomía - **6.** [indicating membership]: **to be on a committee** estar en un comité - **7.** [indicating influence] en, sobre; **the impact on the environment** el impacto en OR sobre el medio ambiente - **8.** [using, supported by]: **to be on social security** cobrar dinero de la seguridad social; **he's on tranquillizers** está tomando tranquilizantes; **to be on drugs** [addicted] drogarse - **9.** [earning]: **she's on £25,000 a year** gana 25.000 libras al año; **to be on a low income** tener bajos ingresos - **10.** [obtained from]: **interest on investments** intereses de OR por inversiones; **a tax on alcohol** un impuesto sobre el alcohol - **11.** [referring to musical instrument] con; **on the violin** con el violín; **on the piano** al piano - **12.** inf [paid by]: **the drinks are on me** yo pago las copas, a las copas invito yo. <> adv - **1.** [indicating covering, clothing]: **put the lid on** pon la tapa; **what did she have on?** ¿qué llevaba encima OR puesto?; **put your coat on** ponte el abrigo - **2.** [being shown]: **what's on at the cinema?** ¿qué echan OR ponen en el cine? - **3.** [working - machine] funcionando; [- radio, TV, light] encendido(da); [- tap] abierto(ta); [- brakes] puesto(ta); **turn on the power** pulse el botón de encendido - **4.** [indicating continuing action]: **we talked/worked on into the night** seguimos hablando/trabajando hasta bien entrada la noche; **he kept on walking** siguió caminando - **5.** [forward]: **send**

my mail **on (to me)** reenvíame el correo; **later on** más tarde, después; **earlier on** antes - **6.** [of transport]: **the train stopped and we all got on** paró el tren y todos nos subimos - **7.** inf [referring to behaviour]: **it's just not on!** ¡es una pasada! - **8.** inf: **to be** OR **go on at sb (to do sthg)** darle la tabarra a alguien (para que haga algo).

◆ **from... on** adv: **from now on** de ahora en adelante; **from that moment/time on** desde aquel momento.

◆ **on about** adv inf: **to go on about sthg** dar la tabarra con algo.

◆ **on and on** adv: **to go on and on** seguir sin parar; **she chattered on and on** no paraba de charlar.

◆ **on and off** adv de vez en cuando.

◆ **on to, onto** (only written as **onto** for senses 4 and 5) prep - **1.** [to a position on top of] encima de, sobre; **she jumped on to the chair** salto encima de OR sobre la silla - **2.** [to a position on a vehicle]: **to get on to a bus/train/plane** subirse a un autobús/tren/avión - **3.** [to a position attached to] a; **stick the photo on to the page** pega la foto a la hoja - **4.** [aware of wrongdoing]: **to be onto sb** andar detrás de alguien - **5.** [into contact with]: **get onto the factory** ponte en contacto con la fábrica.

ON abbr of **Ontario**.

ONC (abbr of **Ordinary National Certificate**) n titulación técnica de enseñanza secundaria en Gran Bretaña.

once [wʌns] ◇ adv - **1.** [on one occasion] una vez; **once a week** una vez a la semana; **once again** OR **more** otra vez; **for once** por una vez; **more than once** más de una vez; **once and for all** de una vez por todas; **once or twice** alguna que otra vez; **once in a while** de vez en cuando - **2.** [previously] en otro tiempo, antiguamente; **once upon a time** érase una vez. ◇ conj una vez que; **once you have done it** una vez que lo hayas hecho.

◆ **at once** adv - **1.** [immediately] en seguida, inmediatamente - **2.** [at the same time] a la vez, al mismo tiempo; **all at once** de repente, de golpe.

once-over n inf: **to give sthg the once-over** echar un vistazo a algo.

oncoming ['ɒn,kʌmɪŋ] adj [traffic] que viene en dirección contraria.

OND (abbr of **Ordinary National Diploma**) n titulación superior que se obtiene tras dos años de formación técnica en Gran Bretaña.

one [wʌn] ◇ num [the number 1] un (una); **I only want one** sólo quiero uno; **one hundred** cien; **one thousand** mil; **one fifth** un quinto, una quinta parte; **one hundred** cien; **one of my friends** uno de mis amigos; **on page a hun-** dred and one en la página ciento uno; **(number) one** el uno; **to arrive in ones and twos** llegar poco a poco OR con cuentagotas. ◇ adj - **1.** [only] único(ca); **it's her one ambition** es su única ambición - **2.** [indefinite]: **one day we went to Athens** un día fuimos a Atenas; **one of these days** un día de éstos - **3.** inf [a]: **one hell of a bang/racket** una explosión/un jaleo de la leche. ◇ pron - **1.** [referring to a particular thing or person] uno (una); **I want the red one** yo quiero el rojo; **the one with the blond hair** la del pelo rubio; **which one do you want?** ¿cuál quieres?; **this one** éste (ésta); **that one** ése (ésa); **another one** otro (otra); **she's the one I told you about** es (ésa) de la que te hablé; **I'm not** OR **I've never been one to gossip, but...** yo no soy de ésos que van por ahí cotilleando, pero... - **2.** fml [you, anyone] uno (una); **to do one's duty** cumplir uno con su deber - **3.** inf [blow] tortazo m, galleta f; **she really thumped him one** le dio un galletón que no veas.

◆ **at one** adv: **to be at one with** estar completamente de acuerdo con.

◆ **for one** adv por lo menos, por mi/tu etc parte; **I for one remain unconvinced** yo, por lo menos OR por mi parte, sigo poco convencido.

◆ **one up on** adv: **to be** OR **have one up on sb** aventajar a alguien.

one-armed bandit n (máquina f) tragaperras f inv.

one-liner n golpe m.

one-man adj individual, en solitario.

one-man band n - **1.** [musician] hombre m orquesta - **2.** [business, operation] aventura f en solitario.

one-night stand n - **1.** [performance] representación f única - **2.** inf [sexual relationship] ligue m de una noche.

one-off inf ◇ adj excepcional. ◇ n caso m excepcional.

one-on-one US = **one-to-one**.

one-parent family n familia f monoparental.

one-piece adj de una pieza.

onerous ['əʊnərəs] adj oneroso(sa), pesado(da).

oneself [wʌn'self] pron - **1.** (reflexive, after prep) uno mismo (una misma); **to buy presents for oneself** hacerse regalos a sí mismo; **to take care of oneself** cuidarse - **2.** (for emphasis): **by oneself** [without help] solo(la).

one-sided [-'saɪdɪd] adj - **1.** [unequal] desigual - **2.** [biased] parcial.

onetime ['wʌntaɪm] adj [former] antiguo(gua).

one-to-one UK, **one-on-one** US adj [relationship] entre dos; [discussion] cara a cara; [tuition] individual.

one-touch dialling *UK,* **one-touch dialing** *US n* marcación *f* automática.

one-upmanship [ˌwʌnˈʌpmənʃɪp] *n habilidad para colocarse en una situación de ventaja.*

one-way *adj* - **1.** [street] de dirección única, de sentido único - **2.** [ticket] de ida.

ongoing [ˈɒnˌɡəʊɪŋ] *adj* [gen] en curso; [problem, situation] pendiente.

onion [ˈʌnjən] *n* cebolla *f.*

online [ˈɒnlaɪn] ⇔ *adj* COMPUT en línea; **to be online** estar conectado a Internet. ⇔ *adv* en línea; **to go online** conectarse a Internet.

online banking *n* banca *f* en línea.

online shopping *n* compras *fpl* en línea.

onlooker [ˈɒnˌlʊkəʳ] *n* espectador *m,* -ra *f.*

only [ˈəʊnlɪ] ⇔ *adj* único(ca); **to be an only child** ser hijo único. ⇔ *adv* - **1.** [exclusively] sólo, solamente; **I was only too willing to help** estaba encantado de poder ayudar; **I only wish I could!** ¡ojalá pudiera!; **it's only natural** es completamente normal; **it's only to be expected** no es de sorprender; **not only... but** no sólo... sino; **only just** apenas. ⇔ *conj* sólo que; **I would go, only I'm too tired** iría, lo que pasa es que estoy muy cansado.

o.n.o., ono (*abbr of* **or near(est) offer):** £50 **o.n.o.** 50 libras negociables.

on-ramp *n US* carril *m* de aceleración *OR* de incorporación.

onrush [ˈɒnrʌʃ] *n* avalancha *f.*

on-screen *adj* & *adv* COMPUT en pantalla.

onset [ˈɒnset] *n* comienzo *m.*

onshore [ˈɒnʃɔːʳ] ⇔ *adj* [wind] procedente del mar; [oil production] en tierra firme. ⇔ *adv* [blow] hacia la tierra; [produce oil] en tierra firme.

onside [ɒnˈsaɪd] *adj* & *adv* SPORT en posición legal *OR* correcta.

onslaught [ˈɒnslɔːt] *n lit* & *fig* acometida *f,* embestida *f.*

Ont. *abbr of* **Ontario.**

Ontario [ɒnˈteərɪəʊ] *n* Ontario.

on-the-job *adj* en el trabajo, práctico(ca).

on-the-spot *adj* en el acto.

onto (*unstressed before consonant* [ˈɒntə], *unstressed before vowel* [ˈɒntu], *stressed* [ˈɒntuː]) = **on to.**

onus [ˈəʊnəs] *n* responsabilidad *f;* **the onus is on you** en ti recae la responsabilidad.

onward [ˈɒnwəd] ⇔ *adj* [in space] hacia delante; [in time] progresivo(va). ⇔ *adv* = **onwards.**

onwards, onward [ˈɒnwədz] *adv* [in space] adelante, hacia delante; [in time]: **from now/then onwards** de ahora/allí en adelante.

onyx [ˈɒnɪks] *n* ónice *m.*

oodles [ˈuːdlz] *npl inf* montones *mpl.*

ooh [uː] *excl inf* ¡oh!

oops [ʊps, uːps] *excl inf* ¡uy!, ¡ay!

ooze [uːz] ⇔ *vt fig* rebosar. ⇔ *vi:* **to ooze (from** *OR* **out of)** rezumar (de); **to ooze with sthg** *fig* rebosar *OR* irradiar algo. ⇔ *n* cieno *m.*

opacity [əˈpæsətɪ] *n* - **1.** [non-transparency] opacidad *f* - **2.** *fig* [obscurity] obscuridad *f.*

opal [ˈəʊpl] *n* ópalo *m.*

opaque [əʊˈpeɪk] *adj* - **1.** [not transparent] opaco(ca) - **2.** *fig* [obscure] oscuro(ra).

open [ˈəʊpn] ⇔ *adj* - **1.** [gen] abierto(ta); [curtains] descorrido(da); [view, road] despejado(da) - **2.** [receptive]: **to be open to** [ideas, suggestions] estar abierto a; [blame, criticism, question] prestarse a; **to lay o.s. open to criticism** quedar expuesto a las críticas - **3.** [frank] sincero(ra), franco(ca) - **4.** [uncovered - car] descubierto(ta); **open fire** chimenea *f* - **5.** [available - subj: choice, chance]: **to be open to sb** estar disponible para alguien. ⇔ *n* - **1.: in the open** [fresh air] al aire libre; **to bring sthg out into the open** sacar a luz algo - **2.** SPORT open *m,* abierto *m.* ⇔ *vt* - **1.** [gen] abrir; **to open fire** abrir fuego - **2.** [curtains] correr - **3.** [inaugurate - public area, event] inaugurar - **4.** [negotiations] entablar. ⇔ *vi* - **1.** [door, flower] abrirse - **2.** [shop, office] abrir - **3.** [event, play] dar comienzo.

🔹 **open on to** *vt insep* dar a.

🔹 **open out** *vi* extenderse.

🔹 **open up** ⇔ *vt sep* abrir. ⇔ *vi* - **1.** [become available] surgir - **2.** [unlock door] abrir.

open-air *adj* al aire libre.

open-and-shut *adj* claro(ra).

opencast [ˈəʊpnkɑːst] *adj* a cielo abierto.

open day *n* jornada *f* de puertas abiertas.

open-ended [-ˈendɪd] *adj* abierto(ta).

opener [ˈəʊpnəʳ] *n* [gen] abridor *m;* [for tins] abrelatas *m inv;* [for bottles] abrebotellas *m inv.*

open-handed [-ˈhændɪd] *adj* generoso(sa).

openhearted [ˌəʊpnˈhɑːtɪd] *adj* franco(ca), sincero(ra).

open-heart surgery *n* cirugía *f* a corazón abierto.

opening [ˈəʊpnɪŋ] ⇔ *adj* inicial. ⇔ *n* - **1.** [beginning] comienzo *m,* principio *m* - **2.** [gap - in fence] abertura *f;* [- in clouds] claro *m* - **3.** [opportunity] oportunidad *f;* **opening for** oportunidad para - **4.** [job vacancy] puesto *m* vacante.

opening hours *npl* horario *m* de apertura).

opening night *n* noche *f* del estreno.

opening time *n UK* hora *f* de abrir.

open letter *n* carta *f* abierta.

openly [ˈəʊpnlɪ] *adv* abiertamente.

open market *n* mercado *m* abierto.

open marriage *n* matrimonio *m* abierto.

open-minded [-ˈmaɪndɪd] *adj* sin prejuicios.

open-mouthed [-'maʊðd] <> *adj* boquiabierto(ta). <> *adv*: **to stare open-mouthed** mirar boquiabierto(ta).

open-necked [-'nekt] *adj* con el cuello abierto.

openness ['əʊpənnɪs] *n* [frankness] franqueza *f*.

open-plan *adj* de planta abierta.

open prison *n* cárcel *f* de régimen abierto.

open sandwich *n* bocadillo con sólo un trozo de pan.

open season *n* temporada *f* (de caza).

open ticket *n* billete *f* abierto.

Open University *n UK*: **the Open University** ≃ la Universidad Nacional de Educación a Distancia.

open verdict *n LAW* fallo en que no se da la causa de la muerte.

opera ['ɒpərə] *n* ópera *f*.

opera glasses *npl* gemelos *mpl* (de teatro).

opera house *n* teatro *m* de la ópera.

opera singer *n* cantante *mf* de ópera.

operate ['ɒpəreɪt] <> *vt* **- 1.** [machine] hacer funcionar **- 2.** [business, system] dirigir; [service] proporcionar. <> *vi* **- 1.** [carry out trade, business] operar, actuar **- 2.** [function] funcionar **- 3.** MED: **to operate (on sb/sthg)** operar (a alguien/de algo).

operatic [,ɒpə'rætɪk] *adj* operístico(ca).

operating profit ['ɒpəreɪtɪŋ-] *n* beneficio *m* de explotación.

operating room ['ɒpəreɪtɪŋ-] *n US* = **operating theatre**.

operating system ['ɒpəreɪtɪŋ-] *n* COMPUT sistema *m* operativo.

operating theatre *UK*, **operating room** *US* ['ɒpəreɪtɪŋ-] *n* quirófano *m*.

operation [,ɒpə'reɪʃn] *n* **- 1.** [planned activity - police, rescue, business] operación *f*; [- military] maniobra *f* **- 2.** [running - of business] administración *f* **- 3.** [functioning - of machine] funcionamiento *m*; **to be in operation** [- machine] estar funcionando; [- law, system] estar en vigor **- 4.** MED operación *f*, intervención *f* quirúrgica; **to have an operation (for/on)** operarse (de).

operational [,ɒpə'reɪʃənl] *adj* **- 1.** [ready for use] en funcionamiento **- 2.** [concerning an operation] de operaciones.

operative ['ɒprətɪv] <> *adj* en vigor, vigente. <> *n* [worker] operario *m*, -ria *f*; [spy] agente *mf*.

operator ['ɒpəreɪtə] *n* **- 1.** TELEC operador *m*, -ra *f*, telefonista *mf* **- 2.** [worker] operario *m*, -ria *f* **- 3.** [company] operadora *f*.

operetta [,ɒpə'retə] *n* opereta *f*.

ophthalmic optician [ɒf'θælmɪk-] *n* óptico *m*, -ca *f*.

ophthalmologist [,ɒfθæl'mɒlədʒɪst] *n* oftalmólogo *m*, -ga *f*.

opinion [ə'pɪnjən] *n* opinión *f*; **to be of the opinion that** opinar OR creer que; **in my opinion** a mi juicio, en mi opinión; **what is her opinion of...?** ¿qué opina de...?

opinionated [ə'pɪnjəneɪtɪd] *adj pej* dogmático(ca).

opinion poll *n* sondeo *m*, encuesta *f*.

opium ['əʊpjəm] *n* opio *m*.

opponent [ə'pəʊnənt] *n* **- 1.** POL adversario *m*, -ria *f*; [of system, approach] opositor *m*, -ora *f* **- 2.** SPORT contrincante *mf*, adversario *m*, -ria *f*.

opportune ['ɒpətjuːn] *adj* oportuno(na).

opportunism [,ɒpə'tjuːnɪzm] *n* oportunismo *m*.

opportunist [,ɒpə'tjuːnɪst] *n* oportunista *mf*.

opportunity [,ɒpə'tjuːnətɪ] (*pl* **-ies**) *n* oportunidad *f*, ocasión *f*, chance *f* Amér; **to take the opportunity to do** OR **of doing sthg** aprovechar la ocasión de OR para hacer algo.

oppose [ə'pəʊz] *vt* oponerse a.

opposed [ə'pəʊzd] *adj* opuesto(ta); **to be opposed to** oponerse a; **as opposed to** en vez de, en lugar de; **I like beer as opposed to wine** me gusta la cerveza y no el vino.

opposing [ə'pəʊzɪŋ] *adj* opuesto(ta), contrario(ria).

opposite ['ɒpəzɪt] <> *adj* **- 1.** [facing - side, house] de enfrente; [- end] opuesto(ta) **- 2.** [very different]: **opposite (to)** opuesto(ta) OR contrario(ria) (a). <> *adv* enfrente. <> *prep* enfrente de. <> *n* contrario *m*; **the opposite** lo contrario; **Janet and John are complete opposites** Janet y John son totalmente diferentes.

opposite number *n* homólogo *m*, -ga *f*.

opposite sex *n*: **the opposite sex** el sexo opuesto.

opposition [,ɒpə'zɪʃn] *n* **- 1.** [gen] oposición *f* **- 2.** [opposing team]: **the opposition** los contrincantes.

➣ **Opposition** *n UK* POL: **the Opposition** la oposición.

oppress [ə'pres] *vt* **- 1.** [persecute] oprimir **- 2.** [depress] agobiar.

oppressed [ə'prest] <> *adj* oprimido(da). <> *npl*: **the oppressed** los oprimidos.

oppression [ə'preʃn] *n* opresión *f*.

oppressive [ə'presɪv] *adj* **- 1.** [unjust] tiránico(ca), opresivo(va) **- 2.** [stifling] agobiante, sofocante **- 3.** [causing unease] opresivo(va), agobiante.

oppressor [ə'presə] *n* opresor *m*, -ra *f*.

opt [ɒpt] <> *vt*: **to opt to do sthg** optar por OR elegir hacer algo. <> *vi*: **to opt for sthg** optar por OR elegir algo.

opt in *vi*: **to opt in (to sthg)** decidir participar (en algo).

opt out *vi*: **to opt out (of sthg)** decidir no participar (en algo).

optic ['ɒptɪk] *adj* óptico(ca).

optical ['ɒptɪkl] *adj* óptico(ca).

optical character reader *n* COMPUT lector *m* óptico de caracteres.

optical character recognition *n* COMPUT reconocimiento *m* óptico de caracteres.

optical fibre *n* fibra *f* óptica.

optical illusion *n* ilusión *f* óptica.

optician [ɒp'tɪʃn] *n* óptico *m*, -ca *f*; **the optician's (shop)** la óptica.

optics ['ɒptɪks] *n (U)* óptica *f*.

optimism ['ɒptɪmɪzm] *n* optimismo *m*.

optimist ['ɒptɪmɪst] *n* optimista *mf*.

optimistic [ˌɒptɪ'mɪstɪk] *adj* optimista; **to be optimistic about** ser optimista respecto a.

optimize, -ise ['ɒptɪmaɪz] *vt* optimizar.

optimum ['ɒptɪməm] *adj* óptimo(ma).

option ['ɒpʃn] *n* opción *f*; **to have the option to do** OR **of doing sthg** tener la opción OR la posibilidad de hacer algo; **to have no option** no tener otra opción.

optional ['ɒpʃənl] *adj* facultativo(va), optativo(va); **optional extra** extra *m* opcional.

opulence ['ɒpjʊləns] *n* opulencia *f*.

opulent ['ɒpjʊlənt] *adj* opulento(ta).

opus ['əʊpəs] *(pl* **-es** OR **opera**) *n* MUS opus *m inv*.

or [ɔːr] *conj* **- 1.** [gen] o; *(before 'o' or 'ho')* u; **or (else)** de lo contrario, si no; **he must be okay or he wouldn't be eating** debe estar bien, si no no comería **- 2.** *(after negative)*: **he cannot read or write** no sabe ni leer ni escribir.

OR *abbr of* **Oregon**.

oracle ['ɒrəkl] *n* oráculo *m*.

oral ['ɔːrəl] <> *adj* **- 1.** [spoken] oral **- 2.** [relating to the mouth] bucal. <> *n* examen *m* oral.

orally ['ɔːrəlɪ] *adv* **- 1.** [in spoken form] oralmente **- 2.** [via the mouth] por vía oral.

orange ['ɒrɪndʒ] <> *adj* naranja *(inv)*. <> *n* **- 1.** [fruit] naranja *f*; **orange tree** naranjo *m* **- 2.** [colour] color *m* naranja.

orangeade [ˌɒrɪndʒ'eɪd] *n* naranjada *f*.

orange blossom *n (U)* azahar *m*.

orange juice *n* zumo *m* de naranja.

Orangeman ['ɒrɪndʒmən] *(pl* **-men** [-mən]) *n* UK orangista *m*.

oration [ɔː'reɪʃn] *n fml* discurso *m*.

orator ['ɒrətər] *n* orador *m*, -ra *f*.

oratorio [ˌɒrə'tɔːrɪəʊ] *(pl* **-s**) *n* oratorio *m*.

oratory ['ɒrətrɪ] *n* oratoria *f*.

orb [ɔːb] *n* esfera *f*.

orbit ['ɔːbɪt] <> *n* órbita *f*; **to be in/go into orbit (around)** estar/entrar en órbita (alrededor de); **to put sthg into orbit (around)** poner algo en órbita (alrededor de). <> *vt* girar alrededor de.

orchard ['ɔːtʃəd] *n* huerto *m*.

orchestra ['ɔːkɪstrə] *n* **- 1.** orquesta *f* **- 2.** [in theatre] platea *f* OR patio *m* de butacas.

orchestral [ɔː'kestrəl] *adj* orquestal.

orchestra pit *n* foso *m* (de la orquesta).

orchestrate ['ɔːkɪstreɪt] *vt fig* & MUS orquestar.

orchestration [ˌɔːke'streɪʃn] *n fig* & MUS orquestación *f*.

orchid ['ɔːkɪd] *n* orquídea *f*.

ordain [ɔː'deɪn] *vt* **- 1.** *fml* [decree] decretar **- 2.** RELIG: **to be ordained** ordenarse (sacerdote).

ordeal [ɔː'diːl] *n* calvario *m*.

order ['ɔːdər] <> *n* **- 1.** [instruction] orden *f*; **to be under orders to do sthg** tener órdenes de hacer algo **- 2.** COMM [request] pedido *m*; **to be on order** estar pedido; **to order** por encargo **- 3.** [in restaurant] ración *f*; **can I take your order now?** ¿ya ha decidido lo que va a tomar? **- 4.** [sequence, discipline, system] orden *m*; **in order** en orden; **out of order** desordenado(da); **in order of importance** por orden de importancia; **to keep order** mantener el orden **- 5.** [fitness for use]: **in working order** en funcionamiento; **'out of order'** 'no funciona'; **to be out of order** [not working] estar estropeado(da); [incorrect behaviour] ser improcedente; **in order** [correct] en regla **- 6.** RELIG orden *f*. <> *vt* **- 1.** [command]: **to order sb (to do sthg)** ordenar a alguien (que haga algo); **to order that** ordenar que **- 2.** [request - drink, taxi] pedir **- 3.** COMM pedir, encargar **- 4.** [put in order] ordenar. <> *vi* pedir.

orders *npl* RELIG: **(holy) orders** órdenes *fpl* sagradas.

in the order of UK, **on the order of** US *prep* del orden de.

in order that *conj* para que.

in order to *conj* para.

order about, order around *vt sep* mangonear.

order book *n* libro *m* de pedidos.

order form *n* hoja *f* de pedido.

orderly ['ɔːdəlɪ] <> *adj* [person, crowd] disciplinado(da), pacífico(ca); [room] ordenado(da). <> *n (pl* **-ies)** **- 1.** [in hospital] auxiliar *mf* sanitario **- 2.** [in army] ordenanza *mf*.

order number *n* número *m* de pedido.

ordinal ['ɔːdɪnl] <> *adj* ordinal. <> *n* ordinal *m*.

ordinarily ['ɔːdənrəlɪ] *adv* ordinario, generalmente.

ordinary ['ɔ:dənrɪ] ⟨⟩ adj - **1.** [normal] corriente, normal - **2.** pej [unexceptional] mediocre, ordinario(ria). ⟨⟩ n: **out of the ordinary** fuera de lo común.

ordinary level n UK examen y calificación sobre una asignatura concreta que se pasaba a los 16 años.

ordinary shares npl UK FIN acciones fpl ordinarias.

ordination [,ɔ:dɪ'neɪʃn] n ordenación f.

ordnance ['ɔ:dnəns] n (U) - **1.** [military supplies] pertrechos mpl de guerra - **2.** [artillery] artillería f.

Ordnance Survey n UK: the Ordnance Survey servicio oficial de topografía y cartografía.

ore [ɔ:ʳ] n mineral m.

oregano [,ɒrɪ'gɑ:nəʊ] n orégano m.

Oregon ['ɒrɪgən] n Oregón.

organ ['ɔ:gən] n [gen, ANAT & MUS] órgano m.

organic [ɔ:'gænɪk] adj - **1.** [gen] orgánico(ca) - **2.** [food] ecológico(ca), orgánico(ca).

organic farming n agricultura f ecológica.

organically [ɔ:'gænɪklɪ] adv orgánicamente.

organic chemistry n química f orgánica.

organism ['ɔ:gənɪzm] n organismo m.

organist ['ɔ:gənɪst] n organista mf.

organization [,ɔ:gənaɪ'zeɪʃn] n organización f.

organizational [,ɔ:gənaɪ'zeɪʃnl] adj organizativo(va).

organize, -ise ['ɔ:gənaɪz] ⟨⟩ vt organizar. ⟨⟩ vi organizarse, sindicarse.

organized ['ɔ:gənaɪzd] adj organizado(da).

organized crime n crimen m organizado.

organizer ['ɔ:gənaɪzəʳ] n organizador m, -ra f.

organza [ɔ:'gænzə] n organza f.

orgasm ['ɔ:gæzm] n orgasmo m.

orgy ['ɔ:dʒɪ] (pl **-ies**) n lit & fig orgía f.

orient ['ɔ:rɪənt] vt esp US = **orientate**.

Orient ['ɔ:rɪənt] n: the Orient el Oriente.

oriental [,ɔ:rɪ'entl] ⟨⟩ adj oriental. ⟨⟩ n oriental mf (atención: el término 'oriental' se considera racista).

orientate ['ɔ:rɪenteɪt], **orient** vt orientar; to orientate o.s. orientarse.

orientation [,ɔ:rɪen'teɪʃn] n orientación f.

orienteering [,ɔ:rɪən'tɪərɪŋ] n deporte m de orientación.

orifice ['ɒrɪfɪs] n orificio m.

origami [,ɒrɪ'gɑ:mɪ] n papiroflexia f.

origin ['ɒrɪdʒɪn] n origen m; **country of origin** país m de origen.

◆ **origins** npl origen m.

original [ə'rɪdʒənl] ⟨⟩ adj original; **the original owner** el primer propietario. ⟨⟩ n original m.

originality [ə,rɪdʒə'nælətɪ] n originalidad f.

originally [ə'rɪdʒənəlɪ] adv [at first] originariamente; [with originality] originalmente.

original sin n pecado m original.

originate [ə'rɪdʒəneɪt] ⟨⟩ vt originar, producir. ⟨⟩ vi: **to originate (in)** nacer OR surgir (de); **to originate from** nacer OR surgir de.

originator [ə'rɪdʒəneɪtəʳ] n autor m, -ra f, inventor m, -ra f.

Orinoco [,ɒrɪ'nəʊkəʊ] n: the (River) Orinoco el (río) Orinoco.

Orkney Islands ['ɔ:knɪ-], **Orkneys** ['ɔ:knɪz] npl: the Orkney Islands las Orcadas.

ornament ['ɔ:nəmənt] n adorno m.

ornamental [,ɔ:nə'mentl] adj ornamental, decorativo(va).

ornamentation [,ɔ:nəmen'teɪʃn] n ornamentación f, adorno m.

ornate [ɔ:'neɪt] adj [style] recargado(da); [decoration, vase] muy vistoso(sa).

ornately [ɔ:'neɪtlɪ] adv vistosamente.

ornery ['ɔ:nərɪ] adj US inf borde.

ornithologist [,ɔ:nɪ'θɒlədʒɪst] n ornitólogo m, -ga f.

ornithology [,ɔ:nɪ'θɒlədʒɪ] n ornitología f.

orphan ['ɔ:fn] ⟨⟩ n huérfano m, -na f. ⟨⟩ vt: **to be orphaned** quedarse huérfano.

orphanage ['ɔ:fənɪdʒ] n orfelinato m, orfanato m.

orthodontist [,ɔ:θə'dɒntɪst] n ortodontista mf.

orthodox ['ɔ:θədɒks] adj ortodoxo(xa).

Orthodox Church n: the Orthodox Church la Iglesia Ortodoxa.

orthodoxy ['ɔ:θədɒksɪ] n ortodoxia f.

orthopaedic, orthopedic [,ɔ:θə'pi:dɪk] adj ortopédico(ca).

orthopaedics [,ɔ:θə'pi:dɪks] n (U) ortopedia f.

orthopaedist [,ɔ:θə'pi:dɪst] n ortopedista mf.

orthopedic [,ɔ:θə'pi:dɪk] = **orthopaedic**.

OS n abbr of Ordnance Survey. abbr of operating system.

Oscar ['ɒskəʳ] n CIN Oscar m.

oscillate ['ɒsɪleɪt] vi lit & fig: **to oscillate (between)** oscilar (entre).

oscilloscope [ɒ'sɪləskəʊp] n osciloscopio m.

OSD (abbr of optical scanning device) n LO m.

OSHA (abbr of Occupational Safety and Health Administration) n organismo estadounidense de seguridad e higiene laborales.

Oslo ['ɒzləʊ] n Oslo.

osmosis [ɒz'məʊsɪs] n ósmosis f inv.

osprey ['ɒsprɪ] (pl **ospreys**) n águila f pescadora.

Ostend [ɒs'tend] n Ostende.

ostensible [ɒ'stensəbl] adj aparente.

ostensibly [ɒ'stensəblɪ] adv aparentemente.

ostentation [ˌɒstən'teɪʃn] n ostentación f.

ostentatious [ˌɒstən'teɪʃəs] adj ostentoso(sa).

osteoarthritis [ˌɒstɪəʊɑː'θraɪtɪs] n osteoartritis f inv.

osteopath ['ɒstɪəpæθ] n osteópata mf.

osteopathy [ˌɒstɪ'ɒpəθɪ] n osteopatía f.

ostracize, -ise ['ɒstrəsaɪz] vt [colleague etc] marginar, hacer el vacío a; POL condenar al ostracismo.

ostrich ['ɒstrɪtʃ] n avestruz m.

OT n - **1.** (abbr of **Old Testament**) A.T. m - **2.** abbr of **occupational therapy**.

OTC (abbr of **Officer Training Corps**) n unidad de formación de oficiales del ejército británico.

other ['ʌðə^r] ⟨⟩ adj otro (otra); **the other one** el otro (la otra); **the other three** los otros tres; **the other day** el otro día; **the other week** hace unas semanas. ⟨⟩ pron - **1.** [different one]: **others** otros(otras) - **2.** [remaining, alternative one]: **the other** el otro (la otra); **the others** los otros (las otras), los demás (las demás); **one after the other** uno tras otro; **one or other** uno u otro; **to be none other than** no ser otro sino.

◆ **something or other** pron una cosa u otra.

◆ **somehow or other** adv de una u otra forma.

◆ **other than** conj excepto, salvo; **other that** por lo demás.

otherwise ['ʌðəwaɪz] ⟨⟩ adv - **1.** [or else] si no - **2.** [apart from that] por lo demás - **3.** [differently] de otra manera; **deliberately or otherwise** adrede o no. ⟨⟩ conj si no, de lo contrario.

other world n: **the other world** el otro mundo, el más allá.

otherworldly [ˌʌðə'wɜːldlɪ] adj espiritual, poco realista.

OTT (abbr of **over the top**) adj UK inf: **it's a bit OTT** eso es pasarse un poco de la raya.

Ottawa ['ɒtəwə] n Ottawa.

otter ['ɒtə^r] n nutria f.

OU n abbr of **Open University**.

ouch [aʊtʃ] excl ¡ay!

ought [ɔːt] aux vb deber; **you ought to go/to be nicer** deberías irte/ser más amable; **she ought to pass the exam** debería aprobar el examen; **it ought to be fun** promete ser divertido.

oughtn't [ɔːtnt] (abbr of = **ought not**), ⟩ **ought**.

Ouija board® ['wiːdʒə-] n tablero m de ouija.

ounce [aʊns] n - **1.** [unit of measurement] = 28,35g, ≈ onza f - **2.** fig [small amount] pizca f.

our ['aʊə^r] poss adj nuestro(tra), nuestros(tras) (pl); **our money** nuestro dinero; **our house** nuestra casa; **our children** nuestros hijos; **it wasn't our fault** no fue culpa nuestra OR nuestra culpa; **we washed our hair** nos lavamos el pelo.

ours ['aʊəz] poss pron nuestro(tra); **that money is ours** ese dinero es nuestro; **those keys are ours** esas llaves son nuestras; **it wasn't their fault, it was OURS** no fue culpa de ellos sino de nosotros; **a friend of ours** un amigo nuestro; **their car hit ours** suyo coche chocó contra el nuestro.

ourselves [aʊə'selvz] pron - **1.** (reflexive) nos mpl & fpl; (after prep) nosotros mpl, nosotras f - **2.** (for emphasis) nosotros mismos mpl, nosotras mismas f; **we did it by ourselves** lo hicimos nosotros solos.

oust [aʊst] vt fml: **to oust sb (from)** [job] desbancar a alguien (de); [land] desalojar a alguien (de).

ouster ['aʊstə^r] n US [from country] expulsión f; [from office] destitución f.

out [aʊt] adv - **1.** [not inside, out of doors] fuera; **we all went out** todos salimos fuera; **I'm going out for a walk** voy a salir a dar un paseo; **they ran out** salieron corriendo; **he poured the water out** sirvió el agua; **out here/there** aquí/allí fuera; **out you go!** ¡hala, afuera! - **2.** [away from home, office] fuera; **John's out at the moment** John está fuera ahora mismo; **don't stay out too late** no estés fuera hasta muy tarde; **an afternoon out** una tarde fuera - **3.** [extinguished] apagado(da); **the fire went out** el fuego se apagó - **4.** [of tides]: **the tide had gone out** la marea estaba baja - **5.** [out of fashion] pasado(da) de moda - **6.** [published, released - book] publicado(da); **they've a new record out** han sacado un nuevo disco - **7.** [in flower] en flor; **the blossom's out already** ya ha florecido - **8.** [visible]: **the moon's out** ha salido la luna - **9.** inf [on strike] en huelga - **10.** [not possible]: **sorry, that's out** lo siento, pero eso no se puede hacer - **11.** [determined]: **to be out to do sthg** estar decidido(da) a hacer algo.

◆ **out of** prep - **1.** [away from, outside] fuera de; **I was out of the country** estaba fuera del país; **to go out of the room** salir de la habitación - **2.** [indicating cause] por; **out of spite/love** por rencor/amor - **3.** [indicating origin, source] de; **a page out of a book** una página de un libro; **to drink out of a glass** beber del vaso; **to get information out of sb** sacar información a alguien **- 4.** [without] sin; **we're out of sugar** estamos sin azúcar, se nos ha acabado el azúcar **- 5.** [made from] de; **it's made out of plastic** está hecho de plástico **- 6.** [using] de; **we can pay for it out of petty cash** podemos pagarlo con el dinero para gastos **- 7.** [sheltered from] a resguardo de; **we're out of the wind here** aquí estamos resguardados del viento **- 8.** [to indicate proportion]: **one out of ten people** una de cada diez personas; **ten out of ten** [mark] diez de OR sobre diez.

out-and-out *adj* [disgrace, lie] infame; [liar, crook] redomado(da).

outback ['aʊtbæk] *n*: **the outback** los llanos del interior de Australia.

outbid [,aʊt'bɪd] (*pt & pp* **outbid**, *cont* **-ding**) *vt*: **to outbid sb (for)** pujar más alto que alguien (por).

outboard (motor) ['aʊtbɔ:d-] *n* (motor *m*) fueraborda *m*.

outbound ['aʊtbaʊnd] *adj* [train, flight] de ida; [traffic] de salida.

outbreak ['aʊtbreɪk] *n* [of war] comienzo *m*; [of crime] ola *f*; [of illness] oleada *f*, epidemia *f*; [of spots] erupción *f*.

outbuildings ['aʊtbɪldɪŋz] *npl* dependencias *fpl*.

outburst ['aʊtbɜ:st] *n* **- 1.** [sudden expression of emotion] explosión *f*, arranque *m* **- 2.** [sudden occurrence] estallido *m*.

outcast ['aʊtkɑ:st] *n* marginado *m*, -da *f*, paria *mf*.

outclass [,aʊt'klɑ:s] *vt* aventajar en OR con mucho.

outcome ['aʊtkʌm] *n* resultado *m*.

outcrop ['aʊtkrɒp] *n* afloramiento *m*.

outcry ['aʊtkraɪ] (*pl* **-ies**) *n* protestas *fpl*.

outdated [,aʊt'deɪtɪd] *adj* anticuado(da), pasado(da) de moda.

outdid [,aʊt'dɪd] *pt* ▷ **outdo**.

outdistance [,aʊt'dɪstəns] *vt lit & fig* dejar atrás.

outdo [,aʊt'du:] (*pt* **-did**, *pp* **-done** [-dʌn]) *vt* aventajar, superar.

outdoor ['aʊtdɔ:r] *adj* [life, swimming pool] al aire libre; [clothes] de calle.

outdoors [aʊt'dɔ:z] *adv* al aire libre; **let's eat outdoors** vamos a comer fuera.

outer ['aʊtər] *adj* exterior, externo(na); **Outer London** las afueras de Londres.

Outer Mongolia *n* Mongolia Exterior.

outermost ['aʊtəməʊst] *adj* [layer] más exterior; [place, planet] más remoto(ta).

outer space *n* espacio *m* exterior.

outfit ['aʊtfɪt] *n* **- 1.** [clothes] conjunto *m*, traje *m* **- 2.** *inf* [organization] grupo *m*, equipo *m*.

outfitters ['aʊt,fɪtəz] *n dated* tienda *f* de confección.

outflank [,aʊt'flæŋk] *vt* **- 1.** MIL sorprender por la retaguardia **- 2.** *fig* [in argument, business] superar.

outgoing ['aʊt,gəʊɪŋ] *adj* **- 1.** [chairman] saliente **- 2.** [train] de salida **- 3.** [sociable] extrovertido(da), abierto(ta).

➤ **outgoings** *npl UK* gastos *mpl*.

outgrow [,aʊt'grəʊ] (*pt* **-grew**, *pp* **-grown**) *vt* **- 1.** [grow too big for]: **he has outgrown his shirts** las camisas se le han quedado pequeñas **- 2.** [grow too old for] ser demasiado mayor para.

outhouse (['aʊthaʊs], *pl* [-haʊzɪz]) *n* dependencia *f*.

outing ['aʊtɪŋ] *n* **- 1.** [trip] excursión *f* **- 2.** [of homosexuals] *revelación de la condición homosexual*.

outlandish [aʊt'lændɪʃ] *adj* extravagante, estrafalario(ria).

outlast [,aʊt'lɑ:st] *vt* sobrevivir a, durar más tiempo que.

outlaw ['aʊtlɔ:] ⬦ *n* proscrito *m*, -ta *f*. ⬦ *vt* **- 1.** [make illegal] ilegalizar **- 2.** [declare an outlaw] proscribir, declarar fuera de la ley.

outlay ['aʊtleɪ] *n* desembolso *m*, inversión *f*.

outlet ['aʊtlet] *n* **- 1.** [for emotions] salida *f*, desahogo *m* **- 2.** [for water] desagüe *m*; [for gas] salida *f* **- 3.** [shop] punto *m* de venta **- 4.** *US* ELEC toma *f* de corriente.

outline ['aʊtlaɪn] ⬦ *n* **- 1.** [brief description] esbozo *m*, resumen *m*; **in outline** en líneas generales **- 2.** [silhouette] contorno *m*. ⬦ *vt* **- 1.** [describe briefly] esbozar, resumir **- 2.** [silhouette]: **to be outlined against** perfilarse contra.

outlive [,aʊt'lɪv] *vt* **- 1.** [subj: person] sobrevivir a **- 2.** [subj: idea, object] durar más tiempo que.

outlook ['aʊtlʊk] *n* **- 1.** [attitude, disposition] enfoque *m*, actitud *f* **- 2.** [prospect] perspectiva *f* (de futuro).

outlying ['aʊt,laɪɪŋ] *adj* [remote] lejano(na), remoto(ta); [on edge of town] periférico(ca).

outmanoeuvre *UK*, **outmaneuver** *US* [,aʊtmə'nu:vər] *vt* superar estratégicamente.

outmoded [,aʊt'məʊdɪd] *adj* anticuado(da), pasado(da) de moda.

outnumber [,aʊt'nʌmbər] *vt* exceder en número.

out-of-date *adj* **- 1.** [clothes, belief] anticuado(da), anticuado(da), pasado(da) de moda **- 2.** [passport, season ticket] caducado(da).

out of doors *adv* al aire libre.

out-of-the-way adj [far away] remoto(ta), aislado(da); [unusual] poco común.

outpace [,aʊt'peɪs] vt lit & fig dejar atrás.

outpatient ['aʊt,peɪʃnt] n paciente externo m, paciente externa f.

outplay [,aʊt'pleɪ] vt superar, jugar mejor que.

outpost ['aʊtpəʊst] n puesto m avanzado.

outpouring ['aʊt,pɔːrɪŋ] n liter efusión f.

output ['aʊtpʊt] ◇ n - **1.** [production] producción f, rendimiento m - **2.** [COMPUT - printing out] salida f; [- printout] impresión f. ◇ vt COMPUT imprimir.

outrage ['aʊtreɪdʒ] ◇ n - **1.** [anger] indignación f - **2.** [atrocity] atrocidad f, escándalo m. ◇ vt ultrajar, atropellar.

outraged ['aʊtreɪdʒd] adj indignado(da).

outrageous [aʊt'reɪdʒəs] adj - **1.** [offensive, shocking] indignante, escandaloso(sa) - **2.** [very unusual] extravagante.

outran [,aʊt'ræn] pt ▷ outrun.

outrank [,aʊt'ræŋk] vt ser de categoría superior a.

outrider ['aʊt,raɪdəʳ] n [on motorcycle] escolta m en moto; [on horse] escolta a caballo.

outright ◇ adj ['aʊtraɪt] - **1.** [categoric] categórico(ca) - **2.** [total - disaster] completo(ta); [- victory, winner] indiscutible. ◇ adv [,aʊt'raɪt] - **1.** [ask] abiertamente; [deny] francamente, categóricamente - **2.** [win, ban] totalmente; [be killed] completamente, en el acto.

outrun [,aʊt'rʌn] (pt -ran, pp -run, cont -ning) vt correr más que.

outsell [,aʊt'sel] (pt & pp -sold) vt vender más que.

outset ['aʊtset] n: at the outset al principio; from the outset desde el principio.

outshine [,aʊt'ʃaɪn] (pt & pp -shone [-'ʃɒn]) vt fig eclipsar.

outside ◇ adj ['aʊtsaɪd] - **1.** [gen] exterior - **2.** [opinion, criticism] independiente - **3.** [chance] remoto(ta). ◇ adv [,aʊt'saɪd] fuera; to go/run/look outside ir/correr/mirar fuera. ◇ prep ['aʊtsaɪd] fuera de; we live half an hour outside London vivimos a media hora de Londres. ◇ n ['aʊtsaɪd] - **1.** [exterior] exterior m - **2.** [limit]: at the outside a lo sumo.
 ◆ outside of prep US [apart from] aparte de.

outside broadcast n UK RADIO & TV emisión f desde exteriores.

outside lane n carril m de adelantamiento.

outside line n línea f exterior.

outsider [,aʊt'saɪdəʳ] n - **1.** [stranger] forastero m, -ra f, desconocido m, -da f - **2.** [in horse race] caballo que no es uno de los favoritos.

outsize ['aʊtsaɪz] adj - **1.** [bigger than usual] enorme - **2.** [clothes] de talla muy grande.

outsized ['aʊtsaɪzd] adj enorme.

outskirts ['aʊtskɜːts] npl: the outskirts las afueras.

outsmart [,aʊt'smɑːt] vt ser más listo(ta) que.

outsold [,aʊt'səʊld] pt & pp ▷ outsell.

outsource ['aʊtsɔːs] vt COMM subcontratar.

outspoken [,aʊt'spəʊkn] adj abierto(ta), franco(ca).

outspread [,aʊt'spred] adj extendido(da), desplegado(da).

outstanding [,aʊt'stændɪŋ] adj - **1.** [excellent] destacado(da) - **2.** [not paid, unfinished] pendiente.

outstay [,aʊt'steɪ] vt: to outstay one's welcome quedarse más tiempo de lo debido.

outstretched [,aʊt'stretʃt] adj extendido(da).

outstrip [,aʊt'strɪp] (pt & pp -ped, cont -ping) vt lit & fig aventajar, dejar atrás.

out-take n CIN & TV descarte m.

outvote [,aʊt'vəʊt] vt: to be outvoted perder en una votación.

outward ['aʊtwəd] ◇ adj - **1.** [journey] de ida - **2.** [composure, sympathy] aparente - **3.** [sign, proof] visible, exterior. ◇ adv US = outwards.

outwardly ['aʊtwədlɪ] adv [apparently] aparentemente, de cara al exterior.

outwards UK ['aʊtwədz], **outward** US adv hacia fuera.

outweigh [,aʊt'weɪ] vt pesar más que.

outwit [,aʊt'wɪt] (pt & pp -ted, cont -ting) vt ser más listo(ta) que.

outworker ['aʊt,wɜːkəʳ] n colaborador externo m, colaboradora externa f.

oval ['əʊvl] ◇ adj oval, ovalado(da). ◇ n óvalo m.

Oval Office n: the Oval Office el Despacho Oval, oficina que tiene el presidente de Estados Unidos en la Casa Blanca.

ovarian [əʊ'veərɪən] adj [gen] ovárico(ca); [cancer] de ovario.

ovary ['əʊvərɪ] (pl -ies) n ovario m.

ovation [əʊ'veɪʃn] n ovación f; a standing ovation una ovación de gala (con el público en pie).

oven ['ʌvn] n horno m.

oven glove n guante m para el horno.

ovenproof ['ʌvnpruːf] adj refractario(ria).

oven-ready adj listo(ta) para meter al horno.

ovenware ['ʌvnweəʳ] n (U) utensilios mpl para el horno.

over ['əʊvəʳ] ◇ prep - **1.** [directly above, on top of] encima de; a fog hung over the river una espesa niebla flotaba sobre el río; put your coat over the chair pon el abrigo encima de la silla - **2.** [to cover] sobre; she wore a veil over her face un velo le cubría el rostro - **3.** [on other side of] al otro lado de; **he lives over the road** vive enfrente - **4.** [across surface of] por encima de; **they sailed over the ocean** cruzaron el océano en barco - **5.** [more than] más de; **over and above** además de - **6.** [senior to] por encima de - **7.** [with regard to] por; **a fight over a woman** una pelea por una mujer - **8.** [during] durante; **over the weekend** (en) el fin de semana. ⬦ *adv* - **1.** [short distance away]: **over here** aquí; **over there** allí - **2.** [across]: **to cross over** cruzar; **to go over** ir - **3.** [down]: **to fall over** caerse; **to push over** empujar, tirar - **4.** [round]: **to turn sthg over** dar la vuelta a algo; **to roll over** darse la vuelta - **5.** [more] más - **6.** [remaining]: **to be (left) over** quedar, sobrar - **7.** [at sb's house]: **over at Mum's** en casa de mamá; **invite them over** invítalos a casa - **8.** RADIO: **over (and out)!** ¡cambio (y cierro)! - **9.** [involving repetitions]: **(all) over again** otra vez desde el principio; **over and over (again)** una y otra vez. ⬦ *adj* [finished] terminado(da). ⬦ *n* en críquet, serie de seis lanzamientos de un mismo jugador.

➡ **all over** ⬦ *prep* por todo(da). ⬦ *adv* [everywhere] por todas partes. ⬦ *adj* [finished] terminado(da), acabado(da).

over- ['əʊvə'] *prefix* sobre-, super-.

overabundance [,əʊvərə'bʌndəns] *n* superabundancia *f*.

overact [,əʊvər'ækt] *vi pej* [in play] sobreactuar, exagerar.

overactive [,əʊvər'æktɪv] *adj* demasiado activo(va).

overall ⬦ *adj* ['əʊvərɔːl] [general] global, total. ⬦ *adv* [,əʊvər'ɔːl] en conjunto, en general. ⬦ *n* ['əʊvərɔːl] - **1.** [gen] guardapolvo *m*, bata *f* - **2.** US [for work] mono *m*.

➡ **overalls** *npl* - **1.** [for work] mono *m* - **2.** US [dungarees] pantalones *mpl* de peto.

overambitious [,əʊvəræm'bɪʃəs] *adj* demasiado ambicioso(sa).

overanxious [,əʊvər'æŋkʃəs] *adj* demasiado preocupado(da).

overarm ['əʊvərɑːm] *adj* & *adv* por encima del hombro.

overate [,əʊvər'et] *pt* ⬡ **overeat**.

overawe [,əʊvər'ɔː] *vt* intimidar.

overbalance [,əʊvə'bæləns] *vi* perder el equilibrio.

overbearing [,əʊvə'beərɪŋ] *adj pej* déspotico(ca).

overblown [,əʊvə'bləʊn] *adj pej* exagerado(da).

overboard ['əʊvəbɔːd] *adv*: **to fall overboard** caer al agua OR por la borda; **to go overboard (about sb/sthg)** *inf* [be over-enthusiastic about] ponerse como loco(ca) (con alguien/algo).

overbook [,əʊvə'bʊk] *vi* hacer overbooking.

overburden [,əʊvə'bɜːdn] *vt*: **to be overburdened with sthg** estar sobrecargado(da) de algo.

overcame [,əʊvə'keɪm] *pt* ⬡ **overcome**.

overcapitalize, -ise [,əʊvə'kæpɪtəlaɪz] *vt* & *vi* FIN sobrecapitalizar.

overcast ['əʊvəkɑːst] *adj* cubierto(ta), nublado(da).

overcharge [,əʊvə'tʃɑːdʒ] ⬦ *vt*: **to overcharge sb (for sthg)** cobrar a alguien en exceso (por algo). ⬦ *vi*: **to overcharge (for sthg)** cobrar en exceso (por algo).

overcoat ['əʊvəkəʊt] *n* abrigo *m*.

overcome [,əʊvə'kʌm] (*pt* -**came**, *pp* -**come**) *vt* - **1.** [deal with] vencer, superar - **2.** [overwhelm]: **to be overcome (by** OR **with)** [fear, grief, emotion] estar abrumado(da) (por); [smoke, fumes] estar asfixiado(da) (por).

overcompensate [,əʊvə'kɒmpənseɪt] *vi*: **to overcompensate (for sthg)** compensar en exceso (por algo).

overconfident [,əʊvə'kɒnfɪdənt] *adj* demasiado confiado(da).

overcook [,əʊvə'kʊk] *vt* hacer demasiado.

overcrowded [,əʊvə'kraʊdɪd] *adj* [room] atestado(da) de gente; [country] superpoblado(da).

overcrowding [,əʊvə'kraʊdɪŋ] *n* [of country] superpoblación *f*; [of prison] hacinamiento *m*.

overdeveloped [,əʊvədə'veləpt] *adj* - **1.** PHOT sobreprocesado(da) - **2.** [too high, too big] excesivo(va).

overdo [,əʊvə'duː] (*pt* -**did** [-dɪd], *pp* -**done**) *vt* - **1.** *pej* [exaggerate] exagerar - **2.** [do too much]: **to overdo one's work/the walking** trabajar/andar demasiado; **to overdo it** pasarse - **3.** [overcook] hacer demasiado.

overdone [,əʊvə'dʌn] ⬦ *pp* ⬡ **overdo**. ⬦ *adj* muy hecho(cha).

overdose ⬦ *n* ['əʊvədəʊs] sobredosis *f inv*. ⬦ *vi* [əʊvə'dəʊs]: **to overdose on** tomar una sobredosis de.

overdraft ['əʊvədrɑːft] *n* [sum owed] saldo *m* deudor; [loan arranged] (giro *m* OR crédito *m* en) descubierto *m*.

overdrawn [,əʊvə'drɔːn] *adj*: **to be overdrawn** tener un saldo deudor.

overdrive ['əʊvədraɪv] *n fig*: **to go into overdrive** ir a marchas forzadas.

overdue [,əʊvə'djuː] *adj* - **1.** [late]: **to be overdue** [train] ir con retraso; [library book] estar con el plazo de préstamo caducado; **I'm overdue (for) a bit of luck** va siendo hora de tener un poco de suerte - **2.** [awaited]: **(long) overdue** (largamente) esperado(da), ansiado(da) - **3.** [unpaid] vencido(da) y sin pagar.

overeager [ˌəʊvər'iːgər] *adj* demasiado ansioso(sa).

overeat [ˌəʊvər'iːt] (*pt* **-ate**, *pp* **-eaten**) *vi* comer con exceso, atracarse.

overemphasize, -ise [ˌəʊvər'emfəsaɪz] *vt* poner demasiado énfasis en.

overenthusiastic [ˈəʊvərɪnˌθjuːzɪ'æstɪk] *adj* demasiado entusiasta.

overestimate [ˌəʊvər'estɪmeɪt] *vt* sobreestimar.

overexcited [ˌəʊvərɪk'saɪtɪd] *adj* sobreexcitado(da).

overexpose [ˌəʊvərɪk'spəʊz] *vt* PHOT sobreexponer.

overfeed [ˌəʊvə'fiːd] (*pt & pp* **-fed** [-fed]) *vt* sobrealimentar.

overfill [ˌəʊvə'fɪl] *vt* llenar demasiado.

overflow ◇ *vi* [ˌəʊvə'fləʊ] **- 1.** [spill over] rebosar; [river] desbordarse **- 2.** [go beyond limits]: **to overflow (into)** rebosar (hacia) **- 3.** [be very full]: **to be overflowing (with)** rebosar (de); **full to overflowing** lleno a rebosar. ◇ *vt* [ˌəʊvə'fləʊ] desbordarse de, salir de. ◇ *n* ['əʊvəfləʊ] [pipe] cañería *f* de desagüe.

overgrown [ˌəʊvə'grəʊn] *adj* cubierto(ta) de matojos.

overhang ◇ *n* ['əʊvəhæŋ] saliente *m*. ◇ *vt* [ˌəʊvə'hæŋ] (*pt & pp* **-hung**) sobresalir por encima de. ◇ *vi* [ˌəʊvə'hæŋ] (*pt & pp* **-hung**) sobresalir.

overhaul ◇ *n* ['əʊvəhɔːl] **- 1.** [of car, machine] revisión *f* **- 2.** [of method, system] repaso *m* general. ◇ *vt* [ˌəʊvə'hɔːl] revisar.

overhead ◇ *adj* ['əʊvəhed] aéreo(a). ◇ *adv* [ˌəʊvə'hed] por lo alto, por encima. ◇ *n* ['əʊvəhed] (*U*) US gastos *mpl* generales.

◆ **overheads** *npl* gastos *mpl* generales.

overhead projector *n* retroproyector *m*.

overhear [ˌəʊvə'hɪər] (*pt & pp* **-heard** [-hɜːd]) *vt* oír por casualidad.

overheat [ˌəʊvə'hiːt] ◇ *vt* recalentar. ◇ *vi* recalentarse.

overhung [ˌəʊvə'hʌŋ] *pt & pp* ▷ **overhang**.

overindulge [ˌəʊvərɪn'dʌldʒ] ◇ *vt* mimar excesivamente. ◇ *vi*: **to overindulge (in sthg)** abusar (de algo).

overjoyed [ˌəʊvə'dʒɔɪd] *adj*: **to be overjoyed (at sthg)** estar encantado(da) (con algo).

overkill ['əʊvəkɪl] *n* exageración *f*, exceso *m*.

overladen [ˌəʊvə'leɪdn] ◇ *pp* ▷ **overload**. ◇ *adj* sobrecargado(da).

overlaid [ˌəʊvə'leɪd] *pt & pp* ▷ **overlay**.

overland ['əʊvəlænd] ◇ *adj* terrestre. ◇ *adv* por tierra.

overlap ◇ *n* ['əʊvəlæp] **- 1.** [similarity] coincidencia *f* **- 2.** [overlapping part, amount] superposición *f*. ◇ *vt* [ˌəʊvə'læp] (*pt & pp* **-ped**,

cont **-ping**) **- 1.** [cover] superponerse a **- 2.** [be similar to] coincidir en parte con. ◇ *vi* [ˌəʊvə'læp] (*pt & pp* **-ped**, *cont* **-ping**) **- 1.** [cover each other] superponerse **- 2.** [be similar]: **to overlap (with sthg)** coincidir en parte (en algo).

overlay [ˌəʊvə'leɪ] (*pt & pp* **-laid**) *vt*: **to be overlaid with** estar revestido(da) de.

overleaf [ˌəʊvə'liːf] *adv* al dorso, a la vuelta.

overload [ˌəʊvə'ləʊd] (*pp* **-loaded** OR **-laden**) *vt* sobrecargar; **to be overloaded (with sthg)** estar sobrecargado (de algo).

overlong [ˌəʊvə'lɒŋ] ◇ *adj* demasiado largo(ga). ◇ *adv* demasiado tiempo.

overlook [ˌəʊvə'lʊk] *vt* **- 1.** [look over] mirar OR dar a **- 2.** [disregard, miss] pasar por alto, no considerar **- 3.** [forgive] perdonar.

overlord ['əʊvələːd] *n fml* señor *m*.

overly ['əʊvəlɪ] *adv* demasiado.

overmanning [ˌəʊvə'mænɪŋ] *n* exceso *m* de mano de obra.

overnight ◇ *adj* ['əʊvənaɪt] **- 1.** [for all of night] de noche, nocturno(na) **- 2.** [for a night's stay - clothes] para una noche; **overnight bag** bolso *m* de viaje **- 3.** [very sudden] súbito(ta), de la noche a la mañana. ◇ *adv* [ˌəʊvə'naɪt] **- 1.** [for all of night] durante la noche **- 2.** [very suddenly] de la noche a la mañana.

overpaid [ˌəʊvə'peɪd] ◇ *pt & pp* ▷ **overpay**. ◇ *adj* pagado(da) en exceso.

overpass ['əʊvəpɑːs] *n* US paso *m* elevado.

overpay [ˌəʊvə'peɪ] (*pt & pp* **-paid**) *vt* pagar en exceso.

overplay [ˌəʊvə'pleɪ] *vt* exagerar.

overpopulated [ˌəʊvə'pɒpjʊleɪtɪd] *adj* superpoblado(da).

overpower [ˌəʊvə'paʊər] *vt* **- 1.** [in fight] vencer, subyugar **- 2.** *fig* [overwhelm] sobreponerse a, vencer.

overpowering [ˌəʊvə'paʊərɪŋ] *adj* arrollador(ra), abrumador(ra).

overpriced [ˌəʊvə'praɪst] *adj* de precio excesivo.

overproduction [ˌəʊvəprə'dʌkʃn] *n* exceso *m* de producción, superproducción *f*.

overprotective [ˌəʊvəprə'tektɪv] *adj* que protege excesivamente.

overran [ˌəʊvə'ræn] *pt* ▷ **overrun**.

overrated [ˌəʊvə'reɪtɪd] *adj* sobreestimado(da).

overreach [ˌəʊvə'riːtʃ] *vt*: **to overreach o.s.** extralimitarse, ir demasiado lejos.

overreact [ˌəʊvərɪ'ækt] *vi*: **to overreact (to sthg)** reaccionar demasiado (a algo).

override [ˌəʊvə'raɪd] (*pt* **-rode**, *pp* **-ridden**) *vt* **- 1.** [be more important than] predominar sobre **- 2.** [overrule] desautorizar.

overriding [,əʊvə'raɪdɪŋ] *adj* predominante.

overripe [,əʊvə'raɪp] *adj* pasado(da), demasiado maduro(ra).

overrode [,əʊvə'rəʊd] *pt* ▷ override.

overrule [,əʊvə'ruː] *vt* [person] desautorizar; [decision] anular; [request] denegar.

overrun [,əʊvə'rʌn] ◇ *vt* (*pt* **-ran**, *pp* **-run**, *cont* **-running**) - **1.** MIL [enemy, army] apabullar, arrasar; [country] ocupar, invadir - **2.** *fig* [cover]: **to be overrun with** estar invadido(da) de. ◇ *vi* (*pt* **-ran**, *pp* **-run**, *cont* **-running**) rebasar el tiempo previsto.

oversaw [,əʊvə'sɔː] *pt* ▷ oversee.

overseas ◇ *adj* ['əʊvəsiːz] - **1.** [in or to foreign countries - market] exterior; [- sales, aid] al extranjero; [- network, branches] en el extranjero - **2.** [from abroad] extranjero(ra). ◇ *adv* [,əʊvə'siːz] [go, travel] al extranjero; [study, live] en el extranjero.

oversee [,əʊvə'siː] (*pt* **-saw**, *pp* **-seen** [-'siːn]) *vt* supervisar.

overseer ['əʊvə,siːəʳ] *n* supervisor *m*, -ra *f*.

overshadow [,əʊvə'ʃædəʊ] *vt* - **1.** [be taller than] ensombrecer, eclipsar - **2.** [be more important than]: **to be overshadowed by** ser eclipsado(da) por - **3.** [mar]: **to be overshadowed by sthg** ser ensombrecido(da) por algo.

overshoot [,əʊvə'ʃuːt] (*pt* & *pp* **-shot**) *vt* [go past] pasarse.

oversight ['əʊvəsaɪt] *n* descuido *m*.

oversimplification ['əʊvə,sɪmplɪfɪ'keɪʃn] *n* simplificación *f* excesiva.

oversimplify [,əʊvə'sɪmplɪfaɪ] (*pt* & *pp* **-ied**) *vt* & *vi* simplificar demasiado.

oversleep [,əʊvə'sliːp] (*pt* & *pp* **-slept** [-'slept]) *vi* no despertarse a tiempo, quedarse dormido(da).

overspend [,əʊvə'spend] (*pt* & *pp* **-spent** [-'spent]) *vi* gastar más de la cuenta.

overspill ['əʊvəspɪl] *n* exceso *m* de población.

overstaffed [,əʊvə'stɑːft] *adj* con exceso de empleados.

overstate [,əʊvə'steɪt] *vt* exagerar.

overstay [,əʊvə'steɪ] *vt*: **to overstay one's welcome** quedarse más tiempo de lo debido.

overstep [,əʊvə'step] (*pt* & *pp* **-ped**, *cont* **-ping**) *vt* pasar de; **to overstep the mark** pasarse de la raya.

overstock [,əʊvə'stɒk] *vt* abarrotar.

overstrike ['əʊvəstraɪk] ◇ *n* COMPUT superposición *f*. ◇ *vt* (*pt* & *pp* **-struck**) COMPUT superponer.

oversubscribed [,əʊvəsʌb'skraɪbd] *adj* suscrito(ta) en exceso.

overt ['əʊvɜːt] *adj* abierto(ta), evidente.

overtake [,əʊvə'teɪk] ◇ *vt* (*pt* **-took**, *pp* **-taken** [-'teɪkn]) - **1.** AUT adelantar - **2.** [subj: event] sorprender, coger de improviso - **3.** [subj: emotion] abrumar, apabullar. ◇ *vi* (*pt* **-took**, *pp* **-taken** [-'teɪkn]) AUT adelantar.

overtaking [,əʊvə'teɪkɪŋ] *n* adelantamiento *m*; **'no overtaking'** 'prohibido adelantar'.

overthrow ◇ *n* ['əʊvəθrəʊ] [of government] derrocamiento *m*, derrumbamiento *m*. ◇ *vt* [,əʊvə'θrəʊ] (*pt* **-threw**, *pp* **-thrown**) - **1.** [oust] derrocar - **2.** [idea, standard] echar abajo.

overtime ['əʊvətaɪm] ◇ *n* (*U*) - **1.** [extra work] horas *fpl* extra - **2.** US SPORT (tiempo *m* de) descuento *m*. ◇ *adv*: **to work overtime** trabajar horas extra.

overtly ['əʊvɜːtlɪ] *adv* abiertamente, públicamente.

overtones ['əʊvətəʊnz] *npl* tono *m*, matiz *m*.

overtook [,əʊvə'tʊk] *pt* ▷ overtake.

overture ['əʊvə,tjʊəʳ] *n* MUS obertura *f*.
➤ **overtures** *npl*: **to make overtures to sb** hacer una propuesta a alguien.

overturn [,əʊvə'tɜːn] ◇ *vt* - **1.** [turn over] volcar - **2.** [overrule] rechazar - **3.** [overthrow] derrocar, derrumbar. ◇ *vi* [vehicle] volcar; [boat] zozobrar.

overuse [,əʊvə'juːz] *vt* usar demasiado.

overview ['əʊvəvjuː] *n* visión *f* general OR de conjunto.

overweening [,əʊvə'wiːnɪŋ] *adj* desmesurado(da).

overweight [,əʊvə'weɪt] *adj* grueso(sa), gordo(da).

overwhelm [,əʊvə'welm] *vt* - **1.** [make helpless] abrumar - **2.** [defeat] aplastar, arrollar.

overwhelming [,əʊvə'welmɪŋ] *adj* - **1.** [despair, kindness] abrumador(ra) - **2.** [defeat, majority] contundente, aplastante.

overwhelmingly [,əʊvə'welmɪŋlɪ] *adv* abrumadoramente.

overwork [,əʊvə'wɜːk] ◇ *n* trabajo *m* excesivo. ◇ *vt* - **1.** [give too much work to] hacer trabajar demasiado - **2.** [overuse] usar demasiado. ◇ *vi* trabajar demasiado.

overwrought [,əʊvə'rɔːt] *adj* *fml* nerviosísimo(ma), sobreexcitado(da).

ovulate ['ɒvjʊleɪt] *vi* ovular.

ovulation [,ɒvjʊ'leɪʃn] *n* ovulación *f*.

ow [aʊ] *excl* ¡ay!

owe [əʊ] *vt*: **to owe sthg to sb, to owe sb sthg** deber algo a alguien.

owing ['əʊɪŋ] *adj* que se debe.
➤ **owing to** *prep* debido a, por causa de.

owl [aʊl] *n* búho *m*, lechuza *f*, tecolote *m* *Amér C* & *Méx*.

own [əʊn] <> *adj*: **my/your/his** *etc* **own car** mi/tu/su *etc* propio coche. <> *pron*: **my own** el mío (la mía); **his/her own** el suyo (la suya); **a house of my/his own** mi/su propia casa; **on one's own** solo(la); **to get one's own back** *inf* tomarse la revancha, desquitarse. <> *vt* poseer, tener.

➥ **own up** *vi*: **to own up (to sthg)** confesar (algo).

own brand *n* COMM marca *f* propia (del comerciante).

owner ['əʊnəʳ] *n* propietario *m*, -ria *f*.

owner-occupier *n esp UK* persona que ha comprado la vivienda en la que habita.

ownership ['əʊnəʃɪp] *n* propiedad *f*.

own goal *n esp UK* - **1.** FTBL gol *m* en propia meta, autogol *m* - **2.** *UK fig* [foolish mistake] metedura *f* de pata, metida *f* de pata *Amér*.

ox [ɒks] (*pl* **oxen**) *n* buey *m*.

Oxbridge ['ɒksbrɪdʒ] *n (U)* las universidades de Oxford y Cambridge.

Oxbridge

Oxbridge designa conjuntamente las Universidades de Oxford y Cambridge, las más antiguas y prestigiosas de Inglaterra. Aparte de éstas, hasta el s. XIX las universidades que había en las Islas Británicas se hallaban en Escocia y Dublín. Oxford y Cambridge experimentaron un gran crecimiento tanto en su tamaño como en sus recursos económicos de la mano de acaudalados benefactores que apadrinaban la fundación de nuevos colegios universitarios. Hoy en día Oxford tiene cuarenta colegios universitarios y Cambrigde treinta y uno; este curioso sistema de agrupación de colegios universitarios las distingue de las demás universidades británicas. Hasta hace poco, un título de Oxbridge era prácticamente indispensable para quien aspirase a una posición prominente entre la clase dirigente. Incluso hoy en día, aunque otras universidades se encuentran a la par o incluso superan a Oxford y Cambridge en determinadas áreas académicas, Oxbridge continúa conservando ese prestigio mitad académico mitad social. Aunque ambas han realizado notables esfuerzos para captar estudiantes provenientes de la enseñanza pública, la verdad es que hoy por hoy la mitad de sus estudiantes vienen del sector privado, el cual, a su vez, reúne únicamente al 10 por ciento de los escolares británicos.

oxen ['ɒksn] *npl* ⊳ **ox**.

Oxfam ['ɒksfæm] *n* sociedad benéfica de ayuda a países subdesarrollados.

oxide ['ɒksaɪd] *n* óxido *m*.

oxidize, -ise ['ɒksɪdaɪz] *vi* oxidarse.

Oxon (*abbr of* **Oxfordshire**) *condado inglés.*

Oxon. (*abbr of* **Oxoniensis**) *de o relativo a Oxford, esp su universidad.*

oxtail soup ['ɒksteɪl-] *n* sopa *f* de rabo de buey.

ox tongue *n* lengua *f* de buey.

oxyacetylene [,ɒksɪə'setɪli:n] <> *n* oxiacetileno *m*. <> *comp* oxiacetilénico(ca).

oxygen ['ɒksɪdʒən] *n* oxígeno *m*.

oxygenate ['ɒksɪdʒəneɪt] *vt* oxigenar.

oxygen mask *n* máscara *f* de oxígeno.

oxygen tent *n* tienda *f* de oxígeno.

oyster ['ɔɪstəʳ] *n* ostra *f*.

oz. *abbr of* **ounce**.

ozone ['əʊzəʊn] *n* ozono *m*.

ozone-friendly *adj* que no daña a la capa de ozono.

ozone layer *n* capa *f* de ozono.

P

p¹ (*pl* **p's** OR **ps**), **P** (*pl* **P's** OR **Ps**) [pi:] *n* [letter] p *f*, P *f*.

p² - **1.** (*abbr of* **page**) p., pág. - **2.** *UK abbr of* **penny, pence.**

pa [pɑ:] *n esp US inf* papá *m*.

p.a. (*abbr of* **per annum**) p.a.

PA <> *n* - **1.** *UK abbr of* **personal assistant** - **2.** *abbr of* **public-address system.** <> *abbr of* **Pennsylvania.**

pace [peɪs] <> *n* paso *m*, ritmo *m*; **she did it at her own pace** lo hizo a su ritmo; **to keep pace (with sthg)** [change, events] mantenerse al corriente (de algo); **to keep pace (with sb)** seguir el ritmo (a alguien). <> *vt* pasearse por. <> *vi*: **to pace (up and down)** pasearse de un lado a otro.

pacemaker ['peɪs,meɪkəʳ] *n* - **1.** MED marcapasos *m inv* - **2.** [in race] liebre *f*.

pacesetter ['peɪs,setəʳ] *n US* [in race] liebre *f*.

pachyderm ['pækɪdɜ:m] *n* paquidermo *m*.

Pacific [pə'sɪfɪk] <> *adj* del Pacífico. <> *n*: **the Pacific (Ocean)** el (océano) Pacífico.

pacification [ˌpæsɪfɪ'keɪʃn] *n fml* - **1.** [calming] apaciguamiento *m* - **2.** [bringing of peace] pacificación *f*.

pacifier ['pæsɪfaɪəʳ] *n US* [for child] chupete *m*.

pacifism ['pæsɪfɪzm] *n* pacifismo *m*.

pacifist ['pæsɪfɪst] *n* pacifista *mf*.

pacify ['pæsɪfaɪ] (*pt & pp* -ied) *vt* - **1.** [person, mob] calmar, apaciguar - **2.** [country, area] pacificar.

pack [pæk] ◇ *n* - **1.** [bundle] lío *m*, fardo *m*; [rucksack] mochila *f* - **2.** *esp US* [packet] paquete *m* - **3.** [of cards] baraja *f* - **4.** [of dogs] jauría *f*; [of wolves] manada *f*; *pej* [of people] banda *f*; **a pack of lies** una sarta de mentira - **5.** [of cyclists, runners] pelotón *m* - **6.** RUGBY delanteros *mpl*. ◇ *vt* - **1.** [for journey - bags, suitcase] hacer; [- clothes etc] meter (en la maleta) - **2.** [put in parcel] empaquetar; [put in container] envasar - **3.** [fill] llenar, abarrotar; **to be packed into sthg** estar apretujados dentro de algo. ◇ *vi* hacer las maletas, hacer el equipaje.

➡ **pack in** *inf* ◇ *vt sep UK* [stop] dejar; **pack it in!** ¡déjalo!, ¡ya basta! ◇ *vi* [break down] escacharrarse.

➡ **pack off** *vt sep inf* enviar, mandar.

➡ **pack up** ◇ *vt sep* - **1.** [for journey] meter en la maleta - **2.** *UK inf* [stop] dejar. ◇ *vi* - **1.** [for journey] hacer las maletas - **2.** *inf* [finish work] terminar de currar - **3.** *UK inf* [break down] escacharrarse - **4.** *inf* [stop] parar.

package ['pækɪdʒ] ◇ *n* [gen & COMPUT] paquete *m*. ◇ *vt* [wrap up] envasar.

package deal *n* convenio *m* OR acuerdo *m* global.

package holiday *n UK* paquete *m* turístico.

packager ['pækɪdʒəʳ] *n* - **1.** [person packaging] empaquetador *m*, -ra *f* - **2.** COMM productora *f* independiente.

package tour *n* paquete *m* turístico, vacaciones *fpl* con todo incluido.

packaging ['pækɪdʒɪŋ] *n* [wrapping] envasado *m*.

packed [pækt] *adj*: **packed (with)** repleto(ta) (de).

packed lunch *n UK* almuerzo preparado de antemano que se lleva uno al colegio, la oficina etc.

packed-out *adj UK inf* a tope, de bote en bote.

packet ['pækɪt] *n* - **1.** [gen] paquete *m*; [of crisps, sweets] bolsa *f* - **2.** *UK inf* [lot of money] dineral *m*; **to cost a packet** costar un dineral; **to earn or make a packet** ganar una fortuna.

pack ice *n* (*U*) banco *m* de hielo.

packing ['pækɪŋ] *n* - **1.** [protective material] embalaje *m* - **2.** [for journey]: **to do the packing** hacer el equipaje.

packing case *n* cajón *m* de embalaje.

pact [pækt] *n* pacto *m*.

pad [pæd] ◇ *n* - **1.** [of material] almohadilla *f*; **shin pad** espinillera *f*; **shoulder pad** hombrera *f* - **2.** [of cotton wool] tampón *m* - **3.** [of paper] bloc *m* - **4.** [of spacecraft]: **(launch) pad** plataforma *f* (de lanzamiento) - **5.** *US* [sanitary napkin] compresa *f*, toalla *f* higiénica *Amér* - **6.** *UK* [of cat, dog] almohadilla *f* - **7.** *inf dated* [home] casa *f*. ◇ *vt* (*pt & pp* -ded, *cont* -ding) acolchar, rellenar. ◇ *vi* (*pt & pp* -ded, *cont* -ding) [walk softly] andar con suavidad.

➡ **pad out** *vt sep* [fill out] meter paja en.

padded ['pædɪd] *adj* [shoulders] con hombreras; [chair] acolchado(da).

padded cell *n* celda *f* acolchada.

padding ['pædɪŋ] *n* (*U*) - **1.** [in jacket, chair] relleno *m* - **2.** [in speech] paja *f*.

paddle ['pædl] ◇ *n* - **1.** [for canoe, dinghy] pala *f*, canalete *m*; *US* [for table tennis] pala *f* - **2.** [walk in sea] paseo *m* por la orilla. ◇ *vt US* remar en. ◇ *vi* - **1.** [in canoe] remar - **2.** [duck] chapotear - **3.** [person - in sea] pasear por la orilla.

paddle boat, paddle steamer *n* vapor *m* de paletas OR ruedas.

paddling pool ['pædlɪŋ-] *n UK* - **1.** [inflatable] piscina *f* inflable - **2.** [in park] piscina *f* infantil.

paddock ['pædək] *n* - **1.** [small field] potrero *m*, corral *m* - **2.** [at racecourse] paddock *m*.

paddy field ['pædɪ-] *n* arrozal *m*.

paddy wagon ['pædɪ-] *n US* [Black Maria] coche *m* celular, furgón *m* policial.

padlock ['pædlɒk] ◇ *n* candado *m*. ◇ *vt* cerrar con candado.

paederast ['pedəræst] *n UK* = **pederast**.

paediatric [ˌpi:dɪ'ætrɪk] *adj UK* = **pediatric**.

paediatrician [ˌpi:dɪə'trɪʃn] *n UK* = **pediatrician**.

paediatrics [ˌpi:dɪ'ætrɪks] *UK* = **pediatrics**.

paedophile ['pi:dəfaɪl] *n UK* = **pedophile**.

paella [paɪ'elə] *n* paella *f*.

paeony ['pi:ənɪ] *n UK* = **peony**.

pagan ['peɪɡən] ◇ *adj* pagano(na). ◇ *n* pagano *m*, -na *f*.

paganism ['peɪɡənɪzm] *n* paganismo *m*.

page [peɪdʒ] ◇ *n* [of book, newspaper] página *f*; **on page ten** en la página diez. ◇ *vt* - **1.** [in hotel, airport] llamar por megafonía - **2.** [using an electronic pager] llamar por el busca.

pageant ['pædʒənt] *n* procesión *f*, desfile *m*.

pageantry ['pædʒəntrɪ] *n* boato *m*, pompa *f*.

page boy *n* - **1.** *UK* [at wedding] paje *m* - **2.** [hairstyle] peinado *m* estilo paje.

pager ['peɪdʒəʳ] *n* busca *m*, buscapersonas *m* *inv*.

pagination [,pædʒɪ'neɪʃn] *n* paginación *f*.

pagoda [pə'gəʊdə] *n* pagoda *f*.

paid [peɪd] ⬦ *pt* & *pp* ⊳ **pay**. ⬦ *adj* [holiday, leave] pagado(da); [work, staff] remunerado(da); **badly/well paid** mal/bien pagado.

paid-up *adj UK*: **a paid-up member** un afiliado.

pail [peɪl] *n* cubo *m*.

pain [peɪn] ⬦ *n* - **1.** [ache] dolor *m*; **to be in pain** sufrir dolor - **2.** [mental suffering] pena *f*, sufrimiento *m* - **3.** *inf* [annoyance - person] pesado *m*, -da *f*; [- thing] pesadez *f*; **a pain in the neck** [- person] un pesado (una pesada); [- thing] una lata, un latazo. ⬦ *vt fml*: **to pain sb (to do sthg)** dolerle a alguien (hacer algo).

⬦ **pains** *npl* [effort, care] esfuerzos *mpl*; **to be at pains to do sthg** afanarse por hacer algo; **to take pains to do sthg** esforzarse en hacer algo; **he got absolutely nothing for his pains** tantas molestias y no obtuvo nada de nada.

pained [peɪnd] *adj* apenado(da).

painful ['peɪnfʊl] *adj* [back, eyes] dolorido(da); [injury, exercise, memory] doloroso(sa); **my shoes are painful** los zapatos me hacen daño; **that's painful** eso me duele.

painfully ['peɪnfʊlɪ] *adv* - **1.** [causing pain] dolorosamente - **2.** [extremely] terriblemente.

painkiller ['peɪn,kɪlə'] *n* analgésico *m*.

painless ['peɪnlɪs] *adj* - **1.** [physically] indoloro(ra) - **2.** [emotionally] sencillo(lla), sin complicaciones.

painlessly ['peɪnlɪslɪ] *adv* - **1.** [without physical pain] sin dolor - **2.** [without emotional pain] sin complicaciones.

painstaking ['peɪnz,teɪkɪŋ] *adj* meticuloso(sa), minucioso(sa).

painstakingly ['peɪnz,teɪkɪŋlɪ] *adv* meticulosamente, minuciosamente.

paint [peɪnt] ⬦ *n* pintura *f*. ⬦ *vt* pintar; **to paint the ceiling white** pintar el techo de blanco; **to paint one's lips/nails** pintarse los labios/las uñas. ⬦ *vi* pintar.

paintbox ['peɪntbɒks] *n* ART caja *f* de acuarelas.

paintbrush ['peɪntbrʌʃ] *n* - **1.** ART pincel *m* - **2.** [of decorator] brocha *f*.

painted ['peɪntɪd] *adj* pintado(da).

painter ['peɪntə'] *n* pintor *m*, -ra *f*; **painter and decorator** pintor *m*, -ra *f* y decorador, -ra *f*.

painting ['peɪntɪŋ] *n* - **1.** [picture] cuadro *m*, pintura *f* - **2.** *(U)* [art form, trade] pintura *f*.

paint stripper *n* quitapinturas *f inv*.

paintwork ['peɪntwɜːk] *n (U)* pintura *f*.

pair [peə'] *n* - **1.** [of shoes, socks, wings] par *m*; [of aces] pareja *f* - **2.** [two-part object]: **a pair of**

scissors unas tijeras; **a pair of trousers** unos pantalones; **a pair of compasses** un compás - **3.** [couple - of people] pareja *f*.

➡ **pair off** ⬦ *vt sep* emparejar. ⬦ *vi* emparejarse.

paisley (pattern) ['peɪzlɪ-] ⬦ *n (U)* cachemira *f (dibujo de una tela)*. ⬦ *comp* de cachemira.

pajamas [pə'dʒɑːməz] *esp US* = **pyjamas**.

Paki ['pækɪ] *n UK v inf término racista que designa a un paquistaní*.

Pakistan [UK ,pɑːkɪ'stɑːn, US ,pækɪ'stæn] *n* (el) Paquistán.

Pakistani [UK ,pɑːkɪ'stɑːnɪ, US ,pækɪ'stænɪ] ⬦ *adj* paquistaní. ⬦ *n* paquistaní *mf*.

pal [pæl] *n inf* - **1.** [friend] amiguete *m*, -ta *f*, colega *mf* - **2.** [as term of address] tío *m*, -a *f*.

palace ['pælɪs] *n* palacio *m*.

palaeontology *UK*, **paleontology** *US* [,pælɪɒn'tɒlədʒɪ] *n* paleontología *f*.

palatable ['pælətəbl] *adj* - **1.** [pleasant to taste] sabroso(sa) - **2.** [acceptable] aceptable, admisible.

palate ['pælət] *n* paladar *m*.

palatial [pə'leɪʃl] *adj* señorial, fastuoso(sa).

palaver [pə'lɑːvə'] *n UK inf* [fuss] lío *m*, follón *m*.

pale [peɪl] ⬦ *adj* - **1.** [colour, clothes, paint] claro(ra); [light] tenue - **2.** [person, skin] pálido(da); **to turn pale** palidecer. ⬦ *vi* palidecer.

pale ale *n tipo de cerveza rubia y amarga*.

paleness ['peɪlnɪs] *n* [lack of brightness] palidez *f*.

Palestine ['pælɪ,staɪn] *n* Palestina.

Palestinian [,pælə'stɪnɪən] ⬦ *adj* palestino(na). ⬦ *n* [person] palestino *m*, -na *f*.

palette ['pælət] *n* paleta *f*.

palette knife *n* espátula *f*.

palimony ['pælɪmənɪ] *n pensión alimenticia pagada al ex-amante*.

palings ['peɪlɪŋz] *npl* cerca *f*, empalizada *f*.

pall [pɔːl] ⬦ *n* - **1.** [of smoke] nube *f*, cortina *f* - **2.** *US* [coffin] féretro *m*. ⬦ *vi* cansar, hacerse pesado(da).

pallbearer ['pɔːl,beərə'] *n* portador *m*, -ra *f* del féretro.

pallet ['pælɪt] *n* palet *m*.

palliative ['pælɪətɪv] *n fml* paliativo *m*.

palliative care *n (U)* MED cuidados *mpl* paliativos.

pallid ['pælɪd] *adj liter* pálido(da).

pallor ['pælə'] *n liter* palidez *f*.

palm [pɑːm] *n* - **1.** [tree] palmera *f* - **2.** [of hand] palma *f*; **to read sb's palm** leerle la mano a alguien.

➤ **palm off** *vt sep inf*: **to palm sthg off on sb** endosar OR encasquetar algo a alguien; **to palm sb off with** despachar a alguien con; **to palm sthg off as** hacer pasar algo por.

palmistry ['pɑːmɪstrɪ] *n* quiromancia *f.*

palm oil *n* aceite *m* de palma.

Palm Sunday *n* Domingo *m* de Ramos.

palmtop ['pɑːmtɒp] *n* COMPUT palmtop *m.*

palm tree *n* palmera *f.*

palomino [ˌpælə'miːnəʊ] (*pl* **-s**) *n* palomino *m.*

palpable ['pælpəbl] *adj* palpable.

palpably ['pælpəblɪ] *adv* evidentemente.

palpitate ['pælpɪteɪt] *vi* **- 1.** [beat quickly] palpitar **- 2.** *fml* [tremble]: **to palpitate (with)** estremecerse (de).

palpitations [ˌpælpɪ'teɪʃənz] *npl* palpitaciones *fpl.*

paltry ['pɔːltrɪ] (*comp* **-ier**, *superl* **-iest**) *adj* mísero(ra).

pampas ['pæmpəz] *n*: **the pampas** la Pampa.

pampas grass *n* cortadera *f.*

pamper ['pæmpər] *vt* mimar.

pamphlet ['pæmflɪt] ⬦ *n* [publicity, information] folleto *m*; [political] panfleto *m.* ⬦ *vi* repartir panfletos.

pamphleteer [ˌpæmflə'tɪər] *n* POL panfletista *mf.*

pan [pæn] ⬦ *n* **- 1.** [saucepan] cazuela *f*, cacerola *f*; [frying pan] sartén *f* **- 2.** *US* [for bread, cakes etc] molde *m.* ⬦ *vt* (*pt & pp* **-ned**, *cont* **-ning**) *inf* [criticize] poner por los suelos. ⬦ *vi* (*pt & pp* **-ned**, *cont* **-ning**) **- 1.** [for gold] extraer **- 2.** CIN: **the camera pans right/left** la cámara se mueve hacia la derecha/la izquierda.

➤ **pan out** *vi inf* [happen succesfully] resultar, salir.

panacea [ˌpænə'sɪə] *n*: **a panacea (for)** la panacea (de).

panache [pə'næʃ] *n* garbo *m*, donaire *m.*

Panama ['pænəˌmɑː] *n* Panamá.

Panama Canal *n*: **the Panama Canal** el canal de Panamá.

Panama City *n* Ciudad de Panamá.

Panamanian [ˌpænə'meɪnɪən] ⬦ *adj* panameño(ña). ⬦ *n* panameño *m*, -ña *f.*

pan-American *adj* panamericano(na).

pancake ['pænkeɪk] *n* torta *f*, crepe *f*, panqueque *m*, panqué *m Amér C & Col*, crepa *f Méx*, panqueca *f Ven.*

Pancake Day *n UK* ≃ Martes *m inv* de Carnaval.

Pancake Tuesday *n* = **Pancake Day.**

pancreas ['pæŋkrɪəs] *n* pancreas *m inv.*

panda ['pændə] (*pl* **panda** OR **-s**) *n* panda *m.*

Panda car *n UK* coche *m* patrulla, auto *m* patrulla *Amér C, Méx & Chile*, patrullero *m*, patrulla *f Col & Méx.*

pandemonium [ˌpændɪ'məʊnjəm] *n* pandemónium *m*, jaleo *m*; **it was pandemonium** fue un auténtico pandemónium.

pander ['pændər] *vi*: **to pander to** complacer a.

pane [peɪn] *n* (hoja *f* de) cristal *m.*

panel ['pænl] *n* **- 1.** [group of people] equipo *m*; [in debates] mesa *f* **- 2.** [of wood, metal] panel *m* **- 3.** [of a machine] tablero *m*, panel *m.*

panel game *n UK* programa *m* concurso de equipos.

panelling *UK*, **paneling** *US* ['pænəlɪŋ] *n* (*U*) [on a ceiling] artesonado *m*; [on a wall] paneles *mpl.*

panellist *UK*, **panelist** *US* ['pænəlɪst] *n* participante *mf.*

pang [pæŋ] *n* punzada *f.*

panic ['pænɪk] ⬦ *n* pánico *m*; **to be in a panic about sthg** ponerse muy nervioso por algo. ⬦ *vi* (*pt & pp* **-ked**, *cont* **-king**) aterrarse, aterrorizarse; **don't panic** que no cunda el pánico.

panicky ['pænɪkɪ] *adj*: **he feels panicky** tiene pánico; **she got panicky** le entró el pánico.

panic stations *n UK inf*: **it was panic stations** cundió el pánico.

panic-stricken *adj* preso(sa) OR víctima del pánico.

pannier ['pænɪər] *n* [on horse, bicycle] alforja *f.*

panorama [ˌpænə'rɑːmə] *n* panorama *m.*

panoramic [ˌpænə'ræmɪk] *adj* panorámico(ca).

pant [pænt] *vi* jadear.

panther ['pænθər] (*pl* **panther** OR **-s**) *n* pantera *f.*

panties ['pæntɪz] *npl US* bragas *fpl*, calzones *mpl Amér*, pantaletas *fpl Amér C & Méx*, bombacha *f R Plata*, blúmer *m Amér C.*

pantihose ['pæntɪhəʊz] = **panty hose.**

panto ['pæntəʊ] (*pl* **-s**) *n UK inf* = **pantomime.**

pantomime ['pæntəmaɪm], **panto** *n* **- 1.** *UK obra musical humorística para niños celebrada en Navidad* **- 2.** [mime] pantomima *f.*

pantry ['pæntrɪ] (*pl* **-ies**) *n* despensa *f.*

pants [pænts] ⬦ *npl* **- 1.** *UK* [underpants] calzoncillos *mpl* **- 2.** *US* [trousers] pantalones *mpl.* ⬦ *adj UK inf* [bad]: **to be pants** ser un churro.

pantsuit ['pæntsuːt] *n* traje *m* pantalón.

panty hose, pantihose ['pæntɪ-] *npl US* medias *fpl.*

papa [*UK* pə'pɑː, *US* 'pæpə] *n* papá *m.*

papadum ['pæpədəm] *n* = **popadum.**

papal ['peɪpl] *adj* papal, pontificio(cia).

paparazzi [ˌpæpə'rætsɪ] *npl pej* paparazzi *mpl.*

papaya [pə'paɪə] *n* papaya *f.*

paper ['peɪpəʳ] <> n - **1.** (U) [material] papel m; **piece of paper** [sheet] hoja f de papel; [scrap] trozo m de papel; **on paper** [written down] por escrito; [in theory] sobre el papel - **2.** [newspaper] periódico m - **3.** UK [in exam] examen m - **4.** [essay - gen] estudio m, ensayo m; [- for conference] ponencia f. <> adj [made of paper] de papel. <> vt empapelar.

➤ **papers** npl - **1.** [official documents] documentación f - **2.** [collected information] documentos mpl.

➤ **paper over** vt insep fig disimular.

paperback ['peɪpəbæk] <> n libro m en rústica; **in paperback** en rústica. <> comp: **paperback book** libro m en rústica.

paperboy ['peɪpəbɔɪ] n repartidor m de periódicos.

paper clip n clip m.

papergirl ['peɪpəgɜːl] n repartidora f de periódicos.

paper handkerchief n pañuelo m de papel, klínex® m inv.

paper knife n abrecartas m inv, cortapapeles m inv.

paper money n (U) papel m moneda.

paper shop n UK quiosco m de periódicos.

paper towel n toallita f de papel.

paper tray n bandeja f de papel.

paperweight ['peɪpəweɪt] n pisapapeles m inv.

paperwork ['peɪpəwɜːk] n papeleo m.

papier-mâché [,pæpjeɪ'mæʃeɪ] <> n cartón m piedra. <> comp de cartón piedra.

papist ['peɪpɪst] n pej papista mf.

paprika ['pæprɪkə] n pimentón m.

Pap smear, Pap test n US citología f.

Papuan ['pæpjuən] <> adj papú, papúa. <> n papú mf, papúa mf.

Papua New Guinea ['pæpjuə] n Papúa Nueva Guinea.

par [pɑːʳ] n - **1.** [parity]: **on a par with** al mismo nivel que - **2.** GOLF par m; **under/over par** bajo/sobre par - **3.** [good health]: **to be below** OR **under par** estar un poco enfermo.

para ['pærə] n UK paracaidista mf (del ejército).

parable ['pærəbl] n parábola f.

parabola [pə'ræbələ] n parábola f.

paracetamol [,pærə'siːtəmɒl] n UK paracetamol m.

parachute ['pærəʃuːt] <> n paracaídas m inv. <> vi saltar en paracaídas.

parade [pə'reɪd] <> n - **1.** [procession] desfile m; **on parade** MIL pasando revista - **2.** UK [street of shops] calle de tiendas. <> vt - **1.** [soldiers] ha-

cer desfilar; [criminals, captives] pasear - **2.** [trophy, medal] pasear - **3.** fig [flaunt] exhibir, hacer alarde de. <> vi desfilar.

parade ground n plaza f de armas.

paradigm ['pærədaɪm] n paradigma m.

paradise ['pærədaɪs] n fig paraíso m.

➤ **Paradise** n [Heaven] el Paraíso.

paradox ['pærədɒks] n paradoja f.

paradoxical [,pærə'dɒksɪkl] adj paradójico(ca).

paradoxically [,pærə'dɒksɪklɪ] adv paradójicamente.

paraffin ['pærəfɪn] n parafina f.

paraffin wax n parafina f.

paragliding ['pærə,glaɪdɪŋ] n parapente m.

paragraph ['pærəgrɑːf] n párrafo m, acápite m Amér.

Paraguay ['pærəgwaɪ] n (el) Paraguay.

Paraguayan [,pærə'gwaɪən] <> adj paraguayo(ya). <> n paraguayo m, -ya f.

parakeet ['pærəkiːt] n periquito m.

paralegal [,pærə'liːgl] n US ayudante de un abogado.

parallel ['pærəlel] <> adj: **parallel (to** OR **with)** paralelo(la) (a). <> n - **1.** [parallel line, surface] paralela f - **2.** [something, someone similar]: **to have no parallel** no tener precedente - **3.** [similarity] semejanza f, paralelo m - **4.** GEOG paralelo m. <> vt ser equiparable a.

parallel bars npl paralelas fpl.

paralyse UK, **paralyze** US ['pærəlaɪz] vt lit & fig paralizar.

paralysed UK, **paralyzed** US ['pærəlaɪzd] adj lit & fig paralizado(da).

paralysis [pə'rælɪsɪs] (pl **-lyses** [-lɪsiːz]) n parálisis f inv.

paralytic [,pærə'lɪtɪk] adj - **1.** MED paralítico(ca) - **2.** UK inf [drunk]: **to be paralytic** estar como una cuba.

paramedic [,pærə'medɪk] n esp US auxiliar sanitario m, auxiliar sanitaria f.

paramedical [,pærə'medɪkl] adj esp US de auxiliar sanitario.

parameter [pə'ræmɪtəʳ] n parámetro m.

paramilitary [,pærə'mɪlɪtrɪ] adj paramilitar.

paramount ['pærəmaʊnt] adj vital, fundamental; **of paramount importance** de suma importancia.

paranoia [,pærə'nɔɪə] n paranoia f.

paranoiac [,pærə'nɔɪæk] <> adj paranoico(ca). <> n paranoico m, -ca f.

paranoid ['pærənɔɪd] adj paranoico(ca).

paranormal [,pærə'nɔːml] adj paranormal.

parapet ['pærəpɪt] n parapeto m.

paraphernalia [,pærəfə'neɪljə] n parafernalia f.

paraphrase [ˈpærəfreɪz] ◇ *n* paráfrasis *f inv.* ◇ *vt* parafrasear.

paraplegic [ˌpærəˈpliːdʒɪk] ◇ *adj* parapléjico(ca). ◇ *n* parapléjico *m*, -ca *f*.

parapsychology [ˌpærəsaɪˈkɒlədʒɪ] *n* parapsicología *f*.

parasite [ˈpærəsaɪt] *n* parásito *m*, -ta *f*.

parasitic [ˌpærəˈsɪtɪk] *adj* parásito(ta).

parasol [ˈpærəsɒl] *n* sombrilla *f*.

paratrooper [ˈpærətruːpəʳ] *n* paracaidista *mf (del ejército)*.

parboil [ˈpɑːbɔɪl] *vt* cocer a medias.

parcel [ˈpɑːsl] *n* paquete *m*, encomienda *f Amér.*
➤ **parcel up** *vt sep* (UK -led, *cont* -ling, US -ed, *cont* -ing) UK empaquetar.

parcel post *n* (servicio *m* de) paquete *m* postal.

parched [pɑːtʃt] *adj* - **1.** [land] abrasado(da); [plant] agostado(da) - **2.** [throat, mouth] muy seco(ca); [lips] quemado(da) - **3.** *inf* [very thirsty] seco(ca).

parchment [ˈpɑːtʃmənt] *n* [paper] pergamino *m*.

pardon [ˈpɑːdn] ◇ *n* - **1.** LAW perdón *m*, indulto *m* - **2.** [forgiveness] perdón *m*; **I beg your pardon?** [showing surprise, asking for repetition] ¿perdón?, ¿cómo (dice)?; **I beg your pardon** [to apologize] le ruego me disculpe, perdón. ◇ *vt* - **1.** [forgive]: **to pardon sb (for sthg)** perdonar a alguien (por algo); **pardon?** ¿perdón?, ¿cómo (dice)?; **pardon me** [touching sb accidentally, belching] discúlpeme, perdón; [excuse me] con permiso - **2.** LAW indultar.

pardonable [ˈpɑːdnəbl] *adj* perdonable.

pare [peəʳ] *vt* [apple] pelar; [fingernails] cortar.
➤ **pare down** *vt sep* recortar.

parent [ˈpeərənt] *n* [father] padre *m*; [mother] madre *f*.
➤ **parents** *npl* padres *mpl*.

parentage [ˈpeərəntɪdʒ] *n (U)* origen *m*, ascendencia *f*.

parental [pəˈrentl] *adj* de los padres.

parent company *n* compañía *f* OR casa *f* matriz.

parenthesis [pəˈrenθɪsɪs] (*pl* -theses [-θɪsiːz]) *n* paréntesis *m inv*; **in parenthesis** entre paréntesis.

parenthood [ˈpeərənthʊd] *n* [fatherhood] paternidad *f*; [motherhood] maternidad *f*.

parenting [ˈpeərəntɪŋ] *n*: **to learn parenting skills** aprender a ser buenos padres.

parent-teacher association *n* asociación de padres y maestros.

pariah [pəˈraɪə] *n pej* paria *mf*.

parish [ˈpærɪʃ] *n* - **1.** [of church] parroquia *f* - **2.** UK [area of local government] ≃ municipio *m*.

parish council *n* UK ≃ consejo *m* parroquial OR municipal.

parishioner [pəˈrɪʃənəʳ] *n* parroquiano *m*, -na *f*.

Parisian [pəˈrɪzjən] ◇ *adj* parisino(na). ◇ *n* parisino *m*, -na *f*.

parity [ˈpærətɪ] *n*: **parity (with/between)** igualdad *f* (con/entre).

park [pɑːk] ◇ *n* parque *m*. ◇ *vt* & *vi* aparcar, estacionar *Amér*, parquear *Amér*.

parka [ˈpɑːkə] *n* parka *f*.

park-and-ride *n* aparcamiento *m* disuasorio *Esp*.

parking [ˈpɑːkɪŋ] *n* aparcamiento *m Esp*, estacionamiento *m Amér*; **'no parking'** 'prohibido aparcar'.

parking brake *n* US freno *m* de mano.

parking garage *n* US aparcamiento OR estacionamiento *Amér m (en edificio)*.

parking light *n* US luz *f* de estacionamiento.

parking lot *n* US aparcamiento *m* (al aire libre).

parking meter *n* parquímetro *m*.

parking place, parking space *n* aparcamiento *m*.

parking ticket *n* multa *f* por aparcamiento indebido, multa *f* por estacionamiento indebido *Amér*.

park keeper *n* UK guarda *mf* del parque.

parkland [ˈpɑːklænd] *n (U)* zonas *fpl* verdes.

parkway [ˈpɑːkweɪ] *n* US avenida *f*.

parky [ˈpɑːkɪ] (*comp* -ier, *superl* -iest) *adj* UK *inf*: **'it's parky'** 'hace fresquito'.

parlance [ˈpɑːləns] *n*: **in common/legal parlance** en el habla común/legal, en el lenguaje común/legal.

parliament [ˈpɑːləmənt] *n* - **1.** [assembly, institution] parlamento *m* - **2.** [session] legislatura *f*.

parliamentarian [ˌpɑːləmənˈteərɪən] *n* parlamentario *m*, -ria *f*.

parliamentary [ˌpɑːləˈmentərɪ] *adj* parlamentario(ria).

parlour UK, **parlor** US [ˈpɑːləʳ] *n dated* salón *m*.

parlour game *n* juego *m* de salón.

parlous [ˈpɑːləs] *adj fml* precario(ria).

Parmesan (cheese) [ˌpɑːmɪˈzæn-] *n* (queso *m*) parmesano *m*.

parochial [pəˈrəʊkjəl] *adj* - **1.** *pej* de miras estrechas - **2.**: **parochial school** US colegio *m* privado religioso.

parody [ˈpærədɪ] ◇ *n* (*pl* -ies) parodia *f*. ◇ *vt* (*pt* & *pp* -ied) parodiar.

parole [pəˈrəʊl] ◇ *n* libertad *f* condicional (bajo palabra); **on parole** en libertad condicional. ◇ *vt* poner en libertad condicional.

paroxysm ['pærəksɪzm] *n* [of anger, laughter] acceso *m*.

parquet ['pɑːkeɪ] *n* parqué *m*.

parrot ['pærət] *n* loro *m*.

parrot fashion *adv* UK como un loro.

parry ['pærɪ] (*pt* & *pp* **-ied**) *vt* **- 1.** [blow] parar; [attack] desviar **- 2.** [question] eludir.

parsimonious [,pɑːsɪ'məʊnjəs] *adj fml* & *pej* mezquino(na), tacaño(ña).

parsley ['pɑːslɪ] *n* perejil *m*.

parsnip ['pɑːsnɪp] *n* chirivía *f*, pastinaca *f*.

parson ['pɑːsn] *n* párroco *m*.

parson's nose *n* UK rabadilla *f* (*del pollo*).

part [pɑːt] <> *n* **- 1.** [gen] parte *f*; **in part** en parte; **the best** OR **better part of** la mayor parte de; **for the most part** en su mayoría; **part and parcel of** parte integrante de **- 2.** [component] pieza *f* **- 3.** THEAT papel *m* **- 4.** [involvement]: **part (in)** participación *f* (en); **to play an important part (in)** desempeñar OR jugar un papel importante (en); **to take part (in)** tomar parte (en); **to want no part in** no querer tener nada que ver con; **for my/his part** por mi/su parte; **on my/his part** por mi/su parte **- 5.** US [hair parting] raya *f*. <> *adv* en parte; **it's part living room, part office** es mitad salón, mitad oficina. <> *vt* **- 1.** [lips, curtains] abrir **- 2.** [hair] peinar con raya. <> *vi* **- 1.** [leave one another] separarse **- 2.** [separate - lips, curtains] abrirse.

◆ **parts** *npl* [place]: **in these parts** por estas tierras.

◆ **part with** *vt insep* desprenderse de, separarse de.

partake [pɑː'teɪk] (*pt* **-took**, *pp* **-taken**) *vi fml*: **to partake of** [wine] beber; [food] comer.

part exchange *n* UK sistema de pagar parte de algo con un artículo usado; **in part exchange** como parte del pago.

partial ['pɑːʃl] *adj* **- 1.** [incomplete, biased] parcial **- 2.** [fond]: **partial to** amigo(ga) de, aficionado(da) a.

partiality [,pɑːʃɪ'ælətɪ] *n* **- 1.** [bias] parcialidad *f* **- 2.** [fondness]: **partiality for** afición *f* a.

partially ['pɑːʃəlɪ] *adv* parcialmente.

participant [pɑː'tɪsɪpənt] *n* participante *mf*.

participate [pɑː'tɪsɪpeɪt] *vi*: **to participate (in)** participar (en).

participation [pɑː,tɪsɪ'peɪʃn] *n* participación *f*.

participle ['pɑːtɪsɪpl] *n* participio *m*.

particle ['pɑːtɪkl] *n* partícula *f*.

particular [pə'tɪkjʊləʳ] *adj* **- 1.** [specific, unique] en particular OR especial; **did you want any particular colour?** ¿quería algún color en particular? **- 2.** [extra, greater] especial **- 3.** [difficult] exigente.

◆ **particulars** *npl* [of person] datos *mpl*; [of thing] detalles *mpl*.

◆ **in particular** *adv* en particular, en especial.

particularly [pə'tɪkjʊləlɪ] *adv* especialmente.

parting ['pɑːtɪŋ] *n* **- 1.** [separation] despedida *f* **- 2.** UK [in hair] raya *f*.

parting shot *n*: **to deliver a parting shot** lanzar un último comentario hiriente antes de marcharse.

partisan [,pɑːtɪ'zæn] <> *adj* partidista. <> *n* [freedom fighter] partisano *m*, -na *f*.

partition [pɑː'tɪʃn] <> *n* **- 1.** [wall] tabique *m*; [screen] separación *f* **- 2.** COMPUT partición *f*. <> *vt* **- 1.** [room] dividir con tabiques **- 2.** [country] dividir **- 3.** COMPUT crear particiones en.

partly ['pɑːtlɪ] *adv* en parte.

partner ['pɑːtnəʳ] <> *n* **- 1.** [spouse, lover] pareja *f* **- 2.** [in an activity] compañero *m*, -ra *f* **- 3.** [in a business] socio *m*, -cia *f* **- 4.** [ally] colega *mf*. <> *vt* ir de pareja de OR con.

partnership ['pɑːtnəʃɪp] *n* **- 1.** [relationship] asociación *f*; **to go into partnership (with)** asociarse (con) **- 2.** [business] sociedad *f*.

part of speech *n* categoría *f* gramatical.

partook [pɑː'tʊk] *pt* ⊳ **partake**.

partridge ['pɑːtrɪdʒ] *n* perdiz *f*.

part-time <> *adj* a tiempo parcial. <> *adv* a tiempo parcial.

part-timer *n* trabajador *m*, -ra *f* a tiempo parcial.

party ['pɑːtɪ] <> *n* (*pl* **-ies**) **- 1.** POL partido *m* **- 2.** [social gathering] fiesta *f* **- 3.** [group] grupo *m* **- 4.** LAW parte *f* **- 5.** [involved person]: **to be a party to** participar en. <> *vi inf* estar de juerga.

party line *n* **- 1.** POL línea *f* (política) del partido **- 2.** TELEC línea *f* (telefónica) compartida.

party piece *n* UK inf número favorito que alguien suele ejecutar siempre para entretener a la gente en fiestas etc.

party political broadcast *n* UK espacio *m* electoral.

party politics *n (U)* política *f* del partidismo.

party wall *n* pared *f* medianera.

pass [pɑːs] <> *n* **- 1.** [in football, rugby, hockey] pase *m*; [in tennis] passing-shot *m* **- 2.** [document, permit] pase *m*; **travel pass** tarjeta *f* OR abono *m* de transportes **- 3.** UK [successful result] aprobado *m* **- 4.** [route between mountains] puerto *m*

▸▸ **to make a pass at sb** intentar ligar con alguien. <> *vt* **- 1.** [gen] pasar; **to pass sthg (to sb), to pass (sb) sthg** pasar OR pasarle algo (a alguien); **pass the string through the hole** pase la cuerda por el agujero **- 2.** [move past -

thing] pasar por (delante de); [- person] pasar delante de; **to pass sb in the street** cruzarse con alguien - **3.** AUT adelantar - **4.** [exceed] sobrepasar - **5.** [exam, candidate, law] aprobar; **to pass sthg fit (for)** dar algo por bueno (para) - **6.** [opinion, judgement] formular; [sentence] dictar. <> *vi* - **1.** [gen] pasar - **2.** AUT adelantar - **3.** [in exam] aprobar - **4.** [occur] transcurrir; **to pass unnoticed** pasar desapercibido.

◆ **pass around** *vt sep* = **pass round**.

◆ **pass as, pass for** *vt insep* pasar por.

◆ **pass away, pass on** *vi* fallecer, pasar a mejor vida.

◆ **pass by** <> *vt sep* [subj: people] hacer caso omiso a; [subj: events, life] pasar desapercibido(da) a; **he felt like life was passing him by** sentía que la vida se le estaba escurriendo de las manos. <> *vi* pasar cerca.

◆ **pass for** *vt insep* = **pass as**.

◆ **pass off** *vt sep*: **to pass sthg/sb off as sthg** hacer pasar algo/a alguien por algo.

◆ **pass on** <> *vt sep*: **to pass sthg on (to)** pasar algo (a). <> *vi* - **1.** [move on] continuar; **to pass on to the next subject** pasar al siguiente tema - **2.** = **pass away**.

◆ **pass out** *vi* - **1.** [faint] desmayarse - **2.** UK MIL graduarse.

◆ **pass over** *vt insep* hacer caso omiso de, pasar por alto.

◆ **pass round, pass around** *vt sep* UK ir pasando, pasar.

◆ **pass to** *vt insep* [be left to] pasar a.

◆ **pass up** *vt sep* dejar pasar OR escapar.

passable ['pɑːsəbl] *adj* - **1.** [satisfactory] pasable, aceptable - **2.** [not blocked] transitable.

passably ['pɑːsəblɪ] *adv* aceptablemente.

passage ['pæsɪdʒ] *n* - **1.** [corridor - between houses] pasadizo *m*, pasaje *m*; [- between rooms] pasillo *m* - **2.** [of music, speech] pasaje *m* - **3.** *fml* [of vehicle, person, time] paso *m* - **4.** [sea journey] travesía *f*.

passageway ['pæsɪdʒweɪ] *n* [between houses] pasadizo *m*, pasaje *m*; [between rooms] pasillo *m*.

passbook ['pɑːsbʊk] *n* ≃ cartilla *f* OR libreta *f* de banco.

passenger ['pæsɪndʒər] *n* pasajero *m*, -ra *f*.

passerby [ˌpɑːsə'baɪ] (*pl* **passersby** [ˌpɑːsəz'baɪ]) *n* transeúnte *mf*.

passing ['pɑːsɪŋ] <> *adj* [fad] pasajero(ra); [remark] de pasada. <> *n* paso *m*, transcurso *m*.

◆ **in passing** *adv* de pasada.

passion ['pæʃn] *n*: **passion (for)** pasión *f* (por).

◆ **Passion** *n*: **the Passion** la Pasión.

passionate ['pæʃənət] *adj* apasionado(da).

passionately ['pæʃənətlɪ] *adv* apasionadamente.

passionfruit ['pæʃənfruːt] *n* granadilla *f*.

passive ['pæsɪv] <> *adj* pasivo(va). <> *n*: **the passive** la pasiva.

passively ['pæsɪvlɪ] *adv* con pasividad.

passive resistance *n* resistencia *f* pasiva.

passive smoker *n* fumador *m* pasivo.

passkey ['pɑːskiː] *n* - **1.** [particular] llave *f* - **2.** [universal] llave *f* maestra.

Passover ['pɑːsˌəʊvər] *n*: **(the) Passover** (la) Pascua judía.

passport ['pɑːspɔːt] *n* pasaporte *m*; **passport to sthg** *fig* pasaporte a algo.

passport control *n* UK control *m* de pasaportes.

password ['pɑːswɜːd] *n* [gen & COMPUT] contraseña *f*.

past [pɑːst] <> *adj* - **1.** [former] anterior - **2.** [most recent] último(ma); **over the past week** durante la última semana - **3.** [finished] terminado(da); **our problems are past** se han acabado nuestros problemas. <> *adv* - **1.** [telling the time]: **it's ten past** son y diez - **2.** [beyond, in front] por delante; **to walk/run past** pasar andando/corriendo. <> *n* - **1.** [time]: **the past** el pasado - **2.** [personal history] pasado *m*. <> *prep* - **1.** [telling the time]: **it's five/half/a quarter past ten** son las diez y cinco/media/cuarto - **2.** [alongside, in front of] por delante de; **to walk/run past sthg** pasar algo andando/corriendo - **3.** [beyond] más allá de; **it's past the bank** está pasado el banco; **to be past it** *inf* estar para el arrastre; **I wouldn't put it past him** *inf* tratándose de él no me extrañaría un pelo.

pasta ['pæstə] *n (U)* pasta *f*.

paste [peɪst] <> *n* - **1.** [smooth mixture] pasta *f* - **2.** [food] paté *m* - **3.** [glue] engrudo *m*. <> *vt* [labels, stamps] pegar; [surface] engomar, engrudar; COMPUT pegar.

pastel ['pæstl] <> *adj* pastel *(inv)*. <> *n* - **1.** [colour] color *m* pastel - **2.** ART [crayon] pastel *m*.

pasteurize, -ise ['pɑːstʃəraɪz] *vt* pasteurizar.

pastiche [pæ'stiːʃ] *n* - **1.** [imitation] imitación *f* - **2.** [mixture] pastiche *m*.

pastille ['pæstɪl] *n* UK pastilla *f*.

pastime ['pɑːstaɪm] *n* pasatiempo *m*, afición *f*.

pasting ['peɪstɪŋ] *n* *inf* paliza *f*.

pastor ['pɑːstər] *n* RELIG pastor *m*.

pastoral ['pɑːstərəl] *adj* - **1.** RELIG pastoral - **2.** [of the country] pastoril, bucólico(ca).

past participle *n* participio *m* pasado.

pastrami [pə'strɑːmɪ] *n* embutido de ternera ahumada.

pastry ['peɪstrɪ] (*pl* **-ies**) *n* - **1.** [mixture] pasta *f*, masa *f* - **2.** [cake] pastel *m*.

past tense *n*: **the past tense** el pasado.

pasture ['pɑːstʃər] n pasto m.

pasty[1] ['peɪstɪ] (comp -ier, superl -iest) adj pálido(da).

pasty[2] ['pæstɪ] (pl -ies) n UK empanada f.

pasty-faced ['peɪstɪ-] adj pálido(da).

pat [pæt] <> adj (comp -ter, superl -test) preparado(da), ensayado(da). <> n - **1.** [gen] golpecito m; [to dog] caricia f; [on back, hand] palmadita f - **2.** [of butter etc] porción f. <> vt (pt & pp -ted, cont -ting) [gen] golpear ligeramente; [dog] acariciar; **to pat sb on the back/hand** darle a alguien una palmadita en la espalda/la mano.

patch [pætʃ] <> n - **1.** [for mending] remiendo m; [on elbow] codera f; [to cover eye] parche m - **2.** [part of surface] área f - **3.** [area of land] bancal m, parcela f - **4.** [period of time] periodo m - **5.** COMPUT parche m
▸▸ **not to be a patch on** UK inf no igualar ni con mucho a. <> vt remendar.

◆ **patch together** vt sep [government, team] formar a duras penas; [agreement, solution] alcanzar a duras penas.

◆ **patch up** vt sep - **1.** [mend] reparar - **2.** [resolve - relationship] salvar; **we have patched things up** hemos hecho las paces.

patchwork ['pætʃwɜːk] <> adj de trozos de distintos colores y formas. <> n fig [of fields] mosaico m.

patchy ['pætʃɪ] (comp -ier, superl -iest) adj - **1.** [uneven - fog, sunshine] irregular; [- colour] desigual - **2.** [incomplete] deficiente, incompleto(ta) - **3.** [good in parts] irregular.

pâté ['pæteɪ] n paté m.

patent [UK 'peɪtənt, US 'pætənt] <> adj [obvious] patente, evidente. <> n patente f. <> vt patentar.

patented [UK 'peɪtəntɪd, US 'pætəntɪd] adj patentado(da).

patentee [UK ˌpeɪtən'tiː, US ˌpætən'tiː] n poseedor m, -ra f de una patente.

patent leather n charol m.

patently [UK 'peɪtəntlɪ, US 'pætəntlɪ] adv evidentemente, patentemente.

paternal [pə'tɜːnl] adj [love, attitude] paternal; [grandmother, grandfather] paterno(na).

paternalistic [pəˌtɜːnə'lɪstɪk] adj pej paternalista.

paternity [pə'tɜːnətɪ] n paternidad f.

paternity leave n permiso m por paternidad.

paternity suit n litigio m de paternidad.

path [pɑːθ] (pl [pɑːðz]) n - **1.** [track, way ahead] camino m; **our paths had crossed before** nuestros caminos se habían cruzado anteriormente - **2.** COMPUT camino m - **3.** [trajectory - of bullet] trayectoria f; [- of flight] rumbo m - **4.** [course of action] curso m.

pathetic [pə'θetɪk] adj - **1.** [causing pity] patético(ca), lastimoso(sa) - **2.** [attempt, person] inútil, infeliz; [actor, film] malísimo(ma).

pathetically [pə'θetɪklɪ] adv - **1.** [causing pity] patéticamente - **2.** [uselessly] lastimosamente.

pathname ['pɑːθneɪm] n camino m.

pathological [ˌpæθə'lɒdʒɪkl] adj patológico(ca).

pathologist [pə'θɒlədʒɪst] n forense mf.

pathology [pə'θɒlədʒɪ] n patología f.

pathos ['peɪθɒs] n patetismo m.

pathway ['pɑːθweɪ] n camino m, sendero m.

patience ['peɪʃns] n - **1.** [quality] paciencia f; **to try sb's patience** poner a prueba la paciencia de alguien - **2.** UK [card game] solitario m.

patient ['peɪʃnt] <> adj paciente. <> n paciente mf.

patiently ['peɪʃntlɪ] adv pacientemente.

patina ['pætɪnə] n pátina f.

patio ['pætɪəʊ] (pl -s) n [paved] área pavimentada al lado de una casa utilizada para el esparcimiento.

patio doors npl puertas de cristal que dan a un patio.

patois ['pætwɑː] (pl patois) n dialecto m.

patriarch ['peɪtrɪɑːk] n [head of family] patriarca m.

patriarchy ['peɪtrɪɑːkɪ] (pl -ies) n patriarcado m.

patrimony [UK 'pætrɪmənɪ, US 'pætrɪməʊnɪ] n fml patrimonio m.

patriot [UK 'pætrɪət, US 'peɪtrɪət] n patriota mf.

patriotic [UK ˌpætrɪ'ɒtɪk, US ˌpeɪtrɪ'ɒtɪk] adj patriótico(ca).

patriotism [UK 'pætrɪətɪzm, US 'peɪtrɪətɪzm] n patriotismo m.

patrol [pə'trəʊl] <> n patrulla f; **on patrol** de patrulla. <> vt (pt & pp -led, cont -ling) patrullar.

patrol car n coche m patrulla, auto m patrulla Amér C, Méx & Chile, patrullero m, patrulla f Col & Méx.

patrolman [pə'trəʊlmən] (pl -men [-mən]) n US policía m, guardia m.

patrol wagon n US coche m celular.

patrolwoman [pə'trəʊlˌwʊmən] (pl -women [-ˌwɪmɪn]) n (mujer f) policía f, guardia f.

patron ['peɪtrən] n - **1.** [of arts] mecenas mf inv - **2.** UK [of charity, campaign] patrocinador m, -ra f - **3.** fml [customer] cliente mf.

patronize, -ise ['pætrənaız] *vt* **- 1.** *pej* [talk down to] tratar con aire paternalista OR condescendiente **- 2.** *fml* [back financially] patrocinar.

patronizing ['pætrənaızıŋ] *adj pej* paternalista, condescendiente.

patron saint *n* santo patrón *m*, santa patrona *f*.

patter ['pætər] ⇔ *n* **- 1.** [of raindrops] repiqueteo *m*; [of feet] golpeteo *m*, pasitos *mpl* **- 2.** [sales talk] charlatanería *f*. ⇔ *vi* [dog, feet] corretear; [rain] repiquetear.

pattern ['pætən] *n* **- 1.** [design] dibujo *m*, diseño *m* **- 2.** [of life, work] estructura *f*; [of illness, events] desarrollo *m*, evolución *f* **- 3.** [for sewing, knitting] patrón *m* **- 4.** [model] modelo *m*.

patterned ['pætənd] *adj* estampado(da).

patty ['pætı] (*pl* **-ies**) *n* **- 1.** [pie] empanada *f* **- 2.** *US* [burger] hamburguesa *f*.

paucity ['pɔːsətı] *n fml* escasez *f*.

paunch [pɔːntʃ] *n* barriga *f*, panza *f*.

paunchy ['pɔːntʃı] (*comp* **-ier**, *superl* **-iest**) *adj* barrigón(ona).

pauper ['pɔːpər] *n* indigente *mf*.

pause [pɔːz] ⇔ *n* pausa *f*. ⇔ *vi* **- 1.** [stop speaking] hacer una pausa **- 2.** [stop moving, doing sthg] detenerse.

pave [peɪv] *vt* pavimentar; **to pave the way for** preparar el terreno para.

paved [peɪvd] *adj* pavimentado(da).

pavement ['peɪvmənt] *n* **- 1.** *UK* [at side of road] acera *f*, andén *m* *Amér C & Col*, vereda *f* *Perú*, banqueta *f* *Amér C & Méx* **- 2.** *US* [roadway] calzada *f*.

pavement artist *n UK* artista callejero que dibuja en las aceras.

pavilion [pə'vɪljən] *n* **- 1.** *UK* [at sports field] vestuarios *mpl* **- 2.** [at exhibition] pabellón *m*.

paving ['peɪvɪŋ] *n* (*U*) pavimento *m*.

paving stone *n* losa *f*.

paw [pɔː] ⇔ *n* [of dog] pata *f*; [of lion, cat] zarpa *f*, garra *f*. ⇔ *vt* **- 1.** [subj: animal] dar zarpazos a; **to paw the ground** piafar **- 2.** *pej* [subj: person] manosear, sobar.

pawn [pɔːn] ⇔ *n* **- 1.** [chesspiece] peón *m* **- 2.** [unimportant person] marioneta *f*. ⇔ *vt* empeñar.

pawnbroker ['pɔːnˌbrəʊkər] *n* prestamista *mf*.

pawnshop ['pɔːnʃɒp] *n* casa *f* de empeños, monte *m* de piedad.

pay [peɪ] ⇔ *vt* (*pt & pp* **paid**) **- 1.** [gen] pagar; **to pay sb for sthg** pagar a alguien por algo; **he paid £20 for it** pagó 20 libras por ello; **to pay one's way** costearse sus propios gastos **- 2.** *UK* [put into bank account]**: to pay sthg into** ingresar algo en; **he paid in his wages** ingresó su sueldo **- 3.** [be advantageous to] ser provechoso(sa) a; **it will pay you not to say any-**

thing más te vale no decir nada **- 4.** [compliment, visit] hacer; [respects] ofrecer; [attention] prestar; [homage] rendir. ⇔ *vi* (*pt & pp* **paid**) **- 1.** [gen] pagar; **to pay by credit card** pagar con tarjeta de crédito; **it pays well** está bien pagado; **to pay dearly for sthg** pagar caro (por) algo **- 2.** [be profitable] ser rentable. ⇔ *n* sueldo *m*, paga *f*.

◆ **pay back** *vt sep* **- 1.** [money] devolver, reembolsar; [person] devolver el dinero a **- 2.** [revenge oneself]: **to pay sb back (for sthg)** hacer pagar a alguien (por algo).

◆ **pay for** *vt insep* pagar.

◆ **pay off** ⇔ *vt sep* **- 1.** [repay - debt] liquidar, saldar **- 2.** [dismiss] despedir con indemnización **- 3.** [bribe] comprar, pagar. ⇔ *vi* [efforts] dar fruto.

◆ **pay out** ⇔ *vt sep* **- 1.** [spend] pagar, desembolsar **- 2.** [rope] ir soltando. ⇔ *vi* [spend money] pagar.

◆ **pay up** *vi* pagar.

payable ['peɪəbl] *adj* **- 1.** [to be paid] pagadero(ra) **- 2.** [on cheque]: **payable to** a favor de.

pay-as-you-go *n* pago *m* por uso.

paybed ['peɪbed] *n UK* cama utilizada por un paciente de pago en un hospital público.

paycheck ['peɪtʃek] *n US* paga *f*.

payday ['peɪdeɪ] *n* día *m* de paga.

PAYE (*abbr of* **pay as you earn**) *n* en el Reino Unido, sistema de retención fiscal de parte del sueldo del trabajador por la empresa.

payee [peɪˈiː] *n* beneficiario *m*, -ria *f*.

pay envelope *n US* sobre *m* de paga.

payer ['peɪər] *n* -ria *f*.

paying guest ['peɪɪŋ-] *n* huésped *mf* de pago.

payload ['peɪləʊd] *n* **- 1.** [gen] carga *f* útil **- 2.** [explosive in missile] carga *f* explosiva.

paymaster ['peɪˌmɑːstər] *n* (oficial *m*) pagador *m*.

payment ['peɪmənt] *n* pago *m*.

payoff ['peɪɒf] *n* **- 1.** [result] resultado *m* **- 2.** [redundancy payment] indemnización *f* (por despido).

payola [peɪˈəʊlə] *n esp US inf* soborno *m*, propina *f*.

payout ['peɪaʊt] *n inf* reparto *m* de dinero.

pay packet *n UK* **- 1.** [envelope] sobre *m* de paga **- 2.** [wages] paga *f*.

pay-per-view *n* pago *m* por visión.

pay phone, pay station *n* teléfono *m* público.

pay rise *n* aumento *m* de sueldo.

payroll ['peɪrəʊl] *n* nómina *f*.

payslip ['peɪslɪp] *n UK* hoja *f* de paga.

pay station *US* = **pay phone**.

pay TV *n* televisión *f* de pago.

PBS (*abbr of* **Public Broadcasting Service**) *n* organización americana que produce y transmite programas de televisión de contenido cultural y educativo.

pc ⟺ *n abbr of* **postcard**. ⟺ (*abbr of per cent*) p.c.

PC ⟺ *n* - **1.** (*abbr of* personal computer) PC *m* - **2.** *UK abbr of* **police constable**. ⟺ *adj abbr of* **politically correct**.

PCB (*abbr of* **printed circuit board**) *n* PCB *m*.

pd *abbr of* **paid**.

PD *abbr of* **police department**.

PDF (*abbr of* **portable document format**) *n* COMPUT PDF *m*.

pdq (*abbr of* **pretty damn quick**) *adv inf* superrápido.

PDT (*abbr of* **Pacific Daylight Time**) *hora de verano de la costa oeste de Estados Unidos*.

PE (*abbr of* **physical education**) *n* educación *f* física.

pea [piː] *n* guisante *m*, arveja *f Andes, Col & Ven*, chícharo *m Amér C & Méx*, petipuá *m Ven*.

peace [piːs] *n* - **1.** [gen] paz *f*; **to be at peace (with)** estar en paz (con) - **2.** [quiet] calma *f*, tranquilidad *f*; **peace of mind** tranquilidad de espíritu - **3.** [freedom from disagreement] orden *m*; **to make (one's) peace (with)** hacer las paces (con).

peaceable [ˈpiːsəbl] *adj* [not aggressive] pacífico(ca).

Peace Corps *n organización estadounidense para la cooperación con los países en vías de desarrollo*.

peaceful [ˈpiːsfʊl] *adj* - **1.** [quiet, calm] tranquilo(la) - **2.** [not aggressive] pacífico(ca).

peacefully [ˈpiːsfʊlɪ] *adv* - **1.** [quietly, calmly] tranquilamente - **2.** [without aggression] pacíficamente.

peace offering *n inf* ofrenda *f* de paz.

peacetime [ˈpiːstaɪm] *n* (U) tiempos *mpl* de paz.

peach [piːtʃ] ⟺ *adj* [in colour] de color melocotón OR durazno Amér. ⟺ *n* - **1.** [fruit] melocotón *m*, durazno *m Amér* - **2.** [colour] color *m* melocotón OR durazno Amér. ⟺ *comp* de melocotón OR durazno Amér.

Peach Melba [-ˈmelbə] *n melocotón servido con helado y zumo de frambuesa*.

peacock [ˈpiːkɒk] *n* pavo *m* real.

peahen [ˈpiːhen] *n* pava *f* real.

peak [piːk] ⟺ *n* - **1.** [mountain top] pico *m*, cima *f* - **2.** [highest point] apogeo *m* - **3.** [of cap] visera *f*. ⟺ *adj* [season] alto(ta); [condition] perfecto(ta). ⟺ *vi* alcanzar el máximo.

peaked [piːkt] *adj* con visera.

peak period *n UK* [of electricity etc] periodo *m* de tarifa máxima; [of traffic] horas *fpl* punta.

peak rate *n* tarifa *f* máxima.

peaky [ˈpiːkɪ] (*comp* **-ier**, *superl* **-iest**) *adj UK inf* pachucho(cha).

peal [piːl] ⟺ *n* [of bells] repique *m*; **peal (of laughter)** carcajada *f*; **peal (of thunder)** trueno *m*. ⟺ *vi* repicar.

peanut [ˈpiːnʌt] *n* cacahuete *m*, maní *m Amér*, cacahuate *m Méx*.

peanut butter *n* manteca *f* de cacahuete OR de maní *R Plata*, mantequilla *f* de maní *Amér OR* de cacahuate *Méx*.

pear [peəʳ] *n* pera *f*.

pearl [pɜːl] *n* perla *f*.

pear-shaped *adj*: **to go pear-shaped** irse a paseo.

peasant [ˈpeznt] *n* - **1.** [in countryside] campesino *m*, -na *f*, guajiro *m*, -ra *f Cuba* - **2.** *pej* [ignorant person] paleto *m*, palurdo *m*.

peasantry [ˈpezntrɪ] *n*: **the peasantry** los campesinos.

peashooter [ˈpiːˌʃuːtəʳ] *n* cerbatana *f*.

peat [piːt] *n* turba *f*.

peaty [ˈpiːtɪ] (*comp* **-ier**, *superl* **-iest**) *adj* [taste] a turba; [whisky] con sabor a turba.

pebble [ˈpebl] *n* guijarro *m*.

pebbledash [ˈpeblˌdæʃ] *n UK* enguijarrado *m*.

peck [pek] ⟺ *n* - **1.** [with beak] picotazo *m* - **2.** [kiss] besito *m*. ⟺ *vt* - **1.** [with beak] picotear - **2.** [kiss] dar un besito a. ⟺ *vi* picotear.

pecking order [ˈpekɪŋ-] *n* jerarquía *f*.

peckish [ˈpekɪʃ] *adj UK inf*: **to feel peckish** estar algo hambriento(ta).

pecs [peks] *npl inf* pectorales *mpl*.

pectin [ˈpektɪn] *n* pectina *f*.

peculiar [pɪˈkjuːljəʳ] *adj* - **1.** [odd] singular, extraño(ña) - **2.** *UK* [slightly ill] raro(ra), indispuesto(ta) - **3.** [characteristic]: **to be peculiar to** ser propio(pia) de.

peculiarity [pɪˌkjuːlɪˈærətɪ] (*pl* **-ies**) *n* - **1.** [eccentricity] extravagancia *f* - **2.** [characteristic] peculiaridad *f* - **3.** [oddness] rareza *f*.

peculiarly [pɪˈkjuːljəlɪ] *adv* - **1.** [especially] particularmente - **2.** [oddly] de una manera extraña.

pedal [ˈpedl] ⟺ *n* pedal *m*. ⟺ *vi* (*UK* **-led**, *cont* **-ling**, *US* **-ed**, *cont* **-ing**) pedalear.

pedal bin *n UK* cubo *m* de basura con pedal.

pedalo [ˈpedələʊ] *n UK* patín *m*.

pedant [ˈpedənt] *n pej* puntilloso *m*, -sa *f*.

pedantic [pɪˈdæntɪk] *adj pej* puntilloso(sa).

peddle [ˈpedl] *vt* - **1.** [drugs] traficar con; [wares] vender de puerta en puerta - **2.** [rumours] divulgar, difundir.

peddler [ˈpedləʳ] *n* - **1.** [drug dealer] traficante *mf* (de drogas) - **2.** *US* = **pedlar**.

pederast, paederast ['pedəræst] n pederasta m.

pedestal ['pedɪstl] n pedestal m; **to put sb on a pedestal** poner a alguien en un pedestal.

pedestrian [pɪ'destrɪən] <> adj pej pedestre. <> n peatón m.

pedestrian crossing n UK paso m de peatones.

pedestrianize, -ise [pɪ'destrɪənaɪz] vt peatonizar, convertir en zona peatonal.

pediatric, paediatric [,pi:dɪ'ætrɪk] adj pediátrico(ca).

pediatrician, paediatrician [,pi:dɪə'trɪʃn] n pediatra mf.

pediatrics, paediatrics [,pi:dɪ'ætrɪks] n pediatría f.

pedicure ['pedɪˌkjuər] n pedicura f.

pedigree ['pedɪgri:] <> adj de raza. <> n - **1.** [of animal] pedigrí m - **2.** [of person] linaje m.

pedlar UK, **peddler** US ['pedlər] n vendedor m, -ra f ambulante.

pedophile, paedophile ['pi:dəfaɪl] n pedófilo m, -la f.

pee [pi:] inf <> n pis m; **to go for a pee** ir a hacer pis. <> vi mear, hacer pis.

peek [pi:k] inf <> n mirada f, ojeada f. <> vi mirar a hurtadillas.

peel [pi:l] <> n [gen] piel f; [of orange, lemon] corteza f; [once removed] mondaduras fpl. <> vt pelar. <> vi [walls, paint] desconcharse; [wallpaper] despegarse; [skin, nose] pelarse.

◆ **peel off** vt sep - **1.** [label] despegar; [cover] quitar - **2.** [clothes] quitarse.

peeler ['pi:lər] n mondador m.

peelings ['pi:lɪŋz] npl peladuras fpl.

peep [pi:p] <> n - **1.** [look] mirada f, ojeada f - **2.** inf [sound] pío m. <> vi [look] mirar furtivamente.

◆ **peep out** vi asomar.

peephole ['pi:phəʊl] n mirilla f.

peeping Tom [,pi:pɪŋ'tɒm] n mirón m.

peep show n mundonuevo m, cosmorama m.

peer [pɪər] <> n - **1.** [noble] par m - **2.** [equal] igual m. <> vi mirar con atención.

peerage ['pɪərɪdʒ] n - **1.** [rank] rango m de par - **2.** [group]: **the peerage** la nobleza.

peeress ['pɪərɪs] n paresa f.

peer group n grupo generacional o social.

peer pressure n presión ejercida por el grupo generacional o social al que uno pertenece.

peeved [pi:vd] adj inf fastidiado(da), disgustado(da).

peevish ['pi:vɪʃ] adj malhumorado(da).

peg [peg] <> n - **1.** UK [for washing line] pinza f - **2.** [on tent] estaca f - **3.** [hook] gancho m. <> vt (pt & pp -ged, cont -ging) - **1.** [prices] fijar, estabilizar - **2.** US [person]: **to peg** identificar a alguien como algo.

◆ **peg out** vi UK inf estirar la pata.

pegboard ['pegbɔ:d] n tablero vertical con agujeros donde se depositan clavijas.

pejorative [pɪ'dʒɒrətɪv] adj peyorativo(va), despectivo(va).

pekinese [,pi:kə'ni:z], **pekingese** [,pi:kɪŋ'i:z] n (pl **pekinese**) [dog] pekinés m.

◆ **Pekinese, Pekingese** <> adj pekinés(esa). <> n (pl **Pekinese**) pekinés(esa).

pekingese n = **pekinese**.

pelican ['pelɪkən] (pl **pelican** OR **-s**) n pelícano m.

pelican crossing n UK paso de peatones con semáforo accionado por el usuario.

pellet ['pelɪt] n - **1.** [small ball] bolita f - **2.** [for gun] perdigón m.

pell-mell [,pel'mel] adv atropelladamente.

pelmet ['pelmɪt] n UK galería f (de cortinas).

pelt [pelt] <> n - **1.** [animal skin] piel f - **2.** [speed]: **(at) full pelt** a toda pastilla, a todo meter. <> vt: **to pelt sb with sthg** acribillar a alguien con algo, arrojar algo a alguien. <> vi - **1.** [rain]: **it was pelting down** OR **with rain** llovía a cántaros - **2.** [run very fast] correr a toda pastilla.

pelvic ['pelvɪk] adj pélvico(ca).

pelvis ['pelvɪs] (pl **-vises** OR **-ves** [-vi:z]) n pelvis f.

pen [pen] <> n - **1.** [ballpoint] bolígrafo m, lapicera f R Plata & Chile; [fountain pen] pluma f; [felt-tip] rotulador m - **2.** [enclosure] redil m, corral m. <> vt (pt & pp **-ned**, cont **-ning**) - **1.** liter [write] escribir - **2.** [enclose] encerrar.

◆ **pen in** vt sep encerrar.

penal ['pi:nl] adj penal.

penalize, -ise UK ['pi:nəlaɪz] vt - **1.** [gen] penalizar; SPORT penalizar, castigar - **2.** [put at a disadvantage] perjudicar.

penal settlement n colonia f penal.

penalty ['penltɪ] (pl **-ies**) n - **1.** [punishment] pena f; **to pay the penalty (for sthg)** fig pagar las consecuencias (de algo) - **2.** [fine] multa f - **3.** SPORT penalty m; **penalty (kick)** FTBL penalty m; RUGBY golpe m de castigo.

penalty area n FTBL área f de castigo.

penalty box n - **1.** FTBL área f de castigo - **2.** [en hockey] banquillo m de castigo.

penalty clause n cláusula f penal.

penalty goal n RUGBY gol m de castigo.

penalty kick ▷ **penalty**.

penance ['penəns] n penitencia f.

pen-and-ink *adj* a pluma.

pence [pens] *UK npl* ▷ **penny**.

penchant [*UK* pɒʃɒ̃, *US* 'pentʃənt] *n*: **to have a penchant for sthg** tener debilidad por algo; **to have a penchant for doing sthg** tener propensión a hacer algo.

pencil ['pensl] ◇ *n* lápiz *m*; **in pencil** a lápiz. ◇ *vt* (*UK* **-led**, *cont* **-ling**, *US* **-ed**, *cont* **-ing**) escribir a lápiz.
- **pencil in** *vt sep* [date, appointment] apuntar provisionalmente.

pencil case *n* estuche *m*, plumero *m Esp*.

pencil sharpener *n* sacapuntas *m inv*.

pendant ['pendənt] *n* [jewel on chain] colgante *m*.

pending ['pendɪŋ] *fml* ◇ *adj* **- 1.** [waiting to be dealt with] pendiente **- 2.** [about to happen] inminente. ◇ *prep* a la espera de.

pending tray *n UK* bandeja *f* OR cajón *m* de asuntos pendientes.

pendulum ['pendjuləm] (*pl* **-s**) *n* [of clock] péndulo *m*.

penetrate ['penɪtreɪt] ◇ *vt* **- 1.** [barrier] salvar, atravesar; [jungle, crowd] adentrarse en, introducirse en; [subj: wind, rain, sharp object] penetrar en **- 2.** [infiltrate - organization] infiltrarse en. ◇ *vi inf* [be understood] hacer mella.

penetrating ['penɪtreɪtɪŋ] *adj* penetrante.

penetration [,penɪ'treɪʃn] *n* **- 1.** [act of penetrating] penetración *f* **- 2.** *fml* [insight] agudeza *f*, perspicacia *f*.

pen friend *n UK* amigo *m*, -ga *f* por correspondencia.

penguin ['peŋgwɪn] *n* pingüino *m*.

penicillin [,penɪ'sɪlɪn] *n* penicilina *f*.

peninsula [pə'nɪnsjulə] (*pl* **-s**) *n* península *f*; **the Iberian Peninsula** la Península Ibérica.

penis ['piːnɪs] (*pl* **penises** ['piːnɪsɪz]) *n* pene *m*.

penitent ['penɪtənt] *adj fml* arrepentido(da).

penitentiary [,penɪ'tenʃərɪ] (*pl* **-ies**) *n US* penitenciaría *f*.

penknife ['pennaɪf] (*pl* **-knives** [-naɪvz]) *n* navaja *f*, chaveta *f Andes*.

pen name *n* seudónimo *m*.

pennant ['penənt] *n* banderín *m*.

penniless ['penɪlɪs] *adj* sin dinero; **to be penniless** estar sin un centavo.

Pennines ['penaɪnz] *npl*: **the Pennines** los Peninos.

Pennsylvania [,pensɪl'veɪnɪə] *n* Pensilvania.

penny ['penɪ] *n* **- 1.** (*pl* **-ies**) *UK* [coin] penique *m*; *US* centavo *m* **- 2.** (*pl* **pence**) *UK* [value] penique *m*; **it was worth every penny** valía realmente la pena
- **a penny for your thoughts** ¿en qué estás pensando?; **as I listened, the penny dropped**

UK inf mientras le escuchaba, caí en la cuenta; **to spend a penny** *UK inf* ir al váter; **they're two** OR **ten a penny** *UK inf* los haya porrillo.

penny-pinching [-,pɪntʃɪŋ] ◇ *adj* tacaño(ña), mezquino(na). ◇ *n* tacañería *f*, miseria *f*.

pen pal *n inf* amigo *m*, -ga *f* por correspondencia.

pension ['penʃn] *n* **- 1.** [gen] pensión *f* **- 2.** [disability pension] subsidio *m*.
- **pension off** *vt sep* jubilar.

pensionable ['penʃənəbl] *adj*: **of pensionable age** en edad de jubilación.

pension book *n UK* libreta *f* de pensiones.

pensioner ['penʃənər] *n*: **(old-age) pensioner** pensionista *mf*.

pension fund *n* fondo *m* de pensiones.

pension plan, pension scheme *n* plan *m* de pensiones.

pensive ['pensɪv] *adj* pensativo(va).

pentagon ['pentəgən] *n* pentágono *m*.
- **Pentagon** *n US*: **the Pentagon** el Pentágono, *sede del ministerio de Defensa estadounidense*.

pentathlon [pen'tæθlən] (*pl* **-s**) *n* pentatlón *m*.

Pentecost ['pentɪkɒst] *n* Pentecostés *m*.

penthouse ['penthaus] (*pl* [-hauzɪz]) *n* ático *m*; **penthouse suite** suite en el ático.

pent up ['pent-] *adj* reprimido(da).

penultimate [pe'nʌltɪmət] *adj* penúltimo(ma).

penury ['penjurɪ] *n fml* miseria *f*, pobreza *f*.

peony ['pɪənɪ] (*pl* **-ies**), **paeony** *n* peonía *f*.

people ['piːpl] ◇ *n* [nation, race] pueblo *m*. ◇ *npl* **- 1.** [gen] gente *f*; [individuals] personas *fpl*; **a table for eight people** una mesa para ocho personas; **people say that...** dice la gente que...; **young people** los jóvenes **- 2.** [inhabitants] habitantes *mpl* **- 3.** POL: **the people** el pueblo. ◇ *vt*: **to be peopled by** OR **with** estar poblado(da) de.

pep [pep] *n inf* vitalidad *f*.
- **pep up** *vt sep* (*pt & pp* **-ped**, *cont* **-ping**) [person] animar; [food] alegrar.

PEP (*abbr of* **personal equity plan**) *n UK plan personal de inversión*.

pepper ['pepər] *n* **- 1.** [spice] pimienta *f*; **black/white pepper** pimienta negra/blanca **- 2.** [vegetable] pimiento *m*; **red/green pepper** pimiento rojo/verde.

peppercorn ['pepəkɔːn] *n* grano *m* de pimienta.

peppered ['pepəd] *adj* **- 1.** [with mistakes, statistics]: **peppered with** salpicado(da) de **- 2.** [with bullets]: **peppered with** acribillado(da) de.

pepper mill *n* molinillo *m* de pimienta.

peppermint ['pepəmɪnt] *n* **- 1.** [sweet] pastilla *f* de menta **- 2.** [herb] menta *f*.

pepper pot *UK,* **peppershaker** *US n* pimentero *m.*

peppery ['pepərɪ] *adj* [spicy] picante.

pep talk *n inf* palabras *fpl* de ánimo.

peptic ulcer ['peptɪk-] *n* úlcera *f* estomacal.

per [pɜːʳ] *prep* [expressing rate, ratio] por; **per hour/kilo/person** por hora/kilo/persona; **per day** al día; **as per instructions** de acuerdo con OR según las instrucciones; **as per usual** como de costumbre.

per annum *adv* al OR por año.

per capita [pə'kæpɪtə] <> *adj* per cápita. <> *adv* por cabeza.

perceive [pə'siːv] *vt* - **1.** [notice] percibir, apreciar - **2.** [understand, realize] advertir, apreciar - **3.** [see]: **to perceive sthg/sb as** ver algo/a alguien como.

per cent *adv* por ciento; **fifty per cent of the population** el cincuenta por ciento de la población.

percentage [pə'sentɪdʒ] *n* porcentaje *m.*

perceptible [pə'septəbl] *adj* perceptible, apreciable.

perception [pə'sepʃn] *n* - **1.** [noticing] percepción *f* - **2.** [insight] perspicacia *f* - **3.** [opinion] idea *f.*

perceptive [pə'septɪv] *adj* perspicaz.

perceptively [pə'septɪvlɪ] *adv* perspicazmente.

perch [pɜːtʃ] <> *n* (*pl* -es) - **1.** [for bird] percha *f,* vara *f* - **2.** [high position] posición *f* elevada - **3.** (*pl* perch) [fish] perca *f.* <> *vi:* **to perch (on)** [bird] posarse (en); [person] sentarse (en).

percolate ['pɜːkəleɪt] *vi lit* & *fig* filtrarse.

percolator ['pɜːkəleɪtəʳ] *n* cafetera *f* eléctrica.

percussion [pə'kʌʃn] *n* MUS percusión *f;* **the percussion** la percusión.

percussionist [pə'kʌʃənɪst] *n* percusionista *mf.*

peremptory [pə'remptərɪ] *adj* perentorio(ria).

perennial [pə'renjəl] <> *adj* [gen & BOT] perenne. <> *n* BOT planta *f* perenne.

perfect <> *adj* ['pɜːfɪkt] perfecto(ta); **he's a perfect stranger to me** me es completamente desconocido; **it makes perfect sense** es totalmente lógico. <> *n* ['pɜːfɪkt] GRAM: **the perfect (tense)** el perfecto. <> *vt* [pə'fekt] perfeccionar.

perfection [pə'fekʃn] *n* perfección *f;* **to perfection** a la perfección.

perfectionist [pə'fekʃənɪst] *n* perfeccionista *mf.*

perfectly ['pɜːfɪktlɪ] *adv* - **1.** [for emphasis] absolutamente; **perfectly well** perfectamente bien - **2.** [to perfection] perfectamente.

perforate ['pɜːfəreɪt] *vt* perforar.

perform [pə'fɔːm] <> *vt* - **1.** [carry out] llevar a cabo, realizar; [duty] cumplir - **2.** [music, dance] interpretar; [play] representar. <> *vi* - **1.** [function - car, machine] funcionar; [- person, team] desenvolverse - **2.** [actor] actuar; [singer, dance] interpretar.

performance [pə'fɔːməns] *n* - **1.** [carrying out] realización *f,* ejecución *f;* [of duty] cumplimiento *m* - **2.** [show] representación *f* - **3.** [of actor, singer etc] interpretación *f,* actuación *f* - **4.** [of car, engine] rendimiento *m.*

performance art *n* arte *m* interpretativo.

performance car *n* coche *m* de altas prestaciones.

performer [pə'fɔːməʳ] *n* [actor, singer etc] intérprete *mf.*

performing arts [pə'fɔːmɪŋ-] *npl:* **the performing arts** las artes interpretativas.

perfume ['pɜːfjuːm] *n* perfume *m.*

perfumed [*UK* 'pɜːfjuːmd, *US* pər'fjuːmd] *adj* perfumado(da).

perfunctory [pə'fʌŋktərɪ] *adj* superficial.

perhaps [pə'hæps] *adv* - **1.** [maybe] quizás, quizá; **perhaps she'll do it** quizás ella lo haga; **perhaps so/not** tal vez sí/no - **2.** [in polite requests, suggestions, remarks]: **perhaps you could help?** ¿te importaría ayudar?; **perhaps you should start again** ¿por qué no empiezas de nuevo? - **3.** [approximately] aproximadamente.

peril ['perɪl] *n liter* peligro *m;* **at one's peril** a su propio riesgo.

perilous ['perələs] *adj liter* peligroso(sa).

perilously ['perələslɪ] *adv* peligrosamente.

perimeter [pə'rɪmɪtəʳ] *n* perímetro *m;* **perimeter fence** OR **wall** cerca *f.*

period ['pɪərɪəd] <> *n* - **1.** [of time] período *m,* periodo *m* - **2.** HIST época *f* - **3.** SCH clase *f,* hora *f* - **4.** [menstruation] período *m;* **to be on one's period** tener el período - **5.** *US* [full stop] punto *m* - **6.** SPORT tiempo *m.* <> *comp* de época.

periodic [,pɪərɪ'ɒdɪk], **periodical** *adj* periódico(ca).

periodical [,pɪərɪ'ɒdɪkl] <> *adj* = **periodic.** <> *n* [magazine] revista *f,* publicación *f* periódica.

periodic table *n* tabla *f* periódica.

period pains *npl* dolores *mpl* menstruales.

period piece *n* obra *f* de época.

peripatetic [,perɪpə'tetɪk] *adj* ambulante, itinerante.

peripheral [pə'rɪfərəl] <> *adj* - **1.** [of little importance] marginal - **2.** [at edge] periférico(ca). <> *n* COMPUT periférico *m.*

periphery [pə'rɪfərɪ] (*pl* -ies) *n* - **1.** [edge] periferia *f* - **2.** [unimportant area] márgenes *mpl.*

periscope [ˈperɪskəʊp] *n* periscopio *m*.

perish [ˈperɪʃ] *vi* - **1.** [die] perecer - **2.** [decay] deteriorarse.

perishable [ˈperɪʃəbl] *adj* perecedero(ra).

➧ **perishables** *npl* productos *mpl* perecederos.

perishing [ˈperɪʃɪŋ] *adj UK inf* - **1.** [cold]: **it's perishing (cold)** hace un frío que pela - **2.** [damn] condenado(da).

peritonitis [ˌperɪtəˈnaɪtɪs] *n (U)* peritonitis *f inv*.

perjure [ˈpɜːdʒər] *vt* LAW: **to perjure o.s.** perjurarse.

perjury [ˈpɜːdʒərɪ] *n* LAW perjurio *m*.

perk [pɜːk] *n inf* extra *m*, beneficio *m* adicional.

➧ **perk up** *vi* animarse.

perky [ˈpɜːkɪ] (*comp* **-ier**, *superl* **-iest**) *adj inf* alegre, animado(da).

perm [pɜːm] ⟨⟩ *n* permanente *f*. ⟨⟩ *vt*: **to have one's hair permed** hacerse la permanente.

permanence [ˈpɜːmənəns] *n* permanencia *f*.

permanent [ˈpɜːmənənt] ⟨⟩ *adj* - **1.** [gen] permanente; [job, address] fijo(ja) - **2.** [continuous, constant] constante. ⟨⟩ *n US* [perm] permanente *f*.

permanently [ˈpɜːmənəntlɪ] *adv* permanentemente.

permeable [ˈpɜːmjəbl] *adj* permeable.

permeate [ˈpɜːmɪeɪt] *vt* impregnar.

permissible [pəˈmɪsəbl] *adj* permisible.

permission [pəˈmɪʃn] *n*: **permission (to do sthg)** permiso *m* (para hacer algo).

permissive [pəˈmɪsɪv] *adj* permisivo(va).

permissiveness [pəˈmɪsɪvnɪs] *n* permisividad *f*.

permit ⟨⟩ *vt* [pəˈmɪt] (*pt & pp* **-ted**, *cont* **-ting**) permitir; **to permit sb sthg/to do sthg** permitir a alguien algo/hacer algo. ⟨⟩ *vi* [pəˈmɪt] (*pt & pp* **-ted**, *cont* **-ting**): **if time permits** si hay tiempo; **weather permitting** si el tiempo lo permite. ⟨⟩ *n* [ˈpɜːmɪt] permiso *m*.

permutation [ˌpɜːmjuːˈteɪʃn] *n* permutación *f*.

pernicious [pəˈnɪʃəs] *adj fml* pernicioso(sa).

pernickety [pəˈnɪkətɪ] *adj inf* quisquilloso(sa).

peroxide [pəˈrɒksaɪd] *n* peróxido *m*.

peroxide blonde *n* rubia *f* oxigenada.

perpendicular [ˌpɜːpənˈdɪkjʊlər] ⟨⟩ *adj* - **1.** MATHS: **perpendicular (to)** perpendicular (a) - **2.** [upright] vertical. ⟨⟩ *n* MATHS perpendicular *f*.

perpetrate [ˈpɜːpɪtreɪt] *vt fml* perpetrar.

perpetration [ˌpɜːpɪˈtreɪʃn] *n fml* perpetración *f*.

perpetrator [ˈpɜːpɪtreɪtər] *n fml* perpetrador *m*, -ra *f*, autor *m*, -ra *f*.

perpetual [pəˈpetʃʊəl] *adj* - **1.** *pej* [constant] constante - **2.** [everlasting] perpetuo(tua).

perpetually [pəˈpetʃʊəlɪ] *adv* - **1.** *pej* [constantly] continuamente, constantemente - **2.** [for ever] perpetuamente.

perpetuate [pəˈpetʃʊeɪt] *vt* perpetuar.

perpetuation [pəˌpetʃʊˈeɪʃn] *n* perpetuación *f*.

perpetuity [ˌpɜːpɪˈtjuːətɪ] *n*: **in perpetuity** *fml* a perpetuidad.

perplex [pəˈpleks] *vt* confundir, dejar perplejo(ja).

perplexed [pəˈplekst] *adj* perplejo(ja).

perplexing [pəˈpleksɪŋ] *adj* desconcertante.

perplexity [pəˈpleksətɪ] *n* perplejidad *f*.

perquisite [ˈpɜːkwɪzɪt] *n fml* beneficio *m* adicional.

per se [pɜːˈseɪ] *adv* en sí.

persecute [ˈpɜːsɪkjuːt] *vt* perseguir.

persecution [ˌpɜːsɪˈkjuːʃn] *n* persecución *f*.

persecutor [ˈpɜːsɪkjuːtər] *n* perseguidor *m*, -ra *f*.

perseverance [ˌpɜːsɪˈvɪərəns] *n* perseverancia *f*.

persevere [ˌpɜːsɪˈvɪər] *vi*: **to persevere (with sthg/in doing sthg)** perseverar (en algo/en hacer algo).

Persian [ˈpɜːʃn] ⟨⟩ *adj* persa. ⟨⟩ *n* [language] persa *m*.

Persian cat *n* gato *m* persa.

Persian Gulf *n*: **the Persian Gulf** el Golfo Pérsico.

persist [pəˈsɪst] *vi* - **1.** [problem, rain] persistir - **2.** [person]: **to persist in doing sthg** empeñarse en hacer algo.

persistence [pəˈsɪstəns] *n* - **1.** [continuation] persistencia *f* - **2.** [determination] perseverancia *f*.

persistent [pəˈsɪstənt] *adj* - **1.** [constant] continuo(nua) - **2.** [determined] persistente.

persistently [pəˈsɪstəntlɪ] *adv* - **1.** [constantly] continuamente - **2.** [determinedly] con persistencia - **3.** [repeatedly] repetidamente.

persnickety [pəˈsnɪkɪtɪ] *adj US* quisquilloso(sa).

person [ˈpɜːsn] (*pl* **people** OR **persons**) *fml n* - **1.** [man, woman] persona *f*; **in person** en persona - **2.** [body]: **to have sthg about one's person** llevar algo encima - **3.** GRAM persona *f*; **in the first person** en primera persona.

persona [pəˈsəʊnə] (*pl* **-s** OR **-ae** [-iː]) *n* imagen *f*.

personable [ˈpɜːsnəbl] *adj* agradable.

personage [ˈpɜːsənɪdʒ] *n fml* personaje *m*.

personal [ˈpɜːsnl] ⟨⟩ *adj* - **1.** [gen] personal - **2.** [private - life, problem] privado(da) - **3.** *pej*

[rude] ofensivo(va); **to be personal** hacer alusiones personales. <> *n US* anuncio *m* personal (por palabras).

personal account *n* cuenta *f* personal.

personal allowance *n* [regular payment] renta *f* personal; [in tax] desgravación *f* personal.

personal assistant *n* secretario *m*, -ria *f* personal.

personal call *n* llamada *f* personal.

personal column *n* sección *f* de asuntos personales.

personal computer *n* ordenador *m* personal.

personal hygiene *n* higiene *f* personal.

personality [,pɜːsə'næləti] (*pl* **-ies**) *n* personalidad *f*.

personalize, -ise ['pɜːsənəlaiz] *vt* personalizar.

personalized ['pɜːsənəlaizd] *adj* personalizado(da).

personally ['pɜːsnəli] *adv* **- 1.** [gen] personalmente; **to take sthg personally** tomarse algo como algo personal **- 2.** [in person] en persona.

personal loan *n* crédito *m* personal.

personal organizer *n* agenda *f* (personal).

personal pension plan *n* plan *m* de jubilación personalizado.

personal pronoun *n* pronombre *m* personal.

personal property *n (U)* bienes *mpl* muebles.

personal stereo *n* walkman® *m inv*.

persona non grata [-'grɑːtə] (*pl* **personae non gratae** [-'grɑːtiː]) *n* persona *f* no grata.

personify [pə'sɒnifai] (*pt & pp* **-ied**) *vt* personificar.

personnel [,pɜːsə'nel] <> *n (U)* [department] departamento *m* de personal. <> *npl* [staff] personal *m*.

personnel department *n* departamento *m* de personal.

personnel manager *n* jefe *m*, -fa *f* de personal.

person-to-person *adj esp US* de persona a persona.

perspective [pə'spektiv] *n* perspectiva *f*; **to get sthg in perspective** *fig* poner algo en perspectiva.

Perspex® ['pɜːspeks] *n UK* ≃ plexiglás® *m*.

perspicacious [,pɜːspi'keiʃəs] *adj fml* perspicaz.

perspiration [,pɜːspə'reiʃn] *n* transpiración *f*.

perspire [pə'spaiə'] *vi* transpirar.

persuade [pə'sweid] *vt*: **to persuade sb (of sthg/to do sthg)** persuadir a alguien (de algo/a hacer algo); **to persuade sb that** convencer a alguien (de) que.

persuasion [pə'sweiʒn] *n* **- 1.** [act of persuading] persuasión *f* **- 2.** [belief] creencia *f*.

persuasive [pə'sweisiv] *adj* persuasivo(va).

persuasively [pə'sweisivli] *adv* de modo persuasivo.

pert [pɜːt] *adj* **- 1.** [person] vivaracho(cha) **- 2.** [part of body] respingón(ona).

pertain [pə'tein] *vi fml*: **pertaining to** relacionado(da) con.

pertinence ['pɜːtinəns] *n* pertinencia *f*.

pertinent ['pɜːtinənt] *adj* pertinente.

perturb [pə'tɜːb] *vt fml* perturbar, inquietar.

perturbed [pə'tɜːbd] *adj fml* perturbado(da), inquieto(ta).

Peru [pə'ruː] *n* (el) Perú.

perusal [pə'ruːzl] *n* [careful reading] lectura *f* detenida; [brief reading] lectura por encima.

peruse [pə'ruːz] *vt* [read carefully] leer detenidamente; [browse through] leer por encima.

Peruvian [pə'ruːvjən] <> *adj* peruano(na). <> *n* [person] peruano *m*, -na *f*.

pervade [pə'veid] *vt* impregnar.

pervasive [pə'veisiv] *adj* **- 1.** [smell] penetrante **- 2.** [influence] dominante.

perverse [pə'vɜːs] *adj* [delight, enjoyment] perverso(sa); [contrary] puñetero(ra).

perversely [pə'vɜːsli] *adv* **- 1.** [ironically] paradójicamente **- 2.** [contrarily] contra toda lógica.

perversion [*UK* pə'vɜːʃn, *US* pə'vɜːrʒn] *n* **- 1.** [sexual deviation] perversión *f* **- 2.** [of justice, truth] tergiversación *f*.

perversity [pə'vɜːsəti] *n* [contrariness] puñetería *f*.

pervert <> *n* ['pɜːvɜːt] pervertido *m*, -da *f*. <> *vt* [pə'vɜːt] **- 1.** [course of justice] tergiversar **- 2.** [corrupt sexually] pervertir.

perverted [pə'vɜːtid] *adj* **- 1.** [sexually deviant] pervertido(da) **- 2.** [twisted] torcido(da).

peseta [pə'seitə] *n* peseta *f*.

peso ['peisəu] (*pl* **-s**) *n* peso *m*.

pessary ['pesəri] (*pl* **-ies**) *n* pesario *m*.

pessimism ['pesimizm] *n* pesimismo *m*.

pessimist ['pesimist] *n* pesimista *mf*.

pessimistic [,pesi'mistik] *adj* pesimista.

pest [pest] *n* **- 1.** [insect] insecto *m* nocivo; [animal] animal *m* nocivo **- 2.** *inf* [annoying person] pesado *m*, -da *f*; [annoying thing] lata *f*.

pester ['pestə'] *vt* dar la lata a, cargosear *Amér*.

pesticide ['pestisaid] *n* pesticida *m*.

pestle ['pesl] *n* mano *f* (de mortero).

pet [pet] <> *adj* [subject, theory] preferido(da); **pet hate** gran fobia *f*. <> *n* **- 1.** [domestic animal] animal *m* doméstico **- 2.** [favourite person] preferido *m*, -da *f*, favorito *m*, -ta *f*. <> *vt* (*pt & pp* **-ted**, *cont* **-ting**) acariciar. <> *vi* (*pt & pp* **-ted**, *cont* **-ting**) pegarse el lote.

petal ['petl] *n* pétalo *m*.

peter ['pi:tər] ◆ **peter out** *vi* [supplies, interest] agotarse; [path] desaparecer.

petit bourgeois [pə,ti:'buəʒwɑ:] <> *adj* pequeño burgués (pequeña burguesa). <> *n* (*pl* **petits bourgeois** [pə,ti:'buəʒwɑ:]) pequeño burgués *m*, pequeña burguesa *f*.

petite [pə'ti:t] *adj* [woman] chiquita.

petit four [,peti-] (*pl* **petits fours** [,peti-]) *n* dulce de bizcocho cubierto de alcorza.

petition [pɪ'tɪʃn] <> *n* petición *f*. <> *vt* presentar una petición a. <> *vi* **- 1.** [campaign]: **to petition for sthg** solicitar algo; **to petition against sthg** presentar una petición contra algo **- 2.** LAW: **to petition for divorce** pedir el divorcio.

petitioner [pɪ'tɪʃənər] *n* solicitante *mf*.

pet name *n* nombre *m* cariñoso.

petrified ['petrɪfaɪd] *adj* [terrified] petrificado(da).

petrify ['petrɪfaɪ] (*pt & pp* **-ied**) *vt* [terrify] petrificar.

petrochemical [,petrəʊ'kemɪkl] *adj* petroquímico(ca).

petrodollar ['petrəʊ,dɒlər] *n* petrodólar *m*.

petrol ['petrəl] *n* UK gasolina *f*, nafta *f* R Plata, bencina *f* Chile.

petrol bomb *n* UK bomba *f* de gasolina.

petrol can *n* UK lata *f* de gasolina OR de nafta R Plata OR de bencina Chile.

petroleum [pɪ'trəʊljəm] *n* petróleo *m*.

petroleum jelly *n* vaselina *f*.

petrol pump *n* UK surtidor *m* de gasolina OR de nafta R Plata OR de bencina Chile, bomba *f* Chile, Col & Ven.

petrol station *n* UK gasolinera *f*, grifo *m* Perú, bomba *f* Chile, Col & Ven, estación *f* de nafta R Plata.

petrol tank *n* UK depósito *m* de gasolina, tanque *m* de gasolina Amér OR de bencina Chile OR de nafta R Plata.

pet shop *n* pajarería *f*.

petticoat ['petɪkəʊt] *n* [underskirt] enaguas *fpl*, enagua *f*, fustán *m* Amér; [full-length] combinación *f*.

pettiness ['petɪnɪs] *n* [small-mindedness] mezquindad *f*.

petting zoo ['petɪŋ'zu:] *n* US parque zoológico en el que los niños pueden acariciar y dar de comer a los animales.

petty ['petɪ] (*comp* **-ier**, *superl* **-iest**) *adj* **- 1.** [small-minded] mezquino(na) **- 2.** [trivial] insignificante.

petty cash *n* dinero *m* para gastos menores.

petty officer *n* sargento *m* de la marina.

petulant ['petjʊlənt] *adj* cascarrabias *(inv)*.

pew [pju:] *n* banco *m*.

pewter ['pju:tər] *n* peltre *m*.

PG (*abbr of* **parental guidance**) para menores acompañados.

PGA (*abbr of* **Professional Golfers' Association**) *n* PGA *f*.

p & h (*abbr of* **postage and handling**) *n* US gastos *mpl* de envío.

pH *n* (*abbr of* **potential of hydrogen**) pH *m*.

phallic ['fælɪk] *adj* fálico(ca); **phallic symbol** símbolo *m* fálico.

phallus ['fæləs] (*pl* **-es** OR **phalli** ['fælaɪ]) *n* falo *m*.

phantom ['fæntəm] <> *adj* ilusorio(ria). <> *n* [ghost] fantasma *m*.

phantom pregnancy *n* embarazo *m* psicológico.

pharaoh ['feərəʊ] *n* faraón *m*.

pharmaceutical [,fɑ:mə'sju:tɪkl] *adj* farmacéutico(ca).

◆ **pharmaceuticals** *npl* productos *mpl* farmacéuticos.

pharmacist ['fɑ:məsɪst] *n* farmacéutico *m*, -ca *f*.

pharmacology [,fɑ:mə'kɒlədʒɪ] *n* farmacología *f*.

pharmacy ['fɑ:məsɪ] (*pl* **-ies**) *n* [shop] farmacia *f*.

phase [feɪz] <> *n* fase *f*. <> *vt* escalonar.

◆ **phase in** *vt sep* introducir progresivamente.

◆ **phase out** *vt sep* retirar progresivamente.

PhD (*abbr of* **Doctor of Philosophy**) *n* **- 1.** [qualification] doctorado *m* **- 2.** [person] doctor *m*, -ra *f*.

pheasant ['feznt] (*pl* **pheasant** OR **-s**) *n* faisán *m*.

phenobarbitone UK [,fi:nəʊ'bɑ:bɪtəʊn], **phenobarbitol** US [,fi:nəʊ'bɑ:bɪtl] *n* fenobarbital *m*.

phenomena [fɪ'nɒmɪnə] *npl* ⊳ **phenomenon**.

phenomenal [fɪ'nɒmɪnl] *adj* extraordinario(ria).

phenomenon [fɪ'nɒmɪnən] (*pl* **-mena**) *n* lit & fig fenómeno *m*.

phew [fju:] *excl* ¡puf!

phial ['faɪəl] *n* frasco *m* (pequeño).

Philadelphia [,fɪlə'delfɪə] *n* Filadelfia.

philanderer [fɪˈlændərəʳ] n tenorio m.

philanthropic [ˌfɪlənˈθrɒpɪk] adj filantrópico(ca).

philanthropist [fɪˈlænθrəpɪst] n filántropo m, -pa f.

philately [fɪˈlætəlɪ] n filatelia f.

philharmonic [ˌfɪlɑːˈmɒnɪk] adj filarmónico(ca).

Philippine [ˈfɪlɪpiːn] adj filipino(na); **the Philippine Islands** las Filipinas.

➡ **Philippines** npl: **the Philippines** las Filipinas.

philistine [UK ˈfɪlɪstaɪn, US ˈfɪlɪstiːn] n fig inculto m, -ta f.

Phillips® [ˈfɪlɪps] comp: **Phillips screw** tornillo m de cabeza en cruz; **Phillips screwdriver** destornillador m de cabeza en cruz.

philosopher [fɪˈlɒsəfəʳ] n filósofo m, -fa f.

philosophical [ˌfɪləˈsɒfɪkl] adj filosófico(ca).

philosophize, -ise [fɪˈlɒsəfaɪz] vi filosofar.

philosophy [fɪˈlɒsəfɪ] (pl -ies) n filosofía f.

phlegm [flem] n [mucus, composure] flema f.

phlegmatic [flegˈmætɪk] adj flemático(ca).

phobia [ˈfəʊbjə] n fobia f; **to have a phobia about sthg** tener fobia a algo.

phoenix [ˈfiːnɪks] n fénix m inv.

phone [fəʊn] ◇ n teléfono m; **to be on the phone** [speaking] estar al teléfono; UK [connected to network] tener teléfono; **to talk about sthg on the phone** discutir algo por teléfono. ◇ comp telefónico(ca). ◇ vt & vi llamar, telefonear.

➡ **phone in** vi llamar.

➡ **phone up** vt sep & vi llamar.

phone book n guía f telefónica.

phone booth n teléfono m público.

phone box n UK cabina f telefónica.

phone call n llamada f telefónica; **to make a phone call** hacer una llamada.

phonecard [ˈfəʊnkɑːd] n tarjeta f telefónica.

phone-in n RADIO & TV programa con llamadas de los oyentes.

phone line n - **1.** [wire] cable m de teléfonos - **2.** [connection] línea f telefónica.

phone number n número m de teléfono.

phone-tapping [-ˌtæpɪŋ] n interceptación f telefónica.

phonetics [fəˈnetɪks] n (U) fonética f.

phoney UK, **phony** US [ˈfəʊnɪ] ◇ adj (comp -ier, superl -iest) inf falso(sa). ◇ n (pl -ies) farsante mf.

phoney war n estado de guerra sin confrontación armada.

phony US adj = phoney.

phosphate [ˈfɒsfeɪt] n fosfato m.

phosphorus [ˈfɒsfərəs] n fósforo m.

photo [ˈfəʊtəʊ] n foto f; **to take a photo (of)** sacar una foto (de).

photocall [ˈfəʊtəʊkɔːl] n cita de una persona famosa con la prensa para que le saquen fotos.

photocopier [ˈfəʊtəʊˌkɒpɪəʳ] n fotocopiadora f.

photocopy [ˈfəʊtəʊˌkɒpɪ] ◇ n (pl -ies) fotocopia f. ◇ vt (pt & pp -ied) fotocopiar.

photoelectric cell [ˌfəʊtəʊɪˈlektrɪk-] n célula f fotoeléctrica.

photo finish n SPORT foto-finish f.

Photofit® [ˈfəʊtəʊfɪt] n: **Photofit (picture)** fotorrobot f.

photogenic [ˌfəʊtəʊˈdʒenɪk] adj fotogénico(ca).

photograph [ˈfəʊtəgrɑːf] ◇ n fotografía f; **to take a photograph (of)** sacar una fotografía (de). ◇ vt fotografiar.

photographer [fəˈtɒgrəfəʳ] n fotógrafo m, -fa f.

photographic [ˌfəʊtəˈgræfɪk] adj fotográfico(ca).

photographic memory n memoria f fotográfica.

photography [fəˈtɒgrəfɪ] n (U) fotografía f.

photojournalism [ˌfəʊtəʊˈdʒɜːnəlɪzm] n periodismo m gráfico.

photon [ˈfəʊtɒn] n fotón m.

photo opportunity n oportunidad de ofrecer una imagen favorable mediante una foto.

photosensitive [ˌfəʊtəʊˈsensɪtɪv] adj fotosensible.

photoshoot [ˈfəʊtəʊʃuːt] n sesión f fotográfica.

Photostat® [ˈfəʊtəstæt] n fotostato m.

➡ **photostat** vt (pt & pp -ted, cont -ting) fotocopiar.

photosynthesis [ˌfəʊtəʊˈsɪnθəsɪs] n fotosíntesis f inv.

phrasal verb [ˈfreɪzl-] n verbo m con preposición.

phrase [freɪz] ◇ n - **1.** [group of words] locución f, frase f - **2.** [expression] expresión f. ◇ vt [apology, refusal] expresar; [letter] redactar.

phrasebook [ˈfreɪzbʊk] n guía f de conversación.

physical [ˈfɪzɪkl] ◇ adj físico(ca). ◇ n [examination] examen m médico.

physical chemistry n fisicoquímica f.

physical education n educación f física.

physical examination n examen m médico.

physical geography n geografía f física.

physical jerks npl UK hum gimnasia f, ejercicios mpl físicos.

physically [ˈfɪzɪklɪ] adv físicamente.

physically handicapped <> *adj* discapacitado físico (discapacitada física). <> *npl*: **the physically handicapped** los discapacitados físicos.

physical science *n (U)* ciencias *fpl* físicas.

physical training *n* preparación *f* física.

physician [fɪ'zɪʃn] *n* médico *mf*.

physicist ['fɪzɪsɪst] *n* físico *m*, -ca *f*.

physics ['fɪzɪks] *n (U)* física *f*.

physio ['fɪzɪəu] *(pl* -s) *n UK inf* - **1.** (*abbr of* **physiotherapist**) fisioterapeuta *mf* - **2.** (*abbr of* **physiotherapy**) fisioterapia *f*.

physiognomy [,fɪzɪ'ɒnəmɪ] *(pl* -ies) *n fml* fisionomía *f*.

physiology [,fɪzɪ'ɒlədʒɪ] *n* fisiología *f*.

physiotherapist [,fɪzɪəu'θerəpɪst] *n* fisioterapeuta *mf*.

physiotherapy [,fɪzɪəu'θerəpɪ] *n* fisioterapia *f*.

physique [fɪ'ziːk] *n* físico *m*.

pianist ['pɪənɪst] *n* pianista *mf*.

piano [pɪ'ænəu] *(pl* -s) *n* (instrument) piano *m*.

piano accordion *n* acordeón-piano *m*.

piccalilli [,pɪkə'lɪlɪ] *n salsa amarilla picante con coliflor y mostaza.*

piccolo ['pɪkələu] *(pl* -s) *n* flautín *m*.

pick [pɪk] <> *n* - **1.** [tool] piqueta *f* - **2.** [for guitar] púa *f* - **3.** [selection]: **take your pick** escoge el que quieras - **4.** [best]: **the pick of** lo mejor de. <> *vt* - **1.** [team, winner] seleccionar; [time, book, dress] elegir; **to pick one's way across** OR **through** andar con tiento por - **2.** [fruit, flowers] coger - **3.** [remove - hairs etc]: **to pick sthg off sthg** quitar algo de algo - **4.** [nose] hurgarse; [teeth] mondarse; [scab, spot] arrancarse - **5.** [provoke]: **to pick a fight/quarrel (with)** buscar pelea/bronca (con) - **6.** [open - lock] forzar (con ganzúa). <> *vi*: **he can afford to pick and choose** puede permitirse el lujo de ser exigente.

➤ **pick at** *vt insep* - **1.** [food] picar, picotear - **2.** [scab, spot] rascarse.

➤ **pick on** *vt insep* meterse con.

➤ **pick out** *vt sep* - **1.** [recognize] reconocer - **2.** [identify] identificar - **3.** [select] escoger, elegir.

➤ **pick up** <> *vt sep* - **1.** [gen] recoger; **she's picking us up at seven** pasará a buscarnos a las siete; **to pick up the pieces** *fig* volver a la normalidad - **2.** [lift up] levantar; [the phone] descolgar - **3.** [buy, acquire] adquirir; **to pick up speed** cobrar velocidad - **4.** [illness, bug] contraer - **5.** [learn - tips, language] aprender; [- habit] adquirir - **6.** [subj: police]: **to pick sb up for sthg** coger a alguien por algo - **7.** *inf* [find partner] ligar con - **8.** RADIO & TELEC captar, reci-

bir - **9.** [start again] reanudar. <> *vi* - **1.** [improve] mejorar - **2.** [start again] seguir - **3.** [wind] aumentar.

pickaxe *UK*, **pickax** *US* ['pɪkæks] *n* piqueta *f*.

picker ['pɪkəʳ] *n* recolector *m*, -ra *f*.

picket ['pɪkɪt] <> *n* piquete *m*. <> *vt* formar piquetes en.

picketing ['pɪkətɪŋ] *n (U)* piquetes *mpl*.

picket line *n* piquete *m* (de huelga).

pickings ['pɪkɪŋz] *npl*: **easy/rich pickings** dinero *m* fácil/a raudales.

pickle ['pɪkl] <> *n* - **1.** [vinegar preserve] encurtido *m*; [sweet vegetable sauce] *salsa espesa agridulce con trozos de cebolla etc*; *US* [cucumber] pepinillos *mpl* en vinagre - **2.** *inf* [difficult situation]: **to be in a pickle** estar en un lío. <> *vt* encurtir.

pickled ['pɪkld] *adj* - **1.** [food] encurtido(da) - **2.** *inf* [drunk] bebido(da).

pick-me-up *n inf* tónico *m*, reconstituyente *m*.

pickpocket ['pɪk,pɒkɪt] *n* carterista *mf*.

pick-up *n* - **1.** [of record player] fonocaptor *m* - **2.** [truck] camioneta *f*, furgoneta *f*.

pick-up truck *n* camioneta *f*, furgoneta *f*.

picky ['pɪkɪ] *(comp* -ier, *superl* -iest) *adj* quisquilloso(sa).

picnic ['pɪknɪk] <> *n* comida *f* campestre, picnic *m*. <> *vi (pt & pp* -ked, *cont* -king) ir de merienda al campo.

picnicker ['pɪknɪkəʳ] *n* excursionista *mf*.

Pict [pɪkt] *n*: **the Picts** los Pictos.

pictorial [pɪk'tɔːrɪəl] *adj* ilustrado(da).

picture ['pɪktʃəʳ] <> *n* - **1.** [painting] cuadro *m*; [drawing] dibujo *m* - **2.** [photograph] foto *f*; [illustration] ilustración *f* - **3.** [on TV] imagen *f* - **4.** [cinema film] película *f* - **5.** [in mind] idea *f*, imagen *f* - **6.** [situation] situación *f* - **7.** [epitome]: **the picture of** la imagen de

▸▸ **to get the picture** *inf* entenderlo; **to put sb in the picture** poner a alguien al corriente; **to be in/out of the picture** estar/no estar en el ajo. <> *vt* - **1.** [in mind] imaginarse - **2.** [in media]: **to be pictured** aparecer en la foto - **3.** [in painting] pintar; [in drawing] dibujar.

➤ **pictures** *npl UK*: **the pictures** el cine.

picture book *n* libro *m* ilustrado.

picture rail *n* moldura *f* para colgar cuadros.

picturesque [,pɪktʃə'resk] *adj* pintoresco(ca).

picture window *n* ventanal *m*.

piddling ['pɪdlɪŋ] *adj inf pej* de poca monta.

pidgin ['pɪdʒɪn] <> *n* lengua *f* híbrida. <> *comp* híbrido(da).

pie [paɪ] *n* [sweet] tarta *f (cubierta de hojaldre)*; [savoury] empanada *f*, pastel *m*; **pie in the sky** castillos en el aire.

piebald ['paɪbɔːld] *adj* pío(a).

piece [piːs] *n* - **1.** [individual part or portion] trozo *m*, pedazo *m*; **to come to pieces** deshacerse; **to be smashed to pieces** ser destrozado; **to take sthg to pieces** desmontar algo; **to tear sthg to pieces** hacer trizas algo; **in pieces** en pedazos; **in one piece** [intact] intacto(ta); [unharmed] sano y salvo (sana y salva); **to go to pieces** *fig* venirse abajo - **2.** *(with U)* [individual object]: **piece of furniture** mueble *m*; **piece of clothing** prenda *f* de vestir; **piece of fruit** fruta *f*; **piece of luggage** bulto *m* de equipaje; **piece of advice** consejo *m*; **piece of news** noticia *f*; **a piece of information** una información; **piece of luck** golpe *m* de suerte; **piece of work** [object] pieza *f*; *inf* [nasty person] elemento *m* - **3.** [in board game] pieza *f*; [in draughts] ficha *f* - **4.** [valuable or interesting object, composition, play] pieza *f* - **5.** [of journalism] artículo *m* - **6.** [coin] moneda *f*.

◆ **piece together** *vt sep* [discover] componer.

pièce de résistance [ˌpjesdərezɪsˈtɑːs] *(pl* **pièces de résistance** [ˌpjesdərezɪsˈtɑːs]*) n* plato *m* principal.

piecemeal ['piːsmiːl] ◇ *adj* poco sistemático(ca). ◇ *adv* [gradually] gradualmente, por etapas.

piecework ['piːswɜːk] *n (U)* trabajo *m* a destajo.

pie chart *n* gráfico *m* de sectores.

pier [pɪəʳ] *n* - **1.** [at seaside] *paseo marítimo en un malecón* - **2.** [for landing boat] embarcadero *m*.

pierce [pɪəs] *vt* - **1.** [subj: bullet, needle] perforar; **to have one's ears pierced** hacerse agujeros en las orejas - **2.** [subj: voice, scream] romper.

pierced [pɪəst] *adj* perforado(da).

piercing ['pɪəsɪŋ] *adj* - **1.** [scream] desgarrador(ra); [sound, voice] agudo(da) - **2.** [wind] cortante - **3.** [look, eyes] penetrante.

piety ['paɪətɪ] *n* piedad *f*.

piffle ['pɪfl] *n (U) inf* tonterías *fpl*.

piffling ['pɪflɪŋ] *adj inf* ridículo(la).

pig [pɪg] *n* - **1.** [animal] cerdo *m*, puerco *m*, chancho *m Amér* - **2.** *inf pej* [greedy eater] tragón *m*, -ona *f*, comilón *m*, -ona *f*; **to make a pig of o.s.** darse un atracón - **3.** *inf pej* [unkind person] cerdo *m*, -da *f*, chancho *m*, -cha *f Amér* - **4.** *inf pej* [policeman] madero *m*; **the pigs** la madera.

◆ **pig out** *vi (pt & pp* **-ged**, *cont* **-ging)** *inf* darse un atracón.

pigeon ['pɪdʒɪn] *(pl* **pigeon** OR **-s)** *n* paloma *f*.

pigeon-chested [-ˌtʃestɪd] *adj* de pecho estrecho y salido.

pigeonhole ['pɪdʒɪnhəʊl] ◇ *n* [compartment] casilla *f*. ◇ *vt* [classify] encasillar.

pigeon-toed [-ˌtəʊd] *adj*: **he is pigeon-toed** tiene las puntas de los pies hacia dentro.

piggish ['pɪgɪʃ] *adj inf* [dirty] cochino(na); [eating too much] cerdo(da).

piggy ['pɪgɪ] ◇ *adj (comp* **-ier**, *superl* **-iest)** [eyes] de cerdito. ◇ *n (pl* **-ies)** *inf* cerdito *m*.

piggyback ['pɪgɪbæk] *n*: **to give sb a piggyback** llevar a alguien a cuestas.

piggybank ['pɪgɪbæŋk] *n* hucha *f* con forma de cerdito.

pigheaded [ˌpɪg'hedɪd] *adj* cabezota.

piglet ['pɪglɪt] *n* cerdito *m*, cochinillo *m*.

pigment ['pɪgmənt] *n* pigmento *m*.

pigmentation [ˌpɪgmən'teɪʃn] *n* pigmentación *f*.

pigmy *adj* & *n* = **pygmy**.

pigpen *US* = **pigsty**.

pigskin ['pɪgskɪn] ◇ *n* piel *f* de cerdo. ◇ *comp* de piel de cerdo.

pigsty ['pɪgstaɪ] *(pl* **-ies)**, **pigpen** *US* ['pɪgpen] *n lit* & *fig* pocilga *f*.

pigswill ['pɪgswɪl] *n* bazofia *f*.

pigtail ['pɪgteɪl] *n* [girl's] trenza *f*; [Chinese, bullfighter's] coleta *f*.

pike [paɪk] *n* - **1.** *(pl* **pike** OR **-s)** [fish] lucio *m* - **2.** *(pl* **-s)** [weapon] pica *f*.

pilaster [pɪ'læstəʳ] *n* pilastra *f*.

Pilates [pɪ'lɑːtiːz] *n* Pilates *m*.

pilchard ['pɪltʃəd] *n* sardina *f*.

pile [paɪl] ◇ *n* - **1.** [heap] montón *m*, ruma *f Andes*; **a pile** OR **piles of** [a lot] un montón de - **2.** [neat stack] pila *f* - **3.** [of carpet, fabric] pelo *m*. ◇ *vt* apilar, amontonar; **a plate piled with food** un plato colmado de comida.

◆ **piles** *npl* MED almorranas *fpl*.

◆ **pile in** *vi inf* entrar en tropel.

◆ **pile into** *vt insep inf* meterse atropelladamente en.

◆ **pile out** *vi inf*: **to pile out (of)** salir en tropel (de).

◆ **pile up** ◇ *vt sep* apilar, amontonar. ◇ *vi* - **1.** [form a heap] apilarse, amontonarse - **2.** [mount up] acumularse.

pile driver *n* martinete *m*.

pileup ['paɪlʌp] *n* accidente *m* en cadena.

pilfer ['pɪlfəʳ] ◇ *vt* sisar. ◇ *vi*: **to pilfer (from)** sisar (de).

pilgrim ['pɪlgrɪm] *n* peregrino *m*, -na *f*.

pilgrimage ['pɪlgrɪmɪdʒ] *n* peregrinación *f*.

pill [pɪl] n - **1.** MED píldora f, pastilla f - **2.** [contraceptive]: **the pill** la píldora (anticonceptiva); **to be on the pill** tomar la píldora.

pillage ['pɪlɪdʒ] ◇ n pillaje m, saqueo m. ◇ vt saquear.

pillar ['pɪlər] n lit & fig pilar m; **to be a pillar of strength** mostrar gran fortaleza.

pillar box n UK buzón m.

pillbox ['pɪlbɒks] n - **1.** [box for pills] cajita f para pastillas - **2.** MIL fortín m.

pillion ['pɪljən] n asiento m trasero; **to ride pillion** ir en el asiento trasero (de una moto).

pillock ['pɪlək] n UK inf gilipollas mf inv.

pillory ['pɪlərɪ] ◇ n (pl -ies) picota f. ◇ vt (pt & pp -ied) poner en la picota.

pillow ['pɪləʊ] n - **1.** [for bed] almohada f - **2.** US [on sofa, chair] cojín m.

pillowcase ['pɪləʊkeɪs], **pillowslip** ['pɪləʊslɪp] n funda f de almohada.

pilot ['paɪlət] ◇ n - **1.** AERON & NAUT piloto m - **2.** TV programa m piloto. ◇ comp [project, study] piloto (inv), de prueba. ◇ vt - **1.** AERON & NAUT pilotar - **2.** [test] poner a prueba.

pilot burner, pilot light n piloto m, luz f indicadora.

pilot scheme n proyecto m piloto.

pilot study n estudio m piloto.

pimento [pɪ'mentəʊ] (pl pimento OR -s) n pimiento m morrón.

pimp [pɪmp] n inf chulo m, padrote m Méx.

pimple ['pɪmpl] n grano m.

pimply ['pɪmplɪ] (comp -ier, superl -iest) adj cubierto(ta) de granos.

pin [pɪn] ◇ n - **1.** [for sewing] alfiler m; **pins and needles** hormigueo m - **2.** [drawing pin] chincheta f - **3.** [safety pin] imperdible m - **4.** [of plug] clavija f; COMPUT pin m - **5.** TECH clavija f - **6.** [in grenade] seguro m. ◇ vt (pt & pp -ned, cont -ning) - **1.** [fasten]: **to pin sthg to** OR **on** [sheet of paper] clavar con alfileres algo en; [medal, piece of cloth] prender algo en - **2.** [trap]: **to pin sb against** OR **to** inmovilizar a alguien contra - **3.** [apportion]: **to pin sthg on** OR **upon sb** cargar algo a alguien.

➤ **pin down** vt sep - **1.** [identify] determinar, identificar - **2.** [force to make a decision]: **to pin sb down (to)** obligar a alguien a comprometerse (a).

➤ **pin up** vt sep - **1.** [fasten with pins] clavar - **2.** [hem] prender con alfileres; [hair] recoger.

PIN [pɪn] (abbr of **personal identification number**) n PIN m.

pinafore ['pɪnəfɔːr] n - **1.** [apron] delantal m - **2.** UK [dress] pichi m.

pinball ['pɪnbɔːl] n millón m, flípper m.

pinball machine n máquina f de millón OR flípper.

pincer movement ['pɪnsə-] n movimiento m de tenazas.

pincers ['pɪnsəz] npl - **1.** [tool] tenazas fpl - **2.** [front claws] pinzas fpl.

pinch [pɪntʃ] ◇ n - **1.** [nip] pellizco m; **to feel the pinch** tener que apretarse el cinturón - **2.** [small quantity] pizca f. ◇ vt - **1.** [nip] pellizcar; [subj: shoes] apretar - **2.** inf [steal] mangar. ◇ vi [shoes] apretar.

➤ **at a pinch** UK, **in a pinch** US adv si no hay más remedio.

pinched [pɪntʃt] adj [thin, pale] demacrado(da); **pinched with** [cold] aterido(da) de; [hunger] muerto(ta) de; **pinched for** [time, money] escaso(sa) de.

pincushion ['pɪn,kuʃn] n acerico m.

pine [paɪn] ◇ n pino m. ◇ comp de pino. ◇ vi: **to pine for** suspirar por.

➤ **pine away** vi morirse de pena.

pineapple ['paɪnæpl] n piña f, ananá m R Plata.

pinecone ['paɪnkəʊn] n piña f.

pine needle n aguja f de pino.

pinetree ['paɪntriː] n pino m.

pinewood ['paɪnwʊd] n - **1.** [forest] pinar m - **2.** [material] madera f de pino.

ping [pɪŋ] ◇ n [of metal] sonido m metálico. ◇ vi producir un sonido metálico.

Ping-Pong® [-pɒŋ] n ping-pong® m.

pinhole ['pɪnhəʊl] n agujero m de alfiler.

pinion ['pɪnjən] ◇ n TECH piñón m. ◇ vt [hold down] inmovilizar.

pink [pɪŋk] ◇ adj rosa. ◇ n - **1.** [colour] rosa m - **2.** [flower] clavel m.

pink gin n UK ginebra f con angostura.

pinkie ['pɪŋkɪ] n US & Scotland dedo m meñique.

pinking scissors, pinking shears ['pɪŋkɪŋ-] npl tijeras fpl dentadas.

pink pound UK, **pink dollar** US n: **the pink pound** el poder adquisitivo de los homosexuales.

pin money n dinero m adicional para gastos menores.

pinnacle ['pɪnəkl] n - **1.** [high point] cumbre f, cúspide f - **2.** [mountain peak] cima f; [spire] pináculo m.

pinny ['pɪnɪ] (pl -ies) n UK inf delantal m.

pinpoint ['pɪnpɔɪnt] vt determinar, identificar.

pinprick ['pɪnprɪk] n - **1.** [mark, hole] marca f de pinchazo - **2.** [slight irritation] pequeña molestia f.

pin-striped [-ˌstraɪpt] *adj* a rayas.

pint [paɪnt] *n* **- 1.** *UK* [unit of measurement] = *0,568 litros; US = 0,473 litros*, ≃ pinta *f* **- 2.** *UK* [beer]: **to go for a pint** salir a tomar una caña.

pinto [ˈpɪntəʊ] *US* ◇ *adj* pinto(ta). ◇ *n* (*pl* **-s** OR **-es**) caballo *m* pinto.

pint-size(d) *adj* *inf* enano(na), muy pequeño(ña).

pinup [ˈpɪnʌp] *n* [of model] *(póster de) mujer medio desnuda*; [of film star etc] *(póster de) una atractiva estrella del pop, del cine etc.*

pioneer [ˌpaɪəˈnɪər] ◇ *n* pionero *m*, -ra *f*. ◇ *vt* iniciar, introducir.

pioneering [ˌpaɪəˈnɪərɪŋ] *adj* pionero(ra).

pious [ˈpaɪəs] *adj* **- 1.** [religious] piadoso(sa) **- 2.** *pej* [sanctimonious] mojigato(ta).

piously [ˈpaɪəslɪ] *adv* *pej* piadosamente.

pip [pɪp] *n* **- 1.** [seed] pepita *f* **- 2.** *UK* [bleep] señal *f*.

pipe [paɪp] ◇ *n* **- 1.** [for gas, water] tubería *f* **- 2.** [for smoking] pipa *f*. ◇ *vt* **- 1.** [transport via pipes] conducir por tuberías **- 2.** [say] decir con voz de pito.

➡ **pipes** *npl* MUS gaita *f*.

➡ **pipe down** *vi* *inf* cerrar la boca.

➡ **pipe up** *vi* *inf*: **to pipe up with a suggestion** saltar con una sugerencia.

pipe cleaner *n* limpiapipas *m inv*.

piped music [paɪpt-] *n* *UK* hilo *m* musical®.

pipe dream *n* sueño *m* imposible, castillos *mpl* en al aire.

pipeline [ˈpaɪplaɪn] *n* tubería *f*; [for gas] gasoducto *m*; [for oil] oleoducto *m*;... **is in the pipeline** hay planes para...

piper [ˈpaɪpər] *n* gaitero *m*, -ra *f*.

piping hot [ˈpaɪpɪŋ-] *adj* humeante, calentito(ta).

piquant [ˈpiːkənt] *adj* **- 1.** [food] picante **- 2.** [story] intrigante; [situation] que suscita un placer mordaz.

pique [piːk] ◇ *n* resentimiento *m*; **a fit of pique** un arrebato de despecho. ◇ *vt* **- 1.** [upset] ofender **- 2.** [arouse] despertar.

piracy [ˈpaɪrəsɪ] *n* **- 1.** [at sea] piratería *f* **- 2.** [illegal copying] piratería *f*.

piranha [pɪˈrɑːnə] *n* piraña *f*.

pirate [ˈpaɪrət] ◇ *adj* [gen & COMPUT] pirata. ◇ *n* **- 1.** [sailor] pirata *mf* **- 2.** [illegal copy] edición *f* pirata. ◇ *vt* piratear.

pirate radio *n* *UK* radio *f* pirata.

pirouette [ˌpɪruˈet] ◇ *n* pirueta *f*. ◇ *vi* hacer piruetas.

Pisces [ˈpaɪsiːz] *n* Piscis *m inv*; **to be (a) Pisces** ser Piscis.

piss [pɪs] *v inf* ◇ *n* **- 1.** [urine] meada *f*; **to take the piss out of** vacilar a **- 2.** [urination]: **to have a piss** mear. ◇ *vi* mear.

➡ **piss about, piss around** *UK* *v inf* ◇ *vt sep* vacilar. ◇ *vi* [waste time] tocarse los huevos; [fool around] hacer el gilipollas.

➡ **piss down** *vi* *UK* llover a cántaros.

➡ **piss off** ◇ *vt sep* cabrear. ◇ *vi* *UK* irse a la mierda; **piss off!** ¡vete a la mierda!

pissed [pɪst] *adj* *vulg* **- 1.** *UK* [drunk] pedo *(inv)*, cocido(da) **- 2.** *US* [annoyed] cabreado(da).

pissed off *adj* *vulg*: **to be** OR **to feel pissed off** estar cabreado(da).

pistachio [pɪˈstɑːʃɪəʊ] (*pl* **-s**) *n* pistacho *m*.

piste [piːst] *n* pista *f* de esquí.

pistol [ˈpɪstl] *n* pistola *f*.

pistol-whip *vt* golpear con la culata de una pistola.

piston [ˈpɪstən] *n* pistón *m*, émbolo *m*.

pit [pɪt] ◇ *n* **- 1.** [large hole] hoyo *m* **- 2.** [small hole - in metal, glass] señal *f*, marca *f*; [- on face] picadura *f*, piquete *m* *Méx* **- 3.** [for orchestra] foso *m* de la orquesta **- 4.** [mine] mina *f* **- 5.** [quarry] cantera *f* **- 6.** *US* [of fruit] hueso *m*, cuesco *m*, carozo *m* *R Plata*, pepa *f* *Col*

▸▸ **the pit of one's stomach** las entrañas. ◇ *vt* (*pt* & *pp* **-ted**, *cont* **-ting**): **to be pitted against** ser enfrentado(da) con; **to pit one's wits against** medirse con.

➡ **pits** *npl* **- 1.** [in motor racing]: **the pits** el box **- 2.** *inf* [awful]: **it's the pits** está fatal.

pitch [pɪtʃ] ◇ *n* **- 1.** SPORT campo *m* **- 2.** MUS tono *m* **- 3.** [level, degree] grado *m*, punto *m* **- 4.** *UK* [selling place] puesto *m* **- 5.** *inf* [sales talk] labia *f* de comerciante **- 6.** [motion - of ship, plane] tumbo *m*, bandazo *m*. ◇ *vt* **- 1.** [throw] lanzar, arrojar; **to be pitched into a situation** encontrarse de la noche a la mañana en una situación **- 2.** [design]: **to be pitched in order to do sthg** estar diseñado para hacer algo **- 3.** [speech] dar un tono a **- 4.** [tent] montar, poner. ◇ *vi* **- 1.** [ball] tocar el suelo; **to pitch forwards** [person] precipitarse hacia delante **- 2.** [ship, plane] dar un bandazo.

➡ **pitch in** *vi* ponerse manos a la obra.

pitch-black *adj* negro(gra) como boca de lobo.

pitched [pɪtʃt] *adj* [sloping] inclinado(da), pendiente.

pitched battle [ˌpɪtʃt-] *n* HIST batalla *f* campal; *fig* [bitter struggle] lucha *f* encarnizada.

pitcher [ˈpɪtʃər] *n* **- 1.** [jug] cántaro *m*, jarro *m* **- 2.** *US* [in baseball] lanzador *m*, pitcher *m*.

pitchfork [ˈpɪtʃfɔːk] *n* horca *f*.

piteous [ˈpɪtɪəs] *adj* lastimero(ra).

piteously [ˈpɪtɪəslɪ] *adv* lastimeramente.

pitfall ['pɪtfɔːl] *n* peligro *m*, escollo *m*.

pith [pɪθ] *n* piel *f* blanca.

pithead ['pɪthed] *n* bocamina *f*.

pith helmet *n* salacot *m*.

pithy ['pɪθɪ] (*comp* -ier, *superl* -iest) *adj* conciso(sa) y contundente.

pitiable ['pɪtɪəbl] *adj* lastimoso(sa).

pitiful ['pɪtɪfʊl] *adj* [condition, excuse, effort] lamentable; [person, appearance] lastimoso(sa).

pitifully ['pɪtɪfʊlɪ] *adv*: **she looks pitifully thin** está tan delgada que da pena; **a pitifully poor excuse** una excusa lamentable.

pitiless ['pɪtɪlɪs] *adj* [person] despiadado(da).

pitman ['pɪtmən] (*pl* -men [-mən]) *n* minero *m*.

pit pony *n UK tipo de poni que antiguamente hacía de animal de carga en las minas británicas.*

pit stop *n* [in motor racing] parada *f* en boxes.

pitta bread ['pɪtə-] *n tipo de pan sin levadura en el que se pone carne, ensalada etc.*

pittance ['pɪtəns] *n* miseria *f*.

pitted ['pɪtɪd] *adj* - **1.** [marked]: **pitted with** picado(da) de - **2.** [olive] sin hueso.

pitter-patter ['pɪtə,pætər] *n* golpeteo *m*.

pituitary [pɪ'tjuɪtrɪ] (*pl* -ies) *n*: **pituitary (gland)** glándula *f* pituitaria.

pity ['pɪtɪ] ◇ *n* - **1.** [compassion] compasión *f*; [shame] pena *f*, lástima *f*; **what a pity!** ¡qué pena!; **to take OR have pity on** compadecerse de. ◇ *vt* (*pt & pp* -ied) compadecerse de, sentir pena por.

pitying ['pɪtɪɪŋ] *adj* compasivo(va).

pivot ['pɪvət] ◇ *n* - **1.** TECH pivote *m*, eje *m* - **2.** *fig* [person] eje *m*. ◇ *vi*: **to pivot (on)** girar (sobre).

pixel ['pɪksl] *n* COMPUT & TV pixel *m*.

pixie, pixy ['pɪksɪ] (*pl* -ies) *n* duendecillo *m*.

pizza ['piːtsə] *n* pizza *f*.

pizzazz [pɪ'zæz] *n inf* vitalidad *f*, energía *f*.

Pl. *abbr of* **Place**.

P & L (*abbr of* **profit and loss**) *n* ganancias y pérdidas *fpl*.

placard ['plækɑːd] *n* pancarta *f*.

placate [plə'keɪt] *vt* aplacar, apaciguar.

placatory [plə'keɪtərɪ] *adj* apaciguador(ra).

place [pleɪs] ◇ *n* - **1.** [gen] lugar *m*, sitio *m*; **place of birth** lugar de nacimiento; **it's good in places** tiene algunas partes buenas - **2.** [proper position] sitio *m*; **to fall into place** encajar; **to put sb in their place** poner a alguien en su sitio - **3.** [suitable occasion, time] momento *m* - **4.** [home] casa *f* - **5.** [specific seat] asiento *m*; [in queue] sitio *m*; THEAT localidad *f* - **6.** [setting at table] cubierto *m* - **7.** [on course, at university] plaza *f* - **8.** [on committee, in team] puesto *m* - **9.** [role, function] papel *m*; **to have an important place in** desempeñar un papel importante en; **it's not my place to question it** no es de mi incumbencia cuestionarlo; **put yourself in my place** ponte en mi lugar - **10.** [position, rank] lugar *m*, posición *f* - **11.** [in book] página *f*; [in speech]: **to lose one's place** no saber (uno) dónde estaba - **12.** MATHS: **decimal place** punto *m* decimal - **13.** [instance]: **in the first place** [from the start] desde el principio; **in the first place... and in the second place...** [firstly, secondly] en primer lugar... y en segundo lugar...

▸▸ **to take place** tener lugar; **to take the place of** sustituir a. ◇ *vt* - **1.** [position, put] colocar, poner; **to be well placed to do sthg** estar en buena posición para hacer algo - **2.** [lay, apportion]: **to place the blame on** echar la culpa a; **to place emphasis on** poner énfasis en; **to place pressure on** ejercer presión sobre - **3.** [identify]: **I recognize the face, but I can't place her** me suena su cara, pero no sé de qué - **4.** [bet, order etc] hacer - **5.** [in horse racing]: **to be placed** llegar entre los tres primeros.

◆ **all over the place** *adv* por todas partes.

◆ **in place** *adv* - **1.** [in proper position] en su sitio - **2.** [established, set up] en marcha OR funcionamiento; **everything is now in place** los preparativos ya están finalizados.

◆ **in place of** *prep* en lugar de.

◆ **out of place** *adv* - **1.** [in wrong position]: **to be out of place** no estar en su sitio - **2.** [inappropriate, unsuitable] fuera de lugar.

placebo [plə'siːbəʊ] (*pl* -s OR -es) *n* placebo *m*.

place card *n* tarjeta *f* (de colocación de los invitados).

placed [pleɪst] *adj* situado(da).

place kick *n* RUGBY puntapié *m* colocado.

place mat *n* mantel *m* individual.

placement ['pleɪsmənt] *n* colocación *f*.

placenta [plə'sentə] (*pl* -s OR -tae [-tiː]) *n* placenta *f*.

place setting *n* cubierto *m*.

placid ['plæsɪd] *adj* - **1.** [even-tempered] apacible - **2.** [peaceful] tranquilo(la).

placidly ['plæsɪdlɪ] *adv* apaciblemente.

plagiarism ['pleɪdʒərɪzm] *n* plagio *m*.

plagiarist ['pleɪdʒərɪst] *n* plagiario *m*, -ria *f*.

plagiarize, -ise ['pleɪdʒəraɪz] *vt* plagiar.

plague [pleɪg] ◇ *n* - **1.** [attack of disease] peste *f* - **2.** [disease]: **(the) plague** la peste; **to avoid sb/sthg like the plague** huir de alguien/algo como de la peste - **3.** [of rats, insects] plaga *f*. ◇ *vt*: **to plague sb with** [complaints, requests] acosar a alguien con; [questions] acribillar a alguien a; **to be plagued by** [ill health] estar acosado de; [doubts] estar atormentado de.

plaice [pleɪs] (*pl* **plaice**) *n* platija *f*.

plaid [plæd] *n* tejido *m* escocés.

Plaid Cymru [ˌplaɪd'kʌmrɪ] *n UK* POL *partido nacionalista galés*.

plain [pleɪn] ⬦ *adj* - **1.** [not patterned] liso(sa) - **2.** [simple - gen] sencillo(lla); [- yoghurt] natural - **3.** [clear] evidente, claro(ra); **to make sthg plain to sb** dejar algo bien claro a alguien - **4.** [speaking, statement] franco(ca) - **5.** [absolute - madness etc] auténtico(ca) - **6.** [not pretty] sin atractivo. ⬦ *adv inf* completamente. ⬦ *n* GEOG llanura *f*, planicie *f*.

plain chocolate *n UK* chocolate *m* amargo.

plain-clothes *adj* vestido(da) de paisano.

plain flour *n UK* harina *f* (sin levadura).

plainly [ˈpleɪnlɪ] *adv* - **1.** [upset, angry] evidentemente - **2.** [visible, audible] claramente - **3.** [frankly] francamente - **4.** [simply] sencillamente.

plain sailing *n*: **it's plain sailing** es coser y cantar.

plainspoken [ˌpleɪn'spəʊkən] *adj* franco(ca).

plaintiff [ˈpleɪntɪf] *n* demandante *mf*.

plaintive [ˈpleɪntɪv] *adj* quejumbroso(sa), lastimero(ra).

plait [plæt] ⬦ *n* trenza *f*. ⬦ *vt* trenzar.

plan [plæn] ⬦ *n* - **1.** [strategy] plan *m*; **to go according to plan** salir según lo previsto - **2.** [of story, essay] esquema *m* - **3.** [of building etc] plano *m*. ⬦ *vt* (*pt & pp* **-ned**, *cont* **-ning**) - **1.** [organize] planear - **2.** [career, future, economy] planificar; **to plan to do sthg** tener la intención de hacer algo; **it wasn't planned** no estaba previsto - **3.** [design, devise] trazar un esquema OR boceto de. ⬦ *vi* hacer planes; **we hadn't planned for that** no lo habíamos previsto.

➤ **plans** *npl* planes *mpl*; **to have plans for** tener planes para.

➤ **plan on** *vt insep*: **to plan on doing sthg** pensar hacer algo.

➤ **plan out** *vt sep* planear.

plane [pleɪn] ⬦ *adj* plano(na). ⬦ *n* - **1.** [aircraft] avión *m* - **2.** GEOM [flat surface] plano *m* - **3.** *fig* [level - intellectual] nivel *m*, plano *m* - **4.** [tool] cepillo *m* - **5.** [tree] plátano *m*. ⬦ *vt* cepillar.

planet [ˈplænɪt] *n* planeta *m*.

planetarium [ˌplænɪˈteərɪəm] (*pl* **-riums** OR **-ria** [-rɪə]) *n* planetario *m*.

planetary [ˈplænɪtrɪ] *adj* planetario(ria).

plane tree *n* plátano *m*.

plank [plæŋk] *n* - **1.** [piece of wood] tablón *m*, tabla *f* - **2.** POL [main policy] punto *m* fundamental.

plankton [ˈplæŋktən] *n* plancton *m*.

planned [plænd] *adj* [crime] planeado(da); [economy] planificado(da).

planner [ˈplænər] *n* planificador *m*, -ra *f*; **town planner** urbanista *mf*.

planning [ˈplænɪŋ] *n* [gen] planificación *f*; **town planning** urbanismo *m*.

planning permission *n* permiso *m* de construcción OR de obras.

plan of action *n* plan *m* de acción.

plant [plɑːnt] ⬦ *n* - **1.** BOT planta *f* - **2.** [factory] planta *f*, fábrica *f* - **3.** [heavy machinery] maquinaria *f*. ⬦ *vt* - **1.** [seed, tree, vegetable]: **to plant sthg (in)** plantar algo (en) - **2.** [field, garden]: **to plant sthg with** sembrar algo de - **3.** [kiss, chair] colocar - **4.** [bomb, bug] colocar secretamente; **to plant sthg on sb** [drugs, weapon] endosar algo a alguien.

➤ **plant out** *vt sep* trasplantar.

plantain [ˈplæntɪn] *n* llantén *m*.

plantation [plæn'teɪʃn] *n* plantación *f*.

planter [ˈplɑːntər] *n* - **1.** [farmer] plantador *m*, -ra *f* - **2.** [container] macetero *m*.

plant pot *n* maceta *f*, tiesto *m*.

plaque [plɑːk] *n* [gen & MED] placa *f*.

plasma [ˈplæzmə] *n* plasma *m*; **plasma display** pantalla *f* de plasma.

plaster [ˈplɑːstər] ⬦ *n* - **1.** [for wall, ceiling] yeso *m* - **2.** [for broken bones] escayola *f*; **in plaster** escayolado(da) - **3.** *UK* [bandage] tirita® *f*. ⬦ *vt* - **1.** [put plaster on] enyesar - **2.** [cover]: **to plaster sthg (with)** cubrir algo (de).

plasterboard [ˈplɑːstəbɔːd] *n* cartón *m* yeso.

plaster cast *n* - **1.** [for broken bones] escayola *f* - **2.** [model, statue] vaciado *m* en yeso.

plastered [ˈplɑːstəd] *adj inf* [drunk] cocido(da).

plasterer [ˈplɑːstərər] *n* yesero *m*, -ra *f*.

plastering [ˈplɑːstərɪŋ] *n* enyesado *m*.

plaster of Paris *n* yeso *m* mate.

plastic [ˈplæstɪk] ⬦ *adj* [made from plastic] de plástico. ⬦ *n* plástico *m*.

plastic bag *n* bolsa *f* de plástico.

plastic bullet *n* bala *f* de goma.

plastic explosive *n* (explosivo *m*) plástico *m*.

Plasticine® [ˈplæstɪsiːn] *n UK* plastilina® *f*.

plastic money *n* (U) plástico *m*.

plastic surgeon *n* cirujano plástico *m*, cirujana plástica *f*.

plastic surgery *n* cirugía *f* plástica.

plastic wrap *n US* [clingfilm] plástico *m* transparente (*para envolver alimentos*).

plate [pleɪt] ⬦ *n* - **1.** [dish, plateful] plato *m*; **to have a lot on one's plate** [be busy] estar hasta el cuello de trabajo; **to hand sthg on a plate**

to sb ponerle algo a alguien en bandeja de plata - **2.** [on machinery, wall, door] placa *f* - **3.** *(U)* [metal covering]: **gold/silver plate** chapa *f* de oro/plata - **4.** [photograph] lámina *f* - **5.** [in dentistry] dentadura *f* postiza. ⬦ *vt*: **to be plated (with)** estar chapado(da) (en *OR* de).

plateau ['plætəʊ] *(pl* -**s** *OR* -**x** [-z]) *n* - **1.** [high, flat land] meseta *f* - **2.** *fig* [steady level]: **to reach a plateau** estancarse.

plateful ['pleɪtfʊl] *n* plato *m*.

plate glass *n* vidrio *m* cilindrado.

plate rack *n* escurreplatos *m inv*.

platform ['plætfɔ:m] *n* - **1.** [gen & COMPUT] plataforma *f*; [stage] estrado *m*; [at meeting] tribuna *f* - **2.** RAIL andén *m*; **platform 12** la vía 12 - **3.** POL programa *m* electoral.

plating ['pleɪtɪŋ] *n* chapeado *m*.

platinum ['plætɪnəm] ⬦ *adj* [colour] platino *(inv)*. ⬦ *n* platino *m*. ⬦ *comp* [made of platinum] de platino.

platinum blonde *n* rubia *f* platino.

platitude ['plætɪtju:d] *n* tópico *m*, cliché *m*.

platonic [plə'tɒnɪk] *adj* platónico(ca).

platoon [plə'tu:n] *n* pelotón *m*.

platter ['plætər] *n* [dish] fuente *f*.

platypus ['plætɪpəs] *(pl* -**es**) *n* ornitorrinco *m*.

plaudits ['plɔ:dɪts] *npl* aplausos *mpl*.

plausible ['plɔ:zəbl] *adj* plausible, admisible.

plausibly ['plɔ:zəblɪ] *adv* plausiblemente.

play [pleɪ] ⬦ *n* - **1.** *(U)* [amusement] juego *m*; **at play** jugando - **2.** [piece of drama] obra *f* - **3.** SPORT: **in play** en juego; **out of play** fuera del campo - **4.** [consideration]: **to come into play** entrar en juego - **5.** [game]: **play on words** juego *m* de palabras - **6.** TECH juego *m*. ⬦ *vt* - **1.** [game, sport] jugar a; [match] jugar; [in specific position] jugar de - **2.** [play game against]: **to play sb (at sthg)** jugar contra alguien (a algo) - **3.** [perform for amusement]: **to play a joke on sb** gastar una broma a; **to play a dirty trick on sb** jugar una mala pasada a - **4.** [act - part, character] representar; **to play a part** *OR* **role in** *fig* desempeñar un papel en; **to play the fool** hacer el tonto - **5.** [instrument, tune] tocar; [record, cassette] poner ▸▸ **to play it safe** actuar sobre seguro; **to play it cool** comportarse con calma. ⬦ *vi* - **1.** [gen]: **to play (with/against)** jugar (con/contra); **to play for sb/a team** jugar para alguien/con un equipo - **2.** [act]: **to play in sthg** actuar en algo - **3.** [be performed, shown - play] representarse; [- film] exhibirse - **4.** [MUS - person] tocar; [- music] sonar.
⬤ **play along** *vi*: **to play along (with)** seguir la corriente (a).

⬤ **play at** *vt insep* jugar a.

⬤ **play back** *vt sep* volver a poner.

⬤ **play down** *vt sep* quitar importancia a.

⬤ **play off** ⬦ *vt sep*: **to play sthg/sb off against** oponer algo/a alguien contra. ⬦ *vi* jugar un partido de desempate.

⬤ **play (up)on** *vt insep* aprovecharse de.

⬤ **play up** ⬦ *vt sep* [emphasize] hacer resaltar, realzar. ⬦ *vi* [machine, part of body, child] dar guerra.

playable ['pleɪəbl] *adj* en condiciones para que se juegue (un partido).

play-act *vi* fingir, hacer comedia.

playback ['pleɪbæk] *n* reproducción *f*.

playbill ['pleɪbɪl] *n* cartel *m* anunciador.

playboy ['pleɪbɔɪ] *n* playboy *m*, fifí *m* *Amér*.

player ['pleɪər] *n* - **1.** [of sport, game] jugador *m*, -ra *f* - **2.** MUS intérprete *mf* - **3.** THEAT actor *m*, actriz *f* - **4.** [important person or organization] protagonista *mf*.

playfellow ['pleɪ,feləʊ] *n* compañero *m*, -ra *f* de juego.

playful ['pleɪfʊl] *adj* juguetón(ona).

playfully ['pleɪfʊlɪ] *adv* de manera juguetona.

playground ['pleɪgraʊnd] *n* - **1.** [at school] patio *m* de recreo - **2.** [in park] zona *f* de juegos.

playgroup ['pleɪgru:p] *n* jardín *m* de infancia, guardería *f*.

playhouse ['pleɪhaʊs] *(pl* [-haʊzɪz]) *n US casita de juguete del tamaño de un niño*.

playing card ['pleɪɪŋ-] *n* naipe *m*, carta *f*.

playing field ['pleɪɪŋ-] *n* campo *m* de juego.

playlist ['pleɪlɪst] *n UK lista de éxitos que pone un disc-jockey en la radio*.

playmate ['pleɪmeɪt] *n* compañero *m*, -ra *f* de juego.

play-off *n* partido *m* de desempate.

playpen ['pleɪpen] *n* parque *m* (de niños) *(tipo cuna)*.

playroom ['pleɪrʊm] *n* cuarto *m* de los juguetes.

playschool ['pleɪsku:l] *n* jardín *m* de infancia, guardería *f*.

plaything ['pleɪθɪŋ] *n lit & fig* juguete *m*.

playtime ['pleɪtaɪm] *n* recreo *m*.

playwright ['pleɪraɪt] *n* autor *m*, -ra *f* de teatro, dramaturgo *m*, -ga *f*.

plaza ['plɑ:zə] *n* [for shopping] centro *m* comercial.

plc *abbr of* **public limited company**.

plea [pli:] *n* - **1.** [appeal] súplica *f*, petición *f* - **2.** LAW *declaración por parte del acusado de culpabilidad o inocencia*.

plea bargaining *n* negociación extrajudicial entre el abogado y el fiscal por la que el acusado acepta su culpabilidad en cierto grado a cambio de no ser juzgado por un delito más grave.

plead [pli:d] ◇ *vt* (*pt & pp* **-ed** OR **pled**) - **1.** LAW [one's cause] defender; **to plead guilty/not guilty** declararse culpable/inocente; **to plead insanity** alegar desequilibrio mental - **2.** [give as excuse] pretender. ◇ *vi* (*pt & pp* **-ed** OR **pled**) - **1.** [beg]: **to plead (with sb to do sthg)** rogar OR implorar (a alguien que haga algo); **to plead for sthg** pedir algo - **2.** LAW declarar.

pleading ['pli:dɪŋ] ◇ *adj* de súplica, implorante. ◇ *n (U)* súplicas *fpl*.

pleasant ['pleznt] *adj* - **1.** [smell, taste, view] agradable; [surprise, news] grato(ta) - **2.** [person, smile, face] simpático(ca), dije *Chile*.

pleasantly ['plezntlɪ] *adv* [smile, say] agradablemente; [be surprised] gratamente.

pleasantry ['plezntrɪ] (*pl* **-ies**) *n*: **to exchange pleasantries** intercambiar cumplidos.

please [pli:z] ◇ *vt* complacer, agradar; **he always pleases himself** él siempre hace lo que le da la gana; **please yourself!** ¡como quieras! ◇ *vi* - **1.** [give satisfaction] satisfacer, agradar - **2.** [think appropriate]: **to do as one pleases** hacer como a uno le parezca; **if you please** si no le importa. ◇ *adv* por favor.

pleased [pli:zd] *adj*: **to be pleased (about/with)** estar contento(ta) (por/con); **to be pleased for sb** alegrarse por alguien; **to be very pleased with o.s.** estar muy satisfecho de sí mismo; **pleased to meet you!** ¡encantado(da) de conocerle!, ¡mucho gusto!

pleasing ['pli:zɪŋ] *adj* agradable, grato(ta).

pleasingly ['pli:zɪŋlɪ] *adv* agradablemente.

pleasurable ['pleʒərəbl] *adj* agradable, grato(ta).

pleasure ['pleʒəʳ] *n* - **1.** [feeling of happiness] gusto *m*; **to take pleasure in doing sthg** disfrutar haciendo algo; **with pleasure** con gusto - **2.** [enjoyment] diversión *f* - **3.** [delight] placer *m*; **it's a pleasure to talk to him** da gusto hablar con él; **it's a pleasure, my pleasure** no hay de qué.

pleat [pli:t] ◇ *n* pliegue *m*. ◇ *vt* plisar.

pleated ['pli:tɪd] *adj* plisado(da).

plebiscite ['plebɪsaɪt] *n* plebiscito *m*.

plectrum ['plektrəm] (*pl* **-s**) *n* púa *f*, plectro *m*.

pled [pled] *pt & pp* ⊏▷ **plead**.

pledge [pledʒ] ◇ *n* - **1.** [promise] promesa *f* - **2.** [token] señal *f*, prenda *f*. ◇ *vt* - **1.** [promise]

prometer - **2.** [commit]: **to pledge sb to sthg** hacer jurar a alguien algo; **to pledge o.s. to** comprometerse a - **3.** [pawn] empeñar.

plentiful ['plentɪful] *adj* abundante.

plenty ['plentɪ] ◇ *n (U)* abundancia *f*. ◇ *pron*: **we've got plenty** tenemos de sobra; **that's plenty** es más que suficiente; **plenty of** mucho(cha); **plenty of reasons** muchas razones; **plenty of time** tiempo de sobra. ◇ *adv* US [very] muy; [a lot] mucho.

plethora ['pleθərə] *n* plétora *f*.

pleurisy ['pluərəsɪ] *n* pleuresía *f*.

Plexiglas® ['pleksɪgla:s] *n* US plexiglás® *m*.

pliable ['plaɪəbl], **pliant** ['plaɪənt] *adj* flexible.

pliers ['plaɪəz] *npl* tenazas *fpl*, alicates *mpl*.

plight [plaɪt] *n* grave situación *f*.

plimsoll ['plɪmsəl] *n* UK playera *f*, zapato *m* de tenis.

plinth [plɪnθ] *n* [for statue] peana *f*; [for pillar] plinto *m*.

PLO (*abbr of* **Palestine Liberation Organization**) *n* OLP *f*.

plod [plɒd] (*pt & pp* **-ded**, *cont* **-ding**) *vi* - **1.** [walk slowly] caminar con paso cansino - **2.** [work steadily]: **to plod away at sthg** trabajar pacientemente en algo.

plodder ['plɒdəʳ] *n pej* persona *f* mediocre pero voluntariosa (en el trabajo).

plonk [plɒŋk] *n (U)* UK *inf* [wine] vino *m* peleón.
 ◆ **plonk down** *vt sep inf* dejar caer.

plop [plɒp] ◇ *n* glup *m*. ◇ *vi* (*pt & pp* **-ped**, *cont* **-ping**) hacer glup.

plot [plɒt] ◇ *n* - **1.** [plan] complot *m*, conspiración *f* - **2.** [story] argumento *m*, trama *f* - **3.** [of land] parcela f **- 4.** US [house plan] plano m básico, plano m inicial. ◇ vt (pt & pp **-ted,** cont **-ting) - 1.** [plan] tramar, urdir **- 2.** [on map, graph] trazar. ◇ vi (pt & pp **-ted,** cont **-ting**): **to plot (to do sthg)** tramar (hacer algo); **to plot against** conspirar contra.

plotter ['plɒtəʳ] n **- 1.** [schemer] conspirador m, -ra f **- 2.** COMPUT plotter m.

plough UK, **plow** US [plaʊ] ◇ n arado m. ◇ vt arar.

◆ **plough into** ◇ vt sep [invest] invertir. ◇ vt insep [hit] chocar contra.

◆ **plough on** vi continuar trabajosamente.

◆ **plough up** vt sep **- 1.** AGRIC arar **- 2.** fig [fill with ruts] llenar de surcos.

ploughman's ['plaʊmənz] (pl **ploughman's**) n UK: **ploughman's (lunch)** queso, cebolletas y ensalada con pan.

ploughshare UK, **plowshare** US ['plaʊʃeəʳ] n reja f del arado.

plow US = **plough**.

ploy [plɔɪ] n táctica f, estratagema f.

pls (abbr of **please**) adv xfa, pf.

pluck [plʌk] ◇ vt **- 1.** [fruit, flower] coger **- 2.** [pull sharply] arrancar **- 3.** [bird] desplumar **- 4.** [eyebrows] depilar **- 5.** [instrument] puntear. ◇ n dated valor m, ánimo m.

◆ **pluck up** vt insep: **to pluck up the courage to do sthg** armarse de valor para hacer algo.

plucky ['plʌkɪ] (comp **-ier**, superl **-iest**) adj dated valiente.

plug [plʌg] ◇ n **- 1.** ELEC enchufe m **- 2.** [for bath or sink] tapón m **- 3.** inf [favourable mention] publicidad f. ◇ vt (pt & pp **-ged**, cont **-ging**) **- 1.** [hole, leak] tapar, taponar **- 2.** inf [mention favourably] dar publicidad a.

◆ **plug in** vt sep enchufar.

plughole ['plʌghəʊl] n desagüe m.

plug-in n COMPUT plug-in m.

plum [plʌm] ◇ adj **- 1.** [colour] de color ciruela **- 2.** [choice]: **plum job** chollo m. ◇ n [fruit] ciruela f.

plumage ['pluːmɪdʒ] n plumaje m.

plumb [plʌm] ◇ adv **- 1.** UK [exactly]: **plumb in the middle** justo en medio **- 2.** US [completely] completamente. ◇ vt: **to plumb the depths of** alcanzar las cotas más bajas de.

◆ **plumb in** vt sep UK instalar.

plumber ['plʌməʳ] n fontanero m, -ra f Esp, plomero m, -ra f Amér, gásfiter mf Chile, gásfitero m, -ra f Perú.

plumbing ['plʌmɪŋ] n (U) **- 1.** [fittings] tuberías fpl **- 2.** [work] fontanería f, plomería f Amér.

plumb line n (hilo m de) plomada f.

plume [pluːm] n **- 1.** [feather] pluma f **- 2.** [decoration, of smoke] penacho m.

plummet ['plʌmɪt] vi caer en picado.

plummy ['plʌmɪ] (comp **-ier**, superl **-iest**) adj UK inf pej [posh] afectado(da).

plump [plʌmp] adj regordete(ta), rollizo(za).

◆ **plump for** vt insep optar OR decidirse por.

◆ **plump up** vt sep ahuecar.

plumpness ['plʌmpnɪs] n rechonchez f.

plum pudding n budín navideño con pasas.

plunder ['plʌndəʳ] ◇ n **- 1.** [stealing, raiding] saqueo m, pillaje m **- 2.** [stolen goods] botín m. ◇ vt saquear.

plunge [plʌndʒ] ◇ n **- 1.** [dive] zambullida f; **to take the plunge** [get married] dar el paso decisivo; [take risk] lanzarse **- 2.** [decrease] caída f vertiginosa. ◇ vt **- 1.** [knife etc]: **to plunge sthg into** hundir algo en **- 2.** [into darkness, water]: **to plunge sthg into** sumergir algo en. ◇ vi **- 1.** [dive] zambullirse **- 2.** [decrease] bajar vertiginosamente.

plunger ['plʌndʒəʳ] n [for blocked pipes] desatascador m.

plunging ['plʌndʒɪŋ] adj: **plunging neckline** escote m pronunciado.

pluperfect [ˌpluːˈpɜːfɪkt] n: **pluperfect (tense)** (pretérito m) pluscuamperfecto m.

plural ['plʊərəl] ◇ adj [gen] plural. ◇ n plural m; **in the plural** en plural.

pluralistic [ˌplʊərəˈlɪstɪk] adj pluralista.

plurality [plʊˈrælətɪ] n **- 1.** [large number] pluralidad f **- 2.** US [majority] mayoría f.

plus [plʌs] ◇ adj **- 1.** [or more]: **35-plus** 35 o más **- 2.** [in marks]: **B-plus** ≃ notable m alto. ◇ n (pl **-es** OR **-ses**) **- 1.** MATHS [sign] signo m más **- 2.** [bonus] ventaja f. ◇ prep más. ◇ conj además.

plus fours npl (pantalones mpl) bombachos mpl.

plush [plʌʃ] adj lujoso(sa).

plus sign n signo m más.

Pluto ['pluːtəʊ] n [planet] Plutón m.

plutocrat ['pluːtəkræt] n plutócrata mf.

plutonium [pluːˈtəʊnɪəm] n plutonio m.

ply [plaɪ] ◇ n [of wood] número m de capas; [of wool, rope] número m de cabos. ◇ vt (pt & pp **plied**) **- 1.** [trade] ejercer **- 2.** [supply, provide]: **to ply sb with sthg** [questions] acosar a alguien con algo; [food, drink] no parar de ofrecer a alguien algo. ◇ vi (pt & pp **plied**) navegar.

plywood ['plaɪwʊd] n contrachapado m.

p.m., pm (abbr of **post meridiem**): **at 3 p.m.** a las tres de la tarde.

PM n abbr of **prime minister**.

PMT, PMS (abbr of **premenstrual tension, premenstrual syndrome**) n tensión f premenstrual.

pneumatic [nju:'mætɪk] *adj* - **1.** [pump, lift] de aire comprimido - **2.** [tyre, chair] neumático(ca).

pneumatic drill *n* martillo *m* neumático.

pneumonia [nju:'məʊnjə] *n (U)* pulmonía *f*.

PO[1] *n abbr of* **Post Office**.

PO[2], **po** *n abbr of* **postal order**.

poach [pəʊtʃ] <> *vt* - **1.** [game] cazar furtivamente; [fish] pescar furtivamente - **2.** [copy] plagiar - **3.** CULIN [salmon] cocer; [egg] escalfar. <> *vi* [for game] cazar furtivamente; [for fish] pescar furtivamente.

poacher ['pəʊtʃə'] *n* [hunter] cazador furtivo *m*, cazadora furtiva *f*; [fisherman] pescador furtivo *m*, pescadora furtiva *f*.

poaching ['pəʊtʃɪŋ] *n* [for game] caza *f* furtiva; [for fish] pesca *f* furtiva.

PO Box (*abbr of* **Post Office Box**) *n* apdo. *m*, casilla *f* (de correos) *Andes*.

pocket ['pɒkɪt] <> *n* - **1.** [in clothes] bolsillo *m*; **to live in each other's pockets** vivir continuamente pegado el uno al otro; **to be £10 out of pocket** salir perdiendo 10 libras; **to pick sb's pocket** vaciar a alguien el bolsillo - **2.** [in car door etc] bolsa *f*, bolsillo *m* - **3.** [of resistance] foco *m*; [of air] bolsa *f*; [on pool, snooker table] tronera *f*. <> *vt* - **1.** [place in pocket] meterse en el bolsillo - **2.** [steal] birlar. <> *adj* de bolsillo.

pocketbook ['pɒkɪtbʊk] *n* - **1.** [notebook] libreta *f* - **2.** *US* [handbag] bolso *m*; [wallet] cartera *f*.

pocket calculator *n* calculadora *f* de bolsillo.

pocketful ['pɒkɪtfʊl] *n* bolsillo *m*.

pocket handkerchief *n* pañuelo *m*.

pocketknife ['pɒkɪtnaɪf] (*pl* **-knives** [-naɪvz]) *n* navaja *f* (de bolsillo).

pocket money *n* - **1.** [from parents] propina *f* - **2.** [for minor expenses] dinero *m* para gastar.

pocket-sized *adj* de bolsillo.

pockmark ['pɒkmɑ:k] *n* marca *f*, señal *f*.

pod [pɒd] *n* - **1.** [of plants] vaina *f* - **2.** [of spacecraft] módulo *m* espacial.

podgy ['pɒdʒɪ] (*comp* **-ier**, *superl* **-iest**), **pudgy** *adj inf* gordinflón(ona).

podiatrist [pə'daɪətrɪst] *n US* podólogo *m*, -ga *f*, pedicuro *m*, -ra *f*.

podium ['pəʊdɪəm] (*pl* **-diums** OR **-dia** [-dɪə]) *n* podio *m*.

poem ['pəʊɪm] *n* poema *m*, poesía *f*.

poet ['pəʊɪt] *n* poeta *mf*.

poetic [pəʊ'etɪk] *adj* poético(ca).

poetic justice *n*: **it was poetic justice that he was sacked too** se llevó su merecido con el despido.

poet laureate *n* poeta *de la corte británica que escribe poemas para ocasiones oficiales.*

poetry ['pəʊɪtrɪ] *n* poesía *f*.

pogo stick *n* palo provisto de un muelle para dar saltos.

pogrom ['pɒgrəm] *n* pogromo *m*.

poignancy ['pɔɪnjənsɪ] *n* patetismo *m*.

poignant ['pɔɪnjənt] *adj* patético(ca), conmovedor(ra).

poinsettia [pɔɪn'setɪə] *n* flor *f* de Pascua.

point [pɔɪnt] <> *n* - **1.** [gen] punto *m*; **point of no return** punto de no retorno; **a sore point** *fig* un asunto espinoso OR delicado - **2.** [in time] momento *m*; **at that point** en ese momento - **3.** [tip] punta *f* - **4.** [detail, argument]: **to make a point** hacer una observación; **to make one's point** explicar la postura de uno; **it proves my point** prueba lo que digo; **to have a point** tener razón; **point taken!** ¡tienes razón! - **5.** [main idea]: **the point is...** lo fundamental es...; **that's the whole point** de eso se trata; **to miss the point of** no coger la idea de; **to get** OR **come to the point** ir al grano; **it's beside the point** no viene al caso; **to be to the point** venir al caso - **6.** [feature] aspecto *m*; **weak/strong point** punto *m* débil/fuerte - **7.** [purpose] sentido *m*; **what's the point?** ¿para qué?; **there's no point in it** no tiene sentido - **8.** [decimal point] coma *f*; **two point six** dos coma seis - **9.** *UK* ELEC toma *f* de corriente - **10.** GEOG punta *f*
⏵⏴ **to make a point of doing sthg** preocuparse de hacer algo. <> *vt*: **to point a gun at sthg/sb** apuntar a algo/alguien con una pistola; **to point one's finger at sthg/sb** señalar algo/a alguien con el dedo. <> *vi* - **1.** [indicate with finger]: **to point at sthg/sb**, **to point to sthg/sb** señalar algo/a alguien con el dedo - **2.** [hands of clock etc]: **to point north/to ten o'clock** indicar el norte/las diez - **3.** *fig* [suggest]: **everything points to her guilt** todo indica que ella es la culpable.
⏵ **points** *npl* - **1.** *UK* RAIL agujas *fpl* - **2.** AUT platinos *mpl*.
⏵ **up to a point** *adv* hasta cierto punto.
⏵ **on the point of** *prep*: **to be on the point of doing sthg** estar a punto de hacer algo.
⏵ **point out** *vt sep* [person, object, fact] señalar, indicar; [mistake] hacer notar.

point-blank <> *adj* - **1.** [refusal etc] categórico(ca) - **2.** [close]: **at point-blank range** a quemarropa. <> *adv* - **1.** [refuse, deny] categóricamente - **2.** [at close range] a quemarropa.

point duty *n UK* control *m* de tráfico en un cruce.

pointed [ˈpɔɪntɪd] *adj* - **1.** [sharp, angular] en punta, puntiagudo(da) - **2.** [cutting, incisive] intencionado(da).

pointedly [ˈpɔɪntɪdlɪ] *adv* intencionadamente.

pointer [ˈpɔɪntəʳ] *n* - **1.** [piece of advice] consejo *m* - **2.** [needle] aguja *f* - **3.** [for map, blackboard] puntero *m* - **4.** COMPUT puntero *m*.

pointing [ˈpɔɪntɪŋ] *n* [on wall] rejuntado *m*.

pointless [ˈpɔɪntlɪs] *adj* sin sentido, inútil; **it's pointless** no tiene sentido.

point of order (*pl* **points of order**) *n*: **to raise a point of order** hacer una moción sobre el acatamiento de las normas.

point of sale (*pl* **points of sale**) *n* punto *m* de venta.

point of view (*pl* **points of view**) *n* - **1.** [opinion] punto *m* de vista - **2.** [aspect, perspective] perspectiva *f*.

point-to-point *n* UK *carrera de caballos por el campo señalizada con banderines.*

poise [pɔɪz] *n* [self-assurance] aplomo *m*, serenidad *f*; [elegance] elegancia *f*.

poised [pɔɪzd] *adj* - **1.** [ready]: **to be poised to do sthg** estar listo(ta) para hacer algo; **to be poised for sthg** estar preparado(da) para algo - **2.** [calm and dignified] sereno(na).

poison [ˈpɔɪzn] ⟨⟩ *n* veneno *m*. ⟨⟩ *vt* - **1.** [generally - intentionally] envenenar; [- unintentionally] intoxicar - **2.** [environment] contaminar - **3.** *fig* [spoil, corrupt] corromper.

poisoning [ˈpɔɪznɪŋ] *n* - **1.** [intentional] envenenamiento *m*; [unintentional] intoxicación *f* - **2.** [of environment] contaminación *f*.

poisonous [ˈpɔɪznəs] *adj* - **1.** [substance, gas] tóxico(ca) - **2.** [snake] venenoso(sa) - **3.** *fig* [influence] pernicioso(sa); [rumours] malintencionado(da).

poison-pen letter *n* anónimo *m* ofensivo.

poke [pəʊk] ⟨⟩ *n* [blow] golpe *m*; [push] empujón *m*; [with elbow] codazo *m*. ⟨⟩ *vt* - **1.** [with finger, stick] empujar; [with elbow] dar un codazo a; [fire] atizar; **to poke sb in the eye** meter el dedo en el ojo de alguien - **2.** [push, stuff]: **to poke sthg into** meter algo en - **3.** [stretch]: **he poked his head round the door** asomó la cabeza por la puerta. ⟨⟩ *vi* - **1.** [protrude]: **to poke out of sthg** sobresalir por algo - **2.** [prod]: **his elbow was poking into my back** me estaba clavando el codo en la espalda.

◆ **poke about, poke around** *vi inf* fisgonear, hurgar.

◆ **poke at** *vt insep* dar golpecitos a.

poker [ˈpəʊkəʳ] *n* - **1.** [game] póker *m* - **2.** [for fire] atizador *m*.

poker-faced [-ˌfeɪst] *adj* con cara inexpresiva.

poky [ˈpəʊkɪ] (*comp* **-ier**, *superl* **-iest**) *adj pej*: **a poky little room** un cuartucho.

Poland [ˈpəʊlənd] *n* Polonia.

polar [ˈpəʊləʳ] *adj* polar.

polar bear *n* oso *m* polar.

polarity [pəʊˈlærətɪ] *n* polaridad *f*.

polarization [ˌpəʊləraɪˈzeɪʃn] *n* polarización *f*.

polarize, -ise [ˈpəʊləraɪz] *vt* polarizar.

Polaroid® [ˈpəʊlərɔɪd] *n* - **1.** [camera] polaroid® *f* - **2.** [photograph] fotografía *f* polaroid.

Polaroids® [ˈpəʊlərɔɪdz] *npl* gafas *fpl* de sol (de polaroid).

pole [pəʊl] *n* - **1.** [rod, post] poste *m*; [for tent, flag] mástil *m*; **telegraph pole** poste *m* telegráfico - **2.** ELEC & GEOG polo *m*; **to be poles apart** *fig* ser polos opuestos.

Pole [pəʊl] *n* polaco *m*, -ca *f*.

poleaxed [ˈpəʊlækst] *adj* atolondrado(da).

polecat [ˈpəʊlkæt] *n* turón *m*.

polemic [pəˈlemɪk] *n fml* [controversy] polémica *f*.

pole position *n* pole-position *f*.

Pole Star *n*: **the Pole Star** la estrella polar.

pole vault *n*: **the pole vault** el salto con pértiga.

◆ **pole-vault** *vi* saltar con pértiga.

pole-vaulter [-ˌvɔːltəʳ] *n* saltador *m*, -ra *f* con pértiga.

police [pəˈliːs] ⟨⟩ *npl* - **1.** [police force]: **the police** la policía - **2.** [policemen, policewomen] policías *mpl* & *fpl*. ⟨⟩ *vt* mantener el orden en, vigilar.

police car *n* coche *m* patrulla, auto *m* patrulla *Amér C, Chile & Méx*, patrullero *m*, patrulla *f* *Col & Méx*.

police constable *n* UK policía *mf*.

police department *n* US jefatura *f* de policía.

police dog *n* perro *m* policía.

police force *n* cuerpo *m* de policía.

policeman [pəˈliːsmən] (*pl* **-men** [-mən]) *n* policía *m*.

police officer *n* agente *mf* de policía.

police record *n*: **(to have a) police record** (tener) antecedentes *mpl* policiales.

police state *n* estado *m* policial.

police station *n* comisaría *f* (de policía).

policewoman [pəˈliːsˌwʊmən] (*pl* **-women** [-ˌwɪmɪn]) *n* (mujer *f*) policía *f*.

policy [ˈpɒlɪsɪ] (*pl* **-ies**) *n* - **1.** [plan, practice] política *f*; **it's not our usual policy to do this** no tenemos por norma hacer esto - **2.** [document, agreement] póliza *f*.

policy-holder *n* asegurado *m*, -da *f*.

polio [ˈpəʊlɪəʊ] *n* polio *f*.

polish ['pɒlɪʃ] <> n - **1.** [for floor, furniture] cera f; [for shoes] betún m; [for metal] abrillantador m; [for nails] esmalte m - **2.** [shine] brillo m, lustre m - **3.** fig [refinement] refinamiento m. <> vt [stone, wood] pulir; [floor] encerar; [shoes, car] limpiar; [cutlery, silver, glasses] sacar brillo a.
◆ **polish off** vt sep inf [food] zamparse; [job] despachar.

Polish ['pəʊlɪʃ] <> adj polaco(ca). <> n [language] polaco m. <> npl: **the Polish** los polacos.

polished ['pɒlɪʃt] adj - **1.** [person, manner] refinado(da) - **2.** [performance, speech] esmerado(da).

polite [pə'laɪt] adj educado(da), cortés; **it is polite to...** es de buena educación...; **polite society** gente f educada.

politely [pə'laɪtlɪ] adv educadamente, con cortesía.

politeness [pə'laɪtnɪs] n educación f, cortesía f.

politic ['pɒlətɪk] adj fml oportuno(na), conveniente.

political [pə'lɪtɪkl] adj - **1.** [concerning politics] político(ca) - **2.** [interested in politics] interesado(da) en política.

political asylum n asilo m político.

political correctness n corrección f política.

political geography n geografía f política.

politically [pə'lɪtɪklɪ] adv políticamente.

politically correct [pə,lɪtɪklɪ-] adj políticamente correcto(ta).

political prisoner n preso político m, presa política f.

political science n (U) ciencias fpl políticas.

politician [,pɒlɪ'tɪʃn] n político m, -ca f.

politicize, -ise [pə'lɪtɪsaɪz] vt politizar.

politics ['pɒlətɪks] <> n (U) política f. <> npl - **1.** [personal beliefs] ideas fpl políticas - **2.** [of a group, area] política f.

polka ['pɒlkə] n polca f.

polka dot n lunar m (en un vestido).

poll [pəʊl] <> n [vote] votación f; [of opinion] encuesta f. <> vt - **1.** [people] sondear - **2.** [votes] obtener.
◆ **polls** npl: **the polls** las elecciones, los comicios; **to go to the polls** acudir a las urnas.

pollen ['pɒlən] n polen m.

pollen count n índice m de polen en el aire.

pollinate ['pɒləneɪt] vt polinizar.

pollination [,pɒlɪ'neɪʃn] n polinización f.

polling ['pəʊlɪŋ] n (U) [votes] votación f.

polling booth ['pəʊlɪŋ-] n cabina f electoral.

polling day ['pəʊlɪŋ-] n UK día m de las elecciones.

polling station ['pəʊlɪŋ-] n colegio m OR centro m electoral.

pollster ['pəʊlstər] n encuestador m, -ra f.

poll tax n impuesto sobre las personas adultas.
◆ **Poll Tax** n UK: **the Poll Tax** ≈ la contribución urbana.

pollutant [pə'lu:tnt] n contaminante m.

pollute [pə'lu:t] vt contaminar.

pollution [pə'lu:ʃn] n (U) - **1.** [process of polluting] contaminación f - **2.** [impurities] sustancias fpl contaminantes.

polo ['pəʊləʊ] n polo m.

polo neck UK n - **1.** [neck] cuello m alto - **2.** [jumper] jersey m de cuello alto.
◆ **polo-neck** adj de cuello alto.

poltergeist ['pɒltəgaɪst] n poltergeist m, espíritu que habita una casa, produciendo ruidos y moviendo objetos.

poly ['pɒlɪ] (pl polys) n UK inf abbr of polytechnic.

polyanthus [,pɒlɪ'ænθəs] (pl -thuses OR -thi [-θaɪ]) n prímula f.

poly bag n UK inf bolsa f de plástico.

polyester [,pɒlɪ'estər] n poliéster m.

polyethylene US = polythene.

polygamy [pə'lɪgəmɪ] n poligamia f.

polygon ['pɒlɪgɒn] n polígono m.

polymer ['pɒlɪmər] n polímero m.

Polynesia [,pɒlɪ'ni:ʒə] n Polinesia.

Polynesian [ˌpɒlɪˈniːʒən] <> *adj* polinesio(sia). <> *n* - **1.** [person] polinesio *m*, -sia *f* - **2.** [language] polinesio *m*.

polyp [ˈpɒlɪp] *n* MED pólipo *m*.

polyphony [pəˈlɪfənɪ] *n* polifonía *f*.

polystyrene [ˌpɒlɪˈstaɪriːn] *n* poliestireno *m*.

polytechnic [ˌpɒlɪˈteknɪk] *n* UK escuela *f* politécnica.

polythene UK [ˈpɒlɪθiːn], **polyethylene** US [ˈpɒlɪˈeθɪliːn] *n* polietileno *m*, politeno *m*.

polythene bag *n* UK bolsa *f* de plástico.

polyunsaturated [ˌpɒlɪʌnˈsætʃəreɪtɪd] *adj* poliinsaturado(da).

polyurethane [ˌpɒlɪˈjʊərəθeɪn] *n* poliuretano *m*.

pom [pɒm] *n Australia inf término a veces peyorativo que designa a un británico.*

pomander [pəˈmændər] *n* bola *f* de loza perfumada.

pomegranate [ˈpɒmɪˌɡrænɪt] *n* granada *f*.

pommel [ˈpɒml] *n* - **1.** [on saddle] perilla *f* - **2.** [on sword] pomo *m*.

pomp [pɒmp] *n* pompa *f*.

pompom [ˈpɒmpɒm] *n* borla *f*, pompón *m*.

pompous [ˈpɒmpəs] *adj* - **1.** [self-important] presumido(da), pretencioso(sa) - **2.** [style] pomposo(sa); [building] ostentoso(sa).

ponce [pɒns] *n* UK *v inf pej* - **1.** [effeminate man] afeminado *m*, maricón *m* - **2.** [pimp] chulo *m*.

poncho [ˈpɒntʃəʊ] *(pl* -**s**) *n* poncho *m*, ruana *f Andes.*

pond [pɒnd] *n* estanque *m*.

ponder [ˈpɒndər] <> *vt* considerar. <> *vi*: **to ponder (on** OR **over)** reflexionar OR meditar (sobre).

ponderous [ˈpɒndərəs] *adj* - **1.** [speech, book] pesado(da) - **2.** [action, walk] lento(ta) y torpe - **3.** [progress] muy lento(ta).

pong [pɒŋ] UK *inf* <> *n* (olor *m* a) peste *f*. <> *vi* apestar.

pontiff [ˈpɒntɪf] *n* pontífice *m*.

pontificate [pɒnˈtɪfɪkeɪt] *vi pej*: **to pontificate (about** OR **on)** pontificar (sobre).

pontoon [pɒnˈtuːn] *n* - **1.** [bridge] pontón *m* - **2.** UK [game] veintiuna *f*.

pony [ˈpəʊnɪ] *(pl* -**ies**) *n* poni *m*.

ponytail [ˈpəʊnɪteɪl] *n* coleta *f* (de caballo).

pony-trekking [-ˌtrekɪŋ] *n* (U): **to go pony-trekking** hacer una excursión en poni.

poodle [ˈpuːdl] *n* caniche *m*.

poof [pʊf] *n* UK *v inf pej* maricón *m*.

pooh [puː] *excl* [said in scorn] ¡bah!; [said in disgust] ¡puaj!

pooh-pooh *vt inf* despreciar, desdeñar.

pool [puːl] <> *n* - **1.** [of water, blood, ink] charco *m*; [pond] estanque *m* - **2.** [swimming pool] piscina *f* - **3.** [of light] foco *m* - **4.** COMM [fund] fondo *m* común - **5.** [of people, things]: **typing pool** servicio *m* de mecanografía; **car pool** parque *m* móvil - **6.** [game] billar *m* americano. <> *vt* [resources, funds] juntar; [knowledge] poner en común.

◆ **pools** *npl* UK: **the pools** las quinielas.

pooped [puːpt] *adj* US hecho(cha) migas OR polvo.

poor [pɔːr] <> *adj* - **1.** [gen] pobre; **poor old John!** ¡el pobre de John!; **you poor thing!** ¡pobrecito! - **2.** [quality, result] malo(la); **to be in poor health** estar mal de salud - **3.** [prospects, chances] escaso(sa). <> *npl*: **the poor** los pobres.

poorhouse [ˈpɔːhaʊs] *(pl* [-haʊzɪz]*)* *n* asilo *m* para pobres.

poorly [ˈpɔːlɪ] <> *adj* UK pachucho(cha). <> *adv* mal; **poorly off** pobre.

poor relation *n fig* pariente *m* pobre.

pop [pɒp] <> *n* - **1.** [music] (música *f*) pop *m* - **2.** (U) *inf* [fizzy drink] gaseosa *f* - **3.** *esp US inf* [father] papá *m* - **4.** [sound] pequeña explosión *f*. <> *vt* (*pt* & *pp* -**ped**, *cont* -**ping**) - **1.** [balloon, bubble] pinchar - **2.** [put quickly]: **to pop sthg into** meter algo en; **he popped his head round the door** asomó la cabeza por la puerta. <> *vi* (*pt* & *pp* -**ped**, *cont* -**ping**) - **1.** [balloon] explotar, reventar; [cork, button] saltar - **2.** [eyes] salirse de las órbitas - **3.** [ears]: **her ears popped** se le destaparon los oídos - **4.** [go quickly]: **I'm just popping round to the shop** voy un momento a la tienda.

◆ **pop in** *vi* entrar un momento.

◆ **pop up** *vi* aparecer de repente.

popadum [ˈpɒpədəm], **papadum** *n tipo de pan indio muy delgado y frito en aceite.*

pop art *n* pop art *m*.

pop concert *n* concierto *m* de música pop.

popcorn [ˈpɒpkɔːn] *n* palomitas *fpl* (de maíz).

pope [pəʊp] *n* papa *m*.

pop group *n* grupo *m* (de música) pop.

poplar [ˈpɒplər] *n* álamo *m*.

poplin [ˈpɒplɪn] *n* popelina *f*.

pop music *n* música *f* pop.

popper [ˈpɒpər] *n* UK [on clothes] corchete *m*.

poppy [ˈpɒpɪ] *(pl* -**ies**) *n* amapola *f*.

poppycock [ˈpɒpɪkɒk] *n* (U) *inf pej* bobadas *fpl*.

Poppy Day *n* UK día en conmemoración de los caídos de las guerras mundiales.

Popsicle® [ˈpɒpsɪkl] *n* US polo *m*.

pop singer *n* cantante *mf* pop.

populace [ˈpɒpjʊləs] *n*: **the populace** [masses] el populacho; [people] el pueblo.

popular ['pɒpjʊləʳ] *adj* - **1.** [gen] popular; [person] estimado(da) - **2.** [belief, attitude, discontent] generalizado(da), común - **3.** [newspaper, politics] para las masas.

popularity [,pɒpjʊ'lærətɪ] *n* popularidad *f*.

popularize, -ise ['pɒpjʊləraɪz] *vt* - **1.** [make popular] popularizar - **2.** [simplify] vulgarizar.

popularly ['pɒpjʊləlɪ] *adv* - **1.** [unofficially]: **popularly known as** conocido(da) popularmente como - **2.** [believed] generalmente.

populate ['pɒpjʊleɪt] *vt* poblar.

populated ['pɒpjʊleɪtɪd] *adj* poblado(da).

population [,pɒpjʊ'leɪʃn] *n* población *f*.

population explosion *n* explosión *f* demográfica.

populist ['pɒpjʊlɪst] *n* populista *mf*.

pop-up *adj* - **1.** [toaster] automático(ca) - **2.** [book & COMPUT] desplegable.

porcelain ['pɔːsəlɪn] *n* porcelana *f*.

porch [pɔːtʃ] *n* - **1.** [entrance] porche *m*, pórtico *m* - **2.** US [verandah] porche *m*.

porcupine ['pɔːkjʊpaɪn] *n* puerco *m* espín.

pore [pɔːʳ] *n* poro *m*.
➤ **pore over** *vt insep* estudiar esmeradamente.

pork [pɔːk] *n* carne *f* de cerdo.

pork chop *n* chuleta *f* de cerdo.

pork pie *n* empanada *f* de carne de cerdo.

porn [pɔːn] (*abbr of* **pornography**) *n inf* porno *m*; **hard/soft porn** porno duro/blando.

pornographic [,pɔːnə'græfɪk] *adj* pornográfico(ca).

pornography [pɔː'nɒgrəfɪ] *n* pornografía *f*.

porous ['pɔːrəs] *adj* poroso(sa).

porpoise ['pɔːpəs] *n* marsopa *f*.

porridge ['pɒrɪdʒ] *n* papilla *f* OR gachas *fpl* de avena.

port [pɔːt] *n* - **1.** [coastal town, harbour] puerto *m* - **2.** NAUT [left-hand side] babor *m*; **to port** a babor - **3.** [drink] oporto *m* - **4.** COMPUT puerto *m*. *comp* - **1.** [relating to a port] portuario(ria) - **2.** NAUT [right-hand] a babor.

portable ['pɔːtəbl] *adj* portátil.

Portacrib® ['pɔːtə,krɪb] *n* US moisés *m*, cuco *m*.

portal ['pɔːtl] *n* - **1.** COMPUT portal *m* - **2.** *liter* pórtico *m*.

portcullis [,pɔːt'kʌlɪs] *n* rastrillo *m*.

portend [pɔː'tend] *vt liter* presagiar, augurar.

portent ['pɔːtənt] *n liter* presagio *m*, augurio *m*.

porter ['pɔːtəʳ] *n* - **1.** UK [in block of flats] portero *m*, -ra *f*; [in public building, hotel] conserje *mf* - **2.** [for luggage] mozo *m* - **3.** US [on train] empleado *m*, -da *f* de coche cama.

portfolio [,pɔːt'fəʊljəʊ] (*pl* **-s**) *n* - **1.** ART, FIN & POL cartera *f* - **2.** [sample of work] carpeta *f*.

porthole ['pɔːthəʊl] *n* portilla *f*.

portion ['pɔːʃn] *n* - **1.** [part, section] porción *f* - **2.** [of chips, vegetables etc] ración *f*.

portly ['pɔːtlɪ] (*comp* **-ier**, *superl* **-iest**) *adj* corpulento(ta).

port of call *n* - **1.** NAUT puerto *m* de escala - **2.** *fig* [on journey] escala *f*, parada *f*.

portrait ['pɔːtrɪt] *n* - **1.** [picture] retrato *m* - **2.** COMPUT formato *m* vertical.

portraitist [p'ɔːtrɪtɪst] *n* retratista *mf*.

portray [pɔː'treɪ] *vt* - **1.** [represent - in a play, film] representar - **2.** [describe] describir - **3.** [paint] retratar.

portrayal [pɔː'treɪəl] *n* - **1.** [representation - in a play, film] representación *f* - **2.** [painting, photograph] retrato *m* - **3.** [description] descripción *f*.

Portugal ['pɔːtʃʊgl] *n* Portugal.

Portuguese [,pɔːtʃʊ'giːz] ◇ *adj* portugués(esa). ◇ *n* [language] portugués *m*. ◇ *npl*: **the Portuguese** los portugueses.

Portuguese man-of-war *n* medusa *f* venenosa.

poser ['pəʊzəʳ] *n* - **1.** *pej* [person] presumido *m*, -da *f* - **2.** *inf* [hard question] pregunta *f* difícil.

poseur [pəʊ'zɜːʳ] *n pej* presumido *m*, -da *f*.

posh [pɒʃ] *adj inf* - **1.** [hotel, area etc] de lujo, elegante - **2.** UK [person, accent] afectado(da).

posit ['pɒzɪt] *vt fml* proponer.

position [pə'zɪʃn] ◇ *n* - **1.** [gen] posición *f* - **2.** [right place] sitio *m*, lugar *m*; **in position** en su sitio - **3.** [status] rango *m* - **4.** [job] puesto *m* - **5.** [in a race, competition] lugar *m* - **6.** [state, situation] situación *f*; **to be in a/no position to do sthg** estar/no estar en condiciones de hacer algo - **7.** [stance, opinion]: **position on** postura *f* respecto a. ◇ *vt* colocar; **to position o.s.** colocarse.

positive ['pɒzətɪv] *adj* - **1.** [gen] positivo(va); **the test was positive** la prueba dio positivo - **2.** [sure]: **to be positive (about)** estar seguro(ra) (de) - **3.** [optimistic, confident]: **to be positive (about)** ser optimista (respecto a) - **4.** [definite - action] decisivo(va); [- decision] categórico(ca) - **5.** [irrefutable - evidence, fact] irrefutable, evidente; [- proof] concluyente - **6.** [for emphasis - delight, nuisance] auténtico(ca), total.

positive discrimination *n* discriminación *f* positiva.

positively ['pɒzətɪvlɪ] *adv* - **1.** [optimistically - think etc] positivamente - **2.** [definitely - act] decisivamente - **3.** [favourably - react, reply] favorablemente - **4.** [irrefutably - prove] irrefutablemente - **5.** [for emphasis - rude, unbearable] realmente.

positive vetting n UK investigación completa a la que es sometido un aspirante a un cargo público relacionado con la seguridad nacional.

positivism ['pɒzɪtɪvɪzm] n positivismo m.

posse ['pɒsɪ] n US **- 1.** [to pursue criminal] grupo m de hombres a caballo **- 2.** [group] grupo m.

possess [pə'zes] vt **- 1.** [gen] poseer **- 2.** [subj: emotion] adueñarse de; **what possessed him to do it?** ¿qué le empujó a hacerlo?

possessed [pə'zest] adj [mad] poseso(sa), poseído(da).

possession [pə'zeʃn] n posesión f; **to have sthg in one's possession, to be in possession of sthg** tener (posesión de) algo.

➠ **possessions** npl bienes mpl.

possessive [pə'zesɪv] <> adj **- 1.** [gen] posesivo(va) **- 2.** pej [selfish] egoísta. <> n GRAM posesivo m.

possessor [pə'zesər] n fml poseedor m, -ra f.

possibility [,pɒsə'bɪlətɪ] (pl -ies) n posibilidad f; **there's a possibility that...** es posible que...

possible ['pɒsəbl] <> adj **- 1.** [gen] posible; **as soon as possible** cuanto antes; **as much as possible** [quantity] todo lo posible; [to the greatest possible extent] en la medida de lo posible; **I go as often as possible** voy siempre que puedo; **it's possible that she'll come** es posible que venga **- 2.** [viable - plan etc] viable, factible. <> n candidato m, -ta f.

possibly ['pɒsəblɪ] adv **- 1.** [perhaps] posiblemente, quizás **- 2.** [within one's power]: **I'll do all I possibly can** haré todo lo que pueda; **could you possibly help me?** ¿te importaría ayudarme? **- 3.** [to show surprise]: **how could he possibly do that?** ¿cómo demonios pudo hacer eso? **- 4.** [for emphasis]: **I can't possibly do it** no puedo hacerlo de ninguna manera.

possum ['pɒsəm] (pl possum OR -s) n US zarigüeya f.

post [pəust] <> n **- 1.** [service]: **the post** el correo; **by post** por correo; **in the post** en el correo **- 2.** (U) [letters etc] cartas fpl **- 3.** [delivery] reparto m **- 4.** UK [collection] colecta f **- 5.** [pole] poste m **- 6.** [position, job] puesto m **- 7.** MIL puesto m

▸▸ **to pip sb at the post** ganar a alguien por los pelos. <> vt **- 1.** [put in letterbox] echar al correo; [send by mail] mandar por correo **- 2.** [transfer] enviar, destinar **- 3.** COMPUT [message, query] enviar

▸▸ **to keep sb posted** mantener a alguien al tanto.

post- [pəust] prefix pos-.

postage ['pəustɪdʒ] n franqueo m, porte m; **postage and packing** gastos mpl de envío.

postage stamp n fml sello m, estampilla f Amér, timbre m Méx.

postal ['pəustl] adj postal.

postal order n giro m postal.

postal vote n voto m por correo.

postbag ['pəustbæg] n **- 1.** UK [bag] saco m postal **- 2.** inf [letters received] cartas fpl.

postbox ['pəustbɒks] n UK buzón m.

postcard ['pəustkɑːd] n postal f.

postcode ['pəustkəud] n UK código m postal.

postdate [,pəust'deɪt] vt poner posfecha a; **a postdated cheque** extender un cheque con fecha posterior.

poster ['pəustər] n cartel m, póster m.

poste restante [,pəust'rɒstɑːnt] n esp UK lista f de correos.

posterior [pɒ'stɪərɪər] <> adj posterior, trasero(ra). <> n hum trasero m.

posterity [pɒ'sterətɪ] n posteridad f.

poster paint n aguada f.

post-free adj esp UK libre de gastos de envío, porte pagado (inv).

postgraduate [,pəust'grædʒuət] <> adj posgraduado(da). <> n posgraduado m, -da f.

posthaste [,pəust'heɪst] adv dated rápidamente, a toda prisa.

posthumous ['pɒstjuməs] adj póstumo(ma).

posthumously ['pɒstjuməslɪ] adv póstumamente.

post-industrial adj postindustrial.

posting ['pəustɪŋ] n destino m.

postman ['pəustmən] (pl -men [-mən]) n cartero m.

postmark ['pəustmɑːk] <> n matasellos m inv. <> vt matasellar.

postmortem [,pəust'mɔːtəm] n **- 1.** [autopsy] autopsia f **- 2.** fig [analysis] reflexión f autocrítica retrospectiva.

postnatal [,pəust'neɪtl] adj posnatal, posparto.

post office n **- 1.** [organization]: **the Post Office** ≃ Correos m inv **- 2.** [building] oficina f de correos.

post office box n apartado m de correos, casilla f de correos Andes & R Plata.

postoperative [,pəust'ɒpərətɪv] adj postoperatorio(ria).

postpaid [,pəust'peɪd] adj libre de gastos de envío, porte pagado (inv).

postpone [,pəust'pəun] vt posponer.

postponement [,pəust'pəunmənt] n aplazamiento m.

postscript ['pəustskrɪpt] n [additional message] posdata f; fig [additional information] postdata f, nota f final.

postulate *fml* ⬦ *n* ['pɒstjʊlət] postulado *m*. ⬦ *vt* ['pɒstjʊleɪt] postular.

posture ['pɒstʃəʳ] ⬦ *n lit & fig* postura *f*; **posture on sthg** postura hacia algo. ⬦ *vi* adoptar poses.

postwar [,pəʊst'wɔːʳ] *adj* de (la) posguerra.

posy ['pəʊzɪ] (*pl* -ies) *n* ramillete *m*.

pot [pɒt] ⬦ *n* - **1.** [for cooking] olla *f* - **2.** [for tea] tetera *f*; [for coffee] cafetera *f* - **3.** [for paint] bote *m*; [for jam] tarro *m* - **4.** [flowerpot] tiesto *m*, maceta *f* - **5.** (*U*) *inf* [cannabis] maría *f*, hierba *f* ▸▸ **to go to pot** ir al traste. ⬦ *vt* (*pt & pp* -ted, *cont* -ting) plantar (en un tiesto).

potash ['pɒtæʃ] *n* potasa *f*.

potassium [pə'tæsɪəm] *n* potasio *m*.

potato [pə'teɪtəʊ] (*pl* -es) *n* patata *f*.

potato crisps *UK*, **potato chips** *US n* patatas *fpl* fritas (*de bolsa*).

potato peeler [-,piːləʳ] *n* pelapatatas *m inv Esp*, pelapapas *m inv Amér*.

pot-bellied [-,belɪd] *adj* - **1.** [from overeating] barrigudo(da), guatón(ona) *Chile* - **2.** [from malnutrition] con el vientre hinchado.

potboiler ['pɒt,bɔɪləʳ] *n* obra *f* con fin comercial (de escaso valor artístico).

potbound ['pɒtbaʊnd] *adj* con muchas raíces.

potency ['pəʊtənsɪ] *n* [gen] potencia *f*; [of argument] fuerza *f*.

potent ['pəʊtənt] *adj* - **1.** [powerful, influential] poderoso(sa) - **2.** [drink, drug] fuerte - **3.** [sexually capable] potente.

potentate ['pəʊtənteɪt] *n* potentado *m*, -da *f*.

potential [pə'tenʃl] ⬦ *adj* potencial, posible. ⬦ *n* (*U*) potencial *m*; **to have potential** tener posibilidades, prometer.

potentially [pə'tenʃəlɪ] *adv* en potencia.

pothole ['pɒthəʊl] *n* - **1.** [in road] bache *m* - **2.** [underground] cueva *f*.

potholer ['pɒt,həʊləʳ] *n UK* espeleólogo *m*, -ga *f*.

potholing ['pɒt,həʊlɪŋ] *n UK* espeleología *f*.

potion ['pəʊʃn] *n* poción *f*.

potluck [,pɒt'lʌk] *n*: **to take potluck** [gen] elegir a ojo; [at meal] conformarse con lo que haya.

pot plant *n* planta *f* de interior.

potpourri [,pəʊ'pʊərɪ] *n* (*U*) [dried flowers] popurrí *m* (*aromático*).

pot roast *n* estofado *m* de carne.

potshot ['pɒt,ʃɒt] *n*: **to take a potshot (at sthg/sb)** disparar (a algo/alguien) sin apuntar.

potted ['pɒtɪd] *adj* - **1.** [plant] en tiesto - **2.** [meat, fish] en conserva - **3.** *UK fig* [biography, history] resumido(da).

potter ['pɒtəʳ] *n* alfarero *m*, -ra *f*, ceramista *mf*.

potter about, potter around *vi UK* entretenerse.

potter's wheel *n* torno *m* de alfarero.

pottery ['pɒtərɪ] (*pl* -ies) *n* - **1.** [gen] cerámica *f*, alfarería *f* - **2.** [factory] fábrica *f* de cerámica.

potting compost ['pɒtɪŋ-] *n* abono *m* para plantas interiores.

potty ['pɒtɪ] *UK inf* ⬦ *adj* (*comp* -ier, *superl* -iest) [person] chalado(da); **to be potty about** estar chalado por. ⬦ *n* (*pl* -ies) orinal *m*.

potty-trained [-,treɪnd] *adj* que ya no lleva pañales.

pouch [paʊtʃ] *n* - **1.** [small bag] bolsa *f* pequeña; [for tobacco] petaca *f* - **2.** [on animal's body] bolsa *f* (abdominal).

pouffe [puːf] *n UK* [seat] puf *m*.

poultice ['pəʊltɪs] *n* cataplasma *f*, emplasto *m*.

poultry ['pəʊltrɪ] ⬦ *n* [meat] carne *f* de pollería. ⬦ *npl* [birds] aves *fpl* de corral.

pounce [paʊns] *vi* - **1.** [leap]: **to pounce (on OR upon)** abalanzarse (sobre) - **2.** *fig* [comment immediately]: **he's quick to pounce on OR upon the slightest error** siempre está a la que salta con el más mínimo error.

pound [paʊnd] ⬦ *n* - **1.** [unit of money, weight] libra *f*; **the pound** la libra (esterlina) - **2.** [for cars] depósito *m* (de coches); [for dogs] perrera *f*. ⬦ *vt* - **1.** [hammer on] golpear - **2.** [pulverize] machacar. ⬦ *vi* - **1.** [hammer]: **to pound on sthg** golpear OR aporrear algo - **2.** [beat, throb] palpitar; **her heart was pounding** le palpitaba el corazón.

pounding ['paʊndɪŋ] *n* - **1.** (*U*) [hammering] golpes *mpl*, aporreamiento *m* - **2.** (*U*) [beating, throbbing] palpitación *f* - **3.** *fig*: **to get OR take a pounding** [team] recibir una soberana paliza; [city] verse sometido a un feroz bombardeo.

pound sterling *n* libra *f* esterlina.

pour [pɔːʳ] ⬦ *vt* - **1.** [cause to flow]: **to pour sthg (into)** echar OR verter algo (en); **to pour sthg down the sink** tirar algo por el fregadero; **to pour sb a drink, to pour a drink for sb** servirle una copa a alguien; **can I pour you a cup of tea?** ¿quieres que te sirva una taza de té? - **2.** *fig*: **to pour money into sthg** invertir mucho dinero en algo. ⬦ *vi* [liquid] chorrear; [smoke] salir a borbotones. ⬦ *impers vb* [rain hard] llover a cántaros; **it's pouring (down)** está lloviendo a cántaros.

⬛ **pour in** *vi* llegar a raudales.

⬛ **pour out** ⬦ *vt sep* - **1.** [empty] echar, vaciar - **2.** [serve] servir - **3.** *fig* [reveal]: **to pour out one's feelings OR heart (to sb)** desahogarse (con alguien). ⬦ *vi* [rush out] salir en manada.

pouring ['pɔːrɪŋ] *adj* [rain] torrencial.

pout [paʊt] <> *n* [showing displeasure] puchero *m*, mohín *m*; [being provocative] gesto *m* provocador (de los labios). <> *vi* [showing displeasure] hacer pucheros; [being provocative] hacer un gesto provocador con los labios.

poverty ['pɒvəti] *n lit* & *fig* pobreza *f*.

poverty line *n* umbral *m* de pobreza.

poverty-stricken *adj* necesitado(da).

poverty trap *n* UK *situación del que gana menos trabajando que en el paro, porque sus ingresos superan por poco el nivel mínimo de contribución fiscal.*

pow [paʊ] *excl inf* ¡pum!, ¡pumba!

POW *n abbr of* prisoner of war.

powder ['paʊdər] <> *n* polvo *m*; [make-up] polvos *mpl*. <> *vt* poner polvos en; **to powder o.s.** darse polvos, empolvarse.

powder compact *n* polvera *f*.

powdered ['paʊdəd] *adj* - **1.** [in powder form] en polvo - **2.** [covered in powder] empolvado(da).

powdered sugar *n* US azúcar *m* glas.

powder puff *n* borla *f*.

powder room *n* servicios *mpl* de señoras, tocador *m*.

powdery ['paʊdərɪ] *adj* [snow] en polvo; [cake etc] harinoso(sa).

power ['paʊər] <> *n* - **1.** *(U)* [authority, control] poder *m*; **to have power over sb** tener poder sobre alguien; **to come to/take power** llegar al/hacerse con el poder; **to be in power** estar en el poder - **2.** [ability] facultad *f*; **it isn't within my power to do it** no está dentro de mis posibilidades hacerlo; **I'll do everything in my power to help** haré todo lo que pueda por ayudar - **3.** [legal authority] autoridad *f*, competencia *f*; **to have the power to do sthg** tener autoridad para hacer algo - **4.** [physical strength] fuerza *f* - **5.** [energy - solar, steam etc] energía *f* - **6.** [electricity] corriente *f*; **to turn the power on/off** dar/cortar la corriente - **7.** [powerful nation, person, group] potencia *f*; **the powers that be** el orden establecido - **8.** [phr]: **to do sb a power of good** sentar de maravilla a alguien. <> *vt* propulsar, impulsar.

powerboat ['paʊəbəʊt] *n* motora *f*.

power cut *n* apagón *m*, corte *m* de corriente.

power failure *n* corte *m* de corriente.

powerful ['paʊəfʊl] *adj* - **1.** [gen] poderoso(sa) - **2.** [blow, voice, drug] potente - **3.** [speech, film] conmovedor(ra).

powerhouse ['paʊəhaʊs] *(pl* [-haʊzɪz]*) n fig* fuente *f* generadora.

powerless ['paʊəlɪs] *adj* - **1.** [helpless] impotente - **2.** [unable]: **to be powerless to do sthg** no poder hacer algo.

power line *n* cable *m* del tendido eléctrico.

power of attorney *n* poder *m*, procuración *f*.

power plant *n* central *f* eléctrica.

power point *n* UK toma *f* (de corriente).

power station *n* central *f* eléctrica.

power steering *n* dirección *f* asistida.

pp *(abbr of* per procurationem) p.p.

p & **p** *abbr of* postage and packing.

PPS *n (abbr of* post postscriptum) PPD.

PR *n abbr of* proportional representation. *abbr of* public relations.

practicable ['præktɪkəbl] *adj* viable, factible.

practical ['præktɪkl] <> *adj* - **1.** [gen] práctico(ca) - **2.** [skilled with hands] hábil, mañoso(sa). <> *n* práctica *f*.

practicality [,præktɪ'kælətɪ] *n* viabilidad *f*.
➤ **practicalities** *npl* aspectos *mpl* prácticos.

practical joke *n* broma *f* pesada.

practically ['præktɪklɪ] *adv* - **1.** [in a practical way] de manera práctica - **2.** [almost] prácticamente, casi.

practice ['præktɪs] *n* - **1.** [training, training session] práctica *f*; SPORT entrenamiento *m*; MUS ensayo *m*; **I'm out of practice** me falta práctica; **practice makes perfect** se aprende a base de práctica - **2.** [reality]: **to put sthg into practice** llevar algo a la práctica; **in practice** [in fact] en la práctica - **3.** [habit, regular activity] costumbre *f* - **4.** [of profession] ejercicio *m* - **5.** [business - of doctor] consulta *f*; [- of lawyer] bufete *m*, despacho *m*.

practiced US = practised.

practicing US = practising.

practise, practice US ['præktɪs] <> *vt* - **1.** SPORT entrenar; MUS & THEAT ensayar - **2.** [religion, economy, safe sex] practicar; **to practise what one preaches** predicar con el ejemplo - **3.** [medicine, law] ejercer. <> *vi* - **1.** [train - gen] practicar; SPORT entrenarse - **2.** [as doctor] practicar; [as lawyer] ejercer.

practised, practiced US ['præktɪst] *adj* experto(ta); **to be practised at doing sthg** ser un experto en hacer algo.

practising, practicing US ['præktɪsɪŋ] *adj* - **1.** [Catholic, Jew etc] practicante - **2.** [doctor, lawyer] en ejercicio - **3.** [homosexual] activo(va).

practitioner [præk'tɪʃnər] *n*: **general practitioner** médico *m*, -ca *f* de cabecera; **medical practitioner** médico *m*, -ca *f*.

pragmatic [præg'mætɪk] *adj* pragmático(ca).

pragmatism ['prægmətɪzm] *n* pragmatismo *m*.

pragmatist ['prægmətɪst] *n* pragmatista *mf*.

prairie ['preərɪ] *n* pradera *f*, prado *m*.

praise [preɪz] <> n (U) elogio m, alabanza f; **to sing sb's praises** cantar alabanzas de alguien. <> vt elogiar, alabar.

praiseworthy ['preɪz,wɜ:ðɪ] adj digno(na) de elogio, encomiable.

pram [præm] n cochecito m de niño.

prance [prɑ:ns] vi - 1. [person] ir dando brincos - 2. [horse] hacer cabriolas.

prank [præŋk] n diablura f, travesura f; **to play a prank on sb** gastarle una broma pesada a alguien.

prat [præt] n UK inf gilipuertas m & f inv.

prattle ['prætl] pej <> n cháchara f. <> vi estar de cháchara; **to prattle on about sthg** rajar sobre algo.

prawn [prɔ:n] n gamba f.

prawn cocktail n cóctel m de gambas.

prawn cracker n corteza f de gambas.

pray [preɪ] vi rezar, orar; **to pray to sb** rogar a alguien; **to pray for sthg/for sthg to happen** lit & fig rogar algo/que pase algo.

prayer [preə^r] n - 1. RELIG oración f; **to say one's prayers** decir uno sus oraciones - 2. fig [strong hope] ruego m, súplica f.

prayer book n devocionario m, misal m.

prayer meeting n reunión de fieles para rezar.

pre- [pri:] prefix pre-.

preach [pri:tʃ] <> vt [gen] predicar; [sermon] dar. <> vi - 1. RELIG: **to preach (to)** predicar (a) - 2. pej [pontificate]: **to preach (at)** sermonear (a).

preacher ['pri:tʃə^r] n - 1. predicador m, -ra f - 2. US [minister] pastor m, -ra f.

preamble [pri:'æmbl] n preámbulo m.

prearrange [,pri:ə'reɪndʒ] vt organizar de antemano.

precarious [prɪ'keərɪəs] adj precario(ria).

precariously [prɪ'keərɪəslɪ] adv precariamente.

precast [,pri:'kɑ:st] adj: **precast concrete** hormigón m en bloques.

precaution [prɪ'kɔ:ʃn] n precaución f; **as a precaution (against)** como precaución (contra).

precautionary [prɪ'kɔ:ʃənərɪ] adj preventivo(va).

precede [prɪ'si:d] vt preceder.

precedence ['presɪdəns] n: **to take precedence over** tener prioridad sobre.

precedent ['presɪdənt] n precedente m.

preceding [prɪ'si:dɪŋ] adj anterior, precedente.

precept ['pri:sept] n precepto m.

precinct ['pri:sɪŋkt] n - 1. UK [shopping area] zona f comercial - 2. US [district] distrito m.

precincts npl recinto m.

precious ['preʃəs] adj - 1. [gen] precioso(sa); **precious little** muy poco - 2. [memories, possessions] preciado(da) - 3. [affected] afectado(da) - 4. iro: **I've heard enough about your precious dog!** ¡ya estoy cansado de tu dichoso perro!

precious metal n metal m precioso.

precious stone n piedra f preciosa.

precipice ['presɪpɪs] n lit & fig precipicio m.

precipitate <> adj [prɪ'sɪpɪtət] fml precipitado(da). <> vt [prɪ'sɪpɪteɪt] precipitar.

precipitation [prɪ,sɪpɪ'teɪʃn] n precipitación f.

precipitous [prɪ'sɪpɪtəs] adj - 1. [very steep] escarpado(da) - 2. [hasty] precipitado(da).

précis [UK 'preɪsɪ:, US 'presɪ:] n resumen m.

precise [prɪ'saɪs] adj preciso(sa), exacto(ta); **to be precise** para ser preciso.

precisely [prɪ'saɪslɪ] adv - 1. [with accuracy] exactamente - 2. [exactly, literally] precisamente - 3. [as confirmation]: **precisely!** ¡eso es!, ¡exactamente!

precision [prɪ'sɪʒn] <> n precisión f. <> comp de precisión.

preclude [prɪ'klu:d] vt fml evitar, impedir; [possibility] excluir; **to preclude sthg/sb from doing sthg** impedir que algo/alguien haga algo.

precocious [prɪ'kəʊʃəs] adj precoz.

precocity [prɪ'kɒsətɪ] n precocidad f.

precognition [,pri:kɒg'nɪʃn] n precognición f.

preconceived [,pri:kən'si:vd] adj preconcebido(da).

preconception [,pri:kən'sepʃn] n idea f preconcebida.

precondition [,pri:kən'dɪʃn] n fml: **precondition (for)** requisito m previo (para).

precooked [pri:'kʊkt] adj precocinado(da).

precursor [,pri:'kɜ:sə^r] n fml precursor m, -ra f; **to be a precursor of** OR **to sthg** ser el precursor de algo.

predate [pri:'deɪt] vt preceder.

predator ['predətə^r] n depredador m, -ra f; fig buitre mf.

predatory ['predətrɪ] adj depredador(ra); fig rapaz, rapiñero(ra).

predecessor ['pri:dɪsesə^r] n antecesor m, -ra f.

predestination [pri:,destɪ'neɪʃn] n predestinación f.

predestine [,pri:'destɪn] vt: **to be predestined to sthg/to do sthg** estar predestinado(da) a algo/a hacer algo.

predetermine [,pri:dɪ'tɜ:mɪn] vt predeterminar.

predetermined [ˌpriːdɪˈtɜːmɪnd] adj predeterminado(da).

predicament [prɪˈdɪkəmənt] n apuro m, aprieto m.

predict [prɪˈdɪkt] vt predecir, pronosticar.

predictable [prɪˈdɪktəbl] adj - **1.** [result etc] previsible - **2.** [film, book, person] poco original.

predictably [prɪˈdɪktəblɪ] adv como era de esperar.

prediction [prɪˈdɪkʃn] n predicción f, pronóstico m.

predilection [ˌpriːdɪˈlekʃn] n: predilection (for) predilección f (por).

predispose [ˌpriːdɪsˈpəʊz] vt: to be predisposed to sthg/to do sthg [by nature] estar predispuesto(ta) a algo/a hacer algo.

predisposition [ˈpriːˌdɪspəˈzɪʃn] n: predisposition to OR towards sthg predisposición f hacia OR propensión f a algo; predisposition to do sthg tendencia f a hacer algo.

predominance [prɪˈdɒmɪnəns] n predominio m.

predominant [prɪˈdɒmɪnənt] adj predominante.

predominantly [prɪˈdɒmɪnəntlɪ] adv fundamentalmente.

predominate [prɪˈdɒmɪneɪt] vi predominar.

preeminent [priːˈemɪnənt] adj preeminente.

preempt [ˌpriːˈempt] vt - **1.** [make ineffective] adelantarse a - **2.** [acquire] apropiarse de.

preemptive [ˌpriːˈemptɪv] adj preventivo(va).

preemptive strike n ataque m preventivo.

preen [priːn] vt - **1.** [subj: bird] arreglar (con el pico); to preen itself atusarse las plumas - **2.** fig [subj: person]: to preen o.s. acicalarse.

prefab [ˈpriːfæb] n inf casa f prefabricada.

prefabricate [ˌpriːˈfæbrɪkeɪt] vt prefabricar.

preface [ˈprefɪs] <> n: preface (to) prólogo m OR prefacio m (a). <> vt: to preface sthg with sthg/by doing sthg introducir algo con algo/haciendo algo.

prefect [ˈpriːfekt] n UK [pupil] delegado m, -da f de curso.

prefer [prɪˈfɜːr] (pt & pp -red, cont -ring) vt: to prefer sthg (to) preferir algo (a); to prefer to do sthg preferir hacer algo.

preferable [ˈprefrəbl] adj: to be preferable (to) ser preferible (a).

preferably [ˈprefrəblɪ] adv preferentemente.

preference [ˈprefərəns] n: preference (for) preferencia f (por); to give sb preference, to give preference to sb dar preferencia a alguien.

preferential [ˌprefəˈrenʃl] adj preferente; to give sb preferential treatment dar tratamiento preferencial a alguien.

preferred [prɪˈfɜːd] adj preferido(da).

preferred stock n US = preference shares.

prefix [ˈpriːfɪks] n prefijo m.

pregnancy [ˈpregnənsɪ] (pl -ies) n embarazo m.

pregnancy test n prueba f del embarazo.

pregnant [ˈpregnənt] adj - **1.** [woman] embarazada - **2.** [animal] preñada - **3.** fig [significant] significativo(va); pregnant with cargado de.

preheated [ˌpriːˈhiːtɪd] adj precalentado(da).

prehistoric [ˌpriːhɪˈstɒrɪk] adj prehistórico(ca).

prehistory [ˌpriːˈhɪstərɪ] n prehistoria f.

pre-industrial adj preindustrial.

prejudge [ˌpriːˈdʒʌdʒ] vt prejuzgar, juzgar de antemano.

prejudice [ˈpredʒʊdɪs] <> n: prejudice (against) prejuicio m (contra); prejudice in favour of predisposición f a favor de. <> vt - **1.** [bias]: to prejudice sb (in favour of/against) predisponer a alguien (a favor de/en contra de) - **2.** [harm] perjudicar.

prejudiced [ˈpredʒʊdɪst] adj parcial; to be prejudiced in favour of/against estar predispuesto a favor de/en contra de.

prelate [ˈprelɪt] n prelado m.

preliminary [prɪˈlɪmɪnərɪ] adj preliminar.

➤ **preliminaries** npl preliminares mpl.

prelims [ˈpriːlɪmz] npl UK [exams] exámenes mpl preliminares.

prelude [ˈpreljuːd] n [event]: prelude (to) preludio m (a).

premarital [ˌpriːˈmærɪtl] adj prematrimonial.

premature [ˈpreməˌtjʊər] adj prematuro(ra).

prematurely [ˌpreməˈtjʊəlɪ] adv antes de tiempo.

premeditated [ˌpriːˈmedɪteɪtɪd] adj premeditado(da).

premenstrual syndrome, premenstrual tension [priːˈmenstrʊəl-] n síndrome m premenstrual.

premier [ˈpremjər] <> adj primero(ra). <> n primer ministro m, primera ministra f.

premiere [ˈpremɪeər] n estreno m.

Premier League n UK FTBL en Inglaterra, máxima división futbolística administrativamente independiente de las demás.

premiership [ˈpremɪəʃɪp] n presidencia f del gobierno.

premise [ˈpremɪs] n premisa f; on the premise that con la idea de que.

➤ **premises** npl local m; on the premises en el local.

premium [ˈpriːmjəm] n prima f; at a premium [above usual value] por encima de su valor; [in great demand] muy solicitado(da); **to put** OR **place a high premium on** sthg dar gran importancia a algo.

premium bond n UK boleto numerado emitido por el Estado que autoriza a participar en sorteos mensuales de dinero hasta su amortización.

premonition [,premə'nɪʃn] n premonición f.

prenatal [,pri:'neɪtl] adj US prenatal.

pre-nup (abbr of **pre-nuptual contract**) n informal acuerdo m prenupcial.

preoccupation [pri:,ɒkjʊ'peɪʃn] n: **preoccupation (with)** preocupación f (por).

preoccupied [pri:'ɒkjʊpaɪd] adj: **preoccupied (with)** preocupado(da) (por).

preoccupy [pri:'ɒkjʊpaɪ] (pt & pp **-ied**) vt preocupar.

preordain [,pri:ɔ:'deɪn] vt predeterminar; **to be preordained to do sthg** estar predestinado a hacer algo.

prep [prep] (abbr of **preparation**) n (U) UK inf tarea f, deberes mpl; **to do one's prep** hacer los deberes.

prepacked [,pri:'pækt] adj empaquetado(da).

prepaid ['pri:peɪd] adj [post paid] porte pagado.

preparation [,prepə'reɪʃn] n - **1.** [act of preparing] preparación f; **in preparation for** en preparación para - **2.** [prepared mixture] preparado m.

➤ **preparations** npl preparativos mpl; **to make preparations for** hacer los preparativos para.

preparatory [prɪ'pærətrɪ] adj preparatorio(ria), preliminar.

preparatory school n [in UK] colegio de pago para niños de 7 a 12 años; [in US] escuela privada de enseñanza secundaria y preparación para estudios superiores.

prepare [prɪ'peə^r] ⟷ vt preparar. ⟷ vi: **to prepare for sthg/to do sthg** prepararse para algo/para hacer algo.

prepared [prɪ'peəd] adj - **1.** [gen] preparado(da); **to be prepared for sthg** estar preparado para algo - **2.** [willing] **to be prepared to do sthg** estar dispuesto(ta) a hacer algo.

preponderance [prɪ'pɒndərəns] n predominio m.

preponderantly [prɪ'pɒndərəntlɪ] adv mayoritariamente.

preposition [,prepə'zɪʃn] n preposición f.

prepossessing [,pri:pə'zesɪŋ] adj fml atractivo(va), agradable.

preposterous [prɪ'pɒstərəs] adj absurdo(da).

preppy ['prepɪ] US inf ⟷ adj pijo(ja). ⟷ n (pl **-ies**) niño m, -ña f bien.

prep school n inf abbr of **preparatory school**.

Pre-Raphaelite [,pri:'ræfəlaɪt] ⟷ adj prerrafaelista. ⟷ n prerrafaelista mf.

prerecorded [,pri:rɪ'kɔ:dɪd] adj pregrabado(da).

prerequisite [,pri:'rekwɪzɪt] n: **prerequisite (for)** requisito m (para).

prerogative [prɪ'rɒgətɪv] n prerrogativa f.

presage ['presɪdʒ] vt fml presagiar.

Presbyterian [,prezbɪ'tɪərɪən] ⟷ adj presbiteriano(na). ⟷ n presbiteriano m, -na f.

presbytery ['prezbɪtrɪ] n [residence] presbiterio m.

preschool ['pri:,sku:l] ⟷ adj preescolar. ⟷ n US parvulario m, escuela f de párvulos.

prescribe [prɪ'skraɪb] vt - **1.** MED recetar - **2.** [order] ordenar, mandar.

prescription [prɪ'skrɪpʃn] n receta f; **on prescription** con receta médica.

prescription charge n UK precio fijo por el coste de los medicamentos recetados por médicos de la seguridad social.

prescriptive [prɪ'skrɪptɪv] adj preceptivo(va).

presence ['prezns] n presencia f; **to be in sb's presence** OR **in the presence of sb** estar en presencia de alguien; **to have presence** tener presencia; **to make one's presence felt** hacer sentir la presencia de uno.

presence of mind n presencia f de ánimo, aplomo m.

present ⟷ adj ['preznt] - **1.** [current] actual; **at the present time** actualmente - **2.** [in attendance] presente; **to be present at sthg** asistir a algo, estar presente en algo. ⟷ n ['preznt] - **1.** [current time]: **the present** el presente; **at present** actualmente; **for the present** de momento, por ahora - **2.** LING: **present (tense)** (tiempo m) presente m - **3.** [gift] regalo m; **to give sb a present** dar un regalo a alguien. ⟷ vt [prɪ'zent] - **1.** [gen] presentar; **to present sb with sthg, to present sthg to sb** [challenge, opportunity] representar algo para alguien; **to present sb to sb** presentar a alguien a alguien; **to present o.s.** [arrive] presentarse - **2.** [give]: **to present sb with sthg, to present sthg to sb** [as present] obsequiar algo a alguien; [at ceremony] entregar algo a alguien - **3.** [play etc] representar.

presentable [prɪ'zentəbl] adj presentable; **to look presentable** tener un aspecto presentable; **to make o.s. presentable** arreglarse.

presentation [,prezn'teɪʃn] n - **1.** [gen] presentación f - **2.** [ceremony] entrega f - **3.** [performance] representación f.

presentation copy n ejemplar m gratuito.

present day *n*: the present day el presente.
➡ **present-day** *adj* actual, de hoy en día.

presenter [prɪ'zentə*r*] *n UK* presentador *m*, -ra *f*.

presentiment [prɪ'zentɪmənt] *n fml* presentimiento *m*.

presently ['prezntlɪ] *adv* - **1.** [soon] dentro de poco - **2.** [now] actualmente, ahora.

preservation [,prezə'veɪʃn] *n* preservación *f*, conservación *f*.

preservation order *n esp UK* orden *f* de protección.

preservative [prɪ'zɜ:vətɪv] *n* conservante *m*.

preserve [prɪ'zɜ:v] <> *vt* conservar. <> *n* [jam] mermelada *f*.
➡ **preserves** *npl* [jam] confituras *fpl*; [vegetables] conserva *f*.

preserved [prɪ'zɜ:vd] *adj* conservado(da).

preset [,pri:'set] (*pt & pp* preset, *cont* -ting) *vt* programar.

preshrunk [,pri:'ʃrʌŋk] *adj* lavado(da) de antemano.

preside [prɪ'zaɪd] *vi*: to preside (over *OR* at sthg) presidir (algo).

presidency ['prezɪdənsɪ] (*pl* -ies) *n* presidencia *f*.

president ['prezɪdənt] *n* presidente *m*, -ta *f*.

President-elect *n* el presidente electo (la presidenta electa).

presidential [,prezɪ'denʃl] *adj* presidencial.

press [pres] <> *n* - **1.** [push]: to give sthg a press apretar algo - **2.** [newspapers, reporters]: the press la prensa; to get a good/bad press tener buena/mala prensa - **3.** [machine] prensa *f*; to go to press entrar en prensa - **4.** [with iron] planchado *m*; to give sthg a press dar un planchado a algo. <> *vt* - **1.** [gen] apretar; to press sthg against sthg apretar algo contra algo - **2.** [grapes, flowers] prensar - **3.** [iron] planchar - **4.** [urge]: to press sb (to do sthg *OR* into doing sthg) presionar a alguien (para que haga algo); to press sb for sthg presionar a alguien en busca de algo - **5.** [force]: to press sthg on *OR* upon sb obligar a alguien a aceptar algo - **6.** [pursue - claim] insistir en; to press charges against sb LAW demandar a alguien. <> *vi* - **1.** [gen]: to press (on sthg) apretar (algo) - **2.** [crowd]: to press forward empujar hacia adelante.
➡ **press for** *vt insep* exigir, reclamar.
➡ **press on** *vi* [continue] proseguir, continuar; to press on (with) seguir adelante (con).

press agency *n* agencia *f* de prensa.

press agent *n* agente *mf* de prensa.

press conference *n* rueda *f* de prensa.

press corps *n US*: the press corps la prensa.

press cutting *n UK* recorte *m* de prensa.

pressed [prest] *adj*: to be pressed (for time/money) andar escaso(sa) (de tiempo/de dinero).

pressing ['presɪŋ] *adj* apremiante, urgente.

pressman ['presmæn] (*pl* -men [-men]) *n UK* periodista *m*.

press officer *n* jefe *m*, -fa *f* de prensa.

press release *n* comunicado *m* de prensa.

press-stud *n UK* automático *m*.

press-up *n UK* flexión *f*.

pressure ['preʃə*r*] <> *n* presión *f*; to put pressure on sb (to do sthg) presionar a alguien (para que haga algo); to be under pressure estar *OR* verse presionado. <> *vt*: to pressure sb to do *OR* into doing sthg presionar a alguien para que haga algo.

pressure cooker *n* olla *f* a presión.

pressure gauge *n* manómetro *m*.

pressure group *n* grupo *m* de presión.

pressurize, -ise ['preʃəraɪz] *vt* - **1.** TECH presurizar - **2.** *UK* [force]: to pressurize sb to do *OR* into doing sthg presionar a alguien para que haga algo.

prestige [pre'sti:ʒ] *n* prestigio *m*.

prestigious [pre'stɪdʒəs] *adj* prestigioso(sa).

prestressed concrete [,pri:'strest-] *n* hormigón *m* pretensado.

presumably [prɪ'zju:məblɪ] *adv*: presumably you've read it supongo que los has leído.

presume [prɪ'zju:m] *vt* suponer; he is presumed dead se supone que está muerto; to presume that suponer que, imaginar que.

presumption [prɪ'zʌmpʃn] *n* - **1.** [assumption] suposición *f*; [of innocence] presunción *f* - **2.** *(U)* [audacity] presunción *f*, osadía *f*.

presumptuous [prɪ'zʌmptʃuəs] *adj* presuntuoso(sa).

presuppose [,pri:sə'pəuz] *vt* presuponer.

pretax [,pri:'tæks] *adj* bruto(ta).

pretence, pretense *US* [prɪ'tens] *n* fingimiento *m*, simulación *f*; to make a pretence of doing sthg fingir hacer algo; under false pretences con engaños, con falsos pretextos.

pretend [prɪ'tend] <> *vt*: to pretend to do sthg fingir hacer algo; she pretended not to notice hizo como si no se hubiera dado cuenta; don't pretend you didn't know! ¡no finjas que no lo sabías! <> *vi* fingir, simular. <> *adj inf* de mentira.

pretense *US* = pretence.

pretension [prɪ'tenʃn] *n* pretensión *f*; to have pretensions to sthg tener pretensiones de algo.

pretentious [prɪ'tenʃəs] *adj* pretencioso(sa).

pretentiously [prɪ'tenʃəslɪ] *adv* de forma pretenciosa.

pretentiousness [prɪˈtenʃəsnɪs] *n* pretenciosidad *f*.

preterite [ˈpretərət] *n* pretérito *m*.

pretext [ˈpriːtekst] *n* pretexto *m*; **on** OR **under the pretext that.../of doing sthg** con el pretexto de que.../de hacer algo.

prettify [ˈprɪtɪfaɪ] (*pt & pp* -**ied**) *vt* embellecer.

prettily [ˈprɪtɪlɪ] *adv* de una forma bonita.

pretty [ˈprɪtɪ] ◇ *adj* (*comp* -**ier**, *superl* -**iest**) bonito(ta). ◇ *adv* bastante; **pretty much** más o menos; **pretty well** [almost] casi.

pretzel [ˈpretsl] *n* galleta *f* salada.

prevail [prɪˈveɪl] *vi* - **1.** [be widespread] predominar, imperar - **2.** [triumph]: **to prevail (over)** prevalecer (sobre) - **3.** [persuade]: **to prevail on** OR **upon sb to do sthg** persuadir a alguien para que haga algo.

prevailing [prɪˈveɪlɪŋ] *adj* predominante.

prevalence [ˈprevələns] *n* predominio *m*.

prevalent [ˈprevələnt] *adj* predominante, imperante.

prevaricate [prɪˈværɪkeɪt] *vi* andarse con evasivas.

prevent [prɪˈvent] *vt* impedir; [event, illness, accident] evitar; **to prevent sthg (from) happening** impedir OR evitar que algo pase; **to prevent sb (from) doing sthg** impedir a alguien que haga algo.

preventable [prɪˈventəbl] *adj* evitable.

preventative [prɪˈventətɪv] *adj* = **preventive**.

prevention [prɪˈvenʃn] *n* prevención *f*.

preventive [prɪˈventɪv], **preventative** *adj* preventivo(va).

preview [ˈpriːvjuː] *n* - **1.** [film] avance *m* - **2.** [exhibition] preestreno *m*.

previous [ˈpriːvjəs] *adj* previo(via), anterior; **the previous week/president** la semana/el presidente anterior; **previous convictions** antecedentes *mpl* penales.

previously [ˈpriːvjəslɪ] *adv* - **1.** [formerly] anteriormente - **2.** [before]: **two years previously** dos años antes.

prewar [ˌpriːˈwɔːr] *adj* de preguerra.

prey [preɪ] *n* presa *f*, víctima *f*; **to fall prey to** ser víctima de.

➤ **prey on** *vt insep* - **1.** [live off] cazar, alimentarse de - **2.** [trouble]: **to prey on sb's mind** atormentar a alguien.

price [praɪs] ◇ *n* *lit & fig* precio *m*; **to go up/down in price** subir/bajar de precio; **you can't put a price on health** la salud no tiene precio; **to pay the price for sthg** pagar el precio de algo; **at any price** a toda costa, a cualquier precio; **at a price** a un alto precio; **to pay a high price for sthg** pagar algo caro. ◇ *vt* poner precio a; **to be wrongly priced** tener el

precio equivocado; **to price o.s. out of the market** salirse del mercado por vender demasiado caro.

price-cutting *n* (*U*) reducción *f* de precios.

price-fixing [-ˌfɪksɪŋ] *n* (*U*) fijación *f* de precios.

priceless [ˈpraɪslɪs] *adj* *lit & fig* que no tiene precio, inestimable.

price list *n* lista *f* OR tarifa *f* de precios.

price tag *n* [label] etiqueta *f* (del precio).

price war *n* guerra *f* de precios.

pricey [ˈpraɪsɪ] (*comp* -**ier**, *superl* -**iest**) *adj* caro(ra).

prick [prɪk] ◇ *n* - **1.** [wound] pinchazo *m* - **2.** *vulg* [penis] polla *f*, pinga *f Andes & Méx* - **3.** *vulg* [stupid person] gilipollas *mf inv*. ◇ *vt* - **1.** [gen] pinchar - **2.** [sting] picar.

➤ **prick up** *vt insep*: **to prick up one's ears** [subj: animal] levantar las orejas; [subj: person] aguzar el oído.

prickle [ˈprɪkl] ◇ *n* - **1.** [thorn] espina *f*, pincho *m* - **2.** [sensation] comezón *f*. ◇ *vi* picar.

prickly [ˈprɪklɪ] (*comp* -**ier**, *superl* -**iest**) *adj* - **1.** [thorny] espinoso(sa) - **2.** *fig* [touchy] susceptible, enojadizo(za).

prickly heat *n* (*U*) sarpullido por causa del calor.

pride [praɪd] ◇ *n* orgullo *m*; **to take pride in sthg/in doing sthg** enorgullecerse de algo/de hacer algo; **to be sb's pride and joy** ser el orgullo de alguien; **to have pride of place** ocupar el lugar de honor; **to swallow one's pride** tragarse el orgullo. ◇ *vt*: **to pride o.s. on sthg** enorgullecerse de algo.

priest [priːst] *n* sacerdote *m*.

priestess [ˈpriːstɪs] *n* sacerdotisa *f*.

priesthood [ˈpriːsthʊd] *n* - **1.** [position, office]: **the priesthood** el sacerdocio - **2.** [priests collectively]: **the priesthood** el clero.

prig [prɪg] *n* mojigato *m*, -ta *f*.

prim [prɪm] (*comp* -**mer**, *superl* -**mest**) *adj* remilgado(da); **prim and proper** remilgado(da).

primacy [ˈpraɪməsɪ] *n* primacía *f*.

prima donna [ˌpriːməˈdɒnə] (*pl* -**s**) *n* - **1.** [female singer] prima donna *f* - **2.** *pej* [self-important person]: **to be a prima donna** ir de estrella.

primaeval [praɪˈmiːvl] *adj* = **primeval**.

prima facie [ˌpraɪməˈfeɪʃɪ] *adj* a primera vista.

primal [ˈpraɪml] *adj* - **1.** [original] primario(ria) - **2.** [most important] primordial.

primarily [ˈpraɪmərɪlɪ] *adv* principalmente.

primary [ˈpraɪmərɪ] ◇ *adj* - **1.** [main] principal - **2.** SCH primario(ria). ◇ *n* (*pl* -**ies**) US POL primaria *f*.

primary colour *n* color *m* primario.

primary election *n* US primaria *f*.

primary school *n* escuela *f* primaria.

primate ['praimeit] *n* ZOOL primate *m*.

prime [praim] <> *adj* **- 1.** [main] primero(ra), principal **- 2.** [excellent] excelente; [quality] primero(ra). <> *n*: **to be in one's prime** estar en la flor de la vida. <> *vt* **- 1.** [inform]: **to prime sb about sthg** preparar a alguien a fondo para algo **- 2.** [surface] preparar **- 3.** [gun, pump] cebar.

prime minister *n* primer ministro *m*, primera ministra *f*.

prime mover [-'mu:vər] *n* fuerza *f* motriz.

prime number *n* número *m* primo.

primer ['praimər] *n* **- 1.** [paint] imprimación *f* **- 2.** [textbook] cartilla *f*.

prime time *n* (U) hora *f* de mayor audiencia.
➡ **prime-time** *adj* de mayor audiencia.

primeval, primaeval [prai'mi:vl] *adj* [ancient] primitivo(va); **primeval forest** bosque *m* virgen.

primitive ['primitiv] *adj* [tribe, species etc] primitivo(va); [accommodation, sense of humour] rudimentario(ria).

primordial [prai'mɔ:djəl] *adj fml* primordial.

primrose ['primrəuz] *n* primavera *f*, prímula *f*.

Primus stove® ['praiməs-] *n* hornillo *m* de camping.

prince [prins] *n* príncipe *m*.
➡ **Prince** *n*: **Prince of Wales** Príncipe de Gales.

Prince Charming *n hum* príncipe *m* azul.

princely ['prinsli] (*comp* -ier, *superl* -iest) *adj*
- 1. [of a prince] principesco(ca) **- 2.** [magnificent] magnífico(ca).

princess [prin'ses] *n* princesa *f*.
➡ **Princess** *n*: **Princess Royal** Princesa Real.

principal ['prinsəpl] <> *adj* principal. <> *n* SCH director *m*, -ra *f*.

principality [,prinsi'pæləti] (*pl* -ies) *n* principado *m*.

principally ['prinsəpli] *adv* principalmente, sobre todo.

principle ['prinsəpl] *n* **- 1.** [gen] principio *m*; **to be against sb's principles** ir contra los principios de alguien **- 2.** (U) [integrity] principios *mpl*; **on principle, as a matter of principle** por principio.
➡ **in principle** *adv* en principio.

principled ['prinsəpld] *adj* de principios.

print [print] <> *n* **- 1.** (U) [type] caracteres *mpl* (de imprenta); **in print** [available] disponible; [in printed characters] en letra impresa; **to be out of print** estar agotado **- 2.** [piece of artwork] grabado *m* **- 3.** [reproduction] reproducción *f* **- 4.** [photograph] fotografía *f* **- 5.** [fabric] estampado *m* **- 6.** [mark - of foot etc] huella *f*. <> *vt*

- 1. TYPO imprimir **- 2.** [produce by printing - book, newspaper] tirar **- 3.** [publish] publicar **- 4.** [decorate - cloth etc] estampar **- 5.** [write in block letters] escribir con letra de imprenta. <> *vi* imprimir.
➡ **print out** *vt sep* COMPUT imprimir.

printed circuit ['printid-] *n* circuito *m* impreso.

printed matter ['printid-] *n* (U) impresos *mpl*.

printer ['printər] *n* **- 1.** [person] impresor *m*, -ra *f*; [firm] imprenta *f* **- 2.** [machine] impresora *f*.

printer cable *n* cable *m* de impresora.

printing ['printiŋ] *n* **- 1.** (U) [act of printing] impresión *f* **- 2.** [trade] imprenta *f*.

printing press *n* prensa *f* (*máquina*).

printout ['printaut] *n* COMPUT salida *f* de impresora.

prior ['praiər] <> *adj* [previous] previo(via); **without prior notice** sin previo aviso; **to have prior commitments** tener compromisos previos; **to have a prior engagement** tener un compromiso previo. <> *n* [monk] prior *m*.
➡ **prior to** *prep* antes de; **prior to doing sthg** con anterioridad a hacer algo.

prioritize, -ise [prai'prɪtaɪz] *vt* dar prioridad a.

priority [prai'prəti] <> *adj* prioritario(ria). <> *n* (*pl* -ies) prioridad *f*; **to have** OR **take priority (over)** tener prioridad (sobre).
➡ **priorities** *npl* prioridades *fpl*; **to get one's priorities right** darse uno cuenta de lo que realmente es importante.

priory ['praiəri] (*pl* -ies) *n* priorato *m*.

prise [praiz] *vt*: **to prise sthg open/away** abrir/separar algo haciendo palanca.

prism ['prizm] *n* prisma *m*.

prison ['prizn] *n* cárcel *f*, prisión *f*; **to be in prison** estar en la cárcel; **to be sentenced to 5 years in prison** ser condenado a cinco años de cárcel. <> *comp*: **to be given a prison sentence** ser condenado a una pena de cárcel; **a prison officer** un funcionario de prisiones.

prison camp *n* campamento *m* de prisioneros.

prisoner ['priznər] *n* **- 1.** [convict] preso *m*, -sa *f* **- 2.** [captive] prisionero *m*, -ra *f*; **to be taken prisoner** ser hecho prisionero.

prisoner of war (*pl* prisoners of war) *n* prisionero *m*, -ra *f* de guerra.

prissy ['prisi] (*comp* -ier, *superl* -iest) *adj* remilgado(da).

pristine ['pristi:n] *adj* prístino(na).

privacy [, UK 'privəsi, US 'praivəsi] *n* intimidad *f*.

private ['praivit] <> *adj* **- 1.** [gen] privado(da); [class] particular; [telephone call, belongings] personal **- 2.** [thoughts, plans] secreto(ta); **a private**

joke un chiste que entienden unos pocos **- 3.** [secluded] retirado(da) **- 4.** [unsociable - person] reservado(da). ◇ *n* **- 1.** [soldier] soldado *m* raso **- 2.**: **(to do sthg) in private** [in secret] (hacer algo) en privado.

➡ **privates** *npl inf* partes *fpl* (pudendas).

private company *n* empresa *f* privada.

private detective *n* detective privado *m*, -da *f*.

private enterprise *n (U)* empresa *f* privada.

private education *n (U)* enseñanza *f* privada.

Private education

Hay más de 2.000 colegios privados en el Reino Unido que son independientes del gobierno, por lo que no tienen que seguir el programa de estudios nacional y suelen ofrecer una educación tradicional que incluye muchas actividades extraescolares, principalmente deportes. La educación en ellos no es gratuita y para atraer a los mejores alumnos algunos ofrecen becas o premios a méritos académicos, musicales o artísticos. Sin embargo, la mayoría de estas becas no cubren la matrícula del colegio. En Inglaterra y Gales algunos de estos centros, como por ejemplo Eton y Harrow, gozan de gran prestigio, pues han sido hasta hace poco los encargados de formar a la élite política, y reciben numerosas solicitudes de ingreso. Son los llamados **public schools**. En EE. UU., y hasta hace poco también en Escocia, el término **public school** se utiliza para designar una escuela pública.

private eye *n* detective privado *m*, -da *f*.

private income *n UK* renta *f* personal.

private investigator *n* detective privado *m*, -da *f*.

privately ['praɪvɪtlɪ] *adv* **- 1.** [not by the state] de forma privada; **privately owned** de propiedad privada **- 2.** [confidentially] en privado **- 3.** [secretly] en el fuero interno de uno.

private parts *npl inf* partes *fpl* (íntimas).

private practice *n UK* ejercicio *m* privado de la medicina.

private property *n* propiedad *f* privada.

private school *n* escuela *f* privada, colegio *m* privado.

private sector *n*: **the private sector** el sector privado.

privation [praɪ'veɪʃn] *n* privación *f*.

privatization [ˌpraɪvɪtaɪ'zeɪʃn] *n* privatización *f*.

privatize, -ise ['praɪvɪtaɪz] *vt* privatizar.

privet ['prɪvɪt] *n* alheña *f*.

privilege ['prɪvɪlɪdʒ] *n* privilegio *m*.

privileged ['prɪvɪlɪdʒd] *adj* privilegiado(da).

privy ['prɪvɪ] *adj*: **to be privy to sthg** estar enterado(da) de algo.

Privy Council *n UK*: **the Privy Council** *en Gran Bretaña, consejo privado que asesora al monarca.*

prize [praɪz] ◇ *adj* de primera. ◇ *n* premio *m*. ◇ *vt*: **to be prized** ser apreciado(da).

prizefight ['praɪzfaɪt] *n* combate *m* de boxeo profesional.

prize-giving [-ˌgɪvɪŋ] *n UK* entrega *f* de premios.

prizewinner ['praɪzˌwɪnər] *n* premiado *m*, -da *f*.

pro [prəʊ] (*pl* **-s**) *n* **- 1.** *inf* [professional] profesional *mf* **- 2.** [advantage]: **the pros and cons** los pros y los contras.

pro- [prəʊ] *prefix* pro-.

PRO [ˌpiːɑːr'əʊ] *n* **- 1.** *UK* (*abbr of* **Public Record Office**) registro *m* del Reino Unido **- 2.** (*abbr of* **public relations officer**), *jefe de relaciones públicas.*

probability [ˌprɒbə'bɪlətɪ] (*pl* **-ies**) *n* probabilidad *f*; **in all probability they'll win** es muy probable que ganen.

probable ['prɒbəbl] *adj* probable; **it is not very probable that it will happen** no es muy probable que ocurra.

probably ['prɒbəblɪ] *adv* probablemente.

probate ['prəʊbeɪt] ◇ *n* LAW legalización *f* de un testamento. ◇ *vt US* legalizar *(un testamento).*

probation [prə'beɪʃn] *n* **- 1.** [of prisoner] libertad *f* condicional; **to put sb on probation** poner a alguien en libertad condicional **- 2.** [trial period] periodo *m* de prueba; **to be on probation** estar en periodo de prueba.

probationary [prə'beɪʃnrɪ] *adj* **- 1.** [teacher, nurse] en periodo de prueba **- 2.** [period] de prueba.

probationer [prə'beɪʃnər] *n* **- 1.** [employee] empleado *m*, -da *f* a prueba **- 2.** [offender] persona *f* en libertad condicional.

probation officer *n encargado de vigilar a los que están en libertad condicional.*

probe [prəʊb] ◇ *n* **- 1.** [investigation]: **probe (into)** investigación *f* (sobre) **- 2.** MED & AERON sonda *f*. ◇ *vt* **- 1.** [investigate] investigar **- 2.** [with tool] sondar; [with finger, stick] hurgar en. ◇ *vi*: **to probe for sthg** investigar para encontrar algo; **to probe into sthg** explorar algo.

probing ['prəʊbɪŋ] *adj* inquisitivo(va).

probity ['prəʊbətɪ] *n fml* probidad *f*.

problem ['prɒbləm] ◇ *n* problema *m*; **no problem!** *inf* ¡por supuesto!, ¡desde luego! ◇ *comp* problemático(ca), difícil.

problematic(al) [ˌprɒbləˈmætɪk(l)] *adj* problemático(ca), difícil.

procedural [prəˈsiːdʒərəl] *adj* de procedimiento.

procedure [prəˈsiːdʒəʳ] *n* procedimiento *m*.

proceed *vi* [prəˈsiːd] **- 1.** [do subsequently]**: to proceed to do sthg** proceder a hacer algo **- 2.** [continue]**: to proceed (with sthg)** proseguir (con algo) **- 3.** *fml* [advance] avanzar.

◆ **proceeds** *npl* [ˈprəʊsiːdz] ganancias *fpl*, beneficios *mpl*.

proceedings [prəˈsiːdɪŋz] *npl* **- 1.** [series of events] acto *m* **- 2.** [legal action] proceso *m*; **to start proceedings against sb** entablar proceso contra alguien.

process [ˈprəʊses] ◇ *n* proceso *m*; **in the process** en el intento; **to be in the process of doing sthg** estar en vías de hacer algo. ◇ *vt* **- 1.** [gen & COMPUT] procesar **- 2.** [application] tramitar.

processed cheese [ˈprəʊsest-] *n* queso *m* fundido.

processing [ˈprəʊsesɪŋ] *n* **- 1.** [gen & COMPUT] procesamiento *m* **- 2.** [of applications etc] tramitación *f*.

procession [prəˈseʃn] *n* desfile *m*; [religious] procesión *f*.

processor [ˈprəʊsesəʳ] *n* **- 1.** COMPUT unidad *f* central (de procesamiento) **- 2.** CULIN procesador *m*.

pro-choice *adj* en favor del derecho de la mujer a decidir en materia de aborto.

proclaim [prəˈkleɪm] *vt* [gen] proclamar; [law] promulgar.

proclamation [ˌprɒkləˈmeɪʃn] *n* [gen] proclamación *f*; [of law] promulgación *f*.

proclivity [prəˈklɪvətɪ] (*pl* **-ies**) *n fml*: **proclivity (to** OR **towards)** propensión *f* OR tendencia *f* (a).

procrastinate [prəˈkræstɪneɪt] *vi* andarse con dilaciones.

procrastination [prəˌkræstɪˈneɪʃn] *n* (U) dilaciones *fpl*.

procreate [ˈprəʊkrɪeɪt] *vi* procrear.

procreation [ˌprəʊkrɪˈeɪʃn] *n* procreación *f*.

procurator fiscal [ˈprɒkjʊreɪtəʳ-] *n Scotland* ≃ fiscal *mf*.

procure [prəˈkjʊəʳ] *vt* [obtain] obtener, conseguir.

procurement [prəˈkjʊəmənt] *n* obtención *f*.

prod [prɒd] ◇ *n* **- 1.** [push, poke] empujoncito *m* **- 2.** *fig* [reminder] toque *m*, aviso *m*. ◇ *vt* (*pt* & *pp* **-ded**, *cont* **-ding**) **- 1.** [push, poke] dar empujoncitos a **- 2.** [remind, prompt]**: to prod sb (into doing sthg)** darle un toque a alguien (para que haga algo).

prodigal [ˈprɒdɪgl] *adj* [son, daughter] pródigo(ga).

prodigious [prəˈdɪdʒəs] *adj* prodigioso(sa).

prodigy [ˈprɒdɪdʒɪ] (*pl* **-ies**) *n* [person] prodigio *m*; **a child prodigy** un niño prodigio.

produce ◇ *n* [ˈprɒdjuːs] (U) productos *mpl* agrícolas; **'produce of France'** 'producto de Francia'. ◇ *vt* [prəˈdjuːs] **- 1.** [gen] producir; [offspring, flowers] engendrar **- 2.** [evidence, argument] presentar **- 3.** [bring out] mostrar, enseñar **- 4.** THEAT poner en escena.

producer [prəˈdjuːsəʳ] *n* **- 1.** [gen] productor *m*, -ra *f* **- 2.** THEAT director *m*, -ra *f* de escena.

product [ˈprɒdʌkt] *n* producto *m*; **to be a product of** ser el resultado OR producto de.

production [prəˈdʌkʃn] *n* **- 1.** [gen] producción *f*; **to put/go into production** empezar a fabricar/fabricarse **- 2.** (U) THEAT puesta *f* en escena.

production line *n* cadena *f* de producción.

production manager *n* **- 1.** THEAT director *m*, -ra *f* de producción **- 2.** [in factory] jefe *m*, -fa *f* de producción.

productive [prəˈdʌktɪv] *adj* **- 1.** [efficient] productivo(va) **- 2.** [rewarding] provechoso(sa).

productively [prəˈdʌktɪvlɪ] *adv* **- 1.** [efficiently] de manera productiva **- 2.** [rewardingly] de manera provechosa.

productivity [ˌprɒdʌkˈtɪvətɪ] *n* productividad *f*.

productivity deal *n* acuerdo *m* sobre la productividad.

Prof. [prɒf] (*abbr of* **Professor**) Catedr.

profane [prəˈfeɪn] *adj* [disrespectful] obsceno(na).

profanity [prəˈfænətɪ] (*pl* **-ies**) *n* **- 1.** [of language, behaviour] obscenidad *f*, indecencia *f* **- 2.** [word] palabrota *f*, taco *m*.

profess [prəˈfes] *vt* **- 1.** [claim]**: to profess (to do sthg)** pretender (hacer algo) **- 2.** [declare] declarar.

professed [prəˈfest] *adj* **- 1.** [avowed] declarado(da) **- 2.** [supposed] pretendido(da).

profession [prəˈfeʃn] *n* profesión *f*; **by profession** de profesión.

professional [prəˈfeʃənl] ◇ *adj* profesional. ◇ *n* profesional *mf*, profesionista *mf Méx*.

professional foul *n* falta *f* profesional.

professionalism [prəˈfeʃnəlɪzm] *n* profesionalismo *m*.

professionally [prəˈfeʃnəlɪ] *adv* **- 1.** [for a profession]**: to be professionally trained/qualified** tener una formación/un título profesional **- 2.** [not as amateur] profesionalmente **- 3.** [skilfully] de manera profesional.

professor [prə'fesər] n - **1.** UK [head of department] catedrático m, -ca f - **2.** US & Canada [lecturer] profesor m, -ra f (de universidad).

professorship [prə'fesəʃɪp] n - **1.** UK [position of head of department] cátedra f - **2.** US & Canada [lectureship] cargo de profesor de universidad.

proffer ['prɒfər] vt: to proffer sthg (to) ofrecer algo (a).

proficiency [prə'fɪʃənsɪ] n: proficiency (in) competencia f (en).

proficient [prə'fɪʃənt] adj: proficient (in OR at) competente (en).

profile ['prəʊfaɪl] n perfil m; high profile notoriedad f; in profile de perfil; to keep a low profile mantenerse en segundo plano.

profit ['prɒfɪt] <> n - **1.** [financial gain] beneficio m, ganancia f; to make a profit sacar un beneficio; to sell sthg at a profit vender algo con beneficios - **2.** [advantage] provecho m. <> vi: to profit (from OR by) sacar provecho (de).

profitability [,prɒfɪtə'bɪlətɪ] n rentabilidad f.

profitable ['prɒfɪtəbl] adj - **1.** [making a profit] rentable - **2.** [beneficial] provechoso(sa).

profitably ['prɒfɪtəblɪ] adv - **1.** [at a profit] con beneficios - **2.** [spend time] de manera provechosa.

profiteering [,prɒfɪ'tɪərɪŋ] n especulación f.

profit-making <> adj con fines lucrativos. <> n obtención f de beneficios.

profit margin n margen m de beneficios.

profit-related pay n remuneración f vinculada a los beneficios.

profit sharing [-,ʃeərɪŋ] n participación f en los beneficios.

profligate ['prɒflɪgɪt] adj - **1.** [extravagant] derrochador(ra) - **2.** [immoral] libertino(na).

pro forma [-'fɔ:mə] adj proforma.

profound [prə'faʊnd] adj profundo(da).

profoundly [prə'faʊndlɪ] adv profundamente.

profuse [prə'fju:s] adj profuso(sa).

profusely [prə'fju:slɪ] adv profusamente; to apologise profusely pedir disculpas cumplidamente.

profusion [prə'fju:ʒn] n profusión f.

progeny ['prɒdʒənɪ] (pl -ies) n progenie f.

progesterone [prə'dʒestərəʊn] n progesterona f.

prognosis [prɒg'nəʊsɪs] (pl -noses [-'nəʊsi:z]) n pronóstico m.

program ['prəʊgræm] <> n - **1.** COMPUT programa m - **2.** US = programme. <> vt (pt & pp -med OR -ed, cont -ming, cont -ing) - **1.** COMPUT programar - **2.** US = programme. <> vi (pt & pp -med OR -ed, cont -ming, cont -ing) COMPUT programar.

programer US = programmer.

programmable [prəʊ'græməbl] adj programable.

programme UK, **program** US ['prəʊgræm] <> n programa m. <> vt: to programme sthg (to do sthg) programar algo (para que haga algo).

programmer UK, **programer** US ['prəʊgræmər] n COMPUT programador m, -ra f.

programming ['prəʊgræmɪŋ] n programación f.

programming language n lenguaje m de programación.

progress <> n ['prəʊgres] - **1.** [gen] progreso m; in progress en curso; to make progress hacer progresos - **2.** [forward movement] avance m. <> vi [prə'gres] - **1.** [gen] progresar; as the year progressed conforme avanzaba el año; [pupil etc] hacer progresos - **2.** [move forward] avanzar - **3.** [move on]: to progress to sthg pasar a algo.

progression [prə'greʃn] n - **1.** [development] evolución f - **2.** [series] sucesión f.

progressive [prə'gresɪv] adj - **1.** [enlightened] progresista - **2.** [gradual] progresivo(va).

progressively [prə'gresɪvlɪ] adv progresivamente.

progress report n [on work, project] informe m sobre el desarrollo del trabajo.

prohibit [prə'hɪbɪt] vt prohibir; to prohibit sb from doing sthg prohibirle a alguien hacer algo; fishing is prohibited prohibido pescar.

prohibition [,prəʊɪ'bɪʃn] n prohibición f.

prohibitive [prə'hɪbətɪv] adj prohibitivo(va).

project <> n ['prɒdʒekt] - **1.** [plan, idea] proyecto m - **2.** SCH: project (on) estudio m OR trabajo m (sobre) - **3.** US: the projects urbanización con viviendas de protección oficial. <> vt [prə'dʒekt] - **1.** [gen] proyectar - **2.** [estimate - statistic, costs] estimar - **3.** [company, person] dar una imagen de; [image] proyectar. <> vi [prə'dʒekt] proyectarse.

projectile [prə'dʒektaɪl] n proyectil m.

projection [prə'dʒekʃn] n - **1.** [gen] proyección f - **2.** [protrusion] saliente m.

projectionist [prə'dʒekʃənɪst] n operador m, -ra f, proyeccionista mf.

projection room n cabina f de proyecciones.

projector [prə'dʒektər] n proyector m.

proletarian [,prəʊlɪ'teərɪən] adj proletario(ria).

proletariat [,prəʊlɪ'teərɪət] n proletariado m.

pro-life adj pro-vida.

proliferate [prə'lɪfəreɪt] vi proliferar.

prolific [prə'lɪfɪk] adj prolífico(ca).

prologue, prolog US ['prəʊlɒg] n prólogo m; **to be the** OR **a prologue to sthg** fig ser el prólogo a algo.

prolong [prə'lɒŋ] vt prolongar.

prom [prɒm] n - **1.** abbr of promenade concert - **2.** UK inf [road by sea] (abbr of promenade) paseo m marítimo - **3.** US [ball] baile m de gala (en la escuela).

promenade [,prɒmə'nɑ:d] n UK [by sea] paseo m marítimo.

promenade concert n UK concierto sinfónico en donde parte del público está de pie.

prominence ['prɒmɪnəns] n - **1.** [importance] importancia f - **2.** [conspicuousness] prominencia f.

prominent ['prɒmɪnənt] adj - **1.** [important] destacado(da), importante - **2.** [noticeable] prominente.

prominently ['prɒmɪnəntlɪ] adv de forma destacada; **to figure prominently in sthg** destacar en algo; **to be prominently displayed** ocupar un lugar destacado.

promiscuity [,prɒmɪs'kju:ətɪ] n promiscuidad f.

promiscuous [prɒ'mɪskjʊəs] adj promiscuo(cua).

promise ['prɒmɪs] <> n promesa f; **to make (sb) a promise** hacer una promesa (a alguien); **to show promise** prometer, ser prometedor. <> vt: **to promise (to do sthg)** prometer (hacer algo); **to promise sb sthg** prometer a alguien algo. <> vi: **I promise** te lo prometo.

promising ['prɒmɪsɪŋ] adj prometedor(ra).

promissory note ['prɒmɪsərɪ-] n pagaré m.

promo ['prəʊməʊ] (pl -s) (abbr of promotion) n inf film m promocional.

promontory ['prɒməntrɪ] (pl -ies) n promontorio m.

promote [prə'məʊt] vt - **1.** [foster] fomentar, promover - **2.** [push, advertise] promocionar - **3.** [in job]: **to promote sb (to sthg)** ascender a alguien (a algo) - **4.** SPORT: **to be promoted** subir.

promoter [prə'məʊtə'] n - **1.** [organizer] organizador m, -ra f - **2.** [supporter] promotor m, -ra f.

promotion [prə'məʊʃn] n - **1.** [in job] ascenso m; **to get** OR **be given promotion** conseguir un ascenso - **2.** [advertising] promoción f - **3.** [campaign] campaña f de promoción.

prompt [prɒmpt] <> adj rápido(da), inmediato(ta); **the injury requires prompt treatment** las heridas requieren un tratamiento inmediato; **to be prompt in doing sthg** hacer algo con prontitud. <> adv en punto; **at 2 o'clock prompt** a las dos en punto. <> vt - **1.** [motivate]: **to prompt sb (to do sthg)** inducir OR impulsar a alguien (a hacer algo) - **2.** [encourage]:

to prompt sb (to do sthg) animar a alguien (a hacer algo) - **3.** THEAT apuntar. <> n THEAT [line] apunte m.

prompter ['prɒmptə'] n apuntador m, -ra f.

promptly ['prɒmptlɪ] adv - **1.** [reply, react, pay] inmediatamente, rápidamente - **2.** [arrive, leave] puntualmente.

promptness ['prɒmptnɪs] n - **1.** [of reply, reaction, payment] rapidez f - **2.** [of arrival, departure] puntualidad f.

promulgate ['prɒmlgeɪt] vt promulgar.

prone [prəʊn] adj - **1.** [susceptible]: **to be prone to sthg/to do sthg** ser propenso(sa) a algo/a hacer algo - **2.** [lying flat] boca abajo.

prong [prɒŋ] n diente m, punta f.

pronoun ['prəʊnaʊn] n pronombre m.

pronounce [prə'naʊns] <> vt - **1.** [gen] pronunciar - **2.** [declare] declarar. <> vi: **to pronounce on sthg** pronunciarse sobre algo.

pronounced [prə'naʊnst] adj pronunciado(da), marcado(da).

pronouncement [prə'naʊnsmənt] n declaración f.

pronunciation [prə,nʌnsɪ'eɪʃn] n pronunciación f.

proof [pru:f] <> n - **1.** [gen & TYPO] prueba f - **2.** [of alcohol]: **to be 10% proof** tener 10 grados. <> adj [secure]: **proof against** a prueba de.

proofread ['pru:fri:d] (pt & pp -read [-red]) vt corregir las pruebas (de imprenta) de.

proofreader ['pru:f,ri:də'] n corrector m, -ra f de pruebas.

prop [prɒp] <> n - **1.** [physical support] puntal m, apoyo m - **2.** fig [supporting thing, person] sostén m. <> vt (pt & pp -ped, cont -ping): **to prop sthg on** OR **against sthg** apoyar algo contra algo.

➤ **props** npl accesorios mpl.

➤ **prop up** vt sep - **1.** [physically support] apuntalar - **2.** fig [sustain] apoyar, sostener.

propaganda [,prɒpə'gændə] n propaganda f.

propagate ['prɒpəgeɪt] <> vt propagar. <> vi propagarse.

propagation [,prɒpə'geɪʃn] n propagación f.

propane ['prəʊpeɪn] n propano m.

propel [prə'pel] (pt & pp -led, cont -ling) vt propulsar, impulsar.

propeller [prə'pelə'] n hélice f.

propelling pencil [prə'pelɪŋ-] n UK portaminas m inv.

propensity [prə'pensətɪ] (pl -ies) n fml: **propensity (for** OR **to sthg)** propensión f (a algo); **to have a propensity to do sthg** tener propensión a hacer algo.

proper [ˈprɒpəʳ] *adj* - **1.** [real] de verdad - **2.** [correct - gen] correcto(ta); [- time, place, equipment] adecuado(da) - **3.** [as emphasis]: **a proper idiot** *inf* un perfecto idiota.

properly [ˈprɒpəlɪ] *adv* - **1.** [satisfactorily, correctly] bien - **2.** [decently] correctamente.

proper noun *n* nombre *m* propio.

property [ˈprɒpətɪ] (*pl* -ies) *n* - **1.** [gen] propiedad *f* - **2.** [estate] finca *f* - **3.** *fml* [house] inmueble *m*.

property developer *n* empresa *f* constructora.

property owner *n* propietario *m*, -ria *f* de un inmueble.

property tax *n* impuesto *m* sobre los bienes raíces.

prophecy [ˈprɒfɪsɪ] (*pl* -ies) *n* profecía *f*.

prophesy [ˈprɒfɪsaɪ] (*pt & pp* -ied) *vt* profetizar.

prophet [ˈprɒfɪt] *n* profeta *mf*.

prophetic [prəˈfetɪk] *adj* profético(ca).

propitious [prəˈpɪʃəs] *adj fml* propicio(cia).

proponent [prəˈpəʊnənt] *n* partidario *m*, -ria *f*, defensor *m*, -ra *f*.

proportion [prəˈpɔːʃn] *n* - **1.** [part] parte *f* - **2.** [ratio, comparison] proporción *f*; **in proportion to** en proporción a; **out of all proportion (to)** totalmente desproporcionado (con relación a) - **3.** [correct relationship]: **in proportion** en proporción; **out of proportion** desproporcionado(da); **to get things out of proportion** *fig* sacar las cosas fuera de quicio; **to keep things in proportion** *fig* no exagerar; **sense of proportion** *fig* sentido *m* de la medida.

proportional [prəˈpɔːʃnl] *adj*: **proportional (to)** proporcional (a), en proporción (a).

proportional representation *n* representación *f* proporcional.

proportionate [prəˈpɔːʃnət] *adj*: **proportionate (to)** proporcional (a).

proposal [prəˈpəʊzl] *n* - **1.** [plan, suggestion] propuesta *f* - **2.** [offer of marriage] proposición *f*.

propose [prəˈpəʊz] <> *vt* - **1.** [suggest] proponer; [motion] presentar; **to propose doing sthg** proponer hacer algo - **2.** [intend]: **to propose doing** OR **to do sthg** tener la intención de hacer algo. <> *vi* [make offer of marriage] declararse; **to propose to sb** pedir la mano de alguien.

proposed [prəˈpəʊzd] *adj* propuesto(ta).

proposition [ˌprɒpəˈzɪʃn] <> *n* - **1.** [statement of theory] proposición *f* - **2.** [suggestion] propuesta *f*; **to make sb a proposition** hacer una propuesta a alguien. <> *vt fml* hacer proposiciones a.

propound [prəˈpaʊnd] *vt fml* exponer, plantear.

proprietary [prəˈpraɪətrɪ] *adj fml* [brand name] registrado(da).

proprietor [prəˈpraɪətəʳ] *n* propietario *m*, -ria *f*.

propriety [prəˈpraɪətɪ] *n* (*U*) *fml* - **1.** [moral correctness] propiedad *f* - **2.** [rightness] conveniencia *f*, oportunidad *f*.

propulsion [prəˈpʌlʃn] *n* propulsión *f*.

pro rata [-ˈrɑːtə] *adj & adv* a prorrata.

prosaic [prəʊˈzeɪɪk] *adj* prosaico(ca).

proscenium [prəˈsiːnjəm] (*pl* -nia [njə] OR -niums) *n*: **proscenium (arch)** proscenio *m*.

proscribe [prəʊˈskraɪb] *vt fml* proscribir.

prose [prəʊz] *n* - **1.** (*U*) LIT prosa *f* - **2.** SCH traducción *f* inversa.

prosecute [ˈprɒsɪkjuːt] <> *vt* procesar, enjuiciar; **to be prosecuted for** ser procesado(da) por. <> *vi* - **1.** [bring a charge] entablar una acción judicial - **2.** [represent in court] representar al demandante.

prosecution [ˌprɒsɪˈkjuːʃn] *n* - **1.** [gen] procesamiento *m* - **2.** [lawyers]: **the prosecution** la acusación.

prosecutor [ˈprɒsɪkjuːtəʳ] *n esp US* fiscal *mf*.

prospect <> *n* [ˈprɒspekt] - **1.** [gen] perspectiva *f*; **it was a pleasant prospect** era una perspectiva agradable; **they were faced with the prospect of losing their jobs** tenían que hacer frente a la perspectiva de perder sus trabajos - **2.** [possibility] posibilidad *f*; **there's little prospect of that happening** hay pocas posibilidades de que eso ocurra. <> *vi* [prəˈspekt]: **to prospect (for)** hacer prospecciones (de).

➡ **prospects** *npl*: **prospects (for)** perspectivas *fpl* (de); **job prospects** perspectivas laborales.

prospecting [prəˈspektɪŋ] *n* (*U*) prospecciones *fpl*.

prospective [prəˈspektɪv] *adj* posible.

prospector [prəˈspektəʳ] *n* prospector *m*, -ra *f*.

prospectus [prəˈspektəs] (*pl* -es) *n* prospecto *m*, folleto *m* informativo.

prosper [ˈprɒspəʳ] *vi* prosperar.

prosperity [prɒˈsperɪtɪ] *n* prosperidad *f*.

prosperous [ˈprɒspərəs] *adj* próspero(ra).

prostate (gland) [ˈprɒsteɪt-] *n* próstata *f*.

prosthesis [prɒsˈθiːsɪs] (*pl* -theses [ˈθiːsiːz]) *n* prótesis *f inv*.

prostitute [ˈprɒstɪtjuːt] *n* prostituta *f*; **male prostitute** prostituto *m*.

prostitution [ˌprɒstɪˈtjuːʃn] *n* prostitución *f*.

prostrate <> *adj* [ˈprɒstreɪt] postrado(da). <> *vt* [prɒˈstreɪt]: **to prostrate o.s. (before sb)** postrarse (ante alguien).

protagonist [prəˈtægənɪst] *n* - **1.** *fml* [supporter] partidario *m*, -ria *f*, defensor *m*, -ra *f* - **2.** [main character] protagonista *mf*.

protect [prə'tekt] *vt*: to protect sthg/sb (against/from) proteger algo/a alguien (contra/de).

protection [prə'tekʃn] *n*: protection (against/from) protección *f* (contra/de).

protectionism [prə'tekʃənɪzm] *n* proteccionismo *m*.

protectionist [prə'tekʃənɪst] *adj* proteccionista.

protection money *n* dinero *m* pagado a cambio de protección.

protective [prə'tektɪv] *adj* protector(ra); **to feel protective towards sb** tener sentimientos protectores hacia alguien.

protective custody *n* detención *f* cautelar; **to be in protective custody** estar detenido(da) cautelarmente.

protectiveness [prə'tektɪvnɪs] *n* sentimiento *m* protector.

protector [prə'tektər] *n* protector *m*, -ra *f*.

protectorate [prə'tektərət] *n* protectorado *m*.

protégé ['prɒteʒeɪ] *n* protegido *m*.

protégée ['prɒteʒeɪ] *n* protegida *f*.

protein ['prəʊtiːn] *n* proteína *f*.

protest <> *n* ['prəʊtest] protesta *f*; **under protest** bajo protesta; **without protest** sin protestar. <> *vt* [prə'test] - **1.** [complain]: **to protest that** quejarse de - **2.** [state] manifestar, aseverar; **he protested his innocence** declaró su inocencia - **3.** *US* [oppose] protestar en contra de. <> *vi* [prə'test]: **to protest (about/against/at)** protestar (por/en contra de/por).

Protestant ['prɒtɪstənt] <> *adj* protestante. <> *n* protestante *mf*.

Protestantism ['prɒtɪstəntɪzm] *n* protestantismo *m*.

protestation [,prɒte'steɪʃn] *n fml* proclamación *f*.

protester [prə'testər] *n* manifestante *mf*.

protest march *n* manifestación *f*.

protocol ['prəʊtəkɒl] *n* protocolo *m*.

proton ['prəʊtɒn] *n* protón *m*.

prototype ['prəʊtətaɪp] *n* prototipo *m*.

protracted [prə'træktɪd] *adj* prolongado(da).

protractor [prə'træktər] *n* transportador *m*.

protrude [prə'truːd] *vi*: **to protrude (from)** sobresalir (de).

protruding [prə'truːdɪŋ] *adj* [chin] prominente; [teeth] salido(da); [eyes] saltón(ona).

protrusion [prə'truːʒn] *n* saliente *m*.

protuberance [prə'tjuːbərəns] *n* protuberancia *f*.

proud [praʊd] <> *adj* - **1.** [gen] orgulloso(sa); **to be proud of** estar orgulloso(sa) de; **that's nothing to be proud of!** ¡yo no estaría orgu-

lloso de eso!; **to be proud of o.s.** estar orgulloso de uno mismo; **to be proud to do sthg** tener el honor de hacer algo - **2.** *pej* [arrogant] soberbio(bia), arrogante. <> *adv*: **to do sb proud** tratar muy bien a alguien.

proudly ['praʊdlɪ] *adv* - **1.** [with satisfaction] orgullosamente - **2.** *pej* [arrogantly] arrogantemente.

provable ['pruːvəbl] *adj* demostrable.

prove [pruːv] <> *vt* (*pp* -d *OR* **proven**) - **1.** [show to be true] probar, demostrar; **events proved her right** los acontecimientos le dieron la razón - **2.** [show oneself to be]: **to prove (to be) sthg** demostrar ser algo; **to prove o.s. to be sthg** resultar ser algo; **to prove o.s.** demostrar (uno) sus cualidades. <> *vi* (*pp* -d *OR* **proven**) resultar; **to prove (to be) interesting/difficult** resultar interesante/difícil.

proven ['pruːvn, 'prəʊvn] <> *pp* ⊳ **prove**. <> *adj* probado(da).

proverb ['prɒvɜːb] *n* refrán *m*, proverbio *m*.

proverbial [prə'vɜːbjəl] *adj* proverbial.

provide [prə'vaɪd] *vt* proporcionar, proveer; **to provide sb with sthg** proporcionar a alguien algo; **to provide sthg for sb** ofrecer algo a alguien.

➤ **provide for** *vt insep* - **1.** [support] mantener - **2.** *fml* [make arrangements for] tomar medidas para.

provided [prə'vaɪdɪd], **providing**
➤ **provided (that)** *conj* con tal (de) que, a condición de que; **you should pass, provided you work hard** aprobarás, con tal de que trabajes duro.

providence ['prɒvɪdəns] *n* providencia *f*.

providential [,prɒvɪ'denʃl] *adj fml* providencial.

provider [prə'vaɪdər] *n* proveedor *m*, -ra *f*.

providing [prə'vaɪdɪŋ] ➤ **providing (that)** *conj* = **provided**.

province ['prɒvɪns] *n* - **1.** [part of country] provincia *f* - **2.** [speciality] campo *m*, competencia *f*.

➤ **provinces** *npl*: **in the provinces** en provincias.

provincial [prə'vɪnʃl] *adj* - **1.** [of a province] provincial - **2.** *pej* [narrow-minded] provinciano(na).

provision [prə'vɪʒn] *n* - **1.** [gen] suministro *m* - **2.** (*U*) [arrangement]: **to make provision for** [eventuality, future] tomar medidas para; [one's family] asegurar el porvenir de - **3.** [in agreement, law] disposición *f*.

➤ **provisions** *npl* [supplies] provisiones *fpl*, víveres *mpl*.

provisional [prə'vɪʒənl] *adj* provisional.

provisional licence *n UK* carné *m* de conducir provisional.

provisionally [prə'vɪʒnəlɪ] *adv* provisionalmente.

proviso [prə'vaɪzəʊ] (*pl* **-s**) *n* condición *f*; **with the proviso that...** con la condición de que...

Provo ['prəʊvəʊ] (*pl* **-s**) (*abbr of* **Provisional**) *n inf*: **the Provos** los provisionales del IRA.

provocation [,prɒvə'keɪʃn] *n* provocación *f*.

provocative [prə'vɒkətɪv] *adj* - **1.** [controversial] provocador(ra) - **2.** [sexy] provocativo(va).

provocatively [prə'vɒkətɪvlɪ] *adv* - **1.** [controversially] provocadoramente - **2.** [sexily] provocativamente.

provoke [prə'vəʊk] *vt* provocar; **to provoke sb to do sthg** OR **into doing sthg** provocar a alguien a que haga algo.

provoking [prə'vəʊkɪŋ] *adj* provocador(ra).

prow [praʊ] *n* proa *f*.

prowess ['praʊɪs] *n fml* proezas *fpl*.

prowl [praʊl] <> *n*: **on the prowl** merodeando. <> *vt* merodear por. <> *vi* merodear.

prowler ['praʊlə^r] *n* merodeador *m*, -ra *f*.

proximity [prɒk'sɪmətɪ] *n fml* proximidad *f*; **in close proximity to** muy cerca de; **in the proximity of** en las proximidades de.

proxy ['prɒksɪ] (*pl* **-ies**) *n*: **by proxy** por poderes.

prude [pru:d] *n* mojigato *m*, -ta *f*.

prudence ['pru:dns] *n fml* prudencia *f*.

prudent ['pru:dnt] *adj* prudente.

prudently ['pru:dntlɪ] *adv* prudentemente.

prudish ['pru:dɪʃ] *adj* mojigato(ta).

prune [pru:n] <> *n* [fruit] ciruela *f* pasa. <> *vt* podar.

prurient ['prʊərɪənt] *adj fml* lascivo(va).

pry [praɪ] (*pt & pp* **pried**) *vi* fisgonear, curiosear; **to pry into sthg** entrometerse en algo.

PS (*abbr of* **postscript**) *n* P.D.

psalm [sɑːm] *n* salmo *m*.

pseud [sjuːd] *n UK inf* intelectualoide *mf*.

pseudo- [,sjuː'dəʊ] *prefix* pseudo-, seudo-.

pseudonym ['sjuːdənɪm] *n* seudónimo *m*.

psoriasis [sɒ'raɪəsɪs] *n* soriasis *f inv*.

psst [pst] *excl* ¡psst!

PST (*abbr of* **Pacific Standard Time**) *hora oficial de la costa del Pacífico en EEUU*.

psych [saɪk] ⏴ **psych up** *vt sep inf* mentalizar; **to psych o.s. up** mentalizarse.

psyche ['saɪkɪ] *n* psique *f*.

psychedelic [,saɪkɪ'delɪk] *adj* psicodélico(ca).

psychiatric [,saɪkɪ'ætrɪk] *adj* psiquiátrico(ca).

psychiatric nurse *n* enfermero psiquiátrico *m*, enfermera psiquiátrica *f*.

psychiatrist [saɪ'kaɪətrɪst] *n* psiquiatra *mf*.

psychiatry [saɪ'kaɪətrɪ] *n* psiquiatría *f*.

psychic ['saɪkɪk] <> *adj* - **1.** [clairvoyant] clarividente - **2.** [mental] psíquico(ca). <> *n* médium *mf*.

psychoanalyse, -yze US [,saɪkəʊ'ænəlaɪz] *vt* psicoanalizar.

psychoanalysis [,saɪkəʊə'næləsɪs] *n* psicoanálisis *m inv*.

psychoanalyst [,saɪkəʊ'ænəlɪst] *n* psicoanalista *mf*.

psychological [,saɪkə'lɒdʒɪkl] *adj* psicológico(ca).

psychological warfare *n (U)* guerra *f* psicológica.

psychologist [saɪ'kɒlədʒɪst] *n* psicólogo *m*, -ga *f*.

psychology [saɪ'kɒlədʒɪ] *n* psicología *f*.

psychopath ['saɪkəpæθ] *n* psicópata *mf*.

psychosis [saɪ'kəʊsɪs] (*pl* **-choses** ['kəʊsiːz]) *n* psicosis *f inv*.

psychosomatic [,saɪkəʊsə'mætɪk] *adj* psicosomático(ca).

psychotherapy [,saɪkəʊ'θerəpɪ] *n* psicoterapia *f*.

psychotic [saɪ'kɒtɪk] <> *adj* psicótico(ca). <> *n* psicótico *m*, -ca *f*.

pt *abbr of* **pint**. *abbr of* **point**.

Pt. (*abbr of* **Point**) [on map] Pta.

PT *n abbr of* **physical training**.

PTA (*abbr of* **parent-teacher association**) *n* ≃ APA *f*.

Pte. *abbr of* **Private**.

PTO <> *n US* (*abbr of* **parent-teacher organization**) ≃ APA. <> (*abbr of* **please turn over**) sigue.

PTV - **1.** (*abbr of* **pay television**), *televisión de pago* - **2.** (*abbr of* **public television**), *televisión pública*.

pub [pʌb] (*abbr of* **public house**) *n* pub *m* (británico).

pub. (*abbr of* **published**) publicado.

pub-crawl *n UK*: **to go on a pub-crawl** ir de bar en bar.

puberty ['pjuːbətɪ] *n* pubertad *f*.

pubescent [pjuː'besnt] *adj* pubescente.

pubic ['pjuːbɪk] *adj* púbico(ca).

public ['pʌblɪk] <> *adj* público(ca); **to be public knowledge** ser del dominio público; **to make sthg public** hacer público algo; **to go public**

COMM constituirse en sociedad anónima (con cotización en Bolsa). <> *n* público *m*; **in public** en público; **the public** el gran público.

Public Access Television

En EE. UU., se llama **Public Access Television** a las cadenas de televisión por cable no comerciales, puestas a disposición de organizaciones sin ánimo de lucro y de los ciudadanos en general. En 1984 el Congreso adoptó el "Cable Communications Policy Act" (Ley de Comunicación por Cable) con el fin de hacer frente al problema de la monopolización de las cadenas por un número reducido de operadores de cable. Esta ley exige a los propietarios de las cadenas por cable que pongan una cadena a disposición de las comunidades locales, así como el correspondiente estudio y material de grabación, y también que contemplen asistencia técnica en caso de ser necesaria.

public-address system *n* sistema *m* de megafonía.

publican ['pʌblɪkən] *n UK* patrón *m*, -ona *f* de un 'pub'.

publication [,pʌblɪ'keɪʃn] *n* publicación *f*.

public bar *n UK* en ciertos pubs y hoteles, bar de sencilla decoración con precios más bajos que los del 'saloon bar'.

public company *n* sociedad *f* anónima (con cotización en Bolsa).

public convenience *n UK* aseos *mpl* públicos.

public holiday *n* fiesta *f* nacional, (dia *m*) feriado *m Amér.*

public house *n UK fml* pub *m* (británico).

publicist ['pʌblɪsɪst] *n* publicista *mf*.

publicity [pʌb'lɪsɪtɪ] <> *n* publicidad *f*. <> *comp* publicitario(ria).

publicity stunt *n* truco *m* publicitario.

publicize, -ise ['pʌblɪsaɪz] *vt* divulgar.

public limited company *n* sociedad *f* anónima (con cotización en Bolsa).

publicly ['pʌblɪklɪ] *adv* públicamente.

public office *n* cargo *m* público.

public opinion *n* (*U*) opinión *f* pública.

public ownership *n* propiedad *f* del estado.

public prosecutor *n* fiscal *mf* del Estado.

public relations <> *n* (*U*) relaciones *fpl* públicas. <> *npl* relaciones *fpl* públicas.

public relations officer *n* agente *mf* de relaciones públicas.

public school *n* - **1.** *UK* [private school] colegio *m* privado - **2.** *US* [state school] escuela *f* pública.

public sector *n* sector *m* estatal.

public servant *n* funcionario *m*, -ria *f*.

public service vehicle *n UK* vehículo *m* de servicio público.

public-spirited *adj* con sentido cívico.

public transport *n* transporte *m* público.

public utility *n* servicio *m* público.

public works *npl* obras *fpl* públicas.

publish ['pʌblɪʃ] <> *vt* - **1.** [gen] publicar - **2.** [make known] hacer público(ca). <> *vi* publicar.

publisher ['pʌblɪʃər] *n* [person] editor *m*, -ra *f*; [firm] editorial *f*.

publishing ['pʌblɪʃɪŋ] *n* (*U*) industria *f* editorial.

publishing company, publishing house *n* (casa *f*) editorial *f*.

pub lunch *n* almuerzo servido en un 'pub'.

puce [pjuːs] *adj* de color morado oscuro.

puck [pʌk] *n* disco *m* (en hockey sobre hielo).

pucker ['pʌkər] <> *vt* fruncir. <> *vi* fruncirse.

pudding ['pʊdɪŋ] *n* - **1.** [sweet] pudín *m*; [savoury] pastel *m* - **2.** (*U*) *UK* [course] postre *m*.

puddle ['pʌdl] *n* charco *m*.

pudgy ['pʌdʒɪ] *adj* = podgy.

puerile ['pjʊərail] *adj fml* pueril.

Puerto Rican [,pwɜːtəʊ'riːkən] <> *adj* puertorriqueño(ña). <> *n* puertorriqueño *m*, -ña *f*.

Puerto Rico [,pwɜːtəʊ'riːkəʊ] *n* Puerto Rico.

puff [pʌf] <> *n* - **1.** [of cigarette, pipe] calada *f*, pitada *f Amér* - **2.** [gasp] jadeo *m* - **3.** [of air] soplo *m*; [of smoke] bocanada *f*. <> *vt* echar. <> *vi* - **1.** [smoke]: **to puff at** OR **on** dar caladas a - **2.** [pant] jadear, resoplar.

➤ **puff out** *vt sep* - **1.** [cheeks, chest] hinchar; [feathers] ahuecar - **2.** [smoke] echar.

➤ **puff up** *vi* hincharse.

puffed [pʌft] *adj* - **1.** [swollen]: **puffed (up)** hinchado(da) - **2.** *UK inf* [out of breath]: **puffed (out)** jadeante.

puffed sleeve *n* manga *f* ablusada.

puffin ['pʌfɪn] *n* frailecillo *m*.

puffiness ['pʌfɪnɪs] *n* hinchazón *f*.

puff pastry, puff paste *US n* hojaldre *m*.

puffy ['pʌfɪ] (*comp* -ier, *superl* -iest) *adj* hinchado(da).

pug [pʌg] *n* doguillo *m*.

pugnacious [pʌg'neɪʃəs] *adj fml* pugnaz, belicoso(sa).

puke [pjuːk] *vi* v *inf* devolver, echar la papilla.

pull [pʊl] ◇ *vt* - **1.** [gen] tirar de; [trigger] apretar - **2.** [tooth, cork] sacar, extraer - **3.** [muscle] sufrir un tirón en - **4.** [attract] atraer - **5.** [gun] sacar y apuntar - **6.** [phr]: **to pull sthg to bits** OR **pieces** hacer pedazos algo. ◇ *vi* tirar. ◇ *n* - **1.** [tug with hand] tirón *m* - **2.** *(U)* [influence] influencia *f*.

◆ **pull ahead** *vi*: **to pull ahead (of)** adelantar (a).

◆ **pull apart** *vt sep* - **1.** [machine etc] desmontar - **2.** [toy, book etc] hacer pedazos.

◆ **pull at** *vt insep* dar tirones de.

◆ **pull away** *vi* - **1.** [from roadside] alejarse (de la acera) - **2.** [in race] despegarse.

◆ **pull back** *vi* retroceder, retirarse.

◆ **pull down** *vt sep* [building] derribar.

◆ **pull in** *vi* [train] pararse (en el andén).

◆ **pull off** *vt sep* - **1.** [clothes] quitarse rápidamente - **2.** [succeed in] conseguir llevar a cabo.

◆ **pull on** *vt sep* [clothes] ponerse rápidamente.

◆ **pull out** ◇ *vt sep* - **1.** [troops] retirar - **2.** [tooth] sacar. ◇ *vi* - **1.** [vehicle] alejarse (de la acera) - **2.** [withdraw] retirarse.

◆ **pull over** *vi* AUT hacerse a un lado.

◆ **pull through** ◇ *vi* recobrarse, reponerse. ◇ *vt sep* ayudar a salir de.

◆ **pull together** ◇ *vt sep*: **to pull o.s. together** calmarse, serenarse. ◇ *vi* *fig* cooperar, aunar fuerzas.

◆ **pull up** ◇ *vt sep* - **1.** [move closer] acercar - **2.** [stop]: **to pull sb up short** parar a alguien en seco. ◇ *vi* parar, detenerse.

pull-down menu *n* COMPUT menú *m* desplegable.

pulley ['pʊlɪ] (*pl* **pulleys**) *n* polea *f*.

pullout ['pʊlaʊt] *n* suplemento *m*.

pullover ['pʊl,əʊvə^r] *n* jersey *m*.

pulp [pʌlp] ◇ *adj* [novel etc] de pacotilla. ◇ *n* - **1.** [soft mass] papilla *f*; **to beat sb to a pulp** hacer papilla a alguien - **2.** [of fruit] pulpa *f* - **3.** [of wood] pasta *f* de papel.

pulpit ['pʊlpɪt] *n* púlpito *m*.

pulsar ['pʌlsɑː^r] *n* púlsar *m*.

pulsate [pʌl'seɪt] *vi* palpitar.

pulse [pʌls] ◇ *n* - **1.** [in body] pulso *m*; **to take sb's pulse** tomarle el pulso a alguien - **2.** TECH impulso *m*. ◇ *vi* latir.

◆ **pulses** *npl* [food] legumbres *fpl*.

pulverize, -ise ['pʌlvəraɪz] *vt* *lit* & *fig* pulverizar.

puma ['pjuːmə] (*pl* **puma** OR **-s**) *n* puma *m*.

pumice (stone) ['pʌmɪs-] *n* piedra *f* pómez.

pummel ['pʌml] (*UK* **-led**, *cont* **-ling**) (*US* **-ed**, *cont* **-ing**) *vt* aporrear.

pump [pʌmp] ◇ *n* - **1.** [machine] bomba *f* - **2.** [for petrol] surtidor *m*. ◇ *vt* - **1.** [convey by pumping] bombear - **2.** *inf* [invest]: **to pump sthg into sthg** inyectar algo en algo - **3.** *inf* [interrogate] sonsacar; **to pump sb for information** sonsacar a alguien. ◇ *vi* latir.

◆ **pumps** *npl* [shoes] zapatillas *fpl* de tenis.

◆ **pump up** *vt* [inflate] inflar.

pumpernickel ['pʌmpənɪkl] *n* pan *m* integral de centeno.

pumpkin ['pʌmpkɪn] *n* calabaza *f*, zapallo *m* *Perú*, auyama *f* *Col*.

pumpkin pie *n* *pastel de calabaza que constituye el postre tradicional de la cena de acción de gracias en Estados Unidos.*

pun [pʌn] *n* juego *m* de palabras.

punch [pʌntʃ] ◇ *n* - **1.** [blow] puñetazo *m* - **2.** [tool - for leather etc] punzón *m*; [- for tickets] máquina *f* para picar billetes - **3.** [drink] ponche *m*. ◇ *vt* - **1.** [hit] dar un puñetazo a, trompear *Amér* - **2.** [ticket] picar - **3.** [hole] perforar.

◆ **punch in** *vi* US fichar (a la entrada).

◆ **punch out** *vi* US fichar (a la salida).

Punch-and-Judy show [-'dʒuːdɪ-] *n* *teatro de guiñol para niños con personajes arquetípicos y representado normalmente en la playa.*

punch bag, punch ball, punching bag *US* ['pʌntʃ-] *n* punching ball *m*.

punch bowl *n* ponchera *f*.

punch-drunk *adj* grogui, aturdido(da).

punch(ed) card [pʌntʃ(t)-] *n* tarjeta *f* perforada.

punching bag *n* US = punch bag.

punch line *n* remate *m* *(de un chiste).*

punch-up *n* *UK* *inf* pelea *f*.

punchy ['pʌntʃɪ] (*comp* **-ier**, *superl* **-iest**) *adj* *inf* efectista, resultón(ona).

punctilious [pʌŋk'tɪlɪəs] *adj* *fml* puntilloso(sa).

punctual ['pʌŋktʃʊəl] *adj* puntual.

punctually ['pʌŋktʃʊəlɪ] *adv* puntualmente.

punctuate ['pʌŋktʃʊeɪt] *vt* - **1.** GRAM puntuar - **2.** [interrupt]: **to be punctuated by** OR **with** ser interrumpido(da) por.

punctuation [,pʌŋktʃʊ'eɪʃn] *n* puntuación *f*.

punctuation mark *n* signo *m* de puntuación.

puncture ['pʌŋktʃə^r] ◇ *n* pinchazo *m*; **to have a puncture** pinchar; [in skin] punción *f*. ◇ *vt* pinchar, ponchar *Guat & Méx*.

pundit ['pʌndɪt] *n* lumbrera *f*, experto *m*, -ta *f*.

pungent ['pʌndʒənt] *adj* - **1.** [strong-smelling] penetrante, fuerte - **2.** *fig* [biting] mordaz.

punish ['pʌnɪʃ] *vt*: to punish sb (for sthg/for doing sthg) castigar a alguien (por algo/por haber hecho algo).

punishable ['pʌnɪʃəbl] *adj* castigable, sancionable; **punishable by death** castigado(da) con la pena de muerte.

punishing ['pʌnɪʃɪŋ] *adj* trabajoso(sa), penoso(sa).

punishment ['pʌnɪʃmənt] *n* - **1.** [for crime] castigo *m* - **2.** [severe treatment]: **to take a lot of punishment** sufrir estragos.

punitive ['pjuːnətɪv] *adj* punitivo(va).

punk [pʌŋk] ◇ *adj* punk. ◇ *n* - **1.** [music]: **punk (rock)** punk *m* - **2.** [person]: **punk (rocker)** punki *mf* - **3.** *US inf* [lout] gamberro *m*.

punnet ['pʌnɪt] *n UK* cajita *f (para fresas etc)*.

punt [pʌnt] ◇ *n* batea *f*. ◇ *vi* navegar en batea.

punter ['pʌntər] *n UK* - **1.** [gambler] apostante *mf* - **2.** *inf* [customer] cliente *m*, -ta *f*.

puny ['pjuːnɪ] *(comp* -ier, *superl* -iest*) adj* [person, limbs] enclenque, raquítico(ca); [effort] penoso(sa), lamentable.

pup [pʌp] *n* - **1.** [young dog] cachorro *m* - **2.** [young seal, otter] cría *f*.

pupil ['pjuːpl] *n* - **1.** [student] alumno *m*, -na *f* - **2.** [follower] pupilo *m*, -la *f* - **3.** [of eye] pupila *f*.

puppet ['pʌpɪt] *n lit & fig* títere *m*.

puppet government *n* gobierno *m* títere.

puppet show *n* teatro *m* de títeres.

puppy ['pʌpɪ] *(pl* -ies*) n* cachorro *m*, perrito *m*.

puppy fat *n inf* gordura *f* infantil.

purchase ['pɜːtʃəs] *fml* ◇ *n* compra *f*, adquisición *f*. ◇ *vt* comprar, adquirir.

purchase order *n* orden *f* de compra.

purchase price *n* precio *m* de compra.

purchaser ['pɜːtʃəsər] *n* comprador *m*, -ra *f*.

purchase tax *n UK* impuesto *m* sobre la venta.

purchasing power ['pɜːtʃəsɪŋ-] *n* poder *m* adquisitivo.

pure [pjʊər] *adj* puro(ra).

purebred ['pjʊəbred] *adj* de pura sangre.

puree ['pjʊəreɪ] *n* puré *m*; **tomato puree** concentrado *m* de tomate.

purely ['pjʊəlɪ] *adv* puramente; **purely and simply** pura y simplemente.

pureness ['pjʊənɪs] *n* pureza *f*.

purgative ['pɜːɡətɪv] *n* purgante *m*.

purgatory ['pɜːɡətrɪ] *n (U) hum* [suffering] purgatorio *m*.

◆ **Purgatory** *n* [place] Purgatorio *m*.

purge [pɜːdʒ] ◇ *n* POL purga *f*. ◇ *vt*: to purge sthg (of) purgar algo (de).

purification [ˌpjʊərɪfɪ'keɪʃn] *n* purificación *f*.

purifier ['pjʊərɪfaɪər] *n* depurador *m*.

purify ['pjʊərɪfaɪ] *(pt & pp* -ied*) vt* purificar.

purist ['pjʊərɪst] *n* purista *mf*.

puritan ['pjʊərɪtən] ◇ *adj* puritano(na). ◇ *n* puritano *m*, -na *f*.

puritanical [ˌpjʊərɪ'tænɪkl] *adj pej* puritano(na).

purity ['pjʊərətɪ] *n* pureza *f*.

purl [pɜːl] ◇ *n (U)* punto *m* del revés. ◇ *vt & vi* tejer con punto del revés.

purloin [pɜː'lɔɪn] *vt fml & hum* hurtar.

purple ['pɜːpl] ◇ *adj* morado(da). ◇ *n* (color *m*) morado *m*.

purport [pə'pɔːt] *vi fml*: to purport to do/be sthg pretender hacer/ser algo.

purpose ['pɜːpəs] *n* - **1.** [gen] propósito *m*; **what is the purpose of your visit?** ¿cuál es el objeto de tu visita?; **for tax purposes** a efectos fiscales; **for one's own purposes** por su propio interés; **it serves no purpose** carece de sentido; **it has served its purpose** ha servido; **to no purpose** en vano - **2.** [determination] resolución *f*.

◆ **on purpose** *adv* a propósito, adrede.

purpose-built *adj* especialmente construido(da).

purposeful ['pɜːpəsfʊl] *adj* resuelto(ta).

purposely ['pɜːpəslɪ] *adv* adrede, a propósito.

purr [pɜːr] ◇ *n* - **1.** [of cat] ronroneo *m* - **2.** [of engine] zumbido *m*. ◇ *vi* - **1.** [cat, person] ronronear - **2.** [engine, machine] zumbar.

purse [pɜːs] ◇ *n* - **1.** [for money] monedero *m* - **2.** *US* [handbag] bolso *m*, bolsa *f Méx*, cartera *f Andes*. ◇ *vt* fruncir (con desagrado); **she pursed her lips** frunció los labios.

purser ['pɜːsər] *n* contador *m*, -ra *f*.

purse snatcher [-ˌsnætʃər] *n US* ladrón *m* que roba dando el tirón.

purse strings *npl*: to hold the purse strings administrar el dinero.

pursue [pə'sjuː] *vt* - **1.** [follow] perseguir - **2.** *fml* [policy] llevar a cabo; [aim, pleasure etc] ir en pos de, buscar; [topic, question] profundizar en; [hobby, studies] dedicarse a.

pursuer [pə'sjuːər] *n* perseguidor *m*, -ra *f*.

pursuit [pə'sjuːt] *n* - **1.** *(U) fml* [attempt to achieve] búsqueda *f* - **2.** [chase, in cycling] persecución *f*; **in pursuit of** en persecución de; **in hot pursuit (of)** pisando los talones (a) - **3.** [occupation, activity] ocupación *f*; **leisure pursuit** pasatiempo *m*.

purveyor [pə'veɪər] *n fml* proveedor *m*, -ra *f*.

pus [pʌs] *n* pus *m*.

push [puʃ] <> *vt* - **1.** [shove] empujar; **to push sth into sth** meter algo en algo; **to push sth open/shut** abrir/cerrar algo empujándolo - **2.** [press - button] apretar, pulsar - **3.** [encourage]: **to push sb (to do sth)** empujar a alguien (a hacer algo) - **4.** [force]: **to push sb (into doing sth)** obligar a alguien (a hacer algo) - **5.** *inf* [promote] promocionar - **6.** *drug sl* pasar, vender. <> *vi* - **1.** [press forward] empujar; [on button] apretar, pulsar - **2.** [move past]: **to push through** abrirse paso (a empujones) entre. <> *n lit & fig* empujón *m*; **at the push of a button** con sólo apretar un botón; **to give sb the push** *inf* [end relationship] dar calabazas a alguien; [from job] dar la patada a alguien; **at a push** apurando mucho.

◆ **push ahead** *vi*: **to push ahead (with sth)** seguir adelante sin parar (con algo).

◆ **push around** *vt sep inf* mandonear.

◆ **push for** *vt insep* [demand] reclamar.

◆ **push in** *vi* [in queue] colarse.

◆ **push off** *vi inf* largarse.

◆ **push on** *vi* seguir adelante sin parar.

◆ **push over** *vt sep* volcar.

◆ **push through** *vt sep* [law etc] conseguir que se apruebe.

pushbike ['puʃbaɪk] *n* UK *inf* bici *f*.

pushcart ['puʃkɑːt] *n* carrito *m*.

pushchair ['puʃtʃeəʳ] *n* UK silla *f* (de paseo).

pushed [puʃt] *adj inf*: **to be pushed for sth** andar corto(ta) de algo; **to be hard pushed to do sth** tenerlo difícil para hacer algo.

pusher ['puʃəʳ] *n inf* camello *m*.

pushing ['puʃɪŋ] *prep inf* alrededor de; **he's pushing 50** ronda los cincuenta.

pushover ['puʃ,əuvəʳ] *n inf*: **it's a pushover** está chupado.

push-start *vt* arrancar empujando.

push-up *n esp* US flexión *f*.

pushy ['puʃɪ] (*comp* -**ier**, *superl* -**iest**) *adj pej* agresivo(va), insistente.

puss [pus], **pussy (cat)** ['pusɪ-] *n inf* gatito *m*, minino *m*.

pussy willow ['pusɪ-] *n* sauce *m* blanco.

put [put] (*pt & pp* **put**, *cont* -**ting**) *vt* - **1.** [gen] poner; **to put sth into sth** meter algo en algo - **2.** [place exactly] colocar - **3.** [send - to prison etc] meter; **to put the children to bed** acostar a los niños - **4.** [express] expresar, formular; **to put it bluntly** hablando claro - **5.** [ask - question] hacer; [- proposal] presentar; **to put it to sb that...** sugerir a alguien que... - **6.** [estimate]: **to put sth at** calcular algo en - **7.** [invest]: **to put money into a project** invertir dinero en un proyecto; **to put money into an account** ingresar dinero en una cuenta; **to put a lot of effort into sth** esforzarse mucho con algo - **8.** [apply]: **to put pressure on** presionar a; **that puts a great responsibility on us** eso nos supone una gran responsabilidad.

◆ **put across, put over** *vt sep* transmitir; **to put o.s. across** hacerse entender.

◆ **put aside** *vt sep* - **1.** [money] ahorrar - **2.** [book, work, differences] dejar a un lado.

◆ **put away** *vt sep* - **1.** [tidy away] poner en su sitio, guardar - **2.** *inf* [lock up] encerrar - **3.** *inf* [consume] tragarse.

◆ **put back** *vt sep* - **1.** [replace] devolver a su sitio - **2.** [postpone] aplazar; [schedule] retrasar - **3.** [clock, watch] atrasar.

◆ **put by** *vt sep* ahorrar.

◆ **put down** *vt sep* - **1.** [lay down] dejar - **2.** [phone] colgar - **3.** [quell] sofocar, reprimir - **4.** *inf* [criticize]: **to put sb down** poner mal a alguien; **to put o.s. down** menospreciarse - **5.** UK [animal] sacrificar - **6.** [write down] apuntar.

◆ **put down to** *vt sep* achacar a.

◆ **put forward** *vt sep* - **1.** [plan, theory, name] proponer, presentar; [proposal] presentar - **2.** [clock, meeting, event] adelantar.

◆ **put in** *vt sep* - **1.** [spend - time] dedicar - **2.** [submit] presentar - **3.** [install] instalar.

◆ **put off** *vt sep* - **1.** [postpone] posponer, aplazar - **2.** [cause to wait] hacer esperar - **3.** [distract] distraer - **4.** [discourage] disuadir, desanimar - **5.** [cause to dislike]: **to put sb off sth** quitarle a alguien las ganas de algo.

◆ **put on** *vt sep* - **1.** [wear] ponerse - **2.** [show, play] representar; [exhibition] hacer; [transport] organizar - **3.** [gain]: **to put on weight** engordar; **I've put on 10 kilos** he engordado 10 kilos - **4.** [radio, light] poner, encender; **to put on the brakes** frenar - **5.** [record, tape] poner - **6.** [start cooking] empezar a hacer OR cocinar; **to put the kettle on** poner el agua a hervir - **7.** [bet] apostar por - **8.** [add] añadir - **9.** [feign - air, accent] fingir - **10.** US *inf* [tease]: **to put sb on** tomar el pelo a alguien.

◆ **put onto** *vt sep* [tell about]: **to put sb onto sth/sb** dirigir a alguien a algo/alguien.

◆ **put out** *vt sep* - **1.** [place outside] sacar - **2.** [issue - statement] hacer público - **3.** [extinguish, switch off] apagar - **4.** [prepare for use - clothes] sacar - **5.** [extend - hand, leg] extender; [- tongue] sacar - **6.** *inf* [injure] dislocarse - **7.** [upset]: **to be put out** estar disgustado(da) - **8.** [inconvenience] causar molestias a; **to put o.s. out** molestarse.

◆ **put over** *vt sep* = **put across**.

◆ **put through** *vt sep* - **1.** TELEC [call] poner; **to put sb through to sb** poner a alguien con alguien - **2.** [cause to suffer]: **to put sb through sth** hacer pasar a alguien por algo.

put together *vt sep* **- 1.** [machine, tool] ensamblar; [team] reunir; [report, strategy] elaborar **- 2.** [combine] mezclar **- 3.** [organize - event] organizar.

put up <> *vt sep* **- 1.** [build] construir; [tent] montar **- 2.** [umbrella] abrir; [flag] izar **- 3.** [raise - hand] levantar **- 4.** [poster] fijar; [painting] pegar, colgar **- 5.** [provide - money] poner **- 6.** [propose - candidate] proponer **- 7.** [increase] subir, aumentar **- 8.** [provide accommodation for] alojar. <> *vt insep* [resistance] ofrecer; **to put up a fight** ofrecer resistencia.

put up to *vt sep*: **to put sb up to sthg** incitar a alguien a hacer algo.

put up with *vt insep* aguantar, soportar.

putative ['pjuːtətɪv] *adj fml* supuesto(ta).

put-down *n inf* desaire *m*, corte *m*.

putrefaction [ˌpjuːtrɪ'fækʃn] *n* putrefacción *f*.

putrefy ['pjuːtrɪfaɪ] (*pt & pp* -**ied**) *vi fml* pudrirse.

putrid ['pjuːtrɪd] *adj fml* putrefacto(ta).

putsch [pʊtʃ] *n* golpe *m* de estado.

putt [pʌt] <> *n* putt *m*. <> *vt & vi* tirar al hoyo.

putter ['pʌtəʳ] *n* [club] putter *m*.

putter about, putter around *vi insep US* entretenerse.

putting green ['pʌtɪŋ-] *n* césped abierto al público en el que se puede jugar a golf con el putter.

putty ['pʌtɪ] *n* masilla *f*.

put-up job *n inf* amaño *m*.

put-upon *adj*: **to feel put-upon** sentirse utilizado(da).

puzzle ['pʌzl] <> *n* **- 1.** [toy, game] rompecabezas *m inv* **- 2.** [mystery] misterio *m*, enigma *m*. <> *vt* dejar perplejo, desconcertar. <> *vi*: **to puzzle over sthg** romperse la cabeza con algo.

puzzle out *vt sep* descifrar, resolver.

puzzled ['pʌzld] *adj* desconcertado(da), perplejo(ja).

puzzling ['pʌzlɪŋ] *adj* desconcertante.

PVC (*abbr of* **polyvinyl chloride**) *n* PVC *m*.

pw (*abbr of* **per week**) *a la semana*.

PX (*abbr of* **post exchange**) *n US* economato militar.

pygmy ['pɪgmɪ] <> *adj* pigmeo(a). <> *n* (*pl* -**ies**) pigmeo *m*, -a *f*.

pyjamas, pajamas [pə'dʒɑːməz] *npl* pijama *m*; **a pair of pyjamas** un pijama.

pylon ['paɪlən] *n* torre *f* (*de conducción eléctrica*).

pyramid ['pɪrəmɪd] *n* pirámide *f*.

pyramid selling *n* venta *f* piramidal.

pyre ['paɪəʳ] *n* pira *f*.

Pyrenean [ˌpɪrə'niːən] *adj* pirenaico(ca).

Pyrenees [ˌpɪrə'niːz] *npl*: **the Pyrenees** los Pirineos.

Pyrex® ['paɪreks] <> *n* pírex® *m*. <> *comp* de pírex.

pyromaniac [ˌpaɪrə'meɪnɪæk] *n* pirómano *m*, -na *f*.

pyrotechnics [ˌpaɪrəʊ'teknɪks] *npl* **- 1.** [show] fuegos *mpl* artificiales **- 2.** [skill] demostración *f* de habilidad extraordinaria.

python ['paɪθn] (*pl* **python** OR -**s**) *n* pitón *m*.

q (*pl* **q's** OR **qs**), **Q** (*pl* **Q's** OR **Qs**) [kjuː] *n* [letter] q *f*, Q *f*.

QC *n abbr of* **Queen's Counsel**.

QED (*abbr of* **quod erat demonstrandum**) Q.E.D.

QM *n abbr of* **quartermaster**.

q.t., QT (*abbr of* **quiet**) *inf*: **I did it on the q.t.** lo hice en secreto.

Q-tip® *n US* hisopo *m* de algodón.

qty (*abbr of* **quantity**) cdad.

quack [kwæk] <> *n* **- 1.** [noise] graznido *m* (*de pato*) **- 2.** *inf* [doctor] matasanos *m inv*. <> *vi* graznar (*el pato*).

quad [kwɒd] *n abbr of* **quadrangle**.

quadrangle ['kwɒdræŋgl] *n* **- 1.** [figure] cuadrángulo *m* **- 2.** [courtyard] patio *m*.

quadrant ['kwɒdrənt] *n* cuadrante *m*.

quadraphonic [ˌkwɒdrə'fɒnɪk] *adj* cuadrafónico(ca).

quadrilateral [ˌkwɒdrɪ'lætərəl] <> *adj* cuadrilátero(ra). <> *n* cuadrilátero *m*.

quadruped ['kwɒdruped] *n* cuadrúpedo *m*.

quadruple [kwɒ'druːpl] <> *adj* cuatro veces mayor. <> *vt* cuadruplicar. <> *vi* cuadruplicarse.

quadruplets ['kwɒdruplɪts] *npl* cuatrillizos *mpl*, -zas *f*.

quads [kwɒdz] *npl inf* cuatrillizos *mpl*, -zas *f*.

quaff [kwɒf] *vt dated* echarse al coleto.

quagmire ['kwægmaɪəʳ] *n* lodazal *m*, cenagal *m*.

quail [kweɪl] ◇ *n* (*pl* **quail** OR **-s**) codorniz *f*. ◇ *vi liter* amedrentarse.

quaint [kweɪnt] *adj* - **1.** [picturesque] pintoresco(ca) - **2.** [odd] singular.

quake [kweɪk] ◇ *n inf* terremoto *m*. ◇ *vi* temblar, estremecerse.

Quaker ['kweɪkəʳ] *n* cuáquero *m*, -ra *f*.

qualification [,kwɒlɪfɪ'keɪʃn] *n* - **1.** [examination, certificate] título *m* - **2.** [ability, skill] aptitud *f* - **3.** [becoming qualified] obtención *f* del título - **4.** SPORT clasificación *f* - **5.** [qualifying statement] condición *f*.

qualified ['kwɒlɪfaɪd] *adj* - **1.** [trained] cualificado(da); **to be qualified to do sthg** estar cualificado para hacer algo - **2.** [limited] limitado(da).

qualify ['kwɒlɪfaɪ] ◇ *vt* (*pt & pp* **-ied**) - **1.** [modify] matizar - **2.** [entitle]: **to qualify sb to do sthg** capacitar a alguien para hacer algo. ◇ *vi* (*pt & pp* **-ied**) - **1.** [pass exams] sacar el título - **2.** [be entitled]: **to qualify (for)** tener derecho (a) - **3.** SPORT clasificarse.

qualifying ['kwɒlɪfaɪŋ] *adj* - **1.** [modifying] calificativo(va) - **2.** [in sport, exam] eliminatorio(ria); **qualifying round** eliminatoria *f*.

qualitative ['kwɒlɪtətɪv] *adj* cualitativo(va).

quality ['kwɒlɪtɪ] (*pl* **-ies**) ◇ *n* - **1.** [standard] calidad *f* - **2.** [characteristic] cualidad *f*. ◇ *comp* de calidad.

quality control *n* control *m* de calidad.

quality press *n* UK: **the quality press** la prensa de calidad.

qualms [kwɑːmz] *npl* remordimientos *mpl*, escrúpulos *mpl*.

quandary ['kwɒndərɪ] (*pl* **-ies**) *n*: **to be in a quandary about** OR **over sthg** estar en un dilema sobre algo.

quango ['kwæŋgəʊ] (*pl* **-s**) (*abbr of* **quasi-autonomous non-governmental organization**) *n* UK pej organismo semiindependiente de la Administración.

quantifiable [kwɒntɪ'faɪəbl] *adj* cuantificable.

quantify ['kwɒntɪfaɪ] (*pt & pp* **-ied**) *vt* cuantificar.

quantitative ['kwɒntɪtətɪv] *adj* cuantitativo(va).

quantity ['kwɒntətɪ] (*pl* **-ies**) *n* cantidad *f*; **in quantity** en cantidad; **unknown quantity** incógnita *f*.

quantity surveyor *n* aparejador *m*, -ra *f*.

quantum leap ['kwɒntəm-] *n* enorme salto *m* adelante.

quantum theory ['kwɒntəm-] *n* la (teoría) cuántica.

quarantine ['kwɒrəntiːn] ◇ *n* cuarentena *f*; **to be in quarantine** estar en cuarentena. ◇ *vt* poner en cuarentena.

quark [kwɑːk] *n* - **1.** PHYS cuark *m* - **2.** CULIN *tipo de queso blando bajo en grasas*.

quarrel ['kwɒrəl] ◇ *n* pelea *f*; **to have no quarrel with sb/sthg** no tener nada en contra de alguien/algo. ◇ *vi* (UK **-led**, *cont* **-ling**, US **-ed**, *cont* **-ing**) pelearse; **to quarrel with sb** pelearse con alguien; **to quarrel with sthg** no estar de acuerdo con algo.

quarrelsome ['kwɒrəlsəm] *adj* pendenciero(ra).

quarry ['kwɒrɪ] ◇ *n* (*pl* **-ies**) - **1.** [place] cantera *f* - **2.** [prey] presa *f*. ◇ *vt* (*pt & pp* **-ied**) extraer.

quart [kwɔːt] *n* cuarto *m* de galón.

quarter ['kwɔːtəʳ] *n* - **1.** [fraction] cuarto *m* - **2.** [in telling time]: **a quarter past two** UK, **quarter after two** US las dos y cuarto; **a quarter to two** UK, **quarter of two** US las dos menos cuarto; **a quarter of an hour** un cuarto de hora - **3.** [of year] trimestre *m* - **4.** US [coin] cuarto *m* de dólar, moneda *f* de 25 centavos - **5.** [four ounces] cuatro onzas *fpl*, cuarto *m* de libra - **6.** [area in town] barrio *m* - **7.** [group of people] lugar *m*, parte *f*; **in some quarters this is seen as lying** algunos ven eso como una mentira.

◆ **quarters** *npl* [rooms] residencia *f*, alojamiento *m*.

◆ **at close quarters** *adv* muy de cerca.

quarterback ['kwɔːtəbæk] *n* US jugador de fútbol americano que lanza la pelota en las jugadas ofensivas.

quarterdeck ['kwɔːtədek] *n* alcázar *m*.

quarterfinal [,kwɔːtə'faɪnl] *n* cuarto *m* de final.

quarter light *n* UK AUT ventanilla *f* triangular (para ventilación).

quarterly ['kwɔːtəlɪ] ◇ *adj* trimestral. ◇ *adv* trimestralmente. ◇ *n* (*pl* **-ies**) trimestral *f*.

quartermaster ['kwɔːtə,mɑːstəʳ] *n* oficial *m* de intendencia.

quarter note *n* US MUS negra *f*.

quarter sessions *npl* audiencia *f* trimestral.

quartet [kwɔː'tet] *n* cuarteto *m*.

quarto ['kwɔːtəʊ] (*pl* **-s**) *n* cuarto *m*.

quartz [kwɔːts] *n* cuarzo *m*.

quartz watch *n* reloj *m* de cuarzo.

quasar ['kweɪzɑːʳ] *n* quasar *m*.

quash [kwɒʃ] *vt* - **1.** [reject] anular, invalidar - **2.** [quell] reprimir, sofocar.

quasi- ['kweɪzaɪ] *prefix* cuasi-.

quaver ['kweɪvəʳ] ◇ *n* - **1.** MUS corchea *f* - **2.** [in voice] trémolo *m*. ◇ *vi* temblar.

quavering ['kweɪvərɪŋ] *adj* trémulo(la).

quay [ki:] *n* muelle *m*.

quayside ['ki:saɪd] *n* muelle *m*.

queasy ['kwi:zɪ] (*comp* **-ier**, *superl* **-iest**) *adj* mareado(da).

Quebec [kwɪ'bek] *n* Quebec.

Quebecer, Quebecker [kwɪ'bekəʳ] *n* quebequés *m*, -esa *f*.

queen [kwi:n] *n* **- 1.** [gen] reina *f* **- 2.** [playing card] dama *f*.

Queen's speech ▬▬▬▬▬

> 🏛 Se trata del discurso pronunciado por la Reina durante la apertura anual del parlamento británico, que habitualmente se lleva a cabo en noviembre, y constituye la ceremonia oficial más importante del año parlamentario en Westminster. En el discurso, pronunciado ante la Cámara de los Lores, se resumen los proyectos legislativos que el gobierno tiene previstos para el año parlamentario que está a punto de comenzar. Aunque el discurso lo pronuncia la Reina, sus contenidos están redactados por una comisión del gobierno y aprobados por el Consejo de Ministros.

Queen Mother *n*: the Queen Mother la reina madre.

Queen's Counsel *n UK* abogado inglés de alto rango.

Queen's English *n UK*: the Queen's English el inglés hablado con mayor corrección en Gran Bretaña.

queen's evidence *n UK*: to turn queen's evidence *testificar un delincuente ante un tribunal en contra de otros a cambio de una reducción de condena.*

queer [kwɪəʳ] <> *adj* **- 1.** [odd] raro(ra), extraño(ña) **- 2.** *inf pej* [homosexual] marica, maricón. <> *n inf pej* marica *m*, maricón *m*, joto *m Méx*.

quell [kwel] *vt* **- 1.** [rebellion] sofocar, reprimir **- 2.** [feelings] dominar, contener.

quench [kwentʃ] *vt* apagar.

querulous ['kwerʊləs] *adj fml* quejumbroso(sa).

query ['kwɪərɪ] <> *n* (*pl* **-ies**) pregunta *f*, duda *f*. <> *vt* (*pt & pp* **-ied**) poner en duda.

quest [kwest] *n liter*: **quest (for)** búsqueda *f* (de).

question ['kwestʃn] <> *n* **- 1.** [query, problem in exam] pregunta *f*; **to ask (sb) a question** hacer una pregunta (a alguien) **- 2.** [doubt] duda *f*; **to bring sthg into question** hacer reflexionar sobre algo; **to call sthg into question** poner algo en duda; **without question** sin duda; **beyond question** fuera de toda duda; **open to question** debatible **- 3.** [issue, matter] cuestión *f*, asunto *m*

▶ **it is a question of staying calm** se trata de mantener la calma; **there's no question of...** es imposible que... <> *vt* **- 1.** [ask questions to] preguntar; [interrogate] interrogar **- 2.** [express doubt about] cuestionar.

◀ **in question** *adv*: **the matter in question** el asunto en cuestión.

◀ **out of the question** *adv* imposible; **that's out of the question!** ¡ni hablar!

questionable ['kwestʃənəbl] *adj* [gen] cuestionable; [taste] dudoso(sa).

questioner ['kwestʃənəʳ] *n* interrogador *m*, -ra *f*.

questioning ['kwestʃənɪŋ] <> *adj* de interrogación, interrogativo(va). <> *n* interrogatorio *m*.

question mark *n* (signo *m* de) interrogación *f*.

question master *esp UK*, **quizmaster** ['kwɪz,mɑːstəʳ] *esp US n* presentador *m*, -ra *f* de un concurso.

questionnaire [,kwestʃə'neəʳ] *n* cuestionario *m*.

question time *n UK* POL *sesión de control parlamentario en la que los diputados realizan preguntas a los miembros del gobierno.*

queue [kju:] *UK* <> *n* cola *f*; **to jump the queue** colarse. <> *vi*: **to queue (up for sthg)** hacer cola (para algo).

queue-jump *vi UK* colarse.

quibble ['kwɪbl] *pej* <> *n* queja *f* OR pega *f* insignificante. <> *vi* quejarse por tonterías; **to quibble over** OR **about** quejarse tontamente por OR de.

quiche [ki:ʃ] *n* quiche *f*.

quick [kwɪk] <> *adj* **- 1.** [gen] rápido(da); **be quick!** ¡date prisa!; **could we have a quick word?** ¿podríamos hablar un momento? **- 2.** [clever - person] espabilado(da); [- wit] agudo(da) **- 3.** [irritable]: **a quick temper** un genio vivo; **to be quick to take offence** ofenderse por nada. <> *adv* rápidamente.

quicken ['kwɪkn] <> *vt* [one's pace] apretar, acelerar. <> *vi* acelerarse.

quickly ['kwɪklɪ] *adv* **- 1.** [rapidly] rápidamente, de prisa **- 2.** [without delay] rápidamente, en seguida.

quickness ['kwɪknɪs] *n* **- 1.** [gen] rapidez *f* **- 2.** [cleverness - of person] inteligencia *f* viva; [- of wit] agudeza *f* **- 3.** [of temper] viveza *f*.

quicksand ['kwɪksænd] *n* arenas *fpl* movedizas.

quicksilver ['kwɪk,sɪlvəʳ] *n* azogue *m*.

quickstep ['kwɪkstep] *n*: the quickstep baile de salón de pasos rápidos.

quick-tempered *adj* de genio vivo.

quick-witted [-'wɪtɪd] *adj* agudo(da).

quid [kwɪd] (*pl* **quid**) *n UK inf* libra *f* (esterlina).

quid pro quo [-'kwəʊ] (*pl* **quid pro quos**) *n* compensación *f*.

quiescent [kwaɪ'esnt] *adj fml* inactivo(va), en reposo.

quiet ['kwaɪət] ◇ *adj* - **1.** [silent - gen] silencioso(sa); [- room, place] tranquilo(la); **to be quiet** [make no noise] no hacer ruido; **be quiet!** ¡cállate!; **in a quiet voice** en voz baja; **to keep quiet about sthg** guardar silencio sobre algo - **2.** [not talkative] callado(da); **to go quiet** callarse - **3.** [tranquil, uneventful] tranquilo(la); **business is quiet** el negocio está un poco apagado - **4.** [unpublicized - wedding etc] privado(da), íntimo(ma) - **5.** [colours] apagado(da). ◇ *n* tranquilidad *f*, silencio *m*; **on the quiet** a escondidas. ◇ *vt US* tranquilizar, calmar.
➼ **quiet down** ◇ *vt sep* tranquilizar, calmar. ◇ *vi* tranquilizarse, calmarse.

quieten ['kwaɪətn] *vt* tranquilizar, calmar.
➼ **quieten down** ◇ *vt sep* tranquilizar, calmar. ◇ *vi* tranquilizarse, calmarse.

quietly ['kwaɪətlɪ] *adv* - **1.** [without noise] silenciosamente, sin hacer ruido; **to speak quietly** hablar en voz baja - **2.** [without moving] sin moverse - **3.** [without excitement] tranquilamente - **4.** [without fuss] discretamente.

quietness ['kwaɪətnɪs] *n* - **1.** [lack of noise] silencio *m* - **2.** [lack of movement] quietud *f*, tranquilidad *f*.

quiff [kwɪf] *n UK* copete *m*, tupé *m*.

quill (pen) [kwɪl-] *n* pluma *f*.

quilt [kwɪlt] *n* edredón *m*.

quilted ['kwɪltɪd] *adj* acolchado(da).

quince [kwɪns] *n* membrillo *m*.

quinine [kwɪ'niːn] *n* quinina *f*.

quins *UK* [kwɪnz], **quints** *US* [kwɪnts] *npl inf* quintillizos *mpl*, -zas *f*.

quintessential [kwɪntə'senʃl] *adj* arquetípico(ca).

quintet [kwɪn'tet] *n* quinteto *m*.

quints *US* = **quins**.

quintuplets [kwɪn'tjuːplɪts] *npl* quintillizos *mpl*, -zas *f*.

quip [kwɪp] ◇ *n* ocurrencia *f*, salida *f*. ◇ *vi* (*pt & pp* **-ped**, *cont* **-ping**) bromear.

quirk [kwɜːk] *n* - **1.** [habit] manía *f*, rareza *f* - **2.** [strange event] extraña coincidencia *f*; **quirk of fate** capricho del destino.

quirky ['kwɜːkɪ] (*comp* **-ier**, *superl* **-iest**) *adj* peculiar, idiosincrásico(ca).

quit [kwɪt] ◇ *vt* (*UK* **quit** OR **-ted**, *cont* **-ting**, *US* **quit**, *cont* **-ting**) - **1.** [resign from] dejar, abandonar - **2.** [stop]: **to quit doing sthg** dejar

de hacer algo - **3.** COMPUT salir de. ◇ *vi* (*UK* **quit** OR **-ted**, *cont* **-ting**, *US* **quit**, *cont* **-ting**) - **1.** [resign] dimitir - **2.** COMPUT salir.

quite [kwaɪt] *adv* - **1.** [completely] totalmente, completamente - **2.** [fairly] bastante; **quite a lot of people** bastante gente - **3.** [after negative]: **it's not quite big enough** no es todo lo grande que tendría que ser; **I'm not quite sure** no estoy del todo seguro; **I don't quite understand/know** no entiendo/sé muy bien - **4.** [to emphasize]: **quite a...** todo un (toda una)...; **quite the opposite** todo lo contrario - **5.** [to express agreement]: **quite (so)!** ¡efectivamente!, ¡desde luego!

quits [kwɪts] *adj inf*: **to be quits (with sb)** estar en paz (con alguien); **to call it quits** dejarlo así.

quitter ['kwɪtər] *n inf pej*: **she's not a quitter** no es de las que abandonan.

quiver ['kwɪvər] ◇ *n* - **1.** [shiver] temblor *m*, estremecimiento *m* - **2.** [for arrows] carcaj *m*, aljaba *f*. ◇ *vi* temblar, estremecerse.

quivering ['kwɪvərɪŋ] *adj* tembloroso(sa).

quixotic [kwɪk'sɒtɪk] *adj liter* quijotesco(ca).

quiz [kwɪz] ◇ *n* (*pl* **-zes**) - **1.** [gen] concurso *m* - **2.** *US* SCH control *m*. ◇ *comp*: **quiz programme** concurso *m*. ◇ *vt* (*pt & pp* **-zed**, *cont* **-zing**): **to quiz sb (about)** interrogar a alguien (sobre).

quizmaster *n esp US* = **question master**.

quizzical ['kwɪzɪkl] *adj* burlón(ona).

quoits [kwɔɪts] *n* el juego de los aros.

Quonset hut ['kwɒnsɪt-] *n US* refugio *m* militar.

quorate ['kwɔːreɪt] *adj UK*: **we are quorate** hay quórum.

quorum ['kwɔːrəm] *n* quórum *m*.

quota ['kwəʊtə] *n* cuota *f*.

quotation [kwəʊ'teɪʃn] *n* - **1.** [citation] cita *f* - **2.** COMM presupuesto *m*.

quotation marks *npl* comillas *fpl*.

quote [kwəʊt] ◇ *n* - **1.** [citation] cita *f* - **2.** COMM presupuesto *m*. ◇ *vt* - **1.** [cite] citar - **2.** [figures, example, price] dar; **he quoted £100** fijó un precio de 100 libras. ◇ *vi* - **1.** [cite]: **to quote (from)** citar (de) - **2.** COMM: **to quote for** dar un presupuesto por.
➼ **quotes** *npl inf* comillas *fpl*.

quoted company ['kwəʊtɪd-] *n UK* compañía *f* cotizada en la Bolsa.

quotient ['kwəʊʃnt] *n* cociente *m*.

qv (*abbr of* **quod vide**) *v*.

qwerty keyboard ['kwɜːtɪ-] *n UK* teclado *m* qwerty.

R

r (*pl* **r's** OR **rs**), **R** (*pl* **R's** OR **Rs**) [ɑːʳ] *n* [letter] r *f*,
R *f*.

➧ **R - 1.** (*abbr of* **right**) dcha. **- 2.** *abbr of* **River**
- 3. US (*abbr of* **restricted**) no recomendada
para menores **- 4.** US *abbr of* **Republican**.

RA (*abbr of* **Royal Academy**) *n academia británica de bellas artes*.

rabbi ['ræbaɪ] *n* rabino *m*.

rabbit ['ræbɪt] *n* conejo *m*.

rabbit hole *n* madriguera *f* de conejos.

rabbit hutch *n* conejera *f*.

rabbit warren *n* madriguera *f* de conejos.

rabble ['ræbl] *n* chusma *f*, populacho *m*.

rabble-rousing *adj* que agita a las masas.

rabid ['ræbɪd, 'reɪbɪd] *adj* **- 1.** [infected with rabies]
rabioso(sa) **- 2.** *pej* [fanatical] fanático(ca).

rabies ['reɪbiːz] *n* rabia *f*.

RAC (*abbr of* **Royal Automobile Club**) *n* aso-
ciación británica del automóvil, ≃ RACE *m*.

raccoon [rə'kuːn] *n* mapache *m*.

race [reɪs] ◇ *n* **- 1.** *lit* & *fig* [competition] carrera *f* **- 2.** [people, descent] raza *f*. ◇ *vt* **- 1.** [com-
pete against] competir con (*corriendo*); **they
raced each other to the door** echaron una
carrera hasta la puerta **- 2.** [cars, pigeons] hacer carreras de; [horses] hacer correr. ◇ *vi*
- 1. [rush] ir corriendo **- 2.** [beat fast] acelerarse.

race car US = **racing car**.

racecourse ['reɪskɔːs] *n* hipódromo *m*.

race driver US = **racing driver**.

racehorse ['reɪshɔːs] *n* caballo *m* de carreras.

race meeting *n* concurso *m* de carreras de
caballos.

race relations *npl* relaciones *fpl* raciales.

race riot *n* disturbio *m* racial.

racetrack ['reɪstræk] *n* [for horses] hipódromo *m*; [for cars] autódromo *m*; [for runners] pista *f* (de carreras).

racewalking ['reɪswɔːkɪŋ] *n* marcha *f* atlética.

racial ['reɪʃl] *adj* racial.

racial discrimination *n* discriminación *f*
racial.

racialism ['reɪʃəlɪzm] *n* = **racism**.

racing ['reɪsɪŋ] *n* carreras *fpl*; **motor racing** carreras de coches.

racing car UK, **race car** US *n* coche *m* de carreras, auto *m* de carrera *Amér*.

racing driver UK, **race driver** US *n* piloto *mf*
de carreras.

racism ['reɪsɪzm], **racialism** *n* racismo *m*.

racist ['reɪsɪst] ◇ *adj* racista. ◇ *n* racista *mf*.

rack [ræk] ◇ *n* **- 1.** [for magazines] revistero *m*;
[for bottles] botellero *m*; [for plates] escurreplatos *m inv*; [for clothes] percha *f* **- 2.** [for lug-
gage] portaequipajes *m inv*. ◇ *vt*: **to be
racked by** OR **with** *liter* estar transido(da) de;
to rack one's brains UK devanarse los sesos.

racket, racquet ['rækɪt] *n* **- 1.** SPORT raqueta *f*
- 2. [noise] jaleo *m*, alboroto *m*, guachafita *f Col*
& *Ven* **- 3.** [swindle] timo *m* **- 4.** [illegal activity] negocio *m* sucio.

racketeering [,rækə'tɪərɪŋ] *n* (U) *pej* estafa *f*, timo *m*.

raconteur [,rækɒn'tɜːʳ] *n persona que sabe
contar anécdotas*.

racquet ['rækɪt] *n* = **racket**.

racy ['reɪsɪ] (*comp* **-ier**, *superl* **-iest**) *adj* entre-
tenido(da) y picante.

RADA ['rɑːdə] (*abbr of* **Royal Academy of Dramatic Art**) *n academia británica de arte dramático*.

radar ['reɪdɑːʳ] *n* radar *m*.

radar trap *n* control *m* de velocidad por radar.

radian ['reɪdjən] *n* radián *m*.

radiance ['reɪdjəns] *n* **- 1.** [of face, smile] lo radiante **- 2.** *liter* [brilliance] resplandor *m*.

radiant ['reɪdjənt] *adj* **- 1.** [happy] radiante
- 2. *liter* [brilliant] resplandeciente.

radiate ['reɪdɪeɪt] ◇ *vt lit* & *fig* irradiar. ◇ *vi*
- 1. [be emitted] ser irradiado(da) **- 2.** [spread
from centre] salir, extenderse.

radiation [,reɪdɪ'eɪʃn] *n* radiación *f*.

radiation sickness *n* enfermedad *f* causada
por la radiación.

radiator ['reɪdɪeɪtəʳ] *n* radiador *m*.

radiator grille *n* rejilla *f* del radiador.

radical ['rædɪkl] ◇ *adj* radical. ◇ *n* POL radical *mf*.

radically ['rædɪklɪ] *adv* radicalmente.

radii ['reɪdɪaɪ] *npl* ⊏➢ **radius**.

radio ['reɪdɪəʊ] ◇ *n* (*pl* **-s**) radio *f*, radio *m Amér*.
◇ *comp* de radio, radiofónico(ca). ◇ *vt* [per-
son] mandar un mensaje por radio a; [message]
transmitir por radio.

radioactive [,reɪdɪəʊ'æktɪv] *adj* radiactivo(va).

radioactive waste *n* (U) residuos *mpl* radiactivos.

radioactivity [ˌreɪdɪəʊæk'tɪvətɪ] n radiactividad f.

radio alarm n radiodespertador m.

radio-controlled [-kən'trəʊld] adj teledirigido(da).

radio frequency n radiofrecuencia f.

radiogram ['reɪdɪəʊˌɡræm] n [apparatus] radiogramola f.

radiographer [ˌreɪdɪ'ɒɡrəfəʳ] n radiógrafo m, -fa f.

radiography [ˌreɪdɪ'ɒɡrəfɪ] n radiografía f.

radiology [ˌreɪdɪ'ɒlədʒɪ] n radiología f.

radiopaging ['reɪdɪəʊˌpeɪdʒɪŋ] n localización f por busca.

radio station n emisora f de radio.

radiotelephone [ˌreɪdɪəʊ'telɪfəʊn] n radioteléfono m.

radiotherapist [ˌreɪdɪəʊ'θerəpɪst] n radioterapeuta mf.

radiotherapy [ˌreɪdɪəʊ'θerəpɪ] n radioterapia f.

radish ['rædɪʃ] n rábano m.

radium ['reɪdɪəm] n radio m.

radius ['reɪdɪəs] (pl radii) n [gen & ANAT] radio m.

radon ['reɪdɒn] n radón m.

RAF [ɑːˈreɪ'ef, ræf] n abbr of **Royal Air Force**.

raffia ['ræfɪə] n rafia f.

raffish ['ræfɪʃ] adj disoluto(ta) pero con encanto.

raffle ['ræfl] ◇ n rifa f, sorteo m. ◇ comp: **raffle ticket** boleto m. ◇ vt rifar, sortear.

raft [rɑːft] n - **1.** [craft] balsa f - **2.** [large number]: **a raft of policies** POL un montón de disposiciones.

rafter ['rɑːftəʳ] n viga f (de armadura de tejado).

rag [ræɡ] n - **1.** [piece of cloth] trapo m; **it was like a red rag to a bull** era una provocación total - **2.** pej [newspaper] periodicucho m.
➡ **rags** npl [clothes] trapos mpl; **from rags to riches** de la pobreza a la riqueza.

ragamuffin ['ræɡəˌmʌfɪn] n golfillo m, galopín m.

rag-and-bone man n trapero m.

ragbag ['ræɡbæɡ] n pej batiburrillo m.

rag doll n muñeca f de trapo.

rage [reɪdʒ] ◇ n - **1.** [fury] rabia f, ira f; **to fly into a rage** montar en cólera - **2.** inf [fashion]: **the rage** la moda; **it's all the rage** es la última moda. ◇ vi - **1.** [behave angrily] estar furioso(sa) - **2.** [subj: storm, sea] enfurecerse; [subj: disease] hacer estragos; [subj: argument, controversy] continuar con violencia.

ragged ['ræɡɪd] adj - **1.** [wearing torn clothes] andrajoso(sa), harapiento(ta) - **2.** [torn] hecho(cha) jirones - **3.** [uneven, poor-quality] desigual.

raging ['reɪdʒɪŋ] adj terrible.

ragout ['ræɡuː] n ragú m.

ragtime ['ræɡtaɪm] n ragtime m.

rag trade n inf: **the rag trade** la industria del vestir.

rag week n UK semana en que los universitarios organizan actividades divertidas con fines benéficos.

raid [reɪd] ◇ n - **1.** [attack] incursión f - **2.** [forced entry - by robbers] asalto m; [- by police] redada f. ◇ vt - **1.** [attack] atacar por sorpresa - **2.** [subj: robbers] asaltar; [subj: police] hacer una redada en.

raider ['reɪdəʳ] n - **1.** [attacker] invasor m, -ra f - **2.** [thief] asaltante mf.

rail [reɪl] ◇ n - **1.** [on staircase] baranda f, barandilla f - **2.** [bar] barra f; **towel rail** toallero m - **3.** (U) [form of transport] ferrocarril m; **by rail** por ferrocarril - **4.** [of railway line] carril m, riel m. ◇ comp ferroviario(ria).

railcard ['reɪlkɑːd] n UK tarjeta que permite algunos descuentos al viajar en tren.

railing ['reɪlɪŋ] n reja f.

railway UK ['reɪlweɪ], **railroad** US ['reɪlrəʊd] n - **1.** [company] ferrocarril m - **2.** [route] línea f de ferrocarril.

railway engine n locomotora f.

railway line n [route] línea f de ferrocarril; [track] vía f férrea.

railwayman ['reɪlweɪmən] (pl -men [-mən]) n UK ferroviario m.

railway station n estación f de ferrocarril.

railway track n vía f férrea.

rain [reɪn] ◇ n lluvia f; **in the rain** bajo la lluvia. ◇ impers vb METEOR llover. ◇ vi caer.
➡ **rain down** vi llover.
➡ **rain off** UK, **rain out** US vt sep: **to be rained off** suspenderse a causa de la lluvia.

rainbow ['reɪnbəʊ] n arco m iris.

rain check n esp US: **I'll take a rain check (on that)** no lo quiero ahora, pero igual me apunto la próxima vez.

raincoat ['reɪnkəʊt] n impermeable m.

raindrop ['reɪndrɒp] n gota f de lluvia.

rainfall ['reɪnfɔːl] n pluviosidad f.

rain forest n bosque m tropical.

rain gauge n pluviómetro m.

rainproof ['reɪnpruːf] adj impermeable.

rainstorm ['reɪnstɔːm] n temporal m de lluvia.

rainwater ['reɪnˌwɔːtəʳ] n agua f de lluvia.

rainy ['reɪnɪ] (comp **-ier**, superl **-iest**) adj lluvioso(sa).

raise [reɪz] ◇ vt - **1.** [lift up] levantar; [flag] izar - **2.** [increase - level] aumentar; **to raise one's voice** levantar la voz - **3.** [improve] elevar - **4.** [obtain - from donations] recaudar; [- by selling, borrowing] conseguir - **5.** [memory, thoughts] traer, evocar; [doubts, fears] levantar - **6.** [bring up, breed] criar - **7.** [crops] cultivar - **8.** [mention] plantear - **9.** [build] construir, erigir. ◇ n US aumento m, subida f.

raisin ['reɪzn] n pasa f.

rajah ['rɑːdʒə] n rajá m.

rake [reɪk] ◇ n - **1.** [implement] rastrillo m - **2.** dated & liter [immoral man] calavera m. ◇ vt - **1.** [smooth] rastrillar - **2.** [gather] recoger con el rastrillo.

➡ **rake in** vt sep inf amasar.

➡ **rake up** vt sep [sb's past] sacar a relucir.

rake-off n inf tajada f.

rakish ['reɪkɪʃ] adj - **1.** [dissolute] libertino(na), disoluto(ta) - **2.** [jaunty] ladeado(da).

rally ['rælɪ] ◇ n (pl **-ies**) - **1.** [meeting] mitin m - **2.** [car race] rally m - **3.** [in tennis etc] peloteo m. ◇ vt (pt & pp **-ied**) reunir. ◇ vi (pt & pp **-ied**) - **1.** [come together] reunirse - **2.** [recover] recuperarse.

➡ **rally round** ◇ vt insep formar una piña con. ◇ vi inf formar una piña.

rallying ['rælɪɪŋ] n rally m.

rallying cry n grito m de guerra.

rallying point n punto m de encuentro.

ram [ræm] ◇ n carnero m. ◇ vt (pt & pp **-med**, cont **-ming**) - **1.** [crash into] embestir - **2.** [force] embutir

➡➡ **to ram sthg home** dejar algo bien claro.

RAM [ræm] (abbr of **random access memory**) n COMPUT RAM f.

Ramadan [,ræmə'dæn] n ramadán m.

ramble ['ræmbl] ◇ n paseo m por el campo. ◇ vi - **1.** [walk] pasear - **2.** [talk] divagar.

➡ **ramble on** vi divagar sin parar.

rambler ['ræmblər] n [walker] excursionista mf.

rambling ['ræmblɪŋ] adj - **1.** [building, house] laberíntico(ca) - **2.** [speech, writing] incoherente.

RAMC (abbr of **Royal Army Medical Corps**) n cuerpo médico de las fuerzas armadas británicas.

ramekin ['ræmɪkɪn] n recipiente m individual para el horno.

ramification [,ræmɪfɪ'keɪʃn] n ramificación f.

ramp [ræmp] n - **1.** [slope] rampa f - **2.** AUT [in road] rompecoches m inv.

rampage [ræm'peɪdʒ] ◇ n: **to go on the rampage** desbandarse. ◇ vi desbandarse.

rampant ['ræmpənt] adj desenfrenado(da).

ramparts ['ræmpɑːts] npl murallas fpl.

ramshackle ['ræm,ʃækl] adj destartalado(da).

ran [ræn] pt ▷ run.

ranch [rɑːntʃ] n rancho m.

rancher ['rɑːntʃər] n ranchero m, -ra f.

ranch house n US - **1.** [house on ranch] hacienda f, estancia f - **2.** [ranch-style house] rancho m.

rancid ['rænsɪd] adj rancio(cia).

rancour UK, **rancor** US ['ræŋkər] n rencor m.

random ['rændəm] ◇ adj - **1.** [arbitrary] hecho(cha) al azar - **2.** TECH aleatorio(ria). ◇ n: **at random** al azar.

random access memory n COMPUT memoria f de acceso aleatorio.

randomly ['rændəmlɪ] adv al azar.

R and R (abbr of **rest and recreation**) n US permiso militar.

randy ['rændɪ] (comp **-ier**, superl **-iest**) adj inf cachondo(da), caliente.

rang [ræŋ] pt ▷ ring.

range [reɪndʒ] ◇ n - **1.** [of missile, telescope] alcance m; [of ship, plane] autonomía f; **to be out of/within range** estar fuera del/al alcance; **at close range** de cerca - **2.** [variety] gama f - **3.** [of prices, salaries] escala f - **4.** [of mountains] cordillera f - **5.** [shooting area] campo m de tiro - **6.** [of voice] registro m. ◇ vt (cont **ranging**) alinear. ◇ vi (cont **ranging**) - **1.** [vary]: **to range from... to..., to range between... and...** oscilar OR fluctuar entre... y...; **prices ranging from $20 to $100** precios que van desde veinte hasta cien dólares - **2.** [deal with, include]: **to range over sthg** comprender algo.

ranger ['reɪndʒər] n guardabosques mf inv.

rangy ['reɪndʒɪ] (comp **-ier**, superl **-iest**) adj zancudo(da).

rank [ræŋk] ◇ adj - **1.** [utter, absolute - bad luck, outsider] absoluto(ta); [- disgrace, injustice] flagrante - **2.** [foul] pestilente. ◇ n - **1.** [position, grade] grado m, rango m; **to pull rank** abusar de su autoridad - **2.** [social class] clase f, categoría f; **the rank and file** las bases - **3.** [row] fila f, hilera f; **to close ranks** cerrar filas. ◇ vt - **1.** [class]: **to be ranked** estar clasificado(da) - **2.** US [outrank] ser de más alta graduación que. ◇ vi: **to rank as** estar considerado(da) (como); **to rank among** encontrarse entre.

➡ **ranks** npl - **1.** MIL: **the ranks** los soldados rasos - **2.** fig [members] filas fpl.

ranking ['ræŋkɪŋ] ◇ n clasificación f. ◇ adj US de alta graduación.

rankle ['ræŋkl] vi doler.

ransack ['rænsæk] vt [search] registrar a fondo; [plunder] saquear.

ransom ['rænsəm] n rescate m; **to hold sb to ransom** fig hacer chantaje a alguien.

rant [rænt] *vi* despotricar.

ranting ['ræntɪŋ] *n* despotrique *m*.

rap [ræp] ⬦ *n* - **1.** [knock] golpecito *m* - **2.** [type of music] rap *m* - **3.** US [legal charge] acusación *f*; **rap sheet** antecedentes *mpl* penales ▸▸ **to take the rap** pagar el pato. ⬦ *vt* (*pt* & *pp* **-ped**, *cont* **-ping**) dar un golpecito en. ⬦ *vi* - **1.** [knock]: **to rap on sthg** dar golpecitos en algo - **2.** [sing rap music] cantar rap.

rapacious [rə'peɪʃəs] *adj fml* [greedy] rapaz.

rape [reɪp] ⬦ *n* - **1.** [crime] violación *f* - **2.** [of countryside etc] destrucción *f* - **3.** BOT colza *f*. ⬦ *vt* - **1.** [person] violar - **2.** [countryside etc] destruir.

rapeseed oil ['reɪpsi:d-] *n* aceite *m* de colza.

rapid ['ræpɪd] *adj* rápido(da).
➤ **rapids** *npl* rápidos *mpl*.

rapid-fire *adj* - **1.** MIL [gun] de tiro rápido - **2.** *fig* [spoken quickly] lanzado uno tras otro (lanzada una tras otra).

rapidity [rə'pɪdətɪ] *n* rapidez *f*.

rapidly ['ræpɪdlɪ] *adv* rápidamente.

rapist ['reɪpɪst] *n* violador *m*, -ra *f*.

rapper ['ræpər] *n* rapero *m*, -ra *f*.

rapport [ræ'pɔ:ʳ] *n* compenetración *f*; **to have a rapport with sb** compenetrarse con alguien.

rapprochement [ræ'prɒʃmã] *n* acercamiento *m*.

rapt [ræpt] *adj* absorto(ta), ensimismado(da).

rapture ['ræptʃəʳ] *n* arrebato *m*, arrobamiento *m*; **to go into raptures over** OR **about** deshacerse en elogios a.

rapturous ['ræptʃərəs] *adj* muy entusiasta.

rare [reəʳ] *adj* - **1.** [scarce] poco común, raro(ra) - **2.** [infrequent] poco frecuente, raro(ra) - **3.** [exceptional] raro(ra), excepcional - **4.** CULIN poco hecho(cha).

rarefied ['reərɪfaɪd] *adj* - **1.** [exalted] exclusivo(va), elevado(da) - **2.** [lacking in oxygen] enrarecido(da).

rarely ['reəlɪ] *adv* raras veces.

rareness ['reənɪs] *n* - **1.** [scarcity] rareza *f* - **2.** [infrequency] infrecuencia *f*.

raring ['reərɪŋ] *adj*: **to be raring to go** estar ansioso(sa) por empezar.

rarity ['reərətɪ] (*pl* **-ies**) *n* rareza *f*.

rascal ['rɑ:skl] *n* pícaro *m*, -ra *f*.

rash [ræʃ] ⬦ *adj* precipitado(da). ⬦ *n* - **1.** MED erupción *f* [cutánea), sarpullido *m*, jiote *m* Méx - **2.** [spate] aluvión *m*.

rasher ['ræʃəʳ] *n* loncha *f*.

rashly ['ræʃlɪ] *adv* precipitadamente.

rashness ['ræʃnɪs] *n* precipitación *f*, impetuosidad *f*.

rasp [rɑ:sp] ⬦ *n* - **1.** [harsh sound] chirrido *m* - **2.** [tool] lima *f* gruesa. ⬦ *vi* [subj: person] hablar con voz áspera y estridente; [subj: voice] tener un sonido áspero y estridente.

raspberry ['rɑ:zbərɪ] (*pl* **-ies**) *n* - **1.** [fruit] frambuesa *f* - **2.** [rude sound] pedorreta *f*.

rasping ['rɑ:spɪŋ] *adj* áspero(ra) y estridente.

rasta ['ræstə] *n inf* rasta *mf*.

rastafarian [,ræstə'feərɪən] *n* rastafari *mf*.

rat [ræt] *n* - **1.** [animal] rata *f*; **I smell a rat** aquí hay gato encerrado - **2.** *pej* [person] canalla *mf*.

ratatouille [,rætə'twi:] *n* ≃ pisto *m*.

ratbag ['rætbæg] *n UK pej* granuja *mf*.

ratchet ['rætʃɪt] *n* trinquete *m*.

rate [reɪt] ⬦ *n* - **1.** [speed] ritmo *m*; **at this rate** a este paso - **2.** [of birth, death] índice *m*; [of unemployment, inflation] tasa *f* - **3.** [price] precio *m*, tarifa *f*; [of interest] tipo *m*. ⬦ *vt* - **1.** [consider]: **to rate sthg/sb (as/among)** considerar algo/a alguien (como/entre); **to rate sthg/sb highly** tener una buena opinión de algo/alguien - **2.** *UK inf* [have good opinion of] valorar mucho - **3.** [deserve] merecer.
➤ **rates** *npl UK* ≃ contribución *f* urbana.
➤ **at any rate** *adv* - **1.** [at least] al menos - **2.** [anyway] de todos modos.

rateable value ['reɪtəbl-] *n UK* valor *m* catastral.

rate of exchange *n* (tipo *m* de) cambio *m*.

ratepayer ['reɪt,peɪəʳ] *n UK* contribuyente *mf*.

rather ['rɑ:ðəʳ] *adv* - **1.** [to quite a large extent] bastante; **I rather thought so** eso es lo que pensaba - **2.** [to a great extent] muy; **it's rather good** está buenísimo - **3.** [to a limited extent] algo; **he's rather like you** se parece (en) algo a ti - **4.** [as preference]: **I would rather wait** preferiría esperar; **I'd rather not stay** prefiero no quedarme; **would you like to come? – I'd rather not** ¿quieres venir? – mejor no - **5.** [more exactly]: **or rather...** o más bien..., o mejor dicho... - **6.** [on the contrary]: **(but) rather...** (sino) más bien OR por el contrario...
➤ **rather than** *conj* en vez de.

ratification [,rætɪfɪ'keɪʃn] *n* ratificación *f*.

ratify ['rætɪfaɪ] (*pt* & *pp* **-ied**) *vt* ratificar.

rating ['reɪtɪŋ] *n* - **1.** [standing] clasificación *f* - **2.** *UK* [sailor] marinero *m*.
➤ **ratings** *npl* índices *mpl* de audiencia.

ratio ['reɪʃɪəʊ] (*pl* **-s**) *n* proporción *f*, relación *f*.

ration ['ræʃn] ⬦ *n* ración *f*. ⬦ *vt* racionar.
➤ **rations** *npl* [supplies] víveres *mpl*.

rational ['ræʃənl] *adj* racional.

rationale [,ræʃə'nɑ:l] *n* lógica *f*, razones *fpl*.

rationalization [,ræʃənəlaɪ'zeɪʃn] *n* racionalización *f*.

rationalize, -ise ['ræʃənəlaɪz] *vt* racionalizar.

rationing ['ræʃənɪŋ] *n* racionamiento *m*.

rat race *n mundo despiadadamente competitivo de los negocios.*

rattle ['rætl] ⟨> *n* - **1.** [of engine, metal] traqueteo *m*; [of chains] crujido *m*; [of glass] tintineo *m*; [of typewriter] repiqueteo *m* - **2.** [for baby] sonajero *m*. ⟨> *vt* - **1.** [make rattle] hacer sonar - **2.** [unsettle] desconcertar. ⟨> *vi* golpetear; [chains] crujir; [glass] tintinear.

⟩ **rattle off** *vt sep* decir de corrido.

⟩ **rattle on** *vi*: **to rattle on (about)** hablar sin parar (sobre).

⟩ **rattle through** *vt insep* acabar en un santiamén.

rattlesnake ['rætlsneɪk], **rattler** *US* ['rætlər] *n* serpiente *f* de cascabel.

ratty ['rætɪ] (*comp* -ier, *superl* -iest) *adj inf* - **1.** *UK* [in bad mood] picajoso(sa), irritable - **2.** *US* [in bad condition - person] desastrado(da); [- thing] destartalado(da).

raucous ['rɔːkəs] *adj* ronco(ca) y estridente.

raunchy ['rɔːntʃɪ] (*comp* -ier, *superl* -iest) *adj* sexy (*inv*).

ravage ['rævɪdʒ] *vt* estragar, asolar.

⟩ **ravages** *npl* estragos *mpl*.

rave [reɪv] ⟨> *adj* muy entusiasta. ⟨> *n* [party] macrofiesta *f* tecno. ⟨> *vt inf*: **to rave it up** divertirse de lo lindo. ⟨> *vi* - **1.** [talk angrily]: **to rave at sb** increpar a alguien; **to rave against sb/sthg** despotricar contra alguien/algo - **2.** [talk enthusiastically]: **to rave about sthg** deshacerse en alabanzas sobre algo.

raven ['reɪvn] ⟨> *adj* negro azabache. ⟨> *n* cuervo *m*.

ravenous ['rævənəs] *adj* [person, animal] famélico(ca), hambriento(ta); [appetite] voraz.

raver ['reɪvər] *n* - **1.** [person at a rave] aficionado *m*, -da *f* al bakalao - **2.** *UK inf* [person who is always partying] juerguista *mf*.

rave-up *n UK inf* juerga *f*.

ravine [rə'viːn] *n* barranco *m*.

raving ['reɪvɪŋ] *adj* [lunatic] de atar; [fantasy] delirante.

⟩ **ravings** *npl* desvaríos *mpl*.

ravioli [,rævɪ'əʊlɪ] *n* (*U*) raviolis *mpl*.

ravish ['rævɪʃ] *vt* [enchant] embelesar.

ravishing ['rævɪʃɪŋ] *adj* [sight, beauty] de ensueño; [person] bellísimo(ma).

raw [rɔː] *adj* - **1.** [uncooked] crudo(da) - **2.** [untreated - silk] crudo(da); [- sewage] sin tratar; [- cane sugar] sin refinar - **3.** [painful - wound] en carne viva - **4.** [inexperienced] novato(ta) - **5.** [cold] crudo(da), frío(a).

raw deal *n*: **to get a raw deal** recibir un trato injusto.

raw material *n* materia *f* prima.

ray [reɪ] *n* rayo *m*; **ray of hope** resquicio *m* de esperanza.

rayon ['reɪɒn] *n* rayón *m*.

raze [reɪz] *vt* destruir por completo, arrasar.

razor ['reɪzər] *n* [wet shaver] navaja *f*; [electric machine] maquinilla *f* de afeitar.

razor blade *n* hoja *f* de afeitar.

razor-sharp *adj* - **1.** [very sharp] muy afilado(da) - **2.** *fig* [very quick] muy agudo(da).

razzle ['ræzl] *n UK inf*: **to go on the razzle** irse de juerga.

razzmatazz ['ræzəmətæz] *n inf* revuelo *m*.

R & B *n abbr of* **rhythm and blues**.

RC *abbr of* **Roman Catholic**.

RCAF (*abbr of* **Royal Canadian Air Force**) *n* fuerzas aéreas canadienses.

RCMP (*abbr of* **Royal Canadian Mounted Police**) *n* policía montada de Canadá.

RCN *n* - **1.** (*abbr of* **Royal College of Nursing**), sindicato británico de enfermeras - **2.** (*abbr of* **Royal Canadian Navy**), armada canadiense.

Rd *abbr of* **road**.

R & D (*abbr of* **research and development**) *n* I + D *f*.

re [riː] *prep* Ref.

RE *n* (*abbr of* **religious education**) religión *f*.

reach [riːtʃ] ⟨> *n* alcance *m*; **he has a long reach** tiene los brazos largos; **within (sb's) reach** [easily touched] al alcance (de alguien); [easily travelled to] a poca distancia (de alguien); **out of** OR **beyond sb's reach** fuera del alcance de alguien. ⟨> *vt* - **1.** [gen] alcanzar, llegar a; **to reach an agreement/a decision** llegar a un acuerdo/una decisión; **to reach an objective** alcanzar un objetivo - **2.** [arrive at - place etc] llegar a - **3.** [get by stretching - object, shelf] alcanzar - **4.** [contact] localizar, contactar con. ⟨> *vi*: **I can't reach** no llego; **to reach out/across** alargar la mano; **to reach down** agacharse.

⟩ **reaches** *npl* [of river]: **upper/lower reaches** parte *f* alta/baja.

reachable ['riːtʃəbl] *adj* - **1.** [place] accesible - **2.** [person, organization] localizable; **he's reachable by phone** se le puede contactar por teléfono.

react [rɪ'ækt] *vi* - **1.** [respond]: **to react (to)** reaccionar (a OR ante) - **2.** [rebel]: **to react against** reaccionar en contra de - **3.** CHEM: **to react with** reaccionar con - **4.** MED: **to react to sthg** sufrir una reacción por algo.

reaction [rɪ'ækʃn] *n*: **reaction (to/against)** reacción *f* (a/contra).

reactionary [rɪ'ækʃənrɪ] ⟨> *adj* reaccionario(ria). ⟨> *n* reaccionario *m*, -ria *f*.

reactivate [rɪˈæktɪveɪt] *vt* reactivar.

reactor [rɪˈæktər] *n* reactor *m*.

read [riːd] ⬦ *vt* (*pt & pp* **read** [red]) - **1.** [gen & COMPUT] leer; **she can't read my writing** no entiende mi letra - **2.** [subj: sign, words] poner, decir - **3.** [subj: thermometer, meter etc] marcar - **4.** [interpret] interpretar - **5.** UK UNIV estudiar. ⬦ *vi* (*pt & pp* **read** [red]) - **1.** [person] leer - **2.** [read aloud]: **to read to sb** leerle a alguien - **3.** [piece of writing]: **to read well** estar bien escrito. ⬦ *n*: **to be a good read** ser una lectura amena; **to give sthg a read** leer algo.

⬦ **read into** *vt sep*: **I wouldn't read too much into it** no le des demasiada importancia.

⬦ **read out** *vt sep* leer en voz alta.

⬦ **read through** *vt sep* leer.

⬦ **read up on** *vt insep* leer OR documentarse sobre.

readable [ˈriːdəbl] *adj* ameno(na).

readdress [ˌriːəˈdres] *vt* reexpedir.

reader [ˈriːdər] *n* - **1.** [person who reads] lector *m*, -ra *f* - **2.** COMPUT lector *m*.

readership [ˈriːdəʃɪp] *n* [total number of readers] lectores *mpl*.

readily [ˈredɪlɪ] *adv* - **1.** [willingly] de buena gana - **2.** [easily] fácilmente.

readiness [ˈredɪnɪs] *n* - **1.** [preparation]: **to be in a state of readiness** estar preparado(da) - **2.** [willingness]: **readiness (to do sthg)** buena disposición *f* (para hacer algo).

reading [ˈriːdɪŋ] *n* - **1.** [gen] lectura *f* - **2.** [recital] recital *m*.

reading lamp *n* flexo *m*.

reading room *n* sala *f* de lectura.

readjust [ˌriːəˈdʒʌst] ⬦ *vt* reajustar. ⬦ *vi*: **to readjust (to)** volverse a adaptar (a).

readmit [ˌriːədˈmɪt] *vt* readmitir.

readout [ˈriːdaʊt] *n* COMPUT visualización *f*.

read-through [riːd-] *n*: **to give sthg a read-through** leer algo.

ready [ˈredɪ] ⬦ *adj* - **1.** [prepared] listo(ta), preparado(da); **to be ready for sthg/to do sthg** estar listo para algo/para hacer algo; **to get ready** [prepare] prepararse; [for going out] arreglarse - **2.** [willing]: **to be ready to do sthg** estar dispuesto(ta) a hacer algo - **3.** [in need of]: **to be ready for sthg** necesitar algo - **4.** [likely]: **to be ready to do sthg** estar a punto de hacer algo - **5.** [smile] pronto(ta). ⬦ *vt* (*pt & pp* **-ied**) preparar; **to ready o.s. for sthg** prepararse para algo.

ready cash *n* dinero *m* contante.

ready-made *adj* - **1.** [products] hecho(cha); [clothes] confeccionado(da) - **2.** *fig* [excuse etc] a la medida.

ready money *n* dinero *m* contante.

ready-to-wear *adj* confeccionado(da).

reaffirm [ˌriːəˈfɜːm] *vt* reafirmar.

reafforest [ˌriːəˈfɒrɪst], **reforest** *vt* repoblar con árboles.

reafforestation [ˈriːəˌfɒrɪˈsteɪʃn], **reforestation** *n* repoblación *f* forestal.

real [ˈrɪəl] ⬦ *adj* - **1.** [not imagined, actual] real; **the real thing** lo auténtico; **this isn't a joke, it's the real thing** esto no va en broma, va en serio; **for real** de verdad; **in real terms** en términos reales - **2.** [genuine, proper] auténtico(ca); **a real friend** un amigo de verdad. ⬦ *adv* US muy.

real ale *n* UK cerveza *f* hecha a la manera tradicional.

real estate *n* propiedad *f* inmobiliaria.

real estate agent *n* US agente inmobiliario *m*, agente inmobiliaria *f*.

realign [ˌriːəˈlaɪn] *vt* volver a alinear.

realignment [ˌriːəˈlaɪnmənt] *n* nueva alineación *f*.

realism [ˈrɪəlɪzm] *n* realismo *m*.

realist [ˈrɪəlɪst] *n* realista *mf*.

realistic [ˌrɪəˈlɪstɪk] *adj* realista; **to be realistic about** ser realista acerca de.

realistically [ˌrɪəˈlɪstɪklɪ] *adv* - **1.** [pragmatically speaking] para ser realistas - **2.** [accurately] con realismo.

reality [rɪˈælətɪ] (*pl* **-ies**) *n* realidad *f*; **in reality** en realidad.

reality TV *n* (U) reality shows *mpl*.

realization [ˌrɪəlaɪˈzeɪʃn] *n* - **1.** [recognition] comprensión *f* - **2.** [achievement] consecución *f*.

realize, -ise [ˈrɪəlaɪz] *vt* - **1.** [become aware of] darse cuenta de; **I realize it isn't easy** ya sé que no es fácil - **2.** [produce, achieve, make profit of] realizar.

reallocate [ˌriːˈæləkeɪt] *vt* redistribuir.

really [ˈrɪəlɪ] ⬦ *adv* - **1.** [for emphasis] de verdad; **really good** buenísimo; **really bad** malísimo; **did you like it? – not really** ¿te gustó? – la verdad es que no - **2.** [actually, honestly] realmente, en realidad - **3.** [to sound less negative] en realidad. ⬦ *excl* - **1.** [expressing doubt]: **really?** [in affirmatives] ¿ah sí?; [in negatives] ¿ah no? - **2.** [expressing surprise, disbelief]: **really?** ¿de verdad?, ¿seguro? - **3.** [expressing anger]: **really!** ¡hay que ver!

realm [relm] *n* - **1.** [field] campo *m*, esfera *f* - **2.** [kingdom] reino *m*.

real-time *adj* COMPUT en tiempo real.

realtor [ˈrɪəltər] *n* US agente inmobiliario *m*, agente inmobiliaria *f*.

ream [riːm] *n* resma *f*.

⬦ **reams** *npl* montones *mpl*.

reap [ri:p] *vt lit* & *fig* cosechar.

reappear [ˌri:ə'pɪə'] *vi* reaparecer.

reappearance [ˌri:ə'pɪərəns] *n* reaparición *f*.

reapply [ˌri:ə'plaɪ] (*pt* & *pp* -ied) *vi*: **to reapply (for)** volver a presentar una solicitud (para).

reappraisal [ˌri:ə'preɪzl] *n* revaluación *f*.

reappraise [ˌri:ə'preɪz] *vt* replantear, reexaminar.

rear [rɪə'] <> *adj* trasero(ra), de atrás. <> *n* - **1.** [back] parte *f* de atrás; **to be at the rear** estar al final; **to bring up the rear** cerrar la marcha - **2.** *inf* [bottom] trasero *m*. <> *vt* criar. <> *vi*: **to rear (up)** encabritarse.

rear admiral *n* contraalmirante *m*.

rearguard action ['rɪəgɑ:d-] *n*: **to fight a rearguard action** MIL atacar desde la retaguardia; *fig* emprender una última tentativa.

rear light *n* luz *f* trasera, calaveras *fpl* Méx.

rearm [ri:'ɑ:m] <> *vt* rearmar. <> *vi* rearmarse.

rearmament [rɪ'ɑ:məmənt] *n* rearme *m*.

rearmost ['rɪəməʊst] *adj* último(ma).

rearrange [ˌri:ə'reɪndʒ] *vt* - **1.** [room, furniture] colocar de otro modo; [system, plans] reorganizar - **2.** [meeting] volver a concertar.

rearrangement [ˌri:ə'reɪndʒmənt] *n* [reorganization] reorganización *f*.

rearview mirror ['rɪəvju:-] *n* (espejo *m*) retrovisor *m*.

reason ['ri:zn] <> *n* - **1.** [cause]: **reason (for)** razón *f* (de); **I don't know the reason why** no sé por qué; **by reason of** *fml* a causa de; **for some reason** por alguna razón - **2.** [justification]: **to have reason to do sthg** tener motivos para hacer algo - **3.** [rationality] razón *f*; **it stands to reason** es lógico; **to listen to reason** avenirse a razones. <> *vt* & *vi* razonar.
➡ **reason with** *vt insep* razonar con.

reasonable ['ri:znəbl] *adj* razonable.

reasonably ['ri:znəblɪ] *adv* razonablemente.

reasoned ['ri:znd] *adj* razonado(da).

reasoning ['ri:znɪŋ] *n* razonamiento *m*.

reassemble [ˌri:ə'sembl] <> *vt* - **1.** [reconstruct] volver a montar - **2.** [regroup] reagrupar. <> *vi* reagruparse.

reassess [ˌri:ə'ses] *vt* revaluar, reconsiderar.

reassessment [ˌri:ə'sesmənt] *n* revaluación *f*.

reassurance [ˌri:ə'ʃʊərəns] *n* - **1.** *(U)* [comfort] palabras *fpl* tranquilizadoras - **2.** [promise] promesa *f*.

reassure [ˌri:ə'ʃʊə'] *vt* tranquilizar.

reassuring [ˌri:ə'ʃʊərɪŋ] *adj* tranquilizador(ra).

reawaken [ˌri:ə'weɪkn] *vt* volver a despertar.

rebate ['ri:beɪt] *n* - **1.** [refund] devolución *f* - **2.** [discount] bonificación *f*.

rebel <> *n* ['rebl] rebelde *mf*. <> *vi* [rɪ'bel] (*pt* & *pp* -led, *cont* -ling): **to rebel (against)** rebelarse (contra), alebrestarse (contra) Col, Méx & Ven.

rebellion [rɪ'beljən] *n* rebelión *f*.

rebellious [rɪ'beljəs] *adj* rebelde.

rebirth [ˌri:'bɜ:θ] *n* renacimiento *m*.

reboot [ˌri:'bu:t] *vt* COMPUT reinicializar.

rebound <> *n* ['ri:baʊnd]: **on the rebound** [ball] de rebote *m*; **to marry on the rebound** casarse por despecho. <> *vi* [rɪ'baʊnd] - **1.** [bounce back] rebotar - **2.** [harm]: **to rebound on** OR **upon sb** volverse contra alguien.

re-brand *vt* relanzar con otra marca.

rebuff [rɪ'bʌf] <> *n* [slight] desaire *m*; [refusal] negativa *f*. <> *vt* [slight] desairar; [reject] rechazar.

rebuild [ˌri:'bɪld] (*pt* & *pp* -built) *vt* reconstruir.

rebuke [rɪ'bju:k] <> *n* reprimenda *f*. <> *vt*: **to rebuke sb (for)** reprender a alguien (por).

rebut [ri:'bʌt] (*pt* & *pp* -ted, *cont* -ting) *vt* rebatir, refutar.

rebuttal [ri:'bʌtl] *n* refutación *f*.

rec. (*abbr of* **received**) recibido.

recalcitrant [rɪ'kælsɪtrənt] *adj* recalcitrante.

recall [rɪ'kɔ:l] <> *n* - **1.** [memory] memoria *f* - **2.** [change]: **beyond recall** inalterable. <> *vt* - **1.** [remember] recordar, acordarse de - **2.** [ambassador] retirar; [goods] retirar del mercado.

recant [rɪ'kænt] <> *vt* [statement, opinion] retractarse de. <> *vi* [deny statement] retractarse; [deny religion] renegar de la fe.

recap ['ri:kæp] *inf* <> *n* resumen *m*, recapitulación *f*. <> *vt* (*pt* & *pp* -ped, *cont* -ping) - **1.** [summarize] recapitular, resumir - **2.** *US* [tyre] recauchutar. <> *vi* (*pt* & *pp* -ped, *cont* -ping) recapitular, resumir.

recapitulate [ˌri:kə'pɪtjʊleɪt] *vt* & *vi* recapitular, resumir.

recapture [ˌri:'kæptʃə'] <> *n* reconquista *f*. <> *vt* - **1.** [experience again] revivir, volver a experimentar - **2.** MIL [regain] reconquistar, volver a tomar - **3.** [criminal] volver a detener.

recd, rec'd (*abbr of* **received**) rbdo.

recede [ri:'si:d] *vi* - **1.** [person, car] alejarse; [coastline] retroceder - **2.** *fig* [disappear] esfumarse - **3.** [hair]: **his hair is receding** empieza a tener entradas.

receding [rɪ'si:dɪŋ] *adj* [chin, forehead] hundida; **to have a receding hairline** tener entradas.

receipt [rɪ'si:t] *n* recibo *m*; **to acknowledge receipt** acusar recibo.
➡ **receipts** *npl* recaudación *f*.

receivable [rɪ'si:vəbl] *adj* - **1.** [able to be received] admisible - **2.** [liable for payment] por cobrar.

receive [rɪ'si:v] ⟨> *vt* - **1.** [gen] recibir; **I received a fine** me pusieron una multa - **2.** [reaction] tener; [injury, setback] sufrir - **3.** [greet]: **to be well/badly received** tener una buena/mala acogida. ⟨> *vi* [in tennis etc] restar.

receiver [rɪ'si:vəʳ] *n* - **1.** [of telephone] auricular *m* - **2.** [radio, TV set] receptor *m* - **3.** [criminal] perista *mf*, receptador *m*, -ra *f* - **4.** FIN síndico *m*, -ca *f*.

receivership [rɪ'si:vəʃɪp] *n* bancarrota *f*.

receiving end [rɪ'si:vɪŋ-] *n*: **to be on the receiving end (of)** ser la víctima de).

recent ['ri:snt] *adj* reciente.

recently ['ri:sntlɪ] *adv* recientemente.

receptacle [rɪ'septəkl] *n* receptáculo *m*.

reception [rɪ'sepʃn] *n* - **1.** [gen] recepción *f* - **2.** [welcome] recibimiento *m*.

reception centre *n* centro *m* de acogida.

reception class *n* UK primer curso *m* de primaria.

reception desk *n* recepción *f*.

receptionist [rɪ'sepʃənɪst] *n* recepcionista *mf*.

reception room *n* salón *m*.

receptive [rɪ'septɪv] *adj* receptivo(va); **to be receptive to sthg** estar abierto a algo.

recess ['ri:ses, UK rɪ'ses] *n* - **1.** [vacation] periodo *m* vacacional; **to be in recess** estar clausurado(da); **to go into recess** suspender las sesiones - **2.** [alcove] nicho *m*, hueco *m* - **3.** US SCH recreo *m*.

⟐ **recesses** *npl* [of mind, heart] recovecos *mpl*; [of building] escondrijos *mpl*.

recessed ['ri:sest, UK rɪ'sest] *adj* empotrado(da).

recession [rɪ'seʃn] *n* recesión *f*.

recessionary [rɪ'seʃənrɪ] *adj* recesivo(va).

recessive [rɪ'sesɪv] *adj* BIOL recesivo(va).

recharge [,ri:'tʃɑ:dʒ] *vt* recargar.

rechargeable [,ri:'tʃɑ:dʒəbl] *adj* recargable.

recipe ['resɪpɪ] *n* fig & CULIN receta *f*.

recipient [rɪ'sɪpɪənt] *n* [of letter, cheque] destinatario *m*, -ria *f*.

reciprocal [rɪ'sɪprəkl] *adj* recíproco(ca).

reciprocate [rɪ'sɪprəkeɪt] ⟨> *vt* corresponder a. ⟨> *vi* corresponder.

recital [rɪ'saɪtl] *n* recital *m*.

recitation [,resɪ'teɪʃn] *n* recitación *f*.

recite [rɪ'saɪt] *vt* - **1.** [poem] recitar - **2.** [list] enumerar.

reckless ['reklɪs] *adj* [gen] imprudente; [driver, driving] temerario(ria).

recklessness ['reklɪsnɪs] *n* imprudencia *f*.

reckon ['rekn] *vt* - **1.** *inf* [think]: **to reckon (that)** pensar que - **2.** [consider, judge]: **to be reckoned to be sthg** ser considerado(da) algo - **3.** [expect]: **to reckon to do sthg** esperar hacer algo - **4.** [calculate] calcular.

⟐ **reckon on** *vt insep* contar con.

⟐ **reckon with** *vt insep* - **1.** [expect] contar con - **2.** [face, deal with]: **he/she** *etc* **is a force to be reckoned with** es alguien a tener muy en cuenta.

⟐ **reckon without** *vt insep* no contar con.

reckoning ['rekənɪŋ] *n* [calculation] cálculo *m*; **by my reckoning** según mis cálculos.

reclaim [rɪ'kleɪm] *vt* - **1.** [claim back] reclamar - **2.** [recover] recuperar; **to reclaim land from the sea** ganarle tierra al mar.

reclamation [,reklə'meɪʃn] *n* [of land] conversión *f* en terreno utilizable.

recline [rɪ'klaɪn] *vi* reclinarse.

reclining [rɪ'klaɪnɪŋ] *adj* [seat] reclinable.

recluse [rɪ'klu:s] *n* solitario *m*, -ria *f*.

reclusive [rɪ'klu:sɪv] *adj* solitario(ria), retraído(da).

recognition [,rekəg'nɪʃn] *n* reconocimiento *m*; **to have changed beyond** OR **out of all recognition** estar irreconocible; **in recognition of** en reconocimiento a.

recognizable ['rekəgnaɪzəbl] *adj* reconocible.

recognize, -ise ['rekəgnaɪz] *vt* reconocer.

recoil ⟨> *vi* [rɪ'kɔɪl] - **1.** [draw back] retroceder, echarse atrás - **2.** *fig* [shrink from]: **to recoil from** OR **at sthg** [truth, bad news] esquivar OR rehuir algo; [idea, suggestion] estremecerse ante algo. ⟨> *n* ['ri:kɔɪl] [of gun] retroceso *m*.

recollect [,rekə'lekt] *vt* & *vi* recordar.

recollection [,rekə'lekʃn] *n* recuerdo *m*; **I have no recollection of it** no lo recuerdo.

recommence [,ri:kə'mens] *vt* & *vi* recomenzar.

recommend [,rekə'mend] *vt* recomendar.

recommendation [,rekəmen'deɪʃn] *n* recomendación *f*.

recommended retail price [,rekə'mendɪd-] *n* precio *m* recomendado.

recompense ['rekəmpens] ⟨> *n*: **recompense (for)** compensación *f* OR indemnización *f* (por). ⟨> *vt*: **to recompense sb (for)** recompensar a alguien (por).

reconcile ['rekənsaɪl] *vt* - **1.** [find agreement between] conciliar; **to reconcile sthg with** hacer compatible algo con - **2.** [make friendly again] reconciliar; **to be reconciled with sb** reconciliarse con alguien - **3.** [accept]: **to reconcile o.s.** to resignarse a.

reconciliation [,rekənsɪlɪ'eɪʃn] *n* - **1.** [accommodation] conciliación *f* - **2.** [forgiveness] reconciliación *f*.

recondite ['rekəndaɪt] *adj fml* abstruso(sa).

reconditioned [,ri:kən'dɪʃnd] *adj* reparado(da).

reconnaissance [rɪ'kɒnɪsəns] *n* reconocimiento *m*.

reconnect [,ri:kə'nekt] *vt* volver a conectar.

reconnoitre *UK*, **reconnoiter** *US* [,rekə'nɔɪtər] ◇ *vt* reconocer. ◇ *vi* hacer un reconocimiento.

reconsider [,ri:kən'sɪdər] *vt* & *vi* reconsiderar.

reconstitute [,ri:'kɒnstɪtjuːt] *vt* **- 1.** [re-form] reconstituir **- 2.** [dried food] rehidratar.

reconstruct [,ri:kən'strʌkt] *vt* **- 1.** [building, crime] reconstruir **- 2.** [system, policy] rehacer.

reconstruction [,ri:kən'strʌkʃn] *n* reconstrucción *f*.

reconvene [,ri:kən'viːn] ◇ *vt* convocar de nuevo. ◇ *vi* volver a reunirse.

record ◇ *n* ['rekɔːd] **- 1.** [of event, piece of information & COMPUT] registro *m*; [of meeting] actas *fpl*; **on record** [on file] archivado; [ever recorded] de que se tiene constancia; **to go/be on record as saying that...** declarar/haber declarado públicamente que...; **off the record** confidencial **- 2.** [vinyl disc] disco *m* **- 3.** [best achievement] récord *m* **- 4.** [past results] resultados *mpl* **- 5.** HIST historial *m*; **criminal record** antecedentes *mpl* penales; **school record** expediente *m* académico

⏩ **to set** OR **put the record straight** dejar las cosas bien claras. ◇ *vt* [rɪ'kɔːd] **- 1.** [write down] anotar **- 2.** [document] documentar **- 3.** [put on tape] grabar. ◇ *vi* [rɪ'kɔːd] grabar. ◇ *adj* ['rekɔːd] récord *(inv)*.

record-breaking *adj* que rompe todos los récords.

recorded delivery [rɪ'kɔːdɪd-] *n* correo *m* certificado.

recorder [rɪ'kɔːdər] *n* **- 1.** [machine] grabadora *f* **- 2.** [musical instrument] flauta *f*.

record holder *n* plusmarquista *mf*.

recording [rɪ'kɔːdɪŋ] *n* grabación *f*.

recording studio *n* estudio *m* de grabación.

record library *n* fonoteca *f*.

record player *n* tocadiscos *m inv*.

recount ◇ *n* ['riːkaʊnt] segundo recuento *m*. ◇ *vt* **- 1.** [rɪ'kaʊnt] [narrate] narrar **- 2.** [,riː'kaʊnt] [count again] volver a contar.

recoup [rɪ'kuːp] *vt* recuperar.

recourse [rɪ'kɔːs] *n fml*: **to have recourse to** recurrir a.

recover [rɪ'kʌvər] ◇ *vt* **- 1.** [retrieve, recoup] recuperar **- 2.** [regain - calm etc] recobrar; **to recover o.s.** reponerse. ◇ *vi*: **to recover (from)** recuperarse (de).

recoverable [rɪ'kʌvrəbl] *adj* FIN recuperable.

recovery [rɪ'kʌvərɪ] *(pl* **-ies)** *n* recuperación *f*.

recovery vehicle *n UK* grúa *f*.

recreate ['riːkrɪˌeɪt] *vt* [reproduce] recrear.

recreation [,rekrɪ'eɪʃn] *n* [leisure] esparcimiento *m*, recreo *m*.

recreational [,rekrɪ'eɪʃənl] *adj* de recreo.

recreational drugs *npl drogas de consumo ocasional y por placer*.

recreation ground *n UK* campo *m* de deportes.

recrimination [rɪ,krɪmɪ'neɪʃn] *n* recriminación *f*.

recruit [rɪ'kruːt] ◇ *n* recluta *mf*. ◇ *vt* **- 1.** [gen] reclutar; **to recruit sb (for sthg/to do sthg)** reclutar a alguien (para algo/para hacer algo) **- 2.** [find, employ] contratar. ◇ *vi* buscar empleados nuevos.

recruitment [rɪ'kruːtmənt] *n* [gen] reclutamiento *m*; [of staff] contratación *f*.

rectangle ['rek,tæŋgl] *n* rectángulo *m*.

rectangular [rek'tæŋgjʊlər] *adj* rectangular.

rectification [,rektɪfɪ'keɪʃn] *n fml* rectificación *f*.

rectify ['rektɪfaɪ] *(pt* & *pp* **-ied)** *vt* rectificar.

rectitude ['rektɪtjuːd] *n fml* rectitud *f*.

rector ['rektər] *n* **- 1.** [priest] párroco *m* **- 2.** *Scotland* [head - of school] director *m*, -ra *f*; [- of college, university] rector *m*, -ra *f*.

rectory ['rektərɪ] *(pl* **-ies)** *n* rectoría *f*.

rectum ['rektəm] *(pl* **-s)** *n* recto *m*.

recuperate [rɪ'kuːpəreɪt] ◇ *vt* recuperar. ◇ *vi*: **to recuperate (from)** recuperarse (de).

recuperation [rɪ,kuːpə'reɪʃn] *n* recuperación *f*.

recur [rɪ'kɜːr] *(pt* & *pp* **-red**, *cont* **-ring)** *vi* repetirse, volver a producirse.

recurrence [rɪ'kʌrəns] *n* repetición *f*.

recurrent [rɪ'kʌrənt] *adj* que se repite, periódico(ca).

recurring [rɪ'kɜːrɪŋ] *adj* **- 1.** [often repeated] que se repite, periódico(ca) **- 2.** MATHS: **3.3 recurring** 3,3 periódico.

recyclable [,riː'saɪkləbl] *adj* reciclable.

recycle [,riː'saɪkl] *vt* reciclar.

recycle bin *n* COMPUT papelera *f*.

red [red] ◇ *adj* (*comp* **-der**, *superl* **-dest**) rojo(ja); **to have red hair** ser pelirrojo(ja); **to go red** [with embarrassment] ponerse colorado(da). ◇ *n* [colour] rojo *m*; **to be in the red** *inf* estar en números rojos; **to see red** ponerse hecho(cha) una furia.

➠ **Red** *pej* ◇ *adj* POL rojo(ja). ◇ *n* POL rojo *m*, -ja *f*.

red alert *n*: (**to be on**) **red alert** (estar en) alerta *f* roja.

red blood cell *n* glóbulo *m* rojo.

red-blooded [-'blʌdɪd] *adj hum* viril.

red-brick *UK adj* [building] de ladrillo rojo.

◆ **redbrick** *adj UK* UNIV: **the redbrick universities** *las universidades británicas de provincias construidas a finales del siglo XIX.*

red card *n* FTBL: **to show sb the red card** mostrarle a alguien (la) tarjeta roja.

red carpet *n*: **to roll out the red carpet for sb** recibir a alguien con todos los honores.

◆ **red-carpet** *adj*: **to give sb the red-carpet treatment** dispensar a alguien un gran recibimiento.

Red Cross *n*: **the Red Cross** la Cruz Roja.

redcurrant ['redkʌrənt] *n* - **1.** [fruit] grosella *f* - **2.** [bush] grosellero *m*.

red deer *n* ciervo *m*.

redden ['redn] ⟨⟩ *vt* [make red] teñir de rojo. ⟨⟩ *vi* [flush] enrojecer.

redecorate [ˌriː'dekəreɪt] *vt* & *vi* volver a pintar *(o empapelar).*

redeem [rɪ'diːm] *vt* - **1.** [save, rescue] salvar, rescatar; **he redeemed himself for his mistake** reparó su error - **2.** RELIG redimir - **3.** *fml* [at pawnbroker's] desempeñar.

redeeming [rɪ'diːmɪŋ] *adj*: **his only redeeming feature** lo único que le salva.

redefine [ˌriː'faɪn] *vt* redefinir.

redemption [rɪ'dempʃn] *n* RELIG redención *f*; **to be beyond** OR **past redemption** *fig* no tener remedio.

redeploy [ˌriːdɪ'plɔɪ] *vt* reorganizar.

redeployment [ˌriːdɪ'plɔɪmənt] *n* reorganización *f*, redistribución *f*.

redesign [ˌriːdɪ'zaɪn] *vt* - **1.** [replan, redraw] rediseñar - **2.** [rethink] elaborar de nuevo.

redevelop [ˌriːdɪ'veləp] *vt* reurbanizar.

redevelopment [ˌriːdɪ'veləpmənt] *n* reurbanización *f*.

red-faced [-'feɪst] *adj* - **1.** [flushed] rojo(ja), colorado(da) - **2.** [with embarrassment] rojo(ja) de vergüenza.

red-haired [-'heəd] *adj* pelirrojo(ja).

red-handed [-'hændɪd] *adj*: **to catch sb red-handed** coger a alguien con las manos en la masa.

redhead ['redhed] *n* pelirrojo *m*, -ja *f*.

red herring *n fig* [unhelpful clue] pista *f* falsa; [means of distracting attention] ardid *m* para distraer la atención.

red-hot *adj* [metal, person, passion] al rojo (vivo).

redid [ˌriː'dɪd] *pt* ▷ **redo**.

Red Indian ⟨⟩ *adj* piel roja. ⟨⟩ *n* piel roja *mf (atención: el término 'Red Indian' se considera racista).*

redirect [ˌriːdɪ'rekt] *vt* - **1.** [retarget] redirigir - **2.** [divert] desviar - **3.** [forward] reexpedir.

rediscover [ˌriːdɪs'kʌvə*] *vt* - **1.** [re-experience] volver a descubrir - **2.** [make popular, famous again]: **to be rediscovered** ser descubierto(ta) de nuevo.

redistribute [ˌriːdɪs'trɪbjuːt] *vt* redistribuir.

red-letter day *n* día *m* memorable.

red light *n* [traffic signal] semáforo *m* rojo.

red-light district *n* barrio *m* chino.

red meat *n* carne *f* roja.

redneck ['rednek] *n US pej* sureño racista y reaccionario, de baja extracción social.

redo [ˌriː'duː] (*pt* **-did**, *pp* **-done**) *vt* - **1.** [do again] volver a hacer - **2.** *inf* [redecorate] volver a pintar *(o empapelar)* - **3.** COMPUT rehacer.

redolent ['redələnt] *adj liter* - **1.** [reminiscent]: **to be redolent of sthg** evocar algo - **2.** [smelling]: **to be redolent of sthg** oler a algo.

redouble [ˌriː'dʌbl] *vt*: **to redouble one's efforts (to do sthg)** redoblar esfuerzos (para hacer algo).

redoubtable [rɪ'daʊtəbl] *adj fml* imponente.

redraft [ˌriː'drɑːft] *vt* volver a redactar.

redraw [ˌriː'drɔː] (*pt* **-drew**, *pp* **-drawn** [-'drɔːn]) *vt* volver a dibujar; COMPUT redibujar.

redress [rɪ'dres] *fml* ⟨⟩ *n* (U) reparación *f*. ⟨⟩ *vt*: **to redress the balance (between)** equilibrar la balanza (entre).

redrew [ˌriː'druː] *pt* ▷ **redraw**.

Red Sea *n*: **the Red Sea** el mar Rojo.

Red Square *n* la plaza Roja.

red squirrel *n* ardilla *f* roja.

red tape *n fig* papeleo *m*.

reduce [rɪ'djuːs] ⟨⟩ *vt* reducir; **to be reduced to doing sthg** verse rebajado OR forzado a hacer algo; **it reduced me to tears** me hizo llorar. ⟨⟩ *vi US* [diet] (intentar) adelgazar.

reduced [rɪ'djuːst] *adj* - **1.** [smaller] reducido(da) - **2.** [poorer]: **in reduced circumstances** venido(da) a menos.

reduction [rɪ'dʌkʃn] *n* - **1.** [gen]: **reduction (in)** reducción *f* (de) - **2.** COMM: **reduction (of)** descuento *m* (de).

redundancy [rɪ'dʌndənsɪ] (*pl* **-ies**) *n UK* [job loss] despido *m*.

redundancy pay *n UK* indemnización *f* (por despido).

redundant [rɪ'dʌndənt] *adj* - **1.** *UK* [jobless]: **to be made redundant** perder el empleo; **to make sb redundant** despedir a alguien - **2.** [not required - equipment, factory] innecesario(ria); [- comment] redundante.

redwood ['redwʊd] *n*: **redwood (tree)** secoya *f*.

reed [riːd] ⟨⟩ *n* - **1.** [plant] carrizo *m*, cañavera *f* - **2.** [of musical instrument] lengüeta *f*. ⟨⟩ *comp* de carrizo.

reeducate [,ri:'edjʊkeɪt] *vt* reeducar.

reedy ['ri:dɪ] (*comp* -ier, *superl* -iest) *adj* [voice] agudo(da), chillón(ona).

reef [ri:f] *n* arrecife *m*.

reek [ri:k] ◇ *n* hedor *m*. ◇ *vi*: **to reek (of)** apestar (a).

reel [ri:l] ◇ *n* - **1.** [of cotton, on fishing rod] carrete *m* - **2.** [of film] rollo *m*. ◇ *vi* - **1.** [stagger] tambalearse - **2.** [whirl - mind] dar vueltas - **3.** [be stunned]: **to reel from sthg** quedarse atónito(ta) por algo.

◆ **reel in** *vt sep* sacar enrollando el carrete (*en pesca)*.

◆ **reel off** *vt sep* recitar al corrido.

reelect [,ri:ɪ'lekt] *vt*: **to reelect sb (as)** reelegir a alguien (como).

reelection [,ri:ɪ'lekʃn] *n* reelección *f*.

reemphasize [,ri:'emfəsaɪz] *vt* recalcar OR subrayar de nuevo.

reenact [,ri:ɪn'ækt] *vt* representar de nuevo.

reenter [,ri:'entə'] *vt* volver a entrar en.

reentry [,ri:'entrɪ] *n* reingreso *m*.

reexamine [,ri:ɪg'zæmɪn] *vt* reexaminar.

reexport [,ri:'ekspɔ:t] ◇ *n* COMM [act of exporting] reexportación *f*. ◇ *vt* COMM reexportar.

ref [ref] *n* - **1.** *inf* SPORT (*abbr of* **referee**) árbitro *m* - **2.** ADMIN (*abbr of* **reference**) ref.

refectory [rɪ'fektərɪ] (*pl* -ies) *n* refectorio *m*.

refer [rɪ'fɜ:r] *vt* (*pt & pp* -red, *cont* -ring) - **1.** [send, direct]: **to refer sb to** [to place] enviar a alguien a; [to source of information] remitir a alguien a - **2.** [report, submit]: **to refer sthg to** remitir algo a.

◆ **refer to** *vt insep* - **1.** [mention, speak about] referirse a - **2.** [consult] consultar.

referee [,refə'ri:] ◇ *n* - **1.** SPORT árbitro *m* - **2.** *UK* [for job application] *persona que proporciona referencias de alguien para un trabajo*. ◇ *vt & vi* SPORT arbitrar.

reference ['refrəns] *n* - **1.** [mention, reference number]: **to make reference to** hacer referencia a; **with reference to** *fml* con referencia a - **2.** *(U)* [for advice, information]: **reference (to)** consulta *f* (a); **for future reference** para consultas futuras - **3.** [for job - letter] referencia *f*; [- person] *persona que proporciona referencias de alguien para un trabajo*.

reference book *n* libro *m* de consulta.

reference library *n* biblioteca *f* de consulta.

reference number *n* número *m* de referencia.

referendum [,refə'rendəm] (*pl* -s OR -da [-də]) *n* referéndum *m*.

referral [rɪ'fɜ:rəl] *n*: **ask for a referral to a specialist** pide que te manden a un especialista; **this patient is a referral from cardiology** a este paciente lo han mandado de cardiología.

refill ◇ *n* ['ri:fɪl] [for pen] recambio *m*; *inf* [of drink]: **would you like a refill?** ¿te apetece otra copa? ◇ *vt* [,ri:'fɪl] volver a llenar.

refillable [,ri:'fɪləbl] *adj* [bottle] rellenable; [pen] recargable.

refine [rɪ'faɪn] *vt* - **1.** [oil, food] refinar - **2.** [plan, speech] pulir.

refined [rɪ'faɪnd] *adj* - **1.** [oil, food, person] refinado(da) - **2.** [equipment, theory] perfeccionado(da).

refinement [rɪ'faɪnmənt] *n* - **1.** [improvement]: **refinement (on)** mejora *f* (de) - **2.** *(U)* [gentility] refinamiento *m*.

refinery [rɪ'faɪnərɪ] (*pl* -ies) *n* refinería *f*.

refit ◇ *n* ['ri:fɪt] [of ship] reacondicionamiento *m*. ◇ *vt* [,ri:'fɪt] (*pt & pp* -ted, *cont* -ting) [ship] reacondicionar.

reflate [,ri:'fleɪt] *vt* ECON reflacionar.

reflation [,ri:'fleɪʃn] *n* ECON reflación *f*.

reflationary [ri:'fleɪʃənrɪ] *adj* ECON reflacionario(ria).

reflect [rɪ'flekt] ◇ *vt* - **1.** [gen] reflejar; **to be reflected in** reflejarse en - **2.** [think, consider]: **to reflect that...** considerar que... ◇ *vi*: **to reflect (on OR upon)** reflexionar (sobre).

reflection [rɪ'flekʃn] *n* - **1.** [gen] reflejo *m* - **2.** [criticism]: **reflection on** crítica *f* de - **3.** [thinking] reflexión *f*; **on reflection** pensándolo bien - **4.** [thought]: **reflections (on)** reflexiones *fpl* (sobre).

reflective [rɪ'flektɪv] *adj* - **1.** [thoughtful] reflexivo(va) - **2.** [shiny] reflectante.

reflector [rɪ'flektə'] *n* reflector *m*.

reflex ['ri:fleks] *n*: **reflex (action)** (acto *m*) reflejo *m*.

◆ **reflexes** *npl* reflejos *mpl*.

reflex camera *n* cámara *f* réflex.

reflexive [rɪ'fleksɪv] *adj* GRAM reflexivo(va).

reflexology [,ri:flek'sɒlədʒɪ] *n* reflexoterapia *f*.

reforest *esp US* [,ri:'fɒrɪst] *vt* = **reafforest**.

reforestation [ri:,fɒrɪ'steɪʃn] = **reafforestation**.

reform [rɪ'fɔ:m] ◇ *n* reforma *f*. ◇ *vt* reformar. ◇ *vi* reformarse.

reformat [,ri:'fɔ:mæt] (*pt & pp* -ted, *cont* -ting) *vt* COMPUT formatear de nuevo.

Reformation [,refə'meɪʃn] *n*: **the Reformation** la Reforma.

reformatory [rɪ'fɔ:mətrɪ] *n* *US* reformatorio *m*.

reformed [rɪ'fɔ:md] *adj* [better behaved] reformado(da).

reformer [rɪ'fɔ:mə'] *n* reformador *m*, -ra *f*.

reformist [rɪ'fɔːmɪst] <> *adj* reformista. <> *n* reformista *mf*.

refract [rɪ'frækt] <> *vt* refractar. <> *vi* refractarse.

refrain [rɪ'freɪn] <> *n* [chorus] estribillo *m*. <> *vi fml*: **to refrain from doing sthg** abstenerse de hacer algo.

refresh [rɪ'freʃ] *vt* [gen & COMPUT] refrescar; **to refresh sb's memory** refrescarle la memoria a alguien.

refreshed [rɪ'freʃt] *adj* descansado(da), vigorizado(da).

refresher course [rɪ'freʃər-] *n* cursillo *m* de reciclaje (*en el mismo trabajo*).

refreshing [rɪ'freʃɪŋ] *adj* [change, honesty, drink] refrescante; [sleep] vigorizante.

refreshments [rɪ'freʃmənts] *npl* refrigerio *m*.

refrigerate [rɪ'frɪdʒəreɪt] *vt* refrigerar.

refrigeration [rɪ,frɪdʒə'reɪʃn] *n* refrigeración *f*.

refrigerator [rɪ'frɪdʒəreɪtər] *n* nevera *f*, refrigerador *m* *Amér*, heladera *f R Plata*, refrigeradora *f Col & Perú*.

refuel [,riː'fjʊəl] <> *vt* (*UK* **-led**, *cont* **-ling**, *US* **-ed**, *cont* **-ing**) llenar de carburante. <> *vi* (*UK* **-led**, *cont* **-ling**, *US* **-ed**, *cont* **-ing**) repostar.

refuge ['refjuːdʒ] *n* refugio *m*; **to seek** OR **take refuge (in)** *fig* buscar refugio (en).

refugee [,refjʊ'dʒiː] *n* refugiado *m*, -da *f*.

refugee camp *n* campamento *m* de refugiados.

refund <> *n* ['riːfʌnd] reembolso *m*. <> *vt* [rɪ'fʌnd]: **to refund sthg to sb, to refund sb sthg** reembolsar algo a alguien.

refurbish [,riː'fɜːbɪʃ] *vt* [building] restaurar; [office, shop] renovar.

refurbishment [,riː'fɜːbɪʃmənt] *n* [of building] restauración *f*; [of office, shop] renovación *f*.

refurnish [,riː'fɜːnɪʃ] *vt* volver a amueblar.

refusal [rɪ'fjuːzl] *n* **- 1.** [disagreement, saying no]: **refusal (to do sthg)** negativa *f* (a hacer algo) **- 2.** [withholding, denial] denegación *f* **- 3.** [nonacceptance]: **to meet with refusal** ser rechazado(da).

refuse[1] [rɪ'fjuːz] <> *vt* **- 1.** [withhold, deny]: **to refuse sb sthg, to refuse sthg to sb** denegar a alguien algo **- 2.** [decline, reject] rechazar **- 3.** [not agree, be completely unwilling]: **to refuse to do sthg** negarse a hacer algo. <> *vi* negarse.

refuse[2] ['refjuːs] *n* [rubbish] basura *f*.

refuse collection ['refjuːs-] *n* recogida *f* de basuras.

refuse collector ['refjuːs-] *n* basurero *m*, -ra *f*.

refuse dump ['refjuːs-] *n* vertedero *m* (de basuras).

refute [rɪ'fjuːt] *vt fml* refutar.

reg., regd. (*abbr of* **registered**): **reg. trademark** marca *f* registrada.

regain [rɪ'geɪn] *vt* [leadership, first place] recuperar; [health, composure] recobrar.

regal ['riːgl] *adj* regio(gia).

regale [rɪ'geɪl] *vt*: **to regale sb with** entretener a alguien con.

regalia [rɪ'geɪljə] *n* (*U*) ropaje *m*, vestiduras *fpl*.

regard [rɪ'gɑːd] <> *n* **- 1.** *fml* [respect, esteem]: **regard (for)** estima *f* OR respeto *m* (por); **to hold sthg/sb in high regard** tener algo/a alguien en gran estima **- 2.** [aspect]: **in this/that regard** a este/ese respecto **- 3.** [consideration]: **with no regard for** sin ninguna consideración por. <> *vt* **- 1.** [consider]: **to regard o.s. as sthg** considerarse algo; **to regard sthg/sb as** considerar algo/a alguien como **- 2.** [look at, view]: **to regard sb/sthg with** ver a alguien/algo con; **to be highly regarded** estar muy bien considerado.

➤ **regards** *npl* [in greetings] recuerdos *mpl*; **give them my regards** salúdales de mi parte.

➤ **as regards** *prep* en cuanto a, por lo que se refiere a.

➤ **in regard to, with regard to** *prep* respecto a, en cuanto a.

regarding [rɪ'gɑːdɪŋ] *prep* respecto a, en cuanto a.

regardless [rɪ'gɑːdlɪs] *adv* a pesar de todo.

➤ **regardless of** *prep* sin tener en cuenta; **regardless of the cost** cueste lo que cueste.

regatta [rɪ'gætə] *n* regata *f*.

Regency ['riːdʒənsɪ] *adj* del estilo regencia.

regenerate [rɪ'dʒenəreɪt] *vt* regenerar.

regeneration [rɪ,dʒenə'reɪʃn] *n* regeneración *f*.

regent ['riːdʒənt] <> *adj* regente. <> *n* regente *mf*.

reggae ['regeɪ] *n* reggae *m*.

regime [reɪ'ʒiːm] *n* régimen *m*.

regiment ['redʒɪmənt] *n* MIL regimiento *m*.

regimental [,redʒɪ'mentl] *adj* MIL del regimiento.

regimented ['redʒɪmentɪd] *adj pej* [life, workers] estrictamente controlado(da); [garden, rows] ordenado(da) en filas.

region ['riːdʒən] *n* región *f*; **in the region of** alrededor de.

regional ['riːdʒənl] *adj* regional.

register ['redʒɪstər] <> *n* [gen] registro *m*; [at school] lista *f*. <> *vt* **- 1.** [record - gen] registrar; [- car] matricular **- 2.** [express] mostrar, reflejar. <> *vi* **- 1.** [be put on official list]: **to register (as/for)** inscribirse (como/para) **- 2.** [book in - at hotel] registrarse; [- at conference] inscribirse

- 3. *inf* [be noticed]: **I told him but it didn't seem to register** se lo dije, pero no pareció que lo captara.

registered ['redʒɪstəd] *adj* **- 1.** [officially listed] inscrito(ta) oficialmente **- 2.** [letter, parcel] certificado(da).

registered nurse *n* enfermera *f* diplomada.

registered post *UK*, **registered mail** *US n* correo *m* certificado.

registered trademark *n* marca *f* registrada.

registrar ['redʒɪstrɑːr] *n* **- 1.** [keeper of records] registrador *m*, -ra *f* oficial **- 2.** UNIV secretario *m*, -ria *f* general **- 3.** [doctor] médico *m*, -ca *f* de hospital.

registration [,redʒɪ'streɪʃn] *n* **- 1.** [gen] registro *m* **- 2.** AUT = **registration number**.

registration document *n* documentos *mpl* de matriculación.

registration number, registration *n* AUT número *m* de matrícula; COMPUT número *m* de registro.

registry ['redʒɪstrɪ] (*pl* -ies) *n* registro *m*.

registry office *n* registro *m* civil.

regress [rɪ'gres] *vi fml*: **to regress (to)** sufrir un retroceso (a).

regression [rɪ'greʃn] *n fml* regresión *f*.

regressive [rɪ'gresɪv] *adj fml* regresivo(va).

regret [rɪ'gret] <> *n* **- 1.** *fml* [sorrow] pesar *m* **- 2.** [sad feeling]: **I've no regrets about it** no lo lamento en absoluto; **he sends his regrets** manda sus excusas. <> *vt* (*pt & pp* -**ted**, *cont* -**ting**) [be sorry about]: **to regret sthg/doing sthg** lamentar algo/haber hecho algo; **we regret to announce...** lamentamos comunicar...

regretful [rɪ'gretful] *adj* [person] pesaroso(sa); [smile, look] de arrepentimiento.

regretfully [rɪ'gretfulɪ] *adv* con pesar; **regretfully, we have to announce...** lamentamos tener que anunciar...

regrettable [rɪ'gretəbl] *adj* lamentable.

regrettably [rɪ'gretəblɪ] *adv* lamentablemente.

regroup [,riː'gruːp] *vi* reagruparse.

regt (*abbr of* **regiment**) regto.

regular ['regjʊlər] <> *adj* **- 1.** [gen] regular **- 2.** [customer] habitual **- 3.** [time, place] acostumbrado(da); [problem] usual, normal **- 4.** *US* [size] normal, mediano(na) **- 5.** *US* [pleasant] legal. <> *n* cliente *m* habitual.

regular army *n* ejército *m* profesional.

regularity [,regjʊ'lærətɪ] *n* regularidad *f*.

regularly ['regjʊləlɪ] *adv* **- 1.** [gen] con regularidad **- 2.** [equally spaced] de manera uniforme.

regulate ['regjʊleɪt] *vt* regular.

regulation [,regjʊ'leɪʃn] <> *adj* [standard] reglamentario(ria). <> *n* **- 1.** [rule] regla *f*, norma *f* **- 2.** *(U)* [control] regulación *f*.

regurgitate [rɪ'gɜːdʒɪteɪt] *vt* **- 1.** [bring up] regurgitar **- 2.** *fig & pej* [repeat] repetir maquinalmente.

rehabilitate [,riːə'bɪlɪteɪt] *vt* rehabilitar.

rehabilitation ['riːə,bɪlɪ'teɪʃn] *n* rehabilitación *f*.

rehash [,riː'hæʃ] *vt inf pej* hacer un refrito de.

rehearsal [rɪ'hɜːsl] *n* ensayo *m*.

rehearse [rɪ'hɜːs] <> *vt* ensayar. <> *vi*: **to rehearse (for)** ensayar (para).

rehouse [,riː'haʊz] *vt* realojar.

reign [reɪn] *lit & fig* <> *n* reinado *m*. <> *vi*: **to reign (over)** reinar (sobre).

reigning ['reɪnɪŋ] *adj* [champion] actual.

reimburse [,riːɪm'bɜːs] *vt*: **to reimburse sb (for sthg)** reembolsar a alguien (algo).

reimbursement [,riːɪm'bɜːsmənt] *n fml*: **reimbursement (for)** reembolso *m* (de OR por).

rein [reɪn] *n fig*: **to give (a) free rein to sb, to give sb free rein** dar rienda suelta a alguien; **to keep a tight rein on sb/sthg** tener muy controlado(da) a alguien/algo.

◆ **reins** *npl* **- 1.** [for horse] riendas *fpl* **- 2.** [for child] andadores *mpl*.

◆ **rein in** *vt sep* refrenar.

reincarnation [,riːɪnkɑː'neɪʃn] *n* reencarnación *f*.

reindeer ['reɪn,dɪər] (*pl* **reindeer**) *n* reno *m*.

reinforce [,riːɪn'fɔːs] *vt* reforzar.

reinforced concrete [,riːɪn'fɔːst-] *n* cemento *m* OR hormigón *m* armado.

reinforcement [,riːɪn'fɔːsmənt] *n* refuerzo *m*.

◆ **reinforcements** *npl* refuerzos *mpl*.

re-install *vt* reinstalar.

reinstate [,riːɪn'steɪt] *vt* **- 1.** [give job back to] restituir OR reintegrar en su puesto a **- 2.** [bring back] restablecer.

reinstatement [,riːɪn'steɪtmənt] *n* [of worker] rehabilitación *f* (*laboral*).

reinterpret [,riːɪn'tɜːprɪt] *vt* reinterpretar.

reintroduce ['riː,ɪntrə'djuːs] *vt* reintroducir.

reintroduction [,riː,ɪntrə'dʌkʃn] *n* reintroducción *f*.

reissue [riː'ɪʃuː] <> *n* reedición *f*. <> *vt* [gen] reeditar; [film] reestrenar, reponer.

reiterate [riː'ɪtəreɪt] *vt fml* reiterar.

reiteration [riː,ɪtə'reɪʃn] *n fml* reiteración *f*.

reject <> *n* ['riːdʒekt] **- 1.** [thing]: **rejects** artículos *mpl* defectuosos **- 2.** *inf* [person] desecho *m*. <> *vt* [rɪ'dʒekt] rechazar.

rejection [rɪ'dʒekʃn] *n* rechazo *m*.

rejig [ˌriːˈdʒɪg] (*pt & pp* **-ged**, *cont* **-ging**) *vt UK inf* modificar un poco.

rejoice [rɪˈdʒɔɪs] *vi*: **to rejoice (at** OR **in)** alegrarse OR regocijarse (con).

rejoicing [rɪˈdʒɔɪsɪŋ] *n*: **rejoicing (at** OR **over)** regocijo *m* (por).

rejoin[1] [ˌriːˈdʒɔɪn] *vt* - **1.** [go back to] volver (a encontrarse) con - **2.** [club] volver a hacerse socio(cia) de; [army] volver a alistarse en.

rejoin[2] [rɪˈdʒɔɪn] *vt liter* [reply] replicar.

rejoinder [rɪˈdʒɔɪndə[r]] *n liter* réplica *f*.

rejuvenate [rɪˈdʒuːvəneɪt] *vt* rejuvenecer.

rejuvenation [rɪˌdʒuːvəˈneɪʃn] *n* renovación *f*.

rekindle [ˌriːˈkɪndl] *vt* reavivar.

relapse [rɪˈlæps] ⬦ *n* recaída *f*. ⬦ *vi*: **to relapse into** volver a caer en.

relate [rɪˈleɪt] ⬦ *vt* - **1.** [connect]: **to relate sthg (to)** relacionar algo (con) - **2.** [tell] contar, relatar. ⬦ *vi* - **1.** [be connected]: **to relate to** estar relacionado(da) con - **2.** [concern]: **to relate to** referirse a - **3.** [empathize]: **to relate (to sb)** tener mucho en común (con alguien).
➡ **relating to** *prep* concerniente OR referente a.

related [rɪˈleɪtɪd] *adj* - **1.** [in same family] emparentado(da); **to be related to sb** ser pariente de alguien - **2.** [connected] relacionado(da).

relation [rɪˈleɪʃn] *n* - **1.** [connection]: **relation (to/between)** relación *f* (con/entre); **to bear no relation to** no tener nada que ver con; **in relation to** [state, size] en relación a; [position] respecto a - **2.** [family member] pariente *mf*, familiar *mf*.
➡ **relations** *npl* [family, race, industrial] relaciones *fpl*.

relationship [rɪˈleɪʃnʃɪp] *n* - **1.** [gen] relación *f*; **a good relationship** buenas relaciones - **2.** [to family member] parentesco *m*.

relative [ˈrelətɪv] ⬦ *adj* relativo(va). ⬦ *n* pariente *mf*, familiar *mf*.
➡ **relative to** *prep fml* con relación a.

relatively [ˈrelətɪvlɪ] *adv* relativamente.

relativity [ˌreləˈtɪvətɪ] *n* relatividad *f*.

relax [rɪˈlæks] ⬦ *vt* - **1.** [gen] relajar - **2.** [loosen - grip] aflojar. ⬦ *vi* - **1.** [gen] relajarse - **2.** [loosen] aflojarse.

relaxation [ˌriːlækˈseɪʃn] *n* - **1.** [recreation] relajación *f*, esparcimiento *m* - **2.** [slackening - of discipline] relajación *f*, relajamiento *m*.

relaxed [rɪˈlækst] *adj* relajado(da).

relaxing [rɪˈlæksɪŋ] *adj* relajante.

relay [ˈriːleɪ] ⬦ *n* - **1.** SPORT: **relay (race)** carrera *f* de relevos; **in relays** *fig* por turnos - **2.** RADIO & TV retransmisión *f*. ⬦ *vt* - **1.** (*pt & pp* **-ed**) [broadcast] retransmitir

- **2.** (*pt & pp* **-ed**) [repeat]: **to relay sthg (to)** transmitir algo (a) - **3.** (*pt & pp* **relaid**) [lay again] volver a poner.

release [rɪˈliːs] ⬦ *n* - **1.** [setting free] puesta *f* en libertad, liberación *f* - **2.** [relief] alivio *m* - **3.** [statement] comunicado *m* - **4.** [emitting - of gas] escape *m*; [- of heat, pressure] emisión *f* - **5.** [thing issued - of film] estreno *m*; [- of record] publicación *f*; **on release** en pantalla; **new releases** novedades. ⬦ *vt* - **1.** [set free]: **to release sb (from)** liberar a alguien (de); **to be released** ser puesto en libertad - **2.** [lift restriction on]: **to release sb from** liberar a alguien de - **3.** [make available - funds, resources] entregar - **4.** [let go - rope, reins, brake, person] soltar; [- grip] aflojar; [- mechanism, trigger] disparar - **5.** [emit - gas, heat] despedir, emitir - **6.** [issue - film] estrenar; [- record] sacar; [- statement] hacer público.

relegate [ˈrelɪgeɪt] *vt* - **1.** [demote]: **to relegate sthg/sb (to)** relegar algo/a alguien (a) - **2.** UK FTBL: **to be relegated** descender (*a una división inferior*).

relegation [ˌrelɪˈgeɪʃn] *n* - **1.** [demotion]: **relegation (to)** relegación *f* (a) - **2.** UK FTBL: **relegation (to)** descenso *m* (a).

relent [rɪˈlent] *vi* [person] ablandarse; [wind, storm] remitir, aminorar.

relentless [rɪˈlentlɪs] *adj* implacable.

relentlessly [rɪˈlentlɪslɪ] *adv* implacablemente.

relevance [ˈreləvəns] *n* pertinencia *f*.

relevant [ˈreləvənt] *adj* - **1.** [connected]: **relevant (to)** pertinente (a) - **2.** [important]: **relevant (to)** importante OR relevante (para) - **3.** [appropriate] pertinente, oportuno(na).

reliability [rɪˌlaɪəˈbɪlətɪ] *n* fiabilidad *f*.

reliable [rɪˈlaɪəbl] *adj* - **1.** [dependable] fiable - **2.** [information] fidedigno(na).

reliably [rɪˈlaɪəblɪ] *adv* - **1.** [dependably] sin fallar - **2.** [correctly]: **to be reliably informed about sthg** saber algo de fuentes fidedignas.

reliance [rɪˈlaɪəns] *n*: **reliance (on)** dependencia *f* (de OR respecto de).

reliant [rɪˈlaɪənt] *adj*: **to be reliant on sb/sthg** depender de alguien/de algo.

relic [ˈrelɪk] *n* - **1.** [gen] reliquia *f* - **2.** [custom still in use] vestigio *m*.

relief [rɪˈliːf] *n* - **1.** [comfort] alivio *m*; **she sighed with relief** suspiró aliviada - **2.** [for poor, refugees] ayuda *f* - **3.** (*U*) US [social security] subsidio *m*.

relief agency *n* organización *f* de ayuda humanitaria.

relief map *n* mapa *m* en relieve.

relief road *n esp UK* desvío *m*.

relieve [rɪ'liːv] *vt* **- 1.** [ease, lessen] aliviar **- 2.** [take away from]: **to relieve sb of sthg** liberar a alguien de algo.

relieved [rɪ'liːvd] *adj* aliviado(da).

religion [rɪ'lɪdʒn] *n* religión *f*.

religious [rɪ'lɪdʒəs] *adj* religioso(sa).

reline [ˌriː'laɪn] *vt* [cupboard, skirt] volver a forrar; [brakes] cambiar el forro de.

relinquish [rɪ'lɪŋkwɪʃ] *vt* [power, claim] renunciar a; **to relinquish one's hold on sthg** soltar algo.

relish ['relɪʃ] <> *n* **- 1.** [enjoyment]: **with (great) relish** con (gran) deleite **- 2.** [pickle] *salsa rojiza agridulce con pepinillo etc.* <> *vt* disfrutar con; **to relish the thought** OR **idea** OR **prospect of doing sthg** disfrutar de antemano con la idea de hacer algo.

relive [ˌriː'lɪv] *vt* revivir.

relocate [ˌriːləʊ'keɪt] <> *vt* trasladar. <> *vi* trasladarse.

relocation [ˌriːləʊ'keɪʃn] *n* traslado *m*.

relocation expenses *npl* gastos *mpl* de traslado.

reluctance [rɪ'lʌktəns] *n* reticencia *f*; **with reluctance** de mala gana.

reluctant [rɪ'lʌktənt] *adj* reacio(cia); **to be reluctant to do sthg** estar poco dispuesto a hacer algo.

reluctantly [rɪ'lʌktəntlɪ] *adv* con desgana.

rely [rɪ'laɪ] (*pt & pp* -ied) ⇒ **rely on** *vt insep* **- 1.** [count on] contar con; **to be able to rely on sb/sthg to do sthg** poder estar seguro de que alguien/algo hará algo **- 2.** [be dependent on]: **to rely on sb/sthg for sthg** depender de alguien/algo para algo.

REM (*abbr of* rapid eye movement) *n* REM *m*.

remain [rɪ'meɪn] <> *vt* continuar como; **to remain the same** continuar siendo igual. <> *vi* **- 1.** [stay] quedarse, permanecer **- 2.** [survive - custom, problem] quedar, continuar **- 3.** [be left]: **to remain to be done/proved** quedar por hacer/probar; **it remains to be seen** queda por ver. ⇒ **remains** *npl* restos *mpl*.

remainder [rɪ'meɪndər] *n* **- 1.** [rest]: **the remainder** el resto **- 2.** MATHS resto *m*.

remaining [rɪ'meɪnɪŋ] *adj* que queda, restante.

remake <> *n* ['riːmeɪk] CIN nueva versión *f*. <> *vt* [ˌriː'meɪk] CIN hacer una nueva versión de.

remand [rɪ'mɑːnd] <> *n* LAW: **on remand** detenido(da) en espera de juicio. <> *vt* LAW: **to be remanded in custody** estar bajo custodia.

remand centre *n* UK centro *m* de prisión preventiva.

remark [rɪ'mɑːk] <> *n* [comment] comentario *m*. <> *vt*: **to remark (that)** comentar que. <> *vi*: **to remark on** hacer una observación sobre.

remarkable [rɪ'mɑːkəbl] *adj* **- 1.** [fantastic] extraordinario(ria) **- 2.** [surprising] sorprendente.

remarkably [rɪ'mɑːkəblɪ] *adv* [extremely] extraordinariamente; [surprisingly] sorprendentemente.

remarry [ˌriː'mærɪ] (*pt & pp* -ied) *vi* volver a casarse.

remedial [rɪ'miːdjəl] *adj* **- 1.** SCH [class, teacher] de refuerzo; [pupil] atrasado(da) **- 2.** [corrective] correctivo(va).

remedy ['remədɪ] <> *n* (*pl* -ies) *lit & fig*: **remedy (for)** remedio *m* (para). <> *vt* (*pt & pp* -ied) remediar, poner remedio a.

remember [rɪ'membər] <> *vt* **- 1.** [gen] recordar, acordarse de; **remember that his eyesight is poor** ten presente que tiene la vista mal; **to remember to do sthg** acordarse de hacer algo; **to remember doing sthg** recordar OR acordarse de haber hecho algo; **he remembered me in his will** me dejó algo en su testamento **- 2.** [as greeting]: **to remember sb to sb** dar recuerdos a alguien de parte de alguien. <> *vi* **- 1.** [gen] recordar, acordarse **- 2.** [not forget] acordarse.

remembrance [rɪ'membrəns] *n fml*: **in remembrance of** en conmemoración de.

Remembrance Day *n* en Gran Bretaña, *día en conmemoración de los caídos en las dos guerras mundiales.*

remind [rɪ'maɪnd] *vt*: **to remind sb (about sthg/to do sthg)** recordar a alguien (algo/que haga algo); **she reminds me of my sister** me recuerda a mi hermana.

reminder [rɪ'maɪndər] *n* **- 1.** [to jog memory] recordatorio *m*, recuerdo *m* **- 2.** [letter, note] notificación *f*, aviso *m*.

reminisce [ˌremɪ'nɪs] *vi*: **to reminisce (about sthg)** rememorar (algo).

reminiscences [ˌremɪ'nɪsənsɪz] *npl* reminiscencias *fpl*.

reminiscent [ˌremɪ'nɪsnt] *adj* [similar to]: **to be reminiscent of** evocar, recordar a.

remiss [rɪ'mɪs] *adj* negligente, remiso(sa); **it was remiss of me** fue una negligencia por mi parte.

remission [rɪ'mɪʃn] *n* (*U*) **- 1.** LAW reducción *f* de condena **- 2.** MED remisión *f*.

remit[1] [rɪ'mɪt] (*pt & pp* -ted, *cont* -ting) *vt* [money] remitir.

remit[2] ['riːmɪt] *n* [responsibility] misión *f*.

remittance [rɪ'mɪtns] *n* giro *m*.

remnant ['remnənt] *n* **- 1.** [remaining part] resto *m* **- 2.** [of cloth] retal *m*.

remodel [ˌriːˈmɒdl] (*UK* **-led**, *cont* **-ling**) (*US* **-ed**, *cont* **-ing**) *vt* remodelar, reformar.

remold *n* & *vt US* = **remould**.

remonstrate [ˈremənstreɪt] *vi fml*: **to remonstrate (with sb about sthg)** reprochar (a alguien algo).

remorse [rɪˈmɔːs] *n (U)* remordimientos *mpl*.

remorseful [rɪˈmɔːsfʊl] *adj* lleno(na) de remordimientos.

remorseless [rɪˈmɔːslɪs] *adj* - **1.** [pitiless] despiadado(da) - **2.** [unstoppable] implacable.

remorselessly [rɪˈmɔːslɪslɪ] *adv* - **1.** [pitilessly] de forma despiadada - **2.** [unstoppably] implacablemente.

remote [rɪˈməʊt] *adj* - **1.** [place, time possibility] remoto(ta) - **2.** [from reality etc]: **remote (from)** apartado(da) *OR* alejado(da) (de).

remote access *n* acceso *m* remoto.

remote control *n* telemando *m*, mando *m* a distancia.

remote-controlled [-kənˈtrəʊld] *adj* teledirigido(da).

remotely [rɪˈməʊtlɪ] *adv* - **1.** [in the slightest]: **not remotely** ni remotamente, en lo más mínimo - **2.** [far off] muy lejos.

remoteness [rɪˈməʊtnɪs] *n* - **1.** [of place] lejanía *f* - **2.** [of person] distanciamiento *m*.

remould *UK*, **remold** *US* [ˈriːməʊld] *n* neumático *m* recauchutado.

removable [rɪˈmuːvəbl] *adj* - **1.** [stain] que se puede quitar - **2.** [detachable] separable - **3.** [hard disk] extraíble.

removal [rɪˈmuːvl] *n* - **1.** *(U)* [act of removing] separación *f*, extracción *f*; [of threat, clause] supresión *f* - **2.** *UK* [change of house] mudanza *f*.

removal man *n UK* encargado *m* de mudanzas.

removal van *n UK* camión *m* de mudanzas.

remove [rɪˈmuːv] *vt* - **1.** [take away, clean away]: **to remove sthg (from)** quitar algo (de) - **2.** [clothing, shoes] quitarse - **3.** [from a job, post]: **to remove sb (from)** destituir a alguien (de) - **4.** [problem, controls] eliminar; [suspicion] disipar.

removed [rɪˈmuːvd] *adj*: **to be far removed from** estar bien lejos de.

remover [rɪˈmuːvər] *n*: **stain remover** quitamanchas *m inv*; **paint remover** quitapinturas *m inv*.

remuneration [rɪˌmjuːnəˈreɪʃn] *n fml* remuneración *f*.

rename [ˌriːˈneɪm] *vt* poner un nombre nuevo a.

rend [ˈrend] (*pt* & *pp* **rent**) *vt liter* desgarrar.

render [ˈrendər] *vt* - **1.** [make]: **to render sthg useless** hacer *OR* volver algo inútil; **to render sb speechless** dejar a alguien boquiabierto - **2.** [give - help, service] prestar.

rendering [ˈrendərɪŋ] *n* - **1.** [rendition] interpretación *f* - **2.** [of carcass] transformación *f*.

rendezvous [ˈrɒndɪvuː] (*pl* **rendezvous**) *n* - **1.** [meeting] cita *f* - **2.** [place] lugar *m* de encuentro.

rendition [renˈdɪʃn] *n* interpretación *f*.

renegade [ˈrenɪgeɪd] <> *adj* renegado(da). <> *n* renegado *m*, -da *f*.

renege [rɪˈniːg] *vi fml*: **to renege on sthg** incumplir algo.

renegotiate [ˌriːnɪˈgəʊʃɪeɪt] *vt* renegociar.

renew [rɪˈnjuː] *vt* - **1.** [attempt, attack] reemprender - **2.** [relationship] reanudar - **3.** [licence, contract, passport] renovar - **4.** [strength, interest] reavivar.

renewable [rɪˈnjuːəbl] *adj* renovable.

renewal [rɪˈnjuːəl] *n* - **1.** [of activity] reanudación *f* - **2.** [of contract, licence, passport] renovación *f*.

rennet [ˈrenɪt] *n* cuajo *m*.

renounce [rɪˈnaʊns] *vt* renunciar a.

renovate [ˈrenəveɪt] *vt* reformar, renovar.

renovation [ˌrenəˈveɪʃn] *n* reforma *f*, renovación *f*.

renown [rɪˈnaʊn] *n* renombre *m*.

renowned [rɪˈnaʊnd] *adj*: **renowned (for)** célebre (por).

rent [rent] <> *pt* & *pp* ⮑ **rend**. <> *n* alquiler *m*. <> *vt* alquilar, rentar *Méx*. <> *vi US* [property] alquilarse; **this apartment rents for $300 a month** este departamento se alquila por 300 dólares al mes.

⮜ **rent out** *vt sep* alquilar, rentar *Méx*.

rental [ˈrentl] <> *adj* de alquiler. <> *n* alquiler *m*.

rent book *n libro que registra la fecha y el pago de alquiler por parte de un inquilino.*

rent boy *n UK inf* chapero *m*.

rented [ˈrentɪd] *adj* alquilado(da).

rent-free <> *adj* exento(ta) de alquiler. <> *adv* sin pagar alquiler.

renunciation [rɪˌnʌnsɪˈeɪʃn] *n* renuncia *f*.

reopen [ˌriːˈəʊpn] <> *vt* - **1.** [gen] volver a abrir - **2.** [court case] rever. <> *vi* - **1.** [gen] volver a abrir - **2.** [start again] volver a iniciarse - **3.** [wound] volver a abrirse.

reorganization [ˈriːˌɔːgənaɪˈzeɪʃn] *n* reorganización *f*.

reorganize, -ise [ˌriːˈɔːgənaɪz] <> *vt* reorganizar. <> *vi* reorganizarse.

rep [rep] *n abbr of* **representative**. *abbr of* **repertory**. *abbr of* **repertory company**.

Rep. US abbr of **Representative**. abbr of **Republican**.

repaid [ri:'peɪd] pt & pp ⊏⟶ **repay**.

repaint [ˌri:'peɪnt] vt repintar.

repair [rɪ'peəʳ] ◇ n reparación f, refacción f Amér; **in good/bad repair** en buen/mal estado; **it's beyond repair** no tiene arreglo. ◇ vt reparar, refaccionar Amér.

repair kit n caja de herramientas de una bicicleta.

repaper [ˌri:'peɪpəʳ] vt volver a empapelar.

reparations [ˌrepə'reɪʃnz] npl indemnizaciones fpl.

repartee [ˌrepɑ:'ti:] n intercambio m de réplicas ingeniosas.

repatriate [ˌri:'pætrɪeɪt] vt repatriar.

repay [ri:'peɪ] (pt & pp **repaid**) vt **- 1.** [money] devolver; [debt, person] pagar; **to repay sb sthg, to repay sthg to sb** devolver a alguien algo **- 2.** [thank] devolver el favor a.

repayment [ri:'peɪmənt] n **- 1.** [act of paying back] devolución f **- 2.** [sum] pago m.

repeal [rɪ'pi:l] ◇ n revocación f, abrogación f. ◇ vt revocar, abrogar.

repeat [rɪ'pi:t] ◇ vt **- 1.** [gen] repetir; **to repeat o.s.** repetirse **- 2.** [TV, radio programme] volver a emitir. ◇ n **- 1.** [recurrence] repetición f **- 2.** [of programme] reposición f.

repeated [rɪ'pi:tɪd] adj repetido(da).

repeatedly [rɪ'pi:tɪdlɪ] adv repetidamente.

repel [rɪ'pel] (pt & pp **-led**, cont **-ling**) vt repeler.

repellent [rɪ'pelənt] ◇ adj repelente. ◇ n espray m antiinsectos.

repent [rɪ'pent] ◇ vt arrepentirse de. ◇ vi: **to repent of** arrepentirse de.

repentance [rɪ'pentəns] n arrepentimiento m.

repentant [rɪ'pentənt] adj [person] arrepentido(da); [smile] de arrepentimiento.

repercussions [ˌri:pə'kʌʃnz] npl repercusiones fpl.

repertoire [ˈrepətwɑ:ʳ] n repertorio m.

repertory [ˈrepətrɪ] n repertorio m.

repertory company n compañía f de repertorio.

repetition [ˌrepɪ'tɪʃn] n repetición f.

repetitious [ˌrepɪ'tɪʃəs], **repetitive** [rɪ'petɪtɪv] adj repetitivo(va).

repetitive strain injury n (U) lesión f por movimiento repetitivo.

rephrase [ˌri:'freɪz] vt reformular.

replace [rɪ'pleɪs] vt **- 1.** [take the place of] sustituir **- 2.** [change for something else]: **to replace sthg (with)** cambiar algo (por) **- 3.** [change for somebody else]: **to replace sb (with)** sustituir a

alguien (por) **- 4.** [supply another]: **they replaced it** me dieron otro **- 5.** [put back] poner en su sitio.

replacement [rɪ'pleɪsmənt] n **- 1.** [act of substituting] sustitución f **- 2.** [something new]: **replacement (for)** sustituto m, -ta f (para) **- 3.** [somebody new]: **replacement (for)** sustituto m, -ta f OR suplente mf (de) **- 4.** [another one]: **they gave me a replacement** me dieron otro.

replacement part n pieza f de recambio.

replay ◇ n [ˈri:pleɪ] repetición f. ◇ vt [ˌri:'pleɪ] **- 1.** [match, game] volver a jugar **- 2.** [film, tape] volver a poner.

replenish [rɪ'plenɪʃ] vt: **to replenish sthg (with)** reaprovisionar OR reponer algo (de).

replete [rɪ'pli:t] adj fml repleto(ta).

replica [ˈreplɪkə] n réplica f.

replicate [ˈreplɪkeɪt] vt reproducir exactamente.

replication [ˌreplɪ'keɪʃn] n **- 1.** [process] reproducción f exacta **- 2.** [copy] réplica f.

reply [rɪ'plaɪ] ◇ n (pl **-ies**): **reply (to)** respuesta f (a); **in reply (to)** en respuesta (a). ◇ vt (pt & pp **-ied**) responder, contestar. ◇ vi (pt & pp **-ied**): **to reply (to sb/sthg)** responder (a alguien/algo).

reply coupon n cupón m de respuesta.

reply-paid adj con porte pagado.

report [rɪ'pɔ:t] ◇ n **- 1.** [gen] informe m, reporte m Amér C & Méx; PRESS & TV reportaje m; [short] información f **- 2.** UK SCH boletín m de evaluación, boletín m de calificaciones OR notas. ◇ vt **- 1.** [say, make known]: **to report that** informar que, reportar que Amér; **to report sthg (to)** informar de algo (a), reportar algo (a) Amér **- 2.** [losses] anunciar **- 3.** [complain about] denunciar; **to report sb (to sb for sthg)** denunciar a alguien (a alguien por algo), reportar a alguien (a alguien por algo) Amér. ◇ vi **- 1.** [give account]: **to report on** informar sobre **- 2.** [present oneself]: **to report to sb/for sthg** presentarse a alguien/para algo, reportarse a alguien/para algo Amér.

➤ **report back** vi: **to report back (to sb)** presentar uninforme (a alguien).

reportage [ˌrepɔ:'tɑ:ʒ] n (U) reportaje m.

report card n US boletín m de evaluación, boletín m de calificaciones OR notas.

reportedly [rɪ'pɔ:tɪdlɪ] adv según se afirma.

reported speech [rɪ'pɔ:tɪd-] n estilo m indirecto.

reporter [rɪ'pɔ:təʳ] n reportero m, -ra f.

repose [rɪ'pəʊz] n liter reposo m.

repository [rɪ'pɒzɪtrɪ] (pl **-ies**) n [store] depósito m, almacén m.

repossess [,ri:pə'zes] *vt* requisar la posesión de.

repossession [,ri:pə'zeʃn] *n* recuperación *f*.

repossession order *n* orden *f* de requisición.

reprehensible [,reprɪ'hensəbl] *adj fml* reprensible.

represent [,reprɪ'zent] *vt* **- 1.** [gen] representar; [person, country] representar a; **to be well** OR **strongly represented** estar bien representado(da) **- 2.** [describe]: **to represent sthg/sb as** describir algo/a alguien como.

representation [,reprɪzen'teɪʃn] *n* representación *f*.

➡ **representations** *npl fml*: **to make representations to** presentar una queja a.

representative [,reprɪ'zentətɪv] <> *adj*: **representative (of)** representativo(va) (de). <> *n* representante *mf*.

repress [rɪ'pres] *vt* reprimir.

repressed [rɪ'prest] *adj* reprimido(da).

repression [rɪ'preʃn] *n* represión *f*.

repressive [rɪ'presɪv] *adj* represivo(va).

reprieve [rɪ'pri:v] <> *n* **- 1.** [delay] tregua *f* **- 2.** [of death sentence] indulto *m*. <> *vt* [prisoner] indultar.

reprimand ['reprɪmɑːnd] <> *n* reprensión *f*. <> *vt* reprender.

reprint <> *n* ['ri:prɪnt] reimpresión *f*. <> *vt* [,ri:'prɪnt] reimprimir.

reprisal [rɪ'praɪzl] *n* represalia *f*.

reproach [rɪ'prəʊtʃ] <> *n* reproche *m*. <> *vt*: **to reproach sb (for** OR **with sthg)** reprochar a alguien (algo).

reproachful [rɪ'prəʊtʃfʊl] *adj* de reproche.

reprobate ['reprəbeɪt] *n hum* libertino *m*, -na *f*.

reproduce [,ri:prə'dju:s] <> *vt* reproducir. <> *vi* BIOL reproducirse.

reproduction [,ri:prə'dʌkʃn] *n* reproducción *f*.

reproductive [,ri:prə'dʌktɪv] *adj* reproductor(ra).

reprogram [,ri:'prəʊɡræm] (*pt* & *pp* **-ed** OR **-med**, *cont* **-ing**, *cont* **-ming**) *vt* volver a programar.

reproof [rɪ'pru:f] *n fml* **- 1.** [words of blame] reprobación *f* **- 2.** [disapproval] reproche *m*.

reproving [rɪ'pru:vɪŋ] *adj* de reprobación, reprobatorio(ria).

reptile ['reptaɪl] *n* reptil *m*.

Repub. US *abbr of* **Republican**.

republic [rɪ'pʌblɪk] *n* república *f*.

republican [rɪ'pʌblɪkən] <> *adj* republicano(na). <> *n* republicano *m*, -na *f*.

➡ **Republican** <> *adj* [in US, Northern Ireland] republicano(na); **the Republican Party** [in US] el partido republicano. <> *n* [in US, Northern Ireland] republicano *m*, -na *f*.

repudiate [rɪ'pju:dɪeɪt] *vt fml* [person, violence] repudiar; [accusation] rechazar.

repudiation [rɪ,pju:dɪ'eɪʃn] *n fml* [of person, violence] repulsa *f*; [of accusation] rechazo *m*.

repugnant [rɪ'pʌɡnənt] *adj* repugnante; **to be repugnant (to sb)** repugnar (a alguien).

repulse [rɪ'pʌls] *vt* rechazar.

repulsion [rɪ'pʌlʃn] *n* repulsión *f*.

repulsive [rɪ'pʌlsɪv] *adj* repulsivo(va).

reputable ['repjʊtəbl] *adj* de buena fama OR reputación.

reputation [,repjʊ'teɪʃn] *n* reputación *f*; **to have a reputation for sthg/for being sthg** tener fama de algo/de ser algo.

repute [rɪ'pju:t] *n fml*: **of good/ill repute** de buena/mala fama; **of repute** de reputación.

reputed [rɪ'pju:tɪd] *adj* supuesto(ta); **to be reputed to be/do sthg** tener fama de ser/hacer algo.

reputedly [rɪ'pju:tɪdlɪ] *adv* según se dice.

reqd *abbr of* **required**.

request [rɪ'kwest] <> *n*: **request (for)** petición *f* (de); **on request** a petición del interesado; **at sb's request** a petición de alguien. <> *vt* solicitar, pedir; **to request sb to do sthg** rogar a alguien que haga algo.

request stop *n* UK parada *f* discrecional.

requiem (mass) ['rekwɪəm-] *n* (misa *f* de) réquiem *m*.

require [rɪ'kwaɪər] *vt* **- 1.** [need] necesitar, requerir **- 2.** [demand] requerir; **to require sb to do sthg** exigir a alguien que haga algo.

required [rɪ'kwaɪəd] *adj* necesario(ria); **if required** si es necesario; **you are required to...** es obligatorio...

requirement [rɪ'kwaɪəmənt] *n* requisito *m*.

requisite ['rekwɪzɪt] *adj fml* preciso(sa).

requisition [,rekwɪ'zɪʃn] *vt* requisar.

reran [,ri:'ræn] *pt* ➪ **rerun**.

reread [,ri:'ri:d] (*pt* & *pp* **reread** [,ri:'red]) *vt* releer.

rerecord [,ri:rɪ'kɔ:d] *vt* volver a grabar.

reroute [,ri:'ru:t] *vt* desviar.

rerun <> *n* ['ri:,rʌn] **- 1.** [film, programme] reposición *f* **- 2.** [repeated situation] repetición *f*. <> *vt* [ri:'rʌn] (*pt* **-ran**, *pp* **-run**, *cont* **-ning**) **- 1.** [race] volver a correr **- 2.** [film, programme] reponer **- 3.** [tape] volver a poner.

resale price maintenance ['ri:seɪl-] *n* UK FIN mantenimiento *m* del precio de reventa.

resat [,ri:'sæt] *pt* & *pp* ➪ **resit**.

reschedule [*UK* ˌriːˈʃedjʊl, *US* ˌriːˈskedʒʊl] *vt* - **1.** [event] cambiar la fecha de - **2.** [debt] renegociar.

rescind [rɪˈsɪnd] *vt* LAW [contract] rescindir; [law] revocar.

rescue [ˈreskjuː] <> *n* rescate *m*; **to go** OR **come to sb's rescue** ir OR acudir al rescate de alguien. <> *vt*: **to rescue sb/sthg (from)** rescatar a alguien/algo (de).

rescue operation *n* operación *f* de rescate.

rescuer [ˈreskjʊər] *n* rescatador *m*, -ra *f*.

reseal [ˌriːˈsiːl] *vt* volver a cerrar.

resealable [ˌriːˈsiːləbl] *adj* que se puede volver a cerrar.

research [rɪˈsɜːtʃ] <> *n (U)*: **research (on** OR **into)** investigación *f* (de OR sobre); **research and development** investigación y desarrollo. <> *vt* investigar. <> *vi*: **to research (into)** hacer una investigación (sobre).

researcher [rɪˈsɜːtʃər] *n* investigador *m*, -ra *f*.

research work *n (U)* investigaciones *fpl*, trabajos *mpl* de investigación.

resell [ˌriːˈsel] (*pt & pp* **resold**) *vt* revender.

resemblance [rɪˈzembləns] *n* parecido *m*, semejanza *f*; **to bear a strong resemblance to** tener un gran parecido con.

resemble [rɪˈzembl] *vt* parecerse a.

resent [rɪˈzent] *vt*: **I resent it** me molesta; **to resent sb** tener celos de alguien.

resentful [rɪˈzentfʊl] *adj* [person] resentido(da); [look] de resentimiento.

resentfully [rɪˈzentfʊlɪ] *adv* con resentimiento.

resentment [rɪˈzentmənt] *n* resentimiento *m*.

reservation [ˌrezəˈveɪʃn] *n* - **1.** [booking] reserva *f* - **2.** [uncertainty]: **without reservation** sin reserva - **3.** *US* [for Native Americans] reserva *f*.
➤ **reservations** *npl* [doubts] reservas *fpl*.

reserve [rɪˈzɜːv] <> *n* - **1.** [gen] reserva *f*; **in reserve** en reserva - **2.** SPORT reserva *mf*, suplente *mf*. <> *vt* - **1.** [save, book] reservar - **2.** [retain]: **to reserve the right to do sthg** reservarse el derecho a hacer algo.

reserve bank *n banco de reserva federal estadounidense.*

reserve currency *n (U) divisas fpl de reserva.*

reserved [rɪˈzɜːvd] *adj* reservado(da).

reserve price *n UK* precio *m* mínimo.

reserve team *n UK* equipo *m* de reserva.

reservist [rɪˈzɜːvɪst] *n* reservista *mf*.

reservoir [ˈrezəvwɑːr] *n* - **1.** [lake] pantano *m*, embalse *m* - **2.** [large supply] cantera *f*.

reset [ˌriːˈset] (*pt & pp* **reset**, *cont* **-ting**) *vt* - **1.** [clock] poner en hora; [meter, controls, computer] reinicializar - **2.** [bone] (volver a) encajar.

resettle [ˌriːˈsetl] <> *vt* reasentar. <> *vi* reasentarse.

resettlement [ˌriːˈsetlmənt] *n* - **1.** [of land] repoblación *f*, nueva colonización *f* - **2.** [of people] reasentamiento *m*.

reshape [ˌriːˈʃeɪp] *vt* [policy, thinking] reformar, rehacer.

reshuffle [ˌriːˈʃʌfl] <> *n* remodelación *f*; **cabinet reshuffle** remodelación del gabinete. <> *vt* remodelar.

reside [rɪˈzaɪd] *vi fml* - **1.** [live] residir - **2.** [be found]: **to reside in** residir en.

residence [ˈrezɪdəns] *n* - **1.** *fml* [house] residencia *f* - **2.** [state of residing]: **to be in residence (at)** residir (a); **to take up residence** instalarse.

residence permit *n* permiso *m* de residencia.

resident [ˈrezɪdənt] <> *adj* - **1.** [settled, living] residente - **2.** [on-site, live-in] que vive en su lugar de trabajo. <> *n* residente *mf*.

residential [ˌrezɪˈdenʃl] *adj* [live-in] en régimen de internado.

residential area *n* zona *f* residencial.

residents' association *n* ≃ asociación *f* de vecinos.

residual [rɪˈzɪdjʊəl] *adj* residual.

residue [ˈrezɪdjuː] *n* residuo *m*.

resign [rɪˈzaɪn] <> *vt* - **1.** [give up] dimitir de, renunciar a - **2.** [accept calmly]: **to resign o.s. to sthg** resignarse a algo. <> *vi* [quit]: **to resign (from)** dimitir (de).

resignation [ˌrezɪgˈneɪʃn] *n* - **1.** [from job] dimisión *f* - **2.** [calm acceptance] resignación *f*.

resigned [rɪˈzaɪnd] *adj*: **resigned (to)** resignado(da) (a).

resilience [rɪˈzɪlɪəns] *n* capacidad *f* de recuperación.

resilient [rɪˈzɪlɪənt] *adj* [person] resistente, fuerte; [rubber] elástico(ca).

resin [ˈrezɪn] *n* resina *f*.

resist [rɪˈzɪst] *vt* - **1.** [refuse to give in to - temptation] resistir - **2.** [refuse to accept] resistir, oponerse a - **3.** [fight against] resistir a.

resistance [rɪˈzɪstəns] *n*: **resistance (to)** resistencia *f* (a).

resistant [rɪˈzɪstənt] *adj* - **1.** [opposed]: **to be resistant to sthg** resistirse a algo - **2.** [immune]: **resistant (to sthg)** resistente (a algo).

resistor [rɪˈzɪstər] *n* ELEC resistencia *f*.

resit *UK* <> *n* [ˈriːsɪt] (examen *m* de) repesca *f*. <> *vt* [ˌriːˈsɪt] (*pt & pp* **-sat**, *cont* **-ting**) volver a presentarse a.

resold [ˌriːˈsəʊld] *pt & pp* ▷ **resell**.

resolute [ˈrezəluːt] *adj* resuelto(ta), determinado(da).

resolutely ['rezəlu:tlı] *adv* con resolución, resueltamente.

resolution [,rezə'lu:ʃn] *n* - **1.** [gen] resolución *f*
- **2.** [vow, promise] propósito *m*.

resolve [rı'zɒlv] <> *n (U)* resolución *f.* <> *vt*
- **1.** [vow, promise]: **to resolve that** resolver
que; **to resolve to do sthg** resolver hacer algo
- **2.** [solve] resolver.

resonance ['rezənəns] *n* resonancia *f*.

resonant ['rezənənt] *adj* resonante.

resonate ['rezəneit] *vi* resonar.

resort [rı'zɔ:t] *n* - **1.** [for holidays] lugar *m* de vacaciones - **2.** [solution]: **as a** OR **in the last resort** como último recurso.
➤ **resort to** *vt insep* recurrir a.

resound [rı'zaund] *vi* - **1.** [noise] resonar, retumbar - **2.** [place]: **the room resounded with
laughter** la risa resonaba por la habitación.

resounding [rı'zaundıŋ] *adj* - **1.** [loud - noise,
knock] retumbante; [- crash] estruendoso(sa)
- **2.** [very great] clamoroso(sa).

resource [rı'sɔ:s] *n* recurso *m*.

resourceful [rı'sɔ:sful] *adj* [person] de recursos;
[solution] ingenioso(sa).

resourcefulness [rı'sɔ:sfulnıs] *n (U)* recursos *mpl*, inventiva *f*.

respect [rı'spekt] <> *n* - **1.** [gen]: **respect (for)**
respeto *m* (por); **with respect** con respeto
- **2.** [aspect] aspecto *m*; **in this respect** a este
respecto; **in that respect** en cuanto a eso.
<> *vt* [admire] respetar; **to respect sb for sthg**
respetar a alguien por algo.
➤ **respects** *npl*: **to pay one's respects (to)**
presentar uno sus respetos (a); **to pay one's
last respects (to)** rendir el último homenaje
(a).
➤ **with respect to** *prep* con respecto a.

respectability [rı,spektə'bılətı] *n* respetabili-
dad *f*.

respectable [rı'spektəbl] *adj* respetable.

respectably [rı'spektəblı] *adv* [correctly] de manera respetable.

respectful [rı'spektful] *adj* respetuoso(sa).

respectfully [rı'spektfulı] *adv* respetuosamen-
te.

respective [rı'spektıv] *adj* respectivo(va).

respectively [rı'spektıvlı] *adv* respectivamente.

respiration [,respə'reıʃn] *n* respiración *f*.

respirator ['respəreıtər] *n* MED respirador *m*.

respiratory [UK rı'spırətrı, US 'respərətɔ:rı] *adj*
respiratorio(ria).

respire [rı'spaıər] *vi* respirar.

respite ['respaıt] *n* - **1.** [lull] respiro *m* - **2.** [delay]
aplazamiento *m*.

resplendent [rı'splendənt] *adj* resplandeciente.

respond [rı'spɒnd] <> *vt* responder. <> *vi*: **to
respond (to)** responder (a); **to respond by
doing sthg** responder haciendo algo.

response [rı'spɒns] *n* respuesta *f*; **in response**
en respuesta.

responsibility [rı,spɒnsə'bılətı] (*pl* -**ies**) *n*: **responsibility (for)** responsabilidad *f* (de); **to
have a responsibility to sb** ser responsable
ante alguien; **to claim responsibility for sthg**
reivindicar algo.

responsible [rı'spɒnsəbl] *adj* - **1.** [gen] responsable; **responsible (for)** responsable (de)
- **2.** [answerable]: **responsible to sb** responsable ante alguien - **3.** [job, position] de responsabilidad.

responsibly [rı'spɒnsəblı] *adv* de manera responsable.

responsive [rı'spɒnsıv] *adj* - **1.** [quick to react]:
to be responsive responder muy bien
- **2.** [aware]: **responsive (to)** sensible OR per-
ceptivo(va) (a).

respray <> *n* ['ri:spreı]: **to give sthg a respray**
volver a pintar algo. <> *vt* [,ri:'spreı] volver a
pintar *(con pistola)*.

rest [rest] <> *n* - **1.** [remainder]: **the rest (of)** el
resto (de); **the rest of us** los demás - **2.** [relax-
ation, break] descanso *m*; **to have a rest**
descansar - **3.** [support - for feet] descanso *m*;
[- for head] respaldo *m*; [- for snooker cue] soporte *m*
▶▶ **to come to rest** pararse. <> *vt* - **1.** [relax -
eyes, feet] descansar - **2.** [support] apoyar,
descansar. <> *vi* - **1.** [relax, be still] descansar
- **2.** [depend]: **to rest on** OR **upon** depender
de - **3.** [duty, responsibility]: **to rest with sb** pesar sobre alguien - **4.** [be supported] apoyarse,
descansar - **5.** *liter* [eyes]: **to rest on** pararse OR
clavarse en
▶▶ **rest assured that...** tenga la seguridad de
que...

rest area *n* US & Australia área *f* de descanso *(en
la autopista)*.

restart <> *n* ['ri:stɑ:t] reanudación *f.* <> *vt*
[,ri:'stɑ:t] - **1.** [vehicle] (volver a) poner en marcha - **2.** [computer] reiniciar. <> *vi* [,ri:'stɑ:t]
- **1.** [play, film] empezar de nuevo - **2.** [vehicle]
(volver a) arrancar.

restate [,ri:'steıt] *vt* - **1.** [intentions, position]
reafirmar - **2.** [problem] replantear.

restaurant ['restərɒnt] *n* restaurante *m*.

restaurant car *n* UK coche *m* OR vagón *m* restaurante, coche *m* comedor.

rest cure *n* cura *f* de reposo.

rested ['restıd] *adj* descansado(da).

restful ['restful] *adj* tranquilo(la), apacible.

rest home *n* [for the elderly] asilo *m* de ancianos; [for the sick] casa *f* de reposo.

resting place ['restɪŋ-] *n* última morada *f*.

restitution [ˌrestɪ'tju:ʃn] *n* fml restitución *f*.

restive ['restɪv] *adj* intranquilo(la), inquieto(ta).

restless ['restlɪs] *adj* - **1.** [bored, dissatisfied] impaciente, desasosegado(da) - **2.** [fidgety] inquieto(ta), agitado(da) - **3.** [sleepless] agitado(da).

restlessly ['restlɪslɪ] *adv* con impaciencia, con desasosiego.

restock [ˌri:'stɒk] <> *vt* [shop, cupboard] reabastecer, reaprovisionar; [lake, river] repoblar. <> *vi* reponer las existencias.

restoration [ˌrestə'reɪʃn] *n* restauración *f*.

restorative [rɪ'stɒrətɪv] *adj* reconstituyente.

restore [rɪ'stɔ:r] *vt* - **1.** [reestablish] restablecer - **2.** [to a previous position or condition]: **to restore sb to sthg** restaurar a alguien en algo; **to restore sthg to sthg** volver a poner algo en algo - **3.** [renovate] restaurar - **4.** [give back] devolver.

restorer [rɪ'stɔ:rər] *n* - **1.** [person] restaurador *m*, -ra *f* - **2.** [substance]: **hair restorer** crecepelo *m*.

restrain [rɪ'streɪn] *vt* controlar; **to restrain o.s. from doing sthg** contenerse para no hacer algo.

restrained [rɪ'streɪnd] *adj* comedido(da).

restraint [rɪ'streɪnt] *n* - **1.** [rule, check] restricción *f*, limitación *f* - **2.** [control] control *m*.

restrict [rɪ'strɪkt] *vt* [limit] restringir, limitar; **to restrict sthg/sb to** restringir algo/a alguien a; **to restrict o.s. to sthg** limitarse a algo.

restricted [rɪ'strɪktɪd] *adj* - **1.** [limited, small] restringido(da), limitado(da); **restricted area** zona *f* de acceso restringido - **2.** [classified, not public] secreto(ta).

restriction [rɪ'strɪkʃn] *n* restricción *f*; **restrictions on** restricciones en OR de.

restrictive [rɪ'strɪktɪv] *adj* restrictivo(va).

restrictive practices *npl* prácticas *fpl* restrictivas.

rest room *n* US servicios *mpl*, aseos *mpl*.

restructure [ˌri:'strʌktʃər] *vt* reestructurar.

result [rɪ'zʌlt] <> *n* resultado *m*; **as a result** como resultado. <> *vi* - **1.** [cause]: **to result (in sthg)** tener como resultado (algo) - **2.** [be caused]: **to result (from)** resultar (de).

resultant [rɪ'zʌltənt] *adj* fml resultante.

resume [rɪ'zju:m] <> *vt* - **1.** [start again] reanudar - **2.** fml [return to] volver a. <> *vi* volver a empezar, continuar.

résumé ['rezju:meɪ] *n* - **1.** [summary] resumen *m* - **2.** US [of career, qualifications] currículum *m* (vitae).

resumption [rɪ'zʌmpʃn] *n* reanudación *f*.

resurface [ˌri:'sɜ:fɪs] <> *vt* pavimentar de nuevo. <> *vi* - **1.** [in water] volver a salir a la superficie - **2.** [reappear] reaparecer.

resurgence [rɪ'sɜ:dʒəns] *n* resurgimiento *m*.

resurrect [ˌrezə'rekt] *vt* resucitar.

resurrection [ˌrezə'rekʃn] *n* resurrección *f*.

➤ **Resurrection** *n*: **the Resurrection** la Resurrección.

resuscitate [rɪ'sʌsɪteɪt] *vt* resucitar, revivir.

resuscitation [rɪˌsʌsɪ'teɪʃn] *n* resucitación *f*.

retail ['ri:teɪl] <> *n* venta *f* al por menor OR al detalle. <> *vt* vender al por menor. <> *vi*: **to retail for** tener un precio de venta al público de. <> *adv* al por menor, al detalle.

retailer ['ri:teɪlər] *n* minorista *mf*, detallista *mf*.

retail outlet *n* punto *m* de venta.

retail price *n* precio *m* de venta al público.

retail price index *n* UK índice *m* de precios al consumo.

retain [rɪ'teɪn] *vt* retener.

retainer [rɪ'teɪnər] *n* - **1.** [fee] anticipo *m* - **2.** [servant] criado *m*, -da *f (con muchos años de servicio en una familia)*.

retaining wall [rɪ'teɪnɪŋ-] *n* muro *m* de contención.

retaliate [rɪ'tælɪeɪt] *vi* - **1.** [react] responder - **2.** [take reprisals] tomar represalias.

retaliation [rɪˌtælɪ'eɪʃn] *n* (U) represalias *fpl*.

retarded [rɪ'tɑ:dɪd] *adj* retrasado(da).

retch [retʃ] *vi* tener arcadas.

retention [rɪ'tenʃn] *n* retención *f*.

retentive [rɪ'tentɪv] *adj* retentivo(va).

rethink <> *n* ['ri:θɪŋk]: **to have a rethink** volver a pensar, reconsiderar. <> *vt* & *vi* [ˌri:'θɪŋk] (*pt* & *pp* **-thought** [-'θɔ:t]) volver a pensar, reconsiderar.

reticence ['retɪsəns] *n* reticencia *f*.

reticent ['retɪsənt] *adj* reservado(da).

retina ['retɪnə] (*pl* **-nas** OR **-nae** [-ni:]) *n* retina *f*.

retinue ['retɪnju:] *n* séquito *m*, comitiva *f*.

retire [rɪ'taɪər] *vi* - **1.** [from work] jubilarse - **2.** fml [to another place, to bed] retirarse.

retired [rɪ'taɪəd] *adj* jubilado(da).

retirement [rɪ'taɪəmənt] *n* [act] jubilación *f*; [time] retiro *m*.

retirement age *n* edad *f* de jubilación.

retirement pension *n* pensión *f* de jubilación.

retiring [rɪ'taɪərɪŋ] *adj* - **1.** [shy] retraído(da), tímido(da) - **2.** [about to retire from work] que está a punto de jubilarse.

retort [rɪ'tɔːt] ◇ *n* [sharp reply] réplica *f*. ◇ *vt*: **to retort (that)** replicar (que).

retouch [ˌriː'tʌtʃ] *vt* retocar.

retrace [rɪ'treɪs] *vt*: **to retrace one's steps** desandar lo andado.

retract [rɪ'trækt] ◇ *vt* - **1.** [withdraw, take back] retractarse de - **2.** [pull in - claws] meter, retraer. ◇ *vi* [subj: claws] meterse, retraerse; [subj: wheels] replegarse.

retractable [rɪ'træktəbl] *adj* [pencil] retráctil; [wheels] replegable.

retraction [rɪ'trækʃn] *n* [of statement] retractación *f*.

retrain [ˌriː'treɪn] ◇ *vt* reciclar. ◇ *vi* reciclarse.

retraining [ˌriː'treɪnɪŋ] *n* reciclaje *m*.

retread ['riːtred] *n* neumático *m* recauchutado.

retreat [rɪ'triːt] ◇ *n* - **1.** MIL: **retreat (from)** retirada *f* (de); **to beat a (hasty) retreat** marcharse a toda prisa - **2.** [backing down]: **retreat (from)** abandono *m* (de) - **3.** [peaceful place] refugio *m*. ◇ *vi* [move away]: **to retreat (from)** [gen] retirarse (de); [from a person] apartarse (de).

retrenchment [rɪ'trentʃmənt] *n fml* reducción *f* de gastos.

retrial [ˌriː'traɪəl] *n* nuevo juicio *m*.

retribution [ˌretrɪ'bjuːʃn] *n (U)* castigo *m* merecido.

retrieval [rɪ'triːvl] *n* [gen & COMPUT] recuperación *f*.

retrieve [rɪ'triːv] *vt* - **1.** [get back] recobrar - **2.** COMPUT recuperar - **3.** [rescue - situation] salvar.

retriever [rɪ'triːvəʳ] *n* perro *m* cobrador.

retro ['retrəʊ] *adj* retro.

retroactive [ˌretrəʊ'æktɪv] *adj fml* retroactivo(va).

retrograde ['retrəʊɡreɪd] *adj fml* [gen] retrógrado(da); [step] hacia atrás.

retrospect ['retrəspekt] *n*: **in retrospect** retrospectivamente, mirando hacia atrás.

retrospective [ˌretrə'spektɪv] ◇ *adj* - **1.** [gen] retrospectivo(va) - **2.** [law, pay rise] con efecto retroactivo. ◇ *n* exposición *f* retrospectiva.

retrospectively [ˌretrə'spektɪvlɪ] *adv* - **1.** [gen] retrospectivamente - **2.** [introduce law, pay rise] de forma retroactiva.

return [rɪ'tɜːn] ◇ *n* - **1.** *(U)* [arrival back] vuelta *f*, regreso *m*; **return to** vuelta a - **2.** [giving back, article given back] devolución *f* - **3.** [in tennis] resto *m* - **4.** *UK* [ticket] billete *m* de ida y vuelta - **5.** [profit] ganancia *f*, rendimiento *m*. ◇ *comp* [journey] de vuelta, de regreso. ◇ *vt* - **1.** [book, visit, compliment, call] devolver - **2.** [reciprocate] corresponder a - **3.** [replace] devolver a su sitio - **4.** LAW [verdict] pronunciar - **5.** POL [candidate] elegir. ◇ *vi*: **to return (from/to)** volver (de/a).

➤ **returns** *npl* COMM rendimiento *m*, réditos *mpl*

▸▸ **many happy returns (of the day)!** ¡feliz cumpleaños!

➤ **in return** *adv* a cambio.

➤ **in return for** *prep* a cambio de.

returnable [rɪ'tɜːnəbl] *adj* retornable.

returning officer [rɪ'tɜːnɪŋ-] *n UK* oficial encargado de organizar las elecciones al Parlamento en su distrito electoral y que anuncia oficialmente los resultados de éstas.

return (key) *n* COMPUT tecla *f* de retorno.

return match *n* partido *m* de vuelta.

return ticket *n UK* billete *m* de ida y vuelta *Esp*, boleto *m* de ida y vuelta *Amér*, boleto *m* redondo *Méx*.

reunification [ˌriːjuːnɪfɪ'keɪʃn] *n* reunificación *f*.

reunion [ˌriː'juːnjən] *n* reunión *f*.

Reunion [ˌriː'juːnjən] *n*: **Reunion (Island)** isla *f* Reunión.

reunite [ˌriːjuː'naɪt] *vt* [people]: **to be reunited with** volver a encontrarse con; [factions, parts] reunir.

reupholster [ˌriːʌp'həʊlstəʳ] *vt* tapizar de nuevo.

reusable [riː'juːzəbl] *adj* reutilizable.

reuse ◇ *n* [ˌriː'juːs] reutilización *f*. ◇ *vt* [ˌriː'juːz] reutilizar.

rev [rev] *inf* ◇ *n* (*abbr of* **revolution**) revolución *f* (motriz). ◇ *vt* (*pt* & *pp* **-ved**, *cont* **-ving**): **to rev sthg (up)** acelerar algo. ◇ *vi* (*pt* & *pp* **-ved**, *cont* **-ving**) [subj: person]: **to rev (up)** acelerar el motor.

Rev [rev] (*abbr of* **Reverend**) *n* R., Revdo.

revalue [ˌriː'væljuː] *vt* - **1.** [currency] revalorizar - **2.** [property] revaluar.

revamp [ˌriː'væmp] *vt inf* renovar.

rev counter *n* contador *m* de revoluciones.

Revd (*abbr of* **Reverend**) *n* R., Revdo.

reveal [rɪ'viːl] *vt* revelar.

revealing [rɪ'viːlɪŋ] *adj* - **1.** [comment, silence] revelador(ra) - **2.** [garment] atrevido(da).

reveille [*UK* rɪ'vælɪ, *US* 'revəlɪ] *n* toque *m* de diana.

revel ['revl] (*UK* **-led**, *cont* **-ling**) (*US* **-ed**, *cont* **-ing**) *vi*: **to revel in** deleitarse en.

revelation [ˌrevə'leɪʃn] *n* revelación *f*.

reveller *UK*, **reveler** *US* ['revələʳ] *n* juergista *mf*.

revelry ['revəlrɪ] *n (U)* juerga *f*.

revenge [rɪ'vendʒ] <> n venganza f; **to take revenge (on sb)** vengarse (de alguien). <> comp por venganza. <> vt vengar; **to revenge o.s. on sb/sthg** vengarse de alguien/en algo.

revenue ['revənjuː] n ingresos mpl.

reverberate [rɪ'vɜːbəreɪt] vi - **1.** [reecho] resonar - **2.** [have repercussions] repercutir.

reverberations [rɪ,vɜːbə'reɪʃnz] npl - **1.** [echoes] reverberaciones fpl - **2.** [repercussions] repercusiones fpl.

revere [rɪ'vɪəʳ] vt venerar, reverenciar.

reverence ['revərəns] n reverencia f.

Reverend ['revərənd] n reverendo m.

Reverend Mother n reverenda madre f.

reverent ['revərənt] adj reverente.

reverential [,revə'renʃl] adj reverencial.

reverie ['revərɪ] n ensueño m.

reversal [rɪ'vɜːsl] n - **1.** [turning around] cambio m total - **2.** [ill fortune] contratiempo m, revés m.

reverse [rɪ'vɜːs] <> adj inverso(sa). <> n - **1.** AUT: **reverse (gear)** marcha f atrás; **to be in reverse** tener puesta la marcha atrás; **to go into reverse** meter la marcha atrás - **2.** [opposite]: **the reverse** lo contrario - **3.** [opposite side, back]: **the reverse** [gen] el revés; [of coin] el reverso; [of piece of paper] el dorso. <> vt - **1.** AUT dar marcha atrás a - **2.** [change usual order] invertir - **3.** [change to opposite] cambiar completamente - **4.** UK TELEC: **to reverse the charges** llamar a cobro revertido. <> vi AUT dar marcha atrás.

reverse-charge call n UK llamada f a cobro revertido, llamada f por cobrar Chile & Méx.

reversible [rɪ'vɜːsəbl] adj reversible.

reversing light [rɪ'vɜːsɪŋ-] n UK luz f de marcha atrás.

reversion [rɪ'vɜːʃn] n vuelta f.

revert [rɪ'vɜːt] vi: **to revert to** volver a.

review [rɪ'vjuː] <> n - **1.** [examination] revisión f; **to come under review** ser revisado; **under review** bajo revisión - **2.** [critique] reseña f. <> vt - **1.** [reexamine] revisar - **2.** [consider] reconsiderar - **3.** [write an article on] reseñar - **4.** US [study again] repasar.

reviewer [rɪ'vjuːəʳ] n crítico m, -ca f, reseñador m, -ra f.

revile [rɪ'vaɪl] vt liter injuriar.

revise [rɪ'vaɪz] <> vt - **1.** [reconsider] revisar - **2.** [rewrite] modificar, corregir - **3.** UK [study] repasar. <> vi UK: **to revise (for sthg)** repasar (para algo).

revised [rɪ'vaɪzd] adj revisado(da).

revision [rɪ'vɪʒn] n - **1.** [alteration] corrección f, modificación f - **2.** UK [study] repaso m.

revisionist [rɪ'vɪʒnɪst] <> adj revisionista. <> n revisionista mf.

revisit [,riː'vɪzɪt] vt volver a visitar.

revitalize, -ise [,riː'vaɪtəlaɪz] vt revivificar.

revival [rɪ'vaɪvl] n - **1.** [of person] resucitación f; [of economy] reactivación f - **2.** [of play] reposición f.

revive [rɪ'vaɪv] <> vt - **1.** [person, plant, hopes] resucitar; [economy] reactivar - **2.** [tradition, memories] restablecer; [play] reponer. <> vi reponerse.

revoke [rɪ'vəʊk] vt fml revocar.

revolt [rɪ'vəʊlt] <> n rebelión f, sublevación f. <> vt repugnar. <> vi: **to revolt (against)** rebelarse OR sublevarse (contra).

revolting [rɪ'vəʊltɪŋ] adj repugnante, asqueroso(sa).

revolution [,revə'luːʃn] n revolución f; **revolution in sthg** revolución en OR de algo.

revolutionary [,revə'luːʃnərɪ] <> adj revolucionario(ria). <> n (pl -ies) revolucionario m, -ria f.

revolutionize, -ise [,revə'luːʃənaɪz] vt revolucionar.

revolve [rɪ'vɒlv] vi [go round] girar; **to revolve around** OR **round** lit & fig girar en torno a.

revolver [rɪ'vɒlvəʳ] n revólver m.

revolving [rɪ'vɒlvɪŋ] adj giratorio(ria).

revolving door n puerta f giratoria.

revue [rɪ'vjuː] n revista f (teatral).

revulsion [rɪ'vʌlʃn] n asco m, repugnancia f.

reward [rɪ'wɔːd] <> n recompensa f. <> vt: **to reward sb (for/with)** recompensar a alguien (por/con).

rewarding [rɪ'wɔːdɪŋ] adj gratificador(ra).

rewind [,riː'waɪnd] (pt & pp **rewound**) vt rebobinar.

rewire [,riː'waɪəʳ] vt cambiar la instalación eléctrica de.

reword [,riː'wɜːd] vt expresar de otra forma.

rework [,riː'wɜːk] vt rehacer.

rewound [,riː'waʊnd] pt & pp ▷ **rewind**.

rewritable [,riː'raɪtəbl] adj COMPUT regrabable.

rewrite [,riː'raɪt] (pt **rewrote** [,riː'rəʊt], pp **rewritten** [,riː'rɪtn]) vt volver a escribir, rehacer.

RFC (abbr of **Rugby Football Club**) n club de rugby.

RGN (abbr of **registered general nurse**) n UK enfermero diplomado m, enfermera diplomada f.

Rh (abbr of **rhesus**) Rh.

rhapsody ['ræpsədɪ] (pl -ies) n - **1.** MUS rapsodia f - **2.** [strong approval]: **to go into rhapsodies over** deshacerse en elogios sobre.

Rhesus ['riːsəs] *n*: **Rhesus positive/negative** Rhesus positivo/negativo.

rhetoric ['retərɪk] *n* retórica *f*.

rhetorical question [rɪ'tɒrɪkl-] *n* pregunta *f* retórica *(a la que no se espera contestación)*.

rheumatic [ruː'mætɪk] *adj* reumático(ca).

rheumatism ['ruːmətɪzm] *n* reumatismo *m*.

rheumatoid arthritis ['ruːmətɔɪd-] *n* reuma *m* articular.

Rhine [raɪn] *n*: **the Rhine** el Rin.

Rhineland ['raɪnlænd] *n* Renania.

rhinestone ['raɪnstəʊn] *n* diamante *m* falso.

rhino ['raɪnəʊ] *(pl* rhino *OR* -s), **rhinoceros** [raɪ'nɒsərəs] *(pl* rhinoceros *OR* -es) *n* rinoceronte *m*.

Rhode Island [rəʊd-] *n* Rhode Island.

rhododendron [ˌrəʊdə'dendrən] *n* rododendro *m*.

Rhône [rəʊn] *n*: **the (River) Rhône** el (río) Ródano.

rhubarb ['ruːbɑːb] *n* ruibarbo *m*.

rhyme [raɪm] <> *n* - **1.** [gen] rima *f* - **2.** [poem] poesía *f*, versos *mpl*; **in rhyme** en verso. <> *vi*: **to rhyme (with)** rimar (con).

rhyming slang ['raɪmɪŋ-] *n UK* rasgo del argot del este de Londres, que consiste en rimar dos palabras que dan el significado de una tercera.

rhythm ['rɪðm] *n* ritmo *m*.

rhythm and blues *n* rhythm *m* and blues.

rhythmic(al) ['rɪðmɪk(l)] *adj* rítmico(ca).

RI <> *n (abbr of* **religious instruction**) religión *f*. <> *abbr of* **Rhode Island**.

rib [rɪb] *n* - **1.** ANAT costilla *f* - **2.** [of umbrella] varilla *f*.

ribald ['rɪbəld] *adj* escabroso(sa), verde.

ribbed [rɪbd] *adj* [sweater] de canalé.

ribbon ['rɪbən] *n* cinta *f*.

rib cage *n* caja *f* torácica.

rice [raɪs] *n* arroz *m*.

rice field *n* arrozal *m*.

rice paper *n* papel *m* de arroz.

rice pudding *n* arroz *m* con leche.

rich [rɪtʃ] <> *adj* - **1.** [gen] rico(ca) - **2.** [full]: **to be rich in** abundar en - **3.** [fertile] fértil - **4.** [indigestible] pesado(da) - **5.** [vibrant - sound, voice] sonoro(ra); [- smell, colour] intenso(sa) - **6.** [sumptuous] suntuoso(sa). <> *npl*: **the rich** los ricos.

➤ **riches** *npl* - **1.** [natural resources] riquezas *fpl* - **2.** [wealth] riqueza *f*.

richly ['rɪtʃlɪ] *adv* - **1.** [rewarded] muy generosamente; **richly deserved** bien merecido - **2.** [plentifully] copiosamente, abundantemente - **3.** [sumptuously] suntuosamente.

richness ['rɪtʃnɪs] *n* - **1.** [gen] riqueza *f* - **2.** [fertility] fertilidad *f* - **3.** [indigestibility] pesadez *f* - **4.** [vibrancy - of sound, voice] sonoridad *f*; [- of smell, colour] intensidad *f* - **5.** [sumptuousness] suntuosidad *f*.

Richter scale ['rɪktər-] *n*: **the Richter scale** la escala Richter.

rickets ['rɪkɪts] *n (U)* raquitismo *m*.

rickety ['rɪkətɪ] *adj* tambaleante, desvencijado(da).

rickshaw ['rɪkʃɔː] *n* jinrikisha *f*.

ricochet ['rɪkəʃeɪ] <> *n* rebote *m*. <> *vi* *(pt & pp* -ed *OR* -ted, *cont* -ing, *cont* -ting): **to ricochet (off)** rebotar (de).

rid [rɪd] <> *adj*: **to be rid of** estar libre de. <> *vt* *(pt* rid *OR* -ded, *pp* rid, *cont* -ding): **to rid sthg/sb of** librar algo/a alguien de; **to rid o.s. of** librarse de; **to get rid of** deshacerse de.

riddance ['rɪdəns] *n inf*: **good riddance!** ¡adiós y viento fresco!

ridden ['rɪdn] *pp* ▷ ride.

riddle ['rɪdl] *n* - **1.** [verbal puzzle] acertijo *m*, adivinanza *f* - **2.** [mystery] enigma *m*.

riddled ['rɪdld] *adj*: **to be riddled with** [mistakes] estar plagado(da) de.

ride [raɪd] <> *n* - **1.** [gen] paseo *m*; **to go for a ride** [on horseback] darse un paseo a caballo; [on bike] darse un paseo en bicicleta; [in car] darse una vuelta en coche; **to take sb for a ride** *inf fig* embaucar a alguien - **2.** [journey] viaje *m*; **it's a short car ride away** está a poca distancia en coche - **3.** [at fair] atracción *f*. <> *vt* *(pt* rode, *pp* ridden) - **1.** [horse] montar a - **2.** [bicycle, motorbike] montar en; **he rode his bike to the station** fue a la estación en bici - **3.** *US* [bus, train] ir en; [elevator] subir/bajar en - **4.** [distance] recorrer. <> *vi (pt* rode, *pp* ridden) - **1.** [on horseback] montar a caballo; **she rode over to see me** vino a verme a caballo - **2.** [on bicycle] ir en bici; [on motorbike] ir en moto - **3.** [in car]: **we rode to London in a jeep** fuimos a Londres en jeep.

➤ **ride out** *vt sep* aguantar.

➤ **ride up** *vi* subirse.

rider ['raɪdər] *n* - **1.** [on horseback] jinete *m*, amazona *f* - **2.** [on bicycle] ciclista *mf*; [on motorbike] motorista *mf*.

ridge [rɪdʒ] *n* - **1.** [on mountain] cresta *f* - **2.** [on flat surface] rugosidad *f*.

ridicule ['rɪdɪkjuːl] <> *n (U)* burlas *fpl*. <> *vt* burlarse de.

ridiculous [rɪ'dɪkjʊləs] *adj* ridículo(la).

ridiculously [rɪ'dɪkjʊləslɪ] *adv* - **1.** [dress, act] de forma ridícula - **2.** [extremely] absurdamente.

riding ['raɪdɪŋ] <> *n* equitación *f*; **to go riding** ir a montar a caballo. <> *comp* de equitación.

riding crop *n* fusta *f*.

riding school *n* escuela *f* de equitación.

rife [raɪf] *adj* extendido(da); **to be rife with** estar lleno de.

riffraff ['rɪfræf] *n* gentuza *f*.

rifle ['raɪfl] <> *n* fusil *m*, rifle *m*. <> *vt* desvalijar.

◆ **rifle through** *vt insep* revolver.

rifle range *n* campo *m* de tiro.

rift [rɪft] *n* **- 1.** GEOL hendidura *f*, grieta *f* **- 2.** [quarrel] desavenencia *f* **- 3.** POL: **rift between/in** escisión *f* entre/en.

rig [rɪg] <> *n* **- 1.**: **(oil) rig** [onshore] torre *f* de perforación; [offshore] plataforma *f* petrolífera **- 2.** *US* [truck] camión *m*. <> *vt* (*pt & pp* **-ged**, *cont* **-ging**) [falsify] amañar, falsificar.

◆ **rig up** *vt sep* construir, armar.

rigging ['rɪgɪŋ] *n* cordaje *m*.

right [raɪt] <> *adj* **- 1.** [correct] correcto(ta); **have you got the right time?** ¿tienes la hora buena?; **to be right (about)** tener razón (respecto a); **he never gets anything right** nunca le salen las cosas bien; **that's right** sí; **to get sthg right** acertar en algo **- 2.** [morally correct, satisfactory, well] bien; **to be right to do sthg** hacer bien en hacer algo; **something isn't right with it** le pasa algo **- 3.** [appropriate] apropiado(da); **it's just right** es perfecto; **the right moment** el momento oportuno **- 4.** [uppermost]: **right side** cara *f* anterior OR de arriba **- 5.** [on right-hand side] derecho(cha) **- 6.** *UK inf* [complete - mess, idiot] auténtico(ca). <> *n* **- 1.** *(U)* [moral correctness] el bien; **to be in the right** tener razón **- 2.** [entitlement, claim] derecho *m*; **by rights** en justicia; **in one's own right** por propio derecho **- 3.** [right-hand side] derecha *f*; **on the right** a la derecha. <> *adv* **- 1.** [correctly] bien, correctamente **- 2.** [to right-hand side] a la derecha **- 3.** [emphatic use]: **right here** aquí mismo; **right at the top** arriba del todo; **right in the middle** justo en el medio; **she crashed right into the tree** chocó de frente contra el árbol **- 4.** [completely] completamente **- 5.** [immediately]: **I'll be right back** ahora mismo vuelvo; **right before/after (sthg)** justo antes/después (de algo); **right now** ahora mismo, ahorita *Amér C & Méx*; **right away** en seguida, luego *Amér*. <> *vt* **- 1.** [correct] corregir, rectificar **- 2.** [make upright] enderezar. <> *excl* ¡bien!

◆ **Right** *n* POL: **the Right** la derecha.

right angle *n* ángulo *m* recto; **at right angles (to)** en ángulo recto (con).

righteous ['raɪtʃəs] *adj* [anger] justo(ta); [person] honrado(da).

righteousness ['raɪtʃəsnɪs] *n* honradez *f*, rectitud *f*.

rightful ['raɪtful] *adj* justo(ta), legítimo(ma).

rightfully ['raɪtfulɪ] *adv* legítimamente, justamente.

right-hand *adj* derecho(cha); **the right-hand side** el lado derecho, la derecha.

right-hand drive *n* vehículo *f* con el volante a la derecha.

right-handed [-'hændɪd] *adj* diestro(tra).

right-hand man *n* brazo *m* derecho.

rightly ['raɪtlɪ] *adv* **- 1.** [correctly] correctamente **- 2.** [appropriately] debidamente, bien **- 3.** [morally] justamente, con razón.

right-minded [-'maɪndɪd] *adj* honrado(da).

righto ['raɪtəu] *excl inf* ¡vale!

right of way *n* **- 1.** AUT prioridad *f* **- 2.** [access] derecho *m* de paso.

right-on *adj inf* progre.

rights issue *n* emisión *f* de derechos de suscripción.

right wing *n*: **the right wing** la derecha.

◆ **right-wing** *adj* de derechas, derechista.

right-winger *n* derechista *mf*.

rigid ['rɪdʒɪd] *adj* **- 1.** [stiff] rígido(da) **- 2.** [harsh, unbending] inflexible.

rigidity [rɪ'dʒɪdətɪ] *n* **- 1.** [stiffness] rigidez *f* **- 2.** [harshness] inflexibilidad *f*.

rigidly ['rɪdʒɪdlɪ] *adv* **- 1.** [without moving] rígidamente **- 2.** [inflexibly] inflexiblemente.

rigmarole ['rɪgmərəul] *n inf pej* **- 1.** [process] ritual *m* **- 2.** [story] galimatías *m inv*.

rigor *US* = rigour.

rigor mortis [-'mɔːtɪs] *n* rigor *m* mortis.

rigorous ['rɪgərəs] *adj* riguroso(sa).

rigorously ['rɪgərəslɪ] *adv* rigurosamente.

rigour *UK*, **rigor** *US* ['rɪgər] *n* [firmness] rigor *m*.

◆ **rigours** *npl* [severe conditions] dureza *f*, rigor *m*.

rig-out *n UK inf* atuendo *m*.

rile [raɪl] *vt* irritar, sacar de quicio.

rim [rɪm] *n* **- 1.** [of container] borde *m* **- 2.** [of spectacles] montura *f*.

rind [raɪnd] *n* [of bacon, cheese] corteza *f*; [of orange, lemon] cáscara *f*.

ring [rɪŋ] <> *n* **- 1.** [telephone call]: **to give sb a ring** llamar a alguien (por teléfono) **- 2.** [sound of doorbell] timbrazo *m* **- 3.** [quality]: **it has a familiar ring** me suena (familiar) **- 4.** [on finger, around planet] anillo *m* **- 5.** [metal hoop] aro *m*; [for curtains, drinks can] anilla *f* **- 6.** [circle - of trees] círculo *m*; [- of people] corro *m* **- 7.** [for boxing] cuadrilátero *m*; [at circus] pista *f* **- 8.** [illegal group] red *f*. <> *vt* **- 1.** (*pt* **rang**, *pp* **rung**) *UK* [phone] llamar por teléfono, telefonear **- 2.** (*pt* **rang**, *pp* **rung**) [bell] tocar **- 3.** (*pt & pp* **ringed**) [draw a circle round] señalar con un círculo **- 4.** (*pt* **rang**, *pp* **rung**) [surround] cercar, rodear; **to be ringed with** estar rodeado de. ⬦ *vi* (*pt* **rang**, *pp* **rung**) **- 1.** *UK* [phone] llamar por teléfono, telefonear **- 2.** [bell] sonar **- 3.** [to attract attention]: **to ring (for)** llamar (para) **- 4.** [resound]: **to ring with** resonar con

▸▸ **to ring true** sonar a ser cierto.

◂ **ring back** *vt sep* & *vi* *UK* llamar más tarde.

◂ **ring off** *vi* *UK* colgar.

◂ **ring out** *vi* **- 1.** [sound] sonar **- 2.** *UK* TELEC llamar.

◂ **ring up** *vt sep* *UK* [telec] llamar (por teléfono).

ring binder *n* carpeta *f* de anillas.

ringer ['rɪŋər] *n*: **to be a dead ringer for sb** ser el vivo retrato de alguien.

ring finger *n* (dedo *m*) anular *m*.

ringing ['rɪŋɪŋ] ⬦ *adj* resonante, sonoro(ra). ⬦ *n* [of bell] repique *m*, tañido *m*; [in ears] zumbido *m*.

ringing tone *n* tono *m* de llamada.

ringleader ['rɪŋ,li:dər] *n* cabecilla *mf*.

ringlet ['rɪŋlɪt] *n* rizo *m*, tirabuzón *m*.

ringmaster ['rɪŋ,mɑ:stər] *n* director *m* de circo, jefe *m* de pista.

ring-pull *n* anilla *f*.

ring road *n* *UK* carretera *f* de circunvalación.

ringside ['rɪŋsaɪd] ⬦ *n*: **the ringside** *espacio inmediato al cuadrilátero o a la pista de circo.* ⬦ *comp* de primera fila.

ring tone *n* [for mobile phone] melodía *f*.

ringway ['rɪŋweɪ] *n* *UK* carretera *f* de circunvalación.

ringworm ['rɪŋwɜ:m] *n* tiña *f*.

rink [rɪŋk] *n* pista *f*.

rinse [rɪns] ⬦ *n* [of dishes, vegetables] enjuague *m*; [of clothes] aclarado *m*. ⬦ *vt* **- 1.** [dishes, vegetables] enjuagar; [clothes] aclarar **- 2.** [wash out]: **to rinse one's mouth out** enjuagarse la boca.

riot ['raɪət] ⬦ *n* disturbio *m*; **to run riot** desbocarse. ⬦ *vi* amotinarse.

rioter ['raɪətər] *n* amotinado *m*, -da *f*.

rioting ['raɪətɪŋ] *n* (*U*) disturbios *mpl*.

riotous ['raɪətəs] *adj* desenfrenado(da).

riot police *npl* brigada *f* antidisturbios.

riot shield *n* escudo *m* antidisturbios.

rip [rɪp] ⬦ *n* rasgón *m*. ⬦ *vt* (*pt* & *pp* **-ped**, *cont* **-ping**) **- 1.** [tear] rasgar, desgarrar **- 2.** [remove violently] quitar de un tirón. ⬦ *vi* (*pt* & *pp* **-ped**, *cont* **-ping**) rasgarse, romperse.

◂ **rip off** *vt sep* *inf* **- 1.** [person] clavar **- 2.** [product, idea] copiar.

◂ **rip up** *vt sep* hacer pedazos.

RIP (*abbr of* **rest in peace**) RIP.

ripcord ['rɪpkɔ:d] *n* cable *m* de apertura manual.

ripe [raɪp] *adj* maduro(ra); **to be ripe (for sthg)** estar listo (para algo).

ripen ['raɪpn] *vt* & *vi* madurar.

ripeness ['raɪpnɪs] *n* madurez *f*.

rip-off *n* *inf* estafa *f*.

ripple ['rɪpl] ⬦ *n* **- 1.** [in water] onda *f*, rizo *m* **- 2.** [of laughter, applause] murmullo *m*. ⬦ *vt* rizar.

rip-roaring *adj* *inf* [party] bullicioso(sa); [success] apoteósico(ca).

rise ⬦ *n* **- 1.** [increase, slope] subida *f* **- 2.** *UK* [increase in salary] aumento *m* **- 3.** [to fame, power, of practice] ascenso *m*

▸▸ **to give rise to sthg** dar origen a algo. ⬦ *vi* [raɪz] (*pt* **rose**, *pp* **risen** ['rɪzn]) **- 1.** [gen] elevarse **- 2.** [price, wage, temperature] subir **- 3.** [sun, moon] salir **- 4.** [stand up, get out of bed] levantarse **- 5.** [street, ground] subir **- 6.** [respond]: **to rise to** reaccionar ante; **to rise to the challenge** estar a la altura de las circunstancias **- 7.** [rebel] sublevarse **- 8.** [move up in status] ascender; **to rise to power/fame** ascender al poder/a la gloria.

◂ **rise above** *vt insep* **- 1.** [handicap, difficulty] superar **- 2.** [jealousy, resentment] estar por encima de.

riser ['raɪzər] *n*: **early riser** madrugador *m*, -ra *f*; **late riser** persona que se levanta tarde.

risible ['rɪzəbl] *adj* *fml* risible.

rising ['raɪzɪŋ] ⬦ *adj* **- 1.** [sloping upwards] ascendente **- 2.** [number, rate] creciente; [temperature, prices] en aumento **- 3.** [increasingly successful] en alza. ⬦ *n* rebelión *f*.

rising damp *n* humedad *f*.

risk [rɪsk] ⬦ *n* [gen] riesgo *m*; [danger] peligro *m*; **a health risk** un peligro para la salud; **to run the risk of sthg/of doing sthg** correr el riesgo de algo/de hacer algo; **to take a risk** arriesgarse; **at your own risk** bajo tu cuenta y riesgo; **at risk** en peligro; **at the risk of** a riesgo de. ⬦ *vt* **- 1.** [put in danger] arriesgar **- 2.** [take the chance of]: **to risk doing sthg** correr el riesgo de hacer algo.

risk capital *n* capital *m* de riesgo.

risk-taking *n* toma *f* de riesgos.

risky ['rɪskɪ] (*comp* **-ier**, *superl* **-iest**) *adj* peligroso(sa), arriesgado(da).

risotto [rɪ'zɒtəʊ] (*pl* **-s**) *n* risotto *m* (*arroz guisado con pollo o verduras etc*).

risqué ['ri:skeɪ] *adj* subido(da) de tono.

rissole ['rɪsəʊl] *n* *UK* especie de albóndiga de carne o verduras.

rite [raɪt] *n* rito *m*.

ritual ['rɪtʃʊəl] ⬦ *adj* ritual. ⬦ *n* ritual *m*.

rival ['raɪvl] ◇ *adj* rival. ◇ *n* rival *mf*. ◇ *vt* (*UK* -led, *cont* -ling, *US* -ed, *cont* -ing) rivalizar con.

rivalry ['raɪvlrɪ] *n* rivalidad *f*.

river ['rɪvəʳ] *n* río *m*.

river bank *n* orilla *f* OR margen *f* del río.

riverbed ['rɪvəbed] *n* cauce *m* OR lecho *m* del río.

riverside ['rɪvəsaɪd] *n*: **the riverside** la ribera OR orilla del río.

rivet ['rɪvɪt] ◇ *n* remache *m*. ◇ *vt* - **1.** [fasten] remachar - **2.** *fig* [fascinate]: **to be riveted by sthg** estar fascinado(da) con algo.

riveting ['rɪvɪtɪŋ] *adj* fascinante.

Riviera [,rɪvɪ'eərə] *n*: **the French Riviera** la Riviera francesa; **the Italian Riviera** la Riviera italiana.

RN *n abbr of* **Royal Navy**. *abbr of* **registered nurse**.

RNA (*abbr of* **ribonucleic acid**) *n* ARN *m*.

RNLI (*abbr of* **Royal National Lifeboat Institution**) *n organización de voluntarios que ofrece un servicio de rescate marítimo en Gran Bretaña e Irlanda.*

roach [rəʊtʃ] *n US* [cockroach] cucaracha *f*.

road [rəʊd] *n* [major] carretera *f*; [street] calle *f*; [path, minor thoroughfare] camino *m*; **to be on the road to recovery** estar en vías de recuperación; **on the road** [car] en circulación; [person] viajando; [rock band] de gira.

road accident *n* accidente *m* de carretera.

road atlas *n* guía *f* de carreteras.

roadblock ['rəʊdblɒk] *n* control *m*.

road-fund licence *n UK* ≃ impuesto *m* de circulación.

road hog *n inf pej* conductor rápido y negligente.

roadholding ['rəʊd,həʊldɪŋ] *n* agarre *m*.

roadie ['rəʊdɪ] *n inf* encargado del transporte y montaje de un equipo musical en gira.

road map *n* mapa *m* de carreteras.

road rage *n* violencia *f* en carretera.

road roller *n* apisonadora *f*.

road safety *n* seguridad *f* en carretera.

road sense *n* buen instinto *m* en la carretera.

roadshow ['rəʊdʃəʊ] *n programa radiofónico transmitido en directo desde un lugar de veraneo por un disc-jockey en gira.*

roadside ['rəʊdsaɪd] ◇ *n*: **the roadside** el borde de la carretera. ◇ *comp* al borde de la carretera.

road sign *n* señal *f* de tráfico.

roadsweeper ['rəʊd,swiːpəʳ] *n* [vehicle] camión *m* limpiacarreteras.

road tax *n* impuesto *m* de circulación.

road test *n* prueba *f* en carretera.

➤ **road-test** *vt* probar en carretera.

road transport *n* transporte *m* por carretera.

roadtrip ['rəʊdtrɪp] *n US* viaje *m* hecho en automóvil.

roadway ['rəʊdweɪ] *n* calzada *f*.

road works *npl* obras *fpl*.

roadworthy ['rəʊd,wɜːðɪ] *adj* apto(ta) para circular.

roam [rəʊm] ◇ *vt* vagar por. ◇ *vi* vagar.

roar [rɔːʳ] ◇ *vi* [make a loud noise] rugir; **to roar with laughter** reírse a carcajadas. ◇ *vt* rugir, decir a voces. ◇ *n* - **1.** [of traffic] fragor *m*, estruendo *m* - **2.** [of lion, person] rugido *m*.

roaring ['rɔːrɪŋ] *adj* - **1.** [loud] clamoroso(sa), fragoroso(sa) - **2.** [fire] muy vivo - **3.** [as emphasis]: **a roaring success** un éxito clamoroso; **to do a roaring trade in sthg** vender algo como rosquillas.

roast [rəʊst] ◇ *adj* asado(da). ◇ *n* asado *m*. ◇ *vt* - **1.** [potatoes, meat] asar - **2.** [nuts, coffee beans] tostar.

roast beef *n* rosbif *m*.

roasting ['rəʊstɪŋ] *inf* ◇ *adj* achicharrante. ◇ *adv*: **it's roasting hot** hace un calor que achicharra.

roasting tin *n* bandeja *f* de asar.

rob [rɒb] (*pt & pp* -bed, *cont* -bing) *vt* robar; [bank] atracar; **to rob sb of sthg** *lit & fig* robar a alguien algo.

robber ['rɒbəʳ] *n* ladrón *m*, -ona *f*; [of bank] atracador *m*, -ra *f*.

robbery ['rɒbərɪ] (*pl* -ies) *n* robo *m*; [of bank] atraco *m*.

robe [rəʊb] *n* - **1.** [towelling] albornoz *m* - **2.** [of student] toga *f* - **3.** [of priest] sotana *f* - **4.** *US* [dressing gown] bata *f*.

robin ['rɒbɪn] *n* petirrojo *m*.

robot ['rəʊbɒt] *n* robot *m*.

robotics [rəʊ'bɒtɪks] *n (U)* robótica *f*.

robust [rəʊ'bʌst] *adj* robusto(ta), fuerte.

robustly [rəʊ'bʌstlɪ] *adv* robustamente, fuertemente.

rock [rɒk] ◇ *n* - **1.** *(U)* [substance, boulder] roca *f* - **2.** [stone] piedra *f* - **3.** [crag] peñasco *m* - **4.** [music] rock *m* - **5.** *UK* [sweet] palo *m* de caramelo. ◇ *comp* [concert, group, singer] de rock. ◇ *vt* - **1.** [cause to move] mecer, balancear - **2.** [shock] sacudir. ◇ *vi* mecerse, balancearse.

➤ **Rock** *n inf* [Gibraltar]: **the Rock** el Peñón.

➤ **on the rocks** *adv* - **1.** [drink] con hielo - **2.** [marriage, relationship] que va mal.

rock and roll, rock'n'roll *n* rock and roll *m*.

rock bottom n: to hit rock bottom tocar fondo.

➤ **rock-bottom** adj: rock-bottom prices precios muy bajos.

rock cake n UK bizcocho con frutos secos.

rock climber n escalador m, -ra f (de rocas).

rock-climbing n escalada f (de rocas).

rock dash n US enguijarrado m.

rocker ['rɒkǝr] n [chair] mecedora f; he's off his rocker inf le falta un tornillo.

rockery ['rɒkǝri] (pl -ies) n jardín m de rocas.

rocket ['rɒkɪt] <> n - 1. [vehicle, weapon, firework] cohete m - 2. [plant] roqueta f. <> vi subir rápidamente.

rocket launcher [-,lɔːntʃǝr] n lanzacohetes m inv.

rock face n pared f de roca.

rockfall ['rɒkfɔːl] n deslizamiento m de montaña.

rock-hard adj duro(ra) como una piedra.

Rockies ['rɒkɪz] npl: the Rockies las Rocosas.

rocking chair ['rɒkɪŋ-] n mecedora f.

rocking horse ['rɒkɪŋ-] n caballo m de balancín.

rock music n música f rock.

rock'n'roll [,rɒkǝn'rǝʊl] = rock and roll.

rock pool n charca f entre las rocas en la playa.

rock salt n sal f gema.

rocky ['rɒkɪ] (comp -ier, superl -iest) adj - 1. [full of rocks] rocoso(sa) - 2. [unsteady] inestable.

Rocky Mountains npl: the Rocky Mountains las montañas Rocosas.

rococo [rǝ'kǝʊkǝʊ] adj rococó.

rod [rɒd] n [wooden] vara f; [metal] barra f; [for fishing] caña f.

rode [rǝʊd] pt ▷ ride.

rodent ['rǝʊdǝnt] n roedor m.

rodeo ['rǝʊdɪǝʊ] (pl -s) n rodeo m.

roe [rǝʊ] n hueva f; hard roe hueva f; soft roe lecha f.

roe deer n corzo m.

rogue [rǝʊg] <> adj - 1. [animal] solitario y peligroso (solitaria y peligrosa) - 2. fig [person] rebelde. <> n - 1. [likeable rascal] picaruelo m, -la f - 2. dated [dishonest person] bellaco m, -ca f.

roguish ['rǝʊgɪʃ] adj picaruelo(la), travieso(sa).

role [rǝʊl] n fig & THEAT papel m; to play an important role in sthg fig desempeñar un papel importante en algo.

role model n modelo m a seguir.

roll [rǝʊl] <> n - 1. [gen] rollo m; [of paper, banknotes] fajo m; [of cloth] pieza f - 2. [of bread] panecillo m - 3. [list] lista f; [payroll] nómina f

- 4. [of drums] redoble m; [of thunder] retumbo m. <> vt - 1. [turn over] hacer rodar; to roll one's eyes poner los ojos en blanco - 2. [roll up] enrollar; rolled into one todo en uno - 3. [cigarette] liar. <> vi - 1. [ball, barrel] rodar - 2. [vehicle] ir, avanzar - 3. [ship] balancearse - 4. [thunder] retumbar; [drum] redoblar.

➤ **roll about, roll around** vi: to roll about OR around (on) rodar (por).

➤ **roll back** vt sep US [prices] bajar.

➤ **roll in** vi inf llegar a raudales.

➤ **roll over** vi darse la vuelta.

➤ **roll up** <> vt sep - 1. [make into roll] enrollar - 2. [sleeves] remangarse. <> vi - 1. [vehicle] llegar - 2. inf [person] presentarse, aparecer.

roll call n: to take a roll call pasar lista.

rolled gold [rǝʊld-] n oro m laminado.

roller ['rǝʊlǝr] n - 1. [cylinder] rodillo m - 2. [curler] rulo m.

Rollerblades® ['rǝʊlǝ,bleɪdz] npl patines mpl en línea.

rollerblade ['rǝʊlǝbleɪd] vi patinar (con patines en línea).

rollerblading ['rǝʊlǝ,bleɪdɪŋ] n patinaje m (con patines en línea); to go rollerblading ir a patinar (con patines en línea).

roller blind n persiana f enrollable.

roller coaster n montaña f rusa.

roller skate n patín m de ruedas.

➤ **roller-skate** vi ir en patines.

rolling ['rǝʊlɪŋ] adj [undulating] ondulante

➤➤ to be rolling in it inf nadar en la abundancia.

rolling mill n taller m de laminación.

rolling pin n rodillo m (de cocina).

rolling stock n material m rodante.

rollneck ['rǝʊlnek] adj de cuello de cisne.

roll of honour n lista f de honor.

roll-on adj [deodorant etc] de bola.

roll-on roll-off adj UK de carga OR transbordo horizontal.

ROM [rɒm] (abbr of read only memory) n ROM f.

romaine lettuce [rǝʊ'meɪn-] n US lechuga f (de hoja larga).

Roman ['rǝʊmǝn] <> adj romano(na). <> n romano m, -na f.

Roman candle n tipo de fuego artificial.

Roman Catholic <> adj católico (romano)(católica (romana)). <> n católico (romano) m, católica (romana) f.

romance [rǝʊ'mæns] n - 1. [romantic quality] lo romántico - 2. [love affair] amorío m - 3. [in fiction - modern] novela f romántica. <> adj: Romance Languages lenguas fpl romance.

Romanesque [,rǝʊmǝ'nesk] adj románico(ca).

Romania, Rumania [ru:'meɪnjə] *n* Rumanía.

Romanian, Rumanian [ru:'meɪnjən] <> *adj* rumano(na). <> *n* - **1.** [person] rumano *m*, -na *f* - **2.** [language] rumano *m*.

Roman numerals *npl* números *mpl* romanos.

romantic [rəʊ'mæntɪk] *adj* romántico(ca).

romanticism [rəʊ'mæntɪsɪzm] *n* romanticismo *m*.

romanticize, -ise [rəʊ'mæntɪsaɪz] <> *vt* poner una nota romántica en. <> *vi* soñar despierto, fantasear.

Romany ['rəʊmənɪ] <> *adj* gitano(na), romaní. <> *n* (*pl* -ies) - **1.** [person] romaní *mf*, gitano *m*, -na *f* - **2.** [language - gen] lengua *f* gitana; [- in Spain] caló *m*.

romp [rɒmp] <> *n* retozo *m*, jugueteo *m*. <> *vi* retozar, juguetear.

rompers ['rɒmpəz] *npl* pelele *m*.

romper suit ['rɒmpə-] *n UK* = **rompers.**

roof [ru:f] *n* - **1.** [of building] tejado *m*; [of vehicle] techo *m*; **under the same roof** bajo el mismo techo; **under one's roof** en la casa de uno; **to have a roof over one's head** tener cobijo; **to go through** OR **hit the roof** [person] subirse por las paredes - **2.** [of mouth] paladar *m*.

roof garden *n* azotea o terraza con flores y plantas.

roofing ['ru:fɪŋ] *n* materiales *mpl* para techar, techumbre *f*.

roof rack *n* baca *f*, portaequipajes *m inv*, parrilla *f Amér.*

rooftop ['ru:ftɒp] *n* tejado *m*.

rook [rʊk] *n* - **1.** [bird] grajo *m* - **2.** [chess piece] torre *f*.

rookie ['rʊkɪ] *n* - **1.** *US inf* [novice] novato *m*, -ta *f* - **2.** *US inf* [military recruit] novato *m*, -ta *f*.

room [ru:m, rʊm] <> *n* - **1.** [in house, building] habitación *f* - **2.** [for conferences etc] sala *f* - **3.** [bedroom] habitación *f*, cuarto *m*, ambiente *m Andes & R Plata* - **4.** (*U*) [space] sitio *m*, espacio *m* - **5.** [opportunity, possibility]: **room for improvement** posibilidad de mejora; **room to** OR **for manoeuvre** espacio para maniobrar. <> *vi sep US*: **room with** compartir alojamiento con.

rooming house ['ru:mɪŋ-] *n US* casa *f* de huéspedes, pensión *f*.

roommate ['ru:meɪt] *n* compañero *m*, -ra *f* de habitación.

room service *n* servicio *m* de habitación.

room temperature *n* temperatura *f* ambiente.

roomy ['ru:mɪ] (*comp* -**ier**, *superl* -**iest**) *adj* espacioso(sa), amplio(plia).

roost [ru:st] <> *n* percha *f*, palo *m*; **to rule the roost** llevar el cotarro. <> *vi* dormir (en una percha).

rooster ['ru:stə-] *n* gallo *m*.

root [ru:t] <> *adj* [fundamental] de raíz. <> *n* lit & fig raíz *f*; **to take root** lit & fig arraigar; **to put down roots** [person] echar raíces, radicarse. <> *vi* [pig etc] hozar; [person] hurgar, escarbar.

➡ **roots** *npl* [origins] raíces *fpl.*

➡ **root for** *vt insep US inf* apoyar a.

➡ **root out** *vt sep* [eradicate] desarraigar, arrancar de raíz.

root beer *n US cerveza sin alcohol hecha de raíces.*

root crop *n* tubérculos *mpl.*

rooted ['ru:tɪd] *adj*: **to be rooted to the spot** quedar inmóvil.

rootless ['ru:tlɪs] *adj* desarraigado(da).

root vegetable *n* tubérculo *m*.

rope [rəʊp] <> *n* [thin] cuerda *f*; [thick] cabuya *f Amér C, Col & Ven*, soga *f*; NAUT maroma *f*, cable *m*; **to know the ropes** saber de qué va el asunto; **to show sb the ropes** poner a alguien al tanto. <> *vt* atar con cuerda.

➡ **rope in** *vt sep inf* arrastrar OR enganchar a; **to rope sb in to do sthg** liar a alguien para hacer algo.

➡ **rope off** *vt sep* acordonar.

rop(e)y ['rəʊpɪ] (*comp* -**ier**, *superl* -**iest**) *adj UK inf* - **1.** [poor-quality] malo(la) - **2.** [unwell] malucho(cha).

rosary ['rəʊzərɪ] (*pl* -ies) *n* rosario *m*.

rose [rəʊz] <> *pt* ▷ **rise.** <> *adj* [pink] rosa, color de rosa. <> *n* [flower] rosa *f*.

rosé ['rəʊzeɪ] *n* rosado *m*.

rosebed ['rəʊzbed] *n* rosaleda *f*.

rosebud ['rəʊzbʌd] *n* capullo *m* de rosa.

rose bush *n* rosal *m*.

rose hip *n* escaramujo *m*.

rosemary ['rəʊzmərɪ] *n* romero *m*.

rosette [rəʊ'zet] *n* [badge] escarapela *f*.

rosewater ['rəʊz,wɔ:tə-] *n* agua *f* de rosas.

rosewood ['rəʊzwʊd] *n* palisandro *m*.

roster ['rɒstə-] *n* lista *f*.

rostrum ['rɒstrəm] (*pl* -**trums** OR -**tra** [-trə]) *n* tribuna *f*.

rosy ['rəʊzɪ] (*comp* -**ier**, *superl* -**iest**) *adj* - **1.** [pink] sonrosado(da) - **2.** [hopeful] prometedor(ra).

rot [rɒt] <> *n* (*U*) - **1.** [of wood, food] podredumbre *f*; [in society, organization] putrefacción *f*, decadencia *f* - **2.** *UK dated* [nonsense] tonterías *fpl*, bobadas *fpl*. <> *vt* (*pt & pp* -**ted**, *cont* -**ting**) pudrir, corromper. <> *vi* (*pt & pp* -**ted**, *cont* -**ting**) pudrirse, corromperse.

rota ['rəʊtə] *n* lista *f* (de turnos).

rotary ['rəʊtərɪ] ⬦ *adj* giratorio(ria), rotativo(va). ⬦ *n* US [roundabout] glorieta *f*, cruce *m* de circulación giratoria.

Rotary Club *n*: the Rotary Club la Sociedad Rotaria.

rotate [rəʊ'teɪt] ⬦ *vt* - **1.** [turn] hacer girar, dar vueltas a - **2.** [jobs] alternar; [crops] cultivar en rotación. ⬦ *vi* - **1.** [turn] girar, dar vueltas - **2.** [jobs] alternarse; [crops] cultivarse en rotación.

rotation [rəʊ'teɪʃn] *n* - **1.** [gen] rotación *f* - **2.** [of jobs] turno *m*; **in rotation** por turno OR turnos.

rote [rəʊt] *n*: **by rote** de memoria.

rote learning *n* aprendizaje *m* de memoria.

rotor ['rəʊtər] *n* rotor *m*.

rotten ['rɒtn] *adj* - **1.** [decayed] podrido(da) - **2.** *inf* [poor-quality] malísimo(ma), fatal - **3.** *inf* [unpleasant] despreciable - **4.** *inf* [unwell]: **to feel rotten** sentirse fatal OR muy mal - **5.** [unhappy]: **to feel rotten (about)** sentirse mal (por).

rotund [rəʊ'tʌnd] *adj fml* orondo(da).

rouble ['ru:bl] *n* rublo *m*.

rouge [ru:ʒ] *n* colorete *m*.

rough [rʌf] ⬦ *adj* - **1.** [not smooth - surface, skin] áspero(ra); [- ground, road] desigual - **2.** [not gentle] bruto(ta) - **3.** [crude, not refined - person, manner] grosero(ra), tosco(ca); [- shelter] precario(ria); [- living conditions] duro(ra) - **4.** [approximate - plan, sketch] a grandes rasgos; [- estimate, translation] aproximado(da); **to write a rough draft of sthg** escribir un borrador de algo - **5.** [unpleasant] duro(ra), difícil - **6.** [wind] violento(ta); [sea] picado(da); [weather, day] embravecido(da), tormentoso(sa), borrascoso(sa) - **7.** [harsh - wine, voice] áspero(ra) - **8.** [violent - area] peligroso(sa); [- person] violento(ta) - **9.** [tired, ill]: **to look/feel rough** tener un aspecto/sentirse fatal. ⬦ *adv*: **to sleep rough** dormir al raso. ⬦ *n* - **1.** GOLF: **the rough** el rough - **2.** [undetailed form]: **in rough** en borrador. ⬦ *vt*: **to rough it** vivir sin comodidades.

roughage ['rʌfɪdʒ] *n* (U) fibra *f*.

rough and ready *adj* tosco(ca).

rough-and-tumble *n* (U) riña *f*.

rough diamond *n* UK *fig* diamante *m* en bruto.

roughen ['rʌfn] *vt* poner áspero(ra).

rough justice *n* injusticia *f*; **it was pretty rough justice** fue un caso de justicia sumaria.

roughly ['rʌflɪ] *adv* - **1.** [approximately] más o menos - **2.** [not gently] brutalmente - **3.** [crudely] toscamente.

roughneck ['rʌfnek] *n* - **1.** [oilworker] *trabajador en una explotación petrolífera* - **2.** US *inf* [ruffian] matón *m*, duro *m*.

roughness ['rʌfnɪs] *n* - **1.** [lack of smoothness] aspereza *f* - **2.** [lack of gentleness] brutalidad *f*.

roughshod ['rʌfʃɒd] *adv*: **to ride roughshod over sthg/sb** tratar algo/a alguien sin contemplaciones.

roulette [ru:'let] *n* ruleta *f*.

round [raʊnd] ⬦ *adj* redondo(da). ⬦ *prep* - **1.** [surrounding] alrededor de; **the reeds round the pond** las cañas alrededor del estanque; **she put her arm round his shoulder** le puso el brazo al hombro - **2.** [near] cerca de; **round here** por aquí - **3.** [all over - the world etc] por todo(da); **we went round the museum** dimos una vuelta por el museo - **4.** [in circular movement]: **round (and round)** alrededor de - **5.** [in measurements]: **she's 30 inches round the waist** mide 30 pulgadas de cintura - **6.** [at or to the other side of]: **they were waiting round the corner** esperaban a la vuelta de la esquina; **to drive round the corner** doblar la esquina; **we went round the lake** rodeamos el lago - **7.** [so as to avoid]: **he drove round the pothole** conduje esquivando el bache. ⬦ *adv* - **1.** [on all sides]: **all round** por todos lados; **to sit round in a circle** sentarse formando un círculo - **2.** [near]: **round about** alrededor, en las proximidades - **3.** [all over]: **to travel round** viajar por ahí - **4.** [in circular movement]: **she passed round a plate of biscuits** pasó un plato de galletas; **round (and round)** en redondo; **to go** OR **spin round** girar - **5.** [to the other side] al otro lado; **we went round to the back of the house** dimos una vuelta hasta la parte de atrás de la casa - **6.** [at or to nearby place]: **he came round to see us** vino a vernos; **I'm going round to the shop** voy un momento a la tienda. ⬦ *n* - **1.** [of talks, drinks, sandwiches] ronda *f*; **a round of toast** una tostada; **a round of applause** una salva de aplausos - **2.** [in championship] vuelta *f* - **3.** [of doctor] visitas *fpl*; [of milkman, postman] recorrido *m* - **4.** [of ammunition] cartucho *m* - **5.** [in boxing] asalto *m* - **6.** [in golf] vuelta *f*, round *m*. ⬦ *vt* doblar.

⬦ **rounds** *npl* [of doctor] visitas *fpl*; **he's out on his rounds** está visitando pacientes; [of postman] recorrido *m*; **to do** OR **go the rounds** [joke, rumour] divulgarse; [illness] estar rodando.

⬦ **round off** *vt sep* terminar.

⬦ **round up** *vt sep* - **1.** [sheep] recoger; [people] reunir - **2.** MATHS redondear al alza.

roundabout ['raʊndəbaʊt] ⬦ *adj* indirecto(ta); **in a roundabout way** después de un largo preámbulo. ⬦ *n* UK - **1.** [on road] glorieta *f*, rotonda *f* - **2.** [at fairground] tiovivo *m*, ca-

ballitos *mpl* - **3.** [at playground] *plataforma giratoria para que los niños la empujen y
monten en ella.*

rounded ['raʊndɪd] *adj* redondeado(da).

rounders ['raʊndəz] *n* UK *juego parecido al
béisbol.*

Roundhead ['raʊndhed] *n seguidor de Oliver
Cromwell en la guerra civil inglesa del siglo
XVII.*

roundly ['raʊndlɪ] *adv* rotundamente.

round-shouldered [-'ʃəʊldəd] *adj* carga-
do(da) de espaldas.

round table *n* mesa *f* redonda.

round-table *adj* en igualdad de condiciones.

round the clock *adv* (durante) las 24 horas
del día.

➽ **round-the-clock** *adj* continuo(nua), 24 horas al día.

round trip ◇ *adj* US de ida y vuelta. ◇ *n*
viaje *m* de ida y vuelta.

roundup ['raʊndʌp] *n* - **1.** [summary] resumen *m*; **news roundup** resumen *m* informativo - **2.** [of criminals] redada *f*.

rouse [raʊz] *vt* - **1.** *fml* [wake up] despertar
- **2.** [impel]: **to rouse sb/o.s. to do sthg** animar a alguien/animarse a hacer algo - **3.** [ex-
cite] excitar; **it roused his interest** le despertó
el interés - **4.** [give rise to] suscitar.

rousing ['raʊzɪŋ] *adj* [speech] conmovedor(ra);
[cheer] entusiasta.

rout [raʊt] ◇ *n* derrota *f* aplastante. ◇ *vt* derrotar, aplastar.

route [ruːt] ◇ *n* [gen] ruta *f*; [of bus] línea *f*, recorrido *m*; [of ship] rumbo *m*; [for deliveries] recorrido *m*, itinerario *m*; [main road] carretera *f*
principal. ◇ *vt* [gen] dirigir; [goods] enviar.

route map *n* plano *m* (del camino).

routine [ruː'tiːn] ◇ *adj* rutinario(ria); **(to
have) a routine checkup** (hacerse) un reconocimiento médico rutinario. ◇ *n* rutina *f*.

routinely [ruː'tiːnlɪ] *adv* rutinariamente.

rove [rəʊv] *liter* ◇ *vt* vagar por. ◇ *vi*: **to rove
around** vagar.

roving ['rəʊvɪŋ] *adj* itinerante; **a roving reporter** un periodista ambulante.

row[1] [rəʊ] ◇ *n* - **1.** [line] fila *f*, hilera *f* - **2.** [suc-
cession] serie *f*; **three in a row** tres seguidos.
◇ *vt* - **1.** [boat] remar - **2.** [people, things] llevar en bote. ◇ *vi* remar.

row[2] [raʊ] ◇ *n* - **1.** [quarrel] pelea *f*, bronca *f*
- **2.** *inf* [noise] estruendo *m*, ruido *m*. ◇ *vi* [quar-
rel] reñir, pelearse.

rowboat ['rəʊbəʊt] *n* US bote *m* de remos.

rowdiness ['raʊdɪnɪs] *n* alboroto *m*, ruido *m*.

rowdy ['raʊdɪ] (*comp* **-ier**, *superl* **-iest**) *adj*
[noisy] ruidoso(sa); [quarrelsome] pendencie-
ro(ra).

rower ['rəʊər] *n* remero *m*, -ra *f*.

row house [rəʊ-] *n* US casa *f* adosada.

rowing ['rəʊɪŋ] *n* remo *m*.

rowing boat *n* UK bote *m* de remo.

rowing machine *n* máquina *f* de remar.

royal ['rɔɪəl] ◇ *adj* real. ◇ *n inf* miembro *m* de
la familia real; **the Royals** la realeza.

Royal Air Force *n*: **the Royal Air Force** las
Fuerzas Aéreas de Gran Bretaña.

royal blue *adj* azul marino.

royal family *n* familia *f* real.

royalist ['rɔɪəlɪst] *n* monárquico *m*, -ca *f*.

royal jelly *n* jalea *f* real.

Royal Mail *n* UK: **the Royal Mail** ≃ Correos *m*.

Royal Marines *npl* UK: **the Royal Marines** la
Infantería de Marina de Gran Bretaña.

Royal Navy *n*: **the Royal Navy** la Armada de
Gran Bretaña.

royalty ['rɔɪəltɪ] *n* realeza *f*.

➽ **royalties** *npl* derechos *mpl* de autor, royalties *mpl*.

RP (*abbr of* **received pronunciation**) *n pronunciación estándar del inglés.*

RPI (*abbr of* **retail price index**) *n* IPC *m*.

rpm (*abbr of* **revolutions per minute**)
r.p.m. *fpl*

RRP *n abbr of* **recommended retail price**.

RSA (*abbr of* **Royal Society of Arts**) *n sociedad británica para el fomento de las artes,
la producción industrial y el comercio.*

RSC (*abbr of* **Royal Shakespeare Company**) *n
compañía de teatro británica.*

RSI (*abbr of* **repetitive strain injury**) *n lesión
muscular producida por ejemplo por el tra-
bajo continuado tecleando en un ordenador.*

RSPB (*abbr of* **Royal Society for the Protection of Birds**) *n sociedad británica para la
protección de las aves en su medio ambiente natural.*

RSPCA (*abbr of* **Royal Society for the Prevention of Cruelty to Animals**) *n sociedad británica protectora de animales,* ≃ SPA *f*.

RSVP (*abbr of* **répondez s'il vous plaît**) s.r.c.

Rt Hon (*abbr of* **Right Honourable**) su Sría.

Rt Rev (*abbr of* **Right Reverend**) muy Rdo.

rub [rʌb] ◇ *vt* (*pt* & *pp* **-bed**, *cont* **-bing**): **to
rub sthg (against** OR **on)** frotar algo (en OR
contra); **to rub sthg on** OR **onto** frotar algo en;
to rub sthg in OR **into** frotar algo en; **to rub
it in** *inf* insistir, machacar; **to rub sb up the**

wrong way *UK*, **to rub sb the wrong way** *US* sacar a alguien de quicio. ◇ *vi* (*pt* & *pp* **-bed**, *cont* **-bing**): **to rub (against sthg)** rozar (algo); **to rub (together)** rozarse.
➣ **rub off on** *vt insep* [subj: quality] influir en.
➣ **rub out** *vt sep* [erase] borrar.

rubber ['rʌbər] ◇ *adj* de goma, de caucho, de hule *Amér*. ◇ *n* - **1.** [substance] goma *f*, caucho *m* - **2.** *UK* [eraser] goma *f* de borrar - **3.** *US inf* [condom] goma *f* - **4.** [in bridge] partida *f* - **5.** *US* [overshoe] chanclo *m*.

rubber band *n US* goma *f* elástica.

rubber plant *n* ficus *m inv*.

rubber boot *n US* bota *f* de agua.

rubber dinghy *n* lancha *f* neumática.

rubberize, -ise ['rʌbəraɪz] *vt* encauchar.

rubberneck ['rʌbənek] *vi US inf* curiosear.

rubber ring *n* flotador *m*.

rubber stamp *n* estampilla *f Esp*, sello *m* de goma, timbre *m* de goma *Chile*.
➣ **rubber-stamp** *vt* aprobar oficialmente.

rubber tree *n* árbol *m* de caucho, árbol gomero.

rubbery ['rʌbərɪ] *adj* elástico(ca), que parece de goma.

rubbing ['rʌbɪŋ] *n dibujo o impresión que se obtiene al frotar un papel, que cubre una superficie labrada, con carbón, ceras etc*.

rubbish ['rʌbɪʃ] ◇ *n* (*U*) - **1.** [refuse] basura *f* - **2.** *inf fig* [worthless matter] porquería *f*; **it was rubbish** fue una porquería - **3.** *inf* [nonsense] tonterías *fpl*, babosadas *fpl Amér C & Méx*; **don't talk rubbish** no digas tonterías. ◇ *vt inf* poner por los suelos.

rubbish bin *n UK* cubo *m* de la basura.

rubbish dump *n UK* vertedero *m*, basurero *m*.

rubbishy ['rʌbɪʃɪ] *adj inf* de mala calidad.

rubble ['rʌbl] *n* (*U*) escombros *mpl*.

rubella [ru:'belə] *n* rubéola *f*.

ruby ['ru:bɪ] (*pl* **-ies**) *n* rubí *m*.

RUC (*abbr of* **Royal Ulster Constabulary**) *n fuerzas de seguridad del gobierno británico en Irlanda del Norte*.

ruched [ru:ʃt] *adj* fruncido(da).

rucksack ['rʌksæk] *n* mochila *f*.

ructions ['rʌkʃnz] *npl inf* bronca *f*, lío *m*.

rudder ['rʌdər] *n* timón *m*.

ruddy ['rʌdɪ] (*comp* **-ier**, *superl* **-iest**) *adj* [reddish] rojizo(za).

rude [ru:d] *adj* - **1.** [impolite - person, manners, word] grosero(ra), liso(sa) *Arg & Perú*; [- joke] verde - **2.** [shocking] violento(ta), brusco(ca).

rudely ['ru:dlɪ] *adv* - **1.** [impolitely] groseramente - **2.** [shockingly] bruscamente, violentamente.

rudeness ['ru:dnɪs] *n* grosería *f*.

rudimentary [,ru:dɪ'mentərɪ] *adj* rudimentario(ria).

rudiments ['ru:dɪmənts] *npl* rudimentos *mpl*, nociones *fpl* básicas.

rue [ru:] *vt* lamentar, arrepentirse de.

rueful ['ru:fʊl] *adj* arrepentido(da).

ruff [rʌf] *n* [on clothes] gola *f*.

ruffian ['rʌfjən] *n* rufián *m*.

ruffle ['rʌfl] *vt* - **1.** [hair] revolver, despeinar; [water] perturbar, agitar; [feathers] encrespar - **2.** [composure, nerves] enervar, encrespar - **3.** [person] poner nervioso(sa) a.

rug [rʌg] *n* - **1.** [carpet] alfombra *f* - **2.** [blanket] manta *f* de viaje.

rugby ['rʌgbɪ] *n* rugby *m*.

Rugby League *n tipo de rugby con equipos de 13 jugadores profesionales*.

Rugby Union *n tipo de rugby con equipos de 15 jugadores aficionados*.

rugged ['rʌgɪd] *adj* - **1.** [wild, inhospitable] escabroso(sa), accidentado(da) - **2.** [sturdy] fuerte - **3.** [roughly handsome] duro y atractivo (dura y atractiva); **his rugged good looks** sus rasgos recios.

ruggedness ['rʌgɪdnɪs] *n* escabrosidad *f*.

rugger ['rʌgər] *n UK inf* rugby *m*.

ruin ['ru:ɪn] ◇ *n* ruina *f*. ◇ *vt* - **1.** [destroy] estropear - **2.** [spoil] arruinar - **3.** [bankrupt] arruinar.
➣ **in ruin(s)** *adv* en ruinas.

ruination [ru:ɪ'neɪʃn] *n* ruina *f*.

ruinous ['ru:ɪnəs] *adj* [expensive] ruinoso(sa).

rule [ru:l] ◇ *n* - **1.** [regulation, guideline] regla *f*, norma *f*; **to bend the rules** hacer una pequeña excepción (con las normas); **to break the rules** violar las normas; **to obey the rules** obedecer las normas - **2.** [norm]: **the rule** la regla, la norma; **as a rule** por regla general - **3.** [government] dominio *m*; **to be under Roman rule** estar bajo dominio romano - **4.** [ruler] regla *f*. ◇ *vt* - **1.** *fml* [control] regir - **2.** [govern] gobernar - **3.** [decide]: **to rule that** decidir *o* ordenar que. ◇ *vi* - **1.** [give decision] decidir, fallar - **2.** *fml* [be paramount] regir, ser primordial - **3.** [govern] gobernar.
➣ **rule out** *vt sep* descartar.

rulebook ['ru:lbʊk] *n* [set of rules]: **the rulebook** el libro de reglamento.

ruled [ru:ld] *adj* rayado(da).

ruler ['ru:lər] *n* - **1.** [for measurement] regla *f* - **2.** [monarch] soberano *m*, -na *f*.

ruling ['ru:lɪŋ] ◇ *adj* en el poder. ◇ *n* fallo *m*, decisión *f*.

rum [rʌm] ◇ *n* ron *m*. ◇ *adj* (*comp* **-mer**, *superl* **-mest**) *UK dated* extraño(ña), raro(ra).

Rumania [ru:'meɪnjə] = **Romania**.

Rumanian [ru:'meɪnjən] = **Romanian**.

rumba ['rʌmbə] *n* rumba *f*.

rumble ['rʌmbl] ⟨⟩ *n* - **1.** [gen] estruendo *m*; [of stomach] ruido *m* - **2.** *US inf* [fight] riña *f* callejera. ⟨⟩ *vt UK inf dated* calar. ⟨⟩ *vi* [gen] retumbar; [stomach] hacer ruido.

rumbustious [rʌm'bʌstʃəs] *adj UK* bullicioso(sa).

ruminate ['ru:mɪneɪt] *vi fml*: **to ruminate (about** OR **on sthg)** rumiar (algo).

rummage ['rʌmɪdʒ] *vi* hurgar, rebuscar; **to rummage around in sthg** revolver en algo.

rummage sale *n US* venta de objetos usados con fines benéficos.

rummy ['rʌmɪ] *n* rum *m*.

rumour *UK,* **rumor** *US* ['ru:mər] *n* rumor *m*; **there's a rumour going around that...** se rumorea que...

rumoured *UK,* **rumored** *US* ['ru:məd] *adj*: **to be rumoured** rumorearse; **she is rumoured to be very rich** se rumorea que es muy rica.

rump [rʌmp] *n* - **1.** [of animal] grupa *f*, ancas *fpl* - **2.** *inf* [of person] trasero *m*, culo *m*.

rumple ['rʌmpl] *vt* [clothes] arrugar; [hair] desordenar.

rump steak *n* filete *m* de lomo, churrasco *m* de cuadril *R Plata*.

rumpus ['rʌmpəs] *n inf* lío *m*, jaleo *m*, despiole *m Arg*.

rumpus room *n US* cuarto *m* de juegos.

run [rʌn] ⟨⟩ *n* - **1.** [on foot] carrera *f*; **to go for a run** ir a correr; **on the run** en fuga; **to make a run for it** tratar de fugarse - **2.** [journey - in car] paseo *m* OR vuelta *f* (en coche); **to go for a run** ir a dar una vuelta; [- in plane, ship] viaje *m* - **3.** [series - of wins, disasters] serie *f*; [- of luck] racha *f* - **4.** THEAT: **the play had a 6-week run** la obra estuvo en cartelera 6 semanas - **5.** [great demand]: **a run on sthg** una gran demanda de algo - **6.** [in tights] carrera *f* - **7.** [in cricket, baseball] carrera *f* - **8.** [for skiing etc] pista *f* - **9.** [term]: **in the short/long run** a corto/largo plazo. ⟨⟩ *vt* (*pt* ran, *pp* run, *cont* -ning) - **1.** [on foot] correr - **2.** [manage - business] dirigir, administrar; [- life, event] organizar - **3.** [operate - computer program, machine, film] poner; [- experiment] montar - **4.** [have and use - car etc] hacer funcionar; **it's cheap to run** es barato de mantener; **it runs on diesel/off the mains** funciona con diesel/electricidad - **5.** [open - tap] abrir; **to run a bath** llenar la bañera - **6.** [publish] publicar - **7.** *inf* [transport by car] llevar; **shall I run you to school?** ¿te llevo al colegio? - **8.** [move]: **to run sthg along** OR **over** pasar algo por. ⟨⟩ *vi* (*pt* ran, *pp* run, *cont* -ning) - **1.** [on foot] correr; **to run for it** echar a correr - **2.** [follow a direction]: **the road runs parallel to the river** la carretera discurre paralela al río - **3.** *esp US* [in election]: **to run (for)** presentarse como candidato(ta) (a); **he's running for president** se presenta a la presidencia - **4.** [factory, machine] funcionar; [engine] estar encendido(da); **to run on** OR **off sthg** funcionar con algo; **to run smoothly** ir bien - **5.** [bus, train] ir - **6.** [flow] correr; **to run dry** secarse, quedarse sin agua - **7.** [tap] gotear; **somebody has left the tap running** alguien se ha dejado el grifo abierto; [nose] moquear; **my nose is running** me moquea la nariz; [eyes] llorar - **8.** [colour] desteñir

▸▸ **feelings were running high** la gente estaba indignada; **to be running late** ir con retraso.

◆ **run across** *vt insep* [meet] encontrarse con.

◆ **run along** *vi dated*: **run along now!** ¡vete!, ¡anda ya!

◆ **run away** *vi* - **1.** [flee]: **to run away (from)** huir OR fugarse (de) - **2.** *fig* [avoid]: **to run away from** [responsibility, subject] evadir; [thought] evitar.

◆ **run away with** *vt insep*: **he lets his enthusiasm run away with him** se deja llevar por el entusiasmo.

◆ **run down** ⟨⟩ *vt sep* - **1.** [run over] atropellar - **2.** [criticize] hablar mal de. ⟨⟩ *vi* [battery] acabarse; [clock] pararse; [project, business] debilitarse, perder energía.

◆ **run into** *vt insep* - **1.** [problem] encontrar; [person] tropezarse con; **to run into debt** endeudarse - **2.** [in vehicle] chocar con - **3.** [blend with]: **to run into each other** mezclarse - **4.** [amount to] ascender a.

◆ **run off** ⟨⟩ *vt sep* [copies, photocopies] sacar. ⟨⟩ *vi*: **to run off (with)** fugarse (con).

◆ **run on** *vi* [continue] continuar.

◆ **run out** *vi* - **1.** [become used up] acabarse - **2.** [expire] caducar.

◆ **run out of** *vt insep* quedarse sin; **we've run out of food** se nos ha acabado la comida.

◆ **run over** *vt sep* atropellar.

◆ **run through** *vt insep* - **1.** [be present in] recorrer, atravesar; **the vein of humour which ran through her work** el tono de humor que está presente en su trabajo - **2.** [practise] ensayar, practicar - **3.** [read through] echar un vistazo a.

◆ **run to** *vt insep* - **1.** [amount to] ascender a; **the bill ran to thousands** la cuenta subía a varios miles - **2.** [afford] permitirse; **I can't run to a new car** no me puedo permitir un nuevo coche.

◆ **run up** *vt insep* [amass] incurrir en, contraer; **he ran up a huge bill** acumuló una factura enorme.

◆ **run up against** *vt insep* tropezar con.

run-around *n inf*: **to give sb the run-around** traerle a alguien al retortero.

runaway ['rʌnəweɪ] ◇ *adj* - **1.** [gen] fugitivo(va); [horse] desbocado(da); [train] fuera de control; [inflation] desenfrenado(da) - **2.** [victory] fácil. ◇ *n* fugitivo *m*, -va *f*.

rundown ['rʌndaʊn] *n* - **1.** [report] informe *m*, resumen *m*; **to give sb a rundown on sthg** poner a alguien al tanto de algo - **2.** [decline] desmantelamiento *m* gradual.

◆ **run-down** *adj* - **1.** [dilapidated] en ruinas, en decadencia - **2.** [tired] agotado(da); **to feel rundown** sentirse débil.

rung [rʌŋ] ◇ *pp* ▷ **ring.** ◇ *n lit & fig* peldaño *m*.

run-in *n inf* altercado *m*, disputa *f*.

runner ['rʌnəʳ] *n* - **1.** [athlete] corredor *m*, -ra *f* - **2.** [smuggler] traficante *mf*, contrabandista *mf* - **3.** [on sledge] carril *m*; [of drawer, sliding seat] carro *m*.

runner bean *n UK* judía *f* verde, chaucha *f R Plata*, vainita *f Ven*, ejote *m Amér C & Méx*, poroto *m* verde *Chile*.

runner-up (*pl* runners-up) *n* subcampeón *m*, -ona *f*.

running ['rʌnɪŋ] ◇ *adj* - **1.** [continuous] continuo(nua) - **2.** [consecutive] seguidos(das); **four days running** cuatro días consecutivos - **3.** [water] corriente. ◇ *n* - **1.** [act of running] el correr; **to go running** hacer footing - **2.** SPORT carreras *fpl* - **3.** [management] dirección *f*, organización *f* - **4.** [operation] funcionamiento *m*

▸▸▸ **to make the running** ir en cabeza; **to be in/out of the running (for sthg)** tener/no tener posibilidades (de algo). ◇ *comp*: **running shoes** zapatillas *fpl* deportivas.

running commentary *n* comentario *m* en directo; **there's no need to give us a running commentary!** *fig* ¡no hace falta que nos hagas un comentario en directo!

running costs *npl* gastos *mpl* corrientes (de mantenimiento).

running mate *n US* candidato *m*, -ta *f* a vicepresidente.

running repairs *npl* reparación *f* temporal.

runny ['rʌnɪ] (*comp* -ier, *superl* -iest) *adj* - **1.** [sauce, gravy] derretido(da) - **2.** [nose] que moquea; [eyes] llorosos(as).

run-of-the-mill *adj* normal y corriente.

runt [rʌnt] *n* - **1.** [animal] cría *f* más pequeña y débil - **2.** *pej* [person] renacuajo *m*.

run-through *n* ensayo *m*.

run-up *n* - **1.** [preceding time] periodo *m* previo; **the run-up to the elections** el periodo previo a las elecciones - **2.** SPORT carrerilla *f*.

runway ['rʌnweɪ] *n* pista *f*.

rupture ['rʌptʃəʳ] ◇ *n* - **1.** MED hernia *f* - **2.** [of relationship] ruptura *f*. ◇ *vt* romper.

rural ['rʊərəl] *adj* rural.

ruse [ruːz] *n* ardid *m*.

rush [rʌʃ] ◇ *n* - **1.** [hurry] prisa *f*; **to be in a rush** tener prisa; **there's no rush** no hay prisa - **2.** [burst of activity]: **rush (for OR on sthg)** avalancha *f* (en busca de algo); **there was a rush to stock up on sugar** hubo una fiebre repentina por almacenar azúcar - **3.** [busy period] hora *f* punta - **4.** [surge - of air] ráfaga *f*; [- of water] torrente *m*; [- mental] arrebato *m*; **to make a rush for sthg** ir en desbandada hacia algo; **there was a rush for the exit** la gente salió apresuradamente. ◇ *vt* - **1.** [hurry] acelerar, apresurar; **don't rush me!** ¡no me metas prisa!; **to rush sb into doing sthg** apresurar a alguien para que haga algo - **2.** [send quickly] llevar rápidamente; **he was rushed to hospital** lo llevaron al hospital a toda prisa - **3.** [attack suddenly] atacar repentinamente. ◇ *vi* - **1.** [hurry] ir de prisa, correr; **to rush into sthg** meterse de cabeza en algo; **there's no need to rush** no hay ninguna prisa; **he rushed to help her** corrió a ayudarla - **2.** [surge] correr, precipitarse.

◆ **rushes** *npl* - **1.** BOT juncos *mpl* - **2.** CIN primeras pruebas *fpl*.

rushed [rʌʃt] *adj* atareado(da).

rush hour *n* hora *f* punta, hora *f* pico *Amér*, hora *f* peack *Chile*.

rush job *n* trabajo *m* precipitado.

rusk [rʌsk] *n galleta que se da a los niños pequeños para que se acostumbran a masticar.*

russet ['rʌsɪt] *adj* rojizo(za).

Russia ['rʌʃə] *n* Rusia.

Russian ['rʌʃn] ◇ *adj* ruso(sa). ◇ *n* - **1.** [person] ruso *m*, -sa *f* - **2.** [language] ruso *m*.

Russian roulette *n* ruleta *f* rusa.

rust [rʌst] ◇ *n* óxido *m*. ◇ *vi* oxidarse.

rustic ['rʌstɪk] *adj* rústico(ca).

rustle ['rʌsl] ◇ *n* - **1.** [of wind, leaves] susurro *m*; [of paper] crujido *m* - **2.** [of silk] roce *m*. ◇ *vt* - **1.** [paper] hacer crujir - **2.** *US* [cattle] robar. ◇ *vi* [wind, leaves] susurrar; [paper] crujir.

rustproof ['rʌstpruːf] *adj* inoxidable.

rusty ['rʌstɪ] (*comp* -ier, *superl* -iest) *adj lit & fig* oxidado(da); **my French is a bit rusty** hace mucho que no practico el francés.

rut [rʌt] *n* [track] rodada *f*; **to get into/be in a rut** *fig* caer/estar metido en una rutina; **to get out of a rut** salir de la rutina.

rutabaga [ˌruːtəˈbeɪgə] *n US* nabo *m* sueco.

ruthless ['ruːθlɪs] *adj* despiadado(da).

ruthlessly ['ruːθlɪslɪ] adv despiadadamente.

ruthlessness ['ruːθlɪsnɪs] n crueldad f.

RV n - **1.** (abbr of revised version), traducción al inglés de la Biblia de finales del siglo XIX - **2.** US (abbr of recreational vehicle) casa-remolque f.

Rwanda [ru'ændə] n Ruanda.

Rwandan [ru'ændən] <> adj ruandés(esa). <> n ruandés m, -esa f.

rye [raɪ] n - **1.** [grain] centeno m - **2.** [bread] pan m de centeno.

rye bread n pan m de centeno.

rye whiskey n whisky m de centeno.

S

s (pl ss OR s's), **S** (pl Ss OR S's) [es] n [letter] s f, S f.
◆ **S** (abbr of south) S.

SA abbr of South Africa. abbr of South America.

Sabbath ['sæbəθ] n: the Sabbath [for Christians] el domingo; [for Jews] el sábado.

sabbatical [sə'bætɪkl] n sabático m; on sabbatical de sabático.

saber US = sabre.

sabotage ['sæbətɑːʒ] <> n sabotaje m. <> vt sabotear.

saboteur [ˌsæbə'tɜːr] n saboteador m, -ra f.

sabre UK, **saber** US ['seɪbər] n sable m.

saccharin(e) ['sækərɪn] n sacarina f.

sachet ['sæʃeɪ] n bolsita f.

sack [sæk] <> n - **1.** [bag] saco m - **2.** UK inf [dismissal]: **to get** OR **be given the sack** ser despedido(da); **to give sb the sack** despedir a alguien. <> vt UK inf despedir, remover Amér.

sackful ['sækfʊl] n saco m.

sacking ['sækɪŋ] n - **1.** [fabric] harpillera f - **2.** [dismissal] despido m.

sacrament ['sækrəmənt] n sacramento m.

sacred ['seɪkrɪd] adj lit & fig sagrado(da).

sacrifice ['sækrɪfaɪs] fig <> n RELIG sacrificio m; **to make sacrifices** sacrificarse. <> vt RELIG sacrificar.

sacrilege ['sækrɪlɪdʒ] n fig & RELIG sacrilegio m.

sacrilegious [ˌsækrɪ'lɪdʒəs] adj sacrílego(ga).

sacrosanct ['sækrəʊsæŋkt] adj sacrosanto(ta).

sad [sæd] (comp -der, superl -dest) adj triste.

sadden ['sædn] vt entristecer.

saddle ['sædl] <> n - **1.** [for horse] silla f (de montar) - **2.** [of bicycle, motorcycle] sillín m, asiento m. <> vt - **1.** [horse] ensillar - **2.** fig [burden]: **to saddle sb with sthg** cargar a alguien con algo; **she was saddled with an elderly patient** le encajaron un pariente anciano.
◆ **saddle up** vt insep & vi ensillar.

saddlebag ['sædlbæg] n alforja f.

saddler ['sædlər] n talabartero m, -ra f.

sadism ['seɪdɪzm] n sadismo m.

sadist ['seɪdɪst] n sádico m, -ca f.

sadistic [sə'dɪstɪk] adj sádico(ca).

sadly ['sædlɪ] adv tristemente.

sadness ['sædnɪs] n tristeza f.

s.a.e., sae n abbr of stamped addressed envelope.

safari [sə'fɑːrɪ] n safari m; **to go on safari** ir de safari.

safari park n safari m, reserva f de animales.

safe [seɪf] <> adj - **1.** [gen] seguro(ra); **a safe place** un lugar seguro; **is this ladder safe?** ¿es segura esta escalera?; **you're safe now** ahora estás seguro; **safe and sound** sano y salvo (sana y salva) - **2.** [without harm] sano y salvo (sano y salva) - **3.** [not causing disagreement]: **it's safe to say that...** se puede afirmar con seguridad que...; **to be on the safe side** por mayor seguridad - **4.** [reliable] digno(na) de confianza; **in safe hands** en buenas manos. <> n caja f (de caudales).

safebreaker ['seɪfˌbreɪkər] n ladrón m, -ona f de cajas.

safe-conduct n salvoconducto m.

safe-deposit box, safety-deposit box n caja f de seguridad.

safeguard ['seɪfgɑːd] <> n salvaguardia f, protección f; **as a safeguard** como protección; **a safeguard against sthg** una protección contra algo. <> vt: **to safeguard sthg/sb (against sthg)** salvaguardar OR proteger algo/a alguien (contra algo).

safe house n piso m franco.

safekeeping [ˌseɪf'kiːpɪŋ] n: **she gave me the letter for safekeeping** me dio la carta para que se la guardara en un lugar seguro.

safely ['seɪflɪ] *adv* - **1.** [with no danger] sin peligro, con seguridad - **2.** [not in danger] seguramente - **3.** [unharmed] sano y salvo (sana y salva) - **4.** [for certain]: **I can safely say that...** puedo decir con toda confianza que...

safe sex *n* sexo *m* sin riesgo.

safety ['seɪftɪ] <> *n* seguridad *f*. <> *comp* de seguridad; **safety regulations** normas *fpl* de seguridad.

safety belt *n* cinturón *m* de seguridad.

safety catch *n* seguro *m*.

safety curtain *n* telón *m* de seguridad.

safety-deposit box = **safe-deposit box**.

safety island *n* US refugio *m*.

safety match *n* cerilla *f* de seguridad, fósforo *m* de seguridad *Amér*, cerillo *m* de seguridad *Amér C, Méx & Ecuad*.

safety net *n* - **1.** [in circus] red *f* de seguridad - **2.** *fig* [means of protection] protección *f*.

safety pin *n* imperdible *m*, seguro *m* *Méx*.

safety valve *n* - **1.** TECH válvula *f* de seguridad - **2.** *fig* [for emotions] válvula *f* de escape.

saffron ['sæfrən] *n* - **1.** [spice] azafrán *m* - **2.** [colour] color *m* azafrán.

sag [sæg] (*pt & pp* -**ged**, *cont* -**ging**) *vi* - **1.** [sink downwards] hundirse, combarse - **2.** *fig* [lessen] decaer.

saga ['sɑ:gə] *n* - **1.** LIT saga *f* - **2.** *pej* [drawn-out account] historia *f*.

sage [seɪdʒ] <> *adj* sabio(bia). <> *n* - **1.** [herb] salvia *f* - **2.** [wise man] sabio *m*.

saggy ['sægɪ] (*comp* -**gier**, *superl* -**giest**) *adj* [bed] hundido(da); [breasts] caído(da).

Sagittarius [,sædʒɪ'teərɪəs] *n* Sagitario *m*; **to be (a) Sagittarius** ser Sagitario.

Sahara [sə'hɑːrə] *n*: **the Sahara (Desert)** el (desierto del) Sáhara.

Saharan [sə'hɑːrən] <> *n* saharaui *mf*. <> *adj* saharaui, sahariano(na).

said [sed] *pt & pp* ▷ **say**.

sail [seɪl] <> *n* - **1.** [of boat] vela *f*; **to set sail** zarpar - **2.** [journey by boat] paseo *m* en barco de vela; **to go for a sail** salir a hacer una excursión en barco de vela. <> *vt* - **1.** [boat, ship] gobernar - **2.** [sea] cruzar. <> *vi* - **1.** [travel by boat] navegar - **2.** [move - boat]: **the ship sailed across the ocean** el barco cruzó el océano - **3.** [leave by boat] zarpar; **we sail at 10 am** zarpamos a las 10 am - **4.** [move]: **she sailed into the room** entró en la habitación con aire de elegancia.

➡ **sail through** *vt insep* hacer con facilidad.

sailboard ['seɪlbɔːd] *n* tabla *f* de windsurf.

sailboat US = **sailing boat**.

sailcloth ['seɪlklɒθ] *n* lona *f*.

sailing ['seɪlɪŋ] *n* - **1.** (*U*) SPORT vela *f*; **to be plain sailing** ser coser y cantar - **2.** [trip by ship] travesía *f*.

sailing boat UK, **sailboat** US ['seɪlbəʊt] *n* barco *m* de vela.

sailing ship *n* (buque *m*) velero *m*.

sailor ['seɪlər] *n* marinero *m*, -ra *f*, marino *m*, -na *f*; **to be a good sailor** no marearse.

saint [seɪnt] *n fig & RELIG* santo *m*, -ta *f*; **he's no saint** no es ningún santo; **to have the patience of a saint** tener más paciencia que un santo.

Saint Lucia [-'luːʃə] *n* Santa Lucía.

saintly ['seɪntlɪ] (*comp* -**ier**, *superl* -**iest**) *adj* santo(ta), piadoso(sa).

sake [seɪk] *n*: **for the sake of** por (el bien de); **to argue for its own sake** discutir por discutir; **for God's** OR **heaven's sake** ¡por el amor de Dios!

salad ['sæləd] *n* ensalada *f*.

salad bowl *n* ensaladera *f*.

salad cream *n* UK salsa parecida a la mahonesa para aderezar la ensalada.

salad dressing *n* aliño *m* (para la ensalada).

salamander ['sælə,mændər] *n* salamandra *f*.

salami [sə'lɑːmɪ] *n* salami *m*.

salaried ['sælərɪd] *adj* [person] asalariado(da); [job] de sueldo fijo.

salary ['sælərɪ] (*pl* -**ies**) *n* sueldo *m*.

salary scale *n* banda *f* salarial.

sale [seɪl] *n* - **1.** [gen] venta *f*; **on sale** en venta; **(up) for sale** en venta; **'for sale'** 'se vende' - **2.** [at reduced prices] liquidación *f*, saldo *m*.

➡ **sales** <> *npl* - **1.** ECON ventas *fpl* - **2.** [at reduced prices]: **the sales** las rebajas. <> *comp* de ventas.

saleroom UK ['seɪlrʊm], **salesroom** US ['seɪlzrʊm] *n* sala *f* de subastas.

sales assistant ['seɪlz-], **salesclerk** US ['seɪlzklɑːrk] *n* dependiente *m*, -ta *f*.

sales conference *n* conferencia *f* de ventas.

sales drive *n* promoción *f* de ventas.

sales force *n* personal *m* de ventas.

salesman ['seɪlzmən] (*pl* -**men** [-mən]) *n* [in shop] dependiente *m*, vendedor *m*; [travelling] viajante *m*.

sales pitch *n* cháchara *f* publicitaria.

sales rep *n inf* representante *mf*.

sales representative *n* representante *mf*.

salesroom US = **saleroom**.

sales slip *n* US [receipt] recibo *m*.

sales tax *n* impuesto *m* de venta.

sales team *n* personal *m* de ventas.

saleswoman ['seɪlz,wʊmən] (*pl* **-women** [-,wɪmɪn]) *n* [in shop] dependienta *f*, vendedora *f*; [travelling] viajante *f*.

salient ['seɪljənt] *adj fml* sobresaliente.

saline ['seɪlaɪn] *adj* salino(na).

saliva [sə'laɪvə] *n* saliva *f*.

salivate ['sælɪveɪt] *vi* salivar.

sallow ['sæləʊ] *adj* cetrino(na), amarillento(ta).

sally ['sælɪ] *n* (*pl* **-ies**) [clever remark] salida *f*.
➡ **sally forth** *vi* (*pt & pp* **-ied**) *hum & liter* salir resueltamente.

salmon ['sæmən] (*pl* **salmon** OR **-s**) *n* salmón *m*.

salmonella [,sælmə'nelə] *n* salmonelosis *f inv*.

salmon pink ◇ *adj* rosa salmón. ◇ *n* color *m* rosa salmón.

salon ['sælɒn] *n* salón *m*.

saloon [sə'luːn] *n* - **1.** UK [car] (coche *m*) utilitario *m* - **2.** US [bar] bar *m* - **3.** UK [in pub]: **saloon (bar)** *en ciertos pubs y hoteles, bar elegante con precios más altos que los del 'public bar'* - **4.** [in ship] salón *m*.

salopettes [,sælə'pets] *npl* pantalones *mpl* de peto para esquiar.

salt [sɔːlt, sɒlt] ◇ *n* sal *f*; **the salt of the earth** la sal de la tierra; **to rub salt into the wounds, he said...** por si fuera poco, encima dijo...; **to take sthg with a pinch of salt** considerar algo con cierta reserva. ◇ *comp* salado(da); **salt fish** pescado *m* salado. ◇ *vt* [food] salar; [roads] echar sal en *(las carreteras etc para evitar que se hielen)*.
➡ **salt away** *vt sep inf* ahorrar, guardar.

SALT [sɔːlt] (*abbr of* **Strategic Arms Limitation Talks/Treaty**) *n* SALT *fpl*.

salt cellar UK, **salt shaker** US [-,ʃeɪkər] *n* salero *m*.

salted ['sɔːltɪd] *adj* salado(da), con sal.

saltpetre UK, **saltpeter** US [,sɔːlt'piːtər] *n* salitre *m*.

salt shaker US = **salt cellar**.

saltwater ['sɔːlt,wɔːtər] ◇ *n* agua *f* de mar, agua salada. ◇ *adj* de agua salada.

salty ['sɔːltɪ] (*comp* **-ier**, *superl* **-iest**) *adj* salado(da), salobre.

salubrious [sə'luːbrɪəs] *adj* salubre, sano(na).

salutary ['sæljʊtrɪ] *adj* saludable.

salute [sə'luːt] ◇ *n* - **1.** [with hand] saludo *m* - **2.** MIL [firing of guns] salva *f*, saludo *m* - **3.** [formal acknowledgement] homenaje *m*. ◇ *vt* - **1.** MIL [with hand] saludar - **2.** [acknowledge formally] reconocer. ◇ *vi* saludar.

Salvadorean, Salvadorian [,sælvə'dɔːrɪən] ◇ *adj* salvadoreño(ña). ◇ *n* salvadoreño *m*, -ña *f*.

salvage ['sælvɪdʒ] ◇ *n (U)* - **1.** [rescue of ship] salvamento *m* - **2.** [property rescued] objetos *mpl* recuperados OR rescatados. ◇ *vt lit & fig*: **to salvage sthg (from)** salvar algo (de).

salvage vessel *n* nave *f* de salvamento.

salvation [sæl'veɪʃn] *n* salvación *f*.

Salvation Army *n*: **the Salvation Army** el Ejército de Salvación.

salve [sælv] ◇ *vt*: **to salve one's conscience (by doing sthg)** apaciguar a la conciencia (haciendo algo). ◇ *n* [ointment] bálsamo *m*.

salver ['sælvər] *n* bandeja *f* (metálica).

salvo ['sælvəʊ] (*pl* **-s** OR **-es**) *n* [of guns, missiles] salva *f*.

Samaritan [sə'mærɪtn] *n*: **good Samaritan** buen alma *f*, buena persona *f*.

samba ['sæmbə] *n* samba *f*.

same [seɪm] ◇ *adj* mismo(ma); **the same colour as his** el mismo color que el suyo; **at the same time** [simultaneously] al mismo tiempo; [yet] aún así; **one and the same** el mismo(la misma). ◇ *pron*: **the same** el mismo (la misma); **she did the same** hizo lo mismo; **the ingredients are the same** los ingredientes son los mismos OR iguales; **his car is the same as yours** su coche es el mismo que el tuyo; **I'll have the same (again)** tomaré lo mismo (que antes); **all** OR **just the same** [nevertheless, anyway] de todos modos; **it's all the same to me** me da igual; **it's not the same** no es lo mismo; **happy Christmas! – the same to you!** ¡feliz Navidad! – ¡igualmente! ◇ *adv*: **the same** lo mismo.

sameness ['seɪmnɪs] *n* uniformidad *f*.

samosa [sə'məʊsə] *n especie de empanadilla rellena de carne verdura etc típica de la cocina india.*

sample ['sɑːmpl] ◇ *n* muestra *f*; **a free sample** una muestra gratuita. ◇ *vt* [food, wine, attractions] probar.

sanatorium (*pl* **-riums** OR **-ria** [-rɪə]), **sanitorium** US (*pl* **-riums** OR **-ria** [-rɪə]) [,sænə'tɔːrɪəm] *n* sanatorio *m*.

sanctify ['sæŋktɪfaɪ] (*pt & pp* **-ied**) *vt* - **1.** RELIG santificar - **2.** [approve] aprobar.

sanctimonious [,sæŋktɪ'məʊnjəs] *adj pej* santurrón(ona).

sanction ['sæŋkʃn] ◇ *n* sanción *f*. ◇ *vt* sancionar.

➤ **sanctions** npl sanciones fpl; **economic sanctions** sanciones económicas; **to impose sanctions on a country** imponer sanciones a un país.

sanctity ['sæŋktətɪ] n santidad f.

sanctuary ['sæŋktʃʊərɪ] (pl -ies) n - **1.** [for wildlife] reserva f; **a bird sanctuary** una reserva de aves - **2.** [refuge] refugio m - **3.** [holy place] santuario m.

sanctum ['sæŋktəm] (pl -s) n [private place] lugar m sagrado, espacio m privado; **the inner sanctum** el sanctasanctórum.

sand [sænd] ◇ n arena f. ◇ vt lijar; **to sand down a surface** lijar una superficie.

➤ **sands** npl arenas fpl.

sandal ['sændl] n sandalia f; **a pair of sandals** unas sandalias.

sandalwood ['sændlwʊd] n sándalo m.

sandbag ['sændbæg] n saco m de arena.

sandbank ['sændbæŋk] n banco m de arena.

sandblast ['sændblɑ:st] vt limpiar con chorro de arena.

sandbox US = **sandpit**.

sandcastle ['sænd,kɑ:sl] n castillo m de arena.

sand dune n duna f.

sander ['sændər] n lijadora f.

sandpaper ['sænd,peɪpər] ◇ n (U) papel m de lija. ◇ vt lijar.

sandpit UK ['sændpɪt], **sandbox** US ['sændbɒks] n cuadro m de arena.

sandstone ['sændstəʊn] n piedra f arenisca.

sandstorm ['sændstɔ:m] n tormenta f de arena.

sand trap n US GOLF bunker m.

sandwich ['sænwɪdʒ] ◇ n [made with roll etc] bocadillo m; [made with sliced bread] sandwich m frío; **a cheese sandwich** un sandwich de queso. ◇ vt fig apretujar; **she was sandwiched between two businessmen** quedó atrapada entre dos hombres de negocios.

sandwich board n cartelón m (de hombre-anuncio).

sandwich course n UK curso universitario que incluye un cierto tiempo de experiencia profesional.

sandy ['sændɪ] (comp -ier, superl -iest) adj - **1.** [covered in sand] arenoso(sa) - **2.** [sand-coloured] rojizo(za).

sane [seɪn] adj - **1.** [not mad] cuerdo(da) - **2.** [sensible] prudente, sensato(ta).

sang [sæŋ] pt ▷ **sing**.

sanguine ['sæŋgwɪn] adj optimista.

sanitary ['sænɪtrɪ] adj - **1.** [connected with health] sanitario(ria) - **2.** [clean, hygienic] higiénico(ca).

sanitary towel, sanitary napkin US n [disposable] compresa f, toalla f higiénica Amér.

sanitation [,sænɪ'teɪʃn] n sanidad f, higiene f.

sanitation worker n US basurero m, -ra f.

sanitize, -ise ['sænɪtaɪz] vt - **1.** [disinfect] desinfectar - **2.** fig descafeinar.

sanitorium US = **sanatorium**.

sanity ['sænətɪ] n - **1.** [saneness] cordura f - **2.** [good sense] sensatez f, prudencia f.

sank [sæŋk] pt ▷ **sink**.

Sanskrit ['sænskrɪt] n sánscrito m.

Santa (Claus) ['sæntə(,klɔːz)] n Papá m Noel.

sap [sæp] ◇ n - **1.** [of plant] savia f - **2.** US inf [gullible person] primo m, -ma f. ◇ vt (pt & pp -ped, cont -ping) [weaken] minar, agotar.

sapling ['sæplɪŋ] n árbol m nuevo, arbolito m.

sapphire ['sæfaɪər] n zafiro m.

Saran wrap® [sə'ræn-] n US plástico m transparente (para envolver alimentos).

sarcasm ['sɑ:kæzm] n sarcasmo m.

sarcastic [sɑ:'kæstɪk] adj sarcástico(ca).

sarcophagus [sɑ:'kɒfəgəs] (pl -gi [-gaɪ] OR -es) n sarcófago m.

sardine [sɑ:'di:n] n sardina f; **to be packed in like sardines** ir como sardinas en lata.

Sardinia [sɑ:'dɪnjə] n Cerdeña.

sardonic [sɑ:'dɒnɪk] adj sardónico(ca).

Sargasso Sea [sɑ:'gæsəʊ-] n: **the Sargasso Sea** el mar de los Sargazos.

sari ['sɑːrɪ] n sari m.

sarong [sə'rɒŋ] n prenda de vestir malaya que se lleva como falda anudada a la cintura o bajo los brazos.

sarsaparilla [,sɑ:spə'rɪlə] n zarzaparrilla f.

sartorial [sɑ:'tɔ:rɪəl] adj fml en el vestir.

SAS (abbr of Special Air Service) n unidad especial del ejército británico encargada de operaciones de sabotaje.

SASE n US abbr of self-addressed stamped envelope.

sash [sæʃ] n faja f.

sash window n ventana f de guillotina.

sassy ['sæsɪ] adj US inf descarado(da), fresco(ca).

sat [sæt] pt & pp ▷ **sit**.

Sat. (abbr of Saturday) sáb.

SAT [sæt] n - **1.** (abbr of Standard Assessment Test), examen de aptitud que se realiza a los siete, once y catorce años en Ingla-

terra y *Gales* - **2.** (*abbr of* **Scholastic Aptitude Test**), *examen de ingreso a la universidad en Estados Unidos.*

SAT

El **SAT** ("Scholastic Aptitude Test") es el examen de acceso a la universidad más extendido en Estados Unidos. Consta de dos partes: una matemática y una verbal, si bien desde 2005 cuenta con tres partes: una escrita, una lectura crítica y una matemática. Este examen tiene lugar varias veces al año y los estudiantes tienen la oportunidad de presentarse más de una vez para intentar mejorar la nota. Como criterio de admisión, las universidades estadounidenses tienen en cuenta los resultados del **SAT**, el expediente académico del alumno, sus actividades extraescolares, una carta de motivación escrita por él y, en ocasiones, referencias de profesores. En el Reino Unido, los **SAT**s examinan a los alumnos al final de cada ciclo educativo (a los 7, 11 y 13 años) del programa de estudios a nivel nacional. En ellos se evalúa la escritura (caligrafía y ortografía), las matemáticas y las ciencias. Su introducción a la temprana edad de los 7 años es reciente y polémica.

Satan ['seɪtn] *n* Satanás *m*, Satán *m*.

satanic [sə'tænɪk] *adj* satánico(ca).

satchel ['sætʃəl] *n* cartera *f*.

sated ['seɪtɪd] *adj fml:* **sated (with)** saciado(da) (de).

satellite ['sætəlaɪt] <> *n lit* & *fig* satélite *m*. <> *comp* - **1.** [link, broadcast] por satélite; **satellite dish** [for TV] antena *f* parabólica - **2.** [dependent] satélite.

satellite TV *n* televisión *f* por satélite.

satiate ['seɪʃɪeɪt] *vt fml* saciar, hartar.

satin ['sætɪn] <> *n* satén *m*, raso *m*. <> *comp* de satén, de raso.

satire ['sætaɪəʳ] *n* sátira *f*.

satirical [sə'tɪrɪkl] *adj* satírico(ca).

satirist ['sætərɪst] *n* escritor satírico *m*, escritora satírica *f*.

satirize, -ise ['sætəraɪz] *vt* satirizar.

satisfaction [,sætɪs'fækʃn] *n* satisfacción *f*; **to do sthg to sb's satisfaction** hacer algo a la satisfacción *OR* al gusto de alguien.

satisfactory [,sætɪs'fæktərɪ] *adj* satisfactorio(ria).

satisfied ['sætɪsfaɪd] *adj* satisfecho(cha); **you're never satisfied!** ¡nunca te conformas con nada!; **a satisfied smile** una sonrisa de satisfacción; **to be satisfied with sthg** estar satisfecho con algo; **to be satisfied that** estar convencido (de) que.

satisfy ['sætɪsfaɪ] (*pt* & *pp* -**ied**) *vt* - **1.** [gen] satisfacer - **2.** [convince] convencer; **to satisfy sb that** convencer a alguien (de) que; **to satisfy o.s. that** convencerse (de) que - **3.** [requirements] cumplir, satisfacer.

satisfying ['sætɪsfaɪŋ] *adj* - **1.** [pleasant] satisfactorio(ria) - **2.** [filling] sustancioso(sa); **a satisfying meal** una comida sustanciosa.

satsuma [,sæt'suːmə] *n* satsuma *f*.

saturate ['sætʃəreɪt] *vt* - **1.** [drench]: **to saturate sthg (with)** empapar algo (de); **he was saturated with sweat** estaba empapado de sudor - **2.** [fill completely] saturar; **to saturate sthg (with)** saturar algo (de).

saturated fat ['sætʃəreɪtɪd-] *n* grasa *f* saturada.

saturation [,sætʃə'reɪʃn] <> *n* saturación *f*. <> *comp* [bombing] por saturación; **TV: saturation coverage** cobertura exhaustiva.

saturation point *n*: **to reach saturation point** llegar al punto de saturación.

Saturday ['sætədɪ] <> *n* sábado *m*; **what day is it? – it's Saturday** ¿a qué estamos hoy? – estamos a sábado; **on Saturday** el sábado; **are you going Saturday?** *inf* ¿te vas el sábado?; **see you Saturday!** *inf* ¡hasta el sábado!; **on Saturdays** los sábados; **last Saturday** el sábado pasado; **this Saturday** este sábado, el sábado que viene; **next Saturday** el sábado de la semana que viene; **every Saturday** todos los sábados; **every other Saturday** cada dos sábados, un sábado sí y otro no; **the Saturday before** el sábado anterior; **the Saturday after next** no este sábado sino el siguiente; **the Saturday before last** hace dos sábados; **Saturday week, a week on Saturday** del sábado en ocho días; **to work Saturdays** trabajar los sábados. <> *comp* del sábado; **Saturday morning/night** la mañana/noche del sábado; **Saturday afternoon/evening** la tarde del sábado; **a Saturday job** un trabajo los sábados.

Saturn ['sætən] *n* Saturno *m*.

sauce [sɔːs] *n* - **1.** CULIN salsa *f* - **2.** *UK inf* [cheek] frescura *f*, descaro *m*.

sauce boat *n* salsera *f*.

saucepan ['sɔːspən] *n* [with two handles] cacerola *f*; [with one long handle] cazo *m*.

saucer ['sɔːsəʳ] *n* platillo *m*.

saucy ['sɔːsɪ] (*comp* -**ier**, *superl* -**iest**) *adj inf* descarado(da), fresco(ca).

Saudi Arabia [,saʊdɪə'reɪbjə] *n* Arabia Saudí.

Saudi (Arabian) ['saʊdɪ-] <> *adj* saudí, saudita. <> *n* [person] saudí *mf*, saudita *mf*.

sauna ['sɔːnə] *n* sauna *f*.

saunter ['sɔːntəʳ] *vi* pasearse (tranquilamente); **he sauntered into the room** entró desenfadadamente en la habitación.

sausage ['sɒsɪdʒ] *n* salchicha *f*.

sausage roll *n* UK *salchicha envuelta en masa como de empanadilla.*

sauté [UK 'səʊteɪ, US səʊ'teɪ] <> *adj* salteado(da). <> *vt* (*pt & pp* **sautéed** OR **sauted**) saltear.

savage ['sævɪdʒ] <> *adj* [cruel, fierce] feroz, salvaje. <> *n pej* salvaje *mf.* <> *vt* - **1.** [subj: animal] embestir, atacar - **2.** [subj: person] atacar con ferocidad.

savageness ['sævɪdʒnɪs], **savagery** ['sævɪdʒrɪ] *n* salvajismo *m*, ferocidad *f.*

savanna(h) [sə'vænə] *n* sabana *f.*

save [seɪv] <> *vt* - **1.** [rescue] salvar, rescatar; **to save sb from sthg** salvar a alguien de algo - **2.** [prevent waste of - time, money, energy] ahorrar - **3.** [set aside - money] ahorrar; [- food, strength] guardar; **why don't you save some of your sweets for later?** ¿por qué no te guardas algunos caramelos para más tarde?; **will you save me some soup?** ¿me guardarás algo de sopa?; **save your strength for later** ahorra fuerzas para más tarde - **4.** [avoid] evitar; **it saves having to go to the bank** ahorra tener que ir al banco; **to save sb from doing sthg** evitar a alguien (el) hacer algo - **5.** SPORT parar - **6.** COMPUT guardar
▶▶ **to save face** salvar las apariencias. <> *vi* ahorrar. <> *n* SPORT parada *f.* <> *prep fml:* **save (for)** excepto.
◆ **save up** *vi* ahorrar.

save as you earn *n* UK *forma de ahorro en que la contribución mensual origina rédito libre de impuestos.*

saveloy ['sævəlɔɪ] *n* UK *salchicha ahumada muy sazonada.*

saver ['seɪvər] *n* - **1.** [thing that prevents wastage]: **a time saver** algo que ahorra tiempo - **2.** FIN ahorrador *m*, -ra *f.*

saving grace ['seɪvɪŋ-] *n* lo único positivo.

savings ['seɪvɪŋz] *npl* ahorros *mpl.*

savings account *n* cuenta *f* de ahorros.

savings bank *n* ≃ caja *f* de ahorros.

saviour UK, **savior** US ['seɪvjər] *n* salvador *m*, -ra *f.*
◆ **Saviour** *n:* **the Saviour** el Salvador.

savoir-faire [sævwa:'feər] *n* tacto *m*, don *m* de gentes.

savour UK, **savor** US ['seɪvər] *vt lit & fig* saborear.

savoury UK (*pl* **-ies**), **savory** US ['seɪvərɪ] <> *adj* - **1.** [not sweet] salado(da) - **2.** US [tasty] sabroso(sa) - **3.** [respectable, pleasant] respetable, agradable; **not a very savoury character** un personaje no muy honesto. <> *n* (*pl* **-ies**) comida *f* de aperitivo.

saw [sɔː] <> *pt* ▷ **see.** <> *n* sierra *f.* <> *vt* (UK **-ed**, *pp* **sawn**, US **-ed**) serrar.

sawdust ['sɔːdʌst] *n* serrín *m.*

sawed-off shotgun US = **sawn-off shotgun.**

sawmill ['sɔːmɪl] *n* aserradero *m.*

sawn [sɔːn] *pp* UK ▷ **saw.**

sawn-off shotgun UK, **sawed-off shotgun** US [sɔːd-] *n* arma *f* de cañones recortados.

sax [sæks] *n inf* saxo *m.*

Saxon ['sæksn] <> *adj* sajón(ona). <> *n* sajón *m*, -ona *f.*

saxophone ['sæksəfəʊn] *n* saxofón *m.*

saxophonist [UK ˌsæks'ɒfənɪst, US 'sæksəfəʊnɪst] *n* saxofón *mf.*

say [seɪ] <> *vt* (*pt & pp* **said**) - **1.** [gen] decir; **she said that...** dijo que...; **you should have said so!** ¡haberlo dicho!; **to say sthg again** repetir algo; **you can say that again!** ¡ya lo creo!; **to say to o.s.** decirse a uno mismo; **to say yes** decir que sí; **he's said to be good** se dice que es bueno; **let's say you were to win** pongamos que ganaras; **shall we say 9.30?** ¿qué tal a las 9.30?; **to say nothing of** sin mencionar; **that goes without saying** ni que decir tiene; **to say the least** por no decir otra cosa; **I'll say this for him/her...** hay que decir OR admitir que él/ella...; **it has a lot to be said for it** tiene muy buenos puntos en su favor; **she didn't have much to say for herself** *inf* era muy reservada - **2.** [indicate - clock, meter] marcar. <> *n:* **to have a/no say in sthg** tener/no tener voz y voto en algo; **let me have my say** déjame decir lo que pienso.
◆ **that is to say** *adv* es decir.

SAYE *n abbr of* **save as you earn.**

saying ['seɪɪŋ] *n* dicho *m.*

say-so *n inf* - **1.** [unproven statement]: **it's only say-so** es algo que se dice, solamente - **2.** [permission] aprobación *f.*

s/c *abbr of* **self-contained.**

scab [skæb] *n* - **1.** MED costra *f* - **2.** *pej* [non-striker] esquirol *m.*

scabby ['skæbɪ] (*comp* **-ier**, *superl* **-iest**) *adj* costroso(sa).

scabies ['skeɪbiːz] *n* (*U*) sarna *f.*

scaffold ['skæfəʊld] *n* - **1.** [around building] andamio *m* - **2.** [for execution] cadalso *m*, patíbulo *m.*

scaffolding ['skæfəldɪŋ] *n* (*U*) andamios *mpl*, andamiaje *m.*

scald [skɔːld] <> *n* escaldadura *f.* <> *vt* escaldar.

scalding ['skɔːldɪŋ] *adj* hirviendo.

scale [skeɪl] <> *n* - **1.** [of map] escala *f*; **to scale** a escala; **not drawn to scale** no hecho(cha) a escala - **2.** [size, extent] tamaño *m*, escala *f*; **on a large scale** a gran escala - **3.** [on measuring equipment] escala f - **4.** [music] escala f - **5.** [of fish, snake] escama f. ⟨⟩ vt - **1.** [climb] escalar - **2.** [remove scales from] escamar.

◆ **scales** npl - **1.** [for weighing food] balanza f - **2.** [for weighing person] báscula f; **bathroom scales** báscula de baño.

◆ **scale down** vt insep reducir.

scale diagram n diagrama m en escala.

scale model n maqueta f.

scallion ['skæljən] n US cebolleta f.

scallop ['skɒləp] ⟨⟩ n ZOOL vieira f. ⟨⟩ vt [decorate edge of] festonear.

scalp [skælp] ⟨⟩ n cuero m cabelludo. ⟨⟩ vt cortar la cabellera a.

scalpel ['skælpəl] n bisturí m.

scaly ['skeɪlɪ] adj [skin] escamoso(sa).

scam [skæm] n inf estratagema f.

scamp [skæmp] n inf bribón m, -ona f, tunante m, -ta f.

scamper ['skæmpər] vi corretear.

scampi ['skæmpɪ] n (U): **(breaded) scampi** gambas fpl a la gabardina.

scan [skæn] ⟨⟩ n exploración f ultrasónica. ⟨⟩ vt (pt & pp -ned, cont -ning) - **1.** [examine carefully] examinar - **2.** [glance at] dar un vistazo a - **3.** ELECTRON & TV registrar - **4.** COMPUT hacer un escáner de. ⟨⟩ vi (pt & pp -ned, cont -ning) - **1.** LIT estar bien medido(da) - **2.** COMPUT hacer un escáner.

scandal ['skændl] n - **1.** [scandalous event, outrage] escándalo m - **2.** [scandalous talk] habladurías fpl.

scandalize, -ise ['skændəlaɪz] vt escandalizar.

scandalous ['skændələs] adj escandaloso(sa).

Scandinavia [ˌskændɪˈneɪvjə] n Escandinavia.

Scandinavian [ˌskændɪˈneɪvjən] ⟨⟩ adj escandinavo(va). ⟨⟩ n [person] escandinavo m, -va f.

scanner ['skænər] n COMPUT & MED escáner m.

scant [skænt] adj escaso(sa).

scanty ['skæntɪ] (comp -ier, superl -iest) adj [amount, resources] escaso(sa); [dress] ligero(ra); [meal] insuficiente.

scapegoat ['skeɪpgəʊt] n cabeza f de turco.

scar [skɑːr] ⟨⟩ n - **1.** [physical] cicatriz f - **2.** fig [mental] señal f. ⟨⟩ vt (pt & pp -red, cont -ring) - **1.** [physically] dejar una cicatriz en; **he was scarred for life** quedó marcado(da) de por vida - **2.** fig [mentally] marcar.

scarce [skeəs] adj escaso(sa); **to make o.s. scarce** esfumarse, quitarse de en medio.

scarcely ['skeəslɪ] adv apenas; **scarcely anyone/ever** casi nadie/nunca.

scarcity ['skeəsətɪ] n escasez f; **it has scarcity value** tiene un gran valor debido a su rareza.

scare [skeər] ⟨⟩ n - **1.** [sudden fear] susto m, sobresalto m - **2.** [public fear] temor m - **3.** [panic]: **there was a bomb scare** hubo una amenaza de bomba. ⟨⟩ vt asustar, sobresaltar.

◆ **scare away, scare off** vt sep ahuyentar.

scarecrow ['skeəkrəʊ] n espantapájaros m inv.

scared ['skeəd] adj - **1.** [frightened] asustado(da); **don't be scared** no te asustes; **to be scared stiff** OR **to death** estar muerto de miedo - **2.** [worried]: **to be scared that** tener miedo que.

scarey ['skeərɪ] = **scary**.

scarf [skɑːf] ⟨⟩ n (pl -s OR scarves) [for neck] bufanda f; [for head] pañuelo m de cabeza. ⟨⟩ vt US [eat]: **scarf (down)** zamparse.

scarlet ['skɑːlət] ⟨⟩ adj color escarlata. ⟨⟩ n escarlata f.

scarlet fever n escarlatina f.

scarves [skɑːvz] npl ▷ **scarf**.

scary ['skeərɪ] (comp -ier, superl -iest), **scarey** adj inf espeluznante.

scathing ['skeɪðɪŋ] adj mordaz; **to be scathing about sthg/sb** criticar duramente algo/a alguien.

scatter ['skætər] ⟨⟩ vt esparcir, desparramar. ⟨⟩ vi dispersarse.

scatterbrained ['skætəbreɪnd] adj inf atolondrado(da).

scattered ['skætəd] adj disperso(sa).

scattering ['skætərɪŋ] n: **a scattering of snow** un poco de nieve.

scatty ['skætɪ] (comp -ier, superl -iest) adj UK inf atolondrado(da).

scavenge ['skævɪndʒ] ⟨⟩ vt - **1.** [subj: animal]: **to scavenge food** buscar carroña - **2.** [subj: person] rebuscar entre las basuras. ⟨⟩ vi - **1.** [animal]: **to scavenge for food** buscar carroña - **2.** [person]: **to scavenge for sthg** rebuscar algo.

scavenger ['skævɪndʒər] n - **1.** [animal] carroñero m, -ra f - **2.** [person] persona f que rebusca en las basuras.

SCE (abbr of **Scottish Certificate of Education**) n título de enseñanza secundaria en Escocia.

scenario [sɪˈnɑːrɪəʊ] (pl -s) n - **1.** [possible situation] situación f hipotética - **2.** [of film, play] resumen m del argumento.

scene [siːn] n - **1.** [gen, theatre] escena f; **behind the scenes** entre bastidores; **and then she appeared on the scene** fig y entonces apareció en escena - **2.** [painting of place] panorama m, paisaje m - **3.** [location] sitio m; **on the scene** en el sitio; **the scene of the crime** la escena del crimen; **a change of scene** un cambio de ambiente OR de aires; **it's not my scene** no es lo mío **- 4.** [show of emotion] jaleo *m*, escándalo *m*; **to make a scene** montar una escena ▸▸ **to set the scene** [for person] describir la escena; [for event] crear el ambiente propicio.

scenery ['si:nərɪ] *n (U)* **- 1.** [of countryside] paisaje *m* **- 2.** THEAT decorado *m*.

scenic ['si:nɪk] *adj* [view] pintoresco(ca); [tour] turístico(ca).

scenic route *n* ruta *f* turística.

scent [sent] ◇ *n* **- 1.** [smell - of flowers] fragancia *f*; [- of animal] rastro *m* **- 2.** *fig* [track] pista *f*; **to lose the scent** perder la pista; **to throw sb off the scent** burlar a alguien **- 3.** [perfume] perfume *m*. ◇ *vt* **- 1.** [subj: animal] olfatear, husmear **- 2.** *fig* [subj: person] percibir.

scented ['sentɪd] *adj* perfumado(da).

scepter US = **sceptre**.

sceptic UK, **skeptic** US ['skeptɪk] *n* escéptico *m*, -ca *f*.

sceptical UK, **skeptical** US ['skeptɪkl] *adj* escéptico(ca); **to be sceptical about** tener muchas dudas acerca de.

scepticism UK, **skepticism** US ['skeptɪsɪzm] *n* escepticismo *m*.

sceptre UK, **scepter** US ['septər] *n* cetro *m*.

schedule [UK 'ʃedjuːl, US 'skedʒʊl] ◇ *n* **- 1.** [plan] programa *m*, plan *m*; **(according) to schedule** según lo previsto; **on schedule** sin retraso; **ahead of schedule** con adelanto; **behind schedule** con retraso **- 2.** [of prices, contents] lista *f*; [of times] horario *m*. ◇ *vt*: **to schedule sthg (for)** fijar algo (para).

scheduled flight [UK 'ʃedjuːld-, US 'skedʒʊld-] *n* vuelo *m* regular.

schematic [skɪ'mætɪk] *adj* esquemático(ca).

scheme [skiːm] ◇ *n* **- 1.** [plan] plano *m*, proyecto *m*; **pension scheme** plan *m* de pensiones **- 2.** *pej* [dishonest plan] intriga *f*, treta *f* **- 3.** [arrangement, decoration - of room] disposición *f*; **colour scheme** combinación *f* de colores ▸▸ **the scheme of things** el orden de las cosas. ◇ *vi pej*: **to scheme (to do sthg)** intrigar (para hacer algo).

scheming ['skiːmɪŋ] *adj* intrigante.

schism ['sɪzm, 'skɪzm] *n* cisma *f*.

schizophrenia [ˌskɪtsə'friːnjə] *n* esquizofrenia *f*.

schizophrenic [ˌskɪtsə'frenɪk] ◇ *adj* esquizofrénico(ca). ◇ *n* esquizofrénico *m*, -ca *f*.

schmal(t)z [ʃmɔːlts] *n inf* sensiblería *f*.

schmuck [ʃmʌk] *n US inf* tonto *m*, -ta *f*.

scholar ['skɒlər] *n* **- 1.** [expert] erudito *m*, -ta *f* **- 2.** *dated* [student] alumno *m*, -na *f* **- 3.** [holder of scholarship] becario *m*, -ria *f*.

scholarship ['skɒləʃɪp] *n* **- 1.** [grant] beca *f* **- 2.** [learning] erudición *f*.

scholastic [skə'læstɪk] *adj fml* escolar.

school [skuːl] *n* **- 1.** [for children] colegio *m*, escuela *f*; **to go to school** ir al colegio, ir a la escuela; **the children are at school** los niños están en el colegio; **art school** escuela *f* de arte; **driving school** autoescuela *f*; **law/medical school** facultad *f* de derecho/medicina **- 2.** US [university] universidad *f* **- 3.** [group of fish, dolphins] banco *m*.

school age *n* edad *f* escolar.

schoolbook ['skuːlbʊk] *n* libro *m* de texto.

schoolboy ['skuːlbɔɪ] *n* colegial *m*, escolar *m*.

schoolchild ['skuːltʃaɪld] (*pl* -children [-tʃɪldrən]) *n* colegial *m*, -la *f*, escolar *mf*.

schooldays ['skuːldeɪz] *npl* años *mpl* de colegio.

school friend *n* amigo *m*, -ga *f* de colegio.

schoolgirl ['skuːlgɜːl] *n* colegiala *f*, escolar *f*.

schooling ['skuːlɪŋ] *n* educación *f* escolar.

schoolkid ['skuːlkɪd] *n inf* colegial *m*, -la *f*, alumno *m*, -na *f*.

school-leaver [-ˌliːvər] *n UK* joven que ha terminado la enseñanza.

school-leaving age [-ˈliːvɪŋ-] *n* edad *f* de finalización de la enseñanza obligatoria.

schoolmaster ['skuːlˌmɑːstər] *n dated* [at primary school] maestro *m*; [at secondary school] profesor *m*.

schoolmistress ['skuːlˌmɪstrɪs] *n dated* [at primary school] maestra *f*; [at secondary school] profesora *f*.

school of thought *n* corriente *f* de opinión.

school report *n* informe *m* escolar.

schoolroom ['skuːlrʊm] *n dated* clase *f*, aula *f*.

schoolteacher ['skuːlˌtiːtʃər] *n* [primary] maestro *m*, -tra *f*; [secondary] profesor *m*, -ra *f*.

school uniform *n* uniforme *m* escolar.

schoolwork ['skuːlwɜːk] *n (U)* trabajo *m* escolar.

school year *n* año *m* escolar.

schooner ['skuːnər] *n* **- 1.** [ship] goleta *f* **- 2.** *UK* [sherry glass] copa *f* larga (para jerez).

sciatica [saɪ'ætɪkə] *n* ciática *f*.

science ['saɪəns] ◇ *n* ciencia *f*; **his best subject is science** su mejor asignatura son las ciencias. ◇ *comp* de ciencias; **science lab** laboratorio de ciencias.

science fiction *n* ciencia *f* ficción.

scientific [ˌsaɪən'tɪfɪk] *adj* científico(ca).

scientist ['saɪəntɪst] *n* científico *m*, -ca *f*.

sci-fi ['saɪfaɪ] (*abbr of* science fiction) *n inf* ciencia *f* ficción.

Scilly Isles ['sɪlɪ-], **Scillies** ['sɪlɪz] npl: the Scilly Isles las islas Sorlinga.

scintillating ['sɪntɪleɪtɪŋ] adj brillante, chispeante.

scissors ['sɪzəz] npl tijeras fpl; **a pair of scissors** unas tijeras.

sclerosis = multiple sclerosis.

scoff [skɒf] ◇ vt UK inf zamparse, tragarse. ◇ vi: **to scoff (at sb/sthg)** mofarse OR burlarse (de alguien/de algo).

scold [skəʊld] vt regañar, reñir.

scone [skɒn] n bollo tomado con té a la hora de la merienda.

scoop [sku:p] ◇ n - **1.** [utensil - for sugar] cucharita f plana; [- for ice cream] pinzas fpl (de helado); [- for flour] paleta f - **2.** [amount - of sugar] cucharilla f; [- of ice cream] bola f - **3.** PRESS exclusiva f; **to make a scoop** conseguir una exclusiva. ◇ vt - **1.** [with hands] recoger - **2.** [with utensil] recoger con cucharilla.
◆ **scoop out** vt sep sacar con cuchara.

scoot [sku:t] vi inf ir pitando; **go on, scoot!** vamos, ¡lárgate!

scooter ['sku:tər] n - **1.** [toy] patinete m - **2.** [motorcycle] escúter m, Vespa® f, motoneta f Amér.

scope [skəʊp] n (U) - **1.** [opportunity] posibilidades fpl; **there is scope for improvement** se puede mejorar - **2.** [range] alcance m.

scorch [skɔ:tʃ] ◇ vt [dress, fabric, grass] chamuscar; [face, skin] quemar. ◇ vi [burn - dress, material] chamuscarse; [face, skin] quemarse.

scorched earth policy [skɔ:tʃt-] n política f de tierra quemada.

scorcher ['skɔ:tʃər] n inf día m abrasador.

scorching ['skɔ:tʃɪŋ] adj inf abrasador(ra).

score [skɔ:r] ◇ n - **1.** [in test] calificación f, nota f; [in competition, game] puntuación f; **are you keeping (the) score?** ¿llevas el tanteo? - **2.** SPORT resultado m; **what's the score?** ¿cómo van?; **the final score was 2 all** el resultado final fue empate a dos - **3.** dated [twenty] veintena f - **4.** MUS partitura f - **5.** [subject]: **on that score** a ese respecto, por lo que se refiere a eso
▸▸ **to have a score to settle with sb** tener una cuenta que saldar con alguien; **to know the score** conocer el percal. ◇ vt - **1.** SPORT marcar - **2.** [achieve - success, victory] obtener - **3.** [cut] grabar. ◇ vi - **1.** SPORT marcar - **2.** [in test etc] obtener una puntuación; **you scored well in part one** obtuviste una buena puntuación en la primera parte - **3.** [win in an argument]: **to score over sb** aventajar a alguien.
◆ **scores** npl [large number]: **scores (of)** montones mpl (de).
◆ **score out** vt sep UK tachar.

scoreboard ['skɔ:bɔ:d] n tanteador m, marcador m.

scorer ['skɔ:rər] n - **1.** [official] tanteador m, -ra f - **2.** [player - in football] goleador m, -ra f; [- in other sports] marcador m, -ra f.

scorn [skɔ:n] ◇ n menosprecio m, desdén m; **to pour scorn on sthg/sb** despreciar algo/a alguien. ◇ vt menospreciar, desdeñar.

scornful ['skɔ:nfʊl] adj despectivo(va), de desdén; **to be scornful of sthg** desdeñar algo.

Scorpio ['skɔ:pɪəʊ] (pl -s) n Escorpión m; **to be (a) Scorpio** ser Escorpión.

scorpion ['skɔ:pjən] n escorpión m, alacrán m.

Scot [skɒt] n escocés m, -esa f.

scotch [skɒtʃ] vt [rumour] poner fin a, desmentir; [idea] desechar.

Scotch [skɒtʃ] n whisky m escocés.

Scotch egg n UK bola de fiambre de salchicha rebozada y con huevo duro en el centro.

Scotch tape® n US ≃ celo® m, cinta f Scotch® Amér, ≃ durex® m Arg, Bol & Méx, ≃ Scotch® m Andes.

scot-free adj inf: **to get off scot-free** salir impune.

Scotland ['skɒtlənd] n Escocia.

Scotland Yard n sede central de la policía londinense.

Scots [skɒts] ◇ adj escocés(esa). ◇ n [dialect] escocés m.

Scotsman ['skɒtsmən] (pl -men [-mən]) n escocés m.

Scotswoman ['skɒtswʊmən] (pl -women [-ˌwɪmɪn]) n escocesa f.

Scottish ['skɒtɪʃ] adj escocés(esa).

Scottish National Party n: **the Scottish National Party** el Partido Nacionalista Escocés.

scoundrel ['skaʊndrəl] n dated sinvergüenza m, canalla m.

scour [skaʊər] vt - **1.** [clean] fregar, restregar - **2.** [search] registrar, batir; **they scoured the countryside looking for the little girl** peinaron el campo en busca de la niña.

scourer ['skaʊərər] n estropajo m.

scourge [skɜ:dʒ] n [cause of suffering] azote m.

scout [skaʊt] n MIL explorador m.
◆ **Scout** n [boy scout] explorador m.
◆ **scout around** vi: **to scout around (for)** explorar el terreno (en busca de).

scowl [skaʊl] ◇ n ceño m fruncido. ◇ vi fruncir el ceño; **to scowl at sb** mirar con ceño a alguien.

scrabble ['skræbl] vi - **1.** [scramble, scrape] escarbar; **to scrabble up/down** subir/bajar escarbando - **2.** [feel around] palpar en busca de algo; **to scrabble around for sthg** hurgar en busca de algo.

Scrabble® ['skræbl] *n* Scrabble® *m*.

scraggy ['skrægɪ] (*comp* -**ier**, *superl* -**iest**) *adj inf* flaco(ca).

scram [skræm] (*pt & pp* -**med**, *cont* -**ming**) *vi inf* largarse; **scram!** ¡lárgate!

scramble ['skræmbl] <> *n* [rush] pelea *f*; **he got hurt in the scramble for the door** resultó herido en la desbandada que hubo hacia la puerta. <> *vi* - **1.** [climb] trepar - **2.** [move clumsily]: **to scramble to one's feet** levantarse rápidamente y tambaleándose; **to scramble out of the way** apartarse atropelladamente.

scrambled eggs ['skræmbld-] *npl* huevos *mpl* revueltos.

scrambler ['skræmblər] *n* COMPUT distorsionador *m* (de frecuencias).

scrap [skræp] <> *n* - **1.** [small piece] trozo *m*, pedazo *m*; **it won't make a scrap of difference** no lo cambiará en lo más mínimo - **2.** (U) [metal] chatarra *f*; **he sold it for scrap** lo vendió para chatarra - **3.** *inf* [fight, quarrel] pelotera *f*; **to have a scrap** pelearse. <> *vt* (*pt & pp* -**ped**, *cont* -**ping**) desechar, descartar.

➡ **scraps** *npl* [food] sobras *fpl*.

scrapbook ['skræpbʊk] *n* álbum *m* de recortes.

scrap dealer *n* chatarrero *m*, -ra *f*.

scrape [skreɪp] <> *n* - **1.** [noise] chirrido *m* - **2.** *dated* [difficult situation] apuro *m*, lío *m*. <> *vt* - **1.** [remove]: **to scrape sthg off sthg** raspar algo de algo - **2.** [vegetables] raspar - **3.** [car, bumper, glass] rayar; [knee, elbow, skin] rasguñar, arañar. <> *vi* [rub]: **to scrape against/on sthg** rozar contra/en algo.

➡ **scrape through** *vt insep* [exam] aprobar por los pelos.

➡ **scrape together, scrape up** *vt sep* juntar (a duras penas).

scraper ['skreɪpər] *n* raspador *m*.

scrap heap *n* montón *m* de chatarra; **to end up on the scrap heap** [idea, plan] ir a parar en el cubo de basura; [person] quedar arrinconado(da); **to throw sthg on the scrap heap** descartar algo.

scrapings ['skreɪpɪŋz] *npl* raspaduras *fpl*.

scrap merchant *n* UK chatarrero *m*, -ra *f*.

scrap metal *n* chatarra *f*.

scrap paper UK, **scratch paper** US *n* (U) papel *m* usado.

scrappy ['skræpɪ] (*comp* -**ier**, *superl* -**iest**) *adj pej* deshilvanado(da), fragmentario(ria).

scrapyard ['skræpjɑːd] *n* [gen] depósito *m* de chatarra; [for cars] cementerio *m* de coches.

scratch [skrætʃ] <> *n* - **1.** [wound] arañazo *m*, rasguño *m* - **2.** [mark] raya *f*, surco *m*

➡➡ **to do sthg from scratch** hacer algo partiendo desde el principio; **to be up to scratch** estar a la altura requerida. <> *vt* - **1.** [wound] arañar, rasguñar - **2.** [mark] rayar - **3.** [rubhead, leg] rascar; **to scratch o.s.** rascarse; **he scratched his head** se rascó la cabeza. <> *vi* - **1.** [make mark]: **to scratch at/against sthg** arañar algo - **2.** [rub] rascarse.

scratch card *n* tarjeta con una zona que hay que rascar para ver si contiene premio.

scratchpad ['skrætʃpæd] *n* US bloc *m* de notas.

scratch paper US = **scrap paper**.

scratchy ['skrætʃɪ] (*comp* -**ier**, *superl* -**iest**) *adj* - **1.** [record] rayado(da); [sound] que chirría - **2.** [material] áspero(ra); [pen] que raspea.

scrawl [skrɔːl] <> *n* garabatos *mpl*. <> *vt* garabatear.

scrawny ['skrɔːnɪ] (*comp* -**ier**, *superl* -**iest**) *adj* flaco(ca).

scream [skriːm] <> *n* - **1.** [cry, shout] grito *m*, chillido *m*; **screams of laughter** carcajadas *fpl* - **2.** [noise] chirrido *m* - **3.** *inf* [funny person]: **she's a scream** ella es la monda. <> *vt* vociferar. <> *vi* - **1.** [person] gritar, chillar; **to scream at sb** gritar a alguien - **2.** [tyres] chirriar; [jet] silbar.

scree [skriː] *n* montón de piedras desprendidas de la ladera de una montaña.

screech [skriːtʃ] <> *n* - **1.** [of person] chillido *m*; [of bird] chirrido *m* - **2.** [of car, tyres] chirrido *m*, rechinar *m*. <> *vt* gritar. <> *vi* - **1.** [person, bird] chillar - **2.** [car, tyres] chirriar, rechinar.

screen [skriːn] <> *n* - **1.** TV, CIN & COMPUT pantalla *f* - **2.** [panel] biombo *m*. <> *vt* - **1.** [show in cinema] proyectar - **2.** [broadcast on TV] emitir - **3.** [shield]: **to screen sthg/sb (from)** proteger algo/a alguien (de) - **4.** [candidate, patient] examinar; **to screen sb for sthg** hacer un chequeo a alguien para algo.

➡ **screen off** *vt sep* separar mediante un biombo.

screen break *n* COMPUT salto *m* de pantalla.

screen door *n* puerta *f* de tela metálica.

screening ['skriːnɪŋ] *n* - **1.** [of film] proyección *f* - **2.** [of TV programme] emisión *f* - **3.** [for security] examen *m*, investigación *f* - **4.** MED [examination] chequeo *m*.

screenplay ['skriːnpleɪ] *n* guión *m*.

screen saver *n* COMPUT salvapantallas *m inv*.

screenshot ['skriːnʃɒt] *n* pantallazo *m*, captura *f* de pantalla.

screen test *n* prueba *f* cinematográfica.

screenwriter ['skriːnˌraɪtər] *n* guionista *mf*.

screw [skru:] ⬦ *n* [for fastening] tornillo *m*. ⬦ *vt* - **1.** [fix]: **to screw sthg to** atornillar algo a - **2.** [twist] enroscar; **to screw a lid on** poner la tapa de rosca - **3.** *vulg* [woman] follar, coger *Amér*. ⬦ *vi*: **the lid screws on/off** la tapa se abre/cierra enroscándola.

➤ **screw up** *vt sep* - **1.** [sheet of paper etc] arrugar - **2.** [eyes] entornar; [face] arrugar - **3.** *v inf* [ruin] jorobar.

screwball ['skru:bɔ:l] *n US* [person] cabeza *mf* loca; **screwball comedy** *US* comedia *f* disparatada.

screwdriver ['skru:,draɪvəʳ] *n* destornillador *m*, desarmador *m Méx*.

screwtop jar ['skru:tɒp-] *n* tarro *m* con tapa de rosca.

screwy ['skru:ɪ] *adj US inf* pirado(da).

scribble ['skrɪbl] ⬦ *n* garabato *m*. ⬦ *vt* & *vi* garabatear.

scribe [skraɪb] *n fml* amanuense *mf*, scriba *f*.

scrimp [skrɪmp] *vi*: **to scrimp and save (to do sthg)** apretarse el cinturón (para hacer algo).

script [skrɪpt] *n* - **1.** [of play, film etc] guión *m* - **2.** [system of writing] escritura *f* - **3.** [handwriting] letra *f*.

scripted ['skrɪptɪd] *adj* con guión.

Scriptures ['skrɪptʃəz] *npl*: **the Scriptures** las Sagradas Escrituras.

scriptwriter ['skrɪpt,raɪtəʳ] *n* guionista *mf*.

scroll [skrəʊl] ⬦ *n* rollo *m* de pergamino/papel. ⬦ *vt* COMPUT desplazar.

➤ **scroll down** *vi* COMPUT desplazarse hacia abajo.

➤ **scroll up** *vi* COMPUT desplazarse hacia arriba.

scroll bar *n* COMPUT barra *f* de desplazamiento.

scrooge [skru:dʒ] *n inf pej* ruin *mf*, tacaño *m*, -ña *f*.

scrotum ['skrəʊtəm] (*pl* -**ta** [-tə] OR -**tums**) *n* escroto *m*.

scrounge [skraʊndʒ] *inf* ⬦ *vt* gorrear, gorronear. ⬦ *vi*: **to scrounge (off sb)** *UK* gorrear OR gorronear (de alguien).

scrounger ['skraʊndʒəʳ] *n inf* gorrón *m*, -ona *f*.

scrub [skrʌb] ⬦ *n* - **1.** [rub] restregón *m*, fregado *m*; **give it a good scrub** dale un buen fregado - **2.** [undergrowth] maleza *f*. ⬦ *vt* (*pt* & *pp* -**bed**, *cont* -**bing**) restregar.

scrubbing brush *UK* ['skrʌbɪŋ-], **scrub brush** *US n* cepillo *m* de fregar.

scruff [skrʌf] *n*: **by the scruff of the neck** por el pescuezo.

scruffy ['skrʌfɪ] (*comp* -**ier**, *superl* -**iest**) *adj* [person] dejado(da); [clothes] andrajoso(sa); [room] desordenado(da).

scrum(mage) ['skrʌm(ɪdʒ)] *n* RUGBY melé *f*.

scrumptious ['skrʌmpʃəs] *adj inf* riquísimo(ma).

scrunch [skrʌntʃ] *inf* ⬦ *vt* estrujar. ⬦ *vi* crujir.

scrunchie ['skrʌntʃɪ], **scrunchy** *n* coletero *m*.

scruples ['skru:plz] *npl* escrúpulos *mpl*.

scrupulous ['skru:pjʊləs] *adj* escrupuloso(sa).

scrupulously ['skru:pjʊləslɪ] *adv* - **1.** [fairly] escrupulosamente - **2.** [thoroughly] completamente, totalmente; **scrupulously clean** impecable.

scrutinize, -ise ['skru:tɪnaɪz] *vt* escudriñar.

scrutiny ['skru:tɪnɪ] *n* (*U*) escrutinio *m*, examen *m*; **to be open to public scrutiny** estar expuesto(ta) al examen del público; **to come under the scrutiny of** ser cuidadosamente examinado(da) por.

scuba diving ['sku:bə-] *n* buceo *m* con botellas de oxígeno.

scud [skʌd] (*pt* & *pp* -**ded**, *cont* -**ding**) *vi liter* deslizarse rápidamente.

scuff [skʌf] *vt* - **1.** [drag] arrastrar - **2.** [damage - shoes] pelar; [- furniture, floor] rayar.

scuffle ['skʌfl] ⬦ *n* refriega *f*, reyerta *f*; **there were scuffles between the police and demonstrators** hubo enfrentamientos entre la policía y los manifestantes. ⬦ *vi*: **to scuffle (with sb)** pelearse (con alguien).

scull [skʌl] ⬦ *n* [oar] remo *m*. ⬦ *vi* remar.

scullery ['skʌlərɪ] (*pl* -**ies**) *n* trascocina *f*, fregadero *m*.

sculpt [skʌlpt] *vt* esculpir.

sculptor ['skʌlptəʳ] *n* escultor *m*, -ra *f*.

sculpture ['skʌlptʃəʳ] ⬦ *n* escultura *f*. ⬦ *vt* esculpir.

scum [skʌm] *n* (*U*) - **1.** [froth] espuma *f* - **2.** *v inf pej* [worthless people] escoria *f*; **to be the scum of the earth** ser la escoria de la sociedad.

scupper ['skʌpəʳ] *vt fig* & NAUT hundir.

scurf [skɜ:f] *n* caspa *f*.

scurrilous ['skʌrələs] *adj fml* injurioso(sa), difamatorio(ria).

scurry ['skʌrɪ] (*pt* & *pp* -**ied**) *vi*: **to scurry off** OR **away** escabullirse.

scurvy ['skɜ:vɪ] *n* escorbuto *m*.

scuttle ['skʌtl] ⬦ *n* cubo *m* del carbón, carbonera *f*. ⬦ *vi* [rush]: **to scuttle off** OR **away** escabullirse.

scythe [saɪð] ⬦ *n* guadaña *f*. ⬦ *vt* guadañar, segar.

SDI (*abbr of* **Strategic Defense Initiative**) *n* IDE *f*.

SDLP (*abbr of* **Social Democratic and Labour Party**) *n partido político norirlandés que defiende la integración pacífica en la república de Irlanda*.

SDP (*abbr of* **Social Democratic Party**) *n* *partido político británico formado como escisión centrista del partido laborista.*

SE (*abbr of* **south-east**) SE.

sea [si:] *n* - **1.** [not land] mar *m o f*; **at sea** en el mar; **by sea** en barco; **by the sea** a orillas del mar; **out to sea** [away from shore] mar adentro; [across the water] hacia el mar - **2.** [not ocean] mar *m* - **3.** *fig* [large number] mar *m*; **a sea of faces** un mar de caras
▸▸ **to be all at sea** estar totalmente perdido(da).
◆ **seas** *npl*: **the seas** los mares; **to sail the seas** surcar los mares.

sea air *n* aire *m* del mar.

sea anemone *n* anémona *f* de mar.

sea bass *n* lubina *f*.

seabed ['si:bed] *n*: **the seabed** el lecho marino.

seabird ['si:bɜ:d] *n* ave *f* marina.

seaboard ['si:bɔ:d] *n* *fml* litoral *m*.

sea breeze *n* brisa *f* marina.

seafaring ['si:,feərɪŋ] *adj* marinero(ra).

seafood ['si:fu:d] *n* *(U)* mariscos *mpl*.

seafront ['si:frʌnt] *n* paseo *m* marítimo.

seagoing ['si:,gəʊɪŋ] *adj* de alta mar.

seagull ['si:gʌl] *n* gaviota *f*.

seahorse ['si:hɔ:s] *n* caballo *m* de mar.

seal [si:l] ◇ *n* (*pl* **seal** OR **-s**) - **1.** [animal] foca *f* - **2.** [official mark] sello *m*; **seal of approval** aprobación *f*, visto *m* bueno; **she has given it her seal of approval** le ha dado el visto bueno; **to put** OR **set the seal on sthg** sellar algo - **3.** [on bottle, meter] precinto *m*; [on letter] sello *m* - **4.** TECH sello *m*. ◇ *vt* - **1.** [envelope] sellar, cerrar - **2.** [opening, tube, crack] tapar, cerrar; **that decision has sealed his** OR **fate** OR **doom** la decisión ha determinado su destino.
◆ **seal off** *vt sep* [entrance, exit] cerrar; [area] acordonar.

sealable ['si:libl] *adj* precintable.

sea lane *n* ruta *f* marítima.

sealant ['si:lənt] *n* [of document, bottle] sello *m*; [for leaks, wood] aislante *m*.

sea level *n* nivel *m* del mar.

sealing wax ['si:lɪŋ-] *n* lacre *m*.

sea lion (*pl* **sea lion** OR **-s**) *n* león *m* marítimo.

sealskin ['si:lskɪn] *n* piel *f* de foca.

seam [si:m] *n* - **1.** SEW costura *f*; **to be bursting at the seams** estar a tope - **2.** [of coal] veta *f*.

seaman ['si:mən] (*pl* **-men** [-mən]) *n* marinero *m*.

seamanship ['si:mənʃɪp] *n* náutica *f*.

sea mist *n* bruma *f*.

seamless ['si:mlɪs] *adj* SEW sin costura.

seamstress ['semstrɪs] *n* costurera *f*.

seamy ['si:mɪ] (*comp* **-ier**, *superl* **-iest**) *adj* sórdido(da).

séance ['seɪɒns] *n* sesión *f* de espiritismo.

seaplane ['si:pleɪn] *n* hidroavión *m*.

seaport ['si:pɔ:t] *n* puerto *m* de mar.

search [sɜ:tʃ] ◇ *n* [gen] búsqueda *f*; [of room, drawer] registro *m*; [of person] cacheo *m*; **search for sthg** búsqueda de algo; **in search of** en busca de. ◇ *vt* [gen] registrar; [one's mind] escudriñar; **to search sthg for sthg** buscar algo en algo. ◇ *vi*: **to search (for sthg/sb)** buscar (algo/a alguien); **he was searched at the airport** lo registraron en el aeropuerto.
◆ **search out** *vt sep* encontrar, descubrir.

search engine *n* COMPUT motor *m* de búsqueda.

searcher ['sɜ:tʃər] *n* buscador *m*, -ra *f*.

searching ['sɜ:tʃɪŋ] *adj* [question] agudo(da); [look] penetrante.

searchlight ['sɜ:tʃlaɪt] *n* reflector *m*, proyector *m*.

search party *n* equipo *m* de búsqueda.

search warrant *n* mandamiento *m* de registro.

searing ['sɪərɪŋ] *adj* - **1.** [pain] punzante; [heat] abrasador(ra) - **2.** [criticism] acerado(da).

sea salt *n* sal *f* marina.

seashell ['si:ʃel] *n* concha *f* (marina).

seashore ['si:ʃɔ:r] *n*: **the seashore** la orilla del mar.

seasick ['si:sɪk] *adj* mareado(da); **to be/feel seasick** estar/sentirse mareado(da).

seaside ['si:saɪd] *n*: **the seaside** la playa.

seaside resort *n* lugar *m* de veraneo (en la playa).

season ['si:zn] ◇ *n* - **1.** [of year] estación *f*; **the four seasons** las cuatro estaciones - **2.** [particular period] época *f*, período *m*; **the planting season** la época de plantar; **the football season** la temporada futbolística; **the holiday season** la temporada de vacaciones; **to book a holiday out of season** reservar unas vacaciones fuera de temporada - **3.** [of fruit etc]: **out of/in season** fuera de/en sazón; **plums are in season** las ciruelas están en temporada - **4.** [of talks, films] temporada *f* - **5.** ZOOL: **to be in season** estar en celo. ◇ *vt* sazonar, condimentar; **season to taste** sazonar a gusto; **season with salt and pepper** salpimentar.

seasonal ['si:zənl] *adj* [work] temporal; [change] estacional.

seasoned ['si:znd] *adj* [experienced] veterano(na); **to be a seasoned traveller** ser un viajero experimentado.

seasoning ['si:znɪŋ] *n* condimento *m*.

season ticket *n* abono *m*.

seat [si:t] ⟨⟩ n - **1.** [in room, on train] asiento m; **is this seat taken?** ¿está ocupado este asiento?; **take a seat, please** siéntese, por favor; **there only are a few seats left** sólo quedan unos pocos asientos - **2.** [of trousers, skirt] trasero m - **3.** POL [in parliament] escaño m - **4.** [centre] sede f; **the seat of government** la sede del gobierno. ⟨⟩ vt - **1.** [sit down] sentar; **be seated!** ¡siéntese!; **to seat o.s.** sentarse - **2.** [subj: building, vehicle] tener cabida para.

seat belt n cinturón m de seguridad.

seated ['si:tɪd] adj sentado(da).

-seater ['si:tər] suffix: **a two-seater car** un coche de dos plazas.

seating ['si:tɪŋ] ⟨⟩ n (U) [capacity] asientos mpl. ⟨⟩ comp: **seating capacity** cabida f; **seating plan** distribución f de asientos.

SEATO ['si:təʊ] (abbr of Southeast Asia Treaty Organization) n OTSEA f.

sea urchin n erizo m de mar.

seawall ['si:'wɔ:l] n dique m.

seawater ['si:,wɔ:tər] n agua f de mar.

seaweed ['si:wi:d] n (U) alga f marina, huiro m Chile.

seaworthy ['si:,wɜ:ði] adj en condiciones de navegar.

sebaceous [sɪ'beɪʃəs] adj sebáceo(a).

sec. (abbr of second) seg.

SEC (abbr of Securities and Exchange Commission) n organismo gubernamental estadounidense que regula las transacciones bursátiles.

secateurs [,sekə'tɜ:z] npl UK podadera f.

secede [sɪ'si:d] vi fml: **to secede (from sthg)** separarse (de algo).

secession [sɪ'seʃn] n fml secesión f.

secluded [sɪ'klu:dɪd] adj apartado(da).

seclusion [sɪ'klu:ʒn] n aislamiento m; **to live in seclusion** vivir aislado(da).

second[1] ['sekənd] ⟨⟩ n - **1.** [of time] segundo m; **can you wait a second?** ¿podrías esperar un momento?; [second gear] segunda f - **2.** UK UNIV ≈ licenciatura f con notable. ⟨⟩ num segundo(da); **to ask for a second chance/opinion** pedir una segunda oportunidad/opinión; **second only to** después de; **Elizabeth the Second** Isabel II. ⟨⟩ vt secundar; see also **sixth**.

⬤ **seconds** npl - **1.** COMM artículos mpl defectuosos - **2.** [of food]: **to have seconds** repetir (en una comida); **are there any seconds?** ¿se puede repetir?

second[2] [sɪ'kɒnd] vt UK [employee] trasladar temporalmente.

secondary ['sekəndrɪ] adj - **1.** [SCH - school] secundario(ria); [- education] medio(dia); [- teacher] de enseñanza media - **2.** [less important]: **to be secondary to** ser secundario(ria) a.

secondary school n escuela f de enseñanza media.

second best ['sekənd-] adj segundo(da) (mejor).

second-class ['sekənd-] ⟨⟩ adj - **1.** [gen] de segunda clase; **to be a second-class citizen** ser un ciudadano de segunda (clase); **second-class mail** servicio postal más barato y lento que el de primera clase - **2.** UK UNIV: **second-class degree** nota global de licenciatura equivalente a un notable o un aprobado alto. ⟨⟩ adv: **to travel second-class** viajar en segunda; **to send a letter second-class** enviar una carta utilizando el correo de segunda clase.

second cousin ['sekənd-] n primo segundo m, prima segunda f.

second-degree burn ['sekənd-] n quemadura f de segundo grado.

seconder ['sekəndər] n persona f que secunda una moción.

second floor ['sekənd-] n UK segundo piso m; US primer piso m.

second-guess ['sekənd-] vt esp US inf juzgar a posteriori.

second hand ['sekənd-] n [of clock] segundero m.

second-hand ['sekənd-] ⟨⟩ adj - **1.** [goods, information] de segunda mano - **2.** [shop] de artículos de segunda mano. ⟨⟩ adv - **1.** [not new] de segunda mano - **2.** fig [indirectly]: **to hear sthg second-hand** oír algo de segunda mano.

second-in-command ['sekənd-] n segundo m en jefe.

secondly ['sekəndlɪ] adv en segundo lugar.

secondment [sɪ'kɒndmənt] n UK traslado m temporal.

second nature ['sekənd-] n (U) hábito muy arraigado en una persona; **it's second nature to him** es algo natural en él.

second-rate ['sekənd-] adj pej de segunda categoría, mediocre.

second thought ['sekənd-] n: **to have second thoughts about sthg** tener dudas acerca de algo; **on second thoughts** UK, **on second thought** US pensándolo bien.

secrecy ['si:krəsɪ] n (U) secreto m; **to be shrouded in secrecy** estar rodeado de un gran secreto.

secret ['si:krɪt] ⟨⟩ adj secreto(ta). ⟨⟩ n secreto m; **in secret** en secreto; **to keep a secret** guardar un secreto; **to tell sb a secret** contar a alguien un secreto; **to make no secret of sthg** no ocultar algo; **the secret of happiness** la clave de la felicidad.

secret agent *n* agente secreto *m*, agente secreta *f*.

secretarial [ˌsekrəˈteərɪəl] *adj* [course, training] de secretariado; [staff] de secretaría, administrativo(va).

secretariat [ˌsekrəˈteərɪət] *n* secretariado *m*.

secretary [UK ˈsekrətrɪ, US ˈsekrəˌterɪ] (*pl* **-ies**) *n* **- 1.** [gen] secretario *m*, -ria *f* **- 2.** POL [minister] ministro *m*.

secretary-general (*pl* **secretaries-general**) *n* secretario *m*, -ria *f* general.

Secretary of State *n* **- 1.** *UK*: **Secretary of State (for)** ministro *m* (de) **- 2.** *US* ministro *m* estadounidense de Asuntos Exteriores.

secrete [sɪˈkriːt] *vt* **- 1.** [produce] secretar, segregar **- 2.** *fml* [hide] esconder, ocultar.

secretion [sɪˈkriːʃn] *n* secreción *f*.

secretive [ˈsiːkrətɪv] *adj* [person] reservado(da); [organization] secreto(ta).

secretly [ˈsiːkrɪtlɪ] *adv* [hope, think] secretamente; [tell] en secreto; **she was secretly pleased** aunque no lo expresara, estaba contenta.

secret police *n* policía *f* secreta.

secret service *n* [in UK] servicio *m* secreto; [in US] *departamento del gobierno de Estados Unidos que se encarga de la protección del presidente y vicepresidente del país y de sus familias.*

sect [sekt] *n* secta *f*.

sectarian [sekˈteərɪən] *adj* sectario(ria).

section [ˈsekʃn] <> *n* sección *f*. <> *vt* seccionar.

sector [ˈsektər] *n* sector *m*.

secular [ˈsekjʊlər] *adj* [education, life] laico(ca), secular; [music] profano(na).

secure [sɪˈkjʊər] <> *adj* **- 1.** [gen] seguro(ra) **- 2.** [house, building] protegido(da), seguro(ra). <> *vt* **- 1.** [obtain] conseguir, obtener **- 2.** [make safe] proteger **- 3.** [fasten] cerrar bien.

securely [sɪˈkjʊəlɪ] *adv* [fixed, locked] firmemente.

security [sɪˈkjʊərətɪ] <> *n* (*pl* **-ies**) **- 1.** seguridad *f* **- 2.** [legal protection]: **security of tenure** cargo *m* vitalicio **- 3.** [for loan] garantía *f*. <> *comp* de seguridad.

◆ **securities** *npl* FIN valores *mpl*, títulos *mpl*.

security blanket *n* manta u otro objeto con el cual un niño se siente protegido.

Security Council *n*: **the Security Council** el Consejo de Seguridad.

security forces *npl* fuerzas *fpl* de seguridad.

security guard *n* guardia *m* jurado OR de seguridad.

security risk *n* persona *f* de dudosa lealtad.

sedan [sɪˈdæn] *n* US (coche *m*) utilitario *m*.

sedan chair *n* silla *f* de manos.

sedate [sɪˈdeɪt] <> *adj* sosegado(da). <> *vt* sedar.

sedation [sɪˈdeɪʃn] *n* (U) sedación *f*; **to be under sedation** estar sedado(da).

sedative [ˈsedətɪv] <> *adj* sedante. <> *n* sedante *m*, calmante *m*.

sedentary [ˈsedntrɪ] *adj* sedentario(ria).

sediment [ˈsedɪmənt] *n* sedimento *m*.

sedition [sɪˈdɪʃn] *n* sedición *f*.

seditious [sɪˈdɪʃəs] *adj* sedicioso(sa).

seduce [sɪˈdjuːs] *vt*: **to seduce sb (into doing sthg)** seducir a alguien (a hacer algo).

seduction [sɪˈdʌkʃn] *n* seducción *f*.

seductive [sɪˈdʌktɪv] *adj* seductor(ra).

see [siː] (*pt* **saw**, *pp* **seen**) <> *vt* **- 1.** [gen] ver **- 2.** [visit - friend, doctor] ir a ver, visitar; **see you soon/later/tomorrow!** ¡hasta pronto/luego/mañana!; **see you!** ¡hasta luego!, ¡chau! *R Plata*; **as I see it** tal y como yo lo veo; **see below/p 10** véase más abajo/pág. 10 **- 3.** [accompany]: **to see sb to the door** acompañar a alguien a la puerta **- 4.** [make sure]: **to see (to it) that...** encargarse de que... <> *vi* [gen] ver; [understand] entender; **I can't see** no veo; **to see if one can do sthg** ver si uno puede hacer algo; **let's see, let me see** vamos a ver, veamos; **you see...** verás, es que...; **I see** ya veo.

◆ **seeing as, seeing that** *conj inf* como.

◆ **see about** *vt insep* **- 1.** [arrange] encargarse de **- 2.** [consider further]: **we'll see about that** ya veremos.

◆ **see off** *vt sep* **- 1.** [say goodbye to] despedir **- 2.** *UK* [chase away] ahuyentar.

◆ **see through** *vt insep* [person] ver claramente las intenciones de; **I can see right through her** veo claramente sus intenciones.

◆ **see to** *vt insep* ocuparse de.

seed [siːd] *n* [of plant] semilla *f*; **to go to seed** *fig* venirse abajo.

◆ **seeds** *npl* *fig* [of doubt] semilla *f*; [of idea] germen *m*.

seedless [ˈsiːdlɪs] *adj* sin pepitas.

seedling [ˈsiːdlɪŋ] *n* plantón *m*.

seedy [ˈsiːdɪ] (*comp* **-ier**, *superl* **-iest**) *adj* [room, area] sórdido(da); [person] desaliñado(da).

seek [siːk] (*pt* & *pp* **sought**) *fml* <> *vt* **- 1.** [look for, try to obtain] buscar **- 2.** [ask for] solicitar **- 3.** [try]: **to seek to do sthg** procurar hacer algo. <> *vi* **- 1.** [look for]: **to seek for sthg** buscar algo **- 2.** [ask for]: **to seek for sthg** solicitar algo.

◆ **seek out** *vt sep* buscar.

seem [si:m] ◇ *vi* parecer; **it seems (to be) good** parece (que es) bueno; **I can't seem to do it** no puedo hacerlo (por mucho que lo intente); **I seem to remember that...** creo recordar que... ◇ *impers vb*: **it seems (that)** parece que; **it seems to me that** me parece que.

seeming ['si:mɪŋ] *adj fml* aparente.

seemingly ['si:mɪŋlɪ] *adv* aparentemente.

seen [si:n] *pp* ▷ **see**.

seep [si:p] *vi* rezumar, filtrarse.

seersucker ['sɪə,sʌkə^r] *n* sirsaca *f*; **a seersucker dress** un vestido de sirsaca.

seesaw ['si:sɔ:] *n* balancín *m*, subibaja *m*.

seethe [si:ð] *vi* - **1.** [person] rabiar - **2.** [place]: **to be seething with** estar a rebosar de.

seething ['si:ðɪŋ] *adj* rabioso(sa).

see-through *adj* transparente.

segment ['segmənt] *n* - **1.** [proportion, section] segmento *m* - **2.** [of fruit] gajo *m*.

segregate ['segrɪgeɪt] *vt* segregar.

segregation [,segrɪ'geɪʃn] *n* segregación *f*.

Seine [seɪn] *n*: **the (River) Seine** el (río) Sena.

seismic ['saɪzmɪk] *adj* sísmico(ca).

seize [si:z] *vt* - **1.** [grab] agarrar, coger - **2.** [capture - control, power, town] tomar, hacerse con - **3.** [arrest] detener - **4.** [take advantage of] aprovechar.

◆ **seize (up)on** *vt insep* valerse de.

◆ **seize up** *vi* agarrotarse.

seizure ['si:ʒə^r] *n* - **1.** MED ataque *m* - **2.** [taking, capturing] toma *f*.

seldom ['seldəm] *adv* raramente.

select [sɪ'lekt] ◇ *adj* selecto(ta). ◇ *vt* - **1.** [gen] elegir, escoger - **2.** [team & COMPUT] seleccionar.

select committee *n* comité *m* de investigación.

selected [sɪ'lektɪd] *adj* escogido(da).

selection [sɪ'lekʃn] *n* - **1.** [gen] selección *f* - **2.** [fact of being selected] elección *f* - **3.** [in shop] surtido *m*; **we have a wide selection of ties** tenemos una amplia selección de corbatas.

selective [sɪ'lektɪv] *adj* selectivo(va).

selector [sɪ'lektə^r] *n* seleccionador *m*, -ra *f*.

self [self] *(pl* **selves)** *n* uno mismo *m*, una misma *f*; **he's his old self again** vuelve a ser el mismo de antes; **she's not her usual self** no estaba como de costumbre; **the self** el yo.

self- [self] *prefix* auto-.

self-addressed envelope [-ə'drest-] *n* sobre *con la dirección de uno mismo.*

self-addressed stamped envelope [-ə,drest'stæmpt-] *n* US sobre con sus señas y *franqueo.*

self-adhesive *adj* autoadhesivo(va).

self-appointed [-ə'pɔɪntɪd] *adj* pej por nombramiento propio.

self-assertive *adj* que se impone ante los demás.

self-assurance *n* confianza *f* en sí mismo (sí misma).

self-assured *adj* seguro de sí mismo (segura de sí misma).

self-catering *adj* sin pensión; **a self-catering holiday/chalet** unas vacaciones/un chalet sin servicio de comidas.

self-centred [-'sentəd] *adj* egocéntrico(ca).

self-cleaning *adj* autolimpiable.

self-confessed [-kən'fest] *adj* confeso(sa).

self-confidence *n* confianza *f* en sí mismo, -ma *f*.

self-confident *adj* [person] seguro de sí mismo (segura de sí misma); [attitude, remark] lleno(na) de seguridad.

self-conscious *adj* cohibido(da).

self-contained [-kən'teɪnd] *adj* independiente; **a self-contained flat** un apartamento independiente.

self-control *n* control *m* de sí mismo/misma.

self-controlled *adj* sereno(na).

self-defence *n* defensa *f* propia, autodefensa *f*; **in self-defence** en defensa propia.

self-denial *n* abnegación *f*.

self-destruct [-dɪs'trʌkt] ◇ *adj* autodestructor(ra). ◇ *vi* autodestruirse.

self-determination *n* autodeterminación *f*.

self-discipline *n* autodisciplina *f*.

self-doubt *n* inseguridad *f*, falta *f* de confianza en uno mismo (una misma).

self-drive *adj* UK alquilado(da) sin chófer.

self-educated *adj* autodidacta.

self-effacing [-ɪ'feɪsɪŋ] *adj* humilde.

self-employed [-ɪm'plɔɪd] *adj* autónomo(ma), que trabaja por cuenta propia.

self-esteem *n* amor *m* propio.

self-evident *adj* evidente, patente.

self-explanatory *adj* evidente, que queda muy claro(ra).

self-expression *n* autoexpresión *f*.

self-focusing [-'fəʊkəsɪŋ] *adj* con enfoque automático.

self-government *n* autogobierno *m*.

self-help *n (U)* ayuda *f* propia.

self-important *adj* pej engreído(da).

self-imposed [-ɪm'pəʊzd] *adj* auto-impuesto(ta).

self-indulgent *adj* pej: **a self-indulgent person** una persona autocomplaciente; **to be self-indulgent** ser autocomplaciente.

self-inflicted [-ɪn'flɪktɪd] *adj* autoinfligido(da).

self-interest n (U) pej interés m propio.
selfish ['selfɪʃ] adj egoísta.
selfishness ['selfɪʃnɪs] n egoísmo m.
selfless ['selflɪs] adj desinteresado(da).
self-locking [-'lɒkɪŋ] adj de cierre automático.
self-made adj: a self-made man un hombre hecho a sí mismo.
self-opinionated adj pej que siempre tiene que decir la suya.
self-perpetuating [-pə'petʃʊeɪtɪŋ] adj que se perpetúa a sí mismo (sí misma).
self-pity n pej lástima f de uno mismo/una misma.
self-portrait n autorretrato m.
self-possessed [-pə'zest] adj dueño de sí mismo (dueña de sí misma).
self-proclaimed [-prə'kleɪmd] adj pej autodenominado(da), supuesto(ta).
self-raising flour UK [-,reɪzɪŋ-], **self-rising flour** US n harina f con levadura.
self-regard n (U) - **1.** pej [self-interest] interés m propio - **2.** [self-respect] propia estima f.
self-regulating [-'regjʊleɪtɪŋ] adj autorregulador(ra).
self-reliant adj independiente.
self-respect n amor m propio.
self-respecting [-rɪs'pektɪŋ] adj que se precie, digno(na); **no self-respecting person would eat this rubbish** nadie con un mínimo de dignidad se comería esa basura.
self-restraint n dominio m de sí mismo/misma.
self-righteous adj pej santurrón(ona).
self-rising flour US = **self-raising flour**.
self-rule n autogobierno m.
self-sacrifice n abnegación f.
selfsame ['selfseɪm] adj mismísimo(ma); **I said the selfsame thing** yo dije exactamente lo mismo.
self-satisfied adj pej [person] satisfecho de sí mismo (satisfecha de sí misma); [smile] lleno(na) de suficiencia.
self-sealing [-'si:lɪŋ] adj [envelope] autoadhesivo(va).
self-seeking [-'si:kɪŋ] pej ⟨⟩ adj interesado(da), egoísta. ⟨⟩ n propio interés m, egoísmo m.
self-service ⟨⟩ n autoservicio m. ⟨⟩ comp de autoservicio; **a self-service restaurant** un autoservicio.
self-starter n - **1.** AUT arranque m automático - **2.** [person] emprendedor m, -ra f.
self-styled [-staɪld] adj pej autodenominado(da), supuesto(ta).

self-sufficient adj: **self-sufficient (in)** autosuficiente (en).
self-supporting [-sə'pɔ:tɪŋ] adj [business, industry] económicamente independiente.
self-taught adj autodidacta.
self-test n COMPUT autotest m.
self-will n pej obstinación f.
sell [sel] ⟨⟩ vt (pt & pp sold) - **1.** [gen] vender; **to sell sthg to sb, to sell sb sthg** vender algo a alguien; **to sell sthg for** vender algo por - **2.** fig [make acceptable, desirable]: **I'm not really sold on it** no estoy convencido(da) de ello; **to sell o.s.** venderse. ⟨⟩ vi (pt & pp sold) - **1.** [subj: businessman, firm] vender - **2.** [subj: merchandise] venderse; **this model sells well** este modelo se vende muy bien; **to sell (for OR at)** venderse (a).
◆ **sell off** vt sep liquidar.
◆ **sell out** ⟨⟩ vt sep [performance]: **to have sold out** estar agotado(da). ⟨⟩ vi - **1.** [shop]: **to sell out (of sthg)** agotar las existencias (de algo) - **2.** [be disloyal, unprincipled] venderse.
◆ **sell up** vi venderlo todo.
sell-by date n UK fecha f de caducidad; **to be past its sell-by date** haber caducado.
seller ['selər] n vendedor m, -ra f.
seller's market n mercado m de demanda OR favorable al vendedor.
selling ['selɪŋ] n (U) venta f.
selling price n precio m de venta.
Sellotape® ['seləteɪp] n UK celo® m, cinta f Scotch® Amér, ≈ durex® m Arg, Bol & Méx, ≈ Scotch® m Andes.
◆ **sellotape** vt pegar con celo etc.
sell-out n [performance, match] lleno m.
selves [selvz] npl ▷ **self**.
semantic [sɪ'mæntɪk] adj semántico(ca).
semantics [sɪ'mæntɪks] n (U) semántica f.
semaphore ['seməfɔ:r] n (U) semáforo m.
semblance ['sembləns] n fml apariencia f.
semen ['si:men] n semen m.
semester [sɪ'mestər] n semestre m.
semi ['semɪ] n - **1.** UK inf (abbr of **semidetached house**) casa f adosada (a otra) - **2.** US abbr of **semitrailer**.
semi- ['semɪ] prefix semi-.
semiautomatic [,semɪ,ɔ:tə'mætɪk] adj semiautomático(ca).
semicircle ['semɪ,sɜ:kl] n semicírculo m; **arranged in a semicircle** poner en semicírculo.
semicircular [,semɪ'sɜ:kjʊlər] adj semicircular.
semicolon [,semɪ'kəʊlən] n punto m y coma.
semiconscious [,semɪ'kɒnʃəs] adj semiconsciente.

semidetached [ˌsemɪdɪ'tætʃt] <> *adj* adosado(da). <> *n UK* casa *f* adosada (a otra).

semifinal [ˌsemɪ'faɪnl] *n* semifinal *f*.

semifinalist [ˌsemɪ'faɪnəlɪst] *n* semifinalista *mf*.

seminar ['semɪnɑːr] *n* seminario *m*.

seminary ['semɪnərɪ] (*pl* -ies) *n* RELIG seminario *m*.

semiprecious ['semɪˌpreʃəs] *adj* semiprecioso(sa).

semiskilled [ˌsemɪ'skɪld] *adj* semicualificado(da).

semi-skimmed [-'skɪmd] *adj* semidesnatado(da).

semitrailer [ˌsemɪ'treɪlər] *n* - **1.** [trailer] remolque *m* - **2.** *US* [lorry] camión *m* articulado.

semolina [ˌsemə'liːnə] *n* sémola *f*.

Sen. (*abbr of* **senator**. *abbr of* **Senior**.

SEN (*abbr of* **State Enrolled Nurse**) *n* enfermero diplomado.

Senate ['senɪt] *n* POL: **the (United States) Senate** el Senado (de los Estados Unidos).

senator ['senətər] *n* senador *m*, -ra *f*.

send [send] *vt* - **1.** [gen] mandar; **to send sb sthg, to send sthg to sb** mandar a alguien algo; **send me a postcard!** ¡mándame una postal!; **send them my best wishes** enviales saludos - **2.** [tell to go] enviar, mandar; **she sent her son to the shop for a newspaper** envió a su hijo a comprar un periódico en la tienda; **he was sent to prison** fue encarcelado - **3.** [subj: explosion, blow]: **to send sthg/sb flying** mandar algo/a alguien por los aires; **to send sb to sleep** dar sueño a alguien.

◆ **send down** *vt sep* [send to prison] encarcelar.

◆ **send for** *vt insep* - **1.** [person] mandar llamar a - **2.** [goods, information] pedir, encargar.

◆ **send in** *vt sep* mandar, enviar.

◆ **send off** *vt sep* - **1.** [by post] mandar (por correo) - **2.** SPORT expulsar.

◆ **send off for** *vt insep* [goods, information] pedir, encargar.

◆ **send up** *vt sep* - **1.** *UK inf* [imitate] parodiar, satirizar - **2.** *US* [send to prison] encarcelar.

sender ['sendər] *n* remitente *mf*.

send-off *n* despedida *f*; **to give sb a good send-off** dar una buena despedida a alguien.

send-up *n UK inf* parodia *f*, sátira *f*.

Senegal [ˌsenɪ'gɔːl] *n* (el) Senegal.

Senegalese [ˌsenɪgə'liːz] <> *adj* senegalés(esa). <> *npl*: **the Senegalese** los senegaleses.

senile ['siːnaɪl] *adj* senil.

senile dementia *n* demencia *f* senil.

senility [sɪ'nɪlətɪ] *n* senilidad *f*.

senior ['siːnjər] <> *adj* - **1.** [highest-ranking] superior, de rango superior - **2.** [higher-ranking]: **senior to sb** superior a alguien - **3.** SCH [pupil] mayor; [class, common room] de los mayores; **senior year** *US* último curso de la enseñanza secundaria y de la universidad en Estados Unidos. <> *n* - **1.** [older person]: **I'm five years his senior** le llevo cinco años; **she's my senior** es mayor que yo - **2.** SCH mayor *mf*.

senior citizen *n* ciudadano *m*, -na *f* de la tercera edad.

senior high school *n US* ≃ instituto *m* de bachillerato (16-18 años).

seniority [ˌsiːnɪ'ɒrətɪ] *n* [degree of importance] categoría *f*.

sensation [sen'seɪʃn] *n* sensación *f*; **to cause a sensation** causar sensación.

sensational [sen'seɪʃənl] *adj* - **1.** [gen] sensacional - **2.** [sensationalist] sensacionalista.

sensationalist [sen'seɪʃnəlɪst] *adj pej* sensacionalista.

sense [sens] <> *n* - **1.** [faculty, meaning] sentido *m*; **to make sense** [have meaning] tener sentido; **to make sense of sthg** entender algo; **I can't make any sense of this** no entiendo esto - **2.** [feeling - of guilt, terror] sentimiento *m*; [- of urgency] sensación *f*; [- of honour, duty] sentido *m* - **3.** [natural ability]: **business sense** talento *m* para los negocios; **dress sense** gusto *m* en el vestir; **sense of humour/style** sentido *m* del humor/estilo - **4.** [wisdom, reason] juicio *m*, sentido *m* común; **to make sense** [be sensible] ser sensato; **to talk sense** hablar con sentido común; **there's no** OR **little sense in arguing** no tiene sentido discutir

▶▶ **to come to one's senses** [see reason] entrar en razón. <> *vt* sentir, percibir; **to sense (that)** percibir OR sentir que.

◆ **in a sense** *adv* en cierto sentido.

senseless ['senslɪs] *adj* - **1.** [stupid] sin sentido - **2.** [unconscious] inconsciente; **the blow knocked him senseless** el golpe lo dejó inconsciente.

sensibilities [ˌsensɪ'bɪlətɪz] *npl* [delicate feelings] sensibilidad *f*; **to offend sb's sensibilities** herir la sensibilidad de alguien.

sensible ['sensəbl] *adj* [person, decision] sensato(ta), razonable; [clothes] práctico(ca).

sensibly ['sensəblɪ] *adv* sensatamente.

sensitive ['sensɪtɪv] *adj* - **1.** [understanding]: **sensitive (to)** comprensivo(va) (hacia) - **2.** [easily hurt, touchy]: **sensitive (to/about)** susceptible (a/acerca de) - **3.** [controversial] delicado(da) - **4.** [easily damaged, tender] sensible; **to have sensitive skin** tener la piel sensible; **sensitive to heat/light** sensible al calor/la luz - **5.** [responsive - instrument] sensible.

sensitivity [ˌsensɪ'tɪvətɪ] *n* **- 1.** [understanding] comprensión *f* **- 2.** [tenderness - of eyes, skin] sensibilidad *f.*

sensor ['sensər] *n* sensor *m.*

sensual ['sensjʊəl] *adj* sensual.

sensuous ['sensjʊəs] *adj* sensual.

sent [sent] *pt* & *pp* ▷ **send**.

sentence ['sentəns] ◇ *n* **- 1.** [group of words] frase *f*, oración *f* **- 2.** LAW sentencia *f*; **a prison sentence** una condena de cárcel. ◇ *vt*: **to sentence sb (to)** condenar a alguien (a); **he was sentenced to death/3 years** lo condenaron a muerte/tres años de cárcel.

sententious [sen'tenʃəs] *adj pej* sentencioso(sa).

sentiment ['sentɪmənt] *n* **- 1.** [feeling] sentimiento *m* **- 2.** [opinion] opinión *f* **- 3.** *(U) pej* [emotion, tenderness] sentimentalismo *m.*

sentimental [ˌsentɪ'mentl] *adj* sentimental.

sentimentality [ˌsentɪmen'tælətɪ] *n pej* sentimentalismo *m.*

sentinel ['sentɪnl] *n* HIST centinela *m.*

sentry ['sentrɪ] *(pl* **-ies)** *n* centinela *m.*

separable ['seprəbl] *adj*: **separable (from)** separable (de).

separate ◇ *adj* ['seprət] **- 1.** [not joined, apart]: **separate (from)** separado(da) (de) **- 2.** [individual, distinct] distinto(ta). ◇ *vt* ['sepəreɪt] **- 1.** [keep or move apart]: **to separate sthg/sb (from)** separar algo/a alguien (de) **- 2.** [distinguish]: **to separate sthg/sb from** diferenciar algo/a alguien de **- 3.** [divide]: **to separate sthg/sb into** dividir algo/a alguien en. ◇ *vi* ['sepəreɪt] **- 1.** [gen]: **to separate (from)** separarse (de) **- 2.** [divide]: **to separate (into)** dividirse (en).

◆ **separates** *npl UK* piezas *fpl (de vestir que combinan).*

separated ['sepəreɪtɪd] *adj* separado(da); **her parents are separated** sus padres están separados; **she's separated from him** está separada de él.

separately ['seprətlɪ] *adv* **- 1.** [on one's own] independientemente **- 2.** [one by one] separadamente, por separado.

separation [ˌsepə'reɪʃn] *n* separación *f.*

separatist ['seprətɪst] *n* separatista *mf.*

sepia ['si:pjə] *adj* sepia, de color sepia.

Sept. *(abbr of* **September)** sep.

September [sep'tembər] *n* septiembre *m*, setiembre *m*; **when are you going? – September** ¿cuándo te vas? – en septiembre; **one of the hottest Septembers on record** uno de los septiembres más calurosos que se recuerdan; **1 September 1992** [in letters etc] 1 de septiembre de 1992; **by/in September** para/en sep-

tiembre; **last/this/next September** en septiembre del año pasado/de este año/del año que viene; **every September** todos los años en septiembre; **during September** en septiembre, durante el mes de septiembre; **at the beginning/end of September** a principios/finales de septiembre; **in the middle of September** a mediados de septiembre.

septic ['septɪk] *adj* séptico(ca); **to go septic** infectarse.

septicaemia *UK*, **septicemia** *US* [ˌseptɪ'si:mɪə] *n* septicemia *f.*

septic tank *n* fosa *f* séptica.

sepulchre *UK* ['sepəlkər], **sepulcher** *US* ['sepʌlkər] *n liter* sepulcro *m.*

sequel ['si:kwəl] *n* **- 1.** [book, film]: **sequel (to)** continuación *f* (de) **- 2.** [consequence]: **sequel (to)** secuela *f* (de).

sequence ['si:kwəns] *n* **- 1.** [series] sucesión *f* **- 2.** [order, of film] secuencia *f*; **in sequence** en secuencia.

sequin ['si:kwɪn] *n* lentejuela *f.*

Serb = **Serbian**.

Serbia ['sɜ:bjə] *n* Serbia.

Serbian ['sɜ:bjən], **Serb** [sɜ:b] ◇ *adj* serbio(bia). ◇ *n* **- 1.** [person] serbio *m*, -bia *f* **- 2.** [dialect] serbio *m.*

Serbo-Croat [ˌsɜ:bəʊ'krəʊaet], **Serbo-Croatian** [ˌsɜ:bəʊkrəʊ'eɪʃn] ◇ *adj* serbocroata. ◇ *n* [language] serbocroata *m.*

serenade [ˌserə'neɪd] ◇ *n* serenata *f.* ◇ *vt* dar una serenata a.

serene [sɪ'ri:n] *adj* sereno(na).

serenely [sɪ'ri:nlɪ] *adv* serenamente.

serenity [sɪ'renətɪ] *n* serenidad *f.*

serf [sɜ:f] *n* HIST siervo *m*, -va *f.*

serge [sɜ:dʒ] *n* sarga *f.*

sergeant ['sɑ:dʒənt] *n* **- 1.** MIL sargento *m* **- 2.** [in police] ≈ subinspector *m* de policía.

sergeant major *n* sargento *m* mayor.

serial ['sɪərɪəl] *n* serial *m.*

serial cable *n* COMPUT cable *m* de serie.

serialize, -ise ['sɪərɪəlaɪz] *vt* publicar por entregas.

serial killer *n asesino que asesina en serie.*

serial number *n* número *m* de serie.

series ['sɪəri:z] *(pl* **series)** *n* serie *f*; **a series of disasters** una serie de catástrofes; **a TV series** una serie televisiva.

serious ['sɪərɪəs] *adj* **- 1.** [gen] serio(ria); **are you serious?** ¿hablas en serio? **- 2.** [very bad] grave.

seriously [ˈsɪərɪəslɪ] *adv* - **1.** [honestly] en serio - **2.** [very badly] gravemente; **to be seriously ill** estar gravemente enfermo - **3.** [in a considered, earnest, solemn manner] seriamente
▸▸ı **to take sthg/sb seriously** tomar algo/a alguien en serio.

seriousness [ˈsɪərɪəsnɪs] *n* - **1.** [gravity] gravedad *f* - **2.** [honesty]: **in all seriousness** seriamente - **3.** [solemnity] seriedad *f*.

sermon [ˈsɜːmən] *n pej* & **RELIG** sermón *m*.

serpent [ˈsɜːpənt] *n liter* serpiente *f*, sierpe *f*.

serrated [sɪˈreɪtɪd] *adj* serrado(da), dentado(da).

serum [ˈsɪərəm] (*pl* **serums** OR **sera**) *n* suero *m*.

servant [ˈsɜːvənt] *n* sirviente *m*, -ta *f*.

serve [sɜːv] ⟨⟩ *vt* - **1.** [work for] servir - **2.** [have effect]: **to serve to do sthg** servir para hacer algo - **3.** [fulfil]: **to serve a purpose** cumplir un propósito - **4.** [provide for] abastecer; **the town is served by three motorways** la ciudad tiene tres autopistas - **5.** [food, drink]: **to serve sthg to sb, to serve sb sthg** servir algo a alguien; **dinner will be served at 8** la cena será servida a las 8 - **6.** [customer] despachar, servir; **are you being served?** ¿lo atienden? - **7.** LAW: **to serve sb with sthg, to serve sthg on sb** entregar a alguien algo - **8.** [prison sentence] cumplir; [apprenticeship] hacer; [term of office] ejercer - **9.** SPORT servir, sacar.
▸▸ı **that serves you right!** ¡bien merecido lo tienes! ⟨⟩ *vi* - **1.** [work, give food or drink] servir - **2.** [function]: **to serve as** servir de - **3.** [in shop, bar etc] despachar - **4.** SPORT sacar. ⟨⟩ *n* saque *m*.
◆ **serve out, serve up** *vt sep* servir.

server [ˈsɜːvəʳ] *n* COMPUT servidor *m*.

service [ˈsɜːvɪs] ⟨⟩ *n* - **1.** [gen] servicio *m*; **in service** en funcionamiento; **out of service** fuera de servicio; **bus/train service** servicio de autobús/tren - **2.** [mechanical check] revisión *f* - **3.** RELIG oficio *m*, servicio *m*; **to hold a service** celebrar un oficio - **4.** [set - of plates etc] servicio *m*, juego *m*; **dinner service** servicio de mesa - **5.** SPORT saque *m* - **6.** [use]: **to be of service (to sb)** servir (a alguien); **to do sb a service** hacer un favor a alguien. ⟨⟩ *vt* [car, machine] revisar.
◆ **services** *npl* - **1.** [on motorway] área *f* de servicios - **2.** [armed forces]: **the services** las fuerzas armadas - **3.** [efforts, work] servicios *mpl*.

serviceable [ˈsɜːvɪsəbl] *adj* útil, práctico(ca).

service area *n* área *f* de servicios.

service charge *n* servicio *m*.

service industries *npl* industrias *fpl* de servicios.

serviceman [ˈsɜːvɪsmən] (*pl* **-men** [-mən]) *n* militar *m*.

service provider *n* proveedor *m* de servicios.

service station *n* estación *f* de servicio.

serviette [ˌsɜːvɪˈet] *n* servilleta *f*.

servile [ˈsɜːvaɪl] *adj* servil.

servility [sɜːˈvɪlətɪ] *n* servilismo *m*.

serving [ˈsɜːvɪŋ] *n* porción *f*.

serving dish *n* fuente *f*.

serving spoon *n* cuchara *f* de servir.

sesame [ˈsesəmɪ] *n* sésamo *m*.

session [ˈseʃn] *n* - **1.** [gen] sesión *f*; **in session** en sesión - **2.** US [school term] trimestre *m*.

set [set] ⟨⟩ *adj* - **1.** [fixed - expression, amount] fijo(ja); [- pattern, method] establecido(da); **set phrase** frase hecha - **2.** UK SCH [text etc] asignado(da) - **3.** [ready, prepared]: **set (for sthg/to do sthg)** listo(ta) (para algo/para hacer algo) - **4.** [determined]: **to be set on sthg/doing sthg** estar empeñado(da) en algo/hacer algo
▸▸ı **to be set in one's ways** tener costumbres muy arraigadas. ⟨⟩ *n* - **1.** [collection - gen] juego *m*; [- of stamps] serie *f* - **2.** [TV, radio] aparato *m* - **3.** THEAT decorado *m*; CIN plató *m* - **4.** TENNIS set *m* - **5.** [hairdressing] marcado *m*. ⟨⟩ *vt* (*pt & pp* **set**, *cont* **-ting**) - **1.** [position, place] poner, colocar - **2.** [fix, insert]: **to set sthg in** OR **into** montar algo en - **3.** [cause to be or start]: **to set free** poner en libertad; **to set fire to** prender fuego a; **to set sthg in motion** poner algo en marcha; **to set sb's mind at rest** tranquilizar a alguien; **to set sb thinking** hacer pensar a alguien - **4.** [trap, table, essay] poner - **5.** [alarm, meter] poner - **6.** [time, wage] fijar - **7.** [example] dar; **to set a good example** dar ejemplo; [precedent] sentar; [trend] imponer, dictar - **8.** [target] fijar - **9.** MED [bones, leg] componer - **10.** [arrange]: **to set sthg to music** poner música a algo - **11.** [book, play, film] situar, ambientar; **the series is set in London** la serie está ambientada en Londres. ⟨⟩ *vi* (*pt & pp* **set**, *cont* **-ting**) - **1.** [sun] ponerse - **2.** [jelly] cuajarse; [glue, cement] secarse, solidificarse.
◆ **set about** *vt insep* [start - task] comenzar; [- problem] atacar; **to set about doing sthg** ponerse a hacer algo.
◆ **set against** *vt sep* - **1.** [lessen effect of] contrarrestar con; **the advantages must be set against the cost** hay que comparar las ventajas con el costo - **2.** [cause to oppose] enemistar con; **she set them against each other** los enemistó.
◆ **set ahead** *vt sep* US [clock] adelantar.
◆ **set apart** *vt sep*: **to set sthg/sb apart from** distinguir algo/a alguien de.
◆ **set aside** *vt sep* - **1.** [keep, save] reservar - **2.** [dismiss - enmity, differences] dejar de lado.

set back vt sep - **1.** [delay] retrasar - **2.** inf [cost]: **this book set me back £10** este libro me costó 10 libras.

set down vt sep - **1.** [write down] poner por escrito - **2.** [drop off] dejar.

set in vi [depression] afianzarse; [winter, infection] comenzar.

set off ⬦ vt sep - **1.** [initiate, cause] provocar - **2.** [ignite - bomb] hacer estallar. ⬦ vi ponerse en camino.

set on vt sep arremeter contra.

set out ⬦ vt sep - **1.** [arrange] disponer - **2.** [explain] exponer. ⬦ vi - **1.** [on journey] ponerse en camino - **2.** [intend]: **to set out to do sthg** proponerse a hacer algo.

set up ⬦ vt sep - **1.** [business] poner, montar; [committee, organization] crear; [procedure] establecer; [interview, meeting] organizar; **to set sb up in business** montar un negocio a alguien; **to set o.s. up** establecerse; **to set up house** OR **home** instalarse - **2.** [statue, roadblock] levantar - **3.** [cause, produce] provocar - **4.** [prepare for use] preparar - **5.** inf [frame] tender una trampa a. ⬦ vi [establish o.s.] establecerse.

setback ['setbæk] n revés m, contratiempo m.

set menu n menú m del día.

set piece n ART & LIT obra f de tema clásico.

setsquare ['setskweər] n UK escuadra f, cartabón m.

settee [se'ti:] n sofá m.

setter ['setər] n [dog] setter m.

setting ['setɪŋ] n - **1.** [surroundings] escenario m - **2.** [of dial, control] posición f.

settle ['setl] ⬦ vt - **1.** [conclude, decide] resolver; **that settles it, she can move out!** ¡no se hable más, que se vaya! - **2.** [pay] ajustar, saldar - **3.** [make oneself comfortable]: **to settle o.s.** acomodarse, sentarse cómodamente - **4.** [calm - nerves] tranquilizar; **this should settle your stomach** esto te asentará el estómago. ⬦ vi - **1.** [stop travelling] instalarse - **2.** [make o.s. comfortable] acomodarse - **3.** [dust, sediment] depositarse, posarse; **the snow has settled** la nieve ha cuajado - **4.** [calm down - person] calmarse - **5.** [bird etc]: **to settle on** posarse en.

settle down vi - **1.** [concentrate on]: **to settle down to doing sthg** ponerse a hacer algo; **to settle down to sthg** concentrarse en algo; **to settle down (for sthg)** prepararse (para algo) - **2.** [become respectable] sentar la cabeza - **3.** [calm oneself] calmarse.

settle for vt insep [choose] conformarse con.

settle in vi [in new home] instalarse; [in new job] adaptarse.

settle on vt insep [choose] decidirse por.

settle up vi: **to settle up (with sb)** ajustar las cuentas (con alguien).

settled ['setld] adj [unchanging] estable.

settlement ['setlmənt] n - **1.** [agreement] acuerdo m - **2.** [village] poblado m.

settler ['setlər] n colono m.

set-up n inf - **1.** [system, organization] sistema m - **2.** [frame, trap] trampa f, lazo m.

seven ['sevn] num siete; see also **six**.

seventeen [,sevn'ti:n] num diecisiete; see also **six**.

seventeenth [,sevn'ti:nθ] num decimoséptimo(ma); see also **sixth**.

seventh ['sevnθ] num séptimo(ma); see also **sixth**.

seventh heaven n: **to be in (one's) seventh heaven** estar en el séptimo cielo.

seventieth ['sevntjəθ] num septuagésimo(ma); see also **sixth**.

seventy ['sevntɪ] num setenta; see also **sixty**.

sever ['sevər] vt - **1.** [cut through] cortar - **2.** [finish completely] romper.

several ['sevrəl] ⬦ adj varios(rias). ⬦ pron varios mpl, -rias fl.

severance ['sevrəns] n fml ruptura f.

severance pay n despido m.

severe [sɪ'vɪər] adj [gen] severo(ra); [pain] fuerte, agudo(da).

severely [sɪ'vɪəlɪ] adv - **1.** [badly] gravemente - **2.** [sternly] severamente, con severidad.

severity [sɪ'verətɪ] n [gen] gravedad f; [of shortage, problem] severidad f.

sew [səʊ] vt & vi (UK sewn, US sewed OR sewn) coser.

sew up vt sep - **1.** [cloth] coser - **2.** inf [arrange, fix]: **to have sthg sewn up** [deal, election etc] tener algo atado y bien atado.

sewage ['su:ɪdʒ] n (U) aguas fpl residuales.

sewage farm n estación f depuradora.

sewer ['suər] n alcantarilla f, cloaca f.

sewerage ['suərɪdʒ] n alcantarillado m.

sewing ['səʊɪŋ] n (U) - **1.** [activity] labor f de costura - **2.** [items] costura f.

sewing machine n máquina f de coser.

sewn [səʊn] pp ➭ **sew**.

sex [seks] n sexo m; **to have sex** tener relaciones sexuales.

sex appeal n atractivo m, sex appeal m.

sex education n educación f sexual.

sexism ['seksɪzm] n sexismo m.

sexist ['seksɪst] ⬦ adj sexista. ⬦ n sexista mf.

sex life n vida f sexual.

sex shop n sex shop m.

sextet [seks'tet] n sexteto m.

sextuplet [seks'tju:plɪt] *n* sextillizo *m*, -za *f*.

sexual ['sekʃʊəl] *adj* sexual.

sexual assault *n* atentado *m* sexual.

sexual harassment *n* acoso *m* sexual.

sexual intercourse *n (U)* relaciones *fpl* sexuales.

sexuality [ˌsekʃʊˈælətɪ] *n* sexualidad *f*.

sexy ['seksɪ] *(comp* -ier, *superl* -iest) *adj inf* sexi *(inv)*.

Seychelles [seɪ'ʃelz] *npl*: **the Seychelles** las islas Seychelles.

SF, sf *n abbr of* **science fiction**.

SG *(abbr of* **Surgeon General**) *n responsable de sanidad pública en Estados Unidos*.

Sgt *(abbr of* **sergeant**) ≃ sarg.

sh [ʃ] *excl* ¡chis!, ¡chitón!

shabby ['ʃæbɪ] *(comp* -ier, *superl* -iest) *adj* - **1.** [clothes, briefcase] desastrado(da); [street] de aspecto abandonado - **2.** [person] andrajoso(sa) - **3.** [treatment etc] mezquino(na).

shack [ʃæk] *n* chabola *f*.

shackle ['ʃækl] *vt* - **1.** [enchain] poner grilletes a - **2.** *liter* [restrict] restringir.

➤ **shackles** *npl* - **1.** [metal rings] grilletes *mpl*, grillos *mpl* - **2.** *liter* [restrictions] trabas *fpl*.

shade [ʃeɪd] ◇ *n* - **1.** *(U)* [shadow] sombra *f*; **in the shade** a la sombra - **2.** [lampshade] pantalla *f* - **3.** [of colour, meaning] matiz *m* - **4.** *US* [blind] persiana *f* - **5.** [little bit]: **a shade too big** un poquito grande. ◇ *vt* [from light] sombrear, dar sombra a; **to shade one's eyes** protegerse del sol con la mano; **the car was shaded from the sun** el coche estaba protegido del sol.

➤ **shades** *npl inf* [sunglasses] gafas *fpl* de sol.

shading ['ʃeɪdɪŋ] *n* sombreado *m*.

shadow ['ʃædəʊ] ◇ *n* - **1.** [dark shape, form] sombra *f* - **2.** [darkness] oscuridad *f*
▸▸ **to be a shadow of one's former self** ser una sombra de lo que uno era; **there's not a** *OR* **the shadow of a doubt** no hay la menor duda; **to be scared of your own shadow** tener miedo hasta de su propia sombra. ◇ *vt* [subj: detective] seguir.

shadow cabinet *n* gobierno *m* en la sombra *(directiva del principal partido de la oposición en Gran Bretaña)*.

shadowy ['ʃædəʊɪ] *adj* - **1.** [dark] sombrío(a) - **2.** [hard to see] vago(ga) - **3.** [unknown, sinister] oscuro(ra).

shady ['ʃeɪdɪ] *(comp* -ier, *superl* -iest) *adj* - **1.** [sheltered from sun] sombreado(da) - **2.** [providing shade] que da sombra - **3.** *inf* [dishonest - businessman] dudoso(sa), sospechoso(sa); [- deal] turbio(bia).

shaft [ʃɑːft] *n* - **1.** [vertical passage] pozo *m* - **2.** [of lift] hueco *m* - **3.** [tech - rod] eje *m* - **4.** [of light] rayo *m* - **5.** [of spear] asta *f*.

shaggy ['ʃægɪ] *(comp* -ier, *superl* -iest) *adj* [dog] peludo(da).

shaggy-dog story *n* chiste largo y pesado.

shake [ʃeɪk] ◇ *vt (pt* **shook**, *pp* **shaken** ['ʃeɪkən]) - **1.** [move vigorously] sacudir, remecer *Méx*; **to shake sb's hand** dar *OR* estrechar la mano a alguien; **to shake hands** darse *OR* estrecharse la mano; **he shook hands with her** le dio la mano; **to shake one's head** [in refusal] negar con la cabeza; [in disbelief] mover la cabeza mostrando incredulidad; **he shook his fist at them** amenazar a alguien con el puño - **2.** [bottle, aerosol] agitar; **shake well before using** agitar antes de usar - **3.** [shock] trastornar, conmocionar; **the disaster which shook the city** el desastre que sacudió la ciudad - **4.** [undermine] quebrantar, hacer flaquear; **it shook her confidence** quebrantó su confianza. ◇ *vi (pt* **shook**, *pp* **shaken** ['ʃeɪkən]) - **1.** [tremble] temblar; **to shake with fear** temblar de miedo - **2.** *inf* [shake hands]: **let's shake on it** venga esa mano. ◇ *n* [of bottle etc] sacudida *f*; [of head in disbelief] movimiento *m* de la cabeza mostrando incredulidad; [of head in disagreement] negación *f* con la cabeza.

➤ **shake off** *vt sep* [pursuer] deshacerse de; [cold] quitarse de encima; [illness] superar.

➤ **shake up** *vt sep* [contents of bottle etc] agitar; [organisation] reestructurar, reorganizar; [person]: **she wasn't hurt, just a bit shaken up** no resultó herida, sólo un poco conmocionada.

shaken ['ʃeɪkn] *pp* ➣ **shake**.

Shakespearean [ʃeɪk'spɪərɪən] *adj* shakesperiano(na).

shake-up *n inf* reestructuración *f*, reorganización *f*.

shaky ['ʃeɪkɪ] *(comp* -ier, *superl* -iest) *adj* - **1.** [weak, nervous] tembloroso(sa); **to feel shaky** encontrarse nervioso - **2.** [unconfident, insecure - start] incierto(ta); [- argument] poco sólido(da); [- finances] precario(ria) - **3.** [wobbly - chair, table] inestable; [- handwriting] tembloroso(sa).

shale [ʃeɪl] *n* esquisto *m*.

shall *(weak form* [ʃəl], *strong form* [ʃæl]*) aux vb* - **1.** *(1st person sing, 1st person pl)* [to express future tense]: **we shall be there tomorrow** mañana estaremos ahí; **I shan't be home till ten** no estaré en casa hasta las diez - **2.** *(esp 1st person sing & 1st person pl)* [in questions]: **shall we go for a walk?** ¿vamos a dar una vuelta?; **shall I give her a ring?** ¿la llamo?; **I'll do that, shall I?** hago esto, ¿vale? - **3.** [will definitely]: **we shall overcome!** ¡venceremos! - **4.** [in orders]: **you**

shall do as I tell you! ¡harás lo que yo te diga!; **no one shall leave until I say so** que nadie salga hasta que yo lo diga.

shallot [ʃəˈlɒt] n chalote m.

shallow [ˈʃæləʊ] adj - **1.** [in size] poco profundo(da) - **2.** pej [superficial] superficial.

➡ **shallows** npl bajío m, bajos mpl.

sham [ʃæm] ⬦ adj fingido(da), simulado(da). ⬦ n farsa f. ⬦ vi (pt & pp -med, cont -ming) fingir, simular.

shambles [ˈʃæmblz] n desbarajuste m, follón m; **in a shambles** patas arriba.

shame [ʃeɪm] ⬦ n - **1.** (U) [remorse] vergüenza f, pena f Andes, Amér C & Méx - **2.** [dishonour]: **to bring shame on** OR **upon sb** deshonrar a alguien - **3.** [pity]: **what a shame!** ¡qué pena OR lástima!; **it's a shame** es una pena OR lástima. ⬦ vt - **1.** [fill with shame] avergonzar, apenar Andes, Amér C & Méx - **2.** [force by making ashamed]: **to shame sb into doing sthg** conseguir que alguien haga algo avergonzándole OR avergonzándolo Amér.

shamefaced [ˌʃeɪmˈfeɪst] adj avergonzado(da).

shameful [ˈʃeɪmfʊl] adj vergonzoso(sa).

shameless [ˈʃeɪmlɪs] adj desvergonzado(da).

shammy [ˈʃæmɪ] (pl -ies) n inf gamuza f.

shampoo [ʃæmˈpuː] ⬦ n (pl -s) - **1.** [liquid] champú m - **2.** [act of shampooing] lavado m (con champú). ⬦ vt (pt & pp -ed, cont -ing) lavar (con champú).

shamrock [ˈʃæmrɒk] n trébol m.

shandy [ˈʃændɪ] (pl -ies) n cerveza f con gaseosa, clara f.

shan't [ʃɑːnt] (abbr of = shall not), ⊳ shall.

shantytown [ˈʃæntɪtaʊn] n barrio m de chabolas, cantegril m Amér.

shape [ʃeɪp] ⬦ n - **1.** [form] forma f; **it's oval in shape** tenía forma ovalada; **biscuits in the shape of stars** galletas con forma de estrellas - **2.** [silhouette] figura f - **3.** [structure] configuración f; **to take shape** tomar forma - **4.** [guise]: **in the shape of** en forma de; **in any shape or form** de ningún tipo - **5.** [form, health]: **to be in good/bad shape** [person] estar/no estar en forma; [business etc] estar en buen/mal estado; **to get back in shape** ponerse en forma; **to lick** OR **knock sb into shape** poner a alguien a punto. ⬦ vt - **1.** [mould]: **to shape sthg (into)** dar a algo forma (de) - **2.** [cause to develop] desarrollar.

➡ **shape up** vi [develop] desarrollarse.

-shaped [ˈʃeɪpt] suffix: **egg/star-shaped** en forma de huevo/estrella.

shapeless [ˈʃeɪplɪs] adj sin forma.

shapely [ˈʃeɪplɪ] (comp -ier, superl -iest) adj bien hecho(cha).

shard [ʃɑːd] n [of glass] esquirla f; [of cup, vase] fragmento m.

share [ʃeəʳ] ⬦ n - **1.** [portion]: **share (of** OR **in)** parte f (de) - **2.** [contribution, quota]: **to have/do one's share of sthg** tener/hacer la parte que a uno le toca de algo. ⬦ vt - **1.** [gen]: **to share sthg (with)** compartir algo (con); **we share a love of opera** nos une la pasión por la ópera - **2.** [reveal]: **to share sthg (with)** revelar algo (a). ⬦ vi compartir.

➡ **shares** npl acciones fpl.

➡ **share out** vt sep repartir, distribuir.

share capital n capital m social.

share certificate n certificado m de acciones.

shareholder [ˈʃeəˌhəʊldəʳ] n accionista mf.

share index n índice m de cotización.

share-out n reparto m.

shareware [ˈʃeəˌweəʳ] n COMPUT shareware m.

shark [ʃɑːk] (pl shark OR -s) n tiburón m; fig estafador m, -ra f.

sharp [ʃɑːp] ⬦ adj - **1.** [not blunt] afilado(da) - **2.** [well-defined - outline] definido(da); [- photograph] nítido(da); [- contrast] marcado(da) - **3.** [intelligent, keen - person] listo(ta), filoso(sa) Amér; [- eyesight] penetrante; [- hearing] fino(na); [- intelligence] vivo(va) - **4.** [abrupt, sudden] brusco(ca), repentino(na) - **5.** [quick, firm - blow] seco(ca) - **6.** [angry, severe] cortante - **7.** [piercing, acute - sound, cry, pain] agudo(da); [- cold, wind] penetrante - **8.** [acid] ácido(da) - **9.** MUS en tono demasiado alto, desafinado(da); **F sharp** fa m sostenido. ⬦ adv - **1.** [punctually]: **at seven o'clock sharp** a las siete en punto - **2.** [quickly, suddenly] bruscamente - **3.** MUS demasiado alto, desafinadamente. ⬦ n MUS sostenido m.

sharpen [ˈʃɑːpn] ⬦ vt - **1.** [make sharp] afilar; [pencil] sacar punta a - **2.** [make keener, quicker, greater] agudizar - **3.** [make angrier - voice]: **to sharpen one's voice** hablar con tono de enfado. ⬦ vi - **1.** [gen] agudizarse - **2.** [become angrier]: **his voice sharpened** se le notaba el enfado en la voz.

sharpener [ˈʃɑːpnəʳ] n [for pencils] sacapuntas m inv; [for knives] afilador m.

sharp-eyed [-ˈaɪd] adj perspicaz.

sharply [ˈʃɑːplɪ] adv - **1.** [distinctly] claramente - **2.** [suddenly] repentinamente - **3.** [harshly] duramente.

sharpness [ˈʃɑːpnɪs] n - **1.** [of point, edge] lo afilado, agudeza f - **2.** [fine definition] nitidez f - **3.** [of intelligence, eyesight, hearing] agudeza f - **4.** [harshness, severity] dureza f, aspereza f - **5.** [loudness, painfulness] agudeza f - **6.** [of pain, cold] intensidad f - **7.** [of lemon, pickle] acritud f.

sharp-witted [-ˈwɪtɪd] adj agudo(da).

shat [ʃæt] *pt* & *pp* ⊏▷ shit.

shatter ['ʃætər] ◇ *vt* - **1.** [smash] hacer añicos - **2.** [hopes etc] destruir, echar por tierra - **3.** [shock, upset]: **to be shattered (by)** quedar destrozado(da) (por). ◇ *vi* hacerse añicos, romperse en pedazos.

shattered ['ʃætəd] *adj* - **1.** [shocked, upset] destrozado(da) - **2.** *UK inf* [very tired] hecho(cha) polvo.

shattering ['ʃætərɪŋ] *adj* - **1.** [shocking, upsetting] terrible - **2.** *UK* [tiring] agotador(ra).

shatterproof ['ʃætəpruːf] *adj* inastillable.

shave [ʃeɪv] ◇ *n* afeitado *m*; **to have a shave** afeitarse; **it was a close shave** nos salvamos por los pelos. ◇ *vt* - **1.** [face, body] afeitar - **2.** [cut pieces off] raspar. ◇ *vi* afeitarse.
➤ **shave off** *vt sep* afeitar.

shaven ['ʃeɪvn] *adj* rapado(da).

shaver ['ʃeɪvər] *n* maquinilla *f* (de afeitar) eléctrica.

shaving brush ['ʃeɪvɪŋ-] *n* brocha *f* de afeitar.

shaving cream ['ʃeɪvɪŋ-] *n* crema *f* de afeitar.

shaving foam ['ʃeɪvɪŋ-] *n* espuma *f* de afeitar.

shavings ['ʃeɪvɪŋz] *npl* virutas *fpl*.

shaving soap ['ʃeɪvɪŋ-] *n* jabón *m* de afeitar.

shawl [ʃɔːl] *n* chal *m*.

she [ʃiː] ◇ *pers pron* - **1.** [referring to woman, girl, animal] ella; **she's tall** es alta; **she loves fish** le encanta el pescado; **I don't like it, but she does** no me gusta, pero a ella sí; **she can't do it** ella no puede hacerlo; **there she is** allí está - **2.** [referring to boat, car, country]: **she's a fine ship** es un buen barco. ◇ *n*: **it's a she** [animal] es hembra; [baby] es (una) niña. ◇ *comp*: **she-elephant** elefanta *f*; **she bear** osa *f*.

sheaf [ʃiːf] (*pl* **sheaves**) *n* - **1.** [of papers, letters] fajo *m* - **2.** [of corn, grain] gavilla *f*.

shear [ʃɪər] *vt* (*pt* -ed, *pp* -ed OR shorn) [sheep] esquilar.
➤ **shears** *npl* - **1.** [for garden] tijeras *fpl* de podar - **2.** [for dressmaking] tijeras *fpl*.
➤ **shear off** ◇ *vt insep* romper. ◇ *vi* romperse.

sheath [ʃiːθ] (*pl* -s) *n* - **1.** [covering for knife] funda *f*, vaina *f* - **2.** *UK* [condom] preservativo *m*, condón *m*.

sheathe [ʃiːð] *vt* - **1.** [put away] envainar, enfundar - **2.** [cover]: **to sheathe sthg in** envolver algo en.

sheath knife *n* cuchillo *m* de monte.

sheaves [ʃiːvz] *npl* ⊏▷ sheaf.

shed [ʃed] ◇ *n* cobertizo *m*, galpón *m* *Andes, Nic & R Plata*. ◇ *vt* (*pt* & *pp* shed, *cont* -ding) - **1.** [skin] mudar de; [leaves] despojarse de - **2.** [discard] deshacerse de - **3.** [accidentally lose]: **a lorry has shed its load on the M1** un

camión ha perdido su carga en la M1 - **4.** [tears, blood] derramar; **to shed blood** derramar sangre.

she'd *(weak form* [ʃɪd], *strong form* [ʃiːd])- **1.** (*abbr of* = she had), ⊏▷ have - **2.** (*abbr of* = she would), ⊏▷ would.

sheen [ʃiːn] *n* brillo *m*, lustre *m*.

sheep [ʃiːp] (*pl* sheep) *n* [animal] oveja *f*.

sheepdog ['ʃiːpdɒg] *n* perro *m* pastor.

sheepish ['ʃiːpɪʃ] *adj* avergonzado(da).

sheepishly ['ʃiːpɪʃlɪ] *adv* tímidamente.

sheepskin ['ʃiːpskɪn] *n* piel *f* de carnero.

sheepskin jacket *n* zamarra *f*, pelliza *f*.

sheer [ʃɪər] *adj* - **1.** [absolute] puro(ra) - **2.** [very steep - cliff] escarpado(da); [- drop] vertical - **3.** [tights] transparente.

sheet [ʃiːt] *n* - **1.** [for bed] sábana *f*; **a double/fitted sheet** una sábana doble/ajustable; **as white as a sheet** blanco como el papel - **2.** [of paper] hoja *f* - **3.** [of glass, metal, wood] lámina *f*.

sheet feed *n* COMPUT alimentador *m* automático de papel.

sheeting ['ʃiːtɪŋ] *n* (U) chapas *fpl*.

sheet lightning *n* (U) fucilazo *m*, relámpago *m*.

sheet metal *n* (U) chapa *f* de metal.

sheet music *n* (U) partituras *fpl* sueltas.

sheik(h) [ʃeɪk] *n* jeque *m*.

shelf [ʃelf] (*pl* shelves) *n* estante *m*; **it's on the top shelf** está en el estante de arriba.

shelf life *n* periodo *m* de conservación.

shell [ʃel] ◇ *n* - **1.** [of egg, nut] cáscara *f* - **2.** [of tortoise, crab] caparazón *m*; [of snail, mussels] concha *f* - **3.** [on beach] concha *f* - **4.** [of building] esqueleto *m*; [of boat] casco *m*; [of car] armazón *m*, chasis *m inv* - **5.** MIL [missile] proyectil *m*. ◇ *vt* - **1.** [peas] desvainar; [nuts, eggs] quitar la cáscara a - **2.** MIL [fire shells at] bombardear.
➤ **shell out** *inf* ◇ *vt sep* aflojar, soltar. ◇ *vi*: **to shell out for** aflojar la pasta para.

she'll [ʃiːl] - **1.** (*abbr of* = she will), ⊏▷ will - **2.** (*abbr of* = she shall), ⊏▷ shall.

shellfish ['ʃelfɪʃ] (*pl* shellfish) *n* - **1.** [creature] crustáceo *m* - **2.** (U) [food] mariscos *mpl*.

shelling ['ʃelɪŋ] *n* MIL bombardeo *m*.

shellshock ['ʃelʃɒk] *n* (U) trauma *m* de guerra.

shell suit *n UK* chandal *m* (de nailon).

shelter ['ʃeltər] ◇ *n* - **1.** [building, protection] refugio *m*; **to seek shelter** buscar refugio; **to take shelter (from)** refugiarse (de); **to run for shelter** correr a refugiarse; **nuclear shelter** refugio nuclear; **bus shelter** marquesina *f* - **2.** [place to live] techo *m*; **their greatest needs are food and shelter** lo que más necesitan es comida y refugio. ◇ *vt* - **1.** [protect]: **to be**

sheltered by/from estar protegido(da) por/de - **2.** [provide place to live for] dar asilo OR cobijo a - **3.** [hide] proteger, esconder. ◇ vi: **to shelter from/in** resguardarse de/en, protegerse de/en.

sheltered [ˈʃeltəd] adj - **1.** [place, existence] protegido(da) - **2.** [accommodation, housing]: **sheltered housing** conjunto de viviendas especialmente diseñado para ancianos o minusválidos.

shelve [ʃelv] vt dar carpetazo a.

shelves [ʃelvz] npl ⊳ shelf.

shelving [ˈʃelvɪŋ] n (U) estantería f.

shepherd [ˈʃepəd] ◇ n pastor m. ◇ vt fig acompañar.

shepherd's pie [ˈʃepədz-] n carne picada cubierta de puré de patatas.

sherbet [ˈʃɜːbət] n - **1.** UK [sweet powder] sidral m - **2.** US [sorbet] sorbete m.

sheriff [ˈʃerɪf] n sheriff m.

sherry [ˈʃerɪ] (pl -ries) n jerez m.

she's [ʃiːz] - **1.** (abbr of = she is), ⊳ be - **2.** (abbr of = she has), ⊳ have.

Shetland [ˈʃetlənd] n: (the) Shetland (Islands) las islas Shetland.

sh(h) [ʃ] excl ¡chis!, ¡chitón!

shield [ʃiːld] ◇ n - **1.** [armour, sports trophy] escudo m - **2.** [protection]: **shield against** protección f contra. ◇ vt: **to shield sb (from)** proteger a alguien (de); **to shield o.s. (from)** protegerse (de).

shift [ʃɪft] ◇ n - **1.** [slight change] cambio m; **a shift in sthg** un cambio en algo - **2.** [period of work, workers] turno m; **the night shift** el turno de noche. ◇ vt - **1.** [furniture etc] cambiar de sitio, mover - **2.** [attitude, belief] cambiar de - **3.** [transfer]: **to shift the blame (on to sb)** echar la culpa (a alguien). ◇ vi - **1.** [person] moverse; [wind, opinion] cambiar - **2.** US AUT cambiar de marcha.

shift key n tecla f de mayúsculas.

shiftless [ˈʃɪftlɪs] adj vago(ga), remolón(ona).

shift work n trabajo m por turnos; **to do shift work** trabajar por turnos.

shifty [ˈʃɪftɪ] (comp -ier, superl -iest) adj inf [person] con pinta deshonesta; [behaviour] sospechoso(sa); [look] huidizo(za).

Shiite [ˈʃiːaɪt] ◇ adj chiíta. ◇ n chiíta mf.

shilling [ˈʃɪlɪŋ] n chelín m.

shilly-shally [ˈʃɪlɪˌʃælɪ] (pt & pp -ied) vi titubear, vacilar.

shimmer [ˈʃɪmər] ◇ n resplandor m trémulo. ◇ vi rielar, brillar con luz trémula.

shin [ʃɪn] n espinilla f.

◆ **shin down** UK, **shinny down** US vt insep (pt & pp -ned, cont -ning) bajar de.

◆ **shin up** UK, **shinny up** US vt insep trepar.

shinbone [ˈʃɪnbəʊn] n espinilla f.

shine [ʃaɪn] ◇ n brillo m. ◇ vt (pt & pp shone) [torch, lamp] dirigir; **she shone a torch into his eyes** la enfocó en los ojos con una linterna. ◇ vi (pt & pp shone) - **1.** [gen] brillar - **2.** [excel]: **to shine at** despuntar en.

shingle [ˈʃɪŋgl] n - **1.** (U) [on beach] guijarros mpl - **2.** US [nameplate] placa f con el nombre; **to hang out one's shingle** abrir un despacho/consultorio.

◆ **shingles** n (U) herpes m inv.

shining [ˈʃaɪnɪŋ] adj - **1.** [gleaming] brillante, brilloso(sa) Amér - **2.** [outstanding] excepcional.

shinny [ˈʃɪnɪ] US ◆ **shinny down** = shin down. ◆ **shinny up** = shin up.

shin pad n espinillera f.

shiny [ˈʃaɪnɪ] (comp -ier, superl -iest) adj brillante.

ship [ʃɪp] ◇ n barco m, buque m. ◇ vt (pt & pp -ped, cont -ping) enviar por barco.

shipbuilder [ˈʃɪpˌbɪldər] n constructor m, -ra f de naves.

shipbuilding [ˈʃɪpˌbɪldɪŋ] n construcción f naval.

shipment [ˈʃɪpmənt] n envío m.

shipper [ˈʃɪpər] n compañía f naviera.

shipping [ˈʃɪpɪŋ] n (U) - **1.** [transport] envío m, transporte m - **2.** [ships] barcos mpl, buques mpl.

shipping agent n agente marítimo m, agente marítima f.

shipping company n compañía f naviera.

shipping forecast n predicción f del estado de la mar.

shipping lane n ruta f marítima.

shipshape [ˈʃɪpʃeɪp] adj en orden.

shipwreck [ˈʃɪprek] ◇ n - **1.** [destruction of ship] naufragio m - **2.** [wrecked ship] barco m náufrago. ◇ vt: **to be shipwrecked** naufragar.

shipwrecked [ˈʃɪprekt] adj náufrago(ga).

shipyard [ˈʃɪpjɑːd] n astillero m.

shire [ʃaɪər] n [county] condado m.

shire horse n percherón m, caballo m de tiro.

shirk [ʃɜːk] vt eludir.

shirker [ˈʃɜːkər] n vago m, -ga f.

shirt [ʃɜːt] n camisa f.

shirtsleeves [ˈʃɜːtsliːvz] npl: **to be in (one's) shirtsleeves** ir en mangas de camisa.

shirttail [ˈʃɜːtteɪl] n faldón m.

shirty [ˈʃɜːtɪ] (comp -ier, superl -iest) adj UK inf de mala uva; **to get shirty** mosquearse.

shit [ʃɪt] (cont -ting) vulg ◇ n - **1.** [excrement] mierda f - **2.** (U) [nonsense] gilipolleces fpl

- 3. [person] hijo *m*, -ja *f* de puta. ⬦ *vi* (*pt & pp* **shit, -ted** OR **shat**) cagar. ⬦ *excl* ¡mierda!

shiver ['ʃɪvəʳ] ⬦ *n* escalofrío *m*, estremecimiento *m*; **to give sb the shivers** dar escalofríos a alguien; **it sent shivers down her spine** le puso los pelos de punta. ⬦ *vi*: **to shiver (with)** [fear] temblar OR estremecerse (de); [cold] tiritar (de).

shoal [ʃəʊl] *n* banco *m*.

shock [ʃɒk] ⬦ *n* **- 1.** [unpleasant surprise, reaction, emotional state] susto *m*; **I got a real shock** me dio un vuelco de corazón; **it came as a shock** fue un duro golpe **- 2.** *(U)* MED: **to be suffering from shock, to be in shock** estar en un estado de choque **- 3.** [impact] choque *m* **- 4.** [electric shock] descarga *f* (eléctrica); **to get a shock from sthg** recibir una descarga de algo **- 5.** [thick mass] mata *f*; **a shock of hair** una mata de pelo. ⬦ *vt* **- 1.** [upset] conmocionar **- 2.** [offend] escandalizar.

shock absorber [-əb,zɔːbəʳ] *n* amortiguador *m*.

shocked [ʃɒkt] *adj* **- 1.** [upset] horrorizado(da) **- 2.** [offended] escandalizado(da), ofendido(da).

shocking ['ʃɒkɪŋ] *adj* **- 1.** [very bad] pésimo(ma) **- 2.** [behaviour, film] escandaloso(sa); [price] de escándalo.

shockproof ['ʃɒkpruːf] *adj* a prueba de choques.

shock tactics *npl* fig & MIL táctica *f* de choque.

shock therapy, shock treatment *n* tratamiento *m* a base de electrochoques.

shock troops *npl* tropas *fpl* de asalto.

shock wave *n* [intense heat, pressure] onda *f* expansiva; fig oleada *f* de turbación.

shod [ʃɒd] ⬦ *pt & pp* ⊳ **shoe**. ⬦ *adj* calzado(da).

shoddy ['ʃɒdɪ] (*comp* **-ier**, *superl* **-iest**) *adj* [work] chapucero(ra); [goods] de pacotilla; fig [treatment] vil, despreciable.

shoe [ʃuː] ⬦ *n* zapato *m*. ⬦ *vt* (*pt & pp* **shod** OR **shoed**) (*cont* **shoeing**) herrar.

shoebrush ['ʃuːbrʌʃ] *n* cepillo *m* para los zapatos.

shoehorn ['ʃuːhɔːn] *n* calzador *m*.

shoelace ['ʃuːleɪs] *n* cordón *m* del zapato, pasador *m* Amér.

shoemaker ['ʃuːˌmeɪkəʳ] *n* zapatero *m*, -ra *f*.

shoe polish *n* betún *m*.

shoe shop *n* zapatería *f*.

shoestring ['ʃuːstrɪŋ] ⬦ *adj* muy reducido(da). ⬦ *n* fig: **on a shoestring** con cuatro cuartos, con muy poco dinero.

shoetree ['ʃuːtriː] *n* horma *f*.

shone [ʃɒn] *pt & pp* ⊳ **shine**.

shoo [ʃuː] ⬦ *vt* [animal] espantar, ahuyentar; **he shooed the cat away** echó al gato; [person] mandar a otra parte. ⬦ *excl* ¡fuera!

shook [ʃʊk] *pt* ⊳ **shake**.

shoot [ʃuːt] ⬦ *n* **- 1.** UK [hunting expedition] cacería *f* **- 2.** [new growth] brote *m*, retoño *m*. ⬦ *vt* (*pt & pp* **shot**) **- 1.** [fire gun at] disparar contra, abalear Andes, Amér C & Ven; [injure] herir a tiros; [kill] matar a tiros; **to shoot o.s.** pegarse un tiro; **he was shot in the leg** le dispararon en la pierna; **to shoot the breeze** US estar de cháchara **- 2.** UK [hunt] cazar **- 3.** [arrow] disparar **- 4.** [direct - glance] lanzar, echar; **she shot him an inquisitive glance** le lanzó una mirada de curiosidad; [- question] disparar **- 5.** CIN rodar, filmar **- 6.** US [play]: **to shoot pool** jugar al billar americano. ⬦ *vi* (*pt & pp* **shot**) **- 1.** [fire gun]: **to shoot (at)** disparar (contra); **don't shoot!** ¡no dispare! **- 2.** UK [hunt] cazar **- 3.** [move quickly]: **to shoot in/out/past** entrar/salir/pasar disparado(da) **- 4.** CIN rodar, filmar **- 5.** SPORT chutar; **he shot at goal** chutó a puerta. ⬦ *excl* US inf **- 1.** [go ahead] ¡venga!, ¡vamos! **- 2.** [damn] ¡ostras!

◆ **shoot down** *vt sep* **- 1.** [plane] derribar **- 2.** [person] matar a tiros.

◆ **shoot up** *vi* **- 1.** [child, plant] crecer rápidamente **- 2.** [prices] dispararse **- 3.** *drug sl* [take drugs] chutarse.

shooting ['ʃuːtɪŋ] *n* **- 1.** [killing] asesinato *m* (*a tiros)* **- 2.** *(U)* [hunting] caza *f*, cacería *f*.

shooting range *n* campo *m* de tiro.

shooting star *n* estrella *f* fugaz.

shoot-out *n* tiroteo *m*.

shop [ʃɒp] ⬦ *n* [store] tienda *f*; **to talk shop** hablar del trabajo. ⬦ *vi* (*pt & pp* **-ped**, *cont* **-ping**) comprar; **to go shopping** ir de compras.

◆ **shop around** *vi* comparar precios.

shop assistant *n* UK dependiente *m*, -ta *f*.

shop floor *n*: **the shop floor** el personal, los obreros.

shopkeeper ['ʃɒpˌkiːpəʳ] *n* tendero *m*, -ra *f*.

shoplifter ['ʃɒpˌlɪftəʳ] *n* ladrón *m*, -ona *f* en una tienda.

shoplifting ['ʃɒpˌlɪftɪŋ] *n* *(U)* robo *m* en una tienda.

shopper ['ʃɒpəʳ] *n* comprador *m*, -ra *f*.

shopping ['ʃɒpɪŋ] *n* *(U)* **- 1.** [purchases] compras *fpl* **- 2.** [act of shopping] compra *f*; **to do some/the shopping** hacer algunas compras/la compra.

shopping bag *n* bolsa *f* de la compra.

shopping basket *n* UK **- 1.** [in supermarket] cesta *f* **- 2.** [for online shopping] cesta *f* de la compra.

shopping cart n US - **1.** [in supermarket] carrito m de la compra - **2.** [for online shopping] cesta f de la compra.

shopping centre UK, **shopping mall** US, **shopping plaza** US [-,plɑːzə] n centro m comercial.

shopping list n lista f de la compra.

shopping mall US, **shopping plaza** US = shopping centre.

shopsoiled UK ['ʃɒpsɔɪld], **shopworn** US ['ʃɒpwɔːn] adj deteriorado(da).

shop steward n enlace mf sindical.

shopwindow [,ʃɒp'wɪndəʊ] n escaparate m.

shopworn US = shopsoiled.

shore [ʃɔːr] n - **1.** [of sea, lake, river] orilla f - **2.** [land]: **on shore** en tierra.
◆ **shore up** vt sep apuntalar.

shore leave n permiso m para bajar a tierra.

shoreline ['ʃɔːlaɪn] n orilla f.

shorn [ʃɔːn] ◇ pp ▷ **shear**. ◇ adj [grass, hair] corto(ta); [head] rapado(da).

short [ʃɔːt] ◇ adj - **1.** [gen] corto(ta); **a short time ago** hace poco - **2.** [not tall] bajo(ja) - **3.** [curt]: **to be short (with sb)** ser seco(ca) (con alguien); **to have a short temper** tener mal genio - **4.** [lacking] escaso(sa); **to be short on sthg** no andar sobrado de algo; **to be short of** estar OR andar mal de; **we're a chair/pound short** nos falta una silla/libra; **to be short of breath** estar sin aliento - **5.** [be shorter form]: **to be short for** ser el diminutivo de. ◇ adv - **1.** [out of]: **we are running short of water** se nos está acabando el agua - **2.** [suddenly, abruptly]: **to cut sthg short** interrumpir algo; **we had to cut short our trip to Cyprus** tuvimos que interrumpir nuestro viaje a Chipre; **to stop short** parar en seco OR de repente; **to bring** OR **pull sb up short** hacer a alguien parar en seco. ◇ n - **1.** UK [alcoholic drink] chupito m - **2.** [film] cortometraje m.
◆ **shorts** npl - **1.** [gen] pantalones mpl cortos, shorts mpl - **2.** US [underwear] calzoncillos mpl.
◆ **for short** adv para abreviar.
◆ **in short** adv en resumen, en pocas palabras.
◆ **nothing short of** prep: **it was nothing short of madness/a disgrace** fue una auténtica locura/vergüenza.
◆ **short of** prep - **1.** [just before] cerca de; **just short of the cliff** casi al borde del precipicio - **2.** [without]: **short of asking, I can't see how you'll find out** salvo que preguntes, no sé cómo lo vas a averiguar.

shortage ['ʃɔːtɪdʒ] n falta f, escasez f; **there was a paper shortage** había falta OR escasez de papel.

short back and sides n UK pelo m corto a los lados y en la nuca.

shortbread ['ʃɔːtbred] n especie de torta hecha de azúcar, harina y mantequilla.

short-change vt [in shop] dar mal el cambio a; fig [reward unfairly] estafar, engañar.

short circuit n cortocircuito m.
◆ **short-circuit** ◇ vt provocar un cortocircuito en. ◇ vi tener un cortocircuito.

shortcomings ['ʃɔːt,kʌmɪŋz] npl defectos mpl.

shortcrust pastry ['ʃɔːtkrʌst-] n pasta f quebrada.

short cut n - **1.** [quick way] atajo m; **to take a short cut** tomar un atajo - **2.** [quick method] método m rápido.

shorten ['ʃɔːtn] ◇ vt acortar. ◇ vi acortarse.

shortening ['ʃɔːtnɪŋ] n CULIN grasa vegetal o animal utilizada para hacer masas pasteleras.

shortfall ['ʃɔːtfɔːl] n: **shortfall (in** OR **of)** déficit m (de).

shorthand ['ʃɔːthænd] n - **1.** [writing system] taquigrafía f - **2.** [short form]: **shorthand (for)** una forma breve (de decir).

shorthanded [,ʃɔːt'hændɪd] adj: **to be shorthanded** estar falto(ta) de personal.

shorthand typist n UK taquimecanógrafo m, -fa f.

short-haul adj [flight] que cubre distancias cortas.

short list n UK [for job] lista f de candidatos seleccionados.
◆ **short-list** vt: **to be short-listed (for)** [job] estar entre los candidatos (para).

short-lived [-'lɪvd] adj efímero(ra).

shortly ['ʃɔːtlɪ] adv - **1.** [soon] dentro de poco; **shortly before/after** poco antes/después de - **2.** [curtly] secamente, bruscamente.

shortness ['ʃɔːtnɪs] n - **1.** [in time] brevedad f - **2.** [in height] baja estatura f; [in length] cortedad f.

short-range adj [aircraft] de corto radio de acción; [missile] de corto alcance.

short shrift [-'ʃrɪft] n: **to give sb short shrift** prestar poca atención a alguien.

shortsighted [,ʃɔːt'saɪtɪd] adj [myopic] miope, corto(ta) de vista; fig [lacking foresight] corto de miras.

short-staffed [-'stɑːft] adj: **to be short-staffed** estar falto(ta) de personal.

shortstop ['ʃɔːtstɒp] n US [baseball] jugador que intenta interceptar bolas entre la segunda y tercera base.

short story n cuento m.

short-tempered [-'tempəd] adj de mal genio, de genio vivo.

short-term adj a corto plazo.

short wave n (U) onda f corta.

shot [ʃɒt] ⬦ pt & pp ▷ **shoot**. ⬦ n
- **1.** [gunshot] tiro m, disparo m; **he fired two
shots** disparó dos tiros; **like a shot** [quickly]
disparado(da) - **2.** [marksman] tirador m, -ra f;
to be a good shot ser un buen tirador - **3.** [in
football] chut m, tiro m; [in golf, tennis] golpe m;
good shot! ¡buen golpe! - **4.** [photograph] foto f
- **5.** CIN plano m, toma f - **6.** inf [try, go] intento m; **go on, have a shot** venga, inténtalo; **to
have a shot at (doing) sthg** intentar (hacer)
algo - **7.** [injection] inyección f - **8.** [of alcohol]
trago m.

shotgun [ʃɒtgʌn] n escopeta f.

shot put n: **the shot put** el lanzamiento de
peso.

should [ʃʊd] aux vb - **1.** [be desirable]: **we
should leave now** deberíamos irnos ya OR
ahora - **2.** [seeking advice, permission]: **should I
go too?** ¿voy yo también? - **3.** [as suggestion]:
I should deny everything yo lo negaría todo
- **4.** [indicating probability]: **she should be home
soon** tiene que llegar a casa pronto - **5.** [have
been expected]: **they should have won the
match** tendrían que OR deberían haber ganado el partido - **6.** [indicating intention, wish]: **I
should like to come with you** me gustaría ir
contigo - **7.** (as conditional): **if you should see
Mary, could you ask her to phone me?** si vie-
ras a Mary, ¿le podrías pedir que me llama-
ra?; **should you decide to accept the job...** si
decide aceptar el trabajo... - **8.** (in 'that' clauses):
we decided that you should do it decidimos
que lo hicieras tú - **9.** [expressing uncertain opin-
ion]: **I should think he's about 50 (years old)**
yo diría que tiene unos 50 (años) - **10.** [express-
ing indignation]: **he tidied up afterwards – so
he should!** después lo limpió – ¡era lo menos
que podía hacer!; **I should hope so!** ¡eso espero!; **I should think so, too!** ¡es lo mínimo
que podía hacer!

shoulder [ʃəʊldər] ⬦ n - **1.** [part of body, cloth-
ing] hombro m; **to look over one's shoulder**
mirar hacia atrás; **a shoulder to cry on** un paño de lágrimas; **to cry on sb's shoulder** llorar en el hombro de nadie; **to rub shoulders
with** codearse con - **2.** CULIN espaldilla f, paleta f Amér. ⬦ vt - **1.** [carry - load] echarse al hombro - **2.** [accept - responsibility] cargar con; **to
shoulder the blame** asumir la responsabilidad.

shoulder bag n bolso m de bandolera Esp, bolso m OR bolsa f Méx OR cartera f con correa para colgar del hombro.

shoulder blade n omóplato m.

shoulder-length adj que llega hasta los
hombros.

shoulder strap n - **1.** [on dress] tirante m, bretel m - **2.** [on bag] correa f, bandolera f.

shouldn't [ʃʊdnt] (abbr of = should
not), ▷ **should**.

should've [ʃʊdəv] (abbr of = should
have), ▷ **should**.

shout [ʃaʊt] ⬦ n grito m; **to let out a shout**
lanzar un grito. ⬦ vt gritar. ⬦ vi: **to shout
(at)** gritar (a).
◆ **shout down** vt sep acallar a gritos.
◆ **shout out** vt sep gritar.

shouting [ʃaʊtɪŋ] n (U) gritos mpl.

shove [ʃʌv] ⬦ n: **(to give sthg/sb) a shove**
(dar a algo/a alguien) un empujón. ⬦ vt empujar; **to shove sthg/sb in** meter algo/a alguien a empujones; **to shove sthg/sb out** sacar algo/a alguien a empujones; **to shove
sthg/sb about** empujar algo/a alguien.
◆ **shove off** vi - **1.** [in boat] alejarse del muelle la orilla etc - **2.** inf [go away] largarse.

shovel [ʃʌvl] ⬦ n pala f. ⬦ vt (UK -led,
cont -ling, US -ed, cont -ing) remover con la
pala OR a paletadas; **to shovel food into one's
mouth** fig zamparse la comida.

show [ʃəʊ] ⬦ n - **1.** [display, demonstration] demostración f; **a show of strength** una demostración de fuerte - **2.** [piece of entertainment -
at theatre] espectáculo m; [- on radio, TV] programa m - **3.** [performance] función f - **4.** [of
dogs, flowers, art] exposición f; **on show** expuesto; **for show** para impresionar. ⬦ vt
(pt -ed, pp shown OR -ed) - **1.** [gen] mostrar;
to show sb sthg, to show sthg to sb enseñar
OR mostrar a alguien algo; **to show sb how to
do sthg** enseñar OR mostrar a alguien cómo
hacer algo; **he has nothing to show for all
his efforts** todos sus esfuerzos han sido en
balde - **2.** [escort]: **to show sb to the door** llevar OR acompañar a alguien hasta algo; **he
showed us to our seats** nos llevó a nuestros
asientos - **3.** [make visible, reveal] dejar ver;
white clothes show the dirt la ropa blanca
deja ver la suciedad; **to show o.s.** dejarse ver;
come on, show yourself! venga, ¡déjate ver!
- **4.** [indicate - increase, profit, loss] arrojar, registrar; **it just goes to show that...** viene a demostrar que... - **5.** [broadcast - film] poner; [- TV
programme] poner, emitir. ⬦ vi (pt -ed,
pp shown OR -ed) - **1.** [indicate, make clear] indicar, mostrar - **2.** [be visible] verse, notarse;
does it show? ¿se ve? - **3.** [film]: **it is showing
at the Odeon** lo ponen en el Odeon.
◆ **show around** = **show round**.
◆ **show off** ⬦ vt sep lucir, presumir de. ⬦ vi
presumir.
◆ **show out** vt sep acompañar hasta la puerta; **show the gentlemen out, please** acompa-
ñe a los caballeros hasta la puerta, por favor.

show round, show around *vt sep*: **to show sb round a flat** enseñarle a alguien un piso.

◆ **show up** ◇ *vt sep* poner en evidencia. ◇ *vi* - **1.** [stand out] resaltar - **2.** [turn up] aparecer.

showbiz [ˈʃəʊbɪz] *inf abbr of* **show business**.

show business *n (U)* mundo *m* del espectáculo.

showcase [ˈʃəʊkeɪs] *n* - **1.** [glass case] vitrina *f* - **2.** *fig* [advantageous setting] escaparate *m*, plataforma *f*.

showdown [ˈʃəʊdaʊn] *n*: **to have a showdown with** enfrentarse abiertamente a OR con.

shower [ˈʃaʊər] ◇ *n* - **1.** [device] ducha *f*, regadera *f Col, Méx & Ven* - **2.** [wash]: **to have** OR **take a shower** ducharse - **3.** [of rain] chubasco *m*, chaparrón *m* - **4.** *US* [party] *fiesta con regalos organizada en honor de una mujer por sus amigas*. ◇ *vt* - **1.** [sprinkle] rociar - **2.** [bestow]: **to shower sb with sthg, to shower sthg on** OR **upon sb** [presents, compliments] colmar a alguien de algo; [insults] acribillar a alguien a algo. ◇ *vi* [wash] ducharse.

shower cap *n* gorro *m* de ducha.

showerproof [ˈʃaʊəpruːf] *adj* impermeable.

showery [ˈʃaʊərɪ] *adj* lluvioso(sa).

showing [ˈʃəʊɪŋ] *n* [of film] pase *m*, proyección *f*; [of paintings] exposición *f*.

show jumping [-ˌdʒʌmpɪŋ] *n* concurso *m* hípico de salto.

showman [ˈʃəʊmən] (*pl* **-men** [-mən]) *n* - **1.** [at fair, circus] empresario *m* - **2.** *fig* [publicity-seeker] showman *m*.

showmanship [ˈʃəʊmənʃɪp] *n* teatralidad *f*, talento *m* teatral.

shown [ʃəʊn] *pp* ▷ **show**.

show-off *n inf* presumido *m*, -da *f*.

show of hands *n*: **to have a show of hands** votar a mano alzada.

showpiece [ˈʃəʊpiːs] *n* pieza *f* de mayor interés.

showroom [ˈʃəʊrʊm] *n* salón *m* OR sala *f* de exposición.

showy [ˈʃəʊɪ] (*comp* **-ier**, *superl* **-iest**) *adj* [person] ostentoso(sa); [clothes, colour] llamativo(va).

shrank [ʃræŋk] *pt* ▷ **shrink**.

shrapnel [ˈʃræpnl] *n* metralla *f*.

shred [ʃred] ◇ *n* [small piece - of material] jirón *m*; [- of paper] trocito *m*, pedacito *m*; *fig* [scrap] ápice *m*, pizca *f*; **there isn't a shred of truth in what he says** no hay una pizca de verdad en lo que dice; **to be in shreds** *lit* & *fig* estar hecho(cha) pedazos. ◇ *vt* (*pt* & *pp* **-ded**, *cont* **-ding**) [paper] hacer trizas; [food] rallar.

shredder [ˈʃredər] *n* [for paper] destructora *f*; [for food] rallador *m*.

shrew [ʃruː] *n* ZOOL musaraña *f*.

shrewd [ʃruːd] *adj* astuto(ta), abusado(da) *Méx*.

shrewdness [ˈʃruːdnɪs] *n* astucia *f*.

shriek [ʃriːk] ◇ *n* chillido *m*, grito *m*. ◇ *vt* chillar, gritar. ◇ *vi*: **to shriek (with** OR **in)** chillar (de).

shrill [ʃrɪl] *adj* [high-pitched] estridente, agudo(da).

shrimp [ʃrɪmp] *n US* gamba *f*, camarón *m Amér*.

shrine [ʃraɪn] *n* santuario *m*.

shrink [ʃrɪŋk] ◇ *vt* (*pt* **shrank**, *pp* **shrunk**) encoger. ◇ *vi* (*pt* **shrank**, *pp* **shrunk**) - **1.** [become smaller] encoger - **2.** *fig* [contract, diminish] disminuir - **3.** [recoil]: **to shrink away from** retroceder OR arredrarse ante - **4.** [be reluctant]: **to shrink from sthg** eludir algo.

shrinkage [ˈʃrɪŋkɪdʒ] *n* [loss in size] encogimiento *m*; *fig* [contraction] reducción *f*.

shrink-wrap *vt precintar o envasar con plástico termoretráctil.*

shrivel [ˈʃrɪvl] (*UK* **-led**, *cont* **-ling**) (*US* **-ed**, *cont* **-ing**) ◇ *vt*: **to shrivel (up)** secar, marchitar. ◇ *vi*: **to shrivel (up)** secarse, marchitarse.

shroud [ʃraʊd] ◇ *n* [cloth] mortaja *f*, sudario *m*. ◇ *vt*: **to be shrouded in sthg** estar envuelto(ta) en algo.

Shrove Tuesday [ˈʃrəʊv-] *n* martes *m inv* de carnaval.

shrub [ʃrʌb] *n* arbusto *m*.

shrubbery [ˈʃrʌbərɪ] *n* (zona *f* de) arbustos *mpl*.

shrug [ʃrʌg] ◇ *n* encogimiento *m* de hombros. ◇ *vt* (*pt* & *pp* **-ged**, *cont* **-ging**): **to shrug one's shoulders** encogerse de hombros. ◇ *vi* (*pt* & *pp* **-ged**, *cont* **-ging**) encogerse de hombros.

◆ **shrug off** *vt sep* quitar importancia a.

shrunk [ʃrʌŋk] *pp* ▷ **shrink**.

shrunken [ˈʃrʌŋkn] *adj* [person] encogido(da).

shucks [ʃʌks] *excl US inf* - **1.** [it was nothing] ¡no es nada! - **2.** [damn] ¡ostras!

shudder [ˈʃʌdər] ◇ *n* escalofrío *m*, estremecimiento *m*. ◇ *vi* - **1.** [tremble]: **to shudder (with)** estremecerse (de); **I shudder to think** me entran escalofríos sólo con pensar - **2.** [shake] temblar, dar sacudidas.

shuffle [ˈʃʌfl] ◇ *n* - **1.** [of feet]: **to walk with a shuffle** andar arrastrando los pies - **2.** [of cards]: **to give the cards a shuffle** barajar las cartas. ◇ *vt* - **1.** [feet] arrastrar - **2.** [cards] ba-

rajar - 3. [sheets of paper] revolver. ◇ *vi* **- 1.** [walk by dragging feet]**: to shuffle in/out/along** entrar/salir/andar arrastrando los pies **- 2.** [fidget] moverse nerviosamente.

shun [ʃʌn] (*pt* & *pp* **-ned**, *cont* **-ning**) *vt* rehuir, esquivar.

shunt [ʃʌnt] *vt* RAIL cambiar de vía; *fig* [move] llevar (de un sitio a otro).

shush [ʃʊʃ] *excl* ¡chis!, ¡chitón!

shut [ʃʌt] ◇ *adj* cerrado(da). ◇ *vt* (*pt* & *pp* **shut**, *cont* **-ting**) cerrar; **shut your mouth** OR **face!** *v inf* ¡cierra el pico! ◇ *vi* (*pt* & *pp* **shut**, *cont* **-ting**) **- 1.** [close] cerrarse **- 2.** [close for business] cerrar.

◆ **shut away** *vt sep* guardar bajo llave; **to shut o.s. away** encerrarse.

◆ **shut down** *vt sep* & *vi* cerrar.

◆ **shut in** *vt sep* encerrar; **to shut o.s. in** encerrarse.

◆ **shut out** *vt sep* **- 1.** [person, cat] dejar fuera a; [light, noise] no dejar entrar **- 2.** [thought, feeling] bloquear.

◆ **shut up** *inf* ◇ *vt sep* [silence] hacer callar. ◇ *vi* callarse; **shut up!** ¡cállate!

shutdown [ˈʃʌtdaʊn] *n* cierre *m*.

shutter [ˈʃʌtər] *n* **- 1.** [on window] postigo *m*, contraventana *f* **- 2.** [in camera] obturador *m*.

shuttle [ˈʃʌtl] ◇ *adj*: **shuttle service** [of planes] puente *m* aéreo; [of buses, trains] servicio *m* regular. ◇ *n* [plane] avión *m* (de puente aéreo). ◇ *vi* ir y venir.

shuttlecock [ˈʃʌtlkɒk] *n* volante *m*.

shy [ʃaɪ] ◇ *adj* **- 1.** [timid] tímido(da) **- 2.** [wary]: **to be shy of doing sthg** no atreverse a hacer algo. ◇ *vi* (*pt* & *pp* **shied**) asustarse, espantarse.

◆ **shy away from** *vt insep*: **to shy away from sthg** huir de algo; **to shy away from doing sthg** negarse a hacer algo.

shyly [ˈʃaɪlɪ] *adv* tímidamente, con timidez.

shyness [ˈʃaɪnɪs] *n* timidez *f*.

Siamese [ˌsaɪəˈmiːz] ◇ *adj* siamés(esa). ◇ *n* (*pl* **Siamese**) ZOOL: **Siamese (cat)** (gato *m*) siamés *m*.

Siamese twins *npl* hermanos *mpl* siameses.

Siberia [saɪˈbɪərɪə] *n* Siberia.

Siberian [saɪˈbɪərɪən] ◇ *adj* siberiano(na). ◇ *n* siberiano *m*, -na *f*.

sibling [ˈsɪblɪŋ] *n* hermano *m*, -na *f*.

Sicilian [sɪˈsɪljən] ◇ *adj* siciliano(na). ◇ *n* [person] siciliano *m*, -na *f*.

Sicily [ˈsɪsɪlɪ] *n* Sicilia.

sick [sɪk] *adj* **- 1.** [ill] enfermo(ma) **- 2.** [nauseous]: **to feel sick** marearse **- 3.** [vomiting]: **to be sick** UK devolver, vomitar **- 4.** [fed up]: **to be sick of sthg/of doing sthg** estar harto(ta) de algo/de hacer algo; **to be sick and tired of (doing) sthg** estar hasta la coronilla de (hacer) algo **- 5.** [angry, disgusted]: **to make sb sick** *fig* poner enfermo(ma) a alguien **- 6.** [joke] de mal gusto.

sickbay [ˈsɪkbeɪ] *n* enfermería *f*.

sickbed [ˈsɪkbed] *n* cama *f* (donde yace un enfermo).

sicken [ˈsɪkn] ◇ *vt* poner enfermo(ma), asquear. ◇ *vi* UK: **to be sickening for sthg** estar cogiendo algo.

sickening [ˈsɪknɪŋ] *adj* **- 1.** [disgusting] asqueroso(sa), repugnante **- 2.** [infuriating] exasperante.

sickle [ˈsɪkl] *n* hoz *f*.

sick leave *n* (*U*) baja *f* por enfermedad.

sickly [ˈsɪklɪ] (*comp* **-ier**, *superl* **-iest**) *adj* **- 1.** [unhealthy] enfermizo(za) **- 2.** [unpleasant] nauseabundo(da).

sickness [ˈsɪknɪs] *n* **- 1.** [illness] enfermedad *f* **- 2.** (*U*) UK [nausea, vomiting] mareo *m*.

sickness benefit *n* (*U*) subsidio *m* por enfermedad.

sick pay *n* (*U*) paga *f* por enfermedad.

sickroom [ˈsɪkrʊm] *n* habitación *f* de un enfermo.

side [saɪd] ◇ *n* **- 1.** [gen] lado *m*; **at** OR **by one's side** al lado de uno; **on every side, on all sides** por todos los lados; **from side to side** de un lado a otro; **side by side** juntos, uno al lado de otro; **to put sthg to** OR **on one side** poner algo a un lado **- 2.** [of person] costado *m*; [of animal] ijada *f* **- 3.** [edge] lado *m*, borde *m* **- 4.** [of hill, valley] falda *f*, ladera *f* **- 5.** [bank] orilla *f* **- 6.** [page] cara *f* **- 7.** [participant - in war, game] lado *m*, bando *m*; [- in sports match] equipo *m* **- 8.** [viewpoint] punto *m* de vista; **you should try to see both sides** deberías considerar las dos caras de la situación; **to take sb's side** ponerse del lado OR de parte de alguien; **to take sides** tomar partido; **to be on sb's side** estar del lado OR de parte de alguien; **whose side are you on?** ¿de qué parte de quién estás? **- 9.** [line of parentage]: **on my father's side** por parte de mi padre **- 10.** [aspect] aspecto *m*; **it does have its comical side** tiene su lado cómico; **to be on the safe side** para estar seguro ▶▶ **on the large/small side** algo grande/pequeño; **to do sthg on the side** hacer algo para sacarse un dinero extra; **to keep** OR **stay on the right side of sb** no llevarle la contraria a alguien. ◇ *adj* lateral.

◆ **side with** *vt insep* ponerse de parte de.

sideboard [ˈsaɪdbɔːd] *n* aparador *m*.

sideboards UK [ˈsaɪdbɔːdz], **sideburns** US [ˈsaɪdbɜːnz] *npl* patillas *fpl*.

sidecar [ˈsaɪdkɑːr] *n* sidecar *m*.

side dish *n* acompañamiento *m*, guarnición *f*.

side effect *n fig* & MED efecto *m* secundario.

sidekick ['saɪdkɪk] *n inf* compinche *mf*, secuaz *mf*.

sidelight ['saɪdlaɪt] *n* luz *f* lateral.

sideline ['saɪdlaɪn] *n* - **1.** [extra business] negocio *m* suplementario - **2.** [on tennis court] línea *f* lateral; [on football pitch] línea de banda - **3.** [periphery]: **on the sidelines** al margen.

sidelong ['saɪdlɒŋ] *adj* & *adv* de reojo OR soslayo; **to give sb a sidelong glance** mirar a alguien de reojo OR soslayo.

side-on ◇ *adj* lateral. ◇ *adv* de lado.

side plate *n* platillo *m* de pan.

side road *n* calle *f* lateral.

sidesaddle ['saɪd,sædl] *adv*: **to ride sidesaddle** montar a sentadillas OR mujeriegas.

sideshow ['saɪdʃəʊ] *n* barraca *f* OR caseta *f* de feria.

sidestep ['saɪdstep] (*pt & pp* -**ped**, *cont* -**ping**) *vt* - **1.** [in football, rugby] regatear - **2.** *fig* [problem, question] esquivar.

side street *n* calle *f* lateral.

sidetrack ['saɪdtræk] *vt*: **to be sidetracked** desviarse OR salirse del tema; **I keep getting sidetracked** me distraigo continuamente.

sidewalk ['saɪdwɔːk] *n* US acera *f*, andén *m* Amér C & Col, vereda *f* Perú, banqueta *f* Méx.

sideways ['saɪdweɪz] ◇ *adj* [movement] de lado, hacia un lado; [glance] de soslayo. ◇ *adv* [move] de lado; [look] de reojo.

siding ['saɪdɪŋ] *n* apartadero *m*, vía *f* muerta.

sidle ['saɪdl] ▸ **sidle up** *vi*: **to sidle up to** acercarse furtivamente a.

siege [siːdʒ] *n* - **1.** [by army] sitio *m*, cerco *m* - **2.** [by police] cerco *m* policial.

Sierra Leone [sɪ'erəlɪ'əʊn] *n* Sierra Leona.

sieve [sɪv] ◇ *n* [utensil] colador *m*; **to have a head** OR **memory like a sieve** tener muy mala memoria. ◇ *vt* [soup] colar; [flour, sugar] tamizar, cerner.

sift [sɪft] ◇ *vt* - **1.** [sieve] tamizar, cerner - **2.** *fig* [examine carefully] examinar cuidadosamente. ◇ *vi*: **to sift through sthg** examinar cuidadosamente algo.

sigh [saɪ] ◇ *n* suspiro *m*; **to heave a sigh of relief** respirar aliviado. ◇ *vi* suspirar.

sight [saɪt] ◇ *n* - **1.** [vision] vista *f* - **2.** [act of seeing]: **her first sight of the sea** la primera vez que vio el mar; **in sight** a la vista; **to disappear out of sight** perderse de vista; **to catch sight of sthg/sb** alcanzar a ver algo/a alguien; **to know sb by sight** conocer a alguien de vista; **to lose sight of** *lit* & *fig* perder de vista; **to shoot on sight** disparar sin esperar; **at first sight** a primera vista; **it was love at first**

sight fue un flechazo - **3.** [something seen] espectáculo *m*; **a beautiful sight** una vista preciosa - **4.** [on gun] mira *f*; **to set one's sights on sthg** echarle el ojo a algo; **it's not a pretty sight** no es muy agradable de ver - **5.** [small amount]: **a sight better/worse** mucho mejor/peor. ◇ *vt* divisar, avistar.

▸ **sights** *npl* atracciones *fpl* turísticas; **to see the sights** ir a ver la ciudad.

sighting ['saɪtɪŋ] *n*: **there had been only two sightings of the bird** el pájaro sólo se había visto dos veces.

sightseeing ['saɪt,siːɪŋ] *n* (U) recorrido *m* turístico; **to go sightseeing** hacer turismo.

sightseer ['saɪt,siːər] *n* turista *mf*.

sign [saɪn] ◇ *n* - **1.** [written symbol] signo *m* - **2.** [horoscope]: **sign of the zodiac** signo del zodiaco - **3.** [gesture] señal *f* - **4.** [of pub, shop] letrero *m*; [on road] señal *f*; [notice] cartel *m* - **5.** [indication] señal *f*, indicio *m*; **it's a good sign** es una buena señal; **there's no sign of him** no se le ve por ninguna parte. ◇ *vt* firmar. ◇ *vi* firmar.

▸ **sign away** *vt sep* ceder.

▸ **sign for** *vt insep* - **1.** [sign receipt for] firmar acusando recibo de - **2.** [sign contract for - football team] fichar por.

▸ **sign in** *vi* firmar en el registro.

▸ **sign on** *vi* - **1.** [enrol, register]: **to sign on (for)** [army] alistarse (en); [job] firmar el contrato (de); [course] matricularse (en) - **2.** [register as unemployed] firmar para cobrar el paro.

▸ **sign out** *vi* firmar al marcharse (de un hotel o club).

▸ **sign up** ◇ *vt sep* [employee] contratar; [recruit] alistar. ◇ *vi*: **to sign up (for)** [army] alistarse (en); [job] firmar el contrato (de); [course] matricularse (en).

signal ['sɪgnl] ◇ *n* señal *f*. ◇ *vt* (UK -**led**, *cont* -**ling**, US -**ed**, *cont* -**ing**) - **1.** [indicate] indicar - **2.** [tell]: **to signal sb (to do sthg)** hacer señas a alguien (para que haga algo) - **3.** *fig* [change, event] señalar. ◇ *adj fml* [triumph] señalado(da); [failure] estrepitoso(sa). ◇ *vi* (UK -**led**, *cont* -**ling**, US -**ed**, *cont* -**ing**) - **1.** AUT señalizar - **2.** [indicate]: **to signal to sb (to do sthg)** hacer señas a alguien (para que haga algo); **to signal for sthg** pedir algo por señas.

signal box UK, **signal tower** US *n* puesto *m* de mando.

signally ['sɪgnəlɪ] *adv fml* [fail] estrepitosamente.

signalman ['sɪgnlmən] (*pl* -**men** [-mən]) *n* RAIL guardavía *m*.

signal tower US = **signal box**.

signatory ['sɪgnətrɪ] (*pl* -**ies**) *n* signatario *m*, -ria *f*, firmante *mf*.

signature [ˈsɪgnətʃəʳ] *n* firma *f*.

signature tune *n* sintonía *f*.

signet ring [ˈsɪgnɪt-] *n* (anillo *m* de) sello *m*.

significance [sɪgˈnɪfɪkəns] *n* trascendencia *f*, importancia *f*; **to attach significance to sthg** atribuir importancia a algo; **to be of little/great/no significance** ser de poca/mucha/ninguna importancia.

significant [sɪgˈnɪfɪkənt] *adj* - **1.** [considerable, meaningful] significativo(va); **to give sb a significant look** mirar a alguien expresivamente - **2.** [important] trascendente.

significantly [sɪgˈnɪfɪkəntlɪ] *adv* - **1.** [considerably, meaningfully] de manera significativa - **2.** [importantly]: **significantly, he was absent** fue significativo el hecho de su ausencia.

signify [ˈsɪgnɪfaɪ] (*pt & pp* -ied) *vt* significar.

signing [ˈsaɪnɪŋ] *n UK* SPORT fichaje *m*.

sign language *n* lenguaje *m* por señas.

signpost [ˈsaɪnpəʊst] *n* letrero *m* indicador.

Sikh [siːk] ⟨⟩ *adj* sij. ⟨⟩ *n* [person] sij *mf*.

silage [ˈsaɪlɪdʒ] *n* ensilaje *m*.

silence [ˈsaɪləns] ⟨⟩ *n* silencio *m*; **to do sthg in silence** hacer algo en silencio. ⟨⟩ *vt* [person, critic] acallar; [gun] hacer callar, silenciar.

silencer [ˈsaɪlənsəʳ] *n* silenciador *m*.

silent [ˈsaɪlənt] *adj* - **1.** [gen] silencioso(sa) - **2.** [not revealing anything]: **to be silent about** quedar en silencio respecto a; **to remain silent** permanecer callado(da) - **3.** CIN & LING mudo(da); **a silent movie** una película muda; **a silent b** una b muda.

silently [ˈsaɪləntlɪ] *adv* - **1.** [without speaking] en silencio - **2.** [noiselessly] silenciosamente.

silent partner *n US* socio comanditario *m*, socia comanditaria *f*.

silhouette [ˌsɪluːˈet] ⟨⟩ *n* silueta *f*. ⟨⟩ *vt*: **to be silhouetted against** perfilarse OR destacarse sobre.

silicon [ˈsɪlɪkən] *n* silicio *m*.

silicon chip [ˌsɪlɪkən-] *n* chip *m* de silicio.

silicone [ˈsɪlɪkəʊn] *n* silicona *f*.

Silicon Valley *pr n* zona industrial californiana en la que se concentra la producción electrónica estadounidense.

silk [sɪlk] ⟨⟩ *n* seda *f*. ⟨⟩ *comp* de seda; **a silk blouse** una blusa de seda.

silk screen printing *n* serigrafía *f*.

silkworm [ˈsɪlkwɜːm] *n* gusano *m* de seda.

silky [ˈsɪlkɪ] (*comp* -ier, *superl* -iest) *adj* [hair, dress, skin] sedoso(sa); [voice] aterciopelado(da).

sill [sɪl] *n* [of window] alféizar *m*.

silliness [ˈsɪlɪnɪs] *n (U)* estupidez *f*.

silly [ˈsɪlɪ] (*comp* -ier, *superl* -iest) *adj* estúpido(da), sonso(sa) *Amér*; **that was a silly thing to say** qué tontería has dicho.

silo [ˈsaɪləʊ] (*pl* -s) *n* silo *m*.

silt [sɪlt] *n* cieno *m*, légamo *m*.

➡ **silt up** *vi* cegarse.

silver [ˈsɪlvəʳ] ⟨⟩ *adj* - **1.** [in colour] plateado(da) - **2.** [made of silver] de plata. ⟨⟩ *n (U)* - **1.** [metal, silverware] plata *f* - **2.** [coins] monedas *fpl* plateadas.

silver foil, silver paper *n (U)* papel *m* de plata.

silver-plated [-ˈpleɪtɪd] *adj* bañado(da) de plata, plateado(da).

silver screen *n inf*: **the silver screen** el cine, las películas.

silversmith [ˈsɪlvəsmɪθ] *n* platero *m*, -ra *f*.

silver surfer *n inf* internauta *mf* de la tercera edad.

silverware [ˈsɪlvəweəʳ] *n (U)* - **1.** [dishes etc] plata *f* - **2.** *US* [cutlery] cubertería *f* de plata.

silver wedding *n* bodas *fpl* de plata.

similar [ˈsɪmɪləʳ] *adj*: **similar (to)** parecido(da) OR similar (a).

similarity [ˌsɪmɪˈlærətɪ] (*pl* -ies) *n*: **similarity (between/to)** parecido *m* (entre/con), semejanza *f* (entre/con).

similarly [ˈsɪmɪləlɪ] *adv* [likewise] asimismo; [equally] igualmente.

simile [ˈsɪmɪlɪ] *n* símil *m*.

simmer [ˈsɪməʳ] *vt & vi* hervir a fuego lento.

➡ **simmer down** *vi inf* calmarse.

simper [ˈsɪmpəʳ] ⟨⟩ *n* sonrisa *f* boba. ⟨⟩ *vi* sonreír con cara de tonto(ta).

simpering [ˈsɪmpərɪŋ] *adj* [person] que sonríe con cara de tonto(ta); [smile] bobo(ba).

simple [ˈsɪmpl] *adj* - **1.** [gen] sencillo(lla) - **2.** *dated* [mentally retarded] simple - **3.** [plain - fact] mero(ra); [- truth] puro(ra).

simple-minded [-ˈmaɪndɪd] *adj* simple.

simpleton [ˈsɪmpltən] *n dated* simplón *m*, -ona *f*.

simplicity [sɪmˈplɪsətɪ] *n* sencillez *f*.

simplification [ˌsɪmplɪfɪˈkeɪʃn] *n* simplificación *f*.

simplify [ˈsɪmplɪfaɪ] (*pt & pp* -ied) *vt* simplificar.

simplistic [sɪmˈplɪstɪk] *adj* simplista.

simply [ˈsɪmplɪ] *adv* - **1.** [merely] sencillamente, simplemente - **2.** [for emphasis]: **you simply must go and see it!** ¡no puedes perdértelo!; **simply dreadful/wonderful** francamente terrible/maravilloso; **I simply can't believe it!** ¡no me lo puedo creer! - **3.** [in a simple way] de manera sencilla.

simulate [ˈsɪmjʊleɪt] *vt* simular.

simulation [ˌsɪmjʊˈleɪʃn] *n* - **1.** [gen & COMPUT] simulación *f* - **2.** [feigning] simulacro *m*.

simulator [ˈsɪmjʊleɪtər] *n* simulador *m*.

simultaneous [*UK* ˌsɪmʊlˈteɪnjəs, *US* ˌsaɪməlˈteɪnjəs] *adj* simultáneo(a).

simultaneously [*UK* ˌsɪmʊlˈteɪnjəslɪ, *US* ˌsaɪməlˈteɪnjəslɪ] *adv* simultáneamente.

sin [sɪn] <> *n* pecado *m*; **to live in sin** vivir en pecado. <> *vi* (*pt & pp* **-ned**, *cont* **-ning**): **to sin (against)** pecar (contra).

since [sɪns] <> *adv* desde entonces; **we haven't been there since** no hemos vuelto allí desde entonces; **long since** hace mucho tiempo. <> *prep* desde; **since last Tuesday** desde el último martes; **since then** desde entonces; **he has worked here since 1975** trabaja aquí desde 1975. <> *conj* - **1.** [in time] desde que; **she's been miserable ever since she married him** desde que se casó con él ha sido desdichada; **it's ages since I saw you** hace siglos que no te veo - **2.** [because] ya que, puesto que.

sincere [sɪnˈsɪər] *adj* sincero(ra).

sincerely [sɪnˈsɪəlɪ] *adv* sinceramente; **Yours sincerely** [at end of letter] atentamente.

sincerity [sɪnˈserətɪ] *n* sinceridad *f*.

sinecure [ˈsaɪnɪˌkjʊər] *n* sinecura *f*.

sinew [ˈsɪnjuː] *n* tendón *m*.

sinewy [ˈsɪnjuːɪ] *adj*: **a sinewy man** un hombre que es pura fibra.

sinful [ˈsɪnfʊl] *adj* - **1.** [person] pecador(ra) - **2.** [thought, act] pecaminoso(sa).

sing [sɪŋ] (*pt* **sang**, *pp* **sung**) *vt & vi* cantar; **to sing along with sb** cantar a coro con alguien.

Singapore [ˌsɪŋəˈpɔːr] *n* Singapur.

singe [sɪndʒ] <> *n* chamusco *m*. <> *vt* (*cont* **singeing**) chamuscar.

singer [ˈsɪŋər] *n* cantante *mf*; **she's a good singer** canta muy bien.

singing [ˈsɪŋɪŋ] <> *adj* de canto; **she has a good singing voice** tiene una excelente voz. <> *n* (*U*) canto *m*.

single [ˈsɪŋgl] <> *adj* - **1.** [only one] solo(la); **not a single person was there** no había ni una sola persona; **not one single time** ni una sola vez - **2.** [individual]: **every single penny** todos y cada uno de los peniques - **3.** [unmarried] soltero(ra); **he's single** está soltero - **4.** *UK* [one-way] de ida. <> *n* - **1.** *UK* [one-way ticket] billete *m* de ida - **2.** MUS [record] sencillo *m*, single *m*.
  - **singles** *npl* TENNIS (partido *m*) individual *m*.
  - **single out** *vt sep*: **to single sb out (for)** escoger a alguien (para).

single bed *n* cama *f* individual.

single-breasted [-ˈbrestɪd] *adj* recto(ta), sin cruzar.

single-click <> *n* clic *m*. <> *vi* hacer clic. <> *vt* hacer clic en.

single cream *n UK* crema *f* de leche, nata *f* líquida.

Single European Market *n*: **the Single European Market** el Mercado Único Europeo.

single file *n*: **in single file** en fila india.

single-handed [-ˈhændɪd] *adv* sin ayuda.

single-minded [-ˈmaɪndɪd] *adj* resuelto(ta); **to be single-minded about** tener un objetivo muy claro respecto a.

single parent *n* padre *m* soltero, madre *f* soltera; **he's a single parent** es padre soltero.

single-parent family *n* familia *f* monoparental.

single room *n* habitación *f* individual.

singles bar *n* bar de encuentro para solteros.

singlet [ˈsɪŋglɪt] *n UK* camiseta *f* sin mangas.

single ticket *n UK* billete *m* de ida.

singsong [ˈsɪŋsɒŋ] *inf* <> *adj* cantarín(ina). <> *n UK*: **to have a singsong** ponerse a cantar.

singular [ˈsɪŋgjʊlər] <> *adj* singular. <> *n* singular *m*; **in the singular** en singular.

singularly [ˈsɪŋgjʊləlɪ] *adv* singularmente.

sinister [ˈsɪnɪstər] *adj* siniestro(tra).

sink [sɪŋk] <> *n* - **1.** [in kitchen] fregadero *m* - **2.** [in bathroom] lavabo *m*. <> *vt* (*pt* **sank**, *pp* **sunk**) - **1.** [cause to go under water] hundir - **2.** [cause to penetrate]: **to sink sthg into** [knife, claws] clavar algo en; [teeth] hincar algo en; **he sank his teeth into the steak** le hincó los dientes al filete. <> *vi* (*pt* **sank**, *pp* **sunk**) - **1.** [go down - ship, sun] hundirse - **2.** [slump - person] hundirse; **she sank into a chair** se desplomó en una silla; **to sink to one's knees** caer de rodillas - **3.** [decrease] bajar - **4.** [become quieter]: **her voice sank** bajó la voz - **5.** *fig* [into poverty, despair]: **to sink into** hundirse en - **6.** [become depressed]: **his heart OR spirits sank** se le cayó el alma a los pies.
  - **sink in** *vi* hacer mella; **it hasn't sunk in yet** todavía no lo tiene asumido.

sink board *n US* escurridero *m*.

sinking [ˈsɪŋkɪŋ] *n* hundimiento *m*; **to have a sinking feeling that** comenzar a preocuparse porque.

sinking fund *n* fondo *m* de amortización.

sink unit *n* fregadero *m* (con mueble debajo).

sinner [ˈsɪnər] *n* pecador *m*, -ra *f*.

sinuous [ˈsɪnjuəs] *adj* sinuoso(sa).

sinus [ˈsaɪnəs] (*pl* **-es**) *n* seno *m*.

sip [sɪp] <> *n* sorbo *m*. <> *vt* (*pt & pp* **-ped**, *cont* **-ping**) beber a sorbos.

siphon, syphon ['saɪfn] <> n sifón m. <> vt - **1.** [liquid] sacar con sifón - **2.** fig [funds] desviar.

◆ **siphon off** vt sep - **1.** [liquid] sacar con sifón - **2.** fig [funds] desviar.

sir [sɜː^r] n - **1.** [form of address] señor m; **thank you, sir** gracias, señor; [in letter]: **Dear sir,** Estimado Señor - **2.** [in titles]: **Sir Philip Holden** Sir Philip Holden.

siren ['saɪərən] n [alarm] sirena f.

sirloin (steak) ['sɜːlɔɪn] n solomillo m, (filete m) de lomo m Andes, Col & Ven.

sissy ['sɪsɪ] (pl -ies) n inf mariquita m.

sister ['sɪstə^r] <> adj [organization, newspaper] hermano(na); [ship] gemelo(la). <> n - **1.** [gen] hermana f - **2.** UK [senior nurse] enfermera f jefe.

sisterhood ['sɪstəhʊd] n hermandad f (entre mujeres).

sister-in-law (pl **sisters-in-law** OR **sister-in-laws**) n cuñada f.

sisterly ['sɪstəlɪ] adj de buena hermana.

sit [sɪt] (pt & pp **sat**, cont **-ting**) <> vi - **1.** [be seated, sit down] sentarse - **2.** [be member]: **to sit on** ser miembro de - **3.** [be in session] reunirse, celebrar sesión - **4.** [be situated] estar emplazado(da)

▸▸ **to sit tight** quedarse quieto(ta). <> vt UK [exam] presentarse a.

◆ **sit about, sit around** vi estar sentado(da) sin hacer nada.

◆ **sit back** vi cruzarse de brazos; **to sit back and do nothing** quedarse de brazos cruzados y no hacer nada.

◆ **sit down** <> vt sep sentar. <> vi sentarse; **sit down, please** siéntese, por favor; **she was sitting down** estaba sentada.

◆ **sit in on** vt insep estar presente en (sin tomar parte).

◆ **sit out** vt sep - **1.** [tolerate] aguantar (hasta el final) - **2.** [not participate in game, discussion] no tomar parte en; **I think I'll sit this one out** [dance] creo que voy a saltarme ésta.

◆ **sit through** vt insep aguantar (hasta el final).

◆ **sit up** vi - **1.** [sit upright] incorporarse; **sit up straight!** siéntate derecho - **2.** [stay up] quedarse levantado(da); **we sat up until midnight** nos quedamos levantados hasta la medianoche.

sitcom ['sɪtkɒm] n inf comedia f de situación.

sit-down <> adj [meal] con los comensales sentados a la mesa; **sit-down strike** huelga f de brazos caídos. <> n UK: **to have a sit-down** sentarse un rato.

site [saɪt] <> n [place] sitio m, lugar m; [of construction work] obra f. <> vt situar.

sit-in n sentada f; **to stage a sit-in** protagonizar una sentada.

sitter ['sɪtə^r] n - **1.** ART modelo mf - **2.** [babysitter] canguro mf.

sitting ['sɪtɪŋ] n - **1.** [serving of meal] turno m (para comer) - **2.** [session] sesión f.

sitting duck n inf blanco m fácil.

sitting room n sala f de estar.

sitting tenant n UK inquilino m, -na f legal.

situate ['sɪtjʊeɪt] vt [locate] situar, emplazar.

situated ['sɪtjʊeɪtɪd] adj [located]: **to be situated** estar situado(da).

situation [,sɪtjʊ'eɪʃn] n - **1.** [gen] situación f - **2.** [job]: **'Situations Vacant'** UK 'Ofertas de trabajo'.

situation comedy n comedia f de situación.

sit-up n abdominal m.

six [sɪks] <> num adj seis (inv); **she's six (years old)** tiene seis años. <> num n - **1.** [the number six] seis m inv; **two hundred and six** doscientos seis; **six comes before seven** el seis va antes que el siete; **my favourite number is six** mi número favorito es el seis - **2.** [in times]: **it's six (thirty)** son las seis (y media); **we arrived at six** llegamos a las seis - **3.** [in temperatures]: **it's six below** hace seis grados bajo cero - **4.** [in addresses]: **six Peyton Place** Peyton Place número seis, el seis de Peyton Place - **5.** [referring to group of six] seis m inv; **we sell them in sixes** se venden de seis en seis; **we need one more to make a six** necesitamos uno más para ser seis; **to form into sixes** formar en grupos de (a) seis - **6.** [in scores]: **six-nil** seis a cero - **7.** [in cards] seis m; **to lay** OR **play a six** jugar un seis. <> num pron seis mf; **I want six** quiero seis; **six of us** seis de nosotros; **there are six of us** somos seis; **groups of six** grupos de seis.

six-shooter [-'ʃuːtə^r] n US revólver m de seis tiros.

sixteen [sɪks'tiːn] num dieciséis; see also **six**.

sixteenth [sɪks'tiːnθ] num decimosexto(ta); see also **sixth**.

sixth [sɪksθ] <> num adj sexto(ta). <> num adv sexto(ta). <> num pron sexto m, -ta f <> n - **1.** [fraction]: **a sixth** OR **one sixth of** un sexto de, la sexta parte de - **2.** [in dates]: **the sixth** el (día) seis; **the sixth of September** el seis de septiembre.

sixth form n UK SCH curso optativo de dos años de enseñanza secundaria con vistas al examen de ingreso a la universidad, ≃ COU m.

sixth form college n UK centro público para alumnos de 16 a 18 años donde se preparan para los 'A levels' o para exámenes de formación profesional.

sixth sense *n* sexto sentido *m*.

sixtieth ['sɪkstɪəθ] *num* sexagésimo(ma); *see also* **sixth**.

sixty ['sɪkstɪ] *num* (*pl* -**ies**) sesenta; *see also* **six**.

➡ **sixties** *npl* - **1.** [decade]: **the sixties** los años sesenta - **2.** [in ages]: **to be in one's sixties** estar en los sesenta - **3.** [in temperatures]: **the temperature was in the sixties** hacía más de sesenta grados (Fahrenheit).

size [saɪz] *n* - **1.** [gen] tamaño *m*; **what size do you take?** ¿cuál es su talla?; **what size shoes do you take?** ¿qué número calza? - **2.** [of clothes] talla *f*; [of shoes] número *m*

▸▸ **to cut sb down to size** bajarle los humos a alguien.

➡ **size up** *vt sep* [situation] evaluar; [person] calar.

sizeable ['saɪzəbl] *adj* considerable.

-sized [saɪzd] *suffix*:...-**sized** de tamaño...

sizzle ['sɪzl] *vi* chisporrotear.

skate [skeɪt] ⬦ *n* - **1.** (*pl* -**s**) [ice skate, roller skate] patín *m* - **2.** (*pl* **skate**) [fish] raya *f*. ⬦ *vi* [on skates] patinar.

➡ **skate over, skate round** *vt insep* [problem] eludir.

skateboard ['skeɪtbɔ:d] *n* monopatín *m*.

skater ['skeɪtə'] *n* patinador *m*, -ra *f*.

skating ['skeɪtɪŋ] *n* patinaje *m*.

skating rink *n* pista *f* de patinaje.

skein [skeɪn] *n* madeja *f*.

skeletal ['skelɪtl] *adj* [emaciated] esquelético(ca).

skeleton ['skelɪtn] *n* ANAT esqueleto *m*; **to have a skeleton in the cupboard** *fig* guardar un secreto vergonzante.

skeleton key *n* llave *f* maestra.

skeleton staff *n* personal *m* mínimo.

skeptic *US* = **sceptic**.

sketch [sketʃ] ⬦ *n* - **1.** [drawing, brief outline] esbozo *m*, bosquejo *m* - **2.** [humorous scene] sketch *m*. ⬦ *vt* esbozar. ⬦ *vi* hacer esbozos *OR* bosquejos.

➡ **sketch in** *vt sep* dar una idea rápida de.

sketchbook ['sketʃbʊk] *n* cuaderno *m* de dibujo.

sketchpad ['sketʃpæd] *n* bloc *m* de dibujo.

sketchy ['sketʃɪ] (*comp* -**ier**, *superl* -**iest**) *adj* incompleto(ta), poco detallado(da).

skewer ['skjʊə'] ⬦ *n* brocheta *f*, broqueta *f*. ⬦ *vt* ensartar en una brocheta.

skew-whiff [ˌskju:'wɪf] *adj UK inf* torcido(da).

ski [ski:] ⬦ *n* esquí *m*. ⬦ *vi* (*pt & pp* **skied**, *cont* **skiing**) esquiar.

ski boots *npl* botas *fpl* de esquí.

skid [skɪd] ⬦ *n* patinazo *m*, derrape *m*. ⬦ *vi* (*pt & pp* -**ded**, *cont* -**ding**) patinar, derrapar.

skid mark *n* huella *f* de un derrape.

skid row [-rəʊ] *n US inf* barrio *m* bajo.

skier ['ski:ə'] *n* esquiador *m*, -ra *f*.

skies [skaɪz] *npl* ⬥ **sky**.

skiing ['ski:ɪŋ] ⬦ *n* (*U*) esquí *m*; **to go skiing** ir a esquiar. ⬦ *comp* [holiday, accident] de esquí; [enthusiast] del esquí.

ski instructor *n* monitor *m*, -ra *f* de esquí.

ski jump *n* - **1.** [slope] pista *f* para saltos de esquí - **2.** [event] saltos *mpl* de esquí.

skilful, skillful *US* ['skɪlfʊl] *adj* hábil.

skilfully, skillfully *US* ['skɪlfʊlɪ] *adv* hábilmente, con habilidad.

ski lift *n* telesilla *m*.

skill [skɪl] *n* - **1.** (*U*) [expertise] habilidad *f*, destreza *f* - **2.** [craft, technique] técnica *f*.

skilled [skɪld] *adj* - **1.** [skilful] habilidoso(sa); **to be skilled (in** *OR* **at doing sthg)** ser experto(ta) (en hacer algo) - **2.** [trained] cualificado(da), especializado(da).

skillet ['skɪlɪt] *n US* sartén *f*.

skillful *US* = **skilful**.

skim [skɪm] ⬦ *vt* (*pt & pp* -**med**, *cont* -**ming**) - **1.** [remove - cream] desnatar, sacar la nata a; [- grease] espumar - **2.** [fly above] volar rozando - **3.** [glance through] hojear, leer por encima. ⬦ *vi* (*pt & pp* -**med**, *cont* -**ming**): **to skim through sthg** hojear algo, leer algo por encima.

skimmed milk [skɪm(d)-mɪlk] *n* leche *f* desnatada.

skimp [skɪmp] ⬦ *vt* [gen] escatimar; [work] hacer de prisa y corriendo. ⬦ *vi*: **to skimp on sthg** [gen] escatimar algo; [work] hacer algo de prisa y corriendo.

skimpy ['skɪmpɪ] (*comp* -**ier**, *superl* -**iest**) *adj* [clothes] muy corto y estrecho (muy corta y estrecha); [meal, facts] escaso(sa).

skin [skɪn] ⬦ *n* - **1.** [gen] piel *f*; [on face] cutis *m*; **to have thick skin** *fig* tener mucho aguante; **to do sthg by the skin of one's teeth** hacerse algo por los pelos; **to jump out of one's skin** *UK* llevarse un susto de muerte; **it makes my skin crawl** me da escalofríos; **to save** *OR* **protect one's own skin** salvar el pellejo - **2.** [on milk, pudding] nata *f*; [on paint] capa *f*, película *f*. ⬦ *vt* (*pt & pp* -**ned**, *cont* -**ning**) - **1.** [animal] despellejar, desollar - **2.** [knee, elbow etc] rasguñarse.

skincare ['skɪnkeə'] *n* (*U*) cuidado *m* de la piel.

skin-deep *adj* superficial.

skin diver *n* submarinista *mf*.

skin diving *n* buceo *m*, submarinismo *m* (sin traje ni escafandra).

skinflint ['skɪnflɪnt] *n* agarrado *m*, -da *f*, roñoso *m*, -sa *f*.

skin graft *n* injerto *m* de piel.
skinhead ['skɪnhed] *n UK* cabeza *m* rapada, skinhead *m*.
skinny ['skɪnɪ] ◇ *adj* (*comp* **-ier**, *superl* **-iest**) *inf* flaco(ca). ◇ *n US*: **the skinny** información *f* confidencial.
skint [skɪnt] *adj UK v inf* pelado(da), sin un duro; **to be skint** estar pelado(da) *OR* sin un duro.
skin test *n* cutirreacción *f*, dermorreacción *f*.
skin-tight *adj* muy ajustado(da).
skip [skɪp] ◇ *n* **- 1.** [little jump] brinco *m*, saltito *m* **- 2.** *UK* [large container] contenedor *m*, container *m*. ◇ *vt* (*pt & pp* **-ped**, *cont* **-ping**) [miss out] saltarse. ◇ *vi* (*pt & pp* **-ped**, *cont* **-ping**) **- 1.** [move in little jumps] ir dando brincos **- 2.** *UK* [jump over rope] saltar a la comba.
ski pants *npl* pantalones *mpl* de esquí.
ski pole *n* bastón *m* para esquiar.
skipper ['skɪpəʳ] *n NAUT & SPORT* capitán *m*, -ana *f*.
skipping ['skɪpɪŋ] *n UK* el saltar a la comba.
skipping rope ['skɪpɪŋ-] *n UK* comba *f*, cuerda *f* de saltar.
ski resort *n* estación *f* de esquí.
skirmish ['skɜːmɪʃ] ◇ *n* lit & fig escaramuza *f*. ◇ *vi MIL* sostener una escaramuza.
skirt [skɜːt] ◇ *n* **- 1.** falda *f*, pollera *f Amér* **- 2.** *US*: (bed) skirt volante *m*. ◇ *vt* **- 1.** [border] rodear, bordear **- 2.** [go round - obstacle] sortear; [- person, group] esquivar **- 3.** [avoid dealing with] evitar, eludir.
◈ **skirt round** *vt insep* **- 1.** [obstacle] sortear **- 2.** [issue, problem] evitar, eludir.
skirting board ['skɜːtɪŋ-] *n UK* zócalo *m*, rodapié *m*.
ski stick *n* bastón *m* para esquiar.
skit [skɪt] *n*: skit (on) parodia *f* (de).
skittish ['skɪtɪʃ] *adj* **- 1.** [person] frívolo(la) **- 2.** [animal] asustadizo(za).
skittle ['skɪtl] *n UK* bolo *m*.
◈ **skittles** *n* (*U*) bolos *mpl*.
skive [skaɪv] *vi UK inf*: **to skive (off)** escaquearse.
skivvy ['skɪvɪ] (*pl* **-ies**) *n UK inf* fregona *f*.
skulduggery [skʌl'dʌgərɪ] *n* (*U*) chanchullos *mpl*.
skulk [skʌlk] *vi* esconderse.
skull [skʌl] *n* [gen] calavera *f*; *ANAT* cráneo *m*.
skullcap ['skʌlkæp] *n* [of priest] solideo *m*; [of Jew] casquete *m*.
skunk [skʌŋk] *n* mofeta *f*.
sky [skaɪ] (*pl* **skies**) *n* cielo *m*.
skydiver ['skaɪ,daɪvəʳ] *n* paracaidista *mf* de estilo.

skydiving ['skaɪ,daɪvɪŋ] *n* paracaidismo *m* de estilo.
sky-high *inf* ◇ *adj* por las nubes. ◇ *adv*: **to blow sthg sky-high** [blow up] volar algo; [destroy] echar por tierra algo; **to go sky-high** ponerse por las nubes.
skylark ['skaɪlɑːk] *n* alondra *f*.
skylight ['skaɪlaɪt] *n* claraboya *f*.
skyline ['skaɪlaɪn] *n* perfil *m* de la ciudad.
sky marshal *n US* policía *destinado en un avión para evitar secuestros.*
skyscraper ['skaɪ,skreɪpəʳ] *n* rascacielos *m inv*.
slab [slæb] *n* [of stone] losa *f*; [of cheese] trozo *m*, pedazo *m*; [of chocolate] tableta *f*.
slack [slæk] ◇ *adj* **- 1.** [rope, cable] flojo(ja) **- 2.** [business] inactivo(va) **- 3.** [person - careless] descuidado(da). ◇ *n* [in rope] parte *f* floja; **to take up the slack** tensar la cuerda.
◈ **slacks** *npl dated* pantalones *mpl* (de esport).
slacken ['slækn] ◇ *vt* [speed, pace] reducir; [rope] aflojar. ◇ *vi* [speed, pace] reducirse.
slag [slæg] *n* [waste material] escoria *f*.
slagheap ['slæghiːp] *n* escorial *m*.
slain [sleɪn] *pp* ⊳ **slay**.
slalom ['slɑːləm] *n* eslálom *m*.
slam [slæm] ◇ *vt* (*pt & pp* **-med**, *cont* **-ming**) **- 1.** [shut] cerrar de golpe; **she slammed the door** dio un portazo **- 2.** [criticize] vapulear, descuerar *Chile* **- 3.** [place with force]: **to slam sthg on** *OR* **onto sthg** dar un golpe con algo contra algo violentamente; **he slammed his fist on the desk** dio un puñetazo en la mesa. ◇ *vi* (*pt & pp* **-med**, *cont* **-ming**) [shut] cerrarse de golpe.
slander ['slɑːndəʳ] ◇ *n* calumnia *f*, difamación *f*. ◇ *vt* calumniar, difamar.
slanderous ['slɑːndrəs] *adj* calumnioso(sa), difamatorio(ria).
slang [slæŋ] ◇ *adj* de argot. ◇ *n* argot *m*, jerga *f*.
slant [slɑːnt] ◇ *n* **- 1.** [diagonal angle] inclinación *f*; **on** *OR* **at a slant** inclinado(da), ladeado(da) **- 2.** [perspective] enfoque *m*. ◇ *vt* [bias] dar un enfoque a. ◇ *vi* inclinarse.
slanting ['slɑːntɪŋ] *adj* inclinado(da).
slap [slæp] ◇ *n* [in face] bofetada *f*; [on back] palmada *f*; **it was a slap in the face** *fig* fue una bofetada; **he gave him a slap on the back** le dio una palmadita en la espalda. ◇ *vt* (*pt & pp* **-ped**, *cont* **-ping**) **- 1.** [person, face] abofetear; **she slapped him round the face** lo abofeteó, le dio una bofetada; [back] dar una palmada a **- 2.** [place with force]: **he slapped the folder on the desk** dejó la carpeta en la mesa dando un golpetazo; **she slapped some paste on the wallpaper** embadurnó el papel

pintado con cola. ⬡ *adv inf* [directly] de narices; **he walked slap into a lamp post** se dio de lleno con una farola; **slap in the middle of...** justo en medio de...

slapstick ['slæpstɪk] *n (U)* payasadas *fpl*; **slapstick comedy** astracanada *f*.

slap-up *adj UK inf*: **slap-up meal** comilona *f*.

slash [slæʃ] ⬡ *n* - **1.** [long cut] raja *f*, tajo *m* - **2.** *esp US* [oblique stroke] barra *f* oblicua; **forward slash** barra inclinada. ⬡ *vt* - **1.** [material, tyre] rasgar; **she slashed her wrists** se cortó las venas - **2.** *inf* [prices etc] recortar drásticamente.

slasher movie *n inf* película *f* sanguinaria.

slat [slæt] *n* tablilla *f*.

slate [sleɪt] ⬡ *n* pizarra *f*. ⬡ *vt* [criticize] poner por los suelos.

slaughter ['slɔːtəʳ] ⬡ *n lit & fig* matanza *f*. ⬡ *vt* matar, carnear *Andes & R Plata*.

slaughterhouse (['slɔːtəhaʊs], *pl* [-haʊzɪz]) *n* matadero *m*.

Slav [slɑːv] ⬡ *adj* eslavo(va). ⬡ *n* eslavo *m*, -va *f*.

slave [sleɪv] ⬡ *n* esclavo *m*, -va *f*; **to be a slave to** *fig* ser un esclavo de. ⬡ *vi* [work hard] trabajar como un negro; **to slave over a hot stove** *hum* pasarse el día bregando en la cocina.

slaver ['sleɪvəʳ] *vi* [salivate] babear.

slavery ['sleɪvərɪ] *n lit & fig* esclavitud *f*.

slave trade *n*: **the slave trade** el comercio OR tráfico de esclavos.

Slavic ['slɑːvɪk] *adj* eslavo *m*, -va *f*.

slavish ['sleɪvɪʃ] *adj pej* [imitation, person] servil; [obedience, devotion] ciego(ga).

slay [sleɪ] (*pt* **slew**, *pp* **slain**) *vt liter* asesinar, matar.

sleazy ['sliːzɪ] (*comp* -**ier**, *superl* -**iest**) *adj* [disreputable] de mala muerte.

sledge [sledʒ], **sled** *US* [sled] *n* trineo *m*.

sledgehammer ['sledʒˌhæməʳ] *n* almádena *f*.

sleek [sliːk] *adj* - **1.** [hair] suave y brillante; [fur] lustroso(sa) - **2.** [shape] de línea depurada.

sleep [sliːp] ⬡ *n* sueño *m*; **to go to sleep** [doze off] dormirse; **my foot has gone to sleep** [become numb] se me ha dormido el pie; **to put to sleep** [animal] matar *(a un animal que es viejo o está enfermo)*. ⬡ *vi* (*pt & pp* **slept**) dormir.

➤ **sleep around** *vi inf pej* acostarse con medio mundo.

➤ **sleep in** *vi* dormir hasta tarde, levantarse tarde.

➤ **sleep off** *vt sep*: **to sleep off a hangover** dormir la borrachera.

➤ **sleep through** *vt insep* [alarm] no despertarse con.

➤ **sleep together** *vi* acostarse, tener relaciones sexuales.

➤ **sleep with** *vt insep euph* acostarse con.

sleeper ['sliːpəʳ] *n* - **1.** [person]: **to be a heavy/ light sleeper** tener el sueño profundo/ligero - **2.** [sleeping compartment] coche-cama *m* - **3.** [train] tren *m* nocturno (con literas) - **4.** *UK* [on railway track] traviesa *f*.

sleepily ['sliːpɪlɪ] *adv* soñolientamente.

sleeping bag ['sliːpɪŋ-] *n* saco *m* de dormir, bolsa *f R Plata*.

sleeping car ['sliːpɪŋ-] *n* coche-cama *m*, coche *m* dormitorio.

sleeping partner ['sliːpɪŋ-] *n UK* socio comanditario *m*, socia comanditaria *f*.

sleeping pill ['sliːpɪŋ-] *n* pastilla *f* para dormir.

sleeping policeman ['sliːpɪŋ-] *n UK inf* rompecoches *m inv*.

sleeping tablet ['sliːpɪŋ-] *n* pastilla *f* para dormir.

sleepless ['sliːplɪs] *adj* [night] en blanco, sin dormir.

sleeplessness ['sliːplɪsnɪs] *n* insomnio *m*.

sleepover ['sliːpˌəʊvəʳ] *n US fiesta infantil en la que los niños pasan la noche en casa de otro niño.*

sleepwalk ['sliːpwɔːk] *vi* [be a sleepwalker] ser somnámbulo(la); [walk in one's sleep] andar mientras uno duerme.

sleepy ['sliːpɪ] (*comp* -**ier**, *superl* -**iest**) *adj* - **1.** [person] soñoliento(ta) - **2.** [place] muerto(ta), poco animado(da).

sleet [sliːt] ⬡ *n* aguanieve *f*. ⬡ *impers vb*: **it's sleeting** cae aguanieve.

sleeve [sliːv] *n* - **1.** [of garment] manga *f*; **to have sthg up one's sleeve** guardar una carta en la manga - **2.** [for record] cubierta *f*.

sleeveless ['sliːvlɪs] *adj* sin mangas.

sleigh [sleɪ] *n* trineo *m*.

sleight of hand [ˌslaɪt-] *n (U) lit & fig* juego *m* de manos.

slender ['slendəʳ] *adj* - **1.** [thin] esbelto(ta) - **2.** [scarce] escaso(sa).

slept [slept] *pt & pp* ➪ **sleep**.

sleuth [sluːθ] *n inf hum* sabueso *m*, detective *mf*.

S-level (*abbr of* **Special level**) *n UK SCH examen que se realiza al mismo tiempo que el A-level, pero de un nivel superior.*

slew [sluː] ⬡ *pt* ➪ **slay**. ⬡ *vi* girar bruscamente.

slice [slaɪs] ⬡ *n* - **1.** [of bread] rebanada *f*; [of cheese] loncha *f*; [of sausage] raja *f*; [of lemon] rodaja *f*; [of meat] tajada *f* - **2.** [of market, glory] parte *f* - **3.** TENNIS golpe *m* con efecto bajo. ⬡ *vt* [gen] cortar; [bread] rebanar. ⬡ *vi*: **to slice through** OR **into sthg** cortar algo.

sliced bread [slaɪst-] *n (U)* pan *m* de molde rebanado.

slick [slɪk] *adj* - **1.** [smooth, skilful] logrado(da) - **2.** *pej* [superficial - talk] aparentemente brillante; [- person] de labia fácil.

slide [slaɪd] <> *n* - **1.** [decline] descenso *m* - **2.** PHOT diapositiva *f* - **3.** [in playground] tobogán *m* - **4.** [for microscope] portaobjeto *m* - **5.** UK [for hair] pasador *m*. <> *vt* (*pt & pp* **slid** [slɪd]) deslizar. <> *vi* (*pt & pp* **slid** [slɪd]) - **1.** [slip] resbalar - **2.** [glide] deslizarse - **3.** [decline gradually] caer; **to let things slide** dejar que las cosas empeoren.

slide projector *n* proyector *m* de diapositivas.

slide rule *n* regla *f* de cálculo.

sliding door [,slaɪdɪŋ-] *n* puerta *f* corredera.

sliding scale [,slaɪdɪŋ-] *n* escala *f* móvil.

slight [slaɪt] <> *adj* - **1.** [improvement, hesitation etc] ligero(ra); [wound] superficial; **not in the slightest** *fml* en absoluto - **2.** [slender] menudo(da), de aspecto frágil. <> *n* desaire *m*. <> *vt* menospreciar, desairar.

slightly [ˈslaɪtlɪ] *adv* - **1.** [to small extent] ligeramente - **2.** [slenderly]: **slightly built** menudo(da).

slim [slɪm] <> *adj* (*comp* **-mer**, *superl* **-mest**) - **1.** [person, object] delgado(da) - **2.** [chance, possibility] remoto(ta). <> *vi* (*pt & pp* **-med**, *cont* **-ming**) (intentar) adelgazar.

slime [slaɪm] *n* [in pond etc] lodo *m*, cieno *m*; [of snail, slug] baba *f*.

slimmer [ˈslɪmər] *n* persona *f* que intenta adelgazar.

slimming [ˈslɪmɪŋ] *n* adelgazamiento *m*.

slimness [ˈslɪmnɪs] *n* delgadez *f*, esbeltez *f*.

slimy [ˈslaɪmɪ] (*comp* **-ier**, *superl* **-iest**) *adj* - **1.** [pond etc] fangoso(sa); [snail] baboso(sa) - **2.** *pej* [servile] empalagoso(sa), zalamero(ra).

sling [slɪŋ] <> *n* - **1.** [for injured arm] cabestrillo *m* - **2.** [for carrying things] braga *f*, honda *f*. <> *vt* (*pt & pp* **slung**) - **1.** [hang roughly] colgar descuidadamente - **2.** *inf* [throw] tirar - **3.** [hang by both ends] colgar.

slingback [ˈslɪŋbæk] *n* zapato abierto en la parte del tacón.

slingshot [ˈslɪŋʃɒt] *n* US tirachinas *m inv*.

slink [slɪŋk] (*pt & pp* **slunk**) *vi*: **to slink (away** OR **off)** escabullirse.

slip [slɪp] <> *n* - **1.** [mistake] descuido *m*, desliz *m*; **a slip of the pen/tongue** un lapsus - **2.** [of paper - gen] papelito *m*; [- form] hoja *f* - **3.** [underskirt] enaguas *fpl*
▶▶ **to give sb the slip** *inf* dar esquinazo a alguien. <> *vt* (*pt & pp* **-ped**, *cont* **-ping**): **to slip**

sthg **into** meter algo rápidamente en; **to slip into** sthg, **to slip** sthg **on** [clothes] ponerse rápidamente algo. <> *vi* (*pt & pp* **-ped**, *cont* **-ping**) - **1.** [lose one's balance] resbalar, patinar - **2.** [slide] escurrirse, resbalar - **3.** [decline] empeorar; **to let** sthg **slip** dejar que las cosas empeoren
▶▶ **to let** sthg **slip** decir algo sin querer.
➤ **slip up** *vi* cometer un error (poco importante).

slip-on *adj* sin cordones.
➤ **slip-ons** *npl* zapatos *mpl* sin cordones.

slipped disc [,slɪpt-] *n* hernia *f* discal.

slipper [ˈslɪpər] *n* zapatilla *f*.

slippery [ˈslɪpərɪ] *adj* resbaladizo(za).

slip road *n* UK [for joining motorway] acceso *m*; [for leaving motorway] salida *f*.

slipshod [ˈslɪpʃɒd] *adj* descuidado(da), chapucero(ra).

slipstream [ˈslɪpstriːm] *n* estela *f*.

slip-up *n inf* desliz *m*; **to make a slip-up** cometer un desliz.

slipway [ˈslɪpweɪ] *n* grada *f*.

slit [slɪt] <> *n* ranura *f*, hendidura *f*. <> *vt* (*pt & pp* **slit**, *cont* **-ting**) abrir, cortar (a lo largo).

slither [ˈslɪðər] *vi* deslizarse; **it slithered away** se marchó deslizándose.

sliver [ˈslɪvər] *n* [of glass] esquirla *f*; [of wood] astilla *f*; [of cheese, ham] tajada *f* muy fina.

slob [slɒb] *n inf* guarro *m*, -rra *f*.

slobber [ˈslɒbər] *vi* babear.

slog [slɒg] *inf* <> *n* - **1.** [work] curro *m*, trabajo *m* pesado - **2.** [journey] viaje *m* pesado. <> *vi* (*pt & pp* **-ged**, *cont* **-ging**) - **1.** [work]: **to slog (away) at** trabajar sin descanso en - **2.** [move] caminar con dificultad.

slogan [ˈsləʊgən] *n* eslogan *m*.

slop [slɒp] <> *vt* (*pt & pp* **-ped**, *cont* **-ping**) derramar. <> *vi* (*pt & pp* **-ped**, *cont* **-ping**) derramarse.
➤ **slops** *npl* bazofia *f*.

slope [sləʊp] <> *n* cuesta *f*, pendiente *f*; **to be on the slippery slope** ir cuesta abajo. <> *vi* inclinarse; **the road slopes down to the beach** la carretera desciende hasta la playa.

sloping [ˈsləʊpɪŋ] *adj* [gen] inclinado(da); [ground] en pendiente.

sloppy [ˈslɒpɪ] (*comp* **-ier**, *superl* **-iest**) *adj* - **1.** [person] descuidado(da); [work] chapucero(ra); [appearance] dejado(da) - **2.** *inf* [sentimental] sensiblero(ra).

slosh [slɒʃ] <> *vt* echar. <> *vi* chapotear; **the paste sloshed around in the bucket** la cola se agitaba ruidosamente en el cubo.

sloshed [slɒʃt] *adj inf*: **to be sloshed** estar como una cuba; **to get sloshed** ponerse como una cuba.

slot [slɒt] *n* - **1.** [opening] ranura *f* - **2.** [groove] muesca *f* - **3.** [place in schedule] espacio *m*.

➤ **slot in** ◇ *vt sep* (*pt & pp* **-ted**, *cont* **-ting**) [into slot] introducir en la ranura; [into timetable etc] hacer un hueco a; **I can slot you in at 1.00** te puedo encajar a la una. ◇ *vi* [fit neatly] encajar.

sloth [sləʊθ] *n* - **1.** [animal] perezoso *m* - **2.** *liter* [laziness] pereza *f*.

slot machine *n* - **1.** [vending machine] máquina *f* automática *(de bebidas, cigarrillos etc)* - **2.** [arcade machine] máquina *f* tragaperras.

slot meter *n UK* contador *m* que funciona con monedas.

slouch [slaʊtʃ] ◇ *n*: **to walk with a slouch** andar con los hombros caídos. ◇ *vi* ir con los hombros caídos.

slough [slʌf] ➤ **slough off** *vt sep* [shed] mudar; *fig* [get rid of] deshacerse de.

Slovak [ˈsləʊvæk] ◇ *adj* eslovaco(ca). ◇ *n* - **1.** [person] eslovaco *m*, -ca *f* - **2.** [language] eslovaco *m*.

Slovakia [sləˈvækɪə] *n* Eslovaquia.

Slovakian [sləˈvækɪən] ◇ *adj* eslovaco(ca). ◇ *n* eslovaco *m*, -ca *f*.

Slovenia [sləˈviːnjə] *n* Eslovenia.

Slovenian [sləˈviːnjən] ◇ *adj* esloveno(na). ◇ *n* esloveno *m*, -na *f*.

slovenly [ˈslʌvnlɪ] *adj* [unkempt] desaliñado(da); [careless] descuidado(da).

slow [sləʊ] ◇ *adj* - **1.** [not fast] lento(ta); **to be a slow reader** leer despacio - **2.** [not prompt]: **to be slow to do sthg** tardar en hacer algo; **to be slow to anger** tarda en enfadarse - **3.** [clock etc] atrasado(da); **my watch is a few minutes slow** mi reloj va atrasado unos cuantos minutos - **4.** [not busy - business] flojo(ja); [- place] poco activo(va) - **5.** [not intelligent] corto(ta) (de alcances) - **6.** [not hot]: **bake in a slow oven** cocinar a horno moderado. ◇ *vt* aminorar, ralentizar. ◇ *vi* ir más despacio.

➤ **slow down, slow up** ◇ *vt sep* [growth] retrasar; [car] reducir la velocidad de. ◇ *vi* - **1.** [walker] ir más despacio; [car] reducir la velocidad - **2.** [take it easy] tomarse las cosas con calma.

slow-acting *adj* de efectos retardados.

slowcoach [ˈsləʊkəʊtʃ], **slow-poke** *US n inf* cachazudo *m*, -da *f*.

slowdown [ˈsləʊdaʊn] *n* - **1.** [slackening off] ralentización *f* - **2.** *US* [go-slow] huelga *f* de celo.

slow handclap *n aplauso lento y rítmico de protesta.*

slowly [ˈsləʊlɪ] *adv* despacio, lentamente; **slowly but surely** lento pero seguro.

slow motion *n*: **in slow motion** a cámara lenta.

➤ **slow-motion** *adj* a cámara lenta.

slow-poke *US* = **slowcoach**.

sludge [slʌdʒ] *n (U)* [mud] fango *m*, lodo *m*; [sewage] aguas *fpl* residuales.

slug [slʌg] ◇ *n* - **1.** [insect] babosa *f* - **2.** *inf* [of alcohol] lingotazo *m* - **3.** *US inf* [bullet] bala *f*. ◇ *vt* (*pt & pp* **-ged**, *cont* **-ging**) *inf* pegar un puñetazo a.

sluggish [ˈslʌgɪʃ] *adj* [movement, activity] lento(ta); [feeling] aturdido(da).

sluice [sluːs] ◇ *n* [passage] canal *m* de desagüe; [gate] compuerta *f*. ◇ *vt* [rinse]: **to sluice down** OR **out** lavar algo con mucha agua.

slum [slʌm] ◇ *n* [area] barrio *m* bajo. ◇ *vt* (*pt & pp* **-med**, *cont* **-ming**): **to slum it** *inf* instalarse de cualquier manera provisionalmente.

slumber [ˈslʌmbə*r*] *liter* ◇ *n* sueño *m*; **slumber party** *US fiesta de adolescentes en que se quedan a dormir en casa de quien la organiza.* ◇ *vi* dormir.

slump [slʌmp] ◇ *n* - **1.** [decline]: **slump (in)** bajón *m* (en) - **2.** ECON crisis *f* económica. ◇ *vi* - **1.** [fall in value] dar un bajón - **2.** [fall heavily - person] desplomarse, dejarse caer; **they found him slumped on the floor** lo encontraron desplomado en el suelo.

slung [slʌŋ] *pt & pp* ▷ **sling**.

slunk [slʌŋk] *pt & pp* ▷ **slink**.

slur [slɜːr] ◇ *n* [insult] agravio *m*, afrenta *f*; **to cast a slur on sb** manchar la reputación de alguien. ◇ *vt* (*pt & pp* **-red**, *cont* **-ring**) mascullar.

slurp [slɜːp] *vt* sorber ruidosamente.

slurred [slɜːd] *adj* indistinto(ta).

slush [slʌʃ] *n* nieve *f* medio derretida.

slush fund, slush money *US n fondos utilizados para actividades corruptas.*

slut [slʌt] *n* - **1.** *inf* [dirty or untidy woman] marrana *f* - **2.** *v inf* [sexually immoral woman] ramera *f*.

sly [slaɪ] ◇ *adj* (*comp* **slyer** OR **slier**, *superl* **slyest** OR **sliest**) - **1.** [look, smile] furtivo(va) - **2.** [person] astuto(ta), ladino(na). ◇ *n*: **on the sly** a escondidas.

slyness [ˈslaɪnɪs] *n (U)* [of person] astucia *f*.

smack [smæk] ◇ *n* - **1.** [slap] cachete *m*, cachetada *f* *Amér* - **2.** [impact] golpe *m*. ◇ *vt* - **1.** [slap] pegar, dar un cachete a - **2.** [place violently] tirar de golpe

▶▶ **to smack one's lips** relamerse. ◇ *vi*: **to smack of sthg** oler a algo. ◇ *adv inf* [directly]: **smack in the middle** justo en medio.

small [smɔ:l] ◇ *adj* [gen] pequeño(ña); [person] bajo(ja); [matter, attention] de poca importancia; [importance] poco(ca); **in a small way** a pequeña escala; **to make sb feel small** hacer que alguien se sienta muy poca cosa; **to get smaller** empequeñecer. ◇ *n*: **the small of the back** la zona lumbar.

➠ **smalls** *npl* UK *inf dated* paños *mpl* menores.

small ads [-ædz] *npl* UK anuncios *mpl* clasificados.

small arms *npl* armas *fpl* portátiles OR de mano.

small change *n* cambio *m*, suelto *m*, calderilla *f Esp*, sencillo *m Andes*, feria *f Méx*, menudo *m Col*.

small fry *n* gente *f* de poco monta.

smallholder ['smɔ:l,həʊldər] *n* UK minifundista *mf*.

smallholding ['smɔ:l,həʊldɪŋ] *n* minifundio *m*.

small hours *npl* primeras horas *fpl* de la madrugada; **in the small hours** en la madrugada.

smallness ['smɔ:lnɪs] *n* [gen] pequeñez *f*; [of rise, amount] escasez *f*.

smallpox ['smɔ:lpɒks] *n* viruela *f*.

small print *n*: **the small print** la letra pequeña.

small-scale *adj* en pequeña escala.

small talk *n* (U) conversación *f* trivial.

small-time *adj* de poca monta.

smarmy ['smɑ:mɪ] (*comp* -ier, *superl* -iest) *adj* cobista.

smart [smɑ:t] ◇ *adj* - **1.** [neat, stylish] elegante - **2.** *esp US* [clever] inteligente - **3.** [fashionable, exclusive] distinguido(da), elegante - **4.** [quick, sharp] rápido(da). ◇ *vi* - **1.** [eyes, wound] escocer - **2.** [person] sentir resquemor.

➠ **smarts** *n US* [intelligence] mollera *f*.

smart card *n* tarjeta *f* inteligente, tarjeta *f* con chip.

smart drug *n* droga *f* inteligente, nootrópico *m*.

smarten ['smɑ:tn] ➠ **smarten up** *vt sep* arreglar; **to smarten o.s. up** arreglarse.

smash [smæʃ] ◇ *n* - **1.** [sound] estrépito *m* - **2.** *inf* [car crash] accidente *m* - **3.** *inf* [success] éxito *m* - **4.** TENNIS mate *m*, smash *m*. ◇ *vt* - **1.** [break into pieces] romper, hacer pedazos - **2.** [hit, crash]: **to smash one's fist into sthg** dar un puñetazo en algo - **3.** *fig* [defeat] aplastar. ◇ *vi* - **1.** [break into pieces] romperse, hacerse pedazos - **2.** [crash, collide]: **to smash through sthg** romper algo atravesándolo; **to smash into sthg** chocar violentamente con algo.

➠ **smash up** *vt sep* romper, hacer pedazos.

smash-and-grab (raid) *n* UK robo rápido después de romper un escaparate.

smashed [smæʃt] *adj inf* [drunk] cocido(da), trompa.

smash hit *n* gran éxito *m*.

smashing ['smæʃɪŋ] *adj inf* fenomenal, estupendo(da).

smash-up *n* choque *m* violento, colisión *f*.

smattering ['smætərɪŋ] *n* nociones *fpl*; **he has a smattering of Spanish** tiene nociones de español.

SME (*abbr of* **small and medium-sized enterprise**) *n* PYME *f*.

smear [smɪər] ◇ *n* - **1.** [dirty mark] mancha *f* - **2.** [smear test] citología *f*, Papanicolau *m Amér* - **3.** [slander] calumnia *f*, difamación *f*. ◇ *vt* - **1.** [smudge] manchar - **2.** [spread]: **to smear sthg onto sthg** untar algo con algo; **the screen was smeared with grease** la pantalla estaba embadurnada de grasa - **3.** [slander] calumniar, difamar.

smear campaign *n* campaña *f* difamatoria.

smear test *n* citología *f*, Papanicolau *m Amér*.

smell [smel] ◇ *n* - **1.** [odour] olor *m* - **2.** [sense of smell] olfato *m*. ◇ *vt* (*pt* & *pp* -ed OR smelt) *lit* & *fig* oler. ◇ *vi* (*pt* & *pp* -ed OR smelt) - **1.** [gen] oler; **to smell of/like** oler a/como; **to smell good/bad** oler bien/mal - **2.** [smell unpleasantly] apestar.

smelly ['smelɪ] (*comp* -ier, *superl* -iest) *adj* maloliente, apestoso(sa).

smelt [smelt] ◇ *pt* & *pp* ▷ **smell**. ◇ *vt* fundir.

smile [smaɪl] ◇ *n* sonrisa *f*. ◇ *vi* sonreír; **to smile at sb** sonreírle a algn. ◇ *vt* mostrar con una sonrisa; **he smiled his approval** mostró su aprobación con una sonrisa.

smiling ['smaɪlɪŋ] *adj* sonriente.

smirk [smɜ:k] ◇ *n* sonrisa *f* desdeñosa. ◇ *vi* sonreír desdeñosamente.

smith [smɪθ] *n* herrero *m*, -ra *f*.

smithereens [,smɪðə'ri:nz] *npl inf*: **to be smashed to smithereens** hacerse añicos; **to smash sthg to smithereens** hacer algo añicos.

smithy ['smɪðɪ] (*pl* -ies) *n* herrería *f*.

smitten ['smɪtn] *adj inf hum*: **to be smitten (with sb)** estar colado(da) (por alguien); **to be smitten (with sthg)** estar entusiasmado(da) (con algo).

smock [smɒk] *n* blusón *m*.

smog [smɒg] *n* niebla *f* baja, smog *m*.

smoke [sməʊk] ◇ *n* - **1.** [gen] humo *m*; **to go up in smoke** ser consumido(da) por las llamas - **2.** [act of smoking]: **to have a smoke** fumar. ◇ *vt* - **1.** [cigarette, cigar] fumar; **to smoke a**

pipe fumar en pipa **- 2.** [fish, meat, cheese] ahumar. ⬦ *vi* **- 1.** [smoke tobacco] fumar; **I don't smoke** no fumo **- 2.** [give off smoke] echar humo.

smoked [sməʊkt] *adj* ahumado(da).

smokeless fuel ['sməʊklɪs-] *n* combustible *m* que no hecha humo.

smokeless zone ['sməʊklɪs-] *n zona en la que se prohíbe el uso de combustible que eche humo.*

smoker ['sməʊkər] *n* **- 1.** [person] fumador *m*, -ra *f* **- 2.** RAIL [compartment] compartimiento *m* de fumadores.

smokescreen ['sməʊkskri:n] *n fig* cortina *f* de humo.

smoke shop *n* US estanco *m*.

smoke signal *n* señal *f* de humo.

smoking ['sməʊkɪŋ] fumar es malo; **to give up smoking** dejar de fumar; **'no smoking'** 'prohibido fumar'.

smoking compartment UK, **smoking car** US *n* compartimiento *m* de fumadores.

smoking gun *n fig* [clue] pista *f*.

smoky ['sməʊkɪ] (*comp* **-ier,** *superl* **-iest**) *adj* **- 1.** [full of smoke] lleno(na) de humo **- 2.** [taste, colour] ahumado(da).

smolder US = **smoulder**.

smooch [smu:tʃ] *vi inf* besuquearse.

smooth [smu:ð] ⬦ *adj* **- 1.** [surface] liso(sa); [skin] terso(sa) **- 2.** [mixture, gravy] sin grumos **- 3.** [movement, taste] suave **- 4.** [flight, ride] tranquilo(la) **- 5.** *pej* [person, manner] meloso(sa) **- 6.** [trouble-free] sin problemas. ⬦ *vt* alisar; **to smooth the way** allanar el camino.

◆ **smooth out** *vt sep* **- 1.** [table cloth, crease] alisar **- 2.** [difficulties] allanar.

◆ **smooth over** *vt insep*: **to smooth things over** limar asperezas.

smoothly ['smu:ðlɪ] *adv* **- 1.** [evenly] suavemente **- 2.** [suavely] sin alterarse **- 3.** [without problems] sin problemas; **everything went smoothly** todo transcurrió sin contratiempos.

smoothness ['smu:ðnɪs] *n* **- 1.** [of surface] lisura *f* **- 2.** [of movement, mixture] suavidad *f* **- 3.** *pej* [of person] melosidad *f*.

smooth-talking *adj* que tiene mucha labia.

smother ['smʌðər] *vt* **- 1.** [cover thickly]: **to smother sthg in** OR **with** cubrir algo de **- 2.** [kill] asfixiar **- 3.** [extinguish] sofocar, apagar **- 4.** *fig* [control] controlar, contener; **to smother a yawn** contener un bostezo **- 5.** [suffocate with love] abrumar de afecto.

smoulder UK, **smolder** US ['sməʊldər] *vi* **- 1.** [fire] arder sin llama **- 2.** *fig* [person, feelings] arder.

SMS (*abbr of* short message service) *n* COMPUT servicio *m* de mensajes cortos.

smudge [smʌdʒ] ⬦ *n* [dirty mark] mancha *f*; [ink blot] borrón *m*. ⬦ *vt* [by blurring] emborronar; [by dirtying] manchar.

smug [smʌg] (*comp* **-ger,** *superl* **-gest**) *adj pej* pagado(da) OR satisfecho(cha) de sí mismo(ma).

smuggle ['smʌgl] *vt* **- 1.** [across frontiers] pasar de contrabando **- 2.** [against rules]: **to smuggle sthg in/out** pasar/sacar algo.

smuggler ['smʌglər] *n* contrabandista *mf*.

smuggling ['smʌglɪŋ] *n* (*U*) contrabando *m*.

smugness ['smʌgnɪs] *n pej* presunción *f*.

smut [smʌt] *n* **- 1.** [dirty mark] tiznón *m*, tiznadura *f* **- 2.** (*U*) *inf pej* [lewd matter] guarrerías *fpl*.

smutty ['smʌtɪ] (*comp* **-ier,** *superl* **-iest**) *adj inf pej* guarro(rra).

snack [snæk] ⬦ *n* bocado *m*, piscolabis *m inv*, botana *f* Guat, Méx & Ven. ⬦ *vi* US picar.

snack bar *n* bar *m*, cafetería *f*.

snag [snæg] ⬦ *n* [problem] pega *f*. ⬦ *vt* (*pt & pp* **-ged,** *cont* **-ging**) engancharse. ⬦ *vi* (*pt & pp* **-ged,** *cont* **-ging**): **to snag (on)** engancharse (en).

snail [sneɪl] *n* caracol *m*; **at a snail's pace** a paso de tortuga.

snail mail *n* correo *m* caracol.

snake [sneɪk] ⬦ *n* [large] serpiente *f*; [small] culebra *f*. ⬦ *vi* serpentear.

snap [snæp] ⬦ *adj* repentino(na); **a snap decision** una decisión repentina. ⬦ *n* **- 1.** [act or sound] crujido *m*, chasquido *m* **- 2.** *inf* [photograph] foto *f* **- 3.** [card game] ≃ guerrilla *f* **- 4.** US [fastener] broche *m* de presión. ⬦ *vt* (*pt & pp* **-ped,** *cont* **-ping**) **- 1.** [break] partir (en dos) **- 2.** [move with a snap]: **to snap sthg open** abrir algo de golpe **- 3.** [speak sharply] decir bruscamente OR de mala manera. ⬦ *vi* (*pt & pp* **-ped,** *cont* **-ping**) **- 1.** [break] partirse (en dos) **- 2.** [move with a snap]: **to snap into place** colocarse con un golpe seco **- 3.** [attempt to bite]: **to snap at sthg/sb** intentar morder algo/a alguien **- 4.** [speak sharply]: **to snap (at sb)** contestar bruscamente OR de mala manera a alguien

▸▸ **to snap out of it** animarse de repente.

◆ **snap up** *vt sep* no dejar escapar.

snappish ['snæpɪʃ] *adj* irritable.

snappy ['snæpɪ] (*comp* **-ier,** *superl* **-iest**) *adj inf* **- 1.** [stylish] con estilo **- 2.** [quick] rápido(da); **make it snappy!** ¡date prisa! **- 3.** [irritable] arisco(ca).

snapshot ['snæpʃɒt] *n* foto *f*.

snare [sneər] ⬦ *n* trampa *f*. ⬦ *vt* [animal] cazar con trampa; [person] hacer caer en la trampa.

snarl [snɑ:l] <> n gruñido m. <> vi gruñir.

snarl-up n [gen] embrollo m; [of traffic] atasco m.

snatch [snætʃ] <> n [of conversation, song] fragmento m. <> vt - **1.** [grab] agarrar; **to snatch sthg from sb** arrancarle OR arrebatarle algo a alguien - **2.** [take as time allows]: **to snatch some sleep** sacar tiempo para dormir; **to snatch an opportunity/a few moments** aprovechar una oportunidad/unos minutos. <> vi: **to snatch at sthg** intentar agarrar algo; **don't snatch!** ¡las cosas no se quitan de las manos!

snazzy ['snæzɪ] (comp -ier, superl -iest) adj inf [stylish] chulo(la); [showy] llamativo(va).

sneak [sni:k] <> n UK inf acusica mf, chivato m, -ta f. <> vt (US **snuck**) pasar a escondidas; **she tried to sneak the cakes out of the cupboard** intentó sacar los pasteles del armario a hurtadillas; **she sneaked him into her bedroom** lo coló en su dormitorio; **to sneak a look at** echar una mirada furtiva a. <> vi (US **snuck**): **to sneak in/out** entrar/salir a escondidas; **he sneaked in without paying** se coló sin pagar; **don't try and sneak off!** ¡no intentes escabullirte!

◆ **sneak up on** vt sep acercarse sigilosamente a.

sneakers ['sni:kəz] npl US zapatos mpl de lona.

sneaking ['sni:kɪŋ] adj secreto(ta); **I have a sneaking feeling that...** tengo la sensación de que...

sneak preview n pase m privado (de una película aún no estrenada).

sneaky ['sni:kɪ] (comp -ier, superl -iest) adj inf solapado(da).

sneer [snɪəʳ] <> n mueca f de desprecio. <> vi - **1.** [smile unpleasantly] sonreír con desprecio - **2.** [ridicule]: **to sneer (at)** burlarse (de).

sneeze [sni:z] <> n estornudo m. <> vi estornudar; **it's not to be sneezed at** inf no es de despreciar.

snicker ['snɪkəʳ] vi US reírse por lo bajo.

snide [snaɪd] adj sarcástico(ca).

sniff [snɪf] <> n: **to give a sniff** sorber por la nariz. <> vt - **1.** [smell] oler - **2.** [drug] esnifar. <> vi - **1.** [to clear nose] sorber por la nariz - **2.** [to show disapproval]: **to sniff at sthg** desdeñar algo.

◆ **sniff out** vt sep - **1.** [detect by sniffing] olfatear - **2.** inf [seek out] descubrir.

sniffer dog ['snɪfəʳ-] n perro entrenado para descubrir drogas o explosivos.

sniffle ['snɪfl] vi [during a cold] sorberse los mocos; [when crying] sorberse las lágrimas.

snigger ['snɪgəʳ] <> n risa f disimulada. <> vi reírse por lo bajo.

snip [snɪp] <> n inf [bargain] ganga f. <> vt (pt & pp -**ped**, cont -**ping**) cortar con tijeras.

snipe [snaɪp] vi - **1.** [shoot]: **to snipe (at)** disparar (sobre) - **2.** [criticize]: **to snipe at sb** criticar a alguien.

sniper ['snaɪpəʳ] n francotirador m, -ra f.

snippet ['snɪpɪt] n retazo m, fragmento m; **snippet of information** un dato aislado.

snivel ['snɪvl] (UK -**led**, cont -**ling**) (US -**ed**, cont -**ing**) vi lloriquear.

snob [snɒb] n esnob mf.

snobbery ['snɒbərɪ] n esnobismo m.

snobbish ['snɒbɪʃ], **snobby** ['snɒbɪ] (comp -ier, superl -iest) adj esnob.

snooker ['snu:kəʳ] <> n snooker m, juego parecido al billar. <> vt UK inf: **to be snookered** estar con las manos atadas.

snoop [snu:p] vi inf: **to snoop (around)** fisgonear.

snooper ['snu:pəʳ] n inf fisgón m, -ona f.

snooty ['snu:tɪ] (comp -ier, superl -iest) adj engreído(da).

snooze [snu:z] <> n cabezada f; **to have a snooze** echar una cabezada. <> vi dormitar.

snore [snɔ:ʳ] <> n ronquido m. <> vi roncar.

snoring ['snɔ:rɪŋ] n (U) ronquidos mpl.

snorkel ['snɔ:kl] n tubo m respiratorio.

snorkelling UK, **snorkeling** US ['snɔ:klɪŋ] n buceo m con tubo; **to go snorkelling** bucear con tubo.

snort [snɔ:t] <> n resoplido m. <> vi resoplar. <> vt drug sl esnifar.

snotty ['snɒtɪ] (comp -ier, superl -iest) adj inf [snooty] altivo(va).

snout [snaʊt] n hocico m.

snow [snəʊ] <> n nieve f. <> impers vb nevar; **it's snowing** está nevando.

◆ **snow in** vt sep: **to be snowed in** estar bloqueado(da) por la nieve.

◆ **snow under** vt sep: **to be snowed under (with)** estar inundado(da) (de).

snowball ['snəʊbɔ:l] <> n bola f de nieve. <> vi fig aumentar rápidamente.

snow blindness n ceguera f de la nieve.

snowboard ['snəʊbɔ:d] n snowboard m.

snowboarding ['snəʊbɔ:dɪŋ] n snowboard m; **to go snowboarding** hacer snowboard.

snowbound ['snəʊbaʊnd] adj bloqueado(da) por la nieve.

snow-capped [-ˌkæpt] adj con el pico cubierto de nieve.

snowdrift ['snəʊdrɪft] n montón m de nieve.

snowdrop ['snəʊdrɒp] n campanilla f blanca.

snowfall ['snəʊfɔ:l] n nevada f.

snowflake ['snəʊfleɪk] n copo m de nieve.

snowman ['snəʊmæn] (*pl* **-men** [-men]) *n* muñeco *m* de nieve.

snow pea *n US* guisante *m* mollar *Esp*, tirabeque *m*, arveja *f* china *Andes*, *Col & Ven*, chícharo *m* chino *Amér C & Méx*.

snowplough *UK*, **snowplow** *US* ['snəʊplaʊ] *n* quitanieves *m inv*.

snowshoe ['snəʊʃu:] *n* raqueta *f* de nieve.

snowstorm ['snəʊstɔ:m] *n* tormenta *f* de nieve.

snowy ['snəʊɪ] (*comp* **-ier**, *superl* **-iest**) *adj* de mucha nieve.

SNP *n abbr of* **Scottish National Party**.

Snr, snr (*abbr of* **senior**) sén.

snub [snʌb] ⟨⟩ *n* desaire *m*. ⟨⟩ *vt* (*pt & pp* **-bed**, *cont* **-bing**) desairar.

snuck [snʌk] *US pt* ⊏⟩ **sneak**.

snuff [snʌf] *n* [tobacco] rapé *m*.

snuffle ['snʌfl] *vi* [during a cold] sorberse los mocos; [when crying] sorberse las lágrimas.

snug [snʌg] (*comp* **-ger**, *superl* **-gest**) *adj* - **1.** [person] cómodo y calentito (cómoda y calentita); [feeling] de bienestar - **2.** [place] acogedor(ra) - **3.** [close-fitting] ajustado(da), ceñido(da).

snuggle ['snʌgl] *vi*: **to snuggle up to sb** arrimarse a alguien acurrucándose; **to snuggle down** acurrucarse.

so [səʊ] ⟨⟩ *adv* - **1.** [to such a degree] tan; **so difficult (that)** tan difícil (que); **don't be so stupid!** ¡no seas bobo!; **I wish he wouldn't talk so much** ojalá no hablara tanto; **I've never seen so much money/many cars** en mi vida he visto tanto dinero/tantos coches; **thank you so much** muchísimas gracias; **he's not so stupid as he looks** no es tan bobo como parece; **we're so glad you could come** estamos tan contentos de que pudieras venir; **it's about so high** es así de alto - **2.** [in referring back to previous statement, event etc]: **so what's the point then?** entonces ¿qué sentido tiene?; **so you knew already?** ¿así que ya lo sabías?; **I don't think so** no creo, me parece que no; **I'm afraid so** me temo que sí; **if so** si es así, de ser así; **is that so?** ¿es cierto?, ¿es así? - **3.** [also] también; **so can I** y yo (también); **so do I** y yo (también); **she speaks French and so does her husband** ella habla francés y su marido también; **as with children so with adults** igual que con los niños, también con los adultos; **just as some people like family holidays so others prefer to holiday alone** igual que hay gente a la que le gustan las vacaciones familiares, otros las prefieren pasar solos - **4.** [in such a way]: **(like) so** así, de esta forma; **it was so arranged as to look impressive** estaba dispuesto de tal manera que pareciera

impresionante - **5.** [in expressing agreement]: **so there is!** ¡pues (sí que) es verdad!, ¡sí que lo hay, sí!; **so I see** ya lo veo - **6.** [unspecified amount, limit]: **they pay us so much a week** nos pagan tanto a la semana; **it's not so much the money as the time involved** no es tanto el dinero como el tiempo que conlleva; **they didn't so much as say thank you** ni siquiera dieron las gracias; **or so** o así; **a year/week or so ago** hace un año/una semana o así. ⟨⟩ *conj* - **1.** [with the result that, therefore] así que, por lo tanto; **he said yes and so we got married** dijo que sí, así que nos casamos - **2.** [to introduce a statement] (bueno) pues; **so what have you been up to?** bueno, ¿y qué has estado haciendo?; **so that's who she is!** ¡anda! ¡o sea que ella!; **so what?** *inf* ¿y qué?; **so there** *inf* ¡(y si no te gusta,) te chinchas!

⟜ **and so on, and so forth** *adv* y cosas por el estilo.

⟜ **so as** *conj* para; **we didn't knock so as not to disturb them** no llamamos para no molestarlos.

⟜ **so far** *conj* [up to now] hasta ahora; **so far, so good** por ahora todo bien.

⟜ **so that** *conj* para que; **he lied so that she would go free** mintió para que ella saliera en libertad.

SO *abbr of* **standing order**.

soak [səʊk] ⟨⟩ *vt* - **1.** [leave immersed] poner en remojo - **2.** [wet thoroughly] empapar, ensopar *Amér*; **to be soaked with** estar empapado de. ⟨⟩ *vi* - **1.** [become thoroughly wet]: **to leave sthg to soak, to let sthg soak** dejar algo en remojo - **2.** [spread]: **to soak into** *OR* **through sthg** calar algo.

⟜ **soak up** *vt sep* [liquid] empapar, absorber.

soaked [səʊkt] *adj* empapado(da); **to be soaked through** *OR* **to the skin** estar empapado hasta los huesos.

soaking ['səʊkɪŋ] *adj* empapado(da); **to be soaking wet** estar empapado.

so-and-so *n inf* - **1.** [to replace a name] fulano *m*, -na *f* de tal - **2.** [annoying person] hijo *m*, -ja *f* de tal.

soap [səʊp] ⟨⟩ *n* - **1.** (*U*) [for washing] jabón *m* - **2.** TV culebrón *m*. ⟨⟩ *vt* enjabonar.

soap dish *n* jabonera *f*.

soap flakes *npl* escamas *fpl* de jabón.

soap opera *n* culebrón *m*.

soap powder *n* jabón *m* en polvo.

soapsuds ['səʊpsʌdz] *npl* espuma *f* de jabón, jabonaduras *fpl*.

soapy ['səʊpɪ] (*comp* **-ier**, *superl* **-iest**) *adj* - **1.** [full of soap] jabonoso(sa) - **2.** [taste] a jabón; [texture] de jabón.

soar [sɔːʳ] *vi* - **1.** [bird] remontar el vuelo - **2.** [rise into the sky] elevarse - **3.** [increase rapidly] alcanzar cotas muy altas - **4.** *liter* [be impressively high] elevarse.

soaring ['sɔːrɪŋ] *adj* - **1.** [rapidly increasing, rising] cada vez más alto(ta) - **2.** [impressively high] altísimo(ma).

sob [sɒb] <> *n* sollozo *m*. <> *vt* (*pt & pp* **-bed**, *cont* **-bing**) decir sollozando. <> *vi* (*pt & pp* **-bed**, *cont* **-bing**) sollozar.

sobbing ['sɒbɪŋ] *n* (*U*) sollozos *mpl*.

sober ['səubəʳ] *adj* - **1.** [gen] sobrio(bria) - **2.** [serious] serio(ria).

➡ **sober up** *vi* pasársele a uno la borrachera.

sobering ['səubərɪŋ] *adj* que hace reflexionar; it was a **sobering thought** dio mucho que pensar.

sobriety [səʊ'braɪətɪ] *n fml* sobriedad *f*.

Soc. *abbr of* **Society**.

so-called [-kɔːld] *adj* - **1.** [expressing scepticism] mal llamado(da), supuesto(ta) - **2.** [widely known as] así llamado(da).

soccer ['sɒkəʳ] *n* (*U*) fútbol *m*.

sociable ['səʊʃəbl] *adj* sociable.

social ['səʊʃl] *adj* social.

social climber *n pej* arribista *mf*.

social club *n* club *m* social.

social conscience *n* conciencia *f* social.

social democracy *n* socialdemocracia *f*.

social fund *n* en *Gran Bretaña*, *fondo de prestaciones en casos de extrema necesidad.*

socialism ['səʊʃəlɪzm] *n* socialismo *m*.

socialist ['səʊʃəlɪst] <> *adj* socialista. <> *n* socialista *mf*.

socialite ['səʊʃəlaɪt] *n* persona *f* que frecuenta fiestas de sociedad.

socialize, -ise ['səʊʃəlaɪz] *vi*: to **socialize (with)** alternar (con).

social life *n* vida *f* social.

socially ['səʊʃəlɪ] *adv* - **1.** [relating to society] socialmente - **2.** [outside business] fuera del trabajo; **we don't speak socially** no tenemos relación fuera del trabajo.

social order *n* orden *m* social.

social science *n* - **1.** (*U*) [in general] ciencias *fpl* sociales - **2.** [individual science] ciencia *f* social.

social security *n* seguridad *f* social.

social services *npl* servicios *mpl* sociales.

social studies *n* estudios *mpl* sociales.

social work *n* (*U*) trabajo *m* social.

social worker *n* asistente *m*, -ta *f* social.

society [sə'saɪətɪ] (*pl* **-ies**) *n* - **1.** [gen] sociedad *f* - **2.** [club, organization] sociedad *f*, asociación *f*.

socioeconomic ['səʊsɪəʊˌiːkə'nɒmɪk] *adj* socioeconómico(ca).

sociological [ˌsəʊsjə'lɒdʒɪkl] *adj* sociológico(ca).

sociologist [ˌsəʊsɪ'ɒlədʒɪst] *n* sociólogo *m*, -ga *f*.

sociology [ˌsəʊsɪ'ɒlədʒɪ] *n* sociología *f*.

sock [sɒk] *n* calcetín *m*, media *f* *Amér*; **to pull one's socks up** *inf* hacer un esfuerzo.

socket ['sɒkɪt] *n* - **1.** ELEC enchufe *m* - **2.** [of eye] cuenca *f*; [of joint] glena *f*.

sod [sɒd] *n* - **1.** [of turf] tepe *m* - **2.** *v inf* [person] cabroncete *m*.

soda ['səʊdə] *n* - **1.** [gen] soda *f* - **2.** *US* [fizzy drink] gaseosa *f*.

soda syphon *n* sifón *m*.

soda water *n* soda *f*.

sodden ['sɒdn] *adj* empapado(da).

sodium ['səʊdɪəm] *n* sodio *m*.

sofa ['səʊfə] *n* sofá *m*.

sofa bed *n* sofá cama *m*.

soft [sɒft] *adj* - **1.** [pliable, not stiff, not strict] blando(da); **to go soft** ablandarse - **2.** [smooth, gentle, not bright] suave - **3.** [caring - person] de buen corazón.

soft-boiled *adj* pasado(da) por agua.

soft drink *n* refresco *m*.

soft drugs *npl* drogas *fpl* blandas.

soften ['sɒfn] <> *vt* suavizar. <> *vi* - **1.** [substance] ablandarse - **2.** [expression] suavizarse, dulcificarse.

➡ **soften up** *vt sep inf* ablandar.

softener ['sɒfnəʳ] *n* suavizante *m*.

soft focus *n*: in soft focus en difuminado.

soft furnishings *UK*, **soft goods** *US npl* artículos del tipo cortinas, cojines, alfombras.

softhearted [ˌsɒft'hɑːtɪd] *adj* de buen corazón.

softly ['sɒftlɪ] *adv* - **1.** [gently] con delicadeza - **2.** [quietly, not brightly] suavemente - **3.** [leniently] con indulgencia.

softness ['sɒftnɪs] *n* - **1.** [gen] suavidad *f* - **2.** [pliability] blandura *f* - **3.** [lenience] indulgencia *f*.

soft sell *n inf sistema de venta en el que no se presiona al posible comprador.*

soft-spoken *adj* de voz suave.

soft toy *n* muñeco *m* de peluche.

software ['sɒftweəʳ] *n* COMPUT software *m*.

software package *n* COMPUT paquete *m* de software.

softy ['sɒftɪ] (*pl* **-ies**) *n inf* - **1.** *pej* [weak person] blandengue *mf* - **2.** [sensitive person] blando *m*, -da *f*.

soggy ['sɒgɪ] (*comp* **-ier**, *superl* **-iest**) *adj inf* empapado(da).

soil [sɔɪl] ◇ n - **1.** [earth] tierra f, suelo m - **2.** fig [territory] territorio m; **on British soil** en territorio británico. ◇ vt ensuciar.

soiled [sɔɪld] adj sucio(cia).

solace ['sɒləs] n liter consuelo m.

solar ['səʊləʳ] adj solar; **solar eclipse** eclipse de sol.

solarium [sə'leərɪəm] (pl **-riums** OR **-ria** [-rɪə]) n solarium m.

solar panel n panel m solar.

solar plexus [-'pleksəs] n: **the solar plexus** el plexo solar.

solar power n energía f solar.

solar system n: **the Solar System** el sistema solar.

sold [səʊld] pt & pp ▷ **sell**.

solder ['səʊldəʳ] ◇ n (U) soldadura f. ◇ vt soldar.

soldering iron ['səʊldərɪŋ-] n soldador m.

soldier ['səʊldʒəʳ] n soldado m.

➡ **soldier on** vi UK seguir adelante a pesar de las dificultades.

sold out adj agotado(da); **the theatre was sold out** se agotaron las localidades; **all the shops were sold out of lemons** se habían agotado los limones en todas las tiendas.

sole [səʊl] ◇ adj - **1.** [only] único(ca) - **2.** [exclusive] exclusivo(va). ◇ n - **1.** (pl **-s**) [of foot] planta f; [of shoe] suela f - **2.** (pl **sole**) [fish] lenguado m.

solely ['səʊllɪ] adv únicamente.

solemn ['sɒləm] adj solemne.

solemnly ['sɒləmlɪ] adv solemnemente, con solemnidad.

sole trader n UK comercio m individual.

solicit [sə'lɪsɪt] ◇ vt fml [request] solicitar. ◇ vi [prostitute] ofrecer sus servicios.

solicitor [sə'lɪsɪtəʳ] n UK LAW abogado que lleva casos administrativos y legales, pero que no acude a los tribunales superiores.

solicitous [sə'lɪsɪtəs] adj fml solícito(ta); **solicitous about** OR **of** OR **for** preocupado(da) por.

solid ['sɒlɪd] ◇ adj - **1.** [gen] sólido(da) - **2.** [rock, wood, gold] macizo(za) - **3.** [reliable, respectable] serio(ria), formal - **4.** [without interruption] sin interrupción; **it rained for two solid weeks** llovió sin parar durante dos semanas. ◇ n sólido m; **to be on solids** [baby] estar tomando alimentos sólidos.

solidarity [ˌsɒlɪ'dærətɪ] n solidaridad f.

solid fuel n combustible m sólido.

solidify [sə'lɪdɪfaɪ] (pt & pp **-ied**) vi solidificarse.

solidly ['sɒlɪdlɪ] adv - **1.** [sturdily] sólidamente; **solidly built** de construcción sólida - **2.** [completely, definitely] enteramente - **3.** [without interruption] sin interrupción.

soliloquy [sə'lɪləkwɪ] (pl **-ies**) n soliloquio m.

solitaire [ˌsɒlɪ'teəʳ] n - **1.** [jewel, board game] solitario m - **2.** US [card game] solitario m.

solitary ['sɒlɪtrɪ] adj solitario(ria).

solitary confinement n: **to be in solitary confinement** estar incomunicado(da) (en la cárcel).

solitude ['sɒlɪtjuːd] n soledad f.

solo ['səʊləʊ] ◇ adj & adv a solas. ◇ n (pl **-s**) solo m.

soloist ['səʊləʊɪst] n solista mf.

solstice ['sɒlstɪs] n solsticio m.

soluble ['sɒljʊbl] adj soluble.

solution [sə'luːʃn] n: **solution (to)** solución f (a).

solve [sɒlv] vt resolver.

solvency ['sɒlvənsɪ] n FIN solvencia f.

solvent ['sɒlvənt] ◇ adj FIN solvente. ◇ n disolvente m.

solvent abuse [-ə'bjuːs] n aspiración por la nariz de gomas o colas.

Somali [sə'mɑːlɪ] ◇ adj somalí. ◇ n - **1.** [person] somalí mf - **2.** [language] somalí m.

Somalia [sə'mɑːlɪə] n Somalia.

sombre UK, **somber** US ['sɒmbəʳ] adj sombrío(a).

some [sʌm] ◇ adj - **1.** [a certain amount, number of]: **would you like some coffee?** ¿quieres café?; **give me some money** dame algo de dinero; **there are some good articles in it** tiene algunos artículos buenos; **I bought some socks** [one pair] me compré unos calcetines; [more than one pair] me compré calcetines - **2.** [fairly large number or quantity of]: **I've known him for some years** lo conozco desde hace bastantes años; **we still have some way to go** nos queda un buen trecho todavía; **I had some difficulty getting here** me costó lo mío llegar aquí - **3.** (contrastive use) [certain] algunos(as); **some jobs are better paid than others** algunos trabajos están mejor pagados que otros; **some people say that...** los hay que dicen que...; **in some ways** en cierto modo - **4.** [in imprecise statements] algún(una); **there must be some mistake** debe haber un OR algún error; **she married some writer or other** se casó con no sé qué escritor; **someday** algún día - **5.** inf [very good] menudo(da); **that's some car he's got** ¡menudo coche tiene!; **some help you are!** iro [not very good] ¡menuda OR valiente ayuda me das! ◇ pron - **1.** [a certain amount]: **can I have some?** [money, milk, coffee etc] ¿puedo coger un poco?; **I've already had some** ya he tomado;

some of parte de **- 2.** [a certain number] algunos(as); **can I have some?** [books, potatoes etc] ¿puedo coger algunos?; **some (of them) left early** algunos se fueron temprano; **some say he lied** hay quien dice que mintió. <> *adv* **- 1.** unos(as); **there were some 7,000 people there** habría unas 7.000 personas **- 2.** *US* [slightly] algo, un poco; **shall I turn it up some?** ¿lo subo algo or un poco?

somebody ['sʌmbədɪ] <> *pron* alguien; **somebody or other** alguien. <> *n*: **he thinks he's somebody** se cree que es alguien.

someday ['sʌmdeɪ] *adv* algún día.

somehow ['sʌmhaʊ], **someway** *US* ['sʌmweɪ] *adv* **- 1.** [by some action] de alguna manera; **somehow or other** de un modo u otro **- 2.** [for some reason] por alguna razón.

someone ['sʌmwʌn] *pron* alguien; **someone or other** alguien, no sé quien.

someplace *US* = **somewhere**.

somersault ['sʌməsɔːlt] <> *n* [in air] salto *m* mortal; [on ground] voltereta *f*. <> *vi* [in air] dar un salto mortal; [on ground] dar una voltereta.

something ['sʌmθɪŋ] <> *pron* algo; **or something** *inf* o algo así; **that's something (at least)** ya es algo; **to be really something** ser de lo que no hay, ser increíble; **she's something of a poet** ella es un poco poeta; **it came as something of a surprise to me** me pilló un poco por sorpresa; **something or other** alguna cosa. <> *adv*: **something like, something in the region of** algo así como.

sometime ['sʌmtaɪm] <> *adj* antiguo(gua). <> *adv* en algún momento; **sometime or other** en algún momento; **sometime next week** durante la semana que viene.

sometimes ['sʌmtaɪmz] *adv* a veces.

someway *US* = **somehow**.

somewhat ['sʌmwɒt] *adv fml* algo.

somewhere *UK* ['sʌmweəʳ], **someplace** *US* ['sʌmpleɪs] *adv* **- 1.** [unknown place - with verbs of position] en alguna parte; [- with verbs of movement] a alguna parte; **it's somewhere else** está en otra parte; **it's somewhere in the kitchen** está en alguna parte de la cocina; **shall we go somewhere else?** ¿nos vamos a otra parte?; **I need somewhere to spend the night** necesito un lugar donde pasar la noche **- 2.** [in approximations]: **somewhere between five and ten** entre cinco y diez; **somewhere around 20** alrededor de 20; **he's somewhere in his fifties** tiene cincuenta años y pico

▸▸▸ **to be getting somewhere** avanzar, ir a alguna parte; **now we're getting somewhere!** ¡parece que las cosas empiezan a funcionar!

son [sʌn] *n* hijo *m*.

sonar ['səʊnɑːʳ] *n* sonar *m*.

sonata [sə'nɑːtə] *n* sonata *f*.

song [sɒŋ] *n* **- 1.** [gen] canción *f*; **they burst into song** se pusieron a cantar; **to make a song and dance about sthg** *inf* armar la de Dios es Cristo sobre algo **- 2.** [of bird] canto *m*

▸▸▸ **for a song** *inf* [cheaply] por cuatro cuartos.

songbook ['sɒŋbʊk] *n* cancionero *m*.

sonic ['sɒnɪk] *adj* sónico(ca).

sonic boom *n* estampido *m* OR boom *m* sónico.

son-in-law (*pl* sons-in-law OR son-in-laws) *n* yerno *m*.

sonnet ['sɒnɪt] *n* soneto *m*.

sonny ['sʌnɪ] (*pl* -ies) *n inf* hijo *m*, chico *m*.

soon [suːn] *adv* pronto; **how soon will it be ready?** ¿para cuándo estará listo?; **soon after** poco después; **as soon as** tan pronto como; **as soon as possible** cuanto antes; **see you soon** hasta pronto; **I'd just as soon...** igual me daría..., no me importaría...

sooner ['suːnəʳ] *adv* **- 1.** [in time] antes; **no sooner did he arrive than...** apenas había llegado cuando...; **no sooner said than done** dicho y hecho; **sooner or later** (más) tarde o (más) temprano; **the sooner the better** cuanto antes mejor **- 2.** [expressing preference]: **I'd sooner (not)...** preferiría (no)...

soot [sʊt] *n* hollín *m*.

soothe [suːð] *vt* **- 1.** [pain] aliviar **- 2.** [nerves etc] calmar.

soothing ['suːðɪŋ] *adj* **- 1.** [pain-relieving] calmante **- 2.** [calming] sedante, relajante.

sooty ['sʊtɪ] (*comp* -ier, *superl* -iest) *adj* cubierto(ta) de hollín.

sophisticated [sə'fɪstɪkeɪtɪd] *adj* **- 1.** [gen] sofisticado(da) **- 2.** [intelligent] inteligente.

sophistication [sə,fɪstɪ'keɪʃn] *n* **- 1.** [gen] sofisticación *f* **- 2.** [intelligence] inteligencia *f*.

sophomore ['sɒfəmɔːʳ] *n US* estudiante *mf* del segundo curso.

soporific [,sɒpə'rɪfɪk] *adj* soporífico(ca).

sopping ['sɒpɪŋ] *adj*: **sopping (wet)** chorreando.

soppy ['sɒpɪ] (*comp* -ier, *superl* -iest) *adj inf pej* sentimentaloide.

soprano [sə'prɑːnəʊ] (*pl* -s) *n* soprano *f*.

sorbet ['sɔːbeɪ] *n* sorbete *m*; **lemon sorbet** sorbete de limón.

sorcerer ['sɔːsərəʳ] *n* mago *m*, -ga *f*, brujo *m*, -ja *f*.

sordid ['sɔːdɪd] *adj* **- 1.** [immoral] obsceno(na) **- 2.** [dirty, unpleasant] sórdido(da).

sore [sɔːʳ] <> *adj* **- 1.** [painful] dolorido(da); **to have a sore throat** tener dolor de garganta **- 2.** *US* [upset] enfadado(da); **to get sore** enfadarse. <> *n* llaga *f*, úlcera *f*.

sorely ['sɔːlɪ] *adv liter* enormemente.

sorority [sə'rɒrətɪ] *n US club de estudiantes universitarias.*

sorrel ['sɒrəl] *n* acedera *f.*

sorrow ['sɒrəʊ] *n* pesar *m*, pena *f.*

sorrowful ['sɒrəfʊl] *adj* apesadumbrado(da), apenado(da).

sorry ['sɒrɪ] ◇ *adj (comp* **-ier,** *superl* **-iest)** - **1.** [expressing apology]**: to be sorry about sthg** sentir OR lamentar algo; **I'm sorry for what I did** siento lo que hice; **I'm sorry** lo siento; **I'm sorry if I'm disturbing you** OR **to disturb you** siento molestarte - **2.** [expressing shame, disappointment]**: to be sorry that** sentir que; **we were sorry about his resignation** sentimos que dimitiera; **to be sorry for** arrepentirse de; **we're sorry to see you go** sentimos que te vayas - **3.** [expressing regret]**: I'm sorry to have to say that...** siento tener que decir que... - **4.** [expressing pity]**: to be** OR **feel sorry for sb** sentir lástima por alguien; **to be** OR **feel sorry for o.s.** sentir lástima de uno mismo (una misma) - **5.** [expressing polite disagreement]**: I'm sorry, but...** perdón, pero... - **6.** [poor, pitiable] lamentable, penoso(sa); **it was a sorry sight** tenía un aspecto horrible. ◇ *excl* - **1.** [I apologise]**: sorry!** ¡perdón! - **2.** [pardon]**: sorry?** ¿perdón? - **3.** [to correct oneself]**: a girl, sorry, a woman** una chica, perdón, una mujer.

sort [sɔːt] ◇ *n* tipo *m*, clase *f*; **what sort of computer have you got?** ¿qué tipo de ordenador tienes?; **all sorts of** todo tipo de; **sort of** más o menos, así así; **a sort of** una especie de; **she did nothing of the sort** no hizo nada por el estilo. ◇ *vt* clasificar.

◆ **sorts** *npl*: **a lawyer of sorts** una especie de abogado; **to be out of sorts** estar bajo(ja) de tono.

◆ **sort out** *vt sep* - **1.** [classify] clasificar - **2.** [solve] solucionar, resolver.

sortie ['sɔːtiː] *n* salida *f*; **to make a sortie** hacer una salida.

sorting office ['sɔːtɪŋ-] *n* oficina *f* de clasificación del correo.

sort-out *n UK inf* limpieza *f* general; **to have a sort-out** hacer limpieza general.

SOS *(abbr of* **save our souls)** *n* SOS *m*; **to send an SOS** lanzar un SOS.

so-so *adj & adv inf* así así.

soufflé ['suːfleɪ] *n* suflé *m*; **a cheese soufflé** un suflé de queso.

sought [sɔːt] *pt & pp* ▷ **seek.**

sought-after *adj* solicitado(da), buscado(da).

soul [səʊl] *n* - **1.** [gen] alma *f*; **she's a good soul** es buena persona; **poor soul!** ¡pobrecito! - **2.** [of nation etc] espíritu *m* - **3.** [music] música *f* soul.

soul-destroying [-dɪ,strɔɪɪŋ] *adj* desmoralizador(ra).

soulful ['səʊlfʊl] *adj* lleno(na) de sentimiento.

soulless ['səʊllɪs] *adj* desangelado(da).

soul mate *n* alma *f* gemela.

soul music *n* música *f* soul.

soul-searching *n (U)* examen *f* de conciencia; **to do a lot of soul-searching** realizar un profundo examen de conciencia.

sound [saʊnd] ◇ *adj* - **1.** [healthy] sano(na) - **2.** [sturdy] sólido(da) - **3.** [reliable] fiable, seguro(ra). ◇ *adv*: **to be sound asleep** estar profundamente dormido(da). ◇ *n* - **1.** [gen] sonido *m* - **2.** [particular noise] ruido *m* - **3.** [impression]**: I don't like the sound of it** no me gusta nada; **by the sound of it** por lo que parece. ◇ *vt* [bell etc] hacer sonar, tocar. ◇ *vi* - **1.** [gen] sonar - **2.** [give impression]: **it sounds interesting** parece interesante; **it sounds like fun** suena divertido; **he sounds like a nice man** parece un hombre simpático.

◆ **sound out** *vt sep*: **to sound sb out (on** OR **about)** sondear a alguien (sobre).

sound barrier *n* barrera *f* del sonido.

sound card *n* COMPUT tarjeta *f* de sonido.

sound effects *npl* efectos *mpl* sonoros.

sounding ['saʊndɪŋ] *n* NAUT sondeo *m* marino.

sounding board *n lit & fig* caja *f* de resonancia.

soundly ['saʊndlɪ] *adv* - **1.** [severely - beat] totalmente - **2.** [deeply] profundamente.

soundness ['saʊndnɪs] *n* [reliability] solidez *f.*

soundproof ['saʊndpruːf] *adj* insonorizado(da).

soundtrack ['saʊndtræk] *n* banda *f* sonora.

sound wave *n* onda *f* sonora.

soup [suːp] *n* [thick] sopa *f*; [clear] caldo *m*, consomé *m.*

◆ **soup up** *vt sep inf* - **1.** [car] trucar - **2.** [book etc] emperifollar.

soup kitchen *n* comedor *m* de beneficiencia.

soup plate *n* plato *m* hondo OR sopero.

soup spoon *n* cuchara *f* sopera.

sour [saʊər] ◇ *adj* - **1.** [acidic] ácido(da) - **2.** [milk, person, reply] agrio(gria). ▶▶ **to go** OR **turn sour** *fig* [evening, plans] irse al traste; [relationship] agriarse. ◇ *vt* agriar. ◇ *vi* agriarse.

source [sɔːs] *n* - **1.** [gen] fuente *f* - **2.** [cause] origen *m* - **3.** [of river] nacimiento *m.*

sour cream *n* nata *f* agria.

sour grapes *n (U) inf*: **it's sour grapes!** ¡están verdes!

sourness ['saʊənɪs] *n* - **1.** [acidity] acidez *f* - **2.** [of milk] agrura *f* - **3.** [of person, relations] acritud *f.*

south [saʊθ] ⬦ *n* **- 1.** [direction] sur *m* **- 2.** [region]: **the South** el sur. ⬦ *adj* del sur. ⬦ *adv*: **south (of)** al sur (de).

South Africa *n*: **(the Republic of) South Africa** (la República de) Suráfrica.

South African ⬦ *adj* surafricano(na). ⬦ *n* [person] surafricano *m*, -na *f*.

South America *n* Sudamérica.

South American ⬦ *adj* sudamericano(na). ⬦ *n* [person] sudamericano *m*, -na *f*.

southbound ['saʊθbaʊnd] *adj* con rumbo al sur.

southeast [,saʊθ'i:st] ⬦ *n* **- 1.** [direction] sudeste *m* **- 2.** [region]: **the Southeast** el sudeste. ⬦ *adj* del sudeste. ⬦ *adv*: **southeast (of)** hacia el sudeste (de).

Southeast Asia *n* el sureste asiático.

southeasterly [,saʊθ'i:stəlɪ] *adj* del sudeste; **in a southeasterly direction** hacia el sudeste.

southeastern [,saʊθ'i:stən] *adj* del sudeste.

southerly ['sʌðəlɪ] *adj* del sur; **in a southerly direction** hacia el sur.

southern ['sʌðən] *adj* del sur, sureño(ña); **the southern hemisphere** el hemisferio sur.

Southerner ['sʌðənəʳ] *n* sureño *m*, -ña *f*.

South Korea *n* Corea del Sur.

South Pole *n*: **the South Pole** el polo Sur.

South Vietnam *n* (el) Vietnam del Sur.

southward ['saʊθwəd] ⬦ *adj* sur. ⬦ *adv* = **southwards**.

southwards ['saʊθwədz], **southward** *adv* hacia el sur.

southwest [,saʊθ'west] ⬦ *n* **- 1.** [direction] suroeste *m* **- 2.** [region]: **the Southwest** el suroeste. ⬦ *adj* del suroeste. ⬦ *adv*: **southwest (of)** hacia el suroeste (de).

southwesterly [,saʊθ'westəlɪ] *adj* del suroeste; **in a southwesterly direction** hacia el suroeste.

southwestern [,saʊθ'westən] *adj* del suroeste.

souvenir [,su:və'nɪəʳ] *n* recuerdo *m*.

sou'wester [saʊ'westəʳ] *n* [hat] sueste *m*.

sovereign ['sɒvrɪn] ⬦ *adj* soberano(na). ⬦ *n* **- 1.** [ruler] soberano *m*, -na *f* **- 2.** [coin] soberano *m*.

sovereignty ['sɒvrɪntɪ] *n* soberanía *f*.

Soviet ['səʊvɪət] ⬦ *adj* soviético(ca). ⬦ *n* [person] soviético *m*, -ca *f*.

Soviet Union *n*: **the (former) Soviet Union** la (antigua) Unión Soviética.

sow[1] [səʊ] (*pt* -ed, *pp* sown OR -ed) *vt lit & fig* sembrar.

sow[2] [saʊ] *n* cerda *f*, puerca *f*, chancha *f* Amér.

sown [səʊn] *pp* ⬦ **sow**.

soya ['sɔɪə] *n* soja *f*.

soy(a) bean ['sɔɪ(ə)-] *n esp US* semilla *f* de soja, frijol *m* de soja Amér, porot *m* de soja Andes.

soy sauce [sɔɪ-] *n esp US* salsa *f* de soja.

sozzled ['sɒzld] *adj UK inf* trompa, mamado(da).

spa [spɑ:] *n* balneario *m*.

spa bath *n* bañera *f* de hidromasaje.

space [speɪs] ⬦ *n* espacio *m*; **to stare into space** tener la mirada perdida; **there isn't enough space for it** no hay suficiente espacio para ello; **in the space of 30 minutes** en el espacio de 30 minutos. ⬦ *vt* espaciar.

➤ **space out** *vt sep* [arrange with spaces between] espaciar.

space age *n*: **the space age** la era espacial.

➤ **space-age** *adj inf* de la era espacial.

space bar *n* [typography] barra *f* espaciadora.

space capsule *n* cápsula *f* espacial.

spacecraft ['speɪskrɑːft] (*pl* spacecraft) *n* nave *f* espacial, astronave *f*.

spaceman ['speɪsmæn] (*pl* -men [-men]) *n inf* astronauta *m*.

space probe *n* sonda *f* espacial.

spaceship ['speɪsʃɪp] *n* nave *f* espacial, astronave *f*.

space shuttle *n* transbordador *m* espacial.

space station *n* estación *f* espacial.

spacesuit ['speɪssuːt] *n* traje *m* espacial.

spacewoman ['speɪs,wʊmən] (*pl* -women [-,wɪmɪn]) *n* astronauta *f*.

spacing ['speɪsɪŋ] *n* TYPO espacio *m*; **double spacing** doble espacio.

spacious ['speɪʃəs] *adj* espacioso(sa).

spade [speɪd] *n* **- 1.** [tool] pala *f* **- 2.** [playing card] pica *f*.

➤ **spades** *npl* picas *fpl*; **the six of spades** el seis de picas.

spadework ['speɪdwɜːk] *n inf* trabajo *m* previo.

spaghetti [spə'getɪ] *n* (U) espaguetis *mpl*.

Spain [speɪn] *n* España *f*.

spam [spæm] ⬦ *n* COMPUT correo *m* basura. ⬦ *vt* (*pt & pp* -med, *cont* -ming) COMPUT enviar correo basura a.

spammer ['spæməʳ] *n* COMPUT spammer *m*.

spamming ['spæmɪŋ] *n* (U) COMPUT spamming *m*, envío *m* de correo basura.

span [spæn] ⬦ *pt* ⬦ **spin**. ⬦ *n* **- 1.** [in time] lapso *m*, periodo *m* **- 2.** [range] gama *f* **- 3.** [of wings] envergadura *f* **- 4.** [of bridge, arch] ojo *m*. ⬦ *vt* (*pt & pp* -ned, *cont* -ning) **- 1.** [in time] abarcar **- 2.** [bridge etc] cruzar, atravesar.

spangled ['spæŋgld] *adj liter*: **spangled (with)** adornado(da) (con).

Spaniard ['spænjəd] *n* español *m*, -la *f*.

spaniel ['spænjəl] *n* perro *m* de aguas.

Spanish [ˈspænɪʃ] <> *adj* español(la). <> *n* [language] español *m*, castellano *m*. <> *npl* [people]: **the Spanish** los españoles.

Spanish America *n* Hispanoamérica.

Spanish American <> *adj* - **1.** [in US] hispano(na) - **2.** [in Latin America] hispanoamericano(na). <> *n* - **1.** [in US] hispano *m*, -na *f* - **2.** [in Latin America] hispanoamericano *m*, -na *f*.

spank [spæŋk] <> *n* azote *m*. <> *vt* dar unos azotes a, zurrar.

spanner [ˈspænəʳ] *n* llave *f* inglesa.

spar [spɑːʳ] <> *n* palo *m*, verga *f*. <> *vi* (*pt & pp* **-red**, *cont* **-ring**) - **1.** [in boxing]: **to spar (with)** entrenarse (con) - **2.** [verbally]: **to spar (with)** discutir amistosamente (con).

spare [speəʳ] <> *adj* - **1.** [surplus] de sobra - **2.** [free - chair, time] libre; **I've got a spare pen you can borrow** tengo un bolígrafo de sobra que te puedo prestar; **have you got a spare minute?** ¿tienes un minuto?; **there's one going spare** sobra uno - **3.** *inf* [crazy]: **to go spare** volverse loco(ca). <> *n* - **1.** [extra one]: **I always carry a spare** siempre llevo uno de sobra - **2.** *inf* [tyre] neumático *m* de recambio - **3.** *inf* [part] pieza *f* de recambio *OR* repuesto, refacción *f* Chile & Méx. <> *vt* - **1.** [time] conceder; [money] dejar; **we can't spare any time/money** no tenemos tiempo/dinero; **to spare** de sobra - **2.** [not harm - person, life] perdonar; **they spared his life** le perdonaron la vida; [- company, city] salvar - **3.** [not use, not take]: **to spare no expense/effort** no escatimar gastos/esfuerzos - **4.** [save from]: **to spare sb sthg** ahorrarle a alguien algo; **you've spared me the trouble** me has ahorrado la molestia.

spare part *n* AUT pieza *f* de recambio *OR* repuesto, refacción *f* Chile & Méx.

spare room *n* habitación *f* de invitados.

spare time *n* tiempo *m* libre.

spare tyre *UK*, **spare tire** *US* *n* - **1.** AUT neumático *m* de recambio - **2.** *hum* [fat waist] michelines *mpl*.

spare wheel *n* rueda *f* de recambio.

sparing [ˈspeərɪŋ] *adj*: **to be sparing with** *OR* **of** ser parco(ca) en.

sparingly [ˈspeərɪŋlɪ] *adv* con moderación.

spark [spɑːk] <> *n* *lit & fig* chispa *f*. <> *vt* provocar; **to spark sthg off** provocar algo.

sparkle [ˈspɑːkl] <> *n* (U) [of diamond] destello *m*; [of eyes] brillo *m*. <> *vi* [star, jewels] centellear; [eyes] brillar.

sparkler [ˈspɑːklər] *n* [firework] bengala *f*.

sparkling wine [ˈspɑːklɪŋ-] *n* vino *m* espumoso.

spark plug *n* bujía *f*.

sparrow [ˈspærəʊ] *n* gorrión *m*.

sparse [spɑːs] *adj* escaso(sa).

spartan [ˈspɑːtn] *adj* espartano(na).

spasm [ˈspæzm] *n* - **1.** MED [state] espasmo *m* - **2.** MED [attack] acceso *m* - **3.** [of emotion] ataque *m*.

spasmodic [spæzˈmɒdɪk] *adj* espasmódico(ca).

spastic [ˈspæstɪk] <> *adj* MED espástico(ca). <> *n* MED espástico *m*, -ca *f*.

spat [spæt] *pt & pp* ⊏ **spit**.

spate [speɪt] *n* cadena *f*, serie *f*.

spatial [ˈspeɪʃl] *adj* *fml* espacial.

spatter [ˈspætər] <> *vt* salpicar. <> *vi*: **to spatter on sthg** salpicar algo.

spatula [ˈspætjʊlə] *n* espátula *f*.

spawn [spɔːn] <> *n* (U) huevas *fpl*. <> *vt* *fig* engendrar. <> *vi* desovar, frezar.

spay [speɪ] *vt* sacar los ovarios a (*un animal*).

SPCA (*abbr of* **Society for the Prevention of Cruelty to Animals**) *n* sociedad estadounidense protectora de animales, ≃ SPA *f*.

SPCC (*abbr of* **Society for the Prevention of Cruelty to Children**) *n* organización estadounidense para la prevención de malos tratos a los niños.

speak [spiːk] <> *vt* (*pt* **spoke**, *pp* **spoken**) - **1.** [say] decir; **to speak ill of** hablar mal de; **to speak one's mind** decir lo que se piensa - **2.** [language] hablar; **can you speak French?** ¿hablas francés? <> *vi* (*pt* **spoke**, *pp* **spoken**) hablar; **to speak to** *OR* **with** hablar con; **to speak to sb (about)** hablar con alguien (de); **to speak about** hablar de; **to speak to sb (on sthg)** [give speech] hablar ante alguien (sobre algo); **to speak well** *OR* **highly of** hablar bien de; **nobody/nothing to speak of** nadie/nada especial; **we aren't speaking** [we aren't friends] no nos hablamos; **is that Mrs Jones? - speaking!** ¿la señora Jones? - sí, soy yo.

➡ **so to speak** *adv* como quien dice, por así decirlo.

➡ **speak for** *vt insep* [represent] hablar en nombre de; **speak for yourself!** ¡eso lo dirás tú!; **it speaks for itself** es evidente.

➡ **speak out** *vi*: **to speak out (against/in favour of)** hablar claro (en contra de/a favor de).

➡ **speak up** *vi* - **1.** [speak out]: **to speak up for** salir en defensa de - **2.** [speak louder] hablar más alto.

speaker [ˈspiːkəʳ] *n* - **1.** [person talking] persona *f* que habla - **2.** [person making a speech - at meal etc] orador *m*, -ra *f*; [- at conference] conferenciante *mf* - **3.** [of a language] hablante *mf*; **English speakers** angloparlantes - **4.** [of radio] altavoz *m*.

speaking ['spi:kɪŋ] <> *adv*: generally speaking en general; **legally speaking** desde una perspectiva legal; **speaking as** [in the position of] hablando como; **speaking of** [on the subject of] hablando de. <> *n* oratoria *f*. <> *adj*: **we are not on speaking terms** no nos dirigimos la palabra.

spear [spɪəʳ] <> *n* [gen] lanza *f*; [for hunting] jabalina *f*. <> *vt* [animal] atravesar; [piece of food] pinchar.

spearhead ['spɪəhed] <> *n* punta *f* de lanza, abanderado *m*, -da *f*. <> *vt* encabezar.

spec [spek] *n* UK *inf*: **to buy on spec** comprar sin garantías; **to go on spec** ir sin haber reservado con anterioridad.

special ['speʃl] <> *adj* - **1.** [gen] especial - **2.** [particular, individual] particular. <> *n* - **1.** [on menu]: **today's special** plato *m* del día - **2.** [TV programme] programa *m* especial.

special agent *n* agente *mf* especial.

special correspondent *n* enviado *m*, -da *f* especial.

special delivery *n* correo *m* urgente.

special effects *npl* efectos *mpl* especiales.

specialist ['speʃəlɪst] <> *adj* [doctor] especialista; [literature] especializado(da). <> *n* especialista *mf*.

speciality [,speʃɪ'ælətɪ] (*pl* -**ies**), **specialty** US ['speʃltɪ] (*pl* -**ies**) *n* especialidad *f*.

specialize, -ise ['speʃəlaɪz] *vi*: **to specialize (in)** especializarse (en).

specially ['speʃəlɪ] *adv* especialmente.

special needs *npl*: **special needs children** niños con necesidades especiales.

special offer *n* oferta *f* especial.

special school *n* escuela *f* especial *(para disminuidos físicos o psíquicos)*.

specialty US = speciality.

species ['spi:ʃi:z] (*pl* **species**) *n* especie *f*.

specific [spə'sɪfɪk] *adj* - **1.** [particular] determinado(da) - **2.** [precise] específico(ca) - **3.** [unique]: **specific to** específico(ca) de.
◆ **specifics** *npl* datos *mpl* específicos.

specifically [spə'sɪfɪklɪ] *adv* - **1.** [particularly] expresamente - **2.** [precisely] específicamente.

specification [,spesɪfɪ'keɪʃn] *n* [plan] especificación *f*.
◆ **specifications** *npl* [of machine etc] datos *mpl* técnicos, descripción *f* técnica.

specify ['spesɪfaɪ] (*pt* & *pp* -**ied**) *vt*: **to specify (that)** especificar (que).

specimen ['spesɪmən] *n* - **1.** [example] espécimen *m*, ejemplar *m* - **2.** [sample] muestra *f*.

specimen copy *n* ejemplar *m* de muestra.

specimen signature *n* muestra *f* de firma.

speck [spek] *n* - **1.** [small stain] manchita *f* - **2.** [small particle] mota *f*.

speckled ['spekld] *adj*: **speckled (with)** moteado(da) (de), con manchas (de).

specs [speks] *npl* UK *inf* [glasses] gafas *fpl*.

spectacle ['spektəkl] *n* [sight] espectáculo *m*; **to make a spectacle of o.s.** dar el espectáculo.
◆ **spectacles** *npl* UK gafas *fpl*.

spectacular [spek'tækjuləʳ] <> *adj* espectacular. <> *n* espectáculo *m*.

spectate [spek'teɪt] *vi* asistir como espectador.

spectator [spek'teɪtəʳ] *n* espectador *m*, -ra *f*.

spectator sport *n* deporte *m* de masas.

spectre UK, **specter** US ['spektəʳ] *n* lit & fig fantasma *m*.

spectrum ['spektrəm] (*pl* -**tra** [-trə]) *n* - **1.** [gen] espectro *m* - **2.** fig [variety] gama *f*, abanico *m*.

speculate ['spekjuleɪt] *vi* especular.

speculation [,spekju'leɪʃn] *n* especulación *f*.

speculative ['spekjulətɪv] *adj* especulativo(va).

speculator ['spekjuleɪtəʳ] *n* FIN especulador *m*, -ra *f*.

sped [sped] *pt* & *pp* ▷ **speed**.

speech [spi:tʃ] *n* - **1.** [gen] habla *f* - **2.** [formal talk] discurso *m*; **to give** OR **make a speech (on sthg to sb)** pronunciar un discurso (sobre algo a alguien) - **3.** [manner of speaking] manera *f* de hablar - **4.** [dialect] dialecto *m*, habla *f*.

speech day *n* UK día *m* de la entrega de premios.

speech impediment *n* defecto *m* en el habla.

speechless ['spi:tʃlɪs] *adj*: **to be speechless (with)** enmudecer (de).

speech therapist *n* logopeda *mf*.

speech therapy *n* logopedia *f*.

speed [spi:d] <> *n* - **1.** [rate of movement] velocidad *f*; **at speed** a gran velocidad; **at top speed** a toda velocidad; **at a speed of 30 mph** a una velocidad de 30 millas por hora - **2.** [rapidity] rapidez *f* - **3.** [gear] marcha *f*. <> *vi* (*pt* & *pp* -**ed** OR **sped**) - **1.** [move fast]: **to speed (along/away/by)** ir/alejarse/pasar a toda velocidad; **to speed by** [hours, years] pasar volando - **2.** AUT [go too fast] conducir con exceso de velocidad.
◆ **speed up** <> *vt sep* [gen] acelerar; [person] meter prisa a. <> *vi* [gen] acelerarse; [person] darse prisa.

speedboat ['spi:dbəut] *n* lancha *f* motora.

speed-dial button *n* [on phone, fax] botón *m* de marcado abreviado.

speed-dialling UK, **speed-dialing** US *n* (U) TELEC marcado *m* rápido.

speeding ['spi:dɪŋ] *n* (U) exceso *m* de velocidad.

speed limit *n* límite *m* de velocidad.

speedometer [spɪ'dɒmɪtəʳ] n velocímetro m.

speed trap n control m policial de velocidad.

speedway ['spi:dweɪ] n - **1.** (U) SPORT carreras fpl de moto - **2.** US [road] autopista f.

speedy ['spi:dɪ] (comp -ier, superl -iest) adj rápido(da).

speleology [,spi:lɪ'ɒlədʒɪ] n fml espeleología f.

spell [spel] <> n - **1.** [of time] temporada f; [of weather] racha f; **sunny spells** intervalos de sol; **to go through a good/bad spell** pasar una buena/mala racha - **2.** [enchantment] hechizo m; **to cast OR put a spell on sb** hechizar a alguien - **3.** [magic words] conjuro m. <> vt (UK spelt OR -ed, US -ed) - **1.** [form by writing] deletrear; **how do you spell that?** ¿cómo se escribe eso? - **2.** fig [signify] significar; **to spell trouble** augurar problemas. <> vi (UK spelt OR -ed, US -ed) escribir correctamente; **I can't spell** cometo muchas faltas de ortografía.

➤ **spell out** vt sep - **1.** [read aloud] deletrear - **2.** [explain]: **to spell sthg out (for OR to sb)** decir algo por las claras (a alguien).

spellbound ['spelbaʊnd] adj hechizado(da), embelesado(da); **to hold sb spellbound** tener hechizado(da) a alguien.

spellcheck ['speltʃek] vt COMPUT pasar el corrector ortográfico a.

spellchecker ['speltʃekəʳ] n COMPUT corrector m ortográfico.

spelling ['spelɪŋ] n ortografía f; **the right/wrong spelling** la grafía correcta/incorrecta; **to be good at spelling** tener buena ortografía; **spelling mistake** falta f de ortografía.

spelt [spelt] UK pt & pp ▷ spell.

spend [spend] (pt & pp spent) vt - **1.** [gen] gastar; **to spend sthg on** gastar algo en - **2.** [time, life] pasar; **to spend one's time doing sthg** pasar el tiempo haciendo algo.

spender ['spendəʳ] n gastador m, -ra f; **to be a big spender** gastar mucho.

spending ['spendɪŋ] n (U) gasto m.

spending money n dinero m para pequeños gastos.

spending power n poder m adquisitivo.

spendthrift ['spendθrɪft] n derrochador m, -ra f, despilfarrador m, -ra f.

spent [spent] <> pt & pp ▷ spend. <> adj [matches, ammunition] usado(da); [patience] agotado(da).

sperm [spɜːm] (pl sperm OR -s) n esperma m.

spermicidal cream [,spɜːmɪ'saɪdl-] n crema f espermicida.

sperm whale n cachalote m.

spew [spju:] <> vt arrojar, escupir. <> vi: **flames spewed out of the volcano** el volcán arrojaba llamas.

sphere [sfɪəʳ] n - **1.** [gen] esfera f - **2.** [of people] círculo m.

spherical ['sferɪkl] adj esférico(ca).

sphincter ['sfɪŋktəʳ] n esfínter m.

sphinx [sfɪŋks] (pl -es) n esfinge f.

spice [spaɪs] <> n - **1.** CULIN especia f - **2.** fig [excitement] sabor m. <> vt - **1.** CULIN: **to spice sthg (with)** condimentar algo (con) - **2.** fig [add excitement to]: **to spice sthg (up)** dar sabor a algo.

spick-and-span [,spɪkən'spæn] adj inmaculado(da).

spicy ['spaɪsɪ] (comp -ier, superl -iest) adj fig [hot and peppery] picante; [with spices] con muchas especias.

spider ['spaɪdəʳ] n araña f.

spider's web, spiderweb US ['spaɪdəweb] n telaraña f.

spidery ['spaɪdərɪ] adj [handwriting] de rasgos largos y finos.

spiel [ʃpiːl] n rollo m.

spike [spaɪk] n - **1.** [on railing etc] punta f; [on wall] clavo m - **2.** [on plant] pincho m; [of hair] pelo m de punta.

➤ **spikes** npl UK zapatillas fpl con clavos.

spiky ['spaɪkɪ] (comp -ier, superl -iest) adj puntiagudo(da); [hair] erizado(da), en punta.

spill [spɪl] <> vt (UK spilt OR -ed, US -ed) derramar, verter. <> vi (UK spilt OR -ed, US -ed) - **1.** [flow] derramarse, verterse - **2.** [flood out]: **to spill out of** salir en masa de.

spillage ['spɪlɪdʒ] n derrame m.

spilt [spɪlt] UK pt & pp ▷ spill.

spin [spɪn] <> n - **1.** [turn] vuelta f - **2.** AERON barrena f - **3.** inf [in car] vuelta f; **to go for a spin** ir a dar una vuelta. <> vt (pt span OR spun, pp spun, cont spinning) - **1.** [cause to rotate] girar, dar vueltas a - **2.** [clothes, washing] centrifugar - **3.** [wool, yarn] hilar. <> vi (pt span OR spun, pp spun, cont spinning) - **1.** [rotate] girar, dar vueltas; **to spin out of control** [vehicle] comenzar a dar trompos - **2.** [feel dizzy]: **my head is spinning** me da vueltas la cabeza - **3.** [make thread, wool, cloth] hilar.

➤ **spin out** vt sep [story] alargar, prolongar; [money] estirar.

spina bifida [,spaɪnə'bɪfɪdə] n espina f bífida.

spinach ['spɪnɪdʒ] n (U) espinacas fpl.

spinal column ['spaɪnl-] n columna f vertebral.

spinal cord n médula f espinal.

spindle ['spɪndl] n - **1.** [machine rod] eje m - **2.** [for spinning] huso m.

spindly ['spɪndlɪ] (comp -ier, superl -iest) adj larguirucho(cha).

spin doctor *n pej* persona encargada de las relaciones con la prensa y de manipular y filtrar la información que se le proporciona.

spin-dry *vt UK* centrifugar.

spin-dryer *n UK* centrifugadora *f*.

spine [spaɪn] *n* - **1.** ANAT espina *f* dorsal - **2.** [of book] lomo *m* - **3.** [spike, prickle] espina *f*, púa *f*.

spine-chilling *adj* escalofriante, espeluznante.

spineless ['spaɪnlɪs] *adj* [feeble] pobre de espíritu.

spinner ['spɪnər] *n* - **1.** [person] hilandera *f* - **2.** [machine] centrifugadora *f*.

spinning ['spɪnɪŋ] *n* hilado *m*.

spinning top *n* peonza *f*.

spin-off *n* [by-product] resultado *m* OR efecto *m* indirecto.

spinster ['spɪnstər] *n* soltera *f*.

spiral ['spaɪərəl] <> *adj* en espiral. <> *n* - **1.** [curve] espiral *f* - **2.** [increase] escalada *f* - **3.** [decrease] descenso *m* rápido. <> *vi* (*UK* **-led**, *cont* **-ling**, *US* **-ed**, *cont* **-ing**) - **1.** [move in spiral curve] moverse en espiral - **2.** [increase rapidly] subir vertiginosamente - **3.** [decrease rapidly]: **to spiral downwards** bajar vertiginosamente.

spiral staircase *n* escalera *f* de caracol.

spire [spaɪər] *n* aguja *f*.

spirit ['spɪrɪt] <> *n* - **1.** [gen] espíritu *m*; **to enter into the spirit of** entrar OR meterse en el ambiente de - **2.** [vigour] vigor *m*, valor *m*. <> *vt*: **to spirit sb in/out** meter/sacar a alguien a escondidas.

⬥ **spirits** *npl* - **1.** [mood] humor *m*; **to be in high/low spirits** estar exultante/alicaído - **2.** [alcohol] licores *mpl*.

spirited ['spɪrɪtɪd] *adj* animado(da), enérgico(ca).

spirit level *n* nivel *m* de burbuja de aire.

spiritual ['spɪrɪtʃʊəl] *adj* espiritual.

spiritualism ['spɪrɪtʃʊəlɪzm] *n* espiritismo *m*.

spiritualist ['spɪrɪtʃʊəlɪst] *n* espiritista *mf*.

spit [spɪt] <> *n* - **1.** [saliva] saliva *f* - **2.** [skewer] asador *m*. <> *vi* (*UK* **spat**, *cont* **-ting**, *US* **spit**, *cont* **-ting**) escupir. <> *impers vb UK* [rain lightly]: **it's spitting** está chispeando.

⬥ **spit out** *vt sep lit* & *fig* escupir; **come on, spit it out!** *fig* venga, ¡suéltalo!

spite [spaɪt] <> *n* rencor *m*; **to do sthg out of** OR **from spite** hacer algo por despecho. <> *vt* fastidiar, molestar.

⬥ **in spite of** *prep* a pesar de; **I did it in spite of myself** [unintentionally] lo hice muy a pesar mío.

spiteful ['spaɪtfʊl] *adj* [person, behaviour] rencoroso(sa); [action, remark] malintencionado(da).

spitting image ['spɪtɪŋ-] *n*: **to be the spitting image of** ser el vivo retrato de.

spittle ['spɪtl] *n* saliva *f*.

splash [splæʃ] <> *n* - **1.** [sound] chapoteo *m* - **2.** [small quantity]: **a splash of lemonade** un chorrito de limonada - **3.** [of colour, light] mancha *f*. <> *vt* salpicar. <> *vi* - **1.** [person]: **to splash about** OR **around** chapotear - **2.** [water, liquid]: **to splash on** OR **against sthg** salpicar algo.

⬥ **splash out** <> *vt sep*: **to splash sthg out on** gastar algo en. <> *vi inf*: **to splash out (on sthg)** gastar un dineral (en algo).

splashdown ['splæʃdaʊn] *n* amerizaje *m*.

splashguard ['splæʃgɑːd] *n US* alfombra *f* salpicadero.

splay [spleɪ] <> *vt* extender, estirar. <> *vi*: **splay (out)** extenderse, estirarse.

spleen [spliːn] *n* ANAT bazo *m*; *fig* [anger] cólera *f*.

splendid ['splendɪd] *adj* - **1.** [marvellous] espléndido(da) - **2.** [magnificent, beautiful] magnífico(ca).

splendidly ['splendɪdlɪ] *adv* - **1.** [marvellously] maravillosamente - **2.** [magnificently] magníficamente.

splendour *UK*, **splendor** *US* ['splendər] *n* esplendor *m*.

splice [splaɪs] *vt* [rope] empalmar; [tape, film] montar.

splint [splɪnt] *n* tablilla *f*.

splinter ['splɪntər] <> *n* [of wood] astilla *f*; [of glass, metal] fragmento *m*. <> *vt*: **to be splintered** [wood] estar astillado(da); [glass, metal] estar fragmentado(da). <> *vi* astillarse.

splinter group *n* grupo *m* disidente.

split [splɪt] <> *n* - **1.** [crack - in wood] grieta *f*; [- in garment] desgarrón *m* - **2.** [division]: **split (in)** escisión *f* (en) - **3.** [difference]: **split (between)** diferencia *f* (entre). <> *vt* (*pt* & *pp* **split**, *cont* **-ting**) - **1.** [tear] desgarrar, rasgar; [crack] agrietar - **2.** [break in two] partir, romper - **3.** [party, organization] escindir - **4.** [share] repartir, dividir; **to split the difference** partir la diferencia. <> *vi* (*pt* & *pp* **split**, *cont* **-ting**) - **1.** [break up - road] bifurcarse; [- object] partirse, romperse - **2.** [party, organization] escindirse - **3.** [wood] partirse, agrietarse; [fabric] desgarrarse, rasgarse - **4.** *US inf* [leave] largarse.

⬥ **splits** *npl*: **to do the splits** hacer el spagat, caer al suelo con las piernas abiertas.

⬥ **split off** <> *vt sep* [break off]: **to split sthg off (from)** separar algo (de). <> *vi* [break off]: **to split off (from)** desprenderse (de).

⬥ **split up** <> *vt sep*: **to split sthg up (into)** dividir algo (en). <> *vi* separarse.

split ends *npl* puntas *fpl* rotas.

split-level *adj* de dos niveles.

split pea *n* guisante *m* seco, arveja *f* seca *Amér*, chícharo *m* seco *Amér C & Méx*.

split personality *n* desdoblamiento *m* de personalidad.

split screen *n* COMPUT pantalla *f* partida.

split second *n* fracción *f* de segundo; **for a split second** por una fracción de segundo.

splitting ['splɪtɪŋ] *adj* [headache] insoportable.

splutter ['splʌtəʳ] <> *n* [of person] balbuceo *m*. <> *vi* **- 1.** [person] balbucear, farfullar **- 2.** [fire, oil] chisporrotear.

spoil [spɔɪl] *vt* (*pt & pp* **-ed** OR **spoilt**) **- 1.** [ruin] estropear, echar a perder **- 2.** [child etc] mimar, regalonear *R Plata & Chile*; **to spoil o.s.** darse un capricho.
➡ **spoils** *npl* botín *m*.

spoiled [spɔɪld] = **spoilt**.

spoilsport ['spɔɪlspɔːt] *n* aguafiestas *m & f inv*.

spoilt [spɔɪlt] <> *pt & pp* ⊳ **spoil**. <> *adj* mimado(da), consentido(da), regalón(ona) *R Plata & Chile*.

spoke [spəʊk] <> *pt* ⊳ **speak**. <> *n* radio *m*.

spoken ['spəʊkn] *pp* ⊳ **speak**.

spokesman ['spəʊksmən] (*pl* **-men** [-mən]) *n* portavoz *m*.

spokesperson ['spəʊks,pɜːsn] *n* portavoz *mf*.

spokeswoman ['spəʊks,wʊmən] (*pl* **-women** [-,wɪmɪn]) *n* portavoz *f*.

sponge [spʌndʒ] <> *n* **- 1.** [for cleaning, washing] esponja *f* **- 2.** [cake] bizcocho *m*. <> *vt* (*UK* **spongeing**, *US* **sponging**) limpiar con una esponja. <> *vi* (*UK* **spongeing**, *US* **sponging**) *inf*: **to sponge off** vivir a costa de.

sponge bag *n UK* neceser *m*.

sponge cake *n* bizcocho *m*, bizcochuelo *m Ven*.

sponge pudding *n UK* pudín *m* de bizcocho hecho al baño maría.

sponger ['spʌndʒəʳ] *n inf pej* gorrón *m*, -ona *f*.

spongy ['spʌndʒɪ] (*comp* **-ier**, *superl* **-iest**) *adj* esponjoso(sa).

sponsor ['spɒnsəʳ] <> *n* patrocinador *m*, -ra *f*. <> *vt* **- 1.** [gen] patrocinar **- 2.** [support] respaldar.

sponsored walk [,spɒnsəd-] *n* marcha *f* benéfica.

sponsorship ['spɒnsəʃɪp] *n* patrocinio *m*.

spontaneity [,spɒntə'neɪətɪ] *n* espontaneidad *f*.

spontaneous [spɒn'teɪnjəs] *adj* espontáneo(a).

spontaneously [spɒn'teɪnjəslɪ] *adv* espontáneamente.

spoof [spuːf] *n*: **spoof (of** OR **on)** parodia *f* (de).

spook [spuːk] *vt US* asustar.

spooky ['spuːkɪ] (*comp* **-ier**, *superl* **-iest**) *adj inf* escalofriante, estremecedor(ra).

spool [spuːl] *n* [gen & COMPUT] bobina *f*.

spoon [spuːn] <> *n* **- 1.** [piece of cutlery] cuchara *f* **- 2.** [spoonful] cucharada *f*. <> *vt*: **to spoon** sthg onto OR **into** poner una cucharada de algo en.

spoon-feed *vt* **- 1.** [feed with spoon] dar de comer con cuchara a **- 2.** *fig* [present in simple form] dar masticado.

spoonful ['spuːnfʊl] (*pl* **-s** OR **spoonsful** ['spuːnzfʊl]) *n* cucharada *f*.

sporadic [spə'rædɪk] *adj* esporádico(ca).

sport [spɔːt] <> *n* [game] deporte *m*. <> *vt* lucir, llevar.
➡ **sports** *comp* deportivo(va).

sporting ['spɔːtɪŋ] *adj lit & fig* deportivo(va); **to give sb a sporting chance** dar a alguien la oportunidad de ganar.

sports car ['spɔːts-] *n* coche *m* deportivo, auto *m* sport, carro *m* sport *Amér*.

sports day *n UK* día *m* dedicado a los deportes.

sports jacket ['spɔːts-] *n* chaqueta *f* de esport.

sportsman ['spɔːtsmən] (*pl* **-men** [-mən]) *n* deportista *m*.

sportsmanship ['spɔːtsmənʃɪp] *n* deportividad *f*.

sports pages *npl* sección *f* OR páginas *fpl* de deportes.

sportswear ['spɔːtsweəʳ] *n* ropa *f* deportiva.

sportswoman ['spɔːts,wʊmən] (*pl* **-women** [-,wɪmɪn]) *n* deportista *f*.

sports utility vehicle *n US* todoterreno *m* utilitario.

sporty ['spɔːtɪ] (*comp* **-ier**, *superl* **-iest**) *adj inf* **- 1.** [fond of sports] aficionado(da) a los deportes **- 2.** [flashy] llamativo(va).

spot [spɒt] <> *n* **- 1.** [stain] mancha *f*, mota *f*; [dot] punto *m* **- 2.** [pimple] grano *m* **- 3.** [drop] gota *f* **- 4.** *inf* [bit, small amount] pizca *f*, miaja *f* **- 5.** [place] lugar *m*; **on the spot** en el lugar; **to do sthg on the spot** hacer algo en el acto **- 6.** RADIO & TV espacio *m*
▶▶ **to have a soft spot for sb** tener debilidad por alguien; **to put sb on the spot** poner a alguien en un aprieto OR contra las cuerdas. <> *vt* (*pt & pp* **-ted**, *cont* **-ting**) [notice] notar, ver.

spot check *n* control *m* aleatorio.

spotless ['spɒtlɪs] *adj* [thing] inmaculado(da); [reputation] intachable.

spotlight ['spɒtlaɪt] *n* [of car] faro *m* auxiliar; [in theatre, home] foco *m*, reflector *m* de luz; **to be in the spotlight** *fig* ser el centro de atención.

spot-on *adj UK inf* exacto(ta), preciso(sa).

spotted ['sppttd] *adj* de lunares, moteado(da).

spotty ['sppti] (*comp* **-ier**, *superl* **-iest**) *adj*
- **1.** *UK* [skin] con granos - **2.** *US* [patchy] irregular.

spouse [spaʊs] *n* cónyuge *mf*.

spout [spaʊt] <> *n* [of teapot] pitorro *m*; [of jug]
pico *m*. <> *vt pej* [churn out] soltar. <> *vi:* **to
spout from** OR **out of** [liquid] salir a chorros de;
[smoke, flames] salir incesantemente de.

sprain [spreɪn] <> *n* torcedura *f*. <> *vt* torcerse.

sprang [spræŋ] *pt* ⊏> spring.

sprat [spræt] *n* espadín *m*.

sprawl [sprɔːl] <> *n* (*U*) urban sprawl desorganización *f* urbana. <> *vi* - **1.** [sit] repantigarse, arrellanarse; [lie] echarse, tumbarse
- **2.** [cover large area] extenderse.

sprawling ['sprɔːlɪŋ] *adj* [city] de urbanización
caótica.

spray [spreɪ] <> *n* - **1.** [small drops - of liquid]
rociada *f*; [- of sea] espuma *f*; [- of aerosol] pulverización *f* - **2.** [pressurized liquid] espray *m*
- **3.** [can, container - gen] atomizador *m*; [- for
garden] pulverizador *m* - **4.** [of flowers] ramo *m*.
<> *vt* rociar, vaporizar. <> *vi:* **water sprayed
all over the room** el agua salpicó toda la habitación.

spray can *n* aerosol *m*, espray *m*.

spray paint *n* pintura *f* en aerosol.

spread [spred] <> *n* - **1.** [soft food] **cheese
spread** queso *m* para untar - **2.** [of fire, disease]
propagación *f* - **3.** [range of products] gama *f*,
surtido *m* - **4.** PRESS **two-page spread** doble
página *f*. <> *vt* (*pt & pp* **spread**) - **1.** [rug, tablecloth] extender; [map] desplegar - **2.** [legs, fingers etc] estirar - **3.** [butter, jam] untar; [glue] repartir; **to spread sthg over sthg** extender
algo por algo - **4.** [disease] propagar; [news] difundir, diseminar - **5.** [in time] **to be spread
over** tener una duración de - **6.** [wealth, work]
repartir equitativamente. <> *vi*
(*pt & pp* **spread**) - **1.** [disease, fire, news] extenderse, propagarse - **2.** [gas, cloud] esparcirse.
◆ **spread out** <> *vt sep* - **1.:** **to be spread
out** [far apart] estar diseminado(da); [sprawling]
extenderse - **2.** [rug, tablecloth, legs] extender;
[map] desplegar. <> *vi* diseminarse, dispersarse.

spread-eagled [-,iːgld] *adj* despatarrado(da).

spreadsheet ['spredʃiːt] *n* COMPUT hoja *f* de cálculo electrónica.

spree [spriː] *n:* **a killing spree** una matanza; **to
go on a shopping spree** salir a comprar a lo
loco.

sprig [sprɪg] *n* ramita *f*.

sprightly ['spraɪtlɪ] (*comp* **-ier**, *superl* **-iest**)
adj ágil, activo(va).

spring [sprɪŋ] <> *n* - **1.** [season] primavera *f*;
in spring en primavera - **2.** [coil] muelle *m*
- **3.** [jump] salto *m* - **4.** [water source] manantial *m*, vertiente *f* R Plata. <> *vt* (*pt* **sprang**,
pp **sprung**) - **1.** [make known suddenly] **to
spring sthg on sb** soltar OR decir de repente
algo a alguien - **2.** [develop] **to spring a leak**
empezar a hacer agua. <> *vi* (*pt* **sprang**,
pp **sprung**) - **1.** [jump] saltar - **2.** [move suddenly] moverse de repente; **she sprang to her
feet** se levantó de un salto; **to spring into action** OR **to life** entrar inmediatamente en acción - **3.** [originate] **to spring from** derivar de.
◆ **spring up** *vi* surgir de repente.

springboard ['sprɪŋbɔːd] *n lit & fig* trampolín *m*.

spring-clean <> *vt* limpiar a fondo. <> *vi* hacer una limpieza general.

spring onion *n UK* cebolleta *f*.

spring roll *n UK* rollito *m* de primavera.

spring tide *n* marea *f* viva.

springtime ['sprɪŋtaɪm] *n:* **in (the) springtime**
en primavera.

springy ['sprɪŋɪ] (*comp* **-ier**, *superl* **-iest**) *adj*
[carpet, mattress, grass] mullido(da); [rubber]
elástico(ca).

sprinkle ['sprɪŋkl] *vt* rociar, salpicar; **to
sprinkle sthg over** OR **on sthg**, **to sprinkle
sthg with sthg** rociar algo sobre algo.

sprinkler ['sprɪŋklər] *n* aspersor *m*.

sprinkling ['sprɪŋklɪŋ] *n* [of water, sand] pizca *f*;
a sprinkling of people unas cuantas personas.

sprint [sprɪnt] <> *n* - **1.** SPORT esprint *m* - **2.** [fast
run] carrera *f*. <> *vi* SPORT esprintar; [run fast]
correr a toda velocidad.

sprinter ['sprɪntər] *n* corredor *m*, -ra *f* de velocidad, esprínter *mf*.

spritzer ['sprɪtsər] *n* vino *m* con gaseosa.

sprocket ['sprɒkɪt] *n* rueda *f* dentada.

sprout [spraʊt] <> *n* - **1.** CULIN (Brussels)
sprouts coles *fpl* de Bruselas - **2.** [shoot] brote *m*, retoño *m*. <> *vt* - **1.** [plant] echar - **2.** [person, animal] **he has sprouted a beard** le ha
salido barba. <> *vi* - **1.** [plants, vegetables] crecer - **2.** [leaves, shoots] brotar - **3.** [hairs, feathers,
horns] salir - **4.** [appear] **to sprout (up)** aparecer rápidamente.

spruce [spruːs] <> *adj* pulcro(cra). <> *n* picea *f*.
◆ **spruce up** *vt sep* arreglar; **to spruce o.s. up**
arreglarse.

sprung [sprʌŋ] *pp* ⊏> spring.

spry [spraɪ] (*comp* **-ier**, *superl* **-iest**) *adj* ágil,
activo(va).

spud [spʌd] *n inf* papa *f*, patata *f*.

spun [spʌn] *pt* & *pp* ▷ **spin**.

spunk [spʌŋk] *n (U) inf* [courage] agallas *fpl*.

spur [spɜːʳ] ◇ *n* - **1.** [incentive]: **spur (to sthg)** estímulo *m* (para conseguir algo) - **2.** [on rider's boot] espuela *f*. ◇ *vt* (*pt* & *pp* **-red**, *cont* **-ring**) [encourage]: **to spur sb to do sthg** animar a alguien a hacer algo.

➡ **on the spur of the moment** *adv* sin pensarlo dos veces.

➡ **spur on** *vt sep*: **to spur sb on** animar a alguien.

spurious ['spʊərɪəs] *adj* falso(sa).

spurn [spɜːn] *vt* rechazar.

spurt [spɜːt] ◇ *n* - **1.** [of water] chorro *m*; [of flame] llamarada *f* - **2.** [of activity, effort] arranque *m* - **3.** [of speed] acelerón *m*; **to put on a spurt** acelerar. ◇ *vi* - **1.** [gush]: **to spurt (out of OR from)** [liquid] salir a chorros de; [flame] salir incesantemente de - **2.** [run] acelerar.

sputter ['spʌtəʳ] *vi* [engine] renquear; [fire, oil] chisporrotear.

spy [spaɪ] ◇ *n* (*pl* **spies**) espía *mf*. ◇ *vt* (*pt* & *pp* **-ied**) *inf* divisar. ◇ *vi* (*pt* & *pp* **-ied**): **to spy (on)** espiar (a), aguaitar (a) *Amér*.

spying ['spaɪɪŋ] *n* espionaje *m*.

Sq., sq. *abbr of* **square**.

squabble ['skwɒbl] ◇ *n* riña *f*. ◇ *vi*: **to squabble (about OR over)** reñir (por).

squad [skwɒd] *n* - **1.** [of police] brigada *f* - **2.** MIL pelotón *m* - **3.** [SPORT - of club] plantilla *f*, equipo *m* completo; [- of national team] selecciona-do *m*; **the England squad** el equipo inglés.

squad car *n US* coche *m* patrulla, auto *m* patrulla *Amér C, Méx & Chile*, patrullero *m*, patrulla *f* *Col & Méx*.

squadron ['skwɒdrən] *n* [of planes] escuadrilla *f*; [of warships] escuadra *f*; [of soldiers] escuadrón *m*.

squadron leader *n UK* ≃ comandante *m* de aviación.

squalid ['skwɒlɪd] *adj* - **1.** [filthy] miserable, sórdido(da) - **2.** [sordid] sórdido(da).

squall [skwɔːl] *n* [storm] turbión *m*.

squalor ['skwɒləʳ] *n (U)* miseria *f*.

squander ['skwɒndəʳ] *vt* [opportunity] desaprovechar; [money] despilfarrar; [resources] malgastar.

square [skweəʳ] ◇ *adj* - **1.** [gen] cuadrado(da); **4 square metres** 4 metros cuadrados; **the kitchen is 4 metres square** la cocina mide 4 metros por 4 - **2.** [not owing money]: **we're square now** ya estamos en paz. ◇ *n* - **1.** [shape] cuadrado *m* - **2.** [in town, city] plaza *f* - **3.** *inf* [unfashionable person] carroza *mf*

▶▶ **to be back to square one** haber vuelto al punto de partida. ◇ *vt* - **1.** MATHS elevar al cuadrado - **2.** [balance, reconcile]: **how can you square that with your principles?** ¿cómo encajas esto con tus principios?; **it doesn't square with the facts** no cuadra con los hechos.

➡ **square up** *vi* - **1.** [settle up]: **to square up with** saldar cuentas con - **2.**: **to square up to** [confront] hacer frente a.

squared [skweəd] *adj* cuadriculado(da).

square dance *n* baile *m* de figuras.

square deal *n* trato *m* justo; **to give sb a square deal** dar a alguien un trato justo.

squarely ['skweəlɪ] *adv* - **1.** [directly] justo, exactamente - **2.** [honestly] abiertamente, honradamente.

square meal *n* comida *f* satisfactoria.

square root *n* raíz *f* cuadrada.

squash [skwɒʃ] ◇ *n* - **1.** [game] squash *m* - **2.** *UK* [drink] zumo *m* - **3.** *US* [vegetable] cucurbitácea *f*. ◇ *vt* [squeeze, flatten] aplastar.

squat [skwɒt] ◇ *adj* (*comp* **-ter**, *superl* **-test**) achaparrado(da). ◇ *n UK* [building] vivienda *f* ocupada. ◇ *vi* (*pt* & *pp* **-ted**, *cont* **-ting**) - **1.** [crouch]: **to squat (down)** agacharse, ponerse en cuclillas - **2.** [be a squatter] vivir en una casa ocupada.

squatter ['skwɒtəʳ] *n UK* ocupante *mf* ilegal, squatter *mf*.

squawk [skwɔːk] ◇ *n* [of bird] graznido *m*, chillido *m*. ◇ *vi* [bird] graznar, chillar.

squeak [skwiːk] ◇ *n* - **1.** [of animal] chillido *m* - **2.** [of hinge] chirrido *m*. ◇ *vi* - **1.** [animal] chillar - **2.** [hinge] chirriar - **3.** [shoes] crujir.

squeaky ['skwiːkɪ] (*comp* **-ier**, *superl* **-iest**) *adj* [voice] chillón(ona); [hinge] chirriante.

squeal [skwiːl] ◇ *n* - **1.** [of person, animal] chillido *m*, grito *m* - **2.** [of brakes, tyres] chirrido *m*. ◇ *vi* - **1.** [person, animal] chillar, gritar - **2.** [brakes] chirriar.

squeamish ['skwiːmɪʃ] *adj* aprensivo(va).

squeeze [skwiːz] ◇ *n* - **1.** [pressure] apretón *m* - **2.** *inf* [squash]: **it was a real squeeze** estábamos totalmente apiñados. ◇ *vt* - **1.** [press firmly] apretar - **2.** [force out - toothpaste] sacar (estrujando); [- juice] exprimir - **3.** [cram]: **to squeeze sthg into sthg** [into place] conseguir meter algo en algo; [into time] arreglárselas para hacer algo en algo - **4.** *fig*: **to squeeze sthg out of sb** [extract] arrancar algo a alguien. ◇ *vi*: **to squeeze into/through** conseguir meterse en/por.

squeezer ['skwiːzəʳ] *n* exprimidor *m*.

squelch [skweltʃ] *vi*: **to squelch through mud** cruzar el barro chapoteando.

squib [skwɪb] n [firework] petardo m; **to be a damp squib** fig ser un chasco.

squid [skwɪd] (pl **squid** OR **-s**) n - **1.** ZOOL calamar m - **2.** (U) [food] calamares mpl.

squiggle ['skwɪgl] n garabato m.

squint [skwɪnt] ◇ n estrabismo m, bizquera f. ◇ vi: **to squint at** mirar con los ojos entrecerrados.

squire ['skwaɪəʳ] n [landowner] terrateniente mf.

squirm [skwɜ:m] vi - **1.** [wriggle] retorcerse - **2.** [wince]: **to squirm (with)** sentirse violento(ta) (por).

squirrel [UK 'skwɪrəl, US 'skwɜ:rəl] n ardilla f.

squirt [skwɜ:t] ◇ vt - **1.** [force out] sacar a chorro de - **2.** [cover with liquid]: **you've squirted me with ketchup, you've squirted ketchup over me** me has echado un chorro de ketchup. ◇ vi: **to squirt out of** salir a chorro.

Sr abbr of **senior**. abbr of **sister**.

Sri Lanka [ˌsri:'læŋkə] n Sri Lanka.

SRN (abbr of **State Registered Nurse**) n UK enfermero diplomado m, enfermera diplomada f.

SS (abbr of **steamship**) barco de vapor.

SSA (abbr of **Social Security Administration**) n organismo estadounidense de la seguridad social.

ssh [ʃ] excl ¡chis!

St - 1. (abbr of **saint**) Sto.(Sta.) - **2.** (abbr of **Street**) c/.

ST (abbr of **Standard Time**) hora oficial.

stab [stæb] ◇ n - **1.** [with knife] puñalada f - **2.** inf [attempt]: **to have a stab (at sthg)** probar (a hacer algo) - **3.** [twinge] punzada f. ◇ vt (pt & pp **-bed**, cont **-bing**) - **1.** [with knife] apuñalar - **2.** [jab] pinchar. ◇ vi (pt & pp **-bed**, cont **-bing**): **to stab at sthg** [with finger] señalar algo con movimientos bruscos del dedo índice.

stabbing ['stæbɪŋ] ◇ adj punzante. ◇ n apuñalamiento m.

stability [stə'bɪlətɪ] n estabilidad f.

stabilize, -ise ['steɪbəlaɪz] ◇ vt estabilizar. ◇ vi estabilizarse.

stabilizer ['steɪbəlaɪzəʳ] n estabilizador m.

stable ['steɪbl] ◇ adj - **1.** [unchanging] estable - **2.** [not moving] fijo(ja) - **3.** MED [condition] estacionario(ria); [mental health] equilibrado(da). ◇ n [building] cuadra f.

stable lad n mozo m de cuadra.

staccato [stə'ka:təu] adj entrecortado(da).

stack [stæk] ◇ n - **1.** [pile] pila m - **2.** inf [a lot, lots]: **stacks** OR **a stack of** montones OR un montón de. ◇ vt - **1.** [pile up] apilar - **2.** [fill]: **to be stacked with** estar amontonado(da) de.

stadium ['steɪdjəm] (pl **-diums** OR **-dia** [-djə]) n estadio m.

staff [sta:f] ◇ n [employees] empleados mpl, personal m. ◇ vt: **the shop is staffed by women** la tienda está llevada por una plantilla de mujeres.

staffing ['sta:fɪŋ] n contratación f de personal.

staff nurse n UK enfermero titulado m, enfermera titulada f.

staff room n sala f de profesores.

Staffs [stæfs] (abbr of **Staffordshire**), condado inglés.

stag [stæg] (pl **stag** OR **-s**) n ciervo m, venado m.

stage [steɪdʒ] ◇ n - **1.** [part of process, phase] etapa f; **to do sthg in stages** hacer algo por etapas - **2.** [in theatre, hall] escenario m, escena f; **on stage** en escena; **to set the stage for** preparar el terreno para - **3.** [acting profession]: **the stage** el teatro. ◇ vt - **1.** THEAT representar - **2.** [event, strike] organizar.

stagecoach ['steɪdʒkəutʃ] n diligencia f.

stage door n entrada f de artistas.

stage fright n miedo m al público.

stagehand ['steɪdʒhænd] n tramoyista mf.

stage-manage vt - **1.** THEAT dirigir - **2.** fig [orchestrate] urdir, maquinar.

stage name n nombre m artístico.

stagger ['stægəʳ] ◇ vt - **1.** [astound] dejar atónito(ta); **to be staggered by sthg** quedarse pasmado(da) por algo - **2.** [arrange at different times] escalonar. ◇ vi tambalearse.

staggering ['stægərɪŋ] adj asombroso(sa).

staging ['steɪdʒɪŋ] n - **1.** THEAT puesta f en escena - **2.** [of event] organización f.

stagnant ['stægnənt] adj lit & fig estancado(da).

stagnate [stæg'neɪt] vi estancarse.

stagnation [stæg'neɪʃn] n estancamiento m.

stag party n despedida f de soltero.

staid [steɪd] adj recatado y conservador (recatada y conservadora).

stain [steɪn] ◇ n mancha f. ◇ vt manchar.

stained [steɪnd] adj - **1.** [marked] manchado(da) - **2.** [coloured - wood] teñido(da).

stained glass [ˌsteɪnd-] n (U) vidrio m de color; **stained glass window** vidriera f.

stainless steel [ˌsteɪnlɪs-] n acero m inoxidable.

stain remover [-rɪˌmu:vəʳ] n quitamanchas m inv.

stair [steəʳ] n peldaño m, escalón m.
➡ **stairs** npl escaleras fpl, escalera f.

staircase ['steəkeɪs] n escalera f.

stairway ['steəweɪ] n escalera f.

stairwell ['steəwel] n hueco m OR caja f de la escalera.

stake [steɪk] <> *n* - **1.** [share]: **to have a stake in** tener intereses en - **2.** [wooden post] estaca *f* - **3.** [in gambling] apuesta *f*. <> *vt* - **1.** [risk]: **to stake sthg (on** OR **upon)** arriesgar OR jugarse algo (en) - **2.** [in gambling] apostar - **3.** [state]: **to stake a claim to sthg** reivindicar algo.
<> **stakes** *npl* - **1.** [prize] premio *m* - **2.** [contest] contienda *f*.
<> **at stake** *adv*: **to be at stake** estar en juego.

stakeout ['steɪkaʊt] *n esp US* [police surveillance] vigilancia *f*.

stalactite ['stæləktaɪt] *n* estalactita *f*.

stalagmite ['stæləgmaɪt] *n* estalagmita *f*.

stale [steɪl] *adj* - **1.** [bread] duro(ra); [food] rancio(cia), pasado(da); [air] viciado(da) - **2.** [athlete] agotado(da); [artist etc] falto(ta) de ideas.

stalemate ['steɪlmeɪt] *n* - **1.** [deadlock] punto *m* muerto - **2.** CHESS tablas *fpl*.

staleness ['steɪlnɪs] *n* [of bread] dureza *f*; [of food] rancidez *f*, deterioro *m*; [of air] lo viciado.

stalk [stɔ:k] <> *n* - **1.** [of flower, plant] tallo *m* - **2.** [of leaf, fruit] pecíolo *m*, rabillo *m*. <> *vt* [hunt] acechar, seguir sigilosamente. <> *vi*: **to stalk in/out** entrar/salir con paso airado.

stall [stɔ:l] <> *n* [in market, at exhibition] puesto *m*, caseta *f*. <> *vt* - **1.** AUT calar - **2.** [delay - person] retener. <> *vi* - **1.** AUT calarse - **2.** [delay] andar con evasivas.
<> **stalls** *npl* UK platea *f*.

stallholder ['stɔ:l,həʊldər] *n* UK propietario *m*, -ria *f* de un puesto (en un mercado).

stallion ['stæljən] *n* semental *m*.

stalwart ['stɔ:lwət] <> *adj* [loyal] leal, incondicional. <> *n* partidario *m*, -ria *f* incondicional.

stamen ['steɪmən] *n* estambre *m*.

stamina ['stæmɪnə] *n* resistencia *f*.

stammer ['stæmər] <> *n* tartamudeo *m*. <> *vi* tartamudear.

stamp [stæmp] <> *n* - **1.** [gen] sello *m*, estampilla *f* Amér, timbre *m* Méx - **2.** [tool] tampón *m*. <> *vt* - **1.** [mark by stamping] timbrar, sellar - **2.** [stomp]: **to stamp one's feet** patear - **3.** [stick stamp on] sellar, poner un sello en, franquear, estampillar Amér, timbrar Méx - **4.** *fig* [identify, mark]: **to stamp sthg/sb as** identificar algo/a alguien como. <> *vi* - **1.** [stomp] patalear, dar patadas - **2.** [tread heavily]: **to stamp on sthg** pisotear OR pisar algo.
<> **stamp out** *vt sep* [custom] erradicar; [fire, revolution] sofocar.

stamp album *n* álbum *m* de sellos OR de estampillas Amér OR de timbres Méx.

stamp collecting [-kə,lektɪŋ] *n* filatelia *f*.

stamp collector *n* coleccionista *mf* de sellos OR de estampillas Amér OR de timbres Méx.

stamp duty *n* UK póliza *f*, impuesto *m* del timbre.

stamped addressed envelope ['stæmptə,drest-] *n* UK sobre *con sus señas y franqueo*.

stampede [stæm'pi:d] <> *n lit & fig* estampida *f*, desbandada *f*. <> *vi* salir de estampida.

stamp machine *n* máquina *f* expendedora de sellos OR de estampillas Amér OR de timbres Méx.

stance [stæns] *n* - **1.** [way of standing] postura *f* - **2.** [attitude]: **stance (on)** postura *f* (ante).

stand [stænd] <> *n* - **1.** [stall] puesto *m*; [selling newspapers] quiosco *m* - **2.** [supporting object] soporte *m*; **coat stand** perchero *m*; **music stand** atril *m* - **3.** SPORT tribuna *f*; **the stands** las gradas - **4.** [act of defence]: **to make a stand** resistir al enemigo - **5.** [publicly stated view] postura *f*; **to take a stand on sthg** adoptar una postura ante OR hacia algo - **6.** US LAW estrado *m*; **to take the stand** subir al estrado. <> *vt* (*pt & pp* **stood**) - **1.** [place upright] colocar (verticalmente) - **2.** [withstand, tolerate] soportar; **I can't stand that woman** no soporto a esa mujer; **he can't stand being beaten** odia perder - **3.** [treat]: **to stand sb sthg** invitar a alguien a algo - **4.** LAW: **to stand trial** ser procesado(da). <> *vi* (*pt & pp* **stood**) - **1.** [be upright - person] estar de pie; [- object] estar *(en posición vertical)*; **try to stand still** procura no moverte; **he doesn't let anything stand in his way** no deja que nada se interponga en su camino - **2.** [get to one's feet] ponerse de pie, levantarse - **3.** [liquid] reposar - **4.** [still be valid] seguir vigente OR en pie - **5.** [be in particular state]: **unemployment stands at three million** la cifra de desempleados es de tres millones; **as things stand** tal como están las cosas - **6.** [have attitude]: **where do you stand on...?** ¿cúal es tu postura ante...? - **7.** [be likely]: **I stand to win/lose** es probable que gane/pierda - **8.** UK POL [be a candidate] presentarse; **to stand for Parliament** presentarse para las elecciones al Parlamento - **9.** US AUT: **'no standing'** 'prohibido aparcar'.
<> **stand aside** *vi* hacerse a un lado.
<> **stand back** *vi* echarse para atrás.
<> **stand by** <> *vt insep* - **1.** [person] seguir al lado de - **2.** [promise, decision] mantener. <> *vi* - **1.** [in readiness]: **to stand by (for sthg/to do sthg)** estar preparado(da) (para algo/para hacer algo) - **2.** [remain inactive] quedarse sin hacer nada.
<> **stand down** *vi* [resign] retirarse.

stand for vt insep **- 1.** [signify] significar; PTO **stands for 'please turn over'** PTO quiere decir 'sigue en la página siguiente' **- 2.** [support - policy, ideas] defender **- 3.** [tolerate] aguantar, tolerar; **I won't stand for it!** ¡no pienso aguantarlo!

stand in vi: **to stand in for sb** sustituir a alguien.

stand out vi sobresalir, destacarse.

stand up <> vt sep inf [boyfriend etc] dejar plantado(da). <> vi **- 1.** [rise from seat] levantarse, pararse Amér **- 2.** [claim, evidence] ser convincente; **it won't stand up in court** no servirá como prueba en un juicio.

stand up for vt insep salir en defensa de.

stand up to vt insep **- 1.** [weather, heat etc] resistir **- 2.** [person] hacer frente a.

standard ['stændəd] <> adj **- 1.** [normal] corriente, estándar **- 2.** [accepted] establecido(da) **- 3.** [basic] clave, fundamental. <> n **- 1.** [acceptable level] nivel m; **to be of a high standard** ser de un excelente nivel; **it's below standard** está por debajo del nivel exigido **- 2.** [point of reference - moral] criterio m; [- technical] norma f **- 3.** [flag] bandera f, estandarte m.

standards npl [principles] valores mpl morales.

standard-bearer n fig portaestandarte mf, abanderado m, -da f.

standardize, -ise ['stændədaɪz] vt normalizar, estandarizar.

standard lamp n UK lámpara f de pie.

standard of living (pl **standards of living**) n nivel m de vida.

standard time n hora f oficial.

standby ['stændbaɪ] (pl **standbys**) <> n recurso m; **to be on standby** estar preparado(da). <> comp: **standby ticket** billete m en lista de espera.

stand-in n [stuntman] doble mf; [temporary replacement] sustituto m, -ta f.

standing ['stændɪŋ] <> adj [permanent] permanente; **a standing joke** la broma de siempre; **standing invitation** invitación abierta. <> n **- 1.** [reputation] reputación f **- 2.** [duration] duración f; **friends of 20 years' standing** amigos desde hace 20 años.

standing committee n comité m permanente.

standing order n domiciliación f de pago Esp, débito m bancario Amér.

standing ovation n ovación f calurosa en pie; **she was given a standing ovation** la ovacionaron de pie.

standing room n (U) [on bus] sitio m para estar de pie, sitio m para ir parado Amér; [at theatre, sports ground] localidades fpl de pie.

standoffish [ˌstændˈɒfɪʃ] adj distante.

standpoint ['stændpɔɪnt] n punto m de vista.

standstill ['stændstɪl] n: **at a standstill** [not moving] parado(da); fig [not active] en un punto muerto, estancado(da); **to come to a standstill** [stop moving] pararse; fig [cease] llegar a un punto muerto, estancarse.

stand-up adj US [decent, honest]: **a stand-up guy** un tipo decente.

stank [stæŋk] pt ▷ **stink**.

stanza ['stænzə] n estrofa f.

staple ['steɪpl] <> adj [principal] básico(ca), de primera necesidad. <> n **- 1.** [item of stationery] grapa f, corchete m Chile **- 2.** [principal commodity] producto m básico OR de primera necesidad. <> vt grapar, corchetear Chile.

staple diet n dieta f básica.

staple gun n grapadora f industrial.

stapler ['steɪplər] n grapadora f, corchetera f Chile.

star [stɑːr] <> n **- 1.** [gen] estrella f **- 2.** [asterisk] asterisco m. <> comp estelar. <> vt (pt & pp **-red**, cont **-ring**): **the film stars Kevin Costner** la película está protagonizada por Kevin Costner. <> vi (pt & pp **-red**, cont **-ring**): **to star (in)** hacer de protagonista en.

stars npl horóscopo m.

star attraction n atracción f principal.

starboard ['stɑːbəd] <> adj de estribor. <> n: **to starboard** a estribor.

starch [stɑːtʃ] n **- 1.** [gen] almidón m **- 2.** [in potatoes etc] fécula f.

starched [stɑːtʃt] adj almidonado(da).

starchy ['stɑːtʃɪ] (comp **-ier**, superl **-iest**) adj [foods] feculento(ta).

stardom ['stɑːdəm] n estrellato m.

stare [steər] <> n mirada f fija. <> vi: **to stare (at sthg/sb)** mirar fijamente (algo/a alguien).

starfish ['stɑːfɪʃ] (pl **starfish** OR **-es**) n estrella f de mar.

stark [stɑːk] <> adj **- 1.** [landscape, decoration, room] austero(ra) **- 2.** [harsh - reality] crudo(da); [- fact] sin tapujos. <> adv: **stark naked** en cueros.

starlight ['stɑːlaɪt] n luz f de las estrellas.

starling ['stɑːlɪŋ] n estornino m.

starlit ['stɑːlɪt] adj iluminado(da) por las estrellas.

starry ['stɑːrɪ] (comp **-ier**, superl **-iest**) adj estrellado(da), lleno(na) de estrellas.

starry-eyed [-'aɪd] *adj* [optimism etc] iluso(sa);
[lovers] encandilado(da).

Stars and Stripes *n*: the Stars and Stripes la
bandera de las barras y estrellas.

star sign *n* signo *m* del horóscopo.

star-studded *adj*: star-studded cast reparto *m* estelar.

start [stɑːt] ◇ *n* - **1.** [beginning] principio *m*, comienzo *m*; **at the start of the year** a principios de año; **to make a good/bad start** tener un buen/mal comienzo; **for a start** para
empezar - **2.** [jerk, jump] sobresalto *m*, susto *m*
- **3.** [starting place] salida *f* - **4.** [time advantage]
ventaja *f*; **to have a start on sb** llevar ventaja
a alguien. ◇ *vt* - **1.** [begin] empezar, comenzar; **to start doing** OR **to do sthg** empezar a
hacer algo - **2.** [turn on - machine, engine] poner
en marcha; [- vehicle] arrancar - **3.** [set up] formar, crear; [business] montar. ◇ *vi* - **1.** [be-
gin] empezar, comenzar; **to start with sb/
sthg** empezar por alguien/algo; **don't start!**
inf ¡no empieces! - **2.** [machine, tape] ponerse
en marcha; [vehicle] arrancar - **3.** [begin journey]
salir, ponerse en camino - **4.** [jerk, jump] asustarse, sobresaltarse.

◆ **start off** ◇ *vt sep* [discussion, rumour] desencadenar; [meeting] empezar; [person]: **this
should be enough to start you off** con esto
tienes suficiente para empezar. ◇ *vi* - **1.** [be-
gin] empezar, comenzar; **to start off by doing
sthg** empezar por hacer algo; **I started off as
a clerk** empecé de oficinista - **2.** [leave on jour-
ney] salir, ponerse en camino.

◆ **start on** *vt insep* empezar con.

◆ **start out** *vi* - **1.** [originally be] empezar, comenzar; **she started out as a journalist** em-
pezó como periodista - **2.** [leave on journey] sa-
lir/ponerse en camino.

◆ **start up** ◇ *vt sep* - **1.** [business] montar;
[shop] establecer, poner; [association] crear, formar - **2.** [car, engine] arrancar, poner en marcha. ◇ *vi* - **1.** [begin] empezar - **2.** [car, engine]
arrancar, ponerse en marcha.

starter ['stɑːtə*r*] *n* - **1.** UK [of meal] primer plato *m*, entrada *f* - **2.** AUT (motor *m* de) arranque *m* - **3.** [person participating in race] participante *mf*, competidor *m*, -ra *f*.

starter motor *n* (motor *m* de) arranque *m*.

starter pack *n* paquete *m* de iniciación.

starting block ['stɑːtɪŋ-] *n* puesto *m* de salida,
bloque *m* de salida *Amér*.

starting point ['stɑːtɪŋ-] *n lit* & *fig* punto *m* de
partida.

startle ['stɑːtl] *vt* asustar.

startling ['stɑːtlɪŋ] *adj* sorprendente, asombro-
so(sa).

start-up *n* nueva empresa *f*.

starvation [stɑːˈveɪʃn] *n* hambre *f*, inanición *f*.

starve [stɑːv] ◇ *vt* - **1.** [deprive of food] privar
de comida, no dar de comer a - **2.** [deprive]:
to starve sb of sthg privar a alguien de algo. ◇ *vi* - **1.** [have no food] pasar hambre; **to
starve to death** morirse de hambre - **2.** *inf* [be
hungry]: **I'm starving!** ¡me muero de hambre!

state [steɪt] ◇ *n* estado *m*; **not to be in a fit
state to do sthg** no estar en condiciones de
hacer algo; **to be in a state** [nervous] tener los
nervios de punta; [untidy] estar hecho un asco.
◇ *comp* [ceremony] oficial, de Estado; [con-
trol, ownership] estatal. ◇ *vt* - **1.** [gen] indicar; [reason, policy] plantear; [case] exponer
- **2.** [time, date, amount] fijar.

◆ **State** *n*: the State el Estado.

◆ **States** *npl*: the States los Estados Unidos.

state-controlled *adj* controlado(da) por el
Estado.

State Department *n US* ≃ Ministerio *m* de
Asuntos Exteriores.

state education *n UK* enseñanza *f* pública.

stately ['steɪtlɪ] (*comp* **-ier**, *superl* **-iest**) *adj*
majestuoso(sa).

stately home *n UK* casa *f* solariega.

statement ['steɪtmənt] *n* - **1.** [gen] declaración *f* - **2.** [from bank] extracto *m* OR estado *m*
de cuenta.

state of affairs *n* situación *f*.

state of emergency *n* estado *m* de emergencia.

state of mind (*pl* **states of mind**) *n* estado *m* de ánimo.

state-of-the-art *adj* vanguardista.

state-owned [-'ɔʊnd] *adj* estatal.

state school *n* escuela *f* pública.

State schools

En el Reino Unido hay dos tipos principales de centros públicos de educación secundaria: las "comprehensive schools" y las "grammar schools". Las primeras fueron introducidas en 1965 por los laboristas, con el fin de democratizar la enseñanza y garantizar la igualdad de oportunidades para todos los estudiantes, cualesquiera que fueran los ingresos de sus padres y su origen social. Hoy en día, el 90% de los alumnos de secundaria asisten a ellas. La calidad de la enseñanza varía enormemente según los centros y es bastante normal que ciertas familias se muden a una zona que tenga una buena escuela. Las "grammar schools", a las que asisten menos del 5% de los estudiantes, imparten una educación más tradicional y se centran en preparar a los alumnos que tienen previsto continuar sus estudios. Para acceder ellas, los alumnos tienen que hacer un examen a los 11 años.

state secret *n* secreto *m* de estado.

stateside ['steɪtsaɪd] *US* ⟨⟩ *adj* estadounidense. ⟨⟩ *adv* [travel] hacia Estados Unidos; [live] en Estados Unidos.

statesman ['steɪtsmən] (*pl* **-men** [-mən]) *n* estadista *m*, hombre *m* de Estado.

statesmanship ['steɪtsmənʃɪp] *n* arte *m* OR habilidad *f* de gobernar.

static ['stætɪk] ⟨⟩ *adj* estático(ca). ⟨⟩ *n* (U) interferencias *fpl*, parásitos *mpl*.

static electricity *n* electricidad *f* estática.

station ['steɪʃn] ⟨⟩ *n* - **1.** [gen] estación *f* - **2.** RADIO emisora *f* - **3.** [centre of activity] centro *m*, puesto *m* - **4.** *fml* [rank] rango *m*. ⟨⟩ *vt* - **1.** [position] situar, colocar - **2.** MIL estacionar, apostar.

stationary ['steɪʃnərɪ] *adj* inmóvil.

stationer's (shop) ['steɪʃnəz] *n* papelería *f*.

stationery ['steɪʃnərɪ] *n* (U) objetos *mpl* de escritorio.

station house *n* US comisaría *f* (de policía).

stationmaster ['steɪʃn,mɑːstər] *n* jefe *m* de estación.

station wagon *n* US ranchera *f*.

statistic [stə'tɪstɪk] *n* estadística *f*.
 statistics *n* (U) estadística *f*.

statistical [stə'tɪstɪkl] *adj* estadístico(ca).

statistician [,stætɪ'stɪʃn] *n* estadístico *m*, -ca *f*.

statue ['stætʃuː] *n* estatua *f*.

statuesque [,stætʃu'esk] *adj* escultural.

statuette [,stætʃu'et] *n* figurilla *f*.

stature ['stætʃər] *n* - **1.** [height] estatura *f*, talla *f* - **2.** [importance] talla *f*, categoría *f*.

status ['steɪtəs] *n* (U) - **1.** [position, condition] condición *f*, estado *m* - **2.** [prestige] prestigio *m*, estatus *m inv*.

status bar *n* COMPUT barra *f* de estado.

status quo [-'kwəʊ] *n*: **the status quo** el statu quo.

status symbol *n* símbolo *m* de posición social.

statute ['stætjuːt] *n* estatuto *m*.

statute book *n*: **the statute book** el código de leyes.

statutory ['stætjʊtrɪ] *adj* reglamentario(ria).

staunch [stɔːntʃ] ⟨⟩ *adj* fiel, leal. ⟨⟩ *vt* restañar.

stave [steɪv] *n* MUS pentagrama *m*.
 stave off *vt sep* (*pt & pp* **-d** OR **stove**) [disaster, defeat] retrasar; [hunger, illness] aplacar temporalmente.

stay [steɪ] ⟨⟩ *vi* - **1.** [not move away] quedarse, permanecer; **to stay put** permanecer en el mismo sitio; **stay put!** ¡no te muevas! - **2.** [as visitor] alojarse, estar - **3.** [continue, remain] permanecer; **to stay away from sb/somewhere** no acercarse a alguien/algún sitio; **to stay out of sthg** mantenerse al margen de algo - **4.** *Scotland* [reside] vivir. ⟨⟩ *n* estancia *f*, permanencia *f*.
 stay in *vi* quedarse en casa.
 stay on *vi* permanecer, quedarse.
 stay out *vi* - **1.** [from home] quedarse fuera, no volver a casa - **2.** [strikers] permanecer en huelga.
 stay up *vi* quedarse levantado(da).

staying power ['steɪŋ-] *n* resistencia *f*.

St Bernard [UK -'bɜːnəd, US -bər'nɑːrd] *n* (perro *m*) San Bernardo *m*.

STD *n* - **1.** (*abbr of* **subscriber trunk dialling**), *sistema de llamadas telefónicas directas de larga distancia* - **2.** (*abbr of* **sexually transmitted disease**) ETS *f*.

stead [sted] *n*: **to stand sb in good stead** servir de mucho a alguien.

steadfast ['stedfɑːst] *adj* [supporter] fiel, leal; [gaze] fijo(ja), imperturbable; [resolve] inquebrantable.

steadily ['stedɪlɪ] *adv* - **1.** [gradually] constantemente - **2.** [regularly - breathe, move] normalmente - **3.** [calmly - look] fijamente; [- speak] con tranquilidad.

steady ['stedɪ] ⟨⟩ *adj* (*comp* **-ier**, *superl* **-iest**) - **1.** [gradual] gradual - **2.** [regular, constant] constante, continuo(nua) **- 3.** [not shaking] firme **- 4.** [voice] sereno(na); [stare] fijo(ja) **- 5.** [relationship] estable, serio(ria); [boyfriend, girlfriend] formal; **a steady job** un trabajo fijo **- 6.** [reliable, sensible] sensato(ta). <> *vt* (*pt & pp* **-ied**) **- 1.** [stop from shaking] mantener firme; **he steadied his hand** dejó de temblar; **to steady o.s.** dejar de temblar **- 2.** [nerves, voice] dominar, controlar; **to steady o.s.** controlar los nervios.

steak [steɪk] *n* **- 1.** (*U*) [meat] bistec *m*, filete *m*, bife *m Andes & R Dom* **- 2.** [piece of meat, fish] filete *m*.

steakhouse (['steɪkhaʊs], *pl* [-haʊzɪz]) *n* restaurante *m* especializado en bistecs.

steal [sti:l] <> *vt* (*pt* **stole**, *pp* **stolen**) [gen] robar; [idea] apropiarse de; **to steal sthg from sb** robar algo a alguien; **to steal a glance at** echar una mirada furtiva a. <> *vi* (*pt* **stole**, *pp* **stolen**) **- 1.** [take illegally] robar, hurtar **- 2.** [move secretly] moverse sigilosamente; **he stole into the bedroom** entró sigilosamente en el dormitorio.

stealing ['sti:lɪŋ] *n* (*U*) robo *m*.

stealth [stelθ] *n* cautela *f*, sigilo *m*.

stealthy ['stelθɪ] (*comp* **-ier**, *superl* **-iest**) *adj* cauteloso(sa), sigiloso(sa).

steam [sti:m] <> *n* (*U*) vapor *m*, vaho *m*; **to let off steam** desfogarse; **to run out of steam** quemarse, quedarse sin fuerzas. <> *vt* CULIN cocer al vapor. <> *vi* [water, food] echar vapor.

<> **steam up** <> *vt sep* **- 1.** [mist up] empañar **- 2.** *fig* [get angry]: **to get steamed up about sthg** mosquearse por algo. <> *vi* empañarse.

steamboat ['sti:mbəʊt] *n* buque *m* de vapor.

steam engine *n* máquina *f* de vapor.

steamer ['sti:mər] *n* **- 1.** [ship] buque *m* de vapor **- 2.** CULIN *tipo de colador para hacer verduras etc al vapor*.

steam iron *n* plancha *f* de vapor.

steamroller ['sti:m,rəʊlər] *n* apisonadora *f*.

steamy ['sti:mɪ] (*comp* **-ier**, *superl* **-iest**) *adj* **- 1.** [full of steam] lleno(na) de vaho **- 2.** *inf* [erotic] caliente, erótico(ca).

steel [sti:l] <> *n* acero *m*. <> *vt*: **to steel o.s. (for sthg)** armarse de valor (para algo).

steel industry *n* industria *f* del acero.

steel wool *n* estropajo *m* de acero.

steelworker ['sti:l,wɜ:kər] *n* obrero *m*, -ra *f* de la siderurgia.

steelworks ['sti:lwɜ:ks] (*pl* **steelworks**) *n* fundición *f* de acero.

steely ['sti:lɪ] (*comp* **-ier**, *superl* **-iest**) *adj* **- 1.** [steel-coloured] acerado(da) **- 2.** [strong, determined] inflexible, duro(ra).

steep [sti:p] <> *adj* **- 1.** [hill, road] empinado(da) **- 2.** [considerable - increase, fall] importante, considerable **- 3.** *inf* [expensive] muy caro(ra), abusivo(va). <> *vt* remojar.

steeped [sti:pt] *adj fig*: **steeped in sthg** empapado(da) OR sumido(da) en algo.

steeple ['sti:pl] *n* aguja *f* (*de un campanario*).

steeplechase ['sti:pltʃeɪs] *n* carrera *f* de obstáculos.

steeply ['sti:plɪ] *adv lit & fig* vertiginosamente.

steer ['stɪər] <> *n* buey *m*. <> *vt* **- 1.** [vehicle] conducir **- 2.** [person, discussion etc] dirigir. <> *vi*: **the car steers well** el coche se conduce bien; **to steer clear of sthg/sb** evitar algo/a alguien.

steering ['stɪərɪŋ] *n* (*U*) dirección *f*.

steering column *n* columna *f* de dirección.

steering committee *n* comité *m* de dirección.

steering wheel *n* volante *m*, timón *m Andes*.

stellar ['stelər] *adj* estelar.

stem [stem] <> *n* **- 1.** [of plant] tallo *m* **- 2.** [of glass] pie *m* **- 3.** GRAM raíz *f*. <> *vt* (*pt & pp* **-med**, *cont* **-ming**) [flow] contener; [blood] detener, restañar.

<> **stem from** *vt insep* derivarse de, ser el resultado de.

stem cell *n* MED célula *f* madre.

stench [stentʃ] *n* hedor *m*.

stencil ['stensl] <> *n* plantilla *f*. <> *vt* (*UK* **-led**, *cont* **-ling**, *US* **-ed**, *cont* **-ing**) estarcir.

stenographer [stə'nɒɡrəfər] *n US* taquígrafo *m*, -fa *f*.

stenography [stə'nɒɡrəfɪ] *n US* taquigrafía *f*.

step [step] <> *n* **- 1.** [gen] paso *m*; **step by step** paso a paso; **to be in/out of step** llevar/no llevar el paso; *fig* estar/no estar al tanto; **to watch one's step** mirar por donde pisa uno; *fig* andarse con cuidado **- 2.** [action] medida *f*; **to take steps to do sthg** tomar medidas para hacer algo **- 3.** [stair, rung] peldaño *m*. <> *vi* (*pt & pp* **-ped**, *cont* **-ping**) **- 1.** [move foot] dar un paso; **watch where you step!** ¡mira dónde pisas!; **he stepped off the bus** se bajó del autobús **- 2.** [tread]: **to step on sthg** pisar algo; **to step in sthg** meter el pie en algo.

<> **steps** *npl* **- 1.** escaleras *fpl* **- 2.** *UK* [stepladder] escalera *f* de tijera.

<> **step aside** *vi* apartarse, hacerse a un lado.

<> **step back** *vi* **- 1.** [move backwards] dar un paso atrás **- 2.** [detach o.s.]: **to step back and think** detenerse a pensar.

<> **step down** *vi* [leave job] renunciar.

<> **step in** *vi* intervenir.

<> **step up** *vt sep* aumentar.

stepbrother ['step,brʌðər] *n* hermanastro *m*.

stepchild ['step$\mathfrak{f}$a$\imath$ld] (*pl* **-children** [-,$\mathfrak{t}$f$\imath$ldr∂n]) *n* hijastro *m*, -tra *f*.

stepdaughter ['step,d$\mathfrak{o}$:t∂'] *n* hijastra *f*.

stepfather ['step,f$\mathfrak{a}$:$\eth$$\partial$'] *n* padrastro *m*.

stepladder ['step,læd∂'] *n* escalera *f* de tijera.

stepmother ['step,m$\Lambda$$\eth$$\partial$'] *n* madrastra *f*.

stepping-stone ['step$\imath$$\eta$-] *n* - **1.** [in river] pasa-dera *f* - **2.** *fig* [to success] trampolín *m*.

stepsister ['step,s$\imath$st∂'] *n* hermanastra *f*.

stepson ['stepsΛn] *n* hijastro *m*.

stereo ['ster$\imath$$\partial$$\upsilon$] $\diamondsuit$ *adj* estéreo (*inv*). $\diamondsuit$ *n* (*pl* **-s**) - **1.** [record player] equipo *m* estereofónico - **2.** [stereo sound] estéreo *m*.

stereotype ['ster$\imath$$\partial$ta$\imath$p] $\diamondsuit$ *n* estereotipo *m*. $\diamondsuit$ *vt* estereotipar.

sterile ['stera$\imath$l] *adj* - **1.** [germ-free] esteriliza-do(da) - **2.** [unable to produce offspring] estéril - **3.** *pej* [unimaginative] improductivo(va).

sterility [ste'r$\imath$l∂t$\imath$] *n* [gen] esterilidad *f*.

sterilization [,ster∂la$\imath$'ze$\imath$$\mathfrak{f}$n] *n* esterilización *f*.

sterilize, -ise ['ster∂la$\imath$z] *vt* esterilizar.

sterilized milk ['ster∂la$\imath$zd-] *n* leche *f* esterili-zada.

sterling ['st$\mathfrak{s}$:l$\imath$$\eta$] $\diamondsuit$ *adj* - **1.** FIN esterlina - **2.** [excellent] excelente. $\diamondsuit$ *n* (*U*) libra *f* ester-lina.

sterling silver *n* plata *f* de ley.

stern [st$\mathfrak{s}$:n] $\diamondsuit$ *adj* severo(ra). $\diamondsuit$ *n* popa *f*.

sternly ['st$\mathfrak{s}$:nl$\imath$] *adv* severamente.

steroid ['st$\imath$$\partial$r$\mathfrak{o}$$\imath$d] *n* esteroide *m*.

stethoscope ['ste$\theta$$\partial$sk$\partial$$\upsilon$p] *n* estetoscopio *m*.

stetson ['stetsn] *n* sombrero *m* de vaquero.

stevedore ['sti:v∂d$\mathfrak{o}$:'] *n* *esp* *US* estibador *m*, -ra *f*.

stew [stju:] $\diamondsuit$ *n* estofado *m*, guisado *m*. $\diamondsuit$ *vt* [meat, vegetables] estofar, guisar; [fruit] hacer una compota de. $\diamondsuit$ *vi*: **to let sb stew** *fig* hacer sufrir a alguien.

steward ['stj$\upsilon$$\partial$d] *n* [on plane] auxiliar *m* de vue-lo; [on ship, train] camarero *m*.

stewardess ['stj$\upsilon$$\partial$d$\imath$s] *n* auxiliar *f* de vuelo, azafata *f*.

stewing steak *UK* ['stju:$\imath$$\eta$-], **stewbeef** *US* ['stju:bi:f] *n* carne *f* para guisar *OR* estofar.

stick [st$\imath$k] $\diamondsuit$ *n* - **1.** [of wood, for playing sport] palo *m* - **2.** [of dynamite] cartucho *m*; [of rock] barra *f* - **3.** [walking stick] bastón *m*
▸▸ **to get the wrong end of the stick** enten-der al revés. $\diamondsuit$ *vt* (*pt* & *pp* **stuck**) - **1.** [push]: **to stick sthg in** *OR* **into sthg** [knife, pin] clavar algo en algo; [finger] meter algo en algo; **to stick sthg through sthg** atravesar algo con al-go - **2.** [make adhere]: **to stick sthg (on** *OR* **to sthg)** pegar algo (en algo) - **3.** *inf* [put] meter - **4.** *UK* *inf* [tolerate] soportar, aguantar; **to stick**

it aguantarlo, soportarlo. $\diamondsuit$ *vi* (*pt* & *pp* **stuck**) - **1.** [adhere]: **to stick (to)** pegarse (a) - **2.** [jam] atrancarse - **3.** [remain]: **to stick in one's mind** permanecer en la mente de uno.
◆ **stick around** *vi* *inf* quedarse.
◆ **stick at** *vt* *insep* perseverar en.
◆ **stick by** *vt* *insep* [person] ser fiel a; [what one has said] reafirmarse en.
◆ **stick out** $\diamondsuit$ *vt* *sep* - **1.** [make protrude] sa-car; **to stick one's tongue out** sacar la lengua - **2.** [endure] aguantar. $\diamondsuit$ *vi* - **1.** [protrude] so-bresalir - **2.** *inf* [be noticeable] llamar la aten-ción, cantar.
◆ **stick out for** *vt* *insep* *UK* insistir hasta con-seguir.
◆ **stick to** *vt* *insep* - **1.** [follow closely] seguir - **2.** [principles] ser fiel a; [promise, agreement] cumplir con; [decision] atenerse a; **if I were you, I'd stick to French** yo que tú, me limitaría al francés.
◆ **stick together** *vi* [friends etc] apoyarse mu-tuamente.
◆ **stick up** $\diamondsuit$ *vt* *sep* [attach] pegar *OR* poner en la pared. $\diamondsuit$ *vi* salir, sobresalir.
◆ **stick up for** *vt* *insep* defender.
◆ **stick with** *vt* *insep* - **1.** [not change from] se-guir con - **2.** [follow closely] seguir.

sticker ['st$\imath$k∂'] *n* [piece of paper] pegatina *f*.

sticking plaster ['st$\imath$k$\imath$$\eta$-] *n* - **1.** [individual] cu-rita® *f*, tirita® *f* - **2.** [tape] esparadrapo *m* *Amér*, tela *f* emplástica.

stick insect *n* insecto *m* palo.

stick-in-the-mud *n* *inf* carroza *mf*.

stickleback ['st$\imath$klbæk] *n* espinoso *m*.

stickler ['st$\imath$kl∂'] *n*: **stickler for sthg** maniáti-co *m*, -ca *f* de algo.

stick-on *adj* adhesivo(va).

stick shift *n* *US* palanca *f* de cambios.

stick-up *n* *inf* atraco *m* a mano armada.

sticky ['st$\imath$k$\imath$] (*comp* **-ier**, *superl* **-iest**) *adj* - **1.** [tacky] pegajoso(sa) - **2.** [adhesive] adhesi-vo(va) - **3.** *inf* [awkward] engorroso(sa) - **4.** [hu-mid] bochornoso(sa).

stiff [st$\imath$f] $\diamondsuit$ *adj* - **1.** [inflexible] rígido(da) - **2.** [door, drawer] atascado(da) - **3.** [aching] agarrotado(da); **to have a stiff neck** tener tor-tícolis; **to be stiff** tener agujetas - **4.** [formal - person, manner] estirado(da); [- smile] rígi-do(da) - **5.** [severe, intense] severo(ra) - **6.** [diffi-cult - task] duro(ra) - **7.** *inf* [strong in alcohol] car-gado(da) - **8.** [breeze] fuerte. $\diamondsuit$ *adv* *inf*: **bored/frozen stiff** muerto(ta) de aburrimien-to/frío.

stiffen ['st$\imath$fn] $\diamondsuit$ *vt* - **1.** [make inflexible - gen] poner rígido(da); [- clothes] almidonar - **2.** [make more severe, intense] reforzar, inten-sificar. $\diamondsuit$ *vi* - **1.** [become inflexible] endurecerse - **2.** [bones] entumecerse; [muscles] agarrotarse - **3.** [become more severe, intense] intensificarse, endurecerse - **4.** [wind] volverse más fuerte.

stiffener ['stɪfnəʳ] n contrafuerte m.

stiffness ['stɪfnɪs] n (U) - **1.** [inflexibility - of material, person] rigidez f - **2.** [inability to move freely] atasco m - **3.** [aching] entumecimiento m - **4.** [severeness, intensity] endurecimiento m - **5.** [difficulty] dureza f, dificultad f.

stifle ['staɪfl] ◇ vt - **1.** [prevent from breathing] ahogar, sofocar - **2.** [yawn etc] reprimir. ◇ vi ahogarse, sofocarse.

stifling ['staɪflɪŋ] adj agobiante, sofocante.

stigma ['stɪgmə] n estigma m.

stigmatize, -ise ['stɪgmətaɪz] vt estigmatizar.

stile [staɪl] n escalones mpl para pasar una valla.

stiletto heel [stɪ'letəʊ-] n UK tacón m fino OR de aguja.

still [stɪl] ◇ adv - **1.** [up to now, up to then, even now] todavía - **2.** [to emphasize remaining amount] aún; **I've still got two left** aún me quedan dos - **3.** [nevertheless, however] sin embargo, no obstante - **4.** [with comparatives] aún; **still bigger** aún más grande - **5.** [motionless] sin moverse; **sit still!** ¡siéntate y no te muevas! ◇ adj - **1.** [not moving] inmóvil - **2.** [calm, quiet] tranquilo(la), sosegado(da) - **3.** [not windy] apacible - **4.** [not fizzy] sin gas. ◇ n - **1.** PHOT vista f fija - **2.** [for making alcohol] alambique m.

stillborn ['stɪlbɔːn] adj nacido muerto (nacida muerta).

still life (pl -s) n bodegón m, naturaleza f muerta.

stillness ['stɪlnɪs] n quietud f.

stilted ['stɪltɪd] adj forzado(da).

stilts [stɪlts] npl - **1.** [for person] zancos mpl - **2.** [for building] pilotes mpl.

stimulant ['stɪmjʊlənt] n estimulante m.

stimulate ['stɪmjʊleɪt] vt [gen] estimular; [interest] excitar.

stimulating ['stɪmjʊleɪtɪŋ] adj [physically] estimulante; [mentally] interesante.

stimulation [,stɪmjʊ'leɪʃn] n estímulo m.

stimulus ['stɪmjʊləs] (pl -li [-laɪ]) n estímulo m.

sting [stɪŋ] ◇ n - **1.** [by bee] picadura f - **2.** [of bee] aguijón m - **3.** [sharp pain] escozor m; **to take the sting out of sthg** suavizar algo. ◇ vt (pt & pp stung) - **1.** [bee, nettle] picar - **2.** [cause sharp pain to] escocer - **3.** fig [criticism] herir. ◇ vi (pt & pp stung) picar.

stinging nettle ['stɪŋɪŋ-] n UK ortiga f.

stingray ['stɪŋreɪ] n pastinaca f.

stingy ['stɪndʒɪ] (comp -ier, superl -iest) adj inf tacaño(ña), roñoso(sa).

stink [stɪŋk] ◇ n peste f, hedor m. ◇ vi (pt stank OR stunk, pp stunk) - **1.** [have unpleasant smell] apestar, heder - **2.** inf fig: **it stinks** da asco.

stink-bomb n bomba f fétida.

stinking ['stɪŋkɪŋ] inf fig ◇ adj asqueroso(sa). ◇ adv: **to have a stinking cold** tener un resfriado horrible; **they're stinking rich** están podridos de dinero.

stint [stɪnt] ◇ n periodo m. ◇ vi: **to stint on sthg** escatimar algo.

stipend ['staɪpend] n estipendio m.

stipulate ['stɪpjʊleɪt] vt estipular.

stipulation [,stɪpjʊ'leɪʃn] n - **1.** [stating of conditions] estipulación f - **2.** [condition] condición f.

stir [stɜːʳ] ◇ n - **1.** [act of stirring]: **to give sthg a stir** remover algo - **2.** [public excitement] revuelo m, sensación f; **to cause a stir** causar revuelo. ◇ vt (pt & pp -red, cont -ring) - **1.** [mix] remover - **2.** [move gently] agitar, mover - **3.** [move emotionally] impresionar, conmover - **4.** [move]: **to stir o.s.** moverse. ◇ vi (pt & pp -red, cont -ring) - **1.** [move gently] moverse, agitarse - **2.** [feeling, idea] despertar el interés.

◆ **stir up** vt sep - **1.** [water, sediment] levantar - **2.** [cause] [excitement, hatred etc] provocar.

stir-fry vt freír rápidamente en aceite muy caliente y removiendo constantemente.

stirring ['stɜːrɪŋ] adj conmovedor(ra).

stirrup ['stɪrəp] n estribo m.

stitch [stɪtʃ] ◇ n - **1.** SEW puntada f - **2.** [in knitting] punto m - **3.** MED punto m (de sutura) - **4.** [stomach pain]: **to have a stitch** sentir pinchazos (en el estómago)

▸▸▸ **to be in stitches** partirse de risa. ◇ vt - **1.** SEW coser - **2.** MED suturar, poner puntos.

stitching ['stɪtʃɪŋ] n costura f.

stoat [stəʊt] n armiño m.

stock [stɒk] ◇ n - **1.** [supply] reserva f - **2.** (U) COMM [reserves] existencias fpl; [selection] surtido m; **in stock** en existencia, en almacén; **out of stock** agotado(da) - **3.** FIN [of company] capital m; **government stock** papel m del estado; **stocks and shares** acciones fpl, valores mpl - **4.** [ancestry] linaje m, estirpe f - **5.** CULIN caldo m - **6.** [livestock] ganado m, ganadería f

▸▸▸ **to take stock (of sthg)** evaluar (algo). ◇ adj estereotipado(da). ◇ vt - **1.** COMM abastecer de, tener en el almacén - **2.** [shelves] llenar; [lake] repoblar.

◆ **stock up** vi: **to stock up (with)** abastecerse (de).

stockade [stɒ'keɪd] n estacada f, empalizada f.

stockbroker ['stɒk,brəʊkəʳ] n corredor m, -ra f de bolsa.

stockbroking ['stɒk,brəʊkɪŋ] *n* corretaje *m* de bolsa.

stock company *n US* ≃ sociedad *f* anónima.

stock cube *n UK* pastilla *f* de caldo.

stock exchange *n* bolsa *f*.

stockholder ['stɒk,həʊldər] *n US* accionista *mf*.

stocking ['stɒkɪŋ] *n* [for woman] media *f*.

stock-in-trade *n* - **1.** [thing important for work] cosa o cualidad indispensable para el trabajo - **2.** *fig* [speciality] especialidad *f*.

stockist ['stɒkɪst] *n UK* distribuidor *m*, -ra *f*.

stock market *n* bolsa *f*, mercado *m* de valores.

stock phrase *n* frase *f* estereotipada.

stockpile ['stɒkpaɪl] <> *n* reservas *fpl*. <> *vt* almacenar, acumular.

stockroom ['stɒkrʊm] *n* almacén *m*.

stock-still *adv* inmóvil.

stocktaking ['stɒk,teɪkɪŋ] *n (U)* inventario *m*, balance *m*.

stocky ['stɒkɪ] (*comp* -ier, *superl* -iest) *adj* corpulento(ta), robusto(ta).

stodgy ['stɒdʒɪ] (*comp* -ier, *superl* -iest) *adj* [indigestible] indigesto(ta).

stoic ['stəʊɪk] <> *adj* estoico(ca). <> *n* estoico *m*, -ca *f*.

stoical ['stəʊɪkl] *adj* estoico(ca).

stoicism ['stəʊɪsɪzm] *n* estoicismo *m*.

stoke [stəʊk] *vt* [fire] avivar, alimentar.

stole [stəʊl] <> *pt* ⊳ **steal**. <> *n* estola *f*.

stolen ['stəʊln] *pp* ⊳ **steal**.

stolid ['stɒlɪd] *adj* impasible, imperturbable.

stomach ['stʌmək] <> *n* - **1.** [organ] estómago *m*; **to do sthg on an empty stomach** hacer algo con el estómago vacío - **2.** [abdomen] vientre *m*. <> *vt* tragar, aguantar; **I can't stomach him** no lo trago.

stomachache ['stʌməkeɪk] *n* dolor *m* de estómago.

stomach pump *n* bomba *f* estomacal.

stomach ulcer *n* úlcera *f* de estómago.

stomach upset [-'ʌpset] *n* trastorno *m* gástrico.

stomp [stɒmp] *vi*: **to stomp in/out** entrar/salir pisando fuerte.

stone [stəʊn] (*pl* -s) <> *n* - **1.** [mineral] piedra *f*; **a stone's throw from** a tiro de piedra de - **2.** [jewel] piedra *f* preciosa - **3.** [seed] hueso *m*, carozo *m R Plata*, cuesco *m*, pepa *f Col* - **4.** (*pl* stone) *UK* [unit of measurement] = 6,35 kilos. <> *vt* apedrear.

Stone Age *n*: **the Stone Age** la Edad de Piedra.

stone-cold *adj* helado(da).

stoned [stəʊnd] *adj v inf* - **1.** [drunk] mamado(da) - **2.** [affected by drugs] colocado(da), puesto(ta).

stonemason ['stəʊn,meɪsn] *n* abañil *m*.

stonewall [,stəʊn'wɔːl] *vi* andarse con evasivas.

stonewashed ['stəʊnwɒʃt] *adj* lavado(da) a la piedra.

stonework ['stəʊnwɜːk] *n* mampostería *f*.

stony ['stəʊnɪ] (*comp* -ier, *superl* -iest) *adj* - **1.** [covered with stones] pedregoso(sa) - **2.** [unfriendly] muy frío(a), glacial.

stood [stʊd] *pt* & *pp* ⊳ **stand**.

stooge [stuːdʒ] *n* - **1.** *inf* [manipulated person] monigote *mf* - **2.** [in comedy act] comparsa *f*.

stool [stuːl] *n* [seat] taburete *m*.

stoop [stuːp] <> *n* - **1.** [bent back]: **to walk with a stoop** caminar encorvado(da) - **2.** *US* [of house] umbral *m* con escaleras. <> *vi* - **1.** [bend] inclinarse, agacharse - **2.** [hunch shoulders] encorvarse - **3.** *fig* [debase oneself]: **to stoop to sthg** rebajarse a algo; **I wouldn't stoop so low as to do that** no caería tan bajo como eso.

stop [stɒp] <> *n* [gen] parada *f*; **to come to a stop** pararse; *fig* detenerse, paralizarse; **to put a stop to sthg** poner fin a algo. <> *vt* (*pt* & *pp* -ped, *cont* -ping) - **1.** [gen] parar; **to stop doing sthg** dejar de hacer algo - **2.** [prevent] impedir; **to stop sb/sthg from doing sthg** impedir que alguien/algo haga algo - **3.** [cause to stop moving] detener - **4.** [not pay - wages] suspender; [- cheque] anular, invalidar - **5.** [block - pipe] tapar, taponar. <> *vi* (*pt* & *pp* -ped, *cont* -ping) [gen] pararse; [rain, music] cesar; **to stop at nothing (to do sthg)** no reparar en nada (para hacer algo).

➡ **stop off** *vi* hacer una parada.

➡ **stop over** *vi* pasar la noche.

➡ **stop up** <> *vt sep* [block] taponar, tapar. <> *vi UK inf* quedarse levantado(da).

stopcock ['stɒpkɒk] *n* llave *f* de paso.

stopgap ['stɒpgæp] *n* [thing] recurso *m* provisional; [person] sustituto *m*, -ta *f*.

stoplight ['stɒplaɪt] *n US* [traffic light] semáforo *m*.

stopover ['stɒp,əʊvər] *n* [gen] parada *f*; [of plane] escala *f*.

stoppage ['stɒpɪdʒ] *n* - **1.** [strike] paro *m*, huelga *f* - **2.** *UK* [deduction] retención *f*.

stopper ['stɒpər] *n* tapón *m*.

stop press *n* noticias *fpl* de última hora.

stopwatch ['stɒpwɒtʃ] *n* cronómetro *m*.

storage ['stɔːrɪdʒ] *n* almacenamiento *m*.

storage heater *n UK* calentador por almacenamiento térmico.

store [stɔːr] ◇ n - **1.** esp US [shop] tienda f - **2.** [supply] provisión f, reserva f - **3.** [place of storage] almacén m
▸▸▸ **to set great store by** OR **on sthg** valorar mucho algo. ◇ vt - **1.** [gen & COMPUT] almacenar - **2.** [keep] guardar.
▸ **in store** adv: **there's a surprise in store for you** te espera una sorpresa.
▸ **store up** vt sep [provisions, goods] almacenar; [information] acumular.

store detective n guardia mf de seguridad.

storehouse (['stɔːhaus], pl [-hauzız]) n esp US [warehouse] almacén m, depósito m.

storekeeper ['stɔːˌkiːpər] n US tendero m, -ra f.

storeroom ['stɔːrum] n [gen] almacén m; [for food] despensa f.

storey UK (pl **storeys**), **story** US (pl **-ies** ['stɔːrɪ]) n planta f.

stork [stɔːk] n cigüeña f.

storm [stɔːm] ◇ n - **1.** [bad weather] tormenta f; **a storm in a teacup** una tormenta en un vaso de agua - **2.** [violent reaction] torrente m. ◇ vt MIL asaltar. ◇ vi - **1.** [go angrily]: **to storm out** salir echando pestes - **2.** [say angrily] vociferar.

storm cloud n liter nubarrón m.

stormy ['stɔːmɪ] (comp **-ier**, superl **-iest**) adj - **1.** [weather] tormentoso(sa) - **2.** [meeting] acalorado(da); [relationship] tempestuoso(sa).

story ['stɔːrɪ] (pl **-ies**) n - **1.** [tale] cuento m, relato m; **it's the (same) old story** es la misma historia de siempre; **to cut a long story short** en resumidas cuentas, para abreviar - **2.** [history] historia f - **3.** [news article] artículo m - **4.** euph [lie] cuento m - **5.** US = **storey**.

storybook ['stɔːrɪbuk] adj de novela, de cuento.

storyteller ['stɔːrɪˌtelər] n - **1.** [teller of story] narrador m, -ra f, cuentista mf - **2.** euph [liar] cuentista mf.

stout [staut] ◇ adj - **1.** [rather fat] corpulento(ta), gordo(da) - **2.** [strong, solid] fuerte, sólido(da) - **3.** [resolute] firme. ◇ n (U) cerveza f negra.

stoutness ['stautnıs] n [portliness] corpulencia f.

stove [stəuv] ◇ pt & pp ▷ **stave**. ◇ n [for heating] estufa f; [for cooking] cocina f.

stow [stəu] vt: **to stow sthg (away)** guardar algo.
▸ **stow away** vi viajar de polizón.

stowaway ['stəuəweı] n polizón m.

straddle ['strædl] vt - **1.** [person] sentarse a horcajadas sobre - **2.** [bridge, town] atravesar, cruzar.

straggle ['strægl] vi - **1.** [sprawl] desparramarse - **2.** [dawdle] rezagarse.

straggler ['stræglər] n rezagado m, -da f.

straggly ['stræglı] (comp **-ier**, superl **-iest**) adj desordenado(da).

straight [streıt] ◇ adj - **1.** [not bent] recto(ta); **sit up straight!** ¡siéntate derecho! - **2.** [hair] liso(sa) - **3.** [honest, frank] franco(ca), sincero(ra) - **4.** [tidy] arreglado(da) - **5.** [choice, swap] simple, fácil - **6.** [alcoholic drink] solo(la), sin mezclar - **7.** inf [conventional] ordinario(ria) - **8.** gay sl [heterosexual] heterosexual. ◇ adv - **1.** [in a straight line - horizontally] directamente; [- vertically] recto(ta); **straight ahead** todo recto; **it was heading straight for me** venía directo hacia mí; **I couldn't see straight** no veía bien - **2.** [directly] directamente; [immediately] inmediatamente; **come straight home** ven directamente a casa - **3.** [frankly] francamente - **4.** [tidy] en orden - **5.** [undiluted] solo(la)
▸▸▸ **let's get things straight** vamos a aclarar las cosas; **to go straight** [criminal] dejar la mala vida. ◇ n [of race track]: **the straight** la recta final.
▸ **straight off** adv en el acto.
▸ **straight out** adv sin tapujos.

straight away [ˌstreıtəˈweı] adv en seguida.

straighten ['streıtn] ◇ vt - **1.** [tidy - room] ordenar; [- hair, dress] poner bien - **2.** [make straight - horizontally] poner recto(ta); [- vertically] enderezar. ◇ vi: **to straighten (up)** enderezarse, ponerse recto(ta).
▸ **straighten out** vt sep [mess] arreglar; [problem] resolver.

straight face n: **to keep a straight face** aguantar la risa.

straightforward [ˌstreıtˈfɔːwəd] adj - **1.** [easy] sencillo(lla) - **2.** [frank - answer] directo(ta); [- person] abierto(ta), sincero(ra).

strain [streın] ◇ n - **1.** [weight] peso m; [pressure] presión f - **2.** [mental stress] tensión f nerviosa; **to be under a lot of strain** estar muy agobiado(da) - **3.** [physical injury] distensión f, torcedura f; **eye strain** vista f cansada - **4.** [variety] tipo m, variedad f. ◇ vt - **1.** [overtax - budget] estirar; [- ceiling] forzar - **2.** [use hard]: **to strain one's eyes/ears** aguzar la vista/el oído - **3.** [injure - eyes] cansar; [- muscle, back] distender, torcerse - **4.** [drain] colar. ◇ vi: **to strain to do sthg** esforzarse por hacer algo.
▸ **strains** npl liter [of music] acordes mpl, compases mpl.

strained [streınd] adj - **1.** [worried] preocupado(da) - **2.** [unfriendly] tirante, tenso(sa) - **3.** [insincere] forzado(da).

strainer ['streınər] n colador m.

strait [streıt] n estrecho m.
▸ **straits** npl: **in dire** OR **desperate straits** en un serio aprieto.

straitened ['streitnd] *adj fml*: **in straitened circumstances** en circunstancias apuradas.

straitjacket ['streit,dʒækit] *n* [garment] camisa *f* de fuerza.

straitlaced [,streit'leist] *adj pej* mojigato(ta), estrecho(cha).

Strait of Gibraltar *n*: **the Strait of Gibraltar** el estrecho de Gibraltar.

strand [strænd] *n* - **1.** [thin piece] hebra *f*; **a strand of hair** un pelo del cabello - **2.** [theme, element] cabo *m*.

stranded ['strændid] *adj* [ship] varado(da), encallado(da); [person] colgado(da).

strange [streindʒ] *adj* - **1.** [unusual] raro(ra), extraño(ña) - **2.** [unfamiliar] desconocido(da).

strangely ['streindʒli] *adv* - **1.** [in an odd manner] de manera extraña - **2.** [unexpectedly] inesperadamente - **3.** [surprisingly]: **strangely (enough)** aunque parezca extraño.

stranger ['streindʒər] *n* - **1.** [unfamiliar person] extraño *m*, -ña *f*, desconocido *m*, -da *f*; **to be a/no stranger to sthg** no estar/estar familiarizado con algo - **2.** [outsider] forastero *m*, -ra *f*.

strangle ['stræŋgl] *vt* - **1.** [kill] estrangular - **2.** *fig* [stifle] ahogar, reprimir.

stranglehold ['stræŋglhəʊld] *n* - **1.** [round neck] collar *m* de fuerza - **2.** *fig* [strong influence] dominio *m* absoluto.

strangulation [,stræŋgjʊ'leiʃn] *n* estrangulamiento *m*.

strap [stræp] *n* [of handbag, watch, case] correa *f*; [of dress, bra] tirante *m*, bretel *m*. *vt* (*pt & pp* **-ped**, *cont* **-ping**) [fasten] atar con correa.

strapless ['stræplis] *adj* sin tirantes.

strapping ['stræpiŋ] *adj* robusto(ta).

strata ['strɑːtə] *npl* ▷ **stratum**.

stratagem ['strætədʒəm] *n* estratagema *f*.

strategic [strə'tiːdʒik] *adj* estratégico(ca).

strategist ['strætidʒist] *n* estratega *mf*.

strategy ['strætidʒi] (*pl* **-ies**) *n* estrategia *f*.

stratified ['strætifaid] *adj* estratificado(da).

stratosphere ['strætə,sfiər] *n*: **the stratosphere** la estratosfera.

stratum ['strɑːtəm] (*pl* **-ta**) *n* estrato *m*.

straw [strɔː] *n* - **1.** AGRIC paja *f* - **2.** [for drinking] pajita *f*, paja *f*, pitillo *m* Col, popote *m* Méx ▸▸ **to clutch at straws** agarrarse a un clavo ardiendo; **the last straw** el colmo.

strawberry ['strɔːbəri] (*pl* **-ies**) *n* fresa *f*, frutilla *f Bol, Ecuad, Andes & R Dom*. *comp* de fresa, de frutilla *f Bol, Ecuad, Andes & R Dom*.

stray [strei] *adj* - **1.** [animal - without owner] callejero(ra); [- lost] extraviado(da) - **2.** [bullet] perdido(da). *n* [animal] animal *m* callejero. *vi* - **1.** [from path] desviarse; [from group] extraviarse - **2.** [thoughts, mind] perderse; **to stray from the point** desviarse del tema, divagar.

streak [striːk] *n* - **1.** [of hair] mechón *m*; **to have streaks in one's hair** tener un mechón en el pelo; [of lightning] rayo *m* - **2.** [in character] vena *f* - **3.** [period]: **a lucky streak** una racha de (buena) suerte. *vi* [move quickly] ir como un rayo.

streaked [striːkt] *adj*: **streaked with** [colour] veteado(da) de; [dirt] manchado(da) de.

streaky ['striːki] (*comp* **-ier**, *superl* **-iest**) *adj* rayado(da), veteado(da).

streaky bacon *n UK* bacon *m* entreverado.

stream [striːm] *n* - **1.** [small river] riachuelo *m*, quebrada *f Amér* - **2.** [of liquid, smoke] chorro *m*; [of light] raudal *m* - **3.** [current] corriente *f* - **4.** [of people, cars] torrente *m* - **5.** [continuous series] sarta *f*, serie *f* - **6.** *UK* SCH grupo *m*. *vi* - **1.** [liquid, smoke, light]: **to stream into** entrar a raudales en; **to stream out of** brotar de - **2.** [people, cars]: **to stream into** entrar atropelladamente en; **to stream out of** salir atropelladamente de - **3.** [phr]: **to have a streaming cold** tener un resfriado horrible. *vt UK* SCH agrupar de acuerdo con el rendimiento escolar.

streamer ['striːmər] *n* [for party] serpentina *f*.

streamline ['striːmlain] *vt* - **1.** [make aerodynamic] dar línea aerodinámica a - **2.** [make efficient] racionalizar.

streamlined ['striːmlaind] *adj* - **1.** [aerodynamic] aerodinámico(ca) - **2.** [efficient] racional.

street [striːt] *n* calle *f*, jirón *m Perú*; **to be right up one's street** *UK inf* ser justo lo que a uno le interesa; **to be streets ahead of sb** *UK* estar muy por delante de alguien; **to be on the streets** estar en la calle.

streetcar ['striːtkɑːr] *n US* tranvía *m*.

street-credibility *n (U) inf* imagen *f*, aceptación *f (entre la gente joven)*.

street lamp, street light *n* farola *f*.

street lighting *n* alumbrado *m* público.

street map *n* plano *m* (de la ciudad).

street market *n* mercado *m* al aire libre.

street plan *n* plano *m* (de la ciudad).

street value *n* precio *m* OR valor *m* en la calle.

streetwise ['striːtwaiz] *adj inf* espabilado(da).

strength [streŋθ] *n* - **1.** [physical or mental power] fuerza *f* - **2.** [power, influence] poder *m*; **to go from strength to strength** tener cada vez más éxito, prosperar - **3.** [quality] punto *m* fuerte - **4.** [solidity - of material structure] solidez *f* - **5.** [intensity - of feeling, smell, wind] intensidad *f*; [- of accent, wine] fuerza *f*; [- of drug] potencia *f* - **6.** [credibility, weight] peso *m*, fuerza *f*; **on the strength of** a partir de, en base a - **7.** *(U)* [in numbers - gen] número *m*; [- army] efectivos *mpl*; **in strength** en gran número; **to be at/below full strength** estar/no estar al completo - **8.** [of currency] valor *m*.

strengthen ['streŋθn] <> *vt* - **1.** [gen] fortalecer - **2.** [reinforce - argument, bridge] reforzar - **3.** [intensify] acentuar, intensificar - **4.** [make closer] estrechar. <> *vi* - **1.** [improve - sales, currency] fortalecerse - **2.** [intensify] acentuarse, intensificarse - **3.** [become closer] estrecharse.

strenuous ['strenjʊəs] *adj* agotador(ra), extenuante.

stress [stres] <> *n* - **1.** [emphasis]: **stress (on)** hincapié *m* OR énfasis *m* *inv* (en) - **2.** [tension, anxiety] estrés *m*, tensión *f* nerviosa; **to be under stress** estar estresado - **3.** [physical pressure]: **stress (on)** presión *f* (en) - **4.** LING [on word, syllable] acento *m*. <> *vt* - **1.** [emphasize] recalcar, subrayar - **2.** *inf* estresar - **3.** LING [word, syllable] acentuar. <> *vi* *inf* estresarse.

◆ **stress out** *vt inf* estresar.

stress-buster *n informal* eliminador *m* de estrés.

stressed [strest] *adj* [anxious] estresado(da).

stressful ['stresfʊl] *adj* estresante.

stress management *n* control *m* del estrés.

stretch [stretʃ] <> *adj* elástico(ca). <> *n* - **1.** [of land, water] extensión *f*; [of road, river] tramo *m*, trecho *m* - **2.** [of time] periodo *m* - **3.** [effort]: **by no stretch of the imagination** ni por asomo - **4.** [to move one's body]: **to have a stretch** estirarse. <> *vt* - **1.** [gen] estirar; **I'm going to stretch my legs** voy a estirar las piernas - **2.** [overtax - person] extender - **3.** [challenge] hacer rendir al máximo. <> *vi* - **1.** [area]: **to stretch over/from...** to extenderse por/desde... hasta - **2.** [person, animal] estirarse - **3.** [clothing] dar de sí.

◆ **at a stretch** *adv* de un tirón, sin interrupción.

◆ **stretch out** <> *vt sep* [foot, leg] estirar; [hand, arm] alargar. <> *vi* - **1.** [lie down] tumbarse - **2.** [reach out] estirarse.

stretcher ['stretʃəʳ] *n* camilla *f*.

stretch limo ['stretʃ'lɪməʊ] *n inf* limusina *f* ampliada.

stretchmarks ['stretʃmɑːks] *npl* estrías *fpl*.

stretchy ['stretʃɪ] (*comp* -**ier**, *superl* -**iest**) *adj* elástico(ca).

strew [struː] (*pt* -**ed**) (*pp* strewn [struːn] OR -**ed**) *vt*: **to be strewn on/over** estar esparcido(da) sobre/por; **to be strewn with** estar cubierto(ta) de.

stricken ['strɪkn] *adj*: **to be stricken by** OR **with** [illness] estar aquejado(da) de; [drought, famine]

estar asolado(da) por; [grief] estar afligido(da) por; [doubts, horror] estar atenazado(da) por; **she was stricken with remorse** le remordía la conciencia.

strict [strɪkt] *adj* - **1.** [gen] estricto(ta) - **2.** [precise] exacto(ta), estricto(ta) - **3.** [faithful, disciplined] riguroso(sa).

strictly ['strɪktlɪ] *adv* - **1.** [severely] severamente - **2.** [absolutely - prohibited] terminantemente; [- confidential] absolutamente, totalmente - **3.** [exactly] exactamente; **strictly speaking** en el sentido estricto de la palabra - **4.** [exclusively] exclusivamente; **this is strictly between you and me** esto debe quedar exclusivamente entre tú y yo.

strictness ['strɪktnɪs] *n* [severity, rigidity] severidad *f*.

stride [straɪd] <> *n* zancada *f*; **to take sthg in one's stride** tomarse algo con calma. <> *vi* (*pt* strode, *pp* stridden ['strɪdn]): **to stride along** andar a zancadas; **he strode off down the road** marchó calle abajo dando grandes zancadas.

◆ **strides** *npl*: **to make strides** hacer progresos.

strident ['straɪdnt] *adj* - **1.** [harsh] estridente - **2.** [vociferous] exaltado(da).

strife [straɪf] *n (U) fml* conflictos *mpl*.

strike [straɪk] <> *n* - **1.** [refusal to work etc] huelga *f*; **to be (out) on strike** estar en huelga; **to go on strike** declararse en huelga - **2.** MIL ataque *m* - **3.** [find] descubrimiento *m*. <> *vt* (*pt & pp* struck) - **1.** *fml* [hit - deliberately] golpear, pegar; [- accidentally] chocar contra - **2.** [disaster, earthquake] asolar; [lightning] fulminar, alcanzar; **she was struck by lightning** le alcanzó un rayo - **3.** [thought, idea] ocurrírsele a - **4.** [give impression]: **to strike sb as sthg** parecer a alguien algo - **5.** [impress]: **to be struck by** OR **with sthg** estar impresionado(da) por OR ante algo - **6.** [deal, bargain] cerrar - **7.** [match] encender - **8.** [find] encontrar; **to strike a balance (between)** llegar a un punto medio (entre); **to strike a serious note** tener un tono de seriedad

▸▸▸ **to be struck blind/dumb** quedarse ciego(ga)/mudo(da); **to strike fear** OR **terror into sb** infundir temor en alguien; **to strike (it) lucky** tener suerte; **to strike it rich** hacerse rico(ca). <> *vi* (*pt & pp* struck) - **1.** [stop working] estar en huelga - **2.** *fml* [hit accidentally]: **to strike against** chocar contra - **3.** [hurricane, disaster] sobrevenir; [lightning] caer - **4.** *fml* [attack] atacar - **5.** [chime] dar la hora; **the clock struck six** el reloj dio las seis.

◆ **strike back** *vi* devolver el golpe.

◆ **strike down** *vt sep* fulminar; **to be struck down with sthg** estar sufriendo de algo.

◆ **strike off** *vt sep*: **to be struck off** ser inhabilitado(da).

◆ **strike out** ◇ *vt sep* tachar. ◇ *vi* [do something different] hacer algo diferente; **to strike out on one's own** establecerse uno por su cuenta.

◆ **strike up** ◇ *vt insep* - **1.** [friendship] trabar; [conversation] entablar - **2.** [tune] empezar a tocar. ◇ *vi* empezar a tocar.

strikebound ['straɪkbaʊnd] *adj* paralizado(da) por la huelga.

strikebreaker ['straɪk,breɪkər] *n* esquirol *mf*.

strike pay *n* (*U*) subsidio *m* de huelga.

striker ['straɪkər] *n* - **1.** [person on strike] huelguista *mf* - **2.** FTBL delantero *m*, -ra *f*.

striking ['straɪkɪŋ] *adj* - **1.** [noticeable, unusual] chocante, sorprendente - **2.** [attractive] llamativo(va), atractivo(va).

striking distance *n*: **to be within striking distance (of)** estar a corta distancia (de).

string [strɪŋ] *n* - **1.** [thin rope] cuerda *f*, piolín *m* *Amér*; **a (piece of) string** un cordón; **(with) no strings attached** sin ninguna condición OR ningún compromiso; **to pull strings** utilizar uno sus influencias - **2.** [of beads, pearls] sarta *f* - **3.** [series] serie *f*, sucesión *f* - **4.** [of musical instrument] cuerda *f*.

◆ **strings** *npl* MUS: **the strings** los instrumentos de cuerda.

◆ **string along** *vt sep* (*pt & pp* **strung**) *inf* [deceive] dar falsas esperanzas a.

◆ **string out** *vt insep*: **to be strung out** alinearse.

◆ **string together** *vt sep* [words] encadenar.

string bean *n* judía *f* verde, chaucha *f* *R Plata*, vainita *f* *Ven*, poroto *m* verde *Chile*, habichuela *f* *Col*.

stringed instrument ['strɪŋd-] *n* instrumento *m* de cuerda.

stringent ['strɪndʒənt] *adj* estricto(ta), severo(ra).

string quartet *n* cuarteto *m* de cuerda.

strip [strɪp] ◇ *n* - **1.** [narrow piece] tira *f*; **to tear a strip off sb, to tear sb off a strip** UK echarle una bronca a alguien - **2.** [narrow area] franja *f* - **3.** UK SPORT camiseta *f*, colores *mpl*. ◇ *vt* (*pt & pp* **-ped**, *cont* **-ping**) - **1.** [undress] desnudar - **2.** [paint, wallpaper] quitar - **3.** [take away from]: **to strip sb of sthg** despojar a alguien de algo. ◇ *vi* (*pt & pp* **-ped**, *cont* **-ping**) - **1.** [undress] desnudarse - **2.** [do a striptease] hacer un striptease.

◆ **strip off** ◇ *vt sep* quitarse. ◇ *vi* desnudarse.

strip cartoon *n* UK historieta *f*, tira *f* cómica.

stripe [straɪp] *n* - **1.** [band of colour] raya *f*, franja *f* - **2.** [sign of rank] galón *m*.

striped [straɪpt] *adj* a rayas.

strip lighting *n* alumbrado *m* fluorescente.

stripper ['strɪpər] *n* - **1.** [performer of striptease] artista *mf* de striptease - **2.** [for paint] disolvente *m*.

strip-search *vt* registrar a alguien haciéndole desnudarse.

striptease ['strɪptiːz] *n* striptease *m*.

stripy ['straɪpɪ] (*comp* **-ier**, *superl* **-iest**) *adj* a rayas, de rayas.

strive [straɪv] (*pt* **strove**, *pp* **striven** ['strɪvn]) *vi fml*: **to strive for sthg** luchar por algo; **to strive to do sthg** esforzarse por hacer algo.

strobe (light) ['strəʊb-] *n* luz *f* de discoteca, luz estroboscópica.

strode [strəʊd] *pt* ▷ **stride**.

stroke [strəʊk] ◇ *n* - **1.** MED apoplejía *f*, derrame *m* cerebral - **2.** [of pen] trazo *m*; [of brush] pincelada *f* - **3.** [in swimming] brazada *f*; [in rowing] palada *f* - **4.** [style of swimming] estilo *m* - **5.** [in tennis, golf etc] golpe *m* - **6.** [of clock] campanada *f* - **7.** UK TYPO [oblique] barra *f* - **8.** [piece]: **a stroke of genius** una genialidad; **a stroke of luck** un golpe de suerte; **not to do a stroke of work** no dar (ni) golpe; **at a stroke** de una vez, de golpe. ◇ *vt* acariciar.

stroll [strəʊl] ◇ *n* paseo *m*; **to go for a stroll** dar un paseo. ◇ *vi* pasear.

stroller ['strəʊlər] *n* US [for baby] sillita *f* (de niño).

strong [strɒŋ] *adj* - **1.** [gen] fuerte; **to be still going strong** [person] conservarse bien; [group] seguir en la brecha; [object] estar todavía en forma - **2.** [material, structure] sólido(da), resistente - **3.** [feeling, belief] profundo(da); [opposition, denial] firme; [support] acérrimo(ma); [accent] marcado(da) - **4.** [discipline, policy] estricto(ta) - **5.** [argument] convincente - **6.** [in numbers]: **the crowd was 2,000 strong** la multitud constaba de 2.000 personas - **7.** [good, gifted]: **I've never been strong at sums** las sumas nunca han sido mi fuerte; **one's strong point** el punto fuerte de uno - **8.** [concentrated] concentrado(da).

strongarm ['strɒŋɑːm] *adj*: **to use strongarm tactics** recurrir a la mano dura.

strongbox ['strɒŋbɒks] *n* caja *f* fuerte.

stronghold ['strɒŋhəʊld] *n fig* [bastion] bastión *m*, baluarte *m*.

strong language *n* (*U*) *euph* lenguaje *m* fuerte.

strongly ['strɒŋlɪ] *adv* - **1.** [sturdily] fuertemente - **2.** [in degree] intensamente - **3.** [fervently]: **to support/oppose sthg strongly** apoyar/oponerse a algo totalmente; **I feel very strongly about that** eso me preocupa muchísimo.

strong man *n* forzudo *m*, hércules *m inv*.

strong-minded [-'maɪndɪd] *adj* firme, decidido(da).

strong room *n* cámara *f* acorazada.

strong-willed [-'wɪld] *adj* tozudo(da).

stroppy ['strɒpɪ] (*comp* -ier, *superl* -iest) *adj* UK *inf* con mala uva; **to get stroppy** cabrearse.

strove [strəʊv] *pt* ⊳ **strive**.

struck [strʌk] *pt* & *pp* ⊳ **strike**.

structural ['strʌktʃərəl] *adj* estructural.

structurally ['strʌktʃərəlɪ] *adv* estructuralmente; **the house is structurally sound** la estructura de la casa está bien.

structure ['strʌktʃər] ⬦ *n* - **1.** [arrangement] estructura *f* - **2.** [building] construcción *f*. ⬦ *vt* estructurar.

struggle ['strʌgl] ⬦ *n* - **1.** [great effort]: **struggle (for sthg/to do sthg)** lucha *f* (por algo/por hacer algo) - **2.** [fight, tussle] forcejeo *m* - **3.** [difficult task]: **it will be a struggle to do it** hacerlo supondrá un gran esfuerzo. ⬦ *vi* - **1.** [make great effort]: **to struggle (for sthg/to do sthg)** luchar (por algo/por hacer algo) - **2.** [to free o.s.]: **to struggle free** forcejear para soltarse - **3.** [fight]: **to struggle (with sb)** pelearse (con alguien) - **4.** [move with difficulty]: **to struggle with sthg** llevar algo con dificultad; **to struggle to one's feet** lograr levantarse a duras penas.

◆ **struggle on** *vi*: **to struggle on (with sthg)** continuar a duras penas (con algo).

struggling ['strʌglɪŋ] *adj* [likely to lose, fail] con dificultades.

strum [strʌm] (*pt* & *pp* -med, *cont* -ming) *vt* & *vi* rasguear.

strung [strʌŋ] *pt* & *pp* ⊳ **string**.

strut [strʌt] ⬦ *n* - **1.** CONSTR puntal *m* - **2.** AERON montante *m*. ⬦ *vi* (*pt* & *pp* -ted, *cont* -ting) andar pavoneándose.

strychnine ['strɪkniːn] *n* estricnina *f*.

stub [stʌb] ⬦ *n* - **1.** [of cigarette] colilla *f*; [of pencil] cabo *m* - **2.** [of ticket] resguardo *m*; [of cheque] matriz *f*. ⬦ *vt* (*pt* & *pp* -bed, *cont* -bing): **to stub one's toe on** darse con el pie en.

◆ **stub out** *vt sep* apagar.

stubble ['stʌbl] *n* - **1.** (*U*) [in field] rastrojo *m* - **2.** [on chin] barba *f* incipiente OR de tres días.

stubborn ['stʌbən] *adj* - **1.** [person] terco(ca), testarudo(da) - **2.** [stain] rebelde, difícil.

stubbornly ['stʌbənlɪ] *adv* tercamente, obstinadamente.

stubby ['stʌbɪ] (*comp* -ier, *superl* -iest) ⬦ *adj* rechoncho(cha). ⬦ *n* Australia *inf* botellín *m* de cerveza.

stucco ['stʌkəʊ] *n* estuco *m*.

stuck [stʌk] ⬦ *pt* & *pp* ⊳ **stick**. ⬦ *adj* - **1.** [jammed - lid, window] atascado(da); [- finger] pillado(da) - **2.** [unable to progress] atascado(da) - **3.** [stranded] colgado(da) - **4.** [in a meeting, at home] encerrado(da).

stuck-up *adj inf pej* engreído(da), que se lo tiene creído.

stud [stʌd] *n* - **1.** [metal decoration] tachón *m* - **2.** [earring] pendiente *m* - **3.** UK [on boot, shoe] taco *m* - **4.** [horse] semental *m*; **to be put out to stud** ser utilizado como semental.

studded ['stʌdɪd] *adj*: **studded (with)** tachonado(da) (con).

student ['stjuːdnt] ⬦ *n* - **1.** [at college, university] estudiante *mf* - **2.** [scholar] estudioso *m*, -sa *f*. ⬦ *comp* estudiantil.

students' union *n* - **1.** [organization] sindicato *m* de estudiantes - **2.** [building] *lugar donde se reúnen los estudiantes*.

stud farm *n* cuadra *f*.

studied ['stʌdɪd] *adj* [look, smile] estudiado(da); [answer] premeditado(da).

studio ['stjuːdɪəʊ] (*pl* -s) *n* estudio *m*.

studio apartment US = **studio flat**.

studio audience *n* público *m* invitado (al estudio).

studio flat UK, **studio apartment** US *n* estudio *m*.

studious ['stjuːdjəs] *adj* estudioso(sa).

studiously ['stjuːdjəslɪ] *adv* cuidadosamente.

study ['stʌdɪ] ⬦ *n* (*pl* -ies) estudio *m*. ⬦ *vt* (*pt* & *pp* -ied) - **1.** [learn] estudiar; **to study for sthg** estudiar para algo - **2.** [examine - report, sb's face] examinar, estudiar. ⬦ *vi* estudiar.

◆ **studies** *npl* estudios *mpl*.

stuff [stʌf] ⬦ *n* (*U*) *inf* - **1.** [things, belongings] cosas *fpl*; **to know one's stuff** saber uno lo que se hace; **and all that stuff** y todo eso - **2.** [substance]: **what's that stuff in your pocket?** ¿qué es eso que llevas en el bolsillo?; **this whisky is good stuff** este whisky es del bueno. ⬦ *vt* - **1.** [push, put] meter - **2.** [fill, cram]: **to stuff sthg (with)** [box, room] llenar algo (de); [pillow, doll] rellenar algo (de) - **3.** [with food]: **to stuff o.s. (with OR on)** *inf* atiborrarse OR hartarse (de) - **4.** CULIN rellenar.

stuffed [stʌft] *adj* - **1.** [filled, crammed]: **stuffed with** atestado(da) de - **2.** *inf* [person - with food] lleno(na), inflado(da) - **3.** CULIN relleno(na) - **4.** [preserved - animal] disecado(da)

▸▸▸ **get stuffed!** UK *v inf* ¡vete al cuerno!

stuffing ['stʌfɪŋ] *n* (*U*) relleno *m*.

stuffy ['stʌfɪ] (*comp* -ier, *superl* -iest) *adj* - **1.** [atmosphere] cargado(da); [room] mal ventilado(da) - **2.** [old-fashioned] retrógrado(da), carca.

stumble ['stʌmbl] *vi* - **1.** [trip] tropezar - **2.** [make mistake in speech] equivocarse; **to stumble at** OR **over sthg** trabársele la lengua con algo; **to stumble through sthg** decir algo sin parar de equivocarse.

➡ **stumble across, stumble on** *vt insep* [thing] dar con; [person] encontrarse con.

stumbling block ['stʌmblɪŋ-] *n* obstáculo *m*, escollo *m*.

stump [stʌmp] ◇ *n* [of tree] tocón *m*; [of limb] muñón *m*. ◇ *vt* - **1.** [question, problem] dejar perplejo(ja); **I'm stumped** no tengo ni idea; **he was stumped for an answer** no sabía qué contestar - **2.** *US* POL [constituency, state] recorrer en campaña electoral.

➡ **stump up** *vt insep UK inf* apoquinar.

stun [stʌn] (*pt & pp* -**ned**, *cont* -**ning**) *vt lit & fig* aturdir.

stung [stʌŋ] *pt & pp* ⊳ **sting**.

stunk [stʌŋk] *pt & pp* ⊳ **stink**.

stunning ['stʌnɪŋ] *adj* - **1.** [very beautiful] imponente - **2.** [shocking] pasmoso(sa).

stunt [stʌnt] ◇ *n* - **1.** [for publicity] truco *m* publicitario - **2.** CIN escena *f* arriesgada OR peligrosa. ◇ *vt* atrofiar.

stunted ['stʌntɪd] *adj* esmirriado(da).

stunt man *n* especialista *m*, doble *m*.

stupefy ['stjuːpɪfaɪ] (*pt & pp* -**ied**) *vt* - **1.** [tire, bore] aturdir, atontar - **2.** [surprise] dejar estupefacto(ta).

stupendous [stjuːˈpendəs] *adj inf* [wonderful] estupendo(da); [very large] enorme.

stupid ['stjuːpɪd] *adj* - **1.** [foolish] estúpido(da), baboso(sa) *Amér* - **2.** *inf* [annoying] puñetero(ra).

stupidity [stjuːˈpɪdətɪ] *n (U)* estupidez *f*.

stupidly ['stjuːpɪdlɪ] *adv* estúpidamente.

stupor ['stjuːpər] *n* estupor *m*, atontamiento *m*.

sturdy ['stɜːdɪ] (*comp* -**ier**, *superl* -**iest**) *adj* [person, shoulders] fuerte; [furniture, bridge] firme, sólido(da).

sturgeon ['stɜːdʒən] (*pl* **sturgeon**) *n* esturión *m*.

stutter ['stʌtər] ◇ *n* tartamudeo *m*. ◇ *vi* tartamudear. ◇ *vt* decir tartamudeando.

sty [staɪ] (*pl* **sties**) *n* [pigsty] pocilga *f*.

stye [staɪ] *n* orzuelo *m*.

style [staɪl] ◇ *n* - **1.** [characteristic manner] estilo *m*; **in the style of** al estilo de - **2.** *(U)* [smartness, elegance] clase *f* - **3.** [design] modelo *m*. ◇ *vt* [hair] peinar.

stylish ['staɪlɪʃ] *adj* elegante, con estilo.

stylist ['staɪlɪst] *n* [hairdresser] peluquero *m*, -ra *f*.

stylized, -ised ['staɪlaɪzd] *adj* estilizado(da).

stylus ['staɪləs] (*pl* -**es**) *n* [on record player] aguja *f*.

stymie ['staɪmɪ] *vt inf* [plan] fastidiar; [person] desconcertar.

styrofoam® ['staɪrəfəʊm] *n US* poliestireno *m*.

suave [swɑːv] *adj* [well-mannered] afable, amable; [obsequious] zalamero(ra).

sub [sʌb] *n inf* - **1.** SPORT (*abbr of* **substitute**) reserva *mf* - **2.** (*abbr of* **submarine**) submarino *m* - **3.** *UK* (*abbr of* **subscription**) subscripción *f*.

sub- [sʌb] *prefix* sub-.

subcommittee ['sʌbkəˌmɪtɪ] *n* [gen] subcomité *m*; POL subcomisión *f*.

subconscious [ˌsʌbˈkɒnʃəs] ◇ *adj* subconsciente. ◇ *n*: **the subconscious** el subconsciente.

subconsciously [ˌsʌbˈkɒnʃəslɪ] *adj* de forma subconsciente.

subcontinent [ˌsʌbˈkɒntɪnənt] *n* subcontinente *m*.

subcontract [ˌsʌbkənˈtrækt] *vt* subcontratar.

subculture ['sʌbˌkʌltʃər] *n* subcultura *f*.

subdivide [ˌsʌbdɪˈvaɪd] *vt* subdividir.

subdue [səbˈdjuː] *vt* - **1.** [enemy, nation] someter, sojuzgar - **2.** [feelings] contener, dominar - **3.** [light, colour] atenuar, suavizar.

subdued [səbˈdjuːd] *adj* - **1.** [person] apagado(da) - **2.** [emotion] ligero(ra) - **3.** [colour, light] tenue.

subeditor [ˌsʌbˈedɪtər] *n* redactor *m*, -ra *f*.

subgroup ['sʌbgruːp] *n* subgrupo *m*.

subheading ['sʌbˌhedɪŋ] *n* subtítulo *m*.

subhuman [ˌsʌbˈhjuːmən] *adj pej* infrahumano(na).

subject ◇ *adj* ['sʌbdʒekt] - **1.** [not independent] subyugado(da) - **2.** [affected]: **subject to** [taxes, changes, law] sujeto(ta) a; [illness] proclive a. ◇ *n* ['sʌbdʒekt] - **1.** [topic] tema *m*; **don't change the subject** no cambies de tema - **2.** GRAM sujeto *m* - **3.** SCH & UNIV asignatura *f* - **4.** [citizen] súbdito *m*, -ta *f*. ◇ *vt* [səbˈdʒekt] - **1.** [bring under control] someter, dominar - **2.** [force to experience]: **to subject sb to sthg** someter a alguien a algo.

➡ **subject to** *prep* dependiendo de; **subject to approval** previa aprobación.

subjection [səbˈdʒekʃn] *n* sometimiento *m*, dominación *f*.

subjective [səbˈdʒektɪv] *adj* subjetivo(va).

subjectively [səbˈdʒektɪvlɪ] *adv* de forma subjetiva.

subject matter ['sʌbdʒekt-] *n (U)* tema *m*, contenido *m*.

subjugate ['sʌbdʒʊgeɪt] *vt fml* - **1.** [conquer] subyugar, sojuzgar - **2.** [treat as less important] supeditar.

subjunctive [səb'dʒʌŋktɪv] *n* GRAM: subjunctive (mood) (modo *m*) subjuntivo *m*.

sublet [,sʌb'let] (*pt & pp* sublet, *cont* -ting) *vt* & *vi* subarrendar.

sublime [sə'blaɪm] *adj* [wonderful] sublime; from the sublime to the ridiculous de lo sublime a lo ridículo.

sublimely [sə'blaɪmlɪ] *adv* absolutamente, completamente.

subliminal [,sʌb'lɪmɪnl] *adj* subliminal.

submachine gun [,sʌbmə'ʃi:n-] *n* metralleta *f*, ametralladora *f*.

submarine [,sʌbmə'ri:n] *n* - **1.** submarino *m* - **2.** US [sandwich] bocadillo OR sandwich hecho con una barra de pan larga y estrecha.

submerge [səb'mɜ:dʒ] ◇ *vt* - **1.** [in water] sumergir - **2.** *fig* [in activity]: to submerge o.s. in sthg dedicarse de lleno a algo. ◇ *vi* sumergirse.

submission [səb'mɪʃn] *n* - **1.** [capitulation] sumisión *f* - **2.** [presentation] presentación *f*.

submissive [səb'mɪsɪv] *adj* sumiso(sa).

submit [səb'mɪt] ◇ *vt* (*pt & pp* -ted, *cont* -ting) presentar. ◇ *vi* (*pt & pp* -ted, *cont* -ting): to submit (to sb) rendirse (a alguien); to submit (to sthg) someterse (a algo).

subnormal [,sʌb'nɔ:ml] *adj* subnormal.

subordinate ◇ *adj* [sə'bɔ:dɪnət] *fml* [less important]: subordinate (to) subordinado(da) (a). ◇ *n* subordinado *m*, -da *f*. ◇ *vt* [sə'bɔ:dɪneɪt] *fml* subordinar.

subordinate clause [sə'bɔ:dɪnət-] *n* oración *f* subordinada.

subordination [sə,bɔ:dɪ'neɪʃn] *n*: subordination (of sthg to sthg) subordinación *f* (de algo a algo).

subpoena [sə'pi:nə] ◇ *n* LAW citación *f*. ◇ *vt* (*pt & pp* -ed) LAW citar.

sub-post office *n* UK estafeta *de correos semiprivada.*

subroutine ['sʌbru:,ti:n] *n* COMPUT subrutina *f*.

subscribe [səb'skraɪb] *vi* - **1.** [to magazine, newspaper]: to subscribe (to) suscribirse (a) - **2.** [to belief]: to subscribe to estar de acuerdo con.

subscriber [səb'skraɪbəʳ] *n* - **1.** [to magazine, newspaper] suscriptor *m*, -ra *f* - **2.** [to service] abonado *m*, -da *f* - **3.** [to charity] donante *mf*.

subscription [səb'skrɪpʃn] *n* [to magazine] suscripción *f*; to take out a subscription to sthg suscribirse a algo; [to service] abono *m*; [to society, club] cuota *f*.

subsection ['sʌb,sekʃn] *n* apartado *m*.

subsequent ['sʌbsɪkwənt] *adj* subsiguiente, posterior; subsequent to this con posterioridad a esto.

subsequently ['sʌbsɪkwəntlɪ] *adv* posteriormente.

subservient [səb'sɜ:vjənt] *adj* - **1.** [servile]: subservient (to sb) servil (ante alguien) - **2.** [less important]: subservient (to sthg) subordinado(da) (a algo).

subside [səb'saɪd] *vi* - **1.** [anger] apaciguarse; [pain] calmarse; [grief] pasarse; [storm, wind] amainar - **2.** [noise] apagarse - **3.** [river] bajar, descender; [building, ground] hundirse.

subsidence [səb'saɪdns, 'sʌbsɪdns] *n* CONSTR hundimiento *m*.

subsidiarity [səbsɪdɪ'ærɪtɪ] *n* subsidiariedad *f*.

subsidiary [səb'sɪdjərɪ] ◇ *adj* secundario(ria). ◇ *n* (*pl* -ies): subsidiary (company) filial *f*.

subsidize, -ise ['sʌbsɪdaɪz] *vt* subvencionar.

subsidy ['sʌbsɪdɪ] (*pl* -ies) *n* subvención *f*.

subsist [səb'sɪst] *vi*: to subsist (on sthg) subsistir (a base de algo).

subsistence [səb'sɪstəns] *n* subsistencia *f*.

subsistence farming *n* agricultura *f* de autoabastecimiento.

subsistence level *n* nivel *m* mínimo de subsistencia.

substance ['sʌbstəns] *n* - **1.** [gen] sustancia *f* - **2.** [essence] esencia *f*.

substandard [,sʌb'stændəd] *adj* deficiente.

substantial [səb'stænʃl] *adj* - **1.** [large, considerable] sustancial, considerable; [meal] abundante - **2.** [solid] sólido(da).

substantially [səb'stænʃəlɪ] *adv* - **1.** [quite a lot] sustancialmente, considerablemente - **2.** [fundamentally] esencialmente; [for the most part] en gran parte.

substantiate [səb'stænʃɪeɪt] *vt* *fml* justificar.

substitute ['sʌbstɪtju:t] ◇ *n* - **1.** [replacement]: substitute (for) sustituto *m*, -ta *f* (de); to be no substitute (for) ser un pobre remedio (de) - **2.** SPORT suplente *mf*, reserva *mf*. ◇ *vt*: to substitute sthg/sb for sustituir algo/a alguien por. ◇ *vi*: to substitute for sb/sthg sustituir a alguien/algo.

substitute teacher *n* US profesor *m*, -ra *f* suplente.

substitution [,sʌbstɪ'tju:ʃn] *n* sustitución *f*.

subterfuge ['sʌbtəfju:dʒ] *n* - **1.** [art of deception] engaño *m* - **2.** [trick] subterfugio *m*.

subterranean [,sʌbtə'reɪnjən] *adj* subterráneo(a).

subtitle ['sʌb,taɪtl] *n* subtítulo *m*.

subtle ['sʌtl] *adj* - **1.** [gen] sutil; [taste, smell] delicado(da) - **2.** [plan, behaviour] ingenioso(sa).

subtlety ['sʌtltɪ] *n* - **1.** [gen] sutileza *f*; [of taste, smell] delicadeza *f* - **2.** [of plan, behaviour] ingenio *m*.

subtly ['sʌtlɪ] *adv* - **1.** [not obviously] sútilmente - **2.** [cleverly] ingeniosamente.

subtotal ['sʌbtəʊtl] *n* subtotal *m*.

subtract [səb'trækt] *vt*: to subtract sthg (from) restar algo (de).

subtraction [səb'trækʃn] *n* resta *f*.

subtropical [ˌsʌb'trɒpɪkl] *adj* subtropical.

suburb ['sʌbɜ:b] *n* barrio *m* residencial.
⇒ suburbs *npl*: the suburbs las afueras.

suburban [sə'bɜ:bn] *adj* - **1.** [of suburbs] de los barrios residenciales - **2.** *pej* [boring] convencional, burgués(esa).

suburbia [sə'bɜ:bɪə] *n (U)* barrios *mpl* residenciales.

subversion [səb'vɜ:ʃn] *n* subversión *f*.

subversive [səb'vɜ:sɪv] ⇔ *adj* subversivo(va). ⇔ *n* subversivo *m*, -va *f*.

subvert [səb'vɜ:t] *vt* subvertir.

subway ['sʌbweɪ] *n* - **1.** *UK* [underground walkway] paso *m* subterráneo - **2.** *US* [underground railway] metro *m*, subte(rráneo) *m* R Plata.

sub-zero *adj* bajo cero; sub-zero temperatures temperaturas bajo cero.

succeed [sək'si:d] ⇔ *vt* suceder a; to succeed sb to the throne suceder a alguien en el trono. ⇔ *vi* - **1.** [gen] tener éxito - **2.** [achieve desired result]: to succeed in sthg/in doing sthg conseguir algo/hacer algo - **3.** [plan, tactic] dar (buen) resultado, salir bien - **4.** [go far in life] triunfar.

succeeding [sək'si:dɪŋ] *adj fml* siguiente.

success [sək'ses] *n* - **1.** [gen] éxito *m*; to be a success tener éxito - **2.** [in career, life] triunfo *m*.

successful [sək'sesfʊl] *adj* [gen] de éxito; [attempt] logrado(da); to be successful in sthg tener éxito en algo.

successfully [sək'sesfʊlɪ] *adv* con éxito.

succession [sək'seʃn] *n* sucesión *f*; to follow in quick OR close succession sucederse rápidamente.

successive [sək'sesɪv] *adj* sucesivo(va), consecutivo(va); he won on 3 successive years ganó durante tres años consecutivos.

successor [sək'sesər] *n* sucesor *m*, -ra *f*.

success story *n* éxito *m*.

succinct [sək'sɪŋkt] *adj* sucinto(ta).

succinctly [sək'sɪŋktlɪ] *adv* sucintamente.

succour *UK*, **succor** *US* ['sʌkər] *n liter* socorro *m*, auxilio *m*.

succulent ['sʌkjʊlənt] *adj* suculento(ta).

succumb [sə'kʌm] *vi*: to succumb (to) sucumbir (a).

such [sʌtʃ] ⇔ *adj* - **1.** [like that] semejante, tal; such stupidity tal OR semejante estupidez; there's no such thing no existe nada seme-

jante - **2.** [like this]: have you got such a thing as a tin opener? ¿tendrías acaso un abrelatas?; such words as 'duty' and 'honour' palabras (tales) como 'deber' y 'honor' - **3.** [whatever]: I've spent such money as I had he gastado el poco dinero que tenía - **4.** [so great, so serious]: there are such differences that... las diferencias son tales que...; such... that tal... que. ⇔ *adv* tan; such a lot of books tantos libros; such nice people una gente tan amable; such a good car un coche tan bueno; such a long time tanto tiempo. ⇔ *pron*: and such (like) y otros similares OR por el estilo; this is my car, such as it is este es mi coche, aunque no sea gran cosa; have some wine, such as there is sírvete vino, si es que aún queda.
⇒ as such *pron* propiamente dicho(cha).
⇒ such and such *adj*: at such and such a time a tal hora.

suchlike ['sʌtʃlaɪk] *pron* [things] cosas por el estilo; [people] gente de este tipo.

suck [sʌk] ⇔ *vt* - **1.** [by mouth] chupar - **2.** [machine] aspirar - **3.** *fig* [involve]: to be sucked into sthg verse envuelto(ta) en algo. ⇔ *vi US v inf* [be bad] [book, film]: that really sucks! ¡es una mierda!
⇒ suck up *vi inf*: to suck up (to) hacer la pelota (a).

sucker ['sʌkər] *n* - **1.** [of animal] ventosa *f* - **2.** *inf* [gullible person] primo *m*, -ma *f*, ingenuo *m*, -nua *f*; to be a sucker for punishment ser un masoquista.

suckle ['sʌkl] ⇔ *vt* amamantar. ⇔ *vi* mamar.

sucrose ['su:krəʊz] *n* sacarosa *f*.

suction ['sʌkʃn] *n* [gen] succión *f*; [by machine] aspiración *f*.

suction pump *n* bomba *f* de aspiración.

Sudan [su:'dɑ:n] *n* (el) Sudán.

Sudanese [ˌsu:də'ni:z] ⇔ *adj* sudanés(esa). ⇔ *n* sudanés *m*, -esa *f*. ⇔ *npl*: the Sudanese los sudaneses.

sudden ['sʌdn] *adj* [quick] repentino(na); [unforeseen] inesperado(da); all of a sudden de repente.

sudden death *n* SPORT muerte *f* súbita.

suddenly ['sʌdnlɪ] *adv* de repente, de pronto.

suddenness ['sʌdnnɪs] *n* [quickness] lo repentino; [unexpectedness] lo inesperado.

suds [sʌdz] *npl* espuma *f* del jabón.

sue [su:] *vt*: to sue sb (for) demandar a alguien (por).

suede [sweɪd] ⇔ *n* [for jacket, shoes] ante *m*; [for gloves] cabritilla *f*. ⇔ *comp* [jacket, shoes] de ante; [gloves] de cabritilla.

suet ['sʊɪt] *n* sebo *m*.

Suez Canal ['suːz] *n*: **the Suez Canal** el canal de Suez.

suffer ['sʌfəʳ] ◇ *vt* sufrir. ◇ *vi* - **1.** [gen] sufrir - **2.** [experience negative effects] salir perjudicado(da) - **3.** MED: **to suffer from** [illness] sufrir OR padecer de.

sufferance ['sʌfrəns] *n*: **he was staying with us on sufferance** se quedó con nosotros porque se lo toleramos.

sufferer ['sʌfrəʳ] *n* enfermo *m*, -ma *f*; **cancer sufferer** enfermo de cáncer; **hay fever sufferer** persona que padece fiebre del heno.

suffering ['sʌfrɪŋ] *n* [gen] sufrimiento *m*; [pain] dolor *m*.

suffice [sə'faɪs] *vi fml* ser suficiente, bastar.

sufficient [sə'fɪʃnt] *adj fml* suficiente, bastante.

sufficiently [sə'fɪʃntlɪ] *adv fml* suficientemente, bastante.

suffix ['sʌfɪks] *n* sufijo *m*.

suffocate ['sʌfəkeɪt] ◇ *vt* asfixiar, ahogar. ◇ *vi* asfixiarse, ahogarse.

suffocation [,sʌfə'keɪʃn] *n* asfixia *f*, ahogo *m*.

suffrage ['sʌfrɪdʒ] *n* sufragio *m*.

suffuse [sə'fjuːz] *vt*: **suffused with** bañado de.

sugar ['ʃʊgəʳ] ◇ *n* azúcar *m* o *f*. ◇ *vt* echar azúcar a.

sugar beet *n* remolacha *f* (azucarera).

sugar bowl *n* azucarero *m*.

sugarcane ['ʃʊgəkeɪn] *n (U)* caña *f* de azúcar.

sugar-coated [-'kəʊtɪd] *adj* [sweets] cubierto(ta) de azúcar; [almonds] garrapiñado(da).

sugared ['ʃʊgəd] *adj* azucarado(da), con azúcar.

sugar lump *n* terrón *m* de azúcar.

sugar refinery *n* refinería *f* de azúcar.

sugary ['ʃʊgərɪ] *adj* - **1.** [high in sugar] azucarado(da), dulce - **2.** *pej* [sentimental] sensiblero(ra).

suggest [sə'dʒest] *vt* - **1.** [propose] sugerir, proponer; **to suggest doing sthg** sugerir hacer algo; **to suggest that sb do sthg** sugerir que alguien haga algo - **2.** [imply] insinuar; **his work suggests a lack of care** su trabajo hace pensar que no se preocupa lo suficiente.

suggestion [sə'dʒestʃn] *n* - **1.** [proposal] sugerencia *f* - **2.** [implication] insinuación *f*; **there was no suggestion of murder** no había nada que indicara que fue un asesinato - **3.** PSYCHOL sugestión *f*.

suggestive [sə'dʒestɪv] *adj* - **1.** [implying sexual connotation] provocativo(va), insinuante - **2.** [implying a certain conclusion]: **suggestive (of)** indicativo(va) (de) - **3.** [reminiscent]: **suggestive of** evocador(ra) (de).

suicidal [suɪ'saɪdl] *adj lit & fig* suicida.

suicide ['suːɪsaɪd] *n lit & fig* suicidio *m*; **to commit suicide** suicidarse.

suicide attempt *n* intento *m* de suicidio.

suit [suːt] ◇ *n* - **1.** [clothes - for men] traje *m*, tenida *f Chile*; [- for women] traje de chaqueta - **2.** [in cards] palo *m* - **3.** LAW pleito *m* ▸▸ **to follow suit** *fig* seguir el ejemplo, hacer lo mismo. ◇ *vt* - **1.** [look attractive on] favorecer, sentar bien a, embonar *Andes, Cuba & Méx*; **it suits you** te favorece, te sienta bien - **2.** [be convenient or agreeable to] convenir, venir bien a; **that suits me fine** por mí, estupendo; **suit yourself!** ¡como quieras! - **3.** [be appropriate to] ser adecuado(da) para; **that job suits you perfectly** ese trabajo te va de perlas.

suitability [,suːtə'bɪlətɪ] *n* [aptness] idoneidad *f*; [convenience] conveniencia *f*.

suitable ['suːtəbl] *adj* adecuado(da); **the most suitable person** la persona más indicada; **to be suitable for sthg** ser adecuado(da) para algo.

suitably ['suːtəblɪ] *adv* adecuadamente; **I was suitably impressed** como era de esperar, estaba impresionado.

suitcase ['suːtkeɪs] *n* maleta *f*, petaca *f Méx*, valija *f R Plata*.

suite [swiːt] *n* - **1.** [of rooms] suite *f* - **2.** [of furniture] juego *m*; **dining-room suite** comedor *m*.

suited ['suːtɪd] *adj*: **suited to/for** adecuado(da) para; **the couple are ideally suited** forman una pareja perfecta.

suitor ['suːtəʳ] *n dated* pretendiente *m*.

sulfate US = **sulphate**.

sulfur US = **sulphur**.

sulfuric acid US = **sulphuric acid**.

sulk [sʌlk] ◇ *n*: **he went into a sulk** le entró un arrebato de mal humor. ◇ *vi* estar de mal humor, enfurruñarse.

sulky ['sʌlkɪ] (*comp* **-ier**, *superl* **-iest**) *adj* malhumorado(da).

sullen ['sʌlən] *adj* hosco(ca), antipático(ca).

sulphate UK, **sulfate** US ['sʌlfeɪt] *n* sulfato *m*.

sulphur UK, **sulfur** US ['sʌlfəʳ] *n* azufre *m*.

sulphuric acid UK, **sulfuric acid** US [sʌl'fjʊərɪk-] *n* ácido *m* sulfúrico.

sultan ['sʌltən] *n* sultán *m*.

sultana [səl'tɑːnə] *n UK* [dried grape] pasa *f* de Esmirna.

sultry ['sʌltrɪ] (*comp* **-ier**, *superl* **-iest**) *adj* - **1.** [hot] bochornoso(sa), sofocante - **2.** [sexual] sensual.

sum [sʌm] *n* suma *f*. ◆ **sum up** *vt sep* & *vi* (*pt* & *pp* **-med**, *cont* **-ming**) [summarize] resumir.

summarily ['sʌmərəlɪ] *adv* sumariamente.

summarize, -ise ['sʌmǝraɪz] *vt* & *vi* resumir.

summary ['sʌmǝrɪ] (*pl* **-ies**) ⟨⟩ *adj fml* sumario(ria). ⟨⟩ *n* resumen *m*.

summation [sʌ'meɪʃn] *n* [sum] suma *f*; [summary] resumen *m*.

summer ['sʌmǝ'] ⟨⟩ *n* verano *m*; **in summer** en verano. ⟨⟩ *comp* de verano.

summer camp *n US* colonia *f* de verano.

summerhouse (['sʌmǝhaʊs], *pl* [-haʊzɪz]) *n* cenador *m*.

summer school *n* escuela *f* de verano.

summertime ['sʌmǝtaɪm] *n*: **(the) summertime** (el) verano.

Summer Time *n UK* hora *f* de verano.

summery ['sʌmǝrɪ] *adj* veraniego(ga), estival.

summing-up [ˌsʌmɪŋ-] (*pl* **summings-up**) *n* LAW resumen *m*.

summit ['sʌmɪt] *n* **- 1.** [mountain-top] cima *f*, cumbre *f* **- 2.** [meeting] cumbre *f*.

summon ['sʌmǝn] *vt* [person] llamar; [meeting] convocar.

➤ **summon up** *vt sep* [courage] armarse de; **to summon up the courage to do sthg** armarse de valor para hacer algo; **to summon up the strength to do sthg** reunir fuerzas para hacer algo.

summons ['sʌmǝnz] ⟨⟩ *n* (*pl* **summonses**) LAW citación *f*. ⟨⟩ *vt* LAW citar.

sumo (wrestling) ['suːmǝʊ-] *n* sumo *m*.

sump [sʌmp] *n* cárter *m*.

sumptuous ['sʌmptʃʊǝs] *adj* suntuoso(sa).

sum total *n* suma *f* total.

sun [sʌn] ⟨⟩ *n* sol *m*; **in the sun** al sol; **everything under the sun** todo lo habido y por haber. ⟨⟩ *vt* (*pt* & *pp* **-ned**, *cont* **-ning**): **to sun o.s.** tomar el sol.

Sun. (*abbr of* Sunday) dom.

sunbathe ['sʌnbeɪð] *vi* tomar el sol.

sunbather ['sʌnbeɪðǝ'] *n* persona *f* que toma el sol.

sunbeam ['sʌnbiːm] *n* rayo *m* de sol.

sunbed ['sʌnbed] *n* camilla *f* de rayos ultravioletas.

sunburn ['sʌnbɜːn] *n (U)* quemadura *f* de sol.

sunburned ['sʌnbɜːnd], **sunburnt** ['sʌnbɜːnt] *adj* quemado(da) por el sol.

sundae ['sʌndeɪ] *n helado con fruta y nueces.*

Sunday ['sʌndɪ] *n* domingo *m*; **Sunday lunch** *comida del domingo que generalmente consiste en carne asada, patatas asadas etc*; *see also* **Saturday**.

Sunday paper *n UK* (periódico *m*) dominical *m*.

Sunday school *n* catequesis *f inv*.

sundial ['sʌndaɪǝl] *n* reloj *m* de sol.

sundown ['sʌndaʊn] *n* anochecer *m*.

sundries ['sʌndrɪz] *npl fml* [gen] artículos *mpl* diversos; FIN gastos *mpl* diversos.

sundry ['sʌndrɪ] *adj fml* diversos(sas); **all and sundry** todos sin excepción.

sunflower ['sʌnˌflaʊǝ'] *n* girasol *m*.

sung [sʌŋ] *pp* ⟩ **sing**.

sunglasses ['sʌnˌɡlɑːsɪz] *npl* gafas *fpl* de sol.

sunhat ['sʌnhæt] *n* pamela *f*.

sunk [sʌŋk] *pp* ⟩ **sink**.

sunken ['sʌŋkǝn] *adj* hundido(da).

sunlamp ['sʌnlæmp] *n* lámpara *f* de rayos ultravioletas.

sunlight ['sʌnlaɪt] *n* luz *f* del sol; **in direct sunlight** a la luz directa del sol.

Sunni ['sʊnɪ] (*pl* **-s**) *n* [doctrine] sunna *f*.

sunny ['sʌnɪ] (*comp* **-ier**, *superl* **-iest**) *adj* **- 1.** [day] de sol; [room] soleado(da) **- 2.** [cheerful] alegre

▸▸ **sunny side up** *US* [egg] frito.

sunrise ['sʌnraɪz] *n* **- 1.** *(U)* [time of day] amanecer *m* **- 2.** [event] salida *f* del sol.

sunroof ['sʌnruːf] *n* [on car] techo *m* corredizo; [on building] azotea *f*.

sunset ['sʌnset] *n* **- 1.** *(U)* [time of day] anochecer *m* **- 2.** [event] puesta *f* del sol.

sunshade ['sʌnʃeɪd] *n* sombrilla *f*.

sunshine ['sʌnʃaɪn] *n* (luz *f* del) sol *m*.

sunspot ['sʌnspɒt] *n* ASTRON mancha *f* solar.

sunstroke ['sʌnstrǝʊk] *n (U)* insolación *f*; **to get sunstroke** coger una insolación.

suntan ['sʌntæn] ⟨⟩ *n* bronceado *m*; **to have a suntan** estar bronceado(da); **to get a suntan** broncearse. ⟨⟩ *comp* [lotion, cream] bronceador(ra).

suntanned ['sʌntænd] *adj* bronceado(da).

suntrap ['sʌntræp] *n* lugar *m* muy soleado.

sunup ['sʌnʌp] *n (U) US inf* salida *f* del sol.

super ['suːpǝ'] ⟨⟩ *adj* **- 1.** *inf* [wonderful] estupendo(da), fenomenal **- 2.** [better than normal - size etc] superior. ⟨⟩ *n US inf* [of apartment building] portero *m*, -ra *f*.

superabundance [ˌsuːpǝrǝ'bʌndǝns] *n* superabundancia *f*.

superannuation ['suːpǝˌrænjʊ'eɪʃn] *n (U)* jubilación *f*, pensión *f*.

superb [suː'pɜːb] *adj* excelente, magnífico(ca).

superbly [suː'pɜːblɪ] *adv* de manera excelente.

Super Bowl *n US*: **the Super Bowl** *la final del campeonato estadounidense de fútbol americano*.

supercilious [ˌsuːpǝ'sɪlɪǝs] *adj* altanero(ra).

superficial [ˌsuːpǝ'fɪʃl] *adj* superficial.

superfluous [suː'pɜːflʊǝs] *adj* superfluo(flua).

superglue ['suːpǝɡluː] *n* cola *f* de contacto.

superhuman [ˌsuːpəˈhjuːmən] *adj* sobrehumano(na).

superimpose [ˌsuːpərɪmˈpəʊz] *vt*: **to superimpose sthg on** superponer OR sobreponer algo a.

superintend [ˌsuːpərɪnˈtend] *vt* supervisar.

superintendent [ˌsuːpərɪnˈtendənt] *n* - **1.** UK [of police] ≃ subjefe *m* (de policía) - **2.** *fml* [of department] supervisor *m*, -ra *f* - **3.** US *inf* [of apartment building] portero *m*, -ra *f*.

superior [suːˈpɪərɪər] ⬦ *adj* - **1.** [gen]: **superior (to)** superior (a) - **2.** *pej* [arrogant] altanero(ra), arrogante. ⬦ *n* superior *mf*.

superiority [suːˌpɪərɪˈɒrətɪ] *n* - **1.** [gen] superioridad *f* - **2.** *pej* [arrogance] altanería *f*, arrogancia *f*.

superlative [suːˈpɜːlətɪv] ⬦ *adj* [of the highest quality] supremo(ma). ⬦ *n* GRAM superlativo *m*.

supermarket [ˈsuːpəˌmɑːkɪt] *n* supermercado *m*.

supernatural [ˌsuːpəˈnætʃrəl] ⬦ *adj* sobrenatural. ⬦ *n*: **the supernatural** lo sobrenatural.

superpower [ˈsuːpəˌpaʊər] *n* superpotencia *f*.

supersede [ˌsuːpəˈsiːd] *vt* suplantar.

supersonic [ˌsuːpəˈsɒnɪk] *adj* supersónico(ca).

superstar [ˈsuːpəstɑːr] *n* superestrella *f*.

superstition [ˌsuːpəˈstɪʃn] *n* superstición *f*.

superstitious [ˌsuːpəˈstɪʃəs] *adj* supersticioso(sa).

superstore [ˈsuːpəstɔːr] *n* hipermercado *m*.

superstructure [ˈsuːpəˌstrʌktʃər] *n* superestructura *f*.

supertanker [ˈsuːpəˌtæŋkər] *n* superpetrolero *m*.

supertax [ˈsuːpətæks] *n* impuesto *m* adicional.

supervise [ˈsuːpəvaɪz] *vt* [person] vigilar; [activity] supervisar.

supervision [ˌsuːpəˈvɪʒn] *n* supervisión *f*; **under supervision** bajo supervisión.

supervisor [ˈsuːpəvaɪzər] *n* [gen] supervisor *m*, -ra *f*; [of thesis] director *m*, -ra *f*.

supper [ˈsʌpər] *n* - **1.** [evening meal] cena *f* - **2.** [before bedtime] *tentempié tomado antes de acostarse.*

supplant [səˈplɑːnt] *vt fml* suplantar.

supple [ˈsʌpl] *adj* flexible.

supplement ⬦ *n* [ˈsʌplɪmənt] suplemento *m*. ⬦ *vt* [ˈsʌplɪment] complementar.

supplementary [ˌsʌplɪˈmentərɪ] *adj* suplementario(ria).

supplier [səˈplaɪər] *n* proveedor *m*, -ra *f*, suministrador *m*, -ra *f*.

supply [səˈplaɪ] ⬦ *n* - **1.** [gen] suministro *m*; [of jokes etc] surtido *m*; **water/electricity supply** suministro de agua/electricidad; **to be in short supply** escasear - **2.** (U) ECON oferta *f*; **supply and demand** la oferta y la demanda. ⬦ *vt*: **to supply sthg (to)** suministrar OR proveer algo (a); **to supply sb (with)** proveer a alguien (de); **to supply sthg with** suministrar a algo de algo.

➡ **supplies** *npl* MIL pertrechos *mpl*; [food] provisiones *fpl*; [for office etc] material *m*.

supply teacher *n* UK profesor *m*, -ra *f* suplente.

support [səˈpɔːt] ⬦ *n* - **1.** (U) [physical, moral, emotional] apoyo *m*; **in support of** en apoyo de - **2.** (U) [financial] ayuda *f* - **3.** (U) [intellectual] respaldo *m* - **4.** TECH soporte *m*. ⬦ *vt* - **1.** [physically] sostener - **2.** [emotionally, morally, intellectually] apoyar - **3.** [financially - oneself, one's family] mantener; [- company, organization] financiar; **to support o.s.** ganarse la vida - **4.** SPORT seguir.

supporter [səˈpɔːtər] *n* - **1.** [gen] partidario *m*, -ria *f* - **2.** SPORT hincha *mf*, seguidor *m*, -ra *f*.

support group *n* grupo *m* de apoyo.

supportive [səˈpɔːtɪv] *adj* comprensivo(va); **she has been very supportive to her** la ha ayudado mucho.

suppose [səˈpəʊz] ⬦ *vt* suponer; **I don't suppose you could help me** [in polite request] ¿crees que podrías ayudarme, por favor?; **you don't suppose she's ill, do you?** [asking opinion] no estará enferma, ¿verdad? ⬦ *vi* suponer; **I suppose (so)** supongo (que sí); **I suppose not** supongo que no; **I suppose you're right** supongo que tienes razón. ⬦ *conj* si; **suppose your father found out?** ¿y si se entera tu padre?

supposed [səˈpəʊzd] *adj* - **1.** [doubtful] supuesto(ta) - **2.** [intended]: **he was supposed to be here at eight** debería haber estado aquí a las ocho - **3.** [reputed]: **it's supposed to be very good** se supone OR se dice que es muy bueno.

supposedly [səˈpəʊzɪdlɪ] *adv* según cabe suponer.

supposing [səˈpəʊzɪŋ] *conj*: **supposing your father found out?** ¿y si se entera tu padre?

supposition [ˌsʌpəˈzɪʃn] *n* suposición *f*.

suppository [səˈpɒzɪtrɪ] (*pl* **-ies**) *n* supositorio *m*.

suppress [səˈpres] *vt* - **1.** [uprising] reprimir - **2.** [information] ocultar - **3.** [emotions] contener.

suppression [səˈpreʃn] *n* - **1.** [gen] represión *f* - **2.** [of information] ocultación *f*.

supremacy [sʊˈpreməsɪ] *n* supremacía *f*.

supreme [sʊˈpriːm] *adj* supremo(ma).

Supreme Court *n*: **the Supreme Court** [in US] el Tribunal Supremo (de los Estados Unidos).

supremely [sʊ'pri:mlɪ] *adv* sumamente.

supremo [sʊ'pri:məʊ] (*pl* **-s**) *n UK inf* jefe supremo *m*, jefa suprema *f*.

Supt. *abbr of* **superintendent**.

surcharge ['sɜ:tʃɑ:dʒ] <> *n*: **surcharge (on)** recargo *m* (en). <> *vt*: **to surcharge sb (on)** cobrar un recargo a alguien (en).

sure [ʃʊə'] <> *adj* - **1.** [gen] seguro(ra); **I'm sure I know him** estoy seguro de que lo conozco; **I'm not sure why he said that** no estoy seguro de por qué dijo eso - **2.** [certain - of outcome]: **to be sure of** poder estar seguro(ra) de; **it's sure to happen** (es) seguro que pasará; **make sure (that) you do it** asegúrate de que lo haces - **3.** [confident]: **to be sure of o.s.** estar seguro(ra) de uno mismo
▸▸ **be sure to lock the door!** ¡no te olvides de cerrar la puerta! <> *adv* - **1.** *esp US inf* [yes] por supuesto, pues claro - **2.** *US* [really] realmente.
➡ **for sure** *adv* con seguridad, a ciencia cierta; **I don't know for sure** no lo sé con total seguridad.
➡ **sure enough** *adv* efectivamente.

surefire ['ʃʊəfaɪə'] *adj inf* seguro(ra).

surefooted [,ʃʊə'fʊtɪd] *adj* [steady on one's feet] de pie firme.

surely ['ʃʊəlɪ] *adv* sin duda; **surely you remember him?** ¡no me digas que no te acuerdas de él!; **surely not!** ¡no puede ser!

sure thing *excl US inf* por supuesto, claro.

surety ['ʃʊərətɪ] *n (U)* fianza *f*.

surf [sɜ:f] <> *n* espuma *f (de las olas).* <> *vt* COMPUT: **to surf the Net** navegar por Internet. <> *vi* hacer surf.

surface ['sɜ:fɪs] <> *n* - **1.** [gen] superficie *f* - **2.** *fig* [immediately visible part]: **on the surface** a primera vista; **below** OR **beneath the surface** debajo de las apariencias
▸▸ **to scratch the surface of sthg** tocar algo por encima. <> *vi* - **1.** [gen] salir a la superficie - **2.** *inf hum* [person] aparecer.

surface mail *n* correo *m* por vía terrestre/marítima.

surface-to-air *adj* tierra-aire *inv*.

surfboard ['sɜ:fbɔ:d] *n* plancha *f* OR tabla *f* de surf.

surfeit ['sɜ:fɪt] *n fml* exceso *m*.

surfer ['sɜ:fə'] *n* surfista *mf*.

surfing ['sɜ:fɪŋ] *n* surf *m*.

surge [sɜ:dʒ] <> *n* - **1.** [of waves, people] oleada *f*; [of electricity] sobrecarga *f* momentánea - **2.** [of emotion] arranque *m*, arrebato *m* - **3.** [of interest, support, sales] aumento *m* súbito. <> *vi* - **1.** [people, vehicles] avanzar en masa; [sea] encresparse; **the blood surged to his head** la sangre se le subió a la cabeza; **the angry mob surged forward** la multitud encolerizada

avanzó en tropel - **2.** [emotion]: **anger surged inside him** la rabia se apoderó de él - **3.** [prices, current] aumentar súbitamente.

surgeon ['sɜ:dʒən] *n* cirujano *m*, -na *f*.

surgery ['sɜ:dʒərɪ] (*pl* **-ies**) *n* - **1.** *(U)* MED [performing operations] cirugía *f* - **2.** *UK* MED [place] consultorio *m*; [consulting period] consulta *f* - **3.** *UK* POL *consultorio de un diputado para atender los problemas de los vecinos.*

surgical ['sɜ:dʒɪkl] *adj* - **1.** [gen] quirúrgico(ca) - **2.** [stocking, boot etc] ortopédico(ca).

surgical spirit *n UK* alcohol *m* de 90°.

surly ['sɜ:lɪ] (*comp* **-ier**, *superl* **-iest**) *adj* hosco(ca), malhumorado(da).

surmise [sɜ:'maɪz] *vt fml* conjeturar.

surmount [sɜ:'maʊnt] *vt* - **1.** [overcome] superar, vencer - **2.** *fml* [top] coronar.

surname ['sɜ:neɪm] *n* apellido *m*.

surpass [sə'pɑ:s] *vt fml* [exceed] superar, sobrepasar.

surplus ['sɜ:pləs] <> *adj* excedente, sobrante; **you are surplus to requirements** ya no requerimos tus servicios. <> *n* [gen] excedente *m*, sobrante *m*; [in budget] superávit *m*.

surprise [sə'praɪz] <> *n* sorpresa *f*; **to take sb by surprise** coger a alguien desprevenido. <> *vt* sorprender.

surprised [sə'praɪzd] *adj* [person, expression] asombrado(da); **we were really surprised** nos quedamos sorprendidos; **I'm surprised you're still here** me sorprende que todavía estés aquí; **she was surprised to find the house empty** se sorprendió al encontrar la casa vacía; **I wouldn't be surprised if she came** no me extrañaría que viniera.

surprising [sə'praɪzɪŋ] *adj* sorprendente.

surprisingly [sə'praɪzɪŋlɪ] *adv* sorprendentemente.

surreal [sə'rɪəl] *adj* surrealista.

surrealism [sə'rɪəlɪzm] *n* surrealismo *m*.

surrealist [sə'rɪəlɪst] <> *adj* surrealista. <> *n* surrealista *mf*.

surrender [sə'rendə'] <> *n* rendición *f*. <> *vt fml* [weapons, passport] rendir, entregar; [claim, right] renunciar a. <> *vi lit & fig*: **to surrender (to)** rendirse OR entregarse (a).

surreptitious [,sʌrəp'tɪʃəs] *adj* subrepticio(cia).

surrogate ['sʌrəgeɪt] <> *adj* sustitutorio(ria). <> *n* sustituto *m*, -ta *f*.

surrogate mother *n* madre *f* de alquiler.

surround [sə'raʊnd] <> *n* borde *m*. <> *vt lit & fig* rodear; **to be surrounded by** estar rodeado(da) de.

surrounding [səˈraʊndɪŋ] *adj* - **1.** [area, countryside] circundante - **2.** [controversy, debate] relacionado(da).

surroundings [səˈraʊndɪŋz] *npl* [physical] alrededores *mpl*; [social] entorno *m*.

surtax [ˈsɜːtæks] *n* recargo *m* (*en los impuestos*).

surveillance [sɜːˈveɪləns] *n* vigilancia *f*.

survey ◇ *n* [ˈsɜːveɪ] - **1.** [of public opinion, population] encuesta *f*, estudio *m* - **2.** [of land] medición *f*; [of building] inspección *f*, reconocimiento *m*. ◇ *vt* [səˈveɪ] - **1.** [contemplate] contemplar - **2.** [investigate statistically] hacer un estudio de - **3.** [examine - land] medir; [- building] inspeccionar.

surveyor [səˈveɪər] *n* [of property] perito *m* tasador de la propiedad; [of land] agrimensor *m*, -ra *f*.

survival [səˈvaɪvl] *n* - **1.** [gen] supervivencia *f* - **2.** [relic] reliquia *f*, vestigio *m*.

survive [səˈvaɪv] ◇ *vt* sobrevivir a. ◇ *vi* - **1.** [person] sobrevivir; **how are you? – surviving** ¿cómo estás? – voy tirando - **2.** [custom, project] perdurar - **3.** *inf* [cope successfully]: **how will you survive?** ¿cómo te las arreglarás?

◆ **survive on** *vt insep* ir tirando con.

survivor [səˈvaɪvər] *n* - **1.** [person who escapes death] superviviente *mf*; **there were no survivors** no hubo supervivientes - **2.** [resilient person] persona *f* que siempre sale adelante.

susceptible [səˈseptəbl] *adj* - **1.** [to pressure, flattery]: **susceptible (to)** sensible (a) - **2.** MED: **susceptible (to)** propenso(sa) (a).

suspect ◇ *adj* [ˈsʌspekt] sospechoso(sa). ◇ *n* [ˈsʌspekt] sospechoso *m*, -sa *f*. ◇ *vt* [səˈspekt] - **1.** [distrust] sospechar - **2.** [think likely] imaginar; **I suspect he's right** imagino que tiene razón - **3.** [consider guilty]: **to suspect sb (of)** considerar a alguien sospechoso(sa) (de).

◆ **suspected** *pp*: **to have a suspected heart attack** haber sufrido un posible infarto; **the suspected culprits** los presuntos culpables.

suspend [səˈspend] *vt* [gen] suspender; [payments, work] interrumpir; [schoolchild] expulsar temporalmente.

suspended animation [səˈspendɪd-] *n* muerte *f* aparente.

suspended sentence [səˈspendɪd-] *n* condena *f* condicional.

suspender belt [səˈspendər-] *n* UK liguero *m*.

suspenders [səˈspendəz] *npl* - **1.** UK [for stockings] ligas *fpl* - **2.** US [for trousers] tirantes *mpl*, tiradores *mpl* Bol & R Plata, suspensores *mpl* Andes & Arg.

suspense [səˈspens] *n* [gen] incertidumbre *f*; CIN suspense *m*; **to keep sb in suspense** mantener a alguien en vilo.

suspension [səˈspenʃn] *n* - **1.** [gen & AUT] suspensión *f* - **2.** [from job, school] expulsión *f* temporal.

suspension bridge *n* puente *m* colgante.

suspicion [səˈspɪʃn] *n* - **1.** [gen] sospecha *f*; [distrust] recelo *m*; **on suspicion of** bajo sospecha de; **to be under suspicion** estar bajo sospecha; **to arouse suspicion** levantar sospechas - **2.** [small amount] pizca *f*.

suspicious [səˈspɪʃəs] *adj* - **1.** [having suspicions] receloso(sa) - **2.** [causing suspicion] sospechoso(sa).

suspiciously [səˈspɪʃəslɪ] *adv* - **1.** [behave] sospechosamente - **2.** [ask, look at] con recelo.

suss [sʌs] ◆ **suss out** UK *inf vt sep* [person] calar; [thing] pillar el tranquillo a; **to suss out how to do sthg** descubrir cómo hacer algo.

sustain [səˈsteɪn] *vt* - **1.** [gen] sostener - **2.** [food, drink] sustentar - **3.** *fml* [injury, damage] sufrir.

sustenance [ˈsʌstɪnəns] *n* (U) *fml* sustento *m*.

suture [ˈsuːtʃər] *n* sutura *f*.

SUV *n* (*abbr of* Sport Utility Vehicle) todoterreno *m* utilitario.

svelte [svelt] *adj* esbelto(ta).

SW - **1.** (*abbr of* short wave) OC - **2.** (*abbr of* south-west) SO.

swab [swɒb] *n* (trozo *m* de) algodón *m*.

swagger [ˈswægər] ◇ *n* pavoneo *m*. ◇ *vi* pavonearse.

Swahili [swɑːˈhiːlɪ] *n* suahili *m*.

swallow [ˈswɒləʊ] ◇ *n* - **1.** [bird] golondrina *f* - **2.** [of food] bocado *m*; [of drink] trago *m*. ◇ *vt* - **1.** [food, drink] tragar - **2.** *fig* [accept, hold back] tragarse; **I find that a bit hard to swallow** me cuesta tragarme eso. ◇ *vi* tragar.

◆ **swallow up** *vt sep* [salary, time] tragarse.

swam [swæm] *pt* ▷ **swim**.

swamp [swɒmp] ◇ *n* pantano *m*, ciénaga *f*. ◇ *vt* - **1.** [flood - boat] hundir; [- land] inundar - **2.** [overwhelm]: **to swamp sthg (with)** [office] inundar algo (de); **to swamp sb (with)** agobiar a alguien (con); **we were swamped with applications** nos vimos inundados de solicitudes.

swan [swɒn] *n* cisne *m*.

swap [swɒp], **swop** ◇ *n* cambio *m*, intercambio *m*. ◇ *vt* (*pt & pp* **-ped**, *cont* **-ping**) - **1.** [of one thing]: **to swap sthg (for/with)** cambiar algo (por/con) - **2.** [of two things]: **to swap sthg (over OR round)** [hats, chairs] cambiarse algo - **3.** *fig* [stories, experiences] intercambiar; **to swap places** cambiarse de sitio. ◇ *vi* (*pt & pp* **-ped**, *cont* **-ping**) hacer un intercambio.

SWAPO ['swɑːpəʊ] (*abbr of* South West Africa People's Organization) *n* SWAPO *f*.

swarm [swɔːm] ⬦ *n* [of bees] enjambre *m*; *fig* [of people] multitud *f*, tropel *m*. ⬦ *vi* **- 1.** [bees] enjambrar **- 2.** *fig* [people] ir en tropel **- 3.** *fig* [place]: **to be swarming (with)** estar abarrotado(da) (de).

swarthy ['swɔːðɪ] (*comp* -ier, *superl* -iest) *adj* moreno(na).

swashbuckling ['swɒʃ,bʌklɪŋ] *adj* [person] intrépido(da); [film] de aventuras.

swastika ['swɒstɪkə] *n* esvástica *f*, cruz *f* gamada.

swat [swɒt] (*pt* & *pp* -ted, *cont* -ting) *vt* aplastar.

swatch [swɒtʃ] *n* muestra *f*.

swathe [sweɪð] *vt liter* [gen] envolver; [in bandages] vendar.

swathed [sweɪðd] *adj liter*: **swathed (in)** envuelto(ta) (en).

SWAT (team) *n* (*abbr of* Special Weapons and Tactics), *unidad armada de la policía estadounidense especializada en intervenciones peligrosas*.

swatter ['swɒtəʳ] *n* matamoscas *m inv*.

sway [sweɪ] ⬦ *vt* **- 1.** [cause to sway] balancear **- 2.** [influence] convencer, persuadir. ⬦ *vi* balancearse. ⬦ *n fml*: **to hold sway (over sthg/ sb)** dominar (algo/a alguien); **to come under the sway of** estar bajo el dominio de.

Swaziland ['swɑːzɪlænd] *n* Suazilandia.

swear [sweəʳ] ⬦ *vt* (*pt* swore, *pp* sworn): **to swear (to do sthg)** jurar (hacer algo); **to swear an oath** prestar juramento; **I could have sworn I saw him** juraría que lo vi. ⬦ *vi* (*pt* swore, *pp* sworn) **- 1.** [state emphatically] jurar; **I couldn't swear to it** no me atrevería a jurarlo **- 2.** [use swearwords] decir tacos, jurar; **to swear at sb** insultar a alguien.

◆ **swear by** *vt insep inf* [method, remedy] confiar totalmente en.

◆ **swear in** *vt sep* LAW tomar juramento a.

swearword ['sweəwɜːd] *n* palabrota *f*, taco *m*.

sweat [swet] ⬦ *n* **- 1.** [perspiration] sudor *m* **- 2.** (*U*) *inf* [hard work] trabajo *m* duro **- 3.** *inf* [state of anxiety]: **to be in a sweat about sthg** tener una neura con algo; **to be in a cold sweat** sentir un sudor frío. ⬦ *vi* **- 1.** [perspire] sudar **- 2.** *inf* [worry] estar aneurado(da). ⬦ *vt* **- 1.** MED: **to sweat out a cold** quitarse un resfriado sudando **- 2.** [in difficult situation]: **to sweat it out** aguantar.

sweatband ['swetbænd] *n* [for head] banda *f*; [for wrist] muñequera *f*.

sweater ['swetəʳ] *n* suéter *m*, jersey *m*, chompa *f Andes*, chomba *f R Plata*.

sweatshirt ['swetʃɜːt] *n* sudadera *f*.

sweatshop ['swetʃɒp] *n fábrica donde se explota al obrero*.

sweatsuit ['swetsuːt] *n US* chándal *m Esp*, buzo *m R Plata*, pants *m Méx*.

sweaty ['swetɪ] (*comp* -ier, *superl* -iest) *adj* **- 1.** [skin] sudoroso(sa); [clothes] sudado(da) **- 2.** [room, atmosphere] cargado(da); [activity] agotador(ra).

swede [swiːd] *n UK* nabo *m* sueco.

Swede [swiːd] *n* sueco *m*, -ca *f*.

Sweden ['swiːdn] *n* Suecia.

Swedish ['swiːdɪʃ] ⬦ *adj* sueco(ca). ⬦ *n* [language] sueco *m*. ⬦ *npl*: **the Swedish** los suecos.

sweep [swiːp] ⬦ *n* **- 1.** [movement - of broom] barrido *m*; [- of arm, hand] movimiento *m* OR gesto *m* amplio **- 2.** [by police] redada *f*. ⬦ *vt* (*pt* & *pp* swept) **- 1.** [with brush] barrer **- 2.** [with light-beam] rastrear; [with eyes] recorrer **- 3.** [move rapidly through - ideas, disease] extenderse rápidamente por **- 4.** [for bugs or bombs] registrar **- 5.** [sea, wave] arrastrar **- 6.** [push]: **she swept the papers off her desk** apartó los papeles de su escritorio. ⬦ *vi* (*pt* & *pp* swept) **- 1.** [wind, rain]: **to sweep over** OR **across sthg** azotar algo **- 2.** [vehicle]: **to sweep along** ir a toda marcha **- 3.** [emotion, laughter, rumour]: **to sweep through sthg** extenderse por algo; **the fire is sweeping through the country** el fuego se está propagando por el país **- 4.** [person]: **to sweep past** pasar como un rayo.

◆ **sweep aside** *vt sep* [objections] rechazar.

◆ **sweep away** *vt sep* [destroy] destruir completamente.

◆ **sweep up** *vt sep* & *vi* barrer.

sweeper ['swiːpəʳ] *n* FTBL líbero *m*.

sweeping ['swiːpɪŋ] *adj* **- 1.** [effect, change] radical **- 2.** [statement] demasiado general **- 3.** [curve] amplio(plia) **- 4.** [gesture] amplio(plia).

sweepstake ['swiːpsteɪk] *n lotería basada en carreras de caballos*.

sweet [swiːt] ⬦ *adj* **- 1.** [gen] dulce; [sugary] azucarado(da) **- 2.** [smell - of flowers, air] fragante, perfumado(da) **- 3.** [sound] melodioso(sa) **- 4.** [character, person] amable **- 5.** *US inf* genial. ⬦ *n UK* **- 1.** [candy] caramelo *m*, golosina *f* **- 2.** [dessert] postre *m*. ⬦ *excl US inf* genial.

sweet-and-sour *adj* agridulce.

sweet corn *n* maíz *m*.

sweeten ['swiːtn] *vt* endulzar.

sweetener ['swiːtnəʳ] *n* **- 1.** [substance] edulcorante *m* **- 2.** *inf* [bribe] especie *f* de soborno.

sweetheart ['swiːthɑːt] *n* **- 1.** [term of endearment] cariño *m* **- 2.** [boyfriend or girlfriend] amor *m*, novio *m*, -via *f*.

sweetness ['swi:tnɪs] *n* - **1.** [gen] dulzura *f* - **2.** [of taste] dulzor *m* - **3.** [of smell] fragancia *f* - **4.** [of sound] melodía *f*.

sweet pea *n* guisante *m* de olor, alverjilla *f* Andes, Col & Ven, chícharo *m* de olor Amér C & Méx, arvejilla *f* R Plata, clarín *m* Chile.

sweet potato *n* batata *f*, camote *m* Andes, Amér C & Méx.

sweet shop *n* UK confitería *f*.

sweet tooth *n inf*: **to have a sweet tooth** ser goloso(sa).

swell [swel] <> *vi* (*pt* -ed, *pp* swollen OR -ed) - **1.** [become larger]: **to swell (up)** hincharse - **2.** [balloon, sails] inflarse - **3.** [population, sound] aumentar. <> *vt* (*pt* -ed, *pp* swollen OR -ed) [numbers etc] aumentar. <> *n* [of sea] oleaje *m*. <> *adj* US *inf* estupendo(da), fenomenal.

swelling ['swelɪŋ] *n* hinchazón *f*; **the swelling has gone down** ha bajado la hinchazón.

sweltering ['sweltərɪŋ] *adj* - **1.** [weather] abrasador(ra), sofocante - **2.** [person] achicharrado(da).

swept [swept] *pt & pp* ⊳ **sweep**.

swerve ['swɜːv] *vi* virar bruscamente.

swift [swɪft] <> *adj* - **1.** [fast] rápido(da) - **2.** [prompt] pronto(ta). <> *n* [bird] vencejo *m*.

swiftly ['swɪftlɪ] *adj* - **1.** [quickly] rápidamente - **2.** [promptly] prontamente, con prontitud.

swiftness ['swɪftnɪs] *n* - **1.** [quickness] rapidez *f*, ligereza *f* - **2.** [promptness] prontitud *f*.

swig [swɪg] *inf* <> *vt* (*pt & pp* -ged, *cont* -ging) beber a grandes tragos. <> *n* trago *m*; **to take a swig of sthg** tomar un trago de algo.

swill [swɪl] <> *n* [pig food] bazofia *f*. <> *vt* UK [wash] enjuagar.

swim [swɪm] <> *n* baño *m*; **to go for a swim** ir a nadar OR a darse un baño. <> *vi* (*pt* swam, *pp* swum, *cont* -ming) - **1.** [in water] nadar - **2.** [head, room] dar vueltas. <> *vt* (*pt* swam, *pp* swum, *cont* -ming): **to swim the English Channel** cruzar el canal de la Mancha a nado; **I swam 20 lengths** nadé veinte largos.

swimmer ['swɪmər] *n* nadador *m*, -ra *f*; **she's a good swimmer** nada bien.

swimming ['swɪmɪŋ] <> *n* natación *f*; **to go swimming** ir a nadar. <> *comp* [club, lesson] de natación.

swimming baths *npl* UK piscina *f* municipal.

swimming cap *n* gorro *m* de baño.

swimming costume *n* UK bañador *m*, traje *m* de baño.

swimming pool *n* piscina *f*, alberca *f* Méx, pileta *f* R Plata.

swimming trunks *npl* bañador *m*.

swimsuit ['swɪmsuːt] *n* bañador *m* Esp, traje *m* de baño, malla *f* R Plata, vestido *m* de baño Col.

swindle ['swɪndl] <> *n* estafa *f*, timo *m*, calote *m* Amér. <> *vt* estafar, timar; **to swindle sb out of sthg** estafar a alguien algo.

swine [swaɪn] *n inf pej* [person] cerdo *m*, -da *f*, canalla *mf*.

swing [swɪŋ] <> *n* - **1.** [child's toy] columpio *m* - **2.** [change] viraje *m*, cambio *m* brusco; **a swing towards the Conservatives** un giro hacia los conservadores - **3.** [sway] meneo *m*, balanceo *m* - **4.** *inf* [blow]: **to take a swing at sb** intentar golpear a alguien

▸▸ **to be in full swing** estar en plena marcha; **to get into the swing of** cogerle la marcha a. <> *vt* (*pt & pp* swung) - **1.** [move back and forth] balancear - **2.** [move in a curve - car etc] hacer virar bruscamente. <> *vi* (*pt & pp* swung) - **1.** [move back and forth] balancearse, oscilar - **2.** [move in a curve] girar; **to swing open** abrirse - **3.** [turn]: **to swing (round)** volverse, girarse - **4.** [hit out]: **to swing at sb** intentar golpear a alguien - **5.** [change] virar, cambiar.

swing bridge *n* puente *m* giratorio.

swing door *n* puerta *f* oscilante.

swingeing ['swɪndʒɪŋ] *adj esp* UK severo(ra).

swinging ['swɪŋɪŋ] *adj inf* - **1.** [lively] alegre - **2.** [uninhibited] liberal.

swipe [swaɪp] <> *n*: **to take a swipe at sthg** intentar golpear algo. <> *vt inf* [steal] birlar. <> *vi*: **to swipe at sthg** intentar golpear algo.

swirl [swɜːl] <> *n* remolino *m*. <> *vt* dar vueltas a. <> *vi* arremolinarse.

swish [swɪʃ] <> *n* [of curtains, dress] frufrú *m*, crujido *m*; [of tail] meneo *m*; [of whip] chasquido *m*. <> *vt* [tail] agitar, menear. <> *vi* [curtains, dress] crujir; [whip] dar un chasquido.

Swiss [swɪs] <> *adj* suizo(za). <> *n* [person] suizo *m*, -za *f*. <> *npl*: **the Swiss** los suizos.

swiss roll *n* UK brazo *m* de gitano.

switch [swɪtʃ] <> *n* - **1.** [control device] interruptor *m*, suiche *m* Amér - **2.** [change] cambio *m* completo, viraje *m* - **3.** US RAIL aguja *f*. <> *vt* - **1.** [change] cambiar de; **to switch one's attention to sthg** dirigir la atención a OR hacia algo - **2.** [swap] intercambiar. <> *vi*: **to switch (to/from)** cambiar (a/de).

◆ **switch off** <> *vt sep* [light, radio etc] apagar; [engine] parar. <> *vi inf* desconectar, dejar de prestar atención.

◆ **switch on** *vt sep* [light, radio etc] encender; [engine] poner en marcha.

Switch® [swɪtʃ] *n* UK tarjeta *f* de débito Switch®.

switchblade ['swɪtʃbleɪd] *n* US navaja *f* automática.

switchboard ['swɪtʃbɔːd] *n* centralita *f*, conmutador *m* Amér.

switchboard operator *n* telefonista *mf*.

Switzerland ['swɪtsələnd] n Suiza.
swivel ['swɪvl] ⟨⟩ vt (UK -led, cont -ling, US -ed, cont -ing) hacer girar. ⟨⟩ vi (UK -led, cont -ling, US -ed, cont -ing) girar.
swivel chair n silla f giratoria.
swollen ['swəʊln] ⟨⟩ pp ⊳ **swell**. ⟨⟩ adj - **1.** [ankle, leg etc] hinchado(da); **my eyes were swollen** tenía los ojos hinchados; **to be swollen with pride** fig estar henchido de orgullo - **2.** [river] crecido(da).
swoon [swu:n] vi liter & hum deshacerse.
swoop [swu:p] ⟨⟩ n - **1.** [of bird] calada f; [of plane] descenso m en picado; **in one fell swoop** de un golpe - **2.** [raid] redada f; **a swoop on a flat** una redada en un apartamento. ⟨⟩ vi - **1.** [move downwards] caer en picado - **2.** [move quickly] atacar por sorpresa.
swop [swɒp] = **swap**.
sword [sɔːd] n espada f; **to cross swords (with)** habérselas (con).
swordfish ['sɔːdfɪʃ] (pl swordfish OR -es) n pez m espada.
swordsman ['sɔːdzmən] (pl -men [-mən]) n espadachín m.
swore [swɔːr] pt ⊳ **swear**.
sworn [swɔːn] ⟨⟩ pp ⊳ **swear**. ⟨⟩ adj - **1.** [committed]: **to be sworn enemies** ser enemigos implacables - **2.** LAW jurado(da).
swot [swɒt] UK inf ⟨⟩ n pej empollón m, -ona f. ⟨⟩ vi (pt & pp -ted, cont -ting): **to swot (for)** empollar (para).
➻ **swot up** inf ⟨⟩ vt sep empollar. ⟨⟩ vi: **to swot up (on sthg)** empollar (algo).
swum [swʌm] pp ⊳ **swim**.
swung [swʌŋ] pt & pp ⊳ **swing**.
sycamore ['sɪkəmɔːr] n - **1.** sicomoro m - **2.** US [plane tree] plátano m.
sycophant ['sɪkəfænt] n adulador m, -ra f.
Sydney ['sɪdnɪ] n Sidney.
syllable ['sɪləbl] n sílaba f.
syllabub ['sɪləbʌb] n postre de nata o leche y claras de huevo.
syllabus ['sɪləbəs] (pl -buses OR -bi [-baɪ]) n programa m (de estudios).
symbol ['sɪmbl] n símbolo m.
symbolic [sɪm'bɒlɪk] adj simbólico(ca); **to be symbolic of** ser un símbolo de.
symbolism ['sɪmbəlɪzm] n simbolismo m.
symbolize, -ise ['sɪmbəlaɪz] vt simbolizar.
symmetrical [sɪ'metrɪkl] adj simétrico(ca).
symmetry ['sɪmətrɪ] n simetría f.
sympathetic [,sɪmpə'θetɪk] adj - **1.** [understanding] comprensivo(va) - **2.** [willing to support] favorable; **sympathetic to** bien dispuesto(ta) hacia - **3.** [likable] agradable.

sympathize, -ise ['sɪmpəθaɪz] vi - **1.** [feel sorry]: **to sympathize (with)** compadecerse (de) - **2.** [understand]: **to sympathize (with sthg)** comprender (algo) - **3.** [support]: **to sympathize with sthg** apoyar algo.
sympathizer, -iser ['sɪmpəθaɪzər] n simpatizante mf.
sympathy ['sɪmpəθɪ] n - **1.** [understanding]: **sympathy (for)** comprensión f (hacia); [compassion] compasión f (por) - **2.** [agreement] solidaridad f; **in sympathy (with)** de acuerdo (con) - **3.** [support]: **in sympathy (with)** en solidaridad (con).
➻ **sympathies** npl - **1.** [support] simpatías fpl - **2.** [to bereaved person] pésame m.
symphonic [sɪm'fɒnɪk] adj sinfónico(ca).
symphony ['sɪmfənɪ] (pl -ies) n sinfonía f.
symphony orchestra n orquesta f sinfónica.
symposium [sɪm'pəʊzjəm] (pl -siums OR -sia [-zjə]) n fml simposio m.
symptom ['sɪmptəm] n lit & fig síntoma m.
symptomatic [,sɪmptə'mætɪk] adj fml: **symptomatic of sthg** sintomático(ca) de algo.
synagogue ['sɪnəgɒg] n sinagoga f.
sync [sɪŋk] n inf: **out of sync** desincronizado(da); **in sync** sincronizado(da).
synchronize, -ise ['sɪŋkrənaɪz] ⟨⟩ vt: **to synchronize sthg (with)** sincronizar algo (con). ⟨⟩ vi ser sincrónico.
synchronized swimming ['sɪŋkrənaɪzd-] n ballet m acuático.
syncopated ['sɪŋkəpeɪtɪd] adj sincopado(da).
syncopation [,sɪŋkə'peɪʃn] n síncopa f.
syndicate ⟨⟩ n ['sɪndɪkət] sindicato m. ⟨⟩ vt ['sɪndɪkeɪt] sindicar.
syndrome ['sɪndrəʊm] n síndrome m.
synonym ['sɪnənɪm] n: **synonym (for OR of)** sinónimo m (de).
synonymous [sɪ'nɒnɪməs] adj: **synonymous (with)** sinónimo(ma) (de).
synopsis [sɪ'nɒpsɪs] (pl -ses [-si:z]) n sinopsis f inv.
syntax ['sɪntæks] n sintaxis f inv.
synthesis ['sɪnθəsɪs] (pl -ses [-si:z]) n síntesis f inv.
synthesize, -ise ['sɪnθəsaɪz] vt sintetizar.
synthesizer ['sɪnθəsaɪzər] n sintetizador m.
synthetic [sɪn'θetɪk] adj - **1.** [man-made] sintético(ca) - **2.** pej [insincere] artificial.
syphilis ['sɪfɪlɪs] n sífilis f inv.
syphon ['saɪfn] = **siphon**.
Syria ['sɪrɪə] n Siria.
Syrian ['sɪrɪən] ⟨⟩ adj sirio(ria). ⟨⟩ n [person] sirio m, -ria f.

syringe [sɪˈrɪndʒ] ⬦ n jeringa f, jeringuilla f.
⬦ vt (cont **syringeing**) jeringar.

syrup [ˈsɪrəp] n (U) - **1.** CULIN almíbar m - **2.** MED
jarabe m; **cough syrup** jarabe para la tos.

system [ˈsɪstəm] n [gen] sistema m; [of central
heating etc] instalación f; **digestive system**
aparato m digestivo; **transport system** red f
de transportes; **to get sthg out of one's system** inf sacarse algo de encima.

systematic [ˌsɪstəˈmætɪk] adj sistemático(ca).

systematize, -ise [ˈsɪstəmətaɪz] vt sistematizar.

system disk n COMPUT disco m del sistema.

systems analyst [ˈsɪstəmz-] n COMPUT analista mf de sistemas.

systems engineer [ˈsɪstəmz-] n COMPUT ingeniero m, -ra f de sistemas.

system software n COMPUT software m del
sistema.

t (pl **t's** OR **ts**), **T** (pl **T's** OR **Ts**) [tiː] n [letter] t f, T f.

ta [tɑː] excl UK inf ¡gracias!

TA n abbr of **Territorial Army**.

tab [tæb] n - **1.** [of cloth] etiqueta f - **2.** [of metal,
card etc] lengüeta f - **3.** US [bill] cuenta f; **to pick
up the tab** inf pagar la cuenta - **4.** COMPUT (abbr
of **tabulator**) tab
▸▸ **to keep tabs on sb** vigilar de cerca a alguien.

tabby [ˈtæbɪ] (pl -ies) n: **tabby (cat)** gato m atigrado.

tabernacle [ˈtæbənækl] n tabernáculo m.

tab key n COMPUT (tecla f del) tabulador m.

table [ˈteɪbl] ⬦ n - **1.** [piece of furniture] mesa f;
[small] mesilla f - **2.** [diagram] tabla f
▸▸ **to turn the tables on** volver las tornas a.
⬦ vt - **1.** UK [propose] presentar - **2.** US [post-
pone] aplazar, posponer.

tableau [ˈtæbləʊ] (pl -x [ˈtæbləʊz] OR -s) n cuadro m vivente.

tablecloth [ˈteɪblklɒθ] n mantel m.

table d'hôte [ˌtɑːblˌdəʊt] n: **the table d'hôte** el
menú.

table lamp n lámpara f de mesa.

table linen n mantelería f.

table manners npl modales mpl en la mesa.

tablemat [ˈteɪblmæt] n salvamanteles m inv.

table salt n sal f de mesa.

tablespoon [ˈteɪblspuːn] n - **1.** [spoon] cuchara f grande - **2.** [spoonful] cucharada f (grande).

tablet [ˈtæblɪt] n - **1.** [pill, piece of soap] pastilla f
- **2.** [piece of stone] lápida f.

table tennis n tenis m de mesa.

table wine n vino m de mesa.

tabloid [ˈtæblɔɪd] n: **the tabloids** los periódicos
sensacionalistas; **tabloid (newspaper)** tabloide m.

Tabloids

Los periódicos británicos y estadounidenses de formato pequeño o tabloide
se dirigen a un público más popular que los periódicos de formato grande, tanto por su contenido como por su estilo. En el Reino Unido,
el principal periódico de formato tabloide es el
"Sun", con una tirada de más de tres millones
de ejemplares diarios, seguido por el "Daily
Mirror", con más de dos millones. En comparación, el periódico de gran formato con mayor tirada es el "Daily Telegraph", con algo
más de un millón de ejemplares diarios. Los
tabloides suelen dedicar muchas columnas a
la vida de personajes televisivos o del mundo
del deporte, a pesar de lo cual se les considera
muy influyentes políticamente, sobre todo durante las elecciones, por lo que algunos políticos escriben regularmente su propia sección en ellos. En EEUU., los llamados "supermarket tabloids" son aún más sensacionalistas, y sus artículos incluyen desde
la vida de los famosos a algunas historias totalmente absurdas. Un buen ejemplo es el
"Weekly World News".

taboo [təˈbuː] ⬦ adj tabú. ⬦ n (pl -s) tabú m.

tabulate [ˈtæbjʊleɪt] vt tabular.

tachograph [ˈtækəgrɑːf] n tacógrafo m.

tachometer [tæˈkɒmɪtə] n tacómetro m.

tacit [ˈtæsɪt] adj fml tácito(ta).

taciturn [ˈtæsɪtɜːn] adj fml taciturno(na).

tack [tæk] ⬦ n - **1.** [nail] tachuela f - **2.** NAUT
bordada f - **3.** fig [course of action] táctica f; **to
change tack** cambiar de táctica. ⬦ vt
- **1.** [fasten with nail] fijar con tachuelas - **2.** [in
sewing] hilvanar. ⬦ vi NAUT virar.
◂ **tack on** vt sep inf añadir.

tackle [ˈtækl] ⬦ n - **1.** FTBL entrada f - **2.** RUGBY
placaje m - **3.** (U) [equipment] equipo m, aparejos mpl - **4.** [for lifting] aparejo m. ⬦ vt

- 1. [deal with - job] emprender; [- problem] abordar **- 2.** FTBL entrar, hacer una entrada a **- 3.** RUGBY placar **- 4.** [attack] atacar, arremeter **- 5.** [talk to]: **to tackle sb about** OR **on sthg** discutir algo con alguien.

tacky ['tækɪ] (comp **-ier**, superl **-iest**) adj **- 1.** inf [cheap and nasty] cutre; [ostentatious and vulgar] hortera **- 2.** [sticky] pegajoso(sa).

taco ['tækəʊ] (pl **-s**) n taco m.

tact [tækt] n (U) tacto m, discreción f.

tactful ['tæktfʊl] adj discreto(ta).

tactfully ['tæktfʊlɪ] adv discretamente.

tactic ['tæktɪk] n táctica f.
⇒ **tactics** n (U) MIL táctica f.

tactical ['tæktɪkl] adj estratégico(ca); [weapons] táctico(ca).

tactical voting n UK votación f táctica.

tactless ['tæktlɪs] adj indiscreto(ta), falto(ta) de tacto.

tactlessly ['tæktlɪslɪ] adv indiscretamente.

tadpole ['tædpəʊl] n renacuajo m.

Tadzhikistan [tɑː,dʒɪkɪ'stɑːn] n (el) Tayikistán.

taffeta ['tæfɪtə] n tafetán m.

taffy ['tæfɪ] (pl **-ies**) n US caramelo m de melaza.

tag [tæg] ⇔ n **- 1.** [of cloth, paper] etiqueta f; **price tag** etiqueta del precio **- 2.** [game] pillapilla m **- 3.** COMPUT código m, etiqueta f. ⇔ vt (pt & pp **-ged**, cont **-ging**) etiquetar.
⇒ **tag question** n cláusula f final interrogativa.
⇒ **tag along** vi inf: **to tag along (with)** pegarse (a), engancharse (a).

Tahiti [tɑː'hiːtɪ] n Tahití.

tail [teɪl] ⇔ n [gen] cola f; [of coat, shirt] faldón m; **with one's tail between one's legs** [person] con el rabo entre las piernas. ⇔ vt inf [follow] seguir de cerca.
⇒ **tails** npl **- 1.** [formal dress] frac m **- 2.** [side of coin] cruz f.
⇒ **tail off** vi **- 1.** [voice] ir debilitándose; [sound] ir disminuyendo **- 2.** [interest, sales etc] ir descendiendo.

tailback ['teɪlbæk] n UK cola f.

tailcoat ['teɪl,kəʊt] n frac m.

tail end n parte f final.

tailgate ['teɪlgeɪt] ⇔ n US [of car] puerta f trasera de un vehículo. ⇔ vt conducir pegado a, pisar los talones a.

taillight ['teɪllaɪt] n luz f trasera, piloto m.

tailor ['teɪlər] ⇔ n sastre m. ⇔ vt adaptar; **it can be tailored to your needs** se puede adaptar a sus necesidades.

tailored ['teɪləd] adj entallado(da).

tailor-made adj hecho(cha) a la medida.

tail pipe n US tubo m de escape.

tailplane ['teɪlpleɪn] n plano m fijo de cola.

tailwind ['teɪlwɪnd] n viento m de cola.

taint [teɪnt] fml ⇔ n mancha f. ⇔ vt viciar.

tainted ['teɪntɪd] adj **- 1.** [reputation] manchado(da) **- 2.** US [food] estropeado(da).

Taiwan [,taɪ'wɑːn] n Taiwán.

Taiwanese [,taɪwəˈniːz] ⇔ adj taiwanés(esa). ⇔ n taiwanés m, -esa f.

take [teɪk] ⇔ vt (pt **took**, pp **taken**) **- 1.** [gen] tomar; **do you take sugar?** ¿tomas azúcar?; **take a seat!** ¡siéntate!; **to take control/command** tomar control/el mando; **to take a photo** hacer OR tomar una foto; **to take a walk** dar un paseo; **to take a bath** bañarse; **to take a test** hacer un examen; **to take sthg seriously/badly/personally** tomarse algo en serio/a mal/personalmente; **to take pity on sb** compadecerse de alguien; **to take offence** ofenderse; **to be taken ill** ponerse enfermo; **take the second turning on the right** toma el segundo giro a la derecha **- 2.** [bring, carry, accompany] llevar **- 3.** [steal] quitar, robar **- 4.** [buy] coger, quedarse con; [rent] alquilar; **I'll take the red one** me quedo con el rojo **- 5.** [take hold of] coger; **let me take your coat** déjeme que le coja el abrigo; **to take sb prisoner** capturar a alguien **- 6.** [accept - offer, cheque, criticism] aceptar; [- advice] seguir; [- responsibility, blame] asumir; **the machine only takes 50p pieces** la máquina sólo admite monedas de 50 peniques; **take my word for it, take it from me** créeme **- 7.** [have room for - passengers, goods] tener cabida para **- 8.** [bear - pain etc] soportar, aguantar; **some people can't take a joke** hay gente que no sabe aguantar una broma **- 9.** [require - time, courage] requerir; [- money] costar; **it will take a week/three hours** llevará una semana/tres horas; **it only took me 5 minutes** sólo me llevó cinco minutos; **it takes guts to do that** hay que tener agallas para hacer eso; **it took 5 people to move the piano** hicieron falta 5 personas para mover el piano **- 10.** [travel by - means of transport, route] tomar, coger **- 11.** [wear - shoes] calzar; [- clothes] usar **- 12.** [consider] considerar; **now, take John for instance...** tomemos a John, por ejemplo...; **to take sb for a fool/a policeman** tomar a alguien por tonto/por un policía **- 13.** [assume]: **I take it (that)...** supongo que... ⇔ vi (pt **took**, pp **taken**) [dye] coger; [vaccine, fire, cutting] prender. ⇔ n CIN toma f.
⇒ **take aback** vt insep dejar atónito(ta); **to be taken aback** estar atónito.
⇒ **take after** vt insep parecerse a.
⇒ **take apart** vt sep [dismantle] desmontar.

◆ **take away** *vt sep* - **1.** [remove] quitar - **2.** [deduct] restar, sustraer.

◆ **take back** *vt sep* - **1.** [return] devolver - **2.** [accept - faulty goods] aceptar la devolución de - **3.** [admit as wrong] retirar - **4.** [in memories]: **it takes me back to when I was a teenager** me hace volver a mi adolescencia.

◆ **take down** *vt sep* - **1.** [dismantle] desmontar - **2.** [write down] escribir, tomar nota de - **3.** [lower - trousers] bajarse; [- picture] bajar.

◆ **take in** *vt sep* - **1.** [deceive] engañar; **to be taken in by sb** ser engañado por alguien - **2.** [understand] comprender, asimilar; **I can't take it all in** no consigo asimilarlo todo - **3.** [include] incluir, abarcar - **4.** [provide accommodation for] acoger.

◆ **take off** ◇ *vt sep* - **1.** [clothes, glasses] quitarse - **2.** [have as holiday]: **to take time off** tomarse tiempo libre - **3.** *UK inf* [imitate] imitar - **4.** *inf* [go away suddenly]: **to take o.s. off** irse, marcharse. ◇ *vi* - **1.** [plane] despegar, decolar *Andes* - **2.** [go away suddenly] irse, marcharse - **3.** [career] consolidarse; [idea, fashion] cuajar.

◆ **take on** ◇ *vt sep* - **1.** [accept - work, job] aceptar; [- responsibility] asumir - **2.** [employ] emplear, coger - **3.** [confront] desafiar. ◇ *vt insep* [assume] tomar.

◆ **take out** *vt sep* - **1.** [from container, pocket] sacar - **2.** [delete] suprimir - **3.** [go out with]: **to take sb out** invitar a salir a alguien; **to take it out** OR **a lot out of one** *inf* agotar a uno.

◆ **take out on** *vt sep* [feelings, anger] descargar contra; **don't take it out on me!** ¡no la tomes conmigo!

◆ **take over** ◇ *vt sep* - **1.** [company, business] absorber, adquirir; [country, government] apoderarse de - **2.** [job] tomar, asumir. ◇ *vi* - **1.** [take control] tomar el poder - **2.** [in job] entrar en funciones.

◆ **take to** *vt insep* - **1.** [feel a liking for - person] coger cariño a; [- activity] aficionarse a - **2.** [begin]: **to take to doing sthg** empezar a hacer algo.

◆ **take up** *vt sep* - **1.** [begin]: **to take up singing** dedicarse a cantar; [job] aceptar, tomar - **2.** [continue] reanudar - **3.** [discuss] discutir - **4.** [use up - time, space] ocupar; [- effort] requerir.

◆ **take upon** *vt sep*: **to take it upon o.s. to do sthg** permitirse hacer algo.

◆ **take up on** *vt sep* - **1.** [accept]: **to take sb up on an offer** aceptar una oferta de alguien - **2.** [ask to explain]: **to take sb up on sthg** pedir que alguien se explique acerca de algo.

takeaway *UK* ['teɪkə,weɪ], **takeout** *US* ['teɪkaʊt] *n* - **1.** [shop] *establecimiento donde se vende comida preparada para llevar* - **2.** [food] comida *f* para llevar.

take-home pay *n* sueldo *m* neto.

taken ['teɪkn] ◇ *pp* ▷ **take**. ◇ *adj*: **taken with** atraído(da) por.

takeoff ['teɪkɒf] *n* [of plane] despegue *m*, decolaje *m* *Amér*.

takeout *US* = **takeaway**.

takeover ['teɪk,əʊvər] *n* - **1.** [of company] adquisición *f* - **2.** [of government] toma *f* del poder.

takeover bid *n* OPA *f*, oferta *f* pública de adquisición de acciones.

taker ['teɪkər] *n* persona *f* interesada *(en comprar algo etc)*; **there were no takers** nadie aceptó la oferta.

takeup ['teɪkʌp] *n* grado *m* de aceptación, respuesta *f*.

takings *npl* [of shop] venta *f*; [of show] recaudación *f*.

talc [tælk], **talcum (powder)** ['tælkəm-] *n* talco *m*.

tale [teɪl] *n* - **1.** [fictional story] cuento *m* - **2.** [anecdote] anécdota *f*.

talent ['tælənt] *n*: **talent (for sthg)** talento *m* (para algo).

talented ['tæləntɪd] *adj* con talento.

talent scout *n* cazatalentos *mf inv*.

talisman ['tælɪzmən] (*pl* -s) *n* talismán *m*.

talk [tɔːk] ◇ *n* - **1.** [conversation] conversación *f*, plática *f* *Amér C & Méx*; **to have a talk** conversar - **2.** *(U)* [gossip] habladurías *fpl* - **3.** [lecture] charla *f*, conferencia *f*, plática *f* *Amér C & Méx*; **to give a talk on sthg** dar una charla sobre algo. ◇ *vi* - **1.** [gen] hablar; **to talk to/of** hablar OR platicar *Amér C & Méx* con/de; **talking of Sarah, I met her mum yesterday** hablando de Sarah, ayer me encontré a su madre; **to talk on** OR **about** hablar OR platicar *Amér C & Méx* acerca de OR sobre; **they aren't talking to each other** no se hablan; **to talk big** fanfarronear, farolear *Esp* - **2.** [gossip] chismorrear. ◇ *vt* hablar de.

◆ **talks** *npl* conversaciones *fpl*.

◆ **talk down to** *vt insep* hablar con aires de suficiencia a.

◆ **talk into** *vt sep*: **to talk sb into doing sthg** convencer a alguien para que haga algo.

◆ **talk out of** *vt sep*: **to talk sb out of doing sthg** disuadir a alguien de que haga algo.

◆ **talk over** *vt sep* discutir, hablar de.

talkative ['tɔːkətɪv] *adj* hablador(ra).

talker ['tɔːkər] *n* hablador *m*, -ra *f*.

talking point ['tɔːkɪŋ-] *n* tema *m* de conversación.

talking-to ['tɔːkɪŋ-] *n* *inf* bronca *f*; **to give sb a (good) talking-to** echar una bronca a alguien.

talk show *US* ◇ *n* programa *m* de entrevistas. ◇ *comp* de programa de entrevistas.

talk time *n (U)* [on mobile phone] tiempo *m* de conversación.

tall [tɔːl] *adj* alto(ta); **she's 2 metres tall** mide 2 metros; **how tall is he?** ¿cuánto mide?

tallboy ['tɔːlbɔɪ] *n* cómoda *f* alta.

tall order *n*: **it's a tall order** es mucho pedir.

tall story *n* cuento *m* (increíble).

tally ['tælɪ] ◇ *n (pl* -ies) cuenta *f*; **to keep a tally** llevar la cuenta. ◇ *vi (pt & pp* -ied) concordar, casar.

talon ['tælən] *n* garra *f*.

tambourine [,tæmbə'riːn] *n* pandereta *f*.

tame [teɪm] ◇ *adj* - **1.** [domesticated] doméstico(ca) - **2.** *pej* [obedient] dócil - **3.** *pej* [unexciting] soso(sa), aburrido(da). ◇ *vt* - **1.** [domesticate] domesticar - **2.** [bring under control] dominar.

tamely ['teɪmlɪ] *adv* dócilmente, sumisamente.

tamer ['teɪmər] *n* domador *m*, -ra *f*.

Tamil ['tæmɪl] ◇ *adj* tamil. ◇ *n* - **1.** [person] tamil *mf* - **2.** [language] tamil *m*.

tamper ['tæmpər] ◆ **tamper with** *vt insep* [lock] intentar forzar; [records, file] falsear; [machine] manipular.

tampon ['tæmpɒn] *n* tampón *m*.

tan [tæn] ◇ *adj* de color marrón claro. ◇ *n* bronceado *m*; **to get a tan** broncearse. ◇ *vi (pt & pp* -ned, *cont* -ning) broncearse.

tandem ['tændəm] *n* [bicycle] tándem *m*; **in tandem** conjuntamente, en colaboración.

tandoori [tæn'dʊərɪ] *n* [cooking method] *método indio de asar la carne en un horno de barro*.

tang [tæŋ] *n* [smell] olor *m* fuerte; [taste] sabor *m* fuerte.

tangent ['tændʒənt] *n* GEOM tangente *f*; **to go off at a tangent** salirse por la tangente.

tangerine [,tæn'dʒəriːn] *n* mandarina *f*.

tangible ['tændʒəbl] *adj* tangible.

tangle ['tæŋgl] ◇ *n* [mass] maraña *f*; *fig* [mess] enredo *m*, embrollo *m*, entrevero *m R Plata*. ◇ *vi* enredarse, enmarañarse; **to get tangled (up)** enredarse.

◆ **tangle with** *vt insep inf* meterse con.

tangled ['tæŋgld] *adj lit & fig* enredado(da).

tango ['tæŋgəʊ] *(pl* -es) *n* tango *m*.

tangy ['tæŋɪ] *(comp* -ier, *superl* -iest) *adj* fuerte.

tank [tæŋk] *n* - **1.** [container] depósito *m*, tanque *m* - **2.** MIL tanque *m*, carro *m* de combate.

tankard ['tæŋkəd] *n* bock *m*.

tanker ['tæŋkər] *n* - **1.** [ship - gen] barco *m* cisterna, tanque *m*; [- for oil] petrolero *m* - **2.** [truck] camión *m* cisterna.

tankful ['tæŋkfʊl] *n* depósito *m* lleno.

tanned [tænd] *adj* bronceado(da).

tannin ['tænɪn] *n* tanino *m*.

Tannoy® ['tænɔɪ] *n* (sistema *m* de) altavoces *mpl*; **his name was called out over the Tannoy** su nombre sonó por megafonía.

tantalize, -ise ['tæntəlaɪz] *vt* atormentar.

tantalizing ['tæntəlaɪzɪŋ] *adj* tentador(ra).

tantamount ['tæntəmaʊnt] *adj*: **tantamount to** equivalente a.

tantrum ['tæntrəm] *(pl* -s) *n* rabieta *f*; **to throw a tantrum** coger una rabieta.

Tanzania [,tænzə'nɪə] *n* Tanzania.

Tanzanian [,tænzə'nɪən] ◇ *adj* tanzano(na). ◇ *n* tanzano *m*, -na *f*.

tap [tæp] ◇ *n* - **1.** [device] grifo *m*, llave *f Amér*, canilla *f R Plata*, paja *f Amér C*, caño *m Perú* - **2.** [light blow] golpecito *m* - **3.** [phr]: **to be on tap** [beer, water] ser de barril; **to have sthg on tap** *fig* tener algo a mano. ◇ *vt (pt & pp* -ped, *cont* -ping) - **1.** [hit] golpear ligeramente; **he tapped his fingers on the table** golpeaba ligeramente la mesa con los dedos - **2.** [strength, resources] utilizar, usar - **3.** [phone] intervenir. ◇ *vi (pt & pp* -ped, *cont* -ping) dar un golpecito; **he tapped on the window** dio unos golpecitos en la ventana.

◆ **taps** *n US* MIL [at funeral] toque *m* de difuntos.

tap dancer *n* bailarín *m*, -ina *f* de claqué.

tap dancing *n* claqué *m*.

tape [teɪp] ◇ *n* - **1.** [cassette, magnetic tape, strip of cloth] cinta *f* - **2.** SPORT [at finishing line] cinta *f* de llegada - **3.** [adhesive plastic] cinta *f* adhesiva. ◇ *vt* - **1.** [on tape recorder, video recorder] grabar - **2.** [with adhesive tape] pegar con cinta adhesiva - **3.** *US* [bandage] vendar.

tape deck *n* pletina *f* del magnetófono.

tape measure *n* cinta *f* métrica.

taper ['teɪpər] ◇ *n* [candle] vela *f*. ◇ *vi* afilarse.

◆ **taper off** *vi* ir disminuyendo.

tape-record [-rɪ,kɔːd] *vt* grabar (en cinta).

tape recorder *n* magnetófono *m*.

tape recording *n* grabación *f* en cinta.

tapered ['teɪpəd] *adj* ahusado(da).

tapestry ['tæpɪstrɪ] *(pl* -ies) *n* - **1.** [piece of work] tapiz *m* - **2.** [craft] tapicería *f*.

tapeworm ['teɪpwɜːm] *n* tenia *f*, solitaria *f*.

tapioca [,tæpɪ'əʊkə] *n* tapioca *f*.

tapir ['teɪpər] *(pl* tapir *OR* -s) *n* tapir *m*.

tar [tɑː] *n* alquitrán *m*.

tarantula [tə'ræntjʊlə] *n* tarántula *f*.

target ['tɑːgɪt] ◇ *n* - **1.** [of missile, goal, aim] objetivo *m* - **2.** [in archery, shooting, of criticism] blanco *m*; **to be on target to do sthg** llevar el ritmo adecuado para hacer algo. ◇ *vt* - **1.** [aim weapon at] apuntar a - **2.** [channel]: **to target funds on** destinar fondos a.

tariff ['tærɪf] *n* tarifa *f*.

Tarmac® ['tɑːmæk] *n* [material] alquitrán *m*.

➤ **tarmac** *n* AERON: **the tarmac** la pista.

tarnish ['tɑːnɪʃ] <> *vt* [make dull] deslustrar; *fig* [damage] empañar, manchar. <> *vi* [become dull] deslustrarse.

tarnished ['tɑːnɪʃt] *adj* [dull] deslustrado(da); *fig* [damaged] manchado(da), empañado(da).

tarot ['tærəʊ] *n*: **the tarot** el tarot.

tarot card *n* carta *f* de tarot.

tarpaulin [tɑːˈpɔːlɪn] *n* lona *f* alquitranada.

tarragon ['tærəgən] *n* estragón *m*.

tart [tɑːt] <> *adj* - **1.** [bitter] agrio(agria) - **2.** [sarcastic] mordaz. <> *n* - **1.** [sweet pastry] tarta *f* - **2.** *v inf* [prostitute] furcia *f*, fulana *f*.

➤ **tart up** *vt sep* UK *inf pej* emperejilar; **to tart o.s. up** emperifollarse.

tartan ['tɑːtn] <> *n* tartán *m*. <> *comp* de tartán.

tartar(e) sauce ['tɑːtər-] *n* salsa *f* tártara.

tartness ['tɑːtnɪs] *n* - **1.** [of taste] acidez *f* - **2.** [of comment] mordacidad *f*, acritud *f*.

task [tɑːsk] *n* tarea *f*.

task force *n* MIL destacamento *m* de fuerzas.

taskmaster ['tɑːskˌmɑːstər] *n*: **a hard taskmaster** un tirano.

Tasmania [tæzˈmeɪnjə] *n* Tasmania.

Tasmanian [tæzˈmeɪnjən] <> *adj* tasmanio(nia). <> *n* tasmanio *m*, -nia *f*.

tassel ['tæsl] *n* borla *f*.

taste [teɪst] <> *n* - **1.** [physical sense, discernment] gusto *m*; **in bad/good taste** de mal/buen gusto - **2.** [flavour] sabor *m* - **3.** [try]: **have a taste** pruébalo - **4.** *fig* [for success, fast cars etc]: **taste (for)** afición *f* (a), gusto *m* (por) - **5.** *fig* [experience] experiencia *f*. <> *vt* - **1.** [notice flavour of] notar un sabor a; **I can't taste the lemon in it** no noto el sabor a limón - **2.** [test, try] probar - **3.** *fig* [experience] conocer. <> *vi* saber; **to taste of** OR **like** saber a.

taste bud *n* papila *f* gustativa.

tasteful ['teɪstfʊl] *adj* elegante, de buen gusto.

tastefully ['teɪstfʊlɪ] *adv* elegantemente, con gusto.

tasteless ['teɪstlɪs] *adj* - **1.** [offensive, cheap and unattractive] de mal gusto - **2.** [without flavour] insípido(da), soso(sa).

taster ['teɪstər] *n* catador *m*, -ra *f*.

tasty ['teɪstɪ] (*comp* **-ier**, *superl* **-iest**) *adj* sabroso(sa).

tat [tæt] *n* (U) UK *inf pej* baratijas *fpl*.

tattered ['tætəd] *adj* [clothes] andrajoso(sa); [paper] desgastado(da).

tatters ['tætəz] *npl*: **in tatters** [clothes] andrajoso(sa); *fig* [confidence, reputation] por los suelos.

tattoo [təˈtuː] <> *n* (*pl* **-s**) - **1.** [design] tatuaje *m* - **2.** UK [military display] desfile *m* militar. <> *vt* tatuar.

tattooist [təˈtuːɪst] *n* tatuador *m*, -ra *f*.

tatty ['tætɪ] (*comp* **-ier**, *superl* **-iest**) *adj* UK *inf pej* desastrado(da).

taught [tɔːt] *pt* & *pp* ➤ **teach**.

taunt [tɔːnt] <> *vt* zaherir a. <> *n* pulla *f*.

Taurus ['tɔːrəs] *n* Tauro *m*; **to be (a) Taurus** ser Tauro.

taut [tɔːt] *adj* tenso(sa).

tauten ['tɔːtn] <> *vt* tensar. <> *vi* tensarse.

tautology [tɔːˈtɒlədʒɪ] *n* tautología *f*.

tavern ['tævn] *n* dated taberna *f*.

tawdry ['tɔːdrɪ] (*comp* **-ier**, *superl* **-iest**) *adj pej* de oropel.

tawny ['tɔːnɪ] *adj* leonado(da).

tax [tæks] <> *n* impuesto *m*, contribución *f*; **pay before** OR **after tax** salario antes/después de impuestos. <> *vt* - **1.** [goods, profits] gravar - **2.** [business, person] imponer contribuciones a - **3.** [strain, test] poner a prueba.

taxable ['tæksəbl] *adj* imponible.

tax allowance *n* desgravación *f* fiscal.

taxation [tækˈseɪʃn] *n* (U) - **1.** [system] sistema *m* tributario - **2.** [amount] impuestos *mpl*, contribuciones *fpl*.

tax avoidance [-əˈvɔɪdəns] *n* evasión *f* fiscal.

tax collector *n* recaudador *m*, -ra *f* de impuestos.

tax cut *n* reducción *f* tributaria.

tax-deductible [-dɪˈdʌktəbl] *adj* desgravable.

tax disc *n* UK *pegatina del impuesto de circulación*.

tax evasion *n* fraude *m* fiscal, evasión *f* de impuestos.

tax-exempt US = **tax-free**.

tax exemption *n* exención *f* de impuestos.

tax exile *n* UK [person] *persona que vive en el extranjero para evitar los impuestos*.

tax-free UK, **tax-exempt** US *adj* exento(ta) de impuestos.

tax haven *n* paraíso *m* fiscal.

taxi ['tæksɪ] <> *n* taxi *m*. <> *vi* [plane] rodar por la pista.

taxicab ['tæksɪkæb] *n* taxi *m*.

taxidermist ['tæksɪdɜːmɪst] *n* taxidermista *mf*.

taxi driver *n* taxista *mf*.

taxing ['tæksɪŋ] *adj* [gen] agotador(ra); [problem, exam] abrumador(ra).

tax inspector *n* ≃ inspector *m* de Hacienda.

taxi rank UK, **taxi stand** *n* parada *f* de taxis.

taxman ['tæksmæn] (*pl* **-men** [-men]) *n* - **1.** [tax collector] recaudador *m*, -ra *f* de impuestos - **2.** *inf* [tax office]: **the taxman** ≃ Hacienda *f*, ≃ el Fisco.

taxpayer ['tæks,peɪər] *n* contribuyente *mf*.

tax relief *n (U)* desgravación *f* fiscal.

tax return *n* declaración *f* de renta.

tax year *n* año *m* fiscal.

TB *n abbr of* **tuberculosis**.

T-bone steak *n* bistec con hueso en forma de T.

tbs., tbsp. (*abbr of* **tablespoon(ful)**) *cucharada grande*.

tea [ti:] *n* - **1.** [drink, leaves] té *m* - **2.** *UK* [afternoon snack] té *m*, merienda *f* - **3.** *UK* [evening meal] merienda cena *f*.

teabag ['ti:bæg] *n* bolsita *f* de té.

tea break *n UK* descanso *m* (*durante la jornada laboral*).

tea caddy [-,kædɪ] *n* bote *m* del té.

teacake ['ti:keɪk] *n UK* bollito *m*.

teach [ti:tʃ] <> *vt* (*pt & pp* **taught**) - **1.** [give lessons to] [student] dar clases a; **to teach sb sthg** enseñar algo a alguien; **to teach sb to do sthg** enseñar a alguien a hacer algo; **to teach (sb) that** inculcar a alguien que; **that will teach you a lesson!** ¡eso te enseñará! - **2.** [give lessons in] [subject] dar clases de - **3.** [advocate, state] preconizar; **to teach sb sthg, to teach sthg to sb** predicar a alguien algo. <> *vi* (*pt & pp* **taught**) ser profesor(ra), dar clases.

teacher ['ti:tʃər] *n* [at primary school] maestro *m*, -tra *f*; [at secondary school] profesor *m*, -ra *f*; **teacher's pet** *pej* enchufado *m*, -da *f* de la clase.

teacher training college *UK*, **teachers college** *US n* escuela *f* normal.

teaching ['ti:tʃɪŋ] *n* enseñanza *f*; **I've got ten hours of teaching** tengo diez horas de clases.

teaching aids *npl* materiales *mpl* pedagógicos.

teaching practice *n (U)* prácticas *fpl* de magisterio.

teaching staff *npl* personal *m* docente, profesorado *m*.

tea cloth *n UK* [tea towel] paño *m* de cocina.

tea cosy *UK*, **tea cozy** *US n* cubretetera *f*.

teacup ['ti:kʌp] *n* taza *f* de té.

teak [ti:k] <> *n* teca *f*. <> *comp* de teca.

tea leaves *npl* hojas *fpl* de té.

team [ti:m] *n* equipo *m*.

◆ **team up** *vi*: **to team up (with)** formar equipo (con).

team games *npl* juegos *mpl* de equipos.

teammate ['ti:mmeɪt] *n* compañero *m*, -ra *f* de equipo.

team spirit *n* espíritu *m* de equipo.

teamster ['ti:mstər] *n US* camionero *m*.

teamwork ['ti:mwɜ:k] *n (U)* trabajo *m* en equipo.

tea party *n* reunión *f* para tomar el té.

teapot ['ti:pɒt] *n* tetera *f*.

tear[1] [tɪər] *n* lágrima *f*; **in tears** llorando.

tear[2] [teər] <> *vt* (*pt* **tore**, *pp* **torn**) - **1.** [rip] rasgar, romper; **to tear sthg open** abrir algo rasgándolo; **to tear sthg to pieces** *fig* poner algo por los suelos - **2.** [remove roughly] arrancar; **she tore a page out of her exercise book** arrancó una página de su libro de ejercicios ▸▸ **to be torn between** vacilar entre. <> *vi* (*pt* **tore**, *pp* **torn**) - **1.** [rip] romperse, rasgarse - **2.** *inf* [move quickly]: **he tore out of the house** salió de la casa a toda pastilla; **they were tearing along** iban a toda pastilla ▸▸ **to tear loose** soltarse de un tirón. <> *n* rasgón *m*, desgarrón *m*.

◆ **tear apart** *vt sep* - **1.** [rip up] despedazar - **2.** *fig* [disrupt greatly] desintegrar - **3.** [upset greatly] desgarrar.

◆ **tear at** *vt insep* tirar de.

◆ **tear away** *vt sep*: **to tear o.s. away from** separarse de.

◆ **tear down** *vt sep* [building, statue] echar abajo.

◆ **tear off** *vt sep* [clothes] quitarse precipitadamente.

◆ **tear up** *vt sep* hacer pedazos.

tearaway ['teərə,weɪ] *n UK inf* alborotador *m*, -ra *f*.

teardrop ['tɪədrɒp] *n* lágrima *f*.

tearful ['tɪəfʊl] *adj* - **1.** [person] lloroso(sa) - **2.** [event] lacrimoso(sa).

tear gas [tɪər-] *n (U)* gas *m* lacrimógeno.

tearing ['teərɪŋ] *adj inf*: **to be in a tearing hurry** tener mucha prisa.

tearjerker ['tɪə,dʒɜ:kər] *n hum* dramón *m*.

tearoom ['ti:rʊm] *n* salón *m* de té.

tease [ti:z] <> *n inf* puñetero *m*, -ra *f*. <> *vt* - **1.** [mock]: **to tease sb (about)** tomar el pelo a alguien (acerca de) - **2.** *US* [hair] cardarse.

tea service, tea set *n* servicio *m* OR juego *m* de té.

tea shop *n* salón *m* de té.

teasing ['ti:zɪŋ] *adj* guasón(ona), burlón(ona).

Teasmaid® ['ti:zmeɪd] *n UK máquina de hacer el té automática*.

teaspoon ['ti:spu:n] *n* - **1.** [utensil] cucharilla *f* - **2.** [amount] cucharadita *f*.

tea strainer *n* colador *m* de té.

teat [ti:t] *n* - **1.** [of animal] tetilla *f* - **2.** [of bottle] tetina *f*.

teatime ['ti:taɪm] *n UK* hora *f* del té.

tea towel *n* paño *m* de cocina, repasador *m R Plata*.

tea urn *n cilindro o barril con grifo para servir té en grandes cantidades.*

technical ['teknɪkl] *adj* técnico(ca).

technical college *n UK* ≃ centro *m* de formación profesional.

technical drawing *n (U)* dibujo *m* técnico.

technicality [,teknɪ'kælətɪ] *(pl* **-ies)** *n* detalle *m* técnico.

technically ['teknɪklɪ] *adv* - **1.** [gen] técnicamente - **2.** [theoretically] teóricamente, en teoría.

technician [tek'nɪʃn] *n* técnico *m*, -ca *f*.

Technicolor® ['teknɪ,kʌlər] *n* tecnicolor® *m*.

technique [tek'ni:k] *n* técnica *f*.

techno ['teknəʊ] *n MUS* tecno *m*.

technological [,teknə'lɒdʒɪkl] *adj* tecnológico(ca).

technologist [tek'nɒlədʒɪst] *n* tecnólogo *m*, -ga *f*.

technology [tek'nɒlədʒɪ] *(pl* **-ies)** *n* tecnología *f*.

technophobe ['teknəfəʊb] *n* tecnófobo *m*, -ba *f*.

teddy ['tedɪ] *(pl* **-ies)** *n*: **teddy (bear)** oso *m* de peluche.

tedious ['ti:djəs] *adj* tedioso(sa).

tedium ['ti:djəm] *n fml* tedio *m*.

tee [ti:] *n* tee *m*.

→ **tee off** *vi GOLF* golpear desde el tee.

teem [ti:m] *vi* - **1.** [rain] llover a cántaros - **2.** [be busy]: **to be teeming with** estar inundado(da) de.

teen [ti:n] *adj inf* adolescente.

teenage ['ti:neɪdʒ] *adj* adolescente.

teenager ['ti:n,eɪdʒər] *n* adolescente *mf*, quinceañero *m*, -ra *f*.

teens [ti:nz] *npl* adolescencia *f*; **he's in his teens** es adolescente.

teeny (weeny) [,ti:nɪ('wi:nɪ)], **teensy (weensy)** [,ti:nzɪ('wi:nzɪ)] *adj inf* pequeñito(ta), chiquitín(ina).

tee-shirt *n* camiseta *f*.

teeter ['ti:tər] *vi lit & fig* tambalearse.

teeter-totter *n US* balancín *m*, subibaja *m*.

teeth [ti:θ] *npl* - **1.** ▷ **tooth** - **2.** *fig* [power] poder *m*.

teethe [ti:ð] *vi* echar los dientes.

teething ring ['ti:ðɪŋ-] *n* chupador *m*.

teething troubles ['ti:ðɪŋ-] *npl fig* problemas *mpl* iniciales.

teetotal [ti:'təʊtl] *adj* abstemio(mia).

teetotaller *UK*, **teetotaler** *US* [ti:'təʊtlər] *n* abstemio *m*, -mia *f*.

TEFL ['tefl] *(abbr of* **teaching of English as a foreign language)** *n* enseñanza de inglés para extranjeros.

Teflon® ['teflɒn] ◇ *n* teflón® *m*. ◇ *comp* de teflón®.

tel. (*abbr of* **telephone)** tfno.

tele- ['telɪ] *prefix* tele-.

telebanking ['telɪbæŋkɪŋ] *n FIN* banca *f* telefónica.

telecast ['telɪkɑ:st] *n* emisión *f* televisiva.

telecom ['telɪkɒm] *n UK inf* telecomunicaciones *fpl*.

telecoms ['telɪkɒmz] *npl* = **telecom**.

telecommunications ['telɪkə,mju:nɪ'keɪʃnz] *npl* telecomunicaciones *fpl*.

telegram ['telɪɡræm] *n* telegrama *m*.

telegraph ['telɪɡrɑ:f] ◇ *n* telégrafo *m*. ◇ *vt* telegrafiar.

telegraph pole, **telegraph post** *UK n* poste *m* de telégrafos.

telepathic [,telɪ'pæθɪk] *adj* telepático(ca).

telepathy [tɪ'lepəθɪ] *n* telepatía *f*.

telephone ['telɪfəʊn] ◇ *n* teléfono *m*; **to be on the telephone** *UK* [connected to network] tener teléfono; [speaking] estar al teléfono. ◇ *vt & vi* telefonear.

telephone banking *n* banca *f* telefónica.

telephone book *n* guía *f* telefónica.

telephone booth *n* teléfono *m* público.

telephone box *n UK* cabina *f* (telefónica).

telephone call *n* llamada *f* telefónica, llamado *m* telefónico *Amér*.

telephone directory *n* guía *f* telefónica.

telephone exchange *n* central *f* telefónica.

telephone number *n* número *m* de teléfono.

telephone operator *n* operador *m*, -ra *f*, telefonista *mf*.

telephonist [tɪ'lefənɪst] *n UK* telefonista *mf*.

telephoto lens [,telɪ'fəʊtəʊ-] *n* teleobjetivo *m*.

teleprinter ['telɪ,prɪntər], **teletypewriter** *US* [,telɪ'taɪp,raɪtər] *n* teletipo *m*, teleimpresor *m*.

Teleprompter® [,telɪ'prɒmptər] *n* teleapuntador *m*.

telesales ['telɪseɪlz] *npl* ventas *fpl* por teléfono.

telescope ['telɪskəʊp] *n* telescopio *m*.

telescopic [,telɪ'skɒpɪk] *adj* - **1.** [magnifying] telescópico(ca) - **2.** [contracting] plegable.

teletext ['telɪtekst] *n* teletexto *m*.

telethon ['telɪθɒn] *n programa televisivo de larga duración destinado a recaudar fondos para una obra benéfica.*

teletypewriter *US* = **teleprinter**.

televideo [telɪ'vɪdɪəu] *n* televídeo *m*.

televise ['telɪvaɪz] *vt* televisar.

television ['telɪ,vɪʒn] *n* televisión *f*; **on television** en televisión; **to watch television** ver la televisión.

television licence *n UK documento que prueba el pago del impuesto que da derecho al uso de un televisor.*

television programme *n* programa *m* de televisión.

television set *n* televisor *m*, (aparato *m* de) televisión *f*.

teleworker ['telɪwɜːkəʳ] *n* teletrabajador *m*, -ra *f*.

telex ['teleks] <> *n* télex *m*. <> *vt* [message] transmitir por télex; [person] mandar un télex a.

tell [tel] <> *vt* (*pt & pp* told) - **1.** [gen] decir; **to tell sb (that)** decir a alguien que; **to tell sb sthg, to tell sthg to sb** decir a alguien algo; **to tell sb to do sthg** decir a alguien que haga algo; **I told you so!** ¡ya te lo dije! - **2.** [joke, story] contar - **3.** [judge, recognize]: **to tell what sb is thinking** saber en qué está pensando alguien; **to tell the time** decir la hora; **there's no telling...** es imposible saber... - **4.** [differentiate]: **to tell the difference between A and B** distinguir entre A y B; **it's hard to tell one from another** son difíciles de distinguir. <> *vi* (*pt & pp* told) [have effect] surtir efecto.

→ **tell apart** *vt sep* distinguir, diferenciar; **I can't tell them apart** no consigo distinguirlos.

→ **tell off** *vt sep esp US* reñir, reprender.

teller ['teləʳ] *n* - **1.** [of votes] escrutador *m*, -ra *f* - **2.** *esp US* [in bank] cajero *m*, -ra *f*.

telling ['telɪŋ] *adj* [remark, incident] revelador(ra).

telling-off (*pl* tellings-off) *n* bronca *f*; **to give sb a (good) telling-off** echar una bronca a alguien.

telltale ['telteɪl] <> *adj* revelador(ra). <> *n* chivato *m*, -ta *f*, acusica *mf*.

telly ['telɪ] (*pl* -ies) (*abbr of* television) *n UK inf* tele *f*; **on telly** en la tele.

temerity [tɪ'merətɪ] *n fml* temeridad *f*.

temp [temp] <> *n UK inf* (*abbr of* temporary (employee)) trabajador *m*, -ra *f* temporal. <> *vi*: **she's temping** tiene un trabajo temporal.

temp. (*abbr of* temperature) temp.

temper ['tempəʳ] <> *n* - **1.** [state of mind, mood] humor *m*; **to keep one's temper** mantener la calma; **to lose one's temper** enfadarse, perder la paciencia; **to have a short temper** te-

ner genio - **2.** [angry state]: **to be in a temper** estar de mal humor - **3.** [temperament] temperamento *m*. <> *vt fml* templar, suavizar.

temperament ['temprəmənt] *n* temperamento *m*.

temperamental [,temprə'mentl] *adj* [volatile] temperamental.

temperance ['temprəns] *n* templanza *f*.

temperate ['temprət] *adj* templado(da).

temperature ['temprətʃəʳ] *n* temperatura *f*; **to take sb's temperature** tomarle a alguien la temperatura; **to have a temperature** tener fiebre.

tempered ['tempəd] *adj* templado(da).

tempest ['tempɪst] *n liter* tempestad *f*.

tempestuous [tem'pestjʊəs] *adj lit & fig* tempestuoso(sa).

tempi ['tempiː] *npl* ⊏▷ **tempo**.

template ['templɪt] *n* plantilla *f*.

temple ['templ] *n* - **1.** RELIG templo *m* - **2.** ANAT sien *f*.

tempo ['tempəʊ] (*pl* -pos *OR* -pi) *n* - **1.** MUS ritmo *m* - **2.** [of an event] tempo *m*.

temporarily [,tempə'rerəlɪ] *adv* temporalmente, provisionalmente.

temporary ['tempərərɪ] *adj* [gen] temporal, temporario *Amér*, provisional, provisorio *Andes, Col & Ven*; [improvement, problem] pasajero(ra).

tempt [tempt] *vt* [entice]: **to tempt sb (to do sthg)** tentar a alguien (a hacer algo); **to be** *OR* **feel tempted to do sthg** estar *OR* sentirse tentado de hacer algo.

temptation [temp'teɪʃn] *n* tentación *f*.

tempting ['temptɪŋ] *adj* tentador(ra).

ten [ten] *num* diez; *see also* **six**.

tenable ['tenəbl] *adj* - **1.** [reasonable, credible] sostenible - **2.** [job, post]: **the post is tenable for one year** el puesto tendrá una duración de un año.

tenacious [tɪ'neɪʃəs] *adj* tenaz.

tenacity [tɪ'næsətɪ] *n* tenacidad *f*.

tenancy ['tenənsɪ] (*pl* -ies) *n* - **1.** [period - of house] alquiler *m*; [- of land] arrendamiento *m* - **2.** [possession] ocupación *f*.

tenant ['tenənt] *n* [of house] inquilino *m*, -na *f*; [of pub] arrendatario *m*, -ria *f*.

tend [tend] *vt* - **1.** [have tendency]: **to tend to do sthg** soler hacer algo, tender a hacer algo; **I tend to think...** me inclino a pensar... - **2.** [look after] cuidar - **3.** *US*: **to tend bar** atender en el bar.

tendency ['tendənsɪ] (*pl* -ies) *n* - **1.** [trend]: **tendency (for sb/sthg to do sthg)** tendencia *f* (de alguien/algo a hacer algo); **tendency towards** tendencia hacia - **2.** [leaning, inclination] inclinación *f*.

tender ['tendə'] <> *adj* [gen] tierno(na); [sore] dolorido(da); **at a tender age** a una edad tierna. <> *n* - **1.** COMM propuesta *f*, oferta *f* - **2.**: **(legal) tender** moneda *f* de curso legal. <> *vt fml* [resignation] presentar.

tenderize, -ise ['tendəraiz] *vt* ablandar.

tenderly ['tendəli] *adv* [caringly] tiernamente, cariñosamente.

tenderness ['tendənis] *n (U)* - **1.** [care, compassion] ternura *f*, dulzura *f* - **2.** [soreness] sensibilidad *f*.

tendon ['tendən] *n* tendón *m*.

tendril ['tendrəl] *n* zarcillo *m*.

tenement ['tenəmənt] *n bloque de viviendas modestas.*

tenet ['tenit] *n fml* principio *m*, dogma *m*.

tenner ['tenə'] *n UK inf* - **1.** [amount] diez libras *fpl* - **2.** [note] billete *m* de diez libras.

tennis ['tenis] *n* tenis *m*.

tennis ball *n* pelota *f* de tenis.

tennis court *n* pista *f* de tenis.

tennis match *n* partido *m* de tenis.

tennis player *n* tenista *mf*.

tennis racket *n* raqueta *f* de tenis.

tenor ['tenə'] <> *adj* de tenor. <> *n* - **1.** [singer] tenor *m* - **2.** *fml* [meaning, mood] tono *m*.

tenpin bowling *UK* ['tenpin-], **tenpins** *US* ['tenpinz] *n (U)* bolos *mpl*.

tense [tens] <> *adj* tenso(sa). <> *n* tiempo *m*. <> *vt* tensar. <> *vi* tensarse, ponerse tenso(sa).

tensed up [tenst-] *adj* tenso(sa), nervioso(sa).

tension ['tenʃn] *n* tensión *f*.

ten-spot *n US* billete *m* de diez dólares.

tent [tent] *n* tienda *f* (de campaña), carpa *f* *Amér.*

tentacle ['tentəkl] *n* tentáculo *m*.

tentative ['tentətiv] *adj* - **1.** [person] indeciso(sa); [step, handshake] vacilante - **2.** [suggestion, conclusion etc] provisional.

tentatively ['tentətivli] *adv* - **1.** [hesitantly] con vacilación - **2.** [not finally] provisionalmente.

tenterhooks ['tentəhuks] *npl*: **to be on tenterhooks** estar sobre ascuas.

tenth [tenθ] *num* décimo(ma); *see also* **sixth**.

tent peg *n* estaca *f*.

tent pole *n* mástil *m* de tienda.

tenuous ['tenjuəs] *adj* [argument] flojo(ja), poco convincente; [evidence, connection] débil, insignificante; [hold] ligero(ra).

tenuously ['tenjuəsli] *adv* ligeramente.

tenure ['tenjə'] *n* - **1.** *(U) fml* [of property] arrendamiento *m* - **2.** [of job] ocupación *f*, ejercicio *m*.

tepee ['ti:pi:] *n* tipi *m*, tienda *f* india.

tepid ['tepid] *adj* - **1.** [liquid] tibio(bia) - **2.** *pej* [welcome] poco caluroso(sa); [performance, speech] poco vehemente.

tequila [tɪ'ki:lə] *n* tequila *m*.

Ter., Terr. *abbr of* **Terrace**.

term [tɜ:m] <> *n* - **1.** [word, expression] término *m* - **2.** SCH & UNIV trimestre *m* - **3.** POL mandato *m*; **term of office** mandato *m* - **4.** [period of time] periodo *m*; **in the long/short term** a largo/corto plazo. <> *vt*: **to term sthg sthg** calificar algo de algo.

◆ **terms** *npl* - **1.** [of contract, agreement] condiciones *fpl* - **2.** [basis]: **in international/real terms** en términos internacionales/reales; **on equal** OR **the same terms** en condiciones de igualdad; **to be on good terms (with sb)** mantener buenas relaciones (con alguien); **to be on speaking terms (with sb)** hablarse (con alguien); **to come to terms with sthg** aceptar algo

▶▶ **to think in terms of doing sthg** pensar hacer algo.

◆ **in terms of** *prep* por lo que se refiere a.

terminal ['tɜ:mɪnl] <> *adj* MED incurable, terminal. <> *n* - **1.** [transport] terminal *f* - **2.** COMPUT terminal *m*.

terminally ['tɜ:mɪnəli] *adv*: **to be terminally ill** ser enfermo terminal.

terminate ['tɜ:mɪneɪt] <> *vt fml* [gen] poner fin a; [pregnancy] interrumpir. <> *vi* - **1.** [bus, train] finalizar el trayecto - **2.** [contract] terminarse.

termination [,tɜ:mɪ'neɪʃn] *n* - **1.** *fml* [ending] terminación *f* - **2.** [abortion]: **termination (of pregnancy)** interrupción *f* del embarazo.

termini ['tɜ:mɪnaɪ] *npl* ▷ **terminus**.

terminology [,tɜ:mɪ'nɒlədʒɪ] *n* terminología *f*.

terminus ['tɜ:mɪnəs] *(pl* **-ni** OR **-nuses**) *n* (estación *f*) terminal *f*.

termite ['tɜ:maɪt] *n* termita *f*.

Terr. = Ter.

terrace ['terəs] *n* - **1.** [gen] terraza *f* - **2.** *UK* [of houses] hilera *f* de casas adosadas.

◆ **terraces** *npl* FTBL: **the terraces** las gradas.

terraced ['terəst] *adj* - **1.** [hillside] a terrazas - **2.** [house, housing] adosado(da).

terraced house *n UK* casa *f* adosada.

terracotta [,terə'kɒtə] *n* terracota *f*.

terrain [te'reɪn] *n* terreno *m*.

terrapin ['terəpɪn] *(pl* **terrapin** OR **-s**) *n* tortuga *f* acuática.

terrestrial [tə'restrɪəl] *adj fml* terrestre.

terrible ['terəbl] *adj* - **1.** [crash, mess, shame] terrible, espantoso(sa) - **2.** [unwell, unhappy, very bad] fatal.

terribly ['terəblɪ] *adv* [sing, play, write] malísima-mente; [injured, sorry, expensive] horriblemente, terriblemente.

terrier ['terɪər] *n* terrier *m*.

terrific [tə'rɪfɪk] *adj* - **1.** [wonderful] fabulo-so(sa), estupendo(da) - **2.** [enormous] enorme, tremendo(da).

terrified ['terɪfaɪd] *adj* aterrorizado(da); **to be terrified (of)** tener terror (a).

terrify ['terɪfaɪ] (*pt & pp* -ied) *vt* aterrorizar.

terrifying ['terɪfaɪŋ] *adj* aterrador(ra), espan-toso(sa).

terrine [te'ri:n] *n* [paté] tarrina *f*.

territorial [,terɪ'tɔ:rɪəl] *adj* territorial.

Territorial Army *n UK*: **the Territorial Army** *el ejército voluntario de Gran Bretaña*.

territorial waters *npl* aguas *fpl* territoria-les, aguas jurisdiccionales.

territory ['terətrɪ] (*pl* -ies) *n* - **1.** [political area] territorio *m* - **2.** [terrain] terreno *m* - **3.** [area of knowledge] esfera *f*, campo *m*.

terror ['terər] *n* - **1.** [fear] terror *m*; **to live in terror** vivir aterrorizado(da); **they ran out of the house in terror** salieron de la casa aterro-rizados - **2.** *inf* [rascal] demonio *m*.

terrorism ['terərɪzm] *n* terrorismo *m*.

terrorist ['terərɪst] *n* terrorista *mf*.

terrorize, -ise ['terəraɪz] *vt* aterrorizar, ate-rrar.

terror-stricken *adj* aterrorizado(da), aterra-do(da).

terse [tɜ:s] *adj* seco(ca).

tersely ['tɜ:slɪ] *adv* secamente.

tertiary ['tɜ:ʃərɪ] *adj fml* terciario(ria).

tertiary education *n* (*U*) estudios *mpl* supe-riores.

Terylene® ['terəli:n] *n* terylene® *m*.

TESL ['tesl] (*abbr of* **teaching of English as a second language**) *n enseñanza de inglés pa-ra extranjeros*.

test [test] ⋄ *n* - **1.** [trial] prueba *f*; **to put sthg to the test** poner algo a prueba - **2.** [examina-tion] examen *m*, prueba *f* - **3.** [of blood, ur-ine] análisis *m inv*; [of eyes] revisión *f*. ⋄ *vt* - **1.** [try out] probar, poner a prueba - **2.** [exam-ine] examinar; **to test sb on** examinar a al-guien de.

testament ['testəmənt] *n* - **1.** [will] testamen-to *m* - **2.** [proof]: **testament to** testimonio *m* de.

test ban *n* suspensión *f* de pruebas nucleares.

test case *n* LAW juicio *m* que sienta jurispru-dencia.

test-drive *vt* someter a prueba de carretera.

tester ['testər] *n* - **1.** [person testing] probador *m*, -ra *f* - **2.** [sample] muestra *f* (*de perfume etc*).

test flight *n* vuelo *m* de prueba.

testicles ['testɪklz] *npl* testículos *mpl*.

testify ['testɪfaɪ] ⋄ *vi* (*pt & pp* -ied) - **1.** LAW prestar declaración - **2.** [be proof]: **to testify to sthg** dar fe de OR atestiguar algo. ⋄ *vt* (*pt & pp* -ied): **to testify that** declarar que.

testimonial [,testɪ'məʊnjəl] *n* [letter] carta *f* de recomendación.

testimony [UK 'testɪmənɪ, US 'testəməʊnɪ] *n* - **1.** LAW testimonio *m*, declaración *f* - **2.** [proof, demonstration]: **testimony to** testimonio *m* de.

testing ['testɪŋ] *adj* duro(ra).

testing ground *n* zona *f* de pruebas.

test match *n UK* SPORT partido *m* internacio-nal.

test paper *n* SCH examen *m*, test *m*.

test pilot *n* piloto *mf* de pruebas.

test tube *n* probeta *f*.

test-tube baby *n* bebé *mf* probeta.

testy ['testɪ] (*comp* -ier, *superl* -iest) *adj* - **1.** [person] irritable, irascible - **2.** [remark, comment] acre, agresivo(va).

tetanus ['tetənəs] *n* tétanos *m inv*.

tetchy ['tetʃɪ] (*comp* -ier, *superl* -iest) *adj* irri-table.

tête-à-tête [,teɪtɑ:'teɪt] *n* conversación *f* confi-dencial (*entre dos personas*).

tether ['teðər] ⋄ *vt* atar. ⋄ *n*: **to be at the end of one's tether** estar uno que ya no pue-de más.

Texan ['teksn] ⋄ *n & adj* tejano(na). ⋄ *n* teja-no *m*, -na *f*.

Texas ['teksəs] *n* Tejas.

text [tekst] ⋄ *n* - **1.** [gen] texto *m* - **2.** [textbook] libro *m* de texto - **3.** [sent by mobile phone] men-saje *m* de texto, SMS *m*. ⋄ *vt* enviar un men-saje de texto a. ⋄ *vi* enviar mensajes de tex-to.

textbook ['tekstbʊk] *n* libro *m* de texto.

textile ['tekstaɪl] ⋄ *n* textil *m*, tejido *m*. ⋄ *comp* textil.

→ **textiles** *npl* industria *f* textil.

texting ['tekstɪŋ] *n inf* mensajes *fpl* de texto.

text message *n* [on mobile phone] mensaje *m* de texto.

text messaging [-'mesɪdʒɪŋ] *n* [on mobile phone] mensajería *f* de texto.

texture ['tekstʃər] *n* textura *f*.

TGWU (*abbr of* **Transport and General Work-ers' Union**) *n sindicato británico de mayor afiliación que acoge a trabajadores de di-versos sectores industriales*.

Thai [taɪ] ⬦ *adj* tailandés(esa). ⬦ *n* - **1.** [person] tailandés *m*, -esa *f* - **2.** [language] tailandés *m*.

Thailand ['taɪlænd] *n* Tailandia.

thalidomide [θə'lɪdəmaɪd] *n* talidomida *f*.

Thames [temz] *n*: **the Thames** el Támesis.

than (*weak form* [ðən], *strong form* [ðæn]) ⬦ *prep* que; **you're older than me** eres mayor que yo; **you're older than I thought** eres mayor de lo que pensaba. ⬦ *conj* que; **I'd sooner read than sleep** prefiero leer que dormir; **no sooner did he arrive than she left** tan pronto llegó él, ella se fue; **more than three/once** más de tres/de una vez; **rather than stay, he chose to go** en vez de quedarse, prefirió irse.

thank [θæŋk] *vt*: **to thank sb (for sthg)** dar las gracias a alguien (por algo), agradecer a alguien (algo); **thank God** OR **goodness** OR **heavens!** ¡gracias a Dios!, ¡menos mal!

➡ **thanks** ⬦ *npl* agradecimiento *m*; **they left without a word of thanks** se marcharon sin dar las gracias. ⬦ *excl* ¡gracias!; **thanks a lot** muchas gracias; **would you like a biscuit? – no thanks** ¿quieres una galleta? – no, gracias; **thanks for** gracias por.

➡ **thanks to** *prep* gracias a.

thankful ['θæŋkfʊl] *adj* - **1.** [relieved] aliviado(da) - **2.** [grateful]: **thankful (for)** agradecido(da) (por).

thankfully ['θæŋkfʊlɪ] *adv* - **1.** [with gratitude] con agradecimiento - **2.** [thank goodness] gracias a Dios.

thankless ['θæŋklɪs] *adj* ingrato(ta).

Thanksgiving ['θæŋks,gɪvɪŋ] *n* US Día *m* de Acción de Gracias *(el cuarto jueves de noviembre)*.

Thanksgiving

Con la celebración del Thanksgiving, el cuarto jueves de noviembre, se conmemora el asentamiento de los primeros colonos en Norteamérica. Se suele celebrar con una cena en familia, que consiste tradicionalmente en un pavo asado con salsa de arándanos, acompañado de boniatos como guarnición, y una tarta de calabaza de postre.

thank you *excl* ¡gracias!; **thank you very much** muchas gracias; **thank you for** gracias por; **to say thank you (for sthg)** dar gracias (por algo); **tea? – no thank you** ¿té? – no, gracias.

➡ **thank you** *n* agradecimiento *m*; **they left without so much as a thank you** se marcharon sin ni siquiera dar las gracias; **a thank you letter** una carta de agradecimiento.

that ([ðæt], *weak form of pron and conj* [ðət]) ⬦ *pron* (*pl* **those**) - **1.** (*demonstrative use: pl* '*those*') ése *m*, ésa *f*, ésos *mpl*, ésas *fpl*; (*indefinite*) eso; **that sounds familiar** eso me resulta familiar; **who's that?** [who is it?] ¿quién es?; **what's that?** ¿qué es eso?; **that's a shame** es una pena; **is that Maureen?** [asking someone else] ¿es ésa Maureen?; [asking person in question] ¿eres Maureen?; **like that** así; **do you like these or those?** ¿te gustan éstos o ésos? - **2.** [further away in distance, time] aquél *m*, aquélla *f*, aquéllos *mpl*, aquéllas *fpl*; (*indefinite*) aquello; **that was the life!** ¡aquello sí que era vida!; **all those who helped me** todos aquellos que me ayudaron - **3.** (*to introduce relative clauses*) que; **a path that led into the woods** un sendero que conducía al bosque; **everything that I have done** todo lo que he hecho; **the room that I sleep in** el cuarto donde OR en (el) que duermo; **the day that he arrived** el día en que llegó; **the firm that he's applying to** la empresa a la que solicita trabajo. ⬦ *adj* (*demonstrative: pl* '*those*') ese(esa), esos(esas) (*pl*); [further away in distance, time] aquel(aquella), aquellos(aquellas) (*pl*); **those chocolates are delicious** esos bombones están exquisitos; **I'll have that book at the back** yo cogeré aquel libro del fondo; **later that day** más tarde ese/ aquel mismo día. ⬦ *adv* tan; **it wasn't that bad** no estuvo tan mal; **it doesn't cost that much** no cuesta tanto; **it was that big** fue así de grande. ⬦ *conj* que; **he recommended that I phone you** aconsejó que te telefoneara; **it's time that we were leaving** deberíamos irnos ya, ya va siendo hora de irse.

➡ **at that** *prep* - **1.** [too]: **she's an artist, and a good one at that** es artista, y además de las buenas - **2.** [on saying/doing that]: **and at that, he left** y en ese momento, se fue.

➡ **that is** *adv* es decir.

➡ **that's it** *adv*: **that's it!, there's no more!** ¡ya está!, ¡ya no quedan más!; **that's it, I'm leaving!** ¡se acabó!, ¡me marcho!

➡ **that's that** *adv* punto, se acabó.

thatched [θætʃt] *adj* con techo de paja.

Thatcherism ['θætʃərɪzm] *n* thatcherismo *m*.

that's [ðæts] (*abbr of* = that is), = **that**.

thaw [θɔ:] ⬦ *vt* [snow, ice] derretir; [frozen food] descongelar. ⬦ *vi* [snow, ice] derretirse; [frozen food] descongelarse; *fig* [people, relations] distenderse. ⬦ *n* deshielo *m*.

the (*weak form* [ðə], *before vowel* [ðɪ], *strong form* [ði:]) *def art* - **1.** (*gen*) el(la); (*pl*) los(las); (*before f nouns beginning with stressed 'a' or 'ha'* = **el**; *'a' + 'el'* = **al**; *'de' + 'el'* = **del**); **the boat** el barco; **the Queen** la reina; **the men** los hombres; **the women** las mujeres; **the water** el agua; **to the end of the world** al fin del mundo; **the highest mountain in the world** la montaña más alta del mundo; **the monkey is a primate** el mono es un primate; **to play the piano** tocar el piano; **the Joneses are coming to supper** los Jones vienen a cenar; **you're not the John Major, are you?** ¿no será usted John Major el político, verdad?; **it's the place to go to in Paris** es el sitio al que hay que ir en París **- 2.** *(with an adj to form a n)*: **the old/young** los viejos/jóvenes; **the impossible** lo imposible **- 3.** [in dates]: **the twelfth of May** el doce de mayo; **the forties** los cuarenta **- 4.** *(in comparisons)*: **the more I see her, the less I like her** cuanto más la veo, menos me gusta; **the sooner the better** cuanto antes mejor **- 5.** [in titles]: **Catherine the Great** Catalina la Grande; **George the First** Jorge Primero.

theatre, theater US [ˈθɪətər] *n* **- 1.** [for plays etc] teatro *m* **- 2.** UK [in hospital] quirófano *m*, sala *f* de operaciones **- 3.** US [cinema] cine *m*.

theatregoer, theatergoer US [ˈθɪətə,gəʊər] *n* aficionado *m*, -da *f* al teatro.

theatrical [θɪˈætrɪkl] *adj* lit & fig teatral.

theft [θeft] *n* [more serious] robo *m*; [less serious] hurto *m*.

their [ðeər] *poss adj* su, sus *(pl)*; **their house** su casa; **their children** sus hijos; **it wasn't their fault** no fue culpa suya OR su culpa; **they washed their hair** se lavaron el pelo.

theirs [ðeəz] *poss pron* suyo(suya); **that money is theirs** ese dinero es suyo; **our car hit theirs** nuestro coche chocó contra el suyo; **it wasn't our fault, it was theirs** no fue culpa nuestra sino suya OR de ellos; **a friend of theirs** un amigo suyo OR de ellos.

them *(weak form* [ðəm]*, strong form* [ðem]*) pers pron pl* **- 1.** *(direct)* los *mpl*, las *fpl*; **I know them** los conozco; **I like them** me gustan; **if I were** OR **was them** si (yo) fuera ellos **- 2.** *(indirect - gen)* les; *(- with other 3rd person pronouns)* se *mpl* & *fpl*; **she sent them a letter** les mandó una carta; **we spoke to them** hablamos con ellos; **I gave it to them** se lo di (a ellos) **- 3.** *(stressed, after prep, in comparisons etc)* ellos *mpl*, ellas *fpl*; **you can't expect them to do it** no esperarás que **ellos** lo hagan; **with/ without them** con/sin ellos; **a few of them** unos pocos; **some of them** algunos; **all of them** todos ellos; **we're not as wealthy as them** no somos tan ricos como ellos.

thematic [θɪˈmætɪk] *adj* temático(ca).

theme [θi:m] *n* **- 1.** [gen] tema *m* **- 2.** [signature tune] sintonía *f*.

theme park *n parque de atracciones que gira alrededor de un tema.*

theme pub *n* UK pub *m* temático.

theme song *n* tema *m* musical.

theme tune *n* tema *m* musical.

themselves [ðem'selvz] *pron* **- 1.** *(reflexive)* se; *(after prep)* sí; **they enjoyed themselves** se divirtieron; **they were talking amongst themselves** hablaban entre ellos **- 2.** *(for emphasis)* ellos mismos *mpl*, ellas mismas *fpl*; **they did it themselves** lo hicieron ellos mismos **- 3.** [alone] solos(las); **they organized it (by) themselves** lo organizaron ellas solas **- 4.** [their usual selves]: **the boys aren't themselves today** hoy los chicos no se están portando como de costumbre.

then [ðen] <> *adv* **- 1.** [not now] entonces; **it starts at 8 – I'll see you then** empieza a las 8 – hasta las 8, entonces; **up until then he had always trusted her** hasta entonces siempre había confiado en ella; **from then on** desde entonces **- 2.** [next, afterwards] luego, después **- 3.** [in that case] entonces; **I'll do it straight away then** entonces lo voy a hacer ahora mismo; **all right then** de acuerdo, pues **- 4.** [therefore] entonces, por lo tanto; **then it must have been her!** ¡entonces tiene que haber sido ella! **- 5.** [furthermore, also] además. <> *adj* entonces; **the then headmistress** la entonces directora; **then again** pero por otra parte.

thence [ðens] *adv dated* [from that place] desde allí.

theologian [θɪəˈləʊdʒən] *n* teólogo *m*, -ga *f*.

theology [θɪˈɒlədʒɪ] *n* teología *f*.

theorem [ˈθɪərəm] *n* teorema *m*.

theoretical [θɪəˈretɪkl] *adj* teórico(ca).

theoretically [θɪəˈretɪklɪ] *adv* en teoría.

theorist [ˈθɪərɪst] *n* teórico *m*, -ca *f*.

theorize, -ise [ˈθɪəraɪz] *vi*: **to theorize (about sthg)** teorizar (sobre algo).

theory [ˈθɪərɪ] *(pl* -ies) *n* teoría *f*; **in theory** en teoría.

therapeutic [,θerəˈpju:tɪk] *adj* terapéutico(ca).

therapeutic cloning *n* MED clonación *f* terapéutica.

therapist [ˈθerəpɪst] *n* terapeuta *mf*.

therapy [ˈθerəpɪ] *n* terapia *f*.

there [ðeər] <> *pron* **- 1.** [indicating existence]: **there is/are** hay; **there's someone at the door** hay alguien en la puerta; **there must be some mistake** debe (de) haber un error; **there are five of us** somos cinco **- 2.** *(with vb)* fml: **there followed an ominous silence** a continuación hubo un silencio amenazador. <> *adv* **- 1.** [referring to place - near speaker] ahí; [- further away] allí, allá; **I'm going there next week** voy para allá OR allí la semana que viene; **there it is** ahí está; **over there** por allí; **it's six miles there and back** hay seis millas entre ir y volver; **we're nearly there** ya casi hemos llegado **- 2.** [in existence, available] ahí; **is anybody there?** ¿hay alguien ahí?; **is John there,**

please? [when telephoning] ¿está John? **- 3.** [point - in conversation, activity] ahí; **I can't agree with you there** ahí no estoy de acuerdo contigo; **we're getting there** estamos ya casi **- 4.** inf phr: **all/not all there** bien/no muy bien de la cabeza. ◇ excl: **there, I knew he'd turn up** ¡mira!, sabía que aparecería; **there, there (don't cry)** ¡venga, venga (no llores)!
◆ **there and then, then and there** adv en el acto.
◆ **there you are** adv **- 1.** [handing over something] ahí tienes/tenéis etc **- 2.** [emphasizing that one is right] ahí está, ahí lo tienes; **there you are, what did I tell you!** ahí lo tienes, ¿qué te dije? **- 3.** [expressing reluctant acceptance]: **it's not ideal, but there you are** no es lo ideal, pero ¿qué le vamos a hacer?

thereabouts [,ðeərə'bauts], **thereabout** US [,ðeərə'baut] adv: **or thereabouts** o por ahí.

thereafter [,ðeər'ɑːftər] adv fml después, a partir de entonces.

thereby [,ðeər'baɪ] adv fml de ese modo.

therefore ['ðeəfɔːr] adv por lo tanto, por consiguiente.

therein [,ðeər'ɪn] adv fml **- 1.** [in that place] allí dentro **- 2.** [in that matter]: **therein lies the problem** ahí radica el problema.

there's [ðeəz] (abbr of = there is), ▷ **there**.

thereupon [,ðeərə'pɒn] adv fml acto seguido.

thermal ['θɜːml] adj térmico(ca).

thermal reactor n reactor m térmico.

thermal underwear n ropa f interior térmica.

thermodynamics [,θɜːməʊdaɪ'næmɪks] n (U) termodinámica f.

thermometer [θə'mɒmɪtər] n termómetro m.

thermonuclear [,θɜːməʊ'njuːklɪər] adj termonuclear.

Thermos (flask) ® ['θɜːməs-] n termo m.

thermostat ['θɜːməstæt] n termostato m.

thesaurus [θɪ'sɔːrəs] (pl -es) n diccionario m de sinónimos y voces afines.

these [ðiːz] pl ▷ **this**.

thesis ['θiːsɪs] (pl theses ['θiːsiːz]) n tesis f inv.

they [ðeɪ] pers pron pl **- 1.** [gen] ellos mpl, ellas fpl; **they're pleased** (ellos) están satisfechos; **they're pretty earrings** son unos pendientes bonitos; **they love fish** les encanta el pescado; **they can't do it** ellos no pueden hacerlo; **there they are** allí están **- 2.** [unspecified people]: **they say it's going to snow** dicen que va a nevar; **they're going to put petrol up** van a subir la gasolina.

they'd [ðeɪd] **- 1.** (abbr of = they had), ▷ **have - 2.** (abbr of = they would), ▷ **would**.

they'll [ðeɪl] **- 1.** (abbr of = they will), ▷ **will - 2.** (abbr of = they shall), ▷ **shall**.

they're [ðeər] (abbr of = they are), ▷ **be**.

they've [ðeɪv] (abbr of = they have), ▷ **have**.

thick [θɪk] ◇ adj **- 1.** [not thin] grueso(sa); **it's 3 cm thick** tiene 3 cm de grueso; **how thick is it?** ¿qué espesor tiene? **- 2.** [dense - hair, liquid, fog] espeso(sa) **- 3.** inf [stupid] corto(ta), necio(cia) **- 4.** [indistinct]: **a voice thick with emotion** una voz velada por la emoción **- 5.** [full, covered]: **to be thick with** estar lleno(na) de. ◇ n: **to be in the thick of** estar en el centro OR meollo de.
◆ **thick and fast** adv: **questions came thick and fast** llovían preguntas de todos los lados.
◆ **through thick and thin** adv a las duras y a las maduras.

thicken ['θɪkn] ◇ vt espesar. ◇ vi **- 1.** [gen] espesarse **- 2.** [forest, crowd] hacerse más denso(sa)
▶ **the plot thickens** la cosa se complica.

thickening ['θɪknɪŋ] n espesante m.

thicket ['θɪkɪt] n matorral m.

thickly ['θɪklɪ] adv **- 1.** [cut bread] a rebanadas gruesas; [spread]: **he spread the butter thickly** untó una buena capa de mantequilla **- 2.** [densely] densamente **- 3.** [indistinctly] con voz poco clara.

thickness ['θɪknɪs] n espesor m.

thickset [,θɪk'set] adj fornido(da), robusto(ta).

thick-skinned [-'skɪnd] adj insensible.

thief [θiːf] (pl thieves) n ladrón m, -ona f.

thieve [θiːv] vt & vi robar, hurtar.

thieves [θiːvz] npl ▷ **thief**.

thieving ['θiːvɪŋ] ◇ adj ladrón(ona). ◇ n (U) robo m, hurto m.

thigh [θaɪ] n muslo m.

thighbone ['θaɪbəʊn] n fémur m.

thimble ['θɪmbl] n dedal m.

thin [θɪn] ◇ adj (comp -ner, superl -nest) **- 1.** [not thick] delgado(da), fino(na) **- 2.** [skinny] delgado(da), flaco(ca) **- 3.** [watery] claro(ra), aguado(da) **- 4.** [sparse - crowd, vegetation, mist] poco denso (poco densa); [- hair] ralo(la); **to be thin on top** estar quedándose calvo. ◇ adv: **to be wearing thin** [joke, story] estar perdiendo interés; **my patience is wearing thin** se me está acabando la paciencia. ◇ vi (pt & pp -ned, cont -ning): **his hair is thinning** se le está empezando a caer el pelo.
◆ **thin down** vt sep [liquid] aclarar.

thin air n: to appear out of thin air aparecer de la nada; **to disappear into thin air** esfumarse.

thing [θɪŋ] n - **1.** [gen] cosa f; **the next thing on the list** lo siguiente de la lista; **the (best) thing to do would be...** lo mejor sería...; **first thing in the morning** a primer hora de la mañana; **last thing at night** a última hora de la noche; **the main thing** lo principal; **the whole thing is a shambles** es un auténtico desastre; **it's a good thing you were there** menos mal que estabas allí; **I thought the same thing** lo mismo pensé yo; **for one thing** en primer lugar; **(what) with one thing and another** entre unas cosas y otras; **the thing is...** el caso es que...; **it's just one of those things** inf son cosas que pasan; **I have a thing about...** inf [like] me gusta muchísimo...; [dislike] no puedo sufrir...; **to make a thing (out) of sthg** inf exagerar algo - **2.** [anything]: **not a thing** nada; **I didn't do a thing** no hice nada - **3.** [person]: **poor thing!** ¡pobrecito! m, -ta f - **4.** inf [fashion]: **the thing** lo último, lo que está de moda.

➥ **things** npl - **1.** [clothes, possessions] cosas fpl, corotos mpl; **things aren't what they used to be** las cosas ya no son lo que eran - **2.** inf [life]: **how are things?** ¿qué tal (van las cosas)?

thingamabob ['θɪŋəmə,bɒb], **thingamajig** ['θɪŋəmədʒɪg], **thingummy(jig)** UK ['θɪŋəmɪ-], **thingy** UK ['θɪŋɪ] n [thing] chisme m; [person] ése m, ésa f, fulano m, -na f.

think [θɪŋk] <> vt (pt & pp thought) - **1.** [believe]: **to think (that)** creer OR pensar que; **I think so** creo que sí; **I don't think so** creo que no - **2.** [have in mind] pensar; **what are you thinking?** ¿en qué piensas?; **I didn't think to ask her** no se me ocurrió preguntárselo - **3.** [imagine] entender, hacerse una idea de; **I can't think what might have happened to them** no quiero ni pensar lo que les podría haber ocurrido; **I thought so** ya me lo imaginaba - **4.** [remember] recordar; **try to think where you saw them last** intenta recordar cuándo los viste por última vez - **5.** [in polite requests]: **do you think you could help me?** ¿cree que podría ayudarme? <> vi (pt & pp thought) - **1.** [use mind] pensar; **let me think** vamos a ver; **to think aloud** pensar en voz alta - **2.** [have stated opinion]: **what do you think of OR about his new film?** ¿qué piensas de su nueva película?; **to think a lot of sthg/sb** tener en mucha estima algo/a alguien; **to think well of sb** tener una buena opinión de alguien

▶▶ **to think better of sthg/doing sthg** pensarse mejor algo/lo de hacer algo; **he thinks nothing of doing it** para él es pan comido hacerlo; **to think twice** pensárselo dos veces. <> n inf: **to have a think (about sthg)** pensarse (algo).

➥ **think about** vt insep pensar en; **I'll have to think about it** tendré que pensarlo; **to think about doing sthg** pensar en hacer algo.

➥ **think back** vi volver la mente atrás; **think back to your childhood** vuelve la mente a tu infancia.

➥ **think of** vt insep - **1.** [consider]: **to think of doing sthg** pensar en hacer algo - **2.** [remember] acordarse de - **3.** [conceive] pensar en; **how did you think of (doing) that?** ¿cómo se te ocurrió (hacer) esto? - **4.** [show consideration for]: **it was kind of you to think of me** fue muy amable de tu parte que te acordaras de mí.

➥ **think out, think through** vt sep [plan] elaborar; [problem] examinar.

➥ **think over** vt sep pensarse, meditar.

➥ **think up** vt sep idear.

thinker ['θɪŋkə'] n pensador m, -ra f.

thinking ['θɪŋkɪŋ] <> adj: **the thinking man** el hombre que piensa. <> n (U) opinión f; **I'll have to do some thinking** tendré que pensármelo; **to my way of thinking** en mi opinión.

think tank n grupo de expertos convocados por una organización para aconsejar sobre un tema determinado.

thinly ['θɪnlɪ] adv - **1.** [slice food] a rebanadas finas; [spread]: **he spread the butter thinly** untó una ligera capa de mantequilla - **2.** [sparsely - forested] escasamente; [- populated] poco.

thinner ['θɪnə'] n disolvente m.

thinness ['θɪnnɪs] n delgadez f.

thin-skinned [-'skɪnd] adj susceptible.

third [θɜːd] <> num adj tercer(ra). <> num n - **1.** [fraction] tercio m - **2.** [in order] tercero m, -ra f - **3.** UNIV ≃ aprobado m (en un título universitario); see also **sixth**.

third-class adj UK UNIV ≃ aprobado.

third-degree burns npl quemaduras fpl de tercer grado.

thirdly ['θɜːdlɪ] adv en tercer lugar.

third party n tercero m.

third party insurance n seguro m a terceros.

third-rate adj pej de poca categoría.

Third World n: **the Third World** el Tercer Mundo.

thirst [θɜːst] n lit & fig: **thirst (for)** sed f (de).

thirsty ['θɜːstɪ] (comp -ier, superl -iest) adj - **1.** [parched]: **to be OR feel thirsty** tener sed - **2.** [causing thirst] que da sed.

thirteen [,θɜː'tiːn] num trece; see also **six**.

thirteenth [ˌθɜː'tiːnθ] ⬦ *num adj* decimotercero(ra). ⬦ *num n* - **1.** [fraction] treceavo *m* - **2.** [in order] decimotercero *m*, -ra *f*; *see also* **sixth**.

thirtieth ['θɜːtɪəθ] *num* trigésimo(ma); *see also* **sixth**.

thirty ['θɜːtɪ] (*pl* -**ies**) *num* treinta; *see also* **sixty**.

thirty-something *adj* típico de ciertas personas que sobrepasan la treintena y viven desahogadamente.

this [ðɪs] ⬦ *pron* (*pl* **these**) [gen] éste *m*, ésta *f*, éstos *mpl*, éstas *fpl*; (*indefinite*) esto; **this is/these are for you** esto es/éstos son para ti; **this can't be true** esto no puede ser cierto; **do you prefer these or those?** ¿prefieres éstos o aquéllos?; **this is Daphne Logan** [introducing another person] ésta es OR te presento a Daphne Logan; [introducing oneself on phone] soy Daphne Logan; **what's this?** ¿qué es eso?; **this and that** esto y lo otro. ⬦ *adj* - **1.** [gen] este(esta), estos(estas) (*pl*); **this country** este país; **these thoughts** estos pensamientos; **I prefer this one** prefiero éste; **this morning/week** esta mañana/semana; **this Sunday/summer** este domingo/verano - **2.** *inf* [a certain] un(una); **there's this woman I know** hay una tía que conozco. ⬦ *adv*: **it was this big** era así de grande; **you'll need about this much** te hará falta un tanto así.

thistle ['θɪsl] *n* cardo *m*.

thither ['ðɪðəʳ] ⊳ **hither**.

tho' [ðəʊ] *inf* = **though**.

thong [θɒŋ] *n* - **1.** [of leather] correa *f* - **2.** US [flip-flop] chancleta *f* - **3.** [underwear] tanga *f*.

thorn [θɔːn] *n* - **1.** [prickle] espina *f*; **to be a thorn in one's flesh** OR **side** ser un engorro para alguien - **2.** [bush, tree] espino *m*.

thorny ['θɔːnɪ] (*comp* -**ier**, *superl* -**iest**) *adj* lit & *fig* espinoso(sa).

thorough ['θʌrə] *adj* - **1.** [investigation etc] exhaustivo(va), completo(ta) - **2.** [person, work] minucioso(sa), concienzudo(da) - **3.** [idiot, waste] completo(ta).

thoroughbred ['θʌrəbred] *n* pura sangre *mf*.

thoroughfare ['θʌrəfeəʳ] *n fml* calle *f* mayor, avenida *f* principal.

thoroughly ['θʌrəlɪ] *adv* - **1.** [fully, in detail] a fondo, exhaustivamente - **2.** [completely, utterly] completamente, totalmente.

thoroughness ['θʌrənɪs] (*U*) *n* - **1.** [exhaustiveness] exhaustividad *f* - **2.** [meticulousness] minuciosidad *f*.

those [ðəʊz] *pl* ⊳ **that**.

though, tho' [ðəʊ] ⬦ *conj* aunque; **difficult though it may be** aunque sea difícil; **even though** aunque; **as though** como si. ⬦ *adv* sin embargo; **she still likes him though** y sin embargo le sigue gustando.

thought [θɔːt] ⬦ *pt* & *pp* ⊳ **think**. ⬦ *n* - **1.** [notion, idea] idea *f* - **2.** [act of thinking]: **after much thought** después de pensarlo mucho - **3.** [philosophy, thinking] pensamiento *m* - **4.** [gesture] detalle *m*; **that was a nice thought** fue un detalle bonito.

◆ **thoughts** *npl* - **1.** [reflections] reflexiones *fpl*; **she keeps her thoughts to herself** no expresa lo que piensa; **to collect one's thoughts** orientarse, concentrarse - **2.** [views] ideas *fpl*, opiniones *fpl*; **what are your thoughts on the subject?** ¿qué piensas sobre el tema?

thoughtful ['θɔːtfʊl] *adj* - **1.** [pensive] pensativo(va) - **2.** [considerate] considerado(da), atento(ta); **that was thoughtful of her** fue muy considerada.

thoughtfulness ['θɔːtfʊlnɪs] *n* (*U*) - **1.** [pensiveness] aire *m* pensativo - **2.** [considerateness] consideración *f*.

thoughtless ['θɔːtlɪs] *adj* desconsiderado(da).

thoughtlessness ['θɔːtlɪsnɪs] *n* desconsideración *f*.

thousand ['θaʊznd] *num* mil; **a** OR **one thousand** mil; **two thousand** dos mil; **thousands of** miles de; **they came in their thousands** vinieron miles de ellos; *see also* **six**.

thousandth ['θaʊzntθ] ⬦ *num adj* milésimo(ma). ⬦ *num n* [fraction] milésima *f*; *see also* **sixth**.

thrash [θræʃ] *vt* lit & *fig* dar una paliza a.

◆ **thrash about, thrash around** *vi* agitarse violentamente.

◆ **thrash out** *vt sep* darle vueltas a, discutir.

thrashing ['θræʃɪŋ] *n* lit & *fig* paliza *f*; **to give sb a thrashing** darle una paliza a alguien.

thread [θred] ⬦ *n* - **1.** [of cotton, argument] hilo *m* - **2.** [of screw] rosca *f*, filete *m*. ⬦ *vt* - **1.** [needle] enhebrar - **2.** [move]: **to thread one's way through** colarse por entre.

threadbare ['θredbeəʳ] *adj* raído(da), gastado(da).

threat [θret] *n*: **threat (to/of)** amenaza *f* (para/de); **they were just empty threats** no eran más que amenazas vanas.

threaten ['θretn] ⬦ *vt* amenazar; **to threaten sb (with)** amenazar a alguien (con); **to threaten to do sthg** amenazar con hacer algo. ⬦ *vi* amenazar.

threatening ['θretnɪŋ] *adj* amenazador(ra).

three [θriː] *num* tres; *see also* **six**.

three-D *adj* tridimensional.

three-dimensional [-dɪ'menʃənl] *adj* tridimensional.

threefold ['θri:fəʊld] <> *adj* triple. <> *adv* tres veces; **to increase threefold** triplicarse.

three-legged race [-'legɪd-] *n carrera por parejas en la que cada corredor tiene una pierna atada a la de su compañero.*

three-piece *adj* de tres piezas; **three-piece suite** tresillo *m*.

three-ply *adj* [wood] de tres capas; [rope, wool] de tres hebras.

three-point turn *n* UK AUT: **to do a three-point turn** hacer la ele.

three-quarter length *adj*: **three-quarter length jacket** tres cuartos *m*.

three-quarters *npl* tres cuartos *mpl*, tres cuartas partes *fpl*.

threesome ['θri:səm] *n* trío *m*.

three-star *adj* de tres estrellas.

three-wheeler [-'wi:lə'] *n* coche *m* de tres ruedas.

thresh [θreʃ] *vt* trillar.

threshing machine ['θreʃɪŋ-] *n* trilladora *f*.

threshold ['θreʃhəʊld] *n* - **1.** [doorway] umbral *m* - **2.** [level] límite *m*; **the pain threshold** el umbral del dolor - **3.** *fig* [verge]: **to be on the threshold of** estar en los umbrales OR a las puertas de.

threshold agreement *n acuerdo concertado para compensar una subida inesperada de la inflación.*

threw [θru:] *pt* ▷ **throw**.

thrift [θrɪft] *n* (U) [gen] frugalidad *f*, economía *f*.

thrift shop *n* US *tienda de una entidad benéfica en la que se venden productos de segunda mano donados por simpatizantes.*

thrifty ['θrɪftɪ] (*comp* -ier, *superl* -iest) *adj* [person] ahorrativo(va); [meal] frugal.

thrill [θrɪl] <> *n* - **1.** [sudden feeling] estremecimiento *m* - **2.** [exciting experience]: **it was a thrill to see it** fue emocionante verlo. <> *vt* entusiasmar. <> *vi*: **to thrill to** entusiasmarse con.

thrilled [θrɪld] *adj*: **thrilled (with sthg/to do sthg)** encantado(da) (de algo/de hacer algo).

thriller ['θrɪlə'] *n* novela *f*/película *f*/obra *f* de suspense.

thrilling ['θrɪlɪŋ] *adj* emocionante.

thrive [θraɪv] (*pt* **throve**) (*pp* **-d**) *vi* [plant] crecer mucho; [person] rebosar de salud; [business] prosperar.

thriving ['θraɪvɪŋ] *adj* [plant] que crece bien.

throat [θrəʊt] *n* garganta *f*; **to have a sore throat** tener dolor de garganta; **to ram** OR **force sthg down sb's throat** *fig* hacerle tragar algo a alguien; **to stick in sb's throat** *fig* atragantársele a alguien; **to be at each other's throats** tirarse los platos a la cabeza.

throaty ['θrəʊtɪ] (*comp* -ier, *superl* -iest) *adj* ronco(ca).

throb [θrɒb] <> *n* [of heart] latido *m*; [of pulse] palpitación *f*; [of engine, music] vibración *f*. <> *vi* (*pt* & *pp* **-bed**, *cont* **-bing**) - **1.** [heart, pulse] latir; [head] palpitar - **2.** [engine, music] vibrar, resonar.

throes [θrəʊz] *npl*: **to be in the throes of** estar en medio de.

thrombosis [θrɒm'bəʊsɪs] (*pl* **-boses** [-si:z]) *n* trombosis *f inv*.

throne [θrəʊn] *n* trono *m*; **the throne** el trono; **to be on the throne** ocupar el trono.

throng [θrɒŋ] <> *n* multitud *f*. <> *vt* llegar en tropel a. <> *vi* llegar en tropel.

throttle ['θrɒtl] <> *n* válvula *f* reguladora. <> *vt* [strangle] estrangular.

through, thru [θru:] <> *adj* [finished]: **to be through with sthg** haber terminado algo. <> *adv* - **1.** [in place] de parte a parte, de un lado a otro; **they let us through** nos dejaron pasar; **I read it through** lo leí hasta el final - **2.** [in time] hasta el final; **we stayed through till Friday** nos quedamos hasta el viernes. <> *prep* - **1.** [relating to place, position] a través de; **to cut/travel through sthg** cortar/viajar por algo - **2.** [during] durante; **all through the night** durante toda la noche; **to go through an experience** pasar por una experiencia - **3.** [because of] a causa de, por - **4.** [by means of] gracias a, por medio de; **I got it through a friend** lo conseguí a través de un amigo - **5.** US [up to and including]: **Monday through Friday** de lunes a viernes.

➤ **through and through** *adv* de pies a cabeza; **to know sthg through and through** conocer algo de arriba abajo.

throughout [θru:'aʊt] <> *prep* - **1.** [during] a lo largo de, durante todo (durante toda) - **2.** [everywhere in] por todo (da). <> *adv* - **1.** [all the time] todo el tiempo - **2.** [everywhere] por todas partes.

throve [θrəʊv] *pt* ▷ **thrive**.

throw [θrəʊ] <> *vt* (*pt* **threw**, *pp* **thrown**) - **1.** [gen] tirar; [ball, hammer, javelin] aventar *Andes, Amér C & Méx*, lanzar; **to throw one's arms around sb** abrazarse a alguien; **to throw o.s.** tirarse, echarse; **to throw o.s. into sthg** *fig* meterse de lleno en algo - **2.** [horse] derribar, desmontar - **3.** *fig* [put]: **we were thrown into confusion** quedamos desconcertados; **they threw him into the job at short notice** le cargaron con el trabajo sin apenas avisarle - **4.** [cast - light, shadow]: **to throw sthg on** proyectar algo sobre - **5.** [have suddenly]: **to throw a tantrum/fit** tener una rabieta/un ataque - **6.** *fig* [confuse] desconcertar. <> *n* lanzamiento *m*, tiro *m*.

◆ **throw away** vt sep [discard] tirar; fig [waste] botar Amér, desperdiciar.

◆ **throw in** vt sep [extra item] incluir.

◆ **throw out** vt sep - **1.** [discard] tirar - **2.** fig [reject] rechazar - **3.** [force to leave] echar.

◆ **throw up** ◇ vt sep [dust] levantar. ◇ vi inf [vomit] vomitar, arrojar.

throwaway ['θrəʊə,weɪ] adj - **1.** [bottle, product] desechable - **2.** [remark, gesture] hecho(cha) como quien no quiere la cosa.

throwback ['θrəʊbæk] n: **throwback (to)** retroceso m (a).

throw-in n UK FTBL saque m de banda.

thrown [θrəʊn] pp ▷ **throw**.

thru [θruː] US inf = **through**.

thrush [θrʌʃ] n - **1.** [bird] tordo m - **2.** MED [vaginal] candidiasis f.

thrust [θrʌst] ◇ n - **1.** [of sword] estocada f; [of knife] cuchillada f; [of troops] arremetida f - **2.** TECH (fuerza f de) propulsión f - **3.** [main meaning] esencia f. ◇ vt (pt & pp thrust) - **1.** [shove]: **he thrust the knife into his enemy** hundió el cuchillo en el cuerpo de su enemigo; **he thrust the book at me** me dio el libro con un movimiento brusco - **2.** [jostle]: **to thrust one's way** abrirse paso a empujones.

◆ **thrust upon** vt insep: **to thrust sthg upon sb** imponer algo a alguien.

thrusting ['θrʌstɪŋ] adj [aggressive] agresivo(va).

thruway ['θruːweɪ] n US autopista f.

thud [θʌd] ◇ n ruido m sordo; **it landed with a thud** cayó haciendo un ruido sordo. ◇ vi (pt & pp -ded, cont -ding) dar un golpe seco.

thug [θʌɡ] n matón m.

thumb [θʌm] ◇ n [of hand] pulgar m; **to twiddle one's thumbs** dar vueltas a los dedos pulgares; fig tocarse OR rascarse la barriga. ◇ vt inf [hitch]: **to thumb a lift** hacer dedo.

◆ **thumb through** vt insep hojear.

thumb index n uñeros mpl (de libro).

thumbnail ['θʌmneɪl] n uña f del pulgar.

thumbnail sketch n descripción f breve.

thumbs down [,θʌmz-] n: **to get** OR **be given the thumbs down** [plan] ser rechazado(da); [play] ser recibido(da) con descontento.

thumbs up [,θʌmz-] n: **we got** OR **were given the thumbs up** nos dieron luz verde OR el visto bueno.

thumbtack ['θʌmtæk] n US chincheta f.

thump [θʌmp] ◇ n - **1.** [blow] puñetazo m, porrazo m - **2.** [thud] golpe m seco. ◇ vt - **1.** [punch] dar un puñetazo a - **2.** [place heavily]: **he thumped the book down on the table** dio un golpe contundente con el libro sobre la mesa. ◇ vi - **1.** [person]: **to thump in/out** entrar/salir con pasos pesados - **2.** [heart, head] latir con fuerza.

thunder ['θʌndər] ◇ n (U) - **1.** METEOR truenos mpl - **2.** fig [loud sound] estruendo m, estrépito m. ◇ vt vociferar. ◇ impers vb METEOR tronar. ◇ vi [make loud sound] retumbar.

thunderbolt ['θʌndəbəʊlt] n rayo m.

thunderclap ['θʌndəklæp] n trueno m.

thundercloud ['θʌndəklaʊd] n nube f de tormenta.

thunderous ['θʌndərəs] adj atronador(ra), ensordecedor(ra).

thunderstorm ['θʌndəstɔːm] n tormenta f, tempestad f.

thunderstruck ['θʌndəstrʌk] adj fig atónito(ta).

thundery ['θʌndərɪ] adj tormentoso(sa).

Thur, Thurs (abbr of Thursday) juev.

Thursday ['θɜːzdɪ] n jueves m inv; see also **Saturday**.

thus [ðʌs] adv fml - **1.** [therefore] por consiguiente, así que - **2.** [in this way] así, de esta manera.

thwart [θwɔːt] vt frustrar.

thyme [taɪm] n tomillo m.

thyroid ['θaɪrɔɪd] n tiroides m inv.

tiara [tɪ'ɑːrə] n tiara f.

Tiber ['taɪbər] n: **the (River) Tiber** el (río) Tíber.

Tibet [tɪ'bet] n (el) Tibet.

Tibetan [tɪ'betn] ◇ adj tibetano(na). ◇ n - **1.** [person] tibetano m, -na f - **2.** [language] tibetano m.

tibia ['tɪbɪə] (pl **-biae** [-biiː] OR **-s**) n tibia f.

tic [tɪk] n tic m.

tick [tɪk] ◇ n - **1.** [written mark] marca f OR señal f de visto bueno - **2.** [sound] tictac m - **3.** inf [credit]: **on tick** a crédito. ◇ vt marcar (con una señal). ◇ vi - **1.** [make ticking sound] hacer tictac - **2.** fig [behave in a certain way]: **what makes her tick?** ¿qué es lo que le mueve?

◆ **tick away, tick by** vi pasar.

◆ **tick off** vt sep - **1.** [mark off] marcar (con una señal de visto bueno) - **2.** [tell off]: **to tick sb off (for sthg)** echar una bronca a alguien (por algo) - **3.** US inf [irritate] fastidiar.

◆ **tick over** vi funcionar al ralentí.

ticked [tɪkd] adj US enfadado(da), afectado(da).

tickertape ['tɪkəteɪp] n (U) cinta de papel que lleva impresa información bursátil.

ticket ['tɪkɪt] n - **1.** [for bus, train etc] billete m, boleto m Amér; [for cinema, football match] entrada f - **2.** [for traffic offence] multa f, parte m Chile - **3.** POL lista f de candidatos.

ticket agency n agencia f de venta de entradas o billetes de tren, avión etc.

ticket collector n UK revisor m, -ra f.

ticket holder *n* poseedor *m*, -ra *f* de billete OR de entrada OR de boleto *Amér*.

ticket inspector *n* UK revisor *m*, -ra *f*.

ticket machine *n* máquina *f* automática para la venta de billetes OR boletos *Amér*.

ticket office *n* taquilla *f*, boletería *f* *Amér*.

ticking off ['tɪkɪŋ-] (*pl* tickings off) *n*: to give sb a ticking off echar una bronca a alguien; to get a ticking off (from sb) recibir una bronca (de alguien).

tickle ['tɪkl] <> *vt* - **1**. [touch lightly] hacer cosquillas a - **2**. *fig* [amuse] divertir. <> *vi*: my feet are tickling tengo cosquillas en los pies.

ticklish ['tɪklɪʃ] *adj* - **1**. [sensitive to touch]: to be ticklish tener cosquillas - **2**. *fig* [delicate] delicado(da), peliagudo(da).

tick-tack-toe *n* US tres *fpl* en raya.

tidal ['taɪdl] *adj* de la marea.

tidal wave *n* maremoto *m*.

tidbit US = titbit.

tiddler ['tɪdlər] *n* UK [fish] pececillo *m*.

tiddly ['tɪdlɪ] (*comp* -ier, *superl* -iest) *adj* UK *inf* - **1**. [tipsy] piripi - **2**. [tiny] pequeñito(ta).

tiddlywinks ['tɪdlɪwɪŋks], **tiddledywinks** US ['tɪdldɪwɪŋks] *n* juego *m* de la pulga.

tide [taɪd] *n* - **1**. [of sea] marea *f*; high/low tide marea alta/baja; the tide is in/out ha subido/bajado la marea; the tide is coming in/going out la marea está subiendo/bajando - **2**. *fig* [of opinion, history] corriente *f* - **3**. *fig* [of protest, feeling] oleada *f*; the rising tide of crime la creciente oleada de crímenes.

➤ **tide over** *vt sep* sacar del bache OR de un apuro.

tidily ['taɪdɪlɪ] *adv* ordenadamente.

tidiness ['taɪdɪnɪs] *n (U)* [of room, desk] orden *m*; [of appearance] pulcritud *f*.

tidings ['taɪdɪŋz] *npl liter* noticias *fpl*.

tidy ['taɪdɪ] <> *adj* (*comp* -ier, *superl* -iest) - **1**. [room, desk etc] ordenado(da) - **2**. [person, dress, hair] arreglado(da) - **3**. *inf* [sum] considerable. <> *vt* (*pt & pp* -ied) ordenar, arreglar.

➤ **tidy away** *vt sep* poner en su sitio.

➤ **tidy up** <> *vt sep* ordenar, arreglar. <> *vi* ordenar las cosas, recoger.

tie [taɪ] <> *n* - **1**. [necktie] corbata *f* - **2**. [string, cord] atadura *f* - **3**. [bond, link] vínculo *m*, lazo *m* - **4**. SPORT [draw] empate *m* - **5**. US RAIL traviesa *f*. <> *vt* (*pt & pp* tied, *cont* tying) - **1**. [attach, fasten]: to tie sthg (to OR onto sthg) atar algo (a algo); to tie sthg round/with sthg atar algo a/con algo - **2**. [do up - shoelaces] atar; [- knot] hacer - **3**. *fig* [link]: to be tied to estar ligado(da) a - **4**. *fig* [limited, restric-

ted]: to be tied to estar atado(da) a. <> *vi* (*pt & pp* tied, *cont* tying) [draw]: to tie (with) empatar (con).

➤ **tie down** *vt sep fig* atar.

➤ **tie in with** *vt insep* concordar con.

➤ **tie up** *vt sep* - **1**. [gen] atar - **2**. *fig* [money, resources] inmovilizar - **3**. *fig* [link]: to be tied up with estar ligado(da) a.

tiebreak(er) ['taɪbreɪk(ər)] *n* - **1**. TENNIS muerte *f* súbita, tiebreak *m* - **2**. [in game, competition] *pregunta adicional para romper un empate*.

tied [taɪd] *adj* SPORT [drawn] empatado(da).

tied up *adj* [busy] ocupado(da).

tie-dye *vt hacerle nudos a una prenda antes de teñirla para lograr un reparto desigual del color*.

tiepin ['taɪpɪn] *n* alfiler *m* de corbata.

tier [tɪər] *n* [of seats] hilera *f*; [of cake] piso *m*.

tiff [tɪf] *n* pelea *f* *(de poca importancia)*.

tiger ['taɪgər] *n* tigre *m*.

tiger cub *n* cachorro *m* de tigre.

tight [taɪt] <> *adj* - **1**. [gen] apretado(da); [shoes] estrecho(cha); it's a tight fit queda muy justo - **2**. [string, skin] tirante - **3**. [painful]: my chest feels tight siento una opresión en el pecho - **4**. [budget, schedule] ajustado(da) - **5**. [rules, restrictions] riguroso(sa) - **6**. [corner, bend] cerrado(da) - **7**. [match, finish] reñido(da) - **8**. *inf* [drunk] cocido(da) - **9**. *inf* [miserly] agarrado(da). <> *adv* - **1**. [hold, squeeze] con fuerza; to hold tight agarrarse (fuerte); to shut OR close sthg tight cerrar algo bien - **2**. [pull, stretch] de modo tirante.

➤ **tights** *npl* medias *fpl*.

tighten ['taɪtn] <> *vt* - **1**. [hold, grip]: to tighten one's hold OR grip on sthg coger con más fuerza algo - **2**. [rope, chain] tensar - **3**. [knot] apretar; [belt] apretarse - **4**. [rules, system] intensificar. <> *vi* [rope, chain] tensarse.

➤ **tighten up** *vt sep* - **1**. [screw, fastening] apretar; [belt] apretarse - **2**. [rules, system, security] intensificar.

tightfisted [,taɪt'fɪstɪd] *adj inf pej* agarrado(da).

tightknit [,taɪt'nɪt] *adj* muy unido (muy unida).

tight-lipped [-'lɪpt] *adj* - **1**. [with lips pressed together] con los labios apretados - **2**. [silent] callado(da).

tightly ['taɪtlɪ] *adv* - **1**. [fit]: the dress fitted her tightly el vestido le iba muy apretado - **2**. [hold, squeeze] con fuerza; [fasten] bien - **3**. [pull, stretch] de modo tirante - **4**. [pack] apretadamente.

tightness ['taɪtnɪs] *n* - **1**. [gen] estrechez *f* - **2**. [of budget] lo ajustado - **3**. [of chest, stomach] opresión *f* - **4**. [of rules, system] rigor *m*.

tightrope ['taɪtrəʊp] *n* cuerda *f* floja, alambre *m*; **to be on** OR **walking a tightrope** andar OR bailar en la cuerda floja.

tightrope walker *n* funámbulo *m*, -la *f*.

tigress ['taɪgrɪs] *n* tigresa *f*.

tilde ['tɪldə] *n* tilde *f*.

tile [taɪl] *n* - **1.** [on roof] teja *f* - **2.** [on floor] baldosa *f*; [on wall] azulejo *m*, baldosín *m*.

tiled [taɪld] *adj* [roof] tejado(da); [floor] embaldosado(da); [wall] alicatado(da).

tiling ['taɪlɪŋ] *n* - **1.** [act of tiling] colocación *f* de tejas/baldosas/azulejos - **2.** [tiled surface - of roof] tejas *fpl*; [- of floor] baldosas *fpl*; [- of wall] azulejos *mpl*, baldosines *mpl*.

till [tɪl] <> *prep* hasta; **till now/then** hasta ahora/entonces. <> *conj* hasta que; **wait till he arrives** espera hasta que llegue. <> *n* caja *f* (registradora).

tiller ['tɪlər] *n* NAUT caña *f* del timón.

tilt [tɪlt] <> *n* inclinación *f*, ladeo *m*. <> *vt* inclinar, ladear. <> *vi* inclinarse, ladearse.

timber ['tɪmbər] *n* - **1.** (*U*) [wood] madera *f* (*para la construcción*) - **2.** [beam - of ship] cuaderna *f*; [- of house] viga *f*.

timbered ['tɪmbəd] *adj* enmaderado(da).

time [taɪm] <> *n* - **1.** [gen] tiempo *m*; **a good time to go** un buen momento de irnos; **ahead of time** temprano; **in good time** con tiempo; **on time** puntualmente; **to take time** llevar tiempo; **it's (about) time to...** ya es hora de...; **to get the time to do sthg** coger el tiempo para hacer algo; **it's high time...** ya va siendo hora de...; **to get time and a half** recibir el pago establecido más la mitad de éste; **to have no time for** no poder con, no aguantar; **to make good time** ir bien de tiempo; **to pass the time** pasar el rato; **to play for time** intentar ganar tiempo; **to take one's time (doing sthg)** tomarse uno mucho tiempo (para hacer algo); **take your time!** ¡tómatelo con calma! - **2.** [as measured by clock] hora *f*; **what time is it?, what's the time?** ¿qué hora es?; **the time is three o'clock** son las tres; **in a week's/year's time** dentro de una semana/un año; **to keep time** ir a la hora; **to lose time** atrasar - **3.** [length of time] rato *m*; **it was a long time before he came** pasó mucho tiempo antes de que viniera; **for a time** durante un tiempo - **4.** [point in time in past, era] época *f*; **at that time** en aquella época; **in ancient times** en la antigüedad; **to be ahead of one's time** adelantarse a su tiempo - **5.** [occasion] vez *f*; **three times a week** tres veces a la semana; **from time to time** de vez en cuando; **time after time, time and again** una y otra vez; **I don't like children at the best of times** ya de entrada no me gustan los niños - **6.** [experience]: **we**
had a good/bad time lo pasamos bien/mal; **I had a hard time making myself understood** me costó mucho hacer que me entendieran - **7.** MUS compás *m*; **to keep time** llevar el compás. <> *vt* - **1.** [schedule] programar - **2.** [race, runner] cronometrar - **3.** [arrival, remark] elegir el momento oportuno para.

<> **times** <> *n*: **four times as much as me** cuatro veces más que yo. <> *prep* MATHS: **4 times 5** 4 por 5.

<> **about time** *adv*: **it's about time** ya va siendo hora.

<> **at a time** *adv*: **for months at a time** durante meses seguidos; **one at a time** de uno en uno.

<> **at (any) one time** *adv* en cualquier momento.

<> **at times** *adv* a veces.

<> **at the same time** *adv* al mismo tiempo.

<> **for the time being** *adv* de momento.

<> **in time** *adv* - **1.** [not late]: **in time (for)** a tiempo (para) - **2.** [eventually] con el tiempo.

time-and-motion study *n* estudio de métodos para mejorar el rendimiento laboral.

time bomb *n* [bomb] bomba *f* de relojería; *fig* [dangerous situation] bomba *f*.

time-consuming [-kən,sjuːmɪŋ] *adj* que requiere mucho tiempo.

timed [taɪmd] *adj* cronometrado(da); **well-timed** oportuno(na); **badly-timed** poco oportuno.

time difference *n* diferencia *f* horaria.

time-honoured *adj* consagrado(da).

timekeeping ['taɪm,kiːpɪŋ] *n* [punctuality] puntualidad *f*; **good/poor timekeeping** mucha/poca puntualidad.

time lag *n* intervalo *m*.

timeless ['taɪmlɪs] *adj* eterno(na).

time limit *n* límite *m* de tiempo, plazo *m*.

timely ['taɪmlɪ] (*comp* -ier, *superl* -iest) *adj* oportuno(na).

time machine *n* máquina *f* del tiempo.

time off *n* tiempo *m* libre; **I'm owed time off (from) work** me deben algunos días en el trabajo.

time out *n* - **1.** US SPORT tiempo *m* muerto - **2.** [break]: **to take time out to do sthg** tomarse tiempo libre para hacer algo.

timepiece ['taɪmpiːs] *n* dated reloj *m*.

timer ['taɪmər] *n* temporizador *m*.

timesaving ['taɪm,seɪvɪŋ] *adj* para ahorrar tiempo.

time scale *n* tiempo *m* de ejecución.

time-share *n* UK multipropiedad *f*.

time sheet *n* ficha *f* (de asistencia al trabajo).

time signal *n* señal *f* horaria.

time switch n interruptor m de reloj.

timetable ['taɪm,teɪbl] n - **1.** [of buses, trains, school] horario m - **2.** [schedule of events] programa m.

time zone n huso m horario.

timid ['tɪmɪd] adj tímido(da).

timidly ['tɪmɪdlɪ] adv tímidamente.

timing ['taɪmɪŋ] n (U) - **1.** [judgment]: **she made her comment with perfect timing** su comentario fue hecho en el momento más oportuno - **2.** [scheduling]: **the timing of the election is crucial** es crucial que las elecciones se celebren en el momento oportuno - **3.** [measuring] cronometraje m.

timpani ['tɪmpənɪ] npl timbales mpl, tímpanos mpl.

tin [tɪn] n - **1.** [metal] estaño m; **tin plate** hojalata f - **2.** UK [can, container] lata f.

tin can n lata f.

tinfoil ['tɪnfɔɪl] n (U) papel m de aluminio.

tinge [tɪndʒ] n - **1.** [of colour] matiz m, toque m - **2.** [of feeling] ligera sensación f.

tinged [tɪndʒd] adj: **tinged with** con un toque de.

tingle ['tɪŋgl] vi: **my feet are tingling** siento hormigueo en los pies; **to tingle with** estremecerse de.

tingling ['tɪŋglɪŋ] n cosquilleo m, hormigueo m.

tinker ['tɪŋkər] vi hacer chapuzas; **to tinker with** enredar con.

tinkle ['tɪŋkl] <> n - **1.** [sound] tintineo m - **2.** UK inf [phone call]: **to give sb a tinkle** llamar a alguien (por teléfono). <> vi [ring] tintinear.

tin mine n mina f de estaño.

tinned [tɪnd] adj UK enlatado(da), en conserva.

tinnitus [tɪ'naɪtəs] n (U) zumbidos mpl (en los oídos).

tinny ['tɪnɪ] (comp -ier, superl -iest) <> adj - **1.** [sound] metálico(ca) - **2.** inf pej [badly made] poco sólido (poco sólida). <> n esp Australia inf lata f de cerveza.

tin opener n UK abrelatas m inv.

tin-pot adj UK pej [country] de mala muerte; [politician, general] de pacotilla.

tinsel ['tɪnsl] n (U) oropel m.

tint [tɪnt] <> n tinte m, matiz m. <> vt [hair] teñir; [windows, glass] ahumar.

tinted ['tɪntɪd] adj [glasses, windows] tintado(da), ahumado(da).

tiny ['taɪnɪ] (comp -ier, superl -iest) adj diminuto(ta), pequeñito(ta).

tip [tɪp] <> n - **1.** [end] punta f; **it's on the tip of my tongue** lo tengo en la punta de la lengua - **2.** UK [dump] vertedero m - **3.** [gratuity] propina f - **4.** [piece of advice] consejo m. <> vt

(pt & pp **-ped**, cont **-ping**) - **1.** [tilt] inclinar, ladear - **2.** [spill, pour] vaciar, verter - **3.** [give a gratuity to] dar una propina a. <> vi (pt & pp **-ped**, cont **-ping**) - **1.** [tilt] inclinarse, ladearse - **2.** [spill] derramarse - **3.** [give a gratuity] dar propina.

◆ **tip off** vt sep informar (confidencialmente).

◆ **tip over** <> vt sep volcar. <> vi volcarse.

tip-off n información f (confidencial).

tipped [tɪpt] adj - **1.** [cigarette] con filtro, emboquillado - **2.** [spear etc]: **tipped with stone/gold** con punta de piedra/oro.

Tipp-Ex® ['tɪpeks] UK <> n Tipp-Ex® m. <> vt corregir con Tipp-Ex®.

tipple ['tɪpl] n inf copa f, bebida f alcohólica.

tipsy ['tɪpsɪ] (comp -ier, superl -iest) adj inf dated piripi.

tiptoe ['tɪptəʊ] <> n: **on tiptoe** de puntillas. <> vi ir de puntillas.

tip-top adj inf dated de primera.

tirade [taɪ'reɪd] n diatriba f.

tire ['taɪər] <> n US = **tyre**. <> vt cansar. <> vi: **to tire (of)** cansarse (de).

◆ **tire out** vt sep agotar.

tired ['taɪəd] adj: **tired (of sthg/of doing sthg)** cansado(da) (de algo/de hacer algo).

tiredness ['taɪədnɪs] n cansancio m.

tireless ['taɪəlɪs] adj incansable.

tiresome ['taɪəsəm] adj pesado(da).

tiring ['taɪərɪŋ] adj cansado(da).

tissue ['tɪʃuː] n - **1.** [paper handkerchief] pañuelo m de papel - **2.** (U) BIOL tejido m - **3.** [paper] papel m de seda

▶▶ **a tissue of lies** una sarta de mentiras.

tissue paper n (U) papel m de seda.

tit [tɪt] n - **1.** [bird] herrerillo m - **2.** vulg [breast] teta f.

titbit UK ['tɪtbɪt], **tidbit** US ['tɪdbɪt] n - **1.** [of food] golosina f - **2.** fig [of news] noticia f breve e interesante.

tit for tat [-'tæt] n: **it's tit for tat** donde las dan las toman.

titillate ['tɪtɪleɪt] vt & vi excitar.

titivate ['tɪtɪveɪt] vt: **to titivate o.s.** emperifollarse, ponerse guapo(pa).

title ['taɪtl] n título m.

titled ['taɪtld] adj con título de nobleza.

title deed n título m de propiedad.

titleholder ['taɪtl,həʊldər] n SPORT campeón m, -ona f.

title page n portada f.

title role n papel m principal.

titter ['tɪtər] vi reírse por lo bajo.

tittle-tattle ['tɪtl,tætl] n (U) inf pej cotilleo m, chismes mpl.

titular ['tɪtjʊlə'] *adj* nominal.

T-junction *n* bifurcación *f* en forma de T.

TM *abbr of* **trademark**.

TNT (*abbr of* **trinitrotoluene**) *n* TNT *m*.

to (*unstressed before consonant* [tə], *unstressed before vowel* [tʊ], *stressed* [tu:]) <> *prep* - **1.** [indicating place, direction] a; **to go to Liverpool/Spain/school** ir a Liverpool/España/la escuela; **to go to the doctor's/John's** ir al médico/a casa de John; **the road to Glasgow** la carretera de Glasgow; **to the left/right** a la izquierda/derecha; **to the east/west** hacia el este/oeste - **2.** (*to express indirect object*) a; **to give sthg to sb** darle algo a alguien; **to talk to sb** hablar con alguien; **a threat to sb** una amenaza para alguien; **we were listening to the radio** escuchábamos la radio - **3.** [as far as] hasta, a; **to count to ten** contar hasta diez; **we work from nine to five** trabajamos de nueve a cinco - **4.** [in expressions of time]: **it's ten/a quarter to three** son las tres menos diez/cuarto - **5.** [per] por; **40 miles to the gallon** un galón (por) cada 40 millas - **6.** [of] de; **the key to the car** la llave del coche - **7.** [for] para; **a letter to my daughter** una carta para OR a mi hija - **8.** [indicating reaction, effect]: **to my surprise** para sorpresa mía; **to be to one's advantage** ir en beneficio de uno; **to be to sb's liking** ser del gusto de alguien - **9.** [in stating opinion]: **to me, he's lying** para mí que miente; **it seemed quite unnecessary to me/him** *etc* para mí/él *etc* aquello parecía del todo innecesario - **10.** [indicating state, process]: **to drive sb to drink** llevar a alguien a la bebida; **to shoot to fame** verse catapultado a la fama; **to lead to trouble** traer problemas - **11.** [accompanied by]: **we danced to the sound of guitars** bailábamos al son de las guitarras. <> *adv* [shut]: **push the door to** cierra la puerta. <> *with inf* - **1.** (*forming simple infinitive*): **to walk** andar - **2.** (*following another vb*): **to begin to do sthg** empezar a hacer algo; **to try/want to do sthg** intentar/querer hacer algo; **to hate to have to do sthg** odiar tener que hacer algo - **3.** (*following an adj*): **difficult to do** difícil de hacer; **ready to go** listos para marchar - **4.** (*indicating purpose*): **I'm doing it to help you** lo hago para ayudarte; **he came to see me** vino a verme - **5.** (*substituting for a relative clause*): **I have a lot to do** tengo mucho que hacer; **he told me to leave** me dijo que me fuera - **6.** (*to avoid repetition of infinitive*): **I meant to call him but I forgot to** tenía intención de llamarle pero se me olvidó - **7.** [in comments]: **to be honest...** para ser honesto...; **to sum up...** para resumir..., resumiendo...

➤ **to and fro** *adv* de un lado para otro, de aquí para allá.

toad [təʊd] *n* sapo *m*.

toadstool ['təʊdstu:l] *n* seta *f* venenosa.

toady ['təʊdɪ] *pej* <> *n* (*pl* **-ies**) pelota *mf*, cobista *mf*. <> *vi* (*pt & pp* **-ied**): **to toady (to)** hacer la pelota OR dar coba (a).

toast [təʊst] <> *n* - **1.** (*U*) [bread] pan *m* tostado; **a slice of toast** una tostada - **2.** [drink] brindis *m*; **to drink a toast to** hacer un brindis por - **3.** [person]: **the toast of the town** el héroe de la ciudad. <> *vt* - **1.** [bread] tostar - **2.** [person] brindar por.

toasted sandwich [,təʊstɪd-] *n* sándwich *m* tostado.

toaster ['təʊstə'] *n* tostador *m*, -ra *f*.

toast rack *n* soporte *m* para tostadas.

tobacco [tə'bækəʊ] *n* tabaco *m*.

toboggan [tə'bɒgən] <> *n* tobogán *m*, trineo *m*. <> *vi* deslizarse en tobogán.

today [tə'deɪ] <> *n* - **1.** [this day] hoy *m*; **today's date** la fecha de hoy; **what is today's date?** ¿qué día es hoy?; **today's paper** el periódico de hoy; **as from today** a partir de hoy - **2.** [nowadays] hoy (en día). <> *adv* - **1.** [this day] hoy; **what's the date today?, what date is it today** ¿qué fecha es hoy?; **today is the 6th of January** hoy es el 6 de enero; **what day is it today?** ¿qué día es hoy?; **it's Sunday today** hoy es domingo; **a week ago today** hoy hace una semana; **a week (from) today** de aquí a una semana - **2.** [nowadays] hoy (en día).

toddle ['tɒdl] *vi* caminar con paso inseguro.

toddler ['tɒdlə'] *n* niño pequeño *m*, niña pequeña *f* (que empieza a andar).

toddy ['tɒdɪ] (*pl* **-ies**) *n* ponche *m*.

to-do (*pl* **-s**) *n inf* jaleo *m*, follón *m*.

toe [təʊ] <> *n* - **1.** [of foot] dedo *m* (del pie) - **2.** [of sock] punta *f*; [of shoe] puntera *f*. <> *vt*: **to toe the line** acatar las normas.

toehold ['təʊhəʊld] *n* [in rock] punto *m* de apoyo; *fig* [in market]: **to gain a toehold in** ganarse un hueco en.

toenail ['təʊneɪl] *n* uña *f* del dedo del pie.

toffee ['tɒfɪ] *n* caramelo *m*.

toffee apple *n* UK manzana *f* acaramelada.

tofu ['təʊfu:] *n* tofu *m*.

toga ['təʊgə] *n* toga *f*.

together [tə'geðə'] <> *adv* - **1.** [gen] juntos(tas); **all together** todos juntos; **to stick together** pegar; **to join together** unir; **to go (well) together** combinar bien - **2.** [at the same time] a la vez, juntos(tas). <> *adj inf* organizado(da).

➤ **together with** *prep* junto con.

togetherness [tə'geðənɪs] *n* (*U*) unión *f*, camaradería *f*.

toggle ['tɒgl] *n* botón *m* de una trenca.

toggle switch n COMPUT & ELECTRON conmutador m de palanca.

togs [tɒgz] npl inf ropa f.

toil [tɔɪl] fml ◇ n trabajo m duro. ◇ vi trabajar sin descanso.
◆ **toil away** vi: **to toil away (at)** trabajar sin descanso (en).

toilet ['tɔɪlɪt] n [at home] wáter m, lavabo m; [in public place] servicios mpl, lavabo m; **to go to the toilet** ir al wáter.

toilet bag n neceser m.

toilet paper n (U) papel m higiénico.

toiletries ['tɔɪlɪtrɪz] npl artículos mpl de tocador.

toilet roll n - **1.** [paper] papel m higiénico - **2.** [roll] rollo m de papel higiénico.

toilet soap n jabón m de tocador.

toilet-trained [-,treɪnd] adj [child] que sabe ir solo al wáter.

toilet water n (agua f de) colonia f.

to-ing and fro-ing [,tu:ɪŋən'frəʊɪŋ] (pl **to-ings and fro-ings**) n (U) idas fpl y venidas.

token ['təʊkn] ◇ adj simbólico(ca). ◇ n - **1.** [voucher] vale m; [disk] ficha f - **2.** [symbol] muestra f, símbolo m; **as a token of our appreciation** como muestra de nuestro agradecimiento.
◆ **by the same token** adv del mismo modo.

told [təʊld] pt & pp ▷ tell.

tolerable ['tɒlərəbl] adj tolerable, pasable.

tolerably ['tɒlərəblɪ] adv medio.

tolerance ['tɒlərəns] n tolerancia f.

tolerant ['tɒlərənt] adj tolerante.

tolerate ['tɒləreɪt] vt - **1.** [put up with] soportar, tolerar - **2.** [permit] tolerar.

toleration [,tɒlə'reɪʃn] n (U) tolerancia f.

toll [təʊl] ◇ n - **1.** [number]: **death toll** número m de víctimas - **2.** [fee] peaje m
▶▶ **to take its toll** hacer mella. ◇ vt tañer, tocar. ◇ vi tocar, doblar.

tollbooth ['təʊlbu:θ] n cabina donde se paga el peaje.

toll bridge n puente m de peaje.

toll-free US ◇ adj gratuito(ta). ◇ adv: **to call a number toll-free** llamar a un número gratis.

tomato [UK tə'mɑ:təʊ, US tə'meɪtəʊ] (pl **-es**) n tomate m, jitomate m Amér C & Méx.

tomb [tu:m] n tumba f, sepulcro m.

tombola [tɒm'bəʊlə] n esp UK tómbola f.

tomboy ['tɒmbɔɪ] n niña f poco feminina.

tombstone ['tu:mstəʊn] n lápida f.

tomcat ['tɒmkæt] n gato m (macho).

tomfoolery [tɒm'fu:lərɪ] n comportamiento m tonto.

tomorrow [tə'mɒrəʊ] ◇ n lit & fig mañana f; **tomorrow is Sunday** mañana es domingo; **the day after tomorrow** pasado mañana; **tomorrow night** mañana por la noche; **he was drinking like there was no tomorrow** bebía como si se fuera a acabar el mundo; **tomorrow's world** el futuro. ◇ adv mañana; **see you tomorrow** hasta mañana; **a week (from) tomorrow** dentro de una semana, a partir de mañana; **it happened a year ago tomorrow** mañana hará un año que ocurrió.

ton [tʌn] (pl **ton** OR **-s**) n - **1.** UK [imperial] = 1016 kg; US = 907,2 kg, ≃ tonelada f - **2.** [metric] = 1000 kg tonelada f
▶▶ **to weigh a ton** inf pesar una tonelada; **to come down on sb like a ton of bricks** [speak angrily] echar la gran bronca a alguien; [punish severely] dar un buen escarmiento a alguien.
◆ **tons** npl inf: **tons (of)** un montón (de).

tonal ['təʊnl] adj tonal.

tone [təʊn] n - **1.** [gen] tono m - **2.** [on phone] señal f
▶▶ **to lower the tone of** dar mal tono a.
◆ **tone down** vt sep suavizar, moderar.
◆ **tone in** vi: **to tone in (with)** ir bien OR armonizar (con).
◆ **tone up** vt sep poner en forma.

tone-deaf adj que no tiene (buen) oído.

toner ['təʊnə'] n - **1.** [for photocopier, printer] virador m - **2.** [cosmetic] tónico m.

tongs [tɒŋz] npl [for coal] tenazas fpl; [for sugar] pinzas fpl, tenacillas fpl.

tongue [tʌŋ] n - **1.** [gen] lengua f; **to have one's tongue in one's cheek** inf no ir en serio; **to hold one's tongue** fig quedarse callado(da); **tongues will wag** seguro que la gente murmurará - **2.** [of shoe] lengüeta f.

tongue-in-cheek adj: **it was only tongue-in-cheek** no iba en serio.

tongue-tied [-,taɪd] adj incapaz de hablar (por timidez o nervios).

tongue twister [-,twɪstə'] n trabalenguas m inv.

tonic ['tɒnɪk] n - **1.** [gen] tónico m - **2.** [tonic water] tónica f.

tonic water n agua f tónica.

tonight [tə'naɪt] ◇ n esta noche f. ◇ adv esta noche.

tonnage ['tʌnɪdʒ] n tonelaje m.

tonne [tʌn] (pl **tonne** OR **-s**) n tonelada f métrica.

tonsil ['tɒnsl] n amígdala f; **to have one's tonsils out** operarse de las amígdalas.

tonsil(l)itis [,tɒnsɪ'laɪtɪs] n (U) amigdalitis f inv.

too [tu:] adv - **1.** [also] también; **me too** yo también - **2.** [excessively] demasiado; **too much** demasiado; **too many things** demasiadas cosas;

it finished all OR only too soon terminó demasiado pronto; **I'd be only too happy to help** me encantaría ayudarte; **not too...** no muy...

took [tʊk] *pt* ▷ take.

tool [tu:l] *n* - **1.** [implement] herramienta *f*; **garden tools** útiles *mpl* del jardín; **to down tools** *UK* dejar de trabajar como protesta - **2.** *fig* [means] instrumento *m*; **the tools of one's trade** los instrumentos de trabajo de uno.

tool bar *n* COMPUT barra *f* de herramientas.

tool box *n* caja *f* de herramientas.

tool kit *n* juego *m* de herramientas.

toot [tu:t] ◇ *n* bocinazo *m*. ◇ *vt* tocar. ◇ *vi* tocar la bocina.

tooth [tu:θ] (*pl* teeth) *n* - **1.** [in mouth, of saw, gear wheel] diente *m*; **to brush one's teeth** cepillarse OR lavarse los dientes; **he had a tooth out** le sacaron un diente; **to be (a bit) long in the tooth for sthg** *UK pej* ser ya (un poco) mayorcito para algo; **to be fed up to the back teeth with sthg** *UK inf* estar hasta la coronilla de algo; **to grit one's teeth** apretar los dientes; **to lie through one's teeth** mentir como un bellaco - **2.** [of comb] púa *f*.

toothache ['tu:θeɪk] *n* dolor *m* de muelas.

toothbrush ['tu:θbrʌʃ] *n* cepillo *m* de dientes.

toothless ['tu:θlɪs] *adj* desdentado(da).

toothpaste ['tu:θpeɪst] *n* pasta *f* de dientes.

toothpick ['tu:θpɪk] *n* palillo *m*.

tooth powder *n* polvos *mpl* dentífricos.

tootle ['tu:tl] *vi inf* [move unhurriedly]: **to tootle off** irse sin prisas.

top [tɒp] ◇ *adj* - **1.** [highest - step, floor] de arriba; [- object on pile] de encima - **2.** [most important, successful] importante; **to be a top model** ser top model; **she got the top mark** sacó la mejor nota - **3.** [maximum] máximo(ma); **at top speed** a máxima velocidad; **to be top secret** ser altamente confidencial. ◇ *n* - **1.** [highest point] parte *f* superior OR de arriba; [of list] cabeza *f*, principio *m*; [of tree] copa *f*; [of hill, mountain] cumbre *f*, cima *f*; **at the top of the stairs** en lo alto de la escalera; **from top to bottom** de pies a cabeza; **on top** encima; **to go over the top** *UK* pasarse (de la raya); **at the top of one's voice** a voz en grito - **2.** [lid, cap - of jar, box] tapa *f*; [- of bottle, tube] tapón *m*; [- of pen] capuchón *m* - **3.** [upper side] superficie *f* - **4.** [blouse] blusa *f*; [T-shirt] camiseta *f*; [of pyjamas] parte *f* de arriba - **5.** [toy] peonza *f* - **6.** [most important level] cúpula *f* - **7.** [of league, table, scale] cabeza *f*. ◇ *vt* (*pt & pp* -ped, *cont* -ping) - **1.** [be first in] estar a la cabeza de - **2.** [better] superar - **3.** [exceed] exceder.

➤ **on top of** *prep* - **1.** [in space] encima de; **to be feeling on top of the world** estar en la gloria - **2.** [in addition to] además de; **on top of that** por si fuera poco - **3.** [in control of]: **to be on top of sthg** tener algo bajo control
▸▸ **to get on top of sb** abrumar a alguien.

➤ **top up** *UK*, **top off** *US vt sep* volver a llenar.

topaz ['təʊpæz] *n* topacio *m*.

top brass *n* (*U*) *inf*: **the top brass** los altos cargos, los mandamases.

topcoat ['tɒpkəʊt] *n* - **1.** [item of clothing] abrigo *m* - **2.** [paint] última mano *f* (de pintura).

top dog *n inf* mandamás *mf*.

top-flight *adj inf* de altos vuelos.

top floor *n* último piso *m*.

top gear *n* directa *f*.

top hat *n* chistera *f*, sombrero *m* de copa.

top-heavy *adj* demasiado pesado(da) en la parte de arriba.

topic ['tɒpɪk] *n* tema *m*, asunto *m*.

topical ['tɒpɪkl] *adj* de actualidad, actual.

topknot ['tɒpnɒt] *n* [in hair] moño *m*.

topless ['tɒplɪs] *adj* en topless.

top-level *adj* de alto nivel.

topmost ['tɒpməʊst] *adj* más alto(ta).

top-notch *adj inf* de primera.

top-of-the-line *adj US* de gama alta.

topography [tə'pɒgrəfɪ] *n* topografía *f*.

topped [tɒpt] *adj*: **topped by** OR **with sthg** con algo encima.

topping ['tɒpɪŋ] *n* capa *f*; **with a topping of cream** cubierto de nata.

topple ['tɒpl] ◇ *vt* [government, pile] derribar; [president] derrocar. ◇ *vi* venirse abajo.

➤ **topple over** *vi* venirse abajo.

top-ranking [-'ræŋkɪŋ] *adj* de alto nivel.

top-secret *adj* sumamente secreto (sumamente secreta).

top-security *adj* de máxima seguridad.

topsoil ['tɒpsɔɪl] *n* capa *f* superficial del suelo.

topsy-turvy [,tɒpsɪ'tɜːvɪ] ◇ *adj* - **1.** [messy] patas arriba *(inv)* - **2.** [haywire] loco(ca). ◇ *adv* [messily] en desorden, de cualquier manera.

top-up *n*: **can I give you a top-up?** ¿quieres que te ponga más?

top-up card *n* [for mobile phone] tarjeta *f* de recarga.

torch [tɔːtʃ] *n* - **1.** *UK* [electric] linterna *f* - **2.** [burning] antorcha *f*.

tore [tɔːʳ] *pt* ▷ tear.

torment ◇ *n* ['tɔːment] tormento *m*; **she waited in torment** esperaba atormentada. ◇ *vt* [tɔː'ment] - **1.** [worry greatly] atormentar - **2.** [annoy] fastidiar.

tormentor [tɔː'mentəʳ] *n* hostigador *m*, -ra *f*.

torn [tɔ:n] *pp* ▷ tear.

tornado [tɔ:'neɪdəʊ] (*pl* **-es** OR **-s**) *n* tornado *m*.

torpedo [tɔ:'pi:dəʊ] ◇ *n* (*pl* **-es**) torpedo *m*. ◇ *vt* torpedear.

torpor ['tɔ:pə^r] *n* apatía *f*.

torque [tɔ:k] *n* par *m* de torsión.

torrent ['tɒrənt] *n* torrente *m*.

torrential [tə'renʃl] *adj* torrencial.

torrid ['tɒrɪd] *adj* [hot] tórrido(da); *fig* [passionate] apasionado(da).

torso ['tɔ:səʊ] (*pl* **-s**) *n* torso *m*.

tortoise ['tɔ:təs] *n* tortuga *f* (de tierra).

tortoiseshell ['tɔ:təʃel] ◇ *adj*: **tortoiseshell cat** gato *m* pardo atigrado. ◇ *n* (*U*) [material] carey *m*, concha *f*. ◇ *comp* de carey OR concha.

tortuous ['tɔ:tʃʊəs] *adj* **- 1.** [twisting] tortuoso(sa) **- 2.** [over-complicated] enrevesado(da), retorcido(da).

torture ['tɔ:tʃə^r] ◇ *n* tortura *f*. ◇ *vt* torturar.

torturer ['tɔ:tʃərə^r] *n* torturador *m*, -ra *f*.

Tory ['tɔ:rɪ] ◇ *adj* tory, del partido conservador (británico). ◇ *n* (*pl* **-ies**) tory *mf*, miembro *m* del partido conservador (británico).

toss [tɒs] ◇ *vt* **- 1.** [throw carelessly] tirar **- 2.** [move from side to side - head, boat] sacudir **- 3.** [salad] remover; [pancake] dar la vuelta en el aire **- 4.** [coin]: **to toss a coin** echar a cara o cruz. ◇ *vi* **- 1.** [with coin] echar a cara o cruz **- 2.** [move rapidly]: **to toss and turn** dar vueltas (en la cama). ◇ *n* **- 1.** [of coin] tirada *f*; **to win/lose the toss** ganar/perder en el sorteo **- 2.** [of head] sacudida *f*.

◆ **toss up** *vi* jugar a cara o cruz.

toss-up *n inf*: **it's a toss-up whether they win or lose** igual ganan que pierden.

tot [tɒt] *n* **- 1.** *inf* [small child] nene *m*, nena *f* **- 2.** [of drink] trago *m*.

◆ **tot up** *vt sep* (*pt & pp* **-ted**, *cont* **-ting**) *inf* sumar.

total ['təʊtl] ◇ *adj* total. ◇ *n* total *m*; **in total** en total. ◇ *vt* (*UK* **-led**, *cont* **-ling**, *US* **-ed**, *cont* **-ing**) **- 1.** [add up] sumar **- 2.** *US inf* [wreck] dejar hecho una ruina. ◇ *vi* (*UK* **-led**, *cont* **-ling**, *US* **-ed**, *cont* **-ing**) [amount to] ascender a.

totalitarian [,təʊtælɪ'teərɪən] *adj* totalitario(ria).

totality [təʊ'tælətɪ] *n* totalidad *f*.

totally ['təʊtəlɪ] *adv* [entirely] totalmente.

tote bag [təʊt-] *n US* bolsa *f* (de la compra).

totem pole ['təʊtəm-] *n* tótem *m*.

toto ['təʊtəʊ] ◆ **in toto** *adv fml* totalmente.

totter ['tɒtə^r] *vi lit & fig* tambalearse.

toucan ['tu:kən] *n* tucán *m*.

touch [tʌtʃ] ◇ *n* **- 1.** [sense, act of feeling] tacto *m* **- 2.** [detail, skill, knack] toque *m*; **to put the finishing touches to sthg** dar el último toque a algo **- 3.** [contact]: **to get/keep in touch (with)** ponerse/mantenerse en contacto (con); **to lose touch (with)** perder el contacto (con); **to be out of touch with** no estar al tanto de **- 4.** SPORT: **in touch** fuera de banda **- 5.** [small amount]: **a touch (of)** un poquito (de) ▷▷ **to be touch and go** ser dudoso OR poco seguro; **to be a soft touch** no saber decir que no. ◇ *vt* **- 1.** [gen] tocar; **you haven't touched your food** no has tocado la comida **- 2.** [emotionally] conmover **- 3.** [equal] igualar; **nobody can touch her for professionalism** nadie la iguala en profesionalismo. ◇ *vi* **- 1.** [with fingers etc] tocar; **don't touch!** ¡no lo toques! **- 2.** [be in contact] tocarse.

◆ **a touch** *adv* [rather] un poco.

◆ **touch down** *vi* [plane] aterrizar, tomar tierra.

◆ **touch on** *vt insep* tocar, tratar por encima.

touch-and-go *adj* dudoso(sa), poco seguro (poco segura).

touchdown ['tʌtʃdaʊn] *n* **- 1.** [of plane] aterrizaje *m* **- 2.** [in American football] ensayo *m*.

touched [tʌtʃt] *adj* **- 1.** [grateful] emocionado(da) **- 2.** *inf* [slightly mad] tocado(da).

touching ['tʌtʃɪŋ] *adj* conmovedor(ra).

touchline ['tʌtʃlaɪn] *n* línea *f* de banda.

touchpaper ['tʌtʃ,peɪpə^r] *n* mecha *f* (de fuego artificial).

touchscreen ['tʌtʃskri:n] *n* pantalla *f* táctil.

touch-type *vi* mecanografiar al tacto.

touchy ['tʌtʃɪ] (*comp* **-ier**, *superl* **-iest**) *adj* **- 1.** [person]: **touchy (about)** susceptible (con) **- 2.** [subject, question] delicado(da).

tough [tʌf] *adj* **- 1.** [resilient] fuerte **- 2.** [hard-wearing] resistente **- 3.** [meat, regulations, policies] duro(ra); **to get tough with sb** ponerse duro(ra) con alguien **- 4.** [difficult to deal with] difícil **- 5.** [rough - area] peligroso(sa) **- 6.** *inf* [unfortunate] injusto(ta); **tough luck** mala suerte.

toughen ['tʌfn] *vt* endurecer.

toughened ['tʌfnd] *adj* endurecido(da).

toughness ['tʌfnɪs] *n* (*U*) **- 1.** [of character, material] resistencia *f* **- 2.** [of meat, regulations, policies] dureza *f* **- 3.** [of problem, decision] dificultad *f*.

toupee ['tu:peɪ] *n* peluquín *m*.

tour [tʊə^r] ◇ *n* **- 1.** [long journey] viaje *m* largo; **to go on a tour of Germany** hacer un recorrido por Alemania **- 2.** [of pop group etc] gira *f* **- 3.** [for sightseeing] recorrido *m*, visita *f*. ◇ *vt* [museum] visitar; [country] recorrer, viajar por. ◇ *vi* estar de gira; **to tour round sthg** viajar por *OR* recorrer algo.

tourer ['tʊərə'] *n* coche *m* grande descapotable.

Tourette's Syndrome, Tourette syndrome *n* MED síndrome *m* de Tourette.

touring ['tʊərɪŋ] ◇ *adj* [exhibition] itinerante; [theatre, music group] que va de gira. ◇ *n* viajes *mpl* turísticos; **to go touring** hacer turismo.

tourism ['tʊərɪzm] *n* turismo *m*.

tourist ['tʊərɪst] *n* turista *mf*.

tourist class *n* clase *f* turista.

tourist (information) office *n* oficina *f* de turismo.

touristy ['tʊərɪstɪ] *adj* pej demasiado turístico(ca).

tournament ['tɔːnəmənt] *n* torneo *m*.

tourniquet ['tʊənɪkeɪ] *n* torniquete *m*.

tour operator *n* touroperador *m*, operador *m* turístico.

tousled ['taʊzl] *adj* despeinado(da), alborotado(da).

tout [taʊt] ◇ *n* revendedor *m*, -ra *f*. ◇ *vt* revender. ◇ *vi*: **to tout for sthg** solicitar algo; **to tout for business** tratar de captar clientes.

tow [təʊ] ◇ *n*: **to give sb a tow** remolcar a alguien; **on tow** UK [car] a remolque; **in tow with sb** acompañado de alguien. ◇ *vt* remolcar.

towards UK [tə'wɔːdz], **toward** US [tə'wɔːd] *prep* - **1.** [gen] hacia; **towards 6 o'clock/the end of the month** hacia las seis/final de mes - **2.** [for the purpose or benefit of] para; **efforts towards peace** esfuerzos encaminados hacia la paz; **£20 towards the blind** 20 libras para los ciegos.

towaway zone ['təʊəweɪ-] *n* US ≃ zona *f* de estacionamiento prohibido.

towbar ['təʊbɑː] *n* barra *f* de remolque.

towel ['taʊəl] *n* toalla *f*.

towelling UK, **toweling** US ['taʊəlɪŋ] ◇ *n (U)* (tejido *m* de) toalla *f*. ◇ *comp* de toalla.

towel rail *n* toallero *m*.

tower ['taʊə'] ◇ *n* torre *f*; **a tower of strength** UK un firme apoyo *OR* pilar. ◇ *vi*: **to tower (over sthg)** elevarse (por encima de algo); **to tower over sb** ser mucho más alto(ta) que alguien.

tower block *n* UK bloque *m* (de pisos u oficinas).

towering ['taʊərɪŋ] *adj* altísimo(ma).

town [taʊn] *n* - **1.** [gen] ciudad *f*; [smaller] pueblo *m* - **2.** [centre of town, city] centro *m* de la ciudad; **to go out on the town** irse de juerga;

to go to town fig [to put in a lot of effort] emplearse a fondo; [spend a lot of money] tirar la casa por la ventana.

town centre *n* centro *m* (de la ciudad).

town clerk *n* secretario del ayuntamiento *m*, secretaria del ayuntamiento *f*.

town council *n* ayuntamiento *m*.

town hall *n* ayuntamiento *m*.

town house *n* [fashionable house] casa *f* lujosa (de un barrio alto).

town plan *n* plano *m* de la ciudad.

town planner *n* urbanista *mf*.

town planning *n* - **1.** [study] urbanismo *m* - **2.** [practice] planificación *f* urbanística.

townsfolk ['taʊnzfəʊk], **townspeople** ['taʊnz,piːpl] *npl*: **the townsfolk** los habitantes (de una ciudad), los ciudadanos.

township ['taʊnʃɪp] *n* - **1.** [in South Africa] zona urbana asignada por el gobierno para la población negra - **2.** [in US] ≃ municipio *m*.

towpath (['təʊpɑːθ], *pl* [-pɑːðz]) *n* camino *m* de sirga.

towrope ['təʊrəʊp] *n* cable *m* de remolque.

tow truck *n* US (coche *m*) grúa *f*.

toxic ['tɒksɪk] *adj* tóxico(ca).

toxin ['tɒksɪn] *n* toxina *f*.

toy [tɔɪ] *n* juguete *m*.

➤ **toy with** *vt insep* [idea] acariciar; [food, coin etc] jugetear con.

toy boy *n* inf joven amante de una mujer mucho mayor que él.

toy shop *n* juguetería *f*.

trace [treɪs] ◇ *n* - **1.** [evidence, remains] rastro *m*, huella *f*; **there's no trace of her** no hay rastro de ella; **without trace** sin dejar rastro - **2.** [small amount] pizca *f*. ◇ *vt* - **1.** [find] localizar, encontrar - **2.** [follow progress of] describir - **3.** [on paper] calcar.

trace element *n* CHEM oligoelemento *m*.

tracer bullet ['treɪsə'-] *n* bala *f* trazadora.

tracing ['treɪsɪŋ] *n* [on paper] calco *m*.

tracing paper ['treɪsɪŋ-] *n (U)* papel *m* de calcar.

track [træk] ◇ *n* - **1.** [path] sendero *m*; **off the beaten track** apartado(da), aislado(da) - **2.** SPORT pista *f* - **3.** RAIL vía *f* - **4.** [mark, trace] rastro *m*, huella *f*; **to hide** *OR* **cover one's tracks** no dejar rastro; **to stop dead in one's tracks** pararse en seco - **5.** [on record, tape] canción *f*

➤➤ **to keep/lose track of sb** no perder/perder la pista a alguien; **to lose/keep track of events** perder el hilo de/seguir los acontecimientos; **I've lost track of how many times I've told you** ya he perdido la cuenta de las veces que te lo he dicho; **to be on the right/**

wrong track ir por el buen/mal camino. ◇ *vt*
- 1. [follow tracks of] rastrear, seguir la pista de
- 2. [with radar] seguir la trayectoria de.
◆ **track down** *vt sep* localizar.

trackball ['trækbɔːl] *n* COMPUT trackball *m*, esfera *f* de arrastre/desplazamiento.

tracker dog ['trækər-] *n* perro *m* rastreador.

track event *n* prueba *f* de atletismo (en pista).

tracking station ['trækɪŋ-] *n* estación *f* de seguimiento.

track record *n* historial *m*; **to have a good track record** tener un buen historial.

track shoes *npl* zapatillas *fpl* de atletismo.

tracksuit ['træksuːt] UK *n* chandal *m*, equipo *m* de deportes, buzo *m* Chile & Perú, pants *mpl* Méx, sudadera *f* Col, jogging *m* R Plata.

tract [trækt] *n* **- 1.** [pamphlet] artículo *m* breve
- 2. [of land, forest] extensión *f* **- 3.** MED: **digestive tract** aparato *m* digestivo.

traction ['trækʃn] *n* tracción *f*; **to have one's leg in traction** tener la pierna escayolada en alto.

traction engine *n* locomotora *f* de tracción.

tractor ['træktər] *n* tractor *m*.

tractor-trailer *n* US camión *m* articulado.

trade [treɪd] ◇ *n* **- 1.** (U) [commerce] comercio *m* **- 2.** [job] oficio *m*; **by trade** de oficio. ◇ *vt* [exchange]: **to trade sthg (for)** cambiar algo (por). ◇ *vi* **- 1.** COMM: **to trade (with)** comerciar (con) **- 2.** US [shop]: **to trade at** OR **with** hacer sus compras en.
◆ **trade in** *vt sep* [exchange] dar como entrada.

trade barrier *n* barrera *f* comercial.

trade deficit *n* déficit *m* (en la balanza) comercial.

trade discount *n* descuento *m* comercial.

trade fair *n* feria *f* de muestras.

trade-in *n* artículo usado que se entrega como entrada al comprar un artículo nuevo.

trademark ['treɪdmɑːk] *n* **- 1.** COMM marca *f* comercial **- 2.** fig [characteristic] rasgo *m* característico.

trade name *n* COMM nombre *m* comercial.

trade-off *n* equilibrio *m*.

trade price *n* precio *m* al por mayor.

trader ['treɪdər] *n* comerciante *mf*.

trade route *n* ruta *f* comercial.

trade secret *n* secreto *m* comercial.

tradesman ['treɪdzmən] (*pl* **-men** [-mən]) *n* [trader] comerciante *m*; [shopkeeper] tendero *m*.

tradespeople ['treɪdz,piːpl] *npl* comerciantes *mpl* & *fpl*.

trade(s) union *n* UK sindicato *m*.

trade(s) unionist *n* UK sindicalista *mf*.

trade wind *n* NAUT viento *m* alisio.

trading ['treɪdɪŋ] *n* (U) comercio *m*.

trading estate *n* UK polígono *m* industrial.

trading stamp *n* cupón *m* del ahorro.

trading standards officer *n* funcionario del organismo británico que vela por el cumplimiento de las normas comerciales.

tradition [trə'dɪʃn] *n* tradición *f*.

traditional [trə'dɪʃənl] *adj* tradicional.

traditionally [trə'dɪʃnəlɪ] *adv* tradicionalmente.

traffic ['træfɪk] ◇ *n* **- 1.** [vehicles] tráfico *m*
- 2. [illegal trade]: **traffic (in)** tráfico *m* (de). ◇ *vi* (*pt* & *pp* **-ked**, *cont* **-king**): **to traffic in** traficar con.

traffic circle *n* US glorieta *f*.

traffic island *n* refugio *m*.

traffic jam *n* embotellamiento *m*, atasco *m*.

trafficker ['træfɪkər] *n*: **trafficker (in)** traficante *mf* (de).

traffic lights *npl* semáforos *mpl*.

traffic offence UK, **traffic violation** US *n* infracción *f* de tráfico.

traffic warden *n* UK ≈ guardia *mf* de tráfico.

tragedy ['trædʒədɪ] (*pl* **-ies**) *n* tragedia *f*.

tragic ['trædʒɪk] *adj* trágico(ca).

tragically ['trædʒɪklɪ] *adv* trágicamente.

trail [treɪl] ◇ *n* **- 1.** [path] sendero *m*, camino *m*; **to blaze a trail** fig marcar la pauta
- 2. [trace, track] rastro *m*, huellas *fpl*; **a trail of smoke** un rastro de humo; **they left a trail of clues** dejaron un rastro de pistas; **to be on the trail of sb/sthg** seguir la pista de alguien/algo; **they are hot on his trail** le están pisando los talones. ◇ *vt* **- 1.** [drag] arrastrar **- 2.** [lose to] ir por detrás de. ◇ *vi* **- 1.** [drag] arrastrarse
- 2. [move slowly] andar con desgana **- 3.** [lose] ir perdiendo.
◆ **trail away, trail off** *vi* apagarse.

trailblazing ['treɪl,bleɪzɪŋ] *adj* pionero(ra).

trailer ['treɪlər] *n* **- 1.** [vehicle for luggage] remolque *m* **- 2.** esp US [for living in] roulotte *m*, caravana *f* **- 3.** CIN trailer *m*.

trailer park *n* US camping *m* para roulottes OR caravanas.

train [treɪn] ◇ *n* **- 1.** RAIL tren *m*; **to go by train** ir en tren **- 2.** [of dress] cola *f*. ◇ *vt* **- 1.** [teach]: **to train sb (to do sthg)** enseñar a alguien (a hacer algo); **to train sb in sthg** preparar a alguien para algo **- 2.** [for job]: **to train sb (as sthg)** formar OR preparar a alguien (como algo) **- 3.** [animal] amaestrar **- 4.** SPORT: **to train sb (for)** entrenar a alguien (para) **- 5.** [direct growth of] guiar **- 6.** [aim - gun] apuntar; [- camera] enfocar; **to train a camera on sb** enfocar a alguien con una cámara. ◇ *vi* **- 1.** [for job]

estudiar, prepararse; **to train as** formarse OR prepararse como; **to train as a doctor** estudiar medicina; **to train to be a teacher** estudiar para ser profesor - **2.** SPORT: **to train (for)** entrenarse (para).

trained [treɪnd] *adj* cualificado(da).

trainee [treɪ'ni:] <> *adj* en período de prácticas. <> *n* aprendiz *m*, -za *f*, persona *f* que está en período de prácticas.

trainer ['treɪnəʳ] *n* - **1.** [of animals] amaestrador *m*, -ra *f* - **2.** SPORT entrenador *m*, -ra *f*.

→ **trainers** *npl* UK zapatillas *fpl* de deporte.

training ['treɪnɪŋ] *n* (U) - **1.** [for job]: **training (in)** formación *f* OR preparación *f* (para) - **2.** SPORT entrenamiento *m*; **to be in training (for sthg)** estar entrenando para algo.

training college *n* UK [gen] centro *m* de formación especializada; [for teachers] escuela *f* normal.

training course *n* cursillo *m* de formación.

training shoes *npl* UK zapatillas *fpl* de deporte.

train of thought *n* hilo *m* del razonamiento.

train set *n* tren *m* eléctrico de juguete.

train spotter [-ˌspɒtəʳ] *n* aficionado a los trenes que en una estación apunta el número de las locomotoras al pasar.

train station *n* US estación *f* de ferrocarril.

traipse [treɪps] *vi* andar con desgana.

trait [treɪt] *n* rasgo *m*, característica *f*.

traitor ['treɪtəʳ] *n*: **traitor (to)** traidor *m*, -ra *f* (a).

trajectory [trə'dʒektərɪ] (*pl* -ies) *n* trayectoria *f*.

tram [træm], **tramcar** ['træmkɑːʳ] *n* UK tranvía *m*.

tramlines ['træmlaɪnz] *npl* UK - **1.** [for trams] vías *fpl* de tranvía - **2.** TENNIS líneas *fpl* de banda.

tramp [træmp] <> *n* - **1.** [homeless person] vagabundo *m*, -da *f* - **2.** US inf [woman] fulana *f*. <> *vi* andar pesadamente.

trample ['træmpl] <> *vt* pisar, pisotear; **to be trampled underfoot** ser pisoteado(da). <> *vi* - **1.** [tread]: **to trample on sthg** pisar algo - **2.** fig [act cruelly]: **to trample on sb** pisar OR pisotear a alguien.

trampoline ['træmpəli:n] *n* cama *f* elástica.

trance [trɑːns] *n* trance *m*; **in a trance** en trance; **to go into a trance** entrar en trance.

tranquil ['træŋkwɪl] *adj liter* tranquilo(la), apacible.

tranquility US = **tranquillity**.

tranquilize US = **tranquillize**.

tranquilizer US = **tranquillizer**.

tranquillity UK, **tranquility** US [træŋ'kwɪlətɪ] *n* tranquilidad *f*.

tranquillize, -ise UK, **tranquilize** US ['træŋkwɪlaɪz] *vt* tranquilizar.

tranquillizer UK, **tranquilizer** US ['træŋkwɪlaɪzəʳ] *n* tranquilizante *m*.

transact [træn'zækt] *vt fml* hacer, llevar a cabo.

transaction [træn'zækʃn] *n* transacción *f*; **money transactions** transacciones de dinero.

transatlantic [ˌtrænzət'læntɪk] *adj* transatlántico(ca).

transceiver [træn'siːvəʳ] *n* transmisor-receptor *m* de radio.

transcend [træn'send] *vt fml* ir más allá de, superar.

transcendental meditation [ˌtrænsen'dentl-] *n* meditación *f* transcendental.

transcribe [træn'skraɪb] *vt* transcribir.

transcript ['trænskrɪpt] *n* US expediente *m* académico.

transept ['trænsept] *n* crucero *m*.

transfer <> *n* ['trænsfɜːʳ] - **1.** [gen] transferencia *f* - **2.** [for job] traslado *m* - **3.** SPORT traspaso *m* - **4.** [design] calcomanía *f* - **5.** US [ticket] *billete válido para transbordar a otro autobús, tren etc.* <> *vt* [træns'fɜːʳ] (*pt & pp* -**red**, *cont* -**ring**) - **1.** [from one place to another] trasladar - **2.** [from one person to another] transferir - **3.** SPORT traspasar. <> *vi* [træns'fɜːʳ] (*pt & pp* -**red**, *cont* -**ring**) - **1.** [to different job etc]: **he transferred to a different department** lo trasladaron a otro departamento - **2.** SPORT: **he transferred to Spurs** fichó por el Spurs.

transferable [træns'fɜːrəbl] *adj* transferible; **not transferable** intransferible.

transference ['trænsfərəns] *n fml* transferencia *f*.

transfer fee *n* UK SPORT traspaso *m*.

transfigure [træns'fɪgəʳ] *vt liter* transfigurar.

transfix [træns'fɪks] *vt* [immobilize] paralizar; **transfixed with** paralizado(da) por.

transform [træns'fɔːm] *vt*: **to transform sthg/sb (into)** transformar algo/a alguien (en).

transformation [ˌtrænsfə'meɪʃn] *n* transformación *f*.

transformer [træns'fɔːməʳ] *n* ELEC transformador *m*.

transfusion [træns'fjuːʒn] *n* transfusión *f*.

transgress [træns'gres] *fml* <> *vt* [limit] traspasar; [law, rules] transgredir. <> *vi* cometer una transgresión.

transgression [træns'greʃn] *n fml* transgresión *f*.

transient ['trænzɪənt] <> *adj fml* [fleeting] transitorio(ria), pasajero(ra). <> *n* US [person] viajero *m*, -ra *f* de paso.

transistor [træn'zɪstəʳ] *n* transistor *m*.

transistor radio n *dated* transistor m.

transit ['trænsɪt] n *US* transporte m; **in transit** en tránsito.

transit camp n campamento m provisional.

transition [træn'zɪʃn] n: **transition (from sthg to sthg)** transición f (de algo a algo); **in transition** en transición.

transitional [træn'zɪʃənl] adj de transición.

transitive ['trænzɪtɪv] adj *GRAM* transitivo(va).

transitory ['trænzɪtrɪ] adj transitorio(ria).

translate [trænsˈleɪt] ⟨⟩ vt - **1.** [languages] traducir - **2.** [transform]: **to translate sthg into** convertir *OR* transformar algo en. ⟨⟩ vi: **it doesn't translate** no se puede traducir; **to translate from sthg into** traducir de algo a.

translation [trænsˈleɪʃn] n traducción f.

translator [trænsˈleɪtər] n traductor m, -ra f.

translucent [trænzˈluːsnt] adj *liter* translúcido(da).

transmission [trænzˈmɪʃn] n transmisión f.

transmit [trænzˈmɪt] (pt & pp **-ted**, cont **-ting**) vt transmitir.

transmitter [trænzˈmɪtər] n *ELECTRON* transmisor m.

transparency [transˈpærənsɪ] (pl **-ies**) n - **1.** [quality] transparencia f - **2.** [slide] diapositiva f.

transparent [trænsˈpærənt] adj - **1.** [see-through] transparente - **2.** [obvious] claro(ra); **that's a transparent excuse** es claramente una excusa.

transpire [trænˈspaɪər] *fml* ⟨⟩ vt: **it transpires that...** resulta que... ⟨⟩ vi [happen] ocurrir, pasar.

transplant ⟨⟩ n ['trænsplɑːnt] trasplante m; **he had a heart transplant** le hicieron un trasplante de corazón. ⟨⟩ vt [trænsˈplɑːnt] [organ, seedlings] trasplantar.

transport ⟨⟩ n ['trænspɔːt] transporte m. ⟨⟩ vt [trænˈspɔːt] transportar.

transportable [trænˈspɔːtəbl] adj transportable.

transportation [ˌtrænspɔːˈteɪʃn] n *esp US* transporte m.

transport cafe ['trænspɔːt-] n *UK* bar m de camioneros.

transporter [trænˈspɔːtər] n camión m para el transporte de vehículos.

transpose [trænsˈpəʊz] vt [change round] invertir.

transsexual [trænsˈsekʃʊəl] n transexual mf.

transvestite [trænzˈvestaɪt] n travestido m, -da f, travestí mf.

trap [træp] ⟨⟩ n trampa f; **to lay a trap (for)** tender una trampa (a). ⟨⟩ vt (pt & pp **-ped**, cont **-ping**) - **1.** [catch - animals, birds] coger con

trampa - **2.** [trick] atrapar, engañar - **3.** [in place, unpleasant situation]: **to be trapped in** estar atrapado(da) en - **4.** [energy, heat] almacenar - **5.** [finger]: **she trapped her fingers in the door** se pilló los dedos en la puerta.

trapdoor [ˌtræpˈdɔːr] n [gen] trampilla f, trampa; *THEAT* escotillón m.

trapeze [trəˈpiːz] n trapecio m.

trapper ['træpər] n trampero m, -ra f.

trappings ['træpɪŋz] npl atributos mpl.

trash [træʃ] n *US lit & fig* basura f.

trashcan ['træʃkæn] n *US* cubo m de la basura.

trashy ['træʃɪ] (comp **-ier**, superl **-iest**) adj inf malísimo(ma), infame.

trauma ['trɔːmə] n trauma m.

traumatic [trɔːˈmætɪk] adj traumático(ca).

traumatize, -ise ['trɔːmətaɪz] vt [shock] traumatizar.

travel ['trævl] ⟨⟩ n (U) viajes mpl; **I'm keen on travel** me gusta viajar. ⟨⟩ vt (*UK* **-led**, cont **-ling**, *US* **-ed**, cont **-ing**) [place] viajar por; [distance] recorrer. ⟨⟩ vi (*UK* **-led**, cont **-ling**, *US* **-ed**, cont **-ing**) viajar.

➤ **travels** npl viajes mpl.

travel agency n agencia f de viajes.

travel agent n empleado m, -da f de una agencia de viajes; **travel agent's** agencia f de viajes.

travel brochure n catálogo m turístico.

traveler *US* = **traveller.**

travelled *UK*, **traveled** *US* ['trævld] adj - **1.** [person] que ha viajado mucho - **2.** [road, route] muy recorrido (muy recorrida).

traveller *UK*, **traveler** *US* ['trævlər] n - **1.** [person on journey] viajero m, -ra f; *UK* **(new age) traveller** *persona que vive en un vehículo y lleva un estilo de vida itinerante* - **2.** [sales representative] viajante mf (de comercio).

traveller's cheque n cheque m de viajero.

travelling *UK*, **traveling** *US* ['trævlɪŋ] adj - **1.** [theatre, showman] ambulante - **2.** [clock, time, allowance] de viaje.

travelling expenses npl gastos mpl *OR* dietas fpl de viaje.

travelling salesman n viajante mf (de comercio).

travelogue *UK*, **travelog** *US* ['trævəlɒg] n - **1.** [talk] conferencia f sobre un viaje - **2.** [film] documental m sobre viajes.

travelsick ['trævəlsɪk] adj que se marea al viajar; **to be** *OR* **feel travelsick** estar mareado(da).

traverse ['trævəs, ˌtrəˈvɜːs] vt *fml* atravesar.

travesty ['trævəstɪ] (pl **-ies**) n burda parodia f.

trawl [trɔːl] <> *n* [fishing net] red *f* barredera. <> *vt*: **to trawl sthg (for)** [fish] rastrear algo (en busca de). <> *vi*: **to trawl for** [fish] pescar al arrastre en busca de.

trawler ['trɔːlər] *n* trainera *f*.

tray [treɪ] *n* bandeja *f*, charola *f Bol, Amér C, Méx & Perú*, charol *m Col & Perú*.

treacherous ['tretʃərəs] *adj* - **1.** [plan, action] traicionero(ra); [person] traidor(ra) - **2.** [dangerous] peligroso(sa).

treachery ['tretʃərɪ] *n* traición *f*.

treacle ['triːkl] *n UK* melaza *f*.

tread [tred] <> *n* - **1.** [on tyre, shoe] banda *f* - **2.** [sound of walking] pasos *mpl*. <> *vt* (*pt* trod, *pp* trodden) [crush]: **to tread sthg into** pisotear algo en; **to tread water** flotar moviendo las piernas. <> *vi* (*pt* trod, *pp* trodden) - **1.** [step]: **to tread on sthg** pisar algo - **2.** [walk] andar; **to tread carefully** *fig* andar con pies de plomo.

treadle ['tredl] *n* pedal *m*.

treadmill ['tredmɪl] *n* - **1.** [wheel] rueda *f* de molino - **2.** *fig* [dull routine] rutina *f*.

treason ['triːzn] *n* traición *f*.

treasure ['treʒər] <> *n lit & fig* tesoro *m*. <> *vt* guardar como oro en paño.

treasure hunt *n* juego *m* de la caza del tesoro.

treasurer ['treʒərər] *n* tesorero *m*, -ra *f*.

treasure trove *n LAW* tesoro *m* escondido OR oculto.

treasury ['treʒərɪ] (*pl* -ies) *n* [room] *habitación donde se guarda el tesoro de un castillo, de una catedral etc.*

➡ **Treasury** *n*: **the Treasury** ≃ el Ministerio de Hacienda.

treasury bill *n* bono *m* del Tesoro.

treat [triːt] <> *vt* - **1.** [gen] tratar; **to treat sb well/badly** tratar bien/mal a alguien; **to treat sb as/like** tratar a alguien como; **to treat sthg as a joke** tomarse algo como si fuera broma; **to treat sb for sthg** MED tratar a alguien de algo - **2.** [give sthg special]: **to treat sb (to)** invitar a alguien (a). <> *n* [something special] regalo *m*; **he took me out to dinner as a treat** me invitó a cenar.

treatise ['triːtɪs] *n fml*: **treatise (on)** tratado *m* (sobre).

treatment ['triːtmənt] *n* - **1.** MED: **treatment (for)** tratamiento *m* (para) - **2.** [manner of dealing] trato *m*.

treaty ['triːtɪ] (*pl* -ies) *n* tratado *m*.

treble ['trebl] <> *adj* - **1.** MUS de tiple - **2.** [with numbers] triple. <> *vt* triplicar. <> *vi* triplicarse.

treble clef *n* clave *f* de sol.

tree [triː] *n BOT & COMPUT* árbol *m*; **to be barking up the wrong tree** equivocarse de medio a medio.

tree-hugger *n inf hum pej* ecologista *mf*.

tree-lined *adj* bordeado(da) de árboles.

tree surgeon *n especialista en el cuidado de los árboles.*

treetop ['triːtɒp] *n* copa *f* (de árbol).

tree-trunk *n* tronco *m* (de árbol).

trek [trek] <> *n* viaje *m* largo y difícil; **it's quite a trek** es toda una caminata. <> *vi* (*pt & pp* -ked, *cont* -king): **we trekked round the museums** nos pateamos los museos.

trellis ['trelɪs] *n* enrejado *m*, espaldera *f*.

tremble ['trembl] *vi* temblar; **to tremble with cold/fear** temblar de frío/miedo.

tremendous [trɪ'mendəs] *adj* - **1.** [impressive, large] enorme, tremendo(da) - **2.** *inf* [really good] estupendo(da), magnífico(ca).

tremendously [trɪ'mendəslɪ] *adv* [impressively, hugely] enormemente.

tremor ['tremər] *n* - **1.** [of person, body, voice] estremecimiento *m* - **2.** [small earthquake] temblor *m*, remezón *m Andes & R Plata*.

tremulous ['tremjʊləs] *adj liter* [voice] trémulo(la); [smile] tímido(da).

trench [trentʃ] *n* - **1.** [narrow channel] zanja *f* - **2.** MIL trinchera *f*.

trenchant ['trentʃənt] *adj fml* mordaz.

trench coat *n* trinchera *f*, gabardina *f*, impermeable *m*.

trench warfare *n (U)* guerra *f* de trincheras.

trend [trend] *n* [tendency] tendencia *f*; [fashion] moda *f*; **to set a trend** establecer una moda.

trendsetter ['trend,setər] *n* iniciador *m*, -ra *f* de modas.

trendy ['trendɪ] *inf* <> *adj* (*comp* -ier, *superl* -iest) [person] moderno(na); [clothes] de moda. <> *n* (*pl* -ies) moderno *m*, -na *f*.

trepidation [,trepɪ'deɪʃn] *n fml*: **in** OR **with trepidation** con ansiedad OR agitación.

trespass ['trespəs] *vi* entrar ilegalmente; **to trespass on** entrar ilegalmente en; **'no trespassing'** 'prohibido el paso'.

trespasser ['trespəsər] *n* intruso *m*, -sa *f*; **'trespassers will be prosecuted'** 'los intrusos serán sancionados por la ley'.

trestle ['tresl] *n* caballete *m*.

trestle table *n* mesa *f* de caballete.

trial ['traɪəl] *n* - **1.** LAW juicio *m*, proceso *m*; **to be on trial (for)** ser procesado(da) (por); **to be brought to trial** ser llevado(da) a juicio - **2.** [test, experiment] prueba *f*; **on trial** de prueba; **by trial and error** a base de probar - **3.** [unpleasant experience] suplicio *m*, fastidio *m*; **trials and tribulations** tribulaciones *fpl*.

trial basis *n*: **on a trial basis** en período de prueba.

trial period *n* período *m* de prueba.

trial run *n* ensayo *m*.

trial-size(d) *adj* en tamaño de muestra.

triangle ['traɪæŋgl] *n* - **1.** GEOM & MUS triángulo *m* - **2.** US [set square] escuadra *f*, cartabón *m*.

triangular [traɪ'æŋgjʊləˈ] *adj* triangular.

triathlon [traɪ'æθlɒn] (*pl* **-s**) *n* triatlón *m*.

tribal ['traɪbl] *adj* tribal.

tribe [traɪb] *n* tribu *f*.

tribulation [,trɪbjʊ'leɪʃn] ▷ **trial**.

tribunal [traɪ'bju:nl] *n* tribunal *m*.

tribune ['trɪbju:n] *n* tribuno *m*.

tributary ['trɪbjʊtrɪ] (*pl* **-ies**) *n* afluente *m*.

tribute ['trɪbju:t] *n* - **1.** [credit] tributo *m*; **to be a tribute to** hacer honor a; **to pay a tribute (to)** hacer un homenaje (a) - **2.** (*U*) [respect, admiration]: **to pay tribute (to)** rendir homenaje (a).

trice [traɪs] *n*: **in a trice** en un dos por tres.

triceps ['traɪseps] (*pl* **triceps** OR **-cepses**) *n* tríceps *m*.

trick [trɪk] ◇ *n* - **1.** [to deceive] truco *m*; [to trap] trampa *f*; [joke] broma *f*; **to play a trick on sb** gastarle una broma a alguien - **2.** [in magic] juego *m* (de manos) - **3.** [knack] truco *m*; **that should do the trick** eso es lo que necesitamos. ◇ *vt* engañar, timar; **to trick sb into doing sthg** engañar a alguien para que haga algo. ◇ *comp* [joke] de broma.

trickery ['trɪkərɪ] *n* (*U*) engaño *m*, fraude *m*.

trickle ['trɪkl] ◇ *n* - **1.** [of liquid] hilo *m* - **2.** [of people, things] sarta *f*, rosario *m*. ◇ *vi* - **1.** [liquid] resbalar *(formando un hilo)* - **2.** [people, things]: **to trickle in/out** llegar/salir poco a poco.

trick question *n* pega *f*, pregunta *f* capciosa.

tricky ['trɪkɪ] (*comp* **-ier**, *superl* **-iest**) *adj* [difficult] difícil, embromado(da) *Amér*.

tricycle ['traɪsɪkl] *n* triciclo *m*.

trident ['traɪdnt] *n* tridente *m*.

tried [traɪd] ◇ *pt* & *pp* ▷ **try**. ◇ *adj*: **tried and tested** probado(da).

trier ['traɪəˈ] *n*: **she's a trier** se esfuerza al máximo.

trifle ['traɪfl] *n* - **1.** UK CULIN *postre de bizcocho con gelatina, crema, frutas y nata* - **2.** [unimportant thing] pequeñez *f*, nadería *f*.

◆ **a trifle** *adv fml* un poco, ligeramente.

◆ **trifle with** *vt insep* tratar sin respeto.

trifling ['traɪflɪŋ] *adj pej* trivial, insignificante.

trigger ['trɪgəˈ] ◇ *n* [on gun] gatillo *m*. ◇ *vt* desencadenar, provocar.

◆ **trigger off** *vt sep* desencadenar, provocar.

trigonometry [,trɪgə'nɒmətrɪ] *n* trigonometría *f*.

trilby ['trɪlbɪ] (*pl* **-ies**) *n* UK sombrero *m* flexible OR de fieltro.

trill [trɪl] ◇ *n* trino *m*. ◇ *vi* [bird] trinar, gorjear; [woman] decir con voz cantarina.

trillions ['trɪljənz] *npl inf*: **trillions (of)** montones *mpl* (de).

trilogy ['trɪlədʒɪ] (*pl* **-ies**) *n* trilogía *f*.

trim [trɪm] ◇ *adj* (*comp* **-mer**, *superl* **-mest**) - **1.** [neat and tidy] limpio y arreglado (limpia y arreglada) - **2.** [slim] esbelto(ta). ◇ *n* - **1.** [of hair] recorte *m*; [of hedge] poda *f* - **2.** [decoration] adorno *m*. ◇ *vt* (*pt* & *pp* **-med**, *cont* **-ming**) - **1.** [nails, moustache] recortar, cortar - **2.** [decorate]: **to trim sthg (with)** adornar algo (con).

◆ **trim away**, **trim off** *vt sep* cortar.

trimmed [trɪmd] *adj*: **trimmed with** adornado(da) con.

trimmings ['trɪmɪŋz] *npl* - **1.** [on clothing] adornos *mpl* - **2.** [with food] guarnición *f*.

Trinidad and Tobago ['trɪnɪdæd-] *n* Trinidad y Tobago.

Trinity ['trɪnətɪ] *n* RELIG: **the Trinity** la Trinidad.

trinket ['trɪŋkɪt] *n* baratija *f*.

trio ['tri:əʊ] (*pl* **-s**) *n* trío *m*.

trip [trɪp] ◇ *n drug sl* [gen] viaje *m*; **to be (away) on a trip** estar de viaje; **a trip to London/the seaside** un viaje a Londres/la costa. ◇ *vt* (*pt* & *pp* **-ped**, *cont* **-ping**) [make stumble] hacer la zancadilla a. ◇ *vi* (*pt* & *pp* **-ped**, *cont* **-ping**) [stumble] tropezar, dar un tropezón; **to trip over sthg** tropezar con algo.

◆ **trip up** *vt sep* - **1.** [make stumble] hacer tropezar, hacer la zancadilla a - **2.** [catch out] coger a, pillar a.

tripartite [,traɪ'pɑ:taɪt] *adj fml* tripartito(ta).

tripe [traɪp] (*U*) *n* - **1.** CULIN callos *mpl* - **2.** *inf* [nonsense] tonterías *fpl*, idioteces *fpl*.

triple ['trɪpl] ◇ *adj* triple. ◇ *adv*: **triple the quantity** el triple. ◇ *vt* triplicar. ◇ *vi* triplicarse.

triple jump *n*: **the triple jump** el triple salto.

triplets ['trɪplɪts] *npl* trillizos *mpl*, -zas *fpl*, triates *mpl Amér*.

triplicate ['trɪplɪkət] *n*: **in triplicate** por triplicado.

tripod ['traɪpɒd] *n* trípode *m*.

tripper ['trɪpəˈ] *n* UK excursionista *mf*.

tripwire ['trɪpwaɪəˈ] *n* cable *m* trampa.

trite [traɪt] *adj pej* trillado(da), manido(da).

triumph ['traɪəmf] ◇ *n* triunfo *m*. ◇ *vi*: **to triumph (over)** triunfar (sobre).

triumphal [traɪ'ʌmfl] *adj fml* triunfal.

triumphant [traɪ'ʌmfənt] *adj* [exultant] triunfante.

triumphantly [trɪ'ʌmfəntlɪ] *adv* triunfalmente.

trivia ['trɪvɪə] *n (U)* trivialidades *fpl*.

trivial ['trɪvɪəl] *adj pej* trivial.

triviality [,trɪvɪ'ælətɪ] *(pl -ies) n* trivialidad *f*.

trivialize, -ise ['trɪvɪəlaɪz] *vt* trivializar.

trod [trɒd] *pt* ▷ **tread**.

trodden ['trɒdn] *pp* ▷ **tread**.

Trojan ['trəʊdʒən] ◇ *adj* HIST troyano(na). ◇ *n* HIST troyano *m*, -na *f*; **to work like a Trojan** *fig* trabajar como un negro.

troll [trəʊl] *n* gnomo *m*, duende *m*.

trolley ['trɒlɪ] *(pl* **trolleys)** *n* **- 1.** UK [for shopping, food, drinks] carrito *m* **- 2.** US [tram] tranvía *m*.

trolleybus ['trɒlɪbʌs] *n* trolebús *m*.

trolley case *n* maleta *f* tipo carrito.

trombone [trɒm'bəʊn] *n* trombón *m*.

troop [tru:p] ◇ *n* [of people] grupo *m*, banda *f*. ◇ *vi* ir en grupo.

◆ **troops** *npl* tropas *fpl*.

◆ **troop in** *vi* entrar en tropel.

◆ **troop out** *vi* salir en tropel.

trooper ['tru:pər] *n* **- 1.** MIL soldado *m* de caballería **- 2.** US [policeman] *miembro de la policía estatal*.

troopship ['tru:pʃɪp] *n* buque *m* de transporte militar.

trophy ['trəʊfɪ] *(pl -ies) n* SPORT trofeo *m*.

tropical ['trɒpɪkl] *adj* tropical.

Tropic of Cancer ['trɒpɪk-] *n:* **the Tropic of Cancer** el trópico de Cáncer.

Tropic of Capricorn ['trɒpɪk-] *n:* **the Tropic of Capricorn** el trópico de Capricornio.

tropics ['trɒpɪks] *npl:* **the tropics** el trópico.

trot [trɒt] ◇ *n* **- 1.** [of horse] trote *m* **- 2.** [of person] paso *m* rápido. ◇ *vi (pt & pp* **-ted,** *cont* **-ting) - 1.** [horse] trotar **- 2.** [person] andar con pasos rápidos.

◆ **on the trot** *adv inf:* **three times on the trot** tres veces seguidas.

◆ **trot out** *vt sep pej:* **he trotted out the same old excuses** repitió las mismas excusas manidas.

Trotskyism ['trɒtskɪɪzm] *n* trotskismo *m*.

trotter ['trɒtər] *n* [pig's foot] pie *m* de cerdo.

trouble ['trʌbl] ◇ *n (U)* **- 1.** [bother] molestia *f*; [difficulty, main problem] problema *m*; **to tell sb one's troubles** contarle a alguien sus problemas; **would it be too much trouble to ask you to...?** ¿tendría inconveniente en...?; **to be in trouble** tener problemas; **to have trouble doing sthg** tener problemas haciendo algo; **to take the trouble to do sthg, to go to the trouble of doing sthg** tomarse la molestia de hacer algo; **the trouble with sb/sthg is...** lo

malo de alguien/algo es...; **to be asking for trouble** estar buscándose problemas; **what seems to be the trouble?** ¿cuál es el problema? **- 2.** *(U)* [pain] dolor *m*; [illness] enfermedad *f*; **heart trouble** problemas cardiacos; **back trouble** problemas de espalda; **I'm having trouble with my leg** me está molestando la pierna **- 3.** *(U)* [violence, unpleasantness] problemas *mpl*. ◇ *vt* **- 1.** [worry, upset] preocupar **- 2.** [disturb, give pain to] molestar.

◆ **troubles** *npl* **- 1.** [problems, worries] problemas *mpl*, preocupaciones *fpl* **- 2.** POL conflicto *m*.

troubled ['trʌbld] *adj* **- 1.** [worried, upset] preocupado(da) **- 2.** [disturbed, problematic] agitado(da), turbulento(ta).

trouble-free *adj* sin problemas.

troublemaker ['trʌbl,meɪkər] *n* alborotador *m*, -ra *f*.

troubleshooter ['trʌbl,ʃu:tər] *n* [in organizations] *persona contratada para resolver problemas*.

troublesome ['trʌblsəm] *adj* molesto(ta), fregado(da) *Amér*.

trouble spot *n* lugar *m* OR punto *m* conflictivo.

trough [trɒf] *n* **- 1.** [for drinking] abrevadero *m*; [for eating] comedero *m* **- 2.** [low point] punto *m* más bajo.

trounce [traʊns] *vt inf* dar una paliza a.

troupe [tru:p] *n* compañía *f*.

trouser press ['traʊzər-] *n* prensa *f* para pantalones.

trousers ['traʊzəz] *npl* pantalones *mpl*.

trouser suit ['traʊzər-] *n* UK traje *m* pantalón.

trousseau ['tru:səʊ] *(pl* **-x** [-z] OR **-s)** *n* ajuar *m*.

trout [traʊt] *(pl* **trout** OR **-s)** *n* trucha *f*.

trove [trəʊv] ▷ **treasure trove**.

trowel ['traʊəl] *n* **- 1.** [for the garden] desplantador *m* **- 2.** [for cement, plaster] paleta *f*, palustre *m*.

truancy ['tru:ənsɪ] *n* el hacer novillos.

truant ['tru:ənt] *n* [child] alumno *m*, -na *f* que hace novillos; **to play truant** hacer novillos.

truce [tru:s] *n:* **truce (between)** tregua *f* (entre).

truck [trʌk] ◇ *n* **- 1.** [lorry] camión *m* **- 2.** RAIL vagón *m* de mercancías. ◇ *vt* US transportar en camión.

truck driver *n esp* US camionero *m*, -ra *f*.

trucker ['trʌkər] *n* US camionero *m*, -ra *f*.

truck farm *n* US *puesto de verduras y frutas para la venta*.

trucking ['trʌkɪŋ] *n* US transporte *m* por camión.

truck stop *n* US restaurante *m* de carretera.

truculent ['trʌkjʊlənt] *adj* agresivo(va), pendenciero(ra).

trudge [trʌdʒ] ⟷ *n* caminata *f* pesada. ⟷ *vi* caminar con dificultad.

true [tru:] *adj* - **1.** [gen] verdadero(ra); **it's true** es verdad; **to come true** hacerse realidad - **2.** [genuine] auténtico(ca); [friend] de verdad - **3.** [exact] exacto(ta) - **4.** [TECH - wheel] centrado(da); [- window-frame] nivelado(da).

true-life *adj* basado(da) en la realidad.

truffle ['trʌfl] *n* trufa *f*.

truism ['tru:ɪzm] *n* truismo *m*.

truly ['tru:lɪ] *adv* verdaderamente; **yours truly** le saluda atentamente.

trump [trʌmp] ⟷ *n* triunfo *m* (*en cartas*). ⟷ *vt* fallar.

trump card *n* fig baza *f*.

trumped-up ['trʌmpt-] *adj* pej inventado(da).

trumpet ['trʌmpɪt] ⟷ *n* trompeta *f*. ⟷ *vi* [elephant] barritar.

trumpeter ['trʌmpɪtər] *n* trompetista *mf*.

truncheon ['trʌntʃən] *n* porra *f*.

trundle ['trʌndl] ⟷ *vt* empujar lentamente. ⟷ *vi* rodar lentamente; **he trundled along to the post office** se arrastró lentamente hasta correos.

trunk [trʌŋk] *n* - **1.** [of tree, person] tronco *m* - **2.** [of elephant] trompa *f* - **3.** [box] baúl *m* - **4.** *US* [of car] maletero *m*, portaequipaje *m*, cajuela *f Méx*, baúl *m Col & R Plata*, maletera *f Perú*.
◆ **trunks** *npl* bañador *m* (de hombre) *Esp*, traje *m* de baño (de hombre).

trunk call *n UK* conferencia *f Esp*, llamada *f* interurbana.

trunk road *n* ≃ carretera *f* nacional.

truss [trʌs] ⟷ *n* - **1.** MED braguero *m* - **2.** CONSTR armazón *m* o *f*. ⟷ *vt*: **truss (up)** atar.

trust [trʌst] ⟷ *vt* - **1.** [believe in] confiar en - **2.** [have confidence in]: **to trust sb to do sthg** confiar en alguien para que haga algo - **3.** [entrust]: **to trust sb with sthg** confiar algo a alguien - **4.** *fml* [hope] esperar; **I trust you slept well** espero que hayas dormido bien - **5.** [accept as safe, reliable] fiarse de. ⟷ *n* - **1.** (*U*) [faith, responsibility]: **trust (in)** confianza *f* (en); **to take sthg on trust** creer algo sin cuestionarlo; **to put OR place one's trust in** confiar en - **2.** FIN trust *m*; **in trust** en fideicomiso.

trust company *n* banco *m* fideicomisario.

trusted ['trʌstɪd] *adj* de confianza.

trustee [trʌs'ti:] *n* FIN & LAW fideicomisario *m*, -ria *f*.

trusteeship [ˌtrʌs'ti:ʃɪp] *n* fideicomiso *m*, administración *f* fiduciaria.

trust fund *n* fondo *m* de fideicomiso.

trusting ['trʌstɪŋ] *adj* confiado(da).

trustworthy ['trʌst,wɜ:ðɪ] *adj* digno(na) de confianza.

trusty ['trʌstɪ] (*comp* **-ier**, *superl* **-iest**) *adj hum* fiel.

truth [tru:θ] *n* verdad *f*; **the truth** la verdad; **in (all) truth** en verdad, verdaderamente.

truth drug *n* suero *m* de la verdad.

truthful ['tru:θʊl] *adj* - **1.** [person] sincero(ra), honesto(ta) - **2.** [story] verídico(ca).

try [traɪ] ⟷ *vt* (*pt & pp* **-ied**) - **1.** [attempt] intentar; **to try to do sthg** tratar de *OR* intentar hacer algo - **2.** [sample, test] probar - **3.** LAW [case] ver; [criminal] juzgar, procesar - **4.** [put to the test - person] acabar con la paciencia de; [- patience] acabar con. ⟷ *vi* (*pt & pp* **-ied**) intentar; **to try for sthg** tratar de conseguir algo. ⟷ *n* (*pl* **-ies**) - **1.** [attempt] intento *m*, tentativa *f*; **to have a try at sthg** intentar hacer algo - **2.** [sample, test]: **to give sthg a try** probar algo - **3.** RUGBY ensayo *m*.
◆ **try on** *vt sep* probarse.
◆ **try out** *vt sep* [car, machine] probar; [plan] poner a prueba; **to try sthg out on sb** probar algo con alguien; **to try out for** *US* presentarse a una prueba de selección para.

trying ['traɪɪŋ] *adj* difícil, pesado(da).

tsar, tzar [zɑːʳ] *n* zar *m*.

T-shirt *n* camiseta *f*, remera *f R Plata*, playera *f Méx*, polera *f Chile*.

tsp. *abbr of* teaspoon.

T-square *n* escuadra *f* en forma de T.

tub [tʌb] *n* - **1.** [container - small] bote *m*; [- large] tina *f* - **2.** *inf* [bath] bañera *f*.

tuba ['tju:bə] *n* tuba *f*.

tubby ['tʌbɪ] (*comp* **-ier**, *superl* **-iest**) *adj inf* regordete(ta), rechoncho(cha).

tube [tju:b] *n* - **1.** [cylinder, container] tubo *m* - **2.** ANAT conducto *m* - **3.** *UK inf* RAIL metro *m*, subte *m*; **by tube** en metro.

tubeless ['tju:blɪs] *adj* sin cámara.

tuber ['tju:bəʳ] *n* tubérculo *m*.

tuberculosis [tju:,bɜ:kjʊ'ləʊsɪs] *n* tuberculosis *f*.

tube station *n UK inf* estación *f* de metro.

tubing ['tju:bɪŋ] *n* (*U*) tubos *mpl*.

tubular ['tju:bjʊləʳ] *adj* tubular.

tuck [tʌk] ⟷ *n* SEW pliegue *m*. ⟷ *vt* [place neatly] meter.
◆ **tuck away** *vt sep* - **1.** [money etc] guardar - **2.** [village, house]: **to be tucked away** estar escondido(da).
◆ **tuck in** ⟷ *vt sep* - **1.** [person - in bed] arropar - **2.** [clothes] meterse. ⟷ *vi inf* comer con apetito.
◆ **tuck up** *vt sep* arropar; **to tuck sb up in bed** arropar a alguien en la cama.

tuck shop *n* UK confitería *f* (*emplazada cerca de un colegio*).

Tudor ['tjuːdəʳ] ◇ *adj* - **1.** HIST de la dinastía Tudor - **2.** ARCHIT de estilo Tudor. ◇ *n* Tudor *mf*.

Tue., Tues. (*abbr of* **Tuesday**) mart.

Tuesday ['tjuːzdɪ] *n* martes *m inv*; *see also* **Saturday**.

tuft [tʌft] *n* [of hair] mechón *m*; [of grass] manojo *m*.

tug [tʌg] ◇ *n* - **1.** [pull] tirón *m* - **2.** [boat] remolcador *m*. ◇ *vt* (*pt & pp* **-ged**, *cont* **-ging**) tirar de, dar un tirón a. ◇ *vi* (*pt & pp* **-ged**, *cont* **-ging**): **to tug (at)** tirar (de).

tugboat ['tʌgbəʊt] *n* remolcador *m*.

tug-of-love *n* UK *inf* lucha por la custodia de un niño.

tug-of-war *n* juego *m* de la cuerda (*en el que dos equipos compiten tirando de ella*).

tuition [tjuːˈɪʃn] *n* enseñanza *f*; **private tuition** clases *fpl* particulares.

tulip ['tjuːlɪp] *n* tulipán *m*.

tumble ['tʌmbl] ◇ *vi* - **1.** [person] caerse (rodando) - **2.** [water] caer a borbotones - **3.** *fig* [prices] caer en picado. ◇ *n* caída *f*.

◆ **tumble to** *vt insep* UK *inf* caerse en la cuenta de, percatarse de.

tumbledown ['tʌmbldaʊn] *adj* ruinoso(sa).

tumble-dry *vt* secar en secadora.

tumble-dryer [-ˌdraɪəʳ] *n* secadora *f*.

tumbler ['tʌmbləʳ] *n* [glass] vaso *m*.

tummy ['tʌmɪ] (*pl* **-ies**) *n* *inf* barriga *f*.

tumour UK**, tumor** US ['tjuːməʳ] *n* tumor *m*.

tumult ['tjuːmʌlt] *n* *fml* tumulto *m*.

tumultuous ['tjuːmʌltjʊəs] *adj* *fml* tumultuoso(sa).

tuna [UK 'tjuːnə, US 'tuːnə] (*pl* **tuna** OR **-s**) *n* atún *m*.

tundra ['tʌndrə] *n* tundra *f*.

tune [tjuːn] ◇ *n* - **1.** [song, melody] melodía *f* - **2.** [harmony]: **in tune** MUS afinado(da); **out of tune** MUS desafinado(da); **to be out of/in tune (with sb/sthg)** *fig* no avenirse/avenirse (con alguien/algo); **to the tune of** *fig* por la friolera de; **to change one's tune** *inf* cambiar de opinión. ◇ *vt* - **1.** RADIO & TV sintonizar; **tune the TV to BBC1** pon la BBC1 (en la tele) - **3.** [engine] poner a punto. ◇ *vi* RADIO & TV: **to tune to sthg** sintonizar algo.

◆ **tune in** *vi* RADIO & TV: **to tune in (to sthg)** sintonizar (algo).

◆ **tune up** *vi* MUS concertar OR afinar los instrumentos.

tuneful ['tjuːnfʊl] *adj* melodioso(sa).

tuneless ['tjuːnlɪs] *adj* poco melodioso(sa).

tuner ['tjuːnəʳ] *n* - **1.** RADIO & TV sintonizador *m* - **2.** MUS afinador *m*, -ra *f*.

tungsten ['tʌŋstən] *n* tungsteno *m*.

tunic ['tjuːnɪk] *n* túnica *f*.

tuning fork ['tjuːnɪŋ-] *n* diapasón *m*.

Tunisia [tjuːˈnɪzɪə] *n* Túnez.

Tunisian [tjuːˈnɪzɪən] ◇ *adj* tunecino(na). ◇ *n* [person] tunecino *m*, -na *f*.

tunnel ['tʌnl] ◇ *n* túnel *m*. ◇ *vi* (UK **-led**, *cont* **-ling**, US **-ed**, *cont* **-ing**) hacer un túnel.

tunnel vision *n* MED visión *f* de túnel; *fig & pej* [narrow-mindedness] estrechez *f* de miras.

tunny ['tʌnɪ] (*pl* **tunny** OR **-ies**) *n* [fish] atún *m*.

turban ['tɜːbən] *n* turbante *m*.

turbid ['tɜːbɪd] *adj* [water] turbio(bia).

turbine ['tɜːbaɪn] *n* turbina *f*.

turbo ['tɜːbəʊ] (*pl* **-s**) *n* turbina *f*.

turbocharged ['tɜːbəʊtʃɑːdʒd] *adj* provisto(ta) de turbina; [car] turbo (*inv*).

turbodiesel [ˌtɜːbəʊˈdiːzl] *n* turbodiésel *m*.

turbojet [ˌtɜːbəʊˈdʒet] *n* turborreactor *m*.

turbot ['tɜːbət] (*pl* **turbot** OR **-s**) *n* rodaballo *m*.

turbulence ['tɜːbjʊləns] *n* (*U*) *lit & fig* turbulencia *f*.

turbulent ['tɜːbjʊlənt] *adj* *lit & fig* turbulento(ta).

tureen [təˈriːn] *n* sopera *f*.

turf [tɜːf] ◇ *n* (*pl* **-s** OR **turves**) - **1.** [grass surface] césped *m* - **2.** [clod] tepe *m*. ◇ *vt* encespedar, cubrir con césped.

◆ **turf out** *vt sep* UK *inf* [person] dar la patada a, echar; [old clothes] tirar.

turf accountant *n* UK *fml* corredor *m*, -ra *f* de apuestas.

turgid ['tɜːdʒɪd] *adj* *fml* [over-solemn] ampuloso(sa).

Turk [tɜːk] *n* turco *m*, -ca *f*.

Turkestan, Turkistan [ˌtɜːkɪˈstɑːn] *n* (el) Turquestán.

turkey ['tɜːkɪ] (*pl* **turkeys**) *n* pavo *m*.

Turkey ['tɜːkɪ] *n* Turquía.

Turkish ['tɜːkɪʃ] ◇ *adj* turco(ca). ◇ *n* [language] turco *m*. ◇ *npl* [people]: **the Turkish** los turcos.

Turkish bath *n* baño *m* turco.

Turkish delight *n* rahat lokum *m*, *dulce de una sustancia gelatinosa, cubierto de azúcar glas*.

Turkistan = **Turkestan**.

turmeric ['tɜːmərɪk] *n* cúrcuma *f*.

turmoil ['tɜːmɔɪl] *n* confusión *f*, alboroto *m*; **the country was in turmoil** reinaba la confusión en el país.

turn [tɜːn] ◇ *n* - **1.** [in road, river] curva *f* - **2.** [of knob, wheel] vuelta *f* - **3.** [change] cambio *m*; **to take a turn for the worse** empeorar - **4.** [in game] turno *m*; **it's my turn** me toca a mí; **in turn** sucesivamente, uno tras otro; **to take (it in) turns (to do sthg)** turnarse (en hacer algo) - **5.** [of year, decade etc] fin *m*; **at the turn of the century** a finales de siglo - **6.** [performance] número *m* - **7.** MED ataque *m*
▸▸ **to do sb a good turn** hacerle un favor a alguien. ◇ *vt* - **1.** [chair, page, omelette] dar la vuelta a - **2.** [knob, wheel] girar - **3.** [corner] doblar - **4.** [thoughts, attention]: **to turn sthg to** dirigir algo hacia - **5.** [change]: **to turn sthg into** convertir OR transformar algo en - **6.** [cause to become]: **the cold turned his fingers blue** se le pusieron los dedos azules por el frío; **to turn sthg inside out** volver algo del revés - **7.** [milk] cortar, agriar. ◇ *vi* - **1.** [car] girar; [road] torcer; [person] volverse, darse la vuelta - **2.** [wheel] dar vueltas - **3.** [turn page over]: **turn to page two** pasen a la página dos - **4.** [thoughts, attention]: **to turn to** dirigirse hacia - **5.** [seek consolation]: **to turn to sb/ sthg** buscar consuelo en alguien/algo; **she has nobody to turn to** no tiene a quien acudir - **6.** [change]: **to turn into** convertirse OR transformarse en - **7.** [become]: **it turned black** se volvió negro; **the demonstration turned nasty** la manifestación se puso violenta - **8.** [go sour] cortarse, agriarse.
◆ **turn against** *vt insep* poner en contra de.
◆ **turn around** *vt sep* = **turn round**.
◆ **turn away** *vt sep* [refuse entry to] no dejar entrar.
◆ **turn back** ◇ *vt sep* [person, vehicle] hacer volver. ◇ *vi* volver, volverse.
◆ **turn down** *vt sep* - **1.** [offer, person] rechazar - **2.** [volume, heating] bajar.
◆ **turn in** *vi inf* [go to bed] irse a dormir.
◆ **turn off** ◇ *vt insep* [road, path] desviarse de, salir de. ◇ *vt sep* [radio, heater] apagar; [engine] parar; [gas, tap] cerrar. ◇ *vi* [leave road] desviarse, salir.
◆ **turn on** ◇ *vt sep* - **1.** [radio, TV, engine] encender; [gas, tap] abrir - **2.** *inf* [excite sexually] poner cachondo(da), excitar. ◇ *vt insep* [attack] atacar.
◆ **turn out** ◇ *vt sep* - **1.** [extinguish] apagar - **2.** *inf* [produce] producir - **3.** [eject] echar - **4.** [empty - pockets, bag] vaciar. ◇ *vt insep*: **to turn out to be** resultar ser; **it turns out that...** resulta que... ◇ *vi* - **1.** [end up] salir - **2.** [arrive]: **to turn out (for)** venir OR presentarse (a).
◆ **turn over** ◇ *vt sep* - **1.** [turn upside down] dar la vuelta a; [page] volver - **2.** [consider] darle vueltas a - **3.** *UK* RADIO & TV cambiar - **4.** [hand over]: **to turn sthg/sb over (to)** entregar algo/a alguien (a). ◇ *vi* [roll over] darse la vuelta.

◆ **turn round, turn around** ◇ *vt sep* - **1.** [gen] dar la vuelta a - **2.** [knob, key] hacer girar. ◇ *vi* [person] darse la vuelta, volverse.
◆ **turn up** ◇ *vt sep* [volume, heating] subir. ◇ *vi inf* aparecer.
turnabout ['tɜːnəbaʊt] *n* cambio *m* radical.
turnaround *US* = **turnround**.
turncoat ['tɜːnkəʊt] *n pej* chaquetero *m*, -ra *f*.
turning ['tɜːnɪŋ] *n* [in road] bocacalle *f*.
turning point *n* momento *m* decisivo.
turnip ['tɜːnɪp] *n* nabo *m*.
turnout ['tɜːnaʊt] *n* número *m* de asistentes, asistencia *f*.
turnover ['tɜːnˌəʊvə'] *n (U)* - **1.** [of personnel] movimiento *m* de personal - **2.** *UK* FIN volumen *m* de ventas, facturación *f*.
turnpike ['tɜːnpaɪk] *n US* autopista *f* de peaje.
turnround ['tɜːnraʊnd] *UK*, **turnaround** ['tɜːnərəʊnd] *US n* - **1.** COMM tiempo *m* de carga y descarga *(de un barco, avión etc)* - **2.** [change] cambio *m* radical.
turnstile ['tɜːnstaɪl] *n* torno *m*, torniquete *m*.
turntable ['tɜːnˌteɪbl] *n* plato *m* giratorio.
turn-up *n UK* [on trousers] vuelta *f*; **a turn-up for the books** *inf* una auténtica sorpresa.
turpentine ['tɜːpəntaɪn] *n* trementina *f*.
turps [tɜːps] (*abbr of* **turpentine**) *n UK inf* trementina *f*.
turquoise ['tɜːkwɔɪz] ◇ *adj* turquesa. ◇ *n* - **1.** [mineral, gem] turquesa *f* - **2.** [colour] turquesa *m*.
turret ['tʌrɪt] *n* torreta *f*, torrecilla *f*.
turtle ['tɜːtl] (*pl* **turtle** OR **-s**) *n* tortuga *f* (marina).
turtledove ['tɜːtldʌv] *n* tórtola *f*.
turtleneck ['tɜːtlnek] *n* cuello *m* (de) cisne.
turves [tɜːvz] *UK npl* ▷ **turf**.
tusk [tʌsk] *n* colmillo *m*.
tussle ['tʌsl] ◇ *n* lucha *f*, pelea *f*. ◇ *vi*: **to tussle (over)** pelearse (por).
tut [tʌt] *excl* ¡vaya!
tutor ['tjuːtə'] ◇ *n* - **1.** [private] profesor particular *m*, profesora particular *f*, tutor *m*, -ra *f* - **2.** UNIV profesor universitario *m*, profesora universitaria *f (de un grupo pequeño)*. ◇ *vt*: **to tutor sb in sthg** dar clases particulares de algo a alguien. ◇ *vi* dar clases particulares.
tutorial [tjuːˈtɔːrɪəl] ◇ *adj*: **tutorial group** *grupo reducido de estudiantes que asiste a una clase.* ◇ *n* tutoría *f*, clase *f* con grupo reducido.
tutu ['tuːtuː] *n* tutú *m*.
tux [tʌks] (*abbr of* **tuxedo**) *n inf* esmoquin *m*.
tuxedo [tʌkˈsiːdəʊ] (*pl* **-s**) *n* esmoquin *m*.

TV (*abbr of* **television**) ⬦ *n* televisión *f*; **on TV** en la televisión. ⬦ *comp* de televisión.

TV dinner *n* comida completa precocinada y lista para el horno.

TV movie *n* telefilm *m*.

twaddle ['twɒdl] *n (U) inf pej* tonterías *fpl*.

twang [twæŋ] ⬦ *n* - **1.** [of guitar] tañido *m*; [of string, elastic] sonido *m* vibrante - **2.** [accent] gangueo *m*, acento *m* nasal. ⬦ *vt* [guitar] tañer; [wire, string] hacer vibrar (tirando y soltando). ⬦ *vi* producir un sonido vibrante.

tweak [twi:k] *vt inf* [nose, ear] pellizcar, dar un tironcito a.

twee [twi:] *adj UK pej* cursi, siútico(ca) *Amér*.

tweed [twi:d] *n* tweed *m*.

tweenage ['twi:neɪdʒ] *adj inf* preadolescente.

tweet [twi:t] *vi inf* piar, hacer pío pío.

tweezers ['twi:zəz] *npl* pinzas *fpl*.

twelfth [twelfθ] *num* duodécimo(ma); *see also* **sixth**.

Twelfth Night *n* Noche *f* de Reyes.

twelve [twelv] *num* doce; *see also* **six**.

twentieth ['twentɪəθ] *num* vigésimo(ma); *see also* **sixth**.

twenty ['twentɪ] (*pl* **-ies**) *num* veinte; *see also* **sixty**.

twenty-one [twentɪ'wʌn] *n US* [game] veintiuna *f*.

twenty-twenty vision *n* vista *f* perfecta.

twerp [twɜ:p] *n inf* imbécil *mf*.

twice [twaɪs] *num adv* dos veces; **twice a week** dos veces por semana; **it costs twice as much** cuesta el doble; **twice as big** el doble de grande; **he's twice her age** le dobla en edad; **think twice** piénsalo dos veces.

twiddle ['twɪdl] ⬦ *vt* dar vueltas a; **to twiddle one's thumbs** *fig* holgazanear. ⬦ *vi*: **to twiddle with** juguetear con.

twig [twɪg] *n* ramita *f*.

twilight ['twaɪlaɪt] *n* crepúsculo *m*, ocaso *m*.

twill [twɪl] *n* sarga *f*.

twin [twɪn] ⬦ *adj* gemelo(la), morocho(cha) *Andes & R Plata*. ⬦ *n* gemelo *m*, -la *f*, morocho *m*, -cha *f Ven*.

twin-bedded [-'bedɪd] *adj* de dos camas.

twin carburettor *n* motor *m* de dos carburadores.

twine [twaɪn] ⬦ *n (U)* bramante *m*. ⬦ *vt*: **to twine sthg round sthg** enrollar algo en algo.

twin-engined [-'endʒɪnd] *adj* bimotor.

twinge [twɪndʒ] *n* [of pain] punzada *f*; [of guilt] remordimiento *m*.

twinkle ['twɪŋkl] ⬦ *n* brillo *m*. ⬦ *vi* - **1.** [star] centellear, parpadear - **2.** [eyes] brillar.

twin room *n* habitación *f* con dos camas.

twin set *n UK* conjunto *m* de jersey y rebeca.

twin town *n* ciudad *f* hermanada.

twin tub *n* lavadora *f* de doble tambor.

twirl [twɜ:l] ⬦ *vt* dar vueltas a. ⬦ *vi* dar vueltas rápidamente.

twist [twɪst] ⬦ *n* - **1.** [in road] vuelta *f*, recodo *m*; [in river] meandro *m* - **2.** [of head, lid, knob] giro *m* - **3.** [shape] espiral *f* - **4.** *fig* [in plot] giro *m* imprevisto. ⬦ *vt* - **1.** [cloth, rope] retorcer; [hair] enroscar - **2.** [face etc] torcer - **3.** [dial, lid] dar vueltas a; [head] volver - **4.** [ankle, knee etc] torcerse - **5.** [misquote] tergiversar. ⬦ *vi* - **1.** [person] retorcerse; [road, river] contorsionarse, serpentear, dar vueltas - **2.** [face] contorsionarse; [frame, rail] torcerse - **3.** [turn - head, hand] volverse.

twisted ['twɪstɪd] *adj pej* retorcido(da).

twister ['twɪstər] *n US inf* tornado *m*.

twisty ['twɪstɪ] (*comp* **-ier**, *superl* **-iest**) *adj inf* lleno(na) de curvas.

twit [twɪt] *n UK inf* imbécil *mf*, gil *m Amér*, gila *f R Plata*.

twitch [twɪtʃ] ⬦ *n* contorsión *f*; **nervous twitch** tic *m* (nervioso). ⬦ *vi* contorsionarse.

twitter ['twɪtər] *vi* - **1.** [bird] gorjear - **2.** *pej* [person] parlotear, cotorrear.

two [tu:] *num* dos; **to break in two** partirse en dos; **to do sthg in twos** hacer algo en pares; **to put two and two together** atar cabos; *see also* **six**.

two-bit *adj US pej* de tres al cuarto.

two-dimensional *adj* en dos dimensiones.

two-door *adj* [car] de dos puertas.

twofaced [,tu:'feɪst] *adj pej* hipócrita.

twofold ['tu:fəʊld] ⬦ *adj* doble; **a twofold increase** un incremento del doble. ⬦ *adv*: **to increase twofold** duplicarse.

two-handed [-'hændɪd] *adj* [sword, axe] que se usa con las dos manos; [backhand] de dos manos.

two-piece *adj* [suit] de dos piezas.

two-ply *adj* de dos capas.

two-seater [-'si:tər] *n* biplaza *m*.

twosome ['tu:səm] *n inf* pareja *f*.

two-stroke ⬦ *adj* [engine] de dos tiempos. ⬦ *n* motor *m* de dos tiempos.

two-time *vt inf* engañar, poner los cuernos a.

two-tone *adj* bicolor.

two-way *adj* - **1.** [traffic] en ambas direcciones; [agreement, cooperation] mutuo(tua) - **2.** TELEC: **two-way radio** aparato *m* emisor y receptor.

two-way street *n* calle *f* de doble sentido.

tycoon [taɪ'ku:n] *n* magnate *m*; **an oil tycoon** un magnate del petróleo.

type [taɪp] ◇ *n* - **1.** [gen] tipo *m*; **he's/she's not my type** *inf* no es mi tipo - **2.** *(U)* TYPO tipo *m*, letra *f*; **in bold/italic type** en negrita/cursiva. ◇ *vt* - **1.** [on typewriter] escribir a máquina, mecanografiar - **2.** [on computer] escribir en el ordenador; **to type sthg into sthg** entrar algo en algo. ◇ *vi* escribir a máquina.
➥ **type up** *vt sep* escribir a máquina, mecanografiar.

typecast ['taɪpkɑːst] *(pt & pp* **typecast)** *vt*: **to typecast sb (as)** encasillar a alguien (como).

typeface ['taɪpfeɪs] *n* tipo *m*, letra *f*.

typescript ['taɪpskrɪpt] *n* copia *f* mecanografiada.

typeset ['taɪpset] *(pt & pp* **typeset,** *cont* **-ting)** *vt* componer.

typewriter ['taɪpˌraɪtəʳ] *n* máquina *f* de escribir.

typhoid (fever) ['taɪfɔɪd-] *n* fiebre *f* tifoidea.

typhoon [taɪ'fuːn] *n* tifón *m*.

typhus ['taɪfəs] *n* tifus *m*.

typical ['tɪpɪkl] *adj*: **typical (of)** típico(ca) (de).

typically ['tɪpɪklɪ] *adv* - **1.** [usually] normalmente - **2.** [characteristically] típicamente.

typify ['tɪpɪfaɪ] *(pt & pp* **-ied)** *vt* tipificar.

typing ['taɪpɪŋ] *n* mecanografía *f*.

typing error *n* error *m* mecanográfico.

typing pool *n* servicio *m* de mecanografía *(en una empresa).*

typist ['taɪpɪst] *n* mecanógrafo *m*, -fa *f*.

typo ['taɪpəʊ] *n inf* error *m* tipográfico.

typographic(al) error [ˌtaɪpə'græfɪk(l)-] *n* error *m* tipográfico.

typography [taɪ'pɒgrəfɪ] *n* - **1.** [process, job] tipografía *f* - **2.** [format] composición *f* tipográfica.

tyrannical [tɪ'rænɪkl] *adj* tiránico(ca).

tyranny ['tɪrənɪ] *n* tiranía *f*.

tyrant ['taɪrənt] *n* tirano *m*, -na *f*.

tyre *UK*, **tire** *US* ['taɪəʳ] *n* neumático *m*.

tyre pressure *n* presión *f* de los neumáticos.

Tyrol, Tirol [tɪ'rəʊl] *n*: **the Tyrol** el Tirol.

Tyrolean [tɪrə'liːən], **Tyrolese** [ˌtɪrə'liːz] ◇ *adj* tirolés(esa). ◇ *n* tirolés *m*, -esa *f*.

Tyrrhenian Sea [tɪ'riːnɪən-] *n*: **the Tyrrhenian Sea** el mar Tirreno.

tzar [zɑːʳ] = **tsar.**

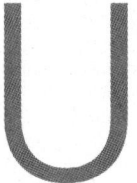

u *(pl* **u's** OR **us)**, **U** *(pl* **U's** OR **Us)** [juː] *n* [letter] u *f*, U *f*.
➥ **U** *adv UK* CIN *(abbr of* **universal)** para todos los públicos.

U-bend *n* sifón *m*.

ubiquitous [juː'bɪkwɪtəs] *adj fml* omnipresente, ubicuo(cua).

UCAS ['juːkæs] *(abbr of* **Universities and Colleges Admissions Service)** *n UK* UNIV & SCH *organización que coordina las admisiones y matrículas en las universidades británicas.*

UDA *(abbr of* **Ulster Defence Association)** *n organización paramilitar protestante que defiende la permanencia de Irlanda del Norte en el Reino Unido.*

udder ['ʌdəʳ] *n* ubre *f*.

UDI *(abbr of* **unilateral declaration of independence)** *n declaración unilateral de independencia.*

UDR *(abbr of* **Ulster Defence Regiment)** *n fuerzas de seguridad de Irlanda del Norte.*

UEFA [juː'eɪfə] *(abbr of* **Union of European Football Associations)** *n* UEFA *f*.

UFO *(abbr of* **unidentified flying object)** *n* OVNI *m*.

Uganda [juː'gændə] *n* Uganda.

Ugandan [juː'gændən] ◇ *adj* ugandés(esa). ◇ *n* [person] ugandés *m*, -esa *f*.

ugh [ʌg] *excl* ¡puf!

ugliness ['ʌglɪnɪs] *n (U)* - **1.** [unattractiveness] fealdad *f* - **2.** *fig* [unpleasantness] lo desagradable.

ugly ['ʌglɪ] *(comp* **-ier,** *superl* **-iest)** *adj* - **1.** [unattractive] feo(a) - **2.** *fig* [unpleasant] desagradable.

UHF *(abbr of* **ultra-high frequency)** UHF.

UHT *(abbr of* **ultra-heat treated)** UHT; **UHT milk** leche uperisada.

UK *(abbr of* **United Kingdom)** *n* RU *m*; **the UK** el Reino Unido.

Ukraine [juː'kreɪn] *n*: **the Ukraine** Ucrania.

Ukrainian [juː'kreɪnjən] ◇ *adj* ucraniano(na). ◇ *n* - **1.** [person] ucraniano *m*, -na *f* - **2.** [language] ucraniano *m*.

ulcer ['ʌlsəʳ] *n* úlcera *f*.

ulcerated [ˈʌlsəreɪtɪd] *adj* ulceroso(sa).

Ulster [ˈʌlstəʳ] *n* (el) Úlster.

Ulster Unionist Party *n* partido político norirlandés que defiende la permanencia de Irlanda del Norte en el Reino Unido.

ulterior [ʌlˈtɪərɪəʳ] *adj*: **ulterior motive** motivo *m* oculto.

ultimata [ˌʌltɪˈmeɪtə] *npl* ⊳ ultimatum.

ultimate [ˈʌltɪmət] ⬦ *adj* - **1.** [final, long-term] final, definitivo(va) - **2.** [most powerful] máximo(ma). ⬦ *n*: **the ultimate in** el colmo de.

ultimately [ˈʌltɪmətlɪ] *adv* finalmente, a la larga.

ultimatum [ˌʌltɪˈmeɪtəm] (*pl* -**s** OR -**ta**) *n* ultimátum *m*; **to issue an ultimatum to sb** dar un ultimátum a alguien.

ultra- [ˈʌltrə] *prefix* ultra-.

ultramarine [ˌʌltrəməˈriːn] *adj* azul de ultramar OR ultramarino *(inv)*.

ultrasonic [ˌʌltrəˈsɒnɪk] *adj* ultrasónico(ca).

ultrasound [ˈʌltrəsaʊnd] *n* ultrasonido *m*.

ultraviolet [ˌʌltrəˈvaɪələt] *adj* ultravioleta.

um [ʌm] *excl* [expressing hesitation] ¡humm!, ¡mm!

umbilical cord [ʌmˈbɪlɪkl-] *n* cordón *m* umbilical.

umbrage [ˈʌmbrɪdʒ] *n*: **to take umbrage (at)** ofenderse (por).

umbrella [ʌmˈbrelə] ⬦ *n* - **1.** [for rain] paraguas *m inv* - **2.** [on beach] parasol *m* - **3.**: **under the umbrella of** *fig* bajo la protección de. ⬦ *adj* que engloba a otros(otras).

umpire [ˈʌmpaɪəʳ] ⬦ *n* árbitro *m*. ⬦ *vt* & *vi* arbitrar.

umpteen [ˌʌmpˈtiːn] *num adj inf*: **umpteen times** la tira de veces.

umpteenth [ˌʌmpˈtiːnθ] *num adj inf* enésimo(ma); **for the umpteenth time** por enésima vez.

UN (*abbr of* United Nations) *n*: **the UN** la ONU.

unabashed [ˌʌnəˈbæʃt] *adj* imperturbable; **to be unabashed** no avergonzarse.

unabated [ˌʌnəˈbeɪtɪd] *adj* incesante; **to continue unabated** continuar sin cesar.

unable [ʌnˈeɪbl] *adj*: **to be unable to do sthg** no poder hacer algo.

unabridged [ˌʌnəˈbrɪdʒd] *adj* íntegro(gra).

unacceptable [ˌʌnəkˈseptəbl] *adj* inaceptable.

unaccompanied [ˌʌnəˈkʌmpənɪd] *adj* - **1.** [child] solo(la), que no va acompañado(da); [luggage] desatendido(da) - **2.** [song] sin acompañamiento.

unaccountable [ˌʌnəˈkaʊntəbl] *adj* - **1.** [inexplicable] inexplicable - **2.** [not responsible]: **unaccountable (for/to)** que no es responsable (de/ante).

unaccountably [ˌʌnəˈkaʊntəblɪ] *adv* inexplicablemente.

unaccounted [ˌʌnəˈkaʊntɪd] *adj*: **12 people are unaccounted for** hay 12 personas aún sin localizar; **£30 is unaccounted for** hay 30 libras que no aparecen.

unaccustomed [ˌʌnəˈkʌstəmd] *adj* - **1.** [unused]: **to be unaccustomed to** no estar acostumbrado(da) a - **2.** *fml* [not usual] desacostumbrado(da), inusual.

unacquainted [ˌʌnəˈkweɪntɪd] *adj*: **to be unacquainted with sthg** no conocer algo.

unadulterated [ˌʌnəˈdʌltəreɪtɪd] *adj* - **1.** [unspoilt] sin adulterar - **2.** [absolute] completo(ta), absoluto(ta).

unadventurous [ˌʌnədˈventʃərəs] *adj* poco atrevido(da).

unaffected [ˌʌnəˈfektɪd] *adj* - **1.** [unchanged]: **to be unaffected (by)** no verse afectado(da) (por) - **2.** [natural] nada afectado(da), natural.

unafraid [ˌʌnəˈfreɪd] *adj* sin miedo.

unaided [ʌnˈeɪdɪd] *adj* & *adv* sin ayuda.

unambiguous [ˌʌnæmˈbɪgjʊəs] *adj* inequívoco(ca).

un-American [ˈʌn-] *adj* antiamericano(na).

unanimity [ˌjuːnəˈnɪmətɪ] *n fml* unanimidad *f*.

unanimous [juːˈnænɪməs] *adj* unánime.

unanimously [juːˈnænɪməslɪ] *adv* unánimemente.

unannounced [ˌʌnəˈnaʊnst] ⬦ *adj* no anunciado(da). ⬦ *adv* sin anunciarlo.

unanswered [ʌnˈɑːnsəd] *adj* sin contestar.

unappealing [ˌʌnəˈpiːlɪŋ] *adj* desagradable.

unappetizing, -ising [ʌnˈæpɪtaɪzɪŋ] *adj* poco apetitoso(sa).

unappreciated [ˌʌnəˈpriːʃɪeɪtɪd] *adj* poco apreciado(da).

unappreciative [ˌʌnəˈpriːʃɪətɪv] *adj* poco apreciativo(va); **to be unappreciative of sthg** no apreciar algo.

unapproachable [ˌʌnəˈprəʊtʃəbl] *adj* inaccesible.

unarmed [ʌnˈɑːmd] ⬦ *adj* desarmado(da). ⬦ *adv* a brazo partido.

unarmed combat *n* lucha *f* OR combate *m* a brazo partido.

unashamed [ˌʌnəˈʃeɪmd] *adj* descarado(da).

unassisted [ˌʌnəˈsɪstɪd] *adj* sin ayuda.

unassuming [ˌʌnəˈsjuːmɪŋ] *adj* sin pretensiones.

unattached [ˌʌnəˈtætʃt] *adj* - **1.** [not fastened, linked] independiente; **unattached to** que no está ligado a - **2.** [without partner] libre, sin compromiso.

unattainable [ˌʌnəˈteɪnəbl] *adj* inalcanzable, inasequible.

unattended [ˌʌnəˈtendɪd] *adj* desatendido(da); **to leave sthg unattended** dejar algo desatendido.

unattractive [ˌʌnəˈtræktɪv] *adj* poco atractivo(va).

unauthorized, -ised [ˌʌnˈɔːθəraɪzd] *adj* no autorizado(da).

unavailable [ˌʌnəˈveɪləbl] *adj*: **to be unavailable** no estar disponible; **he was unavailable for comment** no quiso hacer ningún comentario.

unavoidable [ˌʌnəˈvɔɪdəbl] *adj* inevitable, ineludible; **unavoidable delays** retrasos inevitables.

unavoidably [ˌʌnəˈvɔɪdəblɪ] *adv* inevitablemente, ineludiblemente.

unaware [ˌʌnəˈweəʳ] *adj* inconsciente; **to be unaware of** no ser consciente de.

unawares [ˌʌnəˈweəz] *adv*: **to catch** OR **take sb unawares** coger a alguien desprevenido(da).

unbalanced [ˌʌnˈbælənst] *adj* desequilibrado(da).

unbearable [ʌnˈbeərəbl] *adj* insoportable, inaguantable.

unbearably [ʌnˈbeərəblɪ] *adv* insoportablemente, inaguantablemente.

unbeatable [ˌʌnˈbiːtəbl] *adj* [gen] insuperable; [prices, value] inmejorable.

unbecoming [ˌʌnbɪˈkʌmɪŋ] *adj fml* [unattractive] poco favorecedor(ra).

unbeknown(st) [ˌʌnbɪˈnəʊn(st)] *adv*: **unbeknown(st) to** sin conocimiento de.

unbelievable [ˌʌnbɪˈliːvəbl] *adj* increíble.

unbelievably [ˌʌnbɪˈliːvəblɪ] *adv* [extremely] increíblemente.

unbend [ˌʌnˈbend] (*pt & pp* **unbent**) *vi* [relax] relajarse.

unbending [ˌʌnˈbendɪŋ] *adj* resoluto(ta).

unbent [ˌʌnˈbent] *pt & pp* ⊳ **unbend**.

unbias(s)ed [ˌʌnˈbaɪəst] *adj* imparcial.

unblemished [ˌʌnˈblemɪʃt] *adj fig* intachable, impecable.

unblock [ˌʌnˈblɒk] *vt* [pipe] desobstruir, desatascar; [road, tunnel] desbloquear, abrir.

unbolt [ˌʌnˈbəʊlt] *vt* [door] abrir el cerrojo de.

unborn [ˌʌnˈbɔːn] *adj* [child] no nacido(da) aún.

unbreakable [ˌʌnˈbreɪkəbl] *adj* irrompible.

unbridled [ˌʌnˈbraɪdld] *adj* desmesurado(da), desenfrenado(da).

unbuckle [ˌʌnˈbʌkl] *vt* deshebillar.

unbutton [ˌʌnˈbʌtn] *vt* desabrochar, desabotonar.

uncalled-for [ˌʌnˈkɔːld-] *adj* injusto(ta), inmerecido(da).

uncanny [ʌnˈkænɪ] (*comp* **-ier**, *superl* **-iest**) *adj* extraño(ña).

uncared-for [ˌʌnˈkeəd-] *adj* abandonado(da), desamparado(da).

uncaring [ˌʌnˈkeərɪŋ] *adj* insensible, falto(ta) de sentimientos.

unceasing [ˌʌnˈsiːsɪŋ] *adj fml* incesante.

unceremonious [ˈʌnˌserɪˈməʊnjəs] *adj* - **1.** [curt] brusco(ca) - **2.** [informal] poco ceremonioso(sa).

unceremoniously [ˈʌnˌserɪˈməʊnjəslɪ] *adj* sin contemplaciones, sin ceremonias.

uncertain [ʌnˈsɜːtn] *adj* [gen] incierto(ta); [undecided, hesitant] indeciso(sa); **it's uncertain whether they will accept the proposals** no se sabe si aceptarán las propuestas; **in no uncertain terms** de forma vehemente.

unchain [ˌʌnˈtʃeɪn] *vt* quitar la cadena a, desencadenar.

unchallenged [ˌʌnˈtʃælɪndʒd] *adj* sin cuestionar.

unchanged [ˌʌnˈtʃeɪndʒd] *adj* sin alterar.

unchanging [ˌʌnˈtʃeɪndʒɪŋ] *adj* inmutable, inalterable.

uncharacteristic [ˈʌnˌkærəktəˈrɪstɪk] *adj* inusual, insólito(ta).

uncharitable [ˌʌnˈtʃærɪtəbl] *adj* mezquino(na).

uncharted [ˌʌnˈtʃɑːtɪd] *adj lit & fig* desconocido(da).

unchecked [ˌʌnˈtʃekt] ◇ *adj* [unrestrained] desenfrenado(da). ◇ *adv* [unrestrained] libremente, sin restricciones.

uncivilized, -ised [ˌʌnˈsɪvɪlaɪzd] *adj* [society] incivilizado(da); [person] inculto(ta).

unclassified [ˌʌnˈklæsɪfaɪd] *adj* no confidencial.

uncle [ˈʌŋkl] *n* tío *m*.

unclean [ˌʌnˈkliːn] *adj* - **1.** [dirty] sucio(cia) - **2.** RELIG impuro(ra).

unclear [ˌʌnˈklɪəʳ] *adj* poco claro(ra); **to be unclear about sthg** no tener claro algo.

unclothed [ˌʌnˈkləʊðd] *adj fml* desnudo(da).

uncomfortable [ˌʌnˈkʌmftəbl] *adj* - **1.** [gen] incómodo(da) - **2.** *fig* [fact, truth] inquietante, desagradable.

uncomfortably [ˌʌnˈkʌmftəblɪ] *adv* - **1.** [in physical discomfort] incómodamente; **to be uncomfortably hot** [person] sentir un calor desagradable - **2.** *fig* [uneasily] inquietantemente.

uncommitted [ˌʌnkəˈmɪtɪd] *adj* no comprometido(da).

uncommon [ʌnˈkɒmən] *adj* - **1.** [rare] poco común, raro(ra) - **2.** *fml* [extreme] sumo(ma).

uncommonly [ʌnˈkɒmənlɪ] adv fml extraordinariamente.

uncommunicative [ˌʌnkəˈmjuːnɪkətɪv] adj poco comunicativo(va), reservado(da).

uncomplicated [ˌʌnˈkɒmplɪkeɪtɪd] adj sencillo(lla), sin complicaciones.

uncomprehending [ˈʌnˌkɒmprɪˈhendɪŋ] adj incomprensivo(va).

uncompromising [ˌʌnˈkɒmprəmaɪzɪŋ] adj inflexible, intransigente.

unconcerned [ˌʌnkənˈsɜːnd] adj [not anxious] indiferente.

unconditional [ˌʌnkənˈdɪʃənl] adj incondicional.

uncongenial [ˌʌnkənˈdʒiːnjəl] adj fml [place] desagradable; [person] antipático(ca).

unconnected [ˌʌnkəˈnektɪd] adj inconexo(xa), sin relación.

unconquered [ˌʌnˈkɒŋkəd] adj [area, country] no conquistado(da); [people] invicto(ta).

unconscious [ʌnˈkɒnʃəs] <> adj inconsciente; **to be unconscious of sthg** ser inconsciente de OR ignorar algo; **he was knocked unconscious by a falling brick** un ladrillo que caía lo dejó inconsciente. <> n inconsciente m.

unconsciously [ʌnˈkɒnʃəslɪ] adv inconscientemente.

unconstitutional [ˈʌnˌkɒnstɪˈtjuːʃənl] adj inconstitucional.

uncontested [ˌʌnkənˈtestɪd] adj [decision, judgment] incontestado(da); [seat, election] ganado(da) sin oposición.

uncontrollable [ˌʌnkənˈtrəʊləbl] adj [gen] incontrolable; [desire, hatred] irrefrenable; [laughter] incontenible.

uncontrolled [ˌʌnkənˈtrəʊld] adj [emotion] desenfrenado(da); [trend] incontrolado(da).

unconventional [ˌʌnkənˈvenʃənl] adj poco convencional.

unconvinced [ˌʌnkənˈvɪnst] adj: **to remain unconvinced** seguir sin convencerse.

unconvincing [ˌʌnkənˈvɪnsɪŋ] adj poco convincente.

uncooked [ˌʌnˈkʊkt] adj crudo(da).

uncooperative [ˌʌnkəʊˈɒpərətɪv] adj nada servicial, no dispuesto(ta) a ayudar.

uncork [ˌʌnˈkɔːk] vt descorchar.

uncorroborated [ˌʌnkəˈrɒbəreɪtɪd] adj sin corroborar.

uncouth [ʌnˈkuːθ] adj grosero(ra).

uncover [ʌnˈkʌvər] vt [gen] descubrir; [jar, tin etc] destapar.

uncurl [ˌʌnˈkɜːl] vi - **1.** [hair] desrizarse; [wire] desenrollarse - **2.** [animal] desovillarse, desenroscarse.

uncut [ˌʌnˈkʌt] adj - **1.** [film] sin cortes - **2.** [jewel] sin tallar, en bruto.

undamaged [ˌʌnˈdæmɪdʒd] adj [gen] intacto(ta); [goods] sin desperfectos.

undaunted [ˌʌnˈdɔːntɪd] adj impávido(da), impertérrito(ta).

undecided [ˌʌndɪˈsaɪdɪd] adj - **1.** [person] indeciso(sa) - **2.** [issue] pendiente, sin resolver.

undemanding [ˌʌndɪˈmɑːndɪŋ] adj - **1.** [task] poco absorbente, que requiere poco esfuerzo - **2.** [person] poco exigente.

undemonstrative [ˌʌndɪˈmɒnstrətɪv] adj poco expresivo(va), reservado(da).

undeniable [ˌʌndɪˈnaɪəbl] adj innegable.

under [ˈʌndər] <> prep - **1.** [beneath] debajo de, abajo de Amér - **2.** [with movement] bajo; **put it under the table** ponlo debajo de OR bajo la mesa; **they walked under the bridge** pasaron bajo OR por debajo del puente - **3.** [subject to, undergoing, controlled by] bajo; **under the circumstances** dadas las circunstancias; **under discussion** en proceso de discusión; **he has 20 men under him** tiene 20 hombres a su cargo - **4.** [less than] menos de; **children under the age of 14** niños menores de 14 años - **5.** [according to] según, conforme a - **6.** [in headings, classifications]: **he filed it under 'D'** lo archivó en la 'D' - **7.** [name, title]: **under an alias** bajo nombre supuesto. <> adv - **1.** [gen] debajo; **to go under** [business] irse a pique - **2.** [less]: **children of 12 years and under** niños menores de 13 años; **£5 or under** cinco libras o menos - **3.** [under water] bajo el agua.

under- [ˈʌndər] prefix - **1.** [beneath] inferior, bajo - **2.** [lower in rank] sub-, segundo(da) - **3.** [insufficiently] insuficientemente.

underachiever [ˌʌndərəˈtʃiːvər] n estudiante que no rinde todo lo que puede.

underage [ˌʌndərˈeɪdʒ] adj [person] menor de edad; [sex, drinking] en menores de edad.

underarm [ˈʌndərɑːm] <> adj [deodorant] corporal, para las axilas. <> adv por debajo del hombro.

underbrush [ˈʌndəbrʌʃ] n (U) US maleza f, monte m bajo.

undercarriage [ˈʌndəˌkærɪdʒ] n tren m de aterrizaje.

undercharge [ˌʌndəˈtʃɑːdʒ] vt cobrar menos del precio estipulado a.

underclothes [ˈʌndəkləʊðz] npl ropa f interior.

undercoat [ˈʌndəkəʊt] n [of paint] primera mano f OR capa f.

undercook [ˌʌndəˈkʊk] vt no guisar suficientemente.

undercover [ˈʌndəˌkʌvər] <> adj secreto(ta). <> adv en la clandestinidad; **to go undercover** pasar a la clandestinidad.

undercurrent [ˈʌndəˌkʌrənt] *n fig* sentimiento *m* oculto.

undercut [ˌʌndəˈkʌt] (*pt* & *pp* **undercut**, *cont* -**ting**) *vt* [in price] vender más barato que.

underdeveloped [ˌʌndədɪˈveləpt] *adj* subdesarrollado(da).

underdog [ˈʌndədɒg] *n*: **the underdog** el que lleva las de perder.

underdone [ˌʌndəˈdʌn] *adj* poco hecho(cha).

underemployment [ˌʌndərɪmˈplɔɪmənt] *n* subempleo *m*.

underestimate ◇ *n* [ˌʌndərˈestɪmət] infravaloración *f*. ◇ *vt* [ˌʌndərˈestɪmeɪt] subestimar, infravalorar.

underexposed [ˌʌndərɪkˈspəʊzd] *adj* PHOT subexpuesto(ta).

underfed [ˈʌndəˈfed] *adj* desnutrido(da).

underfinanced [ˌʌndəˈfaɪnænst] *adj* insuficientemente financiado(da).

underfoot [ˌʌndəˈfut] *adv* debajo de los pies; **it's wet underfoot** el suelo está mojado.

undergo [ˌʌndəˈgəʊ] (*pt* -**went**, *pp* -**gone**) *vt* [pain, change, difficulties] sufrir, experimentar; [operation, examination] someterse a.

undergraduate [ˌʌndəˈgrædʒʊət] ◇ *adj* [course, studies] de licenciatura; [gown, prospectus] para estudiantes no licenciados. ◇ *n* estudiante universitario no licenciado *m*, estudiante universitaria no licenciada *f*.

underground ◇ *adj* [ˈʌndəgraʊnd] - **1.** [below the ground] subterráneo(a) - **2.** *fig* [secret, illegal] clandestino(na). ◇ *adv* [ˌʌndəˈgraʊnd]: **to go underground** pasar a la clandestinidad; **to be forced underground** tener que pasar a la clandestinidad. ◇ *n* [ˈʌndəgraʊnd] - **1.** *UK* [railway system] metro *m*, subte(rráneo) *m R Plata* - **2.** [activist movement] resistencia *f*, movimiento *m* clandestino.

undergrowth [ˈʌndəgrəʊθ] *n (U)* maleza *f*, monte *m* bajo.

underhand [ˌʌndəˈhænd] *adj* turbio(bia), poco limpio(pia).

underinsured [ˌʌndərɪnˈʃʊəd] *adj que no está asegurado por una cantidad suficiente.*

underlay [ˈʌndəleɪ] *n* refuerzo *m*.

underline [ˌʌndəˈlaɪn] *vt* subrayar.

underlying [ˌʌndəˈlaɪɪŋ] *adj* subyacente.

undermanned [ˌʌndəˈmænd] *adj* sin suficiente personal.

undermentioned [ˌʌndəˈmenʃnd] *adj fml* abajo citado(da).

undermine [ˌʌndəˈmaɪn] *vt fig* minar, socavar; **to undermine sb's confidence/authority** minar la confianza/autoridad de alguien.

underneath [ˌʌndəˈniːθ] ◇ *prep* - **1.** [beneath] debajo de - **2.** [with movement] bajo. ◇ *adv*

- **1.** [under, below] debajo - **2.** *fig* [fundamentally] por dentro, en el fondo. ◇ *adj inf* inferior, de abajo. ◇ *n* - **1.** [underside]: **the underneath** la superficie inferior - **2.** *fig* [true personality]: **on the underneath** en el fondo.

undernourished [ˌʌndəˈnʌrɪʃt] *adj* desnutrido(da).

underpaid ◇ *pt* & *pp* [ˌʌndəˈpeɪd] ▷ **underpay**. ◇ *adj* [ˈʌndəpeɪd] mal pagado(da).

underpants [ˈʌndəpænts] *npl* calzoncillos *mpl*.

underpass [ˈʌndəpɑːs] *n* paso *m* subterráneo.

underpay [ˌʌndəˈpeɪ] (*pt* & *pp* -**paid**) *vt* pagar mal.

underpin [ˌʌndəˈpɪn] (*pt* & *pp* -**ned**, *cont* -**ning**) *vt* apoyar, sostener.

underplay [ˌʌndəˈpleɪ] *vt* [minimize the importance of] minimizar.

underprice [ˌʌndəˈpraɪs] *vt* marcar con un precio muy por debajo del valor real.

underprivileged [ˌʌndəˈprɪvɪlɪdʒd] *adj* desvalido(da), desamparado(da).

underproduction [ˌʌndəprəˈdʌkʃn] *n* producción *f* insuficiente.

underrated [ˌʌndəˈreɪtɪd] *adj* subestimado(da), infravalorado(da).

underscore [ˌʌndəˈskɔːr] *vt lit* & *fig* subrayar.

undersea [ˈʌndəsiː] *adj* submarino(na).

undersecretary [ˌʌndəˈsekrətərɪ] (*pl* -**ies**) *n* subsecretario *m*, -ria *f*.

undersell [ˌʌndəˈsel] (*pt* & *pp* -**sold**) *vt* [sell at lower prices than] vender a precio más bajo que; **we are never knowingly undersold** vendemos más barato que nadie.

undershirt [ˈʌndəʃɜːt] *n US* camiseta *f*.

underside [ˈʌndəsaɪd] *n*: **the underside** la superficie inferior.

undersigned [ˈʌndəsaɪnd] *n fml*: **the undersigned** el/la abajo firmante; **we, the undersigned...** nosotros, los abajo afirmantes...

undersize(d) [ˌʌndəˈsaɪz(d)] *adj* más pequeño(ña) de lo normal.

underskirt [ˈʌndəskɜːt] *n* enaguas *fpl*.

undersold [ˌʌndəˈsəʊld] *pt* & *pp* ▷ **undersell**.

understaffed [ˌʌndəˈstɑːft] *adj*: **to be understaffed** no tener suficiente personal.

understand [ˌʌndəˈstænd] (*pt* & *pp* -**stood**) ◇ *vt* - **1.** [gen] comprender, entender; **do you understand French?** ¿entiendes francés?; **to make o.s. understood** hacerse entender; **is that understood?** ¿queda claro? - **2.** [know all about] entender de - **3.** *fml* [be informed]: **to understand that** tener entendido que - **4.** [assume]: **it is understood that...** se entiende que... ◇ *vi* comprender, entender.

understandable [ˌʌndə'stændəbl] *adj* comprensible.

understandably [ˌʌndə'stændəblɪ] *adv* naturalmente, comprensiblemente; **she was understandably upset** como es lógico estaba disgustada.

understanding [ˌʌndə'stændɪŋ] ◇ *n* - **1.** [knowledge] entendimiento *m*, comprensión *f* - **2.** [sympathy] comprensión *f* mutua - **3.** [interpretation]: **it is my understanding that...** tengo la impresión de que... - **4.** [informal agreement] acuerdo *m*, arreglo *m*; **on the understanding that** a condición de que; **we have a little understanding** tenemos un pequeño acuerdo. ◇ *adj* comprensivo(va).

understate [ˌʌndə'steɪt] *vt* minimizar, atenuar.

understatement [ˌʌndə'steɪtmənt] *n* - **1.** [inadequate statement] atenuación *f*; **it's an understatement to say he's fat** decir que es gordo es quedarse corto - **2.** (U) [quality of understating]: **he's a master of understatement** puede quitarle importancia a cualquier cosa.

understood [ˌʌndə'stʊd] *pt & pp* ▷ understand.

understudy [ˈʌndəˌstʌdɪ] (*pl* **-ies**) *n* suplente *mf*.

undertake [ˌʌndə'teɪk] (*pt* **-took**, *pp* **-taken**) *vt* - **1.** [task] emprender; [responsibility, control] asumir, tomar - **2.** [promise]: **to undertake to do sthg** comprometerse a hacer algo.

undertaker [ˈʌndəˌteɪkə^r] *n* director *m*, -ra *f* de pompas fúnebres.

undertaking [ˌʌndə'teɪkɪŋ] *n* - **1.** [task] tarea *f*, empresa *f* - **2.** [promise] promesa *f*.

undertone [ˈʌndətəʊn] *n* - **1.** [quiet voice] voz *f* baja; **in an undertone** en voz baja - **2.** [vague feeling] matiz *m*.

undertook [ˌʌndə'tʊk] *pt* ▷ undertake.

undertow [ˈʌndətəʊ] *n* resaca *f* (marítima).

undervalue [ˌʌndə'vælju:] *vt* [person] subestimar, menospreciar; [house] subvalorar.

underwater [ˌʌndə'wɔːtə^r] ◇ *adj* submarino(na). ◇ *adv* bajo el agua.

underwear [ˈʌndəweə^r] *n* ropa *f* interior.

underweight [ˌʌndə'weɪt] *adj* flaco(ca), que no pesa lo suficiente.

underwent [ˌʌndə'went] *pt* ▷ undergo.

underworld [ˈʌndəˌwɜːld] *n* [criminal society]: **the underworld** el hampa, los bajos fondos.

underwrite [ˌʌndə'raɪt] (*pt* **-wrote**, *pp* **-written**) *vt* - **1.** *fml* [guarantee] suscribir - **2.** [in insurance] asegurar.

underwriter [ˈʌndəˌraɪtə^r] *n* asegurador *m*, -ra *f*.

underwritten [ˈʌndəˌrɪtn] *pp* ▷ underwrite.

underwrote [ˈʌndərəʊt] *pt* ▷ underwrite.

undeserved [ˌʌndɪ'zɜːvd] *adj* inmerecido(da).

undeserving [ˌʌndɪ'zɜːvɪŋ] *adj* [person]: **to be undeserving of sthg** no merecer algo.

undesirable [ˌʌndɪ'zaɪərəbl] *adj* indeseable.

undeveloped [ˌʌndɪ'veləpt] *adj* [country] subdesarrollado(da).

undid [ˌʌn'dɪd] *pt* ▷ undo.

undies [ˈʌndɪz] *npl inf* paños *mpl* menores.

undignified [ʌn'dɪgnɪfaɪd] *adj* indecoroso(sa).

undiluted [ˌʌndaɪ'ljuːtɪd] *adj* - **1.** [joy etc] puro(ra) - **2.** [liquid] sin diluir.

undiplomatic [ˌʌndɪplə'mætɪk] *adj* poco diplomático(ca), indiscreto(ta).

undischarged [ˌʌndɪs'tʃɑːdʒd] *adj* - **1.** [debt] sin liquidar - **2.** [person]: **undischarged bankrupt** *persona en quiebra no rehabilitada.*

undisciplined [ʌn'dɪsɪplɪnd] *adj* indisciplinado(da).

undiscovered [ˌʌndɪ'skʌvəd] *adj* no descubierto(ta); **it remained undiscovered for years** permaneció sin descubrir durante años.

undisputed [ˌʌndɪ'spjuːtɪd] *adj* indiscutible.

undistinguished [ˌʌndɪ'stɪŋgwɪʃt] *adj* mediocre.

undivided [ˌʌndɪ'vaɪdɪd] *adj* entero(ra), íntegro(gra); **you have my undivided attention** tienes toda mi atención.

undo [ˌʌn'duː] (*pt* **-did**, *pp* **-done**) *vt* - **1.** [unfasten - knot] desatar, desanudar; [- button, clasp] desabrochar; [- parcel] abrir - **2.** [nullify] anular, deshacer - **3.** COMPUT deshacer.

undoing [ˌʌn'duːɪŋ] *n* (U) *fml* ruina *f*, perdición *f*; **it was his undoing** fue su perdición.

undone [ˌʌn'dʌn] ◇ *pp* ▷ undo. ◇ *adj* - **1.** [coat] desabrochado(da); [shoes] desatado(da); **to come undone** desatarse - **2.** *fml* [not done] por hacer.

undoubted [ʌn'daʊtɪd] *adj* indudable.

undoubtedly [ʌn'daʊtɪdlɪ] *adv fml* indudablemente, sin duda (alguna).

undreamed-of [ʌn'driːmdɒv], **undreamt-of** [ʌn'dremtɒv] *adj* inimaginable.

undress [ˌʌn'dres] ◇ *vt* desnudar. ◇ *vi* desnudarse.

undressed [ˌʌn'drest] *adj* desnudo(da); **to get undressed** desnudarse.

undrinkable [ˌʌn'drɪŋkəbl] *adj* - **1.** [unfit to drink] no potable - **2.** [disgusting] imbebible.

undue [ˌʌn'djuː] *adj fml* indebido(da), excesivo(va).

undulate [ˈʌndjʊleɪt] *vi fml* ondular.

unduly [ˌʌnˈdjuːlɪ] *adv fml* indebidamente, excesivamente.

undying [ʌnˈdaɪɪŋ] *adj liter* imperecedero(ra).

unearned income [ˌʌnˈɜːnd-] *n (U)* renta *f* (no salarial).

unearth [ˌʌnˈɜːθ] *vt* [dig up] desenterrar; *fig* [discover] descubrir.

unearthly [ʌnˈɜːθlɪ] *adj* - **1.** [ghostly] sobrenatural, misterioso(sa) - **2.** *inf* [hour] intempestivo(va).

unease [ʌnˈiːz] *n* malestar *m*.

uneasy [ʌnˈiːzɪ] (*comp* -ier, *superl* -iest) *adj* - **1.** [person, feeling] intranquilo(la) - **2.** [peace] inseguro(ra).

uneatable [ˌʌnˈiːtəbl] *adj* incomible.

uneaten [ˌʌnˈiːtn] *adj* sin comer.

uneconomic [ˈʌnˌiːkəˈnɒmɪk] *adj* poco rentable.

uneducated [ˌʌnˈedjʊkeɪtɪd] *adj* ignorante, inculto(ta).

unemotional [ˌʌnɪˈməʊʃənl] *adj* [person, voice] impasible; [statement, report] objetivo(va).

unemployable [ˌʌnɪmˈplɔɪəbl] *adj* que difícilmente puede encontrar trabajo.

unemployed [ˌʌnɪmˈplɔɪd] <> *adj* parado(da), desempleado(da). <> *npl*: **the unemployed** los parados.

unemployment [ˌʌnɪmˈplɔɪmənt] *n* desempleo *m*, paro *m*.

unemployment benefit *UK*, **unemployment compensation** *US n* subsidio *m* de desempleo OR paro.

unenviable [ˌʌnˈenvɪəbl] *adj* poco envidiable.

unequal [ˌʌnˈiːkwəl] *adj* desigual.

unequalled *UK*, **unequaled** *US* [ˌʌnˈiːkwəld] *adj* sin par, inigualado(da).

unequivocal [ˌʌnɪˈkwɪvəkl] *adj fml* inequívoco(ca).

unerring [ʌnˈɜːrɪŋ] *adj* infalible.

UNESCO [juːˈneskəʊ] (*abbr of* **United Nations Educational, Scientific and Cultural Organization**) *n* UNESCO *f*.

unethical [ʌnˈeθɪkl] *adj* poco ético(ca).

uneven [ˌʌnˈiːvn] *adj* - **1.** [not flat - road] lleno(na) de baches; [- land] escabroso(sa) - **2.** [inconsistent, unfair] desigual.

uneventful [ˌʌnɪˈventfʊl] *adj* tranquilo(la), sin incidentes.

unexceptional [ˌʌnɪkˈsepʃənl] *adj* normal, corriente.

unexpected [ˌʌnɪkˈspektɪd] *adj* inesperado(da).

unexpectedly [ˌʌnɪkˈspektɪdlɪ] *adv* inesperadamente.

unexplained [ˌʌnɪkˈspleɪnd] *adj* inexplicado(da).

unexploded [ˌʌnɪkˈspləʊdɪd] *adj* [bomb] sin explotar.

unexpurgated [ˌʌnˈekspəgeɪtɪd] *adj* sin expurgar, íntegro(gra).

unfailing [ʌnˈfeɪlɪŋ] *adj* indefectible.

unfair [ˌʌnˈfeəʳ] *adj* injusto(ta).

unfair dismissal *n* despido *m* improcedente.

unfairness [ˌʌnˈfeənɪs] *n* injusticia *f*.

unfaithful [ˌʌnˈfeɪθfʊl] *adj* [sexually] infiel.

unfamiliar [ˌʌnfəˈmɪljəʳ] *adj* - **1.** [not well-known] desconocido(da), nuevo(va) - **2.** [not acquainted]: **to be unfamiliar with sthg/sb** desconocer algo/a alguien.

unfashionable [ˌʌnˈfæʃnəbl] *adj* [clothes, ideas] pasado(da) de moda; [area of town] poco popular.

unfasten [ˌʌnˈfɑːsn] *vt* [garment, buttons] desabrochar; [rope, tie] desatar, soltar; [door] abrir.

unfavourable *UK*, **unfavorable** *US* [ˌʌnˈfeɪvrəbl] *adj* desfavorable.

unfeeling [ʌnˈfiːlɪŋ] *adj* insensible.

unfinished [ˌʌnˈfɪnɪʃt] *adj* sin terminar.

unfit [ˌʌnˈfɪt] *adj* - **1.** [injured] lesionado(da); [in poor shape] que no está en forma - **2.** [not suitable - thing] impropio(pia); [- person]: **unfit to** incapaz de; **unfit for** no apto para.

unflagging [ˌʌnˈflægɪŋ] *adj* incansable.

unflappable [ˌʌnˈflæpəbl] *adj esp UK* imperturbable.

unflattering [ˌʌnˈflætərɪŋ] *adj* poco favorecedor(ra).

unflinching [ʌnˈflɪntʃɪŋ] *adj* impávido(da).

unfold [ʌnˈfəʊld] <> *vt* - **1.** [open out] desplegar, desdoblar - **2.** [explain] exponer, revelar. <> *vi* [become clear] revelarse.

unforeseeable [ˌʌnfɔːˈsiːəbl] *adj* imprevisible.

unforeseen [ˌʌnfɔːˈsiːn] *adj* imprevisto(ta).

unforgettable [ˌʌnfəˈgetəbl] *adj* inolvidable.

unforgivable [ˌʌnfəˈgɪvəbl] *adj* imperdonable.

unformatted [ˌʌnˈfɔːmætɪd] *adj* COMPUT sin formato.

unfortunate [ʌnˈfɔːtʃnət] *adj* - **1.** [unlucky] desgraciado(da), desdichado(da), salado(da) *Amér* - **2.** [regrettable] inoportuno(na).

unfortunately [ʌnˈfɔːtʃnətlɪ] *adv* desgraciadamente, desafortunadamente.

unfounded [ˌʌnˈfaʊndɪd] *adj* infundado(da).

unfriendly [ˌʌnˈfrendlɪ] (*comp* -ier, *superl* -iest) *adj* poco amistoso(sa).

unfulfilled [ˌʌnfʊlˈfɪld] *adj* - **1.** [not yet realized] incumplido(da), sin realizar - **2.** [unsatisfied] insatisfecho(cha).

unfurl [ˌʌnˈfɜːl] *vt* desplegar.

unfurnished [ˌʌnˈfɜːnɪʃt] *adj* sin muebles, desamueblado(da).

ungainly [ʌnˈɡeɪnlɪ] *adj* torpe, desgarbado(da).

ungenerous [ˌʌnˈdʒenərəs] *adj* **- 1.** [parsimonious - person] poco generoso(sa); [- amount] miserable **- 2.** [uncharitable] poco caritativo(va).

ungodly [ˌʌnˈɡɒdlɪ] *adj* **- 1.** [irreligious] impío(a) **- 2.** *inf* [hour] intempestivo(va); **at an ungodly hour** a una hora intempestiva.

ungrateful [ʌnˈɡreɪtful] *adj* desagradecido(da), ingrato(ta).

ungratefulness [ʌnˈɡreɪtfulnɪs] *n* ingratitud *f*.

unguarded [ˌʌnˈɡɑːdɪd] *adj* **- 1.** [not guarded] sin protección **- 2.** [careless]: **in an unguarded moment** en un momento de descuido.

unhappily [ʌnˈhæpɪlɪ] *adv* **- 1.** [sadly] tristemente **- 2.** *fml* [unfortunately] lamentablemente, desafortunadamente.

unhappiness [ʌnˈhæpɪnɪs] *n* (U) tristeza *f*, desdicha *f*.

unhappy [ʌnˈhæpɪ] (*comp* **-ier**, *superl* **-iest**) *adj* **- 1.** [sad] triste; [wretched] desdichado(da), infeliz **- 2.** [uneasy]: **to be unhappy (with OR about)** estar inquieto(ta) (por) **- 3.** *fml* [unfortunate] desafortunado(da).

unharmed [ˌʌnˈhɑːmd] *adj* [person] ileso(sa); [thing] indemne; **he escaped unharmed** salió ileso.

UNHCR (*abbr of* **United Nations High Commission for Refugees**) *n* ACNUR *m*.

unhealthy [ʌnˈhelθɪ] (*comp* **-ier**, *superl* **-iest**) *adj* **- 1.** [in bad health] enfermizo(za) **- 2.** [causing bad health] insalubre **- 3.** *fig* [interest etc] morboso(sa).

unheard [ˌʌnˈhɜːd] *adj*: **to be OR go unheard** pasar sin ser oído(da).

unheard-of [ʌnˈhɜːd-] *adj* **- 1.** [unknown, completely absent] inaudito(ta) **- 2.** [unprecedented] sin precedente.

unheeded [ˌʌnˈhiːdɪd] *adj*: **her warning went unheeded** nadie hizo caso de su advertencia.

unhelpful [ˌʌnˈhelpful] *adj* **- 1.** [unwilling to help] poco servicial **- 2.** [not useful] inútil.

unhindered [ʌnˈhɪndəd] *adj*: **unhindered (by)** no estorbado(da) (por).

unhook [ˌʌnˈhuk] *vt* **- 1.** [unfasten hooks of] desabrochar **- 2.** [remove from hook] descolgar, desenganchar.

unhurt [ˌʌnˈhɜːt] *adj* ileso(sa).

unhygienic [ˌʌnhaɪˈdʒiːnɪk] *adj* antihigiénico(ca).

UNICEF [ˈjuːnɪˌsef] (*abbr of* **United Nations International Children's Emergency Fund**) *n* UNICEF *f*.

unicorn [ˈjuːnɪkɔːn] *n* unicornio *m*.

unicycle [ˈjuːnɪsaɪkl] *n* monociclo *m*.

unidentified [ˌʌnaɪˈdentɪfaɪd] *adj* sin identificar, no identificado(da).

unidentified flying object *n* objeto *m* volador no identificado.

unification [ˌjuːnɪfɪˈkeɪʃn] *n* unificación *f*.

uniform [ˈjuːnɪfɔːm] <> *adj* uniforme, constante. <> *n* uniforme *m*.

uniformity [ˌjuːnɪˈfɔːmətɪ] *n* uniformidad *f*.

uniformly [ˈjuːnɪfɔːmlɪ] *adv* de modo uniforme.

unify [ˈjuːnɪfaɪ] (*pt* & *pp* **-ied**) *vt* unificar, unir.

unifying [ˈjuːnɪfaɪɪŋ] *adj* unificador(ra).

unilateral [ˌjuːnɪˈlætərəl] *adj* unilateral.

unimaginable [ˌʌnɪˈmædʒɪnəbl] *adj* inimaginable, inconcebible.

unimaginative [ˌʌnɪˈmædʒɪnətɪv] *adj* poco imaginativo(va).

unimpaired [ˌʌnɪmˈpeəd] *adj* [gen] intacto(ta); [health] inalterado(da).

unimpeded [ˌʌnɪmˈpiːdɪd] *adj* sin estorbos, libre.

unimportant [ˌʌnɪmˈpɔːtənt] *adj* sin importancia, insignificante.

unimpressed [ˌʌnɪmˈprest] *adj* no impresionado(da); **he was unimpressed by her performance** no le impresionó su actuación.

uninhabited [ˌʌnɪnˈhæbɪtɪd] *adj* deshabitado(da), desierto(ta).

uninhibited [ˌʌnɪnˈhɪbɪtɪd] *adj* desinhibido(da).

uninitiated [ˌʌnɪˈnɪʃɪeɪtɪd] *npl*: **the uninitiated** los no iniciados.

uninjured [ˌʌnˈɪndʒəd] *adj* ileso(sa).

uninspiring [ˌʌnɪnˈspaɪrɪŋ] *adj* nada inspirador(ra).

uninstall [ˌʌnɪnˈstɔːl] *vt* desinstalar.

unintelligent [ˌʌnɪnˈtelɪdʒent] *adj* poco inteligente.

unintentional [ˌʌnɪnˈtenʃənl] *adj* involuntario(ria).

uninterested [ˌʌnˈɪntrəstɪd] *adj* no interesado(da).

uninterrupted [ˈʌnˌɪntəˈrʌptɪd] *adj* ininterrumpido(da); **to continue uninterrupted** continuar sin interrupción.

uninvited [ˌʌnɪnˈvaɪtɪd] *adj* no invitado(da); **they turned up uninvited** llegaron sin haber sido invitados.

union [ˈjuːnjən] <> *n* **- 1.** [trade union] sindicato *m* **- 2.** [alliance] unión *f*, alianza *f*. <> *comp* sindical.

Unionist [ˈjuːnjənɪst] *n* UK POL unionista *mf* (*partidario de que Irlanda del Norte siga siendo parte del Reino Unido*).

unionize, -ise [ˈjuːnjənaɪz] *vt* sindicar.

Union Jack n: **the Union Jack** la bandera del Reino Unido.

union shop n US taller fábrica etc donde todos los empleados tienen que pertenecer a un sindicato.

unique [juːˈniːk] adj - **1.** [gen] único(ca) - **2.** fml [peculiar, exclusive]: **unique to** peculiar de.

uniquely [juːˈniːklɪ] adv - **1.** fml [exclusively] exclusivamente - **2.** [exceptionally] excepcionalmente.

unisex [ˈjuːnɪseks] adj unisex (inv).

unison [ˈjuːnɪzn] n unísono m; **in unison** [simultaneously] al unísono.

UNISON [ˈjuːnɪzn] n sindicato grande que acoge a la gran mayoría de los funcionarios británicos.

unit [ˈjuːnɪt] n - **1.** [gen] unidad f - **2.** [piece of furniture] módulo m, elemento m.

unit cost n costo m unitario.

unite [juːˈnaɪt] <> vt [gen] unir; [country] unificar. <> vi unirse, juntarse.

united [juːˈnaɪtɪd] adj unido(da); **to be united in** estar todos(das) de acuerdo en.

United Arab Emirates npl: **the United Arab Emirates** los Emiratos Árabes Unidos.

united front n: **to present a united front (on)** hacer frente común (ante).

United Kingdom n: **the United Kingdom** el Reino Unido.

United Kingdom

Así se denomina en contextos oficiales la entidad política que comprende Inglaterra, Gales, Escocia e Irlanda del Norte, a la que a menudo se hace referencia simplemente con la abreviatura UK. Su nombre completo es "United Kingdom of Great Britain and Northern Ireland".

United Nations n: **the United Nations** las Naciones Unidas.

United States n: **the United States (of America)** los Estados Unidos (de América).

unit price n precio m unitario.

unit trust n UK fondo m de inversión mobiliaria.

unity [ˈjuːnətɪ] n (U) unidad f, unión f.

Univ. abbr of **University**.

universal [ˌjuːnɪˈvɜːsl] adj universal.

universe [ˈjuːnɪvɜːs] n: **the universe** el universo.

university [ˌjuːnɪˈvɜːsətɪ] (pl -ies) <> n universidad f. <> comp universitario(ria); **university student** (estudiante) universitario m, (estudiante) universitaria f.

unjust [ˌʌnˈdʒʌst] adj injusto(ta).

unjustifiable [ʌnˈdʒʌstɪˌfaɪəbl] adj injustificable.

unjustified [ʌnˈdʒʌstɪfaɪd] adj injustificado(da).

unkempt [ˌʌnˈkempt] adj [person] desaseado(da); [hair] despeinado(da); [clothes] descuidado(da).

unkind [ʌnˈkaɪnd] adj - **1.** [uncharitable] poco amable, cruel - **2.** fig [inhospitable] riguroso(sa).

unkindly [ʌnˈkaɪndlɪ] adv cruelmente.

unknown [ˌʌnˈnəʊn] <> adj desconocido(da); **unknown to him** sin que él lo supiera. <> n - **1.** [thing]: **the unknown** lo desconocido - **2.** [person] desconocido m, -da f.

unlace [ˌʌnˈleɪs] vt [clothes] desenlazar; [shoes] desatar los cordones de.

unladen [ˌʌnˈleɪdn] adj vacío(a), sin carga.

unlawful [ˌʌnˈlɔːfʊl] adj ilegal, ilícito(ta).

unleaded [ˌʌnˈledɪd] adj sin plomo.

unleash [ˌʌnˈliːʃ] vt liter desatar, desencadenar.

unleavened [ˌʌnˈlevnd] adj ázimo, sin levadura.

unless [ənˈles] conj a menos que; **unless I say so** a menos que yo lo diga; **unless I'm mistaken** si no me equivoco.

unlicensed, unlicenced US [ˌʌnˈlaɪsənst] adj - **1.** [without a licence - person, vehicle] sin permiso; [- activity] sin licencia - **2.** [not licensed to sell alcohol] no autorizado(da).

unlike [ˌʌnˈlaɪk] prep - **1.** [different from] distinto(ta) a, diferente a - **2.** [differently from] a diferencia de - **3.** [not typical of] impropio(pia) de, poco característico(ca) de; **that's unlike him** no es propio de él.

unlikely [ʌnˈlaɪklɪ] adj - **1.** [not probable] improbable, poco probable; **it's unlikely that he'll come now, he's unlikely to come now** ahora es poco probable que venga; **to be highly unlikely** ser muy poco probable - **2.** [bizarre] inverosímil.

unlimited [ʌnˈlɪmɪtɪd] adj ilimitado(da), sin límites.

unlisted [ʌnˈlɪstɪd] adj US [phone number] que no figura en la guía telefónica.

unlit [ˌʌnˈlɪt] adj - **1.** [not burning] sin encender - **2.** [dark] no iluminado(da).

unload [ˌʌnˈləʊd] vt - **1.** [goods, car] descargar - **2.** fig [unburden]: **to unload sthg on** OR **onto sb** descargar algo en alguien.

unlock [ˌʌnˈlɒk] vt abrir (con llave).

unloved [ˌʌnˈlʌvd] adj: **to be/feel unloved** no ser/sentirse amado(da) por nadie.

unluckily [ʌnˈlʌkɪlɪ] adv desgraciadamente.

unlucky [ʌnˈlʌkɪ] (comp -ier, superl -iest) adj - **1.** [unfortunate] desgraciado(da); **to be un-**

lucky tener mala suerte **- 2.** [number, colour etc] de la mala suerte; **to be unlucky** traer mala suerte.

unmanageable [ˌʌnˈmænɪdʒəbl] *adj* [vehicle, parcel] difícil de manejar; [situation] muy difícil, incontrolable.

unmanly [ˌʌnˈmænlɪ] (*comp* -ier, *superl* -iest) *adj* cobarde.

unmanned [ˌʌnˈmænd] *adj* no tripulado(da).

unmarked [ˌʌnˈmɑːkt] *adj* **- 1.** [uninjured] ileso(sa), sin un rasguño **- 2.** [unidentified - box, suitcase] sin marcar; **unmarked police car** coche camuflado de la policía.

unmarried [ˌʌnˈmærɪd] *adj* que no se ha casado.

unmask [ˌʌnˈmɑːsk] *vt* [gen] desenmascarar; *fig* [truth etc] descubrir, exponer.

unmatched [ˌʌnˈmætʃt] *adj* incomparable, sin par.

unmentionable [ʌnˈmenʃnəbl] *adj* que no se puede mencionar.

unmetered [ʌnˈmiːtəd] *adj* ilimitado(da).

unmistakable [ˌʌnmɪˈsteɪkəbl] *adj* inconfundible.

unmitigated [ʌnˈmɪtɪɡeɪtɪd] *adj* absoluto(ta).

unmoved [ˌʌnˈmuːvd] *adj*: **to be unmoved by** permanecer impasible ante.

unnamed [ˌʌnˈneɪmd] *adj* anónimo(ma).

unnatural [ʌnˈnætʃrəl] *adj* **- 1.** [unusual, strange] anormal **- 2.** [affected] afectado(da).

unnecessary [ʌnˈnesəsərɪ] *adj* innecesario(ria).

unnerving [ˌʌnˈnɜːvɪŋ] *adj* desconcertante.

unnoticed [ˌʌnˈnəʊtɪst] *adj* inadvertido(da), desapercibido(da); **to go unnoticed** pasar desapercibido(da).

UNO (*abbr of* **United Nations Organization**) *n* ONU *f*.

unobserved [ˌʌnəbˈzɜːvd] *adj* inadvertido(da), desapercibido(da).

unobtainable [ˌʌnəbˈteɪnəbl] *adj* inasequible.

unobtrusive [ˌʌnəbˈtruːsɪv] *adj* discreto(ta).

unoccupied [ˌʌnˈɒkjʊpaɪd] *adj* **- 1.** [place, seat] libre; [area] despoblado(da); [house] deshabitado(da) **- 2.** [person] desocupado(da).

unofficial [ˌʌnəˈfɪʃl] *adj* extraoficial, oficioso(sa).

unopened [ʌnˈəʊpənd] *adj* sin abrir.

unorthodox [ˌʌnˈɔːθədɒks] *adj* poco convencional, poco ortodoxo(xa).

unpack [ˌʌnˈpæk] <> *vt* **- 1.** [box] desempaquetar, desembalar; [suitcases] deshacer **- 2.** [clothes] sacar (de la maleta). <> *vi* deshacer las maletas.

unpaid [ˌʌnˈpeɪd] *adj* **- 1.** [person, job, leave] no retribuido(da) **- 2.** [not yet paid] por pagar.

unpalatable [ˌʌnˈpælətəbl] *adj* [food] incomible; [drink] imbebible; *fig* [difficult to accept] desagradable.

unparalleled [ˌʌnˈpærəleld] *adj* incomparable, sin precedente.

unpatriotic [ˈʌnˌpætrɪˈɒtɪk] *adj* antipatriótico(ca).

unpick [ˌʌnˈpɪk] *vt* descoser.

unpin [ˌʌnˈpɪn] (*pt & pp* -ned, *cont* -ning) *vt* [sewing] quitar los alfileres de; [clothes] desabrochar; [hair] quitar las horquillas de.

unplanned [ˌʌnˈplænd] *adj* **- 1.** [event] imprevisto(ta) **- 2.** [pregnancy] no planeado(da).

unpleasant [ʌnˈpleznt] *adj* **- 1.** [disagreeable] desagradable **- 2.** [unfriendly, rude - person] antipático(ca); [- remark] mezquino(na).

unpleasantness [ʌnˈplezntnɪs] *n* **- 1.** [disagreeableness] lo desagradable **- 2.** [rudeness - of person] antipatía *f*; [- of remark] mezquindad *f*.

unplug [ʌnˈplʌɡ] (*pt & pp* -ged, *cont* -ging) *vt* desenchufar, desconectar.

unpolished [ˌʌnˈpɒlɪʃt] *adj* **- 1.** [furniture] sin encerar; [shoes] sin lustrar **- 2.** [style etc] tosco(ca).

unpolluted [ˌʌnpəˈluːtɪd] *adj* sin contaminar.

unpopular [ˌʌnˈpɒpjʊləʳ] *adj* impopular, poco popular; **she was unpopular with the other girls** las otras chicas no le tenían mucho aprecio.

unprecedented [ʌnˈpresɪdəntɪd] *adj* sin precedentes, inaudito(ta).

unpredictable [ˌʌnprɪˈdɪktəbl] *adj* imprevisible.

unprejudiced [ˌʌnˈpredʒʊdɪst] *adj* imparcial.

unprepared [ˌʌnprɪˈpeəd] *adj*: **to be unprepared (for)** no estar preparado(da) (para).

unprepossessing [ˈʌnˌpriːpəˈzesɪŋ] *adj* poco atractivo(va).

unpretentious [ˌʌnprɪˈtenʃəs] *adj* sin pretensiones, modesto(ta).

unprincipled [ʌnˈprɪnsəpld] *adj* sin principios.

unprintable [ˌʌnˈprɪntəbl] *adj fig* que no se puede repetir (en la prensa).

unproductive [ˌʌnprəˈdʌktɪv] *adj* [land, work] improductivo(va); [discussion, meeting] infructuoso(sa).

unprofessional [ˌʌnprəˈfeʃənl] *adj* poco profesional.

unprofitable [ˌʌnˈprɒfɪtəbl] *adj* [company, product] no rentable.

unprompted [ˌʌnˈprɒmptɪd] *adj* espontáneo(a).

unpronounceable [ˌʌnprəˈnaʊnsəbl] *adj* impronunciable.

unprotected [ˌʌnprə'tektɪd] *adj* sin protección, desprotegido(da).

unprovoked [ˌʌnprə'vəʊkt] *adj* no provocado(da).

unpublished [ˌʌn'pʌblɪʃt] *adj* inédito(ta), no publicado(da).

unpunished [ˌʌn'pʌnɪʃt] *adj*: **to go unpunished** escapar sin castigo.

unqualified [ˌʌn'kwɒlɪfaɪd] *adj* - **1.** [not qualified] sin título, no cualificado(da) - **2.** [total, complete] incondicional, completo(ta).

unquestionable [ʌn'kwestʃənəbl] *adj* incuestionable, indiscutible.

unquestioning [ʌn'kwestʃənɪŋ] *adj* incondicional.

unravel [ʌn'rævl] (*UK* -**led**, *cont* -**ling**) (*US* -**ed**, *cont* -**ing**) *vt lit* & *fig* desenmarañar.

unreadable [ˌʌn'ri:dəbl] *adj* - **1.** [difficult, tedious to read] pesado(da) de leer - **2.** [illegible] ilegible.

unreal [ˌʌn'rɪəl] *adj* irreal.

unrealistic [ˌʌnrɪə'lɪstɪk] *adj* [person] poco realista; [idea, plan] impracticable, fantástico(ca).

unreasonable [ʌn'ri:znəbl] *adj* - **1.** [person, behaviour, decision] poco razonable - **2.** [demand, price] excesivo(va).

unrecognizable [ˌʌn'rekəgnaɪzəbl] *adj* irreconocible.

unrecognized [ˌʌn'rekəgnaɪzd] *adj* no reconocido(da).

unrecorded [ˌʌnrɪ'kɔ:dɪd] *adj* no registrado(da).

unrefined [ˌʌnrɪ'faɪnd] *adj* - **1.** [not processed] no refinado(da) - **2.** [vulgar - person] vulgar; [- manner] poco refinado(da).

unrehearsed [ˌʌnrɪ'hɜ:st] *adj* improvisado(da).

unrelated [ˌʌnrɪ'leɪtɪd] *adj*: **to be unrelated (to)** no tener conexión (con).

unrelenting [ˌʌnrɪ'lentɪŋ] *adj* implacable, inexorable.

unreliable [ˌʌnrɪ'laɪəbl] *adj* que no es de fiar.

unrelieved [ˌʌnrɪ'li:vd] *adj* crónico(ca), constante.

unremarkable [ˌʌnrɪ'mɑ:kəbl] *adj* ordinario(ria), corriente.

unremitting [ˌʌnrɪ'mɪtɪŋ] *adj* incesante, continuo(nua).

unrepeatable [ˌʌnrɪ'pi:təbl] *adj* irrepetible.

unrepentant [ˌʌnrɪ'pentənt] *adj* impenitente.

unrepresentative [ˌʌnreprɪ'zentətɪv] *adj*: **unrepresentative (of)** poco representativo(va) (de).

unrequited [ˌʌnrɪ'kwaɪtɪd] *adj* no correspondido(da).

unreserved [ˌʌnrɪ'zɜ:vd] *adj* - **1.** [wholehearted] incondicional, absoluto(ta) - **2.** [not reserved] libre, no reservado(da).

unresolved [ˌʌnrɪ'zɒlvd] *adj* sin resolver, pendiente.

unresponsive [ˌʌnrɪ'spɒnsɪv] *adj*: **to be unresponsive to** ser insensible a.

unrest [ˌʌn'rest] *n (U)* malestar *m*, inquietud *f*.

unrestrained [ˌʌnrɪ'streɪnd] *adj* incontrolado(da), desenfrenado(da).

unrestricted [ˌʌnrɪ'strɪktɪd] *adj* sin restricción.

unrewarding [ˌʌnrɪ'wɔ:dɪŋ] *adj* que no ofrece satisfacción.

unripe [ˌʌn'raɪp] *adj* verde, que no está maduro(ra).

unrivalled *UK*, **unrivaled** *US* [ʌn'raɪvld] *adj* incomparable, sin par.

unroll [ˌʌn'rəʊl] *vt* desenrollar.

unruffled [ˌʌn'rʌfld] *adj* [calm] imperturbable.

unruly [ʌn'ru:lɪ] (*comp* -**ier**, *superl* -**iest**) *adj* - **1.** [person, behaviour] revoltoso(sa) - **2.** [hair] rebelde.

unsafe [ˌʌn'seɪf] *adj* [gen] inseguro(ra); [risky] arriesgado(da).

unsaid [ˌʌn'sed] *adj*: **to leave sthg unsaid** dejar algo sin decir.

unsaleable, unsalable *US* [ˌʌn'seɪləbl] *adj* invendible.

unsatisfactory ['ʌnˌsætɪs'fæktərɪ] *adj* insatisfactorio(ria).

unsavoury, unsavory *US* [ˌʌn'seɪvərɪ] *adj* desagradable.

unscathed [ˌʌn'skeɪðd] *adj* ileso(sa).

unscheduled [*UK* ˌʌn'ʃedjʊld, *US* ˌʌn'skedʒʊld] *adj* imprevisto(ta).

unscientific ['ʌnˌsaɪən'tɪfɪk] *adj* poco científico(ca).

unscrew [ˌʌn'skru:] *vt* - **1.** [lid, top] abrir - **2.** [sign, hinge] desatornillar.

unscripted [ˌʌn'skrɪptɪd] *adj* sin guión, improvisado(da).

unscrupulous [ʌn'skru:pjʊləs] *adj* desaprensivo(va), poco escrupuloso(sa).

unseat [ˌʌn'si:t] *vt* - **1.** [rider] derribar, desarzonar - **2.** *fig* [depose] deponer.

unseeded [ˌʌn'si:dɪd] *adj* que no es cabeza de serie.

unseemly [ʌn'si:mlɪ] (*comp* -**ier**, *superl* -**iest**) *adj* impropio(pia), indecoroso(sa).

unseen [ˌʌn'si:n] *adj* [person, escape] inadvertido(da).

unselfish [ˌʌn'selfɪʃ] *adj* desinteresado(da), altruista.

unselfishly [ˌʌn'selfɪʃlɪ] *adv* desinteresadamente, altruistamente.

unsettle [ʌn'setl] *vt* perturbar, inquietar.

unsettled [ʌn'setld] *adj* - **1.** [person] nervioso(sa), intranquilo(la) - **2.** [weather] variable, inestable - **3.** [argument, matter, debt] pendiente - **4.** [situation] inestable.

unsettling [ʌn'setlɪŋ] *adj* inquietante, perturbador(ra).

unshak(e)able [ʌn'ʃeɪkəbl] *adj* inquebrantable.

unshaven [ʌn'ʃeɪvn] *adj* sin afeitar.

unsheathe [ʌn'ʃiːð] *vt* desenvainar.

unsightly [ʌn'saɪtlɪ] *adj* [building] feo(a); [scar, bruise] desagradable.

unskilled [ʌn'skɪld] *adj* [person] no cualificado(da); [work] no especializado(da).

unsociable [ʌn'səʊʃəbl] *adj* insociable, poco sociable.

unsocial [ʌn'səʊʃl] *adj*: **to work unsocial hours** trabajar a horas intempestivas.

unsold [ʌn'səʊld] *adj* sin vender.

unsolicited [ˌʌnsə'lɪsɪtɪd] *adj* no solicitado(da).

unsolved [ʌn'sɒlvd] *adj* no resuelto(ta), sin resolver.

unsophisticated [ˌʌnsə'fɪstɪkeɪtɪd] *adj* - **1.** [person] ingenuo(nua) - **2.** [method, device] rudimentario(ria).

unsound [ʌn'saʊnd] *adj* - **1.** [conclusion, method] erróneo(a) - **2.** [building, structure] defectuoso(sa).

unspeakable [ʌn'spiːkəbl] *adj* [crime] incalificable; [pain] indecible.

unspeakably [ʌn'spiːkəblɪ] *adv* indescriptiblemente.

unspecified [ʌn'spesɪfaɪd] *adj* sin especificar.

unspoiled [ʌn'spɔɪld], **unspoilt** [ʌn'spɔɪlt] *adj* sin estropear.

unspoken [ʌn'spəʊkən] *adj* - **1.** [not expressed openly] no expresado(da) - **2.** [tacit] tácito(ta).

unsporting [ˌʌn'spɔːtɪŋ] *adj* poco deportivo(va).

unstable [ʌn'steɪbl] *adj* inestable.

unstated [ʌn'steɪtɪd] *adj* no expresado(da).

unsteady [ʌn'stedɪ] (*comp* -**ier**, *superl* -**iest**) *adj* [gen] inestable; [hands, voice] tembloroso(sa); [footsteps] vacilante.

unstinting [ʌn'stɪntɪŋ] *adj* pródigo(ga).

unstoppable [ʌn'stɒpəbl] *adj* irrefrenable, incontenible.

unstrap [ʌn'stræp] (*pt & pp* -**ped**, *cont* -**ping**) *vt* desabrochar (las correas de).

unstructured [ʌn'strʌktʃəd] *adj* poco organizado(da).

unstuck [ʌn'stʌk] *adj*: **to come unstuck** [notice, stamp, label] despegarse, desprenderse; *fig* [plan, system, person] fracasar.

unsubscribe [ˌʌnsəb'skraɪb] *vi*: **to unsubscribe (from sth)** cancelar la suscripción (de algo).

unsubstantiated [ˌʌnsəb'stænʃɪeɪtɪd] *adj* no corroborado(da), sin probar.

unsuccessful [ˌʌnsək'sesfʊl] *adj* [person] fracasado(da); [attempt, meeting] infructuoso(sa); **to be unsuccessful** [person] no tener éxito.

unsuccessfully [ˌʌnsək'sesfʊlɪ] *adv* sin éxito, en vano.

unsuitable [ʌn'suːtəbl] *adj* inadecuado(da), inapropiado(da); **he is unsuitable for the job** no es la persona indicada para el trabajo; **I'm afraid 3 o'clock would be unsuitable** lo siento, pero no me va bien a las 3.

unsuited [ʌn'suːtɪd] *adj* - **1.** [not appropriate]: **to be unsuited to** OR **for** ser inepto(ta) para - **2.** [not compatible]: **to be unsuited (to each other)** ser incompatibles (uno con el otro).

unsung [ˌʌn'sʌŋ] *adj* no celebrado(da).

unsure [ʌn'ʃɔːr] *adj* - **1.** [not confident]: **to be unsure of o.s.** sentirse inseguro(ra) - **2.** [not certain]: **to be unsure (about** OR **of)** no estar muy seguro (de).

unsurpassed [ˌʌnsə'pɑːst] *adj* insuperado(da).

unsuspecting [ˌʌnsə'spektɪŋ] *adj* desprevenido(da), confiado(da).

unsweetened [ʌn'swiːtnd] *adj* sin azúcar.

unswerving [ʌn'swɜːvɪŋ] *adj* firme, inquebrantable.

unsympathetic ['ʌn,sɪmpə'θetɪk] *adj*: **unsympathetic to** indiferente a.

untamed [ʌn'teɪmd] *adj* - **1.** [animal] indomado(da) - **2.** [place, land] sin cultivar - **3.** [person] indómito(ta).

untangle [ʌn'tæŋgl] *vt* desenmarañar.

untapped [ʌn'tæpt] *adj* sin explotar.

untaxed [ʌn'tækst] *adj* antes de impuestos.

untenable [ʌn'tenəbl] *adj* insostenible.

unthinkable [ʌn'θɪŋkəbl] *adj* impensable, inconcebible.

unthinkingly [ʌn'θɪŋkɪŋlɪ] *adv* sin pensar, irreflexivamente.

untidy [ʌn'taɪdɪ] (*comp* -**ier**, *superl* -**iest**) *adj* [room, desk] desordenado(da); [person, appearance] desaliñado(da).

untie [ˌʌn'taɪ] (*cont* **untying**) *vt* desatar.

until [ən'tɪl] ◇ *prep* hasta; **until now/then** hasta ahora/entonces. ◇ *conj* - **1.** [gen] hasta que; **wait until everybody is there** espera a que haya llegado todo el mundo - **2.** *(after negative)*: **don't leave until you've finished** no te vayas hasta que hayas terminado.

untimely [ʌn'taɪmlɪ] *adj* - **1.** [premature] prematuro(ra) - **2.** [inappropriate] inoportuno(na).

untiring [ʌn'taɪərɪŋ] *adj* incansable.

untold [ˌʌnˈtəʊld] *adj* [incalculable, vast] incalculable; [suffering, joy] indecible.

untouched [ˌʌnˈtʌtʃt] *adj* - **1.** [scenery, place] no estropeado(da); [building etc] intacto(ta) - **2.** [food] sin probar.

untoward [ˌʌntəˈwɔːd] *adj* [event] adverso(sa); [behaviour] fuera de lugar.

untrained [ˌʌnˈtreɪnd] *adj* - **1.** [person, worker] no cualificado(da) - **2.** [voice, mind] no educado(da); **to the untrained eye/ear** para el ojo/oído poco avezado.

untrammelled *UK,* **untrammeled** *US* [ʌnˈtræməld] *adj fml* - **1.** [unbounded - joy etc] sin límites - **2.** [unrestricted]: **untrammelled by** libre de.

untranslatable [ˌʌntrænsˈleɪtəbl] *adj* intraducible.

untreated [ˌʌnˈtriːtɪd] *adj* - **1.** [illness, person] que no ha sido tratado(da) - **2.** [waste, effluent] sin tratar.

untried [ˌʌnˈtraɪd] *adj* no probado(da).

untroubled [ˌʌnˈtrʌbld] *adj*: **to be untroubled by** no estar afectado(da) por.

untrue [ˌʌnˈtruː] *adj* - **1.** [not true] falso(sa) - **2.** [unfaithful]: **to be untrue to** ser infiel OR desleal a.

untrustworthy [ˌʌnˈtrʌstˌwɜːðɪ] *adj* indigno(na) de confianza.

untruth [ˌʌnˈtruːθ] *n* mentira *f*.

untruthful [ˌʌnˈtruːθʊl] *adj* falso(sa), mentiroso(sa).

untutored [ˌʌnˈtjuːtəd] *adj* no educado(da).

unusable [ˌʌnˈjuːzəbl] *adj* inútil, inservible.

unused *adj* - **1.** [ˌʌnˈjuːzd] [not previously used] nuevo(va), sin usar - **2.** [ʌnˈjuːst] [unaccustomed]: **to be unused to sthg/to doing sthg** no estar acostumbrado(da) a algo/a hacer algo.

unusual [ʌnˈjuːʒl] *adj* [rare] insólito(ta), poco común.

unusually [ʌnˈjuːʒəlɪ] *adv* - **1.** [exceptionally] extraordinariamente; **the exam was unusually difficult** el examen fue extraordinariamente difícil - **2.** [surprisingly] sorprendentemente.

unvarnished [ʌnˈvɑːnɪʃt] *adj fig* [straightforward] sin adornos.

unveil [ˌʌnˈveɪl] *vt* - **1.** [statue, plaque] descubrir - **2.** *fig* [plans, policy] revelar.

unwaged [ˌʌnˈweɪdʒd] *adj UK* desempleado(da).

unwanted [ˌʌnˈwɒntɪd] *adj* [clothes, furniture] superfluo(flua); [child, pregnancy] no deseado(da).

unwarranted [ʌnˈwɒrəntɪd] *adj* injustificado(da).

unwavering [ʌnˈweɪvərɪŋ] *adj* [determination, feeling] firme, inquebrantable; [concentration] constante; [gaze] fijo(ja).

unwelcome [ʌnˈwelkəm] *adj* inoportuno(na).

unwell [ˌʌnˈwel] *adj*: **to be/feel unwell** estar/sentirse mal.

unwholesome [ˌʌnˈhəʊlsəm] *adj* - **1.** [unhealthy] insalubre - **2.** [unpleasant, unnatural] malsano(na).

unwieldy [ʌnˈwiːldɪ] (*comp* **-ier**, *superl* **-iest**) *adj* - **1.** [object] abultado(da); [tool] poco manejable - **2.** *fig* [system, organization] poco eficiente.

unwilling [ˌʌnˈwɪlɪŋ] *adj* no dispuesto(ta); **to be unwilling to do sthg** no estar dispuesto a hacer algo.

unwind [ˌʌnˈwaɪnd] (*pt & pp* **unwound**) ◇ *vt* desenrollar. ◇ *vi fig* [person] relajarse.

unwise [ˌʌnˈwaɪz] *adj* imprudente, poco aconsejable.

unwitting [ʌnˈwɪtɪŋ] *adj fml* inconsciente.

unwittingly [ʌnˈwɪtɪŋlɪ] *adv fml* inconscientemente, sin darse cuenta.

unworkable [ˌʌnˈwɜːkəbl] *adj* impracticable.

unworldly [ˌʌnˈwɜːldlɪ] *adj* poco mundano(na).

unworthy [ʌnˈwɜːðɪ] (*comp* **-ier**, *superl* **-iest**) *adj* [undeserving]: **to be unworthy of** no ser digno(na) de.

unwound [ˌʌnˈwaʊnd] *pt & pp* ▷ **unwind**.

unwrap [ʌnˈræp] (*pt & pp* **-ped**, *cont* **-ping**) *vt* [present] desenvolver; [parcel] desempaquetar.

unwritten law [ˌʌnˈrɪtn-] *n* ley *f* no escrita.

unyielding [ʌnˈjiːldɪŋ] *adj* inflexible.

unzip [ˌʌnˈzɪp] (*pt & pp* **-ped**, *cont* **-ping**) *vt* abrir la cremallera de.

up [ʌp] ◇ *adv* - **1.** [towards a higher position] hacia arriba; [in a higher position] arriba; **to throw sthg up** lanzar algo hacia arriba; **she's up in her room** está arriba en su cuarto; **we'll be up in just a moment** subiremos en un minuto; **we walked up to the top** subimos hasta arriba del todo; **a house up in the mountains** una casa arriba en las montañas; **put it up there** ponlo ahí arriba - **2.** [into an upright position]: **help me up** ayúdame a levantarme; **up you get!** ¡arriba! - **3.** [northwards]: **I'm going up to York next week** voy a subir a York la semana próxima; **up north** en el norte - **4.** [along a road or river] adelante; **their house is 100 metres further up** su casa está 100 metros más adelante - **5.** [close up, towards]: **to walk up to sb** acercarse a alguien. ◇ *prep* - **1.** [towards a higher position]: **we went up the mountain** subimos por la montaña; **let's go up this road** vamos por esta carretera; **I went up the stairs** subí las escaleras - **2.** [in a higher position] en lo alto de; **up a tree** en un árbol; **halfway**

up a mountain en mitad de la subida a una montaña - **3.** [at far end of] al final de; **they live up the road from us** viven más adelante en nuestra misma calle - **4.** [against current of river]: **up the Amazon** Amazonas arriba. ⬦ *adj* - **1.** [out of bed] levantado(da); **I was up at six today** hoy me levanté a las seis - **2.** [at an end] terminado(da); **time's up** se acabó el tiempo - **3.** [under repair]: **'road up'** 'carretera en obras' - **4.** *inf* [wrong]: **is something up?** ¿pasa algo?, ¿algo va mal?; **what's up?** ¿qué pasa? ⬦ *n*: **ups and downs** altibajos *mpl*. ⬦ *vt* (*pt & pp* **-ped**, *cont* **-ping**) *inf* [price, cost] subir.

◆ **up against** *prep*: **we came up against a lot of opposition** nos enfrentamos con mucha oposición; **to be up against it** vérselas y deseárselas.

◆ **up and down** ⬦ *adv*: **to jump up and down** saltar para arriba y para abajo; **to walk up and down** andar para un lado y para otro. ⬦ *prep*: **she's up and down the stairs all day** lleva todo el día subiendo y bajando por las escaleras; **she looked up and down the ranks of soldiers** inspeccionó las filas de soldados de arriba a abajo; **we walked up and down the avenue** estuvimos caminando arriba y abajo de la avenida.

◆ **up to** *prep* - **1.** [indicating level] hasta: **it could take up to six weeks** podría tardar hasta seis semanas; **it's not up to standard** no tiene el nivel necesario - **2.** [well or able enough for]: **to be up to doing sthg** sentirse con fuerzas (como) para hacer algo; **my French isn't up to much** mi francés no es gran cosa - **3.** *inf* [secretly doing something]: **what are you up to?** ¿qué andas tramando? - **4.** [indicating responsibility]: **it's not up to me to decide** no depende de mí el decidir; **it's up to you** de ti depende.

◆ **up until** *prep* hasta.

up-and-coming *adj* prometedor(ra), con futuro.

up-and-up *n*: **on the up-and-up** *UK* [improving] cada vez mejor; *US* [honest] de confianza.

upbeat ['ʌpbiːt] *adj* optimista.

upbraid [ʌp'breɪd] *vt*: **to upbraid sb (for)** reprender a alguien (por).

upbringing ['ʌp,brɪŋɪŋ] *n* educación *f*.

update [,ʌp'deɪt] *vt* actualizar.

upend [ʌp'end] *vt* volcar.

upfront [,ʌp'frʌnt] ⬦ *adj*: **to be upfront (about)** ser franco(ca) (sobre). ⬦ *adv* [in advance] por adelantado.

upgrade [,ʌp'greɪd] ⬦ *vt* [job, status] ascender, subir de categoría; [facilities] implementar mejoras a; **COMPUT** actualizar. ⬦ *vi* implementar mejoras.

upheaval [ʌp'hiːvl] *n* trastorno *m*, agitación *f*.

upheld [ʌp'held] *pt & pp* ⊳ **uphold**.

uphill [,ʌp'hɪl] ⬦ *adj* [rising] empinado(da), cuesta arriba; *fig* [difficult] arduo(dua), difícil. ⬦ *adv* cuesta arriba.

uphold [ʌp'həʊld] (*pt & pp* **-held**) *vt* sostener, apoyar.

upholster [ʌp'həʊlstər] *vt* tapizar.

upholstery [ʌp'həʊlstərɪ] *n* tapicería *f*, tapizado *m*.

upkeep ['ʌpkiːp] *n* mantenimiento *m*.

upland ['ʌplənd] *adj* de la meseta.

◆ **uplands** *npl* tierras *fpl* altas.

uplift [ʌp'lɪft] *vt* inspirar.

uplifting [ʌp'lɪftɪŋ] *adj* inspirador(ra).

up-market *adj* de clase superior, de categoría.

upon [ə'pɒn] *prep fml* en, sobre; **upon entering the room** al entrar en el cuarto; **question upon question** pregunta tras pregunta; **summer is upon us** ya tenemos el verano encima.

upper ['ʌpər] ⬦ *adj* superior. ⬦ *n* [of shoe] pala *f*.

upper class *n*: **the upper class** la clase alta.

◆ **upper-class** *adj* de clase alta.

uppercut ['ʌpəkʌt] *n* gancho *m*, uppercut *m*.

upper hand *n*: **to have/gain the upper hand (in)** llevar/empezar a llevar la ventaja (en).

uppermost ['ʌpəməʊst] *adj* - **1.** [highest] más alto(ta) - **2.** [most important]: **to be uppermost in one's mind** ser lo más importante para uno.

uppity ['ʌpətɪ] *adj inf* engreído(da), arrogante.

upright ['ʌpraɪt] ⬦ *adj* - **1.** [erect - person, chair] derecho(cha) - **2.** [standing vertically - object] vertical - **3.** *fig* [honest] recto(ta), honrado(da). ⬦ *adv* erguidamente. ⬦ *n* poste *m*.

upright piano *n* piano *m* vertical.

uprising ['ʌp,raɪzɪŋ] *n* sublevación *f*, alzamiento *m*.

uproar ['ʌprɔːr] *n* - **1.** (*U*) [commotion] alboroto *m* - **2.** [protest] escándalo *m*.

uproarious [ʌp'rɔːrɪəs] *adj* [noisy] estrepitoso(sa).

uproot [ʌp'ruːt] *vt* - **1.** [person] desplazar, mudar; **to uproot o.s.** mudarse - **2.** **BOT** [plant] desarraigar.

upset [ʌp'set] ⬦ *adj* - **1.** [distressed] disgustado(da), afectado(da); **to get upset** disgustarse - **2.** **MED**: **to have an upset stomach** sentirse mal del estómago. ⬦ *n*: **to have a stomach upset** sentirse mal del estómago. ⬦ *vt* (*pt & pp* **upset**, *cont* **-ting**) - **1.** [distress] disgustar, perturbar - **2.** [mess up] dar al traste con, estropear - **3.** [overturn, knock over] volcar.

upsetting [ʌp'setɪŋ] *adj* inquietante, perturbador(ra).

upshot ['ʌpʃɒt] *n* resultado *m*.

upside down [ˌʌpsaɪd-] <> *adj* al revés. <> *adv* al revés; **to turn sthg upside down** revolver algo, desordenar algo.

upstage [ˌʌp'steɪdʒ] *vt* eclipsar a.

upstairs [ˌʌp'steəz] <> *adj* de arriba. <> *adv* arriba. <> *n* el piso de arriba.

upstanding [ˌʌp'stændɪŋ] *adj* ejemplar.

upstart ['ʌpstɑ:t] *n* advenedizo *m*, -za *f*.

upstate [ˌʌp'steɪt] *US* <> *adj*: **upstate New York** la parte norteña del Estado de Nueva York. <> *adv* en/hacia el norte del Estado.

upstream [ˌʌp'stri:m] <> *adj*: **to be upstream (from)** estar río arriba (de). <> *adv* río arriba, corriente arriba.

upsurge ['ʌpsɜ:dʒ] *n*: **upsurge of** OR **in** aumento *m* considerable de.

upswing ['ʌpswɪŋ] *n*: **upswing (in)** mejora *f* notable OR alza *f* (en).

uptake ['ʌpteɪk] *n*: **to be quick on the uptake** cogerlas al vuelo; **to be slow on the uptake** ser un poco torpe.

uptight [ʌp'taɪt] *adj inf* tenso(sa), nervioso(sa).

up-to-date *adj* - **1.** [modern] moderno(na) - **2.** [most recent] actual, al día - **3.** [informed]: **to keep up-to-date with** mantenerse al día de.

up-to-the-minute *adj* de última hora.

uptown [ˌʌp'taʊn] *US* <> *adj* alejado(da) del centro. <> *adv* [live, work] en las afueras; [go] a las afueras.

upturn ['ʌptɜ:n] *n*: **upturn (in)** mejora *f* (de).

upturned [ˌʌp'tɜ:nd] *adj* - **1.** [nose] respingón(ona) - **2.** [upside down] volcado(da).

upward ['ʌpwəd] <> *adj* hacia arriba. <> *adv US* = **upwards**.

upwardly mobile ['ʌpwədlɪ-] *adj* ascendiendo socialmente.

upwards ['ʌpwədz], **upward** *adv* hacia arriba.
➡ **upwards of** *prep* más de.

upwind [ˌʌp'wɪnd] *adj*: **to be upwind** estar en el lado de donde sopla el viento.

Urals ['jʊərəlz] *npl*: **the Urals** los Urales.

uranium [jʊ'reɪnjəm] *n* uranio *m*.

Uranus ['jʊərənəs] *n* Urano *m*.

urban ['ɜ:bən] *adj* urbano(na).

urbane [ɜ:'beɪn] *adj* cortés, urbano(na).

urbanize, -ise ['ɜ:bənaɪz] *vt* urbanizar.

urban renewal *n* renovación *f* urbana.

urchin ['ɜ:tʃɪn] *n dated* pilluelo *m*, -la *f*.

Urdu ['ʊədu:] *n* urdu *m*.

urge [ɜ:dʒ] <> *n* impulso *m*, deseo *m*; **to have an urge to do sthg** desear ardientemente hacer algo. <> *vt* - **1.** [try to persuade]: **to urge sb to do sthg** instar a alguien a hacer algo - **2.** [advocate] recomendar encarecidamente.

urgency ['ɜ:dʒənsɪ] *n (U)* urgencia *f*.

urgent ['ɜ:dʒənt] *adj* - **1.** [pressing] urgente - **2.** [desperate] apremiante.

urgently ['ɜ:dʒəntlɪ] *adv* - **1.** [as soon as possible] urgentemente - **2.** [desperately] con insistencia.

urinal [ˌjʊə'raɪnl] *n* [place] urinario *m*; [vessel] orinal *m*.

urinary ['jʊərɪnərɪ] *adj* urinario(ria).

urinate ['jʊərɪneɪt] *vi* orinar.

urine ['jʊərɪn] *n* orina *f*.

URL (*abbr of* **uniform resource locator**) *n* COMPUT URL *m*.

urn [ɜ:n] *n* - **1.** [for ashes] urna *f* - **2.** [for tea, coffee] *cilindro o barril con grifo para servir té o café en grandes cantidades*.

Uruguay ['jʊərəgwaɪ] *n* Uruguay.

Uruguayan [ˌjʊərə'gwaɪən] <> *adj* uruguayo(ya). <> *n* uruguayo *m*, -ya *f*.

us [ʌs] *pers pron* - **1.** (direct, indirect) nos; **can you see/hear us?** ¿puedes vernos/oírnos?; **it's us** somos nosotros; **he sent us a letter** nos mandó una carta; **she gave it to us** nos lo dio - **2.** (stressed, after prep, in comparisons etc) nosotros(tras); **you can't expect us to do it** no esperarás que lo hagamos **nosotros**; **with/without us** con/sin nosotros; **they are more wealthy than us** son más ricos que nosotros; **all of us** todos (nosotros); **some of us** algunos de nosotros.

US (*abbr of* **United States**) *n* EEUU *mpl*.

USA *n* - **1.** (*abbr of* **United States of America**) EEUU *mpl* - **2.** (*abbr of* **United States Army**), *fuerzas armadas estadounidenses*.

usable ['ju:zəbl] *adj* utilizable, aprovechable.

USAF (*abbr of* **United States Air Force**) *n fuerzas aéreas estadounidenses*.

usage ['ju:zɪdʒ] *n* uso *m*.

USB port *n* COMPUT puerto *m* USB.

USDI (*abbr of* **United States Department of the Interior**) *n ministerio estadounidense del interior*.

use <> *n* [ju:s] uso *m*; **to be in use** usarse; **to be out of use** no usarse; **'out of use'** 'no funciona'; **to make use of sthg** utilizar OR aprovechar algo; **he still has the use of his legs** todavía le funcionan las piernas; **to let sb have the use of sthg** dejar a alguien usar algo; **to**

be of/no use ser útil/inútil; **what's the use (of doing sthg)?** ¿de qué sirve (hacer algo)? ◇ *aux vb* [juːs] soler, acostumbrar; **I used to go swimming** solía OR acostumbraba ir a nadar; **he used to be fat** antes estaba gordo. ◇ *vt* [juːz] - **1.** [utilize, employ] usar, emplear - **2.** [exploit] usar, manejar.
➡ **use up** *vt sep* agotar.

used *adj* - **1.** [juːzd] [dirty, second-hand] usado(da) - **2.** [juːst] [accustomed]: **to be used to** estar acostumbrado(da) a; **to get used to** acostumbrarse a.

useful ['juːsfʊl] *adj* - **1.** [handy] útil, provechoso(sa); **to come in useful** servir, ser útil - **2.** [helpful - person] valioso(sa).

usefulness ['juːsfʊlnɪs] *n (U)* utilidad *f*, valor *m*.

useless ['juːslɪs] *adj* - **1.** [gen] inútil - **2.** *inf* [hopeless] incompetente.

uselessness ['juːslɪsnɪs] *n (U)* inutilidad *f*.

user ['juːzər] *n* usuario *m*, -ria *f*.

user-friendly *adj* fácil de utilizar.

usher ['ʌʃər] ◇ *n* [at wedding] ujier *m*; [at theatre, concert] acomodador *m*, -ra *f*. ◇ *vt*: **to usher sb in** hacer pasar a alguien; **to usher sb out** acompañar a alguien hasta la puerta.

usherette [ˌʌʃə'ret] *n* acomodadora *f*.

USN (*abbr of* **United States Navy**) *n armada estadounidense*.

USS (*abbr of* **United States Ship**) *buque de guerra estadounidense*.

USSR (*abbr of* **Union of Soviet Socialist Republics**) *n*: **the (former) USSR** la (antigua) URSS.

usu. *abbr of* **usually**.

usual ['juːʒəl] *adj* habitual; **as usual** [as normal] como de costumbre; [as often happens] como siempre.

usually ['juːʒəlɪ] *adv* por regla general, normalmente; **we usually go to church on Sunday** solemos ir a misa el domingo; **more than usually** más que de costumbre.

usurp [juː'zɜːp] *vt fml* usurpar.

usury ['juːʒʊrɪ] *n fml* usura *f*.

Utah ['juːtɑː] *n* Utah.

utensil [juː'tensl] *n* utensilio *m*.

uterus ['juːtərəs] (*pl* **-ri** [-raɪ] OR **-ruses**) *n* útero *m*.

utilitarian [ˌjuːtɪlɪ'teərɪən] *adj* - **1.** [gen] utilitario(ria) - **2.** [functional] funcional.

utility [juː'tɪlətɪ] (*pl* **-ies**) *n* - **1.** [gen] utilidad *f* - **2.** [public service] servicio *m* público.
➡ **utilities** *n US* [service charges] empresa *f* de servicios públicos.

utility room *n* trascocina *f*.

utilize, -ise ['juːtəlaɪz] *vt* utilizar.

utmost ['ʌtməʊst] ◇ *adj* mayor, supremo(ma). ◇ *n*: **to do one's utmost** hacer lo imposible; **to the utmost** al máximo, a más no poder.

utopia [juː'təʊpjə] *n* utopía *f*.

utter ['ʌtər] ◇ *adj* puro(ra), completo(ta). ◇ *vt* [word] pronunciar; [sound, cry] emitir.

utterly ['ʌtəlɪ] *adv* completamente, totalmente.

U-turn *n lit & fig* giro *m* de 180°; **to do a U-turn** [in car] cambiar de sentido; *fig* dar un giro radical.

UV (*abbr of* **ultraviolet**) UV.

Uzbekistan [ʊzˌbekɪ'stɑːn] *n* (el) Uzbekistán.

v[1](*pl* **v's** OR **vs**), **V** (*pl* **V's** OR **Vs**) [viː] *n* [letter] v *f*, V *f*.

v[2] - **1.** (*abbr of* **verse**) v - **2.** (*abbr of* **volt**) v - **3.** [cross-reference] (*abbr of* **vide**) v. - **4.** *abbr of* **versus**.

vacancy ['veɪkənsɪ] (*pl* **-ies**) *n* - **1.** [job, position] vacante *f* - **2.** [room available] habitación *f* libre; **'no vacancies'** 'completo'.

vacant ['veɪkənt] *adj* - **1.** [room, chair, toilet] libre - **2.** [job, post] vacante - **3.** [look, expression] distraído(da).

vacant lot *n* terreno *m* disponible.

vacantly ['veɪkəntlɪ] *adv* distraídamente.

vacate [və'keɪt] *vt* - **1.** [job, post] dejar vacante - **2.** [room, seat, premises] desocupar.

vacation [və'keɪʃn] *US* ◇ *n* vacaciones *fpl*; **to be on vacation** estar de vacaciones. ◇ *vi* pasar las vacaciones.

vacationer [və'keɪʃənər] *n US*: **summer vacationer** veraneante *mf*.

vaccinate ['væksɪneɪt] *vt*: **to vaccinate sb (against sthg)** vacunar a alguien (de OR contra algo).

vaccination [ˌvæksɪ'neɪʃn] *n* vacunación *f*.

vaccine [*UK* 'væksiːn, *US* væk'siːn] *n* vacuna *f*.

vacillate ['væsəleɪt] *vi*: **to vacillate (between)** dudar OR vacilar (entre).

vacuum ['vækjʊəm] <> n - **1.** fig & TECH vacío m - **2.** [cleaner] aspiradora f. <> vt pasar la aspiradora por.

vacuum cleaner n aspiradora f.

vacuum-packed adj envasado(da) al vacío.

vacuum pump n bomba f neumática.

vagabond ['vægəbɒnd] n liter vagabundo m, -da f.

vagaries ['veɪgəɪz] npl fml caprichos mpl.

vagina [və'dʒaɪnə] n vagina f.

vagrancy ['veɪgrənsɪ] n vagabundeo m.

vagrant ['veɪgrənt] n vagabundo m, -da f.

vague [veɪg] adj - **1.** [imprecise] vago(ga), impreciso(sa) - **2.** [person] poco claro(ra) - **3.** [feeling] leve - **4.** [evasive] evasivo(va); **to be vague about** ser impreciso respecto a - **5.** [absent-minded] distraído(da) - **6.** [outline] borroso(sa).

vaguely ['veɪglɪ] adv - **1.** [imprecisely] vagamente - **2.** [slightly, not very] levemente - **3.** [indistinctly]: **I could vaguely make out a ship** apenas distinguía un barco a lo lejos.

vain [veɪn] adj - **1.** pej [conceited] vanidoso(sa) - **2.** [futile] vano(na).
➡ **in vain** adv en vano.

vainly ['veɪnlɪ] adv vanamente.

valance ['væləns] n - **1.** [on bed] volante m - **2.** US [over window] galería f de cortina.

vale [veɪl] n liter valle m.

valedictory [,vælɪ'dɪktərɪ] adj fml de despedida.

valentine card ['væləntaɪn-] n tarjeta f que se manda el Día de los Enamorados.

valet ['væleɪ 'vælɪt] n ayuda m de cámara.

valet parking n aparcamiento del coche realizado por un mozo.

valet service n - **1.** [for clothes] servicio m de lavandería - **2.** [for cars] lavado m y limpieza.

valiant ['væljənt] adj valeroso(sa).

valid ['vælɪd] adj - **1.** [argument, explanation] válido(da) - **2.** [ticket, driving licence] en vigor; **to be valid for six months** ser válido(da) durante seis meses.

validate ['vælɪdeɪt] vt validar, dar validez a.

validity [və'lɪdətɪ] n validez f.

Valium® ['vælɪəm] n valium® m.

valley ['vælɪ] (pl **valleys**) n valle m.

valour UK, **valor** US ['vælər] n (U) fml & liter valor m.

valuable ['væljʊəbl] adj valioso(sa).
➡ **valuables** npl objetos mpl de valor.

valuation [,væljʊ'eɪʃn] n - **1.** [pricing, estimated price] evaluación f, valuación f - **2.** [opinion, judging of worth] valoración f.

value ['vælju:] <> n valor m; **to lose/gain (in) value** disminuir/aumentar de valor; **to place**

a high value on conceder mucha importancia a; **to be good value** estar muy bien de precio; **to be value for money** estar muy bien de precio; **to take sthg/sb at face value** tomarse algo/a alguien en su sentido literal. <> vt - **1.** [estimate price of] valorar, tasar; **a necklace valued at £300** un colar valorado en 300 libras - **2.** [cherish] apreciar.
➡ **values** npl [morals] valores mpl morales, principios mpl.

value-added tax [-ædɪd-] n impuesto m sobre el valor añadido.

valued ['vælju:d] adj estimado(da), apreciado(da).

value judg(e)ment n juicio m de valor.

valuer ['væljʊər] n tasador m, -ra f.

valve [vælv] n [in pipe, tube] válvula f.

vamoose [və'mu:s] vi US inf: **vamoose!** ¡largo OR fuera de aquí!

vampire ['væmpaɪər] n vampiro m.

van [væn] n - **1.** AUT furgoneta f, camioneta f - **2.** UK RAIL furgón m.

V and A (abbr of **Victoria and Albert Museum**) n gran museo londinense de artes decorativas.

vandal ['vændl] n vándalo m, gamberro m, -rra f.

vandalism ['vændəlɪzm] n vandalismo m, gamberrismo m.

vandalize, -ise ['vændəlaɪz] vt destruir, destrozar.

vanguard ['vænɡɑ:d] n vanguardia f; **in the vanguard of** a la vanguardia de.

vanilla [və'nɪlə] <> n vainilla f. <> comp de vainilla.

vanish ['vænɪʃ] vi desaparecer.

vanishing point ['vænɪʃɪŋ-] n punto m de fuga.

vanity ['vænətɪ] n pej vanidad f.

vanquish ['væŋkwɪʃ] vt liter vencer.

vantage point ['vɑ:ntɪdʒ,pɔɪnt] n posición f ventajosa.

vapour UK, **vapor** US ['veɪpər] n (U) vapor m.

vapour trail n estela f de humo.

variable ['veərɪəbl] <> adj variable. <> n variable f.

variance ['veərɪəns] n fml: **at variance (with)** en desacuerdo (con).

variant ['veərɪənt] <> adj variante. <> n variante f.

variation [,veərɪ'eɪʃn] n: **variation (in/on)** variación f (en/sobre).

varicose veins ['værɪkəʊs-] npl varices fpl.

varied ['veərɪd] adj variado(da).

variety [vəˈraɪətɪ] (pl -ies) n - **1.** [gen] variedad f; **for a variety of reasons** por razones varias; **a wide variety of** una gran diversidad de - **2.** (U) THEAT variedades fpl.

variety show n espectáculo m de variedades.

various [ˈveərɪəs] adj - **1.** [several] varios(rias) - **2.** [different] diversos(sas).

varnish [ˈvɑːnɪʃ] <> n barniz m. <> vt [with varnish] barnizar; [with nail varnish] pintar.

varnished [ˈvɑːnɪʃt] adj barnizado(da).

vary [ˈveərɪ] (pt & pp -ied) <> vt variar. <> vi: **to vary (in/with)** variar (de/con).

varying [ˈveərɪɪŋ] adj variado(da), diverso(sa).

vascular [ˈvæskjʊlər] adj MED vascular.

vase [UK vɑːz, US veɪz] n florero m.

vasectomy [vəˈsektəmɪ] (pl -ies) n vasectomía f.

Vaseline® [ˈvæsəliːn] n vaselina® f.

vast [vɑːst] adj enorme, inmenso(sa).

vastly [ˈvɑːstlɪ] adv enormemente.

vastness [ˈvɑːstnɪs] n inmensidad f.

vat [væt] n cuba f, tina f.

VAT [væt viːeɪˈtiː] (abbr of value added tax) n IVA m.

Vatican [ˈvætɪkən] n: **the Vatican** el Vaticano.

Vatican City n Ciudad del Vaticano.

vault [vɔːlt] <> n - **1.** [in bank] cámara f acorazada - **2.** [in church] cripta f - **3.** [roof] bóveda f - **4.** [jump] salto m. <> vt saltar. <> vi: **to vault over sthg** saltar por encima de algo.

vaulted [ˈvɔːltɪd] adj abovedado(da).

vaulting horse [ˈvɔːltɪŋ-] n potro m.

vaunted [ˈvɔːntɪd] adj fml: **much vaunted** ensalzado(da).

VC n - **1.** (abbr of vice-chairman), vicepresidente - **2.** (abbr of Victoria Cross), (titular de la) máxima distinción británica al valor.

VCR (abbr of video cassette recorder) n US aparato m de vídeo.

VD (abbr of venereal disease) n ETS f.

VDU (abbr of visual display unit) n monitor m.

veal [viːl] n (U) ternera f.

veer [vɪər] vi virar.

veg [vedʒ] n inf - **1.** (abbr of vegetable); **:meat and two veg** carne y dos tipos de verdura - **2.** (abbr of vegetables) verduras fpl.

vegan [ˈviːgən] n vegetariano que no consume ningún producto que provenga de un animal, como huevos, leche etc.

vegetable [ˈvedʒtəbl] <> n - **1.** BOT vegetal m - **2.** [food] hortaliza f, legumbre f; **vegetables** verduras fpl. <> adj vegetal.

vegetable garden n huerto m.

vegetable knife n cuchillo m de verdura.

vegetable oil n aceite m vegetal.

vegetarian [ˌvedʒɪˈteərɪən] <> adj vegetariano(na). <> n vegetariano m, -na f.

vegetarianism [ˌvedʒɪˈteərɪənɪzm] n vegetarianismo m.

vegetate [ˈvedʒɪteɪt] vi pej vegetar.

vegetation [ˌvedʒɪˈteɪʃn] n vegetación f.

veggie [ˈvedʒɪ] (abbr of vegetarian) n UK inf vegetariano m, -na f.

veggieburger [ˈvedʒɪbɜːgər] n hamburguesa f vegetariana.

vehement [ˈviːəmənt] adj [person, denial] vehemente; [attack, gesture] violento(ta).

vehemently [ˈviːəməntlɪ] adv [deny, refuse] con vehemencia; [attack] violentamente.

vehicle [ˈviːəkl] n - **1.** [for transport] vehículo m - **2.** fig [medium]: **a vehicle for** un vehículo para.

vehicular [vɪˈhɪkjʊlər] adj fml [traffic] rodado(da).

veil [veɪl] <> n lit & fig velo m. <> vt cubrir con un velo.

veiled [veɪld] adj velado(da).

vein [veɪn] n - **1.** ANAT & BOT vena f - **2.** [of mineral] filón m, veta f - **3.** [style, mood] estilo m; **he continued in this vein** continuó en el mismo tono; **in a lighter vein** en un tono más ligero.

Velcro® [ˈvelkrəʊ] n velcro® m.

vellum [ˈveləm] n vitela f.

velocity [vɪˈlɒsətɪ] (pl -ies) n velocidad f.

velour [vəˈlʊər] n veludillo m.

velvet [ˈvelvɪt] <> n terciopelo m. <> comp de velludillo.

vendetta [venˈdetə] n enemistad f mortal.

vending machine [ˈvendɪŋ-] n máquina f de venta.

vendor [ˈvendɔːr] n vendedor m, -ra f.

veneer [vəˈnɪər] n [of wood] chapa f; fig [appearance] apariencia f; **a veneer of** una apariencia de.

venerable [ˈvenərəbl] adj fml venerable.

venerate [ˈvenəreɪt] vt fml & RELIG venerar.

venereal disease [vɪˈnɪərɪəl-] n enfermedad f venérea.

Venetian [vɪˈniːʃn] adj veneciano(na).

venetian blind n persiana f veneciana.

Venezuela [ˌvenɪzˈweɪlə] n Venezuela.

Venezuelan [ˌvenɪzˈweɪlən] <> adj venezolano(na). <> n venezolano m, -na f.

vengeance [ˈvendʒəns] n venganza f; **with a vengeance** con creces.

vengeful [ˈvendʒfʊl] adj liter vengativo(va).

venison [ˈvenɪzn] n carne f de venado.

venom [ˈvenəm] n [poison] veneno m; fig [spite] malevolencia f.

venomous ['venəməs] *adj* [poisonous] veneno-so(sa); *fig* [spiteful] malvado(da).

vent [vent] ◇ *n* [opening] abertura *f* de escape; [grille] rejilla *f* de ventilación; **to give vent to sthg** dar rienda suelta a algo. ◇ *vt*: **to vent sthg (on)** desahogar algo (contra).

ventilate ['ventɪleɪt] *vt* ventilar.

ventilation [ˌventɪ'leɪʃn] *n* ventilación *f*.

ventilator ['ventɪleɪtər] *n* ventilador *m*.

ventriloquist [ven'trɪləkwɪst] *n* ventrílocuo *m*, -cua *f*.

venture ['ventʃər] ◇ *n* empresa *f*; **business venture** empresa comercial. ◇ *vt* aventurar; **to venture an opinion** aventurarse a dar una opinión; **to venture to do sthg** aventurarse a hacer algo. ◇ *vi* - **1.** [go somewhere danger-ous]: **she ventured outside** se atrevió a salir - **2.** [take a risk]: **to venture into** lanzarse a.

venture capital *n* capital *m* de riesgo.

venue ['venju:] *n* lugar *m* (en que se celebra algo).

Venus ['vi:nəs] *n* [planet] Venus *m*.

veracity [və'ræsətɪ] *n fml* veracidad *f*.

veranda(h) [və'rændə] *n* veranda *f*.

verb [vɜ:b] *n* verbo *m*.

verbal ['vɜ:bl] *adj* verbal.

verbally ['vɜ:bəlɪ] *adv* verbalmente.

verbatim [vɜ:'beɪtɪm] ◇ *adj* literal. ◇ *adv* li-teralmente, palabra por palabra.

verbose [vɜ:'bəʊs] *adj fml* [person] verboso(sa); [report] prolijo(ja).

verdict ['vɜ:dɪkt] *n* - **1.** LAW veredicto *m*, fa-llo *m*; **a verdict of guilty/not guilty** un vere-dicto de culpabilidad/inocencia - **2.** [opinion]: **verdict (on)** juicio *m* OR opinión *f* (sobre).

verge [vɜ:dʒ] *n* - **1.** [edge, side] borde *m* - **2.** [brink]: **on the verge of sthg** al borde de algo; **to be on the verge of doing sthg** estar a punto de hacer algo.

◆ **verge (up)on** *vt insep* rayar en.

verger ['vɜ:dʒər] *n* sacristán *m*.

verification [ˌverɪfɪ'keɪʃn] *n* verificación *f*, comprobación *f*.

verify ['verɪfaɪ] (*pt* & *pp* **-ied**) *vt* - **1.** [check] ve-rificar, comprobar - **2.** [confirm] confirmar.

veritable ['verɪtəbl] *adj hum* & *fml* verdade-ro(ra).

vermilion [və'mɪljən] ◇ *adj* bermejo(ja). ◇ *n* bermellón *m*.

vermin ['vɜ:mɪn] *npl* [insects] bichos *mpl*, saban-dijas *fpl*; [animals] alimañas *fpl*.

vermouth ['vɜ:məθ] *n* vermut *m*.

vernacular [və'nækjʊlər] ◇ *adj* vernáculo(la). ◇ *n*: **the vernacular** la lengua vernácula.

verruca [və'ru:kə] (*pl* **-cas** OR **-cae** [-kaɪ]) *n* ve-rruga *f*.

versa ▷ vice versa.

versatile ['vɜ:sətaɪl] *adj* - **1.** [person] polifacéti-co(ca) - **2.** [machine, tool] que tiene muchos usos.

versatility [ˌvɜ:sə'tɪlətɪ] *n* - **1.** [of person] carác-ter *m* polifacético - **2.** [of machine, tool] diver-sidad *f* de usos.

verse [vɜ:s] *n* - **1.** (U) [poetry] versos *mpl*, poe-sía *f* - **2.** [stanza] estrofa *f* - **3.** [in Bible] versícu-lo *m*.

versed [vɜ:st] *adj*: **well versed in** versado(da) en.

version ['vɜ:ʃn] *n* versión *f*.

versus ['vɜ:səs] *prep* - **1.** SPORT contra - **2.** [as op-posed to] en oposición a.

vertebra ['vɜ:tɪbrə] (*pl* **-brae** [-bri:]) *n* vérte-bra *f*.

vertebrate ['vɜ:tɪbreɪt] *n* vertebrado *m*.

vertical ['vɜ:tɪkl] *adj* vertical.

vertically ['vɜ:tɪklɪ] *adv* verticalmente.

vertigo ['vɜ:tɪgəʊ] *n* vértigo *m*.

verve [vɜ:v] *n* brío *m*, entusiasmo *m*.

very ['verɪ] ◇ *adv* - **1.** [as intensifier] muy; **he's not very intelligent** no es muy inteligente; **very much** mucho; **I don't go out very often** OR much no salgo mucho; **is it good? – not very** ¿es bueno? – no mucho - **2.** [emphatic]: **the very same/next day** justo ese mismo día/al día siguiente; **the very first** el primero de todos; **the very best** el mejor (de todos); **at the very least** como muy poco; **a house of my very own** mi propia casa. ◇ *adj*: **in the very middle of the picture** en el mismísimo cen-tro del cuadro; **the very thing I was looking for** justo lo que estaba buscando; **the very thought makes me ill** sólo con pensarlo me pongo enfermo; **fighting for his very life** lu-chando por su propia vida; **the very idea!** ¡va-ya idea!

◆ **very well** *adv* muy bien; **you can't very well stop him now** es un poco tarde para im-pedírselo.

vespers ['vespəz] *n* (U) vísperas *fpl*.

vessel ['vesl] *n fml* - **1.** [boat] nave *f* - **2.** [contain-er] vasija *f*, recipiente *m*.

vest [vest] *n* - **1.** UK [undershirt] camiseta *f* - **2.** US [waistcoat] chaleco *m*.

vested interest ['vestɪd-] *n*: **vested interest (in)** intereses *mpl* creados (en).

vestibule ['vestɪbju:l] *n* - **1.** *fml* [entrance hall] vestíbulo *m* - **2.** US [on train] fuelle *m*.

vestige ['vestɪdʒ] *n fml* vestigio *m*.

vestry ['vestrɪ] (*pl* **-ies**) *n* sacristía *f*.

Vesuvius [vɪ'su:vjəs] *n* Vesubio *m*.

vet [vet] ⬦ *n* **- 1.** UK (*abbr of* **veterinary surgeon**) veterinario *m*, -ria *f* **- 2.** US (*abbr of* **veteran**) excombatiente *mf*. ⬦ *vt* (*pt & pp* **-ted**, *cont* **-ting**) someter a una investigación.

veteran ['vetrən] ⬦ *adj* veterano(na). ⬦ *n* veterano *m*, -na *f*.

veteran car *n* UK coche *m* de época (*de antes de 1905*).

Veteran's Day *n* 11 de noviembre, día en que Norteamérica conmemora el final de las dos guerras mundiales.

veterinarian [ˌvetərɪˈneərɪən] *n* US veterinario *m*, -ria *f*.

veterinary science ['vetərɪnrɪ-] *n* veterinaria *f*.

veterinary surgeon ['vetərɪnrɪ-] *n* UK *fml* veterinario *m*, -ria *f*.

veto ['viːtəʊ] ⬦ *n* (*pl* **-es**) veto *m*. ⬦ *vt* (*pt & pp* **-ed**, *cont* **-ing**) vetar.

vetting ['vetɪŋ] *n* (*U*) investigación *f* (*del historial de una persona*).

vex [veks] *vt fml* molestar.

vexed question [ˌvekst-] *n* manzana *f* de la discordia.

vg (*abbr of* **very good**) MB.

VGA (*abbr of* **video graphics array**) *n* COMPUT VGA *m*.

vgc (*abbr of* **very good condition**) m.b.e.

VHF (*abbr of* **very high frequency**) VHF.

VHS (*abbr of* **video home system**) *n* VHS *m*.

VI *abbr of* **Virgin Islands**.

via ['vaɪə] *prep* **- 1.** [travelling through] vía **- 2.** [by means of] a través de, por; **via satellite** por satélite.

viability [ˌvaɪəˈbɪlətɪ] *n* viabilidad *f*.

viable ['vaɪəbl] *adj* viable.

viaduct ['vaɪədʌkt] *n* viaducto *m*.

vibrant ['vaɪbrənt] *adj* **- 1.** [colour, light] fuerte, vivo(va) **- 2.** [voice] vibrante; [person] dinámico(ca); [city, atmosphere] animado(da).

vibrate [vaɪˈbreɪt] *vi* vibrar.

vibration [vaɪˈbreɪʃn] *n* vibración *f*.

vicar ['vɪkəʳ] *n* [in Church of England] párroco *m*; [in Roman Catholic Church] vicario *m*.

vicarage ['vɪkərɪdʒ] *n* casa *f* del párroco.

vicarious [vɪˈkeərɪəs] *adj* indirecto(ta).

vice [vaɪs] *n* **- 1.** [immorality, moral fault] vicio *m* **- 2.** [tool] torno *m* de banco.

vice- [vaɪs] *prefix* vice-.

vice-admiral *n* vicealmirante *m*.

vice-chairman *n* vicepresidente *m*.

vice-chancellor *n* UNIV rector *m*, -ra *f*.

vice-president *n* vicepresidente *m*, -ta *f*.

vice squad *n* brigada *f* antivicio.

vice versa [ˌvaɪsɪˈvɜːsə] *adv* viceversa.

vicinity [vɪˈsɪnətɪ] *n*: **in the vicinity (of)** cerca (de).

vicious ['vɪʃəs] *adj* [dog] furioso(sa); [person, ruler] cruel; [criticism, attack] depravado(da), despiadado(da).

vicious circle *n* círculo *m* vicioso.

viciousness ['vɪʃəsnɪs] *n* [of dog] ferocidad *f*; [of person, system] crueldad *f*, perversidad *f*; [of crime] brutalidad *f*.

vicissitudes [vɪˈsɪsɪtjuːdz] *npl fml* vicisitudes *fpl*.

victim ['vɪktɪm] *n* víctima *f*.

victimize, -ise ['vɪktɪmaɪz] *vt* [retaliate against] tomar represalias contra; [pick on] mortificar.

victor ['vɪktəʳ] *n liter* vencedor *m*, -ra *f*.

Victoria Cross [vɪkˈtɔːrɪə-] *n condecoración militar británica*.

Victoria Falls [vɪkˈtɔːrɪə-] *npl* las cataratas Victoria.

Victorian [vɪkˈtɔːrɪən] *adj* victoriano(na).

Victoriana [ˌvɪktɔːrɪˈɑːnə] *n* (*U*) antigüedades *fpl* victorianas.

victorious [vɪkˈtɔːrɪəs] *adj* victorioso(sa).

victory ['vɪktərɪ] (*pl* **-ies**) *n*: **victory (over)** victoria *f* (sobre).

video ['vɪdɪəʊ] ⬦ *n* (*pl* **-s**) **- 1.** [recording, medium, machine] vídeo *m* **- 2.** [cassette] videocasete *m*. ⬦ *vt* (*pt & pp* **-ed**, *cont* **-ing**) **- 1.** [using video recorder] grabar en vídeo **- 2.** [using camera] hacer un vídeo de.

video camera *n* videocámara *f*.

video cassette *n* videocasete *m*.

videoconference ['vɪdɪəʊˌkɒnfərəns] *n* videoconferencia *f*.

videoconferencing ['vɪdɪəʊˌkɒnfərənsɪŋ] *n* (*U*) videoconferencias *fpl*.

videodisc UK, **videodisk** US ['vɪdɪəʊdɪsk] *n* videodisco *m*.

video game *n* videojuego *m*, juego *m* de vídeo.

video machine *n* vídeo *m*.

video on demand *n* (*U*) TV vídeo *m* a la carta.

videophone ['vɪdɪəʊfəʊn] *n* videófono *m*, videoteléfono *m*.

videorecorder ['vɪdɪəʊrɪˌkɔːdəʳ] *n* vídeo *m*.

video recording *n* grabación *f* en vídeo.

video shop *n* tienda *f* de vídeos.

videotape ['vɪdɪəʊteɪp] *n* videocinta *f*.

vie [vaɪ] (*pt & pp* **vied**, *cont* **vying**) *vi*: **to vie (with sb for sthg/to do sthg)** competir (con alguien por algo/para hacer algo).

Viennese [ˌvɪəˈniːz] ⬦ *adj* vienés(esa). ⬦ *n* vienés *m*, -esa *f*.

Vietnam [UK ˌvjetˈnæm, US ˌvjetˈnɑːm] *n* (el) Vietnam.

Vietnamese [ˌvjetnəˈmiːz] ◇ *adj* vietnamita. ◇ *n* - **1.** [person] vietnamita *mf* - **2.** [language] vietnamita *m*.

view [vjuː] ◇ *n* - **1.** [opinion] parecer *m*, opinión *f*; **what is your view on...?** ¿cuál es tu opinión sobre...?; **in my view** en mi opinión; **to take the view that** pensar que - **2.** [attitude]: **view (of)** actitud *f* (frente a) - **3.** [scene] vista *f*, panorama *m* - **4.** [field of vision] vista *f*; **to come into view** aparecer. ◇ *vt* - **1.** [consider] ver, considerar - **2.** *fml* [examine, look at - stars etc] observar; [- house, flat] visitar, ver.
◆ **in view of** *prep* en vista de.
◆ **with a view to** *conj* con miras OR vistas a.

viewdata [ˈvjuːˌdeɪtə] *n* videotexto *m*.

viewer [ˈvjuːər] *n* - **1.** [person] espectador *m*, -ra *f* - **2.** [apparatus] visionador *m*.

viewfinder [ˈvjuːˌfaɪndər] *n* visor *m*.

viewpoint [ˈvjuːpɔɪnt] *n* - **1.** [opinion] punto *m* de vista - **2.** [place] mirador *m*.

vigil [ˈvɪdʒɪl] *n* - **1.** [watch] vigilia *f*; **to keep (a) vigil** observar vigilia - **2.** RELIG Vigilia *f*.

vigilance [ˈvɪdʒɪləns] *n* vigilancia *f*.

vigilant [ˈvɪdʒɪlənt] *adj* vigilante.

vigilante [ˌvɪdʒɪˈlæntɪ] *n* persona que extraoficialmente patrulla un área para protegerla tomándose la justicia en sus manos.

vigor US = vigour.

vigorous [ˈvɪɡərəs] *adj* enérgico(ca).

vigour UK, **vigor** US [ˈvɪɡər] *n* vigor *m*, energía *f*.

Viking [ˈvaɪkɪŋ] ◇ *adj* vikingo(ga). ◇ *n* vikingo *m*, -ga *f*.

vile [vaɪl] *adj* [person, act] vil, infame; [food, smell] repugnante; [mood] de perros.

vilify [ˈvɪlɪfaɪ] (*pt* & *pp* -**ied**) *vt* *fml* infamar.

villa [ˈvɪlə] *n* [in country] villa *f*; [in town] chalet *m*.

village [ˈvɪlɪdʒ] *n* aldea *f*, pueblecito *m*.

villager [ˈvɪlɪdʒər] *n* aldeano *m*, -na *f*.

villain [ˈvɪlən] *n* - **1.** [of film, book] malo *m*, -la *f* - **2.** *dated* [criminal] canalla *mf*, criminal *mf*.

vinaigrette [ˌvɪnɪˈɡret] *n* vinagreta *f*.

vindicate [ˈvɪndɪkeɪt] *vt* justificar; **his decision was vindicated by the result** el resultado dio la razón a su decisión.

vindication [ˌvɪndɪˈkeɪʃn] *n* justificación *f*.

vindictive [vɪnˈdɪktɪv] *adj* vengativo(va).

vine [vaɪn] *n* [on ground] vid *f*; [climbing plant] parra *f*.

vinegar [ˈvɪnɪɡər] *n* vinagre *m*.

vineyard [ˈvɪnjəd] *n* viña *f*, viñedo *m*.

vintage [ˈvɪntɪdʒ] ◇ *adj* - **1.** [wine] añejo(ja) - **2.** [classic] clásico(ca) - **3.** [outstanding]: **a vintage year** un año excepcional. ◇ *n* cosecha *f* (de vino).

vintage car *n* UK coche *m* de época (*de entre 1919 y 1930*).

vintage wine *n* vino *m* añejo.

vinyl [ˈvaɪnɪl] ◇ *n* vinilo *m*. ◇ *comp* de vinilo.

viola [vɪˈəʊlə] *n* viola *f*.

violate [ˈvaɪəleɪt] *vt* - **1.** [law, treaty, rights] violar, infringir - **2.** [peace, privacy] invadir - **3.** [tomb, grave] profanar.

violation [ˌvaɪəˈleɪʃn] *n* - **1.** [of law, treaty, rights] violación *f* - **2.** [of peace, privacy] invasión *f* - **3.** [of tomb, grave] profanación *f*.

violence [ˈvaɪələns] *n* violencia *f*.

violent [ˈvaɪələnt] *adj* - **1.** [gen] violento(ta) - **2.** [emotion, anger] intenso(sa); **to have a violent dislike for sb** sentir una enorme antipatía hacia alguien - **3.** [weather] borrascoso(sa).

violently [ˈvaɪələntlɪ] *adv* - **1.** [gen] violentamente - **2.** [dislike] intensamente - **3.** [swear, react] furiosamente.

violet [ˈvaɪələt] ◇ *adj* violeta, violado(da). ◇ *n* - **1.** [flower] violeta *f* - **2.** [colour] violeta *m*.

violin [ˌvaɪəˈlɪn] *n* violín *m*.

violinist [ˌvaɪəˈlɪnɪst] *n* violinista *mf*.

VIP (*abbr of* **very important person**) *n* VIP *mf*.

viper [ˈvaɪpər] *n* víbora *f*.

viral [ˈvaɪrəl] *adj* vírico(ca).

virgin [ˈvɜːdʒɪn] ◇ *adj liter* - **1.** [spotless] virgen - **2.** [olive oil] virgen. ◇ *n* virgen *mf*.

Virginia [vəˈdʒɪnjə] *n* Virginia.

Virgin Islands *npl*: **the Virgin Islands** las islas Vírgenes.

virginity [vəˈdʒɪnətɪ] *n* virginidad *f*.

Virgo [ˈvɜːɡəʊ] (*pl* -**s**) *n* Virgo *m*; **to be (a) Virgo** ser Virgo.

virile [ˈvɪraɪl] *adj* viril.

virility [vɪˈrɪlətɪ] *n* virilidad *f*.

virtual [ˈvɜːtʃʊəl] *adj*: **it's a virtual certainty** es casi seguro.

virtually [ˈvɜːtʃʊəlɪ] *adv* prácticamente, casi.

virtual memory *n* COMPUT memoria *f* virtual.

virtual reality *n* realidad *f* virtual.

virtue [ˈvɜːtjuː] *n* - **1.** [morality, good quality] virtud *f* - **2.** [benefit] ventaja *f*; **there's no virtue in** no hay ninguna ventaja en.
◆ **by virtue of** *prep fml* en virtud de.

virtuoso [ˌvɜːtjʊˈəʊzəʊ] (*pl* -**sos** OR -**si** [-siː]) *n* virtuoso *m*, -sa *f*.

virtuous [ˈvɜːtʃʊəs] *adj* virtuoso(sa).

virulent [ˈvɪrʊlənt] *adj lit* & *fig* virulento(ta).

virus [ˈvaɪrəs] *n* COMPUT & MED virus *m*.

visa [ˈviːzə] *n* visado *m*, visa *f Amér*.

vis-à-vis [ˌviːzɑːˈviː] *prep fml* con relación a.

viscose [ˈvɪskəʊs] *n* viscosa *f*.

viscosity [vɪˈskɒsətɪ] *n* CHEM viscosidad *f*.

viscount ['vaɪkaʊnt] n vizconde m.

viscous ['vɪskəs] adj CHEM viscoso(sa).

vise [vaɪs] n US torno m de banco.

visibility [,vɪzɪ'bɪlətɪ] n visibilidad f.

visible ['vɪzəbl] adj visible.

visibly ['vɪzəblɪ] adv visiblemente.

vision ['vɪʒn] n - 1. (U) [ability to see] visión f, vista f - 2. fig [foresight] clarividencia f - 3. [impression, dream] visión f - 4. (U) TV imagen f.

visionary ['vɪʒənrɪ] ⟨⟩ adj con visión de futuro. ⟨⟩ n (pl -ies) visionario m, -ria f.

visit ['vɪzɪt] ⟨⟩ n visita f; **to pay sb a visit** hacer una visita a alguien; **on a visit** de visita. ⟨⟩ vt visitar.

➤ **visit with** vt insep US - 1. [talk with] hablar OR charlar con - 2. [go and see] visitar, ir a ver.

visiting card ['vɪzɪtɪŋ-] n tarjeta f de visita.

visiting hours ['vɪzɪtɪŋ-] npl horas fpl de visita.

visitor ['vɪzɪtə r] n - 1. [to one's home, hospital] visita f; **we've got visitors** [at home] tenemos visitas - 2. [to museum, town etc] visitante mf.

visitors' book n libro m de visitas.

visor ['vaɪzə r] n visera f.

vista ['vɪstə] n [view] vista f, perspectiva f; fig [wide range] perspectiva.

visual ['vɪʒʊəl] adj [gen] visual; [of the eyes] ocular.

visual aids npl medios mpl visuales.

visual display unit n monitor m.

visualize, -ise ['vɪʒʊəlaɪz] vt visualizar; **to visualize (sb) doing sthg** imaginar (a alguien) haciendo algo.

visually ['vɪʒʊəlɪ] adv visualmente; **visually handicapped person** persona f con problemas visuales; **to be visually impaired** tener una discapacidad visual.

vital ['vaɪtl] adj - 1. [essential] vital, esencial - 2. [full of life] enérgico(ca), lleno(na) de vida.

vitality [vaɪ'tælətɪ] n vitalidad f.

vitally ['vaɪtəlɪ] adv sumamente.

vital statistics npl inf medidas fpl (del cuerpo de la mujer).

vitamin [UK 'vɪtəmɪn, US 'vaɪtəmɪn] n vitamina f; **vitamin C** vitamina C.

vitamin pill n pastilla f vitamínica.

vitriolic [,vɪtrɪ'ɒlɪk] adj fml virulento(ta), mordaz.

viva ['vaɪvə] = **viva voce**.

vivacious [vɪ'veɪʃəs] adj vivaz, animado(da).

vivacity [vɪ'væsətɪ] n vivacidad f.

viva voce [,vaɪvə'vəʊsɪ], **viva** n examen m oral.

vivid ['vɪvɪd] adj - 1. [colour] vivo(va) - 2. [description, memory] vívido(da).

vividly ['vɪvɪdlɪ] adv - 1. [brightly] con colores muy vivos - 2. [clearly] vívidamente.

vivisection [,vɪvɪ'sekʃn] n vivisección f.

vixen ['vɪksn] n zorra f.

viz [vɪz] (abbr of vide licet) v. gr.

VLF (abbr of very low frequency) VLF.

V-neck n - 1. [sweater, dress] jersey m con cuello de pico - 2. [neck] cuello m de pico.

VOA (abbr of **Voice of America**) n emisora gubernamental estadounidense que promociona la cultura estadounidense en el mundo.

vocabulary [və'kæbjʊlərɪ] (pl -ies) n vocabulario m.

vocal ['vəʊkl] adj - 1. [outspoken] vociferante - 2. [of the voice] vocal.

➤ **vocals** npl: **on vocals** cantando.

vocal cords npl cuerdas fpl vocales.

vocalist ['vəʊkəlɪst] n [in orchestra] vocalista mf; [in pop group] cantante mf.

vocation [vəʊ'keɪʃn] n vocación f; **to have a vocation for** tener vocación de.

vocational [vəʊ'keɪʃənl] adj profesional.

vociferous [və'sɪfərəs] adj fml ruidoso(sa).

vodka ['vɒdkə] n [drink] vodka m.

vogue [vəʊg] ⟨⟩ adj de moda. ⟨⟩ n moda f; **there's a vogue for......**está de moda; **in vogue** en boga, de moda.

voice [vɔɪs] ⟨⟩ n voz f; **to raise/lower one's voice** elevar/bajar la voz; **to keep one's voice down** no levantar la voz; **to give voice to** expresar. ⟨⟩ vt [opinion, emotion] expresar.

voice box n caja f laríngea.

voice mail n correo m de voz; **to send/receive voice mail** mandar/recibir un mensaje de correo de voz; **to check one's voice mail** verificar el correo de voz.

voice-over n voz f en off.

void [vɔɪd] ⟨⟩ adj - 1. [invalid] inválido(da), ▷ **null** - 2. fml [empty]: **void of** falto(ta) de. ⟨⟩ n liter vacío m.

voile [vɔɪl] n (U) gasa f.

vol. (abbr of **volume**) vol.

volatile [UK 'vɒlətaɪl, US 'vɒlətl] adj [situation] volátil; [person] voluble, inconstante.

vol-au-vent ['vɒləʊvɒ̃] n volován m.

volcanic [vɒl'kænɪk] adj volcánico(ca).

volcano [vɒl'keɪnəʊ] (pl -es OR -s) n volcán m.

vole [vəʊl] n campañol m.

volition [və'lɪʃn] n fml: **of one's own volition** por voluntad propia.

volley ['vɒlɪ] ⟨⟩ n (pl volleys) - 1. [of gunfire] ráfaga f, descarga f - 2. fig [rapid succession] torrente m - 3. SPORT volea f. ⟨⟩ vt volear.

volleyball ['vɒlibɔ:l] n balonvolea m, voleibol m.

volt [vəʊlt] n voltio m.

voltage ['vəʊltɪdʒ] n voltaje m.

voluble ['vɒljʊbl] adj fml locuaz.

volume ['vɒlju:m] n volumen m; **to speak volumes** decir mucho.

volume control n botón m del volumen.

voluminous [və'lu:mɪnəs] adj fml voluminoso(sa).

voluntarily [UK 'vɒləntrɪlɪ, US ,vɒlən'terəlɪ] adv voluntariamente.

voluntary ['vɒləntrɪ] adj voluntario(ria); **voluntary organization** organización f benéfica.

voluntary liquidation n liquidación f voluntaria.

voluntary redundancy n UK despido m voluntario.

volunteer [,vɒlən'tɪər] ⟨⟩ n [person who volunteers] voluntario m, -ria f. ⟨⟩ vt - **1.** [offer of one's free will]: **to volunteer to do sthg** ofrecerse para hacer algo - **2.** [information, advice] dar, ofrecer. ⟨⟩ vi - **1.** [freely offer one's services]: **to volunteer (for)** ofrecerse (para) - **2.** MIL alistarse.

voluptuous [və'lʌptjʊəs] adj voluptuoso(sa).

vomit ['vɒmɪt] ⟨⟩ n vómito m. ⟨⟩ vi vomitar.

voracious [və'reɪʃəs] adj [appetite, eater] voraz; [reader] ávido(da).

vortex ['vɔ:teks] (pl **-texes** OR **-tices** [-tɪsi:z]) n - **1.** [whirlpool, whirlwind] vórtice m - **2.** fig [of events] torbellino m.

vote [vəʊt] ⟨⟩ n - **1.** [gen] voto m; **vote for/against** voto a favor de/en contra de - **2.** [session, ballot, result] votación f; **to put sthg to the vote, to take a vote on sthg** someter algo a votación - **3.** [votes cast]: **the vote** los votos. ⟨⟩ vt - **1.** [person, leader] elegir - **2.** [choose]: **to vote to do sthg** votar hacer algo. ⟨⟩ vi: **to vote (for/against)** votar (a favor de/en contra de).

➡ **vote in** vt sep elegir.

➡ **vote out** vt sep rechazar.

vote of confidence (pl **votes of confidence**) n voto m de confianza.

vote of no confidence (pl **votes of no confidence**) n voto m de censura.

vote of thanks (pl **votes of thanks**) n palabras fpl de agradecimiento.

voter ['vəʊtər] n votante mf.

voting ['vəʊtɪŋ] n votación f.

vouch [vaʊtʃ] ➡ **vouch for** vt insep - **1.** [person] responder por - **2.** [character, accuracy] dar fe de.

voucher ['vaʊtʃər] n vale m.

vow [vaʊ] ⟨⟩ n RELIG voto m; [solemn promise] promesa f solemne. ⟨⟩ vt: **to vow to do sthg** jurar hacer algo; **to vow that** jurar que.

vowel ['vaʊəl] n vocal f.

voyage ['vɔɪɪdʒ] n viaje m.

voyeur [vwɑ:'jɜ:r] n mirón m, -ona f, voyeur mf.

voyeurism [vwɑ:'jɜ:rɪzm] n voyeurismo m.

VP abbr of vice-president.

vs abbr of versus.

VSO (abbr of Voluntary Service Overseas) n organización británica de voluntarios que ayuda a países en vías de desarrollo.

vulgar ['vʌlgər] adj - **1.** [in bad taste] ordinario(ria), vulgar - **2.** [offensive] grosero(ra), guarango(ga) Chile & R Plata.

vulgarity [vʌl'gærətɪ] n (U) - **1.** [poor taste] ordinariez f, vulgaridad f - **2.** [offensiveness] grosería f.

vulnerability [,vʌlnərə'bɪlətɪ] n vulnerabilidad f.

vulnerable ['vʌlnərəbl] adj: **vulnerable (to)** vulnerable (a).

vulture ['vʌltʃər] n lit & fig buitre m.

w (pl **w's** OR **ws**), **W** (pl **W's** OR **Ws**) ['dʌblju:] n [letter] w f, W f.

➡ **W - 1.** (abbr of west) O - **2.** (abbr of watt) w.

WA abbr of Washington.

wacky ['wækɪ] (comp **-ier**, superl **-iest**) adj inf estrafalario(ria).

wad [wɒd] n - **1.** [of paper] taco m - **2.** [of banknotes, documents] fajo m - **3.** [of cotton, cotton wool, tobacco] bola f.

wadding ['wɒdɪŋ] n relleno m.

waddle ['wɒdl] vi caminar como un pato.

wade [weɪd] vi caminar por el agua.

➡ **wade through** vt insep fig: **he was wading through the documents** le costaba mucho leer los documentos.

wadge [wɒdʒ] n UK inf [of food] tajada f; [of papers] fajo m; [of cotton wool] bola f.

wading pool ['weɪdɪŋ-] n US piscina f para niños.

wafer ['weɪfər] n [thin biscuit] barquillo m.

wafer-thin adj finísimo(ma), delgadísimo(ma).

waffle ['wɒfl] <> n - **1.** CULIN gofre m - **2.** UK inf [vague talk] paja f. <> vi enrollarse; **to waffle on about sthg** enrollarse sobre algo.

waft [wɑːft wɒft] vi flotar.

wag [wæg] (pt & pp -ged, cont -ging) <> vt menear; **the dog was wagging its tail** el perro meneaba la cola. <> vi menearse.

wage [weɪdʒ] <> n [gen] salario m; [daily] jornal m. <> vt: **to wage war** hacer la guerra.
◆ **wages** npl [gen] salario m; [daily] jornal m.

wage claim n reivindicación f salarial.

wage differential n diferencia f salarial.

wage earner [-,ɜːnər] n asalariado m, -da f.

wage freeze n congelación f salarial.

wage packet n UK - **1.** [envelope] sobre m de pago - **2.** fig [pay] paga f.

wager ['weɪdʒər] n apuesta f.

waggle ['wægl] inf <> vt menear. <> vi menearse.

waggon ['wægən] UK = **wagon.**

wagon, waggon ['wægən] n - **1.** [horse-drawn vehicle] carro m - **2.** UK RAIL vagón m.

waif [weɪf] n liter niño abandonado m, niña abandonada f.

wail [weɪl] <> n lamento m, gemido m. <> vi lamentarse, gemir.

wailing ['weɪlɪŋ] n (U) gemidos mpl, lamentos mpl.

waist [weɪst] n cintura f.

waistband ['weɪstbænd] n cinturilla f.

waistcoat ['weɪskəʊt] n esp US chaleco m.

waistline ['weɪstlaɪn] n cintura f, talle m.

wait [weɪt] <> n espera f; **to lie in wait for sb** estar al acecho de alguien. <> vi: **to wait (for sthg/sb)** esperar (algo/a alguien); **I can't wait for the holidays/to see her** estoy impaciente por comenzar las vacaciones/verla; **(just) you wait!** ¡me las pagarás!; **to wait and see** esperar y ver lo que pasa; **wait a minute OR second OR moment!** [interrupting sb] ¡espera un minuto OR segundo OR momento!; [interrupting o.s.] ¡espera!; **keys cut while you wait** se hacen llaves en el acto. <> vt US [delay] retrasar.
◆ **wait about, wait around** vi esperar.
◆ **wait for** vt insep esperar.
◆ **wait on** vt insep [serve food to] servir.
◆ **wait up** vi - **1.** quedarse despierto(ta) esperando - **2.** US: **wait up!** ¡un momento!

waiter ['weɪtər] n camarero m, mesero m Amér, mesonero m Ven, mozo m Andes & R Dom.

waiting game ['weɪtɪŋ-] n: **to play a waiting game** esperar el momento oportuno.

waiting list ['weɪtɪŋ-] n lista f de espera.

waiting room ['weɪtɪŋ-] n sala f de espera.

waitress ['weɪtrɪs] n camarera f, mesera f Amér, mesonera f Ven, moza f Andes & R Dom.

waive [weɪv] vt fml [rule] no aplicar.

waiver ['weɪvər] n LAW renuncia f.

wake [weɪk] <> n [of ship, boat] estela f; **in its wake** fig tras de sí; **in the wake of** fig tras. <> vt (pt woke OR -d, pp woken OR -d) despertar. <> vi (pt woke OR -d, pp woken OR -d) despertarse.
◆ **wake up** <> vt sep despertar. <> vi - **1.** [wake] despertarse - **2.** fig [become aware]: **to wake up to** darse cuenta de, tomar conciencia de.

waken ['weɪkən] fml <> vt despertar. <> vi despertarse.

waking hours ['weɪkɪŋ-] npl horas fpl de vigilia.

Wales [weɪlz] n (el país de) Gales.

walk [wɔːk] <> n - **1.** [way of walking] andar m, paso m - **2.** [journey on foot] paseo m; **to go for a walk** dar un paseo; **it's ten minutes' walk away** está a diez minutos andando - **3.** [route for walking]: **there are some nice walks here** se pueden hacer unas buenas caminatas por aquí. <> vt - **1.** [accompany on foot]: **to walk sb home** acompañar a alguien a casa - **2.** [dog] pasear - **3.** [streets] andar por; [distance] recorrer, andar. <> vi - **1.** [move on foot] andar, caminar - **2.** [for pleasure] pasear.
◆ **walk away with** vt insep inf llevarse.
◆ **walk in on** vt insep [meeting] interrumpir; [person] sorprender.
◆ **walk off** vt sep [headache, cramp] aliviar dando un paseo; **to walk off one's lunch/dinner** dar un paseo para bajar la comida/cena.
◆ **walk off with** vt insep inf llevarse.
◆ **walk out** vi - **1.** [leave suddenly] salirse - **2.** [go on strike] declararse en huelga.
◆ **walk out on** vt insep dejar, abandonar.
◆ **walk over** vt insep: **to walk all over sb** pisotear a alguien.

walkabout ['wɔːkə,baʊt] n UK: **to go walkabout** [Queen, president etc] pasearse entre la gente.

walker ['wɔːkər] n caminante mf, paseante mf.

walkie-talkie [,wɔːkɪ'tɔːkɪ] n walki-talki m.

walk-in adj - **1.** [cupboard] empotrado y suficientemente grande para entrar en él - **2.** US [easy] fácil.

walking ['wɔːkɪŋ] ⇔ n (U) [for sport] marcha f; [for pleasure] andar m; **he does a lot of walking** camina mucho. ⇔ adj: **he's a walking disaster** hum es un desastre andante.

walking shoes npl zapatos mpl para caminar.

walking stick n bastón m.

Walkman® ['wɔːkmən] n walkman® m.

walk of life (pl **walks of life**) n: **people from all walks of life** gente de toda condición.

walk-on adj de figurante.

walkout ['wɔːkaʊt] n huelga f.

walkover ['wɔːkˌəʊvəʳ] n victoria f fácil.

walkup [':wɔːkʌp] n US [building] edificio m sin ascensor f.

walkway ['wɔːkweɪ] n [on ship, machine] pasarela f; [between buildings] paso m.

wall [wɔːl] n - **1.** [inside building, of cell, stomach] pared f - **2.** [outside] muro m; **to come up against a brick wall** llegar a un callejón sin salida; **to drive sb up the wall** volverle loco a alguien; **it's like talking to a brick wall** le entra por un oído y le sale por el otro.

wallaby ['wɒləbɪ] (pl **-ies**) n ualabí m.

wallchart ['wɔːltʃɑːt] n (gráfico m) mural m.

wall cupboard n armario m de pared.

walled [wɔːld] adj amurallado(da).

wallet ['wɒlɪt] n cartera f, billetera f.

wallflower ['wɔːlˌflaʊəʳ] n - **1.** [plant] alhelí m - **2.** inf fig [person] persona tímida que queda al margen de una fiesta.

wallop ['wɒləp] inf ⇔ n [to person] torta f; [to thing] golpazo m. ⇔ vt [child] pegar una torta a; [ball] golpear fuerte.

wallow ['wɒləʊ] vi - **1.** [in liquid] revolcarse - **2.** [in emotion]: **to wallow in self-pity** revolcarse en la autocompasión.

wall painting n mural m.

wallpaper ['wɔːlˌpeɪpəʳ] ⇔ n - **1.** [on walls] papel m pintado - **2.** COMPUT papel m tapiz. ⇔ vt empapelar.

Wall Street n Wall Street f, zona financiera neoyorquina.

wall-to-wall adj: **wall-to-wall carpet** moqueta f.

wally ['wɒlɪ] (pl **-ies**) n UK inf majadero m, -ra f, imbécil mf.

walnut ['wɔːlnʌt] n - **1.** [nut] nuez f - **2.** [wood, tree] nogal m.

walrus ['wɔːlrəs] (pl **walrus** OR **-es**) n morsa f.

waltz [wɔːls] ⇔ n vals m. ⇔ vi - **1.** [dance] bailar el vals - **2.** inf dated [walk confidently]: **to waltz in/out** entrar/salir tan fresco(ca).

wan [wɒn] (comp **-ner**, superl **-nest**) adj pálido(da).

wand [wɒnd] n: **(magic) wand** varita f mágica.

wander ['wɒndəʳ] vi vagar; **my mind kept wandering** se me iba la mente en otras cosas.

wanderer ['wɒndərəʳ] n errante mf.

wandering ['wɒndərɪŋ] adj [musician, nomad] ambulante.

wanderlust ['wɒndəlʌst] n pasión f por viajar.

wane [weɪn] ⇔ n: **on the wane** en el ocaso. ⇔ vi [influence, interest] disminuir, decrecer.

wangle ['wæŋgl] vt inf agenciarse, conseguir.

wanna ['wɒnə] esp US - **1.** (abbr of = want a), = **want** - **2.** (abbr of want to), ⊏> **want**.

want [wɒnt] ⇔ n fml - **1.** [need] necesidad f - **2.** [lack] falta f; **for want of** por OR a falta de - **3.** [deprivation] indigencia f, miseria f. ⇔ vt - **1.** [desire] querer; **to want to do sthg** querer hacer algo; **to want sb to do sthg** querer que alguien haga algo - **2.** inf [need - subj: person] tener que; [- subj: thing] necesitar, requerir; **you want to be more careful** tienes que tener más cuidado; **the house wants cleaning** hace falta hacer limpieza en la casa.

want ad n US inf anuncio m por palabras.

wanted ['wɒntɪd] adj: **to be wanted (by the police)** ser buscado(da) (por la policía).

wanting ['wɒntɪŋ] adj fml deficiente; **to be wanting in sthg** carecer de algo; **to be found wanting** no dar la talla.

wanton ['wɒntən] adj fml gratuito(ta), sin motivo.

WAP [wæp] (abbr of **wireless application protocol**) n WAP m.

war [wɔːʳ] ⇔ n lit & fig guerra f; **to go to war** entrar en guerra; **to be at war** estar en guerra; **the war on drugs** la guerra contra las drogas; **to have been in the wars** UK estar maltrecho. ⇔ vi (pt & pp **-red**, cont **-ring**) estar en guerra.

War., Warks. (abbr of **Warwickshire**), condado inglés.

warble ['wɔːbl] vi liter [bird] trinar, gorjear.

war crime n crimen m de guerra.

war criminal n criminal mf de guerra.

war cry n [in battle] grito m de guerra.

ward [wɔːd] n - **1.** [in hospital] sala f - **2.** UK POL distrito m electoral - **3.** LAW pupilo m, -la f.
◆ **ward off** vt insep protegerse de.

war dance n danza f guerrera.

warden ['wɔːdn] n - **1.** [of park] guarda mf - **2.** UK [of youth hostel, hall of residence] encargado m, -da f - **3.**: **(traffic) warden** ≃ guardia mf de tráfico - **4.** US [prison governor] director m, -ra f.

warder ['wɔːdəʳ] n [in prison] carcelero m, -ra f.

ward of court *n* menor *mf* bajo tutela judicial.

wardrobe ['wɔːdrəʊb] *n* - **1.** [piece of furniture] armario *m*, guardarropa *m* - **2.** [collection of clothes] guardarropa *m*, vestuario *m*.

warehouse (['weəhaʊs], *pl* [-haʊzɪz]) *n* almacén *m*.

wares [weəz] *npl liter* mercancías *fpl*.

warfare ['wɔːfeəʳ] *n (U)* guerra *f*.

war game *n* - **1.** [military exercise] maniobras *fpl*, ejercicio *m* de maniobras - **2.** [game of strategy] juego *m* de estrategia militar.

warhead ['wɔːhed] *n* ojiva *f*, cabeza *f*.

warily ['weərəlɪ] *adv* con cautela, cautelosamente.

Warks. = War.

warlike ['wɔːlaɪk] *adj* belicoso(sa).

warm [wɔːm] <> *adj* - **1.** [pleasantly hot - gen] caliente; [- weather, day] caluroso(sa); [lukewarm] tibio(bia), templado(da); **it's/I'm warm** hace/tengo calor; **to get warm** [person, room] calentarse; **they tried to keep warm** intentaron mantenerse calientes; **are you warm enough?** no tendrás frío, ¿verdad? - **2.** [clothes etc] que abriga - **3.** [colour, sound] cálido(da) - **4.** [friendly - person, atmosphere, smile] afectuoso(sa); [- congratulations] efusivo(va). <> *vt* calentar.

◆ **warm over** *vt sep US* calentar.

◆ **warm to** *vt insep* [person, place] tomar simpatía a; **we warmed to the idea at once** en seguida nos hizo gracia la idea.

◆ **warm up** <> *vt sep* calentar. <> *vi* - **1.** [gen] entrar en calor; [weather, room, engine] calentarse - **2.** [sportsperson] calentar.

warm-blooded [-'blʌdɪd] *adj* de sangre caliente.

war memorial *n* monumento *m* a los caídos.

warm front *n* frente *m* cálido.

warm-hearted [-'hɑːtɪd] *adj* afectuoso(sa), cariñoso(sa).

warmly ['wɔːmlɪ] *adv* - **1.** [in warm clothes]: **to dress warmly** vestirse con ropa de abrigo - **2.** [in a friendly way] efusivamente, calurosamente.

warmness ['wɔːmnɪs] *n* [friendliness] cordialidad *f*, efusión *f*.

warmonger ['wɔː,mʌŋgəʳ] *n* belicista *mf*.

warmth [wɔːmθ] *n* - **1.** [heat] calor *m* - **2.** [of clothes] abrigo *m* - **3.** [friendliness] cordialidad *f*, efusión *f*.

warm-up *n* precalentamiento *m*.

warn [wɔːn] <> *vt* prevenir, advertir; **to warn sb of sthg** prevenir a alguien algo; **to warn sb**

not to do sthg, warn sb against doing sthg advertir a alguien que no haga algo. <> *vi*: **to warn of sthg** prevenir contra algo.

warning ['wɔːnɪŋ] <> *adj* de aviso, de advertencia. <> *n* aviso *m*, advertencia *f*; **to give sb a warning** hacer una advertencia a alguien; **without warning** sin previo aviso.

warning light *n* piloto *m*.

warning triangle *n UK* triángulo *m* de avería.

warp [wɔːp] *vi* alabearse, combarse.

warpath ['wɔːpɑːθ] *n*: **to be** OR **go on the warpath** *fig* estar buscando guerra.

warped [wɔːpt] *adj* - **1.** [wood] combado(da), alabeado(da) - **2.** [person] retorcido(da).

warrant ['wɒrənt] <> *n* orden *f* OR mandamiento *m* judicial. <> *vt fml* merecer.

warrant officer *n* grado intermedio entre suboficial y oficial.

warranty ['wɒrəntɪ] (*pl* -ies) *n* garantía *f*; **to be under warranty** estar en garantía.

warren ['wɒrən] *n* red *f* de madrigueras.

warring ['wɔːrɪŋ] *adj* contendiente.

warrior ['wɒrɪəʳ] *n* guerrero *m*, -ra *f*.

warship ['wɔːʃɪp] *n* buque *m* de guerra.

wart [wɔːt] *n* verruga *f*.

wartime ['wɔːtaɪm] *n* tiempos *mpl* de guerra.

war widow *n* viuda *f* de guerra.

wary ['weərɪ] (*comp* -ier, *superl* -iest) *adj*: **wary (of)** receloso(sa) (de).

was (*weak form* [wəz], *strong form* [wɒz]) *pt* ⊳ **be**.

wash [wɒʃ] <> *n* - **1.** [act of washing] lavado *m*, lavada *f*; **to have a wash** lavarse; **to give sthg a wash** lavar algo - **2.** [things to wash] ropa *f* para lavar, ropa sucia - **3.** [from boat] estela *f*. <> *vt* - **1.** [gen] lavar; [hands, face] lavarse; **she's washing her hair** se está lavando el pelo - **2.** [carry - subj: waves etc] arrastrar, llevarse; **it was washed ashore** el mar lo arrastró hasta la costa. <> *vi* - **1.** [clean oneself] lavarse - **2.** [waves, oil]: **to wash over sthg** bañar algo.

◆ **wash away** *vt sep* - **1.** [water, waves] llevarse, barrer - **2.** [dirt] quitar.

◆ **wash down** *vt sep* - **1.** [food] regar, rociar - **2.** [clean] lavar.

◆ **wash out** *vt sep* - **1.** [stain, dye] quitar lavando - **2.** [container] enjuagar.

◆ **wash up** <> *vt sep* - **1.** *UK* [dishes] lavar, fregar - **2.** [sea, river]: **to wash sthg up on the shore** arrojar algo a la playa. <> *vi* - **1.** *UK* [wash the dishes] fregar OR lavar los platos - **2.** *US* [wash o.s.] lavarse.

washable ['wɒʃəbl] *adj* lavable.

wash-and-wear *adj* de lava y pon.

washbasin UK ['wɒʃ,beɪsn], **washbowl** US ['wɒʃbəʊl] n lavabo m.

washcloth ['wɒʃ,klɒθ] n US toallita f para lavarse la cara.

washed-out [wɒʃt-] adj - **1.** [pale] pálido(da), descolorido(da) - **2.** [exhausted] rendido(da).

washed-up [wɒʃt-] adj inf [person] acabado(da); [business, project] fracasado(da).

washer ['wɒʃər] n - **1.** TECH arandela f - **2.** [washing machine] lavadora f.

washer-dryer n lavadora-secadora f.

washing ['wɒʃɪŋ] n (U) - **1.** [operation] colada f; **to do the washing** hacer la colada - **2.** [clothes - dirty] ropa f sucia OR para lavar; [- clean] colada f; **to hang up the washing** tender la colada.

washing line n tendedero m.

washing machine n lavadora f.

washing powder n UK detergente m, jabón m en polvo.

Washington ['wɒʃɪŋtən] n - **1.** [state]: **Washington State** Estado m de Washington - **2.** [town]: **Washington D.C.** ciudad f de Washington.

washing-up n - **1.** UK [crockery, pans etc] platos mpl para fregar - **2.** [operation] fregado m; **to do the washing-up** fregar los platos.

washing-up liquid n UK lavavajillas m inv.

washout ['wɒʃaʊt] n inf desastre m, fracaso m.

washroom ['wɒʃrʊm] n US lavabo m, aseos mpl.

wasn't [wɒznt] (abbr of = was not), ▷ be.

wasp [wɒsp] n [insect] avispa f.

Wasp, WASP [wɒsp] (abbr of White Anglo-Saxon Protestant) n inf persona de raza blanca, origen anglosajón y protestante.

WASP ▬▬▬▬▬▬▬▬▬▬▬▬▬▬▬

⚏ Este término se usa en Estados Unidos, a veces con tono despectivo, para referirse a una persona de raza blanca con antepasados protestantes originarios del norte de Europa, principalmente del Reino Unido. A pesar de la imagen de crisol de culturas que proyecta el país americano, los WASP han constituido tradicionalmente la élite social y política, manteniendo el monopolio del poder. Tanto ha sido así que la victoria de John F. Kennedy, católico de origen irlandés, en las elecciones a la presidencia de 1962, fue vista como un hito histórico, signo de que las personas de un origen social o étnico distinto ya no eran ciudadanos de segunda.

waspish ['wɒspɪʃ] adj mordaz, punzante.

wastage ['weɪstɪdʒ] n desperdicio m.

waste [weɪst] ◇ adj [land] yermo(ma); [material, fuel] de desecho. ◇ n - **1.** [misuse, incomplete use] desperdicio m, derroche m; **to go to waste** perderse; **a waste of time** una pérdida de tiempo - **2.** (U) [refuse] desperdicios mpl; [chemical, toxic etc] residuos mpl. ◇ vt [time] perder; [money] malgastar, derrochar; [food, energy, opportunity] desperdiciar; **it would be wasted on me** no sabría aprovecharlo.

➤ **wastes** npl liter yermos mpl.

wastebasket US = **wastepaper basket**.

waste disposal unit n triturador m de basuras.

wasteful ['weɪstfʊl] adj derrochador(ra).

waste ground n (U) descampados mpl.

wasteland ['weɪst,lænd] n yermo m.

waste paper n papeles mpl viejos OR usados.

wastepaper basket [,weɪst'peɪpər-], **wastepaper bin** [,weɪst'peɪpər-], **wastebasket** US ['weɪst,bɑːskɪt] n papelera f.

watch [wɒtʃ] ◇ n - **1.** [timepiece] reloj m - **2.** [act of watching]: **to keep watch** estar de guardia; **to keep watch on sthg/sb** vigilar algo/a alguien - **3.** MIL [group of people] guardia f. ◇ vt - **1.** [look at - gen] mirar; [- sunset] contemplar; [- football match, TV] ver - **2.** [spy on] vigilar - **3.** [be careful about] tener cuidado con, vigilar; **watch what you say** ten cuidado con lo que dices; **watch it!** inf ¡cuidado!, ¡ojo! ◇ vi mirar, observar.

➤ **watch out** vi tener cuidado, estar atento(ta).

➤ **watch over** vt insep [look after] vigilar.

watchdog ['wɒtʃdɒg] n - **1.** [dog] perro m guardián - **2.** fig [organization] comisión f de vigilancia.

watchful ['wɒtʃfʊl] adj atento(ta).

watchmaker ['wɒtʃ,meɪkər] n relojero m, -ra f.

watchman ['wɒtʃmən] (pl -men [-mən]) n vigilante m, guarda m, rondín m Andes.

watchword ['wɒtʃwɜːd] n lema m.

water ['wɔːtər] ◇ n - **1.** [gen] agua f; **to pour OR throw cold water on** echar un jarro de agua fría sobre; **that's water under the bridge** esto es agua pasada - **2.** [urine]: **to pass water** orinar. ◇ vt regar. ◇ vi - **1.** [eyes]: **my eyes are watering** me lloran los ojos - **2.** [mouth]: **my mouth is watering** se me hace la boca agua.

➤ **waters** npl aguas fpl.

➤ **water down** vt sep - **1.** [dilute] diluir, aguar - **2.** pej [moderate] suavizar.

water bed n cama f de agua.

water bird n ave f acuática.

water biscuit n tipo de galleta sin azúcar.

waterborne ['wɔːtəbɔːn] adj [disease] transmitido(da) a través del agua.

water bottle n cantimplora f.

water buffalo n búfalo m de agua.

water cannon n cañón m de agua.

water chestnut n castaña f de agua.

watercolour ['wɔːtəˌkʌlər] n acuarela f.

water-cooled [-ˌkuːld] adj refrigerado(da) por agua.

watercourse ['wɔːtəkɔːs] n cauce m.

watercress ['wɔːtəkres] n berro m.

watered-down [ˌwɔːtəd-] adj pej suavizado(da).

waterfall ['wɔːtəfɔːl] n cascada f, salto m de agua.

waterfront ['wɔːtəfrʌnt] n muelle m.

water heater n calentador m de agua.

waterhole ['wɔːtəhəʊl] n balsa f (donde acuden a beber los animales).

watering can ['wɔːtərɪŋ-] n regadera f.

water jump n ría f (en carreras de caballos).

water level n nivel m del agua.

water lily n nenúfar m.

waterline ['wɔːtəlaɪn] n NAUT línea f de flotación.

waterlogged ['wɔːtəlɒgd] adj inundado(da).

water main n cañería f principal.

watermark ['wɔːtəmɑːk] n - **1.** [in paper] filigrana f - **2.** [showing water level] marca f del nivel del agua.

watermelon ['wɔːtəˌmelən] n sandía f.

water pipe n [in house, building] tubería f OR cañería f de agua.

water pistol n pistola f de agua.

water polo n water-polo m, polo m acuático.

waterproof ['wɔːtəpruːf] <> adj impermeable. <> n impermeable m. <> vt impermeabilizar.

water rates npl UK tarifa f del agua.

water-resistant adj resistente al agua.

watershed ['wɔːtəʃed] n fig momento m decisivo.

waterside ['wɔːtəsaɪd] <> adj ribereño(ña). <> n: **the waterside** la orilla.

water skiing n esquí m acuático.

water-soluble adj soluble en agua.

water supply n reserva f de agua.

water table n nivel m del agua.

water tank n reserva f de agua.

watertight ['wɔːtətaɪt] adj - **1.** [waterproof] hermético(ca) - **2.** fig [agreement, plan] perfecto(ta); [argument, excuse] irrecusable, irrebatible.

water tower n arca f de agua.

waterway ['wɔːtəweɪ] n vía f navegable.

waterworks ['wɔːtəwɜːks] (pl **waterworks**) n [building] central f de agua.

watery ['wɔːtərɪ] adj - **1.** [food] soso(sa); [drink] aguado(da) - **2.** [pale] desvaído(da), pálido(da).

watt [wɒt] n vatio m.

wattage ['wɒtɪdʒ] n potencia f en vatios.

wave [weɪv] <> n - **1.** [of hand] ademán m OR señal f (con la mano) - **2.** [of water] ola f - **3.** [of emotion, nausea, panic] arranque m; [of immigrants, crime etc] oleada f - **4.** [of light, sound, heat] onda f - **5.** [in hair] ondulación f. <> vt - **1.** [move about as signal] agitar - **2.** [signal to] hacer señales OR señas a; **she waved them in** les hizo una señal para que entraran. <> vi - **1.** [with hand - in greeting] saludar con la mano; [- to say goodbye] decir adiós con la mano; **to wave at** OR **to sb** saludar a alguien con la mano; **he waved hello to us** nos saludó con la mano - **2.** [flag] ondear; [trees] agitarse.

◆ **wave aside** vt sep fig [dismiss] desechar.

◆ **wave down** vt sep hacer señas para que se pare.

waveband ['weɪvbænd] n banda f de frecuencias.

wavelength ['weɪvleŋθ] n longitud f de onda; **to be on the same wavelength** fig estar en la misma onda.

waver ['weɪvər] vi - **1.** [falter - resolution, confidence] flaquear; [- person] vacilar, dudar - **2.** [hesitate] dudar, vacilar - **3.** [fluctuate] oscilar.

wavy ['weɪvɪ] (comp **-ier**, superl **-iest**) adj ondulado(da).

wax [wæks] <> n cera f. <> vt encerar. <> vi dated & hum [become] ponerse; **to wax and wane** subir y bajar.

waxen ['wæksən] adj [pale] pálido(da).

wax paper n esp US papel m de cera.

waxworks ['wæksˌwɜːks] (pl **waxworks**) n museo m de cera.

way [weɪ] <> n - **1.** [manner, method] manera f, modo m; **ways and means** medios mpl; **in the same way** del mismo modo, igualmente; **this/that way** así; **in a way** en cierto modo; **in a big/small way** a gran/pequeña escala; **she has fallen for him in a big way** está locamente enamorada de él; **to get** OR **have one's way** salirse uno con la suya; **to have everything one's own way** salirse siempre uno con la suya; **to have a way with people** tener don de gentes; **to have a way with words** tener un pico de oro; **he had a way of making people laugh** tenía la costumbre de hacer reír a la gente; **to be in a bad way** estar bastante mal - **2.** [route, path] camino m; **to lose one's way** perderse; **to find one's way around** orientarse; **the way back** OR **home** el camino de vuelta a casa; **way in** entrada *f*; **way out** salida *f*; **it's out of my way** no me pilla de camino; **it's out of the way** [place] está algo aislado; **on the** OR **on one's way** de camino; **I'm on my way** voy de camino; **across** OR **over the way** enfrente; **to be under way** [meeting] estar en marcha; **to get under way** [meeting] ponerse en marcha; **to be in the way** estar en medio; **to get in the way** ponerse en medio; **to get out of the way** quitarse de en medio; **to get sthg out of the way** [task] quitarse algo de encima; **to go out of one's way to do sthg** tomarse muchas molestias para hacer algo; **to keep out of the way** mantenerse alejado; **to keep out of sb's way** mantenerse alejado de alguien; **to make one's way to** dirigirse hacia; **to make way for** dar paso a; **to stand in sb's way** *fig* interponerse en el camino de alguien; **to work one's way to** conseguir llegar a **- 3.** [direction] dirección *f*; **come this way** ven por aquí; **go that way** ve por ahí; **which way do we go?** ¿hacia dónde vamos?; **which way is it to the cathedral?** ¿por dónde se va a la catedral?; **the wrong way up** OR **round** al revés; **the right way up** OR **round** del derecho **- 4.** [distance]: **all the way** todo el camino OR trayecto; **we're with you all the way** *fig* te apoyamos incondicionalmente; **most of the way** casi todo el camino OR trayecto; **it's a long way away** está muy lejos; **we have a long way to go** queda mucho camino por recorrer; **to go a long way towards doing sthg** *fig* contribuir enormemente a hacer algo; **we've come a long way since then** *fig* hemos avanzado mucho desde entonces

▸▸▸ **to give way** [under weight, pressure] ceder; **'give way'** UK AUT 'ceda el paso'; **no way!** ¡ni hablar! ◇ *adv inf* [far] mucho; **it's way too big** es tela de grande.

◆ **ways** *npl* [customs, habits] costumbres *fpl*, hábitos *mpl*; **sb's funny little ways** las curiosas costumbres de alguien.

◆ **by the way** *adv* por cierto.

◆ **by way of** *prep* **- 1.** [via] (pasando) por **- 2.** [as a sort of] a modo de, como.

◆ **in the way of** *prep*: **what do you have in the way of wine?** ¿qué clases de vino tiene?

waylay [ˌweɪˈleɪ] (*pt & pp* -**laid**) *vt* abordar.

way of life *n* modo *m* de vida.

wayside [ˈweɪsaɪd] *n* [roadside] borde *m* del camino; **to fall by the wayside** *fig* quedarse a mitad de camino.

wayward [ˈweɪwəd] *adj* [person, behaviour] incorregible.

WC (*abbr of* water closet) WC.

we [wiː] *pers pron* nosotros *mpl*, -tras *f*; **we can't do it** nosotros no podemos hacerlo; **here**

we are aquí estamos; **as we say in France** como decimos en Francia; **we British** nosotros los británicos.

weak [wiːk] *adj* **- 1.** [gen] débil; **to grow weak** debilitarse **- 2.** [material, structure] frágil **- 3.** [argument, tea etc] flojo(ja) **- 4.** [lacking knowledge, skill]: **to be weak on sthg** estar flojo(ja) en algo.

weaken [ˈwiːkn] ◇ *vt* debilitar. ◇ *vi* **- 1.** [become less determined] ceder, flaquear **- 2.** [physically] debilitarse.

weak-kneed [-ˈniːd] *adj inf pej* pusilánime.

weakling [ˈwiːklɪŋ] *n pej* enclenque *mf*.

weakly [ˈwiːklɪ] *adv* débilmente.

weak-minded [-ˈmaɪndɪd] *adj* débil de carácter.

weakness [ˈwiːknɪs] *n* **- 1.** [gen] debilidad *f*; **to have a weakness for sthg** tener debilidad por algo **- 2.** [imperfect point] defecto *m*.

weal [wiːl] *n* verdugón *m*.

wealth [welθ] *n* **- 1.** [riches] riqueza *f* **- 2.** [abundance] profusión *f*, abundancia *f*; **a wealth of sthg** abundancia de algo.

wealth tax *n* UK impuesto *m* sobre el patrimonio.

wealthy [ˈwelθɪ] (*comp* -**ier**, *superl* -**iest**) *adj* rico(ca), platudo(da) *Amér*.

wean [wiːn] *vt* **- 1.** [from mother's milk] destetar **- 2.** [discourage]: **to wean sb from** OR **off sthg** apartar gradualmente a alguien de algo.

weapon [ˈwepən] *n* arma *f*.

weaponry [ˈwepənrɪ] *n* (*U*) armamento *m*.

weapons of mass destruction *npl* armas *fpl* de destrucción masiva.

wear [weə^r] ◇ *n* (*U*) **- 1.** [use] uso *m*; **I've had a lot of wear out of this jacket** le he sacado mucho partido a esta chaqueta; **to be the worse for wear** [thing] estar deteriorado; [person] estar hecho un trapo **- 2.** [damage] desgaste *m*; **wear and tear** desgaste **- 3.** [type of clothes] ropa *f*; **children's wear** ropa de niños; **evening wear** ropa de noche. ◇ *vt* (*pt* **wore**, *pp* **worn**) **- 1.** [clothes, hair, perfume] llevar; [shoes] calzar; **to wear red** vestirse de rojo **- 2.** [damage] desgastar; **to wear a hole in sthg** acabar haciendo un agujero en algo. ◇ *vi* (*pt* **wore**, *pp* **worn**) **- 1.** [deteriorate] desgastarse **- 2.** [last]: **to wear well/badly** durar mucho/poco

▸▸▸ **to wear thin** [joke] dejar de ser gracioso.

◆ **wear away** ◇ *vt sep* desgastar. ◇ *vi* desgastarse.

◆ **wear down** ◇ *vt sep* **- 1.** [reduce size of] desgastar **- 2.** [weaken] agotar. ◇ *vi* desgastarse.

◆ **wear off** *vi* desaparecer, disiparse.

◆ **wear on** *vi* transcurrir.

◆ **wear out** ◇ *vt sep* - **1.** [shoes, clothes] gastar - **2.** [person] agotar. ◇ *vi* gastarse.

wearable ['weərəbl] *adj* que se puede llevar.

wearily ['wɪərɪlɪ] *adv* fatigosamente.

weariness ['wɪərɪnɪs] *n* fatiga *f*, cansancio *m*.

wearing ['weərɪŋ] *adj* [exhausting] fatigoso(sa).

weary ['wɪərɪ] (*comp* -ier, *superl* -iest) *adj* fatigado(da), cansado(da); **to be weary of sthg/of doing sthg** estar cansado de algo/de hacer algo.

weasel ['wiːzl] *n* comadreja *f*.

weather ['weðər] ◇ *n* tiempo *m*; **what's the weather like?** ¿qué tal tiempo hace?; **to make heavy weather of sthg** complicar algo innecesariamente; **to be under the weather** no encontrarse muy bien. ◇ *vt* [crisis etc] superar. ◇ *vi*: **to weather the well** ser resistente.

weather-beaten [-,biːtn] *adj* - **1.** [face, skin] curtido(da) - **2.** [building, stone] deteriorado(da) *(por la intemperie)*.

weathercock ['weðəkɒk] *n* veleta *f*.

weathered ['weðəd] *adj* deteriorado(da) *(por la intemperie)*.

weather forecast *n* parte *m* meteorológico, pronóstico *m* del tiempo.

weatherman ['weðəmæn] (*pl* -men [-men]) *n* hombre *m* del tiempo.

weather map *n* mapa *m* del tiempo.

weatherproof ['weðəpruːf] *adj* [clothing] impermeable; [building] resistente a la intemperie.

weather report *n* [on radio, TV] parte *m* meteorológico; [in newspaper] información *f* meteorológica.

weather vane [-veɪn] *n* veleta *f*.

weave [wiːv] ◇ *n* tejido *m*. ◇ *vt* (*pt* wove, *pp* woven) - **1.** [using loom] tejer - **2.** [move along]: **to weave one's way (through)** colarse (por entre). ◇ *vi* (*pt* wove, *pp* woven) [move]: **to weave through** colarse por entre; **to weave in and out of the traffic** avanzar zigzagueando en el tráfico.

weaver ['wiːvər] *n* tejedor *m*, -ra *f*.

weaving ['wiːvɪŋ] *n* tejeduría *f*.

web [web] *n* - **1.** [cobweb] telaraña *f* - **2.** *fig* [of lies etc] urdimbre *f*, entramado *m* - **3.** COMPUT: **the Web** la Web.

webbed [webd] *adj* palmeado(da).

webbing ['webɪŋ] *n* (U) reps *m inv*.

web browser *n* COMPUT navegador *m*.

webcam ['webkæm] *n* cámara *f* web.

web designer *n* diseñador *m*, -ra *f* de páginas Web.

web-footed [-fʊtɪd] *adj* palmípedo(da).

web page *n* página *f* web.

web site *n* sitio *m* Web.

wed [wed] (*pt & pp* -ded OR wed) *liter* ◇ *vt* desposar. ◇ *vi* desposarse.

we'd [wiːd] - **1.** (*abbr of* = we had), ▷ **have** - **2.** (*abbr of* = we would), ▷ **would**.

Wed. (*abbr of* Wednesday) miérc.

wedded ['wedɪd] *adj* [committed]: **wedded to** sthg entregado(da) a algo.

wedding ['wedɪŋ] *n* boda *f*, casamiento *m*.

wedding anniversary *n* aniversario *m* de boda.

wedding cake *n* tarta *f* nupcial, pastel *m* de bodas, torta *f* de boda OR matrimonio OR novios *Andes, Col & Ven*, torta *f* de casamiento *R Plata* OR de novia *Chile*.

wedding dress *n* traje *m* de novia.

wedding reception *n* fiesta *f* de bodas.

wedding ring *n* anillo *m* de boda, argolla *f Amér*.

wedge [wedʒ] ◇ *n* - **1.** [for steadying or splitting] cuña *f*; **to drive a wedge between** dividir a; **the thin end of the wedge** la punta del iceberg - **2.** [triangular slice] porción *f*, trozo *m*. ◇ *vt*: **to wedge sthg open/shut** dejar algo abierto/cerrado con una cuña.

wedlock ['wedlɒk] *n* (U) *liter* desposorio *m*.

Wednesday ['wenzdɪ] *n* miércoles *m inv*; *see also* **Saturday**.

wee [wiː] ◇ *adj Scotland* pequeño(ña); **a wee bit** un poquito. ◇ *n v inf* pipí *m*; **to do a wee** hacer pipí. ◇ *vi v inf* hacer pipí.

weed [wiːd] ◇ *n* - **1.** [wild plant] mala hierba *f* - **2.** *UK inf* [feeble person] canijo *m*, -ja *f*. ◇ *vt* desherbar, escardar.

◆ **weed out** *vt sep* extirpar.

weeding ['wiːdɪŋ] *n* escarda *f*, limpieza *f* de malas hierbas; **to do the weeding** escardar.

weedkiller ['wiːd,kɪlər] *n* herbicida *m*.

weedy ['wiːdɪ] (*comp* -ier, *superl* -iest) *adj* - **1.** [overgrown with weeds] cubierto(ta) de malas hierbas - **2.** *UK inf* [feeble] enclenque.

week [wiːk] *n* [gen] semana *f*; **a week on Saturday, Saturday week** del sábado en ocho días; **this/next week** esta/la próxima semana; **in 2 weeks' time** en dos semanas; **we haven't seen him for weeks** hace semanas que no lo vemos.

weekday ['wiːkdeɪ] *n* día *m* laborable.

weekend [,wiːk'end] *n* fin *m* de semana.

weekend bag *n* bolsa *f* de fin de semana.

weekly ['wiːklɪ] ◇ *adj* semanal. ◇ *adv* semanalmente. ◇ *n* semanario *m*, periódico *m* semanal.

weep [wiːp] ◇ *n*: **to have a weep** llorar. ◇ *vt* (*pt & pp* wept) derramar. ◇ *vi* (*pt & pp* wept) llorar.

weeping willow [ˌwiːpɪŋ-] *n* sauce *m* llorón.

weepy [wiːpɪ] ◇ *adj* (*comp* **-ier,** *superl* **-iest**) [tearful] lloroso(sa); **to feel weepy** estar lloroso(sa). ◇ *n* [film] película *f* lacrimógena.

weigh [weɪ] *vt* - **1.** [gen] pesar - **2.** [consider carefully] sopesar; **she weighed her words** sopesó sus palabras.

◆ **weigh down** *vt sep* - **1.** [physically] sobrecargar - **2.** [mentally]: **to be weighed down by** OR **with** estar abrumado(da) de OR por.

◆ **weigh (up)on** *vt insep* abrumar; **it weighed on his mind** le pesaba en la conciencia.

◆ **weigh out** *vt sep* pesar.

◆ **weigh up** *vt sep* - **1.** [consider carefully] sopesar - **2.** [size up] hacerse una idea de.

weighbridge [ˈweɪbrɪdʒ] *n UK* puente *m* basculante.

weighing machine [ˈweɪɪŋ-] *n* báscula *f*.

weight [weɪt] ◇ *n* - **1.** [gen] peso *m*; **to put on** OR **gain weight** engordar; **to lose weight** adelgazar; **to carry weight** tener peso; **it's a weight off my mind** me ha quitado un peso de encima; **to pull one's weight** poner (uno) de su parte; **to take the weight off one's feet** descansar; **to throw one's weight about** comportarse de manera autoritaria - **2.** [metal object] pesa *f*. ◇ *vt*: **to weight sthg (down)** sujetar algo con un peso.

weighted [ˈweɪtɪd] *adj*: **to be weighted in favour of/against** inclinarse a favor/en contra de.

weighting [ˈweɪtɪŋ] *n prima por vivir en una ciudad con alto coste de vida.*

weightlessness [ˈweɪtlɪsnɪs] *n* ingravidez *f*.

weightlifter [ˈweɪtˌlɪftər] *n* levantador *m* de pesos.

weightlifting [ˈweɪtˌlɪftɪŋ] *n* levantamiento *m* de pesos, halterofilia *f*.

weight training *n* levantamiento *m* de pesos.

weighty [ˈweɪtɪ] (*comp* **-ier,** *superl* **-iest**) *adj* [serious] de peso.

weir [wɪər] *n* presa *f*, dique *m*.

weird [wɪəd] *adj* raro(ra), extraño(ña).

weirdo [ˈwɪədəʊ] (*pl* **-s**) *n inf* bicho *m* raro.

welcome [ˈwelkəm] ◇ *adj* - **1.** [guest] bienvenido(da); **to make sb welcome** acoger bien a alguien - **2.** [free]: **you're welcome to come** si quieres, puedes venir - **3.** [appreciated]: **to be welcome** ser de agradecer - **4.** [in reply to thanks]: **you're welcome** de nada. ◇ *n* bienvenida *f*; **to give sb a warm welcome** dar una calurosa bienvenida a alguien. ◇ *vt* - **1.** [receive] dar la bienvenida a - **2.** [approve, support] recibir bien. ◇ *excl* ¡bienvenido(da)!

welcoming [ˈwelkəmɪŋ] *adj* cordial.

weld [weld] ◇ *n* soldadura *f*. ◇ *vt* soldar.

welder [ˈweldər] *n* soldador *m*, -ra *f*.

welfare [ˈwelfeər] ◇ *adj* de asistencia social. ◇ *n* - **1.** [state of wellbeing] bienestar *m* - **2.** *US* [income support] subsidio *m* de la seguridad social; **to be on welfare** recibir un subsidio.

well [wel] ◇ *adj* (*comp* **better,** *superl* **best**) bien; **to be well** [healthy] estar bien (de salud); **I don't feel well** no me siento bien; **to get well** mejorarse; **all is well** todo va bien; **(that's all) well and good** (eso está) muy bien; **(it's) just as well** menos mal; **it would be as well to check first** sería mejor comprobar primero. ◇ *adv* - **1.** [satisfactorily, thoroughly] bien; **to go well** ir bien; **he's doing very well at his new school** le va muy bien en el nuevo colegio; **well done!** ¡muy bien!; **well and truly** completamente; **to be well in with sb** *inf* ser muy amiguete de alguien; **to be well out of sthg** *inf* tener la suerte de haberse salido de algo - **2.** [definitely, certainly] claramente, definitivamente; **it was well worth it** sí que valió la pena - **3.** [as emphasis]: **you know perfectly well (that)** sabes de sobra (que) - **4.** [very possibly]: **it could well rain** es muy posible que llueva. ◇ *n* pozo *m*. ◇ *excl* - **1.** [gen] bueno; **oh well!** ¡en fin! - **2.** [in surprise] ¡vaya!

◆ **as well** *adv* - **1.** [in addition] también - **2.** [with same result]: **you may** OR **might as well (do it)** ¿y por qué no (lo haces)?

◆ **as well as** *conj* además de.

◆ **well up** *vi* brotar.

we'll [wiːl] - **1.** (*abbr of* = **we will**), ▷ **will** - **2.** (*abbr of* = **we shall**), ▷ **shall**.

well-adjusted *adj* muy integrado(da).

well-advised [-ədˈvaɪzd] *adj* sensato(ta); **you would be well-advised to do it** sería aconsejable que lo hicieras.

well-appointed [-əˈpɔɪntɪd] *adj* bien equipado(da).

well-balanced *adj* equilibrado(da).

well-behaved [-bɪˈheɪvd] *adj* formal, bien educado(da); **to be well-behaved** portarse bien.

wellbeing [ˌwelˈbiːɪŋ] *n* bienestar *m*.

well-bred [-ˈbred] *adj* bien educado(da).

well-built *adj* fornido(da).

well-chosen *adj* atinado(da), acertado(da).

well-disposed *adj*: **to be well-disposed to sb/sthg, to be well-disposed towards sb/sthg** tener buena disposición hacia alguien/para algo.

well-done *adj* [thoroughly cooked] muy hecho(cha).

well-dressed [-ˈdrest] *adj* bien vestido(da).

well-earned [-ˈɜːnd] *adj* bien merecido(da).

well-established *adj* [custom, tradition] arraigado(da); [company] de sólida reputación.

well-fed *adj* bien alimentado(da).

well-groomed [-ˈgruːmd] *adj* bien arreglado(da).

well-heeled [-hiːld] *adj inf* ricachón(ona).

wellies [ˈwelɪz] *npl UK inf* botas *fpl* de agua.

well-informed *adj*: **to be well-informed (about** OR **on)** estar bien informado(da) (sobre).

wellington boots [ˈwelɪŋtən-], **wellingtons** [ˈwelɪŋtənz] *npl* botas *fpl* de agua.

well-intentioned [-ɪnˈtenʃnd] *adj* bienintencionado(da).

well-kept *adj* **- 1.** [neat, tidy] bien cuidado(da) **- 2.** [not revealed] bien guardado(da).

well-known *adj* conocido(da).

well-mannered [-ˈmænəd] *adj* de buenos modales, educado(da).

well-meaning *adj* bienintencionado(da).

well-nigh [-naɪ] *adv* casi.

well-off *adj* **- 1.** [rich] acomodado(da), rico(ca) **- 2.** [well-provided]: **to be well-off for sthg** tener bastante de algo; **not to know when one is well-off** *inf* no saber uno la suerte que tiene.

well-paid *adj* bien pagado(da).

well-preserved *adj* bien conservado(da).

well-proportioned [-prəˈpɔːʃnd] *adj* bien proporcionado(da).

well-read [-ˈred] *adj* instruido(da), culto(ta).

well-rounded [-ˈraʊndɪd] *adj* [varied] completo(ta).

well-spoken *adj* bienhablado(da).

well-thought-of *adj* de buena reputación; **to be well-thought-of** tener prestigio.

well-thought-out *adj* bien pensado(da).

well-timed *adj* oportuno(na).

well-to-do *adj* de dinero, adinerado(da).

wellwisher [ˈwel.wɪʃər] *n* simpatizante *mf* (que da muestras de apoyo).

well-woman clinic *n UK* centro sanitario para mujeres o tiempo dedicado a la atención sanitaria a mujeres en ambulatorios.

Welsh [welʃ] ◇ *adj* galés(esa). ◇ *n* [language] galés *m*. ◇ *npl*: **the Welsh** los galeses.

Welshman [ˈwelʃmən] (*pl* **-men** [-mən]) *n* galés *m*.

Welsh rarebit [-ˈreəbɪt] *n* tostada cubierta de queso fundido.

Welshwoman [ˈwelʃ.wʊmən] (*pl* **-women** [-.wɪmɪn]) *n* galesa *f*.

welter [ˈweltər] *n* revoltijo *m*, batiburrillo *m*.

welterweight [ˈweltəweɪt] *n* peso *m* wélter.

wend [wend] *vt liter*: **to wend one's way towards** encaminar (uno) sus pasos hacia.

wendy house [ˈwendɪ-] *n UK* casita de juguete del tamaño de un niño.

went [went] *pt* ⊳ **go**.

wept [wept] *pt* & *pp* ⊳ **weep**.

were [wɜːr] *pt* ⊳ **be**.

we're [wɪər] (*abbr of* = we are), ⊳ **be**.

weren't [wɜːnt] (*abbr of* = were not), = **be**.

werewolf [ˈwɪəwʊlf] (*pl* **-wolves** [-wʊlvz]) *n* hombre *m* lobo.

west [west] ◇ *n* **- 1.** [direction] oeste *m* **- 2.** [region]: **the West** el Oeste. ◇ *adj* del oeste. ◇ *adv*: **west (of)** al oeste (de).
◆ **West** *n* POL: **the West** el Occidente.

West Bank *n*: **the West Bank** Cisjordania.

westbound [ˈwestbaʊnd] *adj* con rumbo al oeste.

West Country *n UK*: **the West Country** el sudoeste de Inglaterra.

West End *n UK*: **the West End** zona central de Londres, famosa por sus teatros, tiendas etc.

westerly [ˈwestəlɪ] *adj* [wind] del oeste; **in a westerly direction** hacia el oeste.

western [ˈwestən] ◇ *adj* occidental. ◇ *n* [film] película *f* del oeste, western *m*.

Westerner [ˈwestənər] *n* POL occidental *mf*.

westernize, -ise [ˈwestənaɪz] *vt* occidentalizar.

West German ◇ *adj* de la Alemania Occidental. ◇ *n* [person] alemán *m*, -ana *f* occidental.

West Germany *n*: **(the former) West Germany** (la antigua) Alemania Occidental.

West Indian ◇ *adj* antillano(na). ◇ *n* [person] antillano *m*, -na *f*.

West Indies [-ˈɪndiːz] *npl*: **the West Indies** las Antillas.

Westminster [ˈwestmɪnstər] *n* barrio londinense en que se encuentra el parlamento británico.

West Virginia *n* Virginia Occidental.

westward [ˈwestwəd] ◇ *adj* hacia el oeste. ◇ *adv* = **westwards**.

westwards [ˈwestwədz], **westward** *adv* hacia el oeste.

wet [wet] ◇ *adj* (*comp* **-ter**, *superl* **-test**) **- 1.** [soaked] mojado(da); [damp] húmedo(da); **to get wet** mojarse **- 2.** [rainy] lluvioso(sa) **- 3.** [paint, cement] fresco(ca); **wet paint** recién pintado(da) **- 4.** [eyes] lleno(na) de lágrimas **- 5.** *UK inf pej* [weak, feeble] ñoño(ña). ◇ *n inf* POL político conservador moderado. ◇ *vt* (*pt* & *pp* **wet** OR **-ted**, *cont* **-ting**) **- 1.** [soak]

mojar; [dampen] humedecer **- 2.** [urinate in]: **to wet the bed** orinarse en la cama; **to wet o.s.** orinarse encima.

wet blanket *n inf pej* aguafiestas *mf*.

wet-look *adj* brillante.

wetness ['wetnɪs] *n* humedad *f*.

wet nurse *n* nodriza *f*, ama *f* de cría.

wet rot *n* pudrimiento *de la madera causado por la humedad*.

wet suit *n* traje *m* de submarinista.

WEU (*abbr of* **Western European Union**) *n* UEO *f*.

we've [wiːv] (*abbr of* = **we have**), = **have**.

whack [wæk] *inf* ⟨> *n* **- 1.** [hit] castañazo *m*, cachetada *f Amér* **- 2.** [share] parte *f*. ⟨> *vt* [person] pegar, zurrar; [object] dar un porrazo a; *US* [murder] liquidar.

whacked [wækt] *adj UK inf* [exhausted] molido(da), hecho(cha) polvo.

whale [weɪl] *n* [animal] ballena *f*; **to have a whale of a time** pasárselo bomba.

whaling ['weɪlɪŋ] *n* caza *f* de ballenas.

wham [wæm] *excl inf* ¡zas!

wharf [wɔːf] (*pl* **-s** OR **wharves** [wɔːvz]) *n* muelle *m*, embarcadero *m*.

what [wɒt] ⟨> *adj* **- 1.** *(in direct, indirect questions)* qué; **what kind of car has she got?** ¿qué coche tiene?; **what shape is it?** ¿qué forma tiene?; **he asked me what shape it was** me preguntó qué forma tenía; **what colour is it?** ¿de qué color es? **- 2.** *(in exclamations)* qué; **what a surprise!** ¡qué sorpresa!; **what a stupid idea!** ¡qué idea más tonta! ⟨> *pron* **- 1.** *(interrogative)* qué; **what are they doing?** ¿qué hacen?; **she asked me what they were doing** me preguntó qué estaban haciendo; **what are they talking about?** ¿de qué están hablando?; **what is it called?** ¿cómo se llama?; **what does it cost?** ¿cuánto cuesta?; **what is it like?** ¿cómo es?; **what's the Spanish for 'book'?** ¿cómo se dice 'book' en español?; **what is this for?** ¿para qué es esto?; **what about another drink/going out for a meal?** ¿qué tal otra copa/si salimos a comer?; **what about me?** ¿y yo qué?; **what if nobody comes?** ¿y si no viene nadie, qué? **- 2.** *(relative)* lo que; **I saw what happened/he did** yo vi lo que ocurrió/hizo; **I don't know what to do** no sé qué hacer; **what we need is...** lo que nos hace falta es... ⟨> *excl* [expressing disbelief] ¿qué?; **what, no milk!** ¿cómo? ¿que no hay leche?

whatever [wɒt'evər] ⟨> *adj* cualquier; **eat whatever food you find** come lo que encuentres; **no chance whatever** ni la más remota posibilidad; **nothing whatever** nada en absoluto. ⟨> *pron* **- 1.** [no matter what]: **whatever**

they may offer ofrezcan lo que ofrezcan; **whatever you like** lo que (tú quieras; **don't touch this, whatever you do** hagas lo que hagas, no toques esto; **whatever happens** pase lo que pase; **whatever the weather** haga el tiempo que haga **- 2.** [indicating surprise]: **whatever do you mean?** ¿qué quieres decir? **- 3.** [indicating ignorance]: **he told me to get a D.R.V., whatever that is** OR **may be** me dijo que consiguiera un D.R.V., sea lo que sea eso; **or whatever** o lo que sea.

whatnot ['wɒtnɒt] *n inf*: **and whatnot** y cosas por el estilo.

whatsoever [,wɒtsəʊ'evər] *adj*: **nothing whatsoever** nada en absoluto; **none whatsoever** ni uno.

wheat [wiːt] *n* trigo *m*.

wheat germ *n* germen *m* de trigo.

wheatmeal ['wiːtmiːl] *n* harina *f* semi-integral.

wheedle ['wiːdl] *vt* decir con zalamería; **to wheedle sb into doing sthg** camelar OR engatusar a alguien para que haga algo; **to wheedle sthg out of sb** sonsacarle algo a alguien.

wheel [wiːl] ⟨> *n* **- 1.** [gen] rueda *f* **- 2.** [steering wheel] volante *m*; **to be at the wheel** estar al volante. ⟨> *vt* empujar *(algo sobre ruedas)*. ⟨> *vi* **- 1.** [move in circle] dar vueltas **- 2.** [turn round]: **to wheel round** darse la vuelta.

wheelbarrow ['wiːl,bærəʊ] *n* carretilla *f*.

wheelchair ['wiːl,tʃeər] *n* silla *f* de ruedas.

wheelclamp ['wiːl,klæmp] *n* cepo *m*.

wheeler-dealer ['wiːlər-] *n pej* zorro *m*.

wheeling and dealing ['wiːlɪŋ-] *n (U) pej* tejemanejes *mpl*.

wheeze [wiːz] ⟨> *n* [sound] resuello *m*. ⟨> *vi* resollar.

wheezy ['wiːzɪ] (*comp* **-ier**, *superl* **-iest**) *adj* que resuella.

whelk [welk] *n* buccino *m*.

when [wen] ⟨> *adv* *(in direct, indirect questions)* cuándo; **when does the plane arrive?** ¿cuándo llega el avión?; **he asked me when I would be in London** me preguntó cuándo estaría en Londres; **I don't know when I'll be back** no sé cuándo volveré; **that was when I knew for sure that...** fue entonces cuando me di cuenta que...; **say when!** ¡di basta! ⟨> *conj* cuando; **tell me when you've read it** avísame cuando lo hayas leído; **on the day when it happened** el día (en) que pasó; **use less oil when frying food** utiliza menos aceite al freír comida; **you said it was black when it was actually white**

dijiste que era negro cuando en realidad era blanco; **how can I buy it when I can't afford it?** ¿cómo voy a comprarlo si no tengo dinero?

whenever [wen'evə^r] ⟨⟩ *conj* [no matter when] cuando; [every time] cada vez que; **whenever you like** cuando quieras; **whenever I call him he runs away** siempre que le llamo se marcha corriendo. ⟨⟩ *adv* cuando sea.

where [weə^r] ⟨⟩ *adv* (in direct, indirect questions) dónde; **where do you live?** ¿dónde vives?; **do you know where he lives?** ¿sabes dónde vive?; **where are you from?** ¿de dónde eres?; **where are we going?** ¿adónde vamos?; **I don't know where to start** no sé por dónde empezar. ⟨⟩ *conj* - **1.** [referring to place, situation] donde; **this is where...** es aquí donde...; **go where you like** vete (a) donde quieras - **2.** [whereas]: **children often understand where adults don't** los niños a menudo entienden en casos en los que los adultos no - **3.** [if]: **where possible** siempre que sea posible.

whereabouts ⟨⟩ *adv* [,weərə'bauts] (por) dónde. ⟨⟩ *npl* ['weərəbauts] paradero *m*; **to know sb's whereabouts** conocer el paradero de alguien.

whereas [weər'æz] *conj* mientras que.

whereby [weə'bai] *conj fml* según, el/la cual, por el/la cual.

whereupon [,weərə'pɒn] *conj fml* tras OR con lo cual.

wherever [weər'evə^r] ⟨⟩ *conj* [no matter where] dondequiera que; **wherever you go** dondequiera que vayas; **sit wherever you like** siéntate donde quieras. ⟨⟩ *adv* - **1.** [no matter where] en cualquier parte - **2.** [indicating surprise]: **wherever did you hear that?** ¿dónde habrás oído eso?

wherewithal ['weəwiðɔːl] *n fml*: **to have the wherewithal to do sthg** disponer de los medios para hacer algo.

whet [wet] (*pt & pp* **-ted**, *cont* **-ting**) *vt*: **to whet sb's appetite (for sthg)** despertar el interés de alguien (por algo).

whether ['weðə^r] *conj* - **1.** [indicating choice, doubt] si; **she doesn't know whether to go or stay** no sabe si quedarse o marcharse; **I doubt whether she'll do it** dudo que lo haga - **2.** [no matter if]: **whether I want to or not** tanto si quiero como si no, quiera o no quiera.

whew [hwju:] *excl* ¡buf!

which [witʃ] ⟨⟩ *adj* - **1.** (in direct, indirect questions) qué; **which house is yours?** ¿cuál es tu casa?, ¿qué casa es la tuya?; **which one?** ¿cuál?; **which ones?** ¿cuáles? - **2.** [to refer back to]: **in which case** en cuyo caso; **we won't arrive until 6, by which time it will be dark** no llega-

remos hasta la 6, hora a la cual ya será de noche. ⟨⟩ *pron* - **1.** (in direct, indirect questions) cuál, cuáles *(pl)*; **which do you prefer?** ¿cuál prefieres?; **I can't decide which to have** no sé cuál coger - **2.** (in relative clause replacing n) que; **the table, which was made of wood,...** la mesa, que OR la cual era de madera,...; **the world in which we live** el mundo en que OR en el cual vivimos - **3.** (to refer back to a clause) lo cual; **she denied it, which surprised me** lo negó, lo cual me sorprendió; **before which** antes de lo cual.

whichever [witʃ'evə^r] ⟨⟩ *adj* - **1.** [no matter which]: **whichever route you take** vayas por donde vayas - **2.** [the one which]: **whichever colour you prefer** el color que prefieras. ⟨⟩ *pron* el que (la que), los que (las que) *(pl)*; **take whichever you like** coge el que quieras.

whiff [wif] *n* [smell] olorcillo *m*; **she caught a whiff of his aftershave** le llegó el olorcillo de su aftershave.

while [wail] ⟨⟩ *n* rato *m*; **it's a long while since I did that** hace mucho que no hago eso; **for a while** un rato; **after a while** después de un rato; **in a while** dentro de poco; **once in a while** de vez en cuando; **to be worth one's while** merecerle la pena a uno. ⟨⟩ *conj* - **1.** [during the time that] mientras - **2.** [whereas] mientras que - **3.** [although] aunque.

➤ **while away** *vt sep* pasar; **to while away the time** pasar el rato.

whilst [wailst] *conj fml* - **1.** [during the time that] mientras - **2.** [whereas] mientras que - **3.** [although] aunque.

whim [wim] *n* capricho *m*.

whimper ['wimpə^r] ⟨⟩ *n* gimoteo *m*, gemido *m*. ⟨⟩ *vt & vi* gimotear.

whimsical ['wimzikl] *adj* [idea, story] fantasioso(sa); [remark] extravagante, poco usual; [look] juguetón(ona).

whine [wain] ⟨⟩ *n* gemido *m*, lloriqueo *m*. ⟨⟩ *vi* - **1.** [child, dog] gemir; [siren] ulular - **2.** [complain]: **to whine (about)** quejarse (de).

whinge [windʒ] (*cont* **whingeing**) *vi UK inf*: **to whinge (about)** quejarse (de).

whip [wip] ⟨⟩ *n* - **1.** [for hitting] látigo *m*; [for horse] guasca *f Amér C*, fusta *f* - **2.** UK POL miembro de un partido encargado de asegurar que otros miembros voten en el parlamento. ⟨⟩ *vt* (*pt & pp* **-ped**, *cont* **-ping**) - **1.** [gen] azotar - **2.** [take quickly]: **to whip sthg out/off** sacar/quitar algo rápidamente - **3.** [whisk] batir.

➤ **whip up** *vt sep* [provoke] levantar.

whiplash injury ['wiplæʃ-] *n* lesión *f* de cervicales por efecto de la inercia.

whipped cream [wipt-] *n* nata *f* montada.

whippet ['wipit] *n tipo de galgo pequeño*.

whip-round n UK inf: **to have a whip-round** hacer una colecta.

whirl [wɜːl] ⬦ n **- 1.** [rotating movement] remolino m; **to be in a whirl** estar aturullado **- 2.** fig [of activity, events] torbellino m

▸▸▸ **let's give it a whirl** inf lancémonos. ⬦ vt: **to whirl sb/sthg round** hacer dar vueltas a alguien/algo. ⬦ vi **- 1.** [move around] arremolinarse; [dancers] girar vertiginosamente **- 2.** fig [head, mind] dar vueltas.

whirlpool ['wɜːlpuːl] n remolino m.

whirlpool bath n bañera f de hidromasaje.

whirlwind ['wɜːlwɪnd] ⬦ adj fig vertiginoso(sa). ⬦ n torbellino m.

whirr [wɜːr] ⬦ n zumbido m. ⬦ vi zumbar.

whisk [wɪsk] ⬦ n CULIN varilla f. ⬦ vt **- 1.** [move quickly]: **to whisk sthg away/out** llevarse/sacar algo rápidamente; **we were whisked off to visit the museum** nos llevaron rápidamente a visitar el museo **- 2.** CULIN batir.

whisker ['wɪskər] n (pelo m del) bigote m.

➡ **whiskers** npl [of person] patillas fpl; [of cat] bigotes mpl.

whisky UK (pl **-ies**), **whiskey** (pl **-s**) US & Ireland ['wɪskɪ] n whisky m.

whisper ['wɪspər] ⬦ n [gen] susurro m; [of voices] cuchicheo m. ⬦ vt susurrar. ⬦ vi cuchichear.

whispering ['wɪspərɪŋ] n (U) cuchicheos mpl.

whist [wɪst] n whist m.

whistle ['wɪsl] ⬦ n **- 1.** [sound] silbido m, pitido m **- 2.** [device] silbato m, pito m. ⬦ vt silbar. ⬦ vi **- 1.** [person] silbar, chiflar Amér; [referee] pitar; [bird] piar **- 2.** [move quickly]: **to whistle past** pasar como un rayo **- 3.** [kettle, train] silbar, pitar.

whistle-stop tour n recorrido rápido con múltiples paradas.

Whit [wɪt] n UK Pentecostés m.

white [waɪt] ⬦ adj **- 1.** [gen] blanco(ca); **to go** OR **turn white** ponerse blanco **- 2.** [coffee, tea] con leche. ⬦ n **- 1.** [colour] blanco m **- 2.** [person] blanco m, -ca f **- 3.** [of egg] clara f **- 4.** [of eye] blanco m.

➡ **whites** npl ropa f blanca (para tenis, críquet).

white blood cell n glóbulo m blanco.

whiteboard ['waɪtbɔːd] n pizarra f blanca, tablero m blanco (para escribir con rotuladores).

white Christmas n Navidad f con nieve.

white-collar adj de oficina; **white-collar worker** oficinista mf.

white elephant n fig mamotreto m (caro e inútil).

white goods npl **- 1.** [household machines] línea f blanca (de electrodomésticos) **- 2.** [linen] lencería f.

white-haired [-'head] adj canoso(sa), de pelo blanco.

Whitehall ['waɪtɔːl] n calle londinense en que se encuentra la Administración británica; por extensión ésta.

white-hot adj candente, incandescente.

White House n: **the White House** la Casa Blanca.

White House ▬▬▬▬▬▬▬▬▬▬▬▬▬

▯▯▯ La Casa Blanca es lugar de trabajo y residencia oficial del presidente de Estados Unidos y su familia en Washington, D.C. Se trata del edificio público más antiguo de la ciudad y el primer presidente en vivir en él fue John Adams a partir del año 1800. Tras el incendio por las tropas británicas en 1814, fue restaurado y pintado de blanco. Sin embargo, y al contrario de lo que muchos creen, la "Casa Blanca" ya recibía este nombre antes de que se pintara en esta ocasión. Su nombre se hizo oficial cuando Theodore Roosevelt lo hizo grabar en el membrete de sus cartas. Por extensión, el término White House se utiliza para referirse a la presidencia y la administración estadounidenses.

white lie n mentira f piadosa.

white light n (U) luz f blanca.

white magic n magia f blanca.

white meat n (U) carnes fpl blancas.

whiten ['waɪtn] ⬦ vt blanquear. ⬦ vi ponerse blanco(ca).

whitener ['waɪtnər] n blanqueador m.

whiteness ['waɪtnɪs] n blancura f.

white noise n (U) ruido m blanco.

whiteout ['waɪtaʊt] n pérdida total de visibilidad a causa de la nieve.

white paper n POL libro m blanco.

white sauce n (salsa f) bechamel f.

white spirit n UK especie de aguarrás.

whitewash ['waɪtwɒʃ] ⬦ n **- 1.** (U) [paint] blanqueo m, lechada f (de cal) **- 2.** pej [cover-up] encubrimiento m. ⬦ vt **- 1.** [paint] blanquear, encalar **- 2.** pej [cover up] encubrir.

whitewater rafting ['waɪt,wɔːtər-] n descenso m (de rápidos) en piragua.

white wedding n boda f de blanco.

white wine n vino m blanco.

whiting ['waɪtɪŋ] (*pl* **whiting** OR **-s**) *n* pescadilla *f*.

Whit Monday *n* lunes *m* de Pentecostés.

Whitsun ['wɪtsn] *n* [day] Pentecostés *m*.

whittle ['wɪtl] *vt* [reduce]: **to whittle down** OR **away** reducir gradualmente.

whiz, whizz [wɪz] <> *n inf*: **to be a whiz at sthg** ser un genio OR prodigio en algo. <> *vi* (*pt & pp* **-zed**, *cont* **-zing**): **to whiz past** OR **by** pasar muy rápido OR zumbando.

whiz(z) kid *n inf* genio *m*, prodigio *m*.

who [hu:] *pron* - **1.** (*in direct, indirect questions*) quién, quiénes (*pl*); **who are you?** ¿quién eres tú?; **who is it?** [at door etc] ¿quién es?; **who did you see?** ¿a quién viste?; **I didn't know who she was** no sabía quién era - **2.** (*in relative clauses*) que; **he's the doctor who treated me** es el médico que me atendió; **those who are in favour** los que están a favor.

WHO (*abbr of* **World Health Organization**) *n* OMS *f*.

who'd [hu:d] - **1.** (*abbr of* = **who had**), = **have** - **2.** (*abbr of* = **who would**), = **would**.

whodun(n)it [,hu:'dʌnɪt] *n inf* historia *f* policíaca de misterio.

whoever [hu:'evər] *pron* - **1.** [unknown person] quienquiera; quienesquiera (*pl*); **whoever finds it** quienquiera que lo encuentre; **tell whoever you like** díselo a quien quieras - **2.** [indicating surprise, astonishment]: **whoever can that be?** ¿quién podrá ser? - **3.** [no matter who]: **come in, whoever you are** pasa, seas quién seas.

whole [həʊl] <> *adj* - **1.** [entire, complete] entero(ra); **we've had enough of the whole thing** ya estamos hartos de todo esto - **2.** [for emphasis]: **a whole lot of** muchísimos(mas); **a whole lot taller** muchísimo más alto; **a whole new idea** una idea totalmente nueva. <> *n* - **1.** [all]: **the whole of the school/summer** el colegio/verano entero - **2.** [unit, complete thing] todo *m*.
◆ **as a whole** *adv* en conjunto, en su totalidad.
◆ **on the whole** *adv* en general.

wholefood ['həʊlfu:d] *n* UK comida *f* integral.

whole-hearted [-'hɑːtɪd] *adj* incondicional.

wholemeal ['həʊlmiːl], **whole wheat** *adj* UK integral.

wholemeal bread *n* (U) UK pan *m* integral.

whole note *n* US semibreve *f*.

wholesale ['həʊlseɪl] <> *adj* - **1.** COMM al por mayor - **2.** *pej* [indiscriminate] indiscriminado(da). <> *adv* - **1.** COMM al por mayor - **2.** *pej* [indiscriminately] indiscriminadamente.

wholesaler ['həʊlˌseɪlər] *n* mayorista *mf*.

wholesome ['həʊlsəm] *adj* sano(na), saludable.

whole wheat US = **wholemeal**.

who'll [hu:l] - **1.** (*abbr of* = **who will**), = **will** - **2.** (*abbr of* = **who shall**), = **shall**.

wholly ['həʊlɪ] *adv* completamente, enteramente.

whom [hu:m] *pron* - **1.** (*in direct, indirect questions*) *fml* quién, quiénes (*pl*); **from whom did you receive it?** ¿de quién lo recibiste?; **for/of/to whom** por/de/a quién - **2.** (*in relative clauses*) que; **the man whom I saw** el hombre que vi; **the man to whom I gave it** el hombre al que se lo di; **several people came, none of whom I knew** vinieron varias personas, de las que no conocía a ninguna.

whoop [wu:p] <> *n* grito *m* alborozado. <> *vi* gritar alborozadamente.

whoopee [wʊ'pi:] *excl* ¡yupi!

whooping cough ['hu:pɪŋ-] *n* tos *f* ferina.

whoops [wʊps] *excl* ¡uy!

whoosh [wʊʃ] *inf* <> *n* [of air] ráfaga *f*; [of water] chorro *m*. <> *vi* - **1.** [water]: **to whoosh out** salir a chorro - **2.** [car, train]: **to whoosh past** pasar a toda pastilla.

whopper ['wɒpər] *n inf* - **1.** [big thing] bestialidad *f* - **2.** [lie] bola *f*, trola *f*.

whopping ['wɒpɪŋ] *inf* <> *adj* enorme. <> *adv*: **a whopping great lorry/lie, a whopping big lorry/lie** un camión/una mentira enorme.

whore [hɔːr] *n pej* puta *f*, cuero *m* Amér.

who're ['hu:ər] (*abbr of* = **who are**), = **be**.

whose [hu:z] <> *pron* (*in direct, indirect questions*) de quién, de quiénes (*pl*); **whose is this?** ¿de quién es esto?; **I wonder whose they are** me pregunto de quién serán. <> *adj* - **1.** (*in direct, indirect questions*) de quién; **whose car is that?** ¿de quién es ese coche? - **2.** (*in relative clauses*) cuyo(ya), cuyos(yas) (*pl*); **that's the boy whose father's an MP** ese es el chico cuyo padre es diputado; **the woman whose daughters are twins** la mujer cuyas hijas son gemelas.

whosoever [,hu:səʊ'evər] *pron dated* quienquiera que.

who's who [hu:z-] *n* [book] Quién es Quién *m*.

who've [hu:v] (*abbr of* = **who have**), = **have**.

why [waɪ] <> *adv* por qué; **why did you lie to me?** ¿por qué me mentiste?; **why don't you all come?** ¿por qué no venís todos?; **why not?** ¿por qué no? <> *conj* por qué; **I don't know why he said that** no sé por qué dijo eso. <> *pron*: **there are several reasons why he left** hay varias razones por las que se marchó; **that's why she did it** por eso es por lo que lo hizo; **I don't know the reason why** no se por qué razón. <> *excl* ¡hombre!, ¡vaya!

➤ **why ever** adv: **why ever did you do that?** ¿pero por qué has hecho eso?

WI - 1. (abbr of **Women's Institute**); **the WI** organización cultural para mujeres **- 2.** (abbr of **West Indies**) las Antillas **- 3.** (abbr of **Wisconsin**) Wisconsin.

wick [wɪk] n mecha f; **to get on sb's wick** UK inf fig sacar de quicio a alguien.

wicked ['wɪkɪd] adj **- 1.** [evil] malvado(da) **- 2.** [mischievous, devilish] travieso(sa) **- 3.** inf [very good] molón(ona), chachi (inv).

wicker ['wɪkəʳ] adj de mimbre.

wickerwork ['wɪkəwɜːk] n (U) artículos mpl de mimbre.

wicket ['wɪkɪt] n CRICKET [stumps] palos mpl.

wicket keeper n guardián mf de los palos.

wide [waɪd] ◇ adj **- 1.** [broad] ancho(cha); **how wide is it?** ¿cuánto mide de ancho?; **it's 50 cm wide** tiene 50 cm de ancho **- 2.** [range, choice etc] amplio(plia) **- 3.** [gap, difference, implications] grande, considerable **- 4.** [eyes] muy abierto(ta) **- 5.** [off-target] desviado(da). ◇ adv **- 1.** [broadly]: **to open/spread sthg wide** abrir/desplegar algo completamente **- 2.** [off target]: **to go** OR **be wide** salir desviado.

wide-angle lens n gran angular m.

wide awake adj completamente despierto(ta).

wide boy n UK inf pej pájaro m de cuenta.

wide-eyed [-'aɪd] adj **- 1.** [surprised, frightened] con los ojos muy abiertos (de miedo o sorpresa) **- 2.** [innocent, gullible] inocente, simple.

widely ['waɪdlɪ] adv **- 1.** [smile, yawn] ampliamente **- 2.** [travel, read] extensamente; **to be widely read/travelled** haber leído/viajado mucho **- 3.** [believed, known, loved] generalmente; **there is a widely held view that...** existe la creencia generalizada de que... **- 4.** [differ, vary] mucho.

widen ['waɪdn] ◇ vt [gen] ampliar; [road, bridge] ensanchar. ◇ vi **- 1.** [gen] ampliarse; [river, road] ensancharse **- 2.** [eyes] abrirse mucho.

wide open adj **- 1.** [window, door] abierto(ta) de par en par **- 2.** [eyes] completamente abierto(ta) **- 3.** [spaces] extenso(sa).

wide-ranging [-'reɪndʒɪŋ] adj [changes, survey, consequences] de gran alcance; [discussion, interests] de gran variedad; [selection] amplio(plia).

widescreen ['waɪdskriːn] adj [television] de pantalla ancha.

widescreen TV ['waɪdskriːn-] n televisor m panorámico, televisor m de pantalla ancha.

widespread ['waɪdspred] adj extendido(da), general.

widow ['wɪdəʊ] n [woman] viuda f.

widowed ['wɪdəʊd] adj viudo(da).

widower ['wɪdəʊəʳ] n viudo m.

width [wɪdθ] n **- 1.** [breadth] anchura f; **it's 50 cm in width** tiene 50 cm de ancho **- 2.** [in swimming pool] ancho m.

widthways ['wɪdθweɪz] adv a lo ancho.

wield [wiːld] vt **- 1.** [weapon] esgrimir; [implement] manejar **- 2.** [power] ejercer.

wife [waɪf] (pl **wives**) n mujer f, esposa f.

wig [wɪg] n peluca f.

wiggle ['wɪgl] inf ◇ n **- 1.** [movement] meneo m; [of hips etc] contoneo m **- 2.** [wavy line] línea f ondulada. ◇ vt menear; [hips etc] contonear. ◇ vi menearse; [hips etc] contonearse.

wiggly ['wɪglɪ] (comp **-ier**, superl **-iest**) adj inf **- 1.** [line] ondulado(da) **- 2.** [tooth, chair leg etc] suelto(ta).

wigwam ['wɪgwæm] n tipi m.

wild [waɪld] ◇ adj **- 1.** [gen] salvaje; [plant, flower] silvestre; [bull] bravo(va), chúcaro(ra) Amér **- 2.** [landscape, scenery] agreste **- 3.** [weather, sea] borrascoso(sa) **- 4.** [crowd, laughter, applause] frenético(ca); **to run wild** descontrolarse **- 5.** [hair] alborotado(da) **- 6.** [hope, idea, plan] descabellado(da) **- 7.** [guess, exaggeration] extravagante **- 8.** inf [very enthusiastic]: **to be wild about** estar loco por. ◇ n: **in the wild** en libertad, en su habitat natural.

➤ **wilds** npl: **the wilds** las tierras remotas.

wild card n COMPUT comodín m.

wildcat ['waɪldkæt] n [animal] gato m montés.

wildcat strike n huelga f salvaje.

wildebeest ['wɪldɪbiːst] (pl **wildebeest** OR **-s**) n ñu m.

wilderness ['wɪldənɪs] n **- 1.** [barren land] yermo m, desierto m **- 2.** [overgrown land] jungla f **- 3.** fig [unimportant place]: **in the political wilderness** en el anonimato político.

wildfire ['waɪld,faɪəʳ] n: **to spread like wildfire** propagarse como un reguero de pólvora.

wild flower n flor f silvestre.

wild-goose chase n inf búsqueda f infructuosa.

wildlife ['waɪldlaɪf] n (U) fauna f.

wildly ['waɪldlɪ] adv **- 1.** [enthusiastically] frenéticamente **- 2.** [without discipline, inaccurately] a lo loco **- 3.** [very] extremadamente **- 4.** [menacingly] salvajemente.

wild west n inf: **the wild west** el salvaje oeste.

wiles [waɪlz] npl artimañas fpl.

wilful _UK_, **willful** _US_ ['wɪlfʊl] _adj_ - **1.** [stubborn] que siempre se tiene que salir con la suya - **2.** [deliberate] deliberado(da), intencionado(da).

will[1] [wɪl] <> _n_ - **1.** [gen] voluntad _f_; **against one's will** contra la voluntad de uno; **to do sthg of one's own free will** hacer algo por propia voluntad; **at will** a voluntad - **2.** [document] testamento _m_; **to make a will** hacer testamento. <> _vt_: **to will sthg to happen** desear mucho que ocurra algo; **to will sb to do sthg** desear mucho que alguien haga algo.

will[2] [wɪl] _modal vb_ - **1.** [to express future tense]: **they say it will rain tomorrow** dicen que lloverá _OR_ va a llover mañana; **I'll be arriving at six** llegaré a las seis; **we will have arrived by midday** habremos llegado a mediodía; **when will we get paid?** ¿cuándo nos pagarán?; **will they come?** - yes, they will/no, they won't ¿vendrán? – sí/no; **you will come, won't you?** _(emphatic)_ vas a venir, ¿no? - **2.** [indicating willingness]: **will you have some more tea?** ¿te apetece más té?; **I won't do it** no lo haré - **3.** [in commands, requests]: **you will leave this house at once** vas a salir de esta casa ahora mismo; **close that window, will you?** cierra la ventana, ¿quieres?; **will you be quiet!** ¿queréis hacer el favor de callaros? - **4.** [indicating possibility, what usually happens]: **the hall will hold up to 1,000 people** la sala tiene cabida para 1.000 personas; **this will stop any draughts** esto evitará las corrientes - **5.** [expressing an assumption]: **that'll be your father** ese va a ser _OR_ será tu padre; **as you'll have gathered, I'm not keen on the idea** como ya os imaginaréis, a mí no me hace gracia la idea - **6.** [indicating irritation]: **well, if you will leave your toys everywhere...** normal, si vais dejando los juguetes por todas partes...; **she will keep phoning me** ¡y venga a llamarme!

willful _US_ = **wilful**.

willing ['wɪlɪŋ] _adj_ - **1.** [prepared]: **to be willing (to do sthg)** estar dispuesto(ta) (a hacer algo) - **2.** [eager] servicial.

willingly ['wɪlɪŋlɪ] _adv_ de buena gana.

willingness ['wɪlɪŋnɪs] _n_: **willingness (to do sthg)** disposición _f_ (para hacer algo).

willow (tree) ['wɪləʊ-] _n_ sauce _m_.

willowy ['wɪləʊɪ] _adj_ esbelto(ta).

willpower ['wɪl,paʊər] _n_ fuerza _f_ de voluntad.

willy ['wɪlɪ] (_pl_ **-ies**) _n UK inf_ pito _m_.

willy-nilly [,wɪlɪ'nɪlɪ] _adv_ [carelessly] a la buena de Dios.

wilt [wɪlt] _vi_ [plant] marchitarse; [person] desfallecer, extenuarse.

Wilts [wɪlts] (_abbr of_ **Wiltshire**) _condado inglés_.

wily ['waɪlɪ] (_comp_ **-ier**, _superl_ **-iest**) _adj_ astuto(ta).

wimp [wɪmp] _n inf pej_ blandengue _mf_.

win [wɪn] <> _n_ victoria _f_, triunfo _m_. <> _vt_ (_pt & pp_ **won**, _cont_ **-ning**) ganar. <> _vi_ (_pt & pp_ **won**, _cont_ **-ning**) ganar; **you/I** _etc_ **can't win** no hay manera.

◆ **win over, win round** _vt sep_ convencer.

wince [wɪns] <> _vi_ hacer una mueca de dolor; **to wince at/with sthg** estremecerse ante/de algo. <> _n_ mueca _f_ de dolor.

winch [wɪntʃ] <> _n_ torno _m_. <> _vt_: **to winch sthg up/out** levantar/sacar algo con torno.

wind[1] [wɪnd] <> _n_ - **1.** METEOR viento _m_ - **2.** [breath] aliento _m_, resuello _m_ - **3.** (_U_) [in stomach] gases _mpl_; **to break wind** _euph_ ventosear - **4.** [in orchestra]: **the wind** los instrumentos de viento.

▶▶I **to get wind of sthg** _inf_ enterarse de algo. <> _vt_ - **1.** [knock breath out of] dejar sin aliento - **2.** _UK_ [baby] hacer que eructe.

wind[2] [waɪnd] <> _vt_ (_pt & pp_ **wound**) - **1.** [string, thread] enrollar; **to wind sthg around sthg** enrollar algo alrededor de algo - **2.** [clock, watch] dar cuerda a

▶▶I **to wind its way** serpentear. <> _vi_ (_pt & pp_ **wound**) serpentear.

◆ **wind down** <> _vt sep_ - **1.** [car window] bajar - **2.** [business] cerrar poco a poco. <> _vi_ - **1.** [clock, watch] pararse - **2.** [person] relajarse, descansar.

◆ **wind up** <> _vt sep_ - **1.** [finish - activity] finalizar, concluir; [business] liquidar - **2.** [clock, watch] dar cuerda a - **3.** [car window] subir - **4.** _UK inf_ [annoy] vacilar, tomar el pelo a. <> _vi_ _inf_ [end up] terminar, acabar; **to wind up doing sthg** acabar haciendo algo.

windbreak ['wɪndbreɪk] _n_ protección _f_ contra el viento.

windcheater _UK_ ['wɪnd,tʃiːtər], **windbreaker** _US_ ['wɪnd,breɪkər] _n_ cazadora _f_.

windchill ['wɪndtʃɪl] _n_: **windchill factor** _efecto por el cual el viento reduce la temperatura efectiva._

winded ['wɪndɪd] _adj_ sin aliento.

windfall ['wɪndfɔːl] _n_ - **1.** [fruit] fruta _f_ caída - **2.** [unexpected gift] dinero _m_ llovido del cielo.

wind farm [wɪnd-] _n_ parque _m_ eólico.

winding ['waɪndɪŋ] _adj_ tortuoso(sa), sinuoso(sa).

wind instrument [wɪnd-] _n_ instrumento _m_ de viento.

windmill ['wɪndmɪl] _n_ molino _m_ de viento.

window ['wɪndəʊ] *n* - **1.** [gen & COMPUT] ventana *f* - **2.** AUT ventanilla *f* - **3.** [of shop] escaparate *m*.

window box *n* jardinera *f* (de ventana).

window cleaner *n* - **1.** [person] limpiacristales *m* & *f inv* - **2.** [product] limpiacristales *m inv*.

window dressing *n (U)* - **1.** [in shop] escaparatismo *m* - **2.** *fig* [non-essentials] pura fachada *f*.

window envelope *n* sobre *m* de ventanilla.

window frame *n* marco *m* de ventana.

window ledge *n* alféizar *m*.

window pane *n* cristal *m* (de la ventana).

window shade *n* US persiana *f*.

window-shopping *n*: to go window-shopping ir de escaparates.

windowsill ['wɪndəʊsɪl] *n* alféizar *m*.

windpipe ['wɪndpaɪp] *n* tráquea *f*.

windscreen UK ['wɪndskriːn], **windshield** US ['wɪndʃiːld] *n* parabrisas *m inv*.

windscreen washer *n* lavaparabrisas *m inv*.

windscreen wiper *n* limpiaparabrisas *m inv*.

windshield US = windscreen.

windsock ['wɪndsɒk] *n* manga *f* de aire.

windsurfer ['wɪnd,sɜːfər] *n* - **1.** [person] windsurfista *mf* - **2.** [board] tabla *f* de windsurf.

windsurfing ['wɪnd,sɜːfɪŋ] *n* windsurf *m*.

windswept ['wɪndswept] *adj* - **1.** [scenery] azotado(da) por el viento - **2.** [person, hair] despeinado(da).

wind tunnel [wɪnd-] *n* túnel *m* aerodinámico.

wind turbine [wɪnd-] *n* aerogenerador *m*.

windy ['wɪndɪ] (*comp* **-ier**, *superl* **-iest**) *adj* [day, weather] ventoso(sa), de mucho viento; [place] expuesto(ta) al viento; **it's windy** hace viento.

wine [waɪn] ⬦ *n* vino *m*; **red/white wine** vino tinto/blanco. ⬦ *vt*: **to wine and dine sb** agasajar a alguien.

wine bar *n* UK *bar de cierta elegancia especializado en vinos y que a veces suele servir comidas.*

wine bottle *n* botella *f* de vino.

wine cellar *n* bodega *f*.

wineglass ['waɪnɡlɑːs] *n* copa *f* OR vaso *m* (de vino).

wine list *n* lista *f* de vinos.

wine merchant *n* UK vinatero *m*, -ra *f*.

winepress ['waɪnpres] *n* lagar *m*.

wine tasting [-,teɪstɪŋ] *n* cata *f* de vinos.

wine waiter *n* sommelier *m*.

wing [wɪŋ] *n* - **1.** [gen] ala *f* - **2.** AUT guardabarros *m inv* - **3.** SPORT [side of pitch] banda *f*; [winger] extremo *m*, ala *m*.

⬦ **wings** *npl* THEAT: **the wings** los bastidores.

wing commander *n* UK ≃ teniente *m* coronel de aviación.

winger ['wɪŋər] *n* SPORT extremo *m*, ala *m*.

wing mirror *n* retrovisor *m*.

wing nut *n* palometa *f*, tuerca *f* de mariposa.

wingspan ['wɪŋspæn] *n* envergadura *f* (de alas).

wink [wɪŋk] ⬦ *n* guiño *m*; **to have forty winks** *inf* echarse un sueñecito; **not to sleep a wink, not to get a wink of sleep** *inf* no pegar ojo. ⬦ *vi* - **1.** [eye]: **to wink (at sb)** guiñar (a alguien) - **2.** *liter* [lights] titilar, parpadear.

winkle ['wɪŋkl] *n* bígaro *m*.

Winnebago® [,wɪnɪ'beɪɡəʊ] *n* autocaravana *f*.

winner ['wɪnər] *n* ganador *m*, -ra *f*.

winning ['wɪnɪŋ] *adj* - **1.** [team, competitor] vencedor(ra), victorioso(sa); [goal, point] de la victoria; [ticket, number] premiado(da) - **2.** [smile, ways] atractivo(va).

⬦ **winnings** *npl* ganancias *fpl*.

winning post *n* meta *f*.

winsome ['wɪnsəm] *adj* *liter* atractivo(va), encantador(ra).

winter ['wɪntər] ⬦ *n (U)* invierno *m*; **in winter** en invierno. ⬦ *comp* de invierno, invernal.

winter sports *npl* deportes *mpl* de invierno.

wintertime ['wɪntətaɪm] *n (U)* invierno *m*; **in wintertime** en invierno.

wint(e)ry ['wɪntrɪ] *adj* [gen] de invierno, invernal; [showers] con nieve.

wipe [waɪp] ⬦ *n*: **give the table a wipe** pásale un trapo a la mesa. ⬦ *vt* [rub to clean] limpiar, pasar un trapo a; [rub to dry] secar.

⬦ **wipe away** *vt sep* [tears, sweat] enjugar.

⬦ **wipe out** *vt sep* - **1.** [erase] borrar - **2.** [eradicate] aniquilar.

⬦ **wipe up** *vt sep* empapar, limpiar.

wiper ['waɪpər] *n* [windscreen wiper] limpiaparabrisas *m inv*.

wire ['waɪər] ⬦ *n* - **1.** [gen] alambre *m*; ELEC cable *m* - **2.** US [telegram] telegrama *m*. ⬦ *vt* - **1.** [connect]: **to wire sthg to sthg** conectar algo a algo - **2.** [ELEC - house] poner la instalación eléctrica de; [- plug] conectar el cable a - **3.** US [send telegram to] enviar un telegrama a.

wire brush *n* cepillo *m* de raíces.

wire cutters *npl* cortaalambres *m inv*.

wirefree ['waɪəfriː] *adj* inalámbrico(ca).

wireless ['waɪəlɪs] *n* *dated* radio *f*.

wire netting *n (U)* tela *f* metálica.

wire-tapping [-,tæpɪŋ] *n (U)* intervención *f* telefónica.

wire wool n UK estropajo m metálico.

wiring ['waɪərɪŋ] n (U) instalación f eléctrica.

wiry ['waɪərɪ] (comp -ier, superl -iest) adj
- **1.** [hair] estropajoso(sa) - **2.** [body, man] nervudo(da).

wisdom ['wɪzdəm] n - **1.** [learning] sabiduría f
- **2.** [good sense] sensatez f.

wisdom tooth n muela f del juicio.

wise [waɪz] adj - **1.** [learned] sabio(bia); **to get
wise to sthg** inf caer en la cuenta de algo;
she's no wiser OR **none the wiser** sigue sin
entender - **2.** [sensible] prudente.
◆ **wise up** vi US enterarse, ponerse al tanto.

wisecrack ['waɪzkræk] n pej broma f, chiste m.

wish [wɪʃ] ◇ n: **wish (for sthg/to do sthg)**
deseo m (de algo/de hacer algo); **to make a
wish** pedir un deseo; **to do sthg against sb's
wishes** hacer algo en contra de los deseos de
alguien. ◇ vt: **to wish to do sthg** fml desear
hacer algo; **to wish sb sthg** desear a alguien
algo; **I wish (that) you had told me before!**
¡ojalá me lo hubieras dicho antes!; **I wish
(that) I were** OR **was rich** ojalá fuera rico; **I
wish (that) you would shut up** ¿por qué no
te callas? ◇ vi [by magic]: **to wish for sthg**
pedir (como deseo) algo.
◆ **wishes** npl: **(with) best wishes** [in letter]
muchos recuerdos.
◆ **wish on** vt sep: **to wish sthg on sb** desearle
algo a alguien.

wishbone ['wɪʃbəʊn] n espoleta f.

wishful thinking [,wɪʃful-] n (U): **it's just
wishful thinking** no son más que (vanas) ilusiones.

wishy-washy ['wɪʃɪ,wɒʃɪ] adj inf pej soso(sa),
insípido(da).

wisp [wɪsp] n - **1.** [of hair] mechón m; [of grass]
brizna f - **2.** [cloud] nubecilla f; [of smoke] voluta f.

wispy ['wɪspɪ] (comp -ier, superl -iest) adj
[hair] ralo(la) y a mechones.

wistful ['wɪstful] adj triste, melancólico(ca).

wit [wɪt] n - **1.** [humour] ingenio m, agudeza f
- **2.** [funny person] chistoso m, -sa f - **3.** [intelligence]: **to have the wit to do sthg** tener el
buen juicio de hacer algo.
◆ **wits** npl: **to have** OR **keep one's wits about
one** mantenerse alerta; **to be scared out of
one's wits** inf estar muerto de miedo; **to be at
one's wits' end** estar a punto de volverse loco.

witch [wɪtʃ] n bruja f.

witchcraft ['wɪtʃkrɑːft] n brujería f.

witchdoctor ['wɪtʃ,dɒktər] n hechicero m, -ra f.

witch-hazel n [liquid] liquidámbar m.

witch-hunt n pej caza f de brujas.

with [wɪð] prep - **1.** [in company of] con; **we
stayed with them for a week** estuvimos con
ellos una semana; **with me** conmigo; **with
you** contigo; **with himself/herself** consigo
- **2.** [indicating opposition] con; **the war with
Germany** la guerra con Alemania - **3.** [indicating means, manner, feelings] con; **I washed it
with detergent** lo lavé con detergente; **he
filled it with wine** lo llenó de vino; **covered
with mud** cubierto de barro; **she was trembling with fear** temblaba de miedo; **"all
right"**, **she said with a smile** "vale", dijo con
una sonrisa - **4.** [having - gen] con; **a man with
a beard** un hombre con barba; **the woman
with the black hair/big dog** la señora del pelo negro/perro grande; **I'm married with six
children** estoy casado con seis hijos - **5.** [regarding] con; **he's very mean with money** es
muy tacaño con el dinero - **6.** [indicating simultaneity]: **I can't do it with you watching me**
no puedo hacerlo contigo ahí mirándome
- **7.** [because of] con; **with the weather as it
is, we have decided to stay at home** con el
tiempo como está hemos decidido quedarnos
en casa; **with my luck, I'll probably lose** con
la suerte que tengo seguro que pierdo - **8.** [indicating understanding]: **are you with me?** ¿me
sigues?; **I'm sorry, I'm not with you** lo siento,
me he perdido - **9.** [indicating support] con; **I'm
with Dad on this** en eso estoy con papá.

withdraw [wɪð'drɔː] ◇ vt (pt -drew,
pp -drawn) - **1.** [gen]: **to withdraw sthg
(from)** retirar algo (de) - **2.** [money] sacar.
◇ vi (pt -drew, pp -drawn): **to withdraw
(from/to)** retirarse (de/a); **to withdraw into
o.s.** encerrarse en uno mismo.

withdrawal [wɪð'drɔːəl] n - **1.** [gen & MIL] retirada f - **2.** [retraction] retractación f - **3.** MED
(síndrome m de) abstinencia f - **4.** FIN reintegro m.

withdrawal symptoms npl síndrome m de
abstinencia.

withdrawn [wɪð'drɔːn] ◇ pp ▷ withdraw.
◇ adj [shy, quiet] reservado(da).

withdrew [wɪð'druː] pt ▷ withdraw.

wither ['wɪðər] ◇ vt marchitar. ◇ vi - **1.** [dry
up] marchitarse - **2.** [become weak] debilitarse,
decaer.

withered ['wɪðəd] adj marchito(ta).

withering ['wɪðərɪŋ] adj [remark] mordaz; [look]
fulminante.

withhold [wɪð'həʊld] (pt & pp -held [-'held]) vt
[gen] retener; [consent, permission] negar.

within [wɪ'ðɪn] ◇ prep - **1.** [gen] dentro de;
within reach al alcance de la mano; **within
sight of** a la vista de - **2.** [less than - distance] a
menos de; [- time] en menos de; **it's within
walking distance** se puede ir andando; **he**

was within five seconds of the leader estaba a cinco segundos del líder; **within the next six months** en los próximos seis meses; **it arrived within a week** llegó en menos de una semana. ⇔ *adv* dentro.

without [wɪð'aʊt] ⇔ *prep* sin; **without sthg/doing sthg** sin algo/hacer algo; **without making any mistakes** sin cometer ningún error; **it happened without my realizing** pasó sin que me diera cuenta. ⇔ *adv*: **to go** OR **do without sthg** pasar sin algo.

withstand [wɪð'stænd] (*pt & pp* **-stood** [-'stʊd]) *vt* resistir, aguantar.

witness ['wɪtnɪs] ⇔ *n* **- 1.** [person] testigo *mf*; **to be witness to sthg** ser testigo de algo **- 2.** [testimony]: **to bear witness to sthg** atestiguar algo, dar fe de algo. ⇔ *vt* **- 1.** [see] presenciar **- 2.** [countersign] firmar (como testigo).

witness box *UK*, **witness stand** *US n* tribuna *f* (de los testigos).

witter ['wɪtər] *vi UK inf pej*: **to witter (on)** parlotear.

witticism ['wɪtɪsɪzm] *n* agudeza *f*, ocurrencia *f*.

witty ['wɪtɪ] (*comp* **-ier,** *superl* **-iest**) *adj* ingenioso(sa), ocurrente.

wives [waɪvz] *npl* ⊳ **wife**.

wizard ['wɪzəd] *n* **- 1.** [magician] mago *m (en cuentos)* **- 2.** [skilled person] genio *m*.

wizened ['wɪznd] *adj* marchito(ta).

wk (*abbr of* **week**) sem.

WO *n abbr of* **warrant officer**.

wobble ['wɒbl] *vi* [gen] tambalearse; [furniture] bambolearse, cojear; [legs] temblar.

wobbly ['wɒblɪ] (*comp* **-ier,** *superl* **-iest**) *adj inf* [jelly, flesh] bamboleante; [handwriting, legs] tembloroso(sa); [furniture] cojo(ja).

woe [wəʊ] *n liter* aflicción *f*, pesar *m*.
◆ **woes** *npl liter & hum* males *mpl*, penas *fpl*.

wok [wɒk] *n* sartén *abombada y profunda con dos asas y sin mango.*

woke [wəʊk] *pt* ⊳ **wake**.

woken ['wəʊkn] *pp* ⊳ **wake**.

wolf [wʊlf] *n* (*pl* **wolves**) ZOOL lobo *m*.
◆ **wolf down** *vt sep inf* zamparse, devorar.

wolf whistle *n* silbido *m (piropo)*.

wolves ['wʊlvz] *npl* ⊳ **wolf**.

woman ['wʊmən] (*pl* **women**) ⇔ *n* **- 1.** [female] mujer *f* **- 2.** [womanhood] la mujer. ⇔ *comp*: **woman doctor** médica *f*; **woman prime minister** primera ministra *f*.

womanhood ['wʊmənhʊd] (*U*) *n* **- 1.** [adult life] edad *f* adulta (de mujer) **- 2.** [all women] la mujer.

womanize, -ise ['wʊmənaɪz] *vi pej* ser un mujeriego.

womanly ['wʊmənlɪ] *adj* femenino(na).

womb [wuːm] *n* matriz *f*, útero *m*.

wombat ['wɒmbæt] *n tipo de oso marsupial.*

women ['wɪmɪn] *npl* ⊳ **woman**.

women's group *n* grupo *m* feminista.

Women's Institute *n UK*: **the Women's Institute** *organización cultural para mujeres.*

women's lib [-'lɪb] *n* liberación *f* de la mujer.

women's liberation *n* liberación *f* de la mujer.

won [wʌn] *pt & pp* ⊳ **win**.

wonder ['wʌndər] ⇔ *n* **- 1.** [amazement] asombro *m*, admiración *f* **- 2.** [cause for surprise]: **it's a wonder (that)...** es un milagro que...; **no** OR **little** OR **small wonder...** no es de extrañar que... **- 3.** [amazing thing, person] maravilla *f*; **to work** OR **do wonders** hacer maravillas OR milagros. ⇔ *vt* **- 1.** [speculate]: **to wonder (if** OR **whether)** preguntarse (si) **- 2.** [in polite requests]: **I wonder if** OR **whether I could ask you a question?** ¿le importaría que le hiciera una pregunta? **- 3.** [be surprised]: **I wonder (that) she hasn't left him** me pregunto cómo es que todavía no lo ha dejado. ⇔ *vi* **- 1.** [speculate]: **I was only wondering** preguntaba sólo por curiosidad; **to wonder about sthg** preguntarse por algo **- 2.** *liter* [be amazed]: **to wonder at sthg** quedarse maravillado ante algo.

wonderful ['wʌndəfʊl] *adj* maravilloso(sa), estupendo(da).

wonderfully ['wʌndəfʊlɪ] *adv* **- 1.** [very well] estupendamente **- 2.** [very] extremadamente.

wonderland ['wʌndəlænd] *n* mundo *m* maravilloso.

wonky ['wɒŋkɪ] (*comp* **-ier,** *superl* **-iest**) *adj UK inf* [table, chair etc] cojo(ja); [picture, tie etc] torcido(da).

wont [wəʊnt] ⇔ *adj*: **to be wont to do sthg** ser dado(da) a hacer algo, soler hacer algo. ⇔ *n dated & liter*: **as is his/her** etc **wont** como de costumbre.

won't [wəʊnt] (*abbr of* = **will not**), = **will**.

woo [wuː] *vt* **- 1.** *liter* [court] cortejar **- 2.** [try to win over] granjearse el apoyo de.

wood [wʊd] ⇔ *n* **- 1.** [timber] madera *f*; [for fire] leña *f*; **touch wood!** ¡toquemos madera! **- 2.** [group of trees] bosque *m*; **I can't see the wood for the trees** *UK* los árboles no me dejan ver el bosque **- 3.** GOLF (palo *m* de) madera *f*. ⇔ *comp* de madera.
◆ **woods** *npl* bosque *m*.

wooded ['wʊdɪd] *adj* arbolado(da).

wooden ['wʊdn] *adj* **- 1.** [of wood] de madera **- 2.** *pej* [actor] envarado(da).

woodland ['wʊdlənd] *n* bosque *m*.

woodpecker ['wʊd,pekər] *n* pájaro *m* carpintero.

wood pigeon n paloma f torcaz.

woodshed ['wʊdʃed] n leñera f.

woodwind ['wʊdwɪnd] n: **the woodwind** los instrumentos de viento de madera.

woodwork ['wʊdwɜːk] n carpintería f.

woodworm ['wʊdwɜːm] n carcoma f.

woof [wuːf] n ladrido m; **woof!** ¡guau!

wool [wʊl] n lana f; **to pull the wool over sb's eyes** inf fig dar a alguien gato por liebre.

woollen UK, **woolen** US ['wʊlən] adj de lana.
◆ **woollens** npl géneros mpl de lana.

woolly ['wʊlɪ] ◇ adj (comp **-ier**, superl **-iest**) - **1.** [woollen] de lana - **2.** inf [fuzzy, unclear] confuso(sa). ◇ n (pl **-ies**) inf prenda f de lana.

woolly-headed ['-hedɪd] adj inf pej de ideas confusas OR vagas.

woozy ['wuːzɪ] (comp **-ier**, superl **-iest**) adj inf mareado(da).

Worcester sauce ['wʊstəʳ-] n (U) salsa f Perrins®.

Worcs. (abbr of **Worcestershire**) antiguo condado inglés.

word [wɜːd] ◇ n - **1.** LING palabra f; **we couldn't understand a word he said** no entendimos ni una sola palabra de lo que dijo; **word for word** palabra por palabra; **in other words** en otras palabras; **in one's own words** (uno) con sus propias palabras; **not in so many words** no con esas palabras; **in a word** en una palabra; **too... for words** de lo más...; **by word of mouth** de palabra; **to put in a (good) word for sb** hablar en favor de alguien; **just say the word** no tienes más que decirlo; **she doesn't mince her words** no tiene pelos en la lengua; **to have a word with sb** hablar con alguien; **to have words with sb** inf tener unas palabritas con alguien; **to have the last word** tener la última palabra; **to put sthg into words** expresar algo con palabras; **to weigh one's words** medir (uno) sus palabras; **I couldn't get a word in edgeways** no pude meter baza - **2.** (U) [news] noticia f; **there is no word from them** no hemos tenido noticias de ellos; **word has it that...** se rumorea que... - **3.** [promise] palabra f; **to give sb one's word** dar (uno) su palabra a alguien; **I give you my word** te lo prometo; **to keep/break one's word** mantener/no cumplir la palabra de uno; **to be as good as one's word, to be true to one's word** cumplir lo prometido. ◇ vt redactar, expresar.

word game n juego a base de palabras.

wording ['wɜːdɪŋ] n (U) términos mpl, forma f (de expresión).

word-perfect adj: **to be word-perfect** saber perfectamente el papel.

wordplay ['wɜːdpleɪ] n (U) juegos mpl de palabras.

word processing n (U) proceso m de textos.

word processor [-'prəʊsesəʳ] n procesador m de textos.

wordwrap ['wɜːdræp] n COMPUT salto m de línea automático.

wordy ['wɜːdɪ] (comp **-ier**, superl **-iest**) adj pej prolijo(ja).

wore [wɔːʳ] pt ▷ **wear**.

work [wɜːk] ◇ n - **1.** (U) [employment] trabajo m, empleo m; **to be in work** tener trabajo; **to be out of work** estar desempleado; **at work** en el trabajo - **2.** [activity, tasks] trabajo m; **at work** trabajando; **to have one's work cut out doing sthg** OR **to do sthg** tenerlo muy difícil para hacer algo - **3.** [of art, literature etc] obra f; **he's a nasty piece of work** es un elemento de cuidado - **4.** [handiwork] obra f; **it was the work of a psychopath** fue obra de un psicópata. ◇ vt - **1.** [employees, subordinates] hacer trabajar; **she works herself too hard** trabaja demasiado - **2.** [machine] manejar, operar - **3.** [wood, metal, land] trabajar - **4.** [cause to become]: **to work o.s. into a frenzy** ponerse frenético - **5.** [force]: **to work one's way through** [crowd etc] abrirse camino por; **to work one's way up** [in career] llegar a un (alto) puesto a fuerza de trabajo. ◇ vi - **1.** [person]: **to work (on sthg)** trabajar (en algo); **he works as a gardener** trabaja de jardinero; **to work for sb** trabajar para alguien - **2.** [machine, system, idea] funcionar - **3.** [drug] surtir efecto - **4.** [have effect]: **to work against sb/sthg** funcionar contra alguien/algo - **5.** [become by movement]: **to work loose** soltarse; **to work free** desprenderse.
◆ **works** ◇ n [factory] fábrica f. ◇ npl - **1.** [mechanism] mecanismo m - **2.** [digging, building] obras fpl - **3.** inf [everything]: **the works** todo completo.
◆ **work off** vt sep [anger, frustration] desahogar.
◆ **work on** vt insep - **1.** [pay attention to] trabajar en - **2.** [take as basis] partir de.
◆ **work out** ◇ vt sep - **1.** [plan, schedule] elaborar - **2.** [total, amount] calcular; [answer] dar con. ◇ vi - **1.** [figure etc]: **to work out at** salir a - **2.** [turn out] resultar, resolverse - **3.** [be successful] salir bien, resultar bien - **4.** [train, exercise] entrenarse, hacer ejercicio.
◆ **work up** ◇ vt sep - **1.** [excite]: **to work o.s. up into a frenzy** ponerse frenético(ca) - **2.** [generate] despertar; **I can't work up much enthusiasm** no consigo entusiasmarme; **to work up an appetite** abrir el apetito. ◇ vi: **to work up to sthg** mentalizarse para algo.

workable ['wɜːkəbl] adj factible, viable.

workaday ['wɜːkədeɪ] *adj pej* prosaico(ca), corriente.

workaholic [,wɜːkə'hɒlɪk] *n* adicto *m*, -ta *f* al trabajo.

workbench ['wɜːkbentʃ] *n* banco *m* de trabajo.

workbook ['wɜːkbʊk] *n* libro *m* de ejercicios.

workday ['wɜːkdeɪ], **working day** *n* - **1.** [day's work] jornada *f* de trabajo - **2.** [not weekend] día *m* laborable.

worked up [,wɜːkt-] *adj* nervioso(sa); **to get worked up** alterarse.

worker ['wɜːkər] *n* [person who works] trabajador *m*, -ra *f*; [manual worker] obrero *m*, -ra *f*; **they're hard/slow workers** trabajan duro/despacio; **a hard/fast worker** una persona que trabaja mucho/a prisa; **office worker** oficinista *mf*.

workforce ['wɜːkfɔːs] *n* mano *f* de obra.

workhouse ['wɜːkhaʊs] *n* UK [poor house] *asilo para pobres en la época victoriana.*

working ['wɜːkɪŋ] *adj* - **1.** [in operation] funcionando - **2.** [having employment] empleado(da); **a working mother** una madre trabajadora - **3.** [relating to work - gen] laboral; [- clothes] de trabajo; [- day] laborable.

➤ **workings** *npl* mecanismo *m*.

Working hours ▬▬▬▬▬

La jornada laboral del Reino Unido es normalmente de 35 a 38 horas a la semana. El horario suele ser de 9 a 5, con una hora de descanso para comer. Si los trabajadores tienen que hacer horas extras, a menudo no son remuneradas. En sectores como la hostelería o los hospitales, se puede llegar a trabajar entre 50 y 60 horas a la semana. Ciertas empresas ofrecen un sistema de horarios flexibles (llamado "flexitime" en Reino Unido o "flextime" en Estados Unidos), que permite a los empleados distribuir con cierta libertad su horario de trabajo: pueden, por ejemplo, empezar o terminar más tarde o trabajar durante la pausa de la comida, siempre y cuando estén presentes a unas horas determinadas por la empresa. En cuanto a las vacaciones, lo normal son 4 ó 5 semanas al año, incluyendo las vacaciones de Navidad, aunque en general no se pueden tomar más de dos semanas seguidas. En Estados Unidos, los empleados trabajan entre 40 y 45 horas a la semana, generalmente de 8 a 5 con una hora de descanso. El "flextime" está menos extendido que en el Reino Unido y las horas extras tampoco se suelen remunerar. Las vacaciones varían entre 1 a 4 semanas y aumentan según la antigüedad del trabajador en la empresa.

working capital *n* - **1.** [assets minus liabilities] capital *m* líquido - **2.** [available money] capital *m* disponible.

working class *n*: **the working class** la clase obrera.

➤ **working-class** *adj* obrero(ra).

working day = workday.

working knowledge *n* conocimientos *mpl* básicos.

working man *n* trabajador *m*.

working model *n* maqueta *f* operativa.

working order *n*: **to be in (good) working order** funcionar (bien).

working party *n* grupo *m* de trabajo, comisión *f* investigadora.

working week *n* semana *f* laboral.

work-in-progress *n* trabajo *m* en curso.

workload ['wɜːkləʊd] *n* cantidad *f* de trabajo.

workman ['wɜːkmən] (*pl* **-men** [-mən]) *n* obrero *m*.

workmanship ['wɜːkmənʃɪp] *n* artesanía *f*.

workmate ['wɜːkmeɪt] *n* compañero *m*, -ra *f* de trabajo, colega *mf*.

work of art *n lit* & *fig* obra *f* de arte.

workout ['wɜːkaʊt] *n* ejercicios *mpl* físicos.

work permit [-,pɜːmɪt] *n* permiso *m* de trabajo.

workplace ['wɜːkpleɪs] *n* lugar *m* de trabajo.

workroom ['wɜːkrʊm] *n* taller *m*.

works council *n* ≃ comité *m* de empresa.

workshop ['wɜːkʃɒp] *n* taller *m*.

workshy ['wɜːkʃaɪ] *adj* UK vago(ga), gandul(la).

workspace ['wɜːkspeɪs] *n* COMPUT espacio *m* de trabajo.

workstation ['wɜːk,steɪʃn] *n* COMPUT estación *f* de trabajo.

work surface *n* superficie *f* de trabajo.

worktable ['wɜːk,teɪbl] *n* mesa *f* de trabajo.

worktop ['wɜːktɒp] *n* UK mármol *m*, encimera *f*.

work-to-rule *n* UK huelga *f* de celo.

world [wɜːld] ◇ *n* mundo *m*; **the best in the world** el mejor del mundo; **the highest mountain in the world** la montaña más alta del mundo; **what/where/why in the world...?** ¿qué/dónde/por qué demonios...?; **all over the world** por todo el mundo; **the world over** en todo el mundo; **to be dead to the world** dormir como un tronco; **to want the best of both worlds** querer estar en misa y repicando; **to think the world of sb** querer a alguien con locura; **to do sb the world of good** venirle de maravilla a alguien; **a world of difference** una diferencia enorme; **to see the world** ver mundo; **it's a small world** el mundo es un pañuelo; **the antique world** el mundo antiguo; **what is the world coming to?** ¿a dónde vamos a ir a parar?; **they are worlds apart** hay un abismo entre ellos; **to have all the time in the world** tener todo el tiempo del mundo. ◇ *comp* mundial.

World Bank *n*: **the World Bank** el Banco Mundial.

world-class *adj* de primera categoría.

World Cup *n* FTBL: **the World Cup** el mundial (de fútbol).

world-famous *adj* famoso(sa) en el mundo entero.

worldly ['wɜ:ldlɪ] *adj liter* mundano(na); **worldly goods** bienes *mpl* materiales.

world music *n* música *f* étnica.

world power *n* potencia *f* mundial.

World Series *n*: **the World Series** *la final de la liga estadounidense de béisbol.*

World Series

La **World Series** o Serie Mundial es la más importante competición de béisbol y uno de los eventos deportivos anuales de mayor relevancia en los Estados Unidos. Consiste en una serie de hasta siete partidos en los que se enfrentan al final de la temporada, en el mes de octubre, los campeones de las dos ligas más importantes de los Estados Unidos (la **National League** y la **American League**). El primer equipo que obtiene cuatro victorias se proclama campeón. Según la tradición, el presidente de la nación inaugura el encuentro lanzando la primera pelota.

World Trade Organization *n* Organización *f* Mundial del Comercio.

World War I *n* la Primera Guerra Mundial.

World War II *n* la Segunda Guerra Mundial.

world-weary *adj* hastiado(da), cansado(da) de la vida.

worldwide ['wɜ:ldwaɪd] ◇ *adj* mundial. ◇ *adv* en todo el mundo, a escala mundial.

World Wide Web *n*: **the World Wide Web** la (World Wide) Web.

worm [wɜ:m] ◇ *n* [animal] gusano *m*; [earthworm] lombriz *f* (de tierra). ◇ *vt*: **to worm one's way into sthg** [move] lograr colarse en algo; [wheedle] lograr atraer para sí algo. ➤ **worms** *npl* [parasites] lombrices *fpl*. ➤ **worm out** *vt sep*: **to worm sthg out of sb** sonsacarle algo a alguien.

worn [wɔ:n] ◇ *pp* ▷ **wear**. ◇ *adj* - **1.** [threadbare] gastado(da) - **2.** [tired] ajado(da).

worn-out *adj* - **1.** [old, threadbare]: **to be worn-out** estar ya para tirar - **2.** [tired] agotado(da).

worried ['wʌrɪd] *adj* preocupado(da); **to be worried (sick) about** estar (muy) preocupado(da) por.

worrier ['wʌrɪər] *n*: **to be a worrier** preocuparse por todo.

worry ['wʌrɪ] ◇ *n* (*pl* **-ies**) preocupación *f*. ◇ *vt* (*pt & pp* **-ied**) [trouble] preocupar. ◇ *vi* (*pt & pp* **-ied**): **to worry (about)** preocuparse (por); **not to worry!** ¡no importa!

worrying ['wʌrɪɪŋ] *adj* preocupante.

worrywart ['wʌrɪwɔ:rt] *n US inf* angustias *mf inv Esp*, angustiado *m*, -da *f*.

worse [wɜ:s] ◇ *adj* peor; **to get worse** empeorar; **to get worse and worse** ir cada vez peor; **to go from bad to worse** ir de mal en peor; **to make things worse** empeorar las cosas; **they are none the worse for their adventure** se sienten perfectamente a pesar de su aventura. ◇ *adv* peor; **worse off** [gen] en peor situación; [financially] peor económicamente; **you could do worse than marry him** no harías tan mal casándote con él. ◇ *n*: **worse was to come** lo peor estaba aún por venir; **so much the worse** tanto peor; **a change for the worse** un cambio para peor; **to take a turn for the worse** empeorar.

worsen ['wɜ:sn] *vt & vi* empeorar.

worsening ['wɜ:snɪŋ] *adj* cada vez peor.

worship ['wɜ:ʃɪp] ◇ *vt* (*UK* **-ped**, *cont* **-ping**, *US* **-ed**, *cont* **-ing**) *lit & fig* adorar. ◇ *n lit & fig*: **worship (of)** culto *m* (a), adoración *f* (por). ➤ **Worship** *n*: **Your/Her/His Worship** su señoría; **his Worship the Mayor** el Excelentísimo Señor alcalde.

worshipper *UK*, **worshiper** *US* ['wɜ:ʃɪpər] *n fig & RELIG* devoto *m*, -ta *f*.

worst [wɜ:st] ◇ *adj* peor; **the worst thing is...** lo peor es que...; **worst of all** lo peor de todo. ◇ *adv* peor; **the worst affected area** la región más afectada. ◇ *n*: **the worst** [thing] lo peor; [person] el peor *m*, la peor *f*; **this is communism at its worst** esto es la peor manifestación del comunismo; **to fear the worst** temer lo peor; **if the worst comes to the worst** en último extremo; **to bring out the worst in sb** sacar lo peor de alguien. ➤ **at (the) worst** *adv* en el peor de los casos.

worsted ['wʊstɪd] *n* estambre *m*.

worth [wɜ:θ] ◇ *prep* - **1.** [having the value of]: **it's worth £50** vale 50 libras; **how much is it worth?** ¿cuánto vale?; **it isn't worth that much** no vale tanto - **2.** [deserving of] digno(na) de, merecedor(ra) de; **the museum is worth**

visiting OR a visit, it's worth visiting the museum el museo merece una visita; **it's not worth it** no vale la pena; **it's worth a try** vale la pena intentarlo; **for what it's worth, I think that...** por si mi opinión sirve de algo, creo que... ◇ *n* - **1.** [amount]: **£50,000 worth of antiques** antigüedades por valor de 50.000 libras; **a month's worth of groceries** provisiones para un mes - **2.** *fml* [value] valor *m*.

worthless ['wɜːθlɪs] *adj* - **1.** [object] sin valor - **2.** [person] despreciable.

worthwhile [ˌwɜːθ'waɪl] *adj* que vale la pena; [cause] noble, digno(na).

worthy ['wɜːðɪ] (*comp* -ier, *superl* -iest) *adj* - **1.** [gen] digno(na) - **2.** [good but unexciting] encomiable.

would [wʊd] *modal vb* - **1.** *(in reported speech)*: **she said she would come** dijo que vendría - **2.** *(in conditional phrases)*: **if she couldn't come she would tell us** si no pudiera venir nos lo diría; **what would you do?** ¿qué harías?; **if he had known, he would have resigned** si lo hubiera sabido, habría dimitido - **3.** *(indicating willingness)*: **she wouldn't go** no quiso/quería ir; **he would do anything for her** haría cualquier cosa por ella - **4.** *(in polite questions)*: **would you like a drink?** ¿quieres beber algo?; **would you mind closing the window?** ¿le importaría cerrar la ventana?; **help me shut this suitcase, would you?** ayúdame a cerrar esta maleta, ¿quieres? - **5.** [indicating inevitability]: **he would say that, wouldn't he?** hombre, era de esperar que dijera eso, ¿no? - **6.** [expressing opinions]: **I would have thought (that) it would be easy** hubiera pensado que sería fácil; **I would prefer...** preferiría...; **I would like...** quiero..., quiero... - **7.** [giving advice]: **I would report it if I were you** yo en tu lugar lo denunciaría - **8.** [indicating habit]: **he would smoke a cigar after dinner** solía fumar un puro después de la cena; **she would often complain about the neighbours** se quejaba a menudo de los vecinos - **9.** [in conjectures]: **it would have been around 2 o'clock** serían las dos.

would-be *adj*: **a would-be author** un aspirante a literato.

wouldn't ['wʊdnt] (*abbr of* = would not), = **would**.

would've ['wʊdəv] (*abbr of* = would have), = **would**.

wound[1] [wuːnd] ◇ *n* herida *f*; **to lick one's wounds** compadecerse de uno mismo tras la derrota. ◇ *vt lit & fig* herir.

wound[2] [waʊnd] *pt & pp* ▷ **wind**.

wounded ['wuːndɪd] ◇ *adj* herido(da). ◇ *npl*: **the wounded** los heridos.

wounding ['wuːndɪŋ] *adj* hiriente.

wove [wəʊv] *pt* ▷ **weave**.

woven ['wəʊvn] *pp* ▷ **weave**.

wow [waʊ] *excl inf* ¡anda!, ¡caramba!

WP *abbr of* **word processing**. *abbr of* **word processor**.

WPC (*abbr of* **woman police constable**) *n* (*mujer del*) *rango más bajo de la policía británica*, ≃ agente *f*; **WPC Roberts** agente Roberts.

wpm (*abbr of* **words per minute**) p.p.m.

WRAC [ræk] (*abbr of* **Women's Royal Army Corps**) *n sección femenina del ejército británico*.

WRAF [ræf] (*abbr of* **Women's Royal Air Force**) *n sección femenina de las fuerzas aéreas británicas*.

wrangle ['ræŋgl] ◇ *n* disputa *f*. ◇ *vi*: **to wrangle (with sb over sthg)** discutir OR pelearse (con alguien por algo).

wrap [ræp] ◇ *vt* (*pt & pp* -ped, *cont* -ping) - **1.** [cover] envolver; **to wrap sthg in sthg** envolver algo en algo; **to wrap sthg around OR round sthg** liar algo alrededor de algo - **2.** [encircle]: **he wrapped his hands around it** lo rodeó con sus manos. ◇ *n* - **1.** [garment] echarpe *m*; **to keep sthg under wraps** *fig* mantener algo en secreto - **2.** US [food] *tipo de bocadillo servido en una torta de maíz y doblado por la mitad*.

◆ **wrap up** ◇ *vt sep* - **1.** [cover] envolver - **2.** *inf* [complete] cerrar, finiquitar - **3.** US [summarize] resumir. ◇ *vi* [put warm clothes on]: **wrap up well** OR **warmly** abrígate bien.

wrapped up [ræpt-] *adj inf*: **to be wrapped up in sthg** estar absorto(ta) en algo; **to be wrapped up in sb** estar embelesado(da) con alguien.

wrapper ['ræpər] *n* envoltorio *m*.

wrapping ['ræpɪŋ] *n* envoltorio *m*.

wrapping paper *n* (U) papel *m* de envolver.

wrath [rɒθ] *n liter* ira *f*, cólera *f*.

wreak [riːk] *vt* causar; **to wreak havoc** hacer estragos; **to wreak revenge** OR **vengeance** tomar la revancha.

wreath [riːθ] *n* corona *f* (de flores).

wreathe [riːð] *vt liter* cubrir, envolver.

wreck [rek] ◇ *n* - **1.** [of car, plane] restos *mpl* del siniestro; [of ship] restos del naufragio - **2.** *inf* [person] guiñapo *m*; **to look a wreck** estar hecho un trapo; **to be a nervous wreck** estar hecho(cha) un manojo de nervios. ◇ *vt*

wreckage

- **1.** [destroy] destrozar - **2.** NAUT hacer naufragar; **to be wrecked** naufragar - **3.** [spoil] dar al traste con; [health] acabar con.

wreckage ['rekɪdʒ] n (U) [of plane, car] restos mpl; [of building] escombros mpl.

wrecker ['rekər] n US [vehicle] camión m grúa.

wren [ren] n chochín m.

wrench [rentʃ] <> n - **1.** US [tool] llave f inglesa - **2.** [injury] torcedura f - **3.** [cause of suffering]: **it was a wrench to leave her** fue doloroso dejarla. <> vt - **1.** [pull violently]: **to wrench sthg (off)** arrancar algo; **to wrench sthg open** abrir algo de un tirón - **2.** [twist and injure] torcer.

wrest [rest] vt liter: **to wrest sthg from sb** arrebatarle algo a alguien.

wrestle ['resl] <> vt luchar con OR contra. <> vi lit & fig: **to wrestle (with)** luchar (con).

wrestler ['reslər] n luchador m, -ra f.

wrestling ['reslɪŋ] n lucha f libre.

wretch [retʃ] n desgraciado m, -da f, infeliz mf.

wretched ['retʃɪd] adj - **1.** [miserable] miserable - **2.** inf [damned] maldito(ta).

wriggle ['rɪgl] <> vt menear. <> vi - **1.** [move about] menearse - **2.** [twist] escurrirse, deslizarse.

➤ **wriggle out of** vt insep: **to wriggle out of sthg/doing sthg** escaquearse de algo/de hacer algo.

wring [rɪŋ] (pt & pp wrung) vt - **1.** [wet clothes etc] estrujar, escurrir - **2.** liter [hands] retorcerse - **3.** [neck] retorcer.

➤ **wring out** vt sep estrujar, escurrir.

wringing ['rɪŋɪŋ] adj: **wringing (wet)** empapado(da).

wrinkle ['rɪŋkl] <> n arruga f. <> vt arrugar. <> vi arrugarse.

wrinkled ['rɪŋkld], **wrinkly** ['rɪŋklɪ] adj arrugado(da).

wrist [rɪst] n muñeca f.

wristband ['rɪstbænd] n [leather] correa f; [metal, plastic] brazalete m, pulsera f.

wristwatch ['rɪstwɒtʃ] n reloj m de pulsera.

writ [rɪt] n mandato m judicial.

write [raɪt] (pt wrote, pp written) <> vt - **1.** [gen & COMPUT] escribir; **to write sb a letter** escribirle una carta a alguien; **to write sb a cheque** extender un cheque a nombre de alguien - **2.** US [person] escribir a. <> vi [gen & COMPUT] escribir; **to write (to sb)** UK escribir (a alguien).

➤ **write away** vi: **to write away for sthg** escribir pidiendo algo.

➤ **write back** vt sep & vi contestar.

➤ **write down** vt sep apuntar.

➤ **write in** vi escribir, mandar cartas.

➤ **write off** <> vt sep - **1.** [plan, hopes] abandonar - **2.** [debt] cancelar, anular - **3.** [person - as failure] considerar un fracaso - **4.** UK inf [wreck] cargarse, destrozar. <> vi: **to write off (to sb)** escribir (a alguien); **to write off for sthg** escribir pidiendo algo.

➤ **write up** vt sep redactar.

write-off n: **the car was a write-off** el coche quedó totalmente destrozado.

write-protect <> adj COMPUT de protección contra la copia. <> vt COMPUT proteger contra la copia.

writer ['raɪtər] n - **1.** [as profession] escritor m, -ra f - **2.** [of letter, article, story] autor m, -ra f.

write-up n inf reseña f.

writhe [raɪð] vi retorcerse.

writing ['raɪtɪŋ] n - **1.** (U) [handwriting] letra f, caligrafía f - **2.** [something written] escrito m; **to put sthg in writing** poner algo por escrito - **3.** [activity] escritura f.

➤ **writings** npl escritos mpl.

writing desk n escritorio m.

writing paper n (U) papel m de carta.

written ['rɪtn] <> pp ▷ **write**. <> adj - **1.** [not oral] escrito(ta) - **2.** [official] por escrito.

WRNS (abbr of Women's Royal Naval Service) n sección femenina de la armada británica.

wrong [rɒŋ] <> adj - **1.** [not normal, not satisfactory] malo(la); **the clock's wrong** el reloj anda mal; **what's wrong?** ¿qué pasa?, ¿qué va mal?; **there's nothing wrong** no pasa nada; **there's nothing wrong with me** no me pasa nada - **2.** [not suitable, not correct] equivocado(da); [moment, time] inoportuno(na); [answer] incorrecto(ta); **I got the wrong number** me equivoqué de número; **he has given me the wrong change** me ha dado el cambio equivocado; **I think we've gone the wrong way** creo que nos hemos equivocado de camino; **I always seem to say the wrong thing** parece que siempre digo lo que no debo; **to be wrong** [person] equivocarse; **to be wrong about sthg/sb** equivocarse con respecto a algo/alguien; **to be wrong to do sthg** cometer un error al hacer algo - **3.** [morally bad] malo(la); **it's wrong to steal/lie** robar/mentir está mal; **what's wrong with being a communist?** ¿qué tiene de malo ser comunista? <> adv [incorrectly] mal; **to get sthg wrong** entender mal algo; **to go wrong** [make a mistake] cometer un error; [stop functioning] estropearse; [plans] salir mal; **don't get me wrong** inf no me malinterpretes. <> n - **1.** [evil] mal m; **to be in the wrong** haber hecho mal; **he can do no**

wrong nada de lo que hace está mal **- 2.** [injustice] injusticia *f.* ◇ *vt* ser injusto(ta) con, agraviar.

wrong-foot *vt UK lit* & *fig* coger a contrapié a.

wrongful ['rɒŋfʊl] *adj* [dismissal] improcedente; [arrest, imprisonment] ilegal.

wrongly ['rɒŋlɪ] *adv* equivocadamente.

wrote [rəʊt] *pt* ▷ **write**.

wrought iron [rɔːt-] *n* hierro *m* forjado.

wrung [rʌŋ] *pt* & *pp* ▷ **wring**.

WRVS (*abbr of* **Women's Royal Voluntary Service**) *n organización británica de mujeres que ayudan voluntariamente a los necesitados y en emergencias.*

wry [raɪ] *adj* [amused] irónico(ca).

wt. *abbr of* **weight**.

WTO [ˌdʌbljuːtiːˈəʊ] (*abbr of* **World Trade Organization**) *n* OMC *f.*

WWW (*abbr of* **World Wide Web**) *n* WWW *f.*

WYSIWYG ['wɪzɪwɪg] (*abbr of* **what you see is what you get**) *n* COMPUT *lo que se ve en la pantalla es lo que aparece en la impresión.*

x (*pl* **x's** *OR* **xs**), **X** (*pl* **X's** *OR* **Xs**) [eks] *n* **- 1.** [letter] x *f inv*, X *f inv* **- 2.** [unknown quantity] equis *f inv*; **x number of...** un número equis de... **- 3.** [in algebra, to mark spot] x *f* **- 4.** [at end of letter] besos.
◆ **X** *n* [unknown name]: **Mr X** el señor X.

xenophobia [ˌzenəˈfəʊbjə] *n* xenofobia *f.*

Xmas ['eksməs] *n* Navidad *f.*

XML [ˌeksemˈel] (*abbr of* **Extensible Markup Language**) *n* COMPUT XML *m.*

X-ray ◇ *n* **- 1.** [ray] rayo *m* X **- 2.** [picture] radiografía *f*; **to have a chest X-ray** hacerse una radiografía. ◇ *vt* examinar con rayos X, radiografiar.

xylophone ['zaɪləfəʊn] *n* xilofón *m.*

y (*pl* **y's** *OR* **ys**), **Y** (*pl* **Y's** *OR* **Ys**) [waɪ] *n* [letter] y *f*, Y *f.*

yacht [jɒt] *n* yate *m*; [for racing] balandro *m.*

yachting ['jɒtɪŋ] *n* balandrismo *m.*

yachtsman ['jɒtsmən] (*pl* **-men** [-mən]) *n* balandrista *m.*

yachtswoman ['jɒts,wʊmən] (*pl* **-women** [-,wɪmɪn]) *n* balandrista *f.*

yak [jæk] *n* yak *m.*

Yale lock® [jeɪl-] *n* cerradura *f* de molinillo.

yam [jæm] *n* **- 1.** boniato *m* **- 2.** *US* [sweet potato] batata *f.*

yank [jæŋk] *vt* dar un tirón a.

Yank [jæŋk] *n inf pej* [estadounidense] yanqui *mf.*

Yankee ['jæŋkɪ] *n US término usado para designar a una persona del noreste de los EEUU.*

Yankee

En sus orígenes, el término inglés **Yankee** o **Yank** se refería a los inmigrantes holandeses que se establecieron principalmente en el noreste de los Estados Unidos. Más tarde se utilizó para referirse a cualquier persona procedente del noreste, por lo que durante la Guerra de Secesión se llamaba "yanquis" (**Yankees**) a los soldados que luchaban en el bando de los estados del norte. En nuestros días, algunos estadounidenses sureños aún utilizan el término en tono despectivo para referirse a la gente del norte. Los no norteamericanos --británicos incluidos-- también lo emplean, generalmente con sentido peyorativo, para designar a cualquier persona de nacionalidad norteamericana..

yap [jæp] (*pt* & *pp* **-ped**, *cont* **-ping**) *vi* **- 1.** [dog] ladrar **- 2.** *pej* [person] parlotear, cotorrear.

yard [jɑːd] *n* **- 1.** [unit of measurement] = *91,44 cm* yarda *f* **- 2.** [walled area] patio *m* **- 3.** [shipyard] astillero *m*; **builder's/goods yard** depósito *m* de materiales/de mercancías **- 4.** *US* [attached to house] jardín *m.*

yardstick ['jɑːdstɪk] *n* criterio *m*, pauta *f.*

yarn [jɑːn] n - **1.** [thread] hilo m, hilaza f - **2.** inf [story]: **to spin sb a yarn** contarle una batallita OR un cuento chino a alguien.

yashmak ['jæʃmæk] n velo m (de musulmana).

yawn [jɔːn] ◇ n - **1.** [when tired] bostezo m - **2.** UK inf [boring event] rollo m. ◇ vi - **1.** [when tired] bostezar - **2.** [gap, chasm] abrirse.

yd abbr of yard.

yeah [jeə] adv inf sí.

year [jɪəʳ] n - **1.** [gen] año m; **year in, year out** año tras año; **he's 25 years old** tiene 25 años; **all (the) year round** todo el año; **over the years** con los años - **2.** SCH curso m; **he's in (his) first year** está en primero.
➤ **years** npl [ages] años mpl; **it's years since I last saw you** hace siglos que no te veo.

yearbook ['jɪəbʊk] n anuario m.

Yearbook ▬▬▬

Al final de cada año académico los centros de enseñanza de Estados Unidos publican un **yearbook** (anuario) que resume lo ocurrido a los alumnos del último curso e incluye sus respectivas fotografías y a menudo predicciones sobre su futuro. Últimamente los **yearbooks** han comenzado a aparecer en sitios Web, con lo que se facilita su actualización y permite a los antiguos alumnos mantenerse en contacto.

yearling ['jɪəlɪŋ] n potro m menor de dos años.

yearly ['jɪəlɪ] ◇ adj anual. ◇ adv - **1.** [once a year] una vez al año - **2.** [every year] cada año.

yearn [jɜːn] vi: **to yearn for sthg/to do sthg** ansiar algo/hacer algo.

yearning ['jɜːnɪŋ] n: **yearning (for sb/sthg)** anhelo m (de alguien/algo).

yeast [jiːst] n levadura f.

yell [jel] ◇ n grito m, alarido m. ◇ vt & vi vociferar.

yellow ['jeləʊ] ◇ adj - **1.** [in colour] amarillo(lla) - **2.** [cowardly] cobarde. ◇ n amarillo m. ◇ vi ponerse amarillo(lla), amarillear.

yellow card n FTBL tarjeta f amarilla.

yellow fever n fiebre f amarilla.

yellow lines n líneas fpl amarillas (de tráfico).

Yellow Pages® npl: **the Yellow Pages** las páginas amarillas.

yelp [jelp] ◇ n aullido m. ◇ vi aullar.

Yemen ['jemən] n Yemen.

Yemeni ['jemənɪ] ◇ adj yemení. ◇ n yemení mf.

yen [jen] n - **1.** (pl yen) [Japanese currency] yen m - **2.** [longing]: **to have a yen for sthg/to do sthg** tener muchas ganas de algo/de hacer algo.

yes [jes] ◇ adv sí; **yes, please** sí, por favor; **to say yes** decir que sí; **to say yes to sthg** consentir algo; **does he speak English? – yes, he does** ¿habla inglés? – sí; **he doesn't speak English – yes he does!** no habla inglés – sí, sí que habla. ◇ n sí m.

yes-man n pej pelotillero m.

yesterday ['jestədɪ] ◇ n ayer m. ◇ adv ayer; **yesterday afternoon** ayer por la tarde; **the day before yesterday** antes de ayer, anteayer.

yet [jet] ◇ adv - **1.** [gen] todavía, aún; **have you had lunch yet?** ¿has comido ya?; **their worst defeat yet** la mayor derrota que han sufrido hasta la fecha; **as yet** de momento, hasta ahora; **not yet** todavía OR aún no - **2.** [even]: **yet another car** otro coche más; **yet again** otra vez más; **yet more** aún más. ◇ conj pero, sin embargo.

yew [juː] n tejo m.

Y-fronts npl UK eslip m.

YHA (abbr of Youth Hostels Association) n asociación internacional de albergues juveniles.

Yiddish ['jɪdɪʃ] ◇ adj yídish (inv). ◇ n yídish m.

yield [jiːld] ◇ n - **1.** AGRIC cosecha f - **2.** FIN rédito m. ◇ vt - **1.** [gen] producir, dar - **2.** [give up] ceder. ◇ vi - **1.** [shelf, lock etc] ceder - **2.** fml [person, enemy] rendirse; **to yield to sb/sthg** claudicar ante alguien/algo - **3.** US AUT [give way]: **'yield'** 'ceda el paso'.

yippee [UK jɪ'pɪ, US 'jɪpɪ] excl ¡yupi!

YMCA (abbr of Young Men's Christian Association) n asociación internacional de jóvenes cristianos.

yob(bo) ['jɒb(əʊ)] n UK inf gamberro m.

yodel ['jəʊdl] (UK -led, cont -ling) (US -ed, cont -ing) vi cantar a la tirolesa.

yoga ['jəʊgə] n yoga m.

yoghourt, yoghurt, yogurt [UK 'jɒgət, US 'jəʊgərt] n yogur m.

yoke [jəʊk] n lit & fig yugo m.

yokel ['jəʊkl] n pej palurdo m, -da f, paleto m, -ta f.

yolk [jəʊk] n yema f.

yonder ['jɒndəʳ] adv liter acullá.

Yorks. [jɔːks] (abbr of Yorkshire) condado inglés.

Yorkshire pudding ['jɔːkʃəʳ-] n masa horneada hecha de harina, huevos y leche que se sirve tradicionalmente con el rosbif.

Yorkshire terrier [ˈjɔːkʃər-] n Yorkshire terrier m.

you [juː] pers pron - **1.** (subject - sing) tú, vos (+ pl vb) Amér C & R Plata; (- formal use) usted; (- pl) vosotros mpl, -tras f Esp; (- formal use) ustedes (pl); **you're a good cook** eres/usted es un buen cocinero; **are you French?** ¿eres/es usted francés?; **you idiot!** ¡imbécil!; **there you are** [you've appeared] ¡ya estás/está usted aquí!; [have this] ahí tienes/tiene; **that jacket isn't really you** esa chaqueta no te/le pega - **2.** (direct object - unstressed - sing) te; (- pl) os OR los/las Amér; (- formal use) le m OR lo Amér, la f; (- pl) les mpl OR los Amér, las fpl; **I can see you** te/os OR los/las Amér veo; **yes, Madam, I understand you** sí, señora, la comprendo - **3.** (direct object - stressed): **I don't expect you to do it** no te voy a pedir que **tú** lo hagas - **4.** (indirect object - sing) te; (- pl) os OR los Amér; (- formal use) le; (- pl) les; **she gave it to you** te/os OR se Amér lo dio; **can I get you a chair, sir?** ¿le traigo una silla, señor? - **5.** (after prep, in comparisons etc - sing) tú OR vos Amér C & R Plata; (- pl) vosotros mpl, -tras f OR ustedes Amér; (- formal use) usted; (- pl) ustedes; **we shall go with/without you** iremos contigo/sin ti OR vos Amér C & R Plata, iremos con/sin vosotros OR ustedes Amér (pl); **I'm shorter than you** soy más bajo que tú OR vos Amér C & R Plata/vosotros OR ustedes Amér - **6.** [anyone, one] uno; **you wouldn't have thought so** uno no lo habría pensado; **exercise is good for you** el ejercicio es bueno.

you'd [juːd] - **1.** (abbr of you had), ▷ **have** - **2.** (abbr of you would), ▷ **would**.

you'll [juːl] - **1.** (abbr of you will), ▷ **will** - **2.** (abbr of you shall), ▷ **shall**.

young [jʌŋ] ◇ adj [not old] joven; **his younger sister** su hermana pequeña; **I'm younger than her** soy más joven que ella; **I'm two years younger than her** soy dos años menor que ella; **the younger generation** la generación más joven. ◇ npl - **1.** [young people]: **the young** los jóvenes - **2.** [baby animals] crías fpl.

youngish [ˈjʌŋɪʃ] adj bastante joven.

young man n joven m.

youngster [ˈjʌŋstər] n joven mf, chico m, -ca f.

young woman n (mujer f) joven f.

your [jɔːr] poss adj - **1.** (everyday use - referring to one person) tu; (- referring to more than one person) vuestro(tra); **your dog** tu/vuestro perro; **your children** tus/vuestros niños; **what's your name?** ¿cómo te llamas?; **it wasn't your fault** no fue culpa tuya/vuestra; **you didn't wash your hair** no te lavaste/os lavasteis el pelo - **2.** (formal use) su; **your dog** su perro; **what are your names?** ¿cuáles son sus nombres? - **3.** (impersonal - one's): **your attitude changes as you get older** la actitud de uno cambia con

la vejez; **it's good for your teeth/hair** es bueno para los dientes/el pelo; **your average Englishman** el inglés medio.

you're [jɔːr] (abbr of you are), ▷ **be**.

yours [jɔːz] poss pron - **1.** (everyday use - referring to one person) tuyo (tuya); (- referring to more than one person) vuestro (vuestra); **that money is yours** ese dinero es tuyo/vuestro; **those keys are yours** esas llaves son tuyas/vuestras; **my car isn't yours** mi coche chocó contra el tuyo/el vuestro; **it wasn't her fault, it was yours** no fue culpa de ella sino **tuya/vuestra**; **a friend of yours** un amigo tuyo/vuestro - **2.** (formal use) suyo (suya).

◆ **Yours** adv: **Yours faithfully/sincerely** [in letter] atentamente.

yourself [jɔːˈself] (pl **-selves** [-ˈselvz]) pron - **1.** (as reflexive - sing) te; (- pl) os; (- formal use) se; **did you hurt yourself?** ¿te hiciste/se hizo daño? - **2.** (after prep - sing) ti mismo (ti misma); (- pl) vosotros mismos (vosotras mismas); (- formal use) usted mismo (usted misma); **with yourself** contigo mismo/misma - **3.** (for emphasis): **you yourself** tú mismo (tú misma); (formal use) usted mismo(ma); **you yourselves** vosotros mismos (vosotras mismas); (formal use) ustedes mismos(mas) - **4.** [without help] solo(la); **did you do it (by) yourself?** ¿lo hiciste solo?

youth [juːθ] n - **1.** [gen] juventud f; **in his youth** en su juventud - **2.** [boy, young man] joven m.

youth club n club m juvenil.

youthful [ˈjuːθfʊl] adj juvenil.

youthfulness [ˈjuːθfʊlnɪs] n juventud f.

youth hostel n albergue m juvenil.

youth hostelling [-ˈhɒstəlɪŋ] n UK: **to go youth hostelling** ir de vacaciones durmiendo en albergues juveniles.

you've [juːv] (abbr of you have), ▷ **have**.

yowl [jaʊl] ◇ n aullido m. ◇ vi aullar.

yo-yo [ˈjəʊjəʊ] n yoyó m.

yr abbr of **year**.

Yucatan [ˌjʌkəˈtɑːn] n Yucatán.

yuck [jʌk] excl inf ¡puaj!

Yugoslav adj = **Yugoslavian**.

Yugoslavia [ˌjuːgəˈslɑːvɪə] n Yugoslavia.

Yugoslavian [ˌjuːgəˈslɑːvɪən], **Yugoslav** [ˌjuːgəˈslɑːv] ◇ adj yugoslavo(va). ◇ n yugoslavo m, -va f.

yuletide [ˈjuːltaɪd] n (U) liter Navidad f.

yummy [ˈjʌmɪ] (comp **-ier**, superl **-iest**) adj riquísimo(ma), para chuparse los dedos.

yuppie, yuppy [ˈjʌpɪ] (pl **-ies**) (abbr of young upwardly mobile professional) n yuppy mf.

YWCA (abbr of **Young Women's Christian Association**) n asociación internacional de jóvenes cristianas.

Z

z (*pl* z's *OR* zs), **Z** (*pl* Z's *OR* Zs) [*UK* zed, *US* zi:] *n* [letter] z *f*, Z *f*.

Zaïre [zɑːˈɪər] *n* (el) Zaire.

Zambia [ˈzæmbɪə] *n* Zambia.

Zambian [ˈzæmbɪən] ⟷ *adj* zambiano(na). ⟷ *n* zambiano *m*, -na *f*.

zany [ˈzeɪnɪ] (*comp* -ier, *superl* -iest) *adj inf* [humour, trick] disparatado(da); [person] loco(ca).

zap [zæp] (*pt & pp* -ped, *cont* -ping) *inf vt* [kill] cargarse, matar.

zeal [ziːl] *n fml* celo *m*.

zealot [ˈzelət] *n fml* fanático *m*, -ca *f*.

zealous [ˈzeləs] *adj fml* entusiasta, infatigable.

zebra [*UK* ˈzebrə, *US* ˈziːbrə] (*pl* zebra *OR* -s) *n* cebra *f*.

zebra crossing *n UK* paso *m* cebra.

zenith [*UK* ˈzenɪθ, *US* ˈziːnəθ] *n fig* & ASTRON cenit *m*.

zeppelin [ˈzepəlɪn] *n* zepelín *m*.

zero [*UK* ˈzɪərəʊ, *US* ˈziːrəʊ] ⟷ *adj* cero (*inv*), nulo(la). ⟷ *n* (*pl* zero *OR* -es) cero *m*; **below zero** bajo cero.

◆ **zero in on** *vt insep* - **1.** [weapon] apuntar a - **2.** [person] centrarse en.

zero-rated [-ˌreɪtɪd] *adj UK* sin IVA.

zest [zest] *n* (*U*) - **1.** [enthusiasm] entusiasmo *m*; **her zest for life** su entusiasmo por vivir - **2.** [of orange, lemon] cáscara *f*.

zigzag [ˈzɪgzæg] ⟷ *n* zigzag *m*. ⟷ *vi* (*pt & pp* -ged, *cont* -ging) zigzaguear.

zilch [zɪltʃ] *n US inf* - **1.** [zero] cerapio - **2.** [nothing] na', nada.

Zimbabwe [zɪmˈbɑːbwɪ] *n* Zimbabue.

Zimbabwean [zɪmˈbɑːbwɪən] ⟷ *adj* zimbabuense. ⟷ *n* zimbabuense *mf*.

Zimmer frame® [ˈzɪmər-] *n* andador *m* ortopédico.

zinc [zɪŋk] *n* cinc *m*, zinc *m*.

Zionism [ˈzaɪənɪzm] *n* sionismo *m*.

Zionist [ˈzaɪənɪst] ⟷ *adj* sionista. ⟷ *n* sionista *mf*.

zip [zɪp] ⟷ *n* - **1.** *UK* [fastener] cremallera *f*, cierre *m Amér*, zíper *m Amér C, Méx & Ven*, cierre *m* relámpago *Perú OR* eclair *Chile* - **2.** COMPUT comprimir. ⟷ *vt* (*pt & pp* -ped, *cont* -ping) cerrar con cremallera *OR* con cierre *Amér OR* con zíper *Amér C, Méx & Ven*. ⟷ *vi* (*pt & pp* -ped, *cont* -ping): **he zipped round the city in half an hour** dio la vuelta a la ciudad tan sólo en media hora.

◆ **zip up** *vt sep* cerrar la cremallera *OR* el cierre *Amér OR* zíper *Amér C, Méx & Ven* de.

zip code *n US* código *m* postal.

Zipdisk® *n* COMPUT disco *m* Zip®.

zip fastener *UK n* cremallera *f*.

zipper [ˈzɪpər] *n US* cremallera *f*.

zit [zɪt] *n esp US inf* grano *m*.

zither [ˈzɪðər] *n* cítara *f*.

zodiac [ˈzəʊdɪæk] *n*: **the zodiac** el zodiaco; **sign of the zodiac** signo del zodiaco.

zombie [ˈzɒmbɪ] *n lit* & *fig* zombi *mf*.

zone [zəʊn] *n* zona *f*.

zoo [zuː] *n* zoo *m*.

zoological [ˌzəʊəˈlɒdʒɪkl] *adj* zoológico(ca).

zoologist [zəʊˈɒlədʒɪst] *n* zoólogo *m*, -ga *f*.

zoology [zəʊˈɒlədʒɪ] *n* zoología *f*.

zoom [zuːm] *vi inf* [move quickly]: **to zoom past** pasar zumbando.

◆ **zoom in** *vi*: **to zoom in (on)** enfocar en primer plano (a).

◆ **zoom off** *vi inf* salir zumbando.

zoom lens *n* zoom *m*.

zucchini [zuːˈkiːnɪ] (*pl* zucchini) *n US* calabacín *m*, calabacita *f Méx*, zapallito *m* (italiano).

Zulu [ˈzuːluː] ⟷ *adj* zulú. ⟷ *n* - **1.** [person] zulú *mf* - **2.** [language] zulú *m*.

CONJUGACIÓN DE LOS VERBOS ESPAÑOLES
VERBOS IRREGULARES INGLESES

SPANISH VERBS
ENGLISH IRREGULAR VERBS

CONJUGACIÓN DE LOS VERBOS ESPAÑOLES

SPANISH VERBS

	1 amar	2 temer	3 partir
pres. de indicativo	amo ama amamos	temo teme tememos	parto parte partimos
pret. imperfecto	amaba amábamos	temía temíamos	partía partíamos
pret. indefinido	amé amó amamos amaron	temí temió temimos temieron	partí partió partimos partieron
fut. de ind.	amaré amará amaremos	temeré temerá temeremos	partiré partirá partiremos
condicional	amaría amaríamos	temería temeríamos	partiría partiríamos
pres. de subj.	ame amemos	tema temamos	parta partamos
imperfecto de subj.	amara, amase amáramos, amásemos	temiera, temiese temiéramos, temiésemos	partiera, partiese partiéramos, partiésemos
imperativo	ama (tú), ame (él, ella, usted) amemos (nosotros) amad (vosotros) amen (ellos, ellas, ustedes)	teme (tú) tema (él, ella, usted) temamos (nosotros) temed (vosotros) teman (ellos, ellas, ustedes)	parte (tú) parta (él, ella, usted) partamos (nosotros) partid (vosotros) partan (ellos, ellas, ustedes)
gerundio, participio	amando, amado	temiendo, temido	partiendo, partido

	4 haber	5 ser
presente de indicativo	he ha hemos	soy es somos
preterito imperfecto	había habíamos	era éramos
preterito indefinido	hube hubo hubimos hubieron	fui fue fuimos fueron
futuro de indicativo	habré habrá habremos	seré será seremos
condicional	habría habríamos	sería seríamos
presente de subjuntivo	haya hayamos	sea seamos
imperfecto de subjuntivo	hubiera, hubiese hubiéramos, hubiésemos	fuera, fuese fuéramos, fuésemos
imperativo	he (tú) haya (él, ella, usted) hayamos (nosotros) habed (vosotros) hayan (ellos, ellas, ustedes)	sé (tú) sea (él, ella, usted) seamos (nosotros) sed (vosotros) sean (ellos, ellas, ustedes)
gerundio, participio	habiendo, habido	siendo, sido

conjugaciones

	6 actuar	7 adecuar
presente de indicativo	actúo actúa actuamos	adecuo adecua adecuamos
preterito imperfecto	actuaba actuábamos	adecuaba adecuábamos
preterito indefinido	actué actuó actuamos actuaron	adecué adecuó adecuamos adecuaron
futuro de indicativo	actuaré actuará actuaremos	adecuaré adecuará adecuaremos
condicional	actuaría actuaríamos	adecuaría adecuaríamos
presente de subjuntivo	actúe actuemos	adecue adecuemos
imperfecto de subjuntivo	actuara, actuase actuáramos, actuásemos	adecuara, adecuase adecuáramos, adecuásemos
imperativo	actúa (tú) actúe (él, ella, usted) actuemos (nosotros) actuad (vosotros) actúen (ellos, ellas, ustedes)	adecua (tú) adecue (él, ella, usted) adecuemos (nosotros) adecuad (vosotros) adecuen (ellos, ellas, ustedes)
gerundio, participio	actuando, actuado	adecuando, adecuado

	8 cambiar	9 guiar
presente de indicativo	cambio cambia cambiamos	guío guía guiamos
preterito imperfecto	cambiaba cambiábamos	guiaba guiábamos
preterito indefinido	cambié cambió cambiamos cambiaron	guié guió guiamos guiaron
futuro de indicativo	cambiaré cambiará cambiaremos	guiaré guiará guiaremos
condicional	cambiaría cambiaríamos	guiaría guiaríamos
presente de subjuntivo	cambie cambiemos	guíe guiemos
imperfecto de subjuntivo	cambiara, cambiase cambiáramos, cambiásemos	guiara, guiase guiáramos, guiásemos
imperativo	cambia (tú) cambie (él, ella, usted) cambiemos (nosotros) cambiad (vosotros) cambien (ellos, ellas, ustedes)	guía (tú) guíe (él, ella, usted) guiemos (nosotros) guiad (vosotros) guíen (ellos, ellas, ustedes)
gerundio, participio	cambiando, cambiado	guiando, guiado

	10 sacar	11 mecer
presente de indicativo	saco saca sacamos	mezo mece mecemos
preterito imperfecto	sacaba sacábamos	mecía mecíamos
preterito indefinido	saqué sacó sacamos sacaron	mecí meció mecimos mecieron
futuro de indicativo	sacaré sacará sacaremos	meceré mecerá meceremos
condicional	sacaría sacaríamos	mecería meceríamos
presente de subjuntivo	saque saquemos	meza mezamos
imperfecto de subjuntivo	sacara, sacase sacáramos, sacásemos	meciera, meciese meciéramos, meciésemos
imperativo	saca (tú) saque (él, ella, usted) saquemos (nosotros) sacad (vosotros) saquen (ellos, ellas, ustedes)	mece (tú) meza (él, ella, usted) mezamos (nosotros) meced (vosotros) mezan (ellos, ellas, ustedes)
gerundio, participio	sacando, sacado	meciendo, mecido

	12 zurcir	13 cazar
presente de indicativo	zurzo zurce zurcimos	cazo caza cazamos
preterito imperfecto	zurcía zurcíamos	cazaba cazábamos
preterito indefinido	zurcí zurció zurcimos zurcieron	cacé cazó cazamos cazaron
futuro de indicativo	zurciré zurcirá zurciremos	cazaré cazará cazaremos
condicional	zurciría zurciríamos	cazaría cazaríamos
presente de subjuntivo	zurza zurzamos	cace cacemos
imperfecto de subjuntivo	zurciera, zurciese zurciéramos, zurciésemos	cazara, cazase cazáramos, cazásemos
imperativo	zurce (tú) zurza (él, ella, usted) zurzamos (nosotros) zurcid (vosotros) zurzan (ellos, ellas, ustedes)	caza (tú) cace (él, ella, usted) cacemos (nosotros) cazad (vosotros) cacen (ellos, ellas, ustedes)
gerundio, participio	zurciendo, zurcido	cazando, cazado

conjugaciones

	14 proteger	15 dirigir
presente de indicativo	protejo protege protegemos	dirijo dirige dirigimos
preterito imperfecto	protegía protegíamos	dirigía dirigíamos
preterito indefinido	protegí protegió protegimos protegieron	dirigí dirigió dirigimos dirigieron
futuro de indicativo	protegeré protegerá protegeremos	dirigiré dirigirá dirigiremos
condicional	protegería protegeríamos	dirigiría dirigiríamos
presente de subjuntivo	proteja protejamos	dirija dirijamos
imperfecto de subjuntivo	protegiera, protegiese protegiéramos, protegiésemos	dirigiera, dirigiese dirigiéramos, dirigiésemos
imperativo	protege (tú) proteja (él, ella, usted) protejamos (nosotros) proteged (vosotros) protejan (ellos, ellas, ustedes)	dirige (tú) dirija (él, ella, usted) dirijamos (nosotros) dirigid (vosotros) dirijan (ellos, ellas, ustedes)
gerundio, participio	protegiendo, protegido	dirigiendo, dirigido

	16 llegar	17 distinguir
presente de indicativo	llego llega llegamos	distingo distingue distinguimos
preterito imperfecto	llegaba llegábamos	distinguía distinguíamos
preterito indefinido	llegué llegó llegamos llegaron	distinguí distinguió distinguimos distinguieron
futuro de indicativo	llegaré llegará llegaremos	distinguiré distinguirá distinguiremos
condicional	llegaría llegaríamos	distinguiría distinguiríamos
presente de subjuntivo	llegue lleguemos	distinga distingamos
imperfecto de subjuntivo	llegara, llegase llegáramos, llegásemos	distinguiera, distinguiese distinguiéramos, distinguiésemos
imperativo	llega (tú) llegue (él, ella, usted) lleguemos (nosotros) llegad (vosotros) lleguen (ellos, ellas, ustedes)	distingue (tú) distinga (él, ella, usted) distingamos (nosotros) distinguid (vosotros) distingan (ellos, ellas, ustedes)
gerundio, participio	llegando, llegado	distinguiendo, distinguido

	18 delinquir	19 acertar
presente de indicativo	delinco delinque delinquimos	acierto acierta acertamos
preterito imperfecto	delinquía delinquíamos	acertaba acertábamos
preterito indefinido	delinquí delinquió delinquimos delinquieron	acerté acertó acertamos acertaron
futuro de indicativo	delinquiré delinquirá delinquiremos	acertaré acertará acertaremos
condicional	delinquiría delinquiríamos	acertaría acertaríamos
presente de subjuntivo	delinca delincamos	acierte acertemos
imperfecto de subjuntivo	delinquiera, delinquiese delinquiéramos, delinquiésemos	acertara, acertase acertáramos, acertásemos
imperativo	delinque (tú) delinca (él, ella, usted) delincamos (nosotros) delinquid (vosotros) delincan (ellos, ellas, ustedes)	acierta (tú) acierte (él, ella, usted) acertemos (nosotros) acertad (vosotros) acierten (ellos, ellas, ustedes)
gerundio, participio	delinquiendo, delinquido	acertando, acertado

	20 tender	21 discernir
presente de indicativo	tiendo tiende tendemos	discierno discierne discernimos
preterito imperfecto	tendía tendíamos	discernía discerníamos
preterito indefinido	tendí tendió tendimos tendieron	discerní discernió discernimos discernieron
futuro de indicativo	tenderé tenderá tenderemos	discerniré discernirá discerniremos
condicional	tendería tenderíamos	discerniría discerniríamos
presente de subjuntivo	tienda tendamos	discierna discernamos
imperfecto de subjuntivo	tendiera, tendiese tendiéramos, tendiésemos	discerniera, discerniese discerniéramos, discerniésemos
imperativo	tiende (tú) tienda (él, ella, usted) tendamos (nosotros) tended (vosotros) tiendan (ellos, ellas, ustedes)	discierne (tú) discierna (él, ella, usted) discernamos (nosotros) discernid (vosotros) disciernan (ellos, ellas, ustedes)
gerundio, participio	tendiendo, tendido	discerniendo, discernido

	22 adquirir	23 sonar
presente de indicativo	adquiero adquiere adquirimos	sueno suena sonamos
preterito imperfecto	adquiría adquiríamos	sonaba sonábamos
preterito indefinido	adquirí adquirió adquirimos adquirieron	soné sonó sonamos sonaron
futuro de indicativo	adquiriré adquirirá adquiriremos	sonaré sonará sonaremos
condicional	adquiriría adquiriríamos	sonaría sonaríamos
presente de subjuntivo	adquiera adquiramos	suene sonemos
imperfecto de subjuntivo	adquiriera, adquiriese adquiriéramos, adquiriésemos	sonara, sonase sonáramos, sonásemos
imperativo	adquiere (tú) adquiera (él, ella, usted) adquiramos (nosotros) adquirid (vosotros) adquieran (ellos, ellas, ustedes)	suena (tú) suene (él, ella, usted) sonemos (nosotros) sonad (vosotros) suenen (ellos, ellas, ustedes)
gerundio, participio	adquiriendo, adquirido	sonando, sonado

	24 mover	25 dormir
presente de indicativo	muevo mueve movemos	duermo duerme dormimos
preterito imperfecto	movía movíamos	dormía dormíamos
preterito indefinido	moví movió movimos movieron	dormí durmió dormimos durmieron
futuro de indicativo	moveré moverá moveremos	dormiré dormirá dormiremos
condicional	movería moveríamos	dormiría dormiríamos
presente de subjuntivo	mueva movamos	duerma durmamos
imperfecto de subjuntivo	moviera, moviese moviéramos, moviésemos	durmiera, durmiese durmiéramos, durmiésemos
imperativo	mueve (tú) mueva (él, ella, usted) movamos (nosotros) moved (vosotros) muevan (ellos, ellas, ustedes)	duerme (tú) duerma (él, ella, usted) durmamos (nosotros) dormid (vosotros) duerman (ellos, ellas, ustedes)
gerundio, participio	moviendo, movido	durmiendo, dormido

	26 pedir	27 sentir
presente de indicativo	pido pide pedimos	siento siente sentimos
preterito imperfecto	pedía pedíamos	sentía sentíamos
preterito indefinido	pedí pidió pedimos pidieron	sentí sintió sentimos sintieron
futuro de indicativo	pediré pedirá pediremos	sentiré sentirá sentiremos
condicional	pediría pediríamos	sentiría sentiríamos
presente de subjuntivo	pida pidamos	sienta sintamos
imperfecto de subjuntivo	pidiera, pidiese pidiéramos, pidiésemos	sintiera, sintiese sintiéramos, sintiésemos
imperativo	pide (tú) pida (él, ella, usted) pidamos (nosotros) pedid (vosotros) pidan (ellos, ellas, ustedes)	siente (tú) sienta (él, ella, usted) sintamos (nosotros) sentid (vosotros) sientan (ellos, ellas, ustedes)
gerundio, participio	pidiendo, pedido	sintiendo, sentido

	28 reír	29 nacer
presente de indicativo	río ríe reímos	nazco nace nacemos
preterito imperfecto	reía reíamos	nacía nacíamos
preterito indefinido	reí rió reímos rieron	nací nació nacimos nacieron
futuro de indicativo	reiré reirá reiremos	naceré nacerá naceremos
condicional	reiría reiríamos	nacería naceríamos
presente de subjuntivo	ría riamos	nazca nazcamos
imperfecto de subjuntivo	riera, riese riéramos, riésemos	naciera, naciese naciéramos, naciésemos
imperativo	ríe (tú) ría (él, ella, usted) riamos (nosotros) reíd (vosotros) rían (ellos, ellas, ustedes)	nace (tú) nazca (él, ella, usted) nazcamos (nosotros) naced (vosotros) nazcan (ellos, ellas, ustedes)
gerundio, participio	riendo, reído	naciendo, nacido

conjugaciones

	30 parecer	31 conocer
presente de indicativo	parezco parece parecemos	conozco conoce conocemos
preterito imperfecto	parecía parecíamos	conocía conocíamos
preterito indefinido	parecí pareció parecimos parecieron	conocí conoció conocimos conocieron
futuro de indicativo	pareceré parecerá pareceremos	conoceré conocerá conoceremos
condicional	parecería paraceríamos	conocería conoceríamos
presente de subjuntivo	parezca parezcamos	conozca conozcamos
imperfecto de subjuntivo	pareciera, pareciese pareciéramos, pareciésemos	conociera, conociese conociéramos, conociésemos
imperativo	parece (tú) parezca (él, ella, usted) parezcamos (nosotros) pareced (vosotros) parezcan (ellos, ellas, ustedes)	conoce (tú) conozca (él, ella, usted) conozcamos (nosotros) conoced (vosotros) conozcan (ellos, ellas, ustedes)
gerundio, participio	pareciendo, parecido	conociendo, conocido

	32 lucir	33 conducir
presente de indicativo	luzco luce lucimos	conduzco conduce conducimos
preterito imperfecto	lucía lucíamos	conducía conducíamos
preterito indefinido	lucí lució lucimos lucieron	conduje condujo condujimos condujeron
futuro de indicativo	luciré lucirá luciremos	conduciré conducirá conduciremos
condicional	luciría luciríamos	conduciría conduciríamos
presente de subjuntivo	luzca luzcamos	conduzca conduzcamos
imperfecto de subjuntivo	luciera, luciese luciéramos, luciésemos	condujera, condujese condujéramos, condujésemos
imperativo	luce (tú) luzca (él, ella, usted) luzcamos (nosotros) lucid (vosotros) luzcan (ellos, ellas, ustedes)	conduce (tú) conduzca (él, ella, usted) conduzcamos (nosotros) conducid (vosotros) conduzcan (ellos, ellas, ustedes)
gerundio, participio	luciendo, lucido	conduciendo, conducido

conjugaciones

	34 comenzar	35 negar
presente de indicativo	comienzo comienza comenzamos	niego niega negamos
preterito imperfecto	comenzaba comenzábamos	negaba negábamos
preterito indefinido	comencé comenzó comenzamos comenzaron	negué negó negamos negaron
futuro de indicativo	comenzaré comenzará comenzaremos	negaré negará negaremos
condicional	comenzaría comenzaríamos	negaría negaríamos
presente de subjuntivo	comience comencemos	niegue neguemos
imperfecto de subjuntivo	comenzara, comenzase comenzáramos, comenzásemos	negara, negase negáramos, negásemos
imperativo	comienza (tú) comience (él, ella, usted) comencemos (nosotros) comenzad (vosotros) comiencen (ellos, ellas, ustedes)	niega (tú) niegue (él, ella, usted) neguemos (nosotros) negad (vosotros) nieguen (ellos, ellas, ustedes)
gerundio, participio	comenzando, comenzado	negando, negado

	36 trocar	37 forzar
presente de indicativo	trueco trueca trocamos	fuerzo fuerza forzamos
preterito imperfecto	trocaba trocábamos	forzaba forzábamos
preterito indefinido	troqué trocó trocamos trocaron	forcé forzó forzamos forzaron
futuro de indicativo	trocaré trocará trocaremos	forzaré forzará forzaremos
condicional	trocaría trocaríamos	forzaría forzaríamos
presente de subjuntivo	trueque troquemos	fuerce forcemos
imperfecto de subjuntivo	trocara, trocase trocáramos, trocásemos	forzara, forzase forzáramos, forzásemos
imperativo	trueca (tú) trueque (él, ella, usted) troquemos (nosotros) trocad (vosotros) truequen (ellos, ellas, ustedes)	fuerza (tú) fuerce (él, ella, usted) forcemos (nosotros) forzad (vosotros) fuercen (ellos, ellas, ustedes)
gerundio, participio	trocando, trocado	forzando, forzado

conjugaciones

	38 avergonzar	**39 colgar**
presente de indicativo	avergüenzo avergüenza avergonzamos	cuelgo cuelga colgamos
pretérito imperfecto	avergonzaba avergonzábamos	colgaba colgábamos
pretérito indefinido	avergoncé avergonzó avergonzamos avergonzaron	colgué colgó colgamos colgaron
futuro de indicativo	avergonzaré avergonzará avergonzaremos	colgaré colgará colgaremos
condicional	avergonzaría avergonzaríamos	colgaría colgaríamos
presente de subjuntivo	avergüence avergoncemos	cuelgue colguemos
imperfecto de subjuntivo	avergonzara, avergonzase avergonzáramos, avergonzásemos	colgara, colgase colgáramos, colgásemos
imperativo	avergüenza (tú) avergüence (él, ella, usted) avergoncemos (nosotros) avergonzad (vosotros) avergüencen (ellos, ellas, ustedes)	cuelga (tú) cuelgue (él, ella, usted) colguemos (nosotros) colgad (vosotros) cuelguen (ellos, ellas, ustedes)
gerundio, participio	avergonzando, avergonzado	colgando, colgado

	40 jugar	**41 cocer**
presente de indicativo	juego juega jugamos	cuezo cuece cocemos
pretérito imperfecto	jugaba jugábamos	cocía cocíamos
pretérito indefinido	jugué jugó jugamos jugaron	cocí coció cocimos cocieron
futuro de indicativo	jugaré jugará jugaremos	coceré cocerá coceremos
condicional	jugaría jugaríamos	cocería coceríamos
presente de subjuntivo	juegue juguemos	cueza cozamos
imperfecto de subjuntivo	jugara, jugase jugáramos, jugásemos	cociera, cociese cociéramos, cociésemos
imperativo	juega (tú) juegue (él, ella, usted) juguemos (nosotros) jugad (vosotros) jueguen (ellos, ellas, ustedes)	cuece (tú) cueza (él, ella, usted) cozamos (nosotros) coced (vosotros) cuezan (ellos, ellas, ustedes)
gerundio, participio	jugando, jugado	cociendo, cocido

	42 regir	**43 seguir**
presente de indicativo	rijo rige regimos	sigo sigue seguimos
preterito imperfecto	regía regíamos	seguía seguíamos
preterito indefinido	regí rigió regimos rigieron	seguí siguió seguimos siguieron
futuro de indicativo	regiré regirá regiremos	seguiré seguirá seguiremos
condicional	regiría regiríamos	seguiría seguiríamos
presente de subjuntivo	rija rijamos	siga sigamos
imperfecto de subjuntivo	rigiera, rigiese rigiéramos, rigiésemos	siguiera, siguiese siguiéramos, siguiésemos
imperativo	rige (tú) rija (él, ella, usted) rijamos (nosotros) regid (vosotros) rijan (ellos, ellas, ustedes)	sigue (tú) siga (él, ella, usted) sigamos (nosotros) seguid (vosotros) sigan (ellos, ellas, ustedes)
gerundio, participio	rigiendo, regido	siguiendo, seguido

	44 argüir	**45 averiguar**
presente de indicativo	arguyo arguye argüimos	averiguo averigua averiguamos
preterito imperfecto	argüía argüíamos	averiguaba averiguábamos
preterito indefinido	argüí arguyó argüimos arguyeron	averigüé averiguó averiguamos averiguaron
futuro de indicativo	argüiré argüirá argüiremos	averiguaré averiguará averiguaremos
condicional	argüiría argüiríamos	averiguaría averiguaríamos
presente de subjuntivo	arguya arguyamos	averigüe averigüemos
imperfecto de subjuntivo	arguyera, arguyese arguyéramos, arguyésemos	averiguara, averiguase averiguáramos, averiguásemos
imperativo	arguye (tú) arguya (él, ella, usted) arguyamos (nosotros) argüid (vosotros) arguyan (ellos, usted, ustedes)	averigua (tú) averigüe (él, ella, usted) averigüemos (nosotros) averiguad (vosotros) averigüen (ellos, ellas, ustedes)
gerundio, participio	arguyendo, argüido	averiguando, averiguado

	46 agorar	47 errar
presente de indicativo	agüero agüera agoramos	yerro yerra erramos
preterito imperfecto	agoraba agorábamos	erraba errábamos
preterito indefinido	agoré agoró agoramos agoraron	erré erró erramos erraron
futuro de indicativo	agoraré agorará agoraremos	erraré errará erraremos
condicional	agoraría agoraríamos	erraría erraríamos
presente de subjuntivo	agüere agoremos	yerre erremos
imperfecto de subjuntivo	agorara, agorase agoráramos, agorásemos	errara, errase erráramos, errásemos
imperativo	agüera (tú) agüere (él, ella, usted) agoremos (nosotros) agorad (vosotros) agüeren (ellos, ellas, ustedes)	yerra (tú) yerre (él, ella, usted) erremos (nosotros) errad (vosotros) yerren (ellos, ellas, ustedes)
gerundio, participio	agorando, agorado	errando, errado

	48 desosar	49 oler
presente de indicativo	deshueso deshuesa desosamos	huelo huele olemos
preterito imperfecto	desosaba desosábamos	olía olíamos
preterito indefinido	desosé desosó desosamos desosaron	olí olió olimos olieron
futuro de indicativo	desosaré desosará desosaremos	oleré olerá oleremos
condicional	desosaría desosaríamos	olería oleríamos
presente de subjuntivo	deshuese desosemos	huela olamos
imperfecto de subjuntivo	desosara, desosase desosáramos, desosásemos	oliera, oliese oliéramos, oliésemos
imperativo	deshuesa (tú) deshuese (él, ella, usted) desosemos (nosotros) desosad (vosotros) deshuesen (ellos, ellas, ustedes)	huele (tú) huela (él, ella, usted) olamos (nosotros) oled (vosotros) huelan (ellos, ellas, ustedes)
gerundio, participio	desosando, desosado	oliendo, olido

	50 leer	51 huir
presente de indicativo	leo lee leemos	huyo huye huimos
preterito imperfecto	leía leíamos	huía huíamos
preterito indefinido	leí leyó leímos leyeron	huí huyó huimos huyeron
futuro de indicativo	leeré leerá leeremos	huiré huirá huiremos
condicional	leería leeríamos	huiría huiríamos
presente de subjuntivo	lea leamos	huya huyamos
imperfecto de subjuntivo	leyera, leyese leyéramos, leyésemos	huyera, huyese huyéramos, huyésemos
imperativo	lee (tú) lea (él, ella, usted) leamos (nosotros) leed (vosotros) lean (ellos, ellas, ustedes)	huye (tú) huya (él, ella, usted) huyamos (nosotros) huid (vosotros) huyan (ellos, ellas, ustedes)
gerundio, participio	leyendo, leído	huyendo, huido

	52 andar	53 asir
presente de indicativo	ando anda andamos	asgo ase asimos
preterito imperfecto	andaba andábamos	asía asíamos
preterito indefinido	anduve anduvo anduvimos anduvieron	así asió asimos asieron
futuro de indicativo	andaré andará andaremos	asiré asirá asiremos
condicional	andaría andaríamos	asiría asiríamos
presente de subjuntivo	ande andemos	asga asgamos
imperfecto de subjuntivo	anduviera, anduviese anduviéramos, anduviésemos	asiera, asiese asiéramos, asiésemos
imperativo	anda (tú) ande (él, ella, usted) andemos (nosotros) andad (vosotros) anden (ellos, ellas, ustedes)	ase (tú) asga (él, ella, usted) asgamos (nosotros) asid (vosotros) asgan (ellos, ellas, ustedes)
gerundio, participio	andando, andado	asiendo, asido

	54 caber	55 caer
presente de indicativo	quepo cabe cabemos	caigo cae caemos
preterito imperfecto	cabía cabíamos	caía caíamos
preterito indefinido	cupe cupo cupimos cupieron	caí cayó caímos cayeron
futuro de indicativo	cabré cabrá cabremos	caeré caerá caeremos
condicional	cabría cabríamos	caería caeríamos
presente de subjuntivo	quepa quepamos	caiga caigamos
imperfecto de subjuntivo	cupiera, cupiese cupiéramos, cupiésemos	cayera, cayese cayéramos, cayésemos
imperativo	cabe (tú) quepa (él, ella, usted) quepamos (nosotros) cabed (vosotros) quepan (ellos, ellas, ustedes)	cae (tú) caiga (él, ella, usted) caigamos (nosotros) caed (vosotros) caigan (ellos, ellas, ustedes)
gerundio, participio	cabiendo, cabido	cayendo, caído

	56 dar	57 decir
presente de indicativo	doy da damos	digo dice decimos
preterito imperfecto	daba dábamos	decía decíamos
preterito indefinido	di dio dimos dieron	dije dijo dijimos dijeron
futuro de indicativo	daré dará daremos	diré dirá diremos
condicional	daría daríamos	diría diríamos
presente de subjuntivo	dé demos	diga digamos
imperfecto de subjuntivo	diera, diese diéramos, diésemos	dijera, dijese dijéramos, dijésemos
imperativo	da (tú) dé (él, ella, usted) demos (nosotros) dad (vosotros) den (ellos, ellas, ustedes)	di (tú) diga (él, ella, usted) digamos (nosotros) decid (vosotros) digan (ellos, ellas, ustedes)
gerundio, participio	dando, dado	diciendo, dicho

	58 erguir	59 estar
presente de indicativo	irgo, yergo	estoy
	irgue, yergue	está
	erguimos	estamos
preterito imperfecto	erguía	estaba
	erguíamos	estábamos
preterito indefinido	erguí	estuve
	irguió	estuvo
	erguimos	estuvimos
	irguieron	estuvieron
futuro de indicativo	erguiré	estaré
	erguirá	estará
	erguiremos	estaremos
condicional	erguiría	estaría
	erguiríamos	estaríamos
presente de subjuntivo	irga, yerga	esté
	irgamos	estemos
imperfecto de subjuntivo	irguiera, irguiese	estuviera, estuviese
	irguiéramos, irguiésemos	estuviéramos, estuviésemos
imperativo	irgue, yergue (tú)	está (tú)
	irga, yerga (él, ella)	esté (él, ella, usted)
	irgamos (nosotros)	estemos (nosotros)
	erguid (vosotros)	estad (vosotros)
	irgan, yergan (ellos, ellas, ustedes)	estén (ellos, ellas, ustedes)
gerundio, participio	irguiendo, erguido	estando, estado

	60 hacer	61 ir
presente de indicativo	hago	voy
	hace	va
	hacemos	vamos
preterito imperfecto	hacía	iba
	hacíamos	íbamos
preterito indefinido	hice	fui
	hizo	fue
	hicimos	fuimos
	hicieron	fueron
futuro de indicativo	haré	iré
	hará	irá
	haremos	iremos
condicional	haría	iría
	haríamos	iríamos
presente de subjuntivo	haga	vaya
	hagamos	vayamos
imperfecto de subjuntivo	hiciera, hiciese	fuera, fuese
	hiciéramos, hiciésemos	fuéramos, fuésemos
imperativo	haz (tú)	ve (tú)
	haga (él, ella, usted)	vaya (él, ella, usted)
	hagamos (nosotros)	vayamos (nosotros)
	haced (vosotros)	id (vosotros)
	hagan (ellos, ellas, ustedes)	vayan (ellos, ellas, ustedes)
gerundio, participio	haciendo, hecho	yendo, ido

conjugaciones

	62 oír	63 placer
presente de indicativo	oigo oye oímos	plazco place placemos
preterito imperfecto	oía oíamos	placía placíamos
preterito indefinido	oí oyó oímos oyeron	plací plació, plugo placimos placieron, pluguieron
futuro de indicativo	oiré oirá oiremos	placeré placerá placeremos
condicional	oiría oiríamos	placería placeríamos
presente de subjuntivo	oiga oigamos	plazca plazcamos
imperfecto de subjuntivo	oyera, oyese oyéramos, oyésemos	placiera, placiese placiéramos, placiésemos
imperativo	oye (tú) oiga (él, ella, usted) oigamos (nosotros) oíd (vosotros) oigan (ellos, ellas, ustedes)	place (tú) plazca (él, ella, usted) plazcamos (nosotros) placed (vosotros) plazcan (ellos, ellas, ustedes)
gerundio, participio	oyendo, oído	placiendo, placido

	64 poder	65 poner
presente de indicativo	puedo puede podemos	pongo pone ponemos
preterito imperfecto	podía podíamos	ponía poníamos
preterito indefinido	pude pudo pudimos pudieron	puse puso pusimos pusieron
futuro de indicativo	podré podrá podremos	pondré pondrá pondremos
condicional	podría podríamos	pondría pondríamos
presente de subjuntivo	pueda podamos	ponga pongamos
imperfecto de subjuntivo	pudiera, pudiese pudiéramos, pudiésemos	pusiera, pusiese pusiéramos, pusiésemos
imperativo	puede (tú) pueda (él, ella, usted) podamos (nosotros) poded (vosotros) puedan (ellos, ellas, ustedes)	pon (tú) ponga (él, ella, usted) pongamos (nosotros) poned (vosotros) pongan (ellos, ellas, ustedes)
gerundio, participio	pudiendo, podido	poniendo, puesto

	66 predecir	**67 querer**
presente de indicativo	predigo predice predecimos	quiero quiere queremos
preterito imperfecto	predecía predecíamos	quería queríamos
preterito indefinido	predije predijo predijimos predijeron	quise quiso quisimos quisieron
futuro de indicativo	prediré predirá prediremos	querré querrá querremos
condicional	prediría prediríamos	querría querríamos
presente de subjuntivo	prediga predigamos	quiera queramos
imperfecto de subjuntivo	predijera, predijese predijéramos, predijésemos	quisiera, quisiese quisiéramos, quisiésemos
imperativo	predice (tú) prediga (él, ella, usted) predigamos (nosotros) predecid (vosotros) predigan (ellos, ellas, ustedes)	quiere (tú) quiera (él, ella, usted) queramos (nosotros) quered (vosotros) quieran (ellos, ellas, ustedes)
gerundio, participio	prediciendo, predicho	queriendo, querido

	68 raer	**69 roer**
presente de indicativo	rao, raigo, rayo rae raemos	roo, roigo, royo roe roemos
preterito imperfecto	raía raíamos	roía roíamos
preterito indefinido	raí rayó raímos rayeron	roí royó roímos royeron
futuro de indicativo	raeré raerá raeremos	roeré roerá roeremos
condicional	raería raeríamos	roería roeríamos
presente de subjuntivo	raiga, raya raigamos, rayamos	roa, roiga, roya roamos, roigamos, royamos
imperfecto de subjuntivo	rayera, rayese rayéramos, rayésemos	royera, royese royéramos, royésemos
imperativo	rae (tú) raiga, raya (él, ella, usted) raigamos, rayamos (nosotros) raed (vosotros) raigan, rayan (ellos, ellas, ustedes)	roe (tú) roa, roiga, roya (él, ella, usted) roamos, roigamos, royamos (nos.) roed (vosotros) roan, roigan, royan (ellos, ellas, us.)
gerundio, participio	rayendo, raído	royendo, roído

	70 saber	71 salir
presente de indicativo	sé sabe sabemos	salgo sale salimos
preterito imperfecto	sabía sabíamos	salía salíamos
preterito indefinido	supe supo supimos supieron	salí salió salimos salieron
futuro de indicativo	sabré sabrá sabremos	saldré sadrá saldremos
condicional	sabría sabríamos	saldría saldríamos
presente de subjuntivo	sepa sepamos	salga salgamos
imperfecto de subjuntivo	supiera, supiese supiéramos, supiésemos	saliera, saliese saliéramos, saliésemos
imperativo	sabe (tú) sepa (él, ella, usted) sepamos (nosotros) sabed (vosotros) sepan (ellos, ellas, ustedes)	sal (tú) salga (él, ella, usted) salgamos (nosotros) salid (vosotros) salgan (ellos, ellas, ustedes)
gerundio, participio	sabiendo, sabido	saliendo, salido

	72 tener	73 traer
presente de indicativo	tengo tiene tenemos	traigo trae traemos
preterito imperfecto	tenía teníamos	traía traíamos
preterito indefinido	tuve tuvo tuvimos tuvieron	traje trajo trajimos trajeron
futuro de indicativo	tendré tendrá tendremos	traeré traerá traeremos
condicional	tendría tendríamos	traería traeríamos
presente de subjuntivo	tenga tengamos	traiga traigamos
imperfecto de subjuntivo	tuviera, tuviese tuviéramos, tuviésemos	trajera, trajese trajéramos, trajésemos
imperativo	ten (tú) tenga (él, ella, usted) tengamos (nosotros) tened (vosotros) tengan (ellos, ellas, ustedes)	trae (tú) traiga (él, ella, usted) traigamos (nosotros) traed (vosotros) traigan (ellos, ellas, ustedes)
gerundio, participio	teniendo, tenido	trayendo, traído

conjugaciones

	74 valer	75 venir
presente de indicativo	valgo vale valemos	vengo viene venimos
pretérito imperfecto	valía valíamos	venía veníamos
preterito indefinido	valí valió valimos valieron	vine vino venimos vinieron
futuro de indicativo	valdré valdrá valdremos	vendré vendrá vendremos
condicional	valdría valdríamos	vendría vendríamos
presente de subjuntivo	valga valgamos	venga vengamos
imperfecto de subjuntivo	valiera, valiese valiéramos, valiésemos	viniera, viniese viniéramos, viniésemos
imperativo	vale (tú) valga (él, ella, usted) valgamos (nosotros) valed (vosotros) valgan (ellos, ellas, ustedes)	ven (tú) venga (él, ella, usted) vengamos (nosotros) venid (vosotros) vengan (ellos, ellas, ustedes)
gerundio, participio	valiendo, valido	viniendo, venido

	76 ver	77 yacer
presente de indicativo	veo ve vemos	yazco, yazgo, yago yace yacemos
pretérito imperfecto	veía veíamos	yacía yacíamos
preterito indefinido	vi vio vimos vieron	yací yació yacimos yacieron
futuro de indicativo	veré verá veremos	yaceré yacerá yaceremos
condicional	vería veríamos	yacería yaceríamos
presente de subjuntivo	vea veamos	yazca, yazga, yaga yazcamos, yazgamos, yagamos
imperfecto de subjuntivo	viera, viese viéramos, viésemos	yaciera, yaciese yaciéramos, yaciésemos
imperativo	ve (tú) vea (él, ella, usted) veamos (nosotros) ved (vosotros) vean (ellos, ellas, ustedes)	yace, yaz (tú) yazca, yazga, yaga (él, ella, usted) yazcamos, yazgamos, yagamos (nos.) yaced (vosotros) yazcan, yazgan, yagan (ellos...)
gerundio, participio	viendo, visto	yaciendo, yacido

conjugaciones

20

Verbos defectivos

	78 abolir	79 balbucir
presente de indicativo	*no se conjuga* – – abolimos abolís –	*no se conjuga* balbuces balbuce balbucemos balbucís balbucen
preterito imperfecto	abolía abolías abolía abolíamos abolíais abolían	balbucía balbucías balbucía balbucíamos balbucíais balbucían
preterito indefinido	abolí aboliste abolió abolimos abolisteis abolieron	balbucí balbuciste balbució balbucimos balbucisteis balbucieron
futuro de indicativo	aboliré abolirás abolirá aboliremos aboliréis abolirán	balbuciré balbucirás balbucirá balbuciremos balbuciréis balbucirán
condicional	aboliría abolirías aboliría aboliríamos aboliríais abolirían	balbuciría balbucirías balbuciría balbuciríamos balbuciríais balbucirían
presente de subjuntivo	*no se conjuga*	*no se conjuga*
imperfecto de subjuntivo	aboliera, aboliese abolieras, abolieses aboliera, aboliese aboliéramos, aboliésemos abolierais, abolieseis abolieran, aboliesen	balbuciera, balbuciese balbucieras, balbucieses balbuciera, balbuciese balbuciéramos, balbuciésemos balbucierais, balbucieseis balbucieran, balbuciesen
imperativo	*no se conjuga* – abolid (vosotros) *no se conjuga* –	balbuce (tú) *no se conjuga* balbucid (vosotros) *no se conjuga* –
gerundio, participio	aboliendo, abolido	balbuciendo, balbucido

80 desolar	81 soler
Se usa solamente en infinitivo y como participio : desolado.	
presente de indicativo	suelo sueles suele solemos soléis suelen
preterito imperfecto	solía solías solía solíamos solíais solían
preterito indefinido	solí soliste solió solimos solisteis solieron
futuro de indicativo	*no se conjuga en ninguna de sus personas*
condicional	*no se conjuga en ninguna de sus personas*
presente de subjuntivo	suela suelas suela solamos soláis suelan
imperfecto de subjuntivo	soliera, soliese solieras, solieses soliera, soliese soliéramos, soliésemos solierais, solieseis solieran, soliesen
imperativo	*no se conjuga en ninguna de sus personas*
gerundio, participio	soliendo, solido

Infinitive	Past Tense	Past Participle
arise	arose	arisen
awake	awoke	awoken
be	was, were	been
bear	bore	born(e)
beat	beat	beaten
become	became	become
begin	began	begun
bend	bent	bent
beseech	besought	besought
bet	bet (*also* betted)	bet (*also* betted)
bid	bid (*also* bade)	bid (*also* bidden)
bind	bound	bound
bite	bit	bitten
bleed	bled	bled
blow	blew	blown
break	broke	broken
breed	bred	bred
bring	brought	brought
build	built	built
burn	burnt (*also* burned)	burnt (*also* burned)
burst	burst	burst
buy	bought	bought
can	could	-
cast	cast	cast
catch	caught	caught
choose	chose	chosen
cling	clung	clung
come	came	come
cost	cost	cost
creep	crept	crept
cut	cut	cut
deal	dealt	dealt
dig	dug	dug
do	did	done
draw	drew	drawn
dream	dreamed (*also* dreamt)	dreamed (*also* dreamt)
drink	drank	drunk
drive	drove	driven
dwell	dwelt	dwelt
eat	ate	eaten
fall	fell	fallen
feed	fed	fed
feel	felt	felt
fight	fought	fought
find	found	found
flee	fled	fled
fling	flung	flung
fly	flew	flown
forbid	forbade	forbidden
forget	forgot	forgotten
forsake	forsook	forsaken
freeze	froze	frozen
get	got	got (*Am* gotten)
give	gave	given

Infinitive	Past Tense	Past Participle
go	went	gone
grind	ground	ground
grow	grew	grown
hang	hung (*also* hanged)	hung (*also* hanged)
have	had	had
hear	heard	heard
hide	hid	hidden
hit	hit	hit
hold	held	held
hurt	hurt	hurt
keep	kept	kept
kneel	knelt (*also* kneeled)	knelt (*also* kneeled)
know	knew	known
lay	laid	laid
lead	led	led
lean	leant (*also* leaned)	leant (*also* leaned)
leap	leapt (*also* leaped)	leapt (*also* leaped)
learn	learnt (*also* learned)	learnt (*also* learned)
leave	left	left
lend	lent	lent
let	let	let
lie	lay	lain
light	lit (*also* lighted)	lit (*also* lighted)
lose	lost	lost
make	made	made
may	might	-
mean	meant	meant
meet	met	met
mistake	mistook	mistaken
mow	mowed	mown (*also* mowed)
pay	paid	paid
put	put	put
quit	quit (*also* quitted)	quit (*also* quitted)
read	read	read
rend	rent	rent
rid	rid	rid
ride	rode	ridden
ring	rang	rung
rise	rose	risen
run	ran	run
saw	sawed	sawn
say	said	said
see	saw	seen
seek	sought	sought
sell	sold	sold
send	sent	sent
set	set	set
shake	shook	shaken
shall	should	-
shear	sheared	shorn (*also* sheared)
shed	shed	shed
shine	shone	shone
shoot	shot	shot
show	showed	shown

Infinitive	Past Tense	Past Participle
shrink	shrank	shrunk
shut	shut	shut
sing	sang	sung
sink	sank	sunk
sit	sat	sat
slay	slew	slain
sleep	slept	slept
slide	slid	slid
sling	slung	slung
slit	slit	slit
smell	smelt (*also* smelled)	smelt (*also* smelled)
sow	sowed	sown (*also* sowed)
speak	spoke	spoken
speed	sped (*also* speeded)	sped (*also* speeded)
spell	spelt (*also* spelled)	spelt (*also* spelled)
spend	spent	spent
spill	spilt (*also* spilled)	spilt (*also* spilled)
spin	spun	spun
spit	spat	spat
split	split	split
spoil	spoiled (*also* spoilt)	spoiled (*also* spoilt)
spread	spread	spread
spring	sprang	sprung
stand	stood	stood
steal	stole	stolen
stick	stuck	stuck
sting	stung	stung
stink	stank	stunk
stride	strode	stridden
strike	struck	struck (*also* stricken)
strive	strove	striven
swear	swore	sworn
sweep	swept	swept
swell	swelled	swollen (*also* swelled)
swim	swam	swum
swing	swung	swung
take	took	taken
teach	taught	taught
tear	tore	torn
tell	told	told
think	thought	thought
throw	threw	thrown
thrust	thrust	thrust
tread	trod	trodden
wake	woke (*also* waked)	woken (*also* waked)
wear	wore	worn
weave	wove (*also* weaved)	woven (*also* weaved)
wed	wedded	wedded
weep	wept	wept
win	won	won
wind	wound	wound
wring	wrung	wrung
write	wrote	written

Imprimé chez Rotolito Lombarda (Italie)
Dépôt légal : mars 2009. 541009/05
N° de projet : 11013258 - Juillet 2013